The Oxford–Hachette French Dictionary
Second Edition

The Oxford French dictionary range includes:

The Oxford–Hachette French Dictionary
The Concise Oxford–Hachette French Dictionary
The Compact Oxford–Hachette French Dictionary
The Pocket Oxford–Hachette French Dictionary
The Oxford Colour French Dictionary
The Oxford Paperback French Dictionary
The Oxford French Minidictionary
The Oxford French Dictionary and Grammar
French Usage
French Grammar
10,000 French Words
French Verbs
French Correspondence
The Oxford–Duden Pictorial French Dictionary, Second Edition

The Oxford–Hachette French Dictionary

Second Edition

French–English · English–French

Edited by

Marie-Hélène Corréard · Valerie Grundy

Second edition edited by

Marie-Hélène Corréard

Oxford New York Toronto

OXFORD UNIVERSITY PRESS

Oxford University Press, Great Clarendon Street, Oxford OX2 6DP

Oxford New York
Athens Auckland Bangkok Bogotá Buenos Aires Calcutta
Cape Town Chennai Dar es Salaam Delhi Florence Hong Kong Istanbul
Karachi Kuala Lumpur Madrid Melbourne Mexico City Mumbai
Nairobi Paris São Paulo Singapore Taipei Tokyo Toronto Warsaw

and associated companies in
Berlin Ibadan

Published in the United States by
Oxford University Press Inc., New York

First Edition 1994
Second Edition 1997

British Library Cataloguing in Publication Data
Data available

Library of Congress Cataloging in Publication Data
Data available

ISBN 0-19-860067-4
ISBN 0-19-860068-2 (thumb index)

10 9 8 7 6 5 4 3

Typeset in Monotype Nimrod by Oxford University Press
Printed on acid-free paper in the United States of America

Preface
Préface

Preface to the Second Edition

Published in 1994, the first edition of the *Oxford–Hachette French Dictionary* is recognized as a landmark in the description of French, marking the beginning of a new age of corpus-based bilingual lexicography. The need for a Second Edition so soon after the first is dictated by new developments in the vocabularies of French and English which merit inclusion and description. Continuously updated, the language databases used for the Dictionary's compilation have produced evidence of new words, phrases and idioms which have gained currency since 1994. New evidence from the systematic study of Oxford's databases of French literature has also been recorded. Hundreds of items have been added, from almost every field of activity, and a new *A–Z of Contemporary France* provides a cultural review of all aspects of modern French society. Together with a new guide to communicating effectively in French, (be it on paper or a postcard, by telephone, or on the Internet), these additions reflect the publishers' continuing aim to provide the most accurate description possible of today's French and English.

Preface to the First Edition

This dictionary is the fruit of six years' sustained co-operation between two of the world's foremost reference publishers. Being a completely original work, it is not constrained by previous editions or prior publications, and so is able to provide a truly fresh and contemporary description of the relationship between French and English.

The work was carried out by a team comprising equal numbers of French and English native-speakers, working together on the same site. Editors worked in bilingual pairs, each working only in his or her native language. Editors were able to consult constantly to establish accurate translations of every item in every entry. This team in turn drew on the resources of many freelance lexicographers, translators, consultants, and terminology specialists in the French- and English-speaking worlds.

This is the first French and English dictionary to have been written using electronic corpora: two huge databases of electronic texts, one of current French and the other of current English. Each database contained over 10 million words of language in use. Access to these databases has provided accounts of words and their translations which are always authentic and often revealing. Users of the dictionary can feel confident that translations presented derive from study of real language as it has actually been used in a wide range of contexts. The resulting text provides modern idiomatic coverage of general French and English, with many new words, extensive treatment of colloquial expressions, and thousands of example sentences showing real language in action. A wide range of literary vocabulary has been included, together with vocabulary from the specialized fields of science, business, technology, and medicine.

Préface de la première édition

Ce dictionnaire est le fruit de six années d'étroite collaboration entre deux grands éditeurs d'ouvrages de référence. C'est une œuvre totalement nouvelle et originale qui offre une description actuelle et moderne des langues anglaise et française, et de leurs relations.

Des rédacteurs anglophones et francophones ont uni leurs compétences et ont constitué des équipes bilingues qui ont travaillé ensemble, en un même lieu. Tout au long de l'élaboration du dictionnaire, chaque rédacteur a travaillé dans sa langue maternelle et a pu vérifier, grâce à un échange constant avec les autres membres de l'équipe, la justesse et la pertinence des traductions. Les rédacteurs ont par ailleurs fait appel à de nombreux collaborateurs extérieurs : lexicographes, traducteurs, consultants et terminologues, tous spécialistes des mondes anglophone et francophone.

Les rédacteurs ont, pour la première fois dans l'histoire de la lexicographie bilingue, utilisé un corpus électronique composé de deux bases de données textuelles de français et d'anglais. Les bases de données française et anglaise comportent chacune plus de 10 millions de mots de la langue usuelle. L'utilisation de ces bases de données a permis un repérage des mots et des traductions, toujours authentique et pertinent. Les utilisateurs peuvent en toute confiance se servir des traductions proposées : elles sont issues de la langue réelle et employées en contexte. Le dictionnaire recense et traite de nombreux mots nouveaux, des expressions familières, des expressions idiomatiques et des tournures actuelles du français et de l'anglais. Il accorde également une large place à la langue littéraire, aux américanismes et au vocabulaire de domaines spécialisés : scientifique, commercial, technologique, médical, . . .

The aim of the Publishers has been to provide translators, students at all levels, teachers, and business people with a reference work that is without rival in authority, currency, and accuracy.

The Publishers
Oxford University Press
Project Director Timothy Benbow
Commissioning Editor Robert Scriven

Les éditeurs se sont fixé un seul but: allier recherche linguistique et effort éditorial afin d'offrir aux traducteurs, étudiants de tous niveaux, enseignants et au monde des affaires, un ouvrage de référence inégalé à ce jour en matière d'autorité, d'actualité et de fiabilité.

Les éditeurs
Hachette Dictionnaires
Direction Mireille Maurin
Responsable d'édition Héloïse Neefs

The Oxford–Hachette French Dictionary

Second Edition

Chief editor

Marie-Hélène Corréard

Editors
Marianne Chalmers
Françoise de Peretti

Associate Editor
Mary O'Neill

Tanslator/ Lexicographer
Susan Steinberg

An A–Z of Contemporary France
Richard Aplin

General advice on writing in French
Natalie Pomier

Proofreaders
Isabelle Lemoine
Genevieve Hawkins

Design
An A–Z of Contemporary France, General advice on writing in French:
Text Matters, Reading, UK

First Edition

Chief editors/Direction éditoriale

Marie-Hélène Corréard · Valerie Grundy

Editors/Rédacteurs
Nicola Addyman
Jennifer Barnes
Marianne Chalmers
Glynnis Chantrell
Rosalind Combley
Gearóid Cronin
Laurence Delacroix
Françoise de Peretti
Janet Gough
Gérard G. Kahn
Pascal Lecler
Jacques Lesca
Mary O'Neill
Catherine Palmer
Martine Pierquin
Georges Pilard
Nicolas Rosec
Catherine Roux
Kathleen Shields
Susan Steinberg
Nicole Truchet

Lexicographical adviser/ Conseiller en lexicographie
Beryl T. Atkins

Lexical usage notes and correspondence/ Notes d'usage lexicales et correspondance
Henri Béjoint
Richard Wakely

Assisted by/Assistés de
Ghislaine Ansieau
Lucy Atkins
Agnès Sauzet

Translator-lexicographers/ Traducteurs-lexicographes
Christopher Dawson
Robert Grundy
Hélène Haenen
Marie-Claude Harrison
Frances Illingworth
Thiên-Nga Lê
Natalie Pomier
Muriel Ranivoalison
Patrick Ros Gorasny
Tamsin Simmil
Thérèse Sepulchre
Jo Waite

Specialist terminology consultants/ Consultants en terminologie
Centre de Recherche en Traduction et Terminologie
Université Lumière-Lyon II
Philippe Thoiron
Malcolm Harvey
University of Brighton
Tony Hartley
Malcolm Slater
Dimity Castellano

Consultants/Consultants
Martyn L. Bird
Rosalind Fergusson
Hélène M. A. Lewis
Janet Whitcut

North American English/Anglo-américain
Charles Lynn Clark
Georgie Boge
Amy Deanne Matthews

French outside France/Français d'ailleurs
Lilliam Hurst
Dominique Péladeau

Phonetics/Phonétique
Isabelle Vodoz
Jane Stuart-Smith

Administration/Administration
Coordination/Coordination
Isabelle Lemoine
Marion Fox
Nadia Jamil

Data-capture/Saisie des données
Senior keyboarder/Responsable de la saisie
Philip Gerrish
Alison Curr
Annie Girardin
Alexander Ions
Fabienne Pearson
Muriel Ranivoalison
Tim Weekes

Proofreaders/Correcteurs
Stephen Curtis
Genevieve Hawkins
Isabelle Lemoine

Freelance lexicographers and translators/ Collaborateurs lexicographes et traducteurs
Marie-Hélène Advielle
Isabelle d'Araquy
Ibelle Azodi
Claudie Balavoine
Richard Bateman
Ilona Bellos
Cyprian Blamires
Marion Brilleaud
Amanda Broad
Marie-Thérèse Brun
Flora Buchanan
Anne Buisson-Champalle
Edwin Carpenter
Denise Cavanaugh
Joan Chapman
Barbara Christie
Colin Cooper
Thomas Crawford
Stephen Curtis
Elizabeth Degouge
Bénédicte Duchet-Filhol
Anne Eddi-Vantal
Nathalie Fourrier
Brigitte Guérin
Helga Harrison
Rosemary Hazlerigg
Richard Illingworth
Malcolm Jones
Nicholas Jones
Isabelle Joyau
Claudie Juillard
Teresa Lander
Jakeline Larrieu
Geneviève Lebaut
Dominique Le Fur
Anne Leignadier
Fabienne Lemaître
Isabelle Lidden-Vallin
Sue Lloyd
Nicole Maindrault
Arabel Mérand
Alain Métro
Lise de Micheaux
Annie Mignard
Laurent Milesi
Marie Milesi
Frank Mullineaux
Josiane Parry
Elaine Pollard
Lise Pomier
Brigitte Ponsart
Elizabeth Portier
Colette Price
Caroline Quinnell
François Rappaz
Joseph Rézeau
Sylvia Robertson
Valerie Robinson
Arthur Root
Patrice Salsa
Eric Schmoll
Karin Soyer
Laurence Tron
Pierre Vincent
Rosemary Whitley
John Williams
Christine Winter

Design/Maquette
Text/texte: Fran Holdsworth
Diagrams/organigrammes: Information Design Unit
Letters/correspondance: Raynor Design

Acknowledgements
Remerciements

The editors would like to extend their warmest thanks to a certain number of people and organizations not mentioned in the list of contributors, particularly Beth Levin of Northwestern University, who allowed us to make use of her work on English verb classification.

We are also indebted to all those who made it possible for us to build the corpus of contemporary French which, with the Oxford Corpus of Modern English, has been the cornerstone of this dictionary. In particular, our thanks go to Manuel Lucbert, Secrétaire Général of *Le Monde*, Jean-François Sailly, Gilbert Compagnon and his team, also from *Le Monde*, Christian Poulin from *Libération*, Joseph Laveille and Aimé Munoz from *Le Progrès de Lyon*.

Our thanks also go to Dora Carpenter, Colin Hope, Anne Judge, Helen Lawrence, Katherine Manville, Alain Pierrot, and Robin Sawers for their contribution at various stages of the project.

Finally we would like to thank all those people, too numerous to mention here, who have given us their support and the benefit of their knowledge in writing this dictionary.

Les auteurs tiennent à remercier un certain nombre de personnes et d'organismes qui n'ont pas été mentionnés dans la liste des collaborateurs du projet, en particulier Beth Levin, de Northwestern University, qui nous a permis d'utiliser son travail sur la classification des verbes anglais. Nous sommes également redevables à tous ceux qui nous ont aidés à constituer le corpus de français contemporain qui, avec le corpus d'anglais moderne d'Oxford, a été la pierre angulaire de ce dictionnaire. Nous remercions tout spécialement Manuel Lucbert, Secrétaire Général du journal *Le Monde*, ses collaborateurs Jean-François Sailly, Gilbert Compagnon et son équipe, Christian Poulin de *Libération*, Joseph Laveille et Aimé Munoz du *Progrès de Lyon*.

Nous remercions également Dora Carpenter, Colin Hope, Anne Judge, Helen Lawrence, Katherine Manville, Alain Pierrot, et Robin Sawers qui ont participé à diverses étapes du projet.

Nous adressons nos remerciements à tous ceux qui, trop nombreux pour être nommés ici, nous ont apporté leur soutien et fait bénéficier de leur savoir tout au long de notre entreprise.

Contents

Introduction

Users of this dictionary will find it an effective tool for tackling practical linguistic tasks. In designing this dictionary we have ensured that every entry provides as much information as possible for each of the following users and tasks:

- the native English speaker trying to understand French,
- the native English speaker trying to write or speak French,
- the native French speaker trying to understand English,
- the native French speaker trying to write or speak English.

Users have different levels of skills and knowledge. For the advanced user, we provide thorough coverage of up-to-date language. We include a wide range of vocabulary in specialist but nonetheless highly topical areas such as business, politics, sport, information technology, marketing, social administration, and the environment.

For intermediate users, we have designed the dictionary to enable them to work with the foreign language, using it correctly and well. Particular care has been taken in the selection of the translations. Our electronic corpora (see p. xv) give us a wealth of examples of words in use in real, everyday circumstances. When one good translation has been identified and checked in many contexts, it will often be given as the only general translation for one sense of the headword. It has been our policy throughout to give two or more translations only in those rare cases where they are consistently interchangeable, and to avoid adding less safe alternatives when one equivalent is adequate. Where appropriate, other equivalents, which have been found to work in more restricted contexts, will be shown in examples.

Where nuances of meaning within a sense of the headword are translated in different ways, these nuances are pinpointed by means of semantic indicators and/or typical collocates. For a step-by-step guide to using this type of information to arrive at the most suitable translation, see the section *Using this dictionary* on p. xxiii.

Translations given in isolation are, however, not enough to enable someone to work in a foreign language: grammatical constructions are also needed if the translation is to be used correctly. For this reason, one of our principal concerns has been to include these constructions wherever they are required. This is a significant feature of our dictionary.

Headwords, compounds, and phrasal verbs stand out clearly on the page. English compounds are found in their proper place within the overall alphabetical order of headwords. Phrasal verbs are given a very full and explicit presentation which avoids ambiguous metalanguage and, for the French user, shows clearly the positioning of the noun object.

The dictionary has a wide coverage of North American as well as British English, and exclusively British or North American usage is marked. Where appropriate, American variants are given in translations of French words and phrases. The existence of standard American spelling variants is indicated in translations in the French–English side of the dictionary.

The needs of users extend beyond the bounds of individual dictionary entries. To make this dictionary an effective aid for somebody working in a language not their own, we offer access to the language in several different ways. The user thumbing through this dictionary will find lexical usage notes, notes on function words, model letters, documents and advertisements, maps, verb tables, and organizational diagrams.

Lexical usage notes

These are boxed notes which appear within the dictionary text. They give the user facts about certain types of words that behave alike, for example, names of countries, languages, colour terms, and days of the week, and provide ways of discussing topics such as age, dates, time, and measurement. A full index to these notes is given on p. 1919.

The purpose of these notes is to make generalizations across lexical items, by summarizing syntactic facts that are common to most members of the set, thus supplementing the coverage of individual entries: in a one-volume dictionary it is not possible to give all the facts at each headword. Cross-references to the notes are given at all relevant entries, normally immediately after the pronunciation of the headword. The reference is to the page in the dictionary on which the usage note appears.

These notes are intended for specific users: people seeking to express themselves in a language not their own. Thus, the usage notes which appear in the English–French half of the dictionary are written in English and present facts about expression in French, and vice versa in the French–English half. Since they are designed to help translation into a foreign language, they do not represent a systematic analysis of linguistic facts, nor do they set out to give a comprehensive survey of all possible translations. Their purpose is to allow someone to say or write specific things accurately and naturally in the foreign language.

Many of the lexical usage notes represent a functional approach to language use, grouping the basic structures and expressions necessary in order to write or talk about a specific topic. Thus, as well as being readily usable reference aids for the individual user, they will also serve as valuable vocabulary-teaching material for teachers of French and English.

Notes on function words

The words of a language may be seen to be of two types: those with lexical meaning like *table* and *slowly* and *jump*, and those with function rather than meaning. The latter are the joints and sinews of the language, uniting the other elements into sentences which carry meaning. Examples of such function words are pronouns like *you* and *it*, verbs such as *be* and *have*, and determiners such as *this* and *that*.

The notes within or near function word entries are again intended for use by the person seeking to work in a foreign language. They provide basic information on grammatical words.

The function word notes are easily identifiable in the dictionary. In cases where the information can be presented fairly briefly, the note will be found at the top of the entry, immediately under the headword. In cases where the necessary information is more lengthy and complex, the notes are boxed and clearly visible, appearing as close as possible to the headword concerned.

Letters and documents

A rich and comprehensive set of model letters and documents is to be found in a special section in the centre of the dictionary. Once again, these are designed for people seeking to write in a language not their own. Thus, the model letters for the English-speakers are written in French but introduced in English.

A list of the types of letters and documents is given on p. 897.

Advertisements

Unlike the rest of the material described above, these are essentially aids to comprehension and as such are intended for the user seeking to make use of small ads in a foreign newspaper, which are often made incomprehensible by their extensive use of abbreviations.

The sample advertisements, with accompanying guides to understanding them, are to be found on pp. 935–40 in the centre of the dictionary.

A corpus-based dictionary

The use of corpus material is the most important innovation in the Oxford–Hachette French dictionary: it is certainly the feature that distinguishes it from all other bilingual dictionaries available today. Some of our editors have been writing dictionaries for twenty years or more, while others cut their lexicographical teeth on this dictionary, and none of us would wish to go back to the bad old days of editing dictionaries without a corpus to help us. We all believe that a corpus is essential to what we are doing when we write a bilingual dictionary—when we try to discover how our own native language works, to line it up against another language and capture the equivalences, to pick out the most useful constructions and phrases and to communicate them in the way that is going to be most helpful to most people.

So, what do we mean when we say that we used a corpus to help us compile this dictionary? What is a corpus? Why do we need one? How do we use it? Does it help? This section tries to answer these questions.

What is a corpus?

When we talk of using a corpus, we mean an *electronic text corpus*—or more exactly, two corpora, one of English and one of French—separate collections of printed and transcribed spoken material held in electronic form in a computer. Corpus contents range from the text of books, newspapers, magazine articles, leaflets, letters, and so on, to transcripts of conversations, lectures, and discussions which have been keyed in specially from the audio recording of the event. The computer can find in a matter of seconds all the occurrences of a particular word in the corpus. It makes a concordance for the word: some of the 1,500-odd concordance lines for the word *measure* are shown in Fig. 1, displayed in a way that allows the lexicographer to see how the word is actually being used.

The numbers at the start of each line identify the text from which the example is drawn: for instance, 052886 shows that the example was found in the *Guardian* newspaper, while 006992 refers to Margaret Forster's novel *Lady's Maid*, and so on. It is important for editors to know this, so that they can base decisions on a consensus view of how a word behaves; twenty examples of a particular usage from twenty different people are much more important than twenty examples from the same person, who may have quirks of language use that we do not wish to reflect in our dictionary.

Fig. 1 shows what the lexicographers see when they start on a new entry: a sample of all the citations for the headword *measure*, set out here in alphabetical order: first, of the various forms of that word, and second, of what comes immediately after it in the sentence. This layout helps us to find the constructions that follow the headword, highlighting as it does the patterns that occur frequently: even a cursory glance at these lines alerts us

```
111836 ord with an extraneous espionage plot thrown in for good measure .PP <hd3> NELSON ALGREN </hd3> A Walk On The Wild
402323 for west Oxfordshire , and that 's been achieve for some measure . .PP <s id=g,sx=M> It 's a strange time to rejoin
221098 ty and tranquillity . The Commonwealth remained in large measure a ceremonial affair after 1960 , with a role for th
289870 n ever-lengthening letters to his brother , and for good measure added lightning sketches from memory . He complaine
211903 er produced a bottle of Bacardi , poured himself a large measure , added some coca cola , looked in the fridge , com
009912 ia . The 296 prisoners were removed as a ` precautionary measure " after unusually high levels of the bacteria were
052886 tralian colleagues ..PP The most effective international measure against apartheid in recent years has been the sque
121666 o an objective agreed by everybody , are valuable beyond measure . </qt> .PP After completing the restructuring of B
052886  . Now it could be compelled by the 1988 Act to accept a measure against his and its policy . </st> .PP THE Energy S
021335 ding interests in the Middle East , partly as a security measure , and partly in conjunction with a Dutch holding co
003401 fastidious Max , within earshot , was embarrassed beyond measure ) and , as a career-woman , had always stressed the
052886 e . " A few paragons who display these qualities in full measure are rated by the committee as ` Exceptionally Well
009912 ar the public from the proceedings as a further security measure , but he was overruled by a higher court . .PP The
310200 physical penetration , or if possession is something you measure by its financial cost , and if possession is acknow
052886 e complaint , though : no fill-up at full price is short measure for the money . .PP GILELS and an Amadeus Quartet b
052886  been designed for easy fitting . ` We have computers to measure fuel consumption , to prove it works . It is a syst
200317  and because of that I agree with rearmament as a safety measure . " ` Give a man a weapon and he 'll use it , " Mr
005581  doing , " Moran seized the can violently and poured the measure himself . .PP ` I didn't ask to do this , " the boy
006992 find some greenery and space for Flush and then for good measure he took a pencil and drew a simple map . Wilson clu
057992 precisely , the circumference of a cabbage . With a tape measure , Hope says } . .PP <p 85> .PP { " Every little um
113999 s of Elizabeth Woodville . Shocked and distressed beyond measure , her worst forebodings realized , she blamed herse
020255  It points out that this was introduced as a ` temporary measure " in 1973 . But the RMIF wants car tax taken out ov
052886 h pub but a decrease of about 12 per cent in the average measure in a Scottish pub " . The junior agriculture minist
133169  Nilsson disc ( the Jones , by comparison , offers short measure ) is drawn from a recital with Geoffrey parsons ( i
003401 us Christ into my life . And I 've been comforted beyond measure . " .PP If only it could be that simple . The relig
229834 ignificant aspect of decentralisation is where a certain measure of local autonomy or local initiative is encouraged
139998 d the prop were overhauled completely . Also as a safety measure , modern radios and circuit breakers were installed
052886 ugh stand paid off , and ministers finally supported the measure . .PP Ms Ruddock 's achievement can be measured by
200088 him . Look at the malice in his eyes . I shall get short measure next time , but only for one drink . His annoyance
052886 he NHS , has passed its final parliamentary hurdle . The measure now returns to the Lords for approval and should ga
009912  global issues and regional issues , we have a very good measure of agreement " . They had covered events in ` regio
```

Fig. 1 (*continues overleaf*)

```
077989  takeovers between 1922 and 1988 . .PP The study 's main measure of an acquisition 's success is the subsequent cour
166340 ians from the land of Prester John . But the price was a measure of autonomy granted to what were now emerging as na
227590  and mentally . You 'll be in no doubt whatsoever that a measure of change in your life is essential now . Take your
052886 egree of ` public embarrassment " that finally lead to a measure of change . With them , she also played Rosalind ,
288665 r drink ? I 'm starving ! " .PP As Taff poured me a good measure of cider and handed me a boiled egg and a chunk of
052886 e South-east , the CSO said they should not be used as a measure of comparative living standards , since regional va
211311 cution of many millions of calculations . .PP The common measure of computer performance , MIPS , refers to the numb
052886  successfully attain the criteria . .PP In return , some measure of discipline is expected . In the specific case of
256579 ass of a cooked chicken . Into his small cup he ladled a measure of fresh goat 's milk from a jug on the window-ledg
@52886 that Matthaus can be both stagehand and leading man is a measure of his impact . Schillaci 's goals have been pricel
052886 is labours he received a cheque for 5,000 , but the true measure of his success is five victories at Beckenham for t
244460  important than the minutiae of psephology . .PP It is a measure of how dangerous the National Front has become in F
009912 , despite the obvious risks , to re-open the border is a measure of how impossible is the choice that the authoritie
402323  gendarmes have been introduced to an Oxford school is a measure of how seriously schools in Oxfordshire are taking
177775 would make the APR more than 5,000 per cent _ at least a measure of how very little use following-on is to her . In
211311 ranked order . .PP The inventory ratio provides a useful measure of how well inventory is being controlled , but it
052886 d its proposal to abolish the right to silence . Another measure of its apathy is its failure to implement reforms l
244999 enses all practically at the last . I think Gode has the measure of most men or women , at least where they are most
052886 or who understood Bowden 's idiosyncracies . .PP It is a measure of Lord Bowden 's success at Manchester that when t
009912 s , but mainly will just to allow the two men to get the measure of one another . <sect> Foreign News Page 10 </sect
402323 et the benefit of what we said to him . But we do have a measure of optimism that they might reflect themselves in f
220797 aluminium company whose arrival in Banbury had brought a measure of prosperity to the town in the years of the Depre
009912 point about the licensing laws is to ensure a reasonable measure of public safety . Even in a large marquee in a fie
037783 sks . ` For me at any rate , ` I reply . There will be a measure of relief even in Anna 's sorrow . I dream that we
052886 ighly commercialised sport in which winning was the only measure of success and the means of a financial reward . Ha
009912 e Lambeth , they do not see a low registration rate as a measure of success . .PP Lambeth 's failure to register its
052886 d successes in the West _ in the sense that detente is a measure of success _ then those successes had much to do wi
052886 at kind of cash . " Money was important to him only as a measure of success , ` to prove that I was a star " . Show
052886  . He has since been nominated for Oscars nine times _ a measure of the respect with which he eventually came to be
228703 ill have to . But it ought to be Rod or Joe , I have the measure of them ) . While the kettle in the first-floor kit
287166 wn . The oil companies , whose business depends in large measure on those cars , spend similar sums persuading us th
098963 itor their progress not only with scales but with a tape measure . One hundred ladies kindly volunteered and eight w
344622  pints ) a day . It may help people to drink more if you measure out this amount into a stock of glasses or cups , s
052886 continuing refusal by BR to set targets against which to measure performance . A 24 per cent increase in complaints
197464 e way people think , talk , act and react . Because they measure performance , they touch upon people 's sensitiviti
224156 ox have chosen . This move has been promoted as a safety measure , permitting slip when the tool bites , but the leg
052886 re are three people in the drawing and that they in some measure represent Picasso 's two competing mistresses , Mar
052886 mentary leader , Mr Aleksander Bentkowski , who for good measure said he preferred Solidarity 's concept for a coali
212161 glish : Oxford 's most popular subject , adding for good measure some Good Thinking on T S Eliot by Lyndall Gordon (
200317 But he 'd done neither ! She silently swore and for good measure swore again . Then she stamped up the stairs . To h
207775 e any samples from Mars , so there is no way that we can measure the age of the Martian rocks directly . But we can
100756  ride around your proposed route and use the odometer to measure the distance between familiar landmarks . Alternati
052886 om laser to moon and back again , allowing scientists to measure the distance between the planets . .PP The distance
000790 n the Toscanini/Koussevitsky tradition , adding for good measure the name of Charles Mu\3nch . The review of the rec
237687  well ask me to simultaneously pinpoint the position and measure the speed of a subatomic particle , but yes , most
207775 ontribute much useful information . It is easy enough to measure the volume of lava flows , but it is only by const
022282 onal knowledge of self . It seeks to help individuals to measure their problems against the social realities , and t
326766 rtant respects from that of the Aristotelians . In large measure , these differences are due to the criticisms of th
052886 boy " in the Government 's ` unseemly rush " to push the measure through . But despite the challenges , the Lords de
222878 e as a Mack truck . As a villain , Nick , you just don't measure up . " .PP I turned and looked at myself in the cra
052886 almost irrelevant . .PP ` He is up there and you have to measure up against him and his memory . " .PP Anthony Sher
310200 ard , you cunning little bitch . You don't even begin to measure up against that gentle creature in The Lollipop . {
009912  , and even being education secretary , but how would he measure up to being chairman , in a party where , in times
009912 ast take advantage of its new opportunities and the West measure up to its new responsibilities . At the moment the
052886 ement ... The Communist party in its present form cannot measure up to the present tasks ... The time for experiment
009912 r of clubs in the Football League whose press facilities measure up to UEFA 's minimum standards . .PP The answer wa
335903 no gainsaying the fact that some American products don't measure up, while there is a strong consumer demand for for
052886 ought the whole thing was so arranged to ensure that the measure was defeated . " .PP The slot for the debate was on
009912 remors 10 times as strong as the 15-second quake , which measured 6.9 on the Richter scale . .PP Local politicians b
052886 r of extinction , Europe has only 29 - a low figure when measured against the Brazilian total of 121 . And one of th
332100 She was led away into a crisp-looking cell where she was measured and weighed ; a careful , polite pair of hands fou
052886 owy Australian stands 6ft 3in those fast hands have been measured by a computer at 119mph . As he is also one of the
104055 ive , rather than an intellectual knowing . It cannot be measured by scientific instruments _ and here we must leave
052886 aid it was ` the first step in a good direction " . This measured comment reflects disappointment , shared by Genera
299968 n to all three and consists of 40 rows and 40 stitches , measured in millimetres . This is because the Form program
052886 hydroplane off course as Lady Arran made two runs over a measured kilometre . .PP The judges stipulated that the boa
319199 to admire his swan-like bearing , high chin and steady , measured pace , the result of thirty-three years of soldier
006992 hes so , I shall not sleep , " and when Wilson dutifully measured out drops of the tincture and gave it to her mistr
077989  married . .PP Mr Murray 's solution is drastic . A more measured response is not to abandon welfare but to shift th
009912  day when there was a black president , Mr Sisulu gave a measured response . ` We believe that in our lifetime there
052886 iety at the Athenaeum Club in London . .PP In tones more measured than some cabinet colleagues , he also linked the
333767 ang end . At that time we picked up a problem report and measured the depth of that de-bond area . The criteria is w
111891  to its height , which could well be true ; also to have measured the distance of a ship off-shore , which is usuall
005581 ke some people , " Moran responded tersely . .PP Michael measured the drench into a small bottle . Moran forced it d
009912 tarts one dapper man in his forties before describing in measured tones the ill-treatment he saw the Soviet militia
052886  a lot when he moves in a leathery sort of way . No half measures about Pesky Polltax . This is a 24 carat , copper
332888 ition in other countries , and concern about retaliatory measures against Japanese imports . 4.5 This sort of inte
141456 ey accorded to incomes policies , reflation , or tougher measures against the trade unions . Willie ( later Lord )
022698 ive , 89/646 , allows the Commission to take retaliatory measures against discrimination , such as blocking takeov
166340 e . Therefore the French parliaments successively passed measures aimed at weakening the church . Then , by a sad ac
009912  Office yesterday revealed details of a # 50m package of measures aimed at speeding up the postal service . The move
022000 purity , clearly demarcated terms of address , and other measures aimed at maintaining the systems of control were i
002096  low intelligence among deprived children may be through measures aimed at improving their nutrition . And since the
378858  town such as Bedford . Mr Badman uses false weights and measures , cheats his debtors through a bogus bankruptcy ,
110487 all have to show goodwill and find appropriate emergency measures . </qt> .PP <qt> Civic Forum was the motor of the
331431 olors . In the United States , colors _ like weights and measures _ have been standardized by the National Bureau of
037783  I different ? I suppose I was never contented with half measures . I am sorry your life is so burdensome , I only w
208444 e essentials of arithmetic and the system of weights and measures . If he was based at a school governed by the Chur
052886 of ignorance and self-delusion . He called for emergency measures , including abandoning of the 90 million City Tech
```

Fig. 1 (*continued*)

```
000790 jan in the Toscanini/Koussevitsky tradition , adding for good measure the name of Charles Muench . The review of
200317 ut . But he 'd done neither ! She silently swore and for good measure swore again . Then she stamped up the stairs
227590 r in the cream and stir well . Give one last beating for good measure . .PP Turn your mixture into the pie shell .
155798 New Europe , with a sprinking of gardening thrown in for good measure , is Weidenfeld and Nicolson with J.M/NP. De
320079 tic red , white , and blue bands with grey thrown in for good measure . The PTEs sport their own colour schemes on
111836 ith Harold Lloyd and Fatty Arbuckle trivia thrown in for good measure ) , revealing that Keaton was , for him , th
212161 ps Durham , Bristol , Edinburgh and Exeter thrown in for good measure . .PP A third explanation , rather less acce
009912 nd the soaps , are figuratively thrown into the ring for good measure . There is the daunting prospect of an hour
006992 k to find some greenery and space for Flush and then for good measure he took a pencil and drew a simple map . Wil
```

Fig. 2

to the frequent use of *measures aimed at*, or *a measure of*, or *measures to halt/help/improve* (etc.), or the phrasal verb *measure up*.

Fig. 2 shows some of the concordance lines set out in alphabetical order of what comes before the word *measure*. This layout is particularly revealing in the case of nouns: phrases like *for good measure* (shown here), *safety measure*, *short measure*, and *half measures* are all stacked together and quickly found in this type of display. Once we notice such a term, we can ask the computer to show us all the examples of it in the corpus: this makes it easy to ensure that the phrase is given in its most frequent form, and that the translation offered fits all contexts.

Why do we need a corpus?

Before lexicography was revolutionized by this wealth of computerized corpus material, dictionary editors had to rely on their own or their colleagues' reading and listening for a perspective on their language. New words and phrases, and new meanings of familiar items, were noted as they were encountered, and often large-scale reading programmes were undertaken in an effort to make sure that as little as possible slipped through the net. Such activities still form an important part of lexicography today, and in most places are still the only source of information about the language, apart of course from the editor's own knowledge and intuitions as a native speaker. But no human reader can capture all the examples of how even one word is used in a single book, let alone in a hundred or a thousand books. A computer does just that, for every word in all the texts. No human being, even with all the time in the world, can be sure of remembering all the ways of using even one small word, let alone discover how other people use it. A computer lets us do just that, for every word in the language. No human being can take ten thousand sentences and put them in alphabetical order of one of their words. A computer does that in a few seconds.

A dictionary has to reflect everybody's use of language, not simply the language of one particular editor. When we write a dictionary without the help of a corpus, we are at the mercy of our own misapprehensions about the way we use our language. By reading and listening and discussing with our colleagues, we try to get an objective view of how our language works, and what its words mean. However, we need more data than any single person can find, even by taking careful notes and discussing conscientiously with others: that is why we need a corpus. It lets us look at how not one but hundreds of native speakers use the word we are interested in. With such a resource to draw on, the dictionary is likely to contain more generally useful facts, more central and typical examples, than a dictionary which essentially reflects the language of a handful of lexicographers. By studying a large corpus we can get a very good idea of what people will be hoping to find in the dictionary. The commoner a phrase is, the more likely it is that someone will want to look it up.

How do we use a corpus?

This dictionary was compiled in a series of different operations, needing different skills, and carried out by different groups of people. The English–French side began when a team of English-speaking lexicographers drew up what we called a 'framework' for each word. This took the form of a very large, extremely detailed dictionary entry (on average, a framework was three times as long as the dictionary entry that was eventually made from it), and was compiled using monolingual dictionaries and other reference books —in fact, the traditional way of writing dictionaries. The French–English side of the dictionary was started at the same time and followed the same method: lexicographers in France compiled the frameworks that would form the basis of the lexicography on the French–English side of the dictionary.

The English frameworks were then translated into French, in France by French translators. Similarly, the French frameworks were translated in Britain, by English translators. The translators often suggested useful additions to the text.

The translated framework then went to a pair of editors (one English- and one French-speaking) in Oxford, who worked together on both English–French and French–English text, each being responsible for his or her own language within the entry. Our golden rule is that only English speakers write English and only French speakers write French in this dictionary. From this point onwards, editors worked with corpus data.

For an English–French entry, the English-speaking editor scanned the English corpus for an overview of the various meanings of the word, for constructions that had to be included, for examples of usage, for common collocations that should not be missed. The French-speaking editor studied the English corpus in order to get a clear idea of the scope and range of meaning of the word. The French corpus offered (see pp. xxi–xxii) the chance of checking out exactly how a French word or phrase was used, and comparing it with the way the headword was used in the English corpus. Was it safe to give a particular French word as a translation of the English headword, or to translate an English phrase or idiom in a particular way? Were the English word and its French equivalent used in the same type of contexts? Did one have informal or technical overtones that the other did not have? We shall look at some real examples of what the corpus contributed to the dictionary in the case of the word *measure*.

measure /ˈmeʒə(r)/ ▶ 1412⌋, 1771⌋, 1068⌋, 1869⌋, 1883⌋, 1703⌋ I *n* **1** (unit) unité *f* de mesure; **weights and ~s** les poids *mpl* et mesures *fpl*; **a ~ of length** une unité de longueur; **liquid ~** mesure *f* de capacité pour les liquides; **to make sth to ~** faire qch sur mesure; **it's made to ~** (garment) c'est fait sur mesure, c'est du sur mesure; **2** (standard amount, container) mesure *f*; **a double ~ of vodka** une double mesure de vodka; **he gave me short ~, I got short ~** il a triché sur la quantité; **3** (device for measuring) instrument *m* de mesure; **4** fig (qualified amount, extent) **some** ou **a certain ~ of** un/-e certain/-e; **a ~ of respect/success/change** un certain respect/succès/changement; **to receive only a small ~ of support** ne recevoir qu'un soutien limité; **a good** ou **wide ~ of autonomy** une grande autonomie; **in large ~** dans une large mesure; **she despised them and envied them in equal ~** elle les méprisait autant qu'elle les enviait; **to distribute praise and blame in equal ~** faire autant de compliments que de critiques; **in full ~** [*feel, possess, fulfil, contribute*] pleinement; [*repay*] entièrement; [*suffer*] profondément; **5** (way of estimating, indication) (of price rises) mesure *f*; (of success, anger, frustration etc) mesure *f*, indication *f*; (of efficiency, performance) critère *m*; **to be the ~ of** donner la mesure de; **to give some ~ of** donner une idée de [*delight, failure, talent, arrogance etc*]; **to use sth as a ~ of** utiliser qch pour mesurer [*effects, impact, success*]; **this is a ~ of how dangerous it is** ceci montre à quel point c'est dangereux; **this is a ~ of how seriously they are taking the situation** ceci montre à quel point ils prennent la situation au sérieux; **that is a ~ of how well the company is run** cela mesure la qualité de la gestion de la société; **6** (assessment) **beyond ~** [*change, increase*] énormément; [*anxious, beautiful, difficult*] extrêmement; **it has improved beyond ~** il y a eu d'énormes progrès; **to take the ~ of sb** jauger qn; **I have the ~ of them** je sais ce qu'ils valent; **7** (action, step) mesure *f* (**against** contre; **to do** pour faire) ; **to take ~s** prendre des mesures; **safety** ou **security ~** mesure de sécurité; **~s aimed at doing** des mesures destinées à faire; **to do sth as a precautionary/an economy ~** faire qch par mesure de précaution/d'économie; **as a preventive ~** à titre préventif; **as a temporary ~** provisoirement; **the ~ was defeated** Pol Jur la mesure a été rejetée; **8** Dance, Mus, Literat mesure *f*.

II *vtr* **1** (by standard system) [*person, instrument*] mesurer [*length, rate, depth, person, waist*]; **to ~ sth in** mesurer qch en [*metres, inches*]; **to get oneself ~d for** faire prendre ses mesures pour; **over a ~d kilometre** Sport sur un kilomètre (*délimité par des balises*); **to ~ sth into** mesurer qch dans [*container*]; **2** (have a measurement of) mesurer; **to ~ four by five metres** mesurer quatre mètres sur cinq; **a tremor measuring 5.2 on the Richter scale** une secousse de 5,2 sur l'échelle de Richter; **3** (assess) mesurer [*performance, ability, success, popularity*]; **they ~ their progress by the number of** ils mesurent leur progrès au nombre de; **4** (compare) **to ~ sth against** comparer qch à [*achievement, standard, effort*].

III *vi* [*person, instrument*] mesurer.

IV *v refl* **to ~ oneself against sb** se mesurer à qn.

IDIOMS **for good ~** pour faire bonne mesure; **to do things by half-~s** se contenter de demi-mesures; **there can be no half-~s** il ne saurait être question de demi-mesures.

■ **measure off**: **~ off [sth]** mesurer [*fabric, ribbon etc*].

■ **measure out**: **~ out [sth]** mesurer [*land, flour, liquid*]; doser [*medicine*]; compter [*drops*].

■ **measure up**: ¶ **~ up** [*person*] avoir les qualités requises; [*product*] être de qualité; **to ~ up against sb** être l'égal de qn; **to ~ up to** être à la hauteur de [*expectations*]; soutenir la comparaison avec [*achievement*]; ¶ **~ up [sth]** mesurer [*room etc*].

Fig. 3

What the corpus brought to the dictionary

First, and perhaps above all else, the corpus reminds the editors of all the really important constructions that are found with the headword and that must be included in the dictionary. These express the word's syntactic and semantic complementation, and it is essential that a bilingual dictionary should set these out clearly and comprehensively, both for the source- and the target-language speaker. The entry for *measure* (Fig. 3) contains many instances of complementation, for example, in sense 7: '**against** contre; **to do** pour faire' after the translation of the headword. The prominence in the corpus (see Fig. 1) of the constructions *measure against* and *measures to halt/help/improve* (etc.) made it impossible for the editor to overlook these usages.

The verb *measure*, like the noun, has certain complementation constructions equally important to English and to French users of the dictionary: you measure something *in* inches, or metres, or kilometres; a room measures three metres *by* four, and so on. Such constructions stand out prominently in the concordance lines (see Fig. 1), and consequently appear in the entry (Fig. 3) in the section labelled **II** *vtr*, which covers transitive uses of the verb. Section **1** contains the phrase '**to measure sth in** mesurer qch en [*metres, inches*]', while section **2** offers '**to measure four by five metres** mesurer quatre mètres sur cinq'. Just beside that phrase we find another phrase drawn directly from the corpus, '**a tremor measuring 5.2 on the Richter scale** une secousse de 5,2 sur l'échelle de Richter'. The very frequent collocation of *Richter scale* with *measure* convinced the editors that the phrase *Richter scale* should appear in the *measure* entry, as well as under *Richter*.

Thus, other words and phrases, although not part of a headword's complementation in the strictest sense, may occur so often with it that it makes sense to include them in its entry in a bilingual dictionary. There are, for instance, so many corpus examples of *measures aimed at countering/reducing/stopping* (etc.) (see Fig. 4) that it was clear this construction had to be included. When the French target-language editor was called on to provide a translation for this phrase, the French corpus produced it at once in the form of an equally frequent French collocation: *mesures destinées à faire*, which appears in sense 7 of the entry in Fig. 3. Fig. 5 shows some of the relevant concordance lines from the French corpus.

Similarly, a study of the concordance lines (sampled in Fig. 1) throws up many instances of *as a* [ADJECTIVE] *measure*—a construction so common that many users will be looking for it in the dictionary. Sense 7 (Fig. 3) therefore offers several examples of it, all of them taken directly from the corpus: in *as a precautionary/an economy measure*, the use of options separated by the oblique indicates that this is a general productive usage, and that the translation given ('par mesure de précaution/d'économie'), exemplifying the mutation from English adjective to French noun, is reasonably safe in most contexts; however, the idiosyncratic nature of the French equivalents of *as a preventive measure* ('à titre préventif') and *as a temporary measure* ('provisoirement') obliged the editors to give a specific example of each.

```
311429  the end of the road for three reasons : <en> Most of the measures aimed at competing in the single market are in t
346651 r understanding of homosexuals is called for and that all measures aimed at countering misunderstanding should be w
009912  with protesters . .PP Earlier , the government announced measures aimed at curbing the black market that is threat
311429 ss . This need is currently most acute in relation to the measures aimed at implementing the Social Charter , in th
052886 European partners agreed on specific energy and transport measures aimed at making real cuts in warming gases . Com
346651  measures , if ` palliation " is taken to mean the use of measures aimed at modifying pathological processes or the
163332 man dignity into the education system and the adoption of measures aimed at promoting these values are essential st
052886 he friar said government confiscations and other coercive measures aimed at redistributing wealth were ` positive "
006081  reduce dependence on cars , but in addition a battery of measures aimed at reducing speeds on residential and main
009912 ted area of environmental protection . .PP There are also measures aimed at reducing street litter by fining offend
009912 elta , is preparing infrastructure developments and other measures aimed at restoring some of this sleepy territory
009912 t Office yesterday revealed details of a # 50m package of measures aimed at speeding up the postal service . The mo
009912 he Slovene government 's earlier declaration of emergency measures aimed at stopping a mass rally by Serbian nation
166340 se . Therefore the French parliaments successively passed measures aimed at weakening the church . Then , by a sad
```

Fig. 4

```
010987          </p> <p>Un plan de dépistage et les mesures destinées à empêcher sa propagation aussitôt mis en place
291422              les allégements de charges et les mesures destinées à encourager l'activité des chefs d'entreprise. L
094566       des Finances, elle va s'accompagner de mesures destinées à maîtriser l'évolution des dépenses. En ligne de
325430           de prendre de «toute urgence» des mesures destinées à mettre fin à la traite des femmes originaires du
210006        Ces opérations sont complétées par des mesures destinées à permettre le départ en vacances des familles
361841     entreprise.</p> <p> s'ajoutent enfin deux mesures destinées à rapprocher les professionnels et les
365531       encore, et encore, prendre de nouvelles mesures destinées à relancer l'appareil économique. La modernisation
201887       bénéficiaires de ces pratiques. Mais les mesures destinées à s'attaquer aux racines du problème restent pour
216174          d'ambiguïté et commence à prendre des mesures destinées à sanctionner Aboul Abbas» (l'organisateur présumé
632122        municipal, les élus ont voté diverses mesures destinées à sauvegarder l'environnement. Un sujet qui leur
```

Fig. 5

There we saw an instance of one English construction (*as a* [ADJECTIVE] *measure*) with a constant meaning which was impossible to cover in a bilingual dictionary in a single example. A different problem occurs when one English phrase has several distinct meanings, for instance *a measure of*. The examples of this phrase (some of which are shown in Fig. 1) had first to be sorted by the editors into sense groupings, and this led them to several larger constructions to which the phrase belongs.

In the sense 'a certain amount of' (*a measure of success/change etc.*) the phrase is synonymous with *a certain measure of* and indeed with *some measure of*, and is shown as such in sense 4 of the entry in Fig. 3, with the translation 'un(e) certain(e)'. Before moving to the second sense of *a measure of*, it is worth noting that the first sense just described also occurs in the phrases *a small/good/wide measure of*, phrases which are therefore included with their various translations in sense 4 ('un soutien limité', 'une grande autonomie'), together with *in large measure* ('dans une large mesure') and *in equal measure* (phrases with 'autant'). The adverbial phrase *in full measure* is also given in the same section: this phrase occurs many times in the corpus, in very varied contexts. A comparison of the English contexts with those of possible French equivalents (essentially, *pleinement* and *entièrement*) convinced the editors that both these French adverbs would have to be offered, with typical contexts specified. In addition, however, several examples were found with *suffer* where neither *pleinement* nor *entièrement* would be suitable, and so we have in the entry in Fig. 3 '**in full measure** [*feel, possess, fulfil, contribute*] pleinement; [*repay*] entièrement; [*suffer*] profondément'.

A second sense of *a measure of* is handled in sense 5 of the entry (Fig. 3), where the many examples are an indication of how complex the relationship is between English and French in this area of language. As the English and French editors checked their corpus examples, and discussed various ways of translating the many different usages of *measure* in this sense, it became apparent that there was no safe single translation to be given for *this is a measure of*, although there were straightforward French equivalents of *to be the measure of* ('donner la mesure de'), *to give some measure of* ('donner une idée de') and *to use sth as a measure of* ('utiliser qch pour mesurer'). To cover the usages of *this is a measure of how* (etc.) the editors worked through the concordance lines and decided to offer two examples of the French *ceci montre à quel point* (etc.), one translating an English adjectival construction (*how dangerous it is*) and one an adverbial construction (*how seriously they are taking the situation*). However, a third French equivalent was needed ('ceci mesure la qualité de gestion de la société') to show that sometimes French uses *mesurer* with a noun object to translate the English phrase *this is a measure of how* (etc.).

The third usage of *a measure of* was fortunately simpler to translate, and sense 2 of the entry in Fig. 3 shows a straightforward translation ('mesure *f*') for the sense that appears in the corpus examples *a measure of fresh goat's milk* and *a good measure of cider*.

Ordering the concordance lines according to the word before the headword ('sorting on left context') highlighted other phrases and idioms for the editors: it was clear, for instance that the phrase *for good measure* was extremely common (Fig. 2 shows some of the 22 examples). The French editor's instinct was to translate it simply by *pour faire bonne mesure*, but even in such apparently straightforward cases the editors carry out routine checks. The translation offered must be adequate for all the contexts in which the English phrase is found, and the editors must satisfy themselves that the French equivalent phrase appears in very similar contexts, i.e. that it does not have a much wider scope, or a much narrower one, than the phrase it is being used to translate. Here again, the French corpus was consulted: there were many examples of *pour faire bonne mesure*, and some of them are shown in Fig. 6. In every case the match between the two phrases was perfect, and the simple equivalence was recorded in the IDIOMS section of the dictionary entry.

```
132887       d'un  fort chômage, ajoutant pour faire bonne mesure, comme dans un récent entretien à «l'Express», qu'une
210760             un sac de plastique... Pour faire bonne mesure, des câbles sont noués entre deux blindés pour les
167781               »,</i> conclut-il. Et pour faire bonne mesure, il décrit une situation calédonienne apocalyptique
154828       yeux émerveillés de Lino et, pour faire bonne mesure, ils ont franchi la ligne presque roue dans roue,
269987           vendue dans le commerce. Pour faire bonne mesure, le commerçant avait ajouté le livre d'Henri Charrière
130087       pas été jugé bon» (pas plus, pour faire bonne mesure, que « le film de Michel Deville »,  côté français). </p>
149468           de l'entreprise.»</p> <p>Pour faire bonne mesure, Renault, comme Peugeot, dispose d'un arsenal de
122476                le 1 avril dernier. Pour faire bonne mesure, sa carte de séjour, ainsi que celle de sa femme, n'ont
299698           la maison, le moulin et, pour faire bonne mesure, treize hectares de terrain autour, de la prairie. Et
```

Fig. 6

In many cases, however, there is not such a neat fit—the phrase *beyond measure* (see Fig. 7) is a case in point. There is of course a common French phrase *outre mesure* (see Fig. 8 for some of the examples in the French corpus). The English-speaking editor and her French-speaking counterpart worked carefully through all the examples from both the English and the French corpora, and came to the conclusion that *outre mesure* and *beyond measure* were *faux amis*: *outre mesure* (always found in negative contexts) should never be given as the translation of *beyond measure*. Furthermore, as the editors compared notes and sought translations for the English examples, it became clear that the French equivalent depended on whether the English phrase modified a verb or an adjective. With verbs (*change* and *increase* were selected as typical verbs for the dictionary entry), the French adverb *énormément* was needed, whereas with adjectives (*anxious, beautiful*, and *difficult* are shown in the dictionary), *extrêmement* is required. Further study of the English corpus made it clear that *improve beyond measure* was very common and had to be covered; however, the French equivalent of *improve* (*faire des progrès*) made it impossible to use the adverb *énormément* in this case. The editors therefore decided to include *it has improved beyond measure* as an example in the entry, with its translation *il y a eu d'énormes progrès*.

Was it worth it?

In this discussion of what the corpus brought to our lexicography, we have had time to look at only a very few instances of a process that continued over the whole life of the dictionary: the corpus formed the dictionary entries, shaping them to meet the needs of today's users, highlighting important constructions, exemplifying difficult meanings, focusing attention on common usages, leading the editors to subtle variations of meaning in English and French parallel constructions, helping them to pick out the best and safest translation for the headwords in all their many and varied uses. The corpus inspired us, disciplined us, and guided us through the immensely complex task of analysing over 350,000 words and phrases, and matching them up with their equivalents in the other language. It proved a severe taskmaster, but an inspiring companion, and one that gave the work its unique personality. We are happy that our dictionary should mark the start of a new age of corpus-based bilingual lexicography.

B. T. S. Atkins

```
003401 sus Christ into my life . And I 've been comforted beyond measure . " .PP If only it could be that simple . The rel
117923  upset ; but she had looked strange and distracted beyond measure . Dora hesitated . She was surrounded by people b
113999 rs of Elizabeth Woodville . Shocked and distressed beyond measure , her worst forebodings realized , she blamed her
003401  fastidious Max , within earshot , was embarrassed beyond measure ) and , as a career-woman , had always stressed t
092563 g his 270 &degree ; penalty turn . .PP Exasperated beyond measure , the now balding { wu\3nderkind } threw his cheq
266095  ability to keep a secret appears to have improved beyond measure over the past two years . Recent rights issues ,
052886 PP But in his year as champion Edberg has improved beyond measure . He always felt his reaching the final in Paris
266095  ability to keep a secret appears to have improved beyond measure over the past two years . Recent rights issues ,
288577 here before six . Get back to bed ! '/'' Irritated beyond measure at the inefficiency of the beat system , Bragg ma
```

Fig. 7

```
053129           Gérard Peyrefitte ne s'inquiète pas outre mesure.</p> <p>«J'étais fou de rage à l'issue du match,
064998       revanche, ne semblaient pas l'inquiéter outre mesure. C'est pourtant sur ce dossier qu'il voit sa "méthode"
224913     d'urgence n'a pas impressionné  M. Mandela outre mesure. «De Klerk a levé un obstacle aux négociations. Il en
148895       L'opinion belge n'en serait pas étonnée outre mesure : elle a l'habitude des atermoiements et des compromis
193211            classique, pas de quoi s'émouvoir outre mesure. En revanche, lundi, au coeur de la nuit, ils ont
176576         »</i>. Mais Mitterrand ne semble pas outre mesure inquiet sur l'issue de la bataille : <i>« J'ai
189444         l'affaire » ne semble pas intéresser outre mesure la police judiciaire. « C'est une histoire d'écoutes et
219888         de sauver la face, sans compromettre outre mesure la suite du processus de paix amorcé par les Américains.
121239        qui ne devrait toutefois pas retarder outre mesure le bouclage de son dossier.</p> <p>Au-delà de son
016947           quelque peu surprise n'émeut pas outre mesure les dirigeants. Si la défense, en effet, a joué à son
267694        petite bataille navale, sans émouvoir outre mesure lesdits marchés.</p><p> En Europe, les tensions
235194      alors il n'y a pas lieu de s'inquiéter outre mesure,  -  ou bien elle a été ordonnée « parce que le roi
143712           Sureau ne semble pas s'angoisser outre mesure sur le succès de <i>l'Indépendance à l'épreuve</i>, son
```

Fig. 8

```
010989       leurs livraisons de céréales. La mesure a été un échec complet. Les paysans n'ont pas fait confiance
132887      velier est un ancien banquier, il mesure à des petits riens, (un cachet revu largement à la hausse,
210660 à l'OIC la proposition d'étendre cette mesure à l'ensemble des pays producteurs a été battue en brèche,
094566   est intervenu ensuite en étendant la mesure à tout le pays. Une décision dictée simplement par
210006  la première mise en application d'une mesure arrêtée en décembre 1989, "visant à faciliter la constitution
361841     Sud était et reste, dans une large mesure, artificielle, d'autant qu'elle enveloppe des gens, Magyars
010989      pour ces derniers, le refus d'une mesure aussi radicale que la rupture des relations diplomatiques ne
632122      llations imposantes, sans commune mesure avec ce qui vient d'être réalisé. Il y a un an environ, les
216174        coût économique proprement dit. Mesure aveugle et aléatoire, fondée sur le seul critère d'âge, la
361841   mot "invasion" et, dans une certaine mesure, celui de l'expression "droit du sang" (contenue dans
267641         américain. Le maintien de cette mesure compromet la tenue de la huitième conférence sur le sida, à
514058        "Les gens ne sont pas encore en mesure d'assumer leur liberté avec un esprit de responsabilité"
201887      compagnie déclare qu'elle sera en mesure d'assurer "la quasi-totalité des vols", dont
149468      professionnel. Vous serez donc en mesure d'échafauder de nouveaux plans, ou d'examiner à fond les
216174         mais aucun officiel n'était en mesure d'indiquer l'heure à laquelle elle serait faite. La
130087    un autre monde que la poésie est en mesure d'opérer grâce à la métaphore. L'assimilation de la poésie
167781   répercussions sur l'emploi sont à la mesure de cette désintégration de l'appareil productif. Aujourd'hui,
291422       doit, selon ces experts, être en mesure de contenir la croissance effrénée du pays. Mais, pour le
299698          la société. Personne n'est en mesure de dessiner une évolution future. "Nous avons déjà survécu à
132887    fois, les experts de l'OCDE sont en mesure de donner une évaluation, en pourcentage du produit intérieur
632122  parfaitement claire". Il pense qu'une mesure de faveur serait justifiée." La constance de ce soutien
053129        espionnage et de subversion". Une mesure de grâce à leur égard serait une manifestation "de la
235194          humanitaires du Nord donne la mesure de l'aggravation sensible de la situation militaire dans ces
219888     fait pour que le contenu soit à la mesure de l'emballage. Selon certaines sources bien informées à
175576              désespéré. Pour prendre la mesure de l'événement, il ne suffit pas de relever - comme l'a fait
224193    le quotidien d'Agen, avait donné la mesure de l'événement: sur trente joueurs retenus pour la prochaine
143712      francs) mais le résultat est à la mesure de l'investissement. La Catalogne dispose désormais d'un
016947        poésie de pureté qui prend la mesure de la condition humaine sans complaisance et sans illusion.
147896     Mais, dès ce moment, on a pris la mesure de la fragilité, de l'émotivité du garde des sceaux. Dès ce
852698     de guerre. Et leur riposte fut à la mesure de la provocation : le Liban fut soumis à un blocus général.
145879  dont le fatalisme est sans doute à la mesure de leur impuissance à peser sur les événements. La
548963     qui leur permettrait de prendre la mesure de leur nouvel univers et de tester leurs choix. Plus
219888          Aujourd'hui personne n'est en mesure de préciser quels "problèmes" n'avaient pas été réglés
193211     déchaînés hier en Italie et aucune mesure de protection n'a été prise contre les tifosis hollandais,
299698         été violée ? Personne n'est en mesure de répondre. Plus gravement, de qui viendront des
132998    de la Haute Cour est en tout cas la mesure de rétorsion la plus dure prise à l'encontre d'un syndicat
010987   décision sans précédent, décidée par mesure de sécurité après la découverte dans un supermarché de la
365531          et affiche un dynamisme à la mesure de ses ambitions européennes. Hausse de l'activité globale de
216174     pour qu'il puisse donner la pleine mesure de ses talents. Peut-être est-ce pour cela qu'il se
456365    antique et se demandait dans quelle mesure de telles normes étaient utiles pour la littérature de son
201887  ce dernier ne serait peut-être pas en mesure de tenir ses promesses. Le calcul inverse l'a visiblement
362122 en homme de parti, je suis un homme de mesure, de tolérance et d'ouverture (...). Il faut que nous soyons
154426      du Nord. Puis nous avions pris la mesure des restructurations nécessaires de l'appareil productif, et
158954    Le maire se défend d'avoir pris une mesure discriminatoire à l'encontre de la population immigrée que
210760  à l'autre de la ville et, au fur et à mesure du morcellement du pays, d'une région à l'autre. Aujourd'hui,
299698    De même que l'immobilité donnait la mesure du mouvement, de même la nature doit partir d'un état de
132887 bronzé plus vous êtes protégé. Dans la mesure du possible, essayez de prendre des couleurs avant de prendre
130087    belge n'en serait pas étonnée outre mesure : elle a l'habitude des atermoiements et des compromis lents
122476     chaque noyau cellulaire, le génome mesure en tout 1,5 mètre - où se trouve, chez les personnes atteintes
210760         Un phénomène étrange dont on mesure encore mal les conséquences. Ce tableau assez noir
526430      où on nous pose des questions sur mesure." Enfin, du côté des médias, l'écho semble plus positif
361841   Discussion (10 points) . Dans quelle mesure estimez-vous que le rôle du journaliste consiste, comme le
269987         La perfection de la phrase, sa mesure exacte, l'enchaînement des répliques et leur phrasé, les
325430         Il avait toutefois réagi avec mesure et avait paru plus s'intéresser à la répartition des
156324 l'élégance de son style, le goût de la mesure et des formes brèves (contes, nouvelles), son anti-
053129  Bourse de Paris. L'indice CAC 40, qui mesure l'évolution des cours des quarante plus grandes valeurs de la
216174     dans le commerce. Pour faire bonne mesure, le commerçant avait ajouté le livre d'Henri Charrière
201887  le mark, le yen et, dans une certaine mesure, le franc suisse). Seule une monnaie européenne pourra
094556   de résoudre ou de ramener à sa juste mesure le problème, ou simplement de vivre avec lui. Chacun, dans ce
224913         corrélé à un magnétomètre qui mesure les variations du champs magnétique naturel. "Le problème,
189444  dur qu'archaïque. Vingt ans après, on mesure mieux pourquoi en France il a fallu que le neuf s'avance
210006    confie : "c'est fondamental dans la mesure où cela remet en question la fiabilité des expertises
130087      naturelle qui est en soi. Dans la mesure où cette curiosité n'existe pas, lire devient un acte
167781      ce n'est pas une surprise dans la mesure où des chiffres de cet ordre circulaient depuis un moment,
210760   pas positif mais insuffisant dans la mesure où elle laisse en suspens des questions importantes"
269987         On pardonnera ce culot dans la mesure où il permet de mettre sur le marché un commentaire inédit
143712 de la rédaction de ces livres. Dans la mesure où il peut lutter contre l'assoupissement, le lecteur notera
598751    d'un texte "éminemment grave dans la mesure où il touche à la loi sur la liberté de la presse, où il
176576     parties, rarement quatre). Dans la mesure où il y a des sous-parties, on doit aller à la ligne. Le
299698 place du mobilier. Un déménagement sur mesure, où l'entreprise peut aller jusqu'à vous construire une
365531   Cet amalgame est intolérable dans la mesure où la Cour de cassation s'est bornée à constater qu'en ce qui
148895  ont dû rester confidentielles dans la mesure où la loi interdit la publication de sondages pendant la
216174 'univers sous un jour nouveau. Dans la mesure où la science est le produit de l'humanité, l'homme prend
361481  centrale vétuste mais décente dans la mesure où les détenus sont seuls ou au pire à deux par cellule
010987 stipule que la Communauté agit dans la mesure où les objectifs "peuvent" être mieux réalisés au niveau
210006  ne conduisent au dérapage que dans la mesure où notre système de santé échappe complètement à la
```

Extract from the French corpus (*continues overleaf*)

016947 né et que je vis à Ouessant, je ne mesure pas mon bonheur par rapport à ceux qui sont à la ville
143712 absence de règles...). Une pilule sur mesure permettant une contraception adaptée à chacune. TABAC et
169589 scientifique s'estompe. Le mérite se mesure plus à la fidélité politique qu'à la compétence. Cette
130087 est aisément démontrable. La deuxième mesure porte sur l'aggravation des peines encourues. Désormais, les
235194 dernier dans la SFIM (instruments de mesure pour le militaire et l'aéronautique). Parallèlement, sa
259862 de pente 1,0: aux incertitudes de mesure près, ceci est tout à fait en accord avec la relation de
267641 La science, dans une certaine mesure, propose des certitudes, mais le savoir qu'elle engendre
019684 Il n'est pourtant pas sûr qu'une telle mesure puisse influer sur les cours du baril, comme cela pouvait
147986 commentaire. Les autres candidats, à mesure qu'ils ont moins de chances d'être élus, doivent se rabattre
154426 Ferrari ne pouvait donner sa pleine mesure que dans un châssis conçu et réalisé dans les locaux de la
125987 les risques d'explosion augmentent à mesure que diminue l'espoir d'une solution politique, estime
147895 cette volonté ne peut que s'affirmer à mesure que l'Allemagne retrouvera sa souveraineté. Si l'on y ajoute
132887 et le poisson se font plus rares à mesure que l'on descend dans la hiérarchie sociale". Un art de faire
158954 par rapport à l'ensemble national. A mesure que le chômage baisse, l'importance relative de ce projet
299698 de rock-star overdosée. Au fur et à mesure que les fans vous oublient, vous descendez d'un cran dans la
154896 Gorbatchev en octobre, est en panne. A mesure que les semaines passent, il devient de moins en moins
362122 de la NASA qui a été brisée. Car, à mesure que se précisaient les causes techniques de la catastrophe,
167781 officiellement de ses fonctions. Une mesure qui ne modifie pas la situation puisque, de fait, faute
130087 Afin de garder le sens de la mesure, retenons ce dernier terme. Une "bande", donc, avec ses
361841 Toutefois, une telle mesure risquerait d'apparaître paradoxale, voire "anti-pédagogique"
216174 que l'administration a dans une large mesure satisfaite par la signature du traité de commerce. M.
224913 Compte-tenu des incertitudes de mesure sur la détermination du volume équivalent et ne devant être
210760 et la fiscalité, dans une moindre mesure sur le commerce extérieur. Avec plus ou moins de bonheur
132887 mobilisés cette semaine pour que la mesure sur les fermetures d'usine soit conservée jusqu'au bout.
852698 sera unifié à 34%. A souligner : cette mesure touche toutes les entreprises, grandes ou petites. Mais pour
219888 ils vous on préparé un cocktail sur mesure : une pincée de poudre d'escampette, une bonne dose d'énergie
189444 doute attentif à ne pas prendre une mesure unilatérale de désarmement nucléaire. Le fait que le missile
365531 MON CONSEIL. Gardez le sens de la mesure. VIERGE DU 24 AOUT AU 23 SEPTEMBRE. Mercure. COEUR. Les soupçons
130087 ou des intellectuels et juger des mesures à court, à moyen et à long terme, qui s'imposent,
526430 il est difficile de prendre des mesures à l'égard d'un problème qui est censé ne pas exister." Tout
193211 ont présenté des rapports sur les mesures à prendre pour éviter que les inégalités ne se creusent. M.
053129 j'entends les réactions hostiles aux mesures anti-tabac prises par M. Evin (bravo pour votre courage,
154426 vous renationaliserez ? Quelles mesures concrètes comptez-vous prendre pour assurer le financement de
210760 que le ministre vient d'annoncer des mesures concrètes, pour cet automne, visant à améliorer le
132887 du marché et éventuellement décider de mesures correctives afin de redresser les cours, a annoncé l'agence
526430 en effet dans le financement des mesures d'âge qui accompagnent les opérations de licenciement
156324 avec M. Chevardnadze, une série de mesures d'aide économique à l'URSS, dont une garantie de crédits
132887 positions, à savoir l'annulation des mesures d'austérité décidées par le gouvernement et l'organisation
143712 déficit laisse supposer que de simples mesures d'économie ne suffiront pas. On risque de déboucher sur une
193211 est "donc prématuré de prononcer des mesures d'expulsion à l'encontre de diplomates iraniens". (AFP)
269879 qu'il était nécessaire de prendre des mesures d'urgence pour préserver l'intégrité de l'État fédéral sur
159684 premier pas dans le renforcement des mesures de contrôle du ministère des finances. Certes, l'amendement
132887 Mais il est possible que d'autres mesures de protection des sociétés françaises soient dans le tuyau,
094556 Par cette déclaration, j'annonce nos mesures de réciprocité et nos contre-propositions."
158954 premiers effets, encore limités, des mesures de restructuration mises en oeuvre depuis novembre 1990"
210760 Le protectionnisme conduit à des mesures de rétorsion et met en danger la croissance mondiale. La
216174 un secret à peu près total entoure les mesures de sécurité. "C'est un sujet dont les Coréens n'aiment pas à
201887 d'enlèvement grâce à la police. Les mesures de sécurité ont été renforcées dans la nuit de mardi à
010989 japonais pendant des mois. Ces mesures de soutien ne font que renforcer la structure déjà très
365531 Un problème d'interprétation de mesures déjà rencontré dans la pyramide de Chéops. C'est en grande
224913 du massacre, si l'on ne prend pas de mesures drastiques, il n'y aura plus de dauphins d'ici quelques
156324 ailleurs." Et de recommander des "mesures économiques et budgétaires adaptées à la situation du
361841 de communication sur les nouvelles mesures en faveur de l'emploi. Le bilan de l'année écoulée est
147896 réseaux de communication ; plusieurs mesures en faveur du logement, de l'urbanisation et du développement
167781 internationale, "deux poids, deux mesures" entre Israël et l'Irak. La présidence égyptienne, dans un
132998 priorité. La première série de mesures envisagées porte sur l'élaboration de documents, écrits et
632122 et économiques et à adopter des mesures favorables au libre échange. -B- Le PNB Définition Le Produit
132998 du Budget 1992 comprend une série de mesures fiscales en faveur des investisseurs et des particuliers.
176576 volonté ne se traduit pas que par des mesures financières. Bien sûr, je n'en fais grief à personne. Ce
325430 compétitivité des entreprises par des mesures horizontales (type fiscalité de l'investissement, autre
122476 il s'est vu contraint de prendre des mesures impopulaires. Mercredi dernier, quelque deux cents
145879 son gouvernement de prendre toutes les mesures nécessaires à la mobilisation des forces de défense de la
299698 de l'alternance. Cinq autres mesures ont pour objectif de développer l'alternance comme
219888 au gouvernement fédéral de prendre des mesures pour augmenter la consommation et l'investissement.
130087 va s'améliorer en 1992 ; les mesures pour l'emploi vont donner des droits dans la seconde partie
010987 Le ministère de la santé annonce des mesures pour remédier à cette situation anormale. Après avoir
148895 a par ailleurs mis au point des mesures pour renforcer la sécurité des installations britanniques
526430 qui permettent de prendre des mesures préventives lorsque la paix civile est menacée. Parmi elle
291422 pouvoirs publics ayant multiplié les mesures propres à limiter cette hausse, dans le but de faciliter le
852698 des pays sont tentés de recourir à des mesures protectionnistes. Mais, pour concilier leur adhésion au
167781 pays de l'ornière, il doit prendre des mesures radicales et donc impopulaires. Mais il hésite, devant
158904 L'objectif était de renforcer les mesures sanitaires pour assurer une meilleure protection des
299698 sera publié, il prendra en compte les mesures sociales prises par l'actuel gouvernement (RMI, crédit-
219888 du plan Bush, propose en outre des mesures sur les armes nucléaires tactiques aéroportées. Or, il
.016947 nous sommes obligés d'appliquer les mesures telles qu'elles existent. L'homosexualité, pour les
235194 la SNCF a donc annoncé trois séries de mesures. Tout d'abord, une réduction du nombre des embauches (4000

Extract from the French corpus (*continued*)

Using this dictionary

Each entry in the dictionary is organized hierarchically, by grammatical category, then sense category. Grammatical categories are always in the same order. In the English–French part of the dictionary, the rule is that if the word has a use as an irregular inflected form, like the entry *left* for example, this will come first. Next will come the noun category, if there is one, then the adjective, then the adverb. Verbs, idioms, and phrasal verbs come last, in that order. The way the entry *kindly* is constructed is shown in the diagram below. To translate *he thought kindly of her*, you would go through the steps shown on the right. The section that follows gives other examples of how to get the best out of the dictionary for various kinds of translation task.

As a general rule, all meanings of a word are to be found in one single entry, provided they are pronounced in the same way, exclusive of stress shifts. English compounds have their own place in the alphabetical order of the dictionary, either as separate entries or, where several fall together in the alphabet, grouped together under the first element.

The French–English entries follow a similar sequence, but adjectives precede nouns and non-hyphenated compounds appear together in a separate category at the end of the entry. French hyphenated compounds are given separate-entry status. On both sides of the dictionary, the order of sense categories reflects frequency of use, the most commonly used coming first. Within sense categories, distinctions between alternative translations are shown by means of sense indicators in round brackets and/or collocates giving typical context, which appear in square brackets.

1 **kindly** /ˈkaɪndlɪ/ **I** *adj* [*person, nature*] gentil/-ille; [*smile, interest*] bienveillant; [*voice*] plein de gentillesse; [*face*] sympathique; **she's a ~ soul** elle est très gentille.
2 **II** *adv* **1** (in a kind, nice way) [*speak, look, treat*] avec gentillesse; **to speak ~ of sb** avoir un mot gentil pour qn; **thank you ~†** tous mes remerciements; **2** (obligingly) gentiment; **she ~ agreed to do** elle a gentiment accepté de faire; **would you ~ do/refrain from doing** auriez-vous l'amabilité de faire/de ne pas faire; **'would visitors ~ do', 'visitors are ~ requested to do'**
3 GB 'les visiteurs sont priés de faire'; **3** (fa-
4 vourably) **to look ~ on** approuver [*activity*];
5 **to think ~ of** avoir une bonne opinion de [*person*]; **to take ~ to** apprécier [*idea, suggestion, person*]; **I don't think he'll take ~ to being kept waiting** je ne crois pas qu'il va apprécier qu'on le fasse attendre.

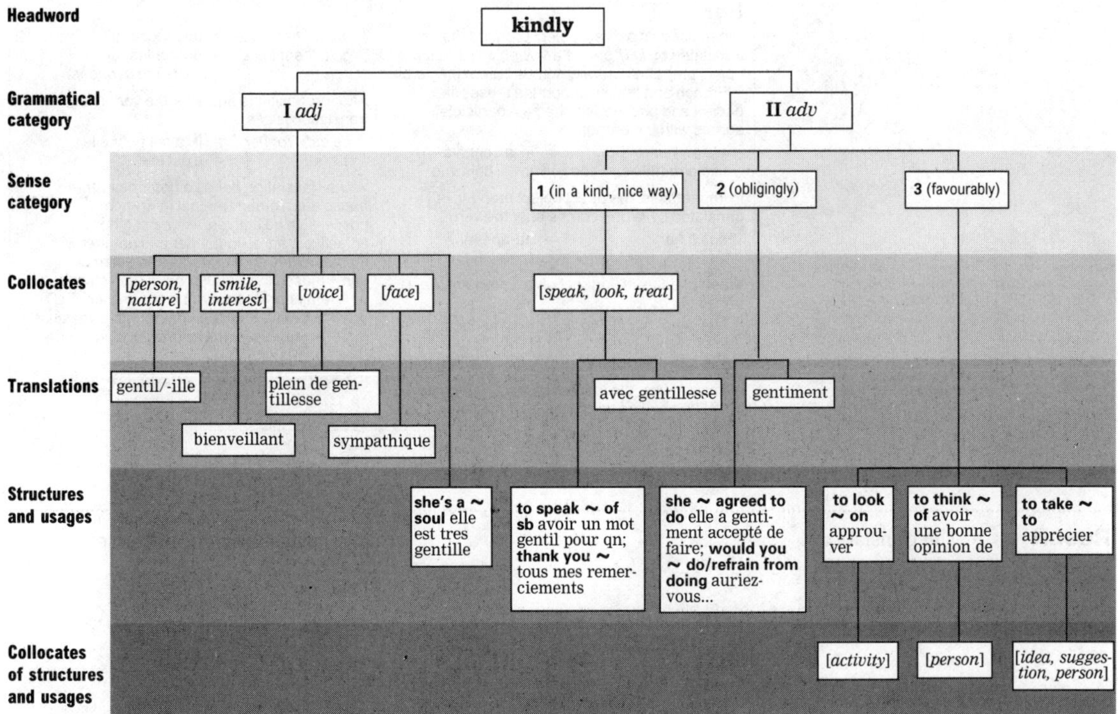

Goal 1 Translate — he treated her kindly

Process

1 Identify the problem word or phrase.

kindly

2 Look up *kindly* and choose the appropriate grammatical category.

II *adv*

kindly /ˈkaɪndlɪ/ **I** *adj* [*person, nature*] gentil/-ille; [*smile, interest*] bienveillant; [*voice*] plein de gentillesse; [*face*] sympathique; **she's a ~ soul** elle est très gentille.
II *adv* **1** (in a kind, nice way) [*speak, look, treat*] avec gentillesse; **to speak ~ of sb**

3 Choose the appropriate sense category.

1 (in a kind, nice way)

II *adv* **1** (in a kind, nice way) [*speak, look, treat*] avec gentillesse; **to speak ~ of sb** avoir un mot gentil pour qn; **thank you ~†** tous mes remerciements; **2** (obligingly) gentiment; **she ~ agreed to do** elle a gentiment accepté de faire; **would you ~ do/refrain from doing** auriez-vous l'amabilité de faire/de ne pas faire; **'would visitors ~ do', 'visitors are ~ requested to do'** GB 'les visiteurs sont priés de faire'; **3** (favourably) **to look ~ on** approuver [*activity*]; **to think ~ of** avoir une bonne opinion de

4 Choose the most appropriate collocate or phrase included in the sense.

treat

II *adv* **1** (in a kind, nice way) [*speak, look, treat*] avec gentillesse; **to speak ~ of sb** avoir un mot gentil pour qn; **thank you ~†** tous mes remerciements; **2** (obligingly) gentiment; **she ~ agreed to do** elle a

5 Note the translation.

avec gentillesse

II *adv* **1** (in a kind, nice way) [*speak, look, treat*] **avec gentillesse**; **to speak ~ of sb** avoir un mot gentil pour qn; **thank you**

6 If necessary look up *treat* in the same way and *her* in the special grammatical note box, near the normal entry for *her*.

her

When used as a direct object pronoun, *her* is translated by *la* (*l'* before a vowel). Note that the object pronoun normally comes before the verb in French and that in compound tenses like perfect and past perfect the past participle agrees with the pronoun:

I know her	= je la connais
I've already seen her	= je l'ai déjà vue

In imperatives, the direct object pronoun is translated by *la* and comes after the verb:

catch her!	= attrape-la! (*note the hyphen*)

When used as an indirect object pronoun, *her* is translated by *lui*:

I've given her the book	= je lui ai donné le livre
I've given it to her	= je le lui ai donné

In imperatives, the indirect object pronoun is translated by *lui* and comes after the verb:

phone her	= téléphone-lui
give them to her	= donne-les-lui (*note the hyphens*)

After prepositions and after the verb *to be* the translation is *elle*:

he did it for her	= il l'a fait pour elle
it's her	= c'est elle

When translating *her* as a determiner (*her house* etc.) remember that in French possessive adjectives, like most other adjectives, agree in gender and number with the noun they qualify; *her* is translated by *son* + masculine singular noun (*son chien*), *sa* + feminine singular noun (*sa maison*) BUT *son* + feminine noun beginning with a vowel or mute 'h' (*son assiette*), and *ses* + plural noun (*ses enfants*).

For *her* used with parts of the body ▶ **1037**

Note the information on agreement.

Result The translation — il l'a traitée avec gentillesse

Goal 2 Translate *a sophisticated nightclub* in the phrase

they spent the rest of the evening in a sophisticated nightclub in Mayfair

Process

1 Look up *nightclub*. English compounds appear in alphabetical order in the wordlist.

~ club

nightcap /ˈnaɪtkæp/ *n* **1** (hat) bonnet *m* de nuit; **2** (drink) **to have a ~** boire quelque chose (avant d'aller se coucher).
night: **~clothes** *npl* vêtements *mpl* pour la nuit; **~club** *n* boîte *f* de nuit.
nightclubbing *n* **to go ~** aller en boîte○.
night: **~dress** *n* chemise *f* de nuit; **~ editor** *n* Journ rédacteur/-trice *m/f* de nuit.
nightfall /ˈnaɪtfɔːl/ *n* tombée *f* de la nuit; **at**

2 Note the translation.

boîte *f* de nuit

Note the usage information in italics. '*f*' indicates feminine gender.

night: **~clothes** *npl* vêtements *mpl* pour la nuit; **~club** *n* **boîte *f* de nuit**.
nightclubbing *n* **to go ~** aller en boîte○.

3 Look up *sophisticated* and select the most appropriate numbered sense category.

1 (smart)

sophisticated /səˈfɪstɪkeɪtɪd/ *adj* **1** **(smart)** [*person*] (worldly, cultured) raffiné, sophistiqué pej; (elegant) chic *inv*; [*clothes, fashion*] recherché; [*restaurant, resort*] chic *inv*; [*magazine*] sophistiqué; **she thinks it's ~ to smoke** elle pense que ça fait chic de fumer; **she was looking very ~ in black** elle était très chic en noir; **2** (discriminating) [*mind, taste*] raffiné; [*audience, public*] averti; **a book for the more ~ student** un livre pour les étudiants plus avancés; **3** (advanced) [*civilization*] évolué; **4** (elaborate, complex)

4 Look for the noun collocate, in square brackets, which is closest to your context.

restaurant

sophisticated /səˈfɪstɪkeɪtɪd/ *adj* **1** (smart) [*person*] (worldly, cultured) raffiné, sophistiqué pej; (elegant) chic *inv*; [*clothes, fashion*] recherché; [***restaurant***, *resort*] chic *inv*; [*magazine*] sophistiqué; **she thinks it's ~ to smoke**

5 Note the translation.

chic

[*person*] (worldly, cultured) raffiné, sophistiqué pej; (elegant) chic *inv*; [*clothes, fashion*] recherché; [*restaurant, resort*] **chic** *inv*; [*magazine*] sophistiqué; **she thinks it's ~ to smoke**

6 Note the usage information in italics.

inv

This means that the form of adjective *chic* does not change in the feminine or the plural.

[*person*] (worldly, cultured) raffiné, sophistiqué pej; (elegant) chic *inv*; [*clothes, fashion*] recherché; [*restaurant, resort*] chic ***inv***; [*magazine*] sophistiqué; **she thinks it's ~ to smoke**

Result The translation of the whole sentence

ils ont fini la soirée dans une boîte de nuit chic de Mayfair

Goal 3		Translate	it's natural for her to want to stay
Process	**1**	Look up *natural* and choose the appropriate grammatical category. **II** *adj*	**natural** /ˈnætʃrəl/ **I** *n* **1**○ (person) **as an actress, she's a ~** c'est une actrice née; **he's a ~ for the role of Hamlet** il est fait pour jouer Hamlet; **2** Mus (sign) bécarre *m*; (note) note *f* naturelle; **3**‡ (simpleton) imbécile *mf*. **II** *adj* **1** (not artificial or man-made) [*phenomenon, force, disaster, harbour, light, resources, process, progression, beauty, material, food*] naturel/-elle; **the ~ world** le monde natu-
	2	Choose the most appropriate numbered sense category. **2** (usual, normal)	**II** *adj* **1** (not artificial or man-made) [*phenomenon, force, disaster, harbour, light, resources, process, progression, beauty, material, food*] naturel/-elle; **the ~ world** le monde naturel; **in its ~ state** à l'état naturel; **2** (usual, normal) naturel/-elle, normal; **it's ~ to do/to be** c'est normal de faire/d'être; **it's ~ for sb to do** c'est normal que qn fasse; **the ~ thing to do would be to protest** la chose la plus normale serait de protester; **it's only ~** c'est tout à fait naturel; **it's not ~!** ce n'est pas normal!; **to die of ~ causes** mourir de mort naturelle or de sa belle mort; **death from ~ causes** Jur mort naturelle; **for the rest of one's ~ life** Jur à vie; **3** (innate) [*gift, talent, emotion, trait*] inné; [*artist, professional, storyteller*] né; [*affinity*] naturel/-elle; **a ~ advantage** (of person, party, country) un atout; **4** (unaffected) [*person, manner*] simple, naturel/-elle; **try**
	3	Look for the basic structure you need. **it's ~ for sb to do**	normal) naturel/-elle, normal; **it's ~ to do/to be** c'est normal de faire/d'être; **it's ~ for sb to do** c'est normal que qn fasse; **the ~ thing to do would be to protest** la
	4	Note the translation. c'est normal que qn fasse	normal) naturel/-elle, normal; **it's ~ to do/to be** c'est normal de faire/d'être; **it's ~ for sb to do** c'est normal que qn fasse; **the ~ thing to do would be to protest** la
	5	Use the translation of the basic structure to translate your sentence, noting that *fasse* is a subjunctive. If you are unsure about the conjugation of the irregular verb *vouloir*, look it up in the French verb tables at the back of the dictionary.	
Result		The translation	c'est normal qu'elle veuille rester

Goal 4 Translate — things were going according to plan

Process

1 Identify the problem word or phrase.

according to plan

2 Look up *plan* and select the appropriate grammatical category.

I *n*

plan /plæn/ **I** *n* **1** (scheme, course of action) plan *m*; **to draw up a six-point ~** dresser un plan en six points; **a ~ of action/of campaign** un plan d'action/de campagne; **the ~ is to leave very early** nous avons prévu de partir très tôt; **the best ~ would be to stay here** le mieux serait de rester ici; **everything went according to ~** tout s'est passé comme prévu; **2** (definite aim) projet *m* (**for** de; **to do** pour faire); **to have a ~ to do** projeter de faire; **3** Archit, Constr, Tech plan *m* (**of** de); **4** (rough outline) (of essay, book) plan *m*; **make a ~ before you start**

3 Scan the sense categories and select the most appropriate one.

1 (scheme, course of action)

plan /plæn/ **I** *n* **1** (scheme, course of action) plan *m*; **to draw up a six-point ~** dresser un plan en six points; **a ~ of action/of campaign** un plan d'action/de campagne; **the ~ is to leave very early** nous avons prévu de partir très tôt; **the best ~ would be to**

4 You know that *to go according to plan* is a fixed expression in English, so you expect to find it in the entry.

everything went according to ~

~ is to leave very early nous avons prévu de partir très tôt; **the best ~ would be to stay here** le mieux serait de rester ici; **everything went according to ~** tout s'est passé comme prévu; **2** (definite aim) projet *m* (**for** de; **to do** pour faire); **to have**

5 Identify the translation.

tout s'est passé comme prévu

~ is to leave very early nous avons prévu de partir très tôt; **the best ~ would be to stay here** le mieux serait de rester ici; **everything went according to ~** **tout s'est passé comme prévu**; **2** (definite aim) projet *m* (**for** de; **to do** pour faire); **to have**

6 Manipulate the translation to suit your context.

Result The translation of the sentence — les choses se passaient comme prévu

Goal 5 Translate — the police have sealed off the area

Process

1 *Seal off* is a phrasal verb, so go to the end of the entry *seal* where you will find the phrasal verbs listed in alphabetical order, each verb clearly signalled by a square bullet.

■ seal off

V sealed *pp adj* [*envelope*] cacheté; [*package*] scellé; [*bid, instructions, orders*] sous pli cacheté; [*jar*] fermé hermétiquement; [*door, vault*] scellé.
■ **seal in** conserver [*flavour*].
■ **seal off**: ~ [sth] off, ~ off [sth] **1** (isolate) isoler [*corridor, wing*]; **2** (cordon off) boucler [*area, building*]; barrer [*street*].
■ **seal up**: ~ [sth] up, ~ up [sth] fermer [qch] hermétiquement [*jar*]; boucher [*gap*].

2 Look for the appropriate phrasal verb pattern.

~ [sth] off, ~ off [sth]

■ **seal off**: ~ [sth] off, ~ off [sth] **1** (isolate) isoler [*corridor, wing*]; **2** (cordon off) boucler [*area, building*]; barrer [*street*].

3 Select the appropriate sense category of the phrasal verb pattern.

2 (cordon off)

■ **seal off**: ~ [sth] off, ~ off [sth] **1** (isolate) isoler [*corridor, wing*]; **2** (cordon off) boucler [*area, building*]; barrer [*street*].

4 Select the appropriate collocate showing context for the translation, in this case typical objects of the verb translations.

area

■ **seal off**: ~ [sth] off, ~ off [sth] **1** (isolate) isoler [*corridor, wing*]; **2** (cordon off) boucler [***area**, building*]; barrer [*street*].

5 Identify the appropriate translation.

boucler

■ **seal off**: ~ [sth] off, ~ off [sth] **1** (isolate) isoler [*corridor, wing*]; **2** (cordon off) **boucler** [*area, building*]; barrer [*street*].

6 If necessary, look up *area* and select the appropriate translation.

quartier *m*

area /ˈeərɪə/ **I** *n* **1** (region) (of land) région *f*; (of sky) zone *f*; (of city) zone *f*; (district) **quartier** *m*; **in the London/Paris ~** dans la région de Londres/de Paris; **residential/rural/slum ~** zone *f* rési-

7 Now construct the translation of the sentence, putting the verb in the correct tense and person.

Result The translation — la police a bouclé le quartier

Goal 6 Translate the sentence *Et quel est l'enjeu commercial?* in this text (taken from an article discussing a large company's advertising strategy).

Mais combien de gens, choqués, se détourneront de la marque et combien de gens, conquis, s'en éprendront? Et quel est l'enjeu commercial?

Process

1 Identify the word or words causing problems of translation.

enjeu

2 Will the word appear in this form in the dictionary? Yes, because it is clearly a noun and not in the plural.

enjeu

enjeu, *pl* **~x** /ɑ̃ʒø/ *nm* **1** Jeux stake; **2** (ce qui est en jeu) what is at stake; **ces programmes seront l'~ de la prochaine bataille** these programmes[GB] will be the focus of the coming battle ou will be what is at stake in the coming battle; **l'~ dépasse maintenant le sort d'une seule personne**

3 Consider the first apparently appropriate translation.

what is at stake

enjeu, *pl* **~x** /ɑ̃ʒø/ *nm* **1** Jeux stake; **2** (ce qui est en jeu) **what is at stake**; **ces programmes seront l'~ de la prochaine bataille** these programmes[GB] will be the

4 If you are unsure about this translation, scan the entry again for a phrase that might help.

un ~ commercial

analyse les ~x des élections the journalist analyses[GB] what is at stake in the elections; **3** (problème) issue; **un ~ économique/politique/commercial** an economic/a political/a commercial issue; **livre consacré aux ~x de l'intelligence artificielle** book devoted to the issues of artificial

5 Note the translation.

a commercial issue

mique/politique/commercial an economic/a political/ commercial issue; **livre consacré aux ~x de l'intelligence artifi-**

6 Which of the two is better? Look at the kind of text you are translating to pick the right phrase. Use your knowledge of your own language to manipulate the phrase to fit the English context.

Result The translation

And what is at stake commercially?

Goal 7 Translate | chat échaudé craint l'eau froide

Process

1 Look up all the words you do not know and find a literal translation. If this does not make sense in your context, ask yourself whether the phrase could be an idiom, saying, or proverb. The answer is yes, because you can see immediately that cats and cold water have no relation to the wider context.

2 Select the word or words that you are least familiar with.

échaudé

3 Will this word appear in this form in the dictionary? No, *échaudé* is part of a verb. Look up the infinitive form.

échauder

échauder /eʃode/ [1] *vtr* **1** (décourager) to put [sb] off; **échaudé par sa première expérience, il décide de**... having had his fingers burned by his first experience, he decides...; **2** (ébouillanter) to scald.
IDIOMES **chat échaudé craint l'eau froide**

4 Look for the phrase in the IDIOMS category.

IDIOMES chat échaudé craint l'eau froide

IDIOMES **chat échaudé craint l'eau froide** Prov once bitten, twice shy Prov.

5 Note the information Prov which tells you that the expression is a proverb in French as its translation is in English.

Prov

decides...; **2** (ébouillanter) to scald.
IDIOMES **chat échaudé craint l'eau froide** Prov once bitten, twice shy Prov.

Result The translation | once bitten, twice shy

Goal 8 Understand the meaning of the acronym *SMIC* in the phrase | ils sont payés au SMIC

Process

1 Look up *SMIC* and follow the indication provided by the arrowed cross-reference.

SME /ɛsɛmə/ *nm*: *abbr* ▶ **système**.
SMIC /smik/ *nm*: *abbr* ▶ **salaire**.
smicard○, **~e** /smikaʀ, aʀd/ *nm,f* person

2 Look up *salaire.*

3 Scan the entry for *SMIC*.
Abbreviations and acronyms will always be in the compound block at the end of the entry.

SMIC

salaire /salɛʀ/ *nm* **1** (paie) salary; (à la journée, à l'heure, à la semaine) (taux) wage; (somme) wages (*pl*); **~ annuel/mensuel** annual/monthly salary; **~ horaire/journalier/hebdomadaire** hourly/daily/weekly wage ou salary; **~ brut/net** gross/take-home pay; **~ au rendement** incentive wages, efficiency wages US; **~ de misère** or **famine** starvation wage; **2** fig (récompense) reward (**de** for); (châtiment) punishment (**de** for).
■ **~ de base** basic salary GB, base pay US; **~ d'embauche** starting salary; **~ minimum interprofessionnel de croissance**, **SMIC** guaranteed minimum wage; **~ unique** single income.

4 Note the full form of the acronym.

salaire minimum interprofessionnel de croissance

US; **~ d'embauche** starting salary; **~ minimum interprofessionnel de croissance**, **SMIC** guaranteed minimum wage; **~ unique** single income.

Result The explanation or, as in this case, the equivalent | guaranteed minimum wage

Structure of Entries

The structure of French–English entries

headword examples part of speech plus gender compounds in block at end of entry idioms in block at end of entry	**bagage** /bagaʒ/ **I** *nm* **1** (effets) luggage; (de soldat) kit; **elle avait un sac pour tout ~** her only luggage was one bag; **envoyer qch en ~ accompagné** to send sth as registered luggage; **2** (sac, valise) piece of luggage; **3** fig (connaissances) knowledge; (diplômes) qualifications (*pl*); (expérience) credentials (*pl*); **avoir un bon/mince ~** to have good/poor qualifications; **il a un excellent ~ de directeur** he has splendid credentials as a manager. **II bagages** *nmpl* (valises, effets) luggage ¢; **faire/défaire ses ~s** to pack/unpack (one's suitcases); **il a amené qn dans ses ~s** fig he's brought sb along with him; **il est toujours dans les ~s du Président** fig the President always takes him along. ■ **~ à main** hand luggage, carry-on baggage US. IDIOMES **plier ~**○ to pack up and go; **partir avec armes et ~s** to up sticks and leave; **se rendre avec armes et ~s** to capitulate; **passer à l'ennemi avec armes et ~s** to defect.	IPA pronunciation uncountable use figurative use swung dash as substitute for headword in examples North American translation
register symbol informal ○ very informal ◑ vulgar or taboo ●	**balader**○ /balade/ [1] **I** *vtr* **1** (à pied) to take [sb] for a walk; (en voiture) to take [sb] for a drive; **je l'ai baladé dans tous les musées** I showed him around all the museums; **2** (emporter avec soi) to carry [sth] around. **II se balader** *vpr* **1** (faire une balade) (à pied) to go for a walk; (plus lent) to go for a stroll; (à moto, vélo) to go for a ride; (en voiture) to go for a drive; **2** (voyager) to travel; **se ~ dans une région** to tour a region; **3** (se déplacer) [*douleur*] to move around; **il y a un écrou qui se balade** there's a loose nut. IDIOMES **envoyer qn ~**○ to send sb packing○; **j'ai envie de tout envoyer ~** I feel like packing everything in○.	Roman grammatical category number Arabic sense number
feminine form of headword	**baladeur, -euse** /baladœʀ, øz/ **I** *adj* [*lampe*] portable. **II** *nm* walkman®, personal stereo. **III baladeuse** *nf* portable lamp. IDIOMES **avoir les mains baladeuses** pej to have wandering hands.	pejorative use
trade mark symbol level of language number of verb group, referring to the French verb tables at the end of the dictionary	**Bison Futé®** /bizɔ̃fyte/ *nm*: ***TV and radio traffic monitoring service.*** **bisou**○ /bizu/ *nm* baby talk kiss; **faire un ~ à qn** to kiss sb, to give sb a kiss; **envoyer des ~s** (avec la main) to blow kisses; (par lettre) to send kisses. **bisque** /bisk/ *nf* Culin bisque. ■ **~ de homard** lobster bisque. **bisquer**○ /biske/ [1] *vi* (enrager) to be mad○, to be furious; **faire ~ qn** to make sb mad○. **bissac** /bisak/ *nm* (huntsman's) pouch. **bissecteur, -trice** /bisɛktœʀ, tʀis/ **I** *adj* [*plan, droite*] bisecting. **II bissectrice** *nf* Math bisector.	explanatory gloss where there is no direct translation equivalent field label IPA pronunciation for feminine form
	BERD /bɛʀd/ *nf*: *abbr* ▶ **banque**. **béret** /beʀɛ/ *nm* beret; **~ basque** Basque beret. **bergamasque** /bɛʀgamask/ *nf* bergamask.	cross-reference

The structure of English–French entries

headword	**mash** /mæʃ/ **I** *n* **1** Agric (for dogs, poultry) pâtée *f*; (for horses) mash *m*; **bran ~** pâtée de son; **2** (in brewing) trempe *f*; **3**○ GB Culin purée *f* (de pommes de terre); **bangers and ~** des saucisses avec de la purée.	Roman grammatical category number Arabic sense numbers
part of speech	**II** *vtr* **1** écraser [*fruit*]; **~ed potatoes/turnips** purée *f* de pommes de terre/de navets; **to ~ potatoes** faire de la purée (de pommes de terre); **2** (in brewing) brasser.	translation
phrasal verb	■ **mash up**: **~ up [sth], ~ [sth] up** écraser [*fruit, potatoes*].	phrasal verb pattern
acronym	**MASH** /mæʃ/ *n* US (*abrév* = **mobile army surgical hospital**) unité *f* médicale de campagne.	
	masher /ˈmæʃə(r)/ *n* (utensil) presse-purée *m inv*.	usage information
IPA pronunciation showing North American variation	**mask** /mɑːsk, US mæsk/ **I** *n* **1** (for face) (for disguise, protection) masque *m*; (at masked ball) loup *m*; **a ~ of indifference** fig un masque d'indifférence; **2** (sculpture) masque *m*; **3** Cosmet **face ~** masque *m*; **4** Electron, Comput masque *m*; **5** Phot cache *m*; **6** Theat masque *m*.	sense indicator
swung dash as substitute for headword in examples		field labels for specialist terms
typical object collocates	**II** *vtr* **1** masquer [*face*]; **2** fig dissimuler [*truth, emotions*]; masquer [*taste*]; **3** Fin déguiser [*losses*]; **4** Phot masquer.	
	mask: **~ed ball** *n* bal *m* masqué; **~ing tape** *n* ruban *m* adhésif.	gender of translation
	MCN *n*: *abrév* ▶ **Micro Cellular Network**.	cross-reference to full form
abbreviation	**MD** *n* **1** Med, Univ (*abrév* = **Doctor of Medicine**) docteur *m* en médecine; **2** US Post *abrév écrite* = **Maryland**; **3** Mgmt (*abrév* = **Managing Director**) directeur *m* général.	
North American usage	**MDT** *n* US *abrév* ▶ **Mountain Daylight Time**.	
North American variant spelling	**meagrely** GB, **meagerly** US /ˈmiːgəlɪ/ *adv* [*eat, live, spread*] chichement.	
	meal /miːl/ *n* **1** (food) repas *m*; **hot/cold/main ~** repas chaud/froid/principal; **they had a ~ in the canteen** ils ont mangé à la cantine; **did you enjoy your ~?** est-ce que vous avez bien mangé?; **to go out for a ~** sortir dîner; **2** (from grain) farine *f*.	examples
idioms in block at end of entry	IDIOMS **don't make a ~ of it**○**!** n'en fais pas tout un plat○!	register symbol ○ informal ◑ very informal ● vulgar or taboo
explanatory gloss for French speaker	**meals on wheels** *n* repas *mpl* (livrés) à domicile (*pour personnes âgées ou handicapées*).	
separate entry for complex compound	**meal ticket** *n* **1** (voucher) ticket-repas *m*; **2**○ fig (quality, qualification) gagne-pain *m*; (person) **I'm just a ~ for you!** pour toi je ne suis qu'un portefeuille!	
compounds in alphabetical order	**meal**: **~time** *n* heure *f* de repas; **~worm** *n* ver *m* de farine.	
	miraculous /mɪˈrækjʊləs/ *adj* **1** (as by miracle) [*cure, escape, recovery, survival*] miraculeux/**-euse**; **2** (great, amazing) [*speed, efficiency etc*] prodigieux/**-ieuse**.	feminine endings in translations
	muscular dystrophy ▶ **1354** *n* dystrophie *f* musculaire.	page number cross-reference to a lexical usage note
	musculature /ˈmʌskjʊlətʃə(r)/ *n* musculature *f*.	
	muse /mjuːz/ **I** *n* muse *f*. **II** *vi* (in silence) songer **(on, over, about** à); (aloud) commenter, l'air songeur.	structures, complementation giving information on how to use the translation

The pronunciation of French

The symbols used in this dictionary for the pronunciation of French are those of the IPA (International Phonetic Alphabet). Certain differences in pronunciation are shown in the phonetic transcription, although many speakers do not observe them—e.g. the long 'a' /ɑ/ in *pâte* and the short 'a' /a/ in *patte*, or the difference between the nasal vowels 'un' /œ̃/ as in *brun* and 'in' /ɛ̃/ as in *brin*.

Transcription
Each entry is followed by its phonetic transcription between slashes, with the following exceptions:

- written abbreviations (*bd, kcal,* etc.)
- cross-references from an inflected to a base form (*yeux, fol*)
- cross-references from a variant spelling to the preferred form (*paraphe/parafe, peinard/pénard, plasticage/plastiquage*).

Alternative pronunciations
Where the speaker has a choice of pronunciations, these are shown in one of the following two ways:

- by the use of brackets e.g. *syllabe* /sil(l)ab/, *déficit* /defisi(t)/
- in full, separated by a comma e.g. *revenir* /ʀəvniʀ, ʀvəniʀ/, *patio* /pasjo, patjo/.

Morphological variations
The phonetic transcription of the plural and feminine forms of certain nouns and adjectives does not repeat the root, but shows only the change in ending. Therefore, in certain cases, the presentation of the entry does not correspond to that of the phonetic transcription e.g. *platonicien, -ienne* /platɔnisjɛ̃, ɛn/.

Phrases
Full phonetic transcription is given for adverbial or prepositional phrases which are shown in alphabetical order within the main headword e.g. *emblée, d'emblée* /dɑ̃ble/, *plain-pied, de plain-pied* /d(ə)plɛ̃pje/.

Consonants
Aspiration of 'h'
Where it is impossible to make a liaison this is indicated by /ˈ/ immediately after the slash e.g. *haine* /ˈɛn/.

Assimilation
A voiced consonant can become unvoiced when it is followed by an unvoiced consonant within a word e.g. *absorption* /apsɔʀpsjɔ̃/.

Vowels
Open 'e' and closed 'e'
A clear distinction is made at the end of a word between a closed 'e' and an open 'e' e.g. *pré* /pʀe/ and *près* /pʀɛ/, *complet* /kɔ̃plɛ/ and *combler* /kɔ̃ble/.

Within a word the following rules apply:

- 'e' is always open in a syllable followed by a syllable containing a mute 'e' e.g. *règle* /ʀɛgl/, *réglementaire* /ʀɛgləmɑ̃tɛʀ/
- in careful speech 'e' is pronounced as a closed 'e' when it is followed by a syllable containing a closed vowel (*y, i, e*) e.g. *pressé* /pʀese/
- 'e' is pronounced as an open 'e' when it is followed by a syllable containing an open vowel e.g. *pressant* /pʀɛsɑ̃/.

Mute 'e'
The pronunciation of mute 'e' varies considerably depending on the level of language used and on the region from which the speaker originates. As a general rule it is only pronounced at the end of a word in the South of France or in poetry and it is, therefore, not shown. In an isolated word the mute 'e' preceded by a single consonant is dropped e.g. *galetas* /galta/, *parfaitement* /paʀfɛtmɑ̃/, but *agréablement* /agʀeabləmɑ̃/.

In many cases the pronunciation of the mute 'e' depends on the surrounding context. Thus one would say *une reconnaissance de dette* /ynʀəkɔnɛsɑ̃sdədɛt/, but, *ma reconnaissance est éternelle* /maʀkɔnɛsɑ̃sɛteteʀnɛl/. The mute 'e' is shown in brackets in order to account for this phenomenon.

Open 'o' and closed 'o'
The difference between open 'o' and closed 'o' is not clear and speakers may hesitate, particularly in the pronunciation of compound words whose first element ends in 'o' e.g. *broncho-pneumonie, sociolinguistique, politologue* etc. It is not possible to opt for one or the other to apply to all cases. Where the word seems to function more like a single word the 'o' tends to be pronounced as an open 'o'. Where the two elements of the compound retain a degree of autonomy, as is often the case when they are hyphenated, the 'o' tends to be pronounced as a closed 'o' e.g. *psychosocial* /psikosɔsjal/, but, *psychologie* /psikɔlɔʒi/.

Stress
There is no real stress as such in French. In normal unemphasized speech a slight stress falls on the final syllable of a word or group of words, providing that it does not contain a mute 'e'. This is not shown in the phonetic transcription of individual entries.

I.V.

Vowels

a	*as in*	patte	/pat/
ɑ		pâte	/pɑt/
ɑ̃		clan	/klɑ̃/
e		dé	/de/
ɛ		belle	/bɛl/
ɛ̃		lin	/lɛ̃/
ə		demain	/dəmɛ̃/
i		gris	/gʀi/
o		gros	/gʀo/
ɔ		corps	/kɔʀ/
ɔ̃		long	/lɔ̃/
œ	*as in*	leur	/lœʀ/
œ̃		brun	/bʀœ̃/
ø		deux	/dø/
u		fou	/fu/
y		pur	/pyʀ/

Semi-vowels

j	*as in*	fille	/fij/
ɥ		huit	/ɥit/
w		oui	/wi/

Consonants

b	*as in*	bal	/bal/
d		dent	/dɑ̃/
f		foire	/fwar/
g		gomme	/gɔm/
k		clé	/kle/
l		lien	/ljɛ̃/
m		mer	/mɛʀ/
n		nage	/naʒ/
ɲ		gnon	/ɲɔ̃/
ŋ	*as in*	dancing	/dɑ̃siŋ/
p		porte	/pɔʀt/
ʀ		rire	/ʀiʀ/
s		sang	/sɑ̃/
ʃ		chien	/ʃjɛ̃/
t		train	/tʀɛ̃/
v		voile	/vwal/
z		zèbre	/zɛbʀ/
ʒ		jeune	/ʒœn/

Abbreviations and symbols
Abréviations et symboles

abbreviation	**abbrev, abrév**	abréviation
accountancy	**Accts**	comptabilité
adjective	**adj**	adjectif
demonstrative adjective	**adj dém**	adjectif démonstratif
exclamatory adjective	**adj excl**	adjectif exclamatif
indefinite adjective	**adj indéf**	adjectif indéfini
interrogative adjective	**adj inter**	adjectif interrogatif
adjectival phrase	**adj phr**	locution adjective
possessive adjective	**adj poss**	adjectif possessif
relative adjective	**adj rel**	adjectif relatif
administration	**Admin**	administration
adverb	**adv**	adverbe
adverbial phrase	**adv phr**	locution adverbiale
advertising	**Advertg**	publicité
aerospace	**Aerosp**	astronautique
agriculture	**Agric**	agriculture
anatomy	**Anat**	anatomie
anthropology	**Anthrop**	anthropologie
antiquity	**Antiq**	antiquité
archeology	**Archeol, Archéol**	archéologie
architecture	**Archit**	architecture
definite article	**art déf**	article défini
indefinite article	**art indéf**	article indéfini
insurance	**Assur**	assurance
astrology	**Astrol**	astrologie
astronomy	**Astron**	astronomie
aerospace	**Astronaut**	astronautique
Australian	**Austral**	anglais d'Australie
automobile	**Aut**	automobile
auxiliary	**aux**	auxiliaire
aviation	**Aviat**	aviation
Belgian French	**B**	belgicisme
biology	**Biol**	biologie
botany	**Bot**	botanique
Canadian French	**C**	canadianisme
European Community	**CEE**	Communauté européenne
chemistry	**Chem**	chimie
cinema	**Cin**	cinéma
civil engineering	**Civ Eng**	génie civil
commerce	**Comm**	commerce
accountancy	**Compta**	comptabilité
computing	**Comput**	informatique
conjunction	**conj**	conjonction
conjunctional phrase	**conj phr**	locution conjonctive
construction	**Constr**	construction, bâtiment
controversial	**controv**	usage critiqué
cosmetics	**Cosmet, Cosmét**	cosmétique
motor-racing	**Courses Aut**	courses automobiles
sewing	**Cout**	couture
culinary	**Culin**	culinaire

dentistry	**Dent**	dentisterie
determiner	**det, dét**	déterminant
indefinite determiner	**dét indéf**	déterminant indéfini
interrogative determiner	**dét inter**	déterminant interrogatif
numerical determiner	**dét num**	déterminant numérique
dialect	**dial**	dialecte
European Community	**EC**	Communauté européenne
ecology	**Ecol, Écol**	écologie
economy	**Econ, Écon**	économie
publishing	**Édition**	édition
electricity	**Elec**	électrotechnique
electronics	**Electron, Électron**	électronique
electricity	**Électrotech**	électrotechnique
management	**Entr**	entreprise
attributive	**épith**	épithète
equitation	**Equit, Équit**	équitation
euphemistic	**euph**	euphémique
exclamation	**excl**	exclamation
feminine	**f**	féminin
fashion	**Fashn**	mode
figurative	**fig**	figuré
finance	**Fin**	finance
tax	**Fisc**	fiscalité
fishing	**Fishg**	pêche
formal	**fml**	soutenu
British English	**GB**	anglais britannique
civil engineering	**Gén Civ**	génie civil
general	**gen, gén**	généralement
geography	**Geog, Géog**	géographie
geology	**Geol, Géol**	géologie
Swiss French	**H**	helvétisme
heraldry	**Herald, Hérald**	héraldique
history	**Hist**	histoire
horticulture	**Hort**	horticulture
humorous	**hum**	humoristique
hunting	**Hunt**	chasse
printing	**Imprim**	imprimerie
industry	**Ind**	industrie
offensive	**injur**	injurieux
insurance	**Insur**	assurance
invariable	**inv**	invariable
Irish	**Ir**	anglais d'Irlande
ironic	**iron**	ironique
journalism	**Journ**	presse
journalese	**journ**	journalistique
law	**Jur**	droit
baby talk	**lang enfantin**	langage enfantin
linguistics	**Ling**	linguistique
literary	**liter, littér**	littéraire
literature	**Literat, Littérat**	littérature
phrase	**loc**	locution
adjectival phrase	**loc adj**	locution adjective
adverbial phrase	**loc adv**	locution adverbiale
conjunctional phrase	**loc conj**	locution conjonctive
noun phrase	**loc nom**	locution nominale
prepositional phrase	**loc prép**	locution prépositive

masculine	**m**	masculin
mathematics	**Math**	mathématique
measure, units etc	**Meas, Mes**	métrologie
mechanics	**Mécan**	mécanique
mechanics	**Mech**	mécanique
medicine	**Med, Méd**	médecine
meteorology	**Meteorol, Météo**	météorologie
management	**Mgmt**	entreprise
military	**Mil**	armée
navy	**Mil Naut**	marine
mineralogy	**Miner, Minér**	minéralogie
noun modifier	**modif**	modificateur
motor-racing	**Motor-racing**	courses automobiles
music	**Mus**	musique
mythology	**Mythol**	mythologie
noun	**n**	nom
nautical	**Naut**	nautisme
feminine noun	**nf**	nom féminin
masculine noun	**nm**	nom masculin
masculine and feminine noun	**nm,f**	nom masculin et féminin
masculine and feminine noun	**nmf**	nom masculin et féminin
proper noun	**npr**	nom propre
nuclear physics	**Nucl**	physique nucléaire
onomatopoeia	**onomat**	onomatopée
computing	**Ordinat**	informatique
pejorative	**pej, péj**	péjoratif
pharmacology	**Pharm**	pharmacie
philosophy	**Philos**	philosophie
phonetics, phonology	**Phon**	phonétique, phonologie
photography	**Phot**	photographie
physics	**Phys**	physique
physiology	**Physiol**	physiologie
plural	**pl**	pluriel
politics	**Pol**	politique
postal services	**Post**	postes
past participle	**pp**	participe passé
past participle adjective	**pp adj**	participe passé adjectif
present participle	**p prés**	participe présent
proper noun	**pr n**	nom propre
prepositional phrase	**prep phr**	locution prépositive
preposition	**prep, prép**	préposition
present participle adjective	**pres p adj**	participe présent adjectif
present	**pres, prés**	présent
preterit	**pret, prét**	prétérit
printing	**Print**	imprimerie
pronoun	**pron**	pronom
demonstrative pronoun	**pron dém**	pronom démonstratif
indefinite pronoun	**pron indéf**	pronom indéfini
interrogative pronoun	**pron inter**	pronom interrogatif
personal pronoun	**pron pers**	pronom personnel
pronominal phrase	**pron phr**	locution pronominale
possessive pronoun	**pron poss**	pronom possessif
relative pronoun	**pron rel**	pronom relatif
social security	**Prot Soc**	protection sociale
proverb	**Prov**	proverbe
psychology	**Psych**	psychologie
advertising	**Pub**	publicité
publishing	**Publg**	édition

something	**qch**	quelque chose
somebody	**qn**	quelqu'un
quantifier	**quantif**	quantificateur
religion	**Relig**	religion
somebody	**sb**	quelqu'un
school	**Sch**	école
sciences	**Sci**	sciences
school	**Scol**	école
Scottish	**Scot**	anglais d'Écosse
singular	**sg**	singulier
social security	**Soc Admin**	protection sociale
sociology	**Sociol**	sociologie
formal	**sout**	soutenu
specialist	**spec, spéc**	spécialiste
statistics	**Stat**	statistique
something	**sth**	quelque chose
technology	**Tech**	technologie
telecommunications	**Telecom, Télécom**	télécommunications
textiles	**Tex**	textile
theatre	**Theat, Théât**	théâtre
always	**tjrs**	toujours
transport	**Transp**	transport
television	**TV**	télévision
university	**Univ**	université
American	**US**	anglais américain
verb	**v**	verbe
impersonal verb	**v impers**	verbe impersonnel
reflexive verb	**v refl**	verbe pronominal
veterinary medicine	**Vet, Vét**	médecine vétérinaire
intransitive verb	**vi**	verbe intransitif
reflexive verb	**vpr**	verbe pronominal
transitive verb	**vtr**	verbe transitif
indirect transitive verb	**vtr ind**	verbe transitif indirect
zoology	**Zool**	zoologie
dated	†	vieilli
archaic	‡	archaïque
trade mark*	®	marque déposée ou nom déposé*
informal	○	familier
very informal	◑	populaire
vulgar or taboo	●	vulgaire ou tabou
countable	**C**	dénombrable
uncountable	**₵**	non dénombrable
swung dash used as substitute for headword	**~**	tiret ondulé de substitution
British spelling only: US spelling varies	GB	graphie britannique: il existe une graphie nord-américaine
indicates an approximate translation equivalent	≈	pour signaler un équivalent approximatif
cross-reference	▶	renvoi

* **Proprietary terms** This dictionary includes some words which are, or are asserted to be, proprietary terms or trade marks. The presence or absence of such assertions should not be regarded as affecting the legal status of any proprietary name or trade mark.

* **Les marques déposées** Les mots qui, à notre connaissance, sont considérés comme des marques ou des noms déposés sont signalés dans cet ouvrage par ®. La présence ou l'absence de cette mention ne peut pas être considérée comme ayant valeur juridique.

An A–Z of Contemporary France

Aa

académie
A geographical administrative division of the state education system, encompassing all levels of the service, headed by a **RECTEUR** and served by **INSPECTEURS**.

Académie des beaux-arts
Founded in its original form in 1648, the national body of wisdom in artistic achievement, composed of distinguished figures from the fields of sculpture, painting, architecture, engraving, musical composition, cinema and television.

Académie des sciences
The most distinguished body of expertise in the field of mathematical, physical, chemical, natural and medical sciences, founded in 1666.

Académie française
The learned body comprising 40 members elected for life, representing the highest achievement in literature and scholarship. One of its best known activities is to prescribe rules on the use of French, and to codify this in the *Dictionnaire de l'Académie française*.

Académie Goncourt
A group of ten authors who award an annual prize in November to a prose writer. The announcement of the prize has become something of a ritual, and gives rise to wide speculation.

Académie nationale de médecine
The highest national body of specialist medical practitioners and bio-medical professionals. It has 130 members, and was founded in 1820.

acte de notoriété
A certificate issued in emergency by a *juge d'instance* which certifies the details of birth or marriage.

agent immobilier
A registered estate agent who works for a local practice or is self-employed.

agrégation
A qualification awarded by **CONCOURS** which provides entry to the highest level of teaching posts in secondary education and higher education. In most subjects the number of candidates is much in excess of the places available.

aide au retour
A government measure to encourage the repatriation of foreign nationals who wish to return to their country of origin.

aide française
The government programme of international aid, mainly directed to French-speaking countries in Africa.

aide judiciaire
Legal aid available to those whose income is below a certain level. This includes awards for the costs of a case and also free initial legal consultations.

alcootest
The test of the level of alcohol in a driver's bloodstream, always carried out if an accident has occurred or if there are suspicions of an offence having been committed, and sometimes at random.

allocation
An allowance payable from the **SÉCURITÉ SOCIALE** or other public funds, if certain conditions are met.

Alsace
The region (**PRÉFECTURE DE RÉGION**: Strasbourg) on the borders of Germany and Switzerland, in area the smallest in France, comprising the two **DÉPARTEMENTS** of Bas-Rhin and Haut-Rhin. The population is about 1.63 million. In some ways, Alsace is more distinctive than other regions, retaining certain minor legal individualities, and with many users of the *Alsacien* dialect. It is mainly an industrial area, although its wines are known world-wide, and many *Alsaciens* commute daily to Germany and Switzerland.

Alsace, l'
The daily newspaper published in Mulhouse.

amende forfaitaire
A fixed penalty payable in the case of a minor motoring offence, either to a police officer or traffic warden, or within 30 days by purchase of a *timbre-amende*.

amnistie
It is usual after the election of the **PRÉSIDENT DE LA RÉPUBLIQUE** for an amnesty to be granted in which certain categories of offenders have their penalties reviewed. This can mean suspension of fines, reduced sentences or early release.

année scolaire
School holidays are fixed nationally, and an **ACADÉMIE** falls into one of three zones so that the starts and ends of holidays are staggered. The year lasts from early September to late June, and main breaks are in early November (*Toussaint*), at Christmas and New Year, mid-February and early April.

ANPE – Agence nationale pour l'emploi
The national agency which provides services to unemployed people and employers seeking labour. Agree-

ment by job-seekers to take training offered by ANPE is a necessary condition for receiving unemployment benefits.

Antenne 2
The former name for **FRANCE 2**, still current among users.

AOC – appellation d'origine contrôlée
The quality control system imposed on the production of higher quality wines. The label identifies the approved name of the area and specifies the vineyard of production.

apprentissage
A nationally structured system of apprenticeships, normally available from age 16, exists in France. The period lasts from one to three years and the employer is bound by contract to include training at a **CFA**, and has to pay the apprentice up to 75% of the **SMIC**.

Aquitaine
The region (**PRÉFECTURE DE RÉGION**: Bordeaux) in south-west France, incorporating the **DÉPARTEMENTS** of Dordogne, Gironde, Landes, Lot-et-Garonne and Pyrénées-Atlantiques. The population is about 2.75 million. Historically, it has often been an area in dispute between England and France.

Modern Aquitaine has seen immigration from Iberia and North Africa. The region is a major producer of energy, is internationally known for its wines, and has received investment in aeronautical, defence and chemical industrial development.

Archives nationales
The state collection of publicly accessible documents, dating back to 1789, and now held in Paris, Aix-en-Provence (overseas archives), Espeyran (microfilm), Fontainebleau (contemporary collection), with plans for a work-related collection at Roubaix. Normally, the archive is secure for 30 years.

arrêté ministériel
A ministerial decision with the force of law, published in the **JOURNAL OFFICIEL**.

arrondissement
A sub-division of a **DÉPARTEMENT**. Each *arrondissement* has a **SOUS-PRÉFET** as local representative of the state administration.

In Paris, Lyon and Marseille, an *arrondissement* is a sub-division of the **COMMUNE**, and has its own **MAIRE** and local council.

Arte
A Franco-German cultural television channel, established in 1992.

Assemblée nationale
The lower house of the French parliament, in which 577 **DÉPUTÉS** are elected for a five-year term. A member, who must be at least 23 years old, has to be elected by at least 50% of the votes cast, and a second round of voting is held if necessary to ensure this.

Affiliation to party groups is indicated by a **DÉPUTÉ**'s allocation to a seat within a left-right gradation in the semi-circular chamber.

The *Assemblée nationale* passes laws, votes on the Budget, questions ministers (who cannot be **DÉPUTÉS**), and passes a **MOTION DE CENSURE** on the government (which automatically entails the fall of the government).

assurance auto obligatoire
The minimum legally required car insurance which covers a driver's liability for passengers and third-party risks. A currently valid insurance certificate has to be displayed on the front windscreen.

Aujourd'hui
A provincial edition of **LE PARISIEN**, introduced at a discount price in 1994.

autorité parentale
Under French law, parents have a joint and equal responsibility for their children, but this is subject to court rulings made by a *juge des enfants* if the welfare of the children is at risk.

autoroutes
The system of motorways, usually subject to tolls outside urban areas. All *autoroutes* are numbered, prefixed by A, and some are named. Tolls repay the loans raised for their construction, and most of the operating companies, once private, are now state-owned.

Auvergne
A region (**PRÉFECTURE DE RÉGION**: Clermont-Ferrand) of central southern France, comprising the **DÉPARTEMENTS** of Allier, Cantal, Haute-Loire and Puy-de-Dôme. Home to 1.3 million people, the Auvergne is primarily agricultural. Clermont-Ferrand is the only significant industrial city. Tourism is of growing importance to the economy, and there is a traditional market in hydrotherapy in certain spa towns of the region.

avocat
A lawyer who practises by preparing cases and defending the accused in court. The *avocat* has to hold a **MAÎTRISE** in law, and may either be part of a group practice or work individually.

Bb

bac + 3
The abbreviation for a course of study successfully completed three years after the **BACCALAURÉAT**.

baccalauréat
The certificate awarded to successful **LYCÉE** students at the end of the **CLASSE DE TERMINALE**, after national examinations. The courses offered are in broad subject groupings, and since 1994, the main series have been L (Littéraire), S (Scientifique) and ES (Économique et social). Series F, G and H are classed as *baccalauréat technologique*. There is also a wide range of specialist vocational qualifications under the broad title of *baccalauréat professionnel*.

bachelier
The holder of the **BACCALAURÉAT**, entitled to enrol for university diploma courses.

Banque de France
The central bank, under state ownership since 1945, which has sole money issuing powers, and a supervisory role over other banks.

Basse-Normandie
The administrative region (**PRÉFECTURE DE RÉGION**: Caen) comprising the **DÉPARTEMENTS** of Calvados, Manche and Orne. A major agricultural producer, Basse-Normandie has a population of 1.39 million. Tourism is becoming an important contributor to the economy.

BCBG – bon chic bon genre
The popular term for the upper bourgeoisie lifestyle, characterized by tastes and behaviour.

Bercy
In the south-east of Paris, on both banks of the Seine, major developments took place after the late 1980s, with the building of the Palais Omnisports, a new headquarters for the Finance Ministry, and the construction of the new **BIBLIOTHÈQUE NATIONALE DE FRANCE**.

Bibliothèque nationale de France
The organization established in 1993, uniting the *Bibliothèque de France*, based at **BERCY**, and the *Bibliothèque nationale*, which retains its premises in central Paris.

Bi-bop
The brand name of message phones sold through **FRANCE TÉLÉCOM**.

bon du Trésor
A government savings certificate, with a minimum investment of 1,000 francs, valid for five years, at a variable interest rate.

Bourgogne
An administrative region (**PRÉFECTURE DE RÉGION**: Dijon) comprising the **DÉPARTEMENTS** of Côte-d'Or, Nièvre, Saône-et-Loire and Yonne. With a population of 1.6 million, the region has mixed industries and is a significant agricultural producer. It is the home of the Charolais breed of cattle and of Burgundy wines.

bourse
A stock exchange (*bourse de valeurs*) of which there are seven in France. Dealing is carried out by *agents de change*. Most operations on the Paris *bourse* are computerized. The index of the 40 most-quoted prices is the CAC-40 (*Compagnie des agents de change*).

Bretagne
A geographically large administrative region (**PRÉFECTURE DE RÉGION**: Rennes) dominated by agriculture and fishing. The **DÉPARTEMENTS** are Côtes-d'Armor, Finistère, Ille-et-Vilaine and Morbihan, with a combined population of 2.79 million. Severe rural depopulation earlier this century has been reversed by immigration, especially of older people in retirement. The Breton language is still used, there are movements for independence from France, and there is a distinct sense of regional cultural identity.

brevet d'études professionnelles – BEP
A vocational qualification awarded after two years of study in a **LYCÉE** *professionnel*, entitling the holder to be classed as an *ouvrier qualifié*.

brevet de technicien – BT
A vocational qualification awarded at the end of a three-year course in a special section of a **LYCÉE**. Selection for the course is rigorous.

brevet de technicien supérieur – BTS
A **BAC + 2** vocational qualification, usually after study in a special section of a **LYCÉE** *professionnel* or *technologique*.

brevet des collèges
A general education qualification taken at the end of studies at a **COLLÈGE**.

Cc

cabinet
The political and administrative office of a minister or **PRÉSIDENT DE LA RÉPUBLIQUE**.

Caisse d'épargne et de prévoyance – CEP
A retail chain of savings banks, controlled by the state, and with a squirrel as its logo.

Caisse des dépôts et consignations
A state-controlled financial institution which oversees the financing of public projects and holds the funds of public institutions.

Caisse nationale d'épargne
The state-owned retail savings institution which operates through post offices to reach its clients.

Canal Plus
The fourth television channel in France, started in 1984, funded mainly by paying subscribers who need a decoder to access the programmes.

canton
An electoral district within a **DÉPARTEMENT**, which elects a member of the **CONSEIL GÉNÉRAL**.

CAPES – certificat d'aptitude au professorat de l'enseignement du second degré
The normal teaching certificate for qualifying as a teacher in a secondary school, following a postgraduate course provided by a **IUFM**. The examination is by **CONCOURS**.

CAPLP – certificat d'aptitude au professorat de lycée professionnel
The teaching qualification entitling teachers to work in a **LYCÉE** *professionnel*.

Carissimo
A concessionary rail card available to those aged 12–25, valid for a year, giving cheap travel for up to four people in off-peak periods.

Carte bleue
A credit card issued by French banks, part of the international Visa network.

carte grise
A motor vehicle's registration papers, which must be carried by the driver.

carte nationale d'identité
A document, valid for ten years, usually issued by the MAIRIE. It is not compulsory but, in practice, many formalities require it.

Carte orange
A season ticket valid for a range of periods and zones for the integrated public transport system in the Paris area.

casier judiciaire
The national database of criminal records and legal judgements. Individuals may obtain copies of their own record.

CDI – centre de documentation et d'information
A school resource and information centre, staffed by a *documentaliste*.

CDS – Centre des démocrates sociaux
A political party of the centre, founded in 1976, part of the grouping known as the UNION POUR LA DÉMOCRATIE FRANÇAISE.

censure
Film censorship is conducted by a joint committee of the industry, representatives of medical and teaching professions and the Ministry of Culture.

Centre
The administrative region (PRÉFECTURE DE RÉGION: Orléans) which comprises the DÉPARTEMENTS of Cher, Eure-et-Loir, Indre, Indre-et-Loire, Loir-et-Cher and Loiret. The overall population of this principally agricultural region is 2.37 million. Cities are small to medium-sized, there are environmental concerns principally about the Sologne wetlands area, and the tourist attractions of the Loire valley sit uneasily alongside a major nuclear electricity generating capacity.

Cérès
The Greek goddess of agriculture, often used as a symbolic representation of France.

césars
The annual prizes awarded to cinema personalities for achievement in the previous year.

CFA – centre de formation d'apprentis
The location for apprentices' general education courses, organized by local chambers of commerce or professional bodies.

CFDT – Confédération française démocratique du travail
A large trade union, in sympathy with catholicism and the PARTI SOCIALISTE, but without formal ties to either.

CFE-CGC – Confédération française de l'encadrement – CGC
A white-collar union, recruiting members from the *cadres*, with about half a million members.

CFTC – Confédération française des travailleurs chrétiens
A moderate with no party affiliations.

CGT – Confédération générale du travail
An influential trade union, whose leadership has traditionally been connected with the PARTI COMMUNISTE FRANÇAIS, but whose membership comes from a wider range of political sympathies.

Chaillot
The Paris home of the TNC, rebuilt in 1975 to include a concert hall. The building overlooks the site of the TOUR EIFFEL.

chambre de commerce et d'industrie – CCI
A local public body, financed largely by the government, representing the interests of the business community, and sometimes managing a public facility.

Champagne-Ardenne
The administrative region in eastern France (PRÉFECTURE DE RÉGION: Châlons-sur-Marne) comprising the DÉPARTEMENTS of Ardennes, Aube, Haute-Marne and Marne. The principal base for the economy in this predominantly rural region is agriculture, with a concentration on cereal and beet crops, but also with the highly lucrative Champagne wine trade. The population of the region is 1.34 million.

Champs-Élysées
The fashionable world-famous shopping and commercial avenue in Paris, on the site of part of the royal hunting forest.

Châtelet-les-Halles
The largest underground railway station in the world, linking six *métro* and RER lines in central Paris.

chef-lieu
The principal town or city of an administrative area.

CHU – centre hospitalier universitaire
A teaching hospital attached to the medical faculty of a university.

Cinquième, la
An educational television channel, inaugurated in 1994, transmitting on the ARTE channel during the daytime.

Cinquième République
The régime established by the constitution of 1958, along the lines laid down by Charles de Gaulle, emphasizing the role of a strong executive and institutions in guaranteeing stability.

Cité de la musique
The site of the *Conservatoire national de musique et de danse*, concert halls and the national music museum at the PARC DE LA VILLETTE.

Cité des sciences et de l'industrie
A museum and exhibition complex at the PARC DE LA VILLETTE, in the north-east of Paris, opened in 1986, distinguished by its active and participatory style of presentation.

classe de neige
A period in which a school class stays in a mountain area for ski tuition and continuation of normal school work.

classe de première
The penultimate class in a LYCÉE, in which students aged 16–17 are following a course towards the BACCALAURÉAT.

classe de seconde
The first year in a LYCÉE, in which a common curriculum with options is followed.

classe de terminale
The final **LYCÉE** year before the **BACCALAURÉAT**.

classes préparatoires
An intensive two-year post-**BACCALAURÉAT** course, usually provided in a **LYCÉE**, working towards the entry **CONCOURS** for a **GRANDE ÉCOLE**.

CNDP – Centre national de documentation pédagogique
The teaching materials and publications office of the *ministère de l'Éducation nationale*.

CNPF – Confédération nationale du patronat français
The organization which represents employers' interests at a national level. It has specialist component sub-groups.

CNRS – Centre national de la recherche scientifique
A nationally financed body which conducts research in its own laboratories or in association with universities or other organizations.

code
The collected legal documents which refer to a particular field of activity.

cohabitation
A period in which the government and the **PRÉSIDENT DE LA RÉPUBLIQUE** come from opposite political camps.

collège
The state school for pupils aged 11–15. The curriculum and organization are nationally prescribed.

Collège de France
A self-governing body of eminent scholars, founded in 1530. The members give free public lectures.

colonie de vacances
A holiday village or summer camp for children, staffed largely by students.

Comédie-Française
The oldest national theatre company, dating back to 1680, with premises in Paris, but also performing on tour.

comité d'entreprise
A representative body of workers and management, required by law in any enterprise with more than 50 employees, and entitled to an annual report from the owners, and consultation on proposed changes.

Comité national d'action laïque – CNAL
An influential pressure group which campaigns against state support for private education.

Comité national de l'enseignement catholique – CNEC
A pressure group which campaigns for further support for private education, especially that connected with Roman Catholic foundations.

commissaire de police
A senior non-uniformed police officer in the **POLICE NATIONALE**.

commissaire-priseur
A professional auctioneer, qualified in law as well as trained in the skills of the post. The number of posts available is fixed by law.

commission mixte paritaire
A committee formed by the **PREMIER MINISTRE**, and drawn from members of both **ASSEMBLÉE NATIONALE** and **SÉNAT** to redraft texts of a parliamentary bill which has been rejected by both houses.

commission permanente
A standing committee of either the **ASSEMBLÉE NATIONALE** or the **SÉNAT** which examines the text of proposed legislation before discussion in the chamber.

commune
The smallest administrative unit, headed by a **MAIRE** and a **CONSEIL MUNICIPAL**. Each village, town and city is a **COMMUNE**, of which there are 36,000.

concours
A competitive selection process for public appointments, or for admission to a course, which usually includes a formal examination.

Confédération générale des petites et moyennes entreprises – CGPME
A small employers' organization forming part of the **CNPF**.

Conseil constitutionnel
The ruling body on the constitutional legality of proposed measures, on disputed election procedures, and on the conduct of the **PRÉSIDENT DE LA RÉPUBLIQUE**.

Conseil d'État
The specialist independent advisory body to the government on proposed legislation, with a watching brief over all public administrative actions.

Conseil des ministres
The weekly meeting of all ministers, held in the **PALAIS DE L'ÉLYSÉE** and chaired by the **PRÉSIDENT DE LA RÉPUBLIQUE**.

Conseil économique et social
A consultative body, protected by the Constitution, representing the major industrial, business and social groups. The role is to liaise with government over the implications of policy and intended measures.

conseil général
The body of elected representatives with the role of managing the implementation of public policy in the **DÉPARTEMENT**. Each *conseiller général* is elected for six years.

conseil municipal
Elected for six years by the inhabitants of a **COMMUNE**, the **CONSEIL MUNICIPAL** in turn elects the **MAIRE**. Its function is to manage local public services.

conseil régional
Members are elected for six years, representing a **DÉPARTEMENT**, and appoint a *président* and an executive team.

Conseil supérieur de l'audiovisuel – CSA
The body which appoints the heads of the public broadcasting systems, licenses private contractors, monitors

advertising and oversees all matters concerning impartiality, freedom of speech, quality and the promotion of French language and culture in the broadcast media.

conseiller d'éducation
A staff member of a secondary school who is responsible for the general discipline of pupils.

conseiller d'orientation
A careers and course adviser, based in a secondary school.

Conservatoire national des arts et métiers
A network of adult education centres providing further professional courses.

constat
A report certified by a **HUISSIER** (or by police in the case of a motor accident) which can be used as evidence in legal proceedings.

contrat initiative-emploi – CIE
A government cash incentive to employers to take on new workers, a measure to reduce unemployment.

Corse
The administrative region covering the island of Corsica (**PRÉFECTURE DE RÉGION:** Ajaccio) and the **DÉPARTEMENTS** of Corse-du-Sud and Haute-Corse. Half its population of a quarter of a million live in the two urban areas (Ajaccio and Bastia), and the overall level of prosperity is considerably less than on the mainland. There is more autonomy than in other regions, but an active independence movement continues to press for change.

Cotisation de charges sociales
The compulsory contributions made by employer and employee to fund the **SÉCURITÉ SOCIALE** scheme.

Coupole
A journalistic term for the **ACADÉMIE FRANÇAISE**, referring to the dome of the *palais de l'Institut de France*.

cour d'appel
The court of appeal in each *région judiciaire*. After its ruling, further appeal is possible only to the **COUR DE CASSATION**.

cour d'assises
A criminal court, presided over by three **JUGES**, where cases are heard before a jury of nine. Judges and jury vote together after hearing the evidence, and the verdict is based on a two-thirds majority. Any appeal is made to the **COUR DE CASSATION**.

Cour de cassation
The highest court of appeal which rules on the legality of decisions in cases referred to it.

Cour de justice de la République
A parliamentary court established in 1993 in which a citizen suffering from illegal activity by a serving minister can bring action.

Cour des comptes
The public body which audits national public expenditure, and the supreme authority in matters of public finance.

Courrier de l'Ouest, le
A daily newspaper published in Angers.

crédit municipal
The network of regulated pawnbrokers, popularly known as **MONT-DE-PIÉTÉ**.

Croix, la
A daily Roman Catholic newspaper published in Paris, with a national circulation.

CROUS – centre régional des œuvres universitaires et scolaires
The student welfare organization attached to each university.

CRS – compagnies républicaines de sécurité
Special units of the **POLICE NATIONALE**, who are trained in riot control and public order techniques, but also have duties policing **AUTOROUTES**, and providing mountain safety and coastal life guard support.

CV – chevaux
The fiscal measure of a vehicle's engine affecting its taxation rate.

cycle d'observation
The first year spent in a **COLLÈGE**, in the *classe de sixième*.

cycle d'orientation
The last year of the **COLLÈGE**, in the *classe de troisième*. The **TRONC COMMUN** is the basis of the curriculum, with certain options available, and an intensive process of counselling occurs to direct the pupil to the most suitable programme in the **LYCÉE**.

cycle élémentaire – CE
The primary school programme for children aged 7–9. Also called *cours élémentaire*.

cycle moyen – CM
The primary school programme for children aged 9–11. Also called *cours moyen*. At the end of the period, the teacher decides whether or not the child should transfer to the **COLLÈGE** immediately or repeat the final year.

cycle préparatoire – CP
The entry year in the **ÉCOLE PRIMAIRE**, for children aged 6–7. Also called *cours préparatoire*.

Dd

Dauphiné Libéré, le
A daily newspaper published in Grenoble.

DEA – diplôme d'études approfondies
An academic qualification taken a year after the **MAÎTRISE** by those who intend to engage in research or work for a doctorate.

Debré, loi
The current law, dating from 1959, which enables state support to be provided for private schools.

décret
A decision of the **PREMIER MINISTRE** which executes a law passed by parliament.

Défense, la
The area immediately to the north-west of Paris, developed as a modern business and residential area from the 1960s to the 1980s.

département
An administrative unit (of which there are 96 in metropolitan France) based on a division in the Revolutionary period. Most are named after rivers or mountains within their border. The main town is the seat of the **PRÉFET**, and is often called the **PRÉFECTURE**.

Dépêche du Midi, la
A daily newspaper published in Toulouse.

dépôt légal
The legal requirement to deposit copies of every publication with the **BIBLIOTHÈQUE NATIONALE DE FRANCE**.

député
A member of the **ASSEMBLÉE NATIONALE**, elected for five years from a constituency within a **DÉPARTEMENT**. The minimum age is 23, and a **DÉPUTÉ** appointed to be a member of the government is replaced by a **SUPPLÉANT**.

Dernières Nouvelles d'Alsace, les
A daily newspaper published in Strasbourg.

DES – diplôme d'études spécialisées
The necessary qualification for medical specialists, awarded after ten years of post-**BACCALAURÉAT** study.

DEUG – diplôme d'études universitaires générales
A qualification awarded after two years of university study in any non-scientific subject.

DEUST – diplôme d'études universitaires de sciences et techniques
A qualification awarded after two years of university study in a range of science courses.

diplôme d'état de docteur en médecine
The professional qualification of a medical practitioner, awarded after eight years of study at medical school.

diplôme d'université
A certificate awarded by a university, but which does not have national recognition in the system of state-prescribed qualifications.

district
A group of **COMMUNES** which have agreed to pool their housing, fire-fighting and possibly other services.

doctorat
An advanced academic qualification, awarded by a university after presentation of a thesis. Entry to doctorate study is via a number of prescribed routes.

DOM – département d'outre-mer
An overseas **DÉPARTEMENT**, which also has the status of a **RÉGION**. The four current DOM are **GUADELOUPE**, **GUYANE**, **MARTINIQUE** and **RÉUNION**.

Drouot
The main auction houses in Paris, taking the name from the original site of the Salle Drouot in the rue Drouot.

DUT – diplôme universitaire de technologie
A qualification awarded after two years of study in an **IUT** including a work placement.

Ee

Échos, les
The Paris daily newspaper which specializes in financial and economic news.

école centrale
Two **GRANDES ÉCOLES**, in Paris and Lyon, which provide post-**BACCALAURÉAT** courses in engineering and general education with a view to producing an élite force of technocrats.

école libre
Private sector school education, predominantly run by the Roman Catholic church. As from 1993, newly appointed teachers have to be trained through the state-directed system.

école maternelle
There are approximately 18,000 *écoles maternelles* providing free nursery education for children from the age of two years. Virtually 100% of children aged four and five years attend, prior to the statutory age of six years, when they transfer to an **ÉCOLE PRIMAIRE**.

école militaire
This term refers both to the eighteenth- century academy in Paris and to the active officer training establishments for the three services, at Coëtquidan (army), Poulmic (navy) and Salon-de-Provence (air force), as well as specialist centres.

École nationale d'administration – ENA
The **GRANDE ÉCOLE**, based in Strasbourg, which trains the élite force of public administrators. There are about 1,500 applicants for 150 places, drawn from graduates of a university or another **GRANDE ÉCOLE**. Entry is by **CONCOURS**, and requires applicants to commit themselves to ten years' work for the state.

École nationale des ponts et chaussées – ENPC
A **GRANDE ÉCOLE**, founded in 1747, which trains public civil engineers and information scientists.

École nationale supérieure agronomique – ENSA
There are eight ENSA which train agricultural and environmental engineers. Entry is by **CONCOURS**.

École nationale supérieure d'arts et métiers – ENSAM
An establishment with regional centres, providing three year courses in design engineering. The final year is always spent in Paris.

École nationale supérieure des arts décoratifs – ENSAD
The most prestigious fine arts and design school in Paris, founded in 1766.

École nationale supérieure des beaux-arts – ENSBA
A leading art school for creative artists, located in Paris.

école normale
The traditional teacher training colleges, which have been absorbed into the **IUFM** network since 1991.

école normale supérieure – ENS
There are four ENS, the most famous being that based in Paris and Montrouge, a training establishment founded

in 1794 for higher education teachers and researchers, senior civil servants and administrators. Entry is by **CONCOURS**, and requires applicants to commit themselves to ten years' work for the state.

École polytechnique
The most prestigious of all the **GRANDES ÉCOLES**, founded in 1794, producing an élite force of engineers who work in industry or public administration. Students, recruited by **CONCOURS**, have the rank of reserve military officers. X, as the *École polytechnique* is nicknamed, is located at Palaiseau.

école primaire
Also called *école élémentaire*, its nineteenth-century name. Attendance is compulsory between the ages of six and eleven, and it incorporates the **CYCLES PRÉPARATOIRE, ÉLÉMENTAIRE**, and **MOYEN** in its programme. The local **COMMUNE** is partly responsible for its funding. A small number of pupils repeat a year if they do not reach the prescribed standard of attainment.

électeur
A French national is entitled to vote in all public elections, if aged 18 or above, unless declared bankrupt or subject to a temporary loss of voting rights as part of a court sentence.

élection
Public elections are held on Sundays, with a week's delay (two weeks in the **ÉLECTIONS PRÉSIDENTIELLES**) between first and second rounds if a clear majority is not achieved immediately. Voters collect slips, and in secret choose the slip containing the name of the favoured candidate or list and place it in an envelope.

élections cantonales
The election for members of the **CONSEIL GÉNÉRAL** held every three years. One member is elected in each **CANTON** by **SCRUTIN UNINOMINAL MAJORITAIRE**.

élections législatives
The election for **DÉPUTÉS** to sit in the **ASSEMBLÉE NATIONALE**. Elections are held every five years, and one member for each **ARRONDISSEMENT** is elected by **SCRUTIN UNINOMINAL MAJORITAIRE**.

élections municipales
The election of the **CONSEIL MUNICIPAL** held every six years. Depending on the size of the **COMMUNE**, either the **SCRUTIN UNINOMINAL MAJORITAIRE** or the **SCRUTIN À MODE MIXTE** method is used.

élections présidentielles
The election for the **PRÉSIDENT DE LA RÉPUBLIQUE** held every seven years. In the second round, only two candidates are left in the contest.

élections régionales
The election for the **CONSEIL RÉGIONAL**, held every six years, using the **SCRUTIN DE LISTE À LA REPRÉSENTATION PROPORTIONNELLE** method.

élections sénatoriales
The election for members of the **SÉNAT**, a third of the seats being renewable every three years. The voters are delegates of elected members of **CONSEILS MUNICIPAUX, GÉNÉRAUX**, and **RÉGIONAUX**, as well as **DÉPUTÉS**, and representatives of French people living abroad.

Élysée, palais de l'
The official residence of the **PRÉSIDENT DE LA RÉPUBLIQUE**, in the **CHAMPS-ÉLYSÉES** in Paris.

Emmaüs
A widely supported charitable foundation which helps underprivileged families and individuals.

Équipe, l'
A daily sports newspaper published in Paris, with national distribution.

Est républicain, l'
A daily newspaper published in Nancy.

état civil
Certified proof of a French citizen's entitlements to civic rights.

état de siège
A state of emergency which allows the **CONSEIL DES MINISTRES** to grant the military authorities exceptional police powers for up to 12 days, renewable with the approval of the **ASSEMBLÉE NATIONALE**.

état d'urgence
A state of emergency, which allows the civil authorities to operate with special powers for up to 12 days in a specified geographical area. Extension is only possible if a special law is passed. It has not been used since the early 1960s.

état-major
The central command of the armed forces, headed by the *Chef d'état-major des armées*, responsible to the **PRÉSIDENT DE LA RÉPUBLIQUE**.

Europe I
A French language commercial radio station, broadcasting a mixture of news, light entertainment, sport and popular music from Saarland, in Germany.

Événement du jeudi, l'
A weekly news magazine published in Paris.

Évin, loi
A 1992 law which bans smoking in public buildings, enclosed workplaces and most public transport as well as advertisements for tobacco products. Smoking zones in hotels and restaurants have to be specifically indicated.

exode rural
The population drift from rural to urban areas which was on a massive scale in the post-war decades.

Express, l'
A weekly news magazine, established in 1953.

externe
A day pupil at a boarding **LYCÉE** or **COLLÈGE**, or an external candidate in a **CONCOURS**.

Ff

famille nombreuse
The designation of a large family, which qualifies for special allowances, discounts, and in some cases honours,

arising from the policy of encouraging population growth.

fauteuil
A designated seat in any theatre, cinema or representative assembly, and a numbered seat in the **ACADÉMIE FRANÇAISE**.

Fédération syndicale unitaire – FSU
A union for teachers, formed in 1993, having links with the **PARTI COMMUNISTE FRANÇAIS**.

fermeture annuelle
The annual summer closure period of many small businesses, often for a calendar month.

fête légale
An official public holiday, of which there are 11 annually in addition to Sundays.

fête nationale
The annual celebrations on 14th July marking the symbolic date of the fall of the Bastille prison in 1789.

Figaro, le
A right-wing daily newspaper published in Paris since 1826, with a national circulation.

flagrant délit
An offence in which the offender is caught red-handed. It allows the police to search premises or a vehicle.

FNAC – Fédération nationale des achats
A chain of discount shops selling books, photographic and hi-fi equipment, records, computers and holidays.

FNSEA – Fédération nationale de syndicats d'exploitants agricoles
The largest grouping of farmers, virtually functioning as the official farmers' union.

Fondation de France
A private charity which supports cultural, scientific and environmental schemes, Third World projects and those in need.

fonds commun de placement – FCP
A unit trust available for individual or company investment.

Force démocrate – FD
The name under which the **CDS** has been known since 1995.

Force ouvrière – FO
A moderate trade union recruiting largely from the lower ranks of public employees.

France 2
The principal public sector television channel, still widely known by its former name, **ANTENNE 2**.

France 3 – FR
A state-owned television channel, regionally based, with the special role of giving access to a diverse range of beliefs and opinions.

France-Culture
A 24-hour **RADIO FRANCE** service featuring serious talk programmes.

France-Dimanche
A tabloid Sunday newspaper with a high national circulation.

France-Info
A 24-hour radio news station run by **RADIO FRANCE**.

France-Inter
The popular light entertainment radio station of **RADIO FRANCE**.

France-Musique
A 24-hour radio station, providing classical music and jazz, run by **RADIO FRANCE**.

France-Soir
A daily Paris newspaper, nationally distributed.

France Télécom
The monopoly provider of telecommunications services, wholly owned by the state.

Franche-Comté
The administrative region (**PRÉFECTURE DE RÉGION**: Besançon) on the border with Switzerland, comprising the **DÉPARTEMENTS** of Doubs, Haute-Saône, Jura, and Territoire de Belfort. The population is almost 1.1 million, and its main employment is industrial, with strengths in the engineering, motor, watchmaking and metallurgy industries. Its aspect is largely rural, however, with substantial forest areas.

Front national – FN
A right-wing political party, established in 1972 by Jean-Marie Le Pen, asserting strongly anti-immigrant policies.

Gg

garde à vue
Police detention for up to 24 hours without a warrant in order to answer questions.

garde des Sceaux
The title of the minister of Justice.

Garde républicaine
A section of the **GENDARMERIE NATIONALE**, with special ceremonial, security and escort duties in connection with prestigious occasions or institutions.

Gendarmerie nationale
A section of the military which provides police service outside major towns.

Génération écologie
A political party founded in 1990 as a breakaway group from the **VERTS**.

Grand-Palais
An exhibition hall in the **CHAMPS-ÉLYSÉES**, completed in 1900, used especially for international touring art exhibitions.

grand projet
The umbrella term identifying the usually presidential schemes for public construction.

Grande arche de la Défense
A huge archway-shaped building at LA DÉFENSE, erected in 1989 to mark the bicentenary of the Revolution.

grande école
A prestigious higher education school recruiting by CONCOURS, considered to be at the summit of the educational system.

grands boulevards
The earliest Paris avenues which took the name Boulevard, laid out on the line of the former city defences.

GRETA – groupement d'établissements pour la formation continue
A local consortium of educational institutions offering post-experience training.

Guadeloupe
A DOM and region (PRÉFECTURE DE RÉGION: Basse-Terre) in the Caribbean since 1946, in French occupation since 1635. The predominantly young population is almost 400,000, and the economy, based on sugar cane, rum, bananas, cement and tourism, is highly dependent on trade with metropolitan France.

Guyane
A DOM and region (PRÉFECTURE DE RÉGION: Cayenne) in the north-east of South America, with a population of about 115,000. The success of the economy is closely linked with the European Ariane space programme. The community, mainly resident on a narrow coastal strip, is dependent on imports for basic foodstuffs.

Hh

Haute-Normandie
The region (PRÉFECTURE DE RÉGION: Rouen) incorporating the DÉPARTEMENTS of Eure and Seine-Maritime, with a population of 1.74 million. It combines a maritime economy, agricultural strength and the outer parts of the Paris commuter belt.

HEC – École des hautes études commerciales
A prestigious GRANDE ÉCOLE run by the Paris CHAMBRE DE COMMERCE ET D'INDUSTRIE. Sited at Jouy-en-Josas, the HEC is a leading business and management school.

HLM – habitation à loyer modéré
Public housing, usually apartments, available for rent, built and managed either by public concerns or by private enterprise supported by state loans, or by cooperatives. About 13 million people live in HLM.

huissier
A legal officer with authority to execute court decisions, to draw up legal contracts, to act as auctioneer, to be an insurance agent, and to seize property in settlement of debts.

Humanité, l'
The daily communist newspaper published in Paris, and distributed nationally.

Ii

Ici Paris
A sensational tabloid weekly newspaper published in Paris.

Île-de-France
The region, previously known as the *Région parisienne*, comprising the city of Paris and the surrounding DÉPARTEMENTS of Essonne, Hauts-de-Seine, Seine-et-Marne, Seine-Saint-Denis and Yvelines. It has a population of 10.69 million, and registers the highest per-capita income and standard of living. A 25-year structure plan from 1992 plans to restrict urban development to five centres – Paris, LA DÉFENSE, Marne-la-Vallée, Roissy, Saclay-Massy.

immatriculation, plaque d'
The registration plate carried on a motor vehicle. The final two figures are the NUMÉRO MINÉRALOGIQUE of the DÉPARTEMENT of the owner's residence, and each vehicle is re-registered at change of ownership, or if the owner moves out of the DÉPARTEMENT.

immunité parlementaire
A DÉPUTÉ or a SÉNATEUR is protected against legal action for voicing opinions, and cannot be arrested during a parliamentary session except for a serious offence or a FLAGRANT DÉLIT, unless the house gives its approval.

impôt sur le revenu – IR
A tax payable on income, paid in three instalments in arrears, or monthly if preferred.

ingénieur-maître
A qualification awarded after a university course which includes professional experience, run by an *Institut Universitaire Professionnalisé.*

INSEE – Institut national de la statistique et des études économiques
The principal statistical office of the government. It carries out surveys and compiles the monthly price index.

inspecteur d'académie
An education inspector, representing the RECTEUR of the ACADÉMIE, usually working within the confines of one DÉPARTEMENT.

inspecteur de l'Éducation nationale – IEN
An education inspector whose main function is to assess the effectiveness of primary school teachers.

inspecteur des finances
A high-ranking civil servant (one of 150) who has the power to audit any area of public finance.

inspecteur général de l'Éducation nationale – IGEN
A high-ranking education inspector concerned with a particular subject area or a specialist aspect of school operations. The main function is to give advice to the ministry about the overall effectiveness of the system.

inspecteur pédagogique régional – IPR
An education inspector who works within a region, and whose main function is to assess the work of secondary school teachers.

Institut d'études politiques de Paris
The prestigious 'Sciences-Po' higher education institution, which offers a course in political science which has higher status than a university LICENCE.

Institut géographique national – IGN
A state-owned map publishing organization which sells its products in the commercial market.

Institut national de la consommation – INC
A state-aided consumer organization which publishes *50 millions de consommateurs* monthly.

Institut Pasteur
A privately funded hospital and medical research organization, operating world-wide.

instituteur
A primary school teacher, trained in an ÉCOLE NORMALE, who qualified before 1991.

interdiction de séjour
A ban on residence in a specified area, imposed by a court of law.

intérêt public, d'
An activity with this title qualifies for government subsidy, recognized as being of benefit to the community.

interpellation
A demand for attendance at a police station, which cannot be refused if the case is one of FLAGRANT DÉLIT.

Itineris
The mobile telephone network operated by FRANCE TÉLÉCOM.

IUFM – institut universitaire de formation des maîtres
A teacher training establishment, introduced in 1990, incorporating the role of the former ÉCOLE NORMALE and providing training for the professional CONCOURS. Each IUFM is attached to a university.

IUT – institut universitaire de technologie
A higher education establishment, attached to a university, which provides post-BACCALAURÉAT courses towards the DUT.

Jj

JO – Journal officiel
The daily gazette in which all laws and DÉCRETS, information about ministerial decisions and official appointments are published.

Journal du dimanche
A popular tabloid Sunday newspaper.

Jours de France
A popular weekly women's magazine.

juge
The president of a court of law, appointed on the recommendation of the GARDE DES SCEAUX. Once appointed, a *juge* cannot be removed without his or her consent.

juge de l'application des peines
A judge who considers all amendments to sentences once a period of imprisonment has begun.

juge d'instruction
An examining magistrate who investigates a criminal case and assembles evidence. The *juge d'instruction* can keep a suspect in prison for up to six months in serious cases. Also known as a *magistrat instructeur*.

juge des tutelles
A judge who rules in the matter of a child's guardianship.

juré
A juror in a COUR D'ASSISES, a registered ÉLECTEUR aged between 23 and 70.

jury
Nine jurors are called for each case in a COUR D'ASSISES. The prosecution can object to four, and the defence to five.

Kk

Keno
A weekly national lottery game, launched in 1993, with the draw televised on FRANCE 3 each Thursday evening.

kilomètre zéro
The point outside Notre-Dame cathedral in Paris, from which all distances to other towns and villages are measured.

Ll

laïcité
The secular nature of the republican state, especially noted in the non-religious nature of state schools.

Languedoc-Roussillon
The southern region (PRÉFECTURE DE RÉGION: Montpellier) comprising the DÉPARTEMENTS of Aude, Gard, Hérault, Lozère and Pyrénées-Orientales, with a population of 2.1 million. The traditional economic base of peasant farming and low-grade wine production has been transformed by massive inward investment in tourism, high-tech industry and urbanization programmes.

Légion d'honneur
The system of honour awarded by the state for meritorious achievement. The PRÉSIDENT DE LA RÉPUBLIQUE is the *Grand maître*. The basic rank is *Chevalier*. They are entitled to wear a small red lapel ribbon.

Légion étrangère
The foreign legion, founded in 1831, and part of the French infantry. About 60% of its members are not of French nationality.

Libération
A left-wing Paris daily newspaper, published since 1973, and distributed nationally.

libération conditionnelle
Early release for a person serving a prison sentence, granted subject to conditions by a **JUGE DE L'APPLICATION DES PEINES** or by the **GARDE DES SCEAUX**.

licence
A degree qualification from a university, awarded after a year's successful study beyond a **DEUG**.

Limousin
The region (**PRÉFECTURE DE RÉGION**: Limoges) in the southern Massif central comprising the **DÉPARTEMENTS** of Corrèze, Creuse and Haute-Vienne. This mainly agricultural area suffered severely from the **EXODE RURAL**, which particularly involved young people. The population is still falling, and there are now 722,615 inhabitants. This is the oldest regional population in the European Union.

Livre de Poche
The largest paperback book series, mainly composed of works which have already appeared under another publisher's imprint.

Livret A
A fixed interest savings account held with the **CAISSE D'ÉPARGNE ET DE PRÉVOYANCE**. Interest is paid tax free, but there is a maximum holding of 90,000 francs.

Livret B
A fixed interest savings account held with the **CAISSE D'ÉPARGNE ET DE PRÉVOYANCE**, interest being taxed before payment.

livret de famille
An official record of family status which is used as proof of family links.

Lorraine
The region in the north-east corner of France (**PRÉFECTURE DE RÉGION**: Metz) with a population of 2.3 million. The north is mainly industrial, but its reliance on traditional heavy industries has led to efforts to restructure and modernize. The south is principally agricultural.

Loto
A national game of chance, with a majority holding by the state.

Louvre
The former royal palace in Paris, now an enormous museum of art and antiquities. An extensive modernization plan is due for completion by 1999.

lycée
A state or private secondary school for students from the age of 15, after studies in a **COLLÈGE**. Most courses lead to the **BACCALAURÉAT**, but there are various course packages available, not all present in each *lycée*. A *lycée professionnel* provides vocational courses, a *lycée technologique* concentrates on technical education. A *lycée polyvalent* combines two or more of these elements within one establishment. Many *lycées* also provide courses beyond the **BACCALAURÉAT**.

Mm

m6
A television channel, privately owned, with an 8% share of the national audience.

Maghreb
The Islamic countries of North Africa which have been a major source of immigration to metropolitan France. Most of them were previously part of the French empire.

Magis
A communications network of personal computers using the **TÉLÉTEL** system.

magistère
A university qualification awarded after three years of study beyond the level of a **DEUG** or a **DUT**.

magistrat
The generic term used for legal officials in public employment, such as judges or state prosecutors.

maire
The chief officer of a **COMMUNE**, elected by the **CONSEIL MUNICIPAL** at the beginning of its term of office. He or she is also the representative of state authority in the area, officiates in marriages and supervises local elections. The *maire* is a politician, usually part-time, although in receipt of an allowance. In larger towns, he or she is full-time and very powerful.

mairie
The administrative headquarters of the **CONSEIL MUNICIPAL** and the office of the **MAIRE**. The building is sometimes called the *hôtel de ville*.

maison des jeunes et de la culture – MJC
A publicly funded centre for young people. There are about 1,500 of them, with a collective membership of almost 700,000.

maître-assistant
A university teacher who gives tutorial help for students working for the **DEUG** and directs demonstrations and practical classes.

maître de conférences
A teacher in a university, recruited by **CONCOURS**, employed to lecture and engage in research activity.

maîtrise
A university qualification which is awarded at the end of two years of study beyond the **DEUG**.

Marianne
One of the symbols of the French Republic is the female allegorical figure of Marianne, who invariably wears the Phrygian cap romanticized in early pictures of the 1789 Revolution. In modern representations, various French film stars have been used as the model for Marianne on postage stamps.

Marseillaise, la
A daily newspaper, published in Marseille, supporting a communist viewpoint.

Marseillaise, la
The popular name of the national anthem, composed by Claude-Joseph Rouget de Lisle in 1792. It was adopted as a marching song by a group of republican volunteers

from Marseille and marked their entry to Paris a month later.

Martinique
An island **DOM** and region (**PRÉFECTURE DE RÉGION**: Fort-de-France) in the Caribbean with a population of about 360,000. The economy is dependent on relations with metropolitan France and the European Union. Unemployment is a severe and continuing problem.

mastère
A qualification given by a **GRANDE ÉCOLE** after four terms of study following the award of a **DEA**.

maternelle
The initial stage of state-provided education. An **ÉCOLE MATERNELLE** or classes in an **ÉCOLE PRIMAIRE** are available to children from the age of two years.

Matignon, hôtel
The official residence and offices of the **PREMIER MINISTRE**, situated in the rue de Varenne, Paris.

Matin, le
A daily newspaper published in Paris, (full title *le Matin de Paris*), founded in 1977.

médiateur de la République
A public official whose office looks into complaints against local or national government or any public service, brought through a **DÉPUTÉ** or a **SÉNATEUR**.

Médicis, prix
An annual literary prize for a recently published novel or short story collection with an innovative approach.

mères, fête des
An officially recognized celebration of motherhood, held annually in May.

Mérite agricole
An honour for people in the agricultural industry. It is awarded to those who have contributed to agricultural development. Its popular name is *le poireau*.

midem
An annual market for records, cassettes and music held in Cannes.

Midi-Pyrénées
A region in the south-west, (**PRÉFECTURE DE RÉGION**: Toulouse) comprising the Ariège, Aveyron, Gers, Haute-Garonne, Hautes-Pyrénées, Lot and Tarn-et-Garonne, with an overall population of 2.4 million. It is the largest region in area, and is generally sparsely populated. The principal sources of employment are agriculture and service industries, and there is a centre of high-tech industrial activity in the Toulouse area.

ministre
Appointed by the **PRÉSIDENT DE LA RÉPUBLIQUE**, on the advice of the **PREMIER MINISTRE**, a *ministre* heads a department of state and becomes a member of the **CONSEIL DES MINISTRES**. The title *ministre d'État* is a recognition that the ministry is of greater than normal significance. In the **CINQUIÈME RÉPUBLIQUE**, a **DÉPUTÉ** has to resign his or her seat in order to take office as a *ministre*.

Minitel
A computer terminal provided by **FRANCE TÉLÉCOM** to its telephone customers, connected to the **TÉLÉTEL** network.

Monde, le
A left-of-centre Paris daily newspaper owned by its staff. Le Monde has an international reputation as a serious commentator. It rather quirkily retains certain traditions, such as an absence of photographs in its editorial matter.

Montagne, la
The principal daily newspaper in the Massif central published in Clermont-Ferrand.

Mont-de-Piété
A popular term for a pawnbroker, now officially known as **CRÉDIT MUNICIPAL**.

motion de censure
An anti-government motion in the **ASSEMBLÉE NATIONALE**, signed by at least 10% of its members, in which only votes for the motion are counted. The government must resign if the motion is carried, but if it is defeated, the same signatories cannot present another *motion de censure* in the same session of the parliament.

Mouvement des radicaux de gauche – MRG
A left-of-centre political grouping which has widespread influence in local politics, if no strong presence at the national level.

musée national
A museum directly under the control of the *ministre de la Culture*.

mutualité
There is a strong tradition of mutual organizations in France, based on common interests of social and economic groups. The most prominent of these is in the field of personal insurance.

Nn

NAP – Neuilly-Auteuil-Passy
The upper bourgeoisie lifestyle typified by residents of these fashionable quarters of western Paris.

nationalisation
The two nationalization programmes of 1945 and 1982, in which public utilities, coal and steel producers, banks, insurance companies, Renault, Air France and Elf-Aquitaine came into state ownership.

navette parlementaire
Texts of new laws pass between the **ASSEMBLÉE NATIONALE** and the **SÉNAT**, if amendments are made by the upper house.

NF – normes françaises
A legally recognized guarantee of quality.

Nice-Matin
A daily newspaper published in Nice.

non-inscrit
A candidate for election who is not officially backed by a recognized political party.

non-lieu
The result of an investigation by a JUGE D'INSTRUCTION if there is insufficient evidence to proceed against a suspect.

Nord-Éclair
A daily newspaper published in Roubaix.

Nord-Matin
A daily newspaper published in Lille.

Nord-Pas-de-Calais
The largely urbanized region (PRÉFECTURE DE RÉGION: Lille) on the Belgian border, comprising the DÉPARTEMENTS of Nord and Pas-de-Calais. The population is 3.96 million, and the economy has traditionally been based on coal production, fishing, cross-channel trade and distribution. Since the mid-1980s, it has been severely affected by unemployment.

notaire
A qualified lawyer who advises clients and deals with legal documents, especially in property transactions.

Nous Deux
A weekly women's magazine.

Nouvel Observateur, le
A radical weekly news magazine.

Nouvelle République, la
A daily newspaper published in Tours.

numéro minéralogique
The two-digit code for the DÉPARTEMENT used on vehicle registration plates, and as the first two digits of postcodes.

numéro vert
A telephone number called free of charge to the caller.

Oo

offense au président
Insulting the PRÉSIDENT DE LA RÉPUBLIQUE either in print or in behaviour is a *délit*.

Office national d'information sur les enseignements et les professions – ONISEP
The national careers and education guidance service, with centres in every DÉPARTEMENT, and representatives in each state LYCÉE.

Officiel des spectacles
A weekly listings magazine giving details of Paris events.

Olympia
A Paris theatre, the venue of pop music and spectacular shows.

Opéra de Paris
The state-supported opera and ballet company based at the Palais Garnier and the Opéra Bastille in Paris.

ordonnance
An extraordinary government decision issued by DÉCRET, valid for only a limited period.

ordonnance pénale
A judgement in a TRIBUNAL DE POLICE in the absence of the defendant, made on the basis of documentary evidence.

ordre des Arts et Lettres
An order of artistic and literary honours.

ordre des Palmes académiques
An order of honours for those working in the national education service.

ordre national du Mérite
An honorary order similar to the LÉGION D'HONNEUR.

orientation scolaire
Advice and guidance offered to pupils and their parents when choosing routes through the education system.

Orly
The international airport south of Paris opened in 1961.

Orsay, musée d'
A fine art museum in the former *gare d'Orsay* railway terminus in Paris, including the Impressionist collection previously held in the *musée du Jeu de Paume*.

Ouest-France
The daily newspaper with the largest circulation in France. Its main edition is published in Rennes, but it has local editions throughout western France.

ouvrier spécialisé – OS
A semi-skilled or unskilled worker.

Pp

palais Bourbon
The eighteenth-century Paris residence on the left bank of the Seine, now the home of the ASSEMBLÉE NATIONALE.

palais du Luxembourg
The home of the SÉNAT in the *jardin du Luxembourg* in Paris.

palais Garnier
The main opera house of the OPÉRA DE PARIS.

palais omnisports Paris-Bercy
An indoor arena, seating 17,000 spectators, in the south-east of Paris.

palais Royal
The seventeenth-century palace of Cardinal Richelieu, later the site of popular promenades, shops, cafés and sideshows.

Panthéon
An eighteenth-century domed former church in Paris which became a civil monument during the Revolution. It houses the tombs of some historical personalities of the Republic.

parc de la Villette
A new cultural centre on the east side of Paris, and a public leisure park with water sports facilities, on the site of the former city abattoir and meat market.

parc des Princes
A sports stadium in the west of Paris, the venue for large events.

Pariscope
A weekly Paris entertainments listings magazine.

Parisien, le
The daily newspaper with the largest circulation in the Paris area, also known as *le Parisien libéré*.

Paris-Match
A weekly magazine which combines features about celebrities with photo-journalism.

Paris-Normandie
A daily newspaper published in Rouen.

Paris-Turf
A daily sports newspaper, with emphasis on horse-racing.

Parti communiste français – PCF
A political party, formerly the largest single political grouping in France, now of declining electoral influence.

Parti radical socialiste
The oldest of the existing political parties, now with relatively little influence, except as a centrist pressure-group within the **UDF**.

Parti républicain – PR
A centre-right political party, part of the **UDF**, originally forming the support base for Valéry Giscard d'Estaing.

Parti socialiste – PS
The largest political party of the left, forming the government majority in 1981–86 and 1988–93. There are strong factions within the party.

Parti socialiste unifié – PSU
A more radical party than the **PARTI SOCIALISTE**, formed in 1960 as a splinter group, now using the title *Alternative rouge et verte*.

Pays de la Loire
The region centred around the lower Loire valley (**PRÉFECTURE DE RÉGION**: Nantes) comprising the **DÉPARTEMENTS** of Loire-Atlantique, Maine-et-Loire, Mayenne, Sarthe and Vendée. The population is 3.06 million. The character of the region is mixed, ranging from a maritime economy to peaceful agricultural areas, with medium-sized urban areas supported by light and increasingly high-tech industries.

permis de conduire
The driving licence issued to those aged 18 and over who have passed theoretical and practical tests. Licences issued since 1992 are on the *permis à points* system, which entails the deduction of points, potentially leading to disqualification, in the case of driving offences.

perquisition
A police search of premises or a vehicle, requiring the permission of the owner, except in the case of a **FLAGRANT DÉLIT** or serious offence.

petite ceinture
The inner ring road in Paris, and the circular bus service which runs along it.

pharmacie d'officine
A licensed and regulated private enterprise pharmacy.

Picardie
The region north of Paris (**PRÉFECTURE DE RÉGION**: Amiens) comprising the **DÉPARTEMENTS** of Aisne, Oise and Somme. The population is 1.8 million. Its place in world history is due to its role in the First World War. Recent economic change has seen a decline in the textile industry and an attempt to rebuild the industrial and agricultural infrastructure.

Plan
The national economic planning instrument, usually lasting four or five years, providing a strategic direction approved by parliament.

plan Orsec
The permanent emergency evacuation and administration plans for implementation in the event of a natural disaster.

Pleyel, salle
The main orchestral concert hall in Paris.

PMU – Pari mutuel urbain
The regulated network of horse-race betting outlets. The most popular form is the *tiercé* which requires the player to predict the first three places.

Point, le
A centre-right weekly news magazine.

Poitou-Charentes
The region (**PRÉFECTURE DE RÉGION**: Poitiers) comprising the **DÉPARTEMENTS** of Charente, Charente-Maritime, Deux-Sèvres and Vienne. The population is 1.6 million. The traditional base of the local economy is the food industry and there is considerable development of administrative services and high-tech industries.

pôle de conversion
An industrialized urban area which receives special aid in combatting declining employment and a poor environment.

police de l'air et des frontières – PAF
The frontier and immigration police force, a section of the **POLICE NATIONALE**, which also has the role of investigating air and rail safety.

police judiciaire – PJ
The regionally administered sections of the **GENDARMERIE NATIONALE** and **POLICE NATIONALE** which deal with organized crime.

police municipale
A local police force carrying out minor or routine policing functions, responsible to the **MAIRE** of a **COMMUNE**.

police nationale
The nationally organized police service, responsible to the *ministre de l'Intérieur*, separate from the **GENDARMERIE NATIONALE**.

préfecture
The administrative headquarters of the **DÉPARTEMENT**, and the town in which these are located.

préfet
The senior administrator of state services in the **DÉPARTEMENT**.

préfet de police de Paris
The head of police services in the capital and coordinator of emergency services in the Paris conurbation.

préfet de région
The *préfet* in the **DÉPARTEMENT** of the *préfecture de région* acts as government representative in negotiations with the **CONSEIL RÉGIONAL**.

premier cycle
The first two-year stage of higher education studies, normally leading to a **DEUG**.

Premier ministre
The chief minister of the government, appointed by the **PRÉSIDENT DE LA RÉPUBLIQUE**, and responsible for the overall management of government affairs.

président de la République
The head of state, elected by universal suffrage for a period of seven years, with a strong executive role in government, and normally taking a direct role in at least the foreign policy.

président du Conseil
The **QUATRIÈME RÉPUBLIQUE**'s equivalent of the **PREMIER MINISTRE**, but with a much weaker role.

prêt conventionné – PC
A loan, repayable over periods up to 20 years, for the purchase, building or rebuilding of living accommodation.

Prévention routière
The public road safety organization.

prévenu
A person accused of an offence which is under investigation by a **JUGE D'INSTRUCTION**.

priorité à droite
Except at roundabouts, and unless there are other indications or regulations in force, drivers must always give way to traffic approaching from their right.

privatisation
The policy of right-wing governments between 1986 and 1988, and after 1993, to sell state-owned enterprises partly or wholly to the private sector.

procès-verbal
A written legal statement alleging facts which can be used in criminal proceedings.

procuration
The power of proxy allowing either voting rights *in absentia* or authorization to take control of another person's affairs.

procureur
A lawyer who is appointed by the **GARDE DES SCEAUX** to act as public prosecutor. There are various ranks, the highest being *Procureur de la République*.

professeur agrégé
A holder of the **AGRÉGATION**, contracted to teach 15–17 hours per week in a **LYCÉE** or higher education institution.

professeur des écoles
A primary school teacher, trained in an **IUFM**, appointed since 1991.

Progrès, le
The principal daily newspaper published in Lyon.

projet de loi
A government proposal for legislation brought to the **ASSEMBLÉE NATIONALE** for debate.

proposition de loi
A proposal for legislation brought to the **ASSEMBLÉE NATIONALE** for debate by a **DÉPUTÉ**.

Provençal, le
A daily newspaper published in Marseille.

Provence-Alpes-Côte-d'Azur – PACA
The south-east coastal region (**PRÉFECTURE DE RÉGION**: Marseille) comprising the **DÉPARTEMENTS** of Alpes-de-Haute-Provence, Alpes-Maritimes, Bouches-du-Rhône, Hautes-Alpes, Var and Vaucluse. The population is 4.27 million. Apart from the industrial zones near Marseille, most of the region's workforce is engaged in service activities, with tourism being an important income-earner. Personal incomes, especially in the Alpes-Maritimes, are higher than the national average.

proviseur
A former **PROFESSEUR AGRÉGÉ** who is the head of a **LYCÉE**.

prud'homme
An elected member of a local industrial tribunal (*conseil de prud'hommes*) which rules in cases of dispute over employment contracts.

Qq

quai Conti
The address of the **ACADÉMIE FRANÇAISE**.

Quai d'Orsay
The address of the *ministère des Affaires étrangères*.

quartier Latin
The original university area in central Paris on the left bank of the Seine.

Quatrième République
The constitutional regime which existed from 1946 to 1958.

Que choisir?
An independent monthly consumer magazine.

Que sais-je?
A paperback imprint in standard format of 128 pages of a wide range of non-fiction titles.

Rr

Radio bleue
A radio service of **RADIO FRANCE**, targeting the over-50 age group, with programmes based on French songs.

Radio France
The state-owned radio broadcasting company, with national and local stations, principally financed by the **REDEVANCE TÉLÉVISION**.

radio libre
A broadcasting radio station not provided by **RADIO FRANCE**.

Radio Monte-Carlo – RMC
A **RADIO PÉRIPHÉRIQUE**, of which the French state is the majority shareholder.

radio périphérique
A radio broadcasting organization independent of **RADIO FRANCE**, controlled and administered from another country.

Radio-Sorbonne
An educational radio service for adult distance-learning students following degree courses.

Radio-Télévision Suisse-Romande
The French language service broadcast from Lausanne, Switzerland.

RATP – Régie autonome des transports parisiens
The Paris public transport authority with a monopoly over the provision of bus, tram and *métro* services.

réclusion à perpétuité
A life imprisonment sentence, with a minimum period of 15 years, and a normal actual maximum of 22 years before **LIBÉRATION CONDITIONNELLE** can be granted.

recteur
The administrative head of the education service within an **ACADÉMIE**.

redevance télévision
The annual television receiving licence, providing income for the state-owned programme-making companies.

redoublement
The repetition of a school year by a pupil in a primary school, when progress in the year has been inadequate.

référé-liberté
An appeal for the release of a person undergoing investigation by a **JUGE D'INSTRUCTION**.

référendum
A referendum may be called by the **PRÉSIDENT DE LA RÉPUBLIQUE** on questions concerning the organization of the state or a matter which might change its nature, or proposed legislation affecting economic and social policy.

régime matrimonial
There are five basic formats of a marriage agreement, the most frequent specifying common ownership only of possessions acquired after marriage.

région
A grouping of **DÉPARTEMENTS**, having played an increasing part since 1982 in planning, education and infrastructure.

rentrée
The beginning of September when normal economic and academic life resumes after the holiday period.

repos obligatoire
The statutory non-working day which must be awarded if Sunday is a working day.

Républicain Lorrain, le
A daily newspaper published in Metz.

République du Centre, la
A daily newspaper published in Orléans.

RER – Réseau express régional
The rapid-transit rail network in the Paris area, run by the **RATP** and **SNCF**, and linked to the *métro*.

Réunion
An island in the Indian Ocean, with the status of **DOM**. The population is about 600,000. The economy is closely linked with that of France, and it suffers severely from unemployment and poverty.

RG – Renseignements généraux
The intelligence-gathering section of the **POLICE NATIONALE**, with a particular mission to watch foreigners and political groups.

Rhône-Alpes
The second most populous region (**PRÉFECTURE DE RÉGION**: Lyon) comprising the **DÉPARTEMENTS** of Ain, Ardèche, Drôme, Haute-Savoie, Isère, Loire, Rhône and Savoie. There are 5.36 million inhabitants, and the economic base of the region is varied, ranging from the intensely industrialized Lyon area to the tourism of the Alpine areas, from the high-tech developments of Grenoble to the declining heavy industry of the Loire.

RMI – revenu minimum d'insertion
An allowance, introduced in 1988, to support the poorest members of society, by bringing them above the poverty line, but also giving them rights of access to other allowances and social security benefits.

Roland-Garros
The tennis stadium in the Bois de Boulogne, in the western part of Paris, the venue for the International Championship in early summer.

route départementale
A major road within a **DÉPARTEMENT**, numbered within a local series, and prefixed by the letter D.

route nationale
A major road within the national framework, with a number prefixed by the letter N.

RPR – Rassemblement pour la République
The largest right-wing political party, founded by Jacques Chirac in 1976 as a successor to the former Gaullist grouping.

RTBF – Radio télévision belge de la communauté française
The French language service provided by the Belgian national broadcasting organization, available to viewers and listeners in the north-east of France.

RTL – Radio-Télé Luxembourg
A private radio network broadcasting throughout France with the largest single audience share, and with a television channel serving eastern France.

Rungis
The wholesale fresh food market for the capital and national distribution, located at Rungis, a southern Paris suburb.

Ss

sapeurs-pompiers
The fire and rescue service, provided by professionals and volunteers. The *brigade de sapeurs-pompiers de Paris* is part of the army.

Sciences et Vie
A popular science magazine first published in 1913.

scrutin à mode mixte
A voting system used for electing the CONSEIL MUNICIPAL in larger COMMUNES, including some element of proportional representation, but allocating half the seats to the list of candidates which wins more than half the votes.

scrutin de liste à la représentation proportionnelle
The system of voting for the CONSEIL RÉGIONAL, by which seats are allocated to lists of candidates in proportion to the votes cast.

scrutin de liste majoritaire
A system of election in which voters choose a list of candidates, and if one list wins more than half the votes, it obtains all the seats.

scrutin uninominal majoritaire
The system of voting used in the ÉLECTIONS PRÉSIDENTIELLES and ÉLECTIONS CANTONALES or where a single candidate is to be chosen. A second round is held if no candidate gains more than 50% of the votes in the first round.

Secours populaire français – SPF
A charitable organization fighting against poverty, with links to the PARTI COMMUNISTE FRANÇAIS.

secrétaire d'État
A junior ministerial post, reporting to a MINISTRE.

section d'éducation spécialisée – SES
A special education unit for children with serious learning difficulties.

Sécurité sociale
The national system for provision of sickness, maternity, child, unemployment, old-age and housing benefits. All employed personnel make contributions in *régimes* or classifications of membership.

Semeuse
The symbolic sower seen on stamps, coins, etc, one of the manifestations of MARIANNE.

Sénat
The upper parliamentary chamber, with 321 SÉNATEURS, elected for nine years. A third of the members are elected every three years by an electoral college within a DÉPARTEMENT. The *président du Sénat* acts in place of the PRÉSIDENT DE LA RÉPUBLIQUE in the latter's incapacity.

sénateur
An elected member of the SÉNAT, at least 35 years of age, representing a DÉPARTEMENT.

Sept, la
A television broadcasting company established in 1986.

Sept d'or
Annual awards for television programmes given at a public ceremony each Spring.

service national
All French males aged 18–35 are liable to serve 10 months' military or 16 months' voluntary service. Proposals for a major reform are under discussion.

SGEN – Syndicat général de l'éducation nationale
A union for teachers from all phases of education, allied to the CFDT.

SMIC – salaire minimum interprofessionnel de croissance
The basic minimum legal wage fixed annually by DÉCRET.

SNALC – Syndicat national des lycées et collèges
A moderate secondary schoolteachers' union.

SNCF – Société nationale des chemins de fer français
The state-owned railway company, with access also to private finance, founded in 1937.

SNES – Syndicat national des enseignants du second degré classique, moderne et technique
A union of secondary school teachers.

SNESUP – Syndicat national de l'enseignement supérieur
A union of teachers in higher education.

SNPMI – Syndicat national des petites et moyennes industries
An organization of small industrial employers.

Socrate
The SNCF's computerized reservation and ticketing system.

soldat inconnu
There are two tombs of the unknown soldier in France, one from the First World War, under the *Arc de Triomphe* in Paris, the other from the Indo-Chinese War at Notre-Dame-de-Lorette, near Arras.

SOS-Racisme
An anti-racist pressure group operating throughout France.

sous-préfecture
The administrative offices of a **SOUS-PRÉFET** situated in the main town of an **ARRONDISSEMENT**.

sous-préfet
The government representative in an **ARRONDISSEMENT**, responsible to the **PRÉFET**.

STS – section de techniciens supérieurs
A specialist section of a **LYCÉE** *professionnel* providing courses for the **BTS**.

Sud-Ouest
A daily newspaper published in Bordeaux.

Sud-Radio
A **RADIO LIBRE** broadcasting in **AQUITAINE**, **LANGUEDOC-ROUSSILLON** and **MIDI-PYRÉNÉES**.

suppléant
A replacement for a sitting **DÉPUTÉ** who is given a ministerial post or who dies during the period of the parliament.

syndicat d'initiative
A local tourist information service funded by municipal authorities and local businesses.

Syndicat enseignant – SE
A teachers' union, drawing most of its membership from the ranks of primary school teachers, with sympathies with the **PARTI SOCIALISTE**.

syndicat intercommunal à vocation unique – SIVU
A joint organization of two or more **COMMUNES** to pool the provision of a particular service.

Tt

tabac
A *débit de tabac*, designated by a red cigar sign, has a licence to sell tobacco products, postage stamps and certain official documents.

taxe d'apprentissage
A payroll tax to support training and apprenticeship schemes.

taxe d'habitation
A local tax based on the value of domestic property.

technicien
A person qualified at *brevet professionnel* level or higher.

technopole
An urban area designated as a centre of high-tech research and development.

Télé 7 Jours
The leading weekly broadcasting and entertainments listings magazine.

Télé Magazine
A weekly listings magazine.

télécarte
A plastic card needed for using a public telephone.

Télégramme de Brest, le
A daily newspaper published in Morlaix.

Télépoche
A weekly broadcasting and entertainments listings magazine.

Télérama
A weekly television magazine.

Télétel
A computerized information network available to all telephone users using a **MINITEL** terminal. Initially used for telephone directory enquiries, it has become an enormous base for commercial and public information.

territoire d'outre-mer – TOM
An overseas territory, constitutionally part of the republic, whose citizens have French nationality.

TF1 – Télévision française 1
A television channel, originally tightly controlled by the state, but privatized since 1987.

TGV – train à grande vitesse
A new generation electric railway passenger train operated by **SNCF**, which can reach speeds of 270kph on specially built track.

théâtre de boulevard
A commercial theatre providing programmes of light entertainment.

Théâtre Français
The eighteenth-century building in Paris which is home to the **COMÉDIE-FRANÇAISE**.

Théâtre national de l'Odéon
A subsidized theatre in Paris with the principal function of performing contemporary works.

tierce opposition
A third party affected by the decision of a civil court may appeal against it, even if not present at the time of the trial.

TNC – Théâtre national de Chaillot
A subsidized theatre in Paris with the principal function of performing contemporary works.

TNP – Théâtre national populaire
A subsidized theatre company based in Villeurbanne, a Lyon suburb.

Tour de France
The annual cycle race, established in 1903, which finishes each year in Paris in the Avenue des **CHAMPS-ÉLYSÉES**.

Tour Eiffel
The steel tower built for the 1889 Paris international exhibition, saved from demolition because of its role as a radio transmitter. It is now owned by the Paris city council, and with extensions for television transmission, is now 320 metres in height.

Tour Maine-Montparnasse
The highest office building (210 metres) within the city limits of Paris.

Trésor public
The state's financial accounting department.

trésorier-payeur général
The senior state finance officer in a **RÉGION**.

tribunal administratif
A tribunal which hears cases of maladministration by national or local government.

tribunal correctionnel
A criminal court where cases are heard before three JUGES, but without a JURY.

tribunal de commerce
A tribunal to hear cases of disputes between businesses, presided over by elected business personnel.

tribunal de grande instance
A civil court for hearing complicated cases with three JUGES.

tribunal d'instance
A civil court for simple cases presided over by one JUGE.

tribunal de police
The criminal court which hears cases of minor offences, in which defendants do not need to engage AVOCATS.

trois jours
The period (actually no more than two days) of selection procedures including medical and aptitude tests prior to SERVICE NATIONAL.

tronc commun
The common core curriculum of the COLLÈGE and the entry year in the LYCÉE.

TVA – taxe sur la valeur ajoutée
A value-added tax, payable at three different rates, depending on the nature of the transaction. Certain activities are exempt.

Uu

UDF – Union pour la démocratie française
A political grouping of the centre right, in which FORCE DÉMOCRATE, PARTI RADICAL SOCIALISTE, PARTI RÉPUBLICAIN and other smaller parties work together at times of elections.

UFR – unité de formation et de recherche
The officially recognized term for the basic unit of university organization.

UNAPEL – Union nationale des associations des parents d'élèves de l'enseignement libre
A pressure group which campaigns for the interests of pupils in private schools and their families.

UNEF – Union nationale des étudiants de France
The major grouping of students' unions.

Union, l'
The daily newspaper published in Reims.

université du troisième âge
A university established to meet the needs of retired people, and not demanding any formal entry qualifications.

université libre
A privately funded university institution.

Vv

VDQS – vin délimité de qualité supérieure
A wine which has passed strict quality controls and is guaranteed to come from a particular area.

vente aux enchères
A sale by auction requires the services of a NOTAIRE, and is traditionally held for the duration of a lighted candle.

Verts, les
A green political party, established in 1984, and since a split with GÉNÉRATION ÉCOLOGIE in 1990, with a left-wing programme.

Vie, la
A weekly Catholic magazine.

Vigipirate
An emergency plan for increased police and military security, bringing increased uniformed presence in public places at times of threatened terrorist attacks, etc.

vignette
A tax on vehicles payable on initial registration and then annually in November until the vehicle is 25 years old. Older vehicles are charged a lower rate. A current disc has to be displayed on the front windscreen.

Voix du Nord, la
A daily newspaper published in Lille.

vote de confiance
A vote, by government request, in the ASSEMBLÉE NATIONALE.

vote par procuration
A proxy vote in an election, subject to formalities having been completed in advance in the presence of a legal officer.

VSD – Vendredi, samedi, dimanche
A popular weekly news and leisure magazine.

Zz

ZAC – zone d'aménagement concerté
A development zone within a locally agreed plan, in which public and private developers collaborate.

French–English dictionary
Dictionnaire français–anglais

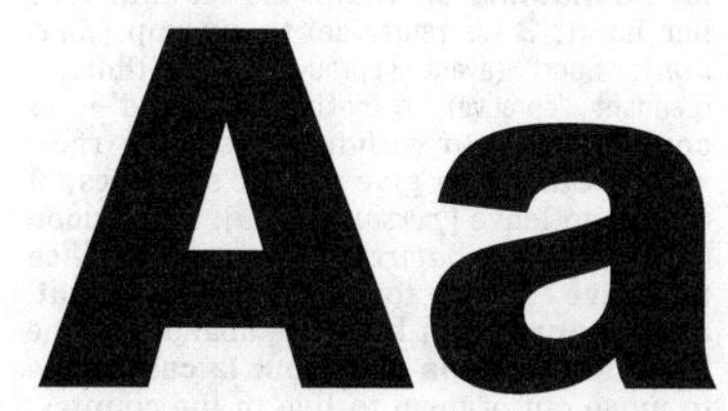

a, **A** /a, ɑ/ **I** *nm inv* (lettre) a, A; **vitamine A** vitamin A; **de A à Z** from A to Z; **le bricolage de A à Z** the A to Z of DIY; **démontrer/prouver qch par A plus B à qn** to demonstrate/prove sth conclusively to sb.

II A *nf* Transp (*abbr* = **autoroute**) **prendre l'A5** take the (motorway GB or freeway US) A5.

■ **a commercial** at sign.

à /a/ *prép*

■ **Note** La préposition *à* se traduit de multiples façons. Les expressions courantes du genre *machine à écrire*, *aller à la pêche*, *difficile à faire etc* sont traitées respectivement sous ***machine***, ***pêche***, ***difficile*** etc.
– Les emplois de *à* avec les verbes *avoir*, *être*, *aller*, *penser etc* sont traités sous les verbes.
– Pour trouver la traduction correcte de *à* on aura intérêt à se reporter aux mots qui précèdent la préposition ainsi qu'aux notes d'usage répertoriées ▶ **1920**.
– On trouvera ci-dessous quelques exemples typiques de traductions de *à*.

1 (avec un verbe de mouvement) **se rendre au travail/~ Paris/~ la campagne** to go to work/to Paris/to the country; **aller de Paris ~ Nevers** to go from Paris to Nevers; **2** (pour indiquer le lieu où l'on se trouve) **~ l'école/la maison** at school/home; **~ Paris/la campagne** in Paris/the country; **3** (dans le temps) **~ l'aube/l'âge de 10 ans** at dawn/the age of 10; **au printemps** in (the) spring; **4** (dans une description) with; **le garçon aux cheveux bruns** the boy with dark hair; **la femme au manteau marron/chapeau noir** the woman with the brown coat/black hat; **5** (employé avec le verbe être) **la maison est ~ louer** the house is for rent ou to let GB; **'~ louer'** 'to let', 'for rent'; **la maison est ~ vendre** the house is for sale; **'~ vendre'** 'for sale'; **il est ~ plaindre** he's to be pitied; **je suis ~ vous tout de suite** I'll be with you in a minute; **maintenant je suis ~ vous** I'm all yours; **c'est ~ qui de jouer?** whose turn is it?; **c'est ~ Emma/~ toi** it's Emma's turn/your turn; **~ moi (de jouer)** my turn (to play); **(c'est) ~ lui de décider** it's up to him to decide; **6** (marquant l'appartenance) **appartenir ~ qn** to belong to sb; **~ qui est cette montre?** whose is this watch?; **elle est ~ moi/lui/elle** it's mine/his/hers; **c'est ~ vous cette voiture?** is this your car?; **une amie ~ moi/eux** a friend of mine/theirs; **encore une idée ~ elle** another of her ideas; **un ami ~ mon père**○ a friend of my father's; **7** (employé avec un nombre) **nous avons fait le travail ~ deux/trois/quatre** two/three/four of us did the work; **(en s'y mettant) ~ deux/dix on devrait y arriver** two/ten of us should be able to manage; **~ nous trois nous avons transporté la malle** the three of us carried the trunk; **~ nous tous on devrait y arriver** between all of us we should be able to manage; **~ trois on est déjà serrés mais ~ quatre c'est impossible** with three people it's crowded but with four it's impossible; **mener 3 ~ 2** to lead 3 (to) 2; **mener par 3 jeux ~ 2** to lead by 3 games to 2; **rouler ~ 100 kilomètres-heure, rouler ~ 100 ~ l'heure**○ to drive at 100 kilometres[GB] per ou an hour; **au 74 de la rue Bossuet** at 74 rue Bossuet; **au 3e étage** on the third GB ou second US floor; **~ quatre kilomètres d'ici** four kilometres[GB] from here; **des bananes ~ 10 francs le kilo** bananas at 10 francs a kilo; **un timbre ~ trois francs** a three-franc stamp; **travailler (de) huit ~ dix heures par jour** to work between eight and ten hours a day, to work eight to ten hours a day; **(de) cinq ~ sept millions de personnes sont concernées** between five and seven million people are concerned, five to seven million people are concerned; **8** (marquant une hypothèse) **~ ce qu'il paraît, ~ ce que l'on prétend, ~ ce que l'on dit** apparently; **~ ce qu'il me semble** as far as I can see; **~ vous entendre, on croirait que** to hear you talk one would think that; **~ y bien réfléchir** when you really think about it; **~ trop vouloir se dépêcher/réclamer on risque de faire** if you hurry too much/ask for too much you run the risk of doing; **~ ne jamais écouter les autres voilà ce qui arrive** that's what happens when you don't listen to other people; **9** (dans phrases exclamatives) **~ nous/notre projet/tes vacances!** (en levant son verre) (here's) to us/our project/your vacation!; **~ ta santé, ~ la tienne!**, **~ la vôtre!** cheers!; **~ tes souhaits** or **amours!** bless you!; **~ toi/vous l'honneur!** (de couper le gâteau) you do the honours!; (après vous) after you!; **~ nous la belle vie!** the good life starts here!; **~ nous (deux)!** (avant un règlement de compte) let's sort this out between us; (de commerçant à client) I'm all yours; **~ demain/ce soir/dans 15 jours** see you tomorrow/tonight/in two weeks; **~ lundi** see you on Monday!; **~ la prochaine** see you next time!; **10** (dans une dédicace) **'~ ma mère'** (dans un livre) 'to my mother'; (sur une tombe) 'in memory of my mother'; **'~ nos chers disparus'** 'in memory of our dear departed'.

Aaron /aaʀɔ̃/ *npr* Aaron.

abaissant, ~e /abɛsɑ̃, ɑ̃t/ *adj* degrading.

abaisse /abɛs/ *nf* Culin rolled-out pastry ¢.

abaisse-langue /abɛslɑ̃g/ *nm inv* spatula, tongue-depressor.

abaissement /abɛsmɑ̃/ *nm* **1** (diminution) (de prix, taux) cut (**de** in); (de seuil, niveau) lowering; **l'~ de l'âge de la retraite à 60 ans** the lowering of the retirement age to 60; **2** (de manette) (en tirant) pulling down; (en poussant) pushing down; **3** (de mur, socle) lowering (**de** of); **4** (avilissement) (de soi-même) self-abasement; (d'autrui) debasement.

abaisser /abese/ [1] **I** *vtr* **1** (diminuer en valeur) to reduce [*prix, taux*] (**à** to; **de** by); to lower [*niveau, seuil*] (**à** to; **de** by); **2** (diminuer en hauteur) to lower [*mur, socle*] (**de** by); **3** (faire descendre) to pull down [*manette, rideau de fer*]; to lower [*pont-levis, rideau de scène*]; **4** Math to draw [*perpendiculaire*]; to bring down [*chiffre de dividende*]; **5** (avilir) liter [*personne*] to humiliate [*adversaire, vaincu*]; [*douleur, vice*] to degrade; **6** (rabattre) to humble [*prétentions, orgueil*]; **7** Culin to roll out [*pâte*].

II s'abaisser *vpr* **1** (descendre) [*rideau de scène*] to fall; **2** (s'avilir) to demean oneself; **s'~ à faire qch** to stoop to doing sth; **ce n'est pas s'~ que de demander de l'aide** it is not demeaning to ask for help.

abaisseur /abɛsœʀ/ *nm* **1** Anat (**muscle**) **~** depressor; **2** Électrotech step-down transformer.

abajoue /abaʒu/ *nf* cheek pouch.

abandon /abɑ̃dɔ̃/ *nm* **1** (état) state of neglect; **état d'~** neglected state; **à l'~** [*maison, domaine*] abandoned, deserted; [*enfant*] running wild; [*jardin*] neglected; **biens à l'~** Jur ownerless property; **laisser à l'~** to allow [sth] to fall into decay [*maison*]; to allow [sth] to become overgrown [*jardin, terres*]; **2** Jur (de véhicule) abandonment; (de personne) desertion; **3** (d'idée, de projet, méthode) abandonment; (de droit, privilège) relinquishment; (de bien) surrender; **faire ~ de** to relinquish [*droit, bien*]; **faire ~ de qch à qn** to make over ou surrender sth to sb; **4** (de cours, d'épreuve) Scol, Sport withdrawal (**de** from) ; (de fonctions) giving up (**de** of); **être contraint à l'~** to be forced to withdraw; **vainqueur par ~** winner by default; **5** (confiance) lack of restraint; **parler avec ~** to talk freely ou without restraint; **6** (attitude détendue) relaxed attitude; **pose pleine d'~** attitude of complete relaxation.

■ **~ de créance** composition between debtor and creditor; **~ du domicile conjugal** desertion of the marital home; **~ d'enfant** abandonment of a child; **~ d'épave** abandonment of a vehicle; **~ d'incapable** abandonment of a person in need of care; **~ de navire** notice of abandonment (of a vessel) ; **~ de poste** desertion (of one's post); **~ des poursuites** abandonment of action, nolle prosequi spéc.

abandonné, ~e /abɑ̃dɔne/ **I** *pp* ▶ **abandonner**.

II *pp adj* **1** (délaissé) [*épouse, famille, ami, cause*] deserted; [*véhicule*] abandoned; [*domaine, maison*] abandoned; [*héros, nation, peuple*] abandoned, forsaken sout; **chef ~ de tous** leader whose supporters have fled; **être ~ à soi-même** to be left to one's own devices; **être ~ par les médecins** to be considered past help by the doctors; **2** (désaffecté) [*chemin, usine, mine*] disused; **3** (qui n'a plus cours) [*théorie, méthode*] discarded; [*modèle, format*] discontinued; **4** (détendu) [*pose, attitude*] gén relaxed; (voluptueusement) abandoned.

abandonner /abɑ̃dɔne/ [1] **I** *vtr* **1** (renoncer à) to abandon, to give up [*projet, théorie, activité, espoir*]; to give up [*habitude*]; to give up, to forsake sout [*confort, sécurité*]; Scol to drop [*matière*]; **~ les recherches** to give up the search; **~ la cigarette/l'alcool** to give up smoking/drinking; **les médecins l'ont abandonné** the doctors have given up on him; **je peignais, mais j'ai abandonné** I used to paint, but I gave it up; **c'est trop dur, j'abandonne** it's too hard, I give up; **~ la partie** or **lutte** to throw in the towel; **2** (céder) to give ou relinquish sout [*bien*] (**à qn** to sb); to hand [sth] over [*gestion*] (**à qn**

to sb); **je vous abandonne le soin d'expliquer** I'm leaving it to you to explain; **elle lui abandonna sa main** she let him take her hand; **3** (se retirer de) to give up [*fonction*]; Sport (avant l'épreuve) to withdraw; (pendant l'épreuve) to retire; **forcé d'~ la course** forced to withdraw from the race; **~ ses études** to give up one's studies; **4** (quitter) to leave [*personne, lieu*]; to abandon [*véhicule, objet, navire*]; **~ Paris pour Nice** to leave Paris for Nice; **il s'enfuit, abandonnant son butin** he abandoned the loot and fled; **~ la ville pour la campagne** to move out of town to live in the country; **~ le terrain** lit to flee; fig to give up; **5** (délaisser) to abandon, to forsake sout [*enfant, famille*]; to abandon [*animal*]; to desert [*foyer, épouse, poste, cause, parti*]; **6** (livrer) **~ qch à** to leave ou abandon sth to; **~ un jardin aux orties** to abandon a garden to the nettles; **~ qn à son sort** to leave ou abandon sb to his/her fate; **7** (faire défaut) [*courage, chance*] to desert [*personne*]; **mes forces m'abandonnent** my strength is failing me; **8** (lâcher) to let go of [*outil, rênes*]; **9** Ordinat to abort.

II s'abandonner *vpr* **1** (se confier) to let oneself go; **2** (se détendre) to let oneself go; **s'~ dans les bras de qn** to sink into sb's arms; **3** (se laisser aller) **s'~ à la passion/au désespoir** to give oneself up ou to abandon oneself to passion/to despair; **s'~ au plaisir de** to lose oneself in the pleasure of; **s'~ au sommeil** to let oneself drift off to sleep; **4** (se donner sexuellement) [*femme*] to give oneself (**à** to).

abaque /abak/ *nm* **1** (graphique) graph; **2** (boulier) abacus.

abasourdir /abazuʀdiʀ/ [3] *vtr* **1** (assourdir) to deafen; **2** (stupéfier) to stun; **être abasourdi** [*personne, groupe*] to be stunned.

abasourdissement /abazuʀdismɑ̃/ *nm* bewilderment, stupefaction.

abâtardir /abɑtaʀdiʀ/ [3] **I** *vtr* to make [sth] degenerate [*être vivant, race*]; to bastardize [*langue*]; to debase, to degrade [*sentiment, vertu, style*].

II s'abâtardir *vpr* [*style*] to become debased; [*race*] to degenerate.

abâtardissement /abɑtaʀdismɑ̃/ *nm* debasement, degeneration.

abat-jour /abaʒuʀ/ *nm inv* lampshade.

abats /aba/ *nmpl* **1** (bœuf, porc, mouton) offal **¢**; **2** (de volaille) giblets.

abat-son /abasɔ̃/ *nm inv* louvre[GB].

abattage /abataʒ/ *nm* **1** (d'arbre) felling; **2** (d'animal de boucherie) slaughter **¢**; **~ rituel** ritual slaughter; **3** (de minerai) mining, working; **~ à l'explosif** blasting; **4**○ (énergie) dynamism; **avoir de l'~** to be very dynamic; **5**○ (prostitution) prostitution with a rapid turnover of clients.

abattant /abatɑ̃/ *nm* (de bureau, secrétaire) (drop) leaf, flap; (de siège de WC) lid.

abattement /abatmɑ̃/ *nm* **1** (état dépressif) despondency; **être plongé dans un ~ profond** to be deeply despondent; **2** (réduction) gén reduction; Fisc allowance.

■ **~ fiscal** tax allowance GB ou deduction US.

abattis /abati/ *nmpl* **1** Culin giblets; **2** Mil abattis; **3**○ (membres) hum limbs; **tu peux numéroter tes ~!** (avant rixe) you're in for a hiding!; **numéroter ses ~** (après accident) to check that one is all in one piece.

abattoir /abatwaʀ/ *nm* slaughterhouse, abattoir; **envoyer qn à l'~** fig to send sb to be slaughtered; **aller à l'~** fig to go to the slaughter.

abattre /abatʀ/ [61] **I** *vtr* **1** (tuer) to slaughter [*animal de boucherie*]; to destroy [*animal dangereux*]; (avec une arme à feu) to shoot [sb] down [*personne*]; to shoot [*animal*]; **c'est l'homme à ~** he is the prime target; fig he is the one to beat; **2** (renverser) to bring [sth/sb] down [*tyran, régime*]; **3** (faire tomber) to pull down [*bâtiment*]; to knock down [*mur, paroi*]; to bring down [*statue*]; to shoot down [*avion*]; to break down [*tabou, préjugé*]; [*personne*] to fell [*arbre*]; [*tempête*] to bring down [*arbre, pylône*]; [*pluie*] to settle [*poussière*]; **4** (découvrir) to show [*carte, jeu*]; **~ ses cartes** or **son jeu** lit, fig to put one's cards on the table; **5** (accabler) (physiquement) to wear [sb] out; (moralement) to demoralize, to get [sb] down○; **être abattu** (physiquement) to be worn out; (moralement) to be demoralized; **on ne va pas se laisser ~!** we're not going to let things get us down!; **ne te laisse pas ~** keep your spirits up!; **6** (accomplir) to get through [*travail*]; **~ de la besogne** to get through a lot of work.

II s'abattre *vpr* **1** [*arbre, construction, rocher*] to come down; [*avion*] to crash; [*personne*] to collapse; **2** (agresser) **s'~ sur** [*orage*] to beat down on; [*oiseau*] to swoop down on; [*léopard*] to pounce on; [*guerre*] to engulf; [*malheur*] to descend upon.

abat-vent /abavɑ̃/ *nm inv* **1** (de cheminée) (chimney) cowl; **2** Agric, Hort wind break.

abbatial, **~e**, *mpl* **-iaux** /abasjal, o/ **I** *adj* abbey (*épith*), abbatial sout.

II abbatiale *nf* abbey church.

abbaye /abei/ *nf* abbey.

abbé /abe/ *nm* **1** (supérieur d'une abbaye) abbot; **le père ~** the abbot; **2** (prêtre) priest; **monsieur l'~** Father; **l'~ Popelin** Father Popelin.

abbesse /abɛs/ *nf* abbess; **mère ~** abbess.

abc /ɑbese/ *nm* (rudiments) ABC, ABC's US, rudiments; **l'~ du jardinage** the ABC ou the rudiments of gardening.

abcès /apsɛ/ *nm inv* abscess; **~ dentaire** (dental) abscess; **crever** or **vider l'~** fig to resolve a crisis.

Abdias /abdjas/ *npr* Obadiah.

abdication /abdikasjɔ̃/ *nf* lit, fig abdication.

abdiquer /abdike/ [1] **I** *vtr* to abdicate [*pouvoir, responsabilité*]; to renounce [*prérogative, sentiment*].

II *vi* **1** [*souverain*] to abdicate (**en faveur de** in favour[GB] of); **2** (renoncer) to surrender (**devant qn/qch** to sb/sth).

abdomen /abdɔmɛn/ *nm* **1** Anat, Zool abdomen; **2** Sport stomach.

abdominal, **~e**, *mpl* **-aux** /abdɔminal, o/ **I** *adj* abdominal.

II abdominaux *nmpl* **1** Anat abdominal muscles; **2** Sport stomach exercises.

abducteur /abdyktœʀ/ *nm* abductor.

abécédaire /ɑbesedɛʀ/ *nm* spelling book, primer†.

abeille /abɛj/ *nf* (honey) bee.

■ **~ maçonne** mason bee; **~ ouvrière** worker bee.

Abel /abɛl/ *npr* Abel.

aber /abɛʀ/ *nm* large estuary.

aberrant, **~e** /abɛʀɑ̃, ɑ̃t/ *adj* **1** (absurde) absurd; **2** (anormal) aberrant.

aberration /abɛʀasjɔ̃/ *nf* **1** (absurdité) aberration; **2** Astron, Phys aberration; **3** Biol aberration; **~ chromosomique** chromosome aberration.

abêtir /abetiʀ/ [3] **I** *vtr* to turn [sb] into a moron○.

II s'abêtir *vpr* to become stupid, to turn into a moron○.

abêtissant, **~e** /abetisɑ̃, ɑ̃t/ *adj* [*travail, spectacle, lecture*] mindless.

abêtissement /abetismɑ̃/ *nm* **1** (processus) stupefying effect; **l'~ du public par les médias** the stupefying effect of the media on the public; **2** (état) mindlessness, stupidity.

abhorrer /abɔʀe/ [1] *vtr* fml to abhor sout, to loathe.

Abidjan /abidʒɑ̃/ **▶ 857** *npr* Abidjan.

abîme /abim/ *nm* **1** (précipice) abyss; **2** (écart) gulf (**entre** between); **un ~ nous sépare** there is a gulf between us; **3** (ruine) ruin; **être au bord de l'~** to be on the verge of ruin; **toucher le fond de l'~** gén to hit rock bottom; (moralement) to be at one's lowest ebb; **sa lente remontée de l'~** his slow recovery from the depths of despair; **4** (haut degré) **un ~ de désespoir** the depths of despair; **plonger qn dans un ~ de perplexité** to make sb deeply perplexed; **être plongé dans des ~s de réflexion** to be deep in thought.

abîmer /abime/ [1] **I** *vtr* to damage [*objet*]; [*froid, produit*] to damage [*peau, mains*]; **les meubles/fruits ont été très abîmés pendant le transport** the furniture/fruit was badly damaged in transit; **être tout abîmé** to be ruined; **des livres tout abîmés** damaged books; **il a eu le nez abîmé dans la bagarre** his nose was injured in the fight.

II s'abîmer *vpr* **1** (se détériorer) [*objet*] to get damaged; [*fruit*] to spoil; **les murs s'abîment à l'humidité** the walls are getting damaged by the damp; **il s'est abîmé l'épaule en tombant** he damaged his shoulder in the fall; **s'~ les mains** to ruin one's hands; **tu vas t'~ la vue/les yeux avec cet éclairage** you'll ruin your eyesight/strain your eyes in this light; **2** (sombrer) liter **s'~ dans la mer** [*bateau, avion*] to be engulfed by the waves; **3** (se plonger) liter **s'~ dans qch** to be lost in sth; **il s'abîmait dans la méditation/prière** he was lost in meditation/prayer; **s'~ dans ses pensées** to be immersed in one's thoughts.

abiotique /abjɔtik/ *adj* abiotic.

abject, **~e** /abʒɛkt/ *adj* despicable, abject; **de façon ~e** despicably.

abjectement /abʒɛktəmɑ̃/ *adv* despicably, abjectly.

abjection /abʒɛksjɔ̃/ *nf* abjectness; **tomber dans l'~** to debase oneself.

abjuration /abʒyʀasjɔ̃/ *nf* abjuration sout.

abjurer /abʒyʀe/ [1] **I** *vtr* to abjure sout [*religion*]; to renounce [*opinion, attitude*].

II *vi* Relig to recant.

ablatif /ablatif/ *nm* Ling ablative; **à l'~** in the ablative.

■ **~ absolu** ablative absolute.

ablation /ablasjɔ̃/ *nf* excision, removal; **avoir une ~ de la rate** to have one's spleen removed.

ablette /ablɛt/ *nf* Zool bleak.

ablution /ablysjɔ̃/ **I** *nf* Relig (du calice) ablution.

II ablutions *nfpl* ablutions; **faire ses ~s** hum to perform one's ablutions.

abnégation /abnegasjɔ̃/ *nf* self-sacrifice, abnegation sout; **faire preuve d'~** to act selflessly.

aboiement /abwamɑ̃/ *nm* **1** (de chien) barking **¢**; **2**○ (de personne) ranting **¢**.

abois /abwa/ *nmpl* **aux ~** Chasse at bay; fig in desperate ou dire straits.

abolir /abɔliʀ/ [3] *vtr* **1** Jur to abolish [*loi, droit*]; **2** (supprimer) to abolish [*monarchie, peine de mort*].

abolition /abɔlisjɔ̃/ *nf* abolition.

abolitionnisme /abɔlisjɔnism/ *nm* abolitionism.

abolitionniste /abɔlisjɔnist/ *adj, nmf* abolitionist.

abominable /abɔminabl/ *adj* [*crime, acte, personne, temps*] abominable; **l'~ homme des neiges** the abominable snowman.

abominablement /abɔminabləmɑ̃/ *adv* (horriblement) abominably; (fortement) terribly.

abomination /abɔminɑsjɔ̃/ *nf* abomination; **dire des ~s** to say abominable things; **avoir qn/qch en ~** to loathe sb/sth.

abominer /abɔmine/ [1] *vtr* liter to abominate sout.

abondamment /abɔ̃damɑ̃/ *adv* [*boire, manger*] copiously; [*illustrer*] copiously; [*pleuvoir*] heavily; [*évoquer, souligner*] at length; **l'événement fut ~ commenté dans la presse** the event was commented on at considerable length in the press; **il était ~ documenté** [*personne*] he was extremely well-informed; [*livre*] it was extremely well-researched; **rincer ~ à l'eau** rinse thoroughly with water.

abondance /abɔ̃dɑ̃s/ *nf* **1** (de produits, renseignements, d'idées) wealth (**de** of); (de récolte, ressources) abundance (**de** of); (de main-d'œuvre) abundant supply (**de** of); **en ~** [*trouver, fournir, produire*] in abundance; **il y a ~ de** there's plenty of; **le vin coulait en ~** wine flowed freely; **2** (aisance) also Écon affluence; **vivre dans l'~** to live in affluence; **parler d'~** liter to speak at great length.

IDIOMES **~ de biens ne nuit pas** Prov wealth does no harm.

abondant, **~e** /abɔ̃dɑ̃, ɑ̃t/ *adj* **1** (en quantité) [*ressources, nourriture, récolte*] plentiful; [*source*] lit, fig abundant; [*commentaires, remarques, illustrations*] numerous; **les pluies ~es ont détrempé le sol** the heavy rainfall has drenched the ground; **une main-d'œuvre ~e** an abundant supply of labour; **il a laissé une ~e correspondance** he left a wealth of correspondence; **le journal a reçu un courrier ~** the newspaper has received a large number of letters; **elle versa des larmes ~es** she wept copious tears; **2** (riche) fml [*style*] rich; **être ~ en** to be rich in [*découvertes, surprises*]; **une bibliothèque ~e en ouvrages rares** a library which has a wealth of rare books; **3** (fourni) [*chevelure*] thick; [*végétation*] lush; **une poitrine ~e** an ample bosom.

abonder /abɔ̃de/ [1] *vi* **1** (être en quantité) [*fruits, produits*] to abound; [*gibier, poisson*] to be plentiful; **les exemples de ce type abondent** examples of this kind abound; **un quartier où abondaient les artistes** an area where artists abounded; **2** (avoir en quantité) **~ en** or **de** to be full of; **la région abonde en gibier/en sites archéologiques** the area is teeming with game/rich in archaeological sites.

IDIOMES **~ dans le sens de qn** to agree wholeheartedly with sb; **j'abondai dans le même sens** I agreed wholeheartedly with this.

abonné, **~e** /abɔne/ **I** *pp* ▸ **abonner**.

II *pp adj* **lecteur ~** subscriber; **spectateur** or **membre ~** season ticket holder; **être ~** Presse, TV to subscribe (**à** to); Mus, Théât, Transp to hold a season ticket; **être ~ au gaz** to be a gas consumer; **être ~ au téléphone** to be on the phone; **je suis ~ à ce journal** I subscribe to this newspaper; **y être ~**○ fig, hum to make a habit of it.

III *nm,f* Presse, TV subscriber; Mus, Théât, Transp season ticket holder; Télécom subscriber; **~ au gaz** gas consumer.

abonnement /abɔnmɑ̃/ *nm* **1** Presse subscription; **prendre** or **souscrire un ~** to take out a subscription (**à** to); **résilier/suspendre/renouveler son ~** to cancel/to suspend/to renew one's subscription; **votre ~ arrive à échéance le** your subscription falls due on; **les frais d'~ à** subscription rates for; **ventes hors ~s** non-subscription sales; **concert hors ~** concert not included on a season ticket; **2** Mus, Théât, Transp (**carte d')~** season ticket (**à** for); **3** (de service) Télécom rental system charge; (pour gaz, électricité) standing charge; **4** TV subscription (**à** to).

abonner /abɔne/ [1] **I** *vtr* **~ qn à qch** Presse to take out a subscription to sth for sb; Mus, Théât to buy sb a season ticket for sth.

II s'abonner *vpr* Presse, TV to subscribe (**à** to); Mus, Théât, Transp to buy a season ticket (**à** for); **je me suis abonné pour un an** Presse I've taken out a year's subscription.

abord /abɔʀ/ **I** *nm* **1** (comportement) manner; **être d'un ~ aimable/facile/difficile** to have a pleasant/an easy/a difficult manner; **sous des ~s grincheux c'est un tendre** his gruff exterior hides a kind heart; **2** (approche) access; **sa théorie est d'un ~ relativement aisé** his theory is relatively accessible; **à l'~ de** on approaching; **3** (contact) **au premier** or **de prime ~** at first sight; **dès l'~** from the outset.

II d'abord *loc adv* **1** (avant autre chose) first; **va d'~ te laver les mains** go and wash your hands first; **nous avons d'~ visité Rome** first we visited Rome; **2** (contrairement à la suite) at first; **j'ai d'~ cru à une mauvaise plaisanterie** at first I thought it was a bad joke; **c'est plus compliqué qu'il n'y paraît d'~** it's more complicated than it seems at first; **3** (primo) firstly, first; **il y a trois stades: d' ~ les maux de tête**... there are three stages: firstly headaches...; **j'ai décidé de partir, d'~ à cause du temps et puis**... I decided to leave, firstly because of the weather and then...; **4** (en priorité) first (of all); **les femmes et les enfants d'~** women and children first; **tout d'~** first of all; **d'~ et avant tout** first and foremost; **5** (avant tout) for a start; **d'~ je refuse de lui parler** for a start I refuse to speak to him.

III abords *nmpl* area (*sg*) around; **les ~s immédiats de qch** the immediate area around sth; **aux ~s de qch** in the area around sth.

abordable /abɔʀdabl/ *adj* **1** [*produit, prix*] affordable; **les chambres sont à des prix très ~s** rooms are very reasonably priced; **2** [*texte, lecture*] accessible; **c'est un problème difficilement ~ en de telles circonstances** it's not an easy subject to talk about in the circumstances; **3** [*personne*] approachable.

abordage /abɔʀdaʒ/ *nm* **1** (collision) collision; **2** (attaque) boarding; **à l'~!** stand by to board!

aborder /abɔʀde/ [1] **I** *vtr* **1** (commencer à traiter) to tackle [*problème, sujet, détails*]; **vous n'abordez pas le problème comme il faut** you're not going about the problem the right way; **2** (approcher) to approach [*personne, obstacle*]; **~ qn dans la rue** to approach sb in the street; **il a abordé le virage trop vite** he approached the bend too fast; **il n'a pas ralenti avant d'~ le virage** he didn't slow down on the approach to the bend; **3** (entamer) to enter; **ils ont abordé la discussion avec méfiance** they entered the discussion cautiously; **la compagnie aborde une période délicate** the company is entering a delicate period; **4** [*voyageur, navire*] to reach [*lieu, rive*]; **5** (heurter) to collide with; (attaquer)† to board†.

II *vi* [*voyageur, navire*] to land; **nous avons abordé à Venise/sur une île** we landed in Venice/on an island.

aborigène /abɔʀiʒɛn/ **I** *adj* **1** (indigène) aboriginal, indigenous; **2** (d'Australie) Aboriginal.

II *nmf* **1** (indigène) aborigine; **2** (d'Australie) Aborigine.

abortif, -ive /abɔʀtif, iv/ **I** *adj* **1** (pour faire avorter) [*produit, effet*] abortifacient; **2** (avorté) [*organe, forme*] abortive.

II *nm* abortifacient.

aboucher /abuʃe/ [1] **I** *vtr* Tech to butt, to place [sth] end to end [*tube, tuyau*].

II s'aboucher *vpr* [*objets*] to be joined (up) to.

Abou Dhabi /abudabi/ ▸ **321** *npr* Abu Dhabi.

abouler◑ /abule/ [1] *vtr* **aboule le fric**◑**, et vite!** quick, hand over the dough○!; **aboule ton assiette si tu veux manger!** hand me your plate if you want something to eat!

aboulie /abuli/ *nf* abulia.

aboulique /abulik/ **I** *adj* abulic.

II *nmf* person suffering from abulia.

Abou Simbel /abusimbɛl/ *npr* Abu Simbel.

about /abu/ *nm* (en bâtiment) end (piece); (en menuiserie) butt (joint).

aboutement /abutmɑ̃/ *nm* (procédé) butt jointing, abutting; (résultat) butt joint.

abouter /abute/ [1] *vtr* to join [sth] end to end, to butt [*objets*].

abouti, **~e** /abuti/ *adj* [*œuvre, film*] accomplished.

aboutir /abutiʀ/ [3] **I aboutir à** *vtr ind* **1** lit **~ à** [*sentier, rue, escalier*] to lead to [*maison, mer, rivière*]; [*personne*] to end up in [*ville, place, rue*]; to end up at [*fontaine, église*]; **2** fig **~ à** to lead to [*compromis, accord, résultat, rupture*]; to end in [*échec*].

II *vi* [*négociations, projet, démarches*] to succeed; **ne pas ~** not to come off.

aboutissants /abutisɑ̃/ *nmpl* **les tenants et les ~ de qch** the ins and outs of sth.

aboutissement /abutismɑ̃/ *nm* (de carrière, rêve, d'évolution) culmination; (de conférence, parcours) (successful) outcome; **la pièce est l'~ de six mois de travail** the play is the culmination of six months' work.

aboyer /abwaje/ [23] **I** *vtr* [*personne*] to bark [*ordres*] (**à** at); to shout [*injures*] (**à** at).

II *vi* **1** [*chien*] to bark (**après, contre** at); ▸ **caravane**; **2** [*personne*] to shout (**après, contre** at).

IDIOMES **chien qui aboie ne mord pas** Prov his/her bark is worse than his/her bite.

aboyeur○ /abwajœʀ/ *nm* (à l'entrée d'une réception) usher (*who announces guests*); (à l'entrée d'un spectacle) barker.

abracadabra /abʀakadabʀa/ *nm* abracadabra.

abracadabrant, **~e** /abʀakadabʀɑ̃, ɑ̃t/ *adj* bizarre; **une histoire ~e** a cock-and-bull story, a bizarre story.

Abraham /abraham/ *npr* Abraham.

abraser /abʀaze/ [1] *vtr* to abrade.

abrasif, -ive /abʀazif, iv/ **I** *adj* abrasive.

II *nm* abrasive.

abrasion /abʀazjɔ̃/ *nf* abrasion; **~ dentaire** wearing down of the teeth.

abrégé /abʀeʒe/ *nm* **1** (de discours, texte) summary; **faire l'~ d'une conférence** to summarize a conference; **en ~** [*mot, expression*] in abbreviated form; [*texte, discours*] in summarized form; **il nous a rapporté, en ~, le contenu des négociations** he gave us a summary of the ground covered by the negotiations; **2** (ouvrage) concise handbook; **un ~ de botanique** a concise handbook of botany.

abrégement /abʀɛʒmɑ̃/ *nm* (de délai, congé) shortening; (de texte, discours) summarizing; (de mot, d'expression) shortening.

abréger /abʀeʒe/ [15] *vtr* **1** (rendre court) to shorten [*mot, expression*]; to summarize [*texte, discours*]; **~ 'télévision' en 'télé'** to shorten 'television' to 'TV'; **donner une version abrégée de qch** to give an abridged version of sth; **donner qch sous une forme abrégée** to give sth in abbreviated form [*terme*]; to give sth in summarized form [*texte*]; **2** (rendre bref) to cut short [sth]; **j'ai dû ~ ma visite** I had to cut short my visit; **une crise cardiaque a abrégé sa carrière** a heart attack cut short his career; **abrège**○! keep it short!; **~ les souffrances de qn** to put an end to sb's suffering; **disons, pour ~, qu'ils se séparent** to cut GB ou make US a long story short, let's just say they are separating.

abreuver /abʀøve/ [1] **I** *vtr* **1** to water [*animal*]; **2** fml to soak [*sol*]; **3** liter **~ qn de qch** to bombard sb with sth [*propagande*]; to shower sb with sth [*compliments*]; **~ qn d'injures** to heap abuse on sb.

II s'abreuver *vpr* liter **1** lit [*animal*] to drink; **2** fig **s'~ de qch** to drink in sth [*aventures*].

abreuvoir /abʀøvwaʀ/ *nm* **1** (lieu) watering place; **2** (récipient) (de bétail) drinking trough; (de poussin, canari) drinking bowl.

abréviation /abʀevjasjɔ̃/ *nf* abbreviation.

abri /abʀi/ *nm* gén shelter; (pour voiture) carport; (cabane) shed; **se faire un ~ de qch, se servir de qch comme ~** (en se mettant derrière) to shelter behind sth; (en se mettant dessous) to shelter under sth; **trouver un ~ provisoire sous/dans** to take shelter temporarily under/in; **températures**

relevées sous ~ Météo temperature in the shade; **à l'~** (à couvert) under cover; (en lieu sûr) safe; **être à l'~** to be sheltered; **être à l'~ de** (d'un mur, d'un arbre) to be sheltered by; (du vent, d'un voleur) to be sheltered from; **se mettre à l'~ d'un arbre** to take shelter under a tree; **se mettre à l'~ des intempéries** to shelter from the weather; **courir se mettre à l'~** to run for shelter; **lire à l'~ d'un mur** to read in the shelter of a wall; **lire à l'~ d'un arbre** to read under a tree; **personne n'est à l'~ d'un accident** accidents can happen to anybody; **personne n'est à l'~ d'une erreur** everybody makes mistakes; **à l'~ de l'humidité** in a dry place.

■ **~ antiaérien** air raid shelter; **~ antiatomique** nuclear (fallout) shelter; **~ météorologique** thermometer screen; **~ souterrain** underground shelter ou bunker.

abribus® /abʀibys/ *nm inv* bus shelter.

abricot /abʀiko/ ▶193 I *adj inv* (couleur) apricot; **couleur ~** apricot-coloured[GB].
II *nm* **1** (fruit) apricot; **confiture d'~s** apricot jam; **à l'~** [*yaourt, tarte*] apricot (*épith*); [*thé*] apricot-flavoured[GB]; **2** (couleur) apricot.

abricoté, **~e** /abʀikɔte/ *adj* [*crème, thé*] apricot-flavoured[GB]; **c'est légèrement ~** it has a slight apricot flavour[GB].

abricotier /abʀikɔtje/ *nm* apricot tree.

abrité, **~e** /abʀite/ I *pp* ▶ **abriter**.
II *pp adj* sheltered.

abriter /abʀite/ [1] I *vtr* **1** [*bâtiment*] to shelter, to provide shelter for [*personnes, animaux*]; to house [*société, organisation, objets*]; to host [*activité, réunion*]; **2** [*pays, région*] to provide a base for [*société, activité*]; to provide a home for [*personnes*]; to provide a habitat for [*animaux, végétaux*]; to harbour[GB] [*malfaiteurs, terroristes, tombe, lieu de culte*].
II **s'abriter** *vpr* (des intempéries) to take shelter (**de** from); (des balles, du feu) to take cover (**de** from); **s'~ derrière le secret professionnel** to shelter ou hide behind professional confidentiality.

abrogation /abʀɔgasjɔ̃/ *nf* repeal, abrogation sout.

abroger /abʀɔʒe/ [13] *vtr* to repeal, to abrogate sout.

abrupt, **~e** /abʀypt/ I *adj* **1** (en pente raide) [*colline, chemin*] steep; (à pic) [*paroi*] sheer; **2** (sans nuances) [*personne, ton*] abrupt; **de manière ~e** [*parler, interrompre*] in an abrupt manner; **le caractère ~ de sa décision** fig the suddenness of his decision.
II *nm* steep slope.

abruptement /abʀyptəmɑ̃/ *adv* **1** (en pente raide) steeply; **2** (soudainement) suddenly; (de manière brusque) abruptly.

abruti, **~e** /abʀyti/ I *pp* ▶ **abrutir**.
II *pp adj* (idiot) [*personne, air*] stupid; **ne prends pas cet air ~!** take that stupid look off your face!
III *nm,f* moron○; **espèce d'~!** you moron○!; **quelle bande d'~s!** what a bunch of morons○!

abrutir /abʀytiʀ/ [3] I *vtr* **1** (rendre passif) [*bruit*] to deafen; [*chaleur*] to wear [sb] out; [*alcool, médicament, fatigue*] to have a numbing effect on; [*coup*] to stun; **être abruti de chaleur** to be overpowered by the heat; **être abruti de fatigue** to be numb with fatigue; **abruti par les médicaments** dopey with medicine; **2** (rendre idiot) **~ qn** [*alcool, tâche répétitive*] to have a numbing effect on sb; **3** (accabler) **~ qn de travail** to load sb with work.
II **s'abrutir** *vpr* **1** (devenir stupide) to turn into a moron○; **2** (s'accabler de) **s'~ de travail** to wear oneself out with work.

abrutissant, **~e** /abʀytisɑ̃, ɑ̃t/ *adj* [*musique, vacarme*] deafening; [*chaleur*] exhausting; [*tâche, activité, travail*] mind-numbing.

abrutissement /abʀytismɑ̃/ *nm* **l'~ des gens** reducing people to a mindless state.

ABS /abeɛs/ I (*written abbr* = **aux bons soins**) c/o.
II *nm inv* Aut **système ~** ABS.

abscisse /apsis/ *nf* abscissa.

abscons, **~e** /apskɔ̃, ɔ̃s/ *adj* fml abstruse.

absence /apsɑ̃s/ *nf* **1** (disparition temporaire) absence; **l'~ de la France à la conférence** the absence of France from the conference; **en l'~ de** in the absence of; **plusieurs ~s injustifiées** gén several absences without a proper justification; Scol repeated unauthorized GB ou unexcused US absences; **'en cas d'~ adressez-vous à côté'** 'if out please enquire next door'; **on a téléphoné ce matin pendant votre ~** somebody phoned this morning while you were out; **nous avons regretté votre ~ à la réunion** we were sorry (that) you didn't attend the meeting; **l'~ de vos bagages est due à** your luggage isn't here because of; **2** (inexistence) absence; **l'~ de témoins** the absence of (any) witnesses; **en l'~ de qch** in the absence of sth; **briller par son ~** hum to be conspicuous by ou in US one's absence hum; **3** (défaut) lack; **l'~ de pluie désespère les agriculteurs** the lack of rain is deeply worrying to farmers; **son ~ totale de réalisme** his total lack of realism; **4** (perte de mémoire) **il a des ~s** or **des moments d'~** at times his mind goes blank; **5** Jur presumption of death.

■ **~ illégale** Mil absence without leave.

absent, **~e** /apsɑ̃, ɑ̃t/ I *adj* **1** (éloigné longtemps) away (*jamais épith*) (**de** from); (éloigné brièvement) out (*jamais épith*) (**de** of); **il est ~ pour deux mois** he's away for two months; **je serai ~ du bureau tout l'après-midi** I'll be out of the office all afternoon; **2** (qui ne s'est pas présenté) [*élève, employé, candidat*] absent; **3** (qui ne participe pas) absent (**de** from); **la France est ~e des débats** France is absent from the debates; **4** (inexistant) absent (**de** from); **mon nom est ~ de la liste** my name is not on ou is absent from the list; **cette espèce est ~e de nos régions** this species is not found in our region; **l'humour était ~ des débats** the debates were lacking in humour[GB]; **5** (absorbé) absent-minded; **elle répondit d'une voix ~e** she replied absent-mindedly.
II *nm,f* **1** gén, Scol absentee; **'~s excusés...'** 'apologies for absence...'; **Pinchon, autre ~ remarqué de la réunion...** Pinchon, also notably absent from the meeting...; **le grand ~ du tournoi, Leconte, était tombé malade la veille** notably absent from the tournament was Leconte, who had fallen ill the day before; **2** (défunt) liter absent one; **il a eu une pensée émue pour les ~s** he thought with emotion of those no longer with him; **3** Jur missing person.

IDIOMES **les ~s ont toujours tort** Prov those who are absent always get the blame.

absentéisme /apsɑ̃teism/ *nm* **1** Admin, Ind, Entr (de travailleurs) absenteeism; **2** Scol gén absenteeism; (école buissonnière) truancy.

absentéiste /apsɑ̃teist/ *nmf* (habitual) absentee.

absenter: **s'absenter** /apsɑ̃te/ [1] *vpr* (longtemps) to go away; (brièvement) to go out; **il s'est absenté pour raisons de santé** he went away for health reasons; **ne vous absentez pas trop longtemps** don't be gone for long; **s'~ de** to go out of, to leave; **je dois m'~ de chez moi/du bureau** I must go out of the house/the office.

abside /apsid/ *nf* Archit apse.

absidial, **~e**, *mpl* **-iaux** /apsidjal, o/ *adj* apsidal.

absidiole /apsidjɔl/ *nf* apsidiole, absidiole.

absinthe /apsɛ̃t/ *nf* Vin, Bot absinthe.

absolu, **~e** /apsɔly/ I *adj* **1** (sans réserve) [*certitude, confiance, pouvoir, souverain*] absolute; **une nécessité ~e** an absolute necessity; **sauf en cas d'~e nécessité** only if absolutely necessary; **défense ~e d'ouvrir cette porte** it is absolutely forbidden to open this door; **je suis dans l'impossibilité ~e de vous aider** it's absolutely impossible for me to help you; **maintenir le secret le plus ~ sur l'affaire** to maintain the utmost secrecy about the deal; **un repos ~** complete rest; **2** (hors du commun) journ [*supériorité*] absolute; [*champion*] undisputed; **3** (non relatif) [*vérité, température, majorité*] absolute; **4** (intransigeant) [*tempérament*] uncompromising; [*règle*] hard and fast; **5** Math [*nombre, valeur*] absolute; **6** Ling [*construction, forme*] absolute; **l'emploi ~ d'un verbe transitif** the use of a transitive verb in the absolute.
II *nm* absolute; **l'~** Philos the Absolute; **dans l'~** in the absolute; **ton besoin/ta quête d'~** your need/your search for absolutes.

absolument /apsɔlymɑ̃/ *adv* absolutely; **'êtes-vous d'accord?'—'~/~ pas!'** 'do you agree?'—'absolutely/absolutely not!'; **je dois ~ finir ce rapport** I absolutely have to finish this report; **tenir ~ à faire qch** to insist (up)on doing sth; **il veut ~ réussir** he's determined to succeed; **des réformes doivent ~ être introduites** it's imperative that reforms be introduced; **film à voir ~** film not to be missed; **il faut ~ que tu visites Versailles** you really must visit Versailles.

absolution /apsɔlysjɔ̃/ *nf* Relig absolution (**de qch** for sth); **donner l'~ à qn** to give sb absolution; **recevoir l'~** to receive absolution.

absolutisme /apsɔlytism/ *nm* absolutism.

absolutiste /apsɔlytist/ *adj, nmf* absolutist.

absorbant, **~e** /apsɔʀbɑ̃, ɑ̃t/ I *adj* **1** [*substance, tissu*] absorbent; **à grand pouvoir ~** highly absorbent; **2** [*travail*] absorbing.
II *nm* absorbent.

absorber /apsɔʀbe/ [1] I *vtr* **1** (s'imbiber) [*matériau*] to absorb, to soak up; **2** (consommer) [*personne*] to take [*nourriture, médicament*]; **3** (retenir) [*organisme, sang, plante*] to absorb; **4** (nécessiter) [*projet, entreprise*] to absorb [*argent*]; [*activité, tâche, problème*] to occupy [*esprit*]; **être absorbé par qch** to be absorbed ou engrossed in sth; **être absorbé dans ses pensées** to be lost in one's thoughts; **avoir l'air absorbé** to look preoccupied; **5** (intégrer) [*entreprise*] to take over [*entreprise*]; [*parti, groupement*] to absorb [*parti, groupuscule*]; [*région, profession, secteur*] to absorb [*population, immigrés*]; **6** (faire face à) to cope with [*dépenses, excédent, déficit*].
II **s'absorber** *vpr* **s'~ dans qch** to be engrossed in sth.

absorption /apsɔʀpsjɔ̃/ *nf* **1** (de nourriture, médicament) taking; **l'~ de ce médicament est déconseillée aux femmes enceintes** pregnant women are advised not to take this medicine; **2** Bot, Physiol absorption; **3** (de liquide, choc, d'ondes) absorption; **4** (d'entreprise) takeover; **5** (de région, population) absorption.

absoudre /apsudʀ/ [75] *vtr* Relig to absolve; **~ les péchés de qn** to absolve sb.

absoute /apsut/ *nf* absolutions (*pl*) of the dead.

abstenir: **s'abstenir** /apstəniʀ/ [36] *vpr* **1** (ne pas voter) to abstain; **2** (éviter) **s'~ de qch/de faire** to refrain from sth/from doing; **s'~ de tout commentaire** to refrain from any comment; **les participants sont priés de s'~ de fumer** participants are kindly requested to refrain from smoking; **abstenez-vous de café** keep off coffee; **'agences s'~'** 'no agencies'; **'pas sérieux s'~'** 'no time-wasters'.

IDIOMES **dans le doute, abstiens-toi** Prov when in doubt, do nowt Prov.

abstention /apstɑ̃sjɔ̃/ *nf* **1** (phénomène) abstention; **lutter contre/prôner l'~** to fight against/to advocate abstention; **une forte ~** a high level of abstention; **2** (personne ne votant pas) abstention; **il y a eu dix**

~s there were ten abstentions; **il y a eu 10% d'~** 10% abstained.

abstentionnisme /apstɑ̃sjɔnism/ *nm* abstentionism.

abstentionniste /apstɑ̃sjɔnist/ **I** *adj* abstentionist.
II *nmf* abstentionist; **rallier les ~s du premier tour** to win over those who abstained in the first round.

abstinence /apstinɑ̃s/ *nf* abstinence (**de** from); **faire ~** (de viande) to abstain from eating meat; (continence sexuelle) to abstain from sexual relations.

abstinent, **~e** /apstinɑ̃, ɑ̃t/ *adj* abstinent.

abstraction /apstʀaksjɔ̃/ *nf* **1** (opération) abstraction; **faire ~ de qch** (de douleur, goût, différence) to forget sth; **2** (chose imaginaire, idée) abstraction; **3** Art **l'~** abstract art; **4** (caractère) abstract style.

abstraire /apstʀɛʀ/ [58] **I** *vtr* to abstract (**de** from).
II s'abstraire *vpr* (s'isoler) to cut oneself off (**de qch** from sth).

abstrait, **~e** /apstʀɛ, ɛt/ **I** *adj* abstract.
II *nm* **1** (opposé à concret) abstract; **dans l'~** [*parler, raisonner*] in the abstract; **2** Art (art) abstract art; (artiste) abstract artist.

abstraitement /apstʀɛtmɑ̃/ *adv* in the abstract.

abstrus, **~e** /apstʀy, yz/ *adj* fml abstruse sout.

absurde /apsyʀd/ **I** *adj* (tous contextes) absurd; **c'est ~** it's absurd (**de faire** to do).
II *nm* absurd; **philosophie de l'~** philosophy of the absurd; **démontrer qch par l'~** gén, Math to prove sth by contradiction; **raisonnement par l'~** Math proof by contradiction.

absurdement /apsyʀdəmɑ̃/ *adv* absurdly.

absurdité /apsyʀdite/ *nf* **1** (caractère) absurdity; **l'~ de ses déclarations/de l'existence** the absurdity of his statements/of existence; **2** (acte, parole) nonsense ¢, absurdity; **quelle ~!** what nonsense!, what an absurdity!; **sa démission est une ~** his resignation is a nonsense; **il ne dit que des ~s** he talks nothing but nonsense; **techniquement c'est une ~** it's a technical nonsense.

abus /aby/ *nm inv* **1** (usage excessif) abuse; **lutter contre l'~ d'alcool et de tabac** to fight against alcohol and tobacco abuse; **'~ dangereux'** 'can seriously damage your health'; **2** (injustice) abuse; **cette loi a donné lieu à de nombreux ~** this law has given rise to a number of abuses; **dénoncer les ~** to denounce abuses; **il y a de l'~**○! that's a bit much○!; **3** (mauvais usage) abuse; **il a été fait un ~ systématique du droit de grève** there has been systematic abuse of the right to strike.
■ **~ d'autorité** abuse of authority; **~ de biens sociaux** Jur fraudulent dealing with a company's assets; **~ de confiance** Jur breach of trust; **~ de droit** Jur abuse of process; **~ de langage** misuse of language; **~ de pouvoir** abuse of power.

abuser /abyze/ [1] **I** *vtr* liter to fool; **ses promesses n'abusent plus personne** his promises no longer fool anyone; **j'ai été abusé par leur ressemblance** I was fooled by their resemblance; **se laisser ~** to be taken in.
II abuser de *vtr ind* **1** (faire usage excessif) **~ de l'alcool** to drink to excess; **~ des tranquillisants** to rely too heavily on tranquillizers[GB]; **~ des sucreries/bonnes choses** to overindulge in sweet things/good things; **~ de ses forces** to overdo it; **2** (profiter) **~ de** to exploit; **~ de la situation** to exploit the situation; **~ de la crédulité/faiblesse des gens** to exploit people's gullibility/weakness; **~ d'un ami/de la patience de qn** to take advantage of a friend/of sb's patience; **je ne voudrais pas ~ (de votre gentillesse)** I don't want to impose (on your kindness); **~ de sa force/son autorité/ses fonctions** to abuse one's strength/one's authority/one's post; **3** (violenter) **~ de qn** to sexually abuse sb.
III *vi* (exagérer) to go too far; **je suis patient mais il ne faut pas ~** I may be patient but don't push me too far.
IV s'abuser *vpr* fml to be mistaken; **si je ne m'abuse** if I'm not mistaken.

abusif, **-ive** /abyzif, iv/ *adj* **1** (exagéré) [*consommation, tarif*] excessive; **simplification abusive** oversimplification; **prescription abusive** inappropriate prescribing; **faire un usage ~ de qch** to use sth excessively; **stationnement ~** illegal parking; **2** (injuste) [*privilège, loi*] unfair; [*licenciement*] unfair, wrongful; [*détention*] wrongful; **les procédés ~s de la concurrence étrangère** the unfair conduct of foreign competitors; **3** (impropre) improper; **emploi ~ d'un terme** improper use of a term; **donner une interprétation abusive de qch** to give a misrepresentation of sth; **4** (possessif) [*parents, mère, époux*] over-possessive.

abusivement /abyzivmɑ̃/ *adv* **1** (exagérément) excessively; **2** (injustement) wrongly; **il a été détenu ~** he was wrongfully detained; **cette œuvre a été ~ attribuée à** this work was wrongly attributed to; **3** (improprement) misguidedly; **il mêle ~ politique et idéologie** he misguidedly mixes politics and ideology; **un terme employé ~** a term improperly used.

abyme /abim/ *nm* **structure** or **composition en ~** Théât play-within-a-play; Art image repeated to infinity; (de roman) 'Chinese boxes' structure.

abyssal, **~e**, *mpl* **-aux** /abisal, o/ *adj* Géog abyssal; **profondeurs ~es** ocean depths.

abysse /abis/ *nm* **les ~s** the abyssal plains.

abyssin, **~e** /abisɛ̃, in/ **I** *adj* Hist Abyssinian.
II *nm* Zool Abyssinian cat.

Abyssin, **~e** /abisɛ̃, in/ *nm,f* Hist Abyssinian.

Abyssinie /abisini/ *nprf* Hist Abyssinia.

acabit /akabi/ *nm* pej **de cet** or **du même ~** of that sort; **les gens de ton ~** people like you; **je connais des gens de leur ~** I've met their sort before.

acacia /akasja/ *nm* **1** (d'Europe) **(faux)** locust tree, false acacia; **miel d'~** acacia honey; **2** (de régions chaudes) acacia.

académicien, **-ienne** /akademisjɛ̃, ɛn/ *nm,f* **1** gén academician; **2** (en France) *member of the Académie française.*

académie /akademi/ *nf* **1** (école) (de billard, danse) school; (de police) academy; **~ de peinture** or **de dessin** art academy; **2** Admin ≈ local education authority GB, school district US; **3** Art (figure) nude; **4** (groupe de personnes) society.

Académie /akademi/ *nf* **l'~ française** the Académie française.

académique /akademik/ *adj* **1** gén academic; (de l'Académie française) of the Académie française; **2** Admin [*service, commission*] ≈ of the local education authority GB ou school district US; **3** Art academic.

académisme /akademism/ *nm* academicism.

Acadie /akadi/ **▶ 692** *nprf* Acadia.

acadien, **-ienne** /akadjɛ̃, ɛn/ **I** *adj* **1** Géog Acadian; **2** Géol acadian.
II ▶ 462 *nm* Ling Acadian.

Acadien, **-ienne** /akadjɛ̃, ɛn/ *nm,f* Acadian.

acajou /akaʒu/ **I** *adj inv* **1 ▶ 193** (couleur) mahogany; **couleur ~** mahogany colour[GB]; **2** (qui imite) **table ~** imitation mahogany table.
II *nm* **1** (arbre) mahogany tree; **2** (bois) mahogany; **table en ~** mahogany table.

acanthe /akɑ̃t/ *nf* Bot acanthus; **feuilles d'~** Archit acanthus leaves.
■ **~ sauvage** scotch thistle.

acariâtre /akaʀjɑtʀ/ *adj* gén cantankerous.

acarien /akaʀjɛ̃/ *nm* dust mite.

accablant, **~e** /akablɑ̃, ɑ̃t/ *adj* **1** (écrasant) [*chaleur, silence*] oppressive; [*tristesse*] overwhelming; **d'une naïveté/laideur ~e** painfully naïve/ugly; **2** (prouvant la culpabilité) [*rapport, témoignage, fait*] damning.

accablement /akabləmɑ̃/ *nm* depression, despondency.

accabler /akable/ [1] *vtr* **1** (écraser) [*chaleur, mauvaise nouvelle*] to devastate [*personne*]; **être accablé par les** or **de soucis** to be overwhelmed with worries; **~ qn de** to overburden sb with [*impôts*]; to bombard sb with [*questions*]; **~ qn d'injures** to heap insults on sb; **~ qn de mépris** to pour scorn on sb; **2** (condamner) [*témoignage, enquête, personne*] to condemn [*personne*].

accalmie /akalmi/ *nf* **1** fig (de lutte, crise) lull; (d'activité) slack period; **les combats ont repris après une ~ de quelques heures** the fighting resumed after a lull of a few hours; **2** Météo, Naut lull.

accaparant, **~e** /akapaʀɑ̃, ɑ̃t/ *adj* [*personne, travail*] very demanding.

accaparement /akapaʀmɑ̃/ *nm* **1** Comm (de marchandises) hoarding; (de marché) cornering; (de moyens de production) monopolizing; **2** fig (de pouvoir, personne) monopolizing.

accaparer /akapaʀe/ [1] *vtr* **1** Comm to hoard [*marchandises*]; to corner [*marché*]; to monopolize [*production*]; **2** fig to monopolize [*personne*]; to preoccupy [*esprit*]; to take up [*temps*]; **~ l'attention générale** to monopolize everyone's attention.

accapareur, **-euse** /akapaʀœʀ, øz/ *nm,f* monopolizer.

accédant, **~e** /aksedɑ̃, ɑ̃t/ *nm,f* **~ à la propriété** first-time home-buyer.

accéder /aksede/ [14] *vtr ind* **1** (atteindre) **~ à** [*personnes*] to reach, to get to [*lieu*]; **2** (obtenir) **~ à** to achieve [*célébrité, gloire*]; to acquire [*responsabilités*]; to obtain [*poste*]; to reach, to attain sout [*fonctions*]; **~ à la propriété** to become a home-owner; **~ au pouvoir** to come to power; **~ au trône** to accede to the throne; **3** fml (satisfaire à) **~ à** to grant, to accede to sout [*demande, prière, désir*]; **4** Ordinat **~ à** to access.

accélérateur, **-trice** /akseleʀatœʀ, tʀis/ **I** *adj* accelerating.
II *nm* Aut accelerator; **câble d'~** accelerator cable; **appuyer sur l'~** to step on the accelerator; **coup d'~** touch on the accelerator; **donner un coup d'~** lit to step on the accelerator; **donner un coup d'~ à qch** fig to give sth a boost, to speed up sth; **jouer un rôle d'~** fig to act as a catalyst.
■ **~ de particules** particle accelerator.

accélération /akseleʀasjɔ̃/ *nf* (de vitesse) acceleration (**de** of); (de croissance, consommation, prix) sharp increase (**de** in); (de processus, travail, projet) speeding-up (**de** of); **l'~ de l'Histoire** the speeding-up of events.

accéléré, **~e** /akseleʀe/ **I** *pp* ▶ **accélérer**.
II *pp adj* accelerated; **à un rythme ~** at an increasingly fast rate; **stage de formation ~e** intensive learning course.
III *nm* Cin fast ou accelerated motion; **en ~** in fast ou accelerated motion.

accélérer /akseleʀe/ [14] **I** *vtr* (hâter) to speed up [*rythme, mouvement*]; to accelerate [*processus, réaction*]; **~ le pas** or **l'allure** to quicken one's step ou pace.
II *vi* **1** Aut [*conducteur*] to accelerate, to speed up; **accélère!** speed up!; **2**○ fig (se dépêcher) to get a move on○.
III s'accélérer *vpr* **1** (aller plus vite) [*pouls, mouvement*] to quicken; **les événements s'accélèrent** the pace of events is quickening; **2** (s'intensifier) [*phénomène, tendance*] to accelerate.

accent /aksɑ̃/ *nm* **1** (façon de parler) accent; **avoir l'~ bordelais** to have a Bordeaux accent; **parler français sans ~/avec un léger ~ anglais** to speak French without an accent/with a slight English accent; **2** (sur une lettre) accent; **~ aigu/grave** acute/grave accent; **~ circonflexe** circumflex (accent); **prendre un ~** [*mot, lettre*] to have an accent; **sourcils en ~ circonflexe** arched eyebrows; **3** Phon **~ (d'intensité)** stress; **~ fixe/libre** fixed/free stress; **l'~ porte sur la dernière syllabe** the stress is ou falls on the last syllable; **mettre l'~ sur qch** fig to put the emphasis on sth, to stress sth; **4** (nuance, note) **il n'y avait pas le moindre ~ de sincérité dans son discours** there wasn't the slightest hint of sincerity in his/her speech; **musique aux ~s mozartiens** music with Mozartian overtones; **un ~ de vérité** a ring of truth.

■ **~ de hauteur** pitch; **~ tonique** stress.

accenteur /aksɑ̃tœʀ/ *nm* **~ mouchet** hedge sparrow.

accentuation /aksɑ̃tɥasjɔ̃/ *nf* **1** (de crise, tension) escalation; (d'inégalités) heightening; (de phénomène) worsening; (de tendance) increase; **2** Phon stress, (en poésie) accentuation; **3** (signes diacritiques) accents (*pl*).

■ **~ d'image** image enhancement.

accentuel, **-elle** /aksɑ̃tɥɛl/ *adj* accentual, stress (*épith*); **groupe ~** stress group; **unité accentuelle** accentual unit.

accentuer /aksɑ̃tɥe/ [1] **I** *vtr* **1** (rendre plus évident) [*mesure, situation*] to accentuate [*inégalités, différences*]; to heighten [*tensions*]; to increase [*tendance*]; **2** (tenter de faire ressortir) [*personne*] to highlight [*différences, trait de caractère, inégalités*]; to emphasize [*aspect*]; **3** Phon to stress, (en poésie) to accentuate [*syllabe*]; **syllabe accentuée/non accentuée** stressed/unstressed syllable, (en poésie) accented/unaccented syllable; **4** (écrire) to put an accent on [*lettre*]; **les lettres accentuées** letters with accents, accented letters.

II s'accentuer *vpr* [*déséquilibre, phénomène, tendance*] to become more marked, to become more pronounced; [*timidité*] to become worse.

acceptabilité /aksɛptabilite/ *nf* acceptability.

acceptable /aksɛptabl/ *adj* **1** (tolérable) [*seuil, norme, condition, comportement*] acceptable; **rendre qch ~** to make sth acceptable (**à** to); **2** (passable) [*travail, qualité*] passable; [*résultat*] satisfactory; **'comment est le nouveau professeur?'—'~'** 'what's the new teacher like?'—'he's/she's all right'.

acceptation /aksɛptasjɔ̃/ *nf* acceptance; **sous réserve d'~** subject to acceptance (**de** of).

accepter /aksɛpte/ [1] **I** *vtr* **1** (bien recevoir) to accept [*invitation, personne, proposition, cadeau*]; **~ qch de qn** to accept sth from sb; **~ de faire qch** to agree to do sth; **~ que** to accept that; **s'il te plaît, accepte!** please say yes!; **je n'accepte pas qu'on m'interrompe!** I will not be interrupted!; **2** (agréer) to agree to [*condition, contrat, devis*]; **3** (relever) to accept, to take up [*défi, pari*]; **4** (admettre) to accept [*excuse, théorie, personne*]; **elle a essayé de faire ~ son fiancé/projet** she tried to get her fiancé/plan accepted; **il aura du mal à se faire ~ par sa belle-famille** he'll have trouble getting himself accepted by his in-laws; **~ l'idée de faire qch** to accept the idea of doing sth; **5** (se résigner à) to accept, to come to terms with [*situation, destin*].

II s'accepter *vpr* **1** (soi-même) **s'~ (tel qu'on est)** to accept oneself (for what one is); **2** (l'un l'autre) **s'~ (mutuellement)** to accept one another.

acception /aksɛpsjɔ̃/ *nf* **1** (sens) sense; **dans toute l'~ du terme** or **mot** in every sense of the word; **2** Jur (distinction) **sans ~ de** irrespective of.

accès /aksɛ/ *nm inv* **1** (moyen, possibilité d'atteindre) access; **moyens d'~** means of access; **être facile d'~** or **d'un ~ facile** to be easy to get to; **être difficile d'~** or **d'un ~ difficile** to be difficult to get to; **être facile d'~ avec une voiture** to be easily accessible ou easy to get to by car; **être d'un ~ facile/difficile** [*personne*] to be approachable/unapproachable; **l'~ au village** (possibilité d'atteindre) access to the village; (moyen d'atteindre) the way into the village, the road leading to the village; **l'~ au roi** access to the king; **cela donne ~ à** (mener) it leads to; **toutes les voies d'~ sont barrées** (portes) all entrances are sealed off; (routes) all approach roads are closed off; **'~ aux quais'** 'to the trains'; **2** (moyen d'entrer) **l'~ à** access to; **les ~ du bâtiment** the entrances to the building; **les ~ de la ville** the approach roads ou approaches to the town; **3** (droit d'entrée) **ne pas avoir ~ à** not to be admitted to; **interdire l'~ aux enfants** not to admit children; **il s'est vu refuser l'~ de la maison** he was not allowed into the house; **'~ interdit'** 'no entry', 'no admittance'; **'~ interdit aux visiteurs'** 'visitors not admitted'; **'~ interdit aux chiens'** 'no dogs (allowed)'; **'~ réservé au personnel** or **au service'** 'staff only'; **4** (possibilité d'obtenir, d'utiliser) access; **avoir ~ à** to have access to [*documents, fonds, soins médicaux*]; **ne pas avoir libre ~ aux médias** not to have free access to the media; **5** (possibilité de participer à) **l'~ à** access to [*profession, cours*]; admission to [*club, grande école*]; **barrer l'~ d'une profession aux femmes** to keep women out of a profession; **ouvrir l'~ d'une profession aux femmes** to open up a profession to women; **faciliter l'~ à une profession** to open up a profession; **6** (possibilité de comprendre) **être d'un ~ facile** to be accessible; **être d'un ~ difficile** not to be very accessible; **7** (crise) **~ de colère** fit of anger; **~ de fièvre** bout of fever; **~ d'enthousiasme** burst of enthusiasm; **par ~** by fits and starts; **8** Ordinat access; **~ aléatoire/séquentiel** random/sequential access; **voie d'~ à** access path to.

accessibilité /aksesibilite/ *nf* **1** (possibilité d'être atteint) accessibility (**de** of); (possibilité d'atteindre) access (**de** to); **2** (droit) right; **l'~ de tous à l'emploi/au droit de vote** everyone's right to a job/to vote; **3** Ling, Psych accessibility.

accessible /aksesibl/ *adj* **1** [*lieu*] accessible; **un site ~ par les transports en commun** a site accessible by public transport; **2** [*emploi*] **~ à** open to; **la culture doit être ~ à tous** culture must be accessible to everyone; **3** [*ouvrage, théorie*] accessible; **un langage ~ à tous** a language which can be understood by everyone; **4** [*prix, tarif*] affordable (**à qn** to sb); **5** [*personne*] (qu'on peut approcher) approachable; (qu'on peut émouvoir) **~ à** susceptible to [*compassion, pitié*].

accession /aksesjɔ̃/ *nf* **1** (fait de parvenir) **~ à** accession to [*pouvoir, trône*]; attainment of [*indépendance*]; **~ à la propriété** home-buying; **2** Jur accession.

accessit /aksesit/ *nm* honourable[GB] mention.

accessoire /akseswaʀ/ **I** *adj* [*problème, détail, avantage*] incidental.

II *nm* **1** (choses non essentielles) **distinguer l'~ de l'essentiel** to distinguish the nonessentials from the essentials; **2** (équipement complémentaire) (d'auto, de moto, vêtement) accessory; (de perceuse, robot ménager, d'aspirateur) attachment; **3** Cin, Théât **~s** props (*pl*).

■ **~s de table** condiments and cutlery; **~s de salle de bains** bathroom accessories; **~s de toilette** toilet requisites.

IDIOMES **ranger qch au magasin des ~s** to shelve sth.

accessoirement /akseswaʀmɑ̃/ *adv* (en plus) incidentally, as it happens; (le cas échéant) if desired; **'je peux amener Paul?'—'oui ~'** 'can I bring Paul along?'—'if you must'.

accessoiriser /akseswaʀize/ [1] *vtr* to accessorize.

accessoiriste /akseswaʀist/ ▶ **510** *nmf* Théât props man/woman.

accident /aksidɑ̃/ *nm* **1** (dommage) accident; **~ grave** serious accident; **en cas d'~ prévenir...** in case of accident (please) notify...; **l'~ a fait deux morts et quinze blessés** two died and fifteen were injured as a result of the accident; **un ~ est si vite arrivé!** accidents can easily happen!; **il y a 10 000 morts par ~ chaque année** 10,000 people die in accidents every year; **il s'est tué par ~ en nettoyant son fusil** he accidentally killed himself while cleaning his gun; **2** (problème) hitch; (événement inhabituel) one off○; hum accident; **une carrière qui évolue sans ~** a career which is progressing without a hitch; **une erreur qui n'est qu'un ~** an error which is just a one-off; **ils ont gagné! c'était un ~!** hum they won! that was an accident!; **~ de parcours**○ hitch; hum accident; **l'arrivée du (petit) dernier est un ~ (de parcours)** the birth of the last one was an accident; **les ~s de l'existence** the unforeseen events of life; **une découverte faite par ~** (par hasard) a chance discovery; **3** Méd accident; **~ cérébral/vasculaire** cerebral/vascular accident; **~ cardiaque** cardiac event; **~ de santé** health problem; **4** (inégalité) **~ de terrain** undulation of the land; **maison cachée par un ~ de terrain** house obscured by an undulation in the land; **le satellite peut repérer le moindre ~ de terrain** the satellite can pick out every contour; **5** Mus accidental; **6** Philos accident.

■ **~ d'avion** plane crash; **~ de chasse** hunting accident; **~ de la circulation** traffic accident; **~ corporel** accident involving injury; **~ domestique** accident in the home; **~ ferroviaire** rail accident; **~ industriel** industrial accident; **~ de montagne** climbing accident; **~ nucléaire** nuclear accident; **~ de la route** road accident; **~ du travail** industrial accident; **~ de voiture** car accident.

accidenté, **~e** /aksidɑ̃te/ **I** *pp* ▶ **accidenter**.

II *pp adj* **1** [*personne*] injured; [*véhicule*] involved in an accident (*après n*); **2** [*chemin, terrain, paysage*] uneven; **3** fig (plein d'événements) chequered GB ou checkered US; **après un parcours ~ il a pris la tête du parti** after a chequered GB ou checkered US career he has taken over leadership of the party.

III *nm,f* casualty, accident victim; **les ~s de la route** road accident victims; **les ~s du travail** people injured at work.

accidentel, **-elle** /aksidɑ̃tɛl/ *adj* accidental; **l'explosion n'avait rien d'~** there was nothing accidental about the explosion.

accidentellement /aksidɑ̃tɛlmɑ̃/ *adv* **1** (dans un accident) [*mourir, tuer*] accidentally; **il s'est tué ~** he accidentally killed himself (**en faisant** while doing); **2** (par hasard) by accident; **le coup (de feu) est parti ~** the shot went off by accident.

accidenter /aksidɑ̃te/ [1] *vtr* to bump [*véhicule*]; **sa camionnette a été accidentée plusieurs fois** he has bumped his van several times.

acclamation /aklamasjɔ̃/ *nf* cheering ¢, acclamation; **sous les ~s de** to the cheering of; **vote par ~** vote by acclamation, voice vote US.

acclamer /aklame/ [1] *vtr* to cheer, to acclaim [*personne, orateur, chef d'État*].

acclimatable /aklimatabl/ *adj* acclimatizable, acclimatable US.

acclimatation /aklimatasjɔ̃/ *nf* acclimatization, acclimation US.

acclimatement /aklimatmɑ̃/ *nm* acclimatization, acclimation US.

acclimater /aklimate/ [1] **I** *vtr* **1** Bot, Zool to acclimatize, to acclimate US [*plante, animal*]; **2** (introduire) to introduce [*mode, idée, procédé*].

II s'acclimater *vpr* **1** Bot, Zool to become acclimatized, to become acclimated US; **2** [*personne*] to adapt; [*idée*] to become accepted.

accointances /akwɛ̃tɑ̃s/ *nfpl* contacts; **avoir des ~ avec qn** to have contacts with sb, to know sb; **il a des ~ en haut lieu** he's got friends in high places.

accolade /akɔlad/ *nf* **1** (embrassade) embrace; **donner l'~ à qn** to embrace sb; **2** Imprim brace; **3** (cérémonie) accolade.

accoler /akɔle/ [1] *vtr* **1** (mettre côte à côte) **~ un bâtiment à qch** to build a building right next to sth; **~ une étiquette/un nom à** to attach a label/a name to; **~ une idée à** to associate an idea with; **2** Imprim to bracket (together) [*lignes, paragraphes*].

accommodant, **~e** /akɔmɔdɑ̃, ɑ̃t/ *adj* [*personne*] accommodating; [*politique*] flexible.

accommodation /akɔmɔdasjɔ̃/ *nf* Physiol, Biol, Psych accommodation.

accommodement /akɔmɔdmɑ̃/ *nm* **1** (transaction) arrangement; **parvenir à un ~ avec qn** to come to an arrangement with sb (**à propos de** about); **2** (expédient) hum agreement; **trouver des ~s avec sa conscience/avec le Ciel** to come to terms with one's conscience/with God.

accommoder /akɔmɔde/ [1] **I** *vtr* **1** Culin to prepare [*aliment, plat*]; **l'art d'~ les restes** the art of using up leftovers; **2** (adapter) to adapt; **il accommode ses propos aux circonstances** he adapts his remarks to suit the circumstances.

II *vi* [*œil*] to focus.

III s'accommoder *vpr* **s'~ de qch** (positif) to make the best of sth; (plus résigné) to put up with sth; **s'~ à** to adapt to.

accompagnateur, **-trice** /akɔ̃paɲatœʀ, tʀis/ *nm,f* **1** ▶510 Mus accompanist; **2** (d'enfants) accompanying adult; (de groupe touristique) courier; **vingt athlètes et ~s** twenty athletes and accompanying personnel.

accompagnement /akɔ̃paɲmɑ̃/ *nm* **1** Mus accompaniment; **sans ~** unaccompanied; **2** Culin accompaniment; **en ~ à** as an accompaniment to; **avec ~ de** served with; **3** (de malade) caring (**de** for); (de touristes) accompanying; **4** (cortège) fig complement; (conséquence) result; **le chômage et son ~ de misères** unemployment and its attendant ills; **5** (soutien) support; **artillerie/aviation d'~** artillery/air support; **mesures/politiques d'~** attendant measures/policies.

■ **~ musical** musical arrangement; **~ social** social measures (*pl*); **crédits d'~ social** social funds.

accompagner /akɔ̃paɲe/ [1] **I** *vtr* **1** (se déplacer avec) (aller) to accompany, to go with; (venir) to accompany, to come with; (conduire) to take (**à** to); **~ un convoi** to accompany a convoy; **accompagne-le au magasin** go with him to the shop GB ou store US; **tu m'accompagnes à la gare?** (à pied) will you come to the station with me? **je vais vous (y) ~** (en voiture) I'll take you (there); (à pied) I'll come with you; **~ un enfant à l'école** to take a child to school; **tous mes vœux vous accompagnent** all my good wishes go with you; **il s'est fait ~ par** ou **d'un ami** he got a friend to go with ou accompany him; **être accompagné de** or **par** to be accompanied by; **20% de réduction à la personne qui vous accompagne** 20% reduction for any person travelling[GB] with you; **ces personnes vous accompagnent?** are these people with you?; **elle les accompagna du regard** her eyes followed them; **elle a accompagné son mari jusqu'à la fin** she stayed by her husband's side until the end; **accompagné/non accompagné** [*bagage, enfant*] accompanied/unaccompanied; **2** (aller de pair avec) to accompany, to go with; **les difficultés qui pourraient ~ la réforme** the difficulties which may accompany the reform; **fièvre accompagnée de maux de tête** fever accompanied by headaches; **une cassette accompagne le livre** there's a cassette with the book; **elle accompagna ces mots d'un sourire/clin d'œil** she smiled/winked as she said this; **CV accompagné de deux photos** CV ou resumé US together with two photographs; **l'inflation et les problèmes qui l'accompagnent** inflation and its attendant problems; **3** (soutenir) to back, to support; **~ la réforme de garanties** to back up the reform with guarantees; **4** Mus to accompany (**à** on); **5** Culin [*sauce, vin, légumes*] (être servi avec) to be served with; (convenir à) to go with; **vin pour ~ un plat** wine to accompany a dish.

II s'accompagner *vpr* **1** Mus to accompany oneself (**à** on); **2** (s'associer à) to be accompanied (**de** by); **la restructuration doit s'~ d'une modernisation** reorganization will have to be accompanied by modernization; **l'accord s'accompagne d'un contrat** the agreement comes with a contract; **3** Culin to be served with.

accompli, **~e** /akɔ̃pli/ **I** *pp* ▶ **accomplir**.

II *pp adj* (parfait) [*personne*] accomplished; (achevé) fulfilled, accomplished; **mission ~e!** mission accomplished!

accomplir /akɔ̃pliʀ/ [3] **I** *vtr* **1** (s'acquitter de) to accomplish [*tâche, mission*]; to fulfil[GB] [*obligation*]; **~ son devoir** to do one's duty; **2** (réaliser) to make [*progrès, effort*]; **~ de grandes choses** to achieve great things; **3** Jur, Admin (faire) to do [*service militaire, peine de prison*]; **~ des démarches/formalités** to go through procedures/formalities.

II s'accomplir *vpr* **1** (se produire) [*événement*] to take place; **2** (se réaliser) [*vœu, souhait, prévisions*] to be fulfilled[GB]; **3** (s'épanouir) [*personne*] to find fulfilment[GB] (**dans** in).

accomplissement /akɔ̃plismɑ̃/ *nm* (d'activité, de mission) accomplishment, fulfilment[GB]; (réalisation) realization, achievement; (épanouissement) (self-)fulfilment[GB].

accord /akɔʀ/ *nm* **1** (consentement) consent (**à** to), agreement (**à** to); **donner son ~ à qch** to give one's consent to sth, to agree to sth; **d'un commun ~** by common consent ou mutual agreement; **2** (pacte) agreement (**portant sur** on); (non formel) understanding; **~ de conciliation/cessez-le-feu** conciliation/ceasefire agreement; **conclure un ~** to enter into an agreement; **~s de commerce** or **commerciaux** trade agreements; **~s bilatéraux** bilateral agreements; **3** (avis partagé, entente) agreement (**sur** on); **décider qch en** or **d'~ avec qn** to decide sth in agreement with sb; **être d'~** to agree; **je suis/je ne suis pas d'~ avec toi là-dessus** I agree/I disagree with you on this; **je suis d'~ que** I agree (that); **Pierre est d'~ pour faire** Pierre has agreed to do; **je suis/je ne suis pas d'~ pour payer** I am/I am not willing to pay; **je ne suis pas d'~ pour que nous fassions** I am not in favour[GB] of our doing; **je demeure d'~ avec vous sur ce point** I am in agreement with you on this point; **se mettre** or **tomber d'~** to come to an agreement; **mettre tout le monde d'~** (du même avis) to bring everybody round[GB] to the same way of thinking; (mettre fin aux querelles) to put an end to the argument; **tu es d'~ pour la plage○?** are you on for the beach○?; **'on signe?'—'d'~'○** 'shall we sign?'—'OK○', 'all right', 'fine'; **4** (entre personnes, couleurs, styles) harmony; **vivre en ~** to live in harmony; **un ~ parfait règne entre eux** they have a very harmonious relationship; **être en ~ avec** (avec écrit, tradition, promesse) to be in keeping ou consistent with; **en ~ avec le reste du mobilier** in keeping with the rest of the furniture; **agir en ~ avec le règlement/ses principes** to act in accordance with the rules/one's principles; **5** Ling agreement; **~ en genre/en nombre** gender/number agreement; **faire l'~** to make the agreement; **6** Mus (notes) chord; (réglage) tuning; **le piano tient l'~** the piano stays in tune.

■ **~ à l'amiable** informal agreement; **~ de contingentement** quota agreement; **~ de gré à gré** mutual agreement; **~ de paiement** Écon trade agreement; **~ de principe** agreement in principle; **~ salarial** Entr wage settlement; **~s de crédit** Fin credit arrangements; **Accord général sur les tarifs douaniers et le commerce** General Agreement on Tariffs and Trade, GATT.

accordable /akɔʀdabl/ *adj* **1** [*prêt*] grantable, which may be granted; **2** Mus [*instrument*] tunable.

accordage /akɔʀdaʒ/, **accordement** /akɔʀd(ə)mɑ̃/ *nm* Mus tuning.

accord-cadre, *pl* **accords-cadres** /akɔʀkadʀ/ *nm* outline agreement.

accordéon /akɔʀdeɔ̃/ ▶534 **I** *nm* accordion; **un air d'~** a tune on the accordion; **en ~** fig [*chaussettes, pantalon*] wrinkled; [*voiture accidentée*] concertinaed; **plier qch en ~** to fold sth into pleats; **être plié en ~** to be folded into a concertina.

II (-)accordéon (*in compounds*) **cloison ~** sliding and folding partition; **porte ~** folding door.

■ **~ chromatique** chromatic accordion; **~ diatonique** diatonic accordion.

accordéoniste /akɔʀdeɔnist/ ▶510, 534 *nmf* accordion-player.

accorder /akɔʀde/ [1] **I** *vtr* **1** (octroyer) **~ qch à qn** to grant sth to sb, to grant sb sth [*faveur, prêt, entretien, permission, droit*]; to give ou award sth to sb, to give ou award sb sth [*indemnité, bourse*]; to give sth to sb, to give sb sth [*réduction, chance, interview*]; **~ une aide financière à qn** to give sb financial assistance; **~ la main de sa fille à qn** to give sb one's daughter's hand in marriage; **m'accorderez-vous cette danse?** may I have this dance?; **peux-tu m'~ quelques instants?** can you spare me a few moments?; **~ sa confiance à qn** to put one's trust in sb; **2** (prêter) to assign, to attach [*importance, valeur*] (**à** to); to pay [*attention*]; **il leur accorda une oreille distraite** he only half-listened to them; **3** (concéder) **~ à qn que** to admit (to sb) that; **je t'accorde bien volontiers que** I freely admit that; **il n'a pas entièrement tort, je te l'accorde** he's not entirely wrong, I'll give you that; **4** (harmoniser) to match [*coloris*] (**avec** with); **~ ses actes à ses principes** to act in accordance with one's principles; **5** Mus to tune [*instrument*]; **6** Ling to make [sth] agree [*mot*] (**avec** with); **7†** (mettre d'accord) to bring [sb] together [*personnes*].

II s'accorder *vpr* **1** (s'octroyer) to give ou allow oneself [*repos, congé*]; **2** (être ou se mettre d'accord) to agree (**sur** about, on); **ils s'accordent à dire/penser/reconnaître que** (tous les deux) they both say/think/acknowledge that; (eux tous) they all say/think/acknowledge that; **ils s'accordent à leur trouver du talent** they agree that they are talented; **3** (s'entendre) [*personnes*] to get on together; **bien/mal s'~ avec qn** to get on/not to get on well with sb; **4** (s'harmoniser) [*couleurs*] to go (together) well; **ces chaises s'accordent bien/ne s'accordent pas avec la table** these chairs go well/do not go with the table; **ça s'accorde avec ce que je disais** it fits in with what I was saying; **leurs caractères s'accordent** they are well matched; **nos sentiments/opinions s'accordent** we feel/think the same; **5** Ling [*adjectif, verbe*] to agree (**avec** with); **6** Mus to tune up.

accordeur /akɔʀdœʀ/ ▶510 *nm* tuner; **~ de pianos/d'orgues** piano/organ tuner.

accordoir /akɔʀdwaʀ/ *nm* tuning hammer, tuning key.

accort, **~e** /akɔʀ, ɔʀt/ *adj* liter winsome littér.

accostable /akɔstabl/ *adj* Naut with easy access.

accostage /akɔstaʒ/ *nm* docking.

accoster /akɔste/ [1] **I** *vtr* **1** Naut to come ou draw alongside [*quai, navire*]; **2** (aborder) to accost [*personne*].

II *vi* Naut to dock, to land.

accotement /akɔtmɑ̃/ *nm* verge; **~ meuble** or **non stabilisé** Gén Civ soft verge GB, soft shoulder.

accoter /akɔte/ [1] **I** *vtr* **1** (étayer) to prop up [*mur, façade*]; **2** (appuyer) to lean (**à, contre** against).

II s'accoter *vpr* to lean (**à, contre** against).

accotoir /akɔtwaʀ/ *nm* arm-rest.

accouchée /akuʃe/ *nf* Méd mother of newborn child.

accouchement /akuʃmɑ̃/ *nm* delivery; **un ~ difficile/facile** a difficult/an easy birth ou delivery; **~ à terme/avant terme** or **prématuré** full-term/premature birth; **préparation à l'~** preparation for birth; **~ simple/multiple** single/multiple birth.

■ **~ aquatique** underwater childbirth; **~ provoqué** induced delivery; **~ psychoprophylactique** or **sans douleur** natural childbirth, psychoprophylaxis spéc; **~ par le siège** breech birth.

accoucher /akuʃe/ [1] **I** *vtr* [*médecin, sage-femme*] to deliver [*femme*].

II accoucher de *vtr ind* **1** Méd **~ de** to give birth to [*enfant*]; **2**○ (produire) **~ de** to produce [*œuvre, idée*]; **alors, t'accouches**○**!** OK, spit it out○!; ▶ **montagne**.

III *vi* to give birth.

accoucheur /akuʃœʀ/ ▶ **510** *nm* **médecin ~** obstetrician.

accoucheuse /akuʃøz/ ▶ **510** *nf* midwife.

accouder: s'accouder /akude/ [1] *vpr* to lean on one's elbows (**à, sur** on); **il était accoudé au bar** he was sitting with his elbows on the bar.

accoudoir /akudwaʀ/ *nm* arm-rest.

accouplement /akupləmɑ̃/ *nm* **1** (pour reproduction) mating; **2** Tech coupling.

accoupler /akuple/ [1] **I** *vtr* **1** (pour reproduction) to mate (**à** with); **2** (mettre par paires) to yoke [*bœufs*]; **3** Tech to couple.

II s'accoupler *vpr* to mate.

accourir /akuʀiʀ/ [26] *vi* to run up; **~ au secours de qn** to rush to sb's aid; **~ pour faire** to rush to do; **les candidats sont accourus de toute la région** candidates came running from all over the area; **dès qu'ils ont entendu les appels à l'aide ils ont accouru sur les lieux de l'accident** as soon as they heard the cries for help they rushed to the spot.

accoutrement /akutʀəmɑ̃/ *nm* pej get-up○, clothes (*pl*); **quel ~ ridicule!** what a ridiculous get-up!

accoutrer /akutʀe/ [1] **I** *vtr* pej **~ qn de qch** to rig sb out in sth.

II s'accoutrer *vpr* to get oneself up (**de** in); **il s'accoutre vraiment n'importe comment!** he dresses any old how!

accoutumance /akutymɑ̃s/ *nf* **1** gén familiarization; **il y a une période d'~** there is an acclimatization period; **2** Méd (à un médicament) addiction (**à** to); **~ aux stupéfiants** drug addiction.

accoutumé, **~e** /akutyme/ **I** *adj* liter (habituel) customary, usual; **avec leur politesse ~e** with their customary politeness.

II comme à l'accoutumée *loc adv* as usual.

accoutumer /akutyme/ [1] **I** *vtr* fml to accustom (**à** to), to get [sb] used (**à** to).

II s'accoutumer *vpr* **s'~ à** to get used to, to grow accustomed to sout; **s'~ à faire qch** to get used to doing sth, to grow accustomed to doing sth; **être accoutumé à qch/à faire** to be used ou accustomed to sth/to doing.

Accra /akʀa/ ▶ **857** *npr* Accra.

accréditation /akʀeditasjɔ̃/ *nf* accreditation (**de** of).

accrédité, **~e** /akʀedite/ *adj* [*représentant*] accredited (**auprès de** to); [*fournisseur*] authorized.

accréditer /akʀedite/ [1] **I** *vtr* **1** (rendre crédible) to give credence to [*opinion, rumeur*]; to lend weight to [*idée, théorie*]; **2** (faire reconnaître) to accredit [*ambassade, représentant*]; **3** Fin (recommander) to accredit [*personne*] (**auprès de** to); (accorder un crédit) to open credit facilities for; **être accrédité auprès d'une banque** to have credit facilities with a bank; **veuillez ~ le porteur** please open a credit to the bearer.

II s'accréditer *vpr* [*nouvelle, rumeur*] to gain currency.

accréditif, **-ive** /akʀeditif, iv/ **I** *adj* accreditive; **lettre accréditive** letter of credit.

II *nm* (lettre) letter of credit; (crédit) credit.

accro○ /akʀo/ **I** *adj* hooked○; **il est complètement ~** he's completely hooked; **être ~ à qch/qn** to be hooked on sth/sb.

II *nmf* addict; **les ~s de la moto/du petit écran** motorcycling/TV addicts.

accroc /akʀo/ *nm* **1** (déchirure) tear; **faire un ~ à qch** to tear sth; **avoir un ~ à** to have a tear in; **2** fig (infraction) breach; (tache) **~ à la réputation de qn** blot on sb's reputation; **se dérouler sans ~(s)** fig to take place without a hitch.

accrochage /akʀɔʃaʒ/ *nm* **1** (affrontement) clash (**entre** between); **2** Aut (légère collision) bump (**avec** with); **3** (de tableau) hanging.

accroche /akʀɔʃ/ *nf* slogan.

accroche-cœur, *pl* **~s** /akʀɔʃkœʀ/ *nm* kiss curl.

accrocher /akʀɔʃe/ [1] **I** *vtr* **1** (suspendre) to hang (**à** from); **2** (attacher) to hook [sth] on [*remorque, wagon*] (**à** to); **la chaîne était mal accrochée** the chain wasn't hooked on properly; **il a accroché le char au tracteur** he hooked the cart onto the tractor; **3** (faire un accroc à) to catch [*bas, pull*] (**à** on); **j'ai accroché mon collant aux ronces** I caught my tights on the brambles; **4** (accoster) [*démarcheur*] to buttonhole○ [*personne, client*]; **5** (heurter) [*voiture, automobiliste*] to bump into [*voiture, piéton*]; **6** (attirer) to catch [*regard, attention*]; **titre qui accroche le lecteur** eye-catching title; **7** Fin, Écon (rattacher) **~ qch à** to tie sth to [*monnaie*]; **~ le dinar au mark** to tie the dinar to the mark.

II *vi* **1** (coincer) [*fermeture*] to stick; [*négociations*] to hit a snag; **2** (attirer) [*titre, image, publicité*] to catch on; **trouver une formule qui accroche** to find a phrase which catches on; **3**○ (apprécier) **~ avec qn** to hit it off○ with sb; **~ avec qch** to go for [*style, musique*]; **je n'accroche pas avec elle** we don't click○, we don't hit it off○.

III s'accrocher *vpr* **1** (se suspendre) lit (à une corniche) to hang on; (à un poteau) to cling (on) (**à** to); fig [*objet*] to cling (on) (**à** to); **accroche-toi à la branche** hang on to the branch; **des villages/chalets accrochés aux pentes** villages/chalets clinging to the slopes; **alpiniste accroché à une corde** climber hanging from a rope; **2** (s'attacher) lit, fig [*personne*] to cling (**à** to); **s'~ au bras de qn** to cling to sb's arm; **l'hameçon s'est accroché à ma veste** the hook got caught on my jacket; **3**○ (tenir bon) **s'~ pour faire** to try hard to do; **accroche-toi!** (sur une moto) hang on to your hat!; (avant histoire, film) brace yourself!; **4** (se disputer) **s'~ avec qn** to have a brush with sb.

IDIOMES **avoir le cœur** or **l'estomac bien accroché** to have a strong stomach.

accrocheur, **-euse** /akʀɔʃœʀ, øz/ *adj* **1** (opiniâtre) [*démarcheur, vendeur*] persistent; **2** (attrayant) [*chanson, air*] catchy; [*image, titre*] eye-catching.

accroire /akʀwaʀ/ *vtr* fml **faire** or **laisser ~ qch à qn** to have sb believe sth; **faire ~ à qn que** to make sb believe that; **en faire ~ à qn** to take sb in; **s'en laisser ~** to be taken in (**par** by).

accroissement /akʀwasmɑ̃/ *nm* growth, increase (**de** in); **un fort/net ~ démographique** a strong/clear demographic growth; **un ~ de 5% par an** an increase of 5% per annum; **être en ~** to be on the increase.

accroître /akʀwɑtʀ/ [72] **I** *vtr* to increase [*quantité, nombre, possibilités, bénéfices*].

II s'accroître *vpr* [*population, pouvoir*] to increase; [*sentiment*] to grow.

accroupi, **~e** /akʀupi/ **I** *pp* ▶ **accroupir**.

II *pp adj* gén squatting (down); (pour se cacher) crouching.

accroupir: s'accroupir /akʀupiʀ/ [3] *vpr* gén to squat (down); (pour se cacher) to crouch (down).

accroupissement /akʀupismɑ̃/ *nm* squatting, crouching.

accru, **~e** /akʀy/ **I** *pp* ▶ **accroître**.

II *pp adj* [*besoin, présence, stabilité*] increased, greater.

accu○ /aky/ *nm* accumulator; **~s** battery (*sg*); **recharger ses ~s** fig to recharge one's batteries.

accueil /akœj/ *nm* welcome, reception; **~ froid** cool reception; **~ chaleureux/enthousiaste** warm/enthusiastic welcome ou reception; **il a reçu le meilleur ~** he received the warmest of welcomes; **faire bon ~ à qn** to make sb welcome; **faire bon ~ à qch** to welcome sth; **faire mauvais ~ à qn/qch** to give sb/sth a cool reception.

accueillant, **~e** /akœjɑ̃, ɑ̃t/ *adj* **1** [*personnes*] hospitable ou welcoming (**à l'égard de** to); **2** [*maison*] homely GB, homey US; [*ville, campagne*] friendly, welcoming; [*appartement, chambre*] inviting.

accueillir /akœjiʀ/ [27] *vtr* **1** (souhaiter la bienvenue) to welcome; **2** (recevoir) to welcome, to receive [*invités, clients, voyageurs*]; to receive [*décision, projet, livre, film*]; **bien/mal ~ qn/qch** to give sb/sth a good/bad reception; **j'ai été bien accueilli** (à l'arrivée) I was given a warm welcome; (pendant le séjour) I was made to feel very welcome; **ils ont été accueillis par des acclamations/sifflets** they were greeted with cheers/whistles; **l'idée a été accueillie avec méfiance/intérêt** the idea was received with suspicion/interest; **3** (contenir) to accommodate [*personnes*]; **4** (prendre en charge) [*organisme, hôpital, maison de retraite*] to cater for [*patients, réfugiés*]; **la Croix rouge est chargée d'~ 200 réfugiés** the Red Cross is responsible for taking care of 200 refugees.

acculer /akyle/ [1] *vtr* **1** (dans un endroit) to drive [sb] back (**contre** against); **les troupes étaient acculées à la mer** the troops were driven back to the edge of the sea; **2** (dans une situation) **~ qn à qch/à faire qch** to force sb into sth/into doing sth; **~ qn à la ruine/au désespoir** to drive sb to ruin/to despair; **~ qn à la faillite** to drive sb into bankruptcy; **se sentir acculé** to feel cornered.

acculturation /akyltyʀasjɔ̃/ *nf* acculturation.

accumulateur /akymylatœʀ/ *nm* accumulator; **batterie d'~s** battery (of accumulators).

■ **~ de chaleur** Tech storage heater.

accumulation /akymylasjɔ̃/ *nf* **1** (action) accumulation, build-up; **l'~ du capital/des richesses** the accumulation of capital/of wealth; **2** (résultat) accumulation, mass; **une ~ de preuves** a mass of evidence; **3** Tech (emmagasinage) storage; **radiateur/chauffe-eau à ~** storage heater/water heater; **4** Géol accumulation.

accumuler /akymyle/ [1] **I** *vtr* **1** (entasser) store (up) [*objets, provisions, réserves*]; **2** (amasser) to accumulate, to amass [*biens, capital, intérêts*]; to let [sth] build up [*colère, ressentiment*]; **3** (répéter) to make a succession ou series of [*erreurs, sottises*]; to have a

string of [*succès*]; **4** (emmagasiner) to store (up) [*énergie, chaleur, électricité*].
II **s'accumuler** *vpr* **1** (s'entasser) [*neige, ordures, commandes*] to pile up; **2** (s'accroître) [*stocks, dettes*] to accrue; [*pression*] to build up.

accusateur, -trice /akyzatœʀ, tʀis/ **I** *adj* **1** [*silence, mot, doigt, ton*] accusing (*épith*); **2** [*inscription, présence, discours*] accusatory.
II *nm,f* accuser.
■ **~ public** Hist public prosecutor.

accusatif /akyzatif/ *nm* Ling accusative; **à l'~** in the accusative.

accusation /akyzasjɔ̃/ *nf* **1** (reproche grave) accusation; Jur (formulation) charge; **porter une ~ contre** to make an accusation against; **répondre d'une ~** to answer an accusation; **mettre qn en ~** (reprocher) to censure sb; Jur to indict sb; **mise en ~ de** gén, Jur indictment of; **2** (ministère public) **l'~** the prosecution.

accusatoire /akyzatwaʀ/ *adj* accusatory.

accusé, ~e /akyze/ **I** *pp* ▶ **accuser**.
II *pp adj* (accentué) [*traits*] strong; [*ride*] deep; [*relief*] marked.
III *nm,f* Jur defendant; **les ~s** the accused; **faites entrer l'~** call the defendant; **'~ levez-vous'** 'will the defendant please rise'.
■ **~ de réception**, **AR** Postes acknowledgement of receipt.

accuser /akyze/ [1] **I** *vtr* **1** Jur [*plaignant*] to accuse (**de** of); [*juge*] to charge (**de** with); **il est accusé du meurtre de sa femme/de meurtre** (par le plaignant, un témoin) he is accused of murdering his wife/of murder; (à l'issue du procès) he is charged with murdering his wife/with murder; ▶ **rage**; **2** (rendre coupable) [*personne*] to accuse [*personne*] (**de (faire)** of (doing)); to blame [*sort, malchance*]; [*fait, preuve*] to point to [*personne*]; **on l'accuse d'espionnage** he is accused of spying; **il est accusé d'avoir provoqué un accident** he is accused of causing an accident; **tout l'accuse** everything points to him; **son silence l'accuse** his silence incriminates him; **voici les photos qui l'accusent** here are the photos which point the finger at him; **~ qn/qch de tous les maux** to put all the blame on sb/sth; **3** (rendre évident) [*traits, expression*] to show [*fatigue, ennui*]; [*ventes, affaires, chiffres*] to show [*baisse, déficit*]; **~ une hausse de 10%** to show a 10% increase; **il accuse son âge** he looks his age; **il accuse (bien) la cinquantaine** he looks all of his fifty years; **4** (accentuer) [*éclairage, maquillage*] to accentuate [*contour, défaut*].
II **s'accuser** *vpr* **1** (se rendre coupable) to take the blame (**de qch** for sth; **d'avoir fait** for doing); **elle s'accuse pour protéger son amant** she took the blame to protect her lover; **2** (l'un l'autre) to accuse each other (**de (faire)** of (doing)); **ils s'accusent mutuellement d'être responsables du conflit** they are accusing each other of being to blame for the conflict; **3** (s'aggraver) [*contour, défaut, différence*] to become more marked ou pronounced.
IDIOMES **~ le coup** to be visibly shaken; **~ réception** to acknowledge receipt (**de** of).

ace /ɛs/ *nm* Sport ace.

acerbe /asɛʀb/ *adj* acerbic.

acéré, ~e /aseʀe/ *adj* **1** lit [*objet*] sharp; **2** fig [*critique, remarque*] cutting, scathing; [*style*] trenchant; [*œil, regard*] sharp, keen; **plume ~e** scathing pen.

acétate /asetat/ *nm* acetate.

acétique /asetik/ *adj* acetic.

acétone /asetɔn/ *nf* acetone.

acétylène /asetilɛn/ *nm* acetylene.

acétylsalicylique /asetilsalisilik/ *adj* **acide ~** acetylsalicylic acid.

ACF /aseɛf/ *nm* (*abbr* = **Automobile Club de France**) *French automobile association*.

achalandé, ~e /aʃalɑ̃de/ *adj* (approvisionné) **bien/mal ~** well-/poorly-stocked.

achaler○ /aʃale/ [1] *vtr* C (importuner) [*personne*] to hassle○ GB, to bug○ US; [*mouche, bruit*] to irritate; **achale-moi pas** don't hassle me.

acharné, ~e /aʃaʀne/ **I** *pp* ▶ **acharner**.
II *pp adj* [*partisan, défenseur*] passionate; [*fumeur, séducteur*] incorrigible; [*travail*] unremitting, relentless; [*lutte, discussion, résistance*] fierce; **c'est un travailleur ~** he works relentlessly.

acharnement /aʃaʀnəmɑ̃/ *nm* (énergie) furious energy; (ténacité) tenacity, determination; **l'~ de qn à faire** sb's determination to do; **son ~ au travail** the fact that he/she works so relentlessly; **lutter avec ~** to fight tooth and nail.
■ **~ thérapeutique** extraordinary or heroic treatment.

acharner: **s'acharner** /aʃaʀne/ [1] *vpr* **1** (s'obstiner) to persevere; **s'~ à faire** to try desperately to do; **à force de s'~ il a fini par réussir son examen** by persevering he eventually passed his exam; **une organisation qui s'acharne à dénoncer les manquements aux droits de l'homme** an organization that is determined to denounce violations of Human Rights; **pourquoi s'acharne-t-il à la faire souffrir?** why is he so determined to make her suffer ou hell-bent on making her suffer?; **s'~ contre** [*personne, groupe*] to fight against [*projet*]; **2** (continuer des violences) **s'~ sur** [*personne, animal*] to keep going at [*victime, proie*]; fig [*personne*] to hound [*enfant, collaborateur*]; [*destin*] to dog [*personne, projet*]; **la fatalité s'acharne sur eux** they're dogged by bad luck.

achat /aʃa/ **I** *nm* **1** (action) buying, purchase; **l'~ de qch** buying sth, the purchase of sth; **un ~** a purchase; **c'est plus cher à l'~** it's more expensive to buy; **j'ai versé 25% à l'~** I paid 25% of the total at the time of purchase; **faire l'~ de qch** to buy ou purchase sth; **consacrer le samedi aux ~s** to spend Saturday shopping; **l'~ sur catalogue** buying by mail order; **faire un ~** to buy something, to make a purchase; **faire des ~s** to do some shopping; **l'~ par téléphone** telephone shopping; **~ d'espace publicitaire** buying advertising space; **2** (objet acheté) purchase; **3** Fin (de devise) buying; (d'action) purchase, buying.
II **achats** *nmpl* (service) buying department, purchasing department.

acheminement /aʃ(ə)minmɑ̃/ *nm* **1** (de troupes, blessés, vivres) transportation (**vers** to); **responsable de l'~ du courrier** responsible for handling the mail; **il y a des retards dans l'~ du courrier** there are postal delays; **2** (fait de se diriger) **l'~ du pays vers la ruine/démocratie** the country's march toward(s) ruin/democracy.

acheminer /aʃ(ə)mine/ [1] **I** *vtr* (transporter) to transport [*troupe, blessés, vivres*] (**vers** to); **~ le courrier** [*service postal*] to handle the mail.
II **s'acheminer** *vpr* **1** [*personne, troupe*] to make one's way (**vers** to ou toward(s)); **2** fig **s'~ vers** [*négociations*] to move toward(s); [*pays, économie*] (aboutissement fâcheux) to head for ou toward(s); (aboutissement positif) to move toward(s).

acheter /aʃte/ [18] **I** *vtr* **1** to buy, to purchase [*objet*]; to buy [*charge, droit, vote, silence*]; **~ qch (au) comptant/à crédit** to buy sth for cash/on credit; **~ à crédit** to buy on credit; **~ qch sur catalogue** to buy sth from a catalogue[GB]; **~ qch par correspondance** to buy sth by mail order; **~ un cadeau à qn** to buy sb a present, to buy a present for sb; **j'ai acheté un livre à ta sœur** (pour elle) I've bought your sister a book ou a book for your sister; (chez elle) I bought a book from your sister; **~ pour 20 francs de qch** to buy 20 francs worth of sth; **~ qch 20 francs** to pay 20 francs for sth, to buy sth for 20 francs; **~ français/japonais** to buy French/Japanese products; **2** (soudoyer) to buy [*juge, politicien*].
II **s'acheter** *vpr* **1** (pour soi) **s'~ qch** to buy oneself sth; **2** (être disponible à l'achat) **cela s'achète où?** where can you get it?; **cela ne s'achète pas** it's something money can't buy.
IDIOMES **s'~ une conduite** to mend one's ways.

acheteur, -euse /aʃtœʀ, øz/ **I** *adj* [*pays*] importing.
II *nm,f* **1** (client) buyer, purchaser; **pour tout ~ du dictionnaire** for anyone who buys the dictionary; **je vends ma voiture, es-tu ~?** I'm selling my car, would you like to buy it?; **à ce prix-là je ne suis pas ~** at that price, I'm not interested; **est-il ~?** is he interested?; **2** ▶ **510** (professionnel) buyer.

achevé, ~e /aʃve/ **I** *pp* ▶ **achever**.
II *pp adj* liter [*œuvre, style, technique*] accomplished; [*exemple, forme, modèle*] perfect; **être d'un ridicule ~/d'une bêtise ~e** to be utterly ridiculous/stupid; **être d'un comique ~/d'une intelligence ~e** [*situation, œuvre*] to be sheer comedy/intelligence; **il est d'une intelligence ~e** he's extremely intelligent; **c'est un snob ~** he's a consummate snob; **c'est un idiot ~** he's a complete idiot.

achèvement /aʃɛvmɑ̃/ *nm* (de travaux, projet, roman) completion; (de rencontre, discussions) conclusion; **en cours** or **voie d'~** nearing completion.

achever /aʃve/ [16] **I** *vtr* **1** (terminer) to finish [*travail, repas, œuvre*]; to conclude [*discussions*]; to complete [*projet, visite, enquête, service militaire*]; to end [*vie*]; **~ de faire** to finish doing; **il avait à peine achevé que tout le monde partait déjà** he had hardly finished speaking when everyone started to leave; **2** (réussir) **l'orage a achevé de décourager les spectateurs** the spectators were dispirited and the storm was the last straw; **il a achevé de me démoraliser avec ses mauvaises nouvelles** I was feeling down-hearted and the bad news he gave me was the last straw; **ta démonstration a achevé de me convaincre** the proof you gave me finally convinced me; **3** (tuer) to destroy [*animal*]; to finish off [*personne*]; **4**○ (épuiser) [*personne, effort*] to wear [sb] out, to finish○; **5**○ (terrasser) [*scandale, ruine*] to finish [sb] off.
II **s'achever** *vpr* to end (**par** with; **sur** on); **le jour s'achève** the day is drawing to a close; **s'~ par un record** to end with a record; **s'~ sur une victoire** to end on a victory.

Achille /aʃil/ *npr* Achilles; **tendon d'~** Achilles tendon.

Achkhabad /aʃkabad/ ▶ **857** *npr* Ashkhabad.

achoppement /aʃɔpmɑ̃/ *nm* **pierre d'~** stumbling block.

achopper /aʃɔpe/ [1] *vi* **~ sur** to stumble over; **les négociations ont achoppé sur ce point** the talks hit a snag over this issue.

achromatique /akʀɔmatik/ *adj* achromatic.

acide /asid/ **I** *adj* **1** (pas assez sucré) [*goût*] acid, sour; (agréablement) [*goût*] sharp; (comme propriété naturelle) [*aliment*] acidic; **2** [*odeur*] acrid; [*couleur*] acid; [*remarque*] acerbic; **3** Chimie acid, acidic.
II *nm* **1** Chimie acid; **~ faible/fort** weak/strong acid; **~ gras** fatty acid; **~ chlorhydrique/sulfurique/urique** hydrochloric/sulphuric[GB]/uric acid; **2**○ (drogue) acid○.
■ **~ aminé** amino acid.

acidification /asidifikasjɔ̃/ *nf* acidification.

acidifier /asidifje/ [2] **I** *vtr* to acidify.
II **s'acidifier** *vpr* to acidify.

acidité /asidite/ *nf* **1** (désagréable) gén acidity, sourness; (pas désagréable) tartness, sharpness; **2** (de personne, réflexion, discours) acerbity; **3** Chimie acidity.

acidulé, **~e** /asidyle/ *adj* **1** lit slightly acid; **2** fig [*parfum*] tangy; [*jaune, vert*] acid.

acier /asje/ **I** ▶**193** *adj inv* **gris/bleu ~** steel(y) grey GB ou gray US/blue.
II *nm* **1** (alliage) steel; **d'~** [*cuve*] steel (*épith*); [*muscle*] of steel; **avoir des nerfs d'~** to have nerves of steel; **avoir un moral d'~** to be made of stern stuff; **2** (industrie) steel industry.
■ **~ inoxydable** stainless steel; **~ rapide** high-speed steel; **~ trempé** tempered steel.

aciérie /asjeʀi/ *nf* steelworks (+ *v sg* ou *pl*).

aciériste /asjeʀist/ *nm* steel maker.

acmé /akme/ *nm* **1** (apogée) liter acme littér; **2** Méd crisis.

acné /akne/ *nf* Méd acne; **~ juvénile** teenage acne; **~ rosacée** acne rosacea.

acolyte /akɔlit/ *nmf* **1** (complice) péj henchman, acolyte; **2** Relig acolyte.

acompte /akɔ̃t/ *nm* (premier versement) down payment; (arrhes) deposit; (versement échelonné) instalment[GB]; (versement partiel) part payment; **~ sur salaire** advance on salary; **verser un ~ de** to make a down payment of; **3 000 francs d'~** or **en ~** a 3,000-franc down payment.
■ **~ provisionnel** Fisc ≈ first instalment[GB].

aconit /akɔnit/ *nm* monkshood.

acoquiner: **s'acoquiner** /akɔkine/ [1] *vpr* **s'~ avec qn** to get thick○ with sb.

Açores /asɔʀ/ ▶**416** *nprfpl* **les ~** the Azores.

à-côté, *pl* **~s** /akote/ *nm* **1** (problème) side issue; **2** (avantages) perk; (gains) **se faire de petits ~s** to make a bit on the side○; **3** (dépenses) extra.

à-coup, *pl* **~s** /aku/ *nm* (secousse) jolt; (de processus, négociations, travail, d'économie) hitch; **les ~s du moteur** the coughs and splutters of the engine; **par ~s** lit, fig by ou in fits and starts; **sans ~s** lit, fig smoothly; **essayez d'éviter les ~s** (dans le travail) try to keep things running smoothly; (dans la vie, les relations) try to keep things on an even keel.

acouphène /akufɛn/ *nm* tinnitus.

acousticien, **-ienne** /akustisjɛ̃, ɛn/ ▶**510** *nm,f* acoustician.

acoustique /akustik/ **I** *adj* acoustic.
II *nf* **1** Phys acoustics (+ *v sg*); **2** (d'un lieu) acoustics (*pl*); **3** Mus acoustic quality.

acquéreur /akeʀœʀ/ *nm* buyer, purchaser; **elle est ~** she's interested; **trouver un ~ pour** to find a buyer for; **se porter ~ de** to state one's intention to buy; **se rendre ~ de** to purchase, to buy.

acquérir /akeʀiʀ/ [35] **I** *vtr* **1** (devenir propriétaire de) to acquire; (en achetant) to purchase; **~ qch par héritage** or **succession** to inherit sth; **2** (arriver à avoir) [*personne*] to acquire [*habitude, connaissance, expérience, réputation*]; **~ une formation** to undergo training; **~ la certitude que** to become convinced that; **~ la preuve de** to gain proof of; **cela vous a acquis l'admiration/le soutien de vos collègues** this has won you your colleagues' admiration/support; **3** (gagner) to acquire; **~ de la valeur** to gain in value; **cela a acquis de l'importance** it has become important; **~ de la vitesse** to gain speed; **4** (au passif) **il est acquis à notre cause** we have his support; **son bon vouloir nous est acquis** we can count on his good will; **il est acquis que** it is accepted that.
II s'acquérir *vpr* **1** (s'obtenir) **s'~ facilement** to be easy to acquire; **s'~ par succession** or **héritage** to be inherited; **2** (s'apprendre) **c'est quelque chose qui s'acquiert** it's something you acquire ou pick up; **l'expérience s'acquiert avec l'âge** experience comes with age.

acquêt /akɛ/ *nm*: *property acquired in common by husband and wife.*

acquiescement /akjɛsmɑ̃/ fml *nm* acquiescence sout; **donner son ~ à qch** to acquiesce to sth.

acquiescer /akjese/ [12] *vi* to acquiesce; **~ d'un signe de tête** to nod in agreement; **et sa fille d'~** and the daughter agrees.

acquis, **~e** /aki, iz/ **I** *pp* ▶ **acquérir**.
II *pp adj* **1** Psych [*comportement, idée*] acquired; **2** (obtenu) [*valeur, expérience, connaissance, conviction*] acquired; **3** (reconnu) [*principe, droit, fait*] accepted, established; **les avantages ~** the gains; **tenir qch pour ~** to take sth for granted ou as read.
III *nm inv* **1** (connaissances) knowledge; **vivre sur ses ~** to draw on one's knowledge; **2** (réussite) achievement; **3** (avantage obtenu) **~ salariaux/syndicaux** wage/union gains; **~ sociaux** social benefits; **c'est un ~** that is one thing gained; **4** Psych, Philos **l'~** acquired knowledge; **l'inné et l'~** nature versus nurture.
IDIOMES **bien mal ~ ne profite jamais** Prov ill-gotten gains never prosper.

acquisition /akizisjɔ̃/ *nf* **1** (achat) purchase, acquisition; **prix d'~** purchase price; **faire l'~ de** to purchase; **2** Ordinat data capture, data acquisition; **temps d'~** data capture time; **3** (de musée, bibliothèque) acquisition, accession spéc; **4** (processus) acquisition; **l'~ du langage** language acquisition; **l'~ automatique de la nationalité** the automatic acquisition of citizenship.

acquit /aki/ *nm* Comm receipt; **pour ~** received.
IDIOMES **par ~ de conscience** to put one's mind at rest.

acquit-à-caution, *pl* **acquits-à-caution** /akiakosjɔ̃/ *nm* (customs and excise) bond.

acquittement /akitmɑ̃/ *nm* **1** Jur acquittal; **2** Fin settlement.

acquitter /akite/ [1] **I** *vtr* **1** Jur to acquit [*personne*]; **faire ~ qn** to get sb acquitted; **2** (payer) to pay [*impôt, loyer*]; to settle, to pay [*dette*]; **3** (dégager) **~ qn d'une dette** to release sb from a debt.
II s'acquitter *vpr* **bien s'~ de son rôle** to fulfil[GB] a role; **s'~ de son devoir** to discharge one's duty; **s'~ d'une dette** lit to pay off a debt; fig to repay a debt of gratitude.

acre /akʀ/ ▶**783** *nf* acre.

âcre /ɑkʀ/ *adj* [*goût, fruit*] sharp; [*fumée, odeur*] acrid; [*remarque*] caustic.

âcreté /ɑkʀəte/ *nf* (de fumée, d'odeur) acridity; (d'aliment, de goût) sharpness.

acrimonie /akʀimɔni/ *nf* liter acrimony littér.

acrimonieux, **-ieuse** /akʀimɔnjø, øz/ *adj* acrimonious.

acrobate /akʀɔbat/ ▶**510** *nmf* lit, fig acrobat.

acrobatie /akʀɔbasi/ *nf* **1** Sport (activité) **l'~** acrobatics (+ *v sg*); **faire de l'~** to do ou perform acrobatics; **un exercice d'~** an acrobatic exercise; **2** (mouvement) **une ~** Sport an acrobatic exercise; **faire des ~s** Sport to do ou perform acrobatics; fig to jump through all sorts of hoops; **elle s'en tire toujours avec une ~** she always wriggles out of it.
■ **~ aérienne** aerobatics (+ *v sg*).

acrobatique /akʀɔbatik/ *adj* acrobatic.

acronyme /akʀɔnim/ *nm* acronym.

Acropole /akʀɔpɔl/ *nprf* **l'~** the Acropolis.

acrostiche /akʀɔstiʃ/ *nm* acrostic.

acrylique /akʀilik/ **I** *adj* acrylic.
II *nm* acrylic; **un pull-over en ~** an acrylic jumper; **c'est de l'~** it's acrylic.

actant /aktɑ̃/ *nm* Ling actor.

acte /akt/ **I** *nm* **1** (action) act; **~ isolé/raciste** isolated/racist act; **~ de guerre/violence** act of war/violence; **l'~ de chair** sexual congress; **un ~ de foi** lit, fig an act of faith; **mes/tes ~s** my/your actions; **être libre de ses ~s** to do as one wishes; **faire ~ d'allégeance/de bravoure/charité** to show allegiance/courage/charity; **faire ~ d'autorité** to exercise one's authority; **faire ~ de candidature** to put oneself forward as a candidate; **faire ~ de citoyen** to perform one's duty as a citizen; **faire ~ de présence** to put in an appearance; **2** Jur deed; **passer des ~s** to execute deeds; **demander/donner ~ de** to ask for/make acknowledgement of; **prendre ~ de** gén to take note of; Jur to take cognizance of; **j'en prends ~** I'll bear it in mind; **dont ~** gén point noted; Jur which is hereby legally certified; **3** Théât act; **pièce en un ~** one-act play; **4** Philos actual; **passer de la puissance à l'~** to go from the potential to the actual; **en ~** in actuality.
II actes *nmpl* **1** (de congrès, réunion) proceedings; **2** Relig acts.
■ **~ d'accusation** bill of indictment; **~ authentique** authenticated deed; **~ de contrition** act of contrition; **~ de décès** death certificate; **~ de l'état civil** *birth, marriage or death certificate*; **~ de foi** act of faith; **~ gratuit** gratuitous act; **~ manqué** parapraxis spéc, Freudian slip; **~ de mariage** marriage certificate; **~ médical** Méd medical treatment; **~ de naissance** birth certificate; **~ notarié** notarial deed; **~ officiel** instrument; **~ de parole** speech act; **~ sexuel** sexual act; **~ de vente** bill of sale; **l'Acte unique européen** Single European Act; **les Actes des apôtres** the Acts of the Apostles.

acteur, **-trice** /aktœʀ, tʀis/ *nm,f* **1** ▶**510** Cin, Théât actor/actress; **~ de cinéma/théâtre** film/stage actor; **les ~s du film/de la pièce** the actors in the film/play; **2** (participant) **~s de la scène politique** actors on the political stage; **tous les ~s de la vie économique** all the parties involved in economic life; **les ~s d'un drame** the protagonists of a tragedy; **3** (agent) agent (**de** of); **~s du changement** agents for change.

actif, **-ive** /aktif, iv/ **I** *adj* **1** (occupé) [*personne, vie*] active; **les femmes actives** working women; **la vie active** working life; **service ~** active service; **l'armée d'active** the regular army; **2** (pas passif) [*association, participation*] active; [*propagande*] vigorous; **jouer/avoir un rôle ~ dans qch** to play/to have an active part in sth; **avoir/prendre une part active à qch** to play/to take an active part in sth; **militant ~** activist; **3** (plein d'énergie) gén active; [*marché, secteur*] buoyant; **4** (agissant) [*substance, principe*] active; **5** Ling **voix active** active voice.
II *nm,f* (qui travaille) working person; **les ~s** the working population.
III *nm* Fin, Compta **l'~** the assets (*pl*); **à l'~ du bilan** on the assets side; **à mettre à l'~ de qn** fig a point in sb's favour[GB].
IV active *nf* **l'armée d'active** the regular army.
■ **~ brut** gross assets (*pl*); **~ disponible** liquid assets (*pl*); **~ immobilisé** fixed assets (*pl*); **~ net** net assets (*pl*).

actinium /aktinjɔm/ *nm* actinium.

action /aksjɔ̃/ *nf* **1** (fait d'agir) action; **il serait temps de passer à l'~** gén it's time to act; (combattre) it's time for action; **entrer en ~** Mil to go into action; **l'entrée en ~ de l'armée** the army's involvement in the conflict; **un homme/une femme d'~** a man/a woman of action; **avoir toute liberté d'~** to have complete freedom of action; **être en ~** [*personne*] to be in action; **en ~** [*machine, mécanisme*] in operation; **mettre qch en ~** to put sth into operation [*mesure, plan*]; **un sportif en (pleine) ~** a sportsman in action; **volonté d'~** will to act; **2** (façon d'agir) action; **programme** or **plan d'~** plan of action; **moyens d'~** courses of action; **avoir une unité d'~** to have a common plan of action; **champ d'~** field of action; **3** (effet) effect; **l'~ du temps** the effects of time; **avoir une ~ bénéfique/néfaste/immunologique** to have a

positive/a negative/an immunizing effect; **sous l'~ de qch** under the effect of sth; **l'~ de qch sur qch/qn** the effect of sth on sth/sb; **l'~ de qn sur qch/qn** sb's influence on sth/sb; **4** (acte) action, act; **une ~ irresponsable/stupide** an irresponsible/a stupid action; **des ~s criminelles/individuelles/racistes** criminal/individual/racist acts; **une ~ d'éclat** a remarkable feat; **faire une ~ d'éclat** to distinguish oneself; **une bonne/mauvaise ~** a good/bad deed; **j'ai fait ma bonne ~ de la journée** I've done my good deed for the day; **5** (initiative) initiative; Mil, Jur action; **une ~ des Nations unies** a UN initiative; **~s culturelles** culturel initiatives; **mener des ~s humanitaires** to carry out a programme[GB] of humanitarian aid; **dégager des ressources pour des ~s sociales** to free money for social programmes[GB]; **entreprendre une ~ militaire offensive** to take offensive action; **intenter une ~ en justice à qn** to take legal action against sb; **intenter une ~ en diffamation** to bring a libel action GB ou suit; **6** (histoire) action; **l'~ se situe à Venise** the action takes place in Venice; **un film d'~** an action film; **un roman d'~** an adventure novel; **j'aime quand il y a de l'~** I like a bit of action; **7** Fin share; **~s et obligations** securities; **une société par ~s** a joint stock company; **~ A/B** A/B share; **~ gratuite** free share; **~ nominative** registered share; **~ ordinaire** ordinary share GB, common share US; **~ préférentielle** preference share GB, preferred share US.
■ **~ de Grâce** thanksgiving.

actionnaire /aksjɔnɛʀ/ *nmf* shareholder, stockholder US; **être ~ à 100%** to be the sole shareholder; **petit/gros ~** minor/major shareholder; **~ majoritaire/minoritaire** majority/minority shareholder.

actionnariat /aksjɔnaʀja/ *nm* **1** (fait d'être actionnaire) shareholding; **2** (ensemble des actionnaires) shareholders (*pl*).

actionner /aksjɔne/ [1] *vtr* **1** (mettre en marche) to activate, to turn on [*sirène, mécanisme*]; **2** (faire fonctionner) to operate [*système, turbine*]; **3** Jur to sue.

activation /aktivasjɔ̃/ *nf* activation.

active ▶ **actif** I, II, IV.

activement /aktivmɑ̃/ *adv* actively; **participer ~ à** to take an active part in.

activer /aktive/ [1] **I** *vtr* **1** (hâter) to speed up [*travail, débat, préparatifs*]; to stimulate [*digestion*]; **2** (intensifier) [*vent*] to stir up [*flamme*]; [*personne*] to stoke [*feu*]; **3** Chimie to activate.
II○ *vi* to get a move on○, to hurry up.
III s'activer *vpr* **1** (s'affairer) to be very busy (**pour faire** doing); **la cuisinière s'activait devant le fourneau** the cook was busy at the stove; **2**○ (se dépêcher) to hurry up.

activisme /aktivism/ *nm* activism.

activiste /aktivist/ *adj, nmf* activist.

activité /aktivite/ *nf* **1** (occupation) activity; **leurs ~s de syndicalistes** their activities as trade unionists; **~ professionnelle** occupation; **c'est une ~ manuelle** it's manual work; **exercer une ~ rémunérée** to be gainfully employed; **l'escroc qui exerçait son ~ sur la côte** the con-man who operated on the coast; **cesser ses ~s** [*entreprise, commerçant*] to stop trading; [*avocat, médecin*] to stop working; **reprendre ses ~s** [*entreprise, commerçant*] to start trading again; [*malade, vacancier*] to go back to work; **entrer en ~** [*entreprise*] to start trading; **l'entrée en ~ de la société en 1993** the company's entry into the market in 1993; **2** (fonctionnement) activity; **~ économique** economic activity; **l'~ de la rue/ville** the bustle of the street/town; **l'~ du volcan** the active state of the volcano; **être en pleine ~** [*atelier*] to be in full production; [*rue, ville, gare*] to be bustling with activity; hum [*personne*] to be very busy; **en ~** [*volcan*] active; [*usine*] in operation; [*travailleur*] working; [*militaire*] in active service GB ou on active duty US; **ses années d'~** his working years; **3** (énergie) (de personne) energy; **être d'une ~ débordante** to be brimming with energy.
■ **~ dirigée** Scol class work.

actrice *nf* ▶ **acteur**.

actuaire /aktɥɛʀ/ ▶ **510** *nmf* actuary.

actualisation /aktɥalizasjɔ̃/ *nf* **1** (mise à jour) (processus) updating ¢; (résultat) update; **2** Fin conversion to current value; **3** Philos actualization; **4** Ling realization.

actualisé, **~e** /aktɥalize/ **I** *pp* ▶ **actualiser**.
II *pp adj* **1** (mis à jour) updated; **2** Fin converted to current value.

actualiser /aktɥalize/ [1] *vtr* **1** (mettre à jour) to update, to bring [sth] up to date [*ouvrage, fichier, méthode*]; **~ ses connaissances** to brush up one's knowledge; **2** Fin to convert [sth] to current value; **3** Philos to actualize; **4** Ling to realize.

actualité /aktɥalite/ **I** *nf* **1** (événements) current affairs (*pl*); **ne pas s'intéresser à l'~** not to be interested in current affairs; **l'~ cinématographique** film news; **coller à l'~** to be up to the minute with the news; **l'~ culturelle** cultural events (*pl*); **être sous les feux de l'~** to be in the spotlight of the media; **être à la une de l'~** to be in the headlines; **2** (d'idées, de débat, livre) topicality; (de réflexion, de pensée) relevance; **sujets d'une brûlante ~** burning issues; **d'~** [*thème, question*] topical; **la démission du Premier ministre n'est plus d'~** the Prime Minister's resignation is no longer at issue; **garder toute son ~** [*texte , question*] to be still relevant today; **3** Philos actuality.
II actualités *nfpl* (à la télévision, radio) news; (au cinéma) newsreel (*sg*); **les ~s télévisées** the television news.

actuariel, **-ielle** /aktɥaʀjɛl/ *adj* Stat [*calcul*] actuarial (*épith*).
■ **taux (d'intérêt) ~ brut** Fin yield to maturity before tax; **taux (d'intérêt) ~ net** Fin yield to maturity after tax.

actuel, **-elle** /aktɥɛl/ *adj* **1** (présent) present, current; **la forme actuelle du traité** the present form of the treaty; **en l'état ~ de l'enquête** at the current stage of the enquiry[GB]; **en l'état ~ des connaissances** in the present state of our knowledge; **en l'état ~ de la science** as far as science extends today; **à l'époque actuelle** in the present day; **dans le monde ~** in today's world; **l'~ territoire de la Pologne** the territory of present-day Poland; **l'Italie actuelle** present-day Italy; **2** (d'actualité) [*œuvre, débat, question*] topical; **3** Philos actual.

actuellement /aktɥɛlmɑ̃/ *adv* (en ce moment précis) at the moment, at present; (à notre époque) currently.

acuité /akɥite/ *nf* **1** (d'intelligence, analyse, de perception) acuteness; **ressentir qch avec ~** to feel sth keenly; **2** (de son) shrillness; **3** (de douleur) intensity; **4** (de problème, crise) seriousness; **le problème se pose avec ~** this is a burning issue.

acupuncteur, **-trice** /akypɔ̃ktœʀ, tʀis/ ▶ **510** *nm,f* acupuncturist.

acupuncture /akypɔ̃ktyʀ/ *nf* acupuncture.

ADAC /adak/ *nm* (*abbr* = **avion à décollage et atterrissage courts**) STOL.

adage /adaʒ/ *nm* saying, adage.

adagio /ada(d)ʒjo/ *nm, adv* adagio.

Adam /adɑ̃/ *npr* Adam; **être en tenue d'~** fig to be in one's birthday suit; ▶ **Ève**.

adamantin, **~e** /adamɑ̃tɛ̃, in/ *adj* liter adamantine.

adaptabilité /adaptabilite/ *nf* adaptability (**à** to).

adaptable /adaptabl/ *adj* **1** (souple) [*personne, caractère, animal*] adaptable (**à** to); **2** (réglable) [*hauteur, équipement*] adjustable; **~ à toutes les circonstances** or **tous les besoins** all-purpose (*épith*).

adaptateur, **-trice** /adaptatœʀ, tʀis/ **I** ▶ **510** *nm,f* Cin, Théât adapter.
II *nm* Tech adapter.

adaptation /adaptasjɔ̃/ *nf* **1** gén, Biol (réajustement) adaptation; **processus/période d'~** process/period of adaptation; **faculté d'~** capacity for adaptation; **~ à** adjustment to; **accomplir un effort d'~** to try to adapt; **avoir des problèmes d'~** to have difficulty in adapting; **2** Cin, Mus, Théât adaptation; **~ au cinéma/à la télévision/au théâtre** film/TV/stage adaptation; **~ d'un roman** adaptation of a novel; **~ libre** loose adaptation.

adapté, **~e** /adapte/ **I** *pp* ▶ **adapter**.
II *pp adj* **1** (approprié) [*logement, emploi, produit, spectacle*] suitable (**à** for); **~ aux circonstances** or **à la situation** suited to the circumstances; **2** (inséré) [*personne*] adjusted (**à** to); **un élève mal ~** a maladjusted pupil; **le personnel est maintenant ~ aux nouveaux horaires** the staff has now got GB ou gotten US used to the new timetable; **3** Cin, Théât adapted (**à, pour** for; **de** from); **4** Tech (modifié) [*équipement, conception, version*] adapted.

adapter /adapte/ [1] **I** *vtr* **1** Tech (poser) to fit [*tuyau, pneu, moteur*] (**à** to); **2** Tech (modifier) to adapt [*équipement*]; **3** (rendre conforme) to adapt [*loi, formation*] (**à** to); **~ l'offre à la demande** to adapt supply to demand; **4** (former) **~ le personnel aux nouvelles technologies** to get the staff to adapt to new technologies; **5** Cin, Théât [*personne*] to adapt [*roman*] (**à, pour** for).
II s'adapter *vpr* **1** Tech (s'insérer) [*outil, pièce*] to fit (**dans** into); **2** (s'habituer) [*personne*] to adapt (**à** to); **3** (être approprié) [*discours, politique, méthode*] to be suited (**à** to).

ADAV /adav/ *nm* (*abbr* = **avion à décollage et atterrissage verticaux**) VTOL.

addenda /adɛ̃da/ *nm inv* addendum; **des ~** addenda.

Addis-Abeba /adisabeba/ ▶ **857** *npr* Addis Ababa.

additif, **-ive** /aditif, iv/ **I** *adj* Math additive.
II *nm* **1** Chimie, Ind (substance) additive; **2** Jur (article, clause) rider (**à** to).

addition /adisjɔ̃/ *nf* **1** Math addition ¢; **il sait déjà faire les ~s** he can already do addition; **faire une erreur d'~** to make a mistake in the addition; **vérifier des ~s** to check sums; **ton ~ est fausse** your sum is wrong; **l'~ des voix** the counting of the votes; **2** Chimie (ajout) addition; **3** (accumulation) accumulation; **l'~ des preuves** the accumulation of evidence; **4** (dans un restaurant) bill, check US; **une ~ de 300 francs** a bill for 300 francs; **5** (dépense) bill; **payer l'~** lit to foot the bill; fig to pay for it; **le projet a représenté une ~ de plusieurs milliards** the project has cost several billion.

additionnel, **-elle** /adisjɔnɛl/ *adj* [*taxe, clause*] additional.

additionner /adisjɔne/ [1] **I** *vtr* **1** Math [*personne, calculatrice*] to add (up) [*chiffres, quantités*]; **~ qch à qch** to add sth to sth; **2** (ajouter) to add; **~ une sauce de cognac** to add cognac to a sauce; **vin additionné de sucre** wine with sugar added; **3** (accumuler) to accumulate [*erreurs, échecs*]; **elle additionne bêtise sur bêtise** she makes one stupid mistake after another.
II s'additionner *vpr* **1** (s'accumuler) [*problèmes, erreurs*] to add up; **2** Math **les fractions s'additionnent** fractions can be added.

additionneur /adisjɔnœʀ/ *nm* Ordinat adder; **~ complet/parallèle/série** full/parallel/serial adder.

adducteur /adyktœʀ/ *nm* adductor.

adduction /adyksjɔ̃/ *nf* Physiol adduction.
■ **~ d'eau** Gén Civ water conveyance; **travaux d'~ d'eau** work on the water supply system.

Adélaïde /adelaid/ ▶ **857** *npr* Adelaide.

Adélie /adeli/ *npr* Géog **terre ~** Adélie Land.

Aden /adɛn/ ▶ 857 *npr* Aden.

adepte /adɛpt/ *nmf* (de secte) follower; (de doctrine) supporter; (de personne) disciple; (de sport, d'activité) enthusiast; **c'est une ~ de la bicyclette** she's a cycling enthusiast.

adéquat, **~e** /adekwa, at/ *adj* **1** (approprié) [*réponse, environnement, choix*] appropriate; [*équipement, outil*] suitable; **2** (suffisant) [*niveau, formation, soins*] adequate.

adéquation /adekwasjɔ̃/ *nf* **1** (conformité) appropriateness (**de** of; **à, avec** to); **en ~ avec qch** in accord with sth; **2** Sci (de modèle) adequacy (**à** to).

adhérence /adeʀɑ̃s/ *nf* **1** Tech (de colle, papier) adhesion (**à** to); (de pneu, semelle) grip; **2** Méd adhesion.

adhérent, **~e** /adeʀɑ̃, ɑ̃t/ **I** *adj* [*matière*] which adheres (**à** to) (*après n*); [*pneu*] with a good grip (*après n*).

II *nm,f* (membre) member; **les ~s du parti/club** the party/club members.

adhérer /adeʀe/ [14] *vtr ind* **1** (coller) [*colle, tissu*] to stick (**à** to), to adhere (**à** to); **le pneu adhère à la route** the tyre GB ou tire US grips the road; **2** (s'inscrire) **~ à** to join [*parti, syndicat, association*]; to become a member of [*organisme*]; (être membre) to be a member of; **3** (se rallier) **~ à** to subscribe to [*doctrine, thèse, politique*].

adhésif, **-ive** /adezif, iv/ **I** *adj* adhesive.

II *nm* (matière) adhesive; **~ thermocollant** iron-on adhesive.

adhésion /adezjɔ̃/ *nf* **1** (appartenance) membership (**à** of GB, in US); **2** (inscription) **l'~ est gratuite** membership is free; **l'~ n'est pas obligatoire** you don't have to join; **l'~ d'un pays à la CEE** the entry of a country into the EEC; **le club vient d'enregistrer dix nouvelles ~s** the club has just enrolled ten new members; **3** (soutien) support (**à** for); **~ à une cause** support for a cause; **mon ~ à votre point de vue est totale** I completely support your point of view.

ad hoc /adɔk/ *loc adj inv* ad hoc.

adieu, *pl* **~x** /adjø/ *nm* goodbye, farewell sout; **se dire ~** to say one's goodbyes, to say goodbye (to each other); **dire ~ à qn, faire ses ~x à qn** to say goodbye to sb, to bid sb farewell sout; **dire ~ à qch** to say goodbye to sth; **un discours/une lettre/un baiser d'~** a farewell speech/letter/kiss; **faire un geste/un sourire d'~** to wave/smile goodbye (**à** to); **donner** or **offrir un pot○/un dîner d'~** to give a farewell drink/dinner; **faire ses ~x à la scène** to take one's leave of the stage; **~ le ski** it's goodbye to skiing.

adipeux, **-euse** /adipø, øz/ *adj* **1** Anat [*tissu, cellule*] fatty, adipose spéc; **2** gén [*personne, visage*] podgy; [*ventre*] fat.

adiposité /adipozite/ *nf* **1** (caractère) adiposity spéc; **2** (amas graisseux) surplus fat ¢.

adjacent, **~e** /adʒasɑ̃, ɑ̃t/ *adj* adjacent (**à** to).

adjectif, **-ive** /adʒɛktif, iv/ **I** *adj* [*forme, locution*] adjectival.

II *nm* adjective; **~ attribut/possessif/qualificatif** predicative/possessive/qualifying adjective; **~ déterminatif** determiner.

adjectival, **~e**, *mpl* **-aux** /adʒɛktival, o/ *adj* adjectival.

adjoindre /adʒwɛ̃dʀ/ [56] **I** *vtr* **on m'a adjoint un nouvel assistant** I've been assigned a new assistant; **~ de nouveaux collaborateurs à son personnel** to take on some extra staff; **~ une pièce au dossier** to attach a document to the file.

II s'adjoindre *vpr* to take on [*collaborateur, équipe*]; **l'organisation vient de s'~ les services d'un juriste** the organization has just engaged the services of a lawyer.

adjoint, **~e** /adʒwɛ̃, ɛ̃t/ **I** *nm,f* Entr assistant; **l'~ du directeur** the manager's assistant.

II *nm* Ling adjunct.

■ **~ au maire** Admin deputy mayor.

adjonction /adʒɔ̃ksjɔ̃/ *nf* addition (**à** to).

adjudant /adʒydɑ̃/ ▶ 390 *nm* Mil (terre) ≈ warrant officer class II GB, ≈ warrant officer US; (air) *intermediate rank between flight sergeant and warrant officer* GB, ≈ warrant officer US; **oui, mon ~** lit yes, sir; fig yes, sergeant.

adjudant-chef, *pl* **adjudants-chefs** /adʒydɑ̃ʃɛf/ ▶ 390 *nm* ≈ warrant officer class I GB, ≈ chief warrant officer US.

adjudicataire /adʒydikatɛʀ/ *nmf* **1** (dans une vente) successful buyer; **2** (de contrat) contractor.

adjudicateur, **-trice** /adʒydikatœʀ, tʀis/ *nm,f* **1** (possesseur) vendor; **2** (intermédiaire) auctioneer.

adjudication /adʒydikasjɔ̃/ *nf* **1** (de biens) auction; **par ~** by auction; **2** (de contrat) tender; **~ ouverte** competitive tender; **par ~** by tender; **3** (d'emprunt) bid.

■ **~ judiciaire** Jur sale by order of the court.

adjuger /adʒyʒe/ [13] **I** *vtr* **1** (vendre aux enchères) to auction; **adjugé 1 000 francs** auctioned for 1,000 francs; **vase adjugé 570 francs à qn** vase sold to sb at auction for 570 francs; **une fois, deux fois adjugé! vendu!** going, going, gone!; **2** (attribuer) to award (**à** to); **prix littéraire adjugé à un jeune écrivain** literary prize awarded to a young writer; **se voir ~ un contrat** to win a contract; **~ une récompense à qn** to give sb a reward.

II s'adjuger *vpr* [*personne*] to grant oneself [*repas, part*]; [*sportif, équipe*] to take [*coupe, titre*]; [*action*] to gain [*plus-value*].

adjuration /adʒyʀasjɔ̃/ *nf* plea.

adjurer /adʒyʀe/ [1] *vtr* to implore (**de faire** to do), to beg (**de faire** to do).

adjuvant /adʒyvɑ̃/ *nm* **1** Méd adjuvant; **2** Chimie additive.

ad libitum /adlibitɔm/ *loc adv* [*jouer, discuter*] ad lib; [*boire*] as much as one likes.

admettre /admɛtʀ/ [60] *vtr* **1** (reconnaître) to accept, to admit [*fait, hypothèse*]; to admit [*tort, échec, erreur*]; **il faut (bien) ~ que la situation est difficile** it has to be admitted that the situation is difficult; **tout en admettant qu'ils ne l'aient pas fait exprès** whilst accepting that they didn't do it deliberately; **je dois ~ que j'ai eu tort/que tu avais raison** I have to admit I was wrong/you were right; **2** (accepter) to accept [*principe, idée, droit*]; to admit [*personne*] (**dans** to); **un club qui admet les enfants** a club which admits children; **avoir du mal à ~ qch** to have difficulty accepting sth; **la société admet mal ce genre de protestation** society does not readily accept this sort of protest; **tant qu'on ne voudra pas ~ cet état de fait** as long as there is a refusal to accept this state of affairs; **ils n'ont jamais bien admis leur nouveau chef** they've never really accepted their new boss; **le plus difficile à ~ pour eux** the most difficult thing for them to accept; **faire ~ qch à qn** to get sb to accept sth; **elle n'a pas réussi à se faire ~ comme déléguée/dans leur société/à ce poste** she didn't get accepted as a delegate/in their company/for this post; **je n'admets pas que l'on soit en retard** I won't tolerate people being late; **nous n'admettrons aucune exception** no exceptions will be made; **je n'admets pas qu'on me traite de cette façon/qu'on me parle sur ce ton** I won't be treated in this way/be spoken to in this way; **3** (supposer) **~ que** to suppose (that); **admettez qu'il vienne plus tôt que prévu** suppose he comes earlier than expected; **admettons que vous ayez raison/qu'il ne se soit rien passé** let's suppose (that) you're right/that nothing happened; **même en admettant que ce soit/que tu puisses** even supposing (that) it is/(that) you can; **'suppose que je gagne'—'bon, admettons'** 'suppose I win!'—'all right then, suppose you do'; **4** Scol, Univ (accepter) to admit (**en** to); **les professeurs n'ont pas voulu m'~ en classe supérieure sans examen** the teachers wouldn't let me move up unless I took an exam; **il n'a pas été admis à se présenter à l'examen** he wasn't allowed to take the exam; **les enfants admis à l'école** children admitted to school; **être admis à l'oral** to get through to the oral; **elle a été admise au concours** she passed the exam; **5** (recevoir) [*personne, local*] to admit (**à** to); **le roi l'admet à sa table** he's admitted to the king's table; **l'huissier m'a admis dans une salle d'attente** the usher showed me into a waiting room; **nos salles de classe ne peuvent ~ que 20 élèves** our classrooms can only hold 20 pupils; **le musée n'admet les visiteurs que par groupes de 20 personnes** visitors are only admitted to the museum in groups of 20; **être admis à la maternité/à l'hôpital** to be admitted to the maternity ward/to hospital; **6** (autoriser) fml **~ qn à faire** to allow sb to do; **7** Tech (laisser passer) to let [sth] through [*liquide, vapeur*].

administrateur, **-trice** /administʀatœʀ, tʀis/ ▶ 510 *nm,f* **1** Admin (d'organisme, de bibliothèque, théâtre) administrator; **~ général** general administrator; **2** Fin (membre du conseil d'administration) director; **~ délégué** executive director; **3** Jur (de fondation, succession) trustee; **4** (gestionnaire) administrator; **avoir des qualités d'~** to have administrative skills.

■ **~ de biens** property manager; **~ civil** ≈ senior civil servant; **~ colonial** Hist colonial administrator; **~ judiciaire** (de faillite) receiver; (de succession) administrator; **~ légal** (des biens d'un mineur) guardian; (d'un patrimoine) trustee; **~ de site Internet** Webmaster.

administratif, **-ive** /administʀatif, iv/ **I** *adj* **1** (relatif à l'administration) [*bâtiment, retard, personnel, réforme*] administrative; **2** (émis par l'administration) official; **courrier/document/rapport ~** official mail/document/report.

II *nm,f* **être un ~** to work in administration; **les ~s** the administrative staff.

administration /administʀasjɔ̃/ *nf* **1** Admin, Pol (appareil) administration; **~ centrale/civile/publique** central/civil/public administration; **~ américaine/française** American/French administration; **2** (fonction publique) civil service; **haute ~** senior civil service; **entrer dans l'~** to go into the civil service; **3** (contrôle) administration; **~ d'une ville** administration of a city; **sous ~ militaire** under military rule; **4** (gestion) management; **~ des entreprises** business management; **5** (octroi) (de médicament, sacrement) administration; (de preuve) furnishing.

■ **~ douanière** customs service; **~ fiscale** Fisc Inland Revenue GB, Internal Revenue US; **~ judiciaire** Jur receivership; **être placé sous ~ judiciaire** to go into receivership; **être sous ~ judiciaire** to be in receivership; **~ légale** Jur trusteeship; **~ militaire** military administration; **~ pénitentiaire** prison service; **~ territoriale** regional administration.

administrativement /administʀativmɑ̃/ *adv* administratively.

administré, **~e** /administʀe/ **I** *pp* ▶ **administrer**.

II *pp adj* **bien/mal ~** well/badly run.

III *nm,f* constituent.

administrer /administʀe/ [1] **I** *vtr* **1** (gérer) to administer [*projet, fonds*]; to run [*économie, pays, compagnie*]; **2** (donner) to administer [*médicament, sacrement*] (**à** to); to produce [*preuve*]; **3** (infliger) **~ une correction à qn** to give sb a good hiding; **~ des coups** to deliver blows.

II s'administrer *vpr* [*médicament*] to be administered.

admirable /admiʀabl/ *adj* admirable; **être ~ de dévouement** to show admirable devotion; **des soldats ~s de courage** soldiers of exemplary courage; **se comporter de manière ~** to behave admirably; **s'exprimer dans une langue ~** to express oneself with admirable elegance.

admirablement /admiʀabləmɑ̃/ *adv* [*s'exprimer, travailler, réussir, jouer*] admirably; [*ouvragé, brodé, vêtu, construit, cuisiné*] superbly.

admirateur, **-trice** /admiʀatœʀ, tʀis/ *nm,f* admirer.

admiratif, **-ive** /admiʀatif, iv/ *adj* [*personne, air, regard*] admiring (*épith*); **tous les spectateurs étaient ~s** all the spectators were full of admiration; **elle poussa un cri ~** she gave a cry of admiration.

admiration /admiʀasjɔ̃/ *nf* admiration (**pour** for); **regarder qn/qch avec ~** to look at sb/sth in admiration; **être en ~ devant qn/qch** to be lost in admiration for sb/sth; **forcer l'~** to command admiration; **remplir qn d'~** to fill sb with admiration; **faire l'~ de qn** to be admired by sb; **avoir de l'~ pour qn** to admire sb; **être digne d'~** to be admirable.

admirativement /admiʀativmɑ̃/ *adv* admiringly.

admirer /admiʀe/ [1] *vtr* to admire; **c'est un homme très admiré** he's much admired; **~ qn de faire** to admire sb for doing.

admis, **~e** /admi, iz/ **I** *pp* ▶ **admettre**.
II *pp adj* (reconnu) [*opinion, pratique, théorie*] accepted, admitted; **selon une idée/thèse généralement ~e** according to a generally accepted idea/theory; **il est généralement ~ que** it is generally accepted ou admitted that; **être bien ~** [*principe, méthode, idée*] to be widely accepted.
III *nm,f* Scol, Univ successful candidate; **publier la liste des ~** to publish the list of successful candidates ou the pass list; **la liste des ~ au concours** the list of successful candidates in the exam.

admissibilité /admisibilite/ *nf* **1** (d'étudiant) eligibility (*to take oral after written examination*); **2** (de preuve, témoignage) admissibility; **3** (d'hypothèse, argument) acceptability.

admissible /admisibl/ *adj* **1** (tolérable) [*dose, seuil, comportement, écart*] acceptable; **2** Jur [*preuve, témoignage*] admissible; **3** Philos, Sci [*théorie, hypothèse, argument*] acceptable; **4** Univ [*étudiant*] eligible (*to take oral after written examination*).

admission /admisjɔ̃/ *nf* **1** (accueil) admission (**à, en** to); **~ d'un patient/élève/candidat** admission of a patient/pupil/candidate; **~ à la CEE/au FMI** admission to the EEC/to the IMF; **~ à l'hôpital/l'enseignement supérieur** admission to hospital/higher education; **~ en maison de retraite** admission to a retirement home; **~ sur examen** admission by entrance examination; **~ sur dossier** admission based on work experience and qualifications; **~ sur titres** admission based on certified qualifications; **demande** or **formulaire d'~** application form; **faire une demande d'~** to fill in an application form; **bureau** or **service des ~s** reception; **2** (droit) **~ à** eligibility for; **~ à l'aide sociale** eligibility for social security; **3** (reconnaissance) admission (**de la part de** by; **que** that); **4** Mécan intake; **régler l'~** to adjust the intake.
■ **~ à la cote** Fin listing; **~ temporaire** Fisc temporary importation.

admonestation /admɔnɛstasjɔ̃/ *nf* admonition; **faire des ~s à qn** to admonish sb.

admonester /admɔnɛste/ [1] *vtr* to admonish.

admonition /admɔnisjɔ̃/ *nf* admonition.

ADN /adeɛn/ *nm* (*abbr* = **acide désoxyribonucléique**) DNA.

ado○ /ado/ *nmf* teenager.

adolescence /adɔlesɑ̃s/ *nf* adolescence; **les premières années de l'~** early adolescence; **à l'~** during adolescence ou the teenage years.

adolescent, **~e** /adɔlesɑ̃, ɑ̃t/ **I** *adj* adolescent, teenage (*épith*).
II *nm,f* teenager, adolescent.

adonis /adɔnis/ *nm inv* fig Adonis.

Adonis /adɔnis/ *npr* Mythol Adonis.

adonner: **s'adonner** /adɔne/ [1] *vpr* **s'~ à** to devote oneself to [*travail, sport, art*]; **s'~ au plaisir** to live a debauched life; **il s'adonnait à la boisson** he used to drink too much.

adopter /adɔpte/ [1] *vtr* **1** Jur to adopt [*enfant*]; **2** (prendre chez soi) to adopt, to take in [*animal, personne*]; **3** (accepter) to accept; **il a vite été adopté par le village** he was soon accepted by the village; **je me suis tout de suite senti adopté par mes nouveaux amis** I immediately felt at home with my new friends; **4** (choisir) to adopt [*méthode, style, attitude, mode*]; **5** (approuver) to take up [*projet*]; to adopt [*proposition, réforme*]; **~ une loi** to pass a law.

adoptif, **-ive** /adɔptif, iv/ *adj* [*enfant*] adopted; [*parent, famille*] adoptive; [*village, pays*] adopted.

adoption /adɔpsjɔ̃/ *nf* **1** Jur adoption; **2** (par choix) adoption; **pays/famille d'~** adopted country/family; **Anglais d'~** English by adoption; **3** (de loi) passing; (de proposition, politique, réforme, texte) adoption.

adorable /adɔʀabl/ *adj* adorable.

adorablement /adɔʀabləmɑ̃/ *adv* [*vêtu*] delightfully; [*naïf*] charmingly.

adorateur, **-trice** /adɔʀatœʀ, tʀis/ *nm,f* **1** (d'un dieu) worshipper[GB]; **2** (d'une personne) fervent admirer.

adoration /adɔʀasjɔ̃/ *nf* **1** (action de rendre hommage) worship, adoration; **être en ~ devant qn/qch** to worship sb/sth; **2** (sentiment) adoration; **avoir de l'~ pour qn** to adore sb.

adorer /adɔʀe/ [1] **I** *vtr* **1** (aimer) to love; (plus fort) to adore; **2** Relig to worship, to adore.
II s'adorer *vpr* **1** (l'un l'autre) to adore one another; **2** (soi-même) **elle s'adore** she thinks she's wonderful.
IDIOMES **brûler ce qu'on a adoré** to turn against what one used to hold dear.

adosser /adose/ [1] **I** *vtr* **1** (appuyer) to lean [sb/sth] (**à** on; **contre** against); **être adossé à qch** [*personne*] to be leaning against sth; **~ un meuble contre un mur** to stand a piece of furniture against a wall; (un peu incliné) to lean a piece of furniture against a wall; **2** (placer à côté) **~ une maison contre qch** to build a house backing on to sth.
II s'adosser *vpr* **1** (s'appuyer) [*personne*] **s'~ à/contre qch** to lean back on/against sth, to lean one's back on/against sth; **2** (être à côté de) [*maison, village*] **s'~ à qch** to back onto sth.

adoubement /adubmɑ̃/ *nm* dubbing.

adouber /adube/ [1] *vtr* **1** (aux échecs) to adjust; **2** Hist to dub.

adoucir /adusiʀ/ [3] **I** *vtr* **1** (rendre plus doux) to soften [*peau, tissu, eau, éclairage, expression*]; to soothe [*gorge*]; to moderate [*son, voix*]; to tone down [*langage*]; to sweeten [*boisson, mets*]; **cette coiffure t'adoucit les traits** this hairstyle softens your features; **~ la réalité** to soften reality; **~ le métal** Tech to soften metal; **~ les angles** to soften the angles; **2** (rendre moins pénible) to alleviate [*misère, conditions*]; to ease [*sort, chagrin*]; to mitigate [*rigueur, régime*].
II s'adoucir *vpr* **1** (devenir plus doux) [*température*] to become milder; [*lumière, voix*] to become softer; [*pente*] to become more gentle; **2** (devenir moins pénible) [*chagrin*] to be soothed; [*conditions*] to be alleviated.
IDIOMES **la musique adoucit les mœurs** music soothes the savage breast.

adoucissant, **~e** /adusisɑ̃, ɑ̃t/ **I** *adj* Cosmét [*lotion, lait*] soothing; **crème ~e** soothing skin cream.
II *nm* Tex softener.

adoucissement /adusismɑ̃/ *nm* (de température) improvement (**de** in); (de conditions) alleviation (**de** of); (de voix) softening (**de** of).

adoucisseur /adusisœʀ/ *nm* **~ d'eau** water softener.

ad patres /adpatʀɛs/ *loc adv* **envoyer qn ~** to send sb to meet his/her maker.

adragante /adʀagɑ̃t/ *nf* **gomme ~** (gum) tragacanth.

adrénaline /adʀenalin/ *nf* adrenalin.

adressable /adʀesabl/ *adj* addressable; **mémoire ~** addressable memory.

adressage /adʀɛsaʒ/ *nm* addressing.

adresse /adʀɛs/ *nf* **1** (domicile) address; **~ postale** postal GB ou mailing US address; **c'est une bonne ~** [*restaurant, magasin*] it's a good place; **faire un changement d'~** to notify one's change of address; **partir sans laisser d'~** to leave without a forwarding address; **se tromper d'~** fig (de personne) to pick the wrong person, to get the wrong number○ US fig; (de lieu) to pick the wrong place; **une remarque lancée à l'~ de qn** a remark directed at sb; **a-t-il dit à l'~ des participants** he said for the benefit of the participants; **2** (habileté physique) dexterity; **jongler avec ~** to juggle with dexterity; **exercer son ~ au tir** to practise[GB] one's shooting; **3** (habileté intellectuelle) skill; **avec ~** skilfully[GB]; **4** (allocution) address; **~ retransmise à la télévision** address broadcast on TV; **5** Ling (en lexicographie) headword; (en sociolinguistique) address; **forme** or **formule d'~** form of address; **6** Ordinat address.

adresser /adʀese/ [1] **I** *vtr* **1** (destiner) to direct [*critique, menace, propos*] (**à** at); to put [*demande, question*] (**à** to); to make [*déclaration*]; to deliver [*ultimatum, message, mise en garde*] (**à** to); to present [*recommandation, pétition, témoignage*] (**à** to); to put out [*appel*] (**à** to); to aim [*coup*] (**à** at); **cette remarque m'était adressée** that remark was directed at me; **~ la parole à qn** to speak to sb; **~ un sourire à qn** to smile at sb; **~ un sourire complice à qn** to give sb a conspiratorial smile; **~ un regard à qn** to look at sb; **~ des éloges** or **louanges à qn** to praise sb; **~ la parole à qn** to speak to sb; **2** (expédier) to send [*lettre, questionnaire*]; **note adressée par télécopie** memorandum sent by fax; **3** (écrire l'adresse) to address [*lettre, colis*]; **lettre bien/mal adressée** correctly/incorrectly addressed letter; **adressé à mon nom** addressed to me personally; **4** (diriger) to refer [*personne*] (**à qn** to sb); **~ un patient à un spécialiste** to refer a patient to a specialist.
II s'adresser *vpr* **1** (parler) **s'~ à qn** to speak to sb; **s'~ à la foule** to speak to ou to address the crowd; **2** (contacter) **s'~ à** to contact; **s'~ au consulat** to contact the consulate; **s'~ à une firme japonaise** to go to a Japanese firm; **pour tous renseignements, s'~ à...** for all information, contact...; **adressez-vous au guichet 2** go to window 2; **adressez-vous au bureau d'information** go and ask at the information desk; **adresse-toi à ton père** ask your father; **pour les visas, adressez-vous au consulat** apply to the consulate for visas; **3** (être destiné) **s'~ à** [*mesure, invention*] to be aimed at; (toucher) **s'~ à** to appeal to [*conscience, instinct*]; **4** (échanger) to exchange [*salut, signe, reproche, lettres*]; **s'~ la parole** to speak to each other.

adret /adʀɛ/ *nm* sunny or south-facing side.

adriatique /adʀijatik/ *adj* [*côte*] Adriatic.

Adriatique /adʀijatik/ ▶ 555 *nprf* **la mer ~, l'~** the Adriatic.

adroit, **~e** /adʀwa, at/ *adj* **1** [*jongleur, bricoleur, tireur, manœuvre*] skilful[GB]; **d'un geste ~** with a deft movement; **avoir des gestes ~s** to be nimble; **être ~ de ses mains** to be good with one's hands; **2** [*homme politique, diplomate*] skilful[GB]; [*réponse, discours*] clever.

adroitement /adʀwatmɑ̃/ *adv* skilfully[GB].

adulateur, **-trice** /adylatœʀ, tʀis/ *nm,f* liter adulator litter; pej flatterer.

adulation /adylasjɔ̃/ *nf* adulation.

aduler /adyle/ [1] *vtr* to worship, to adulate.

adulte /adylt/ **I** *adj* [*personne, comportement, relation*] adult, grown-up; [*démocratie, nation, électorat*] mature; [*animal, plante*] full-grown; **l'âge ~** adulthood.
II *nmf* adult, grown-up.

adultère /adyltɛʀ/ **I** *adj* adulterous.
II *nmf* adulterer/adulteress.
III *nm* adultery.

adultérin, **~e** /adylteʀɛ̃, in/ *adj* [*enfant*] born of adultery (*après n*).

advenir /advəniʀ/ [36] *v impers* fml **1** (se produire) to happen; **quoi qu'il advienne** no matter what happens; **advienne que pourra** come what may; **2** (devenir) **~ de** to become of; **qu'adviendra-t-il de la démocratie?** what will become of democracy?

adventice /advɑ̃tis/ *adj* adventitious.

adventiste /advɑ̃tist/ *adj, nmf* Adventist.

adverbe /advɛʀb/ *nm* adverb; **~ de temps/de lieu/de manière** adverb of time/place/manner.

adverbial, **~e**, *pl* **-iaux** /advɛʀbjal, o/ *adj* adverbial.

adverbialement /advɛʀbjalmɑ̃/ *adv* adverbially.

adversaire /advɛʀsɛʀ/ *nmf* gén opponent; Mil adversary.

adversatif, **-ive** /advɛʀsatif, iv/ *adj* adversative.

adverse /advɛʀs/ *adj* [*équipe*] opposing; [*thèse*] opposite; [*attaque, manœuvre*] from the opposite camp; **partie** or **camp ~** opposite camp.

adversité /advɛʀsite/ *nf* adversity.

ad vitam æternam○ /advitametɛʀnam/ *loc adv* till kingdom come.

AELE /aəɛlə/ *nf* (*abbr* = **Association européenne de libre échange**) EFTA.

aérage /aeʀaʒ/ *nm* Mines ventilation.

aérateur /aeʀatœʀ/ *nm* ventilator.

aération /aeʀasjɔ̃/ *nf* (en ouvrant une fenêtre) airing; (avec un appareil) ventilation; **conduit d'~** airduct.

aéré, **~e** /aeʀe/ **I** *pp* ▶ **aérer**.
II *pp adj* **1** lit (**bien**) **~** [*pièce, chambre*] airy, well-ventilated; [*mine*] well-ventilated; **mal ~** [*pièce, chambre*] stuffy, badly-ventilated; [*mine*] badly-ventilated; **2** (espacé) [*document, texte*] **bien ~** nicely spaced out; **mal ~** cramped.

aérer /aeʀe/ [14] **I** *vtr* **1** (en ouvrant) to air [*pièce, draps*]; [*appareil*] to ventilate; **2** (faire prendre l'air) **ça m'aère un peu** it gets me out into the fresh air; **3** (sur papier) to space out [*devoir, document, lettre*]; **4** Agric to aerate [*terre, champ*].
II s'aérer *vpr* [*personne*] to get some fresh air; **s'~ l'esprit** to think about something different for a change.

aérien, **-ienne** /aeʀjɛ̃, ɛn/ *adj* **1** Aviat [*transport, désastre, base, attaque, carte*] air (*épith*); [*photographie*] aerial; **liaison aérienne** air link; **2** Météo [*courant, phénomène*] air (*épith*); **3** (en l'air) [*câble, circuit*] overhead; [*racine, plante*] aerial; **métro ~** elevated section of the underground GB ou subway US; **4** (léger) [*démarche*] floating; [*grâce*] exquisite; [*musique*] ethereal.

aérobic /aeʀɔbik/ ▶ **449** *nm* aerobics (+ *v sg*).

aérobie /aeʀobi/ **I** *adj* aerobic.
II *nm* aerobe.

aérobiose /aeʀobjoz/ *nf* aerobiosis.

aéro-club, *pl* **~s** /aeʀoklœb/ *nm* flying club.

aérodrome /aeʀodʀom/ *nm* aerodrome GB, (small) airfield.
■ **~ de dégagement** alternate aerodrome ou airfield.

aérodynamique /aeʀodinamik/ **I** *adj* aerodynamic.
II *nf* aerodynamics (+ *v sg*).

aérodynamisme /aeʀodinamism/ *nm* (de voiture, d'avion) aerodynamic properties.

aérofrein /aeʀofʀɛ̃/ *nm* air brake.

aérogare /aeʀogaʀ/ *nf* (air) terminal; **~ 2** terminal 2.

aéroglisseur /aeʀoglisœʀ/ *nm* hovercraft.

aérogramme /aeʀogʀam/ *nm* aerogram, air letter.

aérographe /aeʀogʀaf/ *nm* airbrush; **peinture à l'~** airbrushing.

aérolithe /aeʀolit/ *nm* aerolite.

aéromaritime /aeʀomaʀitim/ *adj* [*compagnie, filiale*] air and sea.

aéromodélisme /aeʀomɔdelism/ *nm* model aircraft making; **un club d'~** a model aircraft club; **faire de l'~** to make model aircraft.

aéromodéliste /aeʀomɔdelist/ *nmf* model aircraft maker.

aéronaute /aeʀɔnot/ *nmf* aeronaut.

aéronautique /aeʀonotik/ **I** *adj* [*construction, industrie*] aeronautics; [*ingénieur*] aeronautical.
II *nf* aeronautics (+ *v sg*); **le marché de l'~** the aeronautics market.

aéronaval, **~e** /aeʀonaval/ **I** *adj* [*opération, forces, base*] air and sea.
II aéronavale *nf* Fleet Air Arm GB, Naval Aviation US.

aéronef /aeʀɔnɛf/ *nm* aircraft.

aérophagie /aeʀɔfaʒi/ ▶ **271** *nf* aerophagia spéc; **faire de l'~** to suffer from aerophagia.

aéroplane† /aeʀɔplan/ *nm* aeroplane GB, airplane US.

aéroport /aeʀɔpɔʀ/ *nm* airport.

aéroporté, **~e** /aeʀɔpɔʀte/ *adj* [*troupes, opération*] airborne; [*missile, arme, matériel*] transported by air.

aéroportuaire /aeʀɔpɔʀtɥɛʀ/ *adj* [*équipement, trafic, capacité*] airport.

aéropostal, **~e**, *mpl* **-aux** /aeʀɔpɔstal, o/ *adj* [*compagnie, service*] airmail.

aérosol /aeʀɔsɔl/ *nm* **1** (suspension) aerosol; **2** (bombe, système) aerosol; **un déodorant/insecticide en ~** an aerosol deodorant/insecticide.

aérospatial, **~e**, *mpl* **-iaux** /aeʀɔspasjal, o/ **I** *adj* [*industrie*] aerospace (*épith*); [*véhicule, lanceur*] space.
II aérospatiale *nf* (industrie) aerospace industry.

aérostat /aeʀɔsta/ *nm* aerostat.

aérostatique /aeʀɔstatik/ **I** *adj* Aviat [*technique*] aerostatic; **un vol ~** a flight in an aerostat.
II *nf* aerostatics (+ *v sg*).

aérostier /aeʀɔstje/ *nm* aerostat pilot.

aéroterrestre /aeʀotɛʀɛstʀ/ *adj* [*division, opération*] air and land.

aérotrain® /aeʀotʀɛ̃/ *nm* hovertrain.

AFAT /afat, aɛfate/ *nf* (*abbr* = **auxiliaire féminin de l'armée de terre**) *women's component of the French army*.

affabilité /afabilite/ *nf* courtesy, affability.

affable /afabl/ *adj* [*personne, attitude, propos*] courteous, affable.

affablement /afabləmɑ̃/ *adv* courteously.

affabulateur, **-trice** /afabylatœʀ, tʀis/ *nm,f* storyteller.

affabulation /afabylasjɔ̃/ *nf* **1** (invention) fabrication **₵**; **ce sont des ~s** that's pure fabrication; **2** Littérat (de roman, récit) construction of the plot.

affabuler /afabyle/ [1] *vi* to tell tall stories.

affacturage /afaktyʀaʒ/ *nm* factoring.

affadir /afadiʀ/ [3] **I** *vtr* **1** lit to make [sth] tasteless ou insipid [*sauce, plat*]; **2** fig [*auteur, corrections*] to make [sth] dull [*texte, personnage*].
II s'affadir *vpr* **1** lit [*plat*] to lose its flavour[GB]; [*odeur*] to fade; **2** fig [*intérêt*] to fade; [*argument*] to lose impact.

affadissement /afadismɑ̃/ *nm* **1** (de nourriture, goût) loss of flavour[GB]; (de couleur, d'odeur) fading; **2** (de style) weakening, loss of impact.

affaiblir /afɛbliʀ/ [3] **I** *vtr* to weaken [*personne, démocratie, sens, monnaie*]; to reduce [*capacité, impact*]; to dull [*intelligence, sentiments*]; **~ les forces de qn** to sap sb's strength; **~ la portée d'un texte de loi** to reduce the scope of a law.
II s'affaiblir *vpr* [*autorité, gouvernement, économie, pont*] to be weakened; [*personne, voix, vue, détermination, volonté*] to get weaker; [*bruit*] to grow fainter; [*force, courage, capacité*] to diminish; [*santé, mémoire*] to deteriorate; **le franc s'affaiblit (face au deutschmark)** the franc is weakening (against the deutschmark); **le franc s'est affaibli face au deutschmark** the franc has fallen against the deutschmark; **le sens du mot s'est affaibli** the meaning of the word has weakened; **sortir affaibli d'une maladie** to be drained by an illness.

affaiblissement /afɛblismɑ̃/ *nm* **1** (de personne, pays, monnaie, sens) (processus) weakening; (état) weakened state; **2** (de bruit, vue, santé) fading; **3** (de volonté, courage, détermination) diminishing; **4** (de style, d'œuvre) **les critiques ont remarqué l'~ de son style dans ses derniers écrits** critics have noted that his style lost its edge in his later writings; **5** (de volume, quantité) reduction (**de** in).

affaire /afɛʀ/ **I** *nf* **1** (ensemble de faits) gén affair; (à caractère politique, militaire) crisis, affair; (à caractère délictueux, scandaleux) (d'ordre général) scandal; (de cas unique) affair; (soumis à la justice) case; **une mystérieuse ~** a mysterious affair; **l'~ des otages** the hostage crisis ou affair; **l'~ de Suez** the Suez crisis; **une ~ politique/de corruption** a political/corruption scandal; **l'~ des fausses factures** the scandal of the bogus invoices; **~ civile/criminelle** civil/criminal case; **il a été condamné pour une ~ de drogue** he was convicted in a drug case; **2** (histoire, aventure) affair; **une ~ délicate** a delicate matter ou affair; **une drôle d'~** an odd affair; **j'ignore tout de cette ~** I don't know anything about the matter; **pour une ~ de cœur** for an affair of the heart; **être mêlé à une sale ~** to be mixed up in some nasty business; **quelle ~!** what a business ou to-do!; **c'est une ~ d'argent/d'héritage** there's money/an inheritance involved; **et voilà toute l'~** and that's that; **3** (occupation, chose à faire) matter, business; **c'est une ~ qui m'a pris beaucoup de temps** it's a matter that has taken up a lot of my time; **il est parti pour une ~ urgente** he's gone off on some urgent business; **c'est toute une ~** it's quite a business; **c'est une (tout) autre ~** that's another matter (entirely); **ce n'est pas une petite** or **mince ~** it's no small ou simple matter; **c'est mon ~, pas la vôtre** that's my business, not yours; **c'est l'~ de tous** it's something which concerns everyone ou us all; **ça ne change rien à l'~** that doesn't change a thing; **l'~ se présente bien/mal** things are looking good/bad; **j'en fais mon ~** I'll deal with it; **4** (spécialité) **il connaît bien son ~** he knows his business; **c'est une ~ d'hommes/de femmes** it's men's/women's business; **c'est une ~ de garçons/filles** it's boys'/girls' stuff péj; **la mécanique/soudure, c'est leur ~** mechanics/welding is their thing; **c'est une ~ de spécialistes** it's a case for the specialists; **5** (transaction) deal; **une bonne/mauvaise ~** a good/bad deal; **conclure une ~** to make ou to strike a deal; **l'~ a été**

conclue or **faite** the deal was settled; **faire ~ avec qn** to make a deal with sb; **la belle ~**○**!** big deal○!; ▸**sac**; **6** (achat avantageux) bargain; **à ce prix-là, c'est une ~** at that price, it's a bargain; **j'ai fait une ~** I got a bargain; **tu y feras des ~s** you'll find bargains there; **on ne fait plus beaucoup d'~s au marché aux puces** there aren't many bargains to be had at the flea market any more; **j'ai acheté cette robe en solde mais je n'ai pas fait une ~** I bought this dress in the sales but it wasn't a good buy; **7** (entreprise) business, concern; **~ commerciale/d'import-export/de famille** commercial/import-export/family business ou concern; **de petites ~s** small businesses ou concerns; **~ industrielle** industrial concern; **leur fils a repris l'~** their son took over the business; **c'est elle qui fait marcher l'~** lit she runs the whole business; fig she runs the whole show; **une ~ en or** fig a gold mine; **8** (question, problème) **c'est une ~ de temps/goût** it's a matter of time/taste; **c'est l'~ de quelques jours/d'un quart d'heure** it'll only take a few days/a quarter of an hour; **c'est ~ de politiciens** it's a matter for the politicians; **c'est l'~ des politiciens** it's the concern of politicians; **il en a fait une ~ personnelle** he took it personally; **en faire toute une ~**○ to make a big deal○ of it ou a fuss○ about it; **on ne va pas en faire une ~ d'État**○**!** let's not make a big issue out of it!; **c'est une ~ de famille** fig it's a family affair; **9** (difficulté, péril) **être hors** or **tiré d'~** [*malade*] to be in the clear; **s'il obtient le poste, il est tiré d'~** if he gets the job, his problems are over; **se tirer d'~** to get out of trouble; **tirer** or **sortir qn d'~** to get sb out of a spot; **on n'est pas encore sortis** or **tirés d'~** we're not out of the woods yet; **10** (relation) **avoir ~ à** to be dealing with [*malfaiteur, fou, drogue, fausse monnaie*]; **nous avons ~ à un escroc/faux** we're dealing with a crook/fake; **je le connais mais je n'ai pas souvent ~ à lui** I know him but I don't have much to do with him; **j'ai eu ~ au directeur lui-même** I saw the manager himself; **tu auras ~ à moi!** you'll have me to contend with!

II affaires *nfpl* **1** (activités lucratives) gén business ¢; (d'une seule personne) business affairs; **être dans les ~s** to be in business; **faire des ~s avec** to do business with; **les ~s sont calmes/au plus bas** business is quiet/at its lowest ebb; **les ~s reprennent** or **marchent mieux** business is picking up; **il gère les ~s de son oncle** he runs his uncle's business affairs; **parler ~s** to talk business; **revenir aux ~s** to go back into business; **avoir le sens des ~s** to have business sense; **voir qn pour ~s** to see sb on business; **voyager pour ~s** to go on a business trip; **le monde des ~s** the business world; **quartier/milieux/lettre/rendez-vous d'~s** business district/circles/letter/appointment; **le français/chinois des ~s** business French/Chinese; **un homme dur en ~s** a tough businessman; **2** (problèmes personnels) business ¢; **ça, c'est mes ~s**○**!** that's my business!; **occupe-toi de tes ~s!** mind your own business!; **se mêler** or **s'occuper des ~s des autres** to interfere ou meddle in other people's business ou affairs; **mettre de l'ordre dans ses ~s** to put one's affairs in order; **parler de ses ~s à tout le monde** to tell everybody one's business; **ça n'arrange pas mes ~s qu'elle vienne** her coming isn't very convenient for me; **3** (effets personnels) things, belongings; **mets tes ~s dans le placard** put your things in the cupboard; **mes ~s de sport/de classe** my sports/school things; **4** Admin, Pol affairs; **~s publiques/sociales/étrangères** public/social/foreign affairs; **les ~s intérieures d'un pays** a country's internal affairs; **les ~s de l'État** affairs of state.

■ **les ~s courantes** gén daily business (*sg*); Jur Pol day-to-day running of a country.

IDIOMES **être à son ~** to be in one's element; **il/ça fera l'~** he'll/that'll do; **il/ça ne peut pas faire l'~** he/that won't do; **ça a très bien fait l'~** it was just the job; **elle fait** or **fera notre ~** she's just the person we need; **ça fera leur ~** (convenir) that's just what they need; (être avantageux) it'll suit them; **faire** or **régler son ~ à qn**○ (tuer) to bump sb off○; (sévir) to sort sb out.

affairé, ~e /afeʀe/ **I** *pp* ▸**affairer**.
II *pp adj* [*personne, air, vie*] busy (**à qch** with sth; **à faire** doing); **avoir l'air ~** to look busy.

affairement /afɛʀmɑ̃/ *nm* bustling activity.

affairer: s'affairer /afeʀe/ [1] *vpr* [*personne*] to bustle about; **s'~ auprès de** or **autour de qn** to fuss over sb; **s'~ à faire** to bustle about doing.

affairisme /afeʀism/ *nm* pej wheeling and dealing○.

affairiste /afeʀist/ *nmf* pej wheeler-dealer○.

affaissé, ~e /afese/ **I** *pp* ▸**affaisser**.
II *pp adj* [*toiture, pont, joues, épaules, tête*] sagging.

affaissement /afɛsmɑ̃/ *nm* **1** (de sol, route) subsidence; (de toit, pont, joues) sagging; **2** (de parti politique, valeurs morales) decline (**de** in).

affaisser: s'affaisser /afese/ [1] *vpr* **1** [*route, terrain*] to subside, to sink; [*visage, épaules, chair, toit, pont*] to sag; **faire ~ le pont** to cause the bridge to sag; **2** (s'effondrer) [*personne*] to collapse (**sur** on; **dans** into); [*tête*] to droop; **3** (se tasser) **un vieillard qui s'affaisse avec l'âge** an old man who is shrinking ou becoming hunched with age; **4** [*ventes, bénéfices*] to decline.

affalé, ~e /afale/ **I** *pp* ▸**affaler**.
II *pp adj* slumped (**dans** in; **sur** on).

affaler /afale/ [1] **I** *vtr* Naut [*personne, marin*] to lower [*voile, cordage*]; **affalez!** lower away!
II s'affaler *vpr* **1**○ [*personne*] (de fatigue) to collapse; (par accident) to fall; **2** Naut [*personne*] to slide; **s'~ par une échelle** to slide down a ladder.

affamé, ~e /afame/ **I** *pp* ▸**affamer**.
II *pp adj* **1** lit starving; **2** fig **~ de** hungry for.
III *nm,f* lit, iron (adulte) starving man/woman; (enfant) starving child; **les ~s** the starving.
IDIOMES **ventre ~ n'a pas d'oreilles** Prov ≈ a hungry man is an angry man.

affamer /afame/ [1] *vtr* to starve [*personne, pays*].

affameur /afamœʀ/ *nm* **1** lit *person who exploits famine situations for financial gain*; **2** fig *employer who pays starvation wages*.

affect /afɛkt/ *nm* Psych affect.

affectation /afɛktasjɔ̃/ *nf* **1** (de bâtiment, matériel, d'argent) allocation (**à** to); **2** (nomination) also Mil (à un emploi, une fonction) appointment (**à** to); (dans un lieu, un pays) posting (**à** to); **recevoir une ~** to receive a posting; **lieu d'~** place of work; **3** (comportement) affectation; **sans ~** unaffectedly, without (any) affectation; **avec ~** in an affected way, affectedly; **4** Compta appropriation; **~s budgétaires** budget appropriations; **5** Math **l'~ d'un signe à un nombre** the modification of a number by a sign.

affecté, ~e /afɛkte/ **I** *pp* ▸**affecter**.
II *pp adj* (non naturel) [*langage, manières, personne*] affected.

affecter /afɛkte/ [1] *vtr* **1** (feindre) to feign, to affect [*pitié, gaieté, indifférence, tristesse*]; to affect [*genre, comportement*]; to take on, to assume [*forme*]; **~ la surprise** to feign surprise; **innocence/gaieté/pondération affectée** feigned innocence/cheerfulness/level-headedness; **~ de faire** to pretend to do; **il affecte de ne pas être ému** he pretends not to be moved; **malgré sa tristesse il affecte la gaieté** despite his unhappiness he's putting on a show of cheerfulness; **~ de grands airs** to put on airs; **2** (allouer) to allocate, to assign [*matériel, lieu*] (**à** to); to allocate [*logement, argent*] (**à qn** to sb; **à qch** to, for sth); **3** (nommer) (à une activité, une fonction, un poste) to appoint (**à** to); (dans un lieu, un pays, une région) to post (**à, en** to); **4** (toucher, affliger) to affect [*pays, marché, cours, autorité, personne*]; **être affecté d'une légère surdité/myopie** to be slightly deaf/short-sighted; **5** Math to modify; **affecté de** modified by.

affectif, -ive /afɛktif, iv/ *adj* gén emotional; Psych affective.

affection /afɛksjɔ̃/ *nf* **1** (tendresse) affection; **avoir beaucoup d'~ pour** to have a lot of affection for; **prendre qn en ~, se prendre d'~ pour qn** to become fond of sb; **2** Méd complaint; **les ~ cardiaques** heart conditions.

affectionné, ~e /afɛksjɔne/ **I** *pp* ▸**affectionner**.
II *pp adj* (dans une lettre) **votre neveu ~** your loving nephew; **votre ~** yours affectionately.

affectionner /afɛksjɔne/ [1] *vtr* to be particularly fond of [*chose, activité*]; to be very fond of [*personne*].

affectivité /afɛktivite/ *nf* feelings (*pl*), affectivity spéc.

affectueusement /afɛktɥøzmɑ̃/ *adv* affectionately, fondly.

affectueux, -euse /afɛktɥø, øz/ *adj* [*personne, geste, lettre, animal*] affectionate; [*caresse, regard*] fond.

afférent, ~e /afeʀɑ̃, ɑ̃t/ *adj* **1** Jur [*héritage*] accruing (**à** to); **2** Anat [*vaisseau, nerf*] afferent (**à** to); **3** [*renseignements, documents*] relative (**à** to), relating (**à** to).

affermage /afɛʀmaʒ/ *nm* leasing.

affermer /afɛʀme/ [1] *vtr* [*propriétaire*] to lease (out) ou rent (out); [*locataire*] to rent ou lease [*terres, domaine*].

affermi, ~e /afɛʀmi/ **I** *pp* ▸**affermir**.
II *pp adj* **1** [*pouvoir, autorité, paix*] consolidated; [*chairs*] firmed up; [*volonté, muscles, voix*] strengthened; [*santé*] better; **2** [*trait, style*] sharpened up, sharpened (up) US; [*écriture*] incisive.

affermir /afɛʀmiʀ/ [3] **I** *vtr* **1** (consolider) to strengthen [*autorité, conviction, volonté, voix*]; to consolidate [*pouvoir, position*]; to firm up [*muscle, chair*]; **2** (rendre plus défini) to sharpen up [*style, écriture*].
II s'affermir *vpr* **1** [*autorité, pouvoir, croissance*] to be consolidated; [*voix*] to become stronger; [*muscle, chair*] to firm up; [*terrain*] to become firmer; [*santé*] to become better; **2** [*style, écriture*] to become sharper.

affermissement /afɛʀmismɑ̃/ *nm* (de pouvoir, reprise) consolidation; (de volonté, muscles, voix) strengthening; (de santé, tendance, d'économie) improvement (**de** in).

affété, ~e /afete/ *adj* liter [*personne, style, manières*] affected.

afféterie /afɛtʀi/ *nf* liter (affectation, manières) affectation; **sans ~** without affectation.

affichage /afiʃaʒ/ *nm* **1** (publicitaire, électoral) billsticking, billposting; **communiqué par voie d'~** [*résultat*] posted (up); **interdit à l'~** [*roman*] not for public display; **campagne d'~** poster campaign; **à ~ numérique** [*réveil*] with digital display; **2** Ordinat display; **3** (de connaissances, savoir) display.
■ **~ à cristaux liquides** liquid crystal display; **~ sauvage** flyposting GB, illegal ou unauthorized posting of bills.

affiche /afiʃ/ *nf* (publicitaire, électorale) poster; (de cinéma, film, d'exposition) poster; (administrative, judiciaire) notice; **à l'~** Cin now showing; Théât on; **plusieurs spectacles sont à l'~ du festival** several shows are on at the festival; **tenir le haut de l'~** to have top billing; **tenir l'~ pendant deux ans** [*pièce*] to run for two years; **la pièce/le film quitte l'~ cette semaine** the play/the film ends its run this week; **une belle ~** a fine cast; **mettre à l'~** to put [sth] on.

■ **~ lumineuse** neon sign; **~ publicitaire** advertisement, advertising poster; **~ de théâtre** playbill.

affiché, ~e /afiʃe/ I *pp* ▶ **afficher**.

II *pp adj* **1** [*photo, annonce*] put up; [*résultat, horaire, information*] posted (up); **2** Écon [*hausse, résultat*] published; [*bénéfice*] declared; **3** fig [*optimisme, volonté, dédain, objectif, opinion*] declared; **4** péj [*liaison*] flaunted; **5** Ordinat [*donnée, texte*] displayed.

afficher /afiʃe/ [1] I *vtr* **1** (coller) to put up [*affiche, photo*]; **'défense d'~'** 'no fly-posting', 'stick no bills'; **2** (faire connaître par voie d'affiche) to display [*prix*]; to post (up) [*décret, résultat*]; **3** Comm, Fin [*entreprise*] to show [*déficit, résultat*]; [*Bourse, marché*] to show [*hausse, baisse, excédent*]; **4** Cin, Théât [*cinéma*] to show [*film*]; [*théâtre*] to have [sth] on [*pièce, spectacle*]; **~ complet** Cin, Théât to be sold out; [*hôtel, voyage*] to be completely full, to be fully booked GB, to be booked up GB; [*parking*] to be full; **5** fig (montrer) to show [*admiration, confiance, détermination*]; to declare [*ambitions*]; to display [*mépris, autorité, opinions*]; to flaunt [*liaison, vie privée*]; **~ le sourire** lit to have a big smile; (feindre) to put on a big smile; **~ sa bonne santé/forme** to show how healthy/fit one is, to flaunt one's health/fitness péj; **6** Ordinat to display [*donnée, résultat*].

II **s'afficher** *vpr* **1** Tech [*résultat, texte, horaire*] to be displayed (**sur** on); **2** (avec ostentation) [*personne*] to flaunt oneself; **s'~ comme catholique** to declare oneself to be a Catholic; **un catholique qui s'affiche comme tel** an out-and-out Catholic; **3** [*sourire, joie*] to appear (**sur** on).

affichette /afiʃɛt/ *nf* (pour information) notice; (électorale) small poster.

afficheur /afiʃœʀ/ *nm* **1** (entreprise) poster display firm; **2** (personne) manager of a poster display firm; **3** (écran) display.

affichiste /afiʃist/ ▶**510** *nmf* poster artist; **~ de cinéma** designer of cinema posters; **~ publicitaire** designer of advertising posters.

affidé, ~e /afide/ *nm,f* littér, péj accomplice, conspirator.

affilage /afilaʒ/ *nm* sharpening.

affilé, ~e /afile/ I *pp* ▶ **affiler**.

II *pp adj* **1** [*couteau, lame, outil*] sharpened; **2** fig [*intelligence*] keen; ▶ **langue**.

III **d'affilée** *loc adv* in a row; **pendant deux semaines d'~e** for two weeks in a row; **parler trois heures d'~e** [*amis*] to talk nonstop for three hours; [*politiciens, directeur*] to talk for three hours without a break; **boire trois verres d'~e** to have three drinks one after the other.

affiler /afile/ [1] *vtr* to sharpen.

affiliation /afiljasjɔ̃/ *nf* affiliation (**à** to).

affilié, ~e /afilje/ *nm,f* affiliated member (**à** of), affiliate; **les ~s à** the affiliated members of.

affilier /afilje/ [2] I *vtr* to affiliate (**à** to).

II **s'affilier** *vpr* to become affiliated (**à** to).

affiloir /afilwaʀ/ *nm* **1** (instrument) gén sharpener; (à couteaux) steel; **2** (pierre) sharpening stone, whetstone.

affinage /afinaʒ/ *nm* Tech (de métal) refining; (de verre) fining; (de fromage) maturing.

affine /afin/ *adj* Math affine.

affinement /afinmɑ̃/ *nm* refinement.

affiner /afine/ [1] I *vtr* **1** lit to refine [*métal*]; to fine [*verre*]; to mature [*fromage*]; **2** fig to refine [*stratégie, politique, idée, style, jugement*]; to sharpen [*ouïe*]; to slim down [*taille, silhouette*].

II **s'affiner** *vpr* [*jugement*] to become keener; [*politique, idée, style, goût*] to become (more) refined; [*personne, taille, silhouette*] to slim down; [*ligne, dessin*] to become (more) refined.

affineur, -euse /afinœʀ, øz/ ▶**510** *nm,f* (de métal) refiner; (de verre) finisher; (de fromage) *person in charge of the maturing process.*

affinité /afinite/ *nf* affinity.

affirmatif, -ive /afiʀmatif, iv/ I *adj* [*proposition, mot, réponse, signe*] affirmative; [*personne, ton*] assertive; **faire un signe de tête ~** to nod agreement.

II *nm* Ling affirmative; **à l'~** in the affirmative.

III *adv* affirmative.

IV **affirmative** *nf* affirmative; **répondre par l'affirmative** to reply in the affirmative; **dans l'affirmative** if so, if the answer is yes.

affirmation /afiʀmasjɔ̃/ *nf* **1** (assertion) assertion; **2** (manifestation) (de sentiment, religion) affirmation; (de personnalité) assertion; **l'~ de soi** assertiveness; **3** Ling assertion.

affirmativement /afiʀmativmɑ̃/ *adv* affirmatively.

affirmer /afiʀme/ [1] I *vtr* **1** (soutenir) to maintain [*fait, vérité, contraire*]; **'je n'ai pas l'intention de démissionner', affirma-t-il** 'I have no intention of resigning,' he declared; **~ faire/avoir fait** to claim to do/to have done; **~ que** to maintain or claim (that); **pouvez-vous l'~?** can you be sure about it?; **la police ne peut encore rien ~** the police are not yet able to make any positive statement; **je vous l'affirme** I can assure you (of it); **2** (prouver) to assert [*talent, personnalité, autorité, originalité, indépendance*]; **3** (proclamer) to declare, to affirm [*volonté, désir*] (**à** to).

II **s'affirmer** *vpr* [*progrès, tendance*] to become apparent; [*majorité*] to be established; [*personnalité, style*] to assert itself; **s'~ comme** [*personne*] to establish oneself as; **s'~ comme une force nouvelle** to establish itself as a new force; **le festival s'affirme comme un événement majeur** the festival is becoming established as a major event.

affixe /afiks/ *nm* Ling affix.

affleurement /aflœʀmɑ̃/ *nm* **1** lit (de roche, minerai) outcrop; (de récif) emergence; **2** fig (d'inconscient, de thème) appearance, surfacing; **3** Tech flushing.

affleurer /aflœʀe/ [1] I *vtr* **1** Tech to make [sth] flush [*planches, battants*]; **2** (arriver au même niveau) **la rivière affleure les quais** the river is almost level with the banks.

II *vi* **1** lit [*roche, glace, récif*] to show on the surface; **~ au niveau du sol** [*eau, pétrole*] to come up to ground level; [*roche, minerai*] to come through the soil, to outcrop spéc; **2** fig [*thème, sentiment*] to surface, to crop up.

affliction /afliksjɔ̃/ *nf* fml affliction; **jeter** or **plonger qn dans l'~** to afflict sb deeply; **être dans l'~** to be in a state of distress.

afflictive /afliktiv/ *adj f* **peine ~** *sentence that strips a person of their civil rights.*

affligé, ~e /afliʒe/ *nm,f* **les ~s** the afflicted.

affligeant, ~e /afliʒɑ̃, ɑ̃t/ *adj* **1** (attristant) distressing; **2** (consternant) pathetic, depressing.

affliger /afliʒe/ [13] I *vtr* **1** (frapper) [*destin, malheur, handicap*] to afflict, to strike; **~ qn de qch** to afflict sb with sth; **être affligé de qch** to be afflicted with sth; **2** (peiner) to distress.

II **s'affliger** *vpr* to be distressed (**de qch** about sth).

affluence /aflyɑ̃s/ *nf* (de personnes) crowd(s); (d'objets) abundance; **l'~ des grands magasins** the crowds in the department stores; **les heures d'~ dans les magasins** peak shopping periods.

affluent /aflyɑ̃/ *nm* Géog tributary.

affluer /aflye/ [1] *vi* [*foule, clients, passagers*] to flock (**à, vers** to); [*eau, air, sang*] to rush (**à, vers** to); [*argent, capitaux*] to flow (**à, vers** to); [*plaintes, lettres de protestation*] to pour in.

afflux /afly/ *nm inv* (de sang) rush; (de personnes) flood; (d'argent, de capitaux, produits) influx; Électron flow.

affolant, ~e /afɔlɑ̃, ɑ̃t/ *adj* (effrayant) [*nouvelle, prix, situation*] frightening, disturbing; **il fume trois paquets par jour, c'est ~!** he smokes three packets a day, it's awful!

affolé, ~e /afɔle/ I *pp* ▶ **affoler**.

II *pp adj* panic-stricken.

affolement /afɔlmɑ̃/ *nm* panic; **être en proie à l'~** to be in a state of panic; **dans l'~** in the panic; **pas d'~!** don't panic!

affoler /afɔle/ [1] I *vtr* to terrify, to throw [sb] into a panic [*personne*].

II **s'affoler** *vpr* **1** [*personne, animal*] to panic; [*aiguille de boussole*] to spin; **ne t'affole pas** don't get into a panic; **2**○ (se dépêcher) to get a move on○; (réagir) [*élève*] to stir oneself.

affouiller /afuje/ [1] *vtr* Tech to undermine.

affranchi, ~e /afʀɑ̃ʃi/ *nm,f* emancipated slave.

affranchir /afʀɑ̃ʃiʀ/ [3] I *vtr* **1** Postes (en collant des timbres) to stamp, to put a stamp ou stamps on; (avec une machine) to frank; **une lettre non affranchie** an unstamped letter; **tu n'as pas suffisamment affranchi le paquet** you haven't put enough stamps on the parcel; **une lettre insuffisamment affranchie** a letter without enough stamps on it; **2** (libérer) lit, fig to free, to liberate [*serf, population, pays*] (**de** from); **3**◑ (informer) to give [sb] the lowdown○; **4** Jeux (aux cartes) to clear.

II **s'affranchir** *vpr* to free oneself (**de** from).

affranchissement /afʀɑ̃ʃismɑ̃/ *nm* **1** Postes (action) (en collant des timbres) stamping; (avec une machine) franking; (coût) postage; **l'~ va augmenter** postage is going up; **2** (libération) (de peuple, pays) liberation; (de serf, d'esclave) freeing; (de groupe, minorité) emancipation.

affres /afʀ/ *nfpl* littér agony; (de douleur) agony; (de faim) pangs; (de jalousie) throes; **les ~ de la mort** death throes.

affrètement /afʀɛtmɑ̃/ *nm* (d'avion, de bateau, camion) chartering.

affréter /afʀete/ [14] *vtr* Transp to charter [*avion, bateau, camion*].

affréteur /afʀetœʀ/ *nm* Comm, Naut charter company.

affreusement /afʀøzmɑ̃/ *adv* **1** [*se conduire, parler*] abominably; [*laid, blessé, défiguré, torturé*] horribly; [*malade*] terribly, dreadfully; **2**○ (extrêmement) terribly; **parler ~ mal** to speak appallingly badly.

affreux, -euse /afʀø, øz/ *adj* **1** (laid) [*personne, visage, vêtement, couleur, style*] ugly, hideous; [*blessure, plaie, monstre*] hideous; **2** (abject) [*crime, attentat, tyrannie, personne*] despicable, dreadful; **3** (désagréable) [*temps, route, voyage, vacances*] awful; [*malentendu*] dreadful, terrible; **c'est ~ ce qu'il est ennuyeux** he really is terribly boring; **c'est ~ le monde qu'il y a** it really is terribly busy; **c'est ~!** it's awful ou dreadful!; **4** (extrême) [*besoin, envie, soif*] terrible; (cruel) [*torture, douleur, accident, blessure*] dreadful, terrible.

affriander /afʀiɑ̃de/ [1] *vtr* to entice, to attract.

affriolant, ~e /afʀiɔlɑ̃, ɑ̃t/ *adj* [*femme*] alluring; [*vêtement*] titillating; [*idée*] tempting.

affrioler /afʀiɔle/ [1] *vtr* to entice.

affriqué, ~e /afʀike/ I *adj* affricative; **consonne ~e** affricate.

II **affriquée** *nf* affricate.

affront /afʀɔ̃/ *nm* affront (**à** to); **rougir sous l'~** to blush at the affront; **faire à qn l'~ de faire** to affront ou insult sb by doing; **il m'a fait l'~ de refuser mon invitation** he insulted me by refusing my invitation.

affrontement /afʀɔ̃tmɑ̃/ *nm* confrontation, clash; **au cours d'~s armés** in armed clashes; **tué dans des ~s avec l'armée** killed in clashes with the army; **des ~s ont eu lieu entre la police et les manifestants** there were clashes between police and demonstrators.

L'âge

Quel âge avez-vous?

L'anglais n'emploie pas le verbe to have (*avoir*) *pour exprimer l'âge, mais le verbe* to be (*être*).

quel âge a-t-il? = how old is he? *ou* what age is he?

Les deux mots years old *peuvent être omis pour les personnes, mais pas pour les choses.*

elle a trente ans = she is thirty years old *ou* she is thirty
il a quatre-vingts ans = he is eighty *ou* he is eighty years old
la maison a cent ans = the house is a hundred years old
atteindre soixante ans = to reach sixty
Nick est plus âgé qu'Isabelle = Nick is older than Isabelle
Isabelle est plus jeune que Nick = Isabelle is younger than Nick
Nick a deux ans de plus qu'Isabelle = Nick is two years older than Isabelle
Isabelle a deux ans de moins que Nick = Isabelle is two years younger than Nick
Louis a le même âge que Mary = Louis is the same age as Mary
Louis et Mary ont le même âge = Louis and Mary are the same age
on te donnerait seize ans = you look sixteen
j'ai l'impression d'avoir seize ans = I feel sixteen
on lui donnerait dix ans de moins = he looks ten years younger

Âgé de

il est âgé de quarante ans = he is forty years of age
un homme de soixante ans = a man of sixty
un enfant de huit ans et demi = a child of eight and a half
une femme âgée de quarante ans = a woman aged forty
M. Stein, âgé de quarante ans = Mr Stein, aged forty
à l'âge de cinquante ans = at fifty *ou* at the age of fifty (*GB*), at age fifty (*US*)
il est mort à vingt-sept ans = he died at twenty-seven *ou* at the age of twenty-seven
un homme âgé de soixante ans = a sixty-year-old man

Noter l'utilisation du trait d'union. Noter aussi que year, *qui fait partie de l'adjectif, ne prend pas la marque du pluriel.*

Lorsque l'on parle d'êtres humains ou d'animaux, le mot qui suit old *peut être sous-entendu. Ainsi, a* three-year-old *peut être un enfant ou un animal (souvent un cheval).*

un enfant de cinq ans et demi = a five-and-a-half-year-old
une course pour les trois ans = a race for three-year-olds

Mais:

un vin de soixante ans d'âge = a sixty-year-old wine

L'âge approximatif

L'anglais emploie indifféremment about *et* around *dans ce cas.*

elle a dans les trente ans = she's about thirty *ou* around thirty
elle a une cinquantaine d'années = she's about fifty *ou* around fifty
il n'a pas encore dix-huit ans = he's not yet eighteen
il vient d'avoir quarante ans = he's just over forty *ou* (*plus familier*) he's just turned forty
il aura bientôt cinquante ans = he's just under fifty
elle a entre trente et quarante ans = she's in her thirties
elle a dans les quarante-cinq ans = she's in her mid-forties
elle va sur ses soixante-dix ans = she's in her late sixties *ou* she's nearly seventy
elle va avoir vingt ans = she's in her late teens *ou* she's almost twenty
il a tout juste dix ans = he's just ten
il a à peine douze ans = he's barely twelve

Les personnes âgées de X ans

les plus de quatre-vingts ans = the over eighties
les moins de dix-huit ans = the under eighteens

Les mots anglais en -arian *sont des noms:*

ce sont des septuagénaires = they're septuagenarians
elle est octogénaire = she's an octogenarian

affronter /afʀɔ̃te/ [1] **I** *vtr* to face, to confront [*adversaire, mort, situation, troupe*]; to brave [*montagne, tempête, froid*].
II s'affronter *vpr* [*adversaires, armées, équipes*] to confront one another; [*idées, points de vue*] to clash; [*politiciens, théoriciens*] to confront one another.

affublement /afybləmɑ̃/ *nm* attire†.

affubler /afyble/ [1] **I** *vtr* péj **~ qn de** to deck sb out in, to dress sb up in [*vêtement, ornement*]; to saddle sb with [*prénom, surnom*]; **elle était affublée d'un chapeau de cow-boy** she was wearing a stupid cowboy hat; **il est affublé d'un prénom ridicule** he's saddled with a ridiculous name.
II s'affubler *vpr* **s'~ de** to deck oneself out in, to dress oneself up in [*vêtement*]; to deck oneself out in [*ornement*]; to take on, to assume [*nom, surnom*].

affût /afy/ *nm* **1** Mil **~ (de canon)** (gun) carriage; **2** Chasse hide GB, blind US; **chasser à l'~** to hunt game from a hide GB ou blind US; **se tenir** or **être à l'~** lit to lie in wait; fig to be on the lookout (**de** for).

affûtage /afytaʒ/ *nm* gén sharpening; (avec une meule) grinding, sharpening.

affûter /afyte/ [1] *vtr* gén to sharpen; (avec une meule) to grind, to sharpen.

affûteur /afytœʀ/ *nm* **1** ▶ 510 (personne) grinder; **2** (outil) sharpener, grinder.

afghan, **~e** /afgɑ̃, an/ ▶ 537, 462 **I** *adj* Afghan.
II *nm* Ling Afghan.

Afghan, **~e** /afgɑ̃, an/ ▶ 537 *nm,f* Afghan.

Afghanistan /afganistɑ̃/ ▶ 321 *nprm* Afghanistan.

afin /afɛ̃/ **I afin de** *loc prép* **~ de faire** in order to do, so as to do; **~ de ne pas faire** so as not to do.
II afin que *loc conj* so that; **faire cuire cinq minutes ~ que la sauce épaississe** cook for five minutes so that the sauce thickens; **prendre des mesures ~ que les jeunes trouvent du travail** to take measures so that young people might find work; **je lui écris régulièrement ~ qu'il ne se sente pas abandonné** I write to him regularly so that he won't feel neglected.

AFME /aɛfɛmə/ *nf*: *abbr* ▶ **agence**.

AFNOR /afnɔʀ/ *nf* (*abbr* = **Association française de normalisation**) AFNOR (*French standards authority*).

afocal, **~e**, *mpl* **-aux** /afɔkal, o/ *adj* Phys afocal.

a fortiori /afɔʀsjɔʀi/ *loc adv* all the more so, a fortiori sout.

AFP /aɛfpe/ *nf* (*abbr* = **Agence France-Presse**) AFP (*French news agency*).

AFPA /afpa/ *nf* (*abbr* = **Association pour la formation professionnelle des adultes**) *adult education and training organization*.

africain, **~e** /afʀikɛ̃, ɛn/ *adj* African.

Africain, **~e** /afʀikɛ̃, ɛn/ *nm,f* African.

africanisation /afʀikanizasjɔ̃/ *nf* Africanization.

africaniser /afʀikanize/ [1] *vtr* to Africanize.

africaniste /afʀikanist/ *nmf* Africanist.

afrikaans /afʀikɑ̃s/ ▶ 462 *nm* Ling Afrikaans.

afrikaner /afʀikanɛʀ/ *adj* Afrikaans.

Afrikaner /afʀikanɛʀ/ *nmf* Afrikaner.

Afrique /afʀik/ ▶ 321 *nprf* Africa; **l'~ australe/du Nord/de l'Ouest/de l'Est** Southern/North/West/East Africa; **l'~ noire** Black Africa; **République d'~ du Sud** Republic of South Africa.

Afrique-Équatoriale /afʀikekwatɔʀjal/ *nprf* Hist **~ française** French Equatorial Africa.

Afrique-Occidentale /afʀikɔksidɑ̃tal/ *nprf* Hist **~ française** French West Africa.

afro /afʀo/ **I** *adj inv* **coiffure ~** Afro haircut.
II○ *nmf* African.

afro- /afʀo/ *préf* **~-brésilien/-cubain** Afro-Brazilian/-Cuban; **~-jazz** African Jazz; **afrophobie** afrophobia; **afrocentrisme** afrocentrism.

afro-américain, **~e**, *mpl* **~s** /afʀoameʀikɛ̃, ɛn/ *adj* Afro-American.

Afro-américain, **~e**, *mpl* **~s** /afʀoameʀikɛ̃, ɛn/ *nm,f* Afro-American.

afro-asiatique /afʀoazjatik/ *adj* Afro-Asian.

Afro-asiatique /afʀoazjatik/ *nmf* Afro-Asian.

AG /aʒe/ *nf*: *abbr* ▶ **assemblée**.

agaçant, **~e** /agasɑ̃, ɑ̃t/ *adj* annoying, irritating.

agacement /agasmɑ̃/ *nm* **1** (ennui) irritation, annoyance; **2** (douleur) irritation.

agacer /agase/ [12] *vtr* **1** (excéder) to annoy, to irritate; **tu commences à m'~** you're starting to annoy me ou get on my nerves; **tu commences à m'~ avec tes cris/pleurs** your shouting/crying is starting to annoy me; **que ça m'agace!** this is really annoying!; **ça m'agace qu'il ne comprenne pas** it annoys me that he doesn't understand; **tu m'agaces à ne jamais écouter ce que je te dis** it annoys me that you never listen to what I say; **tu m'agaces à te ronger les ongles** it annoys me when you bite your nails; **2** (lanciner) to set [sth] on edge [*dent*]; to grate on [*nerf*].
IDIOMES **~ les nerfs de qn** to set sb's nerves on edge.

Agamemnon /agamɛmnɔ̃/ *npr* Agamemnon.

agapes /agap/ *nfpl* feast (*sg*), banquet (*sg*).

agar-agar /agaʀagaʀ/ *nm* agar-agar.

agate /agat/ *nf* **1** Minér agate; **une coupe d'~** an agate cup; **des yeux d'~** (couleur) agate-coloured[GB] eyes; **2** (bille) marble.

agave /agav/ *nm* agave.

âge /ɑʒ/ *nm* **1** (nombre d'années) age; **quel ~ a-t-il?** how old is he?; **ils sont du même ~** they are the same age; **il est mort à l'~ de 25 ans** he died at the age of 25; **depuis l'~ de 12 ans** from the age of 12; **faire** or **paraître son ~** to look one's age; **paraître plus/moins que son ~** to look older/younger than one's years; **bien porter son ~** to be good for one's age; **être sans ~, ne pas avoir d'~** to be ageless; **un homme d'un certain ~** a middle-aged man; **une personne d'un ~ avancé** or **d'un grand ~** an elderly person; **~ avancé, grand ~** great age; **avoir l'~** or **être en ~ de faire** to be old enough to do, to be of an age to do; **il est mort à 95 ans, c'est un bel ~** he died at 95, a fine old age; **30 ans, c'est le bel ~** 30 is a good age;

en ~ de se marier of marriageable age; ▶ **artère**; **2** (vieillesse) (old) age; **le respect dû à l'~** the respect due to age; **s'assagir avec l'~** to calm down as one gets older; **être vieux avant l'~** to be old before one's time; **prendre de l'~** to grow old; **le doyen d'~** the most senior person; **3** (période de la vie) age; **à tout ~**, **à tous les ~s** at any age; **être entre deux ~s** to be middle-aged; **être à un ~ critique** to be at a critical age; **être à l'~ critique** (ménopause) to be at the change of life; **avoir passé l'~ de faire** to be past the age when one does, to be past the age for doing; **être encore/ne plus être en ~ de faire** to be still young enough/ to be too old to do, to be still/no longer of an age to do; **ce n'est plus de mon ~ de faire** I'm too old to do; **qch n'est plus de mon ~** I'm too old for sth; **va t'amuser, c'est de ton ~!** go and have fun, you're young!; **4** (époque) Géol age; Hist age, era; **à travers les ~s** through the ages; **tradition qui nous vient du fond des ~s** tradition which has come down to us through the ages; **idées d'un autre ~** ideas from another age.

■ **l'~ adulte** adulthood; **l'~ bête** the awkward ou difficult age; **l'~ du bronze** the Bronze age; **l'~ critique** the change of life; **l'~ du fer** the Iron age; **l'~ d'homme** manhood; **l'~ ingrat** the awkward ou difficult age; **~ légal** legal age; **~ mental** mental age; **l'~ mûr** maturity; **d'~ mûr** mature; **l'~ d'or** the golden age; **l'~ de la pierre** the Stone age; **l'~ de la pierre polie** the neolithic age; **l'~ de la pierre taillée** the palaeolithic age; **l'~ de raison** the age of reason; **l'~ de la retraite** retirement age; **l'~ scolaire** school age; **l'~ tendre** youth; **l'~ viril** manhood.

âgé, ~e /ɑʒe/ *adj* [*femme, homme*] old, elderly; **les personnes ~es** old ou elderly people; **~ de 12 ans** 12 years old; **les personnes ~es de 15 à 35 ans** people aged between 15 and 35.

agence /aʒɑ̃s/ *nf* **1** Comm agency; **2** Admin agency, bureau; **3** (de banque) branch.

■ **~ bancaire** branch of a bank; **~ commerciale** local branch; **~ consulaire** consular agency; **~ immobilière** estate agents (*pl*) GB, real-estate agency US; **~ d'intérim** temporary employment agency; **~ matrimoniale** marriage bureau; **~ de placement** employment agency; **~ postale** sub post office GB, branch post office US; **~ de presse** news agency; **~ publicitaire** or **de publicité** advertising agency; **~ de renseignements commerciaux** trade bureau; **~ spatiale européenne**, **ASE** European Space Agency, ESA; **~ de voyage** travel agency, travel agents (*pl*) GB; **Agence française pour la maîtrise de l'énergie**, **AFME** *energy conservation agency*; **Agence nationale pour l'emploi**, **ANPE** *national employment agency*, ≈ Job Centre GB.

agencement /aʒɑ̃smɑ̃/ *nm* (d'appartement, de magasin) layout; (de mots, phrases) arrangement; (de couleurs, motifs, d'éléments) setting out; **l'~ des pièces n'est pas fonctionnel** the layout of the rooms is not practical.

agencer /aʒɑ̃se/ [12] **I** *vtr* **1** (disposer) to lay out [*cuisine, salle de bains*]; to put together [*éléments, motifs, couleurs*]; **un magasin bien agencé** a well-laid-out shop GB ou store US; **2** (structurer) to construct [*intrigue, scénario*].

II s'agencer *vpr* **les parties du tableau s'agencent harmonieusement** the various elements of the picture are harmoniously set out; **les bureaux du nouveau bâtiment s'agencent mal** the offices in the new building are not very well laid out.

agenda /aʒɛ̃da/ *nm* **1** (carnet prédaté) diary; **~ électronique/de poche/de bureau** electronic/pocket/desk diary; **2** Pol (programme) agenda.

agenouiller: **s'agenouiller** /aʒnuje/ [1] *vpr* **1** (se mettre à genoux) to kneel (down); **être agenouillé** to be kneeling; **2** fig (se soumettre) **s'~ devant** to bow to [*décision, pouvoir*]; to kowtow to [*personne*].

agenouilloir /aʒnujwaʀ/ *nm* hassock.

agent /aʒɑ̃/ *nm* ▶ **510** **1** (de l'État) Admin official, official; Pol agent; **~ du gouvernement** government official; **~ secret/double** secret/double agent; **2** Comm agent; **~ exclusif** sole agent; **~ agréé** authorized dealer; **3** (employé) Admin, Entr employee; **~ qualifié/non qualifié** skilled/unskilled employee; **~s contractuels/temporaires** contract/temporary staff; **~s de santé** health workers; **4** Chimie, Ling, Sci agent.

■ **~ artistique** Théât theatrical agent; **~ d'assurances** insurance broker; (vendeur) insurance salesman; **~ de bureau** office worker, clerk; **~ de change** stockbroker; **~ de la circulation** traffic policeman; **~ de classement** filing clerk; **~ commercial** sales representative; **~ comptable** Admin accountant; **~ consulaire** consular agent; **~ de dissuasion** deterrent; **~ en douane** customs officer; **~ économique** economic agent; **~ hospitalier** nursing auxiliary GB, nurse's aide US; **~ immobilier** estate agent GB, real-estate agent US; **~ de liaison** liaison officer; **~ de maîtrise** supervisor; **~ maritime** shipping agent; **~ de police** policeman; **~ provocateur** agent provocateur; **~ de publicité** advertising agent; **~ de recouvrement** (de dette) debt collector; (d'impôt) tax collector; **~ de renseignements** intelligence agent; **~ technique** technician; **~ de transmission** messenger, dispatch rider; **~ de voyage** travel agent.

aggiornamento /aʒjɔʀnamɛnto/ *nm* **1** Relig aggiornamento; **2** fig modernization, aggiornamento.

agglomérat /aglɔmeʀa/ *nm* **1** Géol, Minér agglomerate; **2** Phon (de consonnes) cluster; **3** (de personnes, d'objets) jumble.

agglomération /aglɔmeʀasjɔ̃/ *nf* **1** (ville) town; (village) village; **l'~ lyonnaise** Lyons and its suburbs; **vitesse maximum en ~** Aut maximum speed in built-up areas; **2** Tech agglomeration (**de** of).

aggloméré /aglɔmeʀe/ *nm* chipboard; **une table en ~** a chipboard table.

agglomérer /aglɔmeʀe/ [14] **I** *vtr* Tech to agglomerate.

II s'agglomérer *vpr* [*personnes*] to gather together; [*habitations*] to be grouped together.

agglutinant, ~e /aglytinɑ̃, ɑ̃t/ *adj* **1** [*langue*] agglutinative; **2** [*sérum*] agglutinant, agglutinative.

agglutination /aglytinasjɔ̃/ *nf* agglutination.

agglutiner /aglytine/ [1] **I** *vtr* to agglutinate.

II s'agglutiner *vpr* **1** (se masser) [*badauds*] to crowd together (**à** at); [*mouches*] to cluster together; **s'~ autour de** [*curieux*] to crowd around; [*maisons*] to be clustered around; **2** Méd [*plaie*] to close; [*microbes*] to agglutinate.

aggravant, ~e /agʀavɑ̃, ɑ̃t/ *adj* Jur [*témoignage, circonstance*] aggravating.

aggravation /agʀavasjɔ̃/ *nf* (de situation, conflit, crise) worsening; (de maladie) aggravation, worsening; (de chômage, dette, déficit) increase (**de** in).

■ **~ de peine** Jur increase in sentence.

aggravé, ~e /agʀave/ **I** *pp* ▶ **aggraver**.

II *pp adj* Jur [*vol, proxénétisme*] aggravated.

aggraver /agʀave/ [1] **I** *vtr* **1** (rendre pire) to aggravate, to make [sth] worse [*situation, souffrance*]; to aggravate [*crise, faute*]; to make [sth] worse [*santé, conditions*]; **~ son cas** to make things worse; **2** (accroître) to increase [*risque, chômage, inflation, déficit*]; **3** Jur to increase [*peine*]; **~ une peine de cinq années supplémentaires** to increase a sentence by five additional years.

II s'aggraver *vpr* **1** (devenir pire) [*situation, crise, conditions*] to get worse, to deteriorate; [*état de santé*] to deteriorate; **la situation va en s'aggravant** the situation is getting worse ou is deteriorating; **2** (augmenter) [*chômage, inflation, dette*] to increase.

agile /aʒil/ *adj* [*personne, animal*] agile; [*doigts, pas, esprit*] nimble.

agilement /aʒilmɑ̃/ *adv* nimbly, with agility.

agilité /aʒilite/ *nf* agility; **~ d'esprit** mental agility; **avec ~** [*grimper, se faufiler*] with agility; **ses doigts courent avec ~ sur le clavier** his/her fingers run nimbly over the keyboard.

agios /aʒjo/ *nmpl* Fin bank charges.

agiotage /aʒjɔtaʒ/ *nm* illegal speculation.

agir /aʒiʀ/ [3] **I** *vi* **1** (accomplir une action) to act; **décider/refuser d'~** to decide/to refuse to act ou to take action; **il a agi sous le coup de la colère** he acted in anger; **assez parlé, maintenant il faut ~!** that's enough talk, now we've got to act ou let's have some action!; **~ comme intermédiaire** to act as an intermediary; **il est urgent d'~** urgent action must be taken; **il parle beaucoup mais agit peu** he's all talk and no action; **~ avec prudence** to proceed with caution; **2** (se comporter) to behave, to act; **bien/mal ~** to behave well/ badly (**envers, avec** towards[GB]); **~ comme un enfant/idiot** to behave childishly/stupidly, to act like a child/fool; **je n'aime pas sa manière** or **façon d'~** I don't like the way he/she behaves; **~ en honnête homme** to behave honourably[GB]; **~ en lâche/gentleman** to act like a coward/ gentleman; **~ comme on l'entend** to do what one likes; **3** (avoir un effet) [*substance, médicament*] to take effect, to work; **le somnifère agit immédiatement** the sleeping pill takes effect ou works ou acts immediately; **le médicament n'a pas agi** the medicine hasn't worked; **~ sur qch/qn** to have an effect on sth/sb; **~ comme un signal d'alarme** to serve as an alarm signal; **~ sur le marché** Fin to influence the market; **4** (intervenir) **~ auprès de** to approach; **~ auprès d'un ministre pour obtenir une faveur** to approach a minister in order to obtain a favour[GB]; **5** Jur **~ contre qn** to take legal action against sb; **~ au civil** to sue; **~ au criminel** to prosecute.

II s'agir de *vpr impers* **1** (il est question de) **de quoi s'agit-il?** what is it about? ; (il y a un problème) what's the matter?; **mais il ne s'agit pas de ça!** but that's not the point!; **mais il s'agit de ton bonheur/ta santé!** but we're talking about your happiness/your health here!, but it's your happiness/your health that's at stake (here)!; **dans ce livre, il s'agit d'une famille d'agriculteurs** this book is about a family of farmers; **il s'agit de votre mari** it's about your husband, it's to do with your husband; **on connaît maintenant les gagnants**: **il s'agit de messieurs X et Y** we now know who the winners are: they're Mr X and Mr Y; **d'après les experts il s'agirait d'un attentat** according to the experts, it would appear to be an act of terrorism; **quand il s'agit de faire le ménage, il n'est jamais là!** when there's cleaning to be done, he's never there ou around!; **quand il s'agit d'argent il est toujours là!** where money' s concerned ou when it comes to money, he's always right in there!; **s'agissant de qch/qn** as regards sth/sb; **il s'agit bien de partir en vacances maintenant que je suis au chômage!** iron now that I'm unemployed it's hardly the (right) time to talk about going on vacation!; **2** (il est nécessaire de) **il s'agit de faire vite** we/you etc must act quickly; **il s'agit de se remettre au travail** we/you etc must get back to work; **il s'agit de vous ressaisir!** you must pull yourself together!; **il s'agit de savoir ce que tu veux!** make up your mind!; **il ne s'agit pas de changer d'avis à la dernière minute!** there's no question of a last-minute change of mind!; **il s'agit pour le gouvernement de redonner confiance aux électeurs/relancer l'économie** what the government must do now is regain the confidence of the electorate/boost the economy; **il s'agirait de se mettre d'accord: vous venez mardi ou jeudi?** we'd better get it straight: are you coming on Tuesday or Thursday?; **il s'agit de ne pas rater notre coup cette fois** we must get it right this time.

III○ **s'agir que** *vpr impers* **il s'agit qu'il obéisse!** he must do as he's told!; **il ne s'agit pas qu'elle soit en retard!** she mustn't be late!

âgisme /aʒism/ *nm* ageism.

agissant, **~e** /aʒisɑ̃, ɑ̃t/ *adj* **1** (efficace) effective; **2** (actif) active.

agissements /aʒismɑ̃/ *nmpl* pej activities, doings; **de tels ~ sont condamnables** such activities are reprehensible.

agitateur, **-trice** /aʒitatœʀ, tʀis/ **I** *nm,f* Pol agitator.

II *nm* (dispositif) agitator; (baguette) stirring rod.

agitation /aʒitasjɔ̃/ *nf* **1** (mouvement) (de mer) choppiness; (d'air) turbulence; (de branche) swaying; (de malade) restlessness; (d'impatient) restlessness, fidgetiness; **2** (affairement) (de maison, rue) bustle (**de** in); (de marché, d'échange) activity; **peu d'~ à la Bourse** little activity on the Stock Exchange; **3** (nervosité) agitation; **4** (malaise social) Pol unrest.

■ **~ magnétique** Géog, Phys geomagnetic disturbance.

agité, **~e** /aʒite/ **I** *pp* ▶ **agiter**.

II *pp adj* **1** (en mouvement) [*mer*] rough; (moins fort) choppy; [*malade, patient*] agitated; [*rue*] bustling; [*vie*] hectic; **2** (troublé) [*esprit, âme, sommeil*] troubled; [*période*] turbulent; [*nuit*] restless.

III *nm,f* **1** Méd agitated mental patient; **les ~s** the mentally disturbed; **2** (indiscipliné) troublemaker, disruptive element.

agiter /aʒite/ [1] **I** *vtr* **1** (remuer) to wave [*main, mouchoir, cigare*]; to shake [*boîte*]; to shake up [*liquide*]; to wag [*queue*]; to flap [*aile*]; **le vent agite les feuilles** the wind is rustling the leaves; **voile agitée par le vent** sail flapping in the wind; **barque agitée par les vagues** boat tossed by the waves; **un tremblement agitait mon corps** my whole body was shaking; **2** (brandir) to raise [*menace, spectre*]; **3** (troubler) to trouble [*esprit, pays, personne*]; **4** (débattre) to debate, to discuss [*problème, question*].

II **s'agiter** *vpr* **1** (remuer) [*personne*] gén to fidget; (au lit) [*malade, insomniaque*] to toss and turn; [*branche*] to sway (in the wind); **2** (s'affairer) to bustle about; **3** (perdre son calme) [*esprit, peuple*] to become agitated ou restless; **4**○ (se dépêcher) [*paresseux, retardataire*] to get a move on○.

agneau, *pl* **~x** /aɲo/ *nm* **1** Zool, Culin lamb; **2** (cuir) lambskin; **des gants en ~** lambskin gloves; **3**○ hum (enfant) **bonjour, mes ~x!** hello dearies! hum.

■ **~ de Dieu** Relig Lamb of God; **l'~ pascal** Relig the paschal lamb.

IDIOMES **être doux comme un ~** to be as meek as a lamb.

agnelage /aɲəlaʒ/ *nm* lambing.

agneler /aɲəle/ [19] *vi* to lamb.

agnelet /aɲəlɛ/ *nm* baby lamb.

agneline /aɲəlin/ *nf* virgin lamb's wool.

agnelle /aɲɛl/ *nf* ewe lamb.

agnosticisme /agnɔstisism/ *nm* agnosticism.

agnostique /agnɔstik/ *adj, nmf* agnostic.

agonie /agɔni/ *nf* **1** (d'être vivant) death throes (*pl*) littér (**de** of); **il est à l'~** he's at death's door, he's dying; **son ~ a été longue/terrible** he/she died a slow/terrible death; **2** (d'un parti, régime) slow death (**de** of); **le régime politique est à l'~** the political regime is dying ou in its death throes.

agonir /agɔniʀ/ [3] *vtr* **~ qn d'injures** to hurl insults at sb; **se faire ~ d'injures** to have insults hurled at one; **en rentrant, il s'est fait ~** when he got home he was told off soundly.

agonisant, **~e** /agɔnizɑ̃, ɑ̃t/ **I** *adj* dying.

II *nm,f* dying person.

agoniser /agɔnize/ [1] *vi* lit, fig to be dying.

agora /agɔʀa/ *nf* agora.

agoraphobe /agɔʀafɔb/ *adj, nmf* agoraphobic.

agoraphobie /agɔʀafɔbi/ *nf* agoraphobia.

agrafage /agʀafaʒ/ *nm* **1** (de vêtement) fastening; **2** (de papiers) stapling; **3** Méd fastening skin clips (*pl*).

agrafe /agʀaf/ *nf* **1** (pour vêtements) hook; **2** (pour papiers) staple; **3** Méd skin clip; **on m'a mis trois ~s au front** they've put three (skin) clips in my forehead.

agrafer /agʀafe/ [1] **I** *vtr* **1** (fermer) to fasten [*vêtement*]; **2** (attacher) to staple (together) [*papiers, tissu*]; **3**◑ (attraper) to nab○, to catch.

II **s'agrafer** *vpr* [*vêtement*] to fasten.

agrafeuse /agʀaføz/ *nf* stapler.

agraire /agʀɛʀ/ *adj* [*société*] agrarian; [*mesure, réforme*] land (*épith*).

agrammatical, **~e**, *mpl* **-aux** /agʀamatikal, o/ *adj* Ling ungrammatical.

agrandir /agʀɑ̃diʀ/ [3] **I** *vtr* **1** (en dimensions) to enlarge [*ville, photo*]; to extend [*pièce, maison, magasin*]; to widen [*tunnel, marge, écart*]; to make [sth] bigger, to enlarge [*trou*]; **il me regardait, les yeux agrandis par la peur** he was looking at me, his eyes wide with fear; **faire ~ une maison** to have an extension built; **faire ~ une photo** to have a photo enlarged; **la peinture blanche agrandit la pièce** white paint makes the room look bigger ou larger; **2** (en importance) to extend [*famille*]; to expand [*entreprise, parti*].

II **s'agrandir** *vpr* **1** (devenir plus grand) [*trou*] to get bigger; [*ville, famille, entreprise*] to expand, to grow; [*marge, écart, yeux*] to widen; **2**○ (dans un logement) to have more room to live in, to have more space; **déménager pour s'~** to move in order to have more space.

agrandissement /agʀɑ̃dismɑ̃/ *nm* **1** Phot enlargement; **2** (de maison, pièce) extension; (d'ouverture) enlargement; (d'entreprise) expansion; **faire des travaux d'~** (dans une maison) to build an extension; (dans un magasin) to extend the floor space.

agrandisseur /agʀɑ̃disœʀ/ *nm* enlarger.

agraphie /agʀafi/ ▶ 271 *nf* agraphia.

agrarien, **-ienne** /agʀaʀjɛ̃, ɛn/ *adj, nm,f* Hist, Pol agrarian.

agréable /agʀeabl/ **I** *adj* nice, pleasant; **avoir un physique ~** to be good-looking; **~ à l'œil/au toucher/à l'oreille** pleasing to the eye/to the touch/to the ear; **~ à vivre** [*personne*] pleasant ou nice to be with; [*ville*] pleasant to live in; **être ~ à qn** [*personne*] to be nice to sb.

II *nm* **l'~ de qch** the agreeable aspect of sth; ▶ **utile**.

agréablement /agʀeabləmɑ̃/ *adv* pleasantly, agreeably.

agréé, **~e** /agʀee/ **I** *pp* ▶ **agréer**.

II *pp adj* [*agence, concessionnaire*] authorized (**par** by); [*médecin, ambulancier, nourrice*] registered (**par** with); [*matériel, association, établissement*] approved (**par** by).

agréer /agʀee/ [11] *vtr* **1** (accepter) to agree to [*demande*]; **faire ~ qch par qn** to have sth agreed by sb; **veuillez ~, Messieurs, mes salutations distinguées** (personne non nommée) yours faithfully; (personne nommée) yours sincerely; **2** (reconnaître officiellement) to recognize [sb] officially [*diplomate*]; to authorize [*concessionnaire*]; to register [*taxi, nourrice, médecin*]; to approve [*matériel, association, établissement*].

agrégat /agʀega/ *nm* **1** Biol, Constr, Écon aggregate; **2** fig jumble (**de** of).

■ **~s monétaires** Écon monetary aggregates.

agrégatif, **-ive** /agʀegatif, iv/ *nm,f*: *candidate for the agrégation.*

agrégation /agʀegasjɔ̃/ *nf* **1** Univ *high-level competitive examination for recruitment of teachers*; **2** (de particules) agregation.

agrégé, **~e** /agʀeʒe/ *nm,f*: *holder of the agrégation.*

agréger: **s'agréger** /agʀeʒe/ [15] *vpr* **1** (se coller) [*particules*] to aggregate; **2** (se joindre) **s'~ à** [*personne, groupe*] to join.

agrément /agʀemɑ̃/ *nm* **1** (validation officielle) approval; **retirer son ~ à une école de langues** to withdraw a language school's accreditation; **2** (accord) agreement; **recevoir l'~ de qn** to obtain sb's agreement; **3** (charme) (d'activité, expérience) pleasure; (de personne, lieu, chose) charm; **un des ~s de la vie à l'étranger** one of the pleasures of living abroad; **c'en est le principal ~** that's its main charm; **trouver de l'~ à une ville** to find a certain charm in a town; **plein d'~** [*séjour*] very pleasant; [*lieu*] full of charm (*après n*); **sans ~** [*séjour, existence*] dull; [*visage, maison*] unattractive; [*décor, pièce*] cheerless; **voyage d'~** pleasure trip.

■ **~ fiscal** tax relief; **~ mélodique** ornament.

agrémenter /agʀemɑ̃te/ [1] **I** *vtr* to liven up [*texte, histoire*] (**de** with); to cheer up [*réunion*] (**de** with); to brighten up [*jardin*] (**de** with); to supplement [*repas, plat*] (**de** with); **les petits plaisirs qui agrémentent l'existence** the little things that brighten up one's life; **un ensemble immobilier agrémenté de nombreux services** a property development offering many facilities; **un texte agrémenté d'illustrations** a text with illustrations; **un chapeau agrémenté d'une voilette** a hat trimmed with a veil; **une pièce agrémentée de tableaux** a room decorated with pictures.

II **s'agrémenter** *vpr* **s'~ de** [*chapeau, vêtement*] to be trimmed with; [*pièce*] to be decorated with; [*conversation*] to be laced with.

agrès /agʀɛ/ *nmpl* **1** Sport apparatus ₵; **aux ~** on the apparatus; **2** Naut tackle.

agresser /agʀese/ [1] *vtr* **1** (physiquement) [*personne*] to attack, to assault [*personne*]; (pour voler) to mug [*personne*]; [*pays, peuple*] to attack [*pays, peuple*]; **se faire ~ dans la rue** to be mugged in the street; **2** (moralement) [*personne*] to be aggressive with [*personne*]; **se sentir agressé** to feel threatened (**par** by); **les images télévisées nous agressent** we are bombarded by pictures on television; **3** (être trop fort) [*shampooing, pluies acides, fumée*] to attack.

agresseur /agʀesœʀ/ *nm* (individu) attacker; (groupe, peuple) aggressor; **le pays ~** the aggressor.

agressif, **-ive** /agʀesif, iv/ *adj* **1** (hostile) [*personne, animal*] aggressive (**avec qn** with sb; **envers qn** toward, towards GB sb); [*tempérament, ton, air, environnement, publicité*] aggressive; **d'un ton ~** aggressively; **2** (trop fort) [*couleur*] violent; [*son*] ear-splitting; [*lumière, shampooing*] harsh; [*images*] threatening; **3** (dynamique) [*politique, campagne, jeu*] aggressive; **mener une politique commerciale agressive** to have an aggressive sales policy.

agression /agʀesjɔ̃/ *nf* **1** (par une personne) attack; (pour voler) mugging; (par un pays) act of aggression; **une ~ raciste** a racist attack; **être victime d'une ~** gén to be attacked; (être volé) to be mugged; **commettre une ~ contre qn** gén to attack sb; (pour voler) to mug sb; **~ à main armée** armed assault; **2** (par un fait) **protégez votre visage contre les ~s** protect your face from the wind and the cold; **les ~s de l'entourage/la vie urbaine** the stresses and strains of one's surroundings/city life; **3** Psych aggression.

agressivement /agʀesivmɑ̃/ *adv* aggressively.

agressivité /agʀesivite/ *nf* **1** gén aggressiveness; **2** Psych aggression.

agreste /agʀɛst/ *adj* liter rustic.

agricole /agʀikɔl/ *adj* [*produit, ouvrier*] farm; [*coopérative*] farming; [*méthode, problème*] agricultural; [*syndicat*] farm workers'.

agriculteur, **-trice** /agʀikyltœʀ, tʀis/ ▶510 *nm,f* farmer; **une famille d'~s** a farming family.

agriculture /agʀikyltyʀ/ *nf* farming, agriculture spéc.

■ **~ biologique** organic farming ou agriculture.

agripper /agʀipe/ [1] **I** *vtr* to grab [*branche, personne*].

II s'agripper *vpr* **s'~ à** to cling to [*paroi, bras*]; **il était agrippé à une branche** he was clinging to a branch.

agro-alimentaire, *pl* **~s** /agʀoalimɑ̃tɛʀ/ **I** *adj* [*industrie, filière, complexe*] food processing; **la recherche ~** food research.

II *nm* food processing industry; **un géant de l'~** a food giant.

agrochimie /agʀoʃimi/ *nf* agro-chemistry.

agronome /agʀɔnɔm/ ▶510 *nmf* agronomist; **ingénieur ~** agronomist.

agronomie /agʀɔnɔmi/ *nf* agronomy.

agronomique /agʀɔnɔmik/ *adj* agronomic.

agrume /agʀym/ *nm* citrus fruit; **les ~s** citrus fruits.

aguerri, **~e** /ageʀi/ **I** *pp* ▶ **aguerrir**.

II *pp adj* **1** Mil (accoutumé à la guerre) seasoned (**par** by); **2** gén (endurci) hardened, inured sout (**à, contre** to).

aguerrir /ageʀiʀ/ [3] **I** *vtr* [*expérience*] to harden [*personne*] (**à qch** to sth); **~ des troupes au combat** to toughen soldiers for battle.

II s'aguerrir *vpr* to become hardened ou inured sout (**à, contre** to).

aguets: **aux aguets** /ozagɛ/ *loc adv* **être aux ~** (à l'affût) to lie in wait; (se méfier) to be on one's guard; (surveiller de près) to be watching like a hawk.

aguichant, **~e** /agiʃɑ̃, ɑ̃t/ *adj* [*personne, pose, sourire*] alluring.

aguicher /agiʃe/ [1] *vtr* (sexuellement) to lead [sb] on; (pour vendre) to attract [*client*].

aguicheur, **-euse** /agiʃœʀ, øz/ **I** *adj* [*personne, propos*] alluring.

II aguicheuse *nf* pej tease péj.

ah /ɑ/ **I** *nm inv* (d'étonnement, admiration) gasp; (de soulagement, satisfaction) sigh.

II *excl* oh!; **~ non alors!** certainly not!; **~, tu vois!** see!; **~! c'est dégoûtant!** ugh! it's revolting!; **~ oui** or **bon?** really?; **~ ~, il est parti en voyage d'affaires?** iron so, it's a business trip, is it? iron; **~ ~ ~!** (rire) ha ha ha!

ahaner /aane/ [1] *vi* (grogner) to grunt with effort; (peiner) to strain, to heave.

ahuri, **~e** /ayʀi/ **I** *pp* ▶ **ahurir**.

II *pp adj* (hébété) dazed; (étonné) stunned.

III *nm,f* pej halfwit péj.

ahurir /ayʀiʀ/ [3] *vtr* [*réponse, nouvelle*] to stun; **j'ai été ahuri d'apprendre que** I was stunned to hear that.

ahurissant, **~e** /ayʀisɑ̃, ɑ̃t/ *adj* [*nouvelle, bruit*] incredible; [*personne, comportement, force*] incredible; [*chiffre*] staggering; **c'est ~!** it's absolutely incredible!

ahurissement /ayʀismɑ̃/ *nm* amazement.

aï /ai/ *nm* three-toed sloth.

aiche = **èche**.

aide /ɛd/ ▶510 **I** *nmf* (dans un travail) assistant.

II *nf* **1** (secours) (d'individu, de groupe) help, assistance; (d'État, organisme) assistance; **appeler à l'~** to call for help; **à l'~!** help!; **avec/sans l'~ de qn** with/without sb's help; **à l'~ de** with the help ou aid of [*tournevis, dictionnaire, police*]; **proposer son ~ à qn** to offer to help sb; **apporter son ~ à qn** to help sb; **il m'a apporté une ~ considérable** he was a great help to me; **venir/aller à l'~ de qn** to come/to go to sb's aid ou assistance; **venir en ~ à qn** (financièrement) to help ou aid sb; **2** (en argent) (à un pays) aid ₵; (aux démunis) aid ₵, allowance C; (à une industrie, un organisme) aid ₵, subsidy C; (pour un projet) aid ₵, grant C; **recevoir des ~s de** to receive financial backing ou aid from [*État, organisme*]; **les ~s à la famille** financial aid for families; **recevoir une ~ de 5 000 francs** to receive 5,000 francs in aid.

■ **~ de camp** aide-de-camp; **~ au développement** foreign aid; **~ à domicile** home help GB, home helper US; **~ familiale** mother's help GB, mother's helper US; **~ judiciaire** legal aid; **~ légale** = **~ judiciaire**; **~ maternelle** = **~ familiale**; **~ médicale** health care; **~ médicale gratuite** free health care; **~ ménagère** = **~ à domicile**; **~ sociale** social security benefits GB, welfare benefits US.

aide-anesthésiste, *pl* **aides-anesthésistes** /ɛdanɛstezist/ ▶510 *nmf* assistant anaesthetist[GB].

aide-bibliothécaire, *pl* **aides-bibliothécaires** /ɛdbiblijɔtekɛʀ/ ▶510 *nmf* assistant librarian.

aide-comptable, *pl* **aides-comptables** /ɛdkɔ̃tabl/ ▶510 *nmf* assistant accountant.

aide-cuisinier, **-ière**, *pl* **aides-cuisiniers, aides-cuisinières** /ɛdkɥizinje, ɛʀ/ ▶510 *nm,f* assistant cook.

aide-électricien, *pl* **aides-électriciens** /ɛdelɛktʀisjɛ̃/ ▶510 *nm* electrician's mate GB, electrician's helper US.

aide-mécanicien, *pl* **aides-mécaniciens** /ɛdmekanisjɛ̃/ ▶510 *nm* mechanic's mate GB, mechanic's helper US.

aide-mémoire /ɛdmemwaʀ/ *nm inv* aide-mémoire sout; **c'est mon ~** I use it to jog my memory.

aider /ede/ [1] **I** *vtr* **1** (prêter son concours à) to help; **il n'aide jamais** he never helps; **~ qn à faire** to help sb to do; **en quoi puis-je vous ~?** how can I help you?; **~ qn financièrement** gén to help sb financially; (une fois) to help sb out financially; **se faire ~ par qn** to get help from sb; **~ qn de ses conseils** to give sb helpful advice; **il m'a aidé par sa présence** the fact he was there helped me; **le vin/la fatigue aidant** wine/tiredness playing its part; **le temps aidant** with time; **2** (subventionner) to aid [*industrie, déshérités*]; to give aid to [*pays pauvre*].

II aider à *vtr ind* to help toward(s) [*compréhension, insertion sociale, financement*]; **~ à faire** to help in doing.

III s'aider *vpr* **1** (soi-même) **s'~ de** to use [*dictionnaire, tableau, outil*]; **marcher en s'aidant d'une canne** to walk with the help of a stick; **2** (les uns les autres) to help each other.

IDIOMES **aide-toi le Ciel t'aidera** Prov God helps those who help themselves Prov.

aide-soignant, **~e**, *pl* **aides-soignants**, **aides-soignantes** /ɛdswaɲɑ̃, ɑ̃t/ ▶510 *nm,f* nursing auxiliary GB, nurse's aide US.

aïe /aj/ *excl* (de douleur) ouch!; (d'inquiétude) **~** (**~ ~**), **que se passe-t-il?** oh dear, what's going on?; (d'anticipation) **~ ~ ~!...** oh NO!...

aïeul, **~e** /ajœl/ *nm,f* liter grandfather/grandmother.

aïeux /ajø/ *nmpl* liter ancestors; **mes ~†!** upon my word†!

aigle /ɛgl/ **I** *nm* **1** Zool eagle; ▶ **petit**; **2** (lutrin) lectern.

II *nf* **1** Zool (female) eagle; **2** Hist Mil eagle; **les ~s romaines** the Roman eagles; **3** Hérald eagle.

■ **~ impérial** imperial eagle; **~ royal** golden eagle.

IDIOMES **ce n'est pas un ~** he's not the brightest.

aiglefin /ɛgləfɛ̃/ *nm* haddock.

aiglon /ɛglɔ̃/ *nm* eaglet.

aigre /ɛgʀ/ *adj* **1** lit [*odeur, goût*] sour; [*vin, lait*] sour; [*fruit*] (acidulé) sharp; (pas mûr) sour; **2** fig [*paroles, ton*] sharp; [*caractère*] sour; **d'un ton ~** sharply; **tourner** or **virer à l'~** [*discussion, plaisanterie*] to turn sour.

aigre-doux, **-douce**, *pl* **aigres-doux**, **aigres-douces** /ɛgʀədu, dus/ *adj* **1** Culin [*fruit, goût*] bitter-sweet; [*cuisine, sauce*] sweet and sour; **2** fig [*propos, communiqué*] barbed.

aigrefin /ɛgʀəfɛ̃/ *nm* swindler.

aigrelet, **-ette** /ɛgʀəlɛ, ɛt/ *adj* **1** lit [*goût*] rather sour; [*fruit*] (acidulé) rather sharp; (pas mûr) rather sour; **un petit vin ~** a sharpish wine; **2** fig [*voix*] shrill.

aigrement /ɛgʀəmɑ̃/ *adv* fig sharply.

aigrette /ɛgʀɛt/ *nf* **1** Zool (oiseau) egret; (plumes) crest; **2** (ornement de coiffure) aigrette; **un casque à ~** a plumed helmet; **3** Bot pappus.

aigreur /ɛgʀœʀ/ *nf* **1** gén (de lait) sourness; (de vin) sharpness; (de fruit) (acidulé) sharpness; (pas mûr) sourness; **2** Méd **des ~s d'estomac** heartburn ₵; **3** fig bitterness.

aigri, **~e** /egʀi/ **I** *pp* ▶ **aigrir**.

II *pp adj* [*personne*] embittered.

aigrir /egʀiʀ/ [3] **I** *vtr* [*expérience*] to embitter [*personne*].

II s'aigrir *vpr* **1** [*personne*] to become embittered; **2** [*vin, aliment*] to turn sour.

aigu, **-uë** /egy/ **I** *adj* **1** (à l'oreille) [*son, voix, note*] high-pitched; **2** Méd, gén (violent) [*maladie, crise, douleur*] acute; [*symptôme, problème*] acute; [*phase*] critical; **3** (intense) [*perception, sens*] keen; **il a un sens ~ du devoir** he's got a keen sense of duty.

II *nm* Mus (de chaîne stéréo) treble; (de voix) high notes (*pl*); **passer du grave à l'~** to go from low notes to high notes.

aigue-marine, *pl* **aigues-marines** /ɛgmaʀin/ *nf* aquamarine.

aiguière /ɛgjɛʀ/ *nf* ewer.

aiguillage /egɥijaʒ/ *nm* **1** Rail (appareil) points (*pl*) GB, switch US; (manœuvre) switching to another line; **une erreur d'~** a signalling[GB] error; **poste d'~** signal box; **2** fig (orientation) **il y a eu une erreur d'~** (confusion) there's been a mix-up; **il y a eu une erreur d'~ dans leurs études** they were led to choose the wrong courses.

aiguille /egɥij/ *nf* **1** (pour coudre) needle; **~ à coudre/broder/repriser** sewing/embroidery/darning needle; **~ à brider** poultry needle; **~ à suture** suture needle; **travail à l'~** needlework; **tirer l'~†** to ply one's needle†; **2** (de seringue) needle; (en acupuncture) needle; **3** (de montre, chronomètre) hand; (de jauge, d'altimètre) needle; (de balance) pointer; **l'~ des minutes/des heures** the minute/hour hand; **dans le sens des ~s d'une montre** clockwise; **dans le sens inverse des ~s d'une montre** anticlockwise; **4** Bot needle; **5** Géog peak; **6** Zool garfish.

■ **~ aimantée** magnetic needle; **~ de pin** pine needle; **~ de radium** radium needle; **~ à tricoter** knitting needle.

IDIOMES **autant chercher une ~ dans une botte** or **meule de foin** it's like looking for a needle in a haystack; **et de fil en ~** and one thing leading to another.

aiguillée /egɥije/ *nf* length of thread (*on a needle*).

aiguiller /egɥije/ [1] *vtr* **1** (vers un endroit) to direct [*personne*] (**vers** toward); to send [*courrier, dossier*] (**vers** to); (vers une profession, des études) to guide, to steer [*personne*] (**vers** toward, towards GB); (orienter) to steer [*conversation*] (**sur** toward, towards GB); **elle a été mal aiguillée dans ses études** she was badly advised about what to study; **c'est ce qui nous a aiguillés dans nos recherches** that's what put us on the right track in our research; **2** Rail **~ un train** to switch a train to a new line; **3** Ordinat to route.

aiguillette /egɥijɛt/ *nf* **1** Culin (de bœuf) *tip of rump steak*; (de volaille) breast fillet; (mince tranche de viande) fillet; **2** Hist Mil aiguillette.
IDIOMES **nouer l'~ à qn** to render sb impotent by witchcraft.

aiguilleur /egɥijœʀ/ ▶**510** *nm* Rail pointsman GB, switchman US.
■ **~ du ciel** Aviat air traffic controller.

aiguillon /egɥijɔ̃/ *nm* **1** Zool sting; **2** (stimulant) incentive; **3** (bâton) goad; **4** Bot thorn.

aiguillonner /egɥijɔne/ [1] *vtr* **1** (stimuler) to spur [*personne*]; to stimulate [*ambition*]; **~ l'action d'un groupe** to spur a group into action; **la faim m'aiguillonnant...** driven by hunger...; **2** lit to goad [*bœuf*].

aiguisage /egizaʒ/ *nm* sharpening.

aiguiser /egize/ [1] *vtr* **1** (rendre tranchant, pointu) to sharpen [*lame, griffes, crocs*]; **2** (rendre plus vif) to whet [*appétit*]; to arouse [*curiosité*]; to heighten [*sentiment*]; to stimulate [*concurrence*]; to sharpen [*intelligence*]; to hone [*style*]; **ton histoire continue d'~ les curiosités** your story still arouses keen interest.

aiguiseur /egizœʀ/ ▶**510** *nm* knife grinder.

aiguisoir /egizwaʀ/ *nm* **1** (pour couteaux) knife sharpener; **2** C (taille-crayons) pencil sharpener.

aïkido /ajkido/ ▶**449** *nm* aikido.

ail, *pl* **~s** or **aulx** /aj, o/ *nm* garlic; **sauce à l'~** garlic sauce; **piquer un gigot d'~** to put slivers of garlic in a leg of lamb.

aile /ɛl/ *nf* **1** (d'oiseau) wing; **~ de poulet** chicken wing; **2** (d'avion) wing; **3** (de bâtiment) wing; **4** Pol (de mouvement) wing; (d'armée) flank; **5** (de moulin) sail; Agric (de charrue) wing; Bot (de plante, fleur) wing; Pêche (de chalut) wing; **6** Sport (au football, rugby) wing; **7** Aut (de voiture) wing GB, fender US; **~ avant droite** front right-hand wing GB ou fender US.
■ **~ de corbeau** (noir) raven black; **~ delta** Aviat delta wing; Sport hang-glider; **~ de l'ilium** Anat ala (ossis) ilii; **~ libre** Sport (engin) hang-glider; (activité) hang-gliding; **~ marchante** Mil moving flank; **~ du nez** Anat wing of the nose, ala nasi spéc; **~ du sacrum** Anat ala sacralis.
IDIOMES **battre de l'~, ne battre que d'une ~** [*croissance*] to have fallen off; [*économie, entreprise*] to be struggling; **se sentir pousser des ~s** to feel exhilarated; **rogner les ~s de qn** to clip sb's wings; **prendre un coup dans l'~** to suffer a setback; **avoir un coup dans l'~**° to be the worse for drink; **voler de ses propres ~s** to stand on one's own two feet; **la peur leur a donné des ~s** fear lent them wings; **vouloir voler avant d'avoir des ~s** to want to run before one can walk.

ailé, **~e** /ele/ *adj* winged.

aileron /ɛlʀɔ̃/ *nm* **1** (d'oiseau) wing tip; (de requin) fin; **soupe aux ~s de requin** shark's fin soup; **2** (d'avion) aileron; **3** Naut (de coque) fin; **4** (de planche de surf) skeg; **5** (de voiture de course) aerofoil GB, airfoil US; **6** Archit console.

ailette /ɛlɛt/ *nf* **1** Tech (de radiateur) fin; (de turbine, ventilateur) blade; **~ de refroidissement** cooling fin; **2** Astronaut, Mil (de fusée, missile) fin; Aviat (d'aile) winglet; **bombe/obus à ~s** Mil fin-stabilized bomb/shell.

ailier /elje/ *nm* **1** (au football) winger; **~ droit/gauche** left/right winger GB ou wing US; **2** (au rugby) wing three-quarter.

aillade /ajad/ *nf* garlic dressing.

ailler /aje/ [1] *vtr* to put garlic into [*salade, gigot*]; **la salade est trop aillée** there's too much garlic in the salad.

ailleurs /ajœʀ/ **I** *adv* elsewhere; **ici comme ~** here as elsewhere; **des artistes venus d'~** artists from other places; **le problème est ~** the problem lies elsewhere; **l'essentiel est ~** that's not the issue; **ce qui se fait ~** what is done elsewhere; **nulle part ~** nowhere else; **partout ~** everywhere else; **quelque part ~** somewhere else; **ici ou ~, ça m'est égal** here or somewhere else, it's all the same to me; ▶**voir**.
II d'ailleurs *loc adv* besides, moreover, what's more; **d'~, je n'étais pas là** besides, I wasn't there; **ils ont d'~ reconnu les faits** besides, they have acknowledged the facts; **il a fait des tentatives, d'~ fort timides** he made some rather feeble attempts; **l'excuse de mon mal de tête, d'~ bien réel, m'a permis de partir plus tôt** the excuse of having a headache, which I might add was true, allowed me to leave earlier.
III par ailleurs *loc adv* **par ~, l'inflation a atteint un taux record** in addition, inflation has reached a record level; **par ~, je n'ai pas encore reçu les marchandises** may I also add that I have not yet received the goods; **des efforts pour comprendre un problème par ~ complexe** efforts to understand a problem which is in some respects complex; **ils se sont par ~ engagés à faire** they have also undertaken to do.
IDIOMES **être ~, avoir l'esprit ~** to be miles away.

ailloli = **aïoli**.

aimable /ɛmabl/ *adj* **1** (sympathique) [*personne*] pleasant; [*mot*] kind; **c'est très ~ à vous** it's very kind of you; **votre ~ invitation** your kind invitation; **nous informons notre ~ clientèle que** we wish to inform our customers that; **trop ~!** how very kind of you!; **2** (poli) [*lettre, propos*] polite; **c'était une façon ~ de refuser** it was a polite way of saying no; **3** littér [*lieu, visage*] pleasant; **4**‡ (digne d'amour) [*personne*] amiable‡.
IDIOMES **être ~ comme une porte de prison** to be a miserable so-and-so.

aimablement /ɛmabləmɑ̃/ *adv* (avec politesse) politely; (avec gentillesse) kindly.

aimant, **~e** /ɛmɑ̃, ɑ̃t/ **I** *adj* affectionate, loving; **être d'une nature ~e** to have an affectionate nature.
II *nm* **1** (corps magnétique) magnet; **2** Minér **~ naturel** magnetite, lodestone.

aimantation /ɛmɑ̃tasjɔ̃/ *nf* magnetization.

aimanter /ɛmɑ̃te/ [1] *vtr* to magnetize.

aimé, **~e** /eme/ **I** *pp* ▶**aimer**.
II *pp adj* [*personne, visage*] beloved; **une femme très ~e** a woman who is greatly ou very much loved.
III *nm,f* liter **mon ~(e)** my beloved littér.

aimer /eme/ [1] **I** *vtr* **1** (d'amour) to love [*homme, femme, enfants, parents, conjoint*]; **~ qn à la folie** to adore sb; ▶**châtier**; **2** (apprécier) to like, to be fond of [*personne, animal, activité, aliment*]; **il t'aime bien/beaucoup** he's fond/very fond of you; **~ faire, ~ à faire**† to like doing, to be fond of doing; **j'aime à croire que** I like to think that; **~ la chasse/les voyages** to like hunting/travelling[GB]; **cette plante aime l'ombre** this plant likes shade; **je n'aime pas beaucoup cet écrivain** I don't like this writer much; **elle n'aime pas le voir soucieux** she doesn't like to see him worried; **je n'aime pas qu'on me dise ce que j'ai à faire/qu'on me réponde sur ce ton** I don't like being told what to do/being spoken to in that tone; **je n'aimerais pas être à sa place** I wouldn't like to be in his/her shoes; **j'aimerais que tu me dises la vérité** I'd like you to tell me the truth; **aimeriez-vous un peu de thé?** would you like some tea?; **j'aime quand tu me fais ça!** I like ou love it when you do that to me!; **j'aime bien l'opéra/mes collègues** I like opera/my colleagues; **il aime autant le vin que la bière** he likes wine as much as he likes beer; **j'aimerais autant rester à la maison ce soir** I'd rather stay at home tonight, I'd sooner stay at home tonight; **j'aime autant te dire que tu vas le regretter/qu'il n'était pas content!** I may as well tell you that you're going to regret it/that he wasn't very pleased!; **~ mieux** to prefer; **j'aime mieux nager que courir** I prefer swimming to running; **j'aimerais mieux que tu ne le leur dises pas** I'd rather you didn't tell them; **elle aurait mieux aimé que je ne sois pas là** she would have preferred me not to be there; **il n'a rien de cassé? j'aime mieux ça!** (ton de soulagement) nothing's broken? thank goodness!; **vous acceptez de me rembourser? j'aime mieux ça!** (ton menaçant) you agree to pay me back? that's more like it!
II s'aimer *vpr* **1** (d'amour) to love each other; **aimez-vous les uns les autres** love one another; **2** (s'apprécier) **elles s'aiment bien** they like each other; **3** (s'apprécier soi-même) **je ne m'aime pas tellement avec les cheveux courts** I don't like my hair short, I don't think short hair suits me; **4** (faire l'amour) to make love; **ils se sont aimés toute la nuit** they made love all night (long).
IDIOMES **qui m'aime me suive** if you love me, follow me; **elle/il m'aime un peu, beaucoup, passionnément, à la folie, pas du tout** she/he loves me, loves me not, loves me...

Ain /ɛ̃/ ▶**357**, **692** *nprm* (rivière, département) **l'~** the Ain.

aine /ɛn/ *nf* groin.

aîné, **~e** /ene/ **I** *adj* (de deux) elder; (de plus de deux) eldest.
II *nm,f* **1** (enfant) (premier de deux) elder son/daughter, elder child; (premier de plus de deux) eldest son/daughter, eldest child; **les deux ~es ont quitté la maison** the two eldest daughters have left home; **2** (frère, sœur) elder ou older brother/sister; **3** (personne plus âgée) elder; (personne la plus âgée) oldest; **c'est mon ~** he's older than me; **j'ai épousé une femme de vingt ans mon ~e** I married a woman twenty years older than me; **l'~ du groupe** the oldest (person) in the group; **les ~s de la tribu** the elders of the tribe.

aînesse /enɛs/ *nf* **droit d'~** the law of primogeniture.

ainsi /ɛ̃si/ **I** *adv* **1** (de cette manière) **c'est ~ que l'on faisait le beurre** that's the way ou how they used to make butter; **est-ce ~ que tu parles à ta mère?** is that the way ou how you speak to your mother?; **le mélange ~ obtenu** the mixture obtained in this way; **je t'imaginais ~** that's how I imagined you; **le monde est ~ fait que** the world is made in such a way that; **elle est ~** that's how ou the way she is; **~ va la vie** such is life, that's the way it goes; **puisque c'est ~** since that's how it is, since that's the way it is; **Charlotte, c'est ~ qu'on m'appelait** Charlotte, that's what they used to call me; **s'il en est ~** if that's how it is ou the way it is; **il n'en est pas ~ de tous nos amis** this is not the case with all our friends; **les mois ont passé ~** thus the months went by; **~ parlait le prophète** thus spoke the prophet; **le jury se compose ~** the panel is made up as follows; **~ fut fait** that's what was done; **~ soit-il** Relig amen; ▶**suite**; **2** (introduisant une conclusion) thus liter, so; **~, depuis 1989...** thus, since 1989...; **l'enfant apprendra ~ à être indépendant** the child will thus learn to be independent; **partez tôt, vous éviterez ~ les embouteillages** leave early, that way you'll avoid the traffic jams; **~ tu nous quittes?** so you're leaving us then?; **~ (donc) vous niez les faits** so you deny the facts (then); **c'est ~ que nous sachant seuls...** and so, knowing (that) we were alone…; **3** (de même) liter **comme un coup de tonnerre éclate, ~ se répandit la nouvelle** like a bolt from the blue, the news spread.

II ainsi que *loc conj* **1** (de même que) as well as; **les employés ~ que leurs conjoints sont invités** employees together with their partners are invited; **l'Italie ~ que quatre autres pays d'Europe participe à ce projet** Italy, along with four other European countries, is taking part in this project; **l'exposition comprend des aquarelles, des huiles ~ que quelques sculptures** the exhibition includes watercolours[GB] and oils as well as some sculptures; **la question portait sur la vie de l'auteur ~ que sur ses influences littéraires** the question concerned the life of the author as well as his literary influences; **2** (comme) as; **~ que nous en avions convenu** as we had agreed; **je vous écris dès mon arrivée, ~ que je l'avais promis** I have just arrived and I am writing to you as I promised; **il a remis sa démission ~ que le réclamaient les chefs du parti** he handed in his resignation as the party leaders were demanding; **elle marchait ~ qu'un automate** she was walking like a robot; **~ que l'a précisé Paul** as Paul pointed out.

aïoli /ajɔli/ *nm*: *provençal garlic mayonnaise.*

air /ɛʀ/ *nm* **1** (que l'on respire) air; **l'~ marin/de la campagne** the sea/country air; **le bon ~** clean air; **l'~ est vif/pollué** the air is bracing/polluted; **l'~ est confiné** it's stuffy; **changer** or **renouveler l'~ d'une pièce** to let some air circulate in a room; **mettre qch à l'~** to put sth out to air [*lit, tapis*]; **se promener les fesses à l'~** to walk around with a bare bottom; **à l'~ libre** outside, outdoors; **faire sécher du linge à l'~** to dry one's washing outside; **concert en plein ~** open-air concert; **activités de plein ~** outdoor activities; **la vie au grand ~** outdoor life; **on manque d'~ ici** it's stuffy in here; **de l'~!** lit let's get some air in here!; (va-t'en)○ get lost○!; **aller prendre l'~** to go out and get some fresh air; **2** (brise, vent) **il y a de l'~** (dans une pièce) there's a draught GB ou draft US; (à l'extérieur) there's a breeze; **il n'y a pas d'~** there's no wind; **un déplacement d'~** a rush of air; **un courant d'~** a draught GB ou draft US; **ça fait de l'~** there's a draught GB ou draft US; **3** (autour de la terre) air; **jeter qch/tirer en l'~** to throw sth/to shoot into the air; **rester en l'~** to stay in the air; **avoir les bras/les pieds en l'~** to have one's arms/one's feet (up) in the air; **monter** or **s'élever dans les ~s** to rise into the air; **planer dans les ~s** to glide into the air; **par les ~s, par ~** by air; **transport par ~** transport by air; **regarder en l'~** to look up; **avoir le nez en l'~** to daydream; **dans l'~** fig [*réforme, idée*] in the air; **il y a un virus dans l'~** there's a virus going around; **en l'~** [*menace, paroles, promesse*] empty; [*projet, idée*] vague; **parler en l'~** to speculate; **envoyer** or **flanquer qch en l'~**○ to send sth flying; **tout mettre en l'~**○ (mettre en désordre) to make a dreadful mess; (jeter) to chuck everything out; (faire échouer) to ruin everything; **ils ont mis (toute) la maison en l'~**○ they made a (dreadful) mess of the house; **4** (manière d'être) manner; (expression) expression; **avec un ~ résolu/prétentieux** in a resolute/pretentious manner; **avoir un drôle d'~** to look odd ou funny; **avoir un ~ très distingué** to look very distinguished; **un ~ bête/intelligent** a stupid/an intelligent expression; **afficher un ~ dégoûté/blasé** to affect an expression of disgust/of indifference; **avec son petit ~ supérieur/coquin** with that superior/mischievous expression of his/hers; **d'un ~ serieux/triste** with a serious/sad expression; **d'un ~ fâché/désolé** angrily/helplessly; **il y a un ~ de famille entre vous deux** you two share a family likeness; **avoir l'~ épuisé/heureux** to look shattered/happy; **elle a eu l'~ fin(e)!** she looked (like) a fool!; **tu as l'~ malin maintenant!** iron you look a right fool now!; **il avait l'~ d'un prince** he looked like a prince; **la maison a l'~ d'un taudis** the house looks like a slum; **leur histoire (m')a (tout) l'~ d'un mensonge** their story sounds like a lie (to me); **cela m'en a tout l'~** it seems ou looks like it to me; **j'aurais l '~ de quoi?** how would that make me look?; **il n'a l'~ de rien mais il…** he doesn't look it but he…; **il est futé sans en avoir l'~** he's sly although he doesn't look it; **cela n'a l'~ de rien mais** it may not look it, but; **il a l'~ de comprendre** he seems to understand; **cela a l'~ d'être bien/solide** it looks good/strong; **cela a l'~ d'être une usine** it looks like a factory; **ils n'ont pas l'~ de se rendre compte** they don't seem to realize; **il a l'~ de vouloir faire beau** it looks as if it's going to be fine ou nice US; **5** (ambiance) **un ~ d'abandon/de déchéance** an air of neglect/of decay; **il règne un ~ de fête** there's a carnival atmosphere; **la réunion avait un ~ de déjà-vu** there was a feeling of déjà-vu about the meeting; **6** (mélodie) tune; **l'~ d'une chanson** the tune of ou to a song; **siffler/fredonner un ~** to whistle/to hum a tune; **un ~ de jazz** a jazz tune; **un ~ d'opéra** an aria; **jouer toujours le même ~** lit to play the same tune over and over again; fig to come out with the same old story; **danser sur un ~ de tango/valse** to dance to a tango/waltz.

■ ~ climatisé conditioned air; **~ comprimé** compressed air; **~ conditionné** (système) air-conditioning; (que l'on respire) conditioned air; **~ liquide** Tech liquid air.

IDIOMES **il ne manque pas d'~**○ he's got a nerve; **brasser** or **remuer de l'~**○ to give the impression of being busy; **prendre** or **se donner des grands ~s** to put on airs; **j'ai besoin de changer d'~** (d'environnement) I need a change of scene; (par agacement) I need to go and do something else.

airain† /ɛʀɛ̃/ *nm* bronze.

air-air /ɛʀɛʀ/ *adj inv* [*missile*] air-to-air.

airbag /ɛʀbag/ *nm* air bag.

aire /ɛʀ/ *nf* **1** (domaine) sphere; **~ économique/culturelle** economic/cultural sphere; **étendre son ~ d'activité** to extend one's sphere of activity; **2** (surface) area; **3** (nid) eyrie.

■ ~ d'atterrissage (pour avions) landing strip; (pour hélicoptère) landing pad; **~ de battage** threshing floor; **~ de chargement** loading bay; **~ continentale** continental shield; **~ de jeu** playground; **~ de lancement** launching pad, launch pad GB; **~ linguistique** linguistic region; **~ de loisirs** recreation area; **~ de pique-nique** picnic area; **~ de repos** rest area; **~ de services** services *pl* GB, motorway GB ou freeway US service station; **~ de stationnement** parking area.

airedale /ɛʀdal/ *nm* Airedale (terrier).

airelle /ɛʀɛl/ *nf* (myrtille) bilberry; (baie rouge) cranberry.

air-mer /ɛʀmɛʀ/ *adj inv* [*missile*] air-to-sea.

air-sol /ɛʀsɔl/ *adj inv* [*missile*] air-to-ground.

air-surface /ɛʀsyʀfas/ *adj inv* [*missile*] air-to-surface.

aisance /ɛzɑ̃s/ *nf* **1** (facilité) ease; **ton ~ à faire** the ease with which you do; **l'~ de tes mouvements/ta démarche** the ease with which you move/walk; **avec ~** [*parler, se mouvoir*] with ease; **manquer d'~** [*style, manières, personne*] to lack ease; **l'~ de ton style** your flowing style; **2** (opulence) comfort, affluence; **vivre dans l'~** to live comfortably; **l'~ financière** or **matérielle** financial security; **3** (en couture) **donner de l'~ à une veste** (à la confection) to make a jacket roomy; (après confection) to let out a jacket.

■ ~ budgétaire affluence (of money); **~ monétaire** = **~ budgétaire**; **~ de trésorerie** abundance of cash.

aise /ɛz/ **I** *adj* liter pleased; **être bien** or **fort ~ de faire** to be very pleased (to do); **je suis bien ~ que tu puisses venir** I am very pleased you can come; **j'en suis fort ~** hum I'm very pleased about it.

II *nf* liter (contentement) pleasure; **d'~** [*sourire, rougir, ronronner*] with pleasure; [*soupirs*] of pleasure; **être comblé** or **transporté d'~** to be filled with pleasure.

III aises *nfpl* **tenir à** or **aimer ses ~s** to like one's creature comforts; **il prenait ses ~s sur le canapé** he was stretched out on the sofa.

IV à l'aise *loc* **être à l'~** or **à son ~** (physiquement) to be comfortable; (financièrement) to be comfortably off; (psychologiquement) to be at ease, to feel comfortable (**avec qn** with sb); **se sentir mal à l'~** (physiquement) to feel uncomfortable; (psychologiquement) to feel uncomfortable ou ill at ease (**avec qn** with sb); **mettre qn à l'~** or **à son ~** to put sb at his/her ease; **mettre qn mal à l'~** to make sb feel ill at ease; **mets-toi à l'~** or **à ton ~** make yourself comfortable; **faire qch à l'~**○ to do sth easily; **'tu arriveras à porter le sac?'—'à l'~○!'** 'will you manage to carry the bag?'—'no problem!'; **en prendre à son ~ avec qch/qn** to make free with sth/sb; **vous en parlez à votre ~** it is easy for you to talk; **à votre ~!** as you wish ou like!

aisé, ~e /eze/ *adj* **1** (simple) [*procédé, tâche*] easy; **il n'est pas ~ de faire qch** it is not easy to do sth; **2** (cossu) [*commerçant, famille, quartier*] wealthy; **être ~** to be well-off, to be comfortably off; **les classes ~es** the well-off; **3** (sans contrainte) [*manières*] easy; [*style*] flowing.

aisément /ezemɑ̃/ *adv* easily.

Aisne /ɛn/ **▶ 357**, **692** *nprm* (rivière, département) **l'~** the Aisne.

aisselle /ɛsɛl/ *nf* armpit.

Aix-la-Chapelle /ɛkslaʃapɛl/ **▶ 857** *npr* Aachen.

aixois, ~e /ɛkswa, az/ **▶ 857** *adj* of Aix-en-Provence.

Aixois, ~e /ɛʀswa, az/ **▶ 857** *nm,f* (natif) native of Aix-en-Provence; (habitant) inhabitant of Aix-en-Provence.

ajonc /aʒɔ̃/ *nm* gorse bush; **dans les ~s** in the gorse, in the gorse bushes.

ajour /aʒuʀ/ *nm* Cout openwork **₵**.

ajouré, ~e /aʒuʀe/ **I** *pp* **▶ ajourer**.

II *pp adj* **1** Cout [*lingerie, dentelle, broderie*] (entier) openwork (*épith*); (bord) hemstitched; **en mailles ~es** with a lacy pattern; **2** Archit [*clocher, balcon*] with ornamental apertures.

ajourer /aʒuʀe/ [1] *vtr* **1** Cout (le bord) to hemstitch; (l'ensemble) to embroider [sth] in openwork [*napperon, lingerie*]; **2** Archit to make ornamental apertures in [*balcon, clocher*].

ajournement /aʒuʀnəmɑ̃/ *nm* (de voyage, décision) postponement; (de débat, procès) adjournment; **~ de peine** or **du prononcé de la peine** *non-imposition of a sentence.*

ajourner /aʒuʀne/ [1] *vtr* to postpone, to put off [*voyage, projet, décision*]; to adjourn [*débat, procès*] **les débats sont ajournés d'une semaine** discussions are adjourned for a week; **un procès ajourné** an adjourned trial.

ajout /aʒu/ *nm* addition; **faire des ~s** to make additions (**à** to).

ajouter /aʒute/ [1] **I** *vtr* to add (**à** to); **je n'ai rien à ~** I've nothing to add; **j'ajouterais que** I would (also) add that; **si l'on ajoute à cela que** if one adds to that the fact that; **permettez-moi d'~ une remarque à ce que vous venez de dire** allow me to make an additional comment on what you've just said; **~ foi à qch** fml to put faith in sth; **ne pas ~ foi à qch** fml to put no faith in sth;

la chaleur ajoutée à la pollution fait que l'air est irrespirable the heat on top of all the pollution means that it is impossible to breathe; **j'ajoute 8** (dans un calcul) add 8; **ajoute une assiette, il reste dîner** put out another plate, he's staying for dinner.

II **ajouter à** *vtr ind* to add to; **des ordres contradictoires ajoutaient à la confusion** contradictory orders added to the confusion; **en parler ne ferait qu'~ à leur peine** talking about it would only add to their grief.

III **s'ajouter** *vpr* to be added to each other; **s'~ à** to be added to; **à cela s'ajoute**... to that may be added...; **les désordres sociaux viennent s'~ aux difficultés économiques** on top of the economic difficulties there is also social unrest.

ajustage /aʒystaʒ/ *nm* fitting.

ajusté, **~e** /aʒyste/ I *pp* ▶ **ajuster**.
II *pp adj* [*veste*] tailored; [*robe, corsage*] close fitting.

ajustement /aʒystəmɑ̃/ *nm* **1** Tech fit; **2** (adaptation) adjustment (**avec** with); **~ des prix** price adjustment; **plan d'~ structurel** structural adjustment programme[GB].

ajuster /aʒyste/ [1] *vtr* **1** (régler) to adjust [*taux, prix, horaire*]; to alter [*robe, chemise*] (**à** to); to calibrate [*balance*]; to tighten [*rênes*]; **~ qch à** or **sur qch** lit to make sth fit sth; **~ un manche à une brosse** to adjust a handle to fit a brush; **~ la théorie à la pratique** to adapt the theory to the practice; **2** (arranger) to arrange [*coiffure*]; to adjust [*tenue*]; **3** (viser) to take aim at [*lapin*]; **~ son tir** or **coup** lit to adjust one's aim; fig to fix a more precise target.

ajusteur /aʒystœʀ/ ▶ 510 *nm* fitter.

akène /akɛn/ *nm* achene.

Alabama /alabama/ ▶ 692 *nprm* Alabama.

alacrité /alakʀite/ *nf* alacrity sout; **avec ~** with alacrity.

Aladin /aladɛ̃/ *npr* Aladdin.

alaise = **alèse**.

alambic /alɑ̃bik/ *nm* Chimie still.

alambiqué, **~e** /alɑ̃bike/ *adj* [*expression, style*] convoluted; [*explication*] tortuous.

alangui, **~e** /alɑ̃gi/ I *pp* ▶ **alanguir**.
II *pp adj* languid.

alanguir /alɑ̃giʀ/ fml [3] *vtr* **1** (rendre langoureux) [*amour, musique*] to make [sb] languid; **2** (rendre languissant) [*maladie*] to sap [sb's] energy; [*chaleur*] to enervate, to make [sb] listless.

alanguissement /alɑ̃gismɑ̃/ *nm* languor.

alarmant, **~e** /alaʀmɑ̃, ɑ̃t/ *adj* alarming.

alarme /alaʀm/ *nf* **1** (appareil) alarm; **sonner l'~** to sound the alarm; **2** (alerte) alarm, alert; **donner l'~** to raise the alarm; **c'est ce qui a donné l'~** that was what made us/them realize something was wrong; **3** (peur) alarm; **une population tenue en ~** a population kept perpetually on its guard; **en état d'~** in a state of perpetual alarm.

alarmer /alaʀme/ [1] I *vtr* to alarm [*personne, population*].
II **s'alarmer** *vpr* to become alarmed (**de qch** about sth); **vous n'avez aucune raison de vous ~** there's no cause for alarm.

alarmisme /alaʀmism/ *nm* alarmism.

alarmiste /alaʀmist/ *adj, nmf* alarmist.

Alaska /alaska/ ▶ 692 *nprm* Alaska.

albanais, **~e** /albanɛ, ɛz/ I ▶ 537 *adj* Albanian.
II ▶ 462 *nm* Ling Albanian.

Albanais, **~e** /albanɛ, ɛz/ ▶ 537 *nm,f* Albanian.

Albanie /albani/ ▶ 321 *nprf* Albania.

albâtre /albɑtʀ/ *nm* alabaster; **un vase en ~** an alabaster vase; **une peau d'~** a skin as white as alabaster.
IDIOMES **blanc comme l'~** as white as alabaster.

albatros /albatʀos/ *nm inv* albatross.

Alberta /albɛʀta/ ▶ 692 *nprm* Alberta.

albigeois, **~e** /albiʒwa, az/ *adj* Albigensian.

Albigeois /albiʒwa/ *nprmpl* **les ~** the Albigenses; **croisade contre les ~** crusade against the Albigenses.

albinisme /albinism/ *nm* albinism.

albinos /albinos/ *adj inv, nmf inv* albino.

Albion /albjɔ̃/ *nprf* Albion; **la perfide ~** perfidious Albion.

album /albɔm/ *nm* **1** (livre illustré) illustrated book; **~ de bandes dessinées** comic strip book; **2** (classeur, cahier) album; **~ de photographies/cartes postales/timbres** photograph/postcard/stamp album; **3** (disque) album; **double ~** double album.
■ **~ à colorier** colouring[GB] book; **~ de famille** family album.

albumen /albymɛn/ *nm* albumen.

albumine /albymin/ *nf* albumin; **avoir de l'~**○ to suffer from albuminuria spéc.

albumineux, **-euse** /albyminø, øz/ *adj* albuminous.

albuminurie /albyminyʀi/ *nf* albuminuria.

alcali /alkali/ *nm* **1** (ammoniaque) ammonia; **~ volatil** ammonia; **2** Chimie alkali.

alcalin, **~e** /alkalɛ̃, in/ *adj* alkaline.

alcalinité /alkalinite/ *nf* alkalinity.

alcaloïde /alkalɔid/ *nm* alkaloid.

Alceste /alsɛst/ *npr* Mythol Alcestis.

alchimie /alʃimi/ *nf* alchemy.

alchimique /alʃimik/ *adj* alchemic.

alchimiste /alʃimist/ *nmf* alchemist.

alcolo○ /alkolo/ *nmf* drunk.

alcool /alkɔl/ *nm* **1** (boisson) alcoholic drink, spirit; **boire de l'~** to drink alcohol; **vous prendrez bien un petit ~?** will you have a little drop of something?; **~ de poire** pear brandy; **sans ~** [*cocktail*] non-alcoholic; [*bière*] alcohol-free; **elle ne tient pas du tout l'~** she cannot take ou hold her drink at all; **l'~ m'est interdit** I'm not allowed to drink alcohol; **2** (alcoolisme) drink; **s'adonner à** or **sombrer dans l'~** to take to drink; **3** (substance) alcohol; **avoir une forte teneur en ~** to have a high alcohol content.
■ **~ absolu** absolute alcohol; **~ blanc** clear fruit brandy; **~ à brûler** methylated spirits, meths○ GB; **~ camphré** camphorated alcohol; **~ éthylique** ethyl alcohol; **~ à 90°** surgical spirit GB, rubbing alcohol US; **~ de menthe** mentholated alcohol.

alcoolat /alkɔla/ *nm* alcohol-based medicine.

alcoolémie /alkɔlemi/ *nf* presence of alcohol in the blood; **contrôle d'~** checking for alcohol in the blood; **taux d'~** level of alcohol in the blood.

alcoolique /alkɔlik/ *adj, nmf* alcoholic.

alcoolisation /alkɔlizasjɔ̃/ *nf* alcoholization.

alcoolisé, **~e** /alkɔlize/ I *pp* ▶ **alcooliser**.
II *pp adj* alcoholic; **une boisson peu/non ~e** a low-alcohol/non-alcoholic drink.

alcooliser /alkɔlize/ [1] I *vtr* to alcoholize.
II **s'alcooliser**○ *vpr* hum to get drunk.

alcoolisme /alkɔlism/ *nm* alcoholism.

alcootest /alkɔtɛst/ *nm* **1** (appareil) Breathalyzer®; **2** (contrôle) breath test.

Alcotest® /alkɔtɛst/ *nm* Breathalyzer®.

alcôve /alkov/ *nf* alcove; **d'~** [*histoires, secrets*] of the boudoir.

alcyon /alsjɔ̃/ *nm* **1** Mythol halcyon; **2** Zool dead man's fingers (+ *v sg*).

aléa /alea/ *nm* (de temps, nature, marché) vagary; (économique, financier) hazard; **les ~s du métier** occupational hazards.

aléatoire /aleatwaʀ/ *adj* **1** [*événements, succès, résultat*] unpredictable; [*profession*] insecure, risky; **le caractère ~ de** the unpredictability of [*résultat*]; the unstable nature of [*emploi*]; **2** Littérat, Mus aleatory; **3** Math, Stat random; **4** Jur [*acte, contrat*] aleatory.

alémanique /alemanik/ ▶ 462 *adj, nm* Alemannic.

ALÉNA /alena/ *nm* (*abbr* = **Accord de libre-échange nord-américain**) NAFTA.

alêne /alɛn/ *nf* awl.

alentour /alɑ̃tuʀ/ I *adv* surrounding; **visite de la ville et de la région ~** visit of the town and surrounding area; **les maisons d'~** the surrounding houses.
II **alentours** *nmpl* (environs) surrounding areas (*sg*); **les ~s de la ferme/ville** the area around the farm/town; **il n'y a personne aux** or **dans les ~s** there is noone in the surrounding area.
III **aux alentours de** *loc prép* **1** (de lieu) around; **aux ~s de la place/Nîmes** around the square/Nîmes; **2** (de chiffre, date) about, around; **aux ~s de l'an 2000** about the year 2000; **il y avait aux ~s de 1 000 personnes** there were about 1,000 people.

aléoute /aleut/ ▶ 462 I *adj* Aleutian.
II *nm* Ling Aleut.

Aléoute /aleut/ *nmf* Aleut.

Aléoutiennes /aleusjɛn/ ▶ 416 *adj fpl* **les îles ~** the Aleutian islands.

alerte /alɛʀt/ I *adj* (vif) [*personne, esprit*] alert; [*démarche*] brisk; [*style, jeu, interprétation*] lively.
II *nf* alert; **être en état d'~** lit to be in a state of alert; fig to be on the alert; **en cas d'~ grave**... in the event of a serious alert...; **donner l'~** to raise the alarm; **donner l'~ à qn** to alert sb; **fausse ~** false alarm; **~ générale** full alert.
■ **~ aérienne** air raid warning; **~ à la bombe** bomb scare.

alerter /alɛʀte/ [1] *vtr* **1** (donner l'alerte) to alert [*police, autorités*]; **2** (informer) to alert [*opinion publique*] (**sur qch** to sth); to inform [*personne, service*]; **les pompiers alertés sont arrivés rapidement** the firemen arrived soon after being alerted.

alésage /alezaʒ/ *nm* **1** (usinage) boring; **2** (partie alésée) bore; **3** Aut (diamètre des cylindres) cylinder bore.

alèse /alɛz/ *nf* undersheet, mattress protector; (imperméable) waterproof undersheet, waterproof mattress protector.

alésé, **~e** /aleze/ *adj* Hérald couped.

aléser /aleze/ [14] *vtr* to bore.

aléseur /alezœʀ/ *nm* **1** ▶ 510 boring-machine operator; **2** Mines reamer; **~ à rouleaux** rotary reamer.

aléseuse /alezœz/ *nf* Mécan boring machine.

aléseuse-fraiseuse, *pl* **aléseuses-fraiseuses** /alezœzfʀɛzœz/ *nf* boring and milling machine.

alésoir /alezwaʀ/ *nm* Mécan reamer.

alevin /alvɛ̃/ *nm* young fish.

alevinage /alvinaʒ/ *nm* stocking with young fish.

Alexandre /alɛksɑ̃dʀ/ *npr* Alexander; **~ le Grand** Alexander the Great.

Alexandrie /alɛksɑ̃dʀi/ ▶ 857 *npr* **1** (en Égypte) Alexandria; **2** (en Italie) Alessandria.

alexandrin /alɛksɑ̃dʀɛ̃/ *adj m, nm* alexandrine.

alezan, **~e** /alzɑ̃, an/ I *adj* [*cheval*] chestnut.
II *nm* chestnut (horse).

alfa /alfa/ *nm* **1** (herbe) esparto grass; **2** (fibre) esparto; **3** (papier) esparto paper, alfa paper.

algarade /algaʀad/ *nf* quarrel; **avoir une ~ avec qn** to have a quarrel with sb.

algèbre /alʒɛbʀ/ *nf* algebra.

algébrique /alʒebʀik/ *adj* algebraic.

algébriquement /alʒebʀikmɑ̃/ *adv* algebraically.

algébriste /alʒebʀist/ ▶ 510 *nmf* algebraist.

Alger /alʒe/ ▶ 857 *npr* Algiers.

Algérie /alʒeʀi/ ▶ 321 *nprf* Algeria.

algérien, **-ienne** /alʒeʀjɛ̃, ɛn/ ▶537 *adj* Algerian.

Algérien, **-ienne** /alʒeʀjɛ̃, ɛn/ ▶537 *nm,f* Algerian.

algérois, **~e** /alʒeʀwa, az/ ▶857 *adj* of Algiers.

Algérois, **~e** /alʒeʀwa, az/ ▶857 *nm,f* (natif) native of Alger; (habitant) inhabitant of Algiers.

algie /alʒi/ *nf* pain; **~ dentaire** toothache, odontalgia spéc.

ALGOL /algɔl/ *nm* (*abbr* = **algorithmic language**) ALGOL.

algonquin /algɔ̃kɛ̃/ ▶462 *nm* Ling **1** (famille de langues) Algonquian languages (*pl*); **2** (langue) Algonquin.

algorithme /algɔʀitm/ *nm* algorithm.

algorithmique /algɔʀitmik/ *adj* algorithmic.

algue /alg/ *nf* **1** Bot (d'eau douce) alga; (marine) seaweed ¢, alga spéc; **des ~s** (marines) seaweed, algae spéc; **2** Culin seaweed ¢. ■ **~s brunes** brown algae; **~s rouges** red algae; **~s vertes** green algae.

alias /aljas/ *adv* alias.

Ali Baba /alibaba/ *npr* **~ et les quarante voleurs** Ali Baba and the forty thieves; **une vraie caverne d'~** a real Aladdin's cave.

alibi /alibi/ *nm* **1** Jur alibi; **fournir un ~ très solide** to give a watertight alibi; **2** (prétexte) excuse; **il a invoqué l'~ d'une importante réunion de travail** he gave an important business meeting as his excuse; **servir d'~** to do as an excuse.

aliénabilité /aljenabilite/ *nf* Jur alienability.

aliénable /aljenabl/ *adj* Jur alienable.

aliénant, **~e** /aljenɑ̃, ɑ̃t/ *adj* alienating.

aliénataire /aljenatɛʀ/ *nmf* Jur alienee.

aliénateur, **-trice** /aljenatœʀ, tʀis/ *nm,f* Jur alienator.

aliénation /aljenasjɔ̃/ *nf* **1** (asservissement) alienation (**de** of); **2** Jur alienation; **3**† Méd **~ (mentale)** insanity, (mental) alienation†.

aliéné, **~e** /aljene/ *nm,f* Méd insane person.

aliéner /aljene/ [14] **I** *vtr* **1** Jur (céder) to alienate [*terre*]; **2** (perdre) to lose [*liberté*]; (par renoncement) to give up: **3** (détourner) **~ qn à qn** to alienate sb from sb; **ces mesures lui ont aliéné une partie du vote socialiste** these measures have lost him a section of the socialist vote; **4** Philos, Sociol to alienate [*personne*].

II s'aliéner *vpr* **1** (détourner) to alienate [*confrères, électorat, opinion publique*]; **s'~ qch** to lose sth; **tu t'es aliéné leur estime** you have lost their esteem; **2** Philos, Sociol to be alienated (**à** from); **s'~ par le travail** to be alienated by work.

aliéniste /aljenist/ *nmf* alienist†, psychiatrist.

aligné, **~e** /aliɲe/ **I** *pp* ▶ **aligner**.

II *pp adj* Pol [*pays*] aligned; **non ~** non-aligned.

alignement /aliɲ(ə)mɑ̃/ **I** *nm* **1** (rang) row, line; **mettre qch à l'~ de qch** to line sth up with sth, to align sth with sth; **se mettre à/sortir de l'~** [*soldat*] to fall into/to step out of line; **~!** Mil fall in!; **2** (mise côte à côte) alignment; **3** (pour la conformité) alignment; **~ de qch sur qch** [*monnaie, salaires, parti, politique*] alignment of sth with sth; **l'~ de sa conduite sur celle de qn d'autre** bringing one's behaviour[GB] into line with sb else's; **4** (de voie publique) alignment.

II alignements *nmpl* Archéol alignments.

aligner /aliɲe/ [1] **I** *vtr* **1** (mettre côte à côte) to put [sth] in a line, to line [sth] up; (mettre en ligne droite) to line [sth] up, to align [*objets, points*]; **alignés contre le mur** lined up ou in a line against the wall; **des objets alignés** objects in a line; **stands alignés le long de la route** rows of stalls along the road; **2** (rendre conforme à) **~ qch sur qch** to bring sth into line with sth; **3** (énumérer) to give a list of [*statistiques, arguments, chiffres*]; (accumuler) to line up [*somme*]; to notch up○ [*kilomètres, bons résultats*]; **4**○ (payer) **tu peux ~ tes 100 balles**○ you can fork out○ your 100 francs; **~ les fautes/les excuses** to make one mistake/excuse after another ou the other; **5** (présenter) to line up [*joueurs, équipe*].

II s'aligner *vpr* **1** (être côte à côte) to be in a line; **2** (se mettre en file) to line up; (en formation militaire) to fall into line; **3 s'~ sur** to align oneself with [*pays, parti, idées*]; **s'~ sur le règlement** to conform with the rules; **4**○ (dans une compétition) **ils peuvent toujours s'~!** they can try but they don't stand a chance!

aligoté /aligɔte/ **I** *adj* [*cépage, vin*] aligoté (*épith*).

II *nm* white wine.

aliment /alimɑ̃/ **I** *nm* **1** (pour êtres humains) food; **un ~ rare** a rare food; **certains ~s** certain foods; **lavez/faites cuire vos ~s** wash/cook your food; **~s énergétiques/surgelés** high-energy/frozen foods; **dans quels ~s trouve-t-on du fer?** which foods contain iron?; **un ~ de base** a staple food; **2** (pour animaux) gén food; (pour animaux d'élevage) feed; **les ~s pour chats/chiens** catfood/dogfood; **les ~s pour volailles** poultry feed; **3** (pour plantes) nutrient; **les plantes puisent leurs ~s dans le sol** plants take their nutrients from the soil; **4** fig **fournir** or **être un ~ à qch** to feed sth.

II aliments *nmpl* Jur alimony, maintenance.

alimentaire /alimɑ̃tɛʀ/ *adj* **1** lit [*besoins, comportement, habitudes*] dietary; [*ration, aide, industrie, pénurie*] food; **prix ~s** food prices; **produits** or **denrées ~s** foodstuffs; **régime ~** diet; **trouble du comportement ~** eating disorder; **2** fig (pour survivre) **un travail purement ~** a job done purely to make a living; **roman ~** potboiler; **il fait de la traduction/peinture ~** he churns out translations/paintings for money.

alimentation /alimɑ̃tasjɔ̃/ *nf* **1** (manière de se nourrir) diet; **avoir une ~ saine** to have a healthy diet; **surveiller son ~** to watch one's diet; **une ~ riche en** a diet rich in; **l'~ de base** staple food; **2** (action de se nourrir) feeding; **~ artificielle** Méd artificial feeding; **être sous ~ artificielle** to be artificially fed; **3** Comm (produits alimentaires) food; (industrie) food industry; (commerce) food retailing; **20% de leur budget est consacré à l'~** 20% of their budget is devoted to food; **le rayon ~** the food section; **magasin d'~** food shop, grocery store; **4** (approvisionnement) (en papier, oxygène) feeding (**de** of); **l'~ en électricité/eau/mazout de qch** the electricity/water/fuel supply of sth; **l'~ d'une arme à feu** loading a firearm.

alimenter /alimɑ̃te/ [1] **I** *vtr* **1** to feed [*personne, animal*]; **~ au biberon** to bottle-feed; **~ qn artificiellement** to feed sb artificially; **2** (approvisionner) [*torrent, eau*] to feed [*lac, rivière, barrage, turbine*]; [*tuyau, système*] to feed [*chaudière, poêle, moteur*]; **~ qch en** to feed sth with [*papier, grain, données*]; **~ une chaudière en mazout** to feed ou supply a stove with oil; **~ un appareil en électricité** to power an appliance with electricity; **la centrale alimente toute la ville** the power station supplies the whole town with electricity; **~ un budget** to fund a budget; **3** fig to fuel [*conversation, hostilité, feu*].

II s'alimenter *vpr* **1** [*personne*] to eat; [*animal*] to feed; **il s'alimente bien/mal** he eats well/badly; **s'~ de** [*personne*] to live on; [*animal*] to feed on; **2** (en eau, gaz, électricité) [*ville, bâtiment*] **s'~ en** to be supplied with; **3** [*conversation, jalousie, haine*] **s'~ de** to thrive on.

alinéa /alinea/ *nm* (rentré) indentation; (ligne rentrée) indented line; (paragraphe) paragraph; **l'article 49, ~ 3 de la Constitution** article 49, paragraph 3 of the Constitution.

alisier /alizje/ *nm* sorb.
■ **~ blanc** whitebeam mountain ash.

alitement /alitmɑ̃/ *nm* bed rest.

aliter: **s'aliter** /alite/ [1] *vpr* to take to one's bed; **être/rester alité** to be/to remain confined to bed.

alizé /alize/ **I** *adj* **vent ~** trade wind.

II *nm* trade wind; **les ~s** trade winds.

Allah /alla/ *npr* Allah.

allaitement /alɛtmɑ̃/ *nm* (humain) feeding ¢; (animal) suckling ¢.
■ **~ artificiel** bottle-feeding; **~ maternel** breast-feeding; **~ mixte** mixed feeding.

allaiter /alete/ [1] *vtr* [*femme*] to breast-feed; [*animal*] to suckle; **~ au biberon** to bottle-feed.

allant, **~e** /alɑ̃, ɑ̃t/ **I** *adj* active, lively.

II *nm* drive, bounce; **avoir de l'~**, **être plein d'~** to have plenty of drive, to be full of bounce; **perdre son ~** to run out of steam.

alléchant, **~e** /aleʃɑ̃, ɑ̃t/ *adj* tempting.

allécher /aleʃe/ [14] *vtr* to tempt; **~ qn avec des promesses** to tempt sb with promises.

allée /ale/ **I** *nf* **1** (chemin) (de jardin, bois, parc) path; (de château) drive; (rue) road; **une petite ~** a little path; **une ~ de peupliers** an avenue of poplars; **les ~s du pouvoir** fig the corridors of power; **2** (entre des rangées de sièges) aisle; **~ (centrale)** aisle; **~ latérale** side aisle; **3** (escalier) staircase.

II allées *nfpl* **~s et venues** comings and goings; **surveiller les ~s et venues de qn** to watch sb's movements; **faire des ~s et venues entre les bureaux** to go back and forth between offices.
■ **~ cavalière** bridleway, bridle path; **~ forestière** forest trail.

allégation /alegasjɔ̃/ *nf* allegation; **~s mensongères** false allegations.

allégé, **~e** /aleʒe/ **I** *pp* ▶ **alléger**.

II *pp adj* [*beurre, yaourt, menu, cuisine*] low-fat; [*sucre, confiture*] diet (*épith*).

allégeance /aleʒɑ̃s/ *nf* allegiance; **faire acte d'~** to pledge one's allegiance.

allégement /alɛʒmɑ̃/ *nm* **1** (en poids) lightening; **2** (réduction) (de dette, charges) reduction; (de contrôles) relaxing; (de structures, procédures) simplification; **~ des effectifs** Scol reduction in numbers; **~ de la fiscalité** tax cuts (*pl*); **~ fiscal** tax relief; **3** Sport (en ski) unweighting; **4** (de conditions de détention) improvement, easing.

alléger /aleʒe/ [15] **I** *vtr* **1** (rendre moins lourd) to lighten [*véhicule, fardeau, bagages*]; **2** (rendre moins important) to reduce [*dette, charges*] (**de** by); to cut [*impôt*]; to simplify [*structure, dispositif, procédure*]; to relax [*contrôle*]; **~ les horaires scolaires** to reduce the school day; **~ les programmes** Scol, Univ to cut the content of courses; **3** (rendre moins pénible) to improve [*conditions de détention*]; to alleviate [*souffrances*].

II s'alléger *vpr* **1** (devenir moins lourd) [*fardeau, véhicule, bagages*] to get lighter; **2** (devenir moins important) [*dette, impôt, charges*] to be reduced; [*dispositif, structure, procédure*] to be simplified; [*embargo, contrôle*] to be relaxed; **3** (devenir moins pénible) [*conditions de détention*] to be improved.

allégorie /alegɔʀi/ *nf* allegory.

allégorique /alegɔʀik/ *adj* allegorical.

allégoriquement /alegɔʀikmɑ̃/ *adv* allegorically.

allègre /alɛgʀ/ *adj* [*texte, style*] light; [*récit, ton*] light-hearted; [*pas, humeur*] buoyant.

allégrement /alegʀəmɑ̃/ *adv* **1** (avec allégresse) joyfully; **2** iron (sans souci) blithely; **elle est partie ~ au Népal** she blithely went off to Nepal; **promettre ~ un allégement des impôts** to promise tax cuts blithely, to make a blithe promise of tax cuts; **mettre ~ qn en prison** to throw sb in jail without a second thought.

allégresse /alegʀɛs/ *nf* joy; **dans l'~** in joyful mood; **participer à l'~ générale** to share in the general rejoicing; **explosion d'~** joyous outburst.

allegretto /alegʀeto/ *nm, adv* allegretto.

allegro /alegʀo/ *adv* allegro.

alléguer /alege/ [14] *vtr* **1** (invoquer) to invoke [*exemple, précédent*]; **2** (prétexter) to allege, to claim.

allèle /alɛl/ *nm* allele.

alléluia /aleluja/ *nm* hallelujah.

Allemagne /almaɲ/ ▶ 321 *nprf* Germany; **la République fédérale d'~** the Federal Republic of Germany; **les deux ~s** the two Germanies; **l'~ unie** unified Germany; **l'ancienne ~ de l'Est** the former East Germany.

allemand, **~e** /almɑ̃, ɑ̃d/ **I** ▶ 537 *adj* German.

II ▶ 462 *nm* Ling German.

III allemande *nf* Danse, Mus allemande.

Allemand, **~e** /almɑ̃, ɑ̃d/ ▶ 537 *nm,f* German; **~ de l'Est/de l'Ouest** East/West German.

aller[1] /ale/ [9] **I** *v aux* **1** (marque le futur) **je vais partir** I'm leaving; **je vais rentrer chez moi/me coucher** I'm going home/to bed; **j'allais partir** I was just leaving; **j'allais partir quand il est arrivé** I was about to leave when he arrived; **l'homme qui allait inventer la bombe atomique** the man who was to invent the atomic bomb; **il allait le regretter** he was to regret it; **il va le regretter** he'll regret it; **elle va avoir un an** she'll soon be one; **il va faire nuit** it'll soon be dark; **ça va ~ mal**○ there'll be trouble; **tu vas me laisser tranquille?** will you please leave me alone!; **2** (marque le futur programmé) **je vais leur dire ce que je pense** I'm going to tell them what I think; **elle va peindre sa cuisine en bleu** she's going to paint her kitchen blue; **j'allais te le dire** I was just going to tell you; **3** (marque le mouvement) **~ rouler de l'autre côté de la rue** to go rolling across the street; **~ valser**○ **à l'autre bout de la pièce** to go flying across the room; **~ atterrir**○ **en plein champ/sur mon bureau** to end up in the middle of a field/on my desk; **4** (marque l'inclination, l'initiative) **qu'est-ce que tu vas imaginer là?** what a ridiculous idea!; **va savoir!** who knows?; **va** or **allez (donc) savoir ce qui s'est passé** who knows what happened?; **qu'es-tu allé te mettre en tête?** where did you pick up that idea?; **qui irait le soupçonner?** who would suspect him?; **vous n'iriez pas leur dire ça?** you're not going to go and say that, are you?; **pourquoi es-tu allé faire ça?** why did you have to go and do that?; **n'allez pas croire une chose pareille!** (pour réfuter) don't you believe it!; (pour tempérer l'enthousiasme) don't get carried away!; **allez y comprendre quelque chose!** just try and work that out!; **5** (marque l'évolution) **la situation va (en) se compliquant** the situation is getting more and more complicated; **~ (en) s'améliorant/s'aggravant** to be improving/getting worse; **la tristesse ira (en) s'atténuant** the grief will diminish.

II *vi* **1** (se porter, se dérouler, fonctionner) **comment vas-tu, comment ça va?** how are you?; **ça va (bien)** I'm fine; **les enfants vont bien?** are the children all right?; **et ta femme/ton épaule, comment ça va?** how's your wife/your shoulder?; **comment va la santé?** how are you keeping?; **ça va la vie**○**?** how's life○?; **ça va les amours**○**?** how's the love life going?; **~ beaucoup mieux** to be much better; **bois ça, ça ira mieux** drink this, you'll feel better; **tout va bien pour toi?** is everything going all right?; **si tout va bien** if everything goes all right; **vous êtes sûr que ça va?** are you sure you're all right?; **les affaires vont bien/mal** business is good/bad; **ça va**

> **aller¹**
>
> Lorsque *aller* fait partie d'une expression figée comme *aller dans le sens de, aller de pair avec* etc., l'expression est traitée sous l'entrée ***sens***, ***pair*** etc.
>
> On notera les différentes traductions de *aller* verbe de mouvement indiquant:
> un déplacement unique dans le temps:
> *je vais au théâtre ce soir* = I'm going to the theatre this evening
> ou une habitude:
> *je vais au théâtre tous les lundis* = I go to the theatre every Monday
>
> ***aller* + infinitif**
> La traduction dépend du temps:
> *je vais apprendre l'italien* = I'm going to learn Italian
> *il est allé voir l'exposition* = he went to see the exhibition
>
> *j'allais me marier quand la guerre a éclaté* = I was going to get married when the war broke out
> *va voir* = go and see
> *va leur parler* = go and speak to them
> *j'irai voir l'exposition demain* = I'll go and see the exhibition tomorrow
> *je vais souvent m'asseoir au bord de la rivière* = I often go and sit by the river
> *il ne va jamais voir une exposition* = he never goes to see exhibitions
>
> On notera que pour les activités sportives on peut avoir:
> *aller nager* = to go swimming *ou* to go for a swim
> *aller faire du vélo* = to go cycling *ou* to go on a bike ride
>
> On trouvera ci-dessous des exemples et des exceptions illustrant *aller* dans ses différentes fonctions verbales.

l'école? how are things at school?; **ça ne va pas très fort** or **bien** (ma santé) I'm not feeling very well; (la vie) things aren't too good; (le moral) I'm feeling a bit low; **ça pourrait ~ mieux, ça va plus ou moins** (réponse) so-so; **ça va mal entre eux** things aren't too good between them; **qu'est-ce qui ne va pas?** what's the matter?; **la voiture a quelque chose qui ne va pas** there's something wrong with the car; **tout va pour le mieux** everything's fine; **tout est allé si vite!** it all happened so quickly!; **ne pas ~ sans peine** or **mal** not to be easy; **ne pas ~ sans hésitations** to take some thinking about; **ça va de soi** or **sans dire** it goes without saying; **ça devrait ~ de soi** it should be obvious; **ainsi vont les choses** that's the way it goes; **ainsi va le monde** that's the way of the world; **ainsi allait la France** this was the state of affairs in France; **l'amour ne va jamais de soi** love is never straightforward; **ça va tout seul** (c'est facile) it's a doddle○ GB, it's as easy as pie; **ça ne va pas tout seul** it's not that easy, it's no picnic○; **les choses vont très vite** things are moving fast; **on fait ~**○ struggling on○; **ça peut ~**○**, ça ira**○ could be worse○; **ça va pas, non**○ or **la tête**○**?** are you mad○ GB ou crazy○?; **ça va pas, non, de crier** or **gesticuler comme ça**○**?** what's the matter with you, carrying on like that○?; ▶ **pis**; **2** (se déplacer) to go; **tu vas trop vite** you're going too fast; **allez tout droit** go straight ahead; **~ et venir** (dans une pièce) to pace up and down; (d'un lieu à l'autre) to run in and out; **la liberté d'~ et venir** the freedom to come and go at will; **je préfère ~ à pied/en avion** I'd rather walk/fly; **les nouvelles vont vite** news travels fast; **~ d'un pas rapide** to walk quickly; **je sais ~ à bicyclette/cheval** I can ride a bike/horse; **où vas-tu?** where are you going?, where are you off○ to?; **je vais en Pologne** I'm going to Poland; **~ au marché/en ville** to go to the market/into town; **~ chez le médecin/dentiste** to go to the doctor's/dentist's; **va dans ta chambre** go to your room; **je suis allé de Bruxelles à Anvers** I went from Brussels to Antwerp; **je suis allé jusqu'en Chine/au marché** (et pas plus loin) I went as far as China/the market; (et c'était loin) I went all the way to China/the market; **je préfère ne pas y ~** I'd rather not go; **allons-y!** let's go!; **je l'ai rencontré en allant au marché** I met him on the way to the market; **~ vers le nord** to head north; **j'y vais** (je m'en occupe) I'll get it; (je pars)○ I'm going, I'm off○; **où va-t-il encore?** where is he off to now○?; **~ sur** or **vers Paris** to head for Paris; **où va-t-on**○**?, où allons-nous**○**?** fig what are things coming to?, what's the world coming to?; **va donc, eh, abruti**○**!** get lost○, you idiot!; ▶ **cruche**; **3** (pour se livrer à une activité, chercher un produit) **~ à l'école/au travail** to go to school/to work; **~ à la chasse/pêche** to go hunting/fishing; **allez-vous à la piscine?** do you go to the swimming pool?; **il est allé au golf/tennis** he's gone to play golf/tennis; **~ aux champignons/framboises** to go mushroom-/raspberry-picking; **~ au pain**○ to go and get the bread; **dans quelle boulangerie allez-vous?** which bakery do you go to?; **~ aux courses**○ or **commissions**○ to go shopping; **~ au ravitaillement** to go and stock up; **~ aux nouvelles** or **informations** to go and see if there's any news; **4** (s'étendre dans l'espace) **la route va au village** the road leads to the village; **la rue va de la gare à l'église** the street goes from the station to the church; **5** (convenir) **ma robe/la traduction, ça va?** is my dress/the translation all right?; **ça va, ça ira**○**, ça peut aller**○ (en quantité) that'll do; (en qualité) it'll do; **ça va comme ça** it's all right as it is; **ça ne va pas du tout** that's no good at all; **ça ne va pas du tout, tu dois mettre une cravate** you can't go like that, you have to wear a tie; **la traduction n'allait pas** the translation was no good; **lundi ça (te) va?** would Monday suit you ou be okay○?; **une soupe, ça (te) va?** how about some soup?; **va pour une soupe**○ soup is okay○; **ça irait si on se voyait demain?** would it be all right if we met tomorrow?; **ça va si je porte un jean?** can I wear jeans?; **si le contrat ne te va pas, ne le signe pas** don't sign the contract if you're not happy with it; **si ça va pour toi, ça va pour moi**○ or **ça me va**○ if it's okay by you, it's okay by me○; **ça n'irait pas du tout** (inacceptable) that would never do; **ma scie ne va pas pour le métal** my saw is no good for metal; **ça te va bien de faire la morale/parler comme ça**○ iron you're hardly the person to preach/make that sort of remark; **6** (être de la bonne taille, de la bonne forme) **~ à qn** to fit sb; **tes chaussures sont trop grandes, elles ne me vont pas** your shoes are too big, they don't fit me; **cette vis/clé ne va pas** this screw/key doesn't fit; **7** (flatter, mettre en valeur) **~ à qn** to suit sb; **le rouge ne me va pas** or **me va mal** red doesn't suit me; **sa robe lui allait (très) bien** her dress really suited her; **le rôle t'irait parfaitement** the part would suit you perfectly; **ta cravate ne va pas avec ta chemise** your tie doesn't go with your shirt; **les tapis vont bien**

ensemble the rugs go together well; **les meubles vont bien ensemble** the furniture all matches; **je trouve que ta sœur et son petit ami vont très bien ensemble** I think your sister and her boyfriend are ideally suited; **8** (se ranger) to go; **les assiettes vont dans le placard** the plates go in the cupboard; **la chaise pliante va derrière la porte de la cuisine** the folding chair goes behind the kitchen door; **9** (faculté) **pouvoir ~ dans l'eau** to be waterproof; **le plat ne va pas au four** the dish is not ovenproof; **10** (dans une évaluation) **la voiture peut ~ jusqu'à 200 km/h** the car can do up to 200 km/h; **certains modèles peuvent ~ jusqu'à 1 000 francs** some models can cost up to 1,000 francs; **une peine allant jusqu'à cinq ans de prison** a sentence of up to five years in prison; **11** (en arriver à) **~ jusqu'au président** to take it right up to the president; **~ jusqu'à mentir/tuer** to go as far as to lie/kill; **leur amour est allé jusqu'à la folie** their love bordered on madness; **12** (dans le temps) **~ jusqu'en 1914** to go up to 1914; **pendant la période qui va du 8 février au 13 mars** between 8 February and 13 March; **la période qui va de 1918 à 1939** the period between 1918 and 1939; **l'offre va jusqu'à jeudi** the offer lasts until Thursday; **le contrat allait jusqu'en 1997** the contract ran until 1997; **va-t-on vers une nouvelle guerre?** are we heading for another war?; **~ sur ses 17 ans** to be going on 17; **13** (agir, raisonner) **vas-y doucement** or **gentiment, le tissu est fragile** careful, the fabric is delicate; **ils n'y sont pas allés doucement avec les meubles**○ they were rather rough with the furniture; **tu vas trop vite** you're going too fast; **vas-y, demande-leur!** (incitation) go on, ask them!; **vas-y, dis-le!** (provocation) come on, out with it!; **allons, allez!** (pour encourager, inciter) come on!; **j'y vais**○ (je vais agir) here we go!; **si tu vas par là** or **comme ça, rien n'est entièrement vrai** if you take that line, nothing is entirely true; **14** (contribuer) **y ~ de sa petite larme** to shed a little tear; **y ~ de sa petite chanson** to do one's party piece; **y ~ de ses économies** to dip into one's savings; **y ~ de sa personne** to pitch in; **y ~ de 100 francs** Jeux to put in 100 francs; **15**○ (se succéder) **ça y va la vodka avec lui** he certainly gets through the vodka; **ça y allait les coups** the fur was flying○; **16** (servir) **où est allé l'argent?** where has the money gone?; **l'argent ira à la réparation de l'église** the money will go toward(s) repairing the church; **l'argent est allé dans leurs poches** they pocketed the money; **17** (enfreindre) **~ contre la loi** [*personne*] to break the law; [*acte*] to be against the law; **je ne peux pas ~ contre ce qu'il a décidé** I can't go against his decision.

III s'en aller *vpr* **1** (partir, se rendre) **il faut que je m'en aille** I must go ou leave; **je m'en vais en Italie cet été** I'm going to Italy this summer; **je m'en vais du Japon l'année prochaine** I'll be leaving Japan next year; **va-t'en!** go away!; **s'en ~ faire les courses/en vacances/au travail** to go off to do the shopping/on vacation/to work; **ils s'en allaient chantant**† they went off singing; **2** (disparaître) **les nuages vont s'en ~** the clouds will clear away; **la tache ne s'en va pas** the stain won't come out; **avec le temps, tout s'en va** everything fades with time; **les années s'en vont** the years go by; **3** fml (mourir) to pass away; **4** (avoir l'intention de, essayer) **je m'en vais leur dire ce que je pense** I'm going to tell them what I think; **ne t'en va pas imaginer une chose pareille** (pour réfuter) don't you believe it!; (pour tempérer l'enthousiasme) don't get carried away!; **va-t'en savoir ce qu'il a voulu dire!** who knows what he meant?

IV *v impers* **1** (être en jeu) **il y va de ma réputation** my reputation is at stake; **il y va de ta santé** your health is at stake, you're putting your health at risk; **2** (se passer) **il en va souvent ainsi** that's often what happens; **tout le monde doit aider et il en va de même pour toi** everyone must help, and that goes for you too; **il en ira de même pour eux** the same goes for them; **il en va autrement en Corée** things are different in Korea; **il en ira de lui comme de ses prédécesseurs** he'll go the same way as his predecessors; **3** Math **40 divisé par 12 il y va 3 fois et il reste 4** 12 into 40 goes 3 times with 4 left over.

aller² /ale/ **I** *adj inv* **1** Transp **billet ~** gén single ticket GB, one-way ticket US; (d'avion) one-way ticket; **billet ~ (et) retour** return ticket GB, round trip (ticket) US; **2** Sport **match** or **rencontre ~** first leg.

II *nm* **1** (trajet) **j'ai fait une escale à l'~** I made a stopover on the way out; **j'ai pris le bus à l'~** (en allant là) I took the bus there; (en venant ici) I took the bus here; **l'~ a pris trois heures** the journey there took three hours; **il n'arrête pas de faire des ~s et retours entre chez lui et son bureau** he keeps running to and fro from his house to the office; **je suis pressé, je ne fais que l'~ et le retour**○ I'm in a hurry, I've just popped in○; **2** (ticket) **~ (simple)** single (ticket); **deux ~s (pour) Lille** two singles to Lille; **~ (et) retour** return ticket; **3** Sport (match) first leg; **à l'~** in the first leg.

allergène /alɛʀʒɛn/ *nm* allergen.

allergie /alɛʀʒi/ *nf* Méd allergy; **avoir une ~ à qch** Méd to have an allergy to sth; fig to be allergic to sth; **une ~ médicamenteuse** an allergy to a medicine; **~ professionnelle** work-related allergy.

allergique /alɛʀʒik/ *adj* Méd, fig allergic (**à** to); **réaction ~** allergic reaction.

allergisant, ~e /alɛʀʒizɑ̃, ɑ̃t/ *adj* Méd [*produit*] allergenic; **sans effet ~** hypoallergenic; **un produit qui a une action ~e** a product which causes allergic reactions.

allergologie /alɛʀgɔlɔʒi/ *nf* Méd study of allergies; **se spécialiser en ~** to specialize in (the study of) allergies.

allergologue /alɛʀgɔlɔg/ **▶510** *nmf* allergist.

alliacé, ~e /aljase/ *adj* [*odeur, plante*] alliaceous.

alliage /aljaʒ/ *nm* **1** (produit) alloy; **en ~** alloy (*épith*); **en ~ d'aluminium** in aluminium GB ou aluminum US alloy (*après n*); **2** (action) formation of an alloy (**de qch avec qch** of sth and sth); **3** fig (association) combination.

alliance /aljɑ̃s/ *nf* **1** (bague) wedding ring; **2** (entente) (entre pays, personnes, groupes) alliance; **faire ~ avec** to form an alliance with; **rompre une ~** to break off an alliance; **~ militaire** military alliance; **3** Relig Covenant; **l'ancienne/la nouvelle ~** the old/the new Covenant; **4** (mariage) fml union sout, marriage; **cousin par ~** cousin by marriage; **5** (combinaison) fml combination; **une ~ d'autorité et de douceur** a combination of authority and gentleness.

■ **l'~ atlantique** the Atlantic Alliance; **~ de mots** Ling oxymoron.

allié, ~e /alje/ **I** *pp* ▶ **allier**.

II *pp adj* (uni) (par un mariage) related by marriage (**à qn** to sb); (par un traité) [*nation, peuple*] allied; **le débarquement ~** the Allied landings.

III *nm,f* (proche) ally; (parent) relative; **il s'en est fait une ~e** he made an ally of her; **parents et ~s** immediate family and other relatives; **les ~s** Mil Hist the Allies.

allier /alje/ [2] **I** *vtr* **1** Tech to alloy [*métaux*] (**à, avec** with); **2** (combiner) to combine (**et, à** with); **elle réussit à ~ fantaisie et rigueur dans ses œuvres** she successfully combines imagination with precision in her works; **3** (par un mariage) to unite [sth] by marriage [*familles*].

II s'allier *vpr* **1** Pol, Mil (s'unir) to form an alliance (**avec, à** with); **2** (s'harmoniser) [*sons, couleurs*] to go (well) together.

Allier /alje/ **▶357**, **692** *nprm* (rivière, département) **l'~** the Allier.

alligator /aligatɔʀ/ *nm* alligator.

allitération /al(l)iteʀasjɔ̃/ *nf* alliteration ₵; **une ~ en s/t** alliterative 's's/'t's.

allô /alo/ *excl* hello!, hallo!; **~? bonjour! ici Alexandre, pourrais-je parler à Sylvaine?** hello, Alexandre here, could I speak to Sylvaine?

allocataire /al(l)ɔkatɛʀ/ *nmf* person entitled to a state benefit.

allocation /al(l)ɔkasjɔ̃/ *nf* **1** (action) allocation, granting; **2** (somme) benefit, benefits (*pl*) US; **verser une ~ à qn** to pay sb benefit ou benefits US; **toucher des ~s** to get benefit ou benefits US; **toucher une ~ de 50 000 francs par an** to get 50,000 francs in benefit ou benefits US a year; **3** Fin (de prêt) granting.

■ **~ chômage** unemployment benefit ou benefits US; **~ de devises** foreign currency allowance; **~ de fin de droits** income support (*after the period of unemployment benefit has ended*); **~ logement** housing benefit ou benefits US; **~ de maternité** maternity benefit ou benefits US; **~ de recherche** Univ research grant; **~ vieillesse** discretionary retirement pension; **~s familiales** family allowance (*sg*).

allocutaire /al(l)ɔkytɛʀ/ *nmf* Ling addressee.

allocution /al(l)ɔkysjɔ̃/ *nf* address; **une ~ de bienvenue/clôture** a welcome/closing address; **prononcer une ~ télévisée** to make a televised address.

allogène /al(l)ɔʒɛn/ **I** *adj* [*population, peuple*] non-indigenous.

II *nmf* non-indigenous person.

allomorphe /alomɔʀf/ *nm* allomorph.

allonge /alɔ̃ʒ/ *nf* **1** (de table) leaf; **2** (électrique) extension cord, extension lead GB; **3** Sport (en boxe) reach; **4** (crochet de boucherie) meat-hook.

allongé, ~e /alɔ̃ʒe/ **I** *pp* ▶ **allonger**.

II *pp adj* **1** (longiforme) elongated; **visage ~** elongated face; **2** Équit [*pas, trot, galop*] extended.

allongement /alɔ̃ʒmɑ̃/ *nm* **1** (de liste, procédure, délais) lengthening; (de vacances) extension; **2** (de voyelle) lengthening; **3** Aviat aspect ratio; **4** Phys (de ressort) extension.

allonger /alɔ̃ʒe/ [13] **I** *vtr* **1** (coucher) to lay [sb] down; **2** (agrandir) to lengthen [*robe, rideau*] (**de** by); to extend [*itinéraire, liste, vacances*] (**de** by); to prolong [*espérance de vie*] (**de** by); **~ le visage de qn** to make sb's face look longer; **~ la silhouette de qn** to make sb look slimmer; **~ le pas** to quicken one's step; **3** (étirer) to stretch [sth] out [*bras, cou, jambes*]; **allonge tes jambes sur le canapé** stretch your legs out on the sofa; **elle avait les jambes allongées** her legs were stretched out; **4** (diluer) to water [sth] down [*café, vin*]; **allongé d'eau** watered down; **5**○ (dans un combat) to floor○ [*adversaire, personne*]; **6**○ (donner) **~ 200 francs** to give 200 francs; **200 francs, allez, allonge!** 200 francs, go on, hand them over!; **~ un coup de poing à qn** to throw a punch at sb.

II *vi* [*jours*] to lengthen.

III s'allonger *vpr* **1** (pour se reposer, dormir) to lie down; (s'étirer) to stretch out; **allongé sur son lit/le dos** lying on his bed/his back; **2** (tomber)○ **s'~ sur le trottoir** to fall flat on the pavement GB ou sidewalk US; **3** (s'agrandir) [*liste, délais*] to get longer; **ta silhouette s'allonge** you look slimmer; **leur pas s'allonge** they are quickening their step.

allopathe /a(l)lɔpat/ *nmf* allopath.

allopathie /al(l)ɔpati/ *nf* allopathy.

allopathique /a(l)lɔpatik/ *adj* [*méthode, traitement*] allopathic.

allophone /alɔfɔn/ **I** *adj* [*personne*] allophonic.

II *nmf* allophone.

III *nm* Ling allophone.

allotropie /al(l)ɔtʀɔpi/ *nf* allotropy.

allotropique /al(l)ɔtʀɔpik/ *adj* [*état, variétés*] allotropic.

allouer /alwe/ [1] *vtr* **1** (donner) to allocate [*somme, pension, prime, budget*] (**à qn** to sb; **à qch** for sth); **la somme qui nous est allouée** the sum allocated to us; **2** (accorder) to grant [*prêt, indemnité, subvention*] (**à qn** to sb; **à qch** for sth); to allot, to allow [*temps*] (**à qn** to sb; **à qch** for sth); **le temps qui nous est alloué** the time allotted to us.

allumage /alymaʒ/ *nm* **1** Aut ignition; **double ~** dual ignition; **2** (de lampe, chauffage) switching on; **l'~ est automatique** it switches on automatically.

allumé○, **~e** /alyme/ **I** *adj* **1** (fou) mad○; **2** (ivre) tipsy○; **être bien ~** to be well oiled○.
II *nm,f* (fou) **c'est un ~** he's mad○; **les ~s du sport** sport fanatics.

allume-cigare(s) /alymsigaʀ/ *nm inv* cigar lighter.

allume-feu /alymfø/ *nm inv* fire-lighter.

allume-gaz /alymgaz/ *nm inv* gas lighter.

allumer /alyme/ [1] **I** *vtr* **1** (par la flamme) to light [*bougie, poêle, briquet, gaz*]; to strike [*allumette*]; to start [*incendie*]; **le feu ne va pas rester allumé** the fire is not going to stay alight GB, lighted US; **2** (électriquement) to switch [sth] on, to turn [sth] on [*lumière, appareil, électricité*]; **~ la chambre** to switch on ou turn on the light in the bedroom; **le couloir est allumé** the light is (switched ou turned) on in the corridor; **laisser ses phares allumés** to leave one's headlights on; **laisser sa chambre allumée** to leave the lights in one's room on; **allume!** switch on ou turn on the light!; **c'est allumé chez elle** her lights are on; **3** (exciter) to stir [*imagination*]; to arouse [*désir, jalousie, colère*]; to turn [sb] on○ [*personne*].
II s'allumer *vpr* **1** (électriquement) [*lampe, radio, chauffage*] to switch on; **le chauffage s'allume automatiquement** the heating switches on automatically; **le couloir s'allume où?** where do you switch on the light in the corridor?; **2** (s'exciter) [*désir, colère*] to be aroused; [*regard*] to light up.

allumette /alymɛt/ *nf* match, matchstick.
■ **~ au fromage** Culin cheese straw GB, cheese stick US; **~ suédoise** or **de sûreté** safety match.
IDIOMES **avoir des jambes commes des ~s** to have legs like matchsticks.

allumeur, **-euse** /alymœʀ, øz/ ▶**510** **I** *nm,f* **1 ~ de réverbères** lamplighter; **2**○ (séducteur) tease.
II *nm* Aut, Mécan distributor.

allure /alyʀ/ *nf* **1** (de marcheur) pace; (de véhicule) speed; **rouler à vive** or **grande/faible ~** to drive at high/low speed; **l'entreprise s'est développée à grande ~** the company expanded at a tremendous pace; **modérer** or **ralentir son ~** to slow down; **presser l'~** (à pied) to quicken one's pace; (en véhicule) to speed up; **à toute ~** (conduire, marcher) at top speed; (réciter, manger, noter) really fast; **partir à toute ~** to speed off; **à cette ~ nous allons être en retard** at this rate we're going to be late; **2** (apparence) (de personne) appearance; (de vêtement) look; (d'événement) aspect; **avoir des ~s de** to look like; **il a une drôle d'~** he's a funny-looking chap; **tu as une ~** or **de l'~ avec ce chapeau!** you look really daft in that hat!; **ses vêtements lui donnent l'~ d'un bandit** his clothes make him look like a gangster; **prendre l'~** or **les ~s de** [*changement, révolte*] to begin to look like; [*personne*] to make oneself out to be; **3** (distinction) style; **elle a beaucoup d'~** she's got a lot of style; **avoir belle ~** to look very stylish; **une personne de belle ~** a distinguished-looking person; **le salon a de l'~** the sitting room is stylish; **avoir fière ~** to cut a fine figure; **4** Naut sailing trim; **5** (d'animal) gait.

allusif, **-ive** /alyzif, iv/ *adj* **1** (qui contient une allusion) [*propos, phrase, réponse*] allusive; **2** (qui parle par allusions) [*personne*] indirect; **elle est restée très allusive** she spoke very indirectly; **répondre de façon allusive** to give an indirect reply, to reply indirectly.

allusion /alyzjɔ̃/ *nf* (évocation, sous-entendu) allusion (**à** to); **faire ~ à** to allude to; **une ~ littéraire** a literary allusion; **une ~ perfide** an innuendo; **sans faire la moindre ~ au conflit** without alluding at all to the conflict; **l'~ n'était pas innocente** it was not an innocent allusion.

allusivement /alyzivmɑ̃/ *adv* [*s'exprimer, répondre*] indirectly.

alluvial, **~e**, *mpl* **-iaux** /alyvjal, o/ *adj* alluvial.

alluvion /alyvjɔ̃/ *nf* alluvium; **des ~s** alluvia.

alluvionnement /alyvjɔnmɑ̃/ *nm* alluviation.

alluvionner /alyvjɔne/ [1] *vi* to deposit alluvia.

Alma-Ata /almaata/ ▶**857** *npr* Alma-Ata.

almanach /almana(k)/ *nm* almanac.

almée /alme/ *nf* Hist, Liter almah.

aloès /alɔɛs/ *nm inv* aloe.

aloi /alwa/ *nm* **un succès de bon/mauvais ~** a well-deserved/an undeserved success; **une plaisanterie de bon/mauvais ~** a joke in good taste/a tasteless joke; **une gaieté de bon ~** a simple cheerfulness.

alopécie /alopesi/ *nf* hair loss, alopecia spéc.

alors /alɔʀ/ **I** *adv* **1** (à ce moment-là) (dans le passé ou dans le futur) then; **nous pourrons ~ réaliser nos projets** then we will be able to carry out our plans; **j'ai les mêmes amis qu'~** I've got the same friends as I had then; **il est aussi timide qu'~** he's as shy as he was then; **il avait ~ 18 ans** he was 18 at the time; **~ seulement tu pourras faire** only then will you be able to do; **~ enfin il put sortir** then at last he could go out; **l'usine, ~ en pleine activité** the factory, which was then at full production; **le président, ~ gravement malade** the president, who was seriously ill at the time; **le pays, ~ sorti de la crise, pourra** the country which by then will be out of recession, will be able to; **la mode/les habitudes d'~** the fashion/the custom in those days; **c'étaient les mœurs d'~** that was the custom in those days; **le propriétaire/patron/premier ministre d'~** the then owner/boss/prime minister; **le premier ministre britannique d'~** the British Prime Minister at the time; **les enfants d'~ craignaient le maître** in those days children were scared of their teachers; **mes amis d'~ étaient surtout des peintres** my friends at the time were mainly painters; **mes toiles/romans d'~** my paintings/novels of the time; **jusqu'~** until then; **il n'avait cessé jusqu'~ de refuser** until then he had kept on refusing; **une organisation terroriste jusqu'~ inconnue** a terrorist organization which nobody had heard of before then; **c'est ~ qu'il prit la parole** it was then that he started to speak; **c'est ~ qu'il prendra une décision** then he'll come to a decision; **c'est seulement ~ que nous saurons s'il est sauvé** only then will we know whether he's been saved or not; **2** (dans ce cas-là) then; **s'il venait à mourir, ~ elle hériterait** if he should die, then she would inherit; **~ je m'en vais** I'm going then; **(mais) ~ cela change tout!** but that changes everything!; **et (puis) ~?** so what?; **~ quoi? on est encore en retard?** what's this? late again are we?; **~ quoi? qu'est-ce que j'entends? on n'est pas content?** what's this I hear? complaining are we?; **~? que faisons-nous?** so? what shall we do?; **~? qu'en penses-tu?** so? what do you think?; **3** (de ce fait) so; **il y avait grève du métro, ~ j'ai pris un taxi** there was a tube GB ou subway US strike, so I took a taxi; **4** (pour résumer) then; **on se voit demain ~?** we'll see each other tomorrow then?; **tu n'as rien trouvé d'autre ~?** you couldn't find anything else then?; **5** (ou bien) **ou ~** or else; **il a oublié le rendez-vous ou ~ il a eu un accident** he's forgotten the appointment, or else he's had an accident; **je serai dans la cuisine ou ~ dans le jardin** I'll be in the kitchen or in the garden; **6**○ (dans un récit) so; **~ il me dit..., ~ je lui dis...** so he said to me..., so I said to him...; **~ le type s'en va** so the guy goes off; **7** (pour renforcer une exclamation) **non mais ~!** honestly!; **ça ~!** (étonnement) good grief!; **~ ça!** (indignation) that's not on!; **chic** or **chouette ~!** (hey) that's great!; **mince** or **zut ~!** (étonnement) wow○!; (colère) blast○! GB, darn○! US.
II alors que *loc conj* **1** (pendant que) while; **j'ai appris la nouvelle ~ que j'étais à Rome** I heard the news while I was in Rome; **il fait chaud ici ~ que dehors il gèle** it's hot in here while outside it's freezing; **2** (tandis que) when; **vous jouez ~ qu'il faudrait travailler** you're playing when you should be working; **tu lui souris ~ que tu le détestes** you smile at him while (in fact) you hate him.
III alors même que *loc conj* even though.

alose /aloz/ *nf* shad.

alouette /alwɛt/ *nf* lark.
■ **~ des champs** skylark.
IDIOMES **attendre que les ~s vous tombent toutes rôties dans le bec** Prov to expect everything just to drop into one's lap.

alourdir /aluʀdiʀ/ [3] **I** *vtr* **1** (rendre plus lourd) [*fardeau*] to weigh [sb] down [*personne*]; [*problème*] to make [sth] tense [*atmosphère*]; **le subjonctif/l'adverbe alourdit la phrase** the subjunctive/the adverb weighs the sentence down; **la valise était alourdie par les livres** the suitcase was weighed down by the books; **un manteau alourdi par la pluie** a coat heavy with rain; **2** (rendre plus important) to increase [*impôt, charges, déficit*]; **le dernier témoignage a alourdi les accusations** the statement by the last witness weighed heavily against the accused.
II s'alourdir *vpr* **1** (devenir plus lourd) [*paupières*] to grow heavy; [*air, atmosphère*] to get heavy; **2** (devenir plus important) [*dépenses, dette*] to increase; **le bilan de victimes s'est alourdi** the death toll has risen.

alourdissement /aluʀdismɑ̃/ *nm* **1** (en poids) heaviness; **2** Fin (de l'impôt, de prélèvement) increase (**de** in).

aloyau /alwajo/ *nm* (Culin) sirloin; **un bifteck dans l'~** a sirloin steak.

alpaga /alpaga/ *nm* (animal, laine) alpaca.

alpage /alpaʒ/ *nm* mountain pasture.

alpaguer○ /alpage/ [1] *vtr* to collar [*personne*]; **se faire ~ par qn** to be collared by sb.

alpe /alp/ *nf* alpine pasture.

Alpes /alp/ ▶**692** *nprfpl* **les ~s** the Alps.

Alpes-de-Haute-Provence /alpdəotpʀɔvɑ̃s/ ▶**692** *nprfpl* (département) **les ~** the Alpes-de-Haute-Provence.

Alpes-Maritimes /alpmaʀitim/ ▶**692** *nprfpl* (département) **les ~** the Alpes-Maritimes.

alpestre /alpɛstʀ/ *adj* alpine.

alpha /alfa/ *nm inv* (lettre) alpha.
IDIOMES **être l'~ et l'omega** to be the alpha and omega.

alphabet /alfabɛ/ *nm* **1** (signes) alphabet; **2** (manuel) ABC (book).
■ **~ morse** Morse alphabet; **~ phonétique international, API** International Phonetic Alphabet, IPA.

alphabétique /alfabetik/ *adj* alphabetical; **dans l'ordre** or **par ordre ~** in alphabetical order.

alphabétiquement /alfabetikmɑ̃/ *adv* alphabetically.

alphabétisation /alfabetizasjɔ̃/ *nf* **1** (enseignement de l'écriture) literacy tuition; **une poli-**

tique d'~ des quartiers déshérités a policy of promoting literacy in deprived areas; un cours d'~ a literacy class; 2 (mise en ordre alphabétique) alphabetizing.

alphabétiser /alfabetize/ [1] *vtr* 1 (enseigner) to teach [sb] to read and write [*personne, groupe*]; to promote literacy in [*population, pays*]; 2 (mettre en ordre alphabétique) to put [sth] in alphabetical order, to alphabetize.

alphanumérique /alfanymeʀik/ *adj* alphanumeric.

Alphapage /alfapaʒ/ *nm* Télécom pager (*for receiving messages*).

alpin, **~e** /alpɛ̃, in/ *adj* alpine.

alpinisme /alpinism/ ▶449 *nm* mountaineering.

alpiniste /alpinist/ *nmf* mountaineer.

Alsace /alzas/ ▶692 *nprf* l'~ Alsace.

alsacien, **-ienne** /alzasjɛ̃, ɛn/ I ▶692 *adj* [*personne*] from Alsace; [*cuisine, population, paysage*] of Alsace.

II ▶462 *nm* Ling Alsatian.

Alsacien, **-ienne** /alzasjɛ̃, ɛn/ *nm,f* Alsatian.

altérable /alteʀabl/ *adj* [*couleur*] unstable; [*revêtement*] easily damaged.

altération /alteʀasjɔ̃/ *nf* 1 (détérioration) (de facultés) impairment (**de** of); (de denrée) spoiling (**de** of); (d'environnement) deterioration (**de** in); (de sentiment, couleur) change (**de** in); **l'~ de sa santé** the deterioration in his health; 2 (falsification) (de texte, faits) distortion; (de monnaie) falsification; 3 Mus **~ (accidentelle)** accidental; **~ constitutive** key signature.

altercation /altɛʀkasjɔ̃/ *nf* altercation.

alter ego /altɛʀego/ *nm inv* alter ego.

altérer /alteʀe/ [14] I *vtr* 1 (détériorer) to impair [*saveur, caractère, relation*]; to affect [*santé*]; to spoil [*denrée*]; to mar [*joie*]; to alter [*sentiment, composition*]; to change [*expression, visage*]; to fade [*couleur*]; **d'une voix altérée** in a faltering voice; 2 (falsifier) to distort [*fait, texte*]; to falsify [*monnaie*]; to adulterate [*substance*]; 3 fml (donner soif) to make [sb] feel parched; **être altéré de sang/de pouvoir** to thirst for blood/power.

II **s'altérer** *vpr* [*santé, faculté, relation, saveur*] to become impaired; [*denrée*] to spoil; [*voix*] to falter; [*sentiments, expression*] to change.

altérité /alteʀite/ *nf* otherness.

alternance /altɛʀnɑ̃s/ *nf* 1 gén alternation; **~ d'ondées et d'éclaircies** showers with intermittent bright spells; **en ~ avec** alternately with; **en ~** alternately; **'l'Avare' se joue en ~** 'l'Avare' is on every other night; **formation en ~** work-based learning ₵; 2 Pol **choisir l'~** [*électorat, pays*] to opt for a change in power.

alternant, **~e** /altɛʀnɑ̃, ɑ̃t/ *adj* alternating.

alternateur /altɛʀnatœʀ/ *nm* Électrotech alternator.

alternatif, **-ive** /altɛʀnatif, iv/ I *adj* 1 gén alternate; 2 Électrotech alternating; 3 Sociol alternative.

II **alternative** *nf* alternative.

alternativement /altɛʀnativmɑ̃/ *adv* alternately, in turn.

alterne /altɛʀn/ *adj* 1 Bot alternate; 2 Math [*angles*] alternate.

alterné, **~e** /altɛʀne/ *adj* alternating.

alterner /altɛʀne/ [1] I *vtr* gén to alternate; **nous alternons cours pratique et cours théorique** we alternate between practical work and lessons in theory; **~ les cultures** to rotate crops.

II *vi* 1 (se succéder) [*périodes, couleurs, objets*] to alternate (**avec** with); 2 (se relayer) [*personnes, groupe*] **~ avec qn pour faire qch** to take turns with sb (at) doing sth; **les deux partis ont alterné au pouvoir pendant 30 ans** the two parties have been alternately in and out of power for 30 years.

altesse /altɛs/ *nf* 1 (titre) highness; **son Altesse royale** His/Her Royal Highness; 2 (personne) prince/princess.

altier, **-ière** /altje, ɛʀ/ *adj* [*personne, attitude, démarche*] haughty; **avoir un port ~** to have a haughty bearing.

altimètre /altimɛtʀ/ *nm* altimeter.

altimétrie /altimetʀi/ *nf* altimetry.

altiport /altipɔʀ/ *nm* mountain landing strip.

altiste /altist/ ▶534, 510 *nmf* viola player GB, violist US.

altitude /altityd/ *nf* 1 (hauteur) altitude; **perdre/prendre de l'~** [*avion, ballon*] to lose/to gain altitude ou height; **à basse/haute ~** [*neiger, voler*] at low/high altitude; **vol à basse/haute ~** low/high altitude flight; **à une ~ de 2 000 mètres** [*avion*] at an altitude of 2,000 metres[GB]; [*montagne, plateau*] at a height of 2,000 metres[GB] (above sea-level), at an altitude of 2,000 metres[GB]; **quelle est l'~ du mont Blanc?** how high is Mont Blanc?, what is the altitude of Mont Blanc?; **des sommets de plus de 6 000 mètres d'~** peaks more than 6,000 metres[GB] high; **avoir une faible ~** [*plateau, ville*] to be close to sea-level; 2 (haute montagne) **en ~** [*pousser, neiger*] high up (in the mountains), at altitude spéc; **station d'~** mountain resort.

alto /alto/ I *adj* [*saxophone, clarinette*] alto.

II *nm* 1 ▶534 (instrument) viola; 2 ▶510 (musicien) viola player GB, violin US; 3 ▶134 (voix) alto.

altocumulus /altokymylys/ *nm inv* altocumulus.

altostratus /altostʀatys/ *nm inv* altostratus.

altruisme /altʀɥism/ *nm* altruism.

altruiste /altʀɥist/ I *adj* altruistic.

II *nmf* altruist.

alu○ /aly/ *nm* aluminium GB, aluminum US; **papier ~** kitchen foil.

aluminate /alyminat/ *nm* aluminate.

alumine /alymin/ *nf* alumina.

aluminer /alymine/ [1] *vtr* to aluminize.

aluminium /alyminjɔm/ *nm* aluminium GB, aluminum US; **d'~** [*resine, production*] aluminium GB, aluminum US; **en ~** [*casseroles, jantes*] aluminium (*épith*) GB, aluminum (*épith*) US.

alun /alœ̃/ *nm* alum.

alunir /alyniʀ/ [3] *vi* controv to land on the moon.

alunissage /alynisaʒ/ *nm* controv moon landing.

alvéolaire /alveɔlɛʀ/ *adj* 1 Anat [*arcade, point*] alveolar; 2 Ling [*consonne, articulation*] alveolar; 3 Géol [*structure*] alveolate.

alvéole /alveɔl/ *nf* 1 (de ruche) alveolus; 2 Anat (de poumon) alveolus; (de dent) tooth socket, alveolus spéc; 3 Géol cavity.

alvéolé, **~e** /alveɔle/ *adj* [*caoutchouc, carton, métal*] honeycombed.

Alzheimer /alzajmœʀ/ ▶271 *npr* **la maladie d'~** Alzheimer's disease.

amabilité /amabilite/ I *nf* 1 (gentillesse) kindness; **avec ~** kindly; **veuillez avoir l'~ de** please; **il est toujours plein d'~** he's always very pleasant; **quelle ~!** iron charming!; 2 (politesse) courtesy; **avec ~** politely, courteously.

II **amabilités** *nfpl* (prévenances) **faire des ~s à qn** to be polite to sb; **se dire des ~s** lit to exchange pleasantries; iron to exchange insults; **après cet échange d'~s** lit after this exchange of pleasantries; iron after this exchange of insults.

amadou /amadu/ *nm* tinder, touchwood.

amadouer /amadwe/ [1] I *vtr* to coax, to cajole [*personne, animal*]; **~ qn pour qu'il fasse qch** to cajole sb into doing sth; **elle cherche à nous ~ avec des promesses** she's trying to cajole us with promises; **se laisser ~** to let oneself be coaxed.

II **s'amadouer** *vpr* [*personne*] to soften.

amaigrir /amegʀiʀ/ [3] *vtr* [*maladie, régime*] to make [sb] thinner [*personne*]; **je l'ai trouvée très amaigrie** I found her much thinner; **un visage amaigri par la maladie** a face made thin by illness.

amaigrissant, **~e** /amegʀisɑ̃, ɑ̃t/ *adj* [*régime, produit*] slimming.

amaigrissement /amegʀismɑ̃/ *nm* weight loss, loss of weight.

amalgamation /amalgamasjɔ̃/ *nf* amalgamation.

amalgame /amalgam/ *nm* 1 (de qualités, sentiments) mixture; (d'idées) pej hotchpotch GB, hodgepodge US; (d'objets, de personnes) mixture; **faire l'~ entre des problèmes/situations** pej to lump together various problems/situations; 2 Dent, Chimie amalgam.

amalgamer /amalgame/ [1] *vtr* 1 (associer) pej to lump together [*idées, problèmes*]; to combine, to mix [*qualité, sentiments*]; to mix [*personnes, communautés*]; 2 (mélanger) to blend, to amalgamate [*ingrédients*].

amande /amɑ̃d/ *nf* Bot 1 (fruit) almond; **en ~** almond-shaped; **yeux en ~** almond(-shaped) eyes; **huile d'~ douce** almond oil; 2 (dans un noyau) kernel.

amandier /amɑ̃dje/ *nm* almond tree.

amandine /amɑ̃din/ *nf* almond tart.

amanite /amanit/ *nf* amanita.

■ **~ phalloïde** death cap; **~ tue-mouche** fly agaric; **~ vireuse** destroying angel.

amant /amɑ̃/ *nm* lover; **prendre un ~** to take a lover.

amante‡ /amɑ̃t/ *nf* mistress†, lover.

amarante /amaʀɑ̃t/ I ▶193 *adj inv* amaranthine.

II *nm* 1 (couleur) red; 2 (arbre) purple heart; **bois d'~** purple heart.

III *nf* 1 (plante) amaranth; 2 (colorant) amaranth.

amariner /amaʀine/ [1] *vtr* 1 (habituer à la mer) to accustom [sb] to life at sea [*personne*]; 2† to commandeer [*navire*].

amarrage /amaʀaʒ/ *nm* 1 (de bateau, dirigeable) mooring; 2 (fixation) tying, fastening; 3 Astronaut docking.

amarre /amaʀ/ *nf* (cordage) rope; **les ~s** moorings; **rompre les ~s** to break its moorings; **larguer les ~s** lit to cast off; fig to set off.

amarrer /amaʀe/ [1] *vtr* 1 Naut to moor; **~ à** to moor alongside [*quai*]; to moor to [*anneau, piquet*]; 2 (attacher) to tie (**à, sur** to).

amaryllis /amaʀilis/ *nf inv* amaryllis.

amas /ama/ *nm inv* 1 (d'objets, de sable, neige) pile; (de tôle, ferraille, ruines) heap; (de sang, graisse) Méd accumulation; 2 Astron cluster; **~ globulaire** globular cluster; 3 Géol mass; **~ de minerai** mass of ore.

amasser /amase/ [1] I *vtr* to amass, to accumulate [*fortune, livres, papiers*]; to lay in [*provisions*]; to acquire [*connaissances*]; to amass [*preuves*]; to collect [*témoignages*]; **tu devrais profiter de ton argent au lieu de l'~** you should use your money, not hoard it.

II **s'amasser** *vpr* [*documents, objets, neige*] to pile up; [*preuves*] to build up.

amateur /amatœʀ/ I *adj inv* [*catégorie, sport, photographe, cinéma*] amateur; **radio ~** radio ham○, amateur radio operator.

II *nm* 1 (connaisseur) (en moto, tennis, photographie) enthusiast; (en vin) connoisseur; **~ d'opéra/de jazz** opera/jazz lover; **c'est un grand ~ de cigares/cuisine japonaise** he's a great lover of cigars/Japanese cooking; **pour les ~s de sensations fortes** for thrill-seekers; **elle est très ~ de chocolat** she loves chocolate; 2 (collectionneur) **~ d'art/d'antiquités** art/antiques collector; 3 (non-professionnel) amateur; **faire du cinéma en ~** to be an amateur filmmaker; **match entre ~s** amateur match; **c'est du travail d'~** it's the work of an amateur; 4 (acheteur éventuel) potential buyer; **il vend sa voiture,**

vous êtes ~? he's selling his car, are you interested?; **avis aux ~s, je vends mon vélo** I'm selling my bike, if anyone's interested; **avis aux ~s de botanique/catch** calling all botany lovers/wrestling fans.

amateurisme /amatœʀism/ *nm* lit, fig amateurism.

a maxima /amaksima/ *loc* **appel ~** *appeal lodged by public prosecutor against too harsh a sentence.*

amazone /amazon/ *nf* **1** (cavalière) horsewoman; **monter en ~** to ride sidesaddle; **tenue d'~** riding habit; **2**○ (prostituée) prostitute (*who solicits from a car*).

Amazone /amazon/ **I** *nf* Mythol Amazon.
II ▶357 *nprm* Géog **l'~** the Amazon (river).

Amazonie /amazɔni/ ▶692 *nprf* Amazon.

amazonien, -ienne /amazɔnjɛ̃, ɛn/ *adj* Amazonian.

ambages: sans ambages /sɑ̃zɑ̃baʒ/ *loc adv* without beating around the bush.

ambassade /ɑ̃basad/ *nf* **1** (lieu, service) embassy; **l'~ de France à Moscou** the French Embassy in Moscow; **2** (employés) embassy staff; (diplomates) embassy officials; **3** (fonction) ambassadorship; **4** (mission diplomatique permanente) embassy; (temporaire) delegation; fig mission; **aller en ~ auprès de qn** fig to go on a mission to sb.

ambassadeur, -drice /ɑ̃basadœʀ, dʀis/ *nm,f* **1** (diplomate) ambassador; **l'~ de France au Chili/en Belgique** the French ambassador to Chile/to Belgium; **~ auprès des Nations unies** ambassador to the United Nations; **~ extraordinaire** ambassador extraordinary; **madame l'~** or **l'ambassadrice** (en s'adressant à elle) Ambassador; **~ itinérant** roving ambassador, ambassador-at-large US; **2** (représentant) representative; **l'~ du rock russe** the representative of Russian rock.

ambiance /ɑ̃bjɑ̃s/ *nf* **1** (atmosphère) atmosphere, ambiance; **musique/lumière/éclairage d'~** atmospheric music/light/lighting; **2** (gaieté) lively atmosphere; **mettre de l'~** [*musique, éclairage*] to give things a bit of atmosphere; **il a mis un disque pour mettre un peu d'~** he played a record to liven things up ou to liven up the atmosphere; **tu peux compter sur lui pour mettre de l'~** you can count on him to liven things up; **cela manque d'~ ici** it's not much fun here, it lacks atmosphere here.

ambiant, ~e /ɑ̃bjɑ̃, ɑ̃t/ *adj* **1** [*air, chaleur, humidité*] surrounding; **à température ~e** at room temperature; **2** [*joie, hostilité, pessimisme*] pervading; [*état d'esprit*] prevailing.

ambidextre /ɑ̃bidɛkstʀ/ *adj* ambidextrous.

ambigu, -uë /ɑ̃bigy/ *adj* [*réponse, mot, discours, situation, prise de position*] ambiguous; [*personnage*] multifaceted; [*sentiment, attitude*] ambivalent.

ambiguïté /ɑ̃bigɥite/ *nf* **1** (de mot, formule, situation) ambiguity; **sans ~** [*question, article, prise de position*] unambiguous; [*situation*] clear-cut; [*définir, dire*] unambiguously; **2** (de mot, d'expression) ambiguity; **3** (de personnage) enigmatic nature; (de sentiment) ambivalence.

ambitieusement /ɑ̃bisjøzmɑ̃/ *adv* ambitiously.

ambitieux, -ieuse /ɑ̃bisjø, øz/ **I** *adj* ambitious.
II *nm,f* ambitious person; **les ~** ambitious people.

ambition /ɑ̃bisjɔ̃/ *nf* ambition; **avoir de l'~** to be ambitious; **ne pas avoir d'~** to have no ambition; **manquer d'~** to lack ambition; **un homme sans ~** a man with no ambition; **avoir l'~ de faire qch** [*personne*] to have an ambition to do sth; **ces réformes ont pour ~ de moderniser l'industrie** the aim ou object of these reforms is to modernize industry; **être plein d'~** to be very ambitious ou full of ambition; **l'~ du pouvoir** the thirst for power; **je n'ai pas l'~ de réformer le système en un mois** I don't aim to change the system in a month.

ambitionner /ɑ̃bisjɔne/ [1] *vtr* to aspire to [*poste, place*]; to be after○, to aim for [*médaille, titre sportif*]; **~ de faire** to aim to do; **il ambitionne d'obtenir 25% du marché européen de l'automobile** his ambition is to win 25% of the European car market.

ambivalence /ɑ̃bivalɑ̃s/ *nf* ambivalence.

ambivalent, ~e /ɑ̃bivalɑ̃, ɑ̃t/ *adj* ambivalent.

amble /ɑ̃bl/ *nm* amble; **aller** or **marcher l'~** to go at an amble.

ambler /ɑ̃ble/ [1] *vi* to go at an amble.

amblyope /ɑ̃blijɔp/ **I** *adj* amblyopic.
II *nmf* person with amblyopia.

amblyopie /ɑ̃blijɔpi/ *nf* amblyopia.

ambre /ɑ̃bʀ/ *nm* **1** Zool, Cosmét **~ (gris)** ambergris; **2** (résine) **~ (jaune)** amber; **couleur d'~** amber; **collier d'~** amber necklace.

ambré, ~e /ɑ̃bʀe/ *adj* **1** ▶193 (couleur d'ambre) amber; **2** (à senteur d'ambre) perfumed with ambergris.

ambroisie /ɑ̃bʀwazi/ *nf* **1** Mythol ambrosia; **2** Bot ragweed.

ambulance /ɑ̃bylɑ̃s/ *nf* ambulance.

ambulancier, -ière /ɑ̃bylɑ̃sje, ɛʀ/ **I** *adj* **service ~** ambulance service.
II ▶510 *nm,f* ambulance driver.

ambulant, ~e /ɑ̃bylɑ̃, ɑ̃t/ *adj* [*musicien, comédien*] itinerant; [*marchand*] mobile; [*cirque*] travelling[GB]; **marchand de fruits et légumes ~** mobile fruit and vegetable man; **théâtre ~** itinerant ou roving† players; **service de restauration ~e** train buffet trolley; **vendeur ~** (dans une gare) snack trolley man; **c'est un (vrai) cadavre/dictionnaire ~**○ he's/she's a walking skeleton/dictionary○.

ambulatoire /ɑ̃bylatwaʀ/ *adj* ambulatory; **malade ~** outpatient.

âme /ɑm/ *nf* **1** Philos, Relig soul; **(que) Dieu ait son ~** (may) God rest his/her soul; ▶**cheviller**; **2** (nature profonde) (de l'homme) soul; (de nation) soul, spirit; **avoir une ~ de poète** to have the soul of a poet ou a poetic soul; **avoir l'~ d'un pionnier/chef** to have the pioneering spirit/the spirit of a leader; **il se sentait l'~ d'un conquérant** he felt in his soul the power of a conqueror; **ville sans ~** soulless town; **3** (siège de la pensée et des émotions) soul; **du fond de l'~** from the (very) depths of one's soul; **avoir l'~ sensible** to be a sensitive soul; **être ému jusqu'au fond de l'~** to be moved to the depths of one's soul; **chanter/jouer avec ~** to sing/play with feeling; **interprétation sans ~** soulless interpretation; **socialiste/musicien dans l'~** a socialist/musician to the core; **4** (conscience morale) soul; **avoir l'~ sereine** to have an easy conscience; **grandeur** or **noblesse d'~** nobility of spirit; **paix de l'~** spiritual peace; **en mon ~ et conscience** in all honesty; **5** (personne, habitant) soul; **~ noble** noble soul; **c'est une ~ généreuse** he/she has great generosity of spirit; **une bonne ~** a kind soul; **une bonne ~, une ~ charitable** also iron some kind soul; **sans voir ~ qui vive** without seeing a (living ou single) soul; **hameau de 25 ~s** hamlet of 25 souls; **6** (de résistance, nation, parti) soul **(de** of); (de complot) moving spirit **(de** in); **7** Tech (de canon, fusil) bore; (de rail, statue, câble) core; (de soufflet) air-valve; (d'instrument à cordes) soundpost; **8**‡ (terme d'affection) **mon ~** dear heart†.
■ **~ damnée** partner in crime; **~ en peine** soul in torment; **errer comme une ~ en peine** to wander around like a lost soul; **~ sœur** soul mate.

améliorable /ameljɔʀabl/ *adj* **résultats ~s** results which can be improved on.

améliorant, ~e /ameljɔʀɑ̃, ɑ̃t/ *adj* **plante ~e** soil improver.

amélioration /ameljɔʀasjɔ̃/ *nf* improvement **(de, dans** in); **faire des ~s dans une maison** to carry out improvements to a house; **des résultats en nette ~** results that show a distinct improvement.

améliorer /ameljɔʀe/ [1] **I** *vtr* to improve [*résultat, performance, travail*]; to increase [*production*]; **cela ne va pas ~ la situation** that won't help ou improve the situation; **~ une maison** to carry out home improvements; **un pique-nique amélioré** hum a superior picnic.
II s'améliorer *vpr* to improve; **cela ne s'améliore pas, ça ne va pas en s'améliorant**○ things aren't getting any better; **je veux m'~** I want to improve my performance.

amen /amɛn/ *nm inv* Relig amen; **dire ~ à tout** fig to agree to everything; **dire ~ à qn** fig to go along with sb.

aménagé, ~e /amenaʒe/ **I** *pp* ▶**aménager**.
II *pp adj* **1** (transformé) [*fermette, grenier*] converted; **2** (équipé) [*cuisine, salle de bains*] equipped; **l'appartement est mal ~** the apartment is not very well appointed.

aménageable /amenaʒabl/ *adj* **1** [*fermette, grenier*] suitable for conversion (*après n*); (en adaptant) **la petite chambre est ~ en bureau** the small room can be converted into a study; **2** [*emploi du temps, horaire*] flexible.

aménagement /amenaʒmɑ̃/ *nm* **1** (de région, ville) development; **~ urbain/régional** urban/regional development; **l'~ du territoire** ≈ town and country planning; **2** (de port de plaisance, routes) construction; (d'espaces verts) creation; (de parc, terrain de sport) laying out; **3** (de fermette, grenier) (en transformant) conversion; (en améliorant) improvement; **l'~ d'une chambre en salle de jeu** the conversion of a bedroom into a playroom; **l'~ d'un coin repas fut difficile** making a dining area was difficult; **4** (en équipant) (de cuisine) equipping; (de magasin) fitting; **5** (de maison, bateau) fitting; **6** (par rapport à règlement, loi) adjustment; **~s fiscaux** tax adjustments; **obtenir des ~s d'horaires** to obtain more flexible working hours; **l'~ du temps de travail** flexible working hours (*pl*).

aménager /amenaʒe/ [13] *vtr* **1** (en transformant) to convert [*fermette, grenier*]; (en améliorant) to do up [*fermette, appartement*]; **~ un grenier en bureau** to convert a loft into a study; **2** (en équipant) to equip [*cuisine, salle de bains*]; to develop [*région, espace rural*]; to fit out [*magasin, musée*]; **3** (créer) to create [*espaces verts*]; to build [*route*]; to make [*coin-repas*]; to lay out [*jardin, terrain de sport*]; **4** (en adaptant) to arrange [*emploi du temps, horaire*]; to adjust [*règlement*].

amendable /amɑ̃dabl/ *adj* **1** Jur [*loi*] subject to amendment (*après n*); **2** Agric [*sol*] which can be enriched (*épith, après n*).

amende /amɑ̃d/ *nf* fine; **une ~ de 2 000 francs** a fine of 2,000 francs, a 2,000-franc fine; **payer 250 francs d'~** to pay a 250-franc fine; **être condamné à 1 000 francs d'~** to be fined 1,000 francs; **défense d'afficher sous peine d'~** billstickers will be prosecuted; **mettre qn à l'~** hum to give sb a forfeit.
IDIOMES **faire ~ honorable** to make amends.

amendement /amɑ̃dmɑ̃/ *nm* **1** Pol amendment **(à** to; **sur** on); **2** Agric (opération) enrichment; (substance) enriching agent.

amender /amɑ̃de/ [1] **I** *vtr* **1** Jur to amend [*loi, texte*]; **2** (moralement) fml to improve; **3** Agric to enrich [*sol*].
II s'amender *vpr* to mend one's ways; **un criminel amendé** a reformed criminal.

amène /amɛn/ *adj* liter affable; **des paroles peu ~s** unkind words.

amenée /amәne/ *nf* **canal d'~** Gén Civ headrace channel.

amener /amne/ [16] **I** *vtr* **1** (mener) **~ qn quelque part** [*personne, bus, train*] to take sb somewhere; **j'ai amené ma fille chez le dentiste** I took my daughter to the dentist's; **2** (venir avec) **~ qn** (**quelque part**) to bring sb (somewhere); **tu peux ~ tes amis** you can bring your friends; **quel bon vent vous amène?** what brings you here?; **3** (apporter) controv **~ qch** (**à qn**) to bring (sb) sth; **amène nous tes photos** bring us your photos; **je vous amène le beau temps** I've brought the fine weather with me; **4** (convoyer) [*personne, organisme*] to bring [*eau, électricité, marchandises*]; **5** (provoquer) to cause [*problèmes, catastrophe, maladie*]; to bring [*pluie, neige*]; to bring [*gloire, victoire*]; to bring about [*renouveau*]; **la hausse des taux a amené l'effondrement des marchés** the rise in rates caused the market to collapse; **6** (aborder) to bring up, to introduce [*sujet, question*]; **il a bien amené la question** he introduced the question skilfully[GB]; **~ qch sur le tapis**○ to bring sth up; **~ la conversation sur un thème** to bring the conversation around to a subject; **être bien amené** [*conclusion*] to be well-presented; [*phrase, remarque*] to be well-timed; **7** (conduire) fig **~ qn à** to lead sb to [*conclusion*]; to bring sb to [*question*]; **cela l'a amené à de meilleures pensées** this made him think along more positive lines; **~ qn à faire** to lead sb to do; **l'entreprise a été amenée à diversifier ses activités** the company was forced to diversify its activities; **nous serons amenés à nous revoir** we shall doubtless meet again; **~ un liquide à la bonne température** to bring a liquid to the right temperature; **8** (tirer vers soi) [*pêcheur*] to pull in [*filet*]; [*navigateur*] to strike [*voile*]; **~ le pavillon** Naut to strike one's flag; fig to surrender.
II s'amener○ *vpr* (venir) to come; (arriver) to show up○, to turn up○ (**avec** with); **amène-toi!** come here!; **ils se sont amenés sur le coup de onze heures du soir** they showed up at eleven o'clock at night.

aménité /amenite/ *nf* liter affability; **traiter qn avec ~** to be affable with sb; **accueillir qn sans ~** to give sb an unfriendly reception.

aménorrhée /amenɔʀe/ *nf* amenorrhea.

amenuisement /amәnɥizmɑ̃/ *nm* dwindling.

amenuiser /amәnɥize/ [1] **I** *vtr* **1** gén to reduce [*réserves, pouvoir, popularité, chance, risque*]; **2** Tech [*personne*] to plane down [*planche*].
II s'amenuiser *vpr* [*réserves, espoir, chance, clientèle*] to dwindle; [*risque*] to lessen; [*temps*] to slip by.

amer, **-ère** /amɛʀ/ **I** *adj* lit, fig bitter; **laisser un goût ~ dans la bouche** lit, fig to leave a bitter taste in one's ou the mouth; **il a un pli ~ au coin des lèvres** his mouth is set in an embittered expression.
II *nm* Naut seamark.

amèrement /amɛʀmɑ̃/ *adv* bitterly.

américain, **~e** /ameʀikɛ̃, ɛn/ **I** ▶**537** *adj* American; **à l'~e** gén in the American style; Culin à l'américaine (*in a tomato sauce*).
II *nm* Ling American English.
III américaine *nf* (automobile) American car.

Américain, **~e** /ameʀikɛ̃, ɛn/ ▶**537** *nm,f* American.

américanisation /ameʀikanizasjɔ̃/ *nf* Americanization.

américaniser /ameʀikanize/ [1] **I** *vtr* to Americanize [*peuple, entreprise*].
II s'américaniser *vpr* [*personne, entreprise, peuple*] to become Americanized.

américanisme /ameʀikanism/ *nm* Americanism.

américaniste /ameʀikanist/ *nmf* specialist in American studies.

américium /ameʀisjɔm/ *nm* americium.

amérindien, **-ienne** /ameʀɛ̃djɛ̃, ɛn/ *adj* Amerindian.

Amérindien, **-ienne** /ameʀɛ̃djɛ̃, ɛn/ ▶**537** *nm,f* Amerindian, American Indian.

Amérique /ameʀik/ ▶**321** *nprf* America; **~ centrale** Central America; **~ latine** Latin America; **~ du Nord** North America; **~ du Sud** South America.

amerlo◑ /amɛʀlo/, **amerloque**◑ /amɛʀlɔk/ *nmf* offensive Yank○ injur.

amerrir /ameʀiʀ/ [3] *vi* [*hydravion*] to land (on water); [*vaisseau spatial*] to splash down.

amerrissage /ameʀisaʒ/ *nm* (d'hydravion) landing (on water); (de vaisseau spatial) splashdown.
■ **~ forcé** ditching.

amertume /amɛʀtym/ *nf* lit, fig bitterness.

améthyste /ametist/ ▶**193** *adj inv, nf* amethyst.

ameublement /amœbləmɑ̃/ *nm* **1** (meubles) furniture; (secteur d'activité) furniture trade ou business; **2** (action) furnishing.

ameublir /amœbliʀ/ [3] *vtr* to break up.

ameuter /amøte/ [1] **I** *vtr* **1** (alerter) [*personne, bruit, événement*] to bring [sb] out; **ses cris avaient ameuté les voisins** his shouts had brought the neighbours[GB] out; **tais-toi, tu vas ~ tout le quartier**○ be quiet or you'll bring the whole area out; **2** (attrouper à des fins hostiles) to stir [sb] up (**contre** against); **3** (pour la chasse) to whip [sth] in [*chiens*].
II s'ameuter *vpr* [*foule, passants*] to mass, to gather.

ami, **~e** /ami/ **I** *adj* [*pays, entreprise, troupe, personne*] friendly; **être ~ avec qn** to be a friend of sb's; **nous sommes très ~s** we are very good friends.
II *nm,f* **1** (camarade) friend; **un ~ à moi** a friend of mine; **se faire des ~s** to make friends; **je m'en suis fait une ~e** I made a friend of her; **grand ~** great friend; **~ fidèle/intime/d'enfance** faithful/close/childhood friend; **c'est un ~ de la maison** he's a friend of the family; **un ~ de longue date** a friend of long standing; **un ~ de 30 ans** a friend of 30 years; **un ~ de toujours** a life-long friend; **'un ~ qui vous veut du bien'** (sur une lettre anonyme) 'a friend who has your best interests at heart', 'a well-wisher'; **en ~** as a friend; **je te parle en ~** I say this as a friend; **être le meilleur ~ de l'homme** to be man's best friend; **m'~e**‡ my love; ▶**faux**; **2** (amateur) friend; **un ~ de la musique/des bêtes** a music/an animal lover; **c'est un ~ de la simplicité** he likes simplicity; **l'association des ~s de Pouchkine, les ~s de Pouchkine** the friends of Pushkin; **3** (forme d'adresse) gén friend; (entre époux) dear.
■ **~ de cœur** soul mate.
IDIOMES **les bons comptes font les bons ~s** a debt paid is a friend kept; **c'est dans le besoin** or **malheur qu'on connaît ses ~s** Prov a friend in need is a friend indeed; **les ~s de mes ~s sont mes ~s** the friends of my friends are my friends too.

amiable /amjabl/ **I** *adj* Jur (de gré à gré) [*transaction*] privately negotiated.
II à l'amiable *loc* [*se séparer*] on friendly terms; [*séparation*] amicable; [*adoption*] by private agreement; [*divorce*] by mutual consent; **s'arranger à l'~** to come to an amicable agreement.

amiante /amjɑ̃t/ *nm* asbestos; **poussière/fibres d'~** asbestos dust/fibres[GB]; **combinaison d'** or **en ~** asbestos suit.

amibe /amib/ *nf* Zool, Méd amoeba.

amibiase /amibjɑz/ *nf* amoebiasis.

amibien, **-ienne** /amibjɛ̃, ɛn/ **I** *adj* amoebic.
II *nm* amoeba.

amical, **~e**, *pl* **-aux** /amikal, o/ **I** *adj* **1** [*personne, geste, relations, ambiance*] friendly; **2** Sport [*match, rencontre*] friendly.
II amicale *nf* association; **~e des anciens combattants** veterans' association.

amicalement /amikalmɑ̃/ *adv* **1** (gentiment) [*conseiller, aider*] kindly; [*accueillir*] warmly; [*concourir*] in a friendly way; **bavarder ~** to chat (away) happily; **2** (en fin de lettre) (**bien**) **~** best wishes.

amidon /amidɔ̃/ *nm* starch; **l'~ du pain/des pâtes** the starch in bread/in pasta.

amidonnage /amidɔnaʒ/ *nm* starching.

amidonner /amidɔne/ [1] *vtr* to starch [*linge*]; **du linge amidonné** starched linen.

amincir /amɛ̃siʀ/ [3] **I** *vtr* **1** (faire paraître mince) [*vêtement*] to make [sb] look slimmer; **cette coupe de manteau amincit toujours** a coat of this cut always has a slimming effect; **2** (avec un outil) to plane down [*planche*].
II s'amincir *vpr* **1** [*personne, visage*] to get slimmer; **2** [*planche, couche*] to get thinner.

amincissant, **~e** /amɛ̃sisɑ̃, ɑ̃t/ *adj* [*produit*] slimming; [*coupe, robe*] that makes you look slim (*après n*).

amincissement /amɛ̃sismɑ̃/ *nm* **1** (de personne) slimming; **produit favorisant l'~** slimming product; **2** (de couche de glace) thinning (down).

aminé, **~e** /amine/ *adj* **acide ~** amino acid.

a minima /aminima/ *loc adj* **appel ~** *appeal lodged by the public prosecutor against too lenient a sentence*.

amiral, **~e**[1], *mpl* **-aux** /amiʀal, o/ **I** *adj* **bateau** or **vaisseau ~** flagship.
II *nm* ▶**390** admiral; **~ de la flotte** ≈ admiral of the fleet GB, fleet admiral US.

amirale[2] /amiʀal/ *nf* admiral's wife.

amirauté /amiʀote/ *nf* **1** (grade) admiralship; **accéder à l'~** to become an admiral; **2** (corps des amiraux) admiralty; (résidence) Admiralty House.

amitié /amitje/ **I** *nf* **1** (sentiment) friendship (**pour** for); **profonde/solide ~** deep/solid friendship; **par ~** out of friendship; **~ entre les peuples** friendship between peoples; **l'~ franco-allemande** Franco-German friendship; **geste/marque/message d'~** gesture/mark/message of friendship; **entretenir l'~** to keep friendship alive; **en toute ~** as a friend; **éprouver de l'~ pour qn** to have friendly feelings toward(s) sb; **prendre qn en ~, se prendre d'~ pour qn** to take a liking to sb; **faire à qn l'~ de faire** to be kind enough to do; ▶**cadeau**; **2** (relation) friendship; **vieille ~** old friendship; **~s durables** lasting friendships; **se lier d'~ avec qn** to strike up a friendship with sb; **nouer des ~s avec** to form friendships with; **trahir une ~** to betray a friendship; **être fidèle en ~** to be a faithful friend.
II amitiés *nfpl* (en fin de lettre) kindest regards; **faire ses ~s à qn** to give one's kindest regards to sb; **toutes mes ~s à** my kindest regards to.
■ **~ particulière** homosexual relationship.

Amman /aman/ ▶**857** *npr* Amman.

ammoniac /amɔnjak/ *nm* (gaz) ammonia.

ammoniacal, **-ale**, *mpl* **-aux** /amɔnjakal, o/ *adj* [*odeur*] of ammonia (*après n*); [*sel*] ammonia (*épith*).

ammoniaque /amɔnjak/ *nf* ammonia.

ammoniaqué, **~e** /amɔnjake/ *adj* [*détergent, produit*] ammonia-based.

ammonite /amɔnit/ *nf* ammonite.

ammonium /amɔnjɔm/ *nm* ammonium; **chlorure/sulfate d'~** ammonium chloride/sulphate[GB].

amnésie /amnezi/ *nf* amnesia; **période/crise d'~** period/attack of amnesia; **il est atteint d'~** he is suffering from amnesia.

amnésique /amnezik/ **I** *adj* [*patient, symptôme*] amnesic.
II *nmf* amnesiac.

amniocentèse /amnjosɛ̃tɛz/ *nf* amniocentesis.

amnios /amnjos/ *nm inv* amnion.

amniotique /amnjɔtik/ *adj* amniotic.

amnistiable /amnistjabl/ *adj* [*peine*] pardonable; [*personne*] who can be given amnesty (*épith, après n*).

amnistie /amnisti/ *nf* amnesty (**en faveur de** for); **loi d'~** amnesty law.

amnistier /amnistje/ [2] *vtr* to grant an amnesty to [*délinquent*]; to grant an amnesty for [*délit*].

amocher○ /amɔʃe/ [1] **I** *vtr* to bash○ [sb/sth] up [*personne, voiture*]; **leur voiture est bien amochée** their car is really bashed up○; **se faire ~** [*personne*] to get oneself bashed up○; **se faire ~ le nez/sa voiture** to get one's nose/car bashed up○.
II s'amocher *vpr* to bash oneself up○; **s'~ le nez/le bras/le visage** to bash up○ one's nose/face/arm.

amoindrir /amwɛ̃dʀiʀ/ [3] **I** *vtr* to reduce [*résistance*]; to weaken [*autorité, personne*]; **il est sorti très amoindri de cette épreuve** he came out of that ordeal a lesser man.
II s'amoindrir *vpr* [*forces, ressources, chances, possibilités*] to diminish; [*différences*] to grow less.

amoindrissement /amwɛ̃dʀismɑ̃/ *nm* (de pouvoir, forces physiques, facultés) weakening; (de fortune, ressources) reduction.

amollir: **s'amollir** /amɔliʀ/ [3] *vpr* **1** (devenir mou) to soften, to go ou become soft; **la cire s'amollit à la chaleur** wax becomes soft when heated; **s'~ dans le luxe** to grow soft in the lap of luxury; **2** (s'affaiblir) [*jambes, courage, résistance, énergie*] to grow weak, to weaken.

amonceler /amɔ̃sle/ [19] **I** *vtr* to pile up [*sable, terre, neige*]; to pile up, to stack [*objets, pierres*]; to amass [*richesses*]; **des nuages amoncelés** banked clouds.
II s'amonceler *vpr* [*nuages, sable, neige*] to build up; [*preuves, soucis, ennuis*] to pile up, to accumulate.

amoncellement /amɔ̃sɛlmɑ̃/ *nm* **1** (entassement) (de sable, neige, terre) piling up; (de richesses, biens) amassing; **2** (pile) (de sable, neige, terre) pile; (de richesses, biens) mass.

amont /amɔ̃/ **I** *adj inv* [*ski*] uphill.
II *nm* **1** Géog (de cours d'eau) upper reaches (*pl*); **en ~** upstream (**de** from); **naviguer d'~ en aval** to sail downstream; **2** (dans un processus) **dès l'~** from the initial stages; **en ~** upstream (**de** of).

amoral, **~e**, *mpl* **-aux** /amɔʀal, o/ *adj* amoral.

amoralisme /amɔʀalism/ *nm* amorality.

amorçage /amɔʀsaʒ/ *nm* (d'obus, de pompe) priming; (de poisson, ligne) baiting; (d'arc à souder) lighting; (de discussions, négociations) initiating; **l'~ de la reprise économique paraît difficile** getting economic recovery underway seems difficult.

amorce /amɔʀs/ *nf* **1** (de processus, discussion, changement) initiation, beginning; (de route, voie ferrée) initial section, beginning; (de pellicule) leader, tongue; **l'~ d'un sourire** the hint of a smile; **2** Pêche (produit) bait; **3** (détonateur) (d'arme) cap, primer; **brûler une ~** to set off a detonator; (de pétard) cap; **pistolet à ~s** cap gun.

amorcer /amɔʀse/ [12] **I** *vtr* **1** (commencer) to begin, to initiate [*dialogue, changement, processus*]; [*avion*] to begin [*descente*]; [*véhicule*] to go into [*virage*]; **il amorça un geste pour ouvrir la fenêtre** he made as if to open the window; **2** Pêche (appâter) to bait [*ligne, poisson*]; **3** Tech (mettre en route) to prime [*pompe*]; to arm, to activate [*arme à feu*].
II s'amorcer *vpr* to begin, to get under way.

amorphe /amɔʀf/ *adj* **1** (apathique) apathetic, lifeless; **2** Chimie [*roche, substance*] amorphous.

amorti /amɔʀti/ *nm* (au tennis) drop shot; (au football) trap; **exécuter un ~ spectaculaire** (au football) to trap the ball spectacularly.

amortir /amɔʀtiʀ/ [3] *vtr* **1** (atténuer) to deaden [*bruit*]; to absorb, to cushion [*choc*]; to break, to cushion [*chute*]; **2** (rentabiliser) **j'ai amorti mon ordinateur en quelques mois** my computer paid for itself in a few months; **pour ~ mon abonnement il faut que j'aille à la piscine deux fois par semaine** to make my season ticket pay I'll have to go to the swimming pool twice a week; **mon investissement/achat est maintenant amorti** my investment/purchase has paid for itself; **3** Fin (rembourser) to redeem, to pay off [*dette, emprunt*]; **4** Sport (au tennis) to kill [*balle*]; (au football) to trap [*ballon*].

amortissable /amɔʀtisabl/ *adj* [*dette, emprunt*] redeemable.

amortissement /amɔʀtismɑ̃/ *nm* **1** (de bruit) deadening; (de choc) absorption; (de chute) cushioning; **~ de vibrations** Phys dampening of vibrations; **2** Fin (de dette) redemption; (d'emprunt, obligation) paying off; **3** Compta (de machines, d'équipement) depreciation; (d'actifs) amortization; **4** Archit amortizement.
■ **~ comptable** depreciation; **~ dégressif** depreciation on a reducing balance; **~ économique** depreciation; **~ financier** amortization; **~ linéaire** straight line depreciation.

amortisseur /amɔʀtisœʀ/ *nm* Mécan shock absorber; Phys damper.
■ **~ d'oscillation** oscillation damper.

amour /amuʀ/ **I** *nm* **1** (affection) love; **~ maternel/paternel** maternal/paternal love; **l'~ filial** filial love; **avec ~** [*regarder, penser*] with love; **2** (inclination personnelle) love; **~ fou/heureux/déçu** passionate/blissful/disappointed love; **c'est le grand ~ entre eux** they are passionately in love; **lettre/poème/histoire d'~** love letter/poem/story; **aimer qn d'~** to be in love with sb; **par ~ pour** out of love for; **faire qch par ~ pour qn** to do sth out of love for sb ou for the love of sb; **faire qch par ~ de l'aventure** to do sth out of a love of adventure ou for the love of adventure; **mourir d'~** to die of a broken heart; **3** (profond attachement) (pour argent, pays, musique) love; **l'~ de la liberté/de l'art** the love of liberty/of art; **l'~ de la patrie** love of one's country; **pour l'~ de l'art** for the sake of art; **pour l'~ de Dieu** lit for the love of God; fig (supplication) for heaven's sake; **pour l'~ de Dieu vas-tu te taire!** for heaven's sake, will you shut up!; **4** (personne aimée) gén love; (forme d'adresse) darling; **mon ~** my darling; **c'était elle mon ~** she was my true love; **premier ~** first love; **c'était un ~ de jeunesse** it was a youthful romance; **5**○ (relations sexuelles) love; **faire l'~**○ **avec** to make love with; **les plaisirs de l'~** the pleasures of lovemaking; **6**○ (charmant) **~ de** adorable; **un ~ d'enfant/de chapeau** an adorable child/hat.
II amours *nmpl* ou *nfpl* **1** Zool mating ¢; **saison des ~s** mating season; **2** (aventures) love affairs; **les ~s de** the amorous adventures of; **~s enfantines** childhood crushes; **comment vont tes ~s?** what news of the affairs of your heart?; **à tes ~s!** (quand on éternue) bless you!
■ **~ courtois** Hist courtly love; **~ d'enfance** childhood sweetheart; **~ libre** free love; **~ physique** physical love.
IDIOMES **vivre d'~ et d'eau fraîche** to live on love alone; **revenir à ses anciennes** or **premières ~s** to return to one's first love.

Amour /amuʀ/ *nprm* **1** Art Cupid; **2** ▶ 357 Géog (fleuve) Amur.

amouracher: **s'amouracher** /amuʀaʃe/ [1] *vpr* **s'~ de** to become infatuated with.

amourette /amuʀɛt/ **I** *nf* passing infatuation.
II amourettes *nfpl* Culin beef marrow ¢.

amoureusement /amuʀøzmɑ̃/ *adv* lovingly.

amoureux, **-euse** /amuʀø, øz/ **I** *adj* **1** (de quelqu'un) [*personne*] in love (*jamais épith*) (**de** with); **femmes amoureuses** women in love; **être/tomber ~** to be/to fall in love (**de** with); **il est encore très ~ d'elle** he's still very much in love with her; **2** (passionné) **être ~ de peinture** to be a lover of painting; **être ~ de sport** to be a sport lover; **3** (qui dénote de l'amour) [*relation, regard*] loving; [*élan, comportement*] of love; **vie amoureuse** love life; **déception amoureuse** disappointment in love.
II *nm,f* **1** (de quelqu'un) lover; **2** (de quelque chose) **un ~ de musique/des livres** a music-/book-lover.

amour-propre /amuʀpʀɔpʀ/ *nm* self-esteem; **il est blessé dans son ~** his pride is hurt.

amovible /amɔvibl/ *adj* [*capuchon, col, housse, doublure*] detachable; [*étagère, siège, cloison*] removable; **mémoire/disque ~** detachable memory/disk.

ampère /ɑ̃pɛʀ/ *nm* Phys amp, ampère; **un fusible de 16 ~s** a 16 amp fuse.

ampèremètre /ɑ̃pɛʀmɛtʀ/ *nm* ammeter.

amphétamine /ɑ̃fetamin/ *nf* amphetamine.

amphi○ /ɑ̃fi/ *nm* lecture theatre[GB] ou hall; **un cours en ~** a class in a lecture theatre[GB], a lecture course US.

amphibie /ɑ̃fibi/ *adj* Zool, Aut amphibious.

amphibien /ɑ̃fibjɛ̃/ *nm* amphibian; **les ~s** amphibians.

amphigourique /ɑ̃figuʀik/ *adj* [*discours, style*] convoluted, amphigoric sout.

amphithéâtre /ɑ̃fiteɑtʀ/ *nm* **1** Antiq, Géog amphitheatre[GB]; **2** Univ lecture theatre[GB] ou hall.
■ **~ morainique** Géol morainic amphitheatre[GB].

amphitryon /ɑ̃fitʀijɔ̃/ *nm* liter host.

amphore /ɑ̃fɔʀ/ *nf* amphora.

ample /ɑ̃pl/ *adj* **1** (large) [*vêtement, manteau*] ample; [*robe*] loose-fitting; [*jupe, manche*] full, ample; [*geste, mouvement*] sweeping; **2** (abondant) [*quantité*] ample; [*récolte*] abundant, rich; [*détails, information*] full; **faire ~ provision de qch** to lay in ample stocks of sth; **je me tiens à votre disposition pour de plus ~s renseignements** or **détails** I would be pleased to provide you with any further information ou details; **3** (puissant) [*style, phrase*] rich; [*voix*] sonorous.

amplement /ɑ̃pləmɑ̃/ *adv* fully, amply; **une victoire ~ méritée** a fully deserved victory; **être ~ renseigné** to be fully informed; **c'est ~ suffisant** that's more than enough!

ampleur /ɑ̃plœʀ/ *nf* (de problème) size, extent; (de projet, sujet, d'étude) scope; (d'événement, de catastrophe, tâche) scale; (de dégâts, réactions) extent; **mesurer l'~ des dégâts** to gauge the extent of the damage; **devant l'~ de la crise** faced with the scale of the crisis; **des manifestations d'une ~ limitée/comparable** demonstrations on a limited/similar scale; **prendre de l'~** [*épidémie, rumeur*] to spread; [*manifestations, parti*] to grow in size; **le mouvement prend de plus en plus d'~** the movement is becoming more and more extensive; **de (très) grande ~** [*marée noire, mobilisation, crise*] on a large ou vast scale.

ampli○ /ɑ̃pli/ *nm* amp○, amplifier.

ampliation /ɑ̃plijasjɔ̃/ *nf* Jur **1** (copie) (certified) true copy; **2** (ajout) amplification.

amplificateur, **-trice** /ɑ̃plifikatœʀ, tʀis/ **I** *adj* [*effet, force*] magnifying.
II *nm* Audio, Phys amplifier.
■ **~ de brillance** Phot image intensifier; **~ de courant** Électrotech current amplifier; **~ de luminance** = **~ de bril-**

lance; **~ magnétique** Électron magnetic amplifier; **~ de tension** Électrotech voltage amplifier.

amplification /ɑ̃plifikasjɔ̃/ *nf* **1** Phys amplification; **2** (extension) (de relations, d'échanges) development; (de grève, revendications) escalation; (de dialogue, débat) expansion.

amplifier /ɑ̃plifje/ [2] **I** *vtr* to amplify [*voix, son, courant*]; to magnify [*geste, mouvement, rumeur*]; to expand, to extend [*mouvement, grève, échanges*].
II s'amplifier *vpr* [*son*] to grow; [*échanges*] to grow, to increase; [*grève, rumeur, scandale*] to intensify; [*tendance, revendication*] to gain momentum.

amplitude /ɑ̃plityd/ *nf* amplitude.
■ **~ thermique** Météo range of temperature.

ampoule /ɑ̃pul/ *nf* **1** Électrotech (light) bulb; **une ~ de 100 watts** a 100-watt bulb; **2** Pharm (buvable) phial; (injectable) ampoule; **3** Méd (lésion) blister, ampulla spéc; **j'ai une ~ au pied** I have a blister on my foot; **4** Anat ampulla; **5** Relig, Antiq ampulla.
■ **~ buvable** phial; **~ électrique** light bulb; **~ de flash** flash bulb; **~ injectable** ampoule.

ampoulé, **~e** /ɑ̃pule/ *adj* pej [*discours, style*] bombastic.

amputation /ɑ̃pytasjɔ̃/ *nf* **1** Méd amputation; **~ d'une jambe** amputation of a leg; **2** (de discours, texte, crédits) drastic cut (**de** in).

amputé, **~e** /ɑ̃pyte/ *nm,f* amputee.

amputer /ɑ̃pyte/ [1] *vtr* **1** Méd to amputate [*membre*]; to perform an amputation on [*personne*]; **il a été amputé du bras droit** he had his right arm amputated; **2** (réduire) to cut [sth] drastically [*texte, crédits, discours*]; **~ qch de qch** to cut sth from sth; **il a amputé son discours d'un long passage** he cut a long passage from ou out of his speech.

Amsterdam /amstɛʀdam/ **▶857** *npr* Amsterdam.

amuïr: **s'amuïr** /amyiʀ/ [3] *vpr* [*lettre, son*] to become mute.

amuïssement /amɥismɑ̃/ *nm* disappearance.

amulette /amylɛt/ *nf* amulet.

amure /amyʀ/ *nf* tack; **courir bâbord/tribord ~s** to go on the port/starboard tack; **point d'~** tack (of sail).

amurer /amyʀe/ [1] *vtr* to haul aboard the tack of [*voile*].

amusant, **~e** /amyzɑ̃, ɑ̃t/ *adj* **1** (distrayant) [*émission, spectacle, soirée, sport*] entertaining; **trouver ~ de faire** to find it entertaining to do, to enjoy doing; **2** (drôle) [*personne, histoire, film, livre*] funny, amusing; **le plus ~ c'est que** the funniest thing is that; **3** (surprenant) [*idée, initiative, détail*] funny; **c'est ~, je n'y aurais pas pensé** that's funny, I wouldn't have thought of that.

amusé, **~e** /amyze/ **I** *pp* ▶ **amuser**.
II *pp adj* [*sourire, regard, air*] amused, of amusement (*après n*); **elle a eu un sourire ~** she smiled in amusement (**à** at), she gave an amused smile.

amuse-gueule /amyzgœl/ *nm inv* **1** (chose à grignoter) cocktail snack GB, munchies (*pl*) US; **des ~** cocktail snacks, nibbles○; **2**○ fig appetizer; **en ~** as an appetizer.

amusement /amyzmɑ̃/ *nm* **1** (action de divertir) entertainment, amusement; **2** (divertissement) entertainment; **prendre qch comme un ~** to treat sth as entertainment; **écouter/regarder qn avec ~** to enjoy listening to/watching sb.

amuser /amyze/ [1] **I** *vtr* **1** (divertir) to entertain [*personne, auditoire, classe*]; (plaire) to amuse [*personne*]; **laisse-le, si ça l'amuse!** let him be, if he's happy; **tes plaisanteries douteuses ne m'amusent plus** your tasteless jokes no longer amuse me; **ce qui m'amuse c'est que** what I find amusing is that; **ça les amuse de faire** they enjoy doing; **tu crois que ça m'amuse de faire les courses tous les jours?** do you think I enjoy doing the shopping every day?; **amuse-le pendant que je me prépare** keep him entertained while I'm getting ready; **2** (détourner l'attention de) [*personne*] to distract [*personne, classe*]; **il ne travaille pas et amuse toute la classe** he doesn't work and he distracts the whole class; **si tu réussis à les ~ je pourrai téléphoner** if you can manage to distract them I'll be able to phone.
II s'amuser *vpr* **1** (jouer) [*enfant, animal*] to play (**avec** with; **dans** in); **pour s'~** for fun; **dépêche-toi, je n'ai pas le temps de m'~** fig hurry up, I haven't got time to mess about○; **ne t'amuse pas à ce petit jeu avec moi** fig don't play that little game with me; **2** (passer du bon temps) [*enfant, adulte*] to have a good time, to enjoy oneself; **ils s'amusent bien tous les deux!** the two of them are having a great time!; **amuse-toi bien!** enjoy yourself!; **il s'amuse à nous faire peur** he gets a kick out of scaring us○; **j'ai fait ça pour m'~** I did it for fun; **3** (s'aviser de) **ne t'amuse pas à faire cela** don't go doing that; **4** (se moquer de) liter **s'~ de qch/qn** to make fun of sth/sb; **on s'amuse de lui en privé** people make fun of him in private.
IDIOMES **s'~ comme des fous**○ to have a great time ou a ball○.

amusette /amyzɛt/ *nf* **1** (distraction) diversion; **2** (aventure amoureuse) fling○, passing fancy iron.

amuseur, **-euse** /amyzœʀ, øz/ *nm,f* lit, fig entertainer; **un ~ public** a public entertainer.

amygdale /ami(g)dal/ *nf* tonsil; **enlever les ~s** to remove the tonsils; **se faire opérer des ~s** to have one's tonsils taken out.

amygdalite /ami(g)dalit/ **▶271** *nf* tonsillitis.

amylacé, **~e** /amilase/ *adj* [*produit, composé, dérivé*] starch (*épith*).

amylase /amilɑz/ *nf* amylase.

an /ɑ̃/ **▶212, 801** *nm* **1** (durée) year; **passer trois ~s en France** to spend three years in France; **trente francs/trois pour cent par ~** thirty francs/three per cent per year; **trois fois par ~** three times a year; **2** (de date) year; **l'~ dernier** or **passé** last year; **l'~ prochain** next year; **tous les ~s** every year; **une fois par ~** or **l'~** once a year; **en l'~ deux mille** in the year two thousand; **en l'~ de grâce 1616** in the year of Our Lord 1616; **l'~ 55 avant/après Jésus-Christ** 55 BC/AD; **3** (pour exprimer l'âge) **avoir huit ~s** to be eight (years old); **les moins de dix-huit ~s** the under-eighteens; **il est mort à 25 ~s** he died at the age of 25; **être âgé de 30 ~s** to be 30 years old; **une fille de 7 ~s** a 7-year-old girl; **whisky de douze ~s d'âge** twelve-year-old whisky; **quand il a eu 12 ~s** when he was 12; **quand j'aurai 20 ~s** when I'm 20.
IDIOMES **bon ~, mal ~** year in, year out.

ana /ana/ *nm inv* ana.

anabaptisme /anabatism/ *nm* Anabaptism.

anabaptiste /anabatist/ *adj, nmf* Anabaptist.

anabolisant, **~e** /anabolizɑ̃, ɑ̃t/ **I** *adj* anabolic.
II *nm* anabolic steroid.

anabolisme /anabɔlism/ *nm* anabolism.

anacarde /anakaʀd/ *nm* cashew nut.

anacardier /anakaʀdje/ *nm* cashew tree.

anachorète /anakɔʀɛt/ *nm* anchorite.

anachronique /anakʀɔnik/ *adj* anachronistic.

anachronisme /anakʀɔnism/ *nm* anachronism.

anacoluthe /anakɔlyt/ *nf* anacoluthia.

anaconda /anakɔ̃da/ *nm* anaconda.

anaérobie /anaeʀɔbi/ **I** *adj* anaerobic.
II *nm* anaerobe.

anaglyphe /anaglif/ *nm* anaglyph.

anagrammatique /anagʀamatik/ *adj* anagrammatical.

anagramme /anagʀam/ *nf* anagram.

anal, **~e**, *mpl* **-aux** /anal, o/ *adj* anal.

analgésie /analʒezi/ *nf* analgesia.

analgésique /analʒezik/ *adj, nm* analgesic.

analogie /analɔʒi/ *nf* analogy.

analogique /analɔʒik/ *adj* analogical.

analogiquement /analɔʒikmɑ̃/ *adv* analogically.

analogue /analɔg/ **I** *adj* similar (**à** to), analogous sout (**à** to).
II *nm* Chimie analogue[GB].

analphabète /analfabɛt/ *adj, nmf* illiterate.

analphabétisme /analfabetism/ *nm* illiteracy.

analysable /analizabl/ *adj* analysable[GB].

analyse /analiz/ *nf* **1** gén (examen) analysis; **~ politique/financière** political/financial analysis; **ton ~ de la situation est très juste** your analysis of the situation is very accurate; **~ d'un produit/d'une substance** analysis of a product/of a substance; **faire l'~ de qch** to analyse[GB] sth; **en dernière ~** in the final analysis; **avoir l'esprit d'~** to have an analytical mind; **2** Méd test; **elle s'est fait faire des ~s** she's had tests done; **3** Math (discipline) calculus; **4** Psych psychoanalysis; **faire une ~, être en ~** to be in analysis.
■ **~ combinatoire** combinatorial analysis; **~ économique** economic analysis; **~ fonctionnelle** functional analysis; **~ grammaticale** parsing; **faire l'~ grammaticale d'une phrase** to parse a sentence; **~ harmonique** harmonic analysis; **~ logique** clause analysis; **~ numérique** numerical analysis; **~ organique** organic analysis; **~ de sang** blood test; **~ spectrale** spectrum analysis; **~ transactionnelle** transactional analysis; **~ d'urine** urine test; **~ vectorielle** vector analysis.

analyser /analize/ [1] *vtr* **1** gén to analyse[GB] [*problème, situation, produit, substance, texte*]; **2** Méd to test [*sang, urine*]; **3** Psych to psychoanalyse[GB]; **se faire ~** to be in analysis.

analyseur /analizœʀ/ *nm* **~ différentiel** Ordinat differential analyser[GB]; **~ d'ondes** Phys wave analyser[GB]; **~ de spectre** Phys spectrum analyser[GB].

analyste /analist/ **▶510** *nmf* **1** gén, Ordinat analyst; **2** Psych analyst.
■ **~ financier** Fin financial analyst.

analyste-programmeur, **-euse**, *mpl* **analystes-programmeurs** /analistpʀɔgʀamœʀ, øz/ **▶510** *nm,f* analyst-programmer.

analytique /analitik/ **I** *adj* **1** gén, Philos analytical; **2** Psych analytic.
II *nf* Philos analytics (+ *v sg*).

analytiquement /analitikmɑ̃/ *adv* analytically.

anamorphose /anamɔʀfoz/ *nf* anamorphosis.

ananas /anana(s)/ *nm inv* pineapple.

anapeste /anapɛst/ *nm* anapaest.

anaphore /anafɔʀ/ *nf* anaphora.

anaphorique /anafɔʀik/ *adj* anaphoric.

anar○ /anaʀ/ *adj inv, nmf* (*abbr* = **anarchiste**) anarchist.

anarchie /anaʀʃi/ *nf* lit, fig anarchy.

anarchique /anaʀʃik/ *adj* lit, fig anarchic.

anarchiquement /anaʀʃikmɑ̃/ *adv* anarchically.

anarchisant, **~e** /anaʀʃizɑ̃, ɑ̃t/ *adj* anarchistic.

anarchisme /anaʀʃism/ *nm* anarchism.

anarchiste /anaʀʃist/ **I** *adj* anarchistic.
II *nmf* anarchist.

anarcho-syndicalisme /anaʀkosɛ̃dikalism/ *nm* anarcho-syndicalism.

anarcho-syndicaliste, *pl* **~s** /anaʀ

kosɛ̃dikalist/ *adj, nmf* anarchosyndicalist.

anastigmatique /anastigmatik/ *adj* anastigmatic.

anastrophe /anastʀɔf/ *nf* anastrophe.

anathème /anatɛm/ *nm* anathema; **prononcer l'~ contre qn, frapper qn d'~** to excommunicate sb; **jeter l'~ sur qn/qch** fig to curse ou anathematize sout sb/sth.

Anatolie /anatɔli/ **▶692** *nprf* Anatolia.

anatolien, -ienne /anatɔljɛ̃, ɛn/ *adj* Anatolian.

anatomie /anatɔmi/ *nf* **1** Anat (science) anatomy; (structure) anatomy; **2**○ (silhouette) figure; **elle a une belle ~** she's got a good figure; **3** (analyse) analysis; **faire l'~ d'une crise économique** to analyse[GB] ou dissect an economic crisis.

■ **~ artistique** (spécialité) life drawing; (œuvre) life study.

anatomique /anatɔmik/ *adj* [*étude, planche, dessin*] anatomical; [*forme, objet*] anatomically designed.

anatomiquement /anatɔmikmɑ̃/ *adv* anatomically.

anatomiste /anatɔmist/ *nmf* anatomist.

ancestral, ~e, *mpl* **-aux** /ɑ̃sɛstʀal, o/ *adj* ancestral.

ancêtre /ɑ̃sɛtʀ/ *nmf* **1** (aïeul) ancestor; **mes ~s** my ancestors, my forebears; **nos ~s les Gaulois** our ancestors the Gauls; **2**○ (personne âgée) old man/woman; **3** (forme ancienne) ancestor; (précurseur) father, forerunner; **l'~ de l'homme/du catamaran** the ancestor of man/of the catamaran.

anche /ɑ̃ʃ/ *nf* Mus reed.

anchois /ɑ̃ʃwa/ *nm inv* anchovy.

ancien, -ienne /ɑ̃sjɛ̃, ɛn/ **I** *adj* **1** (qui a été autrefois) [*champion, mari, président, coiffeur, toxicomane, capitale*] former; **mon ancienne école** my old school; **2** (vieux) [*église, connaissance, modèle, famille*] old; **dans l'~ temps** in the old days; **3** Antiq [*histoire, langue, civilisation*] ancient; **la Grèce ancienne** ancient Greece; **l'~ français** Old French; **4** Art, Comm [*style, monnaie, tableau*] old; [*voiture*] vintage; [*meuble*] antique; [*livre*] old, antiquarian; **5** (dans une profession, une fonction, un grade) senior.

II *nm* **1** (vétéran) (de congrégation, tribu) elder; (d'entreprise) senior member; **les ~s du village** the village elders; **les ~s** (les personnes âgées) the older people; **2** (qui a été membre) (d'école, entreprise) old member; (de grande école) graduate; **3** (immobilier) **l'~** older property; **4** Comm (vieilles choses) antiques (*pl*); **acheter de l'~** to buy antiques; **5** (pour distinguer des générations) elder; **Caton l'~** Cato the Elder.

III anciens *nmpl* Antiq ancients; **littérature des ~s** literature of the ancients.

IV ancienne *nf* **à l'ancienne** [*confiture, meuble*] traditional; [*préparé, fabriqué*] in the traditional way.

■ **~ combattant** veteran; **~ élève** Scol old boy; Univ graduate; **~ franc** old franc; **l'~ monde** the Old World; **l'Ancien Régime** the Ancien Régime; **l'Ancien Testament** the Old Testament.

anciennement /ɑ̃sjɛnmɑ̃/ *adv* formerly.

ancienneté /ɑ̃sjɛnte/ *nf* **1** (de personne) seniority (**dans** in); **elle a plus d'~ que lui** she has more seniority than him; **avoir peu d'~** to have little seniority; **promotion à l'~** promotion based on seniority; **trois mois/ans d'~** three months'/years' service; **jour d'~** Entr, Ind service-related leave ou holiday GB; **~ dans le chômage** average period of unemployment; **2** (de tradition, relique) antiquity; **3** (âge) age; **4** (temps écoulé depuis) **l'~ de leur immigration** the time elapsed since they immigrated; **en raison de l'~ des faits** because the events happened a long time ago.

ancillaire /ɑ̃silɛʀ/ *adj* **amours ~s** amorous liaisons with the servants.

ancrage /ɑ̃kʀaʒ/ *nm* **1** Naut (action d'ancrer) anchoring; (mouillage) anchorage; **2** Constr (de mur) cramping.

ancre /ɑ̃kʀ/ *nf* **1** Naut anchor; **jeter l'~** lit to cast anchor; fig to settle down; **lever l'~** lit to weigh anchor; fig○ to get a move on○; **être à l'~** to be ou lie ou ride at anchor; **2** Tech (dans le bâtiment) cramp-iron; (en horlogerie) anchor escapement.

■ **~ de salut** or **miséricorde** sheet anchor.

ancrer /ɑ̃kʀe/ [1] **I** *vtr* **1** Naut to anchor [*navire*]; **les navires ancrés dans la baie** the ships lying at anchor ou anchored in the bay; **2** (fixer) **~ une idée dans les esprits** to fix an idea in people's minds; **~ un parti dans une région** to establish a party in an area; **~ qch dans la réalité** to anchor sth to reality; **3** Constr to cramp [*bâtiment*].

II s'ancrer *vpr* **1** Naut to anchor, to cast anchor; **2** fig [*idée*] to become fixed (**dans** in); [*parti, coutume*] to become established (**dans** in); **tradition bien ancrée** well-established tradition; **société trop ancrée dans ses habitudes** society which is too set in its ways.

andain /ɑ̃dɛ̃/ *nm* swathe.

andalou, -ouse /ɑ̃dalu, uz/ *adj* Andalusian.

Andalou, -ouse /ɑ̃dalu, uz/ *nm,f* Andalusian.

Andalousie /ɑ̃daluzi/ **▶692** *nprf* Andalusia.

andante /ɑ̃dɑ̃t(e)/ *nm, adv* andante.

Andes /ɑ̃d/ *nprfpl* **les ~** the Andes.

andin, ~e /ɑ̃dɛ̃, in/ *adj* Andean.

andorran, ~e /ɑ̃dɔʀɑ̃, an/ **▶537** *adj* Andorran.

Andorran, ~e /ɑ̃dɔʀɑ̃, an/ **▶537** *nm,f* Andorran.

Andorre /ɑ̃dɔʀ/ **▶321** *nprf* Andorra.

andouille /ɑ̃duj/ *nf* **1** Culin andouille; **2**○ fool; **faire l'~** to act the fool GB, to goof around US.

andouiller /ɑ̃duje/ *nm* branch of an antler, tine spéc.

andouillette /ɑ̃dujɛt/ *nf* andouillette (*small sausage made from chitterlings*).

androgène /ɑ̃dʀɔʒɛn/ **I** *adj* androgenic.

II *nm* androgen.

androgyne /ɑ̃dʀɔʒin/ **I** *adj* androgynous.

II *nm* androgyne.

androïde /ɑ̃dʀɔid/ *nm* android.

Andromaque /ɑ̃dʀɔmak/ *npr* Andromache.

andropause /ɑ̃dʀɔpoz/ *nf* male menopause.

âne /ɑn/ *nm* **1** Zool donkey, ass; **2**○ (personne stupide) dimwit○; Scol dunce.

■ **~ bâté** stupid clot.

IDIOMES **faire l'~ pour avoir du son** to act dumb to find out more; **être comme l'~ de Buridan** to be chronically indecisive.

anéantir /aneɑ̃tiʀ/ [3] **I** *vtr* **1** (détruire) to ruin [*récoltes*]; to lay waste to [*ville, région*]; to wipe out [*peuple, armée*]; to shatter [*espoir, rêve, autorité*]; **2** (abattre) [*nouvelle, chagrin*] to crush; [*effort, fatigue*] to exhaust; [*chaleur*] to overwhelm; **anéanti par la fatigue** utterly exhausted.

II s'anéantir *vpr* [*espoir, rêve*] to be shattered.

anéantissement /aneɑ̃tismɑ̃/ *nm* **1** (de ville, pays) destruction; (de peuple, armée) annihilation; (de récolte) devastation; **2** (d'espoir) shattering; (d'une personne) total collapse; **la nouvelle a provoqué l'~ de tous leurs espoirs** the news completely shattered all their hopes.

anecdote /anɛkdɔt/ *nf* anecdote; **ton article tient plus de l'~ que de l'analyse** your article is more anecdotal than analytical; **un auteur qui se perd dans l'~** an author who digresses on trivial topics; **pour l'~** as a matter of interest.

anecdotique /anɛgdɔtik, anɛkdɔtik/ *adj* anecdotal.

anémie /anemi/ *nf* **1** **▶271** Méd anaemia; **2** fig weakness.

■ **~ pernicieuse** pernicious anaemia.

anémier /anemje/ [2] **I** *vtr* **1** Méd to make [sb] anaemic [*personne*]; **2** fig to weaken.

II s'anémier *vpr* **1** Méd to become anaemic; **2** fig to grow feeble.

anémique /anemik/ *adj* **1** Méd anaemic; **2** fig weak, anaemic.

anémomètre /anemɔmɛtʀ/ *nm* anemometer.

anémone /anemɔn/ *nf* anemone.

■ **~ de mer** Zool sea anemone.

ânerie /ɑnʀi/ *nf* (parole) silly remark; (action) silly blunder; **dire des ~s** to talk rubbish○ ou nonsense; **faire des ~s** to do silly things.

anéroïde /aneʀɔid/ *adj* **baromètre ~** aneroid barometer.

ânesse /ɑnɛs/ *nf* she-ass, female donkey; **lait d'~** asses' milk.

anesthésiant, ~e /anɛstezjɑ̃, ɑ̃t/ *adj* **1** Méd anaesthetic; **2** fig stupefying.

anesthésie /anɛstezi/ *nf* **1** Méd anaesthesia; **provoquer une ~** to induce anaesthesia; **faire une ~ locale/générale** to give sb a local/general anaesthetic; **sous ~ locale/générale** under local/general anaesthetic; **il ne supporterait pas l'~** he would not tolerate the anaesthetic; **2** fig (de l'opinion publique, de la population) anaesthetizing.

anesthésier /anɛstezje/ [2] *vtr* **1** Méd to anaesthetize; **2** fig to anaesthetize [*opinion publique, population*].

anesthésique /anɛstezik/ *adj, nm* anaesthetic.

anesthésiste /anɛstezist/ **▶510** *nmf* (spécialiste) anaesthetist GB, anesthesiologist US.

aneth /anɛt/ *nm* dill.

anévrisme /anevʀism/ *nm* aneurysm.

anfractuosité /ɑ̃fʀaktɥozite/ *nf* crevice.

ange /ɑ̃ʒ/ *nm* **1** Relig angel; **être le bon ~ de qn** fig to be sb's good angel; **être le mauvais ~ de qn** fig to be a bad influence on sb; **être un ~ de beauté** to be angelically beautiful; **être un ~ de patience** to be patience itself; **2** (terme d'affection) angel, darling; **va me chercher mes cigarettes, tu seras un ~!** be an angel and get my cigarettes for me!

■ **~ déchu** fallen angel; **~ exterminateur** avenging angel; **~ gardien** guardian angel; **~ de mer** angel shark; **~ de la mort** Angel of Death; **~ de la route** motorbike patrolman.

IDIOMES **être aux ~s** to be in seventh heaven, to be walking on air; **'un ~ passe!'** 'somebody's walked over my grave!'; **un ~ passa** there was a lull in the conversation; **sourire aux ~s** to smile serenely; **il est beau comme un ~** he looks like a cherub; **être patient comme un ~** to have the patience of a saint; **être doux comme un ~** to be sweet-natured; **discuter sur le sexe des ~s** to count how many angels can dance on the head of a pin.

angélique /ɑ̃ʒelik/ **I** *adj* angelic.

II *nf* Bot, Culin angelica.

angéliquement /ɑ̃ʒelikmɑ̃/ *adv* angelically.

angélisme /ɑ̃ʒelism/ *nm* angelism.

angelot /ɑ̃ʒlo/ *nm* cherub.

angélus /ɑ̃ʒelys/ *nm inv* Relig angelus.

angevin, ~e /ɑ̃ʒvɛ̃, in/ **▶857** *adj* Angevin (*épith*), of Anjou (*après n*).

Angevin, ~e /ɑ̃ʒvɛ̃, in/ *nm,f* **1** **▶857** (natif d'Angers) native of Angers; (habitant d'Angers) inhabitant of Angers; **2** **▶692** (natif de l'Anjou) native of Anjou; (habitant de l'Anjou) inhabitant of Anjou.

angine /ɑ̃ʒin/ **▶271** *nf* Méd throat infection.

■ **~ diphtérique** angina diphtherica; **~ de poitrine** angina pectoris; **~ rouge** tonsillitis; **~ de Vincent** Vincent's angina ou disease.

angiographie /ɑ̃ʒjɔgʀafi/ *nf* angiography.

angiome /ɑ̃ʒjom/ ▶271 *nm* angioma.

anglais, **~e** /ɑ̃glɛ, ɛz/ **I** *adj* English.
II ▶462 *nm* Ling English; **parler l'~** to speak English.
III anglaise *nf* **1** (écriture) slanted script; **2** (boucle) ringlet.
IDIOMES **filer à l'~e** to take French leave.

Anglais, **~e** /ɑ̃glɛ, ɛz/ *nm,f* Englishman/ Englishwoman; **les ~** the English.

angle /ɑ̃gl/ *nm* **1** Math angle; **~ de 90°** ninety-degree angle; **2** (coin) corner; **être à** or **faire l'~ de deux rues** to be at the corner of two streets; **le bâtiment qui fait l'~** the building on the corner; **bibliothèque/cheminée d'~** corner bookcase/ fireplace; **faire un ~** [*rue*] to bend; **3** (point de vue) angle; **prendre une photo sous le bon ~** to take a photo from the right angle; **vu sous cet ~** viewed from this angle.
■ **~ aigu** Math acute angle; **~ d'arrivée** Mil angle of incidence; **~ d'attaque** Astronaut, Aviat angle of attack; Tech (d'un outil) angle of clearance; **~ de braquage** Aut steering lock; **~ de carrossage** Aut camber angle; **~ de champ** Phot angle of field; **~ de contingence** Math angle of contingence; **~ de déphasage** Phys phase angle; **~ droit** Math right angle; **faire un ~ droit avec qch** to make a right angle with sth; **se couper à ~ droit** to intersect at right angles; **~ d'éclairage** Phot angle of reflection; **~ de gîte** Naut angle of list; **~ de hausse** (au tir) angle of elevation, elevation firing angle; **~ horaire** Aviat, Phot angle of incidence; **~ d'inclinaison** Aviat bank angle; Phot angle of tilt; **~ de montée** Aviat angle of climb; **~ mort** Aut, Aviat blind spot; Mil dead angle; **~ obtus** Math obtuse angle; **~ d'ouverture** Phot, Phys aperture angle; **~ plat** Math straight angle; **~ de prise de vue** viewing angle; **~ de réflexion** Phot, Phys angle of reflection; **~ de réfraction** Phys angle of refraction; **~ rentrant** Math reentrant angle; **~ de route** Aviat track angle; **~ saillant** Math salient angle; **~ solide** Math solid angle; **~ de tir** Mil firing angle; **~ visuel** Phot visual angle; **~s adjacents** Math adjacent angles; **~s alternes externes** Math alternate exterior angles; **~s complémentaires** Math complementary angles; **~s opposés par le sommet** Math opposite angles; **~s supplémentaires** Math supplementary angles.

Angleterre /ɑ̃glətɛʀ/ ▶692 *nprf* Géog England.

anglican, **~e** /ɑ̃glikɑ̃, an/ *adj, nm,f* Anglican.

anglicanisme /ɑ̃glikanism/ *nm* Anglicanism.

anglicisation /ɑ̃glisizasjɔ̃/ *nf* anglicization.

angliciser /ɑ̃glisize/ [1] **I** *vtr* to anglicize.
II s'angliciser *vpr* to become anglicized.

anglicisme /ɑ̃glisism/ *nm* Anglicism.

angliciste /ɑ̃glisist/ *nmf* (spécialiste) Anglicist; (étudiant) student of English.

anglo-américain, **~e**, *mpl* **~s** /ɑ̃gloameʀikɛ̃, ɛn/ **I** *adj* gén Anglo-American; Ling American English (*épith*).
II ▶462 *nm* Ling American English.

anglomanie /ɑ̃glomani/ *nf* Anglomania.

anglo-normand, **~e**, *mpl* **~s** /ɑ̃glonɔʀmɑ̃, ɑ̃d/ **I** *adj* Hist Anglo-Norman.
II *nm* Ling Anglo-Norman.

Anglo-Normande /ɑ̃glonɔʀmɑ̃d/ ▶416 *adj f* **les îles ~s** the Channel Islands.

anglophile /ɑ̃glɔfil/ *adj, nmf* Anglophile.

anglophone /ɑ̃glɔfɔn/ **I** *adj* [*pays, province, groupe, personne*] English-speaking; **littérature ~** Univ literature of the English-speaking countries; **civilisations ~s** Univ the English-speaking world.
II *nmf* gén English speaker; (au Canada) Anglophone.

anglo-saxon, **-onne**, *mpl* **~s** /ɑ̃glosaksɔ̃, ɔn/ **I** *adj* **1** Hist, Ling Anglo-Saxon; **2** (de langue anglaise) [*littérature*] English language (*épith*).
II ▶462 *nm* Ling Anglo-Saxon.

Anglo-Saxon, **-onne**, *mpl* **~s** /ɑ̃glosaksɔ̃, ɔn/ *nm,f* Anglo-Saxon.

angoissant, **~e** /ɑ̃gwasɑ̃, ɑ̃t/ *adj* (alarmant) [*question, futur, réalité*] alarming; (effrayant) [*silence, film, pénombre*] frightening.

angoisse /ɑ̃gwas/ *nf* **1** gén, Psych anxiety (**devant, de** about); **vivre dans l'~ permanente** to live in a state of perpetual anxiety; **ce boulot c'est l'~**°! this work is torture!; **je suis arrivée tôt dans l'~ de rater mon avion** I arrived early for fear of missing my plane; **2** (crise d'anxiété) anxiety; **tous les soirs elle a des ~s** she suffers from anxiety every night; **3** Philos anguish, angst.

angoissé, **~e** /ɑ̃gwase/ **I** *pp* ▶ **angoisser**.
II *pp adj* [*voix, visage, personne*] anxious.
III *nm,f* worrier.

angoisser /ɑ̃gwase/ [1] **I** *vtr* [*personne, situation, question*] to worry [*personne*]; **ma santé m'angoisse** my health is a source of worry ou anxiety to me.
II° *vi* to be anxious ou nervous; **j'ai angoissé toute la nuit avant l'examen** I was anxious all night before my exam.
III s'angoisser *vpr* to get anxious (**de faire** doing).

Angola /ɑ̃gɔla/ ▶321 *nprm* Angola.

angolais, **~e** /ɑ̃gɔlɛ, ɛz/ ▶537 *adj* Angolan.

Angolais, **~e** /ɑ̃gɔlɛ, ɛz/ ▶537 *nm,f* Angolan.

angora /ɑ̃gɔʀa/ **I** *adj* [*animal, laine*] angora (*épith*).
II *nm* Tex angora; **pull-over en ~** angora sweater.

angström /ɑ̃gstʀœm/ *nm* angstrom.

anguille /ɑ̃gij/ *nf* Zool, Culin eel.
■ **~ de mer** conger eel; **~ des sables** sand eel.
IDIOMES **il y a ~ sous roche** there's something going on; **se faufiler comme une ~** to slip in and out; **filer** or **glisser comme une ~** to be as slippery as an eel.

angulaire /ɑ̃gylɛʀ/ *adj* Math, Phys angular.

anguleux, **-euse** /ɑ̃gylø, øz/ *adj* [*visage, traits, coude*] bony; [*aspect, contours*] jagged; [*personne, caractère, esprit*] prickly.

angusture /ɑ̃gystyʀ/ *nf* angostura.

anhydre /anidʀ/ *adj* anhydrous.

anhydride /anidʀid/ *nm* anhydride.

anicroche /anikʀɔʃ/ *nf* hitch; **sans ~(s)** without a hitch.

ânier, **-ière** /ɑnje, ɛʀ/ ▶510 *nm,f* donkey-driver.

aniline /anilin/ *nf* aniline.

animal, **~e**, *mpl* **-aux** /animal, o/ **I** *adj* **1** Biol [*espèce, comportement, graisses*] animal (*épith*); **protéines d'origine ~e** animal proteins; **2** (digne de l'animal) [*foule*] savage; [*comportement*] brutish.
II *nm* Biol, Zool animal.
■ **~ de compagnie** pet; **~ domestique** domestic animal; **~ familier** = **~ de compagnie**; **~ de laboratoire** laboratory animal; **~ nuisible** pest; **~ sauvage** wild animal; **~ utile** useful animal.

animalcule /animalkyl/ *nm* animalcule.

animalerie /animalʀi/ *nf* **1** (dans un laboratoire) animal house; **2** ▶510 (magasin) pet shop GB, pet store US.

animalier, **-ière** /animalje, ɛʀ/ **I** *adj* [*parc, artiste*] wildlife (*épith*).
II *nm,f* ▶510 (dans laboratoire) animal keeper.
III *nm* ▶510 Art wildlife artist.

animalité /animalite/ *nf* animality.

animateur, **-trice** /animatœʀ, tʀis/ ▶510 *nm,f* **1** (de groupe de vacanciers, club) coordinator; (de groupe d'études, d'association) leader; (de projet, congrès, festival) organizer; **~ des ventes** sales coordinator; **~ socioculturel** coordinator of sociocultural activities; **2** (présentateur) host, presenter, emcee US; **~ sportif** sports presenter, sportscaster US; **3** Cin (technicien) animator; **4** Scol *organizer of extra-curricular activities*.

animation /animasjɔ̃/ *nf* **1** (de groupe, d'émission, exposition) organization; (de ventes, service commercial) coordination; (de festival, cérémonie) orchestration; **elle a été chargée de l'~ du tournoi/stand** she's in charge of running the tournament/stand; **~ culturelle/sportive** promotion of cultural/sporting activities; **2** (entrain) life, vitality; **mettre de l'~ dans une réception** to liven up a reception; **le tourisme crée de l'~ au village** tourism puts a bit of life into the village; **ville/spectacle qui manque d'~** town/show that lacks vitality ou lacking in vitality; **une soirée sans ~** a lacklustre[GB] party; **discuter avec ~** to discuss animatedly, to have a lively discussion; **3** (de rue, marché, lieu de travail) hustle and bustle; (de personnes) excitement; **l'~ de la Bourse au lendemain des événements** the excitement on the Stock Exchange the day after the events; **il règne encore une grande ~ dans le quartier après minuit** there's still a lot going on in the area after midnight; **4** (activité dirigée) organized activity; **5** Cin animation.

animé, **~e** /anime/ **I** *pp* ▶ **animer**.
II *pp adj* **1** (vivant) [*débat, soirée, expression, regard*] lively; [*présentateur, orateur*] lively, dynamic; [*période, journées, époque*] lively, busy; [*rue, marché, ville*] bustling; **le marché des valeurs est très ~ en ce moment** the securities market is very brisk ou active at the moment; **2** (inspiré) **~ de bonnes/mauvaises intentions** spurred on by good/bad intentions; **3** Ling, Philos animate.

animer /anime/ [1] **I** *vtr* **1** (diriger) to lead [*débat, groupe, atelier, cérémonie*]; to run [*stage, séjour, exposition, festival*]; to present, to host, to emcee US [*émission, spectacle*]; to run [*revue, association, club*]; **animé par** [*groupe, spectacle, atelier*] organized by; [*mouvement*] led by; TV hosted by, presented by; **2** (rendre vivant) to liven up [*quartier, ville, région*]; to brighten up, to liven up [*récit, réunion, conversation*]; **3** (inspirer) [*sentiment, désir, volonté*] to drive (on) [*personne, équipe, peuple, entreprise*]; **4** (rendre brillant) [*excitant, joie*] to put a sparkle into [*regard, expression*]; **une lueur d'intérêt anima son visage** his/her face brightened with interest; **5** (insuffler la vie) lit [*âme, vie*] to animate [*corps, matière*]; fig [*artiste, lumière*] to bring [sth] to life [*œuvre*].
II s'animer *vpr* **1** (devenir vif) [*conversation, débat*] to become lively; [*réunion, jeu*] to liven up; [*visage, expression*] to light up; [*orateur, participant*] to become animated; **elle s'animait au fur et à mesure de la discussion** she became more animated as the discussion went on; **2** (s'agiter) [*lieu public, auditoire*] to come to life; **le quartier commence à s'~ dès huit heures** from eight o'clock onwards the area begins to liven up; **3** (prendre vie) to come to life; **un film où les objets s'animent** a film in which (the) objects come to life.

animisme /animism/ *nm* animism.

animiste /animist/ **I** *adj* [*religion*] animistic; [*société*] animist (*épith*).
II *nmf* animist.

animosité /animɔzite/ *nf* animosity (**envers** toward, towards GB; **entre** between); **avoir de l'~ contre** or **à l'égard de** or **envers qn** to be hostile toward(s) sb.

anion /anjɔ̃/ *nm* anion.

anis /ani/ *nm inv* **1** Bot (plante) anise; (graine) aniseed; **à l'~** (biscuit, bonbon) aniseed (*épith*); (boisson) aniseed-flavoured[GB]; **2** (bonbon) aniseed drop.

■ **~ étoilé** Chinese ou star anise; **~ vert** anise.

aniser /anize/ [1] *vtr* to flavour[GB] [sth] with aniseed; **goût anisé** aniseed flavour[GB].

anisette /anizɛt/ *nf* anisette.

Anjou /ɑ̃ʒu/ ▶ 692 *nprm* **l'~** Anjou.

Ankara /ɑ̃kaʀa/ ▶ 857 *npr* Ankara.

ankylose /ɑ̃kiloz/ *nf* ankylosis.

ankyloser: **s'ankyloser** /ɑ̃kiloze/ [1] *vpr* [*personne, jambes, bras*] to get stiff; **j'ai les jambes ankylosées** my legs are stiff.

annales /anal/ *nfpl* **1** (de pays, période, d'activité) annals; **ça restera** or **c'est à inscrire dans les ~** fig that will go down in history; **2** (d'un examen) book of past papers; **3** (revue) **'~ littéraires/politiques'** 'literary/political review'.

annamite /anamit/ *adj* Annamese.

Annamite /anamit/ *nmf* Annamese.

anneau, *pl* **~x** /ano/ **I** *nm* **1** (bijou) ring; **2** (pour attacher) ring; **~x de rideau** curtain rings; **3** Astron ring; **les ~s de Saturne** the rings of Saturn; **4** Zool ring, segment spéc; **5** Bot annulus; **6** Gén Civ ring road GB, beltway US.

II anneaux *nmpl* Sport rings; **aux ~x** on the rings.

■ **~ épiscopal** Relig episcopal ring; **~ de mariage** wedding ring; **~ nuptial** = **~ de mariage**; **~ oculaire** Tech Ramsden circle; **~ de vitesse** Sport (en patinage) speed-skating oval; (en sport automobile) racetrack; **~x de Newton** Newton's rings; **~x olympiques** Olympic rings.

année /ane/ ▶ 801 *nf* year; **l'~ en cours** this year, the current year; **en quelle ~ le disque est-il sorti?** what year was the album released?; **~ de naissance** year of birth; **il y a des ~s que je ne l'ai pas vue** I haven't seen her for years; **avec les ~s** over the years; **d'~ en ~** year by year; **d'une ~ à l'autre** from one year to the next; **l'~ 1962** the year 1962; **l'~ Mozart** the Mozart year; **ces dix dernières ~s** over the last ten years; **il a fait une ~ de droit** he has done one year of law; **dans le courant de l'~** in the course of the year; **souhaiter la bonne ~ à qn** to wish sb a happy new year; **tout le long de l'~** throughout the year; **en quelques ~s** within the space of a few years; **dans quelques ~s** in a few years; **au début/à la fin de l'~** at the beginning/at the end of the year; **en début/fin d'~** early/late in the year; **(dans) les ~s 80** (in) the eighties; **abonnement/location à l'~** annual subscription/rent; **il est décédé dans sa soixante-neuvième ~** he died in his sixty-ninth year.

■ **~ bissextile** leap year; **~ civile** calendar year; **~ financière** financial year GB, fiscal year US; **~ fiscale** tax year; **~ de référence** base year; **~ sabbatique** sabbatical year; **prendre une ~ sabbatique** to take a one-year sabbatical; **~ sainte** Holy Year; **~ scolaire** school year; **~ séculaire** last year of the century; **~ sidérale** sidereal year ; **~ solaire** solar year; **~ tropique** tropical year; **~ universitaire** academic year; **les Années folles** the Roaring Twenties.

année-lumière, *pl* **années-lumière** /anelymjɛʀ/ *nf* light-year.

annelé, **~e** /anle/ *adj* **1** Zool [*ver*] ringed; **2** Archit [*colonne*] annulated.

annexe /anɛks/ **I** *adj* **1** (contigu) [*local, salle*] adjoining; **2** (complémentaire) [*questions, déclaration, activités, budget*] additional; [*fiche, dossier*] attached.

II *nf* **1** (bâtiment) annexe GB, annex US; **l'~ de l'école/de la mairie** the school/town hall annexe GB ou annex US; **2** (document complémentaire) appendix; **mettre qch en ~** to put sth in an appendix.

annexer /anɛkse/ [1] **I** *vtr* **1** Pol [*État, pays*] to annex [*territoire, pays*]; **2** (joindre) to append (**à** to).

II s'annexer *vpr* (s'approprier) to appropriate [*part, droit*].

annexion /anɛksjɔ̃/ *nf* Pol annexation (**par** by).

annexionnisme /anɛksjɔnism/ *nm* annexationism.

annexionniste /anɛksjɔnist/ *adj, nmf* annexationist.

Annibal /anibal/ *npr* Hannibal.

annihilation /aniilasjɔ̃/ *nf* **1** gén (d'espoirs) death; (d'efforts) destruction; **2** Phys Nucl (destruction) annihilation.

annihiler /aniile/ [1] **I** *vtr* to destroy [*efforts, espoirs*]; to cancel out [*effet, résultats*].

II s'annihiler *vpr* [*pouvoirs, forces*] to cancel each other out.

anniversaire /anivɛʀsɛʀ/ **I** *adj* **date** or **jour ~ de** anniversary of.

II *nm* **1** (de personne, d'entreprise) birthday; **bon** or **joyeux ~!** happy birthday! **gâteau/cadeau/bougies d'~** birthday cake/present/candles; **2** (d'événement) anniversary; **le dixième ~ de sa naissance/mort** the tenth anniversary of his birth/death.

annonce /anɔ̃s/ *nf* **1** (action) announcement; **l'~ des résultats/de son arrestation** the announcement of the results/of his arrest; **à/dès/après l'~ du déficit il décida** when/as soon as/after the deficit was announced he decided; **un jour avant l'~ de leur départ** a day before they announced (that) they were leaving; **2** (message oral ou écrit) advertisement, advert○ GB, ad○; **une ~ publicitaire** or **commerciale** an advert○; **faire passer une ~** to place an advertisement (**dans** in); **trouver du travail par ~** to find a job through an advertisement; ▶ **petit**; **3** Jeux declaration; **faire une ~** (au bridge) to bid; **4** (indice) sign.

■ **~ classée** classified ad○; **~ immobilière** property ou real-estate US ad○; **~ matrimoniale** lonely hearts advertisement (*for marriage partner*).

annoncer /anɔ̃se/ [12] **I** *vtr* **1** (faire savoir) to announce [*nouvelle, décision, événement*] (**qch à qn** sth to sb); **M. et Mme X sont heureux de vous ~ la naissance de Julie** Mr and Mrs X are pleased to announce the birth of Julie; **elle nous a annoncé son départ** she informed us that she was leaving; **~ à qn que** to announce that; **il a annoncé publiquement qu'il démissionait** he publicly announced that he was resigning; **ils annoncent qu'ils ne participeront pas au colloque** they are announcing that they won't attend the symposium; **j'ai une triste nouvelle à vous ~** I have some sad news for you; **ils nous ont annoncé la nouvelle** gén they told us the news; (mauvaise nouvelle) they broke the news to us; **2** (signaler l'arrivée de) to announce; **veuillez m'~ à** please announce me to; **qui dois-je ~?** what name shall I give?; **se faire ~ (par qn)** to be announced (by sb); **3** (prédire) to forecast [*phénomène, événement*]; **on nous annonce de la pluie pour demain** rain is forecast for tomorrow; **on annonce une reprise de l'inflation** another rise in inflation is forecast; **4** (être l'indice de) [*événement, signal*] to herald [*événement*]; **~ un refroidissement** to herald a return of the cold weather; **n'~ rien de bon** to be a bad sign; **5** Jeux (au bridge) to bid; **~ trois sans atout** to bid three no trumps; **~ la couleur** (aux cartes) to call trumps; fig to lay one's cards on the table; **6** (prêcher) to preach.

II s'annoncer *vpr* **1** (se manifester) [*crise, tempête*] to be brewing; **2** (se présenter) **la saison/le programme s'annonce bien** the season/the programme is off to a good start; **l'été s'annonce chaud/pluvieux** the summer looks like being a hot/rainy one; **la récolte 92 s'annonce excellente** the '92 harvest promises to be very good; **la semaine s'annonce (comme une semaine) difficile** it looks as if this week is going to be difficult; **comment s'annonce la réunion?** how do things look for the meeting?; **3** (prévenir de sa venue) **Oncle Paul s'est annoncé** Uncle Paul said he was coming.

annonceur /anɔ̃sœʀ/ *nm* Pub advertiser.

annonciateur, **-trice** /anɔ̃sjatœʀ, tʀis/ **I** *adj* [*ange*] herald (*épith*); [*signe, signal*] warning (*épith*) (**de qch** of sth); **des problèmes ~s de qch** problems heralding sth.

II *nm,f* herald.

Annonciation /anɔ̃sjasjɔ̃/ *nf* Relig **l'~** the Annunciation.

annotateur, **-trice** /anɔtatœʀ, tʀis/ *nm,f* annotator.

annotation /anɔtasjɔ̃/ *nf* annotation.

annoter /anɔte/ [1] *vtr* to annotate [*ouvrage*]; to write notes on [*copie, devoir*]; **un exemplaire annoté de la main de l'auteur** a copy annotated in the author's own hand.

annuaire /anɥɛʀ/ *nm* **1** (d'adresses, du téléphone) directory; **consulter l'~** to consult ou look in the directory; **ne pas être dans l'~** not to be in the phone book GB, to have an unlisted number; **2** (recueil) yearbook.

■ **~ électronique** Télécom electronic directory; **~ professionnel** professional directory; **~ téléphonique** telephone directory, phone book GB.

annualité /anɥalite/ *nf* yearly basis.

annuel, **-elle** /anɥɛl/ *adj* **1** (de chaque année) [*rapport, bénéfice, congés*] annual, yearly; **2** (qui dure un an) [*abonnement*] annual, one-year (*épith*); [*contrat*] one-year (*épith*).

annuellement /anɥɛlmɑ̃/ *adv* annually, yearly.

annuité /anɥite/ *nf* **1** Fin (dette) annuity; **2** Admin (année de service) year of pensionable service.

annulable /anylabl/ *adj* Jur annullable.

annulaire /anylɛʀ/ **I** *adj* annular.

II *nm* Anat ring finger.

annulation /anylasjɔ̃/ *nf* **1** gén (de mesure) abolition; (de sanction, loi) repeal; (d'événement) cancellation[GB]; **l'Europe propose l'~ de la dette du tiers monde** Europe suggests writing off Third World debts; **2** Jur (de procédure) quashing; (d'élection) cancellation[GB]; (de traité) revocation; (de mariage) annulment; **~ de permis de conduire** removal of driving licence[GB].

annuler /anyle/ [1] **I** *vtr* **1** (supprimer) to cancel [*rendez-vous, vol, spectacle*]; to write off [*dette, créance*]; to discount [*résultat sportif*]; **2** Jur to declare [sth] void [*élection, contrat*]; to revoke [*testament, jugement*]; to quash [*procédure*]; to repeal [*loi*]; **~ le permis de conduire de qn** to remove sb's driving licence[GB].

II s'annuler *vpr* [*questions, forces*] to cancel each other out.

anoblir /anɔbliʀ/ [3] *vtr* to ennoble.

anoblissement /anɔblismɑ̃/ *nm* ennoblement.

anode /anɔd/ *nf* anode.

anodin, **~e** /anɔdɛ̃, in/ *adj* (insignifiant) [*personne*] insignificant; (sans risques) [*substance*] harmless, innocuous; [*remède*] mild; [*sujet*] safe, neutral; [*question, plaisanterie*] innocent.

anodiser /anɔdize/ [1] *vtr* to anodize.

anomal, **~e**, *mpl* **-aux** /anɔmal, o/ *adj* anomalous.

anomalie /anɔmali/ *nf* gén anomaly; Astron, Sci anomaly; Biol abnormality; Tech fault; **~ magnétique** magnetic anomaly.

anomie /anɔmi/ *nf* anomie.

ânon /anɔ̃/ *nm* **1** (petit de l'âne) donkey foal; **2** (petit âne) little donkey.

anone /anɔn/ *nf* annona.

ânonnement /anɔnmɑ̃/ *nm* (récitation hésitante) faltering delivery; (récitation monotone) monotonous delivery; (ton monotone) drone.

ânonner /anɔne/ [1] *vtr* (en hésitant) to stumble through [*texte, leçon*]; (sans expression) (lire) to read [sth] in a drone; (réciter) to recite [sth] in a drone.

anonymat /anɔnima/ *nm* gén anonymity; (discrétion) confidentiality; **sous le couvert de l'~** anonymously; **garder l'~** to remain anonymous; **sortir de l'~** (dire son nom) to reveal one's identity; (devenir célèbre) to emerge from obscurity.

anonyme /anɔnim/ **I** *adj* **1** (sans nom) [*auteur, lettre, don*] anonymous; **2** (neutre) [*décor, style*] impersonal.
II *nmf* unknown man/woman; **les ~s** anonymous people.

anonymement /anɔnimmɑ̃/ *adv* anonymously.

anophèle /anɔfɛl/ *nm* anopheles.

anorak /anɔʀak/ *nm* anorak.

anorexie /anɔʀɛksi/ *nf* anorexia.
■ **~ mentale** anorexia nervosa.

anorexique /anɔʀɛksik/ *adj, nmf* anorexic.

anormal, **~e**, *mpl* **-aux** /anɔʀmal, o/ *adj* **1** (inhabituel) [*saignement, usure, taux, température*] abnormal; [*événement*] unusual; **il est ~ qu'il neige en juin** it's unusual for it to snow in June; **2** (injuste) unfair; **je trouve ~ qu'il parte ainsi** I think it's unfair that he should leave like this; **3**○ (déficient) [*enfant*] abnormal.

anormalement /anɔʀmalmɑ̃/ *adv* abnormally.

anormalité /anɔʀmalite/ *nf* abnormality.

anoxie /anɔksi/ *nf* anoxia.

anoxique /anɔksik/ *adj* anoxic.

ANPE /aɛnpeœ/ *nf* (*abbr* = **Agence nationale pour l'emploi**) *national employment agency*.

anse /ɑ̃s/ *nf* **1** (de tasse, panier) handle; **2** Géog cove; **3** Anat loop.
■ **~ de panier** Archit basket arch.
IDIOMES **faire danser** or **valser l'~ du panier** to be on the fiddle○.

antagonique /ɑ̃tagɔnik/ *adj* [*personnes, forces*] antagonistic; [*intérêts*] conflicting.

antagonisme /ɑ̃tagɔnism/ *nm* antagonism (**entre** between).

antagoniste /ɑ̃tagɔnist/ **I** *adj* **1** [*groupes, forces*] opposing; [*méthodes, conceptions, intérêts*] conflicting; **2** Anat [*muscles*] antagonist.
II *nmf* antagonist.

antan: **d'antan** /dɑ̃tɑ̃/ *loc adj* liter [*guerres, fêtes, guinguettes*] of old (*après n*); [*prestige, splendeur*] former; **les métiers/la ville d'~** the old trades/town; **le Lyon d'~** the Lyons of yesteryear littér.

Antarctide /ɑ̃taʀktid/ *nprf* Antarctica.

antarctique /ɑ̃taʀktik/ *adj* Antarctic.

Antarctique /ɑ̃taʀktik/ *nprm* **1** **▶ 321** (continent et eaux) Antarctic; (continent seul) Antarctica; **2** **▶ 555** (océan) **océan ~** Antarctic Ocean.

antécédent, **~e** /ɑ̃tesedɑ̃, ɑ̃t/ **I** *adj* (précédent) previous (*épith*).
II *nm* **1** (fait du passé) past history; **elle a un ~ judiciaire** she has a criminal record; **2** Méd medical history; **des ~s cardiaques** a (medical) history of heart trouble; **y a-t-il des ~s d'allergie dans votre famille?** do you have a family history of allergy?; **3** Ling, Math antecedent.

antéchrist /ɑ̃tekʀist/ *nm* Antichrist.

antédiluvien, **-ienne** /ɑ̃tedilyvjɛ̃, ɛn/ *adj* antediluvian.

anténatal, **~e**, *mpl* **~s** /ɑ̃tenatal/ *adj* antenatal.

antenne /ɑ̃tɛn/ **I** *nf* **1** Télécom (de radio, télévision) aerial; (de radar, satellite) antenna; **~ collective** community antenna; **~ directive** directional antenna; **~ parabolique** parabolic antenna, satellite dish; **~ télescopique** telescopic aerial; **2** Radio, TV (liaison) **être sur** or **à l'~** to be on the air; **passer à l'~** to go on the air; **être interdit d'~** to be banned from broadcasting; **l'~ est à vous** over to you; **je te rends l'~** back to you; **garder l'~** to stay on the air; **c'est à toi, l'~ dans dix secondes** get ready, on the air in ten seconds; **3** (poste détaché) branch; **~s locales/régionales** local/regional branches; **~s commerciales** commercial outlets; **~ universitaire** outpost of the university GB, branch campus US; **~ médicale** medical unit; **~ chirurgicale** Méd mobile surgical unit; Mil advanced surgical unit; **4** Zool (d'insecte, crustacé) antenna; **avoir des ~s** fig to have a sixth sense.

antépénultième /ɑ̃tepenyltjɛm/ **I** *adj* antepenultimate.
II *nf* antepenultimate syllable.

antéposé, **~e** /ɑ̃tepoze/ *adj* Ling **en anglais l'adjectif est ~** in English the adjective comes before the noun.

antérieur, **~e** /ɑ̃teʀjœʀ/ *adj* **1** (précédent) [*salaire, situation, œuvre*] previous; **le texte est ~ à 1986** the text was written prior to 1986; **toutes les estimations sont ~es au lundi noir** all the estimates were made prior to Black Monday; **sa nomination est très ~e à la guerre** his nomination dates back to long before the war; **2** (placé devant) [*partie, face*] front; [*membre, ligament*] anterior; **3** Phon [*voyelle*] front.

antérieurement /ɑ̃teʀjœʀmɑ̃/ *adv* previously; **~ à** prior to.

antériorité /ɑ̃teʀjɔʀite/ *nf* anteriority; **l'~ de qch sur** the anteriority of sth in relation to.

anthologie /ɑ̃tɔlɔʒi/ *nf* anthology.

anthozoaire /ɑ̃tozɔɛʀ/ *nm* anthozoan; **les ~s** Anthozoa.

anthracite /ɑ̃tʀasit/ **I** **▶ 193** *adj inv* (couleur) charcoal grey GB ou gray US.
II *nm* anthracite.

anthrax /ɑ̃tʀaks/ *nm inv* Méd carbuncle.

anthropocentrisme /ɑ̃tʀɔposɑ̃tʀism/ *nm* anthropocentrism.

anthropoïde /ɑ̃tʀɔpɔid/ **I** *adj* anthropoid.
II *nm* (singe) anthropoid ape.

anthropologie /ɑ̃tʀɔpɔlɔʒi/ *nf* anthropology.

anthropologique /ɑ̃tʀɔpɔlɔʒik/ *adj* anthropological.

anthropologiste /ɑ̃tʀɔpɔlɔʒist/, **anthropologue** /ɑ̃tʀɔpɔlɔg/ **▶ 510** *nmf* anthropologist.

anthropométrie /ɑ̃tʀɔpɔmetʀi/ *nf* anthropometry.
■ **~ judiciaire** criminal anthropometry.

anthropométrique /ɑ̃tʀɔpɔmetʀik/ *adj* anthropometric; **service ~** anthropometry department.

anthropomorphique /ɑ̃tʀɔpɔmɔʀfik/ *adj* anthropomorphic.

anthropomorphisme /ɑ̃tʀɔpɔmɔʀfism/ *nm* anthropomorphism.

anthroponymie /ɑ̃tʀɔpɔnimi/ *nf* anthroponomy.

anthropophage /ɑ̃tʀɔpɔfaʒ/ **I** *adj* cannibalistic, anthropophagous spéc.
II *nmf* cannibal, anthropophagite spéc.

anthropophagie /ɑ̃tʀɔpɔfaʒi/ *nf* cannibalism, anthropophagy spéc.

anthropopithèque /ɑ̃tʀɔpɔpitɛk/ *nm* Anthropopithecus.

antiacide /ɑ̃tiasid/ *adj inv, nm* antacid.

antiadhésif, **-ive** /ɑ̃tiadezif, iv/ *adj* nonstick.

antiaérien, **-ienne** /ɑ̃tiaeʀjɛ̃, ɛn/ *adj* [*défense, missile*] antiaircraft (*épith*).

antialcoolique /ɑ̃tialkɔlik/ *adj* **mesure/campagne ~** anti-alcohol measure/campaign; **ligue ~** temperance league; **centre de cure ~** (alcohol) detoxification centre[GB].

antiallergique /ɑ̃tialɛʀʒik/ *adj* antiallergic.

anti-apartheid /ɑ̃tiapaʀtɛd/ *adj* antiapartheid.

antiatomique /ɑ̃tiatɔmik/ *adj* [*vêtement*] (anti-)radiation (*épith*); **abri ~** nuclear fallout shelter.

antiaveuglant, **~e** /ɑ̃tiavøglɑ̃, ɑ̃t/ *adj* Aut antiglare, antidazzle.

antibactérien, **-ienne** /ɑ̃tibakteʀjɛ̃, ɛn/ *adj* antibacterial.

antibalistique /ɑ̃tibalistik/ *adj* antiballistic.

antibiothérapie /ɑ̃tibjoteʀapi/ *nf* antibiotic therapy.

antibiotique /ɑ̃tibjɔtik/ *adj, nm* antibiotic; **traiter qn aux ~s** to treat sb with antibiotics; **être sous ~s** to be on antibiotics.

antiblocage /ɑ̃tiblɔkaʒ/ *adj inv* **système ~ des roues** anti-lock braking system, ABS.

antibrouillard /ɑ̃tibʀujaʀ/ Aut **I** *adj inv* **phare ~** fog lamp GB, fog light.
II *nm* fog lamp GB, fog light.

antibruit /ɑ̃tibʀɥi/ *adj inv* [*mur, revêtement*] soundproof.

antibuée /ɑ̃tibye/ *adj inv* **dispositif ~** demister.

anticalcaire /ɑ̃tikalkɛʀ/ *adj* **agent** or **produit ~** water softener.

anticancéreux, **-euse** /ɑ̃tikɑ̃seʀø, øz/ *adj* [*traitement*] cancer (*épith*); [*médicament*] anticancer (*épith*); **centre ~** (hôpital) cancer hospital; (laboratoire) cancer research centre[GB].

antichambre /ɑ̃tiʃɑ̃bʀ/ *nf* lit, fig anteroom, antechamber; **faire ~** to wait in the anteroom; **l'~ de la gloire** fig the way to stardom.

antichar /ɑ̃tiʃaʀ/ *adj* antitank (*épith*).

antichoc /ɑ̃tiʃɔk/ *adj inv* **1** (protecteur) **casque ~** crash helmet; **2** (incassable) [*montre*] shockproof.

anticipation /ɑ̃tisipasjɔ̃/ *nf* **1** (prévision) anticipation; **faire qch par ~** to do sth in advance; **2** Cin, Littérat **film/roman d'~** science fiction film/novel.

anticipé, **~e** /ɑ̃tisipe/ **I** *pp* ▶ **anticiper**.
II *pp adj* [*départ, élection, libération*] early; **il a demandé à partir en retraite ~e** he asked for early retirement; **avec mes remerciements ~s** thanking you in advance; **faire qch de façon ~e** to do sth in advance.

anticiper /ɑ̃tisipe/ [1] **I** *vtr* **1** (prévoir) to anticipate [*réaction, coup, victoire, changement*]; to foresee [*invention*]; **~ qch de plusieurs années/trois mois** to anticipate sth by several years/three months; **n'anticipons pas!** let's not get ahead of ourselves!; **2** (effectuer à l'avance) to bring [sth] forward [*paiement, remboursement, construction*]; **ils ont anticipé la construction du pont d'un an** they brought the building of the bridge forward by a year.
II **anticiper sur** *vtr ind* to anticipate [*événements, évolution, mouvement*]; **vous anticipez sur le récit en révélant ce détail** by mentioning that detail you are anticipating the next part of the story.
III *vi* Jeux, Sport (au tennis, aux échecs) to think ahead.

anticlérical, **~e**, *mpl* **-aux** /ɑ̃tikleʀikal, o/ *adj, nm,f* anticlerical.

anticléricalisme /ɑ̃tikleʀikalism/ *nm* anticlericalism.

anticlinal, **~e**, *mpl* **-aux** /ɑ̃tiklinal, o/ **I** *adj* anticlinal.
II *nm* anticline.

anticoagulant, **~e** /ɑ̃tikɔagylɑ̃, ɑ̃t/ **I** *adj* anticoagulant.
II *nm* anticoagulant.

anticolonialisme /ɑ̃tikɔlɔnjalism/ *nm* anticolonialism.

anticolonialiste /ɑ̃tikɔlɔnjalist/ *adj, nmf* anti-colonialist.

anticommunisme /ɑ̃tikɔmynism/ *nm* anticommunism.

anticommuniste /ɑ̃tikɔmynist/ *adj, nmf* anti-communist.

anticonceptionnel, **-elle** /ɑ̃tikɔ̃sɛpsjɔnɛl/ *adj* [*pilule, méthode*] contraceptive; [*propagande*] birth control (*épith*).

anticonformisme /ɑ̃tikɔ̃fɔʀmism/ *nm* nonconformism.

anticonformiste /ɑ̃tikɔ̃fɔʀmist/ *adj, nmf* nonconformist.

anticonstitutionnel, **-elle** /ɑ̃tikɔ̃stitysjɔnɛl/ *adj* unconstitutional.

anticonstitutionnellement /ɑ̃tikɔ̃stitysjɔnɛlmɑ̃/ *adv* unconstitutionally.

anticorps /ɑ̃tikɔʀ/ *nm inv* antibody; **fabriquer des ~** to produce antibodies.

anticorrosion /ɑ̃tikɔʀɔzjɔ̃/ *adj inv* rustproof.

anti-crevaison /ɑ̃tikʀəvɛzɔ̃/ *adj inv* **bombe ~** Aut puncture sealant spray.

anticyclone /ɑ̃tisiklon/ *nm* anticyclone, high.

anticyclonique /ɑ̃tisiklɔnik/ *adj* anticyclonic.

antidater /ɑ̃tidate/ [1] *vtr* to antedate.

antidéflagrant, **~e** /ɑ̃tideflagʀɑ̃, ɑ̃t/ *adj* explosion-proof.

antidémocratique /ɑ̃tidemɔkʀatik/ *adj* undemocratic.

antidépresseur /ɑ̃tidepʀesœʀ/ *nm* antidepressant.

antidérapant, **~e** /ɑ̃tideʀapɑ̃, ɑ̃t/ *adj* [*pneu, chaussée*] nonskid; [*semelle*] nonslip.

antidétonant, **~e** /ɑ̃tidetɔnɑ̃, ɑ̃t/ **I** *adj* antiknock.

II *nm* antiknock.

antidiphtérique /ɑ̃tidifteʀik/ *adj* diphtheria (*épith*).

antidiscriminatoire /ɑ̃tidiskʀiminatwaʀ/ *adj* antidiscriminatory.

antidopage /ɑ̃tidɔpaʒ/ *adj* [*contrôle, test*] dope; [*mesure, lutte*] against doping (*après n*); **subir un contrôle ~** to be dope-tested.

antidote /ɑ̃tidɔt/ *nm* lit, fig antidote (**contre** against; **à, de** for).

antidrogue /ɑ̃tidʀɔg/ *adj inv* antidrug.

antiéconomique /ɑ̃tiekɔnɔmik/ *adj* uneconomical.

antiémeute /ɑ̃tiemøt/ *adj inv* **police/véhicule ~** riot police/vehicle.

antienne /ɑ̃tjɛn/ *nf* **1** (refrain) refrain; **2** Relig antiphon.

antiesclavagisme /ɑ̃tiɛsklavaʒism/ *nm* opposition to slavery; (aux États-Unis) abolitionism.

antiesclavagiste /ɑ̃tiɛsklavaʒist/ **I** *adj* anti-slavery; (aux États-Unis) abolitionist.

II *nmf* opponent of slavery; (aux États-Unis) abolitionist.

antifasciste /ɑ̃tifaʃist/ *adj, nmf* antifascist.

antifatigue /ɑ̃tifatig/ *adj inv* [*bas, collant*] support (*épith*).

anti-g /ɑ̃tiʒe/ *adj invar* anti-g; **combinaison ~** G suit.

antigang /ɑ̃tigɑ̃g/ *adj inv* **brigade ~** crime squad.

antigel /ɑ̃tiʒɛl/ *adj inv, nm* antifreeze.

antigène /ɑ̃tiʒɛn/ *nm* antigen.

Antigone /ɑ̃tigɔn/ *npr* Antigone.

antigouvernemental, **~e**, *mpl* **-aux** /ɑ̃tiguvɛʀnəmɑ̃tal, o/ *adj* anti-government.

Antigue et Barbude /ɑ̃tigebaʀbyd/ ▶ **321**, **416** *nprf* Antigua and Barbuda.

antihausse /ɑ̃tios/ *adj inv* anti-inflationary.

antihéros /ɑ̃tieʀo/ *nm inv* anti-hero.

antihistaminique /ɑ̃tiistaminik/ *adj, nm* antihistamine.

antihygiénique /ɑ̃tiiʒjenik/ *adj* unhygienic.

anti-inflammatoire, *pl* **~s** /ɑ̃tiɛ̃flamatwaʀ/ *adj, nm* anti-inflammatory.

anti-inflation /ɑ̃tiɛ̃flasjɔ̃/ *adj inv* anti-inflation (*épith*).

antilimaces /ɑ̃tilimas/ *adj inv* **granulés ~** slug pellets.

antillais, **~e** /ɑ̃tijɛ, ɛz/ *adj* West Indian.

Antillais, **~e** /ɑ̃tijɛ, ɛz/ ▶ **692** *nm,f* West Indian.

Antilles /ɑ̃tij/ ▶ **692** *nprfpl* **les ~** the West Indies; **les ~ françaises** the French West Indies; **les Petites/Grandes ~** the Lesser/Greater Antilles.

■ **~ néerlandaises** Netherlands Antilles.

antilope /ɑ̃tilɔp/ *nf* antelope.

antimatière /ɑ̃timatjɛʀ/ *nf* antimatter.

antimilitarisme /ɑ̃timilitaʀism/ *nm* antimilitarism.

antimilitariste /ɑ̃timilitaʀist/ *adj, nmf* antimilitarist.

antimissile /ɑ̃timisil/ *adj* antimissile.

antimite /ɑ̃timit/ **I** *adj* moth-repellent.

II *nm* moth repellent.

antimoine /ɑ̃timwan/ *nm* antimony.

antimonarchique /ɑ̃timɔnaʀʃik/ *adj, nmf* antimonarchist.

antimonarchiste /ɑ̃timɔnaʀʃist/ *nmf* antimonarchist.

antinational, **~e**, *mpl* **-aux** /ɑ̃tinasjɔnal, o/ *adj* antinational.

antinomie /ɑ̃tinɔmi/ *nf* antinomy.

antinomique /ɑ̃tinɔmik/ *adj* [*lois, éléments*] antinomic; [*idées, concepts*] paradoxical.

antinucléaire /ɑ̃tinykleɛʀ/ *adj* antinuclear.

Antioche /ɑ̃tjɔʃ/ ▶ **857** *npr* Antioch.

antioxydant, **~e** /ɑ̃tiɔksidɑ̃, ɑ̃t/ **I** *adj* antioxidant.

II *nm* antioxidant.

antipape /ɑ̃tipap/ *nm* antipope.

antiparasitage /ɑ̃tipaʀazitaʒ/ *nm* interference suppression.

antiparasite /ɑ̃tipaʀazit/ *adj inv* anti-interference; **dispositif ~** suppressor.

antiparasiter /ɑ̃tipaʀazite/ [1] *vtr* to fit a suppressor to.

antiparlementaire /ɑ̃tipaʀləmɑ̃tɛʀ/ *adj* antiparliamentary.

antiparlementarisme /ɑ̃tipaʀləmɑ̃taʀism/ *nm* antiparliamentarianism.

antipathie /ɑ̃tipati/ *nf* antipathy (**pour** toward, towards GB, to; **entre** between); **j'éprouve de l'~ pour eux** I dislike them.

antipathique /ɑ̃tipatik/ *adj* [*personne, défaut*] unpleasant; **je le trouve ~** I find him unpleasant; **il m'est ~** I dislike him.

antipatriotique /ɑ̃tipatʀijɔtik/ *adj* unpatriotic.

antipatriotisme /ɑ̃tipatʀijɔtism/ *nm* antipatriotism.

antipelliculaire /ɑ̃tipɛlikylɛʀ/ *adj* [*shampooing, lotion*] dandruff (*épith*).

antipersonnel /ɑ̃tipɛʀsɔnɛl/ *adj inv* antipersonnel.

antiphrase /ɑ̃tifʀɑz/ *nf* antiphrasis; **employer une expression par ~** to use an expression ironically.

antipode /ɑ̃tipɔd/ **I** *nm* Géog antipodes (*pl*); **être l'~ de** to be the antipodes of; **être aux ~s de** lit to be the antipodes of; fig to be the exact opposite of.

II antipodes *nmpl* (pays lointain) **les ~s** the other side of the world.

antipoétique /ɑ̃tipɔetik/ *adj* antipoetic.

antipoison /ɑ̃tipwazɔ̃/ *adj inv* **centre ~** poisons unit.

antipoliomyélitique /ɑ̃tipɔljɔmjelitik/ *adj* [*vaccin*] polio (*épith*).

antipollution /ɑ̃tipɔlysjɔ̃/ *adj inv* **la lutte ~** the fight against pollution; **barrage ~** oil-trapping boom; **impôt ~** pollution tax.

antiprotectionniste /ɑ̃tipʀɔtɛksjɔnist/ **I** *adj* antiprotectionist, free-trade (*épith*).

II *nmf* antiprotectionist, free-trader.

antipsychiatrie /ɑ̃tipsikjatʀi/ *nf* antipsychiatry.

antipuces /ɑ̃tipys/ *adj inv* **collier ~** flea collar.

antipyrétique /ɑ̃tipiʀetik/ *adj, nm* antipyretic.

antipyrine /ɑ̃tipiʀin/ *nf* antipyrine.

antiquailles○ /ɑ̃tikɑj/ *nfpl* pej old junk○ ¢.

antiquaire /ɑ̃tikɛʀ/ *nmf* ▶ **510** antique dealer; **la rue/le quartier des ~s** the street/the area which is full of antique shops GB ou stores US.

antique /ɑ̃tik/ **I** *adj* **1** Hist Antiq [*cité, théâtre, période*] ancient; **la Rome/Grèce ~** ancient Rome/Greece; **2** liter (ancien) [*croyance, demeure*] age-old (*épith*); **3** (démodé) [*véhicule*] antiquated; [*costume*] old-fashioned.

II *nm* Art **l'~** classical art.

antiquité /ɑ̃tikite/ **I** *nf* **1** (objet) antique; **un magasin d'~s** an antique shop; **elle adore les ~s** she loves antiques; **2** (de coutume) ancientness.

II antiquités *nfpl* Art antiquities.

Antiquité /ɑ̃tikite/ *nf* antiquity; **dans l'~** in antiquity; **cela remonte à la plus haute ~** that goes back to ancient times.

antirabique /ɑ̃tiʀabik/ *adj* [*vaccin*] rabies (*épith*).

antirachitique /ɑ̃tiʀaʃitik/ *adj* antirachitic.

antiraciste /ɑ̃tiʀasist/ *adj* antiracist.

antiradar /ɑ̃tiʀadaʀ/ *adj inv* antiradar.

antireflet /ɑ̃tiʀəflɛ/ *adj inv* [*surface, verre*] nonreflective; Phot antiflare.

antirejet /ɑ̃tiʀəʒɛ/ *adj inv* immunosuppressive.

antireligieux, **-ieuse** /ɑ̃tiʀəliʒjø, jøz/ *adj* antireligious.

antirépublicain, **~e** /ɑ̃tiʀepyblikɛ̃, ɛn/ *adj* antirepublican.

antiretour /ɑ̃tiʀətuʀ/ *adj inv* **clapet ~** check valve.

antirévolutionnaire /ɑ̃tiʀevɔlysjɔnɛʀ/ *adj* antirevolutionary.

antirides /ɑ̃tiʀid/ *adj inv* anti-wrinkle (*épith*).

antirouille /ɑ̃tiʀuj/ **I** *adj* (pour protéger) rust-proofing (*épith*); (pour enlever) rust-removing (*épith*).

II *nm* (pour protéger) rust inhibitor; (pour enlever) rust remover.

antiroulis /ɑ̃tiʀuli/ *adj inv* [*dispositif, aileron*] roll-damping.

antiscorbutique /ɑ̃tiskɔʀbytik/ *adj* antiscorbutic.

antisèche○ /ɑ̃tisɛʃ/ *nf* students' slang crib○.

antiségrégationniste /ɑ̃tisegʀegasjɔnist/ *adj* antisegregationist.

antisémite /ɑ̃tisemit/ **I** *adj* anti-Semitic.

II *nmf* anti-Semite.

antisémitisme /ɑ̃tisemitism/ *nm* anti-Semitism.

antisepsie /ɑ̃tisɛpsi/ *nf* antisepsis.

antiseptique /ɑ̃tisɛptik/ *adj, nm* antiseptic.

antisocial, **~e**, *mpl* **-iaux** /ɑ̃tisɔsjal, o/ *adj* antisocial.

anti-sous-marin, **~e**, *mpl* **~s** /ɑ̃tisumaʀɛ̃, in/ *adj* anti-submarine.

antispasmodique /ɑ̃tispasmɔdik/ *adj, nm* antispasmodic.

antisportif, **-ive** /ɑ̃tispɔʀtif, iv/ *adj* (contraire à l'esprit du sport) unsporting.

antistatique /ɑ̃tistatik/ *adj* antistatic.

antistrophe /ɑ̃tistʀɔf/ *nf* antistrophe.

antisubversif, **-ive** /ɑ̃tisybvɛʀsif, iv/ *adj* antisubversive.

antitabac /ɑ̃titaba/ *adj inv* antismoking.

antitache /ɑ̃titaʃ/ *adj inv* **traité ~** stain-resistant.

antiterroriste /ɑ̃titɛʀɔʀist/ *adj* antiterrorist; **la lutte ~** the fight against terrorism.

antitétanique /ɑ̃titetanik/ *adj* [*vaccin*] tetanus (*épith*).

antithèse /ɑ̃titɛz/ *nf* gén Littérat antithesis; **elle est l'~ de son frère** fig she's the exact opposite of her brother.

antithétique /ɑ̃titetik/ *adj* antithetical.

antitoxine /ɑ̃titɔksin/ *nf* antitoxin.

antitoxique /ɑ̃titɔksik/ *adj* antitoxic.

antitrust /ɑ̃titʀœst/ *adj inv* anti-monopoly GB, antitrust US.

antituberculeux, **-euse** /ɑ̃titybɛʀkylø, øz/ *adj* [*vaccin*] tuberculosis (*épith*); **timbre ~** stamp in aid of tuberculosis research.

antitussif, **-ive** /ɑ̃titysif, iv/ **I** *adj* **sirop ~** cough mixture GB, cough syrup GB ou sirup US.

II *nm* cough medicine.

antivariolique /ɑ̃tivaʀjɔlik/ *adj* [*vaccin*] smallpox (*épith*).

antivénéneux, **-euse** /ɑ̃tivenenø, øz/ *adj* antidotal.

antivenimeux, **-euse** /ɑ̃tivənimø, øz/ *adj* **produit/sérum ~** product/serum for use against snake-bite, antivenin product/serum.

antivol /ɑ̃tivɔl/ **I** *adj inv* **dispositif ~** antitheft device.

II *nm* (de vélo, moto) lock; (de voiture) steering lock, anti-theft device.

antonomase /ɑ̃tɔnɔmɑz/ *nf* antonomasia.

antonyme /ɑ̃tɔnim/ *nm* antonym.

antonymie /ɑ̃tɔnimi/ *nf* antonymy.

antre /ɑ̃tʀ/ *nm* **1** (d'animal) den, lair; **2** fig den, lair; **3** Anat antrum.

Antrim *npr* **le comté d'~** Antrim.

anus /anys/ *nm inv* anus.

■ **~ artificiel** colostomy.

ANVAR /ɑ̃vaʀ/ *nf* (*abbr* = **Agence nationale de valorisation de la recherche**) *national council for the promotion of research in industry*.

Anvers /ɑ̃vɛʀ/ ▶ 857, 692 *npr* Antwerp; **la province d'~** Antwerp (province).

anxiété /ɑ̃ksjete/ *nf* anxiety; **l'~ de l'attente** the anxiety of waiting; **être dans l'~** to be very anxious ou worried; **état d'~** anxiety state; **crise d'~** panic attack; **avec ~** anxiously.

anxieusement /ɑ̃ksjøzmɑ̃/ *adv* anxiously.

anxieux, **-ieuse** /ɑ̃ksjø, øz/ **I** *adj* [*personne, voix, attente*] anxious; [*attitude*] concerned; **~ de savoir** anxious to know.

II *nm,f* worrier.

AOC /aose/ *nf*: *abbr* ▶ **appellation**.

aoriste /aɔʀist/ *nm* aorist.

aorte /aɔʀt/ *nf* aorta.

aortique /aɔʀtik/ *adj* aortic.

Aoste /aɔst/ ▶ 857 *npr* Aosta; **le Val d'~** Valle d'Aosta.

août /u(t)/ ▶ 521 *nm* August.

aoûtat /auta/ *nm* harvest mite GB, chigger US.

aoûtien, **-ienne** /ausjɛ̃, ɛn/ *nm,f* August holidaymaker GB ou vacationer US.

AP /ape/ *nf* **1** (*abbr* = **Associated Press**) AP; **2** *abbr* ▶ **assistance**.

apache○† /apaʃ/ *nm* (voyou) hooligan.

Apache /apaʃ/ *nprm* (Indien) Apache.

apaisant, **~e** /apɛzɑ̃, ɑ̃t/ *adj* **1** (lénifiant) [*paroles, voix, personne*] soothing; [*influence*] calming; [*déclaration*] conciliatory; **2** Cosmét, Pharm [*lotion, crème*] soothing.

apaisement /apɛzmɑ̃/ *nm* **1** (de foule, personne) calming down; (de querelle) quietening down; **geste/mesure d'~** calming gesture/measure; **politique d'~** policy of appeasement; **tentative/volonté d'~** attempt/willingness to appease; **2** (calme) calm; **éprouver un profond ~** to have a feeling of deep calm.

apaiser /apeze/ [1] **I** *vtr* (calmer) to pacify, to appease [*personne, militants*]; to ease [*conflit, rivalité*]; to calm, to appease [*colère, inquiétude*]; to satisfy, to appease [*faim, soif, désir*]; to soothe [*brûlure, douleur*]; **dire qch pour ~ les esprits** to say sth to ease people's minds; **il est revenu, l'esprit apaisé** he came back, his mind at rest.

II s'apaiser *vpr* [*vent, orage, colère, troubles*] to die down; [*débat*] to quieten down, to calm down; [*curiosité, désir, faim, douleur*] to subside.

apanage /apanaʒ/ *nm* prerogative; **être l'~ de qch/qn** to be the prerogative of sth/sb; **avoir l'~ de qch** to have a monopoly on sth.

aparté /apaʀte/ *nm* **1** (entretien privé) private conversation; **dire qch à qn en ~** to say sth to sb in private; **2** (remarque, commentaire) gén, Théât aside; **en ~** in an aside.

apartheid /apaʀtɛd/ *nm* apartheid.

apathie /apati/ *nf* (personnelle) apathy; (politique) indifference, apathy; (économique) stagnation; (sportive) lethargy.

apathique /apatik/ **I** *adj* (mou) apathetic; (indifférent) indifferent, apathetic; (stagnant) stagnant; (indolent) lethargic.

II *nmf* apathetic person.

apatride /apatʀid/ **I** *adj* stateless.

II *nmf* stateless person; **les ~s** stateless people.

APEC /apɛk/ *nf* (*abbr* = **Agence pour l'emploi des cadres**) *executive employment agency*.

Apennins /apɔnɛ̃/ *nprmpl* **les ~** the Apennines.

aperception /apɛʀsepsjɔ̃/ *nf* apperception.

apercevoir /apɛʀsəvwaʀ/ [5] **I** *vtr* **1** (voir) [*personne*] to make out [*montagne, clocher, silhouette*]; to see, to catch sight of [*personne, voiture*]; **laisser ~ qch** to reveal sth; **2** (prévoir) [*personne*] to see [*difficultés, possibilités*].

II s'apercevoir *vpr* **1** (se rendre compte) **s'~ que** to notice that, to realize that; **s'~ de** to notice [*erreur, supercherie*]; **personne ne s'est aperçu de ton absence/de ton départ** nobody noticed that you weren't there/that you had left; **il fait des gaffes sans s'en ~** he makes blunders without realizing; **2** (sans se parler) to catch sight of each other; (en se parlant) to meet briefly.

aperçu /apɛʀsy/ *nm* **1** (échantillon) (de talent, caractère) glimpse (**de** of); (de variété, soirée, course) taste (**de** of); (de politique, situation) outline (**de** of); **2** (point de vue) insight (**sur** on).

apéritif, **-ive** /apeʀitif, iv/ **I** *adj* [*boisson, promenade*] which stimulates the appetite (*épith, après n*).

II *nm* aperitif GB, drink; **prendre l'~** to have an aperitif GB ou a drink; **en ~** as an aperitif; **je vous offre un ~?** can I get you an aperitif GB ou a drink?

apéro○ /apeʀo/ *nm*: *abbr* = **apéritif II**.

aperture /apɛʀtyʀ/ *nf* aperture.

apesanteur /apəzɑ̃tœʀ/ *nf* weightlessness; **en état d'~** in a state of weightlessness.

à-peu-près /apøpʀɛ/ *nm inv* vague approximation, (rough) guess.

apeuré, **~e** /apœʀe/ *adj* (effrayé) frightened; (craintif) timid.

apex /apɛks/ *nm inv* **1** Astron, Zool apex; **2** Anat tip of the tongue; **3** Ling macron.

aphasie /afazi/ *nf* aphasia.

aphasique /afazik/ *adj, nmf* aphasic.

aphérèse /afeʀɛz/ *nf* apheresis.

aphone /afɔn/ *adj* voiceless; **être ~** to have lost one's voice.

aphonie /afɔni/ *nf* aphonia.

aphorisme /afɔʀism/ *nm* aphorism; **parler par ~s** to speak ou talk in aphorisms.

aphrodisiaque /afʀɔdizjak/ *adj, nm* aphrodisiac.

Aphrodite /afʀɔdit/ *npr* Aphrodite.

aphte /aft/ *nm* mouth ulcer, aphtha spéc.

aphteuse /aftøz/ ▶ 271 *adj f* **fièvre ~** foot-and-mouth disease.

api: **d'api** /dapi/ *loc adj* **pomme d'~** small apple.

API /apei/ *nm*: *abbr* ▶ **alphabet**.

à-pic /apik/ *nm inv* sheer drop; **un ~ de plus de 800 mètres** a sheer drop of more than 800 metres[GB].

apical, **~e**, *mpl* **-aux** /apikal, o/ *adj* apical; **r ~** trilled r.

apico-alvéolaire, *pl* **~s** /apikoalveɔlɛʀ/ **I** *adj* palato-alveolar.

II *nf* palato-alveolar consonant.

apico-dental, **~e**, *mpl* **-aux** /apikodɑ̃tal, o/ **I** *adj* dental.

II *nf* dental consonant.

apicole /apikɔl/ *adj* beekeeping (*épith*), apiarian spéc.

apiculteur, **-trice** /apikyltœʀ, tʀis/ ▶ 510 *nm,f* beekeeper, apiarist spéc.

apiculture /apikyltyʀ/ *nf* beekeeping, apiculture spéc.

apitoiement /apitwamɑ̃/ *nm* pity (**sur** for).

apitoyer /apitwaje/ [23] **I** *vtr* to move [sb] to pity [*personne*]; **~ qn sur qn** to make sb feel sorry for sb; **n'essaie pas de m'~** don't try to get my sympathy.

II s'apitoyer *vpr* **s'~ sur (le sort de) qn** to feel sorry for sb; **ils s'apitoient sur la malchance de Paul** they feel sorry for Paul on account of his bad luck.

APL /apeɛl/ *nf* **1** (*abbr* = **aide personnalisée au logement**) ≈ housing benefit; **2** (*abbr* = **Armée populaire de libération**) PLA.

aplanir /aplaniʀ/ [3] **I** *vtr* **1** Constr, Gén Civ [*personne, bulldozer*] to level [*terrain, chemin*]; **2** (éliminer) to iron out [*difficultés, problèmes*]; to ease [*tensions*].

II s'aplanir *vpr* fig [*difficultés*] to be ironed out; [*tensions*] to ease.

aplanissement /aplanismɑ̃/ *nm* **1** Constr, Gén Civ levelling[GB]; **2** (de situation financière) levelling[GB] out; (d'obstacle) elimination; (de difficultés) ironing out.

aplati, **~e** /aplati/ **I** *pp* ▶ **aplatir**.

II *pp adj* [*sphère, forme*] oblate; [*fruit, tuyau*] flattened; [*nez*] flat; **la Terre est ~e aux pôles** the Earth is oblate at the poles.

aplatir /aplatiʀ/ [3] **I** *vtr* (rendre plat) to flatten [*carton, tôle*]; to smooth out [*coussin, oreiller*]; to smooth down [*cheveux*]; to press [*coutures, plis*]; **mon chapeau est tout aplati!** my hat is all squashed!

II *vi* (au rugby) to score a try.

III s'aplatir *vpr* **1**○ (tomber) [*personne*] to fall flat (**sur** on); **2**○ (s'immobiliser) [*personne*] to flatten oneself (**contre** against, **dans** in); **aplatis dans le fossé, ils attendaient** they waited, lying flat in the ditch; **3** (devenir plat) [*chapeau*] to get squashed; [*carton*] to be flattened; **4**○ (s'écraser) **s'~ contre** [*voiture, conducteur*] to smash into [*arbre, mur*]; **5**○ (être servile) **s'~ devant qn** to grovel in front of sb.

aplomb /aplɔ̃/ **I** *nm* **1** (de personne) (confiance en soi) confidence; (équilibre) balance; **manquer d'~** to lack confidence; **avoir de l'~** to be confident; **avec ~** confidently, with aplomb; **vous ne manquez pas d'~!** you've got a nerve!; **retrouver son ~** to regain one's balance ou confidence; **2** (de mur) perpendicularity; **à l'~ de qch** directly below sth.

II d'aplomb *loc adv* **1** (en équilibre) [*étagère, armoire*] straight; [*personne*] steady; **attends! je ne suis pas d'~** wait! I'm off balance; **2**○ (en bonne santé) **tu te sens d'~?** do you feel well?; **je ne suis pas bien d'~** I don't feel very well; **prends ça, ça va te remettre d'~** have this, it will put you back on your feet.

III aplombs *nmpl* (du cheval) conformation (*sg*) of the legs.

apnée /apne/ *nf* apn(o)ea; **plonger en ~** to dive without an aqualung.

apocalypse /apɔkalips/ *nf* (fin du monde) apocalypse; **vision/paysage d'~** apocalyptic vision/landscape.

Apocalypse /apɔkalips/ *nprf* **l'~** the Apocalypse.

apocalyptique /apɔkaliptik/ *adj* apocalyptic.

apocope /apɔkɔp/ *nf* apocope.

apocryphe /apɔkʀif/ **I** *adj* apocryphal.

II *nm* book of the Apocrypha; **les ~** the Apocrypha.

apodictique /apɔdiktik/ *adj* apodictic.

apogée /apɔʒe/ *nm* **1** (paroxysme) peak (**de** of); **atteindre** or **connaître son ~** to peak; **2** Astron, Hist apogee.

apolitique /apɔlitik/ *adj* apolitical.

apolitisme /apɔlitism/ *nm* **l'~ de qch** the apolitical nature of sth; **l'~ de qn** the fact that sb is apolitical.

apollon /apɔlɔ̃/ *nm* good-looking man, hunk○; **quel ~!** he looks like a Greek god!

Apollon /apɔlɔ̃/ *npr* Apollo.

apologétique /apɔlɔʒetik/ **I** *adj* **1** (qui loue) laudatory; (qui justifie) justificatory; **2** Relig apologetic.

II *nf* apologetics (+ *v sg*).

apologie /apɔlɔʒi/ *nf* (pour louer) panegyric (**de** of); (pour justifier) apologia (**de** for); **faire l'~ de qch** (justifier) to justify sth; (louer) to applaud sth; **faire l'~ de qn** (louer) to praise sb.

apologiste /apɔlɔʒist/ *nmf* (qui justifie) Relig apologist; (qui loue) eulogist.

apologue /apɔlɔg/ *nm* apologue.

apophyse /apɔfiz/ *nf* apophysis.

apoplectique /apɔplɛktik/ *adj* apoplectic.

apoplexie /apɔplɛksi/ *nf* apoplexy; **crise d'~** lit, fig apoplectic fit; **elle était au bord de l'~** fig she was on the verge of having an apoplectic fit.

apostasie /apɔstazi/ *nf* apostasy.

apostasier /apɔstazje/ [2] *vi* to apostatize.

apostat, **~e** /apɔsta, at/ *adj, nm,f* apostate.

a posteriori /apɔsteʀjɔʀi/ **I** *loc adj inv* [*connaissances*] inductive.

II *loc adv* [*se justifier, décider*] after the event; **~, il semblerait que** with hindsight, it would appear that.

apostille /apɔstij/ *nf* apostil.

apostiller /apɔstije/ [1] *vtr* to add an apostil (to).

apostolat /apɔstɔla/ *nm* **1** Relig apostolate; **2** (activité désintéressée) apostolic mission.

apostolique /apɔstɔlik/ *adj* (des apôtres) apostolic; (papal) Apostolic.

apostrophe /apɔstʀɔf/ *nf* **1** (marquant une élision, en rhétorique) apostrophe; **mot mis en ~** word used in apostrophe; **2** (remarque vive) remark.

apostropher /apɔstʀɔfe/ [1] *vtr* to heckle.

apothème /apɔtɛm/ *nm* apothem.

apothéose /apɔteoz/ *nf* **1** (moment fort) (de spectacle) high point; (d'événement) grand finale; (d'œuvre) supreme achievement; (de carrière) culmination; **finir** or **s'achever en ~** [*spectacle*] to end in a blaze of glory; **l'arrivée de ma belle-mère a été l'~!** iron my mother-in-law's arrival was the last straw!; **2** Antiq apotheosis.

apothicaire‡ /apɔtikɛʀ/ *nm* apothecary‡; **des comptes d'~** fig complicated calculations.

apôtre /apotʀ/ *nm* lit, fig apostle; **se faire l'~ de la non-violence** to become an apostle of nonviolence.

IDIOMES **faire le bon ~** to play the saint.

Appalaches /apalaʃ/ **▶ 692** *nprfpl* **les ~** the Appalachians, the Appalachian mountains.

appalachien, **-ienne** /apalaʃjɛ̃, ɛn/ *adj* Appalachian.

apparaître /apaʀɛtʀ/ [73] **I** *vi* **1** (devenir visible) [*personne, spectre, bouton, problèmes, produit*] to appear; [*lune, soleil*] to come out; **~ à la télévision** to appear on television; **~ en public** to appear in public; **soudain une silhouette apparut dans le brouillard/la nuit** suddenly a shape appeared out of the fog/the darkness; **l'homme est apparu sur Terre** man (first) appeared on Earth; **laisser ~** to reveal; **voir ~ un spectre** to see a ghost; **~ à qn** to appear to sb; **2** (se révéler) [*idée, courage, misère, désaccord*] to become apparent; **laisser ~** [*analyse, compte, rapport, enquête*] to show; **faire ~** (montrer) to show; (révéler) to reveal; **~ comme une victime** to be seen as a victim; **3** (sembler) to appear (to be); **~ à qn** to appear to sb to be; **~ (à qn) comme** to appear (to sb) to be; **~ comme un gâchis** to seem a waste; **~ comme excessif/comme un anachronisme** to appear excessive/anachronistic.

II *v impers* **il apparaît que** it appears that; **il apparut certain que** it appeared certain that.

apparat /apaʀa/ *nm* **1** (faste, luxe) grandeur; (cérémonial) pomp, ceremonial; **d'~** (luxueux) sumptuous; (de cérémonie) ceremonial; **en grand ~** [*fêter*] with pomp and ceremony; [*être habillé*] (pour une cérémonie) in ceremonial regalia; (de façon luxueuse) in one's finery, sumptuously; **2** Littérat **~ critique** apparatus criticus.

apparatchik /apaʀatʃik/ *nm* lit, fig apparatchik.

appareil /apaʀɛj/ *nm* **1** (machine, instrument) device; (pour la maison) appliance; **~ de mesure/de contrôle** measuring/control device; **~ de radio/télévision** radio/television set; **~ de projection** projector; **~ de prise de vues** or **de cinéma** cine GB ou movie US camera; **~ photographique** or **(de) photo** camera; **~ électroménager** household appliance; **2** (téléphone) telephone; **qui est à l'~?** who's calling please?; **on te demande à l'~** you're wanted on the phone; **passe-moi l'~** give me the phone; **Vladimir à l'~** (this is) Vladimir speaking; **3** (avion) plane; **4** Méd (bagues) braces (*pl*); (en chirurgie) brace; **~ (dentaire)** (dentier) dentures (*pl*); (tige métallique) brace; **~ auditif** hearing aid; **~ orthopédique** orthopaedic appliance; **poser** or **mettre un ~ dentaire à qn** to fit sb with dentures; **5** Anat system; **l'~ digestif/circulatoire/respiratoire/phonateur** the digestive/circulatory/respiratory/vocal system; **6** (système) apparatus; **l'~ d'État/du parti/scolaire/administratif** the state/party/educational/administrative apparatus; **7** Archit, Constr bond; **8** (ensemble de notes) **~ critique** or **de notes** critical apparatus; **9** liter (apparence) trappings; **funèbre ~** funeral pomp; **pompeux ~** pompous trappings; **modeste** or **simple ~** simple apparel; **dans le plus simple ~** in one's birthday suit; **10** Culin mixture.

■ **~ d'appui** Constr bearing apparatus; **~ distributeur** vending machine; **~ de production** productive capacity; **~ à sous** slot machine.

appareillage /apaʀɛjaʒ/ *nm* **1** Naut (départ) casting off; (préparations) fitting out; **prêt pour l'~!** ready to cast off!; **2** (appareils) equipment; **3** Méd (pose) fitting; (appareil) surgical appliances (*pl*).

appareiller /apaʀeje/ [1] **I** *vtr* **1** (assembler) to match (up) [*objets*]; to match [*personnes, joueurs*]; **2** (préparer) to fit out [*bateau*]; **3** Méd **~ un bras/une jambe** (mettre une prothèse) to fit an artificial arm/leg; **4** Archit, Constr to dress [*pierre*]; **5** (accoupler) to mate [*animaux*].

II *vi* [*bateau*] to cast off.

apparemment /apaʀamɑ̃/ *adv* **1** (selon toute apparence) apparently; **~ pas!** apparently not!; **2** (en apparence seulement) seemingly.

apparence /apaʀɑ̃s/ *nf* **1** gén (extérieur) appearance; **ne jugez pas sur les ~s** don't judge by appearances; **ne vous fiez pas aux ~s** appearances are deceptive; **pour sauver les ~s** to keep up appearances; **il est bon, malgré les** or **en dépit des ~s** he is kind, despite appearances to the contrary; **contre toute ~** despite every indication to the contrary; **malgré certaines ~s** despite certain indications to the contrary; **il est jeune d'~** he looks young; **homme d'~** or **à l'~ jeune** young-looking man; **elle n'est calme qu'en ~** she only looks ou seems calm; **il n'a que l'~ de la bonté** he only looks ou seems kind; **en ~** seemingly; **sous l'~ de la bonté** under the guise of kindness; **sous des ~s raisonnables** behind a façade of reasonableness; **selon toute ~, ils sont d'accord** it would seem that they agree; **'ils sont d'accord?'—'selon toute ~'** 'they agree?'—'it would seem so'; **'ils sont d'accord'—'en ~ (seulement)'** 'they agree'—'only on the surface'; **des personnes en ~ si différentes** people outwardly so different; **2** Philos **l'~** appearance.

apparent, **~e** /apaʀɑ̃, ɑ̃t/ *adj* **1** (visible) [*signe, partie, bouton, couture*] visible; [*trouble, fragilité*] apparent; **sans raison ~e** for no apparent reason; **sans cause ~e** without any apparent cause; **2** (trompeur) [*facilité, indulgence*] seeming.

apparenté, **~e** /apaʀɑ̃te/ **I** *pp* **▶ apparenter**.

II *pp adj* [*personne, famille*] related (**à** to); [*entreprise*] allied; **maire/sénateur ~ socialiste** mayor/senator allied to the socialist party.

apparentement /apaʀɑ̃tmɑ̃/ *nm* Pol *electoral alliance under proportional representation.*

apparenter: **s'apparenter** /apaʀɑ̃te/ [1] *vpr* **1** (ressembler à) **s'~ à** to resemble; **ma méthode s'apparente à celle d'un sculpteur** my method resembles that of a sculptor; **le film s'apparente à un conte** the film resembles a fairy tale; **2** (s'allier à) **s'~ à** (par mariage) to marry into [*aristocratie*]; (politiquement) to ally with [*parti*].

apparier /apaʀje/ [2] *vtr* fml to match [*gants, bas*].

appariteur /apaʀitœʀ/ *nm* **1** Univ (gardien) ≈ porter GB, *college staff member who handles mail and reception duties*; (surveillant d'examen) invigilator GB, proctor US; **2** (de laboratoire) laboratory technician.

apparition /apaʀisjɔ̃/ *nf* (de personne, bouton, problème, planète, produit) appearance; (de Vierge, spectre) apparition (**à qn** to sb); (de mouvement, mode, science, technologie) emergence; (d'invention) advent; **faire une courte ~** to make a brief appearance; **faire son ~** to turn up; **refaire son ~** to reappear; **faire sa première ~** [*acteur*] to make one's first appearance; **avoir une ~** or **des ~s** to see things.

apparoir /apaʀwaʀ/ *v impers* fml **il appert de ceci que** it appears from this that.

appartement /apaʀtəmɑ̃/ **I** *nm* flat GB, apartment; **la vie en ~** living in a flat GB ou apartment; **de nombreux parisiens vivent en ~** many Parisians live in flats GB ou apartments; **chien/chat/lapin d'~** small dog/cat/rabbit suited to life in an apartment; **plante d'~** houseplant.

II appartements *nmpl* (de château) apartments; **se retirer dans ses ~s** to retire to one's chamber liter.

■ **~ témoin** show flat GB, show apartment US.

appartenance /apaʀtənɑ̃s/ *nf* **1** gén (à un parti, syndicat) membership; (à un groupe non officiel) **il ne dissimule pas son ~ au movement** he doesn't conceal the fact that he belongs to the movement; **condamné pour ~ à un groupe terroriste** condemned for being a member of a terrorist organization; **quelle est son ~ politique?** what are his political sympathies?; **un sentiment d'~** a sense of belonging; **2** Math membership (**à** of); **relation d'~** membership relation.

appartenir /apaʀtəniʀ/ [36] **I appartenir à** *vtr ind* **1** (être la propriété) **~ à** [*objet, propriété, capital*] to belong to; [*projet*] to be the responsibility of; **ce stylo m'appartient** this pen belongs to me ou is mine; **2** (revenir) **~ à** [*victoire*] to belong to; **la décision/le choix t'appartient** the decision/the choice is yours; **3** (faire partie) **~ à** [*personne*] to be a member of; **cesser d'~ à un club** to cease to be a member of a club.

II s'appartenir *vpr* liter **1** [*amants*] to live for each other; **2** (soi-même) **ne plus s'~** not to have a minute to oneself.

III *v impers* (être du ressort de) **il appartient à qn de faire** it is up to sb to do; **il appartient au syndicat de décider/définir** it is up to the union to decide/define; **il m'appartient de choisir une solution** it is up to me to choose a solution.

appas† /apɑ/ *nmpl* liter charms (*pl*).

appât /apɑ/ *nm* **1** Chasse, Pêche bait ₵; **attirer avec un ~** to lure with bait; **mettre** or **fixer un ~ à l'hameçon** to bait the hook; **2** (attrait) lure; **l'~ du gain/de la réussite** the lure of profit/of success.

appâter /apɑte/ [1] *vtr* **1** Chasse, Pêche to lure [*poisson, gibier*]; to bait [*hameçon, piège*]; **2** (attirer) to lure, to entice [*personne*] (**par, avec** with; **en** by).

appauvrir /apovʀiʀ/ [3] **I** *vtr* lit, fig to impoverish.

II s'appauvrir *vpr* to become impoverished.

appauvrissement /apovʀismɑ̃/ *nm* lit, fig impoverishment (**de** of).

appeau, *pl* **~x** /apo/ *nm* decoy.

appel /apɛl/ *nm* **1** (invitation pressante) call; **'dernier ~ pour Tokyo'** 'last call for Tokyo'; **~ au secours** lit call for help; fig cry for help; **les enfants se sont enfuis à l'~ de leur mère** the children ran away when they heard their mother calling; **l'~ des syndicats n'a pas été entendu** the call of the trade unions was not heeded; **il m'a fait un ~ du regard** he signalled[GB] to me with his eyes; **l'~ des fidèles à la messe** calling the faithful to mass; **l'~ de la cloche le dimanche** the ringing of church bells on Sundays; **2** (supplique) appeal, plea; **un ~ pathétique/solennel** a pathetic/solemn appeal; **lancer un ~ (en faveur de)** to make an appeal (on behalf of); **~ à l'aide** plea ou appeal for aid; **répondre** or **se rendre à l'~ de** to respond to the appeal of; **lancer un ~ à la télévision/à la radio** to put out an appeal on television/on the radio; **3** (incitation) **~ à** call for [*solidarité*]; appeal for [*calme*]; call to [*révolte*]; plea for [*clémence*]; **~ à la grève** strike call; **lancer un ~ à** to call for [*solidarité, grève*]; to appeal for [*calme*]; to call to [*révolte, armes*]; **~ au meurtre** death threat; **lancer un ~ au meurtre contre qn** to call for sb's assassination; **4** Télécom call; **~ téléphonique** phone call; **~ radio** radio call; **un ~ de Londres pour vous** a call from London for you; **prendre/recevoir un ~** to take/to get a call; **5** (recours) **~ à** appeal to [*personne, générosité, bon sens*]; **faire ~ à** [*personne*] to call [*pompiers, police, spécialiste*]; to bring in [*artiste, architecte*]; to call up [*capitaux*]; [*gouvernement*] to call in [*armée, police, puissance étrangère*]; to call for [*intervention*]; [*tâche*] to call for [*connaissances, notions*]; **faire ~ à la justice** to go to court; **6** (vérification) gén roll call; Scol registration; **faire l'~** gén to take the roll call; Scol to take the register; **manquer à l'~** gén to be absent at the roll call; Scol to be absent at registration; **7** Mil (convocation) call up GB, draft US; **8** (attirance) **l'~ de** the call of [*large, chair, forêt*]; **9** Jur appeal; **faire ~** to appeal; **faire ~ d'un jugement** to appeal against a decision; **perdre en ~** to lose an appeal; **juger en ~** to hear an appeal; **sans ~** lit without further right of appeal; **une décision sans ~** fig a final decision; **condamner sans ~** fig to condemn out of hand; **10** Sport take off; **prendre son ~** to take off; **jambe/pied d'~** take-off leg/foot; **11** Jeux (aux cartes) signal; **faire un ~** to signal for a card; **faire un ~ à cœur** to ask for a return in hearts; **12** Ordinat call; **d'~** [*programme, station, séquence*] calling (*épith*); [*demande, indicatif, mot*] call (*épith*); **13** Comm **prix d'~** loss-leader price; **produit** or **article d'~** loss leader.

■ **l' ~ du 18 juin** Hist *General de Gaulle's appeal of 18 June 1940*; **~ d'air** draught GB ou draft US; **créer** or **faire un ~ d'air** to create a draught GB ou draft US; **~ des causes** Jur roll call of matters listed; **~ de fonds** Fin call for capital; **faire un ~ de fonds** to call for capital, to call up capital; **~ d'offres** Admin invitation to tender; **lancer un ~ d'offres** to invite tenders; **~ de phares** flash of headlights GB ou high beams US; **faire un ~ de phares** to flash one's headlights GB ou high beams US; **~ du pied**○ veiled invitation, discreet appeal.

appelant, **~e** /aplɑ̃, ɑ̃t/ **I** *adj* **1** Jur appellate, appellant; **2** Ordinat **programme ~** calling routine.

II *nm,f* Jur appellant.

appelé, **~e** /aple/ **I** *pp* ▶ **appeler**.

II *pp adj* (destiné) **~ à qch** destined for sth; **jeune homme ~ à un brillant avenir** young man destined for a brilliant future; **~ à faire** destined to do.

III *nm* Mil conscript, draftee US; **les ~s du contingent** the conscripts.

appeler /aple/ [19] **I** *vtr* **1** (dénommer) to call [*personne, chose*]; **comment ont-ils appelé leur fille?** what did they call their daughter?; **~ un roi 'Majesté'** to call a king 'Your Majesty'; **comme appelles-tu cet arbre?** what's this tree called?; **comment appelle-t-on cela en français?** what's that called in French?; **il se fait ~ Robert** (pour son plaisir) he likes to be called Robert; (par sécurité) he goes by the name of Robert; **2** (attirer l'attention) to call; **~ ses enfants pour dîner** to call one's children for dinner; **~ qn par l'interphone** to call sb on the intercom; **~ les fidèles à la prière** to call the faithful to prayer; **~ à l'aide** to call for help; **~ qn à son aide** or **à l'aide** to call for sb to help one; **3** (téléphoner) to phone GB, to call; **je t'appelle demain** I'll phone you tomorrow; **4** (faire venir) to call [*docteur, ambulance, pompier, taxi*]; to call [*ascenseur*]; to send for [*employé, élève*]; **~ un médecin auprès d'un malade** to call a doctor to see a sick person; **il est temps d'~ un prêtre** it's time to call a priest; **le docteur a été appelé à l'extérieur** the doctor is out on a call; **le docteur a été appelé trois fois la nuit dernière** the doctor was called out three times last night; **le devoir m'appelle** duty calls; **~ un témoin** Jur to call a witness; **~ qn à comparaître (devant le juge/les tribunaux)** to summon sb to appear (before the judge/the court); **~ qn en justice** to summon sb to appear in court; **5** (inciter) **~ qn à** to incite sb to [*révolte*]; to call sb out on [*grève*]; **~ qn à l'abstention** to call on sb to abstain; **les syndicats ont appelé à la grève** unions have called for strike action; **~ qn à faire** to call on sb to do; **~ à manifester** to call for a demonstration; **6** (destiner) **~ qn à** to assign sb to [*charge, fonction*]; to appoint sb to [*poste*]; **il a été appelé à de hautes fonctions** he was called to high office; **ses compétences l'appellent à ce poste** his skills make him ideal for the job; **mon travail m'appelle à beaucoup voyager** my work involves a lot of travel; **7** (qualifier de) to call; **j'appelle ça du vol** I call that robbery; **c'est ce que j'appelle une idiotie/une gaffe!** now that's what I call stupid/a blunder!; **8** (réclamer) **~ qch sur qn** to call sth down on sb [*malédiction*]; **~ la mort sur qn** fml to wish death on sb; **~ l'attention de qn sur qch** to draw sb's attention to sth; **cette question appelle toute notre attention** this issue calls for our full attention; **9** (entraîner) [*crime, comportement*] to call for [*sanction*]; **la violence appelle la violence** violence begets violence; **10** Mil to call [sb] up [*contingent*]; **~ qn sous les drapeaux** to call sb up.

II en appeler à *vtr ind* **1** (s'adresser) **en ~ à** to appeal to [*générosité, bon sens, population*]; **2** fml (contester la validité) **en ~ de** to dispute [*jugement, décision*].

III *vi* (crier) [*personne*] to call; **en cas de besoin, appelez** if you need anything, just call.

IV s'appeler *vpr* **1** (se dénommer) [*objet, fleur, oiseau*] to be called; **comment s'appelle cette fleur en latin?** what is this flower called in Latin?, what is this flower's Latin name?; **comment t'appelles-tu?** what's your name?; **je m'appelle Paul** my name's Paul; **voilà ce qui s'appelle une belle voiture!** now, that's what you call a nice car!; **voilà qui s'appelle jouer/cuisiner/faire une gaffe!** now that's what you call acting/cooking/a blunder!; **voilà qui s'appelle parler!** well said!; **2** (entre personnes, animaux) to call each other, to call to one another; (au téléphone) to phone each other GB, to call each other; **nous nous appelons par nos prénoms** we call each other by our first names; **on s'appelle demain?** shall one of us give the other a ring tomorrow?; **on s'appelle!** we'll be in touch!

IDIOMES **beaucoup seront appelés mais peu seront élus** many are called but few are chosen; **ça s'appelle reviens**○**!** don't forget to give it back!; **~ les choses par leur nom** or **un chat un chat** to call a spade a spade.

appellatif, **-ive** /apɛlatif, iv/ Ling **I** *adj* appellative.

II *nm* appellative.

appellation /apɛlɑsjɔ̃/ *nf* name, appellation sout; **~ d'origine (de produit)** indication of country of origin.

■ **~ d'origine contrôlée**, **AOC** Vin appellation contrôlée (*with a guarantee of origin*).

appendice /apɛ̃dis/ *nm* **1** Anat appendix; **~ nasal** Zool proboscis sout, nasal appendage; **2** (d'ouvrage) appendix; **3** (de système, bâtiment) annexe GB, annex US.

appendicite /apɛ̃disit/ ▶**271** *nf* appendicitis; **se faire opérer de l'~**○ to have one's appendix removed; **avoir une crise d'~** to have appendicitis.

appentis /apɑ̃ti/ *nm inv* (bâtiment) (adossé) lean-to; (non adossé) shed.

Appenzell /apɛnzɛl/ ▶**692** *nprm* **le canton d'~**, **l'~** the canton of Appenzell.

appert /apɛʀ/ ▶ **apparoir**.

appesantir /apəzɑ̃tiʀ/ [3] **I** *vtr* **1** (engourdir) [*âge, froid*] to slow down [*démarche*]; [*inactivité*] to dull [*esprit*]; **2** (augmenter) [*personne, régime*] to strengthen [*autorité, domination*].

II s'appesantir *vpr* **1** (insister) [*orateur, invité*] to dwell on the subject; **s'~ sur** to dwell on; **ne vous appesantissez pas sur des détails** don't dwell on details; **2** (devenir pesant) [*démarche*] to slow.

appesantissement /apəzɑ̃tismɑ̃/ *nm* fml (de démarche) slackening; (de vivacité) (action) dulling; (résultat) dullness.

appétence /apetɑ̃s/ *nf* fml appetence sout.

appétissant, **~e** /apetisɑ̃, ɑ̃t/ *adj* **1** [*mets*] appetizing, tempting; **un plat peu ~** an unappetizing dish; **2**○ [*personne*] appealing.

appétit /apeti/ *nm* **1** (de mangeur) appetite; **le bon air donne de l'~** fresh air gives you an appetite; **perdre l'~** to lose one's appetite; **j'en ai perdu l'~** it made me lose my appetite; **mettre qn en ~** lit, fig to whet sb's appetite; **avoir un ~ modeste/robuste** to have a small/hearty appetite; **ouvrir l'~ de qn** to give sb an appetite; **couper l'~ de qn** to take sb's appetite away; **avoir un ~ d'oiseau** to eat like a bird; **manger avec ~** to eat heartily ou with relish; **manger sans ~** to eat without feeling hungry; **bon ~!** enjoy your meal!; **2** (désir naturel) appetite; **~ sexuel** sexual appetite; **3** (de plaisirs, culture) appetite (**de** for); (de gloire, pouvoir) hunger (**de** for); **on craint les ~s des concurrents** the competitors' acquisitiveness ou greed is causing some concern; **les ~s de conquête du pays** the country's expansionist ambitions.

IDIOMES **l'~ vient en mangeant** Prov appetite comes with eating.

applaudimètre○ /aplodimɛtʀ/ *nm* **1** lit applause meter, clapometer○ GB; **2** fig **à l'~ les féministes l'ont emporté** judging by the applause the feminists won.

applaudir /aplodiʀ/ [3] **I** *vtr* **1** lit [*personne, public*] to applaud [*musicien, chanson*]; **ils ont été très applaudis par le public** they

got a big round of applause from the audience; **on les applaudit bien fort** let's have a big round of applause; **2** fig (approuver) [*personne, groupe*] to applaud [*message, décision*].
II applaudir à *vtr ind* fml to applaud [*choix, décision, résultat*].
III *vi* **1** lit [*personne, foule*] to applaud, to clap; **l'assistance ravie applaudit** the delighted audience applauded ou clapped; **~ des deux mains** to applaud heartily; **le public a applaudi le spectacle à tout rompre** the show brought the house down; **2** fig (approuver) to approve.
IV s'applaudir *vpr* (se féliciter) to congratulate oneself (**de qch** on sth; **de faire qch** on doing sth).

applaudissement /aplodismɑ̃/ *nm* **1** lit applause ₵; **ton discours a suscité de vifs ~s** your speech was greeted with loud applause; **elle a quitté la salle sous un tonnerre d'~s** she left the room to thunderous applause; **2** fig (approbation) acclaim ₵; **le livre a reçu l'~ de la critique** the book has met with critical acclaim.

applicabilité /aplikabilite/ *nf* applicability.

applicable /aplikabl/ *adj* **1** [*loi, règle, sanction*] applicable (**à** to); **facilement/difficilement ~** [*idée, mesure*] easy/difficult to implement; **2** [*peinture, vernis*] **~ sur bois** which can be applied to wood.

applicateur /aplikatœʀ/ *nm* applicator.

application /aplikasjɔ̃/ *nf* **1** (soin) care; **coudre/écrire avec ~** to sew/to write with care; **~ à faire/à qch** the care one takes to do/over sth; **travailler avec/manquer d'~** to work with/to lack application; **2** (de loi, règlement, d'accord) (respect) application; (mise en œuvre) implementation; (de peine) administration; **étendre le champ d'~ de qch** to extend the application of sth [*allocation, découverte, loi*]; to widen the parameters of sth [*loi, dispositif*]; **mettre en ~** to apply [*théorie*]; to implement [*loi, règlement*]; **la loi/réforme entrera en ~ le 2 janvier** the law/reform will come into force on 2 January; **en ~ de l'article 5** in accordance with article 5; **3** Ind, Méd, Tech application; **4** (de vernis, peinture) application (**sur** to; **à** to); **5** Ordinat (programme) application program; **6** Math mapping.

applique /aplik/ *nf* **1** (lampe) wall light; **2** Cout appliqué.

appliqué, **~e** /aplike/ **I** *pp* ▸ **appliquer**.
II *pp adj* **1** [*élève*] hardworking; [*travail, écriture*] careful; **2** [*science*] applied.
III *nm* Cout appliqué.

appliquer /aplike/ [1] **I** *vtr* **1** (enduire de) to apply [*vernis, fond de teint*] (**sur** to); **2** (poser) to apply [*compresse, feuille d'or*] (**sur** to); to put [*cachet, tampon*] (**sur** on); **~ son nez contre une vitre** to press one's nose against a window; **3**° (donner) to give [*coup, baiser, sobriquet*] (**à qn** to sb); **4** (mettre en œuvre) to implement [*politique, ordres, décision*]; **5** (respecter) to apply [*loi, règlement*]; to follow [*quotas*]; (faire subir) **~ une peine à qn** to administer a sentence on sb; **6** (utiliser) to apply [*technique, raisonnement, traitement*] (**à** to); **~ ses talents/son intelligence à qch** to apply one's talents/one's intelligence to sth; **7** (en géométrie) to apply.
II s'appliquer *vpr* **1** (faire avec soin) to take great care (**à faire** to do); **elle ne s'applique pas** [*élève*] she doesn't take much care, she doesn't apply herself; **s'~ à écrire lisiblement** to take care to write legibly; **2** (concerner) **s'~ à qch/qn** [*loi, taux, remarque*] to apply to sth/sb; **3** [*vernis, fond de teint*] to be applied.

appogiature /apo(d)ʒjatyʀ/ *nf* appoggiatura.

appoint /apwɛ̃/ *nm* **1** (somme d'argent) exact change; **je n'ai pas l'~** I haven't got the exact change; **prière de faire l'~** please tender GB ou provide US the exact change; **2** (complément) support; **équipe d'~** support team; **jouer le rôle d'~** to play a supporting role; **mon salaire est juste un salaire d'~** my salary just constitutes a supplementary income; **chauffage d'~** additional heating GB, space heater US.

appointements /apwɛ̃tmɑ̃/ *nmpl* fml salary (*sg*).

appointer /apwɛ̃te/ [1] *vtr* fml to pay a salary to.

appondre /apɔ̃dʀ/ [6] *vtr* H (attacher) to attach.

appontage /apɔ̃taʒ/ *nm* landing (on an aircraft carrier).

appontement /apɔ̃tmɑ̃/ *nm* landing stage.

apponter /apɔ̃te/ [1] *vi* to land (on an aircraft carrier).

apport /apɔʀ/ *nm* **1** (action) **l'~ de** the provision of [*aide financière, solution, modifications*]; the bringing-in of [*idées nouvelles*]; **grâce à l'~ d'engrais/d'eau** thanks to the provision of fertilizers/of water; **2** Jur Comm, Fin (bien concret) contribution; **~ de capitaux** capital contribution ou contribution of capital; **~ (immobilier)** Jur *goods contributed by a partner in a joint estate*; **3** (bénéfice) benefit; (contribution) contribution; **les ~s pédagogiques/nutritionnels de qch** the educational/nutritional benefits of sth; **les ~s de l'Asie à l'art européen** Asia's contribution to European art; **~ calorique/alimentaire** caloric/dietary intake.
■ **~ quotidien recommandé**, **AQR** recommended daily amount, RDA.

apporter /apɔʀte/ [1] *vtr* **1** (transporter) to bring; **apporte ton livre** bring your book; **apporte-moi mon livre** bring me my book; **apporte-leur un livre** take them a book; **apporté par avion** [*primeurs, produits exotiques*] brought in by plane, flown in; **2** (fournir pour sa part) to give [*soutien, aide, coopération technique*]; to bring [*savoir-faire*]; to bring in [*fonds, revenus*]; **~ de l'aide à qn** to help sb; **~ son concours à qch** to help with sth; **~ sa contribution à qch** to contribute to sth; **3** (fournir en plus) to give [*précision, explication, raisons*] (**à qn** to sb); to bring [*idées nouvelles, amélioration, bonnes nouvelles*] (**à qn/qch** to sb/sth); **~ la preuve de qch** to bring proof of sth; **~ des modifications à qch** to modify sth; **les modifications apportées** the modifications made; **4** (créer) to bring [*gloire, ennuis*] (**à qn** to sb); to produce [*émotions fortes*] (**à qn** in sb); **~ une sensation de bien-être** to give a feeling of well-being; **ce stage ne m'a rien apporté** I didn't get anything out of this course; **cet homme ne peut rien t'~** this man has nothing to offer you; **5** (employer) to bring [*courage, sensibilité*] (**à qch** to sth); **~ beaucoup de soin à son travail** to do one's work with great care; **6** (causer) to bring about [*changement, révolution*]; to bring [*liberté, maladie*].

apposer /apoze/ [1] *vtr* fml to affix [*affiche, autocollant*] (**à** to; **sur** on); **~ un visa sur un passeport** to stamp a visa in a passport; **~ sa signature** to affix one's signature.

apposition /apozisjɔ̃/ *nf* **1** Ling apposition; **en ~** in apposition; **2** (action) **l'~ d'un visa** the stamping of a visa.

appréciable /apʀesjabl/ *adj* [*différence*] considerable, appreciable; [*niveau, marge*] considerable; [*soutien, progrès, avantage*] noticeable; **il y avait un nombre ~ de spectateurs** there were a good many spectators; **un grand jardin en ville, c'est ~** it's nice to have a big garden in the centre[GB] of town.

appréciatif, **-ive** /apʀesjatif, iv/ *adj* (approbateur) [*jugement, regard*] appreciative; (évaluatif) [*coup d'œil*] appraising.

appréciation /apʀesjɑsjɔ̃/ *nf* **1** (de distance, résultat, proposition) estimate; (financière) evaluation; **faire une erreur d'~** to make a misjudgment; **2** (jugement) assessment; **émettre une ~ favorable/défavorable** to give a favourable[GB]/an unfavourable[GB] assessment; **c'est une question d'~** it's a question of taste; **être laissé à l'~ de qn** to be left to sb's discretion; **3** (de monnaie) appreciation.

apprécier /apʀesje/ [2] **I** *vtr* **1** (juger favorablement) to appreciate [*musique, vin, calme*]; to like [*personne*]; to appreciate [*efforts, initiative, talent*]; **je n'apprécie pas qu'on se mêle de mes affaires** I don't appreciate people interfering in my affairs; **elle n'a pas apprécié** euph she was not very pleased; **un chercheur des plus appréciés** a highly valued researcher; **ce que j'apprécie en** or **chez elle, c'est**... what I like about her is...; **2** (évaluer) to value [*objet*]; to estimate [*prix, valeur, distance, vitesse*]; **3** (juger) to assess [*conséquences, résultat, événement*]; **ce sera à vous d'~ la situation** it will be up to you to assess the situation.
II s'apprécier *vpr* **1** (s'aimer) [*personnes*] to like one another; **2** (augmenter de valeur) [*monnaie*] to appreciate.

appréhender /apʀeɑ̃de/ [1] *vtr* **1** (arrêter) [*police*] to arrest, to apprehend sout [*malfaiteur, suspect*]; **2** (redouter) to dread [*rencontre, avenir, examen*]; **~ de faire** to dread doing; **elle appréhende de voyager seule** she dreads travelling[GB] on her own; **tu appréhendes qu'il vienne te voir?** are you frightened that he might come and see you?; **j'appréhende toujours un peu les examens** I'm always a bit apprehensive before exams; **3** (concevoir) fml to comprehend [*phénomène, art, univers*].

appréhension /apʀeɑ̃sjɔ̃/ *nf* **1** (crainte) apprehension; **avoir une ~ irraisonnée/soudaine** to have an irrational/a sudden apprehension; **attendre/faire qch avec ~** to wait for/to do sth apprehensively; **2** (conception) apprehension.

apprenant, **~e** /apʀənɑ̃, ɑ̃t/ *nm,f* learner.

apprendre /apʀɑ̃dʀ/ [52] **I** *vtr* **1** (étudier) to learn; **~ qch par cœur** to learn sth by heart, to learn sth off by heart GB; **le bonheur d'~** the joy of learning; **~ à écrire/à conduire** to learn to write/to drive; **~ l'italien** to learn Italian; **~ à reconnaître qch/à se servir de qch** to learn (how) to recognize sth/to use sth; **~ qch sur qch** to learn sth about sth; **2** (être informé de) to hear, to learn [*nouvelle, vérité, décision*] (**par qn** from sb); to hear [*rumeur*]; (de façon indirecte) to hear of ou about [*décision*]; **~ la mort de qn** to learn of ou hear of sb's death; **~ qch par qn** to hear about sth through sb; **~ qch par la radio** to hear sth on the radio; (sujet plus vaste) to hear about sth on the radio; **~ qch par la presse** to see sth in the papers; **~ qch sur qn** to hear ou learn sth about sb; **~ que** to hear ou learn that; **~ qch par téléphone** to be told sth over the phone; **3** (enseigner) to teach; **~ qch à qn** to teach sb sth; **~ à conduire à qn** to teach sb (how) to drive; **cela t'apprendra (à ne pas faire ça)!** that'll teach you (not to do that)!; **ce n'est pas à toi que je l'apprendrai** you don't need me to tell you; **4** (faire savoir) [*personne, journal*] to tell; **~ qch à qn** to tell sb sth; **tu ne m'apprends rien** you're not telling me anything new.
II s'apprendre *vpr* **qch qui s'apprend facilement/difficilement** sth which is easy/difficult to learn; **la patience, cela s'apprend** patience is something you can learn.

apprenti, **~e** /apʀɑ̃ti/ **I** *nm,f* gén trainee; (d'artisan) apprentice; **être ~ chez qn** gén to train with sb; (avec un artisan) to serve as an apprentice ou to do an apprenticeship with sb; **entrer comme ~ chez qn** to be apprenticed to sb.
II apprenti(-), **apprentie(-)** (*in compounds*) **1** gén trainee; (de métier artisanal) apprentice; **~ boulanger** baker's apprentice; **~ forgeron** blacksmith's apprentice; **~ serveur** trainee waiter; **2** (sans expérience) **~-ministre** novice minister; **~ poète** novice poet.
■ **~ sorcier** sorcerer's apprentice; **jouer les ~s sorciers** to open a Pandora's box.

apprentissage /apʀɑ̃tisaʒ/ *nm* **1** gén training; (de métier artisanal) apprenticeship; (chez un artisan) **faire son ~ chez Vladeau** to train with Vladeau, to do one's apprenticeship ou to serve as an apprentice with Vladeau; **faire son ~ de boulanger** to train as a baker; **être en ~** gén to be a trainee; (chez un artisan) to be an apprentice; **entrer en ~ chez qn/dans un atelier** to be apprenticed to sb/to a company; **être placé en ~** to be apprenticed; **2** (étude) learning; **l'~ d'une langue/de la lecture** learning a language/to read; **faire l'~ de la démocratie** to take the first steps toward(s) democracy; **faire l'~ de la vie** to learn about life.

apprêt /apʀɛ/ *nm* **1** Tech (pour cuir, tissu) dressing, finishing; **2** Constr (sur mur, plafond) size; (sur bois) primer; **couche d'~** coat of size ou primer; **3** (affectation) affectation; **un style sans ~** an unaffected style.

apprêtage /apʀɛtaʒ/ *nm* (d'étoffe) dressing, finishing.

apprêté, **~e** /apʀete/ **I** *pp* ▶ **apprêter**.
II *pp adj* [*style*] affected; [*coiffure*] fussy.

apprêter /apʀete/ [1] **I** *vtr* Tech to dress, to finish [*étoffe*]; to size [*mur, plafond*]; to prime [*bois*].
II s'apprêter *vpr* **s'~ à faire** to get ready to do.

apprêteur, **-euse** /apʀɛtœʀ, øz/ ▶ **510** *nm,f* dresser, finisher.

apprivoisable /apʀivwazabl/ *adj* tamable.

apprivoisé, **~e** /apʀivwaze/ **I** *pp* ▶ **apprivoiser**.
II *pp adj* [*animal*] tame.

apprivoisement /apʀivwazmɑ̃/ *nm* taming.

apprivoiser /apʀivwaze/ [1] **I** *vtr* to tame [*animal*]; to win [sb] over [*enfant, personne*].
II s'apprivoiser *vpr* to become tame; **un animal qui ne peut pas s'~** an untamable animal.

approbateur, **-trice** /apʀɔbatœʀ, tʀis/ *adj* [*sourire, clin d'œil*] approving, of approval (*épith, après n*).

approbatif, **-ive** /apʀɔbatif, iv/ *adj* [*mimique, signe de tête*] approving, of approval (*épith, après n*).

approbation /apʀɔbasjɔ̃/ *nf* approval (**de** of); **présenter** or **soumettre qch à l'~ de qn** to present ou submit sth for sb's approval; **la décision a reçu l'~ générale** the decision met with general approval.

approchable /apʀɔʃabl/ *adj* **il n'est guère ~** (distant) he's rather unapproachable; (occupé) one never gets to see him.

approchant, **~e** /apʀɔʃɑ̃, ɑ̃t/ *adj* (comparable) [*problème, mot*] similar; (proche) [*valeur*] approximate; [*résultat*] close; **chercher quelque chose d'~** to look for something similar.

approche /apʀɔʃ/ **I** *nf* **1** (arrivée) approach (**de** of); **il s'est enfui à mon ~** he ran off as I approached; **2** (imminence, proximité) approach (**de** of); **à l'~** or **aux ~s de l'hiver** as winter approaches; **la campagne s'intensifia à l'~ du scrutin** the campaign intensified as the election drew nearer ou approached; **il partit à l'~ de la nuit** he left as night was falling; **à l'~** or **aux ~s de la trentaine il décida que...** as he neared thirty, he decided that...; **ralentis à l'~ du virage** slow down as you approach the bend; **3** (manière d'aborder) approach (**de** to); **~ commerciale/romantique** commercial/romantic approach; **leur nouvelle ~ du problème** their new approach to the problem; **marche d'~** (en alpinisme) approach; **travail d'~** (manœuvres) Mil, fig approaches (*pl*); (préparation) groundwork; **d'~ difficile/aisée** [*lieu*] hard/easy to get to; [*œuvre, auteur*] hard/easy to get to grips with; **personne d'~ difficile** unapproachable person; **personne d'~ aisée** friendly person; **ce n'est qu'une ~ de la théorie** it's only an introduction to the theory; **4** Aviat approach; **procédure d'~** approach procedure; **5** Sport (au golf) approach shot; **6** Imprim (espace) spacing.
II approches *nfpl* (accès) approaches (**de** to); (alentours) gén (general) vicinity (**de** of); (de ville) outskirts (**de** of); **aux ~s de la ville** on the outskirts of town; **aux ~s de la côte** near the coast.

approché, **~e** /apʀɔʃe/ *adj* approximate.

approcher /apʀɔʃe/ [1] **I** *vtr* **1** (déplacer) **~ qch de qch** (placer près de) to move ou bring sth close to sth; (placer plus près de) to move ou bring sth closer to sth; **~ les lits l'un de l'autre** to push the beds closer together; **~ le bureau de la fenêtre** to move ou bring the desk close ou closer to the window; **approche une chaise du lit** bring ou draw a chair up to the bed; **il approcha ses lèvres des siennes** he moved his lips close to hers; **approche ta chaise** pull up your chair, bring your chair closer; **~ la cuillère/le verre de ses lèvres** to raise the spoon/the glass to one's lips; **2** (aller près de) to go up to [*personne*]; (venir près de) to come up to [*personne*]; fig (aborder) to approach [*personne*] (**au sujet de** about); **ne les approche pas** don't go near them, keep away from them; **ne m'approche pas** don't come near me, keep away from me; **on ne peut pas les ~** (occupés) you can never get to see them; (trop distants) they're unapproachable; **dans ce travail, on approche des gens importants** in this job, you come into contact ou you rub shoulders with important people.
II approcher de *vtr ind* to near, to get near [*endroit*]; to be (getting) close to [*but, solution*]; to be close to [*vérité, perfection*]; **nous approchons du but** lit, fig we're nearly there; **il approche de la soixantaine** he's getting on for sixty, he's close to sixty; **nous approchons du marché unique** the single market will soon be with us; **la température approche du zéro** the temperature is near zero; **j'approchais du 100 km à l'heure** I was going at nearly 100 km an hour.
III *vi* [*saison, date, événement*] to approach, to draw near; [*personne, avion, orage*] to approach, to come nearer; **sentir la mort ~** to feel death drawing near; **l'heure du départ approchait** it was nearly time to leave; **approche, que je te voie** come closer ou nearer, so I can see you; **la nuit approche** it's getting dark.
IV s'approcher *vpr* **1 s'~ de qn/qch** (aller) to go up to sb/sth; (venir) to come up to sb/sth; **il s'approcha pour mieux m'examiner** he came up to me to get a better look at me; **l'ennemi s'approchait** the enemy was approaching; **ne t'approche pas du bord** (ne va pas) don't go near the edge; (ne viens pas) don't come near the edge; **2** (ressembler) **ça s'approche de la vérité** it's close to ou not far from the truth; **3** (être imminent) [*saison, date, événement*] to approach, to draw near.

approfondi, **~e** /apʀɔfɔ̃di/ *adj* [*examen, recherche, discussion*] detailed; [*enquête, étude, connaissances*] in-depth (*épith*); **étudier qch de façon très ~e** to study sth in great detail.

approfondir /apʀɔfɔ̃diʀ/ [3] **I** *vtr* **1** fig to go into [sth] in depth [*sujet*]; **vous auriez pu ~** you could have gone into the subject in greater depth; **inutile d'~** don't go into detail; **~ ses connaissances en littérature** to improve one's knowledge of literature; **2** lit to deepen [*canal, trou*].
II s'approfondir *vpr* **1** [*crevasse, trou*] to deepen; **2** [*problèmes*] to get worse.

approfondissement /apʀɔfɔ̃dismɑ̃/ *nm* **1** lit deepening (**de** of); **2** fig improvement; **l'~ de ses connaissances** the improvement of one's knowledge; **l'~ d'une question/d'un débat** the development of an issue/of a debate; **l'~ européen** European consolidation.

appropriation /apʀɔpʀijasjɔ̃/ *nf* taking over, appropriation sout (**de** of).

approprié, **~e** /apʀɔpʀije/ **I** *pp* ▶ **approprier**.
II *pp adj* [*moyens, technique, régime*] appropriate.

approprier: **s'approprier** /apʀɔpʀije/ [2] *vpr* **1** (s'accaparer) to take, to appropriate sout [*chose, œuvre, idée*]; to seize [*pouvoir*]; to steal [*gloire*]; to take the credit for [*succès*]; **2** (être adapté) [*ton*] to be appropriate.

approuver /apʀuve/ [1] *vtr* **1** gén to approve of [*action, décision, projet*]; **je t'approuve totalement** (sur une idée, opinion) I quite agree with you; **je t'approuve d'avoir accepté/d'avoir parlé** I think you were right to accept/to speak up; **je les approuve d'avoir acheté cette maison** I approve of their buying this house; **2** Admin, Pol [*commission, ministres*] to approve [*texte, projet, budget*]; [*parlement*] to pass [*projet de loi, décret*].

approvisionnement /apʀɔvizjɔnmɑ̃/ *nm* **1** (activité) supply (**en** of); **assurer l'~ d'une ville en eau potable** to ensure the supply of drinking water to a town; **l'~ de la ville en eau soulève de graves problèmes** supplying the town with water raises serious problems; **2** (marchandises) **service des ~s** supplies department; **3** (source) supplier; **les industriels diversifient leurs ~s** industrialists vary their suppliers.

approvisionner /apʀɔvizjɔne/ [1] **I** *vtr* **1** (fournir) to supply [*ville, marché*] (**en** with); to load [*arme automatique*]; **une boutique mal approvisionnée** a badly stocked shop; **2** (verser de l'argent à) to pay money into [*compte en banque*]; **votre compte n'est plus approvisionné depuis trois mois** your account has not been in credit for three months.
II s'approvisionner *vpr* **1** (faire des provisions) to stock up (**en** on, with); **2** (acheter) **la compagnie s'approvisionne en papier directement auprès de l'usine** the company gets its supplies of paper directly from the factory.

approximatif, **-ive** /apʀɔksimatif, iv/ *adj* [*devis, coût, croquis, chiffre*] rough; [*traduction*] approximate; **dans un anglais ~** in broken English.

approximation /apʀɔksimasjɔ̃/ *nf* **1** (résultat grossier) (chiffre) rough estimate; (traduction, concept) approximation; **2** (caractère) imprecision; **l'~ de ta traduction/ton tir/ton anglais** the inaccuracy of your translation/your shot/your English; **3** Math approximation.

approximativement /apʀɔksimativmɑ̃/ *adv* approximately.

appui /apɥi/ *nm* **1** (soutien) lit, fig support; **il se sert du tabouret comme ~ pour sa jambe cassée** he uses the stool to support his broken leg; **prendre ~ sur** to lean on [*objet, personne*]; **~ financier** financial backing; **~ matériel/moral** material/moral support; **il bénéficie d'~s puissants** he has the support ou backing of powerful people; **avoir l'~ de qn** to have sb's support; **mon ~ vous est acquis!** you have my support!; **à l'~ de** in support of; **à l'~ de cette thèse il y a de nombreuses statistiques** there are numerous statistics in support of this theory; **une accusation sans preuves à l'~** an accusation which has no proof to support it ou to back it up; **point d'~** Phys fulcrum; **2** Constr **~ (de fenêtre)** window sill, window ledge; **3** Mil support; **~ aérien/tactique/de feu** air/tactical/fire support; **4** Mus (de voix) placing.

appui-bras, *pl* **appuis-bras** /apɥibʀa/ *nm* armrest.

appui-main, *pl* **appuis-main** /apɥimɛ̃/ *nm* maulstick, mahlstick.

appui-tête, *pl* **appuis-tête** /apɥitɛt/ *nm* **1** (de confort) headrest; **2** (de protection) antimacassar.

appuyé, **~e** /apɥije/ **I** *pp* ▶ **appuyer**.
II *pp adj* [*regard*] intent; [*plaisanterie*] heavy; [*politesse*] laboured[GB], overdone.

appuyer /apɥije/ [22] **I** *nm* Équit half-pass.
II *vtr* **1** (poser) to lean, to rest [*objet, partie du corps*] (**sur** on; **contre** against); **~ ses coudes sur la table** to rest ou lean one's elbows on the table; **~ sa tête sur un oreiller** to rest one's head on a pillow; **~ une échelle/bicyclette contre un mur** to lean a ladder/bicycle against a wall; **il dormait, la tête appuyée contre la vitre du train** he was asleep, his head resting against the train window; **2** (presser) to press (**contre** against; **sur** on); **il a appuyé son doigt sur l'endroit douloureux** he pressed his finger on the painful spot; **elle appuyait sa cuisse contre la mienne** she was pressing her thigh against mine; **3** (baser) to support, to back up [*argumentation, démonstration, raisonnement, théorie*] (**sur** with); **~ une démonstration sur des faits irréfutables** to support a demonstration with irrefutable facts; **4** (soutenir) to back [*personne, candidat*]; to support [*action, projet*]; **5** Mil [*artillerie, aviation, blindés*] to support [*assaut, offensive*].
III appuyer sur *vtr ind* **1** (presser) **~ sur** (avec le doigt) to press [*interrupteur, bouton, sonnette, endroit sensible*]; (avec le pied) to put one's foot on [*pédale, frein, levier*]; **appuie sur l'accélérateur!** put your foot down!; **~ sur la détente** to pull ou press the trigger; **il faut ~ sur ton stylo pour que l'encre coule** you have to press on your pen to make the ink flow; **2** (insister) **~ sur** to stress [*syllabe*]; to stress, to emphasize [*mot*]; to accentuate [*note de musique*]; to emphasize [*aspect, argument, qualités, résultats*]; **il appuyait lourdement sur les défauts de son collaborateur** he put heavy emphasis on ou he dwelled on his collaborator's shortcomings; **3** (se porter sur) [*véhicule, automobiliste*] **~ sur la droite/gauche** to bear right/left.
IV s'appuyer *vpr* **1** (prendre appui) to lean (**sur** on; **contre** against); **s'~ sur une canne/le bras de qn** to lean on a stick GB ou cane/sb's arm; **s'~ contre un mur** to lean against a wall; **l'édifice s'appuie sur ces colonnes** the building is supported by these columns, these columns bear the weight of the building; **2** (se fonder) **s'~ sur** to depend on, to rely on [*personne, ami*]; to rely on [*argument, théorie, démonstration, témoignage*]; to draw on [*loi, texte, enquête, rapport*]; to be based on [*connaissance, concept*]; **3**○ (faire, subir) **s'~ qch** to be stuck ou lumbered○ with sth; **s'~ qn** to be stuck ou lumbered○ with sb; **c'est toujours moi qui m'appuie la vaisselle** I'm always the one who gets stuck ou lumbered○ with doing the dishes; **je me suis appuyé le trajet à pied** I was forced to go on foot.

âpre /ɑpʀ/ *adj* **1** (désagréable) [*goût, fruit*] bitter; [*voix*] harsh; [*froid, vent*] bitter; **2** (acharné) [*lutte, concurrence*] fierce; [*dispute, discussion*] bitter; **~ au gain** grasping.

âprement /ɑpʀəmɑ̃/ *adv* [*lutter, défendre*] fiercely; [*discuter*] bitterly.

après[1] /apʀɛ/ **I** *adv* **1** (dans le temps) afterwards; **viens manger, tu finiras ~** come and eat your dinner, you can finish afterwards; **aussitôt** or **tout de suite ~ il s'est mis à pleuvoir** straight after that ou afterwards it started raining; **~ seulement, il a appelé les pompiers** only afterwards did he call the fire brigade; **j'ai compris longtemps ~** I understood a long time after ou afterwards; **il a mangé au restaurant et (puis) ~ il est allé au cinéma** he ate in a restaurant and afterwards went to the cinema; **on verra ça ~** we'll come to that later; **je te le dirai ~** I'll tell you later; **et ~ que s'est-il passé?** and then what happened?, and what happened next?; **peu/bien ~** shortly/long after(wards); **une heure/deux jours/quatre ans ~** one hour/two days/four years later; **la semaine/le mois/l'année d'~** the week/the month/the year after; **pas ce week-end celui d'~** not this weekend, the one after; **pas la semaine prochaine celle d'~** not next week, the week after next; **la fois d'~ nous nous sommes perdus** the next time we got lost; **le bus/train d'~** the next bus/train; **l'instant d'~ il avait déjà oublié** a moment later he had already forgotten; **j'ai regardé le film mais je n'ai pas vu l'émission d'~** I watched the film but I didn't see the programme[GB] after it; **2** (dans l'espace) **tu vois le croisement, j'habite (juste) ~ à droite** can you see the crossroads? I live (just) past ou beyond it on the right; **peu ~ il y a un lac** a bit further on there's a lake; **'c'est après le village?'—'oui juste ~'** 'is it after the village?'—'yes just after'; **la page/le chapitre d'~** the next page/chapter; **3** (dans une hiérarchie) **~ il y a le S puis le T** S comes after and then T; **les loisirs d'abord, le travail passe ~** leisure first, work comes after; **4** (utilisé seul en interrogation) **~?** and what next?; **deux kilos de carottes, ~○?** two kilos of carrots and what else?; **5** (marquant l'agacement) **et ~?** so what○?; **oui je suis rentré à 4 h du matin, et ~?** yes, I came home at 4 am, so what?
II *prép* **1** (dans le temps) after; **sortir/passer ~ qn** to go out/to go after sb; **~ 22 h/12 jours** after 10 pm/12 days ; **~ mon départ** after I left; **~ quelques années ils se sont revus** a few years later they saw each other again; **~ une croissance spectaculaire** after spectacular growth; **~ tant de passion/violence** after so much passion/violence; **~ déduction/impôt** after deductions/tax; **~ cela** after that; **~ tout** after all; **~ tout c'est leur problème** after all it's their problem; **~ quoi** after which; **jour ~ jour** day after day, day in day out; **livre ~ livre** book after book; **~ tout ce qu'il a fait pour toi** after all (that) he's done for you; **j'irai ~ avoir fait la sieste** I'll go after I've had a nap; **~ avoir pris la parole il se rassit** after he had spoken he sat down again; **il est conseillé de boire beaucoup ~ avoir couru** it is advisable to drink a lot after you have been running; **~ manger/déjeuner/dîner/souper** after eating ou meals/lunch/dinner/supper; **peu ~ minuit** shortly after midnight; **2** (dans l'espace) after; **~ l'église/la sortie de la ville** after the church/you come out of the town; **bien/juste ~ l'usine** well/just after the factory; **je suis ~ toi sur la liste** I'm after you on the list; **~ vous!** (par politesse) after you!; **être ~ qn**○ to be getting at sb○; **il est toujours ~ son fils** he's always on at his son○; **en avoir ~ qn**○ to have it in for sb○; **3** (dans une hiérarchie) after; **la dame vient ~ le roi** the Queen comes after the King; **c'est le grade le plus important ~ celui de général** it's the highest rank after that of general; **faire passer qn/qch ~ qn/qch** to put sb/sth after sb/sth.
III d'après *loc prép* **1** (selon) **d'~ moi/toi/nous/vous** in my/your/our/your opinion; **d'~ lui/elle/eux** according to him/her/them ou in his/her/their opinion; **d'~ les journalistes/le gouvernement** according to the journalists/the government; **d'~ la météo il va faire beau** according to the weather forecast it's going to be fine; **d'~ la loi** under the law; **d'~ mes calculs/mes estimations/ma montre** by my calculations/my reckoning/my watch; **d'~ ce qu'elle a dit/mon expérience** from what she said/my experience; **2** (en imitant) from; **un tableau peint d'~ une photo** a painting made from a photograph; **d'~ un dessin de Gauguin** from a drawing by Gauguin; **3** (adapté de) based on; **un film d' ~ un roman de Simenon** a film based on a novel by Simenon.
IV après que *loc conj* after; **~ que je leur ai annoncé la nouvelle** after I told them the news; **~ qu'il eut parlé** after he had spoken.

après[2] /apʀɛ/ *nm* **l'~** the future; **il n'y aura pas d'~** there won't be an afterwards.

> **après**[1]
>
> *après* adverbe se traduit généralement par *afterwards* et *après* préposition par *after*.
>
> Les expressions telles que *courir après qn/qch, crier après qn* etc. sont traitées respectivement sous ***courir***, ***crier*** etc.
>
> *après* entre dans la composition de nombreux mots qui s'écrivent avec un trait d'union (*après-demain, après-guerre, après-midi* etc.). Ces mots sont des entrées à part entière et on les trouvera dans la nomenclature du dictionnaire. Utilisé avec un nom, propre ou commun, pour désigner la période suivant un événement ou la disparition d'une personne il se traduit par *post* et forme alors un groupe adjectival que l'on fait suivre du nom approprié:
>
> *l'après-Gorbatchev* = the post-Gorbachev period
> *l'après-crise* = the post-recession period
> *l'après-1789* = the post-1789 period
>
> On notera:
>
> *l'après-8 mai* = the period following 8 May
> *la France de l'après-de Gaulle* = post-de Gaulle France

après-demain /apʀɛdmɛ̃/ *adv* the day after tomorrow; **la technologie de demain et celle d'~** the technology of tomorrow and beyond.

après-guerre, *pl* **~s** /apʀɛgɛʀ/ *nm* ou *f* postwar period, postwar years (*pl*); **les générations d'~** postwar generations.

après-midi /apʀɛmidi/ *nm* ou *f inv* afternoon; **en début/fin d'~** early/late in the afternoon; **j'y vais le samedi ~** I go there on Saturday afternoons; **à 2 heures de l'~** at 2 in the afternoon, at 2 pm.

après-rasage, *pl* **~s** /apʀɛʀazaʒ/ *nm* after-shave.

après-ski /apʀɛski/ *nm inv* **1** (chaussure) snowboot, moon boot; **2** (moment) après-ski.

après-soleil /apʀɛsɔlɛj/ *nm inv* after-sun lotion; **une crème ~** an after-sun cream.

après-vente /apʀɛvɑ̃t/ *adj inv* **service ~** (département) after-sales service department; (activité) after-sales service.

âpreté /ɑpʀəte/ *nf* **1** (acharnement) (de lutte, concurrence) fierceness; (de discussion) bitterness; **discuter avec ~** to argue bitterly; **son ~ au gain** his/her greed for gain; **2** (de fruit) liter bitterness.

a priori /apʀijɔʀi/ **I** *loc adj inv* [*jugement, raisonnement, preuves*] a priori.
II *loc adv* **1** (à première vue) on the face of it; **~, ça ne devrait pas poser de problèmes** on the face of it there shouldn't be any problems; **~ je ne connais personne qui puisse faire ce travail** offhand I can't think of anybody who could do this job; **~ je ne peux rien décider** right now I can't make a decision; **2** (sans réfléchir) out of hand; **rejeter ~ une proposition** to reject a proposal out of hand; **3** Philos a priori.
III *nm inv* a priori assumption.

apriorisme /apʀijɔʀism/ *nm* **1** gén, pej a priori reasoning; **2** Philos apriorism.

à-propos /apʀɔpo/ *nm inv* **1** (art d'arriver au bon moment) timing; (d'intervention) timeliness; **interrompre avec ~** to make a well-timed interruption; **cette déclaration manque d'~** this declaration is badly timed; **2** (pertinence) aptness, relevance; **intervenir avec ~ dans une discussion** to make a pertinent remark ou observation in a discussion; **répondre avec ~** to make an apt reply; **parler/agir avec ~** to say/to do the right thing; **ta remarque manque d'~** your remark is off the point; **3** (présence d'esprit) presence of mind; **réagir avec (beaucoup d')~** to react with great presence of mind.

apte /apt/ *adj* **1** (capable) capable (**à** of); **2** (ayant les qualifications requises) qualified (**à** for; **à faire** to do); (ayant les qualités requises) suitable (**à** for); (présentant les conditions requises) fit (**à** for; **à faire** to do); **3** Mil fit; **être déclaré ~** to be declared fit (**à** for); **4** Jur **être ~ à qch** to have legal capacity to do sth.

aptitude /aptityd/ *nf* **1** (capacité) competence (**à, pour** for), ability (**à faire** to do); (don) aptitude (**à** for); **2** Mil **~ au service** fitness to serve; **signer l'~ de qn** to pass sb as fit to serve; **3** Jur legal capacity.

apurement /apyʀmɑ̃/ *nm* (de comptes) audit; (de dette, passif) discharge.

apurer /apyʀe/ [1] *vtr* to audit [*comptes*]; to discharge [*dette, passif*].

AQR /akyɛʀ/ *nm*: *abbr* ▶ **apport**.

aquaculture /akwakyltyʀ/ *nf* aquaculture.

aquagym /akwaʒim/ ▶ 449 *nf* aquarobics, aquafitness.

aquaplanage /akwaplanaʒ/ *nm* Aut aquaplaning GB, hydroplaning US.

aquaplane /akwaplan/ *nm* **1** (planche) aquaplane; **2** ▶ 449 (activité) aquaplaning.

aquaplaning /akwaplaniŋ/ *nm* controv Aut aquaplaning GB, hydroplaning US.

aquarelle /akwaʀɛl/ *nf* **1** (procédé) watercolours[GB] (*pl*); **2** (œuvre) watercolour[GB].

aquarelliste /akwaʀelist/ *nmf* painter in watercolours[GB], aquarellist spéc.

aquariophile /akwaʀjɔfil/ *nmf*: *person who keeps exotic fish as a hobby*.

aquarium /akwaʀjɔm/ *nm* aquarium, fish tank.

aquatique /akwatik/ *adj* **1** [*flore, faune*] aquatic; **2** [*jardin, sport*] water (*épith*).

aqueduc /akdyk/ *nm* **1** Constr aqueduct; **2** Anat duct; **~ du limaçon** cochlear duct.

aqueux, ~euse /akø, øz/ *adj* aqueous.

aquifère /akɥifɛʀ/ **I** *adj* water-bearing, aquiferous spéc.
II *nm* aquifer.

aquilin /akilɛ̃/ *adj m* [*nez, profil*] aquiline.

aquilon /akilɔ̃/ *nm* liter north wind.

aquitain, ~e /akitɛ̃, ɛn/ ▶ 692 *adj* of Aquitaine; **le bassin ~** the Aquitaine Basin.

Aquitaine /akitɛn/ ▶ 692 *nprf* **l'~** Aquitaine.

AR *written abbr* ▶ **accusé**.

ara /aʀa/ *nm* macaw.

arabe /aʀab/ **I** *adj* [*architecture, civilisation*] Arab; [*chiffre, dialecte, écriture*] Arabic.
II ▶ 462 *nm* Ling Arabic; **~ classique/littéral** classical/written Arabic.

Arabe /aʀab/ *nmf* Arab.

arabesque /aʀabɛsk/ *nf* arabesque.

arabica /aʀabika/ *nm* arabica.

Arabie /aʀabi/ ▶ 321, 692 *nprf* Arabia; **désert d'~** Arabian desert.
■ **~ Saoudite** Saudi Arabia.

arabique /aʀabik/ *adj* (d'Arabie) Arabian.

arabisant, ~e /aʀabizɑ̃, ɑ̃t/ *nm,f* Arabist.

arabisation /aʀabizɑsjɔ̃/ *nf* Arabization.

arabiser /aʀabize/ [1] *vtr* to Arabize.

arabisme /aʀabism/ *nm* Arabism.

arable /aʀabl/ *adj* arable.

arachide /aʀaʃid/ *nf* groundnut; **huile d'~** groundnut oil.

arachnéen, -éenne /aʀakneɛ̃, ɛn/ *adj* **1** lit arachnidan; **2** fig, liter gossamer (*épith*).

arachnide /aʀaknid/ *nm* arachnid; **les ~s** Arachnida.

arachnoïde /aʀaknɔid/ *nf* arachnoid.

araignée /aʀeɲe/ *nf* **1** Zool (arachnide) spider; **2** Tech (crochet) grapnel.
■ **~ de mer** spider crab.
IDIOMES **avoir une ~ au plafond**° to have a screw loose°, to have bats in the belfry°.

araire /aʀɛʀ/ *nm* ard plough.

aralia /aʀalja/ *nm* aralia.

araméen, -éenne /aʀameɛ̃, ɛn/ **I** *adj* [*architecture, civilisation*] Aramean; [*alphabet, langue*] Aramaic.
II ▶ 462 *nm* Ling Aramaic.

Araméen, -éenne /aʀameɛ̃, ɛn/ *nm,f* Aramean.

araser /aʀaze/ [1] *vtr* Constr to level off [*mur*]; Tech to plane down [*tenon*]; Géol to wear down [*relief*].

aratoire /aʀatwaʀ/ *adj* ploughing GB, plowing US.

araucaria /aʀokaʀja/ *nm* monkey puzzle tree, araucaria spéc.

arbalète /aʀbalɛt/ *nf* crossbow.

arbalétrier /aʀbaletʀije/ *nm* **1** Hist, Sport crossbowman; **2** Constr top chord.

arbitrage /aʀbitʀaʒ/ *nm* **1** (de différend) arbitration; **soumettre un litige à l'~ d'un tiers** to submit a dispute to arbitration by a third party; **2** Sport (en boxe, football, rugby) refereeing; (en baseball, cricket, tennis) umpiring; **3** Fin arbitrage.

arbitraire /aʀbitʀɛʀ/ **I** *adj* arbitrary; **le côté ~ de la décision** the arbitrariness of the decision.
II *nm* **1** (autorité) arbitrary power; **l'~ administratif** the arbitrary power of administration; **2** Ling **l'~ du signe** the arbitrary nature of the sign.

arbitrairement /aʀbitʀɛʀmɑ̃/ *adv* arbitrarily.

arbitral, ~e, *mpl* **-aux** /aʀbitʀal, o/ *adj* arbitration (*épith*).

arbitralement /aʀbitʀalmɑ̃/ *adv* Jur by arbitration.

arbitre /aʀbitʀ/ *nm* **1** Sport (en boxe, football, rugby) referee; (en baseball, cricket, tennis) umpire; ▶ **libre**; **2** fig (expert) arbiter; **l'~ suprême** the Supreme Arbiter; **elle est l'~ des élégances** she's the arbiter of all things elegant; **être l'~ d'une consultation électorale** to hold the balance of power in an election; **3** Jur (de différend) arbitrator.

arbitrer /aʀbitʀe/ [1] **I** *vtr* **1** Sport to referee [*match de boxe, football, rugby*]; to umpire [*match de baseball, cricket, tennis*]; **2** (régler) to arbitrate in [*différend, situation*].
II *vi* to arbitrate (**entre** between).

arboré, ~e /aʀbɔʀe/ *adj* [*terrain*] planted with trees (*après n*).

arborer /aʀbɔʀe/ [1] *vtr* **1** (porter avec ostentation) [*personne*] to sport [*objet*]; **2** (montrer) to wear [*sourire, air*]; to parade [*attitude, idée*]; **3** (porter normalement) [*personne, groupe*] to bear [*enseigne, couleur*]; [*navire, avion, bâtiment*] to fly [*pavillon, drapeau*].

arborescence /aʀbɔʀesɑ̃s/ *nf* **1** (de végétal) tree-like aspect, arborescence spéc; **2** (de veines, branches) branching; **3** Math, Ordinat tree diagram.

arborescent, ~e /aʀbɔʀesɑ̃, ɑ̃t/ *adj* Bot, Ordinat tree (*épith*).

arboretum /aʀbɔʀetɔm/ *nm* arboretum.

arboricole /aʀbɔʀikɔl/ *adj* [*animal*] tree-dwelling, arboreal spéc; [*technique*] arboricultural.

arboriculteur, -trice /aʀbɔʀikyltœʀ, tʀis/ ▶ 510 *nm,f* arboriculturist.

arboriculture /aʀbɔʀikyltyʀ/ *nf* arboriculture.

arborisation /aʀbɔʀizasjɔ̃/ *nf* tree-like pattern, arborization spéc.

arborisé, ~e /aʀbɔʀize/ *adj* dendritic.

arbouse /aʀbuz/ *nf* arbutus berry.

arbousier /aʀbuzje/ *nm* arbutus (tree).

arbre /aʀbʀ/ *nm* **1** (végétal) tree; ▶ **forêt**; **2** (diagramme) tree (diagram); **3** Tech shaft.
■ **~ à cames** Aut camshaft; **~ généalogique** family tree; **~ d'hélice** Naut propeller shaft; **~ de Judée** Bot Judas tree; **~ de la liberté** Hist *tree planted during the French Revolution as a symbol of liberty*; **~ de Noël** (sapin) Christmas tree; (de puits de pétrole) Christmas tree; **~ à pain** Bot breadfruit; **~ de transmission** Aut transmission shaft, propeller shaft; **~ de vie** Bible tree of life.
IDIOMES **grimper à l'~**° to be taken for a ride°; **entre l'~ et l'écorce il ne faut pas mettre le doigt** Prov never meddle in other people's affairs.

arbrisseau, *pl* **~x** /aʀbʀiso/ *nm* small tree.

arbuste /aʀbyst/ *nm* shrub.

arc /aʀk/ *nm* **1** Chasse, Sport bow; **tendre** or **bander un ~** to bend a bow back; **2** (courbe) curve; **en (forme d') ~** arched; **3** Math arc; **~ de cercle** arc of a circle; **4** Archit arch; **5** Électrotech arc; **~ électrique** electric arc.
■ **~ en accolade** ogee arch; **~ brisé** lancet arch; **~ de décharge** discharging arch; **~ plein cintre** round arch; **~ rampant** rampant arch; **~ trilobé** trefoil arch; **~ de triomphe** triumphal arch; **~ Tudor** Tudor arch.
IDIOMES **avoir plus d'une corde à son ~** to have more than one string to one's bow.

arcade /aʀkad/ *nf* **1** Archit arcade; **~ aveugle** blind arcade; **~s** (arches) arcades; (ensemble) archways; **2** Anat arch; **~ dentaire** dental arch; **~ sourcilière** arch of the eyebrow.

Arcadie /aʀkadi/ ▶ 692 *nprf* **l'~** Arcadia.

arcadien, -ienne /aʀkadjɛ̃, ɛn/ *adj* Arcadian.

arcanes /aʀkan/ *nmpl* liter mysteries; **les ~ de la politique** the mysteries of politics.

arcature /aʀkatyʀ/ *nf* arcature.

arc-boutant, *pl* **arcs-boutants** /aʀkbutɑ̃/ *nm* flying buttress.

arc-bouter /aʀkbute/ [1] **I** *vtr* to buttress.
II s'arc-bouter *vpr* to brace oneself (**contre** against).

arceau, *pl* **~x** /aʀso/ *nm* **1** (de voûte) arch; **2** (de tonnelle, croquet) hoop; **3** Aut (de voiture) roll bar; **4** (de lit) cradle.

arc-en-ciel, *pl* **arcs-en-ciel** /aʀkɑ̃sjɛl/ *nm* rainbow.

archaïque /aʀkaik/ *adj* archaic.

archaïsant, ~e /aʀkaizɑ̃, ɑ̃t/ *adj* [*style, œuvre, écrivain*] archaistic.

archaïsme /aʀkaism/ *nm* archaism.

archange /aʀkɑ̃ʒ/ *nm* archangel.

arche /aʀʃ/ *nf* **1** Archit arch; **2** Relig Ark; **~ d'alliance** Ark of the Covenant; **~ de Noé** Noah's Ark.

archéologie /aʀkeɔlɔʒi/ *nf* archaeology.

archéologique /aʀkeɔlɔʒik/ *adj* archaeological.

archéologue /aʀkeɔlɔg/ ▶ 510 *nmf* archaeologist.

archer /aʀʃe/ *nm* archer.

archet /aʀʃɛ/ *nm* Mus bow.

archétype /aʀketip/ *nm* archetype; **c'est l'~ du héros/méchant** he's the archetypal hero/villain.

archevêché /aʀʃəveʃe/ *nm* **1** (domaine) archdiocese; **2** (dignité) archbishopric; **3** (siège) archbishop's palace.

archevêque /aʀʃəvɛk/ *nm* ▶ 813 archbishop.

archibondé°, **~e** /aʀʃibɔ̃de/ *adj* [*salle, bus*] absolutely packed.

archiconnu°, **~e** /aʀʃikɔny/ *adj* really well-known.

archidiaconat /aʀʃidjakɔna/ *nm* archdeaconate.

archidiacre /aʀʃidjakʀ/ ▶ 813 *nm* archdeacon.

archidiocèse /aʀʃidjɔsɛz/ *nm* archdiocese.

archiduc /aʀʃidyk/ ▶ 813 *nm* archduke.

archiduchesse /aʀʃidyʃɛs/ ▶ 813 *nf* archduchess.

archiépiscopal, ~e, *mpl* **-aux** /aʀʃiepiskɔpal, o/ *adj* archiepiscopal.

archiépiscopat /aʀʃiepiskɔpa/ *nm* archiepiscopate.

archimandrite /aʀʃimɑ̃dʀit/ *nm* archimandrite.

Archimède /aʀʃimɛd/ *npr* Archimedes.

archipel /aʀʃipɛl/ *nm* archipelago; **l'~ des Baléares** the Balearic archipelago.

archiphonème /aʀʃifɔnɛm/ *nm* archiphoneme.
archiprêtre /aʀʃipʀɛtʀ/ *nm* archpriest.
architecte /aʀʃitɛkt/ ▶510 *nmf* lit, fig architect; **~ naval** naval architect.
architectonique /aʀʃitɛktɔnik/ **I** *adj* architectonic.
II *nf* architectonics (+ *v sg*).
architectural, **~e**, *mpl* **-aux** /aʀʃitɛktyʀal, o/ *adj* architectural.
architecture /aʀʃitɛktyʀ/ *nf* **1** lit, Ordinat architecture; **2** fig structure.
■ **~ industrielle** industrial architecture; **~ paysagère** landscape architecture.
architrave /aʀʃitʀav/ *nf* architrave.
archivage /aʀʃivaʒ/ *nm* archiving.
archiver /aʀʃive/ [1] *vtr* to archive.
archives /aʀʃiv/ *nfpl* archives, records; **~ communales** parish records; **classé aux ~** filed in the archives; **fouiller dans les ~** to go through the archives; **je vais fouiller dans mes ~** hum I'll go through my (old) papers.
■ **~ sonores** sound archives.
archiviste /aʀʃivist/ ▶510 *nmf* archivist.
archivolte /aʀʃivɔlt/ *nf* archivolt.
arçon /aʀsɔ̃/ *nm* Équit tree; **bois d'~** saddle tree; **vider les ~s** to fall off one's horse; **cheval d'~s** pommel horse.
arctique /aʀktik/ *adj* arctic.
Arctique /aʀktik/ *nprm* **1** ▶692 (région) Arctic; **2** ▶555 (océan) **l'océan ~** the Arctic Ocean.
Ardèche /aʀdɛʃ/ ▶357, 692 *nprf* (rivière, département) **l'~** the Ardèche.
ardemment /aʀdamɑ̃/ *adv* [*aimer, désirer*] passionately; [*défendre*] fiercely, passionately; **être ~ républicain** to be an ardent republican.
Ardennes /aʀdɛn/ ▶692 *nprfpl* (département) **les ~** the Ardennes.
ardent, **~e** /aʀdɑ̃, ɑ̃t/ *adj* **1** [*braise*] glowing; [*tison*] red-hot; [*flamme, soleil, chaleur*] blazing; [*fièvre, soif*] burning, raging; fig [*regard, couleur*] fiery; **d'un rouge ~** fiery red; **2** (intense) [*foi, conviction*] burning, passionate; [*ambition, désir, passion*] burning; [*vœu, souhait, prière, piété*] fervent; [*lutte*] fierce; [*zèle, défense, discours, appel*] impassioned; [*supplications*] urgent; **3** (fougueux) [*nature, amant, partisan, défenseur*] passionate; [*militant, patriote*] fervent; [*jeunesse*] hot-blooded; **être ~ au combat** to fight fiercely; **être ~ au travail** to be an enthusiastic worker.
ardeur /aʀdœʀ/ *nf* **1** (chaleur) heat; **2** (fougue) (d'amant, enthousiasme) ardour[GB]; (de foi, patriotisme) fervour[GB]; (de néophyte) keenness GB, enthusiasm; (de combattant, révolutionnaire) fervour[GB], eagerness; **les ~s de la passion** fig the flames of passion; **modérer** or **calmer les ~s de qn** to cool sb's ardour[GB]; **cheval plein d'~** fiery steed†; **3** (zèle) zeal; **~ révolutionnaire** revolutionary zeal; **ton ~ au travail** your enthusiasm for work; **travailler avec ~** to work hard; **redoubler d'~** to try twice as hard.
ardillon /aʀdijɔ̃/ *nm* **1** (de boucle) prong; **2** (d'hameçon) barb.
ardoise /aʀdwaz/ **I** ▶193 *adj inv* slate-grey GB, slate-gray US.
II *nf* **1** Minér slate; **2** (tuile) slate; **toit d'~(s)** slate roof; **3** (d'écolier) slate; **4**○ (dette) debt; **régler une ~** to settle a debt, to wipe the slate clean; **avoir une ~ chez un commerçant** to owe a shopkeeper money.
■ **~ magique** magic drawing board; **~ électronique** notepad computer.
ardoisé, **~e** /aʀdwaze/ ▶193 *adj* (couleur) slate-grey.
■ **peinture ~e** blackboard paint.
ardoisier, **-ière** /aʀdwazje, ɛʀ/ **I** *adj* [*gîte, roche*] slaty; [*carrière*] slate (*épith*).
II ▶510 *nm* **1** (ouvrier) slate worker; **2** (patron) slate quarry owner.
III ardoisière *nf* slate quarry.
ardu, **~e** /aʀdy/ *adj* **1** (difficile) [*tâche, travail*] arduous, laborious; [*négociations, problème*] taxing, difficult; **2** (escarpé) [*montée, perte*] steep.
are /aʀ/ ▶783 *nf* one hundred square metres[GB], are.
arec /aʀɛk/ *nm* areca.
arène /aʀɛn/ *nf* **1** (dans un amphithéâtre) arena; (au cirque) ring; (pour corridas) bullring; fig arena; **l'~ politique/internationale** the political/international arena; **2** (amphithéâtre) **~s** Antiq amphitheatre[GB] (*sg*); (pour corridas) bullring (*sg*); **3** Géol coarse sand, arenite spéc.
IDIOMES **entrer** or **descendre dans l'~** to enter the ring.
arénicole /aʀenikɔl/ *nf* sandworm.
aréole /aʀeɔl/ *nf* areola.
aréomètre /aʀeɔmɛtʀ/ *nm* hydrometer.
aréométrie /aʀeɔmetʀi/ *nf* hydrometry.
aréopage /aʀeɔpaʒ/ *nm* fig prestigious assembly.
Aréopage /aʀeɔpaʒ/ *nm* **l'~** the Areopagus.
aréquier /aʀekje/ *nm* areca (palm ou tree).
arête /aʀɛt/ *nf* **1** Zool fishbone; **c'est plein d'~s** it's full of bones; **retirer les ~s d'un poisson** to bone a fish; **sans ~s** boned; **pavage en ~ de poisson** herringbone paving; **2** (de toit, montagne) ridge; (de voûte) groin; (de prisme, roche) edge; (de nez) bridge; **3** Bot (d'un épi) **~s** awns.
argent /aʀʒɑ̃/ ▶46 *nm* **1** (monnaie) money; **~ facile/frais/sale** easy/ready/dirty money; **~ public** public funds (*pl*) ou money; **déposer de l'~ à la banque** to deposit money in the bank; **retirer de l'~ à la banque** to withdraw money from the bank; **l'~ me fond dans les mains** money just runs through my fingers; **ça rapporte peu d'~** it doesn't bring in much money; **faire de l'~** to make money; **se faire de l'~ en vendant qch/par la spéculation/sur le dos des autres** to make money by selling sth/through speculation/at the expense of others; **dépenser son ~ sans compter** to spend one's money like water○; **pour de l'~** for money; **perdre son ~ au jeu** to gamble one's money away; **en avoir/vouloir pour son ~** to get/to want one's money's worth; **parler d'~** to talk about money (matters); **l'~ de la drogue** drug money; ▶**bonheur**, **fenêtre**, **odeur**, **serviteur**; **2** (métal) silver; **en ~** [*bracelet, couvert*] silver (*épith*); **d'~** [*fil, feuille*] silver (*épith*); **3** Hérald argent.
■ **~ liquide** cash; **~ de poche** pocket money.
IDIOMES **le temps c'est de l'~** time is money; **prendre qch pour ~ comptant** to take sth at its face value.
argenté, **~e** /aʀʒɑ̃te/ **I** *pp* ▶ **argenter**.
II *pp adj* (plaqué d'argent) silver-plated; **un bougeoir en métal ~** a silver-plated candlestick.
III *adj* **1** (couleur d'argent) silvery; **2**○ (fortuné) flush○, loaded○; **n'être pas très ~** to be hard up○.
argenter /aʀʒɑ̃te/ [1] *vtr* lit, fig to silver.
argenterie /aʀʒɑ̃tʀi/ *nf* silverware, silver.
argentier /aʀʒɑ̃tje/ *nm* **1** Hist treasurer; ▶**grand**; **2** (meuble) display case (*for storing silverware*).
argentifère /aʀʒɑ̃tifɛʀ/ *adj* argentiferous.
argentin, **~e** /aʀʒɑ̃tɛ̃, in/ *adj* **1** [*son*] silvery; **2** ▶537 (d'Argentine) Argentinian; **la République ~e** the Argentine Republic.
Argentin, **~e** /aʀʒɑ̃tɛ̃, in/ **I** ▶537 *nm,f* Argentinian.
II ▶321 **Argentine** *nprf* Argentina.
argenture /aʀʒɑ̃tyʀ/ *nf* **1** (action d'argenter) (de miroir) silvering; (d'objet) silver-plating; **~ électrolytique** electro-plating with silver; **2** (couche d'argent) silver plate.
argile /aʀʒil/ *nf* clay; **~ sédimentaire/à silex** sedimentary/siliceous clay; ▶**colosse**.
argileux, **-euse** /aʀʒilø, øz/ *adj* clayey.
argon /aʀgɔ̃/ *nm* argon.
argonaute /aʀgɔnot/ *nm* Zool argonaut.
Argonautes /aʀgɔnot/ *nprmpl* Argonauts.
argot /aʀgo/ *nm* slang; **un mot d'~** a slang word.
argotique /aʀgɔtik/ *adj* (propre à l'argot) slang (*épith*); (peu raffiné) slangy.
argotisme /aʀgɔtism/ *nm* (mot) slang word; (expression) slang expression.
argousin† /aʀguzɛ̃/ *nm* péj (agent de police) copper◑, policeman.
Argovie /aʀgɔvi/ ▶692 *npr* **le canton d'~** the canton of Aargau.
arguer /aʀge/ [1] **I** *vtr* **1** fml (conclure, déduire) to deduce, to infer; **~ qch de qch** to deduce ou infer sth from sth; **2** (prétexter) **~ qch** to give sth as a reason (**pour faire** for doing); **~ que** to claim that.
II arguer de *vtr ind* (prétexter) to give [sth] as a reason (**pour faire** for doing); **arguant du fait que** pointing to the fact that; **~ de faux** Jur *to assert that an item is forged*.
argument /aʀgymɑ̃/ *nm* **1** (raison) argument (**en faveur de** for; **contre** against); **~ choc** or **massue** decisive ou clinching argument; **~ décisif** deciding factor; **présenter** or **trouver de bons ~s en faveur de/contre qch** to make a good case for/against sth; **les ~s présentés étaient faibles** the case he/they etc made was weak; **tirer ~ de qch** to use sth as an argument ou excuse (**pour faire** for doing); **2** Comm, Pub **~ de vente** selling point; **~ électoral** electoral issue GB, campaign issue US; **3** Littérat, Math argument.
IDIOMES **recourir aux ~s frappants** hum to resort to blows.
argumentaire /aʀgymɑ̃tɛʀ/ *nm* **1** Comm sales talk; **2** (arguments) arguments (*pl*).
argumentation /aʀgymɑ̃tasjɔ̃/ *nf* (arguments) line of argument; **une ~ sans faille** a flawless line of argument.
argumenter /aʀgymɑ̃te/ [1] *vi* to argue (**sur** about; **contre** against); **défense solidement argumentée** soundly argued defence[GB]; **condamnation argumentée en quatre points** condemnation resting on four points.
argus /aʀgys/ *nm inv* **1** Aut *used car prices guide*; **2** Presse **~ (de la presse)** press-cutting agency GB, clipping service; **3** Tech **verre ~** one-way glass.
argutie /aʀgysi/ *nf* pej quibble; **se perdre en ~s** to get lost in a lot of quibbles.
aria /aʀja/ *nf* aria.
Ariane /aʀjan/ *npr* Mythol Ariadne.
arianisme /aʀjanism/ *nm* Arianism.
aride /aʀid/ *adj* **1** [*terre, climat*] arid; **2** [*matière, sujet*] dry; **c'est un texte d'une lecture ~** it makes very dry reading.
aridité /aʀidite/ *nf* **1** (de terre, climat) aridity; **2** (de lecture, statistiques) dryness.
Ariège /aʀjɛʒ/ ▶357, 692 *nprf* (rivière, département) **l'~** the Ariège.
arien, **-ienne** /aʀjɛ̃, ɛn/ *adj* Arian.
ariette /aʀjɛt/ *nf* arietta, ariette.
Arioste /aʀjɔst/ *npr* **l'~** Ariosto.
ariser /aʀize/ [1] *vtr* to reef.
aristo○ /aʀisto/ *nmf* (*abbr* = **aristocrate**) pej aristocrat, toff○.
aristocrate /aʀistɔkʀat/ *nmf* aristocrat.
IDIOMES **les ~s à la lanterne!** string up the aristocrats!
aristocratie /aʀistɔkʀasi/ *nf* aristocracy.
aristocratique /aʀistɔkʀatik/ *adj* aristocratic.
Aristophane /aʀistɔfan/ *npr* Aristophanes.
Aristote /aʀistɔt/ *npr* Aristotle.
aristotélicien, **-ienne** /aʀistɔtelisjɛ̃, ɛn/ *adj, nm,f* Aristotelian.
aristotélisme /aʀistɔtelism/ *nm* Aristotelianism.

L'argent et les monnaies

Pour la prononciation des nombres en anglais ▶ 545 .

L'argent en Grande-Bretagne

écrire	dire
1p	one p ([pi:]) *ou* one penny *ou* a penny
2p	two p *ou* two pence
5p	five p *ou* five pence
20p	twenty p *ou* twenty pence
£1*	one pound *ou* a pound
£1.03	one pound three pence† *ou* one pound three p‡
£1.20	one pound twenty *ou* one pound twenty pence *ou* one pound twenty p
£1.99	one pound ninety-nine
£10	ten pounds
£200	two hundred pounds
£1,000§	one thousand pounds *ou* a thousand pounds
£1,000,000	one million pounds *ou* a million pounds

L'argent aux États-Unis

1c	one cent *ou* a cent
2c	two cents
5c	five cents
10c	ten cents
25c	twenty-five cents
$1*	one dollar *ou* a dollar
$1.99	one dollar ninety-nine
$10	ten dollars
$200	two hundred dollars
$1,000	one thousand dollars§ *ou* a thousand dollars
$1,000,000	one million dollars¶ *ou* a million dollars

L'argent en France

0,25 F	twenty-five centimes
1 F	one franc
1,50 F	one franc fifty centimes *ou* one franc fifty
2 F	two francs
2,75 F	two francs seventy-five centimes *ou* two francs seventy-five†
20 F	twenty francs
100 F	one hundred francs *ou* a hundred francs
200 F	two hundred francs
1 000 F	one thousand francs *ou* a thousand francs
2 000 F	two thousand francs
1 000 000 F	one million francs *ou* a million francs
2 000 000 F	two million francs

* *L'anglais place les abréviations £ et $ avant le chiffre, jamais après.*
† *On ne dit jamais* point *pour les sommes d'argent.*
‡ *Si le chiffre des* pence *est inférieur ou égal à 19, on n'omet pas* pence *ou* p: one pound nineteen pence, *mais* one pound twenty.
§ *Noter que l'anglais utilise une virgule là où le français a un espace.*
¶ *Les numéraux français* millier *ou* million, *qui sont des noms, se traduisent en anglais par des adjectifs:* deux millions de francs = two million francs. *Pour plus de détails,* ▶ 545 .

il y a 100 pennies dans une livre	= there are 100 pence in a pound
il y a 100 cents dans un dollar	= there are 100 cents in a dollar
il y a 100 centimes dans un franc	= there are 100 centimes in a franc

Les pièces et les billets

Attention: billet *se dit* note *en anglais britannique, et* bill *en anglais américain.*

Noter l'ordre des mots dans les adjectifs composés anglais, et l'utilisation du trait d'union. Noter aussi que pound, dollar *etc. qui font partie de l'adjectif composé, ne prennent pas la marque du pluriel:*

un billet de 10 livres	= a ten-pound note (*GB*)
un billet de 50 dollars	= a fifty-dollar bill (*US*)
un billet de 100 F	= a hundred-franc note (*GB*) *ou* a hundred-franc bill (*US*)
une pièce de 20 pennies	= a 20p piece (*dire* [ə twɛntɪ pi: pi:s])
une pièce de 50 pennies	= a 50p piece
une pièce d'une livre	= a pound coin

Noter que pièce *se traduit par* coin *pour l'unité monétaire et au-delà, et par* piece *pour toute fraction de l'unité monétaire.*

une pièce de 50 centimes	= a 50-centime piece
une pièce de 1 F	= a one-franc coin
une pièce de 10 F	= a ten-franc coin

Mais aux États-Unis:

une pièce de 5 cents	= a nickel
une pièce de 10 cents	= a dime
une pièce de 25 cents	= a quarter

Les prix

combien ça coûte?	= how much does it cost? *ou* how much is it?
ça coûte 200 livres	= it costs £200 *ou* it is £200
le prix de l'appareil est de 200 livres	= the price of the camera is £200
à peu près 200 livres	= about £200
presque 200 livres	= almost £200
jusqu'à 20 dollars	= up to $20
100 francs le mètre	= a hundred francs a metre

Noter l'absence d'équivalent anglais de la préposition française de *avant le chiffre dans les expressions de ce genre.*

plus de 200 livres	= over £200 *ou* more than £200
moins de 300 livres	= less than £300
un peu moins de 250 livres	= just under £250

Noter l'ordre des mots dans les adjectifs composés anglais et l'utilisation du trait d'union. Noter aussi que franc, cent *etc. qui font partie de l'adjectif composé, ne prennent pas la marque du pluriel:*

un timbre à 10 F	= a ten-franc stamp
un timbre à 75 cents	= a seventy-five-cent stamp
un billet de théâtre à 10 livres	= a £10 theatre ticket (*dire* a ten-pound theatre ticket)
une bourse de deux mille livres	= a £2,000 grant (*dire* a two-thousand-pound grant)
une voiture à 50 000 dollars	= a $50,000 car (*dire* a fifty-thousand-dollar car)

L'anglais considère parfois une somme d'argent comme une unité indissociable, et donc comme un singulier:

ça coûte dix livres de plus	= it is an extra ten pounds
encore dix livres	= another ten pounds
dix livres, ça fait beaucoup d'argent	= ten pounds is a lot of money
prends tes 100 F, ils sont sur la table	= take your hundred francs, it's on the table

Le maniement de l'argent

payer en livres	= to pay in pounds
50 livres en liquide	= £50 in cash
un chèque de 500 livres	= a £500 cheque
un chèque de voyage en dollars	= a dollar travelers' check
un chèque de voyage en livres	= a sterling travellers' cheque
changer des livres en francs	= to change pounds into francs
le dollar vaut six francs	= there are six francs to the dollar
faire la monnaie d'un billet de 100 dollars	= to change a 100-dollar bill

Le système *lsd*

Le système non-décimal utilisé en Grande-Bretagne jusqu'en 1971 reposait sur la livre, le shilling *et le* penny. *Le* penny (*pluriel* pence) *était abrégé en* d., *à cause du latin* denarius. *Il y avait douze* pence *dans un* shilling *et vingt* shillings *dans une livre.*

arithméticien, -ienne /aʀitmetisjɛ̃, ɛn/ ▶ 510 *nm,f* arithmetician.

arithmétique /aʀitmetik/ **I** *adj* arithmetical.
II *nf* arithmetic.

arithmétiquement /aʀitmetikmɑ̃/ *adv* **1** lit arithmetically; **2** fig mathematically.

Arizona /aʀizona/ ▶ 692 *nprm* Arizona.

Arkansas /aʀkɑ̃sas/ ▶ 692 *nprm* Arkansas.

arlequin /aʀləkɛ̃/ *nm* harlequin.

arlequinade /aʀləkinad/ *nf* harlequinade.

arlésien, -ienne /aʀlezjɛ̃, ɛn/ ▶ 857 *adj* of Arles.

Arlésien, -ienne /aʀlezjɛ̃, ɛn/ ▶ 857 *nm,f* (natif) native of Arles; (habitant) inhabitant of Arles.

armada /aʀmada/ *nf* **1** (armée) hum army; **l'invincible Armada** Hist the Spanish Armada; **2**° (grand nombre) **une ~ de** an avalanche of [*touristes, photographes*]; a huge fleet of [*camions*].

Armagh *npr* **le comté d'~** Armagh.

armagnac /aʀmaɲak/ *nm* armagnac.

armateur /aʀmatœʀ/ *nm* (propriétaire) shipowner.

armature /aʀmatyʀ/ *nf* **1** (de tente, store, d'abat-jour) frame; (de soutien-gorge) underwiring **₵**; (de voûte) arch reinforcement; (de béton armé) reinforcing steel rods (*pl*); **à ~** [*soutien-gorge*] underwired; **sans ~** [*soutien-gorge*] light control (*épith*); **2** (de région, de parti, d'entreprise) infrastructure; **l'~ commerciale de la région** the region's commercial infrastructure; **3** (de roman, pièce de théâtre) structure; **4** Mus key signature; **5** Électrotech armament; **6** (d'aimant) armature.

arme /aʀm/ **I** *nf* **1** (objet) weapon; **~ automatique/de guerre/de chasse** automatic/military/hunting weapon; **l'~ absolue** lit, fig the ultimate weapon; **l'~ du crime** the murder weapon; **porter une ~ sur soi** to carry a weapon; **avoir l'~ au poing** to be holding a weapon; **charger une ~** to load a gun; ▶ **bagage, gauche**; **2** fig (moyen) weapon; **la calomnie est une ~ redoutable** slander is a formidable weapon; **une ~ à double tranchant** a two-edged sword; **3** Mil (corps d'armée) branch of the armed services; **dans quelle ~ as-tu fait ton service?** which branch of the armed services did you do your military service in?
II armes *nfpl* **1** Mil arms (*pl*); **aux ~s!** to arms!; **présentez/reposez ~s!** present/order arms!; **portez ~s!** slope arms! GB, shoulder arms! US; **lancer un appel** or **appeler aux ~s** to call to arms; **prendre les ~s** (guerre) to take up arms; (insurrection) to rise up in arms; **conquérir un pays par la force des ~s** to conquer a country by force of arms; **jeter** or **rendre les ~s** lit to lay down (one's) arms; fig to surrender; **en ~s** [*peuple, soldats, insurgés*] armed; **être/rester en ~s** to be/remain armed; **mourir**

les ~s à la main to die fighting; **passer qn par les ~s** to execute sb by firing squad; **prendre le pouvoir/régler un différend par les ~s** to take power/to settle a dispute by force; **à ~s égales** lit, fig on equal terms; **donner** or **fournir des ~s contre soi** fig to provide ammunition against oneself; **faire ses premières ~s** Mil to begin one's military career; fig to start out; **j'ai fait mes premières ~s dans l'enseignement** I started out as a teacher; **2** Sport (escrime) fencing; **faire des ~s** to fence; **3** Hérald (armoiries) coat (*sg*) of arms; **aux ~s de la ville** bearing the town's coat of arms.

■ **~ blanche** *weapon with a blade*; **~ de destruction massive** weapon of mass destruction; **~ d'épaule** rifle; **~ à feu** firearm; **~ de poing** handgun; **~ de service** standard issue weapon.

armé, **~e** /aʀme/ **I** *pp* ▶ **armer**.
II *pp adj* **1** lit (muni d'armes) [*homme, groupe, conflit, révolte*] armed (**de** with); **~ jusqu'aux dents** armed to the teeth; **agression/attaque/vol à main ~e** armed assault/attack/robbery; **2** fig (pourvu) equipped (**de** with; **contre** against); **~ pour faire** [*personne*] equipped ou in a position to do; [*objet*] designed to do; **il est bien ~ pour réussir dans la vie** he's well equipped to succeed in life; **il est bien ~ pour répondre à leurs arguments** he's well armed to answer their arguments.
III *nm* (d'arme à feu) cocked position.
IV armée *nf* **1** lit army; **l'~e française/américaine** the French/US army ou armed forces (*pl*); **~e de libération** army of liberation; **~e de volontaires** volunteer army; **être à l'~e** to be doing one's military service; **être dans l'~e** to be in the army; **2** (troupe nombreuse) (de serviteurs, figurants, sauterelles) army; (d'incapables, de fainéants) pej bunch.
■ **~e d'active** regular army; **~e de l'air** air force; **~e régulière** = **~e d'active**; **l'~e de réserve** the reserves (*pl*); **l'~e de terre** the army; **l'Armée des ombres** Hist *the French Resistance in World War Two*; **l'Armée rouge** the Red Army ; **l'Armée du Salut** the Salvation Army.

armement /aʀməmɑ̃/ *nm* **1** (apport d'armes) (de recrue, nation, d'armée) arming; **2** (moyens armés) gén armament; (de personne, troupe) weapons (*pl*); (d'unité mobile) weaponry; **~ léger/lourd** light/heavy armament; **leur supériorité dans ce type d'~** their superiority in this kind of armament ou weaponry; **3** (ensemble d'armes) arms (*pl*); **réduction des ~s** arms reduction; **ventes/dépenses d'~** arms sales/expenditure; **4** (mise en état de marche) (d'arme) arming; (d'appareil photo) winding on; **5** Naut (de navire marchand) fitting out.

Arménie /aʀmeni/ ▶ **321** *nprf* Armenia.

arménien, **-ienne** /aʀmenjɛ̃, ɛn/ **I** ▶ **537** *adj* Armenian.
II **462** *nm* Ling Armenian.

Arménien, **-ienne** /aʀmenjɛ̃, ɛn/ ▶ **537** *nm,f* Armenian.

armer /aʀme/ [1] **I** *vtr* **1** (munir d'armes) to arm [*personne, troupe, véhicule, lieu*] (**de** with; **contre** against); **2** (garnir) (pour renforcer) to reinforce [*objet, béton*] (**de** with); (pour faire une arme) to arm, to fit [*objet, canne*] (**de** with); **3** (prémunir) to arm (**contre** against); **4** Naut (équiper) to fit out [*navire marchand*]; **5** (mettre en ordre de marche) to arm [*arme*]; to wind on [*appareil photo*]; to set [*piège*]; **~ un fusil** to cock a rifle.
II s'armer *vpr* **1** (se munir d'armes) to arm oneself (**de** with); **les rebelles s'étaient armés jusqu'aux dents** the rebels were armed to the teeth; **2** (se munir) **s'~ de courage/patience** to summon up one's courage/patience.

armistice /aʀmistis/ *nm* armistice.

armoire /aʀmwaʀ/ *nf* gén cupboard; (pour vêtements) wardrobe; **~ vitrée** glass-fronted cupboard.
■ **~ chauffante** hot cupboard; **~ électrique** switchgear cubicle; **~ frigorifique** cold store; **~ à glace** lit wardrobe with a full-length mirror; **c'est une ~ à glace**○ fig he/she is built like a tank○; **~ à linge** linen cupboard, linen closet US; **~ métallique** metal locker; **~ normande** large wardrobe (*in traditional Norman style*); **~ à pharmacie** medicine cabinet; **~ de toilette** bathroom cabinet.

armoiries /aʀmwaʀi/ *nfpl* arms.

armorial, **~e**, *mpl* **-iaux** /aʀmɔʀjal, o/ *adj* armorial.

armoricain, **~e** /aʀmɔʀikɛ̃, ɛn/ *adj* **1** Hist, Géog Armorican; **2** Culin **à l'~e** *in a sauce made from tomatoes and garlic*.

armorié, **~e** /akmɔʀje/ *adj* [*vaisselle*] (de famille) with the family coat of arms (*épith, après n*); (de société) with the company coat of arms (*épith, après n*); [*papier à lettres*] crested (*épith*).

Armorique /aʀmɔʀik/ *nprf* **l'~** Armorica.

armure /aʀmyʀ/ *nf* **1** Hist Mil armour^{GB}; fig form of protection; **chevalier en ~** knight in armour; **2** Tex weave; **3** (de câble) protective sleeving; (de machine) protective metal casing.

armurerie /aʀmyʀʀi/ *nf* **1** ▶ **510** (magasin, atelier) gunsmith's; **2** Mil (pièce) gun room.

armurier /aʀmyʀje/ ▶ **510** *nm* **1** (qui vend, répare) gunsmith; **2** (dans l'armée) armourer^{GB}.

ARN /aɛʀɛn/ *nm* (*abbr* = **acide ribonucléique**) RNA.

arnaque◑ /aʀnak/ *nf* swindle.

arnaquer◑ /aʀnake/ [1] *vtr* to swindle, to rip [sb] off○ [*personne*]; **se faire ~** to be had○, to be ripped off○; **se faire ~ 500 francs** to be conned out of 500 francs.

arnaqueur◑, **-euse** /aʀnakœʀ, øz/ *nm,f* swindler; **ne va pas dans cette boutique, ce sont des ~s** don't go to that shop GB ou store US, they'll rip you off○.

arnica /aʀnika/ *nf* arnica.

aromate /aʀɔmat/ *nm* (épice) spice; (basilic, persil, menthe etc) herb; **des ~s** (aromatic) herbs and spices.

aromathérapie /aʀɔmateʀapi/ *nf* aromatherapy.

aromatique /aʀɔmatik/ *adj* aromatic.

aromatiser /aʀɔmatize/ [1] *vtr* to flavour^{GB}; **aromatisé au citron** lemon-flavoured^{GB}.

arôme /aʀom/ *nm* **1** (odeur) aroma; **2** (additif alimentaire) flavouring^{GB}; **à l'~ de fruit** fruit-flavoured^{GB}; **'~ naturel'** 'natural flavour^{GB}'; **'~ citron'** 'lemon flavour^{GB}'.

aronde /aʀɔ̃d/ *nf* **assemblage à queue d'~** dovetailing.

arpège /aʀpɛʒ/ *nm* arpeggio.

arpéger /aʀpeʒe/ [15] *vtr* **~ un accord** to play a chord in arpeggio; **accord arpégé** broken chord.

arpent /aʀpɑ̃/ *nm* Hist arpent; **quelques ~s de terre** a few acres of land.

arpentage /aʀpɑ̃taʒ/ *nm* surveying.

arpenter /aʀpɑ̃te/ [1] *vtr* **1** (parcourir) to stride along [*rues, couloirs*]; to travel the length and breadth of [*région*]; **2** (aller et venir) to pace up and down [*couloirs, pièce, terrain*]; **3** (mesurer) to survey.

arpenteur /aʀpɑ̃tœʀ/ ▶ **510** *nm* (land) surveyor.

arpète /aʀpɛt/ *nmf* apprentice.

arpion◑ /aʀpjɔ̃/ *nm* foot.

arqué, **~e** /aʀke/ *adj* [*sourcils*] arched; [*nez*] hooked; **avoir les jambes ~es** to have bandy ou bow legs, to be bow-legged.

arquebuse /aʀkəbyz/ *nf* arquebus.

arquebusier /aʀkəbyzje/ *nm* (soldat) arquebusier.

arquer /aʀke/ [1] **I** *vtr* to bend, to curve [*poutrelle, barre*]; **~ le dos** to arch one's back.
II *vi* **1** [*objet*] to bend, to curve; [*poutre*] to sag; **2**◑ (marcher) to walk.
III s'arquer *vpr* [*poutrelle, barre*] to become bowed.

arrachage /aʀaʃaz/ *nm* (de récolte) picking; (de dent, poteau) pulling out; (de broussailles, souche) digging out; **~ des mauvaises herbes** weeding.

arraché /aʀaʃe/ *nm* Sport snatch; **à l'~** with a snatch; **obtenir qch à l'~** fig to snatch sth; **emporter la première place à l'~** to snatch first place; **réussir une vente à l'~** to manage to bring off a sale; **vol à l'~** bag snatching.

arrache-clou, *pl* **~s** /aʀaʃklu/ *nm* claw hammer.

arrachement /aʀaʃmɑ̃/ *nm* **1** (douleur morale) wrench; **l'~ des adieux** the wrench of parting; **2** (séparation) **~ d'un enfant à sa mère** separating a child from his/her mother.

arrache-pied: **d'arrache-pied** /daʀaʃpje/ *loc adv* **travailler d'~** to work flat out.

arracher /aʀaʃe/ [1] **I** *vtr* **1** (déraciner) [*personne*] to dig up [*légumes*]; to dig out [*broussailles, souche, poteau*]; to uproot [*arbre*]; [*ouragan*] to uproot [*arbre, poteau*]; **~ les mauvaises herbes** to weed; **2** (détacher vivement) [*personne*] to pull [sth] out [*poil, cheveu, dent, ongle, clou*] (**de** from); to tear [sth] down [*affiche*]; to rip [sth] out [*feuillet, page*]; to tear [sth] off [*bandeau, masque*] (**de** from); [*vent*] to blow [sth] off [*feuilles d'arbre*]; to rip [sth] off [*toit, tuiles*] (**de** from); **la machine/l'obus lui a arraché le bras** the machine/the shell ripped his/her arm off; **3** (ôter de force) to snatch [*personne, objet*] (**de, à** from); **~ qch des mains de qn** to snatch sth out of sb's hands; **elle s'est fait ~ son sac** she had her bag snatched; **~ qn à la mort/au désespoir** to snatch sb from the jaws of death/from despair; **~ qn à la misère** to rescue sb from poverty; **~ qn à sa famille/à son pays** to tear sb from the bosom of his/her family/from his/her native land; **4** (tirer brutalement) **~ qn à** to rouse sb from [*rêve, torpeur, pensées*]; to drag sb away from [*travail*]; **5** (soutirer) to force [*augmentation, compromis*] (**à qn** out of sb); to extract [*secret, précision, consentement, confession*] (**de, à qn** from sb); to get [*mot, sourire*] (**de, à qn** from sb); **ils leur ont arraché la victoire** they snatched victory from them; **~ un nul** Sport to manage to draw GB ou tie; **la douleur lui a arraché un cri** he/she cried out in pain; **la douleur lui a arraché des larmes** the pain brought tears to his/her eyes.
II s'arracher *vpr* **1** (ôter à soi-même) **s'~ les cheveux blancs** to pull out one's grey GB ou gray US hairs; **s'~ les poils du nez** to pluck the hairs from one's nose; **2** (se disputer pour) to fight over [*personne*]; to fight over, to scramble for [*produit*]; **on** or **tout le monde se les arrache** everyone is crazy for them; **3** (se séparer) **s'~ à** to rouse oneself from [*pensées, rêverie*]; to tear oneself away from [*travail, occupation, étreinte*]; **4**○ (partir) **s'~ d'un lieu** to tear oneself away from a place ; **viens, on s'arrache** come on, let's split○.
IDIOMES **~ les yeux à** or **de qn** to scratch sb's eyes out; **c'est à s'~ les cheveux**○! (difficile) it's enough to make you tear your hair out!; **s'~ les cheveux de désespoir** to tear one's hair out in despair; **s'~ les yeux** to fight like cat and dog.

arracheur /aʀaʃœʀ/ *nm* **~ de dents** quack.
IDIOMES **mentir comme un ~ de dents** to be a born liar.

arracheuse /aʀaʃøz/ *nf* Agric picker.

arraisonnement /aʀɛzɔnmɑ̃/ *nm* Naut, Aviat boarding and inspection (**de** of).

arraisonner /aʀɛzɔne/ [1] *vtr* Naut, Aviat to board and inspect [*navire, avion*].

arrangeant, **~e** /aʀɑ̃ʒɑ̃, ɑ̃t/ *adj* obliging.

arrangement /aʀɑ̃ʒmɑ̃/ *nm* **1** (accord) arrangement, agreement; **arriver/parvenir à un ~** to come to/to reach an agreement; **2** (de bouquets, personnages, fleurs) arrangement; **3** (d'objets, de mots) arrangement; (de maison) lay out; **4** Math permutation; **~ de cinq objets pris deux à deux** permutation of five things taken two at a time; **5** Mus arrangement.

arranger /aʀɑ̃ʒe/ [13] **I** *vtr* **1** (organiser) [*personne*] to arrange [*voyage, réunion*]; to organize [*vie*]; **~ des rencontres entre hommes d'affaires** to arrange meetings between businessmen; **2** (régler) to settle [*différend, querelle, conflit*]; to sort out [*difficulté, malentendu, affaires*]; **cela ne va pas ~ les choses** that won't help matters; **ça n'arrange rien de se mettre en colère** getting angry isn't going to help matters; **pour ne rien ~, pour tout ~** iron to make matters worse; **le temps arrangera peut-être les choses** perhaps things will improve with time; **3** (disposer) to arrange [*objets, fleurs, bouquet, pièce*]; **~ des livres sur une étagère** to arrange books on a shelf; **elle a joliment arrangé sa chambre** she arranged her bedroom nicely; **4** (remettre en ordre) to tidy [*cheveux, coiffure*]; to straighten [*écharpe, châle, gilet*]; **~ son chapeau (sur sa tête)** to straighten one's hat; **~ sa tenue** to make oneself presentable; **5** (modifier) (en améliorant) to rearrange [*texte, plan, article*]; iron (en déformant) to doctor [*histoire, faits*]; **6** (réparer) to put right, to fix [*mécanisme, montre*]; to fix [*jouet*]; **'mon ourlet est défait'—'donne, je vais (t')~ ça'** 'my hem's come down'—'here, I'll mend it for you'; **faire ~ une montre** to have a watch mended ou fixed; **cela ne t'a pas arrangé de veiller si tard○!** it hasn't done you much good staying up so late!; **7** (convenir) [*fait, événement*] to suit [*personne, affaires*]; **leur faillite nous arrange** their bankruptcy suits us fine; **tu dis ça parce que ça t'arrange** you say that because it suits you; **ton retard m'arrange** it's quite convenient for me that you're late; **ça n'arrange pas mes affaires** that's really inconvenient for me; **il est difficile d'~ tout le monde** it's difficult to please everybody; **il ne garde que ce qui l'arrange** he keeps only what suits him; **ça m'arrangerait que tu viennes plus tôt, tu m'arrangerais en venant plus tôt** it would suit me better if you came earlier; **si cela peut vous ~** if it's all right with you; **remboursez-moi le mois prochain si cela vous arrange** pay me back next month if that's easier for you; **si ça ne vous arrange pas, on peut changer la date** if it's inconvenient for you, we can change the date; **8○** iron (maltraiter) [*personne, vent, pluie*] to make a right GB ou complete mess of○ [*coiffure, plantes*]; [*critique*] to lay into [*auteur, œuvre*]; **ton coiffeur t'a bien arrangé!** your hairdresser has made a right mess of your hair!; **9○** (battre) to give [sb] a good going-over○; **se faire ~** to get a good going-over; **10** Mus to arrange [*morceau de musique*].

II s'arranger *vpr* **1** (s'améliorer) [*situation, temps*] to get better; [*santé*] to improve; **elle ne s'est pas arrangée depuis la dernière fois!** fig, hum she hasn't got GB ou gotten US any better ou hasn't improved since the last time; **s'~ avec l'âge** fig, hum to improve with age; **tout finira par s'~** things will sort themselves out in the end; **2** (se mettre d'accord) **s'~ avec qn** to arrange it with sb; **s'~ avec qn pour faire** to arrange with sb to do; **elle s'est arrangée avec sa voisine pour la garde des enfants** she arranged with her neighbour[GB] to look after the children; **s'~ à l'amiable** to come to a friendly agreement; **3** (prendre des dispositions) **arrange-toi comme tu voudras, mais sois ici à midi** do as you like but be here by 12; **s'~ pour faire** to make sure one does; **arrange-toi pour être à l'heure** make sure you're on time; **arrangez-vous pour que la pièce soit propre d'ici demain** make sure that the room is tidy by tomorrow; **il s'est arrangé pour ne pas partir en même temps que moi** he managed not to leave at the same time as me; **4** (se débrouiller) **il n'y a que trois lits mais on s'arrangera** there are only three beds but we'll sort it out; **je paye tout et on s'arrangera après** I'll pay for everything and we'll sort it out later; **5** (se contenter de) **s'~ de** to make do with; **il s'arrange du peu d'argent qu'il a** he makes do with what little money he has; **son bureau est petit mais il s'en arrange** his study is small but he makes do; **arrange-toi avec ça** try and make do with that; **6○** (s'habiller) **elle ne sait pas s'~** she doesn't know how to do herself up nicely; **7** (être réparé) **ta montre ne peut pas s'~** your watch can't be mended ou fixed.

arrangeur, **-euse** /aʀɑ̃ʒœʀ, øz/ *nm,f* Mus arranger.

arrérages /aʀeʀaʒ/ *nmpl* arrears.

arrestation /aʀɛstasjɔ̃/ *nf* arrest; **ordonner l'~ de qn** to order sb's arrest; **être en état d'~** to be under arrest; **mettre qn en état d'~** to place sb under arrest; **procéder à l'~ de qn** to arrest sb.

arrêt /aʀɛ/ **I** *nm* **1** (de véhicule) stopping; (de combats) cessation; (de livraison, transaction) cancellation; (de production, distribution) halt; (de croissance économique) cessation; **attendez l'~ complet du train/de l'avion** wait until the train/plane has come to a complete stop; **faire un ~ de deux heures** to stop for two hours; **nous ferons plusieurs ~s** we'll make several stops; **demander l'~ des hostilités/essais nucléaires** to call for an end to hostilities/nuclear testing; **décider l'~ de la construction/production de qch** to decide to halt the building/production of sth; **sans ~** (sans escale) nonstop; (sans interruption) constantly; **je suis dérangée sans ~** I'm continually being disturbed; **ce train est sans ~ jusqu'à Toulouse** this train goes nonstop to Toulouse; **tousser/interrompre/se défaire sans ~** to cough/to interrupt/to come undone constantly; **nous sommes sans ~ dérangés** we are constantly being disturbed; **il a plu sans ~ pendant une semaine** it rained continuously for a week; **il faut sans ~ répéter la même chose** the same thing has to be repeated over and over again; **il faut sans ~ que je te répète la même chose** I have to tell you the same thing over and over again; **à l'~** [*voiture, camion, train*] stationary; [*machine*] (prête à fonctionner) idle; (hors tension) off; **'Dijon: trois minutes d'~!'** 'this is Dijon, there will be a 3-minute stop'; **marquer un temps d'~** to pause; **un coup d'~** a halt; **donner un coup d'~ à** (à construction, concurrence, progression) to stop ou halt; **2** (dans les transports en commun) stop; **un ~ de bus** a bus stop; **tu descends à quel ~?** which stop are you getting off at?; **~ facultatif/fixe** request/compulsory stop; **3** C (sur un panneau) stop; **4** Jur ruling; **rendre un ~** to give ou pass a ruling; **5** Chasse **chien d'~** pointer; **être en ~** [*chien*] to point; **être en ~ devant qch** fig to stand with one's tongue hanging out in front of sth.

II arrêts *mpl* Mil arrest ₵; **être aux ~s, garder les ~s** to be under arrest.

■ **~ du cœur** heart failure; **~ sur image** freeze-frame, still; **faire un ~ sur image** to freeze a frame; **~ de jeu** Sport stoppage time; **jouer les ~s de jeu** to play injury time; **~ maladie** (événement) sick leave; (document) sick note; **être en ~ de maladie** to be on sick leave; **~ pipi○** break in a journey (*to go to the toilet*); **~ de porte** doorstop; **~ sur salaire** Admin, Jur writ of attachment of earnings; **~ de travail** (pour grève) stoppage of work; (pour maladie) (événement) sick leave ₵; (document) sick note; **être en ~ de travail** to be on sick leave; **j'ai un ~ de travail de dix jours** I have a sick note for ten days; **~ de volée** (au rugby) mark; **~s de forteresse** Mil confinement ₵; **~s de rigueur** Mil close arrest ₵; **~s simples** Mil open arrest ₵.

arrêté, **~e** /aʀete/ **I** *pp* ▶ **arrêter**.

II *pp adj* **1** (convenu) **c'est une chose ~e** it's settled; **l'affaire est ~e** the matter has been settled; **la décision est ~e** the decision has been taken; **2** (inébranlable) [*idée, principe*] fixed; **avoir des idées trop ~es (sur qch)** to have very fixed ideas (about sth).

III *nm* Admin order, decree; **~ ministériel** ministerial decree; **~ d'expulsion** (contre un étranger) expulsion order, deportation order; (contre un locataire) eviction notice ou order; **~ municipal** bylaw; **~ préfectoral** bylaw (*issued by a prefecture*).

■ **~ de compte** settlement of account.

arrêter /aʀete/ [1] **I** *vtr* **1** (empêcher d'avancer) lit, fig [*personne, groupe*] to stop [*personne, véhicule, cheval*]; to stop [*chronomètre*]; **~ sa voiture le long du trottoir** to pull up along the kerb GB ou curb US, to stop one's car by the kerb GB ou curb US; **arrêtez-la!** stop her!; **rien ne les arrête** fig (pour faire un voyage, pour s'amuser) there's no stopping them; péj (pour obtenir de l'argent) they'd stop at nothing; **fais-le, qu'est-ce qui t'arrête?** just do it, what's stopping you?; **c'est le prix du billet qui m'arrête** I'd go if it weren't for the cost of the ticket; **une plaine immense où rien n'arrête le regard** a vast plain where there's nothing as far as the eye can see; **2** (éteindre) [*personne, mécanisme*] to stop, to switch off [*machine, moteur*]; to switch off [*ventilateur, réveil, radio*]; **arrêtez votre moteur** stop your engine; **3** (mettre fin à) to stop [*fuite, hémorragie, circulation*]; to stop [*guerre, massacre, invasion*]; to halt [*processus, production, transaction, construction*]; **~ la marche** or **le cours du temps** to halt the passage of time; **les travaux ont été arrêtés** work has been halted; **~ qn** (dans une conversation) to stop sb; **je vous arrête tout de suite** I'll stop you straight away; **~ de faire** to stop doing; **arrête de te plaindre/de mentir** stop complaining/lying; **il n'a pas arrêté de pleuvoir** it didn't stop raining; **le téléphone n'arrête pas de sonner** the phone never stops ringing; **elles n'arrêtent pas de bavarder** they never stop talking; **~ de travailler** (définitivement) to stop work; **le trafic est arrêté sur la ligne B en raison d'un accident** service has been suspended on the B line due to an accident; **arrête!** (tu m'ennuies) stop it!; (je ne te crois pas) I don't believe you!; **arrête tes bêtises!** (tais-toi) stop talking nonsense!; (cesse de faire des bêtises) stop fooling around!; (je ne te crois pas) I don't believe you!; **je n'arrête pas en ce moment!** (je suis très occupé) I'm always on the go○ these days!; **'tu n'as qu'à travailler!'—'mais je n'arrête pas!'** 'you should work!'—'but that's what I'm doing!'; **4** (renoncer à) to give up [*études, compétition, activité, alcool*]; **~ la danse/le piano** to give up dance/(playing) the piano; **~ de faire** to give up doing; **~ de fumer/de boire/de se droguer** to give up smoking/drinking/taking drugs; **5** (appréhender) [*police*] to arrest; **13 personnes ont été arrêtées lors de la manifestation** 13 people were arrested at the demonstration; **6** (signer un arrêt de travail pour) [*médecin*] to give [sb] a sick note; **être arrêté pour trois semaines** to be given a sick note for three weeks; **7** Cout to fasten off [*couture*]; (en tricot) to cast off [*mailles*]; **8** (déterminer) to fix [*lieu, date*]; to make [*décision*]; to decide on [*plan, principe, mesure*]; to formulate [*clause, décret*].

II *vi* (faire arrêt) to stop (**à** at); (cesser) [*bruit, cri*] to stop ; **le téléphone n'arrête pas** the phone hasn't stopped (ringing).

III s'arrêter *vpr* **1** (faire un arrêt) [*personne*] to stop (**pour faire** to do); [*voiture, bus, train*] to stop; **arrête-toi ici** stop here; **sans s'~** without stopping; **s'~ pour se reposer** to stop for a rest; **s'~ dans un restau-**

rant to stop at a restaurant; **s'~ à Grenoble** [*personne*] to stop off in Grenoble; [*train, car*] to stop in Grenoble; **je me suis arrêté chez un ami** I stopped off at a friend's house; **il était arrêté au feu rouge** he had stopped at the red light; **2** (cesser de fonctionner) [*montre, pendule, machine*] to stop; [*radio, télévision*] to go dead ou off; [*cassette, disque*] to be finished; **3** (cesser) [*hémorragie, pluie, neige, musique*] to stop; [*émission*] to end; **s'~ de faire** to stop doing; **s'~ de bouger/de pleurer** to stop moving/crying; **s'~ de travailler** to stop working; **ils ne vont pas s'~ là** fig they won't stop there; **4** (renoncer à) to give up (**de faire** doing); **s'~ de boire/de fumer** to give up drinking/smoking; **5** (se terminer) [*enquête, recherche, histoire*] to end; [*voie ferrée, chemin, champ, jardin*] to end; **la ressemblance entre les deux s'arrête là** any similarity between the two ends there; **l'affaire aurait pu s'~ là** that could have been the end of the matter; **6** (fixer son attention sur) **s'~ sur** to dwell on [*texte, point, proposition*]; **s'~ à** to focus on [*détails, essentiel*]; **ce dernier point mérite qu'on s'y arrête** this last point merits some attention.

arrhes /aʀ/ *nfpl* Comm deposit (*sg*); **verser des ~** to put down ou pay a deposit.

arriération /aʀjeʀasjɔ̃/ *nf* backwardness.

arrière /aʀjɛʀ/ **I** *adj inv* [*poche*] back; Mil [*base*] rearguard; Aut [*vitre, portière, roue, feux, frein*] rear; [*banquette*] back; **siège ~** (de voiture) back seat; (de moto) pillion; **les places ~** (de véhicule) the back seats; **la partie ~ du fuselage/bâtiment** the rear of the fuselage/building; **sur le côté ~ gauche du crâne** on the left side of the skull at the back.

II *nm* **1** (partie) (de voiture, bâtiment) back, rear; (de train, navire) rear; **à l'~** (dans une voiture) in the back; (dans un train, bus, avion) at the back ou rear; (sur un bateau) in the stern; (au rugby, football) at the back; **une bicyclette était fixée à l'~ de la camionnette** there was a bicycle on the back of the van; **le capitaine est à l'~ du bateau** the captain is aft; **le moteur est à l'~** the engine is at the back; **une voiture avec le moteur à l'~** a rear-engine car; **en ~** (direction) gén backward(s); **faire un pas en ~** to take a step backward(s); **un pas en avant mais deux en ~** one step forward, two steps back; **il est tombé en ~** he fell over backward(s); **se pencher en ~** to lean backward(s); **pencher la tête en ~** to tilt one's head back; **rester en ~** (parmi les spectateurs) to stand back; (après le départ des autres) to stay behind; (par sécurité, crainte) to keep back; (traîner) to lag behind; **jeter un regard** or **regarder en ~** lit, fig to look back; **remonter de deux ans en ~** to go back two years; **il faut remonter loin en ~** one has to go back a long way; **revenir en ~** [*personne, politique*] lit, fig to go back; (sur un enregistrement) to rewind; **ce qui est fait est fait, on ne peut pas revenir en ~** what's done is done, you can't turn back the clock; **faire un bond en ~** to leap back; **avoir les cheveux tirés en ~** to have one's hair pulled back; **se coiffer en ~** to wear one's hair off the face; **en ~ de** (derrière) behind; **la maison est un peu en ~ de la voie ferrée** the house is set back a bit from the railway line; **vers l'~** backwards; **tendez la jambe vers l'~ en inspirant** stretch your leg backward(s) and breathe in; **2** Sport (au rugby, hockey) fullback; (au football) defender; (au basket) guard; (au volley) backline player; **~ gauche/droit** (au football, hockey) left/right back; **il joue ~** (au rugby) he plays fullback; (au football) he's a defender; **les ~s** (au rugby) the backs; (au football) the defence[GB]; **3** Mil (territoire) civilian zone; (population) civilian population.

III‡ *excl* begone!

IV arrières *nmpl* Mil rear (*sg*); **ils ont attaqué nos ~s** they attacked us in the rear; **surveiller ses ~s** lit, fig to watch one's rear; **assurer ses ~s** fig to cover one's back.

arriéré, **~e** /aʀjeʀe/ **I** *adj* **1** (rétrograde) [*idées, pratique*] outdated; [*pays, société*] backward; [*personne*] behind the times (*jamais épith*); **2** Psych retarded; **3** Comm, Fin [*dette*] outstanding; [*paiement, intérêts*] overdue (*jamais épith*); **loyer ~** arrears (*pl*).

II *nm* arrears (*pl*).

arrière-ban, *pl* **~s** /aʀjɛʀbɑ̃/ *nm* ▶ **ban**.

arrière-boutique, *pl* **~s** /aʀjɛʀbutik/ *nf* back of the shop.

arrière-cour, *pl* **~s** /aʀjɛʀkuʀ/ *nf* (enclosed) backyard.

arrière-cuisine, *pl* **~s** /aʀjɛʀkɥizin/ *nf* scullery.

arrière-garde, *pl* **~s** /aʀjɛʀgaʀd/ *nf* Mil rearguard; **combat d'~** rearguard action; **d'~** [*idée, principe*] regressive.

arrière-goût, *pl* **~s** /aʀjɛʀgu/ *nm* lit, fig aftertaste.

arrière-grand-mère, *pl* **arrière-grands-mères** /aʀjɛʀgʀɑ̃mɛʀ/ *nf* great-grandmother.

arrière-grand-oncle, *pl* **arrière-grands-oncles** /aʀjɛʀgʀɑ̃tɔ̃kl, *pl* gʀɑ̃zɔ̃kl/ *nm* great-great-uncle.

arrière-grand-père, *pl* **arrière-grands-pères** /aʀjɛʀgʀɑ̃pɛʀ/ *nm* great-grandfather.

arrière-grands-parents /aʀjɛʀgʀɑ̃paʀɑ̃/ *nmpl* great-grandparents.

arrière-grand-tante, *pl* **arrière-grands-tantes** /aʀjɛʀgʀɑ̃tɑ̃t/ *nf* great-great-aunt.

arrière-main, *pl* **~s** /aʀjɛʀmɛ̃/ *nf* hindquarters (*pl*).

arrière-neveu, *pl* **~x** /aʀjɛʀn(ə)vø/ *nm* great-nephew.

arrière-nièce, *pl* **~s** /aʀjɛʀnjɛs/ *nf* great-niece.

arrière-pays /aʀjɛʀpei/ *nm inv* back country, hinterland spéc; **acheter une maison dans l'~** to buy a house inland.

arrière-pensée, *pl* **~s** /aʀjɛʀpɑ̃se/ *nf* ulterior motive (**de faire** of doing); **sans ~** without reservation; **non sans ~** not without ulterior motives.

arrière-petite-fille, *pl* **arrière-petites-filles** /aʀjɛʀpətitfij/ *nf* great-granddaughter.

arrière-petite-nièce, *pl* **arrière-petites-nièces** /aʀjɛʀpətitnjɛs/ *nf* great-great-niece.

arrière-petit-fils, *pl* **arrière-petits-fils** /aʀjɛʀpətifis/ *nm* great-grandson.

arrière-petit-neveu, *pl* **arrière-petits-neveux** /aʀjɛʀpətin(ə)vø/ *nm* great-great-nephew.

arrière-petits-enfants /aʀjɛʀpətizɑ̃fɑ̃/ *nmpl* great-grandchildren.

arrière-plan, *pl* **~s** /aʀjɛʀplɑ̃/ *nm* lit, fig background; **en ~**, **à l'~** in the background.

arriérer /aʀjeʀe/ [14] *vtr* to defer [*paiement*].

arrière-saison, *pl* **~s** /aʀjɛʀsɛzɔ̃/ ▶ **738** *nf* late autumn GB, late fall US.

arrière-salle, *pl* **~s** /aʀjɛʀsal/ *nf* backroom (*in café, restaurant*).

arrière-train, *pl* **~s** /aʀjɛʀtʀɛ̃/ *nm* **1** (d'animal) hindquarters (*pl*); **2**○ (d'humain) behind.

arrimage /aʀimaʒ/ *nm* **1** Naut (action) stowing, stowage; **2** Astronaut docking.

arrimer /aʀime/ [1] **I** *vtr* **1** (sur un bateau, une voiture) to stow [sth] away; **~ qch à** or **sur qch** to fasten sth to sth; **2** Astronaut to dock (**à** with).

II s'arrimer *vpr* fig **s'~ à** [*pays, communauté*] to bind itself to.

arrimeur /aʀimœʀ/ ▶ **510** *nm* stevedore, docker GB, longshoreman US.

arrivage /aʀivaʒ/ *nm* **1** Comm delivery, consignment; **attendre un ~** to expect a delivery; **le dernier ~ de fruits** the last delivery of fruit; **un nouvel ~** a new delivery; **2** (de personnes) influx.

arrivant, **~e** /aʀivɑ̃, ɑ̃t/ *nm,f* **les premiers/derniers ~s** the first/last to arrive; **un nouvel ~** a newcomer, a new arrival.

arrivé, **~e** /aʀive/ **I** *pp* ▶ **arriver**.

II *pp adj* **1** (parvenu au but) **le premier/dernier ~** the first/last person to arrive; **le premier ~ aura un livre** the first person to arrive will get a book; **2** (qui a réussi socialement) **être ~** to have made it; **se croire ~** to think one has made it; **tous ces politiciens ~s** all these politicians who have made it ou arrived.

III arrivée *nf* **1** (moment) arrival; **à/dès/après mon ~e** when/as soon as/after I arrived; **l'~e au pouvoir de la gauche** the left's accession to power; **depuis son ~e au pouvoir** since he/she came to power; **il a fait une ~e remarquée** he made quite an entry; **l'~e du printemps/de l'hiver** the coming of spring/of winter; **attendre l'~e de qn** to wait for sb to arrive; **guetter l'~e du courrier** to watch out for the post; **~e à Londres Heathrow, 18 h 30** arrival at London Heathrow, 18.30; **trains à l'~e** arrivals; **je t'attendrai à l'~e (du train)** I'll meet you off GB ou at US your train; **quelle est la gare d'~e?** what station does the train arrive at?; **2** Sport, Turf finish; **à/avant l'~e** at/before the finish; **je n'aurai rien de plus à l'~e** fig I'll be no better off at the end of the day; **3** Tech inlet; **~e d'air/d'eau** air/water inlet; **le tuyau d'~e d'eau** the water supply pipe.

arriver /aʀive/ [1] **I** *vi* **1** (dans l'espace) [*personne, avion, train, colis, lettre*] to arrive; [*nuage, pluie*] to come; **~ de** [*personne, train, bus*] to come from; **~ par** [*eau, gaz*] to come through; **~ ensemble** to arrive together; **elle n'est pas encore arrivée** she hasn't arrived yet; **~ à 13 h à Paris** to arrive in Paris at 1 pm; **~ dans le centre ville/sur la berge** to reach the town centre[GB]/the bank; **~ par bateau/avion/le train** to arrive by boat/plane/train; **je suis arrivé chez moi** I got home; **j'arriverai chez toi dans l'après-midi/tard** I'll get to ou arrive at your place in the afternoon/late; **appelle-nous dès que tu seras arrivé** give us a call as soon as you arrive ou get there; **~ en avance/en retard/à l'heure** to arrive early/late/on time; **~ juste au bon moment** to arrive ou come at just the right moment; **je suis arrivée avant/après toi** I got here before/after you; **elle est arrivée au Japon en 1982** she came to Japan in 1982; **dépêche-toi, le train arrive!** hurry up, the train is coming!; **regarde qui arrive** look who's coming; **le mauvais temps arrive par le nord** the bad weather is coming from the north; **l'eau arrive par ce tuyau** the water comes in through this pipe; **j'arrive!** I'm coming!; **j'arrive du centre ville** I've just come from the city centre[GB]; **j'arrive de Londres** I've just come from London; **~ en courant** to come running up; **~ sur qn** [*orage, cyclone*] to hit sb; [*personne*] to descend on sb; **l'eau nous arrivait aux chevilles** the water came up to our ankles, we were ankle-deep in water; **l'eau arrivait au niveau de la fenêtre** the water came up to the window; **ma jupe m'arrive aux chevilles** my skirt comes down to my ankles; **~ (jusqu')à qn** [*nouvelle, rumeur, odeur*] to reach sb; **heureusement cela n'est pas arrivé jusqu'à lui** or **jusqu'à ses oreilles**○ luckily it didn't reach him ou his ears; **~ sur scène** [*chanteur, acteur*] to come on stage; **~ sur le marché** [*personnes, produits*] to come on the market; **2** (dans le temps) **~ en tête/en queue** to come first/last; **en arrivant au ministère** when he/she became minister; **il est arrivé le premier** he arrived first, he was the first to arrive; **~ dans les premiers** (en compétition) to be among the first to finish; (à une soirée) to be among the first to arrive; **de nombreux signes montrent qu'on arrive à la fin d'une période** a number of signs show that we are coming to the end of an era; **~ à son terme** [*contrat*] to expire; [*projet*] to come to an end; **ce plan arrive au moment où** this plan comes at a time when; **maintenant j'arrive au problème de la drogue** now, I'll come to the problem of drugs; **'qu'en est-il du chômage?'—'j'y arrive'** 'what about unemployment?'—'I'm coming to that'; **tu arrives à un âge où** you are getting to an age when; **3** (avec un raisonnement, après une suite d'événements) **~ à une somme** to come to an amount; **~ à des résultats** to achieve results; **~ à une solution** to find a solution; **~ à une conclusion** to come to a conclusion; **~ à un accord** to reach an agreement; **4** (réussir) **~ à faire** to manage to do, to succeed in doing; **je n'arrive pas à faire** I can't do; **il n'arrive plus à la suivre** he can't keep up with her; **j'essaie, mais je n'y arrive pas** I'm trying, but I can't do it; **je n'arrive à rien** I'm getting nowhere; **~ à ses fins** to achieve one's ends; **5** (aboutir) **on en arrive à des absurdités** you end up with nonsense; **comment peut-on en ~ là?** how could it have come to this?; (parlant d'un pays, d'une économie) how did things get into that state?; **j'en arrive à croire que/à me demander si...** I'm beginning to think that/to wonder if...; **6** (survenir) [*accident, catastrophe*] to happen; **ce sont des choses qui arrivent** these things happen, it's just one of those things; **cela n'était pas arrivé depuis longtemps** it hadn't happened for a long time; **ça arrive mais c'est rare** it does happen, but not very often; **tout peut ~** anything can happen; **ça n'arrive qu'aux autres** it only happens to other people; **on ne sait jamais ce qui peut ~** you never know what may happen; **un accident est si vite arrivé** accidents happen so easily; **voilà ce qui arrive quand on ne fait pas attention** that's what happens when you don't pay attention; **la même chose m'est arrivée il y a un mois** the same thing happened to me a month ago; **tu vois, tout arrive!** I told you, you should never give up hope!; **7** (réussir socialement) [*personne*] to succeed; **faire n'importe quoi pour ~** to do anything to succeed.

II *v impers* **il est arrivé quelque chose** something has happened (**à** to); **il arrive toujours quelque chose** something always happens; **qu'est-il arrivé?** what happened?; **il n'est rien arrivé** nothing happened; **il n'arrive jamais rien ici** nothing ever happens around here; **il arrive un moment où** there comes a time when; **il arrive que qn fasse** sometimes sb does; **il m'arrive d'être en retard/d'aller à l'opéra** sometimes I'm late/I go to the opera; **est -ce qu'il arrive que le courrier se perde?** does the mail ever go missing GB ou get lost?; **est-ce qu'il t'arrive d'y penser?** do you ever think about it?; **qu'est-il arrivé à ta voiture?** what happened to your car?; **que t'arrive-t-il?** what's wrong with you?; **il m'est arrivé une chose bizarre** something odd happened to me; **quoi qu'il arrive** whatever happens; **je t'appellerai quoi qu'il arrive** I'll call you whatever happens ou come what may; **que peut-il ~ au pays?** what can happen to the country?

arrivisme /aʀivism/ *nm* ruthless ambition.

arriviste /aʀivist/ **I** *adj* [*attitude, personne*] ruthlessly ambitious.

II *nmf* go-getter, arriviste GB.

arrogance /aʀɔɡɑ̃s/ *nf* arrogance.

arrogant, **~e** /aʀɔɡɑ̃, ɑ̃t/ **I** *adj* arrogant.

II *nm,f* arrogant person.

arroger: **s'arroger** /aʀɔʒe/ [13] *vpr* to appropriate [*titre*]; to assume, to arrogate sout [*droit, privilège, pouvoir*]; to assume [*fonction*]; to arrogate sout [*monopole*]; **s'~ le monopole de** fig to claim a monopoly on; **s'~ le droit de faire** to assume the right to do; **s'~ des prérogatives** to claim ou appropriate prerogatives.

arroi /aʀwa/ *nm* liter **en grand ~** in full array; **en mauvais ~** fig [*affaires*] in disarray.

arrondi, **~e** /aʀɔ̃di/ **I** *pp* ▶ **arrondir**.

II *pp adj* **1** [*objet*] rounded; [*visage*] round; **femme aux formes ~es** shapely woman; **2** Cout [*encolure*] round; **3** [*chiffre*] round; **4** Phon [*voyelle*] rounded.

III *nm* **1** (d'objet, de visage) roundness; (d'épaule) curve; **l'~ de ses formes** her shapely figure; **2** Cout (de jupe, robe) hemline; **l'~ du col/de l'emmanchure** the shape of the neck/of the armhole; **3** Aviat flare out; **atterrissage avec ~** flared landing.

arrondir /aʀɔ̃diʀ/ [3] **I** *vtr* **1** (rendre rond) to round [sth] off [*objet*]; to round off [*bord*]; to open [sth] wide [*yeux*]; to make the hem of [sth] even [*jupe*]; **~ la bouche** to purse one's lips; **cette coiffure lui arrondit le visage** that hairstyle makes her face look round; **~ les bras au dessus de la tête** to arch one's arms above one's head; **2** (adoucir) to make [sth] softer [*mouvement*]; to polish [*phrase*]; **~ le caractère de qn** to make sb a more rounded character; **3** (dans un calcul) to round off [*chiffre, résultat*]; **on arrondit?** shall we round it off?; **~ au franc supérieur/inférieur** to round up/down to the nearest franc; **en arrondissant** in round figures; **4** (augmenter) to increase [*fortune, patrimoine*] ; **~ son revenu** or **ses fins de mois** to supplement one's income (**en faisant** by doing); **5** Naut to round [*cap*]; **6** Phon to round [*voyelle*].

II s'arrondir *vpr* **1** (devenir rond) [*objet*] to become round(ed); [*personne, visage, ventre*] to fill out; [*yeux*] to widen; **2** (s'adoucir) [*personne*] to mellow; **3** (augmenter) [*fortune, patrimoine*] to be growing.

IDIOMES **~ les angles** to smooth the rough edges.

arrondissement /aʀɔ̃dismɑ̃/ *nm* **1** (de ville) arrondissement; **2** (petite région) *administrative division in France, larger than a canton but smaller than a department.*

arrosage /aʀozaʒ/ *nm* **1** (de plante, champ) watering; (de sol) spraying; **2** Mil (bombardement) bombardment; **3**○ (corruption) palm-greasing○; **4**○ (célébration) celebratory drink.

arroser /aʀoze/ [1] **I** *vtr* **1** (avec de l'eau) [*personne*] (avec un arrosoir, un tuyau) to water [*plante, champ*]; (avec un arroseur) to sprinkle [*plante, champ*]; [*personne, arroseuse*] to spray [*rue, trottoir*]; [*pluie*] to water; **région bien/peu arrosée** region with a lot of/very little rainfall; **un orage arrive, on va se faire ~**○**!** there's a storm coming on, we're going to get soaked!; **2** (avec un autre liquide) **~ qch d'essence** to douse sth with petrol GB ou gasoline US; **~ qch de sang** to cover sth with blood; **~ qch de ses larmes** liter to bathe sth with one's tears; **3** [*rivière*] to water [*région, ville*]; **4** Culin to baste [*rôti*]; to sprinkle [*gâteau*] (**de** with); to lace [*cocktail, café*] (**de** with); **5** (avec une boisson) [*personne*] to wash [sth] down with drink [*repas, plat*]; to drink to [*promotion, victoire*]; **un repas arrosé au bourgogne** a meal washed down with Burgundy; **il faut ~ ça** we must drink to that; **une soirée un peu trop arrosée** a rather over-alcoholic evening; **6** (avec des balles) to spray; (avec des obus) to bombard; **7**○ (corrompre) **~ qn** to grease sb's palm○; **toutes les entreprises de la région ont été arrosées par le candidat** the candidate has bought off all the companies in the area.

II s'arroser○ *vpr* (se fêter) **ça s'arrose** that calls for a drink; **un succès comme ça doit s' ~ au champagne** such success calls for champagne.

arroseur /aʀozœʀ/ *nm* (appareil) sprinkler.

IDIOMES **c'est l'~ arrosé** he's been hoisted by his own petard.

arroseuse /aʀozøz/ *nf* (véhicule) (mobile) street sprinkler.

arrosoir /aʀozwaʀ/ *nm* watering can.

arsenal, *pl* **-aux** /aʀsənal, o/ *nm* **1** Naut (chantier naval) naval shipyard; **2** Mil (dépôt, fabrique d'armes) arsenal; **3** (matériel) gear ₵, paraphernalia ₵; **4** (grand nombre) **tout un ~ de** a whole battery of.

arsenic /aʀsənik/ *nm* arsenic; **empoisonné à l'~** poisoned with arsenic; **empoisonnement à l'~** arsenic poisoning.

arsenical, **~e**, *mpl* **-aux** /aʀsənikal, o/ *adj* arsenical.

art /aʀ/ **I** *nm* **1** (création, œuvres) art; **l'~ abstrait/chinois/nègre** abstract/Chinese/Negro art; **l'~ du Moyen-Âge** the art of the Middle Ages; **l'~ pour l'~** art for art's sake; **d'~** [*amateur, livre, galerie*] art (*épith*); ▶ **grand**; **2** (savoir-faire) art; (habileté) skill; **c'est tout un ~ de créer un parfum** creating a perfume is an art in itself; **c'est du grand ~** it's a real art; **il nous a enseigné l'~ du mime/du trucage/de faire des sauces** he taught us the art of mime/of special effects/of sauce-making; **l'~ de l'écrivain/du jardinier** the writer's/gardener's art; **ils ont un ~ consommé du compromis** they have perfected the art of compromise; **avoir l'~ et la manière** to have the skill and the style (**de faire qch** to do sth); **avec ~** (artistement) artistically ; (habilement) skilfully[GB]; **elle joue/s'exprime avec un ~ consommé de la nuance** she plays/expresses herself with a fine command of nuance; **3** (don) knack; **elle a l'~ de convaincre/de plaire** she has the knack of convincing/of pleasing people; **il a l'~ de parler pour ne rien dire** he's very good at talking without saying anything.

II arts *nmpl* arts; ▶ **école**.

■ **~ contemporain** contemporary art; **~ déco** art deco; **un meuble ~ déco** a piece of art deco furniture; **~ dramatique** drama; **~ floral** flower-arranging; **~ de la guerre** art of war; **~ lyrique** opera; **~ martial** martial art; **~ nouveau** art nouveau; **un vase ~ nouveau** an art nouveau vase; **~ oratoire** public speaking; **~ poétique** (versification, ouvrage) art of poetry; **~ de la table** art of entertaining; **~ de vivre** art of living; **être célibataire c'est plus que vivre seul, c'est un ~ de vivre** there's more to being a bachelor than living on your own, it's an art; **~s appliqués** applied arts; **~s décoratifs** decorative arts; **~s graphiques** graphic arts; **~s libéraux** liberal arts; **~s mécaniques** mechanical arts; **~s ménagers** home economics; **le Salon des Arts Ménagers** ≈ the Ideal Home Exhibition GB, the Home Show US; **~s plastiques** fine arts.

Artaban /aʀtabɑ̃/ *npr* **fier comme ~** proud as a peacock.

Artémis /aʀtemis/ *npr* Artemis.

artère /aʀtɛʀ/ *nf* **1** Anat artery; **~ axillaire/humérale/pulmonaire** axillary/brachial/pulmonary artery; **2** (voie) artery; **grande ~**, **~ principale** (rue) main thoroughfare ou street; (route) arterial road.

IDIOMES **on a l'âge de ses ~s** there's no getting away from one's actual physical age.

artériel, **-ielle** /aʀteʀjɛl/ *adj* arterial.

artériole /aʀteʀjɔl/ *nf* arteriole.

artériosclérose /aʀteʀjoskleʀoz/ ▶ **271** *nf* arteriosclerosis.

artérite /aʀteʀit/ ▶ **271** *nf* arteritis.

artésien /aʀtezjɛ̃/ *adj m* **puits ~** artesian well.

arthrite /aʀtʀit/ ▶ **271** *nf* Méd arthritis; **avoir de l'~** to have arthritis.

arthritique /aʀtʀitik/ *adj, nmf* arthritic.

arthritisme /aʀtʀitism/ *nm* arthritism.

arthropode /aʀtʀɔpɔd/ *nm* arthropod; **les ~s** Arthropoda.

arthrose /aʀtʀoz/ ▶ **271** *nf* osteoarthritis; **avoir de l'~** to suffer from osteoarthritis.

artichaut /aʀtiʃo/ *nm* (globe) artichoke.

IDIOMES **avoir un cœur d'~** to be fickle (*in love*).

article /aʀtikl/ **I** *nm* **1** Presse article (**sur** about, on); **dans un ~ publié dans le Monde** in an article published in le Monde; **série d'~s consacrés à** series of articles about; **l'~ de M. Berne/de Libération** the article by M. Berne/in Libération; **2** Ling article; **~ défini/indéfini** definite/indefinite article; **3** Édition (de dictionnaire) entry; **4** Comm (pris individuellement) item; **quels ~s sont les plus demandés?** which items are most in demand?; **~s de consommation courante** basic consumer items; **faire l'~ à qn** (pour vendre) to give sb the sales pitch; fig to try to win sb over; **5** Jur (de loi, traité, convention) article; (de contrat) clause; **il est très strict sur cet ~** he's very particular about that; **6** Fin, Ordinat item; **7** Bot, Zool segment.
II articles *nmpl* Comm goods (*pl*); **catalogue d'~s de luxe/voyage** catalogue[GB] of luxury/travel goods; **~s de pêche/sport** fishing/sports equipment; **tous les ~s de sport** all sports equipment **¢**; **~s de toilette** toiletries.
■ **~ de fond** feature article; **~ de synthèse** synthesis; **~ de tête** editorial.
IDIOMES **être à l'~ de la mort** to be at death's door.

articulaire /aʀtikylɛʀ/ *adj* articular.

articulation /aʀtikylasjɔ̃/ *nf* **1** Anat (jointure) joint, articulation spéc; (mouvement) articulation; **~ du coude/de la hanche** elbow/hip joint; **~ mobile/semi-mobile/immobile** mobile/cartilaginous/fused joint; **2** Mécan mobile joint; **3** Phon articulation; **point/mode d'~** place/manner of articulation; **double ~** Ling double articulation; **4** (élément) (de phrase) linking sentence; (de paragraphe) linking paragraph; **5** (structure) (d'argumentation) (logical) connection; (de dissertation, discours) structure, logical ordering; **6** Jur ≈ statement of claims.

articulatoire /aʀtikylatwaʀ/ *adj* articulatory.

articulé, **~e** /aʀtikyle/ **I** *pp* ▶ **articuler**.
II *pp adj* [*trolleybus, autobus, membre*] articulated; [*glace*] adjustable; [*son*] articulate.
III *nm* **1** Zool arthropod; **2** Dent **~ dentaire** dental occlusion.

articuler /aʀtikyle/ [1] **I** *vtr* **1** (prononcer) to articulate [*mot, phonème, son*]; to utter [*phrase*]; **articule quand tu parles!** speak clearly!; **2** Mécan (assembler) to connect [*pièce*] (**sur** to); **3** (structurer) to structure [*idées, discours*]; **j'ai articulé mon discours/le débat autour de deux thèmes** I structured my speech/the discussion around two themes.
II s'articuler *vpr* **1** Anat **s'~ à** or **avec** [*os*] to articulate with [*os*]; **2** Mécan **s'~ à** or **sur** [*pièce*] to connect to [*axe*]; **3** (être structuré) **s'~ autour de** [*débat, action*] to be based on [*idées, thème*].

artifice /aʀtifis/ *nm* **1** (ruse) (ingenious) trick; **user d'~s pour...** to use (all sorts of) tricks to...; **les ~s d'un grand séducteur** the ploys of a great charmer; **2** (moyen ingénieux) device; **les ~s du style** stylistic devices; **3** (résultat ingénieux) effect; **~s scéniques/d'éclairage** stage/lighting effects; **4** (procédé) artifice; **sans ~** [*être*] unpretentious; [*agir*] unpretentiously.

artificiel, **-ielle** /aʀtifisjɛl/ *adj* **1** (fabriqué) gén [*intelligence, lumière, fibre*] artificial; [*port, colline*] man-made; **lac ~** artificial lake; **2** (faux) pej [*besoins*] artificial; [*vie, plaisirs*] superficial; [*gaieté, rire*] forced; [*enthousiasme*] false; **3** (arbitraire) [*notion, classification*] arbitrary; [*argumentation*] contrived.

artificiellement /aʀtifisjɛlmɑ̃/ *adv* **1** (en fabriquant) [*produire*] by artificial means, artificially; **fibre fabriquée ~** man-made fibre[GB]; **2** (arbitrairement) [*résoudre, différencier*] arbitrarily.

artificier /aʀtifisje/ **▶510** *nm* **1** (fabricant) (de feux d'artifice) fireworks manufacturer; (d'explosifs) explosives manufacturer; **2** (qui désamorce) bomb disposal expert.

artificieusement /aʀtifisjøzmɑ̃/ *adv* liter in a deceitful way.

artificieux, **-ieuse** /aʀtifisjø, øz/ *adj* liter [*paroles, procédés*] deceitful; [*compliments*] insincere.

artillerie /aʀtijʀi/ *nf* Mil **1** (matériel) artillery; **~ lourde/de campagne** heavy/field artillery; **2** (corps de l'armée) artillery; **il est dans l'~** he's in ou with the artillery; **~ navale** naval guns (*pl*); **~ antiaérienne** anti-aircraft guns (*pl*); **3**○ (arme à feu) gun.
IDIOMES **sortir la grosse ~** to bring out the big guns.

artilleur /aʀtijœʀ/ *nm* Mil artilleryman, gunner.

artimon /aʀtimɔ̃/ *nm* Naut (voile) mizzen; (mât) mizzen(mast); **mât d'~** mizzenmast.

artisan /aʀtizɑ̃/ **▶510** *nm* **1** (travailleur) artisan, (self-employed) craftsman; **il est ~ menuisier** he's a self-employed carpenter ou joiner; **2** (auteur) architect; **être l'~ de qch** to be the architect of sth; **être l'~ de son propre malheur** to bring about one's own misfortune.

artisanal, **~e**, *mpl* **-aux** /aʀtizanal, o/ *adj* **activités/professions ~es** craft industries/professions; **foire/tradition ~e** craft fair/tradition; **méthode ~e** traditional method; **petites entreprises ~es** cottage industries; **ils sont restés à un stade très ~** they are still at the cottage industry stage; **de fabrication ~e** [*objet*] handcrafted; [*charcuterie, pain, moutarde*] made by traditional methods; [*jambon*] home-cured; [*bombe*] home-made.

artisanalement /aʀtizanalmɑ̃/ *adv* **fabriqué ~** [*objet*] hand-crafted; [*charcuterie, pain*] made by traditional methods.

artisanat /aʀtizana/ *nm* **1** (activité) craft industry, cottage industry; **l'~ connaît un renouveau** the craft industry is making a comeback; **2** (groupe social) artisans (*pl*).
■ **~ d'art** arts and crafts.

artiste /aʀtist/ **▶510** **I** *adj* **1** (créatif) artistic; **2** (peu sérieux) **il est un peu ~** he's a bit of a clown.
II *nmf* **1** (créateur) artist; **une sensibilité d'~** an artistic sensibility; **2** (chanteur, danseur, musicien) artist performer; (de music-hall) artiste; **~ dramatique** actor; **~ de cinéma** film actor; **~ lyrique** opera singer; **~ invité** or **en représentation** guest artist; **3** (bon à rien) clown; **salut l'~**○†! hello there!
■ **~ peintre** painter.

artistement /aʀtistəmɑ̃/ *adv* artistically.

artistique /aʀtistik/ *adj* artistic.

artistiquement /aʀtistikmɑ̃/ *adv* artistically.

artothécaire /aʀtɔtekɛʀ/ **▶510** *nmf* librarian at an art lending library.

artothèque /aʀtɔtɛk/ *nf* art lending library.

arum /aʀɔm/ *nm* arum lily.

aryen, **-enne** /aʀjɛ̃, ɛn/ *adj* Aryan.

Aryen, **-enne** /aʀjɛ̃, ɛn/ *nm,f* Aryan.

arythmie /aʀitmi/ *nf* arrhythmia.

as /ɑs/ *nm inv* **1** Jeux (aux cartes, dés, dominos) ace; (au loto, tiercé) **l'~** number one; **~ de cœur/trèfle** ace of hearts/clubs; **2**○ (champion) ace○; **~ du volant** ace○ ou crack driver; **~ du ciel** flying ace; **être un ~ en cuisine** to be an ace○ ou brilliant○ cook; **tu es un ~!** you're brilliant○!; **pour faire des bêtises tu es vraiment un ~** when it comes to doing stupid things you're the best ou the world champion; **3** Sport (au tennis) ace.
■ **~ de pique** lit ace of spades; fig○ [*croupion*] parson's nose; **être ficelé** or **fagoté comme l'~ de pique**○ to look a mess.
IDIOMES **être plein aux ~**○ to be loaded○, to be stinking rich○; **passer à l'~**○ (être gaspillé) [*somme d'argent*] to be ou to go down the drain; (être annulé) [*projet, augmentation, vacances*] to go by the board; (ne pas être compté) [*consommations*] gén to be overlooked; (sur une facture) to be left off the bill; **passer qch à l'~** (ne pas compter) to forget about sth deliberately.

AS /ɑɛs/ *nf* **1** (*abbr* = **Armée secrète**) Secret Army; **2** *abbr* ▶ **association**.

asbeste /asbɛst/ *nm* asbestos.

asbestose /asbɛstoz/ **▶271** *nf* Méd asbestosis.

ascaris /askaʀis/ *nm inv* roundworm.

ascendance /asɑ̃dɑ̃s/ *nf* **1** (ligne généalogique) descent; **il est d'~ normande** he is of Norman descent; **2** (ancêtres) ancestry; **3** Aviat, Météo thermal; **4** Astron rising.

ascendant, **~e** /asɑ̃dɑ̃, ɑ̃t/ **I** *adj* [*courbe, trait*] rising; [*mouvement*] upward; [*astre*] ascending; [*aorte, colon*] ascending; **dans sa phase ~e** Astron during its ascent; ▶ **courant II**.
II *nm* **1** (ancêtre) ancestor; (parent) Jur ascendant; **2** (pouvoir) influence (**sur** over); **avoir de l'~ sur qn** to have influence over sb, to have a hold on sb; **prendre de l'~ sur qn** to gain influence over sb; **3** Astrol ascendant; **elle est scorpion, ~ sagittaire** she's a Scorpio with a Sagittarius ascendant.

ascenseur /asɑ̃sœʀ/ *nm* lift GB, elevator US; **immeuble sans ~** building without a lift GB, walk-up building US.
IDIOMES **renvoyer l'~** to return the favour[GB].

ascension /asɑ̃sjɔ̃/ *nf* **1** (en montagne) ascent; **la première ~ hivernale** the first winter ascent; **faire l'~ de** to climb [*montagne, sommet*]; **il commence son ~ du col** he's beginning to climb the pass; **2** (dans les airs) (d'avion) ascent, climb; (d'aérostat, de fusée) ascent; **l'avion était en pleine ~ quand...** the aeroplane GB ou airplane US was climbing when...; **3** fig (dans une hiérarchie) rise; **les prix sont en pleine ~** prices are rising sharply; **son ~ sociale** his/her rise in social status, his/her social advancement; **son ~ professionnelle** his/her climb up the professional ladder.

Ascension /asɑ̃sjɔ̃/ **I** *nf* Relig (fête) Ascension; **l'~** the Ascension; (jour) Ascension Day.
II **▶416** *nprf* Géog **île de l'~** Ascension Island.

ascensionnel, **-elle** /asɑ̃sjɔnɛl/ *adj* [*mouvement*] upward; [*vitesse*] climbing.

ascèse /asɛz/ *nf* **1** Relig asceticism; **2** fig (façon de vivre) form of asceticism.

ascète /asɛt/ *nmf* Relig ascetic.

ascétique /asetik/ *adj* Relig ascetic.

ascétisme /asetism/ *nm* asceticism.

ASCII /aski/ *nm* Ordinat (*abbr* = **American Standard Code for Information Interchange**) ASCII.

ascorbique /askɔʀbik/ *adj* ascorbic.

ASE /ɑɛsə/ *nf*: *abbr* ▶ **agence**.

asepsie /asɛpsi/ *nf* asepsis.

aseptique /asɛptik/ *adj* aseptic.

aseptisation /asɛptizasjɔ̃/ *nf* (de pièce) disinfection; (d'instrument) sterilization.

aseptisé, **~e** /asɛptize/ **I** *pp* ▶ **aseptiser**.
II *pp adj* [*musique, art*] sanitized; [*vie, monde*] sterile; [*décor, ambiance*] impersonal.

aseptiser /asɛptize/ [1] *vtr* to disinfect [*plaie, pièce*]; to sterilize [*instrument*].

asexué, **~e** /asɛksɥe/ *adj* Biol, Zool asexual.

ashkénaze /aʃkenaz/ *nmf* Ashkenazi.

asiate /azjat/ *nmf* offensive Asian.

asiatique /azjatik/ *adj* Asian.

Asiatique /azjatik/ *nmf* Asian.

Asie /azi/ **▶321** *nprf* Asia; **~ Mineure** Asia Minor.

asile /azil/ *nm* **1** gén refuge; Pol asylum; Relig sanctuary; **terre d'~** land of refuge; **chercher ~** to seek refuge; **offrir ~ pour la nuit** to offer shelter for the night; **trouver ~ chez qn** to find refuge in sb's house; **de-**

mander l'~ politique to seek political asylum; **donner ~ (politique) à qn** to grant sb political asylum; **droit d'~** Pol right of asylum; Relig right to sanctuary; **droit d'~ politique/diplomatique** right to political/diplomatic asylum; **trouver ~ dans une église** to find sanctuary in a church; **2** (établissement) **~ de vieillards** old people's home; **~ d'aliénés** lunatic asylum; **~ de nuit** night shelter; **il est bon pour l'~**° he should be locked up°.

asociabilité /asɔsjabilite/ *nf* Sociol antisocial behaviour[GB].

asocial, ~e, *pl* **-iaux** /asɔsjal, o/ **I** *adj* Sociol antisocial.

II *nm,f* social misfit.

asparagus /aspaʀagys/ *nm inv* asparagus fern.

aspartam(e) /aspaʀtam/ *nm* aspartame.

aspect /aspɛ/ *nm* **1** (perspective) side; **voir qch sous son ~ positif** to see the good side of sth; **je ne connaissais pas Paul sous cet ~** I didn't know that side of Paul; **examiner la question sous tous ses ~s** to examine the question from every angle; **je n'avais pas vu la situation sous cet ~** I hadn't seen the situation in that light; **prendre un ~ inquiétant/bizarre** to take an alarming/a strange turn; **2** (facettes) aspect; **cet ~ du problème** that aspect of the problem; **par bien des ~s** in many respects; **3** (apparence) appearance; **leur ~ physique** their physical appearance; **changer d'~** to change in appearance; **reprendre son ~ normal** to look normal again; **d'~ redoutable** formidable-looking; **une femme d'~ engageant** a pleasant-looking woman; **avoir l'~ du cuir/bois** to look like leather/wood; **garder l'~ du neuf** to stay looking new; **4** Ling, Astrol aspect.

asperge /aspɛʀʒ/ *nf* **1** (légume) asparagus; **2**° (personne) pej beanpole°, string bean US.

asperger /aspɛʀʒe/ [13] **I** *vtr* **1** (avec un jet) to spray (**de** with); (accidentellement) to splash (**de** with); (pour humecter) to sprinkle (**de** with); **se faire ~ par une voiture** to get splashed by a (passing) car; **2** Relig **~ un cercueil/un malade/les fidèles d'eau bénite** to sprinkle a coffin/a sick person/the congregation with holy water.

II s'asperger *vpr* to splash oneself (**de** with); **s'~ le visage d'eau froide** to splash one's face with cold water; **le vainqueur s'est aspergé de champagne** the winner sprayed champagne all over himself; **il s'est aspergé en manipulant le tuyau d'arrosage** he got sprayed by the hosepipe.

aspérité /aspeʀite/ *nf* **1** (saillie) (de sol, planche) bump (**de** in); (de paroi rocheuse) protrusion sout (**de** on); **2** (de voix, caractère) asperity, harshness.

aspersion /aspɛʀsjɔ̃/ *nf* **1** (avec un tuyau, produit) spraying; **2** Relig (avant la messe) asperges (+ *v sg*); (au baptême) aspersion.

aspersoir /aspɛʀswaʀ/ *nm* aspersorium, aspergillum.

asphaltage /asfaltaʒ/ *nm* asphalting.

asphalte /asfalt/ *nm* asphalt.

asphalter /asfalte/ [1] *vtr* to asphalt.

asphodèle /asfɔdɛl/ *nm* asphodel.

asphyxiant, ~e /asfiksjɑ̃, ɑ̃t/ *adj* [*gaz, vapeurs*] asphyxiating.

asphyxie /asfiksi/ *nf* **1** Méd death by suffocation, asphyxia; **2** Bot asphyxiation; **3** (arrêt d'activité) [*de réseau routier, d'entreprise*] paralysis.

asphyxier /asfiksje/ [2] **I** *vtr* **1** Méd to asphyxiate, to suffocate to death; **mourir asphyxié** to die of suffocation; **tu nous asphyxies avec ta fumée de cigarette!** you're choking us to death with your cigarette smoke!; **2** fig (gêner) to paralyse[GB].

II s'asphyxier *vpr* **1** Méd to suffocate to death; (avec un gaz) to asphyxiate; **on va s'~ avec tous ces fumeurs!** we'll choke to death with all these people smoking!; **2** [*pays, économie*] to become paralysed.

aspic /aspik/ *nm* **1** Zool (serpent) asp; **2** Culin aspic; **~ de viande/poisson/légumes** meat/fish/vegetables in aspic; **faire des ~s** to make aspic dishes.

aspirant, ~e /aspiʀɑ̃, ɑ̃t/ **I** *adj* [*pompe*] suction; [*ventilateur*] extractor.

II *nm,f* (candidat) candidate (**à** for).

III ▶390 *nm* Mil (armée de terre, de l'air) ≈ senior officer cadet; (marine) ≈ midshipman cadet.

aspirateur /aspiʀatœʀ/ *nm* **1** (appareil ménager) vacuum cleaner, hoover® GB; **passer l'~ (dans une pièce)** to hoover GB ou vacuum (a room); **donner un coup° d'~ dans le salon** to give the sitting room a quick hoover GB ou vacuum; **~ industriel** industrial vacuum cleaner; **2** Méd aspirator.

aspirateur-balai, *pl* **aspirateurs-balais** /aspiʀatœʀbalɛ/ *nm* electric broom.

aspirateur-traîneau, *pl* **aspirateurs-traîneaux** /aspiʀatœʀtʀeno/ *nm* cylinder vacuum cleaner.

aspiration /aspiʀasjɔ̃/ *nf* **1** (désir) aspiration (**à** for); **2** Tech (de poussière) sucking up; (de liquide) drawing up; (d'air) drawing in; **nettoyage par ~** vacuum extraction; **3** Physiol inhalation; **pendant l'~** when inhaling, when breathing in; **4** Méd (gastrique, endo-utérine) vacuum extraction.

aspiré, ~e /aspiʀe/ **I** *pp* ▶ **aspirer**.

II *pp adj* aspirated.

III aspirée *nf* aspirate.

aspirer /aspiʀe/ [1] **I** *vtr* **1** (inhaler) [*personne*] to breathe in [*air*]; to inhale [*fumée*]; **aspirez, expirez!** breathe in, breathe out!; **2** (avec une paille, un tuyau) to suck up [*boisson, essence*]; (avec un aspirateur) to suck up [*poussière*]; to vacuum [*tapis, pièce*]; (avec une pompe) (pour extraire) to pump [sth] up [*liquide*]; (pour vider) to pump [sth] out [*liquide*]; **3** Ling to aspirate.

II aspirer à *vtr ind* liter to yearn for [*calme, liberté*]; to aspire to [*honneurs, gloire, fonction*]; **~ à faire** to desire to do.

aspirine® /aspiʀin/ *nf* aspirin; **un comprimé** or **cachet d'~** an aspirin; **prenez trois ~s** take three aspirins GB ou aspirin.

IDIOMES **être blanc comme un cachet d'~** to be lily white.

aspiro-batteur, *pl* **~s** /aspiʀobatœʀ/ *nm* (upright) vacuum cleaner.

assagir /asaʒiʀ/ [3] **I** *vtr* to quieten GB ou quiet US [sb] down [*personne*].

II s'assagir *vpr* (devenir sage) to quieten down GB, to quiet down US; (se ranger) to settle down.

assaillant, ~e /asajɑ̃, ɑ̃t/ **I** *adj* [*force, armée*] attacking (*épith*).

II *nm,f* attacker, assailant; **les ~s** Mil the attacking forces.

assaillir /asajiʀ/ [28] *vtr* **1** (attaquer) [*ennemi*] to attack; [*pluie, orage, grêle*] to buffet; **2** fml (envahir) [*mélancolie*] to plague, to assail sout; **être assailli par le doute** to be assailed by doubts; **3** (se précipiter sur) [*mendiant*] to assail; [*journaliste*] to set upon [*personne*]; **nous avons été assaillis par les médias** we were set upon by the media; **~ qn de questions** to bombard sb with questions.

assainir /aseniʀ/ [3] **I** *vtr* **1** (rendre sain) to clean up [*maison, rivière, région*]; to purify [*air, atmosphère*]; **2** (améliorer) to clean up, to rehabilitate [*quartier, rue*]; to clean up [*organisation*]; **3** Écon to stabilize [*marché, économie, situation, climat social*]; to streamline [*entreprise, gestion*]; **~ les finances** to make the finances healthier.

II s'assainir *vpr* [*atmosphère, environnement*] to become healthier; [*marché, économie, monnaie, situation*] to stabilize.

assainissement /asenismɑ̃/ *nm* **1** lit (de logement, rivière, région) cleaning up; (d'air, atmosphère, eau) purification; **2** fig (d'économie, de monnaie) stabilization; (d'entreprise, administration) streamlining; (de situation) improvement.

assaisonnement /asɛzɔnmɑ̃/ *nm* **1** (vinaigrette) dressing; (sel, poivre, épices) seasoning; **2** (addition d'ingrédients) seasoning; **l'~ d'une viande se fait avant la cuisson** meat should be seasoned before cooking.

assaisonner /asɛzɔne/ [1] *vtr* **1** (avec du sel, du poivre, des épices) to season (**de** with); (avec de la vinaigrette) to dress (**de** with); (dans une recette) 'add seasoning'; **~ avec du citron** sprinkle with lemon juice; **la salade est assaisonnée?** is there dressing on the salad?; **une sauce bien assaisonnée** a well-seasoned sauce; **2** (rendre plus vivant) to spice (**de** with); **3**° (critiquer) to tick [sb] off°; (escroquer) to rip [sb] off°, to rob.

assassin, ~e /asasɛ̃, in/ **I** *adj* [*main, regard*] murderous; [*campagne*] vicious; **la remarque assassine lancée par** the poisoned arrow launched by; **lancer une œillade ~e à qn** hum to look daggers at sb; **faire** or **lancer une remarque ~e à qn** to make a scathing remark to sb.

II *nm* gén murderer; (par idéologie) assassin; **'à l'~!'** 'murder!'

assassinat /asasina/ *nm* gén murder; (idéologique, politique) assassination.

assassiner /asasine/ [1] *vtr* **1** (tuer) to murder [*personne*]; to assassinate [*homme d'État, personnage important*]; **2** (détruire) to destroy; **3**° (critiquer) to slate°; **4**° (financièrement) to squeeze [sb] dry, to bleed [sb] white [*personne*].

assaut /aso/ *nm* gén attack (**de** on); (de place forte) assault (**de** on); **donner l'~, partir** or **monter à l'~** to attack; **se lancer** or **partir** or **monter à l'~ de** to launch an attack on [*village, marché, buts adverses*]; [*candidat*] to set out to win [*électeurs*]; [*soliste*] to launch into [*œuvre*]; **prendre d'~** [*soldats, touristes*] to storm; **subir un double/triple ~** to be attacked on two/three fronts; **le buffet a été pris d'~** the buffet was besieged; **la prise d'~ de** the storming of; **à l'~!** attack!; fig **les ~s du froid/de la tempête** the onslaught of cold weather/of the storm.

assèchement /asɛʃmɑ̃/ *nm* **1** Agric, Tech (en drainant) draining; (en vidant) emptying; (dû au climat) drying up ou out; **2** (de marché financier, caisses publiques) (par les responsables) draining; (dû aux circonstances) drying up.

assécher /aseʃe/ [14] **I** *vtr* **1** (drainer) to drain [*marais, sol*]; (vider) to empty [*étang, puits*]; (dessécher) [*vent, chaleur*] to dry up [*marais, sol*]; **2** fig [*responsables*] to drain [*économie, caisses d'État*]; [*récession, phénomène*] to dry [sth] up [*marchés financiers*].

II s'assécher *vpr* [*étang, puits*] to dry up; [*marais, sol*] to dry out.

ASSEDIC /asedik/ *nf* (*abbr* = **Association pour l'emploi dans l'industrie et le commerce**) *organization managing unemployment contributions and payments.*

assemblage /asɑ̃blaʒ/ *nm* **1** (montage) Tech (de pièces, machine, meuble) assembly (**de** of); Édition (de feuilles) gathering; Cout (de pièces, vêtement) sewing together; **l'~ des pièces par soudure** the welding together of parts; **procéder à l'~ de qch** to assemble sth; **l'~ du moteur nous a pris deux heures** it took us two hours to assemble the engine; **2** (structure) **un livre est un ~ de feuilles** a book is an assembly of pages; **3** (en menuiserie) joint; **~ à onglet/entaille** mitre/halving joint; **4** (réunion) (d'objets, idées, de données) collection, assemblage; (de couleurs, sons) combination; **5** Ordinat assembly; **6** Vin assemblage (*blending wines of the same vintage*); **7** Art assemblage.

assemblé /asɑ̃ble/ *nm* Danse assemblé.

assemblée /asɑ̃ble/ *nf* **1** (foule) gathering; Relig **~ (de fidèles)** congregation; **une grande** or **nombreuse ~** a large gathering; **à la fureur de l'~** to the fury of those present; **2** (réunion convoquée) meeting; **se réunir en ~** to assemble for a meeting; **convoquer une ~ générale/extraordinaire** to call a general/an extraordinary

meeting; **3** Pol (groupe élu) assembly; **~ législative/constituante** legislative/constituent assembly.
■ **l'Assemblée européenne** the European Assembly; **~ générale**, **AG** general meeting; **~ générale ordinaire** ordinary general meeting; **~ générale extraordinaire** extraordinary general meeting; **l'Assemblée nationale** the French National Assembly.

assembler /asɑ̃ble/ [1] **I** *vtr* **1** (monter) to assemble, to put [sth] together [*éléments, pièces, moteur*]; to make up, to sew [sth] together [*vêtement, pull*]; **~ des pièces par collage** to glue pieces together; **2** (disposer ensemble) to put [sth] together, to combine [*idées, mots*]; to combine [*couleurs, sons*]; **~ des mots pour faire une phrase** to put words together ou to combine words in a sentence; **3** Ordinat to assemble [*programme*].
II s'assembler *vpr* [*foule*] to gather; [*conseillers, députés*] to assemble.
IDIOMES **qui se ressemble s'assemble** Prov birds of a feather stick together Prov.

assembleur, **-euse** /asɑ̃blœʀ, øz/ **I** ▶**510** *nm,f* **1** Ind fitter; **2** Édition gatherer.
II *nm* Ordinat (programme, langage) assembler.
III assembleuse *nf* Édition (machine) gathering machine.

asséner /asene/ [14] *vtr* **1** (donner) **~ un coup à qn/qch** lit, fig to deal sb/sth a blow; **~ un coup de poing/matraque à qn** to punch/cosh sb; **2** fig (lancer) to hurl [*questions, injures*] (**à** at); to fling [*remarque*]; to fling back [*réplique*]; **la propagande qu'on nous assène** the propaganda we are bombarded with; **une réplique bien assénée** a well-aimed retort.

assentiment /asɑ̃timɑ̃/ *nm* (accord) assent, consent; (approbation) approval; **donner son ~ à** to give one's assent ou consent ou approval to.

asseoir /aswaʀ/ [41] **I** *vtr* **1** (sur un siège) to sit [*personne debout*]; to sit [sb] up [*personne allongée*]; **~ qn sur ses genoux** to sit ou take sb on one's knee; **faire ~ qn** (contraindre) to make sb sit down; (convier) to offer a seat to sb; **~ l'héritier sur le trône** fig to install the heir on the throne; **2** Constr to seat, to bed [*fondations*]; **3** (établir) to establish [*régime, autorité, réputation, conclusion*]; to set up [*argument*]; **~ sa réputation sur qch** to build one's reputation on sth; **4** Admin, Fisc to base [*cotisation, impôt*] (**sur** on); **5**○ (sidérer) to stagger○; **ça m'a assise** I was staggered.
II s'asseoir *vpr* **1** [*personne debout*] to sit (down); [*personne allongée*] to sit up; **s'~ sur une chaise/dans un fauteuil/par terre** to sit on a chair/in an armchair/on the floor; **je me suis assise dessus** I sat on it; **s'~ en tailleur** to sit cross-legged; **voulez-vous vous ~?** would you like to sit down?; **il n'y a rien pour s'~** there's nothing to sit on; **asseyez-vous** (invitation) do sit down, do take a seat GB, please be seated; (ordre) sit down; **s'~ à une** or **autour d'une table** lit to sit down at a table; fig to sit down at the negotiating table; **s'~ sur le trône** to come to the throne; **2**○ (mépriser) **s'~ sur** not to give a damn about○.

assermenté, **~e** /asɛʀmɑ̃te/ *adj* [*témoin, expert*] sworn (*épith*), on oath (*jamais épith*).

assertion /asɛʀsjɔ̃/ *nf* assertion.

asservir /asɛʀviʀ/ [3] *vtr* to enslave [*peuple, personne*]; to subjugate [*pays*] (**à** to); to control [*presse*]; **être asservi à** to be a slave to.

asservissant, **~e** /asɛʀvisɑ̃, ɑ̃t/ fml *adj* [*loi, règle*] oppressive; [*travail*] exacting, demanding.

asservissement /asɛʀvismɑ̃/ *nm* fml **1** (action) (de pays) subjugation; (de peuple) enslavement; (de presse) control; **2** (état) subjection (**à** to); **maintenir un pays dans l'~** to keep a country enslaved; **3** fig (de personne) subservience; **l'~ de qn à un parti politique** sb's subservience to a political party; **l'~ de la jeunesse à la mode vestimentaire** youth's slavish following of fashion, youth's enslavement to fashion; **4** Tech (action) servoing; (dispositif) servo control; (système) servosystem, servomechanism.

assesseur /asesœʀ/ *nm* Jur magistrate's assistant.

assez /ase/ ▶**662** *adv*

■ **Note** Lorsqu'il signifie 'suffisamment', *assez* se traduit par *enough*: *les pommes ne sont pas assez mûres* = the apples are not ripe enough; *tu ne manges pas assez* = you don't eat enough.
– On notera la place de *enough* avec un adjectif: *assez grand (pour faire)* = tall enough (to do). ▶ 1 ci-dessous.
– Lorsqu'il est utilisé pour atténuer un jugement *assez* se traduit par *quite*: *il est assez grand* = he's quite tall. ▶ 2 ci-dessous.

1 (évaluation) enough; **~ fort** strong enough; **~ fort/stupide pour faire** strong/stupid enough to do; **tu n'es pas ~ grand pour atteindre l'interrupteur** you're not tall enough to reach the switch; **~ bien/couramment** well/fluently enough; **avoir ~ de temps/tasses pour tout le monde** to have enough time/cups for everybody; **~ de temps pour finir** enough time to finish; **est-ce qu'il y a ~ de potage pour tout le monde?** is there enough soup for everyone?; **il y en avait à peine ~** there was barely ou hardly enough; **nous avons bien ~ de soucis comme ça** we've got quite enough problems as it is; **~!** that's enough (of that)!; **~ de promesses, nous voulons des actes** that's enough talk, we want action; **serons-nous ~?** will there be enough of us?; **il ne travaille pas ~** he doesn't work hard enough; **j'en aurai ~ de quatre** four will be quite enough (for me); **en avoir ~** to be fed up○ (**de** with); **j'en ai ~ de tes mensonges** I've had enough of ou I'm fed up○ with your lies; **j'en ai ~ qu'il pleuve tous les jours** I'm getting fed up○ with it raining every day; **il a fini par en avoir ~** he eventually got fed up with it; **il n'y en avait ni trop ni pas ~** there was neither too much nor too little; **je ne vous dirai jamais ~ toute ma reconnaissance** I can't thank you enough; **avez-vous ~ mangé?** have you had enough to eat?; **2** (jugement) quite; **~ jeune/lourd** quite young/heavy; **~ souvent** quite often, fairly often; **je suis ~ pressé** I'm in rather a hurry; **leurs notes sont ~ bonnes** their grades are quite or fairly good; **il cuisine ~ bien** he cooks quite well, he's quite a good cook; (plus positif) he cooks rather well; **l'hôtel coûte ~ cher** hotels are rather expensive; **je suis ~ d'accord** I tend to agree; **je les trouve ~ ennuyeux** I find them rather boring.

assidu, **~e** /asidy/ *adj* [*travail*] diligent; [*soins*] unremitting; [*présence, fréquentation, visites*] regular; [*élève*] diligent, assiduous; [*employé, chercheur*] hard-working; [*amateur de théâtre, lecteur*] devoted, assiduous; [*amoureux*] devoted; [*soins*] constant; **faire une cour ~e à qn** to court sb assiduously fml.

assiduité /asidɥite/ **I** *nf* **1** (application) diligence; **avec ~** [*travailler*] diligently; [*s'entraîner*] assiduously; [*lire, regarder*] regularly; [*courtiser*] assiduously; **2** (fréquentation régulière) regular attendance.
II assiduités *nfpl* assiduities.

assidûment /asidymɑ̃/ *adv* [*travailler*] diligently; [*fréquenter un lieu*] regularly, assiduously; [*s'entraîner*] assiduously.

assiégé, **~e** /asjeʒe/ *nm,f* **les ~s** the besieged.

assiégeant, **~e** /asjeʒɑ̃, ɑ̃t/ *nm,f* besieger; **les ~** the besiegers.

assiéger /asjeʒe/ [15] *vtr* **1** Mil to besiege, to lay siege to [*ville, troupe*]; **la ville/population assiégée** the besieged town/population; **la ville a été assiégée pendant six mois** the town was under siege ou besieged for six months; **2** fig (assaillir) to besiege [*magasin, bureau de réclamations*]; **~ la maison de qn** [*journalistes, créanciers*] to lay siege to sb's house; **~ qn** [*créanciers, journalistes*] to besiege sb; **~ qn de questions** to besiege sb with questions; **assiégé de remords** assailed by remorse.

assiette /asjɛt/ *nf* **1** (vaisselle) plate; (contenu) plate (**de** of); **finis ton ~** finish what's on your plate; **il n'a pas touché à son ~** he hasn't touched his food; **2** (base) (de route, voie ferrée) bed; **3** Équit seat; **avoir une bonne ~** to have a good seat; **perdre son ~** to become unseated; **prendre son ~** to settle into the saddle; **4** Fisc (d'imposition) **~ (fiscale)** tax base; **détermination de l'~ fiscale** tax assessment; **5** (de véhicule) stability.
■ **~ anglaise** Culin assorted cold meats (*pl*); **~ creuse** soup plate; **~ à dessert** dessert plate; **~ en carton** paper plate; **~ plate** dinner plate; **~ à soupe** = **~ creuse**.
IDIOMES **ne pas être dans son ~** to be out of sorts.

assiettée /asjɛte/ *nf* plateful.

assignable /asiɲabl/ *adj* fml ascribable (**à** to).

assignat /asiɲa/ *nm* Hist *banknote issued during the French Revolution*.

assignation /asiɲasjɔ̃/ *nf* **1** (attribution de crédits) allocation; **2** Jur (à défendeur) summons (*sg*); (à témoin) subpoena; **l'huissier lui a délivré une ~** (au défendeur) the bailiff served him with a summons; **~ devant le tribunal de grande instance** (à témoin) subpoena to appear before the high court.
■ **~ à comparaître** (à défendeur) summons (*sg*); (à témoin) subpoena; **~ en justice** summons to appear before the court; **~ en référé** urgent summons (*to appear before the court within three days*); **~ à résidence** house arrest.

assigner /asiɲe/ [1] **I** *vtr* **1** (attribuer) to assign [*tâche, rôle*] (**à** to); to allocate [*crédits*] (**à** to); **2** (déterminer) to fix [*date, limite*] (**à** to); to ascribe [*valeur*] (**à** to); **3** Jur **~ à comparaître** to summons [*défendeur*]; to subpoena [*témoin*]; **~ qn en justice** to summons sb to appear before the court; **~ qn à résidence** to put sb under house arrest.
II s'assigner *vpr* **~ un objectif/un but** to set oneself an objective/a goal.

assimilable /asimilabl/ *adj* **1** (comparable) **~ à** comparable to; **2** Jur (équivalent) **~ à** [*personne*] deemed; [*avantage, pratique*] deemed equivalent to; **les résidents étrangers sont ~s aux nationaux du point de vue fiscal** foreign residents are deemed nationals for tax purposes; **les primes sont ~s à des salaires** bonuses are deemed equivalent to salaries; **3** (par l'esprit) **des notions ~s dès l'âge de cinq ans** ideas which can be assimilated from the age of five; **4** (intégrable) [*minorité, peuple*] easily assimilated; **5** Physiol [*aliment, substance*] easily assimilated (**par** by).

assimilateur, **-trice** /asimilatœʀ, tʀis/ *adj* [*pigment, fonction*] assimilative.

assimilation /asimilasjɔ̃/ *nf* **1** (comparaison) comparison (**de qch à qch** between sth and sth); **il refuse l'~ de son association à une secte** he rejects the comparison between his organization and a sect; **2** Jur (équivalence) **accepter/refuser l'~ d'un couple d'homosexuels à un couple marié** to accept/to refuse to deem a homosexual couple to be a married couple; **3** (de connaissances, langue) assimilation; **ses capacités d'~ sont faibles** his ability to assimilate knowledge is poor; **4** (intégration) (de minorité, peuple) assimilation; **5** Physiol assimilation; **6** Phon assimilation.
■ **~ chlorophyllienne** Bot photosynthesis.

assimilé, **~e** /asimile/ **I** *pp* ▶ **assimiler**.
II *pp adj* **1** (intégré socialement) [*milieu, mino-*

rité] assimilated; **2** (de même catégorie) **les médicaments et produits ~s** medicines and similar products.

III *nm* **cadres et ~s** management and those in the same category.

assimiler /asimile/ [1] I *vtr* **1** (considérer équivalent) **~ l'embargo à une déclaration de guerre/leur silence à un refus** to consider the embargo tantamount to a declaration of war/their silence tantamount to a refusal; **~ les travailleurs à des machines** to treat workers as machines; **~ le livre aux périodiques** to make no distinction between books and periodicals; **2** Jur (considérer équivalent juridiquement) **~ une prime à un salaire** to consider a bonus equivalent to a salary; **être assimilé cadre** to have executive status; **3** (comparer) **~ qch/qn à** to liken sth/sb to; **nous ne voulons pas être assimilés à des délinquants** we don't want to be likened to delinquents; **4** (intégrer) to assimilate [*minorité, communauté*]; **5** (apprendre) to assimilate [*leçon, langue*]; to learn [*métier*]; to adopt [*réflexe, geste*]; **6** Physiol to assimilate [*aliment, substance*].

II **s'assimiler** *vpr* **1** (être comparable) [*style, méthode*] to be comparable (**à** to); **2** (se comparer) [*personne*] to compare oneself (**à** to); **3** (s'intégrer) [*communauté, minorité*] to become assimilated; **4** Physiol [*aliments, substances*] to be assimilated.

assis, **~e** /asi, iz/ I *pp* ▶ **asseoir**.

II *pp adj* **1** (position) **être ~** (et non debout) to be sitting down; (et non allongé) to be sitting up; (installé sur un siège) to be sitting down ou seated; **j'étais ~ à mon bureau/dans le jardin** I was sitting at my desk/in the garden GB ou yard US; **je l'ai trouvée ~e par terre** I found her sitting on the floor; **il était ~ dans son lit** he was sitting up in bed; **rester ~** to remain seated; **rester ~ des heures à attendre/ne rien faire** to sit about waiting for hours/for hours doing nothing; **les enfants, ça ne peut pas rester ~** children can't sit still; **reste ~** (ne te lève pas) don't get up; (ne bouge pas) sit still; **~!** (à un chien) sit!; **on est bien/mal ~ dans cette voiture** the seats in this car are comfortable/uncomfortable; **2** (affirmé) [*situation, réputation*] well-established (*épith*); **son autorité est bien ~e** his authority is well established; **régime ~ sur des bases solides** solidly based regime; **3**○ (époustouflé) staggered; ▶ **chaise**.

III *adj* [*personne, position*] seated; **portrait de femme ~e** portrait of (a) seated woman.

IV **assise** *nf* **1** (confort) seating; **ce sofa offre une bonne ~e** this is a comfortable sofa; **2** (fondement) basis, foundation; **3** Constr (pour fondations) bedding, hardcore; (rangée) **~e de briques** course of bricks; **4** Géol (couche) stratum; (de montagne, rocher) step; **5** Biol, Bot layer (of cells).

V **assises** *nfpl* **1** (réunion) gén meeting; Pol conference; **le comité tiendra ses ~es à Paris** the committee will meet ou hold its meeting in Paris; **2** Jur assizes; **envoyer qn aux ~es** to send sb for trial; **c'est ce qu'il soutiendra aux ~es** this is what he will say in court.

Assise /asiz/ ▶ 857 *npr* Assisi.

assistanat /asistana/ *nm* **1** (fonction) Univ assistantship; Cin, Théât position as assistant; **2** pej (aide de l'État) charity.

assistance /asistɑ̃s/ *nf* **1** (secours) gén assistance; (à l'étranger) aid; **~ financière** financial assistance; **~ militaire/technique** (à l'étranger) military/technical aid; **demander l'~ d'un avocat** to ask for legal representation; **~ médicale** medical care; **~ judiciaire** legal aid; **porter** or **prêter ~ à qn** to assist sb; **2** (auditoire) audience; **3** (présence) attendance (**à** at); **4** Aut **~ à la direction/au freinage** power steering/brakes.

■ **l'Assistance publique**, **AP** ≈ welfare services; **~ respiratoire** artificial respiration.

assistant, **~e** /asistɑ̃, ɑ̃t/ ▶ 510 *nm,f* **1** (aide) Cin, TV assistant; Scol (language) assistant; Méd assistant doctor; **2** (personne présente) person present; **l'un des ~s s'est évanoui** one of those present fainted.

■ **~ de production** Cin, TV production assistant; **~ réalisateur** Cin, TV assistant director; **~e maternelle** (nourrice) childminder GB, babysitter US; (dans une crèche) crèche worker; **~e sociale** social worker.

assisté, **~e** /asiste/ I *pp* ▶ **assister**.

II *pp adj* **1** [*personne*] gén assisted (**de** by); (par l'État) receiving benefit GB, on welfare US; **2** Ordinat aided; **~ par ordinateur** computer-aided (*épith*); **3** Aut [*freins, direction*] power (*épith*).

III *nm,f person receiving benefit* GB ou *welfare* US; **avoir une mentalité d'~** pej to think one can live on government handouts pej.

assister /asiste/ [1] I *vtr* **1** (aider) to assist (**de, par** by; **dans** with); **il se fait ~ de plusieurs stagiaires** he has several trainees to assist him; **elle m'assiste dans mon travail** she assists me with my work; **2** (secourir) to aid [*réfugiés, pays*].

II **assister à** *vtr ind* **1** (être présent) **~ à** to be at [*mariage, spectacle*]; to be present at [*couronnement*]; to attend [*réunion, cours, messe*]; **2** (observer) **~ à** to witness [*accident*]; **on assiste à une recrudescence du racisme** we are witnessing a new upsurge in racism.

associatif, **-ive** /asɔsjatif, iv/ *adj* **1** Ling, Math, Psych [*rapport, loi, lien*] associative; **mémoire associative** associative memory; **2** Jur, Sociol [*personne*] belonging to an association; [*réseau, tissu*] of associations; **militant ~** association activist; **responsable ~** association office-holder; **les milieux ~s** associations; **mouvement ~** (ensemble) association; (tendance) trend toward(s) the forming of associations; **à structure associative** with association status; **vie associative** community life.

association /asɔsjasjɔ̃/ *nf* **1** Jur (corps constitué) association; **~ de défense des consommateurs** consumer protection association; **2** (regroupement) association; **en ~ avec** in association with; **3** Psych (rapprochement) association; **libre ~** free association; **~ verbale** verbal association; **~ d'idées** association of ideas; **4** (de couleurs, styles, substances) combination; **5** (groupe) Astron, Biol, Chimie, Géol association.

■ **~ à but non lucratif** non-profitmaking organization GB, non-profit organization US; **~ déclarée** *association that has registered with the prefecture, and is therefore entitled to receive subsidies or take court action*; **~ (de type) loi de 1901** non-profitmaking organization GB, non-profit organization US (*conforming to a law passed in 1901*); **~ familiale** *registered association with the aim of protecting the interests of families*; **~ de malfaiteurs** Jur criminal conspiracy; **~ sportive**, **AS** sports association; **~ syndicale de propriétaires** association of property owners.

associationnisme /asɔsjasjɔnism/ *nm* Philos, Psych associationism.

associationniste /asɔsjasjɔnist/ *adj, nmf* Philos, Psych associationist.

associativité /asɔsjativite/ *nf* Math associativeness.

associé, **~e** /asɔsje/ I *pp* ▶ **associer**.

II *pp adj* (*after n*) [*membre, directeur, professeur*] associate (*épith*); [*entreprises, organismes*] associated (*épith*); **être ~ à qch/qn** to be associated with sth/sb.

III *nm,f* associate, partner; **les ~s européens** Pol the European partners.

associer /asɔsje/ [2] I *vtr* **1** (réunir) to bring together [*personnes*]; **une coproduction qui associe plusieurs éditeurs** a coproduction which brings together several publishers; **2** (faire partager) **~ qn/qch à** to include sb/sth in; **3** (combiner) to combine [*objets, forces, sentiments*] (**à** or **et** with); **4** (rapprocher) to associate (**à** with); **~ une couleur à un son** to associate a colour[GB] with a sound.

II **s'associer** *vpr* **1** (s'unir) [*personnes, sociétés*] to go into partnership, to link up (**à, avec** with); **s'~ pour faire** to join forces to do; **2** (se rallier) [*personne, entité*] **s'~ à** to join [*mouvement, manifestation, campagne*]; to join in [*projet, vote, décision, opération*]; to join in (with) [*proposition, accord, activité*]; **s'~ aux efforts de qn** to join in sb's efforts; **3** (partager) **s'~ à la joie/à la peine/à l'indignation de qn** to share in sb's joy/sorrow/indignation; **4** (se combiner) (matériellement) to combine, to be combined (**à** with; **pour faire** in order to do); (abstraitement) to be associated (**à** with; **pour faire** to do).

assoiffé, **~e** /aswafe/ I *pp* ▶ **assoiffer**.

II *pp adj* **1** lit thirsty; (plus fort) parched○; **2** fig (avide) **~ de** thirsting ou hungry for [*pouvoir, liberté*]; **~ de sang** bloodthirsty.

assoiffer /aswafe/ [1] *vtr* to make [sb/sth] thirsty [*personnes, animal*].

assolement /asɔlmɑ̃/ *nm* rotation of crops.

assoler /asɔle/ [1] *vtr* **~ des terres** to rotate crops.

assombri, **~e** /asɔ̃bʀi/ I *pp* ▶ **assombrir**.

II *pp adj* [*ciel, paysage*] darkened; [*visage, regard*] gloomy.

assombrir /asɔ̃bʀiʀ/ [3] I *vtr* **1** lit [*arbres, papier peint, couleur*] to make [sth] dark [*lieu*]; [*nuages*] to darken [*ciel*]; **2** fig [*nouvelle, événement*] to cast a shadow over [*période, conjoncture, soirée*]; to spoil [*atmosphère*]; [*tristesse*] to cloud [*visage*].

II **s'assombrir** *vpr* **1** lit [*ciel, paysage, horizon*] to darken; **2** fig [*visage, regard*] to become gloomy; [*conjoncture, perspectives*] to become gloomy.

assombrissement /asɔ̃bʀismɑ̃/ *nm* (tous contextes) darkening.

assommant○, **~e** /asɔmɑ̃, ɑ̃t/ *adj* **1** (ennuyeux) [*travail, soirée, livre, personne*] deadly boring○; **c'est ~ de faire la vaisselle** it's a real drag○ doing the dishes; **2** (agaçant) **tu es ~ avec tes questions/conseils** you're a real pain○ with your questions/advice.

assommer /asɔme/ [1] *vtr* **1** (étourdir) to knock [sb] senseless; **~ qn à coups de massue** to club sb senseless; **il a reçu un coup à ~ un bœuf** he got a blow that would have felled an ox; **2**○ (ennuyer) to bore [sb] to tears○; **ça m'assomme d'aller chez eux/de faire ce travail** going to see them/this work bores me to tears; **ça m'assomme d'aller à cette réunion!** what a drag○ having to go to that meeting!; **3**○ (agacer) **il nous assomme avec ses histoires** he gets on our nerves with his stories; **4**○ (accabler) [*nouvelle*] to stagger; [*chaleur*] to overcome.

assommoir‡ /asɔmwaʀ/ *nm* **1** (arme) club; **2** (débit de boissons) low class bar, grogshop† GB.

Assomption /asɔ̃psjɔ̃/ *nf* Relig **l'~** the Assumption.

assonance /asɔnɑ̃s/ *nf* assonance.

assonant, **~e** /asɔnɑ̃, ɑ̃t/ *adj* assonant.

assorti, **~e** /asɔʀti/ I *pp* ▶ **assortir**.

II *pp adj* **1** (en harmonie) [*couleurs, vêtements, linge*] matching; **draps et serviettes ~es** matching sheets and towels; **un couple bien/mal ~** a well-/an ill-matched couple; **un abat-jour ~ aux rideaux** a lampshade that matches the curtains; **2** (varié) [*chocolats, bonbons*] assorted; **pâtisseries ~es** assorted cakes; **3** Comm **une boutique bien/mal ~e** a well-/badly-stocked shop GB ou store US.

assortiment /asɔʀtimɑ̃/ *nm* **1** (ensemble) (d'outils, de pinceaux) set; (de fromages, charcuterie, légumes) assortment; (de produits de beauté) selection; **2** (harmonie) (de tons, couleurs) match; **3** Comm stock.

assortir /asɔʀtiʀ/ [3] **I** *vtr* **1** (harmoniser) to match [*couleurs, vêtements*] (**à** to; **avec** with); to match [*convives*]; **~ sa cravate à** or **avec ses chaussettes** to match one's tie with one's socks; **son sac à main est assorti à ses chaussures** her handbag matches her shoes; **2** (compléter) **~ qch de qch** to add sth to sth; **ils ont assorti leurs propositions de deux conditions** they added two conditions to their proposals; **3** Comm (approvisionner) to stock [*magasin*].
II s'assortir *vpr* **1** (s'harmoniser) [*couleurs, objets, vêtements*] to match; **s'~ à** or **avec qch** to match sth; **2** (être complété) **s'~ de qch** to come with; **la condamnation s'assortit d'une mise à l'épreuve de trois ans** the sentence comes with a three-year probationary period.

assoupir /asupiʀ/ [3] **I** *vtr* **1** (endormir) to make [sb] drowsy [*personne*]; **2** (atténuer) to dull [*passion, remords, sens*].
II s'assoupir *vpr* **1** lit [*personne*] to doze off; **il était assoupi devant la télévision** he was dozing off in front of the television; **2** fig [*enthousiasme, passion*] to wane; [*haine*] to abate; [*querelle*] to die down; [*activité économique*] to be in a lull; [*ville*] to be sleepy.

assoupissement /asupismɑ̃/ *nm* (somnolence) drowsiness; (sommeil) doze; **lutter contre l'~** to fight against drowsiness.

assouplir /asupliʀ/ [3] **I** *vtr* **1** (rendre moins rigide) to make [sth] supple [*cuir*]; to soften [sth] up [*chaussures*]; to soften [*linge, lainage*]; to make [sth] more supple [*corps, membres*]; to loosen [*muscles*]; fig **~ qn** or **le caractère de qn** to make sb more accommodating; **2** (rendre moins strict) to relax [*règlement, politique, sanctions*]; to make [sth] more flexible [*méthode, système*]; to make [sth] less strict [*régime alimentaire*]; **~ sa position/son attitude** to adopt a more flexible position/attitude; **un régime fiscal assoupli** a more flexible system of taxation.
II s'assouplir *vpr* **1** (devenir moins rigide) [*cuir*] to become supple; [*chaussures*] to soften up; [*linge, lainage*] to get softer; [*corps, membres*] to become more supple; fig [*caractère, personne*] to become more accommodating; **2** (devenir moins strict) [*règlement*] to become more relaxed; [*régime politique*] to relax; [*méthode, système*] to become more flexible; [*position, attitude*] to become less rigid.

assouplissant, **~e** /asuplisɑ̃, ɑ̃t/ **I** *adj* **liquide** or **produit ~** fabric softener.
II *nm* fabric softener.

assouplissement /asuplismɑ̃/ *nm* **1** (de cuir, lainage) softening; (de linge) conditioning; **2** Sport **faire des ~s** or **des exercices d'~** to limber up; **3** (de règlement, politique, attitude) relaxing; **s'attendre à un ~ de la politique d'austérité** to expect a relaxation of the austerity measures; **prendre des mesures d'~ des horaires de travail** to take steps to make working hours more flexible.

assouplisseur /asuplisœʀ/ *nm* fabric conditioner.

assourdir /asuʀdiʀ/ [3] **I** *vtr* **1** (rendre sourd) to deafen [*personne*]; **2** (atténuer) [*tapis, rideau, neige*] to muffle [*bruit*]; **la musique nous parvenait assourdie** muffled music reached us.
II s'assourdir *vpr* **1** [*bruit*] to become muffled; **2** Phon to become voiceless.

assourdissant, **~e** /asuʀdisɑ̃, ɑ̃t/ *adj* **1** [*bruit*] deafening; **2** [*bavard, discours*] tiresome.

assourdissement /asuʀdismɑ̃/ *nm* **1** (de personne) (action) deafening; (état) temporary deafness; **2** (de bruit) muffling; **3** Phon devoicing.

assouvir /asuviʀ/ [3] *vtr* to satisfy [*faim, désir, curiosité*]; to assuage [*colère, passion*]; **~ sa vengeance** to satisfy one's desire for vengeance.

assouvissement /asuvismɑ̃/ *nm* **1** (action) (de faim, désir, curiosité) satisfying; (de colère) assuaging; **2** (résultat) satisfaction.

assuétude /asɥetyd/ *nf* **1** (tolérance) tolerance; **2** (dépendance) addiction.

assujetti, **~e** /asyʒeti/ **I** *adj* **~ à** liable for; **les personnes ~es à l'impôt sur le revenu** persons liable for income tax; **être ~ à la sécurité sociale** to be obliged to participate in the French national health and pensions system.
II *nm,f* (à un impôt) person liable for tax; (à une cotisation) contributor.

assujettir /asyʒetiʀ/ [3] **I** *vtr* **1** (astreindre) to subject (**à** to); **2** (soumettre) to subjugate, to subdue [*pays, peuple*]; **un peuple assujetti** a subjugated people; **~ qn par la violence** to subdue sb by violence; **3** (fixer) to secure [*étagère, chargement*].
II s'assujettir *vpr* [*personne*] to submit (**à** to).

assujettissant, **~e** /asyʒetisɑ̃, ɑ̃t/ *adj* fml [*travail, tâche*] demanding; [*devoirs*] exacting.

assujettissement /asyʒetismɑ̃/ *nm* subjection (**à** to); **~ à l'impôt** Fisc liability for tax.

assumer /asyme/ [1] **I** *vtr* **1** (prendre en charge) to take [*responsabilité*]; to hold [*fonctions*]; to meet [*coûts, dépenses*]; **il assume la gestion de l'entreprise** he manages the firm on his own; **je ne peux ~ seul les frais de son éducation** I can't take on the cost of his/her education on my own; **2** (accepter) to come to terms with [*condition, identité, passé*]; to accept [*conséquences*]; **elle a du mal à ~ sa maternité** she's finding it difficult to accept that she's become a mother.
II○ *vi* to cope.
III s'assumer *vpr* to come to terms with oneself.

assurable /asyʀabl/ *adj* insurable; **non ~** uninsurable.

assurage /asyʀaʒ/ *nm* Sport belay.

assurance /asyʀɑ̃s/ *nf* **1** (aisance, aplomb) (self-)confidence, self-assurance; (maîtrise) assurance; **avoir** or **montrer de l'~** to be self-confident; **prendre de l'~** to gain confidence, to become more confident; **perdre (de) sa belle ~** to lose (some of) one's self-confidence; **regard/air plein d'~** confident look/appearance; **avec ~** confidently; **2** (promesse) assurance; (certitude) certainty; **obtenir** or **recevoir l'~ que** to be assured that; **donner à qn l'~ que** to assure sb that; **donnez-moi l'~ que** give me your assurance that; **il n'a accepté de partir qu'avec l'~ que** he agreed to leave only on the assurance that; **avoir l'~ de perdre/gagner** to be certain to lose/win; **il est innocent, j'en ai l'~** I'm convinced or certain that he is innocent; **ils avaient l'~ de ne pas être dérangés** they could be sure of not being disturbed; **veuillez agréer l'~ de mes sentiments distingués/ma considération** (à une personne nommée) yours sincerely; (à une personne non nommée) yours faithfully; **3** Assur (garantie) insurance (**contre** against); (contrat) insurance (policy); (compagnie) insurance company; (prime) insurance (premium); (secteur) **l'~**, **les ~s** insurance; **~ sur la vie** life insurance; **contracter** or **souscrire une ~ contre l'incendie** to take out insurance ou to insure against fire; **avoir une bonne ~** to be well insured; **4** Prot Soc (prestations) benefit ₵ GB, benefits (*pl*) US; **5** (en alpinisme) belaying.
■ **~ automobile** car insurance; **~ chômage** (système) unemployment insurance; (prestations) unemployment benefit GB ou benefits (*pl*) US; **~ incendie** fire insurance; **~ individuelle accident** personal accident insurance; **~ maladie** (système) health insurance; (prestations) sickness benefit GB ou benefits (*pl*) US; **~ maritime** marine insurance; **~ maternité** maternity benefit GB ou benefits (*pl*) US; **~ mixte** endowment policy ou insurance; **~ multirisque** comprehensive insurance; **~ multirisque habitation** comprehensive household insurance; **~ mutuelle** (association) mutual insurance society; **~ responsabilité civile** third-party insurance; **~ scolaire** pupil's personal accident insurance; **~s sociales** social insurance ₵; **~ au tiers** third-party insurance; **~ tous risques** comprehensive insurance; **~ vieillesse** state pension; **~ voyage** travel insurance.

assurance-crédit, *pl* **assurances-crédit** /asyʀɑ̃skʀedi/ *nf* credit insurance.

assurance-vie, *pl* **assurances-vie** /asyʀɑ̃svi/ *nf* life insurance.

assuré, **~e** /asyʀe/ **I** *pp* ▶ **assurer**.
II *pp adj* **1** (sûr) [*personne*] sure, certain; **être ~ de qch/de trouver qch** to be sure ou certain of sth/of finding sth; **~ qu'il était de ne jamais les revoir** since he was sure ou certain he would never see them again; **elle se dit ~e du succès de l'entreprise** she says she is sure ou certain that the venture will succeed; **se sentir mal ~ de l'avenir** to feel uncertain of the future; **tenir qch pour ~** to take sth as certain, to be certain ou confident of sth; **75% des voix leur sont ~es** they are sure of 75% of the vote; **soyez ~ de ma reconnaissance** I am very grateful to you; **2** Assur [*personne, marchandise*] insured; **la personne ~e** the insured party; **non ~** uninsured.
III *adj* **1** (plein d'assurance) [*démarche, air*] confident; [*main*] steady; **dit-il d'une voix ~e** or **d'un ton ~** he said confidently; **mal ~** [*pas, main*] unsteady; [*geste, ton*] nervous; [*voix*] unsteady, trembling; **sa démarche est encore mal ~e** he's/she's still rather unsteady on his/her legs; **2** (garanti) [*échec, réussite*] certain; [*situation, succès*] assured; **il a son avenir ~ dans l'entreprise** his future in the firm is assured; **avoir la subsistance ~e** to have a secure livelihood; **leur statut professionnel est mal ~** their professional status is rather shaky; **maintenant que sa collaboration nous est ~e** now that we are sure of his/her cooperation; **opération dont la réussite est ~e** operation which is sure to succeed, sure-fire operation.
IV *nm,f* Assur insured party.
■ **~ social** Prot Soc social insurance contributor.

assurément /asyʀemɑ̃/ *adv* gén definitely; (pour autoriser) most certainly; **tu n'as ~ rien à leur envier** you definitely have no reason to envy them; **~ pas** gén definitely not; (pour refuser) certainly not.

assurer /asyʀe/ [1] **I** *vtr* **1** (affirmer) **~ à qn que** to assure sb that; **cela marchera, m'assura-t-il** he assured me it would work; **le journal assure qu'il est mort** the paper claims that he's dead; **ce n'est pas drôle, je t'assure** believe me, it's no joke; **qu'est-ce que tu es maladroit, je t'assure**○**!** you really are clumsy!; **2** (faire part à) **~ qn de** to assure sb of [*affection, soutien*]; **3** Assur to insure [*biens*] (**contre** against); **~ sa voiture contre le vol/qn sur la vie** to insure one's car against theft/sb's life; **4** (effectuer) to carry out [*maintenance, tâche*]; to provide [*service*]; (prendre en charge) to see to [*livraison*]; **ils n'assurent que les réparations urgentes** they only carry out urgent repairs; **le service après-vente est assuré par nos soins** we provide the after-sales service; **~ l'approvisionnement en eau d'une ville** to supply a town with water; **le service ne sera pas assuré demain** there will be no service tomorrow; **sa propulsion est assurée par deux turboréacteurs** it is propelled by two turbojets; **le centre assure la conservation des embryons** the centre[GB] stores embryos; **~ la liaison entre** [*train, car*] to run between; [*ferry*] to sail between; [*compagnie*] to operate between; **un vol quotidien assure la liaison entre les capitales** a daily flight links the two capitals;

~ la gestion/défense/sauvegarde de to manage/to defend/to safeguard; **~ sa propre défense** Jur to conduct one's own defence[GB]; **~ les fonctions de directeur/président** to be director/chairman; **5** (garantir) to ensure [*bonheur, gloire*]; to ensure, to secure [*victoire, paix, promotion*]; to give [*monopole, revenu*]; (par des efforts, une intervention) to secure [*droit, situation*] (**à qn** for sb); to assure [*position, avenir*]; to protect [*frontière*]; **pour ~ le succès commercial** (in order) to ensure commercial success; **cela ne suffira pas à ~ son élection** that won't get him/her elected; **il est là pour ~ la bonne marche du projet** his role is to make sure ou to ensure that the project runs smoothly; **~ sa qualification en finale** to get into the final; **ce rachat assure à l'entreprise le monopole** the takeover gives the company a guaranteed monopoly; **il veut leur ~ une vieillesse paisible** he wants to give them a peaceful old age; **mon travail m'assure un revenu confortable** my job provides me with ou gives me a comfortable income; **il assure une rente à son fils** he gives his son an allowance; **le soutien de la gauche lui a assuré la victoire** the support of the left secured his/her victory; **il a réussi à leur ~ un poste** he managed to secure a position for them; **l'exposition devrait ~ 800 emplois** the exhibition ought to create 800 jobs; **~ ses vieux jours** to provide for one's old age; **6** (rendre stable) to steady [*escabeau*]; (fixer) to secure [*corde*]; to fasten [*volet*]; **~ son pas** to steady oneself; **7** Sport (ne pas risquer) **~ une balle/un service** to play a safe ball/service; **8** Sport (en alpinisme) to belay [*grimpeur*].

II *vi* **1**○ (être à la hauteur) to be up to the mark○, to be up to snuff○ US; **~ en chimie** to be good at chemistry; **~ avec les filles** to have a way with the girls; **2** Sport to play it safe.

III **s'assurer** *vpr* **1** (vérifier) **s'~ de qch** to make sure of sth, to check on sth; **s'~ que** to make sure that, to check that; **il vaut mieux s'~ de leur présence** we had better check that they're there; **je vais m'en ~** I'll make sure, I'll check; **2** (se procurer) to secure [*avantage, bien, aide, monopole*]; **s'~ les services de** to enlist the services of; **s'~ une bonne retraite** to arrange to get a good pension; **s'~ une position de repli** to make sure one has a fall-back position; **3** Assur to take out insurance (**contre** against); **s'~ contre l'incendie/sur la vie** to take out fire/life insurance; **4** (se prémunir) **s'~ contre** to insure against [*éventualité, risque*]; **5** (se stabiliser) [*voix*] to steady; [*personne*] to steady oneself; **s'~ en selle** Équit to steady oneself in the saddle; **6** Sport (en alpinisme) to belay oneself; **7**† (se rendre sûr de) **s'~ de qn/de qch** to make sure of sb/about sth.

assureur /asyʀœʀ/ **▶510** *nm* (contractant) underwriter; (intermédiaire) insurance agent; (compagnie) insurance company.

■ **~ conseil** insurance adviser ou consultant.

Assyrie /asiʀi/ *nprf* Assyria.

assyrien, **-ienne** /asiʀjɛ̃, ɛn/ **▶462** I *adj* [*personne, ville, style, art*] Assyrian.

II *nm* Ling Assyrian.

Assyrien, **-ienne** /asiʀjɛ̃, ɛn/ *nm,f* Assyrian.

astasie /astasi/ **▶271** *nf* astasia.

aster /astɛʀ/ *nm* aster.

astérie /asteʀi/ *nf* starfish.

astérisque /asteʀisk/ *nm* asterisk; **marqué d'un ~** asterisked.

astéroïde /asteʀɔid/ *nm* asteroid.

asthénie /asteni/ *nf* asthenia.

asthénique /astenik/ *adj, nmf* asthenic.

asthmatique /asmatik/ *adj, nmf* asthmatic.

asthme /asm/ **▶271** *nm* asthma; **avoir une crise d'~** to have an asthma attack.

asticot /astiko/ *nm* maggot.

asticoter○ /astikɔte/ [1] *vtr* to needle○ [*personne*]; **cesse de m'~**○ stop needling○ me; **il m'a asticoté jusqu'à ce que j'accepte** he goaded me into accepting.

astigmate /astigmat/ *adj* astigmatic.

astigmatisme /astigmatism/ *nm* astigmatism.

astiquage /astikaʒ/ *nm* polishing.

astiquer /astike/ [1] *vtr* to polish.

astragale /astʀagal/ *nm* **1** Bot astragalus, milk vetch; **2** Archit astragal; **3** Anat astragalus.

astrakan /astʀakɑ̃/ *nm* astrakhan; **manteau d'~** astrakhan coat.

astral, **~e**, *mpl* **-aux** /astʀal, o/ *adj* astral.

astre /astʀ/ *nm* star; **l'~ du jour** liter the sun; **l'~ de la nuit** the moon.

astreignant, **~e** /astʀɛɲɑ̃, ɑ̃t/ *adj* [*tâche, horaires*] demanding; [*discipline, mesures*] strict.

astreindre /astʀɛ̃dʀ/ [55] I *vtr* **~ qn à qch** [*personne*] to force sth upon sb; [*réglementation*] to bind sb to sth; **être astreint au secret professionnel** to be bound by the rules of professional confidentiality; **mon taux de cholestérol m'astreint à un régime sévère** my high cholesterol level keeps me on a strict diet; **~ qn à faire** to compel sb to do.

II **s'astreindre** *vpr* **s'~ à qch** to subject oneself to sth; **s'~ à faire** (par autodiscipline) to make oneself do; (par obligation) to force oneself to do.

astreinte /astʀɛ̃t/ *nf* **1** Jur periodic penalty payment, daily fine for delay (*in performance of contract or in payment of debt*); **2** liter (contrainte) constraint.

astringent, **~e** /astʀɛ̃ʒɑ̃, ɑ̃t/ *adj* astringent.

astrolabe /astʀɔlab/ *nm* astrolabe.

astrologie /astʀɔlɔʒi/ *nf* astrology.

astrologique /astʀɔlɔʒik/ *adj* astrological.

astrologue /astʀɔlɔg/ **▶510** *nmf* astrologer.

astronaute /astʀonot/ **▶510** *nmf* astronaut.

astronautique /astʀonotik/ *nf* astronautics (+ *v sg*).

astronef /astʀonɛf/ *nm* spacecraft.

astronome /astʀonɔm/ **▶510** *nmf* astronomer.

astronomie /astʀonɔmi/ *nf* astronomy.

astronomique /astʀonɔmik/ *adj* lit, fig astronomical.

astrophysicien, **-ienne** /astʀofizisjɛ̃, ɛn/ **▶510** *nm,f* astrophysicist.

astrophysique /astʀofizik/ I *adj* astrophysical.

II *nf* astrophysics (+ *v sg*).

astuce /astys/ *nf* **1** (ingéniosité) gén cleverness; (sagacité) shrewdness, astuteness; **être plein d'~** [*enfant*] to be very clever; **avoir beaucoup d'~** [*adulte*] to be extremely shrewd; **2** (truc) trick; **il doit y avoir une ~** there must be some trick to it; **toute l'~ consiste à faire** the trick's in doing; **une ~ juridique** a crafty legal manoeuvre GB ou maneuver US; **3** (jeu de mots) pun; (plaisanterie) joke; **~ vaseuse** awful pun.

astucieusement /astysjøzmɑ̃/ *adv* (ingénieusement) cleverly; (avec sagacité) shrewdly.

astucieux, **-ieuse** /astysjø, øz/ *adj* (ingénieux) clever; (sagace) sharp, shrewd.

asymétrie /asimetʀi/ *nf* asymmetry.

asymétrique /asimetʀik/ *adj* asymmetrical.

asymptomatique /asɛ̃ptɔmatik/ *adj* asymptomatic.

asymptote /asɛ̃ptɔt/ I *adj* asymptotic (**à** to).

II *nf* asymptote; **en ~** asymptotically.

asynchrone /asɛ̃kʀon/ *adj* asynchronous.

asyndète /asɛ̃dɛt/ *nf* asyndeton.

atavique /atavik/ *adj* atavistic.

atavisme /atavism/ *nm* atavism.

ataxie /ataksi/ *nf* ataxia.

■ **~ cérébellaire** cerebellar ataxia; **~ locomotrice** locomotor ataxia.

atchoum /atʃum/ *nm* (*also onomat*) atishoo.

atèle /atɛl/ *nm* spider monkey.

atelier /atəlje/ *nm* **1** (local) (d'artisan, de bricoleur) workshop; (d'artiste) studio; (de couturier) design studio; **2** Ind (dans usine) shop, workshop; **~ de réparation/montage** repair/assembly shop; **3** (groupe de travail) working group; (séance de travail) workshop; **4** Art (groupe autour d'un maître) studio; **l'~ de David** the studio of David; **œuvre d'~** studio work.

■ **~ protégé** Jur training centre[GB] for the disabled.

atermoiement /atɛʀmwamɑ̃/ *nm* procrastination ¢; **après bien des ~s** after much procrastination.

atermoyer /atɛʀmwaje/ [23] *vi* to procrastinate.

athée /ate/ I *adj* atheistic.

II *nmf* atheist.

athéisme /ateism/ *nm* atheism.

Athènes /atɛn/ **▶857** *npr* Athens.

athénien, **-ienne** /atenjɛ̃, ɛn/ *adj* Athenian.

Athénien, **-ienne** /atenjɛ̃, ɛn/ *nm,f* Athenian.

athérome /ateʀom/ **▶271** *nm* atheroma.

athérosclérose /ateʀɔskleʀoz/ **▶271** *nf* atherosclerosis.

athlète /atlɛt/ *nmf* athlete; **c'est un bel ~** he's a splendid athlete; **carrure/corps d'~** athletic build/body.

athlétique /atletik/ *adj* athletic.

athlétisme /atletism/ **▶449** *nm* athletics (+ *v sg*) GB, track and field events; **championnat d'~** athletics championship GB, track and field championship US; **~ en salle** indoor athletics GB, indoor track and field events; **faire de l'~** to do athletics.

atlante /atlɑ̃t/ *nm* Archit telamon, atlas.

Atlantide /atlɑ̃tid/ *nprf* **l'~** Atlantis.

atlantique /atlɑ̃tik/ *adj* Atlantic.

Atlantique /atlɑ̃tik/ **▶555** *nprm* **l'(océan) ~** the Atlantic (Ocean).

atlantisme /atlɑ̃tism/ *nm* Atlanticism.

atlantiste /atlɑ̃tist/ *adj, nmf* Atlanticist.

atlas /atlas/ *nm inv* **1** (livre) atlas; **2** (vertèbre) atlas.

Atlas /atlas/ *nprm* Géog, Mythol Atlas.

atmosphère /atmɔsfɛʀ/ *nf* lit, fig atmosphere; **j'ai besoin de changer d'~** I need a change of air.

atmosphérique /atmɔsfeʀik/ *adj* atmospheric.

atoll /atɔl/ *nm* atoll; **l'~ de Mururoa** (the) Mururoa atoll; **sur un ~ du Pacifique** on an atoll in the Pacific.

atome /atom/ *nm* (particule, système) atom; **un ~ d'hydrogène** a hydrogen atom.

IDIOMES **ne pas avoir un ~ de bon sens/courage** not to have an ounce of common sense/courage; **avoir des ~s crochus avec qn**○ to hit it off with sb○.

atomique /atɔmik/ *adj* [*énergie, centrale, arme*] nuclear; [*bombe, nombre, structure*] atomic.

atomisation /atɔmizasjɔ̃/ *nf* **1** (de pouvoir, parti, société) fragmentation, atomization; **2** (destruction) nuclear annihilation.

atomiser /atɔmize/ [1] I *vtr* **1** (détruire) to annihilate [sth] with nuclear weapons [*ville*]; **2** (morceler) to shatter [*pouvoir*]; to fragment [*secteur, parti*]; to annihilate [*concurrence*]; **3** Nucl to atomize [*corps, métal*].

II **s'atomiser** *vpr* [*parti, État, pouvoir*] to fragment.

atomiseur /atɔmizœʀ/ *nm* spray, atomizer; **~ à parfum** perfume spray ou atomizer.

atomisme /atɔmism/ *nm* atomism.

atomiste /atɔmist/ I *adj* **1** Nucl [*savant, cher-*

cheur] nuclear; [*structure, théorie*] atomic; **2** Philos atomist.

II *nmf* **1** ▶**510** Nucl nuclear ou atomic scientist; **2** Philos atomist.

atonal, **~e** /atɔnal/ *adj* atonal.

atonalité /atɔnalite/ *nf* atonality.

atone /atɔn/ *adj* **1** (apathique) [*vie, pays, groupe*] apathetic; [*personne*] lifeless; **2** (inexpressif) expressionless; **3** Méd atonic; **4** Phon unstressed, unaccented.

atonie /atɔni/ *nf* **1** (de personne, pouvoir, marché) sluggishness, apathy; (de regard, voix) lifelessness; **2** Phon, Méd atony.

atonique /atɔnik/ *adj* atonic.

atours† /atuʀ/ *nmpl* finery ₵; **mettre ses plus beaux ~** to deck oneself out in all one's finery.

atout /atu/ *nm* **1** Jeux (carte) trump; (couleur) trumps (*pl*); **le valet/dix d'~** the jack/ten of trumps; **~ maître** master trump; **c'est ~ cœur** hearts are trumps; **avoir de l'~** to have trumps ou trump cards; **jouer ~** to play a trump; (en début de partie) to lead trumps; **deux sans ~** two no trumps; **2** fig (avantage) asset; (avantage sur les autres) trump card; **ton principal ~, c'est ton charme** your greatest asset is your charm; **jouer son ~/son dernier ~** to play one's trump card/one's last card; **~ supplémentaire** additional advantage; **avoir tous les ~s en main** or **dans son jeu** to hold all the aces; **avoir un ~ en réserve** to have an ace up one's sleeve; **mettre tous les ~s dans son jeu** to leave nothing to chance.
■ **~ sec** singleton trump.

ATP /atepe/ *nf* **1** Sport (*abbr* = **association des tennismen professionnels**) APT; **2** Biol (*abbr* = **adénosinetriphosphate**) ATP.

atrabilaire† /atʀabilɛʀ/ *adj* bad-tempered, atrabilious sout.

âtre /ɑtʀ/ *nm* hearth.

Atrée /atʀe/ *npr* Atreus.

Atrides /atʀid/ *nprmpl* **les ~** the Atreids.

atrium /atʀijɔm/ *nm* atrium.

atroce /atʀɔs/ *adj* **1** (horrible) [*blessure, sentiment, nouvelle*] dreadful; [*souffrance, douleur*] atrocious; [*peur*] terrible; [*supplice*] horrific; [*crime, vengeance, mort*] horrible; [*acte, spectacle*] horrifying; **2**○ (mauvais) [*nourriture, temps, accent*] atrocious, appalling; **il est d'une ~ bêtise** he's appallingly stupid; **tu es ~!** you are dreadful!

atrocement /atʀɔsmɑ̃/ *adv* **1** (horriblement) [*mutiler*] dreadfully; [*souffrir*] horribly, terribly; [*punir*] horribly; **mourir ~** to die a horrible death; **j'ai ~ mal** I'm in agony; **elle a ~ mal aux dents** she has a dreadful toothache; **2**○ (excessivement) [*ennuyeux, bête*] dreadfully, terribly; [*laid*] atrociously.

atrocité /atʀɔsite/ *nf* **1** (caractère) atrocity; **2** (crime) atrocity; **3** (calomnie) **dire des ~s sur qn** to say dreadful things about sb; **4**○ (chose laide) hideous monstrosity; **5** (laideur) **c'est d'une ~!** it's absolutely hideous!

atrophie /atʀɔfi/ *nf* (tous contextes) atrophy.

atrophier /atʀɔfje/ [2] **I** *vtr* Méd, fig to atrophy.
II s'atrophier *vpr* **1** Méd to atrophy; **bras atrophié** wasted arm; **2** fig [*facultés*] to atrophy; [*économie, marché, secteur industriel*] to decline; **une industrie atrophiée** an industry that has declined.

atropine /atʀɔpin/ *nf* atropine.

attabler: **s'attabler** /atable/ [1] *vpr* to sit down at the table; **être attablé** to be sitting at table.

attachant, **~e** /ataʃɑ̃, ɑ̃t/ *adj* [*personne*] charming, engaging; [*caractère*] charming; [*animal*] sweet.

attache /ataʃ/ *nf* **1** gén tie; (ficelle) string; (corde) rope; (courroie) strap; **être à l'~** [*animal*] to be tied up; [*bateau*] to be moored; **2** Anat (articulation) joint; (de muscle) point of attachment; **avoir des ~s fines** to have delicate ankles and wrists; **3** (lien) tie; **il n'a aucune ~ nulle part** he has no ties anywhere; **il a des ~s en Normandie** he has ties in Normandy.
■ **~ parisienne** paper fastener.

attaché, **~e** /ataʃe/ ▶**510** **I** *pp* ▶ **attacher**.
II *pp adj* (lié par l'affection) **être ~ à** to be attached to [*personne, animal, idée, lien*].
III *nm,f* attaché; **~ militaire/culturel/commercial** military/cultural/commercial attaché; **~ d'ambassade** attaché.
■ **~ d'administration** administrative assistant; **~ de presse** press attaché.

attaché-case /ataʃekɛs/ *nm* attaché case.

attachement /ataʃmɑ̃/ *nm* **1** (sentimental) attachment (**à** to); **2** (de principe) commitment (**à** to).

attacher /ataʃe/ [1] **I** *vtr* **1** (joindre à l'aide d'un lien) to tie [*personne*] (**à** to); (avec une corde, laisse) to tie [*chien*] (**à** to); (avec une chaîne) to chain [*chien*] (**à** to); to lock [*bicyclette*] (**à** to); to tether, to fasten [*laisse, corde*] (**à** to); **~ les mains/pieds de qn** to tie sb's hands/feet; **~ ses cheveux** to tie one's hair back; **2** (entourer d'un lien) to tie up [*personne, paquet, colis*]; **~ des lettres avec un élastique** to tie up letters with an elastic band; **~ qn à un poteau** to tie sb to a stake; **~ ses lacets** to tie (up) one's laces; **~ ses chaussures** to do up one's shoes; **3** (fermer) to fasten [*ceinture, collier, vêtement*]; **veuillez ~ vos ceintures** please fasten your seat belts; **n'oublie pas d'~ ton vélo** don't forget to lock your bike; **4** (accorder) **~ de l'importance à qch** to attach importance to sth; **~ du prix** or **de la valeur à qch** to attach great value to sth; **~ une signification à un geste/un regard** to read something into a gesture/an expression; **5** (employer) **~ qn à son service** to take sb into one's service, to employ sb; **6** (associer) **les privilèges attachés à un poste** the privileges attached to a post; **médecin attaché à un hôpital** Admin doctor attached to a hospital; **~ son nom à une découverte/un événement** to link one's name to a discovery/an event; **son nom est attaché à cette découverte** his/her name is linked to ou associated with this discovery.
II *vi* [*aliment, plat, récipient*] to stick (**à** to); **le sucre a attaché au fond de la casserole** the sugar stuck to the bottom of the pan; **cette poêle n'attache pas** this is a nonstick frying-pan.
III s'attacher *vpr* **1** (se fixer par un lien) to fasten, to do up; **robe qui s'attache par derrière** dress which fastens ou does up at the back; **2** (s'accrocher) **le lierre s'attache aux pierres** ivy clings to stones; **s'~ aux pas de qn** to dog sb's footsteps; **3** (s'efforcer) **s'~ à faire** to set out to do; **s'~ à analyser/prouver/démontrer qch** to set out to analyse[GB]/to prove/to demonstrate sth; **4** (se lier affectivement) **s'~ à qn/qch** to become attached to sb/sth, to grow fond of sb/sth.

attaquable /atakabl/ *adj* **1** [*lieu, place*] **facilement/difficilement ~** easy/difficult to attack; **la ville n'est ~ que par le sud** the town can only be attacked from the south; **2** [*théorie, position*] shaky; **3** [*testament*] contestable.

attaquant, **~e** /atakɑ̃, ɑ̃t/ *nm,f* **1** Mil attacker; **2** Sport gén attacker; (au football) striker; **3** Fin raider.

attaque /atak/ *nf* **1** Mil attack; **~ aérienne/terrestre** air/land attack; **~ surprise** surprise attack; **~ en force** attack in force; **passer à l'~** to move onto the attack; **lancer une ~** to launch an attack (**contre** on); **à l'~!** charge!; **2** (crime) (de banque, magasin) raid; (de personne) attack; **~ à main armée** armed raid; **3** fig (critique) attack; **il s'est livré à une ~ en règle contre la presse** he launched into a full-scale attack on the press; **pas d'~s personnelles!** no personal comments!; **4** Méd (d'apoplexie) stroke; (cardiaque) attack; **5** Sport (au football, rugby) break; (en course) spurt; (au tennis, golf) drive; (en alpinisme) attempt; (à la rame) beginning of a stroke; **l'ailier a un bon jeu d'~/est reparti à l'~** the winger GB ou wing US has a good attacking style/is attacking again; **6** Mus striking up.
IDIOMES **être** or **se sentir d'~/tout à fait d'~** to feel on GB ou in US form/on GB ou in US top form; **être** or **se sentir (assez) d'~ pour faire qch** to feel up to doing sth; **je ne me sens pas très d'~ le matin** I don't feel too lively in the morning.

attaquer /atake/ [1] **I** *vtr* **1** Mil to attack [*troupe, pays*]; **~ de front/par derrière/sur tous les fronts** to attack from the front/from behind/on all sides; **nous avons été attaqués par surprise** a surprise attack was made on us; **nos positions sont attaquées au sud** our positions are under attack from the south; **2** (agresser) to attack [*personne*]; to raid [*banque, magasin, train*]; **'attaque!' dit-il à son chien** 'at 'em' GB ou 'sic!' US he said to his dog; **3** (critiquer) to attack [*ministre, projet*]; **4** Jur to contest [*contrat, testament*]; **~ qn en justice** to bring an action against sb GB, to lawsuit sb US; **5** (dégrader) [*produit chimique, médicament*] to attack; **6** (commencer) to launch into [*discours*]; to make a start on [*lecture, rédaction*]; to get going on [*tâche*]; to attack [*plat, dessert*]; to attempt [*escalade*]; **7** (affronter) to tackle [*problème, difficulté*]; **8** Mus to strike up [*air*]; to attack [*note*].
II *vi* **1** Sport (au football, rugby) to break; (au tennis, golf) to drive; [*coureur*] to put on a spurt; **2** (commencer) to begin (brusquely); **'personne ne possède la vérité,' attaqua-t-il** 'nobody has an exclusive right to the truth,' he began brusquely.
III s'attaquer *vpr* **s'~ à** to attack [*personne, œuvre, politique*]; to make a start on [*tâche, lecture*]; to tackle [*problème, difficulté*]; **tu t'attaques à plus fort que toi** you're taking on sb who is more than a match for you.

attardé, **~e** /ataʀde/ **I** *pp* ▶ **attarder**.
II *pp adj* **1** (en retard) late; **quelques passants ~s** some people out late; **2** pej (démodé) [*idées, personne*] old-fashioned; **3** pej (mentalement déficient) [*personne*] retarded.
III *nm,f* pej (handicapé mental) mentally retarded person.

attarder /ataʀde/ [1] **I** *vtr* (mettre en retard) to delay [*personne*]; **être attardé par qch** to be delayed by sth.
II s'attarder *vpr* **1** lit (rester) to stay; (traîner) to linger; **ne t'attarde pas au bureau** don't stay too late at the office; **je me suis attardée en chemin** I lingered on my way; **la caméra s'attarde sur un visage** the camera lingers on a face; **2** fig (s'arrêter) to take one's time; **s'~ sur** to dwell on [*contenu, point, aspect, chiffres*]; **je suis navré de m'~ sur ce point** I'm really sorry at having to dwell on this point; **s'~ à expliquer/examiner** to spend time explaining/examining.

atteindre /atɛ̃dʀ/ [55] **I** *vtr* **1** (arriver à) to reach [*lieu, âge*]; to reach [*niveau, valeur, somme, vitesse*]; [*personne, réforme*] to achieve [*but*]; [*projectile*] to reach [*but, cible*]; **la température peut ~ 30° à l'ombre** the temperature can get up to ou reach 30° in the shade; **arbre qui peut ~ 40 mètres** tree which can grow up to 40 metres[GB] high; **~ des proportions massives** to reach huge proportions; **2** (frapper) [*projectile, tireur*] to hit [*personne, animal, cible*]; **3** (affecter) [*maladie, malheur*] (de façon durable) to affect [*personne, groupe*]; (brusquement) to hit [*personne, groupe*]; [*parole blessante*] to affect [*personne*]; **ses critiques ne m'atteignent pas** I'm impervious to his/her criticism; **~ qn dans son honneur** to cast a slur on sb's honour[GB]; ▶ **crapaud**; **4** (toucher) to reach [*public*].
II atteindre à fml *vtr ind* to achieve [*connaissance, style, succès*].

atteint, **~e** /atɛ̃, ɛ̃t/ **I** *pp* ▶ **atteindre**.
II *pp adj* **1** (affecté) affected (**de, par** by); **les personnes légèrement/gravement ~es** the people slightly/seriously affected; **une région très ~e par la pollution** a region badly affected by pollution; **être ~ de** (de façon durable) to be suffering from [*maladie*]; **les plus ~s** the worst affected; **2** (frappé) hit (**de/par** by); **un passant ~ d'une balle/par un éclat d'obus** a passer-by hit by a bullet/by shrapnel; **3**○ (timbré) **être ~** to be touched○; **un peu ~** a bit touched (*jamais épith*); **complètement ~** off one's rocker○ (*jamais épith*).
III atteinte *nf* **1** (attaque) **~e à** attack on; **il considérait cela comme une ~e à sa virilité** he considered it an attack on his virility; **hors d'~e** [*personne, paix, poste*] beyond reach; [*cible*] out of range; [*rester, sembler*] out of reach; **porter ~e à** to undermine [*crédit, prestige, dignité*]; to damage [*réputation, honneur*]; to endanger [*sécurité, sûreté*]; to infringe [*droit*]; to threaten [*région, environnement*]; **~e aux droits de l'Homme** infringement of human rights; **~e à la liberté/aux droits** (**de l'individu**) Jur infringement of civil liberties/of personal rights; **~e à l'ordre public** Jur public order offence[GB]; **~e à la sécurité** or **sûreté de l'État** Jur breach of national security; **~e à la vie privée** Jur breach of the right to privacy; **2** (affection) problem; **~e pulmonaire** lung problem; **~e de** attack of; **les ~es du froid** the effects of cold; **les premières ~es de la maladie** the onset ou first effects of the disease.

attelage /atlaʒ/ *nm* **1** (système) (de cheval) harness; (de bœuf) yoke; (de wagon) coupling; (de remorque) towing attachment; (de fusée) docking ou coupling device; **2** (animaux) (de chevaux, chiens, bœufs) team; (de deux bœufs) yoke; **3** (équipage) horse-drawn carriage; **~ à deux/quatre chevaux** carriage and pair/four GB, two-/four-horse carriage; **4** (sport) **l'~** (carriage) driving; **5** (action, manière d'atteler) (de cheval) harnessing; (de bœuf) yoking; (de remorque) hitching up; (de wagon) coupling.

atteler /atle/ [19] **I** *vtr* (attacher) to harness [*cheval*] (**à** to); to yoke [*bœuf*]; to hitch up [*remorque*] (**à** to); to couple [*wagon*] (**à** to); **~ deux wagons ensemble** to couple two carriages (together); **~ qn à une tâche** fig to put sb on a job; **~ une charrette à un cheval** or **un cheval à une charrette** to harness a horse to a cart; **le cocher n'a pas attelé** the coachman hasn't harnessed up; **charrette attelée** harnessed cart.
II s'atteler *vpr* **s'~ à une tâche/à faire** to get down to a job/to doing.

attelle /atɛl/ *nf* Méd splint; **mettre des ~s à qn** to put splints on sb.

attenant, **~e** /atnɑ̃, ɑ̃t/ *adj* **1** (accolé) [*pièce*] adjacent (**à** to); **2** (associé) [*problème*] related (**à** to).

attendre /atɑ̃dʀ/ [6] **I** *vtr* **1** (processus qui dure) [*personne*] to wait for [*personne*]; to wait for, to await sout [*événement*]; to wait until ou till [*date*] (**pour faire** to do); **~ l'arrivée de qn** to wait for sb to arrive, to await sb's arrival; **j'attends le bus** I'm waiting for the bus; **j'ai attendu le bus** (**pendant**) **dix minutes** I waited for the bus for ten minutes, I waited ten minutes for the bus; **j'attends le bus depuis dix minutes** I've been waiting for the bus for ten minutes, I've been waiting ten minutes for the bus; **je t'ai attendu jusqu'à 8 heures** I waited for you until 8 o'clock; **~ la fin d'une émission** to wait till the end of a programme[GB]; **n'attends pas demain/la nuit pour le réparer** don't wait until ou till tomorrow/dark to mend it; **~ le bon moment pour agir** to wait for the right moment ou until the time is right to act; **~ la pluie pour semer** to wait for the rain before sowing; **j'attends qu'il finisse** or **ait fini** I'm waiting for him to finish; **j'attends qu'on me serve** or **d'être servi** I'm waiting to be served; **elle n'attendait que ça!** that's just what she was waiting for; **il attend impatiemment Noël/leur départ** he can't wait for Christmas/for them to leave; **il n'attend qu'une chose, c'est de prendre sa retraite** he can't wait to retire; **~ son tour** to wait one's turn; **on n'attend plus qu'elle pour commencer** we're just waiting for her and then we can start; **aller ~ un train/qn au train/qn à la gare** to (go and) meet a train/sb off a train/sb at the station; **attends qu'il écrive pour** or **avant de décider** wait until ou till he writes ou wait for him to write before you decide; **attends d'avoir vu l'autre pour commander** wait until ou till you've seen the other one before you order; **qu'attends-tu pour partir/répondre?** why don't you leave/answer?; **j'attends de voir pour y croire** I'll believe it when I see it; **se faire ~** to keep people waiting; **le serveur/chèque se fait ~** the waiter/cheque GB ou check US is taking a long time ou is a long time coming; **le printemps se fait ~** spring is late, spring is slow to arrive; **la réaction ne se fit pas ~** the reaction was instantaneous; **~ son jour** or **heure** to bide one's time; **reste ici en attendant de trouver mieux/que la pluie cesse/l'heure du départ** stay here until you find sth better/the rain stops/it's time to go; **en attendant mieux** until something better turns up; **où étais-tu, on ne t'attendait plus!** where were you? we'd given up on you!; **si je n'attendais que toi pour m'aider/ça pour vivre!** iron it's a good thing I'm not relying on you to help/that to keep me going!; **c'est là que je l'attends**○! I'm ready and waiting!, I'm right here!; ▶ **ferme**; **2** (être prêt, préparé) [*voiture, taxi*] to be waiting for [*personne*]; [*chambre, appartement*] to be ready for [*personne*]; **une lettre vous attend à la réception** there's a letter (waiting) for you at reception; **un délicieux repas m'attendait** a delicious meal awaited me; **le déjeuner vous attend!** lunch is ready!; **3** (être prévu, prévisible) [*succès, aventure*] to await, to be in store for [*personne*]; **une surprise désagréable les attendait à leur arrivée** there was a nasty surprise awaiting them when they arrived; **je ne sais pas ce qui m'attend** I don't know what's in store for me; **quel avenir nous attend?** what does the future hold (in store) for us?; **un brillant avenir les attendait** a brilliant future lay ahead of them; **les élections sont attendues comme un test** the elections are being viewed as a test; **4** (compter sur) **je les attends pour 5 heures** I'm expecting them at five; **elle attend un bébé** or **un enfant** she's expecting a baby, she's expecting○; **~ qch de qn/qch** to expect sth from sb/sth; **~ de qn qu'il fasse** to expect sb to do; **on attend beaucoup de ce nouveau traitement** great things are expected of this new treatment; **j'attendais mieux de vous** I expected more of you; **j'attendais mieux de ce roman** I found the novel rather disappointing.
II *vi* to wait; (au téléphone) to hold; **attends un instant** wait a moment, hang on (a minute)○; **la ligne est occupée, voulez-vous ~?** the line is engaged GB ou busy US, do you want to hold?; **attends un peu!** wait a moment; (menace) just (you) wait!; **attends voir**○ wait a minute, let's see; **faire ~ qn** to keep sb waiting; **sans plus ~** without further delay; **la lettre attendra** the letter can wait; **ce plat n'attend pas** this dish has to be served immediately; **en attendant** (pendant ce temps) in the meantime; (néanmoins) all the same, nonetheless; **en attendant, je ferai mes courses** in the meantime, I'll do my shopping; **ce n'est peut-être pas grave mais, en attendant, ça fait mal** it may not be serious but all the same it's painful ou it's painful nonetheless; **tu ne perds rien pour ~**○! I'll get you, just you wait!
III s'attendre *vpr* **s'~ à qch/à faire** to expect sth/to do; **je m'attendais au pire/à mieux** I was expecting the worst/something better; **attends-toi à être interrogé** you'll no doubt be grilled; **au moment où je m'y attendais le moins** (just) when I was least expecting it; **s'~ à ce que qn fasse/qch se produise** to expect sb to do/sth to happen; **il fallait s'y ~** it was to be expected; **avec lui, il faut s'~ à tout** with him, anything can happen; **ça alors, si je m'attendais à te retrouver professeur!** I must say I'm surprised to find you in teaching!; **quelle bonne surprise! si je m'attendais**○! what a nice surprise! who would've thought it!; ▶ **cent**.
IDIOMES **tout vient à point pour qui sait ~** Prov everything comes to him who waits Prov.

attendri, **~e** /atɑ̃dʀi/ **I** *pp* ▶ **attendrir**.
II *pp adj* **1** (ému) [*sourire, regard*] fond, tender; **le cœur tout ~** feeling very moved; **être ~ par qch** to be touched ou moved by sth; **2** (viande) tenderized.

attendrir /atɑ̃dʀiʀ/ [3] **I** *vtr* **1** (émouvoir) to touch, to move [*personne*]; to touch [*cœur*]; **se laisser ~** to soften; **tu ne vas pas te laisser ~ par lui!** you're not going to let him soften you up!; **2** Culin to tenderize [*viande*].
II s'attendrir *vpr* **1** (s'émouvoir) [*personne*] to feel moved; **son regard s'attendrit** his/her eyes softened; **s'~ sur qn/soi-même** to feel sorry for sb/oneself; **s'~ sur ses malheurs** to lament one's misfortunes; **2** Culin [*viande*] to become tender.

attendrissant, **~e** /atɑ̃dʀisɑ̃, ɑ̃t/ *adj* [*spectacle, mots*] touching, moving; [*candeur*] endearing; **être ~ de naïveté** to be endearingly naïve.

attendrissement /atɑ̃dʀismɑ̃/ *nm* (affectueux) tenderness; (ému) emotion; **laisser percevoir son ~** to show one's emotion; **pleurer d'~** to be moved to tears; **avec ~** tenderly; **allons, pas d'~!** now, now, let's not get emotional!

attendrisseur /atɑ̃dʀisœʀ/ *nm* tenderizer; **passer qch à l'~** to tenderize sth.

attendu[1] /atɑ̃dy/ **I** *prép* given, considering.
II attendu que *loc conj* given ou considering that; Jur whereas.

attendu[2], **~e** /atɑ̃dy/ **I** *adj* **1** (prévu) [*personne, résultat, réaction*] expected; **2** (souhaité) **le jour/moment** (**tant**) **~** the long-awaited day/moment.
II *nm* Jur **~s d'un jugement** grounds for a decision.

attenir /at(ə)niʀ/ [36] *vi* **~ à** to adjoin.

attentat /atɑ̃ta/ *nm* **1** (contre un individu) assassination attempt (**contre** on); (contre un groupe, bâtiment) attack (**contre** on); **~ terroriste/raciste** terrorist/racist attack; **~ à la bombe** bomb attack; **commettre** or **perpétrer un ~ contre** to carry out an assassination attempt against, to make an attempt on the life of [*individu*]; to carry out an attack against [*groupe, bâtiment*]; **2** Jur **~ à la vie de qn** attempted murder of sb, attempt on sb's life.
■ **~ à la pudeur** Jur indecent assault.

attentatoire /atɑ̃tatwaʀ/ *adj* prejudicial (**à** to).

attente /atɑ̃t/ *nf* **1** (processus) waiting ¢; (période) wait; **l'~ du verdict est angoissante** waiting for the verdict is agonizing; **l'~ n'en finissait pas** the wait was interminable; **il y a deux heures d'~** there's a two-hour wait; **mon ~ a été vaine** I waited in vain ou for nothing; **vivre dans l'~ du facteur** to spend one's life waiting for the postman GB ou mailman US; **vivre dans l'~ des repas** to live in anticipation of the next meal; **dans l'~ de notre rencontre/de vous lire** looking forward to our meeting/to hearing from you; **en ~** [*passager*] waiting; [*dossier, demande, affaire*] pending (*jamais épith*); Télécom [*appel, demandeur*] on hold (*épith, après n*);

commandes en ~ Comm back orders; **le dossier est resté en ~** the file is pending ou is being held over; **employé en ~ de mutation** employee awaiting transfer; **commande en ~ d'exécution** order waiting to be filled; **en ~ de la décision du juge** pending a decision from the judge; **mettre un avion en ~** to stack a plane; **laisser 23 mailles en ~** (au tricot) to leave 23 stitches on a holder; **2** (espoir) expectations (*pl*); **répondre à/dépasser l'~ de qn** to come up to/to exceed sb's expectations; **contrairement à/contre toute ~** contrary to/against all expectations.

attenter /atɑ̃te/ [1] *vtr ind* **~ à** to cast a slur on [*dignité*]; to seek to undermine [*droit*]; to be an affront to [*intelligence*]; Jur to offend against [*pudeur, mœurs*]; to infringe [*liberté, sécurité, autorité*]; **~ à ses jours** to attempt suicide; **~ à la vie de qn** to make an attempt on sb's life.

attentif, **-ive** /atɑ̃tif, iv/ *adj* **1** (vigilant) [*auditeur, spectateur, élève*] attentive; **être ~ à** to pay attention to [*propos, consignes, détail, évolution*]; to be mindful of [*convenances*]; **il est plus/très ~ aux détails** he pays closer/a lot of attention to detail; **être ~ à son travail** to be careful in one's work; **être ~ à ce que qch soit fait** to make sure that sth is done; **être ~ à faire** to be careful to do; **sous l'œil** or **le regard ~ de leur mère** under the watchful eye of their mother; **prêter une oreille attentive à qn** to listen carefully to sb; **2** (minutieux) [*lecture, travail, description*] careful; [*examen*] close; [*soin*] special; **un examen plus ~ du dossier** a closer look at ou examination of the file; **3** (attentionné) [*soins*] special; **être ~ aux autres/besoins de qn** to be attentive to others/sb's needs.

attention /atɑ̃sjɔ̃/ **I** *nf* **1** (vigilance) attention; **demander beaucoup d'~** to require a lot of attention; **porter son ~ sur qch/qn** to turn one's attention to sth/sb; **à l'~ de F. Pons** for the attention of F. Pons; **faire ~ à qch** (prendre garde à) to mind [*voitures, piège, marche*]; to watch out for [*faux billets, fatigue, verglas*]; to be careful of [*soleil*]; to consider [*conséquences*]; (prendre soin de) to take care of [*affaires, vêtements*]; to watch [*alimentation, santé*]; (s'intéresser à) to pay attention to [*actualité, mode, évolution, détails*]; **ne faites pas ~ à ce qu'elle dit** don't take any notice of what she says; **fais ~ à ce que tu fais/dis/écris** be careful what you do/say/write; **faire ~ à qn** (écouter) to pay attention to sb; (surveiller) to keep an eye on sb; (remarquer) to take notice of sb; **faites ~ aux voleurs** watch out for ou beware of thieves; **fais ~ à toi** take care of yourself; **il faut faire ~ avec elle** you've got to be careful with her; **fais ~ que tout soit en ordre** make sure (that) everything is in order; **fais ~ de ne pas confondre les deux** take care not to confuse the two; **avec (beaucoup d')~** [*suivre, écouter, lire, examiner*] (very) carefully; **je n'ai pas fait ~** (je n'ai pas remarqué) I didn't notice; (je n'écoutais pas) I wasn't paying attention; (j'ai été maladroit) I wasn't paying attention; **fais ~, c'est très dangereux/tu mets de la peinture partout** be careful, it's very dangerous/you're getting paint everywhere; **2** (marque de gentillesse) **j'ai été touché par toutes ces ~s** I was touched by all these kind gestures; **être plein d'~s pour qn** to be very attentive to sb; **il a eu la délicate ~ de faire** he was thoughtful enough to do.

II *excl* **1** (pour avertir) (cri) look out!, watch out!; (écrit) gén attention!; (en cas de danger) warning!; (panneau routier) caution!; **~ à la peinture/marche/voiture** mind the paint/step/car; **~, les dossiers d'inscription doivent être retirés avant lundi** please note that application forms must be collected by Monday; **mais ~, il faut réserver à l'avance** however, you must book GB ou reserve in advance; **~ les yeux**○! watch out!; **2** (pour se justifier) **~, je ne veux pas dire**... don't get me wrong, I don't mean...; **mais ~, je ne vous parle pas de politique** now don't get me wrong, I'm not talking about politics here.

attentionné, **~e** /atɑ̃sjɔne/ *adj* [*personne*] attentive, considerate (**pour, envers qn** toward, towards GB, to sb); [*soins*] special.

attentisme /atɑ̃tism/ *nm* wait-and-see attitude; **faire de l'~** to play a waiting game.

attentiste /atɑ̃tist/ **I** *adj* [*attitude*] cautious, wait-and-see (*épith*).

II *nmf* person who adopts a wait-and-see attitude ou policy.

attentivement /atɑ̃tivmɑ̃/ *adv* [*écouter, suivre*] attentively; [*examiner, regarder*] carefully.

atténuantes /atenɥɑ̃t/ *adj fpl* **circonstances ~** Jur mitigating ou extenuating circumstances.

atténuateur /atenɥatœʀ/ *nm* attenuator.

atténuation /atenɥasjɔ̃/ *nf* (de douleur, tension) alleviation, relief; (de nuisance) reduction; (d'effet) mitigation; (de rigueur) relaxation.

atténuer /atenɥe/ [1] **I** *vtr* (amoindrir) to ease [*douleur, tension, chagrin*]; to lessen [*mal, rancune, désespoir, dissensions*]; to weaken [*sensation, impression, effet*]; to soften [*choc*]; to reduce [*rides, rougeur*]; to reduce [*violence, risques, inégalités, gravité*]; to tone down [*reproche, critique*]; to relax [*sévérité, rigueur*]; to dim [*lumière*]; to tone down [*couleur, éclat*]; to make [sth] less strong [*odeur, goût*]; to mitigate [*faute*].

II s'atténuer *vpr* (s'amoindrir) [*douleur*] to ease; [*colère, chagrin, violence*] to subside; [*corruption, pessimisme*] to be lessened; [*tendance*] to become less pronounced; [*inégalités, écarts*] to be reduced; [*ride, couleur*] to fade; [*tempête, bruit*] to die down; [*lumière*] to dim.

atterrant, **~e** /ateʀɑ̃, ɑ̃t/ *adj* **1** (consternant) [*bêtise*] appalling; **2** (choquant) [*image, nouvelle*] shattering.

atterré, **~e** /ateʀe/ **I** *pp* ▸ **atterrer**.

II *pp adj* **1** (consterné) appalled; **d'un air ~** aghast; **2** (en état de choc) shattered.

atterrement /atɛʀmɑ̃/ *nm* consternation.

atterrer /ateʀe/ [1] *vtr* to leave [sb] aghast.

atterrir /ateʀiʀ/ [3] *vi* **1** Aviat to land; **~ en catastrophe/sur le ventre** to make a crash landing/a belly landing; **2** (toucher le sol) [*personne, objet*] to land; **3**○ (aboutir) [*dossier, personne*] to land up○; **~ sur le bureau de qn** to land up on sb's desk; **4**○ (se ressaisir) **il atterrit, cela fait six mois que nous en parlons** it's finally dawned on him, we've been talking about it for six months; **atterris!** wake up!; **5** Naut to make landfall.

atterrissage /ateʀisaʒ/ *nm* landing; **~ en catastrophe** crash landing; **~ en douceur/forcé/d'urgence/sans visibilité** soft/forced/emergency/blind landing.

attestation /atɛstasjɔ̃/ *nf* **1** (déclaration) attestation; (sous serment) affidavit Jur; (certificat) certificate; **~ d'assurance/du médecin** insurance/doctor's certificate; **2** (marque) **être une ~ de qch** to be proof of sth, to prove sth; **3** Ling (d'emploi) attestation.

attester /atɛste/ [1] *vtr* **1** (certifier) to vouch for [*vérité, innocence, fait*]; (témoigner) to testify to [*vérité, innocence*]; **~ que** to vouch for the fact that; (témoigner) to testify that; **j'atteste qu'il était présent** I can vouch for the fact that he was there; **fait attesté** attested fact; **ce fait est attesté par plusieurs témoins** several witnesses can vouch for the fact; **forme attestée/non attestée** Ling attested/unattested form; **2** (être preuve de) [*fait, déclaration*] to prove, to attest to; **les chiffres attestent leur succès** the figures prove their success; **~ la bonne foi de qn** to prove sb's good faith; **3** (prendre à témoin) liter **j'atteste le Ciel/les dieux que** I call heaven/the gods to witness that; **j'en atteste le Ciel** as God is my judge.

attiédir /atjediʀ/ [3] liter **I** *vtr* **1** (réchauffer) to warm [*pièce*]; (refroidir) to cool [*liquide*]; **2** (modérer) to cool [*amour, désir*].

II s'attiédir *vpr* **1** [*liquide, terre*] (se réchauffer) to warm up; (se refroidir) to cool down; **2** (se modérer) [*ardeur, enthousiasme*] to cool down, to wane; [*goût*] to wane.

attifé○, **~e** /atife/ **I** *pp* ▸ **attifer**.

II *pp adj* rigged out○ (**de** in), dressed (**de** in).

attifer○ /atife/ [1] **I** *vtr* to rig [sb] out○ (**de** or **avec** in).

II s'attifer *vpr* to rig oneself out○ (**de** or **avec** in).

attiger○† /atiʒe/ [13] *vi* to go too far, to go over the top○.

attique /atik/ **I** *adj* Attic.

II ▸ **462** *nm* Ling Attic dialect.

Attique /atik/ ▸ **692** *nprf* Géog Attica.

attirail /atiʀaj/ *nm* **1** (équipement) gear; **~ de campeur** camping gear; **~ de pêche** fishing tackle; **l'~ du parfait bricoleur** the well-equipped DIY enthusiast's tool kit; **2**○ (objets encombrants) hum paraphernalia; **tout l'~** all the paraphernalia.

attirance /atiʀɑ̃s/ *nf* attraction (**pour** for); **éprouver** or **avoir de l'~ pour** to feel drawn toward(s), to be attracted to; **l'~ du vide** the fascination ou lure of the abyss.

attirant, **~e** /atiʀɑ̃, ɑ̃t/ *adj* attractive.

attirer /atiʀe/ [1] **I** *vtr* **1** (faire venir) gén, Phys to attract [*foudre, personne, animal, capitaux, convoitises*]; to draw, to attract [*foule, attention*]; **le film attire les foules** the film draws ou attracts the crowds, the film is a big draw ou crowd-puller; **~ l'attention** or **l'œil de qn sur qch** to draw sb's attention to sth; **~ qn vers/à/contre soi** to draw sb toward(s)/to/against oneself; **le bruit l'attira dans le jardin** the noise drew him to the garden GB ou yard US; **c'est ce qui les a attirés l'un vers l'autre** it's what drew them together; **~ qn dans un coin** to take sb into a corner; **~ qn dans un piège** to lure sb into a trap; **~ qn par des promesses** to entice sb with promises; **2** (séduire) [*personne, pays*] to attract; [*études, métier*] to appeal to [*personne*]; **les brunes l'attirent** he goes for brunettes; **3** (susciter) to bring [sth] [*reproche, critique*] (**à qn** on sb); to bring [sth] down [*colère*] (**à qn** on sb); to bring [sth] [*honte, mépris*] (**sur qn** on sb); **~ des ennuis à qn** to cause sb problems; **son échec ne lui a pas attiré de compliments** his failure earned him no congratulations; **~ sur soi** or **sa tête la colère du patron** to bring the boss down on one's head; **ça va lui ~ des jalousies** people are going to be jealous of him.

II s'attirer *vpr* **s'~ des ennemis** to make enemies; **s'~ l'estime/les compliments de qn** to earn sb's respect/praise; **s'~ le soutien de qn** to win sb's support; **s'~ la colère/les reproches de qn** to incur sb's anger/reproaches; **le livre s'est attiré de nombreuses critiques** the book has attracted a lot of criticism; **s'~ des ennuis** to get into trouble.

attiser /atize/ [1] *vtr* **1** (exciter) to kindle [*sentiment, convoitises*]; to fuel [*discorde*]; to stir up [*haine*]; **2** (aviver) to fan [*feu*].

attitré, **~e** /atitʀe/ *adj* **1** (officiel) official; **chauffeur ~** official driver; **détaillant ~** authorized dealer; **représentant ~** accredited representative; **2** (habituel) regular; **client ~** regular customer.

attitude /atityd/ *nf* **1** (du corps) (maintien) bearing; (position) attitude, posture; (pose) pose; **~ raide** stiff bearing; **~ de (la) soumission/de la rébellion** submissive/rebellious attitude; **2** (conduite) attitude (**à l'égard de** or **à l'encontre de** or **vis-à-vis de** or **envers qch/qn** to sth/to ou toward sb); **changer d'~** to change one's attitude; **prendre une ~** to adopt an attitude; **3** (affectation) pose; **ce n'est qu'une ~** it's just a pose; **se composer une ~** to adopt a pose; **4** Danse attitude.

attouchement /atuʃmɑ̃/ *nm* **1** (sexuel) (sans consentement) (sexual) interfering ¢, molesting ¢; (avec consentement) fondling ¢; **se livrer à des ~s sur qn** to interfere (sexually) with sb; **2** (de guérisseur) laying on ¢ of hands.

attractif, -ive /atʀaktif, iv/ *adj* **1** gén, Phys attractive; **2** controv [*spectacle*] entertaining.

attraction /atʀaksjɔ̃/ *nf* **1** (force) gén, Ling, Phys attraction; **Paris exerce une forte ~ sur sa région** Paris acts as a magnet for the surrounding area; **elle exerce une grande ~ sur les hommes** men find her very attractive; **2** (élément qui attire) attraction; **~ touristique** tourist attraction; **centre d'~** centre[GB] of attraction; **principale ~ de la région** main ou star attraction of the area; **3** (de fête, foire) attraction; (numéro d'un spectacle) act, turn; **~ déshabillée** strip show; **elle passe en ~ ce soir au casino** she is appearing tonight at the casino.
■ **~ terrestre** Earth's attraction; **~ universelle** gravitation.

attrait /atʀɛ/ **I** *nm* **1** (de personne, paysage, projet, vie) appeal, attraction; (de l'inconnu, de la nouveauté, du pouvoir) appeal, lure; (de l'interdit) lure; **plein d'~** very attractive; **avoir de l'~ pour qn** to appeal to sb; **exercer de l'~ sur** to appeal to; **manquer d'~** to have no appeal, to be unattractive; **je ne leur trouve aucun ~** they don't appeal to me (in the least); **les actions perdent de leur ~** the shares are ou the stock is no longer so attractive; **banlieue sans ~** dreary suburb; **2** (goût) **l'~ de qn pour qch/qn** sb's liking for sth/sb; **éprouver de l'~ pour qch/qn** to feel attracted ou drawn to sth/sb.
II attraits *nmpl* (charmes) liter charms.

attrape /atʀap/ *nf* trick, joke.

attrape-couillon◑, *pl* **~s** /atʀapkujɔ̃/ *nm* con○, con trick○.

attrape-mouches /atʀapmuʃ/ *nm inv* **1** (plante) flytrap; **2** (piège) gén flytrap; (papier collant) flypaper.

attrape-nigaud, *pl* **~s** /atʀapnigo/ *nm* con○; **tomber dans un ~** to fall for a con; **se laisser prendre à un ~** to be conned○.

attraper /atʀape/ [1] **I** *vtr* **1** (saisir en mouvement) to catch [*personne, animal, ballon*]; **tiens, attrape!** here, catch!; **~ qch au vol** to catch sth in mid air; **2** (capturer) to catch [*malfaiteur, animal*]; **~ une vache au lasso** to catch a cow with a lasso, to lasso a cow; **se faire ~** to get caught; **attrapez-le!** stop him!; **3** (prendre) to catch hold of [*corde, main, jambe*]; **~ qch à deux mains** to catch hold of sth with both hands; **~ qn par le bras/la manche** to catch hold of sb by the arm/the sleeve; **~ une bouteille par le goulot** to pick up a bottle by the neck; **tu peux ~ le livre sur l'étagère?** can you reach and get the book from the shelf?; **4**○ (contracter) [*personne*] to catch [*maladie, virus*]; to get [*coup de soleil*]; to pick up [*manie, accent*]; **~ froid** to catch cold; **~ un torticolis** to get a stiff neck; **j'ai attrapé mal dans le dos/mal à la tête** I got a backache/a headache; **il a attrapé l'accent de la région** he's picked up the local accent; **tu vas ~ du mal!** you'll catch something!; **5**○ (surprendre) to catch [sb] out [*personne*]; **il a été bien attrapé d'apprendre que** he was really caught out by the news that; **~ qn à faire** or **en train de faire** fig to catch sb doing; **6**○ (réprimander) to tell [sb] off [*personne*]; **se faire ~ (par qn)** to get told off (by sb); **7**○ (recevoir) to get [*coup, punition, amende*]; **8**○ (saisir par la pensée) to catch [*mots, phrase*]; to pick up [*idées*].
II s'attraper *vpr* [*maladie*] to be caught.

attrayant, ~e /atʀɛjɑ̃, ɑ̃t/ *adj* gén attractive; [*lecture*] pleasant; **peu ~** gén unattractive; [*tâche, lecture*] unappealing.

attribuable /atʀibɥabl/ *adj* attributable (**à** to).

attribuer /atʀibɥe/ [1] **I** *vtr* **1** (octroyer) to allocate [*quota, place, numéro, logement, tâche*] (**à qn** to sb); to grant [*droit, statut, garde*] (**à qn** to sb); to award [*prix, médaille, bourse*] (**à qn** to sb); Fin to allot [*actions*]; **2** (donner comme cause à) **~ qch à la fatigue/malchance** to put sth down to tiredness/bad luck; **3** (blâmer pour) **~ la responsabilité de qch à qn/qch** to hold sb/sth responsible for sth, to blame sb/sth for sth; **~ un accident au mauvais temps** to blame the bad weather for an accident, to blame an accident on the bad weather; **4** (prêter) **~ qch à qn** to credit sb with sth [*invention, qualité, mérite, bonne intention*]; to ascribe sth to sb [*œuvre*]; **on attribue ce tableau à Poussin** this painting is attributed to Poussin; **~ de l'importance/un sens à qch** to lend importance/meaning to sth.
II s'attribuer *vpr* **s'~ la meilleure part/la meilleure place** to give oneself the largest share/the best seat; **s'~ tout le mérite** to claim ou take all the credit for oneself.

attribut /atʀiby/ *nm* **1** (propriété) attribute; (symbole) symbol; **2** Ling complement; **adjectif ~** predicative adjective; **nom ~** complement.

attributaire /atʀibytɛʀ/ *nmf* recipient of a state benefit.

attribution /atʀibysjɔ̃/ **I** *nf* **1** gén (de crédits, numéro, place, rôle) allocation (**à** to); (de prix, bourse, d'avantage) awarding (**à** to); (de nom, surnom) giving (**à** to); (d'actions) allotment (**à** to); (de nationalité) granting (**à** to); **2** Art, Littérat, Mus (d'œuvre) attribution (**à** to).
II attributions *nfpl* (de personne) remit (*sg*); (de tribunal) competence; **ça ne fait pas partie de** ou **ça n'entre pas dans mes ~s** it doesn't come within my remit.

attristant, ~e /atʀistɑ̃, ɑ̃t/ *adj* **1** (peinant) distressing, upsetting; **2** (consternant) depressing; **d'une bêtise/médiocrité ~e** depressingly stupid/mediocre.

attristé, ~e /atʀiste/ *adj* sad; **condoléances ~es** heartfelt condolences.

attrister /atʀiste/ [1] **I** *vtr* (peiner) to sadden; **j'ai été attristé d'apprendre** I was sorry to hear.
II s'attrister *vpr* **1** (exprimer sa tristesse) to lament (**de** about); **2** (être peiné) to be saddened (**de** by).

attroupement /atʀupmɑ̃/ *nm* gathering; **~ de manifestants** crowd of demonstrators; **causer un ~** to cause a crowd to gather.

attrouper /atʀupe/ [1] **I** *vtr* [*accident*] to attract [*passants*].
II s'attrouper *vpr* [*personnes, groupe*] to gather (**devant** or **autour de** around).

atypique /atipik/ *adj* atypical.

au /o/ *prép* = (**à le**) ▶ **à**.

aubade /obad/ *nf* **1** (à la femme aimée) dawn serenade; **donner l'~ à qn** to serenade sb (at dawn); **2** (en l'honneur de quelqu'un) (little) concert.

aubaine /obɛn/ *nf* **1** (chance inespérée) godsend; **véritable ~** real godsend; **quelle ~!** what a godsend!; **ne pas laisser passer une ~** not to miss an opportunity; **profiter d'une ~** to make the most of an opportunity; **2** (bonne affaire) bargain.

aube /ob/ *nf* **1** (point du jour) dawn; **à l'~** at dawn; **à l'~ du 6 juin** at dawn on 6 June; **avant l'~** before dawn; **dès l'~** at the crack of dawn; **2** (début, approche) dawn; **à l'~ de** at the dawn of; **à l'~ des années 20** in the early twenties; **3** Tech (en bois) paddle; (en métal) blade; **bateau/roue à ~s** paddle boat/wheel; **4** Relig (de prêtre) alb; (d'enfant de chœur) cassock; (pour la communion solennelle) alb.

Aube /ob/ ▶**357**, **692** *nprf* (rivière, département) **l'~** the Aube.

aubépine /obepin/ *nf* hawthorn; **haie d'~s** hawthorn hedge; **fleurs d'~** may ou hawthorn blossom.

aubère /obɛʀ/ *adj, nm* strawberry roan.

auberge /obɛʀʒ/ *nf* inn; **~ rurale** country inn; **ce n'est pas une ~ ici!** this isn't a hotel you know!
■ **~ de jeunesse** youth hostel.
IDIOMES **c'est l'~ espagnole ici** if you want anything around here, you have to bring it yourself; **tu n'es pas sorti de l'~**○! you're not out of the wood yet!

aubergine /obɛʀʒin/ **I** *adj inv* aubergine.
II *nf* **1** Bot, Culin aubergine, eggplant US; **2**○ (auxiliaire de police) (female) traffic warden GB, meter maid US.

aubergiste /obɛʀʒist/ ▶**510** *nmf* innkeeper.

aubier /obje/ *nm* sapwood.

aubrietia /obʀijesja/ *nf* aubrietia.

auburn /obœʀn/ *adj inv* auburn.

aucun, ~e /okœ̃, yn/ **I** *adj* **1** (dans une phrase négative) no, not any; **elle n'a ~ défaut** she has no faults, she hasn't got any faults; **il n'a ~ talent** he has no talent, he hasn't got any talent; **il n'y aura ~es représailles** there won't be any reprisals; **elle n'aura ~e difficulté à s'adapter** she won't have any trouble adapting; **il n'y a plus ~ espoir** there's no hope left; **ils n'ont ~e raison de refuser** they have no reason ou haven't got any reason to refuse; **je n'ai ~e nouvelle de lui** I haven't heard from him; **je n'ai eu ~ mal à le convaincre** I had no trouble persuading him, I didn't have any trouble persuading him; **il parle français sans ~ accent** he speaks French without any accent; **elle l'a fait sans ~e hésitation** or **sans hésitation ~e** she did it without any hesitation; **sans ~e aide du gouvernement** without any aid from the government; **en ~e façon** in no way; **2** liter (quelque) **je l'aime plus qu'~e autre** I love her more than anybody; **je doute qu'~ employé accepte tes conditions** I doubt that any employee would accept your conditions.
II *pron* **1** (dans une phrase négative) **il a trois voitures, ~e n'est en état de marche** he has three cars, none of them work; **je ne connais ~ de ses amis** I don't know any of his friends; **je n'ai lu ~ de vos livres** I haven't read any of your books; **~ de ses arguments n'est convaincant** none of his arguments are convincing; **~ des soldats n'est revenu vivant** none of the soldiers came back alive; **'tu as reçu beaucoup de lettres?'—'~e!'** 'did you receive many letters?'—'not one!'; **2** liter (quiconque) **il est plus compétent qu'~ d'entre nous** he's more competent than any of us; **je doute qu'~ d'entre eux réussisse** I doubt that any of them will succeed; **d'~s** some; **d'~s ont suggéré que** it has been suggested by some that.

aucunement /okynmɑ̃/ *adv* in no way; **je n'avais ~ l'intention de vous froisser** I in no way meant to hurt your feelings, in no way did I mean to hurt your feelings; **il ne voulait ~ la critiquer** he in no way meant to criticize her; **je ne suis ~ surpris** I'm not surprised in the least, I'm not at all surprised; **'est-ce que je vous dérange?'—'~!'** 'am I disturbing you?'—'not in the least!'; **il n'a ~ l'intention de l'épouser** he hasn't got the slightest intention of marrying her.

audace /odas/ *nf* **1** (hardiesse) boldness (**face à** in the face of), daring; **il faut (avoir) de l'~** you have to be bold ou daring; **œuvre d'une grande ~** very bold ou daring work; **avec une grande ~** very boldly, with great daring; **il manque d'~** he's not very daring; **2** (effronterie) audacity, nerve○; (de geste, propos) impudence; **avoir l'~ de faire qch** to have the audacity ou nerve○ to do sth; **il ne manque pas d'~** he's got a nerve○; **mentir avec ~** to tell a bare-faced lie; **3** (innovation) **une ~** a daring ou bold innovation; **les ~s des couturiers/architectes** the daring creations of designers/architects; **~s stylistiques** stylistic daring ¢.

audacieusement /odasjøzmɑ̃/ *adv* (hardiment) boldly; (en innovant) daringly.

audacieux, **-ieuse** /odasjø, øz/ **I** *adj* (hardi) audacious, daring; (effronté) bold.
II *nm,f* daring ou bold person.
IDIOMES **la fortune sourit aux ~** Prov fortune favours[GB] the brave Prov.

Aude /od/ ▶357, 692 *nprf* (fleuve, département) **l'~** the Aude.

au-dedans /odədɑ̃/ **I** *adv* lit, fig inside.
II au-dedans de *loc prép* **~ de** inside; **~ de la maison** inside the house.

au-dehors /odəɔʀ/ *adv* **1** lit outside; **il a des contacts ~** he has contacts outside; **il pleuvait ~** it was raining outside; **le liquide s'écoule ~** the liquid is oozing out; **'ne pas se pencher ~'** 'do not lean out of the window'; **2** fig outwardly; **~ elle paraît froide mais elle est en fait très chaleureuse** outwardly she appears cold, but she is in fact very warm.

au-delà /od(ə)la/ **I** *nm* Relig beyond, hereafter; **dans l'~** in the beyond ou hereafter.
II *adv* beyond; **un peu/très ~** a bit/far beyond; **20% est la limite, ils n'iront pas ~** 20% is the limit, they won't go beyond ou over that; **c'est un problème de financement, et ~, d'organisation générale** it's a problem of funding, and beyond that, of general organization; **je veux bien aller jusqu'à 1000 francs mais pas ~** I'm quite prepared to go up to 1,000 francs but no more; **il a eu ce qu'il voulait et ~** he got what he wanted and more besides; **il est allé ~ dans sa réflexion** he carried his thoughts further; **aller ~ dans l'amélioration** to make further improvements.
III au-delà de *loc prép* beyond; **~ de cette limite** beyond that point; **~ des frontières** beyond the borders; **~ des mers** over ou beyond the seas; **~ d'un certain délai** beyond a certain period; **~ de 20%/10000 francs** over 20%/10,000 francs; **~ de ces questions/ce débat idéologique** beyond these questions/this ideological debate; **~ de cet objectif** beyond this objective.

au-dessous /odəsu/ **I** *adv* **1** (plus bas) below; **la maison est sur le plateau, la mer est ~** the house is on the plateau, the sea is below; **tu vois le dictionnaire, mon livre est ~** you see the dictionary, my book is underneath; **l'étagère ~** the shelf below; **va voir à l'étage ~** go and have a look downstairs; **mon appartement est calme, il n'y a personne ~** my apartment is quiet, there's no one living on the floor below; **il habite juste ~** he lives one floor down; **2** (marquant une infériorité) under; **les enfants de 10 ans et ~** children of 10 years and under.
II au-dessous de *loc prép* **1** (plus bas que) **~ de la fenêtre/du tableau** under ou below the window/the painting; **~ de chez eux** (dans la rue) in the street below them; (à l'étage inférieur) on the floor below them; **~ du genou** below the knee; **2** (inférieur à) **température ~ de zéro** temperature below zero; **~ de ce niveau, il y a un risque de pollution** below this level, there is a risk of pollution; **les notes ~ de 10** marks GB ou grades US below 10; **les enfants ~ de 13 ans** children under 13, the under-thirteens; **les chèques ~ de 100 francs** cheques for under 100 francs; **le dollar est tombé ~ de 5 francs** the dollar has fallen below 5 francs; **il est ~ de sa tâche/son rôle** he isn't up to his task/his role; **être ~ de tout**○ (ne pas être à la hauteur) to be absolutely useless; (moralement) to be despicable.

au-dessus /odəsy/ **I** *adv* **1** (plus haut) above; **le village est en bas, la station de ski est ~** the village is at the foot of the mountain, the ski resort is above (it); **ne prends pas ce livre, prends celui qui est ~** don't take that book, take the one on top (of it); **l'étagère ~** the shelf above; **il habite l'étage ~** he lives on the next floor up ou on the floor above; **il y a plusieurs étages ~** there are several floors above; **~ il y a trois chambres** there are three bedrooms upstairs; **2** (marquant une supériorité) above; **les enfants de 10 ans et ~** children of 10 and over, the over-tens; **la taille ~** the next size up; **les billets de 100 francs et ~** notes GB ou bills US of 100 francs and over; **3** fig **être ~** [*œuvre, auteur*] to be better; **il n'a rien écrit qui soit ~** he hasn't written anything better.
II au-dessus de *loc prép* **1** (plus haut que) above; **~ du tableau/de la ville/de Paris** above the painting/the town/Paris; **~ de la cheminée** above the mantlepiece; **~ des nuages** (up) above the clouds; **~ de chez moi** in the flat GB ou apartment above me; **deux étages ~ de chez moi** two floors up from me; **~ du genou/de la ceinture** above the knee/the waist; **~ de toi** above you; **un pont ~ de la rivière** a bridge over ou across the river; **se pencher ~ de la table** to lean across the table; **2** (supérieur à) above; **~ de zéro** above zero; **~ de 5%** above ou over 5%; **les enfants ~ de 3 ans** children over 3 years old, the over-threes; **~ de la moyenne** above average; **les chèques ~ de 1000 francs** cheques GB ou checks US for over 1,000 francs; **le paiement par carte est accepté ~ de 100 francs** payment by card is accepted for purchases over 100 francs; **elle est ~ de lui dans la hiérarchie** she's above him in the hierarchy; **mettre qn/qch ~ de qn/qch** to place sb/sth above sb/sth; **il met sa fierté ~ de tout** he places his pride above everything else; **un spectacle ~ de tout éloge/toute critique** a show beyond praise/criticism; **il veut se situer ~ des partis/des querelles du groupe** he wants to put himself above the political parties/the internal quarrels; **le débat doit être ~ des considérations politiques** the debate must rise above political considerations; **il est (bien) ~ de ça** fig he's (well) above that.

au-devant: **au-devant de** /odəvɑ̃də/ *loc prép* (à la rencontre) **aller ~ de qn** lit to go to meet sb; **aller ~ des clients** fig to go out looking for custom; **aller ~ des désirs/demandes de qn** fig to anticipate sb's wishes/requests; **aller ~ des ennuis/du danger** fig to let oneself in for trouble/danger.

audibilité /odibilite/ *nf* audibility.

audible /odibl/ *adj* audible.

audience /odjɑ̃s/ *nf* **1** Jur hearing; **'l'~ est suspendue'** 'the hearing is adjourned'; **lever l'~** to close the hearing; **salle d'~** courtroom; **~ publique** public hearing; **2** (entretien) audience sout; **accorder une ~ à qn** to grant sb an audience; **3** (succès, attention) success; **jouir d'une grande ~ auprès des jeunes** to have a lot of success with young people; **~ électorale/nationale** electoral/national success; **4** TV, Radio (ensemble des gens) audience; (chiffres) audience ratings (*pl*); **indicateurs d'~** audience ratings; **32% d'~** 32% in the audience ratings.

audimat® /odimat/ *nm* audience ratings (*pl*); **records d'~** ratings records; **12 points d'~** 12% of the TV audience.

audimètre /odimɛtʀ/ *nm* (appareil) audience research device.

audio /odjo/ *adj inv* [*bande, enregistrement, équipement*] audio.

audiocassette /odjokasɛt/ *nf* audio cassette.

audioconférence /odjokɔ̃feʀɑ̃s/ *nf* audioconference.

audiofréquence /odjofʀekɑ̃s/ *nf* audiofrequency.

audiogramme /odjogʀam/ *nm* audiogram.

audiologie /odjolɔʒi/ *nf* audiology.

audiomètre /odjɔmɛtʀ/ *nm* audiometer.

audiométrie /odjɔmetʀi/ *nf* audiometry.

audionumérique /odjonymeʀik/ *adj* **disque ~** digital audio disc, compact disc.

audio-oral, **~e**, *mpl* **-aux** /odjooʀal, o/ *adj* audio-oral.

audioprothésiste /odjɔpʀɔtezist/ ▶510 *nmf* specialist in hearing aids.

audiotypiste /odjɔtipist/ ▶510 *nmf* audiotypist.

audiovisuel, **-elle** /odjɔvizɥɛl/ **I** *adj* **1** Radio, TV broadcasting; **techniques audiovisuelles** broadcasting technology; **2** Ling, Vidéo audiovisual.
II *nm* **1** Radio, TV broadcasting; **l'~ public** public service broadcasting; **2** (équipement) audiovisual equipment; **3** (méthodes) audiovisual methods (*pl*).

audit /odit/ *nm* **1** (contrôle) audit; **~ interne** internal audit; **cabinet d'~** audit firm; **l'~ des comptes** the auditing of the accounts; **2** (contrôleur) auditor.

auditer /odite/ [1] *vtr* to audit.

auditeur, **-trice** /oditœʀ, tʀis/ *nm,f* **1** gén, Radio listener; (dans un auditorium) member of the audience, listener; **il s'est tourné vers ses ~s** he turned toward(s) the audience; **2** Fin auditor; **3** Ling hearer.
■ **~ libre** Univ *person following a university course with no obligation to take the exam.*

auditif, **-ive** /oditif, iv/ *adj* Anat [*nerf, conduit*] auditory; [*troubles, appareil*] hearing (*épith*); [*mémoire*] aural.

audition /odisjɔ̃/ *nf* **1** Physiol (perception) hearing; **troubles de l'~** hearing troubles; **2** (écoute) hearing; **3** (essai) Cin, Mus, Théât audition; **passer une ~** to be auditioned, to go for an audition; **faire passer une ~ à qn** to audition sb; **4** Jur hearing, examination; **procéder à l'~ des témoins** to examine the witnesses.

auditionner /odisjɔne/ [1] *vtr, vi* to audition.

auditoire /oditwaʀ/ *nm* audience.

auditorium /oditɔʀjɔm/ *nm* auditorium.

auge /oʒ/ *nf* **1** (d'animal) trough; **2**○ (assiette) plate; **3** (de maçon) board; **4** Géog U-shaped valley; **~ glaciaire** glacial valley.

Augias /oʒjas/ *npr* Augeas; **les écuries d'~** the Augean stables.

augment /ogmɑ̃/ *nm* augment.

augmentatif, **-ive** /ogmɑ̃tatif, iv/ **I** *adj* augmentative.
II *nm* augmentative.

augmentation /ogmɑ̃tasjɔ̃/ *nf* **1** (accroissement) increase; (action) increasing; **l'~ des effectifs/du nombre de** the increase in staff/in the number of; **~ de 3%** 3% increase; **~ de 200 francs** increase of 200 francs; **l'~ du capital de 100 millions de francs** the increase in capital of 100 million francs; **2** (majoration) (de salaire) rise GB, raise US, increase; (de prix, loyer, d'impôt, allocation) increase; **l'~ des prix/loyers** the increase in prices/rents; **l'~ des impôts par le gouvernement** the raising of taxes by the government; **une ~ (de salaire)** a pay rise GB ou raise US; **j'ai eu une ~ de 10%** I got a 10% rise GB ou raise US; **~ des prix de 3% en avril** a 3% price increase in April; **~ des tarifs pétroliers de 6%** a 6% increase in oil; **3** (en tricot) increase; **faire une ~** to increase.

augmenter /ogmɑ̃te/ [1] **I** *vtr* **1** (accroître) to raise ou increase [*nombre, salaire, charge, volume*] (**de** by); to turn up ou increase [*son*]; to increase [*valeur, production, participation, capital*] (**de** by); to extend [*durée*] (**de** by); to increase [*risque, chance, joie, impatience*] (**de** by); **~ le loyer de qn** to put sb's rent up; **~ ses revenus** to supplement one's income (**en faisant** by doing); **2** (majorer les appointements de) to give [sb] a rise GB ou raise US [*employé*]; **~ qn de 1000 francs/5%** to give sb a rise GB ou raise US of 1,000 francs/5%; **3** (en tricot) to increase; **~ de deux mailles** increase two stitches.
II *vi* **1** (devenir plus élevé) [*impôts, charges, loyer*] to increase (**de** by), to go up (**de** by); [*température*] to rise (**de** by), to go up (**de**

by); [*revenus*] to increase (**de** by); [*prix, nombre*] to rise (**de** by), to increase (**de** by), to go up (**de** by); [*surface, volume, capacité*] to increase (**de** by); **le nombre des attentats/chômeurs a augmenté** the number of attacks/unemployed people has risen; **le train a augmenté** train fares have gone up; **le cinéma va ~** the price of cinema tickets is going to go up; **le gaz/l'électricité va ~** the price of gas/electricity is going to go up; **les timbres ont augmenté** stamps have gone up; **~ en valeur** to increase in value; **2** (s'intensifier) [*sentiment, danger, faim, force*] to increase; **l'absentéisme ne cesse d'~** absenteeism keeps increasing.

III **s'augmenter** *vpr* **l'entreprise s'est augmentée d'un nouveau service** a new department has been added to the company.

augure /ogyʀ/ *nm* **1** (devin) Antiq augur; fig, hum soothsayer, oracle; **consulter les ~s** Antiq to consult the augurs; fig to consult the oracle; **2** (signe) omen; Antiq augury; **être de bon/mauvais ~ pour qch/qn** to be a good/bad omen for sth/sb.

augurer /ogyʀe/ [1] *vtr* **1** (attendre) **que peut-on ~ de cette attitude?** what should we expect from this attitude?; **j'augure mal** or **je n'augure rien de bon de cette rencontre** I can't see any good coming of this meeting; **cela augure bien/mal de l'avenir** it bodes/doesn't bode well for the future; **cela laisse ~ une difficulté** this suggests we can anticipate a difficulty; **me laissant ~ que** giving me to understand that; **2** (annoncer) [*signe*] to herald.

auguste /ogyst/ I *adj* [*personne*] august; [*maison*] venerable; [*démarche, geste*] noble.

II *nm* (clown) circus clown.

Auguste /ogyst/ *npr* Augustus; **le siècle d'~** the Augustan age.

augustin, ~e /ogystɛ̃, in/ I *adj* Augustinian.

II *nm,f* Augustinian friar/nun.

Augustin /ogystɛ̃/ *npr* Relig **Saint ~** Saint Augustine.

augustinien, -ienne /ogystinjɛ̃, ɛn/ *adj, nm,f* Augustinian.

aujourd'hui /oʒuʀdɥi/ *adv* **1** (ce jour) today; **il arrive ~** he's arriving today; **dans le journal d'~** in today's newspaper; **~ en huit/quinze** a week/two weeks (from) today; **à partir** ou **à dater d'~** as from today; **dès ~** from today; **~ même** just today; **voilà** or **il y a un an ~ que** it's a year ago today that; **pourquoi n'en parles-tu qu'~?** why didn't you mention it before now?; **alors, c'est pour ~ (ou pour demain)**○**?** come on, we haven't got all day!; **2** (de nos jours) today, nowadays; **la jeunesse d'~** the youth of today; **la France d'~** present-day France; **ça ne date pas d'~** [*objet*] it's quite old; [*problème, attitude*] that's nothing new; **~ que la société est mondialement connue** now that the company is known throughout the world.

aulne /on/ *nm* alder.

■ **~ blanc** grey GB ou gray US alder; **~ glutineux** common alder.

aulx ▸ **ail**.

aumône /omon/ *nf* **1** (aux pauvres) hand-out, alms† (*pl*); **faire l'~ à** to give alms to; **demander l'~** to ask for charity; **2** (somme dérisoire) pittance.

aumônerie /omonʀi/ *nf* **1** (lieu) chaplaincy; **2** (charge) chaplainship.

aumônier /omonje/ ▸ **510** *nm* chaplain; **~ militaire** army chaplain.

aumônière /omonjɛʀ/ *nf* (de dame) purse; (de gentilhomme) pouch.

aune /on/ I *nm* = **aulne**.

II *nf* Mes ≈ ell; **à l'~ de** by the yardstick of.

auparavant /opaʀavɑ̃/ *adv* **1** (avant) before; **comme ~** as before; **nous ferons comme ~** we'll do as we did before; **peu (de temps) ~** shortly before; **un an ~** a year before ou earlier; **moins/plus qu'~** less/more than before; **2** (précédemment) previously; **il était ~ ambassadeur** previously he was ambassador; **3** (autrefois) formerly; **~ elle avait été chanteuse** she had formerly been a singer; **4** (en premier lieu) beforehand; **non sans avoir ~ vérifié** not without having checked beforehand.

auprès /opʀɛ/ I *adv* liter nearby.

II **auprès de** *loc prép* **1** (à côté de) next to, beside; (aux côtés de) with; **allongé ~ d'elle** lying down next to her; **il faut rester ~ de lui, il est souffrant** you must stay with him, he's ill; **il s'est rendu ~ de sa tante** he went to see his aunt; **2** (en comparaison de) compared with; **mes problèmes ne sont rien ~ des tiens** my problems are nothing compared with yours; **3** (en s'adressant à) to; **se plaindre/se justifier/s'excuser ~ de qn** to complain/to justify oneself/to apologize to sb; **renseigne-toi ~ de la mairie** ask for information at the town hall; **un sondage effectué ~ de 2 000 personnes** a poll carried out among 2,000 people; **4** fml (en relation avec) to; **représentant ~ de l'ONU** representative to the UN; **négociateur du Canada ~ de la CEE** Canadian negotiator with the EC; **5** (dans l'opinion de) to; **il passe pour riche/un malotru ~ d'eux** to them he's rich/a lout; **il a perdu toute crédibilité ~ des électeurs/de l'opinion** he has lost all credibility among voters/the public; **l'émission a du succès ~ des téléspectateurs/du public** the programme[GB] is a success with TV viewers/the public.

auquel ▸ **lequel**.

aura /oʀa/ *nf* aura; **bénéficier d'une ~ de respect** to enjoy an aura of respect.

auréole /ɔʀeɔl/ *nf* **1** (tache) ring; **laisser une ~** to leave a ring; **2** (d'un astre) halo; **3** (couronne) halo; **~ de cheveux blancs** halo of white hair; **4** (prestige) glory; **paré** or **entouré de l'~ de** crowned with the glory of; **5** Art, Relig halo.

auréoler: **s'auréoler** /ɔʀeɔle/ [1] *vpr* **s'~ de** to take on an aura of; **auréolé de** basking in the glow of.

auréomycine® /ɔʀeɔmisin/ *nf* aureomycin®.

auriculaire /oʀikylɛʀ/ I *adj* auricular.

II *nm* little finger, pinkie.

auriculothérapie /oʀikyloteʀapi/ *nf* auriculotherapy.

aurifère /oʀifɛʀ/ I *nf* Fin gold stock.

II *adj* **1** Géol auriferous; **2** Fin **valeurs ~s** gold stocks.

aurification /oʀifikasjɔ̃/ *nf* Dent gold filling.

aurifier /oʀifje/ [2] *vtr* Dent to fill [sth] with gold.

aurige /oʀiʒ/ *nm* Auriga.

Aurigny /oʀiɲi/ ▸ **416** *nf* Alderney; **à ~** in Alderney.

aurochs /oʀɔk/ *nm inv* aurochs.

aurore /oʀɔʀ/ I *adj inv* rosy gold.

II *nf* **1** (lever du soleil) dawn ₵; **l'~** dawn; **à l'~** at dawn; **aux ~s** (tôt) with the lark; (trop tôt) at an ungodly hour; **dès l'~** at first light; **2** fml (début) dawn; **à l'~ de** at the dawn of; **à l'~ des années 30** in the early thirties.

■ **~ australe** aurora australis; **~ boréale** Northern Lights (*pl*), aurora borealis; **~ polaire** polar lights.

auscultation /ɔskyltasjɔ̃/ *nf* **1** Méd examination with a stethoscope, auscultation spéc; **2** fig (examen approfondi) thorough examination; **3** Tech auscultation.

ausculter /ɔskylte/ [1] *vtr* **1** Méd to sound, to examine [sb] with a stethoscope; **se faire ~** to be examined with a stethoscope; **2** (examiner) to examine thoroughly; **3** Tech to sound.

auspices /ospis/ *nmpl* **1** (augures) auspices; **sous d'heureux/de mauvais/les meilleurs ~** under favourable[GB]/bad/the best auspices; **2** (protection) **sous les ~ de** (patronage institutionnel) under the aegis ou auspices of; (protection personnelle) under the patronage of; (protection symbolique) under the auspices of; **3** Antiq auspices.

aussi /osi/ I *adv* **1** (également) too, as well, also; **moi ~, j'ai du travail** I have work too; **il sera absent et moi ~** he'll be away and so will I; **je suis allée à Paris, à Lyon et ~ à Montpellier** I went to Paris, Lyons and Montpellier too ou as well, I went to Paris, Lyons and also Montpellier; **'j'adore le jazz'—'moi ~'** 'I love jazz'—'me too', 'so do I'; **elle est professeur, elle ~** she's a teacher too ou as well; **mon père ~ était vétérinaire** my father was a vet too ou as well; **nous partons ~** we're leaving too ou as well; **c'est ~ notre opinion** that's our opinion too ou as well, that's also our opinion; **il est peintre et ~ musicien** he's a painter and also a musician, he's a painter and a musician too ou as well; **'bonne journée!'—'merci, toi ~!'** 'have a nice day!'—'thanks, you too!'; **2** (dans une comparaison) **~ âgé/gentil/ennuyeux/débordé que** as old/kind/boring/overloaded as; **~ étrange/ridicule que cela puisse paraître** (as) strange/ridiculous as it may seem; **~ riche soit-elle** (as) rich as she may be; **~ riche qu'elle soit** rich though she is, however rich she is; **cette émission concerne les femmes ~ bien que les hommes** this programme[GB] concerns women as well as men; **~ longtemps que** as long as; **c'est ~ bien** it's just as well; **c'est ~ bien comme cela** lit it's just as good like that; fig it's just as well; **3** (si, tellement) so; **je ne savais pas qu'il était ~ vieux** I didn't know he was so old; **je n'ai jamais rien vu d'~ beau** I've never seen anything so beautiful; **on n'en fait plus d'~ beaux aujourd'hui** they don't make such nice ones nowadays; **dans une ~ belle maison** in such a nice house; **après une ~ longue absence** after such a long absence, after being away so long; **obtenir d'~ bons résultats** to get such good results.

II *conj* **1** (en conséquence) so, consequently; **sa voiture n'a pas démarré, ~ elle a été en retard** her car wouldn't start, so she was late; **il a beaucoup travaillé, ~ a-t-il réussi** he worked hard, so ou consequently he succeeded; **je m'en doutais, ~ ne suis-je guère surprise** I suspected it, so I'm not entirely surprised; **2**○ (mais, d'ailleurs) **'on lui a volé son sac'—'quelle idée ~ de le laisser traîner!'** 'her bag was stolen'—'well, it was stupid to leave it lying about!'; **mais ~, pourquoi est-ce que tu y es allée?** why on earth did you go there?

aussitôt /osito/ I *adv* **1** (immédiatement) [*partir, arriver, s'endormir, reconnaître*] immediately, straight away; **il se tut ~** he shut up immediately ou straight away; **je m'en voulus ~ de m'être mise en colère** I was immediately cross with myself for having lost my temper; **presque ~** almost immediately; **~ après** straight after, immediately after; **je passerai chez toi ~ après l'avoir vu** I'll come to your place straight ou immediately after I've seen him; **~ après ton départ** straight ou immediately ou just after you left; **il est arrivé ~ après** he arrived straight ou immediately afterwards; **2** (juste après) **~ arrivé/descendu de l'avion** as soon as ou the moment he arrived/got off the plane; **un tableau, ~ acheté, n'a plus d'intérêt pour lui** no sooner has he bought a painting than he loses interest in it; **elle n'avait pas ~ quitté la pièce qu'il entra** no sooner had she left the room than he came in; **~ dit ~ fait** no sooner said than done.

II **aussitôt que** *loc conj* as soon as, the moment; **~ qu'il m'a vue, il m'a souri** as soon as ou the moment he saw me, he smiled at me; **je viendrai ~ que possible** I'll come as soon as possible; **elle partit ~ qu'elle put** she left as soon as she could.

austère /ɔstɛʀ, ostɛʀ/ *adj* [*personne, éducation, allure, vie, économie*] austere; [*expression, visage*] stern; [*vêtement*] severe; [*monument, lieu*] forbidding; [*livre*] dry.

austèrement /ostɛʀmɑ̃/ *adv* austerely.

austérité /osteʀite/ *nf* **1** (d'allure, économie, éducation, de lieu, personnne, vie) austerity; **mesures/plan d'~** austerity measures/plan; **politique d'~** policy of austerity; **2** (de vêtement, visage) severity; **3** (d'œuvre) dryness.

austral, **~e**, *mpl* **~s** /ostʀal/ *adj* **1** (du sud) austral; **vents ~s** austral winds; **2** (de l'hémisphère Sud) southern; **été ~** southern summer.

Australasie /ostʀalazi/ *nprf* Australasia; **d'~** Australasian.

Australie /ostʀali/ ▶ **321** *nprf* Australia.

Australie-Méridionale /ostʀalimeʀidjɔnal/ ▶ **692** *nprf* Southern Australia.

australien, **-ienne** /ostʀaljɛ̃, ɛn/ ▶ **537** *adj* Australian.

Australien, **-ienne** /ostʀaljɛ̃, ɛn/ ▶ **537** *nm,f* Australian.

Australie-Occidentale /ostʀaliɔksidɑ̃tal/ ▶ **692** *nprf* Western Australia.

australopithèque /ostʀalɔpitɛk/ *nm* Australopithecus.

austro-hongrois, **~e**, *mpl* **~** /ostʀoɔ̃gʀwa, az/ *adj* Austro-Hungarian.

autant /otɑ̃/ **I** *adv* **comment peut-il manger/dormir ~?** how can he eat/sleep so much?; **il n'a jamais ~ neigé/plu** it has never snowed/rained so much; **je t'aime toujours ~** I still love you as much; **essaie** or **tâche d'en faire ~** try and do the same; **je ne peux pas en dire ~** I can't say the same; **triste ~ que désagréable** as sad as it is unpleasant; **~ elle est gentille, ~ il peut être désagréable** she's as nice as he's unpleasant; **~ je comprends leur chagrin, ~ je déteste leur façon de l'étaler** as much as I understand their grief, I hate the way they parade it; **cela m'agace ~ que toi** it annoys me as much as it does you; **ma mère ~ que mon père déteste voyager** my mother hates travelling[GB] as much as my father does; **je les hais tous ~ qu'ils sont** I hate every single one of them; **je me moque de ce que vous pensez tous ~ que vous êtes** I don't care what any of you think; **j'aime ~ partir tout de suite** I'd rather leave straight away, I'd just as soon leave straight away; **j'aime ~ ne pas attendre pour le faire** I'd rather not wait to do it, I'd just as soon not wait to do it; **j'aime ~ te dire qu'il n'était pas content** believe me, he wasn't pleased; **~ dire que la réunion est annulée** in other words the meeting is cancelled[GB]; **~ parler à un mur** you might as well be talking to the wall; **donnez-m'en encore ~** give me as much again; **tout ~** just as much; **il risque tout ~ de faire** he equally runs the risk of doing; **~ que faire se peut** as much as possible, as far as possible; **~ que je sache** as far as I know; **~ que tu peux/veux** (comme tu peux/veux) as much as you can/like; (aussi longtemps que tu peux/veux) as long as you can/like; **tu peux changer le motif ~ que tu veux** you can change the pattern as much as you like.

II autant de *dét indéf* **1** (avec un nom dénombrable) **~ de cadeaux/de gens/d'erreurs** so many presents/people/mistakes; **leurs promesses sont ~ de mensonges** their promises are just so many lies; **il les considère comme ~ de clients potentiels** he considers them as so many potential customers; **il y a ~ de femmes que d'hommes** there are as many women as (there are) men; **je n'ai pas eu ~ d'ennuis que lui** I haven't had as many problems as he has; **2** (avec un nom non denombrable) **~ d'énergie/d'argent/de temps** so much energy/money/time; **~ de gentillesse/stupidité** such kindness/stupidity; **ce sera toujours ~ de fait** that'll be done at least; **je n'ai pas eu ~ de chance que lui** I haven't had as much luck as he has, I haven't been as lucky as he has; **je n'ai plus ~ de force qu'avant** I'm not as strong as I used to be; **~ à boire qu'à manger** as much to drink as to eat; **je n'avais jamais vu ~ de monde** I'd never seen so many people; **il y a ~ de place qu'ici** there's as much space as there is here; **il a révélé ~ de gentillesse que d'intelligence** he showed as much kindness as he did intelligence.

III d'autant *loc adv* **cela va permettre de réduire d'~ les coûts de production** this will allow an equivalent reduction in production costs; **les salaires ont augmenté de 3% mais les prix ont augmenté d'~** salaries have increased by 3% but prices have increased by just as much; **les informations seront décalées d'une heure et les émissions suivantes retardées d'~** the news will be broadcast an hour later than scheduled as will the following programmes[GB]; **d'~ plus!** all the more reason!; **d'~ mieux!** all the better, even better!; **d'~ moins** even less, all the less; **d'~ moins contrôlable** even less easy to control; **il pouvait d'~ moins ignorer les faits que**... it was all the more difficult for him to ignore the facts since...; **n'étant pas jalouse moi-même je le comprends d'~ moins** not being jealous myself I find it even harder to understand; **d'~ que** all the more so as; **il était furieux d'~ (plus) que personne ne l'avait prévenu** he was all the more furious as nobody had warned him; **d'~ plus heureux/grand que**... all the happier/bigger as...; **une histoire d'~ moins vraisemblable que**... a story all the more implausible since...; **la mesure a été d'~ mieux admise que**... the measure was all the more welcome since...

IV pour autant *loc adv* gén for all that; (en début de phrase) but for all that; **sans pour ~ faire** without necessarily doing; **je ne vais pas abandonner pour ~** I'm not going to give up for all that; **sans pour ~ tout modifier** without necessarily changing everything; **sans pour ~ que les loyers augmentent** without rents necessarily increasing.

V pour autant que *loc conj* **pour ~ que** as far as; **pour ~ qu'ils se mettent d'accord** if they agree; **pour ~ que je sache** as far as I know.

autarcie /otaʀsi/ *nf* autarky; **~ relative** relative autarky; **vivre en ~** to be self-sufficient.

autarcique /otaʀsik/ *adj* autarkic(al).

autel /otɛl/ *nm* altar; **sur l'~ de** on the altar of; **mener** or **conduire sa fille à l'~** to give one's daughter away; **être immolé sur l'~ de** to be sacrificed on the altar of.

auteur /otœʀ/ *nm* **1** (qui a écrit) author; **les grands ~s** the great authors; **relire un ~** to re-read an author; **du même ~** by the same author; **2** (créateur) (de chanson) composer; (de tableau, d'œuvre artistique) artist; **film d'~** art film; **cinéma d'~** art-house cinema GB ou movies (*pl*) US; **photographie d'~** art photography; **3** (de réforme, loi) author; (de découverte) inventor; (de crime, délit, d'attentat) perpetrator; (de coup d'État) leader; **l'~ du canular** the hoaxer; **l'~ de mes jours** hum (mère) my revered mother; (père) my revered father.

■ **~ de chansons** songwriter; **~ dramatique** playwright.

auteur-compositeur, *pl* **auteurs-compositeurs** /otœʀkɔ̃pozitœʀ/ *nm* songwriter.

auteur-compositeur-interprète, *pl* **auteurs-compositeurs-interprètes** /otœʀkɔ̃pozitœʀɛ̃tɛʀpʀɛt/ ▶ **510** *nm* singer-songwriter.

authenticité /otɑ̃tisite/ *nf* (de document, fait) authenticity; (de sentiment) genuineness.

authentifier /otɑ̃tifje/ [2] *vtr* to authenticate.

authentique /otɑ̃tik/ *adj* **1** (vrai) [*fait, récit, histoire*] true; [*tableau, document*] authentic, genuine; [*sentiment*] genuine; **ça s'est passé hier, ~**○**!** it happened yesterday, it really did! ou that's the honest truth!; **2** (conforme) [*document*] authentic; **acte ~** authenticated deed.

authentiquement /otɑ̃tikmɑ̃/ *adv* **1** (sincèrement) genuinely; **2**○ (absolument) totally, utterly.

autisme /otism/ *nm* autism.

autiste /otist/ **I** *adj* autistic.

II *nm,f* autistic person.

autistique /otistik/ *adj* autistic.

auto /auto/ **I** *adj inv* **assurance ~** car ou motor insurance GB, automobile insurance US.

II *nf* car, automobile US.

■ **~ tamponneuse** bumper car, dodgem.

auto-adhésif, **-ive**, *pl* **~s** /otoadezif, iv/ *adj* self-adhesive.

auto-allumage /otoalymaʒ/ *nm* pre-ignition.

autobiographie /otobjogʀafi/ *nf* autobiography.

autobiographique /otobjogʀafik/ *adj* autobiographical.

autobloquant, **~e** /otoblɔkɑ̃, ɑ̃t/ *adj* **pavé ~** paverprint.

autobloqueur /otoblɔkœʀ/ *nm* jammer.

auto-bronzant, **~e** /otobʀɔ̃zɑ̃, ɑ̃t/ *adj* [*crème*] self-tanning.

autobus /otobys/ *nm inv* bus.

autocar /otɔkaʀ/ *nm* coach GB, bus US.

auto-caravane, *pl* **autos-caravanes** /otokaʀavan/ *nf* motorhome, camper US.

autocassable /otokasabl/ *adj f* **ampoule ~** easy to open phial.

autocensure /otosɑ̃syʀ/ *nf* self-censorship.

autocensurer: **s'autocensurer** /otosɑ̃syʀe/ [1] *vpr* to practise[GB] self-censorship.

autochauffant, **~e** /otoʃofɑ̃, ɑ̃t/ *adj* self-heating.

autochenille /otoʃnij/ *nf* half-track.

autochtone /otɔkton/ **I** *adj* **1** Anthrop native, autochthonous spéc; **2** Géol autochthonous.

II *nmf* native, autochthon spéc.

autoclave /otɔklav/ **I** *adj* **fermeture ~** pressure seal.

II *nm* autoclave.

autocollant, **~e** /otɔkɔlɑ̃, ɑ̃t/ **I** *adj* self-adhesive.

II *nm* sticker.

autocommutateur /otɔkɔmytatœʀ/ *nm* private automatic exchange, PAX.

autoconsommation /otokɔ̃sɔmasjɔ̃/ *nf* home consumption; **ils tirent de l'~ le quart de leur alimentation** a quarter of their food is home-produced.

autocontrôle /otokɔ̃tʀol/ *nm.* **1** (gestion) (d'entreprise) self-regulation; **2** Fin holding by a company of its own shares.

autocopiant, **~e** /otokɔpjɑ̃, ɑ̃t/ *adj* carbonless, self-copying.

autocorrection /otokɔʀɛksjɔ̃/ *nf* autocorrection.

autocouchettes /otokuʃɛt/ *adj inv* **train ~** motorail train.

autocrate /otokʀat/ **I** *adj* autocratic.

II *nmf* autocrat.

autocratie /otokʀasi/ *nf* autocracy.

autocratique /otokʀatik/ *adj* autocratic.

autocritique /otokʀitik/ *nf* self-criticism ₵; **faire son ~** to go through a process of self-criticism.

autocuiseur /otokɥizœʀ/ *nm* pressure cooker.

autodafé /otodafe/ *nm* **1** Hist (cérémonie)

auto-da-fé; **2** (destruction par le feu) book-burning; **faire un ~ de qch** fig to throw sth on the bonfire.

autodéfense /otodefɑ̃s/ *nf* gén self-defence; Méd auto-immunity.

autodestructeur, **-trice** /otodɛstʀyktœʀ, tʀis/ *adj* self-destructive.

autodestruction /otodɛstʀyksjɔ̃/ *nf* self-destruction.

autodétention /otodetɑ̃sjɔ̃/ *nf* holding by a company of its own shares.

autodétenu, **~e** /otodetny/ *adj* [*actions*] held by the issuing company.

autodétermination /otodetɛʀminasjɔ̃/ *nf* self-determination.

autodéterminer: **s'autodéterminer** /otodetɛʀmine/ [1] *vpr* to exercise self-determination.

autodétruire: **s'autodétruire** /otodetʀɥiʀ/ [69] *vpr* [*person*] to destroy oneself; [*cassette*] to self-destruct; [*missile*] to auto-destruct.

autodidacte /otodidakt/ **I** *adj* gén self-educated; (dans un domaine) self-taught.
II *nmf* self-educated person, autodidact sout.

autodiscipline /otodisiplin/ *nf* self-discipline; **en ~** without supervision.

autodrome /otodʀom/ *nm* racetrack.

auto-école, *pl* **~s** /otoekɔl/ *nf* driving school.

auto-érotisme /otoeʀɔtism/ *nm* auto-eroticism.

autofécondation /otofekɔ̃dɑsjɔ̃/ *nf* self-fertilization.

autofinancement /otofinɑ̃smɑ̃/ *nm* self-financing.

autofinancer: **s'autofinancer** /otofinɑ̃se/ [1] *vpr* to be self-financing.

autofocus /otofɔkys/ **I** *adj inv* autofocus.
II *nm inv* (appareil) autofocus camera.

autogène /otoʒɛn/ *adj* **soudage ~** welding; **soudure ~** weld; ▶ **training**.

autogérer: **s'autogérer** /otoʒeʀe/ [14] *vpr* [*entreprise*] to be run on a cooperative basis; **usine autogérée** factory run as a cooperative; **autogéré par les ouvriers** run by the workers themselves.

autogestion /otoʒɛstjɔ̃/ *nf* (d'entreprise) worker management, cooperative management; (de collectivité) collective management.

autogestionnaire /otoʒɛstjɔnɛʀ/ *adj* involving worker management (*après n*).

autogire /otoʒiʀ/ *nm* autogiro.

autogonflable /otogɔ̃flabl/ *adj* self-inflating.

autographe /otɔgʀaf/ **I** *adj* original, autograph (*épith*).
II *nm* **1** (texte) original manuscript; **2** (signature) autograph.

autogreffe /otogʀɛf/ *nf* Méd autograft.

autoguidage /otogidaʒ/ *nm* (de missile) homing guidance; (d'avion) automatic guiding.

autoguidé, **~e** /otogide/ *adj* self-guided.

auto-immunisation, *pl* **~s** /otoimynizasjɔ̃/ *nf* autoimmunity.

auto-induction /otoɛ̃dyksjɔ̃/ *nf* self-induction.

auto-intoxication /otoɛ̃tɔksikasjɔ̃/ *nf* auto-intoxication.

autolimitation /otolimitasjɔ̃/ *nf* voluntary restraint.

autologue /otɔlɔg/ *adj* autologous.

automate /otɔmat/ *nm* lit, fig robot, automaton; **gestes d'~** robotic ou robot-like movements; **comme un ~** like a robot.

automation /otɔmɑsjɔ̃/ *nf* controv automation.

automatique /otɔmatik/ **I** *adj* **1** [*réflexe, appareil, voiture, arme, remboursement*] automatic; [*montre*] self-winding; **l'arrêt est ~** it stops automatically; **2**° (certain) **c'est ~** you can bet on it°.
II *nm* **1** Télécom **l'~** STD, subscriber trunk dialling[GB]; **2** (revolver) automatic (revolver); **3** Phot automatic camera.
III *nf* Tech automation.

automatiquement /otɔmatikmɑ̃/ *adv* **1** (de façon automatique) automatically; **2**° (inévitablement) inevitably.

automatisation /otɔmatizɑsjɔ̃/ *nf* automation.

automatiser /otɔmatize/ [1] *vtr* to automate.

automatisme /otɔmatism/ *nm* (de personne, fonction, réaction) automatism; (de machine) automatic functioning; **les ~s boursiers/économiques** automatic stock exchange/economic triggers; **acquérir des ~s** to acquire automatic reflexes.

automédication /otomedikasjɔ̃/ *nf* self-medication.

automitrailleuse /otomitʀajøz/ *nf* armoured[GB] car.

automnal, **~e**, *mpl* **-aux** /otɔnal, o/ *adj* autumnal.

automne /otɔn/ **▶ 738** *nm* autumn GB, fall US; **en ~** in autumn GB, in the fall US; **l'~ prochain/dernier** next/last autumn GB, next/last fall US; **l'~ de leur vie** the autumn of their lives.

automobile /otomɔbil/ **I** *adj* **1** [*véhicule*] motorized; **voiture ~** (motor) car; **2** [*industrie, assurance*] car, motor, automobile US; [*accessoire, constructeur*] car (*épith*); **3** Sport [*course*] motor (*épith*); [*circuit*] motor racing (*épith*).
II *nf* **1** (voiture) (motor) car, automobile US; **2** (industrie) **l'~** the car ou motor industry GB, the automobile industry US.

automobiliste /otomɔbilist/ *nmf* motorist.

automoteur, **-trice** /otomɔtœʀ, tʀis/ **I** *adj* [*véhicule, bateau*] self-propelled, motor (*épith*).
II *nm* self-propelled barge.
III automotrice *nf* electric railcar.

autonettoyant, **~e** /otonetwajɑ̃, ɑ̃t/ *adj* self-cleaning.

autonome /otɔnɔm/ *adj* **1** Pol [*région, république*] autonomous; **2** (autogéré) [*filiale, gestion*] independent, autonomous; [*syndicat*] nonaffiliated, independent; [*personne*] self-sufficient; [*vie*] independent; **variable ~** Écon independent variable; **3** (non connecté) [*moteur*] independent; Ordinat [*unité*] stand-alone; [*système, équipement*] off-line; **4** Philos [*volonté*] autonomous.

autonomie /otɔnɔmi/ *nf* **1** Admin, Fin, Philos, Pol autonomy; **2** Aut, Aviat range; **~ de vol** flight range.
■ **~ de marche** Tech running time.

autonomiste /otɔnɔmist/ *adj, nmf* separatist.

autoplastie /otoplasti/ *nf* Méd autoplasty.

autopollinisation /otopɔlinizasjɔ̃/ *nf* self-pollination.

autopompe /otopɔ̃p/ *nf* fire engine.

autopont /otopɔ̃/ *nm* flyover.

autoportrait /otopɔʀtʀɛ/ *nm* self-portrait.

autoproduit, **~e** /otoprɔdɥi, it/ *adj* made at one's own expense.

autopropulsé, **~e** /otopʀɔpylse/ *adj* self-propelled.

autopropulsion /otopʀɔpylsjɔ̃/ *nf* self-propulsion.

autoprotection /ɔtɔpʀɔtɛksjɔ̃/ *nf* automatic burglar alarm; **dispositif d'~** automatic alarm system.

autopsie /otɔpsi/ *nf* postmortem (examination), autopsy; **faire une ~** to carry out a postmortem (examination), to perform an autopsy; **faire l'~ de la défaite électorale** fig to hold a postmortem on why the election was lost.

autopsier /otɔpsje/ [2] *vtr* to carry out a postmortem (examination) on, to perform an autopsy on [*cadavre*].

autopunition /otopynisjɔ̃/ *nf* self-punishment.

autoradio /otoʀadjo/ *nm* car radio.

autorail /otoʀɑj/ *nm* rail car.

auto-réversible /otoʀevɛʀsibl/ *adj* [*cassette*] with auto-reverse (*après n*).

autorisation /otɔʀizɑsjɔ̃/ *nf* **1** (accord) gén permission (**de faire** to do); (officielle) authorization (**de faire** to do); **donner à qn l'~ de faire** to give sb permission to do; (officiellement) to give ou grant sb authorization to do; **avoir l'~ de faire** to have permission to do; **sans l'~ du gouvernement** without government authorization; **entrée interdite sans ~** no unauthorized entry; **2** Admin, Comm, Jur licence[GB]; **sans ~** without a licence[GB]; **avoir l'~ d'exporter des armes** to have a licence for exporting weapons, to be licensed to export weapons; **3** (document) permit; (licence) licence[GB].
■ **~ administrative de licenciement** Admin *administrative fiat for a company's redundancy plan*; **~ de crédit** Fin overdraft facility; **~ d'étalage** stallholder's permit; **~ de mise sur le marché** product licence[GB]; **~ de mise sur le marché français** product licence[GB] in France; **~ parentale** parental consent; **~ de prélèvement** direct-debit form; Comm release for shipment; **~ de programme** authorization bill; **~ de sortie** Scol *consent form allowing a pupil to leave the school building*; **~ de sortie du territoire** parents' authorization for an unaccompanied minor to travel abroad; **~ de vol** Aviat flight clearance.

autorisé, **~e** /otɔʀize/ **I** *pp* ▶ **autoriser**.
II *pp adj* **1** (approuvé) [*biographie, édition, agent*] authorized; [*parti*] legal; [*représentant*] Comm accredited; **non ~** unauthorized; **2** (officiel) [*personne*] authorized; **milieux ~s** official circles; **de source ~e** from official sources; **3** (qualifié) [*avis, ouvrage*] authoritative; **4** (toléré) [*tension, pression*] permitted; **poids maximum en charge ~** maximum permitted load.

autoriser /otɔʀize/ [1] **I** *vtr* **1** (donner une permission) [*personne*] to allow [*visite*]; [*autorités*] to authorize [*paiement, visite*]; **~ qn à faire** to give sb permission to do, to authorize sb to do; **~ le café à qn** to allow sb coffee; **~ que les prix augmentent** to permit ou allow prices to rise; **2** (donner un droit) [*événement, loi*] **~ qn à faire** to entitle sb to do; **ce qui autorise à penser que** which makes it reasonable ou legitimate to think that; **rien ne vous autorise à agir ainsi** you have no right to behave like that; **3** (rendre possible) [*situation, conditions*] to make [sth] possible, to allow (of) [*réalisation, innovation*]; **la situation n'autorise aucune baisse des prix** the situation doesn't allow of any price reductions; **4** (donner une raison) [*événement, état*] to give grounds for [*espoir, optimisme*]; to justify [*sentiment, réaction*]; **rien n'autorise ce pessimisme** there are no grounds for such pessimism.
II s'autoriser *vpr* **s'~ de qch** (prétexter) to use sth as an excuse (**pour faire** to do); (s'appuyer sur) **je me suis autorisé de votre lettre pour solliciter leur aide** in view of what you wrote in your letter I asked them to help; **s'~ d'un précédent pour faire qch** to rely on precedent in doing sth.

autoritaire /otɔʀitɛʀ/ *adj, nmf* authoritarian.

autoritairement /otɔʀitɛʀmɑ̃/ *adv* in an authoritarian way.

autoritarisme /otɔʀitaʀism/ *nm* authoritarianism.

autorité /otɔʀite/ *nf* **1** (domination) authority (**sur** over); **exercer son ~ sur qn** to exercise authority over sb; **être sous l'~ de qn** to be under sb's authority; **faire acte d'~** to impose one's authority; **de sa propre ~** on one's own authority; **agir avec ~** to act decisively; **faire qch d'~** (de façon impérieuse) to do sth decisively; (sans consulter) to take it upon oneself to do sth; **il**

a été désigné d'~ comme porte-parole it has been decided that he will be appointed as a spokesman; **2** (ascendant) authority; **avoir de l'~ sur qn** to have influence ou authority over sb; **il n'a aucune ~ sur ses enfants/élèves** he has no control over his children/pupils; **faire ~** [*personne*] to be an authority (**en, en matière de** on); [*ouvrage*] to be authoritative; **parler avec ~ de qch** to speak authoritatively on sth; **3** (spécialiste) authority, expert; **4** Admin (pouvoir établi) authority; (personnel) **les ~s** the authorities; **défier l'~** to defy authority; **les ~s monétaires** the monetary authorities; **5** Jur jurisdiction; **territoire soumis à** or **placé sous l'~ de** territory within the jurisdiction of; **placer qch sous l'~ de** to place sth under the authority of [*ministère, conseil*]; **l'~ de la loi** the force of the law; **l'~ de la chose jugée** Jur res judicata; **par ~ de justice** by order of the court.

■ **~ parentale** parental authority.

autoroute /otoʀut/ *nf* motorway GB, freeway US; **~ de dégagement** bypass GB, freeway US; **~ de l'information** Ordinat information (super)highway; **~ à péage** toll motorway; **~ urbaine** urban motorway.

autoroutier, **-ière** /otoʀutje, ɛʀ/ *adj* motorway (*épith*) GB, freeway (*épith*) US.

autosatisfaction /otosatisfaksjɔ̃/ *nf* self-satisfaction.

auto-stop /otostɔp/ *nm* hitchhiking; **faire de l'~** to hitchhike; **aller à Paris en ~** to hitchhike to Paris; **faire la France en ~** to hitchhike around France; **prendre qn en ~** to pick up a hitchhiker; **je l'ai prise en ~** I gave her a lift GB ou ride US.

auto-stoppeur, **-euse**, *mpl* **~s** /otostɔpœʀ, øz/ *nm,f* hitchhiker; **prendre un ~** to pick up a hitchhiker.

autosubsistance /otosybzistɑ̃s/ *nf* self-sufficiency.

autosuffisance /otosyfizɑ̃s/ *nf* self-sufficiency.

autosuffisant, **~e** /otosyfizɑ̃, ɑ̃t/ *adj* self-sufficient.

autosuggestion /otosygʒɛstjɔ̃/ *nf* autosuggestion.

autotracté /ototʀakte/ *adj* self-propelled.

autotransfusion /ototʀɑ̃sfyzjɔ̃/ *nf* autologous transfusion.

autour[1] /otuʀ/ **I** *adv* **un parterre de fleurs avec des pierres ~** a flowerbed with stones around it; **tout ~** all around.

II autour de *loc prép* **1** (marquant le lieu) around, round GB; **~ de la table/du soleil** around the table/the sun; **2** (marquant une approximation) around, round GB; **~ de 10 h/200 francs** around 10 o'clock/200 francs; **3** (au sujet de) **un débat/une conférence ~ du thème du pouvoir** a debate/a conference on the theme of power; **un débat ~ de cinq thèmes** a debate centred[GB] around five themes; **la publicité organisée ~ de cet événement** fig the publicity organized around this event.

autour[2] /otuʀ/ *nm* goshawk.

autre[1] /otʀ/

■ **Note** Lorsqu'il est adjectif indéfini et employé avec un article défini *autre* se traduit par *other*: *l'autre rue* = the other street.
– On notera que *un autre* se traduit par *another* en un seul mot.
– Les autres emplois de l'adjectif ainsi que le pronom indéfini sont traités ci-dessous.
– Les expressions comme *entre autres, nul autre, personne d'autre etc* se trouvent respectivement à ***entre***, ***nul***, ***personne*** etc. De même les expressions telles que *comme dit l'autre, en voir d'autres, avoir d'autres chats à fouetter etc* se trouvent respectivement sous ***dire***, ***voir***, ***fouetter*** etc.
– En revanche *l'un... l'autre* et ses dérivés sont traités ci-dessous.

I *adj indéf* **1** (indiquant la différence) **l'~ côté/solution/bout** the other side/solution/end; **l'~ jour** the other day; **une ~ idée/histoire** another idea/story; **je ferai ça un ~ jour** I'll do that some other day; **pas d'~ place/solution** no other space/solution; **il n'y a pas d'~s exemples** there aren't any other examples; **une (tout) ~ conception** an altogether ou a completely different design; **allumettes, briquets et ~s gadgets** matches, lighters and other gadgets; **bien** or **beaucoup d'~s problèmes** many other problems; **quelque chose/rien d'~** something/nothing else; **quoi d'~?** what else?; **quelqu'un/personne d'~** someone/no-one else; **personne d'~ que lui n'aurait accepté** no-one but him would have accepted; **l'actrice principale n'est ~ que la fille du metteur en scène** the leading actress is none other than the director's daughter; **mon livre préféré n'est ~ que la Bible** my favourite[GB] book is none other than the Bible; **2** (supplémentaire) **tu veux un ~ bonbon?** do you want another sweet GB ou candy US?; **ils ne veulent pas d'~ enfant, ils ne veulent pas d'~s enfants** they don't want another child, they don't want any more children; **donnez-moi dix ~s timbres** give me another ten stamps; **3** (différent) different; **être ~** to be different; **l'effet obtenu est tout ~** the effect produced is completely different; **dans des circonstances ~s** in ou under other circumstances; **un produit ~ que l'éther** a product other than ether; **4**○ (après un pronom personnel) **nous ~s/vous ~s** we/you; **nous ~s professeurs/Français** we teachers/French.

II *pron indéf* **1** (indiquant la différence) **où sont les autres?** (choses) where are the other ones?; (personnes) where are the others?; **je t'ai pris pour un ~** I mistook you for someone else; **certains estiment que c'est juste, d'~s non** some (people) think it's fair, others don't; **elle est pourrie cette pomme, prends-en une ~** this apple is rotten, have another one; **tu n'en as pas d'~s?** haven't you got any others?; **penser aux ~s** to think of others ou other people; **je me fiche**○ **de ce que pensent les ~s** I don't care what other people think; **l'un est souriant l'~ est grognon** one is smiling, the other one is grumpy; **l'une est pliante mais pas l'~** one is folding, the other one isn't; **ce qui amuse l'un agace l'~** what amuses one annoys the other; **certains sont ravis d'~s moins** some people are thrilled, others less so; **aussi têtus l'un que l'~** as stubborn as each other, both equally stubborn; **des récits plus vivants les uns que les ~s** stories each more lively than the one before; **loin l'un de l'~, loin les uns des ~s** far away from each other, far apart; **nous sommes dépendants l'un de l'~, nous sommes dépendants les uns des ~s** we're dependent on each other ou one another; **ils se respectent les uns les ~s** they respect each other; **'aimez-vous les uns les ~s'** 'love one another'; **l'un après/devant/derrière l'~, les uns après/devant/derrière les ~s** one after/in front of/behind the other; **c'est l'un ou l'~!** it's got to be either one or the other!; **quand ce n'est pas l'un c'est l'~** if it isn't one of them, it's the other; **chez lui c'est tout l'un ou tout l'~** he goes to extremes; **ni l'un ni l'~** neither one nor the other, neither of them; **il est où l'~**○**?** where's what's-his-name○ got to?; **l'~ il est gonflé**○**!** he's got a nerve, that one!; **à d'~s**○**!** pull the other one (it's got bells on○)!, go and tell it to the marines○! US; **2** (indiquant un supplément) **prends-en un ~ si tu aimes ça** have another one if you like them; **si je peux je t'en apporterai d'~s** if I can I'll bring you some more; **ils ont deux enfants et n'en veulent pas d'~s** they have two children and don't want any more.

III autre part *loc adv* somewhere else; ▶ **part**.

autre[2] /otʀ/ *nm* Philos **l'~** the other.

autrefois /otʀəfwa/ *adv* gén in the past; (précédemment) before, formerly sout; (en un temps révolu) in the old days, in days gone by littér; **~ c'était possible** it used to be possible; **c'est là que je travaillais ~** that's where I worked before ou I used to work; **~, il n'y avait pas d'électricité** in the old days, there was no electricity; **~, quand Paris s'appelait Lutèce** long ago, when Paris was called Lutetia; **elle ~ si riche** she, who used to be so wealthy; **mes habitudes/ma vie d'~** my former habits/life; **les coutumes/légendes d'~** old customs/legends; **les voitures d'~** cars of an earlier era; **les maisons d'~ étaient solides** in the old days, houses were well built.

autrement /otʀəmɑ̃/ *adv* **1** (de façon autre) [*faire, voir, agir*] differently, in a different way; [*décider, conclure*] otherwise; [*nommé, appelé*] otherwise; **le sort en a voulu ~** fate decided otherwise; **ça ne s'explique pas ~** there's no other explanation for it; **un escroc n'aurait pas agi ~** it's the sort of thing you would expect from a crook; **on ne peut les qualifier ~** that's all you can say about them; **parlez-moi ~, je vous prie** don't talk to me like that, please; **il en est** or **va (tout) ~ des films** it's quite different for films; **il n'en est pas ~ des films** it's no different for films; **il ne peut (pas) en être ~** that's the way it has to be; **c'est comme ça, et pas ~** that's just the way it is; **on ne peut pas faire ~** there's no other way; **comment aurait-elle pu faire ~?** what else could she have done?; **je n'ai pas pu faire ~ que de les inviter** I had no alternative but to invite them; **on ne peut y accéder ~ que par bateau** you can only get there by boat; **je ne l'ai jamais vue ~ qu'en jean** I've never seen her in anything but jeans; **ça s'est passé ~ que prévu** it did not turn out as expected; **~ dit** in other words; **2** (sans quoi) otherwise; **~ ne compte pas sur moi** otherwise don't count on me; **3**○ (à part cela) otherwise, apart from that; **4**○ (spécialement) **pas ~** not particularly ou unduly; **je n'en serais pas ~ surpris** I wouldn't be particularly ou unduly surprised; **5**○ (beaucoup plus) **~ grave** (much) more serious; **~ aimable** (much) nicer; **c'est ~ plus petit qu'ici** it's much smaller than here.

Autriche /otʀiʃ/ ▶ **321** *nprf* Austria.

Autriche-Hongrie /otʀiʃɔ̃gʀi/ *nprf* Hist Austro-Hungary.

autrichien, **-ienne** /otʀiʃjɛ̃, ɛn/ ▶ **537** *adj* Austrian.

Autrichien, **-ienne** /otʀiʃjɛ̃, ɛn/ ▶ **537** *nm,f* Austrian.

autruche /otʀyʃ/ *nf* ostrich.

IDIOMES **avoir un estomac d'~** to have a cast-iron stomach; **faire l'~, jouer les ~s, pratiquer la politique de l'~** to bury one's head in the sand.

autrui /otʀɥi/ *pron indéf* others (*pl*), other people (*pl*); **les biens d'~** other people's property; **la vie d'~** other people's lives (*pl*); **sans l'aide d'~** without the help of others, without other people's help.

auvent /ovɑ̃/ *nm* (de maison) canopy; (de tente, caravane) awning.

auvergnat, **~e** /ovɛʀɲa, at/ ▶ **692** *adj* of the Auvergne.

Auvergnat, **~e** /ovɛʀɲa, at/ ▶ **692** *nm,f* (natif) native of the Auvergne; (habitant) inhabitant of the Auvergne.

Auvergne /ovɛʀɲ/ ▶ **692** *nprf* **l'~** the Auvergne.

aux /o/ *prép* (=**à les**) ▶ **à**.

auxerrois, **~e** /osɛʀwa, az/ ▶ **857** *adj* of Auxerre.

Auxerrois, **~e** /osɛʀwa, az/ ▶ **857** *nm,f* (natif) native of Auxerre; (habitant) inhabitant of Auxerre.

auxiliaire /oksiljɛʀ/ **I** *adj* **1** Ling auxiliary; **2** (accessoire) [*machine*] auxiliary; [*motor*]

back-up (*épith*); [*service*] supplementary; [*cause*] secondary; [*moyen*] additional; Ordinat [*mémoire*] additional; **bureau ~** sub-office; **3** ▶510 (non-titulaire) **maître ~** assistant teacher; **infirmier ~** nursing auxiliary GB, aide US.
II *nmf* assistant helper.
III *nm* **1** (moyen, objet) aid; **2** Ling auxiliary verb.
IV **auxiliaires** *nmpl* Naut auxiliary equipment ¢.
■ **~ de justice** representative of the law; **~ médical** medical auxiliary GB, aide US.

auxiliairement /ɔksiljɛʀmɑ̃/ *adv* **1** Ling as an auxiliary verb; **2** fig less importantly.

auxquels, **auxquelles** ▶ **lequel**.

avachi, **~e** /avaʃi/ I *pp* ▶ **avachir**.
II *pp adj* **1** [*valise, chaussure*] which has lost its shape (*épith, après n*); [*fauteuil*] shapeless; **2** [*traits, visage*] flabby.

avachir /avaʃiʀ/ [3] I *vtr* to wear out [*poche, chaussure*].
II **s'avachir** *vpr* **1** [*fauteuil*] to sag; fig [*personne*] to let oneself go; **2** (s'écrouler) **aussitôt rentré il s'est avachi dans un fauteuil** as soon as he got in he flopped into an armchair; **elle était avachie devant la télévision** she was slumped in front of the television.

avachissement /avaʃismɑ̃/ *nm* (fatigue) sluggishness; **~ intellectuel** intellectual flabbiness.

AVAE /aveaə/ *nm* (*abbr* = **appelé volontaire pour l'action extérieure**) *conscript who volunteers for military service abroad*.

aval /aval/ I *adj inv* Sport downhill.
II *nm* **1** Géog (de cours d'eau) downstream part; **en ~** downstream (**de** from); **2** Géog (de pente) lower slopes (*pl*); **en ~** lower down (**de** from); **3** (de processus) **en ~** downstream (**de** from); **4** Fin (engagement de payer) guarantee; **'Bon pour ~'** 'Guaranteed by'; **donner son ~ à** to endorse; **donneur d'~** guarantor; **5** (approbation) **vous avez mon ~** I'm behind you; **avoir reçu l'~ de qn** to have sb behind one; **donner son ~ à qn** to give sb one's approval.

avalanche /avalɑ̃ʃ/ *nf* **1** Géog, Météo avalanche; **2** (grande quantité) (de critiques, sondages, scandales, questions, réformes) flood; (de projectiles, coups) avalanche; (de compliments) shower.

avaler /avale/ [1] *vtr* **1** (ingurgiter) [*personne*] to swallow [*aliment, sirop, médicament*]; [*machine*] to swallow [*ticket, carte de crédit*]; fig [*entreprise*] to swallow up [*petite entreprise*]; **'ne pas ~'** Pharm 'not to be taken internally'; **~ sa salive** to swallow; **j'ai avalé de travers** it went down the wrong way; **j'ai avalé mon vin de travers** my wine went down the wrong way; **~ ses mots** fig to swallow one's words; **~ un livre** fig to devour a book; **~ l'obstacle** Sport to make nothing of an obstacle; **2** (inhaler) to inhale [*fumée, vapeur*]; **tu avales la fumée?** do you inhale?; **3**○ (admettre) to swallow [*histoire, récit, mensonge*]; **faire ~ qch à qn** to make sb swallow sth; **on te ferait ~ n'importe quoi** they'd make you swallow anything; **c'est dur à ~**○ it's difficult to swallow.
IDIOMES **tu as avalé ta langue?** hum have you lost your tongue?; **il a avalé son parapluie** or **sa canne** hum he's so stiff and starchy.

avaleur /avalœʀ/ ▶510 *nm* **~ de sabres** sword swallower.

avaliseur /avalizœʀ/ *nm* Fin guarantor.

à-valoir /avalwaʀ/ *nm inv* Fin instalment[GB].

avance /avɑ̃s/ I *nf* **1** (progression) advance; **fuir devant l'~ des rebelles** to flee before the advance of the rebels; **ralentir/contenir l'~ de l'ennemi** to slow/to contain the enemy's advance; **2** (avantage) lead; **conserver son ~** to keep one's lead; **~ technologique** technological advance; **avoir une ~ de 3% dans les sondages** [*parti, candidat*] to have a 3% lead in the opinion polls; **prendre de l'~ sur** [*personne, pays, entreprise*] to pull ahead of; **avoir de l'~ sur** [*personne, pays, entreprise*] to be ahead of; **3** Fin (acompte) advance; **une ~ sur salaire** an advance on one's salary.
II **à l'avance** *loc adv* in advance; **faire qch à l'~** to do sth in advance; **ils ont eu connaissance des sujets à l'~** they knew the subjects in advance.
III **d'avance** *loc adv* already; **il a perdu d'~** he has already lost; **ça me déprime d'~** I'm already depressed about it; **c'est acquis d'~, elle sera augmentée** it's already been agreed, she will get a rise GB ou raise US; **il faut payer d'~** you have to pay in advance; **d'~ je vous remercie** I thank you in advance; **avoir cinq minutes d'~** to be five minutes early.
IV **en avance** *loc adv* **1** (sur l'heure) early; **être en ~** to be early; **arriver/partir en ~** to arrive/to leave early; **2** (sur les autres) **le Japon est en ~ sur l'Europe** Japan is ahead of Europe; **il est en ~ pour son âge** he's advanced for his age; **leur fille est très en ~ dans ses études** their daughter is very advanced in her studies.
V **par avance** *loc adv* already; **l'opposition dénonce par ~ les résultats de l'élection** the opposition is denouncing the election results before they're even out.
VI **avances** *nfpl* advances; **faire des ~s à qn** to make advances to sb, to come on to sb○ US; **répondre aux ~s de qn** to respond to sb's advances.
■ **~ rapide** fast-forward.

avancé, **~e** /avɑ̃se/ I *pp* ▶ **avancer**.
II *pp adj* **1** (précoce) [*enfant, élève*] advanced; **2** (évolué) [*technique, niveau de vie*] advanced; [*opinion, idée*] progressive; **3** (qui s'abîme) [*poire, tomate, camembert*] overripe; **le poisson a l'air un peu ~** the fish looks as if it's going off GB ou bad; **4** (loin du début) advanced; **dans un état de décomposition ~e** in an advanced state of decomposition; **être bien ~** [*travail, recherche, construction*] to be well advanced; **la saison est bien ~e** it's late in the season; **la nuit était bien ~e** it was late at night; **je ne suis pas plus ~** I'm none the wiser; **te voilà bien ~!** iron that's done you a lot of good! iron; **être à un stade ~** [*maladie, détérioration*] to be at an advanced stage; **à une heure ~e de la nuit** late at night; **5** Mil [*poste*] advanced.
III **avancée** *nf* **1** (de toit, rocher) overhang; **le belvédère forme une ~e sur le ravin** the belvedere projects over the ravine; **2** (progression) (de monnaie, technologie) advance (**sur** over); (sur le terrain) Mil advance (**de** of); **les sondages confirment l'~e du candidat** the opinion polls confirm the candidate's progress; **l'~e des connaissances en ce domaine** advances made in this field of knowledge; **l'~e du désert** the advance of the desert.

avancement /avɑ̃smɑ̃/ *nm* **1** (dans une carrière) promotion; **obtenir de l'~** to get promotion; **il a reçu de l'~** he was promoted; **demander de l'~** to ask for promotion; **2** (dans des travaux, des connaissances) progress; **un rapport sur l'état d'~ du projet** a progress report on the project; **3** (d'une limite) **~ de l'âge de la retraite** lowering of the retirement age.

avancer /avɑ̃se/ [12] I *vtr* **1** (dans l'espace) to move [sth] forward [*chaise, assiette, échelle*]; **~ le cou** to crane one's neck (forward); **~ une main timide** to hold one's hand out shyly; **~ un siège à qn** to pull ou draw up a seat for sb; **la voiture de Monsieur est avancée** your car awaits, sir; **2** (dans le temps) to bring forward [*départ, voyage, réunion, heure, élections*]; **un match avancé** a game that has been brought forward; **3** (faire progresser) to get ahead with [*travail, tricot*]; **tous ces problèmes ne font pas ~ vos affaires** all these problems aren't improving matters for you; **classe les fiches, ça m'avancera** sort out the cards, it'll help me get on more quickly; **ils ont embauché un intérimaire pour les ~ un peu** they have taken on a temp○ to speed things up a bit; **toutes ces récriminations ne nous avancent pas beaucoup** all these recriminations aren't getting us very far; **à quoi ça t'avance d'avoir deux voitures?** where does it get you, having two cars?; **cela ne nous avance à rien** that doesn't get us anywhere; **4** (prêter) **~ de l'argent à qn** [*banque*] to advance money to sb; [*parent, ami*] to lend money to sb; **pourriez-vous m'~ 1 000 francs sur mon salaire?** could you advance me 1,000 francs out of my salary?; **5** (changer l'heure) **~ sa montre de cinq minutes** to put one's watch forward (by) five minutes; **6** (affirmer) to put forward [*accusation, argument, théorie*]; to propose [*chiffre*]; **~ que** to suggest that.
II *vi* **1** (progresser dans l'espace) [*personne, véhicule, navire*] to move (forward); [*armée, troupes*] to advance; **~ d'un mètre** to move forward (by) one metre; **~ vers la sortie** to move toward(s) the exit; **je ne peux plus ~** I can't go any further; **allez, avance!** go on!; **~ au pas** [*voiture, cavalier*] to move at walking pace; **~ d'un pas** to take one step forward; **~ en boitant** to limp forward; **elle poussait mon frère pour le faire ~** she was pushing my brother forward; **elle avança vers moi** she came up to me; **elle avança vers le guichet** (elle alla) she went up to the ticket office; (elle vint) she came up up to the ticket office; **2** (progresser) [*personne*] to make progress; [*travail, construction, recherche*] to progress; **le travail avance vite/péniblement** the work is making good/halting progress; **j'ai bien avancé dans mon travail ce matin** I've made good progress with my work this morning; **ce pull n'avance guère** this sweater isn't coming on ou progressing very quickly; **et votre projet? ça avance**○**?** and your project? how is it coming along?; **faire ~ une enquête/les négociations** to speed up an inquiry/the negotiations; **faire ~ la science** to further science; **~ en âge** to be getting on (in years); **plus on avance dans la vie** the longer one lives; **la matinée/l'hiver avançait** the morning/the winter was wearing on; **3** (par rapport à l'heure réelle) **j'avance de dix minutes** I am ten minutes fast; **ma montre avance de deux minutes** my watch is two minutes fast; **4** (faire saillie) [*menton, dents*] to stick out, to protrude; [*cap, presqu'île*] to jut out (**dans** into); [*balcon, plongeoir*] to jut out, to project (**au-dessus de** over).
III **s'avancer** *vpr* **1** (physiquement) **s'~ vers qch** to move toward(s) sth; **s'~ vers qn** (aller) to go toward(s) sb; (venir) to come up to sb; **elle s'avança jusqu'à la porte** she went up to the door; **ne t'avance pas trop près du bord** don't go too near the edge; **s'~ dans le bois** to go further into the woods; **s'~ dans le couloir** to go down the corridor; **la mer s'avance dans les terres** the sea goes (a long way) inland; **2** (dans une tâche) to get ahead; **je me suis bien avancé (dans mon travail)** I've got well ahead (with my work); **je me suis avancée pour la semaine prochaine** I'm ahead with my work for next week; **3** (faire saillie) to jut out, to protrude (**dans** into; **sur, au-dessus de** over); **4** (donner son point de vue) to commit oneself; **s'~ sur un terrain glissant** fig to be on slippery ground fig; **je me suis un peu avancé en te promettant le dossier pour demain** I shouldn't have committed myself by promising you I'd have the file ready for tomorrow; **en disant cela je m'avance peut-être un peu trop** maybe I am exaggerating a bit in saying that; **il s'est**

avancé jusqu'à dire que he went as far as to say that.

avanie /avani/ *nf* **faire des ~s à qn** to humiliate sb; **subir des ~s** to suffer humiliation.

avant[1] /avɑ̃/ **I** *adv* **1** (dans le temps) gén before, beforehand; (d'abord) first; **que faisait-il ~** what was he doing before?; **tu n'aurais pas pu le dire ~?** couldn't you have said so before(hand)?; **si j'avais su cela ~ j'aurais**... if I'd known that before(-hand) I would have...; **quelques heures/jours ~** a few hours/days before; **la nuit/la semaine/le mois ~** the night/the week/the month before; **peu ~** not long before (that); **bien ~** long before; **le bus/train d'~** the previous bus/train; **les locataires d'~** the previous tenants; **le cours/la séance d'~** the previous lesson/performance; **repose-toi ~ tu partiras ensuite** rest first and then go; **laquelle de ces lettres veux-tu que je tape ~?** which of these letters would you like me to type first?; **~ nous n'avions pas l'électricité** we didn't have electricity before; **aussitôt ~** just before; **j'avais compris longtemps ~** I had understood a long time before; **ce n'était pas ce lundi mais celui d'~** it was not this Monday but the previous one; **la fois d'~ nous nous étions déjà perdus** we got lost the last time as well; **j'ai vu le film mais pas l'émission d'~** I saw the film GB ou movie US but not the programme[GB] before it; **2** (dans l'espace) before; **tu vois l'église, j'habite (juste) ~** can you see the church? I live (just) before it; **'c'est ~ l'église?'—'oui juste ~'** 'is it before the church?'—'yes just before it'; **il l'a mentionné ~ dans l'introduction** he mentioned it earlier in the introduction; **je crois que la dame était ~** I think this lady was first; **il est inutile de creuser plus ~** lit, fig there's no point in digging any further; **refuser de s'engager plus ~** lit to refuse to go any further; fig to refuse to get any more involved; **3** (dans une hiérarchie) before; **le T vient ~** T comes before; **son travail passe ~** his work comes first.

II *prép* **1** (dans le temps) before; **partir/arriver ~ qn** to leave/to arrive before sb, to leave/to arrive before sb does; **~ mon départ/retour** before I leave/come back; **les enfants ~ les adultes** children before adults; **je suis partie ~ la fin** I left before the end; **~ l'ouverture/la fermeture des magasins** before the shops GB ou stores US open/close; **peu ~ minuit** shortly before midnight; **ne viens pas ~ 5 heures** don't come before 5 o'clock; **rentrer ~ la nuit/le dîner** to come back before nightfall/dinner; **la situation d'~ la crise/révolution** the situation before the crisis/revolution; **~ le 1er juillet** by 1 July; **le travail doit être fini ~ l'été/la fin de l'année/19 heures** the work must be completed by the summer/the end of the year/7 pm; **j'aurai fini ~ une semaine/un mois** I'll have finished within a week/a month; **nous partons à 11 heures, ~ cela je vais travailler un peu** we're leaving at 11, I'm going to do a bit of work before then; **~ peu** shortly; **vous serez informé ~ peu des nouvelles consignes** you will be informed of the new orders shortly; **bien/peu ~ 16 heures** well/a little before 4 pm; **bien ~ ta naissance** long ou well before you were born ; **~ toute explication/considération** before explaining/considering anything; **~ déduction/impôt** before deductions/tax; **2** (dans l'espace) before; **~ le croisement/la poste** before the crossing/the post office; **bien/juste ~ le pont** well/just before the bridge; **j'étais ~ vous** I was in front of ou before you; ▶ **charrue**; **3** (dans une hiérarchie) before; **le grade de capitaine vient ~ celui de colonel** the rank of captain comes before that of colonel; **faire passer qn/qch ~ qn/qch** to put sb/sth before sb/sth; **~ tout, ~ toute chose** (surtout) above all; (d'abord) first and foremost; **il recherche ~ tout la tranquillité** above all he wants peace and quiet; **il s'agit ~ tout de comprendre le principe** above all, it is a matter of understanding the principle; **je suis ~ tout un peintre** I am first and foremost a painter.

III en avant *loc adv* **1** (dans l'espace) forward(s); **se pencher/faire un pas en ~** to lean/to take a step forward(s); **faire deux pas en ~** to take two steps forward(s); **partir en ~** to go ahead; **en ~!, en ~ la musique**○**!** off we go!; **en ~, marche!** Mil, fig forward march!; **en ~ toute!** Naut, fig full steam ahead!; **mettre qch en ~** to put sth forward; **mettre en ~ le fait que** to point out the fact that; **mettre qn en ~** to put sb forward; **se mettre en ~** to push oneself forward; **2** (dans le temps) ahead.

IV avant de *loc prép* **~ de faire** before doing; **réfléchis ~ de prendre ta décision** think about it before making a decision ou before you make a decision; **c'est juste ~ d'arriver dans le village** it's just before you get to the village; **agiter ~ de servir** shake before serving.

V avant que *loc conj* **~ qu'il ne soit trop tard/qu'elle ne dise non** before it's too late/she says no; **essaie de rentrer ~ qu'il ne fasse nuit** try to come back before dark; **il est parti un jour ~ que je n'arrive** he left one day before I arrived; **le gouvernement a démissionné ~ que la révolte n'éclate** the government resigned before the rebellion broke out.

VI en avant de *loc prép* ahead of [*groupe, cortège*].

> **avant¹**
>
> Lorsque *avant* est adverbe il se traduit par *before* sauf lorsqu'il signifie 'en premier lieu, d'abord'; il se traduit alors par *first*:
>
> *si tu prends la route, mange quelque chose avant* = if you're going to drive, have something to eat first
>
> Lorsque *avant* est préposition il se traduit par *before* sauf dans le cas où une limite de temps est précisée; il se traduit alors par *by*:
>
> *à retourner avant le 30 mars* = to be returned by 30 March
>
> *avant* entre dans la composition de nombreux mots qui s'écrivent avec un trait d'union (*avant-hier, avant-guerre, avant-coureur* etc.). Ces mots sont des entrées à part entière et on les trouvera dans la nomenclature du dictionnaire. Utilisé avant un nom pour désigner une période précédant un événement ou l'avènement d'une personne il se traduit par *pre-* et forme alors un groupe adjectival que l'on fait suivre du nom approprié:
>
> *l'avant-1945* = the pre-1945 period
> *l'avant-Thatcher* = the pre-Thatcher era
> *l'avant-sommet* = the pre-summit discussions

avant[2] /avɑ̃/ **I** *adj inv* [*roue, siège, patte*] front; **la partie ~ de qch** the front part of sth.

II *nm* **1** (partie antérieure) **l'~** the front; **tout l'~ du véhicule est à refaire** the whole of the front of the vehicle will have to be repaired; **à l'~** in (the) front; **à l'~ du train** [*passager, locomotive*] at the front of the train; **à l'~ du bateau** at the front of the boat; **d'~ en arrière** backward(s) and forward(s); **aller de l'~** to forge ahead; **aller de l'~ dans ses projets** to forge ahead with one's plans; **c'est une femme qui va de l'~** she's very go-ahead; **2** Sport forward; **la ligne des ~s** gén the forward line; (au rugby) the front line.

avantage /avɑ̃taʒ/ *nm* **1** (point positif) advantage; **les deux méthodes ont chacune leurs ~s** the two methods each have their advantages; **offrir/présenter de grands ~s** to offer/to have great advantages; **2** (supériorité) advantage; **prendre l'~** Mil, Sport, fig to have the advantage (**sur** over); **avoir/reprendre l'~** Mil, Sport, fig to have/to regain the advantage ou upper hand; **perdre/conserver son ~** to lose/to keep one's advantage (**sur** over); **tirer parti de son ~** to exploit one's advantage; **avoir l'~ de l'âge/du nombre** to have the advantage of age/in numbers; **avoir l'~ de faire** gén to have the advantage of doing; **avoir un ~ sur qn/qch** to have an advantage over sb/sth; **elle a sur toi l'~ de parler anglais** she has the advantage over you in that she speaks English; **3** (faveur) advantage; **être à l'~ de qn** [*situation, transaction*] to be to sb's advantage; [*coiffure, vêtement*] to suit sb; [*propos, attitude*] to be in sb's favour[GB]; **se sortir d'une situation à son ~** to come out of a situation well; **tourner à l'~ de qn** to turn to sb's advantage; **tourner qch à son ~** to turn sth to one's advantage; **être/se montrer à son ~** to be/to show oneself at one's best; **paraître à son ~** to look one's best; **4** (profit) advantage; **tirer ~ de qch** to take advantage of sth; **retirer un ~ de qch** to profit from sth; **je les ai beaucoup aidés, mais je n'en ai retiré aucun ~** I helped them a lot, but I didn't get anything out of it; **avoir ~ à faire** to be better off doing; **il aurait ~ à accepter le poste** he'd be better off accepting the post; **tu aurais ~ à prendre un emprunt** you'd be better off taking out a loan; **5** Sport (au tennis) advantage; **'~, Leconte'** 'advantage, Leconte'; **6** Entr benefit; **~s acquis** vested benefits; **~s financiers/commerciaux** financial/trade benefits; **~s sociaux** benefits package (*sg*); **~s en nature** benefits in kind; **~ fiscaux** tax benefits.

avantager /avɑ̃taʒe/ [13] *vtr* **1** (favoriser) [*personne*] to favour[GB]; [*situation*] to be to the advantage of; **~ Pierre par rapport à/au détriment de Paul** to favour[GB] Pierre over/to the detriment of Paul; **être avantagé par rapport à qn** to be at an advantage compared with sb; **être avantagé dès le départ** [*personne, entreprise*] to have a head start; **la nature ne l'a pas avantagé** hum nature hasn't favoured[GB] him; **2** (mettre en valeur) [*vêtement, parure*] to show [sb] off to advantage; **sa robe n'avantageait pas sa silhouette** her dress didn't show her figure off to advantage; **le rouge avantage les brunes** red really is more flattering to women with dark hair.

avantageusement /avɑ̃taʒøzmɑ̃/ *adv* **1** (sous un jour favorable) [*dépeindre*] favourably[GB]; **l'article ne le dépeignait pas ~** the article did not depict him in the best light; **2** (honorablement) **ce système remplace ~ le précédent** this system is an improvement on the previous one; **il a ~ tiré parti de la situation** he exploited the situation to his advantage.

avantageux, -euse /avɑ̃taʒø, øz/ *adj* **1** (intéressant) [*condition, offre, solution, marché*] favourable[GB], advantageous; [*taux, prix, placement*] attractive; [*produit, article*] good value (*jamais épith*); **il est ~ de faire** it is advantageous to do; **trouver ~ de faire** to find it advantageous to do; **être ~ pour qn** to be advantageous to sb; **au tarif le plus ~** at a most attractive rate; **tirer un parti ~ de qch** to profit from sth; **le grand paquet est plus ~** the large packet is more economical; **l'achat en gros est plus ~** it's cheaper to buy wholesale; **2** (flatteur) [*opinion, aspect*] favourable[GB]; [*description, termes, vêtement*] flattering; [*physique*] super-

avec

La préposition *avec* se traduit presque toujours par *with* quand elle marque:

l'accompagnement:

danser avec qn	=	to dance with sb
du vin blanc avec du cassis	=	white wine with blackcurrant

la possession:

la dame avec le chapeau noir	=	the lady with the black hat
une chemise avec un grand col	=	a shirt with a large collar

la relation:

être d'accord avec qn	=	to agree with sb
avec lui c'est toujours pareil	=	it's always the same with him

la simultanéité:

se lever avec le soleil	=	to get up with the sun

l'opposition:

se battre avec qn	=	to fight with sb
être en concurrence avec qn	=	to be in competition with sb

l'identité de vue:

je suis avec toi	=	I'm with you

le moyen:

avec une fourchette	=	with a fork
avec une canne	=	with a stick
avec de l'argent	=	with money

Quand elle désigne la manière elle se traduit souvent par un adverbe formé à partir du nom qui la suit:

avec attention	=	carefully
avec passion	=	passionately

On trouvera ces expressions sous ***attention, passion*** etc.

On notera toutefois que *avec beaucoup d'attention, avec une grande passion* se traduisent: with great care, with a lot of passion. Les expressions telles que *avec l'âge/l'expérience/les années* etc. sont traitées respectivement sous ***âge, expérience, année*** etc.

On trouvera ci-dessous des exceptions et des exemples supplémentaires.

ior; **présenter qch sous un jour ~** to present sth in a favourable[GB] light; **en termes très ~** in very flattering terms; **il se fait une idée trop avantageuse de lui-même** he has an over-inflated opinion of himself; **3** (vaniteux) liter [*air, ton, attitude*] conceited; **prendre un air ~** to assume an air of superiority.

avant-bras /avɑ̃bʀa/ *nm inv* forearm.

avant-centre, *pl* **avants-centres** /avɑ̃sɑ̃tʀ/ *nm* centre[GB] forward; **jouer ~** to play centre[GB] forward.

avant-contrat, *pl* **~s** /avɑ̃kɔ̃tʀa/ *nm* preliminary contract.

avant-coureur, *pl* **~s** /avɑ̃kuʀœʀ/ *adj m* **signes ~s** early warning signs.

avant-dernier, **-ière**, *pl* **~s** /avɑ̃dɛʀnje, ɛʀ/ **I** *adj* **l'~ champion/disque/film** the last champion/record/film but one; **arriver ~** to come last but one.

II *nm,f* the last but one; **l'~ d'une famille de cinq enfants** the second youngest of five children.

avant-garde, *pl* **~s** /avɑ̃gaʀd/ *nf* **1** (mouvement novateur) Art, Littérat avant-garde; **d'~** avant-garde; **cinéma d'~** avant-garde cinema; **être d'~** to be avant-garde; **2** (pointe) **à l'~** in the vanguard; **à l'~ de la recherche** in the vanguard of research; **3** Mil vanguard.

avant-gardisme, *pl* **~s** /avɑ̃gaʀdism/ *nm* avant-gardism.

avant-gardiste, *pl* **~s** /avɑ̃gaʀdist/ **I** *adj* avant-garde.

II *nmf* avant-gardist.

avant-goût, *pl* **~s** /avɑ̃gu/ *nm* foretaste.

avant-guerre, *pl* **~s** /avɑ̃gɛʀ/ **I** *nm* ou *f* **l'~** the prewar period; **remonter à l'~** to date from before the war; **d'~** prewar; **l'Espagne d'~** prewar Spain.

II *adv* before the war.

avant-hier /avɑ̃tjɛʀ/ *adv* the day before yesterday; **toute la journée d'~** the whole of the day before yesterday; **~ matin/soir** two mornings/evenings ago.

avant-midi /avɑ̃midi/ *nm inv* C (matin) morning.

avant-port, *pl* **~s** /avɑ̃pɔʀ/ *nm* outer harbour[GB].

avant-poste, *pl* **~s** /avɑ̃pɔst/ *nm* **1** Mil outpost; **2** fig **être aux ~s** to be in the vanguard.

avant-première, *pl* **~s** /avɑ̃pʀəmjɛʀ/ *nf* preview.

avant-projet, *pl* **~s** /avɑ̃pʀɔʒɛ/ *nm* draft; **~ de loi** draft bill.

avant-propos /avɑ̃pʀɔpo/ *nm inv* foreword.

avant-rasage /avɑ̃ʀazaʒ/ *adj inv* pre-shave; **lotion ~** pre-shave lotion.

avant-scène, *pl* **~s** /avɑ̃sɛn/ *nf* (partie de scène) forestage; (loge) box.

avant-toit, *pl* **~s** /avɑ̃twa/ *nm* eaves (*pl*).

avant-veille, *pl* **~s** /avɑ̃vɛj/ *nf* **1** (deux jours avant) **l'~** two days before; **l'~ du couronnement** two days before the coronation; **2** (journée) **l'~** the day two days before; **l'~ avait été pluvieuse** the day two days before had been rainy.

avare /avaʀ/ **I** *adj* mean with money GB, miserly; **~ de qch** sparing with; **être ~ de son temps** to give one's time to people sparingly; **être ~ de paroles** to use words sparingly; **il n'est pas ~ de compliments** he's generous with his compliments.

II *nmf* miser.

IDIOMES **à père ~, fils prodigue** Prov a miser will father a spendthrift son.

avarice /avaʀis/ *nf* meanness with money GB, miserliness.

avaricieux, **-ieuse** /avaʀisjø, øz/ *adj* miserly.

avarie /avaʀi/ *nf* **1** Naut problem; **2** Assur, Comm, Jur (dommage matériel) damage ₵; (dommage de transport maritime) average ₵.

■ **~ commune** Assur, Jur general average; **~ particulière** Assur, Jur particular average.

avarié, **~e** /avaʀje/ **I** *pp* ▶ **avarier**.

II *pp adj* **1** (gâté) [*viande, poisson*] rotten; **2**† (endommagé) [*navire, avion*] damaged.

avarier /avaʀje/ [2] **I**† *vtr* (endommager) to damage [*navire, véhicule*].

II s'avarier *vpr* (se gâter) [*viande, poisson*] to go rotten.

avatar /avataʀ/ *nm* **1** (mésaventure) mishap; **2** (changement) change; **connaître des ~s** to undergo changes; **3** Relig (réincarnation) reincarnation.

Ave /ave/ *nm* Relig **~ (Maria)** Ave Maria; **dire** or **réciter un ~ (Maria)** to say an Ave Maria.

avec /avɛk/ **I**○ *adv* **mon chapeau lui a plu, elle est partie ~** she liked my hat and went off with it; **si tu lui donnes tes bijoux, il va jouer ~** if you give him your jewels he'll play with them; **quand j'enlève le papier peint le plâtre vient ~** when I take the wallpaper off, the plaster comes away with it.

II *prép* **viens ~ tes amis** bring your friends with you; **une maison ~ jardin/piscine** a house with a garden GB ou yard US/swimming pool; **je suis arrivée ~ la pluie** it started raining when I arrived; **~ cette chaleur** in ou with this heat; **~ ce brouillard il va y avoir des accidents** there are going to be some accidents with this fog; **se marier ~ qn** to marry sb, to get married to sb; **et ~ cela, que désirez-vous?** what else would you like?; **je fais tout son travail et ~ ça il n'est pas content!** I do all his work and he's still not happy!; **sa séparation** or **son divorce d'~ son mari** her separation from her husband.

aveline /avlin/ *nf* Bot, Culin filbert.

aven /avɛn/ *nm* Géog, Géol sinkhole.

avenant, **~e** /avnɑ̃, ɑ̃t/ **I** *adj* [*air, personne*] pleasant; [*maison, façade*] attractive; **peu ~** [*air, personne*] rather unpleasant; [*maison, façade*] rather unattractive.

II *nm* **1** Assur endorsement (**à** to); **faire un ~ à** to add an endorsement to; **2** (de contrat) codicil.

III à l'avenant *loc adv* **être à l'~** to be in keeping; **la suite était à l'~** the rest was in keeping.

avènement /avɛnmɑ̃/ *nm* **1** (de souverain) accession; (d'homme politique, ère) advent; **~ au trône** accession to the throne; **2** Relig Advent; ▶ **second**.

avenir /avniʀ/ *nm* **1** (futur) future; **à l'~** in future GB, in the future US; **dans un ~ proche/immédiat** in the near/immediate future; **projet d'~** future plan; **seul l'~ nous le dira** only time will tell; **préparer l'~ de qn** to plan sb's future; **vivre dans la crainte de l'~** to live in fear of what the future may bring; **il y va de ton ~** your future is at stake; **avoir de l'~** to have a future; **avoir beaucoup d'~** to have a great future; **d'~** [*métier, technique, science*] of the future; **2** Jur writ of summons to opposing counsel.

IDIOMES **l'~ appartient à ceux qui se lèvent tôt** Prov the early bird catches the worm Prov.

avent /avɑ̃/ *nm* **l'~** Advent; **premier/deuxième dimanche de l'~** first/second Sunday in Advent; **calendrier de l'~** Advent calendar.

aventure /avɑ̃tyʀ/ **I** *nf* **1** (épopée) adventure; **esprit d'~** spirit of adventure; **partir à l'~** to set off in search of adventure; **2** (péripétie) adventure; **les ~s de Tintin et Milou** the adventures of Tintin and Milou; **une drôle d'~** a strange adventure; **3** (entreprise risquée) venture; **se lancer dans une ~** to throw oneself into a venture; **l'~ européenne** the European venture; **tenter l'~** to try one's luck; **4** (intrigue amoureuse) affair.

II d'aventure *loc adv* by chance; **si d'~ il venait...** if by chance he should come...

IDIOMES **dire la bonne ~ à qn** to tell sb's fortune.

aventuré, **~e** /avɑ̃tyʀe/ **I** *pp* ▶ **aventurer**.

II *pp adj* [*hypothèse, affirmation*] bold.

aventurer /avɑ̃tyʀe/ [1] **I** *vtr* to risk [*argent*].

II s'aventurer *vpr* lit, fig to venture (**dans** in; **sur** onto; **jusqu'à** to); **s'~ à faire** to venture doing.

aventureusement /avɑ̃tyʀøzmɑ̃/ *adv* adventurously.

aventureux, **-euse** /avɑ̃tyʀø, øz/ *adj* [*personne, esprit*] adventurous; [*vie, jeunesse*] adventurous; [*entreprise, investissement*] risky.

aventurier, **-ière** /avɑ̃tyʀje, ɛʀ/ **I** *adj* [*esprit, humeur*] adventurous.

II *nm,f* gén, péj adventurer/adventuress.

aventurisme /avɑ̃tyʀism/ *nm* adventurism.

aventuriste /avɑ̃tyʀist/ *adj, nmf* adventurist.

avenu, **~e** /avny/ **I** *adj* **nul et non ~** null and void.
II avenue *nf* lit, fig avenue.

avéré, **~e** /aveʀe/ **I** *pp* ▶ **avérer**.
II *pp adj* [*fait, échec, goût*] recognized; [*maladie*] confirmed; **il est ~ que** it is proven ou confirmed that.

avérer: **s'avérer** /aveʀe/ [14] *vpr* to prove to be [*indispensable, insuffisant, efficace*]; **le téléphone s'avère (être) un outil indispensable** the telephone is proving (to be) an indispensable tool; **il s'avère que** it transpires that, it turns out that.

avers /avɛʀ/ *nm inv* obverse.

averse /avɛʀs/ *nf* lit, fig shower.
■ **~ de neige** C snow shower.

aversion /avɛʀsjɔ̃/ *nf* aversion (**pour qch/qn** to sb/sth); **avoir qn/qch en ~** to have a loathing for sb/sth; **prendre qn/qch en ~** to develop a loathing for sb/sth.

averti, **~e** /avɛʀti/ **I** *pp* ▶ **avertir**.
II *pp adj* **1** (avisé) [*lecteur, visiteur*] informed; **2** (expérimenté) [*professionnel*] experienced.
IDIOMES **un homme ~ en vaut deux** Prov forewarned is forearmed Prov.

avertir /avɛʀtiʀ/ [3] *vtr* **1** (informer) to inform [*personne*] (**de qch** of sth; **que** that); **2** (lancer une menace à) to warn [*personne*] (**de qch** of sth; **que** that); **je t'avertis, si je t'attrape**... I warn you, if I catch you...

avertissement /avɛʀtismɑ̃/ *nm* **1** gén, Jur, Scol warning; **le ministre a adressé un ~ à** the minister gave a warning to; **dernier ~** Scol final warning; (sur une facture) final demand; **2** Fisc notification; **3** Sport caution; **4** Édition foreword.

avertisseur /avɛʀtisœʀ/ **I** *adj m* [*panneau*] warning (*épith*).
II *nm* gén alarm; Aut horn; **~ d'incendie** fire alarm; **~ lumineux** warning light.

aveu, *pl* **~x** /avø/ *nm* **1** (de méfait) confession; **arracher des ~x à qn** to extract a confession from sb; **faire des ~x** to make a confession; **faire des ~x complets** to make a full confession; **faire l'~ de** to confess to [*crime, faute*]; **passer aux ~x** to confess; **2** (sans action blâmable) admission; **un ~ d'échec/de faiblesse** an admission of failure/of weakness; **de l'~ de qn** on the admission of sb; **de son propre ~** on his own admission; **c'est un ~ d'impuissance** it's an admission of powerlessness; **après de tendres ~x** liter after tender avowals of love littér.

aveuglant, **~e** /avœglɑ̃, ɑ̃t/ *adj* [*clarté, éclat*] blinding; fig [*preuve*] glaring; [*vérité, fait*] glaringly obvious.

aveugle /avœgl/ **I** *adj* **1** (sans vue) blind; **devenir ~** to go blind; **~ d'un œil** blind in one eye; **il est ~ de naissance** he has been blind from birth, he was born blind; **2** (sans lucidité) [*personne, confiance, passion, ambition*] blind; [*politique*] blinkered; (sans discernement) [*violence, tir*] indiscriminate; **avoir une foi ~ en qn** to have blind faith in sb; **la passion/l'ambition le rend ~** he's blinded by passion/ambition; **3** (sans ouverture) [*façade*] blank; [*couloir*] windowless; [*fenêtre*] blocked-up.
II *nmf* blind person; **les ~s** the blind; **en ~** [*se lancer*] blindly; **jouer en ~** (échecs) to play blind; **traitement en ~** Méd single-blind treatment; **en double ~** Méd double-blind (*épith*); ▶ **royaume**.

aveuglement /avœgləmɑ̃/ *nm* liter (égarement) blindness; **faire preuve d'un ~ coupable** to be shamefully unaware.

aveuglément /avœglemɑ̃/ *adv* blindly.

aveugler /avœgle/ [1] **I** *vtr* **1** (rendre aveugle) lit, fig to blind; (éblouir) lit, fig to dazzle, to blind; **la passion les aveugle** they're blinded by passion; **2** Constr to block up [*fenêtre*]; to stop up [*voie d'eau*].
II s'aveugler *vpr* to hide the truth from oneself; **s'~ sur ses défauts/possibilités** to be blind to one's shortcomings/limitations.

aveuglette: **à l'aveuglette** /alavœglɛt/ *loc adv* **1** (à tâtons) **avancer à l'~** to grope one's way along; **se diriger à l'~ vers la sortie** to grope one's way towards the exit; **2** (au hasard) [*tirer, se lancer*] blindly; [*choisir, distribuer*] at random; [*décider, agir*] in an inconsidered way.

aveulir /avøliʀ/ [3] *vtr* liter to enervate.

aveulissement /avølismɑ̃/ *nm* enervation.

Aveyron /avɛʀɔ̃/ ▶ **357**, **692** *nprm* (rivière, département) **l'~** the Aveyron.

aviateur, **-trice** /avjatœʀ, tʀis/ ▶ **510** *nm,f* **1** (pilote) airman/woman pilot; **les premiers ~s** the first aviators; **2** Mil ≈ aircraftman GB, ≈ airman US.

aviation /avjasjɔ̃/ *nf* **1** (civile) (secteur) aviation; (industrie de fabrication) aircraft industry; **l'~ civile/commerciale** civil/commercial aviation; **compagnie d'~** aviation company; **2** Mil (armée, avions) **l'~** the air force; **3** (activité du pilote, activité sportive) **l'~** flying; **faire de l'~** to fly.
■ **~ de bombardement** bomber command; **~ de chasse** fighter command; **~ navale** carrier-based aviation.

aviatrice *nf* ▶ **aviateur**.

avicole /avikɔl/ *adj* **1** (de volailles) [*ferme, élevage*] poultry (*épith*); **2** (d'oiseaux) [*exposition, élevage*] bird (*épith*).

aviculteur, **-trice** /avikyltœʀ, tʀis/ ▶ **510** *nm,f* **1** (de volailles) poultry farmer; **2** (d'oiseaux) aviculturist.

aviculture /avikyltyʀ/ *nf* **1** (de volailles) poultry farming; **2** (d'oiseaux) aviculture.

avide /avid/ *adj* (vorace) [*mangeur, yeux*] greedy; [*lecteur*] avid; (cupide) greedy; **~ de** avid for [*pouvoir*]; eager for [*plaisirs, affection, honneurs, nouvelles, connaissances, vengeance*]; **~ de faire** eager to do; **tendre une oreille ~** to listen eagerly; **~ de sang** bloodthirsty; **économie ~ de pétrole** oil-guzzling economy.

avidement /avidmɑ̃/ *adv* **1** (voracement) [*manger*] greedily; [*lire, écouter*] avidly; **2** (avec ardeur) [*chercher*] eagerly.

avidité /avidite/ *nf* **1** (cupidité) greed (**de** for); **avec ~** [*manger*] greedily; **2** (vif désir) eagerness (**de** for); **leur ~ d'information** their eagerness for information; **avec ~** eagerly.

avignonnais, **~e** /aviɲɔnɛ, ɛz/ ▶ **857** *adj* of Avignon.

Avignonnais, **~e** /aviɲɔnɛ, ɛz/ ▶ **857** *nm,f* (natif) native of Avignon; (habitant) inhabitant of Avignon.

avilir /aviliʀ/ [3] **I** *vtr* to demean [*personne*]; to debase [*monnaie*]; to bring down the price of [*marchandise*].
II s'avilir *vpr* [*personne*] to demean oneself; [*marchandise, monnaie*] to depreciate; **la langue écrite s'avilit** the written language is being debased.

avilissant, **~e** /avilisɑ̃, ɑ̃t/ *adj* [*conduite, spectacle*] demeaning; [*effet*] debasing.

avilissement /avilismɑ̃/ *nm* (de personne) degradation; (de monnaie, marchandise) depreciation.

aviné, **~e** /avine/ *adj* liter [*personne*] inebriated littér; [*regard, visage*] drunken; **il avait une haleine ~e** you could smell wine on his breath.

avion /avjɔ̃/ *nm* **1** (appareil) (aero)plane GB, airplane US, aircraft (*inv*); **dans l'~** on the plane; **constructeur d'~s** aircraft manufacturer; **aller à Rome en ~** to go to Rome by air, to fly to Rome; **faire 100 000 kilomètres par an en ~** to fly 100,000 kilometres a year; **faire les lacs en ~** to do an aerial tour of the lakes; **envoyer qch par ~** Postes to send sth air mail; **'par ~'** Postes 'by air mail'; **2** (vol) flight; **ton ~ est à quelle heure?** what time is your flight?; **3** (activité) **l'~** flying; **je déteste (prendre) l'~** I hate flying; **il n'a jamais pris l'~** he's never been on a plane, he's never flown.
■ **~ bombardier d'eau** fire-fighting plane ; **~ de chasse** fighter (plane); **~ de combat** combat aircraft; **~ à flèche variable** variable-geometry aircraft; **~ de fret** cargo plane; **~ furtif** stealth bomber; **~ de ligne** civil aircraft, liner; **~ en papier** paper aeroplane GB ou airplane US; **~ pompier** fire-fighting plane; **~ postal** mail plane; **~ à réaction** jet (plane); **~ de reconnaissance** reconnaissance plane; **~ sanitaire** air ambulance; **~ spatial** spacecraft; **~ de tourisme** light passenger aircraft; **~ de transport** transport ou freight plane.

avion-cargo, *pl* **avions-cargos** /avjɔ̃kaʀgo/ *nm* cargo plane.

avion-cible, *pl* **avions-cibles** /avjɔ̃sibl(ə)/ *nm* target aircraft (*inv*).

avion-citerne, *pl* **avions-citernes** /avjɔ̃sitɛʀn/ *nm* tanker aircraft (*inv*).

avion-école, *pl* **avions-école** /avjɔ̃ekɔl/ *nm* training aircraft (*inv*).

avion-espion, *pl* **avions-espions** /avjɔ̃ɛspjɔ̃/ *nm* spy plane.

avion-fusée, *pl* **avions-fusées** /avjɔ̃fyze/ *nm* rocket powered aircraft (*inv*).

avionique /avjɔnik/ *nf* avionics (+ *v sg*).

avionneur /avjɔnœʀ/ *nm* aircraft manufacturer.

avion-suicide, *pl* **avions-suicide** /avjɔ̃sɥisid/ *nm* kamikaze plane.

avion-taxi, *pl* **avions-taxis** /avjɔ̃taksi/ *nm* air taxi.

aviron /aviʀɔ̃/ *nm* **1** ▶ **449** Sport rowing; **course d'~** rowing race; **faire de l'~** to row; **la course d'~ entre Oxford et Cambridge** the Oxford-Cambridge Boat Race; **2** (rame) oar; **coup d'~** stroke.

avis /avi/ *nm inv* **1** (opinion) opinion (**sur** on, about); **à mon ~** in my opinion; **je ne partage pas votre ~** I don't share your opinion; **les ~ sur la question sont partagés** opinions differ; **je suis de ton ~** I agree with you; **je suis du même ~** I agree, I think the same, I'm of the same opinion; **je suis d'un ~ contraire** I disagree, I think differently, I'm of the opposite opinion; **être d'~ que** to be of the opinion that; **donner son/un ~ sur qch** to give one's/an opinion on sth; **de l'~ général** in most people's opinion; **de** or **selon l'~ des spécialistes** in the opinion of specialists; **de l'~ même des spécialistes** in the specialists' own opinion; **demander son ~ à qn** to ask sb his/her opinion; **on ne leur a pas demandé leur ~!** nobody asked for their opinion!; **changer d'~** to change one's mind; **tu ne me feras pas changer d'~** you won't make me change my mind; ▶ **chemise**; **2** (conseil) advice (**sur** on, about); **sans ~ médical** without consulting your doctor; **sauf ~ contraire** unless you hear to the contrary, unless otherwise informed sout (**de qn** by sb); **3** (de jury, commission etc) recommendation; **~ favorable/défavorable** favourable[GB]/unfavourable[GB] recommendation; **4** (annonce) notice; **~ à la population** (affiche) public notice; (cri) public announcement; **'cet ~ tient lieu de faire-part'** (dans journal) 'no individual announcements will be sent'; **'~ de recherche'** 'wanted'; **lancer/faire paraître un ~ de recherche** (pour un disparu) to issue/to publish a description of a missing person; (pour un malfaiteur) to issue/to publish a description of a wanted person.
■ **~ de coup de vent** Météo Naut gale warning; **~ de crédit** credit advice ou note; **~ de débit** debit advice ou note; **~ de décès** death notice; **~ d'échéance** Assur renewal notice; **~ au lecteur** foreword; **~ de mise en recouvrement** demand for payment (*of money owed to the Treasury*); **~ de passage** calling card (*left by meter reader, postman etc*).

avoir[1]

Généralités

Dans la plupart des situations exprimant la possession, la disponibilité *avoir* sera traduit par *to have* ou *to have got*:

j'ai des livres = I have (got) books
j'ai des enfants = I have (got) children
j'ai des employés = I have (got) employees
je n'ai pas assez de place = I don't have (*ou* I haven't got) enough room
je n'ai pas assez de temps = I don't have (*ou* I haven't got) enough time
la maison a l'électricité = the house has electricity
la maison a cinq pièces = the house has five rooms
j'aurai mon visa demain = I'll have my visa tomorrow
ils vont/elle va avoir un bébé en mai = they're/she's having a baby in May

Les autres sens de *avoir*, verbe transitif simple (obtenir, porter, triompher de etc.), sont traités dans l'entrée plus bas.

On notera qu'en règle générale les expressions figées du type *avoir raison*, *avoir beau*, *en avoir marre*, *il y a belle lurette*, *il y a de quoi* etc. seront traitées respectivement sous ***raison***, ***beau***, ***marre***, ***lurette***, ***quoi*** etc.

On pourra également consulter les diverses notes d'usage répertoriées **▶ 1920**, notamment celles consacrées à l'expression de ***l'âge***, aux ***douleurs et maladies***, à l'expression de ***l'heure*** etc.

On trouvera ci-dessous les divers emplois de *avoir* pour lesquelles une explication est nécessaire.

avoir = verbe auxiliaire

avoir verbe auxiliaire se traduit toujours par *to have* sauf dans le cas du passé composé:

ils avaient révisé les épreuves quand je suis parti = they had revised the proofs when I left
quand ils eurent (ou *ont eu*) *révisé les épreuves, ils sont partis* = when they had revised the proofs, they left
ils auront fini demain = they will have finished tomorrow
il aurait (ou *eût*) *aimé parler* = he would have liked to speak

Lorsqu'on a un passé composé en français, il sera traduit soit par le prétérit:

ils ont révisé les épreuves en juin = they revised the proofs in June
ils ont révisé les épreuves avant ma démission = they revised the proofs before I resigned
je suis sûr qu'il l'a laissé là en partant = I'm sure he left it here when he left

soit par le 'present perfect':

ils ont révisé les épreuves plusieurs fois = they have revised the proofs several times

avoir = verbe semi-auxiliaire

De même, *avoir* semi-auxiliaire dans les tournures attributives du type *avoir le cœur malade*/*les genoux cagneux*, se traduit de façon variable (*to be* ou *to have*) selon la structure adoptée par l'anglais pour rendre ces tournures; voir, en l'occurrence, les entrées ***cœur*** et ***cagneux***; mais c'est en général sous l'adjectif que ce problème est traité.

Emplois avec à

avoir à + infinitif

Exprimant l'obligation ou la convenance, cette locution verbale se rend généralement par *to have to* suivi de l'infinitif:

j'aurais à ajouter que … = I would have to add that …
tu auras à rendre compte de tes actes = you'll have to account for your actions
je n'ai pas à vous raconter ma vie = I don't have to tell you my life-story
vous n'aviez pas à le critiquer = you didn't have to criticize him
il n'a pas à te parler sur ce ton = he shouldn't speak to you in that tone of voice
j'ai beaucoup à faire = I have a lot to do *ou* I've got a lot to do
tu n'as rien à faire? = don't you have anything to do? *ou* haven't you got anything to do?
j'ai à faire un rapport ou *j'ai un rapport à faire* = I have to write a report *ou* I have a report to write

n'avoir qu'à

Quand cette locution équivaut à *suffir*, plusieurs possibilités de traduction se présentent:

tu n'avais qu'à = *tu aurais dû*

Elle se rend par *should have* suivi du participe passé

tu n'as qu'à leur écrire = you only have to write to them *ou* you've only got to write to them, *ou* all you have to do is write to them
tu n'auras que cinq minutes à attendre = you'll only have to wait five minutes
tu n'avais qu'à faire attention = you should have paid attention
tu n'avais qu'à me le dire = you should have told me
tu n'avais qu'à partir plus tôt = you should have left earlier

Emplois avec en

On trouvera sous ***assez***, ***marre*** etc. les expressions figées *en avoir assez*, *en avoir marre* etc. Voir aussi les emplois avec *il y a* plus bas.

Expression du temps: **en avoir pour**

L'anglais distingue généralement entre une tâche précise (*to take*) et une activité ou absence indéterminée (*to be*):

vous en avez (ou *aurez*) *pour combien de temps?* (à faire ce travail) = how long will it take you?
(à me faire attendre) = how long are you going to be?
j'en ai pour cinq minutes (je reviens) = I'll be five minutes
je n'en ai pas pour longtemps = I won't be long
j'en ai eu pour deux heures = it took me two hours

Expression du coût: **en avoir pour**

Se traduit par *to cost* suivi du pronom personnel complément correspondant au pronom sujet français (voir aussi ***argent***):

j'en ai eu pour 500 francs = it cost me 500 francs
nous en aurons pour combien? = how much will it cost us?

☛ Voir page suivante

IDIOMES **deux ~ valent mieux qu'un** two heads are better than one.

avisé, **~e** /avize/ **I** *pp* ▶ **aviser**.
II *pp adj* [*personne, conseil*] sensible; **être bien/mal ~** to be well-/ill-advised; **le gouvernement serait (bien) ~ de faire** the government would be well-advised ou wise to do.

aviser /avize/ [1] **I** *vtr* **1** (prévenir) to notify [*personne, famille*] **(de qch** of sth; **que** that); **2†** (apercevoir) to catch sight of.
II *vi* (réfléchir) **nous aviserons plus tard** we'll decide later; **'et s'il n'est pas là?'—'j'aviserai'** 'and if he's not there?'—'I'll see'.
III s'aviser *vpr* **1** (se rendre compte) **s'~ que** to realize that; **s'~ de qch** to notice sth; **2** (oser) **ne t'avise pas de recommencer** don't do that again.

aviso /avizo/ *nm* escort vessel.

avitaminose /avitaminoz/ *nf* vitamin deficiency, avitaminosis spéc.

aviver /avive/ [1] **I** *vtr* **1** (exciter) to intensify [*chagrin, désir, colère*]; to increase [*intérêt*]; to stir up [*querelle*]; to make [sth] more acute [*douleur physique*]; **2** (rehausser) to liven up [*couleur*]; to brighten up [*teint*]; **3** (attiser) to kindle [*feu*]; **un vent violent avivait l'incendie** a strong wind fanned the flames; **4** Méd **~ une plaie** to remove the damaged tissue from a wound; **5** Tech to polish [*métal, marbre*].
II s'aviver *vpr* fig [*chagrin*] to deepen; [*désir, colère, intérêt*] to grow stronger; [*douleur physique*] to become more acute; **la concurrence s'avive** competition is becoming keener.

avocaillon /avɔkajɔ̃/ *nm* pej small-time lawyer.

avocassier○, **-ière** /avɔkasje, ɛʀ/ *adj* péj legal-eagle○ (*épith*).

avocat /avɔka/ **▶ 510** *nm* **1** Jur gén lawyer, solicitor GB, attorney (at law) US; (au barreau) barrister GB, (trial) lawyer US; **elle est ~** she is a solicitor; (elle plaide) she is a barrister; **consulter un ~** to consult a solicitor ou lawyer, to seek legal advice; **~ de la défense** counsel for the defence, defence counsel, defense attorney US; **~ de l'accusation** counsel for the prosecution, prosecuting counsel; **~ commis d'office** court-appointed lawyer, prosecuting attorney US; **2** fig (d'une idée) advocate (**de** of); (d'une cause, personne) champion (**de** of); **se faire l'~ de qn/qch** to champion sb/sth; **3** Bot, Culin avocado (pear).
■ **~ d'affaires** business lawyer; **~ commercial** commercial lawyer; **~ à la cour** barrister GB, (trial) lawyer US allowed to plead at a court of appeals; **l'~ du diable** the devil's advocate; **se faire l'~ du diable** to play devil's advocate; **~ d'entreprise** company ou corporate lawyer GB, corporation lawyer US; **~ général** Advocate-General.

avocat-conseil, *pl* **avocats-conseils** /avɔkakɔ̃sɛj/ **▶ 510** *nm* legal consultant.

avocate /avɔkat/ *nf* female lawyer.

avocatier /avɔkatje/ *nm* avocado (pear) tree.

avocette /avɔsɛt/ *nf* avocet.

avoine /avwan/ *nf* oats (*pl*); **manger de l'~** to eat oats; **champ d'~** field of oats; **récolte d'~** crop of oats, oat crop; ▶ **fou**.

avoir[1] /avwaʀ/ [8] *vtr* **1** (obtenir) to get [*objet, rendez-vous*]; to catch [*train, avion*]; **j'ai pu vous ~ votre visa** I managed to get your visa for you; **j'ai eu ce vase pour cinq francs** I got this vase for five francs; **pouvez-vous m'~ un des traducteurs?** can you get me one of the translators?; **je n'ai pas eu mon train** I didn't catch my train; **il l'a eue**◑ **le soir même** he had○ her that very evening; **2** (au téléphone) **j'ai réussi à l'~** I managed to get through to him; **essayer d'~ le ministre** to try to get through to the minister; **pouvez-vous m'~ son adjoint/Hongkong** can you put me through to ou get me his assistant/Hong Kong; **3** (porter) to wear, to have [sth] on; **elle avait une robe bleue à son mariage** she wore a blue dress at her wedding; **elle a toujours une écharpe autour du cou** she's always got a scarf round her neck; **il avait un béret (sur la tête)** he had a beret on ou he was wearing a beret; **4**○ (triompher) to beat, to get○, to have; **l'équipe de Marseille nous a eus** the Marseilles team beat us; **ne**

avoir¹

Expression de l'existence

il y a du lait dans le réfrigérateur	= there's some milk in the fridge
il y a des souris au grenier	= there are mice in the attic
il n'y a pas de riz	= there's no rice *ou* there isn't any rice
il n'y a plus de riz	= there's no more rice *ou* there isn't any more rice
il doit y avoir des souris dans le grenier ou *il y aura des souris dans le grenier*	= there must be mice in the attic
il n'y a pas eu moins de 50 concurrents	= there were no less than 50 competitors
il y a chapeau et chapeau	= there are hats and hats
il y aura Paul, Marie, …	= there will be Paul, Marie, …
et il y aura Paul et Marie!	= and Paul and Marie will be there!
il n'y a pas de raison de faire	= there's no reason to do
il n'y a pas de raison que tu fasses	= there's no reason for you to do
il a dû y avoir quelque chose de grave	= something serious must have happened
qu'est-ce qu'il y a? (qui ne va pas)	= what's wrong?
(qui se passe)	= what's going on?
il y a qu'elle m'énerve	= she's getting on my nerves, that's what's wrong
il y a que l'ordinateur est en panne	= the computer has broken down

Attention, un mot singulier en français peut être traduit par un mot fonctionnant comme un pluriel en anglais:

- *il y a beaucoup de monde* = there are a lot of people
- *y avait-il du monde?* = were there many people?

Expression du temps

- *il est venu il y a longtemps* = he came a long time ago
- *il est venu il y a cinq ans* = he came five years ago
- *il y a cinq ans que j'habite ici* = I have been living here for five years
- *il y aura cinq ans demain que j'ai pris ma retraite* = it will be five years tomorrow since I retired
- *il y aura deux mois mardi que je travaille ici* = I will have been working here for two months on Tuesday
- *il n'y a que deux mois que je suis ici* = I have only been here for two months
- *il n'y a que deux mois que je travaille ici* = I have only been working here for two months
- *il n'y a pas cinq minutes qu'il est parti* = he left less than five minutes ago
- *il n'y a pas 200 ans que l'espèce est éteinte* = the species has been extinct for no more than 200 years
- *il y a combien de temps que tu habites ici?* = how long have you lived here?
- *il y a combien d'années que tu habites ici?* = how many years have you lived here?
- *il y a combien de temps qu'on ne s'est vus?* = how long is it since we last met?
- *il y a combien d'années qu'on ne s'est vus?* = how many years has it been since we last met?

Expression de la distance

Elle se fait généralement à l'aide du verbe *to be*:

- *combien y a-t-il jusqu'à la gare?* = how far is it to the station?
- *combien y a-t-il d'ici à la gare?* = how far is it to the station from here?
- *combien y a-t-il encore jusqu'à la gare?* = how much further is it to the station?
- *il y a 15 kilomètres jusqu'à la gare* = the station is 15 kilometres away
- *il y a 15 kilomètres d'ici à la gare* = the station is 15 kilometres away from here
- *il y a au moins 15 kilomètres* = it's at least 15 kilometres away
- *il y a encore 15 kilomètres* = it's another 15 kilometres
- *il n'y a pas 200 mètres d'ici à la gare* = it's less than 200 metres from here to the station
- *il n'y a que 200 mètres d'ici à la gare* = it's only 200 metres from here to the station

***il y a à* + infinitif**

- *il y a à manger pour quatre* = there's enough food for four
- *il y a (beaucoup) à faire* = there's a lot to be done (ceci traduit également *il y a de quoi faire*)
- *souligner le danger qu'il y a à faire* = to stress how dangerous it is to do
- *souligner l'avantage qu'il y a à faire* = to stress how advantageous it is to do
- *les risques qu'il y avait/aurait à faire* = how risky it was/would be to do
- *il n'y a pas à hésiter* = there's no need to hesitate
- *il n'y a pas à s'inquiéter* = there's no need to worry
- *il n'y a pas à discuter!* = no arguments!
- *'il n'y a qu'à le repeindre!'* = 'all you have to do is repaint it!'
- *'y a qu'à, c'est facile à dire!'* = 'just repaint it! easier said than done!'

il y en a qui, il y en a pour

L'existence se rend par *there is/are*, le temps par *to take*, et le coût par *to cost* ou *to come to*:

- *il y en a qui n'ont pas peur du ridicule!* = there are some people who aren't afraid of being laughed at!
- *il y en a toujours pour se plaindre* (ou *qui se plaignent*) = there's always someone who complains
- *il y en a (ou aura) pour deux heures* = it'll take two hours
- *il y en a eu pour deux heures* = it took two hours
- *il y en aurait eu pour deux heures* = it would have taken two hours
- *il n'y en a plus que pour deux heures* = it'll only take another two hours
- *il y en a encore pour combien de temps?* = how much longer will it take?
- *il y en a (ou aura) pour 200 francs* = it'll cost (*ou* come to) 200 francs
- *il y en a eu pour 200 francs* = it cost (*ou* came to) 200 francs

Noter aussi:

- *il n'y en a que pour leur chien* = they only think of their dog *ou* their dog comes first

Remarque: certaines formes personnelles du verbe *avoir* sont équivalentes au présentatif *il y a*. En corrélation avec le relatif *qui*, elles ne se traduisent pas; directement suivies de l'objet présenté, elles se traitent comme *il y a*:

- *j'ai mon stylo qui fuit* = my pen is leaking
- *elle avait les larmes aux yeux* = there were tears in her eyes
- *j'ai ma cicatrice qui me fait souffrir* = my scar is hurting
- *à droite, vous avez une tapisserie d'Aubusson* = on your right, there's an Aubusson tapestry

nous laissons pas avoir par la concurrence let's not let the competition beat us; **cette fois-ci, on les aura** this time, we'll get ou have them; **5** (duper) to have○; (par malveillance) to con○; **j'ai été eu** I've been had○; **il t'a bien eu!** (l'escroc) he conned○ you!; (le plaisantin) he was having you on○! GB, he put one over on you○!; **elle s'est fait** ou **laissée ~** she's been had○; **j'ai failli me faire ~** I was nearly conned○; **je ne me laisserai pas ~ par un abruti**○ I won't be conned○ by a moron; **6** (éprouver moralement) to feel; **~ du chagrin/de la haine** to feel sorrow/hate; **qu'est-ce que tu as?** what's wrong ou the matter with you?; **j'ai qu'il m'énerve** he's getting on my nerves, that's what's wrong; **qu'est-ce que tu as à crier comme ça?** what are you shouting like that for?; **j'ai que mon ordinateur ne marche pas** because my computer doesn't work; **qu'est-ce qu'il a à conduire comme ça?** why is he driving like that?; **il a qu'il est soûl** because he's drunk, that's why; **7** (servant à exprimer l'âge, des sensations physiques) **j'ai 20 ans/faim/froid** I am 20 years old/hungry/cold; **la salle a 20 mètres de long** the room is 20 metres[GB] long.

IDIOMES **en ~**○ to have balls◑; **ne pas en ~**○ to have no balls◑.

avoir² /avwaʀ/ *nm* **1** Comm (somme) credit; (attestation) credit note; **2** (possessions) assets (*pl*), holdings (*pl*); **~s à l'étranger** foreign assets ou holdings; **~s en caisse** cash holdings; **~s en dollars** dollar-based assets; **3** Compta (notion) assets (*pl*); (tire d'entrée) credit.
■ **~ fiscal** tax credit.

avoirdupois /avwaʀdypwa/ *nm* avoirdupois.

avoisinant, ~e /avwazinɑ̃, ɑ̃t/ *adj* neighbouring[GB].

avoisiner /avwazine/ [1] *vtr* **1** [*coûts, somme*] to be close to, to be about; **~ les 20%** to be close to ou about 20%; **~ (les) 200 francs** to be close to 200 francs; **2** [*ferme, village*] to be near [*forêt, route*].

Avon *nprm* **l'~** Avon.

avortement /avɔʀtəmɑ̃/ *nm* **1** Méd abortion; **~ spontané** miscarriage; **~ thérapeutique** termination of pregnancy (*on medical grounds*); **2** (échec) collapse (**de** of).

avorter /avɔʀte/ [1] *vi* **1** Méd (par intervention) to have an abortion; (spontanément) to abort, to miscarry; **se faire ~** to have an abortion; **faire ~ qn** [*personne*] to carry out an abortion on sb; [*pilule*] to induce abortion in sb; **2** [*projet, révolution*] to abort.

avorteur, -euse /avɔʀtœʀ, øz/ *nm,f* pej abortionist péj.

avorton /avɔʀtɔ̃/ *nm* pej (personne, animal, plante) runt.

avouable /avwabl/ *adj* [*sentiment*] worthy; [*motif, raison*] respectable; **méthode peu ~** rather dubious method.

avoué, ~e /avwe/ **I** *pp* ▶ **avouer**.
II *pp adj* [*ennemi, revenu*] declared; [*thème*] stated; [*ambition, but, intention*] avowed; [*terroriste, socialiste*] self-confessed; **le mobile ~ du crime** the motive given for the crime; **de manière ~e ou non** overtly or otherwise.
III ▶ **510** *nm* Jur ≈ solicitor GB, attorney(-at-law) US.

avouer /avwe/ [1] **I** *vtr* **1** (confesser) to confess [*amour, haine*] (**à qn** to sb); to confess (to) [*crime*]; (admettre) to admit [*incartade, faiblesse*] (**à qn** to sb); to admit ou confess [*ignorance, dépit, peur*] (**à qn** to sb); **~ un penchant pour qch** to admit (to) a weakness for sth; **'je ne sais pas,' avoua-t-il** 'I don't know,' he admitted; **avoue(-le), tu as triché** admit it, you cheated; **~ avoir fait qch** to admit ou confess to having done sth; **elle avoue ne pas travailler** she admits that she isn't working; **j'avoue m'être trompé** I admit I made a mistake; **~ que** to admit ou confess (that); **(il est) impossible de lui faire ~ que** you'll never get him to admit that; **2** (reconnaître) to admit;

c'est cher, je l'avoue I must admit, it's expensive; **avoue** or **tu avoueras que c'est ridicule** you must admit, it's ridiculous; **j'avoue qu'il fait chaud** I must admit (that) it's hot.

II *vi* (faire des aveux) [*inculpé, suspect*] to confess; [*fautif*] to own up.

III s'avouer *vpr* **1** (se déclarer) **s'~ rassuré/satisfait** to say one feels reassured/ satisfied; **s'~ coupable** to admit one's guilt; **s'~ battu** or **vaincu** to admit defeat; **2** (à soi-même) to admit [sth] to oneself [*motif*].

IDIOMES **faute avouée est à moitié pardonnée** a fault confessed is half redressed.

avril /avʀil/ **▶521** *nm* April.

IDIOMES **en ~, ne te découvre pas d'un fil, en mai fais ce qu'il te plaît** Prov ne'er cast a clout till May be out Prov.

axe /aks/ *nm* **1** Anat, Astron, Math axis; **2** Mécan axle; **3** (route) major road; **les grands ~s routiers** the major trunk roads GB, the major highways US; **l'~ Paris–Metz** the main Paris–Metz road; **4** (prolongement) **dans l'~ du bâtiment** straight along the road from the building; **la cible est dans l'~ du viseur** the target is lined up in the sights; **dans l'~ de sa politique** fig in line with his policy; **5** (ligne directrice) (de projet, plan) main line; (de discours) central theme; **6** Hist **l'Axe** the Axis.

■ **~ de rotation** axis of rotation; **~ rouge** urban clearway GB, urban thruway US.

axer /akse/ [1] *vtr* **1** lit to centre[GB] [*vis*]; to line up [*pièce*]; **2** fig (baser) to base (**sur** on); (concentrer) to centre[GB] (**sur** on); **~ ses recherches sur un thème** to focus one's research on a theme; **film axé sur les problèmes sociaux** film which focuses on social problems; **projet axé sur la clientèle étrangère** scheme aimed at foreign customers.

axial, **~e**, *mpl* **-iaux** /aksjal, o/ *adj* axial; **éclairage ~** centre[GB]-hung (street) lighting.

axillaire /aksilɛʀ/ *adj* axillary.

axiomatique /aksjɔmatik/ **I** *adj* Philos, Math axiomatic.

II *nf* Math axiomatics (+ *v sg*).

axiome /aksjom/ *nm* axiom.

axis /aksis/ *nm inv* axis.

axone /aksɔn/ *nm* axon.

ayant cause, *pl* **ayants cause** /ɛjɑ̃koz/ *nm* Jur assign, cessionary.

ayant droit, *pl* **ayants droit** /ɛyɑ̃dʀwa/ *nm* **1** (à une prestation, une allocation) legal claimant, beneficiary; **2** (ayant cause) assign.

ayatollah /ajatɔla/ **▶813** *nm* ayatollah.

azalée /azale/ *nf* azalea.

Azerbaïdjan /azɛʀbajdʒɑ̃/ **▶321** *nprm* Azerbaijan.

azerbaïdjanais /azɛʀbajdʒanɛ, ɛz/ **I ▶537** *adj* Azerbaijani.

II ▶462 *nm* Ling Azerbaijani.

Azerbaïdjanais, **~e** /azɛʀbajdʒanɛ, ɛz/ **▶537** *nm,f* Azerbaijani.

azéri /azeʀi/ **I ▶537** *adj* Azerbaijani.

II ▶462 *nm* Ling Azerbaijani.

Azéri /azeʀi/ **▶537** *nmf* Azerbaijani.

AZERTY /azɛʀti/ *adj inv* **clavier ~** AZERTY keyboard.

azimut /azimyt/ *nm* **1** Astron, Géog azimuth; **2** fig **défense tous ~s** Mil total defence[GB]; **une offensive tous ~s** Mil an all-out offensive; **négociations/débat tous ~s** wide-ranging negotiations/debate; **arrestations tous ~s** extensive ou wholesale arrests; **dans tous les ~s** everywhere, all over the place.

■ **~ magnétique** magnetic azimuth.

azimutal, **~e**, *mpl* **-aux** /azimytal, o/ *adj* azimuthal.

azimuté○, **~e** /azimyte/ *adj* crazy○.

Azincourt /azɛ̃kuʀ/ *npr* Agincourt.

azote /azɔt/ *nm* nitrogen.

azoté, **~e** /azɔte/ *adj* nitrogenous.

aztèque /astɛk/ *adj* Aztec.

Aztèque /astɛk/ *nmf* Aztec.

azur /azyʀ/ *nm* **1 ▶193** (couleur) azure; **un ciel d'~** an azure sky; **2** (ciel) liter azure, skies (*pl*).

azurant /azyʀɑ̃/ *nm* optical brightener.

azuré, **~e** /azyʀe/ *adj* azure (*épith*).

azuréen, **-éenne** /azyʀeɛ̃, ɛn/ *adj* French Riviera (*épith*).

azurer /azyʀe/ [1] *vtr* [*personne, produit*] to blue [*linge*]; to give a bluish tinge to [*papier*].

azyme /azim/ *adj* unleavened.

■ **pain ~** gén unleavened bread; (en pâtisserie) rice paper; (Relig juive) matzo; **galette de pain ~** matzo.

Bb

b, B /be/ *nm inv* b, B; **le b a ba** the rudiments.

BA /bea/ *nf* (*abbr* = **bonne action**) good deed.

BAB (*written abbr* = **bord à bord**) FIO.

baba /baba/ **I**○ *adj inv* **en être** or **rester ~** to be flabbergasted○.
II *nm* **1** Culin **~ (au rhum)** (rum) baba; **2**○ (personne) **~ (cool)** hippie.
IDIOMES **il l'a eu dans le ~**◑ he was really had○.

Babel /babɛl/ *npr* Babel; **la tour de ~** the tower of Babel.

babeurre /babœʀ/ *nm* buttermilk.

babiche○ /babiʃ/ *nf* C (visage) face.

babil /babil/ *nm* (d'oiseau) twittering, chattering; (d'enfants, de ruisseau, source) babbling; (bavardage) chattering.

babillage /babijaʒ/ *nm* (d'enfants) babbling.

babiller /babije/ [1] *vi* [*bébé, ruisseau*] to babble; [*personne, oiseau*] to chatter.

babines /babin/ *nfpl* Zool chops; **s'en lécher les ~** fig to lick one's chops.

babiole /babjɔl/ *nf* **1** (objet sans valeur) trinket; **2** (chose sans importance) trifle; **ne t'en fais pas, c'est une ~!** don't worry about it, it's nothing!

bâbord /babɔʀ/ *nm* port (side); **à ~** (position) on the port side; (direction) to port; **terre à ~!** land to port!

babouche /babuʃ/ *nf* oriental slipper.

babouin /babwɛ̃/ *nm* baboon.

baby-boom, *pl* **~s** /bebibum/ *nm* baby boom.

baby-foot /babifut/ **▶449** *nm inv* table football GB, table soccer.

Babylone /babilɔn/ *npr* Babylon.

babylonien, **-ienne** /babilɔnjɛ̃, ɛn/ *adj*, *nm* Babylonian.

baby-sitter, *pl* **~s** /bebisitœʀ/ *nmf* babysitter.

baby-sitting /bebisitiŋ/ *nm* babysitting; **faire du ~** to babysit.

bac /bak/ *nm* **1**○ Scol (*abbr* = **baccalauréat**) baccalaureate; (dans une annonce) **'~ + 2'** baccalaureate plus 2 years' higher education; **2** (bateau) ferry; **3** (cuve) gén tub; Ind vat; Phot tray; **évier à deux ~s** double sink.
■ **~ blanc** Scol mock baccalaureate; **~ à fleurs** plant tub; **~ à glace** ice tray; **~ à légumes** vegetable compartment (in fridge), crisper US; **~ professionnel** Scol ≈ GNVQ (*secondary school vocational diploma*); **~ à sable** sandpit GB, sandbox US; **~ à shampooing** shampoo basin; **~ à voitures** car-ferry.

baccalauréat /bakalɔʀea/ *nm* Scol baccalaureate (*school leaving certificate taken at 17–18*).

baccara /bakaʀa/ **▶449** *nm* baccarat.

baccarat /bakaʀa/ *nm* Baccarat crystal.

bacchanale /bakanal/ **I** *nf* **1** Art bacchanal; **2** Danse bacchanal, bacchanalian dance; **3**† (débauche tapageuse) drunken orgy, bacchanalian orgy.
II bacchanales *nfpl* Antiq Bacchanalia.

bacchante /bakɑ̃t/ **I** *nf* Antiq bacchante.
II bacchantes○ *nfpl* moustache (*sg*) GB, mustache (*sg*) US.

Bacchus /bakys/ *npr* Bacchus.

bâchage /baʃaʒ/ *nm* covering (*with sheets*), sheeting over; **nous allons procéder au ~ des camions** we are going to sheet over ou cover the trucks.

bâche /baʃ/ *nf* tarpaulin; **toile de ~** canvas sheet.
IDIOMES **se prendre une ~**◑ to get a slap in the face.

bachelier, **-ière** /baʃəlje, ɛʀ/ *nm,f*: *holder of the (French) baccalaureate*.

bâcher /baʃe/ [1] *vtr* to cover [sth] with tarpaulin [*véhicule*]; **un camion bâché** a covered truck.

bachi-bouzouk, *pl* **~s** /baʃibuzuk/ *nm* bashibazouk.

bachique /baʃik/ *adj* **1** Antiq [*culte, rite*] bacchic; **2** (relatif au vin) drinking (*épith*); **chanson ~** drinking song.

bachot /baʃo/ *nm* **1**○ Scol = **baccalauréat**; **2** (bateau) skiff.

bachotage○ /baʃɔtaʒ/ *nm* Scol cramming; **faire du ~** to cram (for an exam).

bachoter /baʃɔte/ [1] *vi* Scol to cram (for an exam).

bacillaire /basilɛʀ/ *adj* **1** (relatif au bacille) bacillary (*épith*); **2** (tuberculeux) consumptive.

bacille /basil/ *nm* bacillus; **~ de Koch** Koch bacillus.

backgammon /bakgamɔn/ **▶449** *nm* backgammon.

bâcler /bakle/ [1] *vtr* to dash [sth] off [*devoirs, travail*]; to rush through [*cérémonie*]; **~ une rédaction en vingt minutes** to dash an essay off in twenty minutes; **il bâcle tout ce qu'il fait** his work is always slapdash; **c'est du travail bâclé** it's a slapdash job; **l'ouvrier a bâclé le travail** the workman did a sloppy job; **après un procès bâclé** after a summary trial.

bacon /bekɔn/ *nm* smoked back bacon.

bactéricide /bakteʀisid/ **I** *adj* bactericidal.
II *nm* bactericide.

bactérie /bakteʀi/ *nf* bacterium; **des ~s** bacteria.

bactérien, **-ienne** /bakteʀjɛ̃, ɛn/ *adj* bacterial.

bactériologie /bakteʀjɔlɔʒi/ *nf* bacteriology.

bactériologique /bakteʀjɔlɔʒik/ *adj* bacteriological.

bactériologue /bakteʀjɔlɔg/ *nmf* bacteriologist.

bactériophage /bakteʀjɔfaʒ/ **I** *adj* bacteriophagous.
II *nm* bacteriophage.

badaboum /badabum/ **I** *nm* crash.
II *excl* crash bang wallop!

badaud, **~e** /bado, od/ *nm,f* (flâneur) passerby; (curieux) onlooker, rubberneck○ US péj.

baderne○ /badɛʀn/ *nf* **vieille ~** old fogey.

badge /badʒ/ *nm* **1** (insigne) badge; **2** (identité) badge, name tag; (avec piste magnétique) swipe card.

badgeuse /badʒøz/ *nf* time clock.

badiane /badjan/ *nf* star anise.

badigeon /badiʒɔ̃/ *nm* **1** (lait de chaux) whitewash; (coloré) colourwash[GB]; **passer un coup de ~ au plafond** to give the ceiling a coat of whitewash; **2**○ (peinture) paint.

badigeonnage /badiʒɔnaʒ/ *nm* **1** (peinture) whitewashing; (avec couleur) colourwashing[GB]; **2** Méd (de gorge) swabbing.

badigeonner /badiʒɔne/ [1] **I** *vtr* **1** (enduire) (de chaux) to whitewash [*mur*]; (en couleur) to paint; **badigeonné de bleu** painted blue; **2** (barbouiller) to daub (**de** with); **3** Méd to paint [*blessure, gorge*] (**de** with); **4** Culin **~ la pâte de lait** to brush the pastry with milk.
II se badigeonner *vpr* **se ~ la gorge** to paint one's throat (**de, à** with).

badin, **~e** /badɛ̃, in/ **I** *adj* [*ton*] bantering, playful; [*esprit, humeur*] playful.
II badine *nf* **1** (baguette) switch; **2** (canne) cane.

badinage /badinaʒ/ *nm* **1** (attitude) bantering; **2** (propos) banter.

badiner /badine/ [1] *vi* to banter, to jest; **pour ~** in jest; **il ne badine pas avec le règlement** he doesn't mess about when it comes to rules; **avec lui, on ne badine pas** that guy means business○ ou doesn't stand for any nonsense.

badinerie /badinʀi/ *nf* liter **1** (comportement) bantering, jesting littér; **2** (parole) **dire des ~s** to jest littér.

badminton /badmintɔn/ **▶449** *nm* badminton.

BAFA /bafa/ *nm* (*abbr* = **brevet d'aptitude aux fonctions d'animateurs**) *diploma taken to be a children's camp instructor*.

baffe○ /baf/ *nf* clout, slap; **il a reçu une paire de ~s** he got his ears boxed; **il m'a donné une ~** he hit ou clouted me.

Baffin /bafɛ̃/ **▶416** *npr* **la terre de ~** Baffin island; **mer** or **baie de ~** Baffin bay.

baffle /bafl/ *nm* (enceinte) speaker; (écran acoustique) baffle.

bafouer /bafwe/ [1] *vtr* to scorn.

bafouillage /bafujaʒ/ *nm* **1** (façon de parler) hesitancy; **2** (propos) gibberish ₵.

bafouille○ /bafuj/ *nf* letter.

bafouiller /bafuje/ [1] **I** *vtr* to mumble [*excuse, réponse*]; **qu'est-ce que tu bafouilles?** what are you mumbling about?; **il ne bafouille que des inepties** he just talks nonsense.
II *vi* **1** [*personne*] to mumble; **2** [*moteur*] to splutter.

bâfrer◑ /bafʀe/ [1] *vi*, **se bâfrer** *vpr* to gorge oneself, to stuff oneself○.

bâfreur◑, **-euse** /bafʀœʀ, øz/ *nm,f* glutton, pig○ péj.

bagage /bagaʒ/ **I** *nm* **1** (effets) luggage; (de soldat) kit; **elle avait un sac pour tout ~** her only luggage was one bag; **envoyer qch en ~ accompagné** to send sth as registered luggage; **2** (sac, valise) piece of luggage; **3** fig (connaissances) knowledge; (diplômes) qualifications (*pl*); (expérience) credentials (*pl*); **avoir un bon/mince ~** to have good/

poor qualifications; **il a un excellent ~ de directeur** he has splendid credentials as a manager.

II bagages *nmpl* (valises, effets) luggage ¢; **faire/défaire ses ~s** to pack/unpack (one's suitcases); **il a amené qn dans ses ~s** fig he's brought sb along with him; **il est toujours dans les ~s du Président** fig the President always takes him along.

■ **~ à main** hand luggage, carry-on baggage US.

IDIOMES **plier ~**○ to pack up and go; **partir avec armes et ~s** to up sticks and leave; **se rendre avec armes et ~s** to capitulate; **passer à l'ennemi avec armes et ~s** to defect.

bagagiste /bagaʒist/ ▶510 *nm* baggage handler.

bagarre /bagaʀ/ *nf* **1** (empoignade) fight (**entre** between); (action de se battre) **la ~** fighting; **~ dans un club** fight ou brawl in a club; **aimer la ~** to like fighting ou a fight; **chercher la ~** to be spoiling ou looking for a fight; **violentes ~s avec la police** violent clashes with the police; **il y a de violentes ~s dans les rues** there's rioting in the streets; **~ générale** free-for-all; **2** fig (lutte) fight, struggle; **c'est la ~ pour leur faire faire leur travail** it's a real fight ou struggle to get them to do their work; **3** (dispute) clash, confrontation (**entre** between); **entrer dans la ~** to join the fray.

bagarrer○ /bagaʀe/ [1] **I** *vi* (se battre, se disputer) to fight; **ça bagarrait dur hier soir** there was a real dingdong fight last night.

II se bagarrer *vpr* to fight (**pour** for).

bagarreur○, **-euse** /bagaʀœʀ, øz/ **I** *adj* (agressif) aggressive; (combatif) **être ~** to like to pick a fight.

II *nm,f* bruiser○, fighter.

bagatelle /bagatɛl/ *nf* **1** (chose sans importance) triviality; **se fâcher pour des ~s** to get angry over trivialities; **~!**† nonsense!; **2** (objet sans valeur) **je lui ai acheté une ~** I bought him/her a little something; **3** (somme d'argent) trifle; **~ de** iron trifling sum of; **la ~ de 70 millions de francs** the trifling sum of 70 million francs; **4**† (amour physique) euph physical love.

Bagdad /bagdad/ ▶857 *npr* Baghdad.

bagnard /baɲaʀ/ *nm* convict.

bagne /baɲ/ *nm* **1** (prison) penal colony; **2** (peine) penal servitude, hard labour[GB]; **faire vingt ans de ~** to do twenty years' hard labour[GB]; **ce travail, c'est le ~**○! fig this job is hell○!

bagnole○ /baɲɔl/ *nf* car; **vieille ~** old banger○ GB ou clunker○ US, old car.

bagou(t)○ /bagu/ *nm* volubility, glibness péj; **avoir du ~** to have the gift of the gab.

baguage /bagaʒ/ *nm* (d'oiseau, arbre) ringing.

bague /bag/ *nf* **1** (anneau) ring; **porter une ~ au doigt** to wear a ring on one's finger; **avoir une ~ à la patte** to have a ring around its foot; **2** (cercle) (de cigare, colonne) band; (de tuyau) collar; **3** Phot ring.

■ **~ de fiançailles** engagement ring; **~ de serrage** Tech jubilee clip.

IDIOMES **avoir la ~ au doigt** to be married; **elle lui a mis** or **passé la ~ au doigt** she got him to the altar.

baguenaude○ /bagnod/ *nf* **être en ~** to be strolling ou sauntering about.

baguenauder○ /bagnode/ [1] *vi*, **se baguenauder** *vpr* to stroll ou saunter about.

baguer /bage/ [1] *vtr* **1** to ring [*oiseau, arbre*]; Tech to collar [*tuyau*]; **doigts bagués** beringed fingers; **2** Cout to baste.

baguette /bagɛt/ *nf* **1** (pain) baguette, French stick; **2** (bâton) stick; (pour manger) chopstick; **~ d'encens** incense stick; **mener** or **faire marcher qn à la ~** fig to rule sb with a rod of iron; **3** Mus (pour percussion) drumstick; **~ de chef d'orchestre** conductor's baton; **l'orchestre jouera sous la ~ de R. Mutti** the orchestra will be conducted by R. Mutti; **4** Constr (moulure) beading; (pour cacher) casing; **poser des fils sous ~s** to conceal wires in casing; **5** Mode (sur bas, chaussettes) clock.

■ **~ de coudrier** hazel switch, divining rod; **~ de fusil** ramrod; **~ magique** magic wand; **d'un coup de ~ magique** with a wave of the magic wand; **~ de protection** Aut side trim; **~ de sourcier** water-divining rod; **~s de tambour** drumsticks; **elle a les cheveux raides comme des ~s de tambour** her hair is dead straight.

bah /ba/ *excl* so what?

Bahamas /baamas/ ▶321, 416 *nprfpl* **les (îles) ~** the Bahamas.

Bahreïn /baʀɛn/ ▶321 *nprm* Bahrain.

bahreïni /baʀeni/ ▶537 *adj* Bahreini.

Bahreïni /baʀeni/ ▶537 *nmf* Bahreini.

bahut /bay/ *nm* **1** (buffet) sideboard; **2**○ (lycée) students' slang school; **3**○ (camion) truck; **4** (malle) chest.

bai, **~e** /bɛ/ **I** ▶193 *adj* bay.

II baie *nf* **1** Géog bay; **2** Bot berry; **3** Archit opening; Constr (fenêtre) **~e (vitrée)** picture window.

baignade /bɛɲad/ *nf* **1** (activité) swimming, bathing†; **la ~ était bonne?** did you have a nice swim?; **'~ interdite'** 'no swimming', 'no bathing'; **après la ~** after swimming; **2** (lieu) bathing spot.

baigner /beɲe/ [1] **I** *vtr* **1** (donner un bain à) to bath GB, bathe US, to give [sb] a bath [*enfant, malade*]; **2** (pour soulager) to bathe [*œil malade, figure, blessure*] (**dans** in; **avec** with); **3** (inonder) **il avait le visage baigné de larmes** his face was bathed with tears; **baigné de sueur** [*front*] bathed in sweat; **baigné de lumière** liter bathed in light; **4** (voisiner avec) liter **la ville est baignée par l'océan** the ocean laps the town's shores.

II *vi* **les saucisses baignent dans l'huile** the sausages are swimming in grease; **ils baignaient dans leur sang** they were in a pool of their own blood; **ils baignent dans la joie** fig they are ecstatic; **la situation baigne dans l'ambiguïté** fig the situation is steeped in ambiguity.

III se baigner *vpr* **1** (dans la mer, une piscine) to have a swim; **allons nous ~** let's go for a swim; **on s'est baigné en haute mer/dans la rivière** we swam in the open sea/in the river; **2** (dans une baignoire) to have GB ou take US a bath.

IDIOMES **ça baigne** or **tout baigne (dans l'huile)** things are going fine.

baigneur, **-euse** /bɛɲœʀ, øz/ **I** *nm,f* (personne) swimmer, bather†.

II *nm* (poupée) baby doll.

baignoire /bɛɲwaʀ/ *nf* **1** (pour se laver) bath GB, bathtub; **2** Théât ground-floor box; **3** (de sous-marin) conning tower.

■ **~ sabot** hip bath.

Baïkal /bajkal/ ▶459 *npr* **le (lac) ~** Lake Baikal.

bail, *pl* **baux**[1] /baj, bo/ *nm* gén lease; (de trois ans ou moins) tenancy agreement; **~ commercial/à construction** commercial/building lease; **donner à ~** to lease out; **prendre à ~** to lease; **renouveler un ~** to renew a lease; **ça fait un ~ qu'on ne s'est pas vus**○! we haven't seen each other for ages○!

baille /baj/ *nf* **1**○ (eau) water; (mer) briny○; **mettre qn à la ~** to push sb into the water; **2**○ Naut (rafiot) old tub○; **3** Naut (baquet) tub, bucket.

bâillement /bajmɑ̃/ *nm* yawn; **étouffer** or **retenir un ~** to stifle a yawn; **avoir un ~** to yawn.

bailler† /baje/ [1] *vtr* **vous me la baillez belle** ou **bonne** you're pulling my leg○.

bâiller /bɑje/ [1] *vi* **1** lit [*personne, animal*] to yawn (**de** from, out of); **~ de fatigue** to yawn from tiredness; **2** fig [*col, chaussure*] to gape (open); [*porte*] to be ajar.

bailleur, **bailleresse** /bajœʀ, bajʀɛs/ *nm,f* lessor.

■ **~ de fonds** Comm backer, silent partner.

bâilleur, **-euse** /bɑjœʀ, øz/ *nm,f* sleepyhead.

bailli /baji/ *nm* Hist bailiff.

bailliage /bajaʒ/ *nm* bailiwick.

bâillon /bɑjɔ̃/ *nm* gag; **il avait un ~** he was gagged; **mettre un ~ à qn/la presse** fig to gag sb/the press.

bâillonnement /bɑjɔnmɑ̃/ *nm* (tous contextes) gagging.

bâillonner /bɑjɔne/ [1] *vtr* lit, fig to gag [*prisonnier, opposition, presse*].

bain /bɛ̃/ *nm* **1** (pour se laver) (eau) bath; **un ~ moussant** a bubble ou foam bath; **prendre un ~** to have GB ou take a bath; **donner un ~ à un enfant** to give a child a bath, to bath GB ou bathe US a child; **être dans son ~** to be in the bath GB ou bathtub; **je te fais couler un ~?** shall I run you a bath?; **2** (baignade) swim; **après le ~** after a swim; **éviter les ~s** to avoid swimming; **3** (bassin) **grand ~** deep end; **petit ~** (séparé) children's GB ou baby pool; (dans le grand bassin) shallow end; **4** (préparation liquide) bath; **5** fig **un ~ linguistique** or **de langue** total immersion ¢ in a language.

■ **~ de bouche** (produit) mouthwash; **faire des ~s de bouche** to rinse one's mouth (out); **~ de boue** mudbath; **~ bouillonnant** whirlpool bath; **~ fixateur** fixing bath; **~ de foule** walkabout; **prendre un ~ de foule** gén to mingle with the crowd; [*personnalité*] to go on a walkabout GB, to mingle with the crowd US; **~ de friture** cooking oil; **à ~ d'huile** oil-immersed; **~ de jouvence** rejuvenating experience; **~ de minuit** midnight swim; **prendre un ~ de minuit** to go for a midnight swim; **faire des ~s de pieds** to soak one's feet; **~ à remous** Jacuzzi®; **~ révélateur** developing bath; **~ de sable** sand bath; **~ de sang** bloodbath; **~ de siège** Méd sitz bath; **~ de soleil** (corsage) suntop; **robe ~ de soleil** sun dress; **prendre un ~ de soleil** to sunbathe; **~ de teinture** (produit) dye; (bac) vat of dye; **~ turc** Turkish bath; **~ de vapeur** steam bath; **~ d'yeux** (produit) eyewash; **faire des ~s d'yeux** to bathe one's eyes with eyewash; **~s de mer** sea bathing ¢; **~s municipaux** or **publics** public baths.

IDIOMES **être dans le ~** to be in the swing of things; **se mettre/se remettre dans le ~** to get/to get back into the swing of things; **mettre qn dans le ~** to implicate sb; ▶ **bébé**.

bain-douche, *pl* **bains-douches** /bɛ̃duʃ/ *nm* public baths.

bain-marie /bɛ̃maʀi/ *nm* **au ~** gén in a bain-marie; (crèmes, sauces) in a double boiler.

baïonnette /bajɔnɛt/ *nf* **1** Mil bayonet; **~ au canon!** (fix) bayonets!; **charger à la ~** to charge with fixed bayonets; **2** Électrotech bayonet fitting; **ampoule à ~** bulb with a bayonet fitting; **douille à ~** bayonet socket; **culot à ~** bayonet cap.

baise● /bɛz/ *nf* screwing●, fucking●.

baise-en-ville◑ /bɛzɑ̃vil/ *nm inv* overnight bag.

baisemain /bɛzmɛ̃/ *nm* hand-kissing ¢; **faire le ~ à qn** to kiss sb's hand.

baisement /bɛzmɑ̃/ *nm* Relig kissing.

baiser /beze/ [1] **I** *nm* kiss; **faire un ~ à qn** to give sb a kiss; **envoyer un ~ à qn** to blow sb a kiss; **bons ~s** love (and kisses); **~ d'adieu** farewell kiss.

II *vtr* **1**† (embrasser) to kiss; **2**● (faire l'amour à) to fuck●; **3**● (tromper, duper) to screw◑; **se faire ~**, **être baisé** to be screwed◑ ou had○.

III● *vi* (faire l'amour) to fuck●; **il/elle baise bien** he/she's a good fuck●.

■ **~ de Judas** Judas kiss; **le ~ de paix** the kiss of peace.

baiseur●, -euse /bɛzœʀ, øz/ *nm,f* **c'est un bon ~** he's a good fuck●; **c'est un sacré ~** he likes fucking● a lot.

baisse /bɛs/ *nf* **1** gén (de température, pression, d'intensité) fall, drop; (de niveau sonore) lowering; (de lumière) (extérieure) fading; (intérieure) dimming (**de** of); (de puissance, d'influence, de qualité, ventes) decline; **une ~ de 10°/de pression** a fall ou drop of 10°/in pressure; **2** Écon, Fin, Stat (décidée) (de prix, taux, salaires, d'impôts) cut (**de** in); (constatée) (de prix, taux) fall, drop (**de** in); (de salaires, d'impôts) decrease (**de** in); (de productivité) drop (**de** in); **la ~ du dollar** the fall in the value of the dollar; **une ~ des loyers de 2%** a 2% drop in rents; **après deux jours de ~, la Bourse s'est reprise légèrement** after two days of losses, the Stock Exchange recovered slightly; **être en ~** [*taux, actions, valeurs*] to be going down; [*résultats*] to be decreasing; **la natalité est en ~** the birthrate is coming down; **l'or est en ~** gold prices are going down; **le marché est à la ~** Fin the market is bearish; **tendance à la ~** downward ou bearish trend; **revoir** or **réviser des prévisions à la ~** to revise estimates downward(s); **opérations/spéculations à la ~** bear transactions/speculations; **spéculateur à la ~** bear; **spéculer à la ~** to go a bear ou for a fall; **les cinémas connaissent une ~ de fréquentation** fewer people are going to the cinema ou the movies US.

baisser /bese/ [1] **I** *vtr* **1** (abaisser) [*personne*] to lower [*volet, store*]; to wind [sth] down [*vitre*]; to pull down [*pantalon, culotte, visière*]; to turn down [*col*]; **les stores étaient baissés** the blinds were down; **~ la tête** (par précaution) to lower one's head; (vivement) to duck one's head; (par soumission, de honte) to bow; **~ les yeux** (**de honte**) to look down (in shame); **~ les bras** lit to lower one's arms; fig to give up; **~ le nez** fig to hang one's head; **je vais leur faire ~ le nez, à ces prétentieux!** I'm going to bring them down a peg or two, those pretentious twits!; **2** (réduire) to turn down [*son, volume*]; to dim [*lumière*]; [*autorité*] to cut [*prix, taux*]; [*circonstances*] to bring down [*prix, taux*].
II *vi* **1** (diminuer de niveau) [*température, pression, tension*] to fall, to drop, to go down (**à** to; **de** by); [*fièvre, volume sonore*] to go down; [*lumière*] to fade, to grow dim; [*eaux*] to subside; [*qualité*] to decline; [*criminalité, délinquance*] to decline, to be on the decline; [*moral*] to fall; [*optimisme*] to fade; **le Rhône continue de ~** water levels in the Rhône are still dropping; **le niveau des étudiants n'a pas baissé** the standard of the students' work has not deteriorated; **~ dans l'estime de qn** to go down in sb's esteem; **~ dans les sondages** [*candidat*] to go down in the polls; **le baromètre baisse** the barometer is falling; **le jour baisse** the light is fading; **~ d'un ton**○ [*personne*] fig to calm down; **2** (diminuer de valeur) [*prix, résultat, taux, production, recettes*] to fall; [*salaires*] to go down; [*pouvoir d'achat*] to decrease; [*chômage, emplois*] to fall, to decrease; [*productivité*] to decline; [*actions, chiffre d'affaires*] to go ou come down, to decrease; [*budget*] to be cut; [*marché*] to decline; [*monnaie*] to slide; **les loyers vont ~** rents are going to go down; **les prix/taux d'intérêt/salaires ont baissé de 2%** prices/interest rates/salaries have come down by 2%; **leur PNB a baissé de moitié** their GNP has dropped by half; **la productivité va ~ de 10%** productivity will fall ou drop by 10%; **la nouvelle de la guerre a fait ~ la Bourse** news of the war caused prices on the Stock Exchange to fall ou drop; **3** (diminuer de qualité) [*vue*] to fail; [*intelligence, ouïe, facultés*] to deteriorate; **ma vue baisse** my sight is failing.
III se baisser *vpr* [*personne*] (pour passer, saisir) to bend down; (pour éviter) to duck; [*levier, mécanisme*] to go down; [*rideau*] Théât to drop; **baisse-toi pour passer sous les barbelés** bend down to get under the barbed wire; **baissez-vous, ils tirent!** duck, they're shooting at us!

baissier, -ière /besje, ɛʀ/ Fin **I** *adj* bearish.
II *nm* bear.

bajoue /baʒu/ *nf* **1** Culin (de porc, veau) cheek; **2**○ (joue humaine) jowl, chop.

bakchich○ /bakʃiʃ/ *nm* backhander GB, bribe.

bakélite® /bakelit/ *nf* Bakelite®.

baklava /baklava/ *nm* baklava.

Bakou /baku/ **▶ 857** *npr* Baku.

bal /bal/ *nm* **1** (cérémonieux) ball; (simple) dance; **donner un ~ en l'honneur de qn** to give a ball in sb's honour[GB]; **ouvrir le ~ avec qn** to open the dance with sb; **ouvrir le ~ avec une valse** to open the ball with a waltz; **conduire** or **mener le ~** lit [*couple*] to be the centre[GB] of attention at the ball; [*femme*] to be the belle of the ball; fig to run the show; **2** (lieu) dancehall; **aller au ~** to go dancing.
■ **~ champêtre** village dance; **~ costumé** fancy-dress ball, costume ball US; **~ masqué** masked ball; **~ musette** dance with accordion music; **~ populaire** dance; **~ public** (lieu) public dancehall.

balade /balad/ *nf* (à pied) walk; (plus lent) stroll; (à moto, vélo) ride; (en voiture) drive; **faire une ~** to go for a walk ou stroll; **être en ~** (**dans une région**) to tour (a region); **ils sont en ~ pour la journée** they've gone on a day trip.

balader○ /balade/ [1] **I** *vtr* **1** (à pied) to take [sb] for a walk; (en voiture) to take [sb] for a drive; **je l'ai baladé dans tous les musées** I showed him around all the museums; **2** (emporter avec soi) to carry [sth] around.
II se balader *vpr* **1** (faire une balade) (à pied) to go for a walk; (plus lent) to go for a stroll; (à moto, vélo) to go for a ride; (en voiture) to go for a drive; **2** (voyager) to travel; **se ~ dans une région** to tour a region; **3** (se déplacer) [*douleur*] to move around; **il y a un écrou qui se balade** there's a loose nut.
IDIOMES **envoyer qn ~**○ to send sb packing○; **j'ai envie de tout envoyer ~** I feel like packing everything in○.

baladeur, -euse /baladœʀ, øz/ **I** *adj* [*lampe*] portable.
II *nm* walkman®, personal stereo.
III baladeuse *nf* portable lamp.
IDIOMES **avoir les mains baladeuses** pej to have wandering hands.

baladin /baladɛ̃/ *nm* strolling player.

balafre /balafʀ/ *nf* (marque) scar; (entaille) (profonde) slash, gash; (superficielle) cut.

balafrer /balafʀe/ [1] *vtr* (intentionnellement) to slash; (accidentellement) to gash.

balai /balɛ/ *nm* **1** (pour le sol) broom; **passer le ~** to sweep the floor; **donner un coup de ~** lit to give the floor a quick sweep; **coup de ~ dans l'entreprise** fig mass redundancies in the company; **2** (d'essuie-glace) blade; **3** Électrotech brush; **4**○ (an) **avoir 50 ~s** to be fifty.
■ **~ mécanique** carpet sweeper.
IDIOMES **du ~**○! go away!, push off○ GB!

balai-brosse, *pl* **balais-brosses** /balɛbʀɔs/ *nm* stiff broom.

balai-éponge, *pl* **balais-éponges** /balɛepɔ̃ʒ/ *nm* squeeze mop.

balaise○ = **balèze**.

balalaïka /balalaika/ **▶ 534** *nf* balalaika.

balance /balɑ̃s/ *nf* **1** Mes scales (*pl*); **monter sur la ~** to get ou step on the scales; **peser lourd dans la ~** fig [*décision, vote, influence*] to carry a lot of weight; **faire pencher la ~** fig to tip the scales (**en faveur de** in favour[GB] of); **2** Compta balance; **3** (équilibre) balance; **la ~ des forces** or **pouvoirs** the balance of power; **4** Audio balance; **5**◑ (dénonciateur) grass○ GB, informer, stool pigeon○ US; **6** Pêche lift net.
■ **~ commerciale** balance of trade; **~ des comptes** = **~ des paiements**; **~ de cuisine** kitchen scales; **~ électronique** electronic scales; **~ de laboratoire** laboratory balance; **~ des paiements** balance of payments; **la ~ des paiements courants** the current balance of payments; **~ à plateaux** balance; **~ de précision** precision balance; **~ de Roberval** Roberval's balance; **~ romaine** steelyard; **~s dollars** dollar balances.

Balance /balɑ̃s/ **▶ 874** *nprf* Libra.

balancé, ~e /balɑ̃se/ **I** *pp* **▶ balancer.**
II *pp adj* **bien ~** [*phrase*] well- ou nicely balanced; [*personne*]○ well-built.

balancelle /balɑ̃sɛl/ *nf* swing seat, garden hammock.

balancement /balɑ̃smɑ̃/ *nm* lit (de branches, corps) swaying ¢; (de bras, jambes, hanches, corde) swinging ¢; (de tête) lolling ¢.

balancer /balɑ̃se/ [12] **I** *vtr* **1** (faire osciller) [*vent*] to sway [*branches*]; to swing [*cordage*]; **~ les bras/jambes** to swing one's arms/legs; **~ la tête** to rock one's head; **~ la queue** to wag its tail; **il balançait la tête de droite à gauche** he was rocking his head from right to left; **2**○ (jeter) to chuck○, to throw [*projectile, ordures*]; **balance-moi le tournevis** chuck ou pitch○ US me the screwdriver; **arrête de ~ des cailloux!** stop chucking stones!; **~ qch par la fenêtre** or **vitre** to chuck ou pitch○ sth out of the window; **~ qch sur qch/qn** to chuck sth at sth/sb; **~ une gifle à qn** to whack sb○; **~ des coups de pied dans qch** to kick sth; **3**○ (se débarrasser de) to chuck out○, to throw out [*vieux habits, objets inutiles*]; **j'ai balancé tous mes bibelots** I've chucked out all my trinkets; **4**○ (dire) (brutalement) to toss off [*phrases, réponse*]; (pêle-mêle) to bandy [sth] about [*chiffres*]; **~ des statistiques/dates à la figure de qn** to fling statistics/dates at sb; **~ une nouvelle à qn** to break the news to sb brutally; **je leur ai balancé: 'je m'en fiche!'** 'I don't give a damn○!' I flung back at them; **5**○ (dénoncer) **~ qn** to squeal on sb◑; **être balancé** or **se faire ~ par qn** to be squealed on by sb; **il a menacé de ~ tout ce qu'il sait** he's threatened to come out with everything he knows; **6** Compta to balance [*compte*].
II *vi* **1** (osciller) [*branches*] to sway; [*corde, trapèze*] to swing; [*bateau*] to rock; **2** (hésiter) **~ entre deux choix/personnes** to hesitate ou be torn between two choices/people; **il balance entre le 'oui' et le 'non'** he is wavering between 'yes' and 'no'; **entre les deux mon cœur balance** my heart is torn between the two.
III se balancer *vpr* **1** (se mouvoir) [*personne, animal*] to sway; [*bateau*] to rock; **elle se balance au rythme de la musique** she is swaying to the rhythm of the music; **se ~ d'un pied sur l'autre** to shift from one foot to the other; **se ~ de gauche à droite** to sway from left to right; **se ~ au bout d'une liane/d'un trapèze** to swing on a creeper/a trapeze; **se ~ sur sa chaise** to rock on one's chair; **cesse de te ~ (sur ta chaise)!** stop rocking on your chair!; **2**○ (se jeter) **se ~ dans le vide** to throw oneself into space; **se ~ du sixième étage** to fling oneself off the sixth GB ou seventh US floor.
IDIOMES **je m'en balance**◑ I don't give a damn◑.

balancier /balɑ̃sje/ *nm* **1** gén (d'horloge, de métronome) pendulum; **mouvement de ~** lit, fig swing of the pendulum; **politique de ~** fig seesaw politics; **2** (pour funambule) balancing pole; **3** Zool haltere.

balançoire /balɑ̃swaʀ/ *nf* **1** (nacelle suspendue) swing; **faire de la ~** to have a swing ou go on the swing; **2** (planche qui bascule) seesaw.

balayage /balɛjaʒ/ *nm* **1** (avec un balai) sweeping; **2** (en coiffure) **se faire faire un ~**

to have highlights put in; **3** Électron scanning.

balayer /baleje/ [21] *vtr* **1** (avec un balai) to sweep [*lieu, plancher*]; to sweep up [*miettes, feuilles*]; **2** (frôler) [*cape, manteau*] **~ le sol** to brush the ground; **3** [*vent, rafale de pluie*] to sweep across [*plaine, carrefour*]; [*faisceau de projecteur*] to sweep [*terrain*]; [*mitrailleuse*] to rake [*place*]; **son regard balaya l'assistance** his gaze swept the audience; **4** (faire disparaître) to sweep [sth] away [*craintes, divergences*]; (faire fi de) to brush [sth] aside [*objections, rumeurs*]; (plus fort) to sweep [sth] aside [*craintes*]; **5** (chasser) [*vent*] to sweep [sth] away [*nuages, feuilles*]; **être balayé par l'opposition** to be swept aside by the opposition; (sans retour) to be swept away by the opposition; **être balayé du pouvoir** to be swept from power; **~ l'ennemi hors de la région** to sweep the enemy out of the area; **6** Électron to scan.

IDIOMES **~ devant sa porte** to put one's own house in order before criticizing other people.

balayette /balɛjɛt/ *nf* (short-handled) brush.

balayeur -euse /balɛjœʀ, øz/ **I** ▶510 *nm,f* (personne) cleaner; **~ (de rues)** street cleaner.

II balayeuse *nf* (machine) mechanical road-sweeper GB, mechanical street-sweeper US.

balayures /balɛjyʀ/ *nfpl* sweepings.

balbutiant, ~e /balbysjɑ̃, ɑ̃t/ *adj* **1** (qui bredouille) [*personne, enfant*] stammering; [*bébé*] babbling; **2** (qui débute) in its infancy.

balbutiement /balbysimɑ̃/ *nm* **1** lit (de personne, d'enfant) stammering ¢; (de bébé) babbling; **2** fig (début) first step; **les ~s d'une découverte/entreprise** the first steps in a discovery/project; **les ~ du cinéma/d'une science** the cinema's/a science's first steps; **la psychanalyse n'en était qu'à ses premiers ~s** psychoanalysis was still in its infancy.

balbutier /balbysje/ [2] **I** *vtr* [*personne, enfant*] to stammer; [*bébé*] to babble.

II *vi* **1** lit (bredouiller) [*enfant, personne*] to stammer; [*bébé*] to babble; **l'émotion le fit ~** emotion caused him to stammer; **2** fig (débuter) to be in its infancy.

balbuzard /balbyzaʀ/ *nm* osprey.

balcon /balkɔ̃/ *nm* **1** Constr balcony; **2** Théât balcony, circle; **fauteuil de ~** seat in the circle; **premier ~** dress circle GB, mezzanine US; **deuxième ~** balcony, upper circle; **3** Naut (rambarde) bow pulpit, stern pulpit; (galerie) Hist stern gallery.

IDIOMES **il y a du monde au ~**○! hum she's well-endowed!

balconnet /balkɔnɛ/ *nm* **1** Constr small balcony; **2** Mode **soutien-gorge à ~** half-cup bra; **un soutien-gorge à ~ pigeonnant** an uplift half-cup bra; **3** (dans un réfrigérateur) shelf (*in fridge door*).

Balconnet® /balkɔnɛ/ *nm* Mode uplift bra.

baldaquin /baldakɛ̃/ *nm* (de lit) canopy; (de trône, catafalque) baldaquin, canopy; **lit à ~** four-poster bed.

Bâle /bɑl/ *npr* **1** ▶857 (ville) Basel; **2** ▶692 (région) **le canton de ~** the canton of Basel; **le demi-canton de ~-ville/~-campagne** the half-canton of Basel-stadt/Basel-land.

Baléares /baleaʀ/ ▶416 *nprfpl* **les (îles) ~** the Balearic Islands, the Balearics.

baleine /balɛn/ *nf* **1** Zool whale; **la chasse à la ~** whaling; **chasser la ~** to go whaling; **2** Mode (pour renforcer) (de corset) whalebone, stay US; (de col) stiffener, stay US.

■ **~ blanche** white whale; **~ bleue** blue whale; **~ à bosse** humpback whale; **~ franche** right whale; **~ de parapluie** umbrella rib.

IDIOMES **rire** or **se tordre comme une ~**○ to laugh one's head off○.

baleiné, ~e /balɛne/ *adj* [*col*] stiffened, with stays (*après n*) US; [*corset*] boned; [*parapluie*] ribbed.

baleineau, *pl* **~x** /balɛno/ *nm* whale calf.

baleinier, -ière /balɛnje, ɛʀ/ **I** *adj* [*bateau, industrie*] whaling.

II ▶510 *nm* (pêcheur) whaler.

III baleinière *nf* (bateau) whaleboat.

balèze○ /balɛz/ **I** *adj* **1** (grand et fort) hefty○; **2** fig [*intellectuel*] fantastic○, brilliant GB; [*sportif*] fantastic○; **être ~ en qch** (intellectuellement) to be hot○ at sth; (physiquement) to be great at sth.

II *nmf* **1** (personne forte) hefty person; **2** fig (as) genius; **un ~ en informatique** a genius at computing.

balisage /balizaʒ/ *nm* **1** Naut (de port, chenal) beaconing; **2** Aviat (de piste d'aviation) runway lighting; **3** Transp (de route) signposting; (de sentier) marking; **4** Sport (de piste de ski) marking-out; **5** Ordinat (de texte) tagging.

balise /baliz/ *nf* **1** Naut (flotteur) beacon, buoy; (émetteur) radio beacon; **2** Aviat beacon, light; **3** Aut signpost, sign; **4** Rail (de voie ferrée) signal; **5** Sport (de piste de ski) marker; **6** (de sentier) marker; **7** Ordinat tag.

baliser /balize/ [1] **I** *vtr* **1** Naut (avec bouées) to buoy, to mark [sth] out with beacons [*port, chenal*]; **2** Aviat to mark [sth] out with beacons [*piste*]; **3** Transp to signpost [*route*]; **4** Rail to mark [sth] out with signals [*voie ferrée*]; **5** Sport to mark out [*piste, sentier*]; **6** Ordinat to tag [*texte*].

II○ *vi* fig (avoir peur) to have the jitters○, to be frightened.

baliseur /balizœʀ/ *nm* (navire) buoy-layer.

baliste /balist/ *nf* Antiq Mil ballista.

balisticien, -ienne /balistisjɛ̃, ɛn/ *nm,f* ballistics expert.

balistique /balistik/ **I** *adj* [*missile*] ballistic; **expert ~** ballistics expert.

II *nf* ballistics (+ *v sg*).

baliveau, *pl* **~x** /balivo/ *nm* Constr staddle.

baliverne /balivɛʀn/ *nf* nonsense ¢; **raconter des ~s** to talk nonsense ou rubbish; **s'amuser à des ~s** to fool around○.

balkanique /balkanik/ *adj* Balkan.

balkanisation /balkanizɑsjɔ̃/ *nf* (de territoire) Balkanization; (d'institution) break-up.

balkaniser /balkanize/ [1] **I** *vtr* to Balkanize.

II se balkaniser *vpr* to become Balkanized.

Balkans /bɑlkɑ̃/ ▶692 *nprmpl* Balkans; **la péninsule des ~** the Balkan Peninsula.

ballade /balad/ *nf* **1** Mus (instrumentale) ballade; (chanson) ballad; **2** Littérat (forme fixe) ballade; (forme libre) ballad.

ballant, ~e /balɑ̃, ɑ̃t/ **I** *adj* **1** [*bras, jambe*] dangling; [*tête*] lolling; **il était là, les bras ~s** there he was with his arms dangling; **2** Naut [*câble, cordage*] slack.

II *nm* **avoir du ~** [*véhicule, charge*] to sway around; [*câble, cordage*] to be slack; **donner du ~** to give some slack.

ballast /balast/ *nm* Naut, Rail ballast; **sur le ~** on the railway track.

balle /bal/ *nf* **1** Jeux, Sport (objet) ball; **~ de tennis/golf/ping-pong**® tennis/golf/table-tennis ball; **~ à terre** (au football) drop ball; **jouer à la ~** to play ball; **la ~ est dans notre camp** fig the ball is in our court; **renvoyer la ~ (à qn)** lit to throw the ball back (to sb); fig to retort (to sb); **se renvoyer la ~** (discuter) to keep a lively argument going; (se rejeter la responsabilité) to keep passing the buck; ▶**bond**; **2** Sport (échange, envoi) shot; **~ coupée** sliced shot; **faire des ~s** to knock up GB, to have a knock up GB, to knock the ball around US; **~ de jeu/de set/de match** game/set/match point; **3** (pour arme) bullet; **~ explosive/en plastique/perdue** explosive/plastic/stray bullet; **fausse ~** dummy bullet; **criblé de ~s** riddled with bullet holes; **tué par ~** shot dead; **tué d'une ~ dans la tête** killed by a gunshot wound in the head; **il a été blessé par ~** he was shot and injured; **4**○ (franc) franc; **5** (de café, foin) bale; (de papier) ream; **6** Agric, Bot husk.

■ **~ à blanc** blank (bullet); **~ au chasseur** Jeux hunter; **~ traçante** tracer (bullet).

IDIOMES **c'est un enfant de la ~** he comes from a family of performers.

ballerine /balʀin/ *nf* **1** ▶510 (danseuse) ballerina, ballet dancer; **2** (chaussures) (de danse) ballet pump; (de ville) ballerina-style shoe.

ballet /balɛ/ *nm* **1** Danse, Mus ballet; **2** (va et vient) **~ de voitures officielles** flurry of official cars; **~ diplomatique** diplomatic comings and goings (*pl*).

■ **~ aquatique** Sport synchronized swimming; **~s bleus** paedophile ring (*involving young boys*); **~s roses** paedophile ring (*involving young girls*).

ballon /balɔ̃/ *nm* **1** (grosse balle) ball; **~ de football** football GB, soccer ball; **~ de rugby** rugby ball; **jouer au ~** to play ball; **2** (plein de gaz, de liquide) (jouet) balloon; Aviat, Météo balloon; **monter en ~** to go up in a balloon; **3** (verre) **(verre) ~** (pour vin) (red) wine glass (*with rounded bowl*); (pour cognac) brandy glass; **un ~ de rouge** (contenu) a glass of red wine; **4** Aut **~ alcootest** Breathalyzer®; **souffler dans le ~** to breathe into the Breathalyzer®; **5** Géog round-topped mountain.

■ **~ captif** tethered ou captive balloon; **~ dirigeable** airship GB, blimp US; **~ d'eau chaude** hot water tank; **~ d'essai** lit pilot balloon, trial balloon; **lançons un ~ d'essai** fig let's test the waters; **~ ovale** (jeu) rugby; (objet) rugby ball; **~ d'oxygène** lit oxygen bottle; fig life-saver; **~ prisonnier** *team game where players hit by the ball become the prisoners of the opposite team*; **~ rond** (jeu) soccer; (objet) football GB, soccer ball.

IDIOMES **avoir du ~**○ to have a potbelly; **attraper le ~**◑ to get knocked up; **avoir le ~**◑ to have a bun in the oven○ GB, to be pregnant.

ballonnement /balɔnmɑ̃/ *nm* bloating; **avoir des ~s (d'estomac)** to have a bloated stomach, to feel bloated; **provoquer des ~s** to cause the stomach to become bloated.

ballonner /balɔne/ [1] *vtr* to bloat [*personne, animal*]; **cela me ballonne le ventre** it makes my stomach bloated; **j'ai trop mangé, je suis ballonné** I've eaten too much, I'm bloated.

ballonnet /balɔnɛ/ *nm* (de gaz, liquide) small balloon; **~ d'oxygène** small oxygen bottle.

ballon-sonde, *pl* **ballons-sondes** /balɔ̃sɔ̃d/ *nm* sounding balloon.

ballot /balo/ *nm* **1** (de marchandises, vêtements) bundle; **2**○ (sot) nerd○, fool.

ballotin /balɔtɛ̃/ *nm* **~ de chocolats** small box of chocolates.

ballottage /balɔtaʒ/ *nm* Pol *absence of an absolute majority in the first round of an election*; **il y a ~** there has to be a runoff (ballot); **être mis en ~** to face a runoff; **~ pour M. X** Mr X goes on to (compete in) a runoff; **~ favorable/défavorable** easy/difficult runoff.

ballottement /balɔtmɑ̃/ *nm* (de bateau) tossing; (de personne, voiture) jolting.

ballotter /balɔte/ [1] **I** *vtr* **1** [*mer*] to toss [sb/sth] around [*personne, embarcation*]; [*cahot*] to jolt [*personne, véhicule*]; **véhicule/radeau ballotté par la tempête** vehicle/raft buffeted by the storm; **2** fig **être ballotté entre qn et qn/entre la France et l'Angleterre** to be tossed back and forth between sb and sb/between France and England; **être ballotté par qch** to be buffeted by sth; **être ballotté entre sa famille et son travail** fig to be torn between one's family and one's job.

II *vi* [*bateau*] to be buffeted; [*voiture, objet, tête*] to jolt.

ballottine /balɔtin/ *nf* ballottine.
ball-trap, *pl* **~s** /baltʀap/ *nm* **1** (appareil) trap (for clay pigeon shooting); **2** (sport) clay pigeon shooting; **3** (séance) clay pigeon shoot.
balluchon = **baluchon**.
balnéaire /balneɛʀ/ *adj* [*station*] seaside.
balnéothérapie /balneɔteʀapi/ *nf* balneotherapy.
balourd, **~e** /baluʀ, uʀd/ **I** *adj* uncouth.
II *nm,f* (personne) oaf.
III *nm* Tech (déséquilibre) unbalance; Aut (de roue) imbalance; **avoir du ~** [*roue*] to be out of balance.
balourdise /baluʀdiz/ *nf* **1** (gaucherie) clumsiness; **2** (gaffe) (acte) blunder, faux-pas; (parole) gaffe, faux-pas.
baloutche /balutʃ/, **baloutchi** /balutʃi/ **▶ 462** **I** *adj* Baluchi.
II *nm* Ling Baluchi.
Baloutche /balutʃ/ *nmf* Géog Baluchi.
Baloutchistan /balutʃistɑ̃/ **▶ 692** *nprm* Baluchistan.
balsa /balza/ *nm* **1** (arbre) balsa; **2** (bois) balsa wood.
balsamier /balzamje/ *nm* balsam tree.
balsamine /balzamin/ *nf* balsam.
balsamique /balzamik/ *adj* balsamic.
balte /balt/ **▶ 692** *adj* Baltic; **les pays ~s** the Baltic States.
Balte /balt/ *nmf* Balt.
balthazar /baltazaʀ/ *nm* (bouteille) Balthazar.
Baltique /baltik/ **▶ 555** *nprf* **la (mer) ~** the Baltic (Sea).
baluchon /balyʃɔ̃/ *nm* bundle.
IDIOMES **faire son ~** to pack one's bags (and leave).
balustrade /balystʀad/ *nf* **1** (en ciment, pierre) parapet; (en métal) railing; **2** (avec colonnettes) balustrade.
balustre /balystʀ/ *nm* Archit baluster.
balutchi = **baloutche**.
balzacien, **-ienne** /balzasjɛ̃, ɛn/ **I** *adj* Balzac (*épith*); **un héros ~** a Balzac hero; **un personnage très ~** a character very much out of Balzac.
II *nm,f* Balzac specialist.
balzane /balzan/ *nf* (de cheval) **petite ~** sock; **grande ~** stocking.
Bamako /bamako/ **▶ 857** *npr* Bamako.
bambin, **~e** /bɑ̃bɛ̃, in/ *nm,f* kid○, child.
bambou /bɑ̃bu/ *nm* bamboo; **des pousses de ~** bamboo shoots; **coup de ~** (facture) steep ou hefty bill; **dans ce magasin, c'est le coup de ~** in that shop GB ou store US, they charge the earth; **avoir le coup de ~** (se comporter bizarrement) to go off one's rocker○; (être fatigué) to be knackered○ GB ou bushed○ US.
bamboula /bɑ̃bula/ *nf* **1**○ (fête) bash○; **faire la ~**○ to have a bash○; **2** Danse, Mus bamboula.
ban /bɑ̃/ **I** *nm* (applaudissements) round of applause (**pour** for); (roulements de tambour) drum roll; (sonnerie) bugle call; **ouvrir/fermer le ~** (de réunion) to start/end the proceedings.
II bans *nmpl* banns; **publier** or **afficher les ~s** to publish the banns.
IDIOMES **mettre qn/un groupe au ~ de la société** to ostracize sb/a group from society; **être mis au ~ des nations civilisées** to be ostracized from civilized nations; **être en rupture de ~** to have broken (**avec** with); **le ~ et l'arrière-ban de la famille** hum every single member of the family.
banal, **~e**, /banal, o/ *adj* **1** (*mpl* **~s**) (courant) [*mot, idée*] commonplace; [*cas, événement, personne*] unremarkable; (trivial) [*roman, spectacle*] banal; **peu** or **pas ~** rather unusual; **2** (*mpl* **-aux**) Hist [*four, moulin, pressoir*] communal.
banalisation /banalizɑsjɔ̃/ *nf* **1** (fait de rendre trivial) trivialization; (fait de rendre courant) **favoriser la ~ de qch** to help sth to become more commonplace; **2** (de voiture, véhicule) **la ~ d'une voiture de police** the removal of distinguishing marks from a police car.
banaliser /banalize/ [1] **I** *vtr* **1** (rendre courant) to make [sth] commonplace; (rendre trivial) to trivialize; **2** [*police, armée*] to remove all distinguishing marks from [*véhicule*]; **voiture banalisée** unmarked car.
II se banaliser *vpr* to become commonplace.
banalité /banalite/ *nf* **1** (caractère courant) (d'histoire, de vie) commonplace nature; (de remarque, d'idée) triteness; **2** (propos, écrit sans originalité) banality, platitude; **ils ont échangé quelques ~s** they exchanged a few banalities ou platitudes; **3** (caractère peu original) banality.
banane /banan/ *nf* **1** Bot banana; **gâteau/yaourt à la ~** banana cake/yoghurt; **parfumé à la ~** banana-flavoured^GB; **2** (coiffure d'homme) quiff; (de femme) French pleat; **3** (sac) money belt, bum-bag○ GB; **4**○ (imbécile) dummy○.
bananeraie /bananʀɛ/ *nf* banana plantation.
bananier, **-ière** /bananje, ɛʀ/ **I** *adj* **culture bananière** banana growing; **région bananière** banana-growing region.
II *nm* **1** Bot banana tree; **2** (bateau) banana boat.
banc /bɑ̃/ *nm* **1** (siège) bench; **~ public** bench; **~ de jardin** garden bench; **nous nous sommes rencontrés sur les ~s de l'école** we met at school; **2** Pol (au Parlement) bench GB, seats (*pl*) US; **3** Zool **~ de poissons** shoal of fish; **~ d'huîtres** oyster bed; **4** Géol (couche) layer, bed; **5** Tech Mécan bench.
■ **~ des accusés** dock; **dans le ~ des accusés** in the dock; **mettre qn au ~ des accusés** fig to put sb in the dock; **au ~ des avocats** at the bar; **~ de brouillard** patch of fog; (en mer) fog bank; **~ de brume** patch of mist; **~ de coraux** coral reef; **~ d'église** pew; **~ d'essai** lit test bench; fig testing ground; **passer qch au ~ d'essai** lit to test sth; fig to put sth to the test; **au ~ de l'infamie** in the dock; **au ~ du ministère public** on the prosecution bench; **~ de nage** thwart; **~ de sable** sandbank; **au ~ des témoins** in the witness box GB, on the witness stand US; **le ~ de touche** the substitutes' bench; **~ de vase** mud bank.
bancable /bɑ̃kabl/ *adj* bankable.
bancaire /bɑ̃kɛʀ/ *adj* **1** [*activité, secteur, service*] banking; **2** [*carte, compte, chèque, prêt*] bank.
bancal, **~e** /bɑ̃kal/ *adj* [*chaise, table*] rickety; [*solution, raisonnement*] shaky; **la dernière phrase est ~e** the last sentence does not really stand up; **des meubles ~s** rickety furniture.
banco /bɑ̃ko/ *nm* **1** (au baccara) banco; **un ~ de 100 000 francs** a banco for 100,000 francs; **faire ~** to go banco; **gagner le ~** fig to make a packet○; **2** (butin) haul.
bandage /bɑ̃daʒ/ *nm* **1** Pharm (objet) bandage; (action) bandaging; **faire un ~ à qn** to bandage sb up; **faire un ~ à un bras** to bandage an arm; **2** Aut tyre.
bandana /bɑ̃dana/ *nm* bandan(n)a.
bandant●, **~e** /bɑ̃dɑ̃, ɑ̃t/ *adj* (sexuellement) [*femme*] hung-looking●; **c'est ~** it's a turn-on○.
bande /bɑ̃d/ *nf* **1** (de malfaiteurs, voyous) gang; **~ armée** armed gang; **la ~ à Léo**○ Leo's gang; **2** (de touristes, jeunes, d'amis) group, crowd; **en ~** [*sortir, se déplacer*] in a group ou crowd; **~ de crétins!** you bunch of idiots!; **ils font ~ à part** they don't join in; **3** (d'animaux sauvages) pack; **en ~** [*vivre, se déplacer*] in packs; **4** (de tissu, papier, cuir) gén strip; (plus large) band; Pharm bandage; (de journal) mailing wrapper; **5** (forme étroite et allongée) gén strip; (qui orne) (rayure) large stripe; (en bordure) band; **~ de terre** strip of land; **6** (support d'enregistrement) tape; Cin film; **~ (magnétique)** (magnetic) tape; **~ démo**○ demo tape○; **~ vidéo** video tape; **7** (au billard) cushion; **8** Naut **donner de la ~** to list.
■ **~ amorce** Phot leader tape; **~ d'arrêt d'urgence**, **BAU** hard shoulder; **~ banalisée** = **~ publique**; **~ dessinée**, **BD**○ (dans les journaux) comic strip; (livre) comic book; (genre) comic strips (*pl*); **~ élastique** Pharm elastic bandage; **~ d'essai** Phot test strip; **~ étalon** Ordinat calibrating tape; **~ de fréquences** waveband; **~ molletière** puttee; **~ originale** Cin original soundtrack; **~ perforée** Ordinat paper tape; **~ publique** Citizens' band, CB; **~ de roulement** Aut tread; **~ rugueuse** Aut rumble strip; **~ sonore** Cin soundtrack; (d'autoroute) rumble strip; **~ Velpeau®** crepe bandage GB, Ace bandage® US.
IDIOMES **apprendre qch par la bande**○ to hear sth on the grapevine; **faire qch par la ~**○ to do sth in a roundabout way.
bande-annonce, *pl* **bandes-annonces** /bɑ̃danɔ̃s/ *nf* trailer.
bandeau, *pl* **~x** /bɑ̃do/ *nm* **1** (pour ne pas voir) blindfold; (d'œil malade) eye patch; **mettre un ~ à qn** to blindfold sb; **avoir un ~ sur les yeux** fig to be blind; **2** (de coiffure) headband; **porter les cheveux en ~** to wear one's hair parted down the middle (and drawn into a bun).
bandelette /bɑ̃dlɛt/ *nf* **1** Archéol, Pharm bandage; **2** (de soie, papier etc) small strip.
bander /bɑ̃de/ [1] **I** *vtr* **1** (panser) to bandage; **2** (avec un bandeau) **~ les yeux à qn** to blindfold sb; **avoir les yeux bandés** to be blindfolded; **3** (tendre) to bend [*tige souple, arc*]; to stretch [*ressort*]; **~ ses muscles** to tense one's muscles.
II● *vi* to have a hard-on●.
banderille /bɑ̃dʀij/ *nf* banderilla.
banderillero /bɑ̃deʀijeʀo/ *nm* banderillero.
banderole /bɑ̃dʀɔl/ *nf* banner.
bande-son, *pl* **bandes-son** /bɑ̃dsɔ̃/ *nm* soundtrack.
bandit /bɑ̃di/ *nm* **1** (malfaiteur) bandit; **2** (homme sans scrupules) crook; **3** (enfant insupportable) rascal; **espèce de petit ~** you little rascal.
■ **~ de grand chemin** highwayman.
banditisme /bɑ̃ditism/ *nm* **le ~** crime; **le grand/petit ~** organized/petty crime.
bandonéon /bɑ̃dɔneɔ̃/ **▶ 534** *nm* bandoneon.
bandoulière /bɑ̃duljɛʀ/ *nf* shoulder strap; **porter qch en ~** (sur l'épaule) to have sth slung over one's shoulder; (sur la poitrine) to have sth slung across one's chest.
bang /bɑ̃g/ **I** *nm* (supersonique) sonic boom.
II *excl* (explosion) bang!, boom!
Bangkok /bɑ̃kɔk/ **▶ 857** *npr* Bangkok.
bangladais, **~e** /bɑ̃gladɛ, ɛz/ **▶ 537** *adj* Bangladeshi.
Bangladais, **~e** /bɑ̃gladɛ, ɛz/ **▶ 537** *nmf* Bangladeshi.
Bangladesh /bɑ̃gladɛʃ/ **▶ 321** *nprm* Bangladesh.
banjo /bɑ̃(d)ʒo/ **▶ 534** *nm* banjo.
Banjul /bɑ̃ʒul/ **▶ 857** *npr* Banjul.
banlieue /bɑ̃ljø/ *nf* **1** (périphérie) suburbs (*pl*); **la proche/moyenne/grande ~** the inner/intermediate/outer suburbs; **~ sud/nord** southern/northern suburbs; **vivre en lointaine ~** to live in the outer suburbs; **Versailles est en ~** Versailles is in the suburbs; **une ville de ~** a suburban town; **université/hôpital/pavillon de ~** suburban university/hospital/house; **le problème des ~s** the social problems of the suburbs; **2** (quartier) suburb; **une ~ résidentielle/industrielle/ouvrière/rouge**○ a

residential/an industrial/a working-class/a communist suburb; ▶ **dortoir**.

banlieusard, **~e** /bɑ̃ljøzaʀ, aʀd/ **I** *adj* suburban.

II *nm,f* person from the suburbs, suburbanite; **c'est un ~** he's from the suburbs.

banne /ban/ *nf* awning.

banni, **~e** /bani/ *nm,f* exile.

bannière /banjɛʀ/ *nf* (tous contextes) banner; **lever la ~ de** to raise the banner of; **se ranger/marcher sous la ~ de** to rally to/to march under the banner of.
banner of.

■ **la ~ étoilée** the star-spangled banner, the Stars and Stripes.

IDIOMES **c'est la croix et la ~** it's hell (**de faire** doing); **c'est la croix et la ~ pour la faire aller à l'école** it's hell getting her to go to school.

bannir /baniʀ/ [3] *vtr* **1** (chasser) to banish [*personne*] (**de** from); **~ qn pour 10 ans** to banish sb for 10 years; **~ qn à vie** to banish sb for life; **il est banni de ma mémoire** he's banished from my memory; **2** (exclure) to ban [*coutume, sujet*].

bannissement /banismɑ̃/ *nm* banishment (**de** from); **~ à vie** life-long banishment.

banque /bɑ̃k/ *nf* **1** (établissement) bank; **mettre son argent à la ~** to put one's money in the bank; **avoir 1000 francs en ~** to have 1,000 francs in the bank; **mettre un chèque à la ~** to pay in ou deposit a cheque GB ou check US; **2** (activité) banking; **les métiers de la ~** banking careers; **3** Jeux bank; **faire sauter la ~** to break the bank; **tenir la ~** to be banker.

■ **~ d'affaires** merchant bank; **~ de dépôt** deposit bank; **~ à domicile** home banking; **~ de données** Ordinat data bank; **~ d'émission** issuing bank; **Banque européenne d'investissement, BEI** European Investment Bank, EIB; **Banque européenne pour la reconstruction et le développement, BERD** European Bank for Reconstruction and Development, EBRD; **~ d'organes** Méd organ bank; **~ du sang** Méd blood bank; **~ de sperme** Méd sperm bank; **Banque mondiale** World Bank; **Banque des règlements internationaux, BRI** Bank for International Settlements, BIS

banquer○ /bɑ̃ke/ [1] *vi* to fork out○.

banqueroute /bɑ̃kʀut/ *nf* **1** Fin bankruptcy; **~ frauduleuse** fraudulent bankruptcy; **faire ~** to go bankrupt; **2** fig (échec) complete failure.

banqueroutier, **-ière** /bɑ̃kʀutje, ɛʀ/ *nm,f* bankrupt; (après fraude) fraudulent bankrupt.

banquet /bɑ̃kɛ/ *nm* **1** (repas d'apparat) banquet; (repas abondant) feast; **un véritable ~** a real feast; **2** fig (avantages) **les miettes du ~** the crumbs from the table; **être exclu du ~ de la croissance** to miss out on one's share of economic growth; **3** Antiq banquet.

banqueter /bɑ̃kte/ [23] *vi* (participer à un banquet) to banquet; (faire bonne chère) to feast.

banquette /bɑ̃kɛt/ *nf* **1** (de restaurant, café) wall seat, banquette US; (de voiture, train) seat; (de piano) stool; **2** (talus) bank; **3** Archit window seat.

banquier, **-ière** /bɑ̃kje, ɛʀ/ **I** ▶ **510** *nm,f* Fin banker.

II *nm* Jeux banker.

banquise /bɑ̃kiz/ *nf* **1** (glace) ice floe; **2** fig (personne) cold fish.

bantou, **~e** /bɑ̃tu/ ▶ **462** **I** *adj* Géog Bantu.

II *nm* Ling Bantu.

Bantou, **~e** /bɑ̃tu/ *nm,f* Bantu.

bantoustan /bɑ̃tustɑ̃/ *nm* homeland.

baobab /baɔbab/ *nm* baobab.

baptême /batɛm/ *nm* **1** Relig baptism, christening; **donner le ~ à qn** to baptize sb; **recevoir le ~** to be baptized; **2** (inauguration) (de bateau) naming GB, christening US; (de cloche) blessing; **3** (initiation) baptism.

■ **~ de l'air** maiden flight; **~ du feu** lit, fig baptism of fire.

baptiser /batize/ [1] *vtr* **1** Relig to baptize, to christen [*personne*]; **se faire ~** to be baptized; **il n'est pas baptisé** he isn't baptized; **2** (donner un nom à) to call, to christen [*enfant, phénomène, projet, invention*]; **comment va-t-il ~ son émission?** what is he going to call his programme[GB]?; **~ qn/qch du nom de Rose** to name ou call sb/sth Rose; **~ qch du nom de qn/qch** to name sth after sb/sth; **ils l'ont baptisée Chouchou** they nicknamed her Chouchou; **3** (inaugurer) to name GB, to christen US [*navire*]; to bless [*cloche*]; **4**○ hum (tacher) to christen [*moquette, vêtement*]; **5**○ (mettre de l'eau dans) to water down [*vin*].

baptismal, **~e**, *mpl* **-aux** /batismal, o/ *adj* [*eau*] baptismal; **les fonts baptismaux** the font (*sg*).

baptisme /batism/ *nm* Baptist doctrine.

baptiste /batist/ *adj, nmf* Baptist.

baptistère /batistɛʀ/ *nm* baptistry.

baquet /bakɛ/ *nm* **1** (récipient) tub; **2** (siège) bucket-seat.

bar /baʀ/ *nm* **1** (lieu) bar; **2** (comptoir) bar; **au ~** at the bar; **3** (meuble) bar; **4** Zool sea bass; **5** Phys bar.

Barabbas /baʀabas/ *npr* Barabbas.

baragouin○ /baʀagwɛ̃/ *nm* gobbledygook○, gibberish.

baragouinage○ /baʀagwinaʒ/ *nm* gibbering.

baragouiner○ /baʀagwine/ [1] **I** *vtr* to gabble [*propos, phrase*]; to speak [sth] badly [*langue*]; **je baragouine quelques mots d'italien** I speak broken Italian.

II *vi* to witter○ GB, to gibber.

baraka○ /baʀaka/ *nf* luck; **avoir la ~** to be lucky.

baraque /baʀak/ *nf* **1** (construction légère) shack; **une ~ en bois** a wooden shack; **2**○ (maison) pad○, house; (en mauvais état) dump○; **je vis dans une vieille ~** I live in a real dump; **3**○ (personne forte) hefty person.

■ **~ de chantier** builder's hut; **~ foraine** fairground stall ou stand US.

IDIOMES **casser la ~**○ to be a resounding success; **casser la ~**○ **à qn** or **de qn** to mess things up for sb○.

baraqué○, **~e** /baʀake/ *adj* [*personne*] hefty, husky US.

baraquement /baʀakmɑ̃/ *nm* **1** (ensemble de constructions) group of huts; (baraque) hut, terrapin; **2** Mil army camp.

baratin○ /baʀatɛ̃/ *nm* (pour vendre) spiel○, sales pitch; (pour séduire) sweet-talk; (pour convaincre) smooth talk○ GB, bullshit○; **arrête ton ~, je ne te crois pas** stop flannelling GB ou bullshitting, I don't believe you; **il a un ~ avec les femmes!** he's great at chatting up the girls; **avoir du ~** to have the gift of the gab; **il m'a eu au ~** he (sweet) talked me into it.

baratiner○ /baʀatine/ [1] **I** *vtr* (pour vendre) to give [sb] the spiel [*client*]; (pour séduire) to chat [sb] up [*personne*]; (pour convaincre) to try to talk [sb] round GB, to try to persuade [*personne*]; **il m'a baratiné jusqu'à ce que j'accepte l'invitation** he went on○ at me until I accepted the invitation.

II *vi* to jabber (on).

baratineur○, **-euse** /baʀatinœʀ, øz/ *nm,f* (beau parleur) smooth talker○; (menteur) liar.

baratte /baʀat/ *nf* churn.

baratter /baʀate/ [1] *vtr* to churn.

Barbade /baʀbad/ ▶ **321**, **416** *nprf* **la ~** Barbados.

barbant○, **~e** /baʀbɑ̃, ɑ̃t/ *adj* boring.

barbaque◑ /baʀbak/ *nf* meat.

barbare /baʀbaʀ/ **I** *adj* **1** (féroce) barbaric; **2** pej (choquant) [*musique, style, langue*] barbaric; **3** (peu civilisé) [*mœurs, coutumes*] barbarian; [*beauté, splendeur*] barbaric; **4** Antiq **les invasions ~s** the barbarian invasions.

II *nmf* **1** (personne féroce) barbarian, savage; **2** (personne non civilisée) barbarian.

barbaresque /baʀbaʀɛsk/ *adj* **États ~s** Barbary states; **pirates ~s** Barbary Coast pirates.

barbarie /baʀbaʀi/ *nf* **1** (férocité) barbarity, barbarism; **un acte de ~** a barbarous deed, a barbaric act; **la ~ nazie** the barbarity of the Nazis; **2** pej (état) barbarism.

Barbarie /baʀbaʀi/ *nprf* Barbary; **les côtes de ~** the Barbary Coast (*sg*).

barbarisme /baʀbaʀism/ *nm* Ling barbarism.

barbe /baʀb/ **I** *adj* [*cheval, jument*] Barbary (*épith*).

II *nm* (cheval) barb.

III *nf* **1** (d'homme) beard; **porter la ~** to have a beard; **se laisser pousser la ~** to grow a beard; **avoir la ~ dure/fournie** to have a bristly/bushy beard; **faire la ~ à qn** (raser) to shave off sb's beard; (égaliser) to trim sb's beard; **se faire faire la ~** (raser) to have one's beard shaved off; (égaliser) to have one's beard trimmed; **une ~ de trois jours** stubble, a three-day growth; **il avait une ~ de huit jours** he hadn't shaved for a week; **une vieille ~** pej an old fogey○[GB]; **parler dans sa ~** fig to mutter into one's beard; **rire dans sa ~** fig to laugh up one's sleeve; **2** Zool (de bouc, chien) beard; (de plume) barb; (de poisson) barbel; **3** Bot (d'épi, de céréale) awn; **4** Tech (de papier) rough edge; (de pièce métallique) burr; **5**○ (chose ennuyeuse) **quelle ~!, c'est la ~!** what a drag○!; **c'est vraiment la ~ de tout recommencer** it's a real drag to have to start all over again.

IV○ *excl* **la ~!** I've had enough!; **la ~ avec leurs consignes!** to hell with their orders○!

■ **~ de capucin** Bot wild chicory; **~ à papa** Culin candyfloss GB, cotton candy US.

IDIOMES **à la ~ de qn** under sb's nose; **avoir de la ~ au menton** to be an adult.

barbeau, *pl* **~x** /baʀbo/ *nm* **1** (fleur) cornflower; **2** (poisson) barbel.

Barbe-bleue /baʀbəblø/ *npr* Bluebeard.

barbecue /baʀbəkju/ *nm* **1** (appareil) barbecue; **faire cuire qch au ~** to barbecue sth; **une côtelette au ~** a barbecued chop; **2** (réception) barbecue.

barbelé, **~e** /baʀbəle/ **I** *adj* [*fil*] barbed.

II *nm* barbed wire ₵; **je me suis accroché dans les ~s** I got caught on the barbed wire.

barber○ /baʀbe/ [1] **I** *vtr* to bore [sb] stiff○.

II se barber *vpr* to be bored stiff○.

Barberousse /baʀbəʀus/ *npr* Barbarossa.

barbet /baʀbɛ/ *nm* water spaniel.

barbiche /baʀbiʃ/ *nf* (d'homme) goatee (beard); (de chèvre) (small) beard.

barbichette /baʀbiʃɛt/ *nf* (small) goatee (beard).

barbichu, **~e** /baʀbiʃy/ **I** *adj* with a goatee (beard) (*épith, après n*).

II *nm* man with a goatee (beard).

barbier /baʀbje/ ▶ **510** *nm* barber.

barbillon /baʀbijɔ̃/ *nm* **1** (petit barbeau) small barbel, small goatfish US; **2** (de poisson) barbel; (de volaille) wattle; (de bétail) barb.

barbiturique /baʀbityʀik/ **I** *adj* barbituric.

II *nm* barbiturate.

barbon† /baʀbɔ̃/ *nm* pej fogey.

barbotage /baʀbɔtaʒ/ *nm* **1** (dans l'eau) (de canard) dabbling; (de personne) paddling; **2**○ (vol) nicking○ GB, filching○; **3** Chimie (de gaz) bubbling.

barboter /baʀbɔte/ [1] **I**○ *vtr* (voler) to nick○ GB, to filch○ [*portefeuille, stylo*] (**à qn** from sb); **se faire ~ qch** to have sth nicked GB ou filched○.

II *vi* **1** (dans l'eau) [*canard*] to dabble;

[*enfant*] to paddle; **2** Chimie **faire ~ un gaz** to bubble a gas through a liquid.

barboteuse /barbɔtøz/ *nf* romper-suit.

barbouillage /barbujaʒ/ *nm* pej (action) daubing; (résultat) daub.

barbouiller /barbuje/ [1] **I** *vtr* **1** (salir) to smear (**de** with); **~ son visage/un meuble de qch** to get sth all over one's face/a piece of furniture, to smear one's face/a piece of furniture with sth; **il est tout barbouillé** his face is all dirty; **il est tout barbouillé de confiture** his face is all smeared with jam; **2** (couvrir) to daub [*surface, support*] (**de** with); **~ un plafond/une porte de peinture verte** to slap green paint on a ceiling/a door, to daub a ceiling/a door with green paint; **~ un pont d'inscriptions** to daub graffiti all over a bridge; **3** (peindre) pej **~ des natures mortes/des paysages** to do daubs of still lives/landscapes péj; **~ du papier** to write drivel péj; **4** (rendre malade) **cela barbouille l'estomac** it makes you feel queasy; **être** or **se sentir barbouillé** to feel queasy.

II se barbouiller *vpr* (se salir) **se ~ le visage/le corps de qch** to get one's face/body all covered in sth, to smear one's face/body with sth.

barbouilleur, -euse /barbujœr, øz/ *nm,f* pej **1** (peintre) dauber; **2** (qui écrit) bad writer.

barbouillis /barbuji/ *nm* pej **1** (écrit) scrawl; **2** (tableau) daub.

barbouze◑ /barbuz/ **I** *nm* ou *f* secret agent.

II *nf* (barbe) beard, fungus○ GB.

barbu, ~e /barby/ **I** *adj* bearded; **il est ~** he has a beard.

II *nm* bearded man.

III barbue *nf* Zool brill.

barcarolle /barkarɔl/ *nf* barcarole.

barcasse /barkas/ *nf* boat.

Barcelone /barsəlɔn/ **▶857** *npr* Barcelona.

barda○ /barda/ *nm* **1** (bagage encombrant) baggage, gear○; **2** Mil (équipement) kit.

barde /bard/ **I** *nm* (chantre) bard.

II *nf* (de lard) bard.

bardé, ~e /barde/ **I** *pp* **▶ barder**.

II *pp adj* **1** fig (couvert) covered; **être ~ de diplômes/médailles** to be covered in diplomas/medals; **2** [*cheval*] barded.

bardeau, *pl* **~x** /bardo/ *nm* **1** Tech shingle; **un toit de ~x** a shingle roof; **2** Zool = **bardot**.

barder /barde/ [1] **I** *vtr* Culin to bard [*rôti, volaille*].

II○ *vi* **ça barde chez les voisins!** sparks are flying next door!; **si je me lève ça va ~!** if I have to get up, sparks will fly!

bardot /bardo/ *nm* hinny.

barème /barɛm/ *nm* (recueil de tableaux) (set of) tables; (méthode de calcul) scale; **~ d'imposition** tax schedule ou scale; **~ de correction** marking-scheme; **~ des prix** price list.

barge /barʒ/ *nf* **1** (embarcation) barge; **2** (oiseau) black-tailed godwit.

baril /baril/ *nm* **1** (récipient) barrel, cask; (pour vin) cask; (pour poudre) keg; (en métal, carton) drum; **2** Comm (unité de capacité) barrel.

barillet /barijɛ/ *nm* **1** Tech (de pistolet, serrure) cylinder; (d'horloge) barrel; **2** Anat middle ear; **3** (petit baril) small barrel.

bariolage /barjɔlaʒ/ *nm* (action) splashing ¢ of colours[GB]; (résultat) mixture of colours[GB], hotchpotch GB ou hodgepodge US of colours[GB].

bariolé, ~e /barjɔle/ *adj* **1** (multicolore) [*habits, tissus*] multicoloured[GB]; pej gaudy; **2** (mélangé) [*foule*] motley.

barjaquer /barʒake/ [1] *vi* H (bavarder) to chatter.

barjo◑ /barʒo/ *adj* nuts○, crazy.

barmaid /barmɛd/ **▶510** *nf* barmaid.

barman, *pl* **barmen** /barman, mɛn/ **▶510** *nm* barman.

barnum /barnɔm/ *nm* **1** (abri) *shelter for newspaper seller*; **2**◑ (chahut) racket○, din.

baromètre /barɔmɛtr/ *nm* **1** Météo barometer; **le ~ monte/descend** the barometer is rising/falling; **2** fig barometer; **le ~ de la conjoncture est au beau fixe** the situation looks to be set fair.

■ ~ enregistreur recording barometer; **~ à mercure** mercury barometer.

barométrique /barɔmetrik/ *adj* barometric.

baron /barɔ̃/ *nm* **1 ▶813** Hist baron; **2** (personne importante) baron; **les ~s de la drogue** the drug barons; **les ~s de la politique** political heavyweights; **3** Culin **~ d'agneau** saddle and hind legs of lamb; **4**○ Jeux (dans un casino) stooge.

baronnage /barɔnaʒ/ *nm* **1** (qualité) barony, baronage; **2** (ensemble des barons) baronage.

baronne /barɔn/ **▶813** *nf* baroness.

baronnet /barɔnɛ/ **▶813** *nm* baronet.

baronnie /barɔni/ *nf* barony.

baroque /barɔk/ **I** *adj* **1** [*style, art, époque*] baroque; **2** (bizarre) [*idée*] bizarre, outlandish; [*personne*] bizarre, weird.

II *nm* **le ~** the baroque.

baroud○ /barud/ *nm* fighting; **aller au ~** to go into battle.

■ ~ d'honneur last-ditch stand.

baroudeur /barudœr/ *nm* **1** (soldat) fighter, warrior; **un vieux ~ de la politique** an old political warrior; **2** (aventurier) adventurer.

barouf○ /baruf/ *nm* (bruit, vacarme) row, racket; (protestation) row, fuss; **faire du ~** to fuss.

barque /bark/ *nf* (small) boat; **promenade en ~** boatride; **~ à moteur** motorboat.

■ ~ de pêche fishing boat.

IDIOMES **mener la ~** to be in charge; **bien/mal mener sa ~** to manage things well/badly.

barquette /barkɛt/ *nf* **1** Culin (tartelette) (small) tart; **2** (récipient) (pour fruits) punnet GB, basket US; (de margarine) tub; (pour plat cuisiné) container.

barracuda /barakyda/ *nm* barracuda.

barrage /baraʒ/ *nm* **1** (pour retenir l'eau) dam (**sur** on); **~ hydroélectrique** hydroelectric dam; **2** (pour faire obstacle) (d'armée, de police, milice) roadblock; (de manifestants) barricade; **~ militaire/de police** military/police roadblock; **forcer/franchir un ~** to break through/to cross a roadblock; **un ~ de voitures en feu** a barricade of burning cars; **former un ~** [*arbre tombé, montagnes*] to form an impassable barrier; **faire ~ à qn/qch** fig to block sb/sth.

■ ~ de feux fire barrage; **~ de fumée** smoke screen.

barre /bar/ *nf* **1** (pièce de métal, bois etc) bar, rod; **~ de fer** iron bar; **~ d'or fin** fine gold bar; **2** (petite tablette) bar; **~ de céréales** cereal bar; **~ de chocolat** chocolate bar GB, candy bar US; **3** Naut tiller, helm; **être à** or **tenir la ~** lit, fig to be at the helm; **prendre la ~** to take the helm; **4** (bande) band; **5** (trait écrit) stroke; **la ~ du t** the cross on the t; **6** Sport (en rugby, football) crossbar; (en saut en hauteur, à la perche) bar; **7** Danse barre; **faire des exercices à la ~** to exercise at the barre; **8** Jur (des avocats) bar; (des témoins) ≈ witness box GB, witness stand US; **être appelé à la ~** to be called to the witness box; **9** (seuil) mark; **passer** or **franchir la ~ du 13%** to go over the 13% mark; **dépasser la ~ des trois millions** to exceed the three-million mark; **tu places la ~ trop haut** you're expecting too much; **10**○ (douleur) **avoir une ~ à la poitrine** to have a pain across one's chest; **11** Géog (dans un estuaire) sandbar; (hautes vagues) tidal wave; **12** Géol ridge; **13** Mus **~ de mesure** bar (line); **14** Zool bar.

■ ~ d'accouplement tie rod; **~ d'appui** safety rail; **~ de commande de direction** steering drag link; **~ de coupe** cutter bar; **~ d'espacement** space bar; **~ fixe** horizontal bar; **~ de fraction** fraction bar; **~ à mine** jumper; **~ oblique** slash, stroke, solidus spéc; **~ de remorquage** tow bar; **~ à roue** wheel, helm; **~ de torsion** torsion bar; **~s asymétriques** asymmetrical bars; **~s parallèles** parallel bars.

IDIOMES **avoir un coup de ~**○ to feel drained all of a sudden; **c'est le coup de ~ dans ce restaurant**○ that restaurant is a rip-off○; **c'est de l'or en ~** it's a golden opportunity.

barreau, *pl* **~x** /baro/ *nm* **1** (de cage, fenêtre, prison) bar; **être derrière les ~x** to be behind bars; **2** (d'échelle) rung; **3** Jur (dans prétoire) bar; **le ~** (avocats) the Bar; **le ~ de Toulouse** barristers practising[GB] in Toulouse.

■ ~ de chaise lit rung of a chair; (cigare)○ fat cigar.

barrer /bare/ [1] **I** *vtr* **1** (obstruer) to block [*voie, accès*] (**avec** with); **la rue est barrée** the street is blocked; **~ le passage à qn** lit, fig to stand in sb's way; **~ la route** or **le chemin à qn** fig to block sb; **'route barrée'** 'road closed'; **2** (rayer) to cross out [*mot, mention, paragraphe*]; **~ un chèque** Fin to cross a cheque; **3** (traverser) **une cicatrice lui barrait le front** he/she had a scar across his/her forehead; **4** Naut (prendre la barre) to take the helm of; (être à la barre) to be at the helm of; (en aviron) to cox; **un quatre barré** a coxed four; **c'est le capitaine qui barrait** the captain was at the helm.

II se barrer◑ *vpr* (se sauver) [*personne*] to clear off○; [*animal*] to run off; (partir) to leave; **elle s'est barrée de chez elle** she left home; **se ~ au Sénégal/avec qn** to go off to Senegal/with sb.

IDIOMES **on est mal barré**◑ we're in big trouble○; **c'est mal barré**◑ it's looking a bit iffy○; **ne pas être barré**○ C to have a lot of nerve.

barrette /barɛt/ *nf* **1** (pour les cheveux) (hair) slide GB, barrette US; **2** (bijou) bar brooch; **3** Relig red biretta; **recevoir la ~** to become a cardinal; **4** (insigne de décoration) ribbon.

barreur, -euse /barœr, øz/ *nm,f* gén helmsman; (en aviron) cox, coxswain; **avec ~** coxed; **sans ~** coxless.

barricade /barikad/ *nf* barricade; **ne pas être du même côté de la ~** fig to be on opposite sides of the fence.

barricader /barikade/ [1] **I** *vtr* to barricade [*rue, passage, fenêtre*].

II se barricader *vpr* **1** (se protéger) to barricade oneself (**dans** in); **2** (s'isoler) to lock oneself up.

barrière /barjɛr/ *nf* **1** (clôture) fence; (porte) gate; (de passage à niveau) Rail level crossing gate GB, grade crossing gate US; **2** (obstacle naturel) barrier; **~ naturelle/montagneuse** natural/mountain barrier; **▶ grand**; **3** fig barrier; **~ de la langue** language barrier; **faire tomber les ~s** to break down the barriers.

■ ~ automatique Rail automatic barrier; **~ corallienne** Géol coral reef; **~ de dégel** Transp *ban on heavy vehicles using a road during a thaw*; **~ métallique** crowd barrier; **~s douanières** or **tarifaires** trade ou tariff barriers.

IDIOMES **être de l'autre côté de la ~** to be on the other side of the fence.

barrique /barik/ *nf* **1** (tonneau) barrel; **2** (personne forte) pej tubby man/woman.

IDIOMES **être plein comme une ~**◑ to be drunk as a lord GB ou skunk US.

barrir /barir/ [3] *vi* [*éléphant*] to trumpet; [*rhinocéros*] to bellow.

barrissement /barismɑ̃/ *nm* (d'éléphant) trumpeting ¢; (de rhinocéros) bellowing ¢.

bar-tabac, *pl* **bars-tabac** /bartaba/ *nm* café (*where stamps and cigarettes can be purchased*).

bartavelle /baʀtavɛl/ *nf* rock partridge.

baryton /baʀitɔ̃/ ▶134 **I** *adj* Mus baritone. **II** *nm* **1** Mus (voix, chanteur) baritone; **2** Ling baritone.

baryton-basse /baʀitɔ̃bas/ ▶134 *nm* (chanteur) bass-baritone.

baryum /baʀjɔm/ *nm* barium.

bas, **basse** /bɑ, bɑs/ **I** *adj* **1** (peu étendu verticalement) [*maison, table, mur*] low; [*salle*] low-ceilinged (*épith*); **2** (en altitude) [*nuage*] low; [*côte, terre, vallée*] low-lying (*épith*); **la partie basse d'un mur** the lower part of a wall; **l'étagère la plus basse** the bottom shelf; **les branches basses** the lower ou bottom branches; **le ciel est ~** the sky is overcast; **3** (dans une échelle de valeurs) [*fréquence, pression, température, prix, salaire, latitude*] low; Mus [*note*] low; [*instrument*] bass; **vendre qch à ~ prix** to sell sth cheap; **un enfant en ~ âge** a very young child; **basses besognes** (ennuyeuses) menial chores; (répugnantes) dirty work ₵; **le moral des joueurs est très ~** the players are in very low spirits; **de ~ niveau** [*produit*] low-grade; [*élève, classe*] at a low level (*après n*); [*style, texte*] low-brow; **être au plus ~ de la hiérarchie** to be at the bottom of the hierarchy; **les cours sont au plus ~** Fin prices have reached rock bottom; **4** (dans une hiérarchie) [*origine, condition*] low, lowly; **les postes les plus ~** the lowest-grade jobs; **5** Géog **le ~ Dauphiné** the Lower Dauphiné; **6** Hist (dans le temps) [*époque, période*] late; **le ~ Moyen Âge** the late Middle Ages (*pl*); **7** (moralement) [*esprit, âme, vengeance, complaisance*] base; **de ~ étage** [*individu*] common; [*plaisanterie*] coarse, vulgar.

II *adv* **1** (à faible hauteur) [*voler, s'incliner*] low; **la lune est ~ dans le ciel** the moon is low in the sky; **tomber** or **descendre très ~** [*thermomètre*] to go down very low; [*prix, cours*] to fall very low; **comment peut-on tomber si ~!** (dans l'abjection) how can one sink to such a low level!; **tu es assis trop ~** your seat is too low; **colle-le plus ~ sur la page** stick it lower down (the page); **loger un étage plus ~** to live one floor below; **plus ~ dans la rue/sur la colline** further down the street/the hill; **2** (dans un texte) **voir plus ~** see below; **3** (doucement) [*parler*] quietly; **tout ~** [*parler*] in a whisper; [*chanter*] softly; **parle plus ~** lower your voice; **ce que chacun pense tout ~** what everyone is thinking privately; **jeter** or **mettre ~** (abattre) to bring [sb/sth] down [*dictateur, régime*]; **mettre ~ les armes** lit (se rendre) to lay down one's arms; fig (renoncer) to give up the fight; ▶ **mettre II**; **4** (mal) **être bien ~** (physiquement) to be very weak; (moralement) to be very low; **être au plus ~** (physiquement) to be extremely weak; (moralement) to be at one's lowest ou at a very low ebb.

III *nm inv* **1** (partie inférieure) (d'escalier, échelle, de mur, montagne, meuble, vêtement, page) bottom; **le ~ du visage** the lower part of the face; **le ~ du corps** the bottom half of the body; **déchiré dans le ~** torn at the bottom; **au ~ de la liste/colline** at the bottom of the list/hill; **le rayon/l'image du ~** the bottom shelf/picture; **les pièces du ~** the downstairs rooms; **vers le ~** [*incliner*] downward(s); **le ~ de son maillot de bain** the bottom part of her swimsuit; **sauter à ~ de sa monture** to jump off one's horse; **2** Mode stocking; **~ de soie** silk stocking; **des ~ nylon®** nylon stockings; **3** Mus ₵ (registre) **chanter dans le ~** to sing bass notes (*pl*).

IV en bas *loc* (au rez-de-chaussée) downstairs; (en dessous) down below; (sur panneau, page) at the bottom; **en ~ de** at the bottom of [*falaise, page*] ; **tomber en ~ de la falaise** to fall to the bottom of the cliff; **il habite en ~ de chez moi** he lives below me; **l'arrêt de bus en ~ de chez moi** the bus stop outside my place; **la cuisine est en ~** the kitchen is downstairs; **en ~ dans la rue** in the street (down) below; **signe en ~ à gauche** sign on the bottom left-hand side; **l'odeur vient d'en ~** the smell is coming from below; **tout en ~** right at the bottom; **jusqu'en ~** right down to the bottom; **passer par en ~** (dans un village) to take the bottom road; (dans une maison) to get in on the ground GB ou first US floor.

V basse ▶134, 534 *nf* Mus (partie, chanteur, instrument) bass; (voix) bass (voice); **basse continue** (bass) continuo; **basse contrainte** ground bass.

■ **~ allemand** Ling Low German; **~ de casse** Imprim lower case; **le ~ clergé** Relig the lower clergy; **~ de contention** Méd support stocking; **~ de gamme** Ind, Comm *adj* low-quality (*épith*); *nm* lower end of the market; **~ de laine** fig nest egg, savings (*pl*); **~ latin** Ling Low Latin; **~ morceaux** Culin cheap cuts; **~ sur pattes** short-legged (*épith*); **le ~ peuple** the lower classes; **les ~ quartiers** the seedy ou poor districts (of a town); **~ à varices** Méd = **~ de contention**; **basse école** Équit basic equitation; **basse fréquence** Phys, Télécom low frequency; **basse saison** Tourisme low season; **basse de viole** Mus viola da gamba; **basses eaux** (de mer) low tide ₵; (de rivière) low water ₵; **pendant les basses eaux** when the waters are low.

IDIOMES **avoir des hauts et des ~** to have one's ups and downs; **à ~ les tyrans!** down with tyrants!; **mettre qn plus ~ que terre** to run sb into the ground.

basal, **~e**, *mpl* **-aux** /bɑzal, o/ *adj* basal.

basalte /bazalt/ *nm* basalt.

basaltique /bazaltik/ *adj* basaltic.

basané, **~e** /bazane/ *adj* **1** (hâlé) sunburned[GB], (sun-)tanned; **2** (à la peau sombre) offensive swarthy, dark-skinned.

bas-bleu, *pl* **~s** /bɑblø/ *nm* bluestocking.

bas-côté, *pl* **~s** /bɑkote/ *nm* **1** (de route) verge GB, shoulder US; **2** (d'église) (side) aisle.

basculant, **~e** /baskylɑ̃, ɑ̃t/ *adj* **pont ~** bascule bridge; **camion à benne ~e** tipper lorry GB, dump truck; **fenêtre ~e** centre[GB] hung side pivot window.

bascule /baskyl/ *nf* **1** Tech rocker; **fauteuil/cheval à ~** rocking chair/horse; **2** (balançoire) seesaw; **jeu de ~** lit, fig seesaw; **politique de ~** fig policy of alternating party alliance; **mouvement de ~** rocking movement; **3** (machine à peser) weighing machine; **4** Électrotech rocker, multivibrator.

basculement /baskylmɑ̃/ *nm* **1** fig (renversement) swing; **2** Gén Civ lane deviation.

basculer /baskyle/ [1] **I** *vtr* Télécom to transfer [*appel*].

II *vi* **1** (tomber) [*objet, personne*] to topple over; [*benne*] to tip up; **~ dans le ravin** to topple into the ravine; **faire ~** to tip up [*benne*]; to tip out [*chargement*]; to knock [sb] off balance [*personne*]; **2** fig [*match, vie, ambiance*] to change radically; [*opinion*] to swing in the opposite direction; **~ à droite/vers l'opposition** Pol to swing over to the right/toward(s) the opposition; **~ dans la guerre** to be plunged into war; **la scène a basculé dans le drame** the scene suddenly turned dramatic; **faire ~** to turn [*match, opinion publique*]; to change the course of [*Histoire*]; **faire ~ le pays dans l'extrémisme** to push the country into extremism.

basculeur /baskylœʀ/ *nm* Tech tip, tipper.

base /bɑz/ *nf* **1** (partie inférieure) base (**de** of); **2** fig (assise de système, théorie) basis (**de** of); (point de départ) basis (**de** for); **sur la ~ de** on the basis of; **servir de ~ à** to serve as a basis for; **jeter les ~s d'un partenariat** to pave the way to ou lay the foundations for a partnership; **reposer sur des ~s solides** to rest on a firm foundation; **à la ~ de qch** at the root ou heart of sth; **ces principes sont à la ~ de la démocratie** there principles lie at the very heart of democracy; **avoir des ~s en chimie** to have a basic grounding in chemistry; **avoir des ~s solides en russe** to have a solid grounding in Russian; **connaissances/salaire/formation de ~** basic knowledge/salary/training; **citoyen/culture de ~** basic citizen/culture; **document/données de ~** source document/data; **ce raisonnement pèche par la ~** this argument is basically unsound; **repartir sur de nouvelles ~s** fig [*personne*] to make a fresh start; **3** (ingrédient essentiel) base (**de** of); **poison à ~ d'arsenic** arsenic-based poison; **alliage à ~ de cuivre** copper alloy; **le riz forme la ~ de leur alimentation** rice is their staple diet; **4** Chimie base; **5** Math **~ de numération** numerical base; **6** Ling (radical) root; **7** (cosmétique) make-up base, foundation; **8** Mil base; **rejoindre sa ~** to return to base; **avoir Lyon pour ~** [*régiment, groupe industriel*] to be based in Lyons; **9** Pol (militants) **la ~** the rank and file; **militant de ~** rank and file member.

■ **~ aérienne** air base; **~ de données** Ordinat data base; **~ de données relationnelles** Ordinat relational database; **~ d'imposition** tax base; **~ de lancement** launching site; **~ de loisirs** leisure centre[GB]; **~ navale** naval base; **~ d'observation de satellites** satellite observation station; **~ spatiale** space station.

base-ball /bɛzbol/ ▶449 *nm* baseball.

Bas-Empire /bɑzɑ̃piʀ/ *nprm* Hist **le ~** the Later Roman Empire.

baser /bɑze/ [1] **I** *vtr* **1** (fonder) to base [*théorie, stratégie, économie*] (**sur** on); **2** (installer) gén, Mil to base [*unité, missile, société*] (**à, en** in); **missiles basés à terre** land-based missiles.

II se baser *vpr* **se ~ sur qch** to go by sth [*chiffres, étude*]; **sur quoi te bases-tu pour affirmer qu'il est coupable?** what grounds do you have for saying he is guilty?

bas-fond, *pl* **~s** /bɑfɔ̃/ **I** *nm* (haut-fond) shoal; (dépression) dip.

II bas-fonds *nmpl* (de société) dregs (of society); (de ville) seedy parts.

basic, **BASIC** /bazik/ *nm* BASIC.

basilic /bazilik/ *nm* **1** (plante) basil; **2** (animal) basilisk.

basilique /bazilik/ *nf* basilica.

basique /bɑzik/ *adj* gén, Chimie basic; Géol basal.

basket /baskɛt/ ▶449 *nm* **1** (sport) basketball; **2** (chaussure de sport) trainer.

IDIOMES **lâcher les ~s à qn**○ to give sb a break○; **être bien** or **à l'aise dans ses ~s**○ to be very together○.

basket-ball /baskɛtbol/ ▶449 *nm* basketball.

basketteur, **-euse** /baskɛtœʀ, øz/ *nm,f* basketball player.

basquaise /baskɛz/ *adj* **poulet ~** *chicken cooked with tomatoes and sweet peppers*; **sauce ~** *sauce made with tomatoes and sweet peppers*.

basque /bask/ ▶462 **I** *adj* Basque; **le Pays ~** the Basque Country.

II *nm* Ling Basque.

III basques *nfpl* Cout, Mode basques.

IDIOMES **être pendu aux ~s de qn**○ to be always hanging on sb's coat-tails.

Basque /bask/ *nmf* Basque.

bas-relief, *pl* **~s** /bɑʀəljɛf/ *nm* bas-relief, low relief.

Bas-Rhin /bɑʀɛ̃/ ▶692 *nprm* (département) **le ~** the Bas-Rhin.

basse ▶ **bas** I, V.

Basse-Californie /bɑskalifɔʀni/ ▶692 *nprf* Lower California GB, Baja California US.

basse-cour, *pl* **basses-cours** /bɑskuʀ/ *nf* **1** (poulailler) poultry-yard; **2** (volailles) poultry.

basse-fosse, *pl* **basses-fosses** /bɑsfos/ *nf* dungeon.

bassement /basmɑ̃/ *adv* [*agir, se conduire*] despicably, basely; [*flatter*] basely; **fins/raisons ~ politiques** base political ends/reasons.

Basse-Normandie /basnɔʀmɑ̃di/ ▶ 692 *nprf* **la ~** Basse-Normandie.

bassesse /basɛs/ *nf* **1** (caractère vil) baseness, lowness; **faire preuve de ~ dans son attitude/ses actes** to show baseness in one's attitude/one's actions; **avec ~** [*se comporter, agir*] basely; **2** (acte vil) base ou despicable act; **commettre des ~s** to commit despicable acts; **prêt à toutes les ~s** prepared to stoop to anything; **obtenir une faveur à force de ~s** to obtain a favour[GB] through base actions.

basset /basɛ/ *nm* basset (hound).

bassin /basɛ̃/ *nm* **1** (de parc) ornamental lake; (plus petit) pond; (fontaine) fountain; (de piscine) pool; **petit/grand ~** small/main pool; **2** (plat creux) bowl; **3** Géog, Géol basin; **4** Anat pelvis; **grand/petit ~** upper/lower pelvis; **5** Méd bedpan; **passer le ~ à un malade** to give a patient the bedpan; **6** Écon area.
■ **~ d'effondrement** fault-basin, rift; **~ d'emploi** labour[GB] pool; **~ houiller** coal field ou basin; **~ hydrographique** drainage basin; **~ hygiénique** bedpan; **~ minier** mineral field ou basin; **~ sédimentaire** sedimentary basin.

bassine /basin/ *nf* (récipient) bowl; (contenu) bowlful.
■ **~ à confitures** preserving pan.

bassiner /basine/ [1] *vtr* **1** (chauffer) to warm [sth] with a warming pan [*lit*]; **2**○ (agacer) **tu nous bassines avec tes histoires!** you're a pain in the neck with your stories!; **3** (humecter) to bathe [*front, visage*]; **4** Agric to spray [*semis, plante*].

bassinet /basinɛ/ *nm* **1** (petite bassine) small bowl; **2** Hist (casque) basnet.
IDIOMES **cracher au ~** to cough up○; **faire cracher qn au ~** to get sb to cough up○.

bassinoire /basinwaʀ/ *nf* warming pan.

bassiste /basist/ ▶ 534, 510 *nmf* bass player.

basson /basɔ̃/ ▶ 534 *nm* **1** (instrument) bassoon; **2** (instrumentiste) bassoonist.

bassoniste /basɔnist/ *nmf* bassoonist.

basta○ /basta/ *excl* **~!** that's enough!

baster /baste/ [1] *vi* H (céder) to give in.

bastiais, ~e /bastjɛ, ɛz/ ▶ 857 *adj* of Bastia.

Bastiais, ~e /bastjɛ, ɛz/ ▶ 857 *nm,f* (natif) native of Bastia; (habitant) inhabitant of Bastia.

bastide /bastid/ *nf* **1** (ville fortifiée) (medieval) fortified town; **2** (maison) country house.

bastille /bastij/ *nf* fortress.

Bastille /bastij/ *nprf* **la ~** the Bastille.

bastingage /bastɛ̃gaʒ/ *nm* (garde-corps) ship's rail; **accoudé au ~** leaning on the ship's rail.

bastion /bastjɔ̃/ *nm* (tous contextes) bastion.

baston◐ /bastɔ̃/ *nm* ou *f* fight.

bastonnade /bastɔnad/ *nf* beating.

bastonner◐ /bastɔne/ [1] **I** *vtr* to bash○, to beat; **se faire ~** to be bashed up○ ou beaten up.
II se bastonner *vpr* to fight.

bastringue /bastʀɛ̃g/ *nm* **1**○ (vacarme) din, racket; **2**○ (attirail) stuff, clobber○ GB; **3**○ (chose quelconque) thingumajig○; **et tout le ~** and the whole caboodle○ ou shebang○; **4**† (salle de bal) dancehall, ballroom; (orchestre) dance band.

bas-ventre, *pl* **~s** /bavɑ̃tʀ/ ▶ 188 *nm* lower abdomen; **recevoir un coup dans le ~** lit, fig to be hit below the belt.

bât /bɑ/ *nm* pack-saddle.
IDIOMES **c'est là que le ~ blesse** that's where the shoe pinches.

bataclan○ /bataklɑ̃/ *nm* stuff, junk○; **et tout le ~** and all the rest of it.

bataille /bataj/ **I** *nf* **1** Mil battle; **livrer ~ à qn** to give battle to sb; **perdre/gagner une ~** to lose/win a battle; **ordre de ~** battle order ou formation; **2** (lutte morale) battle, war; **~ électorale** electoral battle; **~ commerciale** trade war; **se jeter dans la ~ du pouvoir/de la succession** to fling oneself into the battle for power/for succession; **mener la ~ contre qn/qch** to wage war against sb/sth; **une ~ d'idées** a war of ideas; **dans la ~ j'ai oublié mon sac**○ with all that was going on I forgot my bag; **3** (lutte physique) fight; **une ~ de boules de neige** a snowball fight; **4** Jeux (aux cartes) ≈ beggar-my-neighbour[GB].
II en bataille *loc adj* **1 les cheveux en ~** dishevelled[GB] hair; **les sourcils en ~** bushy eyebrows; **2 stationnement en ~** perpendicular parking.
■ **~ navale** naval battle; **~ rangée** lit, fig pitched battle.

batailler /bataje/ [1] *vi* (lutter) fig to fight, to battle (**pour faire** to do; **pour qch** for sth); **il a fallu ~ pour les convaincre** I had a battle to persuade them.

batailleur, -euse /batajœʀ, øz/ **I** *adj* [*enfant*] aggressive; [*tempérament*] belligerent.
II *nm,f* fighter.

bataillon /batajɔ̃/ *nm* lit, fig battalion; **un ~ de supporters** a battalion of supporters; **X?, inconnu au ~** hum X?, never heard of him.

bâtard, ~e /bɑtaʀ, aʀd/ **I** *adj* **1** fig [*solution, œuvre, style*] hybrid; [*statut*] ill-defined; [*couleur*] indefinite; **2** Zool [*chien*] crossbred; **3** (né hors mariage) offensive [*enfant*] bastard injur.
II *nm,f* **1** (chien) mongrel; **2** (enfant) offensive bastard injur.
III *nm* Culin (pain) small loaf of bread.
IV bâtarde *nf* (écriture) bastard hand.

bâtardise /bɑtaʀdiz/ *nf* bastardy.

batavia /batavja/ *nf* batavia.

bateau, *pl* **~x** /bato/ **I** *adj inv* **un sujet/une question ~** a hackneyed subject/question.
II *nm* **1** Naut, Transp gén boat; (navire) ship; **~ à voile/moteur/vapeur** sailing/motor/steam boat; **prendre le ~** to take the boat; **faire un voyage en ~** to take a boat trip; **aller en** or **par ~** to go by boat; **faire du ~** gén to go boating; (voile) to go sailing; **2** Mode **encolure ~** boat neck; **3**○ (plaisanterie) joke; **monter un ~ à qn** to take sb for a ride; **mener qn en ~** to take sb in; **4** (sur un trottoir) dropped kerb GB ou curb US (*in front of an entrance*).
■ **~ amiral** flagship; **~ de commerce** cargo boat, merchant ship; **~ de guerre** warship; **~ de pêche** fishing boat; **~ de plaisance** pleasure boat; **~ pneumatique** rubber dinghy; **~ de sauvetage** lifeboat.

bateau-citerne, *pl* **bateaux-citernes** /batositɛʀn/ *nm* tanker.

bateau-école, *pl* **bateaux-écoles** /batoekɔl/ *nm* training ship.

bateau-feu, *pl* **bateaux-feux** /batofø/ *nm* lightship.

bateau-lavoir, *pl* **bateaux-lavoirs** /batolavwaʀ/ *nm* washhouse.

bateau-mouche, *pl* **bateaux-mouches** /batomuʃ/ *nm*: *large river boat for sightseeing*.

bateau-phare, *pl* **bateaux-phares** /batofaʀ/ *nm* lightship.

bateau-pilote, *pl* **bateaux-pilotes** /batopilɔt/ *nm* pilot boat.

bateau-pompe, *pl* **bateaux-pompes** /batopɔ̃p/ *nm* fireboat.

bateleur, -euse /batlœʀ, øz/ *nm* **1** lit tumbler, juggler; **2** fig, pej buffoon.

batelier, -ière /batəlje, ɛʀ/ ▶ 510 *nm,f* boatman/boatwoman.

batellerie /batɛlʀi/ *nf* inland water shipping; **la ~ de la Seine** shipping on the Seine.

bâter /bɑte/ [1] *vtr* to put a pack-saddle on.

bat-flanc /baflɑ̃/ *nm inv* (dans une écurie) stall partition; (dans un dortoir) wooden partition.

bath○† /bat/ *adj inv* great, smashing.

bathymètre /batimɛtʀ/ *nm* bathymeter.

bathymétrie /batimetʀi/ *nf* bathymetry.

bathymétrique /batimetʀik/ *adj* bathymetric.

bathyscaphe /batiskaf/ *nm* bathyscaph.

bâti, ~e /bɑti/ **I** *pp* ▶ **bâtir**.
II *pp adj* **1** [*maison, édifice*] built, constructed; **terrain ~** developed site; **2** [*histoire, scénario*] constructed; **un homme bien ~** a well-built man; **il est bien ~** he's well built; **un petit homme mal ~** a small man of irregular build.
III *nm* **1** (terrain bâti) developed site; **2** (de fenêtre, porte) frame; **3** (de machine) frame; **4** Cout tacking.
■ **~ dormant** fixed frame.

batifolage /batifɔlaʒ/ *nm* romping ou larking○ about.

batifoler /batifɔle/ [1] *vi* **1** (jouer) to romp ou lark○ about; **2** (flirter) to flirt.

batik /batik/ *nm* batik.

bâtiment /bɑtimɑ̃/ *nm* **1** (construction) building; **~s administratifs/d'exploitation/universitaires** administrative/farm/university buildings; **2** (métier) building trade; **travailler dans le ~** to work in the building trade; **géant du ~** giant of the building trade; **quand le ~ va, tout va** when the building trade is doing well, everything is doing well; **3** (navire) ship.
■ **~ de guerre** battleship.

bâtir /bɑtiʀ/ [3] **I** *vtr* **1** Constr to build [*édifice*]; **~ qch de ses propres mains** to build sth with one's own hands; **faire ~ sa maison par qn** to have one's house built by sb; **terrain à ~** building land; **2** (établir) to build [*fortune, réputation, avenir, Europe*]; to develop [*stratégie, pays*]; to establish [*paix*]; to build up [*équipe, structure*]; to base [*argumentation, rapport*] (**sur** on); **3** Cout to tack [*vêtement, ourlet*]; ▶ **Espagne**.
II se bâtir *vpr* [*personne*] to build oneself [*maison, cabane*]; to build up [*fortune*]; [*maison, fortune*] to be built.

bâtisse /bɑtis/ *nf* (maison) house; (bâtiment) building.

bâtisseur, -euse /bɑtisœʀ, øz/ *nm* **1** Hist Constr (maçon) master-builder; **les ~s de cathédrales** cathedral master-builders; **2** fig (créateur) builder; **~ d'empire** empire builder; **un roi qui fut un grand ~** a king who commissioned a great number of buildings.

batiste /batist/ *nf* batiste.

bâton /bɑtɔ̃/ *nm* **1** (bout de bois) stick; **un coup de ~** a blow with a stick; **donner un coup de ~ à qn** to hit sb with a stick; **donner des coups de ~ à qn** to beat sb with a stick; **faire donner du ~ à qn** to have sb beaten; **retour de ~** backlash; ▶ **parquet**; **2** (objet allongé) stick; **un ~ de cire/réglisse/colle/dynamite** a stick of wax/liquorice GB ou licorice US/glue/dynamite; **3** (trait vertical) vertical stroke; (pour compter) bar; **4**○ (dix mille francs) ten thousand francs.
■ **~ blanc** baton (*used for directing traffic*); **~ de commandement** baton (*of office*); **~ de craie** stick ou piece of chalk; **~ de maréchal** lit marshal's baton; fig pinnacle of one's career; **~ de rouge (à lèvres)** lipstick; **~ de ski** ski stick.
IDIOMES **être le ~ de vieillesse de qn** to be sb's support in their old age; **mener une vie de ~ de chaise** to lead a wild life; **discuter à ~s rompus** to talk about this and that; **conversation à ~s rompus** general conversation; **mettre des ~s dans les roues de qn** to put a spoke in sb's wheel.

bâtonner /bɑtɔne/ [1] *vtr* to beat [sb] with a stick.

bâtonnet /bɑtɔnɛ/ *nm* **1** (petit bâton) stick; **2** (de rétine) (retinal) rod.
■ **~ ouaté** cotton bud GB, cotton swab US; **~ de poisson** fish finger GB, fish stick US.

bâtonnier /bɑtɔnje/ **▶813⌋** *nm* ≈ president of the Bar.

batracien /batʀasjɛ̃/ *nm* batrachian.

battage /bataʒ/ *nm* **1**○ Pub publicity, hype○; **~ publicitaire** advertising hype○; **faire du ~ autour de qch** to hype sth○, give sth the hard sell; **2** (action de battre) beating; Agric threshing; **le ~ de l'or** Tech gold beating; **le ~ du blé** Agric wheat threshing; **le ~ du beurre** Tech butter churning.

battant, **~e** /batɑ̃, ɑ̃t/ **I** *adj* **~ neuf** brand new; **à deux heures ~es** on the stroke of two; **le cœur ~** with a beating heart; **▶porte**.
II *nm,f* fighter.
III *nm* **1** (de porte, fenêtre) hinged section; (de table, comptoir) leaf; **le ~ droit de la porte** the right-hand door (*of a double door*); **ouvre les deux ~s de la fenêtre** open both sides of the window; **porte à deux ~s** double door; **2** (de cloche) clapper; **3** (de pavillon, drapeau) fly.

batte /bat/ *nf* Sport bat GB, paddle US.

battement /batmɑ̃/ *nm* **1** (pulsation) (de cœur, pouls) beating ¢, beat; **les ~s réguliers du cœur** Méd regular heartbeat (*sg*); **avoir des ~s de cœur** to have palpitations; **2** (de pluie, tambour) beating ¢; **entendre des ~s de tambour** to hear drums; **le ~ des volets contre le mur** the banging of the shutters against the wall; **3** Mus, Phys beat; **4** (mouvement) (d'ailes) flutter; (de cils) fluttering ¢; (de paupières) blinking ¢; (de danseur) battement; (de nageur) (en crawl) flutter kick ¢; (en brasse) frog kick ¢; **5** (entre deux activités) break; (attente) wait; (période creuse) gap; **les professeurs ont du ~ entre les cours** teachers have some free time (in) between lessons; **6** Phon flap.

batterie /batʀi/ *nf* **1** Mus (de grand orchestre) percussion section; (de jazz, rock) drum kit; **être à la ~** (dans un grand orchestre) to be on percussion; (dans un orchestre de jazz, rock) to be on the drums; **morceau de ~** drum break; **2** Mil (artillerie, régiment) battery; **~ de canons** gun battery; **~ ennemie/antichars** enemy/antitank battery; **dresser ses ~s** fig to prepare for the assault; **changer ses ~s** fig to change one's strategy; **démasquer** or **dévoiler ses ~s** fig to show one's hand; **3** Aut, Électrotech battery; **recharger ses ~s** fig to recharge one's batteries; **4** (série) (de caméras, missiles, tests) battery; (de projecteurs) bank; (de satellite) array; (d'avocats, experts) battery.
■ **~ de cuisine** Culin pots and pans (*pl*).

batteur /batœʀ/ **▶510⌋** *nm* **1** Mus (de grand orchestre) percussionist; (de jazz, rock) drummer; **2** (ouvrier) Agric thresher; Tech **~ d'or/d'étain** gold-/pewter-beater; **3** Sport (au cricket) batsman; (au baseball) batter; **4** Culin whisk; **~ à œufs** egg whisk.
■ **~ électrique** hand mixer.

batteuse /batøz/ *nf* **1** Agric threshing machine, thresher; **2** Tech, Ind beating machine, beater.

battoir /batwaʀ/ *nm* **1** (instrument) beater; **~ à tapis** carpet beater; **2**○ (main) paw○, hand.

battre /batʀ/ [61] **I** *vtr* **1** (l'emporter) to beat, defeat [*adversaire*]; to break [*record*]; **~ qn à un jeu/en une matière** to beat sb at a game/in a subject; **je le bats au tennis/en chimie** I beat him at tennis/in chemistry; **elle me bat à la course** she beats me in running; **~ qn aux élections** to beat sb in the elections; **se faire ~ par 6 à 2** to lose 6–2; **ne pas se tenir pour battu** not to admit defeat; **▶couture**; **2** (frapper) to beat [*personne, animal*]; **il bat son chien** he beats his dog; **~ qn à coups de balai** to beat sb with a broom; **~ qn à coups de pied/poing** to kick/punch sb repeatedly; **battu à mort** beaten to death; **▶plâtre**; **3** (taper sur) to beat [*matelas, tapis*]; Tech to beat [*métal*]; Agric to thresh [*blé*]; Chasse to beat [*taillis*]; **~ l'air/l'eau de ses bras** to thrash the air/the water with one's arms; **ma jupe me bat les talons** my skirt is flapping about my heels; **~ monnaie** to mint coins; **~ le briquet**† to strike a light; **4** (heurter) [*pluie*] to beat ou lash against [*vitre*]; [*mer*] to pound ou beat against [*rocher*]; [*artillerie*] to pound [*mur, position*]; **battu des vents/par la pluie** lashed by the wind/by the rain; **5** Culin to whisk [*œuf*]; to churn [*crème*]; **~ les œufs en neige** beat the egg whites until stiff; **~ les œufs en omelette** beat the eggs; **6** Jeux to shuffle [*cartes*]; **7** Mus **~ la mesure** to beat time; **~ le tambour** Mil to beat the drum; fig to shout from the rooftops; Mil [*tambour*] to beat; **~ la retraite** to beat the retreat; **8** (parcourir) to scour [*pays, forêt*]; **~ les chemins** or **sentiers** or **routes** to travel the roads; **▶pavillon**.
II battre de *vtr ind* **1** (agiter) **~ des ailes** to flap its wings; **~ des cils** to flutter one's eyelashes; **~ des mains** to clap (one's hands); **~ des paupières** to blink; **2** (jouer) **~ du tambour** to beat the drum.
III *vi* **1** (palpiter) [*cœur, pouls*] to beat; **la joie/l'émotion me faisait ~ le cœur** my heart was pounding fast with joy/emotion; **le sang me battait aux tempes** I could feel my temples throbbing; **2** (claquer) [*porte, volet*] to bang; **le vent fait ~ les volets** the wind is banging the shutters; **la pluie bat contre la vitre** the rain is lashing against the window; **▶verge**.
IV se battre *vpr* **1** (lutter) to fight (**contre** against; **avec** with); **se ~ au couteau** to fight with knives ou a knife; **se ~ en duel** to fight a duel; **se ~ avec qn** to fight with sb; **se ~ pour obtenir qch** fig to fight for sth; **se ~ avec une serrure** hum to struggle with a lock; **se ~ contre un champion/une équipe** Jeux, Sport to fight (against) a champion/a team; **se ~ contre la corruption** to fight (against) corruption; **2** (échanger des coups) to fight; **leurs enfants n'arrêtent pas de se ~** their children are always fighting; **3** (se frapper) **se ~ la poitrine** to beat one's breast.
IDIOMES **~ en retraite** to beat a retreat; **~ en retraite devant qch/qn** to retreat before sth/sb; **~ son plein** to be in full swing; **je m'en bats l'œil**○ I don't give a damn○.

battu, **~e** /baty/ **I** *pp* **▶battre**.
II *pp adj* **1** (maltraité) [*enfant, femme, prisonnier*] battered; fig [*mine, air*] tired; **2** Danse battu (*épith, après n*); **▶terre**.
III battue *nf* Chasse beat.

bau, *pl* **baux**[2] /bo/ *nm* Naut beam; **maître ~** midship beam.

BAU /beay/ *nf*: *abbr* **▶bande**.

baud /bod/ *nm* baud.

baudelairien, **-ienne** /bodlɛʀjɛ̃, ɛn/ *adj* Baudelairian.

baudet /bodɛ/ *nm* ○(âne) donkey, ass.
IDIOMES **être chargé comme un ~** to be loaded down like a mule.

baudrier /bodʀije/ *nm* **1** (d'uniforme) shoulder strap; **2** (d'alpinisme) harness.
■ **~ réfléchissant** Sam Browne Belt.

baudroie /bodʀwa/ *nf* angler fish, monkfish.

baudruche /bodʀyʃ/ *nf* **1** (de caoutchouc) (matière) rubber skin; (ballon) balloon; **2** fig (homme faible) pej wimp○ péj.
IDIOMES **se dégonfler comme une ~** to lose one's nerve.

bauge /boʒ/ *nf* **1** (de sanglier) wallow; **2** (lieu sale) pigsty; **3** (torchis) cob, clay and straw mortar.

baume /bom/ *nm* Chimie, Pharm balm, balsam.
IDIOMES **mettre du ~ au cœur de qn** to be a solace to sb.

baux /bo/ *nmpl* **▶bail, bau**.

bauxite /boksit/ *nf* bauxite.

bavard, **~e** /bavaʀ, aʀd/ **I** *adj* **1** (qui parle beaucoup) [*personne*] talkative; **2** (qui commet des indiscrétions) **on ne peut pas lui faire confiance, il est trop ~** he can't be trusted, he talks too much ou he can't keep his mouth shut; **3** pej (prolixe) [*roman, film, critique*] long-winded péj.
II *nm,f* **1** (personne qui parle beaucoup) chatterbox; **un ~ impénitent** an incorrigible chatterbox; **2** (personne qui commet des indiscrétions) indiscreet person, bigmouth○.

bavardage /bavaʀdaʒ/ *nm* **1** (action) chattering; **2** (indiscrétions) gossip ¢; **les ~s vont bon train** tongues are wagging; **3** (propos, discussion) idle chatter.

bavarder /bavaʀde/ [1] *vi* **1** péj (parler beaucoup) to talk, to chatter; **2** (s'entretenir avec) to chat (**avec** with); **3** (médire) to gossip (**sur** about); **on bavardait beaucoup sur lui** there was a lot of gossip about him.

bavarois, **~e** /bavaʀwa, az/ **I** *adj* Bavarian.
II *nm* Culin Bavarian cream, bavarois.

Bavarois, **~e** /bavaʀwa, az/ **▶692⌋** *nm,f* Bavarian.

bavasser○ /bavase/ [1] *vi* to babble on○.

bave /bav/ *nf* **1** (salive) (de personne, bébé) dribble; (de crapaud) spittle; (de chien enragé) froth; (d'animal) slaver, slobber; **2** (sécrétion) (d'escargot, de limace) slime; **▶crapaud**.

baver /bave/ [1] *vi* **1** [*personne, bébé*] to dribble, to drool; [*chien enragé*] to froth at the mouth; [*animal*] to slaver, to slobber; **~ d'envie à la vue de qch** to drool over sth; **~ d'admiration** to be open-mouthed with admiration; **2** (couler) [*stylo*] to leak; [*pinceau*] to dribble; [*encre, peinture*] to run; **3**○ (dénigrer) **~ sur qn/qch** to put sb/sth down○.
IDIOMES **en ~ (des ronds de chapeau)**○ to have a hard time; **il leur en a fait ~**○ he gave them a hard time, he put them through the mill○ ou wringer○ US.

bavette /bavɛt/ *nf* **1** (de tablier, salopette) bib; (pour bébé) bib; **2** Culin flank; **3** Aut mudflap.
IDIOMES **tailler une ~ avec qn**○ to have a good chat with sb.

baveux, **-euse** /bavø, øz/ **I** *adj* **1** [*enfant, bouche*] dribbling; **2** [*omelette*] runny.
II○ *nm,f* C (personne arrogante) show-off○.

Bavière /bavjɛʀ/ **▶692⌋** *nprf* Bavaria.

bavoir /bavwaʀ/ *nm* bib.

bavolet /bavɔlɛ/ *nm* storm flap.

bavure /bavyʀ/ *nf* **1** (tache, aussi en imprimerie) smudge; **2** (erreur) blunder; **~ policière** police blunder; **c'est un travail net et sans ~** it's a clean job with no botches.

bayadère /bajadɛʀ/ **I** *adj inv* Tex bayadere.
II *nf* (danseuse) bayadere.

bayer /baje/ [21] *vi* **~ aux corneilles** to gape.

bayonnais, **~e** /bajɔnɛ, ɛz/ **▶857⌋** *adj* of Bayonne.

Bayonnais, **~e** /bajɔnɛ, ɛz/ **▶857⌋** *nm,f* (natif) native of Bayonne; (habitant) inhabitant of Bayonne.

Bayonne /bajɔn/ **▶857⌋** *npr* Bayonne.

bazar /bazaʀ/ *nm* **1** (magasin) general store, bazaar; **2**○ (désordre) mess; **quel ~ dans cette pièce** what a mess this room is; **rangez-moi ce ~** clear this mess up; **ils ont mis le ~ dans toute la maison** they messed up the whole house; **3**○ (affaires) clutter; **il est parti avec son ~** he left with all his clutter; **et tout le ~** and all the rest; **4** (marché oriental) bazaar.

bazarder○ /bazaʀde/ [1] *vi* (jeter) to throw out; (vendre) to sell off.

bazarette /bazaʀɛt/ *nf* convenience store.

bazooka /bazuka/ *nm* bazooka.

bazou○ /bazu/ *nm* C (voiture) banger○ GB, crate○ US.

BCBG○ /besebeʒe/ *adj* (*abbr* = **bon chic bon genre**) iron chic and conservative.

BCG /beseʒe/ *nm* (*abbr* = **bacille bilié de Calmette et Guérin**) Méd BCG; **on leur a fait le ~** they had their BCG.

bd *written abbr* = **boulevard 1**.

BD○ /bede/ *nf*: *abbr* ▶ **bande**.

bê /bɛ/ *nm* (*also onomat*) baa.

beagle /bigl/ *nm* beagle.

béant, **~e** /beɑ̃, ɑ̃t/ *adj* [*plaie, trou, sac*] gaping.

Béarn /beaʀn/ ▶ **692** *nprm* **le ~** the Béarn.

béarnais, **~e** /beaʀnɛ, ɛz/ **I** *adj* **1** Géog from the Béarn; **2** Culin [*sauce*] Béarnaise.
II béarnaise *nf* Béarnaise sauce.

Béarnais, **~e** /beaʀnɛ, ɛz/ ▶ **692** *nm,f* person from the Béarn.

béat, **~e** /bea, at/ *adj* [*personne*] blissfully happy; [*sourire, air, expression*] blissful, beatific hum; **être d'un optimisme ~** to be blindly optimistic; **être ~ devant qch** to be enraptured by sth; **rester ~ devant qch** to gaze enraptured at sth; **être** or **rester ~ d'admiration devant qn/qch** to be wide-eyed with admiration for sb/sth.

béatement /beatmɑ̃/ *adv* blissfully, rapturously.

béatification /beatifikasjɔ̃/ *nf* Relig beatification.

béatifier /beatifje/ [2] *vtr* to beatify.

béatitude /beatityd/ **I** *nf* **1** (bonheur) bliss, beatitude; **plonger qn dans la ~** to fill sb with bliss; **2** Relig (bonheur des élus) beatitude.
II béatitudes *nfpl* Relig **les ~s** the Beatitudes.

beatnik /bitnik/ *nmf* beatnik.

beau (**bel** *before vowel or mute h*), **belle**, *mpl* **~x** /bo, bɛl/ **I** *adj* **1** (esthétiquement) [*enfant, femme, visage, yeux, cheveux*] beautiful; [*homme, garçon*] handsome; [*jambes*] nice; [*corps, silhouette, dents*] good; [*couleur, son, musique, maison, jardin, objet*] beautiful; **tu es belle** (extraordinairement) you're beautiful; (normalement) you look lovely; **c'est une belle fille** she's very nice-looking; **c'est une belle femme** she's a beautiful woman; **avoir belle allure** [*personne*] to cut a fine figure; [*maison, voiture*] to be fine-looking; **se faire ~** to do oneself up; **faire ~ qn** to smarten sb up; **ce n'est pas (bien) ~ à voir**○**!** it's not a pretty sight!; **peindre qch sous de belles couleurs** to make sth sound wonderful; ▶ **fille**; **2** (qualitativement) [*vêtements, machine, performance, match, spectacle*] good; [*œuvre, collection, bijou, spécimen*] fine; [*travail, poste, cadeau, anniversaire*] nice; [*temps, jour*] fine, nice; [*journée, promenade, rêve*] lovely; [*promesse, débat, discours, projet*] fine; [*effort, victoire, exemple, manière*] nice; [*geste, sentiment, âme*] noble; [*pensée*] beautiful; [*carrière*] successful; [*succès, avenir, optimisme*] great; **fais de ~x rêves!** sweet dreams!; **il fait ~** the weather is fine; **il n'est pas ~ de faire** it's not nice to do; **un ~ jour/matin/soir** one fine day/morning/evening; **au ~ milieu de** right in the middle of; **rien n'est trop ~ pour lui/eux** nothing is too good for him/them; **c'est bien ~ tout ça, mais**○ that's all very fine, but; **trop ~ pour être vrai** too good to be true; **ça serait trop ~**○**!** one should be so lucky○!; **ce ne sont que de belles paroles** it's all talk; **assez de belles paroles, dites ce que vous avez à dire** enough of your fine words, say what you have to say; **il y a ~ temps qu'il n'est pas venu** he hasn't been here for ages; ▶ **démener**, **pluie**; **3** (quantitativement) [*somme, héritage*] tidy; [*salaire*] very nice; [*appétit*] big; **belle pagaille** absolute mess; **~ mensonge** whopping lie, whopper○; **bel égoïste** awful egoist; **~ salaud**◑ real bastard◑.
II *nm* **1** (choses intéressantes) **qu'est-ce que tu as fait de ~?** done anything interesting?; **tu n'as rien de ~ à nous raconter?** anything interesting to tell us?; **le plus ~ (de l'histoire) est que** the best part (of the story) is that; **2** Philos (beauté) **le ~** beauty; **goût/recherche/sentiment du ~** taste/quest/feeling for beauty; **3** (bonne qualité) best quality; **n'acheter que du ~** to buy only the best quality; **4** (homme) dandy; **jouer les ~x** to be a dandy; ▶ **vieux**; **5** Météo **le temps est/se met au ~** the weather is/is turning fine.
III avoir beau *loc verbale* **j'ai ~ essayer/travailler, je n'y arrive pas** it's no good my trying/working, I can't do it; **l'économie a ~ se développer, le chômage progresse** even if the economy does develop, unemployment is still growing; **on a ~ dire, ce n'est pas si simple** no matter what people say, it's not that easy.
IV bel et bien *loc adv* **1** (irréversiblement) well and truly; **bel et bien fini** well and truly over; **2** (indiscutablement) definitely; **il était bel et bien coupable** he was definitely guilty.
V belle *nf* **1** (femme) **courtiser les belles** to go courting the ladies; **ma belle** darling, love○ GB, doll○ US; **2** (maîtresse) lady friend; **avoir rendez-vous avec sa belle** to have a date with one's lady friend; **3** Jeux decider; **faire la belle** to play the decider.
VI de plus belle *loc adv* with renewed vigour[GB]; **les hostilités ont repris de plus belle** hostilities resumed with renewed vigour[GB]; **la pluie a repris de plus belle** it started raining again harder than ever; **frapper de plus belle** to hit harder than ever; **crier de plus belle** to shout louder than ever.
VII belles○ *nfpl* (paroles) stories; **j'en ai appris** or **entendu de belles à ton sujet** I have been hearing stories about you; **on en raconte de belles sur elle** there are quite a few stories about her.
■ **~ fixe** Météo fine weather; **être au ~ fixe** [*temps, baromètre*] to be set fair; [*affaire, relation*] to be going well; **avoir le moral au ~ fixe**○ to be on a high○; **~ gosse**○ looker○, doll○ US; **être ~ gosse** to be dishy○ GB, to be a looker○; **~ linge**○ high society; **fréquenter le ~ linge** to hang out○ with society types; **~ parleur** smooth talker; **~ parti** (homme) eligible bachelor; (femme) good match; **épouser un ~ parti** to marry money; **~ sexe** fair sex; **~x jours** (beau temps) fine weather ¢; (belle époque) good days; **les ~x jours sont arrivés** the fine weather is here; **c'étaient les ~x jours** those were the days; **Beau Danube bleu** Mus Blue Danube; **bel esprit** bel esprit; **la Belle au Bois dormant** Sleeping Beauty; **Belle Époque** Belle Époque; **style Belle Époque** Belle Époque style; **belle page** Imprim right-hand page; **belle plante**○ gorgeous specimen○; **belle vie** life of ease; **c'est la belle vie!** this is the life!; **avoir la belle vie** to live it up; **belles années** happy years.
IDIOMES **faire le ~** [*chien*] to sit up and beg; [*personne*] to show off; **(se) faire la belle**○ (s'évader) to do a bunk○ GB, to take a powder○ US; **l'avoir belle**○ to have an easy life; **en faire voir de belles**○ **à qn** to give sb a hard time; **c'est du ~**○**!** iron lovely! iron; **tout ~ (tout ~)!** (pour calmer) easy (, easy)!; **il ferait ~ voir**○ **(qu'il vienne)** I'd like to see the day (when he shows up)○.

Beauce /bos/ ▶ **692** *nprf* **la ~** the Beauce.

beauceron, **-onne** /bosʀɔ̃, ɔn/ *adj* from the Beauce.

Beauceron, **-onne** /bosʀɔ̃, ɔn/ *nm,f* person from the Beauce.

beaucoup /boku/ ▶ **662** **I** *adv* **1** (modifiant un verbe) a lot; (dans les phrases interrogatives et négatives) much; **gagner/écrire/risquer ~** to earn/to write/to risk a lot ou a great deal; **je vous remercie ~** thank you very much; **aimer ~ qn/qch** to like sb/sth a lot ou a great deal; **elle va ~ au théâtre** she goes to the theatre[GB] a lot ou a great deal; **je n'apprécie pas ~ leur comportement** I don't much care for their behaviour[GB]; **la fin du roman surprend ~** the ending of the novel is very surprising; **s'intéresser ~ à qch** to be very interested in sth; **il a ~ changé** he has changed a lot ou a great deal; **j'ai ~ aimé le concert** I enjoyed the concert a lot ou very much ou a great deal; **je n'ai pas ~ aimé le concert** I didn't enjoy the concert very much; **il n'écrit plus ~** he doesn't write much any more; **a-t-il ~ joué ces derniers temps?** has he played much recently?; **~ à boire** a lot to drink; **il a encore ~ à apprendre** he still has a lot to learn; **vous avez déjà fait ~ pour moi** you've already done a lot ou a great deal for me; **c'est ~ dire** that's going a bit far; **c'est ~ pour ton âge** it's a lot for your age; **ils sont 40 élèves par classe, c'est ~** there are 40 pupils in each class, that's a lot; **c'est déjà ~ qu'elle soit venue** it's already quite something that she came; **c'est déjà ~ s'il ne nous met pas dehors** it'll already be something if he doesn't throw us out; **2** (modifiant un adverbe) much, far; **elle va ~ mieux** she's much ou a lot better; **~ moins** much less; **~ moins d'argent** far ou much less money; **~ moins de gens/de livres** far fewer people/books; **c'est ~ moins difficile qu'avant** it's much easier than before, it's much less difficult than before; **~ plus** much more, a lot more; **~ plus d'argent** far ou much more money; **il travaille ~ plus vite que moi** he works much faster than I do; **~ trop** far too much, much too much; **il est resté ~ trop longtemps** he stayed far ou much too long; **c'est ~ trop grand** it's far ou much too big; **j'en ai déjà ~ trop dit** I've already said far ou much too much; **3** (un grand nombre) **~ de** a lot of, lots of○ [*objets, problèmes, idées*]; (dans les phrases interrogatives et négatives) much, many; (une grande quantité) **~ de** a lot of, a great deal of [*argent, eau, bruit, chaleur*] ; **j'ai mangé ~ de cerises** I've eaten a lot of cherries; **il y a ~ de moustiques cette année** there are a lot of mosquitoes this year; **il ne reste plus ~ de places pour le concert** there aren't many seats left for the concert; **des gens intéressants j'en ai rencontré ~ au cours de mes voyages** I met a lot of interesting people during my travels; **a-t-il gagné ~ de matchs?** did he win many matches?; **cela ne m'a pas pris ~ de temps** it didn't take me much time; **il ne reste plus ~ de pain** there isn't much bread left; **il n'y a pas ~ de monde** there aren't many ou a lot of people; **avec ~ de gentillesse** very kindly; **avec ~ de soin** very carefully, with great care; **il a du courage et même ~** he has courage, and a lot of it; **4** (avec valeur pronominale) many; **parmi ces gâteaux, ~ me tentent** I find many ou a lot of these cakes tempting; **~ des lieux que nous avons visités** many ou a lot of the places we visited; **~ de ces gens/d'entre eux** many ou a lot of these people/of them; **~ sont retraités** many are pensioners; **le soir certains lisent, ~ regardent la télévision** in the evenings some read, many watch television; **~ sont tentés de le croire** many are inclined to believe it.
II de beaucoup *loc adv* by far; **elle le surpasse de ~** she surpasses him by far; **elle est de ~ la plus intelligente** she's by far the most intelligent; **je préfère de ~ la musique baroque** I prefer baroque music by far, I much prefer baroque music; **ma montre retarde de ~** my watch is very slow; **il s'en faut de ~ qu'elle ait le niveau** she's nowhere near up to standard; **il ne s'en est pas fallu de ~ qu'il remportât le championnat** he came very close to winning the championship.
III pour beaucoup *loc adv* **il compte pour ~ dans la réussite du projet** he counts for a lot in the success of the project; **ta réussite est due pour ~ à** your success

is largely due to; **être pour ~ dans** to have a lot to do with.

beauf○ /bof/ *nm* **1** (*abbr* = **beau-frère**) brother-in-law; **2** (rustre) pej boor○, redneck○ US.

beau-fils, *pl* **beaux-fils** /bofis/ *nm* **1** (gendre) son-in-law; **2** (fils du conjoint) stepson.

beau-frère, *pl* **beaux-frères** /bofʀɛʀ/ *nm* brother-in-law.

beaujolais, **~e** /boʒɔlɛ, ɛz/ **I** *adj* from Beaujolais.
II *nm inv* Beaujolais; **le ~ nouveau** Beaujolais nouveau.

Beaujolais /boʒɔlɛ/ ▶ **692** *nprm* **le ~** the Beaujolais.

beau-papa, *pl* **beaux-papas** /bopapa/ *nm* father-in-law.

beau-père, *pl* **beaux-pères** /bopɛʀ/ *nm* **1** (père du conjoint) father-in-law; **2** (conjoint de la mère) stepfather.

beaupré /bopʀe/ *nm* (**mât de**) **~** bowsprit.

beauté /bote/ *nf* **1** (esthétique) beauty; **la ~ idéale** ideal beauty; **la ~ d'un paysage/d'une femme** the beauty of a landscape/of a woman; **la ~ d'un homme** a man's good looks (*pl*); **éblouissant/étonnant de ~** dazzlingly/amazingly beautiful; **d'une ~ remarquable/surprenante** amazingly/strikingly beautiful; **d'une grande ~** very beautiful; **de toute ~** exquisite; **être en ~** to look really good; **avoir la ~ du diable** to be in the bloom of youth; **mise en ~** beauty treatment; **se faire une ~** to do oneself up; **2** (qualité) (de geste, sacrifice, sentiments) nobility; (d'œuvre) beauty; **~ de la vie** beauty of life; **les ~s de la rhétorique/la Grèce/la nature** the beauties of rhetoric/Greece/nature; **faire qch pour la ~ du geste** to do sth because it is a nice thing to do; **commencer/s'achever** or **finir en ~** to start/to end with a flourish; **3** (belle personne, belle chose) **elle se prend pour une ~** she thinks she's a great beauty; **les ~s du village** the local lovelies; **ta voiture est une ~** your car is a beauty; **salut, ~**○ hello, love○ GB, hi, doll○ US.

beaux-arts /bozaʀ/ *nmpl* fine arts and architecture.

beaux-parents /bopaʀɑ̃/ *nmpl* parents-in-law.

bébé /bebe/ *nm* (tous contextes) baby; **des cheveux de ~** baby hair; **shampooing/aliments pour ~s** baby shampoo/food; **~ phoque/éléphant** baby seal/elephant; **attendre un ~** to be expecting a baby; **ne fais pas le ~** don't be a baby; **être resté très ~** to be babyish.
IDIOMES **refiler le ~**○ to pass the buck○; **jeter le ~ avec l'eau du bain**○ to throw the baby out with the bathwater.

bébé-éprouvette, *pl* **bébés-éprouvette** /bebeepʀuvɛt/ *nm* test-tube baby.

bébé-nageur, *pl* **bébés-nageurs** /bebenaʒœʀ/ *nm* **séances pour bébés-nageurs** swim-sessions for babies.

bébête○ /bebɛt/ **I** *adj* childish, silly.
II *nf* baby talk creepy-crawly○ GB, insect.

bec /bɛk/ *nm* **1** (d'oiseau) beak, bill; (de tortue, poisson) beak; (de dauphin) snout; **donner des coups de ~** to peck (**dans** at); (**nez en**) **~ d'aigle** hooked nose; **2**○ (bouche) mouth; **essuie ton ~!** wipe your mouth!; **il a toujours la cigarette/pipe au ~** he's always got a cigarette/pipe stuck in his mouth; **3** (de pichet, casserole) lip; (de théière) spout; **4** (d'instrument à vent) mouthpiece; **5** (de stylo) nib; **6** Géog bill, headland; **7** C, H (baiser) kiss.
■ **~ Bunsen** Bunsen burner; **~ fin** gourmet; **~ à gaz** gas burner; **~ de gaz** gas street-lamp; **~ verseur** pourer(-spout).
IDIOMES **clouer** or **clore le ~ à qn**○ to shut sb up○; **se retrouver le ~ dans l'eau**○ to be stuck, to be left high and dry; **tomber sur un ~**○ to come across a snag; ▶ **ongle**.

bécane○ /bekan/ *nf* **1** (deux-roues) bike○; **2** (équipement) gear○, machine.

bécarre /bekaʀ/ *nm* natural; **ré ~** D natural.

bécasse /bekas/ *nf* **1** (oiseau) woodcock; **2** (sotte) featherbrain○.

bécasseau, *pl* **~x** /bekaso/ *nm* **1** (oiseau de rivage) sandpiper; **2** (jeune bécasse) young woodcock.

bécassine /bekasin/ *nf* **1** (oiseau) snipe; **2** (sotte) silly goose○.

bec-croisé, *pl* **becs-croisés** /bɛkkʀwaze/ *nm* crossbill.

bec-de-cane, *pl* **becs-de-cane** /bɛkdəkan/ *nm* (serrure) spring lock; (poignée) door handle.

bec-de-lièvre, *pl* **becs-de-lièvre** /bɛk dəljɛvʀ/ *nm* harelip.

bêchage /bɛʃaʒ/ *nm* digging.

béchamel /beʃamɛl/ *nf* béchamel sauce.

bêche /bɛʃ/ *nf* (à lame pleine) spade; (à dents) garden fork.

bêcher /beʃe/ [1] *vtr* to dig [sth] (with a spade) [*jardin*].

bêcheur○, **-euse** /bɛʃœʀ, øz/ **I** *adj* stuck-up○.
II *nm,f* stuck-up○ person.

bécot○ /beko/ *nm* kissie○, kiss.

bécoter○ /bekɔte/ [1] **I** *vtr* to bill and coo○ with.
II se bécoter *vpr* to bill and coo○, kiss.

becquée /beke/ *nf* beakful; **donner la ~ à** to feed [*oisillon*].

becquet /bɛkɛ/ *nm* **1** Imprim paster; **2** Aut spoiler.

becquetance◑ /bɛktɑ̃s/ *nf* grub○, food.

becqueter /bɛkte/ [20] *vtr* **1** Zool to peck at; **2**◑ (manger) to eat; **il n'y a rien à ~?** isn't there anything to eat, isn't there any grub○?

bedaine○ /bədɛn/ *nf* paunch.

bedeau, *pl* **~x** /bədo/ *nm* verger.

Bedfordshire ▶ **692** *nprm* **le ~** Bedfordshire.

bedon○ /bədɔ̃/ *nm* baby talk tummy.

bedonnant○, **~e** /bədɔnɑ̃, ɑ̃t/ *adj* [*personne*] paunchy, pot-bellied○.

bédouin, **~e** /bedwɛ̃, in/ *adj*, *nm,f* Bedouin.

bée /be/ *adj f* **être bouche ~** to gape (**devant** at); **j'en suis resté bouche ~** I stood there open-mouthed ou gaping; **être bouche ~ d'admiration/d'étonnement/de stupéfaction** to be gaping in wonder/in astonishment/in stupefaction.

béer /bee/ [11] *vi* **1** (être grand ouvert) to gape; **2** (regarder avec étonnement) to gape (**de** in); **~ de surprise/d'étonnement/d'admiration** to gape in surprise/in astonishment/in wonder.

beffroi /befʀwa/ *nm* **1** Archit belfry; **2** Mil (tour de guet) watchtower; (tour mobile) belfry; **3** Gén Civ gantry.

bégaiement /begɛmɑ̃/ *nm* **1** (trouble) stammer, stutter; **2** fig (répétition) repetition, recurrence; **les ~s de l'histoire** the repetitions of history.

bégayer /begeje/ [21] *vtr*, *vi* to stammer, to stutter.

bégonia /begɔnja/ *nm* begonia.

bègue /bɛg/ **I** *adj* **être ~** to stammer, to stutter.
II *nmf* stammerer, stutterer.

bégueule /begœl/ **I** *adj* prudish; **elle n'est pas ~** she is no prude.
II *nf* prude.

bégueulerie /begœlʀi/ *nf* prudishness.

béguin /begɛ̃/ *nm* **1**○ (personne, sentiment) crush; **avoir le ~ pour qn** to have a crush on sb; **2** (bonnet) bonnet.

béguinage /beginaʒ/ *nm* Relig Beguine convent.

béguine /begin/ *nf* Relig Beguine.

behaviorisme /beaviɔʀism/, **behaviourisme** /beavjuʀism/ *nm* behaviourism[GB].

behavioriste /beavjɔʀist/, **behaviouriste** /beavjuʀist/ *adj*, *nmf* behaviourist[GB].

Behring *nprm* = **Béring**.

BEI /bəi/ *nf*: *abbr* ▶ **banque**.

beige /bɛʒ/ ▶ **193** *adj*, *nm* beige.

beigne /bɛɲ/ **I** *nm* C **1** (beignet) doughnut GB, donut US; **2**○ (idiot) fool GB, dummy US.
II○ *nf* (coup) clout○, belt○; **filer**○ **une ~ à qn** to give sb a clout○ ou a belt○, to wallop○ sb.

beignet /bɛɲɛ/ *nm* gén fritter; (à la pâte levée) doughnut, donut○ US; **~ au sucre** doughnut; **~ de** or **aux pommes** apple fritter.
■ **~s de crevettes** prawn crackers.

bel *adj m* ▶ **beau I, IV**.

bêlant, **~e** /bɛlɑ̃, ɑ̃t/ *adj* **1** [*animal*] bleating; **2** [*personne*] pej plaintive.

bêlement /bɛlmɑ̃/ *nm* bleating ₵.

bêler /bɛle/ [1] **I** *vtr* pej to bleat out [*chanson*].
II *vi* to bleat.

belette /bəlɛt/ *nf* weasel.

Belfort /bɛlfɔʀ/ ▶ **692** *npr* (département) **le Territoire de ~** Territoire de Belfort.

belfortain, **~e** /bɛlfɔʀtɛ̃, ɛn/ ▶ **857** *adj* of Belfort.

Belfortain, **~e** /bɛlfɔʀtɛ̃, ɛn/ ▶ **857** *nm,f* (natif) native of Belfort; (habitant) inhabitant of Belfort.

belge /bɛlʒ/ ▶ **537** *adj* Belgian.

Belge /bɛlʒ/ ▶ **537** *nmf* Belgian.

belgicisme /bɛlʒisism/ *nm* Belgian French expression.

Belgique /bɛlʒik/ ▶ **321** *nprf* Belgium.

Belgrade /bɛlgʀad/ ▶ **857** *npr* Belgrade.

bélier /belje/ *nm* **1** Zool ram; **2** Mil, Hist battering ram; **3** Tech **coup de ~** water hammer.
■ **~ hydraulique** hydraulic ram.

Bélier /belje/ ▶ **874** *nprm* Aries.

Belize /beliz/ ▶ **321** *nprm* Belize.

bélizien, **-ienne** /belizjɛ̃, ɛn/ ▶ **537** *adj* Belizean.

Bélizien, **-ienne** /belizjɛ̃, ɛn/ ▶ **537** *nm,f* Belizean.

belladone /bɛladɔn/ *nf* **1** Bot (plante) deadly nightshade, belladonna; **2** Méd (extrait) belladonna.

bellâtre /bɛlɑtʀ/ *nm* handsome hunk.

belle *adj f*, *nf* ▶ **beau I, V, VI, VII**.

belle-de-jour, *pl* **belles-de-jour** /bɛl dəʒuʀ/ *nf* Bot morning glory.

belle-de-nuit, *pl* **belles-de-nuit** /bɛl dənɥi/ *nf* **1** Bot four-o'clock; **2** (prostituée) lady of the night.

belle-doche◑, *pl* **belles-doches** /bɛldɔʃ/ *nf* mother-in-law.

belle-famille, *pl* **belles-familles** /bɛl famij/ *nf* in-laws (*pl*).

belle-fille, *pl* **belles-filles** /bɛlfij/ *nf* **1** (bru) daughter-in-law; **2** (fille du conjoint) stepdaughter.

belle-maman○, *pl* **belles-mamans** /bɛlmamɑ̃/ *nf* mother-in-law.

belle-mère, *pl* **belles-mères** /bɛlmɛʀ/ *nf* **1** (mère du conjoint) mother-in-law; **2** (conjointe du père) stepmother.

belles-lettres /bɛllɛtʀ/ *nfpl* literature ₵, belles lettres ₵.

belle-sœur, *pl* **belles-sœurs** /bɛlsœʀ/ *nf* sister-in-law.

bellicisme /bɛl(l)isism/ *nm* warmongering.

belliciste /bɛl(l)isist/ **I** *adj* [*politicien, discours, opinion*] warmongering (*épith*); [*gouvernement, parti*] hawkish.
II *nmf* warmonger.

bellifontain, **~e** /bɛlifɔ̃tɛ̃, ɛn/ ▶ **857** *adj* of Fontainebleau.

Bellifontain, **~e** /bɛlifɔ̃tɛ̃, ɛn/ ▶ **857** *nm,f* (natif) native of Fontainebleau; (habitant) inhabitant of Fontainebleau.

belligérance /bɛl(l)iʒeʀɑ̃s/ *nf* state of belligerence, state of war; **reconnaissance de ~** Jur recognition of belligerence.

belligérant, **~e** /bɛl(l)iʒeʀɑ̃, ɑ̃t/ **I** *adj* [*puissance, pays*] belligerent; [*troupes*] combatant; **les États non ~s** the nonbelligerent states; **les parties ~es** Jur the warring parties.
II *nm* **1** (pays) belligerent, warring party; **2** (combattant) combatant.

belliqueux, **-euse** /bɛl(l)ikø, øz/ *adj* **1** (guerrier) warlike, bellicose fml; **2** (agressif) aggressive, belligerent.

belon /bəlɔ̃/ *nf* Belon oyster.

belote /bəlɔt/ **▶ 449** *nf* belote (*card game*); **jouer à la ~** to play belote.

bélouga /beluga/ *nm* beluga.

béluga /belyga/ *nm* beluga.

belvédère /bɛlvedɛʀ/ *nm* **1** (point de vue) panoramic viewpoint; **2** Archit (pavillon) belvedere, gazebo.

bémol /bemɔl/ *nm* **1** Mus flat; **mi ~** E flat; **2** (atténuation) damper; **mettre un ~ à qch** to put a damper on sth; **un ~ les enfants**○! pipe down children!

bénédicité /benedisite/ *nm* Relig grace; **réciter** or **dire le ~** to say grace.

bénédictin, **~e** /benediktɛ̃, in/ **I** *adj* Benedictine.
II *nm,f* Benedictine; **un couvent de ~es** a Benedictine convent; **un travail de ~** fig a painstaking task.

bénédiction /benediksjɔ̃/ *nf* **1** (geste) lit, fig blessing; **donner sa ~ à qn** to give sb one's blessing; **recevoir la ~ de qn** to be given sb's blessing; **avoir la ~ de qn** to have sb's blessing; **avec la ~ des autorités** with the full blessing ou approval of the authorities; **2** (consécration) (d'une église) consecration; **3** (grâce accordée par Dieu) blessing; **implorer la ~ de Dieu** to implore God's blessing; **4** (événement heureux) godsend; **cet emploi est une ~ du ciel** that job is a godsend; **c'est une ~!** it's a miracle!
■ **~ nuptiale** wedding ceremony; **~ papale** papal blessing; **~ Urbi et Orbi** Urbi et Orbi blessing.

bénef◑ /benɛf/ *nm* profit.

bénéfice /benefis/ *nm* **1** (gain financier) profit; **~ brut/net** gross/net profit; **~ consolidé** consolidated profit; **~ courant** profit for the year; **~s distribués et non distribués** distributed and retained profits; **faire des ~s** to make profits ou a profit; **faire un ~ de 15 millions de francs, faire 15 millions de ~** to make a profit of 15 million francs (**sur** on); **vendre à ~** to sell at a profit; **c'est tout ~**○ it's all profit; **2** (action bénéfique) benefit; **les ~s du sommeil/d'une bonne alimentation** the benefits of sleep/of a good diet; **tu as perdu tout le ~ de tes vacances** all the good that your vacation did you has been undone; **3** (avantage) advantage; **le ~ de l'ancienneté** the advantage of seniority; **tirer ~ de qch** to gain advantage from sth; **il n'en tire aucun ~** he doesn't gain anything from it, he doesn't get anything out of it; **au ~ de qch/qn** (en faveur de) in favour[GB] of sth/sb, to the advantage of sth/sb; **faire qch au ~ de qch/qn** (pour faire bénéficier) to do sth to benefit sth/sb; **organiser qch au ~ d'une œuvre caritative** to organize sth in aid of a charity; **accorder** or **laisser à qn le ~ du doute** to give sb the benefit of the doubt; **~ des circonstances atténuantes** benefit of extenuating circumstances; **le ~ de l'âge** the prerogative of age.

bénéficiaire /benefisjɛʀ/ **I** *adj* [*affaire, entreprise*] profitable; **marge ~** profit margin.
II *nmf* beneficiary.

bénéficier /benefisje/ [2] *vtr ind* **~ de** to receive [*bourse, aide financière, formation, appui*]; to enjoy [*immunité diplomatique, soutien populaire, avantages importants*]; [*économie, industrie*] to have the advantage of, to benefit from [*conjoncture favorable*]; **~ d'un traitement de faveur** to receive ou enjoy special treatment; **il n'a bénéficié d'aucune publicité** he did not get ou receive any publicity; **~ d'un tarif réduit** to get a reduction; **faire ~ qn de** to give sb [*tarif réduit, bourse*].

bénéfique /benefik/ *adj* beneficial; **cela a un effet** or **pouvoir ~** it's beneficial; **être ~ à qn/qch** to be good for sb, to be beneficial to sb/sth.

Bénélux /benelyks/ *nprm* Benelux.

benêt /bənɛ/ **I** *adj m* simple, simpleminded; **il est un peu ~** he's a bit simple.
II *nm* half-wit; **espèce de grand ~!** you great half-wit!

bénévolat /benevɔla/ *nm* voluntary ou volunteer work.

bénévole /benevɔl/ **I** *adj* [*travail, service*] voluntary, volunteer; [*travailleur*] voluntary, volunteer.
II *nmf* voluntary ou volunteer worker, volunteer.

bénévolement /benevɔlmɑ̃/ *adv* voluntarily; **travailler ~ pour** to do voluntary ou volunteer work for; **rendre des services ~** to carry out work ou to help out on a voluntary basis.

Bengale /bɛ̃gal/ **▶ 692** *nprm* Bengal; **le golfe du ~** the Bay of Bengal.

bengali /bɛ̃gali/ **▶ 462** **I** *adj* Bengali.
II *nm* **1** Ling Bengali; **2** Zool waxbill.

Bengali /bɛ̃gali/ *nmf* Bengali.

bénigne *adj f* ▶ **bénin**.

bénignité /beniɲite/ *nf* **1** Méd (de maladie) mildness; (de tumeur) nonmalignancy; **2** (d'erreur, de faute) harmlessness; (de remarque, critique) mildness.

bénin, **-igne** /benɛ̃, iɲ/ *adj* **1** (sans gravité) [*maladie, blessure*] minor; [*tumeur*] benign; [*faute, erreur*] harmless, minor; **2** fml (bienveillant) [*air, sourire, humour*] benign sout.

Bénin /benɛ̃/ **▶ 321** *nprm* Benin.

béninois, **~e** /beninwa, az/ **▶ 537** *adj* Beninese.

Béninois, **~e** /beninwa, az/ **▶ 537** *nm,f* Beninese.

béni-oui-oui○ /beniwiwi/ *nm inv* yes-man.

bénir /beniʀ/ [3] *vtr* **1** gén to bless [*fidèle, mariage, objet*]; **(que) Dieu vous** or **te bénisse** gén God bless you; (quand on éternue) bless you!; **2** (louer) to praise [*Dieu*]; **~ Dieu pour** or **de qch** to praise God for sth; **je bénis le ciel de, béni soit le ciel de** thank God for; **~ qn de qch** to be (eternally) grateful to sb for sth; **3** (se féliciter de) to be grateful for, to thank God for [*moment, occasion*]; **je bénis le jour où je l'ai rencontré** I bless ou I thank God for the day I met him; **je bénissais l'arrivée de la police** I thanked God when the police arrived; **4**○ iron (maudire) **elle a dû me ~** I bet she thanked me for that iron.

bénit, **~e** /beni, it/ *adj* [*pain, médaille, cierge*] blessed; [*water*] holy.

bénitier /benitje/ *nm* holy water font, stoup.
IDIOMES **se démener comme un diable dans un ~** to struggle like mad (to get oneself out of a predicament).

benjamin, **~e** /bɛ̃ʒamɛ̃, in/ **I** *adj* Sport ≈ junior (*aged 10-11*).
II *nm,f* **1** (dans une famille) youngest son/daughter; (dans un groupe) youngest member; **2** Sport ≈ junior player (*aged 10-11*).

benjoin /bɛ̃ʒwɛ̃/ *nm* benzoin.

benne /bɛn/ *nf* **1** (de chantier) skip GB, dumpster® US; (de mine) (colliery) wagon; (contenu) wagon(ful); **2** (de camion) skip GB, dumpster® US; **3** (cabine) (de téléphérique) (cable) car; (de mine) (pit) cage.
■ **~ à béton** concrete mixer; **~ à ordures** (camion) waste disposal GB ou garbage US truck; (conteneur) skip GB, dumpster® US; **~ preneuse** (de grue) grab-bucket GB, bucket US.

benoît, **~e** /bənwa, at/ *adj* sanctimonious.

benoîtement /bənwatmɑ̃/ *adv* sanctimoniously.

benzène /bɛ̃zɛn/ *nm* benzene.

benzine /bɛ̃zin/ *nf* benzine.

benzol /bɛ̃zɔl/ *nm* benzol.

Béotie /beɔsi/ *nprf* Boeotia.

béotien, **-ienne** /beɔsjɛ̃, ɛn/ **I** *adj* Antiq, Géog Boeotian.
II *nm,f* fml (ignorant) ignoramus.

Béotien, **-ienne** /beɔsjɛ̃, ɛn/ *nm,f* Boeotian.

BEP /bɛp/ *nm*: *abbr* ▶ **brevet**.

BEPA /bepa/ *nm* (*abbr* = **Brevet d'études professionnelles agricoles**) *certificate of agricultural studies* (*age 17*).

BEPC /beəpese, bɛps/ *nm* (*abbr* = **Brevet d'études du premier cycle**) *former examination at the end of the first stage of secondary education*.

béquille /bekij/ *nf* **1** Méd crutch; **marcher avec des ~s** to walk ou be on crutches; **2** Tech (de bicyclette, moto) kickstand; Naut shore; (d'avion) tailskid; (d'arme) bipod.

ber /bɛʀ/ *nm* cradle.

berbère /bɛʀbɛʀ/ **▶ 462** **I** *adj* Berber.
II *nm* Ling Berber.

Berbère /bɛʀbɛʀ/ *nmf* Berber.

bercail /bɛʀkaj/ *nm* **1** Relig fold; **ramener une brebis au ~** to bring a lost sheep back to the fold; **2**○ (foyer) home.

berçante /bɛʀsɑ̃t/ C **I** *adj f* **chaise ~** rocking chair.
II *nf* rocking chair.

berceau, *pl* **~x** /bɛʀso/ *nm* **1** (de bébé) cradle; **dès** or **depuis le ~** from the cradle; **du ~ jusqu'à la tombe** from the cradle to the grave; **il prend ses petites amies au ~, il les prend au ~** fig he's a cradle snatcher; **2** (lieu d'origine) (de personne, famille) birthplace; (de religion, civilisation, peuple) cradle; **3** Tech, Mil, Naut cradle; **4** Archit barrel vault; **5** (voûte de feuillage) bower, arbour[GB].

bercelonnette /bɛʀsəlɔnɛt/ *nf* rocking cradle.

bercement /bɛʀsəmɑ̃/ *nm* rocking (movement).

bercer /bɛʀse/ [12] **I** *vtr* **1** (balancer) to rock, to lull [*enfant*]; **~ un enfant pour l'endormir** to rock ou lull a baby to sleep; **2** (imprégner) **ces musiques/ces contes ont bercé mon enfance** I was brought up with this music/those stories; **3** fml (apaiser) to soothe [*personne, douleur, chagrin*]; **4** (tromper) **~ qn de** to string sb along ou delude sb with [*promesses, paroles*].
II se bercer *vpr* **se ~ de** to delude oneself with [*idées fausses, vains espoirs*]; **se ~ d'illusions** to delude oneself.

berceuse /bɛʀsøz/ *nf* **1** (chanson) lullaby; (morceau de musique) berceuse, lullaby; **2** (siège) rocking chair.

BERD /bɛʀd/ *nf*: *abbr* ▶ **banque**.

béret /beʀɛ/ *nm* beret; **~ basque** Basque beret.

bergamasque /bɛʀgamask/ *nf* bergamask.

bergamote /bɛʀgamɔt/ *nf* **1** (poire) bergamot (pear); **2** (agrume) bergamot (orange); **essence de ~** essence of bergamot; **thé à la ~** earl grey tea.

bergamotier /bɛʀgamɔtje/ *nm* bergamot.

berge /bɛʀʒ/ *nf* **1** (de rivière, canal) bank; **la ~ du canal** the canal bank; **voie sur ~** quayside road; **2**◑ (an) year (of age); **elle a 20 ~s** she's 20 years old.

berger, **-ère** /bɛʀʒe, ɛʀ/ **▶ 510** **I** *nm,f* lit (personne) shepherd/shepherdess.
II bergère *nf* (fauteuil) wing chair.
■ **~ allemand** German shepherd (dog), Alsatian GB; **~ belge** Belgian sheepdog ou shepherd; **~ des Pyrénées** Pyrenean sheepdog.
IDIOMES **la réponse du ~ à la bergère** a settling of accounts.

bergerie /bɛʀʒəʀi/ *nf* (abri) sheep barn.

IDIOMES **faire entrer le loup dans la ~** to set the fox to mind the geese.

bergeronnette /bɛʀʒəʀɔnɛt/ *nf* wagtail.

béribéri /beʀibeʀi/ ▶ 271 *nm* beriberi.

Béring /beʀiŋ/ *npr* **le détroit/la mer de ~** the Bering Strait(s)/Sea.

berk○ /bɛʀk/ *excl* yuk○!

berkélium /bɛʀkeljɔm/ *nm* berkelium.

Berlin /bɛʀlɛ̃/ ▶ 857 *npr* Berlin; **~-Est/-Ouest** East/West Berlin.

berline /bɛʀlin/ *nf* **1** (automobile) four-door saloon GB, sedan US; **2** Mines (wagonnet) (colliery) wagon; **un train de ~s** a string of wagons ou tubs; **3** (attelage) berlin.

berlingot /bɛʀlɛ̃go/ *nm* **1** (bonbon) *twisted hard mint*; **2** (emballage) soft plastic carton.

berlinois, **~e** /bɛʀlinwa, az/ ▶ 857 *adj* Berlin (*épith*); **est-/ouest-~** East/West Berlin (*épith*).

Berlinois, **~e** /bɛʀlinwa, az/ ▶ 857 *nm,f* Berliner; **les ~ de l'Est/l'Ouest** East/West Berliners.

berlue○ /bɛʀly/ *nf* **avoir la ~** to be seeing things; **donner la ~ à qn** to make sb see things.

berme /bɛʀm/ *nf* (de canal) path; (de fossé) verge.

bermuda /bɛʀmyda/ *nm* bermudas (*pl*).

Bermudes /bɛʀmyd/ ▶ 416 *nprfpl* **les ~s** Bermuda (*sg*).

bernacle /bɛʀnakl/ *nf* **~ cravant** brent (goose); **~ nonnette** barnacle goose; **~ du Canada** Canada goose.

bernardin, **~e** /bɛʀnaʀdɛ̃, in/ *nm,f* Bernardine.

bernard-l'(h)ermite /bɛʀnaʀlɛʀmit/ *nm inv* hermit-crab.

berne /bɛʀn/ *nf* **en ~** [*drapeau*] at half-mast; [*enthousiasme*] flagging; **mettre les drapeaux en ~** to put flags at half-mast.

Berne /bɛʀn/ *npr* **1** ▶ 857 (ville) Bern; **2** ▶ 692 (région) **le canton de ~** the canton of Bern.

berner /bɛʀne/ [1] *vtr* to fool, to deceive.

Bernin /bɛʀnɛ̃/ *npr* Bernini.

bernique /bɛʀnik/ **I** *nf* limpet.
II† *excl* nothing doing○!

bernois, **~e** /bɛʀnwa, az/ ▶ 857 *adj* of Bern.

Bernois, **~e** /bɛʀnwa, az/ ▶ 857 *nm,f* (natif) native of Berne; (habitant) inhabitant of Berne.

berrichon, **-onne** /bɛʀiʃɔ̃, ɔn/ ▶ 692 *adj* of Berry.

Berrichon, **-onne** /bɛʀiʃɔ̃, ɔn/ ▶ 692 *nm,f* (natif) native of Berry; (habitant) inhabitant of Berry.

berruyer, **-ère** /bɛʀyje, ɛʀ/ ▶ 857 *adj* of Bourges.

Berruyer, **-ère** /bɛʀyje, ɛʀ/ ▶ 857 *nm,f* (natif) native of Bourges; (habitant) inhabitant of Bourges.

Berry /bɛʀi/ ▶ 692 *nprm* **le ~** Berry.

béryl /beʀil/ *nm* beryl.

berzingue◑: **à toute berzingue** /atutbɛʀzɛ̃g/ *loc adv* flat out○, at top speed.

besace /bəzas/ *nf* (huntsman's) pouch; **avoir qch dans la** or **sa ~** fig (avantage) to have sth under one's belt; (surprise) to have sth up one's sleeve.

bésef◑ /bezɛf/ *adv* **(il n')y a pas ~ de** there's not a whole lot of○; **ça ne fait pas ~** it's not a whole lot○.

besicles† /bezikl/ *nfpl* spectacles.

bésigue /bezig/ ▶ 449 *nm* bezique.

besogne /bəzɔɲ/ *nf* job; **une rude/sale ~** a tough/dirty job; **une basse ~** a menial chore; **abattre de la ~** to get through a lot of work.
IDIOMES **tu vas vite en ~, toi!** you don't waste any time, do you!

besogner /bəzɔɲe/ [1] **I**○ *vtr* (posséder sexuellement) to get one's leg over○.
II† *vi* (travailler) to toil.

besogneux, **-euse** /bəzɔɲø, øz/ **I** *adj* **1** pej (laborieux) plodding (*épith*); **2**† (pauvre) poor.
II *nm,f* **1** (tâcheron) drudge; **2**† (pauvre) needy person.

besoin /bəzwɛ̃/ **I** *nm* **1** (exigence) need; **exprimer un ~** to express a need; **satisfaire un ~** to satisfy a need; **répondre à un ~** to meet a need; **répondre aux ~s de qn** to meet sb's needs; **au ~, si ~ est** if need be; **en cas de ~** if the need arises; **au ~ on prendra deux voitures** if need be, we'll take two cars; **le ~ de qch** the need for sth; **le ~ de faire** the need to do; **j'étais poussée par le ~ de comprendre/savoir** I was driven by the need to understand/know; **avoir ~ de qch/qn** to need sth/sb; **merci, je n'ai ~ de rien** I don't need anything, thank you; **j'ai bien ~ de ça**○! iron that's all I need! iron; **avoir ~ de faire** to need to do; **elle a ~ d'être réconfortée/d'en parler à qn** she needs to be comforted/to talk it over with sb; **j'ai ~ de changer d'air** I need a change of scene; **ai-je ~ de préciser/de rappeler/d'ajouter que...?** need I specify/remind you/add that...?; **tu as ~ qu'on te parle/s'occupe de toi** you need somebody to talk to you/take care of you; **parle-lui, il en a bien ~** go and talk to him, he really needs it right now; **nous avons ~ qu'ils acceptent le contrat** we need them to accept the contract; **il n'est pas ~ de faire** fml there is no need to do; **est-il ~ de venir** or **que je vienne?** fml is it necessary for me to come?; **est-il ~ de le dire** need I remind you, I hardly need to remind you; **éprouver** or **ressentir le ~ de faire** to feel a need to do; **elle n'éprouve pas le ~ de déménager** she doesn't feel a need to move; **si le ~ se fait sentir nous ouvrirons le dimanche** if there is a demand for it we'll open on Sundays; **ils se sont unis pour les ~s de la cause** they got together for the good of the cause; **2** (pauvreté) poverty; **être dans le ~** to be in need; **être à l'abri du ~** to be free from want.
II besoins *nmpl* needs; **pour s'adapter aux ~s actuels/des utilisateurs** to adapt to today's/the users' needs; **on se crée des ~s** people invent needs; **subvenir aux ~s de sa famille** to provide for one's family; **les ~s en équipement/gaz/eau** equipment/gas/water requirements; **quels sont leurs ~s en personnel/main-d'œuvre?** what are their personnel/man-power requirements?
IDIOMES **faire ses ~s**○ [*personne*] to relieve oneself; [*animal*] to do its business.

Bessarabie /besaʀabi/ ▶ 692 *nprf* Bessarabia.

bestiaire /bɛstjɛʀ/ *nm* bestiary.

bestial, **~e**, *mpl* **-iaux** /bɛstjal, o/ *adj* brutish, bestial.

bestialement /bɛstjalmɑ̃/ *adv* [*se comporter*] brutishly; [*assassiner*] brutally.

bestialité /bɛstjalite/ *nf* **1** (caractère bestial) brutality; **2** (zoophilie) bestiality.

bestiaux /bɛstjo/ *nmpl* gén livestock ¢; (bovins) cattle (+ *v pl*).

bestiole○ /bɛstjɔl/ *nf* (insecte) bug; (animal) animal.

bêta, **-asse** /beta, as/ **I**○ *adj* silly.
II○ *nm,f* (personne niaise) silly billy○.
III *nm inv* (lettre) beta; **rythme ~** beta rhythm.

bêta-bloquant, **~e** /betablɔkɑ̃, ɑ̃t/ **I** *adj* beta-blocking.
II *nm* beta-blocker.

bétail /betaj/ *nm* gén livestock ¢; (bovins) cattle (+ *v pl*); **aliments pour le ~** cattle feed ¢; ▶ **gras**.

bétaillère /betajɛʀ/ *nf* cattle truck.

bêtasse ▶ **bêta**.

bête /bɛt/ **I** *adj* **1** (pas intelligent) [*personne, air, idée, question*] stupid; **ce que tu peux être ~!** you can be so stupid sometimes!; **il est loin d'être ~** he's far from stupid; **il n'est pas ~** he's no fool; **tiens ce n'est pas ~ ça!** hey that's not a bad idea!; **suis-je ~!** how stupid of me!; **c'est ~ à pleurer** it's too stupid for words; **tu es bien ~ d'avoir accepté** it was really stupid of you to accept; **je suis restée toute ~** I was dumbfounded; **~ et méchant** [*personne, plaisanterie*] nasty; **il est ~ et discipliné** he just does as he's told; **2** (très simple) [*problème, objet*] simple; **j'ai une question toute ~** I have a very simple question; **c'est tout ~** it's quite simple; **tu prends une boîte toute ~** you just take an ordinary box; **3** (regrettable) [*accident*] silly; **c'est (trop) ~ d'échouer/d'en arriver là** it's (such) a shame to fail/that things should come to this; **c'est ~, je ne peux pas venir** it's (such) a shame I can't come.
II *nf* **1** Zool (quadrupède) animal; (insecte) insect, bug; **la sale ~ m'a mordue** the wretched animal bit me; **on n'est pas des ~s!** we're not animals!; **la Belle et la ~** Beauty and the beast; **nos amis les ~s** our four-legged friends; **2** Agric (vache) cow; (taureau) bull; **il a une cinquantaine de ~s** he has around 50 head of cattle; **3** (en parlant d'une personne) animal; **une vraie ~** a real animal; **sale ~!** stupid thing!; **4**○ (personne talentueuse) **au tennis/en musique c'est une (vraie) ~!** he's/she's (really) brilliant at tennis/ music; **une ~ de scène/du rock** a brilliant actor/rock star; **une ~ de travail** a workaholic.
■ **~ à bon Dieu** Zool ladybird GB, ladybug US; **~ à concours**○ exam fiend○; **~ à cornes** Zool horned animal; **~ curieuse** freak; **regarder qn comme une ~ curieuse** to look at sb as if he/she were a freak; **~ féroce** Zool ferocious animal; **~ noire** bête noire GB, pet hate, pet peeve US; **être la ~ noire de qn** [*personne, sujet, problème*] to be sb's bête noire GB ou pet hate; **~ sauvage** Zool wild animal; **~ de somme** Zool beast of burden.
IDIOMES **il est ~ comme ses pieds**○ or **une oie** he's (as) thick as two short planks○ GB; **elle est ~ à manger du foin**○ or **de la paille**○ she's got nothing between her ears; **bon et ~ commencent par la même lettre** kind souls are easily duped; **chercher la petite ~**○ to nit-pick○; **reprendre du poil de la ~**○ to perk up; **travailler comme une ~**○ to work like crazy○.

bétel /betɛl/ *nm* betel; **noix de ~** betel nut; **mâcher du ~** to chew betel.

bêtement /bɛtmɑ̃/ *adv* **1** (de façon peu intelligente) [*ricaner, se conduire*] stupidly; **2** (simplement) simply; **il suffit (tout) ~ de faire** you simply need to do; **3** (absurdement) [*se blesser, heurter, échouer*] stupidly.

Béthanie /betani/ ▶ 857 *nprf* Bethany.

Bethléem /bɛtleɛ/ ▶ 857 *npr* Bethlehem.

Bethsabée /bɛtsabe/ *npr* Bathsheba.

bêtifiant, **~e** /bɛtifjɑ̃, ɑ̃t/ *adj* [*ouvrage, paroles, émission*] idiotic.

bêtifier /bɛtifje/ [2] *vi* to say stupid things.

bêtise /bɛtiz/ *nf* **1** (défaut d'intelligence) stupidity; **je ne supporte pas la ~** I can't stand stupidity; **il est d'une ~ incroyable** he's incredibly stupid; **c'est de la ~ de dire une chose pareille** it's stupid to say such a thing; **tu as eu la ~ de le faire** you were stupid enough to do it; **2** (acte stupide) act of stupidity; (parole irréfléchie) mistake; (parole stupide) nonsense ¢; **faire une ~** [*enfant, adulte*] to do something stupid ou a stupid thing; **excusez-moi, j'ai dit une ~** I'm sorry, I said something stupid; **arrête de dire des ~s** stop talking nonsense; **j'ai fait une ~ en acceptant** I was stupid to accept; **surtout pas de ~s!** be good now!; **faire une grosse ~** to do something really stupid; **3** (futilité) **se fâcher pour une ~** to get angry over nothing.
■ **~ de Cambrai** Culin mint.

bêtisier /betizje/ *nm* collection of howlers○.

béton /betɔ̃/ *nm* concrete; **de** or **en ~**

[*barrage, pont*] concrete (*épith*); [*argument, dossier*] watertight; **gencives en ~** strong and healthy gums.
■ **~ armé** reinforced concrete; **~ précontraint** prestressed concrete.
IDIOMES **laisse ~**○! (laisse-moi tranquille) lay off○!; (n'en parle plus) drop it○!

bétonnage /betɔnaʒ/ *nm* Constr concreting.

bétonner /betɔne/ [1] *vtr* Constr to concrete.

bétonnière /betɔnjɛʀ/ *nf* concrete mixer.

bette /bɛt/ *nf* Swiss chard.

betterave /bɛtʀav/ *nf* beet, beetroot.
■ **~ fourragère** mangel-wurzel; **~ potagère** or **rouge** beetroot; **~ sucrière** sugar beet.

betteravier, **-ière** /bɛtʀavje, ɛʀ/ I *adj* beet (*épith*).
II ▶ 510 *nm,f* beet grower.

beuglant†○ /bøglɑ̃/ *nm*: *café with live music*.

beuglante /bøglɑ̃t/ *nf* 1◐ (protestation) outburst; **pousser une ~** to hit the roof○; 2○ (chanson) raucous song.

beuglement /bøgləmɑ̃/ *nm* 1 (de vache) mooing; (de bœuf, taureau) bellowing; 2○ (de personne) bawling, yelling.

beugler /bøgle/ [1] I *vtr* to bellow (out) [*chanson, ordre, injures*].
II *vi* 1 [*vache*] to moo; [*bœuf, taureau*] to bellow; 2○ (hurler) [*personne*] to yell; [*haut-parleur, télévision*] to blare out.

beur○ /bœʀ/ *nmf* second-generation North African (*living in France*).

beurk /bœʀk/ = **berk**.

beurre /bœʀ/ *nm* 1 (du lait) butter; **~ demi-sel/doux** salted/unsalted butter; **~ clarifié** clarified butter; **~ composé** compound butter; **cuisiner au ~** to cook with butter; ▶ **inventer**; 2 (pâte) **~ de cacahuètes/de cacao** peanut/cocoa butter; **~ d'anchois/de saumon** anchovy/salmon paste.
■ **~ blanc** *sauce made of butter, vinegar and shallots*; **~ d'escargot** garlic and parsley butter; **~ maître d'hôtel** maître d'hôtel butter; **~ manié** Culin kneaded butter; **~ noir** Culin black butter; **raie au ~ noir** skate in black butter; **œil au ~ noir** black eye.
IDIOMES **faire son ~**○ to make a packet○; **compter pour du ~**○ to count for nothing; **vouloir le ~ et l'argent du ~**○ to want to have one's cake and eat it; **entrer dans qch comme dans du ~**○ to go into sth like a knife through butter; ▶ **épinard**.

beurré, **~e** /bœʀe/ I *pp* ▶ **beurrer**.
II○ *pp adj* (soûl) plastered○.

beurre-frais /bœʀfʀɛ/ ▶ 193 *adj inv* off-white.

beurrer /bœʀe/ [1] I *vtr* to butter [*pain, tartine*]; to grease [sth] with butter [*moule à gâteau*].
II **se beurrer**○ *vpr* to get plastered○.

beurrier /bœʀje/ *nm* butter dish.

beuverie /bœvʀi/ *nf* drinking session, booze-up◐ GB.

bévue /bevy/ *nf* blunder; **commettre une ~** to make a blunder.

bey /bɛ/ *nm* bey.

Beyrouth /bɛʀut/ ▶ 857 *npr* Beirut.

bézef *adv* ▶ **bésef**.

Béziers /bezje/ ▶ 857 *npr* Béziers.

Bhoutan /butɑ̃/ ▶ 321 *nprm* Bhutan.

bi /bi/ *nm* **grand ~** penny-farthing.

biacide /biasid/ *adj* diacid.

Biafra /bjafʀa/ *nprm* Hist Biafra.

biafrais, **~e** /bjafʀɛ, ɛz/ *adj* Biafran.

Biafrais, **~e** /bjafʀɛ, ɛz/ *nm,f* Biafran.

biais /bjɛ/ I *nm inv* 1 Cout, Tex (sens) bias; (bande de tissu) bias binding; 2 (moyen) way; péj dodge○; **trouver un ~ pour éviter de payer** to find a way to get out of paying; **par le ~ de qn** through sb; **par le ~ d'un amendement** by means of an amendment.
II **de biais**, **en biais** *loc adv* **couper une étoffe en ~** to cut material on the bias; **regards en ~** fig sidelong glances; **jeter des regards en ~ à qn** to cast sidelong glances at sb; **prendre un problème de ~** fig to tackle a problem in a roundabout way.

biaiser /bjɛze/ [1] *vi* to hedge.

biarrot, **~e** /bjaʀo, ɔt/ ▶ 857 *adj* of Biarritz.

Biarrot, **~e** /bjaʀo, ɔt/ ▶ 857 *nm,f* (natif) native of Biarritz; (habitant) inhabitant of Biarritz.

biathlon /biatlɔ̃/ *nm* biathlon.

bibelot /biblo/ *nm* ornament.

biberon /bibʀɔ̃/ *nm* (baby's) bottle GB, (nursing) bottle US; **nourrir au ~** to bottle-feed; **c'est l'heure du ~** it's time for his/her feed.

biberonner○ /bibʀɔne/ [1] *vi* to booze○, to drink.

bibi○ /bibi/ I† *nm* woman's hat.
II *pron* hum muggins○ GB, me.

bibine○ /bibin/ *nf* pej cheap wine, plonk○ GB.

bible /bibl/ *nf* (tous contextes) bible; **la Bible** the Bible.

bibliobus /biblijɔbys/ *nm inv* mobile library GB, bookmobile US.

bibliographe /biblijɔgʀaf/ ▶ 510 *nmf* bibliographer.

bibliographie /biblijɔgʀafi/ *nf* bibliography.

bibliographique /biblijɔgʀafik/ *adj* bibliographical.

bibliomanie /biblijɔmani/ *nf* bibliomania.

bibliophile /biblijɔfil/ *nmf* bibliophile.

bibliophilie /biblijɔfili/ *nf* bibliophily spéc.

bibliothécaire /biblijɔtekɛʀ/ ▶ 510 *nmf* librarian.

bibliothèque /biblijɔtɛk/ *nf* 1 (endroit) library; **~ publique/universitaire** public/university library; **~ de prêt/de consultation** lending/reference library; 2 (meuble) bookcase; **~ vitrée** glass-fronted bookcase; 3 (collection de livres) library.
■ **~ nationale de France**, **BNF** *national library in Paris*; **~ publique d'information**, **BPI** *main library of the Pompidou Centre in Paris*.

biblique /biblik/ *adj* biblical.

bibliquement /biblikmɑ̃/ *adv* **connaître qn ~** hum to know sb biblically hum.

bic® /bik/ *nm* biro®.

bicaméral, **~e**, *mpl* **-aux** /bikameʀal, o/ *adj* [*système, assemblée*] bicameral, two-chamber (*épith*).

bicaméralisme /bikameʀalism/, **bicamérisme** /bikameʀism/ *nm* bicameralism.

bicarbonate /bikaʀbɔnat/ *nm* Chimie bicarbonate.
■ **~ de soude** Méd bicarbonate of soda; Culin bicarbonate of soda GB, baking soda.

bicarré, **~e** /bikaʀe/ *adj* biquadratic.

bicentenaire /bisɑ̃tnɛʀ/ I *adj* two-hundred-year-old (*épith*); **être ~** to be two hundred years old.
II *nm* bicentenary GB, bicentennial US; **célébrer le ~ de la naissance de X** to celebrate the bicentenary of X's birth.

bicéphale /bisefal/ *adj* two-headed, bicephalous spéc.

biceps /bisɛps/ *nm inv* biceps; **avoir des ~** to have muscular arms; **jouer des ~** to flex one's muscles.

biche /biʃ/ *nf* 1 Zool doe; 2 (terme d'affection) **ma ~** my pet GB, honey US.

bicher○ /biʃe/ [1] *vi* 1 (aller bien) **ça biche?** how's tricks○?; 2 (être content) to be pleased with oneself.

bichette○ /biʃɛt/ *nf* **ma ~** my poppet.

Bichkek /biʃkɛk/ ▶ 857 *npr* Bishkek.

bichlorure /biklɔʀyʀ/ *nm* dichloride.

bichonner○ /biʃɔne/ [1] I *vtr* 1 (dorloter) to pamper [*personne, animal*]; 2 (parer) to dress [sb] up, to doll up péj.
II **se bichonner** *vpr* 1 (se dorloter) to pamper oneself; 2 (se parer) to get dressed up.

bichromate /bikʀɔmat/ *nm* dichromate.

bicolore /bikɔlɔʀ/ *adj* 1 [*drapeau*] two-coloured[GB] (*épith*); [*étoffe*] two-tone; 2 (au bridge) two-suited.

biconcave /bikɔ̃kav/ *adj* biconcave.

biconvexe /bikɔ̃vɛks/ *adj* biconvex.

bicoque○ /bikɔk/ *nf* little house, dump○ péj.

bicorne /bikɔʀn/ I *adj* 1 Anat [*utérus*] bicornuate; 2 Zool [*rhinocéros*] two-horned.
II *nm* (chapeau) cocked hat.

bicot /biko/ *nm* 1● offensive North African Arab, wog● GB injur; 2○ (chevreau) kid, young of goat.

bi-cross /bikʀɔs/ ▶ 449 *nm inv* 1 (discipline) BMX; 2 (vélo) BMX.

bicycle /bisikl/ *nm* penny-farthing GB, ordinary US.

bicyclette /bisiklɛt/ *nf* 1 (objet) bicycle, bike○; **il sait monter à ~** he can ride a bicycle; **un tour à ~** a bike ou cycle GB ride; **aller au travail à ~** to cycle to work, to go to work by bike; **faire de la ~** to cycle; **il vient de passer à ~** he's just cycled past GB, he just rode by on his bike US; 2 (activité) cycling.

bidasse○ /bidas/ *nm* soldier.

bide /bid/ *nm* 1◐ (ventre) stomach; **avoir du ~** or **un gros ~** to have a paunch; 2○ (échec) flop; **faire un ~** to be a flop.

bidet /bidɛ/ *nm* 1 (de salle de bains) bidet; 2○ (cheval) nag.

bidirectionnel, **-elle** /bidiʀɛksjɔnɛl/ *adj* bidirectional.

bidoche◐ /bidɔʃ/ *nf* meat.

bidon /bidɔ̃/ I○ *adj inv* [*candidat, affaire, compagnie*] bogus; [*adresse, numéro*] false, bogus; [*excuse, histoire*] phoney; **chèque ~** dud cheque.
II *nm* 1 (récipient) (portatif) can; (baril) drum; (gourde) flask; **~ d'essence** (contenant) petrol can GB, gas can US; (contenu) can of petrol GB ou gas US; **~ de peinture** tin GB ou can of paint; 2◐ (ventre) stomach; 3○ (bluff) **cette histoire/ton plan, c'est du ~** that story/your plan is a load of hogwash○; **c'est pas du ~** no kidding○.
■ **~ à lait** milk churn GB, milk can US.

bidonnant○, **~e** /bidɔnɑ̃, ɑ̃t/ *adj* hilarious, killing○.

bidonner○: **se bidonner** /bidɔne/ [1] *vpr* to laugh, to fall about○.

bidonville /bidɔ̃vil/ *nm* shanty town.

bidouiller◐ /biduje/ [1] *vtr* to fiddle with [*appareil, mécanisme*].

bidule○ /bidyl/ *nm* 1 (objet) thingy○ GB, whatsit○ GB, thingamajig○; 2 (femme) what's-her-name○; (homme) what's-his-name○; (à qn) what's-your-name; 3 (de taxi) (taxi) sign.

bief /bjɛf/ *nm* reach.

bielle /bjɛl/ *nf* (de locomotive, d'automobile) connecting rod; **couler une ~** to run a big end; **j'ai coulé une ~** the big end has gone.
■ **~ de connexion** track rod.

biellette /bjelɛt/ *nf* small connecting rod.

biélorusse /bjelɔʀys/ ▶ 537 *adj* Byelorussian.

Biélorusse /bjelɔʀys/ ▶ 537 *nmf* Byelorussian.

Biélorussie /bjelɔʀysi/ ▶ 321 *nprf* Byelorussia.

bien /bjɛ̃/ I *adj inv* 1 (convenable) **être ~ dans un rôle** to be good in a part; **être ~ de sa personne** to be good-looking; **il n'y a rien de ~ ici** there's nothing of interest here; **voilà qui est ~** that's good; **ce n'est pas ~ de mentir** it's not nice to lie; **ce serait ~ si on pouvait nager** it would be nice if we could swim; **ça fait ~ d'aller à l'opéra**○ it's the done thing to go to the opera; **les roses font ~ sur la terrasse** the roses look nice ou good on the terrace; **tout est ~ qui finit ~** all's well that ends well; 2 (en bonne santé) well; **ne pas se**

sentir ~ not to feel well; **non, mais, t'es pas ~**○! you're out of your mind○!; **3** (à l'aise) comfortable; **je suis ~ dans ces bottes** these boots are comfortable; **on est ~ sur cette chaise!** what a comfortable chair!; **on est ~ au soleil!** isn't it nice in the sun!; **je me trouve ~ ici** I like it here; **suis mes conseils, tu t'en trouveras ~** take my advice, it'll serve you in good stead; **nous voilà ~!** iron we're in a fine mess!; **4**○ (de qualité) **un quartier ~** a nice district; **des gens ~** respectable people; **un type ~** a gentleman; **un film ~** a good film.

II *adv* **1** (correctement) [*équipé, fait, géré, s'exprimer, dormir, choisir, se souvenir, danser*] well; [*fonctionner*] properly; [*libeller, diagnostiquer, interpréter*] correctly; **~ payé** well paid; **~ joué!** lit well played!; fig well done!; **aller ~** [*personne*] to be well; [*affaires*] to go well; **ça s'est ~ passé** it went well; **la voiture ne marche pas ~** the car isn't running properly ou right; **ni ~ ni mal** so-so; **parler (très) ~ le chinois** to speak (very) good Chinese, to speak Chinese (very) well; **il travaille ~** (élève) his work is good; (artisan) he does a good job; **un travail ~ fait** a good job; **il est ~ remis** (malade) he's made a good recovery; **~ se tenir à table** to have good table manners; **~ employer son temps** to make good use of one's time; **j'ai cru ~ faire** I thought I was doing the right thing; **il fait ~ de partir** he's right to leave; **c'est ~ fait pour elle!** it serves her right!; **tu ferais ~ d'y aller** it would be a good idea for you to go there; **pour ~ faire, il faudrait acheter une lampe** the thing to do would be to buy a lamp; **~ m'en a pris de refuser** it's a good thing I refused; **2** (complètement) [*arroser, décongeler, laver, mélanger, propre, cuit*] thoroughly; [*remplir, sécher, sec, fondu*] completely; [*lire, examiner, écouter, regarder*] carefully; **marche ~ à droite** keep well over to the right; **mets-toi ~ dans le coin/devant** stand right in the corner/at the front; **~ profiter d'une situation** to exploit a situation to the full; **3** (agréablement) [*présenté, situé*] well; [*s'habiller*] well, smartly; [*décoré, meublé*] tastefully; [*logé, installé, vivre*] comfortably; **femme ~ faite** shapely woman; **aller ~ ensemble** to go well together; **aller ~ à qn** [*couleur, style*] to suit sb; **se mettre ~ avec qn** to get on good terms with sb; **~ prendre une remarque** to take a remark in good part; **4** (hautement) [*aimable, triste*] very; [*apprécier, craindre*] very much; [*simple, vrai, certain, évident*] quite; **il s'est ~ mal comporté** he behaved very ou really badly; **il y a ~ longtemps de ça** that was a very long time ago; **c'est ~ loin pour nous** it's rather far for us; **merci ~** thank you very much; **tu as ~ raison** you're quite ou absolutely right; **c'est ~ dommage** it's a great ou real pity; **~ rire/s'amuser/se reposer** to have a good laugh/time/rest; **tu as l'air ~ pensif** you're looking very pensive; **c'est ~ promis?** is that a promise?; **c'est ~ compris?** is that clear?; **~ au contraire** on the contrary; **c'est ~ beau** ou **joli tout ça, mais** that's all very well, but; **~ mieux/moins/pire** much ou far better/less/worse; **~ trop laid/tard** much too ugly/late; **~ plus riche/cher** much ou far richer/more expensive; **~ plus, il la vole!** not only that, he also takes her money; **~ sûr** of course; **~ entendu** or **évidemment** naturally; **~ souvent** quite often; **5** (volontiers) **j'irais ~ à Bali** I wouldn't mind going to Bali; **j'en prendrais ~ un autre** I wouldn't mind another; **je veux ~ t'aider** I don't mind helping you; **j'aimerais ~ essayer** I would love to try; **je te dirais ~ de rester/venir, mais** I would ask you to stay/come but; **je verrais ~ un arbre sur la pelouse** I think a tree would look nice on the lawn; **je le vois ~ habiter à Paris** I can just imagine him living in Paris; **6** (malgré tout) **il faut ~ le faire/que ça finisse** it has to be done/to come to an end; **il faudra ~ s'y habituer** we'll just have to get used to it; **elle sera ~ obligée de payer** she'll just have to pay; **tu aurais ~ pu me le dire** you could at least have told me; **il finira ~ par se calmer** he'll calm down eventually; **7** (pour souligner) **ça prouve/montre ~ que** it just goes to prove/show that; **j'espère ~ que** I do hope that; **je vois/comprends ~** I do see/understand; **je sais/crois ~ que** I know/think that; **insiste ~** make sure you insist; **dis-le lui ~** make sure you tell him/her; **on verra ~** well, we'll see; **sache ~ que je n'accepterai jamais** let me tell you that I will never accept; **crois ~ que je n'hésiterais pas!** you can be sure ou I can assure you that I would not hesitate!; **je m'en doutais ~!** I thought as much!; **je t'avais ~ dit de ne pas le manger!** I told you not to eat it!; **il le fait ~ lui, pourquoi pas moi?** if he can do it, why can't I?; **veux-tu ~ faire ce que je te dis!** will you do as I tell you!; **tu peux très ~ le faire toi-même** you can easily do it yourself; **il se pourrait ~ qu'il pleuve** it might well rain; **que peut-il ~ faire à Paris?** what on earth can he be doing in Paris?; **8** (réellement) definitely; **c'est ~ lui/mon sac** it's definitely him/my bag, it's him/my bag all right○; **j'ai vérifié: il est ~ parti** I checked, he's definitely gone ou he's gone all right○; **c'est ~ ce qu'il a dit/vu** that's definitely ou exactly what he said/saw; **et c'est ~ lui qui conduisait?** and it was definitely him driving?; **il ne s'agit pas d'une erreur, mais ~ de fraude** it's not a mistake, it's fraud; **c'est ~ mardi aujourd'hui?** today is Tuesday, isn't it?; **c'est ~ ici qu'on vend les billets?** this is where you get tickets, isn't it?; **tu as ~ pris les clés?** are you sure you've got the keys?; **est-ce ~ nécessaire?** is it really necessary?; **s'agit-il ~ d'un suicide?** was it really suicide?; **c'est ~ de lui!** it's just like him!; **voilà ~ la politique!** that's politics for you!; **c'est ~ le moment!** iron great timing!; **c'est ~ le moment de partir!** iron what a time to leave!; **9** (au moins) at least; **elle a ~ 40 ans** she's at least 40, she's a good 40 years old; **ça pèse ~ dix kilos** it weighs at least ten kilos, it weighs a good ten kilos; **ça vaut ~ le double** it's worth at least twice as much; **10** (beaucoup) **c'était il y a ~ des années** that was a good many years ago; **~ des fois** often, many a time; **~ des gens** lots of people; **il s'est donné ~ du mal** he's gone to a lot or a great deal of trouble; **il s'en faut ~!** far from it!; **mon fils me donne ~ du souci** my son is a great worry to me; **avoir ~ de la chance** to be very lucky; **je te souhaite ~ du plaisir!** iron I wish you joy!

III *nm* **1** (avantage) good; **pour le ~ du pays** for the good of the country; **pour le ~ de tous** for the general good; **c'est pour ton ~** it's for your own good; **ce serait un ~** it would be a good thing; **sacrifier son propre ~ à celui d'autrui** to put others first; **le ~ et le mal** good and evil; **faire le ~** to do good; **il a fait beaucoup de ~ autour de lui** he has done a lot of good; **ça fait du ~ aux enfants/plantes** it's good for the children /plants; **ça fait/ça leur fait du ~** it does you/them good; **mon repos m'a fait le plus grand ~** my rest did me a world of good; **grand ~ vous fasse!** iron much good may it do you!; **vouloir le ~ de qn** to have sb's best interests at heart; **vouloir du ~ à qn** to wish sb well; **'un ami qui vous veut du ~'** (dans une lettre anonyme) 'from a well-wisher', 'one who has your best interests at heart'; **dire du ~ de qn** to speak well of sb; **on dit le plus grand ~ du maire/musée** people speak very highly of the mayor/museum; **on a dit le plus grand ~ de toi** a lot of nice things were said about you; **parler en ~ de qn** to speak favourably[GB] of sb; ▶ **ennemi**, **honneur**; **2** (possession) possession; (maison, terres) property; (domaine) **~(s)** estate; (ensemble des possessions) **~(s)** property ¢; (patrimoine) **~(s)** fortune; (avoirs) **~s** assets; **perdre tous ses ~s dans un incendie** to lose all one's possessions in a fire; **ce livre est mon ~ le plus précieux** this book is my most precious possession; **les ~s de ce monde** material possessions; **un petit ~ en Corse** a small property in Corsica; **hériter des ~s paternels** to inherit one's father's property ou estate; **dilapider son ~** to squander one's fortune; **avoir du ~** (maisons, terres) to own property; (argent) to be wealthy; **des ~s considérables** substantial assets; **la santé/liberté est le plus précieux des ~s** you can't put a price on good health/freedom; ▶ **abondance**, **acquis**.

IV *excl* **1** (approbatif) **~! voyons le reste** good! let's see the rest; **2** (impatient) **~! ~! j'arrive!** all right! all right! ou OK! OK○! I'm coming!

V bien que *loc conj* although, though; **~ qu'il le sache** although he knows; **~ qu'elle vive maintenant en Floride, je la vois régulièrement** although she lives in Florida, I see her regularly; **il est venu travailler ~ qu'il soit grippé** he came in to work, although he had flu; **~ que très différentes en apparence, les deux œuvres ont des points communs** although very different in appearance, the two works have common features; **il joue un rôle important ~ que discret** he plays an important role, albeit a discreet one; ▶ **aussi**, **ou**, **si**.

■ **~s de consommation** consumer goods; **~s durables** consumer durables; **~s d'équipement** capital goods; **~s d'équipement ménager** household goods; **~s fonciers** land ¢; **~s immeubles** immovables; **~s immeubles par destination** fixtures; **~s immobiliers** real estate ¢; **~s mobiliers** personal property ¢; **~s personnels** private property ¢; **~s propres** separate estate (*sg*); **détenir qch en ~ s propres** to hold sth as separate estate; **~s publics** public property ¢; **~s sociaux** corporate assets.

bien-être /bjɛ̃nɛtʀ/ *nm* **1** (sensation agréable) well-being; **un sentiment de ~** a feeling of well-being; **le ~ social** the well-being of society; **2** (protection sociale) welfare (**de** of); **préserver le ~ des enfants** to ensure the children's welfare; **3** (situation matérielle satisfaisante) comforts (*pl*); **~ matériel** material comforts.

bienfaisance /bjɛ̃fəzɑ̃s/ *nf* charity; **société de ~** charity, charitable organization; **c'est pour une œuvre de ~** it's for charity; **soirée de ~** charity gala.

bienfaisant, ~e /bjɛ̃fəzɑ̃, ɑ̃t/ *adj* **1** [*traitement, influence*] beneficial; **2** [*personne*] beneficent.

bienfait /bjɛ̃fɛ/ *nm* **1** (acte généreux) kind deed; **c'est un ~ du ciel** it's a godsend; **2** (effet bénéfique) beneficial effect.

IDIOMES **un ~ n'est jamais perdu** a good turn is never wasted.

bienfaiteur /bjɛ̃fɛtœʀ/ *nm* benefactor.

bienfaitrice /bjɛ̃fɛtʀis/ *nf* benefactress.

bien-fondé /bjɛ̃fɔ̃de/ *nm* **1** gén (d'idée) validity; **2** Jur (de demande) legitimacy.

bienheureux, -euse /bjɛ̃nøʀø, øz/ **I** *adj* **1** liter blessed, happy; **2** Relig blessed, blest; **~ les pauvres en esprit** blessed are the poor in spirit.

II *nm,f* Relig **le ~ Adrien** the Blessed Adrian; **les ~** the blessed; **Basile le ~** St Basil the Blessed.

biennal, ~e, *mpl* **-aux** /bjenal, o/ **I** *adj* biennial.

II biennale *nf* biennial event; **~e de la danse** biennial festival of dance.

bien-pensant, ~e, *mpl* **~s** /bjɛ̃pɑ̃sɑ̃, ɑ̃t/ **I** *adj* [*personne*] right-thinking; péj self-righteous.

II *nm,f* right-thinking person; péj self-righteous person.

bienséance /bjɛ̃seɑ̃s/ *nf* fml propriety sout; **les règles de la ~** the rules of polite society.

bienséant, ~e /bjɛ̃seɑ̃, ɑ̃t/ *adj* fml seemly.

bientôt /bjɛ̃to/ *adv* **1** (dans peu de temps, peu de temps après) soon; **je reviens** or **reviendrai ~** I'll be back soon; **ce départ, c'est pour ~?** are you leaving soon?; **~, on pourra aller sur la lune** before long ou soon we'll be able to travel to the moon; **à ~** see you soon; **on est ~ servis?** are we going to be served soon?; **à ~ le plaisir de vous lire** I look forward to hearing from you soon; **mais, ~, tout recommença** but soon it all started again; **2** (presque) nearly; **c'est ~ Noël** it's nearly Christmas, it'll soon be Christmas; **on est ~ arrivés?** are we nearly there?; **voilà ~ 2 ans qu'il est parti** it's nearly 2 years since he left; **ça fait ~ 2 ans que je travaille** I've been working for nearly 2 years.

bienveillance /bjɛ̃vɛjɑ̃s/ *nf* benevolence (**envers** to); **avec ~** [*regarder, parler, sourire*] benevolently; **par ~** out of kindness; **étudier une requête avec ~** to look at a request favourably[GB]; **je sollicite de votre haute ~** fml may I respectfully request.

bienveillant, ~e /bjɛ̃vɛjɑ̃, ɑ̃t/ *adj* benevolent.

bienvenu, ~e /bjɛ̃vəny/ **I** *adj* welcome.

II *nm,f* **être le ~** to be welcome; **soyez la ~e** welcome!

III bienvenue *nf* welcome (**à, dans** to); **~e dans notre pays** welcome to our country; **souhaiter la ~e à qn** to welcome sb; **en signe de ~e** in welcome.

bière /bjɛʀ/ *nf* **1** (boisson) beer; **de la ~** beer; **deux ~s** two beers; **~ en bouteille** bottled beer; **~ (à la) pression** or **en fût** C draught GB or draft US beer; **2** (cercueil) coffin, casket US; **mettre qn en ~** to lay sb in a coffin; **mise en ~** laying in the coffin.

■ **~ blonde** lager, light ale GB; **~ brune** stout; **~ rousse** bitter; (plus fort) brown ale.

IDIOMES **c'est de la petite ~** it's (pretty) small beer GB ou small potatoes US; **ce n'est pas de la petite ~** it's something quite important.

biface /bifas/ **I** *adj* bifacial.

II *nm* biface.

biffer /bife/ [1] *vtr* to cross out.

biffure /bifyʀ/ *nf* (action) crossing out; (trait) crossing-out GB, erasure US.

bifidus /bifidys/ *nm inv* bifidus.

bifocal, ~e, *mpl* **-aux** /bifɔkal, o/ *adj* bifocal; **des lunettes ~es** bifocals.

bifteck /biftɛk/ *nm* steak; **~ de cheval** horsemeat steak.

■ **~ haché** beefburger.

IDIOMES **gagner son ~**○ to earn a living ou crust GB; **défendre son ~**○ to look out for number one○.

bifurcation /bifyʀkasjɔ̃/ *nf* **1** (de route, voie ferrée) fork, junction; **2** Bot, Anat branching, bifurcation spéc; **3** (dans des études) option.

bifurquer /bifyʀke/ [1] *vi* **1** [*route, voie ferrée*] to fork, to branch off; [*tige, artère*] to branch, to bifurcate; **2** [*automobiliste*] to turn off; **~ sur** or **vers la gauche** to turn off to the left; **3** (dans ses études, sa carrière) to change tack.

bigame /bigam/ **I** *adj* bigamous.

II *nmf* bigamist.

bigamie /bigami/ *nf* bigamy.

bigarade /bigaʀad/ *nf* Seville orange, bitter orange; **sauce ~** orange sauce.

bigaradier /bigaʀadje/ *nm* Seville orange tree, bitter orange tree.

bigarré, ~e /bigaʀe/ *adj* **1** (multicolore) [*tissu*] multicoloured[GB]; [*foule*] colourful[GB]; **2** (varié) [*foule, société*] colourful[GB].

bigarreau, *pl* **~x** /bigaʀo/ *nm* bigarreau, cherry.

bigarrure /bigaʀyʀ/ *nf* multicoloured[GB] pattern; **les ~s de sa robe** the multicoloured[GB] patterns on her dress.

big-bang /bigbɑ̃g/ *nm inv* big bang.

bigleux○, **-euse** /biglø, øz/ *adj* pej poor-sighted; **il était complètement ~** he was as blind as a bat.

bigophone◑ /bigɔfɔn/ *nm* phone, horn○ US.

bigophoner◑ /bigɔfɔne/ [1] **I** *vtr* to give sb a buzz○, to call sb.

II se bigophoner *vpr* to call ou phone each other.

bigorneau, *pl* **~x** /bigɔʀno/ *nm* winkle.

bigorner◑ /bigɔʀne/ [1] *vtr* to prang○ GB, to bang up US [*voiture*].

bigot, ~e /bigo, ɔt/ **I** *adj* pej zealously religious.

II *nm,f* religious zealot.

bigoterie /bigɔtʀi/ *nf* pej religious bigotry.

bigoudi /bigudi/ *nm* curler, roller; **en ~s** in curlers ou rollers; **mettre des ~s** to put curlers ou rollers in; **~s chauffants** heated rollers.

bigre○† /bigʀ/ *excl* hum crikey○, my goodness!

bigrement○† /bigʀəmɑ̃/ *adv* hum jolly○ GB, extremely.

biguine /bigin/ *nf* biguine (*type of Caribbean dance*).

bihebdomadaire /biɛbdɔmadɛʀ/ **I** *adj* twice-weekly.

II *nm* twice-weekly publication.

bijectif, -ive /biʒɛktif, iv/ *adj* bijective.

bijection /biʒɛksjɔ̃/ *nf* bijection.

bijou, *pl* **~x** /biʒu/ *nm* piece of jewellery GB ou jewelry US; (de très grande valeur) jewel; **~x en or** gold jewellery GB ou jewelry US; **~x (de) fantaisie** costume jewellery GB ou jewelry US; **boîte à ~x** jewellery GB ou jewelry US box; **~ de famille** piece of family jewellery GB ou jewelry US; **~x de famille** family jewels also hum; **leur maison est un vrai ~** their house is an absolute gem; **un petit ~ mécanique** a marvel of engineering.

bijouterie /biʒutʀi/ **▶510** *nf* **1** (magasin) jeweller's GB, jewellery shop GB, jewelry store US; **2** (bijoux, art) jewellery GB, jewelry US; **3** (commerce) jewellery GB ou jewelry US trade.

bijoutier, -ière /biʒutje, ɛʀ/ **▶510** *nm,f* jeweller[GB]

bikini® /bikini/ *nm* bikini®.

bilabiale /bilabjal/ *adj f, nf* bilabial.

bilame /bilam/ *nm* bimetallic strip.

bilan /bilɑ̃/ *nm* **1** Compta balance sheet; **~ provisoire** interim balance sheet; **dresser** or **établir un ~** to draw up a balance sheet; **~ de fin d'exercice/de vérification** closing/trial balance; **déposer son ~** to file a petition in bankruptcy; **demander un dépôt de ~** to file for bankruptcy; **hors ~** [*passif*] off balance sheet; **2** (aboutissement) outcome; **3** (de catastrophe, d'accident) toll; **le ~ des feux de forêt** the toll of forest fires; **~ officiel** official toll; **'accident de voiture, ~: deux morts'** 'two killed in a car accident'; **4** (évaluation) assessment; **faire** or **dresser le ~ de qch** to assess sth; **quel ~ tirez-vous de...?** what is your assessment of...?; **quel est le ~ de l'année?** how did the year turn out?; **5** (compte-rendu) report; **le ~ d'activité du comité pour 1990** the committee's annual report for 1990; **présenter un ~ des ventes** to report on sales.

■ **~ de liquidation** statement of affairs (in a bankruptcy petition); **~ médical** = **~ de santé**; **~ professionnel** performance appraisal; **~ de santé** check-up; **se faire faire un ~ de santé** to have a check-up; **~ social** Entr social balance sheet; gén (d'une politique) social consequences.

bilatéral, ~e, *mpl* **-aux** /bilateʀal, o/ *adj* [*négociations, traité, contrat*] bilateral; **stationnement ~** parking on both sides of the street.

bilboquet /bilbɔkɛ/ **▶449** *nm* cup-and-ball.

bile /bil/ *nf* bile.

IDIOMES **se faire de la ~**○ to worry, to fret (**pour qch** over sth); **déverser** or **cracher sa ~**○ to vent one's spleen; **échauffer la ~ de qn**○ to make sb's blood boil, to rile○ sb.

biler: se biler○ /bile/ [1] *vpr* to worry, to fret (**pour qch** about qch).

bileux○, **-euse** /bilø, øz/ **I** *adj* **être ~, avoir un caractère ~** to be a worrier; **ne pas être ~** not to let things get to one.

II *nm,f* worrier.

bilharziose /bilaʀzjoz/ **▶271** *nf* bilharziasis.

biliaire /biljɛʀ/ *adj* biliary.

bilieux, -ieuse /biljø, øz/ **I** *adj* **1** Méd bilious; **2** (coléreux) irritable.

II *nm,f* (personne colérique) irritable person.

bilingue /bilɛ̃g/ *adj* [*texte, personne*] bilingual.

bilinguisme /bilɛ̃gɥism/ *nm* bilingualism.

billard /bijaʀ/ **▶449** *nm* (jeu) billiards (+ *v sg*); (salle) billiard room; (table) billiard table.

■ **~ américain** pool; **~ anglais** snooker; **~ électrique** pinball machine.

IDIOMES **c'est du ~**○ it's a doddle○ GB ou cinch○; **passer sur le ~**○ to have an operation.

bille /bij/ *nf* **1 ▶449** Jeux (d'enfant) marble; (au billard) (billiard) ball; **jouer aux ~s** to play GB ou shoot US marbles; **2** (petite boule) Tech ball; **roulement à ~s** ball bearing; **déodorant à ~** roll-on deodorant; **3** (bois) cut length of tree trunk; **4**○ (tête) mug○, face; **5**○ (idiot) twit○ GB, nitwit.

IDIOMES **reprendre** or **retirer ses ~s**○ to pull out; **placer ses ~s**○ to stake out one's position; **il a mal placé ses ~s**○ he backed the wrong horse; **foncer ~ en tête**○ to go blindly ahead.

billet /bijɛ/ *nm* **1** (argent) (bank)note, bill US; **~ de 100 francs** 100-franc note; **faux ~** forged (bank)note ou bill; **2** Transp ticket; **~ de bus/d'avion** bus/plane ticket; **~ circulaire/collectif** round-trip/group ticket; **~ à prix réduit** cheap ticket; **j'ai perdu mon ~ de retour** I've lost my return ticket; **3** (d'admission) ticket; **~ de théâtre/parking/loterie** theatre/car park/lottery ticket; **4** Comm note, bill; **5** Presse short article; **6** (lettre) †or liter note.

■ **~ de banque** banknote, bank bill US; **~ doux** love letter; **~ de faveur** complimentary ticket; **~ de logement** Mil billet; **~ à ordre** Comm promissory note; **~ au porteur** bearer order ; **~ à présentation** bill payable on demand; **~ de retard** Scol late note; Admin, Entr *note from transport company explaining delay to worker's employer*; **~ de trésorerie** Fin commercial paper; **~ vert**○ dollar, greenback○ US.

IDIOMES **je te fiche mon ~ que**○ I bet you anything that.

billetterie /bijɛtʀi/ *nf* **1** (de billets de banque) cash dispenser; **2** (de billets de théâtre, voyage) ticket agency; **3** (activité) issuing of tickets.

■ **~ automatique** ticket machine.

billettiste /bijɛtist/ **▶510** *nmf* **1** Journ writer of short articles; **2** (employé) ticket clerk.

billevesées /bilvəze, bijvəze/ *nfpl* fml nonsense ¢.

billion /biljɔ̃/ **▶545** *nm* (mille milliards) billion GB, trillion US.

billot /bijo/ *nm* block; **▶ tête**.

bilobé, ~e /bilɔbe/ *adj* bilobate.

bimane /biman/ *adj* bimanous.

bimbeloterie /bɛ̃blɔtʀi/ *nf* **1** (objets) knick-knacks (*pl*); Comm fancy goods (*pl*); **2** (commerce) fancy goods trade.

bimensuel, **-elle** /bimɑ̃sɥɛl/ **I** *adj* fortnightly GB, semimonthly US.
II *nm* (journal) fortnightly paper GB, semimonthly US; (revue) fortnightly magazine GB, semimonthly US.

bimensuellement /bimɑ̃sɥɛlmɑ̃/ *adv* fortnightly GB, twice a month.

bimestriel, **-ielle** /bimɛstʀijɛl/ **I** *adj* bimonthly.
II *nm* (revue) bimonthly magazine.

bimétallique /bimetalik/ *adj* bimetallic.

bimétallisme /bimetalism/ *nm* bimetallism.

bimoteur /bimɔtœʀ/ **I** *adj* twin-engined.
II *nm* (avion) twin-engined plane.

binage /binaʒ/ *nm* hoeing.

binaire /binɛʀ/ *adj* binary.

biner /bine/ [1] *vtr* to hoe.

binette /binɛt/ *nf* **1** (outil) hoe; **2**○ (visage) face.

bing /biŋ/ *excl* bang.

bingo /biŋo/ **I** ▶ 449 *nm* ≈ bingo.
II *excl* bingo!

biniou /binju/ *nm* Breton bagpipes (*pl*).

binoclard○, **~e** /binɔklaʀ, aʀd/ **I** *adj* pej four-eyed○.
II *nm,f* pej four-eyes○.

binocle /binɔkl/ **I** *nm* pince-nez.
II binocles○ *nfpl* specs○, glasses.

binoculaire /binɔkylɛʀ/ *adj* binocular.

binôme /binom/ *nm* **1** Math binomial; **2** students' slang (personne) partner (*for practical work in science*); **travailler en ~** to work in pairs.

binomial, **~e**, *mpl* **-iaux** /binɔmjal, o/ *adj* [*loi, nomenclature*] binomial.

bio[1] /bjo/ *préf* bio; **bioclimatologie** bioclimatology; **biogéographie** biogeography; **bioluminescence** bioluminescence.

bio[2] /bjo/ **I** *adj inv* (naturel) **aliments ~** health foods; **produits ~** organic produce ¢; **avoir des goûts ~** to be a health food freak; **yaourt ~** bio yoghurt.
II○ *nf* (biographie) biography.

biocapteur /bjokaptœʀ/ *nm* biosensor.

biocarburant /bjokaʀbyʀɑ̃/ *nm* bio-fuel.

biochimie /bjoʃimi/ *nf* biochemistry.

biochimique /bjoʃimik/ *adj* [*composé, réaction*] biochemical; **usine ~** biochemicals factory ou plant.

biochimiste /bjoʃimist/ ▶ 510 *nmf* biochemist.

biodégradable /bjodegʀadabl/ *adj* biodegradable.

bioénergie /bjoenɛʀʒi/ *nf* bioenergetics (+ *v sg*).

bioéthique /bjoetik/ **I** *adj* bioethical.
II *nf* bioethics (+ *v sg*).

biographe /bjɔgʀaf/ *nmf* biographer.

biographie /bjɔgʀafi/ *nf* biography.

biographique /bjɔgʀafik/ *adj* biographical.

biologie /bjɔlɔʒi/ *nf* biology.

biologique /bjɔlɔʒik/ *adj* **1** Biol biological; **2** Agric [*ferme, produit, pain*] organic.

biologiste /bjɔlɔʒist/ ▶ 510 *nmf* biologist.

biomasse /bjomas/ *nf* biomass.

biomatériau, *pl* **~x** /bjomateʀjo/ *nm* biocompatible material.

biomédecine /bjomedsin/ *nf* biomedicine.

biomédical, **~e**, *mpl* **-aux** /bjomedikal, o/ *adj* biomedical.

bionique /bjɔnik/ *nf* bionics (+ *v sg*).

biophysicien, **-ienne** /bjofizisjɛ̃, ɛn/ ▶ 510 *nm,f* biophysicist.

biophysique /bjofisik/ *nf* biophysics (+ *v sg*).

biopsie /bjɔpsi/ *nf* biopsy.

biorythme /bjoʀitm/ *nm* biorhythm.

biosphère /bjosfɛʀ/ *nf* biosphere.

biosynthèse /bjosɛ̃tɛz/ *nf* biosynthesis.

biotechnologie /bjotɛknɔlɔʒi/ *nf* biotechnology.

biotope /bjɔtɔp/ *nm* biotope.

bioxyde† /biɔksid/ *nm* dioxide.

bip /bip/ *nm* **1** (son) beep; **~ sonore** tone; **2** (appareil) beeper; **appeler qn au ~** to beep sb.

biparti, **~e** /bipaʀti/ = **bipartite**.

bipartisme /bipaʀtism/ *nm* two-party system.

bipartite /bipaʀtit/ *adj* **1** Bot bipartite; **2** Pol two-party, bipartite.

bipède /bipɛd/ *nm* biped.

biper /bipe/ [1] *vtr* to beep.

biphasé, **~e** /bifɑze/ *adj* two-phase.

biplace /biplas/ *adj, nm* two-seater.

biplan /biplɑ̃/ **I** *adj m* **avion ~** biplane.
II *nm* biplane.

bipolaire /bipɔlɛʀ/ *adj* bipolar.

bipolarisation /bipɔlaʀizasjɔ̃/ *nf* Pol bipolarization.

bipolarité /bipɔlaʀite/ *nf* bipolarity.

bique○ /bik/ *nf* **1** (chèvre) nanny-goat; **2** (femme) pej bag○, nasty woman; **une vieille ~** an old bag○; **une (grande) ~** a great ninny.

biquet○ /bikɛ/ *nm* **1** Zool (chevreau) kid; **2** (terme d'affection) **mon ~** sweetheart○.

biquette○ /bikɛt/ *nf* **1** (jeune chèvre) young female goat; **2** (terme d'affection) **ma ~** sweetheart○.

biquotidien, **-ienne** /bikɔtidjɛ̃, ɛn/ *adj* twice-daily.

birbe‡ /biʀb/ *nm* **un vieux ~** an old fogey[GB].

biréacteur /biʀeaktœʀ/ *nm* twin-engined jet.

biréfringent, **~e** /biʀefʀɛ̃ʒɑ̃, ɑ̃t/ *adj* birefringent.

birème /biʀɛm/ *nf* bireme.

birman, **~e** /biʀmɑ̃, an/ ▶ 462, 537 **I** *adj* Burmese.
II *nm* Ling Burmese.

Birman, **~e** /biʀmɑ̃, an/ ▶ 537 *nm,f* Burmese.

Birmanie /biʀmani/ ▶ 321 *nprf* Burma.

bis[1] /bis/ **I** *adv* **1** (dans une adresse) **15 ~** 15 bis; **2** Mus (indication) bis, repeat.
II *nm inv* (œuvre supplémentaire) encore; **l'orchestre a donné** or **joué trois ~** the orchestra did three encores; **le ténor a donné un air de Mozart en ~** the tenor sang a Mozart aria as an encore.

bis[2], **~e** /bi, biz/ ▶ 193 **I** *adj* [*couleur*] greyish GB ou grayish US brown.
II bise *nf* **1**○ (baiser) kiss; **une grosse ~e** a smacker○, a big kiss; **donner** or **faire une ~e à qn** to give sb a kiss, to kiss sb; **faire la ~e à qn** to kiss sb on the cheeks; **se faire la ~e** to kiss each other on the cheeks; **2** Météo (vent) North wind.

bisaïeul, **~e** /bizajœl/ *nm,f* fml great-grandfather/-grandmother.

bisannuel, **-elle** /bizanɥɛl/ *adj* biennial.

bisbille○ /bizbij/ *nf* quarrel; **être en ~ avec qn** to be on bad terms with sb.

biscornu, **~e** /biskɔʀny/ *adj* [*esprit, idée, architecture*] quirky, cranky○.

biscotte /biskɔt/ *nf* continental toast.

biscuit /biskɥi/ *nm* **1** (petit gâteau sec) biscuit GB, cookie US; (gâteau) sponge cake; **2** (porcelaine) biscuit, bisque; (objet) piece of biscuit ware.
■ **~ apéritif** cocktail biscuit GB ou cracker US; **~ pour chien** dog biscuit; **~ à la cuiller** sponge GB ou lady US finger; **~ salé** cracker; (petit) cocktail biscuit GB ou cracker US; **~ de Savoie** sponge cake.
IDIOMES **s'embarquer sans ~** to launch into something with no backup.

biscuiterie /biskɥitʀi/ *nf* (fabrication) biscuit GB ou cookie US making; (fabrique) biscuit GB ou cookie US factory.

bise ▶ **bis**[2].

biseau, *pl* **~x** /bizo/ *nm* **1** (bord) bevel (edge); **tailler en ~** to bevel; **glace en ~** bevelled[GB] mirror; **2** (outil) bevel; **tailler au ~** to bevel.

biseautage /bizotaʒ/ *nm* bevelling[GB].

biseauter /bizote/ [1] *vtr* **1** Tech to bevel; **2** (aux cartes) to mark [*carte*]; **cartes biseautées** marked cards.

bisexualité /bisɛksɥalite/ *nf* bisexuality.

bisexué, **~e** /bisɛksɥe/ *adj* bisexual.

bisexuel, **-elle** /bisɛksɥɛl/ *adj, nm,f* bisexual.

bismuth /bismyt/ *nm* bismuth.

bison /bizɔ̃/ *nm* (d'Europe) bison; (d'Amérique) buffalo, American bison.

Bison Futé® /bizɔ̃fyte/ *nm*: *TV and radio traffic monitoring service.*

bisontin, **~e** /bizɔ̃tɛ̃, in/ ▶ 857 *adj* of Besançon.

Bisontin, **~e** /bizɔ̃tɛ̃, in/ *nm,f* (natif) native of Besançon; (habitant) inhabitant of Besançon.

bisou○ /bizu/ *nm* baby talk kiss; **faire un ~ à qn** to kiss sb, to give sb a kiss; **envoyer des ~s** (avec la main) to blow kisses; (par lettre) to send kisses.

bisque /bisk/ *nf* Culin bisque.
■ **~ de homard** lobster bisque.

bisquer○ /biske/ [1] *vi* (enrager) to be mad○, to be furious; **faire ~ qn** to make sb mad○.

bissac /bisak/ *nm* (huntsman's) pouch.

bissecteur, **-trice** /bisɛktœʀ, tʀis/ **I** *adj* [*plan, droite*] bisecting.
II bissectrice *nf* Math bisector.

bisser /bise/ [1] *vtr* **1** (répéter) [*musicien, orchestre*] to do an encore of, to play [sth] again [*morceau*]; [*comédien, troupe*] to do an encore of, to perform [sth] again [*scène*]; **2** (faire répéter) [*public*] to encore, to ask [sb] for an encore [*musicien, orchestre, comédien*].

bissextile /bisɛkstil/ *adj* **année ~** leap year, bissextile year.

bistouri /bistuʀi/ *nm* bistoury.
■ **~ électrique** diathermy knife.

bistre /bistʀ/ ▶ 193 **I** *adj* [*couleur*] yellowish brown; [*peinture*] bistre[GB]; [*peau*] swarthy.
II *nm* (couleur) bistre[GB].

bistré, **~e** /bistʀe/ ▶ 193 *adj* [*couleur*] yellowish brown; [*peau*] swarthy.

bistro(t)○ /bistʀo/ *nm* bistro, café.

bistroquet○ /bistʀɔkɛ/ *nm* bistro.

bit /bit/ *nm* bit.

BIT /beite/ *nm* (*abbr* = **Bureau international du travail**) International Labour Office.

bite● *nf* = **bitte 2**.

biter● [1] *vtr* = **bitter**.

biterrois, **~e** /bitɛʀwa, az/ ▶ 857 *adj* of Béziers.

Biterrois, **~e** /bitɛʀwa, az/ ▶ 857 *nm,f* (natif) native of Béziers; (habitant) inhabitant of Béziers.

bitoniau○ /bitonjo/ *nm* whatsit○.

bitte /bit/ *nf* **1** (sur un navire) bitt; (sur un quai) **~ d'amarrage** mooring bollard; **2**● (pénis) prick●, cock●.

bitter● /bite/ [1] *vtr* **ne rien ~ à** to understand fuck all● ou zilch○ of [*discours*]; to understand fuck● all ou zilch○ about [*sujet*].

bitumage /bitymaʒ/ *nm* asphalting, blacktopping US.

bitume /bitym/ *nm* **1** Chimie, Minér bitumen; **2** Transp Tarmac®, asphalt, blacktop US.

bitumer /bityme/ [1] *vtr* to asphalt, to tarmac, to blacktop US [*route*]; to coat [sth] with bitumen [*toile*].

bitumineux, **-euse** /bityminø, øz/ *adj* bituminous.

biture○ /bityʀ/ *nf* **quelle ~!** what a booze-up○ GB ou bender○!; **tenir/prendre une (bonne) ~** to be/to get plastered○ ou drunk.

biturer: **se biturer** /bityʀe/ [1] *vpr* to get plastered○, to get drunk.

biunivoque /biynivɔk/ *adj* Math [*correspondance*] bi-uniform, one-to-one.

bivalent, **~e** /bivalɑ̃, ɑ̃t/ *adj* bivalent.

bivalve /bivalv/ *adj, nm* bivalve.

bivouac /bivwak/ *nm* bivouac.

bivouaquer /bivwake/ [1] *vi* to bivouac.

bizarre /bizaʀ/ **I** *adj* **1** (inhabituel) [*objet, parole, événement, acte, attitude*] strange, odd; **il leur est arrivé une aventure ~** something strange ou odd happened to them; **comme c'est ~** how strange ou odd; **2** (étrange) [*personne*] strange, peculiar; **il est ~** he's strange ou peculiar.
II *nm* (d'idée, d'acte, de parole) strangeness, oddity; **le ~ dans cette affaire est que** what is strange ou odd about this business is that.

bizarrement /bizaʀmɑ̃/ *adv* strangely; **~, elle a préféré partir** strangely enough, she thought it better to go.

bizarrerie /bizaʀʀi/ *nf* **1** (caractère étrange) strangeness (**de** of); **2** (chose étrange) quirk; **une ~ du destin** a quirk of fate; **une ~ de l'Histoire** a strange turn of history; **une ~ de la langue** a peculiarity of the language.

bizarroïde○ /bizaʀɔid/ *adj* weird○.

bizut(h) /bizy/ *nm* **1** (étudiant) fresher○ GB, freshman US; **2** (novice) newcomer, rookie○.

bizutage /bizytaʒ/ *nm* students' slang ragging○ GB ¢, hazing○ US ¢.

bizuter /bizyte/ [1] *vtr* to rag○, to haze○ US [*étudiant*]; (brimer) to bully [*nouveau*]; **se faire ~** [*étudiant*] to be ragged○ GB ou hazed○ US.

blabla○ /blabla/ *nm inv* waffle○ GB, hogwash○ US; **tout ça, c'est du ~!** what a load of waffle! GB ou hogwash! US.

blackbouler○ /blakbule/ [1] *vtr* to blackball [*personne, candidat*].

black-out /blakaut/ *nm inv* blackout.

blafard, **~e** /blafaʀ, aʀd/ *adj* [*teint, visage*] pallid; [*paysage, lumière, aube*] pale, wan.

blague /blag/ *nf* **1**○ (plaisanterie, histoire) joke; (mensonge) fib○; **c'est pas des ~s** I'm not kidding○, no kidding○; **ne me raconte pas de ~s** tell me the truth; **sans ~!** no kidding○!; **~ à part** seriously, joking apart; **2**○ (farce) practical joke, trick; **faire une ~ à qn** to play a joke ou a trick on sb; **pas de ~!** no messing around!; **3** (tabatière) **~ (à tabac)** tobacco pouch.

blaguer○ /blage/ [1] *vi* **1** (plaisanter) to joke, to crack jokes; **il dit ça pour ~** he's kidding○; **arrête de ~** stop kidding around○; **2** (bavarder) to chat.

blagueur○, **-euse** /blagœʀ, øz/ *nm,f* joker.

blair◑ /blɛʀ/ *nm* snout○, nose.

blaireau, *pl* **~x** /blɛʀo/ *nm* **1** (animal) badger; **2** (pour rasage) shaving brush; **3** (pinceau) badger-hair brush.

blairer◑ /bleʀe/ [1] *vtr* to stick○ GB, to stand [*personne*]; **je ne peux pas le ~** I can't stick○ GB ou stand him.

blâmable /blɑmabl/ *adj* blameworthy.

blâme /blɑm/ *nm* **1** (désapprobation) criticism; **2** (sanction) official warning; **infliger un ~ à qn** to give sb an official warning.

blâmer /blɑme/ [1] *vtr* (désapprouver) to criticize; **~ qn pour qch** to criticize ou censure sb for sth; **le public n'a pas applaudi, on ne peut pas le ~** the public did not applaud and you can't blame them; **ils sont plus à plaindre qu'à ~** they're more to be pitied than condemned.

blanc, **blanche** /blɑ̃, blɑ̃ʃ/ ▶ 193 **I** *adj* **1** (couleur) white; **fleurs/dents/chaussettes blanches** white flowers/teeth/socks; **~ mat/brillant** matt/glossy white; **devenir ~** to go ou turn white; **~ de peur** white with fear; ▶ **aspirine**, **cheveu**, **coudre**, **crapaud**, **loup**, **patte**; **2** (occidental) gén white; Anthrop Caucasian; **homme/quartier ~** white man/district; **race/domination blanche** white race/domination; **3** (innocent) **il n'est pas ~ dans l'histoire** he was certainly mixed up in it; **ne pas être ~** to have a less than spotless reputation; **4** (vierge) blank; **page/feuille blanche** blank page/sheet; **rendre feuille** or **copie ~** Scol, Univ to give in a blank script; **5** Vin [*vin*] white; **Bordeaux/Bourgogne ~** white Bordeaux/Burgundy.
II *adv* [*laver*] white; **laver plus ~** to wash whiter; **il gèle ~** there's a hoarfrost.
III *nm* **1** (couleur) white; **un beau ~** a beautiful white; **un ~ éclatant** a dazzling white; **2** (peinture) white paint; **un tube de ~** a tube of white paint; **peindre en ~**, **passer au ~** to paint [sth] white [*mur, meuble*]; **3** (linge) household linen; **promotion de ~** household linen promotional sales; **quinzaine du ~** household linen sales period; **4** (vêtements) white; **porter du ~** to wear white; **être habillé en ~** to be dressed in white; **5** Culin (de volaille) white meat; (de poireau) white part; (d'œuf) white; **battre les ~s** beat the whites; **un ~ de poulet** a chicken breast; **je préfère le ~** I prefer white meat; ▶ **neige**; **6** Vin (vin) white wine; (verre de vin) glass of white wine; **préférer le ~** to prefer white wine; **7** Imprim (espace entre des mots) (volontaire) blank; (involontaire) gap; **laisser un ~** to leave a blank; **remplir les ~s** to fill in the blanks; **il y a un ~ dans le texte** there's a gap in the text; **laisser en ~** to leave [sth] blank [*nom, adresse*]; **8**○ (liquide pour corriger les erreurs) correction fluid, Tipp-Ex®, white-out US; **mettre du ~ sur qch** to Tipp-Ex sth out, to white sth out US [*texte, erreur*]; **9** (temps mort) lull; **10** Psych (dans la tête) **j'ai eu un ~** my mind went blank; **11** Cosmét (poudre) white powder; **12** Bot (moisissure) powdery mildew.
IV à blanc *loc* Mil (sans projectile offensif) **coup à ~** blank shot; **tirer à ~** to fire blanks; **charger à ~** to load [sth] with blanks.
V blancs *nmpl* Jeux (aux échecs, aux dames) white (*sg*); **les ~s gagnent** white wins; **je prends les ~s** I'll be white.
VI blanche *nf* **1** Mus minim GB, half note US; **2** Jeux (au billard) white (ball); **3**○ (eau-de-vie) brandy; **4**◑ (héroïne) smack○, horse○; (cocaïne) snow○.
■ **~ de baleine** spermaceti; **~ de blanc** blanc de blancs; **~ cassé** off-white; **~ de céruse** white lead; **~ de chaux** whitewash; **~ crémeux** cream; **~ d'Espagne** whiting; **~ laiteux** milk white; **~ de l'œil** white of the eye; **~ d'œuf** egg white; **~ de plomb** flake white; **~ de zinc** zinc oxide.
IDIOMES **c'est écrit noir sur ~** it's there in black and white; **quand l'un dit ~, l'autre dit noir** they can never agree on anything; **avec lui/elle, c'est (toujours) tout ~ ou tout noir** he/she sees everything in black-and-white terms; **c'est un jour à marquer d'une pierre** or **croix blanche** it's a red-letter day, it's a day to remember; **regarder qn dans le ~ des yeux** to look sb straight in the eye; **se regarder dans le ~ des yeux** to gaze into each other's eyes.

Blanc, **Blanche** /blɑ̃, blɑ̃ʃ/ *nm,f* gén white man/woman; Anthrop Caucasian; **école pour ~s** all-white school.

blanc-bec, *pl* **blancs-becs** /blɑ̃bɛk/ *nm* pej greenhorn.

blanchâtre /blɑ̃ʃɑtʀ/ ▶ 193 *adj* whitish.

blanche ▶ **blanc I, VI**.

Blanche-Neige /blɑ̃ʃnɛʒ/ *npr* Littérat Snow White.

blancheur /blɑ̃ʃœʀ/ *nf* **1** (couleur) whiteness; **2** (innocence) innocence.

blanchiment /blɑ̃ʃimɑ̃/ *nm* **1** Fin (d'argent) laundering; **le ~ de l'argent de la drogue** laundering (of) drug money; **2** Chimie, Ind (de tissu, pâte à papier) bleaching; **un ~ rapide** fast bleaching; **agent de ~** bleaching agent; **3** (badigeonnage) whitewashing; **4** Culin blanching; **5** (de chaussures) whitening.

blanchir /blɑ̃ʃiʀ/ [3] **I** *vtr* **1** gén (rendre blanc) (avec une couche colorée) to whiten [*chaussures, surface*]; (avec de la lumière) to light up [*ciel, route*]; **la gelée blanchit les prés** the frost turns the meadows white; **la lune blanchit la route** the moonlight turns the road white; **~ (à la chaux)** to whitewash [*mur, plafond*]; **2** (laver) **donner son linge à ~** to send one's linen to the laundry; ▶ **logé**; **3** Chimie, Ind to bleach [*textile, pâte à papier, farine*]; to refine [*sucre*]; **papier non blanchi** unbleached paper; **farine non blanchie** unbleached flour; **4** Culin to blanch [*légumes, viande, amandes*]; **5** (disculper) to clear [*accusé, nom*] (**de** of); **blanchi de tout soupçon** cleared of all suspicion; **6** Fin to launder [*argent sale*]; **argent blanchi** laundered money.
II *vi* **1** (devenir blanc) [*cheveux*] to turn grey GB ou gray US; [*ciel*] to grow light; **~ de rage/peur** to go white with rage/fear; **~ aux tempes** to go grey GB ou gray US at the temples; **cheveux blanchis** silvery hair; **2** Culin **faire ~** to blanch [*légumes, viande, amandes*]; **battre le mélange jusqu'à ce qu'il blanchisse** beat the mixture until it turns white.
III se blanchir *vpr* (se disculper) to clear oneself (**de** of; **auprès de** in the eyes of).

blanchissage /blɑ̃ʃisaʒ/ *nm* **1** (du linge) (action) laundering; **service de ~** laundry service; **le ~ coûte cher** laundering is expensive; **2** Ind (du sucre) refining.

blanchissant, **~e** /blɑ̃ʃisɑ̃, ɑ̃t/ *adj* bleaching; **poudre ~e** bleaching powder; **produit ~** bleaching product; **agent ~** bleaching agent.

blanchissement /blɑ̃ʃismɑ̃/ *nm* **1** (des cheveux) greying GB ou graying US; **un ~ précoce des cheveux** hair going grey GB ou gray US early ou prematurely; **2** (disculpation) exoneration.

blanchisserie /blɑ̃ʃisʀi/ ▶ 510 *nf* laundry.

blanchisseur, **-euse** /blɑ̃ʃisœʀ, øz/ ▶ 510 **I** *nm,f* **1** (personne) laundry worker; **2** (magasin) laundry; **le ~ est en face** the laundry is across the street; **aller chez le ~** to go to the laundry.
II blanchisseuse *nf* (femme qui fait des lessives) laundress.

blanc-manger /blɑ̃mɑ̃ʒe/ *nm* blancmange.

blanc-seing, *pl* **blancs-seings** /blɑ̃sɛ̃/ *nm* **1** fig free hand; **donner un ~ à qn** to give carte blanche ou a free hand to sb; **2** Jur blank endorsement; **signer un ~** to endorse in blank.

blanquette /blɑ̃kɛt/ *nf* Culin blanquette; **~ de veau** blanquette of veal.

blase◑ /blaz/ *nm* (nez) conk◑ GB, schnoz◑ US, nose.

blasé, **~e** /blaze/ **I** *pp* ▶ **blaser**.
II *pp adj* blasé; **être ~ de qch/de faire** to be blasé about sth/about doing.
III *nm,f* blasé person; **jeunes ~s** blasé young people; **jouer les ~s, faire le ~** to affect a blasé attitude.

blaser /blaze/ [1] *vtr* to make [sb] blasé.

blason /blazɔ̃/ *nm* Hérald **1** (armoiries) coat of arms, blazon spéc; **2** (discipline) **le ~** heraldry.
IDIOMES **redorer son ~** to restore one's reputation.

blasphémateur, **-trice** /blasfematœʀ, tʀis/ *nm,f* blasphemer.

blasphématoire /blasfematwaʀ/ *adj* blasphemous.

blasphème /blasfɛm/ *nm* blasphemy ¢.

blasphémer /blasfeme/ [1] **I** *vtr* to blaspheme [*nom de Dieu*].
II *vi* to blaspheme (**contre** against).

blatte /blat/ *nf* cockroach.

blazer /blazɛʀ/ *nm* blazer.

blé /ble/ *nm* **1** Agric (céréale) wheat; **grain de ~** grain of wheat; **épi de ~** ear of wheat; **semer du ~** to sow wheat; **~ tendre/dur** soft/hard wheat; **faire du ~**○ to grow wheat; **du ~ en herbe** wheat in the blade; **le ~ est en herbe** the wheat is (still) in the blade; **2**◑ (argent) dough○, money; **avoir**

du ~◑ (être riche) to be rolling in it○; **gagner, (se) faire du ~◑** to rake it in○.
■ **~ cornu** rye affected with ergot; **~ d'Inde** C (maïs) maize GB, corn US; **~ noir** buckwheat.
IDIOMES **manger son ~ en herbe** to spend one's money before one gets it.

bled○ /blɛd/ *nm* village; **passer ses vacances dans un ~ perdu** to spend one's holiday in a godforsaken hole○ GB, to spend one's vacation in the boondocks US.

blême /blɛm/ *adj* **1** (naturellement) [*visage, teint*] pallid; **2** (sous le coup de l'émotion) ashen (**de** with); **3** littér [*lumière, matin*] pale, wan.

blêmir /blemiʀ/ [3] *vi* [*personne, visage*] to pale; **~ de peur/rage** to go white with fear/rage.

blennorragie /blenɔʀaʒi/ ▶ 271 *nf* gonorrhea.

blèsement /blɛzmɑ̃/ *nm* Ling lisping.

bléser /bleze/ [16] *vi* fml to lisp.

blessant, ~e /blesɑ̃, ɑ̃t/ *adj* [*propos*] hurtful, cutting.

blessé, ~e /blese/ *nm,f* (par accident) injured man/woman; (par arme) wounded man/woman; Mil wounded soldier, casualty; **les ~s** gén the injured; Mil the wounded; **l'explosion a fait 20 ~s** 20 people were injured in the explosion; **il n'y a pas de ~s** nobody has been hurt; Mil there are no casualties.
■ **~ de guerre** person wounded in the war; **les ~s de guerre** the war wounded; **~ de la route** road accident victim.

blesser /blese/ [1] **I** *vtr* **1** (par accident) to injure, to hurt; (dans un conflit armé) to wound; **il a été blessé à la tête** (par accident) he received ou sustained head injuries; (par balle, agression) he received head wounds; **~ qn d'un coup de couteau** to stab sb (with a knife); **~ qn d'un coup de revolver** to shoot sb (with a gun); **il a été blessé par balle/un coup de couteau** he received a bullet/a stab wound; **2** (en irritant) [*chaussure, menotte*] to hurt, to make [sth] sore [*personne, pied*]; **3** (offenser) to hurt, to upset [*personne*]; to hurt, to wound [*amour-propre*]; **musique qui blesse l'oreille** music which grates on ou offends the ear; **il s'est senti blessé dans ses sentiments/son orgueil** his feelings were/his pride was hurt; **~ qn au vif** to cut sb to the quick; **un rien la blesse** she's easily hurt; **4** liter (porter atteinte à) to offend against [*convenances, pudeur*].
II se blesser *vpr* (se faire mal) to injure ou hurt oneself; **je me suis blessé au bras en tombant** I fell and hurt my arm.
IDIOMES **il n'y a que la vérité qui blesse** Prov nothing hurts like the truth.

blessure /blesyʀ/ *nf* **1** (lésion) injury; (plaie) wound; **une ~ à la tête/jambe** a head/leg injury ou wound; **~ légère/grave** minor/serious injury ou wound; **2** fig wound; **~ d'amour-propre** wounded pride ¢.

blet, blette /blɛ, blɛt/ **I** *adj* overripe.
II blette *nf* Swiss chard.

blettir /bletiʀ/ [3] *vi* **1** (sur l'arbre) to over-ripen; **2** (dans une corbeille) to get overripe.

bleu, ~e /blø/ **I** *adj* **1** ▶ 193 (couleur) blue; **des yeux ~s** blue eyes; **~ vert** blue-green; **j'ai les lèvres toutes ~es** my lips are all blue; **~ de froid** [*personne, doigts*] blue with cold; **~ de peur** white with fear; ▶ **grand**; **2** Culin [*entrecôte, viande*] very rare.
II *nm* **1** ▶ 193 (couleur) blue; **le ciel était d'un ~ magnifique** the sky was a magnificent blue; **2** (ecchymose) bruise; **avoir un ~ sur le bras/la cuisse** to have a bruise on one's arm/thigh; **être couvert de ~s** to be covered in bruises; **se faire un ~** to bruise oneself; **3** (vêtement) **~ (de travail)** (combinaison) overalls (*pl*); (veste et pantalon) *workman's blue cotton jacket and trousers*; **4** (fromage) blue cheese; **5**○ (nouvelle recrue) soldiers' slang rookie○; (débutant) beginner, greenhorn○; **se faire avoir comme un ~** to be completely conned.
■ **~ ardoise** slate blue; **~ azur** azure blue; **~ canard** peacock blue; **~ ciel** sky blue; **~ de cobalt** cobalt blue; **~ électrique** electric blue; **~ horizon** sky blue; **~ lavande** lavender blue; **~ marine** navy blue; **~ de méthylène** methylene blue; **~ noir** blue-black; **~ nuit** midnight blue; **~ océan** ocean blue; **~ outremer** ultramarine; **~ pétrole** petrol-blue; **~ de Prusse** Prussian blue; **~ roi** royal blue; **~ saphir** sapphire blue; **~ turquoise** turquoise blue.
IDIOMES **avoir une peur ~e de qch** to be scared stiff○ of sth; **j'ai eu une peur ~e** I had a bad scare.

bleuâtre /bløɑtʀ/ ▶ 193 *adj* pej bluish.

bleuet /bløɛ/ *nm* **1** Bot cornflower; **2** (réchaud) picnic stove; **3** C (myrtille) blueberry.

bleuir /bløiʀ/ [3] **I** *vtr* [*froid*] to turn [sth] blue [*mains, objets*]; **le froid lui a bleui les doigts** the cold turned his fingers blue.
II *vi* (tous contextes) to turn blue.

bleuissement /bløismɑ̃/ *nm* **on observe un ~ des lèvres** one can observe that the lips turn blue.

bleusaille○ /bløzaj/ *nf* soldiers' slang **1** (nouvelle recrue) rookie○; **2** (collectif) rookies○.

bleuté, ~e /bløte/ ▶ 193 *adj* bluish.

blindage /blɛ̃daʒ/ *nm* **1** (revêtement) (de porte) reinforcement, armour[GB] plating; (de véhicule, coffre-fort) armour[GB] plating; (pose, revêtement) reinforcing, armour[GB] plating; **2** Mil (revêtement) armour[GB] plate; (pose) armour[GB] plating; **3** Nucl (dispositif) shield; (installation du dispositif) shielding.

blindé, ~e /blɛ̃de/ **I** *adj* **1** Mil [*division, unité, corps*] armoured[GB]; **2** (renforcé) **porte ~e** security door; **3◑** (soûl) pissed○ GB, sloshed○.
II *nm* armoured[GB] vehicle; **un ~ léger** an armoured[GB] car.

blinder /blɛ̃de/ [1] **I** *vtr* **1** (protéger) to reinforce [*porte*]; Mil to armour[GB]; Nucl to shield [*réacteur*]; Électron, Télécom to shroud; **2**○ (endurcir) to harden [*personne*].
II se blinder○ *vpr* (s'endurcir) to become hardened.

blini /blini/ *nm* blini.

blinquer /blɛ̃ke/ [1] *vi* B (briller) to shine; **faire ~** to polish.

blizzard /blizaʀ/ *nm* blizzard; **un coup de ~** a blizzard.

bloc /blɔk/ **I** *nm* **1** (masse solide) block (**de** of); **statue faite d'un seul ~** (en bois) statue made from a single piece of wood; (en marbre) statue made from a single piece of marble; **se retourner tout d'un ~** to pivot round GB ou around US; **2** (de personnes) group (**de** of); Pol bloc; **le ~ socialiste** the socialist bloc; **faire ~** to side together; **faire ~ avec qn** to side with sb; **faire ~ contre qn** (s'unir) to unite against sb; (être unis) to be united against sb; **3** (pour écrire) notepad; **~ de papier à lettres** writing pad; **4** Fin (d'actions, de titres) block (**de** of); **5** Ordinat block; **6**○ (prison) nick○.
II à bloc *loc adv* [*serrer, visser, fermer*] tightly; [*charger, gonfler*] fully.
III en bloc *loc adv* **1** (entièrement) **admettre/rejeter/nier qch en ~** to admit/reject/deny sth outright; **2** Comm **acheter en ~** to buy in bulk.
■ **~ de contrôle** controlling[GB] block; **~ de départ** starting block; **~ monétaire** monetary block; **~ opératoire** surgical unit; **~ optique** Aut headlamp GB ou headlight unit; **~ sanitaire** toilet block; **~ de touches** Ordinat keypool.

blocage /blɔkaʒ/ *nm* **1** (coincement) (de roue, mécanisme) locking; (d'écrou) overtightening; **~ de direction** Aut locking of the steering wheel; **assurer le ~ d'une pièce** to ensure that a part is locked into place; **2** (de route, véhicule, marchandise) blocking (**de** of); **~ des vins italiens dans le port** blockade of Italian wines in the port; **3** Écon, Fin, Pol (action) (d'opération, de fonds, négociations) blocking (**de** of); (de compte, prix) freezing (**de** of); (état) (de situation, négociations) deadlock (**de** in); (d'opération) block (**de** on); (de prix) freeze; **~ de la vente des armes** ban on sales of arms; **situation de ~** deadlock situation; **~ des prix/salaires** price/wage freeze; **4** (mental) (mental) block; **avoir** or **faire un ~** to have a (mental) block; **5** Constr rubble(-filler).
■ **~ articulaire** Méd joint locking; **~ de direction** Aut (antivol) steering lock.

bloc-calendrier, *pl* **blocs-calendriers** /blɔkkalɑ̃dʀije/ *nm* tear-off calendar.

bloc-cuisine, *pl* **blocs-cuisines** /blɔkkɥizin/ *nm* kitchen unit.

bloc-cylindre, *pl* **blocs-cylindres** /blɔksilɛ̃dʀ/ *nm* cylinder block.

bloc-diagramme, *pl* **blocs-diagrammes** /blɔkdjagʀam/ *nm* block diagram.

blockhaus /blɔkos/ *nm inv* blockhouse.

bloc-moteur, *pl* **blocs-moteurs** /blɔkmɔtœʀ/ *nm* engine block.

bloc-notes, *pl* **blocs-notes** /blɔknɔt/ *nm* notepad.

bloc-système, *pl* **blocs-systèmes** /blɔksistɛm/ *nm* block system.

blocus /blɔkys/ *nm inv* blockade; **~ économique** economic blockade; **imposer un ~** to impose a blockade; **forcer/lever le ~** to run/lift the blockade.

blond, ~e /blɔ̃, ɔ̃d/ ▶ 193 **I** *adj* [*cheveux, barbe*] fair, blonde GB, blond US; [*femme*] fair-haired, blonde GB, blond US; [*homme*] fair-haired, blond; [*caramel, épi*] golden; [*tabac*] Virginia, light; **des cigarettes ~es** Virginia tobacco cigarettes; **bière ~e** lager, light ale GB; **les/nos chères têtes ~es** the/our little darlings.
II *nm,f* (femme) fair-haired woman, blonde GB, blond US; (homme) fair-haired man, blond(e); ▶ **faux**.
III *nm* (couleur) blond.
IV blonde *nf* **1** (cigarette) Virginia tobacco cigarette; **2** (bière) lager, light ale GB; **3** C (petite amie) girlfriend.
■ **~ vénitien** strawberry blond; **~e décolorée** peroxide blonde.

blondasse○ /blɔ̃das/ **I** *adj* [*cheveux*] dirty○ blond(e).
II *nf* **une ~** pej a brassy blonde péj.

blondeur /blɔ̃dœʀ/ *nf* (de cheveux) blond(e)-ness, fairness.

blondinet /blɔ̃dinɛ/ *nm* blond(e) ou fair-haired boy.

blondinette /blɔ̃dinɛt/ *nf* blond(e) ou fair-haired girl.

blondir /blɔ̃diʀ/ [3] **I** *vtr* [*soleil*] to lighten, to turn [sth] blonde GB ou blond US [*hair*].
II *vi* [*cheveux, personne*] to turn ou go blonde GB ou blond US; [*épi, champ*] to turn golden; **faire ~** Culin to brown [sth] lightly [*sauce, beurre, caramel*]; **quand le beurre commence à ~** when the butter is lightly browned.

bloque○ /blɔk/ *nf* B students' slang (bachotage) cramming.

bloqué, ~e /blɔke/ **I** *pp* ▶ **bloquer**.
II *pp adj* **1** (obstrué) blocked; Méd **avoir les reins ~s** to have a blockage in the kidneys; **2** (immobilisé) [*mécanisme, porte*] jammed; [*voyageur, véhicule*] stuck; (par la neige) snowbound; **je suis ~ à Paris par la grève** I'm stuck in Paris because of the strike; **il a le dos ~** his back has seized up; **3** fig **être ~** [*activité, carrière, négociations*] to be at a standstill; [*situation*] to be deadlocked; **sans cet accord, je suis ~** without this agreement, I'm stuck; **4** Fin [*fonds, compte*] frozen; **5** (mentalement) **être ~** to have a (mental) block (**sur** about).

bloquer /blɔke/ [1] **I** *vtr* **1** (obstruer) to block [*route, entrée, porte*]; Mil to blockade [*ville, port*]; **~ la route** lit to block the road; fig to block the way; **des difficultés inattendues le bloquent** fig unforeseen difficulties are holding him back ou standing in his way; **2** (coincer) (accidentellement) to jam [*mécanisme, porte*]; to lock [*volant, roue*]; to overtighten [*écrou*]; (volontairement) to lock [sth] into place [*pièce*]; to put a block under [*roues*]; to wedge [*porte*]; to tighten [*écrou*]; **~ les freins** to jam on the brakes; **3** (immobiliser) to stop, to hold [sth] up [*véhicule, voyageur, circulation, marchandise*]; Sport to catch [*ballon*]; Jeux (au billard) to jam, to wedge [*bille*]; **4** Écon, Fin to freeze [*compte, salaires, crédit, dépenses*]; to peg [*prix*]; to stop [*chèque*]; **~ des capitaux** to lock up capital; **5** (enrayer) to stop [*initiative, projet, contrat*]; to prevent [*ovulation*]; to prevent [sth] from going ahead [*travaux*]; **6** (grouper) to lump [sth] together [*heures, jours, personnes*]; Comm to bulk [*commandes*]; **7** fig (paralyser) **les examens/ses parents la bloquent** she can't handle exams/being with her parents.

II *vi* **1** (coincer) to jam, to stick; **il y a quelque chose qui bloque** there's something jamming ou sticking; **2** (ne pas progresser) [*dossier*] to be held up; **3** Psych to have a block (**sur** about); **4**○ B students' slang (étudier) to swot○ GB, to bone up○ US.

III se bloquer *vpr* **1** lit [*frein, mécanisme, porte*] to jam; [*volant, roue*] to lock; **2** fig [*personne*] to freeze, to tense up.

bloqueur, **-euse**○ /blɔkœʀ, øz/ *nm,f* B students' slang (étudiant zélé) swot○ GB, grind○ US.

blottir /blɔtiʀ/ [3] **I**○ *vtr* **~ sa tête contre qn/qch** to press one's head against sb/sth; **sa tête était blottie contre mon épaule** his/her head was pressed against my shoulder.

II se blottir *vpr* to nestle; **le chien était blotti sous la table** the dog was nestling under the table; **se ~ contre qn/qch** (par affection) to snuggle up against sb/sth; (par peur, froid) to huddle up against sb/sth; **se ~ dans les bras de qn** (par affection) to snuggle up in sb's arms; (par peur, froid) to huddle up in sb's arms; **le village était blotti au pied de la montagne** the village nestled at the foot of the mountain.

blousant, **~e** /bluzɑ̃, ɑ̃t/ *adj* [*robe, chemisier*] full.

blouse /bluz/ *nf* **1** (tablier) overall; (de dentiste, médecin) **~ blanche** white coat; **2** (chemisier) blouse; **3** (tunique de paysan) smock.

blouser /bluze/ [1] *vtr* **1**○ (tromper) to take [sb] for a ride○; **se faire ~** to be taken for a ride○; **2** (au billard) to pocket [*bille*].

blouson /bluzɔ̃/ *nm* jacket, blouson.

■ **~ d'aviateur** bomber jacket; **~ noir** ≈ rocker GB.

blue-jean, *pl* **~s** /bludʒin/ *nm* jeans (*pl*).

blues /bluz/ *nm inv* **1** (genre) blues; **chanter du** or **le ~** to sing the blues; **2** (morceau) **jouer un ~** to play a blues song.

IDIOMES **avoir le ~**○ to have the blues.

bluet /blyɛ/ *nm* cornflower.

bluff /blœf/ *nm* bluff; **ce n'est que du ~** it's only a bluff; **avoir qn au ~** to bluff sb.

bluffer○ /blœfe/ [1] **I** *vtr* **1** (au poker) to bluff [*adversaire*]; **2** (tromper) to bluff, to have [sb] on○ GB, to put [sb] on○ US.

II *vi* to bluff.

bluffeur○, **-euse** /blœfœʀ, øz/ *nm,f* bluffer.

blush /blœʃ/ *nm* blusher.

blutage /blytaʒ/ *nm* flour dressing.

BN /beɛn/ *nf* (*abbr* = **Bibliothèque nationale**) *national library in Paris*.

BNF /beɛnɛf/ *nf*: *abbr* ▶ **bibliothèque**.

boa /bɔa/ *nm* **1** (serpent) boa; **2** (parure) boa.

■ **~ constricteur** boa constrictor.

bob /bɔb/ *nm* **1**○ *abbr* = **bobsleigh**; **2** (chapeau) (sailor's) sunhat.

bobard○ /bɔbaʀ/ *nm* fib○, tall story.

bobèche /bɔbɛʃ/ *nf*: *part of a candleholder which catches drips*.

bobinage /bɔbinaʒ/ *nm* **1** Tech winding (*onto a bobbin*); **2** Électrotech (enroulement de fils) (coil-)winding; (fils enroulés) winding.

bobine /bɔbin/ *nf* **1** (de fil, câble, film) reel; (bobineau) bobbin; (de métier à tisser) bobbin; (de machine à écrire) spool; **2** Électrotech coil; **3**◑ (visage) face; **il fait une drôle de ~** he looks pretty fed up○.

■ **~ d'allumage** Aut ignition coil; **~ solénoïde** solenoid.

bobiner /bɔbine/ [1] *vtr* to wind (*onto a bobbin*).

bobinette† /bɔbinɛt/ *nf* (wooden) latch.

bobineuse /bɔbinøz/ *nf* **1** Électrotech spooling machine; **2** (en papeterie) winder; **3** Tex winding frame.

bobinoir /bɔbinwaʀ/ *nm* Tex winding frame.

bobinot /bɔbino/ *nm* Tex reel, bobbin.

bobo○ /bobo/ *nm* baby talk **1** (douleur physique) pain; **se faire ~** to hurt oneself; **j'ai** or **ça fait ~** it hurts; **2** (petite plaie) scratch; **se faire un ~** to get a scratch.

bobonne○ /bɔbɔn/ *nf* pej little housewife péj; **il est arrivé avec sa ~** he turned up with his missus○.

bobsleigh /bɔbslɛg/ ▶ **449** *nm* **1** (engin) bobsleigh, bobsled US; **2** (activité) bobsleighing.

bocage /bɔkaʒ/ *nm* hedged farmland.

bocal, *pl* **-aux** /bɔkal, o/ *nm* **1** (récipient) jar; **mettre qch en bocaux** to preserve sth; **faire des bocaux** to make preserves; **2** (aquarium) bowl; **3**○ (tête) nut○, noodle○, head; **il a rien dans le ~**○ he's got nothing between the ears○.

■ **~ gradué** measuring jug.

bock /bɔk/ *nm* **1** (chope) beer glass; **2** (bière) glass of beer.

IDIOMES **aller pisser un ~**◑ to go for a pee○.

Boers /buʀ/ *nmpl* Boers; **la guerre des ~** the Boer War.

bœuf /bœf, *pl* bø/ *nm* **1** (animal) (de boucherie) bullock GB, steer US; (de trait) ox; **un ~ de labour** or **trait** a draft ox; **2** (viande) beef; **le ~** beef; **3**○ Mus jam (session); **faire un ~**○ lit to have a jam; fig to be a great success.

■ **~ bourguignon** beef bourguignon; **~ gros sel** boiled beef; **~ (à la) mode** braised beef; **~ musqué** Zool musk ox.

IDIOMES **qui vole un œuf vole un ~** Prov once a thief, always a thief; **fort comme un ~**○ as strong as an ox; **souffler comme un ~**○ to huff and puff; **faire un effet ~**○ to make a fantastic○ impression.

bof○ /bɔf/ *excl* **'c'est un bon acteur'—'~, pas terrible!'** 'he's a good actor'—'hmm, not so hot○!'; **'tu aimes la soupe?'—'~, pas vraiment!'** 'do you like soup?'—'hmm, not particularly'; **'tu préfères la mer ou la montagne?'—'~!'** 'which do you prefer the sea or the mountains?'—'I don't mind'.

bog(g)ie /bɔgi/ *nm* Rail bogy, bogie US.

Bogota /bogota/ ▶ **857** *npr* Bogota.

bogue /bɔg/ *nf* **1** Ordinat bug; **2** Bot chestnut bur.

bohème /bɔɛm/ **I** *adj* [*personne, caractère*] bohemian.

II *nf* (milieu artiste) **la ~** bohemia; (style de vie) bohemian lifestyle; **vie de ~** bohemian lifestyle.

Bohême /bɔɛm/ ▶ **692** *nf* Bohemia.

bohémien, **-ienne** /bɔemjɛ̃, ɛn/ *nm,f* **1** (tzigane) Bohemian, Romany; **2** (vagabond) tramp, vagabond.

boire /bwaʀ/ [70] **I** *nm* drink; **le ~ et le manger** food and drink; **il en a perdu le ~ et le manger** fig it has taken over his whole life.

II *vtr* **1** (consommer) [*personne*] to drink; **~ dans un verre/bol** to drink out of a glass/bowl; **elle ne boit que de l'eau** she only drinks water; **~ à la santé de qn** to drink to sb's health; **je bois à la réussite de notre projet** I drink to the success of our project; **ce vin n'est pas encore bon à ~** this wine isn't ready to drink yet; **un vin à ~ frais** a wine which should be drunk chilled; **~ un verre** or **un coup**○ to have a drink; **il a bu un coup de trop**○ he's had one too many○; **donner/verser à ~ à qn** to give/pour sb a drink; **faire ~ qn** to give sb a drink; **il ne m'a même pas fait ~ un café** he didn't even offer me a coffee; **allons ~ un verre** let's go for a drink; **j'ai soif, je boirais bien une bière** I'm thirsty, I'd like a beer; **~ les paroles de qn** fig to lap up sb's words○; **il y a à ~ et à manger dans leur théorie** fig there's both good and bad in their theory; ▶ **lie**, **vin**; **2** (avec excès) to drink; **il boit pour oublier** he drinks to forget; **il s'est mis/remis à ~** he's taken to drink/to drinking again; **il m'a fait ~ pour obtenir des renseignements** he got me drunk to get some information out of me; **3** (absorber) [*plante*] to drink; [*papier, buvard, moquette*] to soak [sth] up [*liquide*].

III se boire *vpr* **ce vin se boit frais** this wine should be drunk chilled; **ce porto se boit bien** or **se laisse ~** this port is very drinkable; **ce punch se boit comme du petit lait!** this punch goes down very easily but it's lethal!

IDIOMES **~ comme un trou**○ to drink like a fish○; **qui a bu boira** Prov once a drinker, always a drinker.

bois /bwa/ **I** *nm inv* **1** (lieu) wood; **~ de chênes/pins** oak/pine wood; **2** (matière) wood; **~ de pin/chêne** pine/oak; **c'est en ~?** is it made of wood?; **~ massif** solid wood; **table en** or **de ~** wooden table; **travailler le ~** to work in wood; **leur visage est resté de ~** they remained impassive; ▶ **déménager**, **loup**; **3** (matériau) (pour menuisier, ébéniste) wood; (pour charpentier, construction) timber; **4** Art (gravure) woodcut; **5** (objet) (manche) handle; (club de golf) wood.

II *nmpl* **1** Zool (de cerf) antlers; **2** Mus **les ~** the woodwind instruments, the woodwind (+ *v pl*); (dans un orchestre) the woodwind section.

■ **~ aggloméré** chipboard; **~ blanc** whitewood, deal; **~ à brûler** firewood; **~ de caisse** softwood; **~ de charpente** timber; **~ de chauffage** firewood; **~ debout** standing timber; **~ d'ébène** lit ebony; Hist fig (esclaves) black slaves (*pl*); **~ des îles** tropical hardwood; **le ~ de justice** the guillotine; **~ de lit** wooden bedstead; **~ mort** firewood; **~ de placage** wood veneer; **~ de rose** rosewood; **~ vert** green wood; (en menuiserie) unseasoned timber.

IDIOMES **être de ~** to be insensitive; **ne pas être de ~** to be only human; **faire un ~** (au tennis) to hit the ball off the wood; **être du ~ dont on fait les flûtes** to be extremely accommodating; **il n'est pas du ~ dont on fait les flûtes** he's not going to let himself be pushed around; **il va voir de quel ~ je me chauffe**○ I'll show him; **faire feu** or **flèche de tout ~** to turn anything to good account; **casser du ~**○ Aviat to crash one's plane.

boisage /bwazaʒ/ *nm* (processus) fixing of timbers; (structure) timber work.

boisé, **~e** /bwaze/ **I** *pp* ▶ **boiser**.

II *pp adj* [*terrain*] wooded; **région très ~e** densely wooded area; **dans les régions ~es** in the woodlands.

boisement /bwazmɑ̃/ *nm* afforestation.

boiser /bwaze/ [1] *vtr* **1** (planter) to afforest, to plant [sth] with trees [*terrain*]; **2** (garnir de bois) to timber [*tunnel, mine*].

boiserie /bwazʀi/ *nf* **1** (montants de porte, de fenêtre) woodwork ¢; **2** (lambris) panelling GB ¢.

boisseau, *pl* **~x** /bwaso/ *nm* (unité) bushel.

IDIOMES **mettre qch sous le ~** to keep sth dark.

boisson /bwasɔ̃/ *nf* drink; **~ alcoolisée/**

non alcoolisée alcoholic/soft drink; **être pris de ~** to be under the influence.

boîte /bwat/ *nf* **1** gén box; (en métal) tin; (de conserve) tin GB, can; **~ de cigares** box of cigars; **~ à chaussures** shoe box; **petits pois en ~** tinned peas GB, canned peas; **mettre des fruits en ~** to can fruit; **mise en ~** Ind canning ¢; ▶ **diable**; **2**○ (cabaret) nightclub; **aller** or **sortir en ~** (une fois) to go out to a nightclub; (d'habitude) to go clubbing; **3**○ (entreprise) firm; (bureau) office; (école) school; **j'en ai marre de cette ~**○ I'm fed up with this place.
■ **~ d'allumettes** (pleine) box of matches; (vide) matchbox; **~ automatique** Aut automatic gearbox GB ou transmission; **~ à bachot**○ Scol crammer○ GB, prep school US; **~ à biscuits** biscuit tin; **~ de conserve** tin GB, can; **~ de couleurs** Art paint box; **~ crânienne** Anat cranium; **~ expressive** Mus swell box; **~ à fusibles** fuse box; **~ à gants** Aut glove compartment; **~ à idées** suggestion box; **~ à** or **aux lettres** Postes post box GB, mailbox US; fig (personne) go-between; (adresse fictive) accommodation address; **~ à** or **aux lettres électronique** electronic mailbox; **~ à malice** bag of tricks; **~ à musique** Mus musical box GB, music box US; **~ noire** Aviat black box; **~ de nuit** nightclub; **~ à œufs** egg box; **~ à onglets** mitre[GB] box; **~ à ordures** (d'intérieur) rubbish bin GB, garbage can US; **~ à outils** toolbox; **~ à ouvrage** Cout sewing box; **~ de Pétri** Biol Petri dish; **~ à pilules** pillbox; **~ postale**, **BP** Postes PO Box; **~ de raccordement** junction box; **~ à rythmes** Mus drum machine; **~ à thé** tea caddy; **~ de vitesses (automatique/mécanique)** (automatic/manual) gearbox.
IDIOMES **mettre qn en ~**○ to tease sb.

boiter /bwate/ [1] *vi* [*personne*] to limp; [*meuble*] to wobble; [*raisonnement*] to be shaky; [*phrase*] (incorrecte) to be badly put together; (maladroite) to be clumsy; **marcher en boîtant** to walk with a limp.

boiteux, **-euse** /bwatø, øz/ **I** *adj* **1** [*personne*] lame; [*meuble*] wobbly; **2** [*raisonnement, alliance, paix*] shaky; [*vers*] lame.
II *nm,f* lame person.

boîtier /bwatje/ *nm* gén case; (d'appareil photo) body; (de téléphone) casing.

boitillant, **~e** /bwatijɑ̃, ɑ̃t/ *adj* [*personne*] with a slight limp (*épith, après n*); **démarche ~e** limping gait.

boitillement /bwatijmɑ̃/ *nm* slight limp.

boitiller /bwatije/ [1] *vi* to limp slightly.

boit-sans-soif○ /bwasɑ̃swaf/ *nmf inv* soak○.

bol /bɔl/ *nm* **1** (récipient, contenu) bowl; **un ~ de café** a bowl of coffee; **2**○ (chance) luck; **coup de ~** stroke of luck; **avoir du ~** to be lucky.
■ **~ d'air** breath of fresh air; **~ alimentaire** bolus.
IDIOMES **se casser le ~**○ to go to a lot of trouble.

bolchevik, **bolchevique** /bɔlʃevik/ *adj, nmf* Bolshevik.

bolchevisme /bɔlʃevism/ *nm* Bolshevism.

bolduc /bɔldyk/ *nm* ≈ gift ribbon.

bolée /bɔle/ *nf* **~ de cidre** bowl of cider.

boléro /bɔleʀo/ *nm* (danse, vêtement) bolero.

bolet /bɔlɛ/ *nm* boletus.

bolide /bɔlid/ *nm* **1** (véhicule) high-powered car; **comme un ~** at high speed; **passer comme un ~** to shoot past; **2** Astron bolide.

Bolivie /bɔlivi/ ▶ **321** *nprf* Bolivia.

bolivien, **-ienne** /bɔlivjɛ̃, ɛn/ ▶ **537** *adj* Bolivian.

Bolivien, **-ienne** /bɔlivjɛ̃, ɛn/ ▶ **537** *nm,f* Bolivian.

bollard /bɔlaʀ/ *nm* Naut bollard.

bolle○ /bɔl/ *nf* C (personne intelligente) brain○; **c'est (toute) une ~ en physique** he's/she's (really) great at physics.

bolognaise /bɔlɔɲɛz/ *adj inv* [*spaghetti*] bolognese (*épith, après n*) GB, with meat sauce (*après n*) US.

Bologne /bɔlɔɲ/ ▶ **857** *npr* Bologna.

bombage /bɔ̃baʒ/ *nm* **1** (action) graffiti spraying; **2** (résultat) sprayed graffiti.

bombance /bɔ̃bɑ̃s/ *nf* **faire ~** to have a feast.

bombarde /bɔ̃baʀd/ *nf* **1** Hist Mil bombard; **2** Mus (bois) bombardon; (jeu d'orgue) bombarde.

bombardement /bɔ̃baʀdəmɑ̃/ *nm* **1** Mil gén bombardment; (avec des bombes) bombing; (d'artillerie) shelling ¢; **~ aérien** air raid; **~ atomique** atom-bomb attack; **~ (à l'arme) chimique** chemical weapons attack; **2** (jet) (de projectiles) pelting; (de questions, critiques) bombardment; **être soumis à un ~ de tomates** to get pelted with tomatoes; **être soumis à un ~ de critiques** to get bombarded with criticism; **3** Phys bombardment; **~ atomique** atomic bombardment.

bombarder /bɔ̃baʀde/ [1] *vtr* **1** Mil gén to bombard; (avec des bombes) to bomb; (avec des obus) to shell; **2** (harceler) **~ qn de tomates** to pelt sb with tomatoes; **~ qn de questions** to bombard sb with questions; **~ qn de coups de fil/lettres** to inundate sb with phone calls/letters; **3** Phys to bombard; **4**○ (nommer) **~ qn à un poste** to catapult sb into a job; **on l'a bombardé président** he was catapulted into the position of president.

bombardier /bɔ̃baʀdje/ *nm* **1** (avion) bomber; **2** (aviateur) bombardier.

Bombay /bɔ̃bɛ/ ▶ **857** *npr* Bombay.

bombe /bɔ̃b/ *nf* **1** Mil bomb; **~ artisanale** homemade bomb; **attaque/attentat à la ~** bomb attack; **l'annonce a fait l'effet d'une ~** the news came as a bombshell; **2** (atomiseur) **~ (aérosol)** spray; **~ de peinture** paint spray; **peindre à la ~** to spray-paint; **3** Équit riding hat.
■ **~ A** A-bomb; **~ antigel** de-icer; **~ atomique** atomic bomb; **avoir la ~ atomique** to have the bomb; **~ autoguidée** homing bomb; **~ à billes** shrapnel bomb; **~ au cobalt** Méd cobalt therapy unit; **~ éclairante** flare bomb; **~ à fission** fission bomb; **~ à fragmentation** fragmentation bomb; **~ gigogne** cluster bomb; **~ glacée** Culin bombe (glacée); **~ à grappes** cluster bomb unit; **~ guidée** = **~ intelligente**; **~ H** H-bomb; **~ à hydrogène** hydrogen bomb; **~ incendiaire** Mil incendiary bomb; (artisanal) incendiary device; **~ insecticide** insecticide spray; **~ intelligente** smart bomb; **~ lacrymogène** Mil teargas grenade; **~ de laque** Cosmét can of hairspray; **~ à neutrons** neutron bomb; **~ perforante** penetration bomb; **~ à retardement** time-bomb; **~ soufflante** air-blast bomb; **~ volcanique** Géol volcanic bomb.
IDIOMES **arriver/partir à toute ~**○ [*personne*] to rush in/off; **arriver comme une ~** [*nouvelle*] to come like a bolt out of the blue○; **faire la ~**○ (s'amuser) to live it up; (dans l'eau) to dive-bomb.

bombé, **~e** /bɔ̃be/ **I** *pp* ▶ **bomber**.
II *pp adj* [*front*] domed; [*forme, vase*] rounded; [*lentille*] convex; [*route*] cambered; [*parquet, mur*] bulging.

bombement /bɔ̃bmɑ̃/ *nm* **1** (de lentille) convexity; (de route) camber; (de mur) bulge; **2 marcher avec des ~s de torse** to walk along with one's chest stuck out.

bomber /bɔ̃be/ [1] **I** *vtr* **1** (gonfler) **~ le torse** lit to thrust out one's chest; fig to swell with pride; **en bombant le torse** with one's chest stuck out; **2**○ (peindre) to spray-paint [*inscription, mur*].
II *vi* **1** [*planche, mur*] to bulge out; **2**○ (rouler vite) to belt along○.

bombyx /bɔ̃biks/ *nm inv* bombyx.
■ **~ du mûrier** silk-worm moth.

bôme /bom/ *nf* Naut boom.

bon, **bonne** /bɔ̃, bɔn/ **I** *adj* **1** (agréable) [*repas, aliment, odeur, matelas, douche*] good; **très ~, ce gâteau!** this cake's very good!; **viens, l'eau est bonne** come on in, the water's lovely ou fine US; ▶ **aventure**; **2** (de qualité) [*objet, système, hôtel, vacances*] good; [*livre, texte, style*] good; [*conseil, métier, travail*] good; [*santé, vue, mémoire*] good; **il n'y a rien de ~ dans ce film** there's nothing good in ou about this film; **un ~ bâton** a good strong stick; **de bonnes chaussures** good strong shoes; **prends un ~ pull** take a warm jumper; **la balle est bonne** (au tennis) the ball is good ou in; **tu as de ~s yeux pour pouvoir lire ça!** you must have good eyesight if you can read that!; **à 80 ans, il a encore de bonnes jambes** at 80, he can still get around; **elle est (bien) bonne, celle-là**○! lit (amusé) that's a good one!; iron (indigné) I like that!; ▶ **raison**, **sang**, **temps**; **3** (supérieur à la moyenne) [*niveau, qualité, client, quantité*] good; **il n'est pas ~ en latin** he's not very good at Latin; **une bonne pointure en plus** a good size bigger; **j'ai attendu un ~ moment/deux bonnes heures** I waited a good while/a good two hours; **une bonne centaine de feuilles** a good hundred sheets; **elle leur a donné une bonne claque** she gave them a good smack; **il a bu trois ~s verres** he's drunk three good ou big glasses; **une bonne rasade de cognac** a big glass of brandy; **ça fait un ~ bout de chemin** it's quite a (long) way; **voilà une bonne chose de faite!** that's that out of the way!; **j'ai un ~ rhume** I've got a rotten cold; **nous sommes ~s derniers** we're well and truly last; **elle est arrivée bonne dernière** she came well and truly last; ▶ **an**, **poids**; **4** (compétent) [*médecin, père, nageur, élève*] good; **en ~ mari/citoyen/écologiste** like a good husband/citizen/ecologist; **en ~ Français (qui se respecte), il passe son temps à râler** like all good Frenchmen, he spends his time moaning; **en ~ fils qu'il est/que tu es** like the good son he is/you are; **elle n'est bonne à rien** she's good for nothing; **il n'est pas ~ à grand-chose** he isn't much use, he's pretty useless; ▶ **ami**, **prince**, **rat**; **5** (avantageux) good; **ce serait une bonne chose** it would be a good thing; **j'ai cru** or **jugé ~ de faire/que qch soit fait** I thought it was a good idea to do/that sth be done; **je n'attends rien de ~ de cette réforme** I don't think any good will come of this reform; **il n'est pas toujours ~ de dire la vérité** it isn't always a good idea to tell the truth; **il est/serait ~ de faire** it is/would be a good thing to do; **il serait ~ qu'on le leur dise/qu'elles le sachent** they ought to be told/to know; **c'est ~ à savoir** that's good to know; **c'est toujours ~ à prendre** it's not to be sneezed at; **à quoi ~?** what's the use ou point?; **6** (efficace) [*remède, climat*] good (**pour, contre** for); **prends ça, c'est ~ pour** or **contre la toux** take this, it's good for coughs ; **ce climat n'est pas ~ pour les rhumatisants** this climate isn't good for people with rheumatism; **ce qui est ~ pour moi l'est pour toi** if it's good enough for me, it's good enough for you; **toutes les excuses lui sont bonnes** he'll/she'll use any excuse; **tous les moyens lui sont ~s pour arriver à ses fins** he'll/she'll do anything to get what he/she wants; **7** (destiné) **~ pour qch** fit for sth; **l'eau n'est pas bonne à boire** the water isn't fit to drink; **ton stylo est ~ à jeter** or **pour la poubelle** your pen is fit for the bin GB ou garbage US; **c'est tout juste ~ pour les chiens!** it's only fit for dogs!; **tu es ~ pour la vaisselle, ce soir!** you're in line for the washing up GB ou for doing the dishes tonight!; **me voilà ~ pour une amende** I'm in for a fine○; **8** (bienveillant) [*personne,* *paroles, geste*] kind (**avec, envers** to); [*sourire*] nice; **il est ~ avec** or **pour les animaux** he's kind to animals; **il a une bonne tête** or **gueule**○ he looks like a nice person ou guy○; **un homme ~ et généreux** a kind and generous man; **tu es trop ~ avec lui** you're too good to him; **c'est un ~ garçon** he's a good lad; **ce ~ vieil Arthur!** good old Arthur!; **avoir ~ cœur** to be good-hearted; **tu es bien ~ de la supporter** it's very good of you to put up with her; **vous êtes (bien) ~!** iron that's (very) good ou noble of you! iron; **il est ~, lui**○! iron it's all very well for him to say that!; ▶ **Dieu, figure**; **9** (correct) [*moment, endroit, numéro, réponse, outil*] right; **j'ai tout ~ à ma dictée**○ I've got everything right in GB ou on US my dictation; **c'est ~, vous pouvez y aller** it's OK, you can go; **c'est ~ pour les jeunes/riches** it's all right for the young/rich; **10** (utilisable) [*billet, bon*] valid; **le lait/pneu/ciment est encore ~** the milk/tyre/cement is still all right; **le pâté n'est plus ~** (périmé) the pâté is past its sell-by date; (avarié) the pâté is off; **le lait ne sera plus ~ demain** the milk will have gone off by tomorrow; **la colle n'est plus bonne** the glue has dried up; **le pneu n'est plus ~** the tyre GB ou tire US is worn, the tyre GB ou tire US has had it○; **11** (dans les souhaits) [*chance, nuit*] good; [*anniversaire*] happy; **~ retour!** (have a) safe journey back!; **bonne journée/soirée!** have a nice day/evening!; **~ séjour/week-end!** have a good ou nice time/weekend!; ▶ **port, pied, race, valet**.

II *nm,f* (personne) **mon ~**† my good man†; **ma bonne**† my good woman†; **les ~s et les méchants** good people and bad people; (au cinéma) the good guys and the bad guys○, the goodies and the baddies○ GB.

III *nm* **1** (ce qui est de qualité) **il y a du ~ dans cet article** there are some good things in this article; **il y a du ~ et du mauvais chez lui** he has good points and bad points; **la concurrence peut avoir du ~** competition can be a good thing ; **la vie de célibataire/sous les tropiques a du ~** being single/in the tropics has its advantages; **2** Comm, Pub (sur un emballage) token GB, coupon; (contremarque) voucher; **cadeau gratuit contre 50 ~s et deux timbres** free gift with 50 tokens GB ou coupons US and two stamps; **~ à valoir sur l'achat de** voucher valid for the purchase of; **échanger un ~ contre** to redeem a voucher against, to exchange a voucher for; **3** Fin bond; **~ indexé/convertible** indexed/convertible bond.

IV *excl* (satisfaction) good; (accord, concession) all right, OK; (intervention, interruption) right, well; **tu as fini? ~, on va pouvoir y aller** have you finished? good, then we can go; **'je vais à la pêche'—'~, mais ne reviens pas trop tard'** 'I'm going fishing'—'all right ou OK, but don't be back too late'; **~, on va pas en faire un drame**○! well, let's not make a fuss about it!; **~, il faut que je parte** right, I must go now; **~, allons-y!** right ou OK, let's go!; **~, si tu veux** well ou OK, if you like; **~, ~, ça va, j'ai compris!** OK, OK, I've got it!; **~, changeons de sujet** right ou well, let's change the subject; **allons ~!** oh dear!

V *adv* **ça sent ~!** that smells good!; **il fait ~ aujourd'hui/en cette saison** the weather's mild today/in this season; **il fait ~ dans ta chambre** it's nice and warm in your room; **il fait ~ vivre ici** it's nice living here; **il ne fait pas ~ le déranger/s'aventurer dans la région** it's not a good idea to disturb him/to venture into the area; ▶ **tenir**.

VI pour de bon *loc adv* (vraiment) really; (définitivement) for good; **je vais me fâcher pour de ~** I'm going to get really cross; **j'ai cru qu'il allait le faire pour de ~** I thought he'd really do it; **je suis ici pour de ~** I'm here for good; **tu dis ça pour de ~?** are you serious?

VII bonne *nf* **1** ▶ **510** (domestique) maid; **je ne suis pas ta bonne!** I'm not the maid!; **2** (plaisanterie) **tu en as de bonnes, toi!** you must be joking!; **il m'en a raconté une bien bonne** he told me a good joke.

■ **~ ami**† boyfriend; **~ de caisse** certificate of deposit; **~ de commande** order form; **~ à composer** final draft; **~ d'échange** voucher; **~ enfant** good-natured; **~ d'essence** petrol GB ou gas US coupon; **~ de garantie** guarantee slip; **~ garçon** nice chap; **être ~ garçon** to be a nice chap; **~ de livraison** delivery note; **~ marché** cheap; **~ mot** witticism; **faire un ~ mot** to make a witty remark (**sur** about); **~ point** lit merit point; fig brownie point○; **~ de réduction** Comm discount voucher; **~ à rien** good-for-nothing; **~ sauvage** noble savage; **~ sens** common sense; **avoir du ~ sens** to have common sense; **un peu de ~ sens, quoi!** use your common sense!; **~ teint** dyed-in-the-wool (*épith*); **une féministe/communiste ~ teint** a dyed-in-the-wool feminist/communist; **~ à tirer** pass for press; **~ de transport** travel voucher; **~ du Trésor** Treasury bill ou bond; **~ usage** good usage; **~ vivant** *adj* jovial; *nm* bon vivant or viveur; **bonne action** good deed; **bonne amie**† girlfriend; **bonne d'enfants** nanny; **bonne femme**○ (femme) woman péj; (épouse) old lady○, wife; **bonne fille** nice person; **être bonne fille** lit to be a nice person; fig [*administration, direction*] to be helpful; **bonne parole** word of God; **bonne pâte** good sort; **bonne sœur**○ nun; **bonne à tout faire** pej skivvy○ GB pej, maid; **bonnes feuilles** advance sheets; **bonnes mœurs** Jur public decency ¢; **bonnes œuvres** good works; **~s offices** good offices; **par les ~s offices de** through the good offices of; **offrir ses ~s offices** to offer one's help and support; **s'en remettre aux ~s offices de qn** to put oneself in the good hands of sb.

IDIOMES **il m'a à la bonne** I'm in his good books.

bonapartisme /bɔnapaʀtism/ *nm* Bonapartism.

bonasse /bɔnas/ *adj* pej meek.

bonbon /bɔ̃bɔ̃/ *nm* sweet GB, candy US; **des ~s** sweets GB, candy US; **~s fourrés** sweets GB ou candy US with a soft centre.

■ **~ acidulé** acid drop GB, sour ball US; **~ anglais** fruit drop; **~ à la menthe** mint; **~ au miel** honey sweet GB, honey candy US.

IDIOMES **coûter ~**◑ to cost a lot; **casser les ~s à qn**◑ to annoy sb, to bug○ sb.

bonbonne /bɔ̃bɔn/ *nf* (en verre) demijohn; (plus grand) carboy; **~ de gaz** gas cylinder; **~ d'oxygène** oxygen cylinder.

bonbonnière /bɔ̃bɔnjɛʀ/ *nf* **1** (boîte) sweet dish GB, candy dish US, bonbonniere spéc; **2** (logement) bijou flat GB, bijou apartment US.

bond /bɔ̃/ *nm* **1** lit, gén (de personne, d'animal) leap, bound; fig (dans le temps) jump; **d'un ~** in one leap ou bound; **d'un ~, il fut à la porte** in one bound, he reached the door; **franchir qch d'un ~** to leap across sth; **se lever d'un ~** to leap to one's feet; **faire un ~ en avant** to leap forward; **faire un ~ en avant de 30 ans** to jump forward 30 years; **le film nous fait faire un ~ en arrière de trois siècles** the film takes us back three centuries; **2** fig (progrès) leap; (hausse) (de prix) jump (**de** in); (de bénéfices, d'exportations) leap (**de** in); **~ en avant** leap forward; (découverte) breakthrough; **faire un ~ en avant** [*technologie, économie*] to make a leap forward; **le chiffre d'affaires/l'action a fait un bond de 50%** the turnover/the share has leaped by 50%; **3** Mil thrust; **progresser par ~s** to progress through a series of thrusts.

IDIOMES **saisir la balle au ~** to seize the opportunity; **faire faux ~ à qn** to let sb down.

bonde /bɔ̃d/ *nf* **1** (orifice) (de piscine) outlet; (d'étang) sluice; (de lavabo) plughole; (de tonneau) bunghole; **2** (bouchon) (de piscine) outlet cover; (d'étang) sluicegate; (de lavabo) plug; (de tonneau) bung.

bondé, **~e** /bɔ̃de/ *adj* packed; **l'endroit est ~ de touristes** the place is packed ou crammed with tourists.

bondieuserie○ /bɔ̃djøzʀi/ *nf* **1** pej (objet) religious souvenir; **2** (religiosité) pej excessive religiosity.

bondir /bɔ̃diʀ/ [3] *vi* **1** (sauter) [*personne, animal, cœur, flamme, torrent*] to leap; **~ de joie** to jump for joy; **~ de surprise/frayeur** to start with surprise/fright; **2** (s'élancer) **~ sur qn/qch** to pounce on sb/sth; **~ vers qn/qch** to rush to sb/sth; **3** (gambader) [*animal*] to leap about; **4** (s'indigner) to react furiously, to hit the roof○; **ça m'a fait ~** it made me sit up○; **~ d'indignation** to be outraged; **~ de colère** to fly into a rage; **5** (augmenter) [*prix, devise*] to soar, to rocket○; **faire ~ les prix** to send prices soaring; **~ de 17%** to jump 17%.

bondissant, **~e** /bɔ̃disɑ̃, ɑ̃t/ *adj* [*animal*] bounding; [*torrent*] leaping.

bondissement /bɔ̃dismɑ̃/ *nm* leap, bound.

bongo /bɔ̃go/ ▶ **534** *nm* bongo drum; **~s** bongos.

bonheur /bɔnœʀ/ *nm* **1** (état de plénitude) happiness; **je vous souhaite beaucoup de ~, tous mes vœux de ~** I wish you every happiness; **être au comble du ~** to be ecstatic; **2** (moment heureux) pleasure; **quel ~ de vous retrouver/boire un bon café** what a pleasure it is to see you again/to drink a nice coffee; **mon plus grand ~ c'est de faire** my greatest pleasure is to do; **faire le ~ de** [*personne, cadeau*] to make [sb] happy [*personne, enfant*]; [*exposition, événement*] to delight [*spectateur, touriste*]; **le nouveau musée fait le ~ des touristes** the new museum is delighting the tourists; **les nouvelles mesures font le ~ de l'industrie** the industry is delighted by the new measures; **pour le plus grand ~ de qn** to the great delight of sb; **3** (chance) pleasure; **c'est un vrai ~ de travailler avec elle** it's a real pleasure to work with her; **avoir le ~ de faire** to have the pleasure of doing; **par ~** fortunately; **au petit ~ (la chance)** [*répondre, décider, chercher*] at random; **tu ne connais pas ton ~!** you don't realize how lucky you are!; **4** fml (réussite) **il manie la métaphore avec ~** he uses metaphor to great effect; **il a répondu avec ~ à toutes nos questions** he answered all our questions felicitously.

IDIOMES **le malheur des uns fait le ~ des autres** Prov one man's meat is another man's poison Prov; **l'argent ne fait pas le ~** Prov money can't buy happiness; **alors, tu as trouvé ton ~○?** did you find what you wanted?

bonheur-du-jour, *pl* **bonheurs-du-jour** /bɔnœʀdyʒuʀ/ *nm* escritoire, writing desk.

bonhomie /bɔnɔmi/ *nf* good-nature; **avec ~** good-naturedly.

bonhomme, *pl* **~s**, **bonshommes** /bɔnɔm, bɔ̃zɔm/ **I** *adj* [*air, propos, gendarme*] good-natured.

II○ *nm* (homme) fellow, chap○; (mari) old man○; (enfant) little man; **découper des ~s de carton** to cut out little cardboard people.

■ **~ de neige** snowman; **~ en pain d'épice** gingerbread man.

IDIOMES **aller** or **suivre son petit ~ de chemin** to go peacefully along.

boni /bɔni/ *nm* **1** (excédent) surplus; **ça nous fait un petit ~** that gives us a small surplus; **2** (prime) bonus.

boniche /bɔniʃ/ *nf* pej skivvy○ GB péj, servant.

bonification /bɔnifikɑsjɔ̃/ *nf* **1** Sport bonus points; (en cyclisme) bonus time; **2** Fin bonus; **3** Agric, Vin improvement.
■ **~ d'intérêt(s)** (action) subsidization of interest; (résultat) interest rebate.

bonifié, **~e** /bɔnifje/ *adj* **prêt à taux ~** (government-)subsidized loan.

bonifier *vtr*, **se bonifier** *vpr* /bɔnifje/ [2] Agric, Vin to improve.

boniment /bɔnimɑ̃/ **I** *nm* (de camelot) sales patter ou pitch; **faire du** or **son ~ à qn** to give sb a sales pitch.
II boniments *nmpl* stories; **raconter des ~s à qn** (mensonges) to give sb some story○ (**à propos de qch** about sth); (flatteries) to smooth-talk sb, to give sb a line○ US; **arrête tes ~s!** don't try that on me!

bonimenter† /bɔnimɑ̃te/ [1] *vi* to make a sales pitch.

bonimenteur /bɔnimɑ̃tœʀ/ *nm* **1** fig smooth talker; **2**† (camelot) street pedlar GB ou peddler US.

bonite /bɔnit/ *nf* bonito.
■ **~ à dos rayé** Atlantic bonito; **~ à ventre rayé** skipjack.

bonjour /bɔ̃ʒuʀ/ *nm* gén hello; (le matin) good morning, hello; (l'après-midi) good afternoon, hello; **faire (un) ~ de la main** to wave hello; **faire un ~ de la tête** to nod; **bien le ~ à votre sœur** say hello to your sister for me, give my regards to your sister; **donnez-leur le ~ de ma part** give them my regards; **tu as le ~ de mon frère** my brother sends his regards; **allô, ~!** hello!
IDIOMES **être simple** or **facile comme ~**○ to be dead easy○ GB, to be easy as pie○; **~**○ **les dégâts** here comes trouble○; **~**○ **l'angoisse**○! it doesn't sound good!; **~**○ **le libéralisme/le progrès!** so much for liberalism/progress!

Bonn /bɔn/ ▶ 857 *npr* Bonn.

bonne ▶ **bon I, II, VII.**

bonne-maman, *pl* **bonnes-mamans** /bɔnmamɑ̃/ *nf* grandma, grandmama.

bonnement /bɔnmɑ̃/ *adv* **tout ~** (quite) simply.

bonnet /bɔnɛ/ *nm* **1** (coiffe) hat; (de bébé) bonnet; ▶ **gros**; **2** (de soutien-gorge) cup; **3** Zool reticulum.
■ **~ d'âne** Scol dunce's cap; **~ de bain** bathing cap; **~ de douche** shower cap; **~ de nuit** lit nightcap; fig wet blanket○; **~ à poils** Mil bearskin.
IDIOMES **prendre qch sous son ~** to make sth one's concern; **avoir la tête près du ~** to be hot-tempered GB ou hotheaded; **c'est blanc ~ et ~ blanc** it's six of one and half a dozen of the other; **être triste comme un ~ de nuit** to be as boring as hell○; ▶ **moulin.**

bonneteau /bɔnto/ *nm inv* three-card trick GB ou monte US.

bonneterie /bɔnɛtʀi/ *nf* **1** Comm, Ind **la ~** hosiery; **2** (magasin) hosiery shop.

bonnetier, **-ière** /bɔntje, ɛʀ/ **I** ▶ 510 *nm,f* Comm hosier.
II bonnetière *nf* (armoire) (small) cupboard.

bonniche = **boniche.**

bon-papa, *pl* **bons-papas** /bɔ̃papa/ *nm* granddad○, grandpapa○.

bonsaï /bɔnzaj/ *nm* bonsai (tree); **un chêne ~** an oak bonsai (tree).

bonshommes ▶ **bonhomme.**

bonsoir /bɔ̃swaʀ/ *nm* (à l'arrivée) good evening, hello; (au départ) good night; (avant le coucher) good night; **on se connaît à peine, bonjour ~** we're just nodding acquaintances.

bonté /bɔ̃te/ **I** *nf* (de personne) kindness (**envers** towards[GB]); (de Dieu, Ciel) goodness; **un homme d'une grande ~** a man of great kindness; **un regard/sourire plein de ~** a look/smile full of kindness; **traiter qn avec ~** to treat sb with kindness; **par ~ d'âme** out of the goodness of one's heart; **c'est mon jour de ~** hum I'm feeling generous today; **voudriez-vous avoir la ~ de faire** fml would you please be kind enough to do; **~ divine!** good heavens!
II bontés *nfpl* (gentillesses) kindness ¢ (**pour** towards[GB]).

bonus /bɔnys/ *nm inv* no-claims bonus.

bonze /bɔ̃z/ *nm* **1** Relig bonze; **2**○ mandarins.

bonzerie /bɔ̃zʀi/ *nf* buddhist monastery.

boogie-woogie, *pl* **~s** /bugiwugi/ *nm* boogie-woogie; **danser le ~** to do the boogie-woogie.

Boole /bul/ *npr* **algèbre de ~** Math Boolean algebra.

booléen, **-éenne** /bɔleɛ̃, ɛn/ *adj* boolean.

boom /bum/ *nm* boom; **~ économique** economic boom; **une industrie en plein ~** a booming industry; **être en plein ~** [*personne*] to be extremely busy.

boomerang /bumʀɑ̃g/ *nm* boomerang; **effet ~** boomerang effect; **faire ~** to boomerang; **revenir en ~** to backfire on sb.

boots /buts/ *nfpl* (avec élastique) jodhpur boots.

boqueteau, *pl* **~x** /bɔkto/ *nm* copse.

borborygme /bɔʀbɔʀigm/ *nm* **1** (bruit) (de faim) rumbling ¢; (de digestion) gurgling ¢; (de tuyauterie) gurgling ¢; **2** (parole indistincte) mumbling ¢.

bord /bɔʀ/ *nm* **1** (limite) gén edge; (de route) side; (de cours d'eau) bank; **le ~ de l'assiette** the edge of the plate; **sur le** or **au ~ de la route** on ou at the side of the road; **au ~ de** lit on ou at the edge of [*chemin, lac, rivière*]; fig on the brink of [*drame, précipice, chaos*]; on the verge of [*faillite, divorce, mort*]; **ils se sont assis au ~ du lac** they sat down by the lake; **au ~ de l'eau** [*restaurant*] waterside (*épith*); [*manger, jouer*] by the waterside; **notre maison est au ~ de l'eau** our house is on the waterside; **au ~ de la mer** [*maison, village, terrain*] by the sea (*après n*); [*activité, vacances*] at the seaside (*après n*) ; **le ~ de la mer** the seaside; **du ~ de mer** [*avenue, village, activité*] seaside (*épith*); **les ~s de (la) Seine** the banks of the Seine; **~ à ~** edge-to-edge; **virage à ~ relevé** bend with a (raised) camber; **2** (pourtour) (de tasse, verre, cratère, lunettes) rim; (de chapeau) brim; **à ~s relevés** [*chapeau*] with a turned-up brim; **soucoupe à large ~** wide-rimmed saucer; ▶ **ras**; **3** (dans un véhicule) **à ~** [*être, travailler, dîner, dormir*] on board, aboard; **monter à ~** to go aboard, to board; **nous sommes restés/avons été retenus à ~** we stayed/have been detained on board; **le travail à ~** work on board; **il y avait 200 passagers à ~** there were 200 passengers on board; **le capitaine/l'hélicoptère les a pris à son ~** the captain/the helicopter took them on board; **à ~ d'un navire/avion/train/bus** on board a ship/plane/train/bus; **un incendie s'est déclaré à ~** a fire broke out on board; **les missiles embarqués à ~ du sous-marin** the missiles on board the submarine; **ils sont partis à ~ de leur voiture/d'une camionnette volée** they left in their car/a stolen van; **par-dessus ~** [*tomber, jeter*] overboard; **de ~** [*instrument, personnel*] on board (*après n*); **on se débrouillera** or **on fera**○ **avec les moyens du ~** we'll make do with what we've got; **4** fig (tendance) side; **je ne suis pas de leur ~** I'm not on their side; **ils sont du même ~** they're on the same side; **des deux/de tous ~s** from both/all sides; **il est un peu anarchiste/alcoolique sur les ~s** he has slightly anarchic/alcoholic tendencies; **5** (côté) side; **ils passaient d'un ~ à l'autre de la frontière** they were crossing from one side of the border to the other; **nous étions projetés d'un ~ à l'autre pendant la tempête** we were thrown from one side to the other during the storm; **de hauts ~s** [*navire*] high-sided (*épith*); **rouler ~ sur ~** [*navire*] to roll in the swell; **tirer des ~s** Naut to tack.
■ **~ d'attaque** Aviat leading edge; **~ de fuite** Aviat trailing edge.

bordage /bɔʀdaʒ/ *nm* **1** Naut (en bois) plank; (en métal) plate; **2** Cout (de vêtement) edging.

bordé /bɔʀde/ *nm* **1** Cout border; **2** Naut (en bois) planking; (en métal) plating.

bordeaux /bɔʀdo/ **I** ▶ 193 *adj inv* burgundy.
II *nm* Vin Bordeaux; **~ rouge** claret.

Bordeaux /bɔʀdo/ ▶ 857 *npr* Bordeaux.

bordée /bɔʀde/ *nf* **1** Mil Naut (décharge) broadside; (canons) broadside; **tirer une ~** lit to fire a broadside; fig to go on a binge○; **2** Naut (route) tack; **tirer des ~s** to tack.
IDIOMES **lâcher une ~ d'injures** to let out a volley of abuse.

bordel● /bɔʀdɛl/ **I** *nm* **1** (maison de prostitution) brothel, whorehouse○; **2** (désordre) shambles (*sg*); **quel ~!** what a shambles!; **mettre le ~** to make a terrible mess; **3** (tapage) racket; **faire le ~** to make a racket.
II *excl* damn○!

bordelais, **~e** /bɔʀdəlɛ, ɛz/ ▶ 857 *adj* of Bordeaux.

Bordelais, **~e** /bɔʀdəlɛ, ɛz/ **I** ▶ 857 *nm,f* (natif) native of Bordeaux; (habitant) inhabitant of Bordeaux.
II ▶ 692 *nprm* Géog **le ~** the Bordeaux region.

bordélique● /bɔʀdelik/ *adj* [*personne*] disorganized; [*lieu*] shambolic○ GB, messy; **c'est ~ ici** this place is a real tip○ GB ou dump○ ou mess.

border /bɔʀde/ [1] *vtr* **1** (suivre un contour) to line (**de** with); **route bordée d'arbres** road lined ou bordered with trees, tree-lined road; **2** (entourer) [*ligne, motif*] to ring [*objet rond*]; [*plage, îles*] to skirt [*côte*]; [*plantes*] to border [*massif, lac*]; **une pelouse bordée de rosiers** a lawn bordered with rose bushes; **3** (longer) [*chemin, cours d'eau*] to border, to run alongside [*maison, terrain*]; [*marin, navire*] to sail along [*côte*]; **sentier bordant la forêt** track bordering the forest; **4** (arranger la literie) to tuck in [*lit*]; to tuck [sb] in [*personne*]; **5** Cout (garnir) to edge [*vêtement, lingerie*] (**de** with); **un mouchoir bordé de dentelle** a handkerchief edged with lace, a lace-trimmed handkerchief; **6** (étarquer) [*marin*] to take up the slack in [*voile*]; **7** (revêtir de bordages) (en bois) to plank; (en métal) to plate; **8** (ramener) [*rameur*] to ship [*avirons*].

bordereau, *pl* **~x** /bɔʀdəʀo/ *nm* **1** (feuille) Admin form, slip; Comm, Fin note; Ordinat sheet; **~ de retrait/de versement** withdrawal/deposit slip; **~ de crédit/d'envoi/d'escompte** credit/dispatch/discount note; **~ de commande** order form; **~ de livraison** delivery slip; **2** (en Bourse) contract; **~ d'achat/de vente** purchase/sale contract; **3** (de dossier juridique) docket.

bordure /bɔʀdyʀ/ **I** *nf* **1** (de terrain, tapis, vêtement) border; **une ~ de dentelle** a lace border; **un jardin/bassin à ~ de fleurs** a garden/pond with a flower border; **une boîte/une enveloppe à ~ rouge** a box/an envelope with a red border; **un manteau à ~ de fourrure** a coat edged ou trimmed with fur; **2** (contour externe) (de route, chemin, quai) edge; (de trottoir) kerb GB, curb US; **3** Naut (de voile) foot.
II en bordure de *loc prép* **1** (sur le bord) (en un point) next to [*parc, terrain*]; (en entourant) on the edge of [*parc, terrain*]; (en longeant) next to, running alongside [*canal, voie ferrée*]; on the side of [*route, chemin*]; **2** (à proximité) just outside [*village, ville*].

bore /bɔʀ/ *nm* boron.

boréal, **~e**, *mpl* **-aux** /bɔʀeal, o/ *adj* boreal; **aurore ~e** aurora borealis.

borgne /bɔʀɲ/ **I** *adj* **1** [*personne*] one-eyed (*épith*); **il est ~** he has only one eye; **2** (bouché) **fenêtre ~** obstructed window;

trou ~ blind hole; **3** (mal famé) [*hôtel, rue*] seedy.

II *nmf* one-eyed man/woman; ▶ **royaume**.

borique /bɔʀik/ *adj* boric.

bornage /bɔʀnaʒ/ *nm* **1** Jur boundary marking; **2**† Naut coastal navigation.

borne /bɔʀn/ I *nf* **1** (sur une route) **~ (kilométrique)** kilometre[GB] marker; **2** (autour d'une propriété) boundary stone; (autour d'un édifice) post; **3** (pour bloquer le passage) bollard GB, post US; **4**○ (kilomètre) kilometre[GB]; **faire 2000 ~s en trois jours** to drive 2000 kilometres[GB] in three days; **5** Électrotech terminal; **~ d'entrée/de sortie** input/output terminal; **6** Math limit; **~ supérieure/inférieure** upper/lower bound.

II **bornes** *nfpl* fig (limites) limits, boundaries; **mettre** or **fixer des ~s** to put limits (**à** on); **une stupidité/tristesse sans ~s** boundless stupidity/sadness; **leur ambition/admiration est sans ~s** their ambition/admiration knows no bounds.

■ **~ d'appel** = **~ téléphonique**; **~ automatique de paiement** electronic pay point; **~ d'incendie** fire hydrant; **~ interactive** electronic communication and information terminal; **~ téléphonique** (sur l'autoroute) emergency telephone; (pour taxis) taxi stand telephone.

IDIOMES **dépasser les ~s** to go too far.

borné, **~e** /bɔʀne/ I *pp* ▶ **borner**.

II *pp adj* [*personne*] narrow-minded; [*esprit, existence*] narrow; [*intelligence*] limited.

borne-fontaine, *pl* **bornes-fontaines** /bɔʀnfɔ̃tɛn/ *nf* C fire hydrant.

Bornéo /bɔʀneo/ ▶ **416** *npr* Borneo.

borner /bɔʀne/ [1] I *vtr* **1** Jur to mark out the boundaries of [*propriété*]; **2** lit [*rivière, montagne*] to border [*pays, région*]; **3** fig to limit [*ambition, désirs*] (**à qch** to sth; **à faire** to doing).

II **se borner** *vpr* **1** (se contenter) **se ~ à faire** [*personne*] to content oneself with doing; **il s'est borné à déclarer/préciser que** he contented himself with declaring/explaining that; **2** (se limiter) **se ~ à qch/à faire** [*rôle, fonctions*] to be limited to sth/to doing; [*personne*] to limit oneself to sth/to doing; **notre rôle se borne à analyser/évaluer** our role is limited to analysing[GB]/evaluating; **je me bornerai à dire que** I'll just say that; **je me suis bornée au strict nécessaire** I kept it down to the absolute essentials.

bosniaque /bɔsnjak/ ▶ **692** *adj* Bosnian.

Bosniaque /bɔsnjak/ *nmf* Bosnian.

Bosnie /bɔsni/ ▶ **692** *nprf* Bosnia.

Bosnie-Herzégovine /bɔsniɛʀzegovin/ ▶ **692** *nprf* Bosnia-Herzegovinia.

boson /bozɔ̃/ *nm* boson.

Bosphore /bɔsfɔʀ/ *nprm* **le ~** Bosphorus; **le détroit du ~** the Bosphorus straits.

bosquet /bɔskɛ/ *nm* (d'arbres) grove.

boss○ /bɔs/ *nm inv* boss.

bossage /bɔsaʒ/ *nm* boss.

bossa-nova, *pl* **bossas-novas** /bɔsanɔva/ *nf* bossa-nova; **danser la ~** to do the bossa-nova.

bosse /bɔs/ *nf* **1** Anat, Zool (sur le dos) hump; (sur le nez) bump; **2** (après un choc) bump; **se faire une ~** to get a bump; **3** (sur un terrain) bump; (sur une piste de ski) mogul, bump; **un parcours en creux et en ~s** a bumpy course; **4** (sur objet) (après choc) dent; (voulue) indentation; **faire une ~ à sa voiture** to dent ou bump one's car.

IDIOMES **avaler les ~s** to zoom over the bumps; **avoir la ~ de** to have a flair for; **rouler sa ~** to knock about.

bosselage /bɔslaʒ/ *nm* embossment.

bosselé, **~e** /bɔsle/ I *pp* ▶ **bosseler**.

II *pp adj* **1** (déformé) [*terrain*] bumpy; [*gobelet*] dented, battered; **2** Art, Tech embossed.

bosseler /bɔsle/ [19] *vtr* **1** (accidentellement) to dent; (volontairement) to make small indentations in; **2** Art, Tech to emboss.

bossellement /bɔsɛlmɑ̃/ *nm* embossing.

bosselure /bɔslyʀ/ *nf* **1** (accidentelle) (small) dent; (voulue) (small) indentation; **2** Art, Tech embossment.

bosser○ /bɔse/ [1] I *vtr* to work on, to swot up○ GB, to cram.

II *vi* to work; **~ comme un fou** to slave away○.

bosseur○, **-euse** /bɔsœʀ, øz/ *nm,f* hard worker, grind○, swot○ GB.

bossoir /bɔswaʀ/ *nm* (d'embarcation) davit; (d'ancre) cathead.

bossu, **~e** /bɔsy/ I *adj* (infirme) hunchbacked; (qui se tient mal) round-shouldered.

II *nm,f* hunchback.

IDIOMES **rire comme un ~** to laugh like a drain.

boston /bɔstɔ̃/ *nm* Mus, Jeux boston.

Boston /bɔstɔ̃/ ▶ **857** *npr* Boston.

bot /bo/ *adj m* **pied ~** club foot; **avoir un pied ~** to be club-footed.

botanique /bɔtanik/ I *adj* botanical; **jardin ~** botanical gardens (*pl*).

II *nf* botany.

botaniste /bɔtanist/ ▶ **510** *nmf* botanist.

Botnie /bɔtni/ ▶ **692** *nprf* Bothnia.

Botswana /bɔtswana/ ▶ **321** *nprm* Botswana.

botte /bɔt/ *nf* **1** (chaussure) boot; **coup de ~**○ kick; ▶ **plein**; **2** Agric (de fleurs, légumes) bunch; (de foin, paille) bale; **3** Sport (en escrime) thrust; (au football, rugby) kick; **4** Univ students' slang **la ~** the top students; **5** Géog **la ~ italienne, la Botte** Italy; ▶ **aiguille**.

■ **~s de caoutchouc** wellington boots, wellingtons; **~s de cheval** riding boots; **~s d'égoutier** waders; **~s de sept lieues** seven league boots.

IDIOMES **sous la ~ de l'ennemi** under the oppressor's heel; **être/se mettre à la ~ de qn** to be/to put oneself under sb's heel.

botté, **~e** /bɔte/ I *pp* ▶ **botter**.

II *pp adj* with boots on; **~ de cuir** leather-booted.

botter /bɔte/ [1] I *vtr* **1** (chausser de bottes) to put [sb's] boots on; **2** (fournir en bottes) to sell boots to; **3**○ (plaire) **ça le botte!** he loves it, he really digs it○; **4** (frapper du pied) to kick; **~ le ballon** to kick the ball; **~ le train** or **le derrière**○ or **les fesses**○ **de qn** to boot sb up the backside○ GB, to kick sb in the ass◐.

II *vi* Équit, Sport to kick.

botteur, **-euse** /bɔtœʀ/ *nm,f* Sport striker.

bottier /bɔtje/ *nm* bootmaker.

bottillon /bɔtijɔ̃/ *nm* bootee.

bottin® /bɔtɛ̃/ *nm* telephone directory, phone book.

bottine /bɔtin/ *nf* ankle-boot.

botulique /bɔtylik/ *adj* botulinic; **bacille ~** botulinum.

botulisme /bɔtylism/ ▶ **271** *nm* botulism.

bouc /buk/ *nm* **1** (animal) billy goat; **2** (barbe) goatee; **porter le ~** to have a goatee (beard).

■ **~ émissaire** scapegoat.

IDIOMES **sentir le ~** to stink.

boucan○ /bukɑ̃/ *nm* **1** (bruit) din, racket○; **faire du ~** to make a din ou racket○; **2** (protestation) fuss (**pour** about); **du ~** a fuss; **faire du ~** [*personne*] to kick up a fuss; [*affaire*] to cause an uproar.

boucanage /bukanaʒ/ *nm* smoke-drying.

boucane○ /bukan/ *nf* C smoke.

boucané, **~e** /bukane/ *adj* [*poisson, viande*] smoke-dried; [*peau*] dried out.

boucaner /bukane/ [1] *vtr* to smoke-dry.

boucanier /bukanje/ *nm* **1** (pirate) buccaneer; **2** (chasseur) hunter of wild ox.

bouchage /buʃaʒ/ *nm* gén sealing; (avec du liège) corking.

bouche /buʃ/ I *nf* **1** (cavité buccale) mouth; **respirer par la ~** to breathe through one's mouth; **ne parle pas la ~ pleine!** don't talk with your mouth full!; **j'avais la ~ sèche** my mouth was dry; ▶ **cul-de-poule**, **eau**, **pain**; **2** (lèvre) mouth, lips (*pl*); **elle a une ~ sensuelle** she has a sensual mouth, she has sensual lips; **s'embrasser à pleine ~** to kiss full on the mouth; **s'embrasser sur la ~** to kiss on the lips; **s'embrasser à ~ que veux-tu** to kiss passionately; **il est arrivé la ~ en cœur** (en minaudant) he came simpering up; **3** (organe de la parole) **ouvrir la ~** to speak; **dès qu'elle ouvre la ~, c'est pour dire une bêtise** every time she opens her mouth, she says something stupid; **il n'a pas ouvert la ~ de toute la soirée** he hasn't said a word all evening; **en avoir plein la ~ de qn/qch** to be unable to stop talking about sb/sth; **il n'a que ce mot à la ~** that word is never off his lips; **il a toujours la critique à la ~** he's always ready to criticize; **dans sa ~, ce n'est pas une insulte** coming from him, that's not an insult; **parler** or **s'exprimer par la ~ de qn d'autre** to use sb else as one's mouthpiece; **il a mis ce mot dans la ~ de Dupont** he put this word into Dupont's mouth; **apprendre qch de la ~ de qn** to hear sth from sb; **apprendre qch de la ~ même de qn** to hear sth from sb's own lips; **être dans la ~ de tout le monde** to be on everyone's lips; **passer/se transmettre de ~ à oreille** [*nouvelle*] to be passed on/to be spread by word of mouth; ▶ **fendre**, **vérité**; **4** (organe du goût) **c'est une fine ~** he's/she's a gourmet; **5** (personne) mouth; **avoir trois ~s à nourrir** to have three mouths to feed; **les ~s inutiles de la société** people who are a burden on society; **6** (de four, volcan) mouth.

II **bouches** *nfpl* (de fleuve) mouth (*sg*); (de golfe, détroit) entrance.

■ **~ d'aération** air vent; **~ de chaleur** hot-air vent; **~ d'égout** manhole; **~ à feu** Hist Mil piece of ordnance; **~ d'incendie** fire hydrant; **~ de métro** tube entrance GB, subway entrance US.

IDIOMES **faire la fine ~ devant qch** to turn one's nose up at sth; **garder qch pour la bonne ~** to keep the best till last; ▶ **sept**.

bouché, **~e** /buʃe/ I *pp* ▶ **boucher**[2].

II *pp adj* **1** lit (obstrué) [*route, tuyau, accès, nez, artère*] blocked; fig [*profession, secteur, discipline*] oversubscribed; **j'ai les oreilles ~es** my ears feel blocked; **tu as les oreilles ~es ou quoi?** iron are you deaf or what○?; **2** Météo [*ciel, temps*] overcast; **l'avenir semble complètement ~** fig the future looks grim; **3** pej (stupide) thick, stupid; **~ à l'émeri** thick○; **4** (en bouteille) [*vin, cidre*] bottled.

III **bouchée** *nf* **1** (contenu de la bouche) mouthful; **pour une ~e de pain** fig for next to nothing; **ne faire qu'une ~e d'un gâteau** to wolf a cake down; **ne faire qu'une ~e d'un adversaire** fig to make short work of an opponent; **mettre les ~es doubles** fig to double one's efforts; **2** Culin **une ~e (au chocolat)** a chocolate; **~e sucrée** petit four.

■ **~e à la reine** vol-au-vent.

bouche-à-bouche /buʃabuʃ/ *nm inv* mouth-to-mouth resuscitation; **faire le ~** to give mouth-to-mouth resuscitation (**à qn** to sb).

bouche-à-oreille /buʃaɔʀɛj/ *nm inv* **le ~** word of mouth.

boucher[1], **-ère** /buʃe, ɛʀ/ I ▶ **510** *nm,f* butcher; **aller chez le ~** to go to the butcher's.

II **bouchère** *nf* (femme de boucher) butcher's wife.

boucher[2] /buʃe/ [1] I *vtr* **1** (mettre un bouchon à) to cork, to put a cork on [*bouteille*]; **2** (obstruer) to block [*tuyau, passage, aération, fenêtre, vue*]; (en encrassant) to clog (up) [*gouttière, artère, pore*]; (en comblant) to fill [*trou, fente*]; **~ les trous** lit to fill the holes; fig (dans un budget, une soirée) to fill the gaps.

II se boucher *vpr* **1** (se fermer) **se ~ le nez** lit to hold one's nose; **se ~ les oreilles** lit (avec doigts) to put one's fingers in one's ears; (avec du coton) to plug one's ears; fig to turn a deaf ear; **2** (s'obstruer) [*lavabo, WC*] to get blocked; [*vaisseaux, artères*] to get clogged up; [*oreilles*] to feel blocked; [*nez*] to get blocked; **3** Météo [*temps*] to become overcast.

IDIOMES **en ~ un coin à qn**○ to amaze sb; **ça t'en bouche un coin que je sache coudre!** you're amazed that I can sew, eh?

boucherie /buʃʀi/ *nf* **1** ▶**510** (magasin) butcher's shop, butcher's; (commerce) butcher's trade, butchery; **2** fig (tuerie) slaughter.

■ **~ chevaline** horsemeat butcher's.

Bouches-du-Rhône /buʃdyʀon/ ▶**692** *nprf pl* (département) **les ~** the Bouches-du-Rhône.

bouche-trou, *pl* **~s** /buʃtʀu/ *nm* stand-in; **jouer les ~s** to be a stand-in.

bouchon /buʃɔ̃/ *nm* **1** (pour boucher) (en liège) cork; (en verre, métal, plastique) stopper; (de baignoire) plug; (qui se visse) (de bidon) cap; (de tube, d'encrier) top, cap; **sentir le ~** [*vin*] to be corked; **2** (obstruction) plug; **~ de cérumen** plug of earwax; **faire ~** to plug; **3** (de la circulation) (en ville) traffic jam; (sur autoroute) traffic jam, tailback; **4** Pêche float; **5** (aux boules) jack.

■ **~ antivol** Aut locking fuel filler cap; **~ de carafe**○ fig gem, rock○; **~ doseur** optic; **~ de réservoir** Aut petrol GB ou gas US cap; **~ de sécurité** safety lid; **~ de vapeur** Mécan air ou vapour[GB] lock; **~ verseur** spout; **~ à vis** screw-top.

IDIOMES **pousser le ~ trop loin** to push it a bit○.

bouchonner /buʃɔne/ [1] **I** *vtr* **1** (frotter) to rub down [*cheval*]; to rub [*personne, visage*]; **2** (cajoler) to pamper.

II *vi* [*circulation*] to get jammed; **ça bouchonne sur les quais** there are traffic jams along the river.

bouchot /buʃo/ *nm* Pêche (parc à moules) mussel bed; **moules de ~** cultivated mussels.

bouclage /buklaʒ/ *nm* **1** (de ceinture) fastening, buckling; **2** (achèvement) (de dossier, d'une affaire) completion; (de périphérique, travaux) completion; **3** Presse **la nouvelle de sa mort est arrivée après le ~** the news of his death arrived after the newspaper had been put to bed; **4** (encerclement) cordoning off; **la police a procédé au ~ du quartier** the police cordoned off the area; **5** Ordinat wrap-around.

boucle /bukl/ *nf* **1** (de ceinture, chaussure) buckle; **une ~ en métal** a metal buckle; **2** (de cheveux) curl; (de lacet, corde) loop; (de lettre) loop; **de belles ~s blondes** lovely blonde curls; **faire une ~ avec une corde** to make a loop with a rope; **la ~ du 'l'** the loop of the 'l'; **3** TV, Vidéo **en ~** in a continuous loop; **4** Ordinat loop.

■ **~ d'oreille** earring.

bouclé, **~e** /bukle/ **I** *pp* ▶ **boucler**.

II *pp adj* [*cheveux, perruque*] curly; [*fourrure*] curled; **elle est toute ~e** she's got very curly hair.

boucler /bukle/ [1] **I** *vtr* **1** (attacher) to fasten [*ceinture de sécurité, valise, bagages*]; **2**○ (fermer) to lock [*porte, issue*]; to lock [*immeuble, pièce*]; to lock [*coffre, armoire*]; **3**○ (encercler) [*police, gendarmes*] to cordon off, surround [*quartier, secteur, territoire*]; to close [*frontière*]; **4** (achever) to complete [*enquête, saison, projet, disque*]; to close [*dossier*]; to sign [*accord*]; **l'enquête a été bouclée en un mois** the enquiry GB ou investigation US was completed in one month; **5** Fin to balance [*budget*]; to settle [*financement*]; **~ un bilan** to balance the books; **~ une OPA** to clinch a takeover bid; **~ le mois/les fins de mois** to make ends meet at the end of the/each month; **6** Presse to put [sth] to bed [*journal, édition*]; **on a bouclé le journal à 19 h** we put the paper to bed at 7 pm; **7**○ (mettre en prison) [*police, justice*] to lock [sb] up [*malfaiteur, meurtrier*]; **faire ~ qn** to get sb locked up.

II *vi* [*cheveux*] to curl; **ses cheveux bouclent naturellement** his/her hair curls naturally; **se faire ~ les cheveux** to have one's hair curled.

IDIOMES **la ~** to shut up; **boucle-la**◐! shut your trap◐!; **~ la boucle** to come full circle; **le héros retrouve son fils, la boucle est bouclée** the hero finds his son and things have come full circle.

bouclette /buklɛt/ *nf* **1** (de cheveux) small curl; **2** Tex (**laine**) **~** bouclé (wool).

bouclier /buklije/ *nm* shield; **~ humain** human shield; **~ thermique** heat shield.

bouddha /buda/ *nm* (représentation) buddha.

Bouddha /buda/ *nprm* Buddha.

bouddhique /budik/ *adj* Buddhist.

bouddhisme /budism/ *nm* Buddhism.

bouddhiste /budist/ *adj, nmf* Buddhist.

bouder /bude/ [1] **I** *vtr* to avoid [*personne*]; to want nothing to do with [*études*]; to stay away from [*spectacle*]; to steer clear of [*marchandise*]; **il ne boude pas le vin/les distractions** he never turns down a glass of wine/a good time.

II *vi* to sulk.

III se bouder *vpr* not to be on speaking terms.

bouderie /budʀi/ *nf* **1** (action) sulking; **2** (manifestation de déplaisir) sulk.

boudeur, **-euse** /budœʀ, øz/ **I** *adj* [*personne, caractère, mine*] sulky.

II *nm,f* sulker.

boudin /budɛ̃/ *nm* **1** Culin ≈ black pudding GB, blood sausage; **~ blanc** ≈ white pudding GB ou sausage; **2**○ pej (femme) lump○; **3** Naut fender.

IDIOMES **s'en aller** or **partir** or **finir en eau de ~** to come to nothing; **faire du ~**○ to sulk.

boudiné, **~e** /budine/ **I** *pp* ▶ **boudiner**.

II *pp adj* **1** (gros) [*doigt, main*] podgy; **2** (serré) squeezed (**dans** into).

boudiner /budine/ [1] **I** *vtr* **1** Tech to coil [*fil de fer*]; **2** Tex to rove [*fil*]; **3** (serrer) **sa robe la boudine** her dress shows every bulge.

II○ **se boudiner** *vpr* to squeeze oneself (**dans** into).

boudoir /budwaʀ/ *nm* **1** (salon) boudoir; **2** (biscuit) sponge finger GB, ladyfinger.

boue /bu/ **I** *nf* **1** (terre) mud; (sédiment) silt; **bain de ~** mudbath; **2** (scandale) muck; **remuer la ~** to muckrake; **traîner qn dans la ~** to drag sb's name through the mud.

II boues *nfpl* (déchet industriel) sludge ¢.

bouée /bwe/ *nf* **1** (gonflable) rubber ring; **2** (balise) buoy; **3**○ (de graisse) spare tyre○ GB ou tire US.

■ **~ de sauvetage** or **de secours** lit lifebelt GB, life preserver US; fig lifeline.

boueux, **-euse** /buø, øz/ **I** *adj* **1** [*terrain, chemin*] muddy; **2** Imprim smudgy.

II○ *nm* dustman GB, bin man GB, garbage man US.

bouffant, **~e** /bufɑ̃, ɑ̃t/ **I** *adj* [*chemisier, pantalon*] baggy; [*manche*] puffed; [*coiffure*] bouffant.

II *nm* (de manche) fullness; **donner du ~ à sa coiffure** to make one's hair look fuller.

bouffarde○ /bufaʀd/ *nf* pipe.

bouffe○ /buf/ *nf* (activité de manger) eating; (nourriture) food, grub○; (repas) meal; **grande ~** blowout○, spread○; **à la ~!** grub's up○!, come and get it○!

bouffée /bufe/ *nf* **1** (souffle) (d'odeur) whiff; (de tabac, vapeur, vent) puff; **une ~ d'air frais** lit, fig a breath of fresh air; **tirer une ~** to have a puff ou drag○; **tirer une ~ de sa pipe** to draw a puff on one's pipe; **le vent soufflait par ~s** the wind blew in gentle gusts; **2** (accès) rush (**de** of); **~ d'orgueil** rush of pride.

■ **~ de chaleur** Méd hot flush GB, hot flash US; **~ délirante** Méd period of hallucination.

bouffer /bufe/ [1] **I**○ *vtr* **1** (manger) to eat; **on dirait qu'il va la ~** it looks as if he's going to strangle her; **2** (accaparer) **~ qn** [*politique, famille*] to take over sb's whole life; **ça me bouffe tout mon temps** it takes up all my time; **se faire/laisser ~** to be/let oneself be taken over (**par** by); **3** (consommer) [*voiture*] to guzzle [*essence*]; [*voiture*] to burn [*huile*]; **4** (dépenser) to throw [sth] away [*argent*]; **5** (utiliser) to take up [*espace*].

II *vi* **1**○ (manger) to eat; (beaucoup) to eat a lot, to stuff oneself○; **2** Mode (gonfler) to billow out.

IDIOMES **~ du curé** to be violently anticlerical; **~ du kilomètre**○ to clock up a lot of mileage; **se ~ le nez**○ to be at each other's throats.

bouffetance◐ /buftɑ̃s/ *nf* grub○, food.

bouffi, **~e** /bufi/ **I** *pp* ▶ **bouffir**.

II *pp adj* **1** (physiquement) puffy; **il a les yeux ~s de sommeil** his eyes are puffy ou swollen with sleep; **il a le visage ~ par l'alcool** his face is swollen from alcohol; **elle est ~e** her face is puffy; **avoir les traits ~s** to have swollen features; **2** (moralement) puffed up (**par** with).

IDIOMES **tu l'as dit, ~**○! you don't say○!

bouffir /bufiʀ/ [3] *vtr* to make [sth] puffy ou swollen [*yeux, visage, peau*].

bouffissure /bufisyʀ/ *nf* **1** (d'œil, de visage) puffiness; **2** (de style) pomposity.

bouffon, **-onne** /bufɔ̃, ɔn/ **I** *adj* farcical.

II *nm* **1** (plaisantin) clown; **faire le ~** to clown about ou around; **2** Hist (de cour) jester; (de théâtre) buffoon.

bouffonnerie /bufɔnʀi/ *nf* **1** (acte) antics (*pl*); **2** (effets comiques) buffoonery; **3** (caractère) ridiculousness; **4** Théât farce.

bougainvillée /bugɛ̃vile/ *nf*, **bougainvillier** /bugɛ̃vilje/ *nm* bougainvillea.

bouge /buʒ/ *nm* (logement) hovel; (café) dive.

bougeoir /buʒwaʀ/ *nm* candleholder; (haut) candlestick.

bougeotte○ /buʒɔt/ *nf* restlessness; **avoir la ~** to be restless.

bouger /buʒe/ [13] **I** *vtr* (tous contextes) to move.

II *vi* **1** (faire un mouvement) [*personne, animal*] to move; **ne bouge pas, j'arrive!** lit, fig don't move, I'm coming!; **il tire sur tout ce qui bouge** he shoots at everything that moves; **ne bougez plus, je prends une photo!** keep still, I'm taking a photo!; **c'est malin, tu m'as fait ~!** well done, you jogged me!; **le vent fait ~ les feuilles** the wind is stirring the leaves; **2** (se déplacer) [*personne, groupe*] to move; **il ne bouge plus de chez lui** he doesn't go out any more; **3**○ (évoluer) [*secteur, entreprise, pays*] to stir; **ça bouge dans l'audiovisuel/en Espagne** things are stirring in the audio-visual world/in Spain; **faire ~ un parti/une entreprise** to shake up a party/a company; **4**○ (être animé) **c'est une ville/un quartier qui bouge** this is a lively town/area; **5**○ (réagir) to show signs of unrest; **le peuple commence à ~** there is some unrest among the people; **6**○ (varier) [*prix, score, prévision*] to change; **le prix/score n'a pas bougé** the price/score hasn't changed; **7**○ Tex **tu peux le laver à la machine, ça ne bougera pas** you can wash it in the machine, it won't shrink; **la couleur ne devrait pas ~** the colour[GB] shouldn't fade.

III se bouger○ *vpr* [*personne*] (se pousser) to get out of the way; (se dépêcher) to move oneself○; (se donner du mal) to put some effort in; ▶ **cul**.

bougie /buʒi/ *nf* **1** (de cire) candle; **~ d'anniversaire** birthday candle; **souffler ses 30 ~s** to celebrate one's 30th birthday; **s'éclairer à la ~** to use candles (for light); **2** Aut sparking plug GB, spark plug.

bougnat○† /buɲa/ *nm* café proprietor (*formerly selling coal*).

bougnoule◑ /buɲul/ *nmf* offensive wog◑ GB injur, North African.

bougon, **-onne** /bugɔ̃, ɔn/ **I** *adj* grumpy. **II** *nm,f* grouch.

bougonnement /bugɔnmɑ̃/ *nm* grouching ¢.

bougonner /bugɔne/ [1] *vi* to grumble.

bougre /bugʀ/ *nm* **1**○ (type) bloke; **le ~!** that so and so!; **bon ~** good sort; **pauvre ~** poor devil; **~ d'imbécile** you bloody GB ou damn○ idiot; **2**† (sodomite) bugger†.

bougrement○ /bugʀəmɑ̃/ *adv* damn○; **~ difficile** damn hard; **se tromper ~** to be absolutely wrong.

bougresse○ /bugʀɛs/ *nf* bird○ GB, chick○, woman.

boui-boui○, *pl* **bouis-bouis** /bwibwi/ *nm* **1** (restaurant) joint○, greasy spoon○, small restaurant; **2** (hotel) cheap hotel, fleabag○ US.

bouif◑ /bwif/ *nm* cobbler.

bouillabaisse /bujabɛs/ *nf* bouillabaisse, fish soup.

bouillant, **~e** /bujɑ̃, ɑ̃t/ *adj* **1** (qui bout) [*eau, huile*] boiling; **faire cuire à l'eau ~e** cook in boiling water; **2**○ (très chaud) [*radiateur, bain, plat, thé*] boiling (hot).

bouille○ /buj/ *nf* face; **quelle ~!** what a face!; **une bonne ~** a nice face.

bouilleur /bujœʀ/ *nm* **~ de cru** home distiller.

bouillie /buji/ *nf* **1** Culin gruel; (pour bébés) baby cereal; **en ~** [*légumes*] pej mushy; **mettre en ~** lit, fig to reduce [sth/sb] to a pulp; **2** (pesticide) spray.

■ **~ bordelaise** Bordeaux mix(ture); **~ bourguignonne** Burgundy mix(ture); **~ explosive** slurry.

bouillir /bujiʀ/ [31] *vi* **1** gén [*eau, lait, préparation*] to boil; **faire ~** to boil, to bring [sth] to the boil; **du lait bouilli** boiled milk; **je vais mettre ces draps à ~** I'm going to boil these sheets; **2** fig (s'emporter) [*personne*] to seethe; **je bouillais intérieurement** I was seething inside; **~ de** to seethe with [*impatience, rage*].

bouilloire /bujwaʀ/ *nf* kettle; **~ électrique** electric kettle.

bouillon /bujɔ̃/ *nm* **1** (potage) broth; **~ de légumes** vegetable broth; ▶ **onze**; **2** (liquide de cuisson, concentré) stock; **~ de poisson/légumes** fish/vegetable stock; **3** (de liquide qui bout) bubble; **au premier ~** as soon as it begins to boil; **bouillir à gros ~s** to boil fiercely; **sortir à gros ~s** [*eau, sang*] to gush out; **4** Cout shirring; **5** Édition **le ~** unsold copies (*pl*); **un ~ important** lots of unsold copies.

■ **~ de culture** Biol nutrient broth; fig hotbed (**pour** of); **~ gras** Culin meat-stock.

IDIOMES **prendre** or **boire un ~** (en nageant) to get a mouthful; (en affaires) to take a tumble○, to sustain losses.

bouillonnant, **~e** /bujɔnɑ̃, ɑ̃t/ *adj* [*liquide*] foaming; [*idées*] bubbling up to the surface; [*milieu, personne*] lively; [*ambition*] boundless; **source ~e** Géol hot spring.

bouillonnement /bujɔnmɑ̃/ *nm* **1** (de liquide) foaming; fig ferment; **2** Géol boil.

bouillonner /bujɔne/ [1] **I** *vtr* Cout to shirr; **store bouillonné** Austrian blind.

II *vi* **1** (faire des bulles) [*liquide*] to bubble; **2** (être dynamique) to be lively; **~ d'activité** to be bustling with activity.

bouillotte /bujɔt/ *nf* hot-water bottle.

boulange○ /bulɑ̃ʒ/ *nf* bakery trade.

boulanger, **-ère** /bulɑ̃ʒe, ɛʀ/ **I** ▶ **510** *nm,f* baker.

II boulangère *nf* (épouse de boulanger) baker's wife.

boulangerie /bulɑ̃ʒʀi/ ▶ **510** *nf* **1** (magasin) bakery, baker's; **2** (activité) bakery trade.

boulangerie-pâtisserie, *pl* **boulangeries-pâtisseries** /bulɑ̃ʒʀipɑtisʀi/ *nf* bakery (*selling cakes and pastries*), *bakery-patisserie* GB.

boulangisme /bulɑ̃ʒism/ *nm* Boulangism.

boulangiste /bulɑ̃ʒist/ *adj, nmf* Boulangist.

boule /bul/ **I** *nf* (de bowling) bowl; (de jeu de boules) boule; (de rampe d'escalier) knob; (de machine à écrire) head; **mettre qch en ~** to roll sth up into a ball; **avoir une ~ dans la gorge** to have a lump in one's throat; **avoir une ~ sur l'estomac** to have a lead weight in one's stomach; ▶ **loto**.

II boules ▶ **449** *nfpl* Jeux boules.

■ **~ de billard** billiard ball; **~ de cristal** crystal ball; **~ de feu** fireball; **~ de gomme** pastille; **~ à légumes** vegetable steamer; **~ de naphtaline** mothball; **~ de neige** snowball; **faire ~ de neige** to snowball; **~ de nerfs**○ bundle of nerves; **~ puante** stink bomb; **~ Quiès®** earplug; **~ à thé** tea ball.

IDIOMES **avoir la ~ à zéro**○ to have no hair left; **il a perdu la ~**○ (définitivement) he's gone mad; (passagèrement) he's lost his marbles○; **être en ~**○ to be furious; **mettre qn en ~**○ to make sb furious; **avoir les ~s**○ (angoisse) to have butterflies○ (in one's stomach); (colère) to be hopping mad○; **ça me fout les ~s**◑ (angoisse) the thought of it makes me sick○; (exaspération) it really gets to me○.

bouleau, *pl* **~x** /bulo/ *nm* birch.

■ **~ blanc** silver birch.

boule-de-neige, *pl* **boules-de-neige** /buldənɛʒ/ *nf* Bot snowball.

bouledogue /buldɔg/ *nm* bulldog.

bouler /bule/ [1] *vi* **~ au bas de l'escalier** to roll down the stairs; **envoyer qn ~**○ to send sb packing○.

boulet /bulɛ/ *nm* **1** (projectile) **~ (de canon)** cannonball; **il est passé comme un ~ de canon** he shot past; **2** (de bagnard) ball and chain; **3** fig millstone; **avoir un ~ au pied** to have a millstone around one's neck; **être un ~ pour qn** to be a millstone around sb's neck; **traîner qch/qn comme un ~** to drag sth/sb around like a ten-ton weight; **4** (de charbon) coal nut; **5** (du cheval) fetlock (joint).

IDIOMES **tirer à ~s rouges sur qn/qch** to launch a bitter attack on sb/sth.

boulette /bulɛt/ *nf* **1** (de pain, papier) pellet; **2**○ (bourde) blunder; **faire une ~** to make a blunder.

■ **~ de viande** Culin meatball.

boulevard /bulvaʀ/ *nm* **1** (avenue) boulevard; **2** Théât farce; **théâtre de ~** farce.

■ **~ périphérique** ring road GB, beltway US.

boulevardier, **-ière** /bulvaʀdje, ɛʀ/ *adj* **esprit ~** bawdy humour[GB].

bouleversant, **~e** /bulvɛʀsɑ̃, ɑ̃t/ *adj* (émouvant) deeply moving; (pénible) distressing.

bouleversement /bulvɛʀsəmɑ̃/ *nm* upheaval; **le ~ du site** the way the whole place has been turned upside down.

bouleverser /bulvɛʀse/ [1] *vtr* **1** (émouvoir) to move [sb] deeply; (affliger) to shatter; **la cérémonie l'a bouleversé** he was deeply moved by the ceremony; **il a été bouleversé par la mort de son ami** he was shattered by the death of his friend; **2** (mettre en désordre) **l'orage a bouleversé le jardin/le paysage** the storm wreaked havoc in the garden/on the countryside; **les cambrioleurs ont bouleversé la maison/les dossiers** the thieves turned the house/the files upside down; **3** (désorganiser) to disrupt; **4** (changer) to change; **les récents événements ont bouleversé le paysage politique** recent events have changed the face of politics.

boulier /bulje/ *nm* abacus.

boulimie /bulimi/ *nf* **1** Psych, Méd bulimia; **2** fig **être pris d'une ~ de lecture** to be devouring books.

boulimique /bulimik/ **I** *adj* **1** Méd bulimic; **2** fig insatiable.

II *nmf* bulimic.

bouliste /bulist/ *nmf* boules player.

boulocher /bulɔʃe/ [1] *vi* [*pull, tissu*] to pill.

boulodrome /bulɔdʀom/ *nm* area for playing boules.

boulon /bulɔ̃/ *nm* (à écrou) bolt; (à clavette) key bolt; **serrer** or **resserrer les ~s** lit to tighten the bolts; fig to tighten things up.

boulonnage /bulɔnaʒ/ *nm* Tech (d'un élément) bolting; (d'éléments entre eux) bolting together.

boulonnais, **~e** /bulɔnɛ, ɛz/ ▶ **857** *adj* of Boulogne.

Boulonnais, **~e** /bulɔnɛ, ɛz/ ▶ **857** *nm,f* (natif) native of Boulogne; (habitant) inhabitant of Boulogne.

boulonner /bulɔne/ [1] **I** *vtr* to bolt [sth] on [*élément*]; to bolt together [*éléments*].

II○ *vi* to work, to slave away.

boulot, **-otte** /bulo, ɔt/ **I** *adj* tubby; **il est un peu ~** he's a bit on the tubby side.

II○ *nm* **1** (tâche) work; **au ~!** (toi) get to work!; (moi, nous) let's get to work!; **tu as fait du bon ~** you've done a good job; **ça va être un sacré ~** it's going to be a helluva○ job; **2** (emploi) job; **chercher du ~** to look for a job; **les petits ~s** casual jobs.

boulotter○ /bulɔte/ [1] *vtr, vi* to eat.

boum /bum/ **I** *nm* **1** (bruit) bang; **il y a eu un gros ~ et puis plus rien** there was an enormous bang and then nothing; **2**○ (développement) **être en plein ~** [*économie, ventes, affaires*] to be booming; **faire un ~** [*naissances*] to boom.

II *nf* (fête) party.

III *excl* **1** (explosion) bang!; **ça va faire ~!** it's going to explode, it'll go 'bang!' lang enfantin; **2** (chute) baby talk **~ (par terre)!** oops a daisy! lang enfantin.

boumer○ /bume/ [1] *vi* **ça boume?** how's it going?; **ça boume!** things are going great○!

bouquet /bukɛ/ *nm* **1** (floral) **~ (de fleurs)** bunch of flowers; (composé) bouquet; (petit) posy; **faire un ~** to make a bouquet; **2** (de feu d'artifice) final flourish; **~ final** crowning piece; **en** or **comme ~ final** fig to crown it all; **3** (d'arbres) clump; **4** (de fines herbes) bunch; **5** (crevette) prawn; **6** Vin bouquet; **7** Comm down payment on a property (*subsequent payments being in the form of an annuity to the owner*).

■ **~ garni** bouquet garni.

IDIOMES **c'est le ~**○! (le comble) that's the limit○!; (le coup de grâce) that's the last straw○!

bouquetière /buktjɛʀ/ ▶ **510** *nf* Comm flower seller.

bouquetin /buktɛ̃/ *nm* ibex.

bouquin○ /bukɛ̃/ *nm* book.

bouquiner○ /bukine/ [1] *vtr, vi* to read.

bouquiniste /bukinist/ ▶ **510** *nmf* second-hand bookseller.

bourbe /buʀb/ *nf* silt, mud.

bourbeux, **-euse** /buʀbø, øz/ *adj* muddy.

bourbier /buʀbje/ *nm* **1** lit quagmire; **2** fig tangle, quagmire.

bourbon /buʀbɔ̃/ *nm* bourbon.

Bourbon /buʀbɔ̃/ *nprm* Bourbon; **les ~** the Bourbons.

bourde /buʀd/ *nf* (bévue) blunder; **faire une ~** to make a blunder, to make a boo-boo○.

bourdon /buʀdɔ̃/ *nm* **1** Zool bumblebee; **2** (cloche) tenor bell; **3** Mus (d'orgue) bourdon; **4** Imprim out; **5** Relig (de pèlerin) pilgrim's staff.

IDIOMES **avoir le ~** to feel depressed, to be down in the dumps○.

bourdonnement /buʀdɔnmɑ̃/ *nm* (d'insecte) buzzing ¢; (de ruche) humming ¢; (de moteur) hum; (d'hélicoptère, avion) drone; (de foule) murmur.

■ **~ d'oreilles** Méd ringing in the ears, tinnitus spéc.

bourdonner /buʀdɔne/ [1] *vi* [*insecte*] to

buzz; [*moteur*] to hum; [*avion, hélicoptère*] to drone; [*foule*] to murmur; **avoir les oreilles qui bourdonnent** to have a ringing in one's ears, to have tinnitus spéc.

bourg /buʀ/ *nm* market town.

bourgade /buʀgad/ *nf* small town.

bourgeois, **~e** /buʀʒwa, az/ **I** *adj* **1** [*libéralisme, idéologie*] bourgeois; péj [*morale, préjugés*] middle-class; **2** (cossu) [*quartier, maison*] bourgeois; **3** Jur [*habitation*] for private use (*après n*).
II *nm,f* **1** (personne de la classe moyenne) middle-class person, bourgeois péj; **2** Hist (sous l'Ancien Régime) bourgeois; (au Moyen Âge) burgher; **les ~ de Calais** the burghers of Calais.

bourgeoisement /buʀʒwazmɑ̃/ *adv* **1** (confortablement) comfortably; **2** Jur for private use (*après n*).

bourgeoisie /buʀʒwazi/ *nf* **1** (classe moyenne) middle classes (*pl*); **la grande** or **haute ~** the upper middle class; **la petite ~** the lower middle class; **2** Hist, Pol bourgeoisie.

bourgeon /buʀʒɔ̃/ *nm* **1** Bot bud; **en ~s** in bud; **2**† (bouton) pimple.

bourgeonnant, **~e** /buʀʒɔnɑ̃, ɑ̃t/ *adj* **1** [*nature*] budding; [*arbre*] burgeoning, in bud (*après n*); **2** fig [*activité*] burgeoning.

bourgeonnement /buʀʒɔnmɑ̃/ *nm* **1** (d'arbre) budding, lit burgeoning; (de graine) burgeoning; **2** fig (développement) burgeoning.

bourgeonner /buʀʒɔne/ [1] *vi* **1** Bot to bud, to burgeon; **2** fig (se développer) to burgeon; **3**○ [*personne*] to get pimples.

bourgmestre /buʀgmɛstʀ/ *nm* burgomaster.

bourgogne /buʀgɔɲ/ *nm* Vin Burgundy.

Bourgogne /buʀgɔɲ/ ▶ **692** *nprf* **la ~** Burgundy.

bourguignon, **-onne** /buʀgiɲɔ̃, ɔn/ **I** *adj* [*personne, activité, lieu*] Burgundian; **la capitale bourguignonne** the capital of Burgundy.
II *nm* Culin beef bourguignon, beef casserole cooked in red wine.

Bourguignon, **-onne** /buʀgiɲɔ̃, ɔn/ ▶ **692** *nm,f* Burgundian.

bourlinguer○ /buʀlɛ̃ge/ [1] *vi* (beaucoup naviguer) to sail the seven seas; (beaucoup voyager) to travel around a lot; **~ dans le monde entier** to travel all over the world.

bourlingueur○, **-euse** /buʀlɛ̃gœʀ, øz/ *nm,f* globetrotter.

bourrache /buʀaʃ/ *nf* (plante) borage; (infusion) borage tea.

bourrade /buʀad/ *nf* (avec la main, l'épaule) shove; (avec le coude) (sharp) nudge; **une ~ amicale** a nudge.

bourrage /buʀaʒ/ *nm* **1** (remplissage) (de fauteuil, coussin) stuffing; (de pipe) filling; (de cartouche) wadding; **2** (engorgement) jamming.
■ **~ de crâne** brainwashing.

bourrasque /buʀask/ *nf* **1** Météo (de vent) gust; (de neige) flurry; **souffler en ~s** to gust; **2** fig whirlwind.

bourratif, **-ive** /buʀatif, iv/ *adj* very filling; (plus lourd et compact) stodgy; **c'est très ~** it's very filling.

bourre /buʀ/ **I**◑ †*nm* (policier) cop○.
II *nf* **1** (pour remplissage) stuffing; (déchets textiles) flock; (de cartouche) wad; **2** Bot down.
IDIOMES **de première ~**○ fig first-rate, top-notch○; **être à la ~**○ to be pushed for time.

bourré, **~e** /buʀe/ **I** *pp* ▶ **bourrer**.
II *pp adj* **1** (plein) [*train, musée*] packed; [*valise, sac*] bulging (**de** with); **c'était ~ de monde** it was packed; **un livre/rapport ~ d'idées** a book/report bursting with ideas; **il est ~ de fric**○ he's stinking rich○; **2**◑ (ivre) sloshed○.
III bourrée *nf* Danse bourrée.

bourreau, *pl* **~x** /buʀo/ *nm* **1** (exécuteur) executioner; **2** (criminel) butcher; (persécuteur) tormenter.
■ **~ des cœurs** lady-killer; **~ d'enfant** child beater; **~ de travail** workaholic.

bourrelé, **~e** /buʀle/ *adj* racked (**de** by).

bourrelet /buʀlɛ/ *nm* **1** Tech (d'étanchéité) weather strip, draught GB ou draft US excluder GB; (amortisseur) pad; **2** (adiposité) **~ (de graisse)** roll of fat.

bourrelier, **-ière** /buʀəlje, ɛʀ/ ▶ **510** *nm,f* (sellier) saddler; (maroquinier) leather craftsman/craftswoman.

bourrellerie /buʀɛlʀi/ *nf* **1** (sellerie) (fabrication) saddlery; (produits) tack; **2** (maroquinerie) (fabrication) making of leather goods; (produits) leather goods (*pl*).

bourrer /buʀe/ [1] **I** *vtr* **1** (remplir) to cram [*valise, caisse*]; to fill [*pipe*]; to fill [sth] up [*poêle*]; to wad [*arme à feu*]; **~ qch de** to cram sth with; **trop ~ une valise** to cram ou stuff too much in a suitcase; **discours bourré de citations** speech crammed with quotations; **pièce bourrée de livres** room crammed with books; **2** (gaver) (de nourriture) to stuff (**de** with); (de médicaments) to dose [sb] up (**de** with); **3** (faire apprendre) **~ (l'esprit de) qn de notions inutiles** to stuff sb's head with idle nonsense; **4**○ (frapper) **~ qn de coups** to lay into sb○; **~ la gueule à qn**◑ to smash sb's face in○.
II *vi* **1**○ (remplir l'estomac) [*aliment*] to be filling; **2**○ (aller vite) [*voiture, automobiliste*] to belt along○; **3** (s'engorger) [*appareil photo, imprimante*] to jam.
III se bourrer *vpr* **1**◑ (s'enivrer) **se ~ (la gueule)** to get sloshed○; **2** (se gaver) **se ~ de** to stuff oneself with [*aliments*]; to dose oneself up with [*médicaments*].

bourriche /buʀiʃ/ *nf* creel.

bourrichon○ /buʀiʃɔ̃/ *nm* **monter le ~ à qn** to get sb worked up; **se monter le ~** (s'échauffer l'esprit) to get oneself into a state; (se faire des illusions) to get carried away.

bourricot /buʀiko/ *nm* donkey.

bourrin○ /buʀɛ̃/ *nm* nag○, horse.

bourrique /buʀik/ *nf* **1** Zool donkey; **2**○ (entêté) pig-headed person.
IDIOMES **faire tourner qn en ~**○ to mess sb around○.

bourru, **~e** /buʀy/ *adj* gruff.

bourse /buʀs/ **I** *nf* **1** Scol, Univ (pour soutien financier) grant GB, scholarship US; (pour mérite) scholarship; (pour un projet particulier) grant; **2** (porte-monnaie) purse; **'la ~ ou la vie'** 'your money or your life'; **3** fig budget; **pour les petites ~s** for limited budgets; **être à la portée de toutes les ~s** to be within everybody's means; **faire ~ commune** to share the expenses; **4** (vente d'objets d'occasion) **~ aux livres/skis/vêtements** second-hand book/ski/clothes sale; **5** Anat bursa.
II bourses *nfpl* Anat scrotum (*sg*).
■ **~ d'étude** grant; **~ de recherche** research grant.

Bourse /buʀs/ *nf* Fin stock exchange; (valeurs cotées) shares (*pl*); **à la ~ de Tokyo** on the Tokyo Stock Exchange; **être coté en ~** to be listed on the stock exchange; **placer de l'argent en ~** to invest money on the stock exchange; **la ~ a chuté de dix points** shares have fallen by ten points; **la ~ de Paris a monté** shares on the Paris Stock Exchange have gone up; **faire son entrée à la ~ de Milan** to become listed on the Milan Stock Exchange; **une société de ~** a broking GB ou brokerage US firm.
■ **~ de commerce** commodity exchange; **~ du travail** Ind *local trade union offices*.

boursicotage /buʀsikɔtaʒ/ *nm* dabbling in stocks and shares.

boursicoter /buʀsikɔte/ [1] *vi* [*personne*] to dabble in stocks and shares.

boursicoteur, **-euse** /buʀsikɔtœʀ, øz/ *nm,f* dabbler in stocks and shares, small-time speculator.

boursier, **-ière** /buʀsje, ɛʀ/ **I** *adj* Fin [*indice, milieu, cotation, activités, valeur*] stock exchange, stock market (*épith*); [*semaine, mois*] trading (*épith*); **sur les grandes places boursières** on the major stock markets; **le krach ~ d'octobre 87** the stock market crash of October '87; **marché ~** stock market; **la nouvelle a stimulé le marché ~** the news stimulated share prices.
II *nm,f* Scol, Univ (pour raisons financières) grant holder GB, scholarship recipient US; (pour mérite) scholar GB, scholarship recipient US; **les étudiants ~s** students on a grant GB, students on financial aid US; (pour mérite) scholarship holders.
III *nm* Fin stock exchange dealer.

boursouflage /buʀsuflaʒ/, **boursouflement** /buʀsufləmɑ̃/ *nm* puffiness.

boursouflé, **~e** /buʀsufle/ **I** *pp* ▶ **boursoufler**.
II *pp adj* **1** (enflé) [*peau, surface*] blistered; [*partie du corps*] puffy; [*corps*] bloated; **2** (emphatique) [*discours*] bombastic.

boursoufler /buʀsufle/ [1] **I** *vtr* **1** (faire gonfler) to cause [sth] to swell [*visage, bras, peau*]; to blister [*papier, peinture*]; **2** (donner de l'emphase à) to blow up [*événement*]; to overdo [*style*].
II se boursoufler *vpr* [*peau, visage*] to swell up; [*papier, peinture*] to blister.

boursouflure /buʀsuflyʀ/ *nf* (de peau) swelling ₵; (de papier, peinture) blister.

bousculade /buskylad/ *nf* **1** (choc) (volontaire) jostling; (involontaire) crush; **2** (précipitation) rush.

bousculer /buskyle/ [1] **I** *vtr* **1** (heurter) (involontairement) to bump into [*personne*]; (volontairement) to knock about [*personne, mobilier*]; **2** (remettre en question) to shake up [*idée, programme*]; **3** (malmener) to jostle [*équipe, parti*]; **4** (presser) to rush [*personne, programme*].
II se bousculer *vpr* **1** (se heurter) to bump into each other; **2** (être nombreux) to fall over each other (**pour faire** to do); **on se bouscule** there are queues GB ou lines US; **on ne se bouscule pas** iron people are not exactly queuing GB ou lining US up; **surtout ne vous bousculez pas pour venir m'aider!** iron don't all rush at once to help me!; ▶ **portillon**.

bouse /buz/ *nf* **1** (substance) cow dung; **2** (fragment) **une ~ (de vache)** a cowpat.

bouseux○, **-euse** /buzø, øz/ *nm,f* pej hick○, country bumpkin○.

bousier /buzje/ *nm* dung beetle.

bousiller○ /buzije/ [1] **I** *vtr* **1** (gâcher) to botch [*travail*]; to ruin [*carrière, vie*]; **2** (détériorer) to wreck [*appareil, moteur, objet*]; to smash up [*véhicule*]; to bust○ [*mécanisme*]; to turn [sb] into a wreck○ [*personne*]; **3** (tuer) to do [sb] in○, to waste○.
II se bousiller *vpr* **se ~ la santé/la vue/l'estomac** to ruin one's health/eyesight/stomach.

boussole /busɔl/ *nf* compass.
IDIOMES **perdre la ~**○ to go round the bend○ GB, to go nuts◑.

boustifaille◑ /bustifɑj/ *nf* grub○, food.

bout[1] /bu/ *nm* **1** (dernière partie) (de nez, queue, branche, ficelle, ligne, table, rue, processus) end; (pointe) (d'épée, aile, de bâton, stylo, langue, doigt) tip; (de chaussure) toe; **au ~ de la jetée** at the end of the pier; **aux deux ~s de la table** at opposite ends of the table; **en ~ de piste** Aviat at the end of the runway; **la maison/le siège du ~** the end house/seat; **tout au ~ de la rue** at the very end of the street; **l'autre ~ de la pièce** the far end of the room; **ciseaux à ~s ronds/pointus** round-ended/pointed scissors; **à ~ rond/carré/rouge** [*bâton, doigt, aile*] round-/square-/red-tipped; **à ~ ferré** [*canne, chaussures*] steel-tipped; **chaussures à ~ pointu/ferré/blanc** pointy-/steel-/white-toed shoes; **au ~ du jardin/champ** at the bottom of the garden/field; **en ~ de table** at the foot of the table; **siège en ~ de rangée** aisle seat; **valser○/projeter qch à l'autre ~ de la pièce** to fly/to fling sth across the room; **mener de ~ en ~** to lead from start to finish; **lire un livre de ~ en ~** to read a book from cover to cover; **parcourir** or **éplucher une liste d'un ~ à l'autre** to scour a list; **d'un ~ à l'autre du spectacle/de l'Europe/de l'année** throughout the show/Europe/the year; **parcourir la Grèce d'un ~ à l'autre** to cover the length and breadth of Greece; **marcher d'un ~ à l'autre de la ville** to walk across the city; **poser/coller ~ à ~** to lay/stick [sth] end to end; **mettre ~ à ~** (additionner) to add up; **être incapable de mettre deux phrases ~ à ~** to be unable to string two sentences together; **mettre des données ~ à ~** to piece data together; **rester jusqu'au ~** to stay until the end; **essayer jusqu'au ~** to try to the end; **je suis/elle est avec vous jusqu'au ~** I'm/she's with you every step of the way; **je te soutiendrai jusqu'au ~** I'm with you all the way; **aller jusqu'au ~** to go all the way; **aller (jusqu')au ~ de** to follow through [*idée, exigence*]; **aller au ~ de soi-même** to push oneself to the limit; **écouter qn jusqu'au ~** to hear sb out; **brûler jusqu'au ~** to burn out; **lutter jusqu'au ~** to fight to the last drop of blood; **je suis/elle est à ~** I/she can't take any more; **je suis à ~ de forces** I can do no more; **ma patience est à ~** my patience is exhausted; **je commence à être à ~ de patience** my patience is wearing thin; **pousser qn à ~** to push sb to the limit; **ne me pousse pas à ~** don't push me; **être à ~ d'arguments** to run out of arguments; **venir à ~ de** to overcome [*problème, difficultés*]; to get through [*tâche, repas*]; to tame [*personne*]; **au ~ d'une semaine/d'un certain temps/de trois chansons** after a week/a while/three songs; **au ~ du compte** ultimately; **à ~ portant** at point-blank range; **2** (morceau) (de pain, chiffon, métal, fil, papier) piece; (de terrain) bit; **j'ai vu un ~ du spectacle** I saw part of the show; **~ de bois** gén piece of wood; (allongé) stick; **~s de papier/ferraille** scraps of paper/metal; **~ de crayon** pencil-stub; **~s d'ongles** nail clippings; **par petits ~s** [*apprendre, manger*] a bit at a time; [*payer, recevoir*] in dribs and drabs; [*occuper, progresser*] little by little; **un ~ de temps** a while; **un petit ~ de temps** a little while; **un bon ~ de temps** quite a long time; **un petit ~ de femme**○ a tiny woman; ▶ **chandelle, discuter**.

■ **~ de l'an** Relig *memorial service on the first anniversary of sb's death*; **~ de chou**○ sweet little thing○; **~ d'essai** Cin screen test; **tourner un ~ d'essai** to do a screen test; **~ filtre** (de cigarette) filter tip; **~ renforcé** Mode (de chaussure) toe cap; **~ de sein**○ Anat nipple; **~ de vergue** Naut yardarm.

IDIOMES **tenir le bon ~**○ to be on the right track; **voir le ~ de qch** to get through sth ; **ne pas être au ~ de ses peines** or **ennuis** not to be out of the woods yet; **ne pas être au ~ de ses surprises** to have still a few surprises in store; **ne pas savoir par quel ~ commencer** not to know where to begin; **ne pas savoir par quel ~ prendre** not to know how to deal with; **prendre qn/qch par le bon/mauvais ~** to handle sb/sth the right/wrong way; **en connaître un ~**○ to know a thing or two○; **mettre les ~s**○ to leave, to clear off○ GB, to split○ US.

bout² /but/ *nm* Naut rope; **filer par le ~** to slip anchor.

boutade /butad/ *nf* **1** (trait d'esprit) witticism; **en forme de ~** as a quip; **2** (caprice) whim.

bout-dehors, *pl* **bouts-dehors** /budəɔʀ/ *nm* Naut boom.

boute-en-train /butɑ̃tʀɛ̃/ *nmf inv* live wire; **~ de la bande** life and soul of the party.

boutefeu, *pl* **~x** /butfø/ *nm* rabble-rouser.

bouteille /butɛj/ *nf* **1** (emballage) bottle; **~ de lait/champagne** (contenant) milk/champagne bottle; (contenu) bottle of milk/champagne; **~ de gaz** cylinder ou bottle of gas; **~ à gaz** gas bottle ou cylinder; **mettre le vin en ~s** to bottle wine; **mis en ~ au château/à la propriété** château/estate bottled; **la mise en ~ du champagne** the bottling of champagne; **l'eau en ~** bottled water; **le lait en ~** milk in bottles; **boire à la ~** to drink out of the bottle; **2** (produit vinicole) bottle; **il nous a offert une de ses meilleures ~s** he served us with one of his best bottles; **sortir une bonne ~** to get out a good bottle of wine; **3** Sport **faire de la plongée** or **plonger avec des/sans ~s** to dive with/without breathing equipment; ▶ **encre, Paris**.

■ **~ isolante** vacuum flask; **~ magnétique** magnetic bottle; **~ d'oxygène** oxygen cylinder.

IDIOMES **être porté sur** or **aimer la ~** to be fond of the bottle; **prendre de la ~**○ (expérience) to have cut one's eyeteeth; (âge) to be getting on; **jeter** or **lancer une ~ à la mer** to make a last despairing bid for help.

bouter† /bute/ [1] *vtr* to drive [*ennemi*] (**hors de** out of).

bouteur /butœʀ/ *nm* bulldozer.

boutique /butik/ *nf* **1** (d'artisan, de commerçant) shop GB, store US; (de prêt-à-porter) boutique; **ouvrir une ~** to open a shop; **ouvrir ~** to set up shop; **tenir ~** to keep shop; **plier** or **fermer ~** lit, fig to shut up shop; **parler ~** to talk shop; **~ hors taxes** duty-free shop GB ou store US; **2**○ (maison, entreprise) place.

boutiquier, **-ière** /butikje, ɛʀ/ **I** *adj* pej [*personne*] small-minded; **avoir l'esprit ~** to be small-minded.

II *nm,f* Comm shopkeeper.

boutoir /butwaʀ/ *nm* snout; **coup de ~** attack.

bouton /butɔ̃/ *nm* **1** Cout, Mode button; **sans ~s** buttonless; **2** Tech (d'appareil) (à tourner) knob; (à presser) button; **appuyer sur le ~ de la sonnette** to ring the bell; **3** Méd spot GB, pimple US; **donner des ~s à qn**○ fig to make sb shudder; **4** Bot bud; **~ floral** flower bud; **en ~** in bud.

■ **~ d'acné** Méd acne ¢; **~ de fièvre** Méd cold sore; **~ de manchette** Mode cuff link; **~ de porte** Constr doorknob.

bouton-d'or, *pl* **boutons-d'or** /butɔ̃dɔʀ/ *nm* Bot buttercup.

boutonnage /butɔnaʒ/ *nm* Cout, Mode **1** (type) **robe à ~ devant/dans le dos** front-/back-buttoning dress; **blazer à ~ croisé** double-breasted blazer; **2** (action) **le ~ de la robe est très long** the dress takes a long time to button up.

boutonner /butɔne/ [1] **I** *vtr* to button [*vêtement*]; **~ qn** to do up sb's buttons; **être boutonné jusqu'au cou** [*vêtement*] to be buttoned right up (to the neck); [*personne*] to have all one's buttons done up; **jupe boutonnée sur le côté** side-buttoning skirt.

II se boutonner *vpr* **1** [*vêtement*] to button up; **robe qui se boutonne devant/derrière** dress which buttons up the front/back; **2** [*personne*] to do up one's buttons.

boutonneux, **-euse** /butɔnø, øz/ *adj* [*visage*] spotty GB, pimply US.

boutonnière /butɔnjɛʀ/ *nf* (de vêtement) buttonhole; **il porte une fleur rouge à la ~** he's wearing a red buttonhole GB ou boutonniere US; **il porte une décoration à la ~** he's wearing a decoration on his lapel.

bouton-poussoir, *pl* **boutons-poussoirs** /butɔ̃puswaʀ/ *nm* push-button.

bouton-pression, *pl* **boutons-pression** /butɔ̃pʀɛsjɔ̃/ *nm* press stud GB, popper GB, snap (fastener).

bout-rimé, *pl* **bouts-rimés** /buʀime/ *nm* poem in set rhymes.

bouturage /butyʀaʒ/ *nm* Hort cutting.

bouture /butyʀ/ *nf* cutting; **faire des ~s** to take cuttings.

bouturer /butyʀe/ [1] **I** *vtr* to take a cutting from [*plante*].

II *vi* [*plante*] to propagate from cuttings.

bouvier /buvje/ *nm* **1** ▶ **510** (personne) oxherd; **2** (chien) bouvier.

bouvreuil /buvʀœj/ *nm* bullfinch.

bovidé /bɔvide/ *nm* bovid; **les ~s** the Bovidae.

bovin, **~e** /bɔvɛ̃, in/ **I** *adj* bovine.

II *nm* bovine; **des ~s** cattle (+ *v pl*); **150 ~s** 150 head of cattle.

bowling /buliŋ/ ▶ **449** *nm* **1** (jeu) tenpin bowling GB, bowling US; **faire un ~** to go bowling; **2** (lieu) bowling alley.

box, *pl* **boxes** /bɔks/ *nm* (pour véhicule) lock-up garage; (pour cheval) stall; (dans un bar) alcove; (dans un dortoir, parloir) cubicle; (de travail) section.

■ **~ des accusés** Jur dock.

boxe /bɔks/ ▶ **449** *nf* boxing; **champion de ~** boxing champion; **faire de la ~** to do boxing, to box.

■ **~ française** savate.

boxer¹ /bɔksɛʀ/ *nm* (chien) boxer.

boxer² /bɔkse/ [1] **I**○ *vtr* (frapper) to punch; **se faire ~** to get thumped.

II *vi* **1** (pratiquer la boxe) to box; **2** (livrer un match de boxe) to have a fight on.

boxeur /bɔksœʀ/ ▶ **510** *nm* boxer.

box-office, *pl* **~s** /bɔksɔfis/ *nm* box office; **être premier au ~** to top the box office.

boxon◑ /bɔksɔ̃/ *nm* **1** (maison de prostitution) whorehouse◑, knocking-shop◑ GB; **2** (désordre) shambles○ (*sg*); **foutre le ~**◑ to create havoc.

boy /bɔj/ *nm* gén boy; (domestique) houseboy.

boyard /bɔjaʀ/ *nm* boyar.

boyau, *pl* **~x** /bwajo/ **I** *nm* **1** (intestin d'animal) gut; **2** (pour raquette, violon) catgut; **3** (pour saucisse) casing; **~ de porc** pork sausage casing; **4** (pneu) tubeless tyre GB ou tire US; **5** (passage) back alley; **6** (tuyau flexible) hose.

II○ **boyaux** *nmpl* (intestins) insides○; **se tordre les ~x (de rire)** to be in stitches○; **ça vous tord les ~x** it's real rotgut○.

■ **~ de chat** catgut.

boycott /bɔjkɔt/, **boycottage** /bɔjkɔtaʒ/ *nm* **1** (mesure) boycott; **2** (action) boycotting; **le ~ de qch par qn** the boycotting of sth by sb.

boycotter /bɔjkɔte/ [1] *vtr* to boycott.

boy-scout†, *pl* **~s** /bɔjskut/ *nm* boy scout.

BP *written abbr* ▶ **boîte**.

BPI /bepei/ *nf*: *abbr* ▶ **bibliothèque**.

brabançon, **-onne** /bʀabɑ̃sɔ̃, ɔn/ *adj* of Brabant.

Brabançon, **-onne** /bʀabɑ̃sɔ̃, ɔn/ **I** *nm,f* (natif) native of Brabant; (habitant) inhabitant of Brabant.

II Brabançonne *nf* **la Brabançonne** (the) Brabançonne (*the Belgian national anthem*).

brabant /bʀabɑ̃/ *nm* half-turn plough GB ou plow US.

Brabant /bʀabɑ̃/ ▶ **692** *nprm* **le ~** Brabant.

bracelet /bʀaslɛ/ *nm* (au poignet) gén bracelet; (large) bangle; (souple) wristband; (au bras, à la cheville) bangle.

■ **~ à breloques** charm bracelet; **~ de force** Sport wristband; **~ d'identification** identity bracelet; **~ de montre** watchstrap.

bracelet-montre, *pl* **bracelets-montres** /bʀaslɛmɔ̃tʀ/ *nm* wristwatch.

brachial, **~e**, *mpl* **-iaux** /bʀakjal, o/ *adj* brachial.

brachiopode /bʀakjɔpɔd/ *nm* brachiopod; **les ~s** the Brachiopoda.

brachycéphale /bʀakisefal/ *adj*, *nmf* brachycephalic.

braconnage /bʀakɔnaʒ/ *nm* poaching.

braconner /bʀakɔne/ [1] *vi* to poach.

braconnier /bʀakɔnje/ *nm* poacher.

bradage /bʀadaʒ/ *nm* lit, fig selling off.

bradé, **~e** /bʀade/ **I** *pp* ▶ **brader**.
II *pp adj* **prix ~s** knockdown prices.

brader /bʀade/ [1] **I** *vtr* **1** (vendre à bas prix) to sell [sth] cheaply; **2** (liquider) to sell off.
II *vi* to slash prices.

braderie /bʀadʀi/ *nf* **1** Comm (marché) street market; (magasin) discount store; **2** (vente) clearance sale; (liquidation) selling off.

bradeur, **-euse** /bʀadœʀ, øz/ *nm,f* **1** lit cheap-jack; **2** fig discarder.

braguette /bʀagɛt/ *nf* Mode flies GB (*pl*), fly US.

brahmane /bʀaman/ *nm* Brahman.

brahmanique /bʀamanik/ *adj* Brahmanic.

brahmanisme /bʀamanism/ *nm* Brahmanism.

Brahmapoutre /bʀamaputʀ/ ▶ **357** *nprm* Brahmaputra.

brai /bʀɛ/ *nm* pitch.

braies /bʀɛ/ *nfpl* breeches, trousers (*worn by the Gauls*).

braillard○, **~e** /bʀɑjaʀ, aʀd/ **I** *adj* (qui crie) yelling (*épith*); (qui pleure) bawling (*épith*).
II *nm,f* loudmouth.

braille /bʀaj/ *nm* Braille; **en ~** in Braille.

braillement○ /bʀɑjmɑ̃/ *nm* (cri) yell, yelling ¢; (pleurs) bawling ¢.

brailler○ /bʀaje/ [1] **I** *vtr* to yell out [*injure*]; to bawl out [*chanson*].
II *vi* (crier) to yell; (chanter fort, pleurer) to bawl.

brailleur○, **-euse** /bʀɑjœʀ, øz/ *adj, nm,f* = **braillard**.

braiment /bʀɛmɑ̃/ *nm* braying ¢.

braire /bʀɛʀ/ [58] *vi* to bray.
IDIOMES **ça me fait ~**○ that gets on my wick○ GB, it bugs me○.

braise /bʀɛz/ *nf* live embers (*pl*); **cuire des pommes de terre sous la ~** to bake potatoes in the embers; **souffler sur les ~s** lit, fig to fan the flames.

braiser /bʀeze/ [1] *vtr* Culin to braise; **chou braisé** braised cabbage.

brame /bʀɑm/ *nm* Chasse, Zool bell.

bramer /bʀɑme/ [1] *vi* **1** [*cerf*] to bell; **2**○ (brailler) to bawl; (se lamenter) to wail.

bran /bʀɑ̃/ *nm* (de son) coarse bran.
■ **~ (de scie)** sawdust.

brancard /bʀɑ̃kaʀ/ *nm* (civière) stretcher; (de charrette) shaft.
IDIOMES **ruer dans les ~s** to rebel.

brancardier /bʀɑ̃kaʀdje/ ▶ **510** *nm* stretcher-bearer.

branchage /bʀɑ̃ʃaʒ/ **I** *nm* branches (*pl*).
II branchages *nmpl* (branches coupées) cut branches.

branche /bʀɑ̃ʃ/ *nf* **1** (d'arbre) branch; **~ maîtresse** limb; **~ charpentière** bough; ▶ **oiseau**, **scier**; **2** Culin **céleri en ~s** sticks of celery; **épinards en ~s** spinach on the stalk; ▶ **vieux**; **3** (secteur) field; **la même ~ d'activité** the same field; **dans chaque ~ professionnelle** in every professional field; **choisir entre la ~ littéraire et la ~ scientifique** to choose the arts or the science subjects; **4** (de famille) branch; **la ~ aînée/cadette** the elder/younger branch; **5** (de nerf, d'artère) branch; **6** (de chandelier) branch; (de compas) arm; (de lunettes) arm; (d'étoile) point; (de ciseaux) blade; **étoile à quatre/cinq ~s** four-/five-pointed star.
IDIOMES **avoir de la ~**○ to have a lot of class.

branché, **~e** /bʀɑ̃ʃe/ **I** *pp* ▶ **brancher**.
II○ *pp adj* trendy○.

branchement /bʀɑ̃ʃmɑ̃/ *nm* **1** (de l'électricité, du gaz, du téléphone) connection; (de nouvel abonné) connecting; **on vous fera le ~ lundi** we'll connect you on Monday; **2** (de deux parties) connection; **3** (conduite d'eau) branch-pipe; (ligne électrique) (service) lead GB, cable US; **4** Rail points (*pl*) GB, switch US; **5** Électron, Ordinat branching.

brancher /bʀɑ̃ʃe/ [1] **I** *vtr* **1** (avec une prise) to plug in [*télévision, téléphone*]; **2** (au réseau) to connect (up) [*eau, gaz, électricité, téléphone*]; to connect [*usager, maison*]; **faire ~ le gaz/téléphone** to have the gas/phone connected; **l'électricité n'est pas encore branchée** the electricity isn't connected (up) yet; **3** Ordinat **~ qn/qch sur un réseau** to connect sb/sth to a network; **4** (aiguiller) **~ qn sur** or **vers** to get sb interested in [*activité*]; to get sb onto [*sujet de conversation*]; **~ qn sur qn** to put sb in touch with sb; **5**○ (plaire à) **ça ne me branche pas** it doesn't do anything for me; **la voile, ça le branche** he's really into○ sailing.
II se brancher *vpr* **1** Radio, TV (capter) **se ~ sur** to tune into [*poste, station*]; **2**○ (s'intéresser à) **se ~ sur** to get into○ [*activité, passe-temps*].

branchette /bʀɑ̃ʃɛt/ *nf* small branch.

branchial, **~e**, *mpl* **-iaux** /bʀɑ̃ʃjal, o/ *adj* branchial.

branchie /bʀɑ̃ʃi/ *nf* gill, branchia spéc.

branchiopode /bʀɑ̃kjɔpɔd/ *nm* branchiopod; **les ~s** the Branchiopoda.

branchu, **~e** /bʀɑ̃ʃy/ *adj* many-branched (*épith*).

brandade /bʀɑ̃dad/ *nf* **~ (de morue)** brandade, dish of flaked salt cod.

brande /bʀɑ̃d/ *nf* **1** Bot (végétation) brush ¢; (terre) heathland ¢; **2** (fagot) brushwood ¢.

brandebourg /bʀɑ̃dbuʀ/ *nm* **1** (ornement) frogging; **à ~s** frogged; **2** (fermeture) frog.

Brandebourg /bʀɑ̃dbuʀ/ ▶ **692**, **857** *nm* Brandenburg; **porte de ~** Brandenburg Gate.

brandebourgeois, **~e** /bʀɑ̃dbuʀʒwa, az/ *adj* of Brandenburg; **concerto ~** Brandenburg Concerto.

brandir /bʀɑ̃diʀ/ [3] *vtr* to brandish [*arme, objet*]; to throw out [*menace, slogan*]; to hold up [*idée*].
IDIOMES **~ l'étendard de la révolte** to be at the vanguard of revolt.

brandon /bʀɑ̃dɔ̃/ *nm* firebrand.
■ **~ de discorde** bone of contention.

brandy /bʀɑ̃di/ *nm* brandy.

branlant, **-e** /bʀɑ̃lɑ̃, ɑ̃t/ *adj* [*meuble, construction*] rickety; [*mur, mât*] unstable, wobbly; [*dent*] loose; [*situation, projet, raisonnement, régime*] shaky.

branle /bʀɑ̃l/ *nm* (oscillation) swing; **mettre qch en ~**, **donner le ~ à qch** to set [sth] in motion [*mesure, projet, convoi*]; **se mettre en ~** [*convoi, personnes*] to get going; [*processus*] to be set in motion.

branle-bas /bʀɑ̃lbɑ/ *nm inv* (agitation) commotion.
■ **~ de combat** Mil, fig action stations; **(c'était le) ~ de combat au village ce matin** it was action stations in the village this morning.

branlement /bʀɑ̃lmɑ̃/ *nm* **approuver d'un ~ de tête** to nod one's approval.

branler /bʀɑ̃le/ [1] **I** *vtr* **1** (hocher) **~ la tête** or **du chef** to nod one's head; **2**● (masturber) to wank● [sb] GB, to jack [sb] off● US, to masturbate [*personne*]; **3**● (faire) **je n'ai rien branlé** I've done fuck all●, I've done nothing; **mais qu'est-ce qu'il branle?** what the fuck● is he doing?
II *vi* (osciller) [*mur*] to wobble; [*escalier, construction, échafaudage, chaise*] to be rickety; [*dent*] to be loose.
III se branler● *vpr* to wank● GB, to jerk off●, to masturbate; **il s'en branle** he doesn't give a fuck●, he couldn't care less.

branlette● /bʀɑ̃lɛt/ *nf* wank● GB, hand job●.

branleur●, **-euse** /bʀɑ̃lœʀ, øz/ *nm, f* (paresseux) lazy sod● GB, bum◑ US.

braquage /bʀakaʒ/ *nm* **1**○ (de supermarché, banque) robbery; **2** Aut (steering) lock, turning circle.

braque /bʀak/ **I**○ *adj* crazy.
II *nm* Zool **~ allemand** German short-haired pointer.

braquemart◑ /bʀakmaʀ/ *nm* dick◑, penis.

braquer /bʀake/ [1] **I** *vtr* **1** (diriger) to point [*arme, caméra*] (**sur, vers** at); to train [*télescope, projecteur*] (**sur, vers** on); to turn ou fix [*yeux*] (**sur, vers** on); **les feux de l'actualité** or **tous les projecteurs sont braqués sur lui** fig he's in the spotlight, the spotlight is on him; **tous les regards sont braqués sur vous** lit, fig all eyes are upon you; **2** Aut to turn [*volant, roues*] (**à gauche/droite** hard left/right); **3**○ (viser) to point a gun at; (plus longtemps) to hold [sb] at gunpoint; **je me suis fait ~** I was held at gunpoint; **4**○ (attaquer) to rob, to make an armed raid on [*banque*]; **5**○ (buter) **~ qn contre qch/qn** to turn sb against sth/sb; **ne le braque pas** don't get his back up; **il est braqué** he's got GB ou gotten US his back up.
II *vi* Aut [*chauffeur*] to turn the wheel full lock GB ou all the way US; [*véhicule*] **bien/mal ~** to have a good/poor lock GB, to turn well/poorly US; **braque à gauche/droite** turn (the wheel) sharply to the left/right.
III se braquer *vpr* **1** (viser) **se ~ sur/vers** [*arme, caméra*] to be pointed at; [*télescope, projecteur*] to be trained on; [*yeux*] to be turned on; **2** (se concentrer) [*personne, attention*] to focus (**sur** on); **3**○ (se buter) to have one's back up; **se ~ contre qn** to turn against sb; **se ~ contre qch** to set one's face against sth.

braquet /bʀakɛ/ *nm* gear ratio; **changer de ~** lit, fig to change gear.

braqueur○ /bʀakœʀ/ *nm* robber.

bras /bʀa/ ▶ **188** *nm inv* **1** Anat arm; **lever/tendre le ~** to raise/stretch one's arm; **avoir les ~ musclés/maigres** to have muscular/thin arms; **prendre qn dans ses ~** to take sb in one's arms; **se jeter/tomber dans les ~ de qn** to throw oneself/fall into sb's arms; **se blottir dans les ~ de qn** to snuggle up in sb's arms; **avoir les ~ en croix** to have one's arms outstretched; **par le ~** [*tenir, prendre*] by the arm; **sous le ~** under one's arm; **au ~ de qn** on sb's arm; **~ dessus ~ dessous** lit, fig arm in arm; **donner le ~ à qn** to give sb one's arm; **accueillir qn à ~ ouverts** to welcome sb with open arms; **elle avait des paquets plein les ~** her arms were full of parcels GB ou packages US; **se retrouver avec** or **avoir qch/qn sur les ~** fig to be lumbered with sth/sb; **porter qch à bout de ~** lit to carry sth with one's arms straight out; fig to keep sth afloat; **baisser les ~** lit to lower one's arms; fig to give up; **en ~ de chemise** in one's shirtsleeves; **les ~ croisés** with one's arms folded; **rester les ~ croisés** to stand idly; **croiser les ~** lit to fold one's arms; fig to twiddle one's thumbs; **viens dans mes ~!** come and have a big hug!; ▶ **tour I 1**; **2** (main-d'œuvre) manpower, labour[GB]; **manquer de ~** to be short of manpower; ▶ **gros**; **3** Géog (de fleuve) branch; **un ~ du Rhin** a branch of the Rhine; **4** Tech (de fauteuil, d'électrophone, ancre) arm; (de brancard) pole; **5** Zool (de cheval) shoulder; (de mollusque) tentacle.
■ **~ droit** fig right hand man; **il est devenu le ~ droit du ministre** he has become the minister's right hand man; **~ de fer** (épreuve physique) arm wrestling; (lutte d'influence) trial of strength; **faire un ~ de fer** or **une partie de ~ de fer avec qn** to arm wrestle with sb; **~ de levier** Phys leverage; **~ de mer** sound; **~ oscillant** swing arm; **le ~ séculier** the secular arm.
IDIOMES **les ~ m'en tombent** I'm absolutely speechless; **avoir le ~ long** to have a lot of influence; **faire un ~ d'honneur à qn** ≈ to give sb the V sign GB ou the finger.

brasage /bʀazaʒ/ *nm* Tech brazing.

braser /bʀaze/ [1] *vtr* Tech to braze.

brasero /bʀazeʀo/ *nm* brazier.

brasier /bʀazje/ *nm* inferno.

Brasilia /bʀazilja/ **▶ 857** *npr* Brasilia.

bras-le-corps: **à bras-le-corps** /abʀalkɔʀ/ *loc adv* **1** lit [*soulever*] bodily; **2** fig head-on; **s'occuper d'un problème à ~** to deal with a problem head-on; **prendre la vie à ~** to live life to the full.

brassage /bʀasaʒ/ *nm* **1** Ind (de bière) brewing; **2** (mélange) (de personnes) intermingling; (d'idées, de cultures) cross-fertilization; (d'air) mixture; **le ~ des populations** the intermingling of populations.

brassard /bʀasaʀ/ *nm* **1** gén armband; **2** Hist Mil arm-piece.

brasse /bʀas/ *nf* **1** Sport (style) breaststroke; (mouvement) stroke; **faire/nager la ~** to do/swim breaststroke; **à la ~** in breaststroke; **traverser en cinq ~s** to cross in five strokes; **2** Hist (160 cm) ≈ 2 yards.
■ **~ anglaise** Naut fathom; **~ coulée** Sport racing breaststroke; **~ papillon** Sport butterfly (stroke).

brassée /bʀase/ *nf* **1** (de fleurs, papier, bois) armful (**de** of); **2** (de chiffres, personnalités) (whole) host (**de** of).

brasser /bʀase/ [1] *vtr* **1** (remuer) [*personne*] to toss [*salade*]; to toss [sth] around [*idées*]; to shuffle [*cartes à jouer*]; to shuffle [sth] around [*papier*]; to gather [sth] up [*feuilles mortes, linge*]; [*vent*] to blow about [*feuilles*]; **les guerres ont brassé les populations d'Europe** war has intermingled the different populations of Europe; **il brasse des millions** he handles big money; **~ des affaires** to do business; **2** Ind to brew [*bière*].
IDIOMES **~ de l'air**○ to talk a lot of hot air○.

brasserie /bʀasʀi/ **▶ 510** *nf* **1** (café, restaurant) brasserie; **2** (usine) brewery; **3** (secteur) brewing industry.

brasseur, **-euse** /bʀasœʀ, øz/ *nm,f* Ind (de bière) brewer.
■ **~ d'affaires** business tycoon.

brassière /bʀasjɛʀ/ *nf* **1** (de bébé) (en coton) baby's vest; (en tricot) baby's top; **2** (soutien-gorge) crop top.

brasure /bʀazyʀ/ *nf* **1** (joint) brazed joint; **2** (alliage) brazing solder.

Bratislava /bʀatislava/ **▶ 857** *npr* Bratislava.

bravache /bʀavaʃ/ **I** *adj* [*personne*] blustering.
II *nmf* show-off○, braggart†; **faire le ~** to brag.

bravade /bʀavad/ *nf* (attitude) bravado; **par ~** out of bravado.

brave /bʀav/ **I** *adj* **1** (gentil) [*personne*] nice; **un ~ homme** a nice man GB ou guy; **de ~s gens** nice people; **ah ma ~ dame**○ **si vous saviez!** well, dear, you can't imagine!; **2** (courageux) [*personne*] brave.
II† *nm* **1** (homme courageux) brave man; **2** (forme d'adresse) **mon ~** my man.
IDIOMES **il n'y a pas d'heure pour les ~s** any time is the right time.

bravement /bʀavmɑ̃/ *adv* **1** (avec courage) bravely; **2** (sans hésiter) boldly.

braver /bʀave/ [1] *vtr* to defy [*personne, ordre, tabou*]; to brave [*tempête, danger*]; **~ la faim et la soif** to brave hunger and thirst.

bravo /bʀavo/ **I** *nm* cheer; **un grand ~ pour** or **à** a big cheer for GB, let's hear it for.
II *excl* **1** (pour applaudir) bravo!; **2** (pour féliciter) also iron well done!

bravoure /bʀavuʀ/ *nf* bravery; **être d'une grande ~** to be very brave; **combattre avec ~** to fight bravely; **faire preuve de ~** to be brave.

break /bʀɛk/ *nm* **1** Aut estate car GB, station wagon US; **2** (d'attelage) (shooting) break.

brebis /bʀəbi/ *nf inv* Zool ewe; **les ~** lit, fig the flock.
■ **~ égarée** lost sheep; **~ galeuse** black sheep.
IDIOMES **à ~ tondue Dieu mesure le vent** Prov God tempers the wind to the shorn lamb Prov.

brèche /bʀɛʃ/ *nf inv* **1** (trou) (dans un mur) hole; (dans une haie) gap; **2** Mil (trouée) breach; **ouvrir une ~ dans un parti/le gouvernement** fig to bring about a split in a party/the government; **3** Géol breccia.
IDIOMES **battre qn/qch en ~** to give sb/sth a pounding; **être sur la ~** to be on the go.

bréchet /bʀeʃɛ/ *nm* wishbone.

brechtien, **-ienne** /bʀɛʃtjɛ̃, ɛn/ *adj* Brechtian.

bredouillant, **~e** /bʀədujɑ̃, ɑ̃t/ *adj* mumbling.

bredouille /bʀəduj/ *adj* lit, fig empty-handed; **revenir ~ de la chasse/de la pêche/d'un championnat** to come back from hunting/from angling/from a championship empty-handed.

bredouillement /bʀədujmɑ̃/ *nm* mumbling ¢.

bredouiller /bʀəduje/ [1] *vtr, vi* to mumble.

bref, **brève** /bʀɛf, bʀɛv/ **I** *adj* **1** (court) [*récit, apparition, séjour*] brief; [*voyelle, son*] short; **soyez ~ s'il vous plaît** please be brief; **dans les plus ~s délais** as soon as possible; **2** (sec) [*ton, voix*] curt; **d'un ton ~** curtly.
II *adv* (pour résumer) **(en) ~** in short.
III *nm* Relig (lettre papale) brief.
IV **brève** *nf* **1** Presse (information) news flash; **2** Littérat, Phon (voyelle, syllabe) short; **deux brèves** two shorts.

brelan /bʀəlɑ̃/ *nm* Jeux three of a kind; **avoir un ~ de 10** to have three tens.

breloque /bʀəlɔk/ *nf* charm; **porter qch en ~** (à un bracelet) to wear sth on a bracelet.
IDIOMES **battre la ~** [*pendule*] to be erratic; [*cœur*] to be none too good; [*personne*] to be a bit batty○.

brème /bʀɛm/ *nf* **1** Zool bream; **2**○ (carte) card.

brésil /bʀezil/ *nm* Bot brazil (wood).

Brésil /bʀezil/ **▶ 321** *nprm* Brazil.

brésilien, **-ienne** /bʀeziljɛ̃, ɛn/ **▶ 537** *adj* **1** Géog Brazilian; **2** Mode [*slip, maillot de bain*] high-cut.

Brésilien, **-ienne** /bʀeziljɛ̃, ɛn/ **▶ 537** *nm,f* Brazilian.

bressan, **~e** /bʀɛsɑ̃, an/ *adj* of Bresse.

Bresse /bʀɛs/ **▶ 692** *nprf* **la ~** Bresse.

brestois, **~e** /bʀɛstwa, az/ **▶ 857** *adj* of Brest.

Brestois, **~e** /bʀɛstwa, az/ **▶ 857** *nm,f* (natif) native of Brest; (habitant) inhabitant of Brest.

Bretagne /bʀətaɲ/ **▶ 692** *nprf* **la ~** Brittany.

bretèche /bʀətɛʃ/ *nf* brattice.

bretelle /bʀətɛl/ **I** *nf* **1** (de robe, maillot) strap; **une ~ de soutien-gorge** a bra-strap; **une robe à ~s** a dress with shoestring straps; **2** (de fusil) sling; **porter l'arme à la ~** to carry a weapon slung over one's shoulder; **3** (de sac à dos, accordéon) strap; **4** Gén Civ (d'autoroute) slip road GB, ramp US; **5** Rail crossover.
II **bretelles** *nfpl* Mode braces GB, suspenders US; **porter des ~s** to wear braces GB ou suspenders US; **une paire de ~s** (a pair of) braces GB ou suspenders US.
■ **~ d'accès** or **d'entrée** Gén Civ access road, entry slip road GB; **~ de raccordement** access road; **~ de sortie** Gén Civ exit, exit slip road GB.
IDIOMES **remonter les ~s à qn**○ to tear sb off a strip○; **se faire remonter les ~s**○ to get told off○.

breton, **-onne** /bʀətɔ̃, ɔn/ **▶ 462** **I** *adj* Breton.
II *nm* Ling Breton.

Breton, **-onne** /bʀətɔ̃, ɔn/ *nm,f* Breton.

bretonnant, **~e** /bʀətɔnɑ̃, ɑ̃t/ *adj* Breton-speaking.

bretteur /bʀɛtœʀ/ *nm* swashbuckler.

bretzel /bʀɛtzɛl/ *nm* pretzel.

breuvage /bʀœvaʒ/ *nm* **1** (boisson étrange) pej brew; **2** C (boisson) beverage.

brève ▶ **bref I, IV**.

brevet /bʀəvɛ/ *nm* **1** (d'invention) **~ (d'invention)** patent; **déposer un ~** to take out a patent (**pour** on); **après le dépôt du ~** after patenting; **2** (diplôme) ≈ certificate; **~ de moniteur de ski/de secourisme** ski instructor's/first aid certificate; **~ de respectabilité** hum social acceptability certificate.
■ **~ des collèges** Scol *certificate of general education*; **~ d'études professionnelles**, **BEP** Scol *certificate of technical education*; **~ de pilote** Aviat pilot's licence[GB]; **~ professionnel** *specialized technical qualification acquired in the workplace*; **~ de technicien supérieur**, **BTS** Univ *advanced vocational diploma*.

brevetable /bʀəvtabl/ *adj* [*invention*] patentable.

breveté, **~e** /bʀəvte/ **I** *pp* ▶ **breveter**.
II *pp adj* **1** (déposé) [*dispositif, invention*] patented; **2** (diplômé) [*personne, pilote*] qualified.

breveter /bʀəvte/ [20] *vtr* **(faire) ~** to patent [*invention*].

bréviaire /bʀevjɛʀ/ *nm* **1** Relig breviary; **2** fig bible.

BRI /beɛʀi/ *nf*: *abbr* ▶ **banque**.

briard, **~e** /bʀijaʀ, aʀd/ Géog **I** *adj* [*produit*] from Brie; [*patrimoine*] of Brie; [*région, population, économie*] Brie (*épith*); **le pays ~** the Brie region.
II *nm* (chien) briard.

bribes /bʀib/ *nfpl* (de conversation, phrase, dialogue) snatches; (de texte, d'histoire, information) bits and pieces; **par ~** bit by bit.

bric: **de bric et de broc** /dəbʀiked(ə)bʀɔk/ *loc adv* [*s'habiller*] any old how; [*meublé*] with bits and pieces; **équipe composée de ~ et de broc** motley crew.

bric-à-brac /bʀikabʀak/ *nm inv* lit bric-à-brac, odds and ends (*pl*); fig bric-à-brac.

brick /bʀik/ *nm* Naut brig.

bricolage /bʀikɔlaʒ/ *nm* **1** (activité) DIY GB, do-it-yourself GB, fixing things US; **magasin de ~** DIY shop GB, hardware store US; **j'adore le ~** I love DIY GB, I love fixing things US; **tout pour le ~** everything for the DIY enthusiast GB ou the do-it-yourselfer US; **2** (travail non professionnel) makeshift job; **c'est du ~ mais ça tiendra** it's a makeshift job but it'll hold.

bricole /bʀikɔl/ *nf* **1** (menu objet) **acheter une ~** to buy a little something; **des ~s** bits and pieces; **2** (bagatelle) **se fâcher pour des ~s** to get angry at the slightest thing; **3** Équit breast harness.

bricoler /bʀikɔle/ [1] **I**○ *vtr* (tenter de réparer) to tinker with [*moteur, appareil*]; (confectionner) to knock up GB, to throw together [*étagère, système*]; (truquer) to fiddle GB ou tamper with US [*compteur, machine*].
II *vi* (faire du bricolage) to do DIY GB, to fix things US.

bricoleur, **-euse** /bʀikɔlœʀ, øz/ **I** *adj* **être ~** to be good with one's hands.
II *nm,f* (personne habile) handyman/handywoman; (personne qui fait du bricolage) DIY enthusiast GB, do-it-yourselfer US.

bride /bʀid/ *nf* **1** Équit bridle; **2** (de boutonnage) button loop; **3** Mécan (fixation) flange; **4** Méd adhesions (*pl*).
IDIOMES **partir à ~ abattue** to dash off; **tourner ~** lit, fig to do a U-turn; **tenir qn/qch en ~** to keep a tight rein on sb/sth; **avoir la ~ sur le cou** to have free rein; **lâcher la ~ à qn** to give sb free rein; **tenir la ~ (haute) à qn** to keep sb on a tight rein.

bridé, **~e** /bʀide/ **I** *pp* ▶ **brider**.
II *pp adj* **yeux ~s** slanting eyes.

brider /bʀide/ [1] *vtr* **1** Équit to bridle [*cheval*]; **2** (contenir) to control [*personne*]; to curb [*élan, liberté, spontanéité*]; **3** Culin to truss [*volaille*]; **4** Tech to flange [*tuyau*].

bridge /bʀidʒ/ *nm* **1** ▶ **449** Jeux bridge; **~ contrat** contract bridge; **~ aux enchères** auction bridge; **2** Dent bridge.

bridger /bʀidʒe/ [13] *vi* Jeux to play bridge.

bridgeur, -euse /bʀidʒœʀ, øz/ *nm,f* Jeux bridge player.

bridon /bʀidɔ̃/ *nm* snaffle.

brie /bʀi/ *nm* Culin Brie (cheese).

Brie /bʀi/ ▶ **692** *nprf* Géog **la ~** Brie, the Brie region.

briefing /bʀifiŋ/ *nm* briefing.

brièvement /bʀijɛvmɑ̃/ *adv* briefly.

brièveté /bʀijɛvte/ *nf* brevity.

brigade /bʀigad/ *nf* **1** Mil brigade; **~ aérienne** airborne brigade; **~ d'infanterie** infantry unit; **2** (dans la police) squad; **3** Admin (groupe de travailleurs) team.

■ **~ antiterroriste** antiterrorist squad; **~ criminelle** crime squad; **~ financière** fraud squad; **~ de gendarmerie** (gendarmes) (small town) police force; (bâtiment) small town police station; **~ des mineurs** juvenile delinquency division; **~ des mœurs** or **mondaine** vice squad; **~ de sapeurs-pompiers** fire brigade GB, fire department US; **~ des stupéfiants** drugs squad GB, drug squad US; **Brigades internationales** Hist International Brigade (*sg*); **Brigades rouges** Hist Red Brigades.

brigadier /bʀigadje/ ▶ **390** *nm* **1** Mil (caporal) ≈ corporal (*in tank, artillery or transport division*); **2** (de sapeurs-pompiers) fire chief; **3** Théât *wooden staff used to give the signal for the beginning of a performance*.

brigadier-chef, *pl* **brigadiers-chefs** /bʀigadjeʃɛf/ ▶ **390** *nm*: *French army rank between corporal and sergeant (in tank, artillery or transport division)*.

brigand /bʀigɑ̃/ *nm* **1** (bandit) brigand, bandit; **2** péj (filou) crook○; **3** (enfant) rascal.

brigandage /bʀigɑ̃daʒ/ *nm* (armed) robbery, banditry†; **commettre des actes de ~** to commit robbery; **c'est du ~!** fig it's daylight ou highway US robbery!

brigantine /bʀigɑ̃tin/ *nf* Naut spanker.

brigue /bʀig/ *nf* liter intrigue; **obtenir qch par ~** to get sth by intrigue.

briguer /bʀige/ [1] *vtr* to crave [*honneur, faveur*]; to set one's sights on [*présidence, poste*]; to solicit [*voix*].

brillamment /bʀijamɑ̃/ *adv* gén brilliantly; **réussir** ou **être reçu ~ à un examen** to pass an exam with flying colours.

brillance /bʀijɑ̃s/ *nf* (d'astre, de diamant) brilliance; (de tissu, papier) sheen.

brillant, ~e /bʀijɑ̃, ɑ̃t/ **I** *adj* **1** (luisant) [*yeux, métal, plumage*] bright; [*surface polie*] shiny; [*surface mouillée*] glistening; [*cheveux*] shiny, glossy; **regard ~ de joie** eyes shining with joy; **2** (admirable) [*personne, carrière, conversation*] brilliant; **pas ~** euph [*résultat, performance*] not brilliant, not very good at all; [*situation*] none too rosy○, quite bad; [*santé, affaires*] none too good, rather poor; **les résultats ne sont pas des plus ~s** the results are not exactly brilliant.

II *nm* **1** (éclat) (de surface polie, cheveux) shine (**de** of); **donner du ~ aux cheveux/meubles** to give hair/furniture a shine; **2** (diamant) (cut) diamond, brilliant.

brillantine /bʀijɑ̃tin/ *nf* brilliantine.

briller /bʀije/ [1] *vi* **1** (luire) [*soleil, lampe*] to shine; [*flamme*] to burn brightly; [*diamant*] to sparkle; [*surface polie, métal*] to shine; (au soleil) to gleam, to shine; [*surface mouillée, neige, larme*] to glisten; [*nez*] to be shiny; [*yeux*] to shine; (pétiller) to sparkle; **tout brillait de propreté** everything was sparkling clean; **faire ~ ses chaussures** to shine one's shoes; **faire ~ l'argenterie** to clean the silver; **shampooing qui fait ~ les cheveux** shampoo which makes your hair shine; **les étoiles brillent** the stars are out; **2** (exprimer) [*yeux, regard*] **~ de** to shine with [*joie, curiosité*]; to blaze with [*colère*]; to burn with [*fièvre, désir*]; to glitter with [*convoitise*]; **3** (se distinguer) [*mondain, causeur*] to shine; [*élève*] (dans une matière) to be brilliant (**en** at), to shine (**en** in); (dans une épreuve) to do brilliantly (**à, en** in); **~ en société** to shine in company; **elle brille par son esprit/talent** she's extremely witty/talented; **elle ne brille pas par son intelligence** euph she's not noted for her intelligence, intelligence isn't her strong point; **il n'a pas brillé par son courage** he wasn't exactly brave; **~ par son absence** to be conspicuous by one's absence; ▶ **or**.

brimade /bʀimad/ *nf* bullying ¢; **être victime de ~s** to be bullied; **faire subir des ~s à qn** to bully sb.

brimborion /bʀɛ̃bɔʀjɔ̃/ *nm* trinket.

brimer /bʀime/ [1] *vtr* to bully [*personne*]; **un enfant brimé par ses camarades** a child who is bullied; **se sentir brimé** to feel frustrated.

brin /bʀɛ̃/ *nm* **1** (tige) **un ~ de muguet/persil** a sprig of lily-of-the-valley/parsley; **un ~ de paille** a wisp of straw; **un ~ d'herbe** a blade of grass; **du muguet à 15 francs le ~** lily-of-the-valley at 15 francs a sprig; **couvert de ~s d'herbe** covered in bits of grass; **2** (peu) **un ~ de** a bit of; **faire un ~ de toilette** to have a quick wash GB, to wash up quickly US; **faire un ~ de causette** to have a little chat; **un ~ exagéré/ennuyeux** a touch exaggerated/boring; **juste un ~** just a touch; **un beau ~ de fille** a gorgeous girl.

brindille /bʀɛ̃dij/ *nf* twig.

bringue○ /bʀɛ̃g/ *nf* **1** (beuverie) booze-up○ GB, drinking party; (fête) rave-up○; **faire la ~** (boire) to have a booze-up○; (faire la fête) to rave it up○, to have a wild time; **2** (fille) (**grande**) **~** beanpole.

brinquebaler /bʀɛ̃kbale/ [1] *vi* [*chargement*] to rattle about; [*véhicule*] to jolt along; [*personne*] to be shaken.

brio /bʀijo/ *nm* (talent) brilliance, panache; Mus brio; **avec ~** brilliantly, with great panache.

brioche /bʀijɔʃ/ *nf* **1** Culin brioche, (sweet) bun; **~ aux raisins** currant bun; **saumon en ~** salmon brioche; **2**○ (ventre) paunch; **prendre de la ~** to develop a paunch.

brioché, ~e /bʀijɔʃe/ *adj* Culin brioche (*épith*).

brique /bʀik/ **I** ▶ **193** *adj inv* [*peinture*] brick red; [*vêtement, objet*] rust-coloured[GB].

II *nf* **1** Constr brick; **mur de** or **en ~s** brick wall; **2** (emballage de lait, jus de fruit) carton; **3**○ (dix mille francs) ten thousand francs; **une ~ et demie** fifteen thousand francs.

■ **~ creuse** hollow block; **~ pleine** brick; **~ de verre** glass block.

briquer /bʀike/ [1] *vtr* to polish up; Naut to scrub down.

briquet /bʀikɛ/ *nm* **1** (de fumeur) (cigarette) lighter; **2** Zool beagle; **3** (sabre) sabre[GB].

briquetage /bʀiktaʒ/ *nm* **1** (en briques) brickwork; **2** (imitation de briques) brick facing ¢.

briqueterie /bʀikɛtʀi/ *nf* **1** (industrie) brickworks (+ *v sg* ou *pl*); **2** (usine) brickyard.

briquette /bʀikɛt/ *nf* briquette GB, briquet US.

briquet-tempête /bʀikɛtɑ̃pɛt/ *nm* windproof lighter.

bris /bʀi/ *nm inv* **1** (rupture) gén, Jur (de matériel, scellés) breaking; **la police ne couvre pas le ~ de glaces** Assur, Aut the policy does not cover broken windows or mirrors; **~ de clôture** Jur breaking and entering; **2** (débris d'objet cassé) fragment.

brisant, ~e /bʀizɑ̃, ɑ̃t/ **I** *adj* high-explosive; **explosif ~** high-explosive charge.

II *nm* (haut-fond) shoal.

III brisants *nmpl* (vagues) breakers.

briscard /bʀiskaʀ/ *nm* lit, fig veteran.

brise /bʀiz/ *nf* breeze; **légère/bonne ~** light/fresh breeze.

brisé, ~e /bʀize/ **I** *pp* ▶ **briser**.

II *pp adj* **1** (fracturé) broken; **2** fig [*personne*] broken; [*élan*] broken; [*rêve, espoir*] shattered; **avoir le cœur ~** to be broken-hearted; **il est ~ par le chagrin** he's broken-hearted; **un vieil homme ~ par la vie** a broken old man; **dit-elle, la voix ~e par l'émotion** she said, her voice breaking with emotion; **3** Hérald [*chevron*] broken.

III *nm* Danse brisé.

IV brisées *nfpl* Chasse broken branches (*to mark the track of an animal*); **aller** or **marcher sur les ~es de qn** fig to poach on sb's territory ou preserve; **suivre les ~es de qn** fig to follow in sb's footsteps.

brise-béton /bʀizbetɔ̃/ *nm inv* Constr jackhammer.

brise-bise /bʀizbiz/ *nm inv* half-curtain.

brise-fer /bʀizfɛʀ/ *nm inv* destructive child.

brise-glace /bʀizglas/ *nm inv* **1** Naut (navire) icebreaker; **2** Constr (de pont) ice-breaker.

brise-jet /bʀizʒɛ/ *nm inv* (rubber) spout.

brise-lames /bʀizlam/ *nm inv* breakwater.

brise-mottes /bʀizmɔt/ *nm inv* harrow.

briser /bʀize/ [1] **I** *vtr* **1** (rompre) to break [*objet, jambe*]; **2** (interrompre) to break [*rythme, volonté, élan*]; to stop [*tentative, attaque, ascension, inflation*]; to break down [*résistance*]; to crush [*révolte*]; [*travailleur*] to break [*grève*]; [*police*] to stop [*grève*]; **3** (mettre fin à) to break [*silence, monopole, accord, isolement*]; to break down [*tabou*]; to bring [sth] to an end [*influence*]; to shatter [*rêve, idylle*]; **4** (détruire) to destroy [*pays, organisation, structure*]; to break [*personne*]; to wreck [*carrière*]; to shatter [*image*]; **cette épreuve a brisé sa vie/ses espoirs** this experience has wrecked his/her life/his/her hopes; **l'émotion lui brisait la voix** his/her voice was breaking with emotion; **5** (épuiser) to shatter [*personne*].

II se briser *vpr* **1** (se rompre) [*vitre, os*] to break; [*vague*] to break (**sur, contre** against); **mes arguments se sont brisés contre son entêtement** fig my arguments were useless in the face of his stubbornness; **2** (s'interrompre) [*élan*] to break; [*rêve*] to be shattered; **3** (s'altérer) [*voix*] to break; **quand il en parle, sa voix se brise** when he talks about it, his voice breaks; **son cœur se brise devant tant de pauvreté** all this poverty is breaking his/her heart.

IDIOMES **il nous les brise**◐ he's bugging us◐.

brise-soleil /bʀizsɔlɛj/ *nm inv* Archit brise-soleil.

brise-tout /bʀiztu/ *nm inv* (personne) butterfingers (*sg*).

briseur, -euse /bʀizœʀ, øz/ *nm,f* wrecker.

■ **~ de chaînes** chain-breaker, strongman in fairground; **~ de grève** strike breaker.

brise-vent /bʀizvɑ̃/ *nm inv* Agric windbreak.

brisquard /bʀiskaʀ/ *nm* = **briscard**.

bristol /bʀistɔl/ *nm* **1** (carton) Bristol (board); **2** (carte de visite) visiting card, calling card US; **3** (carton d'invitation) invitation card.

brisure /bʀizyʀ/ *nf* **1** (fêlure) crack; (débris) fragment; **2** Tech (joint) break; **3** Hérald mark of cadency.

britannique /bʀitanik/ ▶ **537** *adj* British.

Britannique /bʀitanik/ ▶ **537** *nmf* Briton, Britisher US; **un/une ~** a British man/woman; **les ~s** the British (people).

Britanniques /bʀitanik/ ▶ **416** *adj fpl* **les îles ~** the British Isles.

broc /bʀo/ *nm* ewer; ▶ **bric**.

brocante /bʀɔkɑ̃t/ *nf* **1** (activité) bric-à-brac trade; **2** (marché) flea market.

brocanteur, -euse /bʀɔkɑ̃tœʀ, øz/ ▶ **510** *nm,f* bric-à-brac trader.

brocard /bʀɔkaʀ/ *nm* **1** Zool brocket; **2**† liter gibe.

brocarder /bʀɔkaʀde/ [1] *vtr* liter to ridicule, to gibe at.

brocart /bʀɔkaʀ/ *nm* Tex brocade; **~ de soie** silk brocade.

brochage /bʀɔʃaʒ/ *nm* **1** Imprim soft binding (with paper); **2** Tex brocading.

broche /bʀɔʃ/ *nf* **1** (bijou) brooch; **2** Culin spit; **faire cuire qch à la ~** to spit-roast sth, to roast sth on a spit; **3** Méd pin; **4** Tech spindle.
■ **~ à glace** Sport ice-piton.

broché, **~e** /bʀɔʃe/ **I** *pp* ▶ **brocher**.
II *pp adj* [*livre*] paperback (*épith*), softcover (*épith*).
III *nm* Tex (tissu) brocade; (technique) brocading.

brocher /bʀɔʃe/ [1] *vtr* **1** Imprim to bind [sth] (with paper) [*livre*]; **2** Tex to brocade.

brochet /bʀɔʃɛ/ *nm* Zool pike.
■ **~ de mer** barracuda.

brochette /bʀɔʃɛt/ *nf* **1** Culin (tige) skewer; (mets) kebab, brochette; **~ de poisson/viande** fish/meat kebab; **2** fig (de personnalités) band (**de** of); (de décorations) row (**de** of).

brocheur, **-euse** /bʀɔʃœʀ, øz/ **I** ▶ **510** *nm,f* book binder.
II brocheuse *nf* (machine) binder, binding machine.

brochure /bʀɔʃyʀ/ *nf* **1** (fascicule) booklet; (de voyage) brochure; (de présentation) prospectus; **2** Imprim binding (with paper).

brocoli /bʀɔkɔli/ *nm* broccoli ȼ.

brodequin /bʀɔdkɛ̃/ **I** *nm* (laced) boot; (autrefois) buskin.
II brodequins *nmpl* (pour torturer) **les ~s** the boot.

broder /bʀɔde/ [1] **I** *vtr* to embroider [*nappe*] (**de** with); to embroider [*motif*]; **brodé à mes initiales** embroidered with my initials.
II *vi* (enrichir de détails) to embroider (**sur** on).

broderie /bʀɔdʀi/ *nf* **1** (art) embroidery; **~ à la main** hand-embroidery; **faire de la ~** to do embroidery; **2** (ouvrage) piece of embroidery, embroidery ȼ; **3** Ind embroidery trade.
■ **~ anglaise** broderie anglaise.

brodeuse /bʀɔdøz/ *nf* Tex **1** (personne) embroiderer; **2** (machine) embroidery machine.

bromate /bʀɔmat/ *nm* bromate.

brome /bʀom/ *nm* Chimie bromine.

broméliacées /bʀɔmeljase/ *nfpl* Bot bromeliads.

bromique /bʀɔmik/ *adj* **acide ~** bromic acid.

bromure /bʀɔmyʀ/ *nm* bromide; **~ d'argent/de potassium** silver/potassium bromide.

bronche /bʀɔ̃ʃ/ *nf* bronchus; **les ~s** the bronchial tubes; **avoir les ~s fragiles** to have a weak chest.
IDIOMES **souffler dans les ~s de qn**○ to tear a strip off sb○ GB, to tell sb off.

broncher /bʀɔ̃ʃe/ [1] *vi* **1** (réagir) **sans ~** without turning a hair; **il n'a pas bronché quand on lui a annoncé les résultats** he took it calmly when they told him the results; **2** Équit [*cheval*] to stumble.

bronchiole /bʀɔ̃kjɔl/ *nf* bronchiole.

bronchique /bʀɔ̃ʃik/ *adj* bronchial.

bronchite /bʀɔ̃ʃit/ ▶ **271** *nf* bronchitis ȼ; **avoir une (bonne) ~** to have (a bad attack of) bronchitis; **~ chronique** chronic bronchitis.

bronchitique /bʀɔ̃ʃitik/ **I** *adj* [*symptôme*] bronchitic; **il est ~** he suffers from bronchitis.
II *nmf* bronchitis sufferer.

broncho-pneumonie, *pl* **~s** /bʀɔ̃kɔpnømɔni/ ▶ **271** *nf* bronchopneumonia.

bronchoscopie /bʀɔ̃kɔskɔpi/ *nf* bronchoscopy.

brontosaure /bʀɔ̃tozɔʀ/ *nm* brontosaurus.

bronzage /bʀɔ̃zaʒ/ *nm* **1** (action de se faire bronzer) (sun-)tanning; (hâle) tan; **~ artificiel** artificial tan; **mon ~ n'a pas tenu** my tan did not last long; **2** Tech (de matière) bronzing.
■ **~ intégral** (action) nude sunbathing; (hâle) all-over tan.

bronze /bʀɔ̃z/ *nm* (matière, objet) bronze; **un (objet de** or **en) ~** a bronze (object).
IDIOMES **couler un ~**● to have a shit●.

bronzé, **~e** /bʀɔ̃ze/ **I** *pp* ▶ **bronzer**.
II *pp adj* (sun-)tanned; **il est revenu tout ~** he came back with a dark tan.
III *nm,f* péj (sur la plage) beach bum○.

bronzer /bʀɔ̃ze/ [1] **I** *vtr* **1** (hâler) to tan [*peau*]; **2** Tech to bronze [*métal*].
II *vi* [*personne*] to get a tan, to go brown; [*peau*] to tan; **il est allé se faire ~ en Italie** he's gone to sun himself in Italy.
IDIOMES **~ idiot**○ to lie around in the sun.

bronzette○ /bʀɔ̃zɛt/ *nf* sunbathing.

bronzeur /bʀɔ̃zœʀ/ *nm* (ouvrier) bronze-smelter, bronzer.

broquette /bʀɔkɛt/ *nf* (tin) tack.

brossage /bʀɔsaʒ/ *nm* (des cheveux, dents) brushing ȼ; (du dos) scrubbing ȼ; (d'un cheval) grooming ȼ.

brosse /bʀɔs/ *nf* **1** gén brush; **donner un coup de ~ à qch** to give sth a brush; **se donner un coup de ~** (se coiffer) to give one's hair a quick brush; **être coiffé en ~, avoir les cheveux (taillés) en ~** to have a crew cut; **2** B (balai) broom.
■ **~ à cheveux** hairbrush; **~ en chiendent** scrubbing brush; **~ à dents** toothbrush; **~ à habits** clothesbrush; **~ métallique** wire brush; **~ à ongles** nail-brush.

brosser /bʀɔse/ [1] **I** *vtr* **1** (frotter) to brush [*vêtements, cheveux, dents*]; to scrub [*dos*]; to brush [sb] down [*personne*]; to groom [*cheval*]; **2** (peindre) to paint [*toile, paysage*]; **3** (décrire) to give a quick outline of; **~ un tableau de la situation** to give an outline of the situation; **4** Sport to spin [*balle*].
II○ *vi* B schoolchildrens' slang (s'absenter) to skip school.
III se brosser *vpr* to brush oneself down; **se ~ les dents/cheveux** to brush one's teeth/hair.
IDIOMES **il peut (toujours aller) se ~**○ he can go and jump in the lake○, he can forget about it.

brou /bʀu/ *nm* (écale) husk.
■ **~ de noix** walnut stain.

broue /bʀu/ *nf* C **1** (bière) beer; **2** (mousse) (de bière) head; (de lait) froth.

brouet /bʀuɛ/ *nm* Culin **1** péj unsubstantial soup hum; **2**‡ (bouillon) broth; **un ~ de poisson** a fish broth.

brouette /bʀuɛt/ *nf* (véhicule) wheelbarrow; (contenu) barrowful; **trois ~s de terre** three barrowfuls of earth; **faire la ~** Jeux to play wheelbarrows.

brouettée /bʀuɛte/ *nf* barrowful.

brouetter /bʀuete/ [1] *vtr* to wheelbarrow, to cart.

brouhaha /bʀuaa/ *nm* hubbub; **un grand ~** a loud hubbub.

brouillage /bʀujaʒ/ *nm* **1** Radio, Télécom (provoqué) jamming; (involontaire) interference; **2** fig (de pistes) covering up; (de données) mixing up.

brouillard /bʀujaʀ/ *nm* **1** Météo fog; **il y a du ~** it's foggy; **un ~ à couper au couteau** a thick fog, a pea-souper GB; **voir tout à travers un ~** to be in a complete daze; **être dans le ~**○ fig to be somewhat in the dark; **foncer dans le ~**○ fig to charge blindly ahead; **2** (pulvérisation) spray; **3** Comm (livre) daybook.
■ **~ givrant** Météo freezing fog.

brouillasser /bʀujase/ [1] *v impers* to drizzle; **il brouillasse** it's drizzling.

brouille /bʀuj/ *nf* (momentanément) quarrel; (durablement) discord; **cinq ans de ~** five years of discord.
■ **~ ancestrale** blood feud.

brouiller /bʀuje/ [1] **I** *vtr* **1** (rendre trouble) [*produit*] to make [sth] cloudy [*liquide*]; [*pluie*] to blur, to smudge [*nom, texte*]; [*larmes*] to blur [*vue*]; [*personne*] to cover (over) [*empreintes*]; **regard brouillé par les larmes** vision blurred by tears; **~ la combinaison d'un coffre** to scramble the combination of a safe; **~ les pistes** or **les cartes** fig to confuse ou cloud the issue; **il ne cesse de ~ les pistes** he keeps confusing the issue; **2** Radio, Télécom [*personne, groupe*] to jam [*signaux, émission*]; [*parasites, appareils ménagers*] to interfere with [*émission, réception*]; **3** (désunir) **l'incident avait brouillé les deux frères** the two brothers had fallen out over the incident; **~ qn avec qn** to turn sb against sb; **rien ne peut ~ leur amitié** fig nothing can get in the way of their friendship.
II se brouiller *vpr* **1** (se fâcher) [*personnes, groupes*] to fall out; **se ~ avec qn** to fall out with sb; **être brouillé avec qn** to have fallen out with sb; **il est brouillé avec tout le monde** he's fallen out with everybody; **ils sont brouillés (à vie)** they've fallen out (for good); **elles sont brouillées depuis deux ans** they fell out two years ago; **être brouillé avec les chiffres/avec les langues** fig to be hopeless with figures/at languages; **2** (devenir trouble) [*liquide*] to become cloudy; [*vue*] to become blurred; [*esprit, souvenirs*] to become confused; **avoir le teint brouillé** to look ill ou liverish; **3** Météo **le temps se brouille, il va pleuvoir** it's clouding over ou the weather is breaking, it's going to rain; ▶ **œuf**.

brouillon, **-onne** /bʀujɔ̃, ɔn/ **I** *adj* **1** (qui manque de soin) [*personne, copie, devoir*] untidy; **essayez d'être moins ~** try to be less untidy; **2** (désorganisé) [*personne*] disorganized; [*esprit, pensée, caractère*] muddled, confused; [*style*] muddled; [*émission, conférence*] disorganized; **son discours était très ~** his speech was very muddled.
II *nm* **1** (première rédaction) (de texte, discours, devoir) rough draft; **montrez-moi le ~ de votre devoir** show me the rough draft of your work; **fais un ~** make a rough draft; **faire qch au ~** to do sth in rough; **2** (papier) ȼ **(papier) ~** rough paper; **donne-moi du ~** give me some rough paper; **une feuille de ~** a sheet of rough paper.

broum /bʀum/ *excl* broom!

broussaille /bʀusaj/ *nf* (dans sous-bois) undergrowth ȼ; (sur terrain inculte) scrub ȼ, brush ȼ; (dans jardin, parc) bushes (*pl*); **sourcils en ~** bushy eyebrows; **cheveux en ~** tousled hair.

broussailleux, **-euse** /bʀusajø, øz/ *adj* **1** [*terrain, région*] covered with bushes; [*jardin*] overgrown; **2** [*barbe, sourcils*] bushy; [*cheveux*] tousled.

broussard /bʀusaʀ/ *nm* bushman.

brousse /bʀus/ *nf* Géog bush; **vivre dans la ~** to live (out) in the bush; **village/taxi de ~** bush village/taxi; **en pleine ~**○ in the middle of nowhere, in the sticks○.

broutement /bʀutmɑ̃/ *nm* **1** Agric grazing; **2** Aut juddering; **3** Tech (d'outil) chattering.

brouter /bʀute/ [1] **I** *vtr* [*vache, mouton*] to graze; [*chèvre*] to nibble.
II *vi* **1** Agric [*vache, mouton*] to graze; [*chèvre*] to nibble; **2** Aut to judder; **3** Tech [*outil*] to chatter.

broutille /bʀutij/ *nf* trifle; **ce n'est qu'une ~** it's nothing.

broyage /bʀwajaʒ/ *nm* grinding, crushing.

broyer /bʀwaje/ [23] *vtr* **1** (écraser) to grind [*grain, couleurs, aliments*]; to crush [*pierre*]; to crush [*bras, pied*]; **2** (anéantir) to crush [*ennemi*].
IDIOMES **~ du noir** [*personne*] to brood; [*entreprise*] to be in the doldrums.

broyeur, **-euse** /bʀwajœʀ, øz/ **I** *adj* grinding, crushing.

II *nm* (machine) crusher, grinder.
■ **~ à cylindres** break roll; **~ de documents** shredder; **~ d'évier** waste disposal unit; **~ à feuilles** leaf shredder; **~ à glace** ice crusher; **~ à rouleaux** roller crusher; **~ de WC** Saniflo® unit.

brrr /bʀʀ/ *excl* brr!

bru /bʀy/ *nf* daughter-in-law.

bruant /bʀyɑ̃/ *nm* Zool bunting.
■ **~ fou** rock bunting; **~ jaune** yellowhammer; **~ lapon** lapland bunting; **~ des roseaux** reed bunting.

brucelles /bʀysɛl/ *nfpl* tweezers.

brucellose /bʀysɛloz/ *nf* ▶ 271 brucellosis.

brugeois, **~e** /bʀyʒwa, az/ ▶ 857 *adj* of Bruges.

Brugeois, **~e** /bʀyʒwa, az/ ▶ 857 *nm,f* (natif) native of Bruges; (habitant) inhabitant of Bruges.

brugnon /bʀyɲɔ̃/ *nm* nectarine.

brugnonier /bʀyɲɔnje/ *nm* nectarine tree.

bruine /bʀɥin/ *nf* drizzle.

bruiner /bʀɥine/ [1] *v impers* to drizzle; **il bruine** it's drizzling.

bruire /bʀɥiʀ/ [3] *vi* liter [*feuille, papier, tissu*] to rustle; [*ruisseau*] to murmur; [*insecte*] to hum; **le vent bruissait dans les feuillages** the wind was rustling through the leaves.

bruissement /bʀɥismɑ̃/ *nm* liter (de feuille, papier, tissu, vent) rustle ¢, rustling ¢; (de ruisseau) murmur(ing) ¢; (d'insecte) humming ¢.

bruit /bʀɥi/ *nm* **1** (son) noise; **entendre un ~** to hear a noise; **on n'entend pas un ~** you can't hear a sound; **~ léger** faint noise; **~ soudain** sudden noise; **~ étouffé** thud; **le ~ de la circulation/d'un train** (au loin) the sound of traffic/of a train; (proche) the noise of traffic/of a train; **un ~ de marteau** hammering; **un ~ de casseroles/d'assiettes** the clatter of saucepans/of plates; **un ~ de ferraille** a clang; **j'entends un ~ de pas/voix** I can hear footsteps/voices; **entendre le ~ des charrettes sur les pavés** to hear carts rattling over the cobbles; **on dirait un ~ de moteur** it sounds like an engine; **il y a un ~ dans le moteur** the engine is making a funny noise; **dans un ~ de tonnerre** with a noise like thunder; **2** (tapage) noise; **la pollution par le ~** noise pollution; **faire du ~** to make a noise, to be noisy; **tu fais trop de ~** you're too noisy, you're making too much noise; **ne fais pas de ~, il dort** don't make any noise, he's asleep; **il y a du ~** it's noisy; **travailler dans le ~** to work in a noisy environment; **faire un ~ infernal** or **d'enfer** [*machine*] to make a terrible din; [*voisins*] to make an awful racket; **sans ~** [*marcher*] silently; [*pleurer*] in silence; [*fonctionner*] without making any noise; **3** fig (commotion) **son film a fait beaucoup de ~** his/her film attracted a lot of attention; **on a fait grand ~ de ce livre** this book caused quite a stir; **faire beaucoup de ~ pour rien** to make a lot of fuss about nothing; **une affaire qui a fait du ~** an affair that caused an uproar; **4** (rumeur) rumour[GB]; **le ~ court que** rumour[GB] has it that, there's a rumour[GB] that; ▶ **faux**; **5** Méd murmur; **~s cardiaques** heart murmur (*sg*); **6** Télécom noise; **7** liter (agitation) **loin du ~ du monde** far from the madding crowd.
■ **~ de couloir** rumour[GB]; **~ de fond** background noise.

bruitage /bʀɥitaʒ/ *nm* Cin, Théât sound effects (*pl*).

bruiteur /bʀɥitœʀ/ *nm* sound effects engineer.

brûlage /bʀylaʒ/ *nm* **1** Agric (de terres) burning; **2** Cosmét (de cheveux) singeing; **3** Tech (de peinture) burning off.

brûlant, **~e** /bʀylɑ̃, ɑ̃t/ *adj* **1** (très chaud) [*fer à repasser, casserole, plat*] hot; [*thé, café, soupe*] boiling hot; [*vent, sable, rocher, asphalte, tuile, radiateur*] burning hot; [*soleil*] blazing; **2** (fiévreux) [*personne, front*] burning hot; **être ~ de fièvre** to be burning with fever; **3** (urgent) [*question, thème*] burning; **un problème ~** a burning issue; **un sujet d'une ~e actualité** a burning issue; **4** (ardent) [*passion*] burning; [*amour*] passionate; [*regard*] blazing; **il lui jeta un regard ~ de passion** he looked at him/her, his eyes ablaze with passion.

brûlé, **~e** /bʀyle/ **I** *pp* ▶ **brûler**.
II *pp adj* (démasqué) **être ~** [*agent secret*] to have one's cover blown.
III *nm,f* Méd **un grand ~** a third degree burns victim; **service des grands ~s** burns unit.
IV *nm* **odeur de ~** smell of burning, a burned smell; **avoir un goût de ~** to taste burned; **ça sent le ~** lit there's a smell of burning; fig things are becoming unpleasant; **je n'aime pas le ~** I won't eat the burned bit.

brûle-gueule◑ /bʀylgœl/ *nm inv* short-stemmed pipe.

brûle-parfum(s) /bʀylpaʀfœ̃/ *nm inv* perfume-burner.

brûle-pourpoint: **à brûle-pourpoint** /abʀylpuʀpwɛ̃/ *loc adv* point-blank; **demander à ~** to ask point-blank.

brûler /bʀyle/ [1] **I** *vtr* **1** (mettre le feu) to burn [*papiers, broussailles*]; to set fire to [*voiture, maison*]; to burn [*encens*]; **~ un cierge à saint Antoine** to light a candle to Saint Anthony; **~ qn vif** to burn sb alive; ▶ **chandelle**; **2** (consommer) to burn [*bois, charbon, mazout*]; to use [*électricité*]; to burn [*calories*]; ▶ **cartouche**; **3** (provoquer une brûlure) [*acide, flamme, huile*] to burn [*personne, peau*]; [*eau, thé*] to scald [*peau, corps*]; [*aliments, alcool*] to burn [*estomac, gorge*]; [*soleil*] to burn [*peau*]; [*soleil*] to scorch [*herbe*]; **être brûlé par une explosion/dans un accident** to get burned in an explosion/in an accident; **l'acide/l'huile m'a brûlé les mains** the acid/the oil burned my hands; **~ sa chemise en la repassant** to burn ou scorch one's shirt while ironing it; **être brûlé au visage/cou** to suffer burns to one's face/neck; **être brûlé au premier/troisième degré** to sustain first/third degree burns; **attention, ça brûle!** careful, it's very hot!; **être brûlé par le soleil** [*personne*] to get sunburned; **l'argent leur brûle les doigts** fig money burns a hole in their pocket; **j'ai les yeux qui me brûlent** my eyes are stinging; **4** Méd to cauterize [*verrue*] (**à** with); **5**○ (ne pas respecter) to ignore [*stop, priorité*]; to miss [*station*]; **~ un feu (rouge)** to jump○ the lights; **6**† (torréfier) to roast [*café*].
II *vi* **1** (se consumer) [*bois, charbon, bougie*] to burn; [*forêt, maison, ville*] to be on fire; **bien/mal ~** [*bois, combustible*] to burn well/badly; **3000 hectares de forêt ont brûlé** 3000 hectares of forest have been destroyed by fire; **faire ~ qch** to burn [sth] down [*papier, bois, pneu, maison*]; **il fait ~ des ronces dans le jardin** he's burning brambles in the garden; **2** Culin [*rôti, tarte, gâteau*] to burn; **j'ai fait** or **laissé ~ mon gâteau** I've burned the cake; **3** (flamber) [*feu*] to burn (**dans la cheminée** in the fireplace); **4** (être fiévreux) [*personne, front, mains*] to be burning hot; **~ de fièvre** to be burning with fever; **5** (désirer) **~ de faire, ~ d'envie** or **d'impatience de faire** to be longing to do; **~ d'amour/de passion pour qn** to be consumed with love/with passion for sb; **~ pour qn** to be consumed with love for sb; **6** Jeux (à cache-tampon) **tu brûles!** you're getting very, very warm!
III se brûler *vpr* [*personne*] to burn oneself (**avec** with; **en faisant** doing); **se ~ la main/langue** to burn one's hand/tongue; **se ~ les ailes** fig to come to grief, to come unstuck; **se ~ les cheveux** to singe one's hair; **se ~ les doigts** fig to get one's fingers burned; ▶ **pont**.

brûlerie /bʀylʀi/ *nf* **1** (usine) coffee-roasting plant; **2** ▶ 510 (magasin) coffee merchant.

brûleur /bʀylœʀ/ *nm* Tech burner.

brûlis /bʀyli/ *nm inv* **1** (procédé) slash-and-burn technique; **2** (terrain) burned land; **culture sur ~** slash-and-burn cultivation.

brûlot /bʀylo/ *nm* **1** Presse scathing article; **2** Hist Mil fireship; **3** Culin *sugar lump flambéed with brandy*; **4** C Zool biting midge.

brûlure /bʀylyʀ/ *nf* **1** Méd burn; **souffrir de ~s** to suffer from burns; **~ du premier/deuxième/troisième degré** first/second/third degree burn; **2** (marque) mark; (sur un tissu) burn; (sur une surface) mark; **~ de cigarette sur le sol** cigarette mark on the floor.
■ **~s d'estomac** Méd heartburn ¢.

brumaire /bʀymɛʀ/ *nm* Brumaire (*second month of the French revolutionary calendar, ≈ November*); **le coup d'État du 18 ~** the coup of 18 Brumaire.

brume /bʀym/ *nf* **1** (brouillard léger) mist; (en mer) (sea) mist; (épaisse) fog; **un banc de ~** a patch of mist; **2** (vapeur) (d'aérosol) mist; **3** (état confus) haze; **sortir des ~s du sommeil/de l'ivresse** to come out of a sleepy/drunken haze.
■ **~ de chaleur** heat haze.

brumeux, **-euse** /bʀymø, øz/ *adj* **1** Météo (de chaleur) hazy; (de froid) misty, foggy; **2** (peu clair) [*esprit, idée*] hazy.

brumisateur® /bʀymizatœʀ/ *nm* facial mister.

brun, **~e** /bʀœ̃, bʀyn/ **I** ▶ 193 *adj* [*peau, tissu, fourrure*] brown, dark; [*cheveux, barbe*] dark; [*yeux*] brown; [*personne*] dark-haired; [*tabac*] black; **cigarette ~e** black tobacco cigarette; **bière ~e** ≈ stout GB; **~ foncé/clair** dark/light brown; **~ de peau** dark-skinned.
II *nm,f* (homme) dark-haired man; (femme) dark-haired woman, brunette.
III *nm* (couleur) brown; **~ clair/foncé** light/dark brown.
IV brune *nf* **1** (cigarette) black tobacco cigarette; **2** (bière) brown ale, stout GB.
V à la brune *loc prép* littér at dusk.
■ **~ Van Dyck** Vandyke brown.

brunante /bʀynɑ̃t/ *nf* C (crépuscule) dusk; **à la ~** at dusk.

brunâtre /bʀynɑtʀ/ ▶ 193 *adj* brownish.

Brunei /bʀynɛi/ ▶ 321 *nprm* Brunei.

brunette /bʀynɛt/ *nf* brunette.

brunir /bʀyniʀ/ [3] **I** *vtr* **1** (bronzer) [*soleil, rayon*] to tan [*personne, peau*]; **2** Tech to burnish.
II *vi* **1** [*personne, peau*] to tan; [*cheveux*] to get darker; **2** Culin to brown; **faire ~** to brown [*sauce, caramel, beurre*]; **plat à ~** browning dish.

brunissage /bʀynisaʒ/ *nm* Tech burnishing.

brunissure /bʀynisyʀ/ *nf* Tech burnish.

brushing /bʀœʃiŋ/ *nm* blow-dry; **faire un ~ à qn** to give sb a blow-dry; **se faire faire un ~** to have a blow-dry.

brusque /bʀysk/ *adj* **1** (bourru) [*personne, ton*] abrupt, brusque; **être ~ avec** or **envers qn** to be abrupt with sb; **2** (imprévu) [*mouvement*] sudden; [*virage*] sharp; **donner un ~ coup de frein** to brake sharply.

brusquement /bʀyskəmɑ̃/ *adv* **1** [*répondre, dire, interrompre*] abruptly; **2** [*agir, ralentir, entrer, mourir*] suddenly; [*freiner, accélérer*] sharply.

brusquer /bʀyske/ [1] *vtr* **1** (traiter sans ménagement) to be brusque with; **2** (précipiter) to rush; **ne pas ~ les choses** not to rush things; **il ne faut pas ~ les choses** it doesn't do to rush things; **une attaque brusquée** a surprise attack; **un départ brusqué** a hurried departure.

brusquerie /bʀyskəʀi/ *nf* **1** (rudesse) brusqueness; **avec ~** brusquely; **2** (soudaineté) suddenness.

brut, **~e** /bʀyt/ **I** *adj* **1** (non traité) [*coton, soie, matière, minerai, métal*] raw; [*pierre précieuse*] rough, uncut; [*marbre, granit*] rough; [*laine*] untreated; [*sucre*] unrefined; **à l'état ~** in its natural state; **métal ~ de coulée** as-cast metal; **métal ~ de laminage** as-rolled metal; **2** Vin [*champagne, vin mousseux*] dry, brut; [*cidre*] dry; **3** Fin, Écon [*salaire, bénéfice*] gross; **4** Transp, Comm [*poids, charge*] gross; **poids ~** gross weight.
II *adv* [*rapporter, gagner, peser*] gross; **rapporter 10% ~** to gross 10%, to make 10% gross; **véhicule pesant ~ 5t** vehicle weighing 5t gross.
III *nm* (pétrole) crude (oil); (champagne) dry ou brut champagne; (mousseux) dry ou brut sparkling wine; (cidre) dry cider.
IV brute *nf* **1** (personne violente) brute; **sale ~e!** dirty brute!; **comme une ~e** savagely; **2** (personne sans culture) lout; **c'est une ~e épaisse** he/she's just a stupid lout; **3** (créature sauvage) beast.
IDIOMES **dormir comme une ~e** to sleep like a log; **travailler comme une ~e** to work like a horse.

brutal, **~e**, *mpl* **-aux** /bʀytal, o/ *adj* **1** (brusque) [*coup, choc*] violent; [*douleur, attaque, mort*] sudden; [*hausse, chute, changement, phénomène*] dramatic; [*coup de frein, d'accélérateur*] sharp; **2** (violent) [*ton, réponse, caractère, franchise, discours, article*] brutal; [*geste*] violent; **employer la force ~e** to use brute force; **être ~ avec qn** (physiquement) to be rough with sb; (en paroles) to be brutal with sb; **3** (choquant) [*réalité*] stark.

brutalement /bʀytalmɑ̃/ *adv* **1** (avec violence) [*agir, réprimer, parler, frapper, se conduire*] brutally; [*fermer, ouvrir, poser*] violently; **2** (brusquement) [*changer, baisser, augmenter*] dramatically; [*mourir, choisir, s'arrêter*] suddenly; [*freiner, virer, accélérer*] sharply.

brutaliser /bʀytalize/ [1] *vtr* to ill-treat [*personne, animal*]; to use [sth] roughly [*machine, appareil*].

brutalité /bʀytalite/ *nf* **1** (violence) brutality; **agir/parler avec ~** to act/speak brutally; **2** (brusquerie) suddenness; **3** (acte de violence) (act of) brutality ¢; **les ~s policières** police brutality.

brute *adj, nf* ▸ **brut**.

Bruxelles /bʀysɛl/ ▸ 857 *npr* Brussels.

bruxellois, **~e** /bʀyselwa, az/ ▸ 857 *adj* of Brussels.

Bruxellois, **~e** /bʀyselwa, az/ ▸ 857 *nm,f* (natif) native of Brussels; (habitant) inhabitant of Brussels.

bruyamment /bʀɥijamɑ̃/ *adv* [*rire, éternuer, protester*] loudly; [*entrer, sortir*] noisily.

bruyant, **~e** /bʀɥijɑ̃, ɑ̃t/ *adj* **1** lit [*conversation, musique*] loud; [*enfant, jeu*] noisy, boisterous; [*pièce, rue*] noisy; **2** fig [*renommée, succès, scandale*] resounding.

bruyère /bʀyjɛʀ/ *nf* **1** (plante) heather; (racine) briar; **une pipe de** or **en ~** a briar pipe; ▸ **terre**; **2** (lieu) heath; **se promener dans la ~** to walk over the heath.

BT (*written abbr* = **basse tension**) low voltage.

BTP /betepe/ *nm* (*abbr* = **bâtiment et travaux publics**) building and civil engineering works.

BTS /beteɛs/ *nm*: *abbr* ▸ **brevet**.

bu, **~e** /by/ *pp* ▸ **boire**.

buanderie /bɥɑ̃dʀi/ *nf* **1** (dans une maison) laundry room; **2** C (laverie automatique) launderette GB, Laundromat® US.

bubon /bybɔ̃/ *nm* bubo.

bubonique /bybɔnik/ *adj* bubonic.

Bucarest /bykaʀɛst/ ▸ 857 *npr* Bucharest.

buccal, **~e**, *mpl* **-aux** /bykal, o/ *adj* oral.

buccin /byksɛ̃/ *nm* **1** (trompette) buccina; **2** (mollusque) whelk.

bucco-dentaire /bykɔdɑ̃tɛʀ/ *adj* [*hygiène*] oral.

bucco-génital, **~e**, *pl* **-aux** /bykoʒenital, o/ *adj* **rapports bucco-génitaux** oral sex ¢.

bûche /byʃ/ *nf* **1** (de bois) log; **2**○ (chute) tumble; **prendre** or **ramasser une ~** to come a cropper○ GB, to fall (flat on one's face); **quelle ~!** what a fall!
■ **~ de Noël** yule log.

bûcher /byʃe/ [1] **I** *nm* **1** (pour un condamné) stake; **condamner qn au ~** to condemn sb to be burned at the stake; **monter sur le ~** to be burned at the stake; **Jeanne au ~** Joan at the stake; **2** (pour un mort) (funeral) pyre; **3** (réserve) woodshed.
II○ *vtr* to slog (away) at○ [*matière*].
III○ *vi* to slog away○; **il a dû ~ pour en arriver là** he had to slog to get where he is.

bûcheron /byʃʀɔ̃/ ▸ 510 *nm* lumberjack.

bûchette /byʃɛt/ *nf* **1** (objet) (pour le feu) stick; **des ~s pour allumer le feu** kindling ¢; **2** (pour compter) counting rod; **3** Culin individual yule log.

bûcheur○, **-euse** /byʃœʀ, øz/ **I** *adj* [*élève, étudiant*] industrious.
II *nm,f* swot○ GB, grind○ US.

Buckinghamshire ▸ 692 *nprm* **le ~** Buckinghamshire.

bucolique /bykɔlik/ **I** *adj* [*scène, rêverie, atmosphère*] bucolic, pastoral; [*poésie, style*] bucolic.
II *nf* (poème) bucolic.

Budapest /bydapɛst/ ▸ 857 *npr* Budapest.

budget /bydʒɛ/ *nm* budget; **gérer un ~** to administer a budget; **un petit ~** a tight budget; **le ~ de l'État** the Budget; **~ familial** household budget; **~ de fonctionnement** operating budget.

budgétaire /bydʒetɛʀ/ *adj* [*prévisions, déficit, excédent*] budget (*épith*); [*contrôle*] budgetary, budget (*épith*); [*contraintes, restrictions*] budgetary; [*année*] financial GB, fiscal US.

budgétisation /bydʒetizasjɔ̃/ *nf* **1** Fin inclusion in the budget; **2** Entr budgeting.

budgétiser /bydʒetize/ [1] *vtr* to include [sth] in the budget [*dépense, recette*].

budgétivore○ /bydʒetivɔʀ/ *adj* hum expensive.

buée /bɥe/ *nf* (de froid) condensation; (d'haleine) steam; **vitres couvertes de ~** steamed up windows, windows covered in condensation; **dégager de la ~** to let off steam.

Buenos Aires /byenɔzɛʀ/ ▸ 857 *npr* Buenos Aires.

buffet /byfɛ/ *nm* **1** (meuble) (de salle à manger) sideboard; (de cuisine) dresser; **2** (de gare) buffet; **rendez-vous au ~ de la gare** let's meet in the station buffet; **3** (table garnie) buffet; **~ froid/campagnard** cold/country-style buffet; **4**◑ (ventre) belly◑; **ne rien avoir dans le ~** to have an empty belly; **5** (d'orgue) (organ) case.
IDIOMES **danser devant le ~** to have nothing to eat.

buffle /byfl/ *nm* buffalo.

buggy, *pl* **buggies** /bygi/ *nm* Aut buggy.

bugle /bygl/ *nm* Bot, Mus bugle.

buis /bɥi/ *nm* **1** (buisson) box tree; (formant une haie) box hedge; **2** (bois) boxwood; **pièces d'échec en ~** boxwood chess pieces; ▸ **faux**.

buisson /bɥisɔ̃/ *nm* (sauvage) bush; (dans jardin) shrub; **~ d'aubépine** hawthorn bush.
■ **~ ardent** Bible burning bush; **~ d'écrevisses** Culin buisson of crayfish.

buissonneux, **-euse** /bɥisɔnø, øz/ *adj* scrub-covered (*épith*); **être ~** to be scrubby; **terrain ~** scrub.

buissonnière /bɥisɔnjɛʀ/ *adj* **faire l'école ~** to play truant GB, to play hooky○ US.

bulbe /bylb/ *nm* **1** (de plante) bulb, corm spéc; **~ d'oignon/de jacinthe** onion/hyacinth bulb; **2** (coupole) onion(-shaped) dome; **église à ~s** onion-domed church; **3** Naut (d'étrave) bulb.
■ **~ dentaire** root of tooth; **~ pileux** hair bulb; **~ rachidien** medulla oblongata.

bulbeux, **-euse** /bylbø, øz/ *adj* bulbous.

bulgare /bylgaʀ/ ▸ 537, 462 *adj, nm* Bulgarian.

Bulgare /bylgaʀ/ ▸ 537 *nmf* **1** Géog Bulgarian; **2** Hist Bulgar.

Bulgarie /bylgaʀi/ ▸ 321 *nprf* Bulgaria.

bulldozer /byldozœʀ/ *nm* bulldozer; **démolir qch à coups de ~** to bulldoze sth.

bulle /byl/ **I** *nm inv* **papier ~** unbleached paper.
II *nf* **1** (d'air, de gaz) bubble; **~ de savon** soap bubble; **faire des ~s** to blow bubbles; **2** (de bande dessinée) balloon; **3** Méd bubble (*providing a sterile environment*); **bébé ~** *immunodeficient baby kept in a sterile environment*; **4** Relig, Hist bull; **~ pontificale** papal bull; **5** Ordinat **~ (magnétique)** (magnetic) bubble; **6** (pour l'emballage) bubble; **film à ~s** bubblewrap; **sachet ~** bubble pack; **enveloppe à ~s** padded envelope.
IDIOMES **coincer la ~**○ to twiddle one's thumbs.

buller○ /byle/ [1] *vi* to lounge (around), to loaf○ (about).

bulletin /byltɛ̃/ *nm* **1** (informations) bulletin, report; **~ météorologique** weather forecast; **~ d'information** TV, Radio news bulletin; **le ~ de la mi-journée/soirée** TV, Radio the lunchtime/evening news; **~ de santé** Méd medical bulletin; **~ scolaire** ou **de notes** school report GB, report card US; **2** (document) certificate; (d'abonnement, adhésion) form; **~ de salaire** or **paie** payslip; **~ d'expédition** Comm certificate of posting; **~ de naissance** birth certificate; **3** (bon) **~ de commande** order form; **~ de participation** Jeux entry form; **4** (publication) bulletin; **Bulletin de la Bourse** Fin ≈ Stock Exchange prices; **5** (rubrique de journal) (colonne) column; (page) page; **~ économique** financial page; **6** Pol (de vote) ballot ou voting paper; **~ blanc** blank vote; **~ nul** spoiled ballot paper; **dépouiller les ~s** to count the votes.
IDIOMES **avaler son ~ de naissance**○ to kick the bucket○, to die.

bulletin-réponse, *pl* **bulletins-réponse** /byltɛ̃ʀepɔ̃s/ *nm* answer coupon.

bulot /bylo/ *nm* whelk.

bunker /bunkɛʀ/ *nm* bunker.

buraliste /byʀalist/ ▸ 510 *nmf* **1** (de bureau de tabac) (vendant des articles pour fumeurs) tobacconist GB, keeper of a smoke shop US; (vendant des cigarettes et journaux) newsagent GB, newsdealer US; **2** (de bureau de paiement) clerk.

bure /byʀ/ *nf* **1** (étoffe) frieze; **2** (vêtement) habit; **porter la ~** to be a monk.

bureau, *pl* **~x** /byʀo/ *nm* **1** (meuble) desk; **2** (pièce individuelle) (chez soi) study; (au travail) office; **immeuble de ~x** office-block; **heures d'ouverture des ~x** office hours; **3** (établissement) office; **ouvrir un ~ à Londres** to open an office in London; **la société va fermer ses ~x de Londres** the company is about to close its London offices; **4** (organe directeur) board; **~ exécutif** executive board; **~ politique** *policy-making committee of a political party*.
■ **~ d'accueil** reception; **~ d'aide sociale** social security office GB, welfare office US; **~ du cadastre** land registry; **~ de change** bureau de change, foreign exchange office; **~ des contributions** tax office; **~ à cylindre** roll-top desk; **~ de douane** customs office; **~ d'enregistrement** stamp duty office; **~ de l'état civil** registry office; **~ d'étude technique** engineering and design department; **~ d'études** (recherche) research department; (conception) design office; **~ de liaison** liaison office; **~ ministre** execut-

ive desk; **~ des objets trouvés** lost property office GB, lost-and-found office US; **~ de placement** agency (*for actors and domestic staff*); **~ de poste** post office; **~ de tabac** (articles pour fumeurs) tobacconist's GB, smoke shop US; (cigarettes, journaux) newsagent GB, news stand US; **~ de tri** sorting office; **~ de vote** polling station; **Bureau international du travail**, **BIT** International Labour Office, ILO.

bureaucrate /byʀokʀat/ *nmf* pej bureaucrat; **une mentalité de ~** a bureaucratic mentality.

bureaucratie /byʀokʀasi/ *nf* (administration) bureaucracy; (pouvoir des bureaucrates) officialdom.

bureaucratique /byʀokʀatik/ *adj* péj bureaucratic.

bureaucratisation /byʀokʀatizasjɔ̃/ *nf* bureaucratization.

bureaucratiser /byʀokʀatize/ [1] *vtr* to bureaucratize.

bureautique /byʀotik/ *nf* office automation; **~ communicante** network computing.

burette /byʀɛt/ *nf* **1** (pour l'huile, le vinaigre) cruet; **2** (de messe) cruet; **3** Mécan oil applicator; (plus grand) oilcan; **4** Chimie (tube d'analyses) burette.

IDIOMES **casser les ~s à qn**◐ to get on sb's tits◐ GB ou nerves.

burin /byʀɛ̃/ *nm* chisel; **à coups de ~** with a chisel; **gravure au ~** engraving, **sculpter au ~** to chisel.

buriné, **~e** /byʀine/ **I** *pp* ▶ **buriner**.

II *pp adj* [*visage*] furrowed, deeply lined; **avoir les traits ~s** to have a deeply furrowed face.

buriner /byʀine/ [1] *vtr* **1** (graver) to engrave; **2** (dégrossir) to chisel out [*statue, bloc*]; **3** (marquer) to furrow [*visage, traits*].

burkinabè /byʀkinabe/ ▶ 537 *adj* of Burkina Faso.

Burkinabè /byʀkinabe/ ▶ 537 *nmf* (natif) native of Burkina Faso; (habitant) inhabitant of Burkina Faso.

Burkina Faso /byʀkinafaso/ ▶ 321 *nprm* Burkina Faso.

burlat /byʀla/ *nm*: *type of cherry*.

burlesque /byʀlɛsk/ **I** *adj* [*tenue, idée, histoire*] ludicrous; [*farce, film, scène*] farcical.

II *nm* Cin, Littérat **le ~** the burlesque.

burlingue◐ /byʀlɛ̃g/ *nm* office.

burnes◐ /byʀn/ *nfpl* balls◐, testicles.

burnous /byʀnu(s)/ *nm* burnous.

IDIOMES **faire suer le ~**○ to use sweated labour^GB.

burundais, **~e** /buʀundɛ, ɛz/ ▶ 537 *adj* of Burundi.

Burundais, **~e** /buʀundɛ, ɛz/ ▶ 537 *nm,f* (natif) native of Burundi; (habitant) inhabitant of Burundi.

Burundi /buʀundi/ ▶ 321 *nprm* Burundi.

bus /bys/ *nm inv* **1** Transp bus; **2** Ordinat bus.

busard /byzaʀ/ *nm* harrier.

■ **~ cendré** Montagu's harrier; **~ des roseaux** marsh harrier; **~ Saint-Martin** hen-harrier.

buse /byz/ *nf* **1** Zool buzzard; **2**○ (idiot) clot○ GB, clod○; **triple ~!** you total ou prize idiot○!; **3** Tech (conduit) pipe, duct; (embout) nozzle.

business○ /biznɛs/ *nm* **1** (affaires commerciales) business; **2** (affaires privées) affairs; **3** (situation embrouillée) business, affair; **je ne comprends rien à tout ce ~** this whole business is a mystery to me.

busqué, **~e** /byske/ *adj* [*nez*] hooked.

buste /byst/ *nm* **1** (sculpture) bust; **2** (torse) chest; **3** (seins) bust.

bustier /bystje/ *nm* **1** (sous-vêtement) longline bra; **2** (vêtement) bustier; **robe ~** bustier dress.

but /by(t)/ *nm* **1** (de randonnée, course) goal; **marcher sans ~** to walk aimlessly; **2** (dans la vie) (objectif) goal; (intention) aim, purpose; (ambition) aim; **atteindre son ~** to reach one's goal; **c'est le ~ à atteindre** it's our/your etc goal; **nous touchons au** or **approchons du ~** our goal is in sight; **il s'est fixé pour ~ la présidence** he has set his sights on the presidency; **mon ~ dans la vie est de m'amuser** my aim in life is to have a good time; **notre ~ est la protection de** or **de protéger la faune** our aim is the protection of ou to protect wildlife; **dans quel ~ est-il venu?** what was his purpose ou object in coming here?; **dans le (seul) ~ de faire** with the (sole) intention ou aim of doing; **dans ce ~** with this aim in view; **faire qch dans un ~ désintéressé** to do sth with no ulterior motive; **faire qch dans un ~ lucratif/publicitaire** to do sth for financial gain/(the) publicity; **aller droit au ~** to go straight to the point; **3** (d'action, de démarche) purpose, object; **le ~ de la publicité est d'inciter à l'achat** the purpose of advertising is to encourage people to buy; **quel est le ~ de leur visite?** what's the purpose ou object of their visit?; **association à ~ lucratif** profit-making association; **association sans ~ lucratif** non profit-making GB ou nonprofit US association; **4** Sport (au football) goal; (au tir) target; **marquer un ~** to score a goal; **par trois ~s à un** by three goals to one.

IDIOMES **demander/déclarer de ~ en blanc** to ask/declare point-blank; **annoncer qch de ~ en blanc à qn** to spring sth on sb.

butane /bytan/ *nm* Calor gas® GB, butane.

butanier /bytanje/ *nm* Naut butane carrier ou tanker.

buté, **~e** /byte/ **I** *pp* ▶ **buter**.

II *pp adj* [*personne, air*] stubborn, obstinate.

III butée *nf* **1** Tech stop; (sur ski) toe piece; **~e d'une porte** doorstop; **2** Archit buttress.

buter /byte/ [1] **I** *vtr* **1** (rendre têtu) to make [sb] even more stubborn; **2** Constr (étayer) to prop up, to support [*mur*]; **3**○ (tuer) to bump [sb] off○, to kill [*personne*].

II *vi* **1** [*personne*] to trip, to stumble; **~ contre qch** (trébucher) to trip over sth; (se heurter) to bump into sth; **~ sur** or **contre** to come up against [*obstacle, difficulté*]; **2** Constr (s'appuyer) to rest against sth, to abut on sth.

III se buter *vpr* **1** (s'obstiner) **il va se ~** he'll be even more stubborn; **2** (se heurter) **se ~ à un problème/un adversaire** to come up against a problem/an opponent.

buteur /bytœʀ/ *nm* (au rugby) (place-)kicker; (au football) leading goal scorer.

butin /bytɛ̃/ *nm* **1** (de guerre) booty, spoils (*pl*); **2** (de vol) haul, loot; **part de ~** share of the loot; **3** (de recherche) fruits (*pl*).

butiner /bytine/ [1] **I** *vtr* **1** [*abeilles*] to gather pollen from [*fleurs*]; **2** fig (glaner) to glean, to pick up [*renseignements*].

II *vi* [*abeilles*] to gather pollen.

butoir /bytwaʀ/ *nm* **1** Rail buffer; **2** Tech stop; **~ de porte** doorstop; **3** (date limite) deadline.

butor /bytɔʀ/ *nm* **1** Zool bittern; **2** (malappris) lout.

buttage /bytaʒ/ *nm* earthing up.

butte /byt/ *nf* mound.

■ **~ témoin** outlier; **~ de tir** butts (*pl*).

IDIOMES **être en ~ à** to come up against [*difficultés*]; to be the butt of [*sarcasmes, moquerie*]; **être en ~ à des critiques** to be heavily criticized.

butter /byte/ [1] *vtr* to earth up.

buvable /byvabl/ *adj* **1** Pharm (à boire) to be taken orally (*après n*); **2** (qu'on peut boire) drinkable; **pas ~** undrinkable; **3**○ (supportable) just about OK○; **elle est gentille, mais son mari n'est pas ~!** she's nice but her husband is a pain○!

buvard /byvaʀ/ *nm* **1** (matière) **(papier) ~** blotting paper ¢; **2** (feuille) sheet of blotting paper; **3** (sous-main) blotter.

buvette /byvɛt/ *nf* **1** (de gare, fête) refreshment area; **2** (de station thermale) pump room.

buveur, **-euse** /byvœʀ, øz/ *nm,f* **1** (alcoolique) drinker, alcoholic; **c'est un gros ~** he's a heavy drinker; **un ~ invétéré** an inveterate drinker; **2** (personne qui boit) drinker; **un ~ de thé/bière** a tea/beer drinker; **3** (consommateur) customer.

Byzance /bizɑ̃s/ ▶ 857 *npr* Byzantium.

IDIOMES **c'est ~!** hum this is real luxury!

byzantin, **~e** /bizɑ̃tɛ̃, in/ *adj* **1** lit Byzantine; **2** fig **discussions/querelles ~es** hairsplitting discussions/quarrels.

BZH (*written abbr* = **Breizh**) Brittany.

Cc

ça[1]

I *ça sert à désigner*

Pour désigner un objet présent, on utilisera *this* si l'objet est proche, *that* s'il est plus éloigné:

aide-moi à plier ça = help me fold this

Pour récapituler, reprendre ce dont il s'agit, on utilisera *that*:

à part ça = apart from that
et tout ça, parce que … = and all that because …
tu n'en as pas envie, je vois ça = you don't feel like it, I can see that
où as-tu entendu ça? = where did you hear that?
me faire/dire ça, à moi! = fancy doing/saying that to me (of all people)!
c'est pour ça qu'il est parti = that's why he left
il ne manquait plus que ça! = that's all we needed!
on dit ça ! = that's what they/you etc. say!

Attention:
sans ça = otherwise

II *ça est sujet du verbe*

(Voir également les verbes ***aller***, ***être***, ***faire***, ***marcher*** ainsi que la note d'usage sur ***la mesure du temps*** pour l'expression *ça fait un an/deux mois que*)

ça représente un objet:

si ça flotte, ce n'est pas une pierre = if it floats, it can't be a stone
ça coûte cher? = is it expensive?

ça représente un fait, une déclaration, une idée déjà mentionnés: si le ton est neutre, on emploiera *it*, mais s'il est emphatique, on utilisera *that*:

ça fait mal = it hurts

lorsqu'il s'agit d'une simple constatation, mais quand il exprime la surprise, l'indignation:

ça fait mal = that hurts!

de même:

ça ne marchera pas = it won't work (est une affirmation neutre)

alors que:

ça ne marchera pas = that won't work (rejette avec force la solution proposée)
ça paraît incroyable = it seems incredible *ou* that seems incredible (selon l'emphase)

Dans les phrases ci-dessous, nettement emphatiques, *that* est la traduction qui s'impose:

ça suffit, voyons! = that's enough!
ça t'a étonné, n'est-ce pas? = that surprised you, didn't it?

ça représente ce qui va être explicité:

ça m'inquiète de la voir dans cet état = it worries me to see her in that state
ça vaut la peine qu'il y aille = it's worth his going
ça n'est pas pour me vanter, mais … = I don't want to boast, but …

On notera cependant:

la rue a ça de bien qu'elle est calme = one good thing about the street is that it is quiet

ça a une valeur impersonnelle:

ça souffle aujourd' hui! = it's windy today!
ça chauffe aujourd' hui! = it's hot today!

ça représente une personne: dans ce cas on utilisera le pronom personnel approprié, *he*, *she* ou *they*:

et ça se croit malin! = and he/she etc. thinks he's/she's etc. clever!

La nature de *ça* n'est pas définie: on pourra souvent traduire par la tournure impersonnelle *there is/are*, comme dans les exemples suivants:

ça sent le brûlé = there's a smell of burning
ça tapait de tous les côtés = there was banging everywhere
ça criait de tous les côtés = there was shouting everywhere

Lorsque *ça* est sujet de rappel, il ne se traduit pas:

la télévision, ça m'ennuie = television bores me;
voyager (ou *les voyages*), *ça revient cher* = travelling is expensive
et le jardin, ça pousse? = how's the (*ou* your) garden doing?

ça a une valeur d'insistance. La tournure est emphatique:

qu'est-ce que c'est que ça? = what's that?
ça, je m'en moque! = I couldn't care less about that!
ça, ça ne compte pas! = that doesn't count!
c'est bizarre, ça ou *ça, c'est bizarre* = that's strange

On notera que les gallicismes *c'est ça qui/que* sont traités sous le verbe ***être***.

Pour renforcer une interrogation:

pourquoi ça? = why's that?
'je l'ai vu' 'quand/où ça?' = 'I saw him' 'when/where was that?'
'tu la connais?' 'qui ça?' = 'do you know her?' 'who do you mean?'
'je ne veux pas' 'comment ça, tu ne veux pas?' = 'I don't want to' 'what do you mean, you don't want to?'
'c'est faisable' 'comment ça?' = 'it can be done' 'how?'

Dans une comparaison (voir également ***comme***):

ce n'est pas si facile que ça = it's not as easy as (all) that *ou* it's not that easy
la dernière fois que je l'ai vu, il n'était pas plus haut que ça! = last time I saw him, he was only so high!

Attention:
tu te lèves toujours aussi tard que ça?
(l'heure qu'il est) = do you always get up this late?
(l'heure mentionnée) = do you always get up that late?

Avec valeur d'interjection:

ça, par exemple! (indigné) = well, honestly!
(surpris) = well I never!
ça, alors! (surpris) = well I never!
ça, oui! = definitely!
ça, non! = no way! *ou* absolutely not!
ça, pour se plaindre, il se plaint! = talk about complain, he does nothing else!
ça, comme bavard, il n'y a pas mieux = he can certainly talk all right!
ça, mon vieux, débrouille-toi! = sort it out for yourself, mate!

c, **C** /se/ *nm inv* c, C; **c cédille** c cedilla.

c' ▶ **ce**.

CA 1 Fin *written abbr* ▶ **chiffre**; **2** Électrotech *written abbr* ▶ **courant**.

ça[1] /sa/ *pron dém*
IDIOMES **elle est bête et méchante avec ~** she's stupid and what's more she's nasty!; **et avec ~?** anything else?; **avec ~ qu'il ne l'a pas pris○!** iron of course he took it!; **rien que ~!** iron is that all! iron; **c'est ~!** that's right!; **eh bien, c'est ~, ne te gêne pas!** iron oh, carry on GB ou keep going, don't mind me! iron; **~ va** or **roule○?** (la vie) how are things?; (l'affaire proposée) is that a deal?; **~ y est, ~ recommence!** here we go again!; **~ y est, j'ai fini!** that's it, I've finished!; **~ y est, oui, je peux m'asseoir?** is that it then, can I sit down?; **~ y est, tu l'as déchiré!** there! you've gone and torn it!; **~ y est, il pleut!** here comes the rain!; **'alors, ~ y est, tu es prêt?'—'non, ~ n'y est pas!'** 'well, are you ready?'—'no, I'm not!'

ça[2] /sa/ *nm* Psych **le ~** the id.

çà /sa/ *adv* **~ et là** here and there.

cabale /kabal/ *nf* **1** (intrigue, intrigants) cabal; **monter une ~ contre qn** to form a cabal against sb; **2** Relig cabbala.

cabalistique /kabalistik/ *adj* lit, fig cabbalistic.

caban /kabɑ̃/ *nm* sailor's jacket.

cabane /kaban/ *nf* **1** (habitation) hut; pej shack péj; **2** (abri) shed; ▶ **lapin**; **3○** (prison) nick○; **mettre qn en ~** to put sb in the nick○; **avoir fait cinq ans de ~** to have done five years in the nick○.

cabanon /kabanɔ̃/ *nm* **1** (abri) shed; **2** (maison en Provence) small house.
IDIOMES **être bon pour le ~**○ to be fit for the loony bin○.

cabaret /kabaʀɛ/ *nm* cabaret.

cabaretier†, **-ière** /kabaʀtje, ɛʀ/ ▶ 510 *nm,f* innkeeper.

cabas /kaba/ *nm* shopping bag.

cabernet /kabɛʀnɛ/ *nm* **1** (cépage) (**cépage**) **~** Cabernet grape; **2** (vin) Cabernet.

cabestan /kabɛstɑ̃/ *nm* capstan.

cabiai /kabjɛ/ *nm* capybara.

cabillaud /kabijo/ *nm* cod; **filet de ~** cod fillet.

cabine /kabin/ *nf* (de bateau, vaisseau spatial) cabin; (de camion, grue) cab; (d'ascenseur, de téléphérique) car; (de laboratoire de langue) booth; (de piscine) cubicle; (pour se changer) changing room.
■ **~ d'aiguillage** Rail signal box; **~ de bain** changing cubicle; **~ de conduite** Rail driver's cab; **~ de douche** shower cubicle; **~ d'essayage** fitting room; **~ de pilotage** Aviat cockpit; **~ de plage** beach hut; **~ de projection** Cin projection room; **~ téléphonique** phone box GB, phone booth.

cabinet /kabinɛ/ I *nm* **1** (local) gén office; (de médecin, dentiste) surgery GB, office US; (d'avocat, de notaire) office; (d'avocat au barreau, de juge) chambers (*pl*); **2** (affaires et clientèle de professions libérales) practice; (cabinet collectif) firm; (de médecins, dentistes) (group) practice; **le ~ du Dr Hallé** Dr Hallé's practice; **avoir/vendre un ~** to have/to sell a practice; **ouvrir un ~** to set up in practice; **~ d'architectes/d'audit** firm of architects/auditors; **~ d'avocats/d'experts-comptables** law/accountancy firm; **~ de médecins/dentistes** medical/dental practice; **3** (agence) agency; **~ de recrutement** recruitment agency; **~ immobilier** estate agent's; (collectif) firm of estate agents; **avoir un ~ d'assurances** to be an insurance broker; **ouvrir un ~ d'assurances** to set up (in) business as an insurance broker; **4** Pol (gouvernement) cabinet; (de ministre, préfet) staff, cabinet US; **~ ministériel** minister's personal staff; **5** (de musée) exhibition room; **~ des estampes/médailles** print/coin room; **6** (pièce) (bureau) study; (réduit) closet†; **7**† (meuble) cabinet.
II **cabinets** *nmpl* toilet (*sg*), loo○ (*sg*) GB, bathroom (*sg*) US.
■ **~ d'aisances**† water closet† GB, lavatory; **~ de consultation** surgery GB, office US; **~ d'instruction** Jur judge's chambers (*pl*); **~ juridique** law firm; **~ de lecture**† reading room ; **~ médical** medical practice; **~ noir** cubbyhole; **~ particulier** private dining room; **~ de toilette** bathroom; **~ de travail** study.

cabinet-conseil, *pl* **cabinets-conseil** /kabinɛkɔ̃sɛj/ *nm* consultancy ou consulting US firm, firm of consultants.

câblage /kɑblaʒ/ *nm* **1** (connexions) wiring; **2** (mise en place) wiring; **3** TV cabling; **faire le ~ d'une ville** to install cable television in a town.

câble /kɑbl/ *nm* **1** (cordage) (en métal, synthétique) cable; (en fibres végétales) rope; **~ de frein** brake cable; **~ armé/coaxial/isolé** armoured[GB]/coaxial/insulated cable; **~ électrique** electric cable; **~ porteur** (de pont) suspension cable; (de téléphérique) carrying cable; **2** TV cable television; **3**† (télégramme) cable.
■ **~ d'amarrage** Naut mooring rope; **~ de démarrage** Aut jump lead GB, jumper cable US; **~ de direction** guide cable; **~ de halage** Naut towrope; **~ optique** optical cable; **~ de remorque** (de navire) towline; (de grue) trailing cable.

câbler /kɑble/ [1] *vtr* **1** (connecter) to wire; **2** TV to install cable television in [*ville, pays*]; **la ville est câblée** the town has cable television; **foyer/immeuble câblé** house/building with cable television; **3** Ordinat to hardwire [*instruction*]; **4** (télégraphier) to cable.

câblerie /kɑbləʀi/ *nf* **1** (usine) cable-manufacturing plant; **2** (métier, commerce) cable industry.

câbleur, **-euse** /kɑblœʀ, øz/ I ▶ 510 *nm,f* (personne) wiring specialist.
II **câbleuse** *nf* (machine) wire-stranding machine.

câblier /kɑblije/ *nm* cable ship.

câblodistributeur /kɑblodistʀibytœʀ/ *nm* TV distributor of cable television.

câblodistribution /kɑblodistʀibysjɔ̃/ *nf* cable television.

câblo-opérateur, *pl* **~s** /kɑblooperatœʀ/ *nm* cable television company.

cabochard○, **~e** /kabɔʃaʀ, aʀd/ I *adj* [*personne*] pigheaded○, stubborn; [*animal*] stubborn.
II *nm,f* pigheaded person○.

caboche /kabɔʃ/ *nf* **1**○ (tête) nut○, head; **avoir la ~ solide** to have a thick skull; **mets-toi ça dans la ~** get that into your thick skull; **2** (clou de chaussure) hobnail.

cabochon /kabɔʃɔ̃/ *nm* **1** (pierre fine) cabochon; **2** (clou) (furnishing) stud.

cabosser /kabɔse/ [1] *vtr* to dent; (**tout**) **cabossé** [*véhicule, casque*] battered.

cabot○ /kabo/ *nm* **1** (chien) pej dog, mutt○ péj; **2** (acteur) pej ham actor.

cabotage /kabɔtaʒ/ *nm* coastal shipping.

caboter /kabɔte/ [1] *vi* Naut to coast.

caboteur /kabɔtœʀ/ *nm* (navire) coaster.

cabotin, **~e** /kabɔtɛ̃, in/ I *adj* **être ~** to like playing to the gallery.
II *nm,f* **1** (acteur) pej ham actor; **2** (poseur) **c'est un ~** he likes playing to the gallery.

cabotinage /kabɔtinaʒ/ *nm* **1** (comportement) **son ~** the way he/she plays to the gallery; **2** (jeu d'acteur) pej ham acting péj.

cabotiner /kabɔtine/ [1] *vi* pej to ham it up○.

cabrer /kabʀe/ [1] I *vtr* **1** Équit to make [sth] rear [*cheval*]; **2** (braquer) **~ qn** to put sb's back up; **3** Aviat to zoom [*avion*].
II **se cabrer** *vpr* **1** [*cheval*] to rear (**devant** at); **mon cheval s'est cabré devant l'obstacle** my horse reared at the jump; **2** [*personne*] to jib; **il se cabre à la moindre remontrance** he jibs at the slightest reproach; **quand on lui a parlé de cela il s'est cabré** it put his back up when we mentioned that; **3** Aviat [*avion*] to zoom.

cabri /kabʀi/ *nm* Zool kid.
IDIOMES **sauter comme un ~** to gambol like a lamb.

cabriole /kabʀijɔl/ *nf* **1** (de clown, d'enfant, animal) capering ¢; **faire des ~s** to caper about; **2** Équit capriole; **3** Danse cabriole.

cabrioler /kabʀijɔle/ [1] *vi* to caper about, to cavort.

cabriolet /kabʀijɔlɛ/ *nm* **1** Aut convertible, cabriolet; **2** (voiture à cheval) cabriolet; **3** (meuble) (**fauteuil**) **~** open armchair with cabriole legs.

cabus /kaby/ *nm* **chou ~** white cabbage.

CAC® /kak/ *nf* (*abbr* = **compagnie des agents de change**) **indice ~ 40**, **le ~ 40** Paris Stock Exchange index.

caca /kaka/ *nm* baby talk poo GB, poop US; **je veux faire ~**! want to do poo-poo!; **il a fait ~ dans sa culotte** he pooed GB ou pooped US in his pants.
■ **~ d'oie** (couleur) greenish yellow.
IDIOMES **mettre à qn le nez dans son ~** to rub sb's nose in it○; **être dans le ~**○ to be in the soup○, to be in a mess○.

cacahuète /kakawɛt/ *nf* peanut; **~s grillées** roasted peanuts.

cacao /kakao/ *nm* **1** (poudre, boisson) cocoa; **2** (fève) cocoa bean.

cacaoté, **~e** /kakaɔte/ *adj* chocolate-flavoured[GB].

cacaotier /kakaɔtje/, **cacaoyer** /kakaɔje/ *nm* cacao tree.

cacarder /kakaʀde/ [1] *vi* [*oie*] to honk.

cacatoès /kakatɔɛs/ *nm* cockatoo.

cacatois /kakatwa/ *nm* royal (sail); (**mât de**) **~** royal mast; ▶ **grand**, **petit**.

cachalot /kaʃalo/ *nm* sperm whale.

cache /kaʃ/ I *nm* **1** (feuille opaque) mask; **se servir d'un ~ pour apprendre une liste de vocabulaire** to cover up ou mask off the answers while learning a list of vocabulary; **2** Cin matte.
II *nf* hiding place; **~ d'armes** arms cache.

caché, **~e** /kaʃe/ I *pp* ▶ **cacher**.
II *pp adj* [*trésor, recoin, charme, beauté, sens*] hidden; [*complot, douleur, désir, amour*] secret; **la face ~e de qch** the hidden face of sth.

cache-cache /kaʃkaʃ/ ▶ 449 *nm inv* hide and seek; **jouer à ~** lit, fig to play hide and seek.

cache-cœur /kaʃkœʀ/ *nm inv* wrap-over top, wrap top.

cache-col /kaʃkɔl/ *nm inv* scarf.

cache-entrée /kaʃɑ̃tʀe/ *nm inv* key-hole cover, escutcheon.

cachemire /kaʃmiʀ/ *nm* cashmere; **de** or **en ~** cashmere (*épith*); **motif ~** paisley pattern.

Cachemire /kaʃmiʀ/ ▶ 692 *nprm* **le ~** Kashmir.

cache-misère○ /kaʃmizɛʀ/ *nm inv* presentable outer garment (*to hide shabby clothes*).

cache-nez /kaʃne/ *nm inv* scarf, muffler.

cache-plaque /kaʃplak/ *nm* hotplate cover.

cache-pot /kaʃpo/ *nm inv* flowerpot holder, planter.

cache-poussière /kaʃpusjɛʀ/ *nm inv* overcoat.

cache-prise /kaʃpʀiz/ *nm inv* socket cover.

cacher /kaʃe/ [1] I *vtr* **1** (soustraire à la vue) to hide [*argent, corps, cartes, prisonnier, réfugié*]; **~ son visage dans ses mains/bras** to hide ou bury one's face in one's hands/arms; **~ sa nudité/ses seins** to cover one's nakedness/one's breasts; **~ son jeu** lit to hide one's cards ou hand; fig to keep one's cards close to one's chest; **2** (barrer) to hide [*paysage, mer, soleil, objet*]; **3** fig (dissimuler) [*personne*] to hide [*larmes*]; to hide, to conceal [*embarras, déception, enthousiasme, faits*]; **~ qch à qn** to conceal ou hide sth from sb; **tu me caches quelque chose!** you're hiding something from me!; **il leur a caché la mort de son chien** he didn't tell them his dog had died; **je ne vous cache pas que je suis inquiète** frankly, I'm worried; **pour ne rien vous ~** to be quite frank.
II **se cacher** *vpr* **1** gén to hide (**dans** in; **derrière** behind); (temporairement) [*personne*] to go into hiding; [*animal*] to go to ground; **le visage caché derrière son voile** her face hidden behind her veil; **se ~ à** or **de qn** to hide from sb; **il ne s'en cache pas** he makes no secret of it; **derrière son sourire se cache une profonde tristesse** behind his/her smile there lies a deep sadness; **quelle organisation se cache derrière les émeutes?** which organization is behind these riots?; **2** (disparaître) [*soleil, lunettes*] to disappear; **où se cache mon stylo?** where has my pen disappeared to?

cache-radiateur /kaʃʀadjatœʀ/ *nm inv* radiator cover.

cache-sexe /kaʃsɛks/ *nm inv* G-string.

cachet /kaʃɛ/ *nm* **1** (comprimé) tablet; **tu veux un ~ d'aspirine**®? do you want an aspirin?; **~ soluble** soluble tablet; **~ à croquer** chewable tablet; **2** (à l'encre) stamp; (de cire) seal; **~ de la poste** postmark; **'le ~ de la poste faisant foi'** 'as attested by date on postmark'; **3** (chic) style; (marque distinctive) cachet; **un village qui a gardé tout son ~** a village which has kept all its

cachet; [*personne, vêtement*] **avoir du ~** to have style; **4** Cin, Théât (paie) fee.
IDIOMES **courir le ~** [*acteur, chanteur*] to be continually looking for work.

cache-tampon /kaʃtɑ̃pɔ̃/ ▶449 *nm inv* hunt the thimble; **jouer à ~** to play hunt the thimble.

cacheter /kaʃte/ [20] *vtr* to seal; **un paquet cacheté à la cire** a parcel sealed with wax.

cachette /kaʃɛt/ *nf* hiding-place; **sortir de sa ~** gén to come out of one's hiding place; [*fugitif*] to come out of hiding; **en ~** [*manger, téléphoner*] on the sly; **il fume en ~ de sa femme** he smokes on the sly without his wife knowing.

cachexie† /kaʃɛksi/ *nf* cachexia.

cachot /kaʃo/ *nm* (de prison moderne) prison cell; (de prison ancienne) dungeon; (pièce exiguë) prison; **faire trois jours de ~** to be locked up alone for three days; **après avoir dormi sur la paille humide des ~s** liter after having been locked up.

cachotterie /kaʃɔtʀi/ *nf* little secret; **elle lui a reproché cette ~** she told him off for keeping this from her; **faire des ~s** to keep little secrets; **faire des ~s à qn** to keep things from sb.

cachottier, **-ière** /kaʃɔtje, ɛʀ/ **I** *adj* secretive.
II *nm,f* secretive person; **petit ~!** you secretive thing!

cachou /kaʃu/ *nm* **1** (pastille) cachou; **2** Pharm, Tex catechu.

cacique /kasik/ *nm* **1** Hist cacique; **2** (personnalité) leading figure.

cacochyme† /kakɔʃim/ *adj* doddery.

cacophonie /kakɔfɔni/ *nf* cacophony.

cacophonique /kakɔfɔnik/ *adj* cacophonous.

cactacées /kaktase/, **cactées** /kakte/ *nfpl* Cactaceae.

cactus /kaktys/ *nm* cactus.

c-à-d (*written abbr* = **c'est-à-dire**) ie.

cadastral, **~e**, *mpl* **-aux** /kadastʀal, o/ *adj* [*plan*] cadastral; [*registre*] land (*épith*).

cadastre /kadastʀ/ *nm* **1** (registre) land register, cadastre[GB]; **2** (administration) land registry.

cadastrer /kadastʀe/ [1] *vtr* to register [sth] with the land registry.

cadavéreux, **-euse** /kadaveʀø, øz/ *adj* [*teint, mine*] deathly pale.

cadavérique /kadaveʀik/ *adj* [*pâleur, odeur*] deathly (*épith*); [*teint*] deathly pale.

cadavre /kadavʀ/ *nm* **1** (de personne) gén corpse; (de victime) body; (d'animal) body, carcass; **on a retiré trois ~s des décombres** three bodies were pulled out of the rubble; **~ ambulant**○ walking skeleton; **2**○ (bouteille vide) dead bottle.
■ **~ exquis** game of consequences.

caddie /kadi/ *nm* **1** (au golf) caddie; **2** ®(de supermarché) shopping trolley GB, shopping cart US.

cade /kad/ *nm* cade; **huile de ~** oil of cade.

cadeau, *pl* **~x** /kado/ **I** *nm* present, gift (**pour** for); **~ d'anniversaire/de Noël/de baptême** birthday/Christmas/christening present; **faire un ~ à qn** to give sb a present; **elle m'a fait ~ d'une montre** she gave me a watch; **je t'en fais ~** (je te l'offre) I'm giving it to you; (je ne veux pas d'argent) I'm making you a present of it; (tu peux le garder) you can keep it; **achetez le canapé, et je vous fais ~ de la housse** buy the sofa, and I'll throw in the cover as well; **vends-le au lieu d'en faire ~** sell it instead of giving it away; **je te fais ~ de la monnaie** you can keep the change; **il ne fait pas de ~x** [*commerçant*] he doesn't give anything away; [*juge, examinateur, professeur*] he's very strict; **les politiciens ne se font pas de ~x** politicians don' t do each other favours[GB]; **se faire un ~** to treat oneself; **les petits ~x entretiennent l'amitié** small gifts keep a friendship going; **et, en ~, un disque** Comm and a record as a free gift; **mon chef/le nouvel ordinateur, c'est pas un ~**○ my boss/the new computer is a pain○.
II (-)cadeau (*in compounds*) gift; **idée(-)~** gift idea; **papier(-)~** wrapping paper.
■ **~ électoral** electoral sweetener; **~ empoisonné** poisoned chalice; **~ d'entreprise** company gift (*given to a customer*); **~ fiscal** present from the taxman.

cadenas /kadna/ *nm* padlock; **fermer qch avec un ~** to padlock sth.

cadenasser /kadnase/ [1] *vtr* to padlock.

cadence /kadɑ̃s/ *nf* **1** (de mouvements, pas) rhythm; **en ~** [*marcher*] in step; [*ramer*] rhythmically; **donner la ~** (pour ramer) to set the stroke; **2** (de sons, poème) cadence; **3** (de travail, production) rate; **~ infernale** infernal rate; **à la ~ de six par semaine** at the rate of six a week; **à une ~ soutenue/réduite** at a sustained/reduced rate; **relâcher/tenir/forcer la ~** to slacken/keep up/force the pace; **4** Mil (de tir) rate; **5** Mus (enchaînement d'accords) cadence; (passage de soliste) cadenza; **~ parfaite/imparfaite** perfect/imperfect cadence.

cadencer /kadɑ̃se/ [12] *vtr* to put rhythm into [*pas, marche*]; to give rhythm to [*phrase, style*]; **les slogans cadencés des manifestants** the rhythmic chanting of the demonstrators; **les gestes cadencés des rameurs** the rhythmic strokes of the rowers.

cadet, **-ette** /kadɛ, ɛt/ **I** *adj* (de deux) younger; (de plus de deux) youngest.
II *nm,f* **1** (enfant) (dernier de deux) younger son/daughter, younger child; (dernier de plus de deux) youngest son/daughter, youngest child; **les deux cadettes sont encore étudiantes** the two youngest daughters are still students; **c'est moi la cadette de la famille** I am the youngest in ou of the family; **2** (frère, sœur) younger brother/sister; **3** (personne plus jeune) junior; (personne la plus jeune) youngest; **le ~ du groupe** the youngest (person) in the group; **un homme de trente ans ton ~** a man thirty years your junior; **il est mon ~** he's younger than me; ▶**souci 3**; **4** Sport *athlete between the ages of 15 and 17*; **5** Mil cadet.

cadmiage /kadmjaʒ/ *nm* cadmium plating.

cadmium /kadmjɔm/ *nm* cadmium; **pile au ~** cadmium cell.

cadogan /kadɔgɑ̃/ = **catogan**.

cadrage /kadʀaʒ/ *nm* **1** (action de cadrer) framing (**de** of); **2** (résultat) composition.

cadran /kadʀɑ̃/ *nm* (de baromètre, montre, boussole) face; (de compteur) dial; **~ solaire** sundial.
IDIOMES **faire le tour du ~**○ to sleep round GB ou around US the clock.

cadre /kadʀ/ **I** *nm* **1** (de tableau, miroir, fenêtre) frame; **2** (lieu) setting; (milieu) surroundings; **dans un ~ agréable/champêtre** in a pleasant/rustic setting; **le théâtre antique servira de ~ à une série de concerts** the amphitheatre[GB] will be the setting for a series of concerts; **hors de son ~ habituel, c'est un autre homme** out of his usual surroundings, he's a different man; **3** (domaine délimité) **cela sort du ~ de mes fonctions** that's not part of my duties; **nous sortons du ~ de notre contrat** we're overstepping the limits of our contract; **sortir du ~ de la légalité** to go outside the law; **4** (structure) framework; **il n'existe aucun ~ juridique à ce problème** there is no legal framework for this problem; **le ~ d'un récit/ouvrage** the framework of a story/book; **étudier une langue en dehors du ~ scolaire** to study a language outside a school context; **5** (employé) executive; **~ moyen/supérieur** middle ranking/senior executive; **les ~s moyens/supérieurs** middle/senior management (+ *v pl*); **passer ~** to be made an executive; ▶**jeune**; **6** (de bicyclette, moto) frame; **7** (dans un formulaire) space, box; **8** Transp, Comm crate; **9** (en apiculture) frame; **10** Naut berth, bunk.
II cadres *nmpl* Entr **faire partie des ~s** to be on the company's books; **être rayé des ~s** to be dismissed.
III dans le cadre de *loc prép* **1** (à l' occasion de) on the occasion of [*voyage, fête, rencontre*]; **dans le ~ de cette journée particulière** on this special occasion; **2** (dans le contexte de) within the framework of [*lutte, politique, négociations, organisation*]; as part of [*enquête, campagne, plan*]; **les manifestations organisées dans le ~ du festival** events organized as part of the festival; **les négociations doivent avoir lieu dans le ~ de la CEE** negotiations must take place within the framework of the EC; **recevoir une formation dans le ~ d'une entreprise/d'une association** to undergo training within a company/an association.
■ **~ conteneur** container; **~ margeur** Phot masking frame; **~ de vie** (living) environment.

cadrer /kadʀe/ [1] **I** *vtr* Phot, Cin to centre[GB] [*image, scène*]; **la photo est mal cadrée** the photo is off-centre[GB]; **photo bien cadrée** well-composed photo.
II *vi* to tally, to fit (**avec** with); **vos déclarations ne cadrent pas avec les faits** your statements don't tally ou fit with the facts; **les témoignages ne cadrent pas** eyewitness accounts do not tally; **ça ne cadre pas** it doesn't fit.

cadreur /kadʀœʀ/ ▶510 *nm* Cin cameraman.

caduc, **caduque** /kadyk/ *adj* **1** (désuet) obsolete; (sans effet) null; **rendre qch ~** to render sth null and void; **2** Bot [*feuille*] deciduous; **arbre à feuilles caduques** deciduous tree; **3** Phon silent; **e ~** silent e; **4** Méd, Zool deciduous; **membrane caduque** decidua (*pl*); **5**† (chancelant) [*personne, construction*] rickety; [*santé*] precarious.

caducée /kadyse/ *nm* caduceus.

cæcum /sekɔm/ *nm* caecum.

cætera ▶**et cætera**.

CAF /seaɛf/ **I** *nf*: *abbr* ▶**caisse**.
II (*written abbr* = **coût, assurance et fret**) CIF.

cafard, **~e** /kafaʀ, aʀd/ **I** *adj* (fourbe) [*air, expression, mine*] shifty.
II *nm,f* **1**○ schoolchildren's slang (dénonciateur) sneak○ GB, tattletell○ US; **2**† (hypocrite) hypocrite.
III *nm* **1**○ (mélancolie) depression; **avoir le ~** to be down in the dumps○; **un coup de ~** a fit of depression; **donner le ~ à qn**○ to get sb down○, to make sb depressed; **2** (blatte) cockroach.

cafardage○ /kafaʀdaʒ/ *nm* schoolchildren's slang taletelling, tattling US.

cafarder○ /kafaʀde/ [1] **I** *vtr* schoolchildren's slang (dénoncer) to tell on.
II *vi* **1** (avoir le cafard) to feel down○; **2** (rapporter) to tell tales GB, to tattle US.

cafardeur○, **-euse**[1] /kafaʀdœʀ, øz/ *nm,f* schoolchildren's slang telltale GB, tattletale US.

cafardeux, **-euse**[2] /kafaʀdø, øz/ *adj* [*personne*] glum; [*nature, tempérament*] gloomy; [*lieu*] depressing.

café /kafe/ **I** ▶193 *adj inv* (couleur) dark brown.
II *nm* **1** (substance) coffee; **~ vert/torréfié** unroasted/roasted coffee; **~ en grains** coffee beans (+ *v pl*); **~ moulu** ground coffee; **~ instantané** or **soluble** instant coffee; **2** (boisson) coffee; **faire du ~** to make coffee; **prendre un ~** to have a coffee; **3** (arôme) coffee; **glace/gâteau au ~** coffee ice cream/cake; **4** Comm (établissement) café; **être à la terrasse d'un ~** to be sitting outside a café; **5** (à la fin d'un repas) **au ~** at the end of the meal.
■ **~ crème** espresso with milk; **~ filtre** filter coffee; **~ au lait** white coffee GB, coffee with milk; **peau ~ au lait** coffee-coloured[GB] skin; **~ noir** black coffee; **le**

~ **du pauvre**○ lovemaking; ~ **turc** Turkish coffee.
IDIOMES **c'est (un peu) fort de** ~○! that's a bit steep○!

café-bar, *pl* **cafés-bar** /kafebaʀ/ *nm* café-bar.

café-concert, *pl* **cafés-concerts** /kafekɔ̃sɛʀ/ *nm* café with live music.

caféier /kafeje/ *nm* coffee tree.

caféière /kafejɛʀ/ *nf* coffee plantation.

caféine /kafein/ *nf* caffeine.

café-restaurant, *pl* **cafés-restaurants** /kafeʀɛstɔʀɑ̃/ *nm* café-restaurant.

café-tabac, *pl* **cafés-tabac** /kafetaba/ *nm* café (*where cigarettes may be purchased*).

cafétéria /kafeteʀja/ *nf* cafeteria.

café-théâtre, *pl* **cafés-théâtres** /kafe teɑtʀ/ *nm* café with live theatre[GB].

cafetier, **-ière** /kaftje, ɛʀ/ I *nm,f* café proprietor.
II **cafetière** *nf* **1** (récipient) coffee pot; (appareil) coffee maker; **2**○ (tête) head; **il n'a rien dans la cafetière** he is brainless.
■ **cafetière électrique** coffee machine; **cafetière à piston** cafetiere.

cafouillage○ /kafujaʒ/ *nm* (confusion) bungling○ ¢; (en sport) blunder.

cafouiller○ /kafuje/ [1] *vi* [*personne*] to get flustered; [*appareil*] to go wrong; [*organisation*] to get in a muddle; **il a fait** ~ **nos projets** he messed up our plans; **ça cafouille** things are in a mess.

cafouilleux○, **-euse** /kafujø, øz/ *adj* [*personne*] clumsy; [*projet, discours*] muddle-headed○; [*orthographe, mise en scène*] slipshod.

cafouillis○ /kafuji/ *nm* mess○.

caftan /kaftɑ̃/ *nm* caftan.

cafter◑ /kafte/ [1] schoolchildren's slang I *vtr* to tell on (**à** to).
II *vi* to tell tales GB, to tattle US; **il a cafté** he went and told.

cafteur◑, **-euse** /kaftœʀ, øz/ *nm,f* schoolchildren's slang telltale GB, tattletale US.

cage /kaʒ/ *nf* **1** (pour animaux sauvages) cage; **en** ~ caged; **mettre en** ~ to cage [*animal*]; to put [sb] behind bars [*personne*]; **mise en** ~ caging; **dans une** ~ **de verre** behind a glass screen; **vivre en** ~ fig to be cooped up○; **2**○ Sport goal.
■ ~ **d'ascenseur** lift shaft GB, elevator shaft US; ~ **d'écureuil** Jeux climbing frame GB, jungle jim US; Électrotech cage winding; ~ **d'escalier** Constr stairwell; ~ **d'extraction** Mines cage; ~ **de Faraday** Phys Faraday cage; ~ **à lapins** lit, fig○ rabbit hutch; ~ **à oiseaux** birdcage; ~ **à poules** lit hen coop; Jeux climbing frame GB, jungle jim US; fig rabbit hutch○; ~ **de roulement à billes** Mécan ball-bearing housing; ~ **thoracique** Anat rib cage.
IDIOMES **être dans la** ~ **aux lions** to be in the lion's den; **tourner comme un ours** or **lion en** ~ to pace up and down like a caged animal.

cageot /kaʒo/ *nm* crate.

cagette /kaʒɛt/ *nf* tray; **acheter une** ~ **de pêches** to buy a tray of peaches.

cagibi /kaʒibi/ *nm* store cupboard.

cagne = **khâgne**.

cagneux, **-euse** /kaɲø, øz/ I *adj* [*cheval*] bowlegged; [*jambes*] crooked; **avoir les genoux** ~ [*personne*] to be knock-kneed.
II *nm,f* = **khâgneux**.

cagnotte /kaɲɔt/ *nf* **1** (caisse commune) kitty; **2** (de loterie, loto) jackpot; **3** (économies) (pour plus tard) nest egg; (plus général) **une jolie** ~ a nice little sum.

cagoule /kagul/ *nf* **1** (passe-montagne) balaclava; **2** (de malfaiteur) balaclava; **deux pirates en** ~ two hooded ou masked hijackers; **3** (de moine) cowl.

cagoulé, ~**e** /kagule/ *adj* wearing a balaclava (*après n*), hooded.

cahier /kaje/ I *nm* **1** (carnet) notebook; Scol exercise book; ~ **à spirales** spiral-bound notebook; **2** Imprim section, signature; **3** Presse supplement.
II **cahiers** *nmpl* (revue) journal (*sg*).
■ ~ **d'appel** register; ~ **de brouillon** roughbook; ~ **des charges** Jur conditions (*pl*) of contract; Tech specifications (*pl*); ~ **de devoirs** homework book; ~ **de doléances** register of grievances; ~ **d'écriture** copybook; ~ **d'exercices** Scol exercise book; ~ **de revendications** Entr list of union demands; ~ **de textes** homework notebook; ~ **de travaux pratiques** lab book, laboratory notebook.

cahin-caha○ /kaɛ̃kaa/ *adv* [*marcher, avancer*] with difficulty; **les affaires vont** ~ business isn't going too well.

cahot /kao/ *nm* (sur terrain inégal) jolt; fig **les** ~**s** the ups and downs.

cahotant, ~**e** /kaɔtɑ̃, ɑ̃t/ *adj* [*route, carrière*] bumpy; [*danse*] jerky; [*œuvre*] lacking coherence (*jamais épith*).

cahoté, ~**e** /kaɔte/ I *pp* ▶ **cahoter**.
II *pp adj* (secoué) shaken about; (éprouvé) buffeted; ~ **par la vie** buffeted by life.

cahotement /kaɔtmɑ̃/ *nm* jolting ¢.

cahoter /kaɔte/ [1] *vi* [*véhicule*] to bounce along.

cahoteux, **-euse** /kaɔtø, øz/ *adj* bumpy.

cahute /kayt/ *nf* (cabane) hut, shack.

caïd /kaid/ *nm* **1** (gangster) boss; **faire le** ~, **jouer les** ~**s** to act tough; **2**○ (personne importante) big shot; (personne supérieure) Scol, Sport star; (personne très compétente) wizard; **c'est un** ~ **en électronique** he is a real electronics wizard; **3** (magistrat) kaid.

caillage /kɑjaʒ/ *nm* curdling.

caillasse /kajas/ *nf* (cailloux) stones.

caille /kɑj/ *nf* **1** Zool quail; **2** (terme d'affection) **ma** ~ pet○, darling.

caillé, ~**e** /kɑje/ I *pp* ▶ **cailler**.
II *pp adj* [*lait*] curdled; [*sang*] congealed.
III *nm* curd; **du** ~ **de brebis** ewe's milk cheese.

caillebotis /kɑjbɔti/ *nm* **1** (en bois) duckboards (*pl*); (en métal) open metal flooring ¢; **2** Naut grating.

cailler /kɑje/ [1] I *vtr* to curdle.
II *vi* **1** (se figer) [*lait*] to curdle; [*sang*] to congeal; **faire** ~ to curdle [*lait*]; **2**○ (avoir froid) [*personne*] to be freezing.
III **se cailler** *vpr* **1** [*lait*] to curdle; [*sang*] to congeal; **2**○ (avoir froid) [*personne*] to be freezing; **se** ~ **les meules** or **les miches**◑ to be freezing; **on se les caille ici**◑ it's cold enough to freeze the balls off a brass monkey●.
IV○ *v impers* **ça caille** it's freezing, it's brass monkey weather◑.

caillette /kajɛt/ *nf* rennet bag, abomasum spéc.

caillot /kajo/ *nm* clot.

caillou, *pl* ~**x** /kaju/ *nm* **1** (pierre) pebble; **gros** ~ stone; **du** ~○ rock ¢; **avoir un** ~ **à la place du cœur** fig to have a heart of stone; **2**○ (pierre précieuse) stone; **3**○ (tête) nut○, head; **ne plus avoir un poil sur le** ~ to be as bald as a coot○; **ne rien avoir dans le** ~ to be brainless; **4**○ (îlot) piece of rock○; **5** (bonbon) sweet GB, candy US (*that looks like a pebble*); **6**◑ drug users' slang (de drogue) rock○.

Caillou /kaju/ *nprm* **le** ~ New Caledonia.

cailloutage /kajutaʒ/ *nm* **1** Gén Civ (couche) road metal GB, gravel US; (processus) metalling GB, graveling US; **2** Constr (mortier) pebbledash GB.

caillouter /kajute/ [1] *vtr* to metal GB, to gravel US [*route*]; to ballast [*voie de chemin de fer*].

caillouteux, **-euse** /kajutø, øz/ *adj* [*sol, route*] stony; [*plage*] pebbly.

cailloutis /kajuti/ *nm inv* Gén Civ road metal GB, gravel US.
■ ~ **glaciaire** Géol glacial deposits (*pl*).

caïman /kaimɑ̃/ *nm* cayman.

Caïmans /kaimɑ̃/ ▶ **416** *nprfpl* **les (îles)** ~ the Cayman Islands.

Caïn /kaɛ̃/ *npr* Cain.

caïque /kaik/ *nm* caïque.

Caire /kɛʀ/ ▶ **857** *npr* **le** ~ Cairo.

cairn /kɛʀn/ *nm* cairn.

cairote /kɛʀɔt/ ▶ **857** *adj* of Cairo.

Cairote /kɛʀɔt/ *nmf* (natif) native of Cairo; (habitant) inhabitant of Cairo.

caisse /kɛs/ *nf* **1** (boîte) gén crate; (de champagne, vin) case, crate; (bac) planter; **2** Tech (de voiture) shell, body; (d'horloge) casing; (de piano, d'orgue) case; **3**◑ (voiture) old banger○; **4** (tambour) drum; ▶ **gros**; **5** (pour l'argent) (tiroir) till; (appareil) cash register; (coffret) cash box; **avoir de l'argent en** ~ lit to have money in the till; fig to have money; **les** ~**s de l'État** the Treasury coffers; **voler la** ~ to steal the takings; **tenir la** ~ Comm (normalement) to be the cashier; (un moment) to be on the cash desk; fig hum to hold the purse strings; **faire sa** ~ to balance one's cash; **petite** ~ petty cash; **6** (guichet) (de magasin) cash desk; (de supermarché) checkout (counter); (de banque) cashier's desk; **passer à la** ~ (pour payer) to go to the cash desk; (pour être payé) to collect one's money; (pour être licencié)○ to be paid off; **7** (capital, organisme gérant un capital) fund; ~ **d'amortissement** sinking fund; ~ **d'assurances sociales** social insurance fund; ~ **de solidarité/retraite** solidarity/pension fund; ~ **de secours** relief fund.
■ ~ **d'allocations familiales, CAF** ≈ Social Security Office; ~ **claire** snare drum; ~ **d'emballage** packing case ou crate; ~ **enregistreuse** cash register; ~ **d'épargne** ≈ savings bank; ~ **noire** slush fund; ~ **à outils** toolbox; ~ **de résonance** sound box; ~ **de tympan** middle ear, tympanic cavity spéc; **Caisse des dépôts et consignations** *French public and investment organization*.
IDIOMES **à fond la** ~○ [*partir, s'en aller*] at breakneck speed; [*mettre la musique*] at full blast.

caissette /kɛsɛt/ *nf* gén small box ou case; (pour fruits) crate.

caissier, **-ière** /kesje, ɛʀ/ ▶ **510** *nm,f* cashier.

caisson /kɛsɔ̃/ *nm* **1** Archit caisson; **plafond à** ~**s** coffered ceiling; **2** (à bouteilles) crate; **3** (pour méditer) flotation tank; **4** Mil (chariot) caisson.
■ ~ **de décompression** decompression chamber; **le mal des** ~**s** decompression sickness, the bends.
IDIOMES **se faire sauter le** ~◑ to blow one's brains out○.

cajoler /kaʒɔle/ [1] *vtr* **1** (être tendre avec) to make a fuss of ou over; **se faire** ~ **par qn** to be made a fuss of by sb; **2** (flatter) to bring [sb] round GB ou around US.

cajolerie /kaʒɔlʀi/ *nf* **1** (caresse) cuddle; (parole) compliment; **faire des** ~**s à un enfant** to cuddle a child; **2**† (flatterie) wheedling.

cajoleur, **-euse** /kaʒɔlœʀ, øz/ I *adj* (tendre) affectionate.
II *nm,f* **1** (séducteur) enticer; **2**† (flatteur) wheedler.

cajou /kaʒu/ *nm* **noix de** ~ cashew nut.

cajun /kaʒœ̃/ ▶ **462** *adj, nm* Cajun.

Cajun /kaʒœ̃/ *nmf* Cajun.

cake /kɛk/ *nm* fruit cake.

cal /kal/ *nm* callus; **avoir des** ~**s aux mains** to have calluses on one's hands.

calabrais, ~**e** /kalabʀɛ, ɛz/ ▶ **692** *adj* Calabrian.

Calabre /kalabʀ/ ▶ **692** *nprf* Calabria.

calage /kalaʒ/ *nm* **1** (d'étai, de poutre) wedging; **2** (de dynamo, d'altimètre) setting; (de moteur) tuning; **3** Imprim setting.

Calais /kalɛ/ ▶ **857** *npr* Calais.

calaisien, **-ienne** /kalɛzjɛ̃, ɛn/ ▶857 *adj* of Calais.

Calaisien, **-ienne** /kalɛzjɛ̃, ɛn/ *nm,f* (natif) native of Calais; (habitant) inhabitant of Calais.

calamar /kalamaʀ/ *nm* squid.

calamine /kalamin/ *nf* **1** Minér calamine GB, smithsonite; **2** Aut (résidu) carbon deposit.

calaminer: **se calaminer** /kalamine/ [1] *vpr* [*moteur, cylindre*] to carbonize, to coke up; **être calaminé** to be coked up.

calamistré, **~e** /kalamistʀe/ *adj* **1** (frisé) [*cheveux, barbe*] waved, curled; **2** (gominé) brilliantined.

calamité /kalamite/ *nf* **1** (malheur) disaster, calamity; **2** (personne insupportable) hum pain○; (catastrophe ambulante) walking disaster.

calamiteux, **-euse** /kalamitø, øz/ *adj* disastrous, calamitous.

calancher◐ /kalɑ̃ʃe/ [1] *vi* to kick the bucket○, to die.

calandre /kalɑ̃dʀ/ *nf* **1** Aut (radiator) grille[GB]; **2** Tech (machine) calender; **3** Nucl calandria.

calandrer /kalɑ̃dʀe/ [1] *vtr* to calender.

calanque /kalɑ̃k/ *nf* deep rocky inlet (*in the Mediterranean*).

calao /kalao/ *nm* hornbill.

■ **~ bicorne** Great Indian hornbill; **~ rhinocéros** rhinoceros hornbill.

calcaire /kalkɛʀ/ **I** *adj* [*sel*] calcium (*épith*); [*eau*] hard; [*minéral*] calcareous; [*terrain*] chalky; [*plateau, roche*] limestone.

II *nm* **1** (roche) limestone; **2** (dépôt blanc) fur GB, sediment US; **enlever le ~ d'une bouilloire** to descale a kettle.

calcanéum /kalkaneɔm/ *nm* heel bone, calcaneum spéc.

calcédoine /kalsedwan/ *nf* chalcedony.

calcif○ /kalsif/ *nm* (caleçon) underpants (*pl*).

calcification /kalsifikasjɔ̃/ *nf* calcification.

calcination /kalsinasjɔ̃/ *nf* calcination.

calciné, **~e** /kalsine/ **I** *pp* ▶ **calciner**.

II *pp adj* **1** (carbonisé) charred; **2** (soumis à une chaleur intense) scorched.

calciner /kalsine/ [1] *vtr* **1** (carboniser) to char; (au four) to burn [sth] to a crisp; **2** Chimie to calcine.

calcium /kalsjɔm/ *nm* calcium.

calcul /kalkyl/ **I** *nm* **1** (opération) calculation; **faire des ~s** to make some calculations; **faire une erreur de ~** to make an error ou a mistake in calculation; **faire le ~ du prix de revient/bénéfice** to calculate the cost price/profit margin; **'à combien est-ce que ça va me revenir?'—'attends, il faut que je fasse le ~'** 'how much will it come to?'—'wait, I'll have to work it out'; **2** (matière) arithmetic; **3** (tactique) calculation; **agir par ~** to act out of self-interest; **être un bon/mauvais ~** to be a good/bad move; **déjouer les ~s de l'ennemi** to upset the enemy's calculations; **4** Méd stone, calculus spéc.

II calculs *nmpl* (estimations) calculations; **d'après mes ~s nous y serons à midi** according to my calculations, we'll get there by noon.

■ **~ algébrique** algebra (calculation); **~ biliaire** gallstone; **~ différentiel** differential calculus; **~ intégral** integral calculus; **~ mental** mental arithmetic; **~ numérique** numerical calculation; **~ de probabilités** calculation of probability; **~ rénal** kidney stone; **~ urinaire** stone in the bladder.

calculable /kalkylabl/ *adj* [*grandeur, conséquence*] calculable.

calculateur, **-trice** /kalkylatœʀ, tʀis/ **I** *adj* [*personne, esprit*] calculating.

II *nm,f* calculating person; **c'est une calculatrice, elle fait tout par intérêt** she's very calculating, she does everything out of self-interest.

III *nm* Ordinat computer.

IV calculatrice *nf* (calculette) (pocket) calculator.

calculer /kalkyle/ [1] **I** *vtr* **1** (compter) to calculate, to work out [*trajectoire, pourcentage, moyenne, surface*]; **j'ai calculé que ça me reviendrait moins cher de prendre l'avion** I worked out that it would be cheaper for me to go by plane; **2** (évaluer) to weigh up [*avantages, chances*]; to gauge [*résultats, effort*]; **~ son élan** Sport to judge one's run-up; **~ son rythme** Sport to pace oneself; **il a mal calculé son geste et il a renversé le vase** he misjudged his movement and knocked over the vase; **tout bien calculé** all things considered; **3** (préméditer) **~ ses effets** to stage things carefully; **~ son coup** to plan one's move.

II *vi* [*personne, machine*] to calculate.

calculette /kalkylɛt/ *nf* pocket calculator.

Caldoche /kaldɔʃ/ *nmf* European New Caledonian.

cale /kal/ *nf* **1** (pour meuble, porte) wedge; (pour roue de voiture, d'avion) chock; (pour surélever) block; **la voiture est sur ~s** the car is on blocks; **2** Naut (ship's) hold; **~ avant/arrière** fore/stern hold; **à fond de ~** down in the hold.

■ **~ de construction** slipway; **~ flottante** floating dock; **~ de lancement** slipway; **~ sèche** dry dock.

calé○, **~e** /kale/ *adj* **1** (instruit) [*personne*] bright, knowledgeable; **être ~ en qch** to be brilliant at sth; **2** (complexe) [*problème*] difficult, thorny; [*manipulation, calcul*] difficult, clever.

calebasse /kalbas/ *nf* **1** Bot calabash, gourd; **2**○ (tête) nut○, head; **se prendre un coup sur la ~** to be bashed○ on the head.

calèche /kalɛʃ/ *nf* barouche, calash.

caleçon /kalsɔ̃/ *nm* **1** (sous-vêtement masculin) boxer shorts (*pl*), underpants (*pl*); **porter un ~, porter des ~s** to wear boxer shorts; **il est en ~** he's in his boxer shorts; **2** (vêtement féminin) leggings (*pl*).

■ **~ long** long johns○ (*pl*).

Calédonie /kaledɔni/ *nprf* Hist Caledonia.

calédonien, **-ienne** /kaledɔnjɛ̃, ɛn/ *adj* **1** ▶692 (de Nouvelle-Calédonie) New Caledonian; **2** (de Calédonie) Caledonian; **plissement ~** Caledonian fold.

Calédonien, **-ienne** /kaledɔnjɛ̃, ɛn/ *nm,f* New Caledonian, inhabitant of New Caledonia.

calembour /kalɑ̃buʀ/ *nm* pun, play on words; **faire** or **dire des ~s** to make puns, to pun.

calembredaine† /kalɑ̃bʀədɛn/ *nf* twaddle○ GB ¢, nonsense ¢; **dire des ~s** to talk twaddle○.

calendaire /kalɑ̃dɛʀ/ *adj* [*année, mois, jour*] calendar.

calendes /kalɑ̃d/ *nfpl* Antiq calends; **les ~ de mars** the calends of March.

IDIOMES **aux ~ grecques** never in a month of Sundays○; **renvoyer qch aux ~ grecques** to postpone sth indefinitely; **renvoyer qch à d'autres ~** to postpone sth to an unspecified date.

calendos◐ /kalɑ̃dos/ *nm* camembert.

calendrier /kalɑ̃dʀije/ *nm* **1** (système) calendar; **~ républicain** French Revolutionary calendar; **~ perpétuel** perpetual calendar; ▶ **grégorien**; **2** (imprimé) calendar; **~ illustré** illustrated calendar; **3** (programme) schedule; **être en avance sur son ~** to be ahead of (one's) schedule; **4** (dates) dates (*pl*); **le ~ des vacances scolaires** the dates of school holidays GB ou vacation US.

cale-pied, *pl* **~s** /kalpje/ *nm* toe clip.

calepin /kalpɛ̃/ *nm* notebook.

caler /kale/ [1] **I** *vtr* **1** (stabiliser) to wedge [*roue, pied de table*]; to steady [*meuble*]; to support [*rangée de livres*]; **~ une bouteille dans un sac** to wedge a bottle in a bag; **~ sa tête sur un oreiller** to rest one's head on a pillow; **~ un malade dans un fauteuil** to prop up a patient in an armchair; **bien calé dans mon fauteuil** nicely settled in my armchair; **2** (régler) to set; **3**○ (remplir) **petit déjeuner qui cale l'estomac** breakfast that fills you up; **le porridge, ça cale!** porridge is filling!; **4** Naut **~ cinq mètres** [*navire*] to draw five metres[GB] of water; **5** Naut (abaisser) to lower [*mât, voile, vergue*].

II *vi* **1** (s'arrêter) [*moteur, voiture*] to stall; **tu as encore calé!** you've stalled again!; **2** (abandonner) [*personne*] to give up; **j'ai calé au dessert** I gave up when it came to the dessert; **~ sur un problème de maths** to get stuck on a maths GB ou math US problem; **3** Naut [*navire*] to draw water.

III se caler *vpr* **1** (s'installer) to settle (**dans** in); **2** (se remplir) **se ~ les joues**○ to stuff oneself○.

caleter = **calter**.

calfatage /kalfataʒ/ *nm* caulking.

calfater /kalfate/ [1] *vtr* to caulk.

calfeutrage /kalføtʀaʒ/, **calfeutrement** /kalføtʀəmɑ̃/ *nm* draught proofing, weather stripping US.

calfeutrer /kalføtʀe/ [1] **I** *vtr* to stop up, to seal [*fissure*]; to draught proof, to weather strip US [*porte, fenêtre*].

II se calfeutrer *vpr* to shut oneself away; **se ~ chez soi** to shut oneself up at home.

calibrage /kalibʀaʒ/ *nm* **1** Tech (de pièce, machine) calibration; **2** Imprim casting-off; **3** Agric (d'œufs, de fruits, légumes) grading, sizing.

calibre /kalibʀ/ *nm* **1** (diamètre) (d'arme à feu, de tuyau, balle) calibre[GB], bore; (de câble) diameter; **arme/balle de ~ 5,56** 5.56 mm (calibre[GB]) gun/bullet; **arme de gros ~** large-bore weapon; **obus de gros ~** large-calibre[GB] shell; **2** (d'œufs, de fruits, légumes) size, grade; **3** Mécan (étalon) gauge; **~ d'épaisseur** thickness gauge; **4** Mécan, Mode (mesure) template, pattern; **5**○ (pistolet) gun, rod○ US; **6** (de personne) calibre[GB]; **être d'un tout autre ~** [*personne*] to be of a different calibre[GB] altogether; [*création, œuvre*] to be in a different class altogether.

calibrer /kalibʀe/ [1] *vtr* **1** (donner le calibre convenable à) to calibrate [*arme, projectile, tuyau*]; **2** (régler) to calibrate [*machine*]; **3** (classer) to grade, to size [*œufs, fruits, légumes*]; to size [*gravier*]; **4** Imprim to cast off [*texte*].

calice /kalis/ *nm* **1** Relig chalice; ▶ **lie**; **2** Anat, Bot calyx.

calicot /kaliko/ *nm* **1** (banderole) banner; **2** Tex calico.

califat /kalifa/ *nm* caliphate.

calife /kalif/ *nm* caliph.

Californie /kalifɔʀni/ ▶692 *nprf* California; **golfe de ~** Gulf of California.

californien, **-ienne** /kalifɔʀnjɛ̃, ɛn/ ▶692 *adj* Californian.

Californien, **-ienne** /kalifɔʀnjɛ̃, ɛn/ *nm,f* Californian.

califourchon: **à califourchon** /akalifuʀʃɔ̃/ *loc adv* astride; **être (assis) à ~ sur une chaise/un mur** to sit astride a chair/a wall; **il s'est assis** or **mis à ~ sur le mur** he sat astride the wall.

câlin, **~e** /kɑlɛ̃, in/ **I** *adj* [*air, regard, ton*] affectionate; [*personne*] cuddly.

II *nm* cuddle; euph lovemaking; **faire un ~ à qn** to give sb a cuddle; **se faire un ~** euph to make love.

câliner /kaline/ [1] *vtr* to cuddle.

câlinerie /kalinʀi/ *nf* **1** (manières câlines) tender ways (*pl*); **2** (caresse) **~s** caresses; **amoureux qui se font des ~s** lovers caressing each other.

calisson /kalisɔ̃/ *nm*: *marzipan sweet.*

calleux, **-euse** /kalø, øz/ *adj* calloused, rough-skinned.

call-girl, *pl* **~s** /kolgœʀl/ *nf* call girl.

calligramme /kaligʀam/ *nm* calligram.

calligraphe /kaligʀaf/ *nmf* calligrapher.

calligraphie /kaligʀafi/ *nf* calligraphy.

calligraphier /kaligʀafje/ [2] *vtr* to write [sth] in a decorative hand [*texte, lettre*].

calligraphique /kaligʀafik/ *adj* calligraphic.

Calliope /kaljɔp/ *npr* Calliope.

callipyge /kalipiʒ/ *adj* callipygous.

callosité /kalozite/ *nf* callus.

calmant, **~e** /kalmɑ̃, ɑ̃t/ **I** *adj* **1** gén [*musique, parole*] soothing; **2** Pharm sedative.
II *nm* sedative; **prendre un ~** to take a sedative.

calmar /kalmaʀ/ *nm* squid.

calme /kalm/ **I** *adj* **1** (paisible) [*mer, temps, situation*] calm; [*ciel, nuit, atmosphère*] still; [*endroit, marché, Bourse, journée, période, vie, personne*] quiet; **2** (maître de soi) [*personne, regard, voix, attitude*] calm; **restons ~s!** let's keep calm!
II *nmf* (personne tranquille) calm person; **c'est un grand ~** he is unflappable.
III *nm* **1** (environnement paisible) peace (and quiet); **j'ai besoin de ~** I need peace and quiet (**pour faire** to do); **travailler/vivre dans le** or **au ~** to work/live in peace (and quiet); **dans le ~ de ma maison** in the quiet of my house; **2** (absence d'agitation) calm; (de foule, d'assemblée) calmness; (de mer, nuit, sanctuaire) stillness; **lancer un appel au ~** to appeal for calm; **c'est le ~ avant la tempête** lit, fig it's the calm before the storm; **retour au ~** return to a state of calm; **en période de ~** in a period of calm; **un ~ de courte durée** a short-lived calm; **le plus grand ~ règne sur le marché** all is quiet on the stock market; **le ~ est revenu** calm has returned; **dans le ~** peacefully; **rétablir le ~** to restore calm; **~ plat** dead calm; **c'est le ~ plat** (sur mer) there's a dead calm; (en affaires) it's dead quiet; **c'est le ~ plat dans ma vie sentimentale** my love life is non-existent; **3** (maîtrise de soi) composure; **perdre son ~** to lose one's composure; **il nous a étonnés par son ~** he amazed us by his composure; **avec le plus grand ~** with the greatest composure; **il restait d'un ~ parfait en toutes circonstances** he remained perfectly composed ou calm in all circumstances; **garder** or **conserver son ~** to keep calm; **avec ~** calmly; **du ~!** (reste tranquille) calm down!; (fais moins de bruit) quiet!; **4** (sérénité) liter inner peace; **5** Météo, Naut calm.

calmement /kalməmɑ̃/ *adv* calmly.

calmer /kalme/ [1] **I** *vtr* **1** (apaiser) to calm [sb/sth] down [*personne, foule, animal*]; to calm [*marché, Bourse*]; to defuse [*situation*]; to tone down [*discussion*]; to subdue [*agitation, révolte, colère*]; to allay [*inquiétude, crainte*]; to quieten [*dissensions*]; **~ le jeu** fig to calm things down; **~ les esprits** to calm people down; **2** (atténuer) to ease, to relieve [*douleur, mal*]; to bring down [*fièvre*]; to dampen [*passions, ardeur, désir*]; to curb [*impatience*]; to take the edge off [*faim, soif*].
II se calmer *vpr* **1** (s'apaiser) [*personne, foule, situation*] to calm down; [*éléments, tempête*] to die down; [*agitation, révolte, passions, colère*] to die down; [*débat, discussion*] to quieten GB ou quiet US down; [*inquiétude, crainte*] to subside; [*ardeur, désir*] to cool; **calme-toi!** (reste tranquille) calm down!; (fais moins de bruit) quieten GB ou quiet US down!; **les choses se calment** things are calming down; **après l'annonce du ministre, les esprits se sont calmés** after the minister's announcement, tempers cooled; **2** (s'atténuer) [*douleur, mal*] to ease, to wear off; [*fièvre, faim, soif*] to die down; [*rire, bruit, tapage*] to subside.

calomel /kalɔmɛl/ *nm* calomel.

calomniateur, **-trice** /kalɔmnjatœʀ, tʀis/ *nm,f* slanderer.

calomnie /kalɔmni/ *nf* (orale) slander; (écrite) libel **₵**, slander; **répandre des ~s** to spread slanders.

calomnier /kalɔmnje/ [2] *vtr* to slander.

calomnieux, **-ieuse** /kalɔmnjø, øz/ *adj* [*propos*] slanderous; [*écrit*] libellous[GB], slanderous.

caloporteur /kalɔpɔʀtœʀ/ *adj m* **fluide ~** Nucl coolant.

calorie /kalɔʀi/ *nf* calorie; **pauvre/riche en ~s** low/high in calories; **régime (à) basses ~s** low-calorie diet.

calorifère /kalɔʀifɛʀ/ **I** *adj* heat-conveying; **tuyau ~** heating pipe.
II *nm* (appareil) (heating) stove.

calorifique /kalɔʀifik/ *adj* calorific.

calorifuge /kalɔʀifyʒ/ **I** *adj* insulating.
II *nm* lagging.

calorifugeage /kalɔʀifyʒaʒ/ *nm* (heat) insulation.

calorifuger /kalɔʀifyʒe/ [13] *vtr* to insulate.

calorimètre /kalɔʀimɛtʀ/ *nm* calorimeter.

calorimétrie /kalɔʀimetʀi/ *nf* calorimetry.

calorimétrique /kalɔʀimetʀik/ *adj* calorimetric.

calorique /kalɔʀik/ *adj* calorie (*épith*); **ration/valeur ~** calorie intake/content.

calot /kalo/ *nm* **1** (couvre-chef) Mil forage cap GB, overseas cap US; Mode brimless hat; **2** Jeux (bille) large marble; **3**◐ (œil) eye; **rouler des ~s**○ to roll one's eyes.

calotin○, **~e** /kalɔtɛ̃, in/ **I** *adj* pej devoutly Catholic.
II *nm,f* pej pious churchgoer, Holy Joe○ péj.

calotte /kalɔt/ *nf* **1** (couvre-chef) skull cap; **la ~ d'un chapeau** the body of a hat; **2**○ Relig (clergé) **la ~** the cloth; **être de la ~**○ to be of the cloth; **3**○ (tape) slap; fig **prendre une bonne ~** to be given a slap; **4** Archit calotte; **la ~ d'une voûte** the calotte of a vault.
■ **~ crânienne** Anat top of the skull, calvarium spéc; **~ glaciaire** Géog icecap; **~ sphérique** Math spherical cap.

calotter○ /kalɔte/ [1] *vtr* **1** (frapper) to slap; **2** (voler) to pinch○, to steal; **~ qch à qn** to pinch sth from sb; **il s'est fait ~ son portefeuille** he had his wallet pinched○.

calquage /kalkaʒ/ *nm* tracing.

calque /kalk/ *nm* **1** (copie) tracing; **2** (papier) tracing paper; **3** (imitation) replica; **4** Ling calque.

calquer /kalke/ [1] **I** *vtr* **1** (imiter) to copy [*comportement*]; **~ qch sur qch** to model sth on sth; **calqué sur** modelled[GB] on; **2** Tech to trace.
II se calquer *vpr* **se ~ sur qch/qn** to model oneself on sth/sb.

calter◐ /kalte/ [1] *vi*, **se calter**◐ *vpr* to beat it○, to scarper○.

calumet /kalymɛ/ *nm* calumet; **~ de la paix** peace pipe; **fumer le ~ de la paix avec qn**○ fig to make (one's) peace with sb.

calva○ /kalva/ = **calvados**.

calvados /kalvados/ *nm* calvados (*apple brandy distilled in Normandy*).

Calvados /kalvados/ ▶ 692 *nprm* (département) **le ~** Calvados.

calvaire /kalvɛʀ/ *nm* **1** (épreuves) ordeal; **2** Relig (monument) wayside cross; (lieu) Calvary; **la montée au ~** the road to Calvary; **3** Art (représentation) Calvary.

Calvin /kalvɛ̃/ *npr* Calvin.

calvinisme /kalvinism/ *nm* Calvinism.

calviniste /kalvinist/ *adj, nmf* Calvinist.

calvitie /kalvisi/ *nf* **1** (affection) baldness; **~ précoce** premature baldness; **avoir un début de ~, avoir une ~ naissante** to be going bald; **2** (résultat) (crâne chauve) bald head; (zone dégarnie) bald patch.

calypso /kalipso/ *nm* calypso.

camaïeu /kamajø/ *nm* **1** Minér cameo; **2** Art monochrome (painting), camaïeu spéc; **en ~** in monochrome; **3** Mode shades (*pl*); **en ~ vert** in green shades.

camail /kamaj/ *nm* **1** Hist Mil camail; **2** Mode (hooded) capelet; **3** Zool hackles (*pl*), neck feathers (*pl*).

camarade /kamaʀad/ *nmf* **1** gén friend, mate○ GB; **~ d'école** schoolfriend, schoolmate GB, classmate US; **~ d'atelier** workmate; **~ de régiment** army pal○ ou buddy○; **2** Pol comrade; **la ~ Markova demande la parole** Comrade Markova wishes to take the floor.

camaraderie /kamaʀadʀi/ *nf* comradeship, camaraderie; **avoir des relations de bonne ~ avec ses collègues de travail** to be on friendly terms with one's colleagues, to get on well with one's colleagues.

camard, **~e** /kamaʀ, aʀd/ liter **I** *adj* [*nez*] pug (*épith*); [*personne*] pug-nosed.
II *nm,f* (personne) pug-nosed person.

Camarde /kamaʀd/ *nf* **la ~** Death, the grim reaper.

camarguais, **~e** /kamaʀgɛ, ɛz/ **I** ▶ 692 *adj* of the Camargue.
II camarguaise *nf* cowboy boot.

Camarguais, **~e** /kamaʀgɛ, ɛz/ *nm,f* (natif) native of the Camargue; (habitant) inhabitant of the Camargue.

Camargue /kamaʀg/ ▶ 692 *nprf* the Camargue.

camarilla /kamaʀija/ *nf* pej cabal, camarilla.

cambiste /kɑ̃bist/ ▶ 510 *nm* foreign exchange dealer ou broker.

Cambodge /kɑ̃bɔdʒ/ ▶ 321 *nprm* Cambodia.

cambodgien, **-ienne** /kɑ̃bɔdʒjɛ̃, ɛn/ ▶ 537, 462 **I** *adj* Cambodian.
II *nm* Ling Cambodian.

Cambodgien, **-ienne** /kɑ̃bɔdʒjɛ̃, ɛn/ ▶ 537 *nm,f* Cambodian.

cambouis /kɑ̃bwi/ *nm* dirty grease.

cambrage /kɑ̃bʀaʒ/ *nm* = **cambrement**.

cambré, **~e** /kɑ̃bʀe/ **I** *pp* ▶ **cambrer**.
II *pp adj* [*dos, reins*] arched; [*pied, chaussure*] with a high instep (*épith, après n*); **avoir le pied ~** to have a high instep; **avoir le pied bien ~** to have a finely arched foot.

cambrement /kɑ̃bʀəmɑ̃/ *nm* (de corps) bending; (de reins) arching; (d'objet) curving.

cambrer /kɑ̃bʀe/ [1] **I** *vtr* to curve [*objet*]; to arch [*chaussure*]; **~ les reins** or **le dos** to arch one's back.
II se cambrer *vpr* [*personne*] to arch one's back.

Cambridgeshire ▶ 692 *nprm* **le ~** Cambridgeshire.

cambrien, **-ienne** /kɑ̃bʀijɛ̃, ɛn/ **I** *adj* Cambrian.
II *nm* Cambrian.

cambriolage /kɑ̃bʀijɔlaʒ/ *nm* burglary.

cambrioler /kɑ̃bʀijɔle/ [1] *vtr* to burgle GB, to burglarize US; **se faire ~** to be burgled GB, to be burglarized US.

cambrioleur, **-euse** /kɑ̃bʀijɔlœʀ, øz/ *nm,f* burglar.

cambrousse○ /kɑ̃bʀus/ *nf* **la ~** the sticks○ (*pl*), the country; **en pleine ~** right out in the sticks○, in the middle of nowhere; **n'être jamais sorti de sa ~** to be a country bumpkin.

cambrure /kɑ̃bʀyʀ/ *nf* **1** (état courbé) bending; **2** (courbe) curve.
■ **~ des pieds** instep; **~ des reins** small of the back.

cambuse /kɑ̃byz/ *nf* **1** Naut storeroom; **2**◐ (chambre, maison) pej dump○, hovel péj.

came /kam/ *nf* **1** Mécan cam; **2**◐ (drogue) drugs (*pl*).

camé◐, **~e**[1] /kame/ **I** *pp* ▶ **camer**.
II *pp adj* (avec drogue, médicament) **être ~** to be on drugs.
III *nm,f* junkie○, drug addict.

camée[2] /kame/ *nm* cameo.

caméléon /kameleɔ̃/ *nm* lit, fig chameleon.

camélia /kamelja/ *nm* camellia; **la Dame aux ~s** the Lady of the Camellias.

camelot○ /kamlo/ ▶ 510 *nm* street vendor.

camelote○ /kamlɔt/ *nf* pej junk○, rubbish GB; **c'est de la ~ cette montre!** this watch is junk ou rubbish!

camembert /kamɑ̃bɛʀ/ *nm* **1** Culin Camembert; **2**○ Ordinat, Stat pie chart.

camer◑ /kame/ [1] **I** *vtr* to dope○, to drug; **~ qn à** or **avec qch** to dope○ ou drug sb with sth.

II se camer *vpr* to be on drugs.

caméra /kameʀa/ *nf* (cine-)camera GB, movie camera US; **~ de télévision** TV camera; **la ~ cachée** TV candid camera.

cameraman, *pl* **-men** /kameʀaman, mɛn/ ▶ **510** *nm* controv cameraman.

camériste /kameʀist/ *nf* **1** (dame d'honneur) lady-in-waiting; **2** (femme de chambre) chambermaid.

Cameroun /kamʀun/ ▶ **321** *nprm* Cameroon.

camerounais, **~e** /kamʀunɛ, ɛz/ ▶ **537** *adj* Cameroonian.

Camerounais, **~e** /kamʀunɛ, ɛz/ ▶ **537** *nm,f* Cameroonian.

caméscope® /kameskɔp/ *nm* camcorder.

camion /kamjɔ̃/ *nm* **1** (véhicule) truck, lorry GB; **2** (récipient de peinture) paint bucket.
■ **~ à benne** tipper truck; **~ de déménagement** removal van; **~ frigorifique** refrigerated truck ou lorry GB; **~ militaire** Mil military truck.

camion-citerne, *pl* **camions-citernes** /kamjɔ̃sitɛʀn/ *nm* tanker.

camionnage /kamjɔnaʒ/ *nm* **1** (transport) road haulage GB, trucking US; **2** (coût) haulage.

camionnette /kamjɔnɛt/ *nf* van, panel truck US; **~ de livraison** delivery van.

camionneur /kamjɔnœʀ/ ▶ **510** *nm* **1** (conducteur) lorry driver GB, truck driver; **2** (entrepreneur) haulage contractor GB, trucker US.

camisole /kamizɔl/ *nf* camisole.
■ **~ chimique** Méd sedatives (*pl*); **~ de force** Méd straitjacket; **mériter la ~ de force** fig to need locking up.

camomille /kamɔmij/ *nf* **1** (plante) camomile; **2** (infusion) camomile tea.

camouflable /kamuflabl/ *adj* concealable.

camouflage /kamuflaʒ/ *nm* **1** Mil (dispositif) camouflage; (action) camouflaging ¢; **tenue de ~** camouflage fatigues (*pl*); **2** fig (dissimulation de la vérité) concealing ¢; (transformation des faits) disguising ¢ (**en** as); **une opération de ~** a cover-up.

camoufler /kamufle/ [1] **I** *vtr* **1** Mil to camouflage; **2** (cacher) to cover up [*crime, défaut, erreur, vérité*]; to conceal [*intention, sentiment*]; **~ un meurtre en suicide** to disguise a murder as a suicide; **3** (mettre en lieu sûr) to hide [*argent*].

II se camoufler *vpr* to hide; **se ~ le visage** to cover one's face.

camouflet /kamuflɛ/ *nm* affront, snub; **infliger un ~ à qn** to snub sb.

camp /kɑ̃/ *nm* **1** Mil (lieu, groupe) camp; **~ militaire** military camp; **~ fortifié** fortified camp; **~ d'entraînement** training camp; **rentrer au ~** to return to (the) camp; **lever le ~** lit to strike camp; fig○ to leave; **2** (prison) camp; **~ de prisonniers** prison camp; **~ de détention** or **réclusion** detention centre[GB]; **3** (campement provisoire) camp; **~ de réfugiés/nudistes/vacances** refugee/nudist/holiday camp; **~ scout** scout camp; **faire un ~** [*scout*] to go on camp; **partir en ~ d'escalade** to go on a climbing holiday; **4** Sport, Pol side; **choisir son ~** to choose one's side; **changer de ~** to change sides; **dans le ~ adverse** on the other side.
■ **~ de concentration** concentration camp; **~ d'extermination** extermination camp; **~ d'internement** internment camp; **~ de la mort** death camp; **~ retranché** entrenched camp; **~ de travail** labour[GB] camp; **Camp du Drap d'or** Field of the Cloth of Gold.
IDIOMES **ficher**○ or **foutre**◑ **le ~** to split○, to leave; **tout fout le ~**◑ everything is falling apart.

campagnard, **~e** /kɑ̃paɲaʀ, aʀd/ **I** *adj* [*vie, fête, accent*] country (*épith*); [*accent, repas, meuble*] rustic.

II *nm,f* country person; **les ~s** country people.

campagne /kɑ̃paɲ/ *nf* **1** (régions rurales) country; (paysage) (open) countryside; **la ~ toscane** the Tuscan countryside; **habiter (à) la ~** to live in the country; **en pleine ~** in the countryside; **en rase ~** in the open countryside; **route/médecin de ~** country road/doctor; **les gens/les habitudes de la ~** country people/habits; **les travaux de la ~** farm work, agricultural labour[GB]; **2** (opération) campaign; **~ électorale/publicitaire** election/advertising campaign; **~ de presse/propagande** press/propaganda campaign; **~ commerciale** sales campaign ou drive; **~ de recrutement/vaccination** recruitment ou recruiting/vaccination drive; **entrer en ~** [*homme politique*] to start one's campaign; **son entrée en ~** the start of his/her campaign; **mener** or **faire ~ pour/contre** to campaign for/against; **~ de saturation** Pub media saturation campaign; **3** (période d'activité) year; **~ viticole/de pêche** winegrowing/fishing year; **~ de commercialisation 1991–92** 1991/92 marketing year; **4** Mil campaign; **la ~ d'Égypte/de Russie** the Egyptian/Russian campaign; **armée en ~** army on campaign ou in the field; **faire ~** to fight (a campaign); **se mettre en ~** Mil to put oneself on a war footing; **se mettre en ~ pour trouver qch** fig to set about finding sth; **artillerie/tenue de ~** field artillery/dress.
■ **Campagne romaine** Campagna.
IDIOMES **battre la ~**○ to be off one's rocker○.

campagnol /kɑ̃paɲɔl/ *nm* vole.

Campanie /kɑ̃pani/ ▶ **692** *nf* Campania.

campanile /kɑ̃panil/ *nm* bell tower, campanile spéc.

campanule /kɑ̃panyl/ *nf* campanula, bellflower.

campement /kɑ̃pmɑ̃/ *nm* **1** (lieu) camp; **établir un ~** to set up camp; **replier le ~** to pack up; **2** (activité) camping; **matériel de ~** camping equipment.

camper /kɑ̃pe/ [1] **I** *vtr* **1** (décrire) to portray [*personnage*]; to depict [*paysage, scène*]; **personnage bien campé** well-portrayed character; **récit bien campé** well-constructed story; **2**○ (quitter) **il m'a campé là** he dumped me there○.

II *vi* to camp; **~ sur ses positions** fig to stand firm.

III se camper *vpr* **se ~ devant qch/qn** to stand squarely in front of sth/sb; **bien campé sur ses jambes** standing firm; **se campant sur ses jambes, il...** standing firm, he...

campeur, **-euse** /kɑ̃pœʀ, øz/ *nm,f* camper.

camphre /kɑ̃fʀ/ *nm* camphor.

camphré, **~e** /kɑ̃fʀe/ *adj* [*alcool, huile*] camphorated.

camphrier /kɑ̃fʀije/ *nm* camphor laurel.

camping /kɑ̃piŋ/ *nm* **1** (activité) camping; **faire du ~** to go camping; **faire du ~ sauvage** to camp rough; **'~ sauvage interdit'** 'no camping'; **~ à la ferme** camping on a farm-based site; **2** (lieu) campsite GB, campground US.

camping-car, *pl* **~s** /kɑ̃piŋkaʀ/ *nm* controv camper.

camping-gaz® /kɑ̃piŋgaz/ *nm inv* (réchaud) camping stove.

campus /kɑ̃pys/ *nm inv* campus; **hors ~** off-campus.

camus, **~e** /kamy, yz/ *adj* [*nez*] snub (*épith*); **il a le nez ~** he's got a snub nose.

canada /kanada/ *nf inv* Bot, Culin ≈ russet (apple).

Canada /kanada/ ▶ **321** *nprm* Canada.

Canadair® /kanadɛʀ/ *nm* water bomber, air tanker.

canadianisme /kanadjanism/ *nm* Canadianism.

canadien, **-ienne** /kanadjɛ̃, ɛn/ ▶ **537** **I** *adj* Canadian.

II canadienne *nf* **1** (veste) sheepskin-lined jacket; **2** (tente) ridge tent.

Canadien, **-ienne** /kanadjɛ̃, ɛn/ ▶ **537** *nm,f* Canadian.

canaille /kanɑj/ **I** *adj* [*air, allure*] mischievous.

II *nf* **1** (personne) villain; **petite ~** rascal; **2**† (racaille) rabble.

canal, *pl* **-aux** /kanal, o/ *nm* **1** (voie navigable) canal; **le Grand Canal** the Grand Canal; **le ~ de Suez** the Suez canal; **au bord du ~** by the canal; **2** (moyen) channel; **le ~ administratif/diplomatique** the administrative/diplomatic channel; **annoncer/apprendre qch par le ~ de la télévision** to announce/to hear sth on television; **3** Anat (tube) duct; **un ~ obstrué** a blocked duct; **4** Géog (bras de mer) channel; **5** Télécom (fréquence) channel.
■ **~ adducteur** water supply channel; **~ d'amenée** headrace channel; **~ biliaire** bile duct; **~ déférent** vas deferens; **~ de dérivation** bypass channel; **~ de diffusion** or **de distribution** distribution channel; **~ de drainage** drop pipe; **~ d'irrigation** irrigation channel; **~ médullaire** medullary canal; **canaux semi-circulaires** semicircular canals.

canalisation /kanalizasjɔ̃/ *nf* **1** (tuyau) pipe; (réseau) mains (*pl*); **les ~s sont bouchées** the pipes are blocked; **2** (aménagement d'un cours d'eau) canalization; **3** (action de diriger) channelling[GB]; **la ~ de l'information** the channelling[GB] of information.

canaliser /kanalize/ [1] *vtr* **1** Gén Civ to canalize [*cours d'eau*]; to carry out the canalization of [*région*]; **2** (diriger) to channel [*argent, circulation, foule, énergie, force*]; to contain [*colère, mécontentement*].

cananéen /kananeɛ̃/ *nm* Ling Canaanitic.

canapé /kanape/ *nm* **1** (siège) sofa, settee; **~ convertible** sofa bed; **2** Culin canapé; **~s au caviar** caviar canapés.

canapé-lit, *pl* **canapés-lits** /kanapeli/ *nm* sofa bed.

canaque /kanak/ *adj* Kanak.

Canaque /kanak/ *nmf* Kanak.

canard /kanaʀ/ *nm* **1** Zool duck; **chasse aux ~s** duck shooting; **~ domestique/sauvage** domestic/wild duck; **marcher en ~** to waddle; ▶ **vilain**; **2** Culin duck; **~ à l'orange/aux olives** duck in orange sauce/with olives; **3**○ (sucre) *sugar lump dipped in coffee or brandy*; **4**○ (journal) rag○, newspaper; **5**○ (fausse nouvelle) false rumour[GB]; **lancer des ~s** to spread false rumours[GB]; **6** Mus (fausse note) wrong note; **7**○ (terme d'affection) darling; **8** C (bouilloire) kettle.
■ **~ de Barbarie** Muscovy duck; **~ boîteux** fig lame duck; **~ laqué** Peking duck; **~ mandarin** mandarin duck.
IDIOMES **ça ne casse pas trois** or **quatre pattes à un ~**○ it's nothing to write home about; **glisser sur qn comme l'eau sur l'aile d'un ~** to be like water off a duck's back to sb; **il ne faut pas prendre les enfants du bon Dieu pour des ~s sauvages**○ you should give people credit for some intelligence.

canardeau, *pl* **~x** /kanaʀdo/ *nm* duckling.

canarder○ /kanaʀde/ [1] **I** *vtr* lit, fig to snipe at [*personne, positions*].

II○ *vi* Mus (en chantant) to sing a wrong note; (en jouant) to play a wrong note.

canardière /kanaʀdjɛʀ/ *nf* **1** (mare) duck pond; **2** (fusil) punt gun.

canari /kanaʀi/ *nm* **1** (oiseau) canary; **2** ▶ **193** (couleur) **jaune ~** canary yellow.

Canaries /kanaʀi/ ▶ **416** *nprfpl* **les (îles) ~** the Canary Islands, the Canaries.

canasson◑ /kanasɔ̃/ *nm* nag○, horse.

canasta /kanasta/ ▶449 *nf* canasta.
Canberra /kɑ̃bɛʀa/ ▶857 *npr* Canberra.
cancan /kɑ̃kɑ̃/ *nm* **1**○ (commérage) gossip ¢; **faire** or **raconter des ~s** to gossip; **faire courir des ~s sur qn** to spread gossip about sb; **2** (danse) **(French) ~** cancan.
cancaner /kɑ̃kane/ [1] *vi* **1**○ [*personne*] to gossip; **2** [*canard*] to quack.
cancanier, **-ière** /kɑ̃kanje, ɛʀ/ **I** *adj* [*personne*] gossipy (*épith*); **il est (très) ~** he's a (real) gossip.
II *nm,f* (personne) gossip.
cancer /kɑ̃sɛʀ/ *nm* **1** ▶271 Méd cancer; **avoir un ~** to have cancer; **un ~ du sein/du poumon/de la peau** breast/lung/skin cancer; **~ du col de l'utérus/du rein** cervical/renal cancer; **~ de l'estomac/de l'œsophage** cancer of the stomach/of the oesophagus; **2** fig cancer.
■ **~ épithélial** carcinoma; **~ glandulaire** adenocarcinoma.
Cancer /kɑ̃sɛʀ/ ▶874 *nprm* Cancer.
cancéreux, **-euse** /kɑ̃seʀø, øz/ **I** *adj* [*tumeur, cellule*] cancerous; [*personne*] with cancer (*épith, après n*).
II *nm,f* gén person with cancer; (sous traitement) cancer patient; **les ~** people with cancer; **c'est un ~** he has cancer.
cancérigène /kɑ̃seʀiʒɛn/ *adj* carcinogenic.
cancérisation /kɑ̃seʀizasjɔ̃/ *nf* cancerization.
cancériser: **se cancériser** /kɑ̃seʀize/ [1] *vpr* to become cancerous; **tissu cancérisé** cancerous tissue.
cancérogène /kɑ̃seʀɔʒɛn/ *adj* carcinogenic.
cancérologie /kɑ̃seʀɔlɔʒi/ *nf* cancer research; **service de ~** cancer ward.
cancérologue /kɑ̃seʀɔlɔg/ ▶510 *nmf* cancer specialist.
cancre /kɑ̃kʀ/ *nm* dunce.
cancrelat /kɑ̃kʀəla/ *nm* cockroach.
candela /kɑ̃dela/ *nf* candela.
candélabre /kɑ̃delabʀ/ *nm* (chandelier) candelabra GB, candelabrum US.
candeur /kɑ̃dœʀ/ *nf* ingenuousness; **yeux pleins de ~** innocent eyes.
candi /kɑ̃di/ *adj m* **fruit ~** candied fruit; **sucre ~** sugar candy, rock candy US.
candidat, **~e** /kɑ̃dida, at/ *nm,f* **1** Pol candidate; **être** or **se porter ~ aux élections** to stand for election GB, to run for office US; **être ~ aux législatives** to stand for election to the Assemblée; **~ désigné** or **officiel** Pol nominee; **2** Admin, Scol, Univ (à un examen) candidate; **les ~s à l'examen** examination candidates; **les ~s au permis de conduire** people taking the driving test; **3** Admin, Entr (à un poste, statut) applicant (**à** for); **le ~ retenu** the successful applicant; **~ à l'immigration** applicant for immigration; **être** or **se porter ~ (à un poste)** to apply (for a post); **4** Jeux contestant (**à** in); **~ à un concours** contestant in a competition; **5** (aspirant) **~ au voyage/à l'emprunt** would-be traveller[GB]/borrower; **~ au suicide** potential suicide; **c'est un ~ à l'infarctus** he's heading for a heart attack; **être ~ à l'émigration** to be considering emigrating; **il n'est pas ~ au mariage/au suicide** he's not the marrying type/the type to commit suicide; **pour la vaisselle, il n'y a pas beaucoup de ~s!** hum when it comes to doing the dishes, there aren't many takers ou volunteers.
candidature /kɑ̃didatyʀ/ *nf* **1** (à une élection) candidacy, candidature GB; **il a annoncé sa ~ aux élections** he has announced his candidacy in the election; **retirer sa ~** to stand down GB, to drop out US; **2** (à un poste, statut) application; **~ spontanée** Entr unsolicited application; **retirer sa ~** to withdraw one's application; **faire acte de ~** to apply (**à** for).
candide /kɑ̃did/ *adj* ingenuous, guileless.
candidement /kɑ̃didmɑ̃/ *adv* ingenuously.
candidose /kɑ̃didoz/ ▶271 *nf* Méd candidiasis.
candir /kɑ̃diʀ/ [3] *vtr* to candy.
cane /kan/ *nf* (female) duck.
canepetière /kanpətjɛʀ/ *nf* little bustard.
caner◑ /kane/ [1] **I** *vtr* (fatiguer) to knacker [sb] out◑; **j'étais cané** I was knackered◑.
II *vi* (mourir) to die, to croak◑.
caneton /kantɔ̃/ *nm* duckling.
canette /kanɛt/ *nf* **1** (bouteille) **~ (de bière)** (small) bottle of beer; **2** (boîte) **~ de bière** can of beer; **3** Tex (de tissage) pirn GB, quill US; Cout (de machine à coudre) spool; **faire une ~** to make up a spool; **4** Zool (female) duckling.
canevas /kanva/ *nm* **1** Tex (toile) canvas; **2** Cout (ouvrage) tapestry work; **3** fig framework.
caniche /kaniʃ/ *nm* poodle; ▶ **grand**.
■ **~ miniature** or **moyen** miniature poodle; **~ nain** toy poodle.
caniculaire /kanikylɛʀ/ *adj* [*chaleur, journée*] scorching.
canicule /kanikyl/ *nf* **1** (chaleur) **hier, c'était la ~** yesterday was a real scorcher○; **sortir en pleine ~** to go out in the scorching heat; **2** (période chaude) dog days (*pl*); (vague de chaleur) heatwave.
canidé /kanide/ *nm* canine; **les ~s** Canidae.
canif /kanif/ *nm* **1** gén penknife, pocketknife; **bois marqué de coups de ~** wood scored by a penknife; **2** Art (de graveur) knife.
IDIOMES **donner un coup de ~ dans le contrat**○ to be unfaithful.
canin, **~e** /kanɛ̃, in/ **I** *adj* Zool [*race*] canine; [*exposition, nourriture*] dog (*épith*).
II canine *nf* (dent) canine (tooth).
caninette® /kaninɛt/ *nf* pooper-scooper○.
canisse /kanis/ *nf* (treillis) reed screening ¢.
caniveau, *pl* **~x** /kanivo/ *nm* (de chaussée) gutter; (pour câbles) trough; Agric (pour excréments) slurry channel.
canna /kana/ *nm* Bot canna.
cannabis /kanabis/ *nm* cannabis.
cannage /kanaʒ/ *nm* **1** (travail) caning ¢; **2** (produit) canework ¢; **faire refaire le ~ d'une chaise** to have a chair re-caned.
canne /kan/ *nf* **1** (pour marcher) (walking) stick, cane; **une ~ à pommeau** a stick with a knob; **donner un coup de ~ à qn** to hit sb with a stick; **2** Bot cane; **3** Ind (de souffleur de verre) blowpipe; **4**◑ (jambe) pin○, leg; **ne pas tenir sur ses ~s** to be a bit unsteady ou wobbly○ on one's feet.
■ **~ anglaise** (forearm) crutch; **~ blanche** (objet) white stick GB, white cane US; (personne) blind person; **~ de golf** golf club; **~ à pêche** fishing rod; **~ de Provence** Bot giant reed; **~ à sucre** sugar cane.
canné, **~e** /kane/ **I** *pp* ▶ **canner**.
II *pp adj* [*fauteuil, chaise*] cane (*épith*).
canneberge /kanbɛʀʒ/ *nf* cranberry.
canne-épée, *pl* **cannes-épées** /kanepe/ *nf* sword stick GB, sword cane US.
cannelé, **~e** /kanle/ *adj* **1** gén [*colonne, verre*] fluted; **2** Hérald invecked.
cannelier /kanəlje/ *nm* cinnamon (tree).
cannelle /kanɛl/ **I** ▶193 *adj inv* (couleur) cinnamon; **couleur ~** cinnamon coloured[GB].
II *nf* **1** Bot, Culin cinnamon; **2** Tech (robinet) spigot.
cannelloni /kanɛlɔni/ *nmpl* Culin cannelloni.
cannelure /kanlyʀ/ *nf* (de colonne) flute; **~s** fluting ¢.
canner /kane/ [1] *vtr* to cane [*siège*].
Cannes /kan/ ▶857 *npr* Cannes; **festival de ~** Cannes film festival.
cannette *nf* = **canette** 1, 2, 3.
canneur, **-euse** /kanœʀ, øz/ ▶510 *nm,f* cane worker, caner.
cannibale /kanibal/ **I** *adj* [*tribu, espèce*] cannibal (*épith*).
II *nmf* cannibal.
cannibaliser /kanibalize/ [1] *vtr* to cannibalize [*machine, véhicule*].
cannibalisme /kanibalism/ *nm* cannibalism.
cannois, **~e** /kanwa, az/ ▶857 *adj* of Cannes.
Cannois, **~e** /kanwa, az/ *nm,f* (natif) native of Cannes; (habitant) inhabitant of Cannes.
canoë /kanɔe/ ▶449 *nm* **1** (embarcation) (Canadian) canoe; **descendre une rivière en ~** to canoe down a river; **2** (sport) canoeing; **faire du ~** to go canoeing.
canoéiste /kanɔeist/ *nmf* (Canadian) canoeist.
canoë-kayak /kanɔekajak/ ▶449 *nm* canoeing.
canon /kanɔ̃/ **I** *adj m inv* **1**◑ (superbe) fantastic○, magnificent; **2** Jur **droit ~** canon law.
II *nm* **1** Mil (arme) (big) gun; (sur un avion) cannon; Hist cannon; **~ de 75 (mm)** 75-mm gun; **tirer un coup de ~** to fire a gun; **entendre des coups de ~** to hear cannon fire; **salué de 21 coups de ~** given a 21-gun salute; **boulet de ~** cannonball; **2** Mil (tube d'arme) barrel; **à ~ lisse** smoothbore (*épith*); **à ~ rayé** rifled; **fusil à ~ double** double-barrelled[GB] shotgun; **fusil à ~ scié** sawn off GB ou sawed off US shotgun; **3** Mus canon; **chanter en ~** to sing in a round; **4** (principe) canon; **les ~s de la beauté** the canons of beauty; **5** Bible, Relig canon; **6** Zool (os) cannon bone; **7**○ (verre) glass (of wine).
■ **~ antiaérien** antiaircraft gun; **~ antichar** antitank gun; **~ arroseur** Agric sprinkler; **~ à corbeaux** Agric bird-scaring device; **~ à eau** water cannon; **~ à électrons** Phys electron gun; **~ mitrailleur** heavy machine gun; **~ à mousse** foam gun; **~ à neige** Sport snow-blower; **~ de perçage** Tech bush GB, bushing US.
cañon /kanjɔ̃, kanjɔn/ *nm* canyon; **~ sous-marin** submarine canyon.
canonicat /kanɔnika/ *nm* canonry.
canonique /kanɔnik/ *adj* **1** Relig [*décret*] canonical; **droit ~** canon law; **d'âge ~** hum of a venerable age; **2** Ling, Math [*phrase, forme, équation, matrice*] canonical.
canonisation /kanɔnizasjɔ̃/ *nf* canonization.
canoniser /kanɔnize/ [1] *vtr* to canonize.
canonnade /kanɔnad/ *nf* cannonade.
canonner /kanɔne/ [1] *vtr* gén to bombard; (avec des obus) to shell.
canonnier /kanɔnje/ *nm* gunner.
canonnière /kanɔnjɛʀ/ *nf* **1** (navire) gunboat; **2** (meurtrière) loophole, eyelet.
canope /kanɔp/ *nm* Canopic jar.
Canossa /kanɔsa/ ▶857 *npr* Canossa.
IDIOMES **aller à ~** to eat humble pie.
canot /kano/ *nm* (small) boat, dinghy.
■ **~ automobile** motorboat; **~ de pêche** (open) fishing boat; **~ pneumatique** rubber ou inflatable dinghy; **~ à rames** rowing boat; **~ de sauvetage** Naut lifeboat; Aviat life raft.
canotage /kanɔtaʒ/ *nm* boating.
canoter /kanɔte/ [1] *vi* to go boating.
canoteur, **-euse** /kanɔtœʀ, øz/ *nm,f* rower.
canotier /kanɔtje/ *nm* (chapeau) boater.
canson® /kɑ̃sɔ̃/ *nm* drawing paper.
cantabile /kɑ̃tabile/ *nm* Mus cantabile.
Cantal /kɑ̃tal/ ▶692 *nprm* (département) **le ~** Cantal.
cantaloup /kɑ̃talu/ *nm* cantaloupe melon.
cantate /kɑ̃tat/ *nf* cantata.
cantatrice /kɑ̃tatʀis/ ▶510 *nf* (d'opéra) opera singer; (de musique classique) (professional) singer.
cantharide /kɑ̃taʀid/ *nf* Zool Spanish fly; **poudre de ~** cantharides (*pl*).
cantilène /kɑ̃tilɛn/ *nf* cantilena.

La capacité

Pour mesurer les liquides, on utilise traditionnellement les pints, les quarts (rares aujourd'hui) et les gallons en Grande-Bretagne et aux États-Unis. Les liquides comme le vin ou l'essence sont vendus de plus en plus au litre, mais cela n'a pas modifié les habitudes des consommateurs. L'automobiliste anglais ou américain achète donc désormais son essence en litres, mais compte toujours sa consommation en gallons.

Pour les mesures en cm³, dm³, m³ *etc. voir* **le volume ▶ 866**. *Pour la prononciation des nombres, voir* **les nombres ▶ 545**.

Les mesures britanniques: équivalences

								dire
1 pint	=	0,57 ℓ		1 litre*	1 ℓ†	=	1.76‡ pt	*pint*
1 quart	=	2 pints	= 1,13 ℓ				0.88 qt	*quarts*
1 gallon	=	8 pints	= 4,54 ℓ				0.22 galls	*gallons*

Les mesures américaines: équivalences

								dire
1 pint	=	0,47 ℓ		1 litre*	1 ℓ†	=	2.12 pts‡	*pints*
1 quart	=	2 pints	= 0,94 ℓ				1.06 qt	*quart*
1 gallon	=	8 pints	= 3,78 ℓ				0.26 galls	*gallons*

* *Attention: on écrit* litre *en anglais britannique, et* liter *en anglais américain.*

† *L'abréviation de litre (ℓ) est la même en anglais qu'en français.*

‡ *Noter que l'anglais utilise un point là où le français a une virgule.*

il y a 1 000 centimètres cubes dans un litre	=	there are 1,000 cubic centimetres in a litre
1 000 centimètres cubes font un litre	=	1,000 cubic centimetres make one litre
il y a huit pintes dans un gallon	=	there are eight pints in a gallon
quelle est la contenance de la bouteille?	=	what is the size of the bottle? *ou (moins familier)* what is the capacity of the bottle?
combien contient-elle?	=	what does it hold?
elle contient 2 litres	=	it holds two litres
elle a une contenance de 2 litres	=	its capacity is two litres
la contenance de la bouteille est de 2 litres	=	the capacity of the bottle is two litres

Noter l'absence d'équivalent anglais de la préposition française de *avant le chiffre dans les deux derniers exemples.*

la bouteille fait 2 litres	=	the bottle holds 2 litres
elle fait à peu près 2 litres	=	it holds about 2 litres
presque 3 litres	=	almost 3 litres
plus de 2 litres	=	more than 2 litres
moins de 3 litres	=	less than 3 litres
A a une plus grande contenance que B	=	A has a greater capacity than B
B a une moins grande contenance que A	=	B has a smaller capacity than A
A a la même contenance que B	=	A has the same capacity as B
A et B ont la même contenance	=	A and B have the same capacity

Noter l'ordre des mots dans les adjectifs composés anglais, et l'utilisation du trait d'union. Noter aussi que litre, *employé comme adjectif, ne prend pas la marque du pluriel.*

une bouteille de deux litres	=	a 2-litre bottle
un réservoir de 200 litres	=	a 200-litre tank

Mais on peut également dire a tank 200 litres in capacity.

deux litres de vin	=	two litres of wine
vendu au litre	=	sold by the litre
ils utilisent 20 000 litres par jour	=	they use 20,000 litres a day
elle fait 8 litres aux 100	=	it does 28 miles to the gallon

En anglais, on compte la consommation d'une voiture en mesurant non pas le nombre de litres nécessaires pour parcourir 100 kilomètres, mais la distance parcourue (en miles) avec 4,54 litres (un gallon) de carburant.

cantilever /kɑ̃tiləvœʀ/ *adj inv* [*suspension, pont*] cantilever; **travée ~** cantilever span.

cantine /kɑ̃tin/ *nf* **1** (restaurant) canteen GB, cafeteria; **je ne mange jamais à la ~** gén I never eat in the canteen GB ou cafeteria; Scol I never have school dinner GB ou school lunch; **2** (malle) tin trunk.
■ **~ ambulante** Mil mobile canteen.

cantinier, -ière /kɑ̃tinje, ɛʀ/ **▶ 510** **I** *nm,f* canteen manager/manageress.
II cantinière *nf* Hist Mil camp follower (*who cooks for army*).

cantique /kɑ̃tik/ *nm* canticle; **le Cantique des ~s** the Song of Songs.

canton /kɑ̃tɔ̃/ *nm* **1** Admin canton; **réputé dans tout le ~**○ famed for miles around; **2** (de route, voie ferrée) section; **3** Hérald canton.
■ **~ dextre du chef** Hérald dexter chief; **~ dextre de pointe** Hérald dexter base; **~ senestre du chef** Hérald sinister chief; **~ senestre de pointe** Hérald sinister base; **~ de voie** Rail block section; **Cantons de l'Est** Eastern Townships.

Canton /kɑ̃tɔ̃/ **▶ 857** *npr* Canton, Guangzhou.

cantonade: **à la cantonade** /alakɑ̃tɔnad/ *loc adv* **parler à la ~** to speak to no-one in particular; Théât to speak off; **dire qch à la ~** to say sth for all to hear; **il raconte ça à la ~** he tells anyone and everyone.

cantonais, ~e /kɑ̃tɔnɛ, ɛz/ **▶ 462** **I** **▶ 857** *adj* Cantonese.
II *nm* Ling Cantonese.

Cantonais, ~e /kɑ̃tɔnɛ, ɛz/ *nm,f* Cantonese.

cantonal, ~e, *mpl* **-aux** /kɑ̃tɔnal, o/ **I** *adj* cantonal.
II cantonale *nf* Pol **~e (partielle)** by-election; **les ~es** cantonal elections.

cantonné, ~e /kɑ̃tɔne/ *adj* Hérald cantoned.

cantonnement /kɑ̃tɔnmɑ̃/ *nm* **1** Mil (stationnement) (dans une ville, région) stationing ℂ; (chez l'habitant) billeting ℂ; (lieu) gén quarters (*pl*); (chez l'habitant) billet; (camp) station; **installer ses ~s** Mil to set up one's quarters; **2** Rail block.
■ **~ de pêche** Pêche fishery reserve.

cantonner /kɑ̃tɔne/ [1] **I** *vtr* **1** Mil gén to station [*troupes*]; (chez l'habitant) to billet [*troupes*] (**chez** with); **régiment cantonné à la frontière** regiment stationed at the border; **2** (restreindre) **~ qn dans un lieu** to confine sb to a place; **~ qn dans le rôle de** to reduce sb to the role of.
II *vi* [*troupes*] to be stationed.
III se cantonner *vpr* **se ~ dans un rôle/style** to restrict oneself to a role/style.

cantonnier /kɑ̃tɔnje/ **▶ 510** *nm* roadmender.

cantonnière /kɑ̃tɔnjɛʀ/ *nf* (de fenêtre) pelmet.

Cantorbéry /kɑ̃tɔʀbeʀi/ **▶ 857** *npr* Canterbury.

canulant○, **~e** /kanylɑ̃, ɑ̃t/ *adj* irritating.

canular /kanylaʀ/ *nm* hoax; **monter un ~** to set up a hoax; **monter un ~ à qn** to hoax sb.

canule /kanyl/ *nf* cannula; **~ de trachéotomie** tracheotomy tube.

canut, -use /kany, yz/ *nm* silk worker (*in Lyons*).

canyon = **cañon**.

CAO /seao/ *nf*: *abbr* ▶ **conception**.

caoua○ /kawa/ *nm* coffee.

caoutchouc /kautʃu/ *nm* **1** (matière) rubber; **de** or **en ~** rubber (*épith*); **être en ~** to be made of rubber; **bottes en ~** rubber boots, wellington boots; **~ mousse/synthétique** foam/synthetic rubber; **2** (de protection) rubber overshoe; **3** (plante) rubber plant; **4** (élastique) rubber band.

caoutchouter /kautʃute/ [1] *vtr* to rubberize.

caoutchouteux, -euse /kautʃutø, øz/ *adj* rubbery.

cap /kap/ *nm* **1** Géog (promontoire) cape; **le ~ Horn** Cape Horn; **doubler** or **franchir un ~** to round a cape; **2** (obstacle) hurdle; **franchir** or **passer un ~** to get over a hurdle; **3** (limite) mark; **le ~ des 1000 abonnés** the 1,000 subscribers mark; **passer le ~ de la cinquantaine** to pass the fifty mark; **4** (orientation) course; **changer de ~** [*navire, capitaine, parti, ministre*] to change course; **tenir** or **garder** or **maintenir le ~** [*navire, capitaine, parti, ministre*] to hold one's course; **mettre le ~ sur** [*capitaine, navire*] to head for; **mettre le ~ au sud** [*navire, capitaine*] to head south.

Cap /kap/ **▶ 857** *npr* **le ~** Cape Town.

CAP /seape/ *nm*: *abbr* ▶ **certificat**.

CAPA /kapa/ *nm*: *abbr* ▶ **certificat**.

capable /kapabl/ *adj* [*personne, machine, test*] capable (**de qch** of sth; **de faire** of doing); **c'est quelqu'un de très ~** he's a very capable person; **il est ~ d'une analyse lucide** he is capable of lucid analysis; **il n'est même pas ~ de faire cuire un œuf dur** he isn't even capable of boiling an egg!, he can't even boil an egg!; **je vais lui montrer de quoi je suis ~!** I'll show him/her what I'm capable of!; **il est ~ de tout pour garder sa place** he would do anything to keep his job; **il doit noter les appels mais je ne sais pas s'il en est ~** he has to note down the calls but I don't know if he is up to it; **c'est une situation grave, ~ d'évoluer vers la guerre** it's a serious situation which could escalate into war; **je ne le crois pas ~ de nous trahir** I don't think he would betray us; **ils sont bien ~s de nous dénoncer/de ne pas nous attendre** I wouldn't put it past them to turn us in/not to wait for us; **'recherchons boulanger, bon salaire si ~'** 'baker required, good salary for the right person'.

capacitance /kapasitɑ̃s/ *nf* capacitance.

capacité /kapasite/ **I** *nf* **1** (aptitude) ability; **~ de qn/qch à faire** capacity of sb/sth to do; **la ~ d'évolution des employés** the employees' capacity to progress; **un chercheur d'une grande ~** a researcher of great ability, a very talented researcher; **tes ~s d'imagination/d'analyse** your capacity for imagining/analysing; **avoir ~ à faire** Jur to be qualified to do; **2** (potentiel) capacity; **~ exportatrice/de production** export/production capacity; **~ d'intervention** Mil intervention capacity; **~ de 100 mégawatts** 100 megawatt capacity; **~s de stockage** storage capacity; **~ de mémoire** Ordinat memory capacity ou size; **3** (contenance) capacity; **un récipient de grande ~** a large capacity container; **~ d'accueil d'un hôtel/d'une prison** capacity of a hotel/of a prison; **un avion d'une ~ de 200 places** a plane with a capacity of 200; **la ~ d'accueil d'une ville touristique** the number of visitors a tourist resort can accommodate; **machine à laver à ~ variable** washing machine with variable load settings.
II capacités *nfpl* (talent) abilities; **~s**

intellectuelles/physiques intellectual/physical abilities; **je ne doute pas de vos ~s** I have no doubts as to your ability ou abilities.
■ **~ civile** civil capacity; **~ électrostatique** capacitance; **~ en droit** Univ, Jur *basic legal qualification*; **~ légale** Jur legal capacity, legal competence; **~ respiratoire** Méd vital capacity; **~ thermique** Phys thermal capacity; **~ thoracique** = **~ respiratoire**.

caparaçon /kapaʀasɔ̃/ *nm* caparison.

caparaçonner /kapaʀasɔne/ [1] *vtr* **1** Hist to caparison; **2** (protéger) to armour[GB].

cape /kap/ *nf* **1** Mode cape; (très longue) cape, cloak; **~ de berger** shepherd's cloak; **film de ~ et d'épée** swashbuckler; **2** (de matador) cape.
IDIOMES **rire sous ~** to laugh up one's sleeve.

capelan /kaplɑ̃/ *nm* (poisson) poor cod.

capeline /kaplin/ *nf* wide-brimmed hat.

CAPES /kapɛs/ *nm* (*abbr* = **certificat d'aptitude professionnelle à l'enseignement secondaire**) *secondary school teaching qualification*.

capésien, **-ienne** /kapesjɛ̃, ɛn/ *nm,f* holder of the CAPES.

capharnaüm /kafaʀnaɔm/ *nm* shambles○ (*sg*); **quel ~, ta chambre!** what a shambles your room is!

cap-hornier /kapɔʀnje/ *nm* **1** (voilier) *clipper which has followed the Cape Horn route*; **2** (marin) *sailor who has sailed the Cape Horn route*.

capillaire /kapilɛʀ/ **I** *adj* **1** (de vaisseau sanguin) capillary; **2** (de cheveu) hair (*épith*); **soins ~s** hair care; **3** Phys capillary.
II *nm* **1** Anat capillary; **2** Bot maidenhair fern.

capillarité /kapilaʀite/ *nf* capillarity.

capilliculteur, **-trice** /kapilikyltœʀ, tʀis/ ▶ **510** *nm,f* hair care specialist.

capilotade○ /kapilɔtad/ *nf* **en ~** in a bad way○; **se mettre le foie en ~** to ruin one's liver.

capitaine /kapitɛn/ ▶ **390** *nm* **1** (grade) (d'armée de terre, de marine) ≈ captain; (d'armée de l'air) ≈ flight lieutenant GB, ≈ captain US; (d'équipe sportive) captain; **2** Zool threadfin.
■ **~ de corvette** Mil Naut ≈ lieutenant commander; **~ de frégate** Mil Naut ≈ commander; **~ d'industrie** captain of industry; **~ au long cours** Naut fully-licensed captain; **~ des pompiers** fire chief; **~ de port** Naut harbour[GB] master; **~ de vaisseau** Mil Naut ≈ captain.

capitainerie /kapitɛnʀi/ *nf* **1** (administration) port authority; **2** (bâtiment) port authority buildings (*pl*).

capital, **~e**, *mpl* **-aux** /kapital, o/ **I** *adj* **1** (fondamental) [*rôle, rencontre, témoignage, œuvre*] key (*épith*), crucial; [*importance*] major; **le dernier chapitre de son livre est ~** the last chapter of his/her book is crucial; **une découverte ~e dans la recherche contre le cancer** a major breakthrough in cancer research; **c'est d'une importance ~e** it's of the utmost importance; **il est ~ de faire** it's essential to do; **il est ~ que tu viennes** it is essential that you (should) come; **2** Imprim [*lettre*] capital; **3** (de mort) **peine ~e** capital punishment.
II *nm* **1** Fin capital; **société au ~ de 50000 francs** company with (a) capital of 50,000 francs; **procéder à une augmentation de ~** to increase capital; **impôt sur le ~** capital levy; **2** Écon capital; **le ~ et le travail** capital and labour[GB]; **3** (ressource) **notre ~ santé** our health; **le ~ humain/industriel** human/industrial resources (*pl*).
III capitaux *nmpl* Fin (fonds) capital ₵, funds; **avoir besoin/manquer de capitaux** to need/to lack capital; **capitaux étrangers** foreign capital; **marché des capitaux** capital markets (*pl*); **mouvements de capitaux** capital movements.
IV capitale *nf* **1** (d'un pays) capital (city); **les ~es européennes** the European capitals; **les rues de la ~e** the streets of the capital; **2** (centre) capital; **une ~e boursière/culturelle** a financial/cultural capital; **Lyon, ~e des gourmets** Lyons, a paradise for gourmets; **3** Imprim capital; **en ~es d'imprimerie** in block capitals.
■ **~ décès** death benefit; **~ fixe** fixed assets (*pl*); **~ propre** equity capital; **~ social** issued capital; **capitaux fébriles** or **flottants** hot money ₵.

capitalisable /kapitalizabl/ *adj* capitalizable.

capitalisation /kapitalizasjɔ̃/ *nf* capitalization.
■ **~ boursière** market capitalization.

capitaliser /kapitalize/ [1] *vtr* to capitalize.

capitalisme /kapitalism/ *nm* capitalism.

capitaliste /kapitalist/ *adj, nmf* capitalist.

capitalistique /kapitalistik/ *adj* capital-intensive.

capital-risque, *pl* **capitaux-risques** /kapitalʀisk, kapitoʀisk/ *nm* venture capital.

capitation /kapitasjɔ̃/ *nf* head tax.

capiteux, **-euse** /kapitø, øz/ *adj* [*alcool, parfum*] heady.

Capitole /kapitɔl/ *nm* **1** (de Rome) (colline) (**mont**) **~** Capitoline; (temple) Capitol; ▶ **Tarpéienne**; **2** (de Washington) Capitol.

capiton /kapitɔ̃/ *nm* **1** (bourre de soie) padding floss; **2** (rembourrage) padding; **3** (graisse) cellulite dimpling.

capitonnage /kapitɔnaʒ/ *nm* padding.

capitonner /kapitɔne/ [1] *vtr* to pad; **capitonné** padded.

capitulaire /kapitylɛʀ/ **I** *adj* Relig [*acte, assemblée*] capitular.
II *nm* Hist capitulary.

capitulard○, **~e** /kapitylaʀ, aʀd/ *adj, nm,f* pej defeatist.

capitulation /kapitylasjɔ̃/ *nf* capitulation (**devant** to); **~ sans conditions** unconditional surrender.

capitule /kapityl/ *nm* Bot capitulum.

capituler /kapityle/ [1] *vi* lit, fig to capitulate (**devant** to).

caporal, *pl* **-aux** /kapɔʀal, o/ ▶ **390** *nm* **1** Mil (de l'armée de terre) ≈ corporal; (de l'armée de l'air) ≈ corporal GB, ≈ sergeant US; **2** (tabac) caporal.

caporal-chef, *pl* **caporaux-chefs** /kapɔʀalʃɛf, kapɔʀoʃɛf/ ▶ **390** *nm* (dans l'armée de terre) *rank between corporal and sergeant*; (dans l'armée de l'air) *rank between corporal and sergeant* GB ou *staff sergeant* US.

capot /kapo/ **I** *adj inv* Jeux **être ~** not to win a trick; **mettre qn ~** to stop sb from winning any tricks.
II *nm* **1** Aut bonnet GB, hood US; **2** (couvercle) cover; **3** Naut (toile) cover; (trou) hatchway.

capotage /kapɔtaʒ/ *nm* (échec) collapse.

capote /kapɔt/ *nf* **1** (manteau) great-coat; **2** (de voiture, landau) hood GB, top; **3**○ (préservatif) **~ (anglaise)** condom, French letter†○.

capoter /kapɔte/ [1] *vi* **1** (échouer) [*négociation, projet*] to collapse; **faire ~** to ruin [*opération, affaire*]; **2** (se retourner) [*voiture*] to overturn; [*navire*] to capsize.

Capoue /kapu/ ▶ **857** *npr* Capua; **les délices de ~** the luxury (*sg*) of Capua.

cappuccino /kaputʃino/ *nm* cappuccino.

câpre /kɑpʀ/ *nf* caper; **sauce aux ~s** caper sauce.

caprice /kapʀis/ *nm* **1** (fantaisie) (de personne) whim; (de temps, marché, nature, voiture) vagaries (*pl*); **sur un ~** on a whim; **céder aux ~s de qn** to indulge sb's whims; **satisfaire un ~** to indulge one's whim; **2** (accès de colère) tantrum; **faire un ~** to throw a tantrum; **3** (amourette) passing fancy; **4** Mus capriccio.

capricieusement /kapʀisjøzmɑ̃/ *adv* **1** (comme un enfant gâté) capriciously; **2** (avec fantaisie) whimsically.

capricieux, **-ieuse** /kapʀisjø, øz/ **I** *adj* [*personne*] capricious; [*mécanisme*] temperamental; [*temps, destin*] fickle; [*cours d'eau*] irregular.
II *nm,f* capricious person; **petit ~** spoiled ou capricious child.

capricorne /kapʀikɔʀn/ *nm* Zool capricorn beetle.

Capricorne /kapʀikɔʀn/ ▶ **874** *nprm* Capricorn.

câprier /kɑpʀije/ *nm* caper shrub.

caprin, **~e** /kapʀɛ̃, in/ **I** *adj* goat (*épith*), caprine spéc.
II *nm* goat; **les ~s** Capra.

capsulage /kapsylaʒ/ *nm* capsule sealing.

capsule /kapsyl/ *nf* **1** (de bouteille) (bouchon) cap; (enveloppe du bouchon) capsule; **2** Pharm capsule; **3** Astronaut capsule; **~ spatiale** space capsule; **4** Anat, Bot capsule; **5** (détonateur) cap; **~ fulminante** percussion cap.

capsuler /kapsyle/ [1] *vtr* to put a cap on [*bouteille*]; to put a capsule on [*bouchon*]; **boisson capsulée** bottled drink.

captable /kaptabl/ *adj* Radio, TV that can be picked up (*épith, après n*); **une station qui n'est pas ~** a station that you can't pick up.

captage /kaptaʒ/ *nm* **1** (extraction) catchment; **zone de ~** catchment area; **2** (site d'extraction) catchment point.

captation /kaptasjɔ̃/ *nf* Jur illegal securement, captation spéc.

capter /kapte/ [1] *vtr* **1** Électrotech, Radio, Télécom, TV (recevoir) to get [*émission, chaîne*]; to pick up [*signal, rayonnement*]; **~ la BBC sur ondes courtes** to get the BBC on short wave; **2** (saisir et exprimer) to capture [*atmosphère, esprit, expression, image*]; **3** (attirer) to catch [*attention*]; **4** (absorber) to take in [*parole, information*]; to soak up [*lumière*]; Phys to capture [*photons, particules*]; **5** Jur to secure illegally [*héritage, fonds*]; **6** Sport (réceptionner) to catch [*ballon*]; to take [*passe*]; **7** (recueillir) to collect [*eaux*].

capteur /kaptœʀ/ *nm* sensor; **~ à infrarouges** infra-red sensor.
■ **~ solaire** solar cell.

captieux, **-ieuse** /kapsjø, øz/ *adj* fml fallacious.

captif, **-ive** /kaptif, iv/ **I** *adj* **1** (enfermé) [*personne, animal*] captive; **2** Comm [*clientèle, marché*] captive.
II *nm,f* captive.

captivant, **~e** /kaptivɑ̃, ɑ̃t/ *adj* [*livre, lecture*] enthralling; [*récit, histoire*] gripping; [*moment, scène*] riveting; [*musique, personnage, ambiance*] captivating.

captiver /kaptive/ [1] *vtr* [*beauté*] to captivate; [*voix, musique*] to enthral[GB]; [*histoire, aventure, programme, personne*] to fascinate.

captivité /kaptivite/ *nf* captivity; **en ~** in captivity; **vingt ans de ~** twenty years in captivity.

capture /kaptyʀ/ *nf* **1** (action d'attraper) capture; **la ~ d'un criminel/d'un animal/d'un navire** the capture of a criminal/of an animal/of a ship; **2** (ce qui est attrapé) catch; **une belle ~** a good catch; **3** Géog, Phys capture.

capturer /kaptyʀe/ [1] *vtr* lit, fig to capture.

capuche /kapyʃ/ *nf* hood; **à ~** with a hood (*épith, après n*).

capuchon /kapyʃɔ̃/ *nm* **1** (de vêtement) hood; **2** (de moine) cowl; **3** (de stylo, seringue) cap; (de cheminée) cowl; **4** Anat hood.

capucin /kapysɛ̃/ *nm* **1** (moine) Capuchin friar; **2** (singe) capuchin (monkey).

capucine /kapysin/ *nf* Bot nasturtium.

cap-verdien, **-ienne**, *mpl* **~s** /kapvɛʀdjɛ̃, ɛn/ ▶ **537** *adj* Cape Verdean.

Cap-verdien, **-ienne**, *mpl* **~s** /kapvɛʀdjɛ̃, ɛn/ ▶ **537** *nm,f* Cape Verdean.

Cap-Vert /kapvɛʀ/ ▶ **416**, **321** *nprm* **îles du ~** Cape Verde islands.

caque /kak/ *nf* herring barrel.
IDIOMES **être serrés comme des harengs**

en ~ to be squashed (in) like sardines; **la ~ sent toujours le hareng** you can't hide your origins.

caquelon /kaklɔ̃/ *nm* heavy saucepan.

caquet /kakɛ/ *nm* **1** (de poule) cackle; **2** (de bavard) prattle; **rabattre son ~**○ to stop crowing○; **rabattre le ~ à qn**○ to put sb in his/her place, to take sb down a peg or two; **se faire rabattre le ~**○ to be put in one's place.

caquetage /kaktaʒ/ *nm* **1** (de poule) cackling; **2** (de bavard) prattling.

caqueter /kakte/ [20] *vi* **1** [*poule*] to cackle; **2** [*bavard*] to prattle.

car[1] /kaʀ/ *conj* because, for.

car[2] /kaʀ/ *nm* (véhicule) coach GB, bus; **prendre le ~** to take the coach; **voyager en ~** to travel by coach.

■ **~ de police** police van; **~ (de ramassage) scolaire** school bus.

carabin○ /kaʀabɛ̃/ *nm* students' slang medical student.

carabine /kaʀabin/ *nf* **1** (arme) rifle; **~ 22 long rifle** .22 rifle; **coup de ~** rifle shot; **à coups de ~** with rifle shots; **~ à air comprimé** air rifle; **~ à plombs** shotgun; **2** (jouet) toy gun; **~ à flèches** pop gun.

carabiné○, **~e** /kaʀabine/ *adj* [*fièvre*] raging; [*migraine*] ferocious; [*rhume*] stinking○; [*café*] ferociously strong; **avoir une cuite**○ **~e** to be as drunk as a skunk○.

carabinier /kaʀabinje/ *nm* **1** (policier italien) carabiniere; **les ~s** the carabinieri; **2** Hist Mil carabineer.

IDIOMES **arriver comme les ~s** to be too late.

carabistouille○ /kaʀabistuj/ *nf* B (sottise) nonsense ¢.

Carabosse /kaʀabɔs/ *npr* **la fée ~** the wicked fairy.

Caracas /kaʀakas/ ▶ 857 *npr* Caracas.

caraco /kaʀako/ *nm* camisole (top).

caracoler /kaʀakɔle/ [1] *vi* **1** (avoir une position favorable) [*personne, parti*] to be well ahead; **~ en tête** to be well in the lead; **~ en tête de** to be well ahead in; **~ dans les premières places** to be well up among the leaders; **2** Équit [*cheval*] to prance; [*cavalier*] to parade.

caractère /kaʀaktɛʀ/ *nm* **1** (signe d'écriture) character; **~s chinois/cyrilliques** Chinese/Cyrillic characters; **2** Imprim character; **~s d'imprimerie** (type d'écriture) block capitals; **en petits/gros ~s** in small/large print; **en ~s gras** in bold type; **3** Ordinat character; **4** (tempérament) nature; **nous n'avons pas le même ~** we haven't got the same character; **ce n'est pas dans son ~ de critiquer** it's not in his/her nature to criticize; **avoir bon ~** to be good-natured; **avoir mauvais ~** to be bad-tempered; **être d'un ~ gai/facile/joueur** to have a cheerful/an easy-going/a playful nature ou temperament; **avoir un fichu**◑ or **sacré**○ **~** (coléreux) to have a foul temper; (difficile) to be absolutely impossible; **5** (forte personnalité) character; **avoir du ~** to have character; **force de ~** strength of character; **il n'a aucun ~** he's got no backbone, he's spineless; **homme/femme de ~** man/woman of character; **6** (de maison, lieu) character; **avoir du ~** to have character; **sans ~** without character, characterless; **'à vendre, fermette de ~'** 'for sale, small farm with character'; **7** (type humain) character; **une étude de ~s** a study of character types; **8** (marque distinctive) characteristic; **9** (côté, valeur) nature; **le ~ provisoire/anormal/complexe/officiel de qch** the provisional/abnormal/complex/official nature of sth; **la manifestation a un ~ politique** the demonstration is of a political nature; **des articles de ~ scientifique/religieux** articles of a scientific/religious nature; **ma demande n'a aucun ~ définitif/personnel** my request has nothing definite/personal about it; **à ~ commercial/éducatif/expérimental** of a commercial/an educational/an experimental nature; **cela a un ~ grave** it's serious; **film à ~ pornographique** pornographic film.

■ **~ acquis** acquired characteristic; **~ dominant** dominant characteristic; **~ récessif** recessive character.

IDIOMES **avoir un ~ de chien** or **cochon**○, **avoir un sale ~** to have a vile temper; **avoir un ~ en or** to have a delightful nature.

caractériel, **-ielle** /kaʀakteʀjɛl/ **I** *adj* [*troubles*] emotional; [*enfant, adolescent, adulte*] disturbed.

II *nm,f* (enfant) disturbed child; (adulte) disturbed person.

caractérisation /kaʀakteʀizasjɔ̃/ *nf* characterization.

caractérisé, **~e** /kaʀakteʀize/ *adj* **c'est du vol ~** it's a blatant act of theft; **c'est une colite ~e** it's a clear case of colitis.

caractériser /kaʀakteʀize/ [1] **I** *vtr* **1** (être typique de) to characterize, to be characteristic of [*personne, société, genre*]; to characterize, to be a characteristic feature of [*situation, conflit*]; **2** (décrire) to characterize.

II se caractériser *vpr* to be characterized (**par** by).

caractéristique /kaʀakteʀistik/ **I** *adj* characteristic (**de** of).

II *nf* characteristics (*pl*); **quelle est la principale ~ de leur politique?** what are the main characteristics of their policy?

caractérologie /kaʀakteʀɔlɔʒi/ *nf* study of character types.

carafe /kaʀaf/ *nf* **1** (récipient) carafe; **vin en ~** wine by the carafe; **2**○ (tête) nut○, head; **ne rien avoir dans la ~**○ to be brainless, to have nothing upstairs○.

IDIOMES **être** or **rester en ~**○ to be stuck○; **tomber en ~**○ to break down.

carafon /kaʀafɔ̃/ *nm* **1** (récipient) small carafe; **2**○ (tête) nut○, head.

caraïbe /kaʀaib/ *adj* Caribbean.

Caraïbes /kaʀaib/ **I** *nmpl* (peuple) Caribs.

II *nprfpl* **1** ▶ 416 (îles) Caribbean (islands); **aller aux ~** to go to the Caribbean; **sous le soleil des ~** under the Caribbean sun; **2** ▶ 555 (mer) **mer des ~** Caribbean Sea.

carambolage /kaʀɑ̃bɔlaʒ/ *nm* **1** (de voitures) pile-up; **2** (au billard) cannon GB, carom US.

caramboler /kaʀɑ̃bɔle/ [1] **I** *vtr* to collide with [*véhicule*].

II se caramboler *vpr* [*véhicules*] to collide with each other; [*idées*] to clash.

carambouillage /kaʀɑ̃bujaʒ/ *nm*, **carambouille** /kaʀɑ̃buj/ *nf* swindling (*by reselling unpaid-for goods*).

caramel /kaʀamɛl/ *nm* **1** (liquide) caramel; **2** (bonbon) toffee GB, toffy US; **~ mou** ≈ fudge.

caramélisation /kaʀamelizasjɔ̃/ *nf* **1** (transformation) caramelization; **2** (enrobage) coating with caramel.

caraméliser /kaʀamelize/ [1] **I** *vtr* **1** (transformer) to caramelize; **2** (recouvrir) to coat [sth] with caramel.

II *vi* to caramelize.

III se caraméliser *vpr* to caramelize.

carapace /kaʀapas/ *nf* **1** Zool shell, carapace; **2** (protection) **~ de béton** concrete shell; fig armour[GB]; **une ~ d'indifférence/d'égoïsme** a wall of indifference/of selfishness; **3** Tech (en métallurgie) shell mould GB ou mold US.

carapater○: **se carapater** /kaʀapate/ [1] *vpr* to scarper○ GB, to beat it○.

carat /kaʀa/ *nm* **1** Mes carat; **en or 18 ~s** 18-carat gold (*épith*); **2**◑ (an) year; **se payer 50 ~s** to be a good 50 years old.

IDIOMES **dernier ~**◑ at the latest.

Caravage /kaʀavaʒ/ *npr* **le ~** Caravaggio.

caravanage /kaʀavanaʒ/ *nm* caravanning GB, camping (*in a trailer*) US.

caravane /kaʀavan/ *nf* **1** (véhicule) caravan GB, trailer US; **2** (de désert) caravan.

■ **~ publicitaire** publicity cars (*pl*).

IDIOMES **les chiens aboient, la ~ passe** sticks and stones may break my bones (but words will never hurt me).

caravanier, **-ière** /kaʀavanje, ɛʀ/ **I** *adj* [*piste*] caravan (*épith*).

II *nm,f* **1** Tourisme caravanner GB, camper (*in a trailer*) US; **2** (nomade) nomad.

caravaning /kaʀavaniŋ/ *nm* caravanning GB, camping (*in a trailer*) US.

caravansérail /kaʀavɑ̃seʀaj/ *nm* caravanserai.

caravelle /kaʀavɛl/ *nf* Naut caravel.

Caravelle /kaʀavɛl/ *nf* Aviat Caravelle.

carbochimie /kaʀbɔʃimi/ *nf* organic chemistry.

carboglace® /kaʀbɔglas/ *nf* dry ice.

carbonade /kaʀbɔnad/ *nf* Culin (viande grillée) carbonado; (ragoût) carbonade.

carbonate /kaʀbɔnat/ *nm* carbonate; **~ de potassium** potassium carbonate; **~ de sodium** washing soda, sodium carbonate.

carbone /kaʀbɔn/ *nm* **1** Chimie carbon; **2** Imprim (papier) carbon paper; (feuille) sheet of carbon paper.

■ **~ 14** carbon 14; **dater qch au ~ 14** to carbon-date sth; **datation de qch au** or **par ~ 14** (radio)carbon dating sth; **~ blanc** correction paper.

carboné, **~e** /kaʀbɔne/ *adj* carbon (*épith*).

carbonifère /kaʀbɔnifɛʀ/ **I** *adj* **1** (contenant du charbon) [*terrain*] carboniferous; **2** Géol **époque ~** Carboniferous period.

II *nm* Géol **le ~** the Carboniferous period.

carbonique /kaʀbɔnik/ *adj* carbonic; **neige ~** carbon snow; **glace ~** dry ice.

carbonisation /kaʀbɔnizasjɔ̃/ *nf* carbonization.

carbonisé, **~e** /kaʀbɔnize/ **I** *pp* ▶ **carboniser**.

II *pp adj* **1** [*véhicule*] burned-out (*épith*), burned out (*jamais épith*); [*forêt*] charred; [*débris, arbre, corps*] charred; **2** Culin burned to a cinder (*jamais épith*), burned.

carboniser /kaʀbɔnize/ [1] *vtr* **1** Chimie to carbonize; **2** (brûler complètement) to burn [sb] to death [*personne*]; to reduce [sth] to ashes [*forêt, maison, corps*]; to char [*objet, arbre, poutre*]; **les poutres ont été carbonisées par l'incendie** the beams were charred by the fire; **3** Culin to burn [sth] to a cinder.

carburant /kaʀbyʀɑ̃/ **I** *adj m* **mélange ~** mixture of petrol GB ou gas US and air.

II *nm* fuel.

carburateur /kaʀbyʀatœʀ/ *nm* carburettor GB, carburetor US; **régler le ~** to adjust the carburettor GB ou carburetor US.

carburation /kaʀbyʀasjɔ̃/ *nf* **1** Aut carburation; **2** Tech carburization.

carbure /kaʀbyʀ/ *nm* carbide; **les ~s** carbides; **~ d'hydrogène** hydrogen carbide.

carburé, **~e** /kaʀbyʀe/ *adj* carburized.

carburer /kaʀbyʀe/ [1] **I** *vtr* Tech, Ind to carburize.

II *vi* **1** Aut **bien/mal ~** to be well/badly tuned; **2**◑ (fonctionner) **il carbure au vin rouge** hum he runs on red wine; **3**○ (travailler dur) to work flat out; **4**○ (aller) **alors, ça carbure?** how is it going?

carburol /kaʀbyʀɔl/ *nm* Tech gasohol.

carcajou /kaʀkaʒu/ *nm* Zool wolverine, carcajou.

carcan /kaʀkɑ̃/ *nm* **1** (entrave) **~ politique/scolaire/administratif** political/educational/administrative constraints (*pl*) ou straitjacket; **le ~ de la discipline/des institutions** disciplinary/institutional rigidity; **briser le ~ de qch** to break free of sth; **enfermer qn/qch dans le ~ de qch** to place sb/sth under the yoke of sth; **2** (objet qui enserre) vice; **le ~ d'un col empesé** the vice-like grip of a starched collar; **3** Hist (instrument, peine) iron collar.

carcasse /kaʀkas/ *nf* **1** (squelette d'animal) carcass; **une ~ de poulet** a chicken carcass; **2**◑ (corps humain) body; **promener** or **traîner sa ~** to bum around◑; **sauver sa ~** to save one's bacon○; **3**○ (épave de véhicule) shell; **4** (armature) (de navire) skeleton; (de bâtiment, hangar) frame.

carcassonnais, ~e /kaʀkasɔnɛ, ɛz/ ▶857 *adj* of Carcassonne.

Carcassonnais, ~e /kaʀkasɔnɛ, ɛz/ *nm,f* (natif) native of Carcassonne; (habitant) inhabitant of Carcassonne.

Carcassonne /kaʀkasɔn/ ▶857 *npr* Carcassonne.

carcéral, ~e, *mpl* **-aux** /kaʀseʀal, o/ *adj* prison (*épith*); **le milieu ~** the prison environment.

carcinogène /kaʀsinɔʒɛn/ *adj* carcinogenic.

carcinome /kaʀsinom/ *nm* carcinoma.

cardage /kaʀdaʒ/ *nm* carding.

cardamome /kaʀdamɔm/ *nf* cardamom.

cardan /kaʀdɑ̃/ *nm* universal joint.

carde /kaʀd/ *nf* **1** Tech (instrument) card; (machine) carding machine, card; **2** Bot, Culin chard stalk.

carder /kaʀde/ [1] *vtr* to card; **machine à ~** carding machine, card.

cardère /kaʀdɛʀ/ *nf* teasel.

cardeur, -euse /kaʀdœʀ, øz/ ▶510 **I** *nm,f* (ouvrier) carder.

II cardeuse *nf* (machine) carding machine, card.

cardiaque /kaʀdjak/ **I** *adj* **1** (ayant rapport au cœur) heart (*épith*), cardiac spéc; **greffe ~** heart transplant; **avoir des ennuis ~s** to have heart trouble; **2** (malade du cœur) [*personne*] **être ~** to have a heart condition.

II *nmf* person with a heart condition.

cardigan /kaʀdigɑ̃/ *nm* cardigan.

cardinal, ~e, *mpl* **-aux** /kaʀdinal, o/ **I** *adj* Ling, Math, Relig cardinal; **vertu ~e** cardinal virtue; **nombre ~** cardinal number.

II *nm* **1** ▶813 Relig cardinal; **le ~ Newman** Cardinal Newman; **il a été nommé ~** he was made a cardinal; **~ in petto** cardinal 'in petto'; **2** Ling, Math cardinal number; **3** Zool cardinal (grosbeak), redbird US.

cardinalat /kaʀdinala/ *nm* cardinalship.

cardinalice /kaʀdinalis/ *adj* of a cardinal; **conférer la dignité** or **la pourpre ~ à qn** to make sb a cardinal.

cardiogramme /kaʀdjɔgʀam/ *nm* cardiogram.

cardiographe /kaʀdjɔgʀaf/ *nm* cardiograph.

cardiographie /kaʀdjɔgʀafi/ *nf* cardiography.

cardiologie /kaʀdjɔlɔʒi/ *nf* cardiology; **service de ~** cardiology ward; **être en ~** [*patient*] to be in the cardiology ward.

cardiologue /kaʀdjɔlɔg/ ▶510 *nmf* cardiologist.

cardiopathie /kaʀdjopati/ *nf* heart disorder.

cardio-pulmonaire, *pl* **~s** /kaʀdjɔpylmɔnɛʀ/ *adj* cardiopulmonary.

cardio-vasculaire, *pl* **~s** /kaʀdjɔvaskylɛʀ/ *adj* cardiovascular.

cardite /kaʀdit/ ▶271 *nf* Méd carditis.

cardon /kaʀdɔ̃/ *nm* cardoon.

Carélie /kaʀeli/ ▶692 *nprf* Karelia.

carême /kaʀɛm/ *nm* Relig **le ~** Lent; **observer** or **respecter le ~** to observe ou keep Lent; **avoir une face de ~** to look as miserable as sin.

carême-prenant /kaʀɛmpʀənɑ̃/ *nm* Shrovetide.

carénage /kaʀenaʒ/ *nm* **1** Naut careening; **2** Tech streamlining.

carence /kaʀɑ̃s/ *nf* **1** Méd deficiency; **maladie par ~** deficiency disease; **~ en vitamines/fer/calcium** vitamin/iron/calcium deficiency; **2** (absence) lack; **~ d'autorité** lack of authority; **3** (manquement) shortcomings (*pl*); **les ~s de la loi** the shortcomings of the law; **4** Jur insolvency; **procès-verbal de ~** statement of insolvency; **5** Admin **délai de ~** waiting period (*for social security benefit*).

■ **~ affective** Psych emotional deprivation.

carène /kaʀɛn/ *nf* **1** Naut hull (*below the waterline*); **abattre** or **mettre un navire en ~** to careen a vessel; **2** Bot carina.

caréner /kaʀene/ [14] *vtr* **1** Naut to careen; **2** Tech to streamline.

caressant, ~e /kaʀɛsɑ̃, ɑ̃t/ *adj* **1** [*enfant, geste, regard, parole*] affectionate; **2** [*brise, vent, rayon*] soft.

caresse /kaʀɛs/ *nf* (à un animal) stroke; (à une personne) caress, stroke; **couvrir qn de ~s** to caress sb all over; **il aime les ~s** he likes being stroked; **faire une ~** or **des ~s à un enfant** to caress ou stroke a child; **faire une** or **des ~s à un animal** to stroke an animal.

caresser /kaʀese/ [1] **I** *vtr* **1** [*personne*] to stroke [*animal, joue, bras, menton, cheveux, barbe*]; to caress [*amant, maîtresse*]; to finger [*objet*]; **~ qn du regard** or **des yeux** to look at sb lovingly ou fondly; **2** (effleurer) liter [*soleil, vent, air, lumière*] to caress [*joue, cheveux*]; **la mer venait ~ les rochers** the sea was lapping against the rocks; **le vent caressait les blés** the corn was caressed by the wind; **3** (nourrir) to entertain [*rêve, espoir*]; to entertain, to toy with [*idée, projet*]; to flatter [*vanité*]; **il caressait l'espoir de pouvoir retourner dans son pays** he entertained the hope that he would be able to return to his country.

II se caresser *vpr* to stroke; **il se caressa la barbe/le menton/la joue** he stroked his beard/chin/cheek.

IDIOMES **~ qn dans le sens du poil** to stay on the right side of sb; **~ la bouteille** to be on the bottle○; **~ les côtes à qn**○ to give sb a hiding○.

caret /kaʀɛ/ *nm* (tortue) loggerhead (turtle).

car-ferry, *pl* **-ies** /kaʀfɛʀi/ *nm* controv ferry.

cargaison /kaʀgɛzɔ̃/ *nf* **1** Transp (chargement) cargo; **2**○ (grande quantité) load; **une ~ d'enfants**○ a load of children○.

cargo /kaʀgo/ *nm* Naut freighter, cargo boat; **~ mixte** passenger-cargo ship.

cargue /kaʀg/ *nf* Naut brails (*pl*).

carguer /kaʀge/ [1] *vtr* to brail in.

cari /kaʀi/ *nm* = **curry**.

cariatide /kaʀjatid/ *nf* caryatid.

caribou /kaʀibu/ *nm* caribou.

caricatural, ~e, *mpl* **-aux** /kaʀikatyʀal, o/ *adj* **1** [*dessin, portrait, masque*] (deliberately) grotesque; **2** [*récit, numéro*] caricatural.

caricature /kaʀikatyʀ/ *nf* **1** (genre) caricature; **2** (dessin) (d'une personne) caricature; (de plusieurs personnes, de situation) cartoon; **dessiner** or **faire une ~** to draw a caricature ou cartoon; **3** (représentation déformée) caricature; **c'est une ~ de la réalité** it's a caricature of reality; **dans ses romans il fait une ~ de la société** his novels caricature society; **4** (parodie) mockery; **c'est une ~ de procès** it's a mockery of a trial.

caricaturer /kaʀikatyʀe/ [1] *vtr* to caricature.

caricaturiste /kaʀikatyʀist/ ▶510 *nmf* caricaturist, cartoonist.

carie /kaʀi/ *nf* **1** (lésion) decay ₵, caries spéc; (trou) cavity; **avoir une ~** to have a cavity, to have a decayed tooth; **j'ai une ~ à une dent** one of my teeth is decayed; **faire soigner une ~** to have a cavity treated ou a decayed tooth treated; **2** Bot (de blé, vigne) blight; (d'arbre) (dry) rot.

carié, ~e /kaʀje/ **I** *pp* ▶ **carier**.

II *pp adj* decayed.

carier /kaʀje/ [2] Dent **I** *vtr* to cause [sth] to decay [*dent*].

II se carier *vpr* [*dent*] to decay.

carillon /kaʀijɔ̃/ *nm* **1** (d'église, de beffroi) (cloches) bells (*pl*); (sonnerie) chimes (*pl*); **le ~ de Notre-Dame a retenti dans toute la ville** the bells of Notre Dame rang out throughout the town; **2** (pendule) (chiming) clock; (sonnerie) chimes (*pl*); **une horloge à ~** a chiming clock; **le ~ sonna neuf heures** the clock struck nine; **le ~ sonne toutes les heures** the clock chimes on the hour; **3** (de porte) (door) chimes (*pl*).

carillonner /kaʀijɔne/ [1] **I** *vtr* **1** [*cloches*] to chime [*minuit, heure*]; to chime (out) [*air*]; to ring ou peal out for [*événement, naissance, fête*]; **~ les heures** to chime the hours; **2**○ (faire savoir) to broadcast [*nouvelle, victoire, succès*].

II *vi* **1** [*cloches*] to ring out; (très fort) to peal out; **2** (à une porte) to ring (loudly); **~ à la porte/chez qn** to ring loudly at the door/at sb's door.

carillonneur /kaʀijɔnœʀ/ *nm* bell-ringer.

cariste /kaʀist/ ▶510 *nmf* forklift truck operator.

caritatif, -ive /kaʀitatif, iv/ *adj* [*action*] charitable; **une association** or **organisation caritative** a charity.

carlin /kaʀlɛ̃/ *nm* pug (dog).

carlingue /kaʀlɛ̃g/ *nf* **1** Aviat cabin; **2** Naut keelson.

carliste /kaʀlist/ *adj, nmf* Hist, Pol Carlist.

carmagnole /kaʀmaɲɔl/ *nf* Hist carmagnole.

carme /kaʀm/ *nm* Carmelite, white friar.

carmel /kaʀmɛl/ *nm* (de carmes) Carmelite monastery; (de carmélites) Carmelite convent.

Carmel /kaʀmɛl/ *nprm* **1** Géog **le (mont) ~** Mount Carmel; **2** Relig (ordre) **le Carmel** the Carmelite order.

carmélite /kaʀmelit/ *nf* Carmelite nun.

carmin /kaʀmɛ̃/ ▶193 **I** *adj inv* carmine; **rouge ~** carmine red.

II *nm* **1** (matière) cochineal; **2** (couleur) carmine.

carminé, ~e /kaʀmine/ ▶193 *adj* carmine.

carnage /kaʀnaʒ/ *nm* carnage ₵, massacre; **ils ont fait un véritable ~** they massacred everyone.

carnassier, -ière /kaʀnasje, ɛʀ/ **I** *adj* carnivorous; **un sourire ~** fig a ferocious smile.

II *nm* carnivore.

III carnassière *nf* **1** Dent carnassial; **2** (gibecière) game bag.

carnation /kaʀnasjɔ̃/ *nf* complexion; **être de ~ délicate** to have a delicate complexion.

carnaval, *pl* **~s** /kaʀnaval/ *nm* **1** (fête) carnival; **jour du ~** carnival day; **masque/char de ~** carnival mask/float; **le ~ de Venise/Rio** the Venice/Rio carnival; **2** (mannequin) (**sa majesté**) **~** King Carnival.

carnavalesque /kaʀnavalɛsk/ *adj* **1** (grotesque) grotesque; **2** (de carnaval) carnival (*épith*).

carne◑ /kaʀn/ *nf* **1** (viande) leathery meat; **cette viande, c'est de la ~** this meat is leathery; **2** (cheval) nag○; **3** (personne) swine◑.

carné, ~e /kaʀne/ *adj* **1** [*régime, alimentation*] meat-based (*épith*); **2** ▶193 (couleur) flesh-coloured[GB].

carnet /kaʀnɛ/ *nm* **1** (calepin) notebook; **publier les ~s d'un écrivain** to publish a writer's notebooks; **2** (groupe de tickets, bons) book; **un ~ de tickets** a book of tickets; **j'achète mes timbres en ~** I always buy a book of stamps.

■ **~ d'adresses** address book; **~ de bal** dance card; **~ de bord** Naut log book; Aut, Sport record book; **~ de chèques** chequebook GB, checkbook US; **~ de commandes** (registre) order book; **notre ~ de commandes s'élève à 40 millions** de francs our orders amount to 40 million francs; ~ de correspondance Scol mark book; ~ du jour Presse 'births, marriages and deaths'; ~ de maternité ≈ maternity records (*pl*); ~ mondain Presse = ~ du jour; ~ de notes = ~ de correspondance; ~ de rendez-vous appointments diary; ~ de route travel journal; ~ de santé health record; ~ à souches counterfoil book; ~ de timbres book of stamps.

carnier /kaʀnje/ *nm* game bag.

carnivore /kaʀnivɔʀ/ I *adj* **1** Zool [*animal, plante*] carnivorous; **2** (qui aime la viande) **être ~** to be a great meat-eater.
II *nm* carnivore; **les ~s** the carnivores, Carnivora spéc.

carnotzet /kaʀnɔtzɛ/ *nm* H (bar) little bar.

Caroline /kaʀɔlin/ I *npr* (prénom) Caroline.
II ▶692 *nprf* Géog **la ~ du Nord/du Sud** North/South Carolina.
III ▶416 **Carolines** *nprfpl* **les (îles) ~s** the Caroline Islands.

carolingien, -ienne /kaʀɔlɛ̃ʒjɛ̃, ɛn/ *adj* Carolingian.

Carolingien, -ienne /kaʀɔlɛ̃ʒjɛ̃, ɛn/ *nm,f* Carolingian.

caroncule /kaʀɔ̃kyl/ *nf* Zool wattle.

carotène /kaʀɔtɛn/ *nf* carotene.

carotide /kaʀɔtid/ *adj, nf* carotid.

carottage /kaʀɔtaʒ/ *nm* Tech core sampling.

carotte /kaʀɔt/ I ▶193 *adj inv* **1** (orange foncé) carrot-coloured[GB]; **2** (roux) [*cheveux, poils*] carroty.
II *nf* **1** Bot, Culin carrot; **manger des ~s** to eat carrots; **~s râpées** grated carrot ¢; **2** Sci, Tech (échantillon) core sample; **prélever une ~** to take a core sample; **3** (enseigne) *tobacconist's street sign*.
IDIOMES **les ~s sont cuites**○ the game is up○; **manier la ~ et le bâton** to use stick-and-carrot tactics.

carotter /kaʀɔte/ [1] *vtr* **1**○ (extorquer) **~ qch à qn** to cheat sb out of sth; **elle m'a carotté 10 francs** she cheated me out of 10 francs; **je me suis encore fait ~** I've been cheated again; **2** Tech to take a core sample (from).

caroube /kaʀub/ *nf* carob.

caroubier /kaʀubje/ *nm* carob tree.

Carpates /kaʀpat/ ▶692 *nprfpl* **les ~** the Carpathians.

carpe /kaʀp/ I *nm* Anat carpus.
II *nf* Zool carp.
IDIOMES **il est resté muet comme une ~** he never said a word; **faire des sauts de ~** to leap about.

carpeau, *pl* **~x** /kaʀpo/ *nm* young carp.

carpette /kaʀpɛt/ *nf* **1** (paillasson) rug; **2**○ (personne) pej doormat○.
IDIOMES **s'aplatir comme une ~ devant qn** to grovel to sb.

carpien, -ienne /kaʀpjɛ̃, ɛn/ *adj* carpal.

carpillon /kaʀpijɔ̃/ *nm* young carp.

carquois /kaʀkwa/ *nm* quiver.

carrare /kaʀaʀ/ *nm* Carrara marble.

carre /kaʀ/ *nf* (de ski, patin) edge.

carré, ~e /kaʀe/ I *adj* **1** gén [*objet, forme*] square; **des chaussures à bout ~** square-toed shoes; **2** (anguleux) [*visage, menton, front, paume*] square; [*silhouette*] stocky; **il est ~ d'épaules** he has broad shoulders, he's broad-shouldered; **3** (direct) [*personne*] straightforward; [*réponse*] straight; [*refus*] outright; **elle est ~e en affaires** she's straight in her business dealings; **4** ▶783 Math, Mes [*mètre, kilomètre, racine*] square; **prix du** or **au mètre ~** price per square metre[GB].
II *nm* **1** (figure) gén square; (de ciel, plantations) patch; (de chocolat) piece; **avoir une coupe au ~** [*femme*] to have one's hair cut in a bob; **je vais lui faire une** or **lui mettre la tête au ~**○ I'll beat the hell out of him/her○; **un lit (fait) au ~** a meticulously made bed; **2** Math square; **le ~ de l'hypoténuse** the square of the length of the hypotenuse; **élever un nombre au ~** to square a number; **le ~ de deux** two squared; **deux au ~ égale quatre** two squared is four; **3** Culin **~ d'agneau** rack of lamb; **4** Mil square; **former le** or **se former en ~** to form up in a square; **5** Naut wardroom; **6** Jeux (au poker) **avoir un ~ de dix/d'as** to have the four tens/aces; **7** C (place) square.
III **carrée**○ *nf* bedroom.
■ **~ blanc** *'suitable for adults only' sign on French TV*; **~ magique** magic square.

carreau, *pl* **~x** /kaʀo/ I *nm* **1** (de sol) (floor) tile; (de mur) (wall) tile; **2** (carrelage) tiled floor; **glisser sur le ~** to slip on the tiles; **3** (vitre) window-pane; **à petits ~x** with small panes; **faire les ~x** to clean the windows; **regarder à travers les ~x** to look out of the window; **4** (carré) (sur du papier) square; (sur du tissu) check; **papier à ~x** squared paper; **tissu/jupe à ~x** check(ed) fabric/skirt; **à ~x bleus et blancs** blue-and-white checked (*épith*); **papier à grands/petits ~x** large-/small-squared paper; **tissu à grands/petits ~x** fabric in large/small check; **5** ▶449 Jeux (carte) diamonds (*pl*); **sept/valet de ~** seven/jack of diamonds; **jouer ~** to play diamonds; **avoir du ~** to be holding diamonds; **6** Hist (marché) market (floor); **7** Mines pithead; **8** (pour broder) lacemaker's pillow; **9** (d'arbalète) bolt.
II **carreaux**○ *nmpl* (lunettes) specs○.
■ **~ de plâtre** plasterboard.
IDIOMES **étendre qn sur le ~**○ to lay sb out○, to floor sb○; **rester sur le ~**○ (dans une bagarre) to be killed; (dans une affaire) to be left high and dry○; (à un examen) to fail; **se tenir à ~**○ to watch one's step.

carrefour /kaʀfuʀ/ *nm* **1** (intersection) gén junction, intersection; (de deux routes) crossroads (*sg*); **~ ferroviaire** railway junction ou intersection; **un ~ dangereux** a dangerous crossroads; **2** (lieu de passage) crossroads (+ *v sg*); (réseau de communications) transport hub; **l'aéroport est un ~ international** the airport is an international meeting point; **une région ~** a transport hub, a centre[GB] of communications; **3** (moment stratégique) crossroads (*sg*); **être à un ~ de qch** to be at a crossroads in sth; **être à un ~ de sa vie** to be at a crossroads in one's life; **la biochimie est au ~ de la biologie et de la chimie** biochemistry is at the meeting point of biology and chemistry; **4** (forum) debate; **assister à un ~ de l'écologie** to attend a debate on ecology.
■ **~ à sens giratoire** roundabout GB, traffic circle US.

carrelage /kaʀlaʒ/ *nm* **1** (sol) tiled floor; **poser un ~** to lay a tiled floor; **le ~ est propre** the floor is clean; **2** (ensemble de carreaux) tiles (*pl*); (pose) tiling.

carreler /kaʀle/ [19] *vtr* to tile; **faire ~ une pièce** to have a room tiled.

carrelet /kaʀlɛ/ *nm* (poisson) plaice.

carreleur /kaʀlœʀ/ ▶510 *nm* tiler.

carrément /kaʀemɑ̃/ *adv* **1** (purement et simplement) [*malhonnête, stupide, désastreux, exotique*] downright; **la situation devient ~ inquiétante** the situation is becoming downright worrying; **ce n'est plus de la prudence, c'est ~ de la lâcheté** it's no longer a question of being cautious, it's downright cowardice; **il vaut ~ mieux les jeter/changer le moteur** it would be better just to throw them out/to change the engine; **2** (complètement) completely; **changer ~ de nom** to change name completely; **on est ~ dans le brouillard** we're completely in the dark; **c'est ~ un désastre/le cauchemar** it's a complete disaster/nightmare; **certaines entreprises ont ~ été exonérées** some companies have been totally exempted; **ils ont ~ engagé des tueurs** they have even hired assassins; **il faudrait ~ louer une camionnette** we should really hire a van; **dans un cas pareil, appelle ~ la police** in such a case, don't hesitate to call the police; **reprenons ~ depuis le début** let's start again right from the beginning; **les réformes ne suffiront pas, il faut ~ changer le système** the reforms will not be enough, it's the system that needs changing; **3** (sans ambages) [*demander, dire*] straight out; [*exprimer*] clearly, in no uncertain terms; **elle m'a ~ accusé de mentir** she accused me straight out of lying; **4** (sans hésiter) **allez-y ~!** go straight ahead!, go for it○!; **il a ~ démissionné** he went straight ahead and resigned; **faute de pouvoir payer son loyer, il a ~ installé un lit de camp dans son bureau** since he was unable to pay the rent, he went and set up a camp bed in his office; **le pétrolier a ~ vidé ses cuves dans le port** the tanker emptied its tanks right in the harbour[GB].

carrer: se carrer /kaʀe/ [1] *vpr* **1** (s'installer) **se ~ dans un fauteuil** to ensconce oneself in an armchair; **2**◑ (se mettre) **ton argent, tu peux te le ~ où je pense!** you know what you can do with your money◑!

carrier /kaʀje/ ▶510 *nm* (ouvrier) quarryman; (entrepreneur) quarry manager.

carrière /kaʀjɛʀ/ *nf* **1** (profession) career; **~ politique/commerciale** political/business career; **une ~ d'écrivain** a career as a writer; **évolution** or **déroulement de ~** career development; **plan/perspectives de ~** career plan/prospects; **en début/fin de ~** at the start/end of one's career; **militaire/officier de ~** career soldier/officer; **combien gagne un professeur en fin de ~?** what would be a teacher's pre-retirement salary?; **faire ~** to make a career; **faire ~ dans l'enseignement/l'armée** to make a career in teaching/the army; **faire toute sa ~ dans qch** to spend one's whole career in sth; **2** (lieu d'extraction) quarry; **~ d'ardoise/de marbre** slate/marble quarry; **~ de sable** sandpit; **3** Équit outdoor arena.

carriérisme /kaʀjeʀism/ *nm* pej careerism.

carriériste /kaʀjeʀist/ *nm,f* pej careerist.

carriole /kaʀjɔl/ *nf* **1** (charrette) cart; **2**○ (voiture) pej jalopy○, car.

carrossable /kaʀɔsabl/ *adj* suitable for motor vehicles (*après n*).

carrosse /kaʀɔs/ *nm* (horse-drawn) coach; ▶**roue**.
IDIOMES **rouler ~** to live in style.

carrossé, ~e /kaʀɔse/ I *pp* ▶**carrosser**.
II *pp adj* (dessiné) designed; **une voiture superbement ~e** a superbly designed car.

carrosserie /kaʀɔsʀi/ *nf* **1** (de voiture) bodywork; **2** Ind (conception) coachbuilding; (réparation) body repair work; **atelier de ~** body repair workshop; **3** (d'électroménager) casing.

carrossier /kaʀɔsje/ ▶510 *nm* **1** (réparateur) coachbuilder, body repair specialist; **2** (concepteur) coachbuilder.

carrousel /kaʀuzɛl/ *nm* **1** Équit carousel; **2** (pour enfants) merry-go-round, carousel; **3** (pour diapositives) carousel.

carrure /kaʀyʀ/ *nf* **1** lit shoulders (*pl*); **avoir une ~ imposante** to have broad shoulders; **tu as vu sa ~?** have you seen how broad his/her shoulders are?; **une ~ de lutteur** a wrestler's shoulders; **2** fig innate qualities (*pl*), calibre[GB]; **avoir la ~ d'un président/champion** to have the necessary qualities to be a president/champion; **il n'a pas la ~ pour diriger l'entreprise** he hasn't got the necessary qualities to run the company.

carry /kaʀi/ *nm* = **curry**.

cartable /kaʀtabl/ *nm* (d'écolier) schoolbag; (avec des bretelles) satchel; (d'adulte) briefcase.

carte /kaʀt/ *nf* **1** (pour écrire) card; **2** (document) gén card; (laissez-passer) pass; **3** ▶449 Jeux card; **~ à jouer** playing card; **jouer aux ~s** to play cards; **mettre ~s sur table** fig to put one's cards on the table; **jouer la ~ de qn** (soutenir) to choose to support sb; (pour obtenir un soutien) to seek the support of sb; **jouer la ~ de la franchise/du dialogue** to opt for sincerity/dialogue; **jouer la ~ de l'Europe** to turn toward(s) Europe; **il possède plus d'une ~ dans son jeu** he's got other cards up his sleeve; **4** Géog map; Astron, Météo, Naut chart; **~ de la Corse** map of Corsica; **~ marine/du ciel** sea/astronomical chart; **5** Biol **~ génétique** genetic map; **6** (au restaurant) menu; **excellente ~** excellent range of (à la carte) dishes; **prendre la ~**, **manger à la ~** to eat à la carte, to order from the menu; **repas à la ~** à la carte meal; **horaire/programme à la ~** fig personalized timetable/programme[GB]; **activités sportives à la ~** choice of sporting activities.

■ **~ d'abonnement** Rail season ticket; **~ d'accès à bord** Aviat boarding pass; **~ d'adhérent** membership card; **~ d'alimentation** ration card; **~ d'ancien combattant** *card issued to war veterans, affording some privileges*; **~ d'anniversaire** birthday card; **~ d'assuré social** ≈ national insurance card; **~ bancaire** bank card; **~ bleue**® credit card; **~ de chemin de fer** season ou commutation US ticket; **~ de correspondance** plain postcard; **~ couple**® *card giving 50% off to second traveller*[GB]; **~ de crédit** credit card; **~ d'électeur** polling card GB, voter registration card US; **~ électronique de stationnement** electronic parking card; **~ d'état-major** Ordnance Survey map GB, Geological Survey map US; **~ d'étudiant** student card, student ID card; **~ de famille nombreuse** *card issued to families with three or more children, entitling them to reductions*; **~ de fidélité** discount card; **~ grise** car registration document ou papers US; **~ d'identité** identity card, ID card; **~ d'identité scolaire** pupil's identity ou ID card; **~ d'immatriculation** registration card; **~ d'immatriculation consulaire** *card issued by the consulate to French nationals living abroad*; **~ Interail** Interail card; **~ d'invalidité** disabled persons' card; **~ jeunes**® (young persons') railcard; Comm (young people's) discount card; **~ kiwi**® ≈ family railcard; **~ de lecteur** library card, reader's ticket GB; **~ magnétique** gén magnetic card; (pour ouvrir une porte) swipe card; **~ maîtresse** lit master card; fig trump card; **~ de membre** membership card; **~ à mémoire** smart card ; **~ à microprocesseur** smart card; **~ nationale d'identité** Admin identity card; **~ de Noël** Christmas card; **~ orange**® season ticket (*in the Paris region*); **~ de paiement** direct debit card; **~ perforée** punch card; **~ postale** postcard; **~ de presse** press pass; **~ privative** store card; **~ professionnelle** identity card (*showing occupation*); **~ à puce** smart card; **~ de rationnement** ration card; **~ de réduction** discount card; **~ routière** roadmap; **~ scolaire** *distribution of the state-run schools in an area*; **~ de sécurité sociale** = **~ d'assuré social**; **~ de séjour** resident's permit; **~ syndicale** union card; **~ de téléphone** phonecard; **~ vermeil**® senior citizen's rail pass; **~ verte**® Assur, Aut green card GB, ≈ certificate of motor insurance; **~ des vins** wine list; **~ de visite** gén visiting ou calling card; Comm, Entr business card; **~ de vœux** greetings card.

IDIOMES **avoir ~ blanche** to have carte blanche ou a free hand; **donner ~ blanche à qn** to give sb carte blanche ou a free hand.

cartel /kaʀtɛl/ *nm* **1** Écon cartel; **le ~ pétrolier/chimique** the oil/chemicals cartel; **les ~s de la drogue** the drug cartels; **2** Pol coalition; **3** (pendule) wall clock.

carte-lettre, *pl* **cartes-lettres** /kaʀtə lɛtʀ/ *nf* letter-card.

cartellisation /kaʀtelizasjɔ̃/ *nf* cartelization.

carter /kaʀtɛʀ/ *nm* **1** Aut (de moteur) crankcase; (de boîte de vitesses) casing; **2** Mécan gén case; (de vélo) chain guard.

carte-réponse, *pl* **cartes-réponses** /kaʀtʀepɔ̃s/ *nf* reply card.

carterie® /kaʀtəʀi/ ▶**510** *nf* card shop.

cartésianisme /kaʀtezjanism/ *nm* Cartesianism.

cartésien, **-ienne** /kaʀtezjɛ̃, ɛn/ *adj, nm,f* Cartesian.

Carthage /kaʀtaʒ/ ▶**857** *npr* Carthage.

carthaginois, **-oise** /kaʀtaʒinwa, az/ *adj* Carthaginian.

Carthaginois, **~e** /kaʀtaʒinwa, az/ *nm,f* Carthaginian.

cartilage /kaʀtilaʒ/ *nm* **1** Anat, Zool cartilage; **2** Culin gristle.

cartilagineux, **-euse** /kaʀtilaʒinø, øz/ *adj* **1** Anat, Zool cartilaginous; **2** Culin gristly.

cartographe /kaʀtɔgʀaf/ ▶**510** *nmf* cartographer.

cartographie /kaʀtɔgʀafi/ *nf* cartography; **~ du génome humain** genetic mapping.

cartographique /kaʀtɔgʀafik/ *adj* cartographic.

cartomancie /kaʀtɔmɑ̃si/ *nf* fortune-telling, cartomancy spéc.

cartomancien, **-ienne** /kaʀtɔmɑ̃sjɛ̃, ɛn/ ▶**510** *nm,f* fortune-teller, cartomancer spéc.

carton /kaʀtɔ̃/ *nm* **1** (matière) cardboard; **de** or **en ~** cardboard (*épith*); **2** (boîte) (cardboard) box; **un ~ de jouets** a box ou boxful of toys; **c'est resté dans les ~s** lit it's still in the box; fig it didn't get past the drawing-board; **ressortir des ~s** lit to be brought out again; fig to be dusted off; **3** (carte) card; **4** Art (modèle) cartoon; **~ de tapisserie** tapestry cartoon; **5** (cible) target.

■ **~ à chapeau** hatbox; **~ à dessin** portfolio; **~ goudronné** roofing felt; **~ d'invitation** invitation card; **~ jaune** Sport yellow card; **~ ondulé** corrugated cardboard; **~ rouge** Sport red card.

IDIOMES **faire un ~**○ (remporter un succès) to do great○; (tirer sur une cible) to shoot at a target; **battre** or **taper le ~**○ to play cards; **prendre** or **ramasser un ~**○ to get a licking○.

cartonnage /kaʀtɔnaʒ/ *nm* **1** (emballage) cardboard packaging; (boîtes) cardboard boxes (*pl*); **2** Ind cardboard industry; **3** (reliure) hard cover.

cartonné, **~e** /kaʀtɔne/ **I** *pp* ▶ **cartonner**.

II *pp adj* **boîte ~e** cardboard box; **cahier ~** hardback notebook; **couverture ~e** (de livre) case-cover; **livre ~** hardback.

cartonner /kaʀtɔne/ [1] **I** *vtr* **1** Imprim to bind; **2**○ to get one over [*adversaire*], to score a point over [*adversaire*].

II○ *vi* **1** (marquer) to score; **2** (jouer aux cartes) to be a keen card player.

cartonnerie /kaʀtɔnʀi/ *nf* **1** (usine) cardboard factory; **2** (secteur) cardboard manufacturing industry.

cartonnier, **-ière** /kaʀtɔnje, ɛʀ/ *nm,f* Art creator of cartoons (*for stained glass etc*).

carton-pâte /kaʀtɔ̃pɑt/ *nm inv* pasteboard; **en** or **de ~** lit pasteboard (épith); fig cardboard (épith).

cartouche /kaʀtuʃ/ **I** *nm* **1** (sur plan) title block; (sur une carte) legend, cartouche spéc; **2** Archéol cartouche.

II *nf* **1** Mil, Chasse cartridge; **2** (recharge) (de stylo plume, d'imprimante) cartridge; (de gaz) refill; **une ~ d'encre** an ink cartridge; **3** (emballage) **~ de cigarettes** carton of cigarettes; **4** Ordinat cartridge.

■ **~ à blanc** Mil blank cartridge.

IDIOMES **brûler ses dernières ~s** to play one's last cards.

cartoucherie /kaʀtuʃʀi/ *nf* cartridge factory.

cartouchière /kaʀtuʃjɛʀ/ *nf* cartridge belt.

carvi /kaʀvi/ *nm* caraway.

caryatide /kaʀjatid/ *nf* caryatid.

caryotype /kaʀjotip/ *nm* karyotype.

cas /kɑ/ **I** *nm inv* **1** (circonstance) case; **dans ce ~** in that case; **dans certains ~** in certain cases; **en pareil ~** in such a case; **auquel ~** in which case; **dans le premier/second ~** in the first/second case; **dans les deux ~** either way, one way or the other, in both cases; **dans tous les ~** in every case; **dans** or **en ce ~(-là)** in that case; **c'est le ~** it is the case; **ce n'est pas le ~** it is not the case; **si tel était le ~**, **si c'était le ~** if that was the case; **au ~ où il viendrait/déciderait** in case he comes/decides; **prends ta voiture, au ~ où** take your car, just in case; **en ~ de panne** in case of breakdown; **en ~ d'urgence** in case of emergency; **en ~ de besoin** if necessary, if need be; **en ~ de décès/d'invalidité/d'accident** in the event of death/of disability/of an accident; **en ~ d'incendie, brisez la glace** in the event of a fire, break the glass; **nous faisons 10% ou 20% de remise, selon le(s) ~** we give a discount of 10% or 20%, as the case may be; **savoir être sévère ou pas selon les ~** to know how to be strict or not, as circumstances dictate; **ne pas déranger sauf pour un ~ grave** do not disturb except in an emergency; **si le ~ se présente** if the case arises; **le ~ ne s'était jamais présenté** the case had never arisen; **le ~ échéant** if need be; **dans le ~ contraire, vous devrez**... should the opposite occur, you will have to...; **dans le meilleur/pire des ~** at best/worst; **c'est un ~ à envisager** it's a possibility we should bear in mind; **en aucun ~** on no account; **ton chagrin ne peut en aucun ~ justifier ta conduite** your grief in no way justifies your behaviour; **n'abusez en aucun ~ des excitants** under no circumstances ou on no account should you take excessive amounts of stimulants; **elle ne veut en aucun ~ quitter son domicile** she doesn't want to ou won't leave her home under any circumstances; **cet argent ne doit en aucun ~ être dépensé pour autre chose** under no circumstances ou on no account should this money be spent on anything else; **il ne s'agit en aucun ~ de tout recommencer** starting all over again is out of the question; **c'est le ~ de le dire!** you can say that again!; **2** (situation particulière) case; **dans mon/ton ~** in my/your case; **étudier le ~ de qn** to look into sb's case; **le ~ de Sophie est spécial** Sophie's is a special case; **au ~ par ~** case by case; **traiter/négocier** qch **au ~ par ~** to deal with/negotiate sth case by case; **être dans le même ~ que qn** to be in the same position as sb; **n'aggrave pas ton ~** don't make things worse for yourself; **3** (occurrence) case; **plusieurs ~ de rage/rubéole** several cases of rabies/German measles; **un ~ rare** a rare occurrence; **c'est vraiment un ~ ta sœur!** hum your sister is a real case○!; **plusieurs ~ de suicide** several cases of suicide; **4** (en grammaire) case; **5** (cause) **c'est un ~ de renvoi** it's grounds for dismissal.

II en tout cas, **en tous les cas** *loc adv* **1** (assurément) in any case, at any rate; **ce n'est pas moi en tout ~** it's not me at any rate; **2** (du moins) at least; **en tout ~ pas pour l'instant** at least not at the moment.

■ **~ de conscience** moral dilemma; **cela me pose un ~ de conscience** it presents me with a moral dilemma; **~ d'école** textbook case; **~ d'espèce** special case; **~ de figure** scenario; **il y a plusieurs ~ de figure** there are several possible scenarios; **~ de force majeure** case of force majeure ou vis major; **~ de guerre** cause for war; **~ limite** borderline case; **~ social** socially disadvantaged person; **~ type** typical case.

IDIOMES **il a fait grand ~ de son avance-**

ment he made a big thing of his promotion; **elle n'a fait aucun ~ de mon avancement** she didn't attach much importance to my promotion.

Casablanca /kazablɑ̃ka/ ▶**857** *npr* Casablanca.

casanier, **-ière** /kazanje, ɛʀ/ **I** *adj* [*personne*] stay-at-home (*épith*); [*existence*] unadventurous; **il est très ~** he's a real stay-at-home ou homebody US.
II *nm,f* stay-at-home, homebody US.

casaque /kazak/ *nf* **1** Turf jersey, silk; **le numéro 10, ~ verte** number 10, green jersey ou silk; **2** Pol (étiquette) label.
IDIOMES **tourner ~** to do a U-turn.

casbah /kazba/ *nf* **1** (citadelle, quartier) kasbah; **2**○ (maison) pad○, house.

cascabelle /kaskabɛl/ *nf* Zool rattle.

cascade /kaskad/ *nf* **1** (chute d'eau) waterfall; **2** Cin stunt; **une ~ de voitures** a car stunt; **3** (succession précipitée) (de rires, d'applaudissements) stream (**de** of); (d'incidents, de réactions) series (+ *v sg*) (**de** of); **une ~ de dévaluations** a series of devaluations; **un rire en ~** peals (*pl*) of laughter; **ses cheveux tombaient en ~ sur ses épaules** liter his/her hair cascaded over her shoulders; **crises/conflits/démissions en ~** series of crises/conflicts/resignations.

cascadeur, **-euse** /kaskadœʀ, øz/ *nm,f* ▶**510** stuntman/stuntwoman.

case /kɑz/ *nf* **1** (maison) hut, cabin; **2** (de damier, monopoly®) square; **sauter une ~** to jump a square; **reculer d'une ~** lit to move ou go back a square; fig to move backward(s); **3** (sur un formulaire, un test) box; **une lettre par ~** one letter per box; **cochez la ~ correspondante** tick the appropriate box; **4** (de boîte, tiroir) compartment.
■ **~ départ** lit start; fig square one; **retour à la ~ départ** back to square one; **repasser par la ~ départ** to pass go; **~ horaire** TV time slot; **~ postale** C, H PO Box.
IDIOMES **il lui manque une ~**○, **il a une ~ en moins**○ he's got a screw loose○.

caséeux, **-éeuse** /kaʒeø, øz/ *adj* caseous.

caséine /kazein/ *nf* casein.

casemate /kazmat/ *nf* (abri) bunker; (ouvrage fortifié) pillbox.

caser○ /kɑze/ [1] **I** *vtr* **1** (placer) to put, to stick○ (**dans** in; **sur** on; **sous** under); **où puis-je ~ mes affaires?** where can I put my things?; **je n'ai pas de place pour ~ mes jambes** I haven't got any leg room; **tu as réussi à ~ ton expression favorite!** you've managed to slip in your favourite[GB] expression!; **2** (marier) [*parents*] to marry off [*enfant*]; **ils aimeraient bien ~ leur fils** they would like to marry off their son; **3** (loger) to put [sb] up; **où vas-tu les ~?** where are you going to put them up?; **4** (trouver un emploi pour) to find a place for; **~ un protégé au service des ventes** to find a place for a protégé in the sales department.
II se caser *vpr* to tie the knot○, to get married; **elle a 29 ans et n'est toujours pas casée!** she's 29 and she still hasn't tied the knot!

caserne /kazɛʀn/ *nf* Mil barracks; **regagner sa ~** to get back to barracks.
■ **~ de gendarmerie** police quarters (*pl*); **~ de sapeurs-pompiers** fire station.

casernement /kazɛʀnəmɑ̃/ *nm* **1** Mil (caserne) barracks; **2** (action de caserner) quartering in barracks.

caserner /kazɛʀne/ [1] *vtr* to quarter [sb] in barracks.

casernier /kazɛʀnje/ *nm* barrack quartermaster.

cash○ /kaʃ/ *adv* cash; **payer ~** to pay cash.

casher /kaʃɛʀ/ *adj inv* kosher.

cash-flow, *pl* **~s** /kaʃflo/ *nm* controv cash flow.

casier /kɑzje/ *nm* **1** (meuble) **~ (de rangement)** rack; **~ à bouteilles/légumes/chaussures** bottle/vegetable/shoe rack; **2** (pour le courrier) pigeonhole; **j'ai mis la lettre dans ton ~** I've put the letter in your pigeonhole; **3** Pêche pot; **~ à langoustes** lobster pot.
■ **~ fiscal** Jur tax record; **~ judiciaire** Jur police record; **avoir un ~** to have a (police) record; **mon ~ judiciaire est vierge** I don't have a police record.

casino /kazino/ *nm* casino.

casoar /kazɔaʀ/ *nm* **1** Zool cassowary; **2** (plumet) plume.

Caspienne /kaspjɛn/ ▶**555** *nprf* **la (mer) ~** the Caspian Sea.

casque /kask/ *nm* **1** (de motard, pilote) crash helmet; (de cycliste) cycle helmet; (pour les sports dangereux, les chantiers) **~ de protection** hard hat, safety helmet; **le port du ~ est obligatoire** crash ou safety helmets must be worn; **2** Mil helmet; **3** Audio, Mus headphones (*pl*); **4** Cosmét (sèche-cheveux) hairdrier GB, hairdryer US; **être sous le ~** to be under the drier GB ou dryer US; **5** Zool, Bot helmet.
■ **~ antibruit** ear protectors (*pl*); **~ colonial** pith helmet; **~ de chantier** safety helmet, hard hat; **~ intégral** Sport full-face crash helmet; **~ de pompier** fireman's helmet; **~ de tranchée** Mil tin hat○; **Casque bleu** Blue Helmet, Blue Beret.

casqué, **~e** /kaske/ **I** *pp* ▶ **casquer**.
II *pp adj* [*policier, soldat, motocycliste*] helmeted; (**être**) **botté et ~** (to be) wearing boots and a helmet.

casquer○ /kaske/ [1] *vi* **1** (payer la note) to foot the bill; **2** (être puni) to carry the can○ GB, to take the rap○.

casquette /kaskɛt/ *nf* **1** Mode (peaked) cap; **~ de base-ball/cuir** base-ball/leather cap; **~ de contrôleur** ticket collector's cap; **2** (fonction) hat; (étiquette) label; **porter plusieurs ~s** to wear several hats.

cassable /kasabl/ *adj* **1** gén breakable; **2** Jur liable to annulment.

Cassandre /kasɑ̃dʀ/ *npr* Mythol Cassandra; **jouer les ~** to spread doom and gloom.

cassant, **~e** /kasɑ̃, ɑ̃t/ *adj* **1** (qui se brise facilement) [*bois, cheveux*] brittle; [*métal*] brittle, short spéc; **2** (tranchant) [*voix, ton, personne*] curt, abrupt; **3**○ (fatigant) backbreaking; **c'est pas ~ comme travail** it's not exactly back-breaking work!

cassate /kasat/ *nf* cassata.

cassation /kasasjɔ̃/ *nf* Jur quashing, annulment.

casse /kɑs/ **I**◑ *nm* break-in, heist○ US; **faire un ~** to break into a bank.
II *nf* **1** (objets cassés) breakage; **payer la ~** to pay for breakage ou for the damage; **il y a eu beaucoup de ~ pendant le déménagement** a lot of things got broken during the move; **sans trop de ~** without causing too much damage; **si les deux bandes se rencontrent il va y avoir de la ~** if the two gangs meet there'll be a bust-up○; **2** (lieu) breaker's yard, scrap yard; **ta voiture est bonne pour la ~!** your car's ready for the breaker's yard ou scrap yard!; **mettre à la ~** to scrap [*voiture, bicyclette, réfrigérateur*]; **3** Imprim case; **haut de ~** upper case; **bas de ~** lower case; **4** Bot cassia; **5** Vin casse.

cassé, **~e** /kase/ **I** *pp* ▶ **casser**.
II *pp adj* [*voix*] hoarse; ▶ **blanc**.

casse-cou /kasku/ **I** *adj inv* [*personne, entreprise*] reckless; [*lieu*] dangerous.
II *nmf inv* (personne) daredevil.
III *nm inv* (lieu) death trap.
IDIOMES **crier ~** to give a warning.

casse-couilles● /kaskuj/ *nmf inv* pain in the arse● GB ou ass◑ US.

casse-croûte /kaskʀut/ *nm inv* snack.

casse-cul● /kasky/ **I** *adj inv* **être ~** [*gêneur*] to be a pain in the arse● GB ou ass◑ US; [*raseur*] to be a bore; [*corvée*] to be a drag○ ou bore.
II *nmf inv* (gêneur) pain in the arse● GB ou ass◑ US; (raseur) bore.

casse-dalle◑ /kasdal/ *nm inv* snack.

casse-graine○ /kasgʀɛn/ *nm inv* snack.

casse-gueule◑ /kasgœl/ **I** *adj inv* [*lieu, opération*] dangerous; [*projet*] risky; [*action*] reckless.
II *nm inv* (entreprise, projet) risky business; (lieu) deathtrap; **aller au ~** Soldiers' slang to go to the front.

casse-noisettes /kasnwazɛt/, **casse-noix** /kasnwa/ *nm inv* nutcrackers (*pl*).

casse-pieds○ /kaspje/ **I** *adj inv* **être ~** [*gêneur*] to be a pain in the neck○; [*raseur*] to be a bore; [*corvée*] to be a drag○ ou bore.
II *nmf inv* (gêneur) pain in the neck○; (raseur) bore.

casse-pipe◑ /kaspip/ *nm inv* **aller au ~** to go to the front.

casser /kase/ [1] **I** *vtr* **1** (briser) to break [*objet, os, membre*]; to crack [*noix, noisette*]; **les vandales ont tout cassé dans la maison** the vandals wrecked the house; **~ un bras/une côte/une dent à qn** to break sb's arm/rib/tooth; **quel maladroit! il casse tout!** he's so clumsy, he breaks everything!; **~ un carreau** to smash ou break a windowpane; **~ le moral de qn** to break sb's spirit; **~ le mouvement syndical** to break the unions; **ça m'a cassé la voix de hurler comme ça** shouting like that has made me hoarse; **~ les prix** Comm to slash prices; **~ le rythme d'une course** to slow down the pace of a race; **~ la figure**○ or **la gueule**◑ **à qn** to beat sb up○; **~**○ **du flic**◑**/du manifestant** to beat up policemen/demonstrators; ▶ **sucre**, **omelette**; **2**○ (dégrader) to demote [*militaire, employé*]; **3** (annuler) to quash [*jugement*]; to annul [*arrêt*]; **4**○ (humilier) to cut [sb] down to size [*personne*]; **le patron l'a cassé devant tous les employés** the boss put him down in front of all the employees.
II *vi* **1** (se briser) [*matière, objet*] to break; [*ficelle, corde, bande enregistrée*] to break, to snap; **la branche a cassé sous le poids des fruits** the branch broke ou snapped under the weight of the fruit; **ça casse très facilement** it breaks very easily; **2**○ (se séparer) [*couple*] to split up; **il a cassé avec sa petite amie** he's split ou broken up with his girlfriend.
III se casser *vpr* **1**○ (partir) to go away; **'bon, je me casse!'** 'right, I'm off○ ou I'm going!'; **2** (se briser) to break; **la clé s'est cassée net** the key snapped in two; **3** (se blesser) **se ~ une jambe/un bras**, **se ~ la jambe/le bras** to break one's leg/one's arm; **se ~ la figure**○ or **gueule**◑ (tomber par terre) [*piéton*] to fall over GB ou down; [*cavalier, motard*] to take a fall; (avoir un accident) [*automobiliste, motard, avion*] to crash; (échouer) [*entreprise, projet*] to fail, to come a cropper○ GB; (se battre) [*personnes*] to have a scrap○; **il ne s'est pas cassé**○, **il ne s'est pas cassé la tête** ○ or **le tronc**○ or **la nénette**○ or **le cul**◑ he didn't exactly strain himself; **se ~ la tête**○ (**sur un problème**) to rack one's brain (over a problem); **se ~ la tête**○ or **le cul**◑ **à faire qch** to go out of one's way to do sth.
IDIOMES **~ les pieds**○ or **les couilles**● **à qn** to annoy sb, to bug○ sb; **il nous les casse**● he's bugging○ us; **~ la croûte** or **la graine**○ to eat, to nosh○ GB, to chock○ US; **ça casse rien**○, **ça casse pas des briques**○ or **trois pattes à un canard**○ it's nothing to write home about○; **il faut que ça passe ou que ça casse** it's make or break; **une fête/un banquet à tout ~**○ a fantastic party/dinner; **ça te prendra trois heures, à tout ~**○ it'll take you three hours at the very most ou at the outside; **il y avait 200 personnes, à tout ~**○ there were 200 people at the very most ou at the outside; **qui casse (les verres) paie** if you cause damage, you pay for it.

casserole /kasʀɔl/ *nf* Culin saucepan, pan;

~ en aluminium/émaillée aluminium GB ou aluminum US/enamelled[GB] saucepan ou pan; **une ~ d'eau chaude** a saucepan ou pan of hot water.
IDIOMES **passer à la ~◐** (se faire disputer) to get into trouble; (subir un rapport sexuel) to be coerced into sex; **chanter/jouer comme une ~○** to sing/play atrociously.

casse-tête /kastɛt/ *nm inv* **1** (problème) headache fig; **2** (jeu, devinette) puzzle; **3** (massue) club.
■ **~ chinois** Jeux Chinese puzzle.

cassette /kasɛt/ *nf* **1** Audio cassette, tape; **~ vierge** blank cassette ou tape; **acheter une ~ de Tom Waits** to buy a Tom Waits cassette ou tape; **~ de musique classique** classical music cassette ou tape; **2** Ordinat cassette, tape; **3** (petit coffret) casket; **4** Hist privy purse.
■ **~ audio** audio cassette tape; **~ vidéo** video (cassette); **j'ai le film en ~ vidéo** I've got the film on video.

casseur /kasœʀ/ *nm* **1** ▶ 510 (ferrailleur) scrap merchant GB ou dealer; **2** (manifestant) rioting demonstrator; **3◐** (cambrioleur) burglar.

cassis /kasis/ *nm inv* **1** Bot (arbre) blackcurrant (bush); **2** Culin (fruit) blackcurrant; **crème de ~** blackcurrant liqueur, crème de cassis; **une glace au ~** a blackcurrant ice cream; **sirop de ~** blackcurrant cordial; **3** (sur la route) dip.

Cassius /kasjys/ *npr* **pourpre de ~** Chimie gold tin purple.

cassolette /kasɔlɛt/ *nf* **1** Culin (récipient) small ovenproof dish; (plat) small dish (**de** of); **2** (brûle-parfum) essential oil burner.

cassonade /kasɔnad/ *nf* soft brown sugar.

cassoulet /kasulɛ/ *nm*: *meat and (haricot) bean stew*.

cassure /kasyʀ/ *nf* **1** (endroit brisé) break; **2** (rupture) split, rupture; **le divorce de mes parents a été une ~ dans ma vie** my parents' divorce turned my life upside down; **3** Géol fracture; **4** Mode crease, fold mark.

castagne○ /kastaɲ/ *nf* fight, scrap○; **il va y avoir de la ~** there's going to be a fight ou scrap○.

castagnettes /kastaɲɛt/ ▶ 534 *nfpl* castanets; **jouer des ~** to play the castanets.

caste /kast/ *nf* **1** Sociol caste; **2** (groupe social) pej class; **la ~ des gouvernants/officiers** the ruling/officer class.

castel /kastɛl/ *nm* small castle.

castillan, **~e** /kastijɑ̃, an/ ▶ 462 **I** *adj* Castilian.
II *nm* Ling Castilian.

Castillan, **~e** /kastijɑ̃, an/ *nm,f* Castilian.

Castille /kastij/ ▶ 692 *nprf* Castile.

casting /kastiŋ/ *nm* (sélection) casting.

castor /kastɔʀ/ *nm* **1** Zool beaver; **2** (fourrure) beaver; **c'est du ~** it's beaver.

castrat /kastʀa/ *nm* **1** Mus castrato; **2** (homme castré) eunuch.

castrateur, **-trice** /kastʀatœʀ, tʀis/ *adj* Psych castrating.

castration /kastʀasjɔ̃/ *nf* castration.

castrer /kastʀe/ [1] *vtr* to castrate [*animal, homme*].

castrisme /kastʀism/ *nm* Castroism.

castriste /kastʀist/ **I** *adj* Castro (*épith*).
II *nmf* Castroist.

casuel, **-elle** /kazɥɛl/ *adj* **1** (fortuit) fml fortuitous; **2** Ling [*langue, flexion*] case (*épith*).

casuiste /kazɥist/ *nm* casuist.

casuistique /kazɥistik/ *nf* casuistry.

CAT /kat, seate/ *nm* (*abbr* = **centre d'aide par le travail**) adult training centre[GB].

catabolisme /katabɔlism/ *nm* catabolism.

catachrèse /katakʀɛz/ *nf* catachresis.

cataclysme /kataklism/ *nm* lit, fig cataclysm.

cataclysmique /kataklismik/ *adj* cataclysmic.

catacombes /katakɔ̃b/ *nfpl* catacombs.

catadioptre /katadjɔptʀ/ *nm* reflector.

catafalque /katafalk/ *nm* catafalque.

catalan, **~e** /katalɑ̃, an/ ▶ 462 **I** *adj* Catalan.
II *nm* Catalan.

Catalan, **~e** /katalɑ̃, an/ *nm,f* Catalan.

catalepsie /katalɛpsi/ *nf* catalepsy; **tomber en ~** to have a cataleptic fit.

cataleptique /katalɛptik/ **I** *adj* cataleptic.
II *nmf* person suffering from catalepsy.

catalogage /katalɔgaʒ/ *nm* cataloguing[GB].

Catalogne /katalɔɲ/ ▶ 692 *nprf* Catalonia.

catalogue /katalɔg/ *nm* **1** (publication) catalogue[GB]; **~ de l'exposition** exhibition catalogue[GB]; **~ de vente par correspondance** mail order catalogue[GB]; **acheter/vendre qch sur ~** to buy/sell sth by mail order; **la vente sur ~** selling by mail order; **2** (de liste) catalogue[GB]; **faire** or **dresser le ~ de** to catalogue[GB].

cataloguer /katalɔge/ [1] *vtr* **1** (dresser la liste de) to catalogue GB, to catalog US; **2** (juger définitivement) to label; **être catalogué comme républicain** to be labelled as a republican; **se sentir catalogué** to feel one is being pigeon-holed.

catalpa /katalpa/ *nm* catalpa.

catalyse /kataliz/ *nf* catalysis; **par ~** by catalysis.

catalyser /katalize/ [1] *vtr* lit, fig to catalyse[GB].

catalyseur /katalizœʀ/ *nm* **1** Chimie catalyst; **2** (pot catalytique) catalytic converter; **3** fig catalyst (**de** for, of); **jouer le rôle de** or **servir de ~** to act as ou be a catalyst.

catalytique /katalitik/ *adj* catalytic.

catamaran /katamaʀɑ̃/ *nm* catamaran.

cataphote® /katafɔt/ *nm* (safety) reflector.

cataplasme /kataplasm/ *nm* poultice; **poser un ~** to apply a poultice.

catapultage /katapyltaʒ/ *nm* catapulting.

catapulte /katapylt/ *nf* Aviat, Hist catapult.

catapulter /katapylte/ [1] *vtr* to catapult; **~ qn à un poste de direction** to catapult sb into a managerial position.

cataracte /kataʀakt/ *nf* **1** Méd cataract; **2** Géog cataract.

catarrhal, **~e**, *mpl* **-aux** /kataʀal, o/ *adj* catarrhal.

catarrhe /kataʀ/ *nm* catarrh.

catarrheux, **-euse** /kataʀø, øz/ *adj* catarrhal.

catastase /katastaz/ *nf* **1** Littérat catastasis; **2** Phon on-glide.

catastrophe /katastʀɔf/ *nf* disaster; **~ aérienne** air disaster; **tourner à la ~** to end in disaster; **aller** or **courir à la ~** to head for disaster; **ce n'est pas une ~** it's not the end of the world; **en ~** [*partir, terminer*] in a (mad) panic; **atterrissage en ~** crash landing.
■ **~ naturelle** gén natural disaster; Assur, Jur act of God.

catastrophé, **~e** /katastʀɔfe/ **I** *pp* ▶ **catastropher**.
II *pp adj* devastated; **avoir l'air ~** to look ou seem devastated.

catastropher /katastʀɔfe/ [1] *vtr* to devastate; **j'ai été catastrophé de voir** I was devastated when I saw.

catastrophique /katastʀɔfik/ *adj* disastrous; (plus fort) catastrophic.

catastrophisme /katastʀɔfism/ *nm* doomwatch.

catatonie /katatɔni/ *nf* catatonia.

catatonique /katatɔnik/ *adj* catatonic.

catch /katʃ/ ▶ 449 *nm* wrestling; **faire du ~** to wrestle.
■ **~ à quatre** tag wrestling.

catcher /katʃe/ [1] *vi* to wrestle.

catcheur, **-euse** /katʃœʀ, øz/ ▶ 510 *nm,f* wrestler; **avoir des épaules de ~** to be built like a wrestler.

catéchèse /kateʃɛz/ *nf* catechesis.

catéchisation /kateʃizasjɔ̃/ *nf* catechization.

catéchiser /kateʃize/ [1] *vtr* **1** Relig to catechize; **2** (endoctriner) to indoctrinate.

catéchisme /kateʃism/ *nm* **1** Relig catechism; **faire le ~ aux enfants** to teach children the catechism; **2** (dogme) dogma.

catéchiste /kateʃist/ *nmf* catechist.

catéchumène /katekymɛn/ *nmf* catechumen.

catégorie /kategɔʀi/ *nf* **1** (type) category; **de première/deuxième ~** top-/low-grade; **2** Admin class; **3** Sociol group; **~ socioprofessionnelle** social and occupational group; **4** Sport class; **hors ~** in a class of one's own; **toutes ~s** all-round; **5** Ling, Philos category.

catégoriel, **-ielle** /kategɔʀjɛl/ *adj* category-specific.

catégorique /kategɔʀik/ *adj* **1** (inébranlable) adamant; **refus ~** adamant ou categoric refusal; **2** (sans ambiguïté) categoric; **règle ~** categoric rule.

catégoriquement /kategɔʀikmɑ̃/ *adv* categorically; **refuser ~** to refuse flatly ou categorically.

catégorisation /kategɔʀizasjɔ̃/ *nf* categorization; péj labelling[GB].

catégoriser /kategɔʀize/ [1] *vtr* to categorize; péj to label.

catelle /katɛl/ *nf* H (carreau) tile.

caténaire /katenɛʀ/ *adj, nf* Rail catenary.

catgut /katgyt/ *nm* catgut.

cathare /kataʀ/ *adj, nmf* Cathar.

catharsis /kataʀsis/ *nf* catharsis.

cathartique /kataʀtik/ *adj* cathartic.

cathédrale /katedʀal/ *nf* cathedral; **silence de ~** cathedral-like silence.

Catherine /katʀin/ *npr* Catherine.
■ **~ d'Aragon** Catherine of Aragon; **~ la Grande** Catherine the Great; **~ de Médicis** Catherine de' Medici.
IDIOMES **coiffer sainte ~** to remain unattached at the age of 25.

catherinette /katʀinɛt/ *nf*: *single woman aged 25*.

cathéter /kateteʀ/ *nm* catheter.

cathétérisme /kateteʀism/ *nm* catheterization.

catho○ /kato/ *adj inv, nmf* (*abbr* = **catholique**) Catholic.

cathode /katɔd/ *nf* cathode.

cathodique /katɔdik/ *adj* **1** Phys cathodic; **rayons ~s** cathode rays; **tube ~** cathode-ray tube; **2** TV televisual.

catholicisme /katɔlisism/ *nm* (Roman) Catholicism.

catholicité /katɔlisite/ *nf* **1** (groupe) the (Roman) Catholics (*pl*); **2** (caractère) Catholicity.

catholique /katɔlik/ **I** *adj* (Roman) Catholic; **l'Église ~** the (Roman) Catholic Church; **ce n'est pas très ~○** hum it's a bit unorthodox; **ne pas avoir l'air très ~○** to look a bit dubious.
II *nmf* (Roman) Catholic.

catimini: **en catimini** /ɑ̃katimini/ *loc adv* on the sly.

catin† /katɛ̃/ *nf* prostitute, strumpet†.

cation /katjɔ̃/ *nm* cation.

catogan /katɔgɑ̃/ *nm* **1** (coiffure) ponytail (*attached at the nape of the neck*); **2** (ruban) bow, hair ribbon.

Caton /katɔ̃/ *npr* Cato; **~ l'Ancien** Cato the Elder; **~ d'Utique** Cato Uticensis.

Catulle /katyl/ *npr* Catullus.

Caucase /kokɑz/ ▶ 692 *nprm* Caucasus.

caucasien, **-ienne** /kokazjɛ̃, ɛn/ *adj* Caucasian.

cauchemar /koʃmaʀ/ *nm* nightmare; **faire un ~** to have a nightmare.

cauchemarder○ /koʃmaʀde/ [1] *vi* to have nightmares.

cauchemardesque /koʃmaʀdesk/ *adj* [*expérience*] nightmare (*épith*); [*scène*] nightmarish.

cauchemardeux, **-euse** /koʃmaʀdø, øz/ *adj* **1** [*sommeil*] disturbed by nightmares (*après n*); **2** [*personne*] subject to nightmares (*après n*).

caudal, **~e**, *mpl* **-aux** /kodal, o/ **I** *adj* [*nageoire*] caudal; [*plume*] tail.
II caudale *nf* caudal fin.

caudines /kodin/ *adj fpl* **fourches ~** Caudine Forks.
IDIOMES **passer sous les fourches ~** to suffer a humiliating defeat.

cauri /ko(ɔ)ʀi/ *nm* cowrie.

causal, **~e**, *mpl* **-aux** /kozal, o/ **I** *adj* Philos, Ling causal.
II causale *nf* Ling causal clause.

causalité /kosalite/ *nf* causality; **rapports** or **liens de ~ entre** causal relations between.

causant○, **~e** /kozɑ̃, ɑ̃t/ *adj* talkative, chatty○.

causatif, **-ive** /kozatif, iv/ Ling **I** *adj* [*conjonction*] causal; [*fonction*] causative.
II *nm* (verbe) causative (verb); (forme) causative (form).

cause /koz/ *nf* **1** (origine) cause (**de** of); **un rapport** or **une relation de ~ à effet entre** a relation of cause and effect between; **il n'y a pas d'effet sans ~** there's no smoke without fire; **à petites ~s grands effets** minor causes can bring about major results; **2** (raison) reason; **j'ignore la ~ de leur colère/départ** I don't know the reason for their anger/departure; **pour une ~ encore indéterminée** for a reason as yet unknown; **il s'est fâché et pour ~** he got angry and with good reason; **sans ~** [*licenciement, chagrin*] groundless; **c'est une ~ de licenciement immédiat** it's a ground for immediate dismissal; **pour ~ économique** for financial reasons; **pour ~ de maladie** because of illness; **fermé pour ~ d'inventaire/de travaux** closed for stocktaking/for renovation; **avoir pour ~ qch** to be caused by sth; **à ~ de** because of; **3** (ensemble d'intérêts) cause; **défendre une/sa ~** to defend a/one's cause; **se battre pour la ~** to fight for the cause; **une ~ juste/perdue** a just/lost cause; **être dévoué à la ~ commune** to be dedicated to the common cause; **être acquis à la ~ de qn** to be won over to sb's cause; **gagner qn à sa ~** to win sb over to one's cause; **pour les besoins de la ~** for the sake of the cause; **prendre fait et ~ pour qn** to take up the cause of sb; **faire ~ commune avec qn** to make common cause with sb; **pour la bonne ~** for a good cause; **4** (affaire) case; **plaider/gagner/perdre une ~** to plead/win/lose a case; **plaider la ~ de qn/sa propre ~** to plead sb's case/one's own case; **la ~ est entendue** Jur the case is closed; fig it's an open and shut case; **les ~s célèbres** the causes célèbres, the famous cases; **être en ~** [*système, fait, organisme*] to be at issue; [*personne*] to be involved; **être hors de ~** to be in the clear; **mettre qn/qch en ~** to implicate sb/sth; **mise en ~** implication; **mettre qn/qch hors de ~** gén to clear sb/sth; [*police*] to eliminate [sb] from an enquiry; **remettre en ~** to call [sth] into question, to challenge [*politique, principe, droit, hiérarchie, décision*]; to cast doubt on [*projet, efficacité, signification*]; to undermine [*efforts, proposition, processus*]; **tout est remis en ~** everything has been thrown back into doubt; **se remettre en ~** to pass one's life under review; **remise en ~** (de soi-même) rethink; (de système) reappraisal; **avoir** or **obtenir gain de ~** to win one's case; **donner gain de ~ à** to decide in favour[GB] of.
IDIOMES **en toute connaissance de ~** in full knowledge of the facts, fully conversant with the facts sout; **en tout état de ~** in any case; **en désespoir de ~** as a last resort.

causer /koze/ [1] **I** *vtr* **1** (provoquer) to cause; **~ la mort de qn** [*accident, conflit*] to cause sb's death; **~ de la peine à qn** to cause sb grief; **elle m'a causé de gros ennuis** she caused me a lot of trouble; **~ des surprises/un scandale** to cause surprise/a scandal; **~ du tort à qn** to wrong sb; **la Bourse/ma santé m'a causé des soucis** the stock exchange/my health has given me cause for concern; **2**○ (discuter de) to talk; **elles ont causé philosophie toute la soirée** they talked philosophy all evening; **~ travail** or **boutique** to talk shop.
II causer de *vtr ind* to talk about (**avec qn** with sb); **~ longuement d'une affaire** to talk about a matter at length; **~ de choses et d'autres** to talk about this and that; **causons un peu de ton avenir** let's have a chat about your future; ▶ **pluie**.
III *vi* to talk (**avec qn** to sb); **à propos de** about); **hé, je te cause**○**!** hey, I'm talking to you!; **cause toujours tu m'intéresses!** iron fascinating, I'm sure! iron.

causerie /kozʀi/ *nf* **1** (entretien organisé) talk; **une ~ télévisée** a television chat show; **2** (entretien libre) chat; **une ~ au coin du feu** a fireside chat.

causette○ /kozɛt/ *nf* chat; **faire la** or **un brin de** or **un bout de ~ avec qn** to have a little chat with sb.

causeur, **-euse** /kozœʀ, øz/ **I** *nm,f* conversationalist; **c'est un brillant ~** he's a brilliant conversationalist; **c'est un ~ insupportable** he talks too much.
II causeuse *nf* (meuble) love seat.

causse /kos/ *nm* limestone plateau.

causticité /kostisite/ *nf* lit, fig causticity.

caustique /kostik/ **I** *adj* caustic.
II *nm* caustic substance.

cautèle /kotɛl/ *nf* fml cunning.

cauteleux, **-euse** /kotlø, øz/ *adj* fml **1** (hypocrite) dissembling sout; **2** (rusé) cunning.

cautère /kotɛʀ/ *nm* cautery.

cautérisation /koteʀizasjɔ̃/ *nf* cauterization.

cautériser /koteʀize/ [1] *vtr* to cauterize.

caution /kosjɔ̃/ *nf* **1** (garantie financière) Comm deposit; Fin guarantee, security; Jur bail; **j'ai versé un mois de ~ pour mon appartement** I paid a deposit of one month's rent on my apartment; **être libéré sous ~** to be released on bail; **demander/accorder la mise en liberté sous ~** to request/to grant bail; **2** (soutien) support, backing (**de** of); **apporter sa ~ à** to lend one's support to [*thèse, politique*]; **3** (garantie morale) guarantee; **leur témoignage est sujet à ~** their testimony is open to doubt ou is to be treated with caution; **4** (garant) **se porter ~ pour qn** Comm, Fin to stand surety or guarantor for sb; Jur to put up bail for sb ; **il aura besoin de la ~ parentale** his parents will have to stand surety GB ou accountable US for him.

cautionnement /kosjɔnmɑ̃/ *nm* **1** (dépôt d'argent) deposit; **2** (soutien) support, backing.

cautionner /kosjɔne/ [1] *vtr* **1** (soutenir) to give one's support to, to give one's approval to [*régime, action, événement*]; **être cautionné par** to have the support of; **terrorisme cautionné par l'État** state-sanctioned terrorism; **2** Comm, Fin to stand surety for [*personne, projet*]; Jur to put up bail for [*personne*].

cavaillon /kavajɔ̃/ *nm* ≈ cantaloupe (melon).

cavalcade /kavalkad/ *nf* **1** (course bruyante) stampede; **on entendit une ~ dans l'escalier** people could be heard stampeding on the stairs; **2** (défilé de cavaliers) cavalcade.

cavale /kaval/ *nf* **1**○ (évasion) escape; **être en ~** to be on the run; **après trois mois de ~** after three months on the run; **2** (jument) mare.

cavaler○ /kavale/ [1] *vi* **1** (courir) to rush about; **~ dans** to rush around [*magasins, ville*]; **~ après qn/qch** to chase after sb/sth; **2** (courir après les femmes) to be a womanizer, to chase after girls; (courir après les hommes) to chase after men.

cavalerie /kavalʀi/ *nf* Mil cavalry; **officier/charge de ~** cavalry officer/charge.

cavaleur○, **-euse** /kavalœʀ, øz/ pej **I** *adj* womanizing (*épith*)/man-chasing (*épith*); **ce** or **qu'est-ce qu'il est ~!** what a womanizer!
II *nm,f* womanizer/man-chaser.

cavalier, **-ière** /kavalje, ɛʀ/ **I** *adj* **1** pej (impertinent) [*personne, procédé*] cavalier; **2** (en dessin) **vue cavalière** bird's eye view; **perspective cavalière** isometric projection; **3** Équit **allée** or **piste cavalière** bridle path.
II *nm,f* **1** Équit horseman/horsewoman; (en promenade) horse rider; **être bon ~** to be a good rider; **2** (pour danser) partner; **changer de ~** to change partners.
III *nm* **1** Mil cavalryman; **2** (aux échecs) knight; **3** (clou) staple (*for wood*); **4** (de fichier) tab.
IDIOMES **faire ~ seul** [*personne, entreprise*] to go it alone; Sport to be ahead.

cavalièrement /kavaljɛʀmɑ̃/ *adv* [*répondre, agir*] in a cavalier fashion.

cavatine /kavatin/ *nf* cavatina.

cave /kav/ **I** *adj* liter (creux) [*yeux, joues*] hollow, sunken.
II○ *nm* sucker○.
III *nf* **1** (sous-sol) cellar; **de la ~ au grenier** high and low; **~ voûtée** vault; **2** (réserve de vin) cellar; **avoir une bonne ~** [*individu*] to have a good cellar; [*restaurant*] to have a good winelist; **3** (entreprise vinicole) cellar; **4** (cabaret) club; **5** (meuble) drinks cabinet GB, liquor cabinet US; **6** (magasin) wine merchant.

caveau, *pl* **~x** /kavo/ *nm* **1** (sépulture) vault; **~ de famille** family vault; **2** (salle) club.

caverne /kavɛʀn/ *nf* **1** (grotte) cavern; **2** Anat cavity.
■ **~ d'Ali Baba** Aladdin's cave.

caverneux, **-euse** /kavɛʀnø, øz/ *adj* **1** [*voix, son*] hollow; **2** Anat cavernous.

caviar /kavjaʀ/ *nm* caviar.
■ **~ d'aubergines** aubergine dip GB, eggplant dip US.
IDIOMES **passer au ~** to blue-pencil.

caviarder○ /kavjaʀde/ [1] *vtr* to blue-pencil.

caviste /kavist/ ▶ **510** *nmf* cellarman/cellarwoman.

cavité /kavite/ *nf* cavity; **~ buccale** oral cavity.

Cayenne /kajɛn/ *nf* **1** Géog Cayenne; **2** Hist Cayenne penal settlement.

CB /sebe/ *nf* (*abbr* = **Citizens' Band**) **bande ~** CB.

cc /sese/ *nm* (*abbr* = **centimètre cube**) cc.

CC *written abbr* ▶ **courant**.

CCP /sesepe/ *nm*: *abbr* ▶ **compte**.

CD /sede/ *nm* **1** Audio, Vidéo (*abbr* = **compact disc**) CD; **2** Admin (*written abbr* = **corps diplomatique**) CD.

CDD /sedede/ *nm*: *abbr* ▶ **contrat**.

CDI /sedei/ *nm*: *abbr* ▶ **centre**.

CD-I /sedei/ *nm inv* (*abbr* = **compact disc interactif**) CD-I.

CDP /sedepe/ *nm*: *abbr* ▶ **centre**.

CD-ROM /sedeʀɔm/ *nm inv* (*abbr* = **compact disc read only memory**) CD-ROM.

ce /sə/ (**c'** /s/ *before e*, **cet** /sɛt/ *before vowel or mute h*), **cette** /sɛt/, *pl* **ces** /se/ **I** *adj dém* **1**○ (avec un sujet redondant) **alors, ~ bébé, ça pousse?** how's the baby doing?; **et ces travaux, ça avance?** how's the work progressing?; **cet entretien, ça s'est bien passé?** how did the interview go?; **et cette grippe?** how's your flu?; **2** (de politesse) **et pour ces dames?** what are the ladies having?; **si ces messieurs veulent bien me suivre** if the gentlemen would care to follow

ce

L'adjectif démonstratif: *ce, cet, cette, ces*

Lorsque *ce* (parfois renforcé par *-ci*) marque la proximité dans l'espace ou le temps, on le traduira par *this*:

prends ce livre(-ci) plutôt que celui-là = take this book, not that one
il a plu ce matin = it rained this morning
ce mois-ci = this month
un de ces jours = one of these days

Lorsque *ce* (parfois renforcé par *-là*) marque l'éloignement, on le traduira par *that*:

cet homme(-là) = that man
cette année-là = that year
en ces temps lointains = in those far-off days

Lorsque le nom n'est pas suivi de *-ci* ou *-là*, on prendra en compte le contexte pour choisir la traduction:

dans cette maison
(celle où l'on se trouve) = in this house
(celle dont on parle) = in that house

j'aime ces endroits calmes
(tels que celui où nous sommes) = I like these quiet places
(tels que celui dont on parle) = I like those quiet places
en ces temps difficiles (maintenant) = in these difficult times
(autrefois) = in those difficult times

On notera que *that* sert aussi à indiquer que le locuteur se distancie d'une chose ou d'une personne, souvent pour marquer sa désapprobation:

tu es ridicule avec ce chapeau! = you look ridiculous in that hat!
ce garçon m'énerve! = that boy gets on my nerves!

Attention aux expressions suivantes:

cette nuit (passée) = last night
(à venir) = tonight
en ce moment = at the moment
(précis) = at this moment in time

Le pronom démonstratif: *ce, c'*

L'emploi du pronom démonstratif avec le verbe être est traité à l'entrée du verbe ***être1***.

Les autres emplois sont traités ci-dessous, voir **II**.

me; **3** (suivi d'une précision) **il a commis cette erreur que commettent beaucoup de gens** he made the mistake so many people make; **il n'est pas de ces hommes qui manquent de parole** he's not the kind of man ou the sort to break his word; **je lui rends cette justice qu'il m'a tenu au courant** I must say in all fairness to him that he kept me informed; **elle a eu cette chance que la corde a tenu** she was lucky in that the rope held; **4** (marquant le degré) **cette arrogance!** what arrogance!; **cette idée!** what an idea!; **ah, ~ repas!** what a meal!; **quand on a ~ talent** when you are as talented as that; **j'ai un de ces rhumes!** I've got an awful cold, I've got such a cold!; **je ne pensais pas qu'il aurait cette chance/audace** I never thought he would be so lucky/cheeky; **tu as de ces idées!** you've got some funny ideas!

II *pron dém* **~ disant** so saying; **~ faisant** in so doing; **~ que voyant** (and) seeing this; **pour ~ faire, je devrais déménager** in order to do that, I would have to move; **il a refusé, et ~, parce que**... he refused, and all because...; **tout s'est bien passé, et ~, grâce à vos efforts** everything went well, and that was all thanks to you; **c'est un peu trop, ~ me semble** it's a bit much, it seems to me; **vous êtes, ~ dit-on/~ m'a-t-on dit** you are, so they say/so I have been told; **sur ~, je vous quitte** with that, I must take my leave; **c'est te dire s'il faisait chaud!** which just goes to show how hot it was; **c'est tout dire** that says it all; **fais ~ que tu veux** do what you like; **ne te fie pas à ~ qu'il dit** don't rely on what he says; **dis-moi ~ qui s'est passé** tell me what happened; **voilà ~ dont tu as besoin** that's what you need; **~ que je veux savoir, c'est qui l'a cassé** what I want to know is who broke it; **c'est ~ à quoi il a fait allusion** that's what he was alluding to; **il faut être riche, ~ que je ne suis pas** you need to be rich, which I am not; **il a fait faillite, ~ qui n'est pas surprenant** he's gone bankrupt, which is hardly surprising; **il a accepté, ~ à quoi je ne m'attendais pas** he accepted, which is something I didn't expect; **~ qui m'étonne, c'est qu'il ait accepté** what surprises me is that he accepted; **je ne m'attendais pas à ~ qu'il écrive** I wasn't expecting him to write; **il n'y a pas de mal à ~ que tu fasses cela** there's no harm in your doing that; **il s'étonne de ~ que tu ne le saches pas** he's surprised (that) you don't know; **il tient à ~ que vous veniez** he's very keen that you should come ou for you to come; **il se plaint de ~ que tu ne l'aies pas consulté** he complains (that) you didn't consult him; **~ que c'est grand/laid!** it's so big/ugly!; **c'est étonnant ~ qu'il te ressemble!** it's amazing how much he looks like you!; **~ qu'il a mangé de** or **comme bonbons!** what a lot of sweets GB ou candy US he ate!; **~ que c'est que d'être vieux/d'avoir étudié!** what it is to be old/to be educated!; **~ que c'est que les enfants!** that's children for you!; **voilà ~ que c'est de se vanter/ne pas écouter!** that's what comes of boasting/not listening!; **~ qu'il ne faut pas accepter/faire!** the things one has to put up with/to do!; **~ que** or **qu'est-~ que**○ **j'ai faim!** I'm so hungry!, I'm starving!; **~ qu'il**○ **pleut/fait froid!** it's pouring down/freezing!

CE /seə/ *nm* **1** Scol *abbr* ▶ **cours**; **2** Entr *abbr* ▶ **comité**; **3** Pol *abbr* ▶ **conseil**.

CEA /seəa/ *nm*: *abbr* ▶ **commissariat**.

céans† /seɑ̃/ *adv* here; **le maître de ~** the master of the house.

CECA /seka/ *nf*: *abbr* ▶ **communauté**.

ceci /səsi/ *pron dém* this; **prenez ~** take this; **à ~ près** with one slight difference; **à ~ près que** except that; **~ n'empêche pas cela** the one doesn't necessarily exclude the other; **~ compense cela** things balance out; **que je fasse ~ ou cela** whether I do one thing or the other; **cet hôtel a ~ de bien que les chambres sont grandes** one good thing about this hotel is that the rooms are big.

cécité /sesite/ *nf* blindness; **être atteint de ~** to be blind; **souffrir de ~ partielle** to be partially sighted.

■ **~ accidentelle** acquired blindness; **~ verbale** word blindness, alexia spéc.

cédant, **~e** /sedɑ̃, ɑ̃t/ **I** *adj* assigning.
II *nm,f* assignor.

céder /sede/ [14] **I** *vtr* **1** (laisser) to give up [*tour, siège, part*] (**à qn** to sb); to yield [*pouvoir, droit*] (**à qn** to sb); Jur to make over [*bien*] (**à** to); **~ le passage** or **la priorité** Aut to give way (**à** to); **il m'a cédé sa place** he let me have his seat; **~ la place** fig to give way (**à** to); **~ le pas** fig to give way (**à** to; **devant** before); **~ du terrain** lit [*armée*] to lose ou yield ground (**à l'ennemi** to the enemy); fig [*monnaie*] to lose ground (**par rapport à** against); [*épidémie*] to recede; [*négociateur*] to make concessions; **ne pas ~ un pouce de terrain** [*armée*] not to yield an inch of ground; [*négociateur*] not to yield an inch; **l'indice Dow Jones a cédé quelques points** Fin the Dow Jones index fell by a few points; **je cède la parole à mon collègue** I'll hand you over to my colleague; **2** (vendre) to sell (**à qn** to sb); **il m'a cédé son studio pour 50 000 francs** he let me have ou he sold me his studio for 50,000 francs; **'cède villa bord de mer'** (dans une annonce) 'for sale: seaside house'; **~ à bail** Jur to lease; **bail à ~** lease for sale; **3** (être inférieur) **ne le ~ en rien à qn/qch** to be on a par with sb/sth; **il ne le cède à personne en courage** when it comes to courage, he's second to none.

II céder à *vtr ind* to give in to [*personne, désir*]; to give in to, to yield to [*tentation, envie, menace, exigences*]; to yield to [*charme*]; to succumb to [*sommeil*].

III *vi* **1** (fléchir) [*personne*] to give in; fig [*colère*] to subside; **faire ~ qn** to make sb give in; **2** (casser) [*poignée, branche*] to give way; (ne plus résister) [*serrure, porte*] to yield; **faire ~ une porte/serrure** to force a door/lock.

cédérom /sedeʀɔm/ *nm* CD-ROM.

cédétiste /sedetist/ *nmf* member of the CFDT (*trade union*).

cedex /sedɛks/ *nm* (*abbr* = **courrier d'entreprise à distribution exceptionnelle**) *postal code for corporate users*.

cédille /sedij/ *nf* cedilla.

cédrat /sedʀa/ *nm* (fruit) citron.

cédratier /sedʀatje/ *nm* (arbre) citron.

cèdre /sɛdʀ/ *nm* **1** (arbre) cedar; **2** (bois) cedar(wood).

■ **~ blanc** white cedar; **~ du Liban** cedar of Lebanon.

CEE /seəə/ *nf*: *abbr* ▶ **communauté**.

CEEA /seəəa/ *nf* (*abbr* = **Communauté européenne de l'énergie atomique**) EAEC.

cégep /seʒɛp/ *nm* C (*abbr* = **collège d'enseignement général et professionnel**) *college of further education in Quebec offering two-year courses*.

cégétiste /seʒetist/ **I** *adj* CGT (*épith*).
II *nmf* member of the CGT.

CEI /seəi/ *nf*: *abbr* ▶ **communauté**.

ceindre /sɛ̃dʀ/ [55] liter **I** *vtr* **1** (entourer) **~ sa taille d'un ruban** to put ou tie a ribbon around one's waist; **une serviette lui ceignait les reins** he/she had a towel tied round his/her waist; **le front ceint d'un bandeau/diadème** wearing a headband/tiara; **château ceint de douves** castle encircled by a moat; **2** (mettre) to put on [*armure*]; to gird [*épée*]; **~ l'écharpe municipale** lit to put on the mayoral sash; fig to become mayor; **~ la couronne** fig to assume the crown.

II se ceindre *vpr* **se ~ d'un pagne** to put a loincloth on; **se ~ la tête d'un bandeau** to put a headband on; **se ~ les reins** to gird (up) one's loins.

ceint, **~e** /sɛ̃, sɛ̃t/ ▶ **ceindre**.

ceinture /sɛ̃tyʀ/ *nf* **1** (accessoire vestimentaire) belt; **porter des clés à la ~** to carry keys on one's belt; **porter un couteau à la ~** to wear a knife on one's belt; **2** (partie de vêtement) waistband; **3** (gaine) girdle; **4** (taille) waist; **nu jusqu'à la ~** stripped to the waist; **avoir de l'eau jusqu'à la ~** to be up to one's waist in water; **coup en dessous de la ~** blow below the belt; **ne pas arriver à la ~ de qn** fig not to be in the same league as sb; **5** Sport (prise) waist hold; (lien) belt; **être ~ noire** to be a black belt (**de**

in); **6** (ce qui entoure) ring; **~ d'arbres/de feu/d'usines** ring of trees/of fire/of factories; **boulevard de ~** ringroad, beltway US; **chemin de fer de ~** circle line; **petite/grande ~** (de ville) inner/outer circle.
■ **~ de chasteté** chastity belt; **~ de flanelle** flannel binder; **~ de grossesse** maternity girdle; **~ herniaire** truss; **~ orthopédique** surgical corset; **~ pelvienne** pelvic girdle; **~ rouge** (banlieue) *ring of communist suburbs around Paris*; **~ de sauvetage** lifebelt; **~ de sécurité** Aut, Aviat safety ou seat belt; **attacher** or **boucler sa ~ (de sécurité)** Aviat to fasten one's seat belt; Aut to fasten one's seat belt, to buckle up○ US; **~ verte** green belt.
IDIOMES **faire ~**○ to go without; **se serrer la ~** to tighten one's belt.

ceinturer /sɛ̃tyʀe/ [1] *vtr* **1** (construire) to surround [*quartier, ville*] (**de** with); **2** (être autour) [*réseau, murailles*] to encircle [*ville, terrain*]; **une écharpe ceinturait sa taille** he/she wore a scarf (tied) round[GB] his/her waist; **3** (maîtriser) to collar○ [*malfaiteur*]; Sport to tackle [*adversaire*].

ceinturon /sɛ̃tyʀɔ̃/ *nm* belt.

CEL /seəl/ *nm: abbr* ▶ **compte**.

cela /səla/ *pron dém*

■ **Note** Dans de nombreux emplois, *cela* et *ça* sont équivalents. On se reportera donc à cette entrée.

1 (pour montrer) that; **ceci est pour nous et ~, dans le coin, est pour vous** this is for us and that, in the corner, is for you; **mais ~ ne vous appartient pas!** but that doesn't belong to you!; **2** (pour faire référence) **~ m'inquiète de la voir dans cet état** it worries me to see her in that state; **~ n'a pas d'importance** it doesn' t matter ; **~ va sans dire** it ou that goes without saying; **~ serait fort surprenant!** that would be very surprising!; **il y a dix ans de ~** that was ten years ago; **qu'entendez-vous par ~?** what do you mean by that?; **quant à ~** as for that; **il a gagné le marathon et ~ à l'âge de 45 ans** he won the marathon at 45 years of age!; **~ dit/fait** having said/done that.
IDIOMES **voyez-vous ~!** did you ever hear of such a thing!

céladon /seladɔ̃/ ▶ **193** *adj inv, nm* celadon.

Célèbes /selɛb/ ▶ **416**, **555** *nprfpl* Celebes; **mer des ~** Celebes Sea.

célébrant /selebʀɑ̃/ *nm* celebrant.

célébration /selebʀasjɔ̃/ *nf* celebration.

célèbre /selɛbʀ/ *adj* famous (**pour, par qch** for sth); **se rendre ~ par qch/pour avoir fait** to become famous for sth/for doing; **tristement ~** notorious.

célébrer /selebʀe/ [14] *vtr* **1** (fêter) to celebrate [*événement*]; **2** (accomplir) to celebrate [*messe, mariage, culte*]; to perform [*rite*]; **3** (vanter) to praise [*personne*]; to remember [*mort, disparu*]; to extol [*qualité*].

célébrissime /selebʀisim/ *adj* extremely famous.

célébrité /selebʀite/ *nf* **1** (gloire) fame; **2** (personnage) celebrity.

celer† /sәle/ [17] *vtr* to conceal.

céleri /sɛlʀi/ *nm* **1** (en branches) celery; **2** (céleri-rave) celeriac.
■ **~ en branches** celery; **~ rémoulade** grated celeriac in a mayonnaise dressing.

céleri-rave, *pl* **céleris-raves** /sɛlʀiʀav/ *nm* celeriac.

célérité /seleʀite/ *nf* **1** (rapidité) fml promptness, celerity sout; **avec ~** promptly, with dispatch sout; **2** Phys (en acoustique) velocity.

célesta /selɛsta/ ▶ **534** *nm* celesta.

céleste /selɛst/ *adj* **1** Astron [*corps, phénomène*] celestial; **2** (divin) [*puissances*] celestial; [*gloire, esprit*] heavenly; [*colère, intervention, messager*] divine; **3** (surnaturel) liter [*beauté, regard*] heavenly.
■ **Céleste Empire** Celestial Empire.

célibat /seliba/ *nm* **1** (état) single status; **vivre dans le ~** to lead a single life; **les joies du ~** the joys of single life; **2** (chasteté) celibacy.

célibataire /selibatɛʀ/ **I** *adj* **1** [*personne*] single; **je suis ~ pour quelques jours** I'm on my own for a few days; **2** Phys [*électron*] unpaired.
II *nmf* (homme) bachelor, single man; (femme) single woman; **mère/père ~** single mother/father; **un ~ endurci** a confirmed bachelor.

celle ▶ **celui**.

celle-ci ▶ **celui-ci**.

celle-là ▶ **celui-là**.

celles-ci ▶ **celui-ci**.

celles-là ▶ **celui-là**.

cellier /selje/ *nm* (wine) cellar.

cellophane® /selɔfan/ *nf* cellophane®.

cellulaire /selylɛʀ/ *adj* **1** Biol (de la cellule) cell (*épith*); (fait de cellules) cellular; **la théorie ~** cell theory; **2** Jur [*régime, système*] of solitary confinement (*épith, après n*); **emprisonnement ~** solitary confinement; **3** Tech [*béton, plastique*] cellular; **4** Télécom [*téléphone*] cellular.

cellule /selyl/ *nf* **1** Biol cell; **~s nerveuses/sanguines/végétales** nerve/blood/plant cells; **culture/greffe de ~s** cell culture/transplant; **2** (de prison, monastère, ruche) cell; **3** (d'isolement) **faire six jours de ~** to do six days in solitary; **4** Sociol unit; **la famille est la ~ élémentaire de la société** the family is the basic social unit; **5** Pol (de parti) cell; **réunion de ~** cell meeting; **6** Phot cell; **~ photoélectrique** photoelectric cell; **7** Tech (d'électrophone) cartridge; **8** Aviat airframe; **9** Ordinat cell.
■ **~ de crise** emergency committee; **~ de lecture** Tech cartridge; **~ de réflexion** think-tank.

cellulite /selylit/ *nf* **1** (graisse) cellulite; **2** (inflammation) cellulitis.

celluloïd® /selylɔid/ *nm* celluloid.

cellulose /selyloz/ *nf* cellulose.

cellulosique /selylozik/ *adj* cellulosic.

celte /sɛlt/ *adj, nm* Celtic.

Celte /sɛlt/ *nmf* Celt.

celtique /sɛltik/ *adj, nm* Celtic.

celui /səlɥi/, **celle** /sɛl/, *mpl* **ceux** /sø/, *fpl* **celles** /sɛl/ *pron dém*

■ **Note** Voir aussi *celui-ci* et *celui-là*.

1 (devant un complément introduit par de) **tes yeux sont bleus, ceux de ton frère sont gris** your eyes are blue, your brother's are grey GB ou gray US; **le train du matin ou ~ de 17 heures?** the morning train or the 5 o'clock one?; **quelle voisine? celle d'en face?** which neighbour[GB]? the one who lives opposite?; **les gens d'à côté ou ceux du premier?** the people next door or the ones on the first GB ou second US floor?; **~ des deux qui finira le premier** the first one to finish; **c'est ~ de tes amis que je préfère** of all your friends, he's the one I like best; **~ d'entre vous que je choisirai** whichever one of you I choose; **ceux d'entre vous qui veulent partir** those of you who want to leave; **sa réaction a été celle d'un homme innocent** his reaction was that of an innocent man; **ce n'est pas le moment d'hésiter, mais ~ d'agir** now is not the time to hesitate, it's the time for action; **2** (devant une proposition relative) the one; **ceux, celles** (personnes) those; (choses) those, the ones; **non, ~ qui parlait** no, the one who was talking; **tous ceux qui étaient absents** all those who were absent; **ces livres ne sont pas ceux que j'avais choisis** these books are not the ones I chose; **ceux qu'ils ont vendus** the ones ou those they sold; **'quel disque?'—'~ dont je parlais'** 'which record?'—'the one I was talking about'; **il/elle est de ceux/celles qui croient tout savoir** he's/she's the sort who thinks he/she knows everything; **faire ~ qui n'entend pas** to pretend not to hear; **~ qui attend trop est toujours déçu** he who expects too much is bound to be disappointed; **heureux ~/ceux qui...** happy is he/are they who...; **3** (devant une proposition relative elliptique) the one; **ceux, celles** (personnes) those; (choses) those, the ones; **pas cette photo, celle prise en mai** not this photograph, the one taken in May; **tous ceux munis d'une carte** all those who have a card; **les siècles passés et ceux à venir** centuries past and those to come.

celui-ci /səlɥisi/, **celle-ci** /sɛlsi/, *mpl* **ceux-ci** /søsi/, *fpl* **celles-ci** /sɛlsi/ *pron dém* **1** (désignant ce qui est proche dans l'espace) this one; **ceux-ci, celles-ci** these; **prends une autre chaise, celle-ci est cassée** take another chair, this one is broken; **le prix n'est pas le même parce que ceux-ci sont doublés et ceux-là non** the price is different because these are lined and the others are not; **2** (annonçant ce qui suit) **je n'ai qu'une chose à dire et c'est celle-ci** I have only one thing to say and it's this; **3** (ce dernier) **elle essaya la fenêtre mais celle-ci était coincée** she tried the window but it was jammed; **il entra, suivi de son père et de son frère; ~ portait un paquet** he came in, followed by his father and his brother, the latter of whom was carrying a parcel; **le frère ou la sœur? celle-ci est très serviable mais celui-là est plus efficace** the brother or the sister? she is very obliging but he's more efficient; **4** (l'un) **ils ont tous apporté quelque chose: ~ une bouteille, celui-là un gâteau** they all brought something: one brought a bottle, another a cake.

celui-là /səlɥila/, **celle-là** /sɛlla/, *mpl* **ceux-là** /søla/, *fpl* **celles-là** /sɛlla/ *pron dém*

■ **Note** Pour les sens 1, 3 et 4 voir aussi *celui-ci*.

1 (désignant ce qui est plus éloigné) that one; **ceux-là, celles-là** those (ones); **'lequel des deux?'—'~ (là-bas)'** 'which one of the two?'—'that one (over there)'; ▶ **même**; **2** (le suivant) **si je n'ai qu'un conseil à te donner, c'est ~** if I only have one piece of advice for you, it's this; **3** (le premier des deux) the former; **4** (l'autre) another; **5** (par rapport aux précédents) **il fit une autre proposition, plus réaliste celle-là** he made another proposal, a more realistic one this time; **6**○ (emphatique) **il exagère, ~!** that fellow○ GB ou guy○ is pushing it a bit○!; **celle-là, alors, quelle idiote!** what an idiot that woman is!; **~, alors!** (admiratif) what a man!; (irrité) that man!; **regardez-moi ~: il n'est même pas rasé!** look at him! he hasn't even shaved!; **7**○ **elle est bien bonne, celle-là!** that's a good one!; **je ne m'attendais pas à celle-là** I didn't expect that!; **~ même qui a écrit le scénario** the very one who wrote the screenplay; **~ même qui a été publié hier** the very one that was published yesterday.

cément /semɑ̃/ *nm* cementum.

cémentation /semɑ̃tasjɔ̃/ *nf* cementation.

cénacle /senakl/ *nm* **1** (groupe restreint) fml inner circle; **~ littéraire** literary circle; **2** Bible Cenacle.

cendre /sɑ̃dʀ/ *nf* ash; **~ de cigarette** cigarette ash; **couleur de ~** ashen; **pommes de terre cuites sous la ~** potatoes baked in the embers; **le feu couve sous la ~** lit the fire is smouldering; fig there's something brewing; **réduire en ~s** to reduce to ashes; ▶ **mercredi**.

cendré, **~e** /sɑ̃dʀe/ **I** ▶ **193** *adj* ash (grey); **des cheveux blond ~** ash blond hair.
II cendrée *nf* **1** Sport (piste) cinder track; **2** Tech lead dress; **3** (petit plomb) (pour la chasse) dust shot GB, mustard seed US; (pour la pêche) shot.

cendreux, **-euse** /sɑ̃dʀø, øz/ *adj* **1** [*teint, visage*] ashen; **2** [*sol*] ashy.

cendrier /sɑ̃dʀije/ *nm* **1** (de fumeur) ashtray; **2** (de foyer) ash pan; **3** (de locomotive) **~ (de foyer)** ash box.

Cendrillon /sɑ̃dʀijɔ̃/ *npr* Cinderella.

Cène /sɛn/ *nf* **la ~** the Last Supper.

cénesthésie /senɛstezi/ *nf* coenesthesia.

cénobite /senɔbit/ *nm* coenobite.

cénotaphe /senɔtaf/ *nm* cenotaph.

cens /sɑ̃s/ *nm* **1** Hist rent (*paid by tenant to feudal landowner*); **2** Antiq census.
■ **~ électoral** Hist *tax quota for voting rights.*

censé, **~e** /sɑ̃se/ *adj* **être ~ faire** to be supposed to do; **les chiffres sont ~s représenter la tendance** the figures are supposed to represent the trend; **je n'étais pas ~e savoir** I was not supposed to know; **nul n'est ~ ignorer la loi** ignorance of the law is no excuse.

censément /sɑ̃semɑ̃/ *adv* supposedly.

censeur /sɑ̃sœʀ/ *nm* **1** Scol *school official in charge of discipline*; **2** (dans une commission) censor; **3** (moraliste) **s'ériger en ~ de qch** to set oneself up as a critic of sth; **4** Fin auditor; **5** Antiq censor.

censitaire /sɑ̃sitɛʀ/ *adj* [*suffrage, système*] based on a tax qualification (*après n*); [*électeur*] who pays tax (*après n*).

censure /sɑ̃syʀ/ *nf* **1** (interdiction) censorship; **commission de ~** board of censors; **son œuvre est menacée par la ~** his/her work is in danger of being censored; **visa de ~** censor's certificate; **2** (commission) board of censors; **le film est interdit par la ~** the film is banned by the board of censors; **3** Pol censure; **procédure de ~** censure procedure; **voter la ~ (du gouvernement)** to pass a vote of censure ou no confidence; **4** Psych, Relig censure.

censurer /sɑ̃syʀe/ [1] *vtr* **1** (expurger) to censor [*œuvre, passage, lettre*]; (interdire) to ban [*œuvre*]; **2** Pol to pass a vote of censure ou no confidence in [*gouvernement*]; **3** Relig to condemn [*personne, doctrine*].

cent[1] /sɑ̃/ ▶ **545**, **212** **I** *adj* gén a hundred, one hundred; **deux/trois ~s** two/three hundred; **deux ~s enfants** two hundred children; **deux ~ trois/vingt-cinq** two hundred and three/twenty-five; **il y avait ~ à deux ~s personnes** there were between a hundred and two hundred people; ▶ **fois, mètre, occasion, raison**.

II *pron* **ils sont venus tous les ~** all one hundred of them came.

III *nm* hundred; **un ~ d'œufs/d'huîtres** Comm a ou one hundred eggs/oysters; **vendre/acheter au ~** to sell/to buy by the hundred; **c'est 12 francs le ~** they're 12 francs a hundred.

IV pour cent *loc adj* per cent; **un emprunt à sept pour ~** or **7%** a loan at seven per cent ou 7%; **un placement à sept pour ~** an investment at seven per cent ou 7%; **dix à vingt pour ~** or **10 à 20% des enseignants** between ten and twenty per cent of teachers; **une jupe ~ pour ~** or **100% coton** a hundred per cent cotton skirt; **une production ~ pour ~ française** a hundred per cent ou 100% French production; **je ne suis pas sûr/convaincu à 100%** I'm not a hundred per cent sure/convinced.

IDIOMES **faire les ~ pas** to pace up and down; **être aux ~ coups**○ to be worried sick○, to be in a state○; **faire les quatre ~s coups** to be a real tearaway; **s'ennuyer à ~ sous de l'heure**○ to be bored stiff○ ou to death; **attendre ~ sept ans**○ to wait for ages; **durer ~ sept ans**○ to last for ages ou forever.

cent[2] /sɛnt/ ▶ **46** *nm* (centième de dollar, florin, rand, shilling) cent.

centaine /sɑ̃tɛn/ *nf* **1** (cent unités) hundred; **la colonne des ~s** the hundreds column; **dans une ~ il y a dix dizaines** in a hundred there are ten tens; **2** (environ cent) about a hundred; **nous étions une ~** there were about a hundred of us; **il y a une ~ de pages** there are about a hundred pages; **il y a une ~ de kilomètres** it's about a hundred kilometres[GB]; **plus d'une ~ de blessés** a hundred injured people or more; **une ~ de milliers de manifestants** about a hundred thousand protesters; **des ~s de femmes et d'enfants** hundreds of women and children; **quelques/plusieurs ~s de tonnes** a few/several hundred tons; **les victimes se comptent par ~s** there are hundreds of victims; **les lettres arrivent par ~s** letters are arriving in hundreds; **3** (âge) **avoir la ~** to be about a hundred; **approcher de la ~** to be getting on for a hundred; **dépasser la ~** to be over a hundred.

centaure /sɑ̃tɔʀ/ *nm* Mythol centaur.

Centaure /sɑ̃tɔʀ/ *npr* Astron Centaurus.

centaurée /sɑ̃tɔʀe/ *nf* Bot centaury.

centenaire /sɑ̃tnɛʀ/ **I** *adj* **1** (de cent ans) [*arbre, objet*] hundred-year-old (*épith*); **plusieurs fois ~** several hundred years old; **2** [*personne*] centenarian; **elle est ~** she's a hundred years old; **3** (se produisant une fois par siècle) **crue ~** one-in-a-hundred-years flood.

II *nmf* (personne) centenarian sout; **c'est une ~** she's a hundred years old.

III *nm* (anniversaire) centenary GB, centennial US.

centésimal, **~e**, *mpl* **-aux** /sɑ̃tezimal, o/ *adj* centesimal.

centiare /sɑ̃tjaʀ/ ▶ **783** *nm* centiare, square metre[GB].

centième /sɑ̃tjɛm/ ▶ **545** **I** *adj* hundredth.

II *nf* Théât **la ~** the hundredth performance.

centigrade /sɑ̃tigʀad/ *adj, nm* centigrade.

centigramme /sɑ̃tigʀam/ ▶ **620** *nm* centigram.

centilitre /sɑ̃tilitʀ/ ▶ **117** *nm* centilitre[GB].

centime /sɑ̃tim/ *nm* **1** ▶ **46** (monnaie) centime; **2** (somme infime) penny, cent US; **pas un ~** not a penny.

IDIOMES **ne plus avoir un ~** not to have a penny left; **calculer au ~ près** to work things out to the last penny; **dépenser jusqu'au dernier ~** to spend one's last penny; **on n'est pas au ~ près** we don't need to count the pennies.

centimètre /sɑ̃timɛtʀ/ *nm* **1** ▶ **477**, **783**, **793**, **860**, **866** (unité) centimetre[GB]; **2** (distance infime) inch; **ne pas avancer d'un ~** not to move an inch; **3** (ruban) tape measure.
■ **~ carré** square centimetre[GB]; **~ cube** cubic centimetre[GB].

centrafricain, **~e** /sɑ̃tʀafʀikɛ̃, ɛn/ ▶ **537** *adj* of the Central African Republic; **République ~e** Central African Republic.

Centrafricain, **~e** /sɑ̃tʀafʀikɛ̃, ɛn/ ▶ **537** *nm,f* (citoyen) citizen of the Central African Republic.

Centrafrique /sɑ̃tʀafʀik/ ▶ **321** *nprm* Central African Republic.

centrage /sɑ̃tʀaʒ/ *nm* centring[GB].

central, **~e**, *mpl* **-aux** /sɑ̃tʀal, o/ **I** *adj* **1** (au centre) [*pouvoir, gare, pilier, banque*] central; **l'Europe/l'Asie/l'Afrique ~e** Central Europe/Asia/Africa; **court ~** (en tennis) centre[GB] court; **ordinateur ~** host computer; **les rues ~es** streets in the centre of town; **l'axe ~ de la ville** the main road through the town; **habiter dans un quartier ~** to live near the centre[GB] of a town; **chercher quelque chose de plus ~** to look for somewhere ou something more central; **2** (principal) [*bureau, commissariat*] main; **elle occupe une position ~e dans l'entreprise** she holds a key position within the company; ▶ **école**.

II *nm* **1** Télécom **~ (téléphonique)** (telephone) exchange; **2** Sport **le ~** centre court.

III centrale *nf* **1** Nucl, Électrotech power station; **~e nucléaire** or **atomique** nuclear power station; **~e hydraulique/thermique** hydroelectric/thermal power station; **~e solaire** solar power station; **2** Entr **~e syndicale** or **ouvrière** confederation of trade unions; **les ~es syndicales** the trade unions; **3** (prison) prison (*for offenders with sentences of more than two years*); **4** Comm **~e d'achat** (groupement) *central purchasing agency*; (magasin) *discount store for students, civil servants etc.*

Centrale○ /sɑ̃tʀal/ *nf* ▶ **école**.

centralien, **-ienne** /satʀaljɛ, ɛn/ *nm,f*: *graduate of the École centrale des Arts et Manufactures.*

centralisateur, **-trice** /sɑ̃tʀalizatœʀ, tʀis/ *adj* [*régime, politique*] centralizing.

centralisation /sɑ̃tʀalizasjɔ̃/ *nf* centralization.

centraliser /sɑ̃tʀalize/ [1] *vtr* to centralize; **pouvoir centralisé** centralized power; **verrouillage centralisé** central locking.

centralisme /sɑ̃tʀalism/ *nm* centralism.

centre /sɑ̃tʀ/ *nm* **1** (milieu) centre[GB]; **au ~ de qch** in the centre[GB] of sth; **en plein ~ de la ville** right in the centre[GB] of town; **habiter dans le ~** to live in the centre[GB]; **le ~ (de la France)** central France; **~ historique** historic centre[GB]; **2** (lieu important) centre[GB]; **un grand ~ culturel/industriel/d'affaires** a large cultural/industrial/business centre[GB]; **3** (établissement, organisme) centre[GB]; **4** (point essentiel, pôle d'attraction) centre[GB]; **c'est au ~ des discussions** it's at the centre[GB] of the discussions; **il se prend pour le ~ du monde** he thinks the whole world revolves around him; **il a peu de ~s d'intérêt** he has few interests; **5** Pol **le ~** the centre[GB]; **les partis du ~** the centre[GB] parties; **être ~ gauche/droit** to be centre[GB] left/right; **elle est au ~** she's in the centre[GB]; **6** Anat centre[GB]; **~ nerveux** Anat, fig nerve centre[GB]; **~ respiratoire** respiratory centre[GB]; **les ~s vitaux** the vital organs; **7** (passe du ballon) centre[GB] pass.
■ **~ d'accueil** reception centre[GB]; **~ aéré** children's outdoor activity centre; **~ d'affaires** business centre[GB]; **~ d'affaires international** international business centre[GB]; **~ d'animation** community centre[GB] (*offering leisure facilities etc*); **~ antipoison** poisons unit; **~ artistique** arts centre[GB]; **~ chorégraphique** dance studio; **~ commercial** shopping centre[GB] ou arcade; **~ de conférences** conference centre[GB]; **~ culturel** cultural centre[GB]; **~ de cure antialcoolique** alcohol detoxification centre[GB]; **~ de dépistage** screening unit ou centre[GB]; **~ de désintoxication** detoxification centre[GB]; **~ de détention** detention centre[GB]; **~ de diagnostic** Méd diagnostic centre[GB]; **~ de documentation** (dans une école) library; (pour professionnels) resource centre[GB]; **~ de documentation et d'information**, **CDI** learning resources centre[GB]; **~ dramatique** arts centre[GB] for theatre[GB]; **~ d'entraînement** training centre[GB]; **~ équestre riding school; ~ d'études économiques** centre[GB] for economic studies; **~ d'études politiques** centre[GB] for political studies; **~ d'examens** Scol examination centre[GB]; **~ d'expérimentation nucléaire** nuclear test centre[GB]; **~ d'exportation** exhibition hall; **~ de formation** training centre[GB]; **~ de formation des apprentis**, **CFA** vocational training centre[GB]; **~ de gériatrie** geriatric hospital; **~ de gestion informatique** administrative data processing centre[GB]; **~ de gravité** centre[GB] of gravity; **~ hospitalier** hospital complex; **~ hospitalier spécialisé**, **CHS** psychiatric hospital ou unit; **~ hospitalier universitaire**, **CHU** ≈ teaching hospital; **~ d'inertie** centre[GB] of inertia; **~ de loisirs** leisure centre[GB]; **~ de masse** centre[GB] of mass; **~ médical** health centre[GB]; **~ opérationnel** operations centre[GB]; **~ d'orthogénie** family

planning clinic ; **~ de planification familiale** family planning clinic; **~ de poussée** centre[GB] of pressure; **~ de presse** Presse press room; **~ de recherches** research centre[GB]; **~ de rééducation** Méd rehabilitation centre[GB]; **~ de remise en forme** health farm; **~ de soins** clinic; **~ social** community centre[GB]; **~ sportif** sports centre[GB]; **~ de table** table centre-piece; **~ de thalassothérapie** thalassotherapy centre[GB]; **~ de traitement** Ordinat processing centre[GB]; **~ de transfusion sanguine** blood transfusion centre[GB]; **~ de tri (postal)** sorting office; **~ universitaire** university; **~ d'usinage** machining centre[GB]; **~ de vacances** holiday GB ou vacation US centre[GB]; **Centre de documentation pédagogique**, **CDP** teachers' reference centre[GB]; **Centre d'information et d'orientation**, **CIO** Scol national careers guidance centre[GB]; **Centre national d'enseignement à distance**, **CNED** national centre[GB] for distance learning.

Centre /sɑ̃tʀ/ ▶ 692 *nprm* **le ~** the Centre.

centrer /sɑ̃tʀe/ [1] *vtr* **1** (fixer par rapport au centre) to centre[GB]; **~ une roue** Mécan to align a wheel; **2** (diriger) **être centré sur qch** [*débat, campagne électorale*] to be centred[GB] around sth; **école centrée sur l'enseignement de la musique** school which focuses on the teaching of music; **3** Sport to centre[GB].

centre-ville, *pl* **centres-villes** /sɑ̃tʀəvil/ *nm* town centre[GB]; (de grande ville) city centre[GB]; **la circulation dans le** or **en ~** the traffic in the town centre[GB]; **magasins/rues du ~** shops GB ou stores US/streets in the town centre[GB].

centrifugation /sɑ̃tʀifygasjɔ̃/ *nf* centrifugation.

centrifuge /sɑ̃tʀifyʒ/ *adj* [*pompe, force*] centrifugal.

centrifuger /sɑ̃tʀifyʒe/ [13] *vtr* to centrifuge.

centrifugeur /sɑ̃tʀifyʒœʀ/ *nm* centrifuge.

centrifugeuse /sɑ̃tʀifyʒøz/ *nf* **1** (en électroménager) juice extractor, juicer; **2** Chimie, Mécan centrifuge.

centripète /sɑ̃tʀipɛt/ *adj* centripetal.

centrisme /sɑ̃tʀism/ *nm* centrism.

centriste /sɑ̃tʀist/ *adj, nmf* centrist.

centuple /sɑ̃typl/ **I** *adj* **une somme ~ d'une autre** an amount a hundred times greater than another.
II *nm* **dix mille est le ~ de cent** ten thousand is a hundred times one hundred; **notre investissement nous a rapporté au ~** lit we got back our investment a hundredfold; **rendre/être récompensé au ~** fig to repay/to be rewarded a hundred times over.

centupler /sɑ̃typle/ [1] **I** *vtr* to multiply [sth] by a hundred [*nombre*]; to increase [sth] a hundredfold [*fortune, production*].
II *vi* to increase a hundredfold.

centurie /sɑ̃tyʀi/ *nf* Antiq century.

centurion /sɑ̃tyʀjɔ̃/ *nm* centurion.

cep /sɛp/ *nm* **~ (de vigne)** vine stock.

CEP /seəpe/ *nm*: *abbr* ▶ **certificat**.

cépage /sepaʒ/ *nm* grape variety; **~ cabernet** Cabernet grape.

cèpe /sɛp/ *nm* cep.

cependant /səpɑ̃dɑ̃/ **I** *conj* (pourtant) yet, however; **son histoire est incroyable et ~ elle est vraie** his/her story is incredible and yet it is true; **votre devoir est bon mais il y a ~ quelques erreurs** your work is good; however, there are a few mistakes; **une ambiguïté subsiste ~** one ambiguity remains, however; **vous avez été très gentil, j'ai un reproche à vous faire ~** you've been very kind; however, I have one criticism to make.
II *adv* liter meanwhile.
III cependant que *loc conj* **~ que** (tandis que) whereas, while.

céphalée /sefale/ *nf* headache.

céphalique /sefalik/ *adj* cephalic.

céphalopode /sefalɔpɔd/ *nm* cephalopod; **les ~s** Cephalopoda.

céphalo-rachidien, **-ienne**, *mpl* **~s** /sefaloʀaʃidjɛ̃, ɛn/ *adj* cerebrospinal; **liquide ~** cerebrospinal fluid.

céramique /seʀamik/ **I** *adj* ceramic.
II *nf* **1** (matière) ceramic; **en ~** [*objet*] ceramic (*épith*); **2** (objet) ceramic; **3** (art, industrie, technique) ceramics (+ *v sg*).

céramiste /seʀamist/ ▶ 510 *nmf* ceramicist, ceramist, potter.

cerbère /sɛʀbɛʀ/ *nm* **1** (garde du corps) minder; **2** (gardien) watchdog.

Cerbère /sɛʀbɛʀ/ *npr* Mythol Cerberus.

cerceau, *pl* **~x** /sɛʀso/ *nm* (d'enfant, de tonneau) hoop; **pousser un ~** to bowl a hoop.

cerclage /sɛʀklaʒ/ *nm* **1** (de colis, malle) strapping; **2** (de tonneau) hooping; **3** Méd **~ du col de l'utérus** cervical stitching; **faire un ~ du col de l'utérus** to put in a cervical stitch.

cercle /sɛʀkl/ *nm* **1** (figure) circle; **en ~** in a circle; **former un ~ autour de** to form a circle ou ring around; **entourez le verbe d'un ~** ring ou circle the verb; **décrire des ~s** [*avion, oiseau*] to circle (overhead); **décrivez de petits ~s rapides avec les jambes** (en gymnastique) move your legs quickly in a small circular motion; **faire ~ autour de qn** to gather around sb; **2** (groupe) circle; **un ~ d'amis** a circle of friends; **maintenir le ~ de ses relations** to keep in touch with one's circle of acquaintances; **le ~ de famille** the family circle; **3** (association) circle, society; Jeux, Sport club; (local) club; **~ littéraire/artistique** literary/art circle ou society; **~ sportif** sports club; **faire un bridge au ~** to play bridge at the club; **4** (étendue) (de connaissances) scope; (d'occupations) range; **5** (de tonneau) hoop.
■ **~ circonscrit** circumcircle, circumscribed circle; **~ exinscrit** escribed circle; **~ horaire** Astron horary circle; **~ inscrit** inscribed circle; **~ polaire** polar circle; **~ polaire antarctique** Antarctic circle; **~ polaire arctique** Arctic circle; **~ de qualité** quality circle; **~ vertueux** virtuous circle; **~ vicieux** vicious circle.

cercler /sɛʀkle/ [1] *vtr* **1** (renforcer) to strap [*colis, caisse*]; to hoop [*tonneau*]; **2** (entourer) to circle [*mot*]; **les noms cerclés de** or **en rouge** the names circled in red; **poignets cerclés de bracelets d'argent** wrists circled with silver bracelets; **lunettes cerclées** rimmed glasses.

cercopithèque /sɛʀkɔpitɛk/ *nm* Old World monkey.

cercueil /sɛʀkœj/ *nm* coffin.

céréale /seʀeal/ **I** *nf* cereal, grain ¢; **cultiver des ~s** to grow cereals; **le sorgho est une ~** sorgho is a cereal.
II céréales *nfpl* Culin cereal ¢; **manger des ~s au petit déjeuner** to eat cereal for breakfast.

céréalier, **-ière** /seʀealje, ɛʀ/ **I** *adj* [*production*] cereal (*épith*); [*région, potentiel*] cereal-growing (*épith*).
II *nm* (producteur) cereal farmer, grain farmer.

cérébelleux, **-euse** /seʀebɛllø, øz/ *adj* cerebellar.

cérébral, **~e**, *mpl* **-aux** /seʀebʀal, o/ **I** *adj* **1** Anat, Méd cerebral; **2** (intellectuel) [*travail*] intellectual; [*fatigue*] mental; [*personne*] cerebral.
II *nm,f* cerebral type.

cérébro-spinal, **~e**, *mpl* **-aux** /seʀebʀospinal, o/ *adj* cerebrospinal.

cérémonial, *pl* **~s** /seʀemɔnjal/ *nm* ceremonial.

cérémonie /seʀemɔni/ **I** *nf* (tous contextes) ceremony; **~ commémorative/officielle/d'ouverture** commemorative/official/opening ceremony; **la ~ religieuse** the religious ceremony; **tenue** or **habit de ~** ceremonial dress.
II cérémonies *nfpl* (politesse exagérée) ceremony ¢; **faire des ~s** to stand on ceremony; **sans ~s** [*repas, invitation*] informal; [*recevoir*] informally.

cérémonieusement /seʀemɔnjøzmɑ̃/ *adv* ceremoniously.

cérémonieux, **-ieuse** /seʀemɔnjø, øz/ *adj* [*ton, personne*] ceremonious; **d'un air ~** ceremoniously.

cerf /sɛʀ/ *nm* stag.

cerfeuil /sɛʀfœj/ *nm* chervil.

cerf-volant, *pl* **cerfs-volants** /sɛʀvɔlɑ̃/ *nm* **1** (jouet) kite; **2** (insecte) stag beetle.

cerisaie /s(ə)ʀizɛ/ *nf* cherry orchard.

cerise /s(ə)ʀiz/ **I** ▶ 193 *adj inv* **(rouge) ~** cherry-red, cerise.
II *nf* cherry.
IDIOMES **se disputer pour des queues de ~s**○ to fall out over a trifle; **c'est la ~ sur le gâteau** it's the icing ou cherry on the cake.

cerisier /s(ə)ʀizje/ *nm* **1** (arbre) cherry (tree); **2** (bois) cherrywood.

cérium /seʀjɔm/ *nm* cerium.

CERN /sɛʀn/ *nm* (*abbr* = **Conseil européen pour la recherche nucléaire**) CERN.

cerne /sɛʀn/ *nm* **1** (autour des yeux) ring; **avoir des ~s** to have rings under one's eyes; **2** Bot tree ring; **3** (auréole) ring.

cerné, **~e** /sɛʀne/ **I** *pp* ▶ **cerner**.
II *pp adj* **avoir les yeux ~s** to have rings under one's eyes.

cerneau, *pl* **~x** /sɛʀno/ *nm* **~x de noix** walnut halves, halved walnuts.

cerner /sɛʀne/ [1] *vtr* **1** (encercler) to surround [*personne, lieu*]; **rendez-vous, vous êtes cernés!** give yourselves up, you're surrounded!; **2** (définir) to work out [*question, problème*]; to make [sb] out [*personne*]; to determine [*qualité, milieu, personnalité, besoins*]; **j'ai du mal à le ~** I can't make him out; **3** (décortiquer) to shell [*noix*].

certain, **~e** /sɛʀtɛ̃, ɛn/ **I** *adj* **1** (convaincu) **~ de** certain ou sure of; **être ~ de qch** to be certain ou sure of sth; **je suis ~ qu'elle est coupable** I'm certain ou sure that she's guilty; **est-ce que tu es ~ d'avoir fermé le gaz?** are your certain ou sure that you turned off the gas?; **nous ne sommes pas ~s qu'elle en a** or **qu'elle en ait envie** we're not certain ou sure that she feels like it; **2** (indiscutable) certain, sure; **tenir qch pour ~** to be certain of sth; **il est ~ qu'elle acceptera** it's certain that she'll accept, she's certain to accept; **il n'est pas ~ qu'il puisse venir** it's not certain ou definite that he'll be able to come; **ce n'est pas là chose ~e** it's not certain ou definite; **c'est sûr et ~**○ it's absolutely certain; **ils vont gagner, c'est ~!** they're bound to win!, they're sure to win!; **il est ~ qu'il n'aurait jamais pu faire ce qu'il a fait sans sa femme** he certainly couldn't have done what he did if it hadn't been for his wife; **ils vont à une mort ~e** they're heading for certain death; **il a sur ses élèves une influence ~e** he has an undeniable ou a definite influence on his pupils; **un homme d'un âge ~** a man of advanced years; **3** Comm [*date, prix*] definite, fixed; [*taux*] fixed.
II *adj indéf* (*before n*) **1** (mal défini) **elle restera à la maison un ~ temps** she'll stay at home for some time ou for a while; **il y a encore dans le texte un ~ nombre d'erreurs** there are still a (certain) number of mistakes in the text; **il représente une ~e image de la France** he represents a certain image of France; **se faire une ~e idée de la vie** to have a certain conception of life; **j'ai malgré tout une ~e admiration pour lui** in spite of everything I've got

a certain admiration for him; **dans une ~e mesure** to a certain ou to some extent; **d'une ~e manière** in a way; **jusqu'à un ~ point** up to a (certain) point; **il est venu un ~ soir que j'étais sorti** he came one evening when I was out; **2** (devant un nom de personne) **un ~ M. Grovagnard** a (certain) Mr Grovagnard; **3** (intensif) some; **il m'a fallu un ~ temps pour comprendre** it took me a while ou some time to understand; **ça demande un ~ entraînement/une ~e adresse** it requires some practice/some skill; **il faut un ~ culot**○ **pour**... it takes some nerve○ to...; **un homme d'un ~ âge** a man who's no longer young; **il avait déjà un ~ âge lorsqu'il a établi ce record** he was already getting on in years when he set this record.

III **certains**, **certaines** *adj indéf pl* some; **à ~s moments** sometimes, at times.

IV **certains**, **certaines** *pron indéf pl* some people; **~s d'entre eux** some of them.

certainement /sɛʀtɛnmɑ̃/ *adv* **1** (sans certitude) most probably; **c'est ~ quelqu'un de très compétent** he/she must be a very competent person; **vous avez ~ remarqué que** you've most probably noticed that; **il arrivera ~ en retard** he'll most probably be late; **2** (avec certitude) certainly; **je n'irai ~ pas!** I certainly won't go!; **tu y es ~ pour quelque chose!** you have certainly got something to do with it!; **3** (pour renforcer) certainly; **'tu peux m'aider?'—'mais ~!'** 'can you help me?'—'certainly' ou 'of course'; **~ pas!** certainly not!

certes /sɛʀt/ *adv* **1** (en signe de concession) admittedly; **ce ne sera ~ pas facile mais**... admittedly it won't be easy but...; **~, je me suis trompé, mais**... admittedly I made a mistake but...; **il est séduisant, ~, mais prétentieux** he is good-looking, certainly, but he is conceited; **2**† (assurément) indeed; **'c'est une question d'honneur?'—'~ non!'** 'is it a question of honour[GB]?'—'certainly not!'

certif○ /sɛʀtif/ *nm* **1** (*abbr* = **certificat**) certificate; **2** *abbr* = **certificat d'études primaires**.

certificat /sɛʀtifika/ *nm* **1** Admin, Comm (document officiel) certificate; **~ attestant de** certificate attesting (to); **~ attestant que** certificate showing that; **2** (document privé) testimonial; **3** (diplôme) certificate; **4** (titre) certificate.

■ **~ d'aptitude à la profession d'avocat**, **CAPA** *postgraduate legal qualification needed to practise[GB] as a solicitor or barrister*; **~ d'aptitude professionnelle**, **CAP** *vocational training qualification*; **~ d'authenticité** certificate of authenticity; **~ de bonne vie et mœurs** ≈ character reference; **~ de décès** death certificate; **~ d'études (primaires)**, **CEP** *basic school-leaving qualification*; **~ de garantie** certificate of guarantee; **~ médical** medical certificate; **~ de naissance** birth certificate; **~ d'origine** certificate of origin; **~ de résidence** proof of residence; **~ de scolarité** proof of attendance (*at school or university*); **~ de travail** *document from a previous employer giving dates and nature of employment*.

certification /sɛʀtifikasjɔ̃/ *nf* certification.

certifié, **~e** /sɛʀtifje/ I *pp* ▶ **certifier**.

II *pp adj* **professeur ~** fully qualified teacher.

III *nm,f* fully qualified teacher.

certifier /sɛʀtifje/ [2] *vtr* **1** gén to certify; Jur to guarantee [*caution*]; to authenticate [*signature*]; Fin to certify [*chèque*]; **~ que quelque chose est conforme à l'original** to certify that something is a true copy; **~ conforme** to authenticate; **copie certifiée conforme** certified true copy; **2** (affirmer) **elle m'a certifié que** she assured me that.

certitude /sɛʀtityd/ *nf* **1** gén, Philos (caractère indubitable) certainty; **c'est maintenant une ~** it's now a certainty; **on sait avec ~ que** we know for certain that; **seule ~, il est parti à midi** all we know for certain is that he left at noon; **2** (conviction) conviction; **rien ne peut ébranler ses ~s** nothing can shake his/her convictions; **avoir la ~ que** to be certain that; **avoir la ~ de faire** to be certain of doing.

céruléen, **-éenne** /seʀyleɛ̃, ɛn/ ▶ **193** *adj* liter cerulean, deep blue.

cérumen /seʀymɛn/ *nm* earwax, cerumen spéc; **bouchon de ~** cerumen blockage.

céruse /seʀyz/ *nf* ceruse, white lead.

Cervantès /sɛʀvɑ̃tɛs/ *npr* Cervantes.

cerveau, *pl* **~x** /sɛʀvo/ *nm* **1** Anat brain; **2** (siège de l'intelligence) mind; **~ débile/puissant** feeble/powerful mind; **3** (personne intelligente) brain○; **importer/attirer des ~x** to import/attract the best brains○; **exode** or **fuite des ~x** brain drain; **la chasse aux ~x** talent hunting; **c'est un ~** he/she has an outstanding mind, he's/she's got brains○; **4** (organisateur) **c'est elle le ~ de l'association** she's the brains of the association; **c'est le ~ du projet/des attentats** he's/she's the brains ou mastermind behind the project/the attacks.

■ **~ antérieur** forebrain; **~ électronique** Ordinat electronic brain; **~ moyen** midbrain; **~ postérieur** hindbrain.

IDIOMES **avoir le ~ fêlé**○ or **dérangé** to be deranged ou cracked○.

cervelas /sɛʀvəla/ *nm* saveloy.

cervelet /sɛʀvəlɛ/ *nm* cerebellum.

cervelle /sɛʀvɛl/ *nf* **1** (substance) brains (*pl*); **se brûler** or **se faire sauter la ~**○ to blow one's brains out○; **~ de veau/d'agneau** Culin calf's/lamb's brains; **2**○ (tête) brain; **cette idée lui trotte dans la ~** he's/she's got this idea on the brain; **il n'a rien dans la ~** he's brainless; **être sans ~** to be scatterbrained; **quand il a** or **se met quelque chose dans la ~**... when he gets an idea in his head...; **c'est une petite ~** he's/she's a pinhead○; **elle a une ~ d'oiseau** she's a birdbrain.

cervical, **~e**, *mpl* **-aux** /sɛʀvikal, o/ *adj* cervical.

cervidé /sɛʀvide/ *nm* cervid; **les ~s** Cervidae.

Cervin /sɛʀvɛ̃/ *nprm* **le (mont) ~** the Matterhorn.

cervoise /sɛʀvwaz/ *nf* (barley) beer.

ces ▶ **ce**.

CES /seəes/ *nm*: *abbr* **1** ▶ **collège**; **2** ▶ **contrat**.

césar /sezaʀ/ *nm* **1** Cin César (*film award*); **2** (dictateur) caesar.

César /sezaʀ/ *nm* **1** = **césar**; **2** Hist **Jules ~** Julius Caesar.

IDIOMES **rendons à ~ ce qui appartient** or **est à ~** render unto Caesar that which is Caesar's.

Césarée /sezaʀe/ ▶ **857** *npr* Caesarea.

césarienne /sezaʀjɛn/ *nf* caesarian (section); **on lui a fait une ~** she had a caesarian.

césium /sezjɔm/ *nm* caesium[GB].

cessante /sesɑ̃t/ *adj f* **toute(s) affaire(s) ~(s)** fml forthwith sout.

cessation /sesasjɔ̃/ *nf* (d'aide, hostilités) suspension, cessation sout; (de poursuites, paiement, travail) suspension.

■ **~ d'activité** gén suspension of activities; (retraite) retirement; Comm closing down; **~ de commerce** Comm closing down; **~ de paiement** insolvency; **être en ~ de paiement** [*commerce, entreprise*] to be unable to meet one's financial obligations, to be insolvent.

cesse /sɛs/ *nf* **elle n'a de ~ de démontrer/répéter/dénoncer**... she's forever demonstrating/repeating/denouncing...; **sans ~** [*parler, changer*] constantly; **un nombre sans ~ grandissant** an ever increasing number; **des machines sans ~ plus puissantes** ever more powerful machines.

cesser /sese/ [1] I *vtr* to cease, to stop [*traitement, livraisons*]; to end [*soutien, répression*]; **~ de faire** to stop doing; **~ toute activité** [*entreprise*] to cease trading; **~ son activité** [*employé*] to stop work; **~ les combats** to stop fighting; **elle n'a jamais cessé son combat contre**... she has fought relentlessly against...; **~ d'aider qn/de s'inquiéter** to stop helping sb/worrying; **~ de fumer/d'espérer** to give up smoking/hope; **~ d'exister** to cease to exist; **ils ont cessé d'être nos clients en 1992** they ceased to be our clients in 1992; **~ de payer** to cease payment; **ils n'ont (pas) cessé de critiquer** they kept on criticizing; **les taux d'intérêt ne cessent d'augmenter/de baisser** interest rates keep (on) rising/falling; **son courage ne cesse de m'étonner** his/her courage never ceases to amaze me.

II *vi* [*activité*] to cease; [*vent*] to drop; [*pluie*] to stop; **faire ~** to put an end to [*rumeur*]; to put a stop to [*répression, combats*]; to end [*poursuites*].

cessez-le-feu /seselfø/ *nm inv* ceasefire; **accord de ~** ceasefire agreement; **un ~ est entré en vigueur hier** a ceasefire came into force yesterday.

cessible /sesibl/ *adj* transferable.

cession /sesjɔ̃/ *nf* Jur, Fin transfer, assignment; **~ de droits/de titres/d'actifs** transfer of rights/of securities/of assets.

cession-bail, *pl* **cessions-bails** /sesjɔ̃baj/ *nf* leaseback.

cessionnaire /sesjɔnɛʀ/ *nmf* transferee, assignee.

c'est-à-dire /setadiʀ/ *loc conj* **1** (pour préciser) that is (to say); **les pays de l'Est, ~**... eastern countries, that is to say...; **2** (ce qui signifie) **~ que** which means (that); **il n'a pas téléphoné, ~ qu'il ne viendra pas** he hasn't phoned, which means (that) he won't come; **'j'ai presque fini'—'~ que tu viens de commencer'** 'I've nearly finished'—'what you mean is that you've barely started'; **'le travail est trop dur'—'~?'** 'the work is too hard'—'what do you mean?'; **3** (pour rectifier, excuser) **~ que** well, actually; **'il ne se rend pas compte'—'~ qu'il est jeune'** 'he doesn't realize'—'well, you know, he's young'; **'tu ne manges pas?'—'~ que je suis au régime'** 'aren't you eating?'—'well, actually, I'm on a diet'.

césure /sezyʀ/ *nf* **1** Littérat caesura; **2** Ordinat, Imprim line break; **3** (rupture) abrupt transition.

cet ▶ **ce**.

CET /seəte/ *nm*: *abbr* ▶ **collège**.

cétacé /setase/ *nm* cetacean; **les ~s** Cetacea.

cette ▶ **ce**.

ceux ▶ **celui**.

ceux-ci ▶ **celui-ci**.

ceux-là ▶ **celui-là**.

Cévennes /sevɛn/ ▶ **692** *nprfpl* **les ~** the Cévennes.

cévenol, **~e** /sevnɔl/ ▶ **692** *adj* of the Cévennes.

Cévenol, **~e** /sevnɔl/ *nm,f* (natif) native of the Cévennes; (habitant) inhabitant of the Cévennes.

Ceylan /sɛlɑ̃/ *nprm* Hist Ceylon; **thé de ~** Ceylon tea.

CFA /seɛfa/ I *adj* (*abbr* = **Communauté financière africaine**) **franc ~** CFA franc.

II *nm*: *abbr* ▶ **centre**.

CFAO /seɛfao/ *nf* (*abbr* = **conception et fabrication assistées par ordinateur**) CADCAM.

CFC /seɛfse/ *nm* (*abbr* = **chlorofluorocarbone**) CFC.

CFDT /seɛfdete/ *nf* (*abbr* = **Confédération**

française démocratique du travail) CFDT (*French trade union*).

CFTC /seeftese/ *nf* (*abbr* = **Confédération française des travailleurs chrétiens**) CFTC (*French trade union*).

CGC /seʒese/ *nf* (*abbr* = **Confédération générale des cadres**) CGC (*French trade union*).

CGT /seʒete/ *nf* (*abbr* = **Confédération générale du travail**) CGT (*French trade union*).

chacal, *pl* **~s** /ʃakal/ *nm* Zool, fig jackal.

cha-cha-cha /tʃatʃatʃa/ *nm* cha-cha; **danser le ~** to cha-cha.

chaconne /ʃakɔn/ *nf* chaconne.

chacun, **~e** /ʃakœ̃, yn/ *pron indéf* **1** (chaque élément) each (one); **~ de** each one of, every one of; **~ d'entre nous** each (one) of us, every one of us; **~ d'entre eux** each (one) of them, every one of them; **il nous a donné un fusil (à) ~** he gave each of us a gun; **ils avaient ~ un œil au beurre noir** they each had a black eye; **ils ont ~ sa** or **leur chambre** they each have their own room, each of them has their own room; **elles ont ~e leurs qualités** they each have their good points, each of them has their good points; **vous avez droit à une boisson ~** you're each entitled to a drink, you're entitled to a drink each; **ils coûtent 100 francs ~** they cost 100 francs each; **nous avons ~ pris notre veste** we all took our jackets; **~ rentra chez soi de son côté** everyone made their own way home; **2** (tout le monde) everyone; **~ a ses défauts** everyone has their faults; **comme ~ sait** as everyone knows; **~ son tour** everyone in turn, each in turn; **~ son tour!** wait your turn!; **~ a le droit de vivre comme il l'entend** everyone has the right to live as he or she chooses ou as they choose; **à ~ selon son mérite** to everyone according to their merits, to each according to his or her merits; **~ ses goûts** every man to his own taste; **~ pour soi (et Dieu pour tous)** every man for himself (and God for us all); **tout un ~** every Tom, Dick and Harry, everyone; **à ~ son métier** every man to his own trade.

chafouin, **~e** /ʃafwɛ̃, in/ *adj* sly.

chagrin, **~e** /ʃagʀɛ̃, in/ **I** *adj* [*personne*] despondent, dejected; [*visage*] doleful; [*temps*] dreary; **être d'humeur ~e** to be despondent ou dejected; **les esprits ~s** the malcontents.

II *nm* **1** (peine) grief, sorrow; **faire du ~ à qn** to cause sb grief; **accablé de ~** grief-stricken; **à mon grand ~** to my (great) sorrow; **avoir du ~** to be sad; **avoir beaucoup de ~** to be very sad; **'M. et Mme Vernet ont l'immense ~ de vous faire part du décès de leur fils Pierre'** 'it is with great sadness that Mr and Mrs Vernet have to inform you of the death of their son Pierre'; **elle a eu de nombreux ~s** she's had many sorrows; **mourir de ~** to die of a broken heart; **avoir un gros ~** [*enfant*] to be very upset; **2** (en reliure) shagreen; **relié plein ~** bound in shagreen.

■ **~ d'amour** unhappy love affair.

chagriner /ʃagʀine/ [1] *vtr* **1** (peiner) to pain, to grieve; **2** (contrarier) to bother, to worry; **il y a quelque chose qui me chagrine dans cette histoire** there's something about this story which bothers me.

chah = **shah**.

chahut /ʃay/ *nm* racket○; **faire du ~** [*fêtard*] to make a racket○; [*élève*] to play up the teacher.

chahuter /ʃayte/ [1] **I** *vtr* **1** [*élève, classe*] to play up [*enseignant, surveillant*]; [*personne, groupe*] to heckle [*orateur*]; **se faire ~ par qn** gén to be heckled by sb; **2** (mettre à mal) **être chahuté** [*monnaie, valeur*] to come under pressure; [*gouvernement*] to be given a hard time; [*emploi du temps*] to be disrupted.

II *vi* to mess around (**avec** with).

chahuteur, **-euse** /ʃaytœʀ, øz/ **I** *adj* disruptive.

II *nm,f* (élève) disruptive child; (adulte) rowdy person.

chai /ʃɛ/ *nm* wine storehouse.

chaînage /ʃɛnaʒ/ *nm* Ordinat chaining.

chaîne /ʃɛn/ **I** *nf* **1** (entrave) chain; **mettre les ~s à qn** to put sb in chains; **attacher qn avec des ~s** to chain sb up; **attacher son chien à une ~** to put one's dog on a chain; **briser ses ~s** to cast off one's chains; **2** Mécan chain; **~ de transmission/de vélo** transmission/bicycle chain; **~ de sécurité** safety chain; **3** Ind assembly line; **être/travailler à la ~** to be/to work on the assembly line; **produire (qch) à la ~** to mass-produce (sth); **production à la ~** mass production; **on n'est pas à la ~○!** fig we're not machines, you know!; **système éducatif à la ~** conveyor-belt education system; **4** (bijou) chain; **~ en or** gold chain; **~ de montre** watch chain; **5** (succession) chain; **des catastrophes en ~** a series of disasters; **réaction en ~** chain reaction; **6** (organisation) network; **~ de solidarité** support network; **faire la ~** to make a chain; **7** Géog chain, range; **~ de montagnes/des Pyrénées** mountain/Pyrenean chain; **8** (de télévision) channel; **~ de télévision** television channel; **deuxième ~** channel 2; **~ câblée/musicale/publique** cable/music/public channel; **9** Comm chain; **~ de magasins** chain of stores; **~ d'hôtels** hotel chain; **10** Audio system; **~ hi-fi** hi-fi system; **~ stéréo** stereo system; **~ compacte** music centre; **11** Chimie chain; **~ moléculaire** molecular chain; **12** Tex warp.

II chaînes *nfpl* Aut snow chains; **mettre les ~s** to put the snow chains on.

■ **~ alimentaire** food chain; **~ d'arpenteur** surveyor's chain; **~ d'assemblage** assembly line; **~ de caractères** character string; **~ de commandement** chain of command; **~ de fabrication** Ind production line; **~ du froid** cold chain; **~ de montage** Ind assembly line; **~ nerveuse** Anat sympathetic chain; **~ des osselets** Anat (chain of) bonelets; **~ parlée** Ling speech chain.

chaîner /ʃene/ [1] *vtr, vi* Aut to put snow chains on.

chaînette /ʃɛnɛt/ *nf* **1** Mécan small chain; **2** Mode chain; **~ en argent** silver chain; **3** Math catenary.

chaînon /ʃɛnɔ̃/ *nm* **1** gén link; **~ manquant** missing link; **2** Géog secondary chain.

chair /ʃɛʀ/ **I** ▶ **193** *adj inv* flesh-coloured[GB]; **soutien-gorge ~** flesh-coloured[GB] bra.

II *nf* **1** Anat flesh ¢; **~s meurtries** bruised flesh; **bien en ~** plump, well-padded○; **2** Culin (de fruit, légume, poisson) flesh; (de volaille) meat; **~ à saucisses** sausage meat; **3** (corps) flesh; **plaisirs de la ~** pleasures of the flesh; **~ de ma ~** my own flesh and blood; **être de ~** to be only human.

■ **~ à canon○** cannon fodder; **~ fraîche** young bodies (*pl*); **~ de poule** gooseflesh, goose pimples (*pl*), goosebumps (*pl*); **avoir la ~ de poule** to have gooseflesh ou goose pimples ou have goosebumps; **donner la ~ de poule à qn** [*froid*] to give sb gooseflesh; [*peur*] to give sb gooseflesh, to make sb's flesh creep.

IDIOMES **transformer qn en ~ à pâté** or **saucisses○** to make mincemeat of sb○; **l'esprit est ardent mais la ~ est faible** the spirit is willing but the flesh is weak.

chaire /ʃɛʀ/ *nf* **1** Relig (tribune) pulpit; (siège) throne; **être en ~** to be in the pulpit; **monter en ~** to step up into the pulpit; **annoncer qch en ~** to announce sth from the pulpit; **~ épiscopale/pontificale** bishop's/papal throne; **2** Univ (poste) chair; **être titulaire d'une ~ d'histoire médiévale** to hold a chair in medieval history; **3** Univ (tribune) rostrum.

chaise /ʃɛz/ *nf* **1** (siège) chair; **~ cannée/pliante** cane/folding chair; **politique de la ~ vide** empty-chair policy; ▶ **bâton**; **2** Mécan (support d'arbre) seating, mounting.

■ **~ d'arbitre** umpire's chair; **~ pour bébé** = **~ haute**; **~ électrique** electric chair; **~ haute** highchair; **~ longue** deckchair; **faire de la ~ longue** fig to take it easy; **~ percée** commode; **~ à porteurs** sedan chair; **~ de poste** post chaise; **~ roulante** wheelchair; **~s musicales** musical chairs.

IDIOMES **être assis** or **avoir le cul○ entre deux ~s** to be in an awkward position.

chaisière /ʃezjɛʀ/ ▶ **510** *nf* chair attendant.

chaland, **~e** /ʃalɑ̃, ɑ̃d/ **I** *nm,f* (client) regular customer.

II *nm* Naut barge.

chaland-citerne, *pl* **chalands-citernes** /ʃalɑ̃sitɛʀn/ *nm* tank barge.

chalandise /ʃalɑ̃diz/ *nf* **zone de ~** catchment area of shop ou shopping centre[GB].

chalazion /ʃalazjɔ̃/ *nm* chalazion, meibomian cyst.

Chalcidique /kalsidik/ ▶ **692** *nprf* Khalkidiki.

chalcopyrite /kalkopiʀit/ *nf* chalcopyrite, fool's gold.

Chaldée /kalde/ *nprf* Chaldea.

chaldéen, **-éenne** /kaldeɛ̃, ɛn/ **I** *adj* Chaldean.

II *nm* Ling Chaldean.

Chaldéen, **-éenne** /kaldeɛ̃, ɛn/ *nm,f* Chaldean, Chaldee.

châle /ʃɑl/ *nm* shawl.

chalet /ʃalɛ/ *nm* **1** (de montagne) chalet; **2** (maison en bois) chalet-style house.

■ **~ de nécessité†** public convenience.

chaleur /ʃalœʀ/ **I** *nf* **1** (sensation physique) heat; (douce) warmth; **la ~ du poêle/soleil** the heat of the stove/sun; **vague de ~** heatwave; **coup de ~** heat stroke; **~ moite/accablante** muggy/oppressive heat; **la douce ~ printanière** the warmth of spring; **pour conserver la ~ dans votre salon** to keep the heat in your living room; **on étouffe de ~, ici!** it's sweltering in here!; **il faisait une ~ moite** it was muggy; **il fait une de ces ~s○!** it's boiling (hot)○!; **elle est sortie en pleine ~** she went out in the hottest part of the day; **2** (cordialité) (de personne, d'accueil) warmth; (de voix, coloris) warmth; **accueillir qn avec ~** to give sb a warm welcome; **dans la ~ de la discussion** in the heat of the discussion; **3** Zool **(être) en ~** (to be) on heat; **les ~s** the heat ¢; **4** Phys heat.

II chaleurs *nfpl* Météo **les ~s** the hot season (*sg*); **les premières/dernières ~s** the first/last days of the hot season; **lors des grandes** or **grosses○ ~s** in the hot season.

■ **~ animale** body heat; **~ de combustion** combustion heat; **~ latente** latent heat; **~ massique** or **spécifique** specific heat.

chaleureusement /ʃaløʀøzmɑ̃/ *adv* [*applaudir, remercier*] warmly; [*soutenir*] wholeheartedly; **accueillir qn ~** to give sb a warm welcome.

chaleureux, **-euse** /ʃaløʀø, øz/ *adj* [*personne, accueil, voix, paroles*] warm; [*public, applaudissements*] enthusiastic; [*soutien, appui*] wholehearted; [*atmosphère*] friendly; [*maison, endroit*] welcoming.

châlit /ʃɑli/ *nm* (cadre) bedstead; (lit) pallet (bed).

challenge /ʃalɑ̃ʒ/ *nm* **1** (défi) challenge; **femme/homme de ~** woman/man who thrives on challenges; **avoir le goût du ~** to like a challenge; **2** Sport (épreuve) tournament; (trophée) trophy.

challenge(u)r /ʃalɑ̃ʒœʀ/ *nm* challenger

chaloir† /ʃalwaʀ/ *v impers* **peu me** or **m'en chaut** it matters little to me; **peu leur chaut mon hostilité/mes critiques** my hostility/my criticism matters little to them.

chaloupe /ʃalup/ *nf* **1** (à rames) rowing boat GB, rowboat US; **2** (à moteur) (motor) launch.

chaloupé, **~e** /ʃalupe/ *adj* [*valse, tango*] swaying; **une démarche ~e** a rolling gait.

chalumeau, *pl* **~x** /ʃalymo/ *nm* **1** (outil) blowtorch; **au ~** with a blowtorch; **~ coupeur** or **à découper** cutting torch; **~ soudeur** or **à souder** welding torch; **~ à acétylène** oxyacetylene torch; **2** ▶ **534** (flûte) pipe; **3** (pour boire) straw.

chalut /ʃaly/ *nm* trawl; **jeter/tirer le ~** to shoot/to haul the trawl; **pêcher** or **draguer au ~** to trawl; **pêcher qch au ~** to trawl for sth.

chalutier /ʃalytje/ *nm* **1** (bateau) trawler; **2** ▶ **510** (marin) trawlerman.

chamade /ʃamad/ *nf* **battre la ~** to beat wildly.

chamailler○: **se chamailler** /ʃamaje/ [1] *vpr* to squabble (**avec** with).

chamaillerie○ /ʃamajʀi/ *nf* squabble.

chamailleur○, **-euse** /ʃamajœʀ, øz/ *adj* quarrelsome.

chaman /ʃaman/ *nm* shaman.

chamanisme /ʃamanism/ *nm* shamanism.

chamarré, **~e** /ʃamaʀe/ **I** *pp* ▶ **chamarrer**.
II *pp adj* **1** (garni d'ornements) [*tissu, vêtement, uniforme*] richly coloured[GB] and brocaded; **~ de** [*vêtement, tissu*] adorned with; **~ d'or** with gold brocade; **2** (multicolore) [*perroquet*] brightly coloured[GB].

chamarrer /ʃamaʀe/ [1] *vtr* to adorn (**de** with).

chamarrure /ʃamaʀyʀ/ *nf* (ornement) rich decoration.

chambard○ /ʃɑ̃baʀ/ *nm* **1** (vacarme, désordre) din, racket○; **ils ont fait un de ces ~s** they made such a dreadful racket○; **2** (bouleversement) upheaval.

chambardement○ /ʃɑ̃baʀdəmɑ̃/ *nm* **1** (bouleversement) shake-up○; **2** (désordre) mess; **quel ~! tu déménages?** what a mess! are you moving house?

chambarder○ /ʃɑ̃baʀde/ [1] *vtr* **1** (mettre sens dessus dessous) to turn [sth] upside down; **ils ont chambardé toute la maison, ils ont tout chambardé dans la maison** they turned the whole house upside down; **2** (modifier) [*personne, événement*] to shake up [*vie*]; to upset [*plans, projets, habitudes*].

chambellan /ʃɑ̃bɛllɑ̃/ *nm* chamberlain; ▶ **grand**.

chambérien, **-ienne** /ʃɑ̃beʀjɛ̃, ɛn/ ▶ **857** *adj* of Chambéry.

Chambérien, **-ienne** /ʃɑ̃beʀjɛ̃, ɛn/ *nm,f* (natif) native of Chambéry; (habitant) inhabitant of Chambéry.

Chambéry /ʃɑ̃beʀi/ ▶ **857** *npr* Chambéry.

chamboulement○ /ʃɑ̃bulmɑ̃/ *nm* **1** (bouleversement) shake-up; **2** (désordre) mess.

chambouler○ /ʃɑ̃bule/ [1] *vtr* **1** (bouleverser) [*personne, événement*] to upset [*programme, projet*]; to shake up [*vie, service, établissement*]; **~ ses habitudes** to change one's way of doing things; **ils ont tout chamboulé** they upset everything; **2** (mettre en désordre) to turn [sth] upside down [*pièce, maison*]; to mess [sth] up [*meuble, bureau*]; (mélanger) to mix [sth] up [*photos, timbres, papiers*]; **ils ont tout chamboulé (dans la maison)** they turned the whole house upside down.

chambranle /ʃɑ̃bʀɑ̃l/ *nm* (de porte, fenêtre) frame; (de cheminée) mantel, fire surround.

chambre /ʃɑ̃bʀ/ *nf* **1** (pour dormir) gén room; (chez soi) bedroom; **~ meublée à louer** furnished room to let; **~ d'hôtel/d'hôpital** hotel/hospital room; **~ individuelle** or **à un lit** or **pour une personne** single room; **~ double** or **pour deux personnes** double room; **~ à deux lits** twin room; **faire ~ à part** to sleep in separate rooms; **avez-vous une ~ de libre?** have you got any rooms free ou vacancies?; **politicien/athlète en ~** hum, pej armchair politician/athlete hum, péj; **2** Mus **musique/orchestre de ~** chamber music/orchestra; **3** Pol (assemblée parlementaire) house; **4** Jur (section d'un tribunal) *division of a court of justice*; **5** Admin (organe professionnel) chamber; **6** Tech (enceinte close) chamber; **~ d'un revolver/appareil photo** chamber of a gun/camera.
■ **~ d'accusation** *criminal division of the court of appeal*; **~ d'agriculture** *farmers' association in each French department*; **~ à air** inner tube; **~ d'amis** guest room; **~ basse** Pol Lower House; **~ de bonne** maid's room; **~ à bulles** Phys Nucl bubble chamber; **~ des cartes** Naut chart room; **~ de chauffe** (de fonderie) fire chamber; Naut stokehold, fire room; **~ civile** *civil appeal division of a superior court*; **~ claire** camera lucida; **~ de combustion** Aut combustion chamber; **~ de commerce (et d'industrie)** chamber of commerce; **~ de compensation** clearing house; **~ du conseil** (local) Judge's Chambers (*used for deliberation*); (magistrats) *magistrates in deliberation after completion of hearing*; **~ à coucher** (pièce) bedroom; (mobilier) bedroom suite; **~ criminelle** criminal court; **~ forte** strong room; **~ frigorifique** or **froide** cold (storage) room; **~ à gaz** gas chamber; **~ haute** Pol Upper House; **~ d'hôte** ≈ room in a guest house; **'~s d'hôte'** guest house (*sg*); **~ d'isolement** Méd isolation room; **~ de métiers** professional association; **~ noire** Phot (boîte) camera obscura; (local) darkroom; **~ pollinique** Bot pollen chamber; **~ de simulation** Astronaut simulation chamber; **~ sourde** Tech anechoic room; **~ syndicale** Employers' federation; **~ de torture** torture chamber; **Chambre des communes** House of Commons; **Chambre des députés** Pol Chamber of Deputies; **Chambre des lords** House of Lords; **Chambre des représentants** House of Representatives.

chambrée /ʃɑ̃bʀe/ *nf* Mil (dortoir, soldats) barracks; **plaisanterie de ~** barrack-room joke GB, ≈ locker-room joke US.

chambrer /ʃɑ̃bʀe/ [1] *vtr* **1** Vin to bring [sth] to room temperature [*vin, bouteille*]; **ce vin rouge se boit chambré** this red wine is drunk at room temperature; **2**○ (se moquer de) to tease, to take the mickey out of○ GB [*personne*]; **se faire ~** to get teased.

chambrette /ʃɑ̃bʀɛt/ *nf* small bedroom.

chambrière† /ʃɑ̃bʀijɛʀ/ *nf* (femme de chambre) chambermaid.

chameau, *pl* **~x** /ʃamo/ *nm* **1** Zool camel; **2**○ (personne désagréable) pej nasty person; **c'est un ~** he's/she's really nasty.

chamelier /ʃaməlje/ ▶ **510** *nm* camel driver.

chamelle /ʃamɛl/ *nf* she-camel.

chamito-sémitique, *pl* **~s** /kamitosemitik/ *adj, nm* Semito-Hamitic.

chamois /ʃamwa/ **I** ▶ **193** *adj inv* (ocre jaune) fawn.
II *nm* **1** Zool chamois; **2** Sport *medal awarded for skiing competence*.

chamoisée /ʃamwaze/ *adj f* **chèvre ~** mountain goat.

chamoniard, **~e** /ʃamɔnjaʀ, aʀd/ ▶ **857** *adj* of Chamonix.

Chamoniard, **~e** /ʃamɔnjaʀ, aʀd/ *nm,f* (natif) native of Chamonix; (habitant) inhabitant of Chamonix.

Chamonix /ʃamɔni/ ▶ **857** *npr* Chamonix.

champ /ʃɑ̃/ **I** *nm* **1** (terre cultivable) field; **dans un ~ de colza** in a field of rapeseed; **des ~s de coton** cotton fields; **couper** or **prendre à travers ~s** to cut across the fields; **travailler aux ~s** to work in the fields; **se promener dans les ~s** to walk in the fields; **en pleins ~s** in open country; **2** (étendue) field; **~ de glace** ice field; **~ de neige** snowfield; **~ pétrolifère** or **de pétrole** oil field; **~ de dunes** dunes (*pl*); **3** (domaine) field; **mon ~ d'action/de recherche** my field of action/of research; **le ~ culturel/politique** the cultural/political arena; **le ~ des polémiques/investigations** the scope of the controversies/investigations; **le ~ est libre, on peut y aller** lit the coast is clear, we can go; fig the way is clear, we can go; **avoir le ~ libre** to have a free hand; **laisser le ~ libre à qn** gén to give sb a free hand; (en se retirant) to make way for sb; **4** Phot, Cin field; **le ~ visuel** the field of vision; **être dans le ~** to be in shot; **entrer dans le/sortir du ~** to come into/go out of shot; **être hors ~** [*personnage*] to be offscreen ou out of shot; **une voix hors ~** an offscreen voice; **prendre du ~** fig to stand back; **5** Phys field; **~ acoustique/électrique/magnétique** sound/electric/magnetic field; **6** Ling field; **~ conceptuel/dérivationnel/lexical/sémantique** conceptual/derivational/lexical/semantic field; **7** Math field; **~ de vecteurs/scalaires/tenseurs** vector/scalar/tensor field; **8** Hérald, Ordinat field.
II à tout bout de champ○ *loc adv* all the time; ▶ **sur-le-champ**.
■ **~ d'aviation** airfield; **~ de bataille** Mil, fig battlefield; **~ de courses** racecourse GB, racetrack; **~ d'épandage** sewage farm; **~ de foire** fairground; **~ de manœuvre** training area; **~ de mines** minefield; **~ opératoire** (linge) sterile towel; (zone) operative field; **~ de tir** (terrain d'exercice) firing range; (portée) range; **~ de tir aérien** bombing range; **~s ouverts** open fields.
IDIOMES **mourir au ~ d'honneur** to be killed in action.

champagne /ʃɑ̃paɲ/ *nm* Vin champagne; **boire du ~** to drink champagne; **~ brut/sec/demi-sec** extra-dry/dry/medium-dry champagne; **~ rosé** pink champagne.

Champagne /ʃɑ̃paɲ/ *nprf* ▶ **692** **la ~** the Champagne region.

champagnisation /ʃɑ̃paɲizasjɔ̃/ *nf* (pour faire du champagne) champagne-making process; (pour faire un mousseux) carbonation by the champagne method.

champagniser /ʃɑ̃paɲize/ [1] *vtr* **1** (pour faire du champagne) to make [sth] into champagne [*vin*]; **2** (pour imiter le champagne) to render [sth] sparkling by the champagne method [*vin*]; **vins champagnisés** sparkling wines.

champenois, **~e** /ʃɑ̃pənwa, az/ *adj* **1** ▶ **692** Géog of the Champagne region; **2** Vin **méthode ~e** champagne method.

Champenois, **~e** /ʃɑ̃pənwa, az/ *nm,f* (habitant) inhabitant of the Champagne region; (natif) native of the Champagne region.

champêtre /ʃɑ̃pɛtʀ/ *adj* [*fête, bal*] village (*épith*); [*scène, paysage, cadre*] rural; **déjeuner/pique-nique ~** lunch/picnic in the country.

champignon /ʃɑ̃piɲɔ̃/ *nm* **1** Culin mushroom, edible fungus; **~ vénéneux** poisonous mushroom, toadstool; **aller aux ~s** to go mushroom picking; **2** Bot, Méd fungus; **avoir un ~**○ to have a fungal infection; **3** (ornement) (porte-manteau) mushroom-shaped peg; (siège) mushroom-shaped stool; (dans un jardin) toadstool; **4**○ Aut (accélérateur) throttle, accelerator; **appuyer sur le ~** to put one's foot down GB, to step on the gas US.
■ **~ atomique** Nucl mushroom cloud; **~ de couche** or **de Paris** button mushroom GB, champignon US; **~ hallucinogène** hallucinogenic mushroom, magic mushroom○.
IDIOMES **pousser comme des ~s** to pop up like mushrooms.

champignonnière /ʃɑ̃piɲɔnjɛʀ/ *nf* mushroom bed.

champion, **-ionne** /ʃɑ̃pjɔ̃, ɔn/ *nm,f* **1** Sport, Jeux (vainqueur) champion; (sportif de haut niveau) leading player; **~ d'Europe/du Monde d'escrime** European/World fencing champion; **~ olympique** Olympic champion; **le ~ en titre** the titleholder; **2**○

(qui excelle) **être ~** [*personne*] to be in a class of one's own; **quand il s'agit de faire des bêtises, tu es ~** when it comes to doing stupid things, you're in a class of your own; **~ de la gaffe** prize fool; **~ de l'imitation/du rire** top impressionist/comedian; **3**○ (leader) **pays ~ de la lutte contre la drogue** country which leads the field in the fight against drugs; **cette région est championne de la production de vin** this region leads the field in wine production; **4**○ (défenseur) champion; **se poser en ~ de la vertu** to set oneself up as a champion of virtue; **se faire le ~ d'une cause** to champion a cause.

championnat /ʃɑ̃pjɔna/ *nm* Sport, Jeux championship; **~s d'Europe d'escrime** European fencing championships; **finale de ~** championship final.

chançard○, **~e** /ʃɑ̃saʀ, aʀd/ **I** *adj* lucky.
II *nm,f* lucky devil○.

chance /ʃɑ̃s/ *nf* **1** (sort favorable) (good) luck; **quelle ~!** what (a piece of) luck!; **c'est bien ma ~!** iron just my luck!; **pas de ~, tu as perdu!** bad luck, you've lost!; **coup de ~** stroke of luck; **~ inespérée** unexpected stroke of luck; **la ~ a voulu que je le croise** as luck would have it, I bumped into him; **la ~ aidant, il a réussi** he was lucky, he succeeded; **la ~ aidant, il réussira** with a bit of luck, he'll succeed; **il y a une belle part de ~ dans sa réussite** luck played quite a part in his/her success; **la ~ leur a souri** fortune smiled on them; **avoir de la ~** to be lucky; **ne pas avoir de ~** to be unlucky; **il n'a pas eu de ~** (à un examen) he was unlucky; (ces derniers temps) he hasn't had much luck; **avoir une ~ du tonnerre**○ or **de cocu**○ to have the luck of the devil; **avoir la ~ de faire** to have the good luck to do; **courir** or **tenter sa ~** to try one's luck; **avoir la ~ de trouver une maison** to be lucky enough to find a house; **c'est une ~ de pouvoir partir** or **que nous puissions partir** we're lucky to be able to leave; **par ~** luckily, fortunately; **2** (possibilité) chance (**de qch** of sth; **de faire** of doing); **il y a (encore) une ~ de paix** there's (still) a chance of peace; **mes recherches ont peu de ~s d'aboutir** my research is unlikely to come to anything; **il y a de fortes ~s (pour) qu'elle vienne** there's every chance that she will come; **il a ses ~s** he stands a good chance; **il n'a aucune ~** he doesn't stand a chance; **mettre toutes les ~s de son côté** to take no chances; **avoir une ~ sur dix de gagner** to have a one in ten chance of winning; **il a une ~ sur deux** he has a fifty-fifty chance; **garder** or **conserver toutes ses ~s** still to have a chance (**de faire** of doing, to do); **'il va pleuvoir?'—'il y a des ~s'** 'is it going to rain?'—'probably'; **3** (fortune) luck; **leur ~ a tourné** their luck has turned; **tenter** or **courir sa ~** to try one's luck; ▶ **bonheur**; **4** (occasion favorable) chance, opportunity; **c'est la ~ de ma vie** it's the chance ou opportunity of a lifetime; **donner** or **laisser une ~ à qn** to give sb a chance; **la CEE est une ~ pour leur pays** the EC represents an opportunity for their country; **saisir sa ~** to seize the opportunity; **c'est la réunion de la dernière ~** the meeting is the last hope.

chancelant, **~e** /ʃɑ̃slɑ̃, ɑ̃t/ *adj* **1** (qui manque d'équilibre) [*démarche, pas*] unsteady; [*pont, objet*] rickety, shaky; [*personne*] staggering; **~ de fatigue** staggering with tiredness; **avancer** or **marcher d'un pas ~** to walk unsteadily; **2** (fragile) [*courage, pouvoir, foi*] wavering; [*moral*] flagging; [*volonté*] faltering; [*empire, trône*] tottering; [*marché*] unstable; **sa santé est** or **il a une santé ~e** his health is rather shaky.

chanceler /ʃɑ̃sle/ [19] *vi* **1** (perdre l'équilibre) [*personne*] to stagger, to reel; [*objet*] to wobble; **le coup le fit ~** the blow made him stagger ou reel; **2** (manquer de fermeté) [*résolution, courage, foi*] to waver; **~ dans ses opinions** to waver; **3** (être menacé) [*pouvoir, gouvernement, trône*] to totter; [*santé*] to be precarious.

chancelier /ʃɑ̃səlje/ *nm* gén chancellor; (d'ambassade) chancery; (en Allemagne, Autriche) Chancellor.
■ **le ~ de l'Échiquier** the Chancellor of the Exchequer.

chancelière /ʃɑ̃səljɛʀ/ *nf* **1** (épouse du chancelier) chancellor's wife; **2** (chauffe-pieds) foot-warmer.

chancellerie /ʃɑ̃sɛlʀi/ *nf* **1** (en France) Ministry of Justice; **2** (en Allemagne, Autriche) Chancellorship; **3** (d'une ambassade, d'un diocèse) chancellery.

chanceux, **-euse** /ʃɑ̃sø, øz/ **I** *adj* (fortuné) lucky.
II *nm,f* C lucky man/woman.

chancre /ʃɑ̃kʀ/ *nm* **1** Méd canker; **2** Bot canker; **3** (fléau) cancer, canker.
■ **~ lépreux** leproma; **~ mou** chancroid, soft chancre; **~ syphilitique** chancre.
IDIOMES **manger** or **bouffer comme un ~**◐ pej to make a pig of oneself○, to pig out◐ US.

chandail /ʃɑ̃daj/ *nm* sweater, jumper GB.

chandeleur /ʃɑ̃dlœʀ/ *nf* Relig Candlemas; **à la ~** at Candlemas.

chandelier /ʃɑ̃dəlje/ *nm* (à une branche) candlestick; (à plusieurs branches) candelabra[GB]; **~ pascal** paschal candlestick; **~ à sept branches** seven-branched candelabra[GB].

chandelle /ʃɑ̃dɛl/ *nf* **1** (bougie) candle; **lire à la lueur d'une ~** to read by candlelight; **s'éclairer à la ~** to use candles for lighting; **un dîner aux ~s** a candlelit dinner; **2** Sport **faire la ~** (en gymnastique) to do a shoulder stand; (au tennis) to hit a lob; (au rugby) to play an up-and-under; (au football) to loft the ball; **3** Aviat **monter en ~** to zoom; **4** ▶ **449** (jeu) *children's party game*; **5**◐ (morve) trickle of snot○; **avoir la ~ au nez** to have a runny nose, to have a snotty○ nose.
■ **~ romaine** (en pyrotechnie) Roman candle.
IDIOMES **devoir une fière ~ à qn** to be hugely indebted to sb; **faire des économies de bouts de ~s** to make cheeseparing economies; **tenir la ~**○ to play gooseberry○; **brûler la ~ par les deux bouts** to burn the candle at both ends; **le jeu n'en vaut pas la ~** the game isn't worth the candle; **la ~ brûle** time is running out; ▶ **trente-six**.

chanfrein /ʃɑ̃fʀɛ̃/ *nm* **1** (de cheval) nose; **2** Constr chamfer.

change /ʃɑ̃ʒ/ *nm* **1** Fin (taux) exchange rate; **~ fixe/flottant** or **flexible** fixed/floating exchange rate; **hausse/baisse du ~** rise/fall in the exchange rate; **le ~ ne nous est pas favorable** the exchange rate is not in our favour[GB]; **2** Fin (opération) (foreign) exchange; **gagner/perdre au ~** lit to make/to lose money on the exchange; fig to make/to lose on the deal; **en quittant son emploi précédent il a gagné** or **il n'a pas perdu au ~** when he left his previous job it was a change for the better; **3** (de bébé) **~ (complet)** disposable nappy GB ou diaper US.
IDIOMES **donner le ~ à qn** to pull the wool over sb's eyes.

changeant, **~e** /ʃɑ̃ʒɑ̃, ɑ̃t/ *adj* **1** (inconstant) [*personne, opinion, humeur, temps*] changeable, fickle; **il est d'humeur ~e** he's moody, he blows hot and cold; **2** (chatoyant) [*tissu*] shimmering; [*couleur, reflet*] changing, shifting.

changement /ʃɑ̃ʒmɑ̃/ *nm* **1** (remplacement) change (**de** of); **~ de stratégie/gérant** change of strategy/manager; **le ~ d'air te fera du bien** the change of air will do you good; **200 francs pour un ~ de roue** 200 francs for a wheel change; **j'attends les ouvriers pour le ~ de la chaudière** I'm waiting for the workmen to come and change the boiler; **2** (modification) change (**de** in); **~ de température/situation/majorité** change in temperature/the situation/the majority; **~ en mieux/pire** change for the better/worse; **'comment va-t-il?'—'pas de ~'** 'how is he?'—'there's no change'; **au ~ de saison** at the turn of the season; **3** (de train, bus, d'avion) change; **il y a un ~ à Varsovie** you have to change at Warsaw; **Bordeaux-Bruxelles sans ~** Bordeaux-Brussels straight through.
■ **~ d'adresse** change of address; **~ de lune** new moon; **~ de décor** Théât, Cin scene change; fig change of scene; **~ d'état** Phys change of state; **~ social** social change; **~ de vitesse** Aut (mécanisme) gears (*pl*); (processus) change of gear; **~ à vue** Théât transformation scene.

changer /ʃɑ̃ʒe/ [13] **I** *vtr* **1** (échanger) to exchange [*objet*] (**pour, contre** for); to change [*secrétaire, emploi*] (**pour, contre** for); **j'ai changé ma bicyclette pour un ordinateur** I've exchanged my bicycle for a computer; **~ un billet de 100 francs en pièces de 10 francs** to change a 100 franc note into 10 franc coins; **on m'a changé mon assistant** I've been given a new assistant; **2** (convertir) to change [*argent*]; to cash [*chèque de voyage*]; **vous pouvez ~ jusqu'à 5 000 francs** you can change up to 5,000 francs; **~ des francs en dollars** to change francs into dollars; **3** (remplacer) to change [*objet, décoration*] (**par, pour** for); to replace [*personne*] (**par, pour** with); **4** (déplacer) **~ qch de place** to move sth; **~ un employé de poste** to move an employee (to another position); **ils ont changé les livres de place** they've moved the books round GB ou around US; **~ un livre d'étagère** to move a book to another shelf; ▶ **épaule**; **5** (modifier) to change [*plan, attitude, habitudes, texte*]; **cette coiffure te change** you look different with your hair like that; **(mais) ça change tout!** that changes everything!; **qu'est-ce que ça change?** what difference does it make?; **il n'a pas changé une virgule au texte** he didn't change a single comma in the text; **tu as changé quelque chose à ta coiffure** you've done something different with your hair; **cela ne change rien à mes sentiments** that doesn't change the way I feel; **ça n'a rien changé à mes habitudes** it hasn't changed my habits in any way; **cela ne change rien (à l'affaire)** that doesn't make any difference; **cela ne change rien au fait que** that doesn't alter the fact that; **tu n'y changerais rien** there's nothing you can do about it; **on ne peut rien y ~, on n'y peut rien ~** fml we can't do anything about it; **~ sa voix** to disguise one's voice; **6** (transformer) **~ qch/qn en** to turn sth/sb into; **essayer de ~ le plomb en or** to try to turn lead into gold; **elle a été changée en statue** she was turned into a statue; **~ un prince en crapaud** to turn a prince into a toad; **7** (rompre la monotonie) **cela nous change de la pluie/du poulet** it makes a change from the rain/from chicken; **ça va le ~ de sa vie tranquille à la campagne** it'll be a change from his quiet life in the country; **pour ~ j'ai fait de l'oie** I've cooked a goose (just) for a change; **pour ~ nous allons en Espagne cet été** for a change we are going to Spain this summer; **pour ne pas ~** as usual; **pour ne pas ~ elle est en retard** she's late as usual; ▶ **idée**; **8** (renouveler les vêtements de) to change.
II changer de *vtr ind* **1** (quitter) **~ de** to change; **~ de main** lit, fig to change hands; **~ de profession/travail** to change professions/jobs; **~ de position** to change position; **~ de place** [*personne*] to change seats (**avec** with); [*objet*] to be moved, to move; **~ de chaussures/vêtements** to change one's shoes/clothes; **nous avons changé de route au retour** we came back by a different route; **~ de rue/quartier** to

Le chant et les chanteurs

Les voix et les chanteurs

soprano	=	soprano*
mezzo-soprano	=	mezzo-soprano
contralto	=	contralto
haute-contre	=	counter-tenor
ténor	=	tenor
baryton	=	baritone
baryton-basse	=	bass-baritone ([beɪs, 'bærɪ,təʊn])
basse	=	bass

* *Pour* une soprano, *on dira* a soprano, *et pour parler d'un jeune garçon on précisera* a boy soprano.

Dans les expressions suivantes, tenor *est pris comme exemple; les autres noms de voix s'utilisent de la même façon.*

il est ténor	=	he's a tenor *ou* he sings tenor

Les expressions françaises avec de *se traduisent par l'emploi du nom de la voix en position d'adjectif.*

une voix de ténor	=	a tenor voice
la tessiture de ténor	=	the tenor range
un solo de ténor	=	a tenor solo

move to another street/district; **~ d'adresse** to move to a new address, to change address; **quand il m'a vu il a changé de trottoir** when he saw me he crossed over to the other side of the road; **elle change d'amant/de bonne tous les mois** she has a new lover/maid every month; **~ d'opinion** or **d'avis** to change one's mind; **à cette nouvelle, il a changé de tête** or **visage** at this news, his expression changed; **changeons de sujet** let's change the subject; **~ de propriétaire** [*maison, immeuble*] to have a change of owner; **~ de locataire** [*propriétaire*] to get a new tenant; **il a changé de caractère** he's changed; **~ de sexe** to have a sex change; ▶**chemise**, **disque**; **2** Transp **~ de** to change; **~ de train/d'avion** to change trains/planes.

III *vi* **1** (se modifier) [*situation, santé, temps*] to change; **il ne change pas, il est toujours le même** he never changes, he's always the same; **rien n'avait changé** nothing had changed; **il a changé en bien/mal** he's changed for the better/worse; **il y a quelque chose de changé ici/dans leur comportement** there's something different here/about their behaviour[GB]; **2** (être remplacé) [*personne, livre*] to be changed; [*horaire*] to change.

IV se changer *vpr* **1** (mettre d'autres vêtements) to get changed, to change; **je vais me ~ et j'arrive** I'm just going to get changed and I'll be with you; **si tu sors, change-toi** if you're going out, get changed first; **2** (se transformer) **se ~ en** [*personne, animal*] to turn ou change into; **se ~ en citrouille** to turn into a pumpkin; **on ne se change pas** people can't change.

IDIOMES **~ d'air** to have a change of air; **~ du tout au tout** to change completely.

changeur, **-euse** /ʃɑ̃ʒœʀ, øz/ **I** ▶**510** *nm,f* Fin money changer.

II *nm* **1** Hist money changer; **2** Comm (appareil) change machine.

■ **~ de disques** record changer; **~ de fréquence** Télécom frequency changer.

channe /ʃan/ *nf* H (broc) (pewter) tankard.

chanoine /ʃanwan/ ▶**813** *nm* canon; **le ~ Kir** Canon Kir.

IDIOMES **être gras comme un ~** to be as round as a barrel; **avoir une mine de ~**○ to look the picture of health and contentment.

chanoinesse /ʃanwanɛs/ ▶**813** *nf* canoness.

chanson /ʃɑ̃sɔ̃/ *nf* **1** (texte chanté) song; **~ folklorique** traditional folk song; **~ paillarde** bawdy song; **2** (genre) song; **la ~ française/pour enfants** French/children's song; **faire carrière dans la ~** to make a career as a singer; **vedette de la ~** singing star; **3**○ (propos) **c'est toujours la même ~** it's always the same old story ou song; **c'est une autre ~** that's another story; **je connais la ~** I've heard it all before; **4** Littérat song, epic (poem); **la Chanson de Roland** the Chanson de Roland.

■ **~ d'amour** love song; **~ à boire** drinking song; **~ de geste** chanson de geste; **~ guerrière** song of battle; **~ de marche** marching song; **~ de marin(s)** sea shanty; **~ populaire** (traditionnelle) traditional song; (moderne) popular song; **~ à succès** hit (song).

IDIOMES **tout finit par des ~s** there's always a happy ending.

chansonnette /ʃɑ̃sɔnɛt/ *nf* (simple) little song; (frivole) light-hearted song.

chansonnier, **-ière** /ʃɑ̃sɔnje, ɛʀ/ **I** *nm* (livre) songbook.

II ▶**510** *nm,f* cabaret artist (*specializing in political and social satire*).

chant /ʃɑ̃/ *nm* **1** (activité) singing; **entendre un ~ mélodieux** to hear the sweet sound of singing; **réveillé par le ~ des oiseaux** woken by the dawn chorus; **aimer le ~** (chanter) to like singing; (écouter) to like songs; **concours/leçon de ~** singing competition/lesson; **2** (sons caractéristiques) (d'oiseau, de baleine) song; (de coq) crow(ing); (de grillon) chirp(ing); (de cigale) shrilling; (de vent, ruisseau, d'instrument) sound; **au ~ du coq** at cockcrow; **3** (composition musicale) song; **~ à plusieurs voix** part-song; **~s profanes/sacrés** profane/sacred songs; **4** (mélodie) melody; **5** (poésie) ode; (division) canto; **~ funèbre** funeral lament; **~ nuptial** marriage song; **épopée en dix ~s** epic in ten cantos; **6** Tech edge; **de** or **sur ~** on edge ou edgeways.

■ **~ choral** choral singing; **~ du cygne** swansong; **~ d'église** hymn; **~ grégorien** Gregorian chant; **~ guerrier** war song; **~ de Noël** Christmas carol; **~ populaire** folk song; **~ des sirènes** siren song.

chantable /ʃɑ̃tabl/ *adj* singable; **pas ~** impossible to sing (*après n*).

chantage /ʃɑ̃taʒ/ *nm* blackmail; **faire du ~** to use blackmail; **faire du ~ à qn** to blackmail sb; **il me fait du ~ au suicide/divorce** he's using threats of suicide/divorce to blackmail me; **~ affectif** emotional blackmail.

chantant, **~e** /ʃɑ̃tɑ̃, ɑ̃t/ *adj* **1** (mélodieux) [*voix, accent*] singsong (*épith*), lilting; **parler avec des intonations ~es** to speak in a lilting ou singsong voice; **2** (qui se chante aisément) [*mélodie*] tuneful.

chantefable /ʃɑ̃təfabl/ *nf* chante fable.

chanter /ʃɑ̃te/ [1] **I** *vtr* **1** Mus to sing [*air, duo*]; **tu nous chantes quelque chose?** will you sing something for us?, will you give us a song?; **messe chantée** sung mass; **spectacle chanté et dansé** musical spectacular; **2** (célébrer) to sing (of), to celebrate [*exploit, héros*]; **~ les louanges de qn** to sing sb's praises; **3**○ (raconter) **qu'est-ce qu'il nous chante?** what's he on about○? GB, what's he talking about?; **~ qch sur tous les tons** to harp on about sth.

II chanter à○ *vtr ind* (plaire) **si le film te chante** if the film appeals to you; **ça te chante d'aller à la campagne?** do you feel like ou fancy○ going to the country?; **ça ne me chante guère de partir** I don't really feel like going; **ça n'a guère chanté à mon père** it didn't go down very well with my father; **je ferai comme il me chantera** I'll do as I please.

III *vi* **1** [*personne*] to sing; (en parlant) to have a lilting voice ou a singsong accent; **~ juste/faux** to sing in tune/out of tune; **il a un accent/une voix qui chante** he has a singsong accent/a lilting voice; **~ en parlant** to talk with a lilt; **2** [*oiseau*] to sing; [*coq*] to crow; [*poule*] to squawk; [*grillon*] to chirp; [*cigale*] to shrill; [*bouilloire*] to sing; [*vent*] (dans les voiles) to sing; (dans les arbres) to rustle; [*source*] to bubble; **3** (subir du chantage) **faire ~ qn** to blackmail sb.

chanterelle /ʃɑ̃tʀɛl/ *nf* **1** Bot chanterelle; **2** Chasse decoy bird; **3** Mus E-string.

chanteur, **-euse** /ʃɑ̃tœʀ, øz/ **I** *adj* **oiseau ~** songbird; ▶**maître**.

II ▶**510** *nm,f* singer; (de groupe) vocalist; **~ d'opéra/de blues** opera/blues singer; **~ (de) rock/folk** rock/folk singer; **~ de cabaret** cabaret singer; **~ de charme** crooner; **~ populaire** *singer of middle-of-the-road popular songs*; **~ des rues** street singer.

chantier /ʃɑ̃tje/ *nm* **1** (site) building ou construction site; **~ de démolition** demolition site; **travailler sur le ~ d'une école en construction** to work on the building site of a school; **le ~ a été ouvert l'été dernier** the building ou construction work began last summer; **'~ interdit au public'** 'no admittance to the public'; **en ~** [*bâtiment*] under construction; [*loi, document*] in the process of being drafted; [*film*] in the process of being made; **la ville est en ~ depuis deux mois** they've been doing building work in the town for two months; **notre maison sera en ~ tout l'hiver** the work on our house will go on all winter; **mettre en ~** to undertake [*réforme, projet, loi*]; **remettre en ~** to resurrect, to dust [sth] off; **des réformes ont été mises en ~ récemment** reforms have recently been undertaken; **on a décidé la mise en ~ de logements neufs** it has been decided to build some new homes; **on espère la mise en ~ de nouveaux programmes/d'une nouvelle loi** we're hoping that new programmes[GB]/a new law will be created; **2** (entrepôt) builder's yard; **3**○ (lieu en désordre) mess, shambles○ (*sg*); **quel ~!** what a mess!; **4** (de tonneau) gantry; **5** Mines face.

■ **~ naval** shipyard.

chantilly /ʃɑ̃tiji/ *nf inv* **(crème) ~** Chantilly cream.

chantonnement /ʃɑ̃tɔnmɑ̃/ *nm* humming.

chantonner /ʃɑ̃tɔne/ [1] **I** *vtr* to hum [sth] to oneself [*mélodie, air*].

II *vi* to hum to oneself.

chantoung = **shantung**.

chantourné, **~e** /ʃɑ̃tuʀne/ **I** *pp* ▶**chantourner**.

II *pp adj* (arrondi) [*tableau*] with a curved top (*épith, après n*); (ajouré) [*écran*] fretted.

chantourner /ʃɑ̃tuʀne/ [1] *vtr* to cut out.

chantre /ʃɑ̃tʀ/ *nm* **1** Relig cantor; **voix de ~** rich and powerful voice; **2** (laudateur) eulogist (**de** of); (poète) bard; **Virgile, le ~ d'Énée** Virgil, the bard who sang of Aeneas.

chanvre /ʃɑ̃vʀ/ *nm* (plante, fibre) hemp; **toile de ~** hempen cloth.

■ **~ d'eau** eupatorium; **~ indien** Indian hemp, cannabis; **~ de Manille** Manila hemp.

chaos /kao/ *nm* **1** (désordre) chaos; **sombrer dans le ~** to descend into chaos; **mettre le ~ dans** to wreak havoc in; **2** Géol blockfield.

■ **~ de glace** hummocked ice.

chaotique /kaɔtik/ *adj* chaotic.

chapardage○ /ʃapaʀdaʒ/ *nm* **1** (fait de chaparder) pilfering; **2** (petit vol) petty theft.

chaparder○ /ʃapaʀde/ [1] *vtr* to pinch○ (**à qn** from sb); **elle chaparde dans les magasins** she pinches things from shops.

chapardeur○, **-euse** /ʃapaʀdœʀ, øz/ **I** *adj* light-fingered.

II *nm,f* pilferer, petty thief.

chape /ʃap/ *nf* **1** Constr (surface étanche) screed GB, screed coat; **~ de béton** concrete screed; **2** (couche) fml **~ de nuages** blanket of cloud; **~ de tristesse** burden of sadness; **3** Aut (de pneu) tread; **4** Relig (manteau) cope.

■ **~ de bielle** bearing case; **~ de poulie** pulley case.

chapeau, *pl* **~x** /ʃapo/ **I** *nm* **1** (couvre-chef) hat; **un ~ à large bord** a wide-brimmed hat; **porter** or **mettre la main au ~** to touch one's hat; ▶**baver**; **2** (de lampe, gâteau) top; (de tuyau de cheminée) hood; **3** Mécan cap; **4** Presse introductory paragraph; **5** Bot (de champignon) cap.

II○ *excl* well done!

■ **~ de cardinal** cardinal's hat; **~ chinois** (coquillage) limpet; Mus Turkish Crescent, Jingling Johnny; **~ claque** opera hat; **~ cloche** cloche (hat); **~ de cow-boy** cowboy hat, Stetson®; **~ de feutre** felt hat; **~ de gendarme** paper hat; **~ haut de forme** top hat; **~ melon** bowler (hat) GB, derby (hat) US; **~ mexicain** sombrero; **~ mou** trilby GB, fedora; **~ de paille** straw hat; **~ de plage** sun hat; **~ de roue** Aut hubcap; **démarrer sur les ~x de roues**○ [*conducteur, voiture*] to shoot off at top speed; [*film, roman, soirée*] to get off to a good ou cracking start; **~ tyrolien** Tyrolean hat.

IDIOMES **porter le ~**○ to carry the can GB, to take the blame ou rap○; **travailler du ~**○ to be a bit cracked○; **coup de ~ à** hats off to; **tirer son ~ à** to take one's hat off to; **saluer ~ bas qn** to take one's hat off to sb.

chapeauté○, **~e** /ʃapote/ **I** *pp* ▶**chapeauter**.

II *pp adj* **1** (qui porte un chapeau) with a hat on (*épith, après n*), wearing a hat (*après n*); **~ et ganté** wearing a hat and gloves; **2** (contrôlé) **service/organisme ~ par un ministère** department/organization under a ministry.

chapeauter○ /ʃapote/ [1] *vtr* (contrôler) [*personne*] to head; **le ministère chapeaute notre équipe** our team works under the ministry.

chapelain /ʃaplɛ̃/ *nm* chaplain.

chapelet /ʃaplɛ/ *nm* **1** Relig (objet, prières) rosary; **2** (d'oignons, de saucisses, villages) string; (d'obus) stick; (d'îlots) chain; (de jurons, reproches) stream; **en ~** in a string; **les îlots étaient en ~** the islets formed a chain; **égrener un ~ d'injures** to reel off a stream of insults.

chapelier, **-ière** /ʃapəlje, ɛʀ/ **I** *adj* [*industrie, commerce*] hat (*épith*).

II ▶**510** *nm,f* hatter.

chapelle /ʃapɛl/ *nf* **1** Relig chapel; **la ~ de l'hôpital** the hospital chapel; **~ expiatoire** expiatory chapel; **la ~ de la Sainte Vierge** the Lady chapel; **la ~ des marins** the sailors' chapel; **2** (groupe) pej clique, coterie; **3** Mus choir.

■ **~ ardente** temporary mortuary (*used as a chapel to mourn the dead*).

chapellerie /ʃapɛlʀi/ *nf* **1** ▶**510** (magasin) hat shop GB ou store US; **2** (entreprise) hat business; **3** (activité) hat trade.

chapelure /ʃaplyʀ/ *nf* breadcrumbs (*pl*).

chaperon /ʃapʀɔ̃/ *nm* **1** (personne) chaperon(e); **2**† (coiffe) hood; **le Petit Chaperon rouge** Little Red Riding Hood; **3** Constr coping.

chaperonner /ʃapʀɔne/ [1] *vtr* **1** (accompagner) to chaperone; **2** Constr to cope [*mur*].

chapiteau, *pl* **~x** /ʃapito/ *nm* **1** (tente) marquee GB, tent; (de cirque) big top; **2** (de colonne) capital; **3** (de buffet) cornice; **4** (d'alambic) still-head.

chapitre /ʃapitʀ/ *nm* **1** (division) (de livre) chapter; (de rapport) section; **2** (rubrique) **et au ~ des faits divers...** and now, other news...; **3** (sujet) subject; **sur ce ~** on this subject; **au ~ de** on the issue of; **sur le ~ de** in the matter of; **4** (période) chapter; **5** Compta (d'un budget) section, item; **~ des dépenses** section on expenditure; **~ des recettes** section on revenue; **voter le budget par ~** to vote on the budget section by section; **6** Relig chapter.

IDIOMES **avoir voix au ~** to have a say in the matter; **ne pas avoir voix au ~** to have no say in the matter.

chapitrer /ʃapitʀe/ [1] *vtr* (réprimander) to tell [sb] off (**à propos de** about); (faire la morale à) to lecture (**sur, à propos de** about); **se faire ~** to get told off, to get a lecture.

chapka /ʃapka/ *nf* fur hat.

chapon /ʃapɔ̃/ *nm* (jeune coq) capon.

chapska = **schapska**.

chaptalisation /ʃaptalizasjɔ̃/ *nf* chaptalization.

chaptaliser /ʃaptalize/ [1] *vtr* to chaptalize.

chaque /ʃak/

■ **Note** Si l'on veut insister sur ce qui fait l'homogénéité d'un ensemble de phénomènes, d'individus ou d'objets on traduit *chaque* par *every*: *chaque année ils allaient faire du ski* = they used to go skiing every year; si l'on veut mettre l'accent sur les phénomènes ou les individus pris séparément on utilisera plutôt *each* (mais *every* ne serait pas faux pour autant): *la situation se détériore chaque année* = each year the situation gets worse.
– On remarquera que *every* ne s'utilise que pour parler de plus de deux personnes, objets ou phénomènes; dans l'exemple suivant, seul *each* est correct: *au volley-ball, chaque équipe est composée de six joueurs* = in volleyball, each team is made up of six players.

I *adj indéf* each, every; **~ matin il fait sa promenade** he goes for a walk every morning; **~ travailleur devrait avoir droit à des congés payés** (dans l'absolu) every worker should be entitled to paid holidays GB ou vacation US; (dans un groupe particulier) each worker should be entitled to paid holidays GB ou vacation US; **~ violon a sa sonorité propre** each ou every violin has its own sound; **~ chose en son temps!** all in good time!; **~ chose à sa place** everything in its place; **~ visite chez le dentiste était pour elle un calvaire** each ou every visit to the dentist's was an ordeal for her; **la situation devient ~ jour plus compliquée** the situation becomes more and more complicated by the day ou each day ou every day; **il me dérange à ~ instant** he's always disturbing me; ▶**suffire**.

II○ *pron* (chacun) each; **il revend ses disques (à) 100 francs ~** he's selling his records for 100 francs each.

char /ʃaʀ/ *nm* **1** Mil tank; **~ léger/lourd** light/heavy tank; **être dans les ~s** to be in a tank regiment; **2** Antiq chariot; **3** Agric cart, wagon; **~ à foin** haycart, haywagon; **4** (de carnaval) float; **le ~ de la reine** the carnival queen's float; **5** fig, liter **le ~ de la nuit** the chariot of night; **le ~ de l'État** the ship of state; **6**○ (bluff) bluff; **arrête ton ~!** come off it!; **7**○ C (voiture) car.

■ **~ d'assaut** Mil tank; **~ à bancs** *horse-drawn wagon with benches*; **~ à bœufs** oxcart; **~ de combat** = **~ d'assaut**; **~ funèbre** hearse; **~ à voile** Sport (sur roues) sand yacht; (sur patins) ice yacht.

charabia○ /ʃaʀabja/ *nm* gobbledygook○, double Dutch.

charade /ʃaʀad/ *nf* riddle.

charançon /ʃaʀɑ̃sɔ̃/ *nm* weevil.

■ **~ des arbres fruitiers** apple blossom weevil.

charançonné, **~e** /ʃaʀɑ̃sɔne/ *adj* weevilly, weevilled GB.

charbon /ʃaʀbɔ̃/ *nm* **1** Minér, Mines coal; **se chauffer au ~** to use coal for heating; **faire griller qch sur des ~s (de bois)** to barbecue sth; **2** Pharm charcoal; **~ animal/végétal** animal/wood charcoal; **3** ▶**271** Méd, Vét anthrax; **4** Bot, Agric smut; **avoir le ~** to have smut; **5** Art charcoal; (dessin) charcoal drawing; **dessin au ~** charcoal drawing; **6** Électron (balai) carbon brush; (électrode) carbon.

■ **~ actif** or **activé** activated charcoal; **~ de bois** charcoal.

IDIOMES **être noir comme du ~** to be as black as coal; **être sur des ~s ardents** to be like a cat on a hot tin roof; **aller au ~**○ (aller au travail) to get to work; (effectuer une tâche pénible) to do the menial work.

charbonnages /ʃaʀbɔnaʒ/ *nmpl* collieries.

charbonner /ʃaʀbɔne/ [1] **I** *vtr* to blacken [*visage, joue, mur*].

II *vi* [*lampe, mèche*] to go black; [*poêle*] to smoke.

III se charbonner *vpr* **se ~ le visage/corps** to blacken one's face/body.

charbonneux, **-euse** /ʃaʀbɔnø, øz/ *adj* **1** (évoquant le charbon) gén sooty; [*paupière*] black with make-up (*jamais épith*); **2** Méd, Vét [*fièvre*] anthracic; **tumeur charbonneuse** anthracic tumour[GB], anthrax; **3** Bot, Agric smutted.

charbonnier, **-ière** /ʃaʀbɔnje, ɛʀ/ **I** *adj* [*centre*] coalmining (*épith*); [*production, industrie*] coal (*épith*).

II ▶**510** *nm,f* (marchand) coalman/coalwoman.

III *nm* Naut collier GB, coaler.

IV charbonnière *nf* **1** Zool (mésange) great tit; **2** (lieu de fabrication du charbon de bois) charcoal burner's clearing.

IDIOMES **avoir la foi du ~** to have a simple faith; **~ est maître chez soi** Prov an Englishman's GB ou a man's US home is his castle.

charcutage○ /ʃaʀkytaʒ/ *nm* (de viande) mangling; (de malade, texte) carving up.

charcutaille○ /ʃaʀkytaj/ *nf* cooked pork meats (*pl*).

charcuter○ /ʃaʀkyte/ [1] **I** *vtr* **1** (opérer) [*chirurgien*] to hack [sb] about [*malade*]; **se faire ~** (par un chirurgien) to get hacked about; **2** (découper) to mangle [*viande*]; **3** (dénaturer) to carve up [*texte*].

II se charcuter *vpr* (se couper) to cut oneself badly.

charcuterie /ʃaʀkytʀi/ *nf* **1** Culin (produits) cooked pork meats (*pl*); **~s variées** assorted cooked pork meats; **2** ▶**510** **~ (traiteur)** (magasin) pork butcher's; (rayon dans un supermarché) delicatessen.

charcutier, **-ière** /ʃaʀkytje, ɛʀ/ **I** ▶**510** *nm,f* (commerçant) pork butcher; **chez le ~** at the pork butcher's; **~ traiteur** pork butcher and caterer.

II charcutière *nf* (épouse du charcutier) pork butcher's wife.

chardon /ʃaʀdɔ̃/ *nm* thistle.

chardonneret /ʃaʀdɔnʀɛ/ *nm* goldfinch.

charentais, **~e** /ʃaʀɑ̃tɛ, ɛz/ **I** ▶**692** *adj* [*personne*] from the Charente region; [*melon*] Charentais.

II charentaise *nf* (pantoufle) carpet slipper.

Charentais, **~e** /ʃaʀɑ̃tɛ, ɛz/ *nm,f* (natif) native of the Charente region; (habitant) inhabitant of the Charente region.

Charente /ʃaʀɑ̃t/ ▶**692** *nprf* (département) **la ~** Charente.

Charente-Maritime /ʃaʀɑ̃tmaʀitim/ ▶**692** *nprf* (département) **la ~** Charente-Maritime.

charge /ʃaʀʒ/ *nf* **I** **1** (fardeau) lit, fig burden, load; (cargaison) (de véhicule) load; (de navire) cargo, freight; Naut (fait de charger) loading; **le mulet peinait sous la ~** the mule laboured[GB] under its load; **sept enfants, quelle lourde ~!** seven children, what a burden!; **prendre qn en ~** [*taxi*] to take sb as a passenger ou fare; **prise en ~** (dans un taxi) minimum fare; **2** Archit, Constr load; **3** (responsabilité) responsibility; **avoir la ~ de qn/qch** to be responsible for sb/sth; **avoir qn à ~** to be responsible for sb; **avoir trois enfants à ~** to have three dependent children; **il a la ~ de faire, il a pour ~ de faire** he's responsible for doing; **c'est à vous que revient la ~ de le mettre au courant** it's up to you ou it's your duty to let him know; **il s'est bien acquitté de sa ~** he carried out his task well; **prendre en ~** [*tuteur*] to take charge of [*enfant*]; [*ser-*

vices sociaux] to take [sb] into care [*enfant*]; [*sécurité sociale*] to accept financial responsibility for [*malade*]; to take care of [*frais, dépenses*]; **les enfants sont entièrement pris en ~** all the expenses for the children will be paid for; **prise en ~** (par la sécurité sociale) agreement to bear medical costs; **prise en ~ à 100%** agreement to bear full medical costs; **prise en ~** (de personnes, frais) undertaking to accept responsibility; **la prise en ~ des réfugiés/dépenses sera assurée par**... the refugees/expenses will be taken care of ou looked after by...; **se prendre en ~** to take care of oneself; **être à la ~ de qn** [*frais*] to be payable by sb; [*personne*] to be dependent upon sb; **mes neveux sont à ma ~** I support my nephews, I have my nephews to support; **ces frais sont à la ~ du client** these expenses are payable by the customer, the customer is liable for these expenses; **à ~ pour lui de faire** but it's up to him to do; **avoir ~ d'âmes** Relig to have the cure of souls; ▶**revanche**; **4** Admin (fonction) office; **~ élective** elective office; **occuper de hautes ~s** to hold high office; **~ de notaire** notary's office; **5** (preuve) evidence; **il n'y a aucune ~ contre lui** there's no evidence against him; **6** Mil (assaut) charge (**contre** against); (d'explosifs) charge; **~ de cavalerie** cavalry charge; **7** Électrotech, Phys charge; **~ positive/négative** positive/negative charge; **être en ~** to be charging up; **mettre en ~** to put [sth] on charge [*batterie, accumulateur*]; **conducteur en ~** live conductor; **8** (contenu) **~ émotionnelle** emotional charge; **~ symbolique** symbolic content; **9** (caricature) caricature; **ce rôle demande à être joué en ~** this role needs to be overacted.

II charges *nfpl* gén expenses, costs; (de locataire, copropriétaire) service charge (*sg*); **les ~s de l'État** government expenditure ¢; **~s directes** direct costs; **~s d'exploitation** running costs ou expenses.

■ **~ d'amorçage** Mil primer; **~ creuse** Mil hollow charge; **~ de famille** Fisc dependent; **~ inerte** Mil inert filling; **~ limite** maximum load; **~ nucléaire** nuclear warhead; **~ de rupture** Constr breaking stress; **~ de travail** workload; **~ utile** Transp payload; **~s fiscales** tax expenses; **~s locatives** maintenance costs (*payable by a tenant*); **~s patronales** employer's social security contributions; **~s sociales** welfare costs.

IDIOMES **retourner** or **revenir à la ~** to try again.

chargé, ~e /ʃaʀʒe/ **I** *pp* ▶ **charger**.

II *pp adj* [*particule*] charged; **être ~ de** [*branches*] to be heavy ou laden (down) with [*fruits, neige*]; [*bras, doigts, personnes*] to be covered with [*bijoux*]; [*ciel*] to be full of [*nuages*]; [*lettres, texte*] to be full of [*ratures*]; **air ~ des senteurs du printemps** air heavy with the scents of spring; **un regard ~ de menaces** a threatening look; **personnage ~ d'honneurs** person laden with honours[GB]; **être ~ de famille** to have dependents.

III *adj* **1** gén [*personne, véhicule*] loaded; [*programmes scolaires, horaires, emploi du temps*] heavy; [*journée*] busy, full; [*décorations*] over-ornate; [*style*] heavy; [*langue*] coated; **trop ~** [*personne, véhicule, programmes scolaires, horaires, emploi du temps*] overloaded; **avoir un casier judiciaire ~** to have had several previous convictions; **2** Postes [*lettre, colis*] registered.

■ **~ d'affaires** Pol chargé d'affaires; **~ de cours** Univ part-time lecturer; **~ de mission** Pol representative; **~ de recherche** researcher; **~ de travaux dirigés** Univ tutor GB, instructor US.

chargement /ʃaʀʒəmɑ̃/ *nm* **1** (objets transportés) gén load; (marchandises) (par avion, bateau) cargo, load; (par camion) load; **elle ne peut pas partir sans tout un ~**○ she can't go away without taking a whole load of baggage; **2** (mise à bord) loading; **le ~ a pris trois jours** the loading took three days; **3** (d'arme, appareil) loading; (de poêle) stoking; (de logiciel, réacteur) loading; **à ~ automatique** with automatic loading; **machine à laver à ~ frontal/par le haut** front-/top-loading washing machine; **4** Électrotech (de batterie) charging.

■ **~ postal** registered mail ¢.

charger /ʃaʀʒe/ [13] **I** *vtr* **1** gén to load [*marchandises*] (**dans** into; **sur** onto); to load [*véhicule, navire, avion, brouette, animal*] (**de** with); **~ des bagages dans une voiture** to load luggage into a car; **péniche chargée de sable** barge loaded with sand; **~ un client** [*taxi*] to pick up a passenger ou fare; **il a chargé le sac sur son dos** he heaved the bag onto his back; **trop ~ qch** to overload sth; **2** (remplir le chargeur) to load [*arme, appareil photo, caméra*]; **3** Ordinat to load [*disquette, programme*] (**dans** into); **4** Électrotech to charge [*batterie, accumulateur*]; **5** (outrer) to overdo [*description, aspect*]; **acteur qui charge un rôle** actor who hams it up○; **6** (confier une mission à) **~ qn de qch** to make sb responsible for sth; **~ qn de faire** to give sb the responsibility of doing, to make sb responsible for doing; **il l'a chargé de répondre au téléphone** he gave him the responsibility ou the job of answering the phone; **elle m'a chargé de vous transmettre ses amitiés** she asked me to give you her regards; **je l'ai chargé d'une mission de confiance** I entrusted him with an important mission; **être chargé de** to be in charge of; **c'est lui qui est chargé de l'enquête** he is in charge of the investigation; **nous sommes chargés de l'évacuation des blessés** or **d'évacuer les blessés** we are in charge of evacuating the wounded; **ils sont chargés de faire respecter la loi** it is their job to enforce the law; **7** (accabler) to bring evidence against [*accusé, suspect*]; **8** (attaquer) to charge at [*foule, manifestants, ennemi*].

II *vi* [*armée, taureau*] to charge.

III se charger *vpr* **1** (s'occuper) **se ~ de** to take responsibility for; **je m'en charge** I'll see to it, I'll look after it; **je me charge de le leur dire** I'll tell them; **apportez à manger, je me charge de la boisson** bring some food, I'll look after the drinks ou I'll take care of the drinks; **nous nous chargerons de vous trouver un logement** we will undertake to find you accommodation; **il s'est chargé de découvrir la vérité** he made it his business to find out (the truth); **2** (prendre des bagages) to weigh oneself down; **ne te charge pas trop** don't weigh yourself down too much; **3** (s'accuser) **se ~ de** to blame oneself for [*faute, crime*]; **4** Mil **se ~ facilement** [*arme*] to be easy to load.

chargeur /ʃaʀʒœʀ/ *nm* **1** Mil (objet) magazine; (personne) loader; **il a vidé son ~ sur le caissier** he fired a full round of bullets at the cashier; **2** Électrotech charger; **3** Photo cartridge; Cin film magazine; **4** Ordinat loader; **5** (débardeur) loader; **6** (expéditeur) loader, shipper.

chargeuse /ʃaʀʒøz/ *nf* Ind loader.

charia /ʃaʀja/ *nf* sharia.

chariot /ʃaʀjo/ *nm* **1** (poussé à la main) trolley GB, cart US; **~ à bagages** luggage trolley GB, luggage cart US; **~ à desserte** service trolley GB, service wagon US; **~ de supermarché** supermarket trolley GB, shopping cart US; **2** (motorisé) truck; **3** (tiré par des chevaux) waggon[GB]; **~ bâché** covered waggon[GB]; **4** (de machine à écrire) carriage; **5** Cin (de caméra) dolly.

■ **~ alsacien** bassinet; **~ élévateur à fourche** forklift truck.

Chariot /ʃaʀjo/ *nprm* **le Petit ~** the Little Bear GB ou Dipper US; **le Grand ~** the Plough GB ou Plow US.

charismatique /kaʀismatik/ *adj* charismatic.

charisme /kaʀism/ *nm* charisma.

charitable /ʃaʀitabl/ *adj* [*personne, pensée, bonté*] charitable (**envers** toward, towards GB, to); **tendre une main ~ à** fig to lend a helping hand to; **un conseil ~** hum a piece of friendly advice.

charitablement /ʃaʀitabləmɑ̃/ *adv* (avec charité) charitably; (gentiment) kindly; **il leur a ~ conseillé de faire** he very kindly advised them to do.

charité /ʃaʀite/ *nf* **1** (aumône) charity; **faire la ~ à qn** to give sb charity; **demander la ~ à qn** lit, fig to ask sb for charity; **je ne veux pas qu'on me fasse la ~** I don't want charity; **un appel à la ~ publique** a charity appeal; **vente/match de ~** charity sale/match; **la ~ s'il vous plaît** spare me some change, please; **2** (bienveillance) kindness; **par (pure) ~** out of the kindness of one's heart; **il a eu la ~ de faire** he was kind enough to do; **3** Relig charity; **la ~ chrétienne** Christian charity.

IDIOMES **~ bien ordonnée commence par soi-même** Prov charity begins at home Prov.

charivari /ʃaʀivaʀi/ *nm* din, racket○.

charlatan /ʃaʀlatɑ̃/ *nm* (guérisseur) quack○, charlatan; (vendeur) trickster, con man; (prêcheur, politicien) fraud, phon(e)y○.

charlatanisme /ʃaʀlatanism/ *nm* charlatanism.

Charlemagne /ʃaʀləmaɲ/ *npr* Charlemagne.

Charles /ʃaʀl/ *npr* Charles.

■ **~ le Bel** Charles the Fair; **~ Quint** Charles the Fifth (of Spain); **~ le Téméraire** Charles the Bold.

charleston /ʃaʀlɛstɔn/ *nm* (danse) Charleston; **danser le ~** to do ou dance the Charleston.

charlot○ /ʃaʀlo/ *nm* clown; **arrête de faire le ~!** stop clowning!

Charlot /ʃaʀlo/ *npr* Charlie (Chaplin); **aller voir un ~** to go and see a Charlie Chaplin film.

charlotte /ʃaʀlɔt/ *nf* **1** (dessert) charlotte; **~ aux pommes** apple charlotte; **2** (bonnet) mobcap.

charmant, ~e /ʃaʀmɑ̃, ɑ̃t/ *adj* **1** (plaisant) [*personne, sourire, accent, décor, lieu, scène*] charming, delightful; [*soirée, enfant*] delightful; [*objet*] charming, lovely; **trois heures de retard, c'est ~!** iron three hours delay, charming ou wonderful! iron; **elle porte le ~ prénom de**... she has the charming name of...; iron she rejoices in the name of... iron; **un ~ bambin** iron a little dear iron; **2** (aimable) very nice (**avec** to; **envers** toward, towards GB); **ils ont été ~s avec nous** they were very nice to us.

charme /ʃaʀm/ **I** *nm* **1** (de personne, sourire, visage) charm; **avoir du ~/beaucoup de ~** to have charm/great charm; **une opération de ~** a public relations exercise; **c'est une véritable offensive de ~ pour convaincre les électeurs** they are really trying to woo the electorate; **faire du ~** to turn on the charm; **faire du ~ à qn** to use one's charms on sb; **faire du ~** or **son numéro de ~ à qn pour qu'il fasse qch** to try to charm sb into doing sth; **2** (de lieu, musique) charm; **cela a le ~ de la nouveauté** it has (a certain) novelty value; **cela a son ~** or **ses ~s** it has its charms; **cela ne manque pas de ~** (mode de vie, roman) it is not without its charms; (proposition) it is not unattractive; **c'est ce qui fait tout son ~** (lieu) it's what makes it so charming; (après-midi, séjour) it's what makes it so delightful; **3** (qui envoûte) spell; **jeter/rompre un ~** to cast/to break a spell; **tenir qn sous son ~** to hold sb under one's spell; **être/tomber sous le ~ de qch** to be/to fall under sb's spell; **4** Bot hornbeam.

II charmes *nmpl* euph physical attributes euph.

IDIOMES **se porter comme un ~** to be as fit as a fiddle.

charmé, **~e** /ʃaʀme/ **I** *pp* ▶ **charmer**.
II *pp adj* delighted.

charmer /ʃaʀme/ [1] *vtr* [*spectacle, artiste*] to charm, to enchant [*auditoire*]; to charm [*serpent*]; **se laisser ~ par** *qn* to fall for ou succumb to sb's charms.

charmeur, **-euse** /ʃaʀmœʀ, øz/ **I** *adj* [*sourire*] winning, engaging; [*attitude*] charming, engaging; [*regard*] engaging; **airs ~s** charming manner (*sg*).
II *nm,f* charmer.
■ **~ de serpents** snake charmer.

charmille /ʃaʀmij/ *nf* bower, arbour[GB].

charnel, **-elle** /ʃaʀnɛl/ *adj* **1** [*plaisirs, amour*] carnal; **l'acte ~** or **l'union charnelle** the carnal act; **2** (corporel) liter physical; **enveloppe charnelle** mortal coil.

charnellement /ʃaʀnɛlmɑ̃/ *adv* **connaître qn ~** to have carnal knowledge of sb.

charnier /ʃaʀnje/ *nm* gén mass grave; Hist (lieu couvert) charnel house.

charnière /ʃaʀnjɛʀ/ **I** *nf* **1** (de porte, coquillage) hinge; **2** fig (lien important) bridge (**entre** between); **3** Anat joint; **4** (en philatélie) stamp hinge.
II **(-)charnière** (*in compounds*) **œuvre(-)~** bridge; **époque(-)~** transitional period; **événement(-)/rôle(-)~** pivotal event/role.

charnu, **~e** /ʃaʀny/ *adj* [*bras, corps, poulet*] plump; [*lèvre*] fleshy, thick; [*fruit*] plump, fleshy; [*feuille*] fleshy, thick; [*crabe*] meaty; **sur la partie la plus ~e de ma personne** hum on my behind.

charognard /ʃaʀɔɲaʀ/ *nm* **1** (hyène, chacal) carrion feeder; (vautour) vulture; **2** (profiteur) vulture péj.

charogne /ʃaʀɔɲ/ *nf* **1** (d'animal) rotting carcass; (d'humain) rotting corpse; **2**◑ bastard◑.

charolais, **~e** /ʃaʀɔlɛ, ɛz/ **▶ 692** *adj* Charolais.

Charolais /ʃaʀɔlɛ/ **▶ 692** *nm* Charolais.

Charon /kaʀɔ̃/ *npr* Charon.

charpente /ʃaʀpɑ̃t/ *nf* **1** Constr (de toit) roof structure; (de bâtiment) framework; (de bateau) structure; **bois de ~** timber; **2** (métier) carpentry; **3** Anat (structure interne) framework; (constitution) build; **~ osseuse** skeleton; **doté d'une robuste ~** sturdily built; **4** (de livre, film) structure.
■ **~ métallique** steel structure.

charpenté, **~e** /ʃaʀpɑ̃te/ *adj* [*vin*] robust; **bien ~** [*personne*] well-built (*épith*); **solidement ~** [*personne*] solidly built; **être bien ~** [*personne*] to be well built.

charpentier /ʃaʀpɑ̃tje/ **▶ 510** *nm* carpenter.

charpie /ʃaʀpi/ *nf* **1** fig **être en ~** to be in shreds; **réduire** or **mettre qch en ~** to tear sth to shreds; **mettre qn en ~** [*adversaire violent*] to beat sb to a pulp○; [*critique*] to make mincemeat of sb; [*animal*] to tear sb limb from limb; [*véhicule*] to mangle sb; **2**‡ lint.

charretée /ʃaʀte/ *nf* cartload; **par ~s** lit, fig by the cartload; **une ~ de** loads (*pl*) of○ [*critiques, honneurs*].

charretier /ʃaʀtje/ **▶ 510** *nm* carter.
IDIOMES **jurer comme un ~** to swear like a trooper.

charrette /ʃaʀɛt/ *nf* **1** (voiture à deux roues) cart; ▶ **roue**; **2** (série) **il a fait partie de la première ~ de licenciés/d'expulsés** he went in the first wave ou round of layoffs/of expulsions; **3**○ (voiture) car, jalopy○.
■ **~ à bras** handcart, barrow; **~ des condamnés** Hist tumbril.
IDIOMES **être (en) ~** to be battling with a deadline.

charrier /ʃaʀje/ [2] **I** *vtr* **1** (avec un chariot, une brouette) to cart; **2** (tirer avec effort) to haul [*troncs d'arbre, blocs de pierre*]; **3** (entraîner) [*cours d'eau, coulée de lave*] to carry [sth] along; **4**○ (se moquer de) to tease [sb] unmercifully.
II○ *vi* to go too far; **elle charrie** (elle exagère) she's going too far; (elle se moque) she must be kidding○; **faut pas ~** that's really pushing it○!

charroi /ʃaʀwa/ *nm* cartage.

charron /ʃaʀɔ̃/ **▶ 510** *nm* cartwright, wheelwright.

charrue /ʃaʀy/ *nf* plough, plow US.
IDIOMES **mettre la ~ avant les bœufs** to put the cart before the horse.

charte /ʃaʀt/ *nf* charter; ▶ **école**.
■ **la ~ des droits de l'homme** the Charter of Human Rights; **la Grande Charte (d'Angleterre)** Magna Carta; **la Charte 77** Charter 77.

charter /ʃaʀtɛʀ/ **I** *adj inv* [*vol, tarif, compagnie, billet*] charter (*épith*).
II *nm* charter plane; **les touristes arrivaient par ~s entiers** whole planeloads of tourists were arriving.

chartisme /ʃaʀtism/ *nm* Chartism.

chartiste /ʃaʀtist/ *nmf* **1** Hist Chartist; **2** Univ *student at the School of Paleography and Archival Studies in Paris*.

chartreuse /ʃaʀtʀøz/ *nf* **1** (monastère) Carthusian monastery, Charterhouse; **2** (liqueur) chartreuse.

chartreux /ʃaʀtʀø/ *nm* (moine) Carthusian monk.

Charybde /kaʀibd/ *npr* Charybdis.
IDIOMES **tomber de ~ en Scylla** to jump out of the frying pan into the fire.

chas /ʃa/ *nm* (d'aiguille) eye.

chasse /ʃas/ *nf* **1** (activité) gén hunting; (au fusil) shooting; **aller à la ~** (au lapin, pigeon etc) to go shooting GB ou hunting US; (à cheval) to go hunting; **aller à la ~ au chevreuil** (à courre) to go deer hunting; (à pied) to go deer stalking; **la ~ au sanglier** boar hunting; **la ~ au renard** (fox) hunting; **la ~ au pigeon/faisan** pigeon/pheasant shooting; **la ~ au lapin** rabbit shooting, rabbiting; **~ au lièvre** hare coursing; **la ~ aux escargots** snail hunting; **la ~ aux papillons** catching butterflies; **~ au trésor** treasure hunt; ▶ **chien**, **cor**, **fusil**, **partie**, **pavillon**, **rendez-vous**, **tableau**; **2** (saison) (avec un fusil) shooting season; (à cheval) hunting season; **la ~ est ouverte/fermée** it's the open/closed season; ▶ **ouverture**; **3** (gibier) **faire (une) bonne ~** to get a good bag; **se partager la ~** to share the game; **4** (domaine) (pour le petit gibier) shoot; (pour le gros gibier) hunting ground; **~ gardée** lit, fig preserve; **c'est la ~ gardée des médecins** it's the preserve of doctors; **cette fille c'est ~ gardée**○! hum hands off, she's private property○!; ▶ **action**; **5** (participants) **la ~** the hunt; **6** (poursuite) chase; **donner la ~ à**, **prendre en ~** to chase; **faire la ~ aux araignées/fourmis** to wage war on spiders/ants; **faire la ~ aux trafiquants** to hunt down traffickers; **faire la ~ aux abus/fraudes** to search out abuses/fraud; **7** (recherche) hunting (**à** for); **~ aux autographes** autograph-hunting; **~ aux emplois/logements** job-/house-hunting; **être à la ~ de** or **à** to be hunting for; **se mettre en ~ pour trouver qch** to go hunting for sth; **faire la ~ au mari/aux images** to be looking for a husband/a good picture; **8** Mil (avions) **la ~**, **l'aviation de ~** fighter planes (*pl*); ▶ **avion**, **pilote**; **9** (de WC) **~ (d'eau)** (toilet) flush; **~ automatique** automatic flush; **actionner la ~** (manette) to flush the toilet; **tirer la ~** (chaîne) to pull the chain; **10** (de roues, d'essieu) play; **donner de la ~ à qch** to loosen sth up a bit.
■ **~ aérienne** Mil aerial pursuit; **~ à l'affût** hunting from a hide GB ou a blind US; **~ à la baleine** whaling; **~ aux cerveaux** head-hunting; **~ à courre** hunting; **~ au faucon** hawking; **~ au furet** ferreting; **~ à l'homme** manhunt; **~ photographique** wildlife photography; **~ aux sorcières** witch-hunt; **~ sous-marine** Sport harpoon fishing, harpooning.
IDIOMES **qui va à la ~ perd sa place** Prov leave your place and you (will) lose it.

châsse /ʃɑs/ *nf* **1** Relig reliquary; **2**◑ (œil) eye.

chassé /ʃase/ *nm* Danse chassé.

chasse-clou, *pl* **~s** /ʃasklu/ *nm* nail punch.

chasse-coin, *pl* **~s** /ʃaskwɛ̃/ *nm* keying hammer.

chassé-croisé, *pl* **chassés-croisés** /ʃasekʀwaze/ *nm* **1** (manœuvres) continual coming and going (**entre** between); **~ de décisions/démarches** series of conflicting decisions/steps; **~ de dossiers entre les ministères** toing and froing of files chasing each other from ministry to ministry; **chassés-croisés amoureux** romantic intrigue (*sg*); **le ~ des automobilistes sur la route des vacances** the flow of departing and returning holidaymakers GB ou vacationers US on the roads; **2** Danse chassé-croisé, set to partners.

chasselas /ʃasla/ *nm* chasselas grape.

chasse-mouches /ʃasmuʃ/ *nm inv* fly swatter.

chasse-neige /ʃasnɛʒ/ *nm inv* **1** (véhicule) snowplough GB, snowplow US; **2** (à skis) snowplough GB, snowplow US; **faire du ~** to snowplough GB, to snowplow US; **descendre une piste en ~** to snowplough down a piste.

chasse-pierres /ʃaspjɛʀ/ *nm inv* fender, cowcatcher US.

chassepot /ʃaspo/ *nm* chassepot (rifle).

chasser /ʃase/ [1] **I** *vtr* **1** [*animal*] to hunt [*proie*]; **le lion chasse les gazelles** lions hunt gazelles; **2** gén to hunt; (au fusil) to shoot GB, to hunt; **~ à courre** to go hunting; **~ à l'affût** to hunt from a hide GB ou a blind US; **~ au filet** to hunt with a net; **~ le renard/le perdreau** to go (fox) hunting/partridge shooting; **~ (le lapin) au furet** to go ferreting; **~ la baleine** to go whaling; ▶ **race**; **3** (éloigner) [*personne*] to chase away [*visiteurs, animal*]; [*bruit, mauvais temps, personne acariâtre*] to drive away [*touristes, client*]; (expulser) to drive out [*immigrant, ennemi*]; (congédier) to fire, to sack○ GB [*domestique, employé*]; **~ qn de quelque part** (de place, rue, terrain) to drive sb out of ou from somewhere; (de lieu fermé) to throw sb out of somewhere; **le bruit nous a chassés de Paris/chez nous** we were driven out of Paris/our home by the noise; **mes parents m'ont chassé de chez eux** my parents have thrown me out (of the house); **être chassé du parti/du pouvoir** to be thrown out of the party/of power; **être chassé de son emploi** (pour incompétence) to be fired ou sacked from one's job; (pour raisons économiques) to be laid off; **je vous chasse** (à un domestique) you're fired; **l'âne chasse les mouches de sa queue** the donkey flicks off the flies with its tail; ▶ **loup**, **galop**; **4** (disperser) to dispel [*fumée, brume, odeur, doute, soucis*]; **~ une idée de son esprit** to banish a thought from one's mind; **5** (faire avancer) to herd [*bétail, oies*]; **6** (déloger) to force [sth] out [*eau*]; to knock [sth] out [*tenon*].
II *vi* **1** (aller à la chasse) gén to go hunting; (avec un fusil) to go shooting GB ou hunting US; **~ sur les terres de qn** fig to poach on sb's territory; ▶ **chien**; **2** (déraper) [*voiture, moto*] to skid; **3** Naut **le navire chasse sur ses ancres** the ship is dragging her anchor; **4** Imprim to compress.

chasseresse /ʃasʀɛs/ *nf* liter huntress littér.

chasseur, **-euse** /ʃasœʀ, øz/ **I** *nm,f* Chasse (animal, personne) hunter; **mon oncle, c'est un ~** gén my uncle goes hunting; (au fusil) my uncle goes shooting GB ou hunting US; **~ de chevreuils/de renards/de sangliers** deer hunter/fox hunter/boar hunter; **c'est un ~ de canards/de lapins** he goes duck shooting/rabbiting, he shoots duck/rabbit;

être un bon ~ (au fusil) to be a good shot; (avec une meute) to be a good huntsman; **j'ai rencontré un ~** I met a man who was out shooting; **un groupe de ~s** (au fusil) a shooting party; (avec une meute) a hunt.

II *nm* **1** Culin **poulet/lapin ~** sautéed chicken/rabbit (*served with a sauce made with mushrooms, tomatoes, shallots and white wine*); ▶**sauce**; **2** Mil (soldat) chasseur; (régiment) **le 2ᵉ ~** the 2nd (regiment of) chasseurs; **3** Mil (avion) fighter (aircraft); (pilote) fighter pilot; **4** (groom) bellboy GB, bellhop US.

■ **~ d'accompagnement** escort fighter; **~ alpin** *soldier trained for mountainous terrain*; **~ d'autographes** autograph hunter GB ou hound; **~ de baleine** whaler; **~ bombardier** fighter bomber; **~ à cheval** light cavalryman; **~ d'images** camera buff; **~ d'interception** interceptor (plane); **~ de mines** minehunter; **~ à pied** light infantryman; **~ de prime** bounty hunter; **~ à réaction** jet fighter; **~ de sons** recording buff; **~ de têtes** lit, fig head-hunter; **les ~s à cheval** (troupe) the light cavalry (*sg*).

chassie /ʃasi/ *nf* rheum.

chassieux, **-ieuse** /ʃasjø, øz/ *adj* rheumy.

châssis /ʃɑsi/ *nm* **1** (de fenêtre) frame; **2** Aut chassis; **~ surbaissé** drop frame chassis; **3** Hort cold frame; **4** Art (pour tapisserie, broderie) frame; (pour toile) chassis; (en sculpture) pointing machine; **5** Rail underframe; **6** Imprim chase; **7** Phot film holder; **8** Théât flat; **9**○ (corps de femme) body.

chaste /ʃast/ *adj* [*vie, amour, baiser, vêtement*] chaste; [*personne*] celibate; [*oreilles*] innocent.

chastement /ʃastəmɑ̃/ *adv* [*aimer*] chastely, in a chaste fashion; [*s'habiller*] modestly, demurely; **vivre ~** to lead a chaste life.

chasteté /ʃastəte/ *nf* chastity; **vivre dans la ~** to lead a chaste ou celibate life.

chasuble /ʃazybl/ *nf* gén tunic; (de prêtre) chasuble; **robe ~** pinafore dress.

chat /ʃa/ *nm* **1** (animal) gén cat; (mâle) tomcat; **~ siamois/birman/persan** Siamese/Burmese/Persian cat; ▶**appeler**; **2**○ (terme d'affection) **mon ~**○ my pet○ GB, honeybunch○ US; **3** ▶**449** Jeux **jouer à ~** to play tag ou tig GB; **c'est toi le ~** you're 'it'.

■ **~ de gouttière** (tigré) tabby cat; (commun) ordinary cat; péj alley cat; **~ à neuf queues** cat-o'-nine-tails (+ *v sg*); **~ perché** Jeux off-ground tag ou tig GB; **~ sauvage** wildcat; **le Chat botté** Puss in Boots.

IDIOMES **écrire comme un ~** to scrawl; **donner sa langue au ~** to give in; **il n'y a pas un ~** the place is deserted; **avoir un ~ dans la gorge** to have a frog in one's throat; **retomber comme un ~ sur ses pattes** to fall on one's feet; **il ne faut pas réveiller le ~ qui dort** Prov let sleeping dogs lie Prov; **être** or **s'entendre comme chien et ~** to fight like cat and dog.

châtaigne /ʃɑtɛɲ/ *nf* **1** Bot (sweet) chestnut; **2**○ (coup de poing) clout○, punch; **filer** or **flanquer une ~ à qn** to clout○ sb, to give sb a clout○.

■ **~ d'eau** water chestnut.

châtaigneraie /ʃɑtɛɲəʀɛ/ *nf* chestnut grove.

châtaignier /ʃɑteɲe/ *nm* (arbre) (sweet) chestnut (tree); **une table de** or **en ~** a chestnut table.

châtain /ʃɑtɛ̃/ ▶**193** *adj m* [*cheveux, barbe*] brown; **des cheveux ~ foncé/clair** dark brown/light brown hair; **il est ~** he's got brown hair.

château, *pl* **~x** /ʃato/ *nm* **1** (forteresse) castle; **~ médiéval** medieval castle; **2** (résidence) (royale) palace; (seigneuriale) castle; **le ~ de Versailles** the palace of Versailles; **les ~x de la Loire** the Châteaux of the Loire; **le Château** (Élysée) the Elysée; **3** (grande demeure) manor; ▶**Espagne**, **lettre**.

■ **~ d'arrière** Naut sterncastle; **~ d'avant** Naut forecastle; **~ de cartes** lit, fig house of cards; **~ d'eau** water tower; **~ fort** fortified castle; **~ de poupe** Naut = **~ d'arrière**; **~ de proue** Naut = **~ d'avant**; **~ de sable** sand castle.

IDIOMES **mener une vie de ~** to live the life of Riley GB, to live like a prince.

chateaubriand, **châteaubriant** /ʃatobʀijɑ̃/ *nm* Culin chateaubriand.

château-la-pompe○ /ʃatolapɔ̃p/ *nm inv* hum tap water.

châtelain, **~e** /ʃɑtlɛ̃, ɛn/ **I** *nm,f* **1** (propriétaire) owner of a manor; **2** Hist lord/lady (of the manor).

II châtelaine *nf* Mode chatelaine.

chat-huant, *pl* **chats-huants** /ʃayɑ̃/ *nm* tawny owl.

châtier /ʃɑtje/ [2] *vtr* liter **1** (punir) to punish [*fautif, criminel*]; to punish [*faute, délit*]; **~ qn pour son insolence**, **~ l'insolence de qn** to punish sb for his/her insolence; **2** (soigner) to polish [*style*]; to refine [*langage*]; **parler un français châtié** to speak very proper French; **3** Relig to mortify [*chair, corps*].

IDIOMES **qui aime bien châtie bien** Prov spare the rod and spoil the child Prov.

chatière /ʃatjɛʀ/ *nf* **1** (porte) catflap; **2** (en spéléologie) crawl.

châtiment /ʃɑtimɑ̃/ *nm* punishment; **infliger un ~ à qn** to punish sb.

■ **~ corporel** corporal punishment.

chatoiement /ʃatwamɑ̃/ *nm* shimmering.

chaton /ʃatɔ̃/ *nm* **1** (petit chat) kitten; **2** (sur les arbres) catkin; **3** (de bague) (monture) setting; (pierre) gem, stone; **4**○ (flocon de poussière) ball of fluff; **5**○ (terme d'affection) **mon ~** my darling.

chatouille /ʃatuj/ *nf* tickle ₵; **faire des ~s à qn** to tickle sb; **craindre les ~s** to be ticklish.

chatouillement /ʃatujmɑ̃/ *nm* (picotement) tickle; (action de chatouiller) tickling ₵; **sentir des ~s dans la gorge** to have a tickle in one's throat.

chatouiller /ʃatuje/ [1] *vtr* **1** lit to tickle; **arrête, ça chatouille!** stop it, it tickles!; **ça me chatouille dans le dos** my back is tickling; **2** (flatter) to titillate [*palais*]; to tickle [*curiosité, vanité*]; to flatter [*orgueil*]; **une bonne odeur de café vint me ~ les narines** or **l'odorat** a lovely smell of coffee reached my nose; **3**○ (énerver) to nettle, to irritate [*personne*]; **ce n'est pas le moment de le ~** don't needle him now; **il ne faut pas le ~ sur ce sujet** he's very touchy about that.

IDIOMES **~ les côtes à qn** euph to tan sb's hide.

chatouilleux, **-euse** /ʃatujø, øz/ *adj* **1** (sensible aux chatouilles) ticklish; **être ~ des pieds** to have ticklish feet; **2** (susceptible) [*personne*] touchy (**sur** about); **il est très ~ sur l'honneur** he's very touchy about points of honour[GB].

chatouillis○ /ʃatuji/ *nm inv* (gentle) tickling ₵; **faire des ~ à qn** to tickle sb.

chatoyant, **~e** /ʃatwajɑ̃, ɑ̃t/ *adj* **1** [*mer, étoffe, couleur, bijou*] shimmering; [*plumage*] iridescent; [*vitrail*] glowing; **2** [*style, écriture*] sparkling.

chatoyer /ʃatwaje/ [23] *vi* [*étoffe, couleur, bijou, plumage, mer*] to shimmer; [*vitrail*] to glow.

châtrer /ʃɑtʀe/ [1] *vtr* **1** (castrer) to neuter [*chat*]; to geld [*cheval*]; to castrate [*homme, taureau, chien*]; **faire ~ un chat** to have a cat neutered; **un cheval châtré** a gelding; **2** (mutiler) liter to mutilate [*article, film*]; **3** Hort to remove the runners from [*fraisier*].

chatte /ʃat/ *nf* **1** (female) cat; **elle a des allures de ~** she's quite feline; **2**○ (terme d'affection) **ma petite ~** my pet○ GB, sweetie○; **3**● (vagin) pussy●.

IDIOMES **être gourmande comme une ~** to be a piggy○; **une ~ n'y retrouverait pas ses petits** it's a real mess.

chatteries† /ʃatʀi/ *nfpl* **1** (caresses) **faire des ~ à son enfant** to give one's child a cuddle; **des amoureux qui se font des ~** lovers cuddling each other; **faire des ~ à qn** fig to be all over sb; **2** (friandises) sweets GB, candy US; **aimer les ~** to have a sweet tooth.

chatterton® /ʃatɛʀtɔn/ *nm* insulating tape.

chaud, **~e** /ʃo, ʃod/ **I** *adj* **1** (à température élevée) hot; (modérément) warm; [*temps, vent, air*] hot ou warm; [*climat, pays, saison, journée*] hot ou warm; [*nourriture, repas, boisson*] hot; [*mer*] warm; [*soleil*] (excessivement) hot; (agréablement) warm; [*moteur, appareil*] (anormalement) hot; (après usage) warm; **à four ~/très ~** in a warm/hot oven; **on nous a servi des croissants tout ~s** we were served piping hot croissants; ▶**fer**, **gorge**, **larme**, **sang**; **2** (qui donne de la chaleur) [*local, pièce*] (agréablement) warm; (excessivement) hot; **emportez des vêtements ~s** take warm clothing; **ma veste est bien/trop ~e** my jacket is really/too warm; **3** (récent) **ma nomination est toute ~e** my appointment is hot news; **'ils sont mariés?'—'oui, c'est tout ~'** 'they're married?'—'yes, it's hot news ou the latest gossip'; **4** (enthousiaste) [*recommandation, félicitations*] warm; [*partisan*] strong; **ils n'ont pas été très ~s pour faire** they were not very keen on doing; **une ~e ambiance entre camarades** a warm and friendly atmosphere among friends; **5** (agité) [*région, période, rentrée sociale*] turbulent; [*dossier, sujet*] sensitive; [*assemblée, réunion, discussion*] heated; **l'automne sera ~ sur le front social** it's going to be a turbulent autumn GB ou fall US on the industrial relations front; **un des points ~s du globe** one of the flash points of the world; **ils ont eu une ~e alerte** they had a narrow escape; **~e ambiance ce soir chez les voisins!** iron things are getting heated next door tonight!; **6** (attrayant) [*coloris, ton, voix*] warm; **7**○ (de prostitution) euph [*quartier*] red light (*épith*); **une des rues les plus ~es de la capitale** one of the most notorious red light districts in the capital.

II *adv* **il fait ~** (agréablement) it's warm; (excessivement) it's hot; **il a fait/fera ~ toute la journée** Météo it has been/will be hot all day; **ça ne me/leur fait ni ~ ni froid** it doesn't matter one way or the other to me/to them; **boire/manger ~** to drink hot drinks/to eat hot foods; **'à boire/manger ~'** 'to be drunk/eaten hot'; **je n'aime pas boire trop ~** I don't like very hot drinks; **'servir ~/très ~'** 'serve hot/very hot'

III *nm* (chaleur) heat; **on crève de ~ ici**○! we're roasting○ in here!; **avoir ~** (modérément) to be warm; (excessivement) to be hot; **as-tu assez ~?** are you warm enough?; **nous avons eu ~** lit we were very hot; fig we had a narrow escape; **donner ~ à qn** [*boisson*] to make sb feel hot; [*course, aventure*] to make sb sweat; **tenir ~ à qn** to keep sb warm; **ça me tient ~ aux pieds** it keeps my feet warm; **reste contre moi, tu me tiens ~** stay right there, you're keeping me warm; **se tenir ~** [*personnes, animaux*] to keep warm; **~ devant**○! watch out!; **coup de ~ à la Bourse** flurry of activity on the stock exchange; **prendre un coup de ~** [*plante, fleur*] to wilt (in the sun); **tenir** or **garder au ~** lit to keep [sb] warm [*personne, malade*]; to keep [sth] hot [*plat, boisson*]; fig (pour parer à une éventualité) to have [sth] on standby [*matériel, projet, remède*]; **au ~/bien au ~ dans mon manteau/lit** snug/snug and warm in my coat/bed; **je préfère rester au ~ devant la cheminée** I prefer to stay in the warm by the fire; ▶**souffler**.

IV à chaud *loc adv* **à ~** [*commenter, analyser, résoudre*] on the spot; [*réaction,* *impression*] immediate; [*étirer, travailler*] Tech under heat; [*opérer*] on the spot; **opérer qn à ~** Méd to carry out an emergency operation (on sb); **soluble à ~** Chimie, Pharm heat-soluble.

■ **~ et froid** Méd chill; **attraper un ~ et froid** to catch a chill.

IDIOMES **souffler le ~ et le froid** to blow hot and cold.

chaudement /ʃodmɑ̃/ *adv* **1** [*vêtu*] warmly; **'comment ça va?'—'~'** hum 'how are you?'—'hot!'; **2** (vivement) [*féliciter*] warmly; [*recommander*] heartily; [*défendre*] hotly; **ma candidature est ~ appuyée par le directeur** my application has the strong support of the director.

chaude-pisse◑, *pl* **chaudes-pisses** /ʃodpis/ *nf* clap◑ ₵, gonorrhea; **attraper une ~** to catch the clap; **filer une ~ à qn** to give sb a dose (of clap)◑.

chaud-froid, *pl* **chauds-froids** /ʃofʀwa/ *nm* chaudfroid.

chaudière /ʃodjɛʀ/ *nf* (de chauffage central, bateau) boiler.

■ **~ à bois** wood-fired boiler; **~ à gaz** gas boiler; **~ à mazout** oil-fired boiler; **~ nucléaire** nuclear steam boiler.

chaudron /ʃodʀɔ̃/ *nm* cauldron.

chaudronnerie /ʃodʀɔnʀi/ *nf* **1** (industrie) boilermaking industry; (métier) boilermaking; **2** (usine) boilerworks (+ *v sg*); **3** (articles) **grosse ~** industrial boilers (*pl*); **petite ~** pots and pans (*pl*).

chaudronnier, -ière /ʃodʀɔnje, ɛʀ/ **▶510** *nm,f* (ouvrier) boilermaker.

chauffage /ʃofaʒ/ *nm* **1** (utilisation de chaleur artificielle) heating; **le ~ est facturé en sus de la location/n'est pas compris dans le loyer** heating is on top of the rent/isn't included in the rent; **une chambre sans ~** an unheated bedroom; **on dépense trop pour le ~** the heating costs are too high; **mettre/allumer le ~** to put/to turn the heating on; **arrêter/éteindre le ~** to put/to turn the heating off; **le ~ de notre maison coûte très cher** the house is very expensive to heat; **pour le ~ des serres on utilise une source d'eau chaude** a hot spring is used to heat the greenhouses; **2** (installations) heating; **~ central/au gaz/par le sol** central/gas/underfloor heating; **notre voisin/leur maison n'a pas le ~** our neighbour[GB]/their house has no heating; **le ~ est en panne** the heating has broken down; **on a rénové le ~ de l'église** the heating system in the church has been modernized; **l'installation du ~ prendra un mois** it will take a month to install the heating; **3** (appareil) heater; **~ d'appoint** extra heater GB, space heater US; **4** (élévation de la température) heating; **après un léger ~, le colorant vire au rouge** after heating gently, the colouring[GB] turns to red; **il suffit d'un léger ~ pour que la réaction se produise** it is only necessary to heat gently to trigger the reaction; **par un ~ continu à 180°C** by continuously heating at 180°C.

chauffagiste /ʃofaʒist/ **▶510** *nmf* heating engineer.

chauffant, ~e /ʃofɑ̃, ɑ̃t/ *adj* [*surface, élément*] heating.

chauffard○ /ʃofaʀ/ *nm* pej reckless driver, road hog○; **(espèce de) ~!** road hog○!

chauffe /ʃof/ *nf* Tech **1** (opération) stoking; **2** (lieu) fire chamber.

chauffe-assiettes /ʃofasjɛt/ *nm inv* plate warmer.

chauffe-bain, *pl* **~s** /ʃofbɛ̃/ *nm* water-heater.

chauffe-biberon /ʃofbibʀɔ̃/ *nm inv* bottle warmer.

chauffe-eau /ʃofo/ *nm inv* water-heater; **~ électrique** immersion heater; **~ électrique instantané pour douche** electric shower; **~ à gaz** gas water-heater; **~ à accumulation** storage water-heater.

chauffe-pieds /ʃofpje/ *nm inv* foot warmer.

chauffe-plat /ʃofpla/ *nm inv* dish warmer.

chauffer /ʃofe/ [1] **I** *vtr* **1** (élever la température de) to heat [*maison, pièce*]; to heat (up) [*métal, objet, liquide, plat*]; to warm (up) [*pâte à modeler*]; **notre maison est bien/mal chauffée** our house is well/poorly heated; **une piscine chauffée** a heated pool; **les salles de classe sont toujours trop chauffées** the classrooms are always overheated; **je ne chauffe presque pas** I hardly ever have the heating on; **~ du fer au rouge/à blanc** to bring iron to a red/white heat; **il a chauffé l'auditoire à blanc** fig he whipped the audience into a frenzy; **~ le public** to warm up the audience; **2** (procurer de la chaleur) [*soleil, alcool*] to warm; **le cognac chauffait ses joues** the brandy warmed his/her cheeks; **▶oreille**; **3** C (conduire) to drive.

II *vi* **1** (devenir chaud) [*aliment, plat*] to heat (up); [*moteur, machine*] to warm up; [*four, fer à repasser*] to heat up; **la soupe est en train de ~** the soup is heating up; **laissez ~ cinq minutes à feu doux** heat for five minutes on a low setting; **ne laisse pas le café ~ trop longtemps** don't leave the coffee on the heat for too long; **faire ~ qch** to heat [*eau, aliment*]; to warm [*assiette, biberon*]; to heat (up) [*fer à repasser, four*]; to warm (up) [*moteur, machine*]; **faites ~ au four** heat up in the oven; **mettre à ~** to put [sth] on to heat [*eau*]; to heat up [*aliment, plat*]; to warm [*biberon*]; **2** (devenir trop chaud) [*appareil, moteur, frein*] to overheat; **évitez de faire ~ l'appareil** don't let the appliance overheat; **ne laissez pas l'appareil ~ toute la nuit** don't leave the appliance running all night; **3** (produire de la chaleur) [*radiateur, four, lampe*] to give out heat; **4**○ fig (être animé) **avec ce groupe, ça va ~!** this group's going to liven things up!; **ça ~ dans le stade/la discothèque!** things are hotting up○ in the stadium/the disco!; **si le patron l'apprend, ça va ~!** if the boss finds out, there'll be big trouble!; **5** Jeux (à cache-tampon) to get warm; **tu chauffes!** you're getting warm!

III se chauffer *vpr* **1** (se donner chaud) to get warm; **se ~ près du poêle/au coin du feu** to warm oneself by the stove/by the fire; **se ~ au soleil** [*personne, animal*] to bask in the sun; **2** (utiliser un chauffage) **nous nous chauffons au charbon** we have coal-fired heating; **▶bois**.

chaufferette /ʃofʀɛt/ *nf* bedwarmer.

chaufferie /ʃofʀi/ *nf* (de bâtiment) boiler room; (de bateau) stokehold.

chauffeur /ʃofœʀ/ *nm* **1** **▶510** Aut gén driver; (de particulier) chauffeur; **~ de camion** or **de poids lourd** lorry driver GB, truck driver; **~ de car** coach driver GB, bus driver US; **~ de taxi** taxi driver, cab driver; **voiture avec/sans ~** chauffeur-driven/self-drive car; **faire le ~ pour qn** to chauffeur sb about; **2** (de chaudière) gén stoker; Rail fireman.

■ **~ du dimanche** pej Sunday driver; **~ de direction** company chauffeur; **~ de maison** or **maître** chauffeur.

chauffeuse /ʃoføz/ *nf* (chaise) low fireside chair; (fauteuil) low armless easy chair.

chaulage /ʃolaʒ/ *nm* **1** Agric (de sol) liming; **2** (de mur) limewashing.

chauler /ʃole/ [1] *vtr* **1** Agric to lime [*sol*]; **2** to limewash [*mur*].

chaume /ʃom/ *nm* **1** Agric (tige) stubble ₵; (champ) stubble field; **2** (pour toiture) thatch; **une maison recouverte de ~** a thatched cottage; **refaire le ~ d'une maison** to rethatch a house.

chaumer /ʃome/ [1] **I** *vtr* to clear stubble from [*champ*].

II *vi* to clear (the) stubble.

chaumière /ʃomjɛʀ/ *nf* **1** (avec toit de chaume) thatched cottage; **2** (petite maison) liter humble cottage; **une ~ et un cœur** fig love with roses around the door; **faire jaser dans les ~s** hum to cause tongues to wag.

chaumine /ʃomin/ *nf* liter small cottage, cot littér.

chaussant, ~e /ʃosɑ̃, ɑ̃t/ *adj* well-fitting; **ces bottes sont très ~es** these boots are a very good fit; **article** or **produit ~** footwear ₵.

chaussée /ʃose/ *nf* **1** (route) road(way) GB, highway; (rue) street; **2** (revêtement) surface; **~ bitumée** tarmac® road surface; **~ glissante** slippery surface; **~ déformée** uneven road surface; **▶pont**; **3** (chemin surélevé) causeway; (remblai) embankment; **la ~ des Géants** Géog the Giants' Causeway.

chausse-pied, *pl* **~s** /ʃospje/ *nm* shoehorn.

chausser /ʃose/ [1] **I** *vtr* **1** (mettre aux pieds) to put [sth] on [*chaussures, skis*]; to put [sth] on [*lunettes*]; Équit to take [*étriers*]; **~ qn de qch** to put sth on sb; **chaussez les étriers!** take your stirrups!; **être bien/mal chaussé** to be well/poorly shod; **elle était chaussée** or **avait les pieds chaussés de pantoufles** she was wearing slippers; **des écoliers chaussés de neuf** schoolchildren in their new shoes; **le nez chaussé de lunettes de soleil** wearing sunglasses; **2** (équiper) to provide [sb] with shoes [*personne, équipe*]; **je n'arrive pas à ~ ma fille pour moins de 300 francs** I can't buy my daughter shoes for less than 300 francs; **c'est la marque qui chausse l'équipe de France** it's the brand of shoes that the French team wear; **se faire ~ par** or **chez** to get one's shoes at; **se faire ~ sur mesure** to have one's shoes made to measure; **3** (être adapté) to fit; **les noires te chaussent mieux/moins bien** the black ones fit you better/don't fit you as well; **4** Agric (butter) to earth up [*plante*]; **5** (garnir de pneus) to fit [sth] with tyres GB ou tires US [*véhicule*].

II **▶793** *vi* **vous chaussez du combien** or **quelle pointure?** what size do you take?; **je chausse du 41** I take a (size) 41; **il chausse un bon 43** he takes at least a size 43; **elle chausse un petit 37** she's a size 37 or smaller; **ces mocassins chaussent grand/petit** these loafers are large-/small-fitting.

III se chausser *vpr* **1** (mettre ses chaussures) to put (one's) shoes on; **se ~ de qch** to put on sth; **elle se chausse de tennis pour aller au travail** she wears trainers to go to work; **2** (s'équiper) to get ou buy (one's) shoes; **chez qui** or **où te chausses-tu?** where do you get ou buy your shoes?; **je me chausse au moment des soldes** I get my shoes in the sales; **elle a du mal à se ~ à cause de sa petite pointure** she has difficulty in buying shoes because her feet are so small.

chausses /ʃos/ *nfpl* chausses.

chausse-trap(p)e, *pl* **~s** /ʃostʀap/ *nf* **1** lit trap; **2** fig pitfall.

chaussette /ʃosɛt/ *nf* **1** (vêtement) sock; **ne reste pas dehors en ~s** don't stay outside in your socks ou your stockinged feet; **2** (de cafetière) cloth filter.

IDIOMES **laisser tomber qn comme une vieille ~**○ to cast sb off like an old rag.

chausseur /ʃosœʀ/ *nm* **1** **▶510** (commerçant) shoe shop GB ou store US; **2** (fabricant) shoemaker.

chausson /ʃosɔ̃/ *nm* (pantoufle) slipper; (de bébé) bootee; (de danse) ballet shoe ou pump; (de sport) pump.

■ **~ d'escalade** rock-climbing boot; **~ de gymnastique** gymnastics slipper; **~ aux pommes** Culin apple turnover.

chaussure /ʃosyʀ/ *nf* **1** (soulier) shoe; (à tige haute) boot; **~ fermée** high shoe; **~ basse** shoe; **~ montante** ankle boot; **~ cloutée** hobnailed boot; **~ de tennis/golf** tennis/golf shoe; **~ de ski** ski boot; **magasin de ~s** shoe shop GB ou store US; **rayon ~s** shoe department; **2** (industrie) footwear industry; (commerce) footwear trade; **travailler dans la ~** to be in footwear.

IDIOMES **trouver ~ à son pied** (compagnon) to find the right person; (travail) to find one's niche.

chaut† /ʃo/ *v impers* ▶ **chaloir**.

chauve /ʃov/ **I** *adj* **1** [*personne, crâne*] bald; **2** fig, liter [*montagne, sommet*] bare.
II *nmf* bald(-headed) man/woman.
IDIOMES **être ~ comme un œuf**○ or **mon genou**○ or **une boule de billard**○ to be as bald as a coot○.

chauve-souris, *pl* **chauves-souris** /ʃovsuʀi/ *nf* Zool bat.

chauvin, **~e** /ʃovɛ̃, in/ **I** *adj* [*personne, attitude, discours, journal*] chauvinistic, jingoistic.
II *nm,f* chauvinist, jingoist.

chauvinisme /ʃovinism/ *nm* chauvinism, jingoism; **faire preuve de ~** to be chauvinistic ou jingoistic.

chaux /ʃo/ *nf* lime; **lait de ~** whitewash; **blanchir** or **passer à la ~** to whitewash.
■ **~ vive** quicklime; **~ éteinte** slaked lime.

chavirer /ʃaviʀe/ [1] **I** *vtr* (bouleverser) to overwhelm; **j'en ai le cœur tout chaviré** I am overwhelmed.
II *vi* **1** [*navire*] to capsize; **faire ~ un navire** to capsize a ship; **2** (vaciller) [*paysage, pièce*] to reel; **tout chavira autour d'elle** everything reeled about her; **faire ~ les cœurs** to be a heartbreaker; **3** (se renverser) [*objets*] to tip over.

chébran◑ /ʃebʀɑ̃/ *adj inv* trendy○.

chèche /ʃɛʃ/ *nm*: *long scarf worn by Arab men, usually around the head.*

chéchia /ʃeʃja/ *nf* ≈ fez.

check-list, *pl* **~s** /tʃɛklist/ *nf* Aviat, Astronaut controv checklist; **faire la ~** to go through the checklist.

check-up /tʃɛkœp/ *nm inv* controv check-up; **se faire faire un ~** to have a check-up; **faire un ~ à qn** to give sb a check-up.

chef /ʃɛf/ **I** *nm* **1** (meneur) leader; **le ~ du parti** the party leader; **le ~ de l'école cubiste** the leader of the Cubist school; **~ de l'opposition** leader of the opposition; **~ de bande** gang leader; **avoir des qualités de ~** to have leadership qualities; **avoir une âme** or **un tempérament de ~** to be a born leader; **2** (supérieur) superior, boss○; Mil (sergent) sergeant; **votre ~ en sera informé** your superior will be informed; **mon ~** my boss○; **salut, ~**○! hi, boss○!; **3** (patron, dirigeant) gén head; Comm (d'un service) manager; **~ de l'Église/de l'exécutif** head of the Church/of the executive branch of government; **l'exemple doit venir des ~s** the example must come from the top; **architecte en ~** chief architect; **commandant en ~** Mil commander-in-chief; ▶ **petit**; **4** Culin **~** (**cuisinier** or **de cuisine**) chef; **pâté du ~** chef's pâté; **5**○ (as, champion) ace; **se débrouiller comme un ~** to manage splendidly; **6**† (tête) head; **de mon/leur** (**propre**) **~** on my/their own initiative, off my/their own bat○ GB; **7** (chapitre) heading; **sous ce ~** under this heading; **au premier ~, leur négligence** primarily ou first and foremost, their negligence; **il importe, au premier ~, de rétablir l'ordre** primarily, we must restore order.
II○ *nf* boss○; **à la maison, c'est elle la ~** at home, she's the boss○.
■ **~ d'accusation** Jur count of indictment; **répondre à un ~ d'accusation** to answer a charge; **~ d'atelier** (shop) foreman; **~ de bataillon** major; **~ de bureau** chief clerk; **~ de cabinet** principal private secretary; **~ de chantier** works GB ou site foreman; **~ de chœur** choirmaster; **~ de clan** chieftain; **~ de classe** ≈ class prefect ou monitor GB, class president US; **~ de clinique** Méd ≈ senior registrar GB; **~ de département** head of department; **~ d'entreprise** head of a company; **~ d'équipe** Entr foreman; Sport team captain; **~ d'escadron** cavalry major; **~ d'établissement** head teacher; **~ d'État** head of state; **~ d'état-major** Chief of Staff; **~ de fabrication** production manager; **~ de famille** head of the family ou household; **~ de file** gén leader; Pol party leader; Fin (de consortium) lead bank; Naut lead ship; **~ de gare** stationmaster; **~ de gouvernement** head of government; **~ indien** Indian chief; **~ mécanicien** engine driver GB, (locomotive) engineer US; **~ de musique** bandmaster; **~ de nage** stroke; **~ d'orchestre** conductor; **~ de patrouille** patrol leader; **~ du personnel** personnel manager; **~ de plateau** Cin, TV floor manager; **~ de produit** Comm product manager; **~ de projet** Entr project manager; **~ de publicité** (d'agence) account executive; (annonceur) advertising manager; (dans les médias) advertising (sales) manager; **~ de rang** chef de rang; **~ de rayon** Comm department supervisor ou manager; **~ de région** area ou regional manager; **~ de réseau** (espionnage) leader of a spy ring; (Résistance) leader of a cell (*in the Resistance movement*); **~ de service** Admin section ou department head; Méd clinical director GB, chief physician US; **~ de train** guard GB, conductor US; **~ de tribu** headman; **~ des ventes** sales manager; **~ de village** village headman.

chef-d'œuvre, *pl* **chefs-d'œuvre** /ʃɛdœvʀ/ *nm* masterpiece, chef-d'oeuvre.

chef-lieu, *pl* **chefs-lieux** /ʃɛfljø/ *nm* (ville) administrative centre.

chef-opérateur, *pl* **chefs-opérateurs** /ʃɛfɔpeʀatœʀ/ *nm* Cin, TV director of photography.

cheftaine /ʃɛftɛn/ *nf* (de louveteaux) cubmistress GB, den mother US; (d'éclaireuses) guide captain GB, girl scout leader US; (de jeannettes) Brown Owl GB, brownie troop leader US.

cheik(h) /ʃɛk/ *nm* sheik(h).

chelem /ʃlɛm/ *nm* **1** (aux cartes) slam; **faire le petit/grand ~** to make a small/grand slam; **2** Sport **gagner** or **faire le grand ~** to win the Grand Slam.

chélidoine /kelidwan/ *nf* greater celandine.

chemin /ʃ(ə)mɛ̃/ *nm* **1** (route) country road; (étroit) lane; (de terre) (pour véhicule) track; (pour piétons) path; **être toujours sur les ~s** to be always on the road; **le ~ du village** the road (that leads) to the village; ▶ **quatre**, **Rome**; **2** (passage) way; **se frayer un ~ à travers les broussailles** to clear a way through the undergrowth; **les obstacles qui sont** or **se trouvent sur mon ~** lit, fig the obstacles which stand in my way; **3** (direction, itinéraire, trajet) way; **indiquer le/demander son** or **le ~ à qn** to tell/to ask sb the way; **se tromper de ~** to go the wrong way; **sur le ~ du retour/ de l'école** on the way back/to school; **reprendre le ~ du bureau** to go back to the office ou to work; **Aix? c'est (sur) mon ~** Aix? it's on my way; **c'est le plus court ~ entre Pau et Oloron** it's the quickest way from Pau to Oloron; **le plus court ~ vers la paix** the shortest path to peace; **on a fait un bout de ~ ensemble** (à pied) we walked along together for a while; (dans la vie) we were together for a while; **continuer** or **passer** or **aller son ~** to continue on one's way; **passez votre ~!** liter go on your way!; **~ faisant, en ~** on ou along the way; **faire tout le ~ à pied/en boitant** to walk/to limp all the way; **il a su trouver le ~ de mon cœur** fig he's found the way to my heart; **avoir du ~ à faire** to have a long way to go; **on a fait du ~** we've come a long way; **cette femme fera/a fait du ~** this woman will go/has come a long way; **l'idée fait/a fait son ~** the idea is gaining/has gained ground; **faire la moitié du ~** (être conciliant) to meet sb halfway; **montrer le ~** (donner l'exemple) to lead the way, to set an example; **être sur le bon ~** gén to be heading in the right direction; [*malade*] to be on the road to recovery; **prendre le ~ de la faillite/l'échec** to be heading for bankruptcy/failure; **il a l'air d'en prendre le ~** he seems to be heading that way; **s'arrêter en ~** lit to stop off on the way; fig to stop; **tu ne vas pas t'arrêter en si bon ~!** don't stop when things are going so well!; **le ~ de la gloire** the path of glory; **le ~ de la célébrité/perdition** the road to fame/ruin; **le destin l'a mis sur mon ~** fate threw him in my path; ▶ **bonhomme**, **droit**; **4** (tapis) (carpet) runner.
■ **~ acoustique sûr** Mil reliable acoustic path; **~ de câbles** cable tray; **~ charretier** cart track; **~ creux** sunken lane; **~ critique** critical path; **le ~ de Damas** Relig the road to Damascus; **trouver son ~ de Damas** to see the light; **le ~ des écoliers** the long way round GB ou around US; **prendre le ~ des écoliers** to take the long way round GB ou around US; **~ de fer** Rail (infrastructure) railway, railroad US; (mode de transport) rail; Jeux chemin de fer; **par ~ de fer** by rail; **~ de halage** towpath; **le ~ de (la) croix** Relig the stations (*pl*) of the Cross; **~ de ronde** path round[GB] the battlements; **~ de roulement** Aviat taxiway; Tech roller conveyor; **~ de table** (table) runner; **~ de terre** (pour véhicule) dirt track; (pour piétons) path; **~ de traverse** path across ou through the fields; **~ vicinal** country lane.

chemineau†, *pl* **~x** /ʃ(ə)mino/ *nm* vagabond, vagrant.

cheminée /ʃ(ə)mine/ *nf* **1** (de maison) (conduit complet) chimney; (sur toit) chimney stack; (foyer) fireplace; (manteau) mantelpiece; **faire un feu dans la ~** to make a fire in the fireplace; **portrait accroché à la ~** picture hung above the mantelpiece; **2** (d'usine) chimney, smokestack US; **3** (de fosse, cave) shaft; **~ d'aération/de ventilation** air/ventilation shaft; **4** (de bateau, locomotive) funnel, smokestack US; **5** Mines chute; **6** (en montagne) chimney.
■ **~ des fées** Géol fairy chimney.

cheminement /ʃ(ə)minmɑ̃/ *nm* **1** (avance) (de personne, véhicule) (slow) progression; Mil advance; **2** (voie suivie) (d'eaux, de lave) course; **3** (démarche) development, evolution; **le ~ de sa pensée** his/her train of thought; **par un long ~** gradually.

cheminer /ʃ(ə)mine/ [1] *vi* liter **1** (marcher) to walk (along); Mil (avancer à couvert) to advance (under cover); **~ à travers bois** to walk through the woods; **~ péniblement à travers la forêt** to plod along through the forest; **2** (avancer) [*ruisseau, sentier*] **~ à travers/entre** to wend its way through/between littér; **3** (progresser) [*idée, pensée*] to progress, to develop.

cheminot /ʃ(ə)mino/ *nm* railway worker GB, railroader US.

chemisage /ʃəmizaʒ/ *nm* jacketting.

chemise /ʃ(ə)miz/ *nf* **1** (pour hommes) shirt; **~ à manches longues/courtes** long-/short-sleeved shirt; **une ~ à carreaux** a checked shirt; **être en bras de ~** to be in one's shirtsleeves; **2** (lingerie) vest GB, undershirt US; **3** (en papeterie) folder; **4** Tech (intérieure) lining; (extérieure) jacket; **5** Constr facing.
■ **~ américaine** envelope-neck vest; **~ de nuit** (pour femme) nightgown, nightdress GB; (pour homme) nightshirt; **Chemises bleues** Hist Blue Shirts; **Chemises brunes** Hist Brown Shirts; **Chemises noires** Hist Blackshirts.
IDIOMES **j'y ai laissé ma ~**○ it broke the bank; **je m'en moque comme de ma première ~**○ I don't give two hoots○ GB ou a hoot○ US; **changer d'avis comme de ~**○ to change one's mind at the drop of a hat; **être (comme) cul et ~**◑ to be inseparable, to be as thick as thieves; **mouiller sa ~**○ to work hard.

chemiser /ʃ(ə)mize/ [1] *vtr* **1** Culin to line [*moule*]; **2** Tech to jacket [*pièce, conduit*].

chemiserie /ʃ(ə)mizʀi/ *nf* (industrie) shirt-making trade; (fabrique) shirt factory; (magasin) shirt shop GB ou store US.

chemisette /ʃ(ə)mizɛt/ *nf* short-sleeved shirt.

chemisier, **-ière** /ʃ(ə)mizje, ɛʀ/ **I** ▶**510** *nm,f* Ind shirt maker.
II *nm* Mode blouse; **~ à manches courtes** short-sleeved blouse.

chênaie /ʃɛnɛ/ *nf* oak grove.

chenal, *pl* **-aux** /ʃənal, o/ *nm* (de fleuve, d'estuaire) channel, fairway; (d'usine) flume; (de moulin) millrace.

chenapan /ʃənapɑ̃/ *nm* hum scallywag○, rascal; **espèce de petit ~** you little rascal.

chêne /ʃɛn/ *nm* **1** (arbre) oak (tree); **forêt de ~s** oak forest; **2** (bois) oak; **table en ~** oak table.
■ **~ blanc d'Amérique** white oak; **~ chevelu** Turkey oak; **~ écarlate** scarlet oak; **~ des marais** pin oak; **~ pédonculé** common ou pedunculate oak; **~ pubescent** downy oak; **~ rouge d'Amérique** red oak; **~ rouvre** sessile oak, durmast (oak); **~ vert** holm oak, ilex.
IDIOMES **être fort comme un ~** to be as strong as an ox.

chéneau, *pl* **~x** /ʃeno/ *nm* gutter.

chêne-liège, *pl* **chênes-lièges** /ʃɛnljɛʒ/ *nm* cork oak.

chenet /ʃənɛ/ *nm* firedog, andiron.

chènevis /ʃɛnvi/ *nm* hempseed.

chenil /ʃənil/ *nm* **1** (niche) kennel; **2** (pension pour chiens) kennels (*sg*).

chenille /ʃənij/ *nf* **1** Zool caterpillar; **2** Aut caterpillar; **véhicule à ~s** tracked vehicle; **3** Tex chenille.

chenillé, **~e** /ʃ(ə)nije/ *adj* Aut tracked; Mil [*bulldozer, char*] with caterpillar tracks.

chenillette /ʃ(ə)nijɛt/ *nf* universal carrier, armoured supply carrier.

chenit○ /ʃni/ *nm* H (désordre) mess; **en ~** messy.

chenu, **~e** /ʃəny/ *adj* liter [*vieillard, tête, barbe*] hoary; [*arbre*] leafless.

cheptel /ʃɛptɛl/ *nm* **1** (ensemble du bétail) **~ (vif)** livestock; **le ~ bovin de la Normandie** the beef ou dairy herd in Normandy; **le ~ ovin/porcin** the sheep/pig population; **2** Jur contract of agistment.
■ **~ mort** (matériel) dead stock, farm equipment.

chèque /ʃɛk/ *nm* cheque GB, check US; **faire un ~** to write a cheque GB ou check US; **un ~ de 1000 francs** a cheque GB ou check US for 1,000 francs; **faire** or **établir un ~ à l'ordre de M. Dawson** to make a cheque GB ou check US out ou payable to Mr Dawson; **'je mets le ~ à quel nom○?'** 'who should I make the cheque GB ou check US out ou payable to?'; **les ~s sont acceptés à partir de 100 francs** cheques GB ou checks US are accepted for 100 francs or more; (dans un magasin) 'no cheques GB ou checks US under 100 francs'; **mettre** or **déposer un ~ à la banque** to pay in a cheque GB ou check US; **barrer un ~** to cross a cheque GB ou check US.
■ **~ bancaire** cheque GB ou check US; **~ en blanc** blank cheque GB ou check US; **donner un ~ en blanc à qn** fig to give sb carte blanche; **~ en bois**○ rubber cheque○ GB ou check US; **il m'a fait un ~ en bois** the cheque GB ou check US he wrote me bounced; **~ certifié** certified cheque GB ou check US; **~ essence** petrol GB ou gas US coupon ou voucher; **~ à ordre** order cheque GB ou check US; **~ au porteur** bearer cheque GB ou check US; **~ postal** ≈ giro cheque; **~ sans provision** bad cheque GB ou check US; **~ de voyage** traveller's cheque GB ou check US; **~s postaux** (service) ≈ National Girobank.

chèque-cadeau, *pl* **chèques-cadeaux** /ʃɛkkado/ *nm* gift-token.

chèque-voyage, *pl* **chèques-voyage** /ʃɛkvwajaʒ/ *nm* traveller's cheque GB ou check US.

chéquier /ʃekje/ *nm* Fin chequebook GB, checkbook US; **être interdit de ~** not to be allowed to use a chequebook GB ou checkbook US.

cher, **chère** /ʃɛʀ/ **I** *adj* **1** (aimé) [*personne*] dear; [*objet, visage*] beloved; **ses amis les plus ~s** his/her dearest friends; **la mort d'un être ~** the death of a loved one; **2** (précieux) **~ à qn** [*thème, principe, idée*] dear to sb (*épith, après n*); **selon un principe qui lui est ~** according to a principle that he/she holds dear; **selon une formule qui lui est chère** as his/her favourite[GB] saying goes; **une image chère à l'artiste** a favourite[GB] image of the artist; **un site ~ au poète/à Byron** a place the poet/Byron was fond of; **3** (pour interpeller) dear; **~ ami/monsieur, vous avez tout à fait raison!** my dear friend/sir, you're absolutely right!; **ah, mais c'est ce ~ Dupont!** well, if it isn't our dear old Dupont!; **4** (dans la correspondance) dear; **~s tous** dear all; **~ monsieur Martin** dear Mr Martin; **5** (onéreux) expensive, dear; **c'est ~ pour ce que c'est** it's expensive ou dear for what it is; **pas ~** [*restaurant, robe*] cheap, inexpensive; **ils ont des robes pas chères du tout** they've got some very cheap ou reasonably-priced dresses; **60 francs le menu, ce n'est vraiment pas ~** 60 francs for the set menu, that's pretty reasonable; **la vie est plus chère** the cost of living is higher; **manifestations contre la vie chère** demonstrations against the high cost of living.
II *nm,f* **mon ~** gén dear; (condescendant, à homme plus jeune) my dear boy; (à homme plus âgé) my dear sir; **ma chère** gén dear; (condescendant, à femme plus jeune) my dear girl; (à femme plus âgée) my dear lady; **que désirez-vous, très chère?** fml what would you like, my dear?
III *adv* **1** lit (en argent) a lot (of money); **coûter/valoir ~** to cost/be worth a lot; **les vêtements en cuir coûtent ~ à nettoyer** having leather clothes cleaned is expensive ou costly; **coûter plus/moins ~** to cost more/less; **coûter ~ en qch** lit, fig to cost a lost in sth; **acheter/vendre ~** to buy/to sell at a high price; **se vendre ~** [*objet*] to fetch a lot; **ses tableaux ne se vendent pas ~** his/her paintings don't fetch much; **je l'ai payé très ~** I paid a lot for it; **je l'ai eu pour pas ~/moins ~** I got it cheap/cheaper; **il y a mieux ailleurs pour moins ~** there's better and cheaper elsewhere; **certains médecins prennent plus ~** some doctors charge more; **ils font payer ~/très ~ leur services** they charge a lot/an awful lot for their services; **c'est/ce n'est pas ~ payé** it's/it's not expensive; **le procédé revient ~/trop ~** the process is expensive/too expensive; **on y mange pour pas ~** you can eat there at a reasonable price ou quite cheaply; **2** fig (en importance) [*coûter, payer*] dearly; **ça nous a coûté ~** it cost us dearly; **ils lui ont fait payer ~ sa négligence** they made him/her pay dearly for his/her negligence; **le blocus a coûté ~ à notre économie/la collectivité** our economy/the community paid a high price for the blockade.
IV chère *nf* fml food, fare; **faire bonne chère** to eat well; **aimer la bonne chère** to appreciate good food ou fare.
IDIOMES **ne pas donner ~ de qn** or **des chances de qn** or **de la peau de qn**○ not to rate sb's chances (highly).

Cher /ʃɛʀ/ ▶**692** *nprm* (département) **le ~** the Cher.

chercher /ʃɛʀʃe/ [1] **I** *vtr* **1** (essayer de trouver) to look for [*personne, objet, vérité*]; to look for, to try to find [*emploi, repos, appartement*]; **cela fait une heure que je vous cherche** I've been looking for you for the past hour; **~ un mot dans le dictionnaire** to look up a word in the dictionary; **~ qn du regard dans la foule** to look (about) for sb in the crowd; **'cherchons vendeuses'** 'sales assistants wanted'; **son regard cherchait celui de sa femme** he sought his wife's eye; **il cherche son chemin** he's trying to find his way; **elle chercha quelques pièces de monnaie dans sa poche** she felt for some coins in her pocket; **cherche mieux** look harder ou more carefully; **tu n'as pas bien cherché** you didn't look hard enough; **~ le sommeil** to try to get some sleep; **~ l'aventure** to look for ou seek adventure; **~ fortune** to seek one's fortune; **ne cherchez plus!** look no further!; **cherche mon chien, cherche!** fetch, boy, fetch!; ▶ **aiguille**, **bête**, **pou**; **2** (s'efforcer) **~ à faire** to try to do; **je cherche à vous joindre depuis ce matin** I've been trying to contact you since this morning; **il cherchait à les impressionner** he was trying to impress them; **je ne cherche plus à comprendre** I've given up trying to understand; ▶ **quatorze**; **3** (quérir) **aller ~ qn/qch** gén to go and get sb/sth; (passer prendre) to pick sb/sth up; **aller ~ qch** [*chien*] to fetch sth; **allez me ~ le patron!** go and get the boss for me!; **aller ~ la balle/les balles** (au tennis) to go for a shot/for the difficult shots (**au filet** at the net); **venir ~ qn/qch** gén to come and get sb/sth; (passer prendre) to pick sth up; **il est venu me ~ à l'aéroport** he came to meet me at the airport; **envoyer qn ~ qch** to send sb to get sth; **4** (réfléchir à) to try to find [*réponse, idées, mot, solution*]; to look for [*prétexte, excuse*]; (se souvenir de) to try to remember [*nom*]; **je cherche mes mots** I'm groping for words; **~ un moyen de faire qch** to try to think of a way to do sth; **il ne cherche pas assez** he doesn't think hard enough about it; **j'ai beau ~, impossible de m'en souvenir** I've thought and thought and still can't remember it; **pas la peine de ~ bien loin, c'est lui le coupable** you don't have to look too far, he's the guilty one; **5** (imaginer) **qu'allez-vous ~!** what are you thinking of!; **où est-il allé ~ cela?** what made him think that?; **où va-t-il ~ tout cela?** how does he come up with all that?; **je me demande où il est allé ~ tous ces mensonges** I wonder how he thought up all these lies; **6** (atteindre) **une maison dans ce quartier, ça va ~ dans les 800 000 francs** 0 **a house in this area must fetch** GB ou get US about 800,000 francs; **un vol à main armée, ça doit/va ~ dans les cinq ans de prison** armed robbery would/could get you about five years in prison; **'combien ça va me coûter?'—'ça ne devrait pas aller ~ loin'** 'how much will that cost me?'—'it shouldn't come to much'; **7** (aller à la rencontre de) to look for [*complications, problèmes*]; **elle t'a giflé mais tu l'as bien cherché** she slapped you but you asked for it; **il a été renvoyé mais il l'a quand même bien cherché** he was fired but he was asking for it; **si tu me cherches, tu vas me trouver**○ if you're looking for trouble, you'll get it.
II se chercher *vpr* **1** (être en quête de soi-même) to try to find oneself; **un écrivain qui se cherche** (raison d'être) a writer trying to find himself; (style, idées) a writer who is feeling his way; **2** (se donner) **se ~ des excuses/un alibi** to try to find excuses/an alibi for oneself; **3**○ (se provoquer) to be out to get each other○.

chercheur, **-euse** /ʃɛʀʃœʀ, øz/ **I** *adj* liter [*esprit*] inquiring.
II ▶**510** *nm,f* researcher; **elle est chercheuse dans un laboratoire** she's a researcher in a lab; **~ en génétique** genetic researcher; **~ en littérature américaine** researcher in American literature.
III *nm* Astron finder.
■ **~ d'or** gold-digger; **~ de trésor** treasure hunter.

chèrement /ʃɛʀmɑ̃/ *adv* (difficilement) **une réforme/une indépendance ~ acquise** a reform/an independence gained at great cost; **la victoire a été ~ payée en vies humaines** the victory was dearly bought in terms of human lives.

IDIOMES **vendre ~ sa peau**○ or **sa vie** to sell one's life dearly.

chéri, **~e** /ʃeʀi/ **I** *pp* ▶ **chérir**.

II *pp adj* beloved; **l'enfant ~ de** the darling of.

III *nm,f* **1** (en adresse) darling; **ma ~e** my darling; **2** (favori) darling; **le ~ de la famille** the darling of the family; **le ~ de ces dames** a favourite[GB] with the ladies; **le ~ à sa maman**○ mummy's boy○; **3**○ (amoureux) baby talk boyfriend/girlfriend.

chérir /ʃeʀiʀ/ [3] *vtr* liter to cherish [*personne*]; to hold [sth] dear [*principe, idée*].

chérot○ /ʃeʀo/ *adj m* (coûteux) pricey○.

cherté /ʃɛʀte/ *nf* (de produit) high cost, dearness; (de terrain, logement) high cost; (de monnaie) high price; **la ~ de la vie sur l'île** the high cost of living on the island.

chérubin /ʃeʀybɛ̃/ *nm* **1** Relig **des ~s** cherubim; **2** Art cherub; **3** (enfant) iron little angel ou cherub.

Cheshire ▶ **692** *nprm* **le ~** Cheshire.

chétif, **-ive** /ʃetif, iv/ *adj* [*enfant*] puny, undeveloped; [*plante*] scrawny, stunted; **un enfant à l'air ~** a puny-looking child.

chevaine /ʃəvɛn/ *nm* Zool chub.

cheval, *pl* **-aux** /ʃ(ə)val, o/ **I** *nm* **1** Zool horse; **~ sauvage** wild horse; **à (dos de) ~** on horseback; **monter à ~** to ride a horse; **à ~!** mount!; **promenade à ~** (horse) ride; **tenue de ~** riding clothes; **remède/traitement de ~** strong medicine; **fièvre de ~** raging fever; **bon ~** fig right choice; **miser sur le bon/mauvais ~** fig to back the right/wrong horse; ▶ **petit**, **sabot**; **2** ▶ **449** (activité) horse-riding; **aimer le ~** to like horse-riding; **faire du ~** to go horse-riding; **3** (viande) horsemeat; **bifteck de ~** horsemeat steak; **4** (personne) real Trojan; **(vieux) ~ de retour** (homme politique) war horse; (récidiviste) habitual offender, old lag○; **5**○ (femme masculine) péj **c'est un vrai ~** she's built like a horse.

II à cheval sur *loc prép* **1** (à califourchon sur) astride; **à ~ sur un mur** astride a wall; **2** (s'étendant sur) spanning; **à ~ sur deux pays/trois décennies** spanning two countries/three decades; **3** (de part et d'autre de) **le domaine est à ~ sur la route** the estate straddles the road; **4** (entre) in between; **à ~ sur le rouge et le violet** in between red and purple; **5** (pointilleux sur) **être à ~ sur les principes/bonnes manières/horaires** to be a stickler for principles/good manners/schedules.

■ **~ d'arçons** pommel horse; **~ à bascule** Jeux rocking horse; **~ de bataille** hobbyhorse; **enfourcher son ~ de bataille** to get on one's hobbyhorse; **~ de course** racehorse; **~ fiscal**, **CV** Fisc *unit for car tax assessment*; **~ de labour** carthorse GB, drafthorse US; **~ de manège** riding school horse; **~ marin** Zool sea horse; **~ pur sang** thoroughbred horse; **~ reproducteur** stud horse; **~ de saut** Sport vaulting horse; **~ de selle** saddle horse; **~ de trait** = **~ de labour**; **~ de Troie** Trojan horse; **chevaux de bois** merry-go-round horses; **chevaux de frise** Mil chevaux-de-frise.

IDIOMES **à ~ donné on ne regarde pas les dents** Prov don't look a gift horse in the mouth; **ne pas être un mauvais ~** not to be such a bad sort; **monter sur ses grands chevaux** to get on one's high horse; **ce n'est pas la mort du petit ~** it's not the end of the world.

chevalement /ʃ(ə)valmɑ̃/ *nm* (de mur) shoring; Mines pit-head frame.

chevaler /ʃ(ə)vale/ [1] *vtr* to shore up [*mur*].

chevaleresque /ʃ(ə)valʀɛsk/ *adj* **1** Littérat [*littérature, poème*] chevaleresque; **2** (courtois) chivalrous.

chevalerie /ʃ(ə)valʀi/ *nf* chivalry.

chevalet /ʃ(ə)valɛ/ *nm* **1** (de peintre) easel; (de menuisier) trestle, sawhorse; **être à son ~** to be at one's easel; **2** (de violon) bridge; **3** (de torture) rack.

■ **~ de levage** Tech hydraulic lift.

chevalier /ʃ(ə)valje/ *nm* (tous contextes) knight; **les Chevaliers de la Table ronde** the Knights of the Round Table; **Chevalier de Malte** Knight of Malta; **armer qn ~** to dub sb knight, to knight sb; **il a été fait Chevalier de la Légion d'honneur** he has been made a chevalier of the Legion of Honour[GB].

■ **~ blanc** Fin white knight; **~ culblanc** Zool green sandpiper; **~ errant** knight errant; **~ gambette** Zool redshank; **~ guignette** Zool common sandpiper; **~ noir** Fin black knight; **~ servant** hum devoted admirer.

chevalière /ʃ(ə)valjɛʀ/ *nf* signet ring.

chevalin, **~e** /ʃ(ə)valɛ̃, in/ *adj* **1** (ayant rapport au cheval) equine; **race ~e** equine breed; **boucherie ~e** horse butcher's; **2** (ressemblant au cheval) **profil/rire ~** horsey profile/laugh.

cheval-vapeur, *pl* **chevaux-vapeur** /ʃ(ə)valvapœʀ, ʃ(ə)vovapœʀ/ *nm* horsepower.

chevauchant, **~e** /ʃ(ə)voʃɑ̃, ɑ̃t/ *adj* [*tuiles, dents*] overlapping (*épith*); [*feuille*] equitant.

chevauchée /ʃ(ə)voʃe/ *nf* ride; **faire une ~** to go for a ride.

chevauchement /ʃ(ə)voʃmɑ̃/ *nm* **1** (recouvrement) overlapping; **2** Géol thrust fault.

chevaucher /ʃ(ə)voʃe/ [1] **I** *vtr* **1** (être assis sur) to sit astride [*animal, objet*]; **2** (recouvrir en partie) to overlap.

II *vi* **1** [*tuiles, dents*] to overlap; **2** Imprim [*caractères*] to become misaligned; **3** liter to ride.

III se chevaucher *vpr* [*tuiles, dents*] to overlap (each other); [*horaires, attributions*] to overlap.

chevau-léger, *pl* **~s** /ʃəvoleʒe/ *nm* (soldat) light-horseman; (compagnie) **les ~s** the Household Cavalry.

chevêche /ʃəvɛʃ/ *nf* Zool little owl.

chevelu, **~e** /ʃəvly/ **I** *adj* **1** [*homme, génération*] pej long-haired (*épith*); **2** Bot [*racine*] hairy, tufted; [*épi*] bearded.

II *nm* (homme) pej long-haired lout péj.

chevelure /ʃəvlyʀ/ *nf* **1** (cheveux) hair ₵; **une abondante ~ bouclée** a mass of curly hair; **2** Astron (de comète) tail.

chevenne *nm*, **chevesne** /ʃəvɛn/ *nm* chub.

chevet /ʃəvɛ/ *nm* **1** (de lit) bedhead; **être/rester au ~ de qn** to be/stay at sb's bedside; **livre de ~** bedside book; **2** (meuble) bedside table; **3** Archit (d'église) chevet.

cheveu, *pl* **~x** /ʃəvø/ **I** *nm* **1** (poil) hair; **avoir quelques ~x blancs** to have a few grey[GB] hairs; **avoir les ~x blancs** to have grey GB ou gray US hair; **il ne lui reste que quelques ~x sur le dessus** he only has a few hairs left on his head; **il n'a plus un ~ sur la tête** he's nearly bald, he hasn't got a single hair left on his head; **un spécialiste du ~** a hair specialist; **avoir le ~ lisse/mal peigné** to have smooth/dishevelled[GB] hair; **avoir le ~ rare** to be a bit thin on top; **2** (petite dimension) hair's breadth; **être à un ~ de qch/de faire** to be within a hair's breadth of sth/of doing; **il s'en est fallu d'un ~ que je fasse** I came within a hair's breadth of doing; **ne tenir qu'à un ~** to hang by a thread.

II cheveux *nmpl* (chevelure) hair ₵; **avoir les ~x longs** or **de longs ~x** to have long hair; **~x gras/secs** greasy/dry hair; **se couper/se laver les ~x** to cut/to wash one's hair; **se faire couper les ~x** to have one's hair cut; **avoir les ~x en broussaille** or **en bataille** to have tousled hair; **une histoire à vous faire dresser les ~x sur la tête** a story that makes your hair stand on end; **se prendre aux ~x** to grab each other by the hair.

■ **~x d'ange** Culin (vermicelle) angel-hair pasta ₵.

IDIOMES **avoir un ~ sur la langue** to have a lisp; **venir/arriver comme un ~ sur la soupe** to come/to arrive at an awkward moment; **se faire des ~x**○ **(blancs)** to worry oneself to death (**pour** about); **couper les ~x en quatre** to split hairs; **avoir mal aux ~x**○ to have a hangover; **être tiré par les ~x** to be far-fetched; **il y a un ~**○ there's a hitch○.

cheveu-de-Vénus, *pl* **cheveux-de-Vénus** /ʃəvødvenys/ *nm* Bot maidenhair fern.

cheville /ʃ(ə)vij/ ▶ **188** *nf* **1** Anat ankle; **avoir la ~ fine/bien prise** to have slender/well-turned ankles; **jupe qui arrive à la ~** ankle-length skirt; **on avait de l'eau jusqu'aux ~s** we were ankle-deep in water; **l'eau nous arrivait aux ~s** the water came up to our ankles; **2** Constr (pour vis) rawplug; (pour assemblage) peg; (en bois) dowel; **3** (d'instrument de musique) peg; **une ~ d'accord** a tuning peg; **4** (de boucherie) butcher's hook; **vente à la ~** wholesale butchery trade; **acheter/vendre à la ~** to buy/sell meat wholesale; **5** (dans poème) pej padding ₵ péj.

■ **~ ouvrière** lit kingpin; fig kingpin○; **être la ~ ouvrière de...** to play a key role in...

IDIOMES **il n'arrive pas à la ~ de sa sœur** he can't hold a candle to his sister; **avoir les ~s qui enflent** to get big-headed; **être en ~ avec qn**○ to be in cahoots with sb○.

cheviller /ʃ(ə)vije/ [1] *vtr* to peg.

IDIOMES **avoir l'âme chevillée au corps** to have a tremendous hold on life.

chevillette† /ʃəvijɛt/ *nf* small peg; ▶ **choir**.

cheviotte /ʃəvjɔt/ *nf* cheviot (wool).

chèvre /ʃɛvʀ/ **I** *nm* (fromage) goat's cheese.

II *nf* **1** Zool goat; (femelle du bouc) nanny-goat; **2** (peau) goatskin; **un tapis en ~** a goatskin rug; **3** Tech (pour levage) hoist; (pour débiter) sawhorse, sawbuck US.

■ **~ angora** Angora goat; **~ du Cachemire** Kashmir goat; **~ chamoisée** mountain goat.

IDIOMES **devenir ~**○ to go round the bend○ GB, go nuts◑; **rendre qn ~**○ to drive sb round the bend○ GB, drive sb nuts◑; **ménager la ~ et le chou** to sit on the fence.

chevreau, *pl* **~x** /ʃəvʀo/ *nm* **1** Zool kid; **2** (cuir) kid; **gants de** or **en ~** kid gloves.

chèvrefeuille /ʃɛvʀəfœj/ *nm* honeysuckle.

chevrette /ʃəvʀɛt/ *nf* **1** Zool (chèvre) young nanny goat; (femelle du chevreuil) (female) roe deer; **2** (trépied) tripod.

chevreuil /ʃəvʀœj/ *nm* **1** Zool roe (deer); (mâle) roebuck; **2** Culin venison.

chevrier, **-ière** /ʃɛ(ə)vʀije, ɛʀ/ ▶ **510** *nm,f* goatherd.

chevron /ʃəvʀɔ̃/ *nm* **1** (poutre) rafter; **2** (motif) chevron; **les ~s** or **le ~** (petits) herringbone pattern; (grands) chevron design; **disposés en ~** [*briques, lattes, lames*] laid in a herringbone pattern; **veste à ~s** herringbone jacket; **3** Archit, Hérald chevron; **chapiteau à ~s** chevron-patterned capital; **4** Mil (galon) chevron, stripe.

chevronné /ʃəvʀɔne/ *adj* **1** [*personne*] experienced, seasoned (*épith*); **peu ~** fairly inexperienced; **2** [*écu*] per chevron; [*tissu*] herringbone (*épith*).

chevrotant, **~e** /ʃəvʀɔtɑ̃, ɑ̃t/ *adj* [*voix*] quavering, tremulous; [*personne*] with a quavering voice (*après n*).

chevrotement /ʃəvʀɔtmɑ̃/ *nm* (de voix) quaver, tremor; (de personne) quavering voice.

chevroter /ʃəvʀɔte/ [1] *vtr, vi* to quaver.

chevrotine /ʃəvʀɔtin/ *nf* buckshot; **abattu d'une décharge de ~s** shot dead with a rifle.

chewing-gum, *pl* **~s** /ʃwiŋgɔm/ *nm* chewing gum ¢.

chez /ʃe/ *prép* **1** (au domicile de) **~ qn** at sb's place; **~ David** at David's (place); **rentre ~ toi** go home; **je reste/travaille/mange ~ moi** I stay/work/eat at home; **tu peux dormir/rester ~ moi** you can sleep/stay at my place; **viens ~ moi** come to my place; **on va ~ toi ou ~ moi?** your place or mine?; **on passe ~ elle en route** we call in on her on the way; **de ~ qn** [*téléphoner, sortir, venir*] from sb's place; **de Paris à ~ moi** from Paris to my place; **je ne veux pas de ça ~ moi!** I'll have none of that in my home!; **fais comme ~ toi** also iron make yourself at home aussi iron; **il a été suivi jusque ~ lui** he was followed home; **derrière ~ eux il y a une immense forêt** there is a huge forest behind their house; **~ qui l'as-tu rencontré?** whose place did you meet him at?; **vous habitez ~ vos parents?** do you live with your parents?; **faire irruption ~ qn** to burst in on sb; **il a retrouvé le livre ~ lui** he found the book at home; **2** ▶ **510** (magasin, usine, cabinet etc) **je ne me sers plus ~ eux** I don't go there any more; **la montre ne vient pas de ~ nous** this watch doesn't come from our shop GB ou store US; **en vente ~ tous les dépositaires** on sale at all agents; **il ne se fait plus soigner les dents ~ elle** he doesn't use her as a dentist any more; **va chez Hallé, c'est un très bon médecin** go to Hallé, he's a very good doctor; **s'habiller ~ un grand couturier** to buy one's clothes from a top designer; **une montre de ~ Lip** a Lip watch; **paru** or **publié ~ Hachette** published by Hachette; **le nouveau parfum de ~ Patou** the new perfume by Patou; **je fais mes courses ~ l'épicier du coin** I do my shopping at the local grocer's; **il travaille ~ Merlin-Gerin** he works at Merlin-Gerin; **'~ Juliette'** (sur une enseigne) 'Juliette's'; **il va passer à la télévision, ~ Rapp** he's going to be on television, on the Rapp show; **être convoqué ~ le patron** (à son bureau) to be called in before the boss; **3** (dans la famille de) **~ moi/vous/eux** in my/your/their family; **comment ça va ~ les Pichon?** how are the Pichons doing?; **ça va bien/mal ~ eux** things are going well/badly for them; **4** (dans le pays, la région de) **~ nous** (d'où je viens) where I come from; (où j'habite) where I live; **c'est une expression de ~ nous** it's a local expression; **chez eux ils appellent ça...** in their part of the world they call th is...; **un nom/fromage bien de ~ nous**○ (de France) a good old French name/cheese; (de notre région) a good old local name/cheese; **5** (parmi) among, **~ les enseignants/les femmes enceintes/les Romains** among teachers/pregnant women/the Romans; **~ les insectes** among insects; **maladie fréquente ~ les bovins** common disease in cattle; **~ l'homme/l'animal** in man/animals; **6** (dans la personnalité de) **qu'est-ce que tu aimes ~ un homme?** what do you like in a man?; **ce que j'aime ~ elle, c'est son humour** what I like about her, is her sense of humour[GB]; **c'est une obsession ~ elle!** it's an obsession with her!; **7** (dans l'œuvre de) in; **~ Cocteau/Mozart/les surréalistes** in Cocteau/Mozart/the surrealists; **un thème récurrent ~ Buñuel/Prévert** a recurrent theme in Buñuel/Prévert.

chez-elle○ /ʃezɛl/ *nm inv* **son ~** her (own) home.

chez-eux○ /ʃezø/ *nm inv* **leur ~** their (own) home.

chez-lui○ /ʃelɥi/ *nm inv* **son ~** his (own) home.

chez-moi○ /ʃemwa/ *nm inv* **mon ~** my (own) home.

chez-nous○ /ʃenu/ *nm inv* **notre ~** our (own) home.

chez-soi○ /ʃeswa/ *nm inv* **son ~** one's (own) home.

chez-toi○ /ʃetwa/ *nm inv* **ton ~** your (own) home.

chez-vous○ /ʃevu/ *nm inv* **votre ~** your (own) home.

chiadé◑, **~e** /ʃjade/ **I** *pp* ▶ **chiader**.
II *pp adj* **1** (bien fait) detailed, elaborate; **2** (ardu) tough.

chiader◑ /ʃjade/ [1] *vtr* to work on, to put a lot of work into [*devoir*]; to swot up (on)○ [*sujet*].

chialer◑ /ʃjale/ [1] *vi* pej to blubber○, to snivel○; **faire ~ qn** to start sb crying ou blubbering○.

chialeur○, **-euse** /ʃjalœʀ, øz/ **I** *adj* pej blubbering○ (*épith*), snivelling○ (*épith*).
II *nm,f* pej crybaby○.

chiant●, **~e** /ʃjɑ̃, ɑ̃t/ *adj* **1** (ennuyeux) bloody◑ GB ou really boring; **2** (pénible, contrariant) **c'est/il est ~** it's/he's a pain○.

chiard◑ /ʃjaʀ/ *nm* pej brat○ péj.

chiasma /kjasma/ *nm* Anat chiasm(a); **~ optique** optic chiasm(a).

chiasme /kjasm/ *nm* Littérat chiasmus.

chiasse● /ʃjas/ *nf* **avoir la ~** to have the runs○; **quelle ~!** (c'est contrariant) fig what a pain○!

chic /ʃik/ **I** *adj* **1** (élégant) [*personne, vêtement*] smart GB, chic; **être ~** to look smart GB ou chic; **2**○ (sophistiqué) [*magasin, école, personne, hôtel, quartier*] chic; **il est ~ de faire** it's chic GB ou fashionable to do; **être bon ~ bon genre** to be chic and conservative; **3**○ (gentil) nice; **c'est ~ de ta part** that's nice of you.
II *nm* chic; **avoir le ~ pour faire** to have a knack for doing; **avec ~** with style; **avoir du ~** to have style; **le dernier ~ est de faire** the in thing○ is to do; **c'est du dernier ~** it's the height of sophistication.
III *adv* [*s'habiller*] smartly GB, stylishly.
IV *excl* great!

chicane /ʃikan/ *nf* **1** (formée par obstacles) chicane; (tracé de route, piste) double bend; (dans conduit) baffle; **en ~** on alternate sides; **2** (tracasserie) bickering ¢; **chercher ~ à qn pour qch** to pick a quarrel with sb over sth; **3** Jur (point de détail) delaying tactics (*pl*); (procédure) pej legal quibbling péj; **4** (au bridge) chicane; **5** C (dispute) fight.

chicaner /ʃikane/ [1] **I** *vtr* **1** (harceler) **~ qn sur qch** to argue with sb about sth; **~ qch à qn** to argue about sth with sb; **2** C (réprimander) to scold.
II *vi* (discuter) to squabble (**sur, pour** over); (faire des manières) to fuss (**sur** about).
III se chicaner *vpr* to squabble (**pour** over).

chicanerie /ʃikanʀi/ *nf* fuss; **que de ~s pour dix francs!** what a fuss over ten francs!

chicaneur, **-euse** /ʃikanœʀ, øz/ **I** *adj* [*personne, esprit*] fussy.
II *nm,f* fusspot○ GB, fussbudget US.

chicanier, **-ière** /ʃikanje, ɛʀ/ **I** *adj* gén fussy; [*fonctionnaire, administration*] pettifogging.
II *nm,f* gén fusspot○ GB, fussbudget US; (fonctionnaire) stickler.

chiche /ʃiʃ/ **I** *adj* **1** (parcimonieux) [*personne, institution*] mean GB, stingy (**sûr** with; **de** with); **2** (minable) [*portion, subvention*] mean GB, stingy; **3**○ (capable) **être ~ de faire qch** to be able to do sth; **t'es pas ~ de le faire** I bet you can't do it; ▶ **pois**.
II *excl* **'je vais le faire'—'~!'** 'I'll do it'—'I dare you!'; **~ que je le fais!** bet you I can do it!

chichement /ʃiʃmɑ̃/ *adv* [*manger, vivre*] frugally; [*donner, accorder*] meanly GB, stingily; [*décorer*] sparsely; [*récompenser, payer*] poorly.

chichi /ʃiʃi/ *nm* fuss ¢; **ils font toujours des tas de ~s** they always make such a fuss; **ne fais pas de ~s pour moi!** don't go to any trouble!; **sans ~(s)** [*personne*] straightforward; [*réception*] informal.

chichiteux○, **-euse** /ʃiʃitø, øz/ **I** *adj* fussy.
II *nm,f* fusspot○ GB; **cesse de faire le ~!** stop being such a fusspot!

chicon /ʃikɔ̃/ *nm* **1** (laitue) cos (lettuce) GB, Romaine US; **2** (endive) chicory.

chicorée /ʃikɔʀe/ *nf* **1** Bot chicory; (salade) endive GB, chicory ¢ US; **2** Culin (poudre) chicory; (boisson) chicory coffee.

chicot /ʃiko/ *nm* **1**○ (dent) stump, snag; **2** (souche) (tree) stump.

chié●, **~e** /ʃje/ **I** *adj* **1** (embêtant) **tu es ~, toi** you've got a bloody◑ nerve GB, you have some nerve○; **2** (bien) bloody◑ marvellous[GB] GB, absolutely terrific; **3** (difficile) bloody◑ GB, absolutely impossible.
II chiée *nf* **une ~e de** loads○ of, a whole slew of US.

chien, **chienne** /ʃjɛ̃, ʃjɛn/ **I**○ *adj* bloody-minded GB, nasty; **il est un peu ~** he's rather bloody-minded GB ou nasty; **~ de temps** wretched weather; **ma chienne de vie** my wretched life; **ne pas être ~** not to be too hard.
II *nm* **1** (animal) dog; **~ enragé** rabid dog; **~ à poil ras/long** short-/long-haired dog; **'~ méchant'** 'beware of the dog'; ▶ **caravane**, **faïence**, **quille**, **rage**, **saucisse**; **2** (de fusil) hammer; **3** Naut **coup de ~** fresh gale.
III○ **de chien** *loc adj* [*métier, temps*] rotten; **vie de ~** dog's life; **avoir un caractère de ~** to have a lousy○ character; **être d'une humeur de ~** to be in a foul mood; **ça me fait un mal de ~** it hurts like hell○.
IV chienne *nf* **1** (animal) bitch; **c'est une chienne** it's a bitch; **il promène sa chienne** he's walking his dog; **2**◑ (femme) bitch◑.
■ **~ d'arrêt** pointer; **~ d'aveugle** guide dog; **~ de berger** sheepdog; **~ de chasse** retriever, gundog; **~ courant** hound; **~ esquimau** husky; **~ fou** fig wild one; **~ de garde** lit guard dog; fig watchdog; **~ de mer** dogfish; **~ policier** police dog; **~ de prairie** prairie dog ou marmot; **~ de race** pedigree dog; **~ savant** performing dog; fig poodle; **~s écrasés** Presse fillers; **la rubrique des ~s écrasés**○ *column made up of filler items*; **~ de traîneau** sled dog.
IDIOMES **traiter qn comme un ~** to treat sb like a dog ou like dirt; **ne pas donner sa part au ~** not to be backward in coming forward; **être comme ~ et chat** to be always at each other's throats; **être couché en ~ de fusil** to be curled up; **entre ~ et loup** at dusk; **elle a du ~** she's got what it takes; **avoir un air de ~ battu** to have a hangdog look; **ce n'est pas fait pour les ~s**○ it's there to be used; **garder à qn un ~ de sa chienne** to bear a grudge against sb; **merci mon ~**○ iron and thank you too; **c'est un temps à ne pas mettre un ~ dehors** it's foul weather.

chien-assis, *pl* **chiens-assis** /ʃjɛ̃asi/ *nm* dormer window.

chien-chien○, *pl* **chiens-chiens** /ʃjɛ̃ʃjɛ̃/ *nm* doggy.

chiendent /ʃjɛ̃dɑ̃/ *nm* Bot couch grass, scutch grass; **brosse de ~** scrubbing brush.
IDIOMES **pousser comme du ~** to grow like a weed.

chienlit /ʃjɑ̃li/ *nf* havoc, chaos; **c'est la ~** it's havoc ou chaos.

chien-loup, *pl* **chiens-loups** /ʃjɛ̃lu/ *nm* Alsatian GB, German shepherd.

chienne ▶ **chien** I, IV.

chiennerie○ /ʃjɛnʀi/ *nf* bloody-mindedness◑ GB, nastiness.

chier● /ʃje/ [2] *vi* **1** (déféquer) to shit●; **2** (contrarier) **faire ~ qn** (contrarier) to piss sb off●; (énerver) to get up sb's nose○ GB; **se faire ~** to have a bloody◑ GB ou really boring time; **se faire ~ sur qch/à faire** to kill oneself over sth/doing○; **envoyer qn ~** to tell sb to piss● off.

IDIOMES **en ~** to go through it; **ça va ~ des bulles** there'll be hell to pay○; **~ dans la colle** to be taking the piss◑.

chiffe /ʃif/ *nf* fig wet blanket○, drip○; **être une vraie ~ molle, être mou comme une ~** to be a real drip ou wet blanket.

chiffon /ʃifɔ̃/ *nm* **1** (morceau d'étoffe) rag, (piece of) cloth; **une poupée de ~s** a rag doll; **des ~s imbibés d'essence** rags soaked in petrol GB ou gas US; **collecte de ~s** collection of old clothes; **à l'arrivée ma robe était un vrai ~** when I arrived my dress was all crumpled up; **2** (pour nettoyer) gén (sec) duster; **donner** or **passer un coup de ~ sur qch** to give sth a quick dust ou wipe; **donner** or **passer un coup de ~** to do some dusting; **elle a toujours le ~ à la main** she's always got a duster in her hand; **nettoyer avec un ~ humide** to clean [sth] with a damp cloth; **3** (document sans valeur) scrap of paper; **cet accord n'est qu'un ~** this agreement isn't worth the paper it's written on.

■ **~ antistatique** antistatic cloth; **~ à chaussures** shoe cloth; **~ à poussière** duster.

IDIOMES **parler** or **causer ~s** to talk (about) clothes; **agiter un ~ rouge devant qn** to goad sb.

chiffonnade /ʃifɔnad/ *nf* Culin chiffonnade.

chiffonné, ~e /ʃifɔne/ **I** *pp* ▶ **chiffonner**.

II *pp adj* **1** (fatigué) [*teint, trait*] tired; [*visage*] tired-looking; **2**○ (chagriné) troubled, ruffled; **il avait l'air ~** he looked ruffled.

chiffonner /ʃifɔne/ [1] **I** *vtr* **1** (froisser) to crumple (up) [*document, papier, feuille*]; to crease, to crumple [*vêtement, tissu*]; **2**○ (chagriner) to bother [*personne*]; **il y a quelque chose qui me chiffonne dans ce que vous dites** something bothers ou is bothering me about what you're saying.

II se chiffonner *vpr* [*vêtement, tissu*] to crease, to crumple.

chiffonnier, -ière /ʃifɔnje, ɛʀ/ **I** ▶**510** *nm,f* rag-and-bone man/woman.

II *nm* (meuble) chiffonnier.

IDIOMES **se battre comme des ~s** to fight like cat and dog; **être habillé comme un ~** to be dressed like a tramp.

chiffrable /ʃifʀabl/ *adj* [*pertes, dégâts*] calculable; [*électorat, effectif*] whose size can be calculated (*épith, après n*); **les conséquences sont difficilement ~s** the consequences are difficult to calculate; **les pertes ne sont pas ~s** it's impossible to put a figure on the losses.

chiffrage /ʃifʀaʒ/ *nm* **1** Fin (de pertes) assessment (**de** of); (de travaux) costing; **2** Mus figuring.

chiffre /ʃifʀ/ *nm* **1** (symbole) figure; (numéro, nombre) number; **trois ~s après la virgule** three figures after the decimal point; **le ~ 7** the figure 7; **écrire le montant en ~s** to write the amount in figures; **un numéro à six ~s** a six-figure ou -digit number; **les ~s, c'est son fort** he/she has a good head for figures; **avoir horreur des ~s** to hate anything to do with figures; **donne-moi un ~ entre 0 et 9** give me a number between 0 and 9; **2** (résultat) figure; **les ~s de ce mois sont mauvais** this month's figures are bad; **3** (statistique) statistic; **les ~s officiels/du chômage** the official/unemployment statistics; **selon les ~s de l'OCDE** according to OECD figures; **4** (total) total; **le ~ des dépenses/victimes** the total expenditure/number of victims; **~ global** total amount; **5** (code) (de message) code; (de coffre) combination; **le (service du) Chiffre** the cipher room; **6** (monogramme) monogram; **brodé** or **gravé à son ~** monogrammed.

■ **~ d'affaires, CA** turnover GB, sales (*pl*) US; **réaliser un ~ d'affaires de 300 millions de francs par an** to have a turnover of 300 million francs a year, to turn over 300 million francs a year; **faire du ~ d'affaires**○ to go for quick turnover; **~ d'affaires prévisionnel** forecast turnover; **~ d'affaires à l'exportation** export sales (*pl*); **~ arabe** Arabic numeral; **en ~s arabes** in Arabic numerals; **~ romain** Roman numeral; **~ de vente** sales (*pl*).

chiffrement /ʃifʀəmɑ̃/ *nm* encoding.

chiffrer /ʃifʀe/ [1] **I** *vtr* **1** (évaluer) to put a figure on, to assess [*coût, dépenses, pertes*]; to cost [*travaux*]; **~ à** to put ou assess [sth] at [*coût, dépenses, pertes*]; to put the cost of [sth] at [*travaux*]; **la dette extérieure est chiffrée à 46 milliards** the foreign debt is put at 46 billion; **données chiffrées** figures; **2** (coder) to encode [*message*]; **3** (marquer) to monogram [*linge, vaisselle*]; **4** (numéroter) to number [*pages*].

II○ *vi* (coûter cher) to add up; **ça chiffre vite** it soon adds up.

III se chiffrer *vpr* **se ~ à** [*réparations, installation, vente*] to amount to, to come to; **la progression des ventes s'est chiffrée à 4,8%** the increase in sales amounted to 4.8%; **les travaux se chiffrent à plusieurs millions** the work comes to several millions; **se ~ par millions** to amount to millions.

chiffreur, -euse /ʃifʀœʀ, øz/ ▶**510** *nm,f* cipher clerk.

chignole /ʃiɲɔl/ *nf* **1** (outil) hand drill; **2**○ péj (voiture) banger○ GB, junker○ US, car.

chignon /ʃiɲɔ̃/ *nm* bun; (plus élégant) chignon; **avoir un ~** to wear one's hair in a bun; **~ sur la nuque** low bun; **le ~ ne lui va pas** a bun doesn't suit her; **coiffer ses cheveux en ~** to put one's hair in a bun ou chignon; **pouvez-vous me faire un ~?** could you put my hair up?

chihuahua /ʃiwawa/ *nm* chihuahua.

chiisme /ʃiism/ *nm* Shiism.

chiite /ʃiit/ Relig *adj, nmf* Shiite.

Chili /ʃili/ ▶**321** *nprm* Chile.

chilien, -ienne /ʃiljɛ̃, ɛn/ ▶**537** *adj* Chilean.

Chilien, -ienne /ʃiljɛ̃, ɛn/ ▶**537** *nm,f* Chilean.

chimère /ʃimɛʀ/ *nf* fml **1** fig wild ou pipe dream, chim(a)era sout; **se forger des ~s** to fill one's head with wild dreams; **se complaire dans des ~s** to live in a dream world; **poursuivre** or **caresser des ~s** to chase rainbows; **de folles/vagues ~s** crazy/vague fantasies; **2** Mythol Chim(a)era, chim(a)era; **3** Biol, Bot chim(a)era; Zool (poisson) chim(a)era.

chimérique /ʃimeʀik/ *adj* **1** (irréalisable) [*projet, espoir*] wild; **2** (irréel) [*animal*] fabulous; **3** (visionnaire) [*personne, esprit*] fanciful; **c'est un esprit ~** he's a dreamer.

chimie /ʃimi/ *nf* **1** chemistry; **~ organique/minérale** organic/inorganic chemistry; **expérience/laboratoire/cours de ~** chemistry experiment/laboratory/class; **2** (transformation) liter alchemy.

chimiothérapie /ʃimjoteʀapi/ *nf* chemotherapy; **suivre une ~** to have chemotherapy treatment.

chimique /ʃimik/ *adj* **1** [*analyse, réaction, industrie, produit*] chemical; [*fibre*] man-made; **armes ~s** chemical weapons; **2** péj [*boisson, nourriture*] synthetic; [*goût*] chemical.

chimiquement /ʃimikmɑ̃/ *adv* chemically.

chimiste /ʃimist/ ▶**510** *nmf* chemist; **ingénieur ~** chemical engineer.

chimpanzé /ʃɛ̃pɑ̃ze/ *nm* chimpanzee.

chinchilla /ʃɛ̃ʃila/ *nm* **1** Zool chinchilla; **lapin/chat ~** chinchilla rabbit/cat; **2** (fourrure) chinchilla.

chine /ʃin/ **I** *nm* **1** (porcelaine) china; **une tasse en ~** a china cup; **2** (papier) rice paper.

II○ *nf* (par un particulier) antique hunting; (brocante) antique dealing.

Chine /ʃin/ ▶**321** *nprf* China; **~ continentale** mainland China; **République populaire de ~** People's Republic of China.

chiner /ʃine/ [1] **I** *vtr* **1** Tex to dye the warp threads of; **tissu chiné** chiné fabric; **une étoffe rouge chinée de jaune** a red fabric with a yellow thread in it; **2**○ (se moquer) to kid○.

II○ *vi* (chercher) to bargain-hunt, to antique US; (vendre) to deal in second-hand goods.

Chinetoque◑ /ʃintɔk/ *nmf* offensive Chinese, Chink◑ injur.

chineur○, **-euse** /ʃinœʀ, øz/ *nm,f* **1** (acheteur) bargain hunter; (vendeur) second-hand dealer; **2** (plaisantin) teaser.

chinois, ~e /ʃinwa, az/ **I** *adj* **1** ▶**537** Géog Chinese; **2**○ (tatillon) nitpicking○.

II *nm* **1** ▶**462** Ling Chinese; **2** Culin conical strainer.

IDIOMES **pour moi c'est du ~** it's double-Dutch GB ou Greek to me.

Chinois, ~e /ʃinwa, az/ ▶**537** *nm,f* Chinese.

chinoiser /ʃinwaze/ [1] *vi* to quibble (**sur** about ou over).

chinoiserie /ʃinwazʀi/ **I** *nf* (bibelot) chinoiserie.

II chinoiseries○ *nfpl* unnecessary complications; **les ~s administratives** red tape ₡.

chintz /ʃints/ *nm* chintz.

chiot /ʃjo/ *nm* puppy, pup.

chiottes● /ʃjɔt/ *nfpl* toilets; **les ~** the bog◑ (*sg*) GB, the shitter● (*sg*) US.

chiourme /ʃjuʀm/ *nf* Hist **1** (galériens) galley slaves (*pl*); **2** (forçats) convicts (*pl*).

chiper○ /ʃipe/ [1] *vtr* to pinch○; **~ qch à qn** to pinch sth from sb; **il m'a chipé mon journal** he's pinched my newspaper.

chipie○ /ʃipi/ *nf* cow○ pej.

chipolata /ʃipɔlata/ *nf* chipolata.

chipoter /ʃipɔte/ [1] **I** *vi* **1** (faire des difficultés) to quibble (**sur** over); **2** (marchander) to haggle (**sur** over); **3** (pour manger) to pick at one's food.

II se chipoter *vpr* to squabble (**à propos de, pour** over).

chipoteur, -euse /ʃipɔtœʀ, øz/ **I** *adj* **1** (exigeant) difficult; **2** (sur prix) **être ~** to haggle over everything; **3** (à table) fussy.

II *nm,f* **1** (personne exigeante) nit-picker; **2** (sur prix) person who haggles over everything; **3** (à table) fussy ou picky○ US eater.

chips /ʃips/ *nf inv* crisp GB, potato chip US.

chique /ʃik/ *nf* plug ou quid GB (of tobacco); **mâcher sa ~** to chew tobacco.

IDIOMES **avoir la ~**○ to have a swollen cheek; **avaler sa ~**○ to kick the bucket; **couper la ~ à qn** (faire taire) to shut sb up○; (surprendre) to leave sb speechless; **mou comme une ~** spineless, wet○.

chiqué○ /ʃike/ *nm* **1** (bluff) **c'est du ~** it's a put-on ou sham○; **c'est du ~, il n'a pas mal** he's putting it on, there's nothing wrong with him; **combat sans ~** no-holds-barred fight; **2** (affectation) airs (*pl*); **faire du ~** to put on ou give oneself airs.

chiquenaude /ʃiknod/ *nf* flick; **d'une ~** with a flick; **donner une ~ sur la joue de qn** to flick sb on the cheek.

chiquer /ʃike/ [1] *vtr* **~ (du tabac)** to chew tobacco; **tabac à ~** chewing tobacco.

chiqueur, -euse /ʃikœʀ, øz/ *nm,f* tobacco-chewer.

chiromancie /kiʀɔmɑ̃si/ *nf* palmistry, chiromancy; **faire de la ~** to read palms.

chiromancien, -ienne /kiʀɔmɑ̃sjɛ̃, ɛn/ ▶**510** *nm,f* palm-reader.

chiropracteur /kiʀopʀaktœʀ/ ▶**510** *nm* chiropractor.

chiropraxie /kiʀopʀaksi/ *nf* chiropractic.

chirurgical, ~e, *mpl* **-aux** /ʃiʀyʀʒikal, o/ *adj* surgical.

chirurgie /ʃiʀyʀʒi/ *nf* surgery; **~ dentaire** dental surgery; **~ endoscopique** keyhole surgery; **~ plastique** or **réparatrice** or **esthétique** plastic surgery.

chirurgien /ʃiʀyʀʒjɛ̃/ ▶ 510 *nm* surgeon.

chirurgien-dentiste, *pl* **chirurgiens-dentistes** /ʃiʀyʀʒjɛ̃dɑ̃tist/ ▶ 510 *nm* dental surgeon.

Chisinau /kiʃinao/ ▶ 857 *npr* Chisinau, Kishinev.

chistera /ʃisteʀa/ *nm* pelota basket.

chitine /kitin/ *nf* chitin.

chitineux, **-euse** /kitinø, øz/ *adj* chitinous.

chiure /ʃjyʀ/ *nf* **~ (de mouche)** flyspeck.

chleuh◑ /ʃlø/ *adj*, *nm* offensive kraut◑ injur.

chlinguer◑ /ʃlɛ̃ge/ [1] *vi* to stink.

chlorate /klɔʀat/ *nm* chlorate; **~ de soude** or **sodium/potasse** or **potassium** sodium/potassium chlorate.

chlore /klɔʀ/ *nm* chlorine.

chlorer /klɔʀe/ [1] *vtr* to chlorinate.

chlorhydrique /klɔʀidʀik/ *adj* hydrochloric.

chlorique /klɔʀik/ *adj* chloric.

chloroforme /klɔʀɔfɔʀm/ *nm* chloroform.

chloroformé, **~e** /klɔʀɔfɔʀme/ **I** *pp* ▶ **chloroformer**.

II *pp adj* [*personne, collectivité*] apathetic.

chloroformer /klɔʀɔfɔʀme/ [1] *vtr* to chloroform.

chlorophylle /klɔʀɔfil/ *nf* chlorophyll; **dentifrice/chewing-gum à la ~** chlorophyll toothpaste/chewing gum.

chlorophyllien, **-ienne** /klɔʀɔfiljɛ̃, ɛn/ *adj* chlorophyllous.

chlorure /klɔʀyʀ/ *nm* chloride; **~ de sodium/potassium** sodium/potassium chloride; **~ de chaux** chloride of lime.

chlorurer /klɔʀyʀe/ [1] *vtr* to chlorinate.

choc /ʃɔk/ **I** *adj inv* **mesures ~** drastic measures; **'prix ~!'** 'huge reductions'; **c'est l'argument ~!** there's no answer to that!; **le film ~ de l'année** the most sensational film of the year.

II *nm* **1** (rencontre brutale) (d'objets) impact, shock; (de vagues) crash; (de personnes) collision; Aut (collision) crash; (sans gravité) bump; **ça s'ébrèche au moindre ~** it chips at the slightest knock; **résister aux ~s** to be shock-resistant; **à cause de la violence du ~** because of the force of the impact; **sous le ~** under the impact; **à la suite d'un ~ avec un attaquant adverse** Sport after colliding with an opponent; ▶ **onde**; **2** (bruit) (violent) crash, smash; (sourd) thud; (métallique) clang; (de verre, vaisselle) clink; **3** (affrontement) (d'adversaires) gén, Mil clash; Sport encounter; fig (d'idées, opinions) clash; **les troupes ont résisté au premier ~** the troops have weathered the first onslaught; **troupe** or **unité de ~** Mil shock troops (*pl*); **de ~** [*journaliste, patron*] ace○; **4** (commotion) shock; **ça m'a fait un ~ de la revoir** it gave me a shock to see her again; **être encore sous le ~** (après une nouvelle) to be still in a state of shock; Méd (après un accident) to be still in shock; **tenir le ~** to cope; **traitement de ~** shock treatment; ▶ **état**.

■ **~ culturel** culture shock; **~ électrique** electric shock; **~ nerveux** (nervous) shock; **~ opératoire** post-operative shock; **~ pétrolier** oil crisis; **~ en retour** return shock; fig backlash; **~ septique** toxic shock.

chochotte○ /ʃɔʃɔt/ *adj*, *nf* la-di-da○.

chocolat /ʃɔkɔla/ **I** ▶ 193 *adj inv* (couleur) chocolate-brown (coloured[GB]).

II *nm* Culin **1** (substance) chocolate; **gâteau au ~** chocolate cake; **~ aux noisettes** hazelnut chocolate; **une tablette de ~** a chocolate bar, a bar of chocolate; **2** (friandise) chocolate; **je peux reprendre un ~?** can I have another chocolate?; **une boîte de ~s** a box of chocolates; **3** (boisson) chocolate; **un ~ chaud** a hot chocolate.

■ **~ blanc** white chocolate; **~ à croquer** plain GB ou dark chocolate; **~ à cuire** cooking chocolate; **~ en poudre** drinking chocolate; **~ au lait** milk chocolate; **~ de ménage** = **~ à cuire**; **~ noir** = **~ à croquer**.

IDIOMES **être ~**○ to feel let down.

chocolaté, **~e** /ʃɔkɔlate/ *adj* [*boisson, bouillie*] chocolate-flavoured[GB].

chocolaterie /ʃɔkɔlatʀi/ *nf* chocolate factory.

chocolatier, **-ière** /ʃɔkɔlatje, ɛʀ/ **I** ▶ 510 *nm,f* chocolate maker; **pâtissier ~** confectioner and chocolate maker.

II chocolatière *nf* hot chocolate jug.

chocottes○ /ʃɔkɔt/ *nfpl* **avoir les ~** to have the jitters○.

chœur /kœʀ/ *nm* **1** (groupe) choir; (d'opéra) chorus; **2** (morceau) chorus; **chanter en ~** to sing in chorus; **reprendre le refrain en ~** to sing the chorus all together; **'reprenons tous en ~'** 'all together now'; **3** (de théâtre) chorus; **4** Archit chancel, choir; **5** fig chorus (**de** of); **le ~ des grévistes** all the strikers (*pl*); **en ~** [*dire, affirmer*] in unison; [*rire, souffrir*] all together.

choir /ʃwaʀ/ [51] *vi* liter to fall; **la bobinette cherra** the latch will drop; **se laisser ~** to flop; **laisser ~ qch** to drop sth; **laisser ~ qn** (se séparer de) to drop sb; (ne plus aider) to let sb down.

choisi, **~e** /ʃwazi/ **I** *pp* ▶ **choisir**.

II *pp adj* **1** (sélectionné) [*morceaux, œuvres*] selected; **des morceaux ~s de Rimbaud** selected passages from Rimbaud; **2** (recherché) [*expressions, terme*] carefully chosen; **expression bien/mal ~e** felicitous ou appropriate/unfortunate choice of expression; **3** (sélect) [*société, clientèle*] select.

choisir /ʃwaziʀ/ [3] *vtr* to choose (**entre** between); **~ l'exil/la fuite** to choose exile/to flee; **~ son camp** fig to choose sides; **~ de faire** to choose to do; **ils ont choisi de ne pas répondre** they chose not to answer; **bien/mal ~** to make the right/wrong choice; **~ qn comme ministre** to pick sb as a minister; **Nice ou Paris? c'est à toi de ~** Nice or Paris? it's up to you; **ça y est, j'ai choisi** I've made my choice.

choix /ʃwa/ *nm inv* **1** (option) choice (**entre** between; **parmi** among); **le sport/film de ton ~** the sport/film of your choice; **avoir le ~ des armes** to have the choice of weapons; **avoir/ne pas avoir le ~** to have a/no choice; **ne pas avoir d'autre ~ que de partir** to have no choice but to leave; **faire le bon/mauvais ~** to make the right/wrong choice; **mon ~ est fait** I've made my choice; **faire le ~ de rester** to choose to stay; **faire un ~ entre** to choose between; **faire ~ de qch** fml to select sth; **trois menus au ~** a choice of three menus; **fromage ou dessert au ~** a choice of cheese or dessert; **couleur au ~ du client** colour[GB] to be chosen by the customer; **être libre de son ~** to be free to choose; **je te laisse le ~ du jour** you decide on the date; **fixer** or **arrêter** or **porter son ~ sur** to settle ou decide on; **tes ~ musicaux/littéraires** your choice of music/literature; **2** (assortiment) choice; **il y a beaucoup de ~ ici** there's plenty of choice here; **le ~ est très limité** there's very little choice; **un très grand ~ de...** a very wide choice ou range of...; **on manque un peu de ~** there's not much choice; **3** (sélection) selection; **un ~ d'images/d'instruments/d'œuvres** a selection of pictures/of instruments/of works; **4** (qualité) **de ~** [*produit*] choice; [*candidat, collaborateur*] first-rate; **les places de ~ sont toutes réservées** the best seats are all reserved; **un morceau de ~** (en boucherie) a prime cut; **de premier ~** [*fruits*] class one; [*viande*] prime, top-grade; **de ~ courant** standard quality; **de second ~** of poorer quality (*après n*).

choléra /kɔleʀa/ ▶ 271 *nm* cholera.

cholérique /kɔleʀik/ *nmf* cholera victim.

cholestérol /kɔlɛsteʀɔl/ *nm* cholesterol; **avoir du ~**○ to have a high cholesterol level; **surveiller son (taux de) ~** to watch one's cholesterol level.

chômage /ʃomaʒ/ *nm* unemployment; **~ saisonnier/de longue durée/des jeunes** seasonal/long-term/youth unemployment; **la lutte contre le ~** the fight against unemployment; **être au** or **en ~** to be unemployed, to be on the dole○ GB; **ça fait un an qu'il est au ~** he has been out of work ou unemployed for a year; **s'inscrire au ~** to sign on ou up US for unemployment benefit, to go on the dole○ GB; **pointer au ~** to sign on GB, to sign up for unemployment US; **mettre qn au** or **en ~** to make sb redundant GB, to lay sb off; **la mise au ~** redundancy GB, laying off; **l'usine a mis 300 personnes au ~** the factory has made 300 people redundant GB ou has laid off 300 people; **taux de ~** unemployment rate.

■ **~ conjoncturel** or **cyclique** cyclical unemployment; **~ d'insertion** youth unemployment (*of young people who have never had a job*); **~ partiel** short time (working); **mettre qn au ~ partiel** to put sb on short time; **~ structurel** structural unemployment; **~ technique** layoffs (*pl*); **mettre les ouvriers au** or **en ~ technique** to lay off the workforce; **500 ouvriers au** or **en ~ technique** 500 workers laid off.

chômé, **~e** /ʃome/ **I** *pp* ▶ **chômer**.

II *pp adj* **jour ~** day off; **fête ~e** national holiday.

chômedu◑ /ʃomdy/ *nm* (inactivité) unemployment; (indemnités) dole○ GB, welfare○ US.

chômer /ʃome/ [1] **I** *vtr* not to work on.

II *vi* **1** (être improductif) [*personne, machine, capital, imagination*] to be idle; **nous ne chômons pas en ce moment!** we're not short of work at the moment!; **laisser ~ les terres** Agric to leave the land fallow; **2** (être sans travail) [*employé*] to be out of work; [*usine, machines*] to stand idle; [*industrie*] to be at a standstill.

chômeur, **-euse** /ʃomœʀ, øz/ *nm,f* unemployed person; **il est ~** he is unemployed; **les ~s** the unemployed; **le nombre de ~s** the number of unemployed; **15%/2 millions de ~s** 15%/2 million unemployed; **les ~s de longue durée** the long-term unemployed; **~s en fin de droit** unemployed people no longer eligible for benefit.

chope /ʃɔp/ *nf* beer mug, tankard.

choper◑ /ʃɔpe/ [1] *vtr* **1** (attraper) to get [*coup, habitude, tic*]; to catch [*maladie, virus*]; **2** (voler) **~ qch à qn** to pinch○ sth from sb; **se faire ~ qch** to have sth pinched; **3** (arrêter) to nab○, to catch [*voleur*]; **se faire ~** to be nabbed.

chopine○ /ʃɔpin/ *nf* **1** (bouteille de vin) bottle of wine; (verre) glass of wine; **2** C (pinte) pint.

choquant, **~e** /ʃɔkɑ̃, ɑ̃t/ *adj* shocking; **~ de brutalité/franchise** shockingly brutal/frank.

choquer /ʃɔke/ [1] **I** *vtr* **1** (scandaliser) to shock [*personne*]; **ça a choqué les lecteurs** it shocked the readers; **ton cynisme me choque** I am shocked by your cynicism; **ça l'a choqué de voir ça** he was shocked to see it; **ça m'a choqué qu'elle refuse** I was shocked that she should refuse; **si le mot choque** if the word is shocking ou causes offence[GB]; **ça choque** it's shocking; **cela risque de ~** (comportement, film, remarque) it might cause offence[GB]; **2** (commotionner) [*événement, nouvelle*] to shake [*personne*]; [*chute, accident*] to shake [sb] (up); **cette nouvelle l'a choqué** he was shaken by the news; **un peu choqué par sa chute** slightly shaken by his fall; **être choqué** Méd to be in shock; **3** (blesser) to offend [*œil, sensibilité*]; to jar on [*oreille*]; to offend against [*bon sens*]; **4** (cogner) to knock [*objet*]; **~ les verres** to clink glasses; **5** Naut to slacken, to loosen [*amarre*].

II se choquer *vpr* (s'offusquer) to be shocked (**de** at, by).

choral, **~e**, *mpl* **~s** or **-aux** /kɔʀal, o/ **I** *adj* choral.

II (*pl* **~s**) *nm* chorale.
III **chorale** *nf* choir.

chorée /kɔʀe/ *nf* chorea; **~ de Sydenham** Sydenham's chorea; **~ de Huntington** Huntington's chorea.

chorégraphe /kɔʀegʀaf/ ▶**510**| *nmf* choreographer.

chorégraphie /kɔʀegʀafi/ *nf* choreography; **composer la ~** to choreograph.

chorégraphier /kɔʀegʀafje/ [2] *vtr* to choreograph.

chorégraphique /kɔʀegʀafik/ *adj* choreographic.

choreute /kɔʀøt/ *nm* member of the chorus.

choriste /kɔʀist/ *nmf* (d'église) chorister; (d'opéra) member of the chorus; (de chorale) member of the choir.

chorus /kɔʀys/ *nm* Mus chorus; **faire ~ avec qn** fig to join in with sb.

chose /ʃoz/ **I**○ *adj* **se sentir/avoir l'air tout ~** to feel/look out of sorts.
II *nf* **1** (objet) thing; **il aime les bonnes ~s** he likes good things; **ils ont acheté beaucoup de ~s pour dîner** they've bought a lot of things for dinner; **quelle autre ~ pourrais-je leur acheter?** what else could I buy them?; **'une bière'—'la même ~ (pour moi)'** 'a beer'—'the same for me'; **la même ~ s'il vous plaît** (pour être resservi) (the) same again, please; ▶**quelque III**; **2** (entité) thing; **c'est une bonne/mauvaise ~ (en soi)** it's a good/bad thing (in itself); **il y a de bonnes ~s dans ce livre** there are some good things in this book; **une seule et unique ~** one thing only; **il ne s'intéresse qu'à une seule et unique ~** he's only interested in one thing; **et, ~ incroyable/aberrante, il a dit oui** and the incredible/absurd thing is that he said yes; **de deux ~s l'une** it's got to be one thing or the other; **il se passe la même ~ ici** the same thing is happening here; **c'est toujours la même ~ ici/avec lui** it's always the same here/with him; **tu seras privé de dessert et même ~ pour ta sœur** you won't get your dessert and the same goes for your sister; **une ~ communément admise** a widely accepted fact; **je pense** or **j'ai pensé à une ~** I've thought of something; **c'est autre ~** that's different; **autre ~, avez-vous pensé à faire...?** another thing, have you thought about doing...?; **et si on parlait d'autre ~** let's talk about something else; **ce n'est pas autre ~ que de la jalousie** it's nothing but jealousy; **c'est ça, ce n'est pas autre ~** it's that and nothing else; **voilà autre ~**○! that's something else!; **c'est une ~ de rentrer tard, c'en est une autre de disparaître pour trois jours** it's one thing to come home late, quite another (thing) to disappear for three days; ▶**dû**; **3** (affaire, activité, message) thing; **j'ai une ou deux ~s à faire en ville** I've got one or two things to do in town; **j'ai une ~/deux ou trois ~s à vous dire** I've got something/two or three things to tell you; **(vous direz) bien des ~s à votre famille/Madame Lemoine** give my best regards to your family/Mrs Lemoine; **c'était la seule ~ à ne pas dire/faire** that was the last thing to say/do; **c'est pas des ~s**○ **à dire/faire** that's the last thing to say/do; **parler de ~s et d'autres** to talk about one thing and another ou this and that; **la pire ~ qui puisse m'arriver** the worst thing that could happen to me; **en mettant les ~s au mieux/au pire** at best/at (the) worst; **mettre les ~s au point** to clear things up; **ce sont des ~s qui arrivent** it's (just) one of those things, these things happen; **on verra plus tard, chaque ~ en son temps** we'll cross that bridge when we come to it; **avant toute ~** (auparavant) before anything else; (surtout) above all else; **la ~ à craindre** the worrying thing; **ce n'est pas ~ facile** or **aisée de faire** it's no easy thing to do; **c'est ~ courante que de faire** it's common to do; **faire bien les ~s** to do things properly; **'avez-vous déménagé?'—'c'est ~ faite'** 'have you moved?'—'it's all done'; **il leur manquait la bombe atomique, c'est désormais ~ faite** they needed the atomic bomb, now they've got it; **il a l'intention de vous écrire si ce n'est pas déjà ~ faite** he intends to write to you if he hasn't already done so; **voilà** or **c'est une bonne ~ de faite** that's one thing out of the way; **4** (ce dont il s'agit) matter; **la ~ en question** the matter in hand; **la ~ est d'importance** the matter is of some importance; **je vais vous expliquer la ~** I'll tell you what it is (all) about; **la ~ dont je vous parle** what I'm talking about; **il a pris la ~ avec humour** he saw the funny side of it; **il a bien/mal pris la ~** he took it well/badly; **comment a-t-il pris la ~?** how did he take it?; **5** (personne) **ce n'est qu'une pauvre ~** he/she is a poor little thing; **6**○ (activités sexuelles) **être un peu porté sur la ~** to like it○, to be keen on sex; **7**○ (nom de substitution) **Chose m'a dit qu'il...** what's-his-name/what's-her-name ou thingummy told me that he...; **un costume de chez Chose** a suit from thingummy's.
III choses *nfpl* **1** (réalité) **la nature des ~s** the nature of things; **les ~s étant ce qu'elles sont** things being what they are; **toutes ~s (étant) égales par ailleurs** other ou all things being equal; **regarder les ~s de plus près** to take a closer look at things; **2** (domaine) **les ~s d'ici bas** or **de ce monde** the things of this world; **les ~s de l'esprit/de la chair** things of the mind/of the flesh; **les ~s de la religion** religious matters; **les ~s de la vie (quotidienne)** the little things in life.
■ **~ imprimée** printed word; **~ jugée** Jur res judicata; **autorité de la ~ jugée** binding force of the res judicata; **~ léguée** Jur bequest; **~ publique** liter res publica, state; **~ en soi** Philos thing-in-itself.
IDIOMES **en toutes ~s il faut considérer la fin** in all matters one must consider the outcome; **il faut prendre les ~s comme elles viennent** Prov take things as they come.

chosifier /ʃozifje/ [2] *vtr* Philos to reify.

chou, *pl* **~x** /ʃu/ **I** *adj inv* [*personne*] sweet; **elle est ~ avec son chapeau** she looks so sweet in her hat.
II *nm* **1** (légume) cabbage; **soupe aux ~x** cabbage soup; **~ farci** stuffed cabbage; ▶**chèvre**, **oreille**, **palmiste**; **2** (pâtisserie) choux bun GB, pastry shell US; **3** (personne aimable) dear; **ferme la porte tu seras un ~** be a dear and close the door; **tu es un ~** you're a little darling.
■ **~ de Bruxelles** Brussels sprout; **~ à la crème** cream puff; **~ rave** kohlrabi; **~ rouge** red cabbage; **~ vert** green cabbage.
IDIOMES **bête comme ~** really easy; **faire ~ blanc**○ to draw a blank; **faire ses ~x gras de qch**○ to use sth to one's advantage; **être dans les ~x**○ to bring up the rear; **aller planter ses ~x**○ to go and live in the country; **aller planter ses ~x ailleurs** to go to pastures new; **rentrer dans le ~**○ **de qn** (physiquement) to beat sb up; (verbalement) to give sb a piece of one's mind.

chouan /ʃwɑ̃/ **I** *adj* Chouan.
II *nm* Chouan (*Royalist insurgent from western France during the Revolution*).

chouannerie /ʃwanʀi/ *nf* **1** (révolte) revolt of the Chouans; **2** (mouvement) Chouan movement.

choucas /ʃuka/ *nm* jackdaw.

chouchou○, **-oute** /ʃuʃu, ut/ **I** *nm,f* (du professeur) pet; (du public, des spectateurs) darling.
II *nm* (pour les cheveux) scrunchie.

chouchouter○ /ʃuʃute/ [1] *vtr* to pamper [*enfant, adulte*]; **se faire ~** to be pampered.

choucroute /ʃukʀut/ *nf* sauerkraut; **~ garnie** sauerkraut with meat.

chouette /ʃwɛt/ **I**○ *adj* great○, neat○ US; **c'est ~ comme sport** it's a great sport; **être ~ avec qn** to be really nice to sb; **c'est ~ de sa part** that's really nice of him/her.
II *nf* Zool owl; **vieille ~** fig pej old harridan.
III *excl* great○! brilliant○! GB, neat○ US!
■ **~ hulotte** tawny owl.

chou-fleur, *pl* **choux-fleurs** /ʃuflœʀ/ *nm* cauliflower.

chouia○ /ʃuja/ *nm* smidgen○, tiny bit; **un ~ de** a smidgen of.

chou-navet, *pl* **choux-navets** /ʃunavɛ/ *nm* swede GB, rutabaga US.

chou-rave, *pl* **choux-raves** /ʃuʀav/ *nm* kohlrabi.

chouraver● /ʃuʀave/, **chourer**● /ʃuʀe/ [1] *vtr* to pinch○; **se faire ~ qch** to have sth pinched.

chow-chow, *pl* **chows-chows** /ʃoʃo/ *nm* chow(-chow).

choyer /ʃwaje/ [23] *vtr* to pamper [*enfant, adulte, client*].

chrême /kʀɛm/ *nm* chrism; **le saint ~** holy chrism.

chrestomathie /kʀɛstɔmati, kʀɛstɔmasi/ *nf* chrestomathy.

chrétien, **-ienne** /kʀetjɛ̃, ɛn/ *adj, nm,f* Christian.

chrétien-démocrate, **chrétienne-démocrate**, *pl* **chrétiens-démocrates**, **chrétiennes-démocrates** /kʀetjɛ̃demɔkʀat, kʀetjɛndemɔkʀat/ *adj, nm,f* Christian Democrat.

chrétiennement /kʀetjɛnmɑ̃/ *adv* **vivre ~** to lead a Christian life; **mourir ~** to die a Christian death; **être enterré ~** to have a Christian burial; **élever ~ ses enfants** to bring up one's children as Christians.

chrétienté /kʀetjɛ̃te/ *nf* **la ~** Christendom.

christ /kʀist/ *nm* Art **un ~** (sculpté) a sculpted Christ; (peint) a figure of Christ; (crucifix) a crucifix; **un ~ en croix** a crucifixion; **~ en gloire** or **majesté** Christ in majesty.

Christ /kʀist/ *npr* **le ~** Christ.
■ **le ~ aux limbes** Christ in Limbo; **le ~ aux outrages** Christ Mocked.

christiania /kʀistjanja/ *nm* Sport christie, christiana.

christianisation /kʀistjanizasjɔ̃/ *nf* Christianization.

christianiser /kʀistjanize/ [1] *vtr* to Christianize.

christianisme /kʀistjanism/ *nm* **le ~** Christianity.

christologie /kʀistɔlɔʒi/ *nf* Christology.

chromage /kʀomaʒ/ *nm* chromium-plating.

chromate /kʀɔmat/ *nm* chromate; **~ rouge** potassium dichromate.

chromatique /kʀɔmatik/ *adj* **1** Mus chromatic; **2** (relatif aux couleurs) chromatic.

chromatisme /kʀɔmatism/ *nm* **1** Mus chromaticism; **2** (ensemble des couleurs) colour[GB] range.

chrome /kʀom/ *nm* **1** Chimie chromium; **2** Aut **faire les ~s** to polish the chrome.

chromer /kʀome/ [1] *vtr* to chrome-plate.

chromolithographie /kʀɔmolitɔgʀafi/ *nf* **1** (procédé) chromolithography; **2** (image) chromolithograph.

chromosome /kʀɔmozom/ *nm* chromosome; **~ X/Y** X/Y chromosome.

chromosomique /kʀɔmozomik/ *adj* chromosome (*épith*).

chronicité /kʀɔnisite/ *nf* chronicity.

chronique /kʀɔnik/ **I** *adj* (tous contextes) chronic.
II *nf* **1** Presse column, page; Radio, TV programme[GB]; **la ~ économique/politique**

the business/political column; **~ mondaine** gossip column; **tenir une ~** Presse to have a column; TV, Radio to have a spot; **2** (bavardages) local gossip; **3** Hist, Littérat chronicle; **le livre des Chroniques** Bible the book of Chronicles.

chroniquement /kʀɔnikmɑ̃/ *adv* chronically.

chroniqueur, **-euse** /kʀɔnikœʀ, øz/ ▶ **510** *nm,f* **1** Presse columnist, editor; Radio, TV commentator; **~ littéraire** book reviewer; **~ dramatique** drama critic; **chroniqueuse de mode** fashion editor; **2** Hist, Littérat chronicler.

chrono○ /kʀono/ *nm* **1** (*abbr* = **chronomètre**) stopwatch; **faire du 120 km/h ~** to do 120 kilometres[GB] an hour; **réussir un bon ~** to make good time; **2** (classeur) chronological correspondence file.

chronobiologie /kʀɔnobjɔlɔʒi/ *nf* chronobiology.

chronologie /kʀɔnɔlɔʒi/ *nf* chronology.

chronologique /kʀɔnɔlɔʒik/ *adj* chronological.

chronologiquement /kʀɔnɔlɔʒikmɑ̃/ *adv* chronologically.

chronométrage /kʀɔnɔmetʀaʒ/ *nm* timing.

chronomètre /kʀɔnɔmɛtʀ/ *nm* **1** (chronographe) stopwatch; **2** (montre de précision) chronometer.

■ **~ de marine** (marine) chronometer.

chronométrer /kʀɔnɔmetʀe/ [14] *vtr* to time.

chronométreur /kʀɔnɔmetʀœʀ/ *nm* timekeeper.

chronométrique /kʀɔnɔmetʀik/ *adj* chronometric.

chronophotographie /kʀonofɔtɔgʀafi/ *nf* chronophotography, sequential photography.

chrysalide /kʀizalid/ *nf* chrysalis.

IDIOMES **sortir de sa ~** fig to come out of one's shell.

chrysanthème /kʀizɑ̃tɛm/ *nm* chrysanthemum.

CHS /seaʃɛs/ *nm*: *abbr* ▶ **centre**.

ch'timi○ /ʃtimi/ **I** *adj* northern French.
II *nm,f* (personne) person from northern France.
III *nm* (patois) northern French dialect.

chtonien, **-ienne** /ktɔnjɛ̃, ɛn/ *adj* chthonian, chthonic.

chtouille◑ /ʃtuj/ *nf* clap◑, gonorrhea.

chu ▶ **choir**.

CHU /seaʃy/ *nm*: *abbr* ▶ **centre**.

chuchotement /ʃyʃɔtmɑ̃/ *nm* (de personnes) whisper; (de ruisseau, vent) murmur; (de feuilles) rustling.

chuchoter /ʃyʃɔte/ [1] **I** *vtr* to whisper; **elle me chuchota quelques mots à l'oreille** she whispered a few words in my ear; **on chuchote de drôles d'histoires en ville** there are some strange stories going around town.
II *vi* [*personne*] to whisper; [*ruisseau, vent*] to murmur; [*feuilles*] to rustle.

chuchotis /ʃyʃɔti/ *nm* (de personnes) faint whispering; (d'eau) murmur.

chuintant, **~e** /ʃɥɛ̃tɑ̃, ɑ̃t/ **I** *adj* **1** **bruit ~** (sifflement) hissing sound; (frottement) swishing sound; **2** Phon [*consonne*] palato-alveolar fricative.
II chuintante *nf* Phon palato-alveolar fricative.

chuintement /ʃɥɛ̃tmɑ̃/ *nm* **1** (de vapeur) hiss; (de pneus, semelles) swish; **2** (en prononciation) ≈ lisp, pronunciation of *s* as *sh*.

chuinter /ʃɥɛ̃te/ [1] *vi* **1** [*vapeur*] to hiss gently; [*pneu, semelle*] to swish; **2** [*personne*] ≈ to lisp, to pronounce *s* as *sh*; **3** [*chouette*] to hoot.

chum○ /tʃœm/ *nm* C (petit ami) boyfriend.

chut /ʃyt/ *excl* shh!, hush!

chute /ʃyt/ *nf* **1** (action de tomber) fall; **faire une ~** [*personne*] to have ou take US a fall; [*objet*] to fall; **faire une ~ de cheval/moto** to fall off a horse/motorbike; **une ~ de 5 mètres** a 5-metre[GB] fall; **faire une ~ de 5 mètres** to fall 5 metres[GB]; **2** (fait de se détacher) (de feuille) fall; **~ des cheveux** hair loss; **attention aux ~s de pierres** look out for falling rocks; **3** (cascade) **~ d'eau** waterfall; **les ~s du Niagara** Niagara Falls; **barrage de haute ~** Électrotech dam with a high head; **4** Météo fall; **fortes ~s de neige/pluie** heavy snowfall (*sg*)/rainfall (*sg*); **5** (baisse) (de température, pression, prix etc) fall (**de** in), drop (**de** in); (des ventes) drop (**de** in); (de monnaie) Fin **~ du franc** fall in the price of the franc; **~ de la Bourse** fall on the stock market; **~ de tension** Méd sudden drop in blood pressure; **il a fait une ~ de tension** his blood pressure dropped suddenly; **~ de 5%** 5% drop; **6** (faillite) (de ministre, gouvernement, régime, d'empire) fall (**de** of); (d'empire commercial) collapse (**de** of); Mil (de ville, forteresse) fall (**de** of); **7** Relig **la ~** the Fall; **8** (fin) (de texte, film) ending; (d'histoire) punch line; **9** (pente) slope; **10** (de tissu, papier, cuir) offcut.

■ **~ des corps** Phys gravity; **~ libre** free-fall; **descendre en ~ libre** [*parachutiste, avion*] to be in free-fall; **tomber en ~ libre** [*personne, objet*] to fall through the air; **économie/prix/popularité en ~ libre** fig plummeting economy/prices/popularity; **la ~ des reins** the small of the back; **~ du rideau** Théât fall of the curtain, end of the play.

chuter /ʃyte/ [1] *vi* **1** (baisser) [*température, tension, prix*] to fall, to drop; [*ventes, production*] to fall; [*valeurs, actions*] to fall; **~ de/à 10 francs** to fall ou drop by/to 10 francs; **la livre a chuté de deux points (par rapport au dollar)** the pound has fallen two points (against the dollar); **faire ~ les cours** to bring prices down, to cause prices to fall; **2**○ (tomber) [*personne*] to fall down ou over, to come a cropper○.

chyle /ʃil/ *nm* Physiol chyle.

chyme /ʃim/ *nm* Physiol chyme.

Chypre /ʃipʀ/ ▶ **416**, **321** *nprf* Cyprus.

chypriote /ʃipʀijɔt/ ▶ **537** *adj* Cypriot.

Chypriote /ʃipʀijɔt/ ▶ **537** *nmf* Cypriot.

ci /si/ **I** *dét dém* **ce côté-~** this side; **cette page-~** this page; **ces mots-/chaises-~** these words/chairs; **ce lundi-/mois-~** this Monday/month; **cette fois-~** this time; **ces jours-~** (récemment) these last few days; (bientôt) in the next few days; (en ce moment) at the moment; **ces temps-~** (récemment) lately; (à présent) at the moment; **à cette heure-~** (de la journée) at this time of day; (de la nuit) at this time of night; **à cette heure-~, tu ne trouveras personne** at this time, there won't be anybody there; **il doit être arrivé à cette heure-~** he must have arrived by now; **vers cette heure-~** around this time.
II *pron dém* this; **l'un dit ~, l'autre dit ça** one says this, the other says that; **~ et ça** this and that; ▶ **comme**.

CI *written abbr* ▶ **circuit**.

ci-annexé, **~e**, *mpl* **~s** /sianɛkse/ **I** *adj* enclosed; **la copie ~e** the enclosed copy.
II *adv* enclosed.

ciao○ /tʃao/ *excl* bye○!, see you○!

ci-après /siapʀɛ/ *adv* gén below; Jur hereinafter; **voir ~** see below, v. infra sout.

cibiche○ /sibiʃ/ *nf* fag○ GB, cigarette.

cibiste /sibist/ *nmf* CB enthusiast.

ciblage /siblaʒ/ *nm* targeting.

cible /sibl/ *nf* Mil, Pub, Sport target; fig (de critique) target; (de moquerie) butt, target; **~ mobile** moving target; **prendre qn/qch pour ~** fig to pick on sb/sth; **servir de ~ aux moqueries de qn** to be the butt of sb's jokes.

cibler /sible/ [1] *vtr* Comm, Pub to target; **ils ont mal ciblé leur clientèle** they didn't target their market properly.

ciboire /sibwaʀ/ *nm* ciborium.

ciboule /sibul/ *nf* spring onion, scallion US.

ciboulette /sibulɛt/ *nf* Bot chive; Culin chives (*pl*).

ciboulot○ /sibulo/ *nm* nut○, head; **il n'a rien dans le ~** he's not very bright.

cicatrice /sikatʀis/ *nf* lit, fig scar.

cicatriciel, **-ielle** /sikatʀisjɛl/ *adj* Méd scar (*épith*).

cicatrisable /sikatʀizabl/ *adj* lit, fig healable.

cicatrisant, **~e** /sikatʀizɑ̃, ɑ̃t/ **I** *adj* [*substance*] healing.
II *nm* cicatrizant spéc, healing product.

cicatrisation /sikatʀizasjɔ̃/ *nf* lit, fig healing.

cicatriser /sikatʀize/ [1] **I** *vtr* lit, fig to heal; **sa blessure est cicatrisée** his/her wound has healed.
II se cicatriser *vpr* lit, fig to heal.

Cicéron /siseʀɔ̃/ *npr* Cicero.

cicérone† /siseʀɔn/ *nm* hum cicerone.

ci-contre /sikɔ̃tʀ/ *adv* opposite.

ci-dessous /sidəsu/ *adv* below; **voir ~** see below, v. infra sout.

ci-dessus /sidəsy/ *adv* above; **voir ~** see above, v. supra sout.

ci-devant /sidəvɑ̃/ **I** *adj inv* former.
II *nmf inv* Hist *former aristocrat*.
III *adv* formerly.

cidre /sidʀ/ *nm* cider; **~ doux/sec** sweet/dry cider.

■ **~ bouché** cider (*in a corked bottle*).

cidrerie /sidʀəʀi/ *nf* **1** (local) cider-works; **2** (fabrication) cider-making.

ciel /sjɛl, sjø/ *nm* **1** (*pl* **ciels**) Météo sky; **~ clair** or **dégagé** clear sky; **les ~s d'Afrique/de Dali** African/Dali's skies; **carte du ~** star chart; **2** (*pl* **cieux**) liter (firmament) sky; **les cieux étoilés** the starry skies, the starry heavens littér; **être suspendu entre ~ et terre** to be hanging in midair; **entre ~ et terre** fig between heaven and earth; **sous d'autres cieux** in other climes; **sous des cieux plus cléments** (climat) liter in a kinder clime, in kinder climes; (lieu plus sûr) in safer pastures; **vivre sous le ~ de Toscane/la Guadeloupe** liter to live in Tuscany/Guadeloupe; **à ~ ouvert** [*piscine, musée*] open-air; [*égout*] open; [*mine*] opencast GB, strip US; **3** (*pl* **cieux**) (paradis) Relig heaven; **être au ~** to be in heaven; **le royaume des cieux** the kingdom of heaven; **notre Père qui êtes aux cieux** our Father, which ou who art in heaven; **4** (providence) liter heaven; **le ~ m'est témoin que** heaven knows that; **remercier le ~** to thank heaven; **le ~ soit loué!** thank heavens!; (juste) **~!** (good) heavens!; **c'est le ~ qui t'envoie** you are a godsend; ▶ **aider**.

■ **~ de carrière** Mines quarry ceiling; **~ de lit** tester.

IDIOMES **remuer ~ et terre** to move heaven and earth (**pour faire** to do).

cierge /sjɛʀʒ/ *nm* **1** (d'église) (church) candle; **brûler un ~ à un saint** to light a candle to a saint; **2** Bot cereus.

cieux ▶ **ciel** 2, 3.

cigale /sigal/ *nf* cicada.

cigare /sigaʀ/ *nm* **1** (à fumer) cigar; **2**○ (tête) noodle○, head; **il n'a rien dans le ~** he hasn't got much upstairs○.

cigarette /sigaʀɛt/ *nf* cigarette; **~ sans filtre** cigarette without a filter; **fumer** or **griller**○ **une ~** to smoke a cigarette; **la ~ du condamné** the condemned man's last cigarette.

■ **~ (à) bout filtre** filter-tip (cigarette).

cigarillo /sigaʀijo/ *nm* cigarillo.

ci-gît /siʒi/ *loc verbale* here lies.

cigogne /sigɔɲ/ *nf* Zool stork.

ciguë /sigy/ *nf* (poison, plante) hemlock.

ci-inclus, **~e** /siɛ̃kly, yz/ **I** *adj* enclosed; **la copie ~e** the enclosed copy.

II *adv* enclosed; **veuillez trouver ~ la pièce demandée** please find enclosed the document requested.

ci-joint, **~e** /siʒwɛ̃, ɛ̃t/ I *adj* enclosed; **la copie ~e** the enclosed copy.
II *adv* enclosed; **vous trouverez ~ les pièces demandées** you will find enclosed the documents requested.

cil /sil/ *nm* **1** Anat eyelash; **2** Biol, Bot cilium.
■ **~s vibratiles** cilia.

ciliaire /siljɛʀ/ *adj* ciliary.

cilice /silis/ *nm* hair shirt; **porter le ~** to wear a hair shirt.

cilié, **~e** /silje/ I *adj* Bot ciliate.
II **ciliés** *nmpl* Zool Ciliograda.

cillement /sijmɑ̃/ *nm* blinking.

ciller /sije/ [1] *vi* **~ (des yeux)** to blink; **sans ~** lit unblinkingly; fig without batting an eyelid.

cimaise /simɛz/ *nf* (de corniche) cyma; (à mi-hauteur) picture rail.

cime /sim/ *nf* top.

ciment /simɑ̃/ *nm* **1** Constr cement; **~ hydraulique** hydraulic cement; **~ à prise rapide** quick-setting cement; **2** fig cement; **leur passé commun est le ~ de leur amitié** their friendship is cemented by their common past.

cimenter /simɑ̃te/ [1] I *vtr* **1** Constr to cement [*mur, briques*]; to concrete [*sol, allée*]; **2** fig to cement [*amitié*].
II **se cimenter** *vpr* [*amitié*] to grow stronger.

cimenterie /simɑ̃tʀi/ *nf* **1** (usine) cement works; **2** (industrie) cement industry.

cimentier /simɑ̃tje/ *nm* **1** (industriel) cement manufacturer; **2** (ouvrier) cement worker.

cimeterre /simtɛʀ/ *nm* scimitar.

cimetière /simtjɛʀ/ *nm* **1** lit cemetery, graveyard; (d'église) churchyard, graveyard; **à conduire comme ça tu vas finir au ~** if you drive like that you'll end up dead; **2** fig graveyard.
■ **~ d'éléphants** elephants' graveyard; **~ de voitures** scrapyard.

cimier /simje/ *nm* crest.

cinabre /sinabʀ/ *nm* cinnabar.

ciné○ /sine/ *nm* cinema GB, pictures○ (*pl*) GB, movies (*pl*) US.

cinéaste /sineast/ ▶ 510 *nmf* film director.

ciné-club, *pl* **~s** /sineklœb/ *nm* (groupe, lieu) film club.

cinéma /sinema/ *nm* **1** (bâtiment) cinema GB, movie theater US; **dans une salle de ~** in a cinema GB ou movie theater US; **aller au ~** to go to the cinema GB ou movies○ US; **2** (art, technique) cinema; (industrie) film industry; **le marché du ~** the film market; **de ~** [*école*] film (*épith*); [*affiche, actrice, séance*] film (*épith*) GB, movie (*épith*) US; [*programme, écran*] cinema (*épith*) GB, movie (*épith*) US; **l'âge d'or du ~** the golden age of the cinema; **faire du ~** to be in films; **le ~ politique/de Truffaut** political/Truffaut's films; **nouvelle adaptée pour le ~** short story adapted for the screen; **3** péj **c'est du ~** (pas vrai) it's just play-acting; **arrête ton ~** (faire semblant) cut out the play-acting; (faire un drame) stop making such a fuss○; **il a fait tout un ~** he really made a fuss○; **se faire tout un ~** to start imagining things.
■ **~ d'animation** animation; **~ d'art et d'essai** (salle) cinema showing art films GB, art house US; (genre) art films (*pl*); **le ~ muet** silent films (*pl*); **le ~ parlant** the talkies○ (*pl*).

CinémaScope® /sinemaskɔp/ *nm* Cinemascope®.

cinémathèque /sinematɛk/ *nf* **1** (collection) film archive; **2** (petite salle) cinematheque.

cinématique /sinematik/ I *adj* kinematic.
II *nf* kinematics (+ *v sg*).

cinématographe /sinematɔgʀaf/ *nm* **1** (appareil) cinematograph GB, motion-picture camera and projector; **2**† (art de faire des films) cinema.

cinématographie /sinematɔgʀafi/ *nf* cinematography.

cinématographique /sinematɔgʀafik/ *adj* [*production, industrie, expérience, version*] film (*épith*) GB, movie (*épith*) US; **œuvres ~s** films; **l'art ~** the art of filmmaking.

cinéma-vérité /sinemaveʀite/ *nm inv* cinéma vérité.

cinémomètre /sinemomɛtʀ/ *nm* ≈ speed camera.

ciné-parc, *pl* **~s** /sinepaʀk/ *nm* drive-in cinema.

cinéphile /sinefil/ I *adj* [*public*] filmgoing (*épith*); **elle est ~** she's a great filmgoer GB ou moviegoer US.
II *nmf* cinema enthusiast GB ou buff○.

cinéraire /sineʀɛʀ/ I *adj* [*urne*] funerary.
II *nf* Bot cineraria.

Cinérama® /sineʀama/ *nm* Cinerama®.

cinétique /sinetik/ I *adj* kinetic.
II *nf* kinetics (+ *v sg*).

cing(h)alais, **~e** /sɛ̃galɛ, ɛz/ ▶ 462 I *adj* Sinhalese.
II *nm* Ling Sinhalese.

Cing(h)alais, **~e** /sɛ̃galɛ, ɛz/ ▶ 537 *nm,f* Sinhalese.

cinglant, **~e** /sɛ̃glɑ̃, ɑ̃t/ *adj* **1** lit [*vent*] biting; [*pluie*] driving (*épith*); **2** fig [*remarque, ironie*] scathing; [*démenti*] stinging; [*défaite, échec*] crushing, ignominious.

cinglé○, **~e** /sɛ̃gle/ I *adj* mad○, crazy○.
II *nm,f* (fou) loony○, nut○; (chauffeur) maniac.

cingler /sɛ̃gle/ [1] I *vtr* **1** [*pluie, vent*] to sting [*visage*]; **2** (avec un fouet) to lash.
II *vi* Naut **~ vers** to head for.

cinoche○ /sinɔʃ/ *nm* **1** (art) cinema GB, pictures○ (*pl*) GB, movies (*pl*) US; **aller au ~** to go to the cinema ou the movies; **2** (salle) cinema GB, movie theater US.

cinoque = **sinoque**.

cinq /sɛ̃k/ ▶ 545, 407, 212 *adj inv, pron, nm inv* five; ▶ **recevoir**.
IDIOMES **je lui ai dit les ~ lettres** I told him/her where to go; **il a dit les ~ lettres** ≈ he said a naughty word.

cinq-à-sept○ /sɛ̃kasɛt/ *nm inv* (rendez-vous) afternoon meeting (*between lovers*).

cinquantaine /sɛ̃kɑ̃tɛn/ *nf* **1** (environ cinquante) about fifty; **une ~ d'étudiants manifestaient** fifty or so students were demonstrating, about fifty students were demonstrating; **avoir une ~ d'années** to be about fifty; **la ~ de passagers qui attendaient** the fifty or so passengers who were waiting; **il y en a une bonne ~** there are well over fifty of them; **il y a une ~ d'années** about fifty years ago; **nous étions une ~/plus d'une ~** there were about fifty of us/more than fifty of us; **il faut compter une ~ de francs** it's going to cost around fifty francs; **2** (âge) **avoir la ~** to be about fifty, to be fiftyish○; **approcher de la ~** to be getting on for fifty; **Bernard, la ~ bedonnante, est employé de bureau** Bernard, fifty and pot-bellied, works in an office.

cinquante /sɛ̃kɑ̃t/ ▶ 545, 212 *adj inv, pron* fifty.

cinquantenaire /sɛ̃kɑ̃tnɛʀ/ I *adj* [*vigne*] fifty-year-old (*épith*), fifty years old (*jamais épith*).
II *nm* fiftieth anniversary.

cinquantième /sɛ̃kɑ̃tjɛm/ ▶ 545 *adj* fiftieth.

cinquième /sɛ̃kjɛm/ ▶ 545, 212 I *adj, nmf* fifth; ▶ **roue**.
II *nf* Scol *second year of secondary school, age 12–13*.
■ **~ colonne** the Fifth Column.

cintrage /sɛ̃tʀaʒ/ *nm* bending.

cintre /sɛ̃tʀ/ I *nm* **1** (pour vêtement) hanger; **2** Archit curve; **(arc) plein ~** round arch; **3** (armature) former.
II **cintres** *nmpl* Théât **les ~s** the flies.

cintré, **~e** /sɛ̃tʀe/ I *pp* ▶ **cintrer**.
II *pp adj* **1** [*manteau*] waisted; [*chemise*] tailored; **2** Archit [*porte, fenêtre*] arched; [*galerie*] vaulted.

cintrer /sɛ̃tʀe/ [1] *vtr* **1** Cout to take [sth] in at the waist [*veste*]; **2** Archit to arch [*porte, fenêtre*]; to vault [*galerie*]; **3** Tech to bend [*tuyau*].

CIO /seio/ *nm*: *abbr* ▶ **centre**.

cirage /siʀaʒ/ *nm* **1** (produit) (shoe) polish; **~ en crème** shoe cream; **2** (activité, méthode) polishing.
IDIOMES **être dans le ~**○ (à demi conscient) to be half-conscious, to be out of it○; (désorienté) to be all at sea; Aviat to be flying blind.

circadien, **-ienne** /siʀkadjɛ̃, ɛn/ *adj* **rythme ~** circadian rhythm.

circaète /siʀkaɛt/ *nm* harrier eagle.

circoncire /siʀkɔ̃siʀ/ [64] *vtr* to circumcise; **faire ~ qn** to have sb circumcised.

circoncision /siʀkɔ̃sizjɔ̃/ *nf* male circumcision.

circonférence /siʀkɔ̃feʀɑ̃s/ *nf* circumference.

circonflexe /siʀkɔ̃flɛks/ *adj* **accent ~** circumflex (accent).

circonlocution /siʀkɔ̃lɔkysjɔ̃/ *nf* circumlocution sout; **s'exprimer par ~s** to have a rather convoluted way of expressing oneself.

circonscription /siʀkɔ̃skʀipsjɔ̃/ *nf* Admin district.
■ **~ électorale** (de député) ≈ electoral constituency GB ou district US; (de conseiller, maire) ≈ electoral ward.

circonscrire /siʀkɔ̃skʀiʀ/ [67] *vtr* **1** Math to circumscribe; **2** (limiter) to contain [*incendie, épidémie*]; to limit [*sujet, domaine*] (**à** to); **3** (délimiter) to define.

circonspect, **~e** /siʀkɔ̃spɛ, ɛkt/ *adj* [*personne, attitude*] cautious, circumspect (**envers qn** toward, towards GB sb; **envers qch** about sth).

circonspection /siʀkɔ̃spɛksjɔ̃/ *nf* caution, circumspection sout (**envers qn** towards sb; **envers qch** about sth); **avec ~** cautiously, circumspectly sout.

circonstance /siʀkɔ̃stɑ̃s/ I *nf* **1** (condition) circumstance; **~s d'une mort** circumstances of a death; **en raison des ~s** under the circumstances; **2** (situation) situation; **~ grave** serious situation; **en pareille ~** in a situation like this; **en toute ~** in any event; **en la ~** in this particular case; **pour la ~** for the occasion; **être à la hauteur des ~s** to be equal to the occasion.
II **de circonstance** *loc adj* [*poème*] for the occasion (*after n*); [*blague, programme*] topical; [*allié, préoccupation*] of the moment; [*loi*] ad hoc; [*sourire, attitude*] artificial; **être de ~** to be fitting; **faire une tête de ~** to assume a fitting expression.
■ **~ aggravante** Jur aggravating circumstance; **~s atténuantes** Jur extenuating ou mitigating circumstances.

circonstancié, **~e** /siʀkɔ̃stɑ̃sje/ *adj* detailed.

circonstanciel, **-ielle** /siʀkɔ̃stɑ̃sjɛl/ I *adj* **1** (de circonstance) incidental; **2** Ling [*complément, proposition*] adverbial.
II **circonstancielle** *nf* adverbial clause.

circonvenir /siʀkɔ̃v(ə)niʀ/ [36] *vtr* fml to circumvent sout, to get round GB ou around US [*personne*].

circonvolution /siʀkɔ̃vɔlysjɔ̃/ *nf* convolution; **décrire des ~s** to twist and turn.

circuit /siʀkɥi/ *nm* **1** Courses Aut circuit; **2** (de tourisme) tour; **~ accompagné/guidé** accompanied/guided tour; **faire le ~ des châteaux de la Loire** to tour the Châteaux of the Loire; **ne pas suivre les ~s touristiques** to go off the beaten track; **3** (d'activité)

circuit; **~ bancaire/financier/parallèle** banking/financial/unofficial circuit; **~ de production/distribution** production/distribution circuit; **~ économique** economic process; **être mis hors ~** [*personne*] to be put on the sidelines, to be sidelined; **je ne suis plus dans le ~**○ I'm out of the swing of things; **remettre qch dans le ~** to put sth back into circulation; **vivre en ~ fermé** to live in a closed world; **4** (itinéraire) **j'ai fait tout un ~** or **un de ces ~s pour arriver ici!** I took a very roundabout route to get here!; **5** Tech circuit; **~ électrique** electric circuit; **~ fermé/ouvert/dérivé** Électrotech closed/open/derived circuit; **~ primaire/secondaire de refroidissement** Nucl primary/secondary coolant circuit.
■ **~ d'alimentation** feed system; **~ hydraulique** hydraulic system; **~ imprimé** printed circuit; **~ intégré**, **CI** integrated circuit, IC; **~ intégré logique** integrated logic circuit.

circulaire /siʀkylɛʀ/ **I** *adj* circular; **de forme ~** circular.
II *nf* (lettre) circular.

circularité /siʀkylaʀite/ *nf* circularity; **la ~ de ton raisonnement** your circular logic.

circulation /siʀkylasjɔ̃/ *nf* **1** (de véhicules) traffic; **~ aérienne/ferroviaire/maritime/routière** air/rail/maritime/road traffic; **rue interdite à la ~** street closed to traffic; **faire la ~** [*agent*] to be on traffic duty; (en cas d'accident) to direct traffic; **accident de la ~** road accident; **2** (déplacement, échange) circulation; **la libre ~ des personnes, des marchandises et des capitaux** the free movement of people, goods and capital; **être en ~** [*billets, produit*] to be in circulation; [*bateau*] to be in operation; [*train*] to be running; **la mise en ~ de** the circulation of [*produit*]; **mettre/remettre qch en ~** to put sth/to put sth back into circulation [*billets, produit*]; **disparaître de la ~** lit, fig [*personne, produit*] to disappear from circulation; **retirer de la ~** to withdraw [sth] from circulation [*billet, produit*]; **3** (d'air, de gaz, sang) circulation; **la ~ sanguine** or **du sang** the circulation of the blood, blood circulation; **avoir une bonne/mauvaise ~** to have good/poor circulation.

circulatoire /siʀkylatwaʀ/ *adj* Physiol [*accident, troubles*] circulation (*épith*); [*appareil, système*] circulatory spéc.

circuler /siʀkyle/ [1] *vi* **1** (être en service) [*train, bus*] to run; [*bateau*] to operate; **interdiction de ~** no traffic, traffic banned; **'ne circule pas le dimanche'** (train, bus) 'does not run on Sundays'; **les camions ne circulent pas le dimanche** there are no trucks on the roads on Sundays; **2** (aller d'un lieu à un autre) to get around; (sans but précis) to move about; (être en voiture) to travel; **je circule en vélo** I get around by bike; **leurs ressortissants peuvent ~ librement** their nationals can move (about) freely; **deux policiers circulaient à bord de la voiture** there were two policemen travelling[GB] in the car; **circulez, il n'y a rien à voir!** move along, there's nothing to see!; **3** (se répandre) [*rumeur, information, plaisanterie, idée*] to circulate, to go around ou about; **faire ~** to circulate [*information, idée*]; to spread, to put about [*rumeur*]; **4** (être distribué) [*marchandises, billets, journal*] to circulate; **faire ~** to put [sth] into circulation [*marchandises, billets, actions*]; to circulate [*journal, publication*]; **5** [*sang, air*] to circulate; **faire ~** to circulate.

circumpolaire /siʀkɔmpɔlɛʀ/ *adj* circumpolar.

cire /siʀ/ *nf* wax; **en ~** wax (*épith*). ▶ **moulage, pain.**
■ **~ d'abeilles** beeswax; **~ à cacheter** sealing wax.

ciré /siʀe/ *nm* oilskin.

cirer /siʀe/ [1] *vtr* to polish [*chaussures, parquet*]; ▶ **toile.**

IDIOMES **~ les pompes de qn**○ to suck up to sb○; **ne rien avoir à ~ de qn/qch**○ not to give a damn about sb/sth○.

cireur, **-euse**[1] /siʀœʀ, øz/ **I** ▶ **510** *nm,f* shoe-shine boy/girl.
II cireuse *nf* (appareil) (floor) polisher.

cireux, **-euse**[2] /siʀø, øz/ *adj* [*aspect, teint*] waxen; [*consistance*] waxy.

cirque /siʀk/ *nm* **1** (spectacle) circus; **un numéro de ~** a circus act; **2**○ (chahut) racket○; (désordre) shambles○ (*sg*); (comédie) carry-on GB; **il a fait le ~ toute la nuit** he made a racket all night; **arrête ton ~!** stop your nonsense!; **c'est le ~ pour se garer à Oxford** it's a real performance parking in Oxford; **3** Géog cirque; **4** Antiq circus; **les jeux du ~** circus games.

cirrhose /siʀoz/ ▶ **271** *nf* cirrhosis.
■ **~ du foie** cirrhosis of the liver.

cirrocumulus /siʀokymylys/ *nm* cirrocumulus.

cirrostratus /siʀostʀatys/ *nm* cirrostratus.

cirrus /siʀys/ *nm* cirrus.

cisaille /sizɑj/ *nf* **1** (de jardinier, ferblantier, d'orfèvre) pair of shears; **~s** shears; **2** (de relieur, d'établi) guillotine.

cisaillement /sizɑjmɑ̃/ *nm* **1** (découpage) (de plaque, tôle) shearing; (de câble, tige) cutting; **2** (entaille) cutting; **3** (rupture) (de pièces) shearing; (de couches géologiques) shear.

cisailler /sizɑje/ [1] *vtr* **1** (avec une cisaille) to shear [*tôle*]; to cut [*câble*]; **2** (par usure) to shear off.

cisalpin, **~e** /sizalpɛ̃, in/ *adj* [*région*] cisalpine; [*Gaule*] Cisalpine.

ciseau, *pl* **~x** /sizo/ **I** *nm* **1** Tech chisel; **2** Sport (saut) scissors jump; (prise de lutte) scissors hold.
II ciseaux *nmpl* scissors (*pl*); (gros et robustes) shears; **saut en ~x** scissors jump; **tailler une étoffe à grands coups de ~x** to cut boldly into a piece of material; **coupe aux ~x** scissor cut; **donner un coup de ~x dans un texte** fig to prune a text.
■ **~ à froid** cold chisel; **~x à broder** embroidery scissors; **~x de couture** sewing scissors; **~x à cranter** pinking shears; **~x à ongles** nail scissors.

ciselage /sizlaʒ/ *nm* **1** Tech chiselling[GB]; **2** Agric *trimming of bad grapes from bunch before sale.*

cisèlement /sizɛlmɑ̃/ *nm* = **ciselage**.

ciseler /sizle/ [17] *vtr* **1** Tech to chase [*métal*]; to chisel [*bois, pierre*]; **ses traits finement ciselés** his/her finely chiselled[GB] features; **2** fig liter to chisel, to polish [*style, discours*]; **3** Agric to trim off bad grapes from a bunch (before sale); **4** Culin to score [*viande*]; to snip [*herbes*].

ciselure /sizlyʀ/ *nf* (de métal) chasing; (de pierre, bois) carving.

Cisjordanie /sisʒɔʀdani/ ▶ **692** *nprf* **la ~** the West Bank (of Jordan).

cistercien, **-ienne** /sistɛʀsjɛ̃, ɛn/ *adj, nm,f* Cistercian.

citadelle /sitadɛl/ *nf* lit, fig citadel.

citadin, **~e** /sitadɛ̃, in/ **I** *adj* city (*épith*).
II *nm,f* city-dweller.

citation /sitasjɔ̃/ *nf* **1** gén quotation; **fin de ~** end of quotation; **2** Jur (d'accusé) summons (+ *v sg*); (de témoin) subpoena; **3** Mil (récompense) commendation.
■ **~ à l'ordre du jour** mention in dispatches.

cité /site/ *nf* **1** Antiq city; (ville) city; (plus petite) town; **2** (ensemble de logements) housing estate; ▶ **dortoir II.**
■ **~ ouvrière** workers' housing development; **la ~ des Papes** Avignon; **~ universitaire** student halls (*pl*) of residence GB, dormitories (*pl*) US; **la Cité du Vatican** the Vatican City.

cité-jardin, *pl* **cités-jardins** /siteʒaʀdɛ̃/ *nf* garden city GB, planned town US.

citer /site/ [1] *vtr* **1** (rapporter exactement) to quote [*personne, phrase, passage*]; **je cite** I quote; **2** (mentionner) to name [*titre, œuvre*]; to cite [*personne, pays*]; to cite [*exemple, fait, chiffres*]; **cite-moi le nom de trois acteurs espagnols** name three Spanish actors; **elle a cité l'exemple de cet homme qui...** she cited the example of the man who...; **3** Jur to summon [*témoin*]; **être cité en justice** to be issued with a summons; **4** Mil to commend [*soldat, général, unité*]; **~ qn à l'ordre du jour** to mention sb in dispatches.

citerne /sitɛʀn/ *nf* tank.

cithare /sitaʀ/ ▶ **534** *nf* zither.

citoyen, **-enne** /sitwajɛ̃, ɛn/ *nm,f* citizen; **un drôle de ~**○ a strange character.
■ **~ d'honneur** ≈ freeman.

citoyenneté /sitwajɛnte/ *nf* citizenship.

citrate /sitʀat/ *nm* citrate.

citrique /sitʀik/ *adj* citric.

citron /sitʀɔ̃/ **I** ▶ **193** *adj inv* lemon; **jaune ~** lemon yellow.
II *nm* **1** Bot, Culin lemon; **jus de ~** lemon juice; **poulet au ~** lemon chicken; **goût/odeur de ~** lemony taste/smell; **2**○ (tête) head, nut○.
■ **~ givré** lemon sorbet (*served inside a lemon*); **~ pressé** freshly squeezed lemon juice (*with sugar*); **~ vert** lime.
IDIOMES **presser qn comme un ~**○ to squeeze sb dry○; **se presser le ~**○ to rack one's brains.

citronnade /sitʀɔnad/ *nf* lemon squash GB, lemonade US.

citronné, **~e** /sitʀɔne/ *adj* [*odeur, goût*] lemony; [*crème, tisane*] lemon(-flavoured[GB]); **eau ~e** water with a dash of lemon juice.

citronnelle /sitʀɔnɛl/ *nf* **1** Bot citronella; **huile de ~** citronella oil; **2** (mélisse) lemon balm; **3** (liqueur) citronella.

citronnier /sitʀɔnje/ *nm* lemon tree.

citrouille /sitʀuj/ *nf* **1** Bot, Culin pumpkin; **2**○ (tête) head, nut○.
IDIOMES **avoir la tête comme une ~**○ to feel as if one's head was going to burst.

cive /siv/ *nf* **1** Bot chive; **2** Culin chives (*pl*).

civet /sivɛ/ *nm* ≈ stew; **~ de lapin/chevreuil** rabbit/venison stew; **~ de lièvre** jugged hare ₡.

civette /sivɛt/ *nf* **1** (ciboulette) Bot chive; Culin chives (*pl*); **2** (mammifère) civet (cat); **3** (musc) civet.

civière /sivjɛʀ/ *nf* stretcher.

civil, **~e** /sivil/ **I** *adj* **1** (non militaire) [*vie, autorités, vêtements*] civilian; (non religieux) [*mariage*] civil; [*enterrement*] non religious; (non pénal) [*droit, tribunal*] civil; **2** (du citoyen) [*droits*] civil; **3**† (courtois) civil (**à l'égard de** to).
II *nm* **1** (personne) civilian; **soldat en ~** soldier in civilian clothes ou in civvies○; **policier en ~** plain-clothes policeman; **se mettre en ~** [*soldier*] to dress in civilian clothes; [*policier*] to dress in plain clothes; **dans le ~** in civilian life, in civvy street○ GB; **2**○ Jur **poursuivre qn au ~** to bring a civil suit against sb.

civilement /sivilmɑ̃/ *adv* **1** (laïquement) **se marier ~** to get married in a registry office GB ou at city hall US; **être enterré ~** to have a non religious funeral; **2**† (courtoisement) in a civil manner; **3** Jur [*poursuivre*] in the civil court; [*responsable*] under civil law.

civilisateur, **-trice** /sivilizatœʀ, tʀis/ *adj* civilizing (*épith*).

civilisation /sivilizasjɔ̃/ *nf* civilization.

civiliser /sivilize/ [1] **I** *vtr* lit, fig to civilize.
II se civiliser *vpr* to become civilized.

civilité /sivilite/ **I**† *nf* (politesse) civility; **les règles de la ~** good manners.
II civilités *nfpl* fml courtesies; **échanger des ~s** to exchange courtesies; **présenter ses ~s à qn** to pay one's respects to sb.

civique /sivik/ *adj* civic; **avoir l'esprit ~** to have a sense of civic responsibility; **instruction** or **éducation ~** civics (+ *v sg*).

civisme /sivism/ *nm* **avoir le sens du/ n'avoir aucun ~** to have a/to have no sense of civic responsibility.

clabaudage /klabodaʒ/ *nm* liter backbiting **¢**.

clabaudeur, **-euse** /klabodœʀ, øz/ *nm,f* liter backbiter.

clac /klak/ *nm* (*also onomat*) (de porte) slam; (de piège à souris) snap; (de fouet) crack.

cladonie /kladɔni/ *nf* reindeer moss.

clafoutis /klafuti/ *nm* fruit baked in batter.

claie /klɛ/ *nf* **1** (à fromages, fruits) wicker rack; **2** (crible) riddle; **3** (clôture) hurdle; **4** (de sac à dos) stretcher frame.

clair, **~e** /klɛʀ/ **I** *adj* **1** (pâle) [*couleur, teinte*] light; [*teint*] (rosé) fair; (frais) fresh; **du tissu gris très ~** very light grey GB ou gray US material; **avoir les yeux ~s** (bleus) to have pale blue ou grey GB ou gray US eyes; **2** (lumineux) [*logement, pièce*] light; **la maison est très ~e** the house is very light; **3** Météo (pas couvert) [*journée, nuit, ciel, temps*] clear; **par temps ~** (de jour) on a clear day; (de nuit) on a clear night; **4** (limpide) [*son, voix, tonalité*] clear; [*eau*] clear; **à l'eau ~e** [*rincer*] in clear water; **5** (intelligible) [*texte, personne, idées, langue*] clear; **en termes plus ~s** in clearer terms; **je n'ai pas les idées ~es aujourd'hui** I'm not thinking very clearly today; **6** (sans équivoque) [*message, décision, situation*] clear; **suis-je ~?** do I make myself clear?; **il faut que les choses soient (bien) ~es** let's get things straight; **pour moi, c'est ~, il est jaloux** it's clear to me that he's jealous; **il a été très ~ sur ce point** he was very clear on this point; **c'est ~ et net, c'est ~ net et précis** it's absolutely clear; **il n'est pas ~ dans cette histoire**○ his role in this affair is not clear; **il est/semble ~ que** it is/seems clear that; **pour moi il est ~ qu'il ment/que ça ne sert à rien** it's clear to me that he's lying/that it's useless; **passer le plus ~ de son temps** or **de sa vie** to spend most of one's time (**à faire** doing; **dans** in); **dépenser le plus ~ de son argent en bêtises** to spend most of one 's money on rubbish; **7** (peu épais) [*soupe*] clear; (trop) thin; **8** (usé) [*vêtement, tissu*] worn through, thin; **9** (pas touffu) [*forêt, blé*] sparse.

II *adv* **il faisait ~** it was already light; **il fait ~ très tôt** it gets light very early; **il fait ~ très tard** it stays light very late; **voir ~** lit to see well; **avec mes lunettes je** or **j'y vois ~** lit with my glasses I can see well ou properly; **il ne** or **n'y voit pas ~** lit his eyesight is not very good; **j'aimerais y voir ~ dans cette histoire** fig I'd like to get to the bottom of this story; **parler ~** fig to speak clearly.

III *nm* **1** (clarté) light; **en ~** TV unscrambled; Mil, Ordinat in clear; (pour parler clairement) to put it clearly; **en ~ cela veut dire qu'il refuse** to put it clearly it means that he refuses; **mettre ses idées au ~** fig to get one's ideas straight; **tirer une histoire** or **une affaire au ~** to get to the bottom of things; **2** (couleur) light colours[GB] (*pl*); **3** Art **les ombres et les ~s d'un tableau** the light and shadow of a painting.

IV claire *nf* (bassin) oyster bed; **fine de ~e** Culin claire oyster.

■ **~ de lune** moonlight; **se promener au ~ de lune** to go for a walk in the moonlight.

IDIOMES **c'est ~ comme le jour** or **de l'eau de roche** it's clear as daylight, it's crystal clear.

clairance /klɛʀɑ̃s/ *nf* Biol, Chimie clearance.

clairement /klɛʀmɑ̃/ *adv* [*apparaître, dire, définir*] clearly; **il apparaît ~ que** it clearly appears that; **elle a ~ défini/expliqué** she clearly defined/explained.

clairet, **-ette** /klɛʀɛ, ɛt/ **I** *adj* [*vin*] thin; [*bouillon, soupe*] thin.

II *nm* Vin light red wine.

III clairette *nf* Vin (vin) sparkling white wine; (cépage) *variety of white grape*.

claire-voie, *pl* **claires-voies** /klɛʀvwɑ/ *nf* **1** (clôture) openwork fence; **à ~** [*volets, porte*] openwork; **2** Archit clerestory.

clairière /klɛʀjɛʀ/ *nf* clearing, glade.

clair-obscur, *pl* **clairs-obscurs** /klɛʀɔbskyʀ/ *nm* **1** Art chiaroscuro; **2** (pénombre) (evening) twilight.

clairon /klɛʀɔ̃/ **▶534** *nm* **1** (instrument) bugle; **sonner du ~** to sound the bugle; **2** (personne) bugler; **3** (jeu d'orgue) clarion stop.

claironnant, **~e** /klɛʀɔnɑ̃, ɑ̃t/ *adj* [*voix*] strident.

claironner /klɛʀɔne/ [1] *vtr* (proclamer) to shout [sth] from the rooftops [*nouvelle*].

clairsemé, **~e** /klɛʀsəme/ *adj* [*arbres, maisons*] scattered; [*cheveux, public, foule*] thin.

clairvoyance /klɛʀvwajɑ̃s/ *nf* perceptiveness; **faire preuve de/manquer de ~** to show/to lack perceptiveness.

clairvoyant, **~e** /klɛʀvwajɑ̃, ɑ̃t/ *adj* fig [*personne*] perceptive; **un esprit ~** a perceptive person.

clam /klam/ *nm* clam.

clamecer◑ /klamse/ [1] *vi* to croak◑ GB, to die.

clamer /klame/ [1] *vtr* to proclaim (**que** that); **~ haut et fort son soutien** to loudly proclaim one's support.

clameur /klamœʀ/ *nf* (de protestation) clamour[GB] **¢**; (d'enthousiasme) roar.

clamser◑ = **clamecer**.

clan /klɑ̃/ *nm* lit, fig clan; **esprit de ~** clan mentality, clannishness.

clandestin, **~e** /klɑ̃dɛstɛ̃, in/ **I** *adj* [*organisation, journal*] underground (*épith*); [*immigration, commerce, travail*] illegal; [*prostitution*] clandestine; **passager ~** stowaway.

II *nm,f* (immigrant) illegal immigrant GB ou alien US; (passager) stowaway.

clandestinement /klɑ̃dɛstinmɑ̃/ *adv* (illégalement) illegally; (en secret) secretly.

clandestinité /klɑ̃dɛstinite/ *nf* **1** (d'activité, organisation) secret ou clandestine nature; **atmosphère de ~** atmosphere of secrecy; **les milieux de la ~** those who operate in secret; **pendant sa ~** during his/her time in hiding; **dans la ~** [*passer, se réfugier*] underground; [*vivre*] in hiding; [*opérer*] in secret; **sortir de la ~** to come out into the open; **2** (situation illégale) **travailler dans la ~** to work illegally.

clanique /klanik/ *adj* clan (*épith*).

clap /klap/ *nm* clapperboard.

clapet /klapɛ/ *nm* **1** (soupape) valve; **2**○ (bouche) mouth, trap○; **ferme ton ~!** shut your trap○!

■ **~ antiretour** check valve, nonreturn valve; **~ d'échappement** exhaust valve; **~ de retenue** check valve.

clapier /klapje/ *nm* rabbit hutch.

clapotement /klapɔtmɑ̃/ *nm* lapping **¢** (**de** of).

clapoter /klapɔte/ [1] *vi* to lap.

clapotis /klapɔti/ *nm* lapping (**de** of).

clappement /klapmɑ̃/ *nm* clicking **¢**.

clapper /klape/ [1] *vi* **faire ~ sa langue** to click one's tongue.

claquage /klakaʒ/ *nm* **1** Méd (action) pulling ou straining (of a muscle); (blessure) pulled ou strained muscle; **se faire un ~** to pull a muscle; **2** Électrotech breakdown.

claquant○, **~e** /klakɑ̃, ɑ̃t/ *adj* exhausting, knackering○ GB.

claque /klak/ **I** *nm* **1** (chapeau) (**chapeau**) **~** opera hat; **2**◑ (maison close) knocking shop◑ GB, whorehouse.

II *nf* **1** (gifle) slap; **donner une ~ à qn** to slap sb; **recevoir une ~** to get a slap; **2**○ (humiliation) slap in the face; (échec) beating; **se prendre une ~ aux élections** to take a beating ou hammering at the elections; **3** Théât claque.

IDIOMES **en avoir sa ~**○ to be fed up (to the back teeth○ GB).

claqué, **~e** /klake/ **I** *pp* ▶ **claquer**.

II○ *pp adj* (épuisé) knackered○ GB, done in○.

claquement /klakmɑ̃/ *nm* (de porte, fenêtre) bang; (de fouet) crack; (de tonnerre) clap; (de langue) cluck; (répété) (de porte, fenêtre) banging **¢**; (de fouet) cracking **¢**; (de langue) clicking **¢**; (de bannière, voile) flapping **¢**; **le ~ des sabots** (de personne) the clatter(ing) of clogs; (de chevaux) the clip-clop of hooves; **après un ~ de talons, il se retira** with a click of his heels, he withdrew; **un perpétuel ~ de volets** a constant sound of banging shutters; **les ~s du fouet** the crack(ing) of the whip.

claquemurer /klakmyʀe/ [1] **I** *vtr* to immure (**dans** in).

II se claquemurer *vpr* to shut oneself away (**dans** in); **elle vit claquemurée dans sa chambre** she lives shut away in her bedroom.

claquer /klake/ [1] **I** *vtr* **1** (fermer) to slam [*porte*]; **~ la porte au nez de qn** lit, fig to slam the door in sb's face; **partir** or **sortir en claquant la porte** lit to storm out slamming the door behind one; **ils sont partis en claquant la porte** (pendant des négociations) they walked out closing the door on further negotiations; **2**○ (épuiser) to exhaust, to wear [sb] out [*personne*]; **la course l'a claqué** he was worn out after the race; **3**○ (dépenser) to (manage to) go through, to blow○ [*argent*]; **~ sa paie au casino/en livres** to blow one's wages at the casino/on books; **4** Sport to pull, to strain [*muscle*]; **5** (gifler) to slap [*personne*]; **6**○ (casser) to break [*appareil*].

II *vi* **1** (faire un bruit) [*porte, volet*] to bang; [*coup de feu*] to ring out; [*bannière, voile*] to flap; **faire ~ la porte** to slam the door; **faire ~ son fouet** to crack one's whip; **la porte claqua** (se ferma) the door slammed shut; **2** (faire un bruit avec une partie du corps) **~ des doigts** to snap one's fingers; **~ des talons** Mil to click one's heels; **~ des mains** or **dans ses mains** to clap (one's hands); **elle claque des dents** her teeth are chattering; **faire ~ ses doigts** to snap one's fingers; **faire ~ sa langue** to click one's tongue; **3**◑ (mourir) to die (**de** from), to snuff it○ GB, to croak○; **le malade lui a claqué dans les doigts** the patient died on him/her○; **4**○ (se casser) [*appareil, machine*] to pack up○ GB, to conk out○; [*corde*] to snap; fig (échouer) [*affaire*] to go bust○; **la télé m'a claqué dans les mains** the TV died on me○.

III se claquer *vpr* **1** Sport **se ~ un muscle** to pull ou strain a muscle; **2**○ (s'épuiser) to wear oneself out (**à faire** doing).

claquette /klakɛt/ **I** *nf* (claquoir) gén clapper; Cin clapper board.

II claquettes *nfpl* Danse tap dancing (*sg*); **faire des ~s** to tap dance.

claquoir /klakwaʀ/ *nm* clapper board.

clarification /klaʀifikasjɔ̃/ *nf* clarification **¢**; **apporter des ~s** to clarify matters (**sur** concerning).

clarifier /klaʀifje/ [2] *vtr* **1** fig to clarify [*position, situation, débat*]; **2** lit to clarify [*mélange, beurre*].

clarine /klaʀin/ *nf* cowbell.

clarinette /klaʀinɛt/ **▶534** *nf* clarinet; **jouer de la ~** to play the clarinet.

clarinettiste /klaʀinetist/ **▶510** *nmf* clarinettist.

clarisse /klaʀis/ *nf* nun of the order of St Clare.

clarté /klaʀte/ **I** *nf* **1** (lumière) light; **une douce ~** a soft light; **manquer de ~** to lack light; **à la ~ de** by the light of [*bougie, lampe*]; **2** (de l'eau, du verre) clarity; (de teint) fairness; **3** (de raisonnement, style, d'exposé) clarity; **avec ~** clearly; **besoin de/manque de ~** need for/lack of clarity;

faire (toute) la ~ sur qch to get to the bottom of sth.

II **clartés** *nfpl* (connaissances) knowledge ¢; **avoir des ~s sur qch** to be knowledgeable about sth.

clash○ /klaʃ/ *nm* clash.

classe /klas/ *nf* **1** Scol (groupe d'élèves) class, form GB; (niveau) year, form GB, grade US; **une ~ turbulente/studieuse** a rowdy/hard-working class ou form GB; **les ~s primaires/de maternelle** primary (school)/nursery classes; **les ~s du secondaire** secondary school classes ou forms GB, ≈ junior high school and high school US; **redoubler une ~** to repeat a year; **passer dans la ~ supérieure** to go up a year; **être le premier/dernier de sa ~** to be ou come top/bottom of the class; **2** Scol (cours) class, lesson; **une ~ de dessin** a drawing class ou lesson; **les élèves de Mme Dupont n'auront pas ~ demain** Mrs Dupont's class won't be having any lessons tomorrow; **parler en ~** to talk in class; **faire la ~** to teach; **le soir après la ~** in the evening after school; **3** Scol (salle) classroom; **il s'est fait mettre à la porte de la ~** he was sent out of the classroom; **4** Sociol, Pol class; **les ~s sociales** the social classes; **la ~ ouvrière/dirigeante** the working/ruling class; **les ~s moyennes** the middle classes; **une société sans ~s** a classless society; **~ politique** political class ou community; **5** (catégorie) class (**de** of); **la ~ des mammifères** the class of mammals; **les artistes sont une ~ à part** artists are a class apart; **~ grammaticale** Ling grammatical class; **6** (rang) gén class; Admin grade; **produits/champagne de première ~** first-class products/champagne; **7** (élégance) class; **avoir de la ~** to have class; **il a beaucoup de ~** he has real class; **ça, c'est la ~**◐**!** now that's class ou style○!; **c'est pas la ~**◐**!** that's not very stylish!; **elle est très ~**◐ she's really classy○; **8** Transp class; **billet de première/seconde ~** first-/second-class ou standard GB ticket; **~ touristes/affaires** economy ou tourist/business class; **voyager en première ~** to travel first class; **9** Mil annual levy ou draft; **la ~ 1990** the 1990 levy ou draft; **faire ses ~s** lit to do one's basic training; fig to start out; **un cinéaste qui a fait ses ~s à la télévision** fig a film director who started out in television.

■ **~ d'adaptation** special needs class; **~ d'âge** age group; **~ de mer** *educational schooltrip to the seaside*; **~ de nature** *educational schooltrip to the countryside*; **~ de neige** *educational schooltrip in the mountains including skiing lessons*; **~ de transition** Scol remedial class; **~ verte** = **~ de nature**; **les ~s creuses** *age groups depleted by low birthrate*; **~s préparatoires (aux grandes écoles)** *preparatory classes for entrance to Grandes Écoles*.

classement /klasmɑ̃/ *nm* **1** (en catégories) classification (**de** of); **faire un ~ alphabétique/chronologique** to put into alphabetical/chronological order; **2** (rangement) filing (**de** of); **vous vous occuperez du ~** you'll be in charge of filing; **elle fait du ~ toute la journée** she spends all day filing; **faire du ~ dans ses papiers** to sort one's papers out; **3** (d'élèves, employés) grading (**de** of); **donner à des élèves leur ~ trimestriel/annuel** to give students their termly/yearly positions (in class); **avoir un bon/mauvais ~** to be in the top/bottom half of the class; **4** Sport ranking (**de** of); **~ individuel/par équipe** individual/team ranking; **prendre la tête du ~** to get first place; **5** (d'hôtel, de restaurant) rating (**de** of); **~ deux/trois étoiles** two-/three-star rating; **6** Jur closing (**de** of); **~ d'une affaire par manque de preuves** closing of a case for lack of evidence.

classer /klase/ [1] **I** *vtr* **1** (catégoriser) to classify [*animaux, documents, livres, objets, papiers*]; **~ par ordre alphabétique** to classify in alphabetical order; **~ des objets par couleur/des livres par auteur** to classify objects by colour[GB]/books by author; **~ des nombres en ordre croissant/décroissant** to place numbers in ascending/descending order; **être classé comme dangereux** to be considered dangerous; **2** (ranger) to file (away) [*documents, archives*] (**dans** in); **3** Jur, Pol to close [*dossier, affaire*]; **c'est une affaire classée** fig the matter is closed; **4** Admin to list [*bâtiment*]; to designate [sth] as a conservation area [*site*]; **~ un château monument historique** to list a castle as a historical monument; **un immeuble classé** a listed building; **une parcelle classée en terrain non constructible** a plot listed as unsuitable for development; **5** (attribuer un rang à) to class [*pays, élèves*]; to rank [*film, chanson, artiste, joueur*] (**parmi** among); **un sportif classé au plan international** a world class sportsman; **un joueur de tennis/d'échecs classé** a ranked ou seeded tennis/chess player; **non classé** unseeded; **6**○ (juger) to size [sb] up; **je l'ai toute de suite classé** I sized him up○ immediately.

II **se classer** *vpr* [*tableau, pays, site*] to rank (**parmi** among); **se ~ comme le pays le plus pauvre** to be listed as the world's poorest country; **se ~ premier/deuxième** Sport [*personne*] to rank first/second.

classeur /klasœʀ/ *nm* **1** (à anneaux) ring binder; (à compartiments) file; **2** (meuble de rangement) filing cabinet.

classicisme /klasisism/ *nm* **1** Art, Littérat classicism; **2** (conformisme) (de tenue, goût) traditionalism (**of** de), conservatism (**de** of).

classificateur, -trice /klasifikatœʀ, tʀis/ **I** *adj* [*méthode, principe*] of classification (*après n*).

II *nm* Chimie classifier.

classification /klasifikasjɔ̃/ *nf* classification (**de** of); **méfiez-vous des ~s hâtives** don't make hasty judgments; **la ~ périodique des éléments** the periodic table (of elements).

classifier /klasifje/ [2] *vtr* to classify.

classique /klasik/ **I** *adj* **1** (gréco-latin) [*auteur, œuvre, culture, études*] classical; **la littérature ~ grecque** classical Greek literature; **faire des études ~s** Scol to do Latin and Greek, to do classics; **la section ~** Scol the classics stream GB ou group; **2** Ling [*langue*] classical; **3** (pour distinguer une époque, un genre) [*période*] classical; [*danse, musique, répertoire*] classical; **théâtre ~ français** French classical theatre; **4** (consacré) [*auteur, œuvre*] classic; **5** (harmonieux, sobre) [*beauté, style, tenue*] classic; **de coupe ~** of classic cut; **6** (courant) [*exemple, histoire, situation*] classic; [*traitement, méthode*] classic, standard; (habituel) [*symptôme, réaction*] classic; [*conséquence*] usual; **c'est ~**○**!** it's typical!; **c'est l'itinéraire ~ d'un élève studieux** it's the path good students usually follow; **c'est le coup ~**○**!** it's the same old story!; **7** (traditionnel) [*grammaire, agriculture*] traditional; [*arme, genre*] conventional.

II *nm* **1** (auteur) classical author; **2** (œuvre) classic; **un ~ de l'écran** a screen classic; **un ~ du genre** a classic of its kind; **je connais mes ~s**○**!** hum I know my classics!; **3** (style) **le ~** Mus classical music; Danse classical ballet; Mode classic clothes (*pl*).

III *nf* Sport classic.

classiquement /klasikmɑ̃/ *adv* (de façon traditionnelle) traditionally; (habituellement) usually.

claudélien, -ienne /klodeljɛ̃, ɛn/ *adj* Claudelian.

claudicant, ~e /klodikɑ̃, ɑ̃t/ *adj* **1** lit [*démarche*] limping; **2** fig [*argumentation*] shaky.

claudication /klodikasjɔ̃/ *nf* **1** (fait de boiter) limping; **2** (infirmité) limp.

claudiquer /klodike/ [1] *vi* to limp.

clause /kloz/ *nf* clause (**sur** on); **~ résolutoire/échappatoire** cancellation[GB]/escape clause; **~ d'indexation/de sauvegarde** escalator/safeguard clause.

■ **~ de conscience** Presse conscience clause; **~ de style** standard formula.

claustra /klostʀa/ *nm* Archit trellis; (cloison mobile) trellised screen.

claustral, ~e, *mpl* **-aux** /klostʀal, o/ *adj* fml monastic.

claustration /klostʀasjɔ̃/ *nf* fml confinement.

claustrer /klostʀe/ [1] **I** *vtr* to confine.

II **se claustrer** *vpr* to shut oneself away (**dans** in); **se ~ dans le mutisme** to retreat into stubborn silence.

claustrophobe /klostʀɔfɔb/ **I** *adj* claustrophobic.

II *nmf* claustrophobia sufferer.

claustrophobie /klostʀɔfɔbi/ *nf* claustrophobia.

clavecin /klavsɛ̃/ ▶534 *nm* harpsichord; **jouer du ~** to play the harpsichord.

claveciniste /klavsinist/ ▶510 *nmf* harpsichordist.

clavette /klavɛt/ *nf* Tech key.

clavicorde /klavikɔʀd/ ▶534 *nm* clavichord.

clavicule /klavikyl/ *nf* collarbone, clavicle spéc.

clavier /klavje/ *nm* keyboard.

■ **~ numérique** numeric keypad.

claviériste /klavjeʀist/ *nmf* keyboard player.

claviste /klavist/ ▶510 *nmf* **1** Imprim typesetter; **2** Ordinat keyboarder.

clayette /klɛjɛt/ *nf* **1** (de réfrigérateur) shelf; **2** (cageot) crate.

clayon /klɛjɔ̃/ *nm* (à fromages, fruits) small wicker rack; (à gâteaux) cake tray.

clayonnage /klɛjɔnaʒ/ *nm* wicker fences (*pl*).

clé /kle/ **I** *nf* **1** Tech (de serrure, mécanisme, conserve) key; **la ~ de la porte d'entrée/du garage** the front-door/garage key; **la ~ de ma chambre** the key to my bedroom; **laisser la ~ sur la porte** to leave the key in the door ou lock; **sous ~** under lock and key; **fermer à ~** to lock [*porte, valise, tiroir*]; **ça ferme à ~?** does it lock?; **usine/projet ~s en main** turnkey factory/project; **solution ~s en main** ready-made solution; **prix ~s en main** Aut on the road price GB, sticker price US; **2** (condition, solution) key (**de** to); **détenir la ~ du bonheur** to know the secret of true happiness; **détenir la ~ du mystère** to have the key to the mystery; **détenir la ~ de la situation** to control the situation; **la ~ des songes** the key to the interpretation of dreams; **roman à ~** roman à clef; **3** (outil) spanner GB, wrench; **4** Mus (de flûte, clarinette) key; (de violon, guitare) peg; (de cor, trompette) valve; (de tambour) tuning screw; (dans une notation) clef; **~ de fa/de sol/d'ut** bass ou F/treble ou G/alto ou C clef; **5** Sport (prise) armlock; **faire une ~ à qn** to get sb in an armlock; **6** Ling (de caractère chinois) key; **7** Hérald key.

II **(-)clé** (*in compounds*) **poste/mot/document(-)~** key post/word/document; **les industries ~s** the key industries; **l'homme(-)~** the key man.

III **à la clé** *loc adv* (comme enjeu) at stake; Mus in the key-signature; **avec, à la ~, une récompense/un beau salaire** with a reward/a fat salary thrown in.

■ **~ d'accès électronique** Télécom digital security coding; **~ d'accordeur** Mus tuning key; **~ anglaise** = **~ à molette**; **~ à bougie** Aut plug spanner GB, spark-plug wrench US; **~ de contact** Aut ignition key; **~ à crémaillère** monkey wrench; **~ à douille** box spanner GB, socket wrench; **~ dynamométrique** torque spanner GB ou wrench US; **~ de mandrin** chuck key; **~ à molette** adjustable spanner GB ou wrench US; **~ à pipe** box spanner GB, socket wrench; **~ plate** (de serrage) open end spanner GB ou wrench US; (de serrure) cylinder key; **~ de poêle** damper; **~ polygonale** ring spanner GB, box end wrench US; **~ de remontage** winding key; **~ à sardines** Culin sardine tin key GB, sardine can key US; **~ de sûreté** (de serrure) Yale® key; **~ pour vis à six pans creux** Allen® key GB ou wrench US; **~ de voûte** Archit, fig keystone; **~s du royaume** Relig keys of the Kingdom of Heaven; **~s de la ville** keys of the city.

IDIOMES **prendre la ~ des champs** to escape; **mettre la ~ sous la porte** or **le paillasson** (partir) to leave; (faire faillite) to go bankrupt.

clean○ /klin/ *adv inv* [*étudiant, style*] squeaky clean○.

clearing /kliʀiŋ/ *nm* clearing; **accord de ~** clearing agreement.

clébard◑ /klebaʀ/, **clebs**◑ /klɛps/ *nm* mutt○ péj, dog.

clef = **clé**.

clématite /klematit/ *nf* clematis.

■ **~ des haies** old man's beard, traveller's joy.

clémence /klemɑ̃s/ *nf* **1** (indulgence) leniency (**envers** to), clemency sout (**envers** to); **~ judiciaire** judicial clemency; **2** (de climat) mildness, clemency sout (**de** of).

clément, **~e** /klemɑ̃, ɑ̃t/ *adj* **1** [*juge*] lenient (**envers** to), clement sout (**envers** to); **se montrer ~** to show clemency (**envers** to); **2** [*température, hiver*] mild, clement sout.

clémentine /klemɑ̃tin/ *nf* clementine.

clenche /klɑ̃ʃ/ *nf* latch.

Cléopâtre /kleɔpatʀ/ *npr* Cleopatra.

clepsydre /klɛpsidʀ/ *nf* water clock, clepsydra.

cleptomane /klɛptɔman/ *adj, nmf* kleptomaniac.

cleptomanie /klɛptɔmani/ *nf* kleptomania.

clerc /klɛʀ/ *nm* **1** ▶ 510 Admin, Jur clerk; **~ (de notaire)** notary's clerk; **2**† Relig cleric; **3**‡ (lettré) scholar; **être (grand) ~ en la matière** to be an expert on the subject; **il ne faut pas être grand ~ pour**... you don't need to be a genius to...; **4** (intellectuel) intellectual.

clergé /klɛʀʒe/ *nm* clergy; **régulier/séculier** regular/secular clergy; **haut/bas ~** upper/lower clergy.

clérical, **~e**, *mpl* **-aux** /kleʀikal, o/ **I** *adj* **1** [*vie, fonction*] clerical; **2** [*parti, presse*] that supports the Church (*épith, après n*).

II *nm,f* supporter of clericalism.

cléricalisme /kleʀikalism/ *nm* clericalism.

Clermont-Ferrand /klɛʀmɔ̃fɛʀɑ̃/ ▶ 857 *npr* Clermont-Ferrand.

clermontois, **~e** /klɛʀmɔ̃twa, az/ ▶ 857 *adj* of Clermont-Ferrand.

Clermontois, **~e** /klɛʀmɔ̃twa, az/ *nm,f* (natif) native of Clermont-Ferrand; (habitant) inhabitant of Clermont-Ferrand.

Cleveland ▶ 692 *nprm* **le ~** Cleveland.

clic /klik/ *nm* **1** (*also onomat*) click (**de** of); **2** (en phonétique) click.

clic-clac /klikklak/ *nm inv* (*also onomat*) (d'appareil photo, de hauts talons) click (**de** of).

cliché /kliʃe/ *nm* **1** Phot (négatif) negative; (photo) snapshot; **prendre un ~** to take a snap; **2** (lieu commun) cliché; **3** Imprim plate.

client, **~e** /klijɑ̃, ɑ̃t/ *nm,f* **1** (personne) (de magasin) customer; (d'avocat, de notaire) client; (d'hôtel) guest, patron; (de taxi) passenger, fare; **être ~ d'un magasin** to be a regular customer in a shop GB ou store US; **je ne suis pas ~e** (de magasin) I'm not a regular customer; (de banque) I am not a customer; **tu es ~?** fig are you interested?; **2** (pays, société) customer, client; **les pays ~s** countries which are customers; **3** Hist client.

IDIOMES **c'est à la tête du ~** it depends whether they like the look of you.

clientèle /klijɑ̃tɛl/ *nf* **1** (de magasin, restaurant) customers (*pl*), clientele; (d'avocat, de notaire) clients (*pl*); (de médecin) patients (*pl*); (d'hôtel) clientele; **la ~ d'affaires** business customers (*pl*); **ils ont surtout une ~ féminine** their customers are mainly women; **avoir une bonne ~** [*magasin, restaurant*] to have a lot of customers; [*avocat, médecin*] to have a large practice; **se faire une ~** to build up a clientele; **ils ont une ~ d'entreprises** they deal with firms; **perdre de la ~** to lose business ou custom; **2** (habitude d'achat) custom; (à plus grande échelle) business; **accorder sa ~ à qn** to give sb one's custom ou business; **je vais lui retirer ma ~** I'll take my custom elsewhere, I'll take my business elsewhere; **3** Hist clients (*pl*).

■ **~ électorale** Pol supporters (*pl*), constituency US.

clientélisme /klijɑ̃telism/ *nm* Pol pej vote-catching.

clignement /kliɲəmɑ̃/ *nm* **~ d'œil** blinking ¢.

cligner /kliɲe/ [1] **I** *vtr* **~ les yeux** (plisser les yeux) to screw up one's eyes; (battre des paupières) to blink; **la lumière lui fit ~ les yeux** the light made him/her blink.

II cligner de *vtr ind* **~ des yeux** (plisser les yeux) to screw up one's eyes; (battre des paupières) to blink; **~ de l'œil** to wink.

III *vi* **ses yeux clignèrent** he/she blinked.

clignotant, **~e** /kliɲɔtɑ̃, ɑ̃t/ **I** *adj* [*étoile*] twinkling; [*feu, lumière, phare*] flashing; [*yeux*] blinking.

II *nm* **1** Aut (pour tourner) indicator GB, turn signal US, blinker US; **mettre son ~** to indicate GB ou signal; **2** Écon warning sign.

clignotement /kliɲɔtmɑ̃/ *nm* (d'étoile) twinkling; (de feu, lumière, phare) flashing; (d'yeux) blinking.

clignoter /kliɲɔte/ [1] *vi* **1** [*lumière*] (une fois) to flash; (longtemps) to flash on and off; [*étoile*] to twinkle; **2** [*personne, yeux*] to blink; **~ des yeux** to blink.

climat /klima/ *nm* **1** Météo, Géog climate; **~ continental/océanique** continental/oceanic climate; **sous d'autres ~s** liter in other climes; **2** (ambiance) climate; **dans un ~ de violence/confiance** in a climate of violence/confidence; **dans un ~ détendu** in a relaxed atmosphere.

climatique /klimatik/ *adj* climatic.

climatisation /klimatizasjɔ̃/ *nf* air-conditioning.

climatiser /klimatize/ [1] *vtr* (maintenir la température de) to air-condition [*pièce*]; (équiper) to install air-conditioning in [*maison*]; **hôtel climatisé** air-conditioned hotel.

climatiseur /klimatizœʀ/ *nm* air-conditioner.

climatologie /klimatɔlɔʒi/ *nf* climatology.

climatologique /klimatɔlɔʒik/ *adj* climatological.

climatologue /klimatɔlɔg/ *nmf* climatologist.

climatothérapie /klimatɔteʀapi/ *nf* climatotherapy.

clin /klɛ̃/ *nm* **~ d'œil** lit wink; fig allusion; **faire un ~ d'œil à qn** lit to wink at sb; **en un ~ d'œil** in a flash, in the wink of an eye littér.

cline /klin/ *nm* cline.

clinfoc /klɛ̃fɔk/ *nm* flying jib.

clinicien, **-ienne** /klinisjɛ̃, ɛn/ *nm,f* clinician.

clinique /klinik/ **I** *adj* clinical.

II *nf* **1** (établissement) private hospital; **2** (médecine) clinical medecine.

■ **~ d'accouchement** maternity hospital ou home GB; **~ vétérinaire** veterinary clinic.

cliniquement /klinikmɑ̃/ *adv* clinically.

clinquant, **~e** /klɛ̃kɑ̃, ɑ̃t/ **I** *adj* [*bijou, intérieur*] flashy○; **discours ~** cheap rhetoric.

II *nm* **1** (paillettes) beading; **2** (faux éclat) (de décor) flashiness○; fig (de discours) cheap rhetoric.

Clio /klijo/ *npr* Clio.

clip /klip/ *nm* **1** (vidéoclip) pop video; **2** (bijou) (broche) clip brooch; (boucle d'oreille) clip-on.

clique /klik/ *nf* **1** (groupe) clique; **2** (fanfare) pipe band.

IDIOMES **prendre ses ~s et ses claques** to pack up and go.

cliquer /klike/ [1] *vi* Ordinat to click (**sur** on).

cliquet /klikɛ/ *nm* (de roue) pawl.

cliqueter /klikte/ [20] *vi* [*clés, pièces de monnaie*] to jingle; [*chaîne, ferraille*] to rattle; [*mécanisme, engrenage*] to go clickety-clack; [*aiguilles à tricoter*] to click; [*couverts*] to clink; [*épées*] to rattle.

cliquetis /klikti/ *nm* (de clés, pièces de monnaie) jingle; (de chaîne, ferraille) rattle; (de mécanisme, d'engrenage, aiguilles à tricoter) clicking; (d'épée) rattle; (de couverts) clinking.

clisse /klis/ *nf* **1** (à fromage) wicker cheese-drainer; **2** (à bouteille) wicker bottle-covering.

clisser /klise/ [1] *vtr* **~ une bouteille** to cover ou case a bottle in wicker.

clitoridectomie /klitɔʀidɛktɔmi/ *nf* clitoridectomy.

clitoridien, **-ienne** /klitɔʀidjɛ̃, ɛn/ *adj* clitoral.

clitoris /klitɔʀis/ *nm* clitoris.

clivage /klivaʒ/ *nm* **1** Géol (faille) cleavage; **2** Minér (de roche) cleavage; **3** Tech (de diamant, cristal) cleaving; **4** (division) divide (**entre** between); **les ~s politiques/sociaux** political/social divides; **le ~ droite-gauche** the left-right divide; **le ~ Nord-Sud** the North-South divide; **le ~ cinéma-TV**○ the divide between cinema and TV; **~ d'opinion** division of opinion.

cliver /klive/ [1] *vtr*, **se cliver** *vpr* to cleave.

cloaque /klɔak/ *nm* **1** fig cesspit; **2** Zool cloaca.

clochard, **~e** /klɔʃaʀ, aʀd/ *nm,f* tramp, down-and-out.

clochardisation /klɔʃaʀdizasjɔ̃/ *nf*: *process by which a person is reduced to vagrancy*; **des jeunes chômeurs en voie de ~** young unemployed people on the road to vagrancy.

clochardiser: **se clochardiser** /klɔʃaʀdize/ [1] *vpr* to become reduced to vagrancy.

cloche /klɔʃ/ **I**○ *adj* [*personne, propos*] silly, stupid.

II *nf* **1** (instrument sonore) bell; **on a entendu dix coups de ~** we heard the bell ring ten times; **en (forme de) ~** bell-shaped; **courbe en ~** Math Gaussian curve, bell curve; ▶**déménager**; **2** (ustensile) Chimie bell jar; Hort cloche; **mettre qch sous ~** to put sth under cloche; **3**○ (imbécile) clot○ GB, clod○, idiot; **4**○ (clochard) tramp; **la ~** the down-and-outs (*pl*).

■ **~ à fromage** Culin cover of cheese dish; **~ de plongée** Naut diving bell; **~ à vide** Phys vacuum bell jar.

IDIOMES **se taper la ~**○ to have a good ou slap-up GB meal, to pig out○; **entendre plusieurs sons de ~** to hear several different versions; **qui n'entend qu'une ~ n'entend qu'un son** if you only listen to one person, you don't get the whole picture; **sonner les ~s à qn** to bawl sb out○; **se faire sonner les ~s** to get bawled out○.

cloche-pied: **à cloche-pied** /aklɔʃpje/ *loc adv* **sauter à ~** to hop.

clocher /klɔʃe/ [1] **I** *nm* **1** (d'église) (en pointe) steeple; (tour) church ou bell tower; **2** fig (pays natal) home town; **il n'a jamais quitté son ~** he has never left his home town; **esprit de ~** parochial ou small-town mentality; **querelle/rivalités de ~** parish-pump GB ou local quarrel/rivalries.

II○ *vi* (être défectueux) [*argumentation*] to be faulty; **il y a quelque chose qui cloche dans l'amplificateur/dans ce que tu dis**

there's something wrong with the amplifier/with what you are saying.

clocheton /klɔʃtɔ̃/ *nm* **1** (ornement) pinnacle; **2** (petit clocher) little steeple.

clochette /klɔʃɛt/ *nf* **1** (petite cloche) (little) bell; **2** (fleur) bell, bell-shaped flower.

clodo○ /klɔdo/ *nm* tramp, down-and-out.

cloison /klwazɔ̃/ *nf* **1** Constr partition; (mobile de bureau) screen; **2** Anat, Bot septum; **3** (d'un émail) metal strip (*in cloisonné*); **4** Naut bulkhead; **~ étanche** lit watertight bulkhead; fig watertight compartment; **5** fig (barrière) barrier (**entre** between).
■ **~ extensible** folding room-divider.

cloisonnage /klwazɔnaʒ/ *nm* Constr partitioning.

cloisonné, **~e** /klwazɔne/ **I** *pp* ▶ **cloisonner**.
II *pp adj* **1** Constr [*bureau*] partitioned; **2** Pol [*structure, parti*] compartmentalized; **3** Art [*émail*] cloisonné (*épith*).
III *nm* Art cloisonné.

cloisonnement /klwazɔnmɑ̃/ *nm* **1** (action, résultat) partitioning; **2** (de la population) division; (de services, d'administration) compartmentalization; **les ~s entre** the barriers between [*services, groupes*].

cloisonner /klwazɔne/ [1] *vtr* **1** Constr to partition [*pièce*]; to divide up [*surface*]; **2** fig to divide up [*société*]; to compartmentalize [*secteurs, administration*]; to erect barriers between [*groupes*].

cloisonnisme /klwazɔnism/ *nm* Art synthetism.

cloître /klwɑtʀ/ *nm* cloister.

cloîtrer /klwatʀe/ [1] **I** *vtr* **1** (enfermer) to shut [sb] away; **il cloître sa fille dans sa chambre** he keeps his daughter shut (away) in her bedroom; **rester cloîtré dans sa chambre** to shut oneself away in one's room; **2** Relig to put [sb] into a monastery [*homme*]; to put [sb] into a convent [*femme*]; **religieuse cloîtrée** nun belonging to an enclosed order.
II se cloîtrer *vpr* **1** (s'enfermer) to shut oneself away (**dans** in); **se ~ dans le silence** to retreat into silence; **2** Relig [*homme*] to enter a monastery; [*femme*] to enter a convent.

clonage /klonaʒ/ *nm* cloning.

clone /klon/ *nm* clone.

cloner /klone/ [1] *vtr* to clone.

clope○ /klɔp/ *nm* ou *f* fag○ GB, ciggy○, cigarette.

clopet○ /klɔpɛ/ *nm* H (sieste) nap.

clopin-clopant○ /klɔpɛ̃klɔpɑ̃/ *loc adv* **1** (en boitant) **marcher ~** to hobble along; **partir ~** to hobble off; **descendre/remonter la rue ~** to hobble down/up the street; **2** (mal) **aller ~** [*économie, affaires*] to limp along.

clopiner /klɔpine/ [1] *vi* to hobble.

clopinettes○ /klɔpinɛt/ *nfpl* **gagner des ~** to earn peanuts○; **des ~!** no way○!

cloporte /klɔpɔʀt/ *nm* woodlouse; **des ~s** woodlice.
IDIOMES **vivre comme un ~** to live like a hermit.

cloque /klɔk/ *nf* **1** (sur la peau) blister; **2** (sur du papier, de la peinture) blister; **3** Hort peach leaf curl.
IDIOMES **être en ~**◑ to be up the spout○ GB, to be knocked up◑, to be pregnant.

cloqué, **~e** /klɔke/ **I** *pp* ▶ **cloquer**.
II *pp adj* **tissu ~** seersucker.
III *nm* Tex seersucker.

cloquer /klɔke/ [1] **I** *vtr* Tex to pucker [*tissu*].
II *vi* **1** [*peinture, peau*] to blister; **2** [*feuille*] to curl.

clore /klɔʀ/ [79] **I** *vtr* **1** (mettre fin à) to close [*débat, scrutin, compte*] (**par** with); **l'exercice clos le 31 décembre** Compta the financial year which ended on 31 December; **2** (être la fin de) to end, to conclude [*programme, congrès*]; to end [*livre*]; **un dîner a clos le congrès** the conference ended with a dinner; **3** (fermer) liter to close [*yeux, volet*]; to block, to seal off [*passage*]; to seal [*enveloppe*]; **4** (enclore) to enclose [*terrain*] (**de** with); **5**† (conclure) to conclude [*accord, marché*].
II se clore *vpr* (se terminer) to end (**par** with).

clos, **~e** /klo, oz/ **I** *pp* ▶ **clore**.
II *pp adj* **1** (fermé) gén closed; [*enveloppe*] sealed; **monde ~** fig self-contained world; **à la nuit ~e** liter after nightfall; **2** (clôturé) [*terrain*] fenced, enclosed.
III *nm* (terrain) fenced ou enclosed field; (verger) orchard; (vigne) vineyard.

clôture /klotyʀ/ *nf* **1** (barrière) (de bois) fence; (de fil de fer) wire fence; (de grillage) chain-link ou wire-mesh fence; (grille) railings (*pl*); (mur) surrounding wall; (haie) hedge; **~ électrique** electric fence; **mur de ~** enclosing wall; **poser une ~ autour d'un terrain** to fence ou enclose a field; **2** (de débat, scrutin, séance, liste) close; (de souscription) closing; (de magasin, bureau) closing; (de saison) close; **discours/séance de ~** closing speech/session; **~ des inscriptions le 3 mai à midi** closing date for registration, noon on 3 May; **le Te Deum de Bizet est programmé en ~ du festival** Bizet's Te Deum is scheduled to close the festival; **3** (de compte) closure; (en Bourse) close; **à la ~** at the close (of the day's trading); **faiblir en ~** to weaken at the close; **prix/stock de ~** closing price/stock; **achat/vente/opération après ~** after-hours buying/selling/trading; **valoir 10 francs en ~** to close at 10 francs; **4** (de monastère) enclosure.

clôturer /klotyʀe/ [1] **I** *vtr* **1** (enclore) to enclose, to fence in [*terrain*]; **il veut ~ son jardin** he wants to fence in his garden GB ou yard US; **il va le ~ avec du fil de fer barbelé/une haie** he's going to surround it with barbed wire/a hedge; **2** (terminer) [*personne*] to close [*débat, séance, liste, compte*]; [*discours, cérémonie*] to end, to bring [sth] to a close [*débat, festival etc*]; **les inscriptions sont clôturées** the closing date for registration has passed; **l'exercice clôturé le 31 décembre** Compta the financial year which ended on 31 December.
II *vi* Fin [*marché, action*] **~ à 3 francs** to close at 3 francs; **~ à la hausse/baisse** to close up/down; **le marché a clôturé sur un gain de 10 points** trading closed on a gain of 10 points.
III se clôturer *vpr* [*congrès*] to end (**par** with).

clou /klu/ **I** *nm* **1** Tech nail; **suspendu à un ~** hung on a nail; **ceinture/veste à ~s** studded belt/jacket; **planter un ~** to hammer in a nail; **2** (attraction) (de spectacle) star attraction; (de soirée) high point; **3**○ (bicyclette) boneshaker○, bicycle; **4** (furoncle) boil; **5**○ (mont-de-piété) **être/mettre au ~** to be at/to take [sth] to the pawnshop.
II clous *nmpl* **1** (passage pour piétons) pedestrian crossing (*sg*) GB, crosswalk (*sg*) US; **2**○ (rien) **des ~s!** no way!
■ **~ à chaussures** shoe tack; **~ de girofle** Bot, Culin clove; **~ sans tête** lost-head nail; **~ de tapissier** upholstery tack.
IDIOMES **un ~ chasse l'autre** one takes over where the other leaves off; **enfoncer le ~** to drive the point home; **ne pas valoir un ~**○ not to be worth a thing ou a brass farthing GB.

clouage /kluaʒ/ *nm* nailing.

clouer /klue/ [1] *vtr* **1** (fixer avec de gros clous) to nail down [*caisse*]; to nail up [*pancarte*]; to nail together [*planches*]; **2** (fixer avec de petits clous) to tack [*moquette, affiche*]; **3** (immobiliser) **~ au sol** to pin [sb] down [*adversaire*]; **les avions sont restés cloués au sol en raison du mauvais temps** the planes were grounded because of the weather; **4** (invalider) (temporairement) **~ au lit/chez soi** to confine [sb] to bed/to one's home; (en permanence) **être** or **rester cloué au lit** to be bedridden; **5** (stupéfier) to stun; **être** or **rester cloué** to be stunned; **~ de stupeur** to stun.

clouté, **~e** /klute/ *adj* studded (**de** with); **passage ~** pedestrian crossing GB, crosswalk US.

clovisse /klɔvis/ *nf* clam.

clown /klun/ *nm* clown; **quel ~!** fig what a comedian!; **faire le ~** to clown about.
■ **~ blanc** whitefaced clown.

clownerie /klunʀi/ *nf* trick; **~s** clowning ₵; **arrête tes ~s** stop clowning about.

clownesque /klunɛsk/ *adj* [*mimique*] exaggerated; [*personnage*] clown-like; [*situation*] farcical.

cloyère /klwajɛʀ, klɔjɛʀ/ *nf* oyster basket.

club /klœb/ *nm* **1** (société, local) club; fig (groupe) group; **2** (au golf) (golf-)club; ▶ **classe**, **fauteuil**.
■ **~ de vacances** holiday camp.

clubiste /klœbist/ *nmf* club member.

cluse /klyz/ *nf* transverse valley.

Clwyd ▶ 692 *nprm* **le ~** Clwyd.

clystère‡ /klistɛʀ/ *nm* clyster‡.

Clytemnestre /klitɛmnɛstʀ/ *npr* Clytemnestra.

cm (*written abbr* = **centimètre**) cm; **cm²** (centimètre carré) cm²; **cm³** (centimètre cube) gén cm³; (pour moteurs) cc.

CM /seɛm/ *nm*: *abbr* ▶ **cours**.

CNDP /seɛndepe/ *nm* (*abbr* = **Centre national de documentation pédagogique**) *teachers' resource centre.*

CNED /knɛd/ *nm*: *abbr* ▶ **centre**.

CNES /knɛs/ *nm* (*abbr* = **Centre national d'études spatiales**) *French national centre for space research.*

CNET /knɛt/ *nm* (*abbr* = **Centre national d'études des télécommunications**) *French telecommunications research centre.*

CNIL /knil/ *nf* (*abbr* = **Commission nationale de l'informatique et des libertés**) *French national data protection agency.*

CNIT /knit/ *nm* (*abbr* = **Centre national des industries et des techniques**) *exhibition and conference centre in Paris.*

CNJA /seɛnʒia/ *nm* (*abbr* = **Centre national des jeunes agriculteurs**) *union for young peasant farmers.*

CNPF /seɛnpeɛf/ *nm* (*abbr* = **Conseil national du patronat français**) *national council of French employers.*

CNRS /seɛnɛʀɛs/ *nm* (*abbr* = **Centre national de la recherche scientifique**) *national centre for scientific research.*

CNUCED /knysɛd/ *nf* (*abbr* = **Conférence des Nations unies pour le commerce et le développement**) UNCTAD.

coaccusé, **~e** /koakyze/ *nm,f* codefendant.

coacquéreur /koakeʀœʀ/ *nm* joint purchaser.

coactionnaire /koaksjɔnɛʀ/ *nmf* joint shareholder.

coadaptateur, **-trice** /koadaptatœʀ, tʀis/ *nmf* co-author (*of an adaptation*).

coadjuteur, **-trice** /koadʒytœʀ, tʀis/ *nm,f* coadjutor/coadjutress.

coadministrateur, **-trice** /koadministratœʀ, tʀis/ *nm,f* **1** Comm joint administrator; **2** Jur joint trustee.

coagulable /kɔagylabl/ *adj* coagulable.

coagulant, **~e** /kɔagylɑ̃, ɑ̃t/ **I** *adj* coagulative.
II *nm* coagulant.

coagulateur, **-trice** /kɔagylatœʀ, -tʀis/ *adj* coagulative.

coagulation /kɔagylasjɔ̃/ *nf* coagulation; **temps de ~** coagulation ou clotting time.

coaguler /kɔagyle/ [1] *vi*, **se coaguler** *vpr* [*sang*] to coagulate; [*lait*] to curdle.

coalisé, **~e** /kɔalize/ **I** *pp* ▶ **coaliser**.

II *pp adj* [*forces, pays, partis*] Mil, Pol allied; [*intérêts*] combined.
III *nm,f* member of the coalition.

coaliser /kɔalize/ [1] **I** *vtr* gén to unite; Pol to unite [sb] in a coalition; **~ un groupe** to unite a group (**contre** against).
II se coaliser *vpr* gén to unite; Pol to form a coalition; **se ~ contre la misère/pollution** to unite to combat poverty/pollution.

coalition /kɔalisjɔ̃/ *nf* coalition; **gouvernement de ~** coalition government.

coaltar /kɔltaʀ, koltaʀ/ *nm* coal tar.
IDIOMES **être dans le ~**○ to be in a daze.

coassement /kɔasmɑ̃/ *nm* croaking ¢.

coasser /kɔase/ [1] *vi* to croak.

coassurance /koasyʀɑ̃s/ *nf* co-insurance.

coauteur /kootœʀ/ *nm* co-author.

coaxial, **~e**, *mpl* **-iaux** /koaksjal, o/ **I** *adj* coaxial.
II *nm* Électrotech Télécom feeder.

COB /kɔb/ *nf* (*abbr* = **Commission des opérations de Bourse**) *Stock Exchange watchdog body*; cf SERC GB, SEC US.

cobalt /kɔbalt/ *nm* cobalt; **bleu ~** cobalt blue; ▶ **bombe**.

cobaye /kɔbaj/ *nm* lit, fig guinea pig; **servir de ~** to act as a guinea pig.

cobelligérant, **~e** /kobɛliʒeʀɑ̃, ɑ̃t/ **I** *adj* cobelligerent.
II *nm* cobelligerent.

COBOL /kɔbɔl/ *nm* COBOL.

cobra /kɔbʀa/ *nm* cobra.

coca /kɔka/ **I** *nm* **1**○ (*abbr* = **coca-cola**®) Coke®; **2** Bot (arbuste) coca.
II *nm* ou *f* (extrait) coca extract.

coca-dollar○, *pl* **coca-dollars** /kɔkadɔlaʀ/ *nm* cocaine dollar.

cocagne /kɔkaɲ/ *nf* **mât de ~** ≈ greasy pole; **pays de ~** land of Cockaigne.

cocaïne /kɔkain/ *nf* cocaine.

cocaïnomane /kɔkainɔman/ *nmf* cocaine addict.

cocarde /kɔkaʀd/ *nf* (sur uniforme) cockade; (emblème national) (sur avion) roundel; (sur véhicule) official badge; **~ tricolore** Hist revolutionary cockade; (en tissu) rosette.

cocardier, **-ière** /kɔkaʀdje, ɛʀ/ pej **I** *adj* jingoistic.
II *nm,f* jingoist.

cocasse /kɔkas/ *adj* comical.

cocasserie /kɔkasʀi/ *nf* (de personnage, d'objet) comical appearance; (de propos) comical nature.

coccinelle /kɔksinɛl/ *nf* **1** (insecte) ladybird, ladybug US; **2**○ (voiture) beetle○, Volkswagen car.

coccyx /kɔksis/ *nm* coccyx.

coche /kɔʃ/ *nm* (diligence) (stage)coach.
■ **~ d'eau** horse-drawn barge.
IDIOMES **manquer le ~** to miss the boat; **faire la mouche du ~** to act as a goad, to make a nuisance of oneself.

cochenille /kɔʃnij/ *nf* **1** (colorant) cochineal; **2** (insecte) cochineal insect.

cocher /kɔʃe/ [1] **I** *nm* (de diligence) coachman; (de fiacre) cabman.
II *vtr* **1** (marquer) to tick GB, to check US; **2** (entailler) to make a notch in.
IDIOMES **fouette, ~**○! make it snappy○!

cochère /kɔʃɛʀ/ *adj f* **porte ~** carriage entrance.

Cochinchine /kɔʃɛ̃ʃin/ *nprf* Cochin China.

cochon, **-onne** /kɔʃɔ̃, ɔn/ **I**○ *adj* **1** (pornographique) [*film*] dirty, blue (*épith*); [*photographie*] dirty, explicit; [*histoire, plaisanterie, magazine*] dirty, smutty; [*personne*] dirty-minded; **2** (malpropre) [*personne*] messy, dirty.
II○ *nm,f* **1** (personne malpropre ou brouillonne) pej pig○, slob○; **manger comme un ~** to eat like a pig; **elle a mis du chocolat partout, la cochonne** she's got chocolate all over the place, the messy thing; **travailler comme un ~** to make a mess of a job, to make a pig's ear of a job○ GB; **travail de ~** botched job; **tour de ~** dirty trick; **2** (personne lubrique) sex maniac; **espèce de vieux ~!** you dirty old man !; **tu n'es qu'une cochonne** you've got a mind like a sewer.
III *nm* **1** Zool pig, hog; ▶ **confiture**, **perle**; **2** Culin pork.
■ **~ d'Inde** Zool Guinea pig; **~ de lait** Agric, Culin sucking pig; **~ de mer** Zool porpoise.
IDIOMES **il ira loin, si les petits ~s ne le mangent pas** he'll go far, if nothing gets in his way; **un ~ n'y retrouverait pas ses petits** it's like a pigsty, it's a real shambles○; **on n'a pas gardé les ~s ensemble** don't get so pally○ GB ou chummy○ ou familiar with me!; **~ qui s'en dédit!** Prov let's shake hands on it!

cochonceté○ /kɔʃɔ̃ste/ *nf* obscenity.

cochonnaille○ /kɔʃɔnaj/ *nf*: *products made from pork such as salami, bacon, pâté and ham.*

cochonner○ /kɔʃɔne/ [1] *vtr* **1** (souiller) to mess up, to dirty [*vêtement, moquette, livre*]; **2** (bâcler) to botch (up) [*travail*].

cochonnerie○ /kɔʃɔnʀi/ *nf* **1** (toute chose de mauvaise qualité) junk○ ¢; **il ne mange que des ~s** he only eats junk food; **c'est de la ~ ce stylo** this pen is crap◑ ou useless; **2** (saleté) mess ¢; **faire des ~s** to make a mess; **3** (obscénité) obscenity; **dire des ~s** to say smutty○ ou dirty things; **faire des ~s** to get up to dirty stuff; **des magazines pleins de ~s** dirty magazines; **4** (sale tour) dirty trick, mean trick; **faire une ~ à qn** to play a dirty trick on sb.

cochonnet /kɔʃɔnɛ/ *nm* **1** Zool piglet; **2** (à la pétanque) jack.

cochylis /kɔkilis/ *nm* cochylis moth.

cocker /kɔkɛʀ/ *nm* (cocker) spaniel.

cockpit /kɔkpit/ *nm* Aviat, Naut cockpit.

cocktail /kɔktɛl/ *nm* **1** (boisson) cocktail; (plat composé) **~ de crevettes/fruits** prawn/fruit cocktail; **2** fig (mélange) mixture; **3** (réception) cocktail party.
■ **~ Molotov** Molotov cocktail.

coco /koko/ **I** *nm* **1** (noix) coconut; **fibre de ~** coconut matting; **huile de ~** coconut oil; **2**○ (terme d'affection) darling, pet○; **3**○ (individu) guy○, customer○ péj; **c'est un drôle de ~ celui-là!** that guy's a bit of an oddball○ ou a strange customer○; **4**○ (communiste) pej commie○ péj, red○ péj; **5** (boisson à la réglisse) *lemon and liquorice* GB ou *licorice* US *drink*; **6**○ (tête) nut○, head; **elle n'a rien dans le ~** she isn't all there○; **7**○ (œuf) baby talk egg.
II○ *nf* (cocaïne) coke○.

cocon /kɔkɔ̃/ *nm* lit, fig cocoon.
IDIOMES **s'enfermer dans son ~** to withdraw into one's shell.

cocorico /kɔkɔʀiko/ *nm* (*also onomat*) cock-a-doodle-do; **faire ~** lit, fig to crow.

cocoteraie /kɔkɔtʀɛ/ *nf* coconut plantation.

cocotier /kɔkɔtje/ *nm* coconut palm.
IDIOMES **secouer le ~** ≈ to clean out the dead wood.

cocotte /kɔkɔt/ *nf* **1**○ (poule) baby talk hen; **2**○ (terme d'affection) **ma ~** honey; **3**○† péj (femme) loose woman; **4** Culin (récipient) casserole dish GB, pot; (**faire**) **cuire qch à la ~** to casserole GB ou stew sth; **bœuf à la ~** beef casserole GB, braised beef; **5** Culin C (cafetière) coffee pot; **6** (à un cheval) **hue ~!** gee-up!
■ **~ en papier** paper hen (*origami style*).

cocotte-minute®, *pl* **cocottes-minute** /kɔkɔtminyt/ *nf* pressure-cooker.

cocotter◑ /kɔkɔte/ [1] *vi* to stink, to pong○ GB.

cocréancier, **-ière** /kokʀeɑ̃sje, ɛʀ/ *nm,f* joint creditor.

cocu◑, **~e** /kɔky/ **I** *adj* **elle est ~e** her husband is unfaithful to her; **elle le fait ~** she is unfaithful to him (**avec** with), she's cheating on him○ (**avec** with).
II *nm,f* lit deceived husband/wife; fig dupe; ▶ **veine**.

cocufier◑ /kɔkyfje/ [2] *vtr* lit to be unfaithful to, to cheat on○; fig to trick.

coda /kɔda/ *nf* coda.

codage /kɔdaʒ/ *nm* coding, encoding.

code /kɔd/ **I** *nm* **1** (recueil) code; **~ de déontologie** code of practice; **2** (conventions) code; **~ de conduite/de l'honneur** code of conduct/of honour[GB]; **s'appuyer sur les ~s du film noir** to follow the conventions of film noir; **3** (écriture, message) code; **~ chiffré** number code; **message en ~** coded message; **mettre qch en ~** to put sth in code, to encode sth; **4** Ordinat code; **~ de contrôle d'erreur** error-checking code; **~ correcteur d'erreurs** error-correcting code.
II codes *nmpl* (phares) dipped GB ou dimmed US (head)lights, low beam (*sg*); **rouler en ~s** to drive with dipped (head)-lights GB ou on low beam; **se mettre en ~s** to dip GB ou dim US one's headlights.
■ **~ (à) barres** Comm bar code; **~ civil** Jur civil code; **~ confidentiel (d'identification)** Fin personal identification number, PIN; **~ génétique** Biol genetic code; **~ Napoléon** Napoleonic code; **~ de la nationalité** Jur regulations (*pl*) as to nationality; **~ pénal** Jur penal code; **~ postal** Postes post code GB, zip code US; **~ de procédure civile** Jur code of civil procedure; **~ de procédure pénale** Jur code of criminal procedure; **~ de la route** Aut highway code GB, rules (*pl*) of the road US; **passer son ~**○ Aut to take the written part of a driving test; **~ secret** secret code.

codébiteur, **-trice** /kodebitœʀ, tʀis/ *nm,f* joint debtor.

codécideur /kodesidœʀ/ *nm* joint decision-maker.

codéine /kɔdein/ *nf* codeine.

codemandeur, **-eresse** /kodəmɑ̃dœʀ, dəʀɛs/ *nm,f* joint plaintiff.

coder /kɔde/ [1] *vtr* to code, to encode.

codétenteur, **-trice** /kodetɑ̃tœʀ, tʀis/ *nm,f* Jur, Sport joint holder (**de** of).

codétenu, **~e** /kodetny/ *nm,f* fellow prisoner.

codeur /kɔdœʀ/ *nm* (appareil) converter.

codevi /kɔdevi/ *nm* (*abbr* = **compte pour le développement industriel**) *savings plan allowing banks to invest in industrial development.*

codex /kɔdɛks/ *nm* **1** Pharm gén pharmacopoeia; (en France) French pharmacopoeia; **2** (manuscrit) codex.

codicillaire /kɔdisilɛʀ/ *adj* Jur codicillary.

codicille /kɔdisil/ *nm* codicil.

codificateur, **-trice** /kɔdifikatœʀ, tʀis/ *adj* codifying.

codification /kɔdifikasjɔ̃/ *nf* codification.

codifier /kɔdifje/ [2] *vtr* to codify [*lois*]; to standardize [*langue, usage*].

codirecteur, **-trice** /kodiʀɛktœʀ, tʀis/ *nm,f* (responsable) joint manager; (administrateur) joint director.

codon /kɔdɔ̃/ *nm* codon.

coédition /koedisjɔ̃/ *nf* coedition.

coefficient /kɔefisjɑ̃/ *nm* **1** (proportion) ratio; **2** (pourcentage indéterminé) margin; **~ d'erreur** margin of error; **~ de sécurité** safety margin; **3** Scol, Univ *weighting factor in an exam*; **l'anglais a un ~ élevé** English results are heavily weighted; **la chimie est au ~ 4** chemistry results are multiplied by 4; **4** Math, Stat coefficient; Phys (d'expansion, absorption) coefficient; (d'élasticité, écrasement) modulus; **5** Admin *points on a salary scale*; **être au ~ 200** to have 200 points.
■ **~ de capitalisation des résultats** Fin price earning ratio, PER; **~ de liquidité** Fin liquid ratio; **~ d'occupation des sols, COS** (en urbanisme) building to plot ratio, site coverage; **~ d'occupation des vols** Aviat proportion of seats sold; **~**

de pénétration dans l'air Aut, Aviat drag coefficient.

cœlacanthe /selakɑ̃t/ *nm* coelacanth.

cœliaque /seljak/ *adj* Anat coeliac; **maladie ~** Méd coeliac disease.

cœlioscopie /seljoskɔpi/ *nf* coelioscopy.

cœnesthésie /senɛstezi/ = **cenesthésie**.

coentreprise /koɑ̃tʀəpʀiz/ *nf* joint venture.

coéquipier, **-ière** /koekipje, ɛʀ/ *nm,f* team mate.

coercible /kɔɛʀsibl/ *adj* [*gaz*] compressible.

coercitif, **-ive** /kɔɛʀsitif, iv/ *adj* coercive.

coercition /kɔɛʀsisjɔ̃/ *nf* coercion.

cœur /kœʀ/ **I** *nm* **1** Anat heart; **il a le ~ malade, il est malade du ~** he has a heart condition; **'qu'est-ce qu'il a?'—'c'est le ~'** 'what's wrong with him?'—'it's his heart'; **opération à ~ ouvert** open-heart surgery; **être opéré à ~ ouvert** to have ou undergo open-heart surgery; **cellules prélevées sur un ~ de veau** cells taken from the heart of a calf; **je la tenais pressée sur mon ~** I held her close; **serrer qn sur** or **contre son ~** to hold sb close; **porter la main à son ~** (en signe de bonne foi) to put one's hand on one's heart; **en forme de ~** heart-shaped (*épith*); **avoir mal au ~** to feel sick GB ou nauseous US; **donner mal au ~ à qn** to make sb feel sick GB ou nauseous US; **lever** or **soulever le ~ de qn** to make sb feel sick GB ou nauseous US; ▶**accrocher**, **joie**, **loin**; **2** Culin heart; **~ d'agneau/de porc/de veau** lamb's/pig's/calf's heart; **~ de bœuf** ox heart; **~s de poulets** chicken hearts; **~ de palmier** palm heart; **3** fig (de fruit, roche, matière, réacteur) core; (de problème, débat, région, bâtiment) heart; (d'arbre) heartwood; **au ~ de** (de région, ville) in the middle of; (de bâtiment, débat, problème, système) at the heart of; **au ~ de l'été** in the height of summer; **au ~ de l'hiver/la nuit** in the dead of winter/night; **ils ont pu pénétrer jusqu'au ~ de la centrale nucléaire** they got to the very heart of the nuclear power station; **4** (personne) **~ simple/pur** unaffected/guileless person; **un ~ fidèle** a faithful friend; **un ~ généreux** a generous spirit; **mon (petit) ~** dear heart, sweetheart; **5** (siège des émotions) heart; **le ~ d'une mère** a mother's heart; **agir selon son ~** to follow one's heart; **écouter son ~** to go by feelings; **avoir le ~ léger** to have a light heart; **avoir le ~ triste** to be sad at heart; **gagner** or **conquérir le ~ de qn** to win sb's heart; **trouver un mari selon son ~** to find the man of one's dreams; **aller droit au ~ de qn** [*attentions, bienveillance, sympathie, spectacle*] to touch sb deeply; [*attaque, remarque*] to cut sb to the quick; **ce tailleur est un coup de ~ de notre magazine** we on the magazine have chosen this suit as our special favourite[GB]; **avoir un coup de ~ pour qch** to fall in love with sth; **faire mal au ~** to be heartbreaking; **ça me fait mal au ~ de voir** it makes me sick at heart to see; **ça me réchauffe le** or **fait chaud au ~ de voir** it's heartwarming to see, it does my heart good to see; **mon ~ se serre** or **j'ai le ~ serré quand**... I feel a pang when...; **fendre** or **briser** or **déchirer le ~ à** or **de qn** to break sb's heart; **avoir le ~ pur** to be guileless; **la noirceur de son ~** the evil within him/her; **problème de ~** emotional problem; ▶**gros**, **net**; **6** (être intime) heart; **ouvrir son ~ à qn** to open one's heart to sb; **venir du ~** to come from the heart; **du fond du ~** from the bottom of one's heart; **je suis de tout ~ avec vous/elle** my heart goes out to you/her; **de tout son ~** with all one's heart; **aimer qn de tout son ~** to love sb dearly; **je t'embrasse de tout mon ~** ≈ with all my love; **parler à ~ ouvert** to speak openly; **7** (siège de la bonté) **avoir du** or **bon** or **grand ~** to be kind-hearted; **avoir un ~ en** or **d'or** to have a heart of gold; **ton bon ~ te perdra** your generosity will be the end of you; **'à votre bon ~ messieurs-dames'** 'can you spare some change?'; **ne pas avoir de ~, être sans ~** to be heartless; **avoir le ~ dur** or **sec** to be hard-hearted; **faire appel au bon ~ de qn** to appeal to sb's better nature; **fermer son ~ à qch** to harden one's heart to sth; **une personne de ~** a kind-hearted person; ▶**fortune**; **8** (courage) courage; **le ~ m'a manqué** my courage failed me; **avoir le ~ de faire qch** to have the courage to do sth; **redonner du ~ à qn** to give sb new heart; **je n'aurai jamais le ~ de me débarrasser du chaton** I'll never have the heart to get rid of the kitten; **tu n'auras pas le ~ de leur dire la vérité** you won't have the heart to tell them the truth; **9** (énergie) heart; **mettre tout son ~ dans qch/à faire** to put one's heart into sth/into doing; **10** (envie) mood; **avoir le ~ à faire** to be in the mood for doing; **je n'ai pas le ~ à plaisanter** I'm not in the mood for jokes; **je n'ai plus le ~ à rien** I don't feel like doing anything any more; ▶**ouvrage**; **11** Jeux (carte) heart; (couleur) hearts (*pl*); **jouer (du) ~** to play hearts; **trois/dame de ~** three/Queen of hearts.

II à cœur *loc adv* **fait** or **moelleux à ~** [*fromage*] fully ripe; **grillé à ~** [*café*] roasted all the way through; **prendre** or **avoir à ~ de faire** to be intent on doing; **prendre qch à ~** (se vexer) to take sth to heart; (être résolu) to take sth seriously; **cela me tient à ~** it's close to my heart.

III de bon cœur *loc adv* willingly; **faire qch de bon ~** to do sth willingly; **il me l'a prêté mais ce n'était pas de bon ~** he lent it to me, but rather unwillingly; **'merci de m'avoir prêté votre voiture'—'c'est de bon ~'** 'thank you for lending me your car'—'you're welcome'; **il brossait le sol et y allait de bon ~** he was scrubbing the floor with a will; **rire de bon ~** to laugh heartily.

IV par cœur *loc adv* by heart; **savoir/apprendre qch par ~** to know/to learn sth by heart; **connaître qn par ~** to know sb inside out.

IDIOMES **tant que mon ~ battra** until my dying day; **rester sur le ~ de qn** [*remarque, attitude*] to rankle with sb; **avoir le ~ au bord de lèvres** to be about to be sick; **avoir du ~ au ventre** to be brave; **être beau** or **joli comme un ~** to be as pretty as a picture; **avoir le ~ sur la main** to be open-handed; **il a un ~ gros** or **grand comme ça**○ he's very big-hearted; **avoir un ~ de pierre** or **marbre** to have a heart of stone; **il ne le porte pas dans son ~** euph he's not his favourite[GB] person euph; **le ~ n'y est pas** my/your etc heart isn't in it; **si le ~ t'en dit** if you feel like it; **avoir qch sur le ~** to be resentful about sth.

cœur-poumon, *pl* **~s** /kœʀpumɔ̃/ *nm* heart-lung machine.

coexistence /koegzistɑ̃s/ *nf* coexistence; **~ pacifique** Pol peaceful coexistence.

coexister /koegziste/ [1] *vi* to coexist.

coffrage /kɔfʀaʒ/ *nm* Constr **1** (moule) formwork GB, form US; **2** (action) formwork preparation; **3** (habillage de conduite) box; **4** (parois de tranchée) shoring.

coffre /kɔfʀ/ *nm* **1** (meuble) chest; **~ à vêtements/à bois** clothes/wood ou log chest; **~ à linge** linen chest; **~ à jouets** toy box; **2** (pour valeurs) gén safe; (individuel dans banque) safety deposit box; **la salle des ~s** the strongroom; **3** Aut boot GB, trunk US; **4** (de piano, d'orgue) case; **un ~ de piano** a piano case; **5**○ (cage thoracique) chest.

■ **~ à bagages** boot GB, trunk US; **~ de sécurité** safe; **les ~s de l'État** the state coffers.

IDIOMES **avoir du ~**○ (avoir du souffle) to be very fit; (avoir une voix puissante) to have a powerful voice.

coffre-fort, *pl* **coffres-forts** /kɔfʀəfɔʀ/ *nm* safe.

coffrer /kɔfʀe/ [1] *vtr* **1**○ (mettre en prison) **~ qn** to put sb inside○; **se faire ~** to be put inside○; **2** Constr to cast [*pilier, dalle*]; to shore [sth] up [*tranchée*].

coffret /kɔfʀɛ/ *nm* **1** (petit coffre) casket; **~ à bijoux** jewellery GB ou jewelry US box; **2** (de disques, cassettes, livres) boxed set; **un ~ de trois disques** a boxed set of three CDs; **3** (de présentation) presentation box.

cofondateur, **-trice** /kofɔ̃datœʀ, tʀis/ *nm,f* co-founder.

cogérance /koʒeʀɑ̃s/ *nf* joint management; **en ~** [*magasin*] under joint management.

cogérant, **~e** /koʒeʀɑ̃, ɑ̃t/ *nm,f* joint manager.

cogérer /koʒeʀe/ [14] *vtr* to co-manage.

cogestion /koʒɛstjɔ̃/ *nf* joint management.

cogitation /kɔʒitasjɔ̃/ *nf* cogitation ₵.

cogiter /kɔʒite/ [1] hum **I**○ *vtr* to dream up [*plan*].

II *vi* to cogitate, to think (**sur** about).

cognac /kɔɲak/ *nm* cognac (*brandy from the Cognac area*).

cognassier /kɔɲasje/ *nm* quince tree.

■ **~ du Japon** japonica.

cogne◑ /kɔɲ/ **I** *nm* (agent) cop○.

II *nf* (bagarre) fight.

cognée /kɔɲe/ *nf* (woodman's) axe GB ou ax US.

IDIOMES **jeter le manche après la ~** to throw in the towel.

cognement /kɔɲəmɑ̃/ *nm* **1** (bruit) knocking sound; **2** Aut knock; **~ de moteur/des soupapes** engine/valve knock.

cogner /kɔɲe/ [1] **I** *vtr* **1** (heurter) (accidentellement) to knock (**contre** against, on); (volontairement) to bang (**contre** against, on); **tu as dû ~ la tasse** you must have given the cup a knock; **~ ses poings contre le mur** to bang on the wall with one's fists; **2**○ (battre) to beat up [*personne*]; **se faire ~** to be ou get beaten up.

II *vi* **1** (frapper) **~ contre** [*volet*] to bang against; [*branche*] to knock against; [*projectile*] to hit; **ma tête/la pierre est allée ~ contre la vitre** my head/the stone hit the window; **~ à la porte/au mur** [*personne*] to knock on the door/on the wall; (violemment) to bang on the door/on the wall; **~ sur** (avec la main, le poing) to bang on; (avec un marteau) to hammer; **2**○ (frapper du poing) [*boxeur, agresseur*] to hit out; **~ dur** or **fort** to hit hard; **ça va ~** there's going to be a brawl; **il ne sait que ~** violence is the only thing he understands; **3**○ (être chaud) [*soleil*] to beat down; **ça cogne sur la plage** it's baking (hot) on the beach; **ça cogne aujourd'hui** it's a scorcher○, it's baking (hot) today; **4** (battre) [*cœur, sang*] to pound; **5** Aut (faire du bruit) [*moteur*] to knock; **6**◑ (sentir mauvais) to stink.

III se cogner *vpr* **1** (se heurter) to bump into something; **se ~ contre** to hit; **se ~ le genou/la tête** to hit ou bump one's knee/head (**contre** on); **se ~ à la tête/au genou** to get a bump on the head/on the knee; **se ~ le pied contre une pierre** to stub one's toe on a stone; ▶**mur**; **2**○ (se battre) to have a punch-up○ GB, to have a fistfight.

cogneur○ /kɔɲœʀ/ *nm* (homme violent) bruiser○.

cogniticien, **-ienne** /kɔgnitisjɛ̃, ɛn/ ▶**510** *nm,f* artificial intelligence ou AI specialist.

cognitif, **-ive** /kɔgnitif, iv/ *adj* cognitive.

cognition /kɔgnisjɔ̃/ *nf* cognition.

cohabitation /koabitasjɔ̃/ *nf* **1** living with somebody, living under the same roof as somebody; **la ~ avec la belle-famille** living with one's in-laws; **2** Pol *situation where the French President is in political opposition to the majority in the National Assembly.*

cohabiter /koabite/ [1] *vi* [*personnes*] to live

together, to live under the same roof; [*choses*] to coexist; **~ avec qn** to live with sb; **le couple ne fait plus que ~** the couple are living together in name only.

cohérence /kɔeʀɑ̃s/ *nf* **1** (de discours, raisonnement) (logique) coherence; (homogénéité) consistency; (de programme, d'attitude) consistency; **manquer de ~** to be inconsistent; **2** (de molécules, d'éléments) cohesion.

cohérent, **~e** /kɔeʀɑ̃, ɑ̃t/ *adj* **1** gén [*raisonnement*] (logique) coherent; (homogène) consistent; [*attitude, programme*] consistent; [*réseau*] integrated; [*gamme de produits*] coordinated; **2** Phys [*lumière*] coherent.

cohéritier, **-ière** /kɔeʀitje, ɛʀ/ *nm,f* joint heir.

cohésif, **-ive** /kɔezif, iv/ *adj* cohesive.

cohésion /kɔezjɔ̃/ *nf* cohesion.

cohorte /kɔɔʀt/ *nf* **1**○ (groupe) band; **2** (en démographie) cohort; **3** Hist Mil cohort.

cohue /kɔy/ *nf* (monde) crowd; (désordre) crush, scramble; **c'est la ~** it's a crush ou scramble.

coi, **coite** /kwa, kwat/ *adj* (silencieux) **rester** or **se tenir ~** to remain quiet; **j'en suis resté ~** it left me speechless.

coiffant, **~e** /kwafɑ̃, ɑ̃t/ *adj* **gel ~** styling gel; **mousse ~e** styling mousse.

coiffe /kwaf/ *nf* **1** (couvre-chef) gén headgear; (de religieuse) wimple; **2** (de chapeau) lining; **3** (de fusée) fairing; **4** (de racine) root cap; **5** (de nouveau-né) caul.

coiffer /kwafe/ [1] **I** *vtr* **1** (arranger les cheveux de) **~ qn** (mettre en forme) to do sb's hair; (peigner) to comb sb's hair; **il coiffe ses cheveux en arrière** he combs his hair back; **il ne coiffe que les hommes** he only does men's hair; **se faire ~ par qn** to have one's hair done by sb; **fais-toi ~ par Georges, il est mieux que Gérard** get George to do your hair, he does it better than Gérard; **elle est bien coiffée** her hair is nicely done; **elle est mal coiffée** her hair is untidy; **tu n'es pas coiffé, tes cheveux ne sont pas coiffés!** you haven't done your hair!; **elle est coiffée court maintenant** she has short hair now; **être coiffée à la Jeanne d'Arc** to have a pageboy hairstyle; **2** (couvrir la tête) to put [sth] on [*chapeau, casque*]; **le chapeau qui la coiffe** the hat she's wearing; **le béret te coiffe bien** a beret suits you; **leurs chapeaux coiffent toujours bien** their hats always look good; **~ qn de qch** to put sth on sb('s head); **ne reste pas coiffé pendant la cérémonie** take your hat off during the ceremony; **coiffé d'une casquette** wearing a cap; **3** (chapeauter) [*entreprise*] to control; [*personne*] to head; **4** (fournir) [*chapelier*] to make hats for; **5** (recouvrir) liter [*neige, mousse*] to cover; **sommets coiffés de brume** mist-capped peaks.

II se coiffer *vpr* **1** (s'arranger les cheveux) to do one's hair; (se peigner) to comb one's hair; **tu t'es coiffé avec un râteau** or **un clou!** you look as if you've been dragged through a hedge backward(s)○!; **les cheveux frisés se coiffent mal** curly hair is difficult to keep tidy; **2** (se couvrir la tête) **se ~ de qch** to put sth on; **il se coiffe toujours d'un chapeau melon** he always wears a bowler hat GB ou a derby hat US.

IDIOMES **être né** or **naître coiffé** to be born with a silver spoon in one's mouth; **~ qn au poteau**○ or **sur le fil** to pip sb at the post GB, to nose sb out.

coiffeur, **-euse** /kwafœʀ, øz/ **▶510** **I** *nm,f* (pour femmes) hairdresser, hairstylist; (pour hommes) hairdresser, barber†; **aller chez le ~** [*femme*] to go to the hairdresser's, to have one's hair done; [*homme*] to have one's hair cut, to go to the barber's.

II coiffeuse *nf* (meuble) dressing table.

coiffure /kwafyʀ/ *nf* **1** (coupe de cheveux) hairstyle; **tu as changé de ~** you've changed your hairstyle; **faites-moi cette ~** do my hair like that; **2** (profession) hairdressing; **apprendre la ~** to learn hairdressing; **3** (élément de costume) headgear ¢.

coin /kwɛ̃/ **I** *nm* **1** (angle) corner; **un ~ de table/serviette** the corner of a table/napkin; **dans un ~** in a corner; **au ~ de la rue** on the corner of the street; **à tous les ~s de rue** everywhere, all over the place; **il y a des policiers/banques à tous les ~s de rue** there's a policeman/bank on every street corner; **un placard/une étagère qui fait le ~** a corner cupboard/shelf; **regarder dans tous les ~s** to look everywhere ou all over the place; **les ~s et les recoins** the nooks and crannies; **aux quatre ~s de la ville/du globe** or **du monde** all over the town/the world; **rester/travailler dans son ~** to stay/to work in one's own little corner; **aller au ~** (punition) to go and stand in the corner; **j'ai dû poser mon sac dans un ~** I must have put my bag down somewhere; **assis au ~ du feu** sitting by the fire; **une causerie au ~ du feu** a fireside chat; **avoir un ~ à soi dans la maison** to have a corner of one's own in the house; **2** (extrémité) (d'œil, de bouche) corner; **s'essuyer le ~ des lèvres** to wipe the corners of one's mouth; **regarder qch/qn du ~ de l'œil** to watch sth/sb out of the corner of one's eye; **un sourire en ~** a half-smile; **un sourire au ~ des lèvres** a smile flickering around one's mouth; **un regard en ~** (sournois) a sidelong glance; (complice) a meaningful look; **3** (morceau) (de terre) plot; (de pelouse) patch; (d'ombre) spot; (de cour) area; **un ~ ensoleillé** a sunny spot; **un ~ de paradis** an idyllic spot; **un ~ de ciel bleu** a patch of blue sky; **un ~ de verdure** a green bit; **dans un ~ de ma mémoire** in my memory; **garder qch dans un ~ de sa mémoire** to remember sth; **4** (lieu d'habitation) part; **un ~ de France/de l'Ardèche** a part of France/of the Ardèche; **dans le ~** (ici) around here, in these parts; (là-bas) around there, in those parts; **il y a beaucoup de vignes dans le ~** there are a lot of vineyards around here; **nous étions dans le même ~** we were in the same area; **le café/boucher du ~** the local café/butcher; **je ne suis pas du ~** I'm not from around here; **de quel ~ est-il?** where does he come from?; **les gens du ~** the locals; **dans un ~ paumé**○ or **perdu** in the middle of the sticks○ ou of nowhere; **dans un ~ perdu de la Lozère** in a remote part of the Lozère; **connaître les bons ~s** to know all the good places to eat; **il connaît les bons ~s pour les champignons** he knows where to find mushrooms; **5** (en papeterie) (pour photos) corner; (pour classeur) reinforcing corner; **6** Tech (pour fendre) wedge.

II coin(-) (*in compounds*) **~-repas/-salon** dining/living area; **~-rangement/-bureau** storage/work area.

IDIOMES **je n'aimerais pas le rencontrer au ~ d'un bois** I wouldn't like to meet him on a dark night ou in a dark alley; **jouer aux quatre ~s** *five players fight it out for four corners.*

coincé, **~e** /kwɛ̃se/ **I** *pp* ▶ **coincer**.

II *pp adj* **1** (incapable de bouger) [*personne, porte, fermeture, tiroir*] stuck; (incapable de sortir) [*personne*] trapped; **la pièce ~e dans la machine** the coin that is stuck in the machine; **rester ~ dans des embouteillages** to be stuck in traffic jams; **~ entre qch et qch** [*meuble, maison*] wedged between sth and sth; **un lit ~ entre une table et le mur** a bed wedged between a table and the wall; **il n'a pas pu se lever, il était ~**○ he couldn't get up, his back had gone○; **2**○ (incapable d'agir) stuck○; **s'il refuse le compromis, nous sommes ~s** if he refuses to compromise, we're stuck; **sans mes outils je suis ~** without my tools I'm stuck; **être ~ entre qch et qch** to be stuck between sth and sth; **il était ~ entre l'opposition et son propre parti** he was caught between the opposition and his own party; **3**○ (mal à l'aise) ill at ease; **4**○ (collet monté) straitlaced, uptight○.

coincement /kwɛ̃smɑ̃/ *nm* jamming.

coincer /kwɛ̃se/ [12] **I** *vtr* **1** (immobiliser) to wedge [*objet*]; (pour maintenir ouvert) to wedge [sth] open [*porte, fenêtre*]; (pour maintenir fermé) to wedge [sth] shut [*porte, fenêtre*]; [*éboulement, neige*] to trap [*personne*]; **il a coincé la porte avec son pied** he put his foot in the door; **ils m'ont coincé contre le mur** they pinned me (up) against the wall; **2** (bloquer) to jam [*objet, clé, fermeture*]; **il y a des papiers qui coincent le tiroir** there are some papers (which are) jamming the drawer; **j'ai coincé ma fermeture** my zip GB ou zipper US is jammed ou caught; **3** (dans une porte, fermeture) to catch [*vêtement, doigt*]; **j'ai coincé mon écharpe dans la fermeture** I've caught my scarf in the zip GB ou zipper US; **4** (insérer) to wedge [*objet*]; **coinçons un des sacs sous le siège** let's wedge one of the bags under the seat; **5**○ (retenir) to catch, to corner [*personne*]; **elle m'a coincé dans le couloir** she caught me in the corridor (**pour faire** to do); **se faire ~ par** to get caught ou cornered by; **6**● (arrêter) [*police*] to pick [sb] up○, to nick○ GB [*criminel*]; **se faire ~** to get oneself ou to be picked up; **7**○ (prendre en défaut) to catch [sb] out [*personne*]; **il m'a coincé sur les coniques** he caught me out on conic sections; **ils n'ont pas réussi à le ~ juridiquement** they failed to catch him out legally.

II *vi* **1** (résister au mouvement) [*fermeture, tiroir*] to stick; **la pellicule coince dans l'appareil** the film is sticking; **2**○ (créer des problèmes) [*relations*] to cause problems; **il y a quelque chose qui coince entre nous** there's something causing problems between us; **le nouveau projet de loi risque de ~ au Parlement** the new bill may cause problems in Parliament; **ça coince** there's a problem.

III se coincer *vpr* **1** (se bloquer) [*objet*] to get stuck ou jammed; **2** (se prendre) **se ~ les doigts** to get one's fingers caught; **se ~ une vertèbre**○ to trap a nerve in one's back; **se ~ un doigt dans une porte** to get a finger caught in a door.

coïncidence /kɔɛ̃sidɑ̃s/ *nf* (tous contextes) coincidence.

coïncident, **~e** /kɔɛ̃sidɑ̃, ɑ̃t/ *adj* coincident.

coïncider /kɔɛ̃side/ [1] *vi* [*figures, dates, événements, idées, dépositions*] to coincide (**avec** with); [*goûts*] to be similar (**avec** with); **faire ~ l'offre et la demande** to make supply and demand match.

coin-coin /kwɛ̃kwɛ̃/ *nm inv* (*also onomat*) quack; **faire ~** to go quack quack; **tu entends ses ~?** can you hear it quacking?

coïnculpé, **~e** /kɔɛ̃kylpe/ *nm,f* (prévenu) coaccused; (au tribunal) codefendant.

coing /kwɛ̃/ *nm* quince.

coït /kɔit/ *nm* coitus; **~ interrompu** coitus interruptus.

coite ▶ **coi**.

coke[1] /kɔk/ *nm* (charbon) coke.

coke[2]○ /kɔk/ *nf* (cocaïne) drug users' slang coke○.

cokéfaction /kɔkefaksjɔ̃/ *nf* coking.

cokéfier /kɔkefje/ [2] *vtr* to coke.

col /kɔl/ *nm* **1** Mode collar; **~ dur/souple** stiff/soft collar; **~ de fourrure/de dentelle** fur/lace collar; **~ de chemise** shirt collar; **chemise sans ~** collarless shirt; **~ rond** round neckline; **~ carré** square neckline; **~ en V** V neckline; ▶ **faux**; **2** Géog pass; **le ~ du Lautaret** the Lautaret pass; **3** (d'objet, de bouteille, vase) neck; **4** Anat (de vessie, fémur) neck; **il s'est cassé le ~ du fémur** he broke his hip(bone); **5**† (cou) neck.

■ **~ blanc** Sociol white-collar worker; **~ bleu** Sociol blue-collar worker; **~ boule** cowl-neck; **~ camionneur** zipped roll neck; **~ cassé** wing collar; **~ châle** shawl collar; **~ cheminée** turtleneck; **pull à ~ cheminée** turtleneck sweater; **~ chemisier** shirt collar; **~ Claudine** Peter Pan collar; **chemisier à ~ Claudine** blouse with a Peter Pan collar; **~ cravate** tie neck; **~ du fémur** Anat neck of the femur; **~ Mao** mandarin collar; **veste à ~ Mao** jacket with a mandarin collar; **~ marin** sailor collar; **~ montant** turtleneck GB, mock turtleneck US; **~ officier** stand-up collar; **veste à ~ officier** jacket with a stand-up collar; **~ polo** polo collar; **~ romain** clerical collar; **~ roulé** roll-neck GB, polo neck GB, turtleneck US; **pull à ~ roulé** polo neck sweater; **~ tailleur** revers collar; **~ de l'utérus** Anat cervix, neck of the womb.

cola /kɔla/ *nm* Bot cola tree; **noix de ~** cola nut.

colback /kɔlbak/ *nm* busby.
IDIOMES **attraper qn par le ~◑** to grab sb by the scruff of the neck.

colchique /kɔlʃik/ *nm* autumn crocus.

col-de-cygne, *pl* **cols-de-cygne** /kɔldəsiɲ/ *nm* **1** Art, Tech (forme) swan neck; **2** (robinet) swan neck tap GB ou faucet US.

colégataire /kolegatɛʀ/ *nmf* joint legatee.

coléoptère /kɔleɔptɛʀ/ *nm* coleopteran spéc, beetle; **les ~s** Coleoptera spéc.

colère /kɔlɛʀ/ *nf* **1** (humeur) anger (**contre qch** at sth; **contre qn** with sb), wrath sout; **~ froide** contained anger; **la ~ divine** or **de Dieu** Divine wrath; **être rouge de ~** to be flushed with anger; **avec ~** in anger; **passer sa ~ sur qn** to take out ou vent one's anger on sb; **sous le coup de la ~** in a fit of anger; **être en ~** to be angry (**contre** with), to be mad○ (**contre** at); **se mettre en ~** to get angry (**contre** with), to get mad○ (**contre** at); **mettre qn en ~** to make sb angry ou mad○; **geste/larmes de ~** angry gesture/tears; **être ~○** to be angry ou mad○; **2** (crise) fit; (caprice) tantrum; **faire** or **piquer○ une ~** (crise) to have a fit; (caprice) to throw a tantrum; **il était dans une ~ noire** he was in a rage; **3** (de la mer) fury, wrath sout; (des cieux) wrath sout; (d'un volcan) fury.
IDIOMES **la ~ est mauvaise conseillère** Prov one should never allow oneself to be influenced by anger.

coléreux, **-euse** /kɔleʀø, øz/ *adj* [*personne*] quick-tempered, irascible; [*tempérament*] irascible.

colibacille /kɔlibasil/ *nm* E coli, Escherichia coli.

colibacillose /kɔlibasiloz/ *nf* Vét colibacillosis; Méd E coli infection.

colibri /kɔlibʀi/ *nm* hummingbird.

colifichet /kɔlifiʃɛ/ *nm* (bijou) trinket; (bibelot) knick-knack.

colimaçon /kɔlimasɔ̃/ *nm* snail.
■ **escalier en ~** spiral staircase.

colin /kɔlɛ̃/ *nm* (merlu) hake; (lieu noir) coley.

colineau, *pl* **~x** = **colinot**.

colin-maillard /kɔlɛ̃majaʀ/ *nm* blind man's buff; **jouer à ~** to play blind man's buff.

colinot /kɔlino/ *nm* (merlu) (small) hake; (lieu noir) (small) coley.

colique /kɔlik/ *nf* **1** (diarrhée) diarrhoea; **avoir la ~** lit to have diarrhoea; fig to have the collywobbles GB ou the willies◑; **2** (douleur abdominale) stomach pain; (chez le bébé) colic ¢; **~s hépatiques/néphrétiques** biliary/renal colic; **être pris de ~s** to have sudden stomach pains; **3◑** (chose, personne ennuyeuse) **quelle ~** what a pain.

colis /kɔli/ *nm* parcel.
■ **~ alimentaire** food parcel; **~ piégé** parcel bomb; **~ postal** parcel sent by mail; **~ postaux** (service) parcel post.

Colisée /kɔlize/ *nprm* **le ~** the Coliseum.

colistier, **-ière** /kolistje, ɛʀ/ *nm,f* fellow candidate GB, running mate US.

colite /kɔlit/ ▶**271** *nf* colitis.

collabo○ /kɔlabo/ *nmf* Hist pej collaborator; **les ~s du pouvoir** those in cahoots with the ruling party.

collaborateur, **-trice** /kɔlabɔʀatœʀ, tʀis/ *nm,f* **1** (collègue) colleague; (assistant) assistant; **les ~s du président** the president's personal staff; **un ~ du ministre** an adviser to the minister; **2** (employé) employee; **3** (journaliste) contributor (**de** to); (coauteur) collaborator; **4** Hist pej collaborator.

collaboration /kɔlabɔʀasjɔ̃/ *nf* **1** (à revue, journal) contribution (**à** to); (à ouvrage, projet) collaboration (**à** on); **en ~ avec** in collaboration with; **2** Hist, Pol collaboration (**avec** with).

collaborationniste /kɔlabɔʀasjɔnist/ *adj* [*journal, discours*] collaborationist.

collaborer /kɔlabɔʀe/ [1] *vi* **1** (participer) **~ à** to contribute to [*journal, revue*]; to collaborate on [*projet, ouvrage*]; **2** (travailler) to collaborate (**avec** with); **~ (à qch) avec qn** to collaborate with sb (on sth), to work with sb (on sth).

collage /kɔlaʒ/ *nm* **1** Art (technique, œuvre) collage; **les ~s de Braque/de Picasso** Braque's/Picasso's collages; **~s photographiques** photo montages; **2** Tech (de papier, d'étoffe) sizing (**de** of); Imprim gluing (**de** of); **brocher un livre par ~** to bind a book by gluing it; **3** (affichage) **le ~ des affiches** billposting GB, putting up posters; **~ sauvage** flyposting; **4** Vin fining (**de** of).

collagène /kɔlaʒɛn/ *nm* collagen.

collant, **~e** /kɔlɑ̃, ɑ̃t/ **I** *adj* **1** (adhésif) [*substance*] sticky; **2** (gluant) [*main, terre, riz, bonbon*] sticky; Sport, Turf [*terrain*] heavy; **3** (moulant) [*robe, pantalon*] skintight, tight-fitting; **4○** (importun) [*personne*] clinging; [*vendeur*] persistant; **qu'est-ce qu'ils sont ~s ces mecs○!** these guys○ just won't leave you alone!
II *nm* tights (*pl*) GB, panty hose (+*v pl*) US; **~ sans pieds** footless tights GB, leggings (*pl*) US; **~ opaque/en mousse** opaque/micromesh tights GB ou panty hose US; **~ à gousset** gusseted tights GB ou panty hose US; **~ de danse** dance tights.

collapsus /kɔlapsys/ *nm* collapse; **~ cardiovasculaire** circulatory collapse; **~ pulmonaire** collapse of the lung.

collatéral, **~e**, *mpl* **-aux** /kɔlateʀal, o/ **I** *adj* **1** Anat [*nerf*] collateral; **2** Jur [*succession, ligne*] collateral; **3** (de côté) [*nef, rue*] side (*épith*).
II collatéraux *nmpl* Jur (famille) collaterals.

collation /kɔlasjɔ̃/ *nf* **1** (repas) light meal; **prendre une ~** to have a light meal; **2** (de manuscrits) collation; (d'épreuves) checking; **3** (de grade) conferment.

collationnement /kɔlasjɔnmɑ̃/ *nm* (de manuscrit, télégramme) collation; (d'épreuves) checking.

collationner /kɔlasjɔne/ [1] *vtr* **1** (comparer) to collate [*textes, manuscrits*] (**avec** with); **2** (vérifier) gén to check [*épreuves, liste*]; (en reliure) to collate.

colle /kɔl/ *nf* **1** (adhésif) gén glue; (pour papier peint) (wallpaper) paste; **mettre de la ~ sur qch** to put glue on sth; **enduisez le papier peint de ~** coat the wallpaper with paste; **~ forte/à bois** strong/wood glue; **2○** (question difficile) poser○; **poser une ~○ à qn** to set sb a poser○; **alors là, tu me poses une ~○!** that's a real poser○!; **3** (retenue) students' slang detention; **Larue, deux heures de ~!** Larue, two hours' detention for you!; **4○** Univ students' slang oral test.
■ **~ blanche** paste.
IDIOMES **vivre à la ~○** to live with sb; **ils vivent à la ~** they live together.

collecte /kɔlɛkt/ *nf* **1** (de fonds, vêtements) collection; **faire une ~** to raise funds (**pour** for); **2** (prière) collect.

collecter /kɔlɛkte/ [1] *vtr* to collect.

collecteur, **-trice** /kɔlɛktœʀ, tʀis/ **I** *adj* **centre ~** collection point; **organisme ~** collecting agency; **égout ~** main sewer.
II *nm,f* (personne) collector.
III *nm* **1** (égout) main sewer; **2** Aut manifold; **3** Électron collector.
■ **~ de fonds** fundraiser; **~ d'impôts** tax collector; **~ solaire** solar panel.

collectif, **-ive** /kɔlɛktif, iv/ **I** *adj* **1** gén [*travail, responsabilités*] collective; [*démissions, licenciements*] mass (*épith*); [*chauffage*] shared; [*billet, assurance*] group (*épith*); **immeuble ~** block of flats GB, apartment building US; **entreprendre une action collective** to act collectively; **donner une punition collective à toute la classe** to punish the whole class; **l'équipe pratique un bon jeu ~** the team plays well together; ▶**convention**, **ferme**; **2** Ling collective.
II *nm* **1** (groupe de personnes) collective; (groupe de pression) action group; **~ d'usagers des trains** train users' action group; **2** Ling collective noun.
■ **~ budgétaire** supplementary finance bill.

collection /kɔlɛksjɔ̃/ *nf* **1** (de timbres, photos) collection (**de** of); (d'échantillons) line; **~ de timbres/tableaux** stamp/art collection; **c'est un timbre/badge de ~** it's a stamp/badge for collectors; **j'ai acheté deux timbres de ~ pour mon frère** I bought two stamps for my brother's collection; **faire ~ de qch** to collect sth; ▶**pièce**; **2○** (groupe) collection; **quelle ~ d'idiots!** what a bunch of idiots!; **3** (ouvrages) (du même genre) series (+ *v sg*); (du même auteur) set; **~ historique** historical series; **toute la ~ de Tintin** the whole set of Tintin books; **4** Cout, Mode collection.

collectionner /kɔlɛksjɔne/ [1] *vtr* **1** lit to collect [*timbres, papillons*]; **2** fig **~ les erreurs/les gaffes** to make one mistake/blunder after another; **~ les maris** to go through○ one husband after another.

collectionneur, **-euse** /kɔlɛksjɔnœʀ, øz/ *nm,f* collector; **~ de tableaux/timbres** art/stamp collector.

collectivement /kɔlɛktivmɑ̃/ *adv* [*gérer, négocier*] collectively; [*démissionner*] en masse, as a body.

collectivisation /kɔlɛktivizasjɔ̃/ *nf* collectivization.

collectiviser /kɔlɛktivize/ [1] *vtr* to collectivize.

collectivisme /kɔlɛktivism/ *nm* collectivism.

collectiviste /kɔlɛktivist/ *adj, nmf* collectivist.

collectivité /kɔlɛktivite/ *nf* **1** (groupe) group; **~ professionnelle** professional body; **2** (ensemble des citoyens) community; **esprit de ~** community spirit; **la ~ nationale** the nation.
■ **~ locale** local authority GB, local government US; **~ territoriale** *region with a measure of autonomy*; **~s publiques** state, regional and local authorities GB, federal, state and local government US.

collège /kɔlɛʒ/ *nm* **1** (école) **~ (d'enseignement secondaire)**, **CES** secondary school GB, junior high school US (*up to age 16*); **2** (assemblée) college; **~ électoral** Pol electoral college.
■ **~ d'enseignement technique**, **CET** *technical secondary school in France*.

collégial, **~e**, *mpl* **-iaux** /kɔleʒjal, o/ **I** *adj* [*église*] collegiate; [*assemblée, pouvoir, système*] collegial.
II collégiale *nf* collegiate church.

collégialement /kɔleʒjalmɑ̃/ *adv* collectively.

collégialité /kɔleʒjalite/ *nf* **1** Pol corporatism; Entr corporate governance, management with collective responsibility; **2** Relig collegiality; **3** Jur *system whereby a number, always uneven, of judges sit in the same court.*

collégien, **-ienne** /kɔleʒjɛ̃, ɛn/ *nm,f* schoolboy/schoolgirl.

IDIOMES **se faire avoir comme un ~** to be completely taken in.

collègue /kɔlɛg/ *nmf* colleague; (dans lettre) **Monsieur et cher ~** Dear Sir.

coller /kɔle/ [1] **I** *vtr* **1** (faire adhérer) to stick, to glue [*bois, papier, carton*]; to paste up [*affiche*]; to hang [*papier peint, tissu mural*]; to stick [sth] on [*étiquette, timbre, rustine®*]; to stick down [*enveloppe*]; to stick [sth] together [*feuilles, morceaux*]; Cin to splice [*film, bande magnétique*]; **repliez la feuille et collez les bords** fold the sheet and glue the edges together; **~ un timbre sur une enveloppe/un colis** to stick a stamp on an envelope/a parcel; **~ des affiches** to stick ou post bills; **~ une photo sur une page** to stick a photograph onto a page; **il avait les cheveux collés par la peinture** his hair was matted with paint; **un ruban thermocollant pour ~ les bords** an iron-on adhesive strip for taking up hems; **ta colle ne colle pas bien le carton** your glue isn't very good for sticking card; **2** (appuyer) **~ qch contre** or **à qch** to press sth against sth; **~ son front/nez contre la vitre** to press one's forehead/nose against the window; **elle a collé son genou contre le mien** she pressed her knee against mine; **il avait un pistolet collé à la tempe** there was a pistol pressed to his head; **il la colla contre le parapet** he pushed her up against the parapet; **3**○ (mettre) to stick○; **je leur ai collé l'article/la facture sous le nez** I stuck○ the article/the bill (right) under their noses; **je lui ai collé le bébé dans les bras** I stuck○ the baby in his/her arms; **à 15 ans, on m'a collé sur une fraiseuse** at 15, they stuck○ me on a milling machine; **ils m'ont collé président de l'association** they made me chairman of the association; **tu vas te faire ~ une amende** you'll get landed○ with a fine; **il lui a collé trois gosses** he got her pregnant three times; **si tu continues, je te colle une gifle** or **je vais t'en ~ une** if you keep on, I'm going to slap you; **on lui colle une étiquette de chanteur engagé** he's being labelled[GB] as a political singer; **4**○ (dans un examen, un jeu) **je me suis fait ~ en physique** I failed ou flunked○ physics; **'comment s'appelle le premier ministre actuel?'—'alors là tu me colles!'** 'what's the present prime minister's name?' —'you've stumped○ ou got me there!'; **5**○ (donner une retenue à) to give [sb] detention [*élève*]; **se faire ~** to have ou get detention; **6** Vin to fine [*vin, liqueur*].

II *vi* **1** (adhérer) [*colle, timbre, enveloppe*] to stick; [*pâtes, riz, semoule*] to stick together; [*boue, substance*] to stick; **ta colle colle bien/ne colle pas bien** your glue sticks well/doesn't stick very well; **~ à la casserole** to stick to the pan; **~ aux chaussures/mains** to stick to one's shoes/hands; **~ aux dents** to stick to one's teeth; **~ à un véhicule** fig to drive close behind a vehicle; **le coureur collait à la roue de son adversaire** fig the runner stuck close to his opponent; **dans une dissertation, collez toujours au sujet** fig in an essay, always stick to the subject; **mon tee-shirt mouillé me collait à la peau/au corps** my wet T-shirt was clinging to my skin/body; **ta réputation/ton passé te colle à la peau** fig your reputation/your past never leaves you; **2**○ (être cohérent) **~ à** to be consistent ou fit with; **ça colle à** or **avec l'idée qu'on se fait d'elle** that's consistent with her image; **leur analyse ne colle pas à la réalité** their analysis doesn't fit with the facts; **leurs témoignages ne collent pas** their evidence doesn't tally; **tout colle!** it's all falling into place!; **3** (en jouant) to be it.

III se coller *vpr* **1** (s'appuyer) **se ~ à** or **contre qn/qch** to press oneself against sb/sth; **j'ai dû me coller au mur pour les laisser passer** I had to press myself against the wall to let them pass; **les voyageurs étaient collés les uns contre les autres** the passengers were pressed against each other; **ils se sont collés au sol** they lay flat on the ground; **l'alpiniste se collait à la paroi** the climber clung to the rockface; **2**○ (pour une activité) **dès qu'il rentre, il se colle devant la télé/son ordinateur** as soon as he comes in he's glued○ to the TV/his computer; **je m'y suis collé à 2 heures et je n'ai pas encore terminé** I got down to it at 2 o'clock and I still haven't finished; **c'est toi qui t'y colles** (à une tâche) it's your turn (to do it).

collerette /kɔlʀɛt/ *nf* **1** Mode ruffle; (fraise) ruff; **2** Culin (pour gigot) frill; **3** Tech (de tube) flange; **4** Bot (de champignon) ring, annulus spéc.

collet /kɔlɛ/ *nm* **1** (piège) snare; **2** Culin (en boucherie) neck; **3**† Mode (col) collar; (fichu) shoulder cape; **prendre** or **saisir qn par le ~** to grab sb by the collar; **4** Bot collar; **5** (de dent) neck; **6** Tech flange.

IDIOMES **être ~ monté** to be prim; **mettre la main au ~ de qn** [*police*] to collar○ sb.

colleter○: **se colleter** /kɔlte/ [20] *vpr* **se ~ avec** to have a fight with [*personne*]; to grapple with [*difficultés*].

colleur, **-euse** /kɔlœʀ, øz/ ▶ **510** **I** *nm,f* **~ (d'affiches)** billposter, billsticker.

II colleuse *nf* Cin splicer.

colley /kɔlɛ/ *nm* collie.

collier /kɔlje/ *nm* **1** (bijou) necklace; (chaîne de chevalier) chain; **~ de perles** string of pearls; **~ de fleurs** garland of flowers; **2** (d'animal) (marque naturelle, lanière) collar; **3** (barbe) **~ (de barbe)** beard (*round jaw*); **4** (en boucherie) neck; **5** Tech (de tuyau) pipe-collar.

■ **~ de serrage** circlip.

IDIOMES **reprendre le ~** to get back into harness; **donner un coup de ~** (intellectuellement) to get one's head down; (manuellement) to put one's back into it.

collimateur /kɔlimatœʀ/ *nm* Tech collimator.

■ **~ de tir** or **de visée** Mil sight; **~s de pilotage** Aviat head-up display.

IDIOMES **avoir qn dans le ~**○ to have it in for sb○; **être dans le ~**○ **de qn** to be in sb's bad books.

colline /kɔlin/ *nf* hill; **au pied de la ~** at the bottom of the hill.

collision /kɔlizjɔ̃/ *nf* **1** (choc) collision; **~ frontale** head-on collision; **entrer en ~ avec** to collide with; **~ en chaîne** pileup; **2** (affrontement) clash, conflict.

collocation /kɔlɔkasjɔ̃/ *nf* **1** Ling collocation; **2** Jur *scheduling of creditors* (*in statement of affairs*).

collodion /kɔlɔdjɔ̃/ *nm* collodion.

colloïdal, **~e**, *mpl* **-aux** /kɔlɔidal, o/ *adj* [*état*] colloidal.

colloïde /kɔlɔid/ *nm* colloid.

colloque /kɔl(l)ɔk/ *nm* conference, symposium (**sur** on).

collusion /kɔlyzjɔ̃/ *nf* collusion (**avec** with).

collutoire /kɔlytwaʀ/ *nm* Pharm throat preparation.

collyre /kɔliʀ/ *nm* eye drops (*pl*).

colmatage /kɔlmataʒ/ *nm* (de fuite) sealing.

colmater /kɔlmate/ [1] *vtr* **1** (boucher) to plug, to seal off [*fuite*]; to seal [*fente*]; **2** fig (réparer) **~ les brèches** to fill in the gaps; Mil **~ une brèche** to seal a gap.

colocataire /kɔlɔkatɛʀ/ *nmf* cotenant.

Colomb /kɔlɔ̃/ *npr* **Christophe ~** Christopher Columbus.

colombage /kɔlɔ̃baʒ/ *nm* half-timbering; **ferme à ~s** half-timbered farmhouse.

colombe /kɔlɔ̃b/ *nf* **1** (oiseau) dove; **2** (partisan de la paix) dove; **3** (terme d'affection) **ma ~** my little love; ▶ **crapaud**.

Colombie /kɔlɔ̃bi/ ▶ **321** *nprf* Colombia.

Colombie-Britannique /kɔlɔ̃bibʀitanik/ ▶ **692** *nprf* British Columbia.

colombien, **-ienne** /kɔlɔ̃bjɛ̃, ɛn/ ▶ **537** *adj* Colombian.

Colombien, **-ienne** /kɔlɔ̃bjɛ̃, ɛn/ ▶ **537** *nm,f* Colombian.

colombier /kɔlɔ̃bje/ *nm* dovecote.

colombin /kɔlɔ̃bɛ̃/ *nm* **1** (en poterie) coil; **2**◑ (étron) turd◑.

colombophile /kɔlɔ̃bɔfil/ **I** *adj* **club ~** pigeon fanciers'club.

II *nmf* pigeon fancier.

colombophilie /kɔlɔ̃bɔfili/ *nf* pigeon fancying.

colon /kɔlɔ̃/ *nm* **1** (de terres inhabitées) colonist; **2** (de colonie de vacances) child (*at children's holiday camp*); **3**○ (colonel) soldiers' slang colonel.

côlon /kolɔ̃/ *nm* colon.

colonel /kɔlɔnɛl/ ▶ **390** *nm* Mil (dans l'armée de terre) ≈ colonel; (dans l'armée de l'air) ≈ group captain GB, ≈ colonel US.

colonelle /kɔlɔnɛl/ *nf* colonel's wife.

colonial, **~e**, *mpl* **-iaux** /kɔlɔnjal, o/ **I** *adj* colonial.

II *nm,f* (habitant) colonial.

III *nm* Hist (soldat) soldier (*in French colonial army*).

IV coloniale○ *nf* Hist (armée) **la ~e** the French colonial army.

colonialisme /kɔlɔnjalism/ *nm* colonialism.

colonialiste /kɔlɔnjalist/ *adj, nmf* colonialist.

colonie /kɔlɔni/ *nf* **1** Pol, Écon colony; **les ~s** the colonies; **2** (groupe) (d'artistes) colony; (ethnique) community; **3** Zool, Biol colony.

■ **~ pénitentiaire**† reformatory†; **~ de vacances** holiday camp (*for children*) GB, summer camp US.

colonisateur, **-trice** /kɔlɔnizatœʀ, tʀis/ **I** *adj* colonizing.

II *nm,f* colonizer.

colonisation /kɔlɔnizasjɔ̃/ *nf* Pol, Écon colonization.

coloniser /kɔlɔnize/ [1] *vtr* Pol, Écon [*colons*] to colonize; péj to take [sth] over.

colonnade /kɔlɔnad/ *nf* colonnade.

colonne /kɔlɔn/ *nf* gén column; (de lit) (bed)post; Archit column, pillar; **défiler en ~ par cinq** to march in fives; **sur cinq ~s à la une** Presse splashed across the front page; **~ d'air** air stream; ▶ **cinquième**.

■ **~ blindée** Mil armoured[GB] column; **~ de direction** Aut steering column; **~ humide** Constr wet standpipe; **~ montante** Constr riser; **~ Morris** theatre[GB] publicity display (*in the form of a cylinder*); **~ de production** Tech tubing; **~ sèche** Constr dry standpipe; **~ de secours** Mil rescue party; **~ vertébrale** Anat spinal column, vertebral column spéc; **les Colonnes d'Hercule** Géog the Pillars of Hercules.

colonnette /kɔlɔnɛt/ *nf* small column.

colopathie /kɔlɔpati/ *nf* colonopathy.

colophane /kɔlɔfan/ *nf* rosin.

coloquinte /kɔlɔkɛ̃t/ *nf* **1** Bot colocynth; **2**○ (tête) nut○, head.

Colorado /kɔlɔʀadɔ/ ▶ **692** *nprm* Colorado.

colorant, **~e** /kɔlɔʀɑ̃, ɑ̃t/ **I** *adj* colouring[GB].

II *nm* gén colouring[GB] agent; (en teinture) dye; Chimie stain; Culin colouring[GB]; (pour cheveux) colourant[GB].

coloration /kɔlɔʀasjɔ̃/ *nf* **1** (action) colouring[GB]; (de textiles) dyeing; (de bois, cellule) staining; (de cheveux) tinting; (permanente) dyeing; **2** (couleur) colour[GB]; (de peau) colouring[GB]; (nuance) shade; **3** (ton de voix) coloration; **4** fig (aspect) complexion; **~ politique** political bent.

colorature /kɔlɔʀatyʀ/ *nf* coloratura.

coloré, **~e** /kɔlɔʀe/ **I** *pp* ▶ **colorer**.

II *pp adj* **1** (teinte) [*objet*] coloured[GB]; [*teint*] (par l'air vif) ruddy; (par l'alcool) florid; **très**

~ [*tissu, jupe*] brightly coloured[GB]; **2** (pittoresque) [*vie, foule*] colourful[GB]; [*style*] lively.

colorer /kɔlɔʀe/ [1] **I** *vtr* **1** (teinter) to colour[GB] [*liquide, aliment, verre*]; to tint [*photo, cheveux*]; to stain [*bois, cellule*]; (teindre) to dye [*textiles, cheveux*]; **~ qch en vert** to colour[GB] sth green; **2** (empreindre) [*nostalgie, regret*] to tinge; **coloré de nostalgie** tinged with nostalgia; **3** (embellir) to embellish [*récit*] (**de** with).
II se colorer *vpr* **1** lit [*visage*] to flush; [*fruit*] to take colour[GB]; **se ~ de vert/rose** liter [*pétale, ciel*] to become flushed with green/pink; **2** fig **se ~ de nostalgie/racisme** to become tinged with nostalgia/racism.

coloriage /kɔlɔʀjaʒ/ *nm* (action) colouring[GB]; (dessin colorié) coloured[GB] picture; (dessin à colorier) picture for colouring[GB] in.

colorier /kɔlɔʀje/ [2] *vtr* to colour in GB, to color US [*dessin*]; **~ qch en rouge** to colour[GB] sth red.

coloris /kɔlɔʀi/ *nm inv* **1** colour[GB]; (nuance) shade; **'existe en 5 ~'** 'available in 5 colours[GB] ou colour[GB] ways'; **2** Art **l'éclat du ~** the brilliance of the colours[GB]; **le ~ du Titien** Titian's use of colour[GB].

coloriser /kɔlɔrize/ [1] *vtr* to colorize.

coloriste /kɔlɔʀist/ *nmf* **1** (d'estampes) colourer[GB]; (peintre) colourist[GB]; **2** (coiffeur) colourist[GB].

coloscopie /kɔlɔskɔpi/ *nf* colonoscopy.

colossal, **~e**, *mpl* **-aux** /kɔlɔsal, o/ *adj* [*bâtiment, force*] colossal, huge; [*fortune, héritage*] enormous.

colosse /kɔlɔs/ *nm* giant.
■ **le ~ de Rhodes** the Colossus of Rhodes.
IDIOMES **un ~ aux pieds d'argile** an idol with feet of clay.

colostrum /kɔlɔstʀɔm/ *nm* colostrum.

colportage /kɔlpɔʀtaʒ/ *nm* hawking.

colporter /kɔlpɔʀte/ [1] *vtr* **1** (répandre) pej to spread, to peddle [*ragots*]; to spread [*fausses nouvelles*]; **2** (vendre) to hawk [*marchandises*].

colporteur, **-euse** /kɔlpɔʀtœʀ, øz/ *nm,f* (marchand) peddler.
■ **colporteuse de ragots** gossip.

colt /kɔlt/ *nm* (pistolet) gun, Colt®.

coltiner○ /kɔltine/ [1] **I** *vtr* to lug○ [*objet lourd*].
II se coltiner *vpr* **1** (porter) to lug○ [*objet lourd*]; **2** (devoir se charger de) to get lumbered with GB, to get stuck with○ [*corvée, personne*].

columbarium /kɔlɔ̃baʀjɔm/ *nm* columbarium.

Columbia /kɔlɔ̃bja/ **▶692** *npr* **district de ~** District of Columbia, DC.

col-vert, *pl* **cols-verts**, **colvert** /kɔlvɛʀ/ *nm* mallard (*inv*).

colza /kɔlza/ *nm* rape; **huile de ~** rapeseed oil.

coma /kɔma/ *nm* coma; **~ éthylique/diabétique** ethylic/diabetic coma; **~ dépassé** irreversible coma; **être dans le ~** to be in a coma.

comateux, **-euse** /kɔmatø, øz/ **I** *adj* [*état*] comatose.
II *nm,f* coma patient.

combat /kɔ̃ba/ *nm* **1** Mil fighting ¢; **violents ~s** fierce fighting; **~s sporadiques** sporadic fighting; **les ~s ont repris** the fighting has broken out again; **cessation des ~s** end to the fighting; **~s aériens/terrestres** air/land battles; **livrer ~** to join battle (**à** with; **contre** against); **envoyer au ~** to send into combat; **mettre hors de combat** to disable; **partir au ~** to set off for battle; **2** Pol struggle (**contre** against; **pour** for); **~ pour l'indépendance** struggle for independence; **~ d'idées/politique** ideological/political struggle; **mener le ~** to lead the struggle; **littérature/presse de ~** militant literature/press; **livrer un ~** to campaign (**contre** against; **pour** for); **3** Sport bout; **~ de boxe/catch** boxing/wrestling bout; (**mettre**) **hors de ~** (to put) out of action.
■ **~ de coqs** cock fight; **~ de gladiateurs** gladiatorial combat; **~ rapproché** close combat; **~ de rue** street fighting; **~ singulier** single combat.

combatif, **-ive** /kɔ̃batif, iv/ *adj* (déterminé) assertive; (agressif) aggressive; [*boxeur, armée*] full of fighting spirit.

combativité /kɔ̃bativite/ *nf* fighting spirit.

combattant, **~e** /kɔ̃batɑ̃, ɑ̃t/ **I** *adj* **1** (combatif) [*ardeur, esprit*] fighting; **2** (de combat) [*troupe, unité*] combat; **non ~** noncombatant; **France ~e** France at arms.
II *nm,f* **1** Mil combatant; **2** Pol fighter; **~ de rue** street fighter.

combattre /kɔ̃batʀ/ [61] **I** *vtr* **1** Mil, Pol to fight [*adversaire, ennemi*]; **2** Cosmét, Pharm to counteract GB, to fight [*déshydratation, vieillissement, stress*].
II *vi* to fight (**contre** against; **pour** for); **~ aux côtés de qn** to fight side by side with sb; **~ contre la délinquance informatique** to fight computer crime.
III se combattre *vpr* to fight.

combe /kɔ̃b/ *nf* coomb.

combien¹ /kɔ̃bjɛ̃/ **I** *adv* **1** **▶477**, **620**, **662**, **793** (dans une interrogation) **~ coûte une bouteille de vin?** how much ou what does a bottle of wine cost?; **~ vaut le livre?** how much ou what is the book worth?; **~ mesure le salon?** how big is the lounge?; **ça fait ~?** (valeur) how much does that come to?; (dimensions) how big is that?; (poids) how heavy is that?; **j'aimerais savoir ~ il a payé son costume** I'd like to know how much ou what he paid for his suit; **~ êtes-vous/sont-ils?** how many of you/them are there?; **à ~ s'évaluent leurs pertes?** how much ou what do their losses come to?; **~ pèse ta valise?** how much ou what does your case weigh?; **2** (adverbe de degré modifiant un verbe) **il est triste de voir ~ la situation s'est dégradée** it's sad to see how the situation has deteriorated; **elle souligne ~ cette approche peut être efficace** she stresses how effective this approach can be; **vous voyez ~ les choses ont changé** you can see how (much) things have changed; **il est difficile d'expliquer ~ je les apprécie** it's difficult to explain how much I appreciate them; **3** (adverbe de degré modifiant un adjectif) **c'est cher mais ~ efficace!** it's expensive but so effective!; **'il est malin!'—'ô ~!'** 'he's smart!'—'isn't he just!'; **le ~ célèbre chanteur** the very famous singer; **un travail intéressant mais ô ~ difficile** an interesting but very difficult job; **montrer ~ étaient dérisoires les efforts des sauveteurs** to show how useless the rescuers' efforts were; **il souligne ~ est précieuse l'aide de ses collègues** he stresses how valuable his colleagues' help is to him; **4** (adverbe de degré modifiant un adverbe) **il a gagné ô ~ brillamment** he won really ou absolutely brilliantly; **~ peu d'idées** how few ideas; **~ peu d'or** how little gold; **~ plus d'argent/plus de personnes** how much more money/many more people; **~ moins d'argent/moins de personnes** how much less money/many fewer people.
II combien de *dét inter* **1** (avec un nom dénombrable) how many; **~ d'élèves accueillerez-vous en janvier?** how many pupils will you receive in January?; **~ de candidatures avez-vous reçu?** how many applications did you receive?; **sais-tu ~ de voitures circulent dans Paris?** do you know how many cars there are in Paris?; **c'est à ~ de kilomètres?** how far away is it?; **~ de kilomètres y a-t-il entre les deux villes?** how far apart are the two towns?; **~ y a-t-il d'ici à la mer?** how far is it to the sea?; **~ de fois** (nombre de fois) how many times; (fréquence) how often; **dans ~ d'années envisages-tu d'avoir des enfants?** in how many years time do you intend to start a family?; **sais-tu ~ de jours il faut pour y aller?** do you know how many days it takes to get there?; **2** (avec un nom non dénombrable) how much; **de ~ de pain as-tu besoin?** how much bread do you need?; **~ de pain reste-t-il?** how much bread is left?; **~ de temps faut-il?** how long does it take?; **tu es là depuis ~ de temps?** how long have you been here?; **on arrive dans ~ de temps?** when will we get there?; **~ de temps as-tu mis pour venir?** how long did it take you to get here?; **dis-moi ~ de temps il faut le faire cuire** tell me how long it takes to cook.

combien² /kɔ̃bjɛ̃/ **▶793** *nmf inv* **1** (par rapport à un ordre) **tu es la ~?** (dans une queue) how many people are before you?; **tu es le ~ à l'école?** where are you in the class?; **vous êtes arrivés les ~ au rallye?** where did you come in the rally?; **'la sixième en partant de la gauche'—'la ~?'** 'the sixth from the left'—'the which?'; **2** (par rapport à une date) **le ~ sommes-nous?, on est le ~○?** what's the date today?; **vous arrivez le ~?** what date are you arriving?; **3** (par rapport à une mesure) **tu chausses du ~?** what size shoes do you take?; **4** (par rapport à la fréquence) **tu le vois tous les ~?** how often do you see him?

combientième○ /kɔ̃bjɛ̃tjɛm/ *adj* **c'est ton ~ accident?** how many accidents have you had?; **vous êtes arrivés les ~s au rallye?** where did you come in the rally?

combinaison /kɔ̃binɛzɔ̃/ *nf* **1** (agencement) (action) combining; (résultat) combination; **2** Chimie, Math combination; **3** (de serrure, coffre-fort) combination; **4** Mode (de femme) (sous-vêtement) (full-length) slip; (tenue sport) jumpsuit; (d'ouvrier) overalls (*pl*) GB, coveralls (*pl*) US.
■ **~ d'astronaute** space suit; **~ d'aviateur** flying suit; **~ ministérielle** Pol all-party cabinet; **~ de plongée** wetsuit; **~ de protection** protective clothing ¢; **~ de ski** ski-suit.

combinard○, **~e** /kɔ̃binaʀ, aʀd/ pej **I** *adj* **il est ~** (débrouillard) he's a fixer○ ou wheeler-dealer○; (magouilleur) he's a schemer.
II *nm,f* (débrouillard) fixer○, wheeler-dealer○; (magouilleur) schemer.

combinat /kɔ̃bina/ *nm* complex.

combinatoire /kɔ̃binatwaʀ/ *adj* Math combinatorial; Ling combinatory.

combine○ /kɔ̃bin/ *nf* **1** (moyen, truc) trick○, wheeze○ GB; (tricherie) fiddle○; (intrigue) (shady) scheme, scam○, hustle○; **j'ai une (bonne) ~** (truc) I know a good wheeze○ GB; **être de** ou **marcher dans la ~** to be in on it; **il n'y a que la ~ qui marche** you have to wangle○ things; **2** Mode (full-length) slip.

combiné /kɔ̃bine/ *nm* **1** Télécom handset, receiver; **~ de bureau** desktop telephone; **2** Mode (sous-vêtement) pantie-corselette; **3** (au ski) combined; **4** Aviat compound helicopter airliner; **5** Tech **~ toaster-gril** combined toaster and grill GB, toaster oven US; **~ robot-mixer** food processor and liquidizer.

combiné(-gaine)-culotte, *pl* **combinés(-gaines)-culottes** /kɔ̃binegɛnkylɔt/ *nm* pantie-corselette.

combiné-gaine, *pl* **combinés-gaines** /kɔ̃binegɛn/ *nm* corselette.

combiner /kɔ̃bine/ [1] **I** *vtr* **1** (réunir) to combine (**à, avec** with); **l'ambition et le talent combinés** a combination of ambition and talent; **2** (calculer) to work out [*horaire, plan*]; to plan [*action, stratégie*]; **~ de faire** to plan to do.
II se combiner *vpr* **1** (se mélanger) [*éléments*] to combine (**à, avec** with); **2** (s'harmoniser) [*couleurs, saveurs*] to go together; **3**○ (s'arranger) [*plan, affaire*] to work out; **si ça se combine bien au bureau** if things work out in the office.

comble /kɔ̃bl/ **I** *adj* [*salle*] packed; **faire**

salle ~ (pour une conférence) to have a capacity audience; (à un spectacle) to play to packed houses; **la mesure est ~, je démissionne!** that's the last straw, I resign!

II *nm* **1** (point extrême) **le ~ de l'injustice/du mauvais goût** the height of injustice/of bad taste; **c'est le ~ de l'horreur/du ridicule** it's absolutely horrific/ridiculous; **il était au ~ de la colère/joie** he was absolutely furious/delighted; **être à son ~** [*émotion, tension, suspense*] to be at its height; **porter qch à son ~** to take sth to its extreme; **être au ~ du désespoir** to be in the depths of despair; **c'est le ~ du paradoxe** it's a complete paradox; **pour ~ de malheur** or **malchance j'ai raté mon avion!** to crown it all ou as if that wasn't enough, I missed my plane!; **et, ~ du raffinement, les draps étaient en soie!** and, as the ultimate in refinement, there were silk sheets!; **c'est un** or **le ~**○**!** that's the limit!; **2** Archit roof space; **faux ~, ~ perdu** Archit lost roof space, unused roof space; **~ aménageable** usable roof space; **de fond en ~** [*fouiller, nettoyer*] from top to bottom; [*changer, détruire*] completely.

III **combles** *nmpl* gén attic (*sg*); Archit eaves.

combler /kɔ̃ble/ [1] *vtr* **1** (remplir) to fill (in) [*fossé, tranchée*]; **2** (pallier) to fill in [*lacunes*]; to make up [*déficit*]; to make up for [*manque, perte*]; **~ le vide que sa mort a laissé** to fill the gap left by his/her death; **~ son retard** to make up (for) lost time; **le pays a comblé son retard technologique** the country has caught up in the field of technology; **3** (satisfaire) to fulfil[GB], to satisfy [*besoin, désir*]; **la vie m'a comblé** I've had a wonderful life; **~ qn** to fill sb with joy ou delight; **~ qn de cadeaux/d'honneurs** to lavish presents/honours[GB] on sb; **merci beaucoup, je suis comblé!** thank you very much, I don't know what to say!; **c'est une femme comblée** she has everything she could possibly want ou wish for; **je suis un professeur comblé** I'm a very lucky teacher.

comburant /kɔ̃byʀɑ̃/ *nm* combustive.

combustibilité /kɔ̃bystibilite/ *nf* combustibility.

combustible /kɔ̃bystibl/ I *adj* combustible.

II *nm* fuel; **~ nucléaire** nuclear fuel.

combustion /kɔ̃bystjɔ̃/ *nf* Chimie combustion; **~ lente/vive** slow/fast combustion; **~ nucléaire** nuclear combustion; **~ organique** cellular combustion.

comédie /kɔmedi/ *nf* **1** Littérat, Théât comedy; **~ de caractère/mœurs** comedy of character/manners; **2** (attitude feinte) play-acting; **c'est de la ~** it's just an act; **jouer la ~** to put on an act; **3**○ (caprice) scene; **faire une ~** to make a scene; **arrête tes ~s** enough of your nonsense; **4**○ (histoire) palaver○; **quelle ~ pour avoir un visa** what a palaver to get a visa; **c'est toute une ~** it's a real palaver.

■ **~ de boulevard** light comedy; **~ dramatique/policière** comedy drama/thriller; **~ d'intrigue** or **de situation** situation comedy; **~ musicale** musical.

IDIOMES **la ~ a assez duré!** that's enough messing around!

Comédie-Française /kɔmedifʀɑ̃sɛz/ *nf* **la ~** the Comédie-Française.

comédien, -ienne /kɔmedjɛ̃, ɛn/ I *adj* **il est (un peu) ~** (simulateur) he puts it on; (hypocrite) he's a sham.

II *nm,f* **1** ▶ 510 (acteur) actor/actress; (acteur comique) comic actor/actress; **2** fig **c'est un ~** (simulateur) he puts it on; (hypocrite) he's a sham.

comédon /kɔmedɔ̃/ *nm* blackhead, comedo spéc.

comestible /kɔmɛstibl/ I *adj* [*aliment, champignon*] edible.

II **comestibles** *nmpl* food ¢; **marchand de ~s** grocer.

comète /kɔmɛt/ *nf* comet.

IDIOMES **tirer des plans sur la ~** to make ambitious plans.

comice /kɔmis/ I *nf* (poire) Comice pear.

II **comices** *nmpl* Agric **~s agricoles** ≈ country fair.

comique /kɔmik/ I *adj* **1** Théât [*genre, personnage*] comic; **2** (amusant) funny; **ça n'a rien de ~** there is nothing funny about it.

II *nmf* (acteur) comic actor/actress; (humoriste) comedian.

III *nm* **1** (pitre) clown; **2** (genre) comedy; **3** (drôlerie) **le ~ de la situation** the funny side of the situation; **le ~, c'est que...** the funny thing is that...; **c'est d'un ~!** it's so funny!; **c'est du plus haut ~** it's absolutely hilarious.

■ **~ de situation** comedy of situation; **~ troupier** coarse humour[GB]

comité /kɔmite/ *nm* **1** Admin committee; **~ exécutif/d'organisation** executive/steering committee; **~ directeur** executive ou management committee; **réunion du ~** committee meeting; **se réunir en ~** to hold a committee meeting; **faire partie d'un ~** to sit on a committee; **2** (groupe) group; **~ restreint** small group; **un dîner en petit ~** an intimate little dinner; **nous sommes en petit ~** there aren't many of us.

■ **~ d'accueil** welcoming committee; **~ central** Pol Central Committee; **~ d'entreprise, CE** works council GB; **~ des fêtes** events committee; **~ de gestion** management committee; **~ de lecture** selection panel.

commandant /kɔmɑ̃dɑ̃/ ▶ 390 *nm* (dans armée de terre) ≈ major; (dans armée de l'air) ≈ squadron leader GB, ≈ major US; **oui mon ~** (à un homme) yes sir; **oui ~** (à une femme) yes ma'am.

■ **~ de bord** Aviat, Naut captain; **~ d'école militaire** ≈ commandant; **~ en chef** Mil ≈ commander-in-chief; **~ en chef des forces armées en Europe** commander-in-chief of the armed forces in Europe; **~ en second** Mil ≈ second-in-command; **~ militaire** Mil ≈ military governor; **~ supérieur** Mil superior commander.

commandante /kɔmɑ̃dɑ̃t/ *nf* major's wife.

commande /kɔmɑ̃d/ *nf* **1** Comm order; **faire** or **passer une ~ (à qn)** to place an order (with sb); **prendre/honorer/différer une ~** to take/honour[GB]/postpone an order; **payable à la ~** cash with order; **fabriquer/travailler sur ~** to make/to work to order; **être en ~** to be on order; **passer ~ de qch (à qn)** to order sth (from sb), to place an order for sth (with sb); **un enthousiasme de ~** fig forced enthusiasm; **2** Littérat, Art commission; **une ~ publique** a state commission; **je ne travaille que sur ~** I only work to GB ou on US commission; **passer ~ de qch à qn** to commission sb to do sth; **écrire un roman sur ~ de son éditeur** to be commissioned by one's publisher to write a novel; **3** Tech control; **tableau/levier/salle de ~** control panel/lever/room; **à ~ automatique** automatically-operated; **à ~ à distance** remote control; **à double ~** dual-control; **être aux** or **tenir les ~s** lit to be at the controls; fig to be in control; **se mettre aux** or **prendre les ~s de qch** lit to take the controls of sth; fig to take control of sth; **passer les ~s à qn** lit to hand over (the controls) to sb; fig to hand over (control) to sb; **4** Ordinat command.

■ **~ d'affichage** display command; **~ de flux** flow control; **~ de processus** process control; **~ numérique** digital control; **à ~ numérique** digitally operated.

commandement /kɔmɑ̃dmɑ̃/ *nm* **1** Mil (direction) command; **sous le ~ de** under the command of; **avoir le ~ de, être au ~ de** to be in command of [*armée, opération, avion, bateau*]; to be in control of [*course, championnat*]; **prendre le ~ de** to take command of [*troupes, avion*]; to take control of [*championnat*]; **2** Mil (ordre) order, command; **à mon ~, feu!** at ou on my command, fire!; **3** (autorités militaires) command; **le ~ local/régional** local/regional command; **le haut ~** high command; **le ~ intégré de l'OTAN** the integrated military command structure of NATO; **le ~ suprême des forces alliées en Europe** supreme headquarters of the Allied powers in Europe; **4** Relig commandment; **les dix ~s** the Ten Commandments; **5** Jur summons (*sg*) ou order to pay.

commander /kɔmɑ̃de/ [1] I *vtr* **1** (demander livraison de) to order [*article, produit*]; **~ qch à qn** to order sth from sb, to place an order with sb for sth; **~ des pièces à un fournisseur** to order parts from a supplier; **~ qch pour qn** to order sth for sb; **je t'ai commandé une veste** I've ordered a jacket for you; **2** (demander l'exécution de) to commission [*livre, sculpture, tableau, étude, sondage*]; **le rapport a été commandé par** the report was commissioned by; **3** (dans un restaurant, café) to order [*boisson, plat*]; **~ une soupe en entrée** to order a soup as a starter; **êtes-vous prêts à ~?** are you ready to order?; **~ qch pour qn** to order sth for sb; **tu me commanderas une pizza** order a pizza for me; **4** Mil (être à la direction de) to command, to be in command of [*armée, troupe, division*]; (faire exécuter) to order [*manœuvre, attaque, repli*]; (contrôler l'accès de) to command [*fort*]; **5** (exercer une autorité sur) **~ qn** to order sb about; **il aime ~ tout le monde** he loves ordering everyone about; **sans te ~, tu peux fermer la porte?** could I ask you to close the door?; **6** (exiger) to command; **sa conduite commande le respect/l'admiration** his/her behaviour[GB] commands respect/admiration; **les circonstances commandent la prudence** the circumstances call for caution; **7** (actionner) [*dispositif, ordinateur*] to control [*mécanisme, manœuvre, levier*]; **la manette commande l'arrêt du moteur** the lever stops the engine.

II **commander à** *vtr ind* **1** (avoir autorité sur) **~ à** to be in command of; **2** (ordonner) **~ à** to order, to command.

III *vi* [*personne, chef*] to give the orders, to be in command; **c'est moi/lui qui commande!** I'm/he's in charge!

IV **se commander** *vpr* **1** (demander livraison de) [*personne*] to order oneself [*article, produit*]; **je me suis commandé un chapeau** I've ordered myself a hat; **2** (être contrôlable) **la passion/l'amitié, ça ne se commande pas** passion/friendship doesn't come to order; **ces choses ne se commandent pas** you can't force these things.

commandeur /kɔmɑ̃dœʀ/ *nm* Hist commander.

commanditaire /kɔmɑ̃ditɛʀ/ *nmf* **1** Jur limited partner; **2** (bailleur de fonds) sleeping partner GB, silent partner US; **3** (sponsor) backer, sponsor; **4** (d'un crime) **le ~ d'un assassinat** the person behind an assassination.

commandite /kɔmɑ̃dit/ *nf* Jur, Fin **société en ~ simple** limited ou special partnership; **société en ~ par actions** partnership limited by shares.

commandité, ~e /kɔmɑ̃dite/ *nm,f* active partner.

commanditer /kɔmɑ̃dite/ [1] *vtr* **1** Jur, Fin to support, to finance [*société*]; **2** (parrainer) to sponsor [*artiste, exposition, projet*]; **3** (organiser) to be behind [*crime, détournement*].

commando /kɔmɑ̃do/ *nm* (groupe) commando unit; **un ~ de huit hommes** an eight-man commando unit; **une opération ~** a commando raid; **deux membres du ~ ont été arrêtés** two members of the commando unit were arrested.

comme /kɔm/ I *adv* how; **~ tu es malin!** how clever you are!; **~ il a raison!** how right he is!; **~ j'aime lire!** how I love reading!; **~ tu as grandi, je ne t'ai pas reconnu** how you've grown, I didn't recognize you.

II *conj* **1** (de même que) **ici ~ en Italie** (exclusivement) here as in Italy; (inclusivement) both here and in Italy; **ils sont bêtes, lui ~ elle** they are both as stupid as each other, he's as stupid as she is; **en France et en Angleterre, ~ dans les autres pays d'Europe** in France and in England as (well as) in the other European countries; **contente-toi de dire ~ moi** just say the same thing as me; **il est paresseux, ~ sa sœur d'ailleurs** he's lazy, just like his sister; **il mange ~ eux** he eats the same things as they do; **elle est sage-femme ~ sa mère et sa grand-mère** she's a midwife, like her mother and grandmother (before her); **fais ~ moi** do as I do; **nous avons fêté Noël chez nous, ~ tous les ans** we spent Christmas at home, as we do every year; **été ~ hiver** all year round, summer and winter alike; **~ toujours** as always; **j'y étais allé ~ chaque matin** I'd gone there as I did every morning; **jolie/légère ~ tout** ever so pretty/light GB, really pretty/light; **2** (dans une comparaison) **il est grand ~ sa sœur** he's as tall as his sister; **les cheveux du bébé sont lisses ~ de la soie** the baby's hair is as smooth as silk; **c'est tout ~**° it comes to the same thing; **rouge ~ une pivoine** as red as a beetroot GB ou beet US; **je leur ai parlé tout ~ je te parle** I spoke to them just like° I'm speaking to you now; **c'est quelqu'un de ~ ça**°**!** he's/she's great!; **il est bête/courageux ~ pas un** he's as stupid/brave as they come; **il boit/travaille ~ pas un** he drinks/works like anything; **~ tu y vas!** that's going a bit far!; **elle me traite ~ un enfant** she treats me like a child, she treats me as if I were a child; **3** (dans une équivalence) **c'est ~ une brioche avec des raisins à l'intérieur** it's like a brioche with currants in it; **un chapeau ~ celui-là** a hat like that one; **je voudrais un manteau ~ le tien** I'd like a coat like yours; **~ pour faire** as if to do; **et ~ pour bien marquer leur refus, ils sont sortis de la salle** and as if to make a point of their refusal, they left the room; **elle a fait un geste ~ pour se protéger** she made a movement as if to protect herself; **4** (dans une illustration, une explication) **des pays industrialisés ~ les États-Unis et le Japon** industrialized countries such as ou like the United States and Japan; **qu'est-ce que vous avez ~ couleurs?** what colours[GB] do you have?; **qu'est-ce qu'il y a ~ vaisselle?** what is there in the way of crockery?; **~ ça** like that; **alors ~ ça tu vas travailler à l'étranger?** so you're going to work abroad then?; **puisque c'est ~ ça** if that's the way it is, if that's how it is; **on va faire ~ si** we're going to pretend that; **il a fait ~ s'il ne me voyait pas** he pretended (that) he hadn't seen me; **c'est ~ si** it's as if; **~ s'il dormait** as if ou as though he was sleeping; **~ si je n'avais que ça à faire!** as if I had nothing better to do!; **~ si j'avais besoin de ça!** that's the last thing I needed!; **'je ne trouve pas ça joli'—'fais ~ si'** 'I don't think it's pretty'—'just pretend you do'; **elle m'a dit, ~ si de rien n'était, que...** she told me, just like that, that...; **se comporter ~ si de rien n'était** to act as if nothing were wrong; **5**° (dans une approximation) **elle a eu ~ un évanouissement** she sort of fainted, she had a kind of fainting fit; **elle semblait ~ gênée** she seemed somewhat embarrassed; **6** (indiquant l'intensité) **avare ~ il est, il ne te donnera rien** he's so mean, he won't give you anything; **maigre ~ elle est** she's so thin; **7** (indiquant une fonction) as; **travailler ~ jardinier** to work as a gardener; **il a été recruté ~ traducteur** he was taken on as a translator; **la phrase est donnée ~ exemple** the sentence is given as an example; **que veux-tu ~ cadeau?** what would you like for ou as a present?; **8** (puisque) as, since; **~ elle était seule** as ou since she was alone; **comme il l'aime, il lui pardonnera** as ou since he loves him/her, he'll forgive him/her; **9** (au moment où) as; **juste ~** just as; **~ il traversait la rue** as he was crossing the road; **elle arrivait ~ je partais** she was coming in as I was going out.

IDIOMES **~ quoi!** which just shows!; **~ ci ~ ça**° so-so°.

commémoratif, -ive /kɔmemɔʀatif, iv/ *adj* [*plaque, timbre*] commemorative; [*cérémonie*] memorial; **la cérémonie ~ du 18 juin** the ceremony to commemorate the 18th of June; **journée commémorative** (de victoire, libération) anniversary; (de morts) day of remembrance.

commémoration /kɔmemɔʀasjɔ̃/ *nf* **1** (action) remembrance; (cérémonie) commemoration; **en ~ d'une bataille** to commemorate a battle; **2** Relig commemoration.

commémorer /kɔmemɔʀe/ [1] *vtr* to commemorate [*victoire, événement*]; to remember [*mort*].

commencement /kɔmɑ̃smɑ̃/ **I** *nm* **1** (phase initiale) beginning; (point de départ) start; **au ~** at the beginning; **dès le ~** from the beginning ou start; **le ~ de la fin** the beginning of the end; **du ~ à la fin** from start to finish, from beginning to end; **commencez par le ~** start ou begin at the beginning; **il y a un ~ à tout** you've got to start somewhere; hum there's a first time for everything; **je n'en suis qu'au ~** I've only just started; **2** (premier signe) **un ~ de solution/mur** the beginnings (*pl*) of a solution/wall.

II commencements *nmpl* **1** (premiers moments) beginnings (*pl*); **~s pénibles** difficult beginnings; **2** (rudiments) rudimentary notions.

■ **~ d'exécution** Jur attempt; **~ de preuve par écrit** Jur prima facie evidence ¢.

commencer /kɔmɑ̃se/ [12] **I** *vtr* **1** (entreprendre) to start, to begin [*travail, séance, discours*]; to open [*bouteille, boîte*]; **c'est lui qui a commencé!** (la dispute, bagarre) he started it!; **il a commencé sa carrière dans la marine** he began his career in the Navy; **elle a commencé le piano à six ans** she started playing the piano when she was six; **'eh bien,' commença-t-elle** 'well,' she began; **~ qch par le haut/commencement** to start ou begin sth at the top/beginning; **tu commences bien l'année/la journée!** that's a good start to the year/the day!; **la phrase qui commence l'article** the sentence at the beginning of the article; **le film est commencé depuis un moment** the film has already started; **2 ~ à** or **de faire** (se mettre à) to start ou begin to do, to start ou begin doing; (entamer un processus) to begin to do; **je commence à travailler à l'usine le 3 mai** I start (work) at the factory on 3 May; **je commence à comprendre/me demander** I'm beginning to understand/wonder; **je commence à en avoir marre**° I'm getting fed up°; **il commence à se faire tard** it's getting late; **ça commence à bien faire**° or **à suffire!** it's getting a bit much!

II *vi* [*année, film, rue*] to start, to begin; [*évolution, processus*] to begin; **ça commence à 8 heures** it starts ou begins at 8 o'clock; **que la fête commence!** let the party begin!; **et, pour ~, une chanson** and, to start with, a song; **pour ~, c'est trop cher** for a start , it' s too expensive; **qu'attends-tu pour ~?** what are you waiting for?; **commencez sans moi** start without me; **ne commence pas!** don't start!; **on commence dans dix minutes** we're starting in ten minutes; **~ par** [*soirée, mot, numéro*] to start with; **commence par le plafond/les manches** start with the ceiling/the sleeves; **par où** or **quoi vais-je ~?** where shall I start?; **~ par qn** to start with sb; **par qui vais-je ~?** who shall I start with?; **~ par faire** to start ou begin by doing; **commence par obéir/te taire!** for a start you can do as you're told/be quiet!; **~ par être** or **comme secrétaire** to start (off) as a secretary; **vous êtes tous coupables à ~ par toi** you're all guilty starting with you; ▶ **bête, charité**.

III *v impers* **il commence à pleuvoir/neiger** it's starting ou beginning to rain/snow.

commensal, ~e, *mpl* **-aux** /kɔmɑ̃sal, o/ **I** *adj* Biol, Zool commensal.

II *nm,f* **1** Biol, Zool commensal; **2** (*pl*) liter table companion.

commensalisme /kɔmɑ̃salism/ *nm* Biol, Zool commensalism.

commensurable /kɔmɑ̃syʀabl/ *adj* commensurable.

comment[1] /kɔmɑ̃/ *adv* **1** (de quelle manière) **~ le sais-tu?** how do you know (that)?; **~ ça s'écrit?** how do you spell it?; **~ allez-vous?** how are you?; **~ veux-tu que je me débrouille?** how do you expect me to manage?; **~ faire?** how can it be done?; **montre-moi ~** show me how; **~ t'y prendras-tu?** how will you go about it? ; **il faut voir ~ il nous a parlé/nous a traités!** you should have seen the way he spoke to us/treated us!; **~ s'étonner qu'il ait échoué?** it's hardly surprising that he failed!; ▶ **importer II**; **2** (pour faire répéter) **~, peux-tu répéter?** sorry, could you say that again?; **Paul ~?** Paul who?; **3** (évaluation) **~ est leur maison/fils?** what's their house/son like?; **~ trouvez-vous ma robe/son mari?** what do you think of my dress/her husband?, how do you like my dress/her husband?; **4** (indignation, surprise)

---

comment[1]

Lorsqu'il signifie 'de quelle manière', *comment* se traduit généralement par *how*:

comment vas-tu au travail? = how do you get to work?
comment as-tu fait pour arriver avant moi? = how did you manage to get here before me?
je ne comprends pas comment tu as pu te perdre = I don't understand how you managed to get lost
dis-moi comment elle a réagi = tell me how she reacted
comment résoudre le problème? = how can this problem be solved?
as-tu compris comment faire? = do you understand how to do it?
il ne sait même pas comment faire cuire un œuf au plat = he doesn't even know how to fry an egg

Attention: certains verbes comme *appeler, nommer* etc. ont une construction différente en anglais:
comment appelles-tu cet objet? = what do you call this object?
On se reportera au verbe.

Lorsqu'il peut être remplacé par 'pourquoi', *comment* se traduit par *why*:
comment ne m'a-t-on pas averti? = why wasn't I told?

Lorsqu'il sert à exprimer l'indignation ou la surprise, *comment* se traduit par *what*:
comment? il est marié? = what? he's married?

Lorsqu'il sert à faire répéter une information, *comment* se traduit par *pardon*:
comment? qu'est-ce que tu dis? = pardon? what did you say?

On trouvera exemples supplémentaires et exceptions ci-dessous.

~ cela? what do you mean?; **~ se fait-il qu'il soit parti?** how is it that ou how come○ he's gone?; **~ se peut-il que...?** how can it be that...?; **~ ça se fait** ○**?** how come○?, how is that?; **~? tu voudrais des excuses?** what? you expect me to apologize?; **~ donc!** but of course!; **et ~**○**!** most certainly!, and how○!; **'tu l'as éjecté**○**?'—'et ~!'** 'you threw him out?'—'I certainly did!' ou 'did I ever○!' ou 'I sure did○' US; **'c'était bon?'—'et ~**○**!'** 'was it nice?'—'it certainly was!' ou 'was it ever○!' ou 'it sure was○' US.

comment[2] /kɔmɑ̃/ *nm* **le ~** the how.

commentaire /kɔmmɑ̃tɛʀ/ *nm* **1** (remarque) comment (**sur** about); **~ enthousiaste/hostile/pessimiste** enthusiastic/hostile/pessimistic comment; **se passer de ~s** to need no comment; **se refuser au moindre ~** to refuse to comment; **s'abstenir de tout ~** to refrain from any comment; **sans (aucun) ~** without any comment; **sans ~!** no comment!; **épargnez-nous vos ~s** spare us your comments; **je vous dispense de vos ~s** I don't need any of your comments; **un scandale qui provoque bien des ~s** a scandal that gives rise to a lot of gossip; **2** Radio, TV commentary (**de** on); **~ en direct** live commentary; **3** Littérat commentary (**de, sur** on).
■ **~ composé** commentary; **~ critique** Littérat critical commentary; **~ de texte** commentary; **faire un ~ de texte** to do ou write a commentary.

commentateur, -trice /kɔmmɑ̃tatœʀ, tʀis/ ▶510 *nm,f* commentator; **~ sportif/politique/de la radio** sports/political/radio commentator.

commenter /kɔmmɑ̃te/ [1] *vtr* **1** (dire son opinion sur) to comment on [*décision, déclaration, événement*]; **commenté par** commented on by; **commenta-t-il** he commented; **2** (donner des explications) to give a commentary on [*film, visite*]; **commenté par** with a commentary by; **3** Radio, TV (décrire) to commentate on [*match, événement*]; **commenté par** commentated on by; **4** Littérat, Scol to comment on [*texte*]; **5** Jur, Relig to interpret [*loi, texte sacré*].

commérage /kɔmeʀaʒ/ *nm* gossip ¢.

commerçant, ~e /kɔmɛʀsɑ̃, ɑ̃t/ **I** *adj* **rue ~e** shopping street; **quartier ~** shopping area; **nation très ~e** great trading nation; **il n'est pas très ~** he's not interested in pleasing the customer.
II ▶510 *nm,f* shopkeeper, storekeeper US; **petit ~** small shopkeeper ou storekeeper US; **grand** or **gros ~** large retailer; **les ~s ferment en août** the shops ou stores US close in August.

commerce /kɔmɛʀs/ *nm* **1** (magasin) shop, store US; **dans le ~** in the shops ou stores US; **tenir un ~** to run a shop GB ou store US; **édition hors ~** privately printed book; **2** (entreprise commerciale) business; **dix mille mètres carrés de ~s** ten thousand square metres[GB] of business space; **3** (activité) trade; **~ mondial** world trade; **~ des armes/de l'art/du tabac** arms/art/tobacco trade; **le ~ ne marche pas très bien en ce moment** trade ou business is slow at the moment; **faire le ~ de** to trade in; **faire ~ de** to sell; **faire du ~** to be in business; ▶**petit**; **4** (fréquentation) liter company; **~ des hommes** company of others; **être d'un ~ agréable/désagréable** to be good/poor company.
■ **~ de détail** retail trade; **~ d'échange** barter; **~ extérieur** foreign trade; **~ de gros** wholesale trade; **~ international** international trade; **~ triangulaire** Hist triangular trade.

commercer /kɔmɛʀse/ [12] *vi* to trade (**avec** with).

commercial, ~e, *mpl* **-iaux** /kɔmɛʀsjal, o/ **I** *adj* **1** Comm commercial; **entreprise/musique/réussite ~e** commercial company/music/success; **carrière ~e** career in sales and marketing; **sourire ~** plastic smile; **2** Écon trade; **accord/embargo/différend ~** trade agreement/embargo/disagreement.
II *nm,f* sales and marketing person; **les commerciaux** sales and marketing people.

commercialement /kɔmɛʀsjalmɑ̃/ *adv* commercially; **~ exploitable** commercially viable.

commercialisable /kɔmɛʀsjalizabl/ *adj* marketable.

commercialisation /kɔmɛʀsjalizasjɔ̃/ *nf* marketing; **~ du riz/de technologies** marketing of rice/of technology.

commercialiser /kɔmɛʀsjalize/ [1] *vtr* to market.

commère /kɔmɛʀ/ *nf* pej gossip; **c'est une vraie ~!** he/she is a real gossip!

commérer /kɔmeʀe/ [14] *vi* to gossip.

commettant /kɔmetɑ̃/ *nm* principal.

commettre /kɔmɛtʀ/ [60] **I** *vtr* **1** (faire) to make [*erreur, gaffe*]; to commit [*délit, crime, péché*]; to carry out [*attentat, agression, massacre*]; **~ une lâcheté/infamie** to do something cowardly/disreputable; **~ une imprudence** to be careless; **le régime a commis des excès** the regime is guilty of excesses; **2** (créer) hum to perpetrate, to be the perpetrator of [*œuvre*]; **3** (préposer) to appoint; **~ qn à un emploi** to appoint sb to a post; **~ un avocat à la défense de qn** to appoint a lawyer to defend sb; **expert commis** appointed expert.
II se commettre *vpr* fml **se ~ avec des indésirables** to consort ou associate with undesirable characters.

comminatoire /kɔminatwaʀ/ *adj* **1** gén menacing, comminatory sout; **2** Jur with a stated penalty for noncompliance.

commis /kɔmi/ ▶510 *nm* (employé) (de ferme) hand; (de bureau) clerk; (de commerce) shop assistant GB, salesclerk US; ▶**grand**.
■ **~ d'agent de change** stockbroker's assistant; **~ greffier** ≈ Registrar's assistant; **~ voyageur** travelling[GB] salesman.

commisération /kɔmizeʀasjɔ̃/ *nf* commiseration.

commissaire /kɔmisɛʀ/ ▶510 *nm* **1** (dans la police) **~ (de police)** ≈ police superintendent; **~ adjoint** ≈ deputy police superintendent; **2** (membre d'une commission) commissioner; **~ à la concurrence/l'environnement, ~ chargé de la concurrence/l'environnement** Competition/Environment Commissioner; **3** (surveillant, organisateur) steward.
■ **~ de l'air** Mil ≈ command supply officer; **~ de bord** Naut purser; **~ aux comptes** auditor; **~ divisionnaire** Chief Superintendent; **~ européen** European Commissioner; **~ européen à la concurrence** European Competition Commissioner; **~ du gouvernement** Admin, Pol government Commissioner; **~ de la marine** chief administrator (*in the Navy*); **~ parlementaire** Parliamentary Commissioner; **~ de la République** prefect.

commissaire-priseur, *pl* **commissaires-priseurs** /kɔmisɛʀpʀizœʀ/ ▶510 *nm* auctioneer.

commissariat /kɔmisaʀja/ *nm* **1** (local) **~ (de police)** police station; **2** (commission) commission; **3** (fonction) **~ de bord** pursership; **~ aux comptes** auditorship.
■ **~ général du plan** ≈ (government's) economic advisory committee; **Commissariat à l'énergie atomique, CEA** *French Atomic Energy Authority*.

commission /kɔmisjɔ̃/ **I** *nf* **1** (groupe de travail) committee; **2** Comm, Fin commission; **elle prend une ~ de 5%** she takes a 5% commission; **être payé à la ~** to be payed on a commission basis; **3** (mission) **faire une ~ pour qn** to do ou run an errand for sb; **4** (message) **faire la ~ à qn** to give sb the message, to pass the message on to sb; **il pourrait faire ses ~s tout seul!** he could do ou run his own errands!
II commissions○ *nfpl* shopping ¢; **faire les ~s** to do one's ou the shopping; **il est parti en ~s** he is out shopping.
■ **~ ad hoc** ad hoc committee; **~ d'arbitrage** arbitration committee; **~ de contrôle** board of enquiry GB ou inquiry US; **~ des Communautés européennes** Commission of the European Communities, EC Commission; **~ des comptes** Fin accounts commission; **~ d'enquête** gén investigating committee, board of enquiry GB ou inquiry US; Pol select committee; **~ d'examen** board of examiners; **~ des Lois** Law commission; **~ paritaire** joint consultative committee; **~ parlementaire** parliamentary committee; **~ permanente** standing committee; **~ rogatoire** rogatory commission; **~ temporaire** temporary committee.
IDIOMES **faire la petite ~**○ baby talk to do number one○; **faire la grosse ~** baby talk to do number two○.

commissionnaire /kɔmisjɔnɛʀ/ ▶510 *nm* **1** Jur, Comm agent, broker; **2** (coursier) messenger; **~ (d'hôtel)** doorman.
■ **~ en douane** customs agent; **~ de transport** forwarding agent.

commissionner /kɔmisjɔne/ [1] *vtr* to commission, to appoint; **~ qn pour faire** to commission ou appoint sb to do.

commissure /kɔmisyʀ/ *nf* corner, comissure spéc; **à la ~ de ses lèvres** at the corner of his/her mouth.

commode /kɔmɔd/ **I** *adj* **1** (pratique) [*instrument, outil*] handy; [*système, télécommande, prétexte, lieu*] convenient; **un four microonde c'est bien ~** microwave ovens are really convenient; **c'est un endroit ~ pour se rencontrer** it's a convenient place to meet; **2** (aisé) easy; **trouver à se loger ce n'est pas ~** it's not easy to find accommodation; **ce serait trop ~** it would be too easy; **3 ne pas être (très) ~** (être strict) to be strict; (être difficile) to be difficult (to deal with).
II *nf* (meuble) chest of drawers.

commodément /kɔmɔdemɑ̃/ *adv* [*situé*] conveniently; [*installé*] comfortably; [*se déplacer*] easily.

commodité /kɔmɔdite/ **I** *nf* (avantage) convenience; **par ~** for (the sake of) convenience; **c'est d'une grande ~** it is very convenient; **pour plus de ~** for greater convenience.
II commodités *fpl* **1** (de quartier) (local) services, facilities; (dans une maison) mod cons○, modern conveniences; **2** (facilités offertes) services; **3**† (toilettes) toilets.

commotion /kɔmosjɔ̃/ *nf* **1** Méd (ébranlement) concussion; **~ cérébrale** concussion (*of the brain*); **2** fig (émotion) shock.

commotionner /kɔmosjɔne/ [1] *vtr* **1** lit to concuss; **2** fig to shake.

commuable /kɔmɥabl/ *adj* [*peine*] commutable (**en** to); **non ~** non-commutable.

commuer /kɔmɥe/ [1] *vtr* to commute [*peine*] (**en** to).

commun, ~e /kɔmœ̃, yn/ **I** *adj* **1** (venant de plusieurs personnes) [*travail, œuvre*] collaborative; [*désir, volonté, accord, préoccupation, conception*] common; [*candidat, politique, projet, revendication, stratégie*] joint (*épith*); **d'un ~ accord** by mutual agreement; **2** (appartenant à plusieurs) [*cour, pièce, équipement, fonds, souvenirs, expérience*] shared; [*ami*] mutual; [*ancêtre, langue, passé, dénominateur, facteur*] common; [*biens*] joint (*épith*); **nous avons des amis ~s** we have mutual friends, we have friends in common; **pour le bien ~** for the common good; **dans l'intérêt ~** in the common interest; **la cuisine est ~e aux locataires** the kitchen is shared by the tenants; **époux ~s en biens** Jur *couple who have become joint owners of property* *through marriage*; **après dix ans de vie ~e** after living together for ten years; **3** (semblable) [*caractéristiques, intérêts, traits*] common (**à** to); [*ambition, objectifs*] shared; **une politique ~e aux deux partis** a policy common to both parties; **n'avoir plus rien de ~ avec qch/qn** no longer to have anything in common with sth/sb; **les événements d'hier sont sans ~e mesure avec les précédents** yesterday's events are on an altogether different scale from previous ones; **4** (courant) [*attitude, opinion, faute, maladie, espèce*] common; **il est ~ de faire** it's common to do; **ce n'est pas un prénom très ~** that's a rather unusual name; **elle est d'une beauté peu ~e** she's uncommonly beautiful; **5** (ordinaire) pej [*goût, personne*] common péj; [*visage*] plain; **c'est/il est d'un ~!** it's/he's so common!

II *nm* ordinary; **sortir du ~** to be out of the ordinary; **les gens du ~** ordinary people; **le ~ des mortels** ordinary ou common mortals (*pl*); **le ~ des auditeurs/lecteurs** the ordinary listener/reader; **tomber dans le ~** to become commonplace ou run-of-the-mill; **hors du ~** exceptional.

III en commun *loc adv* [*écrire, travailler, produire*] jointly, together; **prendre ses repas en ~** to eat together; **avoir qch en ~** to have sth in common (**avec qn** with sb); **mettre ses moyens** or **ressources en ~** to pool one's resources; **nous mettons tout en ~** we share everything.

IV communs *nmpl* outbuildings (*pl*).

V commune *nf* **1** Admin (village) village; (ville) town, district; **dans la ~e de Melay** in the village of Melay; **2** Hist **la Commune (de Paris)** the (Paris) Commune.

VI communes *nfpl* Pol **les Communes**, **la Chambre des communes** the (House of) Commons.

■ **~e rurale** Admin rural district; **~e urbaine** Admin urban district.

communal, **~e**, *mpl* **-aux** /kɔmynal, o/ **I** *adj* Admin [*budget, gestion, ressources*] local council GB, local government US; [*bâtiment*] local council GB, community US; [*cimetière, fête*] village; **un employé ~** a council worker GB, a town maintenance worker US; **un lotissement ~** a council estate GB, a government-subsidized housing development US; **chemin ~** ≈ public track; **terrain ~** common land.

II communale *nf* state primary school.

communard, **~e** /kɔmynaʀ, aʀd/ **I** *adj* Hist [*mouvement*] Communard.

II *nm,f* **1** Hist Communard; **2** (communiste) pej commie○ péj, communist.

communautaire /kɔmynotɛʀ/ *adj* **1** Pol, CEE [*budget, droit*] Community; [*population*] of the Community (*après n*); **2** (d'une collectivité) **la vie ~** life in a community; **les règles ~s** the rules of a community; **des affrontements ~s** communal violence (*sg*).

communauté /kɔmynote/ ▶321| *nf* **1** (groupe humain) community; **~ culturelle/ethnique** cultural/ethnic community; **la ~ chypriote/musulmane** the Cypriot/Muslim community; **la ~ nationale/internationale** the national/international community; **la ~ scientifique/politique** the scientific/political community; **2** (collectivité) commune; **~s hippies** hippy communes; **vivre en ~** to live in a commune; **la vie en ~** communal life; **3** Relig community; **4** Jur **~ (de biens)** joint ownership; **~ (légale)** or **réduite aux acquêts** joint ownership of property upon marriage; **se marier sous le régime de la ~** to marry on terms of joint ownership of property; **5** (identité) community; **~ de vues/goûts** shared views/tastes; **une ~ d'idées/de valeurs** shared ideas/values.

■ **~ thérapeutique** therapeutic community; **~ urbaine** Admin metropolitan district ou area; **Communauté économique du charbon et de l'acier**, **CECA** European Coal and Steel Community, ECSC; **Communauté économique européenne**, **CEE** European Economic Community, EEC; **Communauté des États indépendants**, **CEI** Commonwealth of Independent States, CIS.

commune ▶ **commun** I, V, VI.

communément /kɔmynemɑ̃/ *adv* [*admettre, désigner*] generally; **une fleur ~ appelée** a flower commonly ou generally known as.

communiant, **~e** /kɔmynjɑ̃, ɑ̃t/ *nm,f* **1** (qui communie) communicant; **2** (qui fait sa première communion) **(premier) ~** child taking his/her first communion; **ce n'est pas une première ~e** hum she's no innocent.

communicable /kɔmynikabl/ *adj* **1** (disponible) [*information*] available to the general public; **données ~s par téléphone** data which can be given over the telephone; **2** (exprimable) [*réalité, sentiment*] which can be conveyed (*épith, après n*); **mon sentiment n'est pas ~** my feeling cannot be conveyed; **3** Méd [*maladie*] communicable.

communicant, **~e** /kɔmynikɑ̃, ɑ̃t/ *adj* **1** Constr [*pièces, porte*] communicating; **salle de bains ~e** communicating ou en suite GB bathroom; **2** Méd [*artère*] communicating.

communicateur /kɔmynikatœʀ/ *nm* communicator.

communicatif, **-ive** /kɔmynikatif, iv/ *adj* **1** [*personne, nature*] talkative; **2** [*gaieté, dynamisme, passion*] infectious.

communication /kɔmynikasjɔ̃/ *nf* **1** Télécom call; **~ téléphonique** telephone call; **~ en PCV** reverse-charge call; **être en ~ avec qn** to be on the line ou talking to sb; **je vous passe la ~** I'll transfer the call to you, I'll put the call through to you; **mettre qn en ~ avec qn** to put sb through to sb; **prix de la ~** cost of a call; **~ longue distance** long-distance call; **~ par satellite** satellite communication; **2** (relations sociales) communications (*pl*); **~ interne** internal communications; **problème de ~** communications problem; **stratégie de ~** communications strategy; **~ entre les individus** interpersonal communications; **améliorer la ~** to promote better communications; **~ de masse** mass communications; **diplôme en ~** degree in communications; **homme de ~** communicator; **3** (transmission) communication; **~ du rapport à tous les membres** a copy of the report will be sent to all members; **donner ~ d'un dossier à qn** to send a file to sb; **demander ~ d'un dossier à qn** to ask sb for a file; **4** (au conseil des ministres) report; (à une conférence) paper; **faire une ~ sur** to give a paper on; **5** (relation personnelle) communication ¢; **~ entre deux personnes** communication between two persons; **problème de ~** communication problem; **être en ~ avec qn** to be in communication with sb; **mettre qn en ~ avec qn** to put sb in touch with sb; **se mettre en ~ avec qn** to get in touch with sb; **6** (média) communications (*pl*); **groupe de ~** communications group; **industrie de la ~** communications industry; **7** (moyens de liaison) **moyens/voies de ~** communications (*pl*); **les ~s ont été coupées** communications have been cut off; **8** Ling communication.

■ **~ de diffusion** Télécom broadcast call; **~ multiple** Télécom conference call.

communicatrice /kɔmynikatʀis/ *nf* communicator.

communier /kɔmynje/ [2] *vi* **1** Relig [*personne*] to receive Communion; **aller ~** to go up for communion; **~ sous les deux espèces** to receive Communion in both kinds; **2** fig to commune (**avec** with); **~ dans la douleur de qn** to share in sb's grief; **~ dans la passion de qch** to share the same passion for sth.

communion /kɔmynjɔ̃/ *nf* **1** Relig Communion; **recevoir la ~** to receive ou take Communion; **donner** or **administrer la ~ à qn** to administer Communion to sb; **2** (accord) communion; **être en étroite ~** to be in close harmony; **se sentir en ~ avec qch/qn** to feel in harmony with sth/sb; **être en ~ d'idées/de sentiments** liter to share the same ideas/feelings; **nous sommes en ~ de goûts** liter we share the same tastes.

■ **~ (privée)** Relig first communion; **faire sa ~** to take ou make one's first communion; **~ solennelle** Relig *solemn declaration of faith made at the age of 11.*

communiqué /kɔmynike/ *nm* **1** (de presse) communiqué, press release; **2** (de parti, gouvernement) statement; **~ commun/final/officiel** common/final/official statement; **~ à la presse** statement to the press; **~ publié hier** statement issued yesterday.

■ **~ de presse** press release.

communiquer /kɔmynike/ [1] **I** *vtr* **1** (faire connaître) [*journaliste*] to announce [*date, décision, résultat*]; [*personne*] to give [*adresse, détail, liste, chiffre*] (**à** to); [*personne*] to declare [*intention*] (**à** to); **~ son enthousiasme à qn** to pass on one's enthusiasm to sb; **2** (transmettre) [*personne*] to pass on [*goût, dossier, proposition, maladie*] (**à** to); [*artiste, interprétation, œuvre*] to convey [*idée, sentiment*] (**à** to); **3** Mécan, Phys to transmit [*mouvement, rayonnement*].

II *vi* **1** Ling, Sociol, Télécom to communicate (**avec** with) ; **~ par signes/lettres/téléphone** to communicate by signs/letters/telephone; **2** Entr, Pub to communicate; **aptitude à ~** communication skills (*pl*); **3** Archit [*pièces*] to be adjoining; **~ avec** to adjoin [*pièce*]; **faire ~** to link.

III se communiquer *vpr* **1** (se transmettre) [*personnes*] to pass on [sth] to each other [*information, nouvelle*]; **2** (se répandre) [*feu, peur, maladie*] to spread (**à** to); **3** (se répercuter) **~ à** [*phénomène*] to affect.

communisant, **~e** /kɔmynizɑ̃, ɑ̃t/ **I** *adj* [*idées*] sympathetic to communism (*après n*); **il a été ~** he was a communist sympathizer.

II *nm,f* communist sympathizer.

communisme /kɔmynism/ *nm* communism.

communiste /kɔmynist/ *adj, nmf* communist.

commutable /kɔmytabl/ *adj* **1** Math commutative; **2** Ling commutable.

commutateur /kɔmytatœʀ/ *nm* **1** Électrotech (de connexion) switch; (de direction, d'intensité) commutator; (interrupteur) (light) switch; **~ conjoncteur/disjoncteur** circuit-closer/-breaker; **2** Télécom switching.

commutatif, **-ive** /kɔmytatif, iv/ *adj* Ling, Math, Jur commutative.

commutation /kɔmytasjɔ̃/ *nf* **1** Jur commutation (**de** of; **en** to); **2** Ling, Math commutation; **loi de ~** commutative law; **3** Ordinat message switching; **4** Télécom switching.

commutativité /kɔmytativite/ *nf* **1** Math commutativity; **2** Ling substitutability on a paradigmatic axis.

commuter /kɔmyte/ [1] **I** *vtr* **1** Math to commute (**avec** with); **2** Ling to substitute, to commute; **3** Électrotech to switch [*courant*].

II *vi* Math to commute (**avec** with).

Comores /kɔmɔʀ/ ▶321|, 416| *nprfpl* **les (îles) ~** the Comoros.

comorien, **-ienne** /kɔmɔʀjɛ̃, ɛn/ ▶537| *adj* Comoran.

Comorien, **-ienne** /kɔmɔʀjɛ̃, ɛn/ ▶537| *nm,f* Comoran.

compacité /kɔ̃pasite/ *nf* **1** (densité) density; **2** (faible encombrement) compactness.

compact, **~e** /kɔ̃pakt/ **I** *adj* **1** (dense) [*brouillard, foule*] dense; [*bois*] close-grained; [*terre*] compact; **2** (peu encombrant) [*meuble*] compact; **sous format ~** [*livre*] in pocket edition; **3** (solide) [*groupe, opposition*] monolithic; [*peloton*] compact.

II *nm* **1** (disque) CD; **2** (chaîne stéréo) compact (stereo) system; **3** (appareil photo) compact camera; **4** Cosmét compact; **5** Sport (ski) compact ski.

III **compacte** *nf* Aut small car, compact.

compagne /kɔ̃paɲ/ *nf* **1** (amie) (female) companion; **~ de toujours** lifelong companion; **~ de voyage** travelling[GB] companion; **2** (femelle) mate.

compagnie /kɔ̃paɲi/ *nf* **1** (présence) company; **attendre/vouloir de la ~** to expect/to want company; **la ~ de** the company of; **tenir ~ à qn** to keep sb company; **être de bonne/mauvaise ~** to be good/bad company; **voyager de ~** to travel together; **en ~ de** together with; **2** (groupe) company; **toute la ~** the entire company; **distraire la ~** to entertain the company; **salut la ~!** hello everybody!; **embrasser/saluer la ~** to kiss/to greet all present; **3** Comm company; **~ privée** private company; **4** Mil company; **5** Danse, Théât company; **~ théâtrale** theatre[GB] company; **~ de danse** dance company; **~ de ballet** ballet company; **6** (colonie animale) **~ de perdrix** covey of partridges.

■ **~ aérienne** airline; **~ d'assurance** insurance company; **~ bancaire** Fin banking corporation; **~ de chemins de fer** railway company; **~ cinématographique** film company; **~ des eaux** water company; **~ financière** Fin finance company; **~ d'infanterie** rifle company; **~ de navigation** shipping line; **~ pétrolière** oil company; **~ de transports** transport company; **Compagnie des agents de change** Fin company of stockbrokers; **Compagnie des Indes** Hist East India Company; **Compagnie de Jésus** Relig Society of Jesus.

compagnon /kɔ̃paɲɔ̃/ *nm* **1** (ami) companion; **~ fidèle** faithful companion; **2** (amant) partner; **3** (mâle) mate; **4** (artisan) journeyman; **5** (franc-maçon) fellow of the craft.

■ **~ d'armes** comrade-in-arms; **~ de captivité** fellow prisoner; **~ d'infortune** companion in misfortune; **~ de route** fellow traveller[GB]; **~ de table** table companion; **~ de voyage** travelling[GB] companion.

compagnonnage /kɔ̃paɲɔnaʒ/ *nm* companionship.

comparable /kɔ̃paʀabl/ *adj* [*prix, qualité, taille*] comparable (**à** to; **avec** with); **il est ~ aux plus grands peintres** he stands comparison with the greatest painters; **ça n'a rien de ~** it's altogether different.

comparaison /kɔ̃paʀɛzɔ̃/ *nf* **1** (rapprochement) comparison (**à, avec** with; **entre** between); **il n'y a pas de ~ (possible)** there's no comparison; **en/par ~** in/by comparison; **en ~ de** by comparison with, compared with; **par ~ avec** or **à** compared with; **si tu fais la ~** if you compare them; **c'est sans ~ le plus confortable** it's far and away the most comfortable; **les deux films ont peu de points de ~** the two films have little in common; **je manque de points de ~** I've no way of making comparisons; **supporter la ~** to stand comparison; **2** (en rhétorique) simile; **3** Ling comparison; **adjectif/adverbe de ~** comparative adjective/adverb; **degré de ~** degree of comparison.

IDIOMES **~ n'est pas raison** Prov comparisons are odious.

comparaître /kɔ̃paʀɛtʀ/ [73] *vi* Jur to appear (**devant** before); **être appelé à ~** to be summoned to appear; **citer qn à ~** to serve sb with a summons; **citation à ~** summons to appear; **défaut de ~** default, failure to appear; **refus de ~** refusal to appear.

comparatif, **-ive** /kɔ̃paʀatif, iv/ I *adj* [*étude, éléments, publicité*] comparative.

II *nm* Ling comparative; **~ d'égalité/d'infériorité/de supériorité** same/lower/higher degree comparative; **au ~** in the comparative.

III **comparative** *nf* Ling comparative clause.

comparatiste /kɔ̃paʀatist/ I *adj* comparative.

II *nmf* (en linguistique) specialist in comparative linguistics; (en littérature) specialist in comparative literature.

comparativement /kɔ̃paʀativmɑ̃/ *adv* comparatively; **~ à** compared with.

comparé, **~e** /kɔ̃paʀe/ I *pp* ▶ **comparer**.

II *pp adj* **1** [*droit, littérature, anatomie*] comparative; **2** [*interprétations, textes*] compared (*épith*); **~ à** compared with.

comparer /kɔ̃paʀe/ [1] I *vtr* (pour évaluer) to compare (**à, avec** with); (assimiler) to compare (**à** to); **~ deux objets/hommes (entre eux)** to compare two things/men; **comparez avant d'acheter** shop around before you buy.

II **se comparer** *vpr* **1** (soi-même) **se ~ à qn/qch** (pour évaluer) to compare oneself with sb/sth; (s'assimiler) to compare oneself to sb; **2** (être comparable) to be comparable; **ça ne se compare pas** there's no comparison.

comparse /kɔ̃paʀs/ *nmf* **1** Théât extra; **rôle de ~** walk-on part; péj minor part; **2** (acolyte) sidekick○; **on n'a arrêté que les ~s** they have only arrested the small fry.

compartiment /kɔ̃paʀtimɑ̃/ *nm* (de meuble, wagon) compartment; **faire des ~s dans qch** lit to divide sth up into compartments; fig to compartmentalize sth.

compartimentage /kɔ̃paʀtimɑ̃taʒ/ *nf* (de service, science, société) compartmentalization.

compartimenter /kɔ̃paʀtimɑ̃te/ [1] *vtr* **1** lit **~ un coffret** to divide a box into compartments; **~ un grenier** to divide up a loft with partitions; **tiroir compartimenté** drawer divided into compartments; **2** fig to compartmentalize [*administration, science*].

comparution /kɔ̃paʀysjɔ̃/ *nf* Jur appearance (**devant** before).

compas /kɔ̃pa/ *nm* **1** (de géométrie) compass, pair of compasses US; **tracé au/sans ~** drawn with a/without a compass; **2** Aviat, Naut compass; **se diriger au ~** to navigate by compass.

■ **~ azimutal** Aviat azimuth compass; **~ à balustre** spring bow compass; **~ d'épaisseur** external callipers[GB] (*pl*); **~ à pointes sèches** dividers (*pl*); **~ à pompe** dropbow compass.

IDIOMES **avoir le ~ dans l'œil** to have a good eye.

compassé, **~e** /kɔ̃pase/ *adj* pej [*personne, attitude*] stuffy; [*air, ton*] prim; [*manières*] affected.

compassion /kɔ̃pasjɔ̃/ *nf* compassion; **avec ~** compassionately.

compatibilité /kɔ̃patibilite/ *nf* **1** gén compatibility; **~ sanguine** Biol compatibility of blood types; **~ tissulaire** Biol histocompatibility; **2** Ordinat compatibility.

compatible /kɔ̃patibl/ *adj* compatible (**avec** with); **~ PC** Ordinat PC compatible; **énoncés ~s** Philos consistent statements or propositions.

compatir /kɔ̃patiʀ/ [3] *vi* to sympathize; **je compatis à votre douleur** fml I feel for you in your sorrow sout.

compatissant, **~e** /kɔ̃patisɑ̃, ɑ̃t/ *adj* compassionate.

compatriote /kɔ̃patʀiɔt/ *nmf* fellow-countryman/-countrywoman, compatriot.

compendium /kɔ̃pɑ̃djɔm, kɔ̃pɛ̃djɔm/ *nm* compendium (**de** of).

compensable /kɔ̃pɑ̃sabl/ *adj* **1** [*dommage, perte*] for which compensation can be obtained (*épith, après n*); **2** Fin **~ à** [*chèque*] to be cleared in.

compensateur, **-trice** /kɔ̃pɑ̃satœʀ, tʀis/ I *adj* [*effet, indemnité*] compensatory; [*pendule*] compensation; [*filtre*] compensatory.

II *nm* **1** Tech (en optique) compensator; **2** Télécom **~ d'affaiblissement** attenuation frequency equalizer; **3** Aviat tab; **4** Audio equalizer.

compensation /kɔ̃pɑ̃sasjɔ̃/ *nf* **1** (action de compenser) compensation; **en ~ ils nous ont payé l'hôtel** as compensation they paid for the hotel; **ils ont reçu une forte somme en ~ des travaux effectués** they received a large sum as compensation for the work carried out; **elle a obtenu 2500 francs en ~** she got 2,500 francs in compensation; **2** (avantage accordé) compensation ₵; **recevoir une ~** to receive compensation; **ils ont obtenu des ~s financières** they obtained financial compensation; **comme** or **à titre de ~** in ou by way of compensation; **ils font des heures supplémentaires sans ~** they are working overtime with no compensation; **3** Écon countertrade, compensation; **4** Fin clearance; ▶ **accord**, **cours**; **5** Méd, Psych compensation.

compensatoire /kɔ̃pɑ̃satwaʀ/ *adj* compensatory; **montants ~s** compensatory amounts.

compensé, **~e** /kɔ̃pɑ̃se/ I *pp* ▶ **compenser**.

II *pp adj* **1** Mode **semelle ~e** wedge heel; **2** Méd compensated.

compenser /kɔ̃pɑ̃se/ [1] I *vtr* **1** gén, Psych, Méd [*personne, groupe, pays*] to compensate for [*manque, défaut, handicap*]; to make up for [*dommages*]; to offset [*inflation, dépenses, pertes*]; **je ne fume plus alors je compense en mangeant plus** I've stopped smoking so I compensate by eating more; **nous souhaitons ~ les pertes par la vente de machines** we want to offset our losses by selling machinery; **pour ~, les banques ont baissé le taux de 3%** to compensate, banks have lowered their rate by 3%; **2** (équilibrer) [*hausse, dédommagement, mesure*] to offset [*perte, inflation*]; [*qualité*] to make up for [*défaut*]; **la hausse des salaires va ~ l'inflation** the wage rise GB ou raise US will offset inflation; **sa timidité est compensée par sa gentillesse** he's/she's very shy but his/her kindness makes up for it.

II **se compenser** *vpr* **les gains et les pertes se compensent** the profits offset the losses; **ses défauts et ses qualités se compensent** his/her good qualities make up for his/her faults.

compère /kɔ̃pɛʀ/ *nm* **1** (partenaire) partner; (dans une tromperie) accomplice; **2** (camarade) mate○ GB, buddy○ US; **3** (individu) **joyeux/rusé ~** cheery/crafty fellow○.

compère-loriot, *pl* **compères-loriots** /kɔ̃pɛʀlɔʀjo/ *nm* **1** Zool golden oriole; **2**† Méd sty.

compétence /kɔ̃petɑ̃s/ *nf* **1** (aptitude) (dans une matière, un domaine) ability; (dans un emploi, une activité) competence, skill; **mes ~s en mécanique sont limitées** my mechanical skills are very limited; **faire preuve de ~** to show ability; **faire la preuve de ses ~s** to show one's competence ou ability; **manquer de ~** to lack competence; **avec une grande ~** very competently; **faire appel aux ~s de qn** to call upon sb's expertise; **2** (aptitude légale) competence; **relever de la ~ de qn** to fall within the competence of sb; **3** (fonction) domain, sphere; **être** or **entrer dans les ~s de qn** to be in sb's domain; **l'entretien du bâtiment n'est pas de mes ~s** I'm not responsible for the upkeep of this building; **4** Ling competence.

compétent, **~e** /kɔ̃petɑ̃, ɑ̃t/ *adj* **1** (qualifié) competent; **être ~ en la matière** to be competent in the subject ou matter; **être assez ~ pour faire** to have the competence ou ability to do; **2** (qui a l'autorité) [*autorité, préfet*] competent; [*administration, service*] appropriate; **tribunal ~** court of competent jurisdiction; **le maire est seul**

~ pour faire the mayor is the only one with the authority to do; **le tribunal de Rennes n'est pas ~ pour juger cette affaire** this case does not come within the jurisdiction of the Rennes court; **remettre un dossier aux autorités ~es** to forward a file to the appropriate authorities ou to the authorities concerned.

compétiteur /kɔ̃petitœʀ/ *nm* competitor.

compétitif, -ive /kɔ̃petitif, iv/ *adj* competitive.

compétition /kɔ̃petisjɔ̃/ *nf* **1** (rivalité) rivalry (**entre** between); **faire naître la ~ entre** to stimulate rivalry between; **se livrer à une ~ acharnée** to be engaged in fierce competition; **être en ~ avec** to be competing with; **en ~ pour** competing for; **entrer en ~ avec** to compete with; **l'esprit de ~** the competitive spirit; **2** (activité) competition; **se retirer de** or **abandonner la ~** (définitivement) to retire from competition; (pour une épreuve) to withdraw from competition; **voiture de ~** competition car; **faire de la ~** to compete; **sport de ~** competitive sport; **3** (épreuve) **~ (sportive)** sporting event; **~ d'athlétisme/de natation/de ski** athletics/swimming/skiing event; **~ automobile** motor GB ou auto US racing event.

compétitivité /kɔ̃petitivite/ *nf* competitiveness.

compétitrice /kɔ̃petitʀis/ *nf* (female) competitor.

compilateur, -trice /kɔ̃pilatœʀ, tʀis/ **I** *nm,f* compiler.
II *nm* Ordinat compiler; **~ de ~s** compiler-compiler; **~ croisé** cross-compiler.

compilation /kɔ̃pilasjɔ̃/ *nf* **1** (action) compilation; **2** (ouvrage, disque) compilation.

compiler /kɔ̃pile/ [1] *vtr* to compile.

complainte /kɔ̃plɛ̃t/ *nf* lament.

complaire: **se complaire** /kɔ̃plɛʀ/ [59] *vpr* **se ~ à faire** to take pleasure in doing; **se ~ dans le malheur** to wallow in misery; **se ~ dans son ignorance** to bask in one's own ignorance.

complaisamment /kɔ̃plɛzamɑ̃/ *adv* **1** (aimablement) obligingly; **2** (avec trop d'indulgence) indulgently; **3** (avec autosatisfaction) complacently.

complaisance /kɔ̃plɛzɑ̃s/ *nf* **1** (volonté de faire plaisir) kindness, readiness to oblige; **avoir la ~ de faire** to be kind enough to do; **faire qch par ~** to do sth to oblige ou out of kindness; **sourire de ~** polite smile; **certificat médical de ~** medical certificate delivered by an obliging doctor; **pavillon de ~** flag of convenience; **2** (indulgence excessive) **la ~ d'un père à l'égard de ses enfants** a father's indulgence toward(s) his children; **leur ~ à l'égard du régime** their soft attitude toward(s) the regime, the fact that they condone the regime; **décrire la situation sans ~** to give an objective assessment of the situation; **un portrait sans ~** a candid portrait; **3** (autosatisfaction) complacency, smugness; **il s'écoute avec ~** he likes the sound of his own voice.

complaisant, ~e /kɔ̃plɛzɑ̃, ɑ̃t/ *adj* **1** (prévenant) obliging; **2** (trop indulgent) pej indulgent (**avec** with); **sa description des faits est trop ~e** he's too uncritical in his account of the facts; **un mari ~** a husband who turns a blind eye; **des oreilles ~es** people who like to listen to gossip; **3** (autosatisfait) pej complacent péj, self-satisfied péj; **se juger d'une manière ~e, se regarder d'un œil ~** to be self-satisfied.

complément /kɔ̃plemɑ̃/ *nm* **1** (allocation) supplementary benefit; **~ de retraite** supplementary pension; **2** (revenu) **~ de salaire** extra payment; **3** (alimentaire, de programme, travail, financement) supplement; **~ de formation** further training; **en ~** as a supplement (**à, de** to); **4** (compagnon) complement (**de** to); **~ naturel** natural complement; **5** Ling complement; **~ d'agent** agent; **~ d'attribution** indirect object; **~ circonstanciel** adverbial phrase; **~ de nom** possessive phrase; **~ d'objet** object; **~ d'objet direct** direct object; **~ d'objet indirect** indirect object; **6** Math complement.
■ **~ d'enquête** Jur further enquiry GB ou inquiry US; **~ d'information** Jur further information.

complémentaire /kɔ̃plemɑ̃tɛʀ/ *adj* **1** (supplémentaire) [*formation, information, examen médical, délai*] further; [*activité, somme*] supplementary; **pour tous renseignements ~s** for further information; **2** (apparié) [*personne, qualité, équipement*] complementary (**de** to); **être ~ l'un de l'autre** to complement each other; **3** Math **arcs/angles ~s** complementary arcs/angles.

complémentarité /kɔ̃plemɑ̃taʀite/ *nf* complementarity.

complet, -ète /kɔ̃plɛ, ɛt/ **I** *adj* **1** (total) [*arrêt, silence, succès, accord, changement, révision*] complete; [*misère, échec, destruction*] total; **2** (sans manques) [*œuvres, liste, exposé, dossier*] complete; [*enquête, formation, spectacle, gamme*] full; [*artiste, athlète*] all-round; **les œuvres complètes de Proust** the complete works of Proust; **la collection complète de** the whole collection of; **c'est un idiot ~** he's a complete idiot; **c'est un homme ~** he's an all-rounder; **c'est ~!** iron it's the last straw!; **3** (approfondi) comprehensive; **très ~** very comprehensive ; **panorama aussi ~ que possible** as comprehensive a survey as possible; **de façon (très) complète** (very) thoroughly; **4** (plein) [*train, autocar, hôtel , salle*] full; **'~'** (dans un hôtel) 'no vacancies'; (dans un théâtre) 'sold out', 'full house'; (dans un stade) 'ground GB ou stadium full'; (dans un parc de stationnement) 'car park full' GB, 'parking lot full' US; **au grand ~** entire (*épith*); **le gouvernement au ~** the entire government; **être (réuni) au (grand) ~** to be all present; **la famille est réunie au grand ~** the whole family is present.
II *nm* Mode suit; **~ deux/trois pièces** two-/three-piece suit.

complètement /kɔ̃plɛtmɑ̃/ *adv* **1** (totalement) completely; **il est ~ fou** he's completely mad; **~ absurde/différent** totally absurd/different; **pas ~** not entirely; **~ guéri** completely cured; **~ réveillé** fully awake; **~ d'accord** in complete agreement; **je suis ~ d'accord** I completely agree; **~ noir** [*pièce*] completely dark; [*mur, situation*] all black; **je m'en moque** or **fiche**○ or **fous**◑ **~** I couldn't care less; **2** (en entier) **j'ai ~ repeint la maison** I've repainted the whole house; **elle a ~ refait son article** she has rewritten her whole article ou her article in its entirety; **lire qch ~** to read sth out in its entirety, to read the whole of sth.

compléter /kɔ̃plete/ [14] **I** *vtr* **1** (s'ajouter à) to complete [*formation, diplôme, collection, enquête*]; to top up [*somme*]; [*arrêté*] to complement [*loi*]; to follow up [*informations*]; to supplement [*connaissances, études*]; **pour ~ le tout** or **tableau** iron to cap it all; **2** (ajouter à) [*personne, entreprise*] to complete [*ensemble*] (**par** by); **~ le financement d'un projet** to complete the funding of a project; **3** (être complémentaire de) [*personne*] to complement [*personne*]; **4** (remplir) [*personne*] to complete [*phrase*]; to complete, to fill in [*questionnaire*]; **'à ~ et à retourner à...'** 'complete and send to...'.
II se compléter *vpr* (l'un l'autre) [*éléments, personnes*] to complement each other.

complétif, -ive /kɔ̃pletif, iv/ **I** *adj* **proposition complétive** object clause; **proposition complétive sujet** subject clause.
II complétive *nf* object clause; **complétive sujet** subject clause.

complet-veston†, *pl* **complets-veston** /kɔ̃plɛvɛstɔ̃/ *nm* suit.

complexe /kɔ̃plɛks/ **I** *adj* (tous contextes) complex.
II *nm* **1** Psych complex; **avoir des ~s** to have complexes; **faire un ~**○ (**à cause de**) to have a complex (about); **donner des ~s à qn** to give sb complexes; **il n'a pas de ~** he hasn't got any hang-ups○, he has no inhibitions; **tu n'as aucun ~ à avoir** (à cause de différence sociale, d'instruction) there's no need to feel inferior (à cause de différence physique) there's no need to feel self-conscious; **2** (ensemble d'installations) complex; **un ~ touristique/hospitalier/sportif** a tourist/hospital/sports complex; **3** Math complex number; **4** Phys, Chimie coordination ou complex compound.
■ **~ de castration** castration complex; **~ d'Électre** Electra complex; **~ d'infériorité** inferiority complex; **~ d'Œdipe** Oedipus complex; **~ de supériorité** superiority complex.

complexé, ~e /kɔ̃plekse/ **I** *pp* ▶ **complexer**.
II○ *pp adj* [*personne*] who has a lot of hang-ups○ (*épith, après n*); **il est très ~** he has a lot of hang-ups○; **vous n'avez aucune raison d'être ~** (moralement) there's no need for you to feel inferior; (physiquement) there's no need for you to feel self-conscious.

complexer /kɔ̃plekse/ [1] *vtr* to give [sb] a complex [*personne*]; **son poids le complexe énormément** he has a terrible complex about his weight; **être complexé par qch** to have a complex about sth, to be self-conscious about sth; **il n'est pas du tout complexé par son accent** he is not in the least self-conscious about his accent.

complexifier /kɔ̃plɛksifje/ [2] **I** *vtr* to make [sth] more complex.
II se complexifier *vpr* to become more complex.

complexion /kɔ̃plɛksjɔ̃/ *nf* **1** (constitution) constitution; **2**† (teint) complexion.

complexité /kɔ̃plɛksite/ *nf* complexity.

complication /kɔ̃plikasjɔ̃/ *nf* **1** (embarras) complication; **par peur des ~s** for fear of complications; **chercher les ~s** to complicate matters; **tu vas chercher des ~s là où il n'y en a pas** you're trying to create problems where there aren't any; **aimer les ~s** to like complicating matters; **2** Méd complication.

complice /kɔ̃plis/ **I** *adj* **1** (qui aide) collusive; **être ~ de qch** to be a party to sth, to be complicit in sth; Jur to be an accessory to sth; **2** (manifestant la connivence) [*air, sourire, silence, regard*] of complicity (*épith, après n*).
II *nmf* **1** (comparse) accomplice (**de qch** in sth); Jur accessory (**de qch** to sth); **être le ~ de qn** to be sb's accomplice; **~ d'un crime** accomplice in a crime; **se faire le ~ de qch** to be a party to sth; **2** hum (de loisirs, d'enfance) companion; (d'activité professionnelle, de réalisation) partner in crime.

complicité /kɔ̃plisite/ *nf* **1** (collaboration) complicity; **être accusé de ~ de vol/d'enlèvement** to be accused of complicity in a robbery/kidnapping GB; **agir en ~ avec qn** to act in complicity ou collusion with sb; **être arrêté pour ~ dans un meurtre** to be arrested for complicity in a murder; **2** (entente) bond; **une tendre ~ les unissait** they shared a deep affection for each other; **un geste/sourire de ~** a gesture/smile of complicity.

complies /kɔ̃pli/ *nfpl* compline (*sg*).

compliment /kɔ̃plimɑ̃/ **I** *nm* **1** (parole de félicitations) compliment; **il lui a retourné** or **renvoyé le ~** he returned the compliment; **ce n'est pas un ~ ce que tu me dis!** that's not very complimentary!; **faire un ~ à qn** to compliment sb ou to pay sb a compliment (**sur** on); **2** (petit discours) (nice little) speech.
II compliments *nmpl* **1** (félicitations) compliments; **elle n'aime pas les ~s** she doesn't like compliments; **(tous) mes ~s!** also iron congratulations!; **faire des ~s à qn** to compliment sb (**sur, pour** on); **je ne te fais pas mes ~s!** I wouldn't say well done!; **adresser ses ~s aux jeunes**

mariés/à la famille to congratulate the newlyweds/the family; **2** (formule de politesse) **avec les ~s de...** with the compliments of...; **faites** or **présentez mes ~s à votre mère** give my regards to your mother.

complimenter /kɔ̃plimɑ̃te/ [1] *vtr* to compliment (**sur**, **pour** on; **pour avoir** or **d'avoir fait** on having done).

compliqué, **~e** /kɔ̃plike/ I *pp* ▶ **compliquer**.
II *pp adj* **1** [*appareil, exercice, dessin*] complicated; [*problème*] complicated, difficult; [*esprit*] tortuous; [*personne*] complicated; **ce n'est pourtant pas ~ de changer un fusible** it's not exactly hard to change a fuse; **ce n'est quand même pas ~ de ranger tes affaires** it wouldn't take much effort to keep your things tidy; **si tu ne t'arrêtes pas de pleurer, ce n'est pas ~, tu vas au lit**○! it's quite simple, if you don't stop crying you'll go straight to bed!; **si ça continue comme ça, ce n'est pas ~, je démissionne**○ if things carry on as they are, I'll simply resign; **'c'est de sa faute alors?'—'c'est un peu plus ~ que cela'** 'so it's his fault?'—'it's not quite as simple as that'; **2** Méd [*fracture*] compound.

compliquer /kɔ̃plike/ [1] I *vtr* to complicate; **ne complique pas les choses avec tes questions** don't complicate things by asking questions; **tu compliques toujours tout** you always complicate things, you always make things (more) complicated; **~ la vie** or **l'existence de qn** to make life difficult for sb.
II **se compliquer** *vpr* **1** (devenir complexe) to get ou become more complicated; **ça se complique!** things are getting complicated!; **2** Méd **la rougeole peut se ~** measles can lead to complications; **3** (rendre plus complexe) **se ~ la vie** or **l'existence** to make life difficult for oneself.

complot /kɔ̃plo/ *nm* (machination, petite intrigue) plot (**contre** against); **ourdir un ~** to hatch a plot; **faire partie du ~** to be in on the plot; **mettre qn dans le ~** to let sb in on the plot.

comploter /kɔ̃plɔte/ [1] I *vtr* to plot [*attentat, ruine*]; to plan [*mauvais coup*].
II *vi* to plot (**contre** against; **de faire** to do).

comploteur, **-euse** /kɔ̃plɔtœʀ, øz/ *nm,f* plotter.

componction /kɔ̃pɔ̃ksjɔ̃/ *nf* **1** (gravité affectée) self-importance; **avec ~** self-importantly; **2** Relig contrition.

componentiel, **-ielle** /kɔ̃pɔnɑ̃sjɛl/ *adj* componential.

comportement /kɔ̃pɔʀtəmɑ̃/ *nm* **1** Psych behaviour^GB; **~ animal/de groupe** animal/group behaviour^GB; **2** (attitude) attitude (**à l'égard de, vis-à-vis de** toward(s)); **~ américain** American attitude; **~ de l'État** attitude of the State; **3** (manières) manner; **~ déplaisant** unpleasant manner; **4** (de sportif, voiture, Bourse) performance.

comportementalisme /kɔ̃pɔʀtəmɑ̃talism/ *nm* behaviourism^GB.

comportementaliste /kɔ̃pɔʀtəmɑ̃talist/ I *adj* [*méthode*] behaviouristic^GB.
II *nmf* **1** (théoricien) behaviourist^GB; **2** (praticien) behaviour^GB therapist.

comporter /kɔ̃pɔʀte/ [1] I *vtr* **1** (inclure entre autres) to include; **~ une bibliographie** to include a bibliography; **ce texte ne doit ~ aucune coupure** there must be no cuts in this text; **2** (être composé de) to comprise; **~ trois parties** to comprise three parts; **3** (présenter) to entail [*risque, inconvénient*]; **avec tout ce que cela comporte comme incertitude** with all the concomitant uncertainty.
II **se comporter** *vpr* **1** [*personne, animal*] to behave, to act; **se ~ en dictateur** to behave like a dictator; **se ~ comme un sauvage** to behave like a savage; **se ~ comme un pays neutre** to act as a neutral power; **2** (fonctionner) [*sportif, voiture, Bourse*] to perform; **bien se ~** to perform well.

composant /kɔ̃pozɑ̃/ *nm* **1** Tech (élément) component; **~ électronique** electronic component; **2** Chimie (élément simple) constituent; **~s de l'eau** constituents of water.

composante /kɔ̃pozɑ̃t/ *nf* **1** gén (élément) element; **2** Pol (de parti) constituent part; (de politique) component; (de pays) element; **3** Math, Phys, Ling component.

composé, **~e** /kɔ̃poze/ I *pp* ▶ **composer**.
II *pp adj* **~ de** made up of; **un groupe ~ à 90% de femmes** a group of which 90% are women; **le groupe est ~ à 90% de femmes** 90% of the group are women; **spectacle ~ de trois parties** show made up of three parts.
III *adj* **1** (fait d'éléments divers) [*bouquet, style*] composite; [*salade*] mixed; **2** (affecté) affected.
IV *nm* **1** Chimie compound; **~ organique** organic compound; **2** Ling compound.
V **composée** *nf* Bot composite; **les ~es** Compositae.

composer /kɔ̃poze/ [1] I *vtr* **1** (constituer) [*éléments, personnes*] to make up; **onze joueurs composent l'équipe** eleven players make up the team; **2** (réaliser) [*personne*] to put [sth] together [*programme, menu*]; to select [*équipe*]; to work out [*décor*]; to make up [*bouquet*]; **3** Art, Littérat, Mus [*personne*] to compose [*morceau, texte*]; to write [*discours*]; to work out the composition of [*tableau*]; **4** to dial [*numéro*]; **~ le 19** to dial 19; **~ son code secret** to enter one's secret code; **5** Imprim to typeset [*page, texte*]; **6** (adopter) fml to assume [*attitude, expression*]; to compose [*visage*].
II fml *vi* (trouver un compromis) to compromise; **~ avec** to come to a compromise with [*personne*]; **~ avec sa conscience** to square it with one's conscience.
III **se composer** *vpr* **1** (être constitué) **se ~ de** to be made up of [*éléments, personnes*]; **2** (adopter) to assume [*attitude, expression*]; **se ~ un personnage** to put on an act.

composite /kɔ̃pozit/ I *adj* **1** (divers) [*société, goûts, parti, livre*] heterogeneous; [*origines*] mixed; **2** Tech [*matériau, verre*] composite; **3** Antiq, Archit [*colonne, ordre*] composite.
II *nm* Tech (matériau) composite.

compositeur, **-trice** /kɔ̃pozitœʀ, tʀis/ ▶ **510** *nm,f* **1** Mus composer; **~ classique** classical composer; **2** Imprim typesetter.

composition /kɔ̃pozisjɔ̃/ *nf* **1** (éléments constitutifs) (de gouvernement, délégation, société) make-up, composition; (d'équipe) line-up, composition; (de produit, d'aliment) ingredients (*pl*); (chimique, pharmaceutique) composition; (de capital) structure; **entrer dans la ~ de** (faire partie de) [*gaz, sel*] to make up part of; (servir à fabriquer) to be used in; **entrer à 40% dans la ~ de** [*gaz, sel*] to make up 40% of; **la farine entre à 90% dans la ~ de ce pain** this bread contains 90% flour; **2** (mise en place) (de gouvernement) formation; (de comité) setting up; (d'équipe) selection; (de liste, menu) drawing up; (de bouquet) making up; **de ma/leur ~** of my/their invention; **3** Art, Littérat, Mus (tous contextes) composition (**de** by); **étudier la ~** to study composition; **~ florale** flower arrangement; **4** Cin, Théât (incarnation) performance (**de** as); **5** Scol (pour classer) end-of-term test; **6** Imprim typesetting; **l'article est à la ~** the article is being typeset; **7** Ling composition.
■ **~ du capital** Fin share structure; **~ française** (devoir) essay; (activité) essay writing; **~ murale** mural.
IDIOMES **être de bonne ~** to be good-natured.

compost /kɔ̃pɔst/ *nm* compost.

compostage /kɔ̃pɔstaʒ/ *nm* **1** (de billet) (au tampon) (date)stamping; (au poinçon) punching; **2** Agric composting.

composter /kɔ̃pɔste/ [1] *vtr* **1** Transp (au tampon) to (date)stamp; (au poinçon) to punch; **2** Agric to compost [*déchets*].

composteur /kɔ̃pɔstœʀ/ *nm* **1** (pour valider) (imprimante) ticket-stamping machine; (poinçon) ticket-punching machine; **2** Imprim composing stick.

compote /kɔ̃pɔt/ *nf* Culin stewed fruit, compote; **~ d'abricots** stewed apricots; **~ de pommes** (en dessert) stewed apples; (avec de la viande) apple sauce; **j'ai les genoux en ~** fig (douloureux) my knees are killing me○; (tremblants) my knees are like jelly; (couverts de bleus) my knees are black and blue; **mettre qn en ~** to beat sb black and blue.

compotier /kɔ̃pɔtje/ *nm* (à compote) compote dish; (à fruits) fruit bowl.

compréhensibilité /kɔ̃pʀeɑ̃sibilite/ *nf* comprehensibility.

compréhensible /kɔ̃pʀeɑ̃sibl/ *adj* **1** [*erreur, réaction, attitude*] understandable; **c'est bien ~** it's quite understandable; **2** (intelligible) [*langage, terme, explication*] comprehensible; **à peine ~** barely comprehensible.

compréhensif, **-ive** /kɔ̃pʀeɑ̃sif, iv/ *adj* **1** gén understanding; **2** Ling [*terme*] comprehensive.

compréhension /kɔ̃pʀeɑ̃sjɔ̃/ *nf* **1** (faculté, aptitude) understanding; **la ~ du monde contemporain** understanding the modern world; **avoir des problèmes de ~** to have trouble understanding, to find it difficult to understand; **2** (possibilité, action de comprendre) (de texte, propos, paroles) comprehension; (de langue) understanding, comprehension; **pour aider à la ~** to make it easier to understand; **je n'ai pas de problèmes de ~ en allemand** I have no problems understanding German; **~ orale/écrite** oral/written comprehension; **3** (indulgence) **faire preuve de ~ à l'égard de** to show understanding toward(s); **une attitude pleine de ~** a sympathetic attitude.

comprendre /kɔ̃pʀɑ̃dʀ/ [52] I *vtr* **1** (saisir le sens de) to understand; **si je comprends bien** if I understand correctly; **je ne comprends rien à ce qu'il raconte** I don't understand a word of what he's saying; **je ne comprends rien aux mathématiques** I don't understand anything about mathematics; **dois-je ~ que tu n'as pas fini?** am I to understand ou to take it that you haven't finished?; **je ne suis pas certain d'avoir bien compris** I'm not sure I got it right; **il m'a dit son nom au téléphone mais je n'ai pas bien compris** he told me his name on the phone but I didn't quite catch it; **ne te mêles pas de cela, tu as compris** or **c'est compris!** keep out of it, do you hear ou understand?; **je ne veux pas que cela se reproduise, tu m'as (bien) compris!** it mustn't happen again, have you got that quite clear?; **est-ce que tu as compris quelque chose au cours?** did you understand any of the lecture?; **'pourquoi a-t-elle fait cela?'—'vas-y ~ quelque chose!'** 'why did she do that?'—'I've no idea!'; **il ne comprend rien à rien** he hasn't got a clue; **c'est à n'y rien ~** it's completely baffling; **mal ~ qn/qch** to misunderstand sb/sth; **être compris comme ironique** to be taken ironically; **être compris comme une menace** to be interpreted as a threat; **~ qch de travers**○ to get sth all wrong; **se faire ~** to make oneself understood; **être lent à ~** to be slow on the uptake; **(qu'est-ce que) tu comprends vite!** iron you're quick! iron; **tu as tout compris!** iron aren't you clever! iron; **tu comprends vite mais il faut t'expliquer longtemps!** hum so the penny's finally dropped!; **comprenne qui pourra!** make of it what you will!; **2** (se rendre compte de) to understand; **faire ~ qch à qn** to make sb understand sth; **faire ~ à qn que** to make it clear to sb that; **ce n'est pas facile, je comprends** it's not easy, I realize that; **je n'ai pas le temps, tu**

comprends you see, I haven't got time; **oui mais tu comprends ils ne paient pas de loyer** yes, but you see they don't pay any rent; **3** (admettre) to understand [*attitude, sentiment*]; (faire preuve de compréhension envers) to understand [*person*]; **je comprends qu'il soit furieux** I can understand his anger; **je suis fatigué tu peux ~ cela?** can't you understand I'm tired?; **je suis prêt à ~ beaucoup de choses, mais n'en abuse pas** I'm usually very understanding, but don't push it○; **essaie de me ~** try to understand; **il n'a jamais rien compris aux femmes** he has never understood a thing about women; **comme je le comprends!** I understand him exactly; **4** (se faire une idée de) to see [*métier, vie, mariage*]; **comment comprends-tu ton rôle dans le projet?** how do you see your role in the project?; **5** (être totalement constitué de) [*comité, salaire*] to be made up of; [*équipement, boite à outils*] to consist of, to comprise; [*méthode d'apprentissage, maison, immeuble, pièce*] to comprise; [*programme, formation*] to consist of, to comprise; [*prix*] to include, to cover; **notre association ne comprend que des médecins** the members of our association are all doctors; **6** (être partiellement constitué de) to include; **l'équipe comprend plusieurs joueurs étrangers** the team includes several foreign players; **7** (compter) to include [*TVA, prix, personnes*].

II se comprendre *vpr* **1** [*personnes*] (l'un l'autre) to understand each other ou one another; **2** (soi-même) **je me comprends** I know what I'm trying to say; **3** (être compréhensible) [*attitude, sentiment*] to be understandable; **4** (être compris) [*terme, mot, expression*] **le terme doit se ~ ici dans son sens large** the term is to be understood ou taken in its broadest sense.

comprenette○ /kɔ̃pʀənɛt/ *nf* **être lent** or **dur à la ~, avoir la ~ lente** or **difficile** to be slow on the uptake○.

compresse /kɔ̃pʀɛs/ *nf* compress.

compresser /kɔ̃pʀese/ [1] *vtr* to compress.

compresseur /kɔ̃pʀesœʀ/ *nm* compressor.

compressibilité /kɔ̃pʀesibilite/ *nf* **1** Phys, Chimie compressibility; **2 la ~ des effectifs/des dépenses** the extent to which manpower/expenses can be reduced.

compressible /kɔ̃pʀesibl/ *adj* **1** Phys, Chimie compressible; **2** (réductible) [*dépenses, effectifs*] reducible.

compression /kɔ̃pʀesjɔ̃/ *nf* **1** Tech compression; **2** (action de réduire) reduction; **la ~ des effectifs se fera progressivement** staff numbers will be reduced gradually; **la ~ des subventions** the cut in subsidies; **3** (diminution effective) cut (**de** in); **~ d'effectifs** cuts in manpower, **~s budgétaires** budget cuts; **~ de crédit** credit squeeze.

comprimé /kɔ̃pʀime/ *nm* Pharm tablet; **~ effervescent/soluble** effervescent/soluble tablet; **~ à croquer** chewable tablet.

comprimer /kɔ̃pʀime/ [1] *vtr* **1** (serrer) to constrict [*ventre, buste*]; to squeeze [*pâte*]; **ils étaient comprimés à l'arrière de la voiture** they were all packed together in the back of the car; **2** Méd (appuyer sur) to compress, to constrict [*objet, organe*]; **3** Tech to compress [*liquide, gaz*]; **air comprimé** compressed air; **4** (réduire) to cut, to reduce [*dépenses, demande, effectifs*]; to cut [*budget*].

compris, **~e** /kɔ̃pʀi, iz/ **I** *pp* ▶ **comprendre**.

II *pp adj* (inclus) including; **loyer de 3000 francs charges ~es/non ~es** rent of 3,000 francs inclusive/exclusive; **service ~/non ~** service included/not included; **TVA ~e/non ~e** including/not including VAT; **être ~ dans** to be included in.

III tout compris *loc adv* in total, all in○ GB; **cela fait 150 francs tout ~** that comes to 150 francs all in; **donnez-moi le prix tout ~** give me the all-in ou inclusive price; **payer 3700 francs de loyer tout ~** to pay a rent of 3,700 francs, inclusive.

IV y compris *loc adv* including; **tout le monde peut se tromper moi/toi y ~** everybody makes mistakes, myself/you included; **y ~ à Paris** in Paris too; **y ~ dans les journaux** even in the newspapers.

compromettant, **~e** /kɔ̃pʀɔmetɑ̃, ɑ̃t/ *adj* [*écrit, situation, passé, présence*] compromising; [*soutien*] damaging; **n'y allez pas, c'est ~** don't go, it will compromise you; **va voir ce qu'il propose, ce n'est pas ~** go and see what he's offering, it won't commit you to anything.

compromettre /kɔ̃pʀɔmɛtʀ/ [60] **I** *vtr* **1** (mettre en danger) to endanger, to jeopardize [*santé, carrière, chances*]; to compromise [*victoire*]; to impair [*efficacité*]; **2** (souiller) to compromise [*personne, femme*]; to damage [*prestige, réputation*]; **~ qn dans qch** to implicate sb in sth.

II *vi* Jur to accept arbitration.

III se compromettre *vpr* **1** (risquer sa réputation) to compromise oneself; **2** (s'engager) to commit oneself.

compromis, **~e** /kɔ̃pʀɔmi, iz/ **I** *pp* ▶ **compromettre**.

II *pp adj* **1** (menacé) [*carrière, résultat, projet*] in jeopardy; [*santé*] at risk; **2** (souillé) [*personne*] compromised; [*réputation, prestige*] damaged; **être ~ dans un scandale** to be involved in a scandal.

III *nm* **1** (arrangement) compromise (**entre** between); (avec un créancier) arrangement; **solution de ~** compromise solution; **plaisir sans ~** pure unadulterated pleasure; **2** Jur arbitration agreement; **mettre une affaire en ~** to refer a dispute to arbitration.

compromission /kɔ̃pʀɔmisjɔ̃/ *nf* (entre personnes) deal; (avec sa conscience) compromise of principle.

comptabilisation /kɔ̃tabilizasjɔ̃/ *nf* **1** (d'erreurs, entrées, de sorties) counting; **2** Compta entering; **faire la ~ de qch** to enter sth.

comptabiliser /kɔ̃tabilize/ [1] *vtr* **1** (additionner) to count (the number of) [*erreurs, personnes, entrées*]; **j'en ai comptabilisé 52** I have counted 52; **2** Compta to enter ou record [sth] in the books.

comptabilité /kɔ̃tabilite/ *nf* **1** (concept, discipline) accountancy; **faire des études de ~** to study accountancy; **2** (profession, activité) accounting; **suivre un stage de ~** to do an accountancy course; **3** (tenue de livres) bookkeeping; **faire sa ~** to do one's accounts; **tenir la ~** to keep the books; **4** (ensemble des comptes) accounts (*pl*); **leur ~ est très mal tenue** their accounts are very badly kept; **5** (service) accounts department.

■ **~ analytique** (d'entreprise) management accounting; (de produit) cost accounting; **~ commerciale** business accounting; **~ d'entreprise** = **~ commerciale**; **~ industrielle** = **~ analytique**; **~ nationale** national accounts (*pl*); **~ publique** (règles) public accounts (*pl*); (service) public accounts office.

comptable /kɔ̃tabl/ **I** *adj* **1** Compta [*document, règle, année*] accounting; [*service*] accounts; **la situation ~ d'un commerce** the state of the accounts of a business; **leur situation ~** the state of their accounts; **agent ~** accountant; **2** Ling [*nom*] countable; **non ~** uncountable; **3** (responsable) fml **être ~ de qch devant qn** to be accountable to sb for sth.

II ▶ **510** *nmf* (spécialiste) accountant; (personne qui tient les livres) bookkeeper.

■ **~ agréé** chartered accountant; **~ du Trésor** Admin *regional governmental treasurer*.

comptage /kɔ̃taʒ/ *nm* counting ₵; **faire le ~ de** to count; **un rapide ~ permet d'affirmer que** a quick count makes it possible to state that; **le ~ des véhicules est effectué à l'entrée du tunnel** vehicles are counted at the tunnel entrance; **système de ~** counting system.

comptant /kɔ̃tɑ̃/ **I** *adj inv* cash; **il m'a versé 300 francs ~** he paid me 300 francs cash; ▶ **argent**.

II *adv* [*payer, régler*] cash; **acheter une maison ~** to pay cash for a house.

III au comptant *loc adv* [*vendre*] for cash.

compte /kɔ̃t/ **I** *nm* **1** (calcul) count; **faire le ~ de qch** to work out [*dépenses, recettes*]; to count (up) [*personnes, objets*]; **si je fais le ~ de ce qu'il me doit** if I work out what he owes me; **le ~ est bon** that works out right; **j'ai fait le ~ des chocolats qui restaient** I counted up how many chocolates were left; **tenir le ~ de qch** to keep count of sth; **elle tient un ~ précis de ses heures supplémentaires** she keeps an exact count of her extra hours; **comment fais-tu ton ~ pour faire...?** fig how do you manage to do...?; **au bout du ~** (pour constater) in the end; **tout ~ fait** (tout bien considéré) all things considered; (en fait) when all is said and done; **en fin de ~** (pour conclure) at the end of the day; **tout ~ fait** or **en fin de ~, c'est lui qui avait raison** when all is said and done, HE was right; **2** (résultat) (d'argent) amount; (d'objets, heures, de personnes) number; **le ~ y est** (en argent) that's the right amount; (en objets, personnes) all present and correct; **le ~ n'y est pas, il n'y a pas le ~** (en argent) that's not the right amount; (en objets, personnes) that's not the right number; **il y a 28 élèves, le ~ y est/n'y est pas** there are 28 pupils, everybody's here/somebody's missing ou (plusieurs personnes) some are missing; **il devrait rester 15 pots de confiture, le ~ n'y est pas** there should be 15 jars of jam left, but they're not all there; **faire le ~** (en argent) to come to the right amount; (en personnes, objets) to come to the right number; **voici 20 francs, cela devrait faire le ~** here's 20 francs, that should be about right; **même si chacun ajoute 20 francs cela ne fera pas le ~** even if everybody puts in another 20 francs, it still won't come to the right amount; **avoir son ~ d'heures de sommeil** to get the right amount of sleep; **il a son ~**○ (battu, tué) he's done for○; (ivre) he's had a drop too much; **nous avons eu notre ~ d'ennuis** fig we've had more than our fair share of problems; **à ce ~-là** (dans ces conditions) in that case; **3** (considération) **prendre qch en ~, tenir ~ de qch** to take sth into account; **~ tenu de** considering; **4** (intérêt personnel) **être à son ~** to be self-employed; **travailler à son ~** to work for oneself; **se mettre** or **s'installler** or **s'établir à son ~** to set up one's own business; **reprendre un commerce à son ~** to take over a business in one's own name; **prendre des jours de congé à son ~** to take a few days off without pay ou to take a few days' unpaid leave; **pour le ~ de qn** on behalf of sb; **y trouver son ~** to get something out of it; **ils ont abandonné l'enquête, beaucoup ont dû y trouver leur ~** they abandoned the enquiry GB ou inquiry US, that must have suited a lot of people; **faire le ~ de qn**† to benefit sb; **les livres publiés à ~ d'auteur** books published at the author's expense; **5** Compta account; **passer** or **mettre en ~** to place [sth] to account [*somme*]; **être en ~ avec qn** to have money matters to settle with sb; **faire ses ~s** [*commerçant, ménagère*] to do one's accounts; **tenir les ~s** [*commerçant, ménagère, comptable*] to keep the accounts; **c'est moi qui tiens les ~s à la maison** I keep the household accounts; ▶ **ami, ligne**; **6** Fin account; **~ bancaire** or **en banque** bank account; **~ gelé/sans mouvement** frozen/dormant account; **avoir un ~ dans une banque** to have an account with a bank; **avoir un ~ en Suisse** to have a Swiss bank account; **avoir 1000 francs sur son ~** to have 1,000 francs in one's account; **verser de l'argent** or **faire un versement sur un ~** to pay money into an account; **retirer de l'argent de son ~** to withdraw (some) money from one's account;

un ~ au nom de... an account in the name of...; 7 Comm (ardoise) account; **j'ai un ~ chez un libraire** I have an account with a bookshop GB ou bookstore; **mettre qch sur le ~ de qn** lit to charge sth to sb's account; fig to put sth down to sb; **il l'a mis sur le ~ de la fatigue** he put it down to tiredness; **8** (somme à payer) **voilà votre ~** here's your money; **demander son ~ à qn** to hand in one's notice to sb; **donner son ~ à qn** to give sb notice; **recevoir son ~** (être payé) to be paid; (être renvoyé) to be given one's notice; **9** (explication, rapport) **rendre ~ de qch à qn** (rapporter) to give an account of sth to sb; (justifier) to account for sth to sb; **je n'ai pas à te rendre ~ de mes actions** I don't have to account for my actions to you; **rendre des ~s à qn** [*responsable*] to be answerable to sb; **je n'ai pas de ~s à te rendre** I don't have to answer to you; **demander des ~s à qn** to ask for an explanation from sb; **10** (notion nette) **se rendre ~ de** (être conscient) to realize; (remarquer) to notice; **il ne s'est pas rendu ~ du mal qu'il avait fait** he didn't realize the harm he had done; **tout cela s'est passé si vite que je ne me suis rendu ~ de rien** it all happened so quickly that I didn't realize what was going on; **tu ne te rends pas ~ que c'est dangereux!** don't you realize how dangerous it is?; **je ne me suis pas rendu ~ de l'heure** I didn't notice the time; **se rendre ~ de la difficulté d'une tâche** to realize how difficult a job is; **je ne me suis jamais rendu ~ que** I never realized that; **11** (sujet) **sur le ~ de qn** about sb; **je ne sais rien sur leur ~** I don't know anything about them; **12** Sport (en boxe) count; **pour le ~** for the count.

II à bon compte *loc adv* lit (à peu de frais) [*acheter*] cheap; [*acquérir, voyager*] cheaply; fig (sans difficulté) the easy way; **avoir qch à bon ~** to get sth cheap; **étudiant qui a obtenu son diplôme à bon ~** student who got his degree the easy way; **s'en tirer à bon ~** to get off lightly; **s'en tirer à bon ~ avec un bras cassé** to get off (lightly) with a broken arm.

■ **~ d'affectation** Compta appropriation account; **~ d'amortissement** Compta depreciation account; **~ de bilan** Compta balance sheet; **~ bloqué** Fin blocked account; **~ chèques** Fin current account GB, checking account US; **~ chèque postal, CCP** Fin, Postes post office account; **~ client** Compta accounts receivable; Fin customer account; **~ courant** Fin = **~ chèques**; **~ de dépôt** Fin deposit account; **~ d'épargne** Fin savings account; **~ d'épargne logement, CEL** Fin *savings account entitling depositor to cheap mortgage*; **~ d'exploitation** Compta trading account; **~ fournisseurs** Compta accounts payable, payables US; **~ joint** Fin joint account; **~ sur livret** Fin savings account; **~ numéroté** Fin numbered account; **~ de pertes et profits** Compta profit and loss account; **ce livre a disparu! encore un à mettre au ~ des pertes et profits!** fig the book has disappeared! another one we can say goodbye to!; **~ à rebours** countdown; **le ~ à rebours de la campagne est commencé** fig the run-up to the elections has started; **~ rémunéré** Fin interest-bearing (current GB ou checking US) account; **~ de résultat** Compta profit and loss account; **~ de situation** = **~ de bilan**; **~ de soutien** Admin, Fin state support fund (**à** for) ; **~ à vue** = **~ chèques**; **~s d'apothicaire** complicated calculations.

compté, ~e /kɔ̃te/ **I** *pp* ▶ **compter**.

II *pp adj* [*jours, heures*] numbered; **ses jours sont ~s, ses heures sont ~es** his/her days are numbered; **le temps est ~** time is short; **le temps nous est ~** we're pressed for time; **à pas ~s** lit with measured steps; fig cautiously.

compte-fils /kɔ̃tfil/ *nm inv* weaver's glass, thread counter.

compte-gouttes /kɔ̃tgut/ *nm inv* dropper; **au ~** lit with a dropper; fig (avec parcimonie) sparingly; (en petite quantité) a little at a time; (en petit nombre à la fois) a few at a time; **il donne le matériel/les stylos au ~** he gives out the supplies/the pens a few at a time.

compter /kɔ̃te/ [1] **I** *vtr* **1** (dénombrer) to count; **~ les jours** to count the days; **'j'ai compté cinq coups à l'horloge'—'j'en ai compté six'** 'I counted five strokes of the clock'—'I counted six'; **'combien y a-t-il de bouteilles?'—'j'en compte 24'** 'how many bottles are there?'—'I make it 24'; **on compte deux millions de chômeurs/3 000 cas de malaria** there is a total of two million unemployed/3,000 cases of malaria; **une heure après le début de l'attaque on comptait déjà 40 morts** an hour after the attack started 40 deaths had already been recorded; **on ne compte plus ses victoires** he/she has had countless victories; **je ne compte plus les lettres anonymes que je reçois** I've lost count of the anonymous letters I have received; **j'ai compté qu'il y avait 52 fenêtres/500 francs** I counted a total of 52 windows/500 francs; **as-tu compté combien il reste d'œufs?** have you counted how many eggs are left?; **2** (évaluer) **~ une bouteille pour trois** to allow a bottle between three people; **pour aller à Caen il faut ~ cinq heures** you must allow five hours to get to Caen; **il faut ~ environ 100 francs** you should reckon on GB ou count on paying about 100 francs; **~ large/très large/trop large** to allow plenty/more than enough/far too much; **j'ai pris une tarte pour huit, je préfère ~ large** I got a tart for eight, I prefer to be on the safe side; **3** (faire payer) **~ qch à qn** to charge sb for sth; **il m'a compté le dollar à 6 francs** he charged me 6 francs to the dollar; **il m'a compté 250 francs de déplacement** he charged a 250 francs call-out fee; **4** (inclure) to count; **je vous ai compté dans le nombre des participants** I've counted you as one of ou among the participants; **nous t'avons déjà compté pour le repas de la semaine prochaine** we've already counted you (in) for the meal next week; **as-tu compté la TVA?** have you counted the VAT?; **15 000 francs par mois sans ~ les primes** 15,000 francs a month not counting bonuses; **sans ~ les soucis** not to mention the worry; **j'ai oublié de ~ le col et la ceinture quand j'ai acheté le tissu** I forgot to allow for the collar and the waistband when I bought the fabric; **je le comptais au nombre de mes amis** I counted him among my friends ou as a friend; **s'il fallait ~ le temps que j'y passe** if I had to work out how much time I'm spending on it; **5** (avoir) to have [*habitants, chômeurs, alliés*]; to have [sth] to one's credit [*victoire, succès*]; **notre club compte des gens célèbres** our club has some well-known people among its members; **un sportif qui compte de nombreuses victoires à son actif** a sportsman who has many victories to his credit; **il compte 15 ans de présence dans l'entreprise** he has been with the company for 15 years; **6** (projeter) **~ faire** to intend to do; **'comptez-vous y aller?'—'j'y compte bien'** 'do you intend to go?'—'yes, I certainly do'; **je compte m'acheter un ordinateur** I'm hoping to buy myself a computer ; **7** (s'attendre à) **il comptait que je lui prête de l'argent** he expected me to lend him some money; **'je vais t'aider'—'j'y compte bien'** 'I'll help you'—'I should hope so too'; **8** (donner avec parcimonie) **il a toujours compté ses sous** he has always watched the pennies; **~ jusqu'au moindre centime** to count every penny; **sans ~** [*donner, dépenser*] freely; **se dépenser sans ~ pour (la réussite de) qch** to put everything one's got into sth.

II *vi* **1** (dire les nombres) to count; **~ jusqu'à 20** to count up to 20; **il ne sait pas ~** he can't count; **il a trois ans mais il compte déjà bien** he's three but he's already good at counting; **~ sur ses doigts** to count on one's fingers; **2** (calculer) to count, to add up; **il sait très bien ~, il compte très bien** he's very good at counting; **cela fait 59 non pas 62, tu ne sais pas ~!** that makes 59 not 62, you can't count!; **~ sur ses doigts** to work sums out on one's fingers; **3** (avoir de l'importance) [*avis, diplôme, apparence*] to matter (**pour qn** to sb); **ce qui compte c'est qu'ils se sont réconciliés** what matters is that they have made it up; **c'est l'intention** or **le geste qui compte** it's the thought that counts; **40 ans dans la même entreprise ça compte/ça commence à ~** 40 years in the same company, that's quite something/it's beginning to add up; **ça compte beaucoup pour moi** it means a lot to me; **je ne compte pas plus pour elle que son chien** I mean no more to her than her dog; **~ dans** to be a factor in [*réussite, échec*]; **le salaire compte beaucoup dans le choix d'une carrière** pay is an important factor in the choice of a career; **cela a beaucoup compté dans leur faillite** it was a major factor in their bankruptcy; **ça fait longtemps que je ne compte plus dans ta vie** it's been a long time since I have meant anything to you; **il connaît tout ce qui compte dans le milieu du cinéma** he knows everybody who is anybody in film circles; **4** (avoir une valeur) [*épreuve, faute*] to count; **~ double/triple** to count double/triple; **~ double/triple par rapport à** to count for twice/three times as much as; **ça ne compte pas, il a triché** it doesn't count, he cheated; **le dernier exercice ne compte pas dans le calcul de la note** the last exercise isn't counted in the calculation of the grade; **la lettre 'y' compte pour combien?** how much is the letter 'y' worth?; **la lettre 'z' compte pour combien de points?** how many points is the letter 'z' worth?; **une faute de grammaire compte pour quatre points** four marks are deducted for a grammatical error; **5** (figurer) **~ au nombre de, ~ parmi** to be counted among; **6 ~ avec** (faire face) to reckon with [*difficultés, concurrence, belle-mère*]; (ne pas oublier) to take [sb/sth] into account [*personne, chose*]; (prévoir) to allow for [*retard, supplément*]; **il doit ~ avec les syndicats** he has to reckon with the unions; **il faut ~ avec l'opinion publique** one must take public opinion into account; **il faut ~ avec le brouillard dans cette région** you should allow for fog in that area; **7 ~ sans** (négliger) to reckon without [*risque, gêne*]; (oublier) not to take [sb/sth] into account [*personne, chose*]; **c'était ~ sans le brouillard** that was without allowing for the fog; **j'avais compté sans la TVA** I hadn't taken the VAT into account; **8 ~ sur** (attendre) to count on [*personne, aide*]; (dépendre, faire confiance) to rely on [*personne, ressource*]; (prévoir) to reckon on [*somme, revenu*]; **vous pouvez ~ sur moi, je viendrai** you can count on me, I'll be there; **tu peux ~ sur ma présence** you can count on me ou on my being there; **vous pouvez ~ sur moi, je vais m'en occuper** you can rely ou count on me, I'll see to it; **ne compte pas sur moi** (pour venir, participer) count me out; **ne compte pas sur moi pour payer tes dettes/faire la cuisine** don't rely on me to pay your debts/do the cooking; **ne compte pas sur eux pour le faire** don't count on them to do it; **le pays peut ~ sur des stocks de vivres en provenance de...** the country can count on stocks of food supplies coming from...; **le pays peut ~ sur ses réserves de blé** the country can rely on its stock of wheat; **je ne peux ~ que sur moi-même** I can only rely on myself; **je leur ferai la commission, compte sur moi** I'll give them the message, you can count on me; **je vais leur dire ce que j'en pense, tu peux ~ là-dessus**○ or **sur moi!** I'll tell them what I think, you can be sure of that!; **quand il s'agit de faire des bêtises, on peut ~ sur toi**○! iron trust you to do something silly!; **~ sur la discrétion de qn** to rely on sb's discretion; **je compte dessus** I'm counting ou relying on it.

III se compter *vpr* **leurs victoires se comptent par douzaines** they have had dozens of victories; **les défections se comptent par milliers** there have been thousands of defections; **leurs chansons à succès ne se comptent plus** they've had countless hits; **les faillites dans la région ne se comptent plus** there have been countless bankruptcies in the area.

IV à compter de *loc prép* as from; **réparations gratuites pendant 12 mois à ~ de la date de vente** free repairs for 12 months with effect from the date of sale.

V sans compter que *loc conj* (en outre) and what is more; (d'autant plus que) especially as; **c'est dangereux sans ~ que ça pollue** it's dangerous and what's more it causes pollution.

IDIOMES **compte là-dessus et bois de l'eau fraîche**○ that'll be the day.

compte(-)rendu, *pl* **comptes(-)rendus** /kɔ̃tʀɑ̃dy/ *nm* (de débat, travaux, d'événement) report; (d'article, de livre) review; **faire le ~ de** to report on [*débat, travaux*]; to review [*article, livre*]; **faire un ~ rapide/détaillé de** to give a brief/detailed report on [*débat, événement*]; to give a short/detailed review of [*livre, thèse*].

compte-tours /kɔ̃ttuʀ/ *nm inv* rev-counter, revolution-counter.

compteur /kɔ̃tœʀ/ *nm* (de fluide) meter; (de distance) clock; **~ d'eau** water meter; **la voiture a 50000 km au ~** the car has 50,000 km on the clock; **il faisait du 90 km/h au ~** he was doing 90 km/h on the speedometer; **remettre le ~ à zéro** lit to reset the meter at ou to zero; fig○ to make a fresh start.

■ **~ kilométrique** ≈ milometer; **~ de vitesse** speedometer.

comptine /kɔ̃tin/ *nf* **1** (pour choisir) counting rhyme; **2** (chansonnette) nursery rhyme.

comptoir /kɔ̃twaʀ/ *nm* **1** (de café) bar; **au ~** at the bar; **prix au ~** *tarif for drinks and snacks at the bar in a café*; **2** (de magasin) counter; **~ parfumerie** perfume counter; **~ frigorifique** refrigerated display counter; **3** Hist trading post; **un ancien ~ des Indes** a former trading post in India; **4** Fin branch (*of the Banque de France*).

■ **~ d'enregistrement** Transp check-in desk.

compulser /kɔ̃pylse/ [1] *vtr* to consult.

compulsif, **-ive** /kɔ̃pylsif, iv/ *adj* compulsive.

compulsion /kɔ̃pylsjɔ̃/ *nf* compulsion.

comte /kɔ̃t/ ▶ **813** *nm* gén count; (titre anglais) earl; **bien, monsieur le ~** very well, my lord.

comté /kɔ̃te/ *nm* **1** (fromage) comté; **2** Admin county; **3** Hist earldom (*land*).

comtesse /kɔ̃tɛs/ ▶ **813** *nf* countess; **bien, madame la ~** very well, your ladyship.

comtois, **~e** /kɔ̃twa, az/ ▶ **692** *adj* of Franche-Comté.

Comtois, **~e** /kɔ̃twa, az/ *nm,f* (natif) native of Franche-Comté; (habitant) inhabitant of Franche-Comté.

con●, **conne** /kɔ̃, kɔn/ **I** *adj* **1** (bête) pej fucking● stupid, bloody◑ GB stupid; **elle est ~** or **conne** she's bloody◑ stupid; **2** (facile) dead○ easy.

II *nm,f* (bête) offensive bloody◑ idiot GB injur, stupid jerk○ injur; **faire le ~** to mess about, to arse around◑; **idée/voiture/ministre à la ~** lousy○ idea/car/minister.

III *nm* (vagin) cunt●.

IDIOMES **être ~ comme la lune** or **un balai** to be as thick as two short planks○.

Conakry /kɔnakʀy/ ▶ **857** *npr* Conakry.

conard● = **connard**.

conasse● = **connasse**.

concassage /kɔ̃kasaʒ/ *nm* crushing.

concasser /kɔ̃kase/ [1] *vtr* **1** Culin, Tech to crush; **2** Mus to mix.

concasseur /kɔ̃kasœʀ/ **I** *adj m* crushing.

II *nm* crusher.

concaténation /kɔ̃katenasjɔ̃/ *nf* concatenation.

concave /kɔ̃kav/ *adj* concave.

concavité /kɔ̃kavite/ *nf* **1** (état) concavity; **2** (partie creuse) hollow.

concédant /kɔ̃sedɑ̃/ *nm* Écon, Jur (de licence) licensor[GB]; (de contrat) contractor.

concéder /kɔ̃sede/ [14] *vtr* **1** Admin, Comm, Écon to grant [*monopole, franchise*] (**à** to); to contract out [*travaux*] (**à** to); **~ un contrat à qn** gén to place a contract with sb; (après un appel d'offres) to award a contract to sb; **autoroute concédée** motorway GB ou freeway US (which is) under private management; **2** (admettre) to concede; **c'est possible, concéda-t-il** it's possible, he conceded; **c'est absurde, concédez-le** you must concede that it is ridiculous; **3** Sport to concede [*défaite, victoire, but*].

concélébrer /kɔ̃selebʀe/ [14] *vtr* Relig to concelebrate.

concentration /kɔ̃sɑ̃tʀasjɔ̃/ *nf* **1** (attention) concentration; **~ d'esprit** (mental) concentration; **j'ai besoin de quelques instants de ~** I need to concentrate for a few moments; **elle manque de ~** she can't concentrate; **2** (accumulation) concentration (**de** of); **~ de troupes aux frontières du pays** build-up of troops on the country's borders; **3** Chimie concentration; **4** Écon concentration; **~ horizontale/verticale** horizontal/vertical integration.

■ **~ urbaine** conurbation.

concentrationnaire /kɔ̃sɑ̃tʀasjɔnɛʀ/ *adj* [*vie, discipline*] concentration camp (*épith*).

concentré, **~e** /kɔ̃sɑ̃tʀe/ **I** *pp* ▶ **concentrer**.

II *pp adj* **1** (attentif) **un air ~** a look of concentration; **un enfant ~** a child who is concentrating (**sur** on); **elle est ~e** she's concentrating; **2** (condensé, rassemblé) concentrated; **lait ~** condensed milk; **3** Mil [*tir*] heavy.

III *nm* **1** Chimie (solution) concentrated solution; **2** (aliment) concentrate; **~ de tomate** tomato purée GB ou paste US; **ses cours, c'est du ~** fig his/her lectures are very condensed; **3** fig (de banalités, vertus) compendium.

concentrer /kɔ̃sɑ̃tʀe/ [1] **I** *vtr* (tous contextes) to concentrate; **~ ses efforts sur qch/à faire qch** to concentrate one's efforts on sth/on doing sth.

II se concentrer *vpr* **1** (être attentif) to concentrate (**sur** on); (se préparer mentalement) to gather one's thoughts; **il n'arrive pas à se ~** he can't concentrate; **se ~ avant un entretien** to gather oneself ou one's thoughts before an interview; **2** (être dirigé) **se ~ sur qch** [*efforts, attention*] to be concentrated on sth; **3** (être rassemblé) [*population, erreurs, usines*] to be concentrated; **4** (se rassembler) **les grévistes se sont concentrés devant l'usine** the strikers gathered outside the factory.

concentrique /kɔ̃sɑ̃tʀik/ *adj* concentric.

concept /kɔ̃sɛpt/ *nm* concept.

concepteur, **-trice** /kɔ̃sɛptœʀ, tʀis/ ▶ **510** *nm,f* **~ maquettiste** graphic designer; **~ rédacteur** advertising copywriter.

conception /kɔ̃sɛpsjɔ̃/ *nf* **1** Biol conception; **2** (formulation d'idée) conception; **la ~ de l'œuvre a été lente** it took a long time to conceive the work; **3** (élaboration de la forme) design; **au stade de la ~** at the design stage; **voiture d'une ~ révolutionnaire** car with a revolutionary design; **4** (idée) idea; (façon de voir) conception; **elle a une ~ bizarre de la fidélité** she has a pretty odd conception ou idea of fidelity; **ils ont une ~ différente du mariage** they don't share the same views on marriage, they have a different conception of marriage.

■ **~ assistée par ordinateur**, **CAO** computer-aided design, CAD; **~ et fabrication assistées par ordinateur**, **CFAO** CAD-CAM; **~ de programmes assistée par ordinateur**, **CPAO** computer-aided software engineering, CASE.

conceptualisation /kɔ̃sɛptɥalizasjɔ̃/ *nf* conceptualization.

conceptualiser /kɔ̃sɛptɥalize/ [1] *vtr* to conceptualize.

conceptuel, **-elle** /kɔ̃sɛptɥɛl/ *adj* Philos, Psych conceptual; **art ~** conceptual art.

concernant /kɔsɛʀnɑ̃/ *prép* **1** (touchant) concerning; **le décret ~ l'élection** the decree concerning the election; **2** (en ce qui concerne) as regards, with regard to; **~ la banque, la situation reste inchangée** as regards the bank ou as far as the bank is concerned, the situation remains unchanged.

concerner /kɔ̃sɛʀne/ [1] *vtr* **1** (viser) to concern; **cette remarque vous concerne** this remark concerns you; **pour affaire vous concernant** in connection with a matter that concerns you; **en ce qui me concerne** as far as I am concerned; **en ce qui concerne le salaire** as regards salary, as far as salary is concerned; **cela ne vous concerne pas** (ne vous vise pas) it does not concern you; (ne vous regarde pas) it's no concern of yours; **se sentir concerné** to feel concerned (**par** about); **2** (toucher) to affect; **cette décision nous concerne tous** this decision affects all of us.

concert /kɔ̃sɛʀ/ **I** *nm* **1** Mus concert; **un ~ de rock/jazz** a rock/jazz concert; **un ~ de musique classique** a concert of classical music; **Max 80 en ~ ce soir** Max 80 in concert tonight; **donner un ~ en plein air** to give an open-air concert; **salle de ~** concert hall; **2** (bruits émis) **~ de klaxons®** a blaring of horns; **~ d'applaudissements** roar of applause; **~ de critiques** barrage of criticism; **~ d'aboiements** dogs barking in unison; **3** (entente) **le ~ des nations** the alliance of nations.

II de concert *loc adv* **ils ont agi de ~** they worked together; **étudier/militer de ~** to study/campaign together; **ils ont protesté de ~ avec les étudiants** they protested in unison with the students.

concertant, **~e** /kɔ̃sɛʀtɑ̃, ɑ̃t/ *adj* concertante; **symphonie ~e** sinfonia concertante; **style ~** concertante style.

concertation /kɔ̃sɛʀtasjɔ̃/ *nf* **1** (discussions) consultation; **un manque de ~** a lack of consultation; **agir en ~ avec** to act in consultation with; **sans ~ préalable** without preliminary consultation; **le projet est en cours de ~** the project is being discussed; **2** (fait de travailler de concert) cooperation; **3** (principe) cooperation, dialogue[GB].

concerté, **~e** /kɔ̃sɛʀte/ **I** *pp* ▶ **concerter**.

II *pp adj* [*plan, action, offensive*] concerted; **fraude ~e** collective fraud.

concerter /kɔ̃sɛʀte/ [1] **I** *vtr* to plan [*action, projet, décision*] (**avec** with).

II se concerter *vpr* to confer (with each other) (**sur** about; **pour faire** (in order) to do).

concertina /kɔ̃sɛʀtina/ *nm* concertina.

concertino /kɔ̃sɛʀtino/ *nm* concertino.

concertiste /kɔ̃sɛʀtist/ ▶ **510** *nmf* concert artist ou performer.

concerto /kɔ̃sɛʀto/ *nm* concerto.

concessif, **-ive** /kɔ̃sesif, iv/ **I** *adj* concessive.

II concessive *nf* concessive clause.

concession /kɔ̃sesjɔ̃/ *nf* **1** (compromis)

concession (**à** to; **sur** on); **film/livre sans ~s** uncompromising ou forthright film/book; **dresser un tableau sans ~s de qch** to give a frank account of sth; **faire des ~s** to make concessions (**à** to); **2** (attribution) concession; **3** (droit d'exploitation) (de mine, territoire, terrain) concession; (de produit) distributorship; Aut dealership; **~ minière** mining concession; **4** Admin (dans un cimetière) burial plot; **~ à perpétuité** burial plot in perpetuity; (pour travaux) **~ de travaux** works contract; **~ de service public** private contract to run a public service; **5** Ling concession; **'bien que' introduit la ~** 'bien que' introduces a concessive clause.

concessionnaire /kɔ̃sesjɔnɛʀ/ **I** *adj* **1** Comm, Écon **société ~** concessionary company; **2** Admin (pour travaux, services publics) **entreprise ~** contract-holder.
II *nmf* **1** (détenteur d'un droit) gén concessionaire; (d'une licence) licensee; (d'une franchise) franchise holder, franchisee; **elle est ~ de parfumerie dans un grand magasin** she runs a perfume concession in a department store; **2** (commerçant) (pour un produit) distributor; (pour un service) agent; Aut dealer.

concevable /kɔ̃s(ə)vabl/ *adj* conceivable; **très ~** quite conceivable.

concevoir /kɔ̃s(ə)vwaʀ/ [5] **I** *vtr* **1** (élaborer) to design [*produit, système, projet*] (**pour qch** for sth; **pour faire** to do); **conçu et réalisé par** designed and produced by; **un système conçu comme flexible** a system which is designed to be adaptable; **notre hôtel a d'abord été conçu comme une maison** we wanted our hotel to be first and foremost a home; **bien/mal conçu** well/badly designed; **conçu en ces termes** phrased in these terms; **2** (procréer) to conceive [*enfant*]; **3** (comprendre) to understand [*attitude, réaction*]; **on conçoit tout à fait que** it is perfectly understandable that; **je conçois très bien que** I fully understand why; **je ne conçois pas de faire** I cannot conceive of ou imagine having to do; **4** Philos to form [*idée*]; **~ une entité** to form an idea of an entity; **5** (considérer) to see [*phénomène, activité*] (**comme** as); **~ la politique comme un métier** to see politics as a job; **la rencontre a été conçue comme une première étape** the meeting was envisaged as a first step; **6** (ressentir) fml to conceive [*haine*]; to have [*doute*].
II se concevoir *vpr* **1** (être imaginable) to be conceivable; **l'avenir ne se conçoit pas sans lui** the future is inconceivable without him; **2** (être compréhensible) [*attitude, réaction*] to be understandable; **cela se conçoit aisément** this is quite understandable; **3** (s'élaborer) to be designed; **se ~ sur ordinateur** to be designed on a computer.

conchyliculture /kɔ̃ʃilikyltyʀ/ *nf* shellfish farming.

concierge /kɔ̃sjɛʀʒ/ **▶510** *nmf* caretaker GB, superintendant US; (dans un immeuble) concierge; **c'est une vraie ~** fig (bavard) he's/she's a real gossip; (curieux) he's/she's a nosy parker○.

conciergerie /kɔ̃sjɛʀʒəʀi/ *nf* caretaker's flat GB, superintendent's apartment US; **la Conciergerie** Hist the Conciergerie.

concile /kɔ̃sil/ *nm* Relig council; **~ œcuménique** ecumenical council.

conciliable /kɔ̃siljabl/ *adj* [*opinions, théories*] reconcilable (**avec** with); [*caractères*] compatible (**avec** with); **nos idées ne sont pas ~s** our ideas are irreconcilable; **ces théories sont difficilement ~s avec celles du gouvernement** these theories are difficult to reconcile with those of the government.

conciliabule /kɔ̃siljabyl/ *nm* **1** (discussion) consultation, confab○; **tenir un ~** to hold a consultation; **être en grand ~** to be deep in discussion; **2†** (réunion) secret meeting.

conciliaire /kɔ̃siljɛʀ/ *adj* [*collection, décision*] conciliar; **père ~** Council Father.

conciliant, **~e** /kɔ̃siljɑ̃, ɑ̃t/ *adj* conciliatory (**avec** toward, towards GB).

conciliateur, **-trice** /kɔ̃siljatœʀ, tʀis/ **I** *adj* conciliatory (*épith*).
II *nm,f* conciliator.
III *nm* Jur conciliator.

conciliation /kɔ̃siljasjɔ̃/ *nf* **1** Jur conciliation; (d'époux) reconciliation; **tentative/esprit de ~** attempt at/spirit of conciliation; **procédure de ~** conciliation procedure; **commission de ~** arbitration committee; **2** (d'intérêts, de besoins) reconciliation, reconciling.

conciliatoire /kɔ̃siljatwaʀ/ *adj* Jur conciliation (*épith*).

concilier /kɔ̃silje/ [2] **I** *vtr* **1** (accorder) to reconcile [*notions, besoins, intérêts*] (**avec** with); **2** Jur (réconcilier) Jur to reconcile [*adversaires*]; **3** (gagner) fml **cette loi lui a concilié l'opinion publique** this law won over public opinion to his/her side.
II se concilier *vpr* (conquérir) to win [*bienveillance, soutien*]; to win over [*opinion publique, personne*]; **se ~ les dieux** to propitiate the gods.

concis, **~e** /kɔ̃si, iz/ *adj* concise.

concision /kɔ̃sizjɔ̃/ *nf* conciseness; **avec ~** concisely.

concitoyen, **-enne** /kɔ̃sitwajɛ̃, ɛn/ *nm,f* **1** (d'un pays) fellow-countryman/fellow-countrywoman; **nos ~s** our fellow-countrymen; **2** (d'une ville) fellow-citizen.

conclave /kɔ̃klav/ *nm* conclave.

concluant, **~e** /kɔ̃klyɑ̃, ɑ̃t/ *adj* conclusive; **peu ~** rather inconclusive.

conclure /kɔ̃klyʀ/ [78] **I** *vtr* **1** (déduire) to conclude (**que** that), to draw the conclusion (**que** that); (parvenir à une opinion) to draw a conclusion (**de** from); **que concluez-vous de ces chiffres?** what conclusion do you draw from these figures?; **il ne faut pas se hâter d'en ~ que** we mustn't jump to the conclusion that; **oui, mais de là à ~ qu'il est coupable**... yes, but to decide from that that he is guilty...; **2** (régler) to conclude [*accord, transaction*]; **~ un marché** to close ou clinch ou strike a deal; **'marché conclu!'** 'it's a deal!'; **3** (mettre fin à) [*personne*] to conclude [*discours, séance*] (**par** with); to finish off [*soirée, match*] (**par** with); **'voilà,' dit-il pour ~** 'that's all,' he concluded; **avant de ~ j'aimerais ajouter que** before concluding I would just like to add that; **4** (être la fin de) [*concert, match*] to bring [sth] to a close [*festival, journée*]; [*phrase*] to bring [sth] to a close ou an end [*discours, chapitre*]; to conclude [*lettre*]; [*but*] to end [*match*].
II conclure à *vtr ind* (décider) **~ à la nécessité/folie de qch** to conclude that sth is necessary/crazy; **~ à la culpabilité de qn** to conclude that sb is guilty; [*jury*] to return a verdict of guilty; **~ au meurtre** to conclude that it was murder; [*jury*] to return a verdict of murder; **~ à l'acquittement** Jur to decide on an acquittal.
III *vi* **1** Jur **~ en faveur de/contre qn** [*témoignage*] to go in favour[GB] of/against sb; [*juge, jury*] to find in favour[GB] of/against sb; **2** Sport [*joueur de tennis*] to end the match.
IV se conclure *vpr* **1** (s'achever) [*soirée, festival, discours*] to end (**par** with); **2** (se régler) [*accord, transaction*] to be concluded; [*marché*] to be clinched ou struck.

conclusion /kɔ̃klyzjɔ̃/ **I** *nf* **1** (déduction) conclusion; (moralité) moral; **en ~** in conclusion; **~, il y a un problème○** in other words, there's a problem; **~, le dîner a été annulé○** so, the dinner was cancelled[GB]; **tirer la ~ qu'il vaut mieux faire**... to draw the conclusion that it's better to do; **tirer les ~s d'une expérience** to learn from an experience; **ne tire pas de ~s hâtives** don't jump to conclusions; **2** (de traité, marché) conclusion; **3** (dénouement) (de discours, session) close; (d'aventure) outcome; **apporter une ~ au débat** to bring the debate to a close.
II conclusions *nfpl* **1** (résultats) (d'analyse, autopsie) results; (d'enquête, de rapport) findings; **2** Jur (d'expert) opinion (*sg*); (de jury) verdict (*sg*) ; (de plaignant) pleadings, submissions; **déposer des ~s auprès d'un tribunal** to file submissions with a court.

concocter○ /kɔ̃kɔkte/ [1] *vtr* to concoct [*dessert, sauce*]; to devise [*réponse, programme*].

concombre /kɔ̃kɔ̃bʀ/ *nm* cucumber.

concomitance /kɔ̃kɔmitɑ̃s/ *nf* concomitance sout.

concomitant, **~e** /kɔ̃kɔmitɑ̃, ɑ̃t/ *adj* concomitant sout.

concordance /kɔ̃kɔʀdɑ̃s/ *nf* **1** (similarité) concordance (**de** between); (compatibilité) compatibility; **la parfaite ~ de leurs témoignages** the fact that their accounts agree in every respect; **s'il y a ~ entre les résultats** if the results tally; **les ~s de vues entre eux** their like-minded attitudes; **mettre en ~ avec** to make [sth] agree ou tally with [*version, témoignage*]; to bring [sth] into line with [*emploi du temps, horaire*]; **2** (index) concordance; **3** Géol conformability.
■ **~ de phase** Phys synchronization; **~ des temps** Ling sequence of tenses.

concordant, **~e** /kɔ̃kɔʀdɑ̃, ɑ̃t/ *adj* **1** [*faits*] corroborating; [*sources, témoignages, informations*] which are in agreement (*épith, après n*); **être ~** to agree ou tally; **2** Géol conformable; **3** Littérat [*vers*] concordant.

concordat /kɔ̃kɔʀda/ *nm* **1** Relig concordat; **2** (avec un créancier) (accord) composition; (attestation) bankrupt's certificate.

concordataire /kɔ̃kɔʀdatɛʀ/ Jur **I** *adj* [*débiteur*] certified; **procédure ~** composition proceedings (*pl*).
II *nmf* certified bankrupt.

concorde /kɔ̃kɔʀd/ *nf* fml harmony, concord.

Concorde /kɔ̃kɔʀd/ *nm* Aviat Concorde; **voyager en** or **prendre le ~** to fly on ou in Concorde.

concorder /kɔ̃kɔʀde/ [1] *vi* **1** [*résultats, descriptions, témoignages*] to tally; [*évaluations*] to agree; **les opinions concordent** everyone agrees; **2** Jur [*débiteur*] to compound (**avec** with).

concourant, **~e** /kɔ̃kuʀɑ̃, ɑ̃t/ *adj* **1** Math [*droites*] convergent; Phys [*forces*] concurrent; **2** [*efforts, tentatives*] concerted (*épith*).

concourir /kɔ̃kuʀiʀ/ [26] **I** *vi* **1** (participer) [*athlète, candidat*] to compete (**pour** for; **dans** in); [*livre, film*] to be entered, to be in the running (**pour** for); **~ aux jeux Olympiques** to compete in the Olympic games; **les films admis à ~ au festival** the films which have been entered for the festival; **2** Math (converger) to converge (**vers** toward, towards GB).
II concourir à *vtr ind* **1** (collaborer pour) **~ à qch** [*facteurs*] to combine to bring about sth; [*personnes*] to work together towards sth; **~ à faire qch** [*facteurs*] to combine to do sth; [*personnes*] to work together to do sth; **2** (contribuer à) [*facteur, personne*] **~ à qch** to help bring about sth; **~ à faire qch** to help do sth.

concours /kɔ̃kuʀ/ *nm* **1** (jeu, compétition) competition; **~ de piano/pêche** piano/angling competition; **~ agricole/floral** agricultural/flower show; **~ d'élégance** fig fashion show; **~ de beauté** beauty contest; **être hors ~** to be ineligible to compete; **2** Admin, Scol competitive examination; **par (voie de) ~** by competitive examination; **~ d'entrée** entrance examination (**à** for); **~ de recrutement** Admin competitive entrance examination; **3** (aide) help, assistance; (appui) support; (collaboration) cooperation; **~ financier** financial assistance; **grâce au ~ du personnel** thanks to the cooperation of the staff; **s'assurer le ~ d'agents qualifiés** to enlist the services of qualified staff; **avec le ~ de l'orchestre des Jeunes** (participation) with the Youth orchestra; **apporter** or **prêter son ~ à qch/qn** to help out with sth/to help sb out; **4** Sport (en athlétisme) field event.

■ **~ de circonstances** combination of circumstances; **~ complet** Équit three-day event; **faire un ~ complet** to go eventing; **~ général** Scol *prestigious competitive examination for pupils in top forms of French secondary schools*; **~ hippique** Équit (sport) show jumping; (épreuve) horse show.

concret, **-ète** /kɔ̃kʀɛ, ɛt/ **I** *adj* **1** (matériel, réel) [*mesure, résultat, détail*] concrete; [*présence*] tangible; **2** (pragmatique) [*esprit, personne*] practical.

II *nm* **le ~ et l'abstrait** the concrete and the abstract; **offrir du ~** to offer something concrete.

concrètement /kɔ̃kʀɛtmɑ̃/ *adv* (en termes réels) in concrete terms; (en pratique) in practical terms; **~, que proposez-vous?** in concrete terms, what are you proposing?; **~, comment t'y prendras-tu?** what are you going to do in practical terms?

concrétion /kɔ̃kʀesjɔ̃/ *nf* concretion.

concrétisation /kɔ̃kʀetizasjɔ̃/ *nf* **1** (résultat) (de domination, d'alliance) concrete expression, concrete manifestation; (d'espoir, de souhait) fulfilment[GB]; (d'ambition) achievement; **2** (action) **quant à la ~ de ce projet** as for turning this project into a reality; **3** Sport (action) scoring; (résultat) score.

concrétiser /kɔ̃kʀetize/ [1] **I** *vtr* **1** (réaliser) to make [sth] a reality [*projet, souhait*]; **2** (exprimer concrètement) to give concrete expression to [*accord, besoin, malaise, notion*]; to make [sth] concrete [*alliance, stratégie*]; **3** Sport (marquer) to score; **~ un avantage** to press home an advantage.

II se concrétiser *vpr* [*projet, rêve*] to become a reality; [*offre*] to materialize; [*espoir, souhait*] to be fulfilled.

concubin, **~e** /kɔ̃kybɛ̃, in/ **I** *nm,f* Jur common law husband/wife.

II concubine *nf* Hist concubine.

concubinage /kɔ̃kybinaʒ/ *nm* cohabitation; **ils vivent en ~** they live together (as husband and wife), they cohabit Admin; **les enfants issus du ~** children born to a cohabiting couple.

■ **~ notoire** Jur cohabitation.

concupiscence /kɔ̃kypisɑ̃s/ *nf* lechery, concupiscence sout.

concupiscent, **~e** /kɔ̃kypisɑ̃, ɑ̃t/ *adj* lecherous, concupiscent sout.

concurremment /kɔ̃kyʀamɑ̃/ *adv* **1** (en collaboration) conjointly sout; **~ avec** in conjunction with; **2** (simultanément) concurrently; **3** (en rivalité) **ils briguent ~ le poste** they are both competing for the post.

concurrence /kɔ̃kyʀɑ̃s/ **I** *nf* **1** (rivalité) competition (**entre** between; **avec** with); **~ déloyale** unfair competition; **être en ~ avec qn/qch** to be in competition with sb/sth; **faire (de la) ~ à qn** to compete with sb; **prix défiant toute ~** unbeatable price; **jeu de la ~** free play of competition; **2** (concurrents) **la ~** competitors (*pl*); **s'aligner sur les prix de la ~** to bring one's prices into line with those of one's competitors.

II jusqu'à ~ de *loc prép* up to a limit of.

concurrencer /kɔ̃kyʀɑ̃se/ [12] *vtr* [*personne, entreprise*] to compete with; [*produit, invention*] to pose a threat to; **être rudement concurrencé par** to come up against fierce competition from; **marché fortement concurrencé** highly competitive market.

concurrent, **~e** /kɔ̃kyʀɑ̃, ɑ̃t/ **I** *adj* **1** Comm, Écon [*produit, compagnie*] rival; **2**† (concourant) [*forces, efforts*] concurrent.

II *nm,f* (pour un avantage, poste) rival; Comm, Sport competitor; Scol, Univ candidate.

concurrentiel, **-ielle** /kɔ̃kyʀɑ̃sjɛl/ *adj* competitive.

concussion /kɔ̃kysjɔ̃/ *nf* Jur misappropriation of public funds.

condamnable /kɔ̃danabl/ *adj* [*attitude, pratique, opinion*] reprehensible; **ce sont les parents qui sont ~s, pas l'enfant** the parents are to blame, not the child.

condamnation /kɔ̃danasjɔ̃/ *nf* **1** Jur (action) conviction; (peine) sentence; **il y a plusieurs types de ~** there are several types of sentence; **elle en est à sa deuxième ~** this is her second conviction; **~ à la prison** prison sentence; **il risque la ~ à mort** he may be condemned to death; **il y a eu trois ~s à mort** three people were condemned to death; **~ à perpétuité/mort** life/death sentence; **~ à dix ans de prison** ten-year prison sentence; **les ~s pour vol/meurtre sont fréquentes** convictions on charges of theft/murder are frequent; **2** (vive critique) condemnation (**de** of); **3** Aut (verrouillage) **~ électronique** or **centralisée des portières** central locking.

condamné, **~e** /kɔ̃dane/ **I** *pp* ▶ **condamner**.

II *pp adj* **1** (très malade) [*personne*] terminally ill; **atteint d'un cancer il se sait ~** he has cancer and he knows it's terminal; **2** (fermé) [*porte, fenêtre*] sealed up.

III *nm,f* convicted prisoner.

■ **~ à mort** condemned man/woman.

condamner /kɔ̃dane/ [1] *vtr* **1** Jur (infliger une peine à) to sentence; **~ qn à une amende** to fine sb; **elle a été condamnée à 1000 francs d'amende** she was fined 1,000 francs; **~ qn à deux ans de réclusion** to sentence sb to two years' imprisonment; **il a été condamné à quatre mois de prison avec sursis** he was given a four-month suspended sentence; **~ qn à mort** to sentence sb to death; **~ qn pour vol** to convict sb of theft; **~ qn par défaut** or **contumace** to sentence sb in absentia; **2** (interdire) [*loi, article*] to punish [*vol, trafic*]; **la législation condamne le racisme/la bigamie** the law punishes racism/bigamy; **3** (désapprouver fortement) [*personne, pays, groupe*] to condemn [*acte, attitude, décision*]; **4** (astreindre à) to condemn (**à** to); **être condamné au silence** to be condemned to silence; **il se voit condamné à un choix difficile/à un rôle secondaire** he's being forced to make a difficult choice/to play a secondary role; **~ qn à faire** to compel sb to do; **il est condamné à attendre/coopérer** he is obliged to wait/cooperate; **5** (bloquer) (définitivement) to seal up [*fenêtre, porte, entrée*]; (fermer à clé) to shut up [*pièce*]; to lock [*portières*]; **6** fig (ruiner) to spell death for [*société, industrie, secteur*]; **les nouvelles technologies ont condamné l'artisanat** the new technologies spell death for the traditional crafts; **7** (déclarer incurable) **les médecins l'ont condamné** the doctors have given up hope of saving him.

condé◐ /kɔ̃de/ *nm* (policier) cop○, policeman.

condensateur /kɔ̃dɑ̃satœʀ/ *nm* condenser.

condensation /kɔ̃dɑ̃sasjɔ̃/ *nf* condensation.

condensé /kɔ̃dɑ̃se/ *nm* (résumé) summary; (recueil) digest.

condenser /kɔ̃dɑ̃se/ [1] **I** *vtr* **1** (abréger) to condense [*texte*]; **2** (liquéfier) to condense [*gaz*]; ▶ **lait**.

II se condenser *vpr* [*vapeur*] to condense.

condenseur /kɔ̃dɑ̃sœʀ/ *nm* condenser.

condescendance /kɔ̃desɑ̃dɑ̃s/ *nf* condescension; **avec ~** condescendingly.

condescendant, **~e** /kɔ̃desɑ̃dɑ̃, ɑ̃t/ *adj* condescending.

condescendre /kɔ̃desɑ̃dʀ/ [6] *vtr ind* **~ à** to condescend to.

condiment /kɔ̃dimɑ̃/ *nm* **1** Culin (à la cuisson) seasoning; (à table) condiment; **2** fig spice.

condisciple /kɔ̃disipl/ *nmf* fellow student.

condition /kɔ̃disjɔ̃/ **I** *nf* **1** (circonstance nécessaire) condition; **~ nécessaire et suffisante** necessary and sufficient condition (**pour faire** to do); **toutes les ~s étaient réunies pour que la cérémonie se passe bien** everything was set for the ceremony to go off well; **mettre/poser une ~** to make/to set a condition (**à** for); **dicter/poser ses ~s** to state/to lay down one's conditions; **poser qch comme ~ à** to impose sth as a condition (up)on; **à une ~** on one condition; **je prends ce modèle à ~ de pouvoir l'échanger** I'll take this model on condition that I can exchange it; **c'est possible à ~ d'avoir le temps** it's possible provided (that) one has the time; **n'importe qui peut y arriver à ~ d'avoir de la patience** anybody can do it provided (that) they have patience; **tu peux le faire à ~ de ne pas perdre de temps** you can do it as long as or provided (that) you don't waste time; **je le ferai mais à ~ que tu m'aides** I'll do it provided (that) you help me; **à la seule ~ que** on the sole condition that; **à la ~ expresse de revenir** or **qu'il revienne tôt** on the strict condition that he comes back early; **je vous prêterai la somme, mais sous ~** I'll lend you the money, but on certain conditions; **sous ~ que** on condition that; **sous ~** [*libéré*] conditionally; **achat sous ~** purchase on approval; **sans ~(s)** [*capitulation*] unconditional; [*capituler*] unconditionally; **imposer ses ~s** to impose one's own terms; **le talent n'est pas la seule ~ de tout succès** talent is not the only requirement for success; **~ préalable** precondition (**à qch** for sth); **~s d'admission** conditions of membership (**à** of GB, in US); **~s d'attribution d'une bourse** eligibility (*sg*) for a grant; **satisfaire** or **répondre aux ~s requises** to fulfil[GB] the necessary conditions; **le cours est ouvert à tout le monde, sans ~ de niveau d'études** the course is open to everyone, irrespective of their educational qualifications; **2** Jur (clause) term; **3** (forme) condition; **être en bonne ~ physique** to be in good physical condition, to be fit; **être en mauvaise ~ (physique)** to be out of condition ou unfit; **mettre qn en ~** (physiquement) to get sb fit; (mentalement) to prepare sb; **se mettre en ~** (physiquement) to get fit; (mentalement) to prepare oneself; **mise en ~** (physique) getting fit; (mentale) preparation; **se maintenir en ~** to keep fit; **4** (situation sociale) condition; **la ~ humaine** the human condition; **la ~ ouvrière** the conditions of working-class life; **la ~ enseignante** the position of teachers in society; **la ~ féminine** or **des femmes** women's position in society; **il s'intéresse beaucoup à la ~ féminine** he's very interested in women's affairs; **5** (niveau social) **~ (sociale)** social status; **vouloir changer de ~ sociale** to want to change one's social status; **accepter sa ~** to accept one's lot in life; **un jeune homme de ~ modeste** a young man from a humble background; **des personnes de toutes ~s** people from all walks of life; **personne de ~**† person of quality†; **se marier au-dessus/au-dessous de sa ~** to marry above/below one's station; **6** Ling conditionality; **'si' exprime la ~** 'si' expresses conditionality.

II conditions *nfpl* **1** (ensemble de circonstances) conditions; **~s atmosphériques** atmospheric conditions; **~s de travail/de logement** working/housing conditions; **~s de vie** living conditions; **~s d'hygiène** sanitary conditions; **ils travaillent dans des ~s difficiles/inhumaines** they are working in difficult/inhuman conditions; **dans ces ~s** (dans cet environnement) in these conditions; (puisque c'est comme ça) in that case; **2** Comm (modalités) terms; **ils ont** or **proposent des ~s très avantageuses** they offer very favourable[GB] terms; **~s générales** general terms; **~s de paiement** terms of payment; **~s de financement** methods of financing.

conditionné, **~e** /kɔ̃disjɔne/ **I** *pp* ▶ **conditionner**.

II *pp adj* **1** Psych [*personne*] conditioned (**à qch** to sth; **à faire** to do); [*animal, réflexe*] conditioned; **2** Comm [*produit*] packaged; **~ sous vide** vacuum-packed.

conditionnel, **-elle** /kɔ̃disjɔnɛl/ **I** *adj* **1** [*soutien, accord*] conditional; **2** Ling conditional.
II *nm* Ling conditional; **~ passé/présent** past/present conditional; **au ~** in the conditional; **prendre qch au ~** fig to regard sth as provisional.
III conditionnelle *nf* Ling conditional clause.

conditionnement /kɔ̃disjɔnmɑ̃/ *nm* **1** (de personne) conditioning; **2** (emballage) packaging ¢; **~s** forms of packaging; **3** (de l'air) conditioning.
■ **~ sous vide** vacuum packing.

conditionner /kɔ̃disjɔne/ [1] *vtr* **1** (influencer) [*milieu, média*] to condition [*personne, comportement*]; to condition [*animal*]; **2** (déterminer) **votre habileté conditionne votre réussite** your success depends on your skill; **leur accord conditionne la réussite du projet** the success of the project depends on their agreement; **3** (emballer) to package (**en** in); **~ qch sous vide** to vacuum-pack sth.

condoléances /kɔ̃dɔleɑ̃s/ *nfpl* condolences; **présenter** or **faire ses ~ à qn** to offer one's condolences to sb; **lettre de ~** letter of condolence; **toutes mes ~** please accept my deepest sympathy.

condom /kɔ̃dɔm/ *nm* condom.

condominium /kɔ̃dɔminjɔm/ *nm* condominium.

condor /kɔ̃dɔʀ/ *nm* condor.

conductance /kɔ̃dyktɑ̃s/ *nf* conductance.

conducteur, **-trice** /kɔ̃dyktœʀ, tʀis/ **I** *adj* **1** Phys conductive; **un matériau peu ~** a poor conductor; **2** (qui guide) [*principe*] guiding.
II ▶510 *nm,f* **1** (de véhicule) driver; **être bon/mauvais ~** to be a good/bad driver; **2** (responsable) (de machine) operator; (de travaux) foreman.
III *nm* Phys conductor; **être un bon/mauvais ~ de la chaleur/de l'électricité** to be a good/poor conductor of heat/of electricity.
■ **~ de bestiaux** drover; **~ de centrale** Électrotech, Nucl power station maintenance supervisor; **~ d'engin** Gén Civ ≈ bulldozer driver; **~ de presse** Imprim pressman; **~ de travaux** clerk of the works GB, foreman.

conductibilité /kɔ̃dyktibilite/ *nf* conductivity.

conductible /kɔ̃dyktibl/ *adj* conductive.

conduction /kɔ̃dyksjɔ̃/ *nf* Phys, Physiol conduction.

conduire /kɔ̃dɥiʀ/ [69] **I** *vtr* **1** (accompagner) to take [*personne*]; (en voiture) to drive [*personne*] (**à** to); **je vais vous ~ à l'hôpital** I'll take ou drive you to the hospital; **se faire ~ quelque part en taxi** to take a taxi somewhere; **conduisez monsieur à sa chambre** show the gentleman to his room; **2** (mener à un lieu) **un bus vous conduira à l'hôtel** a bus will take you to the hotel; **le chemin conduit à l'église** the path leads to the church; **les traces de pneus conduisaient à une clairière** the tyre-tracks GB ou tire-tracks US led to a clearing; **mon voyage m'a conduit dans cinq pays/à Paris** my trip took me to five countries/to Paris; **la route qui conduit à Oxford** the road that goes to Oxford; **~ qn à l'échafaud** to lead sb to the scaffold; **3** (faire aboutir) **~ à qch** to lead to sth; **~ qn à faire** to lead sb to do; **les résultats nous ont conduits à réviser notre programme** the results led us to modify our programme[GB]; **~ à une amélioration de qch/à la fermeture de qch** to lead to an improvement in sth/to the closing of sth; **~ à améliorer qch/à fermer qch** to lead to improvements in sth/to the closing of sth; **~ qn à la faillite** to make sb bankrupt; **~ qn à la folie/au désespoir/au suicide** to drive sb to madness/to despair/to suicide; **4** (être aux commandes de) to drive [*auto, camion, train*]; to ride [*moto*]; **je n'aime pas ~ la nuit/en ville** I don't like driving at night/in town; **je ne te laisserai pas ~** I won't let you drive; **5** (guider) to lead [*personne, animal*] (**à** to); **se laisser ~ par qn/par un chien** to be led by sb/by a dog; **6** (faire évoluer) to conduct [*recherches, négociations*]; to pursue [*politique*]; to carry out [*projet*]; to run [*affaire commerciale*]; **7** (être à la tête de) to lead [*délégation, troupe*]; **~ la marche/le deuil** to lead the march/the mourners; **il a conduit la nation pendant la guerre** he led the nation during the war; **il a conduit le pays d'une poigne de fer** he ruled the country with a rod of iron; **la liste conduite par le candidat socialiste** the list headed by the socialist candidate; **8** (faire passer) [*canalisation*] to carry [*eau, gaz, pétrole*]; [*fil*] to conduct [*électricité*]; [*corps*] to conduct [*chaleur*].
II se conduire *vpr* to behave; **il ne sait pas se ~ en société** he doesn't know how to behave in company; **se ~ bien/mal** to behave well/badly (**avec** or **envers qn** toward, towards GB sb); **se ~ comme un enfant/imbécile** to behave like a child/fool.

conduit /kɔ̃dɥi/ *nm* **1** Constr conduit; **2** Anat canal.
■ **~ d'air chaud** hot-air duct; **~ auditif externe** external auditory canal ou meatus; **~ auditif interne** internal auditory meatus; **~ de fumée** flue; **~ de ventilation** ventilation shaft.

conduite /kɔ̃dɥit/ *nf* **1** (manière d'être) gén behaviour[GB] (**avec, envers qn** to, toward(s) sb); (d'écolier) conduct; **ma peine a été réduite pour bonne ~** my sentence was reduced for good behaviour ou conduct; **elle a eu un zéro de ~** she got a black mark for bad behaviour[GB]; **avoir une ~ bizarre** to behave oddly; **ils n'accepteront pas qu'on leur dicte leur ~** they will not put up with being told what to do; **hésiter sur la ~ à tenir** to be uncertain what to do; **2** (d'enquête) conducting; (de travaux) supervision; (de carrière, d'entreprise) management; (de nation, d'armée) leadership; **sous la ~ de** under the supervision of; **mon père m'a laissé la ~ des affaires** my father left me to run the business; **elle leur a confié la ~ du projet** she put them in charge of the project; **3** (d'auto, de camion, train) driving; (de moto) riding; **la ~ de nuit/jour** night/daytime driving; **la ~ en ville/sur route** driving in town/on the open road; **~ en état d'ivresse** driving under the influence of alcohol, drunk GB ou drunken US driving; **n'oubliez pas la ~ à droite!** don't forget to drive on the right!; ▶ **sportif**; **4** Aut (colonne de direction) **voiture avec ~ à droite/à gauche** right-/left-hand drive car; **ma voiture a la ~ à droite** my car is right-hand drive; **5** (examen) driving test; **j'ai eu le code mais j'ai raté la ~** I passed the written test but I failed the road test; **6** (canalisation) pipe.
■ **~ accompagnée** driving accompanied by a qualified driver; **~ forcée** Gén Civ pressure pipeline.

condyle /kɔ̃dil/ *nm* condyle.

cône /kon/ *nm* cone; **objet en forme de ~** cone-shaped object; **objet en forme de ~ inversé** object shaped like an inverted cone; **taillé en forme de ~** trimmed into a conical shape.
■ **~ de déjection** Géol alluvial fan; **~ de lumière** Phys cone of light; **~ d'ombre** Astron cone of shadow; **~ de pin** Bot pine cone.

confection /kɔ̃fɛksjɔ̃/ *nf* **1** Comm, Mode **la ~** (industrie) the clothing industry; (vêtements) ready-to-wear clothes (*pl*); **costume de ~** ready-to-wear suit; **s'habiller en ~** to buy one's clothes off the peg GB ou off the rack US; **2** (élaboration) making.

confectionner /kɔ̃fɛksjɔne/ [1] *vtr* to make [*gâteau, vêtement*]; to prepare [*repas*].

confectionneur, **-euse** /kɔ̃fɛksjɔnœʀ, øz/ ▶510 *nm,f* manufacturer of ready-to-wear clothing.

confédéral, **~e**, *mpl* **-aux** /kɔ̃fedeʀal, o/ *adj* confederal.

confédération /kɔ̃fedeʀasjɔ̃/ *nf* confederation.
■ **Confédération helvétique** Switzerland.

confédéré, **~e** /kɔ̃fedeʀe/ **I** *pp* ▶ **confédérer**.
II *pp adj* [*États*] confederate; [*syndicats*] confederated.
III confédérés *nmpl* Hist **les ~s** the Confederates.

confédérer /kɔ̃fedeʀe/ [14] *vtr* to confederate.

conférence /kɔ̃feʀɑ̃s/ *nf* **1** (discours, cours) lecture (**sur** on, about); **faire** or **donner une ~** to give a lecture; **2** (congrès) conference (**sur** on); **la ~ de Genève** the Geneva Conference; **se réunir en ~** to hold a conference; **être en ~** to be in conference; **les participants à la ~** the conference delegates; **3** (discussion) debate.
■ **~ épiscopale** Bishops' Conference; **~ de presse** press conference; **~ au sommet** summit meeting; **Conférence sur** or **pour la sécurité et la coopération en Europe**, **CSCE** Conference on Security and Cooperation in Europe.

conférence-débat, *pl* **conférences-débats** /kɔ̃feʀɑ̃sdeba/ *nf* round table (discussion) (**sur** on).

conférencier, **-ière** /kɔ̃feʀɑ̃sje, ɛʀ/ ▶510 *nm,f* gén speaker; Univ lecturer.

conférer /kɔ̃feʀe/ [14] **I** *vtr* **1** (remettre) [*personne, institution*] to confer [*diplôme, droit, statut, ordres*] (**à** on); to award [*décoration*] (**à** on); **~ le baptême à qn** to baptize sb; **2** (donner) fml [*fonction, âge, fortune*] to give [*droit, privilège*] (**à** to); **l'aisance que confère la compétence** the confidence that comes with skill.
II *vi* fml (s'entretenir) to confer (**sur qch** on sth; **de qch** about sth).

confesse○ /kɔ̃fɛs/ *nf* confession; **être/aller à ~** to be at/to go to confession.

confesser /kɔ̃fese/ [1] **I** *vtr* **1** (avouer) to confess [*péché, ignorance*] (**à** to); (proclamer)† **~ sa foi** to confess one's faith; **2** (entendre en confession) **~ qn** to hear sb's confession; **3**○ (faire parler) to get [sb] to talk [*enfant, malfaiteur, témoin*].
II se confesser *vpr* **1** Relig to go to confession; **se ~ à un prêtre** to make one's confession to a priest; **se ~ de qch** to confess (to) sth; **2** (se confier) **se ~ à un ami** to confide in a friend.

confesseur /kɔ̃fesœʀ/ *nm* confessor.

confession /kɔ̃fesjɔ̃/ *nf* **1** (aveu) confession; **faire une ~ à** to make a confession to; **2** Relig (sacrement) confession; **entendre qn en ~** to hear sb's confession; **avouer qch en ~** to confess sth to a priest; **3** (foi) faith; **être de ~ juive** to be of the Jewish faith.
IDIOMES **on te donnerait le bon Dieu sans ~** you look as if butter wouldn't melt in your mouth.

confessionnal, *pl* **-aux** /kɔ̃fesjɔnal, o/ *nm* confessional.

confessionnel, **-elle** /kɔ̃fesjɔnɛl/ *adj* gén denominational; [*école*] denominational GB, parochial US; **non ~** non denominational; [*querelles*] interdenominational.

confetti /kɔ̃feti/ *nm* confetti ¢; **un ~** a piece of confetti; **des ~s** confetti.

confiance /kɔ̃fjɑ̃s/ *nf* **1** (foi en l'honnêteté) trust (**en** in); **la ~ réciproque** mutual trust; **ma ~ en elle** my trust in her; **placer** or **mettre sa ~ en qn** to put one's trust in sb; **gagner/perdre la ~ de qn** to win/lose sb's trust; **en toute ~** [*acheter, prêter*] with complete confidence; **de ~** [*personne*] trustworthy; [*mission*] which requires (the utmost) trust (*après n*); **poste de ~** position of trust; **avoir ~ en qn, faire ~**

à qn to trust sb; **j'y penserai, fais-moi** or **tu peux me faire ~** I'll remember, trust me ou you can trust me; **il va tricher, tu peux lui faire ~!** iron you can rely on him to cheat! iron; **j'ai ~ en l'avenir** I feel confident about the future; **faire ~ en son intuition** to trust one's intuition; **2** (foi en la compétence) confidence (**en** in); **faire ~ à qn** to have confidence in sb; **avoir ~ dans** to have confidence in [*technologie, méthode, médecine*] **3** (assurance) confidence; **~ en soi** (self-)confidence; **avoir ~ en soi** to be self-confident; **tu manques de ~ en toi** you lack self-confidence; **cet homme/cette banque ne m'inspire pas ~** I don't have much confidence in that man/that bank; **ces champignons ne m'inspirent pas ~** I don't feel altogether happy about these mushrooms; **mettre qn en ~** to put sb at ease; **être/se sentir en ~ avec qn** to be/feel at ease with sb; **4** Pol **voter la ~** to pass a vote of confidence.

confiant, ~e /kɔ̃fjɑ̃, ɑ̃t/ *adj* **1** (certain) confident; **être ~ dans** to be confident about [*avenir, succès d'une opération*]; to have confidence in [*capacités, système judiciaire*]; **2** (assuré) (self-)confident; **3** (se fiant aux autres) [*personne, caractère, regard*] trusting; **être ~ de nature** to have a trusting nature.

confidence /kɔ̃fidɑ̃s/ *nf* secret, confidence; **dire qch en ~** to say sth in confidence; **être dans la ~** to be in on the secret; **mettre qn dans la ~** to let sb in on the secret; **faire une ~ à qn** to tell sb a secret, to confide sth to sb; **faire des ~s à qn sur qch** to confide in sb about sth; **je ne reçois pas ses ~s** he/she doesn't confide in me; **elle m'a expliqué sur le ton de la ~, que** she explained, confidentially, that.
■ **~s sur l'oreiller** pillow talk ¢.

confident /kɔ̃fidɑ̃/ *nm* **1** gén, Théât confidant; **2** (fauteuil) tête-à-tête.

confidente /kɔ̃fidɑ̃t/ *nf* gén, Théât confidante.

confidentialité /kɔ̃fidɑ̃sjalite/ *nf* confidentiality.

confidentiel, -ielle /kɔ̃fidɑ̃sjɛl/ *adj* [*dossier, ton*] confidential; **'~'** (sur un pli) 'confidential'.

confidentiellement /kɔ̃fidɑ̃sjɛlmɑ̃/ *adv* in confidence, confidentially.

confier /kɔ̃fje/ [2] **I** *vtr* **1** (remettre) **~ qch à qn** to entrust sth to sb, to entrust sb with sth [*mission, poste*]; to entrust sth to sb [*argent*]; to leave sth in sb's care, to entrust sth to sb [*lettres, valise*]; **~ (la garde d')un enfant à qn** to leave a child in sb's care; **~ à qn le soin de faire** to entrust sb with the task of doing; **~ qch aux soins de qn** to leave sth in sb's care; **confiez-nous votre voiture/vos pellicules photo**○ leave your car/your films to us; **on m'a confié la direction du projet** I have been put in charge of the project; **~ son sort au hasard** to entrust one's fate to chance; **2** (dire en confidence) **~ à qn** to confide [sth] to sb [*peines, intentions*]; **~ un secret à qn** to tell sb a secret.
II se confier *vpr* to confide (**à** in); **je n'ai personne à qui me ~** I have nobody to confide in; **elle se confie peu** she doesn't confide in people much.

configuration /kɔ̃figyʀasjɔ̃/ *nf* **1** (aspect) shape; **la ~ du terrain** the lie of the land; **2** (disposition) configuration; (situation) set-up; **la ~ du marché/de la majorité** the configuration of the market/of the majority; **la ~ administrative/politique** the administrative/political set-up; **la ~ des lieux** the layout of the premises; **3** Ordinat configuration; **4** Chimie configuration.

confiné, ~e /kɔ̃fine/ **I** *pp* ▶ **confiner**.
II *pp adj* **1** (enfermé) **~ dans une pièce** confined to a room; **esprit ~ dans la routine** mind stuck in a rut; **2** (renfermé) [*atmosphère*] lit, fig stuffy; [*air*] stale; **3** (limité) [*espace*] confined, restricted.

confinement /kɔ̃finmɑ̃/ *nm* **1** (de prisonnier, bétail) confinement; **2** Tech (de produit) containment.

confiner /kɔ̃fine/ [1] **I** *vtr* **1** (enfermer) **~ qn dans une pièce** to confine sb to a room; **2** (restreindre) **~ qn à une tâche/un poste** to restrict sb to a task/a post; **ce phénomène n'est pas confiné à la France** this phenomenon is not confined ou restricted to France.
II confiner à *vtr ind* lit, fig to border on [*territoire*]; **~ à la caricature/l'absurde** to border ou verge on caricature/the absurd.
III se confiner *vpr* (s'enfermer) to shut oneself away ou up (**dans** in); **se ~ dans le silence** to immure oneself in silence; **se ~ dans un rôle** to restrict oneself to a role.

confins /kɔ̃fɛ̃/ *nmpl* (de domaine, territoire) boundaries; (de forêt, désert) edges; **aux ~ de l'empire** on the outer edges of the empire; **aux ~ de l'Europe et de l'Asie** on the borders of Europe and Asia; **aux ~ de la psychologie** fig on the borders of psychology; **aux ~ de la réalité** fig on the border(s) between the real and the imaginary; **aux ~ de la science et de l'art** fig in the area between science and art; **être aux ~ du mauvais goût** fig to border on bad taste.

confire /kɔ̃fiʀ/ [64] *vtr* Culin **~ qch dans de la graisse** to preserve sth in fat; **~ des fruits dans du sucre** to crystallize fruit; **~ des cornichons dans du vinaigre** to pickle gherkins in vinegar.

confirmand, ~e /kɔ̃fiʀmɑ̃, ɑ̃d/ *nm,f* candidate for confirmation, confirmand.

confirmatif, -ive /kɔ̃fiʀmatif, iv/ *adj* [*arrêt*] confirmative; [*jugement*] affirmative.

confirmation /kɔ̃fiʀmasjɔ̃/ *nf* **1** (ratification) confirmation (**de** of; **que** that); **attendre ~ d'une commande** to await confirmation of an order; **pour** or **en ~** in confirmation (**de** of); **exiger une lettre de ~** to demand written confirmation; **être la ~ de qch, apporter la ~ de qch** to confirm sth; **2** Relig confirmation; **recevoir la ~** to be confirmed.

confirmer /kɔ̃fiʀme/ [1] **I** *vtr* **1** (rendre certain) to confirm [*commande, fait, jugement*]; to uphold [*décision, verdict*]; to bear out [*témoignage*]; to be evidence of [*attitude, qualité*]; to affirm [*intention, volonté*]; **~ que** to confirm that; **2** (conforter) **~ qn dans son opinion** to reinforce sb's opinion; **3** Relig to confirm.
II se confirmer *vpr* **1** [*bruit, nouvelle*] to be confirmed; [*témoignage*] to be corroborated; **2 il se confirme comme l'un de nos meilleurs acteurs** he's established himself as one of our best actors; **3 il se confirme que** it is becoming increasingly certain that.

confiscable /kɔ̃fiskabl/ *adj* confiscable, liable to confiscation; **non ~** non-confiscable.

confiscation /kɔ̃fiskasjɔ̃/ *nf* confiscation, seizure Jur.

confiscatoire /kɔ̃fiskatwaʀ/ *adj* [*mesure, imposition*] confiscatory.

confiserie /kɔ̃fizʀi/ *nf* **1** ▶ **510** (magasin) confectioner's (shop), sweetshop GB, candy store US; **2** (fabrication, commerce) confectionery; **3** (produits) confectionery ¢, sweets (*pl*) GB, candy ¢ US.

confiseur, -euse /kɔ̃fizœʀ, øz/ ▶ **510** *nm,f* confectioner.

confisquer /kɔ̃fiske/ [1] *vtr* **1** (prendre) gén, Jur to confiscate [*bien, propriété, film*] (**à** from); **2** fig (accaparer) to monopolize [*gestion*]; **~ la direction** or **le pouvoir de** to take control of.

confit, ~e /kɔ̃fi, it/ **I** *pp* ▶ **confire**.
II *pp adj* **1** Culin [*fruits*] crystallized; [*cornichon*] pickled; [*canard*] preserved; **2** fig, pej smug; **être ~ en dévotion/dans des préjugés** to be steeped in piety/in prejudice.
III *nm* confit; **~ de canard** confit of duck.

confiture /kɔ̃fityʀ/ *nf* Culin jam, preserve; (d'agrumes) marmalade; **~ de fraises/de rhubarbe** strawberry/rhubarb jam; **~ d'oranges** marmalade; **faire de la ~** to make jam.
IDIOMES **donner de la ~ aux cochons** or **pourceaux** to cast pearls before swine; **mettre qn en ~**○ to make mincemeat○ of sb; **mettre qch en ~**○ to wreck sth○.

confiturerie /kɔ̃fityʀʀi/ *nf* **1** (usine) jam factory; **2** (industrie) jam manufacture.

confiturier, -ière /kɔ̃fityʀje, ɛʀ/ **I** *adj* jam (*épith*).
II ▶ **510** *nm,f* (fabricant) jam-producer.
III *nm* (récipient) jam pot (*for serving*).

conflagration /kɔ̃flagʀasjɔ̃/ *nf* conflagration.

conflictuel, -elle /kɔ̃fliktɥɛl/ *adj* [*sujet*] controversial, contentious; [*influences, tendances*] conflicting; [*rapport, relations*] confrontational; **c'est une situation conflictuelle** it's a source of conflict; (potentiellement) it's a potential source of conflict.

conflit /kɔ̃fli/ *nm* gén conflict (**entre** between); Entr dispute; **~ d'intérêts** conflict of interests; **~ de compétence** demarcation dispute; **être en/entrer en ~ avec qn** to be in/to come into conflict with sb.
■ **~ armé** Mil armed conflict; **~ de générations** generation gap; **~ social** industrial strife; **~ du travail** Entr industrial dispute.

confluence /kɔ̃flyɑ̃s/ *nf* **1** (de rivières) confluence; **2** (de courants de pensée) convergence.

confluent /kɔ̃flyɑ̃/ *nm* Géog confluence.

confluer /kɔ̃flye/ [1] *vi* **1** Géog to meet, to join; **~ avec** to flow into; **2** fig (troupes) to converge (**vers** on); **tous les efforts confluent vers le même but** all efforts are directed towards the same goal.

confondant, ~e /kɔ̃fɔ̃dɑ̃, ɑ̃t/ *adj* staggering; **il est d'une ignorance ~e** his ignorance is staggering.

confondre /kɔ̃fɔ̃dʀ/ [53] **I** *vtr* **1** (ne pas distinguer) to mix up, to confuse; **je l'ai confondu avec son cousin** I got him mixed up with his cousin, I mistook him for his cousin; **~ le sel avec le sucre** to mistake the salt for the sugar; **tu confonds la science et la technologie** you are confusing science with technology; **ce n'était pas moi, vous devez ~** it wasn't me, you must be confusing me with somebody else; **tu confonds tout!** you're getting it all mixed up!; **tous partis/secteurs confondus** all parties/sectors taken together; **toutes catégories confondues** all categories taken together; **2** (mêler) liter to merge; **les projecteurs confondent leurs faisceaux** the beams of the floodlights merge; **dans son œuvre, l'architecte et le sculpteur confondent leur art** his/her works bring architecture and sculpture together; **3** (décontenancer) fml to stagger; **il a confondu les journalistes par son érudition** he staggered the journalists with his learning; **leur ignorance me confondait** I found their ignorance staggering; **4** (démasquer) to expose, to confound sout [*accusé, traître, fraudeur*].
II se confondre *vpr* **1** (se mêler) [*formes, couleurs*] to merge; [*événements, faits*] to become confused; **se ~ avec qch** to merge with sth; **la mer et le ciel se confondent à l'horizon** sea and sky merge on the horizon; **les deux dates se sont confondues dans mon esprit** the two dates have become confused in my mind; **les caméléons se confondent avec leur environnement** chameleons merge with their background; **2** (être identique) [*intérêts, espoirs, points de vue*] to coincide; **notre avenir se confond avec celui de l'Europe** our future is bound up with that of Europe; **sa vie se confond/ne se confond pas avec son œuvre** his/her life and his/her work are one/are separate; **3** (se répandre) fml **il s'est confondu en excuses** he apologized profusely; **il s'est confondu**

en remerciements/politesses he was effusive in his thanks/courtesies.

conformable /kɔ̃fɔʀmabl/ *adj* [*semelles*] conformable.

conformation /kɔ̃fɔʀmasjɔ̃/ *nf* conformation.

conforme /kɔ̃fɔʀm/ *adj* **1** (en accord) **être ~ à** to be in keeping with [*loi, tradition, principes*]; to comply with [*normes, règlement*]; **radiateur ~ (aux normes de sécurité)** radiator which complies with safety standards; **la qualité de l'eau n'est pas ~ aux normes européennes** the water quality does not comply with European standards; **2** (identique) **être ~ à un modèle/l'original** to conform to a model/the original; **photocopie certifiée ~** Admin certified copy.

conformé, **~e** /kɔ̃fɔʀme/ **I** *pp* ▶ **conformer**.
II *pp adj* **bien ~** normally formed; **mal ~** malformed.

conformément /kɔ̃fɔʀmemɑ̃/ *adv* **~ à** in accordance with.

conformer /kɔ̃fɔʀme/ [1] **I** *vtr* **1** (rendre conforme) **il est essentiel qu'il conforme sa décision aux directives gouvernementales** it's essential that his decision should comply with government directives; **2** Tech (donner une forme à) to shape.
II se conformer *vpr* (à un usage) to conform (**à** to); (à un règlement, une norme) to comply (**à** with).

conformisme /kɔ̃fɔʀmism/ *nm* **1** péj conformity, conventionality; **elle est d'un ~!** she's such a conformist!, she's so conventional!; **2** Relig conformity.

conformiste /kɔ̃fɔʀmist/ *adj, nmf* gén, Relig conformist.

conformité /kɔ̃fɔʀmite/ *nf* **1** (par rapport aux règles) **~ à la loi/aux normes de sécurité** compliance with the law/with safety standards; **en ~ avec** [*agir*] in accordance with; **mettre qch en ~ avec qch** to make sth comply with sth; **2** (de deux objets) close correspondence; **vérifier la ~ de la traduction à l'original** to check that the translation is faithful to the original; **3** (de goûts, points de vue) correspondence.

confort /kɔ̃fɔʀ/ *nm* comfort; **le ~ moderne** modern conveniences (*pl*); **maison avec tout le ~, maison tout ~** house with all mod cons○ GB ou with all modern conveniences; **installer le ~** to install electricity, plumbing, heating etc; **il me faut mon ~** I must have my creature comforts; **ça va déranger ton ~** it'll disturb your cosy GB ou cozy US existence; **~ d'écoute** quality of reception; **~ d'utilisation** user-friendliness; **~ de conduite** driver comfort.

confortable /kɔ̃fɔʀtabl/ *adj* **1** (agréable) [*hôtel, lit, vêtement*] comfortable; **pas ~** uncomfortable; **peu ~** rather uncomfortable; **2** (aisé) [*existence, situation*] comfortable; **3** (considérable) [*revenus, majorité, avance*] comfortable; **une marge ~ d'une seconde** Sport a comfortable lead of one second; **une marge ~ de vingt sièges** Pol an easy margin of twenty seats.

confortablement /kɔ̃fɔʀtabləmɑ̃/ *adv* comfortably.

conforter /kɔ̃fɔʀte/ [1] *vtr* **1** to consolidate [*position, régime*]; to reinforce [*situation*]; **2 ~ qn dans une opinion** to confirm sb in his/her opinion.

confraternel, **-elle** /kɔ̃fʀatɛʀnɛl/ *adj* fraternal.

confraternellement /kɔ̃fʀatɛʀnɛlmɑ̃/ *adv* fraternally.

confrère /kɔ̃fʀɛʀ/ *nm* (de travail) colleague; (d'association) fellow member; **ses ~s musiciens/acteurs** his/her fellow musicians/actors; **dans un entretien accordé à un ~ de la presse écrite** in an interview given to a newspaper.

confrérie /kɔ̃fʀeʀi/ *nf* brotherhood.

confrontation /kɔ̃fʀɔ̃tasjɔ̃/ *nf* **1** (de témoins, d'idées) confrontation (**entre** between; **avec** with); **2** (débat) debate; (affrontement) clash; **3** (de textes, d'écritures) comparison (**de** of); **travaux de ~ des données chiffrées** work on comparing statistical data.

confronter /kɔ̃fʀɔ̃te/ [1] **I** *vtr* **1** (opposer) to confront [*témoins, théories*]; **être confronté avec qn/à qch** to be confronted with sb/sth; **2** (comparer) to compare [*expériences, textes*]; (pour vérifier) **~ qch avec qch** to check sth against sth.
II se confronter *vpr* **se ~ à qch** to be confronted with sth.

confucéen, **-éenne** /kɔ̃fyseɛ̃, ɛn/ *adj* Confucian.

confucianisme /kɔ̃fysjanism/ *nm* Confucianism.

confucianiste /kɔ̃fysjanist/ *adj, nmf* Confucian.

Confucius /kɔ̃fysjys/ *npr* Confucius.

confus, **~e** /kɔ̃fy, yz/ *adj* **1** (indistinct) [*formes, mouvements, bruits*] confused; **un mélange ~** a hotchpotch GB, a hodgepodge US; **2** (obscur) [*situation, affaire, texte, style, esprit*] confused; [*déclaration, explication, débat, discours*] confused, muddled; **son raisonnement devient/paraît ~** his/her reasoning becomes/seems confused; **3** (vague) [*sentiment, crainte*] vague; **4** (navré) sorry; (gêné) embarrassed; **nous sommes ~ de ce retard** we apologize for the delay; **il avait l'air tout ~ de sa méprise** he looked really embarrassed about his mistake; **5** (touché) embarrassed; **merci, dit-il avec un sourire ~** thank you, he said with an embarrassed smile; **je suis ~ de votre générosité** I am overcome by your generosity.

confusément /kɔ̃fyzemɑ̃/ *adv* [*requérir, expliquer*] confusedly; [*sentir*] vaguely; **savoir ~ que** to be vaguely aware that.

confusion /kɔ̃fyzjɔ̃/ *nf* **1** (désordre) confusion; **il règne la plus grande ~ dans...** complete confusion reigns in...; **finir dans la ~ générale/la plus totale** to end in general/complete and utter confusion; **jeter la ~ dans** or **parmi qch** to throw sth into confusion; **jeter la ~ dans les esprits** to throw people into confusion; **situation d'une incroyable ~** incredibly confused situation; ▶ **prêter**; **2** (gêne) embarrassment; **à ma grande ~** to my great embarrassment; **elle était rouge de ~** she was blushing with embarrassment; **ma ~ était visible** I was visibly embarrassed; **vous la plongez dans la ~** you're embarrassing her; **3** (méprise) mix-up; **il y a eu une ~ de noms** there has been a mix-up with the names; **à la suite d'une regrettable ~** owing to an unfortunate mix-up.
■ **~ des genres** Philos overlapping of categories; **~ de peines** Jur concurrency of sentences; **~ des pouvoirs** Pol non-separation of powers.

congé /kɔ̃ʒe/ *nm* **1** (arrêt de travail) leave ¢; **prendre quatre jours de ~** to take four days' leave ou four days off; **être en ~** to be off; **être en ~ pour trois jours** to be away for three days; **se mettre en ~ pour trois jours** to take three days' leave; **se mettre en ~** to take some time off; **il me reste deux jours de ~ à prendre** I still have two days' leave due to me; **accorder six jours de ~ à qn** to grant sb six days' leave; **être en ~ de maladie/maternité** to be on sick/maternity leave; **~ de longue maladie** extended sick leave; **se mettre en ~ de maladie** to go on sick leave; **avoir ~ le lundi** to have Mondays off; **2** Scol holiday GB, vacation US; **être en ~** to be on holiday GB ou vacation US; **en France les écoles ont ~ le mercredi** in France there is no school on Wednesdays; **3** Jur (fin de contrat) notice; **donner (son)** or **signifier son ~ à qn** to give sb notice; **demander son ~** to hand in one's notice; **4** Fisc clearance from bond.
■ **~ de conversion** paid leave for retraining; **~ individuel de formation** personal leave for training; **~ parental d'éducation** parental child-rearing leave; **~ sans solde** unpaid leave; **~s annuels** annual leave; **~s payés** paid leave; **~s scolaires** school holidays GB ou vacation US.
IDIOMES **prendre ~ de qn** to take leave of sb.

congédier /kɔ̃ʒedje/ [2] *vtr* to dismiss.

congelable /kɔ̃ʒlabl/ *adj* suitable for home freezing (*après n*).

congélateur /kɔ̃ʒelatœʀ/ *nm* freezer, deep-freeze; (dans un réfrigérateur) freezer compartment.
■ **~ armoire** upright freezer; **~ bahut** chest freezer.

congélation /kɔ̃ʒelasjɔ̃/ *nf* gén freezing; (d'huile) congelation; **point de ~** freezing point.

congelé, **~e** /kɔ̃ʒle/ **I** *pp* ▶ **congeler**.
II *pp adj* frozen; **produits ~s** frozen foods.
III *nm* frozen foods (*pl*).

congeler /kɔ̃ʒle/ [17] *vtr*, **se congeler** *vpr* to freeze.

congénère /kɔ̃ʒenɛʀ/ **I** *adj* **1** gén congeneric; **2** Ling [*mot*] cognate.
II *nmf* (d'animal) fellow creature; (de personne) **vous et vos ~s** pej you and your like.

congénital, **~e**, *mpl* **-aux** /kɔ̃ʒenital, o/ *adj* [*maladie, malformation*] congenital.

congère /kɔ̃ʒɛʀ/ *nf* snowdrift.

congestif, **-ive** /kɔ̃ʒɛstif, iv/ *adj* [*état, disposition*] congestive.

congestion /kɔ̃ʒɛstjɔ̃/ *nf* **1** Méd congestion; **2** (encombrement) congestion; **~ de la circulation** traffic congestion.
■ **~ cérébrale** stroke; **~ pulmonaire** congestion of the lungs.

congestionner /kɔ̃ʒɛstjɔne/ [1] **I** *vtr* **1** Méd to congest [*poumon, muqueuse*]; **~ qn/le visage** to cause sb/the face to flush; **il est** or **son visage est tout congestionné** he's all flushed; **2** (encombrer) to congest [*rue, ville*].
II se congestionner *vpr* [*personne, visage*] to flush.

conglomérat /kɔ̃glɔmeʀa/ *nm* **1** Écon, Géol conglomerate; **2** fig (mélange) conglomeration.

conglomération /kɔ̃glɔmeʀasjɔ̃/ *nf* conglomeration.

conglomérer /kɔ̃glɔmeʀe/ [14] *vtr* Géol to conglomerate.

Congo /kɔ̃go/ ▶ **321**, **357** *nprm* (pays, fleuve) **le ~** the Congo.

congolais, **~e** /kɔ̃gɔlɛ, ɛz/ **I** ▶ **537** *adj* Congolese.
II *nm* Culin (small) coconut cake.

Congolais, **~e** /kɔ̃gɔlɛ, ɛz/ ▶ **537** *nm,f* Congolese.

congratulations† /kɔ̃gʀatylasjɔ̃/ *nfpl* congratulations.

congratuler† /kɔ̃gʀatyle/ [1] **I** *vtr* to congratulate.
II se congratuler *vpr* **1** (soi-même) to congratulate oneself; **2** (l'un l'autre) to congratulate one another.

congre /kɔ̃gʀ/ *nm* conger eel.

congrégation /kɔ̃gʀegasjɔ̃/ *nf* **1** Relig congregation; **2** (assemblée) hum assembly.

congrès /kɔ̃gʀɛ/ *nm* **1** (réunion) conference; **~ de radiologie** radiology conference; **2** Pol (aux États-Unis) **Congrès** Congress.

congressiste /kɔ̃gʀesist/ *nmf* (conference) delegate.

congru, **~e** /kɔ̃gʀy/ *adj* Math congruent (**à** with); ▶ **portion**.

congruence /kɔ̃gʀyɑ̃s/ *nf* Math congruence.

congruent, **~e** /kɔ̃gʀyɑ̃, ɑ̃t/ *adj* **1** [*idée, propos*] compatible (**à** with); **2** Math congruent.

conifère /kɔnifɛʀ/ *nm* conifer.

conique /kɔnik/ **I** *adj* Math conical; **de forme ~** cone-shaped.

II *nf* conic.

conjectural, **~e**, *mpl* **-aux** /kɔ̃ʒɛktyʀal, o/ *adj* conjectural.

conjecture /kɔ̃ʒɛktyʀ/ *nf* conjecture ¢; **se perdre en ~s** to lose oneself in conjecture; **en être réduit aux ~s** to be reduced to conjecture; **vaines ~s** idle speculation ¢.

conjecturer /kɔ̃ʒɛktyʀe/ [1] *vtr* fml to speculate (**que** that).

conjoint, **~e** /kɔ̃ʒwɛ̃, ɛ̃t/ **I** *adj* **1** [*démarche, déclaration, legs, débiteur*] joint (*épith*); [*questions, situations*] linked; **2** Bot [*feuilles*] compound; **3** Ling conjunct.
II *nm,f* spouse; **les ~s** the husband and wife; **féliciter les (futurs) ~s** to congratulate the happy couple.

conjointement /kɔ̃ʒwɛ̃tmɑ̃/ *adv* **1** (de concert) [*agir, déclarer*] jointly; **~ et solidairement** Jur jointly and severally; **2** (en même temps) at the same time; **~ avec** together with.

conjonctif, **-ive** /kɔ̃ʒɔ̃ktif, iv/ **I** *adj* **1** Anat conjunctival; **2** Ling conjunctive.
II conjonctive *nf* Anat conjunctiva.

conjonction /kɔ̃ʒɔ̃ksjɔ̃/ *nf* (tous contextes) conjunction; **en ~ avec qn** in conjunction with sb.
■ **~ de coordination** Ling coordinating conjunction; **~ de subordination** Ling subordinating conjunction.

conjonctivite /kɔ̃ʒɔ̃ktivit/ ▶**271** *nf* conjunctivitis.

conjoncture /kɔ̃ʒɔ̃ktyʀ/ *nf* situation; **~ politique/économique** political/economic situation; **dans la ~ actuelle** in the present circumstances; **bonne/mauvaise ~** favourable[GB]/unfavourable[GB] conjunction of circumstances.

conjoncturel, **-elle** /kɔ̃ʒɔ̃ktyʀɛl/ *adj* [*déficit, politique*] short-term; [*situation, fluctuations*] economic; [*crise*] temporary, cyclical; [*prélèvement*] temporary; **évolution conjoncturelle** current trends (*pl*); **politique conjoncturelle adaptée à la situation** economic policy in line with the situation.

conjoncturiste /kɔ̃ʒɔ̃ktyʀist/ *nmf* economic forecaster.

conjugable /kɔ̃ʒygabl/ *adj* conjugable.

conjugaison /kɔ̃ʒygɛzɔ̃/ *nf* **1** Biol, Ling conjugation; **2** fig (réunion) combination; **grâce à la ~ de leurs efforts** thanks to their joint efforts.

conjugal, **~e**, *mpl* **-aux** /kɔ̃ʒygal, o/ *adj* [*amour, fidélité*] conjugal; [*drame*] marital; [*bonheur, vie*] married; ▶**devoir**, **domicile**.

conjugalement /kɔ̃ʒygalmɑ̃/ *adv* **vivre ~** to live together as man and wife.

conjugaliser /kɔ̃ʒygalize/ [1] *vtr* Admin, Fisc **~ un avantage fiscal** to extend a tax advantage to married couples.

conjugué, **~e** /kɔ̃ʒyge/ **I** *pp* ▶**conjuguer**.
II *pp adj* **1** [*éléments, efforts, facteurs*] combined; **dû à plusieurs facteurs ~s** due to a combination of factors; **2** Math conjugate.
III conjuguées *nfpl* Bot freshwater algae.

conjuguer /kɔ̃ʒyge/ [1] **I** *vtr* **1** Ling to conjugate [*verbe*]; **2** (combiner) to combine, to unite [*efforts*].
II se conjuguer *vpr* **1** Ling [*verbe*] to be conjugated (**avec** with); **2** (se combiner) [*facteurs, efforts*] to combine.

conjurateur, **-trice** /kɔ̃ʒyʀatœʀ, tʀis/ *nm,f* chief conspirator.

conjuration /kɔ̃ʒyʀasjɔ̃/ *nf* **1** (complot) conspiracy; **2** (d'influences maléfiques) conjuration.

conjuré, **~e** /kɔ̃ʒyʀe/ *nm,f* conspirator.

conjurer /kɔ̃ʒyʀe/ [1] *vtr* **1** (écarter) to avert [*crise, accident, inflation*]; to ward off [*danger, démon, sort*]; to banish [*angoisse, solitude*]; **~ le (mauvais) sort** to ward off ill fortune; **2** (supplier) **~ qn de faire qch** to beg sb to do sth; **je vous en conjure** I beg you; **3†** (comploter) to plot [*perte, ruine*].

connaissable /kɔnɛsabl/ *adj, nm* knowable.

connaissance /kɔnɛsɑ̃s/ **I** *nf* **1** (savoir) knowledge (**de** of); **~ abstraite/pratique/sensorielle** abstract/practical/sensory knowledge; **avoir une bonne ~ de l'espagnol/la musique** to have a good knowledge of Spanish/music; **à ma/notre/leur ~** to (the best of) my/our/their knowledge; **pas à ma ~** not to my knowledge, not as far as I know; **avoir ~ de qch** to know something about sth; **ne pas avoir ~ de qch** to have no knowledge of sth; **il a une profonde ~ de la psychologie humaine** he has a deep understanding of the way the human mind works; **ils ont ~ de nos intentions** they know of our intentions; **prendre ~ d'un texte/d'une information** to acquaint oneself with a text/a piece of information; **'confirme avoir pris ~ des conditions générales de vente'** Comm 'confirm that I have read the conditions of sale'; **donner ~ de qch à qn** to inform sb of sth; **porter à la ~ de qn que** fml to advise sb that; **il a été porté à notre ~ que** it has been drawn ou brought to our attention that; **en ~ de cause** with full knowledge of the facts; **2** (conscience) consciousness; **perdre ~** to lose consciousness; **reprendre ~** to regain consciousness; **rester sans ~** to be unconscious; **tomber sans ~** to faint; **3** (sur le plan social) acquaintance; **faire de nouvelles ~s** to make new acquaintances; **j'ai fait leur ~ hier** I met them yesterday; **un architecte de ma ~** an architect of my acquaintance, an architect I know; **(je suis) heureux de faire votre ~** (I'm) pleased to meet you; **faire (plus ample) ~ avec qn** to get to know sb (better), to become ou get (better) acquainted with sb; **ils ont lié ~ au cours d'un dîner** they struck up an acquaintance during a dinner; **faire faire ~ à deux personnes** to introduce two people (to each other); **un visage de ~** a familiar face; **se retrouver en pays de ~** (avec des gens que l'on connaît) to be among familiar faces; (dans un domaine familier) to find oneself on familiar ground.
II connaissances *nfpl* (théoriques) knowledge ¢; (pratiques) experience ¢; **~s élémentaires/théoriques/solides** elementary/theoretical/sound knowledge; **posséder quelques ~s/des ~s approfondies en** or **sur qch** to have some knowledge/a good knowledge of sth; **approfondir/élargir ses ~s** to deepen/broaden one's knowledge; **'~s en informatique souhaitées'** 'computing experience desirable'.

connaissement /kɔnɛsmɑ̃/ *nm* bill of lading, B/L.

connaisseur, **-euse** /kɔnɛsœʀ, øz/ **I** *adj m* [*air, œil*] expert; **jeter un coup d'œil ~ sur un meuble ancien** to cast an expert eye over a piece of antique furniture.
II *nm,f* expert, connoisseur; **~ en vin/art** wine/art connoisseur; **~ en peinture** connoisseur of painting; **nous avons une clientèle de ~s** our customers are all connoisseurs; **regarder qch en ~** to look at sth with an expert eye; **juger qch en ~** to be a discerning judge of sth.

connaître /kɔnɛtʀ/ [73] **I** *vtr* **1** (avoir connaissance de) to know [*fait, nom, événement, résultat*]; **ne pas ~ sa force** not to know one's own strength; **vous connaissez la suite** you know the rest; **je connais les raisons de ta colère** I know why you're angry; **il nous a fait ~ son avis/ses intentions** he made his opinion/his intentions known (to us); **tu connais l'histoire de Toto qui...** do you know the one about Toto who...; **il ne tient jamais ses promesses, c'est (bien) connu** it is common knowledge that he never keeps his promises; **tes promesses, on connaît!** we know all about your promises!; **la rue de la Glacière? connais pas**○**!** rue de la Glacière? never heard of it!; **je lui connais de grands talents** I know that he/she is very talented; **je ne leur connais aucun vice** I don't know them to have any vices; **on te connaît plusieurs amants** we know you to have several lovers; **ne ~ ni le pourquoi ni le comment de qch** not to know the whys and the wherefores of sth; **leur vie privée est connue de tous** everybody knows about their private life; **tu connais la nouvelle?** have you heard the news?; **tu ne connais pas ta chance** you don't know how lucky you are; **j'en connais long sur ton passé** I know a lot about your past; **ne ~ que son plaisir/devoir** to think of nothing but one's pleasure/duty; ▶**Dieu**, **loup**; **2** (pour avoir étudié) to know, to be acquainted with [*sujet, méthode, auteur*]; **la mécanique, je ne connais que ça** or **ça me connaît!** I know quite a bit about mechanics; **elle connaît tout du solfège** she knows all about music theory; **c'est lui qui m'a fait ~ la musique cajun** it was he who introduced me to Cajun music; **~ un poème/une partition musicale par cœur** to know a poem/a score (off) by heart; **en ~ un rayon**○ **en histoire/théâtre** to know one's stuff○ when it comes to history/the theatre[GB]; **3** (faire l'expérience de) to know, to experience [*faim, froid, pauvreté, amour*]; to experience [*crise, défaite, échec*]; to enjoy [*gloire, succès*]; to have [*difficultés, problèmes*]; **il connaît l'humiliation de la défaite** he knows ou has experienced the humiliation of defeat; **ils ont connu la défaite** they were defeated; **il a connu la prison** he's been to prison before; **il ne connaît pas la pitié/la honte** he knows no pity/shame; **c'est un homme qui connaît la vie** he's a man who knows what life is about; **~ les femmes/hommes** to know something about women/men; **il a connu son heure de gloire** he has had his hour of glory; **les problèmes d'argent, ça me connaît**○**!** I could tell you a thing or two○ about money problems!; **~ des hauts et des bas** to have one's/its ups and downs; **~ une fin tragique** to come to a tragic end; **~ une situation difficile** to be in a difficult situation; **~ une forte croissance** to show a rapid growth; **le club sportif connaît un nouvel essor** the sports club is having a new lease of GB ou on US life; **ils auraient pu ~ un meilleur sort** they could have had a better fate; **4** (de réputation) to know [*personne, acteur*]; **elle est très connue** she's (very) well-known; **~ qn de nom/vue** to know sb by name/sight; **je le connais de réputation mais je ne l'ai jamais rencontré** I know ou I've heard of him but I've never met him; **une œuvre connue/peu connue** a well-known/little-known work (**de** by); **être d'abord connu comme violoniste** to be chiefly known as a violinist; **5** (personnellement) to know [*ami, parent, relation*]; **je le connais depuis longtemps** I've known him for a long time; **vous ne me connaissez pas** you don't know me; **j'ai appris à ~ mon père en grandissant** I got to know my father as I grew up; **j'aimerais bien la ~** I'd really like to get to know her; **c'est bien mal la ~ que de croire que...** they/you're misjudging her if they/you think that...; **je le connais trop bien** I know him only too well; **faire ~ qn à qn** to introduce sb to sb; **mes parents? je les connais, ils seront ravis!** my parents? if I know them, they'll be delighted; **Bernadette? je ne connais qu'elle!** Bernadette? I know her very well!; **il ne me connaît plus depuis qu'il est passé officier** he ignores me now that he's an officer; **6†** (coucher avec) to know†, to have a sexual relationship with; **7** Jur **~ de** to have jurisdiction over [*affaire, cause*]; **avoir à ~ de** to judge ou hear [*cas*].
II se connaître *vpr* **1** (soi-même) to know oneself; **il se connaît mal** he doesn't know himself very well; **'connais-toi toi-même'**

'know thyself'; **il ne se connaissait plus de joie** fml he was beside himself with joy; **quand il a bu, il ne se connaît plus** when he's drunk, he goes berserk; **2** (l'un l'autre) to know each other; **nous nous sommes connus chez des amis communs** we met (each other) at the home of some mutual friends; **3** (être compétent) **s'y ~ en électricité/théâtre** to know all about electricity/theatre; **c'est le carburateur qui est bouché ou je ne m'y connais pas** if I know anything about it, it's the carburettor GB ou carburetor US that's blocked.

IDIOMES **on connaît la chanson** or **musique!** we've heard it all before!, it's the same old story!; **c'est un air connu** it's the same old story!

connard● /kɔnaʀ/ *nm* offensive stupid bastard◐ injur.

connasse● /kɔnas/ *nf* offensive silly bitch◐ injur.

conne ▶ **con** I, II.

connecter /kɔnɛkte/ [1] **I** *vtr* to connect (**à** to); **être/ne pas être connecté** Ordinat to be on/off line.

II se connecter *vpr* **1** [*appareil*] to be connected (**à** to); **2** Ordinat [*utilisateur*] **se ~ à** to log on to.

connecteur /kɔnɛktœʀ/ *nm* **1** (cordon) connector cable; **2** (composant) connector; **3** (en logique) connective.

Connecticut /kɔnɛktikyt/ ▶ **692** *nprm* Connecticut.

connerie● /kɔnʀi/ *nf* **1** (stupidité) stupidity; **2** (action, remarque) **il a sorti une ~** he came out with a bloody◐ stupid remark GB ou crass remark; **faire une ~** to do a bloody◐ stupid thing GB, to fuck up●; **dire des ~s** to talk bullshit●.

connétable /kɔnetabl/ *nm* Hist *supreme commander of the French armies*.

connexe /kɔnɛks/ *adj* related (**à** to).

connexion /kɔnɛksjɔ̃/ *nf* lit, fig connection (**entre** between; **avec** with).

connivence /kɔnivɑ̃s/ *nf* (complicité) connivance ¢; (accord tacite) tacit agreement; **signe/regard de ~** sign/look of complicity; **être** or **agir de ~ avec qn** to connive with sb.

connotatif, **-ive** /kɔnɔtatif, iv/ *adj* connotative; **l'effet ~ d'un mot** the connotation(s) of a word.

connotation /kɔnɔtasjɔ̃/ *nf* connotation.

connoter /kɔnɔte/ [1] *vtr* to connote.

conque /kɔ̃k/ *nf* **1** Zool (mollusque, coquille) conch; **en ~** cupped, shell-shaped; **mettre sa main en ~** to cup one's hand; **2** Anat (de l'oreille) concha; **3** Archit conch.

conquérant, **~e** /kɔ̃keʀɑ̃, ɑ̃t/ **I** *adj* [*peuple*] conquering; fig [*air*] triumphant.

II *nm,f* (guerrier) conqueror.

conquérir /kɔ̃keʀiʀ/ [35] *vtr* to conquer [*pays, sommet*]; to capture [*marché*]; to gain [*pouvoir*]; to win [*amitié, cœur, personne, titre, position*]; to win over [*lecteur, auditoire*]; **leur talent/charme a conquis Paris** they captivated Paris with their talent/charm; **des régions conquises sur** areas captured from.

IDIOMES **se croire en pays** or **terrain conquis** to lord it over everyone.

conquête /kɔ̃kɛt/ *nf* **1** (de pays, sommet, pouvoir) conquest; **faire la ~ d'un pays** to conquer a country; **~ de l'espace** conquest of space; **~s sociales/syndicales** social/trade union victories; **partir à la ~ de** to set out to conquer [*pays, sommet, pouvoir*]; to set out to capture [*marché*]; to set out to achieve [*bonheur*]; **2** (séduction) conquest; (personne séduite) conquest; **faire la ~ d'une femme** to win the heart of a lady; **tu vas faire des ~s dans cette robe** you are going to be a hit○ in that dress.

■ **la Conquête de l'Ouest** Hist the conquest of the Wild West.

conquis, **~e** /kɔ̃ki, iz/ ▶ **conquérir**.

conquistador /kɔ̃kistadɔʀ/ *nm* conquistador.

consacré, **~e** /kɔ̃sakʀe/ **I** *pp* ▶ **consacrer**.

II *pp adj* **1** (ratifié par l'usage) **formule** or **expression ~e** time-honoured[GB] expression; **selon la formule ~e** as the expression goes; **2** (reconnu) **artiste/talent ~** recognized artist/talent; **être ~ joueur de l'année** to be designated player of the year.

consacrer /kɔ̃sakʀe/ [1] **I** *vtr* **1** (accorder) to devote [*texte, effort, vie, ressources, exposition*] (**à** to); **~ du temps et de l'argent à qch** to devote time and money to sth; **~ 20 millions à qch** to devote 20 million to sth; **2** (sanctionner) to sanction [*rupture, alliance*]; **l'usage a consacré le mot** the word has gained acceptance through use; **3** Relig to consecrate [*basilique, hostie, évêque*]; to ordain [*prêtre*]; **jour consacré** holy day.

II se consacrer *vpr* **se ~ à qch/à faire** to devote oneself to sth/to doing; **il pourra désormais se ~ à son passe-temps favori** from now on he'll be able to devote himself to his favourite[GB] hobby.

consanguin, **~e** /kɔ̃sɑ̃gɛ̃, in/ **I** *adj* **1** (entre proches parents) **union ~e**, **mariage ~** marriage between blood relations; **2** (du même père) **frère ~** half brother (*having the same father*).

II consanguins *nmpl* **les ~s** blood relations.

consanguinité /kɔ̃sɑ̃gɥinite/ *nf* **1** (union consanguine) Biol inbreeding; **2** (filiation) consanguinity.

consciemment /kɔ̃sjamɑ̃/ *adv* consciously.

conscience /kɔ̃sjɑ̃s/ *nf* **1** (morale) conscience; **selon ta ~** according to your conscience; **en toute ~** in all conscience; **écouter (la voix de) sa ~** to follow one's conscience; **avoir bonne/mauvaise ~** to have a clear/a guilty conscience; **avoir la ~ tranquille** to be at peace with one's conscience; **faire qch pour se donner bonne ~** to do sth as a salve to one's conscience ou to ease one's conscience; **j'ai ma ~ pour moi** my conscience is clear; **avoir qch sur la ~** to have sth on one's conscience; **2** (connaissance, intuition) awareness; **avoir ~ de qch/d'être** to be aware of sth/of being; **avoir ~ que** to be aware that; **prendre ~ de/que** to become aware of/that; **prise de ~** realization; **campagne de prise de ~** public awareness campaign; **~ de soi** self-awareness; **3** (de collectivité) consciousness ¢; **~ collective/nationale/politique** collective/national/political consciousness; **4** (siège des sentiments) **scruter les ~s** to read people's thoughts; **5** (lucidité) consciousness ¢; **perdre/reprendre ~** to lose/to regain consciousness; **avoir toute sa ~** to be fully lucid.

■ **~ de classe** class consciousness; **~ professionnelle** conscientiousness.

consciencieusement /kɔ̃sjɑ̃sjøzmɑ̃/ *adv* **1** (avec sérieux) conscientiously; **2** (comme il se doit) dutifully.

consciencieux, **-ieuse** /kɔ̃sjɑ̃sjø, øz/ *adj* gén conscientious; [*enfant, époux*] dutiful.

conscient, **~e** /kɔ̃sjɑ̃, ɑ̃t/ **I** *adj* **1** (au fait) **~ de qch/que** aware of sth/that; **être ~ de qch** to be aware ou conscious of sth; **je suis ~ de choquer** I am aware that I shock people; **2** Psych (qui est fait sciemment) conscious; **personne/attitude ~e** conscious person/attitude; **de façon** or **manière ~e** consciously; **politiquement ~** politically aware; **3** (lucide) conscious; **être ~ jusqu'à la fin** to be conscious to the end.

II *nm* conscious; **le ~ et l'inconscient** the conscious and the unconscious.

conscription /kɔ̃skʀipsjɔ̃/ *nf* conscription; **armée de ~** conscript army.

conscrit /kɔ̃skʀi/ *nm* **1** Mil conscript GB, draftee US; **2** (de la même année) **c'est mon ~** he was born in the same year as me.

consécration /kɔ̃sekʀasjɔ̃/ *nf* **1** (reconnaissance) (de personne) recognition; **connaître la ~** to win recognition; **~ suprême** ultimate recognition; **2** Relig (de basilique, d'évêque) consecration; (de prêtre) ordination.

consécutif, **-ive** /kɔ̃sekytif, iv/ *adj* **1** gén consecutive; **remporter le championnat pour la quatrième année consécutive** to win the championship for the fourth consecutive year; **retards ~s à la modernisation** delays resulting from modernization; **série de procès ~s au scandale** series of court cases following the scandal; **2** Ling **proposition consécutive** consecutive clause.

consécutivement /kɔ̃sekytivmɑ̃/ *adv* consecutively; **les points perdus ~ à la défaite** the points lost following the defeat.

conseil /kɔ̃sɛj/ *nm* **1** (avis) advice ¢; **un ~** a piece of advice; **des ~s** some advice; **beaucoup de ~s** a lot of advice; **donner un ~ à qn** to give sb advice; **demander ~ à qn** to ask (for) sb's advice; **suivre/écouter les ~s de qn** to follow/to listen to sb's advice; **un petit ~** a little piece of advice; **un bon ~** a piece of good advice; **~ d'ami** piece of friendly advice; **un ~ gratuit** a piece of free advice; **quelques ~s de prudence** a few words of caution ou warning; **sur les ~s de qn** on sb's advice; **donner à qn le ~ de faire** to advise sb to do; **il est de bon ~** he always gives good advice; **~s d'entretien** cleaning ou care instructions; ▶ **nuit**; **2** (assemblée) council; **réunir le ~** to convene the council; **tenir ~** to hold a meeting; **3** (conseiller) consultant; **~ en gestion** management consultant.

■ **~ d'administration** Entr board of directors; **~ de classe** Scol staff meeting (*for all those teaching a given class*); **~ de discipline** Admin, Mil, Scol disciplinary committee; **~ de famille** Jur Board of Guardians; (non officiel) family meeting ou gathering; **~ général** Pol *council of a French department*; **~ de guerre** Mil council of war; **~ des ministres** Pol gén council of ministers; (au Royaume-Uni) Cabinet meeting; **~ municipal** Pol town council; **~ régional** Pol regional council; **~ de révision** Mil medical board (*assessing fitness for military service*); **~ de surveillance** Entr supervisory board; **~ d'université** Univ senate; **Conseil constitutionnel** Jur Constitutional Council; **Conseil économique et social** Pol Economic and Social Council; **Conseil d'État** Pol Council of State (*advising government on administrative matters*); **Conseil de l'Europe**, **CE** Pol Council of Europe; **Conseil de sécurité (de l'ONU)** Pol (UN) Security Council; **Conseil supérieur de l'audiovisuel**, **CSA** Radio, TV *body which monitors broadcasting*; **Conseil supérieur de la langue française** *body responsible for the regulation and advancement of the French language*; **Conseil supérieur de la magistrature**, **CSM** Jur High Council for the Judiciary.

conseillé, **~e** /kɔ̃seje/ **I** *pp* ▶ **conseiller**.

II *pp adj* [*modèle, activité*] recommended; **il est ~ de faire** it is advisable to do.

conseiller, **-ère** /kɔ̃seje, ɛʀ/ [1] **I** *nm,f* **1** (expert) adviser[GB]; **~ militaire/politique/fiscal** military/political/tax adviser; **~ du président** presidential adviser; **~ en communication** communications adviser; **2** (guide) counsellor[GB]; **bon/mauvais/sage ~** good/bad/wise counsellor[GB]; ▶ **colère**.

II *nm* **1** (membre de conseil, de cour) councillor[GB]; **2** (diplomate) counsellor[GB].

III *vtr* **1** (proposer) to recommend [*lieu, activité, mesure, personne*] (**à** to); **dans ces cas-là je conseille de prendre un avocat** in such cases I advise people to get a lawyer; **~ à qn de faire** to advise sb to do; **~ la prudence** to recommend caution; **2** (servir d'expert à) to advise [*personne*] (**en matière de, sur** on); **être mal conseillé** to be badly advised; **il n'a pas été conseillé** nobody advised him; **se faire ~ par qn** to seek advice from sb.

■ **~ commercial** commercial counsellor[GB]; **~ culturel** cultural counsellor[GB]; **~ (principal) d'éducation** Scol chief supervisor; **~ d'État** member of the Council of State; **~ général** Pol *councillor*[GB] *for a French department*; **~ municipal** town councillor[GB]; **~ d'orientation** Scol, Univ careers adviser; **~ régional** regional councillor[GB].

consensuel, -elle /kɔ̃sɛ̃sɥɛl/ *adj* [*politique*] consensual; [*réforme*] based on consensus (*après n*); **de manière consensuelle** by common consensus.

consensus /kɔ̃sɛ̃sys/ *nm* consensus (**sur** on; **autour de** on; **avec** with); **un ~ s'est fait** consensus has been reached.

consentant, ~e /kɔ̃sɑ̃tɑ̃, ɑ̃t/ *adj* [*personne*] willing; Jur consenting; **s'il est ~** if he is willing; **entre adultes ~s** Jur between consenting adults; **les parents doivent être ~s** the parents must give their consent; **sourire ~** smile of consent; **visage ~** face expressing consent.

consentement /kɔ̃sɑ̃tmɑ̃/ *nm* consent (**à** to); **donner** or **accorder son ~** to give one's consent; **divorce par ~ mutuel** Jur divorce by consent GB, no-fault divorce US; **arracher le ~ de qn** to wrest agreement from sb.

consentir /kɔ̃sɑ̃tiʀ/ [30] **I** *vtr* to grant [*permission, augmentation*] (**à qn** to sb); to allow [*avantage*] (**à qn** to sb); to agree to make [*effort*]; **~ un délai/une remise à qn** to allow sb extra time/a discount; **~ un prêt à qn** [*banque*] to grant sb a loan.

II consentir à *vtr ind* **~ à qch/à faire** to agree to sth/to do; **je consens à ce que tu y ailles** I agree to your going.

IDIOMES **qui ne dit mot consent** Prov silence means consent Prov.

conséquemment /kɔ̃sekamɑ̃/ *adv* **1** (par conséquent) consequently; **~ à** as a result of; **2**† (responsablement) responsibly.

conséquence /kɔ̃sekɑ̃s/ *nf* consequence (**pour** for; **sur** to); **~ logique/pratique** logical/practical consequence; **~s désastreuses/financières** disastrous/financial consequences; **être la ~ de** to be the consequence of; **être lourd de ~s** to have serious consequences; **sans ~(s)** of no consequence; **supporter les ~s** to suffer ou bear the consequences; **tirer les ~s de qch** to learn one's lesson from sth; **ne pas tirer à ~** to be of no consequence; **~ heureuse** happy result; **avoir pour ~ de faire** to have the effect of doing; **avoir pour ~ le chômage/la hausse des prix** to result in unemployment/an increase in prices; **en ~ (de quoi)** as a result (of which); **agir en ~** to act accordingly; **avoir des qualifications et un salaire en ~** to have qualifications and a corresponding salary; **par voie de ~** consequently, by way of consequence.

conséquent, ~e /kɔ̃sekɑ̃, ɑ̃t/ **I** *adj* **1** (important) substantial; **aide ~e** substantial aid; **2** (cohérent) consistent (**avec** with); **être ~ avec soi-même** to be consistent; **3** Géog [*rivière, percée*] consequent; **4** Ling, Philos [*proposition*] consequent.

II *nm* Ling, Philos, Mus consequent.

III par conséquent *loc adv* therefore, as a result.

conservateur, -trice /kɔ̃sɛʀvatœʀ, tʀis/ **I** *adj* **1** Pol conservative; **2** Chimie preservative.

II *nm,f* **1** Pol conservative; **2** ▶**510** Admin (dans un musée) curator; (dans une bibliothèque) chief GB ou head US librarian.

III *nm* **1** Chimie preservative; **'garanti sans ~s'** 'no preservatives'; **2** (appareil ménager) ≈ freezer compartment.

■ **~ des hypothèques** land registrar.

conservation /kɔ̃sɛʀvasjɔ̃/ *nf* **1** (protection) (d'espèce, de patrimoine) conservation; (de livres, tableaux) preservation; **la ~ des manuscrits** the preservation of manuscripts; **état de ~** state of preservation; **2** Chimie (d'aliment, de sperme, d'embryon) preservation; **lait/crème longue ~** long life milk/cream GB; **la ~ des peaux** the preservation of skins; **3** Phys conservation.

■ **~ des hypothèques** Admin land registry.

conservatisme /kɔ̃sɛʀvatism/ *nm* conservatism ¢; **les ~s** conservative attitudes.

conservatoire /kɔ̃sɛʀvatwaʀ/ **I** *adj* Jur protective.

II *nm* academy; **~ de musique** conservatoire of music.

■ **Conservatoire national des arts et métiers** (musée) *museum of technology*; (centre d'études) *institute for engineering studies*.

conserve /kɔ̃sɛʀv/ **I** *nf* **1** Ind canned ou tinned GB food; **numéro un de la ~** market leader in canned food; **se nourrir de ~s** to live on canned foods; **~s de poissons** canned fish; **fruits/petits pois en ~** canned fruit/peas; **boîte de ~** can, tin GB; **2** Culin preserve; **faire des ~s** to make preserves; **des ~s de haricots verts** green bean preserves.

II de conserve *loc adv* [*agir*] in concert; [*naviguer*] in convoy.

conserver /kɔ̃sɛʀve/ [1] **I** *vtr* **1** (garder) to keep [*brouillon, tableau, emploi*]; to retain [*influence, liens, majorité, titre*]; **~ ses habitudes** to retain one's habits; **~ un rythme** to keep a rythm; **~ son calme** to keep calm; **~ l'anonymat** to remain anonymous; **2** Culin to preserve [*aliment*]; **~ qch dans du vinaigre** to pickle sth; **'à ~ au frais'** 'keep refrigerated'; **3** (maintenir jeune) [*sport*] to keep [sb] young [*personne*]; **homme bien conservé** well-preserved man; **elle est bien conservée** she is well-preserved.

II se conserver *vpr* **1** [*aliment*] to keep; **2** [*personne*] to keep young.

conserverie /kɔ̃sɛʀvəʀi/ *nf* **1** (usine) cannery; **2** (secteur) canning industry.

considérable /kɔ̃sideʀabl/ *adj* **1** (très grand) [*fortune, quantité, difficulté, retard*] considerable; **l'émotion est ~** feelings are running high; **2** (de grande importance) [*résultat, rôle, événement*] significant; **l'enjeu est ~** the stakes are high.

considérablement /kɔ̃sideʀabləmɑ̃/ *adv* considerably, significantly.

considérant /kɔ̃sideʀɑ̃/ *nm* Jur grounds (*pl*).

considération /kɔ̃sideʀasjɔ̃/ *nf* **1** (facteur) consideration; **des ~s budgétaires/politiques/techniques** budgetary/political/technical considerations; **prendre qch en ~** to take sth into consideration; **mériter ~** to merit consideration; **avant toute autre ~** before any other consideration; **en ~ de** in view of; **sans ~ de** irrespective of; **2** (respect) consideration, respect (**à l'égard de, pour** for); **par ~ de** or **pour** out of respect for; **jouir d'une ~ unanime** to be respected by all; **3** (remarque) reflection (**sur** on); **~s sur l'histoire** reflections on history; **~s inutiles** idle reflections.

considéré, ~e /kɔ̃sideʀe/ **I** *pp* ▶ **considérer**.

II *pp adj* (en question) under consideration; **gérer les projets ~s** to manage the projects under consideration.

considérer /kɔ̃sideʀe/ [14] **I** *vtr* **1** (juger) **~ qn/qch comme (étant)** to consider sb/sth to be; **~ que** to consider that; **je le considère comme un ami** I consider him a friend, I consider him to be a friend; **être considéré comme le successeur de Rousseau** to be seen as Rousseau's successor; **~ être/ne pas être** to consider oneself to be/not to be; **je les considère comme compétents** I consider them to be competent; **~ un tableau comme un chef-d'œuvre** to consider a painting to be a masterpiece; **~ comme criminels ceux qui polluent l'atmosphère** to regard those who pollute the atmosphere as criminals; **~ que le gouvernement fait preuve d'incompétence** to consider that the government shows incompetence; **il considère comme acquise sa victoire électorale** he sees himself as having already won the election; **on considère généralement que** it is generally considered that; **2** (envisager) to regard [*personne*]; to consider [*chose*]; **~ un adversaire avec respect** to regard an opponent with respect; **~ les choses sous un angle différent** to consider things from a different angle; **si l'on considère les derniers chiffres** if we consider the latest figures; **~ une question sous tous ses aspects** to consider a matter from every angle; **à tout bien ~** all things considered; **3** (respecter) to have a high regard for; **personne/profession bien considérée** highly regarded person/profession; **4** (examiner) to consider; **~ qn/qch très attentivement** to consider sb/sth very carefully; **5** (regarder attentivement) to look at [*personne, spectacle*].

II se considérer *vpr* **1** (soi-même) **se ~ (comme)** to consider oneself (to be); **se ~ (comme) privilégié** to consider oneself (to be) privileged; **2** (l'un l'autre) **se ~ (comme)** to regard one another as being; (s'étudier) to gaze at each other.

consignataire /kɔ̃siɲatɛʀ/ *nmf* **1** Jur, Fin depositary; **2** Comm, Naut consignee.

consignation /kɔ̃siɲasjɔ̃/ *nf* **1** Jur, Fin deposit; **2** Comm **en ~** on consignment.

consigne /kɔ̃siɲ/ *nf* **1** (ordre) orders (*pl*), instructions (*pl*); **donner ~ de faire** to give orders to do; **avoir pour ~ de faire** to have orders to do; **appliquer** or **respecter la ~** to comply with orders; **suivre des ~s** to follow orders; **c'est la ~** those are the orders; **donner** or **lancer une ~ de grève** to issue strike orders; **donner** or **lancer une ~ de boycott** to order a boycott; **la police a reçu des ~s de silence pour cette affaire** the police were instructed to keep silent on the matter; **le mouvement n'a donné aucune ~ de vote à ses adhérents** the movement did not instruct its members how to vote; **~ leur a été donnée de ne rien dire** they were instructed to say nothing; **passer la ~ à qn** to pass the word on to sb; **'~s à suivre en cas d'incendie'** 'fire regulations'; **2** (pour les bagages) (comptoir) left luggage office GB, baggage checkroom US; **mettre** or **laisser** or **déposer qch à la** or **en ~** to put sth in left luggage GB, to check sth (in) US; **3** (de bouteilles, d'emballages) deposit (**de** of).

■ **~ automatique** left luggage lockers (*pl*) GB, baggage lockers (*pl*) US.

consigné, ~e /kɔ̃siɲe/ **I** *pp* ▶ **consigner**.

II *pp adj* [*bouteille, emballage*] returnable; **non ~** nonreturnable.

consigner /kɔ̃siɲe/ [1] *vtr* **1** (conserver par écrit) to record, to write [sth] down [*fait, souvenir*] (**dans** in); **2** (retenir dans un lieu) Mil to confine [*soldat*] (**dans, à** to); Scol to give [sb] detention [*élève*]; **3** (mettre en dépôt) to consign [*objet, marchandise*].

consistance /kɔ̃sistɑ̃s/ *nf* **1** (de pâte, sauce, peinture) consistency; **de ~ molle** of a soft consistency; **avoir de la/manquer de ~** [*sauce, peinture*] to be quite thick/too runny; **prendre ~** to thicken; **donner de la ~ à qch** to thicken sth; **2** (d'argument, de théorie) substance, weight; **prendre de la ~** [*rumeur, théorie*] to gain weight; **sans ~** [*personne*] spineless; [*rumeur*] without substance; [*bonheur*] with no basis in reality.

consistant, ~e /kɔ̃sistɑ̃, ɑ̃t/ *adj* **1** (copieux) [*repas*] substantial; [*plat*] nourishing; [*augmentation, investissement*] substantial; **2** (épais) [*sauce, peinture*] thick; **3** (solide) [*livre*] with some substance (*épith, après n*); [*argument*] solid; **4** (fondé) [*rumeur*] well-founded.

consister /kɔ̃siste/ [1] *vi* **1** (résider) **~ en** or **dans qch** to consist in sth, to lie in sth; **~ à faire** to consist in doing; **le bonheur consiste à accepter son sort** happiness consists in accepting one's fate; **en quoi**

consiste mon erreur? where have I gone wrong?; **2** (être fait) **~ en** to consist of [*éléments, parties*]; **l'examen consiste en deux épreuves/un oral** the examination consists of two papers/an oral; **en quoi consiste cette aide?** what form does this aid take?

consistoire /kɔ̃sistwaʀ/ *nm* consistory; **en ~ secret** in private consistory.

consœur /kɔ̃sœʀ/ *nf* **1** (d'une personne) female colleague; **2** (d'une banque, organisation) counterpart.

consolant, **~e** /kɔ̃sɔlɑ̃, ɑ̃t/ *adj* comforting; **c'est ~ de faire** there is some comfort in doing.

consolateur, **-trice** /kɔ̃sɔlatœʀ, tʀis/ liter **I** *adj* comforting.

II *nm,f* comforter.

consolation /kɔ̃sɔlasjɔ̃/ *nf* consolation; **en guise de ~** by way of consolation; **c'est une maigre** or **piètre ~** it's small consolation; **lot** or **prix de ~** consolation prize.

console /kɔ̃sɔl/ *nf* console.

■ **~ de jeu vidéo** games console; **~ de mixage** Audio, Tech mixing desk.

consoler /kɔ̃sɔle/ [1] **I** *vtr* to console [*personne*] (**de** for); to soothe away [*peine*]; **cela console de savoir que** it is some consolation to know that; **si ça peut te ~** if it is any comfort to you.

II se consoler *vpr* **1** (soi-même) to find consolation, to get over it; **se ~ de qch** to get over sth; **se ~ d'avoir fait** to get over doing; **il s'est vite consolé de son échec** he soon got over his failure; **il s'en consolera vite** he'll soon get over it; **2** (réciproquement) to console each other.

consolidable /kɔ̃sɔlidabl/ *adj* **1** [*dette*] fundable; **2** [*structure*] reinforceable.

consolidation /kɔ̃sɔlidasjɔ̃/ *nf* **1** (de mur, chaise) strengthening; (de position) consolidation; **2** Fin (de dette) consolidation, funding; (de chiffre d'affaires, cours, d'usufruit) consolidation; (de monnaie) strengthening; **3** Compta (de bilan) consolidation; **4** Méd (de fracture) mending.

consolidé, **~e** /kɔ̃sɔlide/ **I** *pp* ▶ **consolider**.

II *pp adj* **1** Fin [*chiffre d'affaires, résultat*] consolidated; **2** (affermi) consolidated; **3** (renforcé) strengthened.

consolider /kɔ̃sɔlide/ [1] **I** *vtr* **1** (renforcer) to strengthen [*mur*]; to consolidate [*position, résultat*]; **2** Fin to consolidate, to fund [*dette*]; to strengthen [*monnaie*]; **~ son avance** [*valeur*] to firm up; **3** Compta to consolidate [*bilan*]; **4** Méd to set [*fracture, tissus*].

II se consolider *vpr* **1** (se renforcer) [*économie*] to get stronger; [*organisation*] to gain strength; [*relation*] to grow stronger; [*position*] to be consolidated; [*structure*] to be strengthened; **2** (s'affermir) to consolidate; **3** Méd [*fracture, tissus*] to mend.

consommable /kɔ̃sɔmabl/ **I** *adj* **1** [*aliment*] edible; [*boisson*] drinkable; **2** Tech expendable.

II consommables *nmpl* Comm, Ordinat consumables.

consommateur, **-trice** /kɔ̃sɔmatœʀ, tʀis/ **I** *adj* Écon [*pays, industrie*] consumer (*épith*); **~ de pétrole/d'énergie** oil-/energy-consuming (*épith*).

II *nm,f* **1** Écon consumer; **gros ~** large consumer; **~ de café/gaz/drogue** consumer of coffee/gas/drugs; **défense des ~s** consumer protection; **organisation de ~s** consumers' association; **2** (de café, bar) customer.

consommation /kɔ̃sɔmasjɔ̃/ *nf* **1** Écon consumption; **~ d'alcool/d'acier** alcohol/steel consumption; **baisse/relance de la ~** drop/stimulation in consumption; **~ intérieure** domestic consumption, home market consumption; **~ des ménages** household consumption; **pour ma ~ personnelle** for my personal use; **faire une grande** or **grosse ~ de** to get through ou use a lot of; **2** (fait de manger, boire) consumption; (fait d'utiliser) **~ d'héroïne/de cocaïne** heroin/cocain use; **la ~ de tabac/d'alcool** tobacco/alcohol consumption; **limitez la ~ d'aliments riches en matières grasses** avoid eating fatty foods; **la trop forte ~ de graisses** excessive intake of fats; **une réduction de la ~ de sodium** eating less salt, a reduction in sodium intake; **3** Comm (boisson) drink; **régler les ~s** to pay for the drinks; **jugé pour ~ de cocaïne** charged with using cocaine; **4** (accomplissement) consummation sout.

consommé, **~e** /kɔ̃sɔme/ **I** *pp* ▶ **consommer**.

II *pp adj* [*art, artiste*] consummate; **avec un sens ~ du spectacle** with a consummate sense of the theatrical.

III *nm* Culin consommé; **~ de poulet** chicken consommé.

consommer /kɔ̃sɔme/ [1] **I** *vtr* **1** ▶ **662** (utiliser) [*personne, pays*] to consume [*produit, énergie, matière*]; [*moteur, voiture*] to consume [*essence, huile*]; **~ peu d'électricité** to consume ou use little electricity; **ma voiture consomme énormément** my car consumes a lot of petrol GB ou gas US; **2** (manger) to eat [*viande, fromage*]; (boire) to drink [*alcool, thé*]; **~ de la drogue** to take drugs; **3** (accomplir) fml to consummate sout [*mariage*]; to complete [*rupture*].

II *vi* **1** Écon to consume; **les Français n'ont jamais autant consommé** the French are consuming more than ever before; **2** Comm (boire) to drink.

III se consommer *vpr* **1** (être mangé) to be eaten; **le gaspacho se consomme froid** gazpacho is eaten cold; **2** (pouvoir être mangé) to be edible; **3** Écon (être utilisé) to be consumed.

consomptible /kɔ̃sɔ̃ptibl/ *adj* Jur expendable.

consomption† /kɔ̃sɔ̃psjɔ̃/ *nf* **1** (dépérissement) decline; **2** (tuberculose) consumption‡.

consonance /kɔ̃sɔnɑ̃s/ *nf* consonance; **un mot aux ~s étrangères** a foreign-sounding word.

consonant, **~e** /kɔ̃sɔnɑ̃, ɑ̃t/ *adj* consonant.

consonantique /kɔ̃sɔnɑ̃tik/ *adj* [*langue*] consonantal; [*groupe*] consonant (*épith*).

consonantisme /kɔ̃sɔnɑ̃tism/ *nm* consonantism.

consonne /kɔ̃sɔn/ *nf* consonant; **~ occlusive/dentale** occlusive/dental consonant; **~ d'appui/de liaison** intrusive/linking consonant.

consort /kɔ̃sɔʀ/ **I** *adj m* **prince ~** prince consort.

II consorts *nmpl* (acolytes) pej **Gérard et ~s** Gérard and his gang; **voleurs, bandits et ~s** thieves, bandits and others of that ilk.

consortium /kɔ̃sɔʀsjɔm/ *nm* consortium; **~ bancaire** consortium of banks.

conspirateur, **-trice** /kɔ̃spiʀatœʀ, tʀis/ **I** *adj* [*activités, air*] conspiratorial.

II *nm,f* conspirator.

conspiration /kɔ̃spiʀasjɔ̃/ *nf* conspiracy (**contre** against); **déjouer une ~** to foil a conspiracy; **une ~ des généraux/de la direction** a conspiracy by the generals/on the part of management.

conspirer /kɔ̃spiʀe/ [1] **I**† *vtr* to plot [*mort, ruine*].

II *vi* (comploter) to conspire, to plot (**contre** against).

III conspirer à *vtr ind* **~ à** to conspire to bring about [*malheur, succès*]; **~ à faire** to conspire to do.

conspuer /kɔ̃spɥe/ [1] *vtr* to boo; **se faire ~** to be booed.

constamment /kɔ̃stamɑ̃/ *adv* **1** (invariablement) always; **il est ~ vainqueur** he always wins; **elle est ~ absente** she's never here; **2** (sans interruption) [*augmenter*] continuously; [*maintenir*] consistently; **elle a fait ~ preuve de courage** she consistently showed courage; **3** (très souvent) [*dérangé, malade*] constantly; **dire/se plaindre ~** to be constantly saying/moaning.

constance /kɔ̃stɑ̃s/ *nf* **1** (caractère stable) (de sentiment, phénomène) constancy; (d'opinion) consistency; **2** (persévérance) steadfastness; (fidélité) constancy†; **aimer avec ~** to love with constancy; **affirmer avec ~ que**... to hold steadfastly that...; **travailler avec ~** to work steadily; **3**○ (patience) patience; **4**† (fermeté, endurance) liter constancy†.

Constance /kɔ̃stɑ̃s/ ▶ **459** *npr* Constance; **le lac de ~** Lake Constance.

constant, **~e** /kɔ̃stɑ̃, ɑ̃t/ **I** *adj* **1** (permanent, très fréquent) constant; **2** (stable) [*vitesse, qualité*] constant; [*personne*] (dans ses affections) constant; (dans ses opinions) consistent; **3** (continu) [*évolution, progression*] continuous; [*hausse, baisse*] continual; **être en hausse/baisse ~e** to be continually rising/falling; **4** (persévérant) liter [*personne*] steadfast; [*résolution*] firm.

■ Note On utilise *continuous* pour décrire une action qui ne cesse pas et *continual* pour décrire une action qui se répète.

II constante *nf* **1** Math, Phys constant; **2** fig (trait) permanent feature.

Constantin /kɔ̃stɑ̃tɛ̃/ *npr* Constantine.

Constantinople /kɔ̃stɑ̃tinɔpl/ ▶ **857** *npr* Constantinople.

constat /kɔ̃sta/ *nm* **1** (procès-verbal) certified ou official report; **dresser un ~** to draw up a report; **2** (bilan) assessment; **3** (preuve) acknowledgement.

■ **~ (à l') amiable** Assur *accident report drawn up by the parties involved*; **~ d'adultère** Jur record of adultery; **~ d'échec** fig admission of failure; **faire un ~ d'échec** to admit failure; **~ d'huissier** Jur bailiff's report.

constatable /kɔ̃statabl/ *adj* observable.

constatation /kɔ̃statasjɔ̃/ **I** *nf* **1** (observation) observation; **faire la ~ suivante** to observe the following (fact); **ce n'est pas une accusation, c'est une simple ~** it's not an accusation, it's simply a statement of fact; **2** (enquête) investigation; (rapport d'enquête) report; **~s d'usage** routine investigations; **procéder à la ~ des pertes** Assur to assess losses.

II constatations *nfpl* (conclusions) findings; **selon les premières ~s des enquêteurs** according to the initial findings of the police.

■ **~ de décès** record of death.

constater /kɔ̃state/ [1] *vtr* **1** (observer) to note, to notice [*fait*]; to notice, to see [*défaut, différence*]; **~ une amélioration/que qch s'est amélioré** to note an improvement/that sth has improved; **~ (par) soi-même** to see for oneself; **comme tu peux le ~** as you can see; **2** (établir) to ascertain, to establish [*fait*]; (consigner) to record [*délit*]; **~ le décès** to certify that death has occurred.

constellation /kɔ̃stɛlasjɔ̃/ *nf* **1** Astron constellation; **2** (groupe) (de partis, villes) cluster; (de firmes) group.

constellé, **~e** /kɔ̃stɛlle/ **I** *pp* ▶ **consteller**.

II *pp adj* **~ de** spangled with [*étoiles, diamants*]; scattered with [*fleurs*]; riddled with [*fautes*]; spotted with [*taches*]; **ciel ~ d'étoiles** starry sky.

consteller /kɔ̃stɛlle/ [1] **I** *vtr* liter **des étoiles constellaient le ciel** the sky was spangled with stars; **des taches constellaient sa jupe** her skirt was spotted with stains; **il constelle ses articles de fautes** his articles are riddled with mistakes.

II se consteller *vpr* liter **le ciel se constelle d'étoiles** the sky is filling up with stars.

consternant, **~e** /kɔ̃stɛʀnɑ̃, ɑ̃t/ *adj* distressing; **être d'une sottise ~e** to be appallingly stupid.

consternation /kɔ̃stɛʀnasjɔ̃/ *nf* consternation, dismay; **jeter** or **semer la ~** to cause consternation; **frapper qn de ~** to fill sb with consternation; **à la ~ générale** to everyone's dismay.

consterner /kɔ̃stɛʀne/ [1] *vtr* to fill [sb] with consternation; **être consterné** to be filled with consternation; **mine consternée** dismayed expression.

constipation /kɔ̃stipasjɔ̃/ *nf* constipation.

constipé, **~e** /kɔ̃stipe/ **I** *pp* ▶ **constiper**.
II *pp adj* **1** Méd constipated; **2**○ fig (contraint) pej **avoir l'air/être ~** to look/to be uptight.
III *nm,f* **1** Méd constipation sufferer; **2**○ fig pej uptight person.

constiper /kɔ̃stipe/ [1] *vtr* to make [sb] constipated; **le chocolat constipe** chocolate causes constipation.

constituant, **~e** /kɔ̃stitɥɑ̃, ɑ̃t/ **I** *adj* [*partie, élément*] constituent.
II *nm* **1** (élément constitutif) constituent (**de** of); **~s de la matière** constituents of matter; **2** Ling constituent; **~ immédiat/ultime** immediate/ultimate constituent; **3** Jur (de procuration, vente) settlor.

Constituante /kɔ̃stitɥɑ̃t/ *nf* Hist, Pol Constituent Assembly.

constitué, **~e** /kɔ̃stitɥe/ **I** *pp* ▶ **constituer**.
II *pp adj* **1** Physiol **personne bien/mal ~e** person of sound/unsound constitution; **2** Pol [*autorité, société*] constituted.

constituer /kɔ̃stitɥe/ [1] **I** *vtr* **1** (être) to be, to constitute; **le vol constitue un délit** theft constitutes an offence[GB]; **2** (mettre en place) [*personne, groupe*] to form [*équipe, commission, alliance*]; to build up [*stocks*]; **la nouvelle société constituée par l'actuelle direction** the new company formed by the existing management; **3** (composer) [*éléments*] to make up [*ensemble*]; **groupe constitué de militants** group made up of militants; **les chômeurs constituent 10% de la population active** unemployed people make up 10% of the working population; **4** Jur to settle [*dot, rente*] (**à, pour** on); **~ qn héritier** to appoint sb as heir.
II se constituer *vpr* **1** (se mettre en place) [*parti, réseau, collection*] to be formed; **2** (créer pour soi) **se ~** to build up [*réseau, clientèle, réserve*]; to get oneself [*alibi*]; **3** (se grouper) **se ~ en** to form [*parti, société*]; **4** (se faire) **se ~ prisonnier** to give oneself up; **se ~ partie civile** to institute a civil action.

constitutif, **-ive** /kɔ̃stitytif, iv/ *adj* **1** (de base) [*élément*] constituent; **2** Pol [*assemblée*] constituent; [*congrès*] founding; [*réunion*] inaugural; [*document, texte*] constitutional.

constitution /kɔ̃stitysjɔ̃/ *nf* **1** (création) **~ d'une société** setting up of a company; **en voie de ~** currently being set up; **~ de capital** capital accumulation; **~ d'un dossier d'inscription** preparing of an application; **~ du plan d'un texte** drafting of an essay; **~ de stocks** stockpiling; **2** Physiol constitution; **bonne ~** sound constitution; **3** Jur (de rente, pension) settling ¢; **~ de partie civile** institution of civil action proceedings.

Constitution /kɔ̃stitysjɔ̃/ *nf* Pol constitution.

constitutionnalité /kɔ̃stitysjɔnalite/ *nf* constitutionality.

constitutionnel, **-elle** /kɔ̃stitysjɔnɛl/ *adj* constitutional.

constitutionnellement /kɔ̃stitysjɔnɛlmɑ̃/ *adv* constitutionally.

constricteur /kɔ̃stʀiktœʀ/ **I** *adj m* **muscle ~** constrictor muscle.
II *nm* Anat constrictor.

constrictif, **-ive** /kɔ̃stʀiktif, iv/ *adj* **1** Méd constrictive; **douleur constrictive** painful constriction; **2** Phon fricative.

constriction /kɔ̃stʀiksjɔ̃/ *nf* constriction.

constrictor /kɔ̃stʀiktɔʀ/ *nm* Zool boa constrictor.

constructeur, **-trice** /kɔ̃stʀyktœʀ, tʀis/ **I** *adj* **1** (créateur) [*force, action*] constructive; **2** Constr **société constructrice** construction company; **3** Zool **animal ~** builder.
II ▶ **510** *nm,f* **1** Ind manufacturer; **~ automobile** or **d'automobiles** car manufacturer; **un ~ aéronautique/informatique/de matériel** an aircraft/a computer/an equipment manufacturer; **~ naval** shipwright; **2** Constr builder; **promoteurs et ~s** planners and builders.

constructible /kɔ̃stʀyktibl/ *adj* [*zone, domaine*] building (*épith*), suitable for development (*après n*); **terrain ~** building land; **être rendu non ~** to be made unsuitable for development.

constructif, **-ive** /kɔ̃stʀyktif, iv/ *adj* constructive.

construction /kɔ̃stʀyksjɔ̃/ *nf* **1** (bâtiment) building; **les ~s gâchent le paysage** the buildings ruin the landscape; **2** (édification) building; **encourager la ~ de logements et de routes** to promote the building of housing and roads; **en (cours de) ~** under construction; **bâtiment de ~ ancienne/récente** old/recent building; **3** Écon (secteur industriel) **la ~** the construction industry; **secteur de la ~** construction sector; **entreprise de ~** construction company; **4** Ind manufacture; **~ de moteurs** engine manufacture; **de ~ japonaise** made in Japan; **~ aéronautique** aircraft manufacturing; **~ automobile** car manufacturing; **~ électrique** electrical engineering; **~ ferroviaire** railway construction; **~ mécanique** mechanical engineering; **~ navale** shipbuilding; **5** Pol construction; **~ européenne/du socialisme** construction of Europe/of socialism; **6** Ling, Math construction; **7** Psych reconstruction; **8** (élaboration) construction; **une pure ~ de l'esprit** pure imagination.

constructivisme /kɔ̃stʀyktivism/ *nm* constructivism.

constructiviste /kɔ̃stʀyktivist/ *adj, nmf* constructivist.

construire /kɔ̃stʀɥiʀ/ [69] **I** *vtr* **1** Constr, Ind to build [*bâtiment, pont, nid, navire*]; to build [*maquette, décor*]; to manufacture [*voiture*]; **faire ~ sa maison par qn** to have one's house built by sb; **se faire ~ une villa** to have a villa built; **2** (établir) to build [*Europe, communisme, avenir*]; to shape [*personnalité, image*]; **3** Ling to construct [*phrase, théorie, modèle*]; **4** Math to construct [*triangle*].
II se construire *vpr* **1** (bâtir pour soi) [*personne*] **se ~ une maison** to build a house for oneself; **se ~ une majorité** fig to build a majority for oneself; **se ~ son identité** fig to shape one's own identity; **2** (être bâti) [*maison*] to be built; **l'Europe se construira** fig Europe will be built; **une image se construit jour après jour** fig an image is shaped day by day; **3** Ling to be constructed; **se ~ avec le subjonctif** to take the subjunctive.

consubstantialité /kɔ̃sypstɑ̃sjalite/ *nf* consubstantiality.

consubstantiation /kɔ̃sypstɑ̃sjasjɔ̃/ *nf* consubstantiation.

consubstantiel, **-elle** /kɔ̃sypstɑ̃sjɛl/ *adj* **être ~ à** Relig to be consubstantial with; fig to be an integral part of.

consul /kɔ̃syl/ *nm* consul; **~ suédois** or **de Suède** Swedish consul.
■ **~ général** consul general.

consulaire /kɔ̃sylɛʀ/ *adj* consular; ▶ **corps**.

consulat /kɔ̃syla/ *nm* **1** Admin consulate; **le ~ d'Italie à Paris** the Italian consulate in Paris; **2** Antiq consulate; **3** Hist **le Consulat** the Consulate.

consultable /kɔ̃syltabl/ *adj* available for consultation (*après n*).

consultant, **~e** /kɔ̃syltɑ̃, ɑ̃t/ ▶ **510** *nm,f* (tous contextes) consultant; **un ~ en gestion** a management consultant.

consultatif, **-ive** /kɔ̃syltatif, iv/ *adj* consultative.

consultation /kɔ̃syltasjɔ̃/ *nf* **1** (heures de réception des malades) surgery hours (*pl*) GB, office hours (*pl*) US; **~ des nourrissons/de planning familial** baby/family planning clinic; **aller à la ~** (au cabinet médical) to go to the surgery GB, to go to the doctor's office US; (à l'hôpital) to go to out-patients; **2** (examen médical) consultation; **elle donne aussi des ~s à l'hôpital** she also gives consultations at the hospital; **3** (fait de prendre un avis) consulting; **après ~ des experts** after consulting the experts; **être en faveur d'une ~ populaire** to be in favour[GB] of consulting the people; **~ électorale** election; **~ juridique** legal consultation; **~ gratuite** free consultation; **4** (délibération) consultation; **être en ~ avec qn** to be in consultation with sb; **5** (de calendrier, livre, document) consultation; **'~ sur place'** (dans une bibliothèque) 'for reference use only'; **la ~ de l'annuaire n'a rien donné** we/they etc looked in the directory but in vain; **une simple ~ du planning montre que** a simple look at the schedule shows that.

consulter /kɔ̃sylte/ [1] **I** *vtr* **1** (pour un diagnostic) [*malade*] to consult [*médecin*]; **2** (pour un conseil) [*gouvernement, individu*] to consult [*expert*]; to ask [sb] for advice [*ami*]; **3** (par un vote) **~ le peuple** to hold a general election, to hold a referendum; **4** (regarder pour information) to consult [*liste, instrument, base de données, agenda, astres, dictionnaire*].
II *vi* Méd (recevoir les patients) to hold surgery GB, to see patients.
III se consulter *vpr* **1** (échanger des vues) [*parents, spécialistes*] to consult together; **se ~ du regard** to exchange glances; **2** (être consultable) **'se consulte sur place'** 'for reference use only'.

consumer /kɔ̃syme/ [1] **I** *vtr* **1** (brûler) to consume [*forêt*]; **2** fig, liter **l'amour le consumait** he was consumed with love; **la maladie qui la consume** the illness which is eating away at her; **il a consumé son temps/sa vie en vains plaisirs** he wasted his time/his life in idle pleasures.
II se consumer *vpr* **1** (brûler) to be burning; **la mèche devrait se ~ en quelques minutes** the fuse should burn out in a few minutes; **2** fig, liter to waste away; **se ~ d'amour** to be consumed with love (**pour** for); **se ~ en vains efforts** to weary oneself in vain efforts.

consumérisme /kɔ̃symeʀism/ *nm* consumerism.

consumériste /kɔ̃symeʀist/ *adj* consumerist.

contact /kɔ̃takt/ *nm* **1** (relation) contact ¢ (**avec** with); **avoir des ~s directs avec qn** to have direct contact with sb; **être en ~** to be in contact; **prendre ~ avec** to make contact with; **garder le ~** to keep in touch; **reprendre ~ avec qn** to get back in touch with sb; **la reprise des ~s avec les émissaires** the renewal of relations with the emissaries; **la première prise de ~ a été encourageante** initial contact was encouraging; **mettre en ~** to put in touch; **entrer en ~ avec** to get in touch with; **avoir un bon ~ avec qn** to get on well with sb; **être d'un ~ agréable/difficile** to be easy/hard to get on with; **elle est devenue plus sociable à ton ~** she's become more sociable through spending time with you; **2** (toucher) contact; **~ physique** physical contact; **en ~** in contact; **'éviter le** or **tout ~ avec les yeux/la peau'** 'avoid any contact with eyes/skin'; **3** Électrotech contact; **mettre/couper le ~** Aut to switch on/switch off the ignition; ▶ **faux**; **4** (personne) contact; **rencontrer son ~** to meet one's contact; **avoir des ~s au gouvernement** to have contacts in the government.

contacter /kɔ̃takte/ [1] **I** *vtr* to contact [*personne, journal, organisme*].

II se contacter *vpr* to get in touch with each other.

contacteur /kɔ̃taktœʀ/ *nm* contactor.

contagieux, **-ieuse** /kɔ̃taʒjø, øz/ **I** *adj* **1** Méd [*malade, maladie*] contagious; **maladie non contagieuse** non-contagious illness; **2** fig [*rire, enthousiasme*] infectious, catching (*jamais épith*); **la peur est contagieuse** fear is catching, fear breeds fear.

II *nm,f* contagious person; **les ~** contagious patients.

contagion /kɔ̃taʒjɔ̃/ *nf* **1** Méd contagion; **2** fig infectiousness; **craindre la ~ de certaines idées** to fear the spread of certain ideas; **les conflits sociaux s'étendent par ~** social unrest spreads like a disease.

contagiosité /kɔ̃taʒjozite/ *nf* contagiousness; **jusqu'à disparition de la ~** until the end of the contagious stage.

container /kɔ̃tenɛʀ/ *nm* controv container.

contamination /kɔ̃taminasjɔ̃/ *nf* (tous contextes) contamination (**par** by).

contaminer /kɔ̃tamine/ [1] *vtr* **1** [*virus, personne*] to infect [*personne, animal*]; [*matière radioactive, agent chimique*] to contaminate [*personne, animal, végétaux, sol, eau*]; **2** fig to contaminate [*esprit, langage*]; **3** Ordinat to contaminate [*programme*].

conte /kɔ̃t/ *nm* **1** Littérat tale, story; **~ de fées** fairy tale; **2** (racontar) story.

contemplateur, **-trice** /kɔ̃tɑ̃platœʀ, tʀis/ **I** *adj* contemplative.

II *nm,f* contemplator.

contemplatif, **-ive** /kɔ̃tɑ̃platif, iv/ **I** *adj* contemplative.

II *nm* contemplative.

contemplation /kɔ̃tɑ̃plasjɔ̃/ *nf* (tous contextes) contemplation; **s'abîmer dans la ~ de qch** to be lost in contemplation of sth; **rester en ~ devant un paysage** to stand contemplating a landscape.

contempler /kɔ̃tɑ̃ple/ [1] **I** *vtr* **1** (du regard) to survey [*spectacle*]; to contemplate [*paysage, monument*]; to look at [*photo, vitrine*]; **2** (par la pensée) to reflect on [*théorie*].

II se contempler *vpr* to gaze at oneself.

contemporain, **~e** /kɔ̃tɑ̃pɔʀɛ̃, ɛn/ **I** *adj* **1** (du présent) [*art, histoire*] contemporary; **2** (du même temps) [*personne*] contemporary; **il était ~ de Dickens** he was Dickens's contemporary; **roman/événement ~ de** novel/event contemporaneous with.

II *nm,f* contemporary (**de** of).

contemporanéité /kɔ̃tɑ̃pɔʀaneite/ *nf* contemporaneousness.

contempteur, **-trice** /kɔ̃tɑ̃ptœʀ, tʀis/ *nm,f* fml denigrator (**de** of).

contenance /kɔ̃t(ə)nɑ̃s/ *nf* **1** ▶117, 866 (volume) capacity; **2** (allure) bearing; **essayer de se donner une ~** to try to appear composed; **perdre ~** to lose one's composure; **faire bonne ~** to keep an air of composure.

contenant /kɔ̃t(ə)nɑ̃/ *nm* packaging.

conteneur /kɔ̃t(ə)nœʀ/ *nm* container.

contenir /kɔ̃t(ə)niʀ/ [36] **I** *vtr* **1** (renfermer) to contain [*substance, erreur*]; **2** ▶117, 866 (avoir une capacité de) to hold [*litre*]; (pouvoir accueillir) to accommodate [*spectateur*]; **3** (stopper) to contain [*foule, colère*].

II se contenir *vpr* to contain oneself.

content, **~e** /kɔ̃tɑ̃, ɑ̃t/ **I** *adj* **1** (heureux) happy, pleased (**de qch** with sth; **de faire** to do; **que** that); **ça te plaît? tu es ~?** do you like it? are you pleased?; **je suis ~ de jouer ce match** I'm happy to be playing in this match; **ne pas avoir l'air très ~** not to look very happy; **je suis ~e que tu sois là** I'm glad you're here; **2** (satisfait) pleased, satisfied (**de** with); **être ~ de soi** to be pleased with oneself; [*vaniteux*] to be self-satisfied; **je suis assez ~ de moi** I'm quite pleased with myself; **maintenant que tu as tout cassé, je suppose que tu es ~?** you've broken everything, are you happy now?; **non ~ de (faire)** not content with (doing); **non ~ de ne rien faire, il s'endette** not content with doing nothing, he is running up debts.

II *nm* **(tout) son ~** [*manger, boire, dormir*] to one's heart's content; **avoir son ~ de** iron to have one's fill of [*ennuis*].

contentement /kɔ̃tɑ̃tmɑ̃/ *nm* contentment, satisfaction; **~ de soi** self-satisfaction.

contenter /kɔ̃tɑ̃te/ [1] **I** *vtr* to satisfy [*clientèle, envie, désir, curiosité*]; **il est facile/difficile à ~** he is easy/hard to please; **on ne peut pas ~ tout le monde** you can't please everybody.

II se contenter *vpr* **se ~ de qch/de faire** to content oneself with sth/with doing; **il s'est contenté d'une remarque/de faire quelques remarques** he contented himself with one remark/with making a few remarks; **je me contente d'un sandwich/de peu** I make do with a sandwich/very little; **je me suis contenté de jeter un coup d'œil au/de feuilleter le rapport** I just glanced at/leafed through the report; **il s'est contenté de rire/d'envoyer des fleurs** he just laughed/sent flowers, all he did was laugh/send flowers.

contentieux, **-ieuse** /kɔ̃tɑ̃sjø, øz/ Jur **I** *adj* contentious.

II *nm* **1** (litige) bone of contention (**avec** with; **entre** between; **sur** about); **un lourd ~** a serious bone of contention; **2** (service) legal department; (affaires) litigation.

contenu, **~e** /kɔ̃t(ə)ny/ **I** *pp* ▶ **contenir**.

II *pp adj* [*sentiment, style*] restrained; [*colère*] suppressed.

III *nm* **1** (de récipient) contents (*pl*); **2** (d'œuvre) content.

conter /kɔ̃te/ [1] *vtr* liter to tell [*histoire*]; to recount, to relate [*aventure, déboires*].

IDIOMES **s'en laisser ~** (une fois) to be taken in; (toujours) to be easily taken in, to be gullible.

contestable /kɔ̃tɛstabl/ *adj* questionable.

contestataire /kɔ̃tɛstatɛʀ/ **I** *adj* [*mouvement, journal*] anti-authority, anti-establishment; **étudiant ~** student protester.

II *nmf* protester.

contestation /kɔ̃tɛstasjɔ̃/ *nf* **1** Pol (de pouvoir) protest (**de** against); (dans une organisation) dissent (**de** from); **2** (de véracité, droit) challenging (**de** of); **être sujet à ~, prêter à ~** to be questionable; **il y a sujet** or **matière à ~** there are grounds for dispute ou contention; **sans ~ possible** beyond dispute; **3** (dispute) dispute.

conteste: **sans conteste** /sɑ̃kɔ̃tɛst/ *loc adv* unquestionably.

contesté, **~e** /kɔ̃tɛste/ **I** *pp* ▶ **contester**.

II *pp adj* [*penalty, territoire*] disputed; [*médicament, thèse*] controversial.

contester /kɔ̃tɛste/ [1] **I** *vtr* to question [*authenticité, bien-fondé, nécessité*]; to contest [*droit, succession, testament*]; to dispute [*chiffre, frontière*]; to dispute, to question [*fait, décision*]; to challenge [*impôt, principe, projet, régime*]; **~ à qn le droit de faire, ~ que qn ait le droit de faire** to contest sb's right to do.

II *vi* **1** (ne pas être d'accord) to raise objections; **2** (faire de l'opposition) to protest.

conteur /kɔ̃tœʀ/ *nm* storyteller.

conteuse /kɔ̃tøz/ *nf* storyteller.

contexte /kɔ̃tɛkst/ *nm* **1** Ling, fig context (**de** of); **dans le ~ politique/économique** in the political/economic context; **hors ~** out of context; **2** (conjoncture) situation; **dans le ~ actuel** in the present situation.

contextuel, **-elle** /kɔ̃tɛkstɥɛl/ *adj* Ling, fig contextual.

contexture /kɔ̃tɛkstyʀ/ *nf* (de tissu) fml texture; (d'os) structure; (de poème) structure.

contigu, **-uë** /kɔ̃tigy/ *adj* **1** [*pièces, jardins*] adjoining; **~ à qch** adjoining sth; **2** [*idées, thèmes*] closely related (**à** to).

contiguïté /kɔ̃tigɥite/ *nf* **1** (de pièces, jardins) contiguity sout; **2** (de notions, thèmes) relatedness; **à cause de la ~ de ces notions** because these ideas are closely related.

continence /kɔ̃tinɑ̃s/ *nf* continence.

continent, **~e** /kɔ̃tinɑ̃, ɑ̃t/ **I** *adj* **1** fml (chaste) continent; **2** Méd continent.

II *nm* Géog **1** (partie du monde) continent; **2** (par opposition à une île) mainland.

■ **le ~ noir** the Dark Continent.

continental, **~e**, *mpl* **-aux** /kɔ̃tinɑ̃tal, o/ *adj* gén continental; (par opposition à un territoire insulaire) mainland (*épith*).

contingence /kɔ̃tɛ̃ʒɑ̃s/ **I** *nf* Philos contingency; **la ~ du monde** the contingent nature of the world.

II contingences *nfpl* (faits imprévus) chance circumstances; (faits sans importance) trivial circumstances.

contingent, **~e** /kɔ̃tɛ̃ʒɑ̃, ɑ̃t/ **I** *adj* contingent.

II *nm* **1** (groupe) contingent; Mil (de conscrits) conscripts (*pl*), draft US; **soldat du ~** conscript; **2** Comm, Écon quota; **3** Jur, fig (quote-part) share.

contingentement /kɔ̃tɛ̃ʒɑ̃tmɑ̃/ *nm* **système de ~** quota system; **le ~ des importations/exportations** the setting of import/export quotas.

contingenter /kɔ̃tɛ̃ʒɑ̃te/ [1] *vtr* (limiter) to fix a quota for [*importations, exportations*]; (répartir) to distribute [sth] using a quota system [*matière première*]; **produit contingenté** product subject to a quota.

continu, **~e** /kɔ̃tiny/ **I** *adj* continuous; **de façon ~e** continuously.

II *nm* continuum.

III en continu *loc adv* [*information*] nonstop; [*fabrication, travail, régulation*] continuous; **suivi en ~** continuous ou constant monitoring; **suivre en ~** to monitor continuously ou constantly.

continuateur, **-trice** /kɔ̃tinɥatœʀ, tʀis/ *nm,f* (de personne) heir; (de tradition, projet) upholder.

continuation /kɔ̃tinɥasjɔ̃/ *nf* continuation; **bonne ~!** all the best!

continuel, **-elle** /kɔ̃tinɥɛl/ *adj* continual.

continuellement /kɔ̃tinɥɛlmɑ̃/ *adv* continually.

continuer /kɔ̃tinɥe/ [1] **I** *vtr* to carry on, to continue [*combat, conversation*]; to continue [*études, voyage*]; **~ son chemin** to continue on one's way; **~ l'œuvre de qn** to carry on sb's work; **continue ton histoire!** carry on with your story!

II *vi* to continue, to go on (**jusqu'à** until); **~ à** or **de faire** to continue doing ou to do; **cela ne peut pas ~** it can't go on; **continua-t-il** he continued; **c'est un bon début, continuez!** it's a good start, keep it up!

III se continuer *vpr* [*soirée, repas*] to continue.

continuité /kɔ̃tinɥite/ *nf* continuity (**de** of); **assurer/garantir la ~** to ensure/guarantee continuity (**de** in).

continûment /kɔ̃tinymɑ̃/ *adv* continuously.

continuum /kɔ̃tinɥɔm/ *nm* continuum.

contondant, **~e** /kɔ̃tɔ̃dɑ̃, ɑ̃t/ *adj* [*arme, instrument*] blunt.

contorsion /kɔ̃tɔʀsjɔ̃/ *nf* lit, fig contortion.

contorsionner: **se contorsionner** /kɔ̃tɔʀsjɔne/ [1] *vpr* [*personne*] to tie oneself in knots; (pour se dégager) to wriggle and writhe; [*serpent*] to writhe.

contorsionniste /kɔ̃tɔʀsjɔnist/ ▶510 *nmf* contortionist.

contour /kɔ̃tuʀ/ **I** *nm* **1** (d'objet, de montagne, bouche, dessin) outline; (de corps, visage, paysage) contour; (de meuble) line; **2** (aspect) (d'expérience, de projet, d'œuvre) outline.

II contours *nmpl* (méandres) (de route, rivière) twists and turns.

contourné, **~e** /kɔ̃tuʀne/ **I** *pp* ▶ **contourner**.
II *pp adj* **1** [*pied de meuble, coquille*] (elaborately) curved; [*jambe*] deformed; **2** [*raisonnement, style*] convoluted.

contournement /kɔ̃tuʀnəmɑ̃/ *nm* (de ville) bypass; **le ~ nord de Lyon** the bypass to the north of Lyons; **le ~ autoroutier de Toulouse** the motorway GB ou freeway US that bypasses Toulouse.

contourner /kɔ̃tuʀne/ [1] *vtr* **1** (passer à côté) to by-pass [*ville, obstacle*]; **2** (faire le tour de) to skirt (around) [*colline*]; **3** lit, fig (éviter) to get round [*obstacle, difficulté*]; **4** (façonner) to shape [*vase*]; (tracer) to trace [*volutes*].

contraceptif, **-ive** /kɔ̃tʀasɛptif, iv/ **I** *adj* contraceptive.
II *nm* contraceptive.

contraception /kɔ̃tʀasɛpsjɔ̃/ *nf* contraception; **~ orale** (moyen) oral contraception; (pilule) oral contraceptive.

contractant, **~e** /kɔ̃tʀaktɑ̃, ɑ̃t/ **I** *adj* contracting.
II *nm,f* contracting party.

contracté, **~e** /kɔ̃tʀakte/ **I** *pp* ▶ **contracter**.
II *pp adj* **1** [*muscles, traits*] contracted (**par** with); **2** [*personne*] tense; **3** Ling contracted.

contracter /kɔ̃tʀakte/ [1] **I** *vtr* **1** (crisper) to contract, to tense [*muscle*]; to tense [*visage*]; to make [sb] tense [*personne*]; **une grimace contracta sa bouche** or **ses traits** he/she grimaced; **l'émotion lui contracta la gorge** his/her throat tightened with emotion; **la peur lui contractait la gorge** his/her throat was tight with fear; **2** Ling to contract [*forme*]; **3** (s'engager dans) to incur [*obligation, dette*]; to conclude [*marché*]; to take out [*assurance, emprunt*]; to enter into [*engagement*]; to form [*amitié, liaison*]; **4** (réduire) to make [sth] contract [*substance*]; **5** Méd to contract [*maladie, virus*].
II se contracter *vpr* **1** (se crisper) [*muscle*] to contract; [*visage, personne*] to tense up; [*gorge*] to tighten; **2** (diminuer) Phys [*substance*] to contract; [*exportations, marché*] to shrink; **3** Ling [*forme, mot*] (si l'on veut) to contract; (obligatoirement) to be contracted.

contractile /kɔ̃tʀaktil/ *adj* contractile.

contractilité /kɔ̃tʀaktilite/ *nf* contractility.

contraction /kɔ̃tʀaksjɔ̃/ *nf* **1** Physiol (état) tenseness; (spasme) contraction; **2** Ling, Phys (action de réduire) contraction; **3** (de marché) shrinking; **la ~ de la demande/l'offre** Écon reduced demand/supplies; **~ des cours** Fin drop in prices.

contractuel, **-elle** /kɔ̃tʀaktɥɛl/ **I** *adj* **1** Jur [*obligation*] contractual; **2** Admin [*personnel*] contract (*épith*); **10% des employés sont ~s** 10% of employees are contract staff.
II *nm,f* **1** (employé) contract employee; **2** ▶ **510** (contrôlant le stationnement) traffic warden GB, meter reader US.

contractuellement /kɔ̃tʀaktɥɛlmɑ̃/ *adv* contractually, by contract.

contracture /kɔ̃tʀaktyʀ/ *nf* **1** Physiol contracture, spasm; **~ musculaire** muscle spasm; **2** Archit contracture.

contradicteur /kɔ̃tʀadiktœʀ/ *nm* (de propos, théorie) opponent (**de** of).

contradiction /kɔ̃tʀadiksjɔ̃/ *nf* **1** (manque de logique) contradiction; **résoudre une ~** to resolve a contradiction; **un raisonnement plein de ~s** an argument full of contradictions; **être en ~ avec qch** to contradict sth; **être en ~ avec soi-même/ses principes** to contradict oneself/one's principles; **2** (contestation) contradiction; **il ne supporte pas la ~** he can't bear to be contradicted; **apporter la ~ à qn** to argue against sb; **porter la ~ dans un débat** to put forward counter-arguments in a debate.

contradictoire /kɔ̃tʀadiktwaʀ/ *adj* [*idées, opinions, témoignages, raisonnement*] contradictory; **être ~ à qch** to be in contradiction to sth; **un débat ~** an open debate.

contraignant, **~e** /kɔ̃tʀɛɲɑ̃, ɑ̃t/ *adj* restrictive.

contraindre /kɔ̃tʀɛ̃dʀ/ [54] **I** *vtr* **1** (obliger) **~ qn à la passivité** or **à demeurer passif** to force ou compel sb to remain passive; **être contraint au repos** or **de se reposer** to be forced ou compelled to rest; **je serai contraint de déménager** I'll have to ou be forced to move; **je me vois contraint de démissionner** I have no option but to resign; **~ par corps** Jur to imprison [sb] for debt; **~ qn par saisie de biens** Jur to distrain sb's property; **2** (réprimer) to restrain [*sentiments, désir*]; to curb [*goût*].
II se contraindre *vpr* **1** (se forcer) **se ~ à faire** to force oneself to do; **se ~ à des exercices/à une vie austère** to force oneself to exercise/to keep to an austere lifestyle; **2** (se contenir) liter to exercise self-control.

contraint, **~e** /kɔ̃tʀɛ̃, ɛ̃t/ **I** *pp* ▶ **contraindre**.
II *pp adj* **1** (obligé) **~ et forcé** Jur under duress; **2** (gêné) [*air*] strained; [*sourire*] forced.
III contrainte *nf* **1** (pression) pressure; (coercition) coercion; **user de ~e à l'égard de qn** to exert ou put pressure on sb; **par la ~e** by force ou coercion; **être empêché par la ~e** to be forcibly prevented; **sous la ~e** under duress; **tenir un peuple dans la ~e** liter to keep a nation in bondage; **2** (exigence) constraint; **~es administratives/budgétaires** administrative/budgetary constraints; **les ~es du marché** the market restrictions; **3** (gêne) strain; **sans ~e** without restraint, freely; **4** Jur duress; **~e par saisie de biens** distress, distraint; **~e par corps** imprisonment for debt.

contraire /kɔ̃tʀɛʀ/ **I** *adj* **1** (inverse) [*effet, sens, décision, attitude*] opposite; Naut [*vent*] contrary; (en conflit) [*avis, intérêts, théories*] conflicting (**à** with); [*forces*] opposite (**à** to); **être ~ à la justice/aux usages/au règlement** to be contrary to justice/to custom/to the regulations; **dans le cas ~** if this shouldn't be the case, (should it be) otherwise; **sauf avis ~** unless otherwise informed, unless you hear anything to the contrary; **2** (défavorable) [*destin, force*] adverse; **le sort leur fut ~** fate was against them.
II *nm* **le ~** the opposite (**de** of); **je pense (tout) le ~** I take the opposite view; **être tout le ~ de qn/qch** to be the complete opposite of sb/sth; **ne dites pas le ~** don't deny it; **je ne dis pas le ~** I don't deny that ou it; **jusqu'à preuve du ~** until there is evidence to the contrary, until proved otherwise; **(bien** or **tout) au ~** on the contrary; **au ~ de tes amis** unlike your friends; **dire tout et son ~** to keep contradicting oneself.

contrairement /kɔ̃tʀɛʀmɑ̃/ *adv* **~ à ce qu'on pourrait penser/à ce qu'il prétend** contrary to what one might think/to what he claims; **~ à une opinion répandue** contrary to popular belief; **~ à qn/à la France** unlike sb/France.

contralto /kɔ̃tʀalto/ ▶ **134** **I** *nm* (voix) contralto.
II *nf* (femme) contralto.

contrapuntique /kɔ̃tʀapɔ̃tik/ *adj* contrapuntal.

contrariant, **~e** /kɔ̃tʀaʀjɑ̃, ɑ̃t/ *adj* **1** [*personne, esprit*] contrary (*jamais épith*); **il n'est pas ~** he is accommodating; **2** [*événement, affaire*] annoying.

contrarier /kɔ̃tʀaʀje/ [2] *vtr* **1** (chagriner) to upset; (fâcher) to annoy; **2** (rendre malade) [*aliment, boisson*] to upset [*personne*]; **3** (contrecarrer) to frustrate, to thwart [*projet, volonté, ambition*]; to hinder [*mouvement, progression*]; **amours contrariées** thwarted love ₵; **~ un gaucher** to make a lefthanded person write with his/her right hand; **4** (alterner) to alternate [*couleurs*]; **couleurs contrariées** alternating colours[GB].

contrariété /kɔ̃tʀaʀjete/ *nf* upset; **éprouver une vive** or **grande ~** to feel very upset.

contrastant, **~e** /kɔ̃tʀastɑ̃, ɑ̃t/ *adj* contrasting (*épith*).

contraste /kɔ̃tʀast/ **I** *nm* (tous contextes) contrast (**entre qch et qch** between sth and sth); **mettre en ~** to contrast; **faire ~ avec** to contrast with; **adoucir les ~s** (de couleurs, photo) to soften the contrast.
II par contraste *loc adv* in contrast (**avec** with), by way of contrast.

contrasté, **~e** /kɔ̃tʀaste/ **I** *pp* ▶ **contraster**.
II *pp adj* **1** (opposé) [*couleurs, périodes*] contrasting; **attitudes très ~es** sharply contrasting attitudes; **2** (nuancé) [*image, photo*] with good contrast (*épith, après n*); [*tableau*] with sharp contrasts (*épith, après n*); **trop ~** with too much contrast (*épith, après n*); **3** (inégal) [*résultats*] uneven; [*semaine, année*] of sharp contrasts (*épith, après n*).

contraster /kɔ̃tʀaste/ [1] **I** *vtr* to contrast [*couleurs, motifs*]; to give contrast to [*photo*].
II *vi* to contrast (**avec** with).

contrastif, **-ive** /kɔ̃tʀastif, iv/ *adj* contrastive.

contrat /kɔ̃tʀa/ *nm* (accord) contract, agreement (**entre** between; **avec** with); Jur (document) contract; fig (pacte) arrangement, understanding; **passer un ~ avec qn** Jur to enter into a contract with sb; fig to come to an arrangement with sb; **signer/rompre un ~** to sign/break a contract; **décrocher un gros ~** to land a large contract; **le ~ prévoit...** the contract provides for...; **sous ~ avec** under contract to; **s'engager par ~ à faire qch** to contract to do sth; **réaliser** or **remplir son ~** (au bridge) to make one's contract; fig to fulfil[GB] one's pledge.
■ **~ d'assurance** contract of insurance; **~ collectif** collective agreement; **~ à durée déterminée**, **CDD** fixed-term contract; **~ à durée indéterminée**, **CDI** permanent contract; **~ emploi solidarité**, **CES** *part-time low-paid work for the long-term unemployed*; **~ de licence** licensing agreement; **~ de location** hire contract GB, rental contract; (pour des locaux) tenancy agreement; **~ de maintenance** service contract; **~ de mariage** marriage contract ou settlement; **~ de prestation de services** contract of services; **~ social** social contract; **~ de société** deed of partnership; **~ de travail** contract of employment; **~ de vente** sale contract.

contravention /kɔ̃tʀavɑ̃sjɔ̃/ *nf* **1** Aut (document) (pour stationnement illicite) parking ticket; (pour excès de vitesse) speeding ticket; (amende) fine; **dresser (une) ~ à qn** gén to take sb's particulars GB, to fine sb; (pour stationnement illicite) to issue a parking ticket; **flanquer**○ or **coller**○ **une ~ à qn** to book○ sb; **2** Jur (infraction) minor offence[GB]; **être en ~ (à la loi)** to be in breach of the law.

contre[1] /kɔ̃tʀ/ **I** *prép* **1** (marquant un contact entre personnes) **viens ~ moi** come to me; **ils étaient couchés l'un ~ l'autre** they were lying close together; **2** (marquant l'opposition) against; **aller ~ la décision de qn** to go against sb's decision; **je ne vais pas aller ~ ce que tu as dit/fait** I won't go against what you have said/done; **c'est ~ mes principes** it's against my principles; **il a tout le monde ~ lui** everyone is against him; **tout est ~ moi** everything is against me; **être seul ~ tous** to stand alone against everyone else; **être ~ une décision/un projet** to be against a decision/a project; **elle est toujours ~ moi** she's always against me; **tu as quelque chose ~ lui/cette idée?** have you got anything against him/this idea?; **je n'ai rien ~ elle** I've got nothing against her; **on ne peut rien ~ ce genre de choses** there's nothing one can do about that kind of thing;

contre¹

En général la préposition *contre* se traduit par *against* lorsqu'elle sert à indiquer:

un contact entre des choses:

pousse le fauteuil contre le mur = push the armchair (up) against the wall

(Les expressions telles que *joue contre joue, pare-chocs contre pare-chocs, furieux contre* sont traitées sous l'élément principal, respectivement ***joue, pare-chocs, furieux*** etc.)

une opposition:

lutter/réagir/voter contre le racisme = to fight/react/vote against racism

une défense:

s'assurer contre le vol = to insure against theft

se protéger contre une attaque = to protect oneself against an attack

On aura toujours intérêt à consulter l'article de l'élément principal.

Lorsque *contre* sert à indiquer la proximité, il se traduit par *next to*:

leur jardin est contre le mien = their garden is next to mine

Lorsque *contre* sert à indiquer un échange, il se traduit par *for*:

changer une chemise trop petite contre une plus grande = to change a shirt which is too small for a larger one

Lorsque *contre* sert à indiquer une comparaison, il se traduit par *as against*:

22% contre 10% le mois dernier = 22% as against 10% last month

On trouvera ci-dessous d'autres exemples de *contre* dans ses diverses fonctions.

dix ~ un (dans un pari) ten to one; **la loi a été adoptée par 230 voix ~ 110** the bill was passed by 230 votes to 110; **Nantes ~ Sochaux** Sport Nantes versus Sochaux, Nantes vs Sochaux; **le procès Bedel ~ Caselli** the Bedel versus Caselli case.

II *adv* **1** (marquant un contact) **il y a un mur et une échelle appuyée ~** there's a wall and a ladder leaning against it; **2** (marquant l'opposition) **la majorité a voté ~** the majority voted against it; **'que penses-tu du projet?'—'je suis ~'** 'what do you think of the plan?'—'I'm against it'; **il refuse cette option, moi je n'ai rien ~** he rejects this option, but I have nothing against it; **si le comité vote en faveur des travaux je n'irai pas ~** if the committee votes for the work to go ahead, I won't go against it.

III par contre *loc adv* on the other hand; **je pense par ~ que** on the other hand I think that; **en France, par ~, il est possible de...** in France, on the other hand, it is possible to...; ▶ **fortune**.

contre² /kɔ̃tʀ/ *nm* **1** (d'opposition) **le pour et le ~** the pros and cons (*pl*); **2** Sport counterattack; **faire un ~** to counter-attack; **3** Jeux (au bridge) double.

contre-accusation, *pl* **~s** /kɔ̃tʀakyzasjɔ̃/ *nf* Jur counter-charge.

contre-alizé, *pl* **~s** /kɔ̃tʀalize/ *nm* anti-trade (wind).

contre-allée, *pl* **~s** /kɔ̃tʀale/ *nf* (de route) service road; (de parc) side path; (d'église) side aisle.

contre-alliance, *pl* **~s** /kɔ̃tʀaljɑ̃s/ *nf* counter alliance.

contre-amiral, *pl* **-aux** /kɔ̃tʀamiʀal, o/ **▶390** *nm* ≈ commodore.

contre-analyse /kɔ̃tʀanaliz/ *nf* counter analysis.

contre-argument, *pl* **~s** /kɔ̃tʀaʀgymɑ̃/ *nm* counter-argument.

contre-attaque, *pl* **~s** /kɔ̃tʀatak/ *nf* counter-attack.

contre-attaquer /kɔ̃tʀatake/ [1] *vi* to counter-attack.

contre-autopsie, *pl* **~s** /kɔ̃tʀotɔpsi/ *nf* second autopsy.

contrebalancer /kɔ̃tʀəbalɑ̃se/ [12] **I** *vtr* **1** (faire équilibre à) to counterbalance [*poids, force*]; **2** (compenser) to offset, to counterbalance [*importance*]; to offset, to make up for [*inconvénient, influence*]; to offset [*sentiment*]; **~ l'influence de la télévision** to offset the influence of television.

II se contrebalancer *vpr* **1** (s'équilibrer) to counterbalance each other; **2**○ (se moquer de) **se ~ de qch** not to give a damn○ about sth; **je m'en contrebalance** I don't give a damn○.

contrebande /kɔ̃tʀəbɑ̃d/ *nf* **1** (activité) smuggling; **faire de la ~** to be a smuggler, to be involved in smuggling; **faire de la ~ de vodka** to smuggle vodka; **faire la ~ d'armes** to smuggle arms; **la ~ d'armes** gun-running; **sortir/introduire qch en ~** (dans un pays) to smuggle sth out of/into the country; **des cigarettes de ~** smuggled cigarettes; **2** (marchandises) smuggled goods (*pl*), contraband; **vendre de la ~** to sell smuggled goods.

contrebandier, **-ière** /kɔ̃tʀəbɑ̃dje, ɛʀ/ *nm,f* smuggler.

contrebas: **en contrebas** /ɑ̃kɔ̃tʀəba/ *loc adv* (down) below; **en ~ de** (de montagne, hauteur) at the foot of; **la rivière coule en ~ de la maison** the stream runs (down) below the house; **la maison est en ~ de la route** the house is at a lower level than the road.

contrebasse /kɔ̃tʀəbas/ *nf* **1** **▶534** (instrument) double bass; **2** **▶510** (musicien) double bass player.

contrebassiste /kɔ̃tʀəbasist/ **▶510** *nmf* double bass player.

contrebasson /kɔ̃tʀəbasɔ̃/ *nm* **1** **▶534** (instrument) contrabassoon; **2** **▶510** (musicien) contrabassoon player.

contre-braquer /kɔ̃tʀəbʀake/ [1] *vi* (pour se garer) to turn the wheel in the opposite direction; (en dérapage) to steer into a skid.

contrecarrer /kɔ̃tʀəkaʀe/ [1] *vtr* to thwart, to foil [*effort, projet*]; to counteract [*influence, décision*]; **il faut ~ l'avancée des troupes ennemies** we must block the enemy's advance.

contrechamp /kɔ̃tʀəʃɑ̃/ *nm* Cin (prise de vue) reverse angle; (plan) reverse shot.

contre-chant, *pl* **~s** /kɔ̃tʀəʃɑ̃/ *nm* counterpoint.

contrechâssis /kɔ̃tʀəʃɑsi/ *nm inv* Tech double windowframe.

contreclé /kɔ̃tʀəkle/ *nf* Archit archstone adjoining the keystone.

contrecœur /kɔ̃tʀəkœʀ/ **I** *nm* **1** (de cheminée) fireback; **2** Rail guard rail, check rail.

II à contrecœur *loc adv* [*donner, prêter*] grudgingly, reluctantly; [*travailler, accepter*] reluctantly; **c'est à ~ que je lui ai prêté ma voiture** I lent him/her my car reluctantly.

contrecollé /kɔ̃tʀəkɔle/ *nm* plywood.

contrecoup /kɔ̃tʀəku/ *nm* (conséquences) effects (*pl*), repercussions (*pl*); **le ~ d'une opération** the after-effects of an operation; **subir le ~ de** to feel the effects of; **par ~** as a result.

contre-courant, *pl* **~s** /kɔ̃tʀəkuʀɑ̃/ *nm* counter-current; **nager à ~** to swim against the current; **aller à ~ de** fig to go against the tide of; **aller à ~ de la mode** to go against the fashion.

contre-culture, *pl* **~s** /kɔ̃tʀəkyltyʀ/ *nf* counterculture.

contredanse /kɔ̃tʀədɑ̃s/ *nf* **1**○ (amende) gén fine; (pour stationnement illicite) parking ticket; **2** (danse) contredanse.

contredire /kɔ̃tʀədiʀ/ [65] **I** *vtr* **1** (dire le contraire) to contradict [*personne, affirmation, déclaration*]; **il ne supporte pas qu'elle le contredise** he can't bear her contradicting him; **2** (démentir) [*personne, fait, situation, déclaration*] to contradict, to belie [*témoignage, thèse, objectif*]; [*document*] to belie [*témoignage, résultat*]; **les résultats contredisent vos prévisions** the results contradict ou belie your predictions.

II se contredire *vpr* **1** (soi-même) to contradict oneself; **2** (l'un l'autre) [*personnes, faits*] to contradict each other; [*témoignages*] to conflict.

contredit: **sans contredit** /sɑ̃kɔ̃tʀədi/ *loc adv* fml indisputably.

contrée /kɔ̃tʀe/ *nf* **1** (pays) liter land, clime littér; **des ~s lointaines** far-off lands; **2** (région) region, district; **le plus grand buveur de toute la ~** the heaviest drinker for miles around.

contre-écrou, *pl* **~s** /kɔ̃tʀekʀu/ *nm* lock-nut.

contre-électromotrice /kɔ̃tʀelɛktʀɔmɔtʀis/ *adj f* **force ~** back electromotive force.

contre-emploi, *pl* **~s** /kɔ̃tʀɑ̃plwɑ/ *nm* Théât, Cin **jouer à ~** to play against type.

contre-enquête, *pl* **~s** /kɔ̃tʀɑ̃kɛt/ *nf* second enquiry GB, second inquiry US.

contre-épreuve, *pl* **~s** /kɔ̃tʀepʀœv/ *nf* **1** (en offset) reproduction proof; **2** (vérification) crosscheck.

contre-espionnage, *pl* **~s** /kɔ̃tʀɛspjɔnaʒ/ *nm* **1** (lutte) counter-intelligence, counter-espionage; **2** (organisation) counter-intelligence service.

contre-essai, *pl* **~s** /kɔ̃tʀesɛ/ *nm* control test.

contre-exemple, *pl* **~s** /kɔ̃tʀɛgzɑ̃pl/ *nm* exception, counter-example.

contre-expertise, *pl* **~s** /kɔ̃tʀɛkspɛʀtiz/ *nf* second opinion; **demander une ~** to seek a second opinion.

contrefaçon /kɔ̃tʀəfasɔ̃/ *nf* **1** (action) (de signature, billet, gravure, carte de crédit) forging; (de pièces) counterfeiting; (d'invention, enregistrement) pirating; (de brevet) infringement; **poursuivre en ~** Jur (pour invention brevetée) to sue for infringement of patent; **2** (résultat) (signature, billet, gravure) forgery; (pièce, montre) counterfeit; (enregistrement, édition) pirated copy; **'se méfier des ~s'** 'beware of imitations'.

contrefacteur /kɔ̃tʀəfaktœʀ/ *nm* (de billets, cartes de crédit, tableau) forger; (de pièces) counterfeiter; (de logiciels, signatures, d'inventions) pirate.

contrefaire /kɔ̃tʀəfɛʀ/ [10] *vtr* **1** Comm, Jur (falsifier) to forge [*signature, billet, carte de crédit*]; to counterfeit [*pièce, montre*]; to pirate [*invention, enregistrement*]; to infringe [*brevet*]; **2** (imiter) liter to imitate [*personne, voix*]; **3** (déguiser) to disguise [*voix, écriture*]; **4**† (simuler) to feign; **5**† (déformer) to distort [*visage*]; to deform [*pied*].

contrefait, **~e** /kɔ̃tʀəfɛ, ɛt/ *adj* (difforme) [*personne, membre*] misshapen.

contre-fenêtre, *pl* **~s** /kɔ̃tʀəfənɛtʀ/ *nf* secondary glazing **¢**.

contre-fer, *pl* **~s** /kɔ̃tʀəfɛʀ/ *nm* iron cap.

contre-feu, *pl* **~x** /kɔ̃tʀəfø/ *nm* **1** (feu de prévention) backfire; **2** (de cheminée) fireback.

contreficher○: **se contreficher** /kɔ̃tʀəfiʃe/ [1] *vpr* not to give a damn○ (**de** about; **que** if).

contre-fil, *pl* **~s** /kɔ̃tʀəfil/ *nm* (irrégularité) cross-grain **¢**; **bois qui présente des ~s** cross-grained wood; **à ~** [*couper, graver*] against the grain.

contre-filet /kɔ̃tʀəfilɛ/ *nm* Culin ≈ sirloin.

contrefort /kɔ̃tʀəfɔʀ/ *nm* **1** Géog foothills (*pl*); **les ~s de l'Atlas** the foothills of the

Atlas Mountains; **2** Archit buttress; **3** (de chaussure) back, counter spéc.

contrefoutre°: **se contrefoutre** /kɔ̃tʀəfutʀ/ [6] *vpr* not to give a shit● (**de** about; **que** if).

contre-indication, *pl* **~s** /kɔ̃tʀɛ̃dikasjɔ̃/ *nf* contraindication; **les ~s d'un médicament** the contraindications of a medicine.

contre-indiqué, **~e**, *mpl* **~s** /kɔ̃tʀ ɛ̃dike/ *adj* [*médicament*] contraindicated; [*activité*] inadvisable.

contre-insurrection, *pl* **~s** /kɔ̃tʀɛ̃syʀɛksjɔ̃/ *nf* counter-insurrection.

contre-interrogatoire, *pl* **~s** /kɔ̃tʀɛ̃teʀɔgatwaʀ/ *nm* cross-examination; **soumettre qn à un ~** Jur to cross-examine sb.

contre-jour, *pl* **~s** /kɔ̃tʀəʒuʀ/ *nm* Phot, Cin **1** (effet) backlighting, contre-jour spéc; **à ~** against ou into the light; **prendre une photo à ~** to take a photograph into ou against the light; **2** (photo) contre-jour ou back-lit photograph.

contre-la-montre /kɔ̃tʀəlamɔ̃tʀ/ *nm inv* Sport time trial; ▶ **montre**.

contremaître, **-esse** /kɔ̃tʀəmɛtʀ, tʀɛs/ ▶ **510** *nm,f* foreman/forewoman.

contre-manifestant, **~e**, *mpl* **~s** /kɔ̃tʀəmanifɛstɑ̃, ɑ̃t/ *nm,f* counter-demonstrator.

contre-manifestation, *pl* **~s** /kɔ̃tʀəmanifɛstasjɔ̃/ *nf* counter-demonstration.

contremarche /kɔ̃tʀəmaʀʃ/ *nf* **1** (d'escalier) riser; **2** Mil countermarch.

contremarque /kɔ̃tʀəmaʀk/ *nf* **1** Théât, Cin pass (*for re-entry into theatre*); **2** Transp *voucher showing that the bearer is travelling on a group ticket*; **3** Admin, Comm counterseal.

contre-mesure, *pl* **~s** /kɔ̃tʀəməzyʀ/ *nf* countermeasure.

■ **~ électronique** Mil electronic countermeasure.

contre-offensive, *pl* **~s** /kɔ̃tʀɔfɑ̃siv/ *nf* counteroffensive.

contre-offre, *pl* **~s** /kɔ̃tʀɔfʀ/ *nf* counter-bid.

contre-OPA /kɔ̃tʀɔpea/ *nf inv* counter-bid, counter-offer; **faire une ~** to make a counter-bid ou counter-offer.

contrepartie /kɔ̃tʀəpaʀti/ *nf* **1** (équivalent) equivalent (**en** in); **2** (contrepoids) **c'est la ~ de la liberté que ça te laisse** it is the price you have to pay for the freedom it gives you; **mais la ~ est que le salaire est élevé** but this is offset by the high salary; **3** (dédommagement) compensation; **en ~** (en compensation) in compensation (**de** for); (en échange) in return (**de** for); **moyennant ~** for a consideration; **4** (inverse) (d'opinion) opposing view; (d'argument) counterargument; **5** Compta (registre) duplicate register; (entrée) contra (item); **en ~** per contra; **6** Fin, Jur (autre partie) other side ou party; **faire de la ~** to operate a suspense account; **7** Mus other part.

contre-pente, *pl* **~s** /kɔ̃tʀəpɑ̃t/ *nf* opposite slope.

contre-performance, *pl* **~s** /kɔ̃tʀəpɛʀfɔʀmɑ̃s/ *nf* poor performance; **~ commerciale** poor commercial performance.

contrepet /kɔ̃tʀəpɛ/ *nm*, **contrepèterie** /kɔ̃tʀəpɛtʀi/ *nf* (deliberate) spoonerism.

contre-pied, *pl* **~s** /kɔ̃tʀəpje/ *nm* **1** fig **prendre le ~ de qn** (en paroles) to say the opposite of what sb says (**de** about, on); **2** Sport **prendre qn à ~** to wrong-foot sb.

contreplaqué /kɔ̃tʀəplake/ *nm* plywood.

contre-plongée, *pl* **~s** /kɔ̃tʀəplɔ̃ʒe/ *nf* low-angle shot; **en ~** from below; **filmer en ~** to film a low-angle shot, to film from below.

contrepoids /kɔ̃tʀəpwa/ *nm* **1** lit, fig counterweight, counterbalance; **faire ~** to act as a counterbalance; **faire ~ à qch** lit, fig to counterbalance sth; **2** (de funambule) balancing pole.

contrepoint /kɔ̃tʀəpwɛ̃/ *nm* **1** Mus counterpoint; **écrit en ~** written in counterpoint; **2** fig counterpoint; **en ~** as a counterpoint (**à** to); **servir de ~ à qch** to counterpoint sth, to serve as a counterpoint to sth.

contrepoison /kɔ̃tʀəpwazɔ̃/ *nm* lit, fig antidote.

contre-porte, *pl* **~s** /kɔ̃tʀəpɔʀt/ *nf* inner door.

contre-pouvoir, *pl* **~s** /kɔ̃tʀəpuvwaʀ/ *nm* forces (*pl*) of opposition.

contre-productif, **-ive** /kɔ̃tʀəpʀɔdyktif, iv/ *adj* counterproductive.

contre-programmation, *pl* **~s** /kɔ̃tʀəpʀɔgʀamasjɔ̃/ *nf* TV *changing of scheduled programmes for competitive purposes*.

contre-projet, *pl* **~s** /kɔ̃tʀəpʀɔʒɛ/ *nm* counter-proposal.

contre-propagande /kɔ̃tʀəpʀɔpagɑ̃d/ *nf* counter-propaganda.

contre-proposition, *pl* **~s** /kɔ̃tʀəpʀɔ pozisjɔ̃/ *nf* counter-proposal.

contre-publicité /kɔ̃tʀəpyblisite/ *nf* adverse publicity.

contrer /kɔ̃tʀe/ [1] **I** *vtr* **1** (se dresser contre) to counter, to fend off [*offensive, armée*]; to counter [*délinquance, accusation*]; to fend off [*concurrent, opposition*]; to combat [*agressivité*]; to oppose [*parti*]; to block [*initiative*]; **2** Sport to block [*adversaire*].

II *vi* Jeux (aux cartes) to double.

contre-rail, *pl* **~s** /kɔ̃tʀəʀɑj/ *nm* guard rail.

Contre-Réforme /kɔ̃tʀəʀefɔʀm/ *nf* Counter-Reformation.

contre-révolution, *pl* **~s** /kɔ̃tʀəʀevɔlysjɔ̃/ *nf* counter-revolution.

contre-révolutionnaire, *pl* **~s** /kɔ̃tʀəʀevɔlysjɔnɛʀ/ *adj, nmf* counter-revolutionary.

contrescarpe /kɔ̃tʀɛskaʀp/ *nf* counterscarp.

contreseing /kɔ̃tʀəsɛ̃/ *nm* countersignature; **apposer son ~** to countersign.

contresens /kɔ̃tʀəsɑ̃s/ *nm* **1** (erreur) misinterpretation; (en traduisant) serious mistranslation; **faire un ~ sur qch** to misinterpret ou misconstrue sth; [*traducteur*] to mistranslate sth; **2** (absurdité) aberration; **3** (sens contraire) **prendre le ~ du trafic** to go against the flow of traffic; **à ~** [*rouler, avancer*] in the opposite direction; (dans le mauvais sens) the wrong way; [*raboter*] against the grain; **agir à ~** to do the precise opposite of what should be done.

contresigner /kɔ̃tʀəsiɲe/ [1] *vtr* to countersign.

contretemps /kɔ̃tʀətɑ̃/ *nm* **1** (difficulté) setback, contretemps sout; **2** Mus syncopation; **à ~** lit [*jouer*] gén on the off-beat; (par erreur) out of time; fig [*agir, parler, intervenir*] at the wrong moment.

contre-terrorisme, *pl* **~s** /kɔ̃tʀətɛʀɔ ʀism/ *nm* counter-terrorism.

contre-terroriste, *pl* **~s** /kɔ̃tʀətɛʀɔʀist/ *adj, nmf* counter-terrorist.

contre-torpilleur, *pl* **~s** /kɔ̃tʀətɔʀpijœʀ/ *nm* destroyer.

contre-ut, *pl* **~(s)** /kɔ̃tʀyt/ *nm* high C.

contre-valeur, *pl* **~s** /kɔ̃tʀəvalœʀ/ *nf* Fin exchange value.

contrevenant, **~e** /kɔ̃tʀəvənɑ̃, ɑ̃t/ *nm,f* offender.

contrevenir /kɔ̃tʀəvəniʀ/ [36] *vtr ind* **~ à** to contravene, to infringe [*loi, règle, accord*]; to contravene [*ordre*].

contrevent /kɔ̃tʀəvɑ̃/ *nm* **1** (volet) shutter; **2** (de charpente) brace, strut.

contre-vérité, *pl* **~s** /kɔ̃tʀəveʀite/ *nf* untruth.

contre-visite, *pl* **~s** /kɔ̃tʀəvizit/ *nf* Méd (examen) second examination; (visite de contrôle) follow-up inspection.

contre-voie, *pl* **~s** /kɔ̃tʀəvwɑ/ *nf* Rail opposite track; **descendre à ~** [*voyageur*] to get out on the wrong side of the track.

contribuable /kɔ̃tʀibɥabl/ *nmf* taxpayer.

contribuer /kɔ̃tʀibɥe/ [1] *vtr ind* **~ à** to contribute to [*frais*]; to contribute to [*projet, résultat*]; **cela y a beaucoup contribué** it was a major factor, it played a large part in it; **~ aux dépenses** to pay one's share of the expenses; **l'argent ne fait pas le bonheur mais il y contribue** money doesn't buy happiness, but it helps.

contributif, **-ive** /kɔ̃tʀibytif, iv/ *adj* Jur [*part*] contributory.

contribution /kɔ̃tʀibysjɔ̃/ **I** *nf* (participation) contribution (**aux frais** toward(s) the costs; **à une entreprise** to an undertaking); **apporter sa ~ au projet** to make one's contribution to the project; **mettre qn à ~** to call upon sb's services.

II contributions *nfpl* **1** (impôts) (à l'État) taxes; (à la commune) local taxes; **2** (bureau) tax office (*sg*).

■ **~ sociale généralisée**, **CSG** *supplementary social security contribution*; **~s directes/indirectes** direct/indirect taxes; **~s foncières** land taxes GB, property taxes US.

contrister /kɔ̃tʀiste/ [1] *vtr* liter to grieve [*personne*]; **être contristé du malheur des autres** to be saddened by other people's misfortunes.

contrit, **~e** /kɔ̃tʀi, it/ *adj* [*personne, air*] contrite, apologetic; **d'un air** or **sur un ton ~** apologetically.

contrition /kɔ̃tʀisjɔ̃/ *nf* liter contrition sout; **acte de ~** act of contrition.

contrôlable /kɔ̃tʀolabl/ *adj* **1** (maîtrisable) [*situation, coût, variable, maladie*] controllable; **2** (pouvant être surveillé) which can be monitored (*après n*); **difficilement ~** difficult to monitor (*après n*); **exportations difficilement ~s** exports which are difficult to monitor.

contrôle /kɔ̃tʀol/ *nm* **1** (maîtrise) control (**de** of; **sur** over); **~ d'une région/société** control of a region/company; **prendre/perdre le ~** to take/to lose control; **prendre le ~ de** Fin to take a controlling interest in; **reprendre le ~ de la situation** to regain control of the situation; **échapper au ~ de** to slip out of the control of; **sous ~** under control; **sous le ~ de** under the control of; **passer sous ~ américain** to come under American control; **~ de l'inflation** control of inflation; **dispositif de ~** control mechanism; **avoir le ~ du ballon** to have control of the ball; **perdre le ~ de son véhicule** to lose control of one's vehicle; **2** Admin check; **~ de police/sécurité** police/security check; **moyen de ~** means of checking ; **~ des billets** ticket inspection; **~ douanier** customs control; **3** Compta audit; **~ annuel** annual audit; **4** (suivi) monitoring ₵; **~ de l'environnement/d'une expérience** monitoring of the environment/of an experiment; **5** Scol, Univ test; **~ de géographie** geography test; **6** Dent, Méd check-up; **~ dentaire** dental check-up; **sous ~ médical** under medical supervision.

■ **~ d'accès** access control; **~ d'altitude** altitude control; **~ antidopage** dope test; **être soumis à un ~ antidopage** to be given a dope test; **~ des changes** Écon exchange controls (*pl*); **~ des connaissances** assessment ; **~ continu (des connaissances)** continuous assessment; **~ fiscal** tax investigation; **~ de gestion** management control; **~ d'identité** identity check; **~ judiciaire** legal restrictions (*pl*) pending trial; **mettre** ou **placer qn sous ~ judiciaire** to impose legal restrictions on sb pending trial; **être placé sous ~ judiciaire** to be subject to legal restrictions pending trial; **~ laitier** milk quality control test; **~ des naissances** birth control; **~ des passeports** (action, guérite) passport control; **~ des passeports s'il vous plaît!** passports please!; **~ phytosanitaire** plant control; **~ des prix** Écon price controls (*pl*); **~ de qualité** Ind quality control; **~ qualité assisté par ordinateur, CQAO** computer-aided quality control; **~ sanitaire** Admin health control; **~ de soi** Psych self-control; **~ technique (des véhicules)** Aut MOT (test); **~ du trafic aérien** Aviat air-traffic control; **~ vétérinaire** animal control.

contrôler /kɔ̃tʀole/ [1] **I** *vtr* **1** Fin, Mil, Pol (exercer son autorité sur) to control [*pays, organisation, entreprise, marché*]; **2** Écon, Psych, Sport (maîtriser) to control [*prix, tremblement, prolifération, ballon*]; **3** (superviser) to monitor [*cessez-le-feu, opération, expérience*]; **4** (vérifier) [*inspecteur*] to check [*identité, voiture, billet*]; [*douanier*] to inspect [*bagage*]; [*comptable*] to audit [*comptes*]; [*contrôleur*] to inspect [*comptes*]; [*percepteur*] to check [*déclaration d'impôt*]; [*employé*] to test [*qualité, produit*]; [*chercheur*] to verify [*résultat, témoignage*]; [*conducteur*] to check [*huile*]; **~ que** to make sure that.

II se contrôler *vpr* (se maîtriser) to control oneself.

contrôleur, **-euse** /kɔ̃tʀolœʀ, øz/ **▶ 510** **I** *nm,f* gén inspector.

II *nm* Électrotech controller; **~ électronique** electronic controller.

■ **~ aérien** air-traffic controller; **~ financier** financial controller; **~ de gestion** management controller; **~ de pression** pressure gauge; **~ de qualité** quality control inspector.

contrordre /kɔ̃tʀɔʀdʀ/ *nm* **1** gén **une série d'ordres et de ~s** a series of conflicting orders; **sauf ~** unless I/you etc hear to the contrary; **il y a ~** there's been a change of plan; **2** Mil counter command; **recevoir un ~** to receive a counter command.

controuvé, **~e** /kɔ̃tʀuve/ *adj* liter fabricated.

controversable /kɔ̃tʀɔvɛʀsabl/ *adj* controversial.

controverse /kɔ̃tʀɔvɛʀs/ *nf* controversy (**sur** about); **soulever une** or **donner lieu à ~** to give rise to controversy; **il a relancé la ~ sur le problème de...** he has stirred up controversy about the problem of...

controversé, **~e** /kɔ̃tʀɔvɛʀse/ *adj* controversial.

contumace /kɔ̃tymas/ *nf* **la procédure de ~** proceedings in the absence of the accused; **condamner qn par ~** to sentence sb in absentia.

contusion /kɔ̃tyzjɔ̃/ *nf* bruise, contusion spéc.

contusionner /kɔ̃tyzjɔne/ [1] *vtr* to bruise [*personne, corps*]; **avoir le visage contusionné** to have a bruised face.

conurbation /kɔnyʀbasjɔ̃/ *nf* conurbation.

convaincant, **~e** /kɔ̃vɛ̃kɑ̃, ɑ̃t/ *adj* **1** (concluant) [*preuve, argument*] convincing; **2** (persuasif) [*personne, discours*] persuasive; **3** Sport [*tactique*] impressive.

convaincre /kɔ̃vɛ̃kʀ/ [57] **I** *vtr* **1** to convince [*incrédule*] (**de** of; **que** that); to persuade [*indécis*] (**de faire** to do); **on a fini par le ~ de rester** we managed to persuade him to stay ou talk him° into staying; **je ne suis pas convaincu** I remain to be convinced; **se laisser ~** to let oneself be persuaded; (à tort) to allow oneself to be persuaded; **crois-tu qu'il se laisserait ~?** do you think that he is open to persuasion?; **2** Jur to prove [sb] guilty (**de** of).

II se convaincre *vpr* to convince oneself (**de** of).

convaincu, **~e** /kɔ̃vɛ̃ky/ **I** *pp* **▶ convaincre**.

II *pp adj* **1** (persuadé) convinced; [*partisan*] staunch; **d'un ton ~** with conviction; **s'adresser à des auditeurs ~s** to preach to the converted; **2** (prouvé coupable) found guilty (**de** of).

convalescence /kɔ̃valesɑ̃s/ *nf* convalescence; **être en ~** to be convalescing; **sortir de ~** to finish convalescing.

convalescent, **~e** /kɔ̃valesɑ̃, ɑ̃t/ **I** *adj* [*personne*] convalescent; [*économie*] on the mend (*jamais épith*).

II *nm,f* convalescent.

convecteur /kɔ̃vɛktœʀ/ *nm* convector heater.

convection /kɔ̃vɛksjɔ̃/ *nf* convection.

convenable /kɔ̃vnabl/ *adj* **1** (approprié) [*solution*] suitable, appropriate; [*endroit*] suitable; **peu ~** [*tenue*] unsuitable; **2** (acceptable) [*résultat, travail*] reasonable, decent; [*salaire, logement*] decent, reasonable; [*vin, repas*] acceptable, decent; **tout juste ~** barely acceptable; **3** (bienséant) [*vêtement*] decent; [*conduite, manières*] proper; **pas ~** [*vêtement*] inappropriate; [*conduite*] improper; **il n'est pas ~ d'arriver en retard** it isn't done to arrive late; **4** (respectable) [*gens, famille*] respectable.

convenablement /kɔ̃vnabləmɑ̃/ *adv* **1** (sans erreur) [*fonctionner, s'exprimer*] properly; **2** (de façon acceptable) [*manger, travailler, payer*] reasonably well; **3** (de façon appropriée) [*vêtu*] properly; **4** (sans choquer) [*se vêtir*] decently; [*se conduire*] properly.

convenance /kɔ̃vnɑ̃s/ **I** *nf* **cette maison est à ma ~** (à mon goût) this house is to my liking; (qui m'arrange) this house suits me; **pour (des motifs de) ~ personnelle** for personal reasons; **lundi ou mardi, à votre ~** on Monday or Tuesday, to suit you ou at your convenience; **un mariage de ~** a marriage of convenience.

II convenances *nfpl* (bienséance) conventions; **respecter/braver les ~s** to respect/ to defy convention ou the conventions; **au mépris des ~s** in defiance of convention; **par souci des ~s** for propriety's sake.

convenir /kɔ̃vniʀ/ [36] **I** *vtr* **1** (concéder) to admit (**que** that); **convenez que c'est faux** you must admit (that) it's wrong; **~ avoir fait** to admit having done; **2** (s'entendre) to agree (**que** that); **nous sommes convenus** or **avons convenu que** we have ou are agreed that.

II convenir à *vtr ind* (plaire à) to suit [*personne, goût*]; (être approprié à) to be suitable for [*circonstance, activité*]; to suit, to be suitable for [*personne*]; (ne pas gêner) [*rendez-vous, horaire*] to be convenient for [*personne*]; [*aliment, climat*] to agree with, to suit [*personne*]; **ce poste m'aurait convenu** that job would have suited me; **si cela vous convient** if it suits you; **la date ne me convient pas** that date isn't convenient for me; (plus catégorique) that date is no good for me; **c'est tout à fait ce qui me convient** it's exactly what I need; **de la taille/couleur qui convient** of a suitable size/colour[GB]; **de la façon qui convient** in the appropriate manner; **l'expression/le geste qui convient** the appropriate expression/ gesture; **l'homme/le mot qui convient** the right man/word.

III convenir de *vtr ind* **1** (reconnaître) **~ de** to admit, to acknowledge [*faute, erreur*]; to acknowledge [*qualité*]; **il convient d'avoir été injuste** he admits ou acknowledges (that) he has been unfair; **j'en conviens** I accept that; **2** (s'accorder sur) **~ de** [*personnes*] to agree on [*date, prix*]; **~ de faire** to agree to do.

IV se convenir *vpr* (être assorti) [*personnes*] to be well suited ou matched.

V *v impers* **1** (il est sage, correct, nécessaire) **il convient de faire** one should do ou ought to do; **il convient que vous fassiez** you should do, you ought to do; **dire ce qu'il aurait convenu de taire** to say what should have been left unsaid; **il aurait convenu de noter** it should have been noted; **2** (il est entendu) fml **il a été/est convenu que** it has been/is agreed that; **il était convenu depuis longtemps que** it had long been agreed that; **il est convenu ce qui suit** it has been agreed as follows; **ce qu'il est convenu d'appeler le réalisme** what is commonly called realism; **comme convenu** as agreed.

convention /kɔ̃vɑ̃sjɔ̃/ **I** *nf* **1** (accord, contrat) gén agreement; (officiel) covenant; (entre nations) convention; (clause) article, clause; **cela n'était pas dans nos ~s** that was not part of our agreement; **sauf ~ contraire** unless otherwise agreed, unless there be a clause to the contrary fml; **2** (usage admis) convention; **c'est par ~ que...** it is a convention that...; **de ~** conventional; **3** Pol (assemblée) convention.

II conventions *nfpl* (convenances) convention ¢; **défier les ~s** to defy convention.

■ **~ collective** Écon ≈ collective labour[GB] agreement; **~ financière** Fin financial covenant; **Convention nationale** National Convention.

convention-cadre, *pl* **conventions-cadres** /kɔ̃vɑ̃sjɔ̃kadʀ/ *nf* outline agreement.

conventionné, **~e** /kɔ̃vɑ̃sjɔne/ *adj* Prot Soc, Admin [*clinique*] registered; **médecin ~** *doctor approved by the Department of Health (whose fees are refunded)*; **médecin non ~** private doctor; **médecin ~ honoraires libres** *doctor approved by the Department of Health (whose private fees may be partially refunded)*; **les tarifs ~s** *charges approved by the Department of Health*.

conventionnel, **-elle** /kɔ̃vɑ̃sjɔnɛl/ **I** *adj* **1** gén conventional; **armes non conventionnelles** nonconventional weapons; **2** Jur [*clause*] contractual.

II *nm* (en histoire de France) **les ~s** the members of the National Convention.

conventionnellement /kɔ̃vɑ̃sjɔnɛlmɑ̃/ *adv* conventionally.

conventionnement /kɔ̃vɑ̃sjɔnmɑ̃/ *nm*: *registration of a doctor with the Department of Health*.

conventuel, **-elle** /kɔ̃vɑ̃tɥɛl/ *adj* [*vie, règle*] conventual.

convenu, **~e** /kɔ̃v(ə)ny/ **I** *pp* **▶ convenir**.

II *pp adj* **1** (décidé) [*date, prix, termes*] agreed; **2** (conventionnel) [*expression, tour*] conventional; [*sourire*] polite, forced.

convergence /kɔ̃vɛʀʒɑ̃s/ *nf* **1** (d'idées, intérêts, de politiques) convergence; **la ~ de leurs efforts a permis de réaliser le projet** their combined efforts have seen the project through; **la ~ des volontés a permis de...** a joint effort of will has made it possible to...; **2** (de faisceaux lumineux, lentille) convergence; (de chemins) meeting, joining; **3** Math convergence.

convergent, **~e** /kɔ̃vɛʀʒɑ̃, ɑ̃t/ *adj* **1** Phys convergent; **2** fig similar, convergent.

converger /kɔ̃vɛʀʒe/ [13] *vi* **1** (dans l'espace) [*chemins, véhicules, personnes*] to converge (**vers** on); **tous les regards convergèrent sur elle** all eyes turned toward(s) her; **2** fig **nos réflexions convergent vers les mêmes conclusions** our thoughts are leading us to the same conclusions; **tous nos efforts doivent ~ vers un seul but, l'Europe!** all of our efforts should be focused on one goal, Europe!; **nos opinions convergent** we're of the same opinion; **3** Math, Phys to converge.

convers, **~e** /kɔ̃vɛʀ, ɛʀs/ *adj* Relig lay.

conversation /kɔ̃vɛʀsasjɔ̃/ *nf* conversation (**avec** with); **une ~ privée/au coin du feu/téléphonique** a private/fireside/telephone conversation; **la ~ mondaine** or **de salon** polite conversation; **être en (grande) ~ (avec qn)** to be (deep) in conversation (with sb); **engager la ~** to strike up a conversation; **faire les frais de la ~** (en être l'objet) to be the chief topic ou subject of conversation; (la mener) to do all the talking;

faire la ~ à qn to make conversation with sb; **rechercher la ~ de qn** to seek sb out for his/her conversation; **n'avoir aucune ~** to have no conversation; **avoir de la ~** to be a good conversationalist; **faire un brin** or **bout de ~** to have a little chat (**à** with); **anglais/français de ~** conversational English/French; **dans la ~ courante** in everyday ou ordinary speech.
■ **~ de bistrot** or **comptoir** bar-room talk; **~ à trois** Télécom three-way calling; **~s diplomatiques** diplomatic talks.

conversationnel, **-elle** /kɔ̃vɛʀsasjɔnɛl/ *adj* Ordinat interactive.

converser /kɔ̃vɛʀse/ [1] *vi* to converse sout (**avec** with).

conversion /kɔ̃vɛʀsjɔ̃/ *nf* **1** Relig, fig conversion (**à** to); **2** (transformation) (d'entreprise) conversion (**en** into); (d'employé) re-training; **prime de ~** conversion premium; **des aides à la ~** incentives for companies changing to a new line of production; **3** (de monnaie, dette) conversion (**en** into); **le taux de ~** the conversion rate; **4** (de degrés, mesures, poids) conversion (**en** into); converting (**en** into); **la ~ de miles en kilomètres** the conversion of miles into kilometres[GB], converting miles into kilometres[GB]; **5** Sport (en ski) kick-turn.

converti, **~e** /kɔ̃vɛʀti/ **I** *pp* ▶ **convertir**.
II *pp adj* converted.
III *nm,f* convert.
IDIOMES **prêcher un ~** to preach to the converted.

convertibilité /kɔ̃vɛʀtibilite/ *nf* Fin (de devise, d'action) convertibility.

convertible /kɔ̃vɛʀtibl/ *adj* **1** Fin [*devise, capital*] convertible (**en** into); **2** Math, Ordinat convertible (**en** to); **3** (transformable) **canapé ~** sofa-bed; **avion ~** convertiplane.

convertir /kɔ̃vɛʀtiʀ/ [3] **I** *vtr* **1** (faire changer d'idée) to convert [*personne, parti, gouvernement*] (**à** to); **~ qn au christianisme** to convert sb to Christianity; **~ qn à l'écologie/au végétarisme** to convert sb to ecological ideals/to vegetarianism; **2** (transformer) to convert [*industrie, logements*] (**en** into); **3** Fin to convert [*devise, prêt, dette*] (**en** into); **4** Math, Ordinat to convert [*fractions, texte*] (**en** to).
II se convertir *vpr* [*personne*] to convert, to become a convert (**à** to); [*entreprise*] to change products; **le pays doit se ~ au libéralisme** the country must go over to GB ou must adopt liberalism.

convertisseur /kɔ̃vɛʀtisœʀ/ *nm* converter.
■ **~ analogique-numérique** Ordinat analogue[GB] to digital converter, ADC; **~ Bessemer** Bessemer converter; **~ de couple** torque converter; **~ d'image** image converter; **~ numérique-analogique** digital to analogue[GB] converter, DAC; **~ de tension** transformer.

convexe /kɔ̃vɛks/ *adj* convex.

convexité /kɔ̃vɛksite/ *nf* convexity.

conviction /kɔ̃viksjɔ̃/ **I** *nf* **1** (certitude) conviction; **avoir la ~ que** to be convinced that; **j'en ai l'intime ~** I am utterly convinced of it; **agir par ~** to act on the strength of one's conviction(s); **2** (fougue, sérieux) conviction; **sans grande/avec ~** without much/with conviction; ▶ **pièce**.
II convictions *nfpl* (opinions) convictions.

convier /kɔ̃vje/ [2] *vtr* **1** (inviter) to invite [*personne*] (**à** to); **2** (engager) to invite [*personne*] (**à faire** to do); to ask [*population, entreprise*] (**à faire** to do); **je vous convie à examiner ce problème** I suggest you look at this problem.

convive /kɔ̃viv/ *nmf* guest.

convivial, **~e**, *mpl* **-iaux** /kɔ̃vivjal, o/ *adj* **1** [*repas, atmosphère, réunion*] friendly, convivial; **2** Ordinat user-friendly.

convivialité /kɔ̃vivjalite/ *nf* **1** (de personne) friendliness, conviviality; (d'atmosphère, de réunion) warmth, friendliness; **la réunion s'est déroulée dans la ~** it was a warm and friendly meeting; **instaurer des rapports de ~** (**entre les gens**) to establish friendly relations (between people); **2** Ordinat user-friendliness.

convocation /kɔ̃vɔkasjɔ̃/ *nf* **1** (appel) (d'assemblée) convening, convocation sout; (d'individu) gén summoning; Mil (de réserviste) calling up; (pour entrevue) invitation; **il n'y a pas eu ~ de tous les participants** not all participants were invited to attend; **se rendre à une ~** gén to attend as instructed; Jur to obey a summons; **se présenter à un bureau sur ~** Admin to call at an office after being requested to do so; **2** (lettre) (ordre) gén notice to attend; Jur summons (*sg*); Mil call-up papers (*pl*); (invitation) invitation; **j'ai reçu une ~ à la mairie** I have received a letter asking me to call at the town hall; **~ aux examens** notification of examination timetables.

convoi /kɔ̃vwa/ *nm* **1** (de véhicules, prisonniers, troupes) convoy; **un ~ militaire** a military convoy; **un ~ de ravitaillement** a supply convoy; **'~ exceptionnel'** Aut 'abnormal load'; **2** Rail train; **un ~ de marchandises** a goods train.
■ **~ funèbre** funeral cortege.

convoiter /kɔ̃vwate/ [1] *vtr* to covet [*objet, honneurs*]; to covet, to lust after [*femme, fortune*].

convoitise /kɔ̃vwatiz/ *nf* gén desire; (péché) covetousness; (ambition, gourmandise) greed; (concupiscence) lust; (cupidité) lust for money; **l'objet de sa ~** the object of his/her desire; **exciter la ~ de qn** to arouse sb's envy; **regard brillant de ~** eyes shining with greed ou lust; **regarder qch avec ~** to cast covetous glances at sth; [*enfant*] to look longingly at sth.

convoler /kɔ̃vɔle/ [1] *vi* hum to marry, to wed†; **~ avec qn** to marry ou wed† sb; **~ en justes noces** to get married.

convoquer /kɔ̃vɔke/ [1] *vtr* **1** (appeler à se réunir) to call, to convene [*réunion, assemblée*]; **la réunion est convoquée pour le 12 juin** the meeting has been called ou convened for 12 June; **2** (appeler à se présenter) to send for, to summon [*élève*]; Jur to summon [*témoin*]; Mil to call [sb] up [*soldat, officier*]; **le ministre les a convoqués dans son bureau** the minister summoned them to his/her office; **~ un témoin à la barre** to summon a witness to give evidence; **être convoqué à un examen** to be asked to attend an exam; **être convoqué pour un entretien** to be called for interview.

convoyage /kɔ̃vwajaʒ/ *nm* (de personnes, troupes, navires) escorting (**de** of); (de marchandises, secours, d'or) transport, transportation (**de** of).

convoyer /kɔ̃vwaje/ [23] *vtr* **1** (escorter) to escort [*prisonnier, navires, troupes*]; (transporter) to transport [*or, marchandises, secours*]; **2** (jusqu'à son lieu d'utilisation) to ferry [*bateau, avion*].

convoyeur, **-euse** /kɔ̃vwajœʀ/ **I** ▶ **510** *nm,f* (de prisonnier) prison escort; (de marchandise) courier.
II *nm* **1** Ind conveyor; **2** Naut **navire ~** escort ship.
■ **~ à bande** Ind conveyor belt; **~ de fonds** security guard; **convoyeuse de l'air** air ambulance nurse.

convulser /kɔ̃vylse/ [1] fml **I** *vtr* **1** (tordre) [*peur, douleur*] to convulse, to contort [*visage*]; to grip [*estomac*]; **il avait le visage convulsé de rage** his face was convulsed ou contorted with rage; **2** (bouleverser) to throw [sth] into turmoil [*pays, société*].
II se convulser *vpr* [*corps, visage*] to be convulsed (**de** with).

convulsif, **-ive** /kɔ̃vylsif, iv/ *adj* **1** [*sanglots, mouvement*] convulsive; [*rire*] nervous; **2** Méd [*toux, maladie*] convulsive.

convulsion /kɔ̃vylsjɔ̃/ *nf* **1** Méd convulsion; **avoir des ~s** to have convulsions; **être pris de ~s** to be seized by convulsions; **2** Pol (troubles) convulsions (*pl*), turmoil ¢.

convulsionnaire /kɔ̃vylsjɔnɛʀ/ **I** *adj* liter convulsionary.
II *nmf* Hist **les ~s** (**de Saint-Médard**) the Convulsionaries.

convulsionner /kɔ̃vylsjɔne/ [1] *vtr* [*maladie, souffrance*] to convulse [*traits, visage, corps*]; **il avait le visage convulsionné de douleur** his face was convulsed ou contorted with pain.

convulsivement /kɔ̃vylsivmɑ̃/ *adv* convulsively.

coobligé, **~e** /koɔbliʒe/ *nm,f* joint debtor.

cooccurrence /kookyʀɑ̃s/ *nf* co-occurrence.

cool○ /kul/ **I** *adj inv* cool○, laidback○.
II *adv* **s'habiller ~** to dress in a laidback○ way.
III *excl* **~ les gars, ça suffit!** come on, cool it, lads GB ou guys, that's enough!

coolie /kuli/ *nm* coolie.

coopérant /koɔpeʀɑ̃/ *nm*: *young man working abroad in lieu of military service.*

coopérateur, **-trice** /koɔpeʀatœʀ, tʀis/ **I** *adj* cooperating.
II *nm,f* **1** (associé) collaborator; **2** (membre d'une coopérative) member of a cooperative.

coopératif, **-ive** /koɔpeʀatif, iv/ **I** *adj* cooperative.
II coopérative *nf* (groupement) cooperative; (magasin) co-op.
■ **coopérative scolaire** school fund.

coopération /koɔpeʀasjɔ̃/ *nf* **1** gén (collaboration) cooperation; **apporter sa ~ à un projet** to cooperate in a project; **2** Mil, Pol *form of national service consisting of working abroad*; **faire son service dans le cadre de la ~** to work abroad in lieu of military service.

coopératisme /koɔpeʀatism/ *nm* cooperation.

coopérer /koɔpeʀe/ [14] **I coopérer à** *vtr ind* to cooperate on ou in.
II *vi* to cooperate.

cooptation /koɔptasjɔ̃/ *nf* co-option; **un membre nommé par ~** a co-opted member; **il a été admis par ~** he was co-opted.

coopter /koɔpte/ [1] *vtr* to co-opt [*personne*].

coordinateur, **-trice** /koɔʀdinatœʀ, tʀis/ **I** *adj* [*bureau, service*] coordinating.
II *nm,f* (personne) coordinator.

coordination /koɔʀdinasjɔ̃/ *nf* **1** gén coordination; **2** (groupe) representative committee.

coordonnant /koɔʀdɔnɑ̃/ *nm* Ling coordinator.

coordonnateur, **-trice** /koɔʀdɔnatœʀ, tʀis/ *nm,f* ▶ **coordinateur**.

coordonné, **~e** /koɔʀdɔne/ **I** *pp* ▶ **coordonner**.
II *pp adj* **1** [*gestes, travail*] coordinated; [*tissus, accessoires, vêtement*] coordinating (*épith*); **2** Ling [*proposition*] coordinate.
III coordonnés *nmpl* (vêtements) coordinates; **les ~s de cuisine** coordinating kitchenware.
IV coordonnées *nfpl* **1** Géog, Math coordinates; **2** (adresse) address and telephone number; **prendre les ~es de qn** to take sb's address and phone number; **je n'ai pas ses ~es** I don't know how to get in touch with him/her; **prendre les ~es d'un magasin** to note the details of a shop.

coordonner /koɔʀdɔne/ [1] *vtr* (tous contextes) to coordinate.

coorganisateur, **-trice** /koɔʀganizatœʀ, tʀis/ *nm,f* co-organizer.

copain○, **copine** /kɔpɛ̃, in/ **I** *adj* pally○ GB, matey○ GB, chummy○.
II *nm,f* (camarade) friend; (acolyte) pej crony; (amoureux) **son ~** her boyfriend; **sa copine** his girlfriend; **c'est un simple ~** he's just a good friend; **on sort en ~s** we go out as friends; **se réunir entre ~s** to get together with friends; (entre hommes) to get together

with one's mates○; **se réunir entre copines** to get together with the girls○.

■ **~ d'école** or **de classe** school friend; **~ de régiment** old army buddy○.

IDIOMES **être ~s comme cochons**○ to be as thick as thieves.

copeau, *pl* **~x** /kɔpo/ *nm* **1** (de bois, métal) shaving; **des ~x de bois** wood shavings; **2** Culin **recouvrez de ~x de parmesan/chocolat** Culin sprinkle with coarsely grated parmesan/chocolate.

Copenhague /kɔpɛnag/ *npr* ▶ **857** Copenhagen.

Copernic /kɔpɛʀnik/ *npr* Copernicus.

copiage /kɔpjaʒ/ *nm* **1** (reproduction) copying; **2** Scol copying (**sur** from).

copie /kɔpi/ *nf* **1** (de document, tableau, logiciel, cassette, film, produit) copy; **être la ~ conforme de qch** to be the exact copy of sth; **être la ~ conforme de qn** to be the spitting image of sb; **~ pirate** pirate copy; **2** (duplication) copying ¢; **3** Scol (feuille) sheet of paper; (devoir) paper; **ramasser les ~s** to collect the papers; **~ d'examen** examination paper; ▶ **blanc**; **4** Imprim copy.

■ **~ certifiée conforme** Jur certified true copy; **~ de jugement** Jur copy of judgment; **~ de sauvegarde** Ordinat backup copy.

IDIOMES **être en mal de ~** [*journaliste*] to be short of copy; **revoir sa ~** to revise one's work.

copier /kɔpje/ [2] *vtr* **1** (transcrire) to copy [*lettre, texte*]; **vous copierez dix fois**... write out ten times...; **il l'a copié dans un livre** he copied it from ou out of a book; **2** (reproduire) to copy [*tableau*]; **3** Scol **~ sur qn** to copy ou crib from sb [*voisin*]; **il copie!** he's copying!

IDIOMES **tu me la copieras (celle-là)**○! I'm not likely to forget that in a hurry!

copieur, -ieuse /kɔpjœʀ, øz/ **I** *nm,f* **1** Scol cheat; **c'est une copieuse** she's a cheat; **2** (plagiaire) imitator.

II *nm* photocopier; **~ couleur** colour[GB] photocopier.

copieusement /kɔpjøzmɑ̃/ *adv* [*manger*] heartily, a lot; [*illustrer*] lavishly; [*annoter*] copiously; **il m'a servi ~** he served ou gave me a generous portion; **un repas ~ arrosé** a meal with lots to drink; **se faire ~ tremper/disputer/insulter** hum to get well and truly soaked/told off/insulted; **il s'est ~ ennuyé toute la soirée** hum he was bored stiff all evening.

copieux, -ieuse /kɔpjø, øz/ *adj* [*repas*] substantial, hearty; [*portion*] generous; [*notes*] copious; [*rapport*] weighty, substantial; **dans ce restaurant c'est bon et c'est ~** it's a good restaurant and the portions are generous; **ce n'est pas très ~** there isn't much of it; **recevoir une copieuse engueulade**◑ to get a good telling off.

copilote /kopilɔt/ *nmf* **1** Aviat, Naut co-pilot; **2** Aut co-driver.

copinage○ /kɔpinaʒ/ *nm* pej cronyism péj.

copine ▶ **copain**.

copiner○ /kopine/ [1] *vi* to be friends (**avec** with).

copiste /kɔpist/ ▶ **510** *nmf* copyist.

copra(h) /kɔpʀa/ *nm* copra.

coprésidence /kopʀezidɑ̃s/ *nf* (d'association, de club) joint presidency, co-presidency; (de comité) joint chairmanship, co-chairmanship; **il assure la ~ de la conférence avec**... he is joint chairperson of the conference with...

coprésident /kopʀezidɑ̃/ *nm* (de société, d'association) joint president, co-president; (de comité, réunion) co-chair, co-chairman.

coprésidente /kopʀezidɑ̃t/ *nf* (de société, d'association) joint president, co-president; (de comité, réunion) co-chair, co-chairwoman.

coprin /kɔpʀɛ̃/ *nm* ink(y) cap, coprinus spéc.

coproducteur, -trice /kopʀɔdyktœʀ, tʀis/ *nm,f* co-producer.

coproduction /kopʀɔdyksjɔ̃/ *nf* co-production; **le spectacle sera réalisé en ~ avec l'Opéra de Toulouse** the show is being produced jointly with the Toulouse opera company.

coproduire /kopʀɔdɥiʀ/ [69] *vtr* to co-produce [*film, spectacle*].

copropriétaire /kopʀɔpʀijetɛʀ/ *nmf* **1** (dans un immeuble) owner (*of a flat in a jointly-owned building*); **2** (de bien, cheval) joint owner, co-owner.

copropriété /kopʀɔpʀijete/ *nf* (à deux) joint ownership; (à plus de deux) co-ownership; **posséder qch en ~** (à deux) to be joint owner of sth; (à plus de deux) to be co-owner of sth; **acheter qch en ~** to buy sth jointly with someone; **la ~ d'un chemin/d'un mur** joint ownership of a road/of a wall; **vendre des appartements en ~** to sell apartments in a block to individual buyers; **un immeuble en ~** a block of individually owned flats GB, a condominium US.

copte /kɔpt/ **I** *adj* Coptic.

II *nmf* Copt; **les ~s** the Copts.

III *nm* Ling Coptic.

copulatif, -ive /kɔpylatif, iv/ *adj* Ling copulative.

copulation /kɔpylasjɔ̃/ *nf* copulation.

copuler /kɔpyle/ [1] *vi* to copulate (**avec** with).

copyright /kɔpiʀajt/ *nm* copyright.

coq /kɔk/ *nm* **1** (de poulailler) cockerel, rooster US; (oiseau mâle) cock; **au chant du ~** at cockcrow; **rouge comme un ~** [*personne*] bright red in the face; **mollets** or **jambes de ~** skinny legs; **le ~ gaulois** the French cockerel (*symbol of the French fighting spirit*); ▶ **grand**; **2** Culin cockerel; **3** Archit (de clocher) weathercock; **4** (jeune séducteur) **le ~ du village** the local Casanova; **5** Naut (ship's) cook.

■ **~ de bruyère** grouse; **~ de combat** fighting cock; **~ faisan** cock pheasant; **~ nain** bantam cock; **~ au vin** coq au vin.

IDIOMES **être comme un ~ en pâte** to be in clover; **sauter du ~ à l'âne** to hop from one subject to another.

coq-à-l'âne, *pl* **coqs-à-l'âne** /kɔkalɑn/ *nm* abrupt change of subject; **faire un ~** to change the subject abruptly; ▶ **coq**.

coquard○, **coquart**○ /kɔkaʀ/ *nm* black eye.

coque /kɔk/ *nf* **1** Naut hull; **~ en bois/en acier** wooden/steel hull; **un bateau à plusieurs ~s** a multi-hulled ship, a multi-hull; **2** Aviat (d'hydravion) fuselage; Aut (car) body; **3** Zool (coquillage) cockle; **4** (coquille) shell.

■ **~ de noix**○ hum leaky old tub.

coquelet /kɔklɛ/ *nm* young cockerel.

coquelicot /kɔkliko/ *nm* poppy.

IDIOMES **être rouge comme un ~** to be as red as a beetroot GB ou beet US.

coqueluche /kɔklyʃ/ *nf* **1** ▶ **271** Méd whooping cough, pertussis spéc; **2**○ fig (chanteur, acteur, sportif) idol; **être la ~ des jeunes** to be the idol of the younger generation.

coquerelle /kɔkʀɛl/ *nf* C (blatte) cockroach.

coquerie /kɔkʀi/ *nf* Naut (à bord) galley; (à terre) canteen, cookhouse US.

coquet, -ette /kɔkɛ, ɛt/ **I** *adj* **1** [*personne*] (effet) well turned-out; (attitude) **être ~** to be particular about one's appearance; **2** [*village*] pretty, well-kept, cute US; [*intérieur, chapeau*] pretty; **3**○ [*revenu, somme*] tidy○ (*épith*); [*héritage*] substantial.

II coquette† *nf* coquette†, flirt.

coquetier /kɔktje/ *nm* eggcup.

IDIOMES **il a gagné le ~!** (réussi) he's hit the jackpot○!; iron he's made a great job of that!

coquettement /kɔkɛtmɑ̃/ *adv* [*regarder*] coquettishly; [*s'habiller*] stylishly; [*meubler*] prettily.

coquetterie /kɔkɛtʀi/ *nf* **1** (souci de plaire) interest in one's appearance; (excessif) vanity; **s'habiller avec ~** to dress stylishly; **par ~** out of vanity; **2** (envers les hommes) coquetry; **3** (maniérisme) affectation; **ses ~s** (minauderies) her coquettish ways; **4** liter (amour-propre) **elle met toute sa ~ à parler leur langue** she prides herself on speaking their language.

IDIOMES **avoir une ~ dans l'œil**○ to have a cast in one's eye.

coquillage /kɔkijaʒ/ *nm* **1** (mollusque) shellfish (*inv*); **2** (coquille) shell.

coquillard◑ /kɔkijaʀ/ *nm* **s'en tamponner le ~** not to give a hoot○ (about it).

coquille /kɔkij/ *nf* **1** (d'œuf, de noix, mollusque) shell; **poussin à peine sorti de sa ~** newly-hatched chick; **rentrer dans/sortir de sa ~** fig to withdraw into/come out of one's shell; **escalier en ~** spiral staircase; **2** Culin (ravier) scallop-shaped dish; (mets) **~ de saumon** scalloped salmon GB, salmon served in a shell US; **3** Imprim misprint, literal spéc; **4** Archit shell; (feston) scallop; **5** Sport box GB, cup US; **6** (d'épée) guard; **7** Méd (plâtre) spinal jacket.

■ **~ de beurre** butter curl; **~ de noix**○ hum cockleshell; **~ d'œuf** (couleur) off-white; **~ Saint-Jacques** scallop; (écaille) scallop shell.

coquillette /kɔkijɛt/ *nf* Culin small macaroni ¢; **des ~s** (small) macaroni.

coquillier, -ière /kɔkije, ɛʀ/ *adj* **1** Agric [*élevage, industrie*] shellfish (*épith*); **2** Géol [*calcaire, roche*] shelly.

coquin, ~e /kɔkɛ̃, in/ **I** *adj* **1** (espiègle) [*enfant, air*] mischievous; **2** [*osé*] [*coup d'œil, film*] naughty, saucy.

II *nm,f* (enfant) scamp; **petit ~!** you little monkey ou scamp!

III‡ *nm* (scélérat) scoundrel, rascal.

IV coquin de sort○ *loc excl* (de surprise) what the devil!; (de dépit) damn it○!

cor /kɔʀ/ *nm* **1** ▶ **534** Mus horn; **sonner** or **donner du ~** to blow the horn; **2** Méd corn; **j'ai un ~ au pied** I've got a corn on my foot; **3** Zool (de cerf) tine; **un (cerf de) six ~s** a 6-point stag, a 6-pointer.

■ **~ anglais** cor anglais; **~ basset** basset horn; **~ de chasse** hunting horn; **~ d'harmonie** French horn; **~ à pistons** valve horn.

IDIOMES **réclamer** or **demander qch à ~ et à cri** to clamour[GB] for sth.

corail, *pl* **-aux** /kɔʀaj, o/ **I** *adj inv* **1** ▶ **193** (couleur) coral(-pink); **une robe ~** a coral-pink dress; **2** Rail **train ~** *inter-city train.*

II *nm* **1** Zool coral; **une barrière de ~** a coral reef; **2** (matière) coral; **un collier en ~** a coral necklace; **3** Culin (de crustacé) coral.

corallien, -ienne /kɔʀaljɛ̃, ɛn/ *adj* coral (*épith*).

Coran /kɔʀɑ̃/ *nm* **le ~** the Koran; **suivre le ~** to follow the teachings of the Koran.

coranique /kɔʀanik/ *adj* [*loi, texte, État*] Koranic; [*préceptes*] of the Koran (*après n*).

corbeau, *pl* **~x** /kɔʀbo/ *nm* **1** Zool crow; **grand ~** raven; **2**○ (auteur de lettres anonymes) poison-pen letter writer; **3**○ (prêtre) offensive priest; **4** Archit corbel; **5** Astron Corvus.

■ **~ corneille** carrion crow; **~ freux** rook.

IDIOMES **être noir comme un ~** to be as black as a crow; **avoir des cheveux (couleur) aile de ~** to have raven black hair.

corbeille /kɔʀbɛj/ *nf* **1** (en vannerie, en plastique) basket; (de bureau) tray; **~ (à courrier) d'arrivée/de départ** in-/out-tray GB, in-/out-box US; **~ de classement/tri** filing/sorting tray; **une ~ en osier** a wicker basket; **une ~ de fleurs/fruits** a basket of flowers/fruit; **2** Théât dress circle; **un fauteuil de ~** a dress circle seat; **3** (à la Bourse) trading floor; **4** Archit bell.

■ **~ à courrier** letter tray; **~ à linge** laundry basket; **~ de mariage** wedding presents (*pl*); **elle a reçu une maison dans sa ~ de mariage** she has been given a house for a wedding present; **~ à pain** bread basket; **~ à papier** (à l'intérieur) (en osier) wastepaper basket; (en métal, en plastique) wastepaper bin; (dans la rue) litter bin GB, trash can US.

corbeille-d'argent, *pl* **corbeilles-d'argent** /kɔʀbɛjdaʀʒɑ̃/ *nf* candytuft.

corbeille-d'or, *pl* **corbeilles-d'or** /kɔʀbɛjdɔʀ/ *nf* yellow alyssum.

corbillard /kɔʀbijaʀ/ *nm* hearse.

cordage /kɔʀdaʒ/ *nm* **1** Naut (corde) rope; **~s** rigging ¢; **2** (de raquette) stringing.

corde /kɔʀd/ *nf* **1** (câble, lien) rope; **avec une ~** with a (piece of) rope; **à semelles de ~** rope-soled; **2** (d'arc, de raquette) string ▶ **arc**; **3** (pendaison) **la ~** hanging; ▶ **cou**; **4** Sport **être à la ~** [*coureur*] to be on the inside; [*cheval*] to be on the rail; **commencer à la ~** [*coureur*] to start in the inside lane; **envoyer un boxeur dans les ~s** to put a boxer against the ropes; **prendre un virage à la ~** to hug a bend; **5** Mus (d'instrument) string; **les (instruments à) ~s** the strings; **à ~s croisées** [*piano*] overstrung; **6** Tex (fil de chaîne) warp thread; **7** Math chord; **8** Aviat **~ de l'aile** wing chord; **9** (mesure) cord.
■ **~ dorsale** spinal cord; **~ à linge** clothes line; **~ lisse** Sport climbing rope; **~ à nœuds** Sport knotted (climbing) rope; **~ raide** lit, fig tightrope; **être sur/marcher sur la ~ raide** to be on/to walk a tightrope; **~ de rappel** Sport abseiling rope; **~ à sauter** skipping rope, jump rope US; **~s du tympan** chorda tympani; **~s vocales** vocal chords.
IDIOMES **pleuvoir** or **tomber des ~s** to rain cats and dogs○; **tirer sur la ~** to push one's luck; **il ne vaut pas la ~ pour le pendre** he's absolutely worthless; **ce n'est pas dans mes ~s**○ it's not my line; **c'est dans tes ~s**○ it's just your sort of thing; **toucher** or **faire vibrer la ~ sensible de qn** to touch on something close to someone's heart; **faire jouer la ~ sensible** to tug at the heartstrings; **quand la ~ est trop tendue, elle casse** Prov (d'une personne) if you push somebody too far, they'll snap; (d'une situation) if you allow a situation to reach a certain point, something's got to give; ▶ **pendu**.

cordeau, *pl* **~x** /kɔʀdo/ *nm* (corde) line; (de jardinier) gardener's line ou cord; **tiré** or **tracé au ~** fig dead straight; **tracer ses lettres au ~** to write very neatly.
■ **~ Bickford** Bickford fuse; **~ détonant** detonator fuse.

cordée /kɔʀde/ *nf* **1** (en alpinisme) roped party (of climbers); **~ de secours** mountain rescue party; **premier de ~** leader; **2**‡ (de bois) cord.

cordelette /kɔʀdəlɛt/ *nf* thin cord.

cordelier /kɔʀdəlje/ *nm* Relig Cordelier.

cordelière /kɔʀdəljɛʀ/ *nf* **1** (corde) cord; **2** Archit cable moulding GB ou molding US.

corder /kɔʀde/ [1] *vtr* **1** Sport to string [*raquette*]; **2** (torsader) to twist; **3** (lier) to tie up [sth] with rope [*ballot, malle*]; to secure [sth] with rope [*cargaison*].

corderie /kɔʀdəʀi/ *nf* **1** (industrie) ropemaking industry; **2** (atelier) rope-works (*pl*).

cordial, **~e**, *mpl* **-iaux** /kɔʀdjal, o/ **I** *adj* [*accueil, relations*] cordial; [*personne*] warm-hearted; [*sentiment*] warm; **une haine ~e** a deep loathing.
II *nm* cordial.

cordialement /kɔʀdjalmɑ̃/ *adv* warmly; **détester qn ~** to dislike sb heartily, to detest sb cordially; **~ (vôtre** or **à vous)** (dans une lettre) yours sincerely.

cordialité /kɔʀdjalite/ *nf* (de relations) warmth, cordiality sout; (de personne, population) friendliness.

cordier, **-ière** /kɔʀdje, ɛʀ/ **I** ▶ **510** *nm,f* (fabricant) ropemaker; (marchand) rope-merchant.
II *nm* Mus tailpiece.

cordillère /kɔʀdijɛʀ/ *nf* cordillera.
■ **la ~ des Andes** the Andes Cordillera; **la ~ australienne** the Great Dividing Range.

cordon /kɔʀdɔ̃/ *nm* **1** (de rideau) cord; (de tablier, bourse, sac) string; (de chaussure) lace; **tenir/dénouer les ~s de la bourse** fig to hold/loosen the purse-strings; **tenir les ~s du poêle** to be a pall-bearer; **2** (d'appareil électrique) flex GB, cord US; **3** (ligne) (d'agents, de troupes) cordon; (d'arbres) row; **4** Anat cord; **5** (décoration) (ruban) ribbon; (écharpe) sash; **~ de la Légion d'honneur** sash of the Legion of Honour[GB]; **6** Hort cordon; **7** Archit (string) course.
■ **~ littoral** offshore bar; **~ médullaire** spinal cord; **~ ombilical** umbilical cord; **couper le ~ (ombilical)** lit, fig to cut the umbilical cord; **~ prolongateur** extension lead GB ou cord US; **~ sanitaire** cordon sanitaire.

cordon-bleu, *pl* **cordons-bleus** /kɔʀdɔ̃blø/ *nm* cordon-bleu cook.

cordonnerie /kɔʀdɔnʀi/ ▶ **510** *nf* **1** (fabrication) shoemaking; (réparation) shoe repairing; **2** (boutique) cobbler's; **aller à la ~** to go to the cobbler's.

cordonnet /kɔʀdɔnɛ/ *nm* **1** (fil solide) buttonhole thread; **2** (petit cordon) thin cord.

cordonnier /kɔʀdɔnje/ ▶ **510** *nm* cobbler; **aller chez le ~** to go to the cobbler's.
IDIOMES **les ~s sont toujours les plus mal chaussés** Prov it's always the baker's children who have no bread Prov.

Cordoue /kɔʀdu/ ▶ **857** *npr* Cordoba.

Corée /kɔʀe/ ▶ **321** *nprf* Korea; **République de ~** Republic of Korea; **République populaire démocratique de ~** Democratic People's Republic of Korea; **la ~ du Nord/Sud** North/South Korea.

coréen, **-éenne** /kɔʀeɛ̃, ɛn/ ▶ **462**, **537** **I** *adj* Korean.
II *nm* Ling Korean.

Coréen, **-éenne** /kɔʀeɛ̃, ɛn/ ▶ **537** *nm,f* Korean; **~ du Nord/Sud** North/South Korean.

coreligionnaire /kɔʀəliʒjɔnɛʀ/ *nmf* fellow believer, coreligionist.

Corfou /kɔʀfu/ ▶ **857** *npr* Corfu.

coriace /kɔʀjas/ *adj* **1** [*personne*] tough, hard-headed; **2** [*viande*] tough.

coriandre /kɔʀjɑ̃dʀ/ *nf* coriander.

coricide /kɔʀisid/ *nm* corn remover.

corindon /kɔʀɛ̃dɔ̃/ *nm* corundum.

Corinthe /kɔʀɛ̃t/ ▶ **857** *npr* Corinth; **raisins de ~** currants.

corinthien, **-ienne** /kɔʀɛ̃tjɛ̃, ɛn/ **I** ▶ **857** *adj* Corinthian.
II *nm* Archit **le ~** the Corinthian order.

Corinthien, **-ienne** /kɔʀɛ̃tjɛ̃, ɛn/ *nm,f* Corinthian.

Coriolan /kɔʀjɔlɑ̃/ *npr* Coriolanus.

cormier /kɔʀmje/ *nm* **1** (arbre) sorb, service tree; **2** (bois) sorb, service wood; **c'est en ~** it's made of sorb ou service wood.

cormoran /kɔʀmɔʀɑ̃/ *nm* cormorant.
■ **~ huppé** crested cormorant.

cornac /kɔʀnak/ *nm* mahout, elephant driver.

cornard● /kɔʀnaʀ/ *nm* cuckold.

corne /kɔʀn/ *nf* **1** (de vache, chamois etc, d'escargot) horn; (de cerf) antler; **animal à ~s** horned animal; **donner un coup de ~ à qn** to butt sb; **blesser qn d'un coup de ~** to gore sb; **tuer qn d'un coup de ~** to gore sb to death; **2** (substance) horn; **peigne de ~** horn comb; **3** ▶ **534** (instrument) horn; **4** (coin) (de page) dog-ear; (de chapeau) point; **faire une ~ à** to turn down ou dog-ear the corner of [*feuille, page*]; to fold down the corner of [*bristol*]; **5**○ (peau durcie) **avoir de la ~ aux pieds** to have calluses on one's feet.
■ **~ d'abondance** horn of plenty, cornucopia; **~ africaine** or **de l'Afrique** horn of Africa; **~ de brume** Naut foghorn; **~ de chasse** hunting horn; **~ à chaussures** shoehorn; **~ de gazelle** gazelle's horn.
IDIOMES **faire les ~s à qn** to jeer at sb (*with a gesture of the hand*); **hou les ~s!** (dit par un enfant) you're no good!; hum shame on you!; **avoir** or **porter des ~s** to be a cuckold†; **faire porter des ~s à** to be unfaithful to, to cheat on○.

cornée /kɔʀne/ *nf* cornea.

cornéen, **-éenne** /kɔʀneɛ̃, ɛn/ *adj* corneal.

corneille /kɔʀnɛj/ *nf* crow.
■ **~ mantelée** hooded crow; **~ noire** carrion crow.

cornélien, **-ienne** /kɔʀneljɛ̃, ɛn/ *adj* [*style, tragédie*] Cornelian; **un choix ~** a Cornelian dilemma, a choice between love and duty.

cornemuse /kɔʀnəmyz/ ▶ **534** *nf* bagpipes (*pl*).

corner[1] /kɔʀne/ [1] **I** *vtr* **1** (plier) to turn down the corner of [*page*]; **page cornée** dog-eared page; **2**† (crier) **~ une nouvelle aux oreilles de qn** to shout a piece of news into sb's ear.
II *vi* **1** (conducteur) to hoot GB, to honk US; **2** (sonneur) to blow a horn.

corner[2] /kɔʀnɛʀ/ *nm* Sport corner-kick.

cornet /kɔʀnɛ/ *nm* **1** (emballage conique) (paper) cone; **feuille de papier roulée en ~** sheet of paper rolled up into a cone; **un ~ de dragées** a cornet of sugared almonds; **2** H (sachet) paper bag; **3** Culin (pour pâtisserie) horn; (pour glace) cone; **~ (à la crème)** cream horn; **un ~** a cone; **une glace en ~** an ice-cream cone; **4** Mus (d'orgue) cornet stop; (petit cor) post horn; **5** Électron, Radio horn antenna.
■ **~ acoustique** ear trumpet; **~ à dés** dice cup; **~ à pistons** cornet.

cornette /kɔʀnɛt/ *nf* **1** (de religieuse) cornet, wimple; **2** Naut burgee; **3** H (coquillette) (small) macaroni ¢.

cornettiste /kɔʀnɛtist/ ▶ **510** *nmf* cornet player, cornetist.

corniaud /kɔʀnjo/ *nm* **1** (chien) mongrel; **2**● (idiot) nitwit○, idiot.

corniche /kɔʀniʃ/ *nf* **1** (de bâtiment) cornice; (de meuble) moulding GB ou molding US, beading; (de plafond) coving; **2** Géog (escarpement) ledge (of rock); **route en ~** (en bord de mer) coastal road; (à la montagne) mountain road; **3** (de neige) cornice.

cornichon /kɔʀniʃɔ̃/ *nm* **1** Bot gherkin; Culin (pickled) gherkin; **2**○ (personne) idiot, nitwit○; **3**○ students' slang *student preparing for the entrance examination for Saint-Cyr*.

cornière /kɔʀnjɛʀ/ *nf* **1** (de tuiles) valley; **2** (équerre) angle iron.

cornique /kɔʀnik/ *nm* Ling Cornish.

Cornouailles /kɔʀnuaj/ ▶ **692** *nprf* Cornwall.

cornouiller /kɔʀnuje/ *nm* **1** (arbre) cornel, dogwood; **2** (bois) dogwood.

cornu, **~e** /kɔʀny/ **I** *adj* [*animal*] horned.
II cornue *nf* (alambic, four) retort.

corollaire /kɔʀɔlɛʀ/ *nm* **1** Math corollary; **2** (conséquence) corollary, consequence; **cette politique ne peut avoir pour ~ que l'inflation** this policy can only result in inflation.

corolle /kɔʀɔl/ *nf* Bot corolla; **en ~** [*jupe*] flared; [*abat-jour, coupe, vase*] flower-shaped.

coron /kɔʀɔ̃/ *nm* miners' terraced houses (*pl*).

coronaire /kɔʀɔnɛʀ/ *adj* [*artère, veine*] coronary.

coronal, **~e**, *mpl* **-aux** /kɔʀɔnal, o/ *adj* [*gaz*] coronal.

coronarien, **-ienne** /kɔʀɔnaʀjɛ̃, ɛn/ *adj* coronary.

corossol /kɔʀɔsɔl/ *nm* soursop.

corporatif, **-ive** /kɔʀpɔʀatif, iv/ *adj* corporate (*épith*).

corporation /kɔʀpɔʀasjɔ̃/ *nf* **1** gén corpora-

Le corps humain

L'anglais utilise souvent l'adjectif possessif avec les noms des parties du corps, là où le français utilise l'article défini.

fermer les yeux = to close one's eyes
je me suis frotté les mains = I rubbed my hands
il a levé la main = he put his hand up
elle se tenait la tête = she was holding her head
il s'est cassé le nez = he broke his nose
elle lui a cassé le nez = she broke his nose

Pour décrire les gens

La tournure française avec avoir (il a le nez long) *peut se traduire en anglais par une tournure avec* to be (his nose is long), *ou par une tournure avec* to have (he has a long nose).

il a les mains sales = his hands are dirty *ou* he has dirty hands
il a mal aux pieds = his feet are sore *ou* he has sore feet
il a le nez qui coule = his nose is running *ou* he has a runny nose
il a les cheveux longs = his hair is long *ou* he has long hair
elle a les yeux bleus = she has blue eyes *ou* her eyes are blue
elle a de beaux cheveux = she has beautiful hair *ou* her hair is beautiful

Noter aussi:

l'homme avec une jambe cassée = the man with a broken leg
l'homme à la jambe cassée = the man with the broken leg
la fille aux yeux bleus = the girl with blue eyes

Noter enfin que les tournures anglaises suivantes ne peuvent être utilisées que pour décrire des caractéristiques durables:

la fille aux yeux bleus = the blue-eyed girl
ceux qui ont de longs cheveux = long-haired people

Pour la taille des personnes, **▶ 793**; *pour le poids,* **▶ 620**; *pour la couleur des yeux, des cheveux* **▶ 193**; *pour les maladies et douleurs* **▶ 271**.

tion; **2** Jur corporate body, body corporate; **3** Hist guild.

corporatisme /kɔʀpɔʀatism/ *nm* corporatism.

corporatiste /kɔʀpɔʀatist/ *adj* corporatist.

corporel, **-elle** /kɔʀpɔʀɛl/ *adj* **1** (du corps) [*besoin, fonction*] bodily; [*température, lotion, soin*] body; [*châtiment*] corporal; **2** Jur (matériel) corporeal; **biens ~s** corporeal property ¢.

corps /kɔʀ/ *nm inv* **1** Anat body; **~ humain** human body; **mouvement/forme du ~** body movement/shape; **qu'est-ce qu'elle a dans le ~?** fig what has got GB ou gotten US into her?; (**combat**) **~ à ~** hand-to-hand combat; **lutter (au) ~ à ~** to fight hand to hand; **se donner ~ et âme à** to give oneself body and soul to; **appartenir ~ et âme à qn** to belong to sb body and soul; **passer sur le ~ de qn** fig to trample sb underfoot; **▶ larme, sain, diable**; **2** Sociol (groupe) body; (profession) profession; **~ professionnel** professional body; **~ d'ingénieurs/de spécialistes** body of engineers/of specialists; **~ médical/enseignant** medical/teaching profession; **le ~ électoral** the electorate; **faire ~ avec** (avec sa famille, un groupe, une profession) to stand solidly behind; (avec la nature) to be at one with; **▶ grand**; **3** Mil corps; **~ d'armée** army corps; **~ blindé** armoured[GB] corps; **~ d'artillerie/d'infanterie/d'élite** artillery/infantry/elite corps; **~ expéditionnaire** expeditionary force; **4** (de doctrine, texte) body; **5** Tech (partie principale) (d'instrument, de machine) body; (de meuble) main part; (de bâtiment) (main) body; **6** (consistance) body; **avoir/donner du ~** to have/give body; **prendre ~** to take shape; **7** (objet) body; **8** Chimie substance; **~ gras** fatty substance; **9** Imprim (de caractère) type size; **10** Mode (de vêtement) bodice; (de cuirasse) breastplate.

■ **~ adipeux** fat body; **~ astral** astral body; **~ de ballet** corps de ballet; **~ de bataille** field forces (*pl*); **~ calleux** corpus callosum; **~ caverneux** corpora cavernosa (*pl*); **~ de chauffe** heater; **~ du Christ** body of Christ; **~ composé** compound; **~ constitué** constituent body; **~ consulaire** consular service; **~ du délit** Jur corpus delicti; **~ diplomatique** diplomatic corps; **~ et biens** Naut with all hands; **~ étranger** foreign body; **~ de ferme** Archit farm building; **~ de garde** guardroom; **~ gazeux** gas; **~ jaune** Anat corpus luteum; **~ judiciaire** Jur judicature; **~ de logis** Archit main building; **~ de métier** corporate body; **~ de moyeu** Mécan hub shell; **~ noir** Phys black body; **~ de pompe** Mécan pump-barrel; **~ de preuves** body of evidence; **~ des sapeurs-pompiers** fire service; **~ simple** element; **~ social** society; **~ spongieux** corpus spongiosum; **~ strié** corpus striatum; **~ de troupe** troop units (*pl*); **~ vitré** vitreous body.

IDIOMES **tenir au ~** to be nourishing; **faire commerce de son ~**, **vendre son ~** to sell one's body.

corps-mort, *pl* **~s** /kɔʀmɔʀ/ *nm* Naut mooring.

corpulence /kɔʀpylɑ̃s/ *nf* stoutness, corpulence; **de faible/forte/moyenne ~** of slight/stout/medium build.

corpulent, **~e** /kɔʀpylɑ̃, ɑ̃t/ *adj* stout, corpulent.

corpus /kɔʀpys/ *nm inv* corpus; **des ~** corpora.

corpuscule /kɔʀpyskyl/ *nm* **1** Anat, Phys corpuscle; **2** (de poussière) particle.

correct, **~e** /kɔʀɛkt/ *adj* **1** (sans erreur) [*calcul, réponse, interprétation, prévisions, résultat*] correct; [*copie*] accurate; **2** (convenable) [*tenue*] proper; [*conduite*] correct; [*personne*] polite; **il ne serait pas ~ d'y aller** it wouldn't be right ou proper to go; **il serait ~ de répondre** it would be polite to answer; **3**○ (de qualité suffisante) [*résultat, vin*] reasonable, decent; [*devoir*] adequate, reasonable; [*logement*] adequate; **4** (honnête) [*personne*] fair, correct; **être ~ vis-à-vis de** or **avec qn** to be fair to ou with sb.

correctement /kɔʀɛktəmɑ̃/ *adv* **1** (sans erreur) correctly; **répondre ~ à une question** to give the right ou correct answer to a question; **2** (convenablement) properly; **3** (raisonnablement) [*manger, loger, traiter*] decently; [*travailler, être payé*] reasonably well.

correcteur, **-trice** /kɔʀɛktœʀ, tʀis/ **I** *adj* corrective; **code ~ d'erreurs** Ordinat, Télécom error correcting code.

II **▶ 510** *nm,f* **1** (d'examen) examiner GB, grader US; **2** Édition proofreader.

III *nm* **1** (pour effacer) correction fluid; **2** Tech controller.

■ **~ d'acidité** Chimie, Ind acidity regulator; **~ automatique d'orthographe** Ordinat automatic spell checker; **~ de fréquence** Audio graphic equalizer; **~ de tonalité** tone control.

correctif, **-ive** /kɔʀɛktif, iv/ **I** *adj* corrective.

II *nm* **1** (amélioration) corrective (**à** to); **2** (rectificatif) qualifier, rider.

correction /kɔʀɛksjɔ̃/ *nf* **1** (action de corriger) gén correcting; Édition (de manuscrit) proofreading; **~ d'épreuves** proofreading; **apporter une ~ à qch** to correct sth; **2** (attribution d'une note) (d'examen) marking GB, grading US; **3** (modification) correction; **~s d'auteur** Édition author's emendations; **4** (punition) gén hiding○; (fessée) spanking; **recevoir une bonne ~** to get a good hiding○; **5** (exactitude) accuracy; (justesse) correctness; **6** (convenance) (de tenue, conduite) propriety, correctness; (politesse) good manners (*pl*); **manquer de ~** to have no manners; **c'est un manque de ~** it's bad manners; **il a été d'une grande ~** he behaved perfectly.

correctionnel, **-elle** /kɔʀɛksjɔnɛl/ **I** *adj* **peine correctionnelle** penalty (imposed by court); **tribunal ~** magistrate's court; **chambre correctionnelle** *division of court judging minor offences*[GB].

II correctionnelle *nf* magistrate's court; **passer en correctionnelle** to go before the magistrate.

Corrège /kɔʀɛʒ/ *npr* **le ~** Correggio.

corrélatif, **-ive** /kɔʀelatif, iv/ **I** *adj* **1** (lié à) correlative (**de** to); **2** Ling correlative.

II *nm* Ling correlative.

corrélation /kɔʀelasjɔ̃/ *nf* correlation (**entre** between); **être en** (**étroite**) **~ avec qn** to be (closely) related ou connected to sth; **mettre deux choses en ~** to establish a connection between two things, to correlate two things.

correspondance /kɔʀɛspɔ̃dɑ̃s/ *nf* **1** Littérat (lettres) letters (*pl*); **la ~ Gide-Paulhan** the Gide-Paulhan correspondence; **2** Postes (courrier) mail; (échange de courrier) correspondence (**entre** between); **réservation/renseignements par ~** reservation ou booking GB/information by mail; **être en ~** to correspond (**avec** with); **faire sa ~** to write one's letters; **avoir une longue ~** to have been corresponding for a long time; **être vendu par ~** to be available by mail order; **faire des études par ~** to do a correspondence course; **étudier qch par ~** to follow a correspondence course in sth; **3** Presse correspondence; **~ de Londres** correspondence from London; **4** (lien, ressemblance) correspondence (**entre** between); **~ entre les sons et les lettres** correspondence between sounds and letters; **5** Transp connection; **rater la ~** to miss the connection; **assurer la ~ entre** to provide a connection between; **autobus en ~ avec le train** bus service connecting with the train; **trains/vols en ~** connecting trains/flights; **voyageurs en ~ pour Sofia** (en train) passengers with a connecting train to Sofia; (en avion) passengers with a connecting flight to Sofia; **6** Math correspondence.

correspondancier, **-ière** /kɔʀɛspɔ̃dɑ̃sje, ɛʀ/ **I** **▶ 510** *nm,f* (employé) correspondence clerk.

II *nm* (classeur) correspondence folder.

correspondant, **~e** /kɔʀɛspɔ̃dɑ̃, ɑ̃t/ **I** *adj* [*avantage, chiffre, emploi, période, reçu*] corresponding; [*étiquette, boulon*] matching.

II *nm,f* **1** (épistolaire) gén correspondent; (dans le cadre d'un passe-temps) penfriend GB, pen pal; **2** Télécom **votre ~** the person you are calling; **3** (responsable) guardian; **4** Admin, Comm, Transp correspondent; **5** Presse correspondent; **~ permanent/de guerre/à l'étranger** permanent/war/foreign correspondent; (d'un institut) corresponding member.

correspondre /kɔʀɛspɔ̃dʀ/ [6] **I** **correspondre à** *vtr ind* **1** (être approprié à) **~ à** to match [*dimension, contenu, formation, programme*]; to suit [*style, goût*]; **~ aux besoins/désirs de qn** to meet sb's needs/wishes; **2** (équivaloir à) **~ à** to correspond to [*valeur, chiffre, travail*]; (coïncider avec) [*élément*] to correspond to; **~ à la description** to match the description; **ce qu'il m'en a dit ne correspond pas du tout à la réalité** what he told me about it bears no relation to reality; **3** (être lié à) **~ à** to correspond to [*événement, caractéristique*].

II *vi* **1** (écrire) to correspond (**avec** with);

2 Télécom (communiquer) to communicate; **~ par téléphone/télécopie** to communicate by phone/fax; **3** [*lieu*] **~ avec** to connect with.

III se correspondre *vpr* [*éléments*] to correspond.

Corrèze /kɔʀɛz/ **▶ 692** *nprf* (département) **la ~** Corrèze.

corrida /kɔʀida/ *nf* **1** lit bullfight; **2**○ fig **ça a été la ~ pour avoir le dernier métro** we had a mad rush to catch the last (underground) train; **c'est la ~ pour se garer à Oxford** it's a real performance parking in Oxford.

corridor /kɔʀidɔʀ/ *nm* **1** (dans un bâtiment) corridor, passage; **2** Géog, Pol corridor.

■ **~ aérien** Aviat air corridor; **le ~ de Dantzig** the Danzig Corridor; **~ de lancement** launching corridor.

corrigé /kɔʀiʒe/ *nm* Scol correct version; **recueil d'exercices avec ~s** collection of exercises with answers.

corriger /kɔʀiʒe/ [13] **I** *vtr* **1** (éliminer les erreurs) gén to correct [*texte*]; Édition to proofread [*manuscrit, texte*]; to read, to correct [*épreuves*]; **édition revue et corrigée** revised edition; **2** (redresser) to correct [*erreur, défaut, jugement, observation*]; to redress [*situation*]; to improve [*manières*]; to correct [*trajectoire, instrument*]; (adapter) to adjust [*position, chiffre*]; to modify [*théorie*]; **~ qn d'un défaut/vice** to cure ou rid sb of a fault/vice; **~ le tir** Mil to alter one's aim; fig to adjust ou modify one's tactics; **en données corrigées des variations saisonnières** taking account of seasonally adjusted figures; **3** Scol to mark GB, to grade US [*copie, examen*]; **4** (tempérer) to soften [*effet*]; to alleviate [*symptômes*]; to mitigate [*influence*]; to dampen [*espoirs*]; (neutraliser) to counter [*effet, influence*]; **~ la sévérité d'un vêtement par une note de couleur** to brighten up an otherwise severe outfit; **pour ~ les injustices/inégalités sociales** to remedy social injustice/inequality; **5** (châtier) gén to give [sb] a hiding○; (fesser) to give [sb] a spanking.

II se corriger *vpr* **1** (en parlant) to correct oneself; **2** (s'améliorer) to mend one's ways; **se ~ d'un défaut** to cure oneself of a fault.

corrigible /kɔʀiʒibl/ *adj* which can be corrected (*épith, après n*).

corroboration /kɔʀɔbɔʀasjɔ̃/ *nf* corroboration.

corroborer /kɔʀɔbɔʀe/ [1] *vtr* to corroborate.

corrodant, **~e** /kɔʀɔdɑ̃, ɑ̃t/ *adj* corrosive.

corroder /kɔʀɔde/ [1] *vtr* to corrode.

corrompre /kɔʀɔ̃pʀ/ [53] **I** *vtr* **1** (soudoyer) to bribe [*policier, juge*]; **2** (pervertir) to corrupt [*jeunesse, mœurs, goût*].

II se corrompre *vpr* [*mœurs, jeunesse*] to become corrupted.

corrompu, **~e** /kɔʀɔ̃py/ **I** *pp* ▶ **corrompre**.

II *pp adj* [*société, juge, gouvernement*] corrupt.

corrosif, **-ive** /kɔʀɔzif, iv/ **I** *adj* **1** (qui attaque) [*substance*] corrosive; **2** (mordant) [*esprit, humour*] caustic; [*remarque*] scathing, caustic.

II *nm* corrosive.

corrosion /kɔʀɔzjɔ̃/ *nf* (de métal) corrosion.

corroyer /kɔʀwaje/ [23] *vtr* to curry [*cuir*]; to weld [*métal*]; to trim [*bois*]; to compact [*talus*].

corrupteur, **-trice** /kɔʀyptœʀ, tʀis/ **I** *adj* [*pensée, influence*] corrupting.

II *nm,f* (qui soudoie) briber; (qui déprave) corrupter.

corruptible /kɔʀyptibl/ *adj* **1** (vénal) corruptible; **est-il ~?** can he be bought ou bribed?; **2** (moralement) **un individu facilement ~** a person who is easily corrupted ou led astray.

corruption /kɔʀypsjɔ̃/ *nf* **1** (avec de l'argent, des cadeaux) bribery (**de** of); **affaire de ~** bribery scandal; **la ~ d'un témoin est sévèrement punie** bribing a witness is a highly punishable offence[GB]; **2** (état) corruption (**de** in); **3** (perversion) corruption (**de** of).

corsage /kɔʀsaʒ/ *nm* **1** (chemisier) blouse; (de robe) bodice; **2** (poitrine) bosom.

corsaire /kɔʀsɛʀ/ **I** *adj* [*bateau, pavillon*] corsair (*épith*).

II *nm* **1** (personne) corsair; **2** (pantalon) pedal pushers (*pl*).

corse /kɔʀs/ **I** **▶ 692** *adj* [*fromage, accent*] Corsican.

II **▶ 462** *nm* Ling Corsican.

Corse /kɔʀs/ **I** *nmf* (habitant) Corsican.

II **▶ 416** *nprf* Corsica.

corsé, **~e** /kɔʀse/ *adj* **1** Culin [*café*] strong; [*vin*] full-bodied; [*sauce*] spicy; **2** (grivois) racy, spicy; **3**○ (difficile) [*problème*] tough; **4**○ (élevé) [*addition, facture*] steep; **c'était plutôt ~** it was a bit steep.

Corse-du-Sud /kɔʀsdysyd/ **▶ 692** *nprf* (département) **la ~** Corse-du-Sud.

corselet /kɔʀsəlɛ/ *nm* corselet.

corser /kɔʀse/ [1] **I** *vtr* **1** (compliquer) to make [sth] more difficult [*exercice, problème*]; **pour ~ l'affaire** (just) to complicate matters; **pour ~ le tout, il a plu toute la journée!** to cap it all○, it rained all day!; **2** (accentuer le goût) to strengthen the flavour[GB] of [*sauce*]; (avec des épices) to make [sth] spicier, to spice up [*sauce, plat*].

II se corser *vpr* (se compliquer) to get more complicated; **ça** or **l'affaire se corse** the plot thickens.

corset /kɔʀsɛ/ *nm* corset.

■ **~ orthopédique** orthopaedic ou surgical corset.

corseter /kɔʀsəte/ [18] *vtr* lit to corset; **l'économie, corsetée par ces mesures...** fig the economy, fettered by these measures...

corsetier, **-ière** /kɔʀsətje, ɛʀ/ **▶ 510** *nm,f* corset-maker.

corso /kɔʀso/ *nm* **~ fleuri** procession of floral floats.

cortège /kɔʀtɛʒ/ *nm* **1** (défilé) procession; **marcher en ~** to walk in procession; **se former en ~** to form a procession; **le ~ des grévistes** the procession of strikers; **suivi d'un ~ d'enfants/de chiens** followed by a troop of children/of dogs; **2** (série) liter **un ~ de souvenirs** a stream of memories; **un ~ de joies et de peines** a succession of joys and sorrows; **la guerre et son ~ de misères** war and its trail of misery.

■ **~ funèbre** (funeral) cortège; **~ nuptial** wedding procession.

cortex /kɔʀtɛks/ *nm* cortex.

cortical, **~e**, *mpl* **-aux** /kɔʀtikal, o/ *adj* cortical.

corticoïdes /kɔʀtikɔid/ *nmpl* corticoids.

corticosurrénal, **~e**, *mpl* **-aux** /kɔʀtikɔsyʀ(ʀ)enal, o/ *adj* of the adrenal cortex (*épith, après n*).

cortisone /kɔʀtizɔn/ *nf* cortisone; **soigner qn à la ~** to treat sb with cortisone.

corvéable /kɔʀveabl/ *adj* required to fulfil[GB] the corvée (*après n*); ▶ **taillable**.

corvée /kɔʀve/ *nf* **1** (activité pénible) chore; **les ~s ménagères** household chores; **aller les voir, quelle ~!** it's a real bore ou grind to have to go and see them; **2** (travail obligatoire) duty; Mil fatigue (duty); **tu es de ~ de patates**○ it's your turn to peel the potatoes; **être de ~ pour faire** to have been roped into doing; **on va être de ~ pour les aider à déménager** we're going to be roped in to helping them move (house); **c'est toujours moi qui suis de ~!** it's always me who has to do the chores!; **3** Hist corvée (*peasant's day of unpaid labour[GB] for feudal lord*).

corvette /kɔʀvɛt/ *nf* corvette.

coryphée /kɔʀife/ *nm* **1** Théât coryphaeus; **2** Danse coryphée.

coryza /kɔʀiza/ **▶ 271** *nm* head cold, coryza spéc.

COS *written abbr* ▶ **coefficient**.

cosaque /kɔzak/ *nm* Cossack.

coscénariste /kosenaʀist/ *nmf* co-writer.

cosécante /kɔsekɑ̃t/ *nf* cosecant.

cosignataire /kosiɲatɛʀ/ *nmf* cosignatory.

cosinus /kɔsinys/ *nm* cosine.

cosmétique /kɔsmetik/ **I** *adj* lit, fig cosmetic.

II *nm* cosmetic ou beauty product; **des ~s** cosmetics.

cosmétologie /kɔsmetɔlɔʒi/ *nf* cosmetology.

cosmétologue /kɔsmetɔlɔg/ **▶ 510** *nmf* cosmetician.

cosmique /kɔsmik/ *adj* lit, fig cosmic.

cosmodrome /kɔsmodʀom/ *nm* cosmodrome.

cosmogonie /kɔsmɔgɔni/ *nf* cosmogony.

cosmographie /kɔsmɔgʀafi/ *nf* cosmography.

cosmologie /kɔsmɔlɔʒi/ *nf* cosmology.

cosmologiste /kɔsmɔlɔʒist/ **▶ 510** *nmf* cosmologist.

cosmonaute /kɔsmɔnot/ **▶ 510** *nmf* cosmonaut.

cosmopolite /kɔsmɔpɔlit/ *adj* [*ville, expérience*] cosmopolitan.

cosmopolitisme /kɔsmɔpɔlitism/ *nm* cosmopolitanism.

cosmos /kɔsmos/ *nm* cosmos.

cossard○, **~e** /kɔsaʀ, aʀd/ **I** *adj* [*personne*] lazy, bone idle○.

II *nm,f* idler, loafer○, lazybones○ (+ *v sg*).

cosse /kɔs/ *nf* **1** Bot (de fève, pois) pod; (de graine) husk; **2** Électrotech terminal; **3**○ (paresse) laziness; **4** Naut eyelet.

■ **~ de batterie** battery clip ou clamp.

cossu, **~e** /kɔsy/ *adj* [*personne*] well-to-do, well-off; [*intérieur*] richly furnished, plush; [*existence*] comfortable; [*maison*] smart, posh○.

costal, **~e**, *mpl* **-aux** /kɔstal, o/ *adj* Anat, Zool costal.

costard○ /kɔstaʀ/ *nm* (costume) suit.

Costa Rica /kɔsta ʀika/ **▶ 321** *nprm* Costa Rica.

costaricain, **~e** /kɔstaʀikɛ̃, ɛn/ **▶ 537** *adj* Costa Rican.

Costaricain, **~e** /kɔstaʀikɛ̃, ɛn/ **▶ 537** *nm,f* Costa Rican.

costaud○ /kɔsto/ **I** *adj* **1** [*personne*] (fort) strong; (vigoureux) sturdy; **il est assez ~** (gros) euph he's pretty hefty○; **tu peux lui dire, elle est ~** (moralement) you can tell her, she's strong ou she can take it; **2** (solide, résistant) [*chaussures, bicyclette*] sturdy; [*matériau, assemblage*] strong; [*mur, maison*] sturdily built; (fort) [*alcool*] strong; [*aliment*] spicy, hot; **c'est du ~ ta machine!** that's a solid machine you have there!; **tâte mes biceps, c'est du ~!** feel my biceps, they're like iron!

II *nm* (homme) sturdily built man.

costume /kɔstym/ *nm* **1** (ensemble veste, pantalon) suit; **il portait un ~, il était en ~** he was wearing a suit; **il est toujours en ~ cravate** he always wears a suit and tie; **2** Théât, Cin, Danse costume; **~ de scène/d'époque** stage/period costume; **elle est apparue en ~ de Pierrot** she appeared in a Pierrot costume; **répéter en ~** to have a dress rehearsal; **3** Hist costume; **les ~s nationaux/régionaux** national/regional costume ou dress ¢.

■ **~ de bain**† swimming costume; **~ de cérémonie** ceremonial dress ¢; **~ marin** sailor suit; **~ trois pièces** three-piece suit.

IDIOMES **en ~ d'Adam/d'Ève** in his/her birthday suit○.

costumer: **se costumer** /kɔstyme/ [1] *vpr* to put on fancy dress; **soirée costumée** fancy-dress party, costume party US.

costumier, **-ière** /kɔstymje, ɛʀ/ ▶ 510 *nm,f* **1** (de troupe) wardrobe master/mistress; (indépendant) costumier; **2** (pour soirées déguisées) **aller chez un ~** to go to a fancy-dress shop GB ou costume store US.

cosy /kɔzi/ *nm*: *corner divan with attached shelves.*

cotangente /kɔtɑ̃ʒɑ̃t/ *nf* cotangent.

cotation /kɔtasjɔ̃/ *nf* Fin quotation; **~ en continu** quotation on the continuous market.

cote /kɔt/ *nf* **1** Fin (valeur en Bourse) quotation; (liste des valeurs) (stock exchange) list; **entrée** or **admission à la ~** stock exchange listing; **inscrit** or **admis à la ~** listed (on the stock exchange); **marché hors ~** curb market, over-the-counter market; **actions hors ~** unlisted shares; **2** Comm (de voiture d'occasion, timbre) quoted value; **3** Turf odds (*pl*); **la ~ est à dix contre un** the odds are ten to one; **4** (de personne, lieu, film) rating; **jouir d'une ~ élevée** to enjoy a high rating; **avoir la ~**○ **auprès de qn** [*célébrité*] to be popular with sb; [*individu*] to be well thought of by sb; **tu as la ~**○**!** you're in favour[GB]!; **ne plus avoir la ~**○ to have fallen from grace; **leur ~ est en baisse** their popularity is waning; **la chimie n'a pas la ~**○ chemistry is unpopular; **5** (sur un plan) dimension; **6** (sur une carte) spot height; **à la ~ plus/moins 20** 20 metres above/below sea level; **7** Mil **~ 451** hill 451; **8** (marque de classement) classification mark; (numéro de livre) pressmark GB, call number US.

■ **~ d'alerte** flood level; fig danger level; **~ d'amour** popularity rating; **~ de crédit** Fin credit rating; **~ foncière** land tax; **~ mal taillée** compromise; **~ mobilière** council tax GB, local rates (*pl*) US; **~ de popularité** = **~ d'amour**.

côte /kot/ **I** *nf* **1** Géog (littoral) coast; **la ~ adriatique** the Adriatic coast; **aller à la ~** [*navire*] to run aground; **2** Géog (pente) hill; **dans une ~** on a hill; **en haut d'une ~** at the top of a hill; **3** Anat rib; **vraie/fausse ~** true/false rib; **~ flottante** floating rib; **4** Culin chop; **~ de porc/d'agneau** pork/lamb chop; **~ première** loin chop; **~ de bœuf** rib of beef; **5** (en tricot) rib; **col à ~s** ribbed collar; **tricoter les ~s** to do the ribbing; **~s simples/doubles** single/double rib; **6** Bot rib.

II côte à côte *loc adv* side by side.

■ **Côte d'Azur** French riviera.

IDIOMES **on lui compte les ~s** he's/she's all skin and bone; **se tenir les ~s** to split one's sides with laughter; **avoir les ~s en long**○ to be bone idle.

coté, **~e** /kɔte/ **I** *pp* ▶ **coter**.

II *pp adj* (prestigieux) **être (très)/mal ~** [*personne, lieu, institution*] to be (very) well/not well thought of.

côté /kote/ **I** *nm* **1** Anat (flanc) side; **être blessé au ~** to be wounded in the side; **porter une arme au ~** to wear a weapon at one's side; **2** (partie latérale) side (**de** of); **être de l'autre ~ de** to be on the other side of; **lancer qch de l'autre ~ du mur** to throw sth over (the other side of) the wall; **sauter de l'autre ~ du mur** to jump over the wall; **de chaque ~ de** on each ou either side of; **du même ~** on the same side; **se garer sur le ~ de la route** to park at the side of the road; **du ~ droit/gauche** on the righthand/lefthand side; **sur** or **d'un seul ~** on one side only; **le ~ face/pile d'une pièce de monnaie** the face/reverse side of a coin; **le ~ nord/sud d'une maison** the north/south side of a house; **le ~ italien des Alpes** the Italian side of the Alps; **chambre ~ cour/rue** room overlooking the courtyard/the street; **~ cour, c'est très calme** the courtyard side is very quiet; **changer de ~** (au tennis) to change ends; **3** (direction) way, direction; **de quel ~ allez-vous?** which way are you going?; **ils sont arrivés des deux ~s** they came from both directions; **je ne vais pas de ce ~** I'm not going that way ou in that direction; **ils sont partis du mauvais ~** they went the wrong way; **4** (aspect) side; **prendre** or **voir les choses du bon ~** to look on the bright side of things; **le bon ~ des choses** the positive side of things; **par certains ~s** in some respects; **d'un ~** (d'une part) on the one hand; (en un sens) in one respect ou way; **d'un autre ~** (d'autre part) on the other hand; (dans un autre sens) in another respect ou way; **~ santé, ça va** healthwise ou on the health side, it's all right; **~ cœur, tout va mal** on the romance side, everything's going badly; **~ travail** as far as work is concerned; **5** (branche familiale) side (**de** of); **du ~ maternel** or **de la mère** on the mother's side; **du ~ de mon mari** on my husband's side; **6** (camp) side; **être du ~ de qn/qch** to be on sb's side/on the side of sth; **du ~ britannique/français** on the British/French side.

II à côté *loc adv* **1** (à proximité) **il habite à ~** he lives nearby ou close by; **tout à ~** very close; **les voisins d'à ~** the next-door neighbours[GB]; **passons (dans la pièce) à ~** let's go into the next room; **2** (en dehors) lit, fig **le ballon est passé à ~** the ball went wide; **répondre à ~** (par erreur) to miss the point; (volontairement) to sidestep the question; **je n'ai rien compris, je suis passée complètement à ~** I didn't understand anything, I missed the point entirely; **3** (en comparaison) by comparison; **4** (simultanément) **elle est étudiante et travaille à ~ (pour payer ses études)** she's a student and she works on the side (to pay for her studies).

III à côté de *loc prép* **1** (à proximité de) next to; **2** (en dehors de) **le ballon est passé à ~ du but** the ball went wide of the goal; **passer complètement à ~ de la question** (par erreur) to miss the point completely; (volontairement) to sidestep the issue; **ils sont passés à ~ de la réalité** they missed the truth; **3** (en comparaison de) compared to; **4** (en plus de) besides; **à ~ de ça**○ (par ailleurs) for all that.

IV de côté *loc adv* **1** (obliquement) **regarder qn de ~** to look sideways at sb, to give sb a sideways ou sidelong look; **faire un pas de ~** to step aside ou to one side; **sauter de ~** to jump aside ou to one side; **2** (sur la partie latérale) side (*épith*) ; **des places de ~** Théât side seats; **3** (en réserve) aside; **mettre de ~** to put [sth] aside ou on one side [*argent, livre, marchandise*]; **je n'ai rien de ~** I haven't got any money put aside; **je n'ai plus rien de ~** I have no money left, the money I had put aside has all gone; **4** (à l'écart) **mettre son travail de ~** to put one's work aside; **mettre sa fierté de ~** to swallow one's pride.

V du côté de *loc prép* **1** (vers) **aller du ~ de Dijon** to head for Dijon, to head Dijon way; **mes parents habitent du ~ de Beaune** my parents live not far from ou live near Beaune; **le bruit vient du ~ de chez eux** the noise is coming from their place; **2** (en ce qui concerne) as for; **le président, de son ~, a dit**... the President, for his part, said...; **il s'amuse, de ce ~-là, il n'y a rien à craindre** he's having fun, as far as that's concerned, there's nothing to worry about; **elle n'a pas été gâtée du ~ de sa famille**○ she hasn't been lucky with her family; **indique-t-on du ~ de la Commission européenne** people in the European Commission are saying; **je regarde beaucoup du ~ de la danse américaine** I take a strong interest in (what is happening in) American dance; **même sévérité du ~ de** same severity on the part of ou from; **des progrès ont été réalisés du ~ de Pretoria** progress has been made by the government in Pretoria; **il se tourne du ~ des dramaturges américains** he's turning toward(s) the American dramatists; **10 morts du ~ des manifestants** 10 dead among the demonstrators.

VI aux côtés de *loc prép* (près de) lit, fig **aux ~s de qn** [*être, rester*] beside sb, at sb's side; **aux ~s de qn/qch** [*se retrouver*] beside ou alongside sb/sth; [*siéger, s'engager, travailler*] alongside sb/sth.

VII de tous (les) côtés *loc adv* (partout) **regarder/courir de tous ~s** to look/to run all over the place; **une ville cernée de tous ~s** a town surrounded on all sides; **ils arrivent de tous ~s** they're coming from all directions.

■ **~ cour** Théât stage left; **~ jardin** Théât stage right.

IDIOMES **ne plus savoir de quel ~ se tourner** not to know which way to turn.

coteau, **~x** /kɔto/ *nm* **1** (pente) hillside; **à flanc de ~** on the hillside; **2** (colline) hill; **3** (vignoble) (sloping) vineyard.

Côte d'Ivoire /kotdivwaʀ/ ▶ 321 *nprf* Ivory Coast; **République de ~** Republic of the Ivory Coast, République de Côte d'Ivoire.

Côte-d'Or /kotdɔʀ/ ▶ 692 *nprf* (département) **la ~** Côte-d'Or.

côtelé, **~e** /kotle/ *adj* **velours ~** corduroy, cord.

côtelette /kotlɛt/ **I** *nf* Culin chop; **~ de mouton/veau** mutton/veal chop.

II côtelettes *nfpl* **1**○ Anat (côtes) ribs; **2**† (moustache) muttonchops.

coter /kɔte/ [1] *vtr* **1** Comm, Fin (fixer le prix de) to quote [*titre, devise*]; to price [*voiture*]; (admettre à la cotation) to list [*titre, voiture*]; **action cotée en Bourse** share listed on the stock market; **~ en hausse/en baisse à la clôture à 392** to close up/down at 392; **2** (valoir) **~ 100 francs** [*titre*] to be quoted at 100 francs; [*voiture, œuvre*] to be priced at 100 francs; **timbre coté cent francs** stamp priced at one hundred francs; **3** (aux courses) to be quoted at; **~ 6 contre 1** to be quoted at 6-1; **4** (numéroter) to give a pressmark GB ou call number US to [*livre*]; **5** Tech to dimension [*dessin industriel*]; to put spot heights on [*carte*].

coterie /kɔtʀi/ *nf* pej circle, clique péj; **~ littéraire/politique** literary/political circle ou clique.

Côtes-d'Armor /kotdaʀmɔʀ/ ▶ 692 *nprfpl* (département) **les ~** Côtes-d'Armor.

cothurne /kɔtyʀn/ *nm* **1** Antiq, Théât buskin, cothurnus; **2**○ students' slang (camarade de chambre) roommate.

côtier, **-ière** /kotje, ɛʀ/ *adj* [*ville, navigation, chemin*] coastal; [*pêche*] inshore.

cotillon /kɔtijɔ̃/ *nm* **1** cotillion; **des accessoires de ~** ou **pour le ~** party accessories; **2** Mode, Hist petticoat.

IDIOMES **courir le ~**† to chase petticoats†.

cotisant, **~e** /kɔtizɑ̃, ɑ̃t/ *nm,f* (à la sécurité sociale, à une caisse de retraite) contributor; (à une assurance, à une association) subscriber, paid-up member.

cotisation /kɔtizasjɔ̃/ *nf* **1** (à la sécurité sociale, à une caisse de retraite) contribution; **une hausse des ~s** a rise in contributions; **~ d'allocations familiales** contribution to a family allowance fund; **~ d'assurance-chômage** unemployment insurance premium ou contribution; **~s patronales/sociales** employer/social security contributions; **~ vieillesse** *contribution to a pension fund*; **2** (à une association) subscription; (à un syndicat) dues (+ *v pl*), subscription; **payer sa ~ syndicale** to pay one's union dues ou subscription; **la ~ est de 500 francs pour l'année** the subscription is 500 francs for the year.

cotiser /kɔtize/ [1] **I** *vi* **1** Prot Soc to pay one's contributions; **cette année, je n'ai pas cotisé** I haven't paid my contributions this year; **~ à une caisse de retraite** to pay one's superannuation contribution; **2** Entr, Pol (à une association) to pay one's subscription (**à** to), to subscribe (**à** to); (à un syndicat) to pay one's dues ou subscription (**à** to); **j'ai décidé de ne plus ~** I've decided to stop paying my subscription.

II se cotiser *vpr* to club together GB, to go in together; **nous nous sommes tous cotisés pour leur faire un cadeau** we all clubbed together GB ou went in together to give them a present.

coton /kɔtɔ̃/ *nm* **1** (plante, fibre) cotton; **drap de** or **en ~** cotton sheet; **2** (ouate) cotton wool GB, cotton US; (morceau d'ouate) piece of cotton wool GB ou cotton US; **avoir du ~ dans les oreilles** lit to have cotton wool in one's ears; fig○ to be cloth-eared; **un ~ imbibé d'eau** a cotton swab ou a piece of cotton wool GB soaked in water.
■ **~ à broder** Cout embroidery thread ou cotton; **~ démaquillant** make-up remover pad; **~ hydrophile** cotton wool GB, absorbent cotton US.
IDIOMES **filer un mauvais ~** (être en mauvaise santé) to be in a bad way; **élever un enfant dans du ~** to give a child a very sheltered upbringing; **elle est ~○, ta question** it's a tricky ou complicated question; **j'ai les jambes en ~** (après un choc) my legs have turned to jelly; (après une maladie) I am wobbly on my legs.

cotonnade /kɔtɔnad/ *nf* Tex cotton fabric; **jupe en ~** a skirt made of cotton fabric.

cotonneux, **-euse** /kɔtɔnø, øz/ *adj* [*brouillard*] like cotton-wool (*après n*); [*nuage*] fleecy, fluffy; [*ciel*] full of fleecy ou fluffy clouds (*après n*).

cotonnier, **-ière** /kɔtɔnje, ɛʀ/ **I** *adj* Tex [*industrie, production*] cotton.
II *nm* Bot cotton plant.

Coton-Tige®, *pl* **Cotons-Tiges** /kɔtɔ̃tiʒ/ *nm* cotton-bud GB, Q-tip®.

côtoyer /kotwaje/ [23] **I** *vtr* **1** (être près de) to be next to; (fréquenter) to move in [*milieu*]; to mix with, to rub shoulders with [*personnes*]; to be in close contact with [*mort, danger*]; **2** (longer) [*piéton*] to walk alongside [*rivière*]; [*route*] to run alongside [*rivière*].
II se côtoyer *vpr* [*personnes*] to mix; [*extrêmes*] to be side by side.

cotre /kɔtʀ/ *nm* Naut cutter.

cottage /kɔtaʒ, kɔtɛdʒ/ *nm* cottage.

cotte /kɔt/ *nf* **1** (vêtement de travail) overalls (*pl*), dungarees (*pl*); **2†** (tunique) tunic coat.
■ **~ d'armes** Hist surcoat; **~ de mailles** Hist coat of mail.

cotutelle /kotytɛl/ *nf* joint guardianship.

cotuteur, **-trice** /kotytœʀ, tʀis/ *nm,f* joint guardian.

cotylédon /kɔtiledɔ̃/ *nm* Bot cotyledon.

cou /ku/ **▶188**, **793** *nm* neck; **il s'est blessé au ~** he has hurt his neck; **j'ai mal au ~** my neck is aching; **avoir un ~ de taureau** to have a bull neck, to be bull-necked; **un animal au long ~** an animal with a long neck; **embrasser qn dans le ~** to kiss sb's neck; **porter un foulard autour du ~** to wear a scarf around one's neck; **avoir des ennuis** or **problèmes jusqu'au ~** fig to be up to one's neck in problems; **être endetté jusqu'au ~** fig to be up to one's eyes in debt.
IDIOMES **se casser** or **rompre le ~** to break one's neck; **se mettre/avoir la corde au ~○** to tie/to have tied the knot○.

couac○ /kwak/ *nm* Mus wrong note; fig jarring note; **faire un ~** Mus to play a wrong note; fig to strike a jarring note.

couard, **~e** /kwaʀ, aʀd/ fml **I** *adj* cowardly.
II *nm,f* coward; **c'est un ~** he's a coward.

couardise /kuaʀdiz/ fml *nf* cowardice; **par ~** out of cowardice.

couchage /kuʃaʒ/ *nm* (organisation) sleeping arrangements (*pl*); (lit) bed; (matériel pour dormir) bedding; **il va y avoir des problèmes de ~** there are going to be problems with the sleeping arrangements; **un studio avec ~ pour six** a studio that sleeps six.

couchant /kuʃɑ̃/ **I** *adj m* **soleil ~** setting sun; **au soleil ~** at sunset.
II *nm* **1** (coucher du soleil) sunset; **au ~** at sunset; **2** (ouest) liter west.

couche /kuʃ/ **I** *nf* **1** (de vernis, peinture, d'apprêt) coat; (d'aliments, de poussière, neige) layer; **passer la deuxième ~** to put on the second coat; **une ~ de crasse/graviers** a layer of filth/gravel; **une ~ d'huile** a film of oil; **2** (strate) stratum, layer; **les ~s atmosphériques** the layers ou strata of the atmosphere; **la ~ d'ozone** the ozone layer; **'préserve la ~ d'ozone'** 'ozone-friendly'; **une ~ argileuse/calcaire** a stratum ou layer of clay/lime; **3** Sociol sector; **les ~s défavorisées/laborieuses** the underprivileged/working classes ou sectors; **toutes les ~s socioprofessionnelles** all the social and occupational sectors; **4** (pour bébés) nappy GB, diaper US; **~ jetable** disposable nappy GB ou diaper US; **5** (lit) liter bed; **partager la ~ de qn** to share sb's bed; **▶ faux**.
II couches† *nfpl* (accouchement) childbirth; **être en ~s** to be giving birth.
IDIOMES **en tenir une (sacrée) ~◑** to be really thick○.

couché, **~e** /kuʃe/ **I** *pp* **▶ coucher**.
II *pp adj* **1** (penché) [*blés, herbes*] flattened; [*écriture*] sloping; **2** (à un chien) **~!** (lie) down!

couche-culotte, *pl* **couches-culottes** /kuʃkylɔt/ *nf* disposable nappy GB ou diaper US.

coucher /kuʃe/ [1] **I** *nm* bedtime; **à l'heure du ~** at bedtime; **le ~ du roi** the King's going-to-bed ceremony.
II *vtr* **1** (allonger) to put [sb] to bed [*malade, enfant*]; to lay out [*blessé, mort*]; **2** (mettre à l'horizontale) to lay [sth] on its side [*armoire, étagère*]; to lay [sth] down [*échelle, planche etc*]; **3** (faire pencher) [*vent, pluie*] to flatten [*blés, herbes*]; **4** (écrire) liter **~ par écrit** to put [sth] down in writing [*idées, phrases*]; **~ qn sur son testament** to name ou mention sb in one's will; **~ une clause dans un contrat/traité** to insert a clause into a contract/treaty.
III *vi* **1** (dormir) to sleep; **~ dans un lit/par terre** to sleep in a bed/on the floor; **~ dans des draps/un sac de couchage** to sleep in sheets/a sleeping bag; **~ avec qn** (partager le lit de) to sleep with sb; **2** (passer la nuit) **~ chez soi/qn** to sleep at home/sb's (house); **j'ai couché chez Eric** I slept at Eric's; **~ à l'hôtel** to sleep at a hotel; **~ sous la tente** to sleep in a tent; **~ sous les ponts** fig to sleep rough GB ou outdoors; **3○** (avoir des relations sexuelles) **~ avec qn** to sleep with sb; **ils couchent ensemble** they're sleeping together; **elle ne couche pas** she doesn't want to have sex.
IV se coucher *vpr* **1** (s'allonger) [*personne, animal*] to lie (down); **je vais me ~ un moment** I'm going to lie down for a while ; **le chien était couché à mes pieds** the dog was lying at my feet; **se ~ sur/dans son lit** to lie (down) on/in one's bed; **couchez-vous sur le divan** lie on the couch; **les vaches sont couchées dans la paille** the cows are lying in the straw; **se ~ sur le dos/côté** to lie on one's back/side; **se ~ sur le ventre** to lie flat on one's stomach; **je dois rester couchée** I have to stay in bed; **2** (aller dormir) [*personne*] to go to bed; **se ~ tôt/tard** to go to bed early/late; **je me suis couchée à 9 heures** I went to bed at nine; **il est retourné se ~** he went back to bed; **les enfants sont couchés** the children are in bed; **va te ~** lit go to bed!; (laisse-moi tranquille)○ clear off○!, get lost○!; **3** (se pencher) [*tige, blés*] to bend; [*voilier*] to list; (chavirer) to keel over; **se ~ sur** [*motard, cycliste*] to lean forward over [*guidon*]; **se ~ sur le côté** [*personne, motocycliste*] to lean (over) to one side, to lean out; **4** (disparaître à l'horizon) [*soleil*] to set, to go down; **le soleil se couche à 20 heures** the sun sets at 8 pm; **le soleil se couche sur la mer/derrière les montagnes** the sun sets over the sea/behind the mountains.
■ **~ de soleil** sunset; **au ~ du soleil** at sunset.

coucherie◑ /kuʃʀi/ *nf* pej casual sexual encounter.

couche-tard○ /kuʃtaʀ/ *nmf inv* night-owl○.

couche-tôt○ /kuʃto/ *nmf inv*: *person who goes to bed early*.

couchette /kuʃɛt/ *nf* (de train) couchette, berth; (de bateau) berth; **nous avons voyagé en ~** we took couchettes; **un train à ~s** a sleeper GB, a Pullman (car) US.

coucheur /kuʃœʀ/ *nm* **mauvais ~** awkward customer.

couci-couça○ /kusikusa/ *adv* so-so○.

coucou /kuku/ **I** *nm* **1** Zool cuckoo; **2** Bot cowslip; **3○** (avion) (old) crate○; **4** (horloge) cuckoo clock.
II○ *excl* (bonjour) cooee!; (en se cachant) peek-aboo!

coude /kud/ **▶188** *nm* **1** Anat elbow; **~s au corps** with elbows tucked in; **donner un coup de ~ à qn** (pour attirer l'attention) to nudge sb, give sb a nudge; (en se battant) to jab sb with one's elbow; **jouer des ~s pour atteindre le buffet** to elbow one's way to the buffet; **2** Cout (partie de manche) elbow; (pièce) elbow patch; **3** (de chemin, tuyau) bend; (de fleuve) bend, elbow; **la route fait un ~** there's a bend in the road; **le tuyau du lave-linge fait un ~** there's a kink in the washing machine waste pipe.
■ **~ à ~** solidarity; **travailler ~ à ~** to work shoulder to shoulder; **être au ~ à ~** to be neck and neck.
IDIOMES **se serrer** or **se tenir les ~s** to stick together; **lever le ~○** to drink a bit; **garder qch sous le ~** to put sth on the back burner.

coudé, **~e** /kude/ **I** *adj* bent at an angle.
II coudée *nf* (mesure) cubit.
IDIOMES **avoir les** or **ses ~es franches** to have elbow room; **être à cent ~es au-dessus de qn** to stand head and shoulders above sb.

cou-de-pied, *pl* **cous-de-pied** /kudpje/ *nm* (dessus du pied) instep; (articulation) ankle joint.

couder /kude/ [1] *vtr* to bend.

coudoiement /kudwamɑ̃/ *nm* close contact.

coudoyer /kudwaje/ [23] *vtr* to come into contact with, to mix with [*personnes*].

coudre /kudʀ/ [76] **I** *vtr* (en couture) to sew [*ourlet*]; (en reliure) to stitch; to sew [sth] on [*bouton, pièce*]; to stitch [sth] on [*semelle*]; to stitch (up) [*robe, plaie*]; **~ un ourlet à la main/à la machine** to sew a hem by hand/by machine; **~ des morceaux de tissu ensemble** to sew pieces of material together; **~ un bouton/une pièce à** or **sur qch** to sew a button/a patch on sth; **~ qch dans l'ourlet** to sew sth inside the hem.
II *vi* to sew; **elle sait très bien ~** she's very good at sewing.
IDIOMES **leur histoire est cousue de fil blanc** you can see through their story; **être cousu d'or†** to be rolling in money; **c'est du cousu main○** that's an expert job.

coudrier /kudʀije/ *nm* hazel (tree); **baguette de ~** divining rod.

Coué /kwe/ *npr* **méthode ~** autosuggestion, Couéism; **employer la méthode ~** to use autosuggestion.

couenne /kwan/ *nf* **1** Culin pork rind; **2◑** (imbécile) jerk◑, fool; **3◑** (peau) skin.

couette /kwɛt/ *nf* **1** (couverture) duvet, continental quilt GB, comforter US; **2** (coiffure) **~s** bunches GB, pigtails US ; **se faire des ~s** to put one's hair (up) in pigtails.

couffin /kufɛ̃/ *nm* (berceau) Moses basket GB, bassinet US; (panier) basket.

couguar /kugaʀ/, **cougouar** /kugwaʀ/ *nm* cougar.

couic /kwik/ *nm* (*also onomat*) squeak.

couille● /kuj/ *nf* **1** (testicule) ball◑, testicle; **avoir/ne pas avoir de ~s** fig to have/to have no balls◑; **2** (problème) cock-up◑ GB, fuck-up●.

■ **~ molle** wimp○.

IDIOMES **partir en ~** to be a complete balls-up◑ GB ou ball-up◑ US.

couillon◑, -onne /kujɔ̃, ɔn/ **I** *adj* bloody stupid◑ GB, fucking stupid●.

II *nm,f* bloody idiot◑ GB, dumb fuck●; **faire le ~** to piss about◑, to fuck around●.

couillonnade◑ /kujɔnad/ *nf* **1** (sottise) **faire des ~s** to piss around◑, to fuck around●; **dire des ~s** to talk crap◑; **2** (tromperie) **c'est de la ~** it's a con○.

couillonner◑ /kujɔne/ [1] *vtr* to con○; **se faire ~** to be conned○.

couinement /kwinmɑ̃/ *nm* (de souris, chaton, jouet) squeak; (de lapin, porc, freins) squeal; (de porte, ressort) creak; (de chien, d'enfant) whine; **pousser un ~** [*souris, chaton*] to squeak; [*lapin, porc*] to squeal; [*chien, enfant*] to whine.

couiner /kwine/ [1] *vi* [*souris, chaton, jouet*] to squeak; [*lapin, porc, freins*] to squeal; [*ressort, porte*] to creak; [*chien, enfant*] to whine.

coulant, ~e /kulɑ̃, ɑ̃t/ **I** *adj* [*camembert*] runny; [*personne*] easy-going; [*style*] flowing.

II *nm* **1** (anneau) belt loop; **2** Bot runner.

coulé, ~e /kule/ **I** *pp* ▶ **couler.**

II *pp adj* **1** (souple) [*mouvement*] fluid, flowing; [*graphisme, écriture*] flowing; [*style*] flowing, fluid; **2** Naut [*navire*] sunken; **touché, ~!** hit and sunk!

III *nm* Mus slide.

IV coulée *nf* **1** (en métallurgie) casting; **2** (d'une substance) **~e de boue/neige** mudslide/snowslide; **~e de lave** lava flow; **~e de peinture** drip of paint; **3** Sport (en natation) glide.

■ **~e arctique** or **polaire** Météo polar flow ou airstream.

coulemelle /kulmɛl/ *nf* Bot common parasol.

couler /kule/ [1] **I** *vtr* **1** (verser) to cast [*métal, verre*]; to pour [*béton*]; **~ une dalle de béton** to make a concrete slab; **2** (fabriquer) to cast [*buste, cloche*]; **~ un bronze** lit to cast a bronze; (déféquer)◑ to have a crap○; **3** (faire sombrer) lit to sink [*navire*]; fig○ to put [sth] out of business [*entreprise, commerce*]; **le supermarché a coulé l'épicerie du quartier** the supermarket has put the corner shop out of business; **4**○ (faire échouer) [*matière, épreuve*] to make [sb] fail [*élève, étudiant*]; **ce sont les maths qui l'ont coulé** it was his maths mark GB ou math grade US that brought him down; **les scandales l'ont coulé** the scandals ruined him○; **5** (glisser discrètement) liter **~ qch dans qch** to slip sth into sth; **il a coulé une lettre dans ma poche** he slipped a letter into my pocket; **~ un regard vers qch/qn** to steal a glance at sth/sb.

II *vi* **1** (se mouvoir) [*eau, ruisseau, boue, larmes, sang*] to flow; [*sève, peinture, colle, maquillage*] to run; **la Saône coule à Lyon** the Saône flows through Lyons; **ton rimmel® a coulé** your mascara has run; **le sang/la sueur coulait sur mon front** blood/sweat was running down my forehead; **~ de** to run ou flow from [*robinet, fontaine, réservoir*]; to run ou flow out of [*plaie*]; **faire ~ qch** to run [*eau*]; to pour [*vin, mazout*]; **faire ~ un bain** to run a bath; **fais-toi couler un bain** run yourself a bath; **2** (se fluidifier) [*fromage*] to go runny; **3** (glisser) [*neige*] to slide; **faire ~ du sable entre ses doigts** to let some sand run through one's fingers; **allez bois, ça coule tout seul!** come on drink it, it just slips down; **4** (fuir) [*robinet, tube, stylo*] to leak; [*nez*] to run; **j'ai le nez qui coule** my nose is running, I've got a runny nose; **5** (sombrer) [*bateau, personne*] to sink; **je coule!** I'm drowning!; **faire ~ un bateau** to sink a boat; **6** (passer paisiblement) liter [*vie, temps*] to slip by; **7** Bot [*fleur, fruit*] to drop; **8**○ (faire faillite) [*entreprise, projet*] to go under, to sink; **faire ~ une société** [*personne, concurrence*] to put a company out of business; **9** (être bien formulé) [*phrases, vers, paroles*] to flow.

III se couler *vpr* (se glisser) **se ~ dans** to slip into [*foule, ouverture*]; to slip between [*draps*]; **se ~ entre** to slip between [*piquets, obstacles, gens*].

IDIOMES **~ des jours heureux** to lead a happy life.

couleur /kulœʀ/ ▶ **193** **I** *nf* **1** gén colour[GB]; **~ primaire/secondaire** primary/secondary colour[GB]; **(de) quelle ~ est ta voiture?** what colour[GB] is your car?; **les feuilles ont pris de belles ~s** the leaves on the trees have turned golden; **sans ~** colourless[GB]; **une veste de ~ verte/marron** a green/brown jacket; **des rideaux de ~ claire/sombre/vive** light-/dark-/brightly-coloured[GB] curtains; **un sac ~ sable/abricot** a sand-/an apricot-coloured[GB] bag; **le linge de ~** coloureds[GB] (*pl*); **avoir la ~ de qch** to be the colour[GB] of sth; **faire prendre ~** Culin to brown; **plein de ~** fig [*récit, description*] vivid, colourful[GB]; **sans ~** dull; **2** Cin, Phot, TV **la ~** colour[GB]; **une télévision ~** a colour[GB] television; **filmer en ~(s)** to film in colour[GB]; **film en ~ (s)** film in colour[GB]; **photo en ~** colour[GB] photograph; **3** (substance colorante) colour[GB], paint; **une boîte de ~s** a paintbox; **un tube de ~** a tube of paint; **4** (coloration des joues) colour[GB]; **changer de ~** to change colour[GB]; **avoir de jolies ~s** to have a good colour[GB]; **tu as pris des ~s!** you've got some colour[GB] in your cheeks!; **ça te redonnera des ~s** it will put some colour[GB] back in your cheeks; **une personne de ~** a coloured[GB] person; **5** Jeux (aux cartes) suit; **quelle est la ~ demandée?** what is the suit?; **fournir à** or **jouer dans la ~** to follow suit; **6** Cosmét haircolour[GB]; **se faire faire une ~** to get one's hair coloured[GB]; **7** (tendance politique) **~ politique** political colour[GB]; **il affiche clairement sa ~** he 's showing his colours[GB] clearly; **8** (aspect) light; **donner une nouvelle ~ à qch** to shed a different light on sth; **sous des ~s trompeuses** in a false light.

II couleurs *nfpl* **1** (drapeau) colours[GB]; **amener/hisser** or **envoyer les ~s** to lower/to hoist the colours[GB]; **2** (marque) colours[GB]; **une écharpe aux ~s de la ville/du club** a scarf in the town's/club's colours[GB]; **un avion aux ~s d'Air France** an aircraft with the Air France livery; **3** (vêtements de couleur) coloureds[GB]; **faire une lessive de ~s** to wash coloureds[GB] ou colour[GB] fabrics.

■ **~ locale** local colour[GB]; **pour faire plus ~ locale** to add some local colour[GB]; **le décor faisait très ~ locale** the decor was full of local colour[GB].

IDIOMES **ne pas voir la ~ de qch**○ never to get a sniff of sth○; **l'héritage? elle n'en a jamais vu la ~** the inheritance? she never got a sniff of it; **avec lui, j'en ai vu de toutes les ~s**○ he really gave me a hard time, he put me through the mill○; **ils leur en ont fait voir de toutes les ~s**○ they really gave them a hard time, they really put them through the mill○; **passer par toutes les ~s (de l'arc-en-ciel)** to change colour[GB]; **sous ~ de faire** under the pretence[GB] ou guise of doing. ▶ **goût**.

couleuvre /kulœvʀ/ *nf* grass snake.

■ **~ à collier** grass snake; **~ vipérine** viperine grass snake.

IDIOMES **être paresseux comme une ~** to be bone idle GB, to be a lazybones○; **avaler des ~s**○ (être humilié) to endure humiliation; (être trompé) to believe anything one is told; **faire avaler des ~s à qn**○ (humilier) to ride roughshod over sb; (tromper) to put one over on sb○.

coulis /kuli/ *nm inv* Culin coulis.

coulissant, ~e /kulisɑ̃, ɑ̃t/ *adj* sliding (*épith*).

coulisse /kulis/ *nf* **1** Théât **les ~s, la ~** (côtés) the wings; (loges) the dressing rooms; **en ~, dans les ~s, dans la ~** (arrière-scène, loges etc) backstage; (côtés) in the wings; fig behind the scenes; **dans les ~s de la politique** behind the political scenes; **2** (rainure) runner; (porte coulissante) sliding door; (cloison coulissante) sliding partition; **à ~** [*porte, cloison*] sliding; **regard en ~** sidelong glance; **3** (ourlet) casing; (cordon) drawstring.

■ **~ à baleine** whalebone casing.

coulissé, ~e /kulise/ **I** *pp* ▶ **coulisser**.

II *pp adj* **points ~s** running stitches; **short ~** or **à la taille ~e** shorts with a drawstring waist.

coulisser /kulise/ [1] *vi* (dans une rainure) to slide; **la porte coulisse mal** the door isn't sliding properly; **faire ~ qch** (pour ouvrir, fermer) to slide sth open/shut.

couloir /kulwaʀ/ *nm* **1** (de bâtiment) corridor GB, hallway US; (de train) corridor; (de station de métro) passage; **conversations de ~s** backstairs gossip; **bruits de ~s** rumours[GB]; **2** Transp **~ (de circulation** or **réservé)** bus (and taxi) lane; **~ de bus** bus lane; **3** (sur stade, en piscine) lane; (sur court) tramlines (*pl*) GB, alley US; **4** Géog corridor.

■ **~ aérien** air (traffic) lane.

coulommiers /kulɔmje/ *nm inv* Coulommiers (*cow's milk cheese*).

coulpe /kulp/ *nf* **battre sa ~** to go around in sackcloth and ashes.

coulure /kulyʀ/ *nf* (de peinture) drip.

country /kuntʀi/ **I** *adj inv* [*musique, style*] country.

II *nm* ou *f* country (music).

coup /ku/ *nm*

■ Note Les expressions comme *coup de barre, coup de maître, coup de téléphone etc* seront normalement dans le dictionnaire sous le deuxième élément donc respectivement sous **barre**, **maître**, **téléphone** etc.

1 (choc physique) (neutre) knock; (brutal) blow, whack○; (dur, par accident) bang; (qui entaille) stroke; (d'un mouvement tranchant) chop; (du plat de la main) smack; (sec et rapide) rap; (léger et direct) tap; (léger et fouettant) flick; (de la pointe) poke, prod, jab; **~ sur la tête** knock ou blow ou bang on the head; **~ à la porte** knock at the door; **~ de marteau** hammer blow; **d'un ~ de hache** [*couper, tuer*] with a single blow from an axe GB ou ax US; **à ~s de hache/machette** [*couper, tuer*] with an axe GB ou ax US/a machete; **frapper qn à ~s de gourdin** to club sb, to beat sb with a club; **assommer qn à ~s de gourdin** to knock sb senseless with a club; **tuer qn à ~s de gourdin** to club sb to death; **casser qch à ~s de gourdin** to take a club to sth; **casser la porte à (grands) ~s de marteau** to break down the door with a hammer; **à ~s de dollars** by forking out dollars; **à ~s de subventions** by means of subsidies; **fièvre combattue à ~s d'antibiotiques** fever controlled with antibiotics; **disperser des manifestants à ~s de gaz lacrymogène** to disperse demonstrators by using ou with teargas; **sous le ~ d'un embargo** under an embargo; **céder sous les ~s de l'ennemi** to cave in under enemy pressure; **donner** or **porter un ~ à qn/qch** gén to hit sb/sth; **donner un ~ de qch à qn** gén to hit ou strike sb with sth; **donner un ~ de poing/pied/coude/dent/couteau à qn** to punch/kick/nudge/bite/stab sb; **recevoir un ~** [*personne*] to get hit; **recevoir un ~ de qch** gén to get hit with sth; **recevoir un ~ de poing/pied/coude/couteau** to be punched/kicked/nudged/stabbed; **prendre un ~** [*personne, appareil, voiture*] to get a knock; **en avoir pris un ~**○ (être très abîmé) to have taken (quite) a punishing; **rendre un ~** to hit back; **rendre ~ pour ~** lit to fight back;

Les couleurs

Attention: certains noms et adjectifs de couleur français ont plusieurs traductions possibles. Par ex., brun *peut être* brown, dark, black *etc. Consulter les articles dans le dictionnaire.*

La couleur des choses

Dans les expressions suivantes, vert *est pris comme exemple; les autres adjectifs et noms de couleurs s'utilisent de la même façon.*

Les adjectifs

de quelle couleur est-il? = what colour is it?
il est vert = it's green
une robe verte = a green dress

Les noms

En anglais, les noms de couleurs n'ont en général pas d'article défini.

j'aime le vert = I like green
je préfère le vert = I prefer green
le vert me va bien = green suits me
porter du vert = to wear green
une gamme de verts = a range of greens
le même vert = the same green
en vert = in green
je t'aime bien en vert = I like you in green
s'habiller en vert = to dress in green
habillé de vert = dressed in green
avez-vous le même modèle en vert? = have you got the same thing in green?

Avec les verbes to paint *(peindre) et* to dye *(teindre), le en français n'est pas traduit:*

peindre la porte en vert = to paint the door green
teindre un chemisier en vert = to dye a blouse green

Les nuances

très vert = very green
vert foncé = dark green
vert clair = light green
vert vif = bright green
vert pâle = pale green
vert pastel = pastel green
vert profond = deep green
vert soutenu = strong green
un chapeau vert foncé = a dark green hat
une robe vert clair = a light green dress
un vert plus foncé = a darker green
la robe était d'un vert plus foncé = the dress was a darker green
un joli vert = a pretty green
un vert affreux = a dreadful green
sa robe est d'un joli vert = her dress is a pretty green

Noter l'absence d'équivalent du de *français.*

En anglais comme en français, on peut exprimer une nuance en utilisant le nom d'une chose dont la couleur est typique. Noter que l'adjectif prend un trait d'union (sky-blue), *mais pas le nom* (sky blue).

bleu ciel = sky blue
une robe bleu ciel = a sky-blue dress
vert tilleul = sage green
vert pomme = apple green
une veste vert pomme = an apple-green jacket

De même, navy-blue *(bleu marine),* midnight-blue *(bleu nuit),* blood-red *(rouge sang) etc. En cas de doute, consulter le dictionnaire. En ajoutant* -coloured *(GB) ou* -colored *(US) à un nom, on obtient un adjectif composé qui correspond au français avec* couleur.

une robe couleur framboise = a raspberry-coloured dress (*GB*)
= a raspberry-colored dress (*US*)
des collants couleur chair = flesh-coloured tights (*GB*)
un papier peint couleur crème = cream-coloured wallpaper (*GB*)

Noter enfin:

bleu-noir = blue-black
verdâtre = greenish
un jaune verdâtre = a greenish yellow

Attention: ces adjectifs n'existent pas pour toutes les couleurs. En cas de doute, consulter le dictionnaire. On peut toujours utiliser shade, *comme on utilise* ton *ou* nuance *en français.*

un joli ton de vert = a pretty shade of green

Les gens (▶ 188)

L'anglais n'utilise pas d'article défini dans les expressions suivantes:

avoir les cheveux blonds = to have fair hair
avoir les yeux bleus = to have blue eyes

Noter les adjectifs composés anglais:

un blond = a fair-haired man
une brune = a dark-haired woman
un enfant aux yeux bleus = a blue-eyed child

Mais on peut aussi dire: a man with fair hair, a child with blue eyes *etc.*

La couleur des cheveux

Les adjectifs des deux langues ne sont pas exactement équivalents, mais les correspondances suivantes sont utiles. Noter que hair *est toujours au singulier.*

les cheveux noirs = black hair
les cheveux bruns = dark hair
les cheveux châtains = brown hair
les cheveux blonds = fair hair (*ou* blond(e): *voir le mot français* blond *dans le dictionnaire*)
les cheveux roux = red hair
les cheveux gris = grey (*GB*) *ou* gray (*US*) hair
les cheveux blancs = white hair

La couleur des yeux

les yeux bleus = blue eyes
les yeux bleu clair = light blue eyes
les yeux gris = grey (*GB*) *ou* gray (*US*) eyes
les yeux verts = green eyes
les yeux gris-vert = greyish green (*GB*) *ou* grayish green (*US*) eyes (grey-green *et* gray-green *sont aussi possibles*)
les yeux marron = brown eyes
les yeux marron clair = light brown eyes
les yeux noisette = hazel eyes
les yeux clairs = light-coloured (*GB*) *ou* light-colored (*US*) eyes
les yeux noirs = dark eyes

fig to give tit for tat; **en venir aux ~s** to come to blows (**pour** over); **frapper trois ~s à la porte** to knock on the door three times, to give three knocks on the door; **les trois ~s** Théât *three knocks signalling*[GB] *that the curtain is about to rise*; **2** (choc moral) gén blow; (plus modéré) knock; **porter un ~ (sévère) à** to deal [sb/sth] a (severe) blow [*personne, organisation, théorie*]; **être un ~ terrible** to be a terrible ou real blow (**pour** to); **sa fierté en a pris un ~** it was a blow to his/her pride; **ce fut un ~ dur pour eux/pour l'économie** it was a great blow for ou to them/for ou to the economy; **porter un ~ très dur à qn** to deal sb a major blow; **en cas de ~ dur** (accident) should anything really bad happen; (difficulté) if things get rough; **ça m'a donné un (sacré) ~**○ it gave me an awful shock; **sous le ~ de la colère** in (a fit of) anger; **sous le ~ de la fatigue/peur** out of tiredness/fear; **être sous le ~ d'une forte émotion** to be in a highly emotional state; **tomber sous le ~ d'une condamnation** to be liable to conviction; **être sous le ~ d'une condamnation** to have a conviction; **être sous le ~ d'une procédure d'extradition** to be facing extradition proceedings; ▶**mauvais**; **3** (bruit) gén knock; (retentissant) bang; (sourd) thump, thud; **j'ai entendu un ~ à la porte** I heard a knock at the door; **au douzième ~ de minuit** on the last stroke of midnight; **sur le ~ de dix heures**○ around ten; **~ de gong** stroke of a gong; **~ de sifflet** whistle blast; **donner un ~ de gong** to strike the gong; **donner un ~ de sifflet** to blow one's whistle; **4** (mouvement rapide) **~ de brosse/peigne** brush/comb; **se donner un (petit) ~ de brosse/peigne** to give one's hair a (quick) brush/comb GB, to brush/comb one's hair (quickly); **donner un (petit) ~ d'aspirateur à une pièce** to give a room a (quick) hoover® GB, to vacuum a room (quickly); **donner un ~ sur la table** to dust the table; **les volets ont besoin d'un ~ de peinture** the shutters need a lick of paint; **d'un ~ d'aile** with a flap of its wings; **5** Jeux, Sport (au tennis, golf, cricket) gén stroke; (dont on juge) shot; (aux échecs, dames) move; (aux dés) throw; (à la boxe) blow, punch; (au karaté) (du poing) punch; (du tranchant) chop; (du pied) kick; **tous les ~s sont permis** lit, fig no holds barred; **~ défendu** Jeux, Sport foul; **6** (d'arme à feu) (décharge , détonation) shot; (munition) round; **chasser qn à ~s de fusil** to scare sb off with gunshots; **blesser qn d'un ~ de fusil** or **pistolet** to shoot and wound sb; **tuer qn d'un ~ de fusil** or **pistolet** to shoot sb dead; **7**○ (action organisée) (opération illégale) job○, racket○; (vilain tour) trick○; (manœuvre) move; **monter un ~** to plan a job○, to set up a racket○; **c'est encore un ~ des enfants!** the children have been up to their tricks again!; **c'était un beau ~ de vendre tes actions** it was a good ou shrewd move to sell your shares; **monter un ~ contre qn** gén to set sb up; (en vue d'une fausse accusation) to frame sb; **c'est un ~ monté!** it's a set-up○!; **monter le ~ à qn** to pull a fast one on sb○; **expliquer le ~ à qn** to put sb in the picture; **mettre qn dans le ~** to bring sb in on the job○, to cut sb in on the racket○ ou deal; **ils m'ont mis sur** or **dans le ~** they've let me in on it ou on the racket○ ou on the deal○; **se mettre dans le ~** to get in on the action○; **mettre qn sur un ~** to put sb in on a job○, to put sb onto a racket○; **être sur un gros ~** to be onto something big○; **préparer un sale** or **mauvais ~** to be up to mischief; **manquer** or **rater**○ or **foirer**◑ **son ~** to blow it○, not to pull it off; **il a raté son ~**○ he blew it○; **réussir son ~** to pull it off; **être dans le ~** (impliqué) to be in on it ou on the racket○ ou on the deal○; (au courant) to be up to date, to know what's going on, to know what's what○; **tu n'es plus dans le ~!** fig you're behind the times!; **être/rester hors du ~** (non impliqué) to have/to keep one's nose clean○; **être sur le ~** (opération d'envergure) to be in on it ou on the job○; **qui a fait le ~?** gén who did it?; (opération minutieuse) whose work is it, who did the job?; **elle m'a fait le ~ de la veuve éplorée** she did the weeping widow act with me; **ce n'est pas la première fois qu'il me fait le ~** it's not the first time he's done that to me; **8** (fois, moment) **essayer un ~/encore un ~** to have a shot/another shot; **du premier ~** (immédiatement) straight off; (à la première tentative) at the first attempt; **au deuxième/troisième ~** at the second/third attempt; **(encore) un ~ pour rien** no go again○; **à chaque ~, à tout ~, à tous les ~s** every time; **ce ~-ci/-là** this/that time; **du ~**○ as a result; **du même ~**○ by the same token; **pour le ~**○ this time; **après ~** afterwards, in restropect; **au ~ par ~** as things come; **~ sur ~** in succession; **tout d'un ~, tout à ~** suddenly, all of a sudden; **d'un ~, d'un seul ~** just like that; **d'un seul ~ d'un seul**○ in one fell swoop; **en un seul ~** in one go○; **sur le ~** (à ce moment-là) at the time; [*mourir, tuer*] instantly, on the spot; **rigoler un bon ~** to have a good laugh; **pleure un bon ~** have a good cry; **mouche-toi un bon ~** give your nose a good blow; **respire un grand ~** take a deep breath; **boire à petits ~s** to sip; **boire à grands ~s** to swig; **9**○ (boisson) drink; **viens, je te paye un ~ (à boire)** come on, I'll buy you a drink; **un ~ de rouge/blanc** a glass of red/white wine; **donne-moi encore un petit ~ de gin** give me another shot○ of gin; **10**● (partenaire sexuel) **un bon** or **beau ~** a good fuck● ou lay●.

■ **~ bas** (en boxe) blow ou punch below the belt; fig blow below the belt; **c'était un ~ bas** fig that was below the belt; **~s et blessures** Jur assault and battery; **~s et blessures volontaires** malicious wounding ¢; **~ droit** (au tennis) (forehand) drive; **faire un ~ droit** (au tennis) to drive; **~ fourré** dirty trick; **~ franc** (au football) free kick.

IDIOMES **tenir le ~** (résister à l'épreuve) [*personne*] to make it○; [*véhicule, appareil, chaussures*] to last out; [*lien, réparation*] to hold; (ne pas abandonner) [*personne*] to hold on; [*forces, armée*] to hold out; (faire face) to cope; **j'ai vu venir le ~** I could see it coming; **faire ~ double** to kill two birds with one stone; **compter les ~s** (rester neutre) to stay ou stand on the sidelines; **en mettre un ~**○ to give it all one's got○; **être aux cent ~s**○ to be worried sick○, to be in a state○; **faire les quatre cents ~s**○ to be up to no good; **les ~s sont bons mais rares**○! any chance of another drop of wine?; **avoir/attraper le ~ pour faire qch**○ to have/to get the knack of doing sth; **tirer un** or **son ~**● to have a screw●.

coupable /kupabl/ **I** *adj* **1** gén, Jur [*personne, entreprise*] guilty (**de qch** of sth; **d'avoir fait** of doing); **non ~** not guilty; **être reconnu ~ de** to be found guilty of; **s'être rendu ~ de qch** to have committed sth; **2** (répréhensible) [*pensées, indifférence*] shameful; [*amour*] illicit.

II *nmf* gén, Jur culprit; (dans un procès) guilty party.

coupage /kupaʒ/ *nm* **1** Vin blending; **2** Tech cutting.

coupant, ~e /kupɑ̃, ɑ̃t/ *adj* **1** [*lame*] sharp; **2** [*ton, remarque*] cutting, sharp.

coup-de-poing, *pl* **coups-de-poing** /kudpwɛ̃/ *nm* **~ américain** knuckle-duster GB, brass knuckles (*pl*) US.

coupe /kup/ **I** *nf* **1** Sport cup; **jouer en ~ Davis** to play in the Davis Cup; **la ~ du monde** the World Cup; **2** (coiffure) haircut; **tu as une jolie ~** you've got a nice haircut; **faire une ~ à qn** to give sb a haircut; **3** Cout (processus) cutting out; (façon) cut; **j'aime le tissu mais pas la ~** I like the fabric ou material but not the cut; **cours de ~ et de couture** dressmaking course; **4** (diminution) cut; **annoncer une ~ de 10% dans le budget** to announce a cut of 10% in the budget; **5** gén cutting (**de** of); **la ~ (des arbres) a commencé ce matin** they started cutting down the trees this morning; **fromage/jambon vendu à la ~** cheese/ham which is not sold pre-packed; **6** (surface d'exploitation) felling area; **7** Cin, Littérat, Presse (censure) (action) cutting; (résultat) cut; **8** (à fruits, dessert) bowl; (à champagne) glass; **une ~ de champagne** a glass of champagne; **9** Sci, Biol section; **une (vue en) ~ de qch** a section of sth; **~ longitudinale/transversale** longitudinal/cross section; **un os vu en ~** a bone seen in section; **10** (aux cartes) void; **avoir une ~ (à cœur/trèfle)** to have a void (in hearts/clubs); **11** Ling boundary; **~ syllabique** syllable boundary, syllabic division; **~ rythmique** rhythm group boundaries (*pl*).

II sous la coupe de *loc prép* **être sous la ~ de l'État** to be under the control of the state; **tomber sous la ~ de qn** to fall under sb's control; **vivre sous la ~ de parents autoritaires** to live under the thumb of authoritarian parents.

■ **~ au bol** pudding GB ou dessert US bowl cut; **~ en brosse** crew cut; **~ claire** lit heavy felling; fig drastic cut; **~ dégradée** layered cut; **~ réglée** periodic felling; **~ à sec** dry cut; **~ sombre** light felling.

IDIOMES **la ~ est pleine** enough is enough; **cette fois, la ~ est pleine!** this time, I've had enough!

coupé /kupe/ *nm* coupé.

coupe-carrelage /kupkaʀlaʒ/ *nm inv* tile-cutter.

coupe-choux○ /kupʃu/ *nm inv* **1** (sabre) short sword; **2** (rasoir) cut-throat razor GB, straight razor US.

coupe-cigare, *pl* **~s** /kupsigaʀ/ *nm* cigar cutter.

coupe-circuit /kupsiʀkɥi/ *nm inv* fuse.

coupe-coupe /kupkup/ *nm inv* machete.

coupée /kupe/ *nf* gangway.

coupe-faim /kupfɛ̃/ *nm inv* appetite suppressant.

coupe-feu /kupfø/ **I** *adj inv* fire-proof; **mur ~** fire wall; **porte ~** fire door.

II *nm inv* (en forêt) firebreak.

coupe-file, *pl* **~s** /kupfil/ *nm* pass.

coupe-frites /kupfʀit/ *nm inv* chip-cutter GB, potato slicer US.

coupe-gorge /kupgɔʀʒ/ *nm inv* (lieu) rough place; (quartier) rough area.

coupe-jambon /kupjɑ̃bɔ̃/ *nm inv* bacon-slicer, ham-slicer.

coupe-jarret† /kupʒaʀɛ/ *nm inv* cut-throat†.

coupe-légumes /kuplegym/ *nm inv* vegetable cutter.

coupelle /kupɛl/ *nf* small dish.

coupe-œuf /kupœf/ *nm inv* egg slicer.

coupe-ongles /kupɔ̃gl/ *nm inv* nail clippers (*pl*).

coupe-papier /kuppapje/ *nm inv* paper knife, letter opener.

couper /kupe/ [1] **I** *vtr* **1** (sectionner) to cut [*ficelle, papier, tissu, fleur*] (**avec** with); to cut down [*arbre*]; to chop [*bois*]; (ôter) to cut [sth] off, to cut off [*frange, branche, tête, membre*]; **~ un fil avec les dents** to bite a thread off; **~ les cheveux/ongles à qn** to cut sb's hair/nails; **se faire ~ les cheveux** to have ou get one's hair cut; **on a dû lui ~ la jambe/le bras** they had to cut his/her leg/arm off; **ils ont coupé les ailes du corbeau pour qu'il ne s'envole pas** they have clipped the crow's wings so it won't fly off; **~ qch en deux/trois** to cut sth in two/three; **le débat a coupé notre pays en deux** the debate has split our country in two; **~ le voyage/la journée** to break up the journey/the day; **j'ai coupé par le bois/par le champ** I cut through the wood/across the field; ▶ **herbe**; **2** Culin to cut (up), to slice [*pain, gâteau*]; to carve [*volaille, rôti*]; to cut (off) [*tranche*]; to cut, to chop [*légumes*]; **~ qch en morceaux** to cut sth up, to cut sth into pieces; **~ une tarte en huit** to cut a tart into eight pieces; **~ qch en lamelles** to cut sth into thin slices; **~ qch en dés** or **cubes** to dice sth, to cut sth into cubes; **~ qch en tranches** to slice sth, to cut sth into slices; **3** Cout (d'après un patron) to cut out [*vêtement*]; (raccourcir) to shorten; **il faut ~ la robe de 3 cm** you've got to shorten the dress by 3 cm; **4** (entamer) [*menottes, lanière*] to cut into [*poignet, chair*]; [*couteau, ciseaux*] to cut [*os, métal, carton*]; **5** Cin to cut; (pour censurer) to cut (out) [*passage, images, scène*]; **6** (croiser) [*route, voie ferrée*] to cut across [*route*]; Math [*droite, courbe*] to intersect with [*axe*]; **~ la route à qn/un véhicule** to cut in on sb/a vehicle; **7** (pour faire obstacle) [*barrage, police*] to cut off [*route, passage*]; **une veste qui coupe bien le vent** a jacket that keeps out the wind; **8** (interrompre) [*agence*] gén to cut off [*électricité, eau, téléphone*]; (pour non-paiement) to disconnect [*électricité, eau, téléphone*]; [*locataire, usager*] to turn off [*chauffage, eau, gaz*]; to switch off [*électricité, contact*]; **ne coupez pas!** don't cut us off!; **un œuf dur coupe la faim** a hard boiled egg takes the edge off your hunger; **~ la fièvre à qn** to bring sb's temperature down; **~ les vivres à qn** lit to cut off sb's food supply; fig to stop giving sb money; **~ l'appétit à qn** to ruin ou spoil sb's appetite; **~ le souffle à qn** lit, fig to take sb's breath away; **~ la parole à qn** to interrupt sb, to cut sb off; **9** (isoler) **~ qn de qn/qch** to cut sb off from sb/sth; **il vit coupé du monde** he lives cut off from the outside world; **10** (mélanger) to dilute [*jus de fruit, vin*]; (à la fabrication) to blend [*vin*]; **11** (au tennis) to slice [*balle, revers*]; **12** Jeux (pour mélanger) to cut; (avec une carte) to trump; **j'ai coupé à trèfle/cœur** I trumped it with a club/heart; **13** Vét to neuter, to castrate [*chat, chien*]; **il a fait ~ son chat** he had his cat neutered.

II *vi* **attention ça coupe!** be careful, it's sharp ou you'll cut yourself!; **ça coupe beaucoup mieux** it cuts a lot better.

III se couper *vpr* **1** (se blesser) to cut oneself (**avec** with); **il s'est coupé au menton/à l'oreille** he cut himself on the chin/on the ear; **il s'est coupé le doigt** (entamé) he cut his finger; (amputé) he cut his finger off; **se ~ les cheveux/ongles** to cut one's hair/nails; **2** (se trahir) to give oneself away; **3** (s'isoler) **se ~ de qn/qch** (volontairement) to cut oneself off from sb/sth; (involontairement) to be cut off from sb/sth; **4** (se fendre) [*cuir*] to crack; [*étoffe*] to tear, to rip; **5** (se tailler) **ça se coupe facilement/difficilement** it's easy/hard to cut; **6** (se croiser) [*lignes, voies*] to cross, to intersect; Math to intersect, to cross.

IDIOMES **c'est ton tour de faire à manger, tu n'y couperas pas** it's your turn to cook, you won't get out of it; **j'en mettrais ma main à ~** or **au feu** I'd stake my life on it; **ça te la coupe**◑, **hein?** that's shut you up○!; ▶ **main**.

couperet /kupʀɛ/ *nm* (de boucher) cleaver; (de guillotine) blade; **la nouvelle est tombée comme un ~** the news came as a bolt from the blue.

couperose /kupʀoz/ *nf* broken veins (*pl*), rosacea spéc.

couperosé, ~e /kupʀoze/ *adj* [*joue, nez*] with broken veins (*épith, après n*), affected by rosacea spéc.

coupe-tomates /kuptɔmat/ *nm inv* tomato slicer.

coupeur, -euse /kupœʀ, øz/ ▶ **510** *nm,f* Cout cutter.

coupe-vent /kupvɑ̃/ *nm inv* **1** (anorak) windcheater GB, windbreaker US; **2** (haie) windbreak.

couplage /kuplaʒ/ *nm* Électrotech, Télécom coupling; Pub joint deal.

couple /kupl/ **I** *nm* **1** (avec lien amoureux) couple; **2** (relation) relationship; **leur ~ n'a pas résisté à ces épreuves** their relationship didn't survive these problems; **3** (paire) (de danseurs) couple, pair; (d'animaux) pair; **le ~ de marcheurs/d'Italiens** the two walkers/Italians; **le ~ franco-allemand** France and Germany; **4** Électrotech, Phys couple; **5** Aviat frame; Naut **~ (de construction)** (transverse) frame.
II *nf* Chasse couple.
■ **~ moteur** engine torque; **~ résistant** resisting torque.

couplé, **~e** /kuple/ **I** *pp* ▶ **coupler**.
II *pp adj* **annonces ~es** Pub ads in a multimedia campaign; **pari ~** Turf reversed forecast; **télémètre ~** Phot coupled rangefinder.
III *nm* Turf reversed forecast.

coupler /kuple/ [1] *vtr* (tous contextes) to couple; **~ des machines** to couple machines (together); **~ qch avec qch** to couple sth (up) with sth.

couplet /kuplɛ/ *nm* (de chanson) verse; Littérat (deux vers) couplet; péj **faire son ~ sur** to trot out the same old stuff about; **y aller de son petit ~** to trot out one's party piece.

coupleur /kuplœʀ/ *nm* Électron, Ordinat coupler; Rail coupling.

coupole /kupɔl/ *nf* Archit cupola, dome.

Coupole /kupɔl/ *nprf* **la ~** the Académie française; **être reçu sous la ~** to become a member of the Académie française.

coupon /kupɔ̃/ *nm* **1** (de tissu) remnant; **2** Théât ticket voucher; **3** Transp multiuse ticket (*in travel pass*); **4** Fin coupon.

couponnage /kupɔnaʒ/ *nm* Fin couponing.

coupon-réponse, *pl* **coupons-réponses** /kupɔ̃ʀepɔ̃s/ *nm* Postes, Pub reply coupon.

coupure /kupyʀ/ *nf* **1** (pause) break; **~ estivale/publicitaire** summer/commercial break; **une ~ d'un quart d'heure** a 15-minute break; **trois jours de congé, ça fait une ~**○ three days off makes a nice break; **2** (fossé) gap; **la ~ entre l'école et le monde du travail** the gap between school and working life; **3** (passage censuré ou éliminé) cut; **ils ont fait plusieurs ~s dans le texte** they have made several cuts in the text; **4** (rupture) break; **je voulais une ~ nette avec mon passé** I wanted to make a clean break with my past; **5** (blessure) cut; **tu as une ~ au doigt/menton** you've got a cut on your finger/chin; **6** (d'eau, de gaz) **une ~ d'électricité** or **de courant** gén a power cut; (pour non-paiement) disconnection of electricity supply; **'~s d'eau pour travaux'** 'the water will be cut off several times during the repairs'; **les ~s de gaz sont rares** it's quite rare for the gas to be cut off; **7** Fin (billet de banque) (bank)note GB, bill US; **petites/grosses ~s** notes of small/large denomination.
■ **~ de journal** or **de presse** (newspaper) cutting ou clipping.

cour /kuʀ/ *nf* **1** (de maison, bâtiment) courtyard; (où l'on joue) playground; (de ferme) yard; **la ~ des grands** lit the older children's playground; fig the big league; **~ de ferme** farmyard; **sur ~** overlooking the courtyard; **2** (de souverain) court; (de personne en vue) entourage; **~ d'Angleterre** English court; **~ royale/pontificale** royal/papal court; **habit de ~** court dress; **le roi et sa ~** the king and his courtiers; **être bien/mal en ~** to be in/out of favour[GB] (**auprès de** with); **3** (à une jeune fille) courtship; **faire la ~ à** to court; **faire sa ~ à** lit, fig to pay court to; **4** Jur court; **devant la ~** before the court; **'messieurs, la ~'** 'all rise'.
■ **~ d'appel** Jur court of appeal GB ou appeals US; **~ d'arrivée** arrivals area; **~ d'assises** Jur criminal court; **~ de caserne** barracks square; **~ constitutionnelle** Admin constitutional court; **~ de départ** departures area; **~ d'école** schoolyard; **~ de gare** station forecourt; **~ d'honneur** main courtyard; **~ d'immeuble** inner courtyard; **~ intérieure** inner courtyard; **~ martiale** Mil court-martial; **passer en ~ martiale** to be court-martialled; **faire passer qn en ~ martiale** to court-martial sb; **~ des Miracles** Hist *area of a city frequented by beggars and thieves*; fig den of thieves; **~ de récréation** playground; **~ de renvoi** court of appeal GB ou appeals US; **Cour de cassation** court of cassation; **Cour des comptes** national audit office; **Cour européenne des droits de l'homme** European Court of Human Rights; **Cour européenne de justice** European Court of Justice; **Cour internationale de justice** International Court of Justice; **Cour de justice des communautés européennes** = **Cour européenne de justice**; **Cour suprême** (des États-Unis) Supreme Court; **Cour de sûreté de l'État** state security court.

courage /kuʀaʒ/ *nm* **1** (devant l'adversité) courage; (devant un danger physique) bravery; **avec ~** courageously, with courage, bravely; **avoir du ~** to be courageous ou brave; **avoir le ~ de faire** to be courageous ou brave enough to do, to have the courage to do; **trouver le ~ de faire** to pluck up the courage to do; **faire preuve de (beaucoup de) ~** to show (great) courage; **il faut du ~ pour faire ça** it takes courage ou guts○ to do that; **donner du ~ à qn** to give sb courage; **avoir le ~ de ses opinions** to have the courage of one's convictions; **2** (énergie) energy; **je n'ai même pas le ~ de me doucher** I don't even have the energy to have a shower; **je n'ai pas eu le ~ de dire non** I didn't have the heart to say no; **'je vais travailler'—'bon ~!'** 'I'm going to work'—'work hard!' ou iron 'good luck to you!'; **~!** don't lose heart!; **perdre/prendre ~** to lose/to take heart; **reprendre ~** to take fresh heart; **cela m'a donné du ~ (pour faire)** it encouraged me (to do); **je mange du chocolat pour me donner du ~** I eat chocolate to keep myself going.
IDIOMES **prendre son ~ à deux mains** to take one's courage in both hands.

courageusement /kuʀaʒøzmɑ̃/ *adv* **1** (face à l'adversité) courageously; (face au danger physique) bravely; **2** (avec décision) with a will; **~, elle se mit au travail** she went to work with a will.

courageux, **-euse** /kuʀaʒø, øz/ *adj* **1** (fort moralement) courageous; (sans peur) brave; **sois ~** gén be brave; (avant une mauvaise nouvelle) be strong; **2** (énergique) **je ne me sens pas très ~ aujourd'hui** I haven't got much energy today; **il est ~, il travaille 16 heures par jour** he's not afraid of hard work, he works 16 hours a day.

couramment /kuʀamɑ̃/ *adv* **1** (avec aisance) [*parler, écrire*] fluently; **il parle ~ le russe, il parle russe ~** he speaks Russian fluently, he speaks fluent Russian; **2** (communément) **cela se fait ~** it's very common; **ça se dit ~** it's a common expression; **se pratiquer ~** to be widely practised[GB]; **~ admis** widely ou generally accepted; **~ utilisé** widely ou extensively used.

courant[1] /kuʀɑ̃/ *prép* some time in; **~ janvier** some time in January.

courant[2], **~e** /kuʀɑ̃, ɑ̃t/ **I** *adj* **1** (fréquent) [*mot, pratique, erreur*] common; **l'expression est de plus en plus ~e** the expression is becoming increasingly common; **il est ~ de faire** it is common to do; **2** (ordinaire) [*langue*] everyday; [*procédure, fonctionnement*] usual, ordinary; Comm [*taille*] standard; **3** (avec référence temporelle) [*semaine, mois, année*] current; **le 15 du mois ~** the 15th of this month, the 15th inst.; **bénéfice ~** profit for the year.
II *nm* **1** (mouvement de l'eau) current; **un ~ fort/faible** a strong/weak current; **il y a beaucoup de ~** there's a strong current; **nager/ramer contre le ~** to swim/to row against the current; **aller contre le ~** fig to go against the tide; **suivre le ~** lit to go with the current, to go downstream; fig to go with the flow; **remonter le ~** [*saumon*] to swim upstream; [*embarcation*] to sail against the current; fig [*personne, entreprise*] to get back on one's feet; **2** Aviat, Météo current; **~ aérien** air current; **3** Électrotech current; **~ électrique** electric current; **il n'y a plus de ~** the power has gone off; **remettre le ~** to switch the power back on; **le ~ passe** lit the power's on; **le ~ ne passe pas** there's no power; **le ~ passe bien entre elle et lui** fig they get on very well; **il faut que le ~ passe avec le public** fig you have to have a good rapport with the audience; **certains soirs le ~ ne passe pas avec le public** fig on some evenings there's just no rapport with the audience; **4** (tendance) trend; **un ~ culturel/politique/religieux** a cultural/political/religious trend; **un ~ de pensée/d'opinion** a current of thought/of opinion; **5** (déplacement) movement; **les ~s migratoires/de population** migratory/population movements; ▶ **plume**; **6** (période) **dans le ~ de** in the course of; **dans le ~ du mois/de l'année/de la journée** in the course of the month/of the year/of the day; **demain, dans le ~ de la journée** some time tomorrow.
III au courant *loc adj* **1** (informé) **être au ~** to know (**de qch** about sth); **tu étais au ~ et tu n'as rien dit!** you knew and you didn't say anything!; **je ne suis pas du tout au ~ de ce qu'il veut faire** I really don't know what he wants to do; **mettre qn au ~** to put sb in the picture, to fill sb in (**de qch** about sth); **il serait préférable de les mettre au ~** it would be better to put them in the picture; **tenir qn au ~** to keep sb posted (**de qch** about sth); **tiens-moi au ~ de l'affaire, ça m'intéresse** keep me posted about the case, I'm interested; **2** (au fait) **être très au ~** to know all about it; **pour les questions techniques demande à Paul, il est très au ~** for technical questions ask Paul, he knows all about it; **pour un spécialiste il n'a pas l'air très au ~** for a specialist he doesn't really seem to know what he's doing; **mettre qn au ~** to bring sb up to date (**de qch** on sth); **nous vous mettrons au ~ du nouveau système** we will bring you up to date on the new system; **se tenir au ~** to keep up to date (**de qch** on sth); **j'essaie de me tenir au ~ de ce qui se fait en informatique** I'm trying to keep up to date with what's happening in computing.
IV courante *nf* **1** Mus, Danse courante; **2**○ (diarrhée) runs◑ (*pl*); **avoir la ~e** to have the runs◑.
■ **~ d'air** draught GB, draft US; **faire ~ d'air** to make a draught (**avec** with); **leur fils est un vrai ~ d'air** hum their son is never in one place for more than five minutes at a time; **~ alternatif, CA** alternating current, AC; **~ ascendant** updraught; **~ atmosphérique** Aviat air flow; Météo air stream; **~ continu, CC** direct current, DC; **~ descendant** Aviat downdraught; **~ d'induction** or **induit** Électrotech induction current; **~ porteur** carrier current.

courant-jet, *pl* **courants-jets** /kuʀɑ̃ʒɛ/ *nm* jet stream.

courbatu, **~e** /kuʀbaty/ *adj* liter stiff; **être tout ~** to be stiff all over; **j'ai les bras ~s** my arms are stiff.

courbature /kuʀbatyʀ/ *nf* ache; **avoir des ~s** to be stiff; **j'ai des ~s dans les jambes** my legs are stiff; **être plein de ~s** to be stiff all over; **donner des ~s à qn/dans le bras de qn** to make sb/sb's arm stiff.

courbaturé, **~e** /kuʀbatyʀe/ *pp adj* (après

effort) stiff; (pendant grippe) aching; **être tout ~ après un match** to be stiff all over after a match; **j'ai le bras ~** my arm is stiff.

courbe /kuʀb/ **I** *adj* curved.
II *nf* **1** (représentation graphique) curve; **~ ascendante du chômage/des prix** rising unemployment/price curve; **~s de rentabilité/boursières** profit/stock exchange graphs; **la ~ de popularité du ministre** the minister's popularity rating; **2** (de rivière) bend; (de route) curve; (plus marqué) bend; (de sourcil) arch; **faire une ~** [*route, voie ferrée*] to curve; (plus marqué) to bend.
■ **~ gauche** Math skew curve; **~ de niveau** Géog contour line; **~ de température** Méd temperature chart.

courbé, **~e** /kuʀbe/ **I** *pp* ▶ **courber**.
II *pp adj* **être ~** (avec l'âge) to be bent with age; (par déformation) to stoop.

courber /kuʀbe/ [1] **I** *vtr* **1** (faire plier) to bend [*rameau, barre*]; **2** (incliner) to bend [*corps, partie du corps*]; **courbant la tête sur son livre** bending over his/her book; **courbant le dos** or **les épaules pour** bending down in order to; **~ la tête** or **le front** or **le dos** fig to bow down.
II *vi* **~ sous le poids** to be bowed down under the weight.
III se courber *vpr* (se baisser) to bend down; (avec l'âge) to become bent with age.

courbette /kuʀbɛt/ *nf* **1** (low) bow; **faire des ~s** fig to bow and scrape (**devant** to); **2** Équit curvet.

courbure /kuʀbyʀ/ *nf* gén curve; **la ~ de mon nez** the curved shape of my nose.

courette /kuʀɛt/ *nf* small courtyard.

coureur, **-euse** /kuʀœʀ, øz/ **I** *adj* **il est ~** he's a womanizer; **elle est coureuse** she's a manhunter○.
II *nm,f* **1** ▶**510** Sport (en course à pied) runner; **2** (séducteur) womanizer/manhunter○.
■ **~ automobile** racing driver; **~ des bois** C (trappeur) trapper; **~ cycliste** (racing) cyclist; **~ de demi-fond** middle-distance runner; **~ de fond** long-distance runner; **~ de haies** hurdler; **~ de jupons** philanderer; **~ motocycliste** motorcycle racer.

courge /kuʀʒ/ *nf* **1** (terme générique) gourd; (fruit) (vegetable) marrow; **2**◑ (imbécile) berk◑ GB, idiot.

courgette /kuʀʒɛt/ *nf* courgette GB, zucchini US.

courir /kuʀiʀ/ [26] **I** *vtr* **1** Sport [*athlète*] to run (in) [*épreuve, marathon*]; [*cycliste*] to ride in [*épreuve*]; [*pilote*] to drive in [*rallye, course*]; [*cheval*] to run in [*épreuve*]; **~ le relais/100 mètres** to run (in) the relay/100 metres[GB]; **2** (parcourir en tous sens) **~ la campagne/les océans/le monde** to roam the countryside/the oceans/the world; **j'ai couru tout Paris pour trouver ton cadeau** I searched the whole of Paris for your present; **~ les boutiques** to go round the shops GB ou stores US; **3** (fréquenter) **~ les cocktails/bals/théâtres** to do the rounds of the cocktail parties/dances/theatres[GB]; **4** (s'exposer à) **~ un (grand) danger** to be in (great) danger; **faire ~ un (grand) danger à qn/qch** to put sb/sth in (serious) danger; **~ un (gros) risque** to run a (big) risk; **je ne veux ~ aucun risque** I don't want to run any risks; **~ le risque de faire** to run the risk of doing; **faire ~ un risque à qn** to put sb at risk; **c'est un risque à ~** it's a risk one has to take; **5**◑ (agacer) **~ qn** to get on sb's nerves ou wick○ GB; **tu nous cours avec tes histoires!** you're getting on our nerves with your stories!; **6**○ (chercher à séduire) **~ les filles/garçons** to chase after girls/boys; ▶ **lièvre**.
II *vi* **1** gén [*personne, animal*] to run; **~ dans le couloir/dans les escaliers** to run in the corridor/on the stairs; **~ à travers champs/à travers bois** to run across the fields/through the woods; **~ vite** (ponctuellement) to run fast; (en général) to be a fast runner; **je ne cours pas vite** I can't run very fast; **ils courent tous les samedis** (en jogging) they go for a run ou go jogging every Saturday; **sortir en courant** to run out; **se mettre à ~** to start running; **~ vers** or **à qn** to run toward(s) sb; **cours chercher de l'aide/ton père** run and get help/your father; **je cours leur dire/les prévenir** I'll run and tell them/warn them; **'va chercher ton frère'—'j'y cours'** 'go and get your brother'—'I'm going'; **tout le monde court voir leur spectacle** everybody is rushing to see their show; **qu'est-ce qui vous fait ~?** fig what makes you tick○?; **les voleurs courent toujours** fig the thieves are still at large; **2** Sport (en athlétisme) to run; (en cyclisme) to ride, to race; (en voiture, moto) to race; (en équitation) to run; **~ sur** to race with [*nom de marque*]; to race on [*nom de vehicule*]; **~ au grand prix du Japon** to race in the Japanese Grand Prix; **on court à Vincennes cet après-midi** Turf there's a race meeting at Vincennes this afternoon; **~ sur une balle** (au tennis) to run for a ball; **3** (se presser) [*personne*] to rush; **j'ai couru toute la journée** I've been rushing about all day; **elle court sans arrêt** she's always rushing about, she's always on the go; **~ au secours de qn** to rush to sb's aid; **en courant** hastily, in a rush; **~ (tout droit) à la catastrophe/faillite** to be heading (straight) for disaster/bankruptcy; **4** (chercher à rattraper) **~ après qn/qch** gén to run after sb/sth; (poursuivre) to chase after sb/sth; **ton chien m'a couru après** your dog chased after me; **~ après un voleur** to chase after a thief; **s'il ne veut pas me voir je ne vais pas lui ~ après** fig if he doesn't want to see me I'm not going to go chasing after him; ▶ **valoir**; **5** (essayer d'obtenir) **~ après qch** to chase after sth; **~ après les honneurs/le succès/la gloire** to chase after honour[GB]/success/glory; **6**○ (essayer de séduire) **~ après qn** to chase after sb; **il te court après** he's chasing after you; **7**○ (apprécier) **ne pas ~ après qch** not to be wild about sth○; **le chou, je ne cours pas après** I'm not wild about cabbage○; **8** (se mouvoir rapidement) [*ruisseau, torrent*] to rush, to run (**dans** through); [*flammes*] to run, to race; [*nuages*] to race (**dans** across); **ses doigts courent sur le clavier** his/her fingers race over the keyboard; **ma plume court sur la feuille** my pen is racing across the page; **laisser ~ sa plume** or **son stylo (sur le papier)** to let one's pen run ou race across the page; **9** (parcourir) **~ le long de** [*sentier*] to run along [*bois, pré*]; [*veine, varice*] to run down [*jambe*]; **les lignes qui courent sur la paume de la main** the lines that run across the palm; **10** (se propager) [*rumeur, bruit*] to go around; **il y a un bruit qui court à leur sujet** there's a rumour[GB] going around about them; **le bruit court que** rumour[GB] has it (that), there's a rumour[GB] that; **c'est un bruit qui court** it's a rumour[GB]; **faire ~ un bruit** to spread a rumour[GB]; **11** (être en vigueur) [*intérêts*] to accrue; [*bail, contrat*] to run (**jusqu'à** to); **12** (s'écouler) **le mois/l'année qui court** the current ou present month/year; **13** Naut [*navire*] to run, to sail.
III se courir *vpr* **1** (avoir lieu) [*tiercé, course à pied*] to be run; [*course de voiture, moto*] to take place; **2** (chercher à se rattraper) **se ~ après** to chase (after) each other; **arrêtez de vous ~ après dans la maison!** stop chasing each other around the house!; **3**○ (se chercher) **se ~ après** to look for each other.
IDIOMES **tu peux toujours ~**○**!** you can go whistle for it○!; **laisser ~**○ to let things ride; **laisse ~, tu vois bien qu'il le fait exprès** forget it, can't you see he's doing it on purpose?; **rien ne sert de ~ il faut partir à point** Prov slow and steady wins the race Prov.

courlis /kuʀli/ *nm* curlew.

couronne /kuʀɔn/ *nf* **1** (de roi) crown; (de noble) coronet; **~ de fleurs d'oranger** garland of orange blossom; **~ d'épines** crown of thorns; **~ de lauriers** laurel wreath; **~ de fleurs** wreath; **~ de roses** wreath of roses; **2** (pour un enterrement) wreath; **~ funéraire** or **mortuaire** funeral wreath; **3** Dent crown; **poser une ~** to crown a tooth; **4** (cercle) ring; **5** (pouvoir) **la ~** the Crown; **les joyaux de la ~** the crown jewels; **prétendre à la ~** to lay claim to the throne; **héritier de la ~** heir to the throne; **6** Astron, Météo corona; Mécan crown wheel; (en numismatique) crown; **7** (pain) ring-shaped loaf; **8** (banlieue de Paris) **la petite ~** *the inner suburbs* (*pl*); **la grande ~** *the outer suburbs* (*pl*).

couronnement /kuʀɔnmɑ̃/ *nm* **1** (de souverain) coronation; (de saint, héros) crowning; **2** (accomplissement) **c'est le ~ de leur carrière** it crowns their career.

couronner /kuʀɔne/ [1] *vtr* **1** (coiffer d'une couronne, sacrer) to crown; **~ qn roi** to crown sb king; **il fut couronné d'épines/de lauriers** he was crowned with thorns/with a laurel wreath; **enfant à la tête couronnée de roses** child wearing a garland of roses on his head; **2** (entourer, surmonter) liter to crown; **couronné de neige** snow-capped; **3** (donner un prix à) to award a prize to [*personne, œuvre*]; (récompenser) **être couronné de succès** to be crowned with success; **cela couronne dix années de recherches** this is the crowning achievement of ten years' research; **et pour ~ le tout** iron and to crown it all; **4** Dent to crown.
IDIOMES **se ~ les genoux** to graze one's knees.

courre /kuʀ/ *vtr* **chasse à ~** hunting.

courrier /kuʀje/ *nm* **1** (lettres) mail, post GB; **faire son ~** to do some letter-writing; **par retour du ~** by return (of post) GB, by return mail; **2** (une lettre) letter; **je vous envoie un ~** you will be receiving a letter from me; **en réponse à votre ~ du** in answer to your letter of; **3** Presse (lettres, rubrique) **~ des lecteurs** readers' letters; (dans journaux d'information) letters to the editor; **4** Postes (avion) mail GB, mail plane; (bateau) mail GB, mail boat; ▶ **long**, **moyen**; **5** (employé en malle-poste) post.
■ **~ d'ambassade** or **diplomatique** diplomatic courier; **~ du cœur** problem page; **~ de la mode/littéraire** fashion/book page; **~ électronique** Ordinat electronic mail.

courriériste /kuʀjeʀist/ *nmf* (chargé de chronique) columnist.

courroie /kuʀwa/ *nf* **1** (lien) strap; **2** Mécan belt.
■ **~ de transmission** lit drive belt; fig communication channel; **~ de ventilateur** Aut fan belt.

courroucé, **~e** /kuʀuse/ *adj* fml wrathful sout, irate; **d'un ton ~** wrathfully sout, angrily; **sous le regard ~ de** under the incensed gaze of.

courroucer /kuʀuse/ [12] *vtr* fml to anger, to incense.

courroux /kuʀu/ *nm* fml wrath sout, ire sout; **être/se mettre en ~** to be/to become irate ou infuriated.

cours /kuʀ/ *nm inv* **1** (session d'enseignement) Scol lesson, class; Univ class; (magistral) lecture; (hors cadre scolaire) class; (en privé) lesson; (ensemble de sessions) course; **avoir ~** to have a class; **je n'ai pas ~ demain** I haven't got any lessons ou classes tomorrow; **prendre des ~ de qch** to take classes in sth; **tu devrais prendre des ~ de diction** you should go to elocution classes; **suivre un ~** to do ou take a course; **il prend des ~ d'espagnol** he's taking Spanish lessons; **je suis un ~ de secrétariat/cuisine/littérature** I'm doing ou taking a secretarial/cookery/literature course; **je suis les ~ du professeur X** I'm attending Professor X's lectures; **le professeur X a publié son ~ sur la traduction** Professor X has published his/her course of lectures on translation; **faire ~** to teach; **qui vous**

fait ~ en maths? who teaches you maths GB ou math US?; **faire un ~ sur qch** (une fois) to give a class in sth; (plusieurs fois) to teach a course in sth; **il nous a fait un véritable ~ sur la gastronomie** he gave us a real lecture on gastronomy; **donner des ~ de français/piano** (dans l'enseignement) to teach French/piano; (en privé) to give French/piano lessons; **2** Scol, Univ (manuel) course book, textbook; (notes) notes (*pl*); **3** (établissement) school; **~ de théâtre** drama school; **4** Fin (taux de négociation) (de denrée, valeur) price; (de devise) exchange rate; **le ~ du change** the exchange rate; **le ~ du dollar** the price of the dollar; **~ légal** official exchange rate; **les ~ boursiers** or **de la Bourse** Stock Exchange prices; **le ~ du marché** the market price; **acheter qch au ~ des halles** to buy sth at wholesale market price; **~ d'ouverture/de clôture** or **fermeture** opening/closing price; **avoir ~** Fin [*monnaie*] to be legal tender; fig [*théorie, pratique*] to be current; [*terme, expression*] to be used; **ne plus avoir ~** Fin [*monnaie*] to be no longer legal tender; fig [*théorie, pratique*] to be no longer accepted; [*terme, expression*] to be no longer used; **5** (de rivière) (parcours) course; (débit) flow; **détourner le ~ d'une rivière** to divert the course of a river; **avoir un ~ lent/rapide** to flow slowly/quickly; **fleuve au ~ rapide** fast-flowing river; **descendre/remonter le ~ d'une rivière** to go down/to go up a river; **6** (enchaînement) (de récit, conflit, carrière, maladie) course; (d'idées) flow; (d'événements) course; **les choses suivent tranquillement leur ~** things are quietly taking their course; **le ~ des choses** the course of events; **reprendre son ~** to resume; **la vie reprend son ~** life returns to normal; **la sonnerie interrompit le ~ de mes pensées** the bell interrupted my train of thought; **donner libre ~ à** to give free rein to [*imagination, fantaisie*]; to give way to [*peine, douleur*]; to give vent to [*colère, indignation*]; **au** or **dans le ~ de** in the course of, during; **dans le ~ du mois prochain** in the course of next month; **dans le ~ du mois** within the month; **en ~** [*mois, semaine, année*] current; [*processus, projet*] under way (*après n*); [*travail, négociations, changements*] in progress (*après n*); **en ~ de journée/saison/séance** in the course of the day/season/session; **en ~ de fabrication/rénovation** in the process of being manufactured/renovated; **le pont en ~ de construction** the bridge being built or under construction; **le pont est en ~ de construction** the bridge is under construction ou in the process of being built; **en ~ de route** along the way; **rajoutez un peu d'eau en ~ de cuisson** add some water during the cooking.

■ **~ accéléré** crash course; **~ de compensation** Fin mark-up price; **~ d'eau** watercourse; **~ élémentaire deuxième année**, **CE2** *third year of primary school, age 8–9*; **~ élémentaire première année**, **CE1** *second year of primary school, age 7–8*; **~ intensif** intensive course; **~ magistral** Univ lecture; **~ moyen deuxième année**, **CM2** *fifth year of primary school, age 10–11*; **~ moyen première année**, **CM1** *fourth year of primary school, age 9–10*; **~ d'initiation** introductory course; **~ intensif** intensive course; **~ par correspondance** correspondence course; **suivre des ~ par correspondance** to take a correspondence course; **~ particulier(s)** private tuition ¢ GB, private tutoring ¢ US (**en, de** in); **donner/suivre des ~ particuliers** to give/to have private tuition ou lessons; **~ de perfectionnement** improvers' course; **~ préparatoire**, **CP** Scol *first year of primary school, age 6–7*; **~ de rattrapage** remedial course; **~ de remise à niveau** refresher course; **~ du soir** evening class.

course /kuʀs/ **I** *nf* **1** (mode de déplacement) running; **être en pleine ~** to be running at full speed; **faire la ~ avec qn** lit, fig to race sb; **viens, on va faire la ~** come on, I'll race you; **être rapide à la ~** to be a fast runner; **2** (trajet) (de personne) run; (de taxi) journey; **une ~ de 15 kilomètres** (à pied) a 15 kilometre[GB] run; (en taxi) a 15 kilometre[GB] journey; **après une ~ effrénée** after a frantic run; **cette ~ m'a épuisé** that run has tired me out; **c'est 50 francs la ~** the fare is 50 francs; **leurs ~s à travers l'Afrique/le monde** their travels around Africa/the world; **3**○ (précipitation) rush; **ça va être la ~ pour rendre le rapport dans les délais** it'll be a rush getting the report in before the deadline; **ça a été la ~ aujourd'hui!** (pour moi) I've been rushing around all day!; **4** (compétition) race; **la ~ au profit/pouvoir** the race for profit/power; **la ~ à la présidence/la Maison Blanche** the race for the presidency/the White House; **se lancer dans la ~ aux voix/au développement** to throw oneself into the race for votes/for development; **être en ~** Sport to be in the race; fig to be in the running; **être hors ~** Sport, fig to be out of the race; **plusieurs entreprises sont en ~ pour ce projet** there are several companies in the running for this project; **5** (activité) (en athlétisme) running; (en alpinisme) climb; (avec un véhicule, animal) racing; (épreuve) race; **~ de motos** (activité) motorcycle racing; **~ de chevaux/lévriers** horse/greyhound race; **6** (démarche) **j'ai une ~ à faire** I've got to get something; **elle est partie faire une ~** she's gone off to get something; **j'ai deux ou trois ~s à faire** I've got some shopping to do; **7** (de pièce mécanique) (mouvement) travel; (distance parcourue) stroke; **~ à vide** idle stroke; **en bout de ~** at full stroke; **8** (trajectoire) (d'astre, de planète, comète) path; (de nuages) passage; (de fusée, projectile) flight path; **9** (passage) liter **la ~ du temps/des années** the passing of time/of the years; **10** Hist Naut privateering; **navire en ~** privateer.

II courses *nfpl* **1** (achats) shopping ¢; **faire des ~s** to go shopping; **je vais faire des ~s** I'm going shopping; **je fais mes ~s au marché/au supermarché** I do my shopping at the market/in the supermarket; **2** Turf races; **jouer/gagner aux ~s** to bet/to win at the races; **quel est le résultat des ~s?** lit what are the racing results?; fig, hum○ can you fill me in?, what's the crack○?

■ **~ aux armements** Pol arms race; **~ automobile** (activité) motor racing; (épreuve) motor race; **faire de la ~ automobile** to race cars; **~ de côte** hill climb; **~ cycliste** (activité) cycle racing; (épreuve) cycle race; **faire de la ~ cycliste** to compete in cycle races; **~ de demi-fond** middle-distance race; **~ de fond** long-distance race; **~ de haies** (en athlétisme) hurdle race, hurdles (*pl*); Équit steeplechase; **~ à handicap** Équit handicap race; **~ landaise** *sport in which a competitor must evade a charging bull controlled by a rope*; **~ contre la montre** race against the clock; **~ d'obstacles** Équit obstacle race; fig hurdle; **~ à pied** running; **~ de plat** Équit (activité) flat racing; (épreuve) flat race; **~ de relais** relay race; **~ en sac** sack race; **~ de taureaux** (corrida) bullfight; (dans la rue) bull run; **~ de trot** Équit trotting race; **~ de vitesse** (en athlétisme) sprint; (en moto) speedway race.

IDIOMES **ne plus être dans la ~** to be out of touch; **être en fin de ~** to be on the decline; **être à bout de ~** to be worn out.

course-croisière, *pl* **courses-croisières** /kuʀskʀwɑzjɛʀ/ *nf* long-distance yacht race.

course-poursuite, *pl* **courses-poursuites** /kuʀspuʀsɥit/ *nf* **1** lit chase; (en voitures) car chase; **2** fig race.

courser○ /kuʀse/ [1] *vtr* to chase [*animal, personne*]; **se faire ~ par qn** (chasser) to be chased off by sb; (poursuivre) to be chased by sb.

coursier, **-ière** /kuʀsje, ɛʀ/ ▶**510** **I** *nm,f* messenger.

II *nm* Hist charger, warhorse.

coursive /kuʀsiv/ *nf* (d'immeuble, de bateau) passageway.

court, **~e** /kuʀ, kuʀt/ **I** *adj* **1** (pas long) [*vêtement, cheveu, texte, période, mémoire, distance, balle*] short; **manches/culottes ~es** short sleeves/trousers GB ou pants US; **dans le délai le plus ~** in the shortest possible time; **de ~e durée** [*victoire, joie, espoir*] short-lived; [*prêt, emploi, maladie*] short-term; **s'arrêter, souffle ~** to get out of breath and stop; **avoir le souffle ~** to get out of breath easily; **avoir la vue ~e** lit, fig to be short-sighted; **~ sur pattes** [*animal*] short-legged; [*personne*]○ shortish; **prendre au plus ~** to take the shortest way; ▶**paille**; **2** (insuffisant) [*connaissances*] limited; **une heure/deux francs/trois pages c'est (un peu) ~** one hour/two francs/three pages, that's not really enough; **3** (faible) [*défaite, victoire, majorité*] narrow; **gagner d'une ~e tête** to win by a short head.

II *adv* **s'habiller ~** to wear short skirts; **jouer ~** to play short balls; **couper qch ~** to cut sth short; **les cheveux coupés ~** with short hair; **couper ~** to cut the conversation short; **couper ~ à qch** (abréger) to cut sth short; (faire cesser) to put paid to sth; **tourner ~** to come to a sudden end; **s'arrêter ~** to stop short.

III *nm* **1** Mode **le ~** short skirts (*pl*); **la mode est au ~** short skirts are in; **2** Sport court; **~ de tennis** tennis court; **~ central** centre[GB] court.

■ **~ métrage** Cin short (film); **~e échelle** leg up; **faire la ~e échelle à qn** to give sb a leg up.

IDIOMES **être à ~ de** to be short of [*argent, munitions*]; to be short on [*arguments, idées*]; **prendre qn de ~** to catch sb on the hop○ GB ou unprepared.

courtage /kuʀtaʒ/ *nm* brokerage.

courtaud, **~e** /kuʀto, od/ *adj* **1** [*personne*] shortish; **2** [*chien, cheval*] with a docked tail.

court-bouillon, *pl* **courts-bouillons** /kuʀbujɔ̃/ *nm* court-bouillon; **au ~** in a court-bouillon.

court-circuit, *pl* **~s** /kuʀsiʀkɥi/ *nm* short-circuit.

court-circuiter /kuʀsiʀkɥite/ [1] *vtr* **1** lit to short-circuit; **2**○ fig to bypass [*intermédiaire*].

courtier, **-ière** /kuʀtje, ɛʀ/ ▶**510** *nm,f* broker; **~ en assurances** insurance broker; **~ maritime** ship-broker.

courtine /kuʀtin/ *nf* curtain.

courtisan /kuʀtizɑ̃/ *nm* **1** (flagorneur) sycophant; **attitude de ~** fawning ¢; **2** Hist courtier.

courtisane /kuʀtizan/ *nf* courtesan.

courtiser /kuʀtize/ [1] *vtr* **1** (flatter) to woo [*électeurs, entreprise, puissants*]; **2**† to court, to woo [*femme*].

court-jus○, *pl* **courts-jus** /kuʀʒy/ *nm* short○, short-circuit.

courtois, **~e** /kuʀtwa, az/ *adj* [*personne, lettre, ton*] courteous (**avec** to); [*genre, tradition*] courtly.

courtoisement /kuʀtwazmɑ̃/ *adv* courteously.

courtoisie /kuʀtwazi/ *nf* courtesy; **visite de ~** courtesy visit; **par ~** out of courtesy.

■ **~ internationale** Jur comity of nations.

court-vêtu, **~e**, *mpl* **~s** /kuʀvety/ *adj* **une femme ~e** a woman in a short skirt.

couru, **~e** /kuʀy/ **I** *pp* ▶**courir**.

II *pp adj* **1** (prisé) [*restaurant, musée, villégiature*] popular.

IDIOMES **c'est ~ d'avance**○ it's a foregone conclusion.

couscous /kuskus/ *nm* couscous.

couscoussier /kuskusje/ *nm* steamer (*for cooking couscous*).

cousette /kuzɛt/ *nf* **1** (matériel) small sewing kit; **2**† (personne) dressmaker's apprentice.

cousin, **~e** /kuzɛ̃, in/ **I** *nm,f* cousin; **~ germain** first cousin; **~s au deuxième degré** second cousins; **un vague ~** a distant relation.

II *nm* Zool mosquito.

IDIOMES **être ~s à la mode de Bretagne** hum to be distantly related; **le roi n'est pas son ~** he thinks he is the cat's whiskers.

cousinage /kuzinaʒ/ *nm* (lien de parenté) cousinhood; (éloigné) distant relationship; **air de ~** similarity (**entre** between).

cousiner /kuzine/ [1] *vi* to be on familiar terms (**avec** with).

coussin /kusɛ̃/ *nm* **1** (pour divan) cushion; **2** Tech (pour protéger) padding.

■ **~ d'air** air cushion; **~ de sécurité** air bag.

coussinet /kusinɛ/ *nm* **1** (de divan) small cushion; **2** Mécan bearing; Rail chair.

■ **~ plantaire** Zool pad.

cousu, **~e** /kuzy/ ▶ **coudre**.

coût /ku/ *nm* cost (**de** of; **en** in); **~ élevé/total** high/total cost; **~ de fonctionnement/production** operating/production cost; **~ économique/politique/social** economic/political/social cost; **~ en vies humaines** cost in human lives.

■ **~ du crédit** Fin lending rate; **~ du travail** labour[GB] costs (*pl*); **~ de la vie** cost of living; **~s salariaux** wage costs; **~s salariaux indirects** non-wage labour[GB] costs.

coûtant /kutɑ̃/ *adj* **prix ~** cost price; **à** or **au prix ~** at cost price.

couteau, *pl* **~x** /kuto/ *nm* **1** gén knife; (de mixeur) blade; **au ~** [*couper, graver*] with a knife; **c'est un coup de ~** (blessure) it's a knife wound; **jouer** or **manier du ~** to use a knife (*in a fight*); **donner un coup de ~ à qn** to stab sb; **tuer qn à coups de ~** to stab sb to death; **il a reçu un coup de ~** he was stabbed; ▶ **brouillard**, **lame**, **plaie**; **2** (coquillage) razor shell GB, razor clam US; **3** (de balance) knife edge; **4** (personne) **premier ~** accomplice; **second ~** henchman.

■ **~ à beurre** butter knife; **~ de boucher** butcher's knife; **~ de chasse** hunting knife ; **~ à cran d'arrêt** flick knife GB, switchblade US; **~ de cuisine** kitchen knife; **~ à découper** carving knife; **~ électrique** electric knife; **~ éplucheur** or **à éplucher** peeler; **~ à pain** bread knife; **~ à palette** Art palette knife; **~ de poche** pocket knife; **~ à poisson** fish knife; **~ de table** table knife.

IDIOMES **être à ~x tirés avec qn** to be at daggers drawn with sb; **avoir le ~ sous la gorge** to have a pistol to one's head; **mettre le ~ sous la gorge de qn** to hold a pistol to sb's head; **tendre la gorge au ~** to lay one's head on the block.

couteau-scie, *pl* **couteaux-scies** /kutosi/ *nm* serrated knife.

coutelas /kutlɑ/ *nm* (de cuisine) large (kitchen) knife; (sabre) cutlass.

coutelier, **-ière** /kutəlje, ɛʀ/ ▶ **510** **I** *nm,f* (marchand, fabricant) cutler.

II coutelière *nf* (étui) knife box.

coutellerie /kutɛlʀi/ *nf* (magasin) cutlery shop; (fabrique) cutlery works (*pl*); (industrie) cutlery industry; (commerce) cutlery trade ou business; (objets) cutlery.

coûter /kute/ [1] **I** *vtr* to cost; **~ son emploi à qn** to cost sb his/her job; **~ la vie à qn** to cost sb his/her life; **cela ne coûte rien de faire** it doesn't cost anything to do.

II *vi* to cost; **~ dix francs** to cost ten francs; **~ beaucoup/une fortune** to cost a lot/a fortune; **me ~ six francs** to cost me six francs; **~ beaucoup à Pierre/au pays** to cost Pierre/the country a lot; **cela a coûté six francs à Paul** it cost Paul six francs; **cela ne te coûtera rien** it won't cost you a penny ou thing; **combien coûte ce livre?** how much is this book?, how much does this book cost?; **cela me coûte d'aller le voir** it's hard for me to go and see him; **~ cher** to be expensive; **ne pas ~ cher** to be cheap, not to cost a lot; **~ cher à qn** lit [*travaux, achat*] to cost sb a lot; fig [*erreur, action*] to cost sb dear(ly).

III *v impers* **ce chien nous coûte cher** this dog costs us a lot; **il en coûte à qn de faire** it's hard for sb to do; **il t'en coûtera d'avoir fait cela** you will pay for doing this; **coûte que coûte**, **quoi qu'il en coûte** at all costs.

IDIOMES **il n'y a que le premier pas qui coûte** the first step is the hardest; **~ la peau des fesses**◑ or **les yeux de la tête**○ to cost an arm and a leg○.

coûteusement /kutøzmɑ̃/ *adv* expensively.

coûteux, **-euse** /kutø, øz/ *adj* **1** (qui entraîne des dépenses) costly; **un bâtiment ~ à rénover** a building which is costly to renovate; **2** (qui entraîne des pertes) costly; **politique coûteuse en temps/pour l'environnement** policy which is costly in terms of time/for the environment.

coutil /kuti/ *nm* (pour vêtement) (cotton) drill; (pour matelas) ticking; **pantalon de ~** twill trousers GB ou pants US.

coutre /kutʀ/ *nm* coulter GB, colter US (of plough GB ou plow US).

coutume /kutym/ *nf* **1** (habitude) custom; **selon la ~** according to custom; **selon sa ~** as is his/her custom; **avoir ~ de faire qch** to be in the habit of doing sth; **la ~ le veut** it is the custom; **la ~ veut que** custom has it that; **de ~** as a rule; **comme de ~** as usual; **plus tôt/tard que de ~** earlier/later than usual; **2** Jur (usage) custom; (recueil) customary.

IDIOMES **une fois n'est pas ~** it does no harm just this once.

coutumier, **-ière** /kutymje, ɛʀ/ **I** *adj* **1** (habituel) customary, usual; **2** Jur [*droit, autorité*] customary.

II *nm* Jur customary.

couture /kutyʀ/ **I** *adj inv* designer.

II *nf* **1** (activité, chose à coudre) sewing; (activité professionnelle) dressmaking; **faire de la ~** to sew; (occasionnellement) to do some sewing; **haute ~** haute couture; **2** (bords cousus) seam; **faire une ~ pour assembler** to stitch [sth] together; **sans ~s** seamless; **avec** or **à ~s** seamed; **~ apparente** visible seam; **~ rabattue** flat seam; **~ anglaise** French seam.

IDIOMES **le petit doigt sur la ~ du pantalon** standing stiffly to attention; **regarder** or **examiner qch sous toutes les ~s** to look at ou scrutinize sth from every angle; **battre qn à plates ~s** to beat sb hollow.

couturé, **~e** /kutyʀe/ **I** *pp* ▶ **couturer**.

II *pp adj* [*visage*] scarred.

couturier /kutyʀje/ *nm* **1** ▶ **510** dress designer; **grand ~** couturier; **2** Anat sartorius (muscle).

couturière /kutyʀjɛʀ/ *nf* **1** ▶ **510** Cout dressmaker; **2** Théât dress rehearsal.

couvain /kuvɛ̃/ *nm* (œufs) brood.

couvaison /kuvɛzɔ̃/ *nf* (action) brooding; (période) incubation (period).

couvée /kuve/ *nf* (d'oisillons, enfants) brood; (d'œufs) clutch.

couvent /kuvɑ̃/ *nm* **1** (pour femmes) convent; (pour hommes) monastery; **entrer au ~** to enter a convent; **2** (école) convent school.

couventine /kuvɑ̃tin/ *nf* (religieuse) conventual; (écolière) convent schoolgirl.

couver /kuve/ [1] **I** *vtr* **1** Zool to brood; **~ trois œufs** to sit on three eggs; **2** (protéger) to overprotect; **tu le couves trop** you are overprotective (of him); **~ qn/qch du regard** (avec tendresse) to look fondly at sb/sth; (avec envie) to gaze longingly at sb/sth; **3** (être atteint de) to be sickening for [*maladie*]; **4** (préparer) to hatch [*complot*]; to plot [*vengeance*].

II *vi* [*révolte*] to brew; [*colère, jalousie*] to smoulder; [*racisme, fanatisme*] to lie dormant; [*feu*] to smoulder.

couvercle /kuvɛʀkl/ *nm* (de boîte, pot, casserole) lid; (qui se visse) screw-top.

couvert, **~e** /kuvɛʀ, ɛʀt/ **I** *pp* ▶ **couvrir**.

II *pp adj* **1** (plein) covered (**de** in, with); **pages ~es d'écriture** closely-written pages; **être ~ de diplômes** to have a lot of qualifications; **2** (en intérieur) [*piscine*] indoor; [*court de tennis*] indoor, covered; [*marché, stade, passage*] covered; **3** Météo [*ciel*] overcast; [*temps*] overcast, cloudy, dull.

III *nm* **1** (accessoires pour un repas) place setting; **un lave-vaisselle pour 12 ~s** a dishwasher for 12 place settings; **retirer un ~** to take away a place setting; **ajouter un ~** to set another place; **une table de six ~s** a table set for six; **mettre le ~** to lay the table; **mettre trois ~s** to lay ou set the table for three; **mets-lui un ~** set a place for him/her; **avoir son ~ chez qn** fig to be a frequent dinner guest at sb's house; **un repas de 12 ~s** a meal for 12 (people); **2** (ustensiles) **mettre les ~s** to put out the knives and forks; **un ~ en argent** a silver knife, fork and spoon; **ils mangent avec des ~s en argent** they eat with silver cutlery; **il manque les ~s** (sur la table) the knives and forks aren't on the table; **~ à dessert** dessert knife, fork and spoon; **un ~ à poisson** a fish knife and fork; **3** Comm (au restaurant) cover charge; **ils ne font pas payer le ~** there's no cover charge; **4** (abri) cover; **sous le ~ d'un arbre/bois** under the cover of a tree/wood; ▶ **gîte 1**.

IV à couvert *loc adv* under cover; **se mettre à ~** to take cover; **mettre sa fortune à ~** to safeguard one's fortune.

V à couvert de *loc prép* **être** or **rester à ~ de la pluie** to be sheltered from the rain; **être** or **rester à ~ d'un bois** to take cover in a wood; **se mettre à ~ de** to shelter from.

VI sous le couvert de *loc prép* **1** (apparence) under the pretence[GB] of; **sous ~ de la plaisanterie** under the guise of a joke; **2** Admin **écrire à X, sous le ~ de Y** to write to X, care of Y.

VII couverte *nf* **1** Imprim covering, facing; **2** Art glaze.

couverture /kuvɛʀtyʀ/ *nf* **1** (de lit) blanket; (plus petit) rug GB, lap robe US; **2** (de livre, cahier, magazine) cover; **en ~** on the (front) cover; **3** (de journaliste, presse) coverage; **assurer la ~ d'un événement** to cover an event; **4** Constr roofing; **~ d'ardoises/de chaume** slate/thatched roofing; **il faut changer toute la ~** the whole roof needs replacing; **5** Assur, Fin, Mil cover; (cachant activités suspectes) cover; **~ aérienne** air cover; **taux de ~** (dans échanges commerciaux) import-export ratio; **6** École **~ (végétale)** plant cover.

■ **~ chauffante** electric blanket; **~ sociale** social security cover; **~ de voyage** travelling rug GB, lap robe US.

IDIOMES **tirer la ~ à soi** to turn a situation to one's own advantage.

couveuse /kuvøz/ *nf* **1** (appareil) incubator; **être en ~** to be in an incubator; **2** (poule) brood hen.

couvrant, **~e** /kuvʀɑ̃, ɑ̃t/ **I** *adj* [*peinture, produit de beauté*] that provides good cover (*épith, après n*); **pouvoir ~ (d'une peinture)** surface coverage (of a paint).

II couvrante◑ *nf* (couverture) blanket.

couvre-chef, *pl* **~s** /kuvʀəʃɛf/ *nm* hum headgear ¢, hat.

couvre-feu, *pl* **~x** /kuvʀəfø/ *nm* curfew;

instaurer le ~ to impose a curfew; **lever le ~** to lift the curfew.

couvre-lit, *pl* **~s** /kuvRəli/ *nm* bedspread.

couvre-matelas /kuvRəmatla/ *nm inv* mattress cover.

couvre-pieds /kuvRəpje/ *nm inv* small quilt.

couvre-plat, *pl* **~s** /kuvRəpla/ *nm* dish cover.

couvre-théière, *pl* **~s** /kuvRətejɛR/ *nm* tea cosy.

couvreur /kuvRœR/ ▶ **510** *nm* roofer.

couvrir /kuvRiR/ [32] **I** *vtr* **1** (recouvrir) gén to cover [*meuble, mur, objet, feu, blessé*] (**de** with); to roof [*maison*]; (aux cartes) to cover; **des boutons couvraient son corps** his/her body was covered in ou with spots GB ou pimples; **~ un toit d'ardoises/de tuiles/de chaume** to slate/tile/thatch a roof; **~ des pages et des pages d'une écriture serrée** to fill page after page in closely written script; **une peinture qui couvre bien** a paint that gives good coverage; **2** (être plus fort que) [*son, musique*] to drown out; **3** (desservir) [*émetteur, radio, inspecteur*] to cover [*région*]; **4** (contre le froid) (avec des vêtements) to wrap [sb] up; (au lit) to cover [sb] up; **il est trop couvert** (vêtu) he's got too many clothes on; (au lit) he's got too many blankets on; **je ne l'ai pas assez couvert** (vêtu) I haven't dressed him warmly enough; (au lit) I haven't put enough blankets on his bed; **5** (donner en grande quantité) **~ qn de coups/d'honneurs** to shower sb with blows/honours[GB]; **~ qn de bijoux/compliments** to shower jewels/compliments on sb; **~ qn d'or** lit to shower sb with gold; fig (enrichir) to make sb wealthy; **~ qn de baisers** to cover sb with kisses; **6** (protéger) to cover up for [*faute, personne*]; (avec une arme) to cover [*complice, soldat, retraite*]; **~ qn de son corps** to shield sb with one's body; **7** (parcourir) [*coureur, véhicule*] to cover [*distance*]; **8** (rendre compte de) [*livre, film*] to cover [*sujet, période*]; [*journaliste, presse*] to cover [*affaire, événement*]; **9** (pourvoir à) **~ les besoins de qn** to meet sb's needs; **10** Fin [*somme*] to cover [*dépenses, coûts*]; **~ une enchère** to make a higher bid; **11** Assur (garantir) to cover [*dégât, risque, personne*]; **12** Zool [*mâle*] to cover [*femelle*]; **faire ~** to get [sth] covered.

II se couvrir *vpr* **1** (s'habiller) to wrap up; (d'un chapeau) to put on a hat; **tu ne te couvres pas assez** you don't wrap up well enough; **elle se couvrit les épaules d'un châle noir** she covered her shoulders with a black shawl; **rester couvert** to keep one's hat on; **2** Météo [*ciel*] to become cloudy ou overcast; **le temps se couvrira un peu cet après-midi** it will cloud over in the afternoon; **3** (se remplir) **se ~ de** (de plaques, boutons) to become covered with; **au printemps la pelouse se couvre de fleurs** in spring the lawn becomes a carpet of flowers; **l'arbre se couvre de fleurs/feuilles** the tree comes into bloom/leaf; **son visage se couvrit de sueur/larmes** sweat/tears poured down his/her face; **4** (se protéger) (de critiques, d'accusations) to cover oneself, to cover one's back; (de coups) to protect oneself; **5** Assur **se ~ contre** to cover oneself against.

covoiturage /kovwatyRaʒ/ *nm* car sharing.

coxalgie /kɔksalʒi/ *nf* coxalgia.

coyote /kɔjɔt/ *nm* coyote.

CP /sepe/ *nm*: *abbr* ▶ **cours**.

CPAO /sepeao/ *nf*: *abbr* ▶ **conception**.

CPR /sepeɛR/ *nm* (*abbr* = **Centre pédagogique régional**) ≈ Teachers' Centre GB; **il fait son (stage de) ~** he is doing his year's teaching practice.

CQAO /sekyao/ *nm*: *abbr* ▶ **contrôle**.

CQFD /sekyɛfde/ (*abbr* = **ce qu'il fallait démontrer**) QED.

crabe /kRab/ *nm* Zool crab; **marcher en ~** to sidle along, to walk crabwise.

crac /kRak/ *nm* (*also onomat*) (cassure) crack; (déchirure) rip; **entendre un ~** to hear a cracking sound; **et puis ~! elle a changé d'idée** and then, bang! she changed her mind.

crachat /kRaʃa/ *nm* **1** spit ¢; **un ~** some spit; **couvert de ~s** covered in spit; **2**○† (décoration) decoration, gong○ GB.

craché○, **~e** /kRaʃe/ *adj* **tu es (le portrait de) ta mère toute ~e** you're the spitting image of your mother; **c'est lui tout ~** that's just like him.

crachement /kRaʃmɑ̃/ *nm* **1** (de salive, etc) spitting ¢, expectorating ¢ spéc; **le ~ de sang indique que** spitting blood is a sign that; **2** (de fumée) belching ¢; (d'étincelles) shower; (de flammes) burst; **3** (bruit à la radio, d'arme, etc) crackling ¢.

cracher /kRaʃe/ [1] **I** *vtr* **1** (ce qui est dans la bouche) to spit out [*noyau, aliment*]; **~ du sang** to spit blood; **crache-le**, **crache** spit it out; **2**○ (payer) to cough up○ [*somme*]; **3** (dire) **~ des injures à qn** to hurl abuse at sb; **'bande d'idiots,' cracha-t-elle** 'you fools,' she hissed; **elle lui cracha à la figure que** she told him/her venomously that; **4** (émettre) to belch out [*flammes, fumée*]; to spit out [*balles*].

II *vi* **1** [*personne*] to spit; **2** fig **~ sur qn** (mépriser) to despise sb; (injurier) to hurl abuse at sb; **je ne cracherais pas dessus**○ I wouldn't say no, I wouldn't turn up my nose at it; **3** [*robinet, stylo*] to splutter; [*radio*] to crackle.

IDIOMES **c'est comme si on crachait en l'air**○ it's a complete waste of time.

cracheur /kRaʃœR/ *nm* **~ de feu** fire-eater.

crachin /kRaʃɛ̃/ *nm* drizzle.

crachiner /kRaʃine/ [1] *v impers* to drizzle.

crachoir /kRaʃwaR/ *nm* spittoon.

IDIOMES **tenir le ~**○ to talk nonstop, to talk a mile a minute US; **tenir le ~ à qn**○ to talk on and on at sb○.

crachotement /kRaʃɔtmɑ̃/ *nm* **1** (de personne) coughing and spluttering ¢; **2** (de radio, micro) crackling ¢.

crachoter /kRaʃɔte/ [1] *vi* **1** [*personne*] to cough and splutter; **2** [*robinet, stylo*] to splutter; **3** [*micro, radio*] to crackle.

crachouiller /kRaʃuje/ [1] *vi* [*personne*] to cough and splutter.

crack /kRak/ *nm* **1** (cheval) champion horse; **2**○ (génie) ace; **c'est un ~ en français** he/she is an ace at French; **c'est un ~ au volant** he/she is an ace driver; **3**○ (drogue) crack○.

cracking /kRakiŋ/ *nm* = **craquage**.

cracra○ /kRakRa/, **cradingue**◐ /kRadɛ̃g/, **crado**○ /kRado/ *adj* [*personne, vêtement*] filthy; [*endroit*] grotty GB, grungy US.

craie /kRɛ/ *nf* (roche, bâton) chalk; **~ (de) tailleur** French chalk, tailor's chalk; **écrire qch à la ~ sur** to chalk sth on.

craignos◐ /kRɛɲos/ *adj* [*personne, lieu, attitude*] scary○; [*situation*] hairy○.

craindre /kRɛ̃dR/ [54] **I** *vtr* **1** (redouter) to fear, to be afraid of [*personne, attaque, réprimande, mort*]; **avoir tout à ~ de qn/qch** to have every reason to fear sb/sth; **n'avoir rien à ~ de qn/qch** to have nothing to fear from sb/sth; **~ une rechute/le pire** to fear a relapse/the worst; **ne craignez rien** don't be afraid; **oui, je le crains** yes, I'm afraid so; **~ pour** to fear for [*vie, réputation*]; **se faire ~** to make oneself feared; **~ de faire** to be afraid of doing; **il craignait d'être attaqué** he was afraid of ou he feared being attacked; **je crains d'avoir à le vendre** I am afraid ou I fear I may have to sell it; **je crains de ne pouvoir y aller** I am afraid ou I fear I may not be able to go; **je crains qu'il ne manque le train** I'm afraid ou I fear that he might miss the train; **je crains qu'il n'ait eu un accident** I'm afraid ou I fear that he may have had an accident; **ne crains-tu pas qu'il refuse?** aren't you afraid he might ou he'll say no?; **je crains que vous ne fassiez erreur** euph I'm afraid you are mistaken; **il est à ~ que l'amélioration ne dure pas** it is to be feared that the improvement won't last; **une explosion est à ~** there's some danger of an explosion; ▶ **échauder**; **2** (regretter) **~ de** to be afraid (that); **~ que** to be afraid (that); **je crains de ne pas savoir** I am afraid (that) I don't know; **je crains que non** I am afraid not; **3** (être sensible à) [*personne*] to be sensitive to [*froid*]; [*plante*] to dislike [*soleil*]; [*peau*] to be sensitive to [*savon*]; **ce produit craint l'humidité/la chaleur** this product must be kept in a dry/cool place.

II○ *vi* **ça craint!** that's bad!

III se craindre *vpr* to be afraid of each other.

crainte /kRɛ̃t/ *nf* **1** (peur) fear (**de** of; **de faire** of doing); **la ~ du ridicule/d'être ridicule** fear of ridicule/of being ridiculous; **sans ~** without fear; **par ~ de qch/de faire** for fear of sth/of doing; **de ~ qu'on ne le voie** for fear of being seen; **de ~ qu'elle ne l'apprenne** for fear that she might find out; **de ~ d'avoir à payer, il n'est pas venu** he didn't come for fear of having to pay ou fearing that he might have to pay; **avec ~** fearfully; **2** (inquiétude) fear; **~s injustifiées** groundless fears; **alimenter/apaiser les ~s** to bolster/to calm fears; **avoir des ~s au sujet de qn** to be worried about sb; **n'ayez ~, soyez sans ~** have no fear.

IDIOMES **la ~ est le commencement de la sagesse** Prov only a fool knows no fear.

craintif, **-ive** /kRɛ̃tif, iv/ *adj* [*personne, attitude, voix*] timorous; [*animal*] timid.

craintivement /kRɛ̃tivmɑ̃/ *adv* timidly.

cramé○ /kRame/ *nm* **ça sent le ~** there is a smell of burning.

cramer○ /kRame/ [1] **I** *vtr* to burn [*rôti*]; to singe [*linge*].

II *vi* [*maison, forêt, meubles*] to go up in flames.

cramique /kRamik/ *nm* B currant loaf.

cramoisi, **~e** /kRamwazi/ ▶ **193** *adj* crimson (**de** with).

crampe /kRɑ̃p/ *nf* cramp; **avoir une ~ à la jambe** to have cramp GB ou a cramp US in one's leg; **des ~s** cramp.

■ **~s d'estomac** stomach cramps.

crampon /kRɑ̃pɔ̃/ **I**○ *adj* [*personne*] clingy○.

II *nm* **1** (d'alpiniste) crampon; **chaussures à ~s** (de football, rugby) boots with studs GB ou cleats US; (de course) spiked shoes; **2**○ (personne) **quel ~!** what a leech!; **3** (pour assembler) cramp (iron), clamp.

cramponner /kRɑ̃pɔne/ [1] **I**○ *vtr* to cling to.

II se cramponner *vpr* to hold on tightly; **se ~ à qch/qn** lit, fig to cling to sth/sb.

cran /kRɑ̃/ **I** *nm* **1** (encoche) notch; (sur ceinture, courroie) hole; **resserrer sa ceinture d'un ~** to tighten one's belt by one notch; **se mettre un ~ à la ceinture** fig to tighten one's belt; **monter d'un ~** [*cote de popularité*] to go up a notch; [*personne*] (dans l'estime) to move up a notch; (dans une hiérarchie) to move up a rung; **pousse-toi d'un ~** move up one (place); ▶ **couteau**; **2** Cout, Imprim (comme repère) nick; **3**○ (courage) **avoir du ~** (courage) to have guts○; **4** (en coiffure) wave; **se faire faire des ~s** to have one's hair crimped.

II à cran *loc adv* **être à ~, avoir les nerfs à ~** (irrité) to be edgy ou on edge; **ne la mets pas à ~** (en colère) don't make her angry.

■ **~ d'arrêt** flick knife GB, switchblade US; **~ de sûreté** safety catch.

crâne /kRɑn/ **I** *adj* [*personne*] gallant; péj cocksure.

II *nm* **1** Anat (boîte osseuse) skull, cranium spéc; **2**○ (tête) head; **avoir mal au ~**○ to have a (splitting) headache; **ne rien avoir**

dans le ~ to have no brains; **avoir le ~ dur** fig to be thick(-skulled)○.
IDIOMES **bourrer le ~ à qn**○ to brainwash sb.

crânement /kʀɑnmɑ̃/ *adv* (bravement) gallantly; (fièrement) proudly; (insolemment) cheekily.

crâner○ /kʀɑne/ [1] *vi* to show off.

crânerie† /kʀɑnʀi/ *nf* gallantry; péj swaggering.

crâneur○, **-euse** /kʀɑnœʀ, øz/ **I** *adj* pretentious; **être ~** to be a show-off, to be pretentious.
II *nm,f* show-off; **faire le ~** to show off.

crânien, **-ienne** /kʀɑnjɛ̃, ɛn/ *adj* cranial; **boîte crânienne** cranium.

craniologie /kʀɑnjɔlɔʒi/ *nf* craniology.

cranter /kʀɑ̃te/ [1] *vtr* **1** (entailler) to notch; **2** (en coiffure) to crimp; **cheveux crantés** crimped hair.

crapahuter○ /kʀapayte/ [1] *vi* soldiers' slang to yomp○.

crapaud /kʀapo/ *nm* **1** Zool toad; **2**○ (enfant) **petit ~!** little monkey○; **3** (de diamant) flaw.
IDIOMES **la bave du ~ n'atteint pas la blanche colombe** hum ≈ sticks and stones (may break my bones but words will never hurt me).

crapaudine /kʀapodin/ *nf* **1** (grille) grating; **2** (palier) hinge bearing.

crapouillot /kʀapujo/ *nm* Hist Mil trench-mortar.

crapule /kʀapyl/ *nf* **1** (individu) crook; **2**○ (enfant espiègle) monkey○.

crapulerie† /kʀapylʀi/ *nf* **1** (acte) dirty trick○; **2** (nature) villainy.

crapuleux, **-euse** /kʀapylø, øz/ *adj* [*acte, personne*] villainous; ▶ **crime**.

craquage /kʀakaʒ/ *nm* Chimie cracking.

craquant○, **~e** /kʀakɑ̃, ɑ̃t/ *adj* [*personne*] irresistible.

craque◑ /kʀak/ *nf* tall story○.

craquèlement /kʀakɛlmɑ̃/ *nm* crackling.

craqueler /kʀakle/ [19] **I** *vtr* gén to crack; (en céramique) to crackle.
II se craqueler *vpr* to crack.

craquelure /kʀaklyʀ/ *nf* crack; **~s** (en céramique) (accidentelles) crazing ¢; (délibérées) crackle ¢; Art craquelure ¢.

craquement /kʀakmɑ̃/ *nm* (produit en pliant) creaking sound, creak; (produit en se brisant) cracking sound, crack; (de feuilles mortes) crackle ¢.

craquer /kʀake/ [1] **I** *vtr* **1** (déchirer) to split [*pantalon, veste, jupe*]; to rip [*collant*]; to burst [*sac*]; to break [*sangle, poignée*]; **2** (frotter) to strike [*allumette*]; **3** Chimie to crack [*pétrole*].
II *vi* **1** (se rompre) [*couture*] to split; [*vêtement*] to split (at the seams); [*collant*] to rip; [*branche, poutre, plaque de verre*] to crack; [*sac*] to burst; **ta veste va ~ sous les bras** your jacket is going to split under the arms; **faire ~ une branche/poutre** to break a branch/beam; **2** (faire un bruit) [*plancher, mât*] to creak; [*neige*] to crunch; [*feuilles*] to rustle; [*branchages, brindilles*] to crack; **qui craque sous la dent** crunchy; **faire ~ ses articulations** to crack one's joints; **3** (pour allumer) **faire ~ une allumette** to strike a match; **4**○ (ne pas résister) [*entreprise*] to collapse; [*personne*] (de tension nerveuse) to break down, to crack up○; (dans effort) to give up; **je craque** (de tension nerveuse) I'm cracking up○; (séduit par qch) I just can't resist; **~ pour qn** (tomber amoureux) to fall for sb○.

crasher○: **se crasher** /kʀaʃe/ [1] *vpr* controv [*avion*] to crash land; [*voiture*] to crash (**dans, contre** into).

crasse /kʀas/ **I** *adj* [*ignorance, stupidité*] crass; [*impolitesse*] gross; **être d'une ignorance ~** to be pig ignorant○.
II *nf* **1** (saleté) grime, filth; **plein de ~** covered in filth; **2**○ (mauvais tour) dirty trick, mean trick; **faire une ~ à qn** to play a dirty trick on sb; **3** Tech (scorie) dross, slag; (résidus) scum ¢.

crasseux, **-euse** /kʀasø, øz/ *adj* filthy, grimy.

crassier /kʀasje/ *nm* slag heap.

cratère /kʀatɛʀ/ *nm* Antiq, Géog crater.

cravache /kʀavaʃ/ *nf* whip; **donner un coup de ~ à** to whip.

cravacher /kʀavaʃe/ [1] **I** *vtr* to whip [*cheval*].
II○ *vi* **1** (rouler vite) to belt along○; **2** (travailler dur) to work like mad○.

cravate /kʀavat/ *nf* **1** (pour chemise) tie; (insigne de décoration) ribbon; **2** (prise de catch) headlock; **3** Naut sling.
■ **~ de chanvre** hum hangman's rope.
IDIOMES **s'en jeter un derrière la ~**◑ to put one down the hatch○, to knock back a drink○.

cravaté, **~e** /kʀavate/ **I** *pp* ▶ **cravater**.
II *pp adj* (portant une cravate) wearing a tie; **~ de soie** wearing a silk tie.

cravater /kʀavate/ [1] *vtr* **1**○ (saisir par le cou) to grab [sb] round the neck; (en sport) to put [sb] in a headlock; **2**◑ (arrêter) [*police*] to collar○, to nab○; [*importun*] to buttonhole; **se faire ~ par qn** to be collared ou buttonholed by sb.

crave /kʀav/ *nm* chough.

crawl /kʀol/ *nm* crawl; **nager le ~** to do ou swim the crawl.

crawler /kʀole/ [1] *vi* to do ou swim the crawl; **dos crawlé** backstroke; **nager le dos crawlé** to do ou swim backstroke.

crayeux, **-euse** /kʀɛjø, øz/ *adj* gén chalky; [*teint*] chalk-white; **d'un blanc ~** chalk-white.

crayon /kʀɛjɔ̃/ *nm* **1** (pour écrire) pencil; **au ~** [*écrire, dessiner*] in pencil; **dessin au ~** pencil drawing, drawing in pencil; **remarque au ~** comment written in pencil, pencilled[GB] remark; **avoir un bon coup de ~** to be good at drawing; **barrer qch d'un coup de ~** to draw a pencil-line through sth; **faire un portrait en trois coups de ~** to quickly sketch a portrait; **2** Cosmét, Pharm pencil, stick; **3** (dessin) pencil drawing; **4** Nucl **~ (combustible)** fuel rod.
■ **~ à bille** ballpoint pen; **~ de couleur** coloured[GB] pencil; **~ feutre** felt-tip pen; **~ gras** soft pencil; **~ à lèvres** lip pencil; **~ noir** lead pencil; **~ optique** or **lumineux** light pen; **~ à papier** lead pencil; **~ pour les yeux** eyeliner; **~ à sourcils** eyebrow pencil.

crayon-feutre, *pl* **crayons-feutres** /kʀɛjɔ̃føtʀ/ *nm* felt-tip pen.

crayon-lecteur, *pl* **crayons-lecteurs** /kʀɛjɔ̃lɛktœʀ/ *nm* bar-code reader.

crayonnage /kʀɛjɔnaʒ/ *nm* (croquis) pencil sketch; (gribouillage) **des ~s** scribbles.

crayonner /kʀɛjɔne/ [1] *vtr* (dessiner) to make a pencil sketch of; (écrire) to scribble down.

créance /kʀeɑ̃s/ *nf* **1** Fin, Jur (somme due) debt (*owed by a debtor*); (titre) letter of credit; **2** (foi) liter credence sout; **mériter ~** to deserve credence; **donner ~ à qch** (croire) to give credence to sth; (rendre croyable) to lend credibility to sth; **perdre ~ auprès de qn** to lose credibility with sb.
■ **~ douteuse** bad debt; **~s à recouvrer** outstanding debts.

créancier, **-ière** /kʀeɑ̃sje, ɛʀ/ *nm,f* creditor; **~ hypothécaire/privilégié** secured/preferential creditor.
■ **~ gagiste** lienor.

créateur, **-trice** /kʀeatœʀ, tʀis/ **I** *adj* creative; **un dieu ~** a god of creation.
II *nm,f* (de parfum, genre littéraire, rôle) creator; (de produit) designer.

Créateur /kʀeatœʀ/ *nm* Relig **le ~** the Creator.

créatif, **-ive** /kʀeatif, iv/ *adj* creative.

création /kʀeasjɔ̃/ *nf* **1** (action de créer, produit original) creation; Comm (action) invention; (produit) product; **la ~ d'une société/d'un comité** the setting up of a company/a committee; **la ~ d'emplois** job creation; **il y aura des ~s d'emplois** new jobs will be created; **on va encourager les ~s d'entreprises** they are going to encourage business start-ups; **2** (univers) **la ~** creation; **3** Théât **c'est une ~** (rôle) the part has never been acted before; (pièce) the play is being staged for the first time.

Création /kʀeasjɔ̃/ *nf* Bible **la ~ (du monde)** the Creation.

créativité /kʀeativite/ *nf* creativity; **elle est d'une grande ~** she is very creative.

créature /kʀeatyʀ/ *nf* gén creature; **une ~ de rêve** a beautiful woman.

crécelle /kʀesɛl/ *nf* (instrument, jouet) rattle; **une voix de ~** a shrill voice.

crécerelle /kʀesʀɛl/ *nf* kestrel.

crèche /kʀɛʃ/ *nf* **1** (garderie) crèche GB, day-nursery; **mon fils va à la ~** my son is at the day-nursery; **2**◑ (logement) pad○; **3** (de Noël) crib.
■ **~ parentale** *crèche run by parents on a voluntary basis.*

crécher◑ /kʀeʃe/ [14] *vi* (loger) to live; (coucher) to crash○, to kip down○ GB.

crédence /kʀedɑ̃s/ *nf* Relig (dans église) credence (table), credenza; (dans maison) credence.

crédibilité /kʀedibilite/ *nf* credibility; **perdre sa ~** to lose credibility (**auprès de** with).

crédible /kʀedibl/ *adj* credible.

crédit /kʀedi/ *nm* **1** (somme allouée) funds (*pl*); **nous disposons d'un ~ de 20000 francs** we have funds of 20,000 francs; **voter un ~** to allocate funds; **nos ~s sont épuisés** we have run out of funds; **injecter des ~s supplémentaires** to pump in additional funds ou money; **les ~s de la recherche/défense** research/defence[GB] funding ou budget; **2** (avance de fonds) credit ¢; **accorder** or **octroyer un ~ à qn** to grant credit terms ou facilities to sb; **conditions de ~** credit terms; **~s à court/long terme** short-term/long-term credit; **organisme** or **société** or **établissement de ~** credit institution; **six mois de ~ gratuit** six months interest-free credit; **faire ~ à qn** to give sb credit; **'la maison ne fait pas ~'** 'no credit given'; **acheter qch à ~** to buy sth on credit; **une offre de ~** a credit offer; **3** Compta credit; **la colonne des débits et des ~s** the debit/credit side; **votre ~ est de 1500 francs** you are 1,500 francs in credit; **porter une somme au ~ de qn** or **d'un compte** Compta to credit sb's account with a sum of money; **4** (considération) credibility; **disposer d'un** or **jouir d'un** or **avoir un grand ~** to have a lot of credibility; **mettre** or **porter qch au ~ de qn** fig to give sb credit for sth; **n'avoir plus aucun ~** not to have any credibility any more.
■ **~ acheteur** buyer credit; **~ bancaire** bank credit; **~ en blanc** unsecured credit; **~ budgétaire** budget appropriation; **~ à la consommation** consumer credit; **~ croisé** cross currency swap; **~ documentaire** documentary credit; **~ de fonctionnement** administrative appropriation; **~ immobilier** homebuyer's loan; **~ d'impôt** tax credit; **~ municipal** pawnshop; **~ permanent** revolving credit; **~ public** public credit.

crédit-bail, *pl* **crédits-bails** /kʀedibaj/ *nm* leasing; **acheter qch en ~** to purchase sth under a leasing agreement.

créditer /kʀedite/ [1] *vtr* Compta to credit [*compte, personne*]; **la somme n'a pas été créditée** the amount has not been credited; **~ un compte/qn de 700 francs** to credit an account/sb's account with 700 francs.

créditeur, **-trice** /kʀeditœʀ, tʀis/ **I** *adj* [*compte, solde*] credit (*épith*); [*client, pays*] in credit (*après n*); **votre compte est ~** your account is in credit.
II *nm,f* (personne) customer in credit; (pays) nation in credit.

crédit-formation, *pl* **crédits-formation** /kʀedifɔʀmasjɔ̃/ *nm*: *government training grant*.

crédit-relais, *pl* **crédits-relais** /kʀediʀəlɛ/ *nm* bridging loan.

credo /kʀedo/ *nm* **1** (principes) creed, credo sout; **2** Relig **le Credo** the Creed.

crédule /kʀedyl/ *adj* gullible, credulous.

crédulité /kʀedylite/ *nf* gullibility, credulity.

créer /kʀee/ [11] **I** *vtr* **1** gén to create [*problème*]; to set up [*compagnie, comité*]; to design, to invent [*produit*]; **le plaisir de ~** the pleasure of creating something; **~ une clientèle** [*médecin, notaire*] to build up a practice; **2** Théât to create [*rôle*]; to put on [sth] (for the first time) [*pièce, spectacle*].
II se créer *vpr* **se ~ du travail** to create work for oneself; **se ~ des problèmes** to store up trouble for oneself.

crémage /kʀemaʒ/ *nm* C (sur un gâteau) icing GB, frosting US.

crémaillère /kʀemajɛʀ/ *nf* **1** Mécan, Tech rack; **ligne à ~** Rail rack railway, cog railway; **2** (de cheminée) trammel, chimney hook.
IDIOMES **pendre la ~** to have a housewarming (party).

crémation /kʀemasjɔ̃/ *nf* cremation.

crématoire /kʀematwaʀ/ *nm* crematorium; **four ~** crematorium furnace.

crématorium /kʀematɔʀjɔm/ *nm* crematorium.

crème /kʀɛm/ **I** ▶ 193 *adj inv* [*peinture, surface, tissu*] cream.
II *nm* **1**○ (café) espresso with milk; **2** ▶ 193 (couleur) cream.
III *nf* **1** (matière grasse) cream; **fraises à la ~** strawberries and cream; **escalope à la ~** escalope with cream; **2** (entremets) cream dessert; (pour fourrer un gâteau) cream; **une ~ au chocolat** a chocolate cream dessert; **un gâteau à la ~** a cream cake; **3** (soupe veloutée) **~ d'asperges/de volaille** cream of asparagus/chicken soup; **4** (liqueur) **~ de cassis/menthe** blackcurrant/peppermint liqueur, crème de cassis/menthe; **5** Cosmét, Pharm cream; **~ pour les mains/le visage** hand/face cream; **~ pour peaux sèches** dry skin cream; **~ à la cortisone** cortisone cream; **le produit existe aussi en ~** the product is also available in a cream ou also comes in a cream; **6**○ (élite) **la ~** (socialement) the cream of society; (professionnellement) the very best (people); **la ~ des linguistes** the very best linguists; **c'est la ~ des hommes/des maris** he's the perfect man/husband; **la ~ de la ~** the crème de la crème.
■ **~ anglaise** ≈ custard; **~ antirides** Cosmét anti-wrinkle cream; **~ au beurre** butter cream; **~ brûlée** crème brûlée; **~ (au) caramel** crème caramel; **~ Chantilly** Chantilly cream; **~ fraîche** crème fraîche, ≈ cream; **~ fraîche allégée** low-fat single cream GB, low-fat cream US; **~ fraîche épaisse** ≈ double cream GB (*thick cream*); **~ (fraîche) liquide** ≈ single cream GB, cream US; **~ fleurette** ≈ whipping cream; **~ fouettée** whipped cream; **~ glacée** dairy ice cream; **~ de gruyère** ≈ cheese spread; **~ de jour** Cosmét day cream; **~ de marrons** chestnut purée; **~ de nuit** Cosmét night cream; **~ pâtissière** confectioner's custard; **~ quotidienne de soin** Cosmét protective day cream; **~ renversée** caramel custard; **~ teintée** Cosmét tinted day cream.

crémerie /kʀɛmʀi/ ▶ 510 *nf* cheese shop GB ou store US; **changer de ~**○ hum to take one's custom ou business elsewhere.

crémeux, **-euse** /kʀemø, øz/ *adj* lit, fig creamy.

crémier, **-ière** /kʀemje, ɛʀ/ ▶ 510 *nm,f* cheese seller.

crémone /kʀemɔn/ *nf* espagnolette (bolt).

créneau, *pl* **~x** /kʀeno/ *nm* **1** Aut parallel parking ¢; **faire un ~** to parallel-park; **2** (moment) **tu as un ~ demain?** do you have any free time tomorrow?; **3** Comm market; **~ porteur** profitable market; **trouver un ~ sur le marché** to find a gap ou a niche in the market; **4** Archit crenel; **les ~x** crenellations.
■ **~ de lancement** Astronaut launch window; **~ publicitaire/horaire** Radio, TV advertising/time slot.
IDIOMES **monter au ~** to intervene.

crénelage /kʀenlaʒ/ *nm* (de fortification) crenellations (*pl*); (de pièce de monnaie) milling.

crénelé, **~e** /kʀenle/ **I** *pp* ▶ **créneler**.
II *pp adj* **1** [*muraille, tour*] crenellated; **2** Bot [*feuille*] crenate; **3** Hérald [*blason*] embattled.

créneler /kʀenle/ [19] *vtr* to crenellate [*tour*]; to mill [*pièce de monnaie*].

crénom† /kʀenɔ̃/ *excl* confound it‡!

créole /kʀeɔl/ **I** *adj* [*accent, cuisine*] creole.
II ▶ 462 *nm* Ling Creole.
III *nf* **1** (boucle d'oreille) hoop earring; **2** Culin **à la ~** creole.

Créole /kʀeɔl/ *nmf* Creole.

créosote /kʀeɔzɔt/ *nf* creosote.

crêpage /kʀɛ(e)paʒ/ *nm* Tech, Tex creping.
■ **~ de chignon**○ fight.

crêpe /kʀɛp/ **I** *nm* **1** Tex (tissu) crepe; **~ de laine** wool crepe; **robe de** or **en ~** crepe dress; **2** (de deuil) (voile) black veil; (brassard) black armband; (ruban) (au revers) black ribbon; (au chapeau) black band; (sur drapeau) black silk; **mettre un ~ à un drapeau** to drape a flag with black silk; **3** (latex) crepe (rubber); **semelles (de** or **en) ~** crepe soles.
II *nf* Culin pancake, crepe; **faire sauter une ~** to toss a pancake.
■ **~ de Chine** Tex crepe de chine; **~ dentelle** Culin very thin pancake; **~ georgette** Tex georgette (crepe); **~ Suzette** Culin crepe Suzette.
IDIOMES **s'aplatir comme une ~**○ pej to grovel (**devant qn** to sb, at sb's feet).

crêper /kʀepe/ [1] **I** *vtr* **1** to backcomb GB, to tease [*cheveux*]; **cheveux crêpés** (naturellement) frizzy hair; (au peigne) backcombed GB ou teased hair; **2** Tex to crepe.
II se crêper *vpr* **1** [*cheveux*] to go frizzy; **2 se ~ les cheveux** to backcomb GB ou tease one's hair.
IDIOMES **se ~ le chignon**○ (physiquement) to scratch each other's eyes out; (verbalement) to have a set-to○, to have a spat○ US.

crêperie /kʀɛpʀi/ *nf* creperie.

crépi, **~e** /kʀepi/ **I** *pp* ▶ **crépir**.
II *pp adj* rendered.
III *nm* rendering.

crépine /kʀepin/ *nf* **1** Culin caul (fat); **2** Tech inlet filter.

crépir /kʀepiʀ/ [3] *vtr* to render.

crépitation /kʀepitasjɔ̃/ *nf* gén crackling ¢; Méd crepitus.

crépitement /kʀepitmɑ̃/ *nm* (de feu, flamme) crackling ¢; (d'huile) sizzling ¢; (de fusillade) crackle ¢; (d'appareils photo) clicking ¢.

crépiter /kʀepite/ [1] *vi* [*feu, bois, marrons*] to crackle; [*huile*] to sizzle; [*pluie, grêle*] to patter; **les applaudissements crépitaient** there was a ripple of applause.

crépon /kʀepɔ̃/ *nm* (tissu) plissé, crepon; (papier) crepe paper.

crépu, **~e** /kʀepy/ *adj* [*personne*] frizzy-haired (*épith*); [*cheveux*] frizzy; **le garçon était ~** the boy had frizzy hair.

crépusculaire /kʀepyskylɛʀ/ *adj* lit, fig [*animal, vision*] crepuscular.

crépuscule /kʀepyskyl/ *nm* lit twilight, dusk; fig twilight.

crescendo /kʀeʃɛndo/ **I** *adv* Mus [*jouer*] crescendo; **aller ~** [*bruit, protestations, douleur*] to intensify; [*colère*] to grow, to mount.
II *nm* Mus crescendo.

cresson /kʀɛsɔ̃, kʀəsɔ̃/ *nm* watercress.

cressonnière /kʀɛsɔnjɛʀ, kʀəsɔnjɛʀ/ *nf* watercress bed.

Crésus /kʀezys/ *npr* Croesus.
IDIOMES **être riche comme ~** to be as rich as Croesus.

crétacé, **~e** /kʀetase/ **I** *adj* Cretaceous.
II *nm* Cretaceous.

crête /kʀɛt/ *nf* **1** Zool (de volaille) comb; (de lézard, d'oiseau) crest; **2** (de montagne, de vague) crest; (de mur, de toit) ridge; **3** Électrotech peak value; ▶ **ligne**.

Crète /kʀɛt/ ▶ 416 *nprf* Crete.

crétin, **~e** /kʀetɛ̃, in/ **I** *adj* **1**○ (idiot) moronic○ péj; **2** Méd cretin.
II *nm,f* moron○ péj.

crétinerie /kʀetinʀi/ *nf* **1**○ (acte) idiotic prank; (parole) idiotic remark; **2** (état) imbecillity.

crétiniser○ /kʀetinize/ [1] *vtr* to turn [sb] into a moron○.

crétinisme /kʀetinism/ *nm* **1**○ péj (sheer) stupidity; **2** Méd cretinism.

crétois, **~e** /kʀetwa, az/ **I** *adj* Cretan.
II *nm* Cretan.

Crétois, **~e** /kʀetwa, az/ *nm,f* Cretan.

cretonne /kʀətɔn/ *nf* cretonne.

Creuse /kʀøz/ ▶ 692 *nprf* (région, département) **la ~** Creuse.

creusement /kʀøzmɑ̃/ *nm* **1** (de sol) digging; **2** (augmentation) widening.

creuser /kʀøze/ [1] **I** *vtr* **1** (ôter de la matière dans) [*personne*] to dig a hole in [*terre*]; to hollow out [*tronc, fruit*]; to drill a hole in [*dent*]; [*bulldozer*] to dig into [*roche*]; [*mer, eau*] to eat into, to erode [*falaise, rochers*]; [*ver*] to burrow through [*terre*]; **2** (pratiquer) [*personne*] to dig [*trou, souterrain, tombe, fossé*]; to sink [*puits, fondations*]; to cut, to dig [*canal, tunnel*]; to plough GB, to plow US [*sillon*] (**dans** in); [*lapin, renard*] to dig [*terrier*]; [*rivière*] to hollow out [*lit*]; **~ un trou à la pelleteuse** to dig a hole with a mechanical digger; **~ sa propre tombe** lit, fig to dig one's own grave; **3** (marquer) [*rides*] to furrow [*front, visage*]; **elle avait le visage creusé par la faim/le chagrin/l'épuisement** her face was gaunt with hunger/grief/exhaustion; **4** (accentuer la cambrure de) **~ le dos** or **les reins** to arch one's back; **5** (accentuer) to deepen, to increase [*déficit, fossé, inégalités*]; **~ l'écart entre** to widen the gap between; **6** (approfondir) [*personne*] to go into [sth] in depth, to research [*question, sujet, théorie*]; **vous ne creusez pas assez votre analyse** your analysis does not go far enough; **si tu creuses un peu, tu t'aperçois vite que** if you scratch the surface you soon realize that.
II *vi* **~ dans la craie/la roche/l'argile** to dig into the chalk/the rock/the clay.
III se creuser *vpr* **1** (devenir concave) [*joues, visage*] to become hollow; [*mer, vagues*] to be whipped up; **2** (s'accentuer) [*rides*] to deepen; [*écart, différence*] to widen.
IDIOMES **ça creuse**○ it really gives you an appetite; **se ~ (la tête** or **la cervelle)**○ to rack one's brains.

creuset /kʀøzɛ/ *nm* **1** (récipient) crucible; **2** (mélange de cultures, d'influences) melting pot; **3** (épreuve) liter crucible; **passer par le ~ du temps/de la souffrance** to pass through the crucible of time/of suffering.

creux, **-euse** /kʀø, øz/ **I** *adj* **1** (vide à l'intérieur) [*tronc, dent, balle, tube*] hollow; **un son ~** a hollow sound; **2** (concave) [*joues, visage*] hollow; **un plat ~** a shallow dish; **assiette creuse** soup dish ou plate; **3** (vide de sens) [*discours*] empty; [*débat, raisonne-*

ment, analyse] shallow; **c'est un beau gosse mais totalement ~!** he's good-looking but he's completely shallow!; **4** (à l'activité réduite) [*heure, période*] off-peak; **pendant la saison creuse** during the off-season; **août est un mois ~ pour les affaires** August is a slack month for business; **un jour ~** a slack day.

II *adv* **sonner ~** lit to make a hollow sound; fig to ring hollow.

III *nm inv* **1** (légère dépression) hollow, dip; **les ~ et les bosses** the hollows and the bumps; **le ~ d'un arbre/rocher** the hollow of a tree/rock; **le ~ de l'épaule** the hollow of one's shoulder; **le ~ des reins** or **du dos** the small of the back; **le ~ de l'aisselle** the armpit; **il l'a frappé au ~ de l'estomac** he hit him in the pit of the stomach; **ça tient dans le ~ de la main** it fits into the palm of the hand; **l'oiseau a mangé/bu dans le ~ de ma main** the bird ate/drank from my hand; **le ~ de la vague** lit the trough of the wave; **être au ~ de la vague** fig to be at rock bottom; **au ~ de la vallée** in the bottom of the valley; **2**○ (petite faim) **avoir un (petit) ~** to feel peckish○ GB, to have the munchies○; **3** Art **en ~** [*fresque, motif*] incised, engraved; **gravure en ~** intaglio engraving; **4** (sur un graphique) trough, dip; **la courbe fait un ~** there is a trough in the curve; **5** (ralentissement d'activité) slack period; **pendant les heures de ~** during slack periods.

crevaison /kʀəvɛzɔ̃/ *nf* puncture; **avoir une ~** to have a puncture.

crevant○, **~e** /kʀəvɑ̃, ɑ̃t/ *adj* **1** (épuisant) [*activité*] killing○, exhausting; [*enfant, journée*] exhausting; **2** (amusant) hilarious; **il/c'est ~** he's/it's a scream○ ou riot○, he's/it's hilarious.

crevard○, **~e** /kʀəvaʀ, aʀd/ *nm,f* **1** (personne chétive) sickly person; **2** (glouton) greedy guts○, hog○ US.

crevasse /kʀəvas/ *nf* **1** (en montagne) crevasse; **2** (dans la terre, sur un mur) crack, fissure; **3** (gerçure) (sur les lèvres, mains) chap; (sur les mamelons) crack.

crevassé, **~e** /kʀəvase/ **I** *pp* ▶ **crevasser**.

II *pp adj* **1** [*terre*] cracked; **2** [*mains, peau*] chapped; [*mamelon*] cracked.

crevasser /kʀəvase/ [1] **I** *vtr* to cause [sth] to crack [*terre, mur*]; to chap [*peau*].

II se crevasser *vpr* [*terre, mur*] to crack; [*peau*] to chap, to become chapped.

crève○ /kʀɛv/ *nf* chill; **avoir la ~** to have a bad cold; **tu vas attraper la ~** you'll catch a chill ou your death of cold.

crevé, **~e** /kʀəve/ **I** *pp* ▶ **crever**.

II *pp adj* **1** (percé) [*ballon, pneu*] punctured; [*tympan*] burst; **2**○ (épuisé) done in○ GB, exhausted; **3** (mort) dead.

crève-cœur /kʀɛvkœʀ/ *nm inv* heartbreak; **c'est un** or **quel ~ de voir ça!** it's heartbreaking to see.

crève-la-faim○ /kʀɛvlafɛ̃/ *nmf inv* (affamé) hungry ou starving person; (clochard) down-and-out.

crever /kʀəve/ [16] **I** *vtr* **1** (percer) to puncture, to burst [*pneu, ballon*]; to burst [*bulle, abcès, tympan*]; **~ les yeux de qn** (accidentellement) to blind sb; (volontairement) to put ou gouge littér sb's eyes out; **ça te crève les yeux** fig it's staring you in the face; **ça crève les yeux** fig it's blindingly obvious; **ça me crève le cœur** fig it breaks my heart; **ça crève le cœur** fig it's heartbreaking; **2**○ (épuiser) [*travail, chaleur*] to wear [sb] out; [*patron*] to work [sb] into the ground; **cet enfant me crève** this child is wearing me out; **~ ses hommes (au travail)** to work one's men into the ground; **~ un animal** (au travail) to work an animal into the ground; **~ un cheval** (au galop) to ride a horse into the ground; **3**○ (être affamé) **la ~**◑, **~ la faim**○ or **la dalle**◑ to be famished; **on la crève**◑ **ici** they're starving us here.

II *vi* **1** (se percer) [*pneu, ballon, bulle, nuage, abcès, tympan*] to burst; [*paquet, sac*] to burst open; **faire ~ les groseilles** cook the redcurrants gently until they burst (open); **2** [*automobiliste, cycliste*] to have a puncture; **j'ai crevé deux fois en route** I had two punctures on the way; **3** (mourir) [*plante, animal*] to die; **laisser ~ des plantes/un chien** to let plants/a dog die; **faire ~ des plantes** to kill plants; **4**◑ (mourir) [*personne*] to snuff it○ GB, to croak○, to die; **qu'il crève!** he can go to hell○!, he can die for all I care!; **plutôt ~ (que de...)** I'd rather die (than...); **~ de faim/froid** to be starving/freezing; **laisser qn ~ de faim/froid** to let sb starve/freeze to death; **on crève de froid/chaleur dans cette maison** it's freezing/baking ou boiling in this house; **il fait un froid/une chaleur à ~** it's terribly cold/hot; **tu veux nous faire ~!** are you trying to finish us off?; **~ de rire** to kill oneself○ laughing; **c'est à ~ de rire** it's hysterically funny○; **~ d'envie/de jalousie** to be eaten up ou consumed with envy/with jealousy; **~ d'orgueil** to be terribly full of oneself.

III se crever *vpr* **1** (se percer) **se ~ un tympan** to burst an eardrum; **il s'est crevé un œil** he put one of his eyes out; **2**◑ (s'épuiser) to wear oneself out; **se ~ au travail** to work oneself to death; **se ~ à faire qch** to wear oneself out ou get worn out doing sth; **je me suis crevé à le peindre** I wore myself out painting it; **je me suis crevé pendant deux ans dans cette usine** I've slaved away for two years in this factory.

IDIOMES **marche ou crève** sink or swim.

crevette /kʀəvɛt/ *nf* **~ grise** shrimp; **~ rose** prawn; **filet à ~s** shrimping net.

crevettier /kʀəvɛtje/ *nm* shrimp boat.

cri /kʀi/ *nm* **1** (de personne) cry; (plus fort) shout; (aigu) scream; **un ~ de douleur/d'effroi/de surprise** a cry of pain/of fright/of surprise; **un ~ de détresse** a cry for help; **des ~s de joie/protestation** cries of joy/protest; **un ~ déchirant** a heart-rending cry; **un ~ perçant** a piercing scream; **un ~ aigu** a shriek; **au ~ de 'vive la révolution'** shouting 'long live the revolution'; **à grands ~s** [*réclamer, protester*] loudly; **un ~ d'amour** a passionate declaration of love; **pousser un ~** to scream (**de** in); **pousser un grand ~** to scream loudly; **pousser des ~s de douleur/plaisir** to cry out in pain/pleasure; ▶ **dernier**; **2** (d'animal) gén cry; (d'oiseau) call; **la pauvre bête poussait des ~s lamentables** the poor creature was crying out pitifully; **comment s'appelle le ~ du renard/paon?** what noise does the fox/peacock make?

■ **~ d'alarme** cry of alarm; **~ du cœur** cry from the heart, cri de cœur; **~ de guerre** lit, fig war cry; **~ primal** Psych primal scream.

IDIOMES **pousser** or **jeter les hauts ~s** to protest loudly.

criaillement /kʀi(j)ɑjmɑ̃/ *nm* **1** (cri désagréable) squeal; **2** Zool (d'oie) honk; (de paon) screech.

criailler /kʀi(j)ɑje/ [1] *vi* **1** (crier souvent) [*enfants*] to shriek; **2** (rouspéter) to grouse (**après** at); **3** Zool [*oie*] to honk; [*paon*] to screech.

criailleries /kʀi(j)ɑjʀi/ *nfpl* grousing ₵; **j'en ai assez de tes ~!** I've had enough of your grousing!

criant, **~e** /kʀijɑ̃, ɑ̃t/ *adj* **1** (manifeste) [*besoin, évidence, preuve*] clear, striking; [*contraste, manque*] striking; **~ de vérité** [*description, peinture, témoignage*] true to life (*jamais épith*); **il est ~ de vérité dans le rôle** he's extremely convincing in the role; **2** (scandaleux) [*inégalité, malhonnêteté, mauvaise foi*] blatant; [*injustice*] glaring; [*abus*] flagrant.

criard, **~e** /kʀiaʀ, aʀd/ *adj* **1** (perçant) [*voix*] shrill; **2** (violent) [*couleur, affiche*] garish; **3** (braillard) **un enfant ~** a child who bawls a lot.

criblage /kʀiblaʒ/ *nm* Tech (de sable) riddling; (de minerai) screening.

crible /kʀibl/ *nm* Tech (pour minerai) screen; (pour sable) riddle; **passer au ~** lit to screen [*minerai*]; fig to sift through [*résultats, chiffres*].

■ **~ mécanique** mechanical screen.

criblé, **~e** /kʀible/ **I** *pp* ▶ **cribler**.

II *pp adj* **~ de** [*corps*] (de balles, trous) riddled with; (de flèches) bristling with; (de taches de rousseur) covered in; [*personne*] (de dettes) crippled with; [*texte*] (de fautes) riddled with.

cribler /kʀible/ [1] *vtr* **1 ~ qn/qch de balles** to riddle sb/sth with bullets; **~ qn/qch de flèches** to rain arrows on sb/sth; **~ qn de coups** to rain blows on sb; **2** (accabler) **~ qn de reproches** to heap reproaches on sb; **3** Tech to screen [*minerai*]; to riddle [*grains, sable*].

cribleur /kʀiblœʀ/ *nm* Agric grader.

cribleuse /kʀibløz/ *nf* = **cribleur**.

cric /kʀik/ *nm* (de voiture) jack; **~ hydraulique** hydraulic jack; **mettre qch sur ~** to jack sth up.

cric-crac /kʀikkʀak/ *excl* click!; **~, je suis enfermé** click, I'm locked in.

cricket /kʀikɛ(t)/ **▶ 449** *nm* Sport cricket.

cricoïde /kʀikɔid/ Anat **I** *adj* cricoid.

II *nm* cricoid cartilage.

cricri /kʀikʀi/ *nm* (*also onomat*) **1** (cri du grillon) chirping; **2** (grillon) cricket.

criée /kʀije/ *nf* auction; **vente à la ~** (de bétail) cattle auction; (de poissons) auction of fish to fishmongers; **vendre à la ~** to auction [*meubles, bétail*]; **acheter à la ~** to buy [sth] at auction [*meubles, bétail*].

crier /kʀije/ [2] **I** *vtr* **1** (pour dire) to shout (**à qn** to sb); **~ des slogans** to shout ou chant slogans; **il m'a crié de m'enfuir** he shouted to me to run away; **elle a crié qu'elle en avait marre○/que c'était fini** she shouted that she'd had enough/that it was over; **2** (pour proclamer) **~ son indignation/dégoût** to proclaim one's indignation/disgust; **~ son innocence** to protest one's innocence.

II crier à *vtr ind* **ils criaient à l'oppression/l'injustice/la provocation** they protested that it was oppression/injustice/provocation; **on a crié au génie quand il a proposé sa théorie** he was proclaimed a genius when he put forward his theory; **~ au vol/au meurtre** to cry ou shout 'stop thief'/'murder'; **on a crié au scandale quand...** there was an outcry when...

III *vi* **1** (forcer la voix) [*personne*] to shout; (en pleurant) to cry; (de peur) to scream; **elle n'arrête pas de ~** [*adulte*] she's always shouting; **ne crie pas, je t'entends!** you don't have to shout, I can hear you!; **~ de joie** to shout for joy; **~ de douleur/peur/plaisir** to cry out in pain/fear/delight; **~ après**○ **qn** to shout at sb; **2** (émettre des sons) [*animal*] to give a cry; [*singe*] to chatter; [*mouette*] to cry; [*porc*] to squeal; **3** (crisser, grincer) [*craie, chaussure*] to squeak; [*planche, marche, gond*] to creak; [*pneu, frein*] to squeal; **la scie criait sur le métal** the saw screeched as it bit into the metal.

IDIOMES **~ comme un cochon qu'on égorge** or **un damné** to squeal like a stuck pig.

crieur, **-ieuse** /kʀijœʀ, øz/ *nm,f* **une foule de ~s de slogans** a crowd of slogan chanters.

■ **~ de journaux** news vendor; **~ public** Hist town crier.

CRIF /kʀif/ *nm* (*abbr* = **Conseil représentatif des institutions juives de France**) *council of French Jewish organizations*.

crime /kʀim/ **I** *nm* **1** (acte criminel) crime; **ce n'est pas un ~!** there's no law against it!; **2** (meurtre) murder; **heure/lieux du ~** time/scene of the murder; **~ crapuleux** murder for money; **~ passionnel** crime of passion, crime passionnel; **~ parfait** perfect crime; **3** (actions criminelles) crime; **le**

~ ne paie pas crime does not pay; **4** (faute) crime; **ce serait un ~ de faire** it would be a crime to do; **ton seul ~ est d'avoir dit oui** your only crime is to have said yes.
II○ *nf* crime squad.
■ **~ contre l'humanité** crime against humanity; **~ d'État** crime against the state; **~ de haute trahison** crime of high treason; **~ organisé** organized crime; **~ de sang** murder; **~s de guerre** war crimes.

Crimée /kʀime/ **▶692** *nprf* Crimea; **guerre/presqu'île de ~** Crimean war/peninsula.

criminaliste /kʀiminalist/ **▶510** *nmf* criminologist.

criminalité /kʀiminalite/ *nf* crime; **grande/petite ~** serious/petty crime; **~ informatique** computer crime; **~ organisée** organized crime.

criminel, -elle /kʀiminɛl/ **I** *adj* criminal; **acte/régime ~** criminal act/regime; **l'origine criminelle de l'accident ne fait pas de doute** there's no doubt that the accident was caused deliberately; **c'est ~ de faire** it's a crime to do.
II *nm,f* **1** (coupable d'actes criminels) criminal; ▶ **droit**; **2** (meurtrier) murderer.
III *nm* **juger/poursuivre au ~** to try/to prosecute before a criminal court.
IV criminelle○ *nf* crime squad.
■ **~ de guerre** war criminal.

criminellement /kʀiminɛlmɑ̃/ *adv* in a criminal way.

criminogène /kʀiminɔʒɛn/ *adj* **environnement ~** environment which is conducive to crime.

criminologie /kʀiminɔlɔʒi/ *nf* criminology.

criminologue /kʀiminɔlɔg/ **▶510** *nmf* criminologist.

crin /kʀɛ̃/ *nm* (de cheval) horsehair; **matelas en** or **de ~** horsehair mattress; **à tout ~** fig dyed-in-the-wool; ▶ **gant**.
■ **~ végétal** leaf fibre.

crincrin○ /kʀɛ̃kʀɛ̃/ *nm* pej scratchy (old) violin.

crinière /kʀinjɛʀ/ *nf* **1** (de lion, cheval) mane; **2**○ (chevelure) mane; **3** (de casque) plume.

crinoline /kʀinɔlin/ *nf* (jupon, robe) crinoline; **robe à ~** crinoline (dress).

crique /kʀik/ *nf* Géog cove.

criquet /kʀikɛ/ *nm* locust.
■ **~ migrateur** migratory locust; **~ pèlerin** desert locust.

crise /kʀiz/ *nf* **1** gén crisis; **~ conjugale/d'adolescence** marital/adolescent crisis; **~ de conscience** crisis of conscience; **~ d'identité** identity crisis; **la ~ de l'Église/de l'Université** the crisis in the Church/in the Universities; **être en ~** [*couple, éducation*] to be in crisis; **traverser/connaître une ~** to undergo/to experience a crisis; **2** Pol, Écon crisis; **~ ministérielle/gouvernementale** ministerial/government crisis; **~ constitutionnelle** constitutional crisis; **~ bancaire/boursière/pétrolière** banking/stock market/oil crisis; **~ agricole** crisis in the agricultural industry; **~ de l'énergie** energy crisis; **en (pleine) ~** [*secteur, pays*] in (the middle of a) crisis; **en période** or **temps de ~** in times of crisis; **être au bord de la ~** to be on the verge of a crisis; **la ~** the economic crisis, the slump; **ressentir les effets de/sortir de la ~** to feel the effects of/to come out of the economic crisis ou the slump; **la ~ de 1929** the Great Depression, the Slump; **3** (pénurie) shortage; **~ de main-d'œuvre** shortage of labour[GB]; **~ de l'emploi** job shortage; **4** Méd attack; **~ d'asthme** asthma attack; **~ de paludisme/d'urticaire** attack of malaria/of hives; **en cas de ~** in case of an attack; **~ d'angoisse** panic ou anxiety attack; **~ d'appendicite** appendicitis; **~ d'épilepsie** epileptic fit; **~ de rhumatisme** bout of rheumatism; **~ de toux** coughing fit; **5** (accès) fit; **~ de colère/jalousie** fit of rage/jealousy; **~ de larmes** crying fit; **elle a été prise d'une ~ de rangement** she had a sudden urge to tidy up; **une ~ de fou rire** (a fit of) the giggles (*pl*); **avoir une ~ de fou rire** to get the giggles; **6**○ (colère) outburst; **ne fais pas attention à mes ~s!** don't take any notice of my outbursts!; **faire/piquer**○ **une** or **sa ~** [*enfant*] to have/to throw a tantrum; [*adulte*] to have/to throw a fit○.
■ **~ cardiaque** heart attack; **~ de foie** indigestion; **~ de nerfs** hysterics (*pl*); **avoir une ~ de nerfs** to have hysterics.

crispant○, **~e** /kʀispɑ̃, ɑ̃t/ *adj* irritating, aggravating○.

crispation /kʀispɑsjɔ̃/ *nf* **1** (contraction) (de muscle, visage) tensing; (de mâchoires, main) clenching; **2** (tension nerveuse) state of tension; **3** fig (durcissement) tension.

crispé, ~e /kʀispe/ **I** *pp* ▶ **crisper**.
II *pp adj* **1** (contracté) [*doigts, mâchoires*] clenched; [*muscles, visage*] tensed; **traits ~s par la douleur/colère** features tense with pain/anger; **2** (tendu) [*personne, sourire*] tense, nervous.

crisper /kʀispe/ [1] **I** *vtr* **1** (contracter) **la colère/l'angoisse crispait son visage** his/her face was tense with anger/worry; **2**○ (irriter) **~ qn** to irritate sb, to get on sb's nerves○.
II se crisper *vpr* **1** (se contracter) [*mains, doigts*] to clench; [*visage, personne*] to tense (up); [*sourire*] to freeze; **son visage se crispait sous l'effet de la colère** his/her face was tense with anger; **ne te crispe pas sur le volant!** don't clutch the wheel so hard!; **2** fig (devenir tendu) [*personne*] to get nervous, to tense up; **3** (se raidir) [*régime, gouvernement*] to take a hard line (**sur** on).

crispin /kʀispɛ̃/ *nm* cuff (of gauntlet); **gant à ~** gauntlet.

criss = **kriss**.

crissement /kʀismɑ̃/ *nm* (de chaussures, craie, d'ongles) squeak; (de neige, sable) crunch; (de freins, pneus) screech; (de stylo à plume) scratching.

crisser /kʀise/ [1] *vi* [*chaussures, craie, ongles*] to squeak; [*gravillons, neige*] to crunch; [*pneus, freins*] to screech; [*stylo à plume*] to scratch.

cristal, *pl* **-aux** /kʀistal, o/ *nm* **1** Chimie, Minér crystal; **~ de Bohême/Baccarat** Bohemian/Baccarat crystal; **~ de soufre** sulphur[GB] crystal; **~ de glace** ice crystal; **~ de neige** snow crystal; **vase de** or **en ~** crystal vase; **2** fig (limpidité d'eau) liter crystal clarity; **eaux d'une limpidité de ~** crystal-clear waters; **voix de ~** crystal-clear voice; **3** (objet) piece of crystalware; **les cristaux** crystal(ware) ₵; **les cristaux du lustre** the crystal droplets of the chandelier.
■ **~ électro-optique** liquid crystal; **~ liquide** liquid crystal; **affichage à cristaux liquides** liquid crystal display, LCD; **~ de plomb** lead crystal; **~ de quartz** quartz crystal; **~ de roche** rock crystal; **cristaux (de soude)** (pour laver) washing soda ₵.
IDIOMES **clair comme le ~** [*yeux, eau*] as clear as crystal; **pur comme le ~** [*voix, son*] as clear as a bell.

cristallerie /kʀistalʀi/ *nf* (fabrication) crystal glassmaking; (objets) crystal; (lieu de fabrication) crystal glassworks.

cristallier /kʀistalje/ **▶510** *nm* glassworker.

cristallin, ~e /kʀistalɛ̃, in/ **I** *adj* **1** Géol [*roche*] crystalline; [*massif*] of crystalline rock (*après n*); **2** Chimie, Phys [*zone, structure*] crystal; **3** (limpide) [*eau*] crystal (*épith*); **elle avait un rire ~** her laugh was as clear as a bell.
II *nm* Anat (crystalline) lens.

cristallisation /kʀistalizasjɔ̃/ *nf* Chimie, gén crystallization.

cristalliser /kʀistalize/ [1] *vtr, vi*, **se cristalliser** *vpr* to crystallize; ▶ **sucre**.

cristallisoir /kʀistalizwaʀ/ *nm* crystallizer.

cristallographie /kʀistalɔgʀafi/ *nf* crystallography.

cristallomancie /kʀistalɔmɑ̃si/ *nf* crystal gazing.

critère /kʀitɛʀ/ *nm* **1** (pour juger, pour sélectionner) criterion; (pour évaluer) standard; (pour identifier) indication, sign; **~s psychologiques** psychological criteria; **les ~s du succès/de l'intelligence** the criteria for success/intelligence; **établir des ~s pour l'attribution d'un prix** to establish the criteria by which a prize can be awarded; **~s de gestion/de confort** standards of management/comfort; **ce n'est pas un ~** that doesn't mean anything; **le prix n'est pas un ~ de qualité** price is no indication of quality; **et si leur réaction est un ~...** and if their reaction is anything to go by ou is any indication...; **le ~ déterminant** the crucial factor; **le seul ~ qui puisse les influencer** the only consideration that could influence them; **2** (stipulation) specification; **les références aux ~s d'âge et de diplôme** the references to specifications of age and qualifications; **répondre aux** or **remplir les ~s d'âge et de diplôme** to meet the requirements as far as age and qualifications are concerned.

critérium /kʀiteʀjɔm/ *nm* Sport (épreuve de classement) heat; (cycliste) rally.

critiquable /kʀitikabl/ *adj* **1** (qu'on peut critiquer) open to criticism (*après n*); **2** (discutable, contestable) questionable.

critique /kʀitik/ **I** *adj* **1** (décisif, alarmant) Méd, Phys [*instant, situation, seuil*] critical; **2** (désapprobateur) critical; **être** or **se montrer ~ à l'égard de** or **envers** to be critical of; **ton esprit ~** your readiness to criticize ou to pick holes in things; **avoir l'esprit ~** to be always criticizing ou ready to criticize; **3** (qui évalue, juge) [*examen, présentation, édition*] critical; **la pensée ~ de notre époque** contemporary critical thought; **d'un œil ~** critically, with a critical eye; **manquer de sens ~** to lack (critical) judgment.
II ▶510 *nmf* (commentateur) critic; **un ~ littéraire/musical** a literary/music critic; **un ~ d'art/de théâtre/de cinéma** an art/a theatre[GB]/a film critic.
III *nf* **1** (reproche) criticism; **accabler qn de ~s** to heap criticism on sb; **tes ~s incessantes** your constant criticism(s); **être l'objet de ~s** to be the butt of criticism; **faire l'objet de vives ~s** to come in for sharp criticism; **faire une ~ à qn, faire des ~s à qn** to criticize sb; **j'ai une ~ à te faire** or **à t'adresser** there is one thing I would criticize you for; **une ~ que je te ferai, c'est que** there is one criticism I might make, which is that; **2** (désapprobation) criticism (**à l'égard** or **l'adresse de** of); **il ne supporte pas la ~** he can't bear criticism; **la ~ est aisée** it's easy to criticize; **3** (art de juger) criticism; **la ~ historique/littéraire/musicale** historical/literary/music criticism; **la nouvelle ~** the new criticism; **4** (de livre, film) review (**de** of); **lis les ~s avant de l'acheter** read the reviews before buying it; **avoir une bonne/mauvaise ~** to get good/bad reviews; **faire la ~ d'une pièce/d'un film** to review a play/a film; **5** (commentateurs) **la ~** the critics (*pl*); **la ~ est unanime, c'est un chef-d'œuvre** the critics all agree that it is a masterpiece.

critiqué, ~e /kʀitike/ **I** *pp* ▶ **critiquer**.
II *pp adj* **1** gén criticized; **très ~** much ou heavily criticized; **2** Ling controversial; **usage ~** controversial usage.

critiquer /kʀitike/ [1] *vtr* **1** (condamner) to criticize; **il ne fait que ~** he finds fault with everything, he criticizes everything; **se faire ~ pour qch** to be criticized for sth; **2**

(analyser) to make a critical study ou appraisal of [*ouvrage*].

croassement /kʀɔasmɑ̃/ *nm* cawing ¢.

croasser /kʀɔase/ [1] *vi* to caw.

croate /kʀɔat/ ▶537, 462 **I** *adj* Croatian.
II *nm* Ling Croatian.

Croate /kʀɔat/ ▶537 *nmf* Croat.

Croatie /kʀɔasi/ ▶321 *nprf* Croatia.

croc /kʀo/ *nm* **1** (d'animal) fang; **montrer les ~s** lit to bare one's fangs; fig to bare one's teeth; **2** Tech (crochet) butcher's hook; (perche) boathook; (fourche) pitchfork.
IDIOMES **avoir les ~s**○ to be starving.

croc-en-jambe, *pl* **crocs-en-jambe** /kʀɔkɑ̃ʒɑ̃b/ *nm* **faire un ~ à qn** lit to trip sb up; fig to set sb up.

croche /kʀɔʃ/ *nf* quaver GB, eighth note US; **double ~** semiquaver GB, sixteenth note US; **triple ~** demisemiquaver GB, thirty-second note US; **quadruple ~** hemidemisemiquaver GB, sixty-fourth note US.

croche-pied○, *pl* **~s** /kʀɔʃpje/ *nm* **faire un ~ à qn** to trip sb up.

crochet /kʀɔʃɛ/ *nm* **1** Tech hook; (d'appareil dentaire) clasp; **~ de grue** crane hook; **pendu à un ~** hung on a hook; **2** (de serrurier) picklock; **3** Cout (instrument) crochet hook; (technique) crochet; (activité) crochet; **faire du ~** to crochet; **faire qch au ~** to crochet sth; **fait au ~** crocheted; **4** Imprim square bracket; **mettre entre ~s** to put [sth] in square brackets; **5** (détour) lit, fig detour; **faire un ~** to make a detour (**par** via); **6** (écart) swerve; **faire un ~** to swerve; **7** Sport (en boxe) hook; **~ du gauche** left hook; **8** Archit crocket; **9** Radio (pour chanteur) talent contest; **10** Zool (de serpent) fang.
■ **~ d'attelage** Rail coupling; **~ de fenêtre** Tech catch; **~ à venin** fang.
IDIOMES **vivre aux ~s**○ **de qn** to sponge off○ sb.

crochetage /kʀɔʃtaʒ/ *nm* (de serrure) lock-picking.

crocheter /kʀɔʃte/ [18] *vtr* **1** Cout to crochet; **2** (ouvrir) to pick [*serrure*]; **~ une porte** to pick the lock on a door; **3** Sport to side-step.

crochu, **~e** /kʀɔʃy/ *adj* [*bec, nez*] hooked; [*doigt, main*] clawed.
IDIOMES **avoir les doigts ~s** to be tight-fisted.

croco○ /kʀɔko/ *nm* (peau) crocodile; **chaussures en ~** crocodile shoes.

crocodile /kʀɔkɔdil/ *nm* (animal, peau) crocodile; **ceinture en ~** crocodile belt; ▶**larme**.

crocus /kʀɔkys/ *nm* crocus; **des ~** crocuses.

croire /kʀwaʀ/ [71] **I** *vtr* **1** (admettre comme vrai) to believe [*histoire, récit*]; **je n'en crois pas un traître mot** I don't believe a single word of it; **il faut le voir pour le ~** it has to be seen to be believed; **faire ~ à qn** to make sb believe [*histoire*]; **2** (faire confiance à) to believe [*personne*]; **je veux bien te ~ mais** I'd like to believe you but; **tu me croiras si tu veux** believe it or not; **je n'en ai pas cru mes yeux/oreilles** I couldn't believe my eyes/ears; ▶**Dieu**; **3** (penser) to think; **j'ai cru mourir/étouffer** I thought I was dying/suffocating; **je crois rêver!** I must be dreaming!; **je crois n'avoir rien oublié** I don't think I've forgotten anything; **je crois pouvoir vous aider** I think I can help you; **~ nécessaire/bon/raisonnable de faire** to think it necessary/a good thing/reasonable to do; **il n'a pas cru bon de vous prévenir** he didn't think it necessary to warn you; **elle croyait bien faire** she thought she was doing the right thing; **~ que** to think (that); **je crois bien que non** I don't think so; **je crois savoir que** I happen to know that; **il faut ~ qu'il avait vraiment besoin de repos** it would seem that he really needed a rest; **il est malin, (il ne) faut pas**○ **~!** he's clever, believe me!; **c'est à ~ qu'elle le fait exprès** anyone would think she was doing it on purpose; **je le croyais malade/disparu/sincère** I thought he was ill/missing/sincere; **je vous croyais en Afrique!** I thought you were in Africa!; **tu le crois capable de garder le secret?** do you think he can keep the secret?; **je ne suis pas celui que vous croyez** I'm not what you think I am; **tu ne crois pas si bien dire** you don't know how right you are; **on croirait de la soie/un diamant** it looks like silk/a diamond; **coiffée comme ça on croirait sa mère** with her hair like that she looks just like her mother; **4** (se fier à) **en ~** to believe; **si l'on en croit l'auteur, à en ~ l'auteur** if we are to believe the author; **si l'on en croit le rapport** if you believe the report; **vous pouvez m'en ~** you can believe me; **à en ~ les sondages, elle va remporter les élections** if the polls are anything to go by, she will win the election; **crois-en mon expérience** take my word for it.
II croire à *vtr ind* **1** (admettre comme vrai) **~ à** to believe [*histoire, mensonge*]; to believe in [*fantômes, esprits*]; **je n'ai pas cru à ton histoire** I didn't believe your story; **personne n'a cru au suicide** no-one believed it was suicide; **nous avons cru à la victoire** we thought we'd win; **'veuillez ~ à ma sympathie'** 'with deepest sympathy'; **faire ~ à un accident/vol** to make people believe ou think it was an accident/it was theft; **2** (être convaincu du mérite de) **~ à** to believe in [*sorcellerie, justice, promesses*]; **~ à la médecine** to have faith in doctors; **~ au bonheur/à l'amour/au progrès** to believe in happiness/in love/in progress.
III croire en *vtr ind* **1** (avoir foi en) **~ en** to believe in [*Dieu, esprit, saint*]; **~ en l'existence de qch/qn** to believe in the existence of sth/sb; **2** (avoir confiance en) **~ en** to believe in; **~ en soi** to believe in oneself.
IV *vi* Relig to believe.
V se croire *vpr* **1** (se considérer) **il se croit beau/libre/seul** he thinks he's handsome/free/alone; **elle se croit tout permis** she thinks she can do what she likes; **il se croit quelqu'un** he thinks he's really somebody; **on se croirait à New York/en Afrique** you'd think you were in New York/Africa; **tu te crois où?** where do you think you are?; **2**○ (être vaniteux) **il se croit un peu, il s'y croit** he thinks he's really somebody.

croisade /kʀwazad/ *nf* **1** Relig, Hist crusade; **partir pour les ~s** to go on the Crusades; **2** fig (lutte) crusade (**contre** against; **pour** for).

croisé, **~e** /kʀwaze/ **I** *pp* ▶**croiser**.
II *pp adj* **1** (se chevauchant) [*bâtons, fils, jambes*] crossed; [*bras, mains*] folded; **châle ~ sur la poitrine** shawl crossed over the chest; **bretelles ~es dans le dos** braces GB ou suspenders US which cross over at the back; **conversations ~es** Télécom crossed lines; **2** (métissé) [*sang*] mixed; [*chien*] crossbred; **race ~e** crossbreed; **pollinisation ~e** cross-pollination; **3** Mode [*costume, veste*] double-breasted; [*dos, corsage*] cross-over (*épith*); **4** (réciproque) [*accords, alliances*] reciprocal; [*taux*] cross (*épith*); **accord de licences ~es** reciprocal licensing agreements; **participations ~es** cross ou reciprocal holdings; **indexation ~e** cross indexing; **5** Littérat [*rimes, vers*] alternate; **6** Sport **volée ~e** cross-court volley; **passe ~e** reverse pass; **7** Tex **tissu ~** twill; **8** Ordinat **compilateur ~** cross-compiler.
III *nm* **1** Hist crusader; **2** Tex twill.
IV croisée *nf* **1** (intersection) junction (**de** of); **à la ~e des chemins** lit, fig at the crossroads; **être à la ~e de deux cultures/mondes** to be poised between two different cultures/worlds; **2** (fenêtre) liter window; (fenêtre à meneaux) casement window; **3** Archit **~e d'ogives** ribbed vault; **~e du transept** transept crossing.

croisement /kʀwazmɑ̃/ *nm* **1** Transp (carrefour) crossroads; (point d'intersection) crossing, junction; **au ~ des (deux) routes** where the (two) roads cross; **au ~ de la rue A et de la rue B** where A Street and B Street cross; **au ~ de la route et de la voie ferrée** where the road crosses the railway line; **au ~ de la modernité et de la tradition** where modernity and tradition meet; **2** (entrecroisement) (de fils, lanières) crossing; **~ des financements** cross-financing; **3** (fait de passer à côté de) **le ~ de deux trains** two trains passing one another; **les ~s ne peuvent s'effectuer qu'ici** this is the only place where vehicles can pass; **4** Biol, Hort, Zool (méthode) crossing ¢ (**avec** with), cross-breeding ¢ (**avec** with); (spécimen obtenu) hybrid, cross(breed); **obtenu par des ~s répétés** obtained by repeated crossbreeding ou hybridization[GB]; **faire des ~s (d'espèces)** to crossbreed species; **faire un ~ entre A et B** to cross A with B; **c'est un ~ de A et B** it's a cross between A and B; **grâce au ~ de plusieurs techniques** fig through the combination of several techniques; **c'est le produit du ~ de deux styles** it is a mixture of two different styles.

croiser /kʀwaze/ [1] **I** *vtr* **1** (mettre l'un sur l'autre) to cross [*objets, câbles*]; **~ les bras/mains** to fold one's arms/hands; **~ les jambes** to cross one's legs; **~ les doigts (pour que ça réussisse)** fig to keep one's fingers crossed; **2** (couper) [*rue, voie*] to cross [*rue, voie*]; **3** (passer à côté de) [*véhicule, piéton*] **~ qn/qch** to pass sb/sth (coming the other way); (rencontrer) to meet; **on a croisé un car** we passed a coach GB ou bus (coming the other way); **j'ai croisé leur bateau en sortant du port** I passed their boat (coming in) as I left the harbour[GB]; **une voiture nous a croisés à vive allure** a car flashed past us in the opposite direction; **mon regard croisa le sien** our eyes met, my gaze met his/hers; **4** Biol to cross(breed) [*espèces, animaux*]; **~ A avec B** to cross A with B; **5** Sport (au tennis) **~ un coup** to play a cross-court stroke; (au football) **~ son tir** to make a diagonal pass.
II *vi* **1** Cout, Mode [*bretelles*] to cross; [*veste*] to cross over; **la veste croise mal parce qu'il a grossi** the jacket pulls across the front because he's put on weight; **2** Naut gén to cruise; (pour surveiller) to be on patrol; **~ dans le golfe** to patrol the gulf; **~ au large des côtes africaines** to cruise off the coast of Africa.
III se croiser *vpr* **1** (passer à côté) [*piétons, véhicules, navires*] to pass each other; [*colis, lettres*] to cross (in the post GB ou mail US); **2** (se couper) [*routes, lignes*] to cross; **nos regards se sont croisés** our eyes met; **3** Hist to go on a crusade.

croiseur /kʀwazœʀ/ *nm* cruiser (warship).

croisière /kʀwazjɛʀ/ *nf* cruise; **faire une/partir en ~** to go/to set off on a cruise; **régime de ~** lit cruising speed; **en allure** or **vitesse** or **régime de ~ nous faisons 850 km à l'heure** we have a cruising speed of 850 km/h; **en régime de ~, nous produirons 10 tonnes par mois** fig once we're up and running○ we'll produce 10 tons a month; **mon rythme** or **régime de ~ est de 10 pages par jour** once I've got GB ou gotten US into my stride, I can do 10 pages a day.

croisiériste /kʀwazjeʀist/ *nmf* (cruise) passenger.

croisillon /kʀwazijɔ̃/ *nm* (de croix, charpente) crosspiece; (de châssis de fenêtre) transom; (d'église) transepts (*pl*); **~s** (de fenêtre) lattice work; (sur une tarte) lattice pattern.

croissance /kʀwasɑ̃s/ *nf* **1** Écon growth; **~ annuelle/économique/rapide** annual/economic/fast growth; **forte/vive ~** sustained/sharp growth; **~ de 7%** 7% growth; **~ démographique** population growth; **en pleine ~** fast-growing (*épith*), growing fast (*jamais épith*); **chiffres en ~ constante** constantly increasing figures; **2** Physiol growth; **~ des plantes/enfants**

plant/children's growth; **pendant sa ~** while growing; **un enfant en période de** or **en pleine ~** a growing child; ▶**prime**, **rythme**.

croissant, **~e** /kʀwasɑ̃, ɑ̃t/ **I** *adj* **1** (en expansion) growing; **besoin/déficit/intérêt/nombre ~** growing need/deficit/interest/number; **doses ~es** increasingly large doses; **de manière ~e** increasingly; **2** Math [*fonction, suite*] monotonic.
II *nm* **1** Culin croissant; **~ ordinaire/pur beurre** plain/all-butter croissant; **2** (forme) crescent; **en forme de ~** crescent-shaped; **3** Hérald crescent; **4** (emblème de l'islam, de la Turquie ottomane) crescent.
■ **~ de lune** crescent moon.

croissanterie® /kʀwasɑ̃tʀi/ **▶510** *nf* croissant shop, croissanterie.

Croissant-Rouge /kʀwasɑ̃ʀuʒ/ *nm* **le ~** the Red Crescent.

croître /kʀwatʀ/ [72] *vi* **1** Physiol, Bot (se développer) [*animal, personne, plante*] to grow; **~ en volume/intelligence** to grow in volume/intelligence; **faire ~** to grow; **croissez et multipliez** be fruitful and multiply; **2** (en nombre, en importance) [*colère, peur, abstentionnisme*] to grow; [*bruit*] to get ou grow louder; **aller ~** to increase; **3** (augmenter) [*production, vente, exportation*] to grow (**de** by); [*jour*] to get longer; **~ de 3%** to grow by 3%; **4** Math [*fonction, valeur*] to increase; **faire ~** to increase.

croix /kʀwa/ *nf inv* **1** (objet) cross; (décoration, emblème) cross; **~ russe/grecque** Russian/Greek Cross; **~ ansée** or **égyptienne** ansate cross, ankh; **~ potencée** cross of Jerusalem; **en ~** crosswise, in the shape of a cross; **disposer des brindilles en ~** to lay twigs crosswise; **être disposé** or **arrangé en ~** to form a cross, to be arranged crosswise; **mettre** or **tendre les bras en ~** to hold one's arms out on either side of the body; **être mis en ~** [*condamné*] to be crucified; **2** (marque) cross; **marquer un nom d'une ~** to put a cross against ou by a name; **signer d'une ~** to sign one's name with a cross; **3** (épreuve) cross (to bear); **cet enfant, c'est une vraie ~** he's a cross I have to bear; **chacun porte sa ~** we all have our cross to bear.
■ **~ celte** or **celtique** Celtic cross; **~ de fer** (décoration) Mil Iron Cross; Sport crucifix; **~ gammée** swastika; **~ de guerre** Mil Croix de guerre; **~ de Lorraine** cross of Lorraine; **~ de Malte** Maltese cross; **~ de Saint-André** St Andrew's cross; **~ de Saint-Pierre** Peter's cross; **~ du Saint-Sépulcre** cross of Jerusalem.
IDIOMES **ton argent, tu peux faire** or **tirer** or **mettre une ~ dessus**○ you can kiss your money goodbye; **la récompense promise, tu peux faire** or **tirer** or **mettre une ~ dessus**○ you can kiss goodbye to the promised reward; **faire une ~ sur son passé** to leave the past behind; **un jour à marquer d'une ~ blanche** a red-letter day, a day to remember; **~ de bois, ~ de fer (si je mens, je vais en enfer)** cross my heart (and hope to die).

Croix-du-Sud /kʀwadysyd/ *nprf* **la ~** the Southern Cross.

Croix-Rouge /kʀwaʀuʒ/ *nprf* **la ~** the Red Cross.

crolle /kʀɔl/ *nf* B (boucle de cheveux) curl.

crollé, **~e** /kʀɔle/ *adj* B (bouclé) curled.

cromorne /kʀɔmɔʀn/ *nm* Mus crumhorn.

croquant, **~e** /kʀɔkɑ̃, ɑ̃t/ **I** *adj* [*salade, pâtisserie*] crunchy.
II *nm,f* Hist *participant in French peasants' revolts of 16th, 17th centuries.*
III *nm* Culin (petit gâteau) *small crunchy almond biscuit*; (cartilage) gristle.

croque: **à la croque au sel** /alakʀɔkosɛl/ *loc adv* with just a sprinkling of salt.

croque-madame /kʀɔkmadam/ *nm inv*: *toasted ham and cheese sandwich topped with a fried egg.*

croquembouche /kʀɔkɑ̃buʃ/ *nm*: *pyramid of cream puffs with caramel.*

croque-mitaine, *pl* **~s** /kʀɔkmitɛn/ *nm* (monstre imaginaire) bogeyman; hum ogre.

croque-monsieur /kʀɔkməsjø/ *nm inv*: *toasted ham and cheese sandwich.*

croque-mort○, *pl* **~s** /kʀɔkmɔʀ/ *nm* undertaker; **avoir une tête de ~** to look like an undertaker.

croquenot○ /kʀɔkno/ *nm* clodhopper○, shoe.

croquer /kʀɔke/ [1] **I** *vtr* **1** (manger) to crunch [*biscuit, pomme*]; **comprimé à ~** Pharm chewable tablet; **2**○ (dilapider) to blow○ [*paie*]; to squander [*fortune, argent*]; **3** (esquisser) to sketch [*personne*]; fig (décrire) to give a thumbnail sketch of [*personne*]; **elle est (jolie** or **belle) à ~** she's as pretty as a picture, she looks good enough to eat.
II *vi* **1** [*pomme, biscuit*] to be crunchy; **pomme qui croque** crunchy apple; **2** [*personne*] **~ dans une pomme** to bite into an apple.

croquet /kʀɔkɛ/ *nm* **1** **▶449** Jeux croquet; **2** Cout rickrack braid GB, rickrack US.

croquette /kʀɔkɛt/ *nf* **1** Culin croquette; **~ de viande/de pomme de terre** meat/potato croquette; **~ de poisson** fishcake; **2** (pour chien) dry dogfood ¢; (pour chat) dry catfood ¢.

croqueuse /kʀɔkøz/ *nf*
■ **~ de diamants**○ gold digger○; **~ d'hommes**○ man-eater○.

croquignolet○, **-ette** /kʀɔkiɲɔlɛ, ɛt/ *adj* cute.

croquis /kʀɔki/ *nm* **1** (dessin) sketch; **faire le ~ d'une maison** to draw a sketch of a house; **2** (description) outline; **faire un ~ de la situation** to give an outline of the situation.

crosne /kʀon/ *nm* Bot Chinese artichoke.

cross(-country) /kʀɔs(kuntʀi)/ *nm* **1** (discipline) (à pied) cross country running; (à cheval) cross country racing; (à moto) motocross; **2** (course) (à pied) cross country race; (à cheval) cross country race; (à moto) motocross event; **3** (parcours) run; **tous les soirs, je fais un ~** every evening, I go for a run.

crosse /kʀɔs/ *nf* **1** (de fusil) butt; (de revolver) grip; **frapper qn à coups de ~** (de fusil) to hit sb with the butt of a rifle; **2** Relig crozier; **~ d'évêque** bishop's crozier; **3** Sport stick; **~ de hockey** hockey stick; **4** (extrémité recourbée) (de fougère) crozier; (de canne) crook; (de violon) head; (d'aorte) arch.
IDIOMES **chercher des ~s**○ **à qn** to pick a fight with sb.

crotale /kʀɔtal/ *nm* rattlesnake.

crotte /kʀɔt/ **I** *nf* **1** (déjection) (de souris, lapin, chèvre, cheval) dropping; **ce sont des ~s** or **c'est de la ~ de souris** they're mouse droppings; **c'est de la ~ de chien/chat** it's dog/cat mess ¢ ou muck ¢; **faire une ~**○ [*personne*] to have a pooh○; [*chien, chat*] to make a mess; **2**† (boue) mud; **être dans la ~**○ fig to be up the creek○.
II○ *excl* **~ (de bique)!** damn○!
■ **~ de bique**○ rubbish ¢; **c'est pas de la ~ de bique**○ it must be worth a pretty penny○; **~ en chocolat** Culin chocolate drop; **~ de nez** bogey○ GB, booger○ US.
IDIOMES **il ne se prend pas pour de la ~**○ he thinks he's the cat's whiskers○.

crotté, **~e** /kʀɔte/ *adj* muddy.

crotter /kʀɔte/ [1] *vtr* to muddy.

crottin /kʀɔtɛ̃/ *nm* **1** (de cheval) dung; **2** (fromage) (*small round*) goat's cheese.

croulant, **~e** /kʀulɑ̃, ɑ̃t/ **I** *adj* **1** (en mauvais état) [*bâtiment*] crumbling; **2**○ (vieux) pej [*personne*] decrepit.
II○ *nm,f* (vieillard) pej old fogey.

crouler /kʀule/ [1] *vi* **1** [*mur, bâtiment*] (s'effondrer) to collapse; (se désagréger) to crumble; [*butte de terre*] to fall down; **se laisser ~ dans un fauteuil** to collapse into an armchair; **2** (aller à la ruine) [*empire, pays, régime*] to collapse; **~ de toutes parts** to collapse on all sides; **3** (être submergé) **~ sous** to be weighed down by [*dettes, travail, projets*]; [*personne*] to be inundated with [*fleurs*]; to be weighed down with [*paquets*]; [*arbre*] to be weighed down with [*fruits*]; [*ville*] to crumble under [*obus*]; **~ sous les applaudissements** [*salle*] to resound with applause; **~ sous le poids de** [*meuble, étagère, table*] to groan under the weight of.

croup /kʀup/ *nm* croup; **faux ~** spasmodic croup.

croupe /kʀup/ *nf* **1** (de cheval) croup; **monter en ~** (à cheval) to ride behind the saddle; (en moto) to ride pillion; **2**○ (postérieur) behind○, posterior hum; **3** (de colline, montagne) (rounded) top.

croupetons: **à croupetons** /akʀuptɔ̃/ *loc adv* squatting; **être à ~** to be squatting; **se mettre à ~** to squat down.

croupi, **~e** /kʀupi/ **I** *pp* ▶ **croupir**.
II *pp adj* [*eau*] stagnant.

croupier /kʀupje/ **▶510** *nm* croupier.

croupière /kʀupjɛʀ/ *nf* crupper.
IDIOMES **tailler des ~s à qn** to put a spanner in the works for sb.

croupion /kʀupjɔ̃/ *nm* **1** (d'oiseau) rump; fig **parti/parlement ~** rump party/parliament; **2** Culin (de volaille) parson's nose; **3**○ (postérieur) hum backside○.

croupir /kʀupiʀ/ [3] *vi* **1** [*eau*] to stagnate; [*détritus*] to rot; **2** [*personne*] **~ en prison** to rot in jail; **~ dans l'ignorance/la misère** to languish in ignorance/poverty.

croupissant, **~e** /kʀupisɑ̃, ɑ̃t/ *adj* [*eau*] stagnant.

croustade /kʀustad/ *nf* ≈ savoury[GB] pie.

croustillant, **~e** /kʀustijɑ̃, ɑ̃t/ *adj* **1** [*pain, peau grillée*] crispy; [*biscuit, toast*] crunchy; **2** [*histoire, détails*] spicy.

croustiller /kʀustije/ [1] *vi* [*pain*] to be crusty; [*viande grillée, chips*] to be crisp; [*chocolat*] to be crunchy.

croûte /kʀut/ *nf* **1** (surface épaisse) (de pain) crust; (de fromage) rind; **une ~ de pain** a crust; **2** (couche) (de peinture) old layers (*pl*); (de glace) crust; **3** Culin (plat) croute, pastry; **agneau/filet/pâté en ~** lamb/fillet/pâté en croute ou in pastry; **4** Méd scab; **5**○ (tableau) daub; **6** (de cuir) split, flesh split.
■ **~ continentale** Géol continental crust; **~ de lait** Méd cradle cap; **~ océanique** Géol oceanic crust; **~ terrestre** Géol earth's crust.
IDIOMES **casser la ~**○ to have a bite to eat; **gagner sa ~**○ to earn a crust○.

croûter○ /kʀute/ [1] *vtr, vi* to eat.

croûton /kʀutɔ̃/ *nm* **1** (extrémité d'un pain) crust; **2** Culin crouton; **3**○ (vieillard) pej **vieux ~** old fossil.

croyable /kʀwajabl/ *adj* **ce n'est pas ~!** (c'est surprenant) it's unbelievable!; (c'est choquant) I don't believe it!; **c'est à peine ~** it's hard to believe.

croyance /kʀwajɑ̃s/ *nf* **1** gén belief; **la ~ collective** or **populaire** popular belief; **2** Relig, Sociol belief (**en** in).

croyant, **~e** /kʀwajɑ̃, ɑ̃t/ **I** *adj* **être ~** to be a believer; **je ne suis pas ~e** I'm not a religious person, I'm a nonbeliever.
II *nm,f* believer.

CRS /seɛʀɛs/ (*abbr* = **compagnie républicaine de sécurité**) **I** *nm member of the French riot police*; **compagnie de ~** ≈ riot squad.
II *nf*: *French riot squad.*

cru, **~e** /kʀy/ **I** *adj* **1** Culin [*viande, poisson, légume*] raw; [*pâte à tarte*] uncooked; [*lait*] unpasteurized; **du fromage au lait ~** cheese made with unpasteurized milk; **se faire manger** or **dévorer tout ~**○ fig to get eaten alive○; **2** (intense) [*lumière, éclairage*] stark, harsh; [*couleur*] garish péj, harsh; **3** (direct) [*description, réalisme, réponse*] blunt; [*détail*] raw; [*représentation*] graphic; [*vérité*] harsh; **en termes un peu ~s** in rather blunt terms; **répondre de façon ~e** to answer bluntly; **il dit les choses toutes ~es**○ he says things straight out○; **4** (osé) [*langage, plaisanterie*] crude; **5** Tech [*métal*] crude; [*soie, chanvre*] raw; [*brique, terre*] unbaked.

II *adv* (sans ménagement) [*parler*] bluntly; **elle le lui a annoncé tout ~!** she told him/her straight○!; **monter à ~** Équit to ride bareback.

III *nm* **1** Vin (vignoble) vineyard; (vin) **un ~** a vintage, a growth spéc; **un nouveau/grand ~** a new/great vintage; **2** (année) vintage year; **le ~ 1987** the 1987 vintage; **de grand** or **du meilleur ~** [*disque, collection*] vintage (*épith*); **du ~** [*vin, spécialités, auteur*] local; **les gens du ~** the locals; **de son (propre) ~** [*procédé, recette*] of one's own invention; [*terme, expression*] of one's coinage; **3** Culin **le ~** raw food.

IV crue *nf* (montée des eaux) rise in water level; (inondation) flood; **il a été emporté par les ~es** he was swept away by the flood waters; **en temps de ~e** in times of flood; **en ~e** in spate; **les ~es ont inondé la plaine** the plain is flooded ou under water.

cruauté /kʀyote/ *nf* **1** (caractère) cruelty (**envers** to); **il est d'une ~ incroyable envers les animaux** he is unbelievably cruel to animals; **traiter qn avec ~** to treat sb cruelly; **2** (action cruelle) act of cruelty; **subir des ~s** to be subjected to cruelty.

cruche /kʀyʃ/ **I**○ *adj* stupid; **avoir l'air ~** to look stupid.

II *nf* **1** (contenant) jug GB, pitcher US; (contenu) jugful GB, pitcherful US; **une ~ en terre** an earthenware jug; **2**○ (personne niaise) dope○, twit○ GB.

IDIOMES **tant va la ~ à l'eau qu'à la fin elle se casse** Prov that's what comes of taking things too much for granted.

cruchon /kʀyʃɔ̃/ *nm* small jug GB, small pitcher US.

crucial, **~e**, *mpl* **-iaux** /kʀysjal, o/ *adj* [*moment, question, année*] crucial.

crucifère /kʀysifɛʀ/ *nf* crucifer.

crucifiement /kʀysifimɑ̃/ *nm* **1** (supplice) crucifixion; **2** (épreuve) torture ¢; **c'est un ~ pour leur mère** it's torture for their mother; **le ~ de la chair** the mortification of the flesh; **3** Art Crucifixion.

crucifier /kʀysifje/ [2] *vtr* lit, fig to crucify.

crucifix /kʀysifi/ *nm* crucifix.

crucifixion /kʀysifiksjɔ̃/ *nf* **1** (supplice) crucifixion; **2** Art Crucifixion.

cruciforme /kʀysifɔʀm/ *adj* gén cruciform; Tech **vis (à tête) ~** cross-head screw; **tournevis ~** Phillips® ou cross-head screwdriver.

cruciverbiste /kʀysivɛʀbist/ *nmf* crossword fan.

crudité /kʀydite/ *nf* **1** (légume) raw vegetable; **servir des ~s** to serve crudités; **2** (d'aliments) rawness; **3** (de couleur) garishness; (de lumière) harshness; **4** (de langage, sentiment) crudeness.

cruel, **-elle** /kʀyɛl/ *adj* **1** [*personne, destin, histoire*] cruel (**envers, avec** to); [*incertitude*] cruel; **2** (intense) [*manque*] desperate; **3** (douloureux) terrible; [*maladie*] painful.

cruellement /kʀyɛlmɑ̃/ *adv* **1** (avec cruauté) [*se venger, réprimer, sacrifier*] cruelly; **2** (beaucoup) desperately; **manquer ~ de qch** to be desperately short of sth; **avoir ~ besoin de qch** to be desperately in need of sth; **le talent lui fait ~ défaut** he's/she's desperately lacking in talent; **les médicaments font ~ défaut** medical supplies are desperately inadequate; **3** (douloureusement) [*éprouver, ressentir*] terribly; **la pénurie de carburant se fait ~ sentir** the fuel shortage is being sorely felt; **les effets de l'embargo se font ~ sentir** the embargo is biting hard; **être ~ ramené à la réalité** to be brought back to earth painfully.

cruiser /kʀuizœʀ/ *nm* cabin cruiser.

crûment /kʀymɑ̃/ *adv* **1** (sans ménagement) bluntly; **répondre ~** to reply bluntly; **2** (de façon choquante) crudely.

crustacé /kʀystase/ *nm* shellfish (*inv*), crustacean spéc.

cryobiologie /kʀijobjolɔʒi/ *nf* cryobiology.

cryochirurgie /kʀijoʃiʀyʀʒi/ *nf* cryosurgery.

cryogène /kʀijoʒɛn/ *adj* cryogenic.

cryogénie /kʀijoʒeni/ *nf* cryogenics (+ *v sg*).

cryogénique /kʀijoʒenik/ *adj* cryogenic.

cryptage /kʀiptaʒ/ *nm* Ordinat encryption; TV scrambling.

crypte /kʀipt/ *nf* crypt.

crypté, **~e** /kʀipte/ *adj* coded; Ordinat encrypted; TV scrambled.

cryptogame /kʀiptɔgam/ **I** *adj* cryptogamic.

II *nm* cryptogam.

cryptogramme /kʀiptɔgʀam/ *nm* cryptogram.

cryptographie /kʀiptɔgʀafi/ *nf* cryptography.

cryptographique /kʀiptɔgʀafic/ *adj* [*message, procédé*] cryptographic.

crypton = **krypton**.

CSA /seɛsa/ *nm*: *abbr* ▶ **conseil**.

CSCE /seɛsseə/ *nf* (*abbr* = **Conférence sur la sécurité et la coopération en Europe**) CSCE.

CSG /seɛsʒe/ *nf*: *abbr* ▶ **contribution**.

CSM /seɛsɛm/ *nm*: *abbr* ▶ **conseil**.

Cuba /kyba/ ▶416, 321 *nprf* Cuba.

cubage /kybaʒ/ *nm* (d'eau, air) volume.

cubain, **~e** /kybɛ̃, ɛn/ ▶537 *adj* Cuban.

Cubain, **~e** /kybɛ̃, ɛn/ ▶537 *nm,f* Cuban.

cube /kyb/ **I** ▶866 *adj* Math, Mes, Phys cubic; **mètre/centimètre ~** cubic metreGB/centimetreGB.

II *nm* **1** Math (polyèdre) cube; (puissance) cube; **le ~ de 3 est 27** 3 cubed is 27; **mettre au ~** to cube; **2** (objet) cube; Culin cube; **couper en ~s** to cut [sth] into cubes [*viande*]; to dice [*légumes*]; **3** (jouet) building block; ▶ **gros**.

cuber /kybe/ [1] **I** *vtr* to gauge [*pierre*].

II ▶866 *vi* [*citerne, cuve, tonneau*] to have a capacity of, to hold.

cubique /kybik/ *adj* **1** Math [*racine*] cubic; **2** gén **de forme ~** cube-shaped.

cubisme /kybism/ *nm* Cubism.

cubiste /kybist/ *adj, nmf* Cubist.

cubitainer® /kybitenɛʀ/ *nm* winebox.

cubital, **~e**, *mpl* **-aux** /kybital, o/ *adj* [*nerf, artère*] ulnar.

cubitus /kybitys/ *nm* Anat ulna.

cucul○ /kyky/ **I** *adj* pej [*histoire, film*] corny○; [*personne*] silly; [*intérieur, jardin*] twee GB, cutesy○ US.

II *nmf* (personne) pej twit○ GB, jerk○ US.

■ **~ la praline** corny○.

cucurbitacée /kykyʀbitase/ *nf* cucurbit; **les ~s** Cucurbitaceae.

cueillette /kœjɛt/ *nf* **1** (ramassage) (de fruits, fleurs) picking; fig (d'idées, de chiffres) gathering together; **~ du coton/des pommes** cotton-/apple-picking; **ils vivent de chasse et de ~** Anthrop they are hunter-gatherers; **2** (produit) (de fruits) crop, harvest; (d'idées) crop.

cueillir /kœjiʀ/ [27] *vtr* **1** (ramasser) to pick [*fruits, fleurs*]; **2** fig to gather [*informations*]; to win [*applaudissements*]; **~ des lauriers** to cover oneself in glory, to win acclaim; **cueillez votre jeunesse/le jour qui passe** liter make the most of your youth/of today; **~ un baiser** liter to steal a kiss; **3**○ (prendre) to pick up○, to arrest [*malfaiteur*]; to pick up○ [*ami*]; **4** (atteindre) [*projectile*] to catch; **se faire ~ à froid** fig to be caught off guard.

cuesta /kwɛsta/ *nf* cuesta.

cui-cui /kɥikɥi/ *nm inv* (*also onomat*) twitter; **faire ~** to go tweet tweet!

cuiller, **cuillère** /kɥijɛʀ/ *nf* **1** (pour manger) spoon; (contenu) spoonful; **petite ~** ≈ teaspoon; **~ en bois** wooden spoon; **une ~ de sucre** a spoonful of sugar; ▶ **serrer**; **2** Mus spoon; **jouer des ~s** to play the spoons; **3** Pêche spoon; **pêche à la ~** spoonbait fishing; **4** Tech (de grenade) safety catch; (de fondeur, verrier) ladle.

■ **~ à café** ≈ teaspoon; (très petite) coffee spoon; **~ à dessert** dessertspoon; **~ à soupe** soupspoon; (pour mesurer) ≈ tablespoon; **une ~ à soupe d'huile** a tablespoon ou tablespoonful of oil; **~ tournante** spinner.

IDIOMES **il n'y va pas avec le dos de la ~**○ (en parlant) he doesn't pull his punches; (en agissant) he doesn't do things by halves; **on l'a ramassée à la petite ~**○ they had to scrape her up off the road; **je suis à ramasser à la petite ~**○ I'm knackered○ GB ou pooped○; **faire qch en deux** or **trois coups de ~ à pot** to do sth in two shakes of a lamb's tail○.

cuillerée /kɥij(ə)ʀe/ *nf* spoonful; **deux ~s à soupe de farine** two tablespoonful(s) of flour.

cuir /kɥiʀ/ *nm* **1** (peau traitée) leather; **c'est du ~** it's leather; **sac en** or **de ~** leather bag; **le travail du ~** leatherwork; **2** (peau non traitée) rawhide; (peau de gros mammifère) hide; **~ de bœuf/vache** oxhide/cowhide; **3**○ (peau humaine) hum hide; **avoir le ~ épais** to be thick-skinned; **4**○ (vêtement) leather○; **5**○ (liaison fautive) incorrect liaison (*by insertion of a t or z sound*); **6**○ (au football) ball.

■ **~ à rasoir** (razor) strop; **~ bouilli** cuir-bouilli; **~ chevelu** Anat scalp; **~ naturel** natural leather, russet leather spéc; **~ de Russie** Russia leather; **~ suédé** suede (leather); **~ verni** patent leather.

cuirasse /kɥiʀas/ *nf* **1** (armure) breast-plate; (blindage) armourGB plating; **2** fig (d'indifférence) front; **3** Zool cuirass.

cuirassé, **~e** /kɥiʀase/ **I** *pp* ▶ **cuirasser**.

II *pp adj* Mil [*soldat*] armourGB-clad; [*véhicule, bateau, division*] armouredGB.

III *nm* battleship.

cuirasser /kɥiʀase/ [1] **I** *vtr* **1** Mil to dress [sb] in armourGB [*chevalier*]; to armourGB [*véhicule, bateau*]; **2** fig (endurcir) to harden [*personne*] (**contre** to).

II se cuirasser *vpr* fig **se ~ contre qch** to harden oneself to sth; **être cuirassé contre qch** to be hardened to sth.

cuirassier /kɥiʀasje/ *nm* **1** (soldat) cuirassier; **2** (régiment) **le premier/deuxième ~** the first/second armouredGB division.

cuire /kɥiʀ/ [69] **I** *vtr* **1** Culin [*personne*] (sur le feu) to cook [*aliment*]; (au four) to bake [*pain, gâteau, poisson, pomme, gratin*]; to roast [*viande*]; to cook [*daube*]; **~ à l'eau/au bouillon/au beurre** to cook in water/in stock/in butter; **~ au bain-marie** to cook in a double-boiler; **~ à la vapeur** to steam; **~ à l'étuvée** to braise; **~ à la poêle** to fry; **~ au gril** to grill, to broil US; **~ au barbecue** to barbecue; **~ au gaz/au charbon de bois** to cook with gas/over charcoal; **~ qch à feu doux** to cook ou simmer sth gently; **~ qch à gros bouillons** to cook sth at full boil; **~ des pommes de terre au four** to bake potatoes; **2** Tech to fire [*porcelaine, brique, émaux*]; **3** (chauffer) [*soleil*] to scorch [*champ, plante*]; to bake [*argile, terre*]; to beat down on [*sable, rocher*]; to burn [*peau*]; **le soleil me cuit le dos** the sun is burning my back.

II *vi* **1** Culin [*aliment, repas*] to cook; **le riz cuit vite** rice cooks quickly; **le rôti est en train de ~** the joint ou roast is cooking; **mets les légumes/la tarte à ~ à 6 heures** put the vegetables/the pie on (to cook) at 6 o'clock; **faire** or **laisser ~ 20 minutes** cook [sth] for 20 minutes; **laissez ~ à petit feu** allow to simmer gently; **faites ~ la pâte à four chaud** bake the pastry case in a hot oven; **faites ~ le poulet**

à four chaud roast the chicken in a hot oven; **tu l'as trop peu/trop fait ~** it's undercooked ou underdone/overcooked; **à ~** [*chocolat, pomme*] cooking; [*fruit*] stewing; **2**○ (avoir chaud) [*personne*] **on cuit sur la plage** it's baking (hot) on the beach; **j'ai cuit au soleil toute la matinée** I spent the morning roasting in the sun; **3** (faire mal) [*écorchure*] to sting; [*alcool sur plaie*] to sting; **ça me cuit** it stings; **les joues me cuisaient** (de honte, après un coup de soleil) my cheeks were burning; (après gifles) my cheeks were stinging ou smarting.
III *v impers* fml **il vous en cuira** you'll rue the day sout; **il lui en a cuit** he/she had good reason to feel sorry.
IDIOMES **laisse-la ~ dans son jus**○ let her stew in her own juice○.

cuisant, **~e** /kɥizɑ̃, ɑ̃t/ *adj* **1** (humiliant) [*défaite, regret, déception*] bitter; [*remarque*] stinging; **2** (douloureux) [*douleur*] (qui brûle) burning; (qui pique) stinging; [*froid*] biting, bitter; **3** (brûlant) [*joue*] (de honte) burning; (après une gifle) stinging.

cuisine /kɥizin/ **I** *nf* **1** (pièce) kitchen; Naut galley; **2** (mobilier) kitchen units (*pl*), kitchen furniture ¢; **ustensiles/meubles de ~** kitchen utensils/furniture ¢; **3** (préparation des aliments) (art) cookery; (activité) cooking; **apprendre la ~** Scol to do cookery, to study cooking US; **apprendre à faire la ~** to learn (how) to cook; **il sait faire la ~** he can cook; **qui fait la ~ chez toi?** who does the cooking in your house?; **les métiers de la ~** catering ¢; ▶ **grand**; **4** (méthode) cooking; (aliments) food; **tu n'aimes pas ma ~?** don't you like my cooking?; **~ au beurre** (méthode) cooking in butter; (aliments) food cooked in butter; **faire de la bonne ~** to be a good cook; **la ~ française** (méthode, art) French cooking ou cuisine; (aliments) French food; **je préfère la ~ épicée** I prefer spicy food ou dishes; **5** (personnel) **la ~** the kitchen staff; **6**○ (magouillage) jiggery-pokery○ GB, intrigues (*pl*); **la ~ électorale** dubious electioneering tactics; **faire sa petite ~** to be on the fiddle○ GB ou on the take○ US.
II cuisines *nfpl* (de restaurant, d'hôpital, école) kitchens.
■ **~ bourgeoise** (good) plain cooking; **~ familiale** home cooking; **~ intégrée** fully fitted kitchen; **~ roulante** Mil field kitchen.

cuisiner /kɥizine/ [1] **I** *vtr* **1** Culin to cook [*plat*]; **viande cuisinée** meat in a sauce; **2**○ (combiner) to fix [*affaire, élection*]; **3**○ (interroger) to grill○ [*suspect*].
II *vi* to cook; **aimer ~** to like cooking; **bien ~** to be a good cook.

cuisinette /kɥizinɛt/ *nf* kitchenette.

cuisinier, **-ière** /kɥizinje, ɛʀ/ **I** ▶ **510** *nm,f* (chez des particuliers) cook; (dans restaurant) chef.
II cuisinière *nf* (à gaz, électrique) cooker GB, stove; **cuisinière à charbon/bois** solid-fuel/wood-burning stove, kitchen range.

cuissage† /kɥisaʒ/ *nm* **droit de ~** droit du seigneur.

cuissard /kɥisaʀ/ *nm* **1** (short) cycling shorts (*pl*); **2** (d'armure) cuisse.

cuissarde /kɥisaʀd/ *nf* (de caoutchouc) wader; (de cuir, daim) thighboot.

cuisse /kɥis/ ▶ **188** *nf* **1** Anat thigh; **2** Culin (de poulet) thigh; (de chevreuil) haunch; **des ~s de grenouille** frogs' legs; **3** (en œnologie) **un vin qui a de la ~** a round full-bodied wine.
IDIOMES **avoir la ~ légère**○ to be an easy lay◑.

cuisseau, *pl* **~x** /kɥiso/ *nm* **~ de veau** haunch of veal.

cuisse-madame, *pl* **cuisses-madame** /kɥismadam/ *nf* (*variety of*) *pear*.

cuissettes /kɥisɛt/ *nfpl* H (short) sports shorts.

cuisson /kɥisɔ̃/ *nf* **1** Culin gén cooking; (au four) (de pain, gâteau, poisson) baking; (de rôti, poulet) roasting; **temps de ~** cooking time; **après dix minutes de ~** after cooking for ten minutes; **la ~ de la viande est très longue** meat takes a long time to cook; **2** Tech (de poterie, d'émaux) firing; **mettre qch à la ~** to fire sth.

cuissot /kɥiso/ *nm* (de chevreuil) haunch.

cuistance◑ /kɥistɑ̃s/ *nf* **1** (préparation) cooking; **2** (aliments) grub○.

cuistot○ /kɥisto/ *nm* cook.

cuistre /kɥistʀ/ *nm* liter **1** (pédant) prig; **2** (malotru) oaf.

cuistrerie /kɥistʀəʀi/ *nf* liter **1** (pédanterie) priggishness; **2** (grossièreté) oafishness.

cuit, **~e** /kɥi, kɥit/ **I** *pp* ▶ **cuire**.
II *pp adj* **1** Culin [*aliment*] cooked; [*viande, poisson, gâteau*] done (*jamais épith*); [*abricot, pruneau*] stewed; **trop ~** [*gigot, steak*] overdone; **bien ~** well done; **pas assez ~** underdone; **2** Tech [*poterie, argile*] fired; **3**○ (par le soleil) [*gazon, plante*] scorched; [*peau*] burned.
III cuite *nf* **1**○ (ivresse) **quelle ~e!** what a booze-up○ GB ou bender○!; **tenir/prendre une ~e** to be/to get plastered○ ou pissed◑ GB, to tie one on○ US; **il a** or **tient une sacrée ~e** he's plastered○ ou completely pissed◑ GB; **2** Tech (cuisson) firing; **mettre qch à la ~e** to fire sth.
IDIOMES **c'est ~**○ we've had it○; **sinon, on était ~s**○ otherwise, we were done for○; **c'est du tout ~**○ (facile) it's a piece of cake○; (assuré) it's in the bag○; **ce n'est pas du tout ~**○ it's not all cut and dried; **elle attend que ça (lui) tombe tout ~**○ she expects things to fall straight into her lap.

cuiter○: **se cuiter** /kɥite/ [1] *vpr* to get plastered○ ou pissed◑ GB.

cuivre /kɥivʀ/ **I** *nm* (métal) **~ (rouge)** copper; **~ (jaune)** brass; **vase en ~** (rouge) copper vase; (jaune) brass vase; **à fond de ~** copper-bottomed; **collection d'objets en ~** collection of copperware.
II cuivres *nmpl* **1** (objets) (en cuivre rouge) copperware; (en cuivre jaune) brass; **2** Mus **les ~s** the brass (*sg*); **ensemble de ~s** brass ensemble.

cuivré, **~e** /kɥivʀe/ **I** *pp* ▶ **cuivrer**.
II *pp adj* **1** ▶ **193** [*peau*] copper-coloured[GB]; (par le soleil) bronzed; **aux reflets ~s** with coppery glints; **2** [*voix*] resonant.

cuivrer /kɥivʀe/ [1] *vtr* **1** (bronzer) to bronze [*peau*]; **2** Tech to copper [*métal*].

cuivreux, **-euse** /kɥivʀø, øz/ *adj* Chimie [*métal, oxyde*] cuprous.

cuivrique /kɥivʀik/ *adj* [*métal, oxyde*] cupric.

cul /ky/ **I**◑ *adj inv* [*personne*] simple; [*film*] twee○.
II *nm* **1**◑ Anat (postérieur) bottom, arse● GB, ass◑ US; **~ nu** (à moitié nu) bare-bottomed; (entièrement nu) stark naked; **~ par-dessus tête** head over heels, arse● GB ou ass◑ US over tit◑; **mon ~!** my foot○!, my arse● GB ou ass◑ US!; ▶ **faux, main, péter, pied, plein, taper**; **2**◑ (sexe) sex; **film/scène de ~** sex film/scene; **histoire de ~** (blague) dirty joke; (texte) dirty story; (liaison) affair; **3** Zool rump; **4**○ (arrière) (de voiture, camion) back end; ▶ **gros**; **5** (base) (de lampe, bouteille) bottom.
■ **~ béni**◑ bigot○; **~ de bouteille** bottom of a bottle; **~ sec**○**!** bottoms up!; **faire ~ sec**○ to down it in one.
IDIOMES **avoir qn au ~**◑ to have sb on one's tail; **l'avoir dans le ~**◑ to be in trouble; **se bouger le ~**◑ (se dépêcher) to get moving○, to shift one's arse● GB ou ass◑ US; (se donner du mal) to get one's arse● GB ou ass◑ US into gear; **se le foutre** or **se le mettre au ~**● to stuff it up one's arse● GB ou ass◑ US; **parle à mon ~, ma tête est malade**◑ you may as well talk to my arse● GB ou ass◑ US for all I care; **en rester** or **tomber sur le ~**◑ to be gobsmacked○; **avoir le ~**◑ **bordé de nouilles** to be a lucky devil○ ou bastard◑.

culasse /kylas/ *nf* **1** (de moteur) cylinder head; **2** (d'arme à feu) breechblock.

culbute /kylbyt/ *nf* **1** (galipette) somersault; **faire une ~** to somersault, to turn a somersault; **2** Sport [*nageur*] somersault turn; **faire une ~** to do a somersault turn; **3** (chute) tumble; **faire une ~ dans l'escalier** to tumble down the stairs; **4** fig (de régime, d'institutions) fall; (de banque, d'entreprise) collapse; **faire la ~** (tout perdre) to come a cropper○, to go bust○; (doubler ses gains) to double one's money.

culbuter /kylbyte/ [1] **I** *vtr* (faire tomber) to knock [sth] over [*objet, personne*]; fig to topple [*régime*]; to break down [*préjugés*]; to overcome [*adversaire*].
II *vi* (se renverser) [*personne*] to take a tumble; [*meuble*] to tip over; [*vase*] to topple; [*véhicule*] to overturn, to somersault; **la voiture a culbuté dans le ravin** the car fell into the ravine.

culbuteur /kylbytœʀ/ *nm* **1** (de récipient) tipper; **2** (de moteur) rocker arm; **3** (jouet) tumbler, tumbling toy.

cul-cul○ = **cucul**.

cul-de-basse-fosse, *pl* **culs-de-basse-fosse** /kyd(ə)bɑsfos/ *nm* dungeon.

cul-de-jatte, *pl* **culs-de-jatte** /kydʒat/ *nmf* person who has had both legs amputated.

cul-de-lampe, *pl* **culs-de-lampe** /kydlɑ̃p/ *nm* Imprim tailpiece.

cul-de-poule, *pl* **culs-de-poule** /kydpul/ *nm* (récipient) mixing bowl.
IDIOMES **avoir la bouche en ~** to have a small pursed mouth.

cul-de-sac, *pl* **culs-de-sac** /kydsak/ *nm* **1** (rue) cul-de-sac; **2** (situation) dead end; (emploi sans avenir) dead-end job.

culer /kyle/ [1] *vi* [*vent*] to veer astern; [*navire*] to go astern.

culinaire /kylinɛʀ/ *adj* culinary; **préparation ~** dish; **l'art ~** the culinary arts (*pl*).

culminant, **~e** /kylminɑ̃, ɑ̃t/ *adj* **point ~** (de montagne) highest point ou peak; (d'astre) culmination; (de carrière) peak; (de gloire, puissance, crise) height; (de réunion, vacances, soirée, spectacle) high point; **être au point ~ de sa carrière** to be at the peak of one's career.

culminer /kylmine/ [1] *vi* **1** Géog [*sommet, massif*] **~ au-dessus de qch** to tower above sth; **l'Everest culmine à 8 848 mètres** Everest reaches 8,848 metres[GB] at its peak; **les Alpes françaises culminent au mont Blanc** Mont Blanc is the highest peak in the French Alps; **2** fig [*inflation, chômage*] to reach its peak, to peak; [*fureur, crise, carrière*] to reach its height ou peak; [*soirée, festival*] to reach its climax; **l'inflation a culminé à 5% en mai** inflation peaked at 5% in May; **3** Astron [*astre*] to reach culmination.

culot /kylo/ *nm* **1**○ (aplomb) cheek○, nerve○; **quel ~!** what (a) cheek○ ou nerve○!; **avoir du ~** to have a cheek○ ou a nerve○; **avoir un sacré ~** or **un ~ monstre** or **tous les ~s** to have the devil's own cheek○, to have a hell○ of a nerve; **avoir le ~ de faire** to have the nerve○ ou cheek○ to do; **y aller au ~** to bluff; **2** Tech (de bougie) shell, body; (de douille, cartouche, d'ampoule) base; **3** (résidu) (de pipe) dottle[GB]; (de creuset) residue.

culotte /kylɔt/ *nf* **1** (sous-vêtement féminin) pants (*pl*) GB, knickers (*pl*) GB, drawers (*pl*), panties (*pl*) US; **une ~/deux ~s** (pour femme) a pair/two pairs of pants GB ou panties US ou drawers; **~ en caoutchouc** plastic pants GB ou panties US ou drawers; **où est la ~ de mon maillot de bain?** where are my bikini bottoms?; **faire dans sa ~**○ (déféquer) to dirty one's pants; (uriner) to wet one's pants; fig to wet oneself; **2** (pantalon mi-long) breeches (*pl*); (pantalon) trousers (*pl*), pants US (*pl*); **en ~(s) courte(s)** in short trousers GB ou pants US.

■ **~ bouffante** bloomers (*pl*); **~ de cheval** (pantalon) riding breeches (*pl*); (cellulite) flabby thighs (*pl*); **~ de golf** plus-fours (*pl*); **~ de peau**○ fig pej old soldier, colonel Blimp○.

IDIOMES **c'est elle qui porte la ~**○ she's the one who wears the trousers GB ou pants US; **baisser ~**○ fig to back down; **(se) prendre une ~**○ Jeux to lose one's shirt (gambling).

culotté○, **~e** /kylɔte/ *adj* [*personne*] cheeky.

culotter /kylɔte/ [1] *vtr* to season [*pipe*]; **une pipe bien culottée** a well-seasoned pipe.

culpabilisation /kylpabilizasjɔ̃/ *nf* (action) making guilty; (résultat) feeling of guilt.

culpabiliser /kylpabilize/ [1] **I** *vtr* to make [sb] feel guilty.

II *vi* to feel guilty.

III se culpabiliser *vpr* to feel guilty.

culpabilité /kylpabilite/ *nf* Jur, Psych guilt; **sentiment de ~** guilt feelings (*pl*); **complexe de ~** guilt complex.

culte /kylt/ **I** *nm* **1** Relig gén cult; (adoration) worship; **~ des morts** cult of the dead; **~ du soleil** sun worship; **~ des ancêtres** ancestor worship; **rendre/vouer un ~ à qn/qch** to worship sb/sth; **2** (ensemble de pratiques) religion; **le ~ catholique/musulman** the Catholic/Muslim religion; **3** (office protestant) (Protestant) service; **4** (adoration profane) cult, worship; **avoir le ~ de qch** to worship sth; **il a le ~ de la réussite sociale** he worships social success.

II (-)culte (*in compounds*) **groupe-/film-/roman-~** cult group/film/novel.

■ **~ de la personnalité** personality cult.

cul-terreux○, *pl* **culs-terreux** /kyterø/ *nm* pej country bumpkin○.

cultivable /kyltivabl/ *adj* cultivable.

cultivateur, **-trice** /kyltivatœr, tris/ **I** ▶ 510 *nm,f* farmer.

II *nm* (machine) cultivator.

cultivé, **~e** /kyltive/ **I** *pp* ▶ **cultiver**.

II *pp adj* **1** Agric [*terre, espèce*] cultivated; **2** (raffiné) [*personne, esprit*] cultured, cultivated.

cultiver /kyltive/ [1] **I** *vtr* **1** Agric to grow [*plante*]; to cultivate [*champ*]; **2** (entretenir) to cultivate [*art, image, tradition, relation, mémoire, don*].

II se cultiver *vpr* **1** (devoir être entretenu) [*beauté, amitié, don, goût*] to need to be cultivated; **2** (s'instruire) [*personne*] to improve one's culture; **3** Agric [*plante*] to be grown; [*terre*] to be cultivated.

cultuel, **-elle** /kyltɥɛl/ *adj* [*association*] religious; **lieu ~** place of worship.

culture /kyltyr/ **I** *nf* **1** Agric (action de cultiver) cultivation; **la ~ du blé** wheat growing; **~ d'un champ** cultivation of a field; **mettre en ~** to bring [sth] under cultivation; **petite/moyenne/grande ~** small-scale/medium-scale/large-scale farming; **aire/terre de ~** farming area/land; **2** Agric (espèce cultivée) crop; **~ d'hiver** winter crop; **~ d'exportation** export crop; **~ céréalière** cereal crop; **3** Biol culture; **~ in vitro** in vitro culture; **4** Anthrop, Sociol culture; **la ~ européenne/chinoise** European/Chinese culture; **~ de masse** mass culture; **~ d'entreprise/de groupe** corporate/group culture; **5** (connaissances) knowledge; **~ encyclopédique/générale/musicale** encyclopedic/general/musical knowledge; **vaste ~** wide knowledge; **~ classique** classical education; **femme/homme de (grande) ~** woman/man of (great) learning; **avoir de la ~** to be cultured; **ne pas avoir de ~** to be uncultured; **6** Écon arts (*pl*); **subventionner la ~** to subsidize the arts; **budget de la ~** arts budget.

II cultures *nfpl* Agric (terres cultivées) cultivated land ¢.

■ **~ extensive** extensive farming; **~ intensive** intensive farming; **~ physique** Scol physical education; Sport physical exercise; **~ de rapport** commercial farming; **~s vivrières** subsistence crops.

culturel, **-elle** /kyltyrɛl/ *adj* cultural.

culturisme /kyltyrism/ ▶ 449 *nm* body-building.

culturiste /kyltyrist/ *nmf* body-builder.

Cumbria ▶ 692 *nprm* **le ~** Cumbria.

cumin /kymɛ̃/ *nm* cumin; **pain/fromage au ~** bread/cheese with cumin seeds.

cumul /kymyl/ *nm* **1** (accumulation) **~ d'avantages/de handicaps** accumulation of advantages/handicaps; **~ de fonctions/charges/mandats** holding of several posts/offices/mandates concurrently; **~ de salaires** drawing several salaries concurrently; **le ~ de la retraite avec un salaire** drawing both a pension and a wage concurrently; **2** Jur **~ d'actions** joinder; **~ d'infractions** multiple counts (*on an indictment*); **~ juridique des peines** ≈ concurrent sentence; **~ des peines** ≈ consecutive sentence; **3** Assur **~ de responsabilités** aggregate liability (*third party*); **~ de risques** accumulation of risks (*credit insurance*).

cumulable /kymylabl/ *adj* [*fonctions, mandats*] which can be held concurrently (*épith, après n*); [*traitement, allocations*] which can be drawn concurrently (*épith, après n*); **cette fonction est ~ avec celle de délégué** this post can be held concurrently with that of delegate.

cumulard○, **~e** /kymylar, ard/ *nm,f* pej *holder of various mandates or remunerative positions.*

cumulatif, **-ive** /kymylatif, iv/ *adj* cumulative.

cumulativement /kymylativmɑ̃/ *adv* **1** (postes occupés, salaires perçus) concurrently; **2** Jur (peines purgées) consecutively.

cumuler /kymyle/ [1] **I** *vtr* **1** (avoir en même temps) to hold [sth] concurrently [*fonctions, titres*]; to draw [sth] concurrently [*salaires, allocations*]; **~ deux pensions** to draw two separate pensions; **il cumule les fonctions de gestionnaire avec celles de concepteur** he combines the post of manager with that of designer; **si vous cumulez tous ces symptômes** if you have a combination of all these symptoms; **2** (accumuler) to accumulate [*handicaps, échecs, diplômes*]; **3** (réunir) to combine [*résultats*]; (ajouter) to total ou add up [*sommes*]; **effets/bilans cumulés** combined effects/balance ¢; **intérêts/dividendes cumulés** Fin accrued interest ¢/dividends; **fréquence cumulée** Stat cumulative frequency; **~ qch avec qch** (réunir) to combine sth with sth; (ajouter) to add sth to sth.

II se cumuler *vpr* **1** (être ajoutés) [*intérêts*] to accrue; [*dettes, sommes, erreurs*] to mount up; **2** (être cumulables) **ces fonctions se cumulent** these posts can be held concurrently; **ces réductions ne peuvent pas se ~** you may claim only one of these discounts.

cumulo-nimbus /kymylonɛ̃bys/ *nm inv* cumulonimbus.

cumulus /kymylys/ *nm inv* cumulus.

cunéiforme /kyneifɔrm/ *adj, nm* cuneiform.

cunnilingus /kynilɛ̃gys/ *nm inv* cunnilingus.

cupide /kypid/ *adj* [*personne, esprit*] grasping.

cupidité /kypidite/ *nf* cupidity.

Cupidon /kypidɔ̃/ *npr* Cupid.

cuprifère /kyprifɛr/ *adj* Minér [*sol*] cupriferous; [*exploitation*] copper.

cupule /kypyl/ *nf* cupule.

curabilité /kyrabilite/ *nf* curability.

curable /kyrabl/ *adj* [*maladie*] curable.

curage /kyraʒ/ *nm* (de puits) cleaning out; (de canal, rivière, d'étang) dredging; Agric (de fumier) mucking out GB, cleaning out.

curare /kyrar/ *nm* curare.

curatelle /kyratɛl/ *nf* Jur ≈ legal guardianship; **placer qn en ~** to place sb under guardianship.

curateur, **-trice** /kyratœr, tris/ *nm,f* guardian (*of adult lacking legal capacity*).

curatif, **-ive** /kyratif, iv/ *adj* curative.

cure /kyr/ *nf* **1** (dans une station thermale) course of treatment in ou at a spa; **faire une ~** to go for a course of treatment in a spa; **2** (traitement) course of treatment; **faire une ~ de vitamines/calcium** to take a course of vitamins/calcium; **3** (grande consommation) **faire une ~ de raisin/fruits** to eat a lot of grapes/fruit; **j'ai fait une ~ de repos/soleil/cinéma** I did nothing but rest/soak up the sun/watch films GB ou movies US; **4** fml (souci) **n'avoir ~ de qch** to care little about sth; **je n'en ai ~!** I care not! sout; **5** (presbytère) presbytery; (charge) cure.

■ **~ d'amaigrissement** slimming course GB, reducing treatment US; **~ de beauté** beauty treatment; **~ de désintoxication** detoxification; **faire une ~ de désintoxication** to go for detoxification; **~ de jouvence** rejuvenation treatment; **subir une ~ de jouvence** [*quartier*] to have a face lift; [*institution*] to be modernized; [*équipe*] to be given an injection of fresh blood; **~ de repos** rest cure; **~ de sommeil** sleep therapy; **faire une ~ de sommeil** to undergo sleep therapy; **~ de thalassothérapie** course of thalassotherapy.

curé /kyre/ *nm* (parish) priest; **se faire ~**○ to become a priest; **les ~s**○ pej the clerics; **aller à l'école chez les ~s** to go to a church school.

■ **~ de campagne** country priest.

IDIOMES **bouffer du ~**○ to be anticlerical.

cure-dents /kyrdɑ̃/ *nm inv* toothpick.

curée /kyre/ *nf* **1** Chasse (portion of) quarry (*fed to hounds*); **donner la ~ aux chiens** to give the hounds their quarry (*to eat*); **sonner la ~** to sound the horn (*for the hounds to eat their quarry*); **2** fig scramble for the spoils; **se précipiter à la ~** to scramble for the spoils.

cure-ongles /kyrɔ̃gl/ *nm inv* nail cleaner, orange-stick.

cure-pipes /kyrpip/ *nm inv* pipe cleaner.

curer /kyre/ [1] **I** *vtr* to clean out [*pipe, étang*].

II se curer *vpr* **se ~ les ongles/oreilles** to clean one's nails/ears; **se ~ les dents/le nez** to pick one's teeth/nose.

curetage /kyrtaʒ/ *nm* Méd D and C, curettage; **on lui a fait un ~** she's had a D and C spéc.

cureter /kyrte/ [20] *vtr* Méd to scrape.

cureton○ /kyrtɔ̃/ *nm* pej priest.

curette /kyrɛt/ *nf* Méd curette.

curie /kyri/ **I** *nm* Phys curie.

II *nf* **1** Antiq curia; **2** Relig **la ~** the Curia.

curiethérapie /kyriterapi/ *nf* radium therapy.

curieusement /kyrjøzmɑ̃/ *adv* **1** (modifiant un verbe ou un adjectif) oddly, strangely, curiously; **2** (adverbe de phrase) curiously enough, oddly enough; **~, on m'a laissé entrer** curiously ou oddly enough, I was let in.

curieux, **-ieuse** /kyrjø, øz/ **I** *adj* **1** (comme défaut) [*personne*] inquisitive, nosy○, curious; [*visage, yeux*] inquisitive; **regarder qn d'un œil ~** to look curiously at sb; **2** (étrange) strange, curious, odd; **individu à l'allure curieuse** strange-looking ou odd-looking individual; **par une curieuse coïncidence** by a strange coincidence; **un ~ paradoxe** a curious paradox; **il est ~ de voir à quel point...** it is strange ou curious to see how much...; **c'est ~, il n'y a**

personne that's strange ou curious, there's nobody there; **ce qui est ~ c'est que** the strange ou curious thing is that; **et, chose curieuse, elle était seule** and, curiously ou oddly enough, she was alone; **3** (intellectuellement) with an inquiring mind (*épith, après n*); **esprit ~** person with an inquiring mind; **être ~ de** to be very interested in; **elle est curieuse de tout** she has a keen interest in everything; **être ~ d'apprendre** to be keen to learn; **je suis ~ de voir**... (une réaction) I am curious to see...; (une collection, un objet) I am keen to see...; **4** (intéressant) interesting; **ce serait ~ à voir** it would be interesting to see.

II *nm,f* **1** (personne indiscrète) **c'est un ~** he's nosy○; **le ~!** the nosy○ thing ou parker GB!; **aller quelque part en ~** to go somewhere (just) out of curiosity; **2** (passant) onlooker.

III *nm* (chose étrange) **le ~ de l'histoire c'est que** the funny ou curious thing about it is that.

curiosité /kyʀjozite/ *nf* **1** (défaut) curiosity; **par ~** out of curiosity; **par pure** or **simple ~** purely ou simply out of curiosity; **il est d'une ~!** he is so curious!; **susciter des ~s** to make a lot of people curious; **la ~ est un vilain défaut** curiosity killed the cat; **2** (désir de connaître) curiosity; **~ intellectuelle** intellectual curiosity; **sa ~ pour** his/her curiosity about; **avec ~** [*dévisager, regarder*] curiously; **se demander avec ~ si** to be curious to know if; **3** (objet) strange object; (de collection) curio, curiosity; **cabinet des ~s** cabinet of curios; **magasin de ~** curiosity shop; **4** (étrangeté) **objet d'une grande ~** very curious object.

curiste /kyʀist/ *nmf* person having hydrotherapy.

curling /kœʀliŋ/ **▶449** *nm* curling; **jouer au ~** to go curling.

curriculum vitae /kyʀikylɔmvite/ *nm inv* curriculum vitae, résumé US.

curry /kyʀi/ *nm* **1** (assaisonnement) curry powder; **riz/poulet au ~** curried rice/chicken; **2** (plat) curry; **~ d'agneau/de bœuf** lamb/beef curry.

curseur /kyʀsœʀ/ *nm* **1** Ordinat cursor; (de règle à calcul) cursor; **2** (de fermeture à glissière) slider.

cursif, -ive /kyʀsif, iv/ **I** *adj* [*écriture*] cursive; [*lecture*] cursory.

II cursive *nf* cursive script.

cursus /kyʀsys/ *nm* programme[GB].

curule /kyʀyl/ *adj* **chaise ~** curule chair.

curviligne /kyʀviliɲ/ *adj* curvilinear.

custode /kystɔd/ *nf* **1** Aut rear quarter panel; **2** Relig pyx.

custom /kœstɔm/ *nm* (voiture) customized car; (moto) customized motorbike.

cutané, ~e /kytane/ *adj* skin (*épith*), cutaneous spéc; **affection/maladie ~e** skin disorder/disease.

cuti /kyti/ *nf* skin test.

IDIOMES **virer sa ~** lit to have a positive reaction to the Heaf test; fig (changer d'opinion) to switch sides; (changer de comportement sexuel) to switch over, to change one's sexual preferences.

cuticule /kytikyl/ *nf* cuticle.

cuti-réaction, *pl* **~s** /kytiʀeaksjɔ̃/ *nf* skin test; (à la tuberculine) Heaf test.

cutter /kytœʀ/ *nm* Stanley® knife.

cuve /kyv/ *nf* (pour fermentation, teinture) vat; (à eau, mazout) tank; (de lave-linge, lave-vaisselle) interior; Phot developing tank.

cuvée /kyve/ *nf* **1** Vin (contenu) vatful; (vin de toute une vigne) vintage; **la ~ 1959** the 1959 vintage; **de la même ~** of the same vintage; **vin de première ~** first-rate wine; **~ du patron** house wine; **2** fig (de romans, films) crop; (d'élèves) year group.

cuver /kyve/ [1] **I**○ *vtr* **~ son vin** to sleep it off○; **~ sa colère** to be simmering down.

II *vi* **1** [*vin, raisin*] to ferment; **2**○ [*personne*] to sleep it off○.

cuvette /kyvɛt/ *nf* **1** (en plastique, métal) bowl; **~ des WC** (lavatory) bowl ou pan; **2** Géog basin; **~ océanique** deep sea floor; **3** Mécan race.

CV /seve/ *nm* **1** (*abbr* = **curriculum vitae**) CV GB, résumé US; **2** (*written abbr* = **cheval-vapeur**) HP.

cyanose /sjanoz/ *nf* cyanosis.

cyanosé /sjanoze/ *adj* cyanotic spéc; **avoir le visage ~** to be blue in the face.

cyanoser: **se cyanoser** /sjanoze/ [1] *vpr* [*peau, personne*] to become cyanotic.

cyanure /sjanyʀ/ *nm* cyanide.

cybercafé /sibɛʀkafe/ *nm* cybercafe.

cyberespace /sibɛʀɛspas/ *nm* cyberspace.

cybernaute /sibɛʀnot/ *nmf* cybernaut.

cybernéticien, -ienne /sibɛʀnetisjɛ̃, ɛn/ **▶510** *nm,f* cyberneticist.

cybernétique /sibɛʀnetik/ **I** *adj* cybernetic.

II *nf* cybernetics (+ *v sg*).

cyclable /siklabl/ *adj* **piste ~** cycle track.

cyclamen /siklamɛn/ *nm* cyclamen.

cycle /sikl/ *nm* **1** (de phénomènes, changements) cycle; **~ solaire/du carbone** solar/carbon cycle; **~ de fonctionnement** operating cycle; **~ infernal** fig vicious cycle; **2** (série) gén series (*sg*); (de conférences) course, series; **deux ~s de dix sessions** two series of ten sessions; **deux ~s de dix semaines** two ten-week courses; **3** Littérat cycle; **~ de la Table ronde** Arthurian cycle; **~ de chansons** song cycle; **4** Scol **premier/second ~** *first four years/last three years of secondary school*; **~ court** nonacademic course (*in secondary school*); **~ long** academic course (*leading to university entrance*) GB, academic course (*for college-bound students*) US; **5** Univ **premier ~** *first two years of a degree course leading to a diploma*; **deuxième ~** *final two years of a degree course*; **troisième ~** postgraduate GB ou graduate US studies; **6** (bicyclette) cycle; **magasin de ~s** cycle shop.

■ **~ de formation** training course.

cyclique /siklik/ *adj* cyclic.

cycliquement /siklikmɑ̃/ *adv* cyclically.

cyclisme /siklism/ **▶449** *nm* gén cycling; (de compétition) cycle racing; **faire du ~** to go cycling ou cycle racing.

cycliste /siklist/ **I** *adj* [*club, saison*] cycling (*épith*); [*course, coureur*] cycle (*épith*).

II *nmf* cyclist; **short de ~** cycling shorts (*pl*).

cyclo-cross /siklokʀɔs/ **▶449** *nm inv* **1** (sport) cyclo-cross; **faire du ~** to do cyclo-cross racing; **2** (épreuve) cyclo-cross event.

cycloïdal, ~e, *mpl* **-aux** /siklɔidal, o/ *adj* cycloidal.

cycloïde /siklɔid/ *nm* cycloid.

cyclomoteur /siklomɔtœʀ/ *nm* moped.

cyclomotoriste /siklomɔtɔʀist/ *nmf* moped rider.

cyclonal, ~e, *mpl* **-aux** /siklɔnal, o/ *adj* cyclonic.

cyclone /siklon/ *nm* **1** Météo (typhon) cyclone; (zone de basse pression) depression; **2** fig whirlwind; **arriver comme un ~** to sweep in like a whirlwind.

Cyclope /siklɔp/ *npr* Cyclops; **travail de ~** or **cyclope** Herculean task.

cyclopéen, -éenne /siklɔpeɛ̃, ɛn/ *adj* **1** Archéol, Mythol Cyclopean; **2** (fig) [*tâche*] Herculean.

cyclo-pousse /siklopus/ *nm inv* trishaw, rickshaw.

cyclothymie /siklotimi/ *nf* cyclothymia.

cyclothymique /siklotimik/ *adj, nmf* cyclothymic.

cyclotourisme /siklotuʀism/ **▶449** *nm* cycle touring; **faire du ~** to go long-distance cycling; **aller faire du ~ en Provence** to go on a cycling tour of Provence.

cyclotouriste /siklotuʀist/ *nmf* (touring) cyclist.

cyclotron /siklotʀɔ̃/ *nm* cyclotron.

cygne /siɲ/ *nm* gén swan; **~ mâle** cob; **~ femelle** pen; **jeune ~** cygnet; **cou de ~** fig swan-like neck; **d'une blancheur de ~** snowy-white.

IDIOMES **chant du ~** swan-song.

cylindrage /silɛ̃dʀaʒ/ *nm* (de route) rolling; (au tour) turning.

cylindre /silɛ̃dʀ/ *nm* **1** (objet cylindrique) cylinder; **2** Tech (pour compresser, laminer) roller; (pour imprimer) cylinder; **~ enregistreur** recording drum; **3** Math cylinder; **~ droit/oblique** right/oblique cylinder; **~ de révolution** cylinder of revolution; **4** Aut, Mécan cylinder.

cylindrée /silɛ̃dʀe/ *nf* **1** (volume) capacity, size; **~ de 1200 cm³** 1200 cc engine, engine capacity of 1200 cc; **voiture de petite/grosse ~** car with a small/powerful engine; **2** (moto, voiture) **petite ~** (voiture) car with a small engine; (moto) light motorcycle; **grosse ~** (voiture) powerful car; (moto) powerful motorcycle.

cylindrer /silɛ̃dʀe/ [1] *vtr* (pour aplatir) to roll.

cylindrique /silɛ̃dʀik/ *adj* cylindrical.

cymbale /sɛ̃bal/ **▶534** *nf* cymbal; **coup de ~s** clash of cymbals.

cymbalier, -ière /sɛ̃balje, ɛʀ/ **▶510** *nm,f* cymbal player, cymbalist.

cynégétique /sineʒetik/ **I** *adj* hunting (*épith*).

II *nf* hunting.

cynique /sinik/ **I** *adj* **1** gén cynical; **2** Philos Cynic.

II *nmf* **1** gén cynic; **2** Philos Cynic.

cyniquement /sinikmɑ̃/ *adv* cynically.

cynisme /sinism/ *nm* **1** gén cynicism; **2** Philos Cynicism.

cynocéphale /sinosefal/ *nm* baboon.

cynodrome /sinodʀom/ *nm* greyhound track.

cynorhodon /sinoʀɔdɔ̃/ *nm* rosehip.

cyprès /sipʀɛ/ *nm* cypress.

cypriote /sipʀijɔt/ **▶537** *adj* Cypriot.

Cypriote /sipʀijɔt/ **▶537** *nmf* Cypriot.

cyrillique /siʀilik/ *adj* Cyrillic.

cystite /sistit/ **▶271** *nf* cystitis ¢; **avoir une ~** to have cystitis.

Cythère /sitɛʀ/ *nprf* Cythera.

cytise /sitiz/ *nm* laburnum.

cytologie /sitɔlɔʒi/ *nf* cytology.

cytologique /sitɔlɔʒik/ *adj* cytological.

cytoplasme /sitɔplasm/ *nm* cytoplasm.

Dd

d, D /de/ *nm inv* d, D; ▶ **système**.
d' ▶ **de**.
dab○ /dab/ *nm* old man○, father; **mes ~s** my parents, my folks○.
DAB /deabe/ *nm*: *abbr* ▶ **distributeur**.
d'abord ▶ **abord**.
dacquois, ~e /dakwa, az/ **▶857** *adj* of Dax.
Dacquois, ~e /dakwa, az/ **▶857** *nm,f* (natif) native of Dax; (habitant) inhabitant of Dax.
dacron® /dakʀɔ̃/ *nm* Dacron®.
dactyle /daktil/ *nm* **1** Littérat dactyl; **2** Bot cocksfoot, orchard grass US.
dactylique /daktilik/ *adj* Littérat dactylic.
dactylo /daktilo/ **I ▶510** *nmf* (*abbr* = **dactylographe**) typist.
II *nf* (*abbr* = **dactylographie**) typing.
dactylographe /daktilɔgʀaf/ *nmf* typist.
dactylographie /daktilɔgʀafi/ *nf* **1** (technique) typing; **2** (texte dactylographié) typewritten text.
dactylographier /daktilɔgʀafje/ [2] *vtr* to type (out).
dactylographique /daktilɔgʀafik/ *adj* typing.
dactyloscopie /daktilɔskɔpi/ *nf* fingerprinting.
dada /dada/ **I** *adj* Art, Littérat Dada.
II *nm* **1**○ (cheval) baby talk horsie○, gee-gee○ GB lang enfantin; **tu veux faire à ~ avec Papa?** do you want Daddy to bounce you up and down on his knee?; **jeu de ~** ≈ ludo GB, Parcheesi® US; **2**○ (passe-temps) hobby; (idée fixe) hobbyhorse; **enfourcher son ~** to get on one's hobbyhorse; **3** (mouvement artistique) Dada.
dadais○ /dadɛ/ *nm* clumsy youth; **espèce de grand ~!** you great oaf!
dadaïsme /dadaism/ *nm* Dadaism.
dadaïste /dadaist/ *adj*, *nmf* Dadaist.
dague /dag/ *nf* **1** (épée courte) dagger; **2** (de cerf) spike.
daguerréotype /dageʀeɔtip/ *nm* daguerreotype.
daguet /dagɛ/ *nm* brocket.
dahlia /dalja/ *nm* dahlia.
dahoméen, -éenne /daɔmeɛ̃, ɛn/ *adj* Dahomean.
Dahoméen, -éenne /daɔmeɛ̃, ɛn/ *nm,f* Dahomean.
Dahomey /daɔme/ *nprm* Hist Dahomey.
dahu /day/ *nm*: *imaginary animal invented in order to lure children in its pursuit*.
daigner /deɲe/ [1] *vtr* to deign (**faire** to do).
daim /dɛ̃/ *nm* **1** (animal) (fallow) deer; **2** (viande) venison; **3** (cuir de daim) buckskin; **4** (cuir de veau) suede; **chaussures/veste en ~** suede shoes/jacket.
daine /dɛn/ *nf* fallow doe.
dais /dɛ/ *nm* (tous contextes) canopy.
Dakar /dakaʀ/ **▶857** *npr* Dakar.
Dakota /dakota/ **▶692** *nprm* Dakota; **~ du Nord/du Sud** North/South Dakota.
dalaï-lama /dalailama/ *nm* Dalai Lama.
Dalila /dalila/ *npr* Delilah.
dallage /dalaʒ/ *nm* **1** (revêtement) paving; **2** (action) flagging, paving.
dalle /dal/ *nf* **1** (de pierre, marbre) slab; (dans église, maison) flagstone; (de trottoir) paving stone; **2** Géol slab; **3** Constr (à même le sol) concrete foundation slab; (d'étage) suspended slab; **~ de moquette** carpet tile; **4** (en alpinisme) wall; **5**○ throat; **avoir la ~ en pente** to be a boozer○; **se rincer la ~** to wet one's whistle○, to have a swig○; **6 que ~**◑ nothing at all, damn○ all GB, zilch○; **on n'y voit que ~** you can't see a damn○ thing.
■ **~ funèbre** or **funéraire** tombstone.
IDIOMES **avoir** or **crever la ~**○ to be ravenous; **casser la ~**○ to eat.
daller /dale/ [1] *vtr* to pave, to lay paving stones on.
dalleur /dalœʀ/ *nm* paver.
dalmate /dalmat/ **I** *adj* Dalmatian.
II *nm* Ling Dalmatian.
Dalmate /dalmat/ *nmf* Dalmatian.
Dalmatie /dalmasi/ **▶692** *nprf* Dalmatia.
dalmatien /dalmasjɛ̃/ *nm* (chien) Dalmatian.
dalmatique /dalmatik/ *nf* dalmatic.
daltonien, -ienne /daltɔnjɛ̃, ɛn/ **I** *adj* colour[GB]-blind.
II *nm,f* colour[GB]-blind person.
daltonisme /daltɔnism/ *nm* colour[GB]-blindness.
dam /dɑ̃, dɑm/ *nm* **au grand ~ de** to the great displeasure of; **il a arrêté ses études, au grand ~ de ses parents** he gave up his studies, to the great displeasure of his parents.
damas /dama(s)/ *nm* **1** (tissu) damask; **2** (acier) Damascus steel; **3** Bot (prune) damson.
Damas /damas/ **▶857** *npr* Damascus.
damasquinage /damaskinaʒ/ *nm* damascening.
damasquiner /damaskine/ [1] *vtr* to damascene.
damassé, ~e /damase/ **I** *pp* ▶ **damasser**.
II *pp adj* **1** [*tissu*] damask (*épith*); **2** [*acier*] damascened steel.
III *nm* Tex damask.
damasser /damase/ [1] *vtr* **1** to damask [*tissu*]; **2** to damascene [*acier*].
dame /dam/ **I** *nf* **1** (femme) lady; (de la noblesse) lady; **une vieille ~** an old lady; **la première ~ de France** France's First Lady; **les ~s des postes** the post office ladies; **il a du succès auprès des ~s** he's very popular with the ladies; **la ~ de son cœur** liter his lady-love; **de ~** [*chapeau, parapluie*] lady's; **pour ~s** [*vêtements, coiffeur*] ladies'; **jouer les grandes ~s** to behave like a princess; **c'est une grande ~ du cinéma** she's a grande dame of the screen; **ma bonne** or **petite ~**○ my dear; **2**○ (épouse) lady; **3** (dans fables, contes) **~ belette/tortue** Old Mother Weasel/Tortoise; **Dame Nature** Mother Nature; **4** Jeux (aux cartes, échecs) queen; (aux dames) King; **aller à ~** (aux dames) to crown a King; **mener un pion à ~** (aux dames) to crown a King; (aux échecs) to queen a pawn; **5** Jur Mrs; (**la**) **~ Durand** Mrs Durand; **6** Tech (pour damer) rammer.
II† *excl* upon my word!; **~ oui!/non!** my word yes!/no!
III dames *nfpl* **1 ▶449** Jeux draughts (+ *v sg*) GB, checkers (+ *v sg*) US; **jouer aux ~s** to play draughts GB ou checkers US; **faire une partie de ~s** to have a game of draughts GB ou checkers US; **2** (inscription) ladies; **3** Sport **le simple/la finale ~s** the women's singles/final; **4** (prostituées) euph ladies of the night.
■ **~ catéchiste** (Catholic) Sunday school teacher; **~ de charité** lady who does charity work; **~ de compagnie** live-in companion; **~ d'honneur** lady-in-waiting; **~ de nage** Naut rowlock; **~ patronnesse** lady who does good works; **une ~ de petite vertu** a woman of easy virtue; **~ pipi**○ (female) toilet attendant; **la Vieille Dame (du quai Conti)** *the French Academy*.
dame-d'onze-heures, *pl* **dames-d'onze-heures** /damdɔ̃zœʀ/ *nf* star-of-Bethlehem.
dame-jeanne, *pl* **dames-jeannes** /damʒɑn/ *nf* demijohn.
damer /dame/ [1] *vtr* **1** (tasser) to ram [*sol*]; to pack [*neige*]; **2** Jeux [*aux dames*] to crown; (aux échecs) to queen.
IDIOMES **~ le pion à qn** to trump sb.
damier /damje/ *nm* draughtboard GB, checkerboard US; **étoffe en** or **à ~** checked material; **rues en ~** streets in a grid pattern; **le ~ des champs** fig the patchwork of the fields.
damnable /danabl/ *adj* Relig [*personne*] damnable; [*acte*] reprehensible.
damnation /danasjɔ̃/ *nf* (tous contextes) damnation.
damné, ~e /dɑne/ **I** *pp* ▶ **damner**.
II *pp adj* **1**○ (maudit) (*before n*) cursed; **2** Relig damned.
III *nm,f* **1** Relig damned soul; **les ~s** the damned; **2** (réprouvé) outcast; **les ~s de la terre** the damned of the earth.
IDIOMES **souffrir comme un ~** to suffer horribly.
damner /dɑne/ [1] **I** *vtr* to damn; **faire ~**○ **qn** to drive sb mad, to try sb's patience.
II se damner *vpr* **1** Relig to damn oneself; **2**○ hum **se ~ pour qn/qch** to sell one's soul for sb/sth.
Damoclès /damɔklɛs/ *npr* Damocles; **épée de ~** sword of Damocles.
damoiseau‡, *pl* **~x** /damwazo/ *nm* Hist squire, page; hum (young) gallant.
damoiselle‡ /damwazɛl/ *nf* Hist (jeune fille) damsel‡; (titre) mistress‡.
dan /dan/ *nm* Sport dan.
Danaïdes /danaid/ *nprfpl* Mythol Danaides; **c'est le tonneau des ~** (tâche sans fin) it's an insurmountable task; (gouffre financier) bottomless pit.
dancing /dɑ̃siŋ/ *nm* dance hall.
dandinement /dɑ̃dinmɑ̃/ *nm* waddling ¢.
dandiner: **se dandiner** /dɑ̃dine/ [1] *vpr* [*canard*] to waddle; **se ~ d'un pied sur**

l'autre to shift from one foot to the other; **se ~ sur une chaise** to shift about in a chair.

dandy /dɑ̃di/ *nm* dandy.

dandysme /dɑ̃dism/ *nm* dandyism.

Danemark /danmaʀk/ ▶ 321 *nprm* Denmark.

danger /dɑ̃ʒe/ *nm* **1** (risque général) danger; **être en ~** to be in danger; **tout ~ est écarté maintenant** the danger is past now; **être hors de ~** to be out of danger; **mettre qn/qch hors de ~** to get sb/sth out of danger; **mettre qn/qch en ~** to endanger sb/sth; **le ~ est imminent** danger is imminent; **sans ~** safe; **(en) ~ de faire** (in) danger of doing; **le ~ d'une politique/doctrine** the danger of a policy/doctrine; **il y a ~ à faire** there's a danger in doing; **(il n'y a) pas de ~ qu'il fasse** no danger of him doing; **(il n'y a) pas de ~ que cela arrive** no danger of that happening; **'~ de chute'** 'Danger: steep drop'; **'~ d'éboulement'** 'risk of landslide'; **'~ de mort'** 'Danger of death'; **'~ de noyade'** 'Danger: unsafe for bathing'; **'attention ~!'** 'Danger!'; **2** (risque ponctuel) danger; (personne) menace, dangerous person; **un ~ grave/mortel** a serious/mortal danger; **au volant c'est un vrai ~** he is a real menace at the wheel; **un ~ pour qn/qch** a danger to sb/sth; **courir un (grand) ~** to be in (great) danger; **faire courir un (grand) ~ à qn** to put sb in (serious) danger; **~ de la route** (obstacle) road hazard; (personne) menace behind the wheel.

■ **~ public** lit danger to the public; fig iron menace.

dangereusement /dɑ̃ʒʀøzmɑ̃/ *adv* dangerously; **se rapprocher ~** to come dangerously close.

dangereux, -euse /dɑ̃ʒʀø, øz/ *adj* [*voyage, virage, activité*] dangerous, hazardous (**pour** to); [*personne, geste, politique, animal, produit*] dangerous (**pour** to); **zone dangereuse** danger zone.

danois, ~e /danwa, az/ **I** ▶ 537 *adj* Danish.

II *nm* **1** ▶ 462 Ling Danish; **2** (chien) Great Dane.

Danois, ~e /danwa, az/ ▶ 537 *nm,f* Dane.

dans /dɑ̃/

■ **Note**

– La préposition *dans* est présentée ici dans ses grandes lignes. Les expressions courantes comme *dans la pénombre*, *dans le monde entier*, *être dans le pétrin etc* sont traitées respectivement dans les articles ***pénombre***, ***monde***, ***pétrin*** etc.

– On trouvera ci-dessous des exemples illustrant les principales utilisations de la préposition mais il sera toujours prudent de consulter l'entrée du nom introduit par *dans*.

– Par ailleurs, la consultation des notes d'usage dont la liste est donnée ▶ 1920 pourra apporter des réponses à certains problèmes bien précis.

prép **1** (lieu, sans déplacement) **être ~ la cuisine/le tiroir/la forêt** to be in the kitchen/the drawer/the forest; **~ cette histoire/son discours/cette affaire** fig in this story/his speech/this business; **être ~ le brouillard/l'eau** to be in the fog/the water; **dans cette région/ville** in this region/town; **être ~ un avion/train/bus/bateau** to be on a plane/train/bus/boat; **être ~ une voiture/un taxi** to be in a car/a taxi; **il y a des fleurs ~ le vase** there are some flowers in the vase; **le paquet est ~ le placard/la chambre** the parcel is in the cupboard/the bedroom; **l'histoire se passe ~ un train/~ un pays lointain** the story takes place on a train/in a distant country; **il est en vacances ~ le Cantal/les Alpes** he's on vacation in the Cantal/the Alps; **j'ai lu ça ~ Proust/un magazine** I read that in Proust/a magazine; **boire ~ un verre** to drink out of a glass; **fouiller ~ un tiroir** to rummage through a drawer; **prendre une casserole ~ un placard** to take a pan out of a cupboard; **vider qch ~ l'évier** to pour sth down the sink; **qu'est-ce que je fais ~ tout ça**○? what am I doing in all this?; **ce n'est pas ~ ton intérêt** it's not in your interest; **~ l'ensemble** by and large; **~ le fond** in fact; **2** (avec des verbes de mouvement) **aller ~ la cuisine/le grenier** to go to the kitchen/the attic; **entrer ~ une pièce** to go into a room; **voler ~ les airs** to fly in the air; **descendre ~ un puits** to go down a well; **monter ~ un avion** to get on a plane; **3** (temps) **~ ma jeunesse/leur adolescence/le futur** in my youth/their adolescence/the future; **~ deux heures/jours/ans** in two hours/days/years; **je t'appellerai ~ la journée** I'll call you during the day; **~ l'immédiat** for the time being; **~ la minute qui a suivi** the next moment; **~ l'heure qui suivit** within the hour; **finir qch ~ les temps**○ to finish sth in time; **4** (domaine) **être ~ les affaires/l'édition/la restauration** to be in business/publishing/the catering business; **5** (état) **~ la misère/le silence** in poverty/silence; **6** (but) **~ un esprit de vengeance** in a spirit of revenge; **~ l'espoir de** in the hope of; **~ l'intention de faire** with the intention of doing; **~ cette optique** from this perspective; **7** (approximation) about, around; **~ les 30 francs/20%/50 ans** about ou around 30 francs/20%/50 years old; **ça coûte ~ les 1000 francs** it costs about ou around 1,000 francs.

dansant, ~e /dɑ̃sɑ̃, ɑ̃t/ *adj* **1** (entraînant) [*rythme*] dance (*épith*); [*reflet*] dancing; **une musique ~e** music that makes you want to get up and dance; **2** (où l'on danse) **dîner/thé ~** dinner/tea dance; **soirée ~e** dance; **nuit ~e** all-night dance.

danse /dɑ̃s/ *nf* **1** (style) dance; (activité) dancing; **la ~ est une forme d'art** dance ou dancing is a form of art; **faire de la ~** to take dancing classes; **je fais de la ~ contemporaine** I go to contemporary dancing classes; **le tango est une ~ argentine** the tango is an Argentinian dance; **ce n'est pas de la ~ c'est de la gymnastique** that isn't dancing it's gymnastics; **accorder une ~ à qn** to give sb a dance; **m'accorderez-vous cette ~?** may I have this dance?; **de ~** [*festival*] of dance; [*club, piste, rythme, salle, troupe*] dance (*épith*); **cours de ~** (pour adultes) dance class; (pour enfants) dancing class; **école de ~** school of dance; **professeur de ~** gén dancing teacher; (de ballet) ballet teacher; **contempler la ~ des flammes dans l'âtre** to watch the flames dancing in the hearth; **2**○ (correction) hiding○; **flanquer une ~ à qn** to give sb a hiding.

■ **~ de caractère** character dancing; **~ classique** classical ballet; **amateur de ~ classique** ballet-lover; **faire de la ~ classique** to do ballet dancing; **~ contemporaine** contemporary dance; **~ du feu/de la pluie** Anthrop (ritual) fire-/rain-dance; **~ folklrique** (action) folk dancing; (spectacle) folk dance; **~ guerrière** war dance; **~ macabre** dance of death; **~ moderne** modern dance; **faire de la ~ moderne** to do modern dance; **~ nuptiale** Zool courtship display; **~ rythmique** rhythmic dancing; **~ de salon** ballroom dancing; **~ du ventre** lit belly dancing; fig seductive manoeuvre GB ou maneuver US.

IDIOMES **entrer dans la ~** lit to join the dance; fig to join in; **mener la ~** fig to run the show fig; **avoir la ~ de Saint-Guy** fig to have the fidgets; Méd to have St Vitus's dance.

danser /dɑ̃se/ [1] **I** *vtr* to dance [*valse, rock*]; **je ne sais pas ~ le tango** I can't do the tango; **un opéra dansé** an opera ballet; **scènes dansées** Cin, Théât dance scenes (**par qn** with sb).

II *vi* **1** [*personne*] to dance; [*abeilles, ours*] to dance; **~ dans un ballet** to dance in a ballet; **~ sur un rythme/une musique** to dance to a rhythm/a tune; **~ de joie** to dance with joy; **faire ~ qn** to have a dance with sb; **2** [*flammes, reflets*] to dance; [*barque*] to bob; ▶ **souris**.

IDIOMES **ne pas savoir sur quel pied ~** not to know what to do.

danseur, -euse /dɑ̃sœʀ, øz/ **I** *nm,f* dancer; **~ classique/de claquettes** ballet/tap dancer; **en danseuse** Sport standing on the pedals; **pédaler en danseuse** to pedal standing up.

II danseuse *nf* hum (maîtresse) mistress; (passe-temps) (expensive) hobby; **entretenir une danseuse** (maîtresse) to keep a mistress; (passe-temps) to indulge in an expensive hobby.

■ **~/danseuse de corde** tightrope walker; **~/danseuse étoile** principal dancer; **danseuse de cabaret** chorus girl.

dantesque /dɑ̃tɛsk/ *adj* Dantesque.

DAO /deao/ *nm: abbr* ▶ **dessin**.

dard /daʀ/ *nm* **1** (aiguillon) sting; **2** (arme) spear.

Dardanelles /daʀdanɛl/ *nprfpl* **les ~** the Dardanelles.

darder /daʀde/ [1] *vtr* **1** to hurl [*javelot*]; to shoot [*flèche*] (**contre** at); **2** liter **le soleil darde ses rayons** the sun is beaming down; **~ sur qn des regards aigus** to shoot piercing glances at sb.

dare-dare○ /daʀdaʀ/ *adv* [*rentrer, rejoindre*] double quick.

darne /daʀn/ *nf* (fish) steak.

dartre /daʀtʀ/ *nf* scurf patch.

darwinien, -ienne /daʀwinjɛ̃, ɛn/ *adj, nm,f* Darwinian.

darwinisme /daʀwinism/ *nm* Darwinism.

darwiniste /daʀwinist/ *adj, nmf* Darwinist.

datable /databl/ *adj* datable.

datation /datasjɔ̃/ *nf* **1** (attribution d'une date) dating; **2** (date attribuée) date.

date /dat/ ▶ 212 *nf* **1** (moment précis) date; **~ de naissance/décès** date of birth/death; **~ d'expiration** expiry date GB, expiration date US; **~ d'arrivée** date of arrival; **~ de départ** departure date; **j'ai reçu les ~s d'examens** I've received the exam dates; **~ de clôture** closing date; **~ butoir** deadline; **prendre ~** to set a date; **à une ~ ultérieure** at some future date; **à ~ fixe** on a set date; **~ anniversaire** anniversary; **depuis 1962, ~ à laquelle...** since 1962, in which year...; **en ~ du 7 février...** of 7 February...; **~ limite** deadline; **~ limite de consommation** eat-by date; **~ limite de vente** sell-by date; **~ limite de dépôt/d'envoi des dossiers** final date for submission of/for sending the documents; **~ limite d'inscription** closing date for registration; **2** (époque) time; **à/depuis cette ~** at/from that time; **jusqu'à une ~ récente** until recently; **un ami de fraîche/longue ~** a recent/longstanding friend; **la réunion était prévue de longue ~** the meeting had been scheduled well in advance; **le premier/dernier scandale en ~** the earliest/latest scandal; **3** (événement marquant) date; **une grande ~ dans** or **de l'histoire** an important date in history; **faire ~** to make its mark.

■ **~ de valeur** *actual date on which an amount is credited to or debited from an account.*

dater /date/ [1] **I** *vtr* **1** (donner une date à) to date [*document*]; **la circulaire est datée du...** the circular is dated the...; **n'oublie pas de ~ et de signer ton chèque** don't forget to date and sign your cheque GB ou check US; **document non daté** undated document; **à ~ du 31 juillet/de demain** as from 31 July/tomorrow; **2** (attribuer une date à) to date [*fossile, objet*].

II *vi* **1** (exister depuis) **~ de** to date from, date back to; **le disque date des années 50** the record dates from the 50's; **de quand date cette réforme?** what was the date of

La date

Noter

- *Les noms de mois et les noms de jours prennent toujours une majuscule en anglais; pour les abréviations des noms de mois et de jours fréquemment utilisées en anglais,* ▶ **521** *et* ▶ **750**.
- *En anglais parlé, on utilise presque toujours le nombre ordinal (par ex.* fifth *et non* five*) pour indiquer le jour du mois; pour les abréviations des nombres ordinaux,* ▶ **545**.

En anglais, il y a quatre façons d'écrire la date, et trois façons de la dire: ces options sont toutes indiquées pour la première date du tableau suivant. Pour écrire la date, les deux premières façons (May 1st *ou* May 1) *sont acceptées dans tous les pays anglophones. Dans le tableau on utilisera indifféremment l'une ou l'autre de ces deux formes.*

Pour dire la date, la première des formes données (May the first) *est acceptée partout, et c'est cette forme qu'on utilisera dans le tableau. Les deux autres ne sont pas aussi répandues.*

	écrire	**dire**
1er mai	May 1 *ou* May 1st (*US & GB*) 1st May *ou* 1 May (*GB*)	May the first (*GB & US*) *ou* the first of May (*GB*) *ou* May first (*US*)
2 avril	April 2 (etc.) *abrév.* Apr 2	April the second (etc.)
lundi 3 mai	Monday, May 3	Monday, May the third
4 mai 1927	May 4th 1927	May the fourth, nineteen twenty-seven
31.7.65	31.7.65* (*GB*) *ou* 7.31.65* (*US*)	July the thirty-first nineteen sixty-five
jeudi 5 mai 1994	Thursday, May 5 1994	Thursday, May the fifth, nineteen ninety-four
1968	1968	nineteen sixty-eight
1900	1900	nineteen hundred
l'an 2000	the year 2000	the year two thousand
2001	2001	two thousand and one
45 ap. J.-C.	45 AD†	forty-five AD [eɪdiː]
250 av. J.-C.	250 BC‡	two hundred and fifty BC [biːsiː]
le XVIe siècle	the 16th§ century	the sixteenth century

* *L'anglais britannique, comme le français, place le chiffre du jour avant celui du mois; l'anglais américain commence par le chiffre du mois.*

† AD *signifie* anno domini (*l'année de notre Seigneur*).

‡ BC *signifie* before Christ (*avant Jésus-Christ*).

§ *Noter que l'anglais utilise les chiffres arabes pour les siècles.*

Pour les dates sur les lettres, voir **activités**.

Quel jour?

le combien sommes-nous aujourd'hui? = what's the date today?
nous sommes le 10 = it's the tenth
nous sommes le lundi 10 = it's Monday 10th (*dire* Monday the tenth)
nous sommes le 10 mai = it's May 10 (*dire* it's the tenth of May)

Pour indiquer la date à laquelle il s'est passé ou se passera quelque chose, l'anglais utilise normalement la préposition on *devant le quantième du mois.*

on se voit le 10 = see you on the 10th
c'est arrivé le 10 = it happened on the 10th
c'est arrivé le 10 décembre = it happened on 10th December (*dire* the tenth of December)
le 10 de chaque mois = on the 10th of every month

L'anglais emploie on *même en début de phrase.*

le lundi 5 mai, il atteignit Tombouctou = on Monday May 5, he reached Timbuktu

Mais on peut aussi utiliser d'autres prépositions:

à partir du 10 = from the 10th onwards
jusqu'au 10 = till *ou* until the 10th
attendez le 10 = wait till the 10th
avant le 10 mai = before May 10 (*dire* before May the tenth)
aux environs du 10 mai = around 10 May (*dire* around the tenth of May)
du 10 au 16 mai = from 10th to 16th May (*GB*) (*dire* from the tenth to the sixteenth of May) *ou* from 10th through 16th May (*US*) (*dire* from the tenth through the sixteenth of May)

Devant les noms de mois et les chiffres des années et des siècles, l'anglais utilise normalement in.

en mai = in May
je suis né en mai 1914 = I was born in May 1914
en 1945 = in 1945
il est mort en 1616 = he died in 1616
Shakespeare (1564–1616) = Shakespeare (1564–1616) (*dire* Shakespeare fifteen sixty-four to sixteen sixteen) *ou* Shakespeare, b. 1564–d. 1616 (*dire* Shakespeare born in fifteen sixty-four and died in sixteen sixteen)

la révolution de 1789 = the 1789 revolution
les émeutes de 68 = the riots of '68 (*dire* of sixty-eight)
en mai 45 = in May '45 (*dire* in May forty-five)
dans les années 50 = in the fifties *ou* in the 1950s (*dire* in the nineteen fifties)
au début des années 50 = in the early fifties
à la fin des années 50 = in the late fifties
au XVIIe siècle = in the 17th century (*dire* in the seventeenth century)
au début du XIIe siècle = in the early twelfth century
à la fin du XIIe siècle = in the late twelfth century

Le mot century *ne peut pas être omis en anglais*:

à partir du XII[e] = from the 12th century onwards (*dire* from the twelfth century onwards)
les romanciers du XIX[e] = 19th-century novelists (*dire* nineteenth century novelists)

this reform?; **de quand date votre séparation/rencontre?** when did you separate/first meet?; **cela ne date pas d'hier**○ it's not exactly new; **2** (être démodé) [*vêtement, personne, roman*] to be dated.

dateur /datœʀ, øz/ **I** *adj* [*tampon, timbre*] date (*épith*).
II *nm* **1** Admin date stamp; **2** (sur montre) date indicator.

datif /datif/ *nm* Ling dative; **au ~** in the dative.

dation /dasjɔ̃/ *nf* **~ (en paiement)** payment in kind.

datte /dat/ *nf* date.

dattier /datje/ *nm* date palm.

daube /dob/ *nf* casserole; **bœuf en ~**, **~ de bœuf** beef casserole.

daubière /dobjɛʀ/ *nf* casserole dish.

dauphin /dofɛ̃/ *nm* **1** Zool dolphin; **2** (successeur) heir apparent; **le président a choisi son ~** the president chose his heir apparent; **3** Hist dauphin.

dauphine /dofin/ *nf inv* **pomme ~** Dauphine potato.

Dauphiné /dofine/ ▶ **692** *nprm* Dauphiné.

dauphinois, **~e** /dofinwa, az/ ▶ **692** *adj* Géog [*club, musée*] Dauphiné (*épith*), from the Dauphiné region.

Dauphinois, **~e** /dofinwa, az/ ▶ **692** *nm,f* **1** (natif) native of the Dauphiné region; **2** (habitant) inhabitant of the Dauphiné region.

daurade /dɔʀad/ *nf* **~ (royale)** gilt-head bream.

davantage /davɑ̃taʒ/ **I** *adv* **1** (plus) more; **il est rusé mais elle l'est ~** he's crafty but she's (even) more so; **il ne travaille pas ~** (en effort) he isn't working any harder; (en quantité) he doesn't do any more work; **je n'en sais pas ~!** I don't know any more than that!, more than that I do not know!; **après trois mois de cours je n'en sais pas ~** after three months of classes I don't know any more than I did before ou I'm none the wiser; **je lui ai répété deux fois la question, mais je crois qu'il n'a pas ~ compris** I repeated the question twice but I don't think he understood any better; **je ne peux pas la supporter et ses enfants pas ~** I can't stand her or her children either; **sinon ~** if not more; **~ que** more than; **rien ne me plaît ~ que** controv I like nothing better than; **maintenant je l'apprécie bien ~** now I like him/her much more; **choisissez l'ouvrage qui vous plaît ~** choose the book you like better; **2** (plus longtemps) longer; **le projet prendra cinq ans et peut-être ~** the project will take five years and perhaps (even) more ou longer; **si vous vous exposez ~ aux radiations** if you are further exposed to radiation.
II *dét indéf* **~ de** more; **en voulez-vous ~?** would you like some more?; **prenez ~ de viande** have some more meat; **créer ~ d'emplois** to create more jobs; **offrir ~ de possibilités** to offer more possibilities; **le système a ~ de succès à la campagne** the system is more successful in the country.

David /david/ *npr* David; **~ et Goliath** David and Goliath.

davier /davje/ *nm* **1** Dent dentist's forceps; **2** Tech cramp; **3** Naut davit.

dB (*written abbr* = **décibel**) dB.

DB /debe/ *nf abbr* ▶ **division**.

DCA /desea/ *nf* (*abbr* = **défense contre les aéronefs**) antiaircraft defence[GB].

DDASS /das/ *nf* (*abbr* = **Direction départementale de l'action sanitaire et sociale**) regional social services department.

DDT /dedete/ *nm* (*abbr* = **dichlorodiphényl-trichloréthane**) DDT.

de (**d'** *before vowel or mute h*) /də, d/ *prép* **1** (indiquant l'origine) from; **leur départ/le train ~ Bruxelles** their departure/the train from Brussels; **il arrive du Japon** he's just come from Japan; **~ la fenêtre, on peut voir...** from the window, one can see...; **à 20 mètres ~ là** 20 metres[GB] from there; **~ ce moment** fml from that moment; **un enfant ~ mon premier mari/mariage** a child by my first husband/from my first marriage; **elle est ~ Taiwan** she's from Taiwan; **un vin ~ Grèce** (rapporté de là-bas) a wine from Greece; (fait là-bas) a Greek wine; **né ~ parents immigrés** born of immigrant parents; **il est ~ père italien et ~ mère chinoise** his father is Italian and his mother Chinese; **le bébé est ~ février** the baby was born in February; **~ méfiant il est devenu paranoïaque** he went from being suspicious to being paranoid; **d'ici là** between now and then; **d'ici la fin du mois**

de

La préposition

Certains emplois de la préposition *de* sont traités ailleurs dans le dictionnaire, notamment:

lorsque *de* introduit le complément de verbes transitifs indirects comme *douter de*, *jouer de*, de verbes à double complément comme *recevoir qch de qn*, de certains noms comme *désir de*, *obligation de*, de certains adjectifs comme *fier de*, *plein de*;

lorsque *de* fait partie de locutions comme *d'abord*, *de travers* ou de composés comme *chemin de fer*, *pomme de terre*;

lorsque *de* est utilisé dans la structure de déterminants indéfinis comme *peu de*, *moins de* etc.;

lorsque *de* fait suite à *être* dans certaines tournures **être**.

D'autres renvois essentiels apparaissent dans l'entrée ci-dessous, mais on se reportera également aux notes d'usage répertoriées **▶ 1920** pour certaines constructions.

L'article indéfini

de article indéfini pluriel est traité avec **un I**.

L'article partitif: de, de l', de la, du

Lorsqu'il exprime une généralité non quantifiée ou une alternative, *de*, article partitif ne se traduit pas:

manger de la viande/du lapin/des œufs = to eat meat/rabbit/eggs
il ne boit jamais de vin = he never drinks wine
tu prends du café au petit déjeuner? = do you have coffee for breakfast?
voulez-vous de la bière ou du vin? = would you like beer or wine?
il ne veut pas de vin mais de la bière = he doesn't want wine, he wants beer

Lorsque l'idée de quantité est présente il se traduit par *some* ou *any*:

achète de la bière = buy some beer
achète des bananes = buy some bananas
voulez-vous de la bière? = would you like some beer?
évidemment, tu leur as donné de l'argent? = of course, you gave them some money?
y a-t-il du soleil? = is there any sun?
il n'y a pas de soleil = there isn't any sun, there's no sun
il y a rarement du soleil = there's seldom any sun
il n'y a jamais de soleil = there's never any sun
il n'y a plus de vin = there isn't any more wine

Et lorsque qu'il s'agit d'une partie déterminée d'un tout, il se traduit par *some of* ou *any of*:

a-t-elle bu du vin que j'ai apporté? = did she drink any of the wine I brought?
je ne prendrai plus de ce mélange = I won't take any more of this mixture

by the end of the month; **▶ par**; **2** (indiquant la progression) **~...à**, **~...en** from...to; **~ 8 à 10 heures** from 8 to 10 (o'clock); **~ mardi à samedi, du mardi au samedi** from Tuesday to Saturday; **du matin au soir** from morning till night; **d'une semaine à l'autre** from one week to the next; **~ Lisbonne à Berlin** from Lisbon to Berlin; **~ l'équateur aux pôles** from the equator to the poles; **~ ville en ville** from town to town; **d'heure en heure** from hour to hour; **~ déception en désillusion** from disappointment to disillusion; **▶ Charybde**, **long**, **moins**, **moment**, **place**, **plus**; **3** (indiquant la destination) to; **le train ~ Paris** the train to Paris, the Paris train; **4** (indiquant la cause) **mourir ~ soif/~ chagrin/d'une pneumonie** to die of thirst/of a broken heart/of pneumonia; **phobie ~ l'eau/la foule** fear of water/crowds; **des larmes ~ désespoir** tears of despair; **un hurlement ~ terreur** a scream of terror; **pleurer ~ rage** to cry with rage; **hurler ~ terreur** to scream with terror; **trembler ~ froid** to shiver with cold; **▶ joie**; **5** (indiquant la manière) in; **parler d'un ton monocorde** to speak in a monotone; **s'exprimer ~ manière élégante** to express oneself in an elegant way; **plaisanterie d'un goût douteux** joke in dubious taste; **tirer ~ toutes ses forces** to pull with all one's might; **il a répondu d'un geste obscène** he answered with an obscene gesture; **▶ beau**, **cœur**, **concert**, **mémoire**, **tac**, **trait**; **6** (indiquant le moyen) with; **pousser qch du pied** to push sth aside with one's foot; **soulever qch d'une main** to lift sth with one hand; **gravure/graver ~ la pointe d'un couteau** engraving/to engrave with the point of a knife; **suspendu des deux mains** hanging by two hands; **déjeuner/vivre ~ saucisses et ~ haricots** to lunch/to live on sausages and beans; **il a fait ~ sa chambre un bureau** he made his bedroom into a study; **▶ coup**, **coude**; **7** (indiquant l'agent) by; **un poème/dessin ~ Victor Hugo** a poem/drawing by Victor Hugo; **avoir un enfant ~ qn** to have a child by sb; **respecté ~ tous** respected by all; **8** (indiquant la durée) **travailler ~ nuit/~ jour** to work at night/during the day; **ne rien faire ~ la journée/semaine** to do nothing all day/week; **~ ma vie je n'avais vu ça** I had never seen such a thing in my life; **▶ temps**; **9** (indiquant l'appartenance, la dépendance) **les chapeaux ~ Paul/~ mon frère/~ mes parents** Paul's/my brother's/my parents' hats; **les oreilles ~ l'ours/~ mon chat** the bear's/my cat's ears; **la politique ~ leur gouvernement/~ la France** their government's/France's policy, the policy of their government/of France; **un élève du professeur Talbin** one of professor Talbin's students; **l'immensité ~ l'espace/la mer** the immensity of space/the sea; **le toit ~ la maison** the roof of the house; **la porte ~ la chambre** the bedroom door; **les rideaux ~ la chambre sont sales** the bedroom curtains are dirty; **j'ai lavé les rideaux ~ la chambre** I washed the bedroom curtains; **le cadran du téléphone** the dial on the telephone; **c'est bien ~ lui** it's just like him; **10** (détermination par le contenant) **le foin ~ la grange** the hay in the barn; **le vin du tonneau** (qui s'y trouve) the wine in the barrel; (qu'on a tiré) the wine from the barrel; **11** (détermination par le contenu) of; **une tasse ~ café** a cup of coffee; **un sac ~ charbon** a sack of coal; **12** (détermination par la quantité) of; **cinq pages ~ roman** five pages of a novel; **deux mètres ~ tissu** two metres[GB] of material; **trois litres ~ vin** three litres[GB] of wine; **une minute ~ silence** one minute of silence, a minute's silence; **quatre heures ~ musique** four hours of music; **deux milliardièmes ~ seconde** two billionths of a second; **le quart ~ mes économies** a quarter of my savings; **la totalité** or **l'ensemble ~ leurs œuvres** the whole of their works; **les sept maisons du hameau** the seven houses of the hamlet; **13** (détermination par le lieu) of; **les pyramides d'Égypte** the pyramids of Egypt; **le roi ~ Brunéi** the King of Brunei; **le premier ministre du Japon** the prime minister of Japan, the Japanese prime minister; **le comte ~ Monte-Cristo** the Count of Monte-Cristo; **14** (détermination par le temps) of; **les ordinateurs ~ demain** the computers of tomorrow; **le 20 du mois** the 20th of the month; **la réunion ~ samedi** Saturday's meeting; **la réunion du 20 juin** the meeting on 20 June; **le train ~ 15 heures** the 3 o'clock train; **les ventes ~ juin** the June sales; **15** (détermination par la dimension, la mesure) **un livre ~ 200 pages** a 200-page book; **un spectacle ~ deux heures** a two-hour show; **une grue ~ 50 tonnes** a 50-tonne crane; **être long ~ 20 mètres**, **avoir 20 mètres ~ long** to be 20 metres[GB] long; **50 francs ~ l'heure** 50 francs an hour; **enceinte ~ trois mois** three months' pregnant; **on aura deux heures d'attente** we'll have a two-hour wait; **on aura deux heures ~ retard** we'll be two hours late; **trop lourd ~ trois kilos** three kilos too heavy; **plus/moins ~ trois** more/less than three; **elle est la plus âgée/jeune ~ deux ans** she's the oldest/youngest by two years; **16** (détermination par la nature, fonction, matière) **un billet ~ train** a train ticket; **une statue ~ cristal** a crystal statue; **un livre ~ géographie** a geography book; **un professeur ~ botanique** a botany teacher; **un chapeau ~ cow-boy** a cowboy hat; **une salle ~ réunion** a meeting room; **une robe ~ coton rouge** a red cotton dress; **une bulle d'air/~ savon** an air/a soap bubble; **un joueur ~ tennis** a tennis player; **un produit ~ qualité** a quality product; **un travail ~ qualité** quality work; **un spécialiste ~ l'électronique** an electronics expert, an expert in electronics; **un homme ~ bon sens** a man of common sense; **la théorie ~ la relativité** the theory of relativity; **▶ bois**, **laine**; **17** (apposition) of; **le mois ~ juillet** the month of July; **la ville ~ Singapour** the city of Singapore; **le titre ~ duc** the title of duke; **le nom ~ Flore** the name Flore; **le terme ~ quark** the term quark; **18** (avec attribut du nom ou du pronom) **trois personnes ~ tuées** three people killed; **une jambe ~ cassée** a broken leg; **un seul ticket ~ valable** only one valid ticket; **deux heures ~ libres** two hours free; **200 francs ~ plus** 200 francs more; **l'ourlet a deux centimètres ~ trop** the hem is two centimetres[GB] too long; **ton imbécile ~ frère** your stupid brother; **quelque chose/rien ~ nouveau** something/nothing new; **je n'ai jamais rien vu ~ semblable** I've never seen anything like it; **c'est quelqu'un ~ célèbre** he's/she's famous; **c'est ça ~ fait**○ that's that out of the way, that's that taken care of; **19** (avec un infinitif) **~ la voir ainsi me peinait** seeing her like that upset me; **ça me peinait ~ la voir ainsi** it upset me to see her like that; **et eux/toute la salle ~ rire** and they/the whole audience laughed; **être content ~ faire** to be happy to do; **20** (après un déverbal) **le filtrage ~ l'eau pose de gros problèmes** filtering water poses big problems; **le remplacement ~ la chaudière a coûté très cher** replacing the boiler was very expensive; **21** (après un superlatif) gén of; (avec un lieu ou ensemble assimilé) in; **le plus jeune des trois frères** the youngest of the three brothers; **le roi des rois** the king of kings; **le plus grand restaurant ~ la ville** the biggest restaurant in the town; **le plus vieux ~ la classe/famille** the oldest in the class/family; **22**○ (en corrélation avec le pronom un, une) **pour une gaffe, c'en est une, ~ gaffe!** as blunders go, that was a real one!; **est-ce que j'en ai une, moi, ~ voiture?** and me, have I got a car?; **23** (dans une comparaison chiffrée) than; **plus/moins ~ 10** more/less than 10.

dé /de/ *nm* **1** Jeux dice (*inv*); **un ~ en bois** a wooden dice; **jeter les ~s** to throw the dice; **les ~s sont jetés** the die is cast; **les ~s sont pipés** the dice are loaded; **couper de la viande/des légumes en ~s** to dice meat/vegetables; **coup de ~** lit, fig throw of the dice; **jouer sa carrière sur un coup de ~** to risk one's career on a toss of the dice; **2** Cout **~ (à coudre)** lit thimble; (mesure) thimbleful.

DEA /deɑa/ *nm* (*abbr* = **diplôme d'études approfondies**) postgraduate certificate (*prior to doctoral thesis*).

dealer○ /dilœʀ/ *nm* pusher○, (drug) dealer.

déambulateur /deɑ̃bylatœʀ/ *nm* zimmer (frame) GB, walker US.

déambulation /deɑ̃bylasjɔ̃/ *nf* wandering.

déambulatoire /deɑ̃bylatwaʀ/ *nm* (d'église) ambulatory; (hall) reception hall.

déambuler /deɑ̃byle/ [1] *vi* to wander (about).

débâcle /debɑkl/ *nf* **1** Géog breaking up; **2** Mil rout; **3** fig (économique) collapse; (générale) rout, collapse.

déballage /debalaʒ/ *nm* **1** (de cartons) unpacking; **2** (désordre) jumble; **3** (aveu public) outpouring.

déballastage /debalastaʒ/ *nm* oil dumping.

déballer /debale/ [1] *vtr* **1** (retirer l'emballage de) to unpack [*marchandise, caisse*]; to open [*paquet, cadeau*]; **2** (étaler) to display [*marchandise*]; **3** (avouer) to pour out; ▶ **linge**.

débandade /debɑ̃dad/ *nf* **1** (déroute) stampede; **manifestants/soldats en pleine ~** demonstrators/soldiers fleeing in disarray; **2** fig disarray; **tout va à la ~** everything's falling apart.

débander /debɑ̃de/ [1] **I** *vtr* **1** (ôter le bandage de) to take the bandage off; **2** (ôter un bandeau de) **~ les yeux de qn** to remove sb's blindfold; (détendre) to loosen [*ressort, arc*].

II● *vi* (ne plus être en érection) to go limp.

III se débander *vpr* (se disperser) to scatter.

IDIOMES **sans ~**○ without pausing for breath.

débaptiser /debatize/ [1] *vtr* to change the name of [*personne*]; to rename [*rue, ville*].

débarbouillage /debaʀbujaʒ/ *nm* wash.

débarbouiller /debaʀbuje/ [1] **I** *vtr* to wash [*enfant, visage*].

II se débarbouiller *vpr* to wash one's face.

débarbouillette /debaʀbujɛt/ *nf* C (petite serviette) face flannel GB, face cloth.

débarcadère /debaʀkadɛʀ/ *nm* landing stage, jetty.

débardage /debaʀdaʒ/ *nm* (en forêt) forwarding; (sur camion) hauling.

débarder /debaʀde/ [1] *vtr* (en forêt) to forward; (sur camion) to haul.

débardeur /debaʀdœʀ/ *nm* **1** (pull sans manches) tank top; (d'été) sleeveless tee-shirt; **2** (ouvrier) forest labourer[GB]; (dans un port) docker.

débarquement /debaʀkəmɑ̃/ *nm* **1** (de marchandises) unloading; (de passagers) disembarkation; **à son ~** on disembarkation; **le ~ des marchandises du bateau** unloading the goods from the ship; **c'est lors de mon ~ (de l'avion) que**... while I was disembarking (from the plane)...; **2** Mil landing; **troupes de ~** landing troops; **le ~ en Normandie** Hist the Normandy landings (*pl*).

débarquer /debaʀke/ [1] **I** *vtr* to unload [*marchandise, véhicule*] (**de** from; **sur** onto); to land, to unload [*passager, troupe*] (**de** from; **sur** onto).

II *vi* **1** (descendre à terre) [*passagers*] to disembark; **~ du train/de l'avion** to get off the train/the plane; **2** Mil to land (**sur** on; **en** in); **3**○ (arriver) (en masse) to descend (**à** upon); (à l'improviste) to turn up○ (**chez qn** at sb's place); (en un lieu inconnu) [*étranger*] to find oneself (**à** in); **4**○ (ne pas être au courant) **il débarque toujours** he never has a clue○ (what's going on); **tu débarques!** where have you been!

débarras /debaʀa/ *nm* **1** (endroit) junk room; **ça me sert de ~** I use it to store things; **2** (action) clearance; **~ de grenier** attic clearance; **bon ~**○**!** good riddance!

débarrasser /debaʀase/ [1] **I** *vtr* **1** (vider) to clear out [*pièce, placard*]; to clear [*bureau, table, jardin*]; **~ une pièce/un placard de qch** to clear sth out of a room/a cupboard; **~ un bureau/une table de qch** to clear sth off a desk/a table; **~ (la table)** (après le repas) to clear the table; **2** (libérer) **~ qn de ses préjugés/complexes** to free sb from ou of their prejudices/complexes; **~ qn d'une obligation/d'une corvée** to release sb from an obligation/from a chore; **~ un pays d'un dictateur** to rid a country of a dictator; **~ un chien de ses puces** to get rid of a dog's fleas; **si tu as besoin de vieux journaux, sers-toi, ça me débarrasse** if you need some old papers, help yourself, it'll get them out of my way; **~ votre peau de ses impuretés** to rid your skin of impurities; **les murs ont été débarrassés des vieux papiers peints** the walls have been stripped of the old wallpaper; **3 ~ qn (de son manteau)** to take sb's coat; **je peux vous ~** can I take your coat?

II se débarrasser *vpr* **1** (se séparer) **se ~ de** to get rid of; **se ~ des déchets** to dispose of waste; **débarrassez-vous du travail en retard d'abord** get rid of the backlog first; **se ~ d'un rhume** to shake off a cold; **2 se ~ (de son manteau)** to take off one's coat; **3** (tuer) **se ~ de** to get rid of.

IDIOMES **~ le plancher**○ to clear off○.

débarrer /debaʀe/ [1] *vtr* C (ouvrir) to unlock [*porte*].

débat /deba/ **I** *nm* **1** (discussion) debate (**sur** on); **conduire un ~** to chair a debate; **entrer dans le cœur du ~** to get to the heart of the matter; **2** (conflit moral) crisis; **~ intérieur** or **de conscience** crisis of conscience.

II débats *nmpl* **1** Pol debates; **2** Jur hearing (*sg*).

III (-)débat (*in compounds*) **dîner(-)~** dinner-debate.

débâter /debɑte/ [1] *vtr* to unsaddle [*mulet*].

débâtir /debɑtiʀ/ [3] *vtr* to take out the basting from [*vêtement, ouvrage*].

débattement /debatmɑ̃/ *nm* Aut clearance.

débattre /debatʀ/ [61] **I** *vtr* **1** (discuter) to discuss [*question*]; **2** (négocier) to negotiate [*prix, conditions*]; **prix/salaire à ~** price/salary negotiable.

II débattre de or **sur** *vtr ind* (discuter) to discuss; (au Parlement, à la télévision) to debate.

III se débattre *vpr* **1** lit [*animal*] to struggle; [*personne*] to put up a struggle; **se ~ contre** to struggle with; **2** fig to struggle (**dans** with; **contre** against).

débauchage /deboʃaʒ/ *nm* (de personne) laying off.

débauche /deboʃ/ *nf* **1** (dépravation) debauchery; **un lieu de ~** a den of vice; **2** (profusion) profusion; **~ de couleur** profusion of colour[GB]; **~ d'énergie/imagination** abundance of energy/imagination.

débauché, **~e** /deboʃe/ **I** *pp* ▶ **débaucher**.

II *pp adj* [*personne*] debauched.

III *nm,f* debauchee; **mener une vie de ~** to lead a dissolute life.

débaucher /deboʃe/ [1] *vtr* **1** (licencier) to lay off [*employé*]; **2** (inciter à la grève) to incite [sb] to strike; **3** (dépraver) to corrupt [*personne*]; **4**○ (distraire) to tempt [sb] away (**pour faire** to do); **je voulais réviser mais il m'a débauchée!** I wanted to revise but he tempted me away!

débe(c)queter○ /debɛkte/ [1] *vtr* to make [sb] gag○; fig to make [sb] sick.

débile /debil/ **I**○ *adj* **1** (idiot) [*personne*] moronic; [*film, raisonnement*] daft○; **c'est ~** it's daft○; **2**† liter (faible) [*enfant*] sickly; [*santé*] weak; [*esprit*] feeble.

II *nmf* **~ mental** Méd retarded person; péj moron○.

débilitant, **~e** /debilitɑ̃, ɑ̃t/ *adj* (physiquement) debilitating; (moralement) demoralizing.

débilité /debilite/ *nf* **1** Méd debility; **2**○ (de film, discours) stupidity.

■ **~ mentale** mental retardation.

débiliter /debilite/ [1] *vtr* **1** (physiquement) to debilitate; **2** (moralement) to demoralize.

débine● /debin/ *nf* **être dans la ~** to be down at heel; **tomber dans la ~** to fall on hard times.

débiner○ /debine/ [1] **I** *vtr* to slag [sb] off○ GB, to badmouth.

II se débiner *vpr* **1** (partir) to clear off○; (pour se dérober à qch) to make oneself scarce○; **2** (se disloquer) [*choses*] to fall apart.

débineur○, **-euse** /debinœʀ, øz/ *nm,f* mudslinger.

débirentier, **-ière** /debiʀɑ̃tje, ɛʀ/ *nm,f* Jur payer of an allowance.

débit /debi/ *nm* **1** Compta debit; **colonne des ~s** debit side; **la somme est inscrite au ~** gén the sum has been debited; (sur un relevé) the sum appears on the debit side; **inscrire** or **porter une somme au ~ d'un compte en banque** to debit a bank account with a sum of money; **porter un achat au ~ de qn** to charge a purchase to sb's account; **mettre** or **porter qch au ~ de qn** fig to count sth against sb; **2** (en parlant, récitant) delivery; **il a un de ces ~s!** (bavard) he never stops talking!; **3** (de cours d'eau) rate of flow; **4** (de liquide) flow, outflow; (de gaz) output; **5** (de ligne d'assemblage) output; **6** (de magasin) turnover (of stock); (de restaurant) customer turnover; **produit qui a un bon ~** product which sells well; **7** (de véhicules) flow; **8** Mil rate of fire; **9** Ordinat **~ d'une unité** data throughput rate; **10** (de pièce de bois) sawing up.

■ **~ de boissons** (bar) bar; **~ cardiaque** cardiac output; **~ de tabac** tobacconist GB; **ils font aussi ~ de tabac** they also sell tobacco.

débitable /debitabl/ *adj* **1** [*compte*] debitable; **2** [*bois*] easy to cut up (*jamais épith*).

débitage /debitaʒ/ *nm* (de bois) sawing.

débiter /debite/ [1] *vtr* **1** Fin to debit [*compte, client*]; **~ un compte de 100 francs** to debit an account with 100 francs, to debit 100 francs from ou to an account; **~ qn de 100 francs** to debit 100 francs to sb; **compte à ~** account which is to be debited; **2** (fournir) to reel off [*texte*]; [*radio, télévision*] to churn out [*musique*]; **~ des bêtises** to talk a lot of nonsense; **~ des mensonges** to spout lies; **3** (découper) to cut up [*animal, tissu, bois, marbre*]; **4** (vendre) to sell, to retail; **5** (produire) to produce; **6** (fournir en liquide) **~ tant par heure** [*cours d'eau*] to have a flow of so much per hour; [*appareil, pompe*] to discharge ou output so much per hour.

débiteur, **-trice** /debitœʀ, tʀis/ **I** *adj* [*compte, solde*] debit (*épith*); [*pays*] debtor (*épith*), which is in debt; [*entreprise*] which is in debt; **il leur est ~ d'un million** he owes them a million.

II *nm,f* Compta, Fin debtor.

déblai /deblɛ/ Tech **I** *nm* (pour dégager) clearing; (en creusant) excavation; (pour niveler) earth-moving.

II déblais *nmpl* (décombres) rubble ₵; (sol) earth ₵.

déblaiement /deblɛmɑ̃/ *nm* clearing.

déblatérer○ /deblateʀe/ [14] *vi* **~ contre** or **sur qch/qn** to rant on about sth/sb○.

déblayage /deblɛjaʒ/ *nm* **1** lit clearing; **2** fig (d'affaires) sorting out.

déblayer /debleje/ [21] *vtr* **1** (dégager) to clear away [*gravats, terre, neige*]; to clear [*passage, lieu, porte*] (**de qch** of sth); (ranger) to tidy up [*pièce*]; **~**○ **le terrain** or **le plancher** to clear off○; **2** (traiter) to sort out [*correspondance*]; (préparer) to do the groundwork on [*affaire*]; **~ une question** to sort out the main issue.

déblocage /deblɔkaʒ/ *nm* **1** (de frein) releasing; (de roue) unlocking; (de machine, mécanisme) unjamming; **2** (de fonds) releasing; (de salaires) unfreezing; (de prix) deregulating; **attendre un ~ de la situation** to wait for an end to the deadlock.

débloquer /deblɔke/ [1] **I** *vtr* **1** Tech to release [*frein*]; to unlock [*volant, roue*]; to unjam [*machine, mécanisme*]; **2** (libérer) to unfreeze [*salaires, prix*]; to release [*fonds, crédits, dossiers, marchandises*]; to break ou end the deadlock in [*situation, négociation*]; to give renewed impetus to [*processus*]; **3** (dégager) to make [sth] available [*crédits, subventions*]; to create [*poste*]; **4** (ouvrir) to clear [*rue, entrée*]; **~ la voie vers un accord commercial** fig to clear the way for a trade agreement; **5**○ (guérir) **~ qn** to straighten sb out.

II○ *vi* to be off one's rocker○.

III se débloquer *vpr* **la situation s'est débloquée** the deadlock has been broken.

débobiner /debɔbine/ [1] *vtr* **1** gén to wind off [*fil*]; to unwind [*bobine*]; **2** Électrotech to remove the coil(s) from [*dispositif*].

débogage /debɔgaʒ/ *nm* debugging.

déboguer /debɔge/ [1] *vtr* to debug.

déboires /debwaʀ/ *nmpl* **1** (déceptions) disappointments; **~ amoureux** disappointments in love; **2** (ennuis) trials, difficulties; **3** (échecs) setbacks; **essuyer des ~ professionnels** to meet with ou suffer professional setbacks.

déboisement /debwazmɑ̃/ *nm* (de région) deforestation; **le ~ de la colline** the clearing of the hill.

déboiser /debwaze/ [1] **I** *vtr* to clear [sth] of trees [*terrain*]; to deforest [*région*].

II se déboiser *vpr* to become deforested.

déboîtement /debwatmɑ̃/ *nm* **1** Méd dislocation; **2** Aut pulling out; **accident dû au ~ d'une voiture** accident caused by a car pulling out.

déboîter /debwate/ [1] **I** *vtr* (déloger) to dislocate [*os*]; to dislodge [*objet*]; to disconnect [*tubes*]; **~ une montre** to take a watch out of its case; **tu m'as déboîté l'épaule** you've dislocated my shoulder.

II *vi* (sortir d'un alignement) [*personne*] to move out of line; [*groupe*] to break out of column; [*voiture*] to pull out.

III se déboîter *vpr* **1 se ~ le genou** to dislocate one's knee; **2** (être luxé) **mon genou s'est déboîté** my knee is dislocated.

débonnaire /debɔnɛʀ/ *adj* [*personne*] (sympathique) good-humoured[GB]; (tolérant) easy-going; [*ambiance, soirée*] relaxed; **il a l'air ~** he has a kindly air about him.

débordant, ~e /debɔʀdɑ̃, ɑ̃t/ *adj* **1** (extrême) [*imagination*] overactive; [*joie*] overflowing; **être d'une activité ~e** to be extremely active; **2** (abondant) **~ de** brimming with; **~ de vitalité/d'énergie** brimming with vitality/with energy; **~ de santé** bursting with health; **3** (qui déborde) lit, fig overflowing (**de** with); **4** Mil, Sport [*manœuvre*] outflanking.

débordé, ~e /debɔʀde/ **I** *pp* ▶ **déborder**.

II *pp adj* **1** (dépassé) overwhelmed; **la police a été ~e** the police were overwhelmed; **~s, les pompiers n'ont pu sauver tout le monde** the firemen were overwhelmed and couldn't save everyone; **2** (surchargé) overloaded; **être ~ de travail** to be snowed under ou overloaded with work; **3** Mil, Sport outflanked (**sur** on).

débordement /debɔʀdəmɑ̃/ **I** *nm* **1** (abondance) (d'insultes, de protestations) flood; (d'enthousiasme) excess; **2** Pol, Entr (dépassement) outflanking; **le ~ d'un parti sur sa droite** the outflanking of a party by its right-wingers; **3** Mil, Sport (contournement) outflanking; **4** (de cours d'eau) overflowing.

II débordements *nmpl* liter excesses.

déborder /debɔʀde/ [1] **I** *vtr* **1** (sortir de) [*problème*] to go beyond [*domaine*]; **~ le cadre de qch** to go beyond the scope ou framework of sth; **cette remarque/votre question déborde le sujet** that remark/your question is outside the scope of the subject; **2** (submerger) to overwhelm [*personne, groupe*]; **se laisser ~** to let oneself be overwhelmed (**par qn/qch** by sb/sth); **3** Entr, Pol (dépasser) to outflank; **le chef du parti s'est fait/laissé ~ sur sa gauche** the party leader was/let himself be outflanked by the left; **4** Mil, Sport (contourner) to outflank; **se faire ~ sur l'aile gauche** to be outflanked on the left wing; **5** (saillir de) to jut out from; **certaines briques débordent le mur de deux centimètres** some of the bricks jut out two centimetres[GB] from the wall; **6** Cout (ôter le bord) to cut the border off [*tapis, napperon*]; **7** (tirer les draps) **~ qn** to untuck sb's bed [*enfant, malade*].

II déborder de *vtr ind* (être plein de) to be overflowing with [*personnes, détails*]; to be brimming over with [*joie, amour*]; to be bursting with [*santé*]; **~ de vie/d'activité** to be full of life/of activity; **il débordait de gratitude** he was overflowing with gratitude.

III *vi* **1** (sortir des bords) [*liquide, rivière*] to overflow; (en bouillant) to boil over; **la rivière a débordé de son lit** the river has overflowed; **faire** or **laisser ~ le lait** to let the milk boil over; **2** (laisser répandre) [*récipient*] to overflow; (en bouillant) to boil over; **la coupe déborde** fig it's the last straw; ▶ **vase**; **3** (dépasser) to spill out; **les vêtements débordent de la valise** the clothes are spilling out of the suitcase; **son ventre débordait de sa ceinture** his/her belly hung over his/her belt; **la foule débordait sur la chaussée** the crowd spilled out onto the street; **les poubelles débordent** the dustbins GB ou garbage cans US are overflowing; **ton rouge à lèvres déborde** your lipstick is smudged; **la terrasse du café déborde sur le trottoir** the café terrace spills out onto the pavement GB ou sidewalk US; **la pierre déborde de dix centimètres** the stone juts out ten centimetres[GB]; **elle déborde en coloriant** she goes over the lines when she's colouring[GB] in; **4** (s'épancher) fml **sa joie déborde** he's/she's bursting with joy; **laisser ~ son cœur** to give way to one's emotions.

IV se déborder *vpr* (perdre ses couvertures) to become untucked; **il s'est débordé en dormant** his covers came off while he was asleep.

débosselage /debɔslaʒ/ *nm* C **atelier de ~** body shop.

débotté /debɔte/ *nm* **surprendre qn au ~** to take sb by surprise, to catch sb with his/her pants down○.

débotter /debɔte/ [1] **I** *vtr* **~ qn** to take off ou remove sb's boots.

II se débotter *vpr* to take off one's boots, to remove one's boots.

débouchage /debuʃaʒ/ *nm* (d'évier) unblocking; (de bouteille) opening.

débouché /debuʃe/ *nm* **1** (ouverture commerciale) (pays, région) market (**dans** in; **pour** for); (créneau) outlet (**dans** in; **pour** for); **trouver de nouveaux ~s à l'exportation** to find new export outlets; **2** (perspective d'avenir) opening, job opportunity (**en** in); **la formation offre peu de ~s** the training course offers few job opportunities; **3** (de vallée) mouth; **au ~ de la rue** where the street opens out; **avoir un ~ sur la mer** to have access to the sea.

déboucher /debuʃe/ [1] **I** *vtr* **1** (dégager) to unblock [*évier, nez, oreilles*]; **2** (ouvrir) to open, to uncork [*bouteille*]; to unstopper [*carafe*]; to uncap [*tube*].

II *vi* **1** lit, fig (arriver) [*personne, véhicule*] to come out (**de** from; **sur** onto; **dans** into); (brusquement) to appear (**de** from; **sur** on; **dans** in); **ils ont débouché sur le marché de l'emploi** fig they appeared on the job market; **2** (ouvrir) **~ sur** or **dans** [*rue, passage*] to open onto; **3** (se jeter) **~ dans** [*cours d'eau*] to flow into; **4** (mener) **~ sur** [*études, négociations, débat*] to lead to; **~ sur un déficit** to result in a deficit.

III se déboucher *vpr* **1** [*évier, conduit*] to come unblocked; **mes oreilles se sont débouchées** my ears popped; **2 se ~ les oreilles/le nez** to unblock one's ears/nose.

déboucheur /debuʃœʀ/ *nm* **1** (instrument) **~ (à ventouse)** plunger; **2** (produit) drain clearing product; **~ liquide** drain clearing fluid.

déboucler /debukle/ [1] *vtr* to unbuckle [*ceinture*].

déboulé /debule/ *nm* **1** Danse déboulé; **2** Chasse (de chien) bolt(ing); (de gibier) breaking cover; **tirer au ~** to shoot as the animal breaks cover; **3** Sport sprint.

débouler /debule/ [1] **I**○ *vtr* (dévaler) to charge down [*pente, escalier*].

II○ *vi* **1** (dégringoler) to tumble down; **2** (venir rapidement) **~ de** to come charging down; **~ sur qn** to burst in on sb; **~ dans l'arène politique** fig to burst onto the political scene; **3** Chasse [*gibier*] to bolt (**de** out of); **4** Sport to sprint.

déboulonnage /debulɔnaʒ/ *nm*, **déboulonnement** /debulɔnmɑ̃/ *nm* (dévissage) unbolting; (pour séparer) removal.

déboulonner /debulɔne/ [1] *vtr* **1** (enlever les boulons de) to remove the bolts from, to unbolt [*roue*]; **~ une statue** [*ouvrier*] to remove a statue; [*manifestants*] to topple a statue; **2**○ (discréditer) to discredit; (renvoyer) to fire, to sack○ GB; (aux élections) to unseat [*élu*].

débourber /debuʀbe/ [1] *vtr* **1** École (assainir) to dredge [*canal, étang*]; **2** Minér (nettoyer) to wash [*minerai*]; **3** Vin to rack [*vin*].

débourrer /debuʀe/ [1] *vtr* Équit to break in.

débours /debuʀ/ **I** *nm inv* **1** gén expense, outlay ₵; **rentrer dans ses ~** to cover one's expenses; **2** Compta disbursement.

II *nmpl* Jur costs.

déboursement /debuʀsəmɑ̃/ *nm* paying out, disbursement sout (**de** of).

débourser /debuʀse/ [1] *vtr* to pay out, to disburse sout; **sans ~ un centime** without paying out a single penny.

déboussoler○ /debusɔle/ [1] *vtr* to throw○, to confuse [*personne*]; **il est complètement déboussolé** he's all at sea○ GB he's totally confused.

debout /dəbu/ **I** *adv, adj inv* **1** (vertical, sur pied) [*personne*] standing; **~ sur une chaise** standing on a chair; **les personnes/trois personnes ~** the people/three people standing; **il reste cinq places ~** there are five standing places left; **'assis: 40, ~:10'** (dans un bus) 'seated: 40, standing: 10'; **la station ~ me fatigue** I find standing up tiring; **nous sommes restés ~ toute la soirée** we stood (up) all evening; **j'ai dû voyager ~** I had to stand all the way; **ne restez pas ~, asseyez-vous** do take a seat; **merci, je préfère rester ~** thanks, but I prefer to stand; **être** or **se tenir ~** to stand; **se mettre ~** to stand up, to get to one's feet, to get up; **le plafond était trop bas pour que je puisse me tenir ~** the ceiling was too low for me to stand upright; **ça bougeait tellement que personne ne pouvait se tenir ~** it was moving so much that no-one could stay on their feet; **je ne tiens plus ~, je vais me coucher** I'm falling asleep on my feet, I'm going to go to bed; **le vieillard/l'ivrogne tient à peine ~ sur ses jambes** the old man/the drunkard can hardly stand; **dès qu'elle a su se tenir ~** as soon as she could stand; **aidez-la à se mettre ~** help her to get up; **2** (hors du lit) [*personne*] up; **tu es déjà ~!** you're already up!; **il est ~ à cinq heures** he's up at five; **je suis resté ~ toute la nuit** I stayed up all night (long); **3** (qui se maintient) [*bâtiment, mur*] standing; **un seul temple/arbre était encore ~** only one temple/tree was still standing; fig **une des rares institu-**

tions restant ~ one of the few institutions still standing; **le bâtiment ne tient plus ~** the building is falling down; **ton histoire tient ~**○ your story seems likely; **leur histoire ne tient pas ~**○ their story doesn't hold water; **4** (vertical, sur une extrémité) [*animal*] on its hind legs; [*objet*] upright; **le chien s'est mis ~ pour attraper le sucre** the dog got up on its hind legs to get the sugar; **poser un tonneau ~** to put a barrel upright; **j'ai mis la table ~ contre le mur** I've stood the table up against the wall; **nous avons remis la statue ~** we stood the statue back up; **5** (guéri) **grâce à votre médicament, il était ~ en deux jours** thanks to your medicine, he was up and about in two days.

II *excl* (hors du lit) get up! , out of bed!; (hors d'un siège) get up!, on your feet!

débouté /debute/ *nm* nonsuit.

débouter /debute/ [1] *vtr* to nonsuit [*plaideur*]; **~ qn de sa demande** to nonsuit a plaintiff in appeal.

déboutonner /debutɔne/ [1] I *vtr* to unbutton, to undo [*vêtement*]; **tu es déboutonné** your buttons are undone.

II **se déboutonner** *vpr* **1** [*personne*] to unbutton ou undo one's clothes; **2** [*vêtement*] to come undone; **3**○ (parler sans réserve) to open up○; **4**● (avouer) to blab○, to spill the beans○.

débraillé, ~e /debʀaje/ I *adj* [*personne*] dishevelled[GB], sloppily dressed; [*tenue, style*] sloppy; [*manières*] slovenly; [*vie*] disorganized; [*conversation*] disjointed; **la poitrine ~e** with his shirt half undone.

II *nm* (de tenue, manières) slovenliness; (de style) sloppiness; **sortir en ~** to go out sloppily dressed.

débranchement /debʀɑ̃ʃmɑ̃/ *nm* **1** gén disconnection; **2** Rail splitting up.

débrancher /debʀɑ̃ʃe/ [1] *vtr* **1** (supprimer le branchement de) to disconnect, to unplug [*appareil*]; to disconnect, to switch off [*système d'alarme*]; to disconnect, to pull out [*prise*]; **2** Rail to split up [*wagons*].

débrayage /debʀɛjaʒ/ *nm* **1** Aut declutching; **manette/pédale de ~** clutch lever/pedal; **2** (grève) stoppage.

débrayer /debʀeje/ [21] I *vtr* Tech to throw [sth] out of gear.

II *vi* **1** Aut to declutch; **2** (cesser le travail) to down tools GB, to stop work.

débridé, ~e /debʀide/ I *pp* ▶ **débrider**.

II *pp adj* [*imagination, optimisme*] unbridled.

débrider /debʀide/ [1] *vtr* **1** (ôter la bride) to unbridle [*cheval*]; **2** (donner libre cours à) to unleash [*imagination*]; **3** (faire tourner plus vite) to race, to rev up○ [*moteur*]; **4** Méd (inciser) **~ un abcès** to lance an abscess; **~ une plaie** to remove the unhealthy tissue from a wound; **5** (ôter la ficelle) to untruss [*volaille*].

débris /debʀi/ I *nm inv* **1** (d'objet brisé) fragment; **des ~ de verre** broken glass ¢; **2** (de véhicule accidenté) piece of wreckage; **parmi les ~ de l'avion** among the debris ou wreckage from the plane; **3**○ (personne, animal) pej **vieux ~** old wreck.

II *nmpl* **1** (ordures) rubbish ¢; (restes) scraps; **2** (humains, fossiles) remains; (d'édifice) ruins, remains; (d'empire, armée, de fortune) remnants.

débrouillard, ~e /debʀujaʀ, aʀd/ I *adj* resourceful; **il est ~** he can look after himself.

II *nm,f* **c'est un ~** he can look after himself; péj he's a crafty one péj.

débrouillardise /debʀujaʀdiz/ *nf* resourcefulness.

débrouille○ /debʀuj/ *nf* resourcefulness.

débrouiller /debʀuje/ [1] I *vtr* **1** (démêler) to disentangle [*fils, écheveau*]; **2** (éclaircir) to solve, to unravel [*énigme, problème*]; **3**○ (enseigner les bases à) to teach [sb] the basics (**en, à** of).

II **se débrouiller** *vpr* **1** (s'arranger) to manage; **je ne sais pas comment il s'est débrouillé mais...** I don't know how he managed it but...; **débrouille-toi comme tu veux, mais sois rentré pour 11 h** do as you like but make sure you're back by eleven; **débrouille-toi avec ça je n'ai rien d'autre** you'll have to make do with that I've got nothing else; **se ~ avec qn** to sort it out with sb; **se ~ pour qch** to sort sth out; **il s'est débrouillé pour les tickets de théâtre** he has sorted out the theatre[GB] tickets; **se ~ pour faire** to manage to do; **se ~ pour obtenir qch** to manage to get sth, to wangle○ sth; **débrouillez-vous pour faire** make sure you do; **se ~ pour que** to arrange it so that; **débrouille-toi pour que** make sure that; **se ~ pour ne pas faire** to weasel out of doing sth○; **il s'est débrouillé pour perdre la clé** he's gone and lost the key; **2** (s'en sortir) to get by; **dans la vie il faut savoir se ~** in life you have to learn to stand on your own two feet; **il se débrouille en espagnol** he gets by in Spanish; **il se débrouille bien en espagnol** he speaks good Spanish; **débrouille-toi tout seul** you'll have to manage on your own; **il se débrouille!** he's doing all right!

débroussaillage /debʀusajaʒ/, **débroussaillement** /debʀusajmɑ̃/ *nm* **1** (d'un chemin) clearing (**de** of); **2** (de texte, problème) spadework (**de** on).

débroussailler /debʀusaje/ [1] *vtr* **1** Agric to clear the undergrowth from [*terrain*]; **2** (éclaircir) to do the groundwork ou spadework on [*texte, problème*].

débroussailleuse /debʀusajøz/ *nf* brushcutter.

débusquer /debyske/ [1] *vtr* **1** (dévoiler) to bring [sth] to light [*erreur*]; **2** (déloger) to flush out [*animal, personne*].

début /deby/ I *nm* (de film, mois, discours) beginning; (de crise, négociations, d'épidémie) start; **au tout** or **tout au ~** at the very beginning; **au ~** at first, initially; **au ~ de** at the beginning of; **~ mars/1990** early in March/1990; **dès le ~** from the outset ou the very beginning ou the start; **depuis le ~ (de)** since the beginning (of); **je le savais depuis le ~** I knew all along; **salaire de ~** starting salary; **en ~ de soirée/semaine/carrière** at the beginning of the evening/the week/one's career; **du ~ (jusqu')à la fin** from start to finish; **ce n'est qu'un ~** this is only the beginning; **il y a un ~ à tout** you have to start somewhere; **pour un ~, ce n'est pas mal** it's not bad for starters; **un ~ de solution/d'explication/de démocratie** the beginnings of a solution/of an explanation/of democracy; **avoir un ~ de calvitie** to have a bald patch.

II **débuts** *nmpl* **1** (de comédien, musicien) debut (*sg*); **faire ses ~s dans le monde** to make one's debut in society; **faire des ~s éblouissants au théâtre** to make a dazzling stage debut; **à mes ~s** when I started out; **2** (de parti politique, média) early stages; **(en être encore) à ses ~s** [*mouvement, projet*] (to be still) in its early stages; **depuis ses ~s en 1962, le mouvement a évolué** since its inception in 1962, the movement has evolved.

débutant, ~e /debytɑ̃, ɑ̃t/ I *adj* [*conducteur, skieur, artiste*] novice (*épith*); [*ingénieur, cadre*] recently qualified; [*diplômé*] recent; **elle est ~e** she's a beginner; **cours d'anglais pour adultes** or **grands ~s** English classes for adult beginners.

II *nm,f* gén beginner (**en** in); Théât, Cin actor/actress making his/her debut; **c'est une ~e** she's a beginner; **'~s acceptés'** 'experience not essential'; ▶ **faux**.

III **débutante** *nf* debutante.

débuter /debyte/ [1] I *vtr* controv to begin, to start [*match, réunion*].

II *vi* **1** (commencer) [*journée, roman, séance*] to begin, to start (**avec, par, sur** with); [*personne*] to start off (**avec, par, sur** with); **2** (faire ses premiers pas) gén to start out (**comme** as); [*acteur, comédien*] to make one's debut (**dans** in); **elle débute dans le métier** she's just starting out in the profession; **~ à 10 000 francs par mois** to start on 10,000 francs per month.

déca○ /deka/ *nm* decaf○, sanka® US.

deçà /dəsa/ I *adv* **~, delà** here and there.

II **en deçà** *loc adv* on this side.

III **en deçà de** *loc prép* **1** (de ce côté-ci de) on this side of [*montagne, rivière*]; **2** fig (en dessous de) below; **en ~ de 2%** below 2%; **être (très) en ~ des prévisions** to be (well) below the forecasts; **le résultat est (très) en ~ de notre objectif/nos attentes** the result falls (far) short of our target/our expectations; **bien** or **très en ~ du seuil des 3%** well below the 3% threshold.

décachetage /dekaʃtaʒ/ *nm* unsealing.

décacheter /dekaʃte/ [20] *vtr* to unseal.

décade /dekad/ *nf* **1** (dix jours) 10-day period; **2** (décennie) controv decade; **3** Littérat decade.

décadenasser /dekadnase/ [1] *vtr* to unpadlock.

décadence /dekadɑ̃s/ *nf* (état) decadence; (déclin) decline; **la ~ de l'empire romain** the decline of the Roman Empire.

décadent, ~e /dekadɑ̃, ɑ̃t/ I *adj* **1** (en état de dégénérescence) decadent; **2** (en déclin) in decline (*après n*); **3** Littérat Decadent.

II *nm,f* Littérat Decadent.

décaèdre /dekaɛdʀ/ I *adj* decahedral.

II *nm* decahedron.

décaféiné, ~e /dekafeine/ I *adj* decaffeinated.

II *nm* decaffeinated coffee.

décaféiner /dekafeine/ [1] *vtr* to decaffeinate.

décagonal, ~e, *mpl* **-aux** /dekagɔnal, o/ *adj* decagonal.

décagone /dekagɔn/ *nm* decagon.

décagramme /dekagʀam/ ▶ **620** *nm* decagram.

décaissement /dekɛsmɑ̃/ *nm* Fin disbursement.

décaisser /dekese/ [1] *vtr* **1** Fin to pay out; **2** Transp to uncrate.

décalage /dekalaʒ/ *nm* **1** (différence) (écart) gap (**entre** between); (désaccord) discrepancy (**entre** between); **~ entre ce qu'il dit et ce qu'il fait** discrepancy between what he says and what he does; **se sentir/être en ~ (par rapport aux autres)** to feel/to be out of step (with the others); **2** (intervalle dans le temps) interval, time-lag (**entre** between); **3** (glissement dans le temps) (avance) move forward; (retard) move back; **à cause du ~ de date** (avance) because the date has been brought forward; (retard) because the date has been put back GB ou moved back US; **4** (dans l'espace) shift; (mouvement vers l'avant) shifting forward; (mouvement en arrière) shifting back; **~ des lignes de départ** Sport staggering of starting lines; **il y a un ~ de 10 centimètres entre les deux tableaux** there's a 10 centimetre[GB] difference in the height at which the two pictures are hung; **5** Ordinat shift.

■ **~ horaire** (entre deux lieux) time difference; **mal supporter le ~ horaire** to suffer from jet-lag.

décalaminage /dekalaminaʒ/ *nm* decarbonization.

décalaminer /dekalamine/ [1] *vtr* to decarbonize.

décalcification /dekalsifikasjɔ̃/ *nf* decalcification.

décalcifier /dekalsifje/ [1] I *vtr* to decalcify.

II **se décalcifier** *vpr* to be decalcified.

décalcomanie /dekalkɔmani/ *nf* transfer GB, decal US.

décalé, ~e /dekale/ I *pp* ▶ **décaler**.

II *pp adj* **salaires ~s par rapport à ceux des pays voisins** salaries out of step with those of neighbouring[GB] countries; **il se sent un peu perdu, ~** he feels a bit lost and out of step ou sorts.

décaler /dekale/ [1] I *vtr* **1** (dans le temps) (avancer) to bring [sth] forward [*date, départ*]; (reculer) to put GB ou move US [sth] back; **~ le départ d'une heure** (avancer) to bring forward the departure time by one hour; **les avions sont tous décalés d'une heure** (en retard) the planes are all taking off an hour later; **réactions décalées** delayed reactions; **2** (dans l'espace) (avancer) to move ou shift [sth] forward [*objet*]; (reculer) to move ou shift [sth] back; **~ qch de 10 centimètres** (avancer) to move ou shift sth 10 centimetres[GB] forward; **~ qn/qch d'un rang** (reculer) to move sb/sth back a row; **poteau décalé (par rapport aux autres)** post out of line (with the others); **lignes décalées** staggered lines.

II **se décaler** *vpr* **se ~ sur la droite/gauche** to move ou shift to the right/left.

décalitre /dekalitʀ/ ▶**117** *nm* **1** (unité) decalitre[GB]; **2** (récipient) decalitre[GB] container.

décalogue /dekalɔg/ *nm* Decalogue[GB].

décalotter /dekalɔte/ [1] *vtr* to take the top off; **~ (le gland)** Physiol to retract the foreskin.

décalquage /dekalkaʒ/ *nm* **1** Art tracing; **2** (imitation) carbon copying; **pur ~** pure imitation.

décalque /dekalk/ *nm* **1** Art tracing; **2** (imitation) carbon copy.

décalquer /dekalke/ [1] *vtr* **1** Art (par transparence) to trace (**sur** from); (reporter) to transfer (**sur** onto); **2** fig (imiter) to copy (**sur** onto).

décamètre /dekamɛtʀ/ *nm* **1** ▶**477** (unité) decametre[GB]; **2** (instrument) 10-metre[GB] tape measure.

décamper○ /dekɑ̃pe/ [1] *vi* (s'enfuir) to scarper○ GB, to run off; (partir) to clear off, to clear out○ US; **faire ~ qn** to get rid of sb.

décan /dekɑ̃/ *nm* decan.

décanat /dekana/ *nm* (fonction) deanship.

décaniller◑ /dekanije/ [1] *vi* to scarper○ GB, to run off.

décantage /dekɑ̃taʒ/ *nm*, **décantation** /dekɑ̃tasjɔ̃/ *nf* **1** (procédé) decantation; **2** (action) (de liquide) (settling and) decanting; **3** (d'idées) clarification.

décanter /dekɑ̃te/ [1] I *vtr* **1** (laisser reposer) to allow [sth] to settle [*liquide*]; to clarify [*eaux usées*]; **2** (éclaircir) to get [sth] straight, to clarify [*idées*].

II **se décanter** *vpr* **1** [*liquide*] to settle; [*eaux usées*] to clarify; **2** [*situation, idées*] to become clearer; **laisser les choses se ~** to allow the dust to settle.

décanteur /dekɑ̃tœʀ/ *nm* sedimentation ou settling tank.

décapage /dekapaʒ/ *nm* **1** (de meuble, plancher) gén cleaning; **~ avec un abrasif** scouring; (avec un produit) stripping; (à la brosse) scrubbing; (à la ponceuse) sanding; **2** Tech (de métal) pickling.

décapant, **~e** /dekapɑ̃, ɑ̃t/ I *adj* **1** (abrasif) scouring; **produit ~** (produit pour enlever la peinture, le vernis) paint stripper; **2** Tech **produit ~** (acide) pickle; **3**○ fig (stimulant) stimulating; (caustique) [*humour*] abrasive, caustic.

II *nm* (abrasif) scouring agent; (pour peinture) paint stripper; (acide) pickle.

décaper /dekape/ [1] *vtr* **1** (nettoyer) gén to clean; (enlever la peinture, le vernis de) to strip [*meuble, plancher*]; **~ à la brosse** to scrub; **~ avec un abrasif** to scour; **~ à la sableuse** to sandblast; **~ une surface au chalumeau** to burn the paint off a surface with a blowtorch; **~ à la ponceuse** to sand; **2**○ [*shampooing, savon*] to be harsh; **3** Tech to pickle [*métal*]; to strip [*chaussée*].

décapitation /dekapitasjɔ̃/ *nf* **1** (de personne) (accident) decapitation; (exécution) beheading, decapitation; **2** (d'arbre, de fleur, d'objet) removal of the top of; (d'organisation) removal of those at the top.

décapiter /dekapite/ [1] *vtr* **1** (tuer) to behead [*personne*]; (accidentellement) to decapitate; **2** (étêter) to cut the top off [*arbre, fleur, objet*]; fig to remove the leaders from [*parti, organisation*]; **être décapité** [*parti, organisation*] to be left leaderless.

décapode /dekapɔd/ *nm* decapod; **les ~s** the Decapoda.

décapotable /dekapɔtabl/ I *adj* **une voiture ~** a convertible; **cette voiture est ~** this car is a convertible.

II *nf* convertible.

décapoté, **~e** /dekapɔte/ I *pp* ▶**décapoter**.

II *pp adj* [*voiture*] with its top down (*épith, après n*); **la voiture est ~e** the car has got its top down.

décapoter /dekapɔte/ [1] *vtr* **~ une voiture** to put the top of a car down.

décapsuler /dekapsyle/ [1] *vtr* to take the top off [*bouteille*].

décapsuleur /dekapsylœʀ/ *nm* bottle-opener.

décarcasser○: **se décarcasser** /dekaʀkase/ [1] *vpr* to put oneself to a lot of trouble (**pour qn** for sb; **pour faire** to do).

décarrer◑ /dekaʀe/ [1] *vi* to leave, to make tracks○; **ils ne voulaient pas ~** they wouldn't go ou leave.

décasyllabe /dekasil(l)ab/ I *adj* decasyllabic.

II *nm* decasyllable.

décasyllabique /dekasil(l)abik/ *adj* decasyllabic.

décathlon /dekatlɔ̃/ ▶**449** *nm* decathlon.

décathlonien /dekatlɔnjɛ̃/ *nm* decathlete.

décati, **~e** /dekati/ *adj* decrepit.

décatir: **se décatir** /dekatiʀ/ [3] *vpr* to become decrepit.

décavé○ /dekave/ *adj* **1** (épuisé) haggard; **2** (ruiné) cleaned out○, ruined.

décéder /desede/ [14] *vi* to die; **Yan récemment décédé** Yan who died recently; **il est décédé d'un cancer** he died of cancer; **la pension du conjoint décédé** the pension of the deceased spouse.

décelable /deslabl/ *adj* detectable.

déceler /desle/ [17] *vtr* **1** (distinguer) to detect; **facile à ~** easily detectable, easy to detect; **l'analyse a permis de ~ des traces de poison** analysis revealed traces of poison; **2** (indiquer) to reveal [*anomalie, sentiment*]; to indicate [*présence*].

décélération /deseleʀasjɔ̃/ *nf* **1** (de rythme) slowdown; **2** (de vitesse) deceleration.

décélérer /deseleʀe/ [14] *vi* to slow down, to decelerate.

décembre /desɑ̃bʀ/ ▶**521** *nm* December.

décemment /desamɑ̃/ *adv* **1** (selon les normes) [*se conduire, être logé*] decently; **2** (avec compétence) [*travailler, jouer*] reasonably well; **faire ~ un travail** to do a decent job, to do a job reasonably well; **3** (raisonnablement) reasonably; **on ne peut ~ le prendre au sérieux** one can't reasonably be expected to take him seriously, it's unreasonable to expect one to take him seriously.

décence /desɑ̃s/ *nf* **1** (bienséance) decency; **il n'a pas eu la ~ de faire** he didn't have the decency to do; **2** (discrétion) sense of decency.

décennal, **~e**, *mpl* **-aux** /desenal, o/ *adj* ten-year; **plan ~** ten-year plan.

décennie /deseni/ *nf* decade.

décent, **~e** /desɑ̃, ɑ̃t/ *adj* **1** (bienséant) [*tenue, conduite*] decent; **arriver à une heure ~e** to arrive at a decent time ou hour; **2** (correct) proper, right; **3** (acceptable) [*travail*] decent, reasonable; **faire qch d'une manière ~e** to do sth reasonably well.

décentralisateur, **-trice** /desɑ̃tʀalizatœʀ, tʀis/ I *adj* [*politique*] of decentralization (*épith, après n*); [*homme politique*] in favour[GB] of decentralization (*après n*).

II *nm,f* advocate of decentralization.

décentralisation /desɑ̃tʀalizasjɔ̃/ *nf* decentralization.

décentralisé, **~e** /desɑ̃tʀalize/ I *pp* ▶**décentraliser**.

II *pp adj* decentralized.

décentraliser /desɑ̃tʀalize/ [1] I *vtr* to decentralize.

II **se décentraliser** *vpr* to become decentralized.

décentrement /desɑ̃tʀəmɑ̃/ *nm* **1** Phot shift; **objectif à ~** shift lens; **2** (décalage) shifting away from the centre[GB].

décentrer /desɑ̃tʀe/ [1] I *vtr* to move [sth] away from the centre[GB]

II **se décentrer** *vpr* to move away (**par rapport à** from); **décentré** off-centre[GB].

déception /desɛpsjɔ̃/ *nf* disappointment (**de faire** at doing); **~s amoureuses** unsuccessful love affairs.

décérébrer /deseʀebʀe/ [14] *vtr* to decerebrate.

décerner /desɛʀne/ [1] *vtr* **1** gén to give [*titre, label*]; to award, to give [*prix*]; **~ qch à qn** to award ou give sth to sb, to award ou give sb sth; **2** Jur to issue [*mandat*].

décès /desɛ/ *nm* death, decease sout; **fermé pour cause de ~** closed owing to bereavement.

décevant, **~e** /desəvɑ̃, ɑ̃t/ *adj* disappointing.

décevoir /desəvwaʀ/ [5] I *vtr* **1** (ne pas répondre aux espoirs de) to disappoint [*personne*]; **tu me déçois (beaucoup)** I'm (very) disappointed in you; **ne pas ~** to come up to expectations; **2** (tromper) to fail to fulfil[GB] [*espoir*]; **~ la confiance de qn** to betray sb's trust.

II *vi* to be disappointing.

déchaîné, **~e** /deʃene/ I *pp* ▶**déchaîner**.

II *pp adj* **1** (violent) [*mer, vent*] raging; [*vagues*] crashing; [*passions, instincts*] unbridled; **2** (très énervé) [*personne, enfant, foule*] wild; [*opinion publique*] stirred up (*jamais épith*); **~ contre qn/qch** furious with sb/sth.

déchaînement /deʃɛnmɑ̃/ *nm* **1** (de tempête) raging; (de flots) crashing; **2** (explosion) **~ de colère/passion** outburst of anger/passion; **~ d'enthousiasme** wave of enthusiasm; **le ~ de l'opinion publique** the public outcry (**contre** against); **je ne comprends pas le ~ de Pierre contre Paul** I don't understand why Pierre is always attacking Paul; **3** (torrent) **~ d'injures/d'idées/de paroles** torrent ou flood of insults/of ideas/of words.

déchaîner /deʃene/ [1] I *vtr* to rouse, to stir up [*passions, sentiments*]; to excite, to make [sb] wild [*personnes, foule*]; **le meurtre a déchaîné (la colère de) l'opinion publique** the murder unleashed a public outcry.

II **se déchaîner** *vpr* **1** [*phénomènes naturels*] to rage; [*sentiments, passions*] to burst out; **2** (devenir très agité) [*personnes, foule*] to go wild; **3** (s'emporter) [*personne*] to fly into a rage (**contre qn/qch** against sb/sth).

déchanter /deʃɑ̃te/ [1] *vi* to become disenchanted; **elle a dû ~** she was brought down to earth; **faire ~** to disappoint.

décharge /deʃaʀʒ/ *nf* **1** (d'arme à feu) discharge; **il a reçu une ~ de fusil de chasse en pleine tête** he was shot in the head with a hunting rifle; **2** (d'ordures) rubbish GB ou garbage US dump; **~ municipale/publique** municipal/public dump ou tip GB; **3** Électrotech (perte brusque) discharge; (dépense progressive) discharging; **recevoir une ~ dans les doigts** to get an electric shock in one's fingers; **4** Jur (d'accusé) acquittal; **à leur ~** fig in their defence[GB]; **5** (libération) (de tâche) release; (de dette) discharge; **~ de l'obligation alimentaire** release from maintenance obligation; **signer une ~** to sign a discharge; **6** Fisc exemption; **7** Tech (dispositif) (d'étang, bassin) overflow; (de barrage) spillway; (citerne) overflow tank; (bassin) overflow basin.

■ **~ de service** reduction in working hours (*for civil servants*).

déchargement /deʃaʀʒəmɑ̃/ *nm* (de véhicule, d'arme à feu) unloading; **commencer le ~ d'une cargaison** to begin unloading a cargo; **je vous aiderai pour le ~ des caisses** I'll help you unload the boxes.

décharger /deʃaʀʒe/ [13] **I** *vtr* **1** (débarrasser de sa charge) to unload [*navire, véhicule, machine à laver*] (**de** from); to relieve [*personne*] (**de** of); **2** (enlever un chargement) to unload [*marchandises, passagers*]; **les dockers déchargeront cet après-midi** the dockers will unload this afternoon; **3** (ôter la charge de) to unload [*arme à feu*]; (tirer avec) to fire [*fusil, arme*]; **4** (libérer) **~ qn de** to relieve sb of [*tâche, obligation*]; to release sb from [*dette*]; **5** (innocenter) [*expertise, témoignage*] to clear [*accusé*] (**de** of); **6** Électrotech [*personne*] to discharge [*appareil, batterie*]; [*faux contact*] to cause [sth] to run down [*batterie*]; **7** (soulager) to unburden [*conscience, cœur*] (**auprès de qn** to sb); to vent [*colère*]; **~ sa colère sur qn** to take one's anger out on sb; **8** (alléger) to take the weight off [*plancher, poutre*].

II *vi* **1** (déteindre) [*tissu*] to lose its colour[GB]; **2**◑ (éjaculer) to shoot one's load◑, to ejaculate.

III se décharger *vpr* **1** (se libérer) **se ~ de qch** to off-load sth (**sur qn** onto sb); **j'ai pu me ~ du dossier/de toute la comptabilité sur un collègue** I managed to off-load the file/all the accounting onto a colleague; **2** Électrotech [*batterie*] to run down; **la batterie est déchargée** the battery is flat.

décharné, **~e** /deʃaʀne/ **I** *pp* ▶ **décharner**.

II *pp adj* **1** (maigre) [*corps, bras, visage*] emaciated; [*doigt*] bony; **2** (sans chair) [*squelette*] fleshless.

décharner /deʃaʀne/ [1] *vtr* to emaciate; **son régime l'a décharné** his diet has left him emaciated ou has left him mere skin and bones.

déchaussé, **~e** /deʃose/ **I** *pp* ▶ **déchausser**.

II *pp adj* [*personne*] barefoot; [*mur*] with exposed foundations; [*arbre*] with exposed roots; **il avait les dents ~es** he had receding gums.

déchaussement /deʃosmɑ̃/ *nm* **1** (de dents) receding of gums; **2** (de mur) exposure of the foundations.

déchausser /deʃose/ [1] **I** *vtr* **1** gén **~ qn** to remove sb's shoes, take sb's shoes off; **2** Sport **~** (**ses skis**) to take off one's skis; **3** to expose the foundations of [*mur*].

II se déchausser *vpr* **1** (ôter ses chaussures) to take off one's shoes, to remove one's shoes; **2** [*dent*] to work loose due to receding gums; **3** [*plante, mur*] to become exposed at the base.

dèche○ /dɛʃ/ *nf* **être dans la ~** to be broke○; **en ce moment, c'est la ~** I'm broke at the moment.

déchéance /deʃeɑ̃s/ *nf* **1** (décadence morale) decline, degeneration; **tomber dans la ~** to go into total decline; **2** (décrépitude) degeneration; **3** (déclin) (d'une nation, civilisation) decline, decay; **4** Jur **~ des droits** forfeiture of rights; **~ de nationalité** loss of nationality; **~ de l'autorité parentale** loss of parental rights; **5** Hist, Pol (de monarque, politicien) deposition.

déchet /deʃɛ/ **I** *nm* **1** (morceau inutilisé) scrap; **~s de viande/métal** scraps of meat/metal; **2** (perte) waste; **il y a du ~** (dans la marchandise) there's some waste; (parmi des candidats) there are failures ou duds○; **3** (incompétent) failure; (épave) wreck; **les ~s de la société** the dregs of society.

II déchets *nmpl* (résidus) waste material ¢; (ordures) waste ¢; **~s ménagers** household refuse ¢ ou waste ¢; **~s industriels/nucléaires/toxiques** industrial/nuclear/toxic waste; **~s de jardin** garden refuse.

déchetterie /deʃɛtʀi/ *nf* waste reception centre[GB].

déchiffonner /deʃifɔne/ [1] *vtr* to smooth out [*papier, robe*].

déchiffrable /deʃifʀabl/ *adj* decipherable.

déchiffrage /deʃifʀaʒ/ *nm* **1** (de message codé) decoding, deciphering; (de texte, d'écriture) deciphering; **2** Mus sight-reading; **~ chanté** sight-singing.

déchiffrement /deʃifʀəmɑ̃/ *nm* (de message codé) decoding; (de texte, d'écriture) deciphering.

déchiffrer /deʃifʀe/ [1] *vtr* **1** (lire) to decipher [*texte, écriture*]; to decode, to decipher [*texte codé*]; **2** (interpréter) to fathom out; **3** Mus to sight-read [*partition*].

déchiffreur, **-euse** /deʃifʀœʀ, øz/ *nm,f* **1** (de texte, d'écriture) decipherer; **2** (de message codé) decoder; **3** Mus sight-reader.

déchiqueté, **~e** /deʃikte/ **I** *pp* ▶ **déchiqueter**.

II *pp adj* [*côte, relief*] jagged, ragged.

déchiqueter /deʃikte/ [20] *vtr* **1** (réduire en lambeaux) to tear [sth] to shreds, tear [sth] to pieces [*étoffe, viande, papier*]; **2** (mutiler) to mutilate, mangle [*membre*]; **des bâtiments déchiquetés par les bombardements** buildings devastated ou wrecked by bombs; **3** (tuer) [*machine, animal*] to tear [sb] to pieces [*victime*]; [*explosion*] to blow [sb] to pieces [*victime*].

déchiqueture /deʃiktyʀ/ *nf* fml **1** (partie déchiquetée) ragged edge; **2** (aspect découpé) jagged outline.

déchirant, **~e** /deʃiʀɑ̃, ɑ̃t/ *adj* **1** (émouvant) [*adieu, cri, lettre, histoire*] heart-rending; **2** (difficile) [*choix, révision*] agonizing; **3** (fratricide) [*lutte*] divisive.

déchirement /deʃiʀmɑ̃/ *nm* **1** (souffrance) heartbreak; **2** (conflit) rift (**entre, de** between); **~ entre deux cultures** rift between two cultures.

déchirer /deʃiʀe/ [1] **I** *vtr* **1** (mettre en morceaux) to tear [sth] up [*papier, tissu*]; to rip [sth] up [*chair*]; to break [sth] up [*surface*]; **~ un contrat/un accord** fig to go back on a contract/an agreement; **~ le voile** fig to lift the veil; **2** (détériorer) to rip, to tear [*vêtement, sac*]; **3** fml (troubler) [*bruit*] to shatter [*silence, nuit*]; [*éclair, lumière*] to rend [*obscurité, ciel*]; [*événement*] to shatter [*vie, illusion*]; **4** (diviser) [*conflit*] to split [*groupe, pays*]; **couple/pays déchiré** divided couple/country; **il était déchiré entre son devoir et son désir de rester** he was torn between his duty and his desire to stay; **déchiré entre sa famille et son travail** torn between his family and his work; **5** (faire souffrir) [*spectacle, douleur, personne*] to torture [*personne*]; **humanité déchirée** tortured humanity.

II se déchirer *vpr* **1** (se rompre) [*papier, tissu, vêtement*] to tear, to rip; **ma robe s'est déchirée** my dress has torn ou ripped; **2** Méd **se ~ un muscle** to tear a muscle; **3** (s'affronter) [*groupes, personnes*] to tear each other apart; **4** fml (souffrir) [*cœur*] to break; [*âme*] to be in torment; **mon cœur se déchire à l'idée de partir** the thought of leaving breaks my heart.

déchirure /deʃiʀyʀ/ *nf* **1** Méd tear; **~ abdominale/intercostale/musculaire** abdominal/intercostal/muscle tear; **~ à la cuisse** muscle tear in the thigh; **2** (accroc) tear (**de** in); **~ d'un tissu/d'une robe** tear in a piece of material/in a dress; **3** (rupture) break (**de** in); **~ de la couche d'ozone** hole in the ozone layer; **4** (conflit) rift (**de** within); **~ du pays** rift within the country.

déchoir /deʃwaʀ/ [51] **I** *vtr* Jur (priver) to strip [sb] of [*droit, privilège*]; **être déchu de ses droits** to be stripped ou deprived of one's rights.

II *vi* **1** (tomber dans un état inférieur) [*personne*] to demean oneself, lower oneself; **vous pouvez accepter sans ~** you can accept without demeaning yourself; **~ de son rang** or **de sa condition** to come down in the world; **2** (s'affaiblir) [*autorité, popularité, influence*] to wane.

déchristianisation /dekʀistjanizasjɔ̃/ *nf* de-christianization.

déchristianiser /dekʀistjanize/ [1] *vtr* to de-christianize.

déchu, **~e** /deʃy/ **I** *pp* ▶ **déchoir**.

II *pp adj* [*monarque, dictateur*] deposed; [*ange*] fallen; **politicien ~** political has-been○, politician who has fallen out of favour[GB]; **une star ~e** a has-been○, a star whose popularity has waned.

de-ci /dəsi/ *adv* **~ de-là** here and there.

décibel /desibɛl/ *nm* decibel.

décidé, **~e** /deside/ **I** *pp* ▶ **décider**.

II *pp adj* **1** (arrêté) **c'est chose ~e** or **c'est ~, je m'en vais** it's settled, I'm leaving; **2** (résolu) [*personne*] determined; [*allure, air*] resolute.

décidément /desidemɑ̃/ *adv* really; **tu as ~ la mémoire courte** you've really got a short memory; **~, tu n'as pas de chance!** you really don't have much luck!

décider /deside/ [1] **I** *vtr* **1** (prendre la décision de) to decide (**de faire** to do; **que** that); **~ l'envoi de troupes/l'utilisation de qch** to decide to send troops/to use sth; **~ une politique** to decide on a policy; **j'ai décidé de ne pas m'en mêler** I decided not to interfere; **cela a été décidé en avril** it was decided in April; **je vous laisse ~** I'll let you decide; **c'est toi qui décides, c'est à toi de ~** it's up to you ou for you to decide; **il a décidé qu'il n'irait pas** he decided (that) he wouldn't go; **~ si** to decide whether; **as-tu décidé si tu les emmènes?** have you decided whether you're taking them?; **~ qui contacter/quelle route prendre** to decide who to contact/which road to take; **c'est à lui de ~ qui il veut inviter** it's up to him to decide who he wants to invite; **c'est ce qui a décidé sa perte** it's what led to his downfall; **2** Jur to decide on [*acquittement*]; **~ le non-lieu** to dismiss a case; **3** (persuader) to persuade (**à faire** to do); **l'approche de l'hiver l'a décidé à déménager** the onset of winter persuaded him to move house.

II décider de *vtr ind* to decide on, to arrange, to set [*date*]; to fix [*prix*]; to decide on [*politique, mesure, lieu*]; **ont-ils décidé de la marche à suivre?** have they decided how to go about it?; **le hasard en décida autrement** fate decided otherwise; **l'événement allait ~ de leur avenir** the event would decide their future; **il faut toujours que tu décides de tout!** you're always the one who makes the decisions!; **~ du sort de qn** to seal sb's fate.

III se décider *vpr* **1** (prendre une décision) to make up one's mind; **tu te décides à parler?** are you going to speak?; **elle s'est enfin décidée à s'excuser** she apologized at last; **ma voiture n'a pas l'air de se ~ à démarrer** my car doesn't seem to want to start; **être/sembler décidé à faire** to be/to seem determined to do; **2** (choisir) **se ~ pour qch/qn** to decide on sth/sb; **elle s'est décidée pour le pull vert** she's decided on the green sweater; **3** (être fixé) [*accord, réunion*] to be decided on; [*date*] to be set, to be arranged; **tout s'est décidé très vite** it all happened very quickly.

décideur /desidœʀ/ *nm* decision-maker.

décigramme /desigʀam/ ▶ **620** *nm* decigram.

décilitre /desilitʀ/ ▶ **117** *nm* decilitre[GB].

décimal, **~e**, *mpl* **-aux** /desimal, o/ **I** *adj* **1** Math [*nombre, système*] decimal; **2** Chimie decinormal; **dilution ~e** decinormal dilution.

II décimale *nf* decimal.

décimalisation /desimalizasjɔ̃/ *nf* decimalization.

décimaliser /desimalize/ [1] *vtr* to decimalize.

décimation /desimasjɔ̃/ *nf* decimation.

décimer /desime/ [1] *vtr* to decimate.

décimètre /desimɛtʀ/ *nm* **1** ▶477 (unité) decimetre[GB]; **2** (instrument) (decimetre[GB]) ruler; **double ~** (20 centimetre[GB]) ruler.

décisif, -ive /desizif, iv/ *adj* gén decisive; [*preuve*] conclusive; [*ton, voix*] authoritative.

décision /desizjɔ̃/ *nf* **1** (résolution) decision (**de faire** to do); **prendre une ~** to make ou take GB a decision; **ma ~ est prise, je reste** I've made my decision, I'm staying; **j'ai pris la ~ de ne plus fumer/de ne plus le voir** I've decided to stop smoking/to stop seeing him; **2** (fait de décider) **avoir le pouvoir de ~** to be the one who makes the decisions; **3** (détermination) decisiveness; **faire preuve de ~** to show decisiveness; **avoir l'esprit de ~** to be decisive; **manquer d'esprit de ~** to be indecisive; **agir avec ~** to act decisively.
■ **~ exécutoire** binding decision; **~ judiciaire** court order.

décisionnaire /desizjɔnɛʀ/ **I** *adj* [*pouvoir, instance*] decision-making (*épith*).
II *nmf* decision-maker.

décisionnel, -elle /desizjɔnɛl/ *adj* [*système, processus*] decision-making (*épith*); **avoir un pouvoir ~** to have the power to make decisions.

déclamateur, -trice /deklamatœʀ, tʀis/ **I** *adj* declamatory.
II *nm,f* **1** péj ranter; **2** Hist declaimer.

déclamation /deklamasjɔ̃/ *nf* Littérat declamation; péj ranting ¢.

déclamatoire /deklamatwaʀ/ *adj* declamatory.

déclamer /deklame/ [1] *vtr* to declaim.

déclarant, ~e /deklaʀɑ̃, ɑ̃t/ *nm,f* Admin declarant; Fisc taxpayer; Assur person making a statement.

déclaratif, -ive /deklaʀatif, iv/ *adj* **1** Jur **jugement ~ de faillite** adjudication order; **2** Ling [*verbe, phrase*] declarative.

déclaration /deklaʀasjɔ̃/ *nf* **1** (communication publique) gén statement; (officielle) declaration (**sur** about); **faire une ~ à la presse** to make a statement to the press; **signer une ~ commune** to sign a common declaration ou statement; **~ solennelle** solemn declaration; **~ d'intention/de principe** statement of intent/of principle; **~ de guerre/d'indépendance** declaration of war/of independence; **~ (d'amour)** declaration of love; **faire sa ~ à qn** to declare one's love to sb; **2** Admin notification; **~ d'accident/de changement de domicile** notification of an accident/of change of address; **~ de naissance** (enregistrement) registration of birth; (information) notification of birth; **~ d'une maladie** notification of a disease; **3** Jur statement; **faire une ~ à la police** to make a statement to the police; **~ de vol/perte** report of theft/loss; **~ sous serment** sworn statement.
■ **~ d'ajudication** declaration of adjudication; **~ d'impôts** or **de revenus** (income-)tax return; **faire** or **remplir sa ~ d'impôts** to fill in one's tax return; **Déclaration universelle des droits de l'homme** Universal Declaration of Human Rights.

déclaratoire /deklaʀatwaʀ/ *adj* declaratory.

déclaré, ~e /deklaʀe/ **I** *pp* ▶ **déclarer**.
II *pp adj* **1** [*ennemi*] avowed; [*haine*] professed; **2** [*maladie*] full-blown.

déclarer /deklaʀe/ [1] **I** *vtr* **1** (faire connaître) to declare [*indépendance, intentions*]; **~ son amour/sa passion** to declare one's love/one's passion; **a-t-il déclaré** he declared; **le président a déclaré** the president declared; **la transaction a été déclarée illégale** the deal was declared illegal; **~ qn responsable/vainqueur/mort** to declare sb responsible/the winner/dead; **il a été déclaré coupable** he was found guilty; **~ la séance ouverte** to declare the meeting open; **il a déclaré vouloir participer/avoir travaillé** he declared that he wanted to take part/that he had worked; **~ que** to declare that; **il s'est contenté de ~ qu'il regrettait son acte** all he did was to declare that he regretted his action; **~ à qn que** to tell sb that; **il a déclaré à la presse qu'il n'était en rien responsable** he told the press that he was in no way responsible; **~ la guerre à qn/qch** lit, fig to declare war on sb/sth; **2** (informer une autorité de) to declare [*marchandise, revenus, employé*]; to report [*vol*]; (faire enregistrer) to register [*naissance, décès*]; **avez-vous qch à ~?** (à la douane) do you have anything to declare?; **elle emploie des gens sans les ~** she employs people without declaring them; **non déclaré** [*somme*] undeclared; [*travail*] illegal.
II se déclarer *vpr* **1** (commencer) [*incendie, épidémie*] to break out; [*fièvre*] to start; [*maladie*] to manifest itself; **2** (faire connaître sa pensée) **se ~ confiant/inquiet/heureux/convaincu** to declare oneself confident/worried /happy/convinced; **elle s'est déclarée prête à relever le défi** she declared herself ready to take up the challenge; **se ~ pour/contre qch** to come out for/against sth; **3** (avouer son amour) to declare one's love; **se ~ à qn** to declare one's love to sb.

déclassé, ~e /deklase/ **I** *pp* ▶ **déclasser**.
II *pp adj* **1** (relégué) [*athlète, équipe*] relegated; [*monument, hôtel, restaurant*] downgraded; **2** (en désordre) [*livres, fiches*] jumbled (*épith*), jumbled up (*jamais épith*); **3** (déchu) [*noble, bourgeois*] who has come down in the world (*épith, après n*).
III *nm,f* dropout.

déclassement /deklasmɑ̃/ *nm* **1** (relégation) (de sportif, club) relegation GB, demotion; (d'hôtel, de monument, restaurant) downgrading; **2** Sociol (dévalorisation) drop in status.

déclasser /deklase/ [1] *vtr* **1** (rétrograder) to downgrade [*personne, concurrent, hôtel*]; Sport to relegate [*équipe, joueur*]; **2** (mettre en désordre) to jumble up [*livres, fiches*]; **3** Ind, Mil (retirer du service) to decommission [*centrale nucléaire, armements*]; **4** (dévaloriser) **~ qn** [*situation, travail*] to lower sb's status; (humilier) to be socially demeaning for [*personne*].

déclenchement /deklɑ̃ʃmɑ̃/ *nm* **1** (de système) triggering; (de mécanisme) release; (d'avalanche) start; **provoquer le ~ de l'alarme** to set off the alarm; **2** (de maladie) onset; (de réaction) start; (de conflit, grève, crise) outbreak.

déclencher /deklɑ̃ʃe/ [1] **I** *vtr* **1** (actionner) to set off [*alarme, mécanisme*]; to cause [*explosion, orgasme*]; to start [*avalanche*]; **2** Ordinat to initiate [*opération*]; **3** (commencer) to launch [*offensive*]; to begin [*hostilités*]; to start [*grève, polémique*]; **4** (entraîner) [*nouvelle, décision, événement*] to spark (off) [*protestation, crise*]; to produce [*réaction*]; to prompt [*action, décision*]; [*médicament, manque*] to cause [*réaction, crise*]; [*dispute, discussion*] to lead to [*colère, larmes*]; to cause [*drame*]; **la déclaration n'a déclenché aucune réaction** the statement produced no reaction; **~ les larmes de qn** to make sb burst into tears; **~ un éclat de rire général** to provoke general laughter.
II se déclencher *vpr* **1** (se mettre en marche) [*alarme*] to go off; [*signal, mécanisme*] to be activated; **la sirène se déclenche automatiquement** the alarm goes off automatically; **2** (commencer) [*douleur, réaction, contractions*] to start; [*grève, guerre*] to break out; [*crise, opération, offensive*] to begin.

déclencheur /deklɑ̃ʃœʀ/ *nm* **1** Phot shutter release; **appuyer sur le ~** to press the shutter; **2** Électrotech release; **3** (événement décisif) trigger; **le ~ de la révolte** the factor which triggered the rebellion.

déclic /deklik/ *nm* **1** (mécanisme) trigger; **actionner** or **faire jouer un ~** to activate a trigger; **2** (bruit) (d'appareil photo, de gâchette) click; **attendre le ~** wait till you hear the click; **3** (moment décisif) turning point; **ma rencontre avec Gandhi a été un ~** my meeting with Gandhi marked a turning point.

déclin /deklɛ̃/ *nm* gén decline; (de sentiment, passion) waning (**de** of); **~ d'une région/civilisation** decline of a region/civilisation; **~ de leur prestige/de la demande/du marché** decline in their prestige/in demand/in the market; **popularité/productivité en ~** declining popularity/productivity; **être en** or **sur le ~** [*civilisation, industrie*] to be in decline; [*talent, intelligence*] to be on the wane; [*popularité, prestige*] to be waning; **être sur le** or **son ~** [*homme d'État*] to be on the way out; **le soleil est à son ~** the sun is going down; **au ~ du jour** liter at the close of day; **au ~ de la vie** liter in the twilight of life littér; **la lune est à son ~** the moon is on the wane.

déclinable /deklinabl/ *adj* **1** Ling [*mot*] declinable; **2** fig **~ en plusieurs coloris** available in several colours.

déclinaison /deklinɛzɔ̃/ *nf* **1** Ling declension; **2** Astron declination; **~ australe/boréale** southing/northing.

déclinant, ~e /deklinɑ̃, ɑ̃t/ *adj* [*courage, pouvoir, forces*] waning; [*santé*] failing.

décliner /dekline/ [1] **I** *vtr* **1** (refuser) to decline [*invitation*]; to turn down [*suggestion, offre*]; **~ toute responsabilité** to disclaim all responsibility; **~ la compétence d'un tribunal** to refuse to recognize the jurisdiction of a court; **2** Ling to decline; **3** fig **modèle décliné en trois coloris** item available in three colours; **4** (dire) to state, to give [*nom, adresse*]; **refuser de ~ son identité** to refuse to give one's name.
II *vi* **1** (faiblir) [*lumière*] to fade; [*vue*] to deteriorate; [*gloire, succès, santé*] to decline; [*talent*] to fade; [*enthousiasme*] to wane; [*malade*] to deteriorate, to grow weaker; **la construction ne cesse de ~ depuis...** the building industry has been in constant decline since...; **2** (descendre) liter [*soleil*] to go down.
III se décliner *vpr* **1** Ling to decline; **2** fig **ce modèle peut se ~** there are several versions available.

déclivité /deklivite/ *nf* (inclinaison) gradient; (pente) slope; **habiter sur une ~** to live on a hill; **avoir une ~ de 20%** to have a gradient of one in five, to have a gradient of 20%.

décloisonnement /deklwazɔnmɑ̃/ *nm* fig opening up.

décloisonner /deklwazɔne/ [1] *vtr* to open up [*service*]; **~ les études** to make studies more interdisciplinary.

déclouer /deklue/ [1] *vtr* to remove the nails from [*planche, coffre*].

décocher /dekɔʃe/ [1] *vtr* to shoot [*flèche*] (**à** at); **~ un coup de poing à qn** to punch sb; **~ un regard mauvais à qn** to give sb a dirty look; **~ des insultes à qn** to hurl insults at sb.

décoction /dekɔksjɔ̃/ *nf* brew, decoction spéc.

décodage /dekɔdaʒ/ *nm* decoding.

décoder /dekɔde/ [1] *vtr* to decode.

décodeur, -euse /dekɔdœʀ, øz/ **I** *nm,f* (personne) decoder.
II *nm* (appareil) Tech, TV decoder.

décoiffer /dekwafe/ [1] **I** *vtr* **1** (dépeigner) **~ qn** to ruffle sb's hair; **elle est décoiffée** her hair is in a mess; **tu me décoiffés** you are messing up my hair; **2** Tech to uncap [*fusée*].
II° *vi* Pub **ça décoiffe** it takes your breath away; **peu décoiffant** uninspiring.

III se décoiffer *vpr* (se découvrir) to doff one's hat.

décoincer /dekwɛ̃se/ [12] **I** *vtr* **1** (débloquer) to unjam [*mécanisme, tiroir, porte*]; to free [*clé, levier*]; to get [sth] back to normal [*dos, cou*]; **2**○ (décomplexer) to put [sb] at ease [*personne*].
II se décoincer *vpr* **1** [*mécanisme, portière*] to come free; **mon dos a fini par se ~** my back eventually went back to normal; **2**○ [*personne*] to relax.

décolérer /dekɔleʀe/ [14] *vi* **ne pas ~ de la soirée** to stay angry all evening; **sans ~** without letting up.

décollage /dekɔlaʒ/ *nm* **1** (d'avion) take-off; (de fusée) lift-off; **au moment du ~** (d'avion) at take-off; (de fusée) at lift-off; **~ vertical** vertical take-off; **2** (démarrage) take-off; **~ économique/en flèche** economic/rapid take-off; **le ~ du projet a été lent** the project was slow to take off; **3** (d'affiche, étiquette) peeling off.

décollation /dekɔlasjɔ̃/ *nf* beheading.

décollement /dekɔlmɑ̃/ *nm* **~ de la rétine** detachment of the retina; **avoir un ~ de la rétine** to have a detached retina.

décoller /dekɔle/ [1] **I** *vtr* (détacher) gén to take ou get off; to peel off [*étiquette, affiche*]; to unstick [*bouts de ruban adhésif*]; to remove [*pansement adhésif*]; **~ une étiquette en la laissant tremper** to soak a label off; **~ à la vapeur** to steam [sth] off [*étiquette, papier*]; to steam [sth] open [*enveloppe*]; **affiche à moitié décollée** peeling poster.
II *vi* **1** (s'envoler) [*avion*] to take off (**de** from); [*fusée*] to lift off (**de** from); **2** (démarrer) [*industrie, région*] to take off; [*spectacle*] to get going; **3**○ (maigrir) to lose weight; **4**○ (partir) [*importun*] to budge; **~ du peloton** Sport to break away from the pack; **5**○ [*drogué*] to get high○.
III se décoller *vpr* **se ~ facilement** to come off easily; **c'est en train de se ~** it's coming off.

décolletage /dekɔltaʒ/ *nm* bar turning.

décolleté, **~e** /dekɔlte/ **I** *pp* ▸ **décolleter**.
II *pp adj* [*vêtement*] low-cut; **pas assez ~** too high-cut; **une robe ~e en V** a V-neck dress.
III *nm* **1** Mode low neckline; **~ plongeant** plunging neckline; **2** (partie du corps) cleavage; **dans son ~** down her cleavage.

décolleter /dekɔlte/ [20] *vtr* **1** Cout **~ une robe devant/dans le dos** to make a dress low-cut at the front/at the back; **2** Ind to cut (from the bar) [*vis, boulons*].

décolleuse /dekɔløz/ *nf* steam stripper.

décolonisateur, **-trice** /dekɔlɔnizatœʀ, tʀis/ *adj* [*mesure, mouvement*] decolonization (*épith*).

décolonisation /dekɔlɔnizasjɔ̃/ *nf* decolonization.

décoloniser /dekɔlɔnize/ [1] *vtr* to decolonize.

décolorant, **~e** /dekɔlɔʀɑ̃, ɑ̃t/ **I** *adj* [*produit, agent*] bleaching (*épith*).
II *nm* bleaching agent.

décoloration /dekɔlɔʀasjɔ̃/ *nf* **1** (perte de la couleur) gén discoloration; (de tissu) fading; **2** Cosmét bleaching; **se faire faire une ~** to have one's hair bleached.

décolorer /dekɔlɔʀe/ [1] **I** *vtr* [*substance*] to bleach [*tissu, cheveux*]; [*lumière, lavage*] to cause [sth] to fade; **se faire ~ (les cheveux)** to have one's hair bleached.
II se décolorer *vpr* **1** [*personne*] to bleach one's hair; **2** [*tapis, rideau*] to fade; **ça s'est décoloré au lavage** it faded in the wash.

décombres /dekɔ̃bʀ/ *nmpl* rubble ₵; **enseveli sous les ~** buried under the rubble.

décommander /dekɔmɑ̃de/ [1] **I** *vtr* to call off [*rendez-vous, soirée*].
II se décommander *vpr* to cry off.

décompensé, **~e** /dekɔ̃pɑ̃se/ *adj* [*cardiopathie*] decompensated.

décomplexer /dekɔ̃plɛkse/ [1] *vtr* **~ qn** [*stage, opération*] to do wonders for sb's self-confidence; **leur simplicité nous a décomplexés** their unpretentiousness soon put us at our ease.

décomposable /dekɔ̃pozabl/ *adj* [*substance, lumière*] decomposable (**en** into); **~ en facteurs** [*nombre*] factorable.

décomposer /dekɔ̃poze/ [1] **I** *vtr* **1** (analyser) to break [sth] down [*raisonnement, argumentation, phrase*] (**en** into); **2** (montrer au ralenti) to break down [*mouvement*]; **3** Chimie, Phys to break down [*eau*]; to disperse [*lumière*]; to resolve [*force*]; **4** Math (en facteurs) to factorize; **5** (putréfier) to cause [sth] to decompose; **6** (par l'émotion) to distort [*traits, visage*]; **son visage décomposé** his/her distraught face; **7** (désorganiser, détruire) to cause [sth] to disintegrate [*société, parti*].
II se décomposer *vpr* **1** [*matière organique*] to decompose; **2** [*société, parti*] to fall apart; **3** [*visage, traits*] to become distorted; **4** [*composé*] to break down (**en** into); **la phrase/le raisonnement se décompose en...** the sentence/the argument can be broken down into ou separated into...

décomposition /dekɔ̃pozisjɔ̃/ *nf* **1** (putréfaction) decomposition; **en ~** decomposing; **2** (de société, parti, système) disintegration; **en ~** [*société*] decaying; **3** (altération passagère) **la ~ de son visage** or **de ses traits** his/her distraught face; **4** (de phrase, raisonnement, mouvement) breaking down (**de** into); **5** Chimie, Phys (d'eau) breakdown (**en** into); (de force) resolution (**en** into).

décompresser○ /dekɔ̃pʀese/ [1] *vi* to unwind, to relax.

décompresseur /dekɔ̃pʀesœʀ/ *nm* decompressor.

décompression /dekɔ̃pʀesjɔ̃/ *nf* decompression; **chambre/palier de ~** decompression chamber/stage; **avoir un accident de ~** to get the bends, to get decompression sickness.

décomprimer /dekɔ̃pʀime/ [1] *vtr* to decompress.

décompte /dekɔ̃t/ *nm* **1** (déduction) deduction, discount; **~ de 5% pour tout achat comptant** 5% discount on all cash purchases; **2** (calcul détaillé) count; **faire le ~ de** to count [sth] up [*votes, points*]; **le ~ des morts** the body count; **3** (relevé) statement.

décompter /dekɔ̃te/ [1] **I** *vtr* **1** (déduire) to deduct (**de** from); **2** (calculer) to calculate, to work out [*frais*]; to count [*votes, points, personnes*].
II *vi* [*horloge*] to strike ou chime at the wrong time.

déconcentration /dekɔ̃sɑ̃tʀasjɔ̃/ *nf* **1** Admin, Ind decentralization; **2** (de personne) loss of concentration.

déconcentré, **~e** /dekɔ̃sɑ̃tʀe/ **I** *pp* ▸ **déconcentrer**.
II *pp adj* (parlant d'une personne) **être ~** to have lost one's concentration.

déconcentrer /dekɔ̃sɑ̃tʀe/ [1] **I** *vtr* **1** Admin to decentralize [*services, administration*]; to decentralize [*quartier, ville, région*]; Ind to disperse [*entreprises*]; **2** (distraire) [*personne, événement*] to distract sb.
II se déconcentrer *vpr* [*personne*] to lose one's concentration.

déconcertant, **~e** /dekɔ̃sɛʀtɑ̃, ɑ̃t/ *adj* [*attitude, fait, personne*] disconcerting; **d'une facilité ~e** disconcertingly easy.

déconcerter /dekɔ̃sɛʀte/ [1] *vtr* [*personne, événement, propos*] to disconcert; **il est vite déconcerté** he is easily disconcerted; **elle ne s'est pas laissé ~ par ma remarque** she didn't allow my remark to put her off.

déconditionnement /dekɔ̃disjɔnmɑ̃/ *nm* (de personne) deconditioning.

déconditionner /dekɔ̃disjɔne/ [1] *vtr* to decondition [*personne, opinion publique*].

déconfit, **~e** /dekɔ̃fi, it/ *adj* **1** [*personne, air, mine*] crestfallen, downcast; **avoir l'air ~** to look crestfallen ou downcast; **2** (vaincu) [*troupe*] routed.

déconfiture /dekɔ̃fityʀ/ *nf* **1** (échec) (de personne) failure; (de parti, d'équipe, de gouvernement) defeat; **un parti politique en pleine ~** a political party that is falling apart; **2** (faillite) (d'entreprise) collapse; **être** or **tomber en pleine ~** to collapse completely; **3** Jur (de personne) insolvency; **4** Mil (déroute) defeat, rout.

décongélation /dekɔ̃ʒelasjɔ̃/ *nf* (d'aliments) defrosting, thawing; **'faire cuire sans ~ préalable'** 'cook from frozen'.

décongelé /dekɔ̃ʒle/ **I** *pp* ▸ **décongeler**.
II *pp adj* [*aliment, produit*] thawed, defrosted.

décongeler /dekɔ̃ʒle/ [17] **I** *vtr* **1** [*personne*] to defrost, to leave [sth] to thaw [*aliment, viande*]; **2** Méd to thaw [*organe, sperme*].
II *vi* [*aliment, plat*] to defrost, to thaw; **laissez** or **faites ~ la viande à température ambiante** leave the meat to defrost ou thaw out at room temperature.

décongestion /dekɔ̃ʒɛstjɔ̃/ *nf* (tous contextes) decongestion, relief of congestion.

décongestionnant, **~e** /dekɔ̃ʒɛstjɔnɑ̃, ɑ̃t/ **I** *adj* decongestant.
II *nm* decongestant.

décongestionner /dekɔ̃ʒɛstjɔne/ [1] **I** *vtr* **1** Méd [*médicament*] to relieve congestion in [*organe*]; to clear, to decongest [*nez*]; **2** fig [*déviation, autoroute*] to relieve congestion in [*rue, ville, zone urbaine*]; [*gouvernement, mesure*] to ease the pressure on [*universités, services administratifs, transports*].
II se décongestionner *vpr* **1** [*nez, poumons*] to clear; **2** [*carrefour, route*] to clear.

déconnecté, **~e** /dekɔnɛkte/ **I** *pp* ▸ **déconnecter**.
II *pp adj* **1** (débranché) Ordinat, Télécom disconnected; Électrotech [*appareil*] disconnected; [*circuit*] broken; **2** fig [*personne*] out of touch (**de** with).

déconnecter /dekɔnɛkte/ [1] *vtr* **1** Ordinat, Télécom to disconnect; Électrotech to disconnect [*appareil*]; to break [*circuit*]; **2** fig to dissociate (**de** from).

déconner◑ /dekɔne/ [1] *vi* **1** [*personne*] (plaisanter) to kid around○; (dire des bêtises) to talk crap◑; (faire l'idiot) to mess around○; (mal agir) to piss around◑ GB; **~ dans son travail** to screw up one's work; **sans ~!** no kidding○!; **faut pas ~!** come off it○!; **2** (dysfonctionner) [*appareil, montre*] to play up○, to act up○.

déconneur◑, **-euse** /dekɔnœʀ, øz/ **I** *adj* [*tempérament*] wacky○, wild.
II *nm,f* (enfant) unruly child; (adulte) joker.

déconseillé, **~e** /dekɔ̃seje/ **I** *pp* ▸ **déconseiller**.
II *pp adj* [*action*] inadvisable; [*médicament, boisson, nourriture*] not recommended; **~ aux enfants de moins de 10 mois** not recommended for children under 10 months; **exposition au soleil ~e aux femmes enceintes** sunbathing is not recommended for pregnant women; **départ ~ samedi entre 8 heures et 15 heures** you are advised not to travel on Saturday between 8 am and 3 pm; **baignade ~e** bathing unsafe.

déconseiller /dekɔ̃seje/ [1] *vtr* **~ qch à qn** to advise sb against sth; **~ à qn de faire** to advise sb against doing; **il nous a vivement déconseillé d'accepter** he strongly advised us not to accept; **l'avion m'est déconseillé** I have been advised not to fly; **à ~ aux âmes sensibles** not recommended for the squeamish.

déconsidération /dekɔ̃sideʀasjɔ̃/ *nf* fml discredit.

déconsidérer /dekɔ̃sideʀe/ [14] **I** *vtr* to discredit.
II se déconsidérer *vpr* [*personne*] to

discredit oneself, to bring discredit upon oneself; [*journal*] to become discredited.

déconsigner /dekɔ̃siɲe/ [1] *vtr* **1** [*voyageur*] to take [sth] out of left-luggage GB ou of the baggage room US [*bagages*]; **2** [*commerçant*] to return the deposit on [*bouteille, emballage*]; **3** Mil to lift the order confining [sb] to barracks [*soldats, unité*].

décontamination /dekɔ̃taminasjɔ̃/ *nf* decontamination.

décontaminer /dekɔ̃tamine/ [1] *vtr* to decontaminate [*personne, eau, matériel, zone*].

décontenancer /dekɔ̃tnɑ̃se/ [12] **I** *vtr* to disconcert, to put [sb] out of countenance sout [*personne*]; **il en faut plus pour le ~** it takes more than that to disconcert him; **il ne se laisse pas facilement ~** he's not easily disconcerted.
II se décontenancer *vpr* [*personne*] to be disconcerted, to lose countenance sout; **avoir une mine décontenancée** to look disconcerted.

décontract○ /dekɔ̃tʀakt/ *adj inv* cool○, laidback○.

décontractant, **~e** /dekɔ̃tʀaktɑ̃, ɑ̃t/ **I** *adj* relaxing.
II *nm* relaxant.

décontracté, **~e** /dekɔ̃tʀakte/ **I** *pp* ▸ **décontracter**.
II *pp adj* **1** (décrispé) [*personne, corps, muscles*] relaxed; **2** (détendu) [*personne, allure, ambiance, soirée*] relaxed; [*tenue vestimentaire, mode*] casual; **3** (désinvolte) [*personne, attitude*] laidback○, casual.

décontracter /dekɔ̃tʀakte/ [1] *vtr*, **se décontracter** *vpr* to relax.

décontraction /dekɔ̃tʀaksjɔ̃/ *nf* **1** (relaxation) relaxation; **une telle ~ est rare chez un débutant** it's rare to see a beginner so relaxed; **2** (aisance) ease; **3** (désinvolture) casual attitude.

déconvenue /dekɔ̃vəny/ *nf* disappointment.

décor /dekɔʀ/ *nm* **1** (de pièce) decor; (d'objet) decoration; **~ de rêve/sans goût** dream/tasteless decor; **2** (extérieur) (cadre) setting; (paysage) scenery; **~ de verdure** green ou lush setting; **j'ai besoin de changer de ~** fig I need a change of scene; **aller** or **rentrer dans le ~**○ Aut to drive off the road; **3** (de l'action) Cin set; Théât **le ~, les ~s** the set, the scenery ¢; **film tourné en ~ naturel** film shot on location; **comme un ~ de théâtre** like a stage setting; **planter le ~** to set the scene; **4** (surface de meuble) finish; **~ imitation chêne** oak finish.

décorateur, **-trice** /dekɔʀatœʀ, tʀis/ ▸ **510** *nm,f* **1** (de maison, d'appartement) interior decorator; (de vitrine) window dresser; **2** Théât (créateur) set designer; (artiste peintre) scene painter; Cin, TV set designer.

décoratif, **-ive** /dekɔʀatif, iv/ *adj* **1** (destiné à la décoration) [*plantes, bougie, casseroles*] ornamental; **2** (qui décore bien) [*vase, assiettes, meubles*] decorative; **ce piano, il est ~ ou bien tu sais en jouer?** hum is that piano purely for decoration or do you know how to play?

décoration /dekɔʀasjɔ̃/ *nf* **1** (action) decoration; **2** (garniture) decoration; **~s de Noël** Christmas decorations; **3** Mil (médaille) decoration; **4** (de pièce) interior design; Cin set design; Théât stage design.
■ **~ florale** flower arranging.

décorder: **se décorder** /dekɔʀde/ [1] *vpr* [*alpiniste*] to unrope.

décoré, **~e** /dekɔʀe/ *nm,f* person honoured[GB] for his/her service; **c'est un ~ de la guerre** he was decorated in the war.

décorer /dekɔʀe/ [1] *vtr* **1** (orner) to decorate (**de** with); Cout to trim (**de** with); **2** Mil to decorate; **il a été décoré de la médaille militaire** he has been awarded the military medal.

décorner /dekɔʀne/ [1] *vtr* **1** to smooth out [*page, photo*]; **2** to dehorn [*animal*].

IDIOMES **il fait un vent à ~ les bœufs** it's blowing a gale.

décorticage /dekɔʀtikaʒ/ *nm* **1** (de crabe, noix) shelling; (de crevette) peeling; Agric (de graine) hulling, husking; **2** (de texte, roman) dissection.

décortication /dekɔʀtikasjɔ̃/ *nf* Hort, Méd decortication.

décortiquer /dekɔʀtike/ [1] *vtr* **1** (débarrasser de la coquille, l'enveloppe) to shell [*noix, crabe*]; to peel [*crevette*]; to hull, to husk [*riz, graine*]; **2** (analyser) to dissect [*texte, discours*]; **3** Méd [*vétérinaire, biologiste*] to decorticate [*animal*]; **4** Hort to decorticate.

décorum /dekɔʀɔm/ *nm* **1** (bienséance) propriety, decorum; **observer/ignorer le ~** to observe/ignore the proprieties; **2** (étiquette) protocol; **le ~ royal** royal protocol.

décote /dekɔt/ *nf* **1** Fisc tax rebate; **2** Fin (réduction) discount (**par** from); (baisse) drop; **des actions vendues avec une ~** shares sold at a loss.

découcher /dekuʃe/ [1] *vi* to spend the night away from home.

découdre /dekudʀ/ [76] **I** *vtr* to take the stitches out of, unstitch [*vêtement, rideau*]; to unstitch, to take off [*bouton*]; to unpick GB, to take out US [*couture, ourlet*].
II *vi* **en ~** to have a fight (**avec** with).
III se découdre *vpr* [*couture, ourlet*] to come unstitched; [*bouton*] to come off.

découler /dekule/ [1] *vi* **1** (s'ensuivre) to follow (**de** from); **des conséquences/décisions qui découlent des derniers conflits sociaux** consequences/decisions which follow from the recent industrial disputes; **2** (provenir) to result (**de** from); **la loi découle d'un rapport** the law is the result of a report; **la maladie qui en découle** the illness which results from it.

découpage /dekupaʒ/ *nm* **1** (de gigot, volaille) carving; (de gâteau) cutting; (de bois, photo) cutting (out); **2** fig (division) division (**en** into); **3** (image découpée) cut-out; **faire des ~s** to make cut-out figures; **4** Cin (action) continuity editing; (script) shooting script.
■ **~ électoral** Pol division into constituencies GB, districting US; **procéder à un nouveau ~ électoral** to redraw the electoral boundaries GB, to redistrict US.

découpe /dekup/ *nf* **1** Cout (coupe décorative) cut; (empiècement décoratif) (de veste, chemise) yoke; (de jupe, pantalon) panel; **à ~ en V** [*robe, T-shirt*] V-neck (*épith*); **une jupe à ~s** a panelled[GB] skirt; **2** Tech (de verre) cutting.

découpé, **~e** /dekupe/ **I** *pp* ▸ **découper**.
II *pp adj* Bot [*feuilles*] serrated.

découper /dekupe/ [1] **I** *vtr* **1** (pour diviser) to cut up [*tarte*]; to carve [*rôti, volaille*]; fig to divide up [*territoire, domaine*]; **~ qch en tranches** to cut sth into slices; **~ une émission en trois épisodes** fig to split a programme[GB] into three episodes; **2** (suivant un contour) to cut out [*article, photo*]; **~ une photo dans un journal** to cut a photo out of a newspaper; **3** liter (déchiqueter) to indent; **de petites baies découpent la côte** small bays indent the coast; **4** liter (profiler) **la lampe découpe des ombres sur le mur** the lamp casts shadows on the wall; **silhouette découpée par les phares** figure picked out by the headlights; **le clocher découpait sa silhouette sur le ciel** the steeple was outlined against the sky; **5** (émonder) to lop [*arbre*].
II se découper *vpr* liter (se profiler) **se ~ sur** to stand out against.

découpeur, **-euse** /dekupœʀ, øz/ **I** *nm,f* (ouvrier) (de bois) jigsaw operator.
II découpeuse *nf* (machine) cutting machine.

découplé, **~e** /dekuple/ *adj* **bien ~** well-proportioned.

découpure /dekupyʀ/ *nf* **1** (chose découpée) cutting; **2** (bord découpé) indented edge.

découragé, **~e** /dekuʀaʒe/ **I** *pp* ▸ **décourager**.
II *pp adj* [*personne*] disheartened, downhearted; [*air*] despondent; [*ton*] dejected.

décourageant, **~e** /dekuʀaʒɑ̃, ɑ̃t/ *adj* disheartening, discouraging.

découragement /dekuʀaʒmɑ̃/ *nm* discouragement, despondency.

décourager /dekuʀaʒe/ [13] **I** *vtr* **1** (déprimer) to discourage, to dishearten; **se laisser ~ par qch** to let oneself be discouraged by sth, to let sth get one down; **avoir l'air découragé** to look discouraged ou disheartened, to look down; **2** (rebuter) to discourage [*épargne, initiative, violence*]; to put [sb] off, to discourage [*personne*]; to discourage, to deter [*malfaiteur*]; **la pluie va en ~ plusieurs** the rain will put some people off; **~ qn de faire** to put sb off doing, to discourage sb from doing.
II se décourager *vpr* to lose heart, to become discouraged ou disheartened; **ne te décourage pas** don't lose heart, don't be discouraged.

découronner /dekuʀɔne/ [1] *vtr* **1** Hist [*peuple, révolution*] to dethrone, to depose [*roi*]; **2** [*vent*] to take the top off [*arbre*].

décours /dekuʀ/ *nm* **1** Méd (de maladie, fièvre) abating; (de crise) easing; **sa fièvre est à son ~** his fever is abating; **2** Astron (de lune) waning.

décousu, **~e** /dekuzy/ **I** *pp* ▸ **découdre**.
II *pp adj* Cout [*vêtement, ourlet*] which has come unstitched (*épith*); **ta chemise est ~e au col** your shirt has come unstitched at the collar.
III *adj* (sans cohésion) [*histoire, discours, exposé, conversation*] rambling; [*propos*] disjointed; [*idées*] disconnected; **travailler d'une façon ~e** to work in a disjointed way.

découvert, **~e** /dekuvɛʀ/ **I** *pp* ▸ **découvrir**.
II *pp adj* **1** (nu) [*épaules*] bare; **avoir la tête ~e** to be bare-headed; **il est resté ~ pendant toute la cérémonie** he stood hat in hand throughout the ceremony; **2** (dégagé) [*terrain, pays*] open; **3** (non fermé) [*camion, wagon*] open; [*voiture*] open-topped.
III *nm* Fin overdraft; **~ budgétaire** budget deficit.
IV à découvert *loc adv* **1** Fin **être à ~** [*client, compte*] to be overdrawn; **vendre à ~** (à la Bourse) to sell short; **2** (ouvertement) [*parler, agir*] openly; **3** (sans couvercle) [*cuire*] uncovered; **4** (à nu) **la marée laisse les rochers à ~** the tide leaves the rocks exposed; **5** (sans protection) [*combattre*] out in the open.
V découverte *nf* discovery; **faire une grande ~e** to make a great discovery; **partir** or **aller à la ~e** to go exploring; **'à la ~e du jazz/de l'art antique'** 'discovering jazz/ancient art'.

découvreur, **-euse** /dekuvʀœʀ, øz/ *nm,f* discoverer; **un ~ de talents** a talent-spotter.

découvrir /dekuvʀiʀ/ [32] **I** *vtr* **1** (trouver ce qui est inconnu) to discover [*remède, pays, fait, artiste*]; **j'ai découvert qu'elle s'intéressait aux sciences** I've discovered ou found out that she's interested in science; **2** (trouver ce qui est perdu, caché) to discover, to find [*objet, fugitif*]; to discover, to find out [*vérité*]; to uncover, to expose [*complot*]; **j'ai découvert par hasard le livre que je cherchais** I discovered, quite by chance, the book I was looking for; **elle a découvert que** she discovered that; **il a été découvert** (dans sa cachette) he was discovered; (dans ses activités occultes) he was found out; ▸ **pot**; **3** (apprendre à apprécier) to discover; **faire ~ à qn** to introduce sb to [*musique, peinture baroque*]; **je vais leur faire ~ Paris** I'm going to show them Paris; **les nouveaux auteurs/ouvrages à ~** new authors/works to be discovered; **4** (révéler) to reveal, to disclose (**à qn** to sb); **~ ses plans à un ami** to disclose one's plans to a friend; **~ son jeu** fig to show one's hand; **5** (dénuder) [*personne*] to bare [*partie du corps*]; to unveil [*statue*]; **6** (laisser voir) to reveal [*vêtement, geste*]; to reveal [*partie du corps, cicatrice*]; **son rictus découvrait des dents jaunies** his/her grin revealed yellow teeth; **7** (priver de protection) to leave [sth] exposed [*frontière, ligne de défense, pièce d'échec*]; **8** (apercevoir) to catch sight of [*château, vallée*]; (voir) to see [*château, vallée*]; **9** (ôter le couvercle) to take the lid off [*casserole, plat*].

II se découvrir *vpr* **1** (enlever son chapeau) to take one's hat off; **2** (trouver en soi) **se ~ avec l'âge** to become more self-aware as one grows older; **elle s'est découvert un talent/une passion** she found she had a talent/a passion; **3** (s'exposer) [*troupe*] to leave oneself exposed; [*boxeur*] to leave oneself open; **4** (perdre ses couvertures) to throw off one's bedclothes; ▶ **avril**; **5** (apparaître) [*lieu, site*] to come into sight; **6** liter (se confier) **se ~ à qn** to confide in sb.

décrassage /dekʀasaʒ/ *nm* **1** (de bougie, moteur) cleaning; **2** (de mur, sol) scrubbing.

décrasser /dekʀase/ [1] **I** *vtr* **1** (nettoyer) to clean [sth] up, to give a good scrubbing to [*animal, enfant*]; (en frottant) to scrub the dirt off [*vêtement, chaussure*]; (en faisant tremper) to soak the dirt out of [*objet, vêtement*]; **2**○ (dégrossir) to take the rough edges off [sb], to give [sb] a bit of polish.

II se décrasser *vpr* **1** (se laver) to clean oneself up, give oneself a good scrub; **se ~ les mains** to scrub one's hands clean; **se ~ les poumons**○ to get some fresh air into one's lungs; **2**○ (se dégrossir) [*personne*] to become more sophisticated.

décrêper /dekʀepe/ [1] *vtr* to straighten [*cheveux*].

décrépir /dekʀepiʀ/ [3] **I** *vtr* to remove roughcast from [*mur, surface*].

II se décrépir *vpr* [*immeuble, maison, façade, mur*] to crumble.

décrépit, ~e /dekʀepi, it/ *adj* **1** [*personne, vieillard*] decrepit; **2** [*bâtiment*] decrepit, dilapidated; [*mur*] crumbling.

décrépitude /dekʀepityd/ *nf* (de mœurs, d'idéologie) degeneration; (de civilisation, régime) decay; (de personne) decrepitude; **tomber en ~** [*idéologie, système*] to degenerate; [*lieu, monument*] to crumble.

decrescendo /dekʀeʃɛndo/ **I** *adv* Mus decrescendo; **aller ~** [*bruit, protestation, colère*] to be waning.

II *nm* Mus decrescendo.

décret /dekʀɛ/ **I** *nm* Jur, Relig order, decree (**sur** on); **légiférer/gouverner par ~s** to legislate/rule by decree; **publier un ~** to issue a decree.

II décrets *nmpl* liter decrees; **les ~s de la Providence** the decrees of Providence; **les ~s de la bienséance** the dictates of etiquette.

■ **~ d'application** implementing decree; **~ présidentiel** or **du président** presidential decree.

décréter /dekʀete/ [14] *vtr* **1** Pol (ordonner par décret) to order; **~ le couvre-feu** to impose a curfew; **~ la mobilisation générale** to order general mobilization; **2** (décider autoritairement) to decree (**que** that); (dire avec force) to announce (**que** that).

décret-loi, *pl* **décrets-lois** /dekʀɛlwa/ *nm* government decree.

décrier /dekʀije/ [2] *vtr* to disparage, to decry sout [*auteur, œuvre, institution*]; **le roman a été très décrié** the novel was much maligned; **après avoir été tant décrié, le mariage redevient à la mode** after being denigrated for so long, marriage has come back into fashion.

décriminaliser /dekʀiminalize/ [1] *vtr* to decriminalize.

décrire /dekʀiʀ/ [67] *vtr* **1** (dépeindre) to describe, to depict; **~ en détail** to describe in detail; **être décrit comme un écologiste** to be described as an ecologist; **2** (suivre) to describe sout [*cercle, courbe*] (**autour de** around); to follow [*trajectoire*].

décrispation /dekʀispasjɔ̃/ *nf* easing of tension; **un climat de ~** a more relaxed atmosphere.

décrisper /dekʀispe/ [1] **I** *vtr* (détendre) to take the strain ou tension out of [*relations, atmosphère*]; to defuse [*situation*]; **les entretiens se déroulent dans un climat décrispé** talks are taking place in a more relaxed atmosphere.

II se décrisper *vpr* **1** (se détendre) [*personne*] to relax; **2** Pol [*relations*] to become less strained; [*situation*] to de-escalate.

décrochage /dekʀɔʃaʒ/ *nm* **1** Radio, TV switch-over; **2** Aviat stalling.

décrochement /dekʀɔʃmɑ̃/ *nm* **1** (discontinuité) (en creux) indentation; (en saillie) projection; **en ~** (en creux) indented; (en saillie) projecting; **présenter un ~** to indent, to project; **2** Géol strike slip.

décrocher /dekʀɔʃe/ [1] **I** *vtr* **1** (détacher) to take down [*tableau, jambon, tenture*]; to uncouple [*wagon*]; **~ son téléphone** (pour répondre, appeler) to pick up the receiver; (pour ne pas être dérangé) to take the phone off the hook; **2**○ (obtenir) to clinch○, to get [*marché*]; to land○, to get [*contrat, poste, rôle*]; to get [*diplôme*]; to win [*titre*].

II *vi* **1**○ (cesser une activité) to give up; **2**○ (en parlant de tabac, drogue) to kick the habit○; **3**○ (cesser de s'intéresser) to switch off GB, to tune out US; **4** Mil to disengage; **5** Aviat to stall; **6** Radio, TV (passer sur un autre canal) to switch; (cesser les programmes) to cease transmission.

III se décrocher *vpr* [*tableau, applique*] to come off its hook; [*rideau*] to come down; [*soutien-gorge, jupe*] to come undone; **le poisson s'est décroché** the fish has got off the hook; **se ~ facilement** [*rideau*] to be easy to take down; ▶ **mâchoire**.

IDIOMES **~ la timbale** or **le gros lot** to hit the jackpot.

décroiser /dekʀwaze/ [1] *vtr* **~ les bras** to unfold one's arms; **~ les jambes** to uncross one's legs; Tech to uncross [*fils*].

décroissance /dekʀwasɑ̃s/ *nf* Admin, Écon decline, fall (**de** in).

décroissant, ~e /dekʀwasɑ̃, ɑ̃t/ *adj* [*bruit*] fading; [*intensité*] lessening; [*fortune, pouvoir*] declining; [*vitesse, nombre*] decreasing, falling; **par** or **en ordre ~** in descending order; **dans l'ordre ~ de vos préférences** in descending order of preference.

décroissement /dekʀwasmɑ̃/ *nm* (des jours) shortening; (de la lune) waning.

décroître /dekʀwatʀ/ [72] *vi* **1** Géog (baisser) [*niveau*] to fall, to drop; [*eau*] to subside; [*rivière*] to subside, to go down; **2** (diminuer) [*jour*] to get shorter; [*lumière, bruit*] to fade; [*inflation, chômage*] to go down; [*influence, force*] to decline; [*dimensions*] to diminish; **3** Astron [*lune*] to wane.

décrotter /dekʀɔte/ [1] *vtr* **1** [*personne*] to scrape the dirt off [*chaussures, semelles*]; **2**○ [*personne, événement*] to civilize○ [*personne*].

décrottoir /dekʀɔtwaʀ/ *nm* shoescraper, mud scraper.

décrue /dekʀy/ *nf* **1** (d'eaux, de fleuve) fall ou drop in the (water) level; **une ~ d'un mètre** a one metre[GB] drop in the water level; **le fleuve est en ~** the (water) level of the river is falling; **un fleuve en ~** a river with a falling water level; **2** (déclin) decline (**de** in).

décryptage /dekʀiptaʒ/ *nm* **1** (décodage) deciphering; **2** (interprétation) interpreting.

décrypter /dekʀipte/ [1] *vtr* **1** (décoder) to decipher [*signes, langue*]; **2** (interpréter) to interpret [*déclaration, propos*].

déçu, ~e /desy/ **I** *pp* ▶ **décevoir**.

II *pp adj* [*personne*] disappointed (**de** or **par** by); [*espoir*] thwarted, foiled; **être ~ dans ses attentes** to feel let down.

III *nm,f* disillusioned person; **un ~ du parti** a disillusioned party member; **les ~s de** those disillusioned with.

déculottée◐ /dekylɔte/ *nf* (défaite) thrashing○, beating○; **infliger/prendre une ~** to give/take a thrashing○.

déculotter /dekylɔte/ [1] **I** *vtr* **~ qn** to take off sb's trousers GB ou pants US.

II se déculotter *vpr* **1** lit to take off one's trousers GB ou pants US; **2**◐ (s'humilier) to grovel○, to crawl○ (**devant** to).

déculpabilisation /dekylpabilizasjɔ̃/ *nf* (de personne) freeing sb of guilt; (d'actes) justification.

déculpabiliser /dekylpabilize/ [1] **I** *vtr* to justify [*actes*]; to free [sb] of guilt [*personne*].

II se déculpabiliser *vpr* [*personne*] to stop feeling guilty.

décuple /dekypl/ **I** *adj* **une somme ~ d'une autre** an amount ten times more than another.

II *nm* **sa mise lui a rapporté le ~** he/she got back ten times more than what he/she had bet.

décuplement /dekypləmɑ̃/ *nm* **1** lit tenfold increase; **2** fig **le ~ de leur énergie** their greatly increased energy.

décupler /dekyple/ [1] **I** *vtr* **1** Math to multiply [sth] by ten; **2** fig to increase ou to multiply [sth] tenfold [*énergie, forces*]; **~ les forces de qn** to give sb the strength of ten.

II *vi* [*population, ressources*] to increase ou to multiply tenfold, to increase greatly.

dédaignable /dedɛɲabl/ *adj* **ce n'est pas ~** it is not to be sneezed at ou despised.

dédaigner /dedeɲe/ [1] *vtr* (mépriser) to despise [*personne, gloire, richesse*]; to scorn [*danger*]; to spurn [*conseil, office*]; (ne pas faire cas de) to disregard, to ignore [*insulte, interruption, danger*]; **ce n'est pas à ~** (somme, titre) it's not to be sneezed at ou despised; (danger) it shouldn't be ignored; **dédaigné de ses contemporains** spurned by his/her contemporaries; **il ne dédaigne pas la bonne chère** he's not averse to good food; **elle dédaigna de se lever** she did not deign to get up; **il ne dédaigne pas de les aider** he doesn't consider it beneath him to help them out.

dédaigneusement /dedɛɲøzmɑ̃/ *adv* [*regarder, parler*] disdainfully; [*accueillir*] with disdain.

dédaigneux, -euse /dedɛɲø, øz/ *adj* [*ton, sourire, air*] disdainful, scornful; **~ de** scornful of [*danger, honneurs*]; **faire une moue dédaigneuse** to curl one's lip.

dédain /dedɛ̃/ *nm* contempt (**de** for), disdain (**de** for); **afficher un ~ complet de la mort** to be utterly disdainful of death; **avec ~** scornfully, disdainfully; **écraser qn de son ~** to be witheringly scornful of sb.

dédale /dedal/ *nm* **1** (de couloirs, bâtiments) maze; **2** (de pensées, lois, formalités, d'intrigues) labyrinth.

Dédale /dedal/ *npr* Daedalus.

dedans /dədɑ̃/ **I** *adv* (à l'intérieur) inside; **il vaut mieux dîner ~** it would be better to eat inside ou indoors; **j'ai perdu mon sac et mes clés étaient ~** I've lost my bag and my keys were in it; **essaie ce fauteuil, on est très bien ~** try this armchair, it's very comfortable; **rouge à l'extérieur et blanc ~** red (on the) outside and white (on the) inside; **jetez les tomates ~**, Culin throw the tomatoes in; **il n'y a rien ~** there's nothing in it ou inside; **de ~, je les entendais parler sous ma fenêtre** from inside, I could hear them talking under my window; **quand on vient de ~, on est ébloui par la lumière** when you come from indoors, the light blinds you.

II en dedans *loc adv* **1** (à l'intérieur) inside; **en ~, la boîte est tapissée de soie** inside, the box is lined with silk; **2** (vers l'intérieur) inwards; **la porte s'ouvre en ~** the door opens inwards; **3**○ (en dessous de ses possibilités) **il joue un peu en ~** he's not playing up to his normal standard, he's playing a bit below par.

III *nm* inside; **les oppositions politiques du dehors et du ~** political opposition from outside and from within; **un mouvement du dehors vers le ~** a movement from the outside in.

IDIOMES **je lui ai mis le nez ~** ◑I really rubbed his/her nose in it○.

dédicace /dedikas/ *nf* **1** (inscription) (imprimée) dedication (**à qn** to sb); (manuscrite) inscription (**à qn** to sb); **faire une ~ à qn** to sign sth for sb; **demander une ~ à un auteur** to ask an author to sign a book; **2** Radio request (**pour qn** for sb); **3** Relig (consécration) consecration, dedication.

dédicacer /dedikase/ [12] *vtr* **1** (dédier) to dedicate (**à** to); **2** (signer) to sign [*ouvrage, photographie*] (**à** for).

dédier /dedje/ [2] *vtr* **1** (offrir en hommage) to dedicate [*roman, œuvre, pensées*] (**à** to); **2** (consacrer) [*personne, organisme*] to dedicate [*vie, efforts*] (**à** to); to devote [*soirée*] (**à** to); **3** Relig to dedicate [*chapelle, autel*] (**à** to).

dédire: **se dédire** /dediʀ/ [65] *vpr* **1** (se rétracter) to retract one's statement; **2** (revenir sur) to back out (**de** of) [*engagement, assurance*]; to go back on, to retract [*promesse*]. ▶ **cochon**.

dédit /dedi/ *nm* **1** (fait de se dédire) retraction; **en cas de ~** in case of default; **2** (somme d'argent) forfeit money, fine (*for breaking a contract*).

dédommagement /dedɔmaʒmɑ̃/ *nm* compensation; **à titre de ~** in compensation (**pour** for); **recevoir une somme en ~ de qch** to get money as ou in compensation for sth.

dédommager /dedɔmaʒe/ [13] **I** *vtr* **1** Assur, Jur (indemniser) to compensate (**de** for); **sa maison a brûlé mais il n'a jamais été dédommagé** his house burned down but he never got compensation; **2** (offrir une compensation à) **~ de qch** to make up for sth; **~ qn de qch** to make it up to sb for sth; **je lui ai offert le restaurant pour le ~ des ennuis que je lui ai causés** I invited him out for a meal to make up for the problems I had caused him.

II se dédommager *vpr* to take what is due to one; **il s'est servi dans la caisse pour se ~** he took money from the till to make up what was owed to him.

dédouanement /dedwanmɑ̃/ *nm* customs clearance; **le ~ de qch** the clearance of [sth] through customs [*biens, marchandises*]; **certificat de ~** customs clearance certificate.

dédouaner /dedwane/ [1] **I** *vtr* **1** Comm to clear [sth] through customs [*marchandises, biens*]; **2** (réhabiliter) to clear; **~ qn d'un soupçon** to clear sb of suspicion (**auprès de** in the eyes of).

II se dédouaner *vpr* fig [*personne*] to clear oneself of responsibility.

dédoublement /dedubləmɑ̃/ *nm* **1** (division) (de groupe) splitting [sth] in two; (de câble, fil) separating [sth] into strands; **2** (doublement) **le ~ d'un train** Rail the running of a relief train; **le ~ de la route** making the road into a dual carriageway.

■ **~ de la personnalité** Méd, Psych split ou dual personality.

dédoubler /deduble/ [1] **I** *vtr* **1** (diviser) to divide ou split [sth] in two [*groupe*]; to separate [sth] into strands [*câble*]; **2** (doubler) **~ un train** Rail to put on ou to run a relief train; **3** Cout to remove the lining of [*vêtement*].

II se dédoubler *vpr* **1** (se diviser) [*groupe*] to split in two; [*ongle*] to split; [*rayon, image*] to split into two; [*fil, laine, câble*] to come apart; **2** Méd, Psych [*personne*] to have a split personality.

dédramatisation /dedʀamatizasjɔ̃/ *nf* (de conflit, maladie) playing down (**de** of).

dédramatiser /dedʀamatize/ [1] *vtr* to make [sth] less traumatic, to take the drama out of [*divorce, examen*]; to play [sth] down [*maladie*]; to take the tension out of [*situation*]; to play down the significance of [*événement*]; **on a vu dans leur discours une volonté de ~** their speech showed their desire to play things down.

déductibilité /dedyktibilite/ *nf* deductibility; **~ fiscale** tax deductibility.

déductible /dedyktibl/ *adj* deductible (**de** from); **~ des impôts** tax-deductible.

déductif, -ive /dedyktif, iv/ *adj* deductive.

déduction /dedyksjɔ̃/ *nf* **1** (raisonnement) deduction; **par ~** by deduction; **2** (conclusion) deduction; **3** (soustraction) deduction; **après ~ de**, **~ faite de** after deducting; **~ fiscale** or **d'impôts** tax deduction; **venir en ~** to be deducted (**de** from).

déduire /dedɥiʀ/ [69] **I** *vtr* **1** (tirer la conséquence) to deduce (**de** from; **que** that); **2** (supposer) to infer (**de** from; **que** that); **3** (soustraire) to deduct (**de** from); **frais déduits, une fois déduits les frais** after deduction of expenses.

II se déduire *vpr* **1** (être induit) to be inferred (**de** from); **2** (découler) to be deduced (**de** from); **3** Compta to be deducted (**de** from); **se ~ des impôts** Fisc to be tax-deductible.

déesse /deɛs/ *nf* goddess; **la ~ de l'amour/la beauté/la justice** the goddess of love/beauty/justice.

de facto /defakto/ *loc adj inv, loc adv* de facto.

défaillance /defajɑ̃s/ *nf* **1** (mauvais fonctionnement) fault; (panne) breakdown (**de** in); **2** (insuffisance) failing, weakness; **avoir des ~s en mathématiques** to have areas of weakness in mathematics; **3** (moment de faiblesse) (physique) blackout; (morale) moment of weakness; **ma mémoire a des ~s** my memory is faulty; **il a eu une ~ à 100 m de l'arrivée** he began to flag ou to lose strength 100 metres[GB] from the line; **travailler sans ~** to work consistently; **faire son devoir sans ~** not to fail in one's duty; **4** Jur default.

■ **~ cardiaque** heart failure.

défaillant, **~e** /defajɑ̃, ɑ̃t/ *adj* **1** (qui fonctionne mal) [*moteur, installation*] faulty; **2** (inefficace) [*organisation, service, pouvoir*] inefficient; **un service public ~ en matière de santé** a public service which fails to provide proper health care; **3** (qui faiblit) [*courage, volonté*] flagging; [*voix, pas*] faltering; [*santé, mémoire*] failing; (près de s'évanouir) fml [*personne*] on the verge of fainting (*après n*).

défaillir /defajiʀ/ [28] *vi* **1** (s'évanouir) to faint; **se sentir ~** to feel faint; **~ de faim/de peur** to feel faint with hunger/with fear; **elle défaillait de bonheur** fig she was overcome with happiness; **2** (faiblir) [*mémoire, santé*] to fail; **soutenir qn sans ~** to show unflinching support for sb.

défaire /defɛʀ/ [10] **I** *vtr* **1** (ce qui est fait) to undo [*paquet, chignon, ourlet, couture, assemblage*]; to unwind [*pelote*]; to unravel [*tricot, écheveau*]; to break [sth] up [*puzzle*]; to muddle up [*classement*]; **je n'ai pas encore défait mon sac** I haven't unpacked (my bag) yet; **~ le lit de qn** (mettre en désordre) to mess up sb's bed; (changer les draps) to strip sb's bed; **arrête! tu défais tout mon lit** stop it, you're messing up my bed!; **le lit n'était pas défait** the bed hadn't been slept in; **tout ce que je fais il le défait** he undoes everything I do; **2** (détacher) to undo [*cravate, bouton, ceinture, soutien-gorge*]; to untie [*lacet, chaussure, nœud*]; **ta jupe est défaite** your skirt has come undone; **3** (casser) to break up [*union, alliance*]; to spoil [*plan, projet*]; **4** (infliger une défaite) to defeat, to rout littér [*armée, ennemi, pays*]; to defeat [*équipe, adversaire*]; **5** (délivrer) liter **~ qn de** to deliver ou free sb from [*chaînes, liens*]; fig to rid sb of [*habitudes, préjugés, illusions*].

II se défaire *vpr* **1** (ce qui était fait) [*nœud, coiffure, jupe, bouton, ourlet, collier*] to come undone; [*couture*] to come apart; **ta couture s'est défaite** your seam has come undone; **2** (se casser) [*alliance, amitié, liaison*] to break up; **3** (se débarrasser) **se ~ de** (volontairement) to get rid of; (à regret) to part with [*objet, voiture, animal*] ; to get [sth] out of one's mind [*pensée, idée*]; to rid oneself of [*croyance, habitude*]; to overcome [*faiblesse*]; to get rid of [*gêneur, importun*]; **4** (se troubler) [*visage, mine*] to fall; **son visage s'est défait en apprenant la nouvelle** his/her face fell when he/she heard the news.

défait, **~e** /defɛ, ɛt/ **I** *pp* ▶ **défaire**.

II *pp adj* **1** [*nœud, chignon*] undone; [*lit*] unmade; **2** [*visage*] haggard; **avoir la mine ~e** to look haggard; **3** [*armée, ennemi*] defeated.

III défaite *nf* defeat.

défaitisme /defetism/ *nm* defeatism.

défaitiste /defetist/ *adj, nmf* defeatist.

défalcation /defalkasjɔ̃/ *nf* deduction.

défalquer /defalke/ [1] *vtr* to deduct (**de** from).

défausser /defose/ [1] **I** *vtr* to straighten [*clé, outil*].

II se défausser *vpr* (aux cartes) to discard; **se ~ à cœur/pique** to discard a heart/spade; **se ~ d'une carte** to throw away a card.

défaut /defo/ **I** *nm* **1** (moral) (de personne) fault, failing; (de caractère) flaw (**de** in); **la paresse est un vilain ~** laziness is a bad fault; **c'est là son moindre ~** that's the least of his/her faults ou failings; **elle a tous les ~s** I can't think of one good thing to say about her; **n'avoir aucun ~** to be perfect; **se mettre en ~** to put oneself in the wrong; **prendre qn en ~** to catch sb out; **2** (physique, matériel, esthétique) gén defect; (de machine, système) defect (**de** in), fault (**de** in); (de tissu, verre, gemme) flaw (**de** in); (de théorie, raisonnement, d'œuvre d'art) flaw (**de** in); **avoir** or **présenter des ~s** [*machine, construction*] to be faulty; [*diamant, roman*] to be flawed, to have flaws; **sans ~** [*système, machine*] perfect; [*rubis, raisonnement*] flawless; **(il) y a comme un ~**○! hum there's something seriously wrong; **3** (insuffisance) shortage (**de** of); (absence) lack (**de** of); **faire ~** [*argent, ressources*] to be lacking; [*signature, document*] to be missing; **les indices ne font pas ~** there's no lack of clues, there are plenty of clues; **le talent/courage leur fait ~** they lack talent/courage; **le courage leur a fait ~** their courage failed them; **la patience/bonne volonté ne leur fait pas ~** they are not lacking in patience/good will; **l'argent ne leur fait pas ~** they're not short of money; **le temps me/m'a fait ~** I don't/didn't have enough time; **4** Jur default; **~ de comparaître** default, failure to appear (in court); **~ de livraison/paiement** non-delivery/non-payment; **par ~** by default; (condamné, jugé) in absentia; **faire ~** [*accusé, témoin*] to fail to appear in court; **5** Math **arrondir (un résultat) par ~** to round (a figure) down.

II à défaut de *loc prép* **à ~ de qch/qn** (en son absence) if sth/sb is not available; **à ~ de miel, utilisez du sucre** if you have no honey, use sugar; **de la soie ou, à ~, du coton** silk or, failing that, cotton; **à ~ de paiement immédiat** failing prompt payment, unless prompt payment is made; **à ~ de quoi vous serez poursuivi** failing which you will be prosecuted; **à ~ de mieux** for want of anything better; **à ~ de pouvoir acheter, elle loue** since she can't buy, she has to rent.

■ **~ de construction** Constr structural defect; **le ~ de la cuirasse de qn** fig the chink in sb's armour[GB]; **~ de fabrication** Tech manufacturing fault; **~ de masse** mass defect; **~ de procédure** procedural error; **~ de prononciation** speech impediment ou defect.

défaut-congé, *pl* **défauts-congés** /defokɔ̃ʒe/ *nm* Jur nonappearance of plaintiff.

défaveur /defavœʀ/ *nf* **1** (perte d'estime) disfavour[GB] sout; **être en ~ auprès de qn** to be out of favour[GB] with sb; **2** (désavantage) **il s'est trompé de 30 francs en ma ~** he overcharged me 30 francs; **mon âge a joué en ma ~** my age worked against me.

défavorable /defavɔʀabl/ *adj* [*situation, conditions*] unfavourable[GB] (**à** to); [*personne, gouvernement*] opposed (**à** to); **émettre un avis ~** to give an unfavourable[GB] response.

défavorablement /defavɔʀabləmɑ̃/ *adv* unfavourably[GB]; **juger ~** to have an unfavourable[GB] opinion of.

défavorisé, **~e** /defavɔʀize/ **I** *pp* ▶ **défavoriser**.
II *pp adj* [*milieu, personne*] underprivileged, disadvantaged; [*région, pays*] disadvantaged, poor.
III *nm,f* underprivileged person; **les ~s** the underprivileged.

défavoriser /defavɔʀize/ [1] *vtr* **1** (léser) [*impôt, mesure sociale*] to discriminate against, to be unfair to [*personne, catégorie sociale*]; **2** (handicaper) [*difformité physique, défaut*] to put [sb] at a disadvantage [*personne*]; **3** (être injuste envers) [*professeur, examinateur*] to put [sb] at an unfair disadvantage, to treat unfairly [*candidat*].

défécation /defekasjɔ̃/ *nf* **1** Chimie defecation, purification; **2** Physiol defecation.

défectif, **-ive** /defɛktif, iv/ *adj* defective.

défection /defɛksjɔ̃/ *nf* **1** (abandon) (d'amis, alliés) desertion (**de** of); (pour un autre parti, pays) defection; **faire ~** to defect; **2** (absence) nonappearance; **faire ~** to back out; **on ne déplore aucune ~** nobody backed out.

défectueux, **-euse** /defɛktɥø, øz/ *adj* [*matériel, article*] faulty, defective; [*raisonnement, logique*] flawed; [*enseignement, organisation, discipline*] poor.

défectuosité /defɛktɥozite/ *nf* fml **1** (état défectueux) defectiveness; **2** (défaut) fault, imperfection.

défendable /defɑ̃dabl/ *adj* Mil [*position, ville*] defensible, defendable; [*thèse, point de vue*] tenable; [*conduite*] justifiable; **pas ~** [*ville*] indefensible; [*thèse*] untenable; [*conduite*] indefensible, inexcusable; **l'accusé/employé n'est pas ~** the accused/employee hasn't got a case.

défendant: **à son corps défendant** /asɔ̃kɔʀdefɑ̃dɑ̃/ *loc adv* against one's will, unwillingly.

défendeur, **-eresse** /defɑ̃dœʀ, dəʀɛs/ *nm,f* Jur defendant.
■ **~ en appel** respondent.

défendre /defɑ̃dʀ/ [6] **I** *vtr* **1** (interdire) **~ qch à qn** to forbid sb sth; **~ que qn fasse**, **~ à qn de faire** to forbid sb to do; **il nous a défendu de sortir** he forbade us to go out; **ne fume pas ici, c'est défendu** you can't smoke here; **l'alcool/le tabac m'est défendu** I'm not allowed alcohol/cigarettes ou to drink/to smoke; **~ sa porte à qn** not to allow sb into one's house; **un panneau défend l'entrée aux civils** there's a sign telling civilians to keep out; **2** (lutter pour) gén, Mil to defend [*personne, pays, honneur, intérêts*] (**contre** against); to fight for [*droit*]; Sport to defend [*titre*]; **~ qn/qch au péril de sa vie** to risk one's life in defence[GB] of sb/sth; **~ une cause** to support ou champion a cause; **3** (protéger) to defend, to protect [*personne, territoire, biens*] (**de** or **contre** from ou against); to protect [*environnement*]; to defend [*démocratie*]; to safeguard [*paix, intérêts*]; Sport to defend [*but*]; **4** (soutenir) to defend [*idée, théorie, stratégie*]; to stand up for [*ami, principe*]; Jur to defend [*accusé*]; ▶ **orphelin**.
II se défendre *vpr* **1** (lutter) gén, Jur, Mil to defend oneself (**contre** against); **2** (résister aux critiques, brimades) [*personne*] to stand up for oneself (**contre** against); [*argument, proposition, thèse*] to be tenable; **cette opinion/stratégie se défend** it's a valid opinion/strategy; **un petit vin qui se défend** a very decent little wine; **il préfère attendre et ça se défend** he'd rather wait and he's got a point; **3** (se protéger) to protect oneself (**de** or **contre** from ou against); **se ~ contre le désespoir/la tentation** to ward off despair/temptation; **4**° (se débrouiller) to get by, to manage; **se ~ en français/au piano** to be quite good at French/at the piano; **il se défend bien en affaires/en classe** he does very well in business/at school; **5** (nier) **se ~ d'être jaloux/vexé** to deny being jealous/offended; **6** (s'empêcher) **se ~ de faire qch** to refrain from doing sth; **ne pouvoir se ~ d'un sentiment de regret** to be unable to repress a feeling of regret; **on ne peut se ~ de penser que**... one can't help thinking that...

défenestration /defənɛstʀasjɔ̃/ *nf* defenestration.

défenestrer /defənɛstʀe/ [1] *vtr* to throw [sb] out of a window.

défense /defɑ̃s/ *nf* **1** (interdiction) **'~ de pêcher/nager/fumer'** 'no fishing/swimming/smoking'; **'~ d'entrer'** 'no entry'; **'~ de toucher'** '(please) do not touch'; **~ d'en parler devant lui** don't mention it in front of him; **ils sont sortis malgré la ~ qui leur en avait été faite** they went out although they had been forbidden to do so; **2** (contre un agresseur) gén, Mil defence[GB] (**contre** against); (moyens, ouvrages) **~s** defences[GB]; **courir à la ~ de qn** to leap to sb's defence[GB]; **le budget de la ~ (nationale)** the defence[GB] budget; **ligne/moyens de ~** line/means of defence[GB]; **position/armes de ~** defensive position/weapons; **assurer la ~ du territoire** to defend the country; **sans ~** (faible) defenceless[GB], helpless; (sans protection) unprotected; ▶ **légitime**; **3** (protection) protection; **la ~ de l'environnement** the protection of the environment; **la ~ du patrimoine/de la langue française** the preservation of the national heritage/of the French language; **association pour la ~ des consommateurs/droits de l'homme/libertés** consumer rights/human rights/civil liberties organization; **faire grève pour la ~ de l'emploi** to strike against job cuts; **prendre la ~ de qn/qch** to stand up for sb/sth; **4** (résistance) Sport defence[GB]; **opposer une ~ énergique** to put up a stubborn defence[GB] ou resistance; **jouer en ~** Sport to play in defence[GB]; **5** Physiol, Psych defence[GB]; **les ~s de l'organisme** the body's defences[GB]; **les ~s immunitaires** the immune system; **6** (justification, plaidoyer) gén, Jur defence[GB]; **pour sa ~, elle a dit que**... in her defence[GB], she said that...; **assurer la ~ d'un accusé** Jur to conduct the case for the defence[GB]; **7** Jur (partie défendante) defence[GB]; (defenseur) defence[GB]; **l'avocat de la ~** counsel for the defence[GB], defense attorney US; **la parole est à la ~** (the counsel for) the defence[GB] may now speak; **8** Zool (d'éléphant, de sanglier, morse) tusk.
■ **~ passive** civil defence[GB].

défense-recours /defɑ̃sʀəkuʀ/ *nf* **garantie ~** *cover against legal costs incurred when personally liable or when claiming against a third party.*

défenseur /defɑ̃sœʀ/ *nm* **1** gén, Mil, Sport defender (**de** of); fig (de cause) champion, defender (**de** of); **se faire le ~ des faibles** to defend the weak; **2** Jur counsel for the defence[GB], defense attorney US.

défensif, **-ive** /defɑ̃sif, iv/ **I** *adj* defensive.
II défensive *nf* **être** or **se tenir sur la défensive** to be on the defensive.

déféquer /defeke/ [14] **I** *vtr* Chimie to defecate, to purify.
II *vi* Physiol to defecate.

déférence /defeʀɑ̃s/ *nf* deference (**pour, envers** to); **par ~** out of ou in deference; **des marques de ~** marks of respect.

déférent, **~e** /defeʀɑ̃, ɑ̃t/ *adj* (respectueux) deferential; **se montrer ~** to show respect (**envers, à l'égard de** for).

déférer /defeʀe/ [14] *vtr* Jur **~ une affaire à la justice** to refer a case to a court; **~ un accusé à la justice/devant un tribunal** to bring a defendant before the courts/before a court.

déferlante /defɛʀlɑ̃t/ **I** *adj f* [*vague*] breaking.
II *nf* breaker.

déferlement /defɛʀləmɑ̃/ *nm* **1** (d'articles, images) flood; (de violence, protestations) upsurge (**de** in); (de passion) surge; (de paroles) torrent; (de louanges) flood; **il y eu un ~ de critiques** there was a barrage of criticism; **2** (de vagues) breaking.

déferler /defɛʀle/ [1] **I** *vtr* Naut to unfurl [*voile, gréement*].
II *vi* **1** fig [*violence, protestations, délinquance*] to erupt; [*injures*] to pour out; [*articles*] to flood in; **~ sur** [*crise, racisme*] to sweep through; **une vague de racisme déferle sur la France** a wave of racism is sweeping through France; **les nouveaux films déferlent sur la ville** a wave of new films has hit the city; **les images déferlent sur** or **à l'écran** pictures flash across the screen; **2** lit [*vague*] to break (**sur** on); **3** (envahir) **~ sur** [*réfugiés, soldats*] to pour into [*ville, pays*]; **~ dans** [*réfugiés, manifestants, touristes*] to pour through [*rues*].

défi /defi/ *nm* **1** (gageure) challenge; **lancer un ~ à qn** to challenge sb; **relever un ~** to take up a challenge; **mettre qn au ~ de faire** to challenge sb to do; **c'est un ~ à la raison/aux lois de l'équilibre** it defies reason/the laws of gravity; **2** (provocation) act of defiance; **a-t-il agi par ~?** was it an act of defiance?; **geste/air de ~** defiant gesture/look.

défiance /defjɑ̃s/ *nf* distrust, mistrust; **avec ~** distrustfully, warily; **sans ~** unsuspectingly, trustingly; **éprouver** or **ressentir de la ~ envers qn** to distrust sb, to be distrustful of sb; **mettre qn en ~** to arouse sb's mistrust.

défiant, **~e** /defjɑ̃, ɑ̃t/ *adj* [*attitude, personne*] distrustful, wary.

déficeler /defisle/ [19] **I** *vtr* to untie [*paquet*].
II se déficeler *vpr* [*paquet*] to come untied.

déficience /defisjɑ̃s/ *nf* **1** Méd deficiency; **~ mentale** mental deficiency; **~ en vitamines/calcium** vitamin/calcium deficiency; **~ physique** physical handicap; **~ musculaire** muscular deficit; **~ cardiaque** heart failure; **~ immunitaire** immunodeficiency; **2** fig deficiency; **pallier les ~s du système** to compensate for the deficiencies of the system; **les ~s du marché** the weak spots of the market; **les ~s de l'intrigue** weaknesses in the plot.

déficient, **~e** /defisjɑ̃, ɑ̃t/ *adj* **1** Méd [*cœur, muscle*] deficient; [*organe*] malfunctioning; **il est mentalement ~** he's mentally deficient; **2** fig (insuffisant) [*système, budget, contrôle*] inadequate; (inapproprié) [*jugement, arbitrage*] faulty.

déficit /defisit/ *nm* **1** Comm, Écon, Fin deficit; **~ budgétaire/commercial** budget/trade deficit; **~ chronique/cumulé/public** chronic/cumulative/public deficit; **combler/enregistrer un ~** to make up/show a deficit; **être en ~** to be in deficit; **2** Méd deficiency; **~ hormonal/intellectuel** hormone/mental deficiency; **3** fig (insuffisance) lack (**en qch** of sth).

déficitaire /defisitɛʀ/ *adj* **1** Comm, Écon, Fin [*budget, compte*] showing a deficit (*jamais épith*); [*affaire, entreprise*] showing a loss (*jamais épith*); [*activité, régime*] loss-making (*épith*); [*secteur, service*] loss-making (*épith*); **2** (insuffisant) [*récolte, ressources*] showing a shortfall (*jamais épith*).

défier /defje/ [2] **I** *vtr* **1** (provoquer) to

challenge [*rival, adversaire*] (**à** to); **~ qn en combat singulier** to challenge sb to single combat; **~ qn de faire** to challenge ou defy sb to do; **je te défie de plonger** I challenge ou dare you to dive; **~ qn du regard** to stare defiantly at sb; **2** (braver) [*personne*] to defy [*danger, mort, opinion*]; [*raisonnement, conclusion*] to defy [*raison, logique*]; **prix défiant toute concurrence** unbeatable price.
II se défier *vpr* **1** (se braver) [*adversaires*] to defy each other; **se ~ du regard** to stare defiantly at each other; **2** (se méfier) **se ~ de qn/qch** fml to distrust sb/sth.

défiguration /defigyʀasjɔ̃/ *nf* lit, fig disfigurement.

défigurer /defigyʀe/ [1] *vtr* **1** lit [*accident, maladie, cicatrice*] to disfigure [*personne*]; [*grimace, peur*] to disfigure [*personne*]; **la douleur le défigurait** he was disfigured by pain; **2** fig (dénaturer) to disfigure [*paysage, monument*]; to mutilate [*texte*]; to distort [*pensée, propos*]; **le front de mer est défiguré par les immeubles** the seafront is disfigured by the buildings.

défilé /defile/ *nm* **1** (de fête) parade, procession; (de manifestants) march; **2** (suite) (de visiteurs, candidats) stream; **3** Géog gorge, defile spéc.
■ **~ aérien** flypast GB, flyover US; **~ militaire** march-past, military parade; **~ de mode** fashion show.

défilement /defilmɑ̃/ *nm* **1** Audio, Cin, TV (de film, bande) running; **2** Ordinat (à l'écran) scrolling (**vers le bas** down; **vers le haut** up); (**touche**) **arrêt ~** scroll lock (key); **3** Mil (technique de camouflage) defilade.
■ **~ horizontal** horizontal hold; **~ vertical** vertical hold.

défiler /defile/ [1] **I** *vi* **1** (marcher en rangs) (pour célébrer) to march, to parade; (pour manifester) to march; **2** (se succéder) [*mannequins, touristes*] to come and go; **j'ai vu ~ 15 candidats ce matin** I saw 15 candidates this morning; **il a vu ~ des générations d'étudiants** he's seen generations of students come and go; **~ devant** (devant cercueil, lieu) to file past; [*mannequin*] to parade in front of; **~ dans** [*clients, malades*] to go through; **les souvenirs défilaient dans ma mémoire** a stream of memories passed through my mind; **3** (s'additionner) [*minutes, kilomètres*] to add up; **4** (se dérouler) [*images, paysage*] to unfold; **~ rapidement** to flash past; **voir ~ sa vie en quelques secondes** to see one's life flash before one's eyes; **laisser** or **faire ~ la bande d'une cassette** (en avant) to fast forward a tape; (en arrière) to rewind a tape; **5** Ordinat [*texte*] to scroll (**vers le bas** down; **vers le haut** up).
II se défiler○ *vpr* (se dérober) **se ~ au moment de faire** to slip away when it comes to doing.

défini, **~e** /defini/ **I** *pp* ▶ **définir**.
II *pp adj* **1** gén defined; **elle n'avait pas de thème ~** she had no clearly defined theme; **mal ~** [*sentiment, goût*] indefinable; [*contour, image, circonstances*] ill-defined; **bien ~** well-defined; **2** Ling [*article*] definite.

définir /definiʀ/ [3] **I** *vtr* **1** gén to define, to specify [*loi, règle*]; **les conditions sont clairement définies dans le contrat** the conditions are clearly specified in the contract; **mieux ~ le but choisi** to define the chosen aim more clearly; **les conditions sont à ~** the conditions are still to be specified; **~ sa politique** to lay down firm political guidelines; **~ comme une priorité la lutte contre l'inflation** to make the fight against inflation one's top priority; **2** (caractériser) to characterize [*personne*]; (résumer) [*personne, qualité*] to define [*personne*] (**comme** as); **~ la gestion comme un art** to see management as an art.
II se définir *vpr* [*personne*] to define oneself (**comme** as); [*mot, sentiment, position*] to be defined.

définissable /definisabl/ *adj* definable; **facilement/difficilement ~** easy/difficult to define.

définitif, **-ive** /definitif, iv/ **I** *adj* **1** (final) [*comptes, rapport, traduction, édition, résultat, choix, plan*] definitive; [*édition d'un journal*] final; [*prix*] set; **2** (irrévocable) [*fermeture, cessez-le-feu, frontière, renvoi, arrêt*] permanent; [*accord, règlement, choix, jugement*] definitive; [*échec, succès*] conclusive; [*refus*] absolute; **rien de ~** nothing definite; **3** (péremptoire) definite.
II *nm* **la fermeture, est-ce du ~?** is the closure permanent?
III en définitive *loc adv* after all is said and done.

définition /definisjɔ̃/ *nf* **1** gén definition; (de mots croisés) clue; **par ~** by definition; **~ des objectifs/du marché** target/market specification; **2** TV definition; **télévision (à) haute ~** high-definition TV; **écran à haute ~ graphique** Ordinat screen with high-resolution graphics.

définitivement /definitivmɑ̃/ *adv* **1** (pour toujours) [*fermer, cesser*] for good; [*abandonner, écarter*] once and for all, definitively; [*adopter, nommer*] definitively; **2** controv (en définitive) definitely.

définitoire /definitwaʀ/ *adj* Ling defining (*épith*).

défiscaliser /defiskalize/ [1] *vtr* to exempt [sth] from taxation; **défiscalisez en faisant** avoid tax by doing; **épargne défiscalisée** tax-exempt savings.

déflagration /deflagʀasjɔ̃/ *nf* (explosion) detonation; (combustion) deflagration.

déflagrer /deflagʀe/ [1] *vi* to deflagrate.

déflation /deflasjɔ̃/ *nf* **1** Écon deflation; **~ monétaire** deflation of the currency; **2** (d'emplois, effectifs) reduction; **3** Géol deflation.

déflationniste /deflasjɔnist/ *adj* [*théorie, système, mesures*] deflationary; [*économiste, ministre*] deflationist.

déflecteur /deflɛktœʀ/ *nm* **1** Aut quarter light GB, vent US; **2** Tech baffle.

déflexion /deflɛksjɔ̃/ *nf* deflection.

défloration /deflɔʀasjɔ̃/ *nf* defloration.

déflorer /deflɔʀe/ [1] *vtr* **1** (trahir) to give away [*sujet, intrigue*]; **2** to deflower [*jeune fille*].

défoliant, **~e** /defɔljɑ̃, ɑ̃t/ **I** *adj* defoliant.
II *nm* defoliant.

défoliation /defɔljasjɔ̃/ *nf* defoliation.

défolier /defɔlje/ [2] *vtr* to defoliate.

défonçage /defɔ̃saʒ/ *nm* Agric (en bêchant) double-digging; (labour) deep-ploughing GB, deep-plowing US.

défonce● /defɔ̃s/ *nf* drug users' slang (usage de la drogue) drug abuse; **~ à la colle** glue-sniffing; **~ aux solvants** solvent abuse.

défoncé, **~e** /defɔ̃se/ **I** *adj* **1** (endommagé) [*fauteuil, divan*] sagging (*épith*); [*chaise*] with a broken seat (*épith, après n*); [*chemin*] potholed, full of potholes (*après n*); [*trottoir*] full of holes (*après n*); **2**● drug users' slang [*personne*] high○ (*jamais épith*).
II○ *nm,f* (drogué) drug users' slang junkie○ péj, drug addict.

défoncer /defɔ̃se/ [12] **I** *vtr* **1** (casser) to smash [*vitrine, barricade*]; to break [sth] down [*porte*]; to break the springs of [*divan, sommier*]; to smash [sth] in [*aile, arrière d'une voiture*]; to dent [*chapeau*]; **il lui a défoncé la mâchoire**○ he broke his jaw; **la pluie a défoncé le terrain** the rain has churned up the ground; **les camions ont défoncé la piste** the lorries have ruined the track ou left the track full of holes; **2** (ôter le fond) to knock the bottom out of [*tonneau, bateau*]; **3** (bêcher) to double-dig; (labourer) to deep-plough GB, to deep-plow US; **4**○ (surpasser) to break [*taux, record*]; **~ les taux d'audience** Radio, TV to break all the ratings records.
II se défoncer *vpr* **1**○ (peiner) **quand il est sur scène il se défonce** when he's on stage he gives it his all; **se ~ pour qn/pour faire** to do everything one possibly can for sb/to do; **2**● (se droguer) drug users' slang to get high○ (**à** on); **se ~ à l'héroïne** to shoot heroin; **se ~ à la colle** to sniff glue.

déforestation /defɔʀɛstasjɔ̃/ *nf* deforestation.

déformant, **~e** /defɔʀmɑ̃, ɑ̃t/ *adj* [*influence*] warping; [*miroir*] distorting.

déformation /defɔʀmasjɔ̃/ *nf* **1** (d'objet, image, de fait, propos) distortion; **2** (difformité) deformity; **~ de la colonne vertébrale** spinal deformity.
IDIOMES **c'est de la ~ professionnelle** it's a habit that comes from the job.

déformé, **~e** /defɔʀme/ **I** *pp* ▶ **déformer**.
II *pp adj* **1** (tordu) [*visage, trait, image*] distorted; [*objet*] warped; [*corps, membre*] deformed, misshapen; (abîmé) [*vêtement*] gén shapeless; [*pantalon, pull-over*] baggy, shapeless; **mains ~es par le travail/l'âge** hands gnarled by work/with age; **chaussée ~e** uneven (road) surface; **2** (faussé) [*fait, pensée, message, vérité*] distorted; **3** (perverti) [*esprit*] warped, twisted; [*mœurs, sens moral*] corrupt; **~ par** warped ou corrupted by.

déformer /defɔʀme/ [1] **I** *vtr* **1** (endommager) to bend [sth] (out of shape) [*pare-chocs, aile d'avion*]; **tu vas le ~** [objet en plastique, en bois] it'll get out of shape, you'll damage it; **tu vas ~ les poches de ta veste** your jacket pockets will lose their shape, you're going to ruin the pockets of your jacket; **2** (transformer) to distort [*image, visage, traits*]; to deform [*corps, doigt*]; **3** (fausser) to distort, to misrepresent [*message, vérité, information, faits*]; to warp [*esprit*]; **on a déformé mes propos** (par erreur) I've been misquoted; (à dessein) my words have been twisted.
II se déformer *vpr* gén to lose its shape; [*pantalon*] to go GB ou become baggy.

défoulement /defulmɑ̃/ *nm* **1** (processus) (dépense d'énergie) letting off steam ¢; (détente) letting one's hair down○ ¢; **2** (résultat) loss of inhibition.

défouler /defule/ [1] **I** *vtr* **1** [*activité*] to release tension in [*personne*]; **ça me défoule** it helps me (to) unwind; **2** [*personne*] **~ sa colère contre qn** to vent one's anger on sb.
II se défouler *vpr* (dépenser de l'énergie) to let off steam; (se détendre) to let one's hair down○; **se ~ sur qn** to take it out on sb.

défourner /defuʀne/ [1] *vtr* to take [sth] out of the oven [*pain*]; to take [sth] out of the kiln [*céramique*].

défraîchi, **~e** /defʀeʃi/ **I** *pp* ▶ **défraîchir**.
II *pp adj* (usé) [*vêtement, rideau*] worn; (passé) [*tissu, beauté, couleur*] faded; **une robe ~e** a dress that has seen better days; **vêtements ~s** Comm shop-soiled GB ou damaged garments.

défraîchir /defʀeʃiʀ/ [3] **I** *vtr* [*temps*] to make [sth] look the worse for wear [*vêtement, tissu*]; [*soleil*] to fade [*couleur, tissu*].
II se défraîchir *vpr* (pâlir) to fade; (s'user) to look worn.

défrayer /defʀeje/ [21] *vtr* **1** (être le sujet de) **~ la conversation** to be the main topic of conversation; **~ la chronique** to be the talk of the town; **2** (rembourser) **~ qn** to pay sb's expenses; **~ qn de son voyage** or **ses frais de voyage** to pay sb's travel costs.

défrichage /defʀiʃaʒ/ *nm*, **défrichement** /defʀiʃmɑ̃/ *nm* **1** Agric clearance (**de** of); **2** (de sujet, problème, texte) groundwork (**de** on).

défricher /defʀiʃe/ [1] *vtr* **1** Agric to clear [*bois, terre*]; **~ le terrain** fig to do the groundwork; **2** (éclaircir) to open up [*problème, domaine*].

défricheur, **-euse** /defʀiʃœʀ, øz/ *nm,f* **1** Agric land-clearer; **2** fig (de sujet, domaine) pioneer.

défriper /defʀipe/ [1] *vtr* to smooth out [*vêtement, papier*].

défrisant, **~e** /defʀizɑ̃, ɑ̃t/ **I** *adj* straightening.

II *nm* hair straightener.

défriser /defʀize/ [1] *vtr* **1** (rendre moins frisé) to straighten [*cheveux*]; **se faire ~** to have one's hair straightened; **2**○ (contrarier) to bug○ [*personne*].

défroisser /defʀwase/ [1] *vtr* to smooth out [*vêtement, papier*].

défroque /defʀɔk/ *nf* **1** (vêtements hors d'usage) cast-offs (*pl*); **2** (vêtements ridicules) ridiculous outfit.

défroqué, **~e** /defʀɔke/ **I** *pp* ▶ **défroquer**.

II *pp adj* [*moine, prêtre*] defrocked.

III *nm* (prêtre) defrocked priest; (moine) defrocked monk.

défroquer /defʀɔke/ [1] **I** *vtr* to defrock [*prêtre*].

II se défroquer *vpr* Relig to leave holy orders.

défunt, **~e** /defœ̃, œ̃t/ **I** *adj* **1** (décédé) [*personne*] late (*épith*); **votre ~ père** your late father; **2** liter [*jeunesse, bonheur*] lost; [*empire, grandeur*] former; [*parti, idéologie*] defunct.

II *nm,f* **le ~, la ~e** the deceased.

dégagé, **~e** /degaʒe/ **I** *pp* ▶ **dégager**.

II *pp adj* **1** [*vue, accès, passage, entrée, chemin*] clear, unobstructed; [*espace, route*] clear, open; [*site*] clear; [*ciel*] clear, cloudless; **2** (dénudé) [*cou, front*] bare; **3** (décontracté) [*air, allure*] casual; **dit-il d'un ton ~** he remarked casually; **parler de qch d'un ton ~** to talk casually about sth.

dégagement /degaʒmɑ̃/ *nm* **1** (d'un lieu) clearing (**de** of); **le ~ de la chaussée s'est effectué rapidement** the road was soon cleared; **2** (de vestiges) digging out (**de** of); **3** Sport (au football) clearance (**de qn** by sb); **~ en touche** kicking a ball out of play; **4** Méd **~ de la tête/des épaules d'un bébé** freeing of the head/of the shoulders of a baby.

■ **~ des cadres** Admin cutting back on managerial staff; Mil cutting back on officers; **~ instantané** gas escape.

dégager /degaʒe/ [13] **I** *vtr* **1** (libérer physiquement) to free; **elle essayait de ~ sa jambe coincée** she was trying to free her trapped leg; **2** (débarrasser) to clear [*bureau, route, passage*]; **~ un camion de la voie publique** to clear a truck off the public highway; **'dégagez le passage, s'il vous plaît'** 'clear the way, please'; **'dégagez, s'il vous plaît'** (ordre de la police) 'move along please'; **dégage**○! clear off○! GB, get lost○!; **demande au coiffeur de te ~ les oreilles/la nuque/le front** ask the hairdresser to cut your hair away from your ears/neck/forehead; **3** (extraire) to bring out [*idée, morale, sens*]; **~ les grands axes d'une politique** to bring out the salient ou main points of a policy; **4** (laisser échapper) [*volcan, voiture*] to emit [*odeur, gaz*]; [*casserole*] to let out [*vapeur*]; **le feu/moteur dégage de la chaleur** the fire/engine gives out ou off heat; **5** Fin **~ des crédits pour la construction d'une école** [*État, ville*] to make funds available ou release funds for a school to be built; **~ des bénéfices** or **profits** to make ou show a profit; **~ un excédent commercial** to show a trade surplus; **6** (racheter ce qui était en gage) **~ une montre du mont-de-piété** to redeem a watch from the pawnbroker; **7** (libérer moralement) **~ qn d'une responsabilité** to relieve sb of a responsibility; **~ qn d'une obligation/d'une promesse** to release ou free sb from an obligation/from a promise; **~ qn de tous soucis** to free sb from all his/her worries, to take all sb's worries away; **8** (au football, rugby) **~ une balle** or **un ballon** to clear a ball; **9** (déboucher) to unblock [*nez, sinus*]; to clear [*bronches*].

II se dégager *vpr* **1** (se libérer) to free oneself; **se ~ d'une situation piégée** to extricate oneself from a tricky situation; **se ~ du contrôle de l'État** to free oneself of state control; **2** Météo [*temps, ciel*] to clear; **3** (émaner) **se ~ de** [*chaleur, gaz, fumée*] to come out of; [*odeur, parfum*] to emanate from; **4** (apparaître) **un charme désuet se dégage du roman** the novel has an (element of) old world charm about it; **il se dégage de vos tableaux une impression de sérénité** there is an impression of calm about your paintings; **une conclusion se dégage: il faut agir** one thing is clear: we have to act; **la conclusion qui se dégage de la discussion est que** the outcome of the debate is (that).

dégaine○ /degɛn/ *nf* (allure) odd appearance; (démarche) odd walk; **tu ne pourras jamais entrer avec cette ~** you'll never be allowed in looking like that; **avoir une ~ de cow-boy** (allure) to look like a cowboy; (démarche) to walk like a cowboy.

dégainer /degene/ [1] *vtr* **1** (sortir de son étui) to draw [*arme*]; **2** Électrotech to strip [*câble*].

déganter /degɑ̃te/ [1] **I** *vtr* **elle déganta sa main droite** she took her right glove off; **une main dégantée** a gloveless hand.

II se déganter *vpr* [*personne*] to take one's gloves off.

dégarni, **~e** /degaʀni/ **I** *pp* ▶ **dégarnir**.

II *pp adj* **1** (sans cheveux) [*personne*] balding; **front ~** receding hairline; **2** (vide) [*rayons, magasin*] bare; [*compte en banque*] empty.

dégarnir /degaʀniʀ/ [3] **I** *vtr* to empty [*rayon, frigo, compte en banque*]; **~ une place forte de ses troupes** Mil to withdraw the garrison from a fortress town.

II se dégarnir *vpr* **1** (perdre ses cheveux) [*personne*] to be going bald, to be losing one's hair; **il a le crâne qui se dégarnit** he's receding, he's got a receding hairline; **2** (se vider) [*rue, salle*] to empty.

dégât /dega/ *nm* **1** (dommage) **~s** damage ¢; **60 millions de francs de ~** 60 million francs' worth of damage; **limiter les ~s** to limit the damage; **faire des ~s** [*personne*] to do damage; [*explosion*] to cause damage; **attention aux ~s causés par le soleil** beware of the damaging effects of the sun; **2** (désordre) mess○; **vous en avez fait du ~**○! you've made a real mess○!

■ **~s des eaux** Jur flood damage ¢.

IDIOMES **attention, il va y avoir des ~s**○ watch out, there's going to be trouble; **arrêtez les ~s**○! stop right there!; **bonjour les ~s**○! here comes trouble○!

dégauchir /degoʃiʀ/ [3] *vtr* **1** (aplanir) to surface [*bois*]; to dress [*pierre*]; **2** (redresser) to straighten [*tringle*].

dégauchissage /degoʃisaʒ/ *nm* (de bois) surfacing; (de pierre) dressing; (de tringle) straightening.

dégauchisseuse /degoʃisøz/ *nf* surface-planer.

dégazage /degazaʒ/ *nm* **1** Chimie degassing; **2** (vidange des cuves) oil dumping.

dégazer /degaze/ [1] **I** *vtr* **1** Chimie to degas; **2** Naut to gas-free [*réservoir*].

II *vi* Naut (vidanger les cuves) to flush out the tanks (at sea).

dégazeur /degazœʀ/ *nm* (de chaudière, de réfrigérateur) deaerator; (de pétrole) degasser.

dégel /deʒɛl/ *nm* **1** Météo thaw; **c'est le ~** it's thawing; **2** (de relations, tensions) thaw; **3** (de crédits) unfreezing; **le ~ économique** the unfreezing of the economy.

dégelée○ /deʒle/ *nf* hiding○, beating; **recevoir une ~** to get a hiding.

dégeler /deʒle/ [17] **I** *vtr* **1** (détendre) to improve [*relations*]; to warm up [*public, spectateur*]; **sa plaisanterie a dégelé l'atmosphère** his/her joke broke the ice; **2** Fin (débloquer) to unfreeze [*crédits*].

II *vi* [*sol, lac*] to thaw (out); **le soleil a fait ~ les flaques** the sun has thawed the puddles.

III se dégeler *vpr* fig [*relations, situation*] to thaw; [*public*] to warm up; [*personne*] to thaw out.

IV *v impers* to thaw; **ça dégèle aujourd'hui** it's thawing today.

dégénératif, **-ive** /deʒeneʀatif, iv/ *adj* degenerative.

dégénéré, **~e** /deʒeneʀe/ **I** *pp* ▶ **dégénérer**.

II *pp adj* **1** Sci [*animal, espèce, plante*] degenerate; [*personne*] degenerate○; **2**○ **il est complètement ~** offensive he's a real moron○.

III *nm,f* **1** Méd degenerate; **2**○ offensive moron○.

dégénérer /deʒeneʀe/ [14] *vi* **1** (mal tourner) [*bagarre, manifestation, incident*] to get out of hand; **~ en** to degenerate into; **les dissensions ont dégénéré en crise politique** the disagreements degenerated into a political crisis; **2** (s'abâtardir) [*race, plante, espèce*] to degenerate; **3** Méd [*tumeur*] to degenerate.

dégénérescence /deʒeneʀesɑ̃s/ *nf* **1** Méd (de tissus) degeneration; (mentale) degeneracy; **~ cancéreuse** cancerous degeneration; **2** (de plante, race) degeneration; **3** (de mœurs, d'idées) degeneration; **en pleine ~** in decline.

dégénérescent, **~e** /deʒeneʀesɑ̃, ɑ̃t/ *adj* Méd [*cellules*] degenerating.

dégermer /deʒɛʀme/ [1] *vtr* to remove the sprouts from [*pomme de terre*]; to degerm [*orge*].

dégingandé, **~e** /deʒɛ̃gɑ̃de/ *adj* lanky.

dégivrage /deʒivʀaʒ/ *nm* **1** Aviat, Aut deicing; **2** (de réfrigérateur) defrosting.

■ **~ automatique** auto defrost.

dégivrant, **~e** /deʒivʀɑ̃, ɑ̃t/ *adj* [*rétroviseur*] heated.

dégivrer /deʒivʀe/ [1] **I** *vtr* **1** Tech to de-ice [*pare-brise, serrure*]; **2** (ôter la glace de) to defrost [*réfrigérateur*].

II *vi* [*réfrigérateur*] to defrost.

dégivreur /deʒivʀœʀ/ *nm* **1** Aut, Aviat de-icing system; **2** (de réfrigérateur) defroster.

déglaçage /deglasaʒ/ *nm* Culin deglazing.

déglacer /deglase/ [12] *vtr* Culin to deglaze; **bien ~** deglaze thoroughly.

déglingué○, **~e** /deglɛ̃ge/ **I** *pp* ▶ **déglinguer**.

II *pp adj* [*ascenseur, vélo, voiture*] clapped out○ GB, dilapidated; [*maison*] dilapidated.

déglinguer○ /deglɛ̃ge/ [1] **I** *vtr* to bust○, to break [*appareil, objet*].

II se déglinguer *vpr* [*mécanisme*] to go wrong; [*appareil, machine*] to go on the blink○, to break down; **se ~ la santé/le foie** to wreck○ one's health/liver.

déglutir /deglytiʀ/ [3] *vtr, vi* to swallow.

déglutition /deglytisjɔ̃/ *nf* swallowing, deglutition spéc.

dégobiller◑ /degɔbije/ [1] **I** *vtr* to puke◑ [sth] up, to vomit.

II *vi* to puke◑, to vomit.

dégoiser○ /degwaze/ [1] pej **I** *vtr* (dire) to spout○, to utter [*âneries, boniments*]; to come out with a stream of○, to shout [*injures*].

II *vi* (parler) to rattle on○, to ramble on.

dégommer○ /degɔme/ [1] *vtr* **1** (licencier) to dismiss, to fire, to sack○ GB; **se faire ~** to be fired; **2** (vilipender) to put [sb] down, to lay into○ [sb]; **se faire ~ (en flèche)** to get a telling off○; **3** (atteindre) to hit (**avec** with).

dégonflage /degɔ̃flaʒ/ *nm* **1** (de pneu) deflation; **2**○ (lâcheté) chickening out○, loss of nerve.

dégonflard○, **~e** /degɔ̃flaʀ, aʀd/ *nm,f* chicken○, coward.

dégonflé, **~e** /degɔ̃fle/ **I** *pp* ▶ **dégonfler**.

II *pp adj* [*ballon*] deflated; [*pneu*] flat.

III○ *nm,f* chicken○, coward.

dégonflement /degɔ̃fləmɑ̃/ *nm* = **dégonflage**.

dégonfler /degɔ̃fle/ [1] **I** *vtr* **1** (vider de son air) to deflate [*bouée*]; to let down, to deflate [*pneu, ballon*]; **2**○ (réduire) to streamline [*effectifs*]; to reduce [*masse monétaire*].

II *vi* (désenfler) [*entorse, cheville, bosse*] to go down.
III **se dégonfler** *vpr* **1** (se vider de son air) [*bouée*] to deflate; [*pneu, ballon*] to go down; **2**○ (manquer de courage) [*personne*] to chicken out○, to lose one's nerve; **3**○ (perdre de l'importance) [*rêve*] to fade; [*mouvement, phénomène*] to fizzle out○, to die.

dégorgement /degɔʀʒəmɑ̃/ *nm* **1** (de liquide) (épanchement) discharge; (évacuation) drainage; **2** (d'égout, de gouttière) (écoulement) overflow; (évacuation) clearing out; **3** (de cuir) soaking; (de laine) scouring.

dégorgeoir /degɔʀʒwaʀ/ *nm* **1** (pour écoulement) overflow; **2** Tech (de menuisier) gouge; **3** Pêche disgorger.

dégorger /degɔʀʒe/ [13] I *vtr* **1** (déverser) [*conduit*] to discharge [*eau*] (**dans** into); [*stade, rue*] to disgorge [*foule*] (**dans** into); **2** (déboucher) to unblock, to clear [*gouttière, évier*]; **3** (nettoyer) to soak [*cuir*]; to scour [*laine*].
II *vi* **1** (se délaver) [*tissu, couleur*] to run; **2** Culin [*légume*] to sweat; [*escargot*] to purge; [*viande*] to soak; **faire ~, mettre à ~** to let [sth] sweat [*légume*]; to let [sth] soak [*viande*].
III **se dégorger** *vpr* [*réservoir*] to flow (**dans** into).

dégot(t)er○ /degɔte/ [1] *vtr* to find.

dégoulinade /degulinad/ *nf* trickle.

dégoulinant, ~e /degulinɑ̃, ɑ̃t/ *adj* **1** [*liquide*] trickling; **2** [*personne, parapluie*] dripping (**de** with); **3**○ (exsudant) oozing; **~ de** oozing [*obséquiosité, hypocrisie*].

dégoulinement /degulinmɑ̃/ *nm* trickling.

dégouliner /deguline/ [1] *vi* **1** [*liquide*] to trickle; **la sueur me dégouline sur le visage et dans le dos** sweat trickles down my face and my back; **2** [*personne, objet*] to drip; **~ de** to drip with [*liquide*]; **3**○ (exsuder) to ooze [*sentiment*].

dégoulinure /degulinyʀ/ *nf* = **dégoulinade**.

dégoupiller /degupije/ [1] *vtr* **~ une grenade** to pull the pin out of a grenade.

dégourdi, ~e /deguʀdi/ I *pp* ▶ **dégourdir**.
II *pp adj* (débrouillard) smart; **tu n'es pas bien ~!** you're useless!

dégourdir /deguʀdiʀ/ [3] I *vtr* **1** (réchauffer) to warm [sth] up [*doigts, mains, pieds*]; to take the chill off [*eau*]; **2** (assouplir) to loosen [sth] up [*doigts, membres*]; **un peu de marche va te ~** a walk will loosen you up; **3** (rendre plus hardi) **~ des enfants** to bring children out of themselves.
II **se dégourdir** *vpr* **1** (se détendre) to unwind; **se ~ les jambes** to stretch one's legs; **2** (devenir plus hardi) to come out of oneself.

dégoût /degu/ *nm* **1** (répulsion) disgust (**devant** at; **pour** for); **éprouver du ~ pour** to feel disgust for; **avec un profond ~** with absolute disgust; **2** (lassitude) weariness; **~ de la vie** world-weariness; **3** (satiété) nausea; **jusqu'au ~** ad nauseam.

dégoûtant, ~e /degutɑ̃, ɑ̃t/ I *adj* **1** (sale) filthy; **des chaussettes ~es** filthy socks; **2**○ (scandaleux) disgusting; (éhonté) sickening (*jamais épith*); **c'est ~** it is disgusting; **il a une chance ~e** his luck is sickening; **3** (obscène) dirty; **revue ~e** dirty magazine; **4** (répugnant) [*habitude*] revolting; [*créature*] disgusting; **il fait un temps ~ aujourd'hui** the weather is foul today.
II *nm,f* revolting man/woman; **vieux ~** dirty old man.

dégoûtation /degutasjɔ̃/ *nf* disgrace.

dégoûté, ~e /degute/ I *pp* ▶ **dégoûter**.
II *pp adj* **1** [*commentaire, ton*] disgusted; **d'un air ~** with disgust; **2 être ~ de qch** to have had enough of sth; **ne pas être ~** to have a strong stomach; **faire le ~** to turn one's nose up.

dégoûter /degute/ [1] I *vtr* **1** (répugner) to disgust; (écœurer) to make [sb] feel sick; **la saleté me dégoûte** filthiness disgusts me; **les rognons me dégoûtent** kidneys make me feel sick; **ça me dégoûte** it's disgusting; **2** (ôter l'envie) to put [sb] off; **~ qn de qch/de faire** to put sb off sth/off doing sth; **3** (scandaliser) to sicken; **ça me dégoûte (de voir) que/de voir comment** it makes me sick (to see) that/the way.
II **se dégoûter** *vpr* **1** (se lasser) **se ~ de** to get tired of; **2** (se répugner) to be disgusted with oneself (**de faire** for doing).

dégoutter /degute/ [1] *vi* **1** (couler) [*pluie, sueur*] to drip (**de** from); **2** (ruisseler) **~ de** [*toit, parapluie, front*] to drip with [*eau*].

dégradant, ~e /degʀadɑ̃, ɑ̃t/ *adj* [*activité, travail*] degrading.

dégradation /degʀadasjɔ̃/ *nf* **1** (dégât provoqué) damage ¢; **commettre des ~s** to cause damage; **la ~ du site par les touristes** the damage caused to the area by tourists; **2** (usure naturelle) deterioration; **le monument/la peinture est dans un état de ~ avancé** the monument/paint is in an advanced state of deterioration; **3** (détérioration) (de conditions, situation, contacts) deterioration (**de** in); (de mœurs) decline (**de** in); **la ~ des conditions de vie/de l'économie** the deterioration in the standard of living/economy; **la ~ du pouvoir d'achat** the erosion in purchasing power; **4** Sci (de matière organique, d'énergie) degradation; (de l'environnement) degradation; (de la couche d'ozone) depletion.
■ **~ civique** loss of civil rights; **~ militaire** dishonourable[GB] discharge.

dégradé, ~e /degʀade/ I *pp* ▶ **dégrader**.
II *pp adj* **tons ~s** shaded tones; **coupe ~e** layered cut.
III *nm* **1** (de couleurs) gradation; (de lumière) fading ¢; **peint en ~** painted in shaded tones; **2** (en coiffure) layered cut.

dégrader /degʀade/ [1] I *vtr* **1** (détériorer) to damage [*site, monument, environnement*]; **2** Mil (destituer) to cashier [*officier*]; **3** Art to use [sth] in gradation [*tons, couleurs*]; **4** (avilir) [*vice*] to degrade [*personne*].
II **se dégrader** *vpr* **1** (se détériorer) [*quartier, météo, situation, santé*] to deteriorate; **2** fml (s'avilir) to demean oneself (**en** by); **3** Phys [*énergie*] to degrade.

dégrafer /degʀafe/ [1] I *vtr* to undo, to unfasten [*corsage, soutien-gorge, collier, ceinture*].
II **se dégrafer** *vpr* (accidentellement) to come undone.

dégraissage /degʀɛsaʒ/ *nm* **1**○ (d'effectifs) reduction (**de** in); (d'entreprise) streamlining ¢ (**de** of); **~s de personnel** staff cuts; **2** (nettoyage à sec) dry-cleaning; **3** (de viande) trimming; **4** (de laine) scouring.

dégraissant, ~e /degʀɛsɑ̃, ɑ̃t/ I *adj* [*produit, liquide*] grease-removing (*épith*).
II *nm* (pour ôter la graisse) grease remover; (pour taches diverses) stain remover.

dégraissé, ~e /degʀese/ I *pp* ▶ **dégraisser**.
II *pp adj* Culin [*jambon, viande*] extra lean; [*bouillon*] with the fat skimmed off (*épith, après n*).

dégraisser /degʀese/ [1] *vtr* **1**○ (réduire le personnel) to streamline [*effectifs, entreprise*]; **son entreprise dégraisse** his company is cutting down on staff; **2** (nettoyer) to dry-clean [*vêtement*]; **j'ai fait ~ mon manteau** I had my coat dry-cleaned; **3** Culin to trim the fat off [*jambon, viande*]; to skim the fat from [*bouillon*]; **4** Tex to scour [*laine*].

degré /dəgʀe/ *nm* **1** ▶ **800** (d'angle, de température) degree; **un angle de 30 ~s** or **30°** an angle of 30 degrees ou 30°; **eau chauffée à 37 ~s** or **37°** water heated to 37 degrees ou 37°; **la température a baissé/monté de cinq ~s** the temperature has fallen/risen (by) five degrees, there has been a five-degree drop/rise in temperature; **il fait 15 ~s dehors** it's 15 degrees outside; **2** (concentration) **~ en** or **d'alcool d'une boisson** proof of an alcoholic drink; **ce vin fait 12°** this wine contains 12% alcohol (by volume); **ce cognac fait 40°** this cognac contains 40% alcohol (by volume) GB, this cognac is 70° proof; **cette boisson fait combien de ~s?** what is the alcohol content of this drink?; **3** (niveau) degree (**de** of), level (**de** of); (stade d'une évolution) stage; **~ de comparaison** Ling degree of comparison; **par ~s** by degrees, gradually; **à des ~s divers** in varying degrees; **à un moindre ~** to a lesser extent ou degree; **jusqu'à un certain ~** to some extent ou degree, up to a point; **susceptible au dernier** or **plus haut ~** extremely touchy; **un tel ~ de cruauté est-il possible?** is it possible that anyone could be so cruel?; **4** (dans un classement) Tech, Sci degree; Admin (rang) grade; (en alpinisme) grade; **paroi du 4e ~** grade 4 wall; **~ de parenté** degree of kinship; **~ de brûlure** degree to which a person is burned; **brûlures du premier/troisième ~** first-/third-degree burns; **équation du premier/second ~** first/second-degree equation; **cousins au premier/second ~** first/second cousins; **enseignant/enseignement du premier/second ~** primary/secondary schoolteacher/education; **5** (dans une interprétation) **premier/deuxième** or **second ~** literal/hidden meaning; **prendre ce que qn dit au premier ~** to take what sb says literally ou at face value; **tout discours politique est à interpréter au deuxième** or **second ~** you need to read between the lines of any political speech; **6** (marche) step; **gravir les ~s de la terrasse** to climb the steps leading to the terrace; **les ~s de la hiérarchie** or **de l'échelle sociale** fig the rungs of the social ladder.
■ **~ Baumé** or **Bé** degree on the Baumé scale; **sirop à 40 ~s Baumé** or **Bé** syrup GB ou sirup US with a 40-degree (Baumé scale) sugar content; **~ Celsius** degree Celsius; **~ Fahrenheit** degree Fahrenheit; **~ prohibé** Jur proscribed degree of kinship.

dégressif, -ive /degʀesif, iv/ *adj* **tarif ~** prices according to quantity of order; [*impôt*] graduated; **système ~ de taxation** graduated taxation; **amortissement ~ d'une dette** repayment of a loan on the basis of a diminishing balance.

dégressivité /degʀesivite/ *nf* degression.

dégrèvement /degʀɛvmɑ̃/ *nm* **~ (fiscal)** tax relief; **avoir droit à un ~** to be entitled to tax relief.

dégrever /degʀəve/ [16] *vtr* Fisc to relieve the tax burden on [*contribuable*]; Jur to disencumber [*propriété*].

dégriffé, ~e /degʀife/ I *adj* **robe/veste ~e** marked-down designer dress/jacket.
II *nm* (vêtements) marked-down designer clothing; **un magasin de ~s** a shop GB ou store US that sells marked-down designer clothes.

dégringolade○ /degʀɛ̃gɔlad/ *nf* **1** (de personne, d'objets) fall; **2** (de cours, prix) collapse; **une ~ de 50%** a drop of 50%.

dégringoler○ /degʀɛ̃gɔle/ [1] I *vtr* [*personne*] to race down [*escalier, pente*].
II *vi* **1** (culbuter) [*personne*] to tumble; [*livres, tuiles*] to tumble down (**de** off); [*pluie*] to pour down; **~ dans les escaliers/le ravin** to tumble on the stairs/into the ravine; **la neige dégringole du toit** the snow tumbles down off the roof; **2** (baisser) [*prix, cours, température*] to fall sharply; [*production*] to drop sharply; [*popularité*] to slump; **~ dans les sondages** to slump in the opinion polls; **3** (être abrupt) [*sentier, escalier*] to plunge down.

dégrippant /degʀipɑ̃/ *nm* penetrating oil.

dégripper /degʀipe/ [1] I *vtr* Aut to lubricate [*moteur*]; Mécan to unjam [*mécanisme*].
II **se dégripper** *vpr* **1** Aut [*moteur*] to loosen up; Mécan [*mécanisme*] to unjam; **2** fig [*administration*] to be set in motion.

dégrisement /degʀizmɑ̃/ *nm* sobering up.

dégriser /degʀize/ [1] **I** *vtr* **1** (dessoûler) to sober [sb] up; **2** (ramener à la réalité) to bring [sb] to his/her senses.

II se dégriser *vpr* **1** (dessoûler) to sober up; **2** (revenir à la réalité) to come to one's senses.

dégrossi, **~e** /degʀosi/ *adj* **1** [*planches*] rough-hewn; **2** pej [*personne*] **mal ~** coarse péj.

dégrossir /degʀosiʀ/ [3] *vtr* **1** Tech [*tailleur de pierre, sculpteur*] to rough-hew [*marbre, pierre*]; **2** (éclaircir) to break the back of [*travail, tâche*]; to get a general idea of [*question, affaire*]; **3** (éduquer) to knock a few corners off [*personne*].

dégrossissage /degʀosisaʒ/ *nm* (de marbre, bois) rough-hewing.

dégrouiller○: **se dégrouiller** /degʀuje/ [1] *vpr* to hurry up, to get a move on○; **dégrouille-toi de partir** hurry up and leave.

dégrouper /degʀupe/ [1] *vtr* to divide into groups.

déguenillé, **~e** /degənije/ *adj* ragged (*épith*), in rags (*après n*).

déguerpir /degɛʀpiʀ/ [3] *vi* to clear off○, to clear out US, to leave; **faire ~ qn** to drive sb off.

dégueulasse◑ /degœlas/ **I** *adj* **1** (sale) [*personne, vêtement, cheveux, lieu, objet*] grotty○ GB, disgusting; **2** (mauvais) [*plat, aliment*] lousy○, disgusting; [*temps*] lousy○, disgusting; [*travail*] shoddy○, disgusting; **c'est pas ~ ce ragoût!** this stew isn't half bad○; **3** (révoltant) [*personne, action*] shitty◑, rotten; **c'est ~ ce qu'ils ont fait** what they did was really rotten; **tu es ~ de dire une chose pareille** what a rotten thing to say.

II *nm* **un vieux ~** a dirty old man○.

dégueulasser◑ /degœlase/ [1] *vtr* to dirty, to mess up○ [*pantalon, feuille*].

dégueuler◑ /degœle/ [1] **I** *vtr* to throw [sth] up, to vomit [*nourriture*].

II *vi* to puke◑, vomit.

dégueulis◑ /degœli/ *nm* puke○, vomit.

déguisé, **~e** /degize/ **I** *pp* ▸ **déguiser**.

II *pp adj* **1** (vêtu d'un déguisement) (pour s'amuser) in fancy dress (*jamais épith*); (pour duper) in disguise (*jamais épith*); **~ en pirate** dressed up as a pirate; **un escroc ~ en policier** a crook disguised as a policeman; **2** (où l'on se déguise) [*soirée, défilé*] fancy dress (*épith*); **3** (camouflé) [*appui, subvention, tentative*] concealed; [*compliment*] disguised; [*critique*] veiled, disguised; **une façon ~e de faire** a roundabout way of doing; **non ~** undisguised.

déguisement /degizmɑ̃/ *nm* **1** (costume) (pour s'amuser) fancy dress, costume; (pour duper) disguise; **sous ce ~ de clown** in that clown's costume; **2** (de pensée, vérité) concealment; **sans ~** openly.

déguiser /degize/ [1] **I** *vtr* **1** (mettre un déguisement à) (pour s'amuser) to dress [sb] up (**en** as); (pour duper) to disguise (**en** as); **2** (altérer) to disguise [*visage, voix, écriture*]; **3** (camoufler) to disguise [*intentions, sentiment, ambition*]; **4** Jur to conceal [*donation*].

II se déguiser *vpr* (pour s'amuser) to dress up (**en** as); (pour duper) to disguise oneself (**en** as).

dégurgiter /degyʀʒite/ [1] *vtr* **1** (vomir) to bring up [*aliment*]; **2** (dire) to spew out [*insultes*]; to regurgitate [*leçon*].

dégustateur, **-trice** /degystatœʀ, tʀis/ *nm,f* Vin wine taster.

dégustation /degystasjɔ̃/ *nf* tasting; **~ d'huîtres** tasting of oysters; **~ de vin(s)/ fromages** wine/cheese tasting; **~ gratuite** free tasting.

déguster /degyste/ [1] **I** *vtr* **1** (savourer) to savour[GB] [*boisson, aliment, victoire*]; to enjoy [*livre, œuvre, spectacle*]; **2** [*dégustateur*] to taste [*vins, liqueurs*].

II◑ *vi* (endurer) to suffer, to go through hell○; **qu'est-ce que j'ai dégusté!** I really went through hell!

déhanché, **~e** /deɑ̃ʃe/ **I** *pp* ▸ **déhancher**.

II *pp adj* **1** [*démarche, allure*] swaying; **2** (infirme) [*corps*] crooked.

déhanchement /deɑ̃ʃmɑ̃/ *nm* **1** (naturel) swaying hips; **2** (d'infirme) lopsidedness; **3** Méd dislocation of the hip.

déhancher: **se déhancher** /deɑ̃ʃe/ [1] *vpr* **1** (en marchant) to sway one's hips; (exagérément) to wiggle one's hips; **2** (sans bouger) to stand with one's weight on one hip.

dehors /dəɔʀ/ **I** *adv* **1** (à l'extérieur) outside; **manger/dormir ~** to eat/to sleep outside ou outdoors; **ne restez pas ~, entrez** don't stay outside, come in; **passer la nuit ~** (occasionnellement) to spend the night outdoors; (habituellement) to sleep rough; **mettre sa bicyclette ~** to put one's bicycle outside; **allez jouer ~!** go and play outside!; **2** (hors de son domicile) out; **j'ai été ~ toute la journée** I was out all day; **je déjeune ~ aujourd'hui** I'm having lunch out today; **mettre** or **flanquer**○ **qn ~** (exclure d'un lieu) gén to throw ou to chuck○ sb out; (d'un cours) to throw sb out; (d'un travail) to fire, to sack○ GB; (d'un établissement scolaire) to expel; **de ~** [*voir, appeler, arriver*] from outside.

II *excl* get out!

III *nm inv* **1** (lieu) **le ~** the outside; **les bruits du ~** noise from outside; **quelqu'un du ~ ne peut pas comprendre** fig an outsider can't understand; **2** (apparence) **ses ~ bourrus cachent un cœur d'or** his/her rough exterior hides a heart of gold; **sous des ~ modestes, il est très orgueilleux** under his modest exterior, he's a very proud man.

IV en dehors *loc adv* **1** (à l'extérieur) outside; **2** fig (exclu) **il a préféré rester en ~** he preferred to stay out of it.

V en dehors de *loc prép* **1** (à l'extérieur de) outside; **en ~ de la ville/du pays** outside the city/the country; **traverser en ~ des passages pour piétons** to cross the street ou road outside the pedestrian crossings; **il fait du tennis en ~ de l'école** he plays tennis outside school; **choisir qn en ~ du groupe/parti** to choose sb from outside the group/party; **l'accident est survenu en ~ de l'autoroute** the accident happened off the motorway GB ou freeway US; **2** (mis à part) apart from; **en ~ de quelques amis, il ne voit personne** apart from a few friends, he sees no one; **il a des indemnités en ~ de son salaire** he has allowances in addition to his salary; **en ~ de certaines dates** outside certain dates; **3** (hors de) outside of; **en ~ des heures d'ouvertures/heures de travail** outside of opening hours/office hours; **il est resté en ~ du coup** or **de cette histoire** he stayed out of the whole business; **c'est en ~ du sujet** Scol it's off the subject; **c'est en ~ de mes attributions** that's outside my jurisdiction sout, that's not my job; **c'est en ~ d'eux qu'il faut chercher la responsabilité** we must look beyond them to find those who are to blame; **en ~ de tout clivage idéologique** beyond all ideological divisions; **la police a agi en ~ des limites de la loi** the police went beyond the limits of the law; **en ~ des repas** between meals; **4**○ (à l'insu de) **faire qch en ~ de qn** to do sth without the knowledge of sb; **la décision a été prise en ~ de moi** the decision was taken without my knowledge.

déhoussable /deusabl/ *adj* [*canapé*] with fully removable covering (*épith, après n*); [*coussin*] with a removable cover (*épith, après n*).

déicide /deisid/ **I** *adj* deicidal.

II *nmf* (personne) deicide.

III *nm* (crime) deicide.

déictique /deiktik/ *adj, nm* deictic.

déification /deifikasjɔ̃/ *nf* **1** (divinisation) deification; **2** (vénération) idolization.

déifier /deifje/ [2] *vtr* **1** (diviniser) to deify [*personne, animal*]; **2** (vénérer) to worship [*argent, progrès*]; to idolize [*jeunesse, vedette*].

déisme /deism/ *nm* deism.

déiste /deist/ **I** *adj* [*personne, théologie*] deistic.

II *nmf* deist.

déité /deite/ *nf* liter **1** (divinité) deity; **2** (idole) idol; **faire de la richesse une ~** to worship money.

déjà /deʒa/ *adv* **1** (dès maintenant) already; **il est ~ tard** it is already late, it is late already; **à trois ans ~, il savait lire** he could already read by the age of three; **sans cela, j'aurais ~ fini** if it hadn't been for that, I would have finished already ou I'd be finished by now; **elle serait ~ mariée, si elle l'avait voulu** she could have been married by now if she'd wanted; **2** (précédemment) before, already; **je te l'ai ~ dit** I told you before, I've already told you once; **3**○ (pour renforcer) **c'est ~ un joli salaire!** that's a pretty good salary!; **être second, c'est ~ très bien!** even to come second is pretty good!; **c'est ~ beaucoup d'avoir la santé** if at least you have your health, that's a good start; **il s'est excusé, c'est ~ quelque chose** at least he apologized, that's something; **4**○ (pour protester) **elle est ~ assez riche (comme ça)!** she's rich enough as it is; **~ qu'il est assommant, s'il faut en plus l'écouter!** he's boring enough as it is without having to listen to him as well; **~ que j'ai la migraine, tu veux que je supporte ce bruit?** with this migraine, how am I supposed to stand that noise?; **5**○ (pour faire répéter) again; **qu'est-ce que tu voulais, ~?** what did you want again?; **il a dit quoi, ~?** what did he say again?; **c'est combien, ~?** how much was it again?

déjanter /deʒɑ̃te/ [1] **I** *vtr* to remove [*pneu*].

II *vi* **1** [*conducteur*] to lose a tyre GB ou tire US; [*pneu*] to come off the rim; **2**○ (devenir fou) to be off one's trolley○; **il déjante complètement!** he's completely off his trolley○!

déjauger /deʒoʒe/ [13] *vi* Naut [*bateau*] to lift out of the water; [*voilier, hors-bord*] to plane; **~ de 12 centimètres** to lift by 12 centimetres[GB].

déjà-vu /deʒavy/ *nm inv* **1**○ **c'est du ~** we've seen it all before; **2** Psych déjà vu.

déjection /deʒɛksjɔ̃/ **I** *nf* Physiol (évacuation) excretion.

II déjections *nfpl* **1** Physiol (matières fécales) excrement ¢, dejecta (*pl*) spéc; **les ~s canines** dog excrement ¢; **2** Géol (de volcan) ejecta spéc.

déjeté, **~e** /deʒ(ə)te/ *adj* [*arbre, mur, personne*] lopsided; [*marche*] out of true; [*planche*] warped; [*colonne vertébrale*] twisted.

déjeuner /deʒœne/ [1] **I** *nm* **1** (repas de midi) lunch; **~ d'affaires/de travail/de famille** business/working/family lunch; **prendre son ~** to have lunch; **inviter qn pour le ~** to invite sb to lunch; **manger de la soupe au ~** or **pour le ~** to have soup for lunch; **c'est l'heure du ~** it's lunchtime; **le ~ est servi** lunch is ready; **à l'heure du ~** at lunchtime; **après ~** after lunch; **2** (le matin) B, C breakfast; **petit ~** breakfast; **3** (objet) breakfast cup and saucer.

II *vi* **1** (prendre le repas de midi) to have lunch; **inviter qn à ~** to invite sb for ou to lunch; **restez (à) ~** stay for ou to lunch; **venez ~ samedi** come and have lunch ou come to lunch on Saturday; **qu'est-ce que tu as eu à ~?** what did you have for lunch?; **~ d'un sandwich** to have a sandwich for lunch; **2** (le matin) dial, B, C to have breakfast.

III déjeuner(-) (*in compounds*) **~-concert** lunchtime concert; **~-conférence** lecture accompanied by lunch.

■ **~ sur l'herbe** picnic lunch.

déjouer /deʒwe/ [1] *vtr* to frustrate [*astuce, précaution*]; to foil [*plan, conspiration*]; to evade [*surveillance, contrôle*]; **~ les pièges de l'ennemi** to avoid the traps set by the enemy; **~ les manœuvres de qn** to outmanoeuvre sb.

déjuger: **se déjuger** /deʒyʒe/ [13] *vpr* fml to go back on one's decision.

delà /dəla/ *adv* **deçà, ~** here and there.

de-là /dəla/ *adv* ▶ **de-ci**.

délabré, ~e /delabʀe/ I *pp* ▶ **délabrer**.

II *pp adj* [*maison, équipement*] dilapidated; [*plafond, mur*] crumbling; [*vêtements*] ragged; fig [*santé, esprit*] damaged; [*affaires*] in a sorry state (*jamais épith*); [*fortune*] depleted.

délabrement /delabʀəmɑ̃/ *nm* (de maison, d'équipement) dilapidation; (de santé, pays, d'affaires, économie) poor state; (de fortune) depletion; (de vêtements) raggedness; (d'esprit) impairment; **état de ~** fig dilapidated state.

délabrer /delabʀe/ [1] I *vtr* to ruin [*maison, équipement, vêtement, santé, économie, pays*]; to deplete [*fortune*].

II **se délabrer** *vpr* **1** [*maison, équipement, économie*] to become run-down; [*affaires*] to go to rack and ruin; [*santé*] to deteriorate; **2 se ~ la santé/l'estomac** to ruin one's health/stomach.

délacer /delase/ [12] I *vtr* to undo [*chaussures*]; to unlace [*corsage, corset*]; **~ qn** to unlace sb.

II **se délacer** *vpr* [*chaussure*] to come undone; [*corsage*] to come unlaced.

délai /delɛ/ *nm* **1** (période accordée) period of time; (date limite) deadline, final date; **tu as un ~ de 10 jours pour payer** you have (a period of) 10 days in which to pay; **dans un ~ de 24 heures/6 mois** within 24 hours/6 months; **faire qch dans le ~ prescrit** to do sth within the allotted ou prescribed time; **rester dans les ~s** to meet the deadline; **les ~s sont trop courts** or **serrés** there isn't enough time; **à l'expiration de ce ~** when the allotted time expires, when the deadline is reached; **fixer un ~** to set a time limit, to fix a deadline; **respecter un ~** to stick to ou meet a deadline; **dernier ~ pour les inscriptions, mardi 2 mai** final date for registration, Tuesday 2 May; **2** (période d'attente) **abaisser** or **réduire** or **raccourcir un ~** to reduce ou shorten the waiting time; **le ~ moyen tourne autour de six mois** the average wait is about six months; **comptez trois semaines de ~ pour l'obtention d'un visa/pour la livraison** allow three weeks to get a visa/for delivery; **le ~ écoulé depuis la demande/commande** the time since the application was made/the order was placed; **dans les meilleurs** or **plus brefs ~s** as soon as possible; **sans ~** [*agir*] without delay, immediately; **demander le retrait sans ~ de l'armée** to demand the immediate withdrawal of the army; **3** (période supplémentaire) extension; **obtenir un ~** to get an extension; **demander/accorder un ~** to ask for extra ou more/grant extra time; **accorder un ~ à un débiteur** to allow a debtor (more) time to pay; **proroger un ~** to extend a deadline; **je t'accorde un ~ de dix jours** I'll give you ten days' grace.

■ **~ d'amortissement** payback period; **~ de grâce** grace period; **~ de livraison** delivery ou lead time (**pour qch** on sth); **~ de préavis** (period of) notice; **~ de réflexion** time to think; **~ de rétractation** Comm cooling-off period; **~ de rigueur** deadline.

délai-congé, *pl* **délais-congés** /delɛ kɔ̃ʒe/ *nm* (period of) notice.

délainage /delɛnaʒ/ *nm* fellmongering.

délainer /delene/ [1] *vtr* to remove the wool from.

délaissé, ~e /delese/ I *pp* ▶ **délaisser**.

II *pp adj* **1** (abandonné) [*épouse*] deserted; [*maîtresse, enfant, coutumes, profession, terres*] abandoned; **2** (négligé) [*personne, profession, méthodes*] neglected.

III *nm,f* **les ~s** those abandoned, those left behind; **les ~s du système scolaire** those whom the education system has left behind.

délaissement /delɛsmɑ̃/ *nm* sout **1** (action) abandonment; **2** (état) state of neglect ou abandonment; **être dans un état de ~ complet** to be completely neglected; **3** Jur (de bien, droit) relinquishment.

■ **~ d'enfant** Jur child neglect.

délaisser /delese/ [1] *vtr* **1** (abandonner) to leave [*épouse, mari*]; to abandon [*lieu, activité*]; **2** (négliger) to neglect [*amis, études*]; **3** Jur to relinquish [*bien, droit*].

délassant, ~e /delɑsɑ̃, ɑ̃t/ *adj* [*bain, activité physique*] relaxing; [*film, loisir*] entertaining.

délassement /delɑsmɑ̃/ *nm* **1** (repos) relaxation; **un lieu de ~** a place for relaxation; **2** (loisir) means of relaxation; **c'est mon ~ préféré** it's my favourite[GB] way of relaxing.

délasser /delɑse/ [1] I *vtr* [*bain*] to relax [*corps*]; [*lecture*] to relax; **cela m'a délassé de faire** I feel more relaxed after doing; **c'est un film qui délasse** it's an entertaining film.

II **se délasser** *vpr* to relax (**en faisant** by doing).

délateur, -trice /delatœʀ, tʀis/ I *adj* **encourager les pratiques délatrices** to encourage informing.

II *nm,f* informer.

délation /delɑsjɔ̃/ *nf* denunciation, informing; **incitations à la ~** encouragement to inform on others; **vivre dans un climat de ~** to live in constant fear of informers.

délavage /delavaʒ/ *nm* **1** (de tissu) fading; (de couleur) watering down; **2** (de terres) waterlogging.

délavé, ~e /delave/ I *pp* ▶ **délaver**.

II *pp adj* **1** (décoloré) [*couleur, ciel*] washed-out; [*jean, affiche*] faded; **2** (imprégné d'eau) [*terre*] waterlogged.

délaver /delave/ [1] *vtr* **1** to water down [*couleur*]; to put a wash on [*aquarelle*]; to fade [*jean, tissu*]; **2** to saturate [*terre*].

Delaware /dəlawɛʀ/ ▶ **692** *nprm* Delaware.

délayage /delɛjaʒ/ *nm* **1** (de peinture, liquide) thinning (**avec** with); (de farine, poudre) mixing (**dans** with); **2**○ péj waffle○; **faire du ~** to waffle○.

délayer /deleje/ [21] *vtr* **1** (diluer) to thin [sth] down, to dilute [*peinture, liquide*] (**avec** with); to mix [*farine*] (**dans** with); **2** (trop étirer) to drag [sth] out [*idées, pensée*]; **un rapport trop délayé** a waffling report○.

delco® /dɛlko/ *nm* Aut distributor; ▶ **tête**.

deleatur /deleatyʀ/ *nm inv* dele.

délébile /delebil/ *adj* washable.

délectable /delɛktabl/ *adj* [*nourriture, vin*] delicious, delectable sout; [*endroit, histoire*] delightful.

délectation /delɛktasjɔ̃/ *nf* liter **1** (plaisir) delight, delectation; **manger/boire avec ~** to eat/to drink with relish; **lire/écouter avec ~** to read/to listen rapturously ou with delight; **2** Relig ecstasy, rapture.

délecter: **se délecter** /delɛkte/ [1] *vpr* liter **se ~ à faire/en faisant** to delight in doing; **se ~ de** to enjoy [sth] thoroughly [*lecture, spectacle*]; to enjoy [sth] thoroughly, to relish [*poires, vin*]; **se ~ à l'avance de qch** to be thoroughly looking forward to sth; **se ~ à la pensée/l'idée de faire** to relish the thought/the idea of doing; **se ~ en apprenant que les résultats sont bons** to be delighted to hear that the results are good.

délégant, ~e /delegɑ̃, ɑ̃t/ *nm,f* Jur principal.

délégataire /delegatɛʀ/ *nmf* Jur agent.

délégation /delegasjɔ̃/ *nf* **1** (groupe de personnes) delegation (**auprès de** to); **~ d'étudiants** student delegation; **aller voir qn en ~** to form a delegation to go and see sb; **2** Jur, Admin authority; **agir en vertu d'une/signer par ~** to act/sign on sb's authority; **recevoir ~ (de qn) pour faire qch** to be authorized to do sth (by sb); **3** (transmission) delegation (**à qn** to sb); **~ de fonctions/pouvoirs** delegation of duties/power.

■ **~ de créance** Jur assignment of debt; **Délégation générale pour l'armement, DGA** *state organization supervising the manufacture and sale of armaments.*

délégué, ~e /delege/ I *pp* ▶ **déléguer**.

II *pp adj* [*administrateur, directeur*] acting (*épith*); **~ à qch** [*adjoint, conseiller*] responsible for sth.

III *nm,f* **1** (à conférence, réunion) delegate; **2** Entr, Admin (responsable) director.

■ **~ de classe** Scol student representative; **~ commercial** sales representative; **~ du personnel** workers' representative; **~ syndical** union representative.

déléguer /delege/ [14] *vtr* **1** (charger d'une mission) to appoint [sb] as a delegate (**auprès de qn** to sb); **~ qn à un congrès** to appoint sb as a delegate to a congress; **2** (transmettre) to delegate [*autorité, responsabilités*] (**à qn** to sb).

délestage /delɛstaʒ/ *nm* **1** (de navire, d'aérostat) unloading of the ballast; **2** (d'axe routier) diversion (*to relieve a road of heavy traffic*); **3** Électrotech power cut; **effectuer un ~** to interrupt the power supply.

délester /delɛste/ [1] I *vtr* **1** (alléger) to get rid of the ballast from [*navire, aérostat*]; **~ un véhicule de six sacs** to take six bags out of a vehicle; **2** (décongestionner) to divert traffic away from [*autoroute, voie*]; **3** (voler) [*voleur*] to relieve (**de** of); **4** Électrotech to interrupt the power supply to.

II **se délester** *vpr* **se ~ de** [*personne*] to get rid of [*bagages*]; to off-load [*responsabilité*] (**sur** onto); [*avion, aérostat*] (lâcher) to release [*bombe*]; (en cas de danger) to jettison [*cargaison, bagages*].

délétère /deletɛʀ/ *adj* fml **1** (nocif) [*gaz, vapeur*] noxious, toxic; **2** (néfaste) [*effet, doctrine, influence*] harmful, deleterious sout.

délétion /delesjɔ̃/ *nf* deletion (**de** of).

Delhi /deli/ ▶ **857** *npr* Delhi.

déliasser /deljase/ [1] *vtr* Ordinat to decollate.

délibérant, ~e /delibeʀɑ̃, ɑ̃t/ *adj* [*assemblée, comité*] deliberative.

délibératif, -ive /delibeʀatif, iv/ *adj* **avoir/avec voix délibérative** Jur to have/with voting powers.

délibération /delibeʀasjɔ̃/ *nf* **1** (discussion) deliberation; **par** or **sur ~ de** after deliberation by; **être en ~** [*jury*] to be deliberating; **mettre qch en ~** to debate sth; **2** (décision) decision; **prendre/annuler une ~** to make/to quash a decision; **3** fml (réflexion) deliberation.

délibéré, ~e /delibeʀe/ I *pp* ▶ **délibérer**.

II *pp adj* **1** (intentionnel) [*acte, pression, violation*] deliberate; **de propos ~** deliberately, on purpose; **2** (résolu) [*choix, volonté, politique*] conscious.

III *nm* Jur deliberation.

délibérément /delibeʀemɑ̃/ *adv* **1** (intentionnellement) [*ignorer, blesser, provoquer*] deliberately; **2** (résolument) [*accepter, choisir*] consciously.

délibérer /delibeʀe/ [14] I **délibérer de** or **sur** *vtr ind* (discuter de) to discuss [*affaire, question*].

II *vi* **1** (tenir conseil) [*jurés, assemblée*] to deliberate; **2** (réfléchir) fml to deliberate, to ponder.

délicat, ~e /delika, at/ I *adj* **1** (fin, subtil) gén delicate; **2** (raffiné) [*mets, manières*] delicate, dainty; [*palais*] discriminating; [*personne*] refined; **3** (plein de tact) tactful; (attentionné) thoughtful; **avoir un geste ~**

pour or **envers qn** to do something thoughtful for sb; **quelle attention ~e!** what a kind thought!; **un homme peu ~ en affaires** a man with few business scruples; **des procédés peu ~s** unscrupulous means; **4** (complexe, difficile) [*équilibre, négociations, tâche*] delicate; [*domaine, affaire, secteur, dossier, point, moment*] sensitive; [*mission, manœuvre*] tricky; **il est ~ pour lui de faire** it's tricky for him to do; **la tâche est ~e** it's a delicate task; **5** (fragile) [*peau*] delicate, sensitive; [*mécanisme, dispositif, instrument*] delicate; [*estomac*] sensitive; **elle est de santé ~e** she's delicate; **6** pej (tatillon) [*personne*] **elle est très ~e sur la nourriture** she's very fussy about her food; **vous êtes bien ~!** (pour choisir) how fussy GB ou picky US you are!; **7** (chaste) [*oreille*] sensitive.
II *nm,f* (tatillon) pej fusspot○ GB, fussbudget; **faire le ~** to be fussy.

délicatement /delikatmɑ̃/ *adv* **1** (avec finesse, subtilité) [*dessiner, graver, sculpter*] finely, delicately; [*parfumer*] delicately; **2** (avec légèreté) [*appuyer, caresser, saisir*] delicately.

délicatesse /delikatɛs/ *nf* **1** (de saveur, coloris, parfum, sentiments) delicacy; (de dentelle) fineness; **la ~ de ses traits** his/her delicate features; **une œuvre sans ~** a crude piece of work; **un style sans ~** a coarse style; **2** (fragilité) gén delicacy; (de peau) sensitivity; **3** (tact) delicacy; **manquer de ~** to be heavy-handed; **ne pas poser une question par ~** to tactfully refrain from asking a question; **il a eu la ~ de ne pas poser la question** he was tactful enough not to ask; **montrer de la ~ à l'égard de qn** to show kindness and consideration to sb; **4** (complexité, difficulté) (d'opération, de négociations) delicacy; (de problème, cas, situation) trickiness; **un problème/une situation d'une grande ~** a very delicate problem/situation; **5** (précaution) **manipuler qch avec ~** to handle sth with care; **6** (attention) **avoir des ~s pour qn** to be very attentive to sb.
IDIOMES **être en ~ avec qn** to be at odds with sb.

délice /delis/ **I** *nm* delight; **avec ~** with delight; **quel ~ de vivre ici!** what a delight to live here!; **un vrai ~ ton poulet** your chicken is quite delicious.
II délices *nfpl* delights; **savourer les ~s de** to savour[GB] the delights of; **faire ses ~s de qch** to delight in sth; **faire les ~s de qn** [*humour, campagne, activité*] to delight sb; **ton cadeau/le disque a fait les ~s de papa** Daddy was delighted with your present/the record.

délicieusement /delisjøzmɑ̃/ *adv* gén delightfully; (au goût) deliciously; **~ parfumé** [*bain, drap*] delightfully perfumed; [*fruit*] sweet-smelling (*épith*).

délicieux, -ieuse /delisjø, øz/ *adj* [*repas, goût, odeur, frisson*] delicious; [*sensation, endroit, humour, souvenir, musique*] delightful; [*joie*] exquisite; [*personne*] sweet; **il fait un temps ~** the weather is really lovely.

délictueux, -euse /deliktɥø, øz/ *adj* [*acte*] criminal.

délié, ~e /delje/ **I** *pp* ▶ **délier**.
II *pp adj* **1** [*taille*] slender; **2** [*foulée, mouvement*] loose; **3** liter [*esprit*] nimble.
III *nm* (en calligraphie) upstroke.
IDIOMES **avoir la langue ~e** to have the gift of the gab○.

délier /delje/ [2] **I** *vtr* **1** (dégager d'un lien) to untie [*personne, gerbe*]; **~ les poignets de qn** to untie sb's wrists; **2** (dénouer) to untie [*lacet, ruban*]; **3** (assouplir) to loosen up [*doigt, jambes*]; **4** (relever) **~ qn de** to release sb from [*promesse, serment*]; **5** Relig to absolve [*pécheur*] (**de** from).
II se délier *vpr* **1** (se dégager) [*prisonnier*] to untie oneself; **il se délia les chevilles** he untied his ankles; **2** (se dénouer) [*lacet*] to come undone; **3** (s'assouplir) **se ~ les doigts** to loosen up one's fingers; **4** (se libérer) **se ~ de** to release oneself from [*obligation, serment, promesse*].
IDIOMES **sans bourse ~** without paying a penny; **~ la langue à qn** to loosen sb's tongue; **les langues se délient** people start talking.

délimitation /delimitasjɔ̃/ *nf* **1** (fait de délimiter) demarcation (**de** of); **2** (frontière) demarcation, boundary (**entre** between).

délimiter /delimite/ [1] *vtr* **1** (déterminer les limites de) [*géomètre*] to demarcate, to delimit [*terrain*]; [*clôture*] to mark the boundary of [*domaine*]; [*montagnes*] to form the boundary of [*pays*]; **2** (définir) [*traité*] to set out [*frontière*] (**entre** between); to define [*rôle, tâches*]; to define the scope of [*sujet, question*]; to define [*idées, paragraphes*]; to circumscribe [*champ d'action*]; **3** Ordinat to delimit.

délinquance /delɛ̃kɑ̃s/ *nf* crime; **la petite ~** petty crime; **la ~ en col blanc** white-collar crime; **~ informatique** computer crime; **la ~ juvénile** juvenile delinquency.

délinquant, ~e /delɛ̃kɑ̃, ɑ̃t/ **I** *adj* delinquent; **la jeunesse/l'enfance ~e** juvenile/child delinquents (*pl*) ou offenders (*pl*).
II *nm,f* delinquent; **un petit ~** a petty criminal.
■ **~ primaire** first offender.

déliquescence /delikesɑ̃s/ *nf* **1** (décomposition) decline (**de** of); **société en ~** society in decline; **être en pleine ~** to be in rapid decline, to be declining rapidly; **2** Chimie deliquescence (**de** of).

déliquescent, ~e /delikesɑ̃, ɑ̃t/ *adj* [*mœurs*] declining; [*style*] lifeless; [*esprit*] failing; [*industrie*] in decline (*après n*).

délirant, ~e /delirɑ̃, ɑ̃t/ *adj* **1** (exubérant) [*accueil, enthousiasme, foule*] delirious; **2**○ (loufoque) [*personne*] nutty○; [*scénario, soirée*] surreal○, wild○; **3** (déraisonnable) [*prix*] outrageous; **4** Méd [*personne, état*] delirious.

délire /delir/ *nm* **1** Méd, Psych delirium; **fièvre accompagnée de ~** fever accompanied by delirium; **en proie au ~** suffering from delirium; **~ obsessionnel** obsessive-compulsive disorder, OCD; **2**○ (folie) madness; **travailler autant, c'est du ~!** it's madness to work that hard; **sur la route hier c'était le ~** it was sheer madness on the road yesterday; **la soirée de Max c'était le ~!** (c'était génial) Max's party was fantastic○; (c'était atroce) Max's party was a nightmare○; **3** (enthousiasme exubérant) frenzy; **au troisième but ce fut le ~** at the third goal the crowd went wild; **foule/salle en ~** crowd/audience in raptures; **4** (frénésie) frenzy; **~ verbal** verbal excess.

délirer /delire/ [1] *vi* **1** Méd to be delirious; **la fièvre le fait ~** the fever is making him delirious; **2**○ fig to be off one's rocker○.

delirium tremens /delirjɔmtremɛ̃s/ *nm inv* delirium tremens.

délit /deli/ *nm* offence[GB]; **~ civil/pénal** civil/criminal offence[GB]; **commettre un ~** to commit an offence[GB]; ▶ **flagrant**.
■ **~ de fuite** failure to report an accident Jur, hit-and-run offence[GB]; **~ d'initié** Fin insider trading; **~ d'opinion** *expression of opinion contrary to that of the ruling party*; **~ de presse** *violation of the laws governing the press.*

déliter: **se déliter** /delite/ [1] *vpr* **1** lit [*roche*] to flake; **2** fig [*groupe*] to fall apart.

délivrance /delivrɑ̃s/ *nf* **1** (soulagement) relief; **quelle ~ de quitter ce pays!** what a relief it is to leave this country!; **la mort fut pour elle une ~** her death was a merciful release; **2** (remise) (de certificat, brevet, passeport) issue; (de diplôme, prix) award; (de marchandises) delivery; (d'ordonnance) issue; **3** Méd, Vét (expulsion du placenta) delivery; (accouchement) liter delivery.

délivrer /delivre/ [1] **I** *vtr* **1** (libérer) to free [*captif, otage*]; to liberate [*pays, peuple*]; **~ qn de** to free sb from [*chaînes*]; to release sb from [*obligation*]; to relieve sb from [*angoisse, obsession*]; **~ qn de qn** liter to free sb from sb; **vous me délivrez d'un grand poids** you have taken a great weight off my shoulders; **délivre-nous du mal** Relig deliver us from evil; **2** (remettre) to issue [*certificat, brevet, passeport*]; to award [*diplôme, prix*]; to deliver [*marchandises*]; to issue [*ordonnance, reçu*]; **3** (dispenser) [*hôpital*] to provide [*soins*].
II se délivrer *vpr* **1** (se libérer) [*captif, otage*] to free oneself; **se ~ de qch** to free oneself from [*chaînes, obligation*]; to rid oneself of [*angoisse, obsession*]; **le pays s'est délivré du joug de l'occupant** the country threw off the occupier's yoke; **2** (être remis) [*document*] to be issued.

délocalisation /delɔkalizasjɔ̃/ *nf* **1** (d'administration) relocation (**de** of); **~ industrielle** relocation of industry (*in search of cheap labour*); **2** (de capitaux) relocation.

délocaliser /delɔkalize/ [1] *vtr* to delocalize.

déloger /delɔʒe/ [13] *vtr* **1** (chasser d'un logement) to evict (**de** from); **2** (d'une position) to shift (**de** from); **3** Mil to flush out [*rebelles*]; **4**○ (enlever) to remove [*poussière*]; **5** Chasse to flush out [*gibier*].

déloyal, ~e, *mpl* **-aux** /delwajal, o/ *adj* **1** (perfide) [*ami, collègue*] disloyal (**envers** to, toward, towards GB); [*concurrence*] unfair; [*acte, conduite, méthode, procédé*] underhand; **agir de manière ~e** to act in an underhand manner; **2** Sport **un coup ~** a foul; **porter un coup ~ à son adversaire** to foul one's opponent.

déloyalement /delwajalmɑ̃/ *adv* disloyally.

déloyauté /delwajote/ *nf* fml disloyalty (**à l'égard de, envers** to, toward, towards GB); (de concurrent) unfairness; **faire acte de ~** to be disloyal.

Delphes /dɛlf/ ▶ **857** *npr* Delphi.

delphinarium /dɛlfinarjɔm/ *nm* dolphinarium.

delphinium /dɛlfinjɔm/ *nm* delphinium.

delta /dɛlta/ *nm inv* **1** Math, Ling delta; **2** Géog delta; **le ~ du Rhône** the Rhône delta; **3** (forme) delta; **un avion à ailes ~** a delta-wing plane.

deltaplane /dɛltaplan/ ▶ **449** *nm* **1** (engin) hang-glider; **2** (activité) hang-gliding; **faire du ~** to go hang-gliding.

deltoïde /dɛltɔid/ *adj, nm* deltoid.

déluge /delyʒ/ *nm* **1** (pluie) downpour, deluge; **2** (profusion) (de coups, d'insultes) hail (**de** of); (de larmes, plaintes) flood (**de** of); (de mots) torrent (**de** of); (de compliments) shower (**de** of); (de fleurs) profusion; (de malheurs) spate (**de** of); **un ~ de malheurs s'est abattu sur eux** they had a spate of misfortunes.

Déluge /delyʒ/ *nm* **le ~** the Flood, the Deluge.
IDIOMES **ça remonte au ~** it goes back to the year dot ou one; **après moi le ~** I don't care what happens after I'm gone, après moi le déluge.

déluré, ~e /delyre/ **I** *pp* ▶ **délurer**.
II *pp adj* **1** (dégourdi) knowing; **il n'est pas très ~** he's not very smart; **2** (effronté) forward; péj fast (*jamais épith*).

délurer /delyre/ [1] **I** *vtr* **1** (dégourdir) to wake [sb] up a bit GB, to wise [sb] up○ US; **2** (dévergonder) to lead [sb] astray.
II se délurer *vpr* **1** (se dégourdir) to shake one's ideas up a bit GB, to wise up; **2** (se dévergonder) to run wild.

délustrer /delystre/ [1] *vtr* to remove the shine from [*vêtement*].

démagnétisation /demaɲetizasjɔ̃/ *nf* demagnetization.

démagnétiser /demaɲetize/ [1] *vtr* Phys to demagnetize.

démagogie /demagɔʒi/ *nf* gén popularity seeking; (électoraliste) electioneering, demagogy sout; **faire de la ~** to try to gain popularity.

démagogique /demagɔʒik/ *adj* gén

popularity-seeking (*épith*); (en politique) electioneering (*épith*).

démagogue /demagɔg/ *nmf* popularity-seeker, demagogue sout.

démailler /demaje/ [1] **I** *vtr* **1** to unravel [*tricot*]; to ladder, run [*bas*]; **2** Naut to unshackle [*ancre*]; Pêche to disentangle [*poisson*].

II se démailler *vpr* [*tricot*] to unravel; [*bas*] to ladder, to run.

démailloter /demajɔte/ [1] *vtr* to unswaddle.

demain /dəmɛ̃/ **I** *adv* **1** (dans un jour) tomorrow; **~ matin/soir** tomorrow morning/evening; **~ toute la journée** all day tomorrow; **~ en huit/en quinze** a week/two weeks tomorrow; **à partir** or **dater de ~** as from tomorrow; **ce sera fait dès ~** it will be done first thing tomorrow; **2** (dans l'avenir) tomorrow; **~ tout peut arriver** anything could happen tomorrow; **~ l'homme pourra vivre sur la lune** one day man will be able to live on the moon.

II *nm* **1** (jour suivant) tomorrow; **dans le journal de ~** in tomorrow's newspaper; **à ~!** see you tomorrow; **d'ici (à) ~ tout peut changer** by tomorrow things might look very different; **2** (avenir) tomorrow; **de quoi ~ sera-t-il fait?** who knows what tomorrow may bring?; **le monde/la jeunesse de ~** the world/the youth of tomorrow; **la voiture/la société/l'Europe de ~** the car/the society/the Europe of the future.

IDIOMES **~ il fera jour** tomorrow is another day; **ce n'est pas ~ la veille!** that's not going to happen in a hurry!; **il ne faut pas remettre à ~ ce que l'on peut faire aujourd'hui** Prov never put off till tomorrow what can be done today.

démanché, **~e** /demɑ̃ʃe/ **I** *pp* ▶**démancher**.

II *pp adj* **1** (sans manche) without a handle (*épith, après n*); **des outils ~s** tools without handles; **le balai/couteau est ~** the handle has come off the broom/knife; **2**○ (disloqué) [*membre, mâchoire*] dislocated.

démancher /demɑ̃ʃe/ [1] **I** *vtr* **1** (ôter le manche de) to take the handle off; **2**○ (disloquer) to dislocate [*membre, mâchoire*].

II se démancher *vpr* **1** (perdre son manche) to come off its handle; **mon balai s'est démanché** the head of my broom has come off its handle; **2**○ (se disloquer) [*membre, mâchoire*] to be dislocated; **il s'est démanché l'épaule au tennis** he dislocated his shoulder playing tennis.

demande /dəmɑ̃d/ *nf* **1** (sollicitation) request; **à la** or **sur (la) ~ de qn** at sb's request; **à la ~ générale** by popular request; **répondre à la ~ de qn** to grant sb's request; **2** (démarche) application; **les ~s de formation/d'abonnements sont nombreuses** there are many applications for training/subscriptions; **leur ~ d'adoption a été rejetée** their adoption application has been turned down; **les ~s (d'adhésion) peuvent se faire ici** applications (for membership) can be made here; **faire une ~ de mutation** to apply for a transfer; **gratuit sur (simple) ~** free on request; **remboursement sur simple ~ écrite** refund on written application; **3** Admin (formulaire) application form; **une ~ de passeport/d'inscription** a passport application/registration form; **envoyez votre ~ de bourse avant le 10 mai** send your grant application before 10 May; **4** Écon demand; **l'offre et la ~** supply and demand; **la ~ de logements** the demand for housing; **5** Assur, Jur **~ (en justice)** claim; **~ de dommages et intérêts** claim for damages; **~ de divorce** petition for divorce.

■ **~ d'asile** application for asylum; **faire une ~ d'asile** to apply for asylum; **~ d'emploi** (démarche) job application; **faire une ~ d'emploi** to apply for a job; **'~s d'emploi'** (rubrique) 'situations wanted'; **faire paraître une ~ d'emploi** to advertise in the situations wanted column; **~ d'extradition** extradition request; **faire une ~ d'extradition** to request extradition; **~ en mariage** marriage proposal; **faire une ~ en mariage à qn** to propose to sb.

demandé, **~e** /dəmɑ̃de/ **I** *pp* ▶**demander**.

II *pp adj* (recherché) **très/peu ~** [*destination, sport, personne*] very/not very popular; [*service, qualification, produit*] in great demand/not in great demand.

demander /dəmɑ̃de/ [1] **I** *vtr* **1** (solliciter) to ask for [*conseil, argent, aide, permission*]; **~ l'addition** or **la note** to ask for the bill GB ou check US; **~ la démission de qn** to ask for sb's resignation; **~ la parole** to ask for permission to speak; **~ de l'argent à qn** to ask sb for money; **~ des renforts** Mil to ask for reinforcements; fig to ask for support; **~ l'autorisation** or **la permission à qn** to ask sb's permission (**de faire** to do); **~ conseil à qn** to ask sb's advice; **~ le report/l'annulation de la réunion, ~ que la réunion soit reportée/annulée** to request that the meeting be postponed/cancelled[GB]; **il a demandé que tout le monde assiste à la réunion** he asked everybody to attend the meeting; **~ que le travail soit terminé** to ask for the work to be completed; **~ l'asile politique** to apply for political asylum; **~ la libération/condamnation de qn** to call for sb's release/conviction; **le policier m'a demandé mes papiers** the policeman asked to see my papers; **~ la main de qn** to ask for sb's hand; **~ qn en mariage** to propose to sb; **'le numéro que vous demandez n'est plus en service'** 'the number you have dialled[GB] is unobtainable'; **on demande un plombier/ingénieur** (dans une offre d'emploi) plumber/engineer required GB ou wanted; **elle a demandé à rester/sortir** she asked if she could stay/go out; **~ à rencontrer qn** to ask to meet sb; ▶**reste**; **2** (enjoindre) **~ à qn de faire** to ask sb to do; **nous vous demandons de ne pas fumer/prendre de photos** may we ask you not to smoke/take photographs; **on a demandé aux spectateurs de rester calme** the audience was told to stay calm; **fais ce qu'on te demande!** do as you're told!; **tout ce que je te demande c'est de faire un effort** all I ask is that you make an effort; **3** (souhaiter) **il demande beaucoup de son personnel** he expects a lot of his staff; **il n'en demandait pas tant** he didn't expect all that; **je/il ne demande pas mieux que de partir** there's nothing I/he would like better than to go; **aller au théâtre? je ne demande pas mieux!** go to the theatre[GB]? I'd love to!; **les aider? mais je ne demande pas mieux** help them? but I'd be delighted to; **je ne demande que ça!** that's exactly what I want!; **il ne demande qu'à travailler/te croire** he'd really like to work/to believe you; **je demande à voir**○ that'll be the day○; **il ne faut pas trop leur en ~** you mustn't expect too much of them; **4** (interroger sur) **~ qch à qn** to ask sb sth; **~ son chemin (à qn)** to ask (sb) the way; **~ l'heure** to ask the time; **il m'a demandé de tes nouvelles** he asked me how you were getting on GB ou along; **demande-lui son nom** ask him/her his name/her name; **~ à qn comment/pourquoi/si** to ask sb how/why/whether; **j'ai demandé à Paul s'il viendrait** I asked Paul if he was coming; **demande-lui comment il a fait** ask him how he did it; **'est-il parti?' demanda-t-il** 'has he left?' he asked; **je ne t'ai rien demandé**○**!** I wasn't talking to you!; **de qui se moque-t-on, je vous le demande**○**!** what do they think they're playing at?, I ask you! GB; **5** (faire venir) to send for [*médecin, prêtre*]; **'un vendeur est demandé à l'accueil'** 'would a salesman please come to the reception'; **le patron vous demande** (dans son bureau) the boss wants to see you ou is asking for you; (au téléphone) the boss wants to speak to you; **on vous demande au parloir/téléphone** you're wanted in the visitors' room/on the phone; **6** (nécessiter) [*travail, tâche*] to require [*effort, attention, qualification*]; [*plante, animal*] to need [*attention*]; **le tennis demande une grande énergie/concentration** tennis requires a lot of energy/concentration; **mon travail demande une attention constante/une formation spécifique** my work requires total concentration/special training; **~ à être revu/discuté/approfondi** [*sujet, texte*] to need revision/discussion/more in-depth treatment; **7** Jur [*tribunal*] to call for [*peine, expertise*]; [*personne*] to sue ou ask for [*divorce*]; to sue for [*dommages-intérêts*]; **elle a décidé de ~ le divorce/des dommages-intérêts** she's decided to sue for divorce/damages.

II se demander *vpr* **1** (s'interroger) **se ~ si/pourquoi/comment/où/ce que** to wonder whether/why/how/where/what; **il se demande quel sera son prochain travail** he wonders what his next job will be; **je me demande ce qu'elle a bien pu devenir** I wonder what on earth○ became of her; **'tu crois qu'elle l'a fait exprès?'—'je me demande'** 'do you think she did it on purpose?'—'I wonder'; **c'est à se ~ si le bonheur existe** it makes you wonder whether there's such a thing as happiness; **tu ne t'es jamais demandé pourquoi?** have you ever wondered why ou asked yourself why?; **2** (être demandé) **ce genre de choses ne se demande pas** it's not the kind of thing you ask; **cela ne se demande même pas!** (c'est évident) what a stupid question!

demandeur[1], **-euse** /dəmɑ̃dœʀ, øz/ *nm,f* **1** gén, Admin applicant; **les couples ~s d'adoption** couples applying for adoption; **2** Comm, Écon **le pays est très ~ de biens de consommation/matières premières** consumer goods/raw materials are very much in demand in the country.

■ **~ d'asile** asylum-seeker; **~ d'emploi** job-seeker; **le nombre de ~s d'emploi a doublé** the number of people looking for work has doubled; **~ de visa** visa applicant.

demandeur[2], **-eresse** /dəmɑ̃dœʀ, d(ə)ʀɛs/ *nm,f* Jur plaintiff.

démangeaison /demɑ̃ʒɛzɔ̃/ *nf* **1** (irritation) itch ¢; **les piqûres de moustiques provoquent des ~s** mosquito-bites cause itching; **avoir des ~s** to be itching; **j'ai des ~s dans le pied** my foot is itching; **2**○ fig (envie) **avoir une ~ de faire** to be itching to do○.

démanger /demɑ̃ʒe/ [13] *vtr* **1** lit (irriter) **ça me/le démange** I'm/he's itchy; **ça me/le démange de partout** I'm/he's itching all over; **ça te démange beaucoup?** is it itching a lot?; **sa jambe/brûlure le démange terriblement** his leg/burn is itching terribly; **ça me/le démange à la jambe** my/his leg is itching; **2** fig **ça me/le démange de faire** I'm/he's itching to do; **l'envie de le gifler me démangeait** I was itching to slap him; **quand elle entend des choses pareilles la main lui démange**○ when she hears things like that she feels like hitting somebody.

IDIOMES **gratter qn où ça le démange** to butter sb up○.

démantèlement /demɑ̃tɛlmɑ̃/ *nm* (de laboratoire, service) dismantling (**de** of); (de forces nucléaires) destruction; **le ~ du gang a pris plusieurs mois** it took several months to smash the gang.

démanteler /demɑ̃tle/ [17] *vtr* to dismantle [*institution, armes, barricades, frontières*]; to break up [*gang*].

démantibuler○ /demɑ̃tibyle/ [1] **I** *vtr* to bust○, to break up [*meuble*].

II se démantibuler *vpr* [*meuble*] to fall to pieces.

démaquillage /demakijaʒ/ *nm* make-up removal.

démaquillant, **~e** /demakijɑ̃, ɑ̃t/ **I** *adj* [*lait, gel*] cleansing (*épith*).
II *nm* make-up remover; **~ pour les yeux** eye make-up remover.

démaquiller /demakije/ [1] **I** *vtr* to remove make-up from; **~ qn** to remove sb's make-up.
II se démaquiller *vpr* to remove one's make-up; **se ~ les yeux** to remove one's eye make-up.

démarcatif, **-ive** /demaʀkatif, iv/ *adj* Ling demarcative.

démarcation /demaʀkasjɔ̃/ *nf* demarcation (**de** of; **entre** between).

démarchage /demaʀʃaʒ/ *nm* door-to-door selling; **~ électoral** canvassing; **~ téléphonique** cold calling.

démarche /demaʀʃ/ *nf* **1** (allure) walk; **~ bizarre** funny walk; **avoir une ~ assurée/lourde** to walk with a confident/heavy step; **avoir une ~ de canard** to waddle like a duck; **2** (tentative) step; **mes ~s pour adopter un enfant** the steps I took to adopt a child; **sa ~ auprès du ministre a abouti** the approaches he made to the minister were successful; **entreprendre des ~s auprès de qn** to apply to sb; **faire** or **tenter une ~ auprès de qn** to approach sb; **faire des ~s pour obtenir qch** to take steps to obtain sth; **multiplier les ~s pour sauvegarder la paix** to step up peace initiatives; **~ commune** or **collective** joint representation (**auprès de** to); **les ~s nécessaires** the appropriate steps; **aider qn dans ses ~s auprès de l'administration** to help sb deal with officialdom; **plusieurs ~s sont possibles** there are several possible courses of action; **les ~s à effectuer sont les suivantes** the correct procedure is as follows; **3** (attitude) approach; **la ~ homéopathique** the homœopathic approach; **4** (raisonnement) reasoning; (évolution) **~ de la pensée/du raisonnement** thought/reasoning process; **analyser la ~ par laquelle l'enfant apprend à parler** to analyse the process by which a child learns to speak; **~ de l'analyse** analytical methodology.
■ **~ qualité** Entr total quality control.

démarcher /demaʀʃe/ [1] *vtr* **1** (vendre) to sell [sth] door-to-door [*produit*]; **2** (solliciter) to canvass [*client, entreprise*].

démarcheur, **-euse** /demaʀʃœʀ, øz/ *nm,f* (door-to-door) salesman.

démarquage /demaʀkaʒ/ *nm* **1** Comm (d'article) marking down (**de** of); **'~ de tous nos appareils ménagers'** 'all household appliances marked down'; **2** (fait de se distinguer) **on observe un ~ de plus en plus net entre les deux candidats** one can see an increasingly clear distinction between the two candidates.

démarque /demaʀk/ *nf* (de marchandises) mark-down (**de** of).

démarquer /demaʀke/ [1] **I** *vtr* **1** (rendre anonyme) **~ un article** to remove the designer's label from an item (*so as to lower the price*); **2** (solder) to mark down [*marchandises*]; **3** Sport to free [sb] from a marker.
II se démarquer *vpr* **1** (se distinguer) **se ~ de qn/qch** to distance oneself from sb/sth; **2** Sport to get free of one's marker, to shake off one's marker.

démarrage /demaʀaʒ/ *nm* **1** (de moteur) starting up; **le ~ est parfois difficile** the car is sometimes difficult to start; **j'ai peur de caler au ~** I'm afraid of stalling as I pull away; **2** (d'activité, d'entreprise) starting up (**de** of); **le ~ de ce film/cette affaire/cet élève est assez lent** this film/business/pupil has made a rather slow start; **le ~ de l'économie a eu lieu dans les années 60** the economy began to take off in the 60's; **3** (en course à pied) spurt, burst of speed.
■ **~ en côte** hill start.

démarrer /demaʀe/ [1] **I** *vtr* **1** (mettre en marche) to start (up) [*moteur, véhicule*]; **2** (débuter) to start [*roman, tableau, émission*]; to get [sth] off the ground [*campagne électorale, projet*].
II *vi* **1** (se mettre en marche) [*véhicule*] to pull away; [*moteur*] to start; **2** (mettre en marche) [*chauffeur*] to drive off, pull away; **3** (débuter) [*affaire, entreprise*] to start up; [*campagne électorale*] to get under way; [*personne*] to start off; **~ dans les affaires** to start up in business; **faire ~ une affaire** to get a business off the ground; **bien/mal ~ en italien** to make a good/poor start in Italian; **4** (en course à pied) to put on a spurt.

démarreur /demaʀœʀ/ *nm* Aut starter.

démasquer /demaske/ [1] **I** *vtr* **1** (révéler) to unmask [*traître, malfaiteur*]; to expose [*hypocrisie, vice*]; to discover [*passage secret*]; to uncover [*complot, dessein*]; **2** (ôter le masque de) **~ qn** to remove sb's mask.
II se démasquer *vpr* **1** (se révéler) (involontairement) to betray oneself; (volontairement) to reveal oneself; **2** (ôter son masque) to remove one's mask.
IDIOMES **~ ses batteries** to show one's hand.

démâter /demɑte/ [1] **I** *vtr* [*équipage*] to unstep the mast of [*navire*]; [*tempête*] to dismast [*navire*].
II *vi* [*voilier*] to lose its mast.

dématérialisation /dematerjalizasjɔ̃/ *nf* Fin (de titres, valeurs) *phasing out of actual share certificates*.

démazouter /demazute/ [1] *vtr* to clean the oil from [*plage*].

démédicaliser /demedikalize/ [1] *vtr* to demedicalize, to stop treating [sth] as a medical problem [*naissance, mort*].

démêlage /demɛlaʒ/ *nm* **1** (de fils, pelote) disentangling; (de cheveux) untangling; (de fibres) carding; **2** (d'énigme, affaire) disentanglement.

démêlant, **~e** /demelɑ̃, ɑ̃t/ *adj* [*baume, shampooing*] detangling.

démêlé /demele/ *nm* wrangle; **il a eu un ~ avec son voisin à propos d'une clôture** he had a wrangle with his neighbour[GB] about a fence; **avoir des ~s avec le fisc/la justice** to get in trouble with the taxman/the law.

démêler /demele/ [1] **I** *vtr* **1** lit to disentangle [*fils, pelote*]; to untangle [*cheveux*]; **2** fig (éclaircir) to sort out [*affaire, situation*]; **~ le vrai du faux** to sort out truth from falsehood; **~ la part de responsabilité de chacun** to sort out everyone's responsibilities; **~ les fils d'une intrigue** to unravel the threads of a plot; **je n'arrive pas à ~ le sens du message** I can't make out what the message means.
II se démêler *vpr* **1** (être clarifié) [*situation*] to get sorted out; **2** (se dépêtrer) [*personne*] **se ~ de qch** to extricate oneself from sth.

démêloir /demelwaʀ/ *nm* wide-toothed comb.

démembrement /demɑ̃bʀəmɑ̃/ *nm* **1** (d'un pays, d'un trust) break-up (**de** of), dismantling (**de** of); **2** Agric division (**de** of).

démembrer /demɑ̃bʀe/ [1] *vtr* **1** (dépecer) to cut up, to joint [*animal*]; **2** (morceler) to divide up, to dismember [*domaine, empire*].

déménagement /demenaʒmɑ̃/ *nm* **1** (action de déménager) move; **c'est mon troisième ~** it's my third move; **ton ~ s'est bien passé?** did your move go well?; **mon ~ est prévu pour le 31** I'm moving house on the 31st; **2** (changement de domicile) moving house ¢; **~ à Paris** moving house to Paris; **nouveau ~** moving house again; **3** (changement de bureaux) relocation (**from** de; **à** to); **4** (transport) removal; (effets transportés) **mon ~ arrive demain** the removals firm is bringing my stuff tomorrow; **le ~ du piano** the removal of the piano; **~s internationaux** international removals; **compagnie** or **entreprise de ~s** removals firm GB, moving company US; **les ~s Solo** Solo Removals; **5** (action de vider) clearing ¢; **le ~ du salon** clearing the lounge.

déménager /demenaʒe/ [13] **I** *vtr* **1** (déplacer) to move [*meubles, livres*] (**de** out of); to relocate [*bureaux*] (**de** from; **à** to); **2** (vider) to clear [*pièce, bâtiment*].
II *vi* **1** (changer de domicile) to move house; **~ de Paris** to move from Paris; **~ à Oxford** to move to Oxford; **2** (changer de bureaux) to relocate; **3**○ (partir) to push off○, to leave; **faire ~** to turf [sb] out○ GB, to make [sb] leave [*personne*]; **4**○ (être fou) to be out to lunch○, to lose one's reason.
IDIOMES **~ à la cloche de bois** to do a moonlight flit GB.

déménageur, **-euse** /demenaʒœʀ, øz/ **I** ▶510 *nm,f* (ouvrier) removal GB ou moving US man/woman; (patron) furniture remover GB ou mover US; **épaules de ~** muscular shoulders; **avoir une carrure de ~** to be built like an ox.
II déménageuse *nf* H (camion) removal van.

démence /demɑ̃s/ *nf* madness, insanity; **avoir une crise de ~** to have a fit of madness; **plaider la ~** Jur to plead insanity.

démener: **se démener** /dem(ə)ne/ [16] *vpr* **1** (s'agiter) to thrash about; [*prisonnier*] to struggle; **l'animal se démène dans sa cage** the animal is running around like mad○ in its cage; **2** (se donner du mal) to put oneself out; **se ~ pour faire** to put oneself to some trouble to do, to do one's damnedest to do○; **elle se démène du matin au soir dans la maison** she slaves away in the house from morning till night; **j'ai beau me ~ je ne trouve pas d'emploi** however hard I try I can't find a job.
IDIOMES **se ~ comme un beau diable** (pour se libérer) to thrash about; (pour avoir qch) to do one's utmost.

dément, **~e** /demɑ̃, ɑ̃t/ **I** *adj* **1** (fou) mad, insane; **2**○ [*spectacle*] terrific○, fantastic○; [*événement*] amazing, incredible; [*prix*] outrageous.
II *nm,f* mentally ill person.

démenti /demɑ̃ti/ *nm* denial; **les faits ont apporté un ~ à ses déclarations** the facts proved his statements false; **cette rumeur est restée sans ~** the rumour[GB] has not been denied; **opposer un ~ formel à qch** to deny sth categorically.

démentiel, **-ielle** /demɑ̃sjɛl/ *adj* **1**○ [*inflation, rythme*] insane; [*prix*] outrageous; **2** Psych insane.

démentir /demɑ̃tiʀ/ [30] **I** *vtr* **1** (nier) to deny [*information, accusation, lien*]; **il dément l'avoir dit** he denies having said it; **sans ~ que** without denying that; **les autorités ont formellement démenti cette rumeur** the authorities have categorically denied this rumour[GB]; **2** (contredire) [*personne*] to refute [*propos, déclaration*]; [*fait*] to give the lie to [*propos, déclaration*]; to contradict [*point de vue, prévision*]; to belie [*apparence*].
II se démentir *vpr* to flag; **son intérêt pour cette cause ne s'est pas démenti un instant** his interest in this cause has never flagged for one moment; **un produit dont le succès ne s'est jamais démenti** an unfailingly successful product.

démerdard◑, **~e** /demɛʀdaʀ, aʀd/ **I** *adj* **il est ~/vraiment pas ~** he's a smart cookie/bloody useless◑.
II *nm,f* smart cookie○.

démerder◑: **se démerder** /demɛʀde/ [1] *vpr* **1** (se débrouiller) to manage; **se ~ pour faire** to manage to do; **se ~ pour obtenir qch** to wangle○ sth; **se ~ avec ses problèmes** to sort out one's own problems; **démerde-toi pour payer** sort the bill GB ou check US out yourself○; **il s'est démerdé pour trouver du travail** he managed to find a job; **2** (se dépêcher) **démerde-toi un peu!** get your arse GB ou ass US in gear◑!

démerdeur○, **-euse** /demɛʀdœʀ, øz/ = **démerdard, ~e**.

démérite /demeʀit/ *nm* liter fault; **il n'y a pas de ~ à agir ainsi** there is no shame in acting this way.

démériter /demeʀite/ [1] *vi* to prove oneself unworthy (**de** of); **~ auprès de** or **aux yeux de qn** to lose sb's respect.

démesure /deməzyʀ/ *nf* **1** (d'ambition, de prétentions) excesses (*pl*); **avoir horreur de la ~** to have a horror of excess; **2** (taille exagérée) excessive size.

démesuré, ~e /deməzyʀe/ *adj* **1** [*taille*] excessive; **d'une hauteur/largeur ~e** excessively high/wide; **2** [*orgueil, appétit*] immoderate; [*ambition*] excessive, inordinate.

démesurément /deməzyʀemɑ̃/ *adv* excessively, inordinately.

démettre /demɛtʀ/ [60] **I** *vtr* **1** (déboîter) **~ l'épaule de qn** to dislocate sb's shoulder, to put sb's shoulder out (of joint); **2** (révoquer) to dismiss [*personne*]; **~ qn de ses fonctions** to relieve sb of his/her duties; **3** Jur (débouter) **~ qn de son appel** to dismiss sb's appeal.
II se démettre *vpr* **1** (se déboîter) **il s'est démis l'épaule en tombant** he dislocated his shoulder when he fell; **2** (démissionner) to resign; **il s'est démis de son poste de président** he resigned his position as chairman.

demeurant: **au demeurant** /odəmœʀɑ̃/ *loc adv* in fact; **un brave homme au ~** a good chap all things considered.

demeure /dəmœʀ/ **I** *nf* **1** (habitation) residence; **une belle ~ du XIXe siècle** a beautiful 19th century residence; **~ ancestrale** ancestral home; ▶ **dernier**; **2** Jur **mettre qn en ~ de faire** gén to require sb to do; Jur to give sb formal notice to do; **se mettre en ~ de faire** to set oneself to doing; **mise en ~** gén demand; Jur formal notice (**de faire** to do).
II à demeure *loc adv* permanently.
IDIOMES **il n'y a pas péril en la ~** there's no rush.

demeuré, ~e /dəmœʀe/ **I** *adj* retarded.
II *nm,f* simpleton.

demeurer /dəmœʀe/ [1] *vi* **1** (résider) (+ *v avoir*) to reside; **demeurant à Paris/25 rue du Bac** residing in Paris/at 25 rue du Bac; **2** (rester) (+ *v être*) to remain; **il est demeuré sourd à nos supplications** he remained deaf to our entreaties; **~ comme un grand homme** to be remembered as a great man; **il n'en demeure pas moins que** nonetheless, the fact remains that.

demi, ~e /d(ə)mi/ ▶ **407** **I et demi, et demie** *loc adj* and a half; **trois et ~ pour cent** three and a half per cent; **trois kilos/jours et ~** three and a half kilos/days; **trois millions et ~ de dollars/victimes** three and a half million dollars/victims; **il est trois heures et ~e** it's half past three; ▶ **malin**.
II *nm,f* half; **cinq ~s** five halves; **un jambon entier, c'est trop, achètes-en un ~** a whole ham will be too much, just buy a half; **je ne veux pas une bouteille entière, vous avez des ~es?** I don't want a whole bottle, have you got any half-bottles?
III *nm* **1** (verre de bière) glass of beer, ≈ half-pint GB; **2** Sport half; **~ de mêlée** scrum half; **~ d'ouverture** stand-off half.
IV à demi *loc adv* half; **je ne suis qu'à ~ satisfait/convaincu/éveillé** I'm only half satisfied/convinced/awake; **elle ne fait pas les choses à ~** she doesn't do things by halves.
V demi- (*in compounds*) **1** (à moitié) half; **une ~-pomme** half an apple; **trois ~-pommes** three half apples; **2** (incomplet) partial; **un ~-succès** a qualified success; **nous n'avons obtenu qu'une ~-victoire** we only won a partial victory; **cela n'a été qu'une ~-surprise** it wasn't a total surprise.
VI demie *nf* (d'heure) half hour; **la ~e vient de sonner** the half hour has just struck; **l'horloge sonne les ~es** the clock strikes on the half hour; **il est déjà la ~e, dépêche-toi!** it's already half past, hurry up!

demi-arrêt, *pl* **~s** /d(ə)miaʀɛ/ *nm* Équit half halt.

demi-botte, *pl* **~s** /d(ə)mibɔt/ *nf* calf-length boot.

demi-bouteille, *pl* **~s** /d(ə)mibutɛj/ *nf* half-bottle.

demi-centre /d(ə)misɑ̃tʀ/ *nm* halfback.

demi-cercle, *pl* **~s** /d(ə)misɛʀkl/ *nm* semicircle; **placez-vous en ~** form a semicircle; **en ~** [*objet*] semicircular.

demi-colonne, *pl* **~s** /d(ə)mikɔlɔn/ *nf* Archit half-column.

demi-deuil, *pl* **~s** /d(ə)midœj/ *nm* **1** (rituel) half-mourning; **une robe ~** a half-mourning dress; **se mettre en ~** to go into half-mourning; **2** Culin demi-deuil (*served with truffles and white sauce*).

demi-dieu, *pl* **~x** /d(ə)midjø/ *nm* demigod.

demi-douzaine, *pl* **~s** /d(ə)miduzɛn/ *nf* **1** (six) half a dozen; **une ~ d'œufs** half a dozen eggs; **une ~ d'œufs coûte 10 francs** half a dozen eggs cost 10 francs; **sa dernière ~ d'œufs** his/her last half-dozen eggs; **2** (environ six) half a dozen or so, about half a dozen; **une ~ de personnes étaient déjà là** about half a dozen people were already there; **la ~ de personnes qui restaient** the last half-dozen people; ▶ **cinquantaine 1**.

demi-droite, *pl* **~s** /d(ə)midʀwat/ *nf* half-line.

demi-échec /d(ə)mieʃɛk/ *nm* partial failure.

demi-écrémé, ~e, *mpl* **~s** /d(ə)miekʀeme/ *adj* semi-skimmed.

demi-finale, *pl* **~s** /d(ə)mifinal/ *nf* semi-final.

demi-finaliste, *pl* **~s** /d(ə)mifinalist/ *nmf* semifinalist.

demi-fond, *pl* **~s** /d(ə)mifɔ̃/ *nm* (spécialité) middle-distance running; **de ~** [*course, coureur*] middle-distance.

demi-franc, *pl* **~s** /d(ə)mifʀɑ̃/ *nm* half a franc, fifty centimes.

demi-frère, *pl* **~s** /d(ə)mifʀɛʀ/ *nm* half-brother.

demi-gros /d(ə)migʀo/ *nm inv* wholesale direct to the public.

demi-heure, *pl* **~s** /d(ə)mijœʀ/ *nf* half an hour; **à intervalles d'une ~** at half-hourly intervals; **je serai prêt dans une ~** I'll be ready in half an hour GB ou in a half-hour US.

demi-jour, *pl* **~(s)** /d(ə)miʒuʀ/ *nm* half-light.

demi-journée, *pl* **~s** /d(ə)miʒuʀne/ *nf* half a day; **à la ~** on a half-day basis; **travailler trois ~s par semaine** to work three half-days a week.

démilitarisation /demilitaʀizasjɔ̃/ *nf* demilitarization.

démilitariser /demilitaʀize/ [1] *vtr* to demilitarize.

demi-litre, *pl* **~s** /d(ə)militʀ/ *nm* half a litre[GB]; **par ~** by the half-litre[GB].

demi-longueur, *pl* **~s** /d(ə)milɔ̃gœʀ/ *nf* half-length; **d'une ~** by a half-length.

demi-lune, *pl* **~s** /d(ə)milyn/ *nf* **1** lit half-moon; **2** (objet) half-circle; **des montures de lunettes (en) ~** half-moon spectacles.

demi-mal /d(ə)mimal/ *nm* **il n'y a que ~** it's not as bad as all that.

demi-mesure, *pl* **~s** /d(ə)mim(ə)zyʀ/ *nf* lit, fig half-measure; **se contenter de ~s** to make do with half-measures.

demi-mondaine†, *pl* **~s** /d(ə)mimɔ̃dɛn/ *nf* demimondaine†.

demi-monde†, *pl* **~s** /d(ə)mimɔ̃d/ *nm* demimonde†.

demi-mort, ~e, *pl* **~s, ~es** /dəmi mɔʀ, mɔʀt/ *adj* half-dead (**de** from ou with).

demi-mot: **à demi-mot** /ad(ə)mimo/ *loc adv* **j'ai compris à ~** I took the hint; **elle me comprend à ~** she can read my mind.

déminage /deminaʒ/ *nm* (de terrain) (land)-mine clearance; (de mer) minesweeping.

déminer /demine/ [1] *vtr* to clear [sth] of mines [*terrain*]; to sweep [sth] of mines [*estuaire*].

déminéraliser /demineʀalize/ [1] **I** *vtr* to demineralize [*eau*].
II se déminéraliser *vpr* [*personne*] to lose essential body salts, to suffer from a mineral deficiency.

démineur /deminœʀ/ *nm* mine clearance expert.

demi-pause, *pl* **~s** /d(ə)mipoz/ *nf* minim rest GB, half rest US.

demi-pension /d(ə)mipɑ̃sjɔ̃/ *nf* **1** (régime, prix) half board; **être en ~** (à l'hôtel) to stay half board; (à l'école) to have school lunches; **2** (hôtel) hotel offering half board; **3** (pour un cheval) half-livery.

demi-pensionnaire, *pl* **~s** /d(ə)mipɑ̃sjɔnɛʀ/ *nmf* Scol pupil who has school lunches.

demi-place, *pl* **~s** /d(ə)miplas/ *nf* **deux ~s, s'il vous plaît** two halves, please; **payer ~** Transp to pay half-fare; (au spectacle) to pay half-price; **une ~ au cinéma** a half-price seat at the cinema.

demi-plan, *pl* **~s** /d(ə)miplɑ̃/ *nm* Math half-plane.

demi-pointe, *pl* **~s** /d(ə)mipwɛ̃t/ *nf* demi-pointe; **faire des ~s** to dance on demi-pointe.

demi-portion○, *pl* **~s** /d(ə)mipɔʀsjɔ̃/ *nf* pej little squirt○ péj.

demi-queue, *pl* **~s** /d(ə)mikø/ *nm* **(piano) ~** boudoir grand piano.

demi-reliure, *pl* **~s** /d(ə)miʀəljyʀ/ *nf* quarter-binding; **~ à coins** half-binding.

démis, ~e /demi, iz/ **I** *pp* ▶ **démettre**.
II *pp adj* [*articulation*] dislocated.

demi-saison, *pl* **~s** /d(ə)misɛzɔ̃/ *nf* **manteau de ~** lightweight coat.

demi-sel /d(ə)misɛl/ *adj inv* [*beurre, fromage*] slightly salted.

demi-siècle, *pl* **~s** /d(ə)misjɛkl/ *nm* half a century.

demi-sœur, *pl* **~s** /d(ə)misœʀ/ *nf* half-sister.

demi-solde, *pl* **~s** /d(ə)misɔld/ *nf* half-pay; **à la ~** on half-pay.

demi-sommeil, *pl* **~s** /d(ə)misɔmɛj/ *nm* **être dans un ~** (somnolence) to be half-asleep; (inactivité) to be slumbering.

demi-soupir, *pl* **~s** /d(ə)misupiʀ/ *nm* quaver rest GB, eighth rest US.

démission /demisjɔ̃/ *nf* **1** lit resignation (**de** from); **donner sa ~** lit to hand in one's resignation; hum to give up; **2** fig failure to take responsibility, cop out○.

démissionnaire /demisjɔnɛʀ/ **I** *adj* **1** (qui a démissionné) resigning (*épith*); **2** (qui abandonne) negligent.
II *nmf* person who has resigned.

démissionner /demisjɔne/ [1] **I**○ *vtr* hum to oust; **être démissionné** to be ousted.
II *vi* **1** (quitter son poste) to resign (**de** from); **2** (renoncer) to give up; (renier ses responsabilités) to abdicate one's responsibilities.

demi-succès /d(ə)misyksɛ/ *nm inv* qualified success.

demi-tarif, *pl* **~s** /d(ə)mitaʀif/ **I** *adj inv* [*billet, place*] half-price (*épith*).
II *adv* **payer ~** to pay half-price.
III *nm* (billet) half-price ticket; **voyager à**

~ to travel half-fare; **avoir droit au ~** to be entitled to travel half-fare.

demi-teinte, *pl* **~s** /d(ə)mitɛ̃t/ *nf* muted colours[GB]; **en ~s** lit in muted colours[GB]; fig in a subdued style.

demi-ton, *pl* **~s** /d(ə)mitɔ̃/ *nm* semitone.

demi-tonneau, *pl* **~x** /d(ə)mitɔno/ *nm* Aviat half-roll.

demi-tour, *pl* **~s** /d(ə)mituʀ/ *nm* **1** (dans l'espace) Aut U-turn; Mil about-turn GB, about face US; **faire ~** gén to turn back; **faire** or **exécuter un ~** Aut to make a U-turn; Mil to about-turn GB, to about-face US; **2** (de serrure) sash.

démiurge /demjyʀʒ/ *nm* Philos demiurge; Littérat creator.

demi-vie, *pl* **~s** /d(ə)mivi/ *nf* Phys half-life.

demi-vierge†, *pl* **~s** /d(ə)mivjɛʀʒ/ *nf* demi-vierge†.

demi-volée, *pl* **~s** /d(ə)mivɔle/ *nf* half-volley.

démobilisable /demɔbilizabl/ *adj* authorized to be demobilized.

démobilisateur, **-trice** /demɔbilizatœʀ, tʀis/ *adj* **1** fig pacifying (*épith*); **2** Mil demobilization (*épith*).

démobilisation /demɔbilizasjɔ̃/ *nf* **1** Mil demobilization; **procéder à la ~** to demobilize; **2** fig demotivation.

démobilisé, **~e** /demɔbilize/ *nm,f* demobilized soldier.

démobiliser /demɔbilize/ [1] **I** *vtr* **1** Mil to demobilize; **2** fig to demotivate [*électorat, partisan*].

II se démobiliser *vpr* (perdre sa combativité) to become demotivated.

démocrate /demɔkʀat/ **I** *adj* **1** gén democratic; **2** (aux États-Unis) [*parti, sénateur*] Democratic; **voter pour le parti ~** to vote Democratic.

II *nmf* **1** gén democrat; **2** (aux États-Unis) Democrat.

démocrate-chrétien, **-ienne**, *pl* **démocrates-chrétiens**, **-iennes** /demɔkʀat kʀetjɛ̃, ɛn/ *adj, nm,f* Christian Democrat.

démocratie /demɔkʀasi/ *nf* democracy; **~ parlementaire/populaire** parliamentary/popular democracy.

démocratique /demɔkʀatik/ *adj* **1** Pol [*régime, débat*] democratic; **2** (accessible à tous) accessible.

démocratiquement /demɔkʀatikmɑ̃/ *adv* democratically.

démocratisation /demɔkʀatizasjɔ̃/ *nf* (tous contextes) democratization.

démocratiser /demɔkʀatize/ [1] **I** *vtr* Pol, fig to democratize [*régime, enseignement*].

II se démocratiser *vpr* **1** Pol [*régime*] to become more democratic; **2** [*enseignement*] to become more accessible to people.

démodé, **~e** /demɔde/ *adj* old-fashioned.

démoder: **se démoder** /demɔde/ [1] *vpr* to go out of fashion.

démographe /demɔgʀaf/ **▶510** *nmf* demographer.

démographie /demɔgʀafi/ *nf* demography.

démographique /demɔgʀafik/ *adj* demographic.

demoiselle /d(ə)mwazɛl/ *nf* **1** (jeune fille) fml or iron young lady; **si ça ne dérange pas ces ~s** if the young ladies don't mind; **2**† (célibataire) single lady; **elle est restée ~** she remained single; **3**† (fille) daughter; **4**† (jeune noble) young noblewoman; **être habillée en ~** to be dressed in one's finery; **elle se prend pour une ~** she gives herself airs and graces; **5** (libellule) damselfly; **6** Tech (pour damer) rammer.

■ **~ coiffée** Géol earth pillar; **~ de compagnie** female companion; **~ d'honneur** (de mariée) bridesmaid; (à la cour) maid of honour[GB].

démolir /demɔliʀ/ [3] **I** *vtr* **1** (détruire) to demolish [*quartier*]; to pull down, to demolish [*bâtiment*]; **2** (rendre inutilisable) to wreck [*appareil, jouet*]; **3** (ruiner) to destroy [*système, doctrine, réputation*]; [*critique*] to demolish [*argumentation*]; **les critiques m'ont démoli** the critics tore me to pieces; **4** (discréditer) to demolish [*politicien*]; **cette histoire a démoli sa carrière** the affair wrecked his/her career; **5**○ (rosser) to beat [sb] up○ [*personne*]; **se faire ~** to get beaten up; **6**○ (épuiser) [*effort*] to whack [sb] out○ [*personne*]; [*produit*] to do [sth] in○ [*organe*]; **l'alcool lui a démoli le foie/la santé** alcohol has wrecked his liver/health.

II se démolir *vpr* **se ~**○ **la santé** to ruin one's health.

démolissage /demɔlisaʒ/ *nm* (de réputation, organisation) destruction; (de bâtiment) demolition.

démolisseur, **-euse** /demɔlisœʀ, øz/ *nm,f* **1** **▶510** (personne) demolition worker; (entreprise) demolition contractor GB, wrecker US; **2** (destructeur) wrecker.

démolition /demɔlisjɔ̃/ **I** *nf* **1** (de maison, construction) demolition; **travaux/chantier/entreprise de ~** demolition works/site/contractor; **bâtiment en (cours de) ~** building under demolition; **2** (de réputation, système, doctrine, d'institution) destruction.

II démolitions *nfpl* rubble **¢**; **les victimes ensevelies sous les ~s** the victims buried under the rubble.

démon /demɔ̃/ *nm* **1** Relig devil; **le ~** the Devil; **2** (esprit) **bon/mauvais ~** good/evil spirit; **poussé par son ~ intérieur** (bon) prompted by his guiding spirit; (mauvais) driven by the demon inside him; **3** (personne) devil; **4** (passion) demon; **le ~ du jeu** the gambling demon; **le ~ de la boisson** or **de l'alcool** the demon drink.

■ **~ de midi** ≈ mid-life crisis.

démonétisation /demɔnetizasjɔ̃/ *nf* demonetization.

démonétiser /demɔnetize/ [1] *vtr* Fin to demonetize.

démoniaque /demɔnjak/ *adj* demonic.

démonologie /demɔnɔlɔʒi/ *nf* demonology.

démonstrateur, **-trice** /demɔ̃stʀatœʀ, tʀis/ **▶510** *nm,f* Comm demonstrator; **être démonstratrice en produits de beauté** to demonstrate beauty products.

démonstratif, **-ive** /demɔ̃stʀatif, iv/ **I** *adj* **1** (expansif) [*personne, caractère*] demonstrative; [*geste*] expressive; [*joie*] uninhibited; **individu peu ~** a rather undemonstrative person; **2** (convaincant) [*argument, expérience*] demonstrative; **3** Ling [*adjectif, pronom*] demonstrative.

II *nm* Ling demonstrative.

démonstration /demɔ̃stʀasjɔ̃/ *nf* **1** (signe extérieur) show **¢**; **faire des ~s d'amitié à qn** to make a show of friendship towards sb; **2** (leçon pratique) demonstration; **~ culinaire/de judo** cookery GB ou cooking US/judo demonstration; **faire une ~ à qn** to give sb a demonstration; **faire la ~ d'un appareil** to demonstrate an appliance; **de ~** [*appareil, matériel*] demonstration; **3** (illustration, preuve) (de loi, théorie, vérité) demonstration; (de théorème) proof; **la ~ en a été faite** this has been proved GB ou proven; **l'organisme a fait la ~ de son utilité** the organization has demonstrated its usefulness; **~ par l'absurde** reductio ad absurdum; **4** (manifestation) display; **~ de force/courage** display of strength/courage; **~ aérienne** Sport air display.

démontable /demɔ̃tabl/ *adj* [*meuble*] that can be taken apart ou dismantled (*après n*), knockdown (*épith*) US.

démontage /demɔ̃taʒ/ *nm* **1** (de tente, d'échafaudage) taking down; (de meuble) taking apart; (de moteur, d'arme) stripping down; (de serrure, pendule) dismantling; (de roue) removal; **le ~ de la tente est très simple** the tent is very easy to take down; **2** fig (explication) **procéder au ~ de mécanismes psychologiques/biologiques** to describe the functioning of psychological/biological mechanisms.

démonté, **~e** /demɔ̃te/ **I** *pp* ▶ **démonter**.

II *pp adj* [*mer*] stormy.

démonte-pneu, *pl* **~s** /demɔ̃t(ə)pnø/ *nm* Aut tyre-lever GB, tire iron US.

démonter /demɔ̃te/ [1] **I** *vtr* **1** (désassembler) to take down [*tente, échafaudage*]; to take apart, to knock down US [*meuble, maquette*]; to strip down [*moteur, arme*]; to dismantle [*pendule, mécanisme*]; to unpick [*vêtement*]; **2** (enlever) to remove [*roue*]; to take off [*porte*]; to take down [*rideau*]; **3**○ (déconcerter) to fluster; **ne pas se laisser ~** to remain unruffled; **sans se laisser ~ il...** unruffled he...; **4** (désarçonner) Équit [*cheval*] to throw [*cavalier*]; **5** Chasse to wing [*oiseau*].

II se démonter *vpr* **1** (être démontable) [*meuble, maquette*] to be able to be taken apart; [*moteur, arme*] to be able to be stripped down; [*pendule, mécanisme*] to be able to be dismantled; [*vêtement*] to be able to be unpicked; **ce buffet se démonte facilement** this sideboard can be taken apart ou knocked down US easily; **2** (se disloquer) to come apart; **3**○ (perdre son sang-froid) to become flustered; **il ne s'est pas démonté devant cette accusation** he wasn't flustered by this accusation.

démontrable /demɔ̃tʀabl/ *adj* demonstrable.

démontrer /demɔ̃tʀe/ [1] *vtr* **1** (avec preuve) to demonstrate [*intérêt, puissance, absurdité*]; to prove [*théorème*]; **~ que** to demonstrate that; **~ qch à qn** to demonstrate sth to sb; **~ à qn que** to demonstrate to sb that; **je lui ai démontré par a plus b qu'il avait tort** I demonstrated to him conclusively that he was wrong; **2** (indiquer) to prove, to demonstrate (**que** that); **l'incident démontre la fragilité des accords** the incident proves how fragile the agreements are.

démoralisant, **~e** /demɔʀalizɑ̃, ɑ̃t/ *adj* demoralizing.

démoralisation /demɔʀalizasjɔ̃/ *nf* demoralization.

démoraliser /demɔʀalize/ [1] **I** *vtr* to demoralize; **se laisser ~** to let oneself get demoralized; **se laisser ~ par qch** to let sth demoralize one.

II se démoraliser *vpr* to get demoralized.

démordre: **démordre de** /demɔʀdʀ/ [6] *vtr ind* **je n'en démords pas** (d'une idée, opinion) I won't let go of it; (d'une déclaration, décision) I'm sticking to it.

Démosthène /demɔstɛn/ *npr* Demosthenes.

démotique /demɔtik/ *adj, nm, nf* demotic.

démotiver /demɔtive/ [1] *vtr* to demotivate.

démoulage /demulaʒ/ *nm* **1** (de pâtisserie) turning out; **avant/pendant le ~** before/when turning out; **2** Art, Tech (d'objet) removal from the mould GB ou mold US; (de moule) turning out of the mould GB ou mold US.

démouler /demule/ [1] **I** *vtr* to turn [sth] out of the tin GB ou pan US [*gâteau*]; to turn [sth] out of the mould[GB] [*flan*]; to remove [sth] from the mould [*statue*].

II se démouler *vpr* **bien/mal se ~** [*gâteau*] to come out of the tin GB ou pan US easily/badly; [*flan, statue*] to come out of the mould easily/badly.

démultiplicateur, **-trice** /demyltiplikatœʀ, tʀis/ **I** *adj* reduction (*épith*).

II *nm* reduction-unit.

démultiplication /demyltiplikasjɔ̃/ *nf* (effet) gearing down; (rapport) reduction ratio.

démultiplier /demyltiplije/ [2] *vtr* **1** to reduce [*vitesse*]; **2** to multiply the number of [*établissements, réseaux*].

démuni, **~e** /demyni/ **I** *pp* ▶ **démunir**.

II *pp adj* **1** (pauvre) impoverished; (à court d'argent) penniless; **2** (vulnérable) helpless (**face à, devant** in the face of); **nous sommes totalement ~s face à leur dé-**

tresse we are helpless when faced with their distress; **3** (à court de stock) out of stock (*jamais épith*); **4** (privé) **~ de** devoid of [*talent*]; lacking [*diplômes*].

démunir /demyniʀ/ [3] **I** *vtr* (dégarnir) to divest (**de** of).

II se démunir *vpr* (se dessaisir) **se ~ de** to leave oneself without [*argent, provisions, biens*]; **je ne veux pas me ~** I don't want to leave myself short.

démystification /demistifikasjɔ̃/ *nf* **1 la ~ de qn** the dispelling of sb's illusions; **2** (d'une discipline) demystification.

démystifier /demistifje/ [2] *vtr* **1** (détromper) **~ qn** to dispel sb's illusions; **2** to demystify [*discipline*].

démythification /demitifikasjɔ̃/ *nf* demythologization.

démythifier /demitifje/ [2] *vtr* to demythologize.

dénasalisation /denazalizasjɔ̃/ *nf* denasalization.

dénasaliser /denazalize/ [1] **I** *vtr* to denasalize.

II se dénasaliser *vpr* to be denasalized.

dénatalité /denatalite/ *nf* fall in the birthrate.

dénationalisation /denasjɔnalizasjɔ̃/ *nf* denationalization.

dénationaliser /denasjɔnalize/ [1] *vtr* to denationalize.

dénaturant, **~e** /denatyʀɑ̃, ɑ̃t/ **I** *adj* [*produit*] denaturing (*épith*).

II *nm* denaturant; (agent traceur) denaturing agent.

dénaturation /denatyʀasjɔ̃/ *nf* **1** Ind, Tech, Sci denaturation; **2** fig distortion.

dénaturé, **~e** /denatyʀe/ **I** *pp* ▶ **dénaturer**.

II *pp adj* **1** [*alcool*] denaturated; **2** (dépravé) warped; **3** (indigne) [*parents, enfants*] unnatural; **4** (déformé) distorted.

dénaturer /denatyʀe/ [1] *vtr* **1** Tech, Ind to denature; **2** (déformer) to distort [*faits*]; **3** (altérer) to spoil [*goût, sauce*].

dénazification /denazifikasjɔ̃/ *nf* denazification.

dénazifier /denazifje/ [2] *vtr* to denazify.

dendrologie /dɑ̃dʀɔlɔʒi/ *nf* dendrology.

dénébuler /denebyle/ [1] *vtr* to disperse fog; **~ une piste** to disperse the fog on a runway.

dénégation /denegasjɔ̃/ *nf* gén, Jur denial.

déneigement /denɛʒmɑ̃/ *nm* clearing of snow.

déneiger /deneʒe/ [13] *vtr* to clear the snow; **~ qch** to clear the snow from sth.

déni /deni/ *nm* denial (**de** of).

déniaiser /denjeze/ [1] **I** *vtr* **1** (dégourdir) to make [sb] more worldly-wise, to wise [sb] up○ US; **2**○ (initier sexuellement) to initiate [sb] sexually.

II se déniaiser *vpr* (devenir débrouillard) to become more worldly-wise, to wise up○.

dénicher /deniʃe/ [1] *vtr* **1**○ (découvrir) to dig out○ [*objet*]; to track down [*personne*]; to discover [*bonne adresse*]; **2** (faire sortir) to flush out [*ennemi, voleur, animal*] (**de** from); **3** lit to take [sth] from the nest.

dénicheur, **-euse** /deniʃœʀ, øz/ *nm,f* **1** (d'objets, de talents) spotter (**de** of); **2** (d'œufs) bird's-nester.

dénicotiniser /denikɔtinize/ [1] *vtr* to make [sth] nicotine-free; **cigarette dénicotinisée** nicotine-free cigarette.

denier /dənje/ **I** *nm* **1** Fin, Hist (français) denier; (romain) denarius; **2** Tex (unité de finesse) denier; **collants de 20 ~s** 20-denier tights GB ou panty hose US.

II deniers *nmpl* money; **payer de ses ~s** to pay with one's own money; **~s publics** or **de l'État** public funds.

■ **~ du culte** Relig *funds collected annually for a parish*; **~ de saint Pierre** Relig Peter's pence.

dénier /denje/ [2] *vtr* to deny; **~ qch à qn** to deny sb sth.

dénigrement /denigʀəmɑ̃/ *nm* denigration; **par ~** disparagingly; **esprit de ~** disparaging mentality.

dénigrer /denigʀe/ [1] *vtr* to denigrate.

dénivelé /denivle/ *nm*, **dénivelée** *nf* difference in altitude (**entre** between); **1 000 mètres de ~** a difference in altitude of 2,000 metres[GB].

déniveler /denivle/ [19] *vtr* **1** (rendre accidenté) to make [sth] uneven; **2** (changer le niveau) to alter the level of.

dénivellation /denivɛlasjɔ̃/ *nf* **1** (écart d'altitude) difference in altitude (**entre** between); (écart de niveau) difference in level; **2** (inclinaison) gradient; **3** (inégalité de terrain) unevenness; **4** (changement du niveau) alteration of level.

dénombrable /denɔ̃bʀabl/ *adj* Math, Ling countable, count (*épith*); **non ~** uncountable.

dénombrement /denɔ̃bʀəmɑ̃/ *nm* **~ de la population** population count; **le ~ des victimes a pris plusieurs jours** it took several days to count the victims.

dénombrer /denɔ̃bʀe/ [1] *vtr* to count; **on dénombre 14 blessés** the number of wounded is 14.

dénominateur /denɔminatœʀ/ *nm* denominator; **~ commun** Math, fig common denominator (**à** of); **plus petit ~ commun** lowest common denominator (**à** of).

dénominatif, **-ive** /denɔminatif, iv/ **I** *adj* denominative.

II *nm* denominative.

dénomination /denɔminasjɔ̃/ *nf* **1** gén name; **2** Relig denomination.

■ **~ commune** Pharm generic name; **~ sociale** Admin registered company name.

dénommé, **~e** /denɔme/ **I** *pp* ▶ **dénommer**.

II *pp adj* Admin **le ~ Pierre** the person by the name of Pierre; **il y avait là un ~ Martin** there was a certain Martin there.

dénommer /denɔme/ [1] *vtr* **1** Jur to name; **2** (appeler) to call; **comment dénommez-vous...?** what do you call...?; **3** (désigner) to designate; **~ d'après** to designate according to.

dénoncer /denɔ̃se/ [12] **I** *vtr* **1** (signaler) to denounce [*personne, coupable*] (**à** to); **il a été dénoncé par ses amis** he was denounced by his friends; **2** (rendre public) to denounce [*abus, répression, scandale, activité*]; **3** Jur (rompre) to terminate [*traité, contrat*].

II se dénoncer *vpr* to give oneself up.

dénonciateur, **-trice** /denɔ̃sjatœʀ, tʀis/ **I** *adj* [*lettre, article*] denunciatory.

II *nm,f* (de coupable) informer; (d'injustice) campaigner (**de** against).

dénonciation /denɔ̃sjasjɔ̃/ *nf* **1** (de coupable) denunciation; **lettre de ~** letter of denunciation; **il a été inculpé sur ~ des voisins** he was convicted on the strength of his neighbours'[GB] denunciation; **2** (d'injustice, de scandale) denunciation; **3** Jur (rupture) termination; (signification légale) notice.

dénotatif, **-ive** /denɔtatif, iv/ *adj* denotative.

dénotation /denɔtasjɔ̃/ *nf* denotation.

dénoter /denɔte/ [1] *vtr* denote.

dénouement /denumɑ̃/ *nm* **1** Théât denouement; **2** (d'une affaire, d'un conflit) outcome, conclusion; **un heureux ~** a happy ending.

dénouer /denwe/ [1] **I** *vtr* **1** (détacher) to undo, untie [*nœud, lacets, ruban*]; to let down [*cheveux*]; to undo [*cravate, ceinture*]; to disentangle [*fils*]; **mes cheveux étaient dénoués** my hair was loose; **2** (débrouiller) to unravel [*intrigue, imbroglio*]; to resolve [*affaire, crise, situation*]; **~ les fils d'une intrigue** to unravel the threads of a plot.

II se dénouer *vpr* **1** [*lacet, ruban, corde*] to come undone; **2** [*crise*] to resolve itself; [*intrigue*] to unravel itself; [*affaire, situation*] to resolve.

dénoyauter /denwajote/ [1] *vtr* to stone GB, to pit US.

dénoyauteuse /denwajotøz/ *nf* fruit-stoner GB, fruit-pitter US.

denrée /dɑ̃ʀe/ *nf* **1** (produit) **~ de base** staple; **~s alimentaires** foodstuffs; **~s congelées** frozen foods; **~s de luxe/périssables** luxury/perishable foodstuffs; **~s de consommation courante/de première nécessité** basic/primary foodstuffs; **2** fig commodity; **une ~ rare** a rare commodity.

dense /dɑ̃s/ *adj* **1** Géog **la population est ~** it is densely populated; **2** Phys [*corps*] dense; **3** [*brouillard, végétation, texte, circulation*] dense; [*réseau*] concentrated; [*programme, tir*] heavy.

densimètre /dɑ̃simɛtʀ/ *nm* densitometer.

densité /dɑ̃site/ *nf* **1** Géog (population) density; **~ rurale/urbaine** rural/urban population density; **~ démographique** density of population; **à forte/faible ~** densely/sparsely populated; **2** Phys relative density; **3** (de végétation, brouillard) denseness; **~ d'un réseau** density of a network; **~ bancaire/policière** number of banks/police; **4** Ordinat density.

dent /dɑ̃/ *nf* **1** Anat, Zool tooth; **~s de devant/de derrière** front/back teeth; **~ en or** gold tooth; **entre les ~s** between one's teeth; **entre ses ~s** [*murmurer, jurer*] under one's breath; **parler entre ses ~s** to mumble; **mal** or **rage de ~s** toothache; **donner un coup de ~ à qn/dans qch** to bite sb/into sth; **à pleines** or **à belles ~s** [*mâcher, déchirer, croquer*] with relish; **rire de toutes ses ~s** to laugh heartily; **manger du bout des ~s** to pick at one's food; **rire du bout des ~s** to laugh half-heartedly; **accepter du bout des ~s** to accept reluctantly; **faire ses (premières) ~s, percer ses ~s** to teethe; **elle vient de percer une ~** she has just cut a tooth; **jusqu'aux ~s** [*s'armer, être armé*] to the teeth; **ne rien avoir à se mettre sous la ~** (à manger) to have nothing to eat; (à lire) to have nothing to read; **montrer les ~s** lit, fig to bare one's teeth; **serrer les ~s** to grit one's teeth; **se faire les ~s (sur qch)** to come to grief (over sth); **2** (de peigne, scie, roue d'engrenage) tooth; (de fourchette, râteau) prong; (de couteau, scie) tooth, serration; (de timbre, feuille) serration; **en ~s de scie** [*bord, lame*] serrated; [*carrière*] full of ups and downs, chequered GB ou checkered US; [*résultats*] which go up and down; **avoir un moral en ~s de scie** to have ups and downs; **3** (sommet) crag.

■ **~ de lait** milk ou baby GB tooth; **~ de sagesse** wisdom tooth; ▶ **faux**.

IDIOMES **avoir** or **conserver une ~ contre qn** to bear sb a grudge; **avoir les ~s longues** to be ambitious; **avoir la ~ dure** to be scathing; **avoir la ~**○ to feel peckish○; **être sur les ~s** (occupé) to be up to one's eyes in work; (tendu) to be on edge; **œil pour œil, ~ pour ~** Prov an eye for an eye and a tooth for a tooth Prov.

dentaire /dɑ̃tɛʀ/ *adj* dental; **faire ~**○ or **des études ~s** to study to be a dentist.

dental, **~e**, *mpl* **-aux** /dɑ̃tal, o/ **I** *adj* dental.

II dentale *nf* dental (consonant).

dent-de-lion, *pl* **dents-de-lion** /dɑ̃də ljɔ̃/ *nf* dandelion.

denté, **~e** /dɑ̃te/ *adj* Tech, Zool toothed; Bot dentate.

dentelé, **~e** /dɑ̃t(ə)le/ **I** *pp* ▶ **denteler**.

II *pp adj* [*côte*] indented; [*crête*] jagged; [*tissu*] pinked; [*papier, lame*] serrated; [*timbre*] perforated; Bot dentate.

denteler /dɑ̃t(ə)le/ [19] *vtr* to pink [*tissu, papier*]; to indent [*côte*]; to give a jagged outline to [*montagne*]; to perforate [*timbre*].

dentelle /dɑ̃tɛl/ *nf* lace; **une ~** a piece of lace; **mouchoir de** or **en ~** lace handkerchief; **~ au fuseau** bobbin lace; **~ de pierre** stone filigree.

IDIOMES **il ne fait pas dans la ~** he's not one to bother with niceties.

dentellerie /dɑ̃tɛlʀi/ *nf* (fabrication) lacemaking; (industrie) lace industry.

dentellier, -ière /dɑ̃təlje, ɛʀ/ **I** *adj* lace.
II dentellière *nf* **1** (personne) lacemaker; **2** (machine) lacemaking machine.

dentelure /dɑ̃tlyʀ/ *nf* (de timbre) perforation; (de tissu) pinked edge; (de papier, lame) serrated edge; (de côte) indentation; (de crête) jagged outline; Bot serration; Archit dentils (*pl*).

dentier /dɑ̃tje/ *nm* dentures (*pl*).

dentifrice /dɑ̃tifʀis/ **I** *adj* **pâte ~** toothpaste; **poudre ~** tooth powder; **eau ~** mouthwash.
II *nm* toothpaste.

dentine /dɑ̃tin/ *nf* dentine[GB].

dentiste /dɑ̃tist/ ▶**510** *nmf* dentist; **aller chez le ~** to go to the dentist's.

dentisterie /dɑ̃tist(ə)ʀi/ *nf* dentistry.

dentition /dɑ̃tisjɔ̃/ *nf* dentition; **avoir une bonne/mauvaise ~** to have good/bad teeth.

denture /dɑ̃tyʀ/ *nf* **1** Dent (disposition) dentition; (dents) set of teeth; **2** Tech teeth (*pl*), cogs (*pl*).

dénucléarisation /denykleaʀizasjɔ̃/ *nf* denuclearization.

dénucléariser /denykleaʀize/ [1] *vtr* to denuclearize.

dénudé, ~e /denyde/ **I** *pp* ▶ **dénuder**.
II *pp adj* gén bare; (crâne) bald.

dénuder /denyde/ [1] **I** *vtr* **1** Électrotech to strip [*câble, fil*]; **2** [*mouvement*] to reveal [*corps*]; **la robe dénudait son épaule** the dress left her shoulder bare; **3** Méd to bare [*nerf, veine*]; to strip [*os*] (**de** of); **4** liter **le vent a dénudé les arbres/la colline** the wind stripped the trees/the hill bare; **~ un arbre de son écorce** to strip a tree of its bark.
II se dénuder *vpr* **1** [*personne*] to strip (off); **se ~ jusqu'à la taille** to strip down to the waist; **2** [*arbre*] to become bare; **3** [*crâne*] to go bald.

dénué, ~e /denɥe/ *adj* lacking (*après n*) (**de** in); **~ d'inventivité** devoid of inventiveness, lacking in inventiveness; **~ de scrupules** completely without scruples, lacking in scruples; **elle n'est pas ~e d'imagination** she is not lacking in imagination; **un acte ~ de sens** a senseless act, an act devoid of sense; **accusation ~e de fondement** groundless accusation; **~ de toute utilité** utterly useless; **~ de tout** destitute.

dénuement /denymɑ̃/ *nm* (de personne) destitution; (de pièce) bareness; **dans le plus grand ~** in a state of utter destitution.

dénutrition /denytʀisjɔ̃/ *nf* malnutrition.

déodorant, ~e /deɔdɔʀɑ̃, ɑ̃t/ **I** *adj* [*savon, lotion*] deodorant.
II *nm* deodorant; **un ~ en bombe** a spray deodorant.

déontologie /deɔ̃tɔlɔʒi/ *nf* (de profession) ethics (+ *v sg*), code of practice GB; Philos deontology; **code de ~ médicale** medical ethics.

déontologique /deɔ̃tɔlɔʒik/ *adj* Philos deontological; **code ~ des médecins** code of practice governing doctors GB, medical code of ethics.

dépailler /depɑje/ [1] **I** *vtr* to strip the rush off [*chaise, fauteuil*].
II se dépailler *vpr* **la chaise se dépaille** the rush seat is wearing out.

dépannage /depanaʒ/ *nm* **1** (réparation) repair; **~s à domicile** home repairs; **~ 24 heures sur 24** 24 hour repair service; **faire un ~** to do a repair job; **2**○ (aide temporaire) **à titre de ~ je leur ai prêté...** to help them out I lent them...

dépanner /depane/ [1] *vtr* **1** (réparer) to fix [*voiture, appareil*]; **le garagiste m'a dépanné** the mechanic fixed my car; **2** (remorquer) to tow away; **3**○ (aider) to help [sb] out.

dépanneur, -euse /depanœʀ, øz/ **I** ▶**510** *nm,f* (personne) engineer.
II *nm* C (magasin) corner shop, convenience store.
III dépanneuse *nf* (véhicule) breakdown truck GB, tow truck US.

dépaqueter /depakte/ [20] *vtr* to unpack.

déparasiter /depaʀazite/ [1] *vtr* Vét to disinfest.

dépareillé, ~e /depaʀeje/ **I** *pp* ▶ **dépareiller**.
II *pp adj* **1** (isolé) odd (*épith*); **un volume ~** an odd volume; **articles ~s** oddments; **2** (disparate) [*service, ensemble*] odd; **un service de verres ~** a set of odd glasses; **3** (incomplet) incomplete.

dépareiller /depaʀeje/ [1] *vtr* **1** (rendre incomplet) to spoil (**en** by); **~ un service à thé en cassant une tasse** to spoil a tea service by breaking a cup; **2** (en mélangeant) **~ un costume** to wear a jacket and trousers from different suits; **~ un service à thé** to mix cups and saucers from different sets.

déparer /depaʀe/ [1] *vtr* to spoil [*lieu, façade*]; to mar [*visage, beauté*].

déparié, ~e /depaʀje/ *adj* odd (*épith*); **mes gants sont ~s** my gloves don't match.

départ /depaʀ/ *nm* **1** (d'un lieu) departure; **retarder son ~** to postpone one's departure; **heures de ~** departure times; **~ des grandes lignes/des lignes de banlieue** Rail (platforms for) main line/suburban departures; **je l'ai vue avant mon ~ pour Paris** I saw her before I left for Paris; **les ~s en vacances** holiday GB ou vacation US departures; **avant mon ~ en vacances** before I set off on holiday GB ou vacation US; **téléphone avant ton ~** phone before you leave; **c'est bientôt le ~, le ~ approche** it'll soon be time to leave; **se donner rendez-vous au ~ du car** (au lieu) to arrange to meet at the coach GB ou bus US; **vols quotidiens au ~ de Nice** daily flights from Nice; **le train a pris du retard au ~ de Lyon** the train was late leaving Lyons; **être sur le ~** to be about to leave; **il n'y a qu 'un ~ du courrier par jour** the post GB ou mail US only goes once a day; **2** (exode) exodus (**vers** to); **le ~ des cadres vers la capitale** the exodus of executives to the capital; **3** (d'une fonction, organisation) departure; (démission) resignation; **son ~ du Parti socialiste** his/her departure from the socialist party, his/her leaving the socialist party; **exiger le ~ du directeur** to demand the manager's resignation; **le ~ en retraite/préretraite** retirement/early retirement; **la restructuration a abouti au ~ de 600 employés** restructuring led to 600 workers being laid off; **4** Sport start; **~ arrêté/décalé/lancé** standing/staggered/flying start; **ligne/position de ~** starting line/position; **donner le (signal du) ~ aux coureurs** to start the race; **prendre le ~** (d'une course) to be among the starters; **prendre un bon/mauvais ~** to get off to a good/bad start; **prendre un nouveau ~** fig to make a fresh start; ▶ **faux**; **5** (début) start; **dès le ~** right from the start; **au ~** (d'abord) at first; (au début) at the outset; **langue de ~** source language; **salaire de ~** starting salary; **capital de ~** start-up capital; **6** liter (séparation) distinction (**entre** between); **faire le ~ entre le bien et le mal** to distinguish between good and evil.

départager /depaʀtaʒe/ [13] *vtr* **1** (trancher parmi) to decide between [*personnes, concurrents, opinions*]; **le vote du président va ~ les voix** the chairman has the casting vote; **~ un jury** to bring the members of a jury to agreement; **2** (séparer) to separate [*terrain*].

département /depaʀtəmɑ̃/ *nm* **1** Admin (administrative) department (*French territorial division*); **2** (d'organisme, d'université, d'administration) department; **ce n'est pas mon ~** lit fig that's not my department; **3** (ministère) department.

départemental, ~e, *mpl* **-aux** /depaʀtəmɑ̃tal, o/ **I** *adj* [*archives, budget, élection*] local, regional; **route ~e** secondary road.
II départementale *nf* (route) secondary road, ≈ B road GB.

départementaliser /depaʀtəmɑ̃talize/ [1] *vtr* **~ un territoire** to give a territory formal status as a department.

départir /depaʀtiʀ/ [30] **I** *vtr* to allot (**qch à qn** sth to sb).
II se départir *vpr* **se ~ de** to lose [*calme, sourire*]; to swerve from [*opinion*]; to abandon [*réserve*]; to break [*silence*].

départ-usine /depaʀyzin/ *adj inv* ex-works.

dépassé, ~e /depase/ **I** *pp* ▶ **dépasser**.
II *pp adj* **1** (qui n'a plus cours) [*idée, méthode, procédé, technique*] outdated, outmoded; **2** (vieux jeu) [*personne*] out-of-date (*épith*); **tu es ~, ça ne se fait plus** you're out of date, it isn't done any more; **3**○ (débordé) [*personne*] overwhelmed; **être ~ par les événements** to be overtaken by events.

dépassement /depɑsmɑ̃/ *nm* **1** Transp overtaking GB, passing US; **en France le ~ se fait à gauche** you overtake GB ou pass US on the left in France; **faire** or **effectuer un ~ dans un virage** to overtake GB ou pass US on a bend; **2** (de valeur) overrun; **~ d'horaire** overrunning the schedule; **le ~ de la dose prescrite peut entraîner des effets secondaires** exceeding the stated dose can produce side-effects; **~ de la vitesse autorisée** exceeding the speed limit; **3** (fait de se surpasser) **~ de soi** surpassing oneself; **avoir le goût de l'aventure et du ~** to have a taste for adventure and challenge.
■ **~ budgétaire** Admin, Fin cost overrun; **~ de capacité** Ordinat overflow.

dépasser /depɑse/ [1] **I** *vtr* **1** (passer devant) [*concurrent, véhicule, automobiliste*] to overtake GB, to pass US; **il a dépassé le tracteur dans un virage** he overtook GB ou passed US the tractor on a bend; **se faire ~** to be overtaken GB ou passed US; **2** (excéder) [*longueur, poids, budget, température*] to exceed; **leur dette dépasse le million de dollars** their debt exceeds the million dollar mark; **elle le dépasse de cinq centimètres/d'une tête** she's five centimetres[GB]/a head taller than him; **~ qch en hauteur/largeur** to be taller/wider than sth; **~ qch en taille/importance** to be larger/more important than sth; **orages qui dépassent en intensité ce qu'on attendait** storms which are fiercer than expected; **certaines classes dépassent 30 élèves** some classes have over 30 pupils; **l'entrevue ne devrait pas ~ une demi-heure** the interview shouldn't take more than ou exceed half an hour; **il a dépassé la cinquantaine** he's over ou past fifty; **nous n'avons plus le temps, les délais sont déjà dépassés de 3 semaines** we've got no more time, we're already 3 weeks over the deadline; **3** (aller au-delà de) lit to go past [*cible, lieu*]; fig to exceed [*espérances, attributions*]; **les résultats dépassent notre attente** the results exceed our expectations; **quand vous aurez dépassé le village, tournez à droite** when you've gone through the village, turn right; **je ne peux pas acheter cette maison, elle dépasse mes moyens** I can' t buy that house, it's more than I can afford ou it's beyond my means; **j'ai dépassé le stade de ces puérilités** I'm past (the stage of) such childishness; **nous avons dépassé les difficultés de base** we have got over the basic difficulties; **~ la mesure** or **les bornes** or **les limites** to go too far; **4** (montrer une supériorité sur) to be ahead of, to outstrip, to surpass; **~ qn en cruauté/bêtise** to be cruellet/more stupid than sb, to surpass sb in cruelty/stupidity; **leurs propositions dépassent en absurdité tout ce qu'on a pu entendre** their proposals are the most ridiculous I've ever heard; **5** (déconcerter) **ça me dépasse!** (incompréhensible) it's beyond me!; (effarant, choquant) it's beyond belief!; **la mode d'aujourd'hui me dépasse** I don't know what to make of today's fashions.

II *vi* **1** (être plus grand) (plus large) to jut out (**de** from); (plus haut) to jut out (**au-dessus** above); **la planche dépasse du coffre** the plank juts out from the boot GB ou trunk US; **~ de 10 centimètres** [*poutre, pierre, motif*] to jut out 10 centimetres[GB]; **2** (sortir) to stick out; **il y a un clou qui dépasse dans le parquet** there's a nail sticking out of the floor; **fais attention de ne pas ~ en coloriant** be careful not to colour[GB] over the lines; **3** (se faire voir) to show; **ton jupon dépasse** your slip is showing; **la robe dépasse sous le manteau** the dress shows underneath the coat; **leurs têtes dépassaient à peine des fauteuils** their heads barely showed above the armchairs.

III se dépasser *vpr* **1** (soi-même) to surpass oneself; **2** (l'un l'autre) to overtake each other; **les concurrents se dépassaient à tour de rôle** the competitors kept overtaking each other.

dépassionner /depasjɔne/ [1] *vtr* to defuse, to take the heat out of [*débat, discussion*]; **style dépassionné** dispassionate style; **réflexion dépassionnée** dispassionate reflection.

dépatouiller○: **se dépatouiller** /depatuje/ [1] *vpr* to get by; **se ~ de** to pull oneself out of [*situation, affaire*]; **qu'il se dépatouille tout seul** he'll just have to get by on his own; **savoir se ~** to be able to manage.

dépavage /depavaʒ/ *nm* taking up of paving stones (**de** from).

dépaver /depave/ [1] *vtr* to take up the paving stones (from).

dépaysé, ~e /depeize/ **I** *pp* ▶ **dépayser**.

II *pp adj* out of place; **il est complètement ~** he's like a fish out of water; **il n'est pas ~ ici** he feels at home here.

dépaysement /depeizmɑ̃/ *nm* (changement volontaire) change of scenery; (changement désagréable) disorientation; **ressentir une impression de ~** to feel disoriented; **c'est une promesse de ~** it promises exotic new surroundings.

dépayser /depeize/ [1] **I** *vtr* (agréablement) to provide with a pleasant change of scenery; (désagréablement) to disorient.

II se dépayser *vpr* **aimer se ~** to like a change of scene.

dépeçage /dep(ə)sаʒ/ *nm* (d'animal) cutting up; (de pays, propriété) carving up.

dépecer /dep(ə)se/ [16] *vtr* to tear [sth] apart [*proie*]; to cut up [*animal, victime*]; to carve up [*pays, propriété*]; to dissect [*ouvrage, cas*].

dépêche /depɛʃ/ *nf* dispatch; **~ d'agence** agency dispatch.

■ **~ d'Ems** Hist Ems telegram.

dépêcher /depeʃe/ [16] **I** *vtr* to dispatch (**à** to); **~ qn auprès de qn** to dispatch sb to see sb; **~ qn sur place** to dispatch sb to the scene; **~ des troupes en renfort** to dispatch troops as reinforcements.

II se dépêcher *vpr* to hurry up; **dépêche-toi de finir ton travail** hurry up and finish your work; **je me dépêche** I'm hurrying.

dépeigné, ~e /depeɲe/ **I** *pp* ▶ **dépeigner**.

II *pp adj* dishevelled[GB].

dépeigner /depeɲe/ [1] **I** *vtr* **~ qn** to make sb's hair untidy.

II se dépeigner *vpr* to make one's hair untidy.

dépeindre /depɛ̃dʀ/ [55] **I** *vtr* to depict (**comme** as).

II se dépeindre *vpr* to depict oneself (**comme** as).

dépenaillé, ~e /depənaje/ *adj* ragged.

dépénalisation /depenalizasjɔ̃/ *nf* decriminalization (**de** of).

dépénaliser /depenalize/ [1] *vtr* to decriminalize.

dépendance /depɑ̃dɑ̃s/ *nf* **1** (d'individu, de pays, d'économie) dependence; **~ économique/administrative** economic/administrative dependence; **être sous la ~ de** to be dependent on; **maintenir qn dans la ~** to keep sb dependent; **2** (lien) link; **3** (de malade, drogué) dependency; **être en état de ~ par rapport à l'alcool** to suffer from alcohol dependency; **4** (bâtiment) outbuilding; **5** Hist, Pol dependency.

dépendant, ~e /depɑ̃dɑ̃, ɑ̃t/ *adj* **1** (pas autonome) gén dependent (**de** on); (l'un de l'autre) interdependent; **être ~ de qn** (dans un emploi) to be responsible to sb; **organisme ~ du ministère** organization under the authority of the ministry; **les personnes ~es** the aged and the infirm; **2** (qui fait partie de) [*bâtiment*] that is part of.

dépendre /depɑ̃dʀ/ [6] **I** *vtr* to take down [*pendu, tableau, décoration, jambon*].

II dépendre de *vtr ind* **1** (reposer sur) **~ de** to depend on; **ton avenir en dépend** your future depends on it; **il dépend de toi que** it depends on you whether; **il ne dépend pas de toi qu'elle vienne** it's not up to you whether she comes or not; **ça dépend de toi** it's up to you; **il dépend de toi d'être prêt** it's up to you to be ready; **ça dépend** it depends; **cela dépend qui/pourquoi** it depends who/why; **2** (avoir besoin de) **~ de** [*personne, pays, économie*] to be dependent on; **~ financièrement de qn** to be financially dependent on sb; **3** (être sous l'autorité de) **~ de** [*organisme, comité, région*] to come under the control of; [*personne*] to be responsible to; **combien de personnes dépendent du ministère?** how many people are employed by the ministry?; **4** (être la responsabilité de) **~ de** [*environnement, dérogations*] to be the responsibility of; **5** (être un territoire de) **~ de** to be a dependency of; **6** (être une dépendance de) **~ de** [*bâtiment, terre, forêt*] to belong to.

dépens /depɑ̃/ *nmpl* **1** (détriment) **aux ~ de** at the expense of; **économiser aux ~ des patients** to save money at the patients' expense; **insister sur la quantité aux ~ de la qualité** to put the emphasis on quantity at the expense of quality; **victoire** or **succès aux ~ de l'équipe favorite** win over the favourite[GB] team; **se qualifier aux ~ d'Auxerre** to qualify by beating Auxerre; **réussir aux ~ des autres** to walk over people to get to the top; **rire aux ~ de qn** to have a laugh at sb's expense; **apprendre/découvrir à ses ~** to learn/to discover to one's cost; **2** (frais) **vivre aux ~ des autres** to live off other people; **s'enrichir/s'engraisser**○ **aux ~ des autres** to get rich/to become prosperous at other people's expense; **3** Jur (frais de justice) legal costs; **être condamné aux ~** to be ordered to pay costs.

dépense /depɑ̃s/ *nf* **1** (emploi d'argent) spending, expenditure; **~s sociales/militaires** welfare/military expenditure; **~s de fonctionnement** operating ou operational expenses; **pousser qn à la ~** to make sb spend money; **ça vaut la ~** it's worth the outlay; **regarder à la ~** (être économe) to watch one's spending; **ne pas regarder à la ~** to spare no expense; **2** (somme déboursée) outlay; **une ~ de 300 francs** an outlay of 300 francs; **avoir beaucoup de ~s** to have a lot of outgoings GB ou expenses; **excédent des ~s sur les recettes** excess of expenditure over income; **faire des ~s inconsidérées** to indulge in reckless spending; **se lancer dans de folles ~s pour faire** to spend an enormous amount of money on doing; **être une source de ~s** to be a drain on one's resources; **participer à la ~** to make a contribution to the cost; **3** (quantité utilisée) consumption; **~ en essence/d'électricité** petrol GB ou gasoline US/electricity consumption; **~ d'énergie physique/nerveuse** expenditure of physical/nervous energy; **cela représente une ~ de temps trop importante** it takes too much time; **ce travail me demande une trop grosse ~ d'énergie** this work takes too much out of me.

■ **la ~ publique** public expenditure; **~s courantes** running costs; **~s de personnel** staff costs.

dépenser /depɑ̃se/ [1] **I** *vtr* **1** (employer de l'argent) to spend [*salaire, fortune*] (**en** or **pour** on); **aimer ~** to enjoy spending money; **~ sans compter** to spend (money) freely; **2** (consommer) [*moteur, machine, chaudière*] to use up [*carburant*]; to use [*tissu, papier*]; to spend [*temps*]; **j'ai dépensé toute mon énergie à essayer de** I've worn myself out trying to; **ils ont dépensé des trésors d'imagination pour faire** they've really used their imagination to do.

II se dépenser *vpr* **1** (faire de l'exercice) to get (enough) exercise; **se ~ beaucoup** to get a lot of exercise; **2** (se donner du mal) **se ~ pour qn/qch** to do a lot for sb/sth; **se ~ pour faire** to put a lot of energy into doing; **dans son travail, il se dépense sans compter** he gives his all to his work.

dépensier, -ière /depɑ̃sje, ɛʀ/ **I** *adj* [*personne, humeur*] extravagant.

II *nm,f* spendthrift.

déperdition /depɛʀdisjɔ̃/ *nf* **1** (perte) loss; **~ de chaleur** heat loss; **~s d'électricité** electricity losses; **2** (baisse) decline; **3** (affaiblissement) weakening.

dépérir /depeʀiʀ/ [3] *vi* [*personne, animal*] lit to waste away; fig to fade away; [*plante*] to wilt; [*économie, région*] to be on the decline; [*civilisation*] to decay.

dépérissement /depeʀismɑ̃/ *nm* (de personne) deterioration; (de plante) wilting; (d'économie, organisation, de région) decline; (de civilisation) decay.

dépersonnalisation /depɛʀsɔnalizasjɔ̃/ *nf* depersonalization.

dépersonnaliser /depɛʀsɔnalize/ [1] **I** *vtr* to depersonalize, to make [sth] impersonal; **dépersonnalisé** depersonalized, impersonal.

II se dépersonnaliser *vpr* **1** [*personne*] to lose one's personality; **2** [*chose*] to be depersonalized, to become impersonal.

dépêtrer /depetʀe/ [1] **I** *vtr* to extricate (**de** from).

II se dépêtrer *vtr* **se ~ de** to extricate oneself from [*situation*]; to get rid of [*personne*].

dépeuplement /depœpləmɑ̃/ *nm* depopulation.

dépeupler /depœple/ [1] **I** *vtr* **1** Géog, Sociol to depopulate; **2** (vider temporairement) to empty; **~ les rues** to empty the streets; **3** Écol to reduce the wildlife in [*forêt, rivière*].

II se dépeupler *vpr* **1** Géog, Sociol to become depopulated; **2** (se vider temporairement) to become deserted; **3** Écol [*forêt, rivière*] to lose its wildlife.

déphasage /defazaʒ/ *nm* **1** (décalage) discrepancy; **2** Électron, Phys phase difference (**entre** between); **3** Télécom phase shift.

déphasé, ~e /defaze/ **I** *pp* ▶ **déphaser**.

II *pp adj* **1**○ (décalé) out of step (**par rapport à** with); **je suis complètement ~e** I'm not with it at all; **2** Phys out of phase.

déphaser /defaze/ [1] **I** *vtr* **1**○ (décaler) to disorientate; **2** Électrotech to shift phase.

II se déphaser *vpr* fig to fall out of step (**de** with).

déphaseur /defazœʀ/ *nm* Électrotech phase shifter.

dépiautage○ /depjotaʒ/ *nm*, **dépiautement**○ /depjotmɑ̃/ *nm* **1** (de document) dissecting; **2** (d'animal) skinning.

dépiauter○ /depjote/ [1] *vtr* **1** (analyser) to dissect [*document*]; **2** (ôter la peau de) to skin [*animal*].

dépierrage /depjɛʀaʒ/ *nm* stone picking.

dépierrer /depjeʀe/ [1] *vtr* to clear the stones from [*chemin, terrain*]; **le chemin a été dépierré** the path has been cleared of stones.

dépigmentation /depigmɑ̃tasjɔ̃/ *nf* **1** Méd depigmentation; **2** Zool, Bot loss of pigmentation.

dépigmenter: **se dépigmenter** /depigmɑ̃te/ [1] *vpr* **1** Méd (totalement) to become depigmented; (partiellement) to become discoloured[GB]; **2** (volontairement) **se ~ la peau** to remove the colour[GB] from one's skin; **3** Zool, Bot to lose pigmentation.

dépilation /depilasjɔ̃/ *nf* **1** (élimination) hair removal, depilation; **2** (chute) hair loss.

dépilatoire /depilatwaʀ/ **I** *adj* [*crème, produit*] depilatory; **crème ~** depilatory ou hair-removing cream.

II *nm* depilatory.

dépiler /depile/ [1] *vtr* **1** Cosmét to depilate; **2**† Méd **~ qn** to make sb's hair fall out.

dépiquer /depike/ [1] *vtr* Cout to unpick.

dépistable /depistabl/ *adj* detectable.

dépistage /depistaʒ/ *nm* (de maladie) screening; **~ systématique du sida** mass screening for Aids; **~ du cholestérol** cholesterol screening; **centre de ~** screening centre GB; **test de ~ du sida** Aids test; **~ précoce** early detection; **test de ~ génétique** genetic testing.

dépister /depiste/ [1] *vtr* **1** (découvrir) to track down [*criminel*]; to identify [*problème*]; to detect [*maladie*]; **2** (détourner) to deflect [*soupçons*]; **3** Chasse to spoor [*gibier*].

dépit /depi/ **I** *nm* (déception) bitter disappointment, chagrin; (ressentiment) pique; **par ~** in ou out of pique; **par ~ amoureux** on the rebound.

II en dépit de *loc prép* in spite of; **en ~ du bon sens** contrary to common sense; **il travaille en ~ du bon sens** the way he works is contrary to common sense.

dépité, **~e** /depite/ **I** *pp* ▶ **dépiter**.

II *pp adj* piqued (**de** at); **avoir une mine ~e** to look really disappointed ou upset; **~ de faire** piqued at doing.

dépiter /depite/ [1] *vtr* [*personne, comportement, échec*] to upset [*personne*].

déplacé, **~e** /deplase/ **I** *pp* ▶ **déplacer**.

II *pp adj* **1** Sociol [*population, personnes*] displaced; **2** (pas adapté) inappropriate; **c'est ~** (malséant) it's out of place; (inopportun) it's uncalled for; **3** (impoli) [*geste, remarque*] improper.

déplacement /deplasmɑ̃/ *nm* **1** (voyage) trip; **au cours de ses ~s il rencontre...** when he is travelling[GB] around he meets...; **les ~s en car/en train sont en hausse** more people are travelling[GB] by car/train; **les ~s urbains** journeys within the city; **son infirmité lui interdit les ~s** his/her disability means he/she is unable to travel; **elle a fait le ~** (pour aller) she made the effort to go; (pour venir) she made the effort to come; **ça vaut le ~!** it's worth the trip!; **2** (pour le travail) business trip; **être en ~** (pour la journée) to be out on business; (pour plus longtemps) to be away on business; **3** (frais) **payer pour le ~** (de médecin, d'artisan) to pay a call-out fee; **4** (action de déplacer) moving; (action de se déplacer) movement; (d'attention, de problème) shifting; (de l'âge de retraite) change; **le ~ des voix sur un autre parti** the swing of votes to another party; **5** (de population) displacement (**vers** to); (d'employé) transfer; (de service) transfer (**vers** to); **6** Ling, Naut, Psych displacement.

■ **~ d'air** air displacement; **~ de vertèbre** slipped disc.

déplacer /deplase/ [12] **I** *vtr* **1** (dans l'espace) (volontairement) to move [*objet, personne, lieu, membre*] (**de** from); (par accident) to dislodge [*tuile*]; to dislocate [*os*]; **2** (dans le temps) to move [*réunion, cours*]; to change [*âge de la retraite*]; **~ ses vacances** to change the dates of one's holidays GB ou vacation US; **3** (faire porter sur autre chose) to shift [*débat, problème, attention*]; to distract [*attention*]; **cela a déplacé des voix du parti X sur le parti Y** this has swung votes from the X party to the Y party; **4** (muter) to move; (faire venir) to call [sb] out [*médecin, artisan*]; (faire migrer) to displace; (attirer) to bring in [*foules*].

II se déplacer *vpr* **1** (changer de position, de place) [*personne, téléphérique, courants*] to move; **2** (être mis ailleurs) [*meuble, bouton*] to be moved; [*tuile*] to be dislodged; **se ~ avec difficulté** [*meuble*] to be difficult to move; **se ~ une vertèbre** to slip a disc; **3** (avancer, marcher) to get about; **se ~ avec des béquilles** to get about on crutches; **se ~ en fauteuil roulant** to be in a wheelchair; **se ~ avec difficulté** to have difficulty getting about; **4** (avec moyen de transport) to get about; (plus loin) to travel; **se ~ en voiture/à bicyclette** to get about by car/by bike; **5** (aller quelque part) to go; (venir) to come; **il ne s'est même pas déplacé** he didn't even bother to come; **ils se déplacent librement** they come and go as they please; **elle ne se déplace qu'avec ses gardes du corps** she never goes anywhere without her bodyguards; **il ne se déplace que la nuit** he only moves around at night; **6** [*médecin, artisan*] to go out on call; **faire ~ qn pour rien** to call sb out for nothing.

IDIOMES **~ de l'air** or **beaucoup d'air**○ to like to make one's presence felt.

déplafonnement /deplafɔnmɑ̃/ *nm* lifting of the ceiling.

déplafonner /deplafɔne/ [1] *vtr* fig to lift the ceiling on; **déplafonné** without ceiling; **les cotisations sont déplafonnées** the ceiling on contributions has been lifted.

déplaire /deplɛʀ/ [59] **I** *vi* **1** (ne pas avoir de succès) **le spectacle a déplu/n'a pas déplu** the show was not well received/was moderately successful; **2** (rebuter) **elle déplaît** she is not liked ou is disliked.

II déplaire à *vtr ind* **cela m'a déplu** I didn't like it; **elle me déplaît** I don't like her; **une vie luxueuse ne me déplairait pas** I wouldn't say no to a life of luxury; **le spectacle m'a profondément déplu** I didn't like the show at all; **la situation n'est pas pour me ~** the situation quite suits me; **tout ceci me déplaît fort** I dislike all this intensely.

III se déplaire *vpr* **1** (ne pas être bien) **je me déplais ici** I don't like it here; **la plante se déplaît à l'ombre** the plant doesn't like to be ou isn't happy in the shade; **2** (l'un l'autre) to dislike each other; **ils se sont déplu** they disliked ou didn't like each other.

IV *v impers* **il me déplairait de vous voir partir** fml I should be sorry to see you go; **il ne me déplaîrait pas de les voir partir** I'd be quite happy to see them go; **je le ferai ne vous en déplaise** fml with all due respect to you I shall do it in any case.

déplaisant, **~e** /deplɛzɑ̃, ɑ̃t/ *adj* unpleasant, disagreeable.

déplaisir /deplezir/ *nm* fml displeasure.

déplanter /deplɑ̃te/ [1] *vtr* to dig up [*plante*]; to clear [*jardin, terrain*]; to pull up [*piquet*]; to take down [*tente*].

déplâtrage /deplɑtʀaʒ/ *nm* **1** Constr stripping of plaster; **~ d'un mur** stripping plaster off a wall; **2** Méd removal of plaster (cast); **~ d'un bras** removal of the plaster (cast) from an arm.

déplâtrer /deplɑtʀe/ [1] *vtr* **1** Constr to strip the plaster off; **2** Méd to remove the cast from.

déplétion /deplesjɔ̃/ *nf* depletion; **~ des réserves** depletion of stocks.

dépliage /deplijaʒ/ *nm* unfolding.

dépliant /deplijɑ̃/ *nm* **1** gén leaflet; **2** Édition gatefold; **~ hors-texte** foldout.

déplier /deplije/ [2] **I** *vtr* to unfold [*mouchoir, journal*]; to open out [*carte*]; to display [*marchandise*]; **~ les jambes** to stretch one's legs out.

II se déplier *vpr* **1** [*parachute*] to unfold; [*feuille, drapeau*] to unfurl; **2**○ [*personne*] to rise to one's feet.

déplisser /deplise/ [1] **I** *vtr* to take the pleats out of [*vêtement plissé*]; to remove the creases from, to smooth out [*vêtement froissé*].

II se déplisser *vpr* [*jupe*] to lose its pleats.

déploiement /deplwamɑ̃/ *nm* **1** (démonstration) display; **~ de force/solidarité** display of force/solidarity; **un ~ considérable de nouvelles mesures** a deployment of a large number of new measures; **2** Mil deployment; **~ de missiles** deployment of missiles; **~ militaire/britannique** deployment of troops/of British troops; **3** (ouverture) (d'aile) spreading; (de drapeau, voile) unfurling; (de panneau) opening out.

déplomber /deplɔ̃be/ [1] *vtr* **1** gén to unseal [*compteur, colis*]; **2** Dent to remove the filling from [*dent*].

déplorable /deplɔʀabl/ *adj* **1** (fâcheux) [*événement, incident, initiative*] regrettable; **2** (très mauvais) [*attitude, exemple, note*] appalling, deplorable; **temps/santé ~** appalling weather/health.

déplorer /deplɔʀe/ [1] *vtr* to deplore [*événement, état de fait*]; **~ que** to lament ou bemoan the fact that; **'nous manquons d'argent,' déplore le maire** 'we're short of money,' laments the mayor; **il est à ~ que...** it's deplorable that...; **trois morts sont à ~** three deaths have been reported.

déployer /deplwaje/ [23] **I** *vtr* **1** (montrer) to display [*activité, talent*]; **~ des trésors de** to display a wealth of; **~ toute son énergie pour faire** to expend all one's energy to do; **~ une activité fébrile pour faire qch** to work really hard to get sth done; **2** Mil to deploy [*chars, troupes*]; **3** (déplier) to spread [*ailes*]; to unfurl [*drapeau, voile*]; to open out [*panneau*].

II se déployer *vpr* **1** (s'éparpiller) [*groupe, policiers*] to fan out; **2** Mil (prendre position) [*chars, troupes*] to be deployed; **3** (se déplier) [*ailes*] to spread; [*drapeau, voile*] to unfurl; [*panneau*] to open out.

déplumer: **se déplumer** /deplyme/ [1] *vpr* **1** [*oiseau*] to lose its feathers; **2**○ [*personne*] to go bald, to lose one's hair.

dépoitraillé○, **~e** /depwatʀaje/ *adj* with one's shirt open to the waist.

dépolarisant, **~e** /depɔlaʀizɑ̃, ɑ̃t/ **I** *adj* depolarizing.

II *nm* depolarizer.

dépolarisation /depɔlaʀizasjɔ̃/ *nf* depolarization.

dépolariser /depɔlaʀize/ [1] *vtr* to depolarize.

dépoli, **~e** /depɔli/ *adj* **verre ~** gén frosted glass; Phot ground glass.

dépolir /depɔliʀ/ [3] **I** *vtr* to frost [*verre*]; to take the gloss off [*vernis*]; to texture [*marbre*].

II se dépolir *vpr* to tarnish.

dépolissage /depɔlisaʒ/ *nm* (de verre) frosting; (de marbre) texturing.

dépolitisation /depɔlitizasjɔ̃/ *nf* depoliticization.

dépolitiser /depɔlitize/ [1] **I** *vtr* to depoliticize [*conflit, débat, personne, groupe*].

II se dépolitiser *vpr* to become depoliticized.

dépolluer /depɔlɥe/ [1] *vtr* to rid [sth] of pollution, to clean up [*rivière, lac*].

dépollution /depɔlysjɔ̃/ *nf* cleanup.

dépolymérisation /depɔlimeʀizasjɔ̃/ *nf* depolymerization.

dépolymériser /depɔlimeʀize/ [1] *vtr*, **se dépolymériser** *vpr* to depolymerize.

déponent, **~e** /depɔnɑ̃, ɑ̃t/ **I** *adj* deponent.

II *nm* deponent verb.

dépopulation /depɔpylasjɔ̃/ *nf* depopulation.

déportation /depɔʀtasjɔ̃/ *nf* **1** (dans un camp

de concentration) internment in a concentration camp; **mourir en ~** to die in a concentration camp; **2** (bannissement) deportation, transportation.

déporté, **~e** /depɔʀte/ *nm,f* **1** (dans un camp de concentration) prisoner interned in a concentration camp; **2** (personne bannie) transported convict.

déportement /depɔʀtəmɑ̃/ *nm* **1** (tendance à se déporter) swerving; **2** (embardée) swerve.

déporter /depɔʀte/ [1] **I** *vtr* **1** (interner) to send [sb] to a concentration camp [*personne*]; **2** (faire dévier d'une trajectoire) to make [sth] swerve [*véhicule*] (**sur la gauche/droite** to the left/right); **3** Hist (bannir) to deport, to transport (**à** to).

II se déporter *vpr* to swerve (**sur la gauche/droite** to the left/right).

déposant, **~e** /depozɑ̃, ɑ̃t/ *nm,f* **1** Fin depositor; **les petits ~s** small savers; **2** Jur (de bien) bailor; (témoin) deponent.

dépose /depoz/ *nf* (retrait) gén removal; (de tapis) taking up; (de tenture, rideau) taking down; (de robinet) taking out.

déposer /depoze/ [1] **I** *vtr* **1** (poser) to put down [*fardeau*]; to dump, to tip GB [*ordures*]; to lay [*gerbe*] (**sur** on); **'défense de ~ des ordures'** 'no dumping', 'no tipping'; **il déposa un baiser sur sa joue** he kissed his/her cheek; **~ les armes** fig to lay down one's arms; **2** (laisser) to leave [*objet, lettre*]; (au passage) to drop off, to leave [*paquet, passager*]; **on a déposé un paquet pour toi** somebody left a parcel for you; **dépose ma jupe au pressing en passant** drop my skirt off at the dry-cleaner's on your way; **le taxi m'a déposé à la gare** the taxi dropped me (off) at the station; **je peux vous ~ quelque part?** can I drop you (off) somewhere?, can I give you a lift GB ou ride US somewhere?; **3** (verser) gén, Fin to deposit [*argent, titre, bijoux*]; **~ de l'argent à la banque/dans un coffre/sur un compte** to deposit money in the bank/in a safe/in an account; **~ sa signature à la banque** to give the bank a specimen signature; **ses œuvres seront déposées au musée de la ville** his/her works will be put into the local museum; **4** (faire enregistrer) to register [*marque, brevet, nom*]; to submit [*rapport, dossier, offre*]; to table GB, to propose [*motion, amendement*]; to introduce [*projet de loi*]; to file [*requête*]; to lodge [*plainte*]; **~ une demande d'extradition** to apply for extradition; **~ son bilan** Fin to file a petition in bankruptcy; **~ sa candidature** [*chercheur d'emploi*] to apply (**à** for); [*homme politique*] to stand GB, to run (**à** for); **~ une motion de censure** Pol to move a vote of no confidence; **~ un préavis de grève** Entr to give notice of strike action; **5** (laisser un dépôt) [*fleuve*] to deposit [*alluvions, sable*]; **6** (destituer) to depose [*souverain, dirigeant*]; **7** (enlever) to remove [*moteur*]; to take up [*tapis*]; to take down [*rideau, tenture*].

II *vi* **1** Jur (devant un juge) to testify, to give evidence (**auprès de** before); (au commissariat) to make a statement; **2** (laisser un dépôt) [*liquide, vin*] to leave a sediment.

III se déposer *vpr* [*poussière, lie*] to settle (**sur** on); [*sels, calcaire, sable*] to collect.

dépositaire /depozitɛʀ/ *nmf* **1** Comm **~ (exclusif)** (sole) agent (**de** for); **~ agréé** authorized dealer; **2** (gardien) (d'objet confié) trustee; Jur (de biens) bailee; fig (de secret) guardian (**de** of).

■ **~ de journaux** newsagent GB, newsdealer US.

déposition /depozisjɔ̃/ *nf* **1** Jur (au tribunal) evidence ¢; (recueillie) statement; (par écrit) deposition; **~ sous serment** sworn statement; **2** (destitution) (de dirigeant, souverain) deposition; (de magistrat) removal from office; **3** Art **~ de croix** Deposition (from the Cross).

déposséder /depɔsede/ [14] *vtr* **~ qn de qch** to dispossess sb of sth, to take sth away from sb.

dépossession /depɔsɛsjɔ̃/ *nf* dispossession.

dépôt /depo/ *nm* **1** (entrepôt) warehouse; (plus petit) store, storehouse US; Rail depot; (à la douane) bonded warehouse; Mil (de garnison) depot; **~ d'autobus** bus depot; **être en ~** (à la douane) to be in a bonded warehouse; **2** Comm (succursale) outlet; **l'épicerie fait ~ de pain** the grocer's sells bread; **la maison a 30 ~s** the firm has 30 outlets; **il y a un ~ de gaz au garage** they sell bottled gas at the garage GB ou service station US; **3** (enregistrement) Admin, Jur (d'acte, de candidature, plainte) filing ¢; (de marque, brevet) registration; (de projet de loi) introduction; (de clause, d'amendement) tabling ¢ GB, proposal; **4** (remise en un lieu) **nous recommandons le ~ des documents chez un notaire** we recommend that the documents be deposited with a notary; **date limite de ~ des déclarations d'impôt/des dossiers de demande de bourse** deadline for income tax returns/grant applications; **5** Fin (de fonds) deposit; (de titres) lodging ¢; **~ en banque/coffre-fort** bank/safe deposit; **banque/compte de ~** deposit bank/account; **en ~** [*fonds*] on deposit; [*bijoux*] in a safe at the bank; **mettre des valeurs en ~** to place securities in a safe deposit; **6** (sédiment) deposit; **~ glaciaire** glacial deposit; **~ de tartre** deposit of tartar; **il y a un ~ de calcaire dans la bouilloire** the kettle is furred up; **7** (prison) police cells; **8** (chose confiée) **restituer un ~** to restore ou return an object entrusted to one.

■ **~ d'armes** arms store; (clandestin) arms cache; **~ de bilan** voluntary liquidation; **entreprises menacées de ~ de bilan** firms threatened with bankruptcy; **~ légal** *formal deposit of a copy of a book, film, record, etc with an institution*; **~ de marchandises** Rail goods GB ou freight US depot; **~ de matériel** Mil depot; **~ de munitions** Mil munitions store; (au rebut) munitions dump; **~ d'ordures** (rubbish) tip ou dump GB, garbage dump US; **~ à terme fixe/à vue** fixed term/demand ou sight deposit.

dépotage /depɔtaʒ/ *nm*, **dépotement** /depɔtmɑ̃/ *nm* **1** Hort removal of a plant from its pot; **2** Tech (déchargement) stripping.

dépoter /depɔte/ [1] *vtr* **1** Hort to remove a plant from its pot; **2** Tech (décharger) to strip.

dépotoir /depɔtwaʀ/ *nm* **1** (décharge) rubbish dump, rubbish tip GB, garbage dump US; **2**○ (lieu en désordre) shambles○ (*sg*); **3** Ind (établissement de traitement) sewage works, sewage plant.

dépôt-vente, *pl* **dépôts-ventes** /depovɑ̃t/ *nm* secondhand shop GB ou store (*where goods are sold on commission*).

dépouille /depuj/ **I** *nf* **1** (peau) skin; (de gros mammifère) hide; **2** Zool (de serpent) slough; (d'insecte) husk; **3** (cadavre) **~ (mortelle)** mortal remains (*pl*).

II dépouilles *nfpl* (butin) spoils; **le système des ~s** US Pol the spoils system.

dépouillé, **~e** /depuje/ **I** *pp* ▶ **dépouiller**.

II *pp adj* **1** (sobre, simple) [*style, formes*] pared down, spare; **2** (écorché) [*animal*] skinned; **3** (dénudé) [*arbre*] bare, leafless.

dépouillement /depujmɑ̃/ *nm* **1** (examen) **le ~ du courrier/des documents** going through the mail/the documents; **assister au ~ du scrutin** or **des voix** to be present when the votes are counted; **procéder au ~ du courrier** to go through the mail; **le ~ du questionnaire sera long** it'll take a long time to analyze the answers to the questionnaire; **2** (ascèse) asceticism; **vivre dans le plus grand ~** to live a very ascetic ou spartan life; **3** (sobriété) sobriety.

dépouiller /depuje/ [1] **I** *vtr* **1** (dépecer) to skin [*animal*]; **2** (dénuder) to strip [*personne*]; to lay [sth] bare [*champ, région*]; **le vent dépouille les arbres (de leurs feuilles)** the wind is stripping the leaves off the trees; **3** (déposséder) to rob [*voyageur*]; hum to fleece○ [*contribuable*]; **~ un héritier** to rob sb of his inheritance; **l'État dépouille ceux qu'il devrait défendre** the State robs those it should protect; **~ qn de qch** to rob sb of sth; **4** (ouvrir) to open [*courrier*]; to count [*scrutin*]; (examiner) to go through [*archives, documents*].

II se dépouiller *vpr* **1** (se démunir) [*personne*] **se ~ de** to shed [*vêtements*]; to divest oneself of [*biens*]; fig to cast off [*morgue, fierté*]; **2** Zool (muer) [*serpent*] to slough; **3** (se dénuder) [*arbre*] to shed its leaves; [*style*] to become spare.

dépourvu, **~e** /depuʀvy/ **I** *adj* **~ de** devoid of, lacking in [*intérêt, charme, finesse, talent, qualités*]; free of [*agressivité, arrière-pensées*]; unequipped with [*accessoire*]; without [*chauffage, rideaux, rampe*]; **elle semble complètement ~e de bon sens** she seems completely devoid of ou lacking in common sense; **des négociations ~es d'ambiguïtés** negotiations free of all ambiguity; **des travailleurs ~s de toute qualification** workers who have no qualifications whatsoever.

II *nm* **prendre qn au ~** to take sb by surprise, to catch sb off-guard.

dépoussiérage /depusjeʀaʒ/ *nm* **1** gén dusting; **2** Tech (procédé) dust extraction, dust removal; **3** (d'organisation, d'idéologie) revamping, retooling US.

dépoussiérant /depusjeʀɑ̃/ *nm* furniture polish.

dépoussiérer /depusjeʀe/ [14] *vtr* **1** gén to dust; **2** Tech to extract dust from; **3** fig to revamp [*idéologie, loi, programme politique*].

dépravation /depʀavasjɔ̃/ *nf* depravity.

dépravé, **~e** /depʀave/ **I** *adj* depraved.

II *nm,f* depraved person; **c'est un ~** he's depraved.

dépraver /depʀave/ [1] **I** *vtr* to deprave.

II se dépraver *vpr* to become depraved.

dépréciation /depʀesjasjɔ̃/ *nf* depreciation.

déprécier /depʀesje/ [2] **I** *vtr* **1** Écon, Fin to depreciate; **2** (rabaisser) to disparage, to depreciate.

II se déprécier *vpr* **1** Écon, Fin to depreciate; **2** (se rabaisser) to put oneself down.

déprédateur -trice /depʀedatœʀ, tʀis/ **I** *adj* destructive.

II *nm,f* vandal.

déprédation /depʀedasjɔ̃/ *nf* **1** (pillage) pillaging ¢; (dégâts) damage ¢; **commettre des ~s** to cause damage; **commettre des ~s dans une pièce** to vandalize a room; **2** Jur embezzlement.

déprendre: **se déprendre** /depʀɑ̃dʀ/ [52] *vpr* littér **se ~ de qn/qch** to free oneself from sb/sth.

dépressif, **-ive** /depʀesif, iv/ *adj, nm,f* depressive.

dépression /depʀesjɔ̃/ *nf* **1** ▶ **271** Méd, Psych (état) depression; **~ nerveuse** nervous breakdown; **faire de la ~** to be depressed; **2** Météo (atmospheric) depression; **une ~ centrée sur le nord de la France** a depression over northern France; **3** Écon depression, slump; **4** Géog depression.

dépressionnaire /depʀesjɔnɛʀ/ *adj* **zone ~** area of low pressure, low.

dépressurisation /depʀesyʀizasjɔ̃/ *nf* (volontaire) depressurization; (accidentelle) loss of pressure.

dépressuriser /depʀesyʀize/ [1] *vtr* to depressurize.

déprimant, **~e** /depʀimɑ̃, ɑ̃t/ *adj* depressing.

déprime○ /depʀim/ *nf* depression; **il est en pleine ~** he's really depressed; **faire de la ~** to get depressed.

déprimé, **~e** /depʀime/ **I** *adj* depressed.

II *nm,f* depressed person, depressive.

déprimer /depʀime/ [1] *vtr* **1** (démoraliser) to depress; **tout ça me déprime** all this is depressing me ou getting me down; **2** (affaisser) to indent, to make a depression in.

depuis

L'adverbe

depuis se traduit généralement par *since*:

elle a démontré, depuis, qu'elle pouvait le faire = she has since demonstrated that she could do it

Lorsqu'on veut insister sur le temps qui s'est écoulé depuis l'action dont on parle on peut renforcer *since* par *ever*:

nous nous sommes disputés hier, depuis il me fait la tête = we had an argument yesterday, he's been sulking ever since

Attention, cette construction ne marche pas à la forme négative:

depuis il ne me parle plus = he hasn't talked to me since

La préposition

depuis préposition de temps se traduit par *since* lorsqu'il sert à indiquer un point de départ, une date, une heure précise:

depuis 1789 = since 1789
depuis 2 heures du matin = since 2 am
depuis le début = since the beginning

et par *for* lorsqu'il sert à indiquer une durée, un nombre de jours, d'heures:

depuis deux heures = for two hours
depuis six ans = for six years
depuis quelques mois = for a few months

depuis + date

j'apprends l'anglais depuis l'âge de 12 ans = I've been learning English since I was 12
cette maison nous appartient depuis 1876 = we've owned this house since 1876
je le connais depuis l'été dernier = I've known him since last summer
je n'ai rien mangé depuis hier soir = I haven't eaten since yesterday evening
il a fait trois films depuis le début de sa carrière = he's made three films since the beginning of his career
il neigeait depuis midi = it had been snowing since midday
il n'avait pas plu depuis dimanche = it hadn't rained since Sunday

On notera l'emploi de la forme progressive:

il habite ici depuis 1990 = he's lived here since 1990 *ou* he's been living here since 1990
il habite ici depuis le mois de janvier = he's been living here since January

depuis + durée

il travaille ici depuis quelques années = he's worked here for a few years
il travaille ici depuis dix ans = he's worked here for ten years
nous marchons depuis deux heures = we've been walking for two hours
je n'ai pas eu de nouvelles depuis six mois = I haven't had any news for six months
je dormais depuis une heure = I had been sleeping for an hour
je ne les avais pas vus depuis cinq ans = I hadn't seen them for five years

On trouvera des exemples supplémentaires et les autres emplois de la préposition *depuis* et de la locution conjonctive *depuis que* dans l'entrée ci-dessous.

déprogrammer /depʀɔgʀame/ [1] *vtr* to cancel.

dépucelage◐ /depyslaʒ/ *nm* losing of virginity.

dépuceler◐ /depysle/ [19] *vtr* to take sb's virginity; **se faire ~** to lose one's virginity (**par** to).

depuis /dəpɥi/ **I** *adv* since; **je ne les ai pas revus ~** I haven't seen them since; **il est parti il y a deux ans, ~ je n'ai plus de nouvelles** he left two years ago, since then I haven't had any news; **elle a été gravement malade l'année dernière, ~ nous sommes inquiets** she was very ill last year and we've been worried ever since.

II *prép* **1** (marquant le point de départ) since; **je fais du courrier ~ 9 heures du matin** I've been writing letters since 9 am; **j'ai écrit trois lettres ~ 9 heures du matin** I've written three letters since 9 am; **j'habite ici ~ le 1er juillet** I've been living here since 1 July; **elle est malade ~ ce matin** she's been ill since this morning; **il n'a pas retravaillé ~ son accident** he hasn't worked since his accident; **elle fait de la danse ~ l'âge de six ans** she has been dancing since she was six years old; **~ ce jour-là** since that day; **~ quand vis-tu là-bas?** how long have you been living there?; **~ quand tu réponds à ta mère?** so you're answering your mother back now, are you?; **~ lors** since then; **~ ta naissance** since you were born; **~ leur réconciliation** since they were reconciled ou since their reconciliation; **~ le jour où je les ai rencontrés** since the day I met them; **~ ce jour, je ne les ai pas revus** since that day I haven't seen them again; **~ les événements de mai 68** since the events of May '68; **~ sa création en 1986, l'entreprise s'est développée** since it was set up in 1986, the company has expanded; **c'est ce que je te répète ~ le début** that's what I've been telling you all along; **~ le début jusqu'à la fin** from start to finish; **2** (marquant la durée) for; **~ deux heures/dix ans/trois siècles** for two hours/ten years/three centuries; **il fait une collection de timbres ~ deux ans** he's been collecting stamps for two years; **ils sont mariés/amis ~ six mois** they've been married/friends for six months; **il pleut ~ trois jours** it's been raining for three days; **nous marchions ~ deux heures lorsque**... we had been walking for two hours when...; **je ne fume plus ~ six mois** I gave up smoking six months ago, I haven't smoked for six months; **~ quand** or **combien de temps est-ce qu'elle enseigne?** how long has she been teaching?; **cela dure ~ des jours/mois/années** it's been going on for days/months/years; **~ longtemps** for a long time; **je le savais ~ longtemps** I had known for a long time; **il n'habite plus ici ~ longtemps** he hasn't lived here for a long time; **~ peu** recently; **il est installé à Caen ~ peu** he has recently settled in Caen; **~ toujours** always; **le travail/les vacances dont il rêve ~ toujours** the job/the vacation he has always dreamed of; **on pratique cette coutume ~ toujours** this custom has been observed from time immemorial; **3** (marquant le lieu) from; **~ ma fenêtre/le belvédère on aperçoit**... from my window/the belvedere you can see...; **~ chez moi/Dijon il faut deux heures** from where I live/Dijon it takes two hours; **le lancement de la fusée sera retransmis ~ Kourou** the launch of the rocket will be broadcast from Kourou; **~ Paris jusqu'à Arles** from Paris to Arles; **4** (dans une série) **tous les métiers ~ caissier jusqu'à infirmier** every job from cashier to nurse; **chemises, robes ~ 50 francs** shirts, dresses from 50 francs; **~ le premier jusqu'au dernier** from first to last; **nous avons toutes les pointures ~ le 34** we have all sizes from 34 upward(s).

III depuis que *loc conj* gén since; (pour renforcer) ever since; **~ qu'il sait nager, il adore l'eau** he has loved the water ever since he learned to swim; **je le vois rarement ~ qu'il habite au Canada** I haven't seen much of him since he went to live in Canada; **elle a changé ~ que sa fille est née** she's changed a lot since her daughter was born; **il pleut ~ que nous sommes arrivés** it's been raining ever since we arrived; **j'ai grossi ~ que je ne fais plus de sport** I've put on weight since I stopped doing any sport; **il dirige l'entreprise ~ qu'il a 20 ans** he's been running the company since he was 20.

dépuratif, **-ive** /depyʀatif, iv/ **I** *adj* depurative.

II *nm* depurative.

députation /depytasjɔ̃/ *nf* **1** (délégation) deputation; **2** (mandat de député) Pol post of deputy; **être candidat à la ~** to stand GB ou run US for the post of deputy.

député /depyte/ *nm* **1** Pol deputy; **élu ~ de Lyon** elected (as) deputy for Lyons; **~ britannique** (British) MP; **être ~ au Parlement européen** to be a Euro-MP GB ou member of the European Parliament; **2** (envoyé) representative, delegate.

député-maire, *pl* **députés-maires** /depytemɛʀ/ *nm* deputy and mayor; **~ de Beaune** deputy and mayor of Beaune.

députer /depyte/ [1] *vtr* **~ qn auprès d'un comité** to send sb as a representative to serve on a committee; **~ qn pour faire qch** to delegate sb to do sth; **la Corse a député Peretti à l'Assemblée nationale** Pol Corsica has elected Peretti to be a deputy in the National Assembly.

déqualification /dekalifikasjɔ̃/ *nf* deskilling.

déqualifier /dekalifje/ [2] *vtr* to deskill.

der○ /dɛʀ/ *nf* last; **la ~ des ~s** Hist the war to end all wars; **dix de ~** Jeux *bonus of 10 points awarded to player who takes the last trick in game of belote*.

déraciné, **~e** /deʀasine/ **I** *adj* lit, fig uprooted.

II *nm,f* uprooted person.

déracinement /deʀasinmɑ̃/ *nm* **1** (d'arbre) uprooting; **2** (d'immigré) (processus) loss of connection with one's roots; (résultat) rootlessness.

déraciner /deʀasine/ [1] *vtr* **1** lit to uproot [*arbre, plante*]; **2** fig to uproot [*personne*]; **3** (faire disparaître) to eradicate [*préjugé, abus*].

déraillement /deʀɑjmɑ̃/ *nm* derailment.

dérailler /deʀɑje/ [1] *vi* **1** Rail to derail, to go off the rails; **faire ~ un train** to derail a train; **2**○ (perdre l'esprit) [*vieillard*] to go senile, to lose one's marbles○; (tenir des propos incohérents) to rave, to ramble; (se tromper) to talk through one's hat○; **mais tu déraille!** you're talking through your hat○!; **3** [*voix*] (chantée) to waver; (parlée) to crack; [*instrument*] to go out of pitch.

dérailleur /deʀɑjœʀ/ *nm* **1** (de bicyclette) derailleur; **2** Rail derailing stop.

déraison /deʀɛzɔ̃/ *nf* fml madness.

déraisonnable /deʀɛzɔnabl/ **I** *adj* (impensable) unrealistic; (peu sage) senseless; (excessif) unreasonable.

II *nm* insanity; **à la limite du ~** bordering on insanity.

déraisonner /deʀɛzɔne/ [1] *vi* not to be compos mentis.

dérangé, **~e** /deʀɑ̃ʒe/ **I** *pp* ▶ **déranger**.
II *pp adj* **1** [*estomac*] upset; **2**○ (fou) **être ~**, **avoir l'esprit ~** to be deranged.

dérangeant, **~e** /deʀɑ̃ʒɑ̃, ɑ̃t/ *adj* [*idée, livre, film*] disturbing.

dérangement /deʀɑ̃ʒmɑ̃/ **I** *nm* **1** (inconvénient) trouble, inconvenience; **c'est trop de ~** it's too much trouble, it's too inconvenient; **excusez le ~** sorry to bother you; **2** (dérèglement) **~ intestinal** stomach upset; **être en ~** [*ascenseur, téléphone*] to be out of order.
II dérangements *nmpl* Télécom fault reporting service (*sg*); **appeler les ~s** to call the fault reporting service.

déranger /deʀɑ̃ʒe/ [13] **I** *vtr* **1** (importuner) [*visiteur, téléphone*] to disturb [*personne*]; **je vous dérange?** am I disturbing you?; **'prière de ne pas ~'** 'do not disturb'; **entrez, vous ne me dérangez pas du tout** come in, you're not disturbing me in the least; **excusez-moi de vous ~** (I'm) sorry to bother you; **2** (gêner) [*bruit, fumée*] to bother [*personne*]; **ça ne me dérange pas du tout** it doesn't bother me at all; **est-ce que la fumée vous dérange?** do you mind if I smoke?; **cela vous dérangerait-il de me le livrer?** would you mind delivering it?; **et alors, ça te dérange que je sorte?** so, what's it to you if I go out?; **3** (surprendre) to disturb [*animal, voleur*]; **4** (faire déplacer) to disturb [*spectateurs assis*]; (faire venir) to call out [*médecin, plombier*]; **~ dix personnes pour arriver à sa place** to disturb ten people getting to one's seat; **on l'a dérangé trois fois cette nuit** he was called out three times last night; **~ qn pour rien** to bother ou disturb sb for nothing; **5** (contrarier) to upset [*personne*]; to upset [*ordre établi, emploi du temps*]; (troubler) to disturb [*personne*]; **le ministre ne veut pas ~ les riches** the minister doesn't want to upset the rich; **ça dérange mes habitudes** it upsets my routine; **le film/la vérité dérange** the film/truth is disturbing; **cet auteur dérange par sa franchise** this writer's frankness is disturbing; **6** (mettre en désordre) to disturb [*affaires, livres*]; to ruffle, to mess up [*coiffure*] ; to turn [sth] upside down [*pièce*]; **7** (dérégler) to upset [*estomac, foie*]; to affect [*esprit*]; **les chagrins lui ont dérangé l'esprit** grief has affected his mind.
II se déranger *vpr* **1** (se déplacer) (aller) to go out; (venir) [*médecin, plombier*] to come out; **téléphone, tu n'as pas besoin de te ~ pour passer une commande** you don't have to go out to place an order, just phone; **ne vous dérangez pas, je vous l'apporte** don't come out, I'll bring it over; **je me suis dérangé pour rien, c'était fermé** I wasted my time going there, it was shut; **2** (se lever) to get up; **ne vous dérangez pas!** please don't get up!; (changer de place) to move; **il ne s'est même pas dérangé pour les laisser passer** he couldn't be bothered to move to let them by; **3** (faire un effort) **il ne se dérangerait pas pour m'aider** he wouldn't lift a finger to help me; **je vous en prie, ne vous dérangez pas pour moi** please don't go to any trouble ou don't put yourself out on my account; **ne vous dérangez pas, je m'en occupe/je vais la raccompagner en voiture** don't put yourself out, I'll see to it/I'll drive her back.

dérapage /deʀapaʒ/ *nm* **1** (de véhicule) skid; **~ contrôlé** controlled skid; **des traces de ~** skid marks; **2** (erreur) blunder; **3** (augmentation) escalation; **~ des prix/salaires** escalation of prices/salaries; **4** (perte de contrôle) loss of control; **les risques de ~ demeurent** the risk of things getting out of control remains; **gare au ~!** don't let it get out of control!; **~ verbal** slip; **5** (sur skis) sideslip; **faire un ~** to sideslip.

déraper /deʀape/ [1] *vi* **1** [*prix, affaire, débat*] to get out of control; **le mouvement dérape à droite** the movement is veering toward(s) the right; **2** [*outil, couteau*] to slip; **3** [*personne, voiture*] to skid; **4** (à skis) to sideslip; **descendre en dérapant** to sideslip down.

dératé○, **~e** /deʀate/ *nm,f* **courir comme un ~** to run like the clappers○ GB, to run like crazy.

dératisation /deʀatizasjɔ̃/ *nf* pest control (*for rats*).

dératiser /deʀatize/ [1] *vtr* to clear [sth] of rats.

derby /dɛʀbi/ *nm* **1** Équit Derby; **2** (en football, rugby) local derby; (en cyclisme) **~ de la route** Bordeaux-Paris race.

Derbyshire **▶ 692** *nprm* **le ~** Derbyshire.

derche◑ /dɛʀʃ/ *nm* arse◑ GB ou ass○ US, buttocks; ▶ **faux**.

derechef /dəʀəʃɛf/ *adv* fml once again.

déréglé, **~e** /deʀegle/ **I** *pp* ▶ **dérégler**.
II *pp adj* [*esprit*] unbalanced; **avoir le sommeil ~** to have a disrupted sleep pattern.

dérèglement /deʀɛgləmɑ̃/ **I** *nm* (de machine) fault; Météo disturbance; (psychologique) disturbance; (physiologique) disorder; (socio-économique) imbalance.
II dérèglements *mpl* fml excesses.

déréglementation /deʀɛgləmɑ̃tasjɔ̃/ *nf* deregulation; **~ aérienne** airline deregulation.

déréglementer /deʀɛgləmɑ̃te/ [1] *vtr* to deregulate.

dérégler /deʀegle/ [14] *vtr* to affect [*temps, organe*]; to upset [*déroulement*]; **~ la radio** to lose the station on the radio; **~ la télévision** to lose the channel on the TV; **~ le réveil** to change the alarm clock to the wrong time.

déresponsabilisation /deʀɛspɔ̃sabilizasjɔ̃/ *nf* lack of any sense of responsibility (**de** on the part of).

déresponsabiliser /deʀɛspɔ̃sabilize/ [1] *vtr* to remove all sense of responsibility from; **déresponsabilisé** with no sense of responsibility.

dérider /deʀide/ [1] **I** *vtr* to cheer [sb] up.
II se dérider *vpr* to start smiling; **il ne s'est pas déridé** he didn't smile once.

dérision /deʀizjɔ̃/ *nf* scorn, derision; **avec ~** scornfully, derisively; **un rire de ~** a derisive laugh; **être un objet de ~** to be the object of derision; **tourner en ~** to greet [sth/sb] with derision.

dérisoire /deʀizwaʀ/ *adj* [*pouvoir, spectacle*] pathetic; [*somme, montant*] trivial, derisory.

dérivable /deʀivabl/ *adj* Math differentiable.

dérivatif, **-ive** /deʀivatif, iv/ **I** *adj* Ling derivative.
II *nm* **1** gén diversion (**à** from); **2** Méd derivative.

dérivation /deʀivasjɔ̃/ *nf* **1** (de cours d'eau) diversion; **un barrage/canal de ~** a diversion dam/channel; **2** (routière) diversion GB, detour US; **mettre en place une ~** to set up a diversion; **3** (de navire, nappe) drifting; **4** Méd (en chirurgie) shunt; **5** Électrotech shunt; **en ~** in parallel; **6** Ling derivation; **~ régressive** back formation; **7** Math differentiation; **8** Mil (en artillerie) drift; (pour armes légères) deflection; **(angle) de ~** drift ou deflection.

dérivationnel, **-elle** /deʀivasjɔnɛl/ *adj* Ling derivational.

dérive /deʀiv/ *nf* **1** (évolution regrettable) drift; **~ nationaliste** nationalist drift; **2** (errance) drift; **à la ~** drifting; **aller** or **partir à la ~** to drift away; **3** Écon slide; **~ budgétaire** budgetary slide; **4** Naut (aileron) centreboard[GB]; (déviation) deviation; **navire à la** or **en ~** ship adrift; **être à la ~** to be adrift; **5** Aviat (déviation) drift; (gouvernail) (vertical) fin; **6** Électron drift; **7** Mil, Sci drift.
■ **~ des continents** Géog continental drift.

dérivé, **~e** /deʀive/ **I** *pp* ▶ **dériver**.
II *pp adj* **1** gén stemming (**de** from); **2** Ind, Chimie derived (**de** from); **3** Ling derived (**de** from).
III *nm* **1** gén spin-off; **2** Ind by-product (**de** of); **~s du pétrole** petroleum by-products; **3** Chimie derivative (**de** of); **4** Ling derivative (**de** of).
IV dérivée *nf* Math derivative; **~e logarithmique/partielle** logarithmic/partial derivative.

dériver /deʀive/ [1] **I** *vtr* **1** (détourner) to divert [*rivière*]; **2** Math to obtain the derivative of [*fonction*].
II dériver de *vtr ind* **1** gén **~ de** to stem from; **2** Ling **~ de** to be derived from.
III *vi* **1** lit, fig to drift (**vers** toward, towards GB); **2** Math to differentiate.

dériveur /deʀivœʀ/ *nm* **1** (de plaisance) (sailing) dinghy; **2** (de pêche) drifter; **3** (voile) stormsail.

dermatite /dɛʀmatit/ **▶ 271** *nf* dermatitis.

dermatologie /dɛʀmatɔlɔʒi/ *nf* dermatology.

dermatologique /dɛʀmatɔlɔʒik/ *adj* dermatological.

dermatologiste /dɛʀmatɔlɔʒist/ *nmf*, **dermatologue** /dɛʀmatɔlɔg/ *nmf* **▶ 510** dermatologist.

dermatose /dɛʀmatoz/ **▶ 271** *nf* dermatosis spéc.

derme /dɛʀm/ *nm* dermis.

dermite /dɛʀmit/ **▶ 271** *nf* dermatitis.

dernier, **-ière** /dɛʀnje, ɛʀ/ **I** *adj* **1** (qui termine une série) [*coureur, jour, paragraphe, bâtiment*] last; [*étage, étagère*] top; **ce fut son ~ roman** it was his/her last novel; **faire un ~ effort** to make one last effort; **la dernière édition de la journée** Presse the last edition of the day; **la dernière édition date de 1920** the last edition came out in 1920; **dernière chance** last chance; **dernière fois** last time; **décision de dernière minute** or **heure** last-minute decision; **attendre la dernière minute** or **le ~ moment pour faire** to wait until the last minute to do; **arriver ~** (dans une course) to come last; **arriver bon ~** to come in last a long way behind; **être bon ~** to come well and truly last; **être classé** or **placé ~** (dans une course) to be in last place; **c'est la toute dernière maison** it's the very last house; **un ~ mot avant que vous ne partiez** a final word before you go; **je voudrais ajouter un ~ mot** I'd like to say one more thing; **troisième et ~ volume** third and final volume; **je les veux jeudi ~ délai** I want them by Thursday at the latest; **la dissertation est pour le 20 juin ~ délai** the deadline for this essay is 20 June; **de la dernière chance** final; **2** (précédent) last; **l'an ~** last year; **jeudi ~** last Thursday; **la nuit dernière** last night; **au siècle ~** in the 19th century; **Noël ~** last Christmas; **les dernières 24 heures ont été éprouvantes** the last 24 hours have been terrible ou awful; **pendant la dernière guerre** during the last war; **son ~ livre** his/her last book; **la dernière édition datait de 1910** the last edition came out in 1910; **3** (le plus récent) [*roman, album, production, nouvelles*] latest; **mon ~ roman paraîtra demain** my latest novel will come out tomorrow; **notre ~ modèle** our latest model; **notre dernière création** our latest creation; **les dernières exigences des ravisseurs** the kidnappers'[GB] latest demands; **nouvelles de dernière heure** latest news; **aux dernières nouvelles on apprenait que** the latest news was that; **ces ~ temps** recently; **ces ~s temps il n'a pas fait beau** the weather hasn't been very good recently ou lately; **4** (extrême) **le ~ degré de** the height of; **c'est ridicule au ~ degré** or **point** it's utterly ou absolutely ridiculous; **être du ~ ridicule** to be utterly ou absolutely ridiculous; **c'est de la dernière impolitesse** it's the height of rudeness;

c'était la dernière chose à faire it was the worst possible thing to do; **c'est bien la dernière personne à qui je ferais des confidences** he/she really is the last person I would confide in; **c'est bien la dernière personne que j'aurais choisie** he/she really is the last person I would have chosen; **le ~ choix** the poorest quality; **c'est la dernière fois que je viens ici** that's the last time I come here; **les trois ~s jours** the last three days.
II *nmf* **1** (qui est à la fin) last; **les ~s** the last; **arriver le ~** to arrive last; **le ~ arrivé** the last to arrive; **le ~ arrivé offre une bouteille de champagne** the last one there has to buy a bottle of champagne; **tu es toujours le ~** you are always last; **c'est le ~ qui me reste** it's my last one; **ce fut le ~ des rois de France** he was the last of the kings of France; **le ~ qui** the last person who; **ce sont les ~s à pouvoir faire** they are the last people who could do; **les premiers seront les ~s** Bible the first shall be last; **c'est bien le ~ de mes soucis** that really is the least of my worries; **être le ~ de la classe** to be bottom of the class; **être le ~ de la liste** to be bottom of the list; **si tu cherches ton nom dans la liste, c'est le ~** if you're looking for your name in the list, it's at the bottom; **la dernière des guerres** the war to end all wars; **le petit ~** the youngest child; **est-ce votre ~?** is that your youngest?; **ce ~, ces ~s** (de plusieurs) the latter; **c'était un fidèle de Grovagnard, et il devint chef du parti à la mort de ce ~** he was a follower of Grovagnard, and became party leader when he died; **elle est venue avec son mari, ce ~ me semblait d'ailleurs pas très à l'aise** she came with her husband, who actually didn't seem very comfortable; **elle est venue avec Pierre et Anne, cette dernière étant seule ce soir là** she came with Pierre and Anne, the latter of whom happened to be alone that evening; **dans ce ~ cas** in the latter case; **2** (le pire) **c'est le ~ des imbéciles** or **idiots** he's a complete idiot; **c'est le ~ des lâches** he's a complete and utter coward; **le ~ des ignorants** or **imbéciles sait cela** any fool knows that; **le ~ des ~s** the lowest of the low.
III **en dernier** *loc adv* last; **je m'en occuperai en ~** I'll deal with that last; **j'irai chez eux en ~** I'll go to them last.
IV **dernière** *nf* **1** (histoire, nouvelle) **la dernière** the latest; **connaissez-vous la dernière?** have you heard the latest?; **2** (d'un spectacle) last performance.
■ **~ cri** latest fashion; **dernière demeure** final resting place; **conduire/accompagner qn à sa dernière demeure** to take/to accompany sb to his/her final resting place; **dernières volontés** final ou dying wish.
IDIOMES **(en) être à sa dernière heure** to be on one's deathbed.

dernièrement /dɛʀnjɛʀmɑ̃/ *adv* recently, lately.

dernier-né, **dernière-née**, *mpl* **derniers-nés** /dɛʀnjene, dɛʀnjɛʀne/ *nm,f* **1** (enfant) youngest; **le ~ de la famille** the youngest in the family; **2** (modèle) latest model.

dérobade /deʀɔbad/ *nf* gén evasion; Équit running out.

dérobé, **~e** /deʀɔbe/ I *pp* ▶ **dérober**.
II *pp adj* [*porte, escalier*] concealed.
III **à la dérobée** *loc adv* furtively.

dérober /deʀɔbe/ [1] I *vtr* **1** liter (voler) to steal [*argent, baiser, secret*] (**à** from); **2** liter (cacher) to hide [*vue, paysage*] (**à** from); **~ qch au regard de qn** to hide sth from sb.
II **se dérober** *vpr* **1** (se soustraire aux questions) to be evasive, to hedge; **2** (se soustraire à son devoir) to shirk responsibility; **3** (se soustraire) **se ~ à** to shirk [*responsabilités, devoir*]; to evade, to avoid [*question*]; to evade [*justice*]; **se ~ à un engagement** to get out of a commitment; **4** (céder) [*sol*] to give way (**sous** under); **le sol se dérobe sous leurs pieds** the ground gives way under their feet; **ses jambes se dérobaient sous elle** her legs were giving way; **5** Équit (s'écarter) to run out; **se ~ devant un obstacle** to run out of a fence.

dérocher /deʀɔʃe/ [1] I *vtr* **1** to pickle [*métal*]; **2** to clear rocks away from [*rivière, terrain*].
II *vi* (en alpinisme) to fall from a rock.

dérogation /deʀɔgasjɔ̃/ *nf* **1** (autorisation) (special) dispensation (**pour faire** to do); **obtenir par ~** to get by dispensation; **des ~s pourront être accordées** dispensations may be granted; **2** (contravention) infringement (**à** of); **par ~ à l'article 1** contrary to article 1.

dérogatoire /deʀɔgatwaʀ/ *adj* [*mesure, arrêté*] derogatory (**à** from); [*régime, cas*] special; **clause ~** derogation clause.

déroger /deʀɔʒe/ [13] *vtr ind* **~ à** [*personne, initiative*] to infringe [*loi, règle, droit*]; to depart from [*principes, politique*]; to break [*habitude*]; to disregard [*obligation*]; to break with [*tradition, usage*]; **~ aux bonnes manières** to breach the rules of etiquette.

dérouillée○ /deʀuje/ *nf* **1** (volée de coups) hiding○, beating; **recevoir** or **prendre une ~** to get a hiding; **2** (défaite sportive) thrashing○, defeat.

dérouiller○ /deʀuje/ [1] I *vtr* (dégourdir) [*sport*] to loosen up [*jambes*]; to limber [sb] up [*personne*]; [*lecture*] to stimulate [*esprit*].
II *vi* (recevoir des coups) to get a hiding○, to get a beating; (souffrir) to go through hell○, to suffer.
III **se dérouiller** *vpr* (se dégourdir) to limber up; **se ~ les jambes** to loosen up one's legs.

déroulant /deʀulɑ̃/ *adj m* Ordinat **menu ~** pulldown menu.

déroulement /deʀulmɑ̃/ *nm* **1** (succession de moments) **tenter de se remémorer le ~ des événements** to try to recall the sequence of events; **veiller au bon ~ de** [*cérémonie, négociations*] to make sure [sth] goes smoothly; **expliquer le ~ de la cérémonie** to explain the procedure for the ceremony; **expliquer le ~ d'une semaine de travail** to explain the organization of the working week; **~ de carrière** career development; **le ~ de l'intrigue** the unfolding of the plot; **2** (fait de progresser) **pendant le ~ du film/du match** during the film/the match, while the film/match was in progress; **3** (fait d'avoir lieu) **le ~ d'élections est encore utopique** the holding of elections is still a pipe-dream; **4** (de corde) uncoiling; (de câble, corde sur un tambour) unwinding; (de manuscrit) unrolling.

dérouler /deʀule/ [1] I *vtr* **1** (étendre) to unroll [*tapis, tuyau, manuscrit*]; to let down [*chevelure*]; to uncoil [*corde*]; (autour d'une bobine) to unwind [*fil, pellicule*]; **~ le tapis rouge** fig to roll out the red carpet (**à, pour** for); **2** fml (présenter) to unfold [*histoire*].
II **se dérouler** *vpr* **1** (avoir lieu) to take place; **la réunion s'est déroulée hier à Damas comme prévu** the meeting took place yesterday in Damascus as planned; **la manifestation s'est déroulée dans le calme** the demonstration went off without incident; **2** (évoluer) [*négociations*] to proceed sout, to go; **cela s'est déroulé comme prévu** it went as expected; **la façon dont les événements se déroulent** the way the situation is unfolding; **une vie qui s'est déroulée sans histoires** a trouble-free life; **3** (être déroulé) [*tapis*] to be unrolled; [*pellicule*] to be unwound; [*carte*] to unroll; **les images qui se déroulent dans ma tête** the images going through my head; **4** (se présenter) **se ~ devant nos yeux** [*panorama, histoire*] to unfold before our eyes.

dérouleur /deʀulœʀ/ *nm* **1** gén holder; **~ de papier hygiénique** toilet paper holder; **2** Tech (de câble, papier) unwinding machine; **3** Ordinat **~ de bande** tape drive.

dérouleuse /deʀuløz/ *nf* **~ de câble** cable drum.

déroutant, **~e** /deʀutɑ̃, ɑ̃t/ *adj* puzzling.

déroute /deʀut/ *nf* **1** (défaite) crushing defeat; **mettre qn en ~** to defeat sb; **2** (débandade) rout; **en ~** in full flight; **mettre en ~** to put [sb] to flight, to rout sb; **3** (crise profonde) disarray; **en ~** in disarray.

déroutement /deʀutmɑ̃/ *nm* Aviat, Naut diversion.

dérouter /deʀute/ [1] I *vtr* **1** (déconcerter) to puzzle; **2** Aviat, Naut to divert.
II **se dérouter** *vpr* to divert (**vers** to).

derrick /deʀik/ *nm* derrick.

derrière[1] /dɛʀjɛʀ/ I *prép* **1** (en arrière de) behind; **une remorque accrochée ~ la voiture** a trailer hitched to the back of the car; **gardez les mains ~ le dos** keep your hands behind your backs; **l'un ~ l'autre** one behind the other; **2** (sous) behind; **il dissimule sa timidité ~ des plaisanteries** he hides his shyness behind a façade of joking remarks; **elle cache sa méchanceté ~ de grands sourires** she hides her nastiness behind a smiling exterior; **~ les apparences** (de chose) under the surface; (de personne) behind the façade; (de situation) beneath the surface.
II *adv* (à l'arrière) (de personne) behind; (dans le fond) at the back; (à l'arrière d'une voiture) in the back; **mets- les ~** (dans une voiture) put them in the back, put them behind; **qu'y a-t-il ~?** fig what's behind it?; **ne poussez pas ~!** stop pushing at the back!, stop pushing back there!
IDIOMES **être toujours ~ le dos de qn** to be always on○ at sb GB, to be always bugging○ sb; **il ne fait rien par lui-même, il faut toujours être ~ lui** he never gets anything done unless you keep after him; **il a les syndicats ~ lui** the unions are behind him; **elle a laissé deux enfants ~ elle** she died leaving two children; **s'abriter** or **se retrancher ~ qn** to hide behind sb.

derrière[2] /dɛʀjɛʀ/ *nm* **1** (de maison, véhicule, d'objet) back; **de ~** [*chambre, porte*] back; **2**○ (de personne, d'animal) behind○, backside○.

Derry ▶ **692** *npr* **le comté de ~** Derry.

derviche /dɛʀviʃ/ *nm* dervish; **~ tourneur** whirling dervish.

des /de/ I *art indéf pl* ▶ **un I**.
II *prép* ▶ **de**.

dès /dɛ/ I *prép* **1** (indique le point de départ dans le temps) from; **~ (l'âge de) huit ans** from the age of eight; **~ aujourd'hui/hier** from today/yesterday; **~ maintenant** or **à présent** from now on; **~ le départ** or **début** (right) from the start ou beginning; **~ 1954 l'économie de la région commença à péricliter** the area's economy started to collapse from 1954 (onwards); **~ l'instant** or **le moment** or **la minute où** from the very moment when; **~ l'instant où il la vit** from the moment he saw her; **~ le lever du soleil il se met à faire chaud** as soon as the sun rises it starts to get hot; **je vous téléphone ~ mon arrivée** I'll phone ou call you as soon as I arrive; **cette boisson était connue ~ l'antiquité** this drink has been known since the earliest times; **~ avant** even before; **je lui en parlerai ~ lundi** I'll talk to him about it on Monday; **2** (indique le point de départ dans l'espace) from; **~ Versailles il y a des embouteillages** from Versailles onwards, there are traffic jams; **vous serez pris en charge par les organisateurs ~ l'aéroport** organizers will take care of you as soon as you get to the airport.
II **dès que** *loc conj* as soon as; **~ que possible** as soon as possible; **~ qu'il m'a**

vue, il m'a souri as soon as ou the moment he saw me, he smiled at me.

III dès lors *loc adv* (à partir de ce moment) from then on, from that time on, henceforth; (de ce fait) therefore, consequently.

IV dès lors que *loc conj* (à partir du moment où) once, from the moment that; (puisque) since.

désabonner: **se désabonner** /dezabɔne/ [1] *vpr* to cancel one's subscription (**à** to).

désabusé, **~e** /dezabyze/ **I** *pp* ▶ **désabuser**.

II *pp adj* [*personne*] disillusioned; [*air, ton, parole*] cynical.

désabusement /dezabyzmɑ̃/ *nm* disenchantment (**quant à** with).

désabuser /dezabyze/ [1] *vtr* **1** (désillusionner) to disenchant (**de** with); **2** (détromper) to disabuse (**de** about)

désacclimaté, **~e** /dezaklimate/ *adj* out of one's element.

désaccord /dezakɔʀ/ *nm* **1** (divergence) disagreement (**avec** with; **sur** over); **sujet de ~** subject of disagreement; **exprimer son ~** to express disagreement; **en ~** in disagreement; **en total ~** in complete disagreement; **être en ~** to disagree (**avec** with; **sur** over); **2** (contradiction) discrepancy; **~s entre différentes versions** discrepancies between various versions.

désaccordé, **~e** /dezakɔʀde/ **I** *pp* ▶ **désaccorder**.

II *pp adj* Mus out-of-tune (*épith*); **ton piano est ~** your piano is out of tune.

désaccorder /dezakɔʀde/ [1] **I** *vtr* [*chaleur, transport*] to make [sth] go out of tune [*piano, violon*].

II se désaccorder *vpr* [*instrument de musique*] to go out of tune.

désaccoupler /dezakuple/ [1] *vtr* gén to uncouple; Électrotech to decouple; Mécan to disengage [*moteur, vitesses*].

désaccoutumance /dezakutymɑ̃s/ *nf* **la ~ à la drogue/l'alcool est progressive** overcoming drug/alcohol addiction is a gradual process.

désaccoutumer /dezakutyme/ [1] **I** *vtr* **~ qn de qch** to cure sb's addiction to sth [*tabac, drogue*]; **~ qn de faire** to cure sb of doing.

II se désaccoutumer *vpr* **se ~ de** to break one's dependence on [*tabac, alcool*]; **se ~ de boire** to break one's dependence on drink; **se ~ de tricher** to break one's habit of cheating.

désacralisation /desakʀalizasjɔ̃/ *nf* **~ de qch** destruction of the sacred aura surrounding sth.

désacraliser /desakʀalize/ [1] *vtr* to destroy the sacred aura surrounding [*valeur, pratique*].

désactivation /dezaktivasjɔ̃/ *nf* Chimie deactivation; Nucl cooling.

désactiver /dezaktive/ [1] *vtr* **1** (neutraliser) to deactivate [*alarme*]; **2** Nucl to cool; **3** Chimie to deactivate; **4** Ind (en pétrochimie) to inhibit.

désaffecté, **~e** /dezafɛkte/ *adj* disused.

désaffection /dezafɛksjɔ̃/ *nf* disaffection.

désagréable /dezagʀeabl/ *adj* unpleasant (**avec, envers** to, toward(s)), disagreeable (**avec, envers** to, toward(s)).

désagréablement /dezagʀeabləmɑ̃/ *adv* unpleasantly.

désagrégation /dezagʀegasjɔ̃/ *nf* **1** (décomposition) disintegration; (écroulement) collapse; (dislocation) break-up; **2** Géol disintegration; **3** Psych collapse; **~ mental** or **psychique** mental collapse.

désagréger /dezagʀeʒe/ [15] **I** *vtr* to disintegrate, to break up.

II se désagréger *vpr* **1** (se décomposer) to disintegrate; (s'écrouler) to collapse; (se disloquer) to break up; **2** Géol to disintegrate.

désagrément /dezagʀemɑ̃/ *nm* **1** (gêne) inconvenience; **cela m'a causé beaucoup de ~** it caused me a lot of inconvenience; **2** (embêtement) annoyance, inconvenience; **les ~s de la vie citadine** the annoyances ou inconveniences of city life; **réserve une place, tu t'éviteras bien des ~s** if you reserve a seat, you'll save yourself a lot of trouble ou inconvenience.

désaimantation /dezɛmɑ̃tasjɔ̃/ *nf* demagnetization.

désaimanter /dezɛmɑ̃te/ [1] *vtr* to demagnetize.

désaltérant, **~e** /dezalteʀɑ̃, ɑ̃t/ *adj* thirst-quenching.

désaltérer /dezalteʀe/ [14] **I** *vtr* **~ qn** to quench sb's thirst; **le thé m'a désaltérée** the tea has quenched my thirst; **les pastèques désaltèrent** watermelons are thirst-quenching.

II se désaltérer *vpr* to quench one's thirst.

désambiguïser /dezɑ̃bigɥize/ [1] *vtr* to disambiguate.

désamorçage /dezamɔʀsaʒ/ *nm* **1** (d'explosif, de crise) defusing; **2** (de pompe) draining.

désamorcer /dezamɔʀse/ [12] *vtr* to defuse [*explosif, crise*]; to drain [*pompe*].

désapparier /dezapaʀje/ [2] *vtr* to break up a pair of.

désappointement /dezapwɛ̃tmɑ̃/ *nm* disappointment.

désappointer /dezapwɛ̃te/ [1] *vtr* to disappoint.

désapprendre /dezapʀɑ̃dʀ/ [52] *vtr* **1** (involontairement) to forget (**à faire** how to do); **2** (volontairement) to unlearn.

désapprobateur, **-trice** /dezapʀɔbatœʀ, tʀis/ *adj* [*regard, ton, remarque*] disapproving; **d'un air ~** disapprovingly.

désapprobation /dezapʀɔbasjɔ̃/ *nf* disapproval; **exprimer sa ~ pour qch** to express one's disapproval of sth.

désapprouver /dezapʀuve/ [1] *vtr* to disapprove of [*projet, conduite, personne, manière*]; **il m'arrive de ~** I sometimes disapprove.

désarçonner /dezaʀsɔne/ [1] *vtr* **1** Équit to throw [*cavalier*]; **2** (déconcerter) to take [sb] aback [*personne*]; **sa remarque m'a désarçonné** his remark took me aback; **être désarçonné** to be taken aback (**par** by); **se faire ~** to be thrown (**par** by).

désargenté○, **~e** /dezaʀʒɑ̃te/ *adj* (pauvre) hard up○, penniless.

désargenter /dezaʀʒɑ̃te/ [1] *vtr* [*lave-vaisselle*] to take the silver plating off [*couverts, plat*]; **les fourchettes sont désargentées** the silver plating has come off the forks.

désarmant, **~e** /dezaʀmɑ̃, ɑ̃t/ *adj* [*franchise, personne*] disarming.

désarmé, **~e** /dezaʀme/ **I** *pp* ▶ **désarmer**.

II *pp adj* **1** Mil [*soldat, pays*] disarmed; [*région*] demilitarized; **2** Naut [*navire*] laid up.

désarmement /dezaʀməmɑ̃/ *nm* **1** Mil (de pays, région) disarmament; **~ conventionnel/chimique** conventional/chemical disarmament; **2** Naut (de navire) laying up.

désarmer /dezaʀme/ [1] **I** *vtr* **1** (rendre inoffensif) to disarm [*malfaiteur, adversaire*]; to disarm [*pays, région*]; to disarm [*arme à feu, mine*]; **2** (décontenancer) to disarm [*personne*]; (désamorcer) to defuse [*colère*]; to allay [*méfiance*]; to invalidate [*reproche*]; to disarm [*critique*]; **face à elle je me sens désarmé** I feel helpless faced with her; **3** Naut to lay up [*navire*]; to ship [*avirons*].

II *vi* **1** Mil to disarm; **2** (abandonner une lutte) [*personne*] to give up the fight; (cesser) [*colère, haine*] to abate.

désarrimage /dezaʀimaʒ/ *nm* **1** Transp (accidentel) shifting; (volontaire) unstowing; **2** Astronaut undocking.

désarrimer /dezaʀime/ [1] **I** *vtr* **1** Transp to unstow; **2** Astronaut to undock.

II se désarrimer *vpr* Transp to shift.

désarroi /dezaʀwa/ *nm* (trouble moral) distress; (désordre) confusion; **sentiment de profond ~** feeling of deep distress; **au grand ~ de** much to the distress of; **le ~ du camp adverse** the confusion in the opposing camp; **jeter qn dans le ~** to throw sb into confusion; **être en plein ~** (moralement) to be very confused; (en désordre) to be in a state of disarray.

désarticulation /dezaʀtikylasjɔ̃/ *nf* **1** (déboîtement) dislocation; **2** (amputation) disarticulation.

désarticulé, **~e** /dezaʀtikyle/ **I** *pp* ▶ **désarticuler**.

II *pp adj* [*fauteuil*] wrecked; [*pantin*] with broken joints (*épith, après n*).

désarticuler /dezaʀtikyle/ [1] **I** *vtr* **1** (déboîter) to dislocate [*membre*]; **2** Méd (amputer) to amputate.

II se désarticuler *vpr* [*acrobate, contorsionniste*] to contort oneself.

désassembler /dezasɑ̃ble/ [1] *vtr* to dismantle [*pièces, planches*].

désassorti, **~e** /dezasɔʀti/ *adj* [*service*] incomplete; [*magasin*] poorly stocked.

désastre /dezastʀ/ *nm* (tous contextes) disaster; **~ écologique/économique/électoral** environmental/economic/electoral disaster; **mesurer l'ampleur** or **l'étendue du ~** to assess the extent of the disaster.

désastreusement /dezastʀøzmɑ̃/ *adv* disastrously.

désastreux, **-euse** /dezastʀø, øz/ *adj* [*incidence, effet, état, bilan*] disastrous.

désavantage /dezavɑ̃taʒ/ *nm* **1** (handicap) disadvantage; **~ intellectuel/physique** intellectual/physical disadvantage; **compenser un ~ intellectuel** to make up for intellectual shortcomings; **avoir un ~ par rapport à qn** to be at a disadvantage compared to sb; **être/tourner au ~ de qn** to be/to turn to sb's disadvantage; **voir qn à son ~** to see sb in an unfavourable[GB] light; **se montrer à son ~** to show oneself in an unfavourable[GB] light; **2** (inconvénient) drawback, disadvantage; **avoir** or **présenter des ~s** to have drawbacks.

désavantager /dezavɑ̃taʒe/ [13] *vtr* **1** (mettre en état d'infériorité) to put [sb/sth] at a disadvantage, to disadvantage [*personne, entreprise*]; **~ qn/qch en faisant** to put sb/sth at a disadvantage by doing; **être le plus désavantagé** to be put at the greatest disadvantage; **il est désavantagé par sa mémoire/son jeune âge** his bad memory/his youth puts him at a disadvantage; **être désavantagé par rapport à qn/qch** to be at a disadvantage compared to sb/sth; **2** Jur to put [sb] at a disadvantage, to disadvantage.

désavantageusement /dezavɑ̃taʒøzmɑ̃/ *adv* unfavourably[GB].

désavantageux, **-euse** /dezavɑ̃taʒø, øz/ *adj* [*contrat, affaire, échange, marché, prix*] unfavourable[GB], disadvantageous; [*jugement*] unfavourable[GB]; [*portrait, description*] unflattering; [*incident*] damaging; **être ~ à** or **pour qn** [*contrat, affaire*] to be unfavourable[GB] to sb.

désaveu, *pl* **~x** /dezavø/ *nm* **1** (reniement) denial; **2** (condamnation) rejection; **encourir le ~ de l'opinion publique** to encounter rejection at the hands of the public.

■ **~ de paternité** Jur denial of paternity.

désavouer /dezavwe/ [1] *vtr* **1** (ne pas reconnaître comme sien) to deny [*acte, propos*]; **il a désavoué les propos qu'il avait tenus** he denied his previous comments; **2** (rejeter) to disown [*personne, candidat*]; **elle a désavoué la conduite/les propos de son ami** she disowned her friend's behaviour[GB]/comments; **3** Jur to disown [*enfant*]; **~ la paternité d'un enfant** to deny that one is the father of a child.

désaxé, **~e** /dezakse/ **I** *pp* ▶ **désaxer**.

II *pp adj* [*personne*] deranged.

III *nm,f* deranged person.

désaxer /dezakse/ [1] *vtr* **1** Tech to put [sth] out of true [*roue*]; **2** (rendre fou) to unbalance [*personne*].

desceller /desele/ [1] **I** *vtr* **1** Constr to work [sth] free [*lavabo*]; **2** (ouvrir) to unseal [*acte, lettre*].

II se desceller *vpr* [*lavabo*] to work loose.

descendance /desɑ̃dɑ̃s/ *nf* **1** (lignée) descendants (*pl*); **une nombreuse ~** many descendants; **2†** (origine familiale) descent.

descendant, **~e** /desɑ̃dɑ̃, ɑ̃t/ **I** *adj* [*cabine, courbe*] downward; **organe ~** Méd descending organ; **voie ~e** Rail down line; **train ~** Rail down train.

II *nm,f* descendant (**de** of).

descendeur, **-euse** /desɑ̃dœʀ, øz/ **I** *nm,f* (en ski) downhill racer, downhiller.

II *nm* Sport (en alpinisme) abseiling device, descendeur.

descendre /desɑ̃dʀ/ [6] **I** *vtr* **1** (transporter) (en bas) gén to take [sb/sth] down [*personne, objet*] (**à** to); (à l'étage) to take [sb/sth] downstairs [*personne, objet*]; (d'en haut) gén to bring [sb/sth] down [*personne, objet*] (**de** from); (de l'étage) to bring [sb/sth] downstairs [*personne, objet*]; **~ les bouteilles à la cave** to take the bottles down to the cellar; **~ les valises du grenier** to bring the suitcases down from the attic; **je peux vous ~ au village** I can take you down to the village; **descends-moi mes pantoufles** bring my slippers down for me; **je leur ai fait ~ les bouteilles à la cave** I had them take the bottles down to the cellar; **j'ai fait ~ le piano dans le salon** I had the piano taken ou brought down to the living room; **faites-moi ~ les dossiers secrets** have the secret files brought down to me; **2** (placer plus bas) to put [sth] down [*objet*]; (en abaissant) gén to lower (**de** by); (avec une manivelle) to wind [sth] down; **descends le store** put the blind down; **j'ai descendu le vase sur l'étagère du bas/de l'étagère du haut** I moved the vase down to the bottom shelf/ from the top shelf; **~ l'étagère d'un cran/ de 20 centimètres** to lower the shelf by one notch/by 20 centimetres[GB]; **~ un seau dans un puits** to lower a bucket into a well; **3** (réussir à mettre plus bas) to get [sth] down [*objet*]; **impossible de ~ le piano par l'escalier/par la fenêtre** it's impossible to get the piano down the stairs/through the window; **comment va-t-on ~ le piano?** (de l'étage) how are we going to get the piano downstairs?; (du camion) how are we going to get the piano out?; **tu peux me ~ cette valise de l'armoire?** can you get this suitcase down from the wardrobe for me?; **4** (parcourir) (en allant) to go down [*pente, rue, marches, fleuve*]; (en venant) to come down [*pente, rue, marches, fleuve*]; **je l'ai vu ~ les escaliers sur le derrière**○ I saw him slide down the stairs on his bottom; **~ la colline en rampant/à bicyclette** to crawl/to cycle down the hill; **~ la rivière en pagayant/à la nage** to paddle/to swim down the river; **je leur ai fait ~ la colline en courant** I made them run down the hill; **il m'a fait ~ les escaliers trois fois** he made me go downstairs ou down the stairs three times; **5**○ (éliminer) to bump off○, to plug○, to kill [*personne*]; to shoot down [*avion*]; **se faire ~** [*personne*] to be bumped off○; [*avion*] to be shot down; **on l'a descendu d'une balle dans la poitrine/tête** he was shot in the chest/head and killed; **6**○ (malmener) to tear [sb/sth] to pieces; **il s'est fait ~ par la presse** the newspapers tore him to pieces; **ils ont descendu ma thèse pendant deux heures** they spent two hours tearing my thesis to pieces; **7**○ (boire) [*personne*] to down [*bouteille, verre*]; **il a descendu son verre en deux secondes** he downed his drink in two seconds flat.

II *vi* **1** (se déplacer) [*personne*] (en allant) gén to go down (**à** to); (de l'étage) to go downstairs; (en venant) gén to come down (**de** from); (de l'étage) to come downstairs; [*train, ascenseur, téléphérique, avion, hélicoptère*] (en allant) to go down; (en venant) to come down; [*oiseau*] to fly down; [*soleil*] to set (**sur** over); [*nuit*] to fall; [*brouillard*] to come down (**sur** over); **reste ici, je descends à la cave** stay here, I'm going down to the cellar; **peux-tu ~ chercher mon sac?** can you go downstairs and get my bag?; **tu peux ~ m'aider à pousser l'armoire?** can you come downstairs and help me push the wardrobe?; **il est descendu fumer** he went downstairs to smoke; **te voilà! tu es descendu par l'ascenseur?** there you are! did you come down in the elevator?; **tu es descendu à pied?** did you walk down?; **je préfère ~ par l'escalier** I prefer to go down by the stairs; **nous sommes descendus par le sentier/la route** (à pied) we walked down by the path/the road; (à cheval) we rode down by the path/the road; **il est descendu du col à bicyclette/en voiture** he cycled/drove down from the pass; **où est l'écureuil? il a dû ~ de l'arbre** where's the squirrel? it must have come down ou climbed down from the tree; **descends, je te suis** go on down, I'll follow you; **descends de là!** get down from there!; **je suis descendu au fond du puits/au bas de la falaise** I went down to the bottom of the well/to the foot of the cliff; **~ de son lit** to get out of bed; **~ de son nid** [*oiseau*] to fly out of its nest; **~ de** [*personne*] to step off [*trottoir, marche*]; [*animal*] to get off [*marche, trottoir*]; [*personne, animal*] to climb down from [*mur, tabouret*]; **il est descendu du toit** [*enfant, chat*] he' s come down from the roof; **~ de l'échelle/l'arbre/la corde** to climb down from the ladder/the tree/the rope; **~ à la verticale** [*paquet, alpiniste*] to descend vertically; **~ aux Enfers** Relig to descend into Hell; **l'air froid fait ~ les ballons/planeurs** cold air makes balloons/gliders drop; **elle m'a fait/ne m'a pas laissé ~ à la cave** she had me/didn't let me go down to the cellar; **faites-les ~** send them down [*clients, marchandises*]; **faire ~ sa jupe/ ses bas/son châle** to pull one's skirt/one's tights/one's shawl down; **2** (d'un moyen de transport) **~ d'une voiture** to get out of a car; **le chien ne veut pas ~** (de la voiture) the dog doesn't want to get out; **~ d'un train/bus/avion** to get off a train/bus/plane; **~ d'avion/de bateau** to get off a plane/a boat; **~ de bicyclette** to get off one 's bicycle; **~ de cheval** to get off one's horse, to dismount sout; **~ à Marseille** (d'avion, de bateau, de bus, de train) to get off at Marseilles; **3** (s'étendre de haut en bas) [*route, voie ferrée*] to go downhill, to go down; [*terrain*] to go down; [*canalisations, ligne téléphonique*] (en allant) to go down; (en venant) to come down; [*rivière*] to flow down; **~ jusqu'à** [*chemin, muraille, escalier*] to go down to; **~ jusqu'à la mer** [*route, rivière*] to go right down to the sea; **~ en lacets** [*route*] to wind its way down; **~ en pente douce** [*terrain, route*] to slope down gently; **~ en pente raide** [*terrain, route*] to drop steeply; **~ brusquement sur 200 mètres** [*pente, route*] to drop sharply for 200 metres[GB]; **4** (atteindre) [*vêtement, cheveux*] to come down (**jusqu'à** to); **robe qui descend jusqu'aux chevilles** dress that comes down to the ankles; **elle avait une robe qui lui descendait aux chevilles** she was wearing an ankle-length dress; **il a les cheveux qui lui descendent sur la nuque/jusqu'à la taille** his hair comes down the nape of his neck/to his waist; **5** (baisser) [*niveau, baromètre, température, pression, prix, taux*] to drop, to go down (**à** to; **de** by); [*marée*] to go out; **le franc est** or **a descendu par rapport à la livre** the Franc has dropped ou gone down against the pound ; **faire ~ les cours de 2%** to bring prices down by 2%; **ça va faire ~ le dollar** it'll send ou put the dollar down; **ça fait ~ la température** gén it lowers the temperature; Méd it brings one's temperature down; **ça ne fera pas ~ le taux de chômage** it won't bring the unemployment rate down; **6** (se rendre, séjourner) **~ à Marseille/dans le Midi** to go down to Marseilles/to the South (of France); **~ en ville** to go into town; **~ dans un hôtel** to stay at a hotel; **~ dans la rue** gén to go outside; Pol to take to the streets; **~ dans un bar/chez qn** [*police*] to raid a bar/sb's place; **7** (être issu) **~ de** gén to come from; (génétiquement) to be descended from; **~ d'une famille de négociants** to come from a family of merchants; **l'homme descend du singe** man is descended from the ape; **8**○ (passer) **boire de l'eau pour faire ~ la viande** to have a drink of water to help the meat down; **un petit vin qui descend bien** a wine which slips down nicely.

descente /desɑ̃t/ *nf* **1** (parcours d'un véhicule, d'une personne) descent; **nous amorçons notre ~ sur Paris** we're beginning our descent toward(s) Paris; **la ~ a été plus dure que la montée** it was much more difficult coming down than going up, the climb down ou descent was more difficult than the climb up; **la ~ a pris une heure** it took an hour to come down; **freiner dans les ~s** to brake going downhill; **la ~ est verglacée/ dangereuse** it's icy/dangerous on the way down; **au milieu de la ~** halfway down; **ralentir/avoir peur dans la ~** to go slower/ be scared on the way down; **tomber dans la ~** to fall on the way down; **au bas de la ~** at the bottom; **faire la ~ d'une rivière en canoë** to canoe down a river; **faire la ~ d'une rivière en péniche** to go down a river by barge; **la ~ du fleuve a été très agréable** sailing down the river was most pleasant; **2** (sortie) **à ma ~ du train/bus/ bateau/de l'avion** when I got off the train/ bus/boat/plane; **accueillir qn à sa ~ d'avion** to meet sb off the plane; **'la ~ se fait à l'avant de l'appareil'** 'please disembark at the front of the aircraft'; **3** Sport (en ski) (épreuve) downhill (event); (parcours) run; **~ hommes/dames** men's/ women's downhill; **faire une ~** to make a run; **c'est ma troisième ~ depuis ce matin** it's my third run since this morning; **4** Sport (en alpinisme, cyclisme, spéléologie) descent; (en parachutisme) drop; **~ en chute libre** free fall; **5** (raid) raid (**dans** en); **~ de police** police raid; **la police a fait une ~ dans l'immeuble/le bar** the police raided the building/bar; **faire une ~ dans la cuisine** hum to raid the kitchen; **6** Pol **~ dans la rue** demonstration; **une ~ à Paris des agriculteurs** a farmers' demonstration in Paris; **7** (exploration) exploration; **~ dans les profondeurs** or **au cœur de l'inconscient** exploration of the depths of the subconscious.

■ **~ de croix** Art, Relig descent from the cross; **~ d'eaux pluviales** Constr downpipe; **~ aux enfers** descent into hell; **~ de lit** (tapis) (bedside) rug; **~ d'organe** Méd prolapse; **~ en rappel** Sport (principe) abseiling **¢**; **une ~ en rappel** a descent.

IDIOMES **il a une bonne ~**○ he can really knock it back○.

descriptible /deskʀiptibl/ *adj* describable; **ne pas être ~** to be indescribable.

descriptif, **-ive** /deskʀiptif, iv/ **I** *adj* (tous contextes) descriptive.

II *nm* (notice explicative) gén detailed description; Constr specification.

description /deskʀipsjɔ̃/ *nf* **1** gén description; **faire une ~ de qch** to give a description of sth, to describe sth; **2** Jur (inventaire) inventory.

descriptivisme /dɛskʀiptivism/ *nm* descriptivism.

descriptiviste /dɛskʀiptivist/ *adj* descriptivist.

désectorisation /desɛktɔʀizasjɔ̃/ *nf* Admin, Scol phasing out of catchment areas.

désectoriser /desɛktɔʀize/ [1] *vtr* to remove [sth] from catchment area restriction [*école*].

déségrégation /desegregasjɔ̃/ *nf* desegregation.

désembourber /dezɑ̃buʀbe/ [1] **I** *vtr* to get [sth] out of the mud [*véhicule*].
II se désembourber *vpr* (sortir de la boue) to get out of the mud.

désembourgeoiser /dezɑ̃buʀʒwaze/ [1] **I** *vtr* to make [sb/sth] less bourgeois [*groupe, mode de vie*].
II se désembourgeoiser *vpr* to become less bourgeois.

désembouteiller /dezɑ̃buteje/ [1] *vtr* to ease congestion in [*rue, voie*].

désembuage /dezɑ̃byaʒ/ *nm* demisting GB, defogging US.

désembuer /dezɑ̃bye/ [1] *vtr* to demist GB, to defog US.

désemparé, **~e** /dezɑ̃paʀe/ **I** *pp* ▶ **désemparer**.
II *pp adj* **1** (dérouté) [*personne*] distraught, at a loss (*jamais épith*); **2** [*avion, navire*] in distress.

désemparer /dezɑ̃paʀe/ [1] **I** *vtr* (dérouter) to throw [sb] into confusion.
II *vi* **sans ~** without let-up.

désemplir /dezɑ̃pliʀ/ [3] **I** *vi* **ne pas ~** to be full; **ce restaurant ne désemplit pas** this restaurant is always full.
II se désemplir *vpr* to empty.

désenchanté, **~e** /dezɑ̃ʃɑ̃te/ **I** *pp* ▶ **désenchanter**.
II *pp adj* disillusioned, disenchanted (**de** with).

désenchantement /dezɑ̃ʃɑ̃tmɑ̃/ *nm* disillusionment, disenchantment.

désenchanter /dezɑ̃ʃɑ̃te/ [1] *vtr* to disillusion.

désenclavement /dezɑ̃klɑvmɑ̃/ *nm* opening up.

désenclaver /dezɑ̃klave/ [1] **I** *vtr* to open up [*région*].
II se désenclaver *vpr* to open up.

désencombrer /dezɑ̃kɔ̃bʀe/ [1] *vtr* to free [*esprit*] (**de** from); to unjam [*ligne téléphonique*]; to clear [*local*]; to ease congestion in [*rue, voie*].

désencrasser /dezɑ̃kʀase/ [1] *vtr* to clean out.

désendettement /dezɑ̃dɛtmɑ̃/ *nm* (partiel) reduction of the debt; (complet) rescuing from debt.

désendetter: **se désendetter** /dezɑ̃dete/ [1] *vpr* (partiellement) to reduce one's debt (**de** or **à hauteur de** by); (complètement) to get out of debt.

désenfler /dezɑ̃fle/ [1] *vi* to become less swollen, to go down.

désenfumage /dezɑ̃fymaʒ/ *nm* smoke extraction; **trappe de ~** smoke extraction hatch.

désenfumer /dezɑ̃fyme/ [1] *vtr* to extract smoke from [*local*].

désengagement /dezɑ̃gaʒmɑ̃/ *nm* **1** Écon, Pol disengagement; **2** Mil withdrawal (**de** from).

désengager /dezɑ̃gaʒe/ [13] Écon, Mil, Pol **I** *vtr* to disengage (**de** from).
II se désengager *vpr* to withdraw (**de** from).

désengorgement /dezɑ̃gɔʀg(ə)mɑ̃/ *nm* **1** (d'organisation) freeing up; **2** (de rue, voie) easing of congestion; **3** (de canalisation) unblocking.

désengorger /dezɑ̃gɔʀʒe/ [13] **I** *vtr* **1** Transp to ease congestion in [*rue, voie*]; **2** Tech to unblock [*canalisation*].
II se désengorger *vpr* **1** [*voie*] to become less congested; **2** [*canalisation*] to clear.

désenivrer /dezɑ̃nivʀe/ [1] **I** *vtr* to sober [sb] up [*personne*].
II *vi* to sober up.

désensabler /dezɑ̃sable/ [1] *vtr* **1** (nettoyer) to dredge [*canal, port*]; **2** (sortir du sable) to get [sth] out of the sand [*auto, bateau*].

désensibilisant, **~e** /desɑ̃sibilizɑ̃, ɑ̃t/ **I** *adj* desensitizing (*épith*).
II *nm* desensitizing substance.

désensibilisateur /desɑ̃sibilizatœʀ/ *nm* Phot desensitizer.

désensibilisation /desɑ̃sibilizasjɔ̃/ *nf* **1** Phot desensitizing; **2** Méd desensitization.

désensibiliser /desɑ̃sibilize/ [1] *vtr* Phot, Méd to desensitize; **se faire ~** to be desensitized.

désensorceler /dezɑ̃sɔʀsəle/ [19] *vtr* to break the spell on.

désentoiler /dezɑ̃twale/ [1] *vtr* to remove the canvas from [*tableau*].

désentortiller /dezɑ̃tɔʀtije/ [1] *vtr* to unravel.

désentraver /dezɑ̃tʀave/ [1] *vtr* to untie.

désenvenimer /dezɑ̃vənime/ [1] *vtr* **1** (apaiser) to defuse [*situation*]; **2** Méd to remove the poison from [*blessure*].

désenvoûtement /dezɑ̃vutmɑ̃/ *nm* breaking of a spell.

désenvoûter /dezɑ̃vute/ [1] *vtr* to break the spell on.

désépaissir /dezepɛsiʀ/ [3] *vtr* **1** Culin to thin [*sauce*]; **2** Cosmét to thin [sth] out [*chevelure*].

déséquilibrant, **~e** /dezekilibʀɑ̃, ɑ̃t/ *adj* fig [*facteur*] destabilizing.

déséquilibre /dezekilibʀ/ *nm* **1** lit (de personne) loss of balance; (de meuble, objet) rocking; **le coup a entraîné un ~ de son adversaire** the blow upset his opponent's balance; **en ~** [*table*] unstable; [*personne*] off balance; **2** fig (d'ordre économique, social, écologique) imbalance; **~ de la balance des paiements** imbalance of payments; **le budget est en ~** the budget is unbalanced; **les marchés sont en ~** the markets are unstable; **3** Psych lack of balance; **on sent chez lui un ~** he seems to be unbalanced.

déséquilibré, **~e** /dezekilibʀe/ **I** *pp* ▶ **déséquilibrer**.
II *pp adj* Psych (perturbé) unbalanced; (fou) crazy.
III *nm,f* Psych lunatic.

déséquilibrer /dezekilibʀe/ [1] *vtr* **1** lit [*personne, choc, coup*] to make [sb] lose his/her balance [*personne*]; [*poids*] to make [sth] unstable [*barque, meuble*]; **le choc a déséquilibré le motocycliste** the jolt made the motorcyclist lose his balance; **être déséquilibré par qch** [*personne*] to be thrown off balance by sth; [*meuble, objet*] to be made unstable by sth; **2** fig to destabilize [*pays*]; to unbalance [*résultats*]; **3** Psych to unbalance [*personne*].

désert, **~e** /dezɛʀ, ɛʀt/ **I** *adj* **1** (inhabité) uninhabited; **île ~e** desert island; **2** (vide) deserted.
II *nm* lit, fig desert; **~ du Sahara/Sinaï** Sahara/Sinaï desert; **~ culturel** cultural desert.
IDIOMES **prêcher dans le ~** to be a voice in the wilderness.

déserter /dezɛʀte/ [1] **I** *vtr* to desert; **ville/station de sports d'hiver désertée** deserted town/ski resort.
II *vi* Mil to desert.

déserteur /dezɛʀtœʀ/ *nm* deserter.

déserticole /dezɛʀtikɔl/ *adj* desert (*épith*).

désertification /dezɛʀtifikasjɔ̃/ *nf* **1** Écol desertification; **2** Sociol (de région) depopulation.

désertifier: **se désertifier** /dezɛʀtifje/ [2] *vpr* **1** Écol to turn into a desert; **2** Sociol to become depopulated.

désertion /dezɛʀsjɔ̃/ *nf* **1** Mil desertion; **2** Pol defection (**vers** to).

désertique /dezɛʀtik/ *adj* **1** (du désert) [*paysage, climat, région*] desert (*épith*); **2** (vide) [*étendue*] barren.

désescalade /desɛskalad/ *nf* de-escalation.

désespérance /dezɛspeʀɑ̃s/ *nf* littér despair.

désespérant, **~e** /dezɛspeʀɑ̃, ɑ̃t/ *adj* [*personne, situation*] hopeless; [*nouvelle*] heartbreaking; **il est d'une idiotie ~e** he's hopelessly stupid; **être d'une lenteur ~e** to be appallingly slow; **il a obtenu des résultats ~s** his results were hopeless.

désespéré, **~e** /dezɛspeʀe/ **I** *pp* ▶ **désespérer**.
II *pp adj* [*personne, population*] in despair (*épith*); [*situation, cas*] hopeless; [*mesure, tentative, parti, aide, appel*] desperate; [*regard, visage, chant, geste*] despairing; **~ d'avoir découvert qch/que** driven to despair by the discovery of sth/that; **~, il voulait** driven to despair, he wanted; **il appelait d'un cri ~** he called out in despair ou despairingly.
III *nm,f* desperate person; **un ~ se jette du haut de la tour Eiffel** man commits suicide by jumping off the Eiffel Tower.

désespérément /dezɛspeʀemɑ̃/ *adv* **1** (avec désespoir) [*pleurer, attendre*] despairingly; [*regretter*] desperately; **2** (avec acharnement) [*tenter, chercher, lutter*] desperately; **3** (à en pleurer) hopelessly; **~ seul/vide** hopelessly lonely/empty.

désespérer /dezɛspeʀe/ [14] **I** *vtr* to fill [sb] with despair, to drive [sb] to despair (**avec, par** with); **~ que qn fasse** to have given up hope that sb will do, to have lost hope of sb doing; **je désespère qu'il réussisse** I have given up hope of his succeeding; **il ne désespère pas qu'elle revienne un jour** he has not given up hope that she will come back one day.
II désespérer de *vtr ind* **~ de qn/qch** to despair of sb/sth; **~ de son fils** to despair of one's son; **~ de l'avenir** to despair of the future; **~ de faire** to despair of doing, to have given up (all) hope of doing; **il ne désespère pas de le sauver** he hasn't given up hope of saving him.
III *vi* to despair, to lose hope; **il ne faut pas ~** don't despair; **c'est à ~** it's hopeless.
IV se désespérer *vpr* to despair, to give way to despair.

désespoir /dezɛspwaʀ/ *nm* despair; **avec ~** despairingly, in despair; **par ~** out of despair; **à mon plus (grand) ~** to my utter despair; **jeter/plonger qn dans le ~** to cast/plunge sb into despair; **mettre** or **réduire qn au ~** to drive sb to despair; **s'abandonner au ~** to sink into despair; **être** or **faire le ~ de** [*enfant, paresse, bêtise*] to be the despair of; **cette décision fait leur ~** they despair at this decision; **être au ~ de faire** to be really sorry to do sth; **en ~ de cause** in ou out of desperation; **commettre un acte de ~** to commit suicide.

désespoir-des-peintres, *pl* **désespoirs-des-peintres** /dezɛspwaʀdepɛ̃tʀ/ *nm* Bot London pride.

désétatisation /dezetatizasjɔ̃/ *nf* (d'économie) removal from state control; (d'entreprise) denationalization.

désétatiser /dezetatize/ [1] *vtr* to remove [sth] from state control [*économie*]; to denationalize [*entreprise*].

déshabillage /dezabijaʒ/ *nm* undressing; **procéder au ~ de qn** to undress sb.

déshabillé, **~e** /dezabije/ **I** *adj* (osé) [*robe, tenue*] revealing.
II *nm* Mode negligee; **un ~ de soie** a silk negligee.

déshabiller /dezabije/ [1] **I** *vtr* **1** (dévêtir) to undress [*personne*]; **il l'a déshabillée du regard** he undressed her with his eyes; **2** (dégarnir) to clear [sth] of ornaments [*mur, salon*]; **3** fig (dépouiller) **~ qn de qch** to strip sb of sth.
II se déshabiller *vpr* **1** (complètement) to undress; **2** (ôter son manteau) to take one's coat off.
IDIOMES **~ Pierre pour habiller Paul** to rob Peter to pay Paul.

déshabituer /dezabitɥe/ [1] **I** *vtr* to get [sb]

out of the habit (**de qch** of sth; **de faire** of doing).

II **se déshabituer** *vpr* to get out of the habit (**de qch** of sth; **de faire** of doing).

désherbage /dezɛʀbaʒ/ *nm* weeding.

désherbant /dezɛʀbɑ̃/ *nm* weedkiller.

désherber /dezɛʀbe/ [1] *vtr* (à la main) to weed [*allée*]; (avec un désherbant) to apply weedkiller to [*allée*].

déshérence /dezeʀɑ̃s/ *nf* Jur escheat; **tomber en ~** to escheat; **succession tombée en ~** escheated inheritance; **une coutume en ~** fig a lapsed custom.

déshérité /dezeʀite/ I *pp* ▶ **déshériter**.

II *pp adj* (pauvre) [*personne*] underprivileged; [*pays*] disadvantaged; [*région, quartier*] deprived.

III *nm,f* **les ~s** the underprivileged.

déshériter /dezeʀite/ [1] *vtr* to disinherit.

déshonneur /dezɔnœʀ/ *nm* disgrace; **il est le ~ de la famille** he is the black sheep of the family.

déshonorant, **~e** /dezɔnɔʀɑ̃, ɑ̃t/ *adj* **1** (pour soi-même) dishonourable[GB]; **il n'y a rien de ~ à faire** there is nothing dishonourable[GB] in doing; **c'est ~ de faire** it's dishonourable[GB] to do; **2** (pour autrui) insulting.

déshonorer /dezɔnɔʀe/ [1] I *vtr* **1** (apporter le déshonneur à) to bring disgrace on [*personne, famille*]; to bring [sth] into disrepute [*doctrine, pays*]; **se sentir déshonoré** to feel disgraced; **être déshonoré** to be in disgrace; **2** fml (enlaidir) [*construction*] to disfigure [*paysage*]; **3**† (séduire) to dishonour[GB] [*femme, jeune fille*].

II **se déshonorer** *vpr* to disgrace oneself.

déshumanisation /dezymanizasjɔ̃/ *nf* dehumanization.

déshumaniser /dezymanize/ [1] I *vtr* to dehumanize [*société, personne*].

II **se déshumaniser** *vpr* [*société, travail*] to become dehumanized.

déshumidificateur /dezymidifikatœʀ/ *nm* dehumidifier.

déshydratant, **~e** /dezidʀatɑ̃, ɑ̃t/ I *adj* dehydrating.

II *nm* dehydrating agent.

déshydratation /dezidʀatasjɔ̃/ *nf* **1** Méd, Cosmét dehydration; **2** Tech drying; **~ à froid** freeze-drying.

déshydraté /dezidʀate/ I *pp* ▶ **déshydrater**.

II *pp adj* **1** Méd, Cosmét dehydrated; **2** Tech [*aliment*] dried.

déshydrater /dezidʀate/ [1] I *vtr* **1** Méd to dehydrate; **ça m'a complètement déshydraté** it left me completely dehydrated; **2** Tech to dry [*aliment*].

II **se déshydrater** *vpr* [*malade*] to dehydrate; [*peau*] to dry out.

déshydrogénation /dezidʀɔʒenasjɔ̃/ *nf* dehydrogenation.

déshydrogéner /dezidʀɔʒene/ [14] *vtr* to dehydrogenate.

déshypothéquer /dezipɔteke/ [14] *vtr* to pay off a mortgage on [*maison, propriété*].

desiderata /dezideʀata/ *nmpl* wishes.

design /dizajn/ I *adj inv* [*mobilier, véhicule*] modern and functional.

II *nm* **1** (stylique) design; **~ industriel/graphique** industrial/graphic design; **~ italien/scandinave** Italian/Scandinavian design; **le ~ des années 80** the 80's style; **2** (ensemble d'objets) modern and functional furnishings (*pl*); **3** (conception) design; **le ~ futuriste d'une voiture** the futuristic design of a car.

désignation /deziɲasjɔ̃/ *nf* **1** (d'un candidat) gén designation; (à un emploi) appointment; (comme candidat électoral) nomination; **2** Ling (appellation) designation; **3** Comm (description) description; **~ du contenu/des lieux/de l'article** description of the contents/of the property/of the item.

designer /dizajnœʀ/ *nm* (stylicien) designer.

désigner /deziɲe/ [1] I *vtr* **1** (faire référence à) [*mot, expression*] to refer to, to designate; [*couleur, triangle*] to represent; **le mot 'baroque' désigne à peu près n'importe quoi** the word 'baroque' can refer to just about anything; **les cercles désignent les villes principales** the circles represent the main cities; **le contrat la désigne comme travailleur temporaire** the contract describes her as a temporary worker; **2** (indiquer) (d'un geste) to point out; (en nommant) to name; **~ qch du menton** or **d'un mouvement de tête** to indicate sth with a jerk of one's head; **~ du doigt** to point to; **~ nommément** to name; **elle a désigné la personne qui** she named the person who; **~ qch à l'attention de qn** to draw sb's attention to sth; **~ qn à l'hostilité générale** fml to signal sb out for public condemnation; **tout le désigne comme coupable** everything points to him as the guilty party; **~ qn comme responsable** to hold sb responsible; **3** (choisir) gén to choose, to designate (**comme**, **en qualité de** as); (à un emploi) to appoint (**comme** as); (comme candidat électoral) to nominate (**comme** as); **~ qn comme son successeur** to designate sb as one's successor; **avoir été désigné comme** to have been designated as; **être tout désigné pour** to be just right for; **c'est la victime toute désignée** he's ou she's the obvious person to go for; **4** (fixer) to set [*date, lieu*].

II **se désigner** *vpr* **il s'est désigné à notre attention en...** fml we noticed him when he...

désillusion /dezil(l)yzjɔ̃/ *nf* disillusion; **éprouver une ~** to be disillusioned.

désillusionner /dezil(l)yzjɔne/ [1] I *vtr* to disillusion.

II **se désillusionner** *vpr* to lose one's illusions.

désincarcération /dezɛ̃kaʀseʀasjɔ̃/ *nf* **la ~ des victimes a pris 3 heures** it took 3 hours to cut the victims free; **matériel de ~** cutting equipment.

désincarcérer /dezɛ̃kaʀseʀe/ [14] *vtr* to cut [sb] free [*personne*].

désincarné, **~e** /dezɛ̃kaʀne/ *adj* **1** Relig disembodied; **2** liter [*théorie*] wild.

désincrustant, **~e** /dezɛ̃kʀystɑ̃, ɑ̃t/ I *adj* **1** Ind, Tech descaling; **2** Cosmét cleanser.

II *nm* **1** Tech descaler; **2** Cosmét cleanser.

désincruster /dezɛ̃kʀyste/ [1] *vtr* **1** Ind, Tech to descale [*chaudière, bouilloire*]; **2** Cosmét to cleanse [*peau*].

désindexation /dezɛ̃dɛksasjɔ̃/ *nf* deindexation (**de** of).

désindexer /dezɛ̃dɛkse/ [1] *vtr* to deindex.

désindustrialisation /dezɛ̃dystʀijalizasjɔ̃/ *nf* deindustrialization.

désinence /dezinɑ̃s/ *nf* Ling ending.

désinfectant, **~e** /dezɛ̃fɛktɑ̃, ɑ̃t/ I *adj* disinfecting.

II *nm* disinfectant.

désinfecter /dezɛ̃fɛkte/ [1] *vtr* to disinfect.

désinfection /dezɛ̃fɛksjɔ̃/ *nf* disinfection.

désinflation /dezɛ̃flasjɔ̃/ *nf* disinflation.

désinformation /dezɛ̃fɔʀmasjɔ̃/ *nf* disinformation; **opération de ~** disinformation campaign; **il y a une ~ du public sur ce point** the public is being deliberately misinformed on that matter.

désinformer /dezɛ̃fɔʀme/ [1] *vtr* to misinform deliberately.

désinsectisation /dezɛ̃sɛktizasjɔ̃/ *nf* pest control.

désinsectiser /dezɛ̃sɛktize/ [1] *vtr* to treat with insecticide.

désintégration /dezɛ̃tegʀasjɔ̃/ *nf* **1** (destruction) disintegration; **2** Nucl disintegration; **3** Géol crumbling.

désintégrer /dezɛ̃tegʀe/ [14] I *vtr* **1** (détruire) to disintegrate, to break up; **2** Nucl to disintegrate.

II **se désintégrer** *vpr* **1** (être détruit) to disintegrate, to break up; **2** Nucl to disintegrate.

désintéressé, **~e** /dezɛ̃teʀese/ I *pp* ▶ **désintéresser**.

II *pp adj* [*personne, acte*] selfless, unselfish; [*conseil, jugement*] disinterested; **son engagement n'est pas totalement ~** his commitment is not wholly disinterested; **il n'était pas ~ en faisant** he had an ulterior motive in doing; **il l'a aidée de façon ~e** he had no ulterior motive for helping her.

désintéressement /dezɛ̃teʀɛsmɑ̃/ *nm* **1** (détachement) disinterestedness; **agir avec ~** to act disinterestedly; **2** Fin (remboursement) paying off.

désintéresser /dezɛ̃teʀese/ [1] I *vtr* **1** (démotiver) to make [sb] lose interest (**de** in); **2** Fin to pay off [*créancier*].

II **se désintéresser** *vpr* **1** (ne plus s'intéresser) **se ~ de qch/qn** to lose interest in sth/sb; **2** (se détacher de) **se ~ de qch/qn** to disassociate oneself from sth/sb; **nous nous désintéressons de la question** we disassociate ourselves from the question.

désintérêt /dezɛ̃teʀɛ/ *nm* (indifférence) lack of interest (**pour** in); (baisse d'intérêt) loss of interest (**pour** in); **faire preuve du** or **marquer le plus total ~ envers** to show complete lack of interest in.

désintoxication /dezɛ̃tɔksikasjɔ̃/ *nf* detoxification; **subir une cure de ~** to go to a detoxification centre[GB].

désintoxiquer /dezɛ̃tɔksike/ [1] *vtr* Méd to detoxify [*alcoolique, toxicomane*]; **se faire ~** to undergo detoxification.

désinvestir /dezɛ̃vɛstiʀ/ [3] I *vtr* **1** Mil to withdraw one's troops from [*ville, région*]; **2** Fin, Écon **il a désinvesti son argent de l'entreprise** he took his money out of the company.

II *vi* Fin, Écon to cut investment; **on désinvestit dans la sidérurgie** investment in the steel industry is being cut.

désinvestissement /dezɛ̃vɛstismɑ̃/ *nm* **1** Écon (dans secteur économique) divestiture; (dans biens d'équipement) disinvestment; **2** Psych withdrawal of cathexis.

désinvolte /dezɛ̃vɔlt/ *adj* [*personne, remarque, geste*] offhand.

désinvolture /dezɛ̃vɔltyʀ/ *nf* offhand manner; **avec ~** in an offhand manner.

désir /deziʀ/ *nm* **1** (souhait) desire (**de** for; **de faire** to do); **~ compréhensible/naturel** understandable/natural desire; **~ d'indépendance du gouvernement** government's desire for independence; **~s du défunt/public** wishes of the deceased/public; **vos ~s sont des ordres** your wish is my command; **prendre ses ~s pour des réalités** to delude oneself; **2** (attirance sexuelle) desire.

désirable /deziʀabl/ *adj* desirable.

désirer /deziʀe/ [1] *vtr* **1** (vouloir) to want (**faire** to do); **s'il le désire** if he wants; **enfant désiré** wanted child; **effets non désirés** unwanted effects; **que désirez-vous?** what would you like? **je/elle désire qu'il parte** I/she would like him to leave; **n'avoir plus rien à ~** to have all one could wish for; **laisser à ~** to leave something to be desired; **laisser beaucoup à ~** to leave much to be desired; **se faire ~** to make oneself wanted; **2** (vouloir sexuellement) to want, to desire.

désireux, **-euse** /deziʀø, øz/ *adj* **~ de faire/que** anxious to do/that.

désistement /dezistəmɑ̃/ *nm* (de candidature, plainte) withdrawal; **~ en faveur de qn** withdrawal in order to allow sb else to stand GB ou to run.

■ **~ d'action** Jur withdrawal of a lawsuit; **~ de demande** Jur waiver of a claim.

désister: **se désister** /deziste/ [1] *vpr* to stand down GB, to withdraw (**en faveur de** in favour[GB] of); **se ~ de sa plainte** Jur to withdraw one's complaint.

désobéir /dezɔbeiʀ/ [3] *vtr ind* to be disobedient, to disobey; **~ à qn/à un ordre** to disobey sb/an order; **~ aux consignes de sécurité** to disregard safety regulations.

désobéissance /dezɔbeisɑ̃s/ *nf* disobedience; **on l'a renvoyé pour ~ à ses professeurs** he was expelled for disobeying his teachers.
■ **~ civile** civil disobedience.

désobéissant, **~e** /dezɔbeisɑ̃, ɑ̃t/ *adj* disobedient.

désobligeance /dezɔbliʒɑ̃s/ *nf* disagreeableness; **avec ~** disparagingly.

désobligeant, **~e** /dezɔbliʒɑ̃, ɑ̃t/ *adj* discourteous.

désobliger /dezɔbliʒe/ [13] *vtr* to put [sb] out [*personne*]; **vous me désobligez!** I'm offended; **vous ne me désobligerez pas en faisant** I wouldn't mind if you did.

désodorisant, **~e** /dezɔdɔʀizɑ̃, ɑ̃t/ **I** *adj* deodorant.
II *nm* (pour la toilette) deodorant; (pour la maison) air freshener.

désodoriser /dezɔdɔʀize/ [1] *vtr* to freshen.

désœuvré, **~e** /dezœvʀe/ **I** *adj* at a loose end○ GB, at loose ends○ (*jamais épith*) US.
II *nm,f* person at a loose end○ GB ou at loose ends○ US.

désœuvrement /dezœvʀəmɑ̃/ *nm* lack of anything to do; **faire qch par ~** to do sth for lack of anything better to do.

désolant, **~e** /dezɔlɑ̃, ɑ̃t/ *adj* **1** (attristant) distressing, upsetting; **2** (consternant) depressing.

désolation /dezɔlasjɔ̃/ *nf* **1** (affliction) grief; **2** (caractère dévasté) desolation.

désolé, **~e** /dezɔle/ **I** *pp* ▶ **désoler**.
II *pp adj* **1** (au regret) sorry; **être ~ que** to be sorry that; **j'en suis ~** I am sorry about that; **je suis ~ d'être en retard!** sorry I'm late!; **il est ~ de ne pas pouvoir venir** he's sorry he can't come; **~ de te faire attendre**○ sorry to keep you waiting; **2** (très affligé) [*personne*] desolate; **3** (vide) [*pays, village, plaine*] desolate; **une région ~e par la peste** a region desolated by the plague.

désoler /dezɔle/ [1] **I** *vtr* **1** (attrister) to upset, to distress; **2** (consterner) to depress; **tu me désoles!** I despair of you!
II se désoler *vpr* to be upset (**de qch** about); **il se désole de ne pas pouvoir venir à la fête** he's upset that he can't come to the party; **il est cassé, se désole Charlotte** it's broken, laments Charlotte.

désolidariser /desɔlidaʀize/ [1] **I** *vtr* Tech to disconnect (**de** from).
II se désolidariser *vpr* to dissociate oneself (**de** from).

désopilant, **~e** /dezɔpilɑ̃, ɑ̃t/ *adj* hilarious; **une histoire ~e** a hilarious story.

désordonné, **~e** /dezɔʀdɔne/ *adj* **1** (désorganisé) [*façon, article, paroles, pensée*] muddled; [*réunion, activité, combat*] disorderly; [*gestes*] uncoordinated; **2** (peu soigné) [*lieu, personne*] untidy; **3** (déréglé) [*conduite, existence*] wild.

désordre /dezɔʀdʀ/ **I**○ *adj inv* **faire ~** to look untidy ou messy; **être très ~** to be very untidy.
II *nm* **1** (fouillis) mess; **beau ~** fine mess; **dans le ~** in a mess; **dans le plus grand ~** in a complete mess; **pièce/maison en ~** untidy room/house; **laisser tout en ~** to leave everything in a mess; **quel ~!** what a mess!; **~ de papiers/livres** mess of papers/books; **il a tout mis en ~** (dans une pièce) he made it all untidy; (papiers, documents) he messed everything up○; **2** (manque de cohérence) chaos ¢; **être dans le ~/le plus grand ~** to be in chaos/utter chaos; **en ~** in chaos; **~ économique** economic chaos; **plonger le pays dans le ~/un ~ accru** to plunge the country into chaos/further chaos; **semer le ~** to cause chaos; **le ~ règne dans les esprits** confusion reigns in people's minds, everyone is utterly confused; **~ des idées** muddled thinking; **se retirer dans le ~** Mil to retire in disorder; **3** (caractère peu soigné) untidiness; **le ~ de sa chevelure/maison** her untidy hair/house; **4** (ordre aléatoire) **dans le ~** in any order; **répondre à des questions dans le ~** to answer questions in no particular ou in any order; **gagner dans le ~** Turf to win with a combination forecast; **5** (trouble) disorder; **~ public** public disorder; **~s sociaux** social disorder; **~s mentaux/du foie** mental/liver disorders; **6** liter (dérèglement) **~ de sa conduite** his/her wild behaviour.

désorganisation /dezɔʀganizasjɔ̃/ *nf* (action) disruption; (résultat) disorganization.

désorganisé, **~e** /dezɔʀganize/ **I** *pp* ▶ **désorganiser**.
II *pp adj* **1** [*économie, fonctionnement, structure*] disorganized; **2** [*personne, service*] disorganized.

désorganiser /dezɔʀganize/ [1] *vtr* to disrupt.

désorienter /dezɔʀjɑ̃te/ [1] *vtr* **1** (déconcerter) to confuse, to bewilder; **2** (faire perdre le sens de l'orientation) to disorientate[GB] [*personne*]; **ils ont été désorientés par la tempête** they lost their bearings in the storm.

désormais /dezɔʀmɛ/ *adv* (au présent) from now on, henceforth; (au passé) from then on, henceforth.

désossé, **~e** /dezɔse/ *adj* **1** Culin boned; **2**○ (très souple) lithe.

désosser /dezɔse/ [1] **I** *vtr* **1** Culin to bone; **2** (analyser) to take [sth] to pieces, to dissect [*texte*].
II se désosser *vpr* (se désarticuler) to contort oneself.

désoxydant /dezɔksidɑ̃/ *nm* deoxydizer.

désoxyder /dezɔkside/ [1] *vtr* to deoxydize.

désoxyribonucléique /dezɔksiʀibɔnykleik/ *adj* deoxyribonucleic.

desperado /dɛspeʀado/ *nm* desperado.

despote /dɛspɔt/ *nm* despot.

despotique /dɛspɔtik/ *adj* despotic.

despotiquement /dɛspɔtikmɑ̃/ *adv* despotically.

despotisme /dɛspɔtism/ *nm* despotism.

desquamation /dɛskwamasjɔ̃/ *nf* desquamation.

desquamer /dɛskwame/ [1] **I** *vi* (tomber) [*peau*] (en lambeaux) to peel off; (en pellicules) to flake off.
II se desquamer *vpr* [*peau*] to peel off.

desquelles ▶ **lequel**.

desquels ▶ **lequel**.

DESS /deəɛsɛs/ *nm inv* (*abbr* = **diplôme d'études supérieures spécialisées**) *postgraduate degree taken after Master's.*

dessaisir /desɛziʀ/ [3] **I** *vtr* **1** (priver) **~ qn de qch** to take sb off sth [*dossier*]; to relieve sb of sth [*responsabilité*]; **~ un juge d'une affaire** Jur to remove a judge from a case; **2** (déposséder) **~ qn de** to divest sb of [*bien*].
II se dessaisir *vpr* **se ~ de** to relinquish.

dessaisissement /desɛzismɑ̃/ *nm* Jur **1** (dans une succession) divestment; **2** (de jury) withdrawal of a case (**de** from); **3** (d'après la loi anti-trust) divestiture.

dessalage /desalaʒ/ *nm* **1** (d'eau de mer) desalination; **2** Naut capsizing.

dessalement /desalmɑ̃/ *nm* **1** (d'eau de mer) desalination; **usine de ~** desalination plant; **2** (de mets) desalting.

dessaler /desale/ [1] **I** *vtr* **1** (initier) to teach [sb] the ways of the world; **2** (extraire le sel de) to desalinate [*eau de mer*]; to desalt [*mets*].
II *vi* **1** Culin to desalt; **2**○ Naut to capsize.
III se dessaler *vpr* to lose one's innocence.

dessangler /desɑ̃gle/ [1] *vtr* (défaire la sangle) to undo the girth of; (relâcher) to loosen the girth of.

dessaouler = **dessoûler**.

desséchant, **~e** /desɛʃɑ̃, ɑ̃t/ *adj* drying; **effet ~** drying effect.

dessèchement /desɛʃmɑ̃/ *nm* **1** (de matière) (état) dryness; (processus) drying-out; **2** (de personne) withering.

dessécher /deseʃe/ [14] **I** *vtr* **1** (déshydrater) to dry [sth] out; **le soleil dessèche la peau** the sun makes your skin dry, the sun dries your skin out; **arbre/fruit desséché** withered tree/fruit; **cheveux desséchés** dry hair; **2** (rendre insensible) to harden [*personne, cœur*]; to deaden [*âme, imagination*].
II se dessécher *vpr* **1** (se déshydrater) [*cheveux, lèvres*] to become dry; [*végétation*] to wither; [*sol*] to dry out; **2** (devenir insensible) [*personne*] to become unfeeling, to harden; **3** (vieillir) [*personne*] to wither; **un vieillard desséché** a withered old man; **un intellectuel desséché** a fusty intellectual.

dessein /desɛ̃/ *nm* (objectif) objective; **grand ~** grand design; **noirs ~s** dark designs; **les ~s de Dieu** God's plans; **avoir/former le ~ de faire** to have/form the intention of doing; **avoir des ~s sur qn** to have designs on sb; **à ~** deliberately, by design; **à ~ de faire** with the intention of doing; **dans le ~ de faire** with a view to doing; **dans ce ~** to this end.

desseller /desele/ [1] *vtr* to unsaddle.

desserrage /desɛʀaʒ/ *nm* loosening.

desserré, **~e** /deseʀe/ **I** *pp* ▶ **desserrer**.
II *pp adj* loose.

desserrement /desɛʀmɑ̃/ *nm* **1** Tech loosening; **2** Écon relaxation; **~ du crédit** relaxation of credit.

desserrer /deseʀe/ [1] **I** *vtr* **1** lit to loosen [*ceinture, col, cravate, écrou, vis*]; to release [*frein*]; to undo [*nœud*]; to space out [*écriture*]; **~ les cordons de la bourse** to loosen one's purse strings; **2** fig to relax [*étau, étreinte*]; to relax [*crédit*]; **~ les rangs** to break ranks.
II se desserrer *vpr* **1** [*ceinture, col, cravate*] to come loose; [*écrou, vis*] to work loose; [*nœud*] to come undone; **2** [*étau, étreinte*] to slacken.
IDIOMES **il n'a pas desserré les dents** he never once opened his mouth.

dessert /desɛʀ/ *nm* **1** (plat) dessert, sweet GB, pudding GB; **en** or **comme ~** for dessert; **2** (moment) **au ~** at dessert; **servir un vin doux au ~** to serve a sweet wine at dessert.

desserte /desɛʀt/ *nf* **1** (service de transport) service; **~ ferroviaire** rail ou train service; **~ de cars** coach GB ou bus US service; **2** (fait de desservir une localité) **la ~ d'une ville par les transports en commun** public transport services to and from a city; **la ~ aérienne des Antilles** flights to and from the Antilles; **chemin de ~** access road; **3** (meuble) sideboard.

dessertir /desɛʀtiʀ/ [3] *vtr* to remove [sth] from its setting [*pierre*].

desservir /desɛʀviʀ/ [30] **I** *vtr* **1** Transp (relier) to serve [*ville, village*]; **quartier bien/mal desservi** well-/badly-served district; **2** (conduire à) to lead to [*chambre, étage*]; **l'ascenseur ne dessert pas le premier étage** the elevator does not stop at the first floor GB ou second floor US; **3** (être au service de) to serve; **l'hôpital dessert la moitié du pays** the hospital serves half of the country; **4** (nuire à) to do a disservice to; **5** (débarrasser) to clear [*table*].
II *vi* (débarrasser la table) to clear the table.

dessiccatif, **-ive** /desikatif, iv/ **I** *adj* desiccative, desiccating.
II *nm* dessicant.

dessiccation /desikasjɔ̃/ *nf* (de ciment) drying out, desiccation; (d'aliment) drying, dessication; **conserver des fruits par ~** to dry fruit.

dessiller /desije/ [1] *vtr* **~ les yeux de qn** fig to open sb's eyes.

dessin /desɛ̃/ *nm* **1** Art (activité) drawing; **le ~ s'apprend** drawing can be learned; **~ au crayon/pinceau** pencil/brush drawing; **~ de paysage/nu** landscape/nude drawing; **~ d'art** drawing; **faire du ~** to draw; **cours de ~** drawing class; **concours de ~** drawing competition; **apprendre le ~** to learn how to draw; **école/professeur de ~** art school/teacher; **2** (résultat) drawing; **~s et eaux-fortes** drawings and etchings; **~s d'enfants** children's drawings; **faire un ~** to do a drawing; **tu veux que je te fasse un ~**○**?** fig, iron do I have to spell it out for you?; **il n'y a pas besoin d'un ~**○**!** fig, iron it's perfectly clear!; **3** Art, Ind (conception) design; **~ d'une voiture/chaise** design of a car/chair; **4** (motif) pattern; **~ floral/géométrique** floral/geometric pattern; **5** (organisation) layout; **~ des rues/d'une ville** layout of the streets/of a city; **6** (contour) outline; **~ des lèvres** outline of the lips; **7** (grandes lignes) outline; **~ d'une intrigue/d'un projet** outline of a plot/a plan.
■ **~ animé** Cin cartoon; **~ d'architecture** architectural drawing; **~ assisté par ordinateur**, **DAO** computer-aided design, CAD; **~ humoristique** Presse cartoon; **~ industriel** technical drawing; **~ à main levée** freehand drawing; **~ mélodique** melodic line.

dessinateur, **-trice** /desinatœʀ, tʀis/ ▶**510** *nm,f* **1** Art draughtsman GB ou draftsman US; **~ de paysages** artist who does landscape drawings; **le ~ Daumier** Daumier, renowned for his drawings; **2** Ind **~ (industriel)** draughtsman[GB]; **3** Art, Ind (concepteur) designer; **~ de bijoux/meubles** jewellery GB ou jewelry US/furniture designer.
■ **~ de bande dessinée** Art (strip) cartoonist; **~ humoristique** Presse cartoonist; **~ de mode** fashion illustrator; **~ de presse** illustrator; **~ publicitaire** commercial artist.

dessiné, **~e** /desine/ **I** *pp* ▶ **dessiner**.
II *pp adj* **bouche bien ~e** well-shaped mouth.

dessiner /desine/ [1] **I** *vtr* **1** Art (représenter) to draw; **~ un nu/un plan** to draw a nude/a map; **~ au crayon/à la plume** to draw in pencil/in pen and ink; **particulièrement bien/mal dessiné** very skilfully[GB]/badly drawn; **2** (en se maquillant) **~ les sourcils** to draw in one's eyebrows; **~ les lèvres** to outline the lips; **3** (concevoir) to design [*tissu, décor, timbre*]; to draw up [*plans*]; **~ les contours** or **les grandes lignes de** to outline [*plan, programme, objectif*]; **4** (faire ressortir) **robe qui dessine la silhouette** figure-hugging dress; **5** (former) **l'ombre des feuilles dessine une dentelle** the shadow of the leaves makes a lacy pattern.
II *vi* Art to draw; **savoir ~** to be able to draw.
III se dessiner *vpr* **1** (se faire jour) [*avenir, aptitude, possibilité, victoire*] to take shape; **un sourire se dessina sur ses lèvres** a smile played across his/her lips; **2** (apparaître) **se ~ à l'horizon** [*ruines, cavalier*] to appear on the horizon; **il se dessinait nettement dans la lumière** he was clearly outlined in the light; **3** (être représenté) to be drawn; **se ~ facilement** to be easy to draw; **4** (se maquiller) **se ~ les lèvres** to outline one's lips.

dessouder /desude/ [1] **I** *vtr* **1** (ôter la soudure de) to unsolder [*pièces*]; **2**◐ (tuer) to do [sb] in○, to kill [*personne*].
II se dessouder *vpr* to come unsoldered.

dessoûler /desule/ [1] **I** *vtr* (faire cesser l'ivresse de) to sober up [*personne*]; **l'air frais l'a dessoûlée** the cool air has sobered her up.
II *vi* (cesser d'être ivre) to sober up; **il n'a pas dessoûlé pendant trois jours** he's been drunk for three days.

dessous /dəsu/ **I** *adv* underneath; **le prix est marqué ~** the price is marked underneath; **j'ai soulevé le livre, mes clés étaient ~** I lifted the book and my keys were underneath; **il ne pouvait pas sauter la barrière alors il s'est glissé ~** he couldn't jump over the gate so he slipped underneath; **quand je vois une échelle, je ne passe jamais ~** when I see a ladder, I never walk under it; **j'ai un parapluie, viens t'abriter ~** I've got an umbrella, why don't you shelter under it?
II *nm* (de langue, vase, d'assiette) underside; (de bras) inside (part); **le ~ du pied** the sole of the foot; **le dossier se trouve dans le ~ de la pile** the file is toward(s) the bottom of the pile; **de ~, du ~** [*drap, couche*] bottom; **l'étagère de** or **du ~** (sous une autre) the shelf below; (la dernière) the bottom shelf; **les voisins du ~** the downstairs neighbours[GB]; **l'étage du ~** the floor below.
III dessous *nmpl* **1** (sous-vêtements) underwear ¢; **porter des ~ en soie** to wear silk underwear; **2** (la face cachée) (de scandale, cas, succès) inside story (*sg*) (**de** on); **les ~ de la campagne électorale** what goes on behind the scenes in the electoral campaign; **on ignore les ~ de l'affaire** we don't know what's behind this affair.
IV‡ *prép* under.
V en dessous *loc adj* (inférieur) **la taille/le modèle en ~** the next size down.
VI en dessous *loc adv* **1** (sous quelque chose) underneath ; **tu vois l'armoire là-bas, la valise est en ~** see that wardrobe over there, the suitcase is underneath; **mets une chemise en ~** put a shirt on underneath; **il n'y a personne en ~** there's no one living on the floor below; **il habite juste en ~** he lives on the floor below; **va voir à l'étage en ~** go and have a look downstairs; **2** (sournoisement) **agir en ~** to do [sth] behind people's backs; **rire en ~** to be laughing up one's sleeve; **regarder qn en ~** to look at sb sidelong, to give sb sidelong glances.
VII par en dessous *loc adv* **1** (sous quelque chose) underneath; **passer par en ~** to go underneath; **ça fuit par ~** it's leaking underneath; **prendre qch par en ~** to lift sth up by the bottom ou from underneath; **2** (de manière sournoise) **il te fait des sourires mais par en ~ il te critique** he's all smiles when he sees you but he criticizes you behind your back.
VIII en dessous de *loc prép* **1** (sous) below; **il habite juste en ~ de chez moi** he lives on the floor below me; **en ~ de la fenêtre** below the window; **2** (à un niveau inférieur) below; **15 degrés en ~ de zéro** 15 degrees below zero; **en ~ d'un salaire minimum/du seuil de pauvreté/de 10%** below a minimum wage/the poverty line/10%; **les producteurs de pétrole travaillent en ~ de leurs possibilités** oil producers are operating below capacity; **les chèques en ~ de 100 francs ne sont pas acceptés** cheques for under 100 francs are not accepted; **les enfants en ~ de 13 ans** children under 13; **tu travailles en ~ de tes possibilités** you're not working to your full potential, you're not giving your all.
IX de dessous *loc prép* (d'un endroit) **on l'a retiré de ~ les décombres** they pulled him from beneath ou out of the rubble; **j'ai retiré le tapis de ~ la table** I pulled the rug from under the table.
IDIOMES **avoir le ~** to be at a disadvantage; **être en ~ de tout**○ (ne pas être à la hauteur) to be absolutely useless○; (moralement) to be despicable.

dessous-de-bouteille /d(ə)sudbutɛj/ *nm inv* drip mat (for bottle).

dessous-de-bras /d(ə)sudbʀɑ/ *nm inv* dress shield.

dessous-de-plat /d(ə)sudpla/ *nm inv* (en vannerie, en bois) table mat; (à pieds) plate stand; (en métal) trivet.

dessous-de-table /d(ə)sudtabl/ *nm inv* (entre particuliers) under-the-counter payment; (pot-de-vin) bribe, backhander○ GB; **recevoir des ~ de qn** to be bribed by sb.

dessous-de-verre /d(ə)sudvɛʀ/ *nm inv* coaster.

dessus /dəsy/

■ **Note** Lorsque *dessus* est utilisé avec un verbe d'action tel que *marcher*, *taper*, *tirer*, *compter etc* on se reportera au verbe correspondant; de même pour certaines expressions telles que *mettre la main dessus*, *avoir le nez dessus etc* on se reportera aux entrées ***main***, ***nez*** etc. Les usages particuliers sont traités dans l'entrée ci-dessous.

I *adv* **passe ~** go over it; **tu vois la pile, le livre doit être ~** see that pile over there, the book should be on top of it; **un gâteau avec du chocolat ~** a cake with chocolate on top, a chocolate-covered cake; **ne mets pas tes doigts ~** gén don't touch it; (sur une photographie) don't put your fingers on it; **le prix est marqué ~** the price is marked on it; **'ton rapport est fini?'—'non , je travaille** or **suis ~'** 'is your report finished?'—'no, I'm working on it'; **il a mis ses meilleurs chercheurs ~** he set his best researchers to work on it; **nous n'avons aucune chance d'emporter le marché, le numéro un mondial est déjà ~** we're not likely to corner the market, the world leader is working on it; **il y en a deux, prends celui de** or **du ~** there are two of them, take the top one.
II *nm* (de chaussure) upper; (de table, tête, panier) top; (de main) back; **les voisins du ~** the upstairs neighbours[GB]; **l'étage du ~** the upper floor, the floor above; **le drap de ~** the top sheet.
IDIOMES **avoir** or **prendre/reprendre le ~** to gain/to regain the upper hand; **avec lui, c'est toujours le poète qui prend le ~** his poetic nature always comes to the fore.

dessus-de-lit /d(ə)sydli/ *nm inv* bedspread.

dessus-de-porte /d(ə)sydpɔʀt/ *nm inv* decorated lintel.

déstabilisation /destabilizasjɔ̃/ *nf* destabilization; **~ monétaire** monetary destabilization; **manœuvres de ~** destabilizing activities; **~ d'un adversaire/opposant** unsettling of an adversary/opponent.

déstabiliser /destabilize/ [1] *vtr* to unsettle [*personne*]; to destabilize [*situation, pays*].

déstalinisation /destalinizasjɔ̃/ *nf* destalinization.

destin /dɛstɛ̃/ *nm* **1** (fatalité) fate; **les arrêts du ~** the dictates of fate; **c'est le ~!** that's life!; **c'est un coup du ~** it's a twist of fate; **2** (existence) destiny; **prendre son ~ en main** to take control of one's (own) destiny.

destinataire /dɛstinatɛʀ/ *nmf* **1** Postes (de lettre) addressee; **2** Ling addressee; **3** (bénéficiaire de crédit, d'aide) beneficiary; (de mandat) payee.

destination /dɛstinasjɔ̃/ **I** *nf* **1** Postes, Télécom, Transp destination; **arriver à ~** [*personne*] to reach one's destination; [*lettre, train*] to reach its destination; **~ inconnue/finale** unknown/final destination; **~s exotiques/européennes** exotic/European destinations; **2** (rôle, fonction) purpose.
II à destination de *loc prép* [*avion, bateau, train*] bound for [*lieu*]; **partir à ~ de** to leave for; **'vol Air France 810 à ~ de Londres'** 'Air France flight 810 to London'.

destiné, **~e** /dɛstine/ **I** *pp* ▶ **destiner**.
II *pp adj* **1** (prévu) **~ à faire** intended to do, meant to do; **un dispositif ~ à encourager l'investissement** a mechanism intended ou meant to encourage investment; **2** (promis) **~ à une belle carrière** destined

for a successful career; **~ à la rencontrer** destined to meet her.

III **destinée** *nf* destiny; **~e d'un peuple/d'un projet** destiny of a people/a project; **présider aux ~es d'une entreprise/d'un club** to control a company's/club's destiny; **prendre en main les ~es du pays** to take control of the country's destiny; **promis aux plus hautes ~es** destined for great things; **unir les ~es de nos enfants** liter to unite our children; **unir sa ~e à qn** to marry sb.

destiner /dɛstine/ [1] I *vtr* **1** (concevoir pour) **~ qch à qn** to design sth for sb; **être destiné à faire** [*objet, système*] to be designed ou intended to do; **l'appareil n'était pas destiné à cet usage** the appliance was not designed for that purpose ou was not intended to be used in that way; **des mesures destinées à faire** measures aimed at doing; **2** (réserver) **l'argent que je destine à mes enfants** the money I intend to leave to my children; **l'argent destiné à mes enfants** the money intended for my children; **la somme que je destinais à mes vacances** the money I had set aside for my holiday GB ou vacation US; **produits destinés à l'exportation** goods (destined) for export; **3** (adresser) **la lettre ne leur était pas destinée** the letter wasn't for them ou meant for them; **lettre destinée à ma sœur** letter for my sister; **la gifle ne t'était pas destinée** the slap wasn't aimed at you; **la bombe était destinée à quelqu'un d'autre** the bomb was meant ou intended for somebody else; **4** (vouer) **être destiné à qch/à faire** [*personne*] to be destined for sth/to do; **son talent la destine à un grand avenir** with her talent she's destined for a great future; **5** (par le destin) **on ne peut pas savoir ce qui nous est destiné** we never know what fate has in store for us.

II **se destiner** *vpr* **elle se destine à une carrière de juriste** she's decided on a legal career.

destituer /dɛstitɥe/ [1] *vtr* to discharge [*officier*]; to depose [*souverain*]; **~ qn de ses fonctions** to relieve sb of his/her duties.

destitution /dɛstitysjɔ̃/ *nf* (d'officier) discharge; (d'homme politique) deposition.

déstockage /destɔkaʒ/ *nm* reduction of stocks.

déstocker /destɔke/ [1] I *vtr* to reduce stocks of [*marchandise*]; **~ des surplus** to reduce surplus stocks.

II *vi* to reduce stocks, to cut down on stocks.

destrier† /dɛstʀije/ *nm* charger†, steed†.

destroyer /dɛstʀwaje/ *nm* Naut destroyer.

destructeur, -trice /dɛstʀyktœʀ, tʀis/ I *adj* destructive; **produits chimiques ~s de la couche d'ozone** chemicals which destroy the ozone layer.

II *nm,f* destroyer.

destruction /dɛstʀyksjɔ̃/ *nf* destruction ¢; **~ partielle/totale/massive** partial/total/mass destruction; **instinct de ~** destructive instinct; **la ~ des cafards/moustiques** the extermination of cockroaches/mosquitoes.

déstructuration /destʀyktyʀasjɔ̃/ *nf* **1** Sociol disintegration; **2** Psych breakdown, disintegration.

désuet, -ète /dezɥɛ, ɛt/ *adj* **1** (vieillot) [*décor, charme*] old-world, quaint; [*manière, style*] old-fashioned; **2** (dépassé) [*mot, expression*] obsolete; [*méthode, technique*] outmoded.

désuétude /dezɥetyd/ *nf* obsolescence; **tomber en ~** to become obsolete.

désuni ,~e /dezyni/ *adj* **1** (en désaccord) [*famille*] divided; [*amants*] estranged; **2** Sport [*athlète*] uncoordinated, off one's stride (*jamais épith*); **3** Équit [*cheval, galop*] disunited.

désunion /dezynjɔ̃/ *nf* **1** (de parti) division, dissension; **2** (dans la famille, le couple) discord.

désunir /dezyniʀ/ [3] I *vtr* (diviser) [*dispute*] to divide, to break up [*famille, groupe*].

II **se désunir** *vpr* [*athlète*] to be off one's stride.

désyndicalisation /desɛ̃dikalizasjɔ̃/ *nf* deunionization.

détachable /detaʃabl/ *adj* **1** (qu'on peut détacher et rattacher) [*pièce, élément, partie de véhicule*] detachable; **2** (qu'on peut ôter et remettre) [*fiche, intercalaire*] removable; **3** (qui se déchire) [*coupon, feuille de calendrier*] tear-off (*épith*); **le coupon est ~** the coupon can be torn off.

détachage /detaʃaʒ/ *nm* **procéder au ~ d'un vêtement** to remove the stains from a piece of clothing; **produit de ~** stain remover.

détachant, ~e /detaʃɑ̃, ɑ̃t/ I *adj* stain-removing (*épith*); **produit ~** stain remover.

II *nm* stain remover.

détaché, ~e /detaʃe/ I *pp* ▶ **détacher**.

II *pp adj* **1** (indifférent) [*air, expression, mine*] detached, unconcerned; **dit-elle d'un ton ~** she said indifferently; **2** Admin [*professeur, diplomate, militaire*] on secondment GB (*après n*), transferred (*jamais épith*) (**auprès de** to); **3** Mus [*note*] detached.

détachement /detaʃmɑ̃/ *nm* **1** (distance) detachment (**de** from); **voir qch avec ~** to view sth with detachment; **2** (indifférence) ¢ indifference; **elle affiche le plus total ~ à l'égard des questions d'argent** she's completely indifferent to money matters; **3** Admin (de fonctionnaire) secondment GB, transfer (**auprès de** to); **être en ~** to be on secondment; **mettre qn en ~** to second sb; **4** Mil (troupe) detachment.

détacher /detaʃe/ [1] I *vtr* **1** (ôter les liens de) to untie [*personne, animal, barque, cheveux, paquet*] (**de** from); **2** (défaire un lien) to unfasten [*agrafe, ceinture, collier*]; to undo [*chaussure, bouton*]; to untie, to undo [*nœud, corde, ficelle, lacet*]; **détachez-lui ses menottes** remove his/her handcuffs; **3** (défaire d'un support) [*personne*] to tear [sth] off [*timbre, coupon, chèque*]; to take down [*affiche, tableau, cadre*]; [*vent*] to tear [sth] off [*affiche*]; to blow [sth] off [*fruits, feuilles, tuiles*]; [*humidité*] to make [sth] come away [*affiche, plâtre*]; **détachez selon** or **suivant le pointillé** tear along the dotted line; **'partie à ~'** 'tear off here'; **~ un fruit/une feuille d'un arbre** [*personne*] to pick a fruit/a leaf from a tree; [*vent*] to blow a fruit/a leaf off a tree; **~ un wagon d'un train** to uncouple a carriage GB ou car US from a train; **4** (éloigner) **~ qn de** [*personne, famille*] to turn ou drive sb away from; [*défaut, mode de vie*] to alienate sb from sb/sth; **son travail l'a détachée de sa vie de famille** her work has drawn her away from her family life; **5** (détourner) **~ les yeux** or **le regard/l'esprit de qch** to take one's eyes/one's mind off sth; **~ son attention/ses pensées de qch** to turn one's attention/one's thoughts away from sth; **6** (affecter) [*administration*] to second GB, to transfer [*enseignant, diplomate, militaire*] (**à, en, auprès de** to; **de** from); **demander à être détaché en Asie** to ask to be seconded to Asia; **se faire ~** to be seconded; **7** (faire ressortir) [*orateur*] to articulate [*mot, syllabe*]; [*musicien*] to detach [*note*]; [*imprimeur, designer*] to make [sth] stand out [*lettre, titre, mot*]; [*peintre*] to make [sth] stand out [*motif*]; **8** (écarter) **~ les bras du corps** to hold one's arms away from one's body; **9** (enlever les taches de) to remove the stain(s) from [*tissu, cuir, vêtement*] (**à** with).

II **se détacher** *vpr* **1** (se défaire de ses liens) [*prisonnier, animal*] to break loose (**de** from); [*bateau*] to come untied (**de** from); [*colis*] to come undone; **2** (se défaire) [*agrafe, nœud, bouton, corde, lacet*] to come undone; **comment se détache cette ceinture?** how does this belt unfasten?; **3** (se séparer d'un support) [*coupon, feuillet*] to come out (**de** of); [*papier peint, affiche*] to come away (**de** from), to peel (**de** off); **les fruits se détachent facilement des branches** the fruit comes off the branches easily; **4** (se désintéresser) **se ~ de** to lose interest in [*vie, activité*]; to turn one's back on [*monde*]; to grow away from [*personne*]; **se ~ des biens terrestres** to turn one's back on worldly goods; **5** (ressortir) [*motif, titre, objet, silhouette*] to stand out (**dans** in; **sur** against); **6** (s'éloigner) **se ~ de** [*individu, invité*] to detach oneself from [*groupe*]; [*coureur, cycliste, cheval*] to pull away from [*groupe*]; [*entreprise*] to pull away from [*concurrent*]; [*personne, œuvre, style*] to break away from [*tradition, genre*]; [*membre, pays*] to break away from [*organisation, union*]; **7** (se distinguer) [*élève, candidat, artiste, œuvre*] to stand out (**de** from).

détail /detaj/ *nm* **1** (petit élément) detail; **~ fâcheux/significatif/troublant** annoying/significant/disturbing detail; **~ sans intérêt** unimportant detail; **~s techniques** technical details; **soigner chaque ~** to pay attention to every detail; **le moindre ~** the slightest detail; **étudier/dépeindre/imaginer dans les moindres ~s** to study/depict/imagine in minute detail; **2** (analyse précise) breakdown; **~ des dépenses** breakdown of expenses; **~ chiffré** breakdown in figures; **expliquer en ~/plus en ~** to explain in detail/in greater detail; **entrer dans le ~** or **les ~s** to go into detail; **ne pas faire dans le ~** not to do in detail; **ils n'ont pas fait de ~, ils ont licencié tout le monde** they didn't use half-measures, they laid everybody off; **avoir un sens/le goût du ~** to have an eye/a liking for detail; **raconter qch en ~** to give a detailed account of sth; **analyse/étude/discussion de ~** detailed analysis/study/discussion; **un point de ~** a minor detail; **'un ~, n'oubliez pas votre manuel la prochaine fois!'** 'just one thing, don't forget your textbook next time!'; **3** Comm retail; **acheter/vendre (qch) au ~** to buy/sell (sth) retail.

détaillant, ~e /detajɑ̃, ɑ̃t/ *nm,f* retailer.

détaillé, ~e /detaje/ I *pp* ▶ **détailler**.

II *pp adj* [*analyse, liste, plan*] detailed; [*facture*] itemized; **très ~** very detailed.

détailler /detaje/ [1] *vtr* **1** (exposer) to detail [*dépenses, projet, problème*]; **2** (regarder) to scrutinize [*personne, objet*].

détaler /detale/ [1] *vi* **1** [*lapin*] to bolt; **2**○ [*personne*] to dash off, to scarper○ GB; **faire ~ des voleurs** to frighten off thieves; **il a détalé à toutes jambes** he made off as fast as his legs could carry him.

IDIOMES **~ comme un lapin** to run off like a startled rabbit.

détartrage /detaʀtʀaʒ/ *nm* **1** (de chaudière, bouilloire) descaling; **2** (de dents) scaling; **se faire faire un ~** to have one's teeth scaled.

détartrer /detaʀtʀe/ [1] *vtr* **1** to descale [*bouilloire, chaudière*]; **2** to scale [*dents*].

détaxation /detaksasjɔ̃/ *nf* tax exemption.

détaxe /detaks/ *nf* Fisc (suppression de taxe) tax removal; (remboursement de taxe) tax refund; (ristourne d'exportation) export rebate.

détectable /detɛktabl/ *adj* detectable.

détecter /detɛkte/ [1] *vtr* to detect.

détecteur, -trice /detɛktœʀ, tʀis/ I *adj* detector (*épith*).

II *nm* detector; **~ de mines** mine detector.

détection /detɛksjɔ̃/ *nf* detection.

détective /detɛktiv/ **▶510** *nm* detective; **~ privé** private detective, private eye○.

déteindre /detɛ̃dʀ/ [55] I *vtr* to fade [*tissu*].

II *vi* **1** (perdre sa couleur) [*vêtement, tissu*] to fade; **~ au lavage** to fade in the wash; **2** (être instable) [*couleur*] to run; **3** (donner sa couleur) [*vêtement*] to run; **ta jupe a déteint sur ma chemise** your skirt has run and the colour[GB] has come out on my shirt; **4** (influer) to rub off (**sur** on).

dételage /detlaʒ/ *nm* (de cheval) unharnessing; (de bœuf) unyoking.

dételer /detle/ [19] I *vtr* to unharness

[*cheval*]; to unyoke [*bœuf*]; to unhitch [*charrue, wagon*].
II○ *vi* (arrêter de travailler) to knock off○; **sans ~** without a break.

détendeur /detɑ̃dœʀ/ *nm* Tech regulator.

détendre /detɑ̃dʀ/ [6] **I** *vtr* **1** (relâcher) to release [*arc, ressort*]; **2** (étirer) to slacken [*ressort, corde*]; to make [sth] lose its shape, to make [sth] baggy○ [*vêtement*]; **3** (reposer) to relax [*muscle*]; to calm [*atmosphère, esprit*]; **~ la situation politique** to defuse the political situation; **4** (distraire) to entertain [*public*].
II *vi* **1** (reposer) [*pause, thé*] to be relaxing; **2** (distraire) [*comédie*] to be entertaining.
III se détendre *vpr* **1** (s'étirer) [*corde, ressort*] to slacken; [*vêtement*] to lose its shape, to go baggy○; **2** (se relaxer) [*personne, muscle*] to relax; **l'atmosphère se détend** the atmosphere is becoming more relaxed.

détendu, **~e** /detɑ̃dy/ **I** *pp* ▶ **détendre**.
II *pp adj* (étiré) [*ressort, corde*] slack; [*vêtement*] shapeless, baggy○.
III *adj* (calme) [*personne, ambiance, relation*] relaxed.

détenir /det(ə)niʀ/ [36] *vtr* **1** (posséder) to keep [*objets*]; to hold [*pouvoir, capital, record*]; to possess [*armes*]; to have [*moyen, secret, preuve*]; **~ la vérité** to possess the truth; **2** Jur to detain [*criminel, suspect*].

détente /detɑ̃t/ *nf* **1** (repos) relaxation; **moment/journée de ~** moment/day of relaxation; **sensation de ~** feeling of relaxation; **~ musculaire** muscle relaxation; **c'est une ~ pour moi** it's a way for me to relax; **2** Pol détente; **~ en Europe** détente in Europe; **l'atmosphère est à la ~** détente is in the air; **3** Écon **~ des taux d'intérêt** relaxation of interest rates; **4** Tech (d'arme) trigger; **appuyer sur la ~** to pull the trigger; **5** Phys (de gaz) expansion; **6** Sport **avoir une bonne ~** [*joueur de tennis, gardien de but*] to have quick reflexes; [*athlète*] to have a good take-off.
IDIOMES **être lent** or **dur à la ~**○ to be slow on the uptake.

détenteur, **-trice** /detɑ̃tœʀ, tʀis/ *nm,f* (d'armes, argent) possessor; (d'actions, autorisation, autorité, de passeport, record) holder; (de secret) guardian.

détention /detɑ̃sjɔ̃/ *nf* **1** (possession) (d'actions, de drogue, passeport, record) holding; (d'armes, de secret) possession; **2** Jur (privation de liberté) detention; **camp de ~** detention camp; **~ illégale** illegal detention.
■ **~ criminelle** Jur imprisonment; **~ préventive** or **provisoire** Jur custody; **placer qn en ~ préventive** to remand sb in custody.

détenu, **~e** /detəny/ *nm,f* prisoner.

détergent, **~e** /detɛʀʒɑ̃, ɑ̃t/ **I** *adj* detergent; **produit ~** detergent.
II *nm* detergent.

détérioration /deteʀjɔʀasjɔ̃/ *nf* **1** (dégât) damage (**de** to); **2** (usure) wear and tear (**de** on); **3** (déclin) deterioration (**de** in).

détériorer /deteʀjɔʀe/ [1] **I** *vtr* to damage.
II se détériorer *vpr* [*économie, équipement, relation, situation, temps*] to deteriorate; [*denrée*] to go bad; [*monnaie*] to weaken.

déterminable /detɛʀminabl/ *adj* determinable.

déterminant, **~e** /detɛʀminɑ̃, ɑ̃t/ **I** *adj* [*rôle, facteur, élément*] decisive.
II *nm* **1** Ling determiner; **2** Math determinant; **3** (facteur) determining factor.

déterminatif, **-ive** /detɛʀminatif, iv/ **I** *adj* **adjectif ~** determiner; **complément ~** postmodifier.
II *nm* Ling determinative.

détermination /detɛʀminasjɔ̃/ *nf* **1** (volonté) determination (**à faire** to do); **avec ~** with determination; **2** (mise en évidence) determination; **~ des causes** determination of the causes; **3** (fixation) determination; **~ du loyer** determination of the rent; **4** Ling determination and modification.

déterminé, **~e** /detɛʀmine/ **I** *pp* ▶ **déterminer**.
II *pp adj* **1** (résolu) [*personne*] determined; **~ à faire** determined to do; **2** (causé) determined (**par** by); **prix ~ par la demande** price determined by demand; **3** (établi) [*corrélation*] demonstrated (*jamais épith*); **il est mort dans des circonstances mal ~es** the circumstances in which he died are not yet clear ou established; **4** (donné) [*durée, objectif*] given; **appartenir à une religion ~e** to belong to a given religion; **5** Philos determinate.
III *nm* Ling determined word, referent.

déterminer /detɛʀmine/ [1] **I** *vtr* **1** (établir) to determine [*raison, responsabilité*]; **~ les causes de l'accident** to determine what caused the accident; **2** (fixer) to work out [*mesures, modalités*]; **~ une politique** to work out a policy; **3** (causer) to determine [*attitude, décision, choix*]; to lead to [*événement, phénomène*]; **4** (pousser) **~ qn à faire** to cause sb to do; **cela l'a déterminé à quitter l'armée** it caused ou led him to leave the army; **5** Ling to determine.
II se déterminer *vpr* **1** (être établi) to be determined; **2** (être fixé) to be worked out; **3** (choisir) [*personne*] to make a choice (**entre** between); (se décider à) **se ~ à** to make up one's mind to.

déterminisme /detɛʀminism/ *nm* determinism.

déterministe /detɛʀminist/ *adj, nmf* determinist.

déterré, **~e** /deteʀe/ **I** *pp* ▶ **déterrer**.
II *pp adj* [*cadavre, plante*] that has been dug up (*après n*).
III *nm,f* **avoir une tête** or **mine de ~** to look like death warmed up.

déterrer /deteʀe/ [1] *vtr* to dig up [*trésor, plante, cadavre, os*].

détersif, **-ive** /detɛʀsif, iv/ Tech **I** *adj* detergent; **produit ~** detergent.
II *nm* detergent.

détersion /detɛʀsjɔ̃/ *nf* cleaning with a detergent.

détestable /detɛstabl/ *adj* [*caractère, style, temps*] appalling; [*habitudes*] revolting.

détestablement /detɛstabləmɑ̃/ *adv* [*écrire, jouer, se comporter*] abominably.

détestation /detɛstasjɔ̃/ *nf* detestation.

détester /detɛste/ [1] **I** *vtr* **1** (exécrer) to detest, loathe [*personne*]; **se faire ~ de qn** to arouse sb's hatred; **2** (ne pas supporter) to hate; **~ faire** to hate doing; **~ que qn fasse** to hate sb doing; **~ cordialement** to cordially detest; **ne pas ~ qch/faire qch** not to be averse to sth/doing sth; **ne ~ rien tant que** to hate nothing so much as.
II se détester *vpr* **1** (soi-même) to hate oneself; **2** (l'un l'autre) to hate each other.

détonant, **~e** /detɔnɑ̃, ɑ̃t/ *adj* lit, fig explosive.

détonateur /detɔnatœʀ/ *nm* **1** (amorce d'explosif) detonator; **2** fig catalyst; **être le ~ de qch** to be the catalyst of sth, to trigger sth off.

détonation /detɔnasjɔ̃/ *nf* detonation.

détoner /detɔne/ [1] *vi* to go off, to detonate.

détonner /detɔne/ [1] *vi* **1** (jurer) [*personne, comportement, meuble*] to be out of place (**au milieu de** among); [*couleur, rideaux*] to clash; **2** Mus (mal chanter) to sing out of tune; (mal jouer) to play out of tune.

détordre /detɔʀdʀ/ [6] *vtr* to untwist [*barre de fer*]; to unwind [*câble*].

détortiller /detɔʀtije/ [1] *vtr* to untwist, to unwind.

détour /detuʀ/ *nm* **1** (trajet) detour; **faire un ~** to make a detour; **faire un ~ par Oxford** to make a detour via Oxford; **ça vaut le ~** it's worth the trip; **faire du cinéma après un ~ par le théâtre** fig to go into films after a brief spell in the theatre[GB]; **les négociations font un ~ par les salaires** fig the negotiations have branched off into discussions about salaries; **2** (moyen indirect) roundabout means; (dans le langage) circumlocution; **user de ~s pour dire qch** to say sth in a roundabout way; **être sans ~s** (explication) to be straight and to the point; (personne) to be plain-speaking; **il nous a parlé sans ~s** he spoke to us frankly; **il me l'a dit sans ~s** he told me straight; **il m'a expliqué son point de vue sans ~s** he told me straight out what his position was; **3** (tournant) bend; **les ~s d'une route/rivière** the bends in a road/river; **au ~ de la route/rivière** at the bend in the road/river; **au ~ de la conversation** fig in the course of the conversation; **faire des ~s** [*route*] to twist and turn; [*rivière*] to meander.

détourné, **~e** /detuʀne/ **I** *pp* ▶ **détourner**.
II *pp adj* [*allusion, sens*] oblique; [*moyen*] indirect; **d'une façon** or **manière ~e** in a roundabout way; **par des chemins ~s** by a circuitous route.

détournement /detuʀnəmɑ̃/ *nm* **1** (de recette, dividendes) misappropriation; **2** (d'avion, de navire) hijacking; **3** (de circulation, rivière) diversion; **4** (subversion) perversion; **~ du processus démocratique** perversion of the democratic process; **5** (d'œuvre, affiche, objet) defacement (**de** of).
■ **~ de fonds** embezzlement, misappropriation of funds; **~ de fonds publics** misuse of public money, peculation; **~ de mineur** (incitation à la débauche) corruption of a minor.

détourner /detuʀne/ [1] **I** *vtr* **1** (écarter) to divert [*attention*] (**de** from); **~ les yeux** or **le regard** or **la tête** to look away (**de** from); **~ les soupçons sur qn** to make suspicion fall on sb else; **2** (éloigner) **~ de** to distract [sb] from [*objectif, études, vrai problème*]; **ils cherchent à te ~ de moi** they are trying to get you away from me; **3** (modifier le cours de) to divert [*rivière, circulation*]; **~ la conversation** to change the subject; **4** (modifier la destination de) to divert [*vol, navire, troupes, ressources*] (**sur, vers** to); **5** (à des fins criminelles) to hijack [*avion , navire*]; to misappropriate, to embezzle [*fonds, somme d'argent*]; **6** Sport to deflect [*balle*]; **~ la balle en corner** to deflect the ball for a corner kick; **7** (subvertir) to twist [*loi*]; **~ l'Histoire à son profit** to rewrite history to serve one's own purposes; **8** (déformer) to deface [*film, affiche, objet*].
II se détourner *vpr* **1** (renoncer) **se ~ de** to turn away from [*client, ami*]; to neglect [*obligation*]; **2** (tourner la tête) to look away.

détracteur, **-trice** /detʀaktœʀ, tʀis/ **I** *adj* [*esprit*] disparaging.
II *nm,f* detractor.

détraqué, **~e** /detʀake/ **I** *pp* ▶ **détraquer**.
II *pp adj* **1** [*mécanisme, moteur*] broken down, on the blink○; [*organisation, système*] broken down; [*temps*] unsettled; **mon ordinateur est ~** my computer is down ou on the blink○; **ma montre est complètement ~e** my watch has gone completely wrong; **2**○ **avoir l'estomac ~** to have stomach problems; **avoir les nerfs ~s** to have bad nerves; **il a le cerveau ~** he's off his rocker○.
III○ *nm,f* deranged person, headcase◑.

détraquer /detʀake/ [1] **I** *vtr* **1** [*personne*] to bust○ [*mécanisme, montre*]; [*poussière, rouille, humidité*] to make [sth] go wrong [*mécanisme, montre*]; **la pollution a détraqué le temps** pollution has upset the weather; **2**○ [*médicament, alcool*] to upset [*foie, estomac, santé*]; **la mort de son fils lui a détraqué le cerveau** his son's death unhinged his mind.
II se détraquer *vpr* **1** [*mécanisme, moteur*] to break down, to go on the blink○; [*montre, horloge*] to go wrong, to pack up○ GB; [*temps*] to break; **2**○ [*nerfs*] to go to pieces;

[*esprit*] to become unhinged; [*santé*] to break down; **se ~ la santé** to ruin one's health (**avec** with).

détrempe /detʀɑ̃p/ *nf* **1** Art (technique, matière) tempera; (œuvre) tempera painting; **peindre à la ~** to paint in tempera; **2** (de l'acier) softening.

détremper /detʀɑ̃pe/ [1] *vtr* **1** (imprégner) to saturate [*sol, vêtement*]; **la pluie a détrempé mon manteau** the rain has soaked my coat; **le terrain est détrempé** the ground is waterlogged; **2** Art (diluer) to dilute [*couleurs*]; **3** Tech to soften [*acier*].

détresse /detʀɛs/ *nf* **1** (angoisse) distress; **sentiment/cri de ~** feeling/cry of distress; **la ~ des réfugiés** the distress of refugees; **2** (difficulté) distress; **dans la ~** in distress; **soulager la ~ de qn** to alleviate sb's distress; **lancer un appel de ~** to send out a distress call; **émettre des signaux de ~** to emit distress signals; **en ~** [*navire, avion*] in distress; [*entreprise, train*] in difficulties; **se porter au secours d'un alpiniste en ~** to go to the aid of a climber in difficulty; **~ respiratoire** respiratory distress syndrome.

détriment: **au détriment de** /odetʀimɑ̃də/ *loc prép* to the detriment of.

détritique /detʀitik/ *adj* Géol detrital.

détritus /detʀity(s)/ **I** *nm inv* (bon à rien) pej wreck péj.

II *nmpl* (ordures) refuse ¢, rubbish GB ¢, garbage US.

détroit /detʀwɑ/ *nm* Géog straits (*pl*); **le ~ de Gibraltar** the Straits of Gibraltar; **le ~ de Magellan** the Magellan Straits; **le ~ des Dardanelles** the Dardanelles.

détromper /detʀɔ̃pe/ [1] **I** *vtr* to disabuse, to set [sb] straight; **j'ai pu la ~ sur ce point** I was able to set her straight on this point.

II se détromper *vpr* **détrompez-vous!** don't you believe it!; **si tu crois qu'il va nous attendre, détrompe-toi!** if you think he's going to wait for us, you'd better think again!

détrôner /detʀone/ [1] *vtr* **1** Hist, Pol to depose, to dethrone [*souverain*]; **2** fig to supplant [*personne, pays*]; to depose [*produit, usage*].

détrousser† /detʀuse/ [1] *vtr* to rob.

détruire /detʀɥiʀ/ [69] **I** *vtr* lit, fig to destroy; **forêt détruite par le feu aux deux tiers** forest two thirds destroyed by fire; **le drame l'a complètement détruit** the tragedy has completely destroyed him; **~ qch à l'explosif** to blow sth up.

II se détruire *vpr* **1** (soi-même) to destroy oneself; **2** (l'un l'autre) to destroy each other.

dette /dɛt/ *nf* **1** (somme due) debt; **~ publique/extérieure** Écon national/foreign debt; **avoir des ~s** to have debts, to be in debt; **avoir 1 000 F de ~s** to have debts of 1,000 francs; **faire des ~s** to run up debts; **être couvert** or **criblé de ~s** to be debt-ridden, to be up to one's eyes in debt○; **~ de jeu** gambling debt; **être en ~ envers qn** lit, fig to be indebted to sb; **2** (obligation morale) debt (**envers** to); **avoir une ~ d'amitié/de reconnaissance envers qn** to owe sb a debt of gratitude/of friendship; **payer sa ~ à la société** to pay one's debt to society; **il leur gardait une ~ de reconnaissance** he remained indebted to them; **payer une vieille ~** to pay off an old debt.

DEUG /dœg/ *nm* (*abbr* = **diplôme d'etudes universitaires générales**) *university diploma taken after two years' study*.

deuil /dœj/ *nm* **1** (décès) bereavement; **être frappé par un ~** to be bereaved, to suffer a bereavement; **un nouveau ~ les afflige** they have suffered another bereavement fml, there has been another death in the family; **elle est en ~?** has she lost somebody?; **2** (douleur) mourning ¢, grief; **jour de ~ national** day of national mourning; **pays plongé dans le ~** country plunged into mourning; **prendre part** or **s'associer au ~ de qn** to share (in) sb's grief ou sorrow; **3** (tenue) mourning (clothes); **être/se mettre en ~** to be in/go into mourning; **être en grand ~** to be in deep mourning; **prendre/porter le ~ de qn** to go into/wear mourning for sb; **la nature est en ~** fig, liter nature is in mourning; **4** (période) period of mourning; **abréger le ~** to cut short a period of mourning; **une année de ~** a year's mourning; **5** (cortège) funeral procession; **le ~ se réunira à l'église** the funeral procession will meet at the church; **mener** or **conduire le ~** to head the funeral procession, to be chief mourner.

IDIOMES **faire son ~ de qch**○ to kiss sth goodbye○; **le contrat, tu peux en faire ton ~** you can kiss ou say goodbye to the contract○.

deus ex machina /deusɛksmakina/ *nm* deus ex machina.

deusio○ = **deuzio**.

deutérium /døteʀjɔm/ *nm* deuterium.

Deutéronome /døteʀɔnɔm/ *nm* **le ~** Deuteronomy.

deux /dø/ **▶ 545**, **407**, **212** **I** *adj inv* **1** (précisément) two; **il a été opéré des ~ yeux** he's had surgery on both (his) eyes; **prendre qch à ~ mains** to take sth with both hands; **ouvrez bien grand les ~ yeux/oreilles** look/listen very carefully; **~ fois** twice; **des ~ côtés de la rue/de la rivière/de l'Atlantique** on either side ou both sides of the street/of the river/of the Atlantic; **tous les ~ jours/ans** every other day/year, every two days/years; **'~ l/m'** (en épelant) 'double l/m'; **balle s'écrit avec ~ l** there are two 'l's in balle; **à nous ~** (je suis à vous) I'm all yours; (parlons sérieusement) let's talk; (à un ennemi) it's just you and me now; **on sera ~** there will be two of us; **▶ à**, **chose**, **doigt**, **par**, **tout**, **trois**, **uni**; **2** (quelques) a few, a couple of; **écrivez-nous ~ ou trois lignes** drop us a few ou couple of lines; **j'en ai pour ~ minutes** I'll be two minutes ou ticks○ GB; **c'est à ~ minutes d'ici** it's a couple of ou two minutes from here; **l'arrêt de bus est à ~ pas** the bus stop is a stone's throw away; **▶ mot**; **3** (dans une date) second.

II *pron* **je vais essayer les ~** I'll try both of them; **elles sont venues toutes les ~** they both came.

III *nm* **1** (chiffre) two; **une fois sur ~** 50% of the time; **il travaille un week-end sur ~** he works every other week-end; **vivre à ~** to live together ou as a couple; **la vie à ~ n'est pas toujours facile** living together ou as a couple is not always easy; **faire qch en moins de ~**○ to do sth very quickly ou in two ticks○ GB; **2** Sport (en aviron) pair; **~ barré/sans barreur** coxed/coxless pair.

IV○ *adv* two, second(ly).

IDIOMES **faire ~ poids, ~ mesures** to have double standards; **un tiens vaut mieux que ~ tu l'auras** Prov a bird in the hand is worth two in the bush Prov; **en ~ temps, trois mouvements** very quickly, in two ticks○ GB; **la couture et moi, ça fait ~** I know nothing about sewing; **lui et moi, ça fait ~** we're two different people; **il est menteur comme pas ~**○ he's the world's biggest liar; **c'est simple comme ~ et ~ font quatre** it's as easy as ABC; **aussi vrai que ~ et ~ font quatre** as true as I'm standing here; **je n'ai fait ni une ni ~** I didn't waste any time, I didn't hang about○.

deux-coups /døku/ *nm inv* (fusil) double-barrelled[GB] shotgun.

deux-deux /dødø/ *nm* Mus two-two; **à ~** in two-two (time).

deux-huit /døɥit/ *nm* Mus two-eight; **à ~** in two-eight (time).

deuxième /døzjɛm/ **▶ 545**, **212** *adj* **1** (dans une séquence) second; **~ fois/partie** second time/part; **dans un ~ temps nous étudierons...** subsequently, we will study...; **c'est à prendre au ~ degré** it is not to be taken literally; **2** (dans une hiérarchie) second; **3** (autre) second; **ma ~ patrie** my second home, my second homeland; **un ~ enfant** a second child.

■ **~ âge** [*produits, vêtements*] for babies from six to twelve months (*épith, après n*); **~ classe** (soldat) private; Transp second class, standard class GB.

deuxièmement /døzjɛmmɑ̃/ *adv* secondly, second.

deux-mâts /dømɑ/ *nm inv* Naut two-master.

deux-points /døpwɛ̃/ *nm inv* Ling colon.

deux-quatre /døkatʀ/ *nm inv* Mus two-four; **à ~** in two-four (time).

deux-roues /døʀu/ *nm inv* two-wheeled vehicle, two-wheeler.

deux-seize /døsɛz/ *nm inv* two-sixteen; **à ~** in two-sixteen (time).

Deux-Sèvres /døsɛvʀ/ **▶ 692** *nprfpl* (département) **les ~** Deux-Sèvres.

deux-temps /døtɑ̃/ *adj, nm inv* Mécan two-stroke; **mélange ~** two-stroke mix.

deuzio○ /døzjo/ *adv* secondly.

dévaler /devale/ [1] **I** *vtr* [*animal, rocher*] to hurtle down [*pente*]; [*personne*] to tear down [*pente, rue*]; **~ les escaliers** to rush downstairs; **elle a dévalé les escaliers/les marches quatre à quatre** she rushed down the stairs/the steps four at a time.

II *vi* **1** (avec mouvement) **les manifestants dévalent dans la rue** the demonstrators go tearing down the street; **la lave dévale vers le village** the lava pours down toward(s) the village; **2** (sans mouvement) to fall away sharply; **le jardin dévalait vers le ravin** the garden sloped away sharply into the ravine.

dévaliser /devalize/ [1] *vtr* **1** (voler) to rob [*personne, banque, coffre*]; to clean out○ [*appartement*]; **on s'est fait ~ pendant le voyage** we were robbed during the journey; **2** (vider) to clean out○; **la boutique de jouets a été dévalisée à l'approche de Noël** the toyshop has been completely cleaned out in the run-up to Christmas; **les soldes ont bien marché, j'ai été dévalisé!** the sales went well, I'm completely cleaned out!; **les enfants ont dévalisé le garde-manger** the children have raided the larder.

dévaloir /devalwaʀ/ *nm* H (vide-ordures) chute.

dévalorisation /devalɔʀizasjɔ̃/ *nf* **1** (de monnaie, compétence) depreciation; **2** (de politique, diplôme) devaluation.

dévaloriser /devalɔʀize/ [1] **I** *vtr* **1** Écon, Fin (diminuer la valeur de) to reduce the value of [*monnaie, produit*]; **2** (diminuer le prestige de) to depreciate [*objet*]; to belittle [*personne*].

II se dévaloriser *vpr* **1** (en valeur) to lose value; (en prestige) to lose prestige; **le métier se dévalorise** the job is losing its prestige; **2** (se déprécier soi-même) to put oneself down.

dévaluation /devalɥasjɔ̃/ *nf* Écon devaluation.

dévaluer /devalɥe/ [1] **I** *vtr* Écon to devalue [*monnaie*].

II se dévaluer *vpr* to become devalued.

devancement /dəvɑ̃smɑ̃/ *nm* **~ d'appel** enlistment before call-up.

devancer /dəvɑ̃se/ [12] *vtr* **1** (avoir de l'avance sur) to be ahead of, to outstrip [*adversaire, concurrent*]; **pour l'instant, il devance son rival de 12 minutes/2 000 voix/100 mètres** at the moment, he is 12 minutes/2 000 votes/100 metres[GB] ahead of his opponent; **un penseur qui a devancé ses contemporains** a thinker who is ahead of his time; **dans la course aux exportations, nous avons été devancés par nos concurrents** our competitors have outstripped us in the exports league; **2** (précéder) **les pompiers ont devancé la police sur les lieux de l'accident** the fire brigade got to the scene of the accident ahead of ou before the police; **3** (anticiper sur) to anticipate [*revendication, désir*]; to forestall, to preempt [*attaque, critiques*]; **4** (faire avant la date prévue) **~ l'appel** to enlist for military service before call-up; **~ l'échéance d'un paiement** to settle a payment before the due date.

devancier, **-ière** /dəvɑ̃sje, ɛʀ/ *nm,f* precursor.

devant[1] /dəvɑ̃/ **I** *prép* **1** (en face de) **~ qn/qch** in front of sb/sth; **la voiture est garée ~ la maison** the car is parked in front of the house; **il est assis ~ la fenêtre** he's sitting at the window; **tu as mis ton pull ~ derrière** you've put your jumper on back to front; **le bus est passé ~ moi sans s'arrêter** the bus went straight past me without stopping; **elle est passée ~ moi**, **elle m'est passée ~**○ (dans une file) she jumped the queue GB ou cut in line US and went ahead of me; **regarder/marcher droit ~ soi** to look/walk straight ahead; **regarde ~ toi quand tu marches!** look where you're going!; **il était assis ~ une bière** he was sitting with a beer in front of him; **pousse -toi de ~ la télévision** move away from the television ; **enlève ça de ~ moi** (obstacle à la vue) move that away, I can't see; (obstacle au passage) move that out of my way; **2** (près de) outside; **on se retrouve ~ le théâtre** let's meet outside the theatre[GB]; **cela s'est passé ~ chez moi** it happened in front of ou outside my house; **il attendait ~ la porte** (à l'extérieur) he was waiting outside the door; (à l'intérieur) he was waiting by the door; **3** (en présence de) **il l'a dit ~ moi** he said it in front of me; **il tremblait ~ le juge** he stood before the judge, trembling; **il doit comparaître ~ la Cour Suprême** he has to appear before the Supreme Court ; **tous les hommes sont égaux ~ la loi** all men are equal in the eyes of the law; **je jure ~ Dieu** I swear before God; **on est toujours ému ~ un tel spectacle** it's always such a moving sight; **il ne fume jamais ~ ses parents** (c'est interdit) he never smokes in front of his parents; **il s'inclina ~ elle** he bowed before her; **cela s'est passé ~ nous/nos yeux** it took place in front of us/before our very eyes; **~ la situation, il faut faire** faced with ou in view of the situation, it's necessary to do; **je m'incline ~ tes arguments** I bow to your arguments; **à la porte, il s'effaça ~ moi** when we got to the door, he stood back to let me pass; **passer ~ le maire** to get married; **4** (face à) **fuir ~ le danger** to run away from danger, to flee in the face of danger; **hésiter ~ le danger** to hesitate in the face of danger; **je recule ~ ce genre de responsabilité** I shy away from that kind of responsibility; **l'égalité ~ l'éducation** equality in education; **~ l'inévitable/la difficulté** faced with the inevitable/difficulty; **l'impuissance des mots ~ le malheur** the inadequacy of language when confronted with misfortune; **la réaction des étudiants ~ le texte** the reaction of the students when faced ou confronted with the text; **ils ont reconnu leur impuissance ~ mon cas** they had to admit they couldn't help me; **5** (en avant de) **la voiture ~ nous** the car ahead ou in front of us; **il était si fatigué qu'il ne pouvait plus mettre un pied ~ l'autre** he was so tired he could hardly put one foot in front of the other; **laisser passer quelqu'un ~ (soi)** to let somebody go first; **6** (de reste) **avoir beaucoup de travail ~ soi** to have a lot of work to do; **avoir du temps ~ soi** to have plenty of time; **avoir de l'argent ~ soi** to have some money to spare; **avoir un mois ~ soi** to have a whole month ahead of one; **avoir toute la vie ~ soi** to have one's whole life ahead of one.

II *adv* **1** (en face) **si tu passes ~, achète-moi un livre** if you're passing it ou the bookshop, buy me a book; **'où est la poste?'—'tu es juste ~'** 'where's the post office?'—'you're right in front of it'; **2** (en tête) **je passe ~, si vous le permettez** (pour montrer le chemin) I'll go ahead of you, if you don't mind; **puis-je passer ~?** (dans une file) do you mind if I go before you?; **pars ~, je te rejoins** go ahead, I'll catch up with you; **3** (à l'avant) (dans une salle, un théâtre) at the front; (dans une voiture) in the front; **j'ai pris des places ~** I've booked GB ou reserved seats at the front.

IDIOMES **sortir les pieds ~**○ to leave feet first; **se retrouver Gros Jean comme ~** to be back at square one, to be back where one started.

devant[2] /dəvɑ̃/ *nm* (de vêtement, maison, scène) front; **une chambre sur le ~** a room at the front; **de ~** [*dents, chambre, porte*] front; ▶ **scène**.

■ **~ de cheminée** fire-screen.

IDIOMES **prendre les ~s** to take the initiative; **il savait qu'on allait le licencier**: **il a pris les ~s et a démissionné** he knew he was going to be made redundant: he preempted it by resigning ou he took the initiative and resigned first.

devanture /dəvɑ̃tyʀ/ *nf* **1** (façade de magasin) front, frontage; **2** (vitrine) shop ou store US window; **3** (étalage) window-dressing; **en ~** on display, in the window.

dévaser /devaze/ [1] *vtr* to dredge.

dévastateur, **-trice** /devastatœʀ, tʀis/ *adj* devastating; **une nouvelle à l'effet dévastateur** a devastating piece of news.

dévastation /devastasjɔ̃/ *nf* devastation ¢, havoc ¢.

dévaster /devaste/ [1] *vtr* **1** (détruire) [*armée*] to lay waste to [*pays*]; [*orage, feu*] to destroy [*récoltes, immeuble*]; **2** (saccager) [*cambrioleur*] to wreck [*habitation*]; **3** (altérer) [*passion, souffrance*] to ravage [*personne, cœur*]; **visage dévasté par la douleur** face ravaged by grief.

déveine○ /devɛn/ *nf* rotten luck○, bad luck; **ça a été mon jour de ~ aujourd'hui** I've had a run of bad luck today; **tu parles d'une** or **d'un coup de ~!** what rotten luck!; **avoir la ~ de faire** to have the bad luck to do.

développable /devlɔpabl/ *adj* gén Math developable.

développateur /devlɔpatœʀ/ *nm* Phot developer.

développé /devlɔpe/ *nm* Sport press.

développement /devlɔpmɑ̃/ *nm* **1** (de faculté, science, pensée, d'organisme) development; **le ~ de l'embryon/du langage** the development of the embryo/of language; **les ~s d'une affaire** the developments in an affair; **surveiller de près le ~ des événements** to keep a close eye on how things develop; **2** (d'entreprise, économie, de pays) development, expansion (**de** of); **pays en voie de ~** developing nation ou country; **l'entreprise a connu un fort ~ dans les années 80** the firm expanded greatly in the eighties; **en plein ~** (pays) rapidly developing (*épith*); (industrie) fast-growing (*épith*); (ville, université) rapidly expanding (*épith*); **3** (croissance) (de mouvement) growth (**de** of), spread (**de** of); (de fraude, chômage) increase (**de** in), rise (**de** in); (d'investissements) increase (**de** in); **4** (de produit, technique, stratégie) development; **le ~ de produits nouveaux** development of new products; **5** Phot developing; **détail qui est apparu au ~** detail which appeared when the picture was developed; **6** (de sujet, thème) development; **entrer dans des ~s oiseux** to ramble; **7** Math (de solide, fonction) development; (d'expression algébrique) simplification, reduction; **8** (en cyclisme) *distance covered for each revolution of the pedal*; **avec un petit ~, on grimpe mieux** it's easier to ride uphill in a low gear.

■ **~ personnel** Psych personal growth.

développer /devlɔpe/ [1] **I** *vtr* **1** (faire croître) to develop [*muscle, faculté, personnalité, pays, économie, technologie, ressources*]; to expand [*importations, réseau, connaissances, activité, projet*]; **muscles bien/peu développés** well-developed/underdeveloped muscles; **2** (amplifier) to develop, to expand [*sujet, chapitre, récit*]; Mus to develop [*thème*]; **3** (innover) to develop [*stratégie, politique, modèle*]; **4** Phot to develop [*cliché*]; **donner qch à ~** to have ou get sth developed; **5** Math to develop [*solide, fonction, série*]; to reduce [*expression*]; **6** Chimie **formule développée** structural formula; **7** (en cyclisme) **vélo qui développe deux mètres** bicycle which covers two metres[GB] for each turn of the pedals.

II se développer *vpr* **1** (s'accroître) [*personne, corps, muscle, faculté*] to develop; [*plante*] to grow; [*entreprise, ville, économie*] to grow, to expand; [*pratique, mœurs, usage*] to become widespread; **2** (évoluer) [*intrigue*] to develop.

devenir /dəvniʀ/ [36] **I** *nm* **1** (avenir) future; **le ~ des minorités/d'une alliance** the future of the minorities/of an alliance; **2** Philos Becoming.

II *vi* to become; **il est devenu riche/protestant/ministre** he has become rich/a Protestant/a minister; **~ réalité** to become a reality; **parti qui allait** or **devait ~ plus tard**... party which was later to become...; **qu'est-ce que je vais ~**○**?, que vais-je ~?** what is to become of me?; **que sont devenues tes belles promesses?** what has become of all your fine promises?; **et Paul, qu'est-ce qu'il devient**○ or **que devient-il?** and what is Paul up to these days?; **il devient urgent de faire** it has become necessary to do; **la concurrence devient sévère** the competition is getting fierce.

déverbal, *pl* **-aux** /devɛʀbal, o/ *nm* deverbal noun.

dévergondage /devɛʀgɔ̃daʒ/ *nm* debauchery, loose living.

dévergondé, **~e** /devɛʀgɔ̃de/ **I** *adj* [*personne, conduite*] debauched, licentious; **vie ~e** loose living.

II† *nm,f* (homme) profligate; (femme) shameless hussy†.

dévergonder: **se dévergonder** /devɛʀgɔ̃de/ [1] *vpr* to lead a debauched life.

déverrouiller /devɛʀuje/ [1] *vtr* to unbolt [*porte*]; to unlock [*portière*]; to open [*arme*].

dévers /devɛʀ/ *nm* (de rails, route) banking; **virage en ~** banked curve.

déversement /devɛʀsəmɑ̃/ *nm* **1** (de trop-plein) draining-off, pouring-out; (d'effluents, de pétrole) dumping; **~ accidentel** spillage; **2** Constr deflection.

déverser /devɛʀse/ [1] **I** *vtr* **1** lit to pour [*liquide*] (**dans** into); to drop [*bombes*] (**sur** on); to dump [*ordures*] (**dans** into; **sur** on); to tip GB, to dump [*sable*] (**sur** onto); to discharge [*effluents*] (**dans** into); to disgorge [*foule, touristes*] (**dans** onto); **~ du pétrole/des produits chimiques** (volontairement) to dump oil/chemicals (**dans** into); (accidentellement) to spill oil/chemicals (**dans** into); **la Seine déverse ses eaux dans la Manche** the Seine flows into the English Channel; **les agriculteurs en colère ont déversé du purin dans les rues** angry farmers dumped manure all over the streets; **2** fig to churn out [*musique*]; to pour out [*insultes*]; **elle a déversé sa colère sur lui** she vented her anger on him.

II se déverser *vpr* [*fleuve, rivière*] to flow (**dans** into); [*égout, foule*] to pour (**dans** into); **tout le contenu du camion-citerne s'est déversé sur la chaussée** the entire contents of the tanker were spilled all over the roadway.

déversoir /devɛʀswaʀ/ *nm* spillway.

■ **~ de fond** outlet-sluice.

dévêtir /devɛtiʀ/ [33] **I** *vtr* to undress.

II se dévêtir *vpr* to get undressed.

déviance /devjɑ̃s/ *nf* deviance ¢.

déviant, **~e** /devjɑ̃, ɑ̃t/ *adj, nm,f* deviant.

déviation /devjasjɔ̃/ *nf* **1** (de circulation, réseau) diversion GB, detour US; **mettre en place une ~** to set up a diversion; **2** (altération) departure (**par rapport à** from); **~ par rapport à la norme** departure from the norm; **3** (de boussole) deviation; **4** (optique) deflection; **5** (d'aiguille) deflection.

■ **~ de la colonne vertébrale** Méd curvature of the spine; **avoir une ~ de la colonne vertébrale** to have curvature of the spine.

déviationnisme /devjasjɔnism/ *nm* deviationism.

déviationniste /devjasjɔnist/ *adj, nmf* deviationist.

dévidage /devidaʒ/ *nm* **1** (de bobine) unwinding; **2** Tex (d'écheveau) winding (up).

dévider /devide/ [1] *vtr* **1** (dérouler) to unwind [*fil, câble, bobine*]; **2** Tex (mettre en écheveau) to wind [sth] into a skein; **~ la soie du cocon** to spin the silk off the cocoon; **3**○ (raconter) to pour out [*histoire, souvenirs*].

dévidoir /devidwaʀ/ *nm* reel.

dévier /devje/ [2] **I** *vtr* to deflect [*ballon, trajectoire*]; to divert [*circulation*]; **~ une attaque** to deflect an attack; **essayer de ~ la conversation** to try to change the subject.

II *vi* **1** [*balle de fusil, ballon*] to deflect; [*véhicule*] to veer off course; **~ à gauche** to veer to the left; **~ de sa course pour éviter un accident** to swerve to avoid an accident; **~ d'une trajectoire** to veer off course; **2** fig **~ de** to deviate from, to depart from [*projet, plan*]; **3** [*outil*] to slip; **4** [*conversation*] to drift.

devin /dəvɛ̃/ *nm* soothsayer, seer; **je ne suis pas ~!** I'm not psychic!

deviner /dəvine/ [1] **I** *vtr* **1** (parvenir à connaître) to guess [*secret*]; to foresee, to tell [*avenir*]; **2** (soupçonner) to sense [*danger*]; **je devine quelque chose de louche là-dessous** I smell a rat; **3** (imaginer) to imagine; **je te laisse ~ leur joie** I leave you to imagine their joy; **4** (apercevoir) to make out; **on devine une maison au loin** you can make out a house in the distance; **sa robe laisse ~ ses rondeurs** you can make out her curves through her dress.

II se deviner *vtr* **1** (être facile à connaître) **la suite du film se devine aisément** it's easy to guess what happens next in the film; **2** (transparaître) [*inquiétude, trouble*] to come out.

devineresse /dəvinʀɛs/ *nf* soothsayer, seer.

devinette /dəvinɛt/ *nf* riddle, conundrum; **poser une ~ à qn** to ask sb a riddle; **cesse** or **arrête de jouer aux ~s!** fig stop talking in riddles!

devis /d(ə)vi/ *nm* estimate, quote; **un ~ de dix millions** an estimate ou a quote of ten million; **établir/faire faire un ~** to draw up/to ask for an estimate ou quote; **~ pour la fabrication de qch** estimate of the cost of making sth; **~ gratuit sur demande** free estimate available on request; **~ descriptif** detailed estimate; **~ de réparation** estimate for repairs.

dévisager /devizaʒe/ [13] *vtr* to stare at [*personne*]; **~ qn avec insistance** to stare hard at sb.

devise /dəviz/ *nf* **1** (monnaie d'un pays) currency; **des ~ européennes** European currencies; **une ~ forte** a strong ou hard currency; **la ~ américaine/allemande** journ the US dollar/the Deutschmark; **2** (monnaie étrangère) (foreign) currency **¢**; **acheter des ~s** to buy foreign currency; **payer en ~s** to pay in foreign currency; **3** (maxime) motto; **ne pas se mêler des affaires des autres, telle est ma ~** don't meddle in other people's affairs, that's my motto; **4** Hérald (emblème) device.

deviser /dəvize/ [1] *vi* to converse (**de** about).

dévissage /devisaʒ/ *nm* **1** (de pièce vissée) unscrewing; **2** (en alpinisme) fall.

dévisser /devise/ [1] **I** *vtr* to unscrew [*couvercle, boulon*].

II *vi* (en alpinisme) to fall; **il a dévissé mortellement sur 1 000 mètres** he fell 1,000 metres[GB] to his death.

III se dévisser *vtr* **1** (être amovible) to unscrew; **2**○ (se tordre) **~ la tête/le cou** to twist one's head/neck around.

de visu /devizy/ *loc adv* [*constater*] for oneself, with one's own eyes.

dévitalisation /devitalizasjɔ̃/ *nf* **~ d'une dent** root canal work.

dévitaliser /devitalize/ [1] *vtr* to do root canal work on [*dent*].

dévoilement /devwalmɑ̃/ *nm* **1** lit unveiling; **2** fig revelation.

dévoiler /devwale/ [1] *vtr* **1** lit to unveil [*statue, plaque*]; to reveal [*partie du corps*]; **~ ses charmes** to reveal one's charms; **2** fig to reveal [*intentions, information, complot*] (**à qn** to sb); to uncover [*scandale, vérité*]; [*compagnie, firme*] to unveil [*nouveau modèle*]; **~ ses batteries** to reveal one's secret intentions.

devoir[1] /dəvwaʀ/ [44]

■ **Note** Lorsque *devoir* est utilisé comme auxiliaire pour exprimer une obligation posée comme directive, une recommandation, une hypothèse ou un objectif, il se traduit par *must* suivi de l'infinitif sans *to*: *je dois finir ma traduction aujourd'hui* = I must finish my translation today; *tu dois avoir faim!* = you must be hungry!
– Lorsqu'il exprime une obligation imposée par les circonstances extérieures, il se traduit par *to have* suivi de l'infinitif: *je dois me lever tous les matins à sept heures* = I have to get up at seven o'clock every morning.
– Les autres sens du verbe auxiliaire, et *devoir* verbe transitif et verbe pronominal, sont présentés ci-dessous.

I *v aux* **1** (obligation, recommandation, hypothèse) **tu dois te brosser les dents au moins deux fois par jour** you must brush your teeth at least twice a day; **je dois aller travailler** I've got to go to work; **je devais aller travailler** I had to go to work; **il doit accepter** he has got to accept; **il a dû accepter** he had to accept; **tu ne dois pas montrer du doigt!** you shouldn't point!; **ces mesures doivent permettre une amélioration du niveau de vie** these measures should allow an improvement in the standard of living; **le texte doit pouvoir être compris de tous** the text should be comprehensible to everyone; **il doit absolument éviter l'alcool** it's imperative that he avoid alcohol, he really must avoid alcohol; **je dois dire/reconnaître que cela ne m'étonne pas** I have to ou I must say/admit I'm not surprised; **je dois avouer que j'ai hésité** I have to ou must admit I did hesitate; **vous devrez être attentif à cela** you'll have to ou you must watch out for that; **tu devrais réfléchir avant de parler** you should think before you speak; **on devrait mettre cet enfant au lit** this child ought to be put to bed; **elle ne doit pas être fière!** she can't be proud of herself!; **ils ne doivent plus lui faire confiance** they can't trust him any more; **je devais avoir 12 ans à ce moment-là** I must have been 12 at the time; **ils doivent arriver d'une minute à l'autre** they're due to arrive any minute; **2** (être dans la nécessité de) **l'entreprise va ~ fermer** the company will have to close, the company is going to have to close; **encore doivent-elles faire leurs preuves** they still have to prove themselves; **dois-je prendre un parapluie?** should I take an umbrella?, do I need to take an umbrella?; **tu ne dois pas venir si tu ne te sens pas bien** you don't have to come if you don't feel well; **dussé-je en mourir** liter even if I die for it; **il a cru ~ partir** he felt obliged to leave; **3** (exprime une prévision) **elles devaient en parler** they were to talk about it; **le contrat doit être signé à 16 heures** the contract is to be signed at 4 pm; **cet argent devait rester disponible** this money was to have remained available; **à quelle heure doit-il rentrer?** what time should he be home?; **à quoi doivent-ils s'attendre ensuite?** what are they to expect next?; **nous ne devons pas partir cet été** we're not intending to go away this summer; **je dois le voir demain** I'll be seeing him tomorrow; **je dois m'absenter prochainement** I'll have to leave shortly; **nous devions partir quand il s'est mis à pleuvoir** we were about to leave when it started raining, we should have left but it started raining; **4** (exprime la fatalité) **10 ans plus tard, il devait sombrer dans la pauvreté** 10 years later, he was to be found languishing in poverty; **ce qui devait arriver arriva** what was to happen, happened; **cela devait arriver** it was bound to happen; **nous devons tous mourir un jour** we all have to die some day; **elle devait mourir dans un accident de voiture** she was to die in a car crash.

II *vtr* **1** (avoir à payer) to owe [*argent, repas*]; **~ qch à qn** to owe sth to sb, to owe sb sth; **il déteste ~ de l'argent** he hates owing money; **combien vous dois-je?** (pour un service) how much do I owe you?; (pour un achat) how much is it?; **j'ai payé la veste mais je dois encore la jupe** I've paid for the jacket but I haven't paid for the skirt yet; **2** (être redevable de) **~ qch à qn** to owe sth to sb, to owe sb sth; **~ qch à qch** to owe sth to sth ; **il doit tout à sa femme** he owes it all to his wife; **je te dois d'avoir gagné** it's thanks to you that I won; **c'est à votre générosité que nous devons de ne pas être morts de faim** it's thanks to your generosity that we didn't die of hunger; ▶**chandelle**; **3** (avoir une obligation morale) **~ qch à qn** to owe sb sth; **il me doit des excuses** he owes me an apology.

III se devoir *vpr* **1** (avoir une obligation morale) **se ~ à qn/son pays** to have a duty to sb/one's country; **je me dois de le faire** it's my duty to do it, I have a duty to do it; **2** (réciproquement) **les époux se doivent fidélité** spouses owe it to each other to be faithful; **3** (par convention) **un homme de son rang se doit d'avoir un chauffeur** a man of his standing has to have a chauffeur.

IV comme il se doit *loc adv* **1** (comme le veut l'usage) **faire qch/agir comme il se doit** to do sth/to act in the correct way; **il plaça les convives comme il se doit** he seated the guests as was proper; **2** (comme prévu) **comme il se doit, elle est en retard!** as you might expect, she's late!

devoir[2] /dəvwaʀ/ **I** *nm* **1** (obligation morale) duty; **avoir le sens du ~** to have a sense of duty; **homme/femme de ~** man/woman of conscience; **agir par ~** to act out of a sense of duty; **faire son ~** to do one's duty; **je n'ai fait que mon ~** I only did my duty; **2** (obligation imposée par la loi ou les convenances) duty; **manquer à tous ses ~s** to fail in all one's duties; **le ~ m'appelle!** duty calls!; **se faire un ~ de faire** to make it one's duty to do; **il est de mon ~ de** it's my duty to; **se mettre en ~ de faire qch** to set about doing sth; **voter est un droit, c'est aussi un ~** voting is not only a right, but also a duty; ▶**réserve**; **3** Scol (exercice écrit) (fait en classe) test; (fait à la maison) homework; **faire ses ~s** to do one's homework; **fais tes ~s avant d'aller jouer** do your homework before going out to play; **j'ai un ~ d'anglais demain** I've got an English test tomorrow; **j'ai un ~ à rendre pour lundi** I have a piece of homework to be handed in on Monday.

II† **devoirs** *nmpl* (hommages) respects; **présenter ses ~s à qn** to pay one's respects to sb; **les derniers ~s rendus à qn** the last respects paid to sb.

■ **~ d'ingérence** Pol *duty to interfere in the affairs of another nation*; **~ surveillé** or **sur table** Scol written test; **~ de vacances** holiday homework (*done from workbooks*).

dévoisé, ~e /devwaze/ *adj* devoiced.

dévoltage /devɔltaʒ/ *nm* reduction in voltage.

dévolter /devɔlte/ [1] *vtr* to reduce the voltage of [*circuit*].

dévolu, ~e /devɔly/ **I** *adj* **1** (échu par droit) devolved (**à** to); **2** (réservé) reserved (**à** for).

II *nm* **jeter son ~ sur** to set one's heart on [*objet*]; to set one's cap at [*personne*].

dévolution /devɔlysjɔ̃/ *nf* devolvement.

devon /dəvɔ̃/ *nm* lure.

Devon ▶692 *nprm* **le ~** Devon.

dévonien, -ienne /devɔnjɛ̃, ɛn/ *adj* [*système*] devonian.

dévorant, ~e /devɔʀɑ̃, ɑ̃t/ *adj* [*faim, flamme*] voracious; [*soif*] raging; [*passion, amour*] all-consuming.

dévorer /devɔʀe/ [1] *vtr* **1** (consommer) to devour [*nourriture, proie, livre*]; **être dévoré par les moustiques** to be eaten alive by mosquitoes; **~ qn de baisers** to smother sb with kisses; **~ qn des yeux** to devour sb with one's eyes; **2** (miner) [*obsession, sentiment*] to consume; **dévoré d'ambition/de chagrin** consumed with ambition/sorrow; **3** (consumer) to go through [*héritage*]; to eat up [*kilomètres*]; to take up [*temps*].

dévot, ~e /devo, ɔt/ **I** *adj* (très pieux) devout.

II *nm,f* pej sanctimonious person.

dévotion /devosjɔ̃/ **I** *nf* **1** (ferveur) devoutness; (culte) devotion (**à** to); **un lieu/livre de ~** a place/book of devotion; **2** (dévouement) **être à la ~ de qn** to be totally devoted to sb; **avec ~** devotedly; **3** (adoration) passion; **elle a une véritable ~ pour la musique** she has a real passion for music.

II dévotions *nfpl* **faire ses ~s** to perform one's devotions.

dévoué, ~e /devwe/ *adj* devoted (**à** to); **votre ~ serviteur**† your devoted servant.

dévouement /devumɑ̃/ *nm* devotion (**à qn/qch** to sb/sth); **avec ~** with devotion.

dévouer: se dévouer /devwe/ [1] *vpr* **1** (se consacrer) to devote oneself (**à** to), to dedicate oneself (**à** to); **2** (faire abnégation) to put oneself out (**pour qn/qch** for sb/sth; **pour faire** to do); **c'est toujours elle qui se dévoue** she's always the one who puts herself out.

dévoyé, ~e /devwaje/ **I** *pp* ▶ **dévoyer**.

II *pp adj* [*personne, esprit*] depraved.

III *nm,f* depraved person.

dévoyer /devwaje/ [23] **I** *vtr* **1** (pervertir) to deprave, to lead [sb] astray [*personne*]; **2** (déformer) to corrupt; **~ le sens d'un mot** to corrupt the meaning of a word.

II se dévoyer *vpr* to go astray; **il s'est dévoyé au contact de ses nouveaux amis** he's been led astray by his new friends.

dextérité /dɛksteʀite/ *nf* (adresse manuelle) dexterity, skill; (adresse de l'esprit) skill; **avec ~** with skill, skilfully[GB].

dextre /dɛkstʀ/ **I** *adj* Hérald dexter.

II† *nf* right hand.

dextrine /dɛkstʀin/ *nf* dextrin.

DG /deʒe/ *nm* (*abbr* = **directeur général**) MD.

DGA /deʒea/ *nm* (*abbr* = **directeur général adjoint**) assistant general manager.

DGLF /deʒeɛlɛf/ *nf*: *abbr* ▶ **délégation**.

dia: **à hue et à dia** /ayeadja/ *loc adv* **tirer à hue et à ~** to pull in opposite directions.

diabète /djabɛt/ ▶271 *nm* diabetes; **avoir du ~** to have diabetes.

diabétique /djabetik/ *adj, nmf* diabetic.

diable /djɑbl/ **I** *nm* **1** Mythol, Relig devil; **le Diable** the Devil; **signer un pacte avec le ~** to make a pact with the devil; **vendre son âme au ~** to sell one's soul to the devil; **avoir un mal du ~** or **de tous les ~s à faire** to have a devil ou a hell○ of a job doing; **se donner un mal de tous les ~s** to take a tremendous amount of trouble (**pour qch** over sth; **pour faire** to do); **du ~** [*courage, peur*] terrific; **il fait un froid du ~** or **de tous les ~s** it's hellishly cold; **un ~ d'homme/de métier** quite a man/job; **cette ~ de fille a vraiment du courage** what a fantastic girl—she really is brave; **en ~** [*difficile*] diabolically; [*beau*] devastatingly; [*intelligent*] fiendishly; ▶ **bénitier**, **démener**, **Dieu**; **2** (enfant) **un (petit) ~** a little devil; **faire le ~** to be up to mischief; **3** (individu) **un pauvre ~** a poor devil; **un bon ~** a decent sort; **ce n'est pas un mauvais ~** he's not a bad sort; **un grand ~** a beanpole; **4** (jouet) **~ (en boîte)** jack-in-the-box; **5** Culin (ustensile) *a high-lidded earthenware cooking vessel*; **6** Tech (chariot) two-wheeled trolley GB, hand truck US.

II *excl* gosh! GB, my God!; **du ~ si** I'm damned if○; **faites un effort, que ~!** make an effort, damn it○!; **pourquoi/comment/qui ~** why/how/who on earth; **au ~ l'avarice!** hang the expense!; **au ~ les scrupules!** to hell○ with scruples!

III à la diable *loc* **1** (hâtivement) any old how; **2** Culin [*volaille, sauce*] devilled[GB].

■ **~ cornu** moloch; **~ de mer** devilfish; **~ de Tasmanie** Tasmanian devil.

IDIOMES **habiter au ~** or **à tous les ~s** to live miles from anywhere; **qu'il aille au ~** or **à tous les ~s** or **aux cinq cents ~s!** he can go to the devil!; **que le ~ t'emporte!** to hell with you!; **(que) le ~ m'emporte si je me trompe** I'll eat my hat if I'm wrong; **à moins que le ~ s'en mêle** unless something weird occurs; **ce n'est pas le ~!** it's not that difficult!; **c'est le ~ pour faire** it's the devil of a job to do; **ce serait bien le ~ si** it would be odd if; **ce serait tenter le ~** that would be asking for it; **avoir le ~ au corps** to be like someone possessed; **tirer le ~ par la queue** to live from hand to mouth; **se faire un sang du ~** to get into a terrible state; **se débattre comme un beau ~** to fight tooth and nail; **surgir comme un ~ de sa boîte** to pop up out of the blue.

diablement /djɑbləmɑ̃/ *adv* [*courageux, sévère*] terrifically; [*intelligent*] fiendishly; [*beau*] devastatingly; **il fait ~ chaud** it's hellishly○ hot.

diablerie /djɑbləʀi/ *nf* mischief ¢; **ses ~s m'exaspèrent** his/her mischievous behaviour drives me mad.

diablesse /djɑblɛs/ *nf* **1** Mythol, Relig she-devil; **2** (enfant) little devil; **3**† (femme méchante) she-devil.

diablotin /djɑblɔtɛ̃/ *nm* **1** Mythol imp; **2** (enfant) little imp; **3** (pétard) ≈ party cracker.

diabolique /djabɔlik/ *adj* **1** Relig [*inspiration, pouvoir*] diabolic; **2** (malveillant) [*personne, sourire*] demonic; [*machination, idée, ruse*] devilish; [*invention*] devilish, diabolical; **3** (pénible, difficile) [*problème, situation*] diabolical; **4** (extrême) [*précision, habileté*] uncanny.

diaboliquement /djabɔlikmɑ̃/ *adv* fiendishly, diabolically.

diaboliser /djabɔlize/ [1] *vtr* to demonize [*personne, entreprise*].

diabolo /djabɔlo/ *nm* (jouet) diabolo.

■ **~ grenadine** grenadine and lemonade GB ou soda US; **~ menthe** mint cordial and lemonade GB ou soda US.

diachronie /djakʀɔni/ *nf* diachrony.

diachronique /djakʀɔnik/ *adj* diachronic.

diacide /diasid/ *adj, nm* diacid.

diaconat /djakɔna/ *nm* diaconate.

diaconesse /djakɔnɛs/ *nf* deaconess.

diacre /djakʀ/ *nm* deacon.

diacritique /djakʀitik/ *adj* diacritic; **signe ~** diacritic mark.

diadème /djadɛm/ *nm* **1** (parure) tiara; **2** Hist diadem.

diagnostic /djagnɔstik/ *nm* **1** Méd diagnosis; **bon/mauvais ~** correct/wrong diagnosis; **~ prénatal/psychiatrique** prenatal/psychiatric diagnosis; **établir** or **poser un ~** to make a diagnosis; **erreur de ~** error in diagnosis; **avoir un bon ~** to be good at making diagnoses; **2** (évaluation) diagnosis; **~ d'un expert** expert opinion.

diagnostique /djagnɔstik/ *adj* diagnostic.

diagnostiquer /djagnɔstike/ [1] *vtr* lit, fig to diagnose.

diagonal, ~e, *mpl* **-aux** /djagɔnal, o/ **I** *adj* diagonal.

II diagonale *nf* diagonal; **en ~e** [*traverser, disposer*] diagonally; **lire qch en ~e** to skim through sth.

diagonalement /djagɔnalmɑ̃/ *adv* diagonally.

diagramme /djagʀam/ *nm* (courbe graphique) graph.

■ **~ de température** Méd temperature chart; **~ d'une phrase** sentence diagram.

dialectal, ~e, *mpl* **-aux** /djalɛktal, o/ *adj* dialectal.

dialecte /djalɛkt/ *nm* dialect.

dialecticien, -ienne /djalɛktisjɛ̃, ɛn/ *nm,f* dialectician.

dialectique /djalɛktik/ **I** *adj* dialectical.

II *nf* dialectic.

dialectiquement /djalɛktikmɑ̃/ *adv* dialectically.

dialectologie /djalɛktɔlɔʒi/ *nf* dialectology.

dialogue /djalɔg/ *nm* dialogue[GB] (**entre** between; **avec** with).

■ **un ~ de sourds** a dialogue[GB] of the deaf.

dialoguer /djalɔge/ [1] **I** *vtr* (mettre en dialogue) to put [sth] into dialogue[GB] [*roman*]; **une scène dialoguée** a conversational scene.

II *vi* to have talks (**avec** with), to enter into dialogue[GB] (**avec**, with); **accepter de ~ avec l'ennemi** to agree to have talks with the enemy; **les deux camps refusent de ~** the two camps are refusing to talk.

dialoguiste /djalɔgist/ ▶510 *nmf* Cin screenwriter, dialogist.

dialyse /djaliz/ *nf* dialysis.

dialysé, ~e /djalize/ *nm,f* dialysis patient.

dialyser /djalize/ [1] *vtr* **1** Méd to perform dialysis on [*malade*]; **être dialysé** to have dialysis treatment; **2** Chimie to dialyse[GB] [*mélange*].

dialyseur /djalizœʀ/ *nm* dialyser[GB].

diamant /djamɑ̃/ *nm* **1** Minér diamond; **~ brut** rough diamond; **2** Audio (de tête de lecture) stylus.

■ **~ de vitrier** glazier's diamond.

diamantaire /djamɑ̃tɛʀ/ ▶510 *nm* (tailleur) diamond cutter; (commerçant) diamond merchant.

diamantifère /djamɑ̃tifɛʀ/ *adj* diamondiferous.

diamétralement /djametʀalmɑ̃/ *adv* diametrically; **des opinions ~ opposées** diametrically opposite opinions; **une opinion ~ opposée à la mienne** an opinion diametrically opposed to mine.

diamètre /djamɛtʀ/ *nm* diameter.

diane /djan/ *nf* Mil reveille; **battre** or **sonner la ~** to sound the reveille.

Diane /djan/ *npr* **~ (chasseresse)** Diana (the Huntress).

diantre† /djɑ̃tʀ/ *excl* **(que) ~!** good heavens!; **où/comment/pourquoi ~?** where/how/why on earth?

diapason /djapazɔ̃/ *nm* Mus **1** (note) diapason; **2** (instrument) **~ (à branches)** tuning fork; **~ à bouche** pitch pipe; **~ électronique** tuner.

IDIOMES **se mettre au ~** to fall in step (**de** with); **être au ~** to be in tune.

diaphane /djafan/ *adj* liter [*teint*] pallid; [*brume*] hazy; [*tissu*] diaphanous; [*papier*] translucent.

diaphragme /djafʀagm/ *nm* **1** Anat, Bot diaphragm; **2** (en contraception) cap, diaphragm; **3** (de haut-parleur) diaphragm; **4** Phot diaphragm, stop.

diaphragmer /djafʀagme/ [1] *vi* Phot to

adjust the aperture; **~ à 16** to adjust the aperture to 16.

diaphyse /djafiz/ *nf* shaft, diaphysis spéc.

diapo○ /djapo/ *nf* (*abbr* = **diapositive**) slide.

diaporama /djapoʀama/ *nm* slide show.

diapositive /djapozitiv/ *nf* slide.

diapré, **~e** /djapʀe/ *adj* liter iridescent.

diaprer /djapʀe/ [1] *vtr* liter to dapple (**de** with).

diaprure /djapʀyʀ/ *nf* liter iridescence.

diarrhée /djaʀe/ *nf* diarrhoea; **avoir la ~** to have diarrhoea.

diarrhéique /djaʀeik/ *adj* diarrhoeic[GB].

diarthrose /djaʀtʀoz/ *nf* diarthrosis.

diaspora /djaspɔʀa/ *nf* diaspora; **la ~ ukrainienne** the Ukrainian diaspora.

Diaspora /djaspɔʀa/ *nf* Hist, Relig **la ~ (juive)** the (Jewish) Diaspora.

diastase /djastɑz/ *nf* diastase.

diastasique /djastazik/ *adj* diastatic.

diastole /djastɔl/ *nf* diastole.

diastolique /djastɔlik/ *adj* diastolic.

diathermie /djatɛʀmi/ *nf* diathermy.

diatomique /diatɔmik/ *adj* diatomic.

diatonique /djatɔnik/ *adj* diatonic.

diatribe /djatʀib/ *nf* diatribe (**contre** against); **se lancer dans une ~** to launch into a diatribe.

dichotomie /dikɔtɔmi/ *nf* dichotomy.

dichotomique /dikɔtɔmik/ *adj* dichotomous, dichotomic.

dichromatique /dikʀɔmatik/ *adj* dichromatic.

dico○ /diko/ *nm* (*abbr* = **dictionnaire**) dictionary.

dicotylédone /dikɔtiledɔn/ **I** *adj* dicotyledonous.

II *nf* dicotyledon.

dictaphone® /diktafɔn/ *nm* Dictaphone®.

dictateur /diktatœʀ/ *nm* dictator; **jouer au ~** fig to behave ou act like a dictator.

dictatorial, **~e**, *mpl* **-iaux** /diktatɔʀjal, o/ *adj* dictatorial.

dictature /diktatyʀ/ *nf* dictatorship; **vivre sous une ~** to live under ou in a dictatorship; **la ~ des sondages en matière de politique** fig the tyranny of opinion polls in politics.

■ **~ du prolétariat** dictatorship of the proletariat.

dictée /dikte/ *nf* **1** Scol (exercice) dictation; **faire une ~** to do a dictation; **faire faire une ~ à qn** to give sb a dictation; **2** (action de dicter) **écrire sous la ~ de qn** [*élève, secrétaire*] to take down sb's dictation; (sous la contrainte) to write down what sb dictates; **agir sous la ~ des événements/circonstances** to act as events/circumstances dictate.

■ **~ musicale** musical dictation.

dicter /dikte/ [1] *vtr* **1** (à haute voix) to dictate [*texte, lettre*]; **~ qch à qn** to dictate sth to sb; **2** (motiver) to motivate, to dictate; **le souci d'aider autrui dicte notre action** our action is motivated by the desire to help others; **3** (imposer) to dictate (**à** to), to impose (**à** on); **les ravisseurs ont dicté leurs conditions à la police** the kidnappers[GB] dictated their conditions to the police; **je ne me laisserai pas ~ ma conduite par cet imbécile** I'm not going to be dictated to by that idiot; **une paix dictée** an imposed peace settlement.

diction /diksjɔ̃/ *nf* **1** gén diction; **avoir une bonne/mauvaise ~** to have good/poor diction; **2** Cin, Théât elocution; **professeur/cours de ~** elocution teacher/lesson.

dictionnaire /diksjɔnɛʀ/ *nm* **1** gén dictionary; **un ~ de langue/synonymes** a dictionary of language/synonyms; **~ bilingue** bilingual dictionary; **~ encyclopédique** encyclopedic dictionary; **~ français-anglais** French-English dictionary; **2** Ordinat dictionary.

■ **~ analogique** ≈ thesaurus; **~ électronique** electronic dictionary; **~ inverse** reverse dictionary.

dicton /diktɔ̃/ *nm* saying; **comme le dit le ~** as the saying goes.

didacticiel /didaktisjɛl/ *nm* educational software program.

didactique /didaktik/ **I** *adj* **1** (instructif) [*ouvrage, ton*] didactic; [*jouet*] educational; **matériel ~** teaching aids (*pl*); **2** (de spécialiste) [*terme, expression, langage*] technical, specialist (*épith*).

II *nf* didactics (+ *v sg*).

didactiquement /didaktikmɑ̃/ *adv* didactically.

didactyle /didaktil/ *adj* didactyle.

didascalie /didaskali/ *nf* stage direction.

Didon /didɔ̃/ *npr* Dido.

Die /di/ ▶ 857 *npr* Die.

dièdre /djɛdʀ/ *adj, nm* dihedral.

Dieppe /djɛp/ ▶ 857 *npr* Dieppe.

dieppois, **~e** /djɛpwa, az/ ▶ 857 *adj* of Dieppe.

Dieppois, **~e** /djɛpwa, az/ ▶ 857 *nm,f* (natif) native of Dieppe; (habitant) inhabitant of Dieppe.

diérèse /djeʀɛz/ *nf* diaeresis; **faire la ~** to pronounce the diaeresis.

dièse /djɛz/ **I** *adj* sharp; **do ~** C sharp.

II *nm* sharp.

diesel /djezɛl/ *nm* **1** (moteur) (**moteur**) **~** diesel (engine); **2** (véhicule) diesel; **fourgonnette/voiture ~** diesel van/car.

diète /djɛt/ *nf* **1** Méd light diet; **mettre qn à la ~** to put sb on a light diet; **être à la ~** to be on a light diet; **2** Hist diet.

diététicien, **-ienne** /djetetisjɛ̃, ɛn/ ▶ 510 *nm,f* dietician.

diététique /djetetik/ **I** *adj* dietary (*épith*); **ce n'est pas très ~ de manger du pain avec des pâtes** it's not very healthy to eat bread with pasta.

II *nf* dietetics (+ *v sg*); **magasin de ~** health food shop GB ou store US.

dieu, *pl* **~x** /djø/ *nm* **1** Relig, Mythol god; **le ~ des mers** the god of the sea; **les ~x égyptiens** the Egyptian gods; **grands ~x!** God almighty!; **vingt ~x**○**!** good God almighty○!; **2** (personne talentueuse) **sur le terrain c'est un ~** he's brilliant on the sports field; **le ~ du tennis/golf** the greatest tennis player/golfer.

IDIOMES **être beau comme un ~** to look like a Greek god; **nager/skier/jouer comme un ~** to be a superb swimmer/skier/player; **jurer ses grands ~x que...** to swear to God that...; **être dans le secret des ~x** to be privy to the secrets of those on high.

Dieu /djø/ *nm* Relig God; **~ le père** God the Father; **le royaume de ~** the kingdom of God; **croire en ~** to believe in God; **le bon ~** the good Lord; **mon ~!** my God!; **grand ~!** God almighty!; **~ du ciel!** God in heaven!; **bon ~**◑**!** for God's sake○!; **bon ~ d'bon ~**◑**!** good God almighty○!; **nom de ~**◑**!** Christ almighty◑!; **~ merci!** thank God!; **~ me pardonne!** God forgive me!; **~ vous entende!** may God hear your prayer!; **~ soit loué** or **béni!** thanks be to God!; **~ te garde!** may God protect you!; **~ m'en garde!** God forbid!; **~ ait son âme!** God rest his/her soul; **c'est pas ~ possible**○**!** good God, it's not possible!; **~ sait si je l'avais prévenu!** goodness ou God knows I warned him!; **~ sait pourquoi/quand!** goodness (only) knows why/when; **~ seul le sait** goodness only knows; **si ~ le veut** God willing; ▶ **confession**, **femme**, **fou**, **homme**.

IDIOMES **se prendre pour ~ le père** to think one is God Almighty; **ne craindre ni ~ ni diable** to fear neither Heaven nor Hell; **ne croire ni à** or **en ~ ni au diable** not to believe in anything; **chaque jour que ~ fait** day in, day out; **chacun pour soi et ~ pour tous** every man for himself (and God for us all); **l'homme propose et ~ dispose** man proposes, God disposes; **il vaut mieux s'adresser à ~ qu'à ses saints** Prov always go straight to the top; **qui donne aux pauvres prête à ~** Prov he who gives to the poor will be rewarded in heaven; **~ reconnaîtra les siens** the Lord looks after his own; **c'est la maison du bon ~ ici!** it's open house here!

diffamant, **~e** /difamɑ̃, ɑ̃t/ *adj* slanderous, defamatory.

diffamateur, **-trice** /difamatœʀ, tʀis/ **I** *adj* **1** gén slanderous, defamatory; **2** Jur [*écrits*] libellous[GB]; [*propos*] slanderous.

II *nm,f* (par écrit) libeller[GB]; (verbalement) slanderer.

diffamation /difamasjɔ̃/ *nf* **1** gén slander, defamation; **2** Jur (par écrit) libel; (verbalement) slander; **plainte en ~** libel suit; **poursuivre qn en ~** to sue sb for libel.

diffamatoire /difamatwaʀ/ *adj* **1** gén slanderous, defamatory; **2** Jur (par écrit) libellous[GB]; (oralement) slanderous; **écrit ~** libel.

diffamer /difame/ [1] *vtr* **1** gén to slander, to defame; **2** Jur (par écrit) to libel; (verbalement) to slander.

différé, **~e** /difeʀe/ **I** *pp* ▶ **différer**.

II *pp adj* **1** (remis) postponed; **2** Fin deferred; **3** Radio, TV pre-recorded.

III *nm* recording; **match Cameroun-Roumanie en ~** recording of the Cameroon-Romania match; **le discours du président sera diffusé en ~** the broadcast of the president's speech will be a recording; **en léger ~** recorded moments before.

différemment /difeʀamɑ̃/ *adv* differently (**de** from); **un peu ~** a little bit differently; **il en va ~ de** or **pour** it's a different matter for.

différence /difeʀɑ̃s/ *nf* **1** (écart) difference (**entre** between); **~ de salaire/d'âge** wage/age difference; **~ de taille/statut** difference in height/status; **~ d'opinion** difference of opinion; **à une ~ près** with one difference; **à quelques petites ~s près** with one or two little differences; **2** (distinction) difference (**entre** between); **faire la ~** to tell the difference; **je suis incapable de faire la ~** I cannot tell the difference; **à la ~ de** unlike; **à la ~ que**, **à cette ~ que** with the difference that; **3** (discrimination) differentiation ¢ (**entre** between); **faire des ~s entre ses enfants** to differentiate between one's children; **4** (spécificité) difference; **le droit à la ~** the right to be different; **faire la ~** to make all the difference; **le style fait la ~** the style makes the difference; **5** Math difference.

■ **~ de potentiel** Phys potential difference.

différenciation /difeʀɑ̃sjasjɔ̃/ *nf* differentiation; **~ cellulaire** Biol cellular differentiation.

différencié, **~e** /difeʀɑ̃sje/ **I** *pp* ▶ **différencier**.

II *pp adj* **1** (varié) [*situation, évolution*] diverse; **2** (bien distinct) distinct; **3** Comm (spécifique) [*produit, service*] differentiated.

différencier /difeʀɑ̃sje/ [2] **I** *vtr* **1** (distinguer) to differentiate (**de** from); **rien ne les différencie** there's no way of telling them apart; **2** (créer une différence) to make [sb/sth] different (**de** from); **leur éducation les a différenciés l'un de l'autre** their education has made them different from each other; **3** (voir une différence) to differentiate between; **être incapable de ~ l'école flamande et l'école hollandaise** or **l'école flamande de l'école hollandaise** to be unable to tell the difference between the Flemish school and the Dutch school; **4** Math to differentiate.

II se différencier *vpr* **1** (se rendre différent) [*personne, parti, organisation*] to differentiate oneself (**de** from); **2** (pouvoir être distingué) to differ, to be different (**de** from); **3** (devenir différent) to become different (**de** from); **4** Biol to differentiate.

différend /difeʀɑ̃/ *nm* disagreement (**entre** between; **sur** over).

différent, **~e** /difeʀɑ̃, ɑ̃t/ *adj* **1** (dissemblable) different (**de** from); **2** (varié) different, various; **il a choisi de ne pas venir pour ~es raisons** he chose not to come for various reasons ou for a number of reasons; **à ~s moments** at various times; **en ~s endroits** in different places; **à ~es heures de la journée** at different times of the day.

différentiation /difeʀɑ̃sjasjɔ̃/ *nf* Math differentiation.

différentiel, **-ielle** /difeʀɑ̃sjɛl/ **I** *adj* (tous contextes) differential.
II *nm* Écon, Mécan differential.
III différentielle *nf* Math differential.

différer /difeʀe/ [14] **I** *vtr* (remettre à plus tard) to postpone [*départ, réunion, décision*]; to defer [*paiement, remboursement*].
II *vi* (être différent) to differ (**de** from); **~ peu** to differ little; **ne ~ en rien** not to differ at all; **~ en ce que** to differ in that; **~ par** to differ in; **~ par le caractère** to differ in character.

difficile /difisil/ *adj* **1** (malaisé, pénible) [*moment, parcours, conditions, atterrissage*] difficult; [*langue, problème, ascension, rôle, passage*] difficult, hard; [*victoire*] hard-won (*épith*); **avoir des débuts ~s** to have a difficult start; **c'est ~ à faire, il est ~ de faire** it's difficult ou hard to do; **le plus ~ reste à faire** the worst is yet to come; **2** (indocile) [*personne, caractère, humeur*] difficult; **un enfant ~ à élever** a difficult child; **être ~ à vivre** to be difficult to live with; **3** (exigeant) fussy; **il ne mange rien, il est trop ~** he doesn't eat anything, he's too fussy ou finicky; **je ne t'achète plus rien, tu es trop ~!** I won't buy you anything else, you're too fussy!; **est-ce que ce cadeau va lui plaire? elle est si ~!** will she like this present? she's so hard to please!; **tu le trouves beau? tu n'es pas ~!** do you think he's good-looking? you're not hard to please!; **être ~ sur** to be fussy about [*choix, nourriture, boisson*]; **faire le ~, faire la ~** to be fussy.

difficilement /difisilmɑ̃/ *adv* [*se lever, atteindre, imaginer, admettre*] with difficulty; **je pouvais ~ dire non** I couldn't very well say no; **la chaleur/douleur est ~ supportable** the heat/pain is hard to bear.

difficulté /difikylte/ *nf* **1** (peine) difficulty; **toute la ~ est là** therein lies the difficulty; **aimer/fuir la ~** to enjoy/to avoid difficulties; **reconnaître la ~ d'une tâche/d'une situation** to admit that a task/a situation is difficult; **avoir/éprouver de la ~ à faire** to have/to experience difficulty (in) doing; **avec ~** with difficulty; **en ~** [*avion, bateau, personne, famille, secteur*] in difficulties ou trouble; **mettre qn/se mettre en ~** to put sb/to put oneself in a difficult position; **2** (obstacle) difficulty, problem; **la principale/seconde ~ a été de faire** the main/second difficulty was to do; **avoir des ~s scolaires** or **à l'école** to have problems at school; **connaître/avoir des ~s financières/techniques** to experience/to have financial/technical difficulties; **ne présenter aucune ~** to present no difficulty; **sans ~(s)** without any difficulty; **non sans ~s** not without difficulty; **avoir des ~s en français/algèbre** to have difficulty with ou in French/algebra; **avoir des ~s à** or **pour faire** to have difficulty (in) doing; **avoir des ~s de stationnement/logement/trésorerie** to have problems parking/with housing/with one's finances; **3** (objection) objection; **faire des ~s** to raise objections (**pour faire** about doing); **elle n'a fait aucune ~** she didn't raise a single objection.

difforme /difɔʀm/ *adj* [*corps, partie du corps*] deformed; [*objet, édifice*] strangely shaped (*épith*); [*arbre*] twisted.

difformité /difɔʀmite/ *nf* deformity.

diffracter /difʀakte/ [1] *vtr* to diffract.

diffraction /difʀaksjɔ̃/ *nf* diffraction.

diffus, **~e** /dify, yz/ *adj* **1** [*lumière, chaleur*] diffuse; **2** [*sentiment, impression*] vague; [*style, exposé*] pej diffuse, loose.

diffuser /difyze/ [1] **I** *vtr* **1** Radio, TV to broadcast [*émission, reportage*]; **le concert a été diffusé en direct** the concert was broadcast live; **émission diffusée sur la deuxième chaîne** programme[GB] broadcast on channel two; **le match de tennis sera diffusé en différé** a recording of the tennis match will be broadcast; **2** (propager) to spread [*nouvelle, mode*]; to disseminate, to spread [*idées*]; **la police a diffusé le signalement du jeune fugueur** the police sent out ou issued a description of the young runaway; **3** Comm (distribuer) to distribute [*article, produit, revue*]; **4** (émettre) to diffuse [*lumière, chaleur*].
II *vi* [*matière, fluide, particules*] to diffuse.
III se diffuser *vpr* [*nouvelle, information*] to spread; [*chaleur, lumière*] to be diffused.

diffuseur /difyzœʀ/ *nm* **1** Comm, Presse (distributeur) distributor; **2** fig (propagateur) disseminator, spreader; **3** (de lumière) diffuser; **4** Radio, TV, Cin broadcaster; **5** Aut jet.
■ **~ d'insecticide** electric insecticide diffuser; **~ de parfum** air freshener.

diffusion /difyzjɔ̃/ *nf* **1** Radio, TV, Cin broadcasting; **à la suite d'incidents techniques, la ~ du match de tennis n'aura pas lieu** due to technical problems, the tennis match will not be broadcast; **la ~ du film a provoqué un scandale** the showing of the film caused a scandal; **2** (de connaissances, d'écrits) dissemination, diffusion; **3** Comm (distribution) distribution; **4** Presse circulation; **à large ~** with a wide circulation; **5** Méd, Phys diffusion.

digérer /diʒeʀe/ [14] *vtr* **1** Physiol to digest; **bien/mal ~** to have good/bad digestion; **un plat difficile à ~** a dish that is difficult to digest; **bois une tisane pour ~** drink some herbal tea to help your digestion; **2** (assimiler) to digest [*lecture, connaissances*]; **une théorie mal digérée** an ill-digested theory; **3**° (accepter) to swallow [*insulte, affront*]; to stomach [*défaite*]; **il a du mal à ~ son échec** he finds it hard to come to terms with his failure.

digest /diʒɛst/ *nm* **1** (résumé) synopsis; **2** (volume) digest.

digeste /diʒɛst/ *adj* easily digestible, easy to digest; **les cours ne sont pas très ~s** fig the lectures are very heavy-going.

digestibilité /diʒɛstibilite/ *nf* digestibility.

digestible /diʒɛstibl/ *adj* digestible.

digestif, **-ive** /diʒɛstif, iv/ **I** *adj* Physiol digestive.
II *nm* (liqueur) liqueur (*taken after dinner*); (eau-de-vie) brandy.

digestion /diʒɛstjɔ̃/ *nf* Chimie, Physiol digestion; **faciliter la ~** to aid digestion; **problèmes de ~** digestive problems.

digicode® /diʒikɔd/ *nm* digital (access) lock.

digipuncture /diʒipɔ̃ktyʀ/ *nf* acupressure.

digital, **~e**, *mpl* **-aux** /diʒital, o/ **I** *adj* **1** (qui appartient aux doigts) [*artères, veines, nerfs*] digital; **2** (numérique) [*affichage, lecture, montre, enregistrement*] digital.
II digitale *nf* Bot digitalis.
■ **~e pourprée** foxglove.

digitaline /diʒitalin/ *nf* digitalin.

digitaliser /diʒitalize/ [1] *vtr* to digitize.

diglossie /diglɔsi/ *nf* diglossia.

digne /diɲ/ *adj* **1** (plein de dignité) [*personne, débat, geste, air, silence*] dignified; **2** (approprié) [*défenseur, émule, représentant, successeur*] worthy; **3** (méritant) **~ de confiance** or **de foi** trustworthy; **~ d'être loué** praiseworthy; **~ d'être souligné** noteworthy; **~ d'envie** enviable; **~ de ce nom** worthy of the name; **4** (à la hauteur de) **~ de** worthy of [*personne, mission*].

dignement /diɲmɑ̃/ *adv* **1** (avec dignité) [*se comporter*] with dignity; **très ~** with great dignity; **2** (comme il convient) [*accueillir, fêter*] fittingly.

dignitaire /diɲitɛʀ/ *nm* dignitary; **hauts ~s de l'État** leading state dignitaries.

dignité /diɲite/ *nf* **1** (qualité) dignity; **mourir dans la ~** to die with dignity; **la cérémonie s'est déroulée dans la ~** the ceremony was very dignified; **~ de l'homme** human dignity; **la ~ des travailleurs** the dignity of the workers; **notre ~ de femmes** our dignity as women; **rendre leur ~ aux détenus** to restore dignity to the prisoners; **avoir sa ~** to have one's pride; **2** (fonction) dignity; **élever/promouvoir à la ~ de** to raise/promote to the dignity of.

digramme /digʀam/ *nm* digraph.

digression /digʀesjɔ̃/ *nf* **1** (s'écartant du sujet) digression (**sur** about); **ne faites pas trop de ~s** let's not have too many digressions; **faire une ~, faire des ~s** to digress; **partir dans une ~** to go off on a tangent; **2** Astron digression.

digue /dig/ *nf* **1** (au bord de la mer) sea wall; (pour polder) dyke GB, dike US; (autour d'un port) harbour[GB] wall; **2** (barrière morale) barrier; **élever une ~ contre** to erect a barrier against.

Dijon /diʒɔ̃/ ▶857 *npr* Dijon.

dijonnais, **~e** /diʒɔnɛ, ɛz/ ▶857 *adj* of Dijon.

Dijonnais, **~e** /diʒɔnɛ, ɛz/ ▶857 *nm,f* (natif) native of Dijon; (habitant) inhabitant of Dijon.

diktat /diktat/ *nm* diktat.

dilapidateur, **-trice** /dilapidatœʀ, tʀis/ *adj, nm,f* spendthrift.

dilapidation /dilapidasjɔ̃/ *nf* (d'argent, de richesses) squandering; (d'énergie, de forces) waste.

dilapider /dilapide/ [1] *vtr* to squander [*argent, fortune*]; to fritter away [*temps, énergie*].

dilatabilité /dilatabilite/ *nf* expansibility, dilatability.

dilatable /dilatabl/ *adj* expansible, dilatable.

dilatateur, **-trice** /dilatatœʀ, tʀis/ **I** *adj* dilative.
II *nm* dilator.

dilatation /dilatasjɔ̃/ *nf* **1** (de corps, gaz) expansion; **2** (de pupille, vaisseau, d'organe, orifice) dilation, dilatation spéc.

dilater /dilate/ [1] **I** *vtr* **1** (agrandir) to dilate [*orifice, pupille, vaisseau*]; to expand [*poumons*]; to distend [*estomac*]; **2** Phys to expand [*corps, gaz*].
II se dilater *vpr* **1** (s'agrandir) [*pupille, vaisseau, orifice*] to dilate (**de** with); [*poumons*] to expand; [*estomac*] to be distended; **2** Phys [*corps, gaz*] to expand; **se ~ sous l'effet de la chaleur** to expand in the heat.

dilatoire /dilatwaʀ/ *adj* **1** (pour gagner du temps) [*tactique*] delaying; [*mesure, réponse, conduite*] intended to gain time; **2** Jur dilatory.

dilemme /dilɛm/ *nm* dilemma; **se laisser enfermer dans un ~** to be caught in a dilemma.

dilettante /dilɛtɑ̃t/ *nmf* gén amateur, dilettante péj; **peindre** or **faire de la peinture en ~** to dabble in painting; **écrire des romans en ~** to be an amateur novelist.

dilettantisme /dilɛtɑ̃tism/ *nm* gén amateurism; péj dilettantism.

diligemment /diliʒamɑ̃/ *adv* diligently.

diligence /diliʒɑ̃s/ *nf* **1** (véhicule) stagecoach; **l'attaque de la ~** the stagecoach hold-up; **2** (empressement) haste; **faire qch avec ~** to do sth posthaste; **mettre beaucoup de ~ à faire qch** to do sth very promptly; **mettre**

peu de ~ dans l'exécution d'un ordre to carry out an order in no great haste; **3** fml (soin attentif) diligence; **avoir de la ~** to be diligent; **4** Jur **à la ~ de qn** at the behest of sb.

diligent, ~e /diliʒɑ̃, ɑ̃t/ *adj* diligent; **être ~ dans son travail** to be a diligent worker; **soins ~s** diligent care.

diligenter /diliʒɑ̃te/ [1] *vtr* to carry out [sth] diligently [*enquête*].

diluant /dilɥɑ̃/ *nm* Tech thinner.

diluer /dilɥe/ [1] **I** *vtr* **1** (diminuer la concentration de) to dilute (**avec** with; **dans** in); **alcool dilué** diluted alcohol; **2** (rendre plus liquide) to thin [sth] down; **~ qch avec qch** to thin sth with sth; **3** (rendre moins dense) to dilute [*énergie, force, idées, réponses*] (**dans** in).

II se diluer *vpr* **1** [*peinture, alcool, vernis*] to be diluted; **2** (se disperser) [*responsabilité*] to attenuate; [*énergie, force*] to attenuate; [*volonté*] to evaporate.

dilution /dilysjɔ̃/ *nf* **1** (pour diminuer la concentration) dilution; (pour liquéfier) thinning down; **2** (solution) solution; **3** (perte de puissance) dilution; **~ des responsabilités** attenuation of responsibility.

diluvien, -ienne /dilyvjɛ̃, ɛn/ *adj* **1** (torrentiel) **pluies diluviennes** torrential rain; **2** Bible diluvian.

dimanche /dimɑ̃ʃ/ **▶750** *nm* Sunday; **habits** or **toilette du ~** Sunday best; **conducteur** or **chauffeur du ~** Sunday driver; **peintre/poète/mécanicien du ~** weekend ou amateur painter/poet/mechanic.

IDIOMES **ce n'est pas tous les jours ~** not every day is a holiday.

dîme /dim/ *nf* tithe.

dimension /dimɑ̃sjɔ̃/ *nf* **1** Math, Phys dimension; **la troisième/quatrième ~** the third/fourth dimension; **espace/object à trois ~s** three-dimensional space/object; **film en trois ~s** three-D film; **2** (mesure) dimension; **prendre** or **noter les ~s de qch** to take (down) ou note the dimensions of sth; **3** (taille, grandeur) size; **de toutes les ~s** of all sizes; **un objet de petite/grande ~** a small/large object; **un matelas de ~s standard** a standard-size mattress; **4** (aspect, caractère) dimension, aspect; **la ~ humaine/spirituelle/politique de qch** the human/spiritual/political dimension ou aspect of sth; **donner** or **conférer une nouvelle ~ à qch** to give sth a new dimension; **5** (importance, ampleur) dimensions (*pl*); **une entreprise de ~ internationale** a company of international dimensions; **prendre la ~** or **les ~s de** to get the measure of [*problème, situation*]; **à la ~ de, aux ~s de** commensurate to ou with.

dimensionner /dimɑ̃sjɔne/ [1] *vtr* Tech to size.

diminué, ~e /diminɥe/ **I** *pp* ▶ **diminuer**.

II *pp adj* **1** (affaibli) [*personne, adversaire*] weak; **je l'ai trouvé physiquement très ~** I found him physically very weak; **je ne pensais pas qu'il était aussi ~** (physiquement) I didn't think that he would be so weak; (intellectuellement) I didn't think that his faculties would be so impaired; **2** Mus [*intervalle*] diminished.

diminuendo /diminɥɛndo/ *adv* diminuendo.

diminuer /diminɥe/ [1] **I** *vtr* **1** (réduire) to reduce [*quantité, intensité, durée, niveau, chances*] (**à** to; **de** by); to lower [*taux, taxe, salaire*]; **pour ~ les frais/pertes/risques** to reduce the cost/losses/risks; **~ sa consommation d'alcool** to reduce one's alcohol intake; **2** (modérer) to dampen [*enthousiasme, courage*]; **le salaire proposé a vite diminué mon ardeur** the salary which was offered soon dampened my enthusiasm; **3** (dénigrer) to diminish [*exploit, succès, réussite*]; **~ les mérites/le talent de qn** to detract from sb's merits/talent; **4** (affaiblir) [*maladie, opération*] to weaken [*personne*]; to sap [*forces*]; **5** (en tricot) to decrease [*mailles*]; **diminuez deux mailles à chaque rang** decrease (by) two stitches on every row; **diminuez de deux mailles** decrease (by) two stitches; **arrêtez de ~** stop decreasing.

II *vi* **1** (se réduire) [*facture, montant, chômage, taux, prix*] to come ou go down (**de** by), to decrease (**de** by); [*écart*] to close; [*réserves, consommation, quantité*] to decrease, to diminish; [*croissance, volume, déficit, différence*] to decrease; [*production, ventes, demande*] to fall off; [*bougie, bouteille*] to go down; **notre pouvoir d'achat/notre salaire a diminué** our purchasing power/our salary has gone down; **les jours diminuent** the days are getting shorter; **2** (faiblir) [*activité, intérêt, attaques, violence*] to fall off; [*pression, tension*] to decrease , to diminish; [*bruit, flamme, orage, rire, rumeurs, colère*] to die down; [*forces, capacités*] to diminish; [*courage*] to fail; [*ardeur*] to cool; [*température, fièvre*] to go down.

diminutif, -ive /diminytif, iv/ **I** *adj* [*suffixe*] diminutive.

II *nm* gén diminutive; (familier) pet name; **Jacquot est le ~ de Jacques** Jacquot is a pet name for ou a diminutive of Jacques.

diminution /diminysjɔ̃/ *nf* **1** (réduction) gén (provoquée ou contrôlée) reduction; (constatée) decrease; (de production, d'activités commerciales) fall-off; **exiger une ~ de la durée du travail** to demand a reduction in working hours; **constater une ~ des accidents** to notice a decrease in the number of accidents; **la ~ des naissances** the decline in the birthrate; **être en ~** gén to be decreasing; [*production, exportations*] to be falling off; **le taux de natalité est en ~** the birthrate is on the decline; **être en ~ de 7%** to be down by 7%; **2** (affaiblissement) diminishing; **3** (en tricot) **commencer les ~s** start decreasing; **faites deux ~s à chaque rang** decrease two at the end of each row.

dimorphe /dimɔʀf/ *adj* Bot, Zool, Chimie dimorphous.

dimorphisme /dimɔʀfism/ *nm* Bot, Zool, Chimie dimorphism.

dinanderie /dinɑ̃dʀi/ *nf* (fabrication) brassmaking; (ustensiles) brasswork ¢.

dinandier /dinɑ̃dje/ **▶510** *nm* brassworker.

dinar /dinaʀ/ **▶46** *nm* dinar.

dînatoire /dinatwaʀ/ *adj* **buffet ~** buffet supper.

dinde /dɛ̃d/ *nf* **1** Zool gén turkey; (femelle) turkey hen; **2** Culin turkey; **~ aux marrons** turkey with chestnuts; **escalope de ~** turkey escalope; **3**○ (femme stupide) (silly) goose○; **petite ~!** you silly goose!

dindon /dɛ̃dɔ̃/ *nm* **1** Zool turkey (cock); **2**○ (homme stupide) dope○, stupid man.

IDIOMES **être le ~ de la farce** to be fooled ou duped.

dindonneau, *pl* **~x** /dɛ̃dɔno/ *nm* **1** Zool (turkey) poult; **2** Culin turkey; **un rôti de ~** turkey roast.

dîner /dine/ [1] **I** *nm* **1** (repas du soir) dinner; **c'est l'heure du ~** it's dinner time; **préparer le ~** to get dinner ready, to fix dinner US; **qu'est-ce qu'il y a pour le ~?** what's for dinner?; **le ~ est servi** dinner is ready ou served; **après ~** after dinner; **2** (repas de midi) dial, B, C lunch.

II *vi* **1** (prendre le repas du soir) to have dinner, to dine; **inviter qn à ~** to invite ou ask sb to dinner; **~ d'une soupe/d'un œuf** to have soup/an egg for dinner, to dine on soup/an egg; **2** (prendre le repas de midi) dial, B, C to have lunch.

IDIOMES **qui dort dîne** Prov when you're asleep you don't feel hungry.

dînette /dinɛt/ *nf* **1** (petit repas simulé) (children's) tea party; **jouer à la ~** to play at tea parties; **2** (service miniature) doll's tea set.

dîneur, -euse /dinœʀ, øz/ *nm,f* diner, person dining in a restaurant.

ding /diŋ/ **I** *excl* ding!

II ding, ding, dong /diŋdɛ̃dɔ̃/ *loc excl* ding dong!

dingo○ /dɛ̃go/ **I** *adj* crazy○, nuts○; **il est devenu complètement ~** he's lost his marbles○.

II○ *nmf* (idiot) nutter○, nutcase○.

III *nm* Zool dingo.

dingue○ /dɛ̃g/ **I** *adj* **1** (idiot) [*personne*] crazy○, nuts○; **2** (fou) [*ambiance, bruit, spectacle, succès*] wild; [*prix, vitesse*] ridiculous; **c'est ~!** (inadmissible) it's crazy!; (incroyable) it's amazing!; **3** (passionné) **être ~ de qch** to be crazy○ ou nuts○ about sth.

II *nmf* **1** (fou) nutcase○, loony○; **il est chez les ~s** he's in a loony bin○; **2** (passionné) **être un ~ de musique/tennis** to be a music/tennis freak○; **c'est un ~ de la vitesse** he's a real speed-merchant ou speed-freak○.

dinguer◑ /dɛ̃ge/ [1] *vi* **aller/venir ~** to go/to come flying; **la pile de livres a failli ~ dans l'escalier** the pile of books nearly went flying down the stairs; **envoyer ~ qn** (pousser) to send sb flying; (chasser) to send sb packing○.

dinosaure /dinozɔʀ/ *nm* dinosaur.

diocésain, ~e /djɔsezɛ̃, ɛn/ *adj, nm,f* diocesan.

diocèse /djɔsɛz/ *nm* diocese.

diode /djɔd/ *nf* diode.

Diogène /djɔʒɛn/ *npr* Diogenes.

diois, ~e /diwa, az/ **▶857** *adj* of Die.

Diois, ~e /diwa, az/ **I ▶857** *nm,f* (natif) native of Die; (habitant) inhabitant of Die.

II ▶692 *nm* **le ~** the Die area.

dionysiaque /djonizjak/ **I** *adj* Dionysian; **culte ~** cult of Dionysus.

II dionysiaques *nfpl* **les ~s** the Dionysia.

Dionysos /djonizɔs/ *npr* Dionysus.

dioptrie /djɔptʀi/ *nf* dioptre[GB].

dioptrique /djɔptʀik/ Phys **I** *adj* dioptric.

II *nf* dioptrics (+ *v sg*).

diorama /djɔʀama/ *nm* diorama.

dioxine /dijɔksin/ *nf* dioxin.

dioxyde /dijɔksid/ *nm* dioxide; **~ de carbone** carbon dioxide.

diphasé, ~e /difɑze/ *adj* diphase.

diphtérie /difteʀi/ **▶271** *nf* Méd diphtheria.

diphtérique /difteʀik/ **I** *adj* diphtherial.

II *nmf* diphtheria sufferer.

diphtongaison /diftɔ̃gɛzɔ̃/ *nf* diphthongization.

diphtongue /diftɔ̃g/ *nf* diphthong.

diphtonguer /diftɔ̃ge/ [1] *vtr*, **se diphtonguer** *vpr* to diphthongize.

diplodocus /diplɔdɔkys/ *nm* diplodocus.

diplomate /diplɔmat/ **I** *adj* diplomatic.

II ▶510 *nmf* diplomat.

III *nm* Culin *dessert of glacé fruits and custard on a sponge base.*

diplomatie /diplɔmasi/ *nf* diplomacy; **faire preuve de ~ dans** to show diplomacy in; **agir avec ~** to act diplomatically.

diplomatique /diplɔmatik/ *adj* diplomatic.

diplomatiquement /diplɔmatikmɑ̃/ *adv* diplomatically.

diplôme /diplom/ *nm* **1** Scol certificate, diploma; **il n'a aucun ~** he hasn't got any qualifications; **quels ~s faut-il pour faire?** what qualifications are needed to do?; **2** (d'université, de grande école) degree; (d'autre institution) diploma; **les ~s universitaires** university degrees; **~ de licence/de maîtrise** ≈ bachelor's degree/Master's (degree); **il possède un ~ d'une école de commerce** he has a degree from a business school; **~ d'enseignement** teaching qualification; **~ d'ingénieur** engineering degree; **~ d'architecte** degree in architecture; **~ d'infirmière** nursing qualification GB ou degree; **3** (dans l'armée, la police) staff exam; **4** (nécessaire à l'exercice d'une activité) certificate; **~ de maître nageur/de secouriste** lifesaver's/first aid certificate;

5 (épreuves) exam; **passer un ~** to take an exam; **6** (document) certificate.

diplômé, ~e /diplome/ **I** *pp* ▶ **diplômer**.
II *pp adj* **il est ~ de l'université de Lille/ d'une école de commerce** he's a graduate of the university of Lille/of a business school; **elle est ~e en droit** she has a degree in law; **il est ~ en mécanique** he has a diploma in mechanics; **une infirmière/sage-femme ~e** a qualified nurse/midwife; **un entraîneur ~** a qualified coach.
III *nm,f* graduate.

diplômer /diplome/ [1] *vtr* gén to award a diploma to; Univ to award a degree to [*étudiant*].

diplopie /diplɔpi/ ▶271 *nf* diplopia.

dipsomane /dipsɔman/ *adj, nmf* Méd dipsomaniac.

dipsomanie /dipsɔmani/ ▶271 *nf* dipsomania.

diptère /diptɛʀ/ **I** *adj* **1** Zool dipterous; **2** Archit dipteral.
II *nm* dipteran; **les ~s** diptera.

diptyque /diptik/ *nm* diptych.

dire /diʀ/ [65] **I** *nm* **au ~ de** according to; **au ~ des experts** according to the experts; **au ~ de tous** by all accounts.
II dires *nmpl* statements; **leurs ~s ne concordent pas** their statements do not agree; **selon les ~s de ta sœur** according to your sister.
III *vtr* **1** (faire entendre) to say [*mots, prière*]; to recite [*poème*]; to read [*leçon*]; to tell [*histoire, blague*]; **~ non** to say no; **dites quelque chose de drôle** say something funny; **'entrez' dit-elle** 'come in,' she said; **j'ai quelque chose à ~ là-dessus** I've got something to say about that; **sans mot ~** without saying a word; **ce n'est pas une chose à ~** you don't say that sort of thing; **~ des bêtises** or **inepties** to talk nonsense; **~ qch à voix basse** to whisper sth; **~ qch entre ses dents** to mutter sth; **ne plus savoir que ~** to be at a loss for words; **avoir son mot à ~** to have one's say; **~ ce qu'on a à ~** to say one's piece; **2** (faire savoir) to tell; **~ des mensonges/la vérité/l'avenir** to tell lies/the truth/the future; **~ qch à qn** to tell sb sth; **dites-moi votre nom** tell me your name; **je le leur dirai** I'll tell them; **dis-le à ton frère** tell your brother; **je vous l'avais bien dit!** I told you so!; **dites-moi, vous aimez l'opéra?** tell me, do you like opera?; **c'est ce qu'on m'a dit** so I've been told; **dis-leur que tu es occupé** tell them you're busy; **je dois vous ~ que**... I have to tell you that...; **faire ~ à qn que** to let sb know that...; **faites ~ à ma femme que je serai en retard** let my wife know that I will be late; **~ ses projets** to describe one's plans; **~ son opinion/sa satisfaction** to express one's opinion/one's satisfaction; **je me suis laissé ~ que**... I heard that...; **tenez-vous le pour dit!** I don't want to have to tell you again!; **c'est moi qui vous le dis**○ I'm telling you; **permets-moi de te ~ que tu vas le regretter**○! you'll regret this, I can tell you!; **je ne te dis que ça**○ I'll say no more; **c'est pas pour ~, mais**○ I don't want to make a big deal of it, but○...; **à qui le dites-vous**○! don't I know it!; **vous m'en direz tant**○! you don't say!; **je ne vous le fais pas ~**○! you don't need to tell me!; **ne pas se le faire ~ deux fois**○ not to need to be told twice; **dis, tu me crois**○? tell me, do you believe me?; **dis donc, où tu te crois**○? hey! where do you think you are?; **dites-donc, il n'est pas valable, votre ticket!** here—did you know your ticket's not valid?; **à vous de ~** Jeux your bid; ▶ **vérité**; **3** (affirmer) to say (**que** that); **elle dit pouvoir le faire** she says she can do it; **~ ce qu'on pense** to say what one thinks; **~ tout haut ce que d'autres pensent tout bas** to say out loud what other people are thinking; **ne fais pas attention, il ne sait pas ce qu'il dit** don't mind him, he doesn't know what he's talking about ou he's talking through his hat; **on dit que**... it is said that...; **on le dit marié/veuf** he is said to be married/a widower; **j'irai jusqu'à ~ que** I'd go as far as to say that; **c'est le moins qu'on puisse ~** that's the least one can say; **le moins qu'on puisse ~ c'est que**... the least one can say is that...; **si l'on peut ~** if one might say so; **si je puis ~** if I may put it like that; **on peut ~ qu'elle a du toupet celle-là!** she's really got a nerve○!; **on ne peut pas ~ qu'il se soit fatigué!** he certainly didn't overtax himself; **autant ~ que** you might as well say that, in other words; **et que ~ de...?** to say nothing of...; **j'ose ~ que**... I'm not afraid to say that...; **si j'ose ~** if I may say so; **ce n'est pas à moi de le ~** it's not for me to say; **cela va sans ~** it goes without saying; **ce n'est pas peu ~** that's saying a lot; **il faut ~ que** one should say that; **c'est (tout) ~!** need I say more?; **cela dit** having said that; **c'est vous qui le dites!** that's what you say!; **tu peux le ~**○! you can say that again○!; **disons, demain** let's say tomorrow; **c'est difficile à ~** it's hard to tell; **je sais ce que je dis** I know what I'm talking about; **à ce qu'il dit** according to him; **vous dites?** pardon?; **à vrai ~** actually; **entre nous soit dit** between you and me; **soit dit en passant** incidentally; **pour tout ~** all in all; **c'est ~ si j'ai raison** it just goes to show I'm right; **c'est beaucoup ~** that's going a bit far; **c'est peu ~** that's an understatement; **c'est vite dit** that's easy for you to say; **ce n'est pas dit** I'm not that sure; **tout n'est pas dit** that's not the end of the story; **c'est plus facile à ~ qu'à faire** it's easier said than done; **il est dit que je ne partirai jamais** I'm destined never to leave; **tu l'as dit**○!, **comme tu dis**○! you said it○!; **que tu dis**○! says you○!; ▶ **envoyer, fontaine**; **4** (formuler) **~ qch poliment/effrontément** to say sth politely/cheekily; **voilà qui est bien dit!** well said!; **il l'a mal dit, mais j'ai compris** he put it badly but I understood; **comment ~?, comment dirais-je?** how shall I put it?; **tu ne crois pas si bien ~** you don't know how true that is; **pour ainsi ~, comme qui dirait**○ so to speak; **autrement dit** in other words; **lent, pour ne pas ~ ennuyeux** slow, not to say boring; **comme dirait l'autre**○ as they say; **disons que je suis préoccupé** let's say I'm worried; **un livre, disons un 'texte', comme dirait Adam** a book, or let's say a 'text', as Adam would have it; **un lien disons social** a link which we could call social; **5** (indiquer) [*loi*] to state (**que** that) ; [*appareil de mesure*] to show (**que** that); [*sourire*] to express (**que** that); **ma calculatrice dit l'heure** my calculator shows the time; **que dit ta montre?** what time is it by your watch?; **vouloir ~** to mean; **qu'est-ce que tu crois qu'il a voulu ~?** what do you think he meant?; **quelque chose me dit que** something tells me that; **qu'est-ce que ça veut ~ tout ce bruit**○? what's the meaning of all this noise?; **qu'est-ce que ça veut ~ de téléphoner à une heure pareille**○? what do you mean by calling me at this time?; **qu'est-ce à ~**†? what is the meaning of this?; **est-ce à ~ que...?** does this mean that...?; ▶ **doigt**; **6** (demander) **~ à qn de faire** to tell sb to do; **dites-leur de venir** tell them to come; **je vous avais dit d'être prudent** I told you to be careful; **qui vous a dit de partir?** who told you to go?; **fais ce qu'on te dit!** do as you're told!; **faites ~ au médecin de venir** have somebody call the doctor; **7** (objecter) **qu'avez-vous à ~ à cela?** what have you got to say to that?; **j'ai beaucoup à ~ sur ton travail** I've quite a lot to say about your work; **je n'ai rien à ~** no comment; **il n'y a pas à ~**○, **elle est belle** you have to admit, she's beautiful; **il n'y a rien à ~, tout est en ordre** nothing to report, everything's fine; **tu n'as rien à ~!** (ne te plains pas) don't complain!; (tais-toi) don't say a word!; **8** (penser) to think; **qu'en dites-vous?** what do you think?; **que dis-tu de mon nouveau sac?** what do you think of my new bag?; **que diriez- vous d'une promenade/d'aller au marché?** how about a walk/going to the market?; **on dirait qu'il va pleuvoir/neiger** it looks as if it's going to rain/to snow, it looks like rain/snow; **on dirait que le vent se lève** the wind seems to be picking up; **on dirait qu'elle me déteste** you'd think she hated me; **on dirait un fou** you'd think he was mad; **on aurait dit qu'elle était déçue** you'd have thought she was disappointed; **on dirait de l'estragon** (à la vue) it looks like tarragon; (au goût) it tastes like tarragon; **on dirait du Bach** it sounds like Bach; **~ qu'hier encore il était parmi nous!** it's odd to think (that) he was still with us yesterday!; **~ que demain à la même heure je serai chez moi** it's odd to think that this time tomorrow I'll be home; **9** (inspirer) **ça ne me/leur dit rien de faire** I /they don't feel like doing; **notre nouveau jardinier ne me dit rien (qui vaille)** I don't think much of our new gardener; **10** Ling **il faut ~ 'excusez-moi' et non 'je m'excuse'** one should say 'excusez-moi', not 'je m'excuse'; **tu dirais 'une professeur', toi?** would you say 'une professeur'?; **comment dis-tu ça en italien?** how do you say that in Italian?
IV se dire *vpr* **1** (penser) to tell oneself (**que** that); **je me suis dit qu'il était trop tard** I told myself that it was too late; **il faut (bien) se ~ que**... one must realize that...; **il faut te ~ que**... you must understand that...; **2** (échanger des paroles) **se ~ des insultes/des mots doux** to exchange insults/sweet nothings; **se ~ adieu** to say goodbye to each other; **3** (se prétendre) to claim to be, to say one is; **il se dit intelligent/innocent/ingénieur** he claims to be intelligent/innocent/an engineer; **elle se dit incapable de marcher** she claims to be unable to walk; **4** (se déclarer) **il s'est dit prêt à participer à la conférence** he said that he was prepared to take part in the conference; **ils se sont dits favorables à cette mesure** they said that they were in favour[GB] of this measure; **elle s'est dite persuadée que**... she said that she was convinced that...; **5** Ling **comment se dit 'voiture' en espagnol?** how do you say 'car' in Spanish?; **'surprise-party' ne se dit plus** people don't say 'surprise-party' any more; **ça ne se dit pas** you can't say that; **6** (être dit) **il ne s'est rien dit d'intéressant à la réunion** nothing of interest was said during the meeting.
IDIOMES **bien faire et laisser ~** Prov do right and fear no man Prov; **dis-moi qui tu hantes, je te dirai qui tu es** you're known by the company you keep; **dis-moi ce que tu manges, je te dirai qui tu es** you are what you eat.

direct /diʀɛkt/ **I** *adj* **1** (sans intermédiaire) [*contact, descendant, rapport, affrontement, allusion, impôt*] direct; [*supérieur, entourage*] immediate; **2** Transp [*route, chemin, liaison, accès*] direct; **l'itinéraire le plus ~** the most direct route; **vol ~** direct flight; **train ~** through train; **ce train est ~ pour Lille** this train is nonstop to Lille; **3** (franc) [*personne, regard, question*] direct; **4** Ling [*discours, style, objet*] direct.
II *nm* **1** Radio, TV live broadcasting ¢; **les avantages et les inconvénients du ~** the advantages and disadvantages of broadcasting live; **en ~ de Prague** live from Prague; **émission diffusée en ~** live broadcast; **2** Sport (en boxe) jab; **~ du gauche/du droit** left/right jab; **3** Rail express (train).

directement /diʀɛktəmɑ̃/ *adv* **1** (sans détour) [*aller, rentrer, venir*] straight; **je suis venu ~** I came straight here; **elle est rentrée ~ chez elle** she went straight home; **je vous rejoindrai ~ à la piscine** I'll meet you at the swimming pool; **2** (personnellement) [*concerner, affecter*] directly; **ça te concerne ~** it concerns you directly ou personally; **ça ne dépend pas ~ de lui** it's not entirely up to him; **3** (sans intermédiaire) [*s'affronter, intervenir, financer*] directly; **~ du producteur au consommateur** straight from the producer to the consumer; **adressez-vous ~ au gérant** go straight to the manager.

directeur, -trice /diʀɛktœʀ, tʀis/ **I** *adj* (central) **principe ~** guiding principle; **idée directrice d'un ouvrage** central theme of a book; **les lignes directrices d'une politique** the guidelines of a policy.
II ▶510 *nm,f* **1** Scol (d'école) head teacher, headmaster/headmistress GB, principal US; (d'établissement privé) principal; **2** Comm (d'hôtel, de cinéma, casino) manager/manageress; **3** Admin, Entr (administrateur) director; (chef) head (**de** of).
III directrice *nf* Math directrix.
■ **~ adjoint** deputy manager; **~ d'agence** branch manager; **~ artistique** artistic director; **~ de banque** bank manager; **~ commercial** sales manager; **~ de conscience** spiritual adviser; **~ exécutif** executive director; **~ financier** financial director; **~ général** managing director GB, chief executive officer US; Admin director general; **~ général adjoint** assistant general manager; **~ gérant** managing director; **~ de journal** newspaper editor; **~ du personnel** personnel manager; **~ de la photographie** director of photography; **~ de prison** prison governor GB, warden US; **~ de projet** project manager; **~ de la publication** Presse editorial director; **~ de recherche** head of research; **~ de la rédaction** Presse managing editor; **~ régional** district ou regional manager; **~ des ressources humaines, DRH** human resources manager; **~ sportif** (team) manager; **~ technique** Ind works ou plant manager, technical manager; **~ de thèse** Univ supervisor GB, adviser US; **~ d'usine** works manager GB, plant manager.

directif, -ive /diʀɛktif, iv/ **I** *adj* **1** Psych [*entretien, méthode*] directive; **non ~** nondirective; **2** Tech [*antenne, micro*] directional.
II directive *nf* Admin (instruction) directive.

direction /diʀɛksjɔ̃/ *nf* **1** (chemin) direction; **se tromper de ~** to go in the wrong direction; **être** or **aller dans la bonne/mauvaise ~** lit, fig to be heading in the right/wrong direction; **changer de ~** lit, fig to change direction; **quelle est la ~ du vent?** which way is the wind blowing?; **quelle ~ ont-ils prise?** which way did they go?; **il a pris la ~ du nord** he headed north; **il faut orienter nos recherches dans une autre ~** we must take a new direction in our research; **dans la ~ de, en ~ de** [*aller, regarder*] toward(s); **un village dans la ~ de Clermont** a village on the way to Clermont; **demander la ~ de la poste/mairie** to ask the way ou for directions to the post office/town hall; **indiquer la ~ à qn** to tell sb the way, to give sb directions; **prenez la ~ Nation** (d'autobus) take the bus going to 'Nation'; (de métro) take the train going to 'Nation'; **la ~ Lille** (route) the Lille road; **train en ~ de Toulouse** Toulouse train; **avion/bateau en ~ de Lisbonne** flight/ship to Lisbon; **faire un pas** or **geste en ~ de qn** fig to make an overture to sb; **2** (fonction de directeur) (gestion) management; (supervision) supervision; (de journal) editorship; (de parti, mouvement) leadership; **on leur a confié la ~ du projet/de l'entreprise/des travaux** they've been put in charge of the project/company/work; **il a été nommé à la ~ de l'usine** he's been appointed manager of the factory; **il veut siéger à la ~** he wants to be on the management team; **assurer la ~ de** to manage, to run [*entreprise, service*]; to be in charge of [*opération, travaux, projet*]; **orchestre sous la ~ de** orchestra conducted by; **thèse /recherches sous la ~ de** thesis/research supervised by; **3** (personnes) management; **la ~ et les ouvriers** management and workers; **la ~ refuse de négocier** the management refuses to negotiate; **allez vous plaindre à la ~** go and complain to the management; **'changement de ~'** 'under new management'; **'la ~ décline toute responsabilité'** 'the management accepts no responsibility'; **4** (lieu) manager's office; (siège social) head office; **les grévistes ont occupé la ~ de l'usine** the strikers took over the factory manager's office; **5** (service) department; **~ commerciale/du personnel** sales/personnel department; **6** Aut, Aviat, Naut steering.
■ **~ assistée** Aut power steering; **~ à crémaillère** Aut rack-and-pinion steering; **~ des ressources humaines, DRH** human resources department.

directionnel, -elle /diʀɛksjɔnɛl/ *adj* directional.

directoire /diʀɛktwaʀ/ *nm* board of directors (*responsible for the actual day-to-day management of a firm*).

Directoire /diʀɛktwaʀ/ *nm* Hist Directoire (*French Regime from 1795 to 1799*); **meubles/style ~** Directoire furniture/style.

directorial, ~e, *mpl* **-iaux** /diʀɛktɔʀjal, o/ *adj* managerial.

directrice ▶ **directeur**.

dirigeable /diʀiʒabl/ **I** *adj* dirigible.
II *nm* dirigible, airship.

dirigeant, ~e /diʀiʒɑ̃, ɑ̃t/ **I** *adj* [*classe*] ruling; [*rôle*] leading; **cadre ~** senior executive; **milieux ~s** executive circles.
II *nm* (de pays, gouvernement, parti, mouvement) leader; (gérant) manager; (administrateur) director.

diriger /diʀiʒe/ [13] **I** *vtr* **1** (être responsable de) to be in charge of [*personnes, ouvriers, équipe*]; to run, to be in charge of [*service*]; to run, to be in charge of [*école*]; to manage, to run [*usine, entreprise, théâtre*]; to lead, to run [*parti, syndicat, pays*]; to lead [*discussion, débat, enquête*]; to direct [*opération, manœuvre*]; to supervise [*recherches, thèse, travaux*]; to run [*journal*]; **mal ~ une entreprise/un projet** to mismanage a business/project; **il veut tout ~** he wants to be in charge of everything; **2** (conduire) to steer [*véhicule*] (**vers** toward, towards GB); to steer, to navigate [*navire*] (**vers** toward, towards GB); to pilot [*avion*] (**vers** toward, towards GB); **il vous dirigera dans la vieille ville** he'll guide you around the old town; **la sonde spatiale est dirigée depuis la Terre** the space probe is guided from earth; **les blessés ont été dirigés vers l'hôpital le plus proche** the wounded were sent ou taken to the nearest hospital; **3** (orienter) lit to turn [*lumière, lampe, projecteur, jet*] (**vers** toward, towards GB; **sur** on); to turn [*regard*] (**vers** toward, towards GB); to point [*arme, canon, télescope*] (**sur** at); fig to direct [*critiques, attaques, sarcasmes*] (**contre** against); **~ son attention vers** or **sur qch** to turn one's attention to sth; **~ des étudiants dans leurs recherches** to guide students in their research; **~ qn vers un service/bureau** to send ou refer sb to a department/an office; **4** (expédier) to dispatch [*colis, marchandises*] (**vers, sur** to); to direct [*convoi*] (**vers, sur** to); **5** (motiver) **la volonté de plaire dirige tous leurs actes** all their actions are motivated by the desire to be liked; **le souci de satisfaire le client dirige notre action** our number one priority is to satisfy the customer; **6** Mus to direct, to conduct [*orchestre*]; to conduct [*symphonie, concerto*]; **7** Cin, Théât to direct [*acteurs*]; to manage [*troupe*].
II se diriger *vpr* **1** (aller) **se ~ vers** to make for, to head for; **se ~ droit sur** to head ou make straight for; **il se dirige vers la porte** he's heading for the door; **le cyclone se dirige vers le Mexique/le nord** the cyclone is heading for ou toward(s) Mexico/is heading northwards; **le météore se dirige droit sur la Terre** the meteorite is heading straight for earth; **tu devrais te ~ dans cette voie** fig that's the way to go; **2** (s'orienter) **se ~ d'après les étoiles** [*navigateur*] to sail ou navigate by the stars; [*promeneur*] to be guided by the stars.

dirigisme /diʀiʒism/ *nm* planned economy.

dirigiste /diʀiʒist/ *adj* [*politicien, gouvernement, État, pays*] in favour[GB] of a planned economy.

discale /diskal/ *adj f* **hernie ~** slipped disc, herniated (intervertebral) disc spéc.

discernable /disɛʀnabl/ *adj* discernible, detectable.

discernement /disɛʀnəmɑ̃/ *nm* judgment, discernment sout; **faire preuve/manquer de ~** to display/to lack judgment; **avoir du ~ dans** to be discerning in; **agir avec/sans ~** to act with/without discretion ou proper judgment; **choisir avec/sans ~** to be discriminating/undiscriminating in one's choice.

discerner /disɛʀne/ [1] *vtr* **1** (par un effort d'attention) to detect [*signe, odeur, expression*]; to make out, to discern fml [*silhouette, bruit*]; **~ un fauteuil** to make out the shape of an armchair; **2** (par un effort de réflexion) to make out [*mobiles, intentions*]; **~ le vrai du faux** to discriminate between truth and untruth; **~ le bien du mal** to be able to tell right from wrong.

disciple /disipl/ *nmf* **1** (partisan) follower, disciple; **2** (élève) disciple; **les ~s de Jésus** the disciples of Jesus.

disciplinaire /disiplinɛʀ/ *adj* [*commission, procédure, mesure*] disciplinary; **cellule ~** punishment cell; **internement ~** Mil military detention.

discipline /disiplin/ *nf* **1** (règle) discipline; **~ budgétaire/de fer** financial/iron discipline; **une stricte ~ de vie** a strictly disciplined way of life; **se plier/ne pas se plier à la ~ de vote** to follow/to ignore the party whip; **2** (spécialité) discipline; **des chercheurs de toutes les ~s** researchers of all disciplines; **les ~s artistiques** the artistic disciplines, the arts; **3** Scol (matière) subject; **une ~ secondaire** a subsidiary subject; **4** Sport sport; **~ olympique** Olympic sport; **5** (fouet) scourge.

discipliner /disipline/ [1] **I** *vtr* **1** (faire obéir) to discipline [*personne, groupe*]; **foule disciplinée** disciplined crowd; **2** (maîtriser) to control, to keep [sb] under control [*troupes*]; to discipline, to control [*pensées, passions*]; **3** (faire tenir en place) to keep [sth] under control [*cheveux*].
II se discipliner *vpr* to discipline oneself.

disc-jockey, *pl* **~s** /diskʒɔkɛ/ ▶510 *nm* disc jockey, DJ.

disco /disko/ **I** *adj inv* disco; **soirée ~** disco night.
II *nm* disco music.

discobole /diskɔbɔl/ *nm* **1** Antiq, Art discobolus; **2** Sport discus thrower.

discographie /diskɔgʀafi/ *nf* discography; **une ~ de Mozart** a Mozart discography.

discoïde /diskɔid/ *adj* discoid, discoidal.

discontinu, ~e /diskɔ̃tiny/ *adj* **1** (intermittent) [*effort, mouvement*] intermittent; [*ligne*] broken, dotted; **2** Math, Ling discontinuous.

discontinuer /diskɔ̃tinɥe/ [1] *vi* **sans ~** without a break, nonstop.

discontinuité /diskɔ̃tinɥite/ *nf* Math, Phys discontinuity.

disconvenir /diskɔ̃v(ə)niʀ/ [36] *vi* fml **ne pas ~ de qch** not to deny sth; **je n'en disconviens pas** I don't deny it; **ne pas ~ que** not to deny that.

discophile /diskɔfil/ *nmf* record collector.

discordance /diskɔʀdɑ̃s/ *nf* **1** (d'opinions) conflict; (de couleurs) clash; **2** (de sons) dissonance; **3** Géol unconformity; **reposer en ~** to be unconformable.

discordant, **~e** /diskɔʀdɑ̃, ɑ̃t/ *adj* **1** (mal assortis) [*caractères, couleurs*] clashing; **2** (désagréable) [*son, instrument*] discordant; [*voix*] strident; **3** (tranchant sur un ensemble) [*opinions*] conflicting; **4** Géol [*formation*] unconformable.

discorde /diskɔʀd/ *nf* discord, dissension; **semer la ~** to sow dissension; **pomme de ~** bone of contention.

discorder /diskɔʀde/ [1] *vi* fml **1** (être discordant) to be discordant, to be dissonant; **2** (être en désaccord) to conflict (**avec** with).

discothécaire /diskɔtekɛʀ/ **▶510** *nmf* music librarian.

discothèque /diskɔtɛk/ *nf* **1** (organisme de prêt) music library; **2** (collection de disques) record collection; **3** (boîte de nuit) discotheque.

discount /diskunt/ *nm* discount; **un ~ de 15%** a discount of 15%; **magasin de ~** discount shop GB ou store, cut-price shop GB ou store; **faire du ~** to offer discounts.

discounter /diskunte/ [1] *vtr* to give ou offer a discount on.

discoureur, **-euse** /diskuʀœʀ, øz/ *nm,f* pej great talker péj.

discourir /diskuʀiʀ/ [26] *vi* **~ de** or **sur qch** to hold forth on sth.

discours /diskuʀ/ *nm* **1** (exposé) speech (**devant** in front of; **sur** on); **faire/prononcer/improviser un ~** to make/to deliver/to improvise a speech; **un ~ inaugural/d'ouverture/de clôture/d'investiture** inaugural/opening/closing/investiture speech; **un ~, un ~!** speech, speech!; **2** (paroles) talk; **assez de ~, des actes!** let's have less talk and more action!, we want deeds not words!; **il nous ennuie avec ses ~** he bores us with his talk; **fais ce que je te dis et pas de ~!** do what I say and no argument!; **tenir de longs ~ sur qch** to talk at great length about sth, to hold forth about sth; **les beaux ~ ne servent à rien** fine words butter no parsnips; **3** (propos) views (*pl*); Pol position; **il tient toujours le même ~** his views haven't changed; **le ~ écologique/des syndicats** the position of the ecologists/the unions; **4** Ling (utilisation de la langue) speech; (unité de comportement) discourse; **~ direct/indirect/rapporté** direct/indirect/reported speech; **l'analyse du ~** discourse analysis.
■ **~ programme** Pol keynote speech.

discourtois, **~e** /diskuʀtwa, az/ *adj* discourteous.

discrédit /diskʀedi/ *nm* disrepute; **en ~** in disrepute; **jeter le ~ sur** to discredit, to bring [sth] into disrepute.

discréditer /diskʀedite/ [1] **I** *vtr* to discredit.
II se discréditer *vpr* **1** (se déconsidérer) to discredit oneself (**auprès de qn, aux yeux de qn** in sb's eyes); **2** (se dévaloriser) to become discredited.

discret, **-ète** /diskʀɛ, ɛt/ *adj* **1** (qu'on remarque peu) [*personne*] unassuming; [*vêtement, couleur*] sober; [*allusion, charme, maquillage*] subtle; [*éclairage*] subdued; [*sourire, signe, surveillance, parfum, bijou*] discreet; [*lieu*] quiet; **2** (qui garde les secrets) discreet (**sur** about); **3** (qui n'est pas curieux) not inquisitive; **4** Ling, Math, Phys, Stat discrete.

discrètement /diskʀɛtmɑ̃/ *adv* (sans publicité) [*agir*] discreetly; (sobrement) [*se vêtir*] soberly; (sans bruit) [*marcher, fermer une porte*] quietly.

discrétion /diskʀesjɔ̃/ **I** *nf* (réserve) discretion; **faire preuve de ~** to show discretion; **dans la plus grande ~** in the greatest secrecy; **entourer qch de (la plus grande) ~** to shroud sth in (the greatest) secrecy; **garder la plus grande ~ sur qch** to keep sth a closely-guarded secret; **~ assurée** discretion assured.
II à discrétion *loc* [*vin, pain*] unlimited; **il y avait à boire et à manger à ~** you could drink and eat as much as you like.
III à la discrétion de *loc prép* at the discretion of.

discrétionnaire /diskʀesjɔnɛʀ/ *adj* discretionary; **pouvoir ~** discretionary power.

discriminant, **~e** /diskʀiminɑ̃, ɑ̃t/ **I** *adj* **1** (qui différencie) [*caractère, facteur*] differential; **2** (discriminatoire) discriminatory.
II *nm* Math discriminant.

discrimination /diskʀiminasjɔ̃/ *nf* **1** (principe) discrimination (**contre, envers, à l'égard de** against); **sans ~ de race ou de religion** without racial or religious discrimination; **~ en fonction de** or **par l'argent** discrimination on grounds of money; **2** (acte) act of discrimination; **subir des ~s** to suffer discrimination.

discriminatoire /diskʀiminatwaʀ/ *adj* discriminatory (**à l'encontre de** against).

discriminer /diskʀimine/ [1] *vtr* fml to categorize [*personnes, objets*].

disculpation /diskylpasjɔ̃/ *nf* fml exculpation sout.

disculper /diskylpe/ [1] **I** *vtr* Jur, gén [*juge, témoignage*] to exculpate.
II se disculper *vpr* to vindicate oneself; **se ~ auprès de qn** to vindicate oneself in sb's eyes.

discursif, **-ive** /diskyʀsif, iv/ *adj* discursive.

discussion /diskysjɔ̃/ *nf* **1** (débat) discussion (**sur** about); **mettre qch en ~** to open sth up for discussion; **le texte est en ~** the text is under discussion; **une réforme en cours de ~** a reform being discussed; **lors de la ~ du budget/du projet de loi** when the budget/law was being discussed; **nous sommes en ~ avec eux** we're having discussions with them; **des ~s sont en cours** there are discussions ou talks in progress; **relancer la ~** to revive the debate; **cela mérite ~** that's worth discussing; **2** (échange de vues) discussion (**sur** about); **prendre part à la ~** to take part in the discussion; **avoir une ~ avec qn** (conversation) to have a discussion with sb; (dispute) to have an argument with sb; **après maintes ~s nous avons décidé de faire** after much discussion we decided to do; **3** (contestation) argument; **obéir sans ~** to obey without any argument; **pas de ~!** no argument!

discutable /diskytabl/ *adj* **1** (prêtant à discussion) [*question, notion, proportion*] debatable, arguable; **2** (critiquable) [*manière, choix, procédé*] questionable; **leur décision est très ~** their decision is very questionable.

discutailler○ /diskytɑje/ [1] *vi* to quibble (**sur** over); **on ne va pas ~ là-dessus** we're not going to quibble over that.

discuté, **~e** /diskyte/ **I** *pp* ▶ **discuter**.
II *pp adj* [*problème, programme, proposition*] controversial; **question très ~e** vexed question.

discuter /diskyte/ [1] **I** *vtr* **1** (examiner) to discuss [*question, point, problème, accord*]; to debate [*texte, projet de loi, mesure*]; **~ le budget** Pol to debate the budget; **2** (contester) to question [*décision, ordre, mesure, autorité*]; **~ l'utilité/le bien-fondé de qch** to question the usefulness of/the grounds for sth.
II discuter de *vtr ind* to discuss [*projet, réforme, crise, prix*]; **~ de la stratégie à adopter** to discuss the strategy to adopt; **le sujet dont nous avons discuté** the subject we discussed; **nous en avons longuement discuté** we discussed it at length; ▶ **ange**, **goût**.
III *vi* **1** (converser) to talk (**avec qn** to sb); **~ toute la nuit** to talk all night; **on peut essayer de ~** we can try to talk; **2** (protester) to argue; **on ne discute pas!** no arguing!; **faites ce qu'on vous dit sans ~!** do what you're told without arguing!; **il a dit trois heures et il n'y a pas à ~** he said three o'clock and that's all there is to it.
IV se discuter *vpr* **ça se discute**, **ça peut se ~** that's debatable.
IDIOMES **~ le coup**○ to have a chat; **~ le bout de gras**○ to chew the fat○, to shoot the breeze○.

disert, **~e** /dizɛʀ, ɛʀt/ *adj* fml **1** (bavard) talkative; **2** (éloquent) eloquent.

disette /dizɛt/ *nf* (famine) famine, food shortage.

diseur, **-euse** /dizœʀ, øz/ *nm,f* **~ de bonne aventure** fortune-teller.

disgrâce /disgʀɑs/ *nf* **1** (défaveur) disgrace; **tomber en ~** to fall into disgrace; **connaître la ~** to be in disgrace; **encourir la ~ de qn** to incur sb's displeasure; **2** (revers de fortune) fml misfortune; **avoir connu de nombreuses ~s** to have met with many misfortunes.

disgracié, **~e** /disgʀasje/ *adj* fml ugly.

disgracier /disgʀasje/ [2] *vtr* fml to dismiss [sb] from one's favour[GB] [*protégé*]; to reject [*amant*].

disgracieux, **-ieuse** /disgʀasjø, øz/ *adj* [*visage, enfant*] ugly; [*bouton, poil*] unsightly; [*démarche*] awkward; [*vêtement*] unbecoming.

disjoindre /disʒwɛ̃dʀ/ [56] **I** *vtr* **1** (écarter) to loosen; **planches disjointes** loose boards; **2** (isoler) to separate; **questions disjointes** separate issues.
II se disjoindre *vpr* to come loose.

disjoint, **~e** /disʒwɛ̃, ɛ̃t/ **I** *pp* ▶ **disjoindre**.
II *pp adj* Ling [*pronom, forme*] disjunctive.

disjoncter /disʒɔ̃kte/ [1] **I** *vtr* Électrotech to trip [*circuit*].
II *vi* **1** Électrotech to trip out; fig [*système, usine*] to grind to a halt; **2**○ [*personne*] (perdre le fil) to go off at GB ou on US a tangent; (divaguer) to go off one's head○.

disjoncteur /disʒɔ̃ktœʀ/ *nm* circuit breaker.

disjonctif, **-ive** /disʒɔ̃ktif, iv/ *adj* disjunctive.

disjonction /disʒɔ̃ksjɔ̃/ *nf* disjunction.

dislocation /dislɔkasjɔ̃/ *nf* **1** (d'empire, de fédération) dismemberment; (de pacte, coalition, conglomérat, groupe) breaking up; (de machine) falling apart; **2** Méd **~ (articulaire)** dislocation (of a joint); **3** Phys dislocation.

disloquer /dislɔke/ [1] **I** *vtr* **1** (démembrer) to dismember [*empire, État*]; **2** (déboîter) to dislocate [*membre*]; **3** (démonter) to break up [*meuble, mécanisme*]; to pull sth off its hinges [*porte, fenêtre*]; **une chaise disloquée** a broken chair.
II se disloquer *vpr* **1** (se démembrer) [*État, groupe*] to break up; **2** (se déboîter) [*personne*] **se ~ l'épaule** to dislocate one's shoulder; **3** (se contorsionner) [*personne*] to contort oneself; **4** (se casser) [*navire, mécanisme*] to break up.

disparaître /dispaʀɛtʀ/ [73] *vi* **1** (devenir invisible) to disappear; **~ de la scène politique** to disappear from the political scene; **disparaissez!** out of my sight!; **le soleil disparaît à l'horizon** the sun is dipping below the horizon; **le village disparaissait sous la neige** the village was hidden by the snow; **faire ~ tout un gâteau** to gobble down○ a whole cake; **2** (devenir introuvable) [*objet, personne*] to disappear; (soudainement) to vanish; **l'avion a disparu au-dessus de l'Atlantique** the plane disappeared somewhere over the Atlantic; **~ sans laisser de traces** to disappear without trace; **des centaines de personnes disparaissent chaque année** hundreds of people go missing every year; **faire ~ qch** to remove sth [*objet*]; **3** (être supprimé) [*douleur, odeur*] to go; [*tache*] to come out; [*difficulté*] to disappear; [*craintes*] to vanish; [*enflure*] to go down; [*fièvre*] to subside; **faire ~** to get rid of [*douleur, symptôme, trouble*]; to remove [*tache*]; to dispel [*crainte*]; to make [sth] go down [*enflure*]; to make [sth] extinct [*espèce*]; to clear [*pellicules, acné*]; to eradicate [*pauvreté, criminalité*]; **4** euph (mourir) to die, to go euph; (cesser d'exister) [*civilisation*] to die out; [*espèce*] to become extinct; **faire ~ qn** euph to get rid of sb; **voir ~ qch** to witness the end of sth [*civilisation, culture*]; **quand j'aurai disparu** when I'm gone; **~ en mer** to be lost at sea; **~ corps et bien** gén to be lost without trace; Naut to sink without trace.

disparate /disparat/ *adj* [*ensemble, mobilier*] ill-assorted; [*foule, groupe*] mixed; [*compétences, expériences*] varied.

disparité /disparite/ *nf* **1** (caractère différent) disparity sout (**de** in); **la ~ des réactions à une nouvelle** the range of reactions to a piece of news; **2** (différence) difference, disparity sout (**entre** between); **~s sociales** social differences ou disparities.

disparition /disparisjɔ̃/ *nf* **1** gén disappearance; (d'espèce) extinction; **une espèce en voie de ~** an endangered species; **en voie de ~** [*culture, civilisation*] fast disappearing, dying (*épith*); [*art, métier*] dying (*épith*); **une race en voie de ~** fig a dying breed; **2** euph (mort) death.

disparu, **~e** /dispary/ **I** *pp* ▶**disparaître**.

II *pp adj* **1** [*personne*] (enlevé, présumé mort etc) missing; **porté ~** Mil missing in action; **être porté ~** to be reported missing; **l'enfant ~ depuis trois jours** the child who has been missing for three days; **2** (perdu) [*civilisation, tradition, peuplade*] lost; [*espèce*] extinct; [*amour, gaieté*] lost; **les œuvres à jamais ~es** works lost forever; **3** euph (mort) dead; **marin ~ en mer** sailor lost at sea; **notre ami ~** our dear friend who is no longer with us.

III *nm,f* **1** (personne introuvable) missing person; **il y a des centaines de ~s chaque année** hundreds of people go missing every year; **neuf morts, un ~** nine dead, one missing; **2** euph (mort) **les ~s** the dead; **nos chers ~s** our dear departed.

dispendieusement /dispɑ̃djøzmɑ̃/ *adv* fml extravagantly, expensively.

dispendieux, **-ieuse** /dispɑ̃djø, øz/ *adj* expensive, extravagant.

dispensaire /dispɑ̃sɛʀ/ *nm* health centre[GB].

dispense /dispɑ̃s/ *nf* **1** (exemption) exemption (**de** from); **2** (certificat d'exemption) certificate of exemption; **3** Relig dispensation.

■ **~ d'âge** Admin exemption from statutory age limit; **~ d'examen** Univ exemption from an examination; **~ de scolarité** Univ permission not to attend classes; **~ de service national** Mil exemption from military service.

dispenser /dispɑ̃se/ [1] **I** *vtr* **1** (donner) to give [*cours, information, conseil, service, soin*] (**à** to); to hand out [*largesses*] (**à** to); to bestow sout [*honneurs, compliment, présent*] (**à** on); **2** (produire) to put out [*musique*]; to give out [*éclairage*]; **3** Jur (exempter) **~ qn de qch/de faire** to exempt sb from sth/from doing; **dispensé de paiement/d'accomplir ses obligations** exempt from payment/from performing one's duties; **4** (épargner) **~ qn de qch/de faire** to excuse sb from sth/doing; **cela ne vous dispense pas d'étudier** this does not make it any the less necessary for you to study; **se faire ~ d'un cours** to be excused from a lesson; **je vous dispense de (tout) commentaire** I don't need any comment from you.

II se dispenser *vpr* **1** (être donné) [*cours, soins*] to be given; **2** (se passer de) **se ~ de qch/de faire** to spare oneself sth/the trouble of doing; **j'ai décidé de me ~ de vos services** I've decided to dispense with your services.

dispersant /dispɛʀsɑ̃/ *nm* Chimie dispersing agent.

dispersé, **~e** /dispɛʀse/ **I** *pp* ▶**disperser**.

II *pp adj* [*personne, esprit*] unsystematic.

disperser /dispɛʀse/ [1] **I** *vtr* to scatter [*objets, documents, cendres, famille*]; to disperse [*foule, manifestants, fumée*]; to break up [*rassemblement, collection*]; **~ ses efforts** or **forces** to spread oneself too thinly; **~ son attention** to lack concentration.

II se disperser *vpr* [*famille*] to disperse, to scatter; [*foule, manifestants*] (volontairement) to disperse; (par nécessité) to scatter; [*fumée*] to disperse; [*rassemblement*] to break up; [*attention, esprit*] to wander; **nos efforts se sont trop dispersés, nous nous sommes trop dispersés** we spread ourselves too thinly.

dispersion /dispɛʀsjɔ̃/ *nf* **1** (de manifestants, foule, collection, fumée) dispersal; (de famille) scattering; **2** (manque de concentration) lack of concentration; **3** Mil (de tir, troupe) dispersion; **4** Chimie, Phys, Math, Stat dispersion.

disponibilité /disponibilite/ **I** *nf* **1** (temps libre) availability; **2** Comm availability; **3** Admin temporary leave of absence; **en ~** on leave of absence; **prendre une ~, se mettre en ~** to take temporary leave of absence; **4** Mil reserve; **en ~** on reserve.

II disponibilités *nfpl* Fin available funds.

disponible /disponibl/ *adj* **1** (libre) available (**pour** for); **esprit ~** open mind; **2** Comm (à disposition) available (**auprès de** from).

dispos, **~e** /dispo, oz/ *adj* (reposé) refreshed; (en bonne forme) in good form; **avoir l'esprit ~** to have a fresh and alert mind; **frais et ~** fresh as a daisy, bright eyed and bushy tailed○.

disposé, **~e** /dispoze/ **I** *pp* ▶**disposer**.

II *pp adj* **1** (agencé) [*meubles, fleurs*] arranged; [*appartement, pièce, jardin*] laid out; **chaises ~es en cercle autour de qch** chairs arranged in a circle around sth; **2** (prêt) **~ à aider/investir** willing to help/invest; **3** (favorable) **être bien/mal ~** to be in a good/bad mood; **être bien/mal ~ l'égard de** or **envers qn** to be well-/ill-disposed toward(s) sb.

disposer /dispoze/ [1] **I** *vtr* **1** (placer) to arrange [*objets*]; [*chef, capitaine*] to position [*personnes*]; **~ des chaises le long d'un mur** to arrange chairs along a wall; **nous étions disposés en cercle autour de lui** we formed a circle around him; **2** fml (prescrire) **~ que** to stipulate that.

II disposer de *vtr ind* **1** (avoir) **~ de** to have, to have at one's disposal [*moyens, instruments, temps*]; **les machines dont nous disposons** the machines we have at our disposal; **vous disposez de cinq minutes pour répondre** you have five minutes to answer; **je ne dispose que de quelques minutes pour vous recevoir** I can only spare you a few minutes; **2** (se servir de) **~ de** to use; **vous pourrez ~ de notre appartement cet été** you can use our apartment this summer; **disposez de moi comme vous voudrez** fml you can employ me as you like; **3** (être maître de) fml **~ de la vie/du sort de qn** to have sb's life/fate in one's hands; **le droit des peuples à ~ d'eux-mêmes** the right of peoples to self-determination; **merci, vous pouvez ~** thank you, you may go; ▶**homme**.

III se disposer *vpr* **1** (se préparer) **se ~ à faire** to be about to do; **je me disposais à vous écrire quand vous avez appelé** I was about to write when you rang GB ou called; **2** (se placer) **nous nous sommes disposés en cercle autour de lui** we formed a circle around him.

dispositif /dispozitif/ *nm* **1** (mécanisme) device; (système) system; **~ d'alarme/de sécurité** warning/safety device; **~ électronique/optique** electronic/optical device; **~ de commande** control system; **2** (ensemble de mesures) operation; **un imposant ~ policier a été mis en place** a large-scale police operation was set up; **~ militaire/de défense/financier** military/defence[GB]/financial operation; **le ~ de sécurité mis en place pour la venue du président** the security operation for the president's visit; **3** Jur (de loi) purview; (de jugement) pronouncement.

disposition /dispozisjɔ̃/ **I** *nf* **1** (arrangement) arrangement; (d'appartement, de salle) layout; (de pions, troupes) position; **arbustes plantés selon une ~ symétrique** symmetrically planted shrubs; **espèces distinguées par la ~ de leurs nageoires** species distinguished by the position of their fins; **2** (possibilité d'utiliser) **c'est à ta ~** it's at your disposal; **j'ai une voiture à ma ~** I have a car at my disposal; **à la ~ du public** for public use; **se tenir à la ~ de qn** to be at sb's disposal (**pour qch** for sth; **pour faire** to do); **je suis à votre entière ~** I am entirely at your disposal; **mettre qch à la ~ de qn** to put sth at sb's disposal; **une voiture sera mise/sera à ~ pour** a car will be made/will be available for; **se mettre à la ~ de la justice** [*témoin*] to make oneself available to the court; **il doit rester à la ~ de la justice** he must remain available to the court; **les dossiers ont été remis à la ~ de la justice** the files were made available to the court; **il a été mis à la ~ de la justice** he was remanded in custody; **3** (mesure) measure, step; **~s fiscales/législatives** tax/legal measures; **j'ai pris mes ~s pour arriver à l'heure** I made arrangements to arrive on time; **4** (tendance) fml tendency (**à** to); **cet enfant a une ~ à la paresse** this child has a tendency to laziness; **5** Assur, Jur (clause) clause.

II dispositions *nfpl* **1** (aptitudes) aptitude; **avoir/montrer des ~s pour qch/pour faire** to have/to show an aptitude for sth/for doing; **2** (humeur) **elle n'était pas dans de bonnes ~s ce jour-là** she wasn't in a good mood that day; **attends qu'il soit dans de meilleures ~s** wait till he's in a better mood; **ses mauvaises ~s à mon égard** his/her ill-feelings toward(s) me.

■ **~ d'esprit** state ou frame of mind.

disproportion /dispʀɔpɔʀsjɔ̃/ *nf* lack of proportion, disproportion sout.

disproportionné, **~e** /dispʀɔpɔʀsjɔne/ *adj* [*effort, demande*] disproportionate; [*réaction*] disproportionate, out of (all) proportion (*jamais épith*); [*nez, bouche*] disproportionately large; [*bras, jambes, tête*] out of proportion with one's body (*jamais épith*); **~ à qch** [*effort, demande, réaction*] out of (all) proportion with sth.

dispute /dispyt/ *nf* **1** (querelle) argument (**sur** about); **un sujet de ~** a cause for argument; **avoir une ~ avec qn** to have an argument with sb; **2** (discussion) debate.

disputé, **~e** /dispyte/ *adj* **1** (objet de lutte) [*épreuve, victoire, titre*] keenly contested (*épith*); **un match très ~** a keenly contested match; **2** (recherché) [*personne, marché, place*] sought-after (**de** by); **3** (contesté) [*question, projet*] controversial.

disputer /dispyte/ [1] **I** *vtr* **1** (participer à) to compete in [*épreuve, tournoi*]; to compete for [*coupe*]; to play [*match*]; to run [*course*]; to take part in [*combat*]; **la finale sera disputée à Rome** the final will be played in Rome; **2** (lutter pour obtenir) **~ qch à qn** to compete with sb for sth [*honneur, prix, place, titre, poste*]; to contend with sb for sth [*trône, pouvoir*]; **3**○ (réprimander) to tell [sb] off [*personne, enfant*]; **se faire ~** to get told off; **4 le disputer à** liter to rival; **le réalisme le dispute au fantastique** realism rivals the fantastic; **elle le dispute en élégance à sa mère** she rivals her mother in ou for elegance.

II disputer de *vtr ind* liter to debate [*question, point*].

III se disputer *vpr* **1** (se quereller) to argue; **cessez de vous ~!** stop arguing!; **nous nous sommes disputés** we had an argument; **se ~ pour qch** to argue over sth [*partage*]; **se ~ avec qn** to argue with sb (**à propos de, sur, au sujet de** about); **2** (lutter pour obtenir) to fight over [*héritage, os*]; to contest [*siège*]; to compete for [*honneur, place de classement*]; to contend for [*trône, titre, pouvoir, suprématie*]; **ils se disputent le contrôle de la société** they are competing for control of the company; **les deux familles se disputent la garde de l'enfant** the two families are fighting for custody of the child; **3** (avoir lieu) [*tournoi, championnat*] to take place; **le championnat se dispute par équipe/région** it's a team/regional championship.

disquaire /diskɛʀ/ **▶510** *nmf* record dealer.

disqualification /diskalifikasjɔ̃/ *nf* disqualification.

disqualifier /diskalifje/ [2] **I** *vtr* **1** (exclure d'une compétition) to disqualify [*sportif, cheval*]; **se faire ~ (par)** to be disqualified (by); **se faire ~ d'office** to put oneself out of the running; **2** (discréditer) [*acte, personne*] to discredit [*personne, institution*]; **~ qn aux yeux de qn** to discredit sb in sb's eyes.

II se disqualifier *vpr* to discredit oneself (**en faisant** by doing).

disque /disk/ *nm* **1** Mus record, disc; **passer un ~** to play a record; **change de ~**○**!** fig give it a rest ou break!; lit put another record on; **2** Tech disc; **3** **▶449** Sport discus; **lancer le ~** to throw the discus; **le lancer du ~** the discus; **4** (objet rond) disc; **le ~ du soleil** the sun's disc; **5** Ordinat disk.

■ **~ audionumérique** digital audio disk; **~ compact** compact disc; **~ dur** Ordinat hard disk; **~ d'embrayage** Aut clutch disc; **~ intervertébral** Anat intervertebral disc; **~ laser** laser disc; **~ noir** vinyl; **~ numérique** digital disk; **~ optique** optical disk; **~ optique compact, doc** CD-ROM; **~ optique numérique, DON** digital optical disk; **~ d'or** gold disc; **~ souple** (de présentation, en cadeau) flexi disc; Ordinat floppy disk, diskette; **~ vidéo** videodisc.

disquette /diskɛt/ *nf* diskette, floppy disk; **~ de sauvegarde** back-up diskette; **lecteur de ~s** disk drive.

disruptif, **-ive** /disʀyptif, iv/ *adj* [*décharge*] disruptive.

dissection /disɛksjɔ̃/ *nf* **1** Méd, Biol dissection; **instruments/table de ~** dissecting instruments/table; **2** (de texte, d'œuvre) dissection, analysis.

dissemblable /disɑ̃blabl/ *adj* dissimilar, different.

dissemblance /disɑ̃blɑ̃s/ *nf* dissimilarity, difference (**de** in).

dissémination /diseminasjɔ̃/ *nf* (de germe, virus) spread; (de pollen, troupes) dispersal; (de maisons) scattering; (d'idée) dissemination.

disséminé, **~e** /disemine/ **I** *pp* **▶disséminer**.

II *pp adj* [*maisons, population, entreprises*] scattered.

disséminer /disemine/ [1] **I** *vtr* to spread [*germe, idée*]; to disperse [*pollen*]; to distribute [*personnes, troupes*].

II se disséminer *vpr* [*personnes*] to scatter; [*germe, idée*] to spread.

dissension /disɑ̃sjɔ̃/ *nf* **1** (discorde) dissension sout, conflict; **être un sujet de ~ entre des personnes** to be the subject of dissension between people; **2** (désaccord) disagreement (**au sein de** within).

dissentiment /disɑ̃timɑ̃/ *nm* fml disagreement (**entre** between).

disséquer /diseke/ [14] *vtr* **1** Méd, Biol to dissect [*cadavre, plante*]; **2** (analyser) to dissect, to analyse[GB] [*texte, œuvre*].

dissertation /disɛʀtasjɔ̃/ *nf* **1** Scol, Univ (devoir) essay; **faire une ~** to write an essay; **sujet de ~** essay subject; **2** (exposé écrit ou oral) paper; **faire une ~ savante sur un sujet** (oralement) to present a paper on a subject; (par écrit) to write a paper on a subject.

disserte○ /disɛʀt/ *nf* essay.

disserter /disɛʀte/ [1] *vi* **1** (discourir) to speak (**sur** on); pej to hold forth (**sur** about); **2** Scol (composer une dissertation) to write (an essay) (**sur** on).

dissidence /disidɑ̃s/ *nf* **1** (opposition) Philos, Relig dissent; Pol dissidence; (insubordination civile) rebellion; **entrer en ~ contre** to enter into rebellion against [*régime*]; to break away from [*parti*]; **être en ~ avec** to have broken away from; **2** (opposants) **la ~** the dissidents; **les ~s religieuses/politiques** religious/political dissidents.

dissident, **~e** /disidɑ̃, ɑ̃t/ **I** *adj* **1** Pol [*personne*] dissident; [*groupe*] break-away; **2** Relig [*secte*] dissenting.

II *nm,f* **1** Pol dissident; **2** Relig, Philos dissenter.

dissimilation /disimilasjɔ̃/ *nf* dissimilation.

dissimilitude /disimilityd/ *nf* dissimilarity.

dissimulateur, **-trice** /disimylatœʀ, tʀis/ **I** *adj* secretive.

II *nm,f* dissembler.

dissimulation /disimylasjɔ̃/ *nf* **1** (de sentiment) dissimulation; **2** (d'information) concealment; **3** (caractère) secretiveness.

dissimulé, **~e** /disimyle/ **I** *pp* **▶dissimuler**.

II *pp adj* concealed; **mal ~** ill-concealed; **fierté non ~e** undisguised pride.

III *adj* [*personne*] secretive.

dissimuler /disimyle/ [1] **I** *vtr* to conceal (**derrière** behind; **à qn** from sb); **mal ~** to conceal badly; **ne pas ~** not to try to conceal.

II se dissimuler *vpr* **1** (se cacher) [*personne*] to hide; **2** (être caché) to be concealed (**derrière** behind); **3** (ne pas vouloir voir) to close one's eyes to [*problème*].

dissipation /disipasjɔ̃/ *nf* **1** (de malentendu) clearing up; **2** Météo (de brouillard, nuages) clearing; **après ~ des brumes matinales** after the early morning mist has cleared; **3** (de patrimoine) squandering; **4** (d'attention) wandering; **5** (d'élève) restlessness; **6**† (de débauché) dissipation.

dissipé, **~e** /disipe/ *adj* **1** [*élève*] restless; **2** [*jeunesse, vie*] dissipated.

dissiper /disipe/ [1] **I** *vtr* to dispel [*menace, doute, illusion, fatigue, malaise*]; to clear up [*malentendu*]; to disperse [*fumée*]; to squander [*patrimoine*]; to distract [*personne*].

II se dissiper *vpr* **1** (disparaître) [*menace*] to recede; [*illusion, doute*] to vanish; [*fatigue*] to wear off; [*malaise*] to vanish, to wear off; [*malentendu*] to be cleared up; [*brume*] to clear; **2** (s'agiter) [*élève*] to grow restless.

dissociable /disɔsjabl/ *adj* [*questions, événements*] dissociable, separable; **les deux causes ne sont pas ~s** the two causes can't be separated.

dissociation /disɔsjasjɔ̃/ *nf* **1** gén dissociation, separation (**de** of); **2** Chimie dissociation; **3** Jur severance.

dissocier /disɔsje/ [2] **I** *vtr* **1** (séparer) to separate (**de** from), to dissociate (**de** from); **2** Chimie to dissociate [*molécules*]; to break down [*substance*].

II se dissocier *vpr* **se ~ de qch/qn** to dissociate oneself from sth/sb.

dissolu, **~e** /disɔly/ *adj* [*vie*] dissolute; [*mœurs*] loose; **mener une vie ~e** to lead a dissolute life.

dissolubilité /disɔlybilite/ *nf* dissolvability.

dissoluble /disɔlybl/ *adj* that can be dissolved (*épith, après n*).

dissolution /disɔlysjɔ̃/ *nf* **1** (d'assemblée, organisation, de mariage, gouvernement) dissolution; (de parti, mouvement) dissolution, disbanding; **2** (de substance) dissolution, dissolving (**dans** in); **absorber les comprimés après ~ complète** take the tablets when they have completely dissolved; **3** (écroulement) (d'empire, de système politique) disintegration; (de famille) break-up; (d'autorité) breakdown, collapse.

dissolvant, **~e** /disɔlvɑ̃, ɑ̃t/ **I** *adj* Chimie solvent; **un produit ~** a solvent.

II *nm* **1** Cosmét nail varnish; **2** Chimie solvent.

dissonance /disɔnɑ̃s/ *nf* **1** Mus dissonance ¢, discord; **musique pleine de ~s** very dissonant ou discordant music; **2** (de mots, syllabes) dissonance; **3** (incohérence) (d'opinions, idées) conflict; (de style) inconsistency; **~s entre** disparities between; **il y a des ~s dans le style de l'auteur** the author's style jars in places.

dissonant, **~e** /disɔnɑ̃, ɑ̃t/ *adj* **1** (discordant) [*voix, sons*] dissonant, discordant; [*notes, accord, harmonie*] dissonant; [*couleurs, tons*] clashing, jarring; **2** (conflictuel) [*idées*] conflicting; **des voix ~es se faisaient entendre au sein du parti** dissenting voices were heard within the party.

dissoudre /disudʀ/ [75] **I** *vtr* **1** Jur, Pol to dissolve [*assemblée, mariage, compagnie*]; to disband [*parti, mouvement*]; **le mouvement dissous** the disbanded movement; **2** Chimie [*eau, acide, dissolvant*] to dissolve [*substance*] (**dans** in); **faire ~ la lessive** to dissolve the washing powder; **3** (briser) to break up [*empire, institutions, alliance*]; to destroy [*cohésion, unité*]; **4** liter [*lumière, éclairage, brouillard*] to blur [*contours, objets*].

II se dissoudre *vpr* **1** Jur, Pol [*organisation, parti*] to disband; [*mariage*] to be dissolved; **2** Chimie [*substance, comprimé*] to dissolve (**dans** in); **3** [*institutions*] to die out; [*société*] to disintegrate; [*unité*] to crumble; [*sentiment*] to fade; [*volonté*] to melt away; **4** liter (devenir flou) to dissolve, to be blurred (**dans** in).

dissuader /disɥade/ [1] *vtr* **~ qn de faire** [*personne*] to dissuade sb from doing, to persuade sb not to do; [*publicité, maladie, temps*] to put sb off doing, to deter sb from doing; **j'aimerais pouvoir t'en ~** I wish I could talk you out of it; **~ l'ennemi** to deter the enemy; **je n'ai pas réussi à la ~** I didn't manage to dissuade her.

dissuasif, **-ive** /disɥazif, iv/ *adj* **1** (qui dissuade) [*argument, idée*] dissuasive; [*armes, force*] deterrent; **avoir un effet ~ sur qn** to act as a deterrent to sb; **les contrôles doivent être ~s** the controls must act as a deterrent; **le temps est plutôt ~** the weather is rather off-putting; **2** (élevé) [*prix, taux d'intérêt*] prohibitive; **à un prix ~** at a prohibitive price.

dissuasion /disɥazjɔ̃/ *nf* **1** Mil, Pol deterrence; **la ~ nucléaire** nuclear deterrence; **stratégie/force de ~** deterrent strategy/force; **2** (action de dissuader) dissuasion.

dissyllabe /disilab/ **I** *adj* disyllabic.

II *nm* disyllable.

dissyllabique /disilabik/ *adj* disyllabic.

dissymétrie /disimetʀi/ *nf* asymmetry.

■ **~ moléculaire** Chimie molecular asymmetry.

dissymétrique /disimetʀik/ *adj* asymmetrical.

distance /distɑ̃s/ **▶477** *nf* **1** (intervalle spatial) distance; **quelle est la ~ entre Paris et Londres?** what is the distance between Paris and London?; **Paris est à quelle ~ de Londres?** what distance ou how far is Paris from London?; **à quelle ~ est-ce?** what distance ou how far is it?; **être à ~ moyenne de** to be a reasonable distance (away) from; **mettre une ~ entre X et Y** to put a distance between X and Y; **parcourir de longues ~s en peu de temps** to cover long distances in a short time; **je ne peux pas courir sur de longues ~s** I can't run long distances; **un avion capable de transporter 100 passagers sur une ~ de 1000 kilomètres** an aeroplane GB ou airplane US capable of transporting 100 passengers over a distance of 1,000 kilometres[GB]; **j'ai couru sur une ~ de deux kilomètres** I ran for two kilometres[GB]; **à 100 mètres de ~, à une ~ de 100 mètres** 100 metres[GB] away; **les deux frères**

vivent à 1000 kilomètres de ~ the two brothers live 1,000 kilometres[GB] apart; **notre maison est à faible ~ du centre** our house isn't far (away) from the centre[GB]; **~ d'un point à un plan** Math distance from a point to a plane; **gardez vos ~s** Aut keep your distance; **prendre ses ~s avec qn/qch** fig to distance oneself from sb/sth; **tenir** or **garder** or **maintenir qn/qch à ~** fig to keep sb/sth at a distance; **tenir** or **garder ses ~s** fig [*supérieur*] to stand aloof; [*inférieur*] to know one's place; **tenir/ne pas tenir la ~** [*sportif*] to stay/not to stay the course; **appel longue ~** Télécom long-distance call; **à ~** [*agir, communiquer, observer*] from a distance; [*commande, accès, manipulation*] remote (*épith*); **rester à bonne ~/à ~ respectueuse/à ~** to keep at a good distance/at a respectful distance/one's distance; **se tenir à bonne ~ de qch** to keep a good distance from sth; **à égale ~ de** at the same distance from; **2** (intervalle temporel) gap; **la ~ entre/qui sépare les deux événements** the gap between/separating the two events; **à une semaine/deux siècles de ~** one week/two centuries apart; **ils sont morts à trois mois de ~** their deaths were three months apart; **une considérable ~ culturelle les sépare** there is a considerable cultural gap between them; **3** (recul) distance; **avec la ~ que donne l'âge/le temps** with the distance conferred by age/time; **à ~, ces événements sont plus faciles à comprendre** with hindsight, those events are easier to understand.

■ **~ focale** focal length; **~ de freinage** braking distance.

distancer /distɑ̃se/ [12] *vtr* (en compétition sportive) gén to outdistance; (en course à pied, à cheval) to outrun; **il a largement distancé son rival** fig he left his rival standing; **se faire** or **se laisser ~** to get left behind.

distanciation /distɑ̃sjasjɔ̃/ *nf* **1** (recul) distance; **2** Théât alienation.

distancier /distɑ̃sje/ [2] **I** *vtr* to distance (**de** from).

II se distancier *vpr* to distance oneself (**de** from).

distant, ~e /distɑ̃, ɑ̃t/ *adj* **1** (éloigné dans l'espace) [*lieu, bruit, lueur*] distant; **un village ~ de trois kilomètres** a village three kilometres[GB] away; **~s de trois kilomètres** three kilometres[GB] apart; **2** (réservé) [*personne*] distant, aloof, stand-offish○; [*regard*] distant; [*attitude, comportement, air*] reserved, stand-offish○; [*rapports, relations*] cool; **être** or **se montrer ~ avec/envers qn** to be distant with/toward(s) sb; **3** (éloigné spirituellement) [*opinions, points de vue*] divergent; **nos opinions sont très ~es** our opinions differ greatly; **son point de vue est très ~ du mien** his/her point of view is far removed from mine; **4** (éloigné dans le temps) **un événement ~ dans ma vie** an event in my remote past; **à une époque ~e de la nôtre** in the distant past; **des événements ~s de plusieurs années** (entre eux) events that are several years apart; (par rapport à aujourd'hui) events that took place several years ago.

distendre /distɑ̃dʀ/ [6] **I** *vtr* **1** (étirer) to distend [*estomac*]; to strain [*ligament, muscle*]; to stretch [*peau, câble, corde*]; to over-stretch [*ressort*]; **2** (relâcher) to weaken [*liens, attaches*]; **cette querelle a distendu nos relations** the quarrel has put a strain on our relationship.

II se distendre *vpr* **1** (se relâcher) [*peau, ligament, ressort, câble, corde*] to slacken; **2** (s'affaiblir) [*liens, relations*] to cool.

distendu, ~e /distɑ̃dy/ **I** *pp* ▶ **distendre**.

II *pp adj* **1** (étiré) [*estomac*] distended; [*peau*] stretched; [*muscle*] strained; [*ressort*] over-stretched; **2** (relâché) [*peau, ressort, câble*] slack; **3** (affaibli) [*liens, relations*] cool.

distension /distɑ̃sjɔ̃/ *nf* (de peau) stretching; (d'estomac) distension; (de muscle, ligament) straining.

distillat /distila/ *nm* distillate.

distillateur /distilatœʀ/ *nm* (personne) distiller.

distillation /distilasjɔ̃/ *nf* **1** Ind, Vin distillation; **par ~** by distillation; **des opérations de ~** distilling operations; **2** fig (de savoir) distillation (**de** of).

■ **~ fractionnée** fractional distillation.

distiller /distile/ [1] **I** *vtr* **1** Chimie to distil[GB] [*fruit, vin, plantes, alcool*]; **2** (secréter) to secrete [*suc, poison, résine*]; **3** (répandre) to disclose [sth] little by little [*informations, confidences, rumeurs, idée*]; **un écrivain qui distille l'ennui** a profoundly boring writer.

II *vi* Chimie to evaporate (**à** at).

distillerie /distilʀi/ *nf* **1** (usine) distillery; **2** (production) distilling; **la ~ du vin** the distilling of wine; **il travaille dans la ~** he works in distilling.

distinct, ~e /distɛ̃, ɛ̃kt/ *adj* **1** (différent) distinct (**de** from); **2** (qui se perçoit nettement) [*forme, son*] distinct; [*voix*] clear; **de façon ~e** [*prononcer*] clearly, distinctly; [*s'exprimer*] clearly; **3** (sans liens) [*société, entreprise*] separate.

distinctement /distɛ̃ktəmɑ̃/ *adv* [*voir, entendre, prononcer*] clearly, distinctly; [*s'exprimer*] clearly.

distinctif, -ive /distɛ̃ktif, iv/ *adj* [*signe, caractère*] distinguishing; [*trait*] distinctive.

distinction /distɛ̃ksjɔ̃/ *nf* **1** (différence) distinction; **faire** or **établir une ~ entre X et Y** to make ou draw a distinction between X and Y; **sans ~** [*agir, récompenser*] without discrimination; [*massacrer, nuire*] indiscriminately; **sans ~ d'origine ou de religion** irrespective of colour[GB] or creed; **2** (récompense) honour[GB]; **la plus haute ~** the highest honour[GB]; **remettre/recevoir une ~** to confer/to be awarded an honour[GB]; **~ honorifique** award; **3** (élégance) distinction ou refinement; **il n'a aucune ~** he lacks refinement; **avoir de la ~** to be distinguished ou refined; **d'une grande ~** [*personne, œuvre*] of great distinction (*épith, après n*).

distingué, ~e /distɛ̃ge/ **I** *pp* ▶ **distinguer**.

II *pp adj* **1** (élégant) [*personne, manières*] distinguished, refined; [*air, allure*] distinguished; **2** (éminent) distinguished; **3** (en correspondance) **veuillez agréer mes salutations ~es** (à une personne non nommée) yours faithfully; (à une personne nommée) yours sincerely.

distinguer /distɛ̃ge/ [1] **I** *vtr* **1** (séparer) [*personne, esprit*] to distinguish between; **il faut ~ deux domaines bien différents** we must distinguish between two very different fields; **~ A et B** to distinguish between A and B; **~ A de B** to tell ou distinguish A from B; **il est difficile de ~ les deux jumeaux** it's difficult to tell the twins apart; **2** (par la vue, l'ouïe) (percevoir les différences) to distinguish [*couleurs, nuances*]; (percevoir avec difficulté) to make out [*contours, sons, différences*]; **3** (percevoir intellectuellement) to discern; **quant aux espèces vénéneuses, on en distingue quatre** there are four poisonous species; **je distinguerais trois points** (dans un exposé) I would like to bring out three main points; **4** (différencier) [*détail, qualité, trait*] to set [sb] apart [*personnes, animaux*]; to make [sth] different [*objets*] (**de** from); **ce qui distingue Paris de Londres** what makes Paris different from London, what distinguishes Paris from London; **à part leur taille, rien ne les distingue** apart from their size, there's nothing that sets them apart; **je vois mal ce qui les distingue** I fail to see what makes them different; **aucune caractéristique physique ne les distingue** physically, they have no distinguishing features; **5** (récompenser) [*personne, jury*] to single out [sb] for an honour[GB] [*personne*]; [*prix, récompense*] to be awarded to [*personne, œuvre*].

II *vi* **il faut savoir ~** you have to be able to tell the difference; **~ s'il s'agit d'un besoin réel ou d'un caprice** to judge whether it's a question of real need or of a whim; **~ entre A et B** to distinguish ou make a distinction between A and B.

III se distinguer *vpr* **1** (différer) **se ~ de** (par ses qualités) to differ from; (par ses actes) to set oneself apart from; **il vaut mieux éviter de se ~** it's best not to be conspicuous; **2** (s'illustrer) [*chercheur, sportif, candidat*] to distinguish oneself; **il s'est surtout distingué en physique théorique** he distinguished himself especially in theoretical physics; **l'auteur se distingue/ne se distingue pas par son originalité** the author is noted/isn't noted for his originality; **3** (être perçu) to be distinguishable; **se ~ à peine dans le brouillard** to be barely distinguishable in the fog; **4** (se faire remarquer) pej to draw attention to oneself; **il faut toujours qu'elle se distingue, celle-là!** she always has to draw attention to herself!

distinguo /distɛ̃go/ *nm* fine distinction; **faire le** or **un ~ entre** to make a fine distinction between.

distique /distik/ *nm* distich.

distordre /distɔʀdʀ/ [6] **I** *vtr* **1** (perturber) to distort [*son, image*]; **2** [*colère, douleur*] to contort [*visage, bouche*]; **être distordu par la douleur** to be contorted with pain.

II se distordre *vpr* **1** [*visage, bouche, traits*] to become contorted; **leur visages se distordaient sous la douleur** their faces were contorted with pain; **2** [*image, son*] to become distorted.

distorsion /distɔʀsjɔ̃/ *nf* **1** (de fait, réalité, d'histoire) distortion (**de** of); **2** (de son, d'image) distortion; **3** (de salaire, prix, taux, d'économie) imbalance; **4** (de visage, bouche) distortion.

distraction /distʀaksjɔ̃/ *nf* **1** (activité) leisure ¢, entertainment ¢; **c'est ma seule ~** it's my only form of leisure; **cette ville manque de ~s** there's not much in the way of entertainment in this town; **les ~s sont rares ici** there's not much to do around here; **2** (détente) recreation; **la lecture est un moyen de ~** reading is a means of relaxation; **j'ai besoin de ~** I need some form of relaxation; **tout a été conçu pour la ~ des membres du club** everything has been designed to keep the club members entertained; **3** (étourderie) absent-mindedness ¢; **par ~** through absent-mindedness; **avec ~** absent-mindedly; **mes professeurs me reprochent ma ~** my teachers tell me off for not paying attention; **4** Jur (de fonds, biens) misappropriation.

distraire /distʀɛʀ/ [58] **I** *vtr* **1** (divertir) (en amusant) to amuse; (en occupant) to entertain; **cela m'a distrait un moment** (amusé) it kept me amused for a while; **2** (soulager) **~ qn de** to take sb's mind off [*problème, chagrin, ennui*]; **3** (déconcentrer) to distract [*personne*] (**de** from; **par** by); **il distrait les autres élèves** he distracts the other pupils; **~ l'attention de qn** to distract sb's attention; **je me suis laissée ~** I let myself be ou get distracted; **4** Jur (détourner) to misappropriate [*argent, fonds*].

II se distraire *vpr* **1** (s'amuser) to amuse oneself; (prendre du bon temps) to enjoy oneself; **que fais-tu pour te ~?** what do you do for entertainment?; **2** (se changer les idées) **j'ai besoin de me ~** I need to take my mind off things; **se ~ de ses problèmes** to take one's mind off one's problems.

distrait, ~e /distʀɛ, ɛt/ **I** *pp* ▶ **distraire**.

II *pp adj* [*personne*] (trait de caractère) absent-minded; (occasionnellement) inattentive; [*élève*] inattentive; [*air, manière*] distracted; [*regard, sourire*] vague; **excusez-moi, j'étais ~** I'm sorry, I wasn't paying attention; **écouter d'une oreille ~e** to listen with only half an ear, to half-listen; **regarder qn d'un œil ~** to look vaguely at sb.

distraitement /distʀɛtmɑ̃/ *adv* [*entrer, verser, déplacer*] absent-mindedly; **regarder ~ qch** to look vaguely at sth; **écouter ~** to listen with half an ear, to half-listen; **il lisait ~ un journal** he was reading a newspaper with half an eye, he was half-reading a newspaper.

distrayant, **~e** /distʀɛjɑ̃, ɑ̃t/ *adj* [*personne, soirée, film*] entertaining, amusing; **c'est (d')une lecture ~e** it's an entertaining read, it makes entertaining reading.

distribuer /distʀibɥe/ [1] **I** *vtr* **1** (donner) to distribute [*prospectus, médicaments*] (**à** to); to pay out [*dividende*] (**à** to); to hand out [*compliments, poignées de main*] (**à** to); to allocate [*crédits, tâches, rôles*] (**à** to); **~ les cartes** Jeux to deal; **~ le courrier** to deliver the mail; **~ les prix** to award the prizes; **~ les récompenses** to give out the awards; **2** Comm (vendre) [*personne*] to distribute [*produit, film*]; [*machine*] to dispense [*tickets, boissons*]; **3** Constr, Gén Civ to supply [*eau, chaleur*]; **4** (organiser) **bâtiments mal distribués le long de l'avenue** buildings poorly distributed along the avenue; **maison bien/mal distribuée** well-/badly-planned house.

II se distribuer *vpr* (se répartir) to be distributed; **se ~ régulièrement** to be evenly distributed.

distributeur, **-trice** /distʀibytœʀ, tʀis/ ▶**510** **I** *adj* **1** Comm distributing; **compagnie distributrice** distributing firm; **2** Tech **flacon ~** dispenser.

II *nm,f* **1** Comm distributor; **~ de films** film distributor; **~ exclusif** sole distributor; **2** (de rue) distributor; **~ de prospectus** leaflet distributor.

III *nm* **1** (machine automatique) dispenser; (payant) vending machine; **~ de mayonnaise** mayonnaise dispenser; **~ de tickets** ticket machine; **~ de billets** (**de banque**) cash dispenser; **~ de boissons/préservatifs/cigarettes** drinks/condom/cigarette vending machine; **2** Aut, Électrotech, Tech distributor; **3** (compagnie du secteur de la distribution) retailing group.

■ **~ automatique de billets**, **DAB** automatic teller machine, ATM; **~ d'engrais** Agric fertilizer spreader.

distributif, **-ive** /distʀibytif, iv/ *adj* Math distributive.

distribution /distʀibysjɔ̃/ *nf* **1** Écon, Fin (secteur) retailing; **secteur de la ~ alimentaire** food retailing sector; **géant de la ~** retailing giant; **chaîne de ~** retailing chain; ▶ **grand**; **2** Comm (commercialisation) distribution; **branche ~** distribution branch; **~ d'un journal/du gin** distribution of a paper/of gin; **se réserver l'exclusivité de la ~** to keep exclusive distribution rights (**de** for); **3** Gén Civ supply; **~ de l'électricité/eau/énergie** electricity/water/energy supply; **4** (fourniture) (d'objets) distribution; (de tâches, rôles) allocation; **~ gratuite de lait aux écoliers** distribution of free milk to schoolchildren; **~ de prospectus** distribution of leaflets; **5** (disposition) distribution; **~ géographique** geographical distribution; **~ d'une maison** layout of a house; **6** Cin, Théât (choix effectué) casting; (liste) cast; **7** Tech valve gear.

■ **~ d'actions gratuites** allocation of bonus shares; **~ automatique** Comm automatic dispensing; **~ des cartes** Jeux deal; **~ complémentaire** Ling complementary distribution; **~ du courrier** Postes postal delivery; **~ de dividendes** Fin payment of dividends; **~ des prix** Scol prizegiving.

distributionnel, **-elle** /distʀibysjɔnɛl/ *adj* Ling distributional.

distributivité /distʀibytivite/ *nf* Math distributivity.

district /distʀik(t)/ *nm* ≈ district (*administrative subdivision of a department of France*).

District of Columbia ▶**692** *nprm* District of Columbia.

dit /di/ *nm* Littérat ditty.

dithyrambe /ditiʀɑ̃b/ *nm* **1** (éloge) fml dithyramb sout; (exagéré) panegyric; **2** Littérat, Antiq (poème) dithyramb.

dithyrambique /ditiʀɑ̃bik/ *adj* [*discours, article, propos*] ecstatic; [*louange*] extravagant; **les critiques ont été ~s sur ce film** the critics gave the film ecstatic reviews.

dito /dito/ *adv* Comm ditto.

diurèse /djyʀɛz/ *nf* diuresis.

diurétique /djyʀetik/ *adj, nm* diuretic.

diurne /djyʀn/ *adj* [*activité, éclairage, programmation*] daytime; [*fleur, animal, fièvre*] diurnal.

diva /diva/ *nf* diva.

divagation /divagasjɔ̃/ *nf* **1** (de fou, malade) ravings (*pl*); **2** (élucubration) rambling ¢; **n'écoute pas leurs ~s** don't listen to their ramblings; **3** Jur (d'animal) straying; **être en état de ~** to be a stray.

divaguer /divage/ [1] *vi* **1** (délirer) [*fou, malade*] to rave; **il divague** he's raving; **la fièvre le fait ~** he's raving with fever; **2** (déraisonner) to ramble; (dire des bêtises) to talk nonsense; **3** Jur [*animaux*] to stray.

divan /divɑ̃/ *nm* **1** (siège) divan; **2** Hist (salle) divan; **3**○ (d'analyste) (shrink's) couch; **passer** or **s'allonger sur le ~** to go to see a psychoanalyst; **mettre qch sur le ~** to analyze sth closely.

dive /div/ *adj f* **la ~ bouteille** hum the bottle○; **être porté sur la ~ bouteille** to be fond of the bottle○.

divergence /divɛʀʒɑ̃s/ *nf* **1** (d'opinions, de points de vue) divergence; **des ~s d'intérêts** divergences of interest; **des ~s politiques/idéologiques** political/ideological differences; **~ de goûts/au sein d'un parti** differences of taste/within a party; **2** Sci divergence.

divergent, **~e** /divɛʀʒɑ̃, ɑ̃t/ *adj* lit, fig divergent.

diverger /divɛʀʒe/ [13] *vi* **1** (être en désaccord) [*idées, intérêts, points de vue*] to diverge (**de** from); [*lois, goûts*] to differ (**de** from; **sur** on); **les règlements divergent d'un pays à l'autre** regulations differ from one country to another; **les témoignages divergent sur l'heure à laquelle le suspect a été vu** testimonies differ as to the time at which the suspect was seen; **2** (se séparer) [*lignes, voies, rayons*] to diverge; **3** Nucl [*réacteur*] to go critical.

divers, **~e** /divɛʀ, ɛʀs/ **I** *adj* **1** (varié) various, diverse; (plusieurs) various, several; **pour des raisons ~es** for various reasons; **pour des raisons très ~es** for very diverse reasons; **par des moyens ~** by various ou diverse means; **des styles/matériaux ~** diverse styles/materials; **les ~ aspects/résultats** the various aspects/results; **les résultats des ~es entreprises** the results of the various companies; **selon ~es sources** according to various ou several sources; **à ~es reprises** on various ou several occasions; **en ~ endroits** in various ou several places; **elle connaît les gens les plus ~** she knows all sorts of people; **2** (indéfini) [*frais*] miscellaneous; **dépenses ~es** sundries; **3** liter (nuancé) [*paysage*] varied; **le film a été accueilli avec un intérêt ~** the film was met with varying degrees of interest.

II *nmpl* (rubrique) miscellaneous.

■ **~ droite** Pol *minor right-wing parties*; **~ gauche** Pol *minor left-wing parties.*

diversement /divɛʀsəmɑ̃/ *adv* variously, in different ways; **le film a été ~ accueilli** the film had a mixed reception.

diversification /divɛʀsifikasjɔ̃/ *nf* diversification; **une politique de ~** a policy of diversification; **une entreprise en voie de ~** a company in the process of diversifying; **la ~ des exportations/produits/investissements** export/product/investment diversification; **une ~ de la clientèle** targeting a wider clientele; **des efforts de ~** efforts at diversification; **la ~ de ses activités a permis à l'entreprise de se développer** by diversifying its activities, the company has been able to develop.

diversifier /divɛʀsifje/ [2] **I** *vtr* **1** (varier) [*personne*] to vary [*occupations, méthodes, lectures, intérêts*]; [*entreprise*] to widen the range of, to diversify [*produits, activités, services*]; to widen [*clientèle*]; [*personne, entreprise*] to diversify [*investissements*]; **des méthodes diversifiées** varied methods; **des produits diversifiés** a wide range of products; **2** Assur to spread [*risques*].

II se diversifier *vpr* [*entreprise*] to diversify; [*produits, activités*] to be diversified.

diversion /divɛʀsjɔ̃/ *nf* **1** Mil diversion; **une manœuvre de ~** a diversionary move; **une tentative de ~** an attempt at diversion; **faire ~** to create a diversion; **2** liter (distraction) diversion, distraction; **trouver une ~ à son ennui** to find something to take one's mind off one's boredom; **pour faire ~, elle offrit du café** she created a diversion by serving coffee.

diversité /divɛʀsite/ *nf* (de personnes, paysages) diversity; (de couleurs, produits, cultures) diversity, variety; (de goûts, d'opinions, intérêts) variety, range; **les ~s ethniques/culturelles** ethnic/cultural diversity; **ils tirent leur force de leur ~** their strength lies in their diversity.

divertir /divɛʀtiʀ/ [3] **I** *vtr* **1** (distraire) (en occupant) to entertain; (en amusant) to amuse [*personne*]; (en changeant les idées) **~ qn** to take sb's mind off things; **le film nous a divertis** we thoroughly enjoyed the film; **2** Jur (détourner) to misappropriate [*fonds, argent, héritage*].

II *vi* to entertain; **le spectacle n'a d'autre ambition que de ~** the show aims purely to entertain.

III se divertir *vpr* [*personne, enfant*] (en s'amusant) to amuse oneself; (en prenant du bon temps) to enjoy oneself; **nous nous sommes bien divertis** we really enjoyed ourselves; **se ~ de qch** to be amused by sth; **faire qch pour se ~** (en jouant, plaisantant) to do sth for fun; (à cause d'ennuis, de problèmes) to do sth to take one's mind off things.

divertissant, **~e** /divɛʀtisɑ̃, ɑ̃t/ *adj* [*personne, activité, jeu, spectacle*] (qui fait rire) amusing; (qui occupe) entertaining; (plaisant) enjoyable.

divertissement /divɛʀtismɑ̃/ *nm* **1** (action) entertainment ¢; **être chargé du ~ des enfants/vieillards** to be in charge of entertaining the children/old people; **la puissance de ~ du roman** the entertainment value of the novel; **2** (distraction) recreation; **la reliure et la photo sont mes ~s favoris** bookbinding and photography are my favourite[GB] recreations; **3** Mus divertimento, divertissement; Théât divertissement; **4** Jur misappropriation.

dividende /dividɑ̃d/ *nm* **1** Fin dividend; **les ~s des actions** dividends from shares, share dividends; **verser/toucher des ~s** to pay out/to receive dividends; **2** Math dividend.

divin, **~e** /divɛ̃, in/ **I** *adj* **1** (de Dieu) divine; **2** (merveilleux) [*temps, écriture, musique, robe, vin*] divine; **tu es ~e ainsi** you look divine; **il y a quelque chose de ~ dans ta musique** there's something divine about your music; **le ~ Mozart** the divine Mozart.

II *nm* **le ~** the divine.

■ **le ~ Enfant** the Holy Child; **la ~e Providence** divine Providence; **le ~ Sauveur** the Divine Saviour[GB]

divinateur, **-trice** /divinatœʀ, tʀis/ *adj* **instinct ~** intuition; **puissance divinatrice** powers of divination.

divination /divinasjɔ̃/ *nf* divination.

divinatoire /divinatwaʀ/ *adj* divinatory.

divinement /divinmɑ̃/ *adv* [*chanter, jouer*] divinely; **elle est ~ belle** she's divinely beautiful.

divinisation /divinizasjɔ̃/ *nf* deification.

diviniser /divinize/ [1] *vtr* (tous contextes) to deify.

divinité /divinite/ *nf* **1** (être divin) deity; **~ agraire** agricultural deity; **2** Relig (nature) divinity; **la ~ du Christ** the divinity of Christ.

divisé, ~e /divize/ **I** *pp* ▶ **diviser**.
II *pp adj* **1** (désuni) [*communauté, opposition*] divided (**sur** over); **l'entreprise semble très ~e sur sa stratégie financière** the company seems very divided over its financial strategy; **2** (séparé) divided (**en** into); **l'exposition est ~e en deux parties** the exhibition is divided into two parts.

diviser /divize/ [1] **I** *vtr* **1** (désunir) to divide; **question qui divise l'opinion** issue which divides opinion; **~ pour régner** divide and rule; **2** (séparer) to divide (**en** into; **entre** between); **~ en trois groupes** to divide into three groups; **~ en deux/dix** to divide in two/ten; **3** Math to divide (**par** by).
II se diviser *vpr* **1** (se désunir) to become divided (**sur** over); **2** (être divisible) **la liberté ne se divise pas** freedom is indivisible; **3** (être séparé) to be divided (**en** into); **le dictionnaire se divise en deux parties** the dictionary is divided into two parts; **se ~ en deux/dix** to be divided into two/ten; **4** Math to be divisible (**par** by); **trente se divise par cinq** thirty is divisible by five; **5** (se ramifier) [*cellule, branche, fleuve*] to divide; [*route*] to fork.

diviseur /divizœʀ/ *nm* Math divisor.

divisibilité /divizibilite/ *nf* Math, Phys divisibility.

divisible /divizibl/ *adj* [*immeuble, nombre, élément*] divisible.

division /divizjɔ̃/ *nf* **1** (désunion) division (**sur** over); **~ du pays/de la population sur les questions sociales** division in the country/among the population over social issues; **~s internes** internal divisions; **2** (répartition) division (**en** into; **entre** between); **~ en salles de classe** division into classrooms; **3** Entr (service) division; **~ communication/environnement** communications/environmental division; **4** Sport division; **jouer en deuxième ~** to play in the second division; **5** Mil division; **6** Math division ¢ (**par** by); **apprendre à faire des ~s** to learn to do division; **faire une erreur de ~** to make a mistake in the division; **ta ~ est fausse** your division is wrong; **~ harmonique** harmonic division; **7** (graduation, partie) division; **la seconde est une ~ de la minute** the second is a division of the minute.
■ **~ blindée, DB** Mil armoured[GB] division; **~ cellulaire** Biol cell division; **~ d'infanterie** Mil infantry division; **~ légère blindée** Mil light armoured[GB] division; **~ militaire territoriale** Mil military region; **~ du travail** Écon division of labour[GB].

divisionnaire /divizjɔnɛʀ/ *adj* **commissaire ~** Admin ≈ Chief Superintendent; **inspecteur de police ~** Admin ≈ detective chief inspector; **monnaie ~** Fin fractional currency.

divorce /divɔʀs/ *nm* **1** Jur divorce (**d'avec** from); **prononcer le ~ entre deux époux** to grant a divorce to a couple; **demander/obtenir le ~** to ask for/to obtain a divorce; **faire une demande en ~** to file for (a) divorce, to file a petition for divorce; **~ par consentement mutuel** divorce by mutual agreement; **~ aux torts de l'un des deux époux** divorce pronounced against one party; **gagner le ~** to win a divorce suit; **être en instance de ~** to be getting divorced ou a divorce; **2** fig (rupture) divorce (**entre** between).

divorcé, ~e /divɔʀse/ **I** *pp* ▶ **divorcer**.
II *pp adj* divorced.
III *nm,f* divorcee.

divorcer /divɔʀse/ [12] *vi* **1** Jur to divorce; **il a divorcé d'avec** or **de sa femme** he has divorced his wife; **elle veut ~** she wants a divorce ou to divorce him; **ils veulent ~** they want a divorce ou to get divorced; **nous sommes divorcés depuis deux ans** we have been divorced for two years; **2** fig (rompre) [*personne, parti, entreprise*] to split (**d'avec, de** from); **les deux entreprises ont divorcé** the two companies have split.

divulgation /divylgasjɔ̃/ *nf* disclosure.

divulguer /divylge/ [1] **I** *vtr* to disclose, to divulge.
II se divulguer *vpr* to become known.

dix /dis, *but before consonant* di, *before vowel* diz/ ▶ 545, 407, 212 *adj inv, pron* ten; ▶ **pied**.
IDIOMES **ne rien savoir faire de ses ~ doigts** to be useless, to be good for nothing; **un de perdu, ~ de retrouvés** Prov there's plenty more fish in the sea Prov.

dix-huit /dizɥit/ ▶ 545, 407, 212 *adj inv, pron* eighteen.

dix-huitième /dizɥitjɛm/ ▶ 212, 545 *adj* eighteenth.

dixième /dizjɛm/ ▶ 212, 545 **I** *adj* tenth.
II *nf* Scol *second year of primary school, age 7–8.*

dix-neuf /diznœf/ ▶ 545, 407, 212 *adj inv, pron* nineteen.

dix-neuvième /diznœvjɛm/ ▶ 212, 545 *adj* nineteenth.

dix-sept /dis(s)ɛt/ ▶ 545, 407, 212 *adj inv, pron* seventeen.

dix-septième /dis(s)ɛtjɛm/ ▶ 212, 545 *adj* seventeenth.

dizain /dizɛ̃/ *nm* Littérat ten-line poem.

dizaine /dizɛn/ *nf* **1** (nombre) ten; **la colonne des ~s** the tens column; **2** (environ dix) about ten; **il y a une ~ de kilomètres** it's about ten kilometres[GB]; **il a une ~ d'années** he's about ten; **il y a une ~ d'années** about ten years ago; **ça a duré une bonne ~ d'années** it went on for over ten years; **nous étions une ~** there were about ten of us; **il y a une ~ de pages** there are about ten pages; **plus d'une ~ de victimes** at least ten casualties; **des ~s de personnes** dozens of people; **les victimes se comptent par ~s** there are dozens of casualties; ▶ **cinquantaine 1**.

djellaba /dʒɛlaba/ *nf* jellaba.

Djibouti /dʒibuti/ ▶ 857, 321 *npr* Djibouti.

djinn /dʒin/ *nm* djinn, jinni.

dm *written abbr* = **décimètre 1**.

DM ▶ 46 (*written abbr* = **Deutsche Mark**) DM.

do /do/ *nm inv* Mus (note) C; (en solfiant) doh.

doberman /dɔbɛʀman/ *nm* Doberman (pinscher).

doc /dɔk/ **I** *nm* CD-ROM.
II○ *nf* information, literature.

docile /dɔsil/ *adj* [*animal, personne, élève*] docile, obedient; péj submissive; [*cheveux*] manageable; **il est d'un caractère ~** he's docile.

docilement /dɔsilmɑ̃/ *adv* [*écouter*] obediently; [*sourire, obéir*] meekly.

docilité /dɔsilite/ *nf* (d'animal, enfant) obedience; (d'employé, adhérent) docility, obedience.

dock /dɔk/ *nm* **1** (bassin de chargement) dock; **2** (entrepôt) warehouse.

docker /dɔkɛʀ/ ▶ 510 *nm* docker.

docte /dɔkt/ *adj* [*ton, réflexions, personne*] learned, erudite.

doctement /dɔktəmɑ̃/ *adv* learnedly, eruditely.

docteur /dɔktœʀ/ ▶ 813 *nm* **1** (en médecine) doctor, GP GB; **le ~ Lagrange** Doctor Lagrange; **jouer au ~** to play doctors and nurses; **2** Univ Doctor; **~ en médecine/droit** Doctor of Medicine/Law; **elle est ~ ès sciences** she has a doctorate in science; **J.P. Bon, ~ ès lettres** J.P. Bon, PhD.
■ **~ de l'Église** Relig Doctor of the Church; **~ de la Loi** Relig Doctor of the Law.

doctoral, ~e, *mpl* **-aux** /dɔktɔʀal, o/ *adj* **1** (pédant) péj [*air, ton*] pompous; **2** Univ [*études, formation*] doctoral.

doctoralement /dɔktɔʀalmɑ̃/ *adv* pej pompously.

doctorat /dɔktɔʀa/ *nm* PhD, doctorate (**ès, en** in).

doctoresse† /dɔktɔʀɛs/ ▶ 510 *nf* (female) doctor.

doctrinaire /dɔktʀinɛʀ/ **I** *adj* [*attitude*] doctrinaire pej; [*ton*] sententious; [*discussion*] doctrinal.
II *nmf* doctrinaire.

doctrinal, ~e, *mpl* **-aux** /dɔktʀinal, o/ *adj* [*revirement, référence*] Relig doctrinal; Pol ideological.

doctrine /dɔktʀin/ *nf* doctrine.

docudrame /dɔkydʀam/ *nm* docudrama.

document /dɔkymɑ̃/ *nm* **1** (pour information, témoignage) document (**sur** on); **~s écrits/photographiques/d'archive** written/photographic/archive documents; **~s secrets** secret documents; **~ sonore/vidéo** audio/video material ¢; **prouver qch avec ~s à l'appui** to prove sth by means of documentary evidence; **l'exposition est un ~ extraordinaire sur notre époque** the exhibition is an extraordinary record ou chronicle of our times; **2** (papier officiel) document, paper; **faux ~s** false documents ou papers; **3** Scol, Univ **vous n'avez droit à aucun ~ pour cette épreuve** no books or notes are allowed for this exam.
■ **~s de bord** Naut ship's papers ou documents.

documentaire /dɔkymɑ̃tɛʀ/ **I** *adj* [*caractère, intérêt*] documentary (*épith*); [*centre, système*] information (*épith*); **à titre ~** for your information.
II *nm* documentary (**sur** on, about).

documentaliste /dɔkymɑ̃talist/ ▶ 510 *nmf* Presse, Entr information officer; TV researcher; Scol (school) librarian.

documentation /dɔkymɑ̃tasjɔ̃/ *nf* **1** (documents) material, information (**sur** on); **~ d'archives** archive material; **nous avons toute une ~ sur la ville** we can provide information ou literature about the town; **2** (information) research; **leur analyse est basée sur une ~ solide** their analysis is based on solid research; **3** (brochures) brochures (*pl*) (**sur** on); **j'ai pris de la ~ pour les vacances** I picked up some holiday GB ou travel brochures; **tous les participants recevront une ~ sur la ville** all the participants will be given an information pack about the city; **4** (activité) Entr information; Presse, TV research; **service de ~** Entr information unit; Presse, TV research unit; **centre de ~** resource centre[GB]; **5** Scol **la ~** the (school) library; **6** Univ (discipline) studies in librarianship.

documenter /dɔkymɑ̃te/ [1] **I** *vtr* **1** (fournir des renseignements à) to provide [sb] with information [*chercheur*]; **elle est mal documentée sur ce sujet** she hasn't got much information on that subject; **2** (fournir des renseignements pour) to research; **une thèse bien documentée** a well-researched thesis.
II se documenter *vpr* **se ~ sur qch** to research sth, to gather information ou material on sth.

dodécaèdre /dɔdekaɛdʀ/ *nm* dodecahedron.

dodécagone /dɔdekagɔn/ *nm* dodecagon.

dodécaphonique /dɔdekafɔnik/ *adj* Mus twelve-tone (*épith*), dodecaphonic.

dodeliner /dɔdline/ [1] *vi* **il dodelinait de**

la tête his head was nodding; **s'endormir en dodelinant de la tête** to nod off.

dodo /dodo/ *nm* **1** baby talk **faire ~** to sleep; **c'est l'heure d'aller faire ~** it's time for beddy-byes langage enfantin, it's bedtime; **chut! fais ~** sssh! go to sleep; **au ~!** off to bed!; **2** Zool dodo.

dodu, **-e** /dɔdy/ *adj* [*personne, épaule, volaille*] plump; [*bébé, joue*] chubby.

doge /dɔʒ/ *nm* doge.

dogmatique /dɔgmatik/ *adj* dogmatic.

dogmatiquement /dɔgmatikmɑ̃/ *adv* dogmatically.

dogmatiser /dɔgmatize/ [1] *vi* to dogmatize (**sur** about).

dogmatisme /dɔgmatism/ *nm* dogmatism.

dogme /dɔgm/ *nm* dogma.

dogue /dɔg/ *nm* mastiff.

doigt /dwa/ ▶**188** *nm* **1** Anat finger; **compter sur ses ~s** to count on one's fingers; **petit ~** little finger GB, pinkie US; **le petit ~ sur la couture du pantalon** fig standing to attention; **lever le ~** to put one's hand up; **bout des ~s** fingertips (*pl*); **du bout des ~s** lit with one's fingertips; fig reluctantly; **être français jusqu'au bout des ~s** to be French through and through; **sur le bout des ~s** lit on one's fingertips; **connaître une ville sur le bout des ~s** to know a city like the back of one's hand; **savoir son vocabulaire sur le bout des ~s** to know one's vocabulary off pat; **désigner** or **montrer du ~** lit to point at; fig to point the finger at; **mettre le ~ sur qch** lit, fig to put one's finger on sth; **tu as mis le ~ dessus** you put your finger on it; **toucher du ~** (vraiment sentir) to experience at first hand; (atteindre) to come close to touching; ▶**bague**, **dix**, **obéir**, **plaie**; **2** (de gant) finger; **3** Mes finger; **mettez-moi deux ~s de vodka** pour me two fingers of vodka.

■ **~ de dieu** Relig hand of God; **~ de pied** Anat toe; ▶**éventail**.

IDIOMES **se brûler les ~s** to get one's fingers burned; **ça se compte sur les ~s de la** or **d'une main** it can be counted on the fingers of one hand; **croiser les ~s** to cross one's fingers; **être à deux ~s de qch/faire** to be a whisker away from sth/doing; **filer entre les ~s** [*affaire, argent, voleur*] to slip through one's fingers; [*temps*] to slip away from sb; **ne pas lever le petit ~** not to lift a finger (**pour qn** for sb; **pour faire** to do); **mon petit ~ me dit que** a little bird tells me that; ; **se mordre les ~s d'avoir fait** to kick oneself for having done; **s'en mordre les ~s** to kick oneself over it; **les ~s dans le nez**○ standing on one's head; **se mettre**○ or **fourrer**◑ **le ~ dans l'œil** (**jusqu'au coude**) to be seriously mistaken; **se faire taper sur les ~s** to get one's knuckles rapped.

doigté /dwate/ *nm* **1** (diplomatie) tact; **faire preuve de/manquer de/demander du ~** to show/to be lacking in/to call for tact; **avoir du ~** to be tactful; **2** (adresse manuelle) light touch; **avoir du ~** to have a light touch; **manquer de ~** to be heavy-handed; **3** Mus fingering.

doigtier /dwatje/ *nm* fingerstall; **~ en latex** rubber fingerstall.

doléance /dɔleɑ̃s/ *nf* complaint; **faire** or **présenter ses ~** to present a list of one's grievances.

dolent, **~e** /dɔlɑ̃, ɑ̃t/ *adj* [*air, voix, personne*] doleful; [*ville*] lifeless.

dolichocéphale /dɔlikosefal/ *adj, nmf* dolichocephalic.

doline /dɔlin/ *nf* sinkhole.

dollar /dɔlaʀ/ ▶**46** *nm* dollar.

dolmen /dɔlmɛn/ *nm* dolmen.

dolomie /dɔlɔmi/ *nf* dolomite.

Dolomites /dɔlɔmit/ ▶**692** *nfpl* **les ~** the Dolomites.

DOM /dɔm/ *nm inv* (*abbr* = **département d'outre-mer**) *French overseas (administrative) department.*

domaine /dɔmɛn/ **I** *nm* **1** (terres) estate; **ils possèdent un vaste ~ dans le Sud-Ouest** they own a large estate in the South West; **~ vinicole** vineyards (*pl*); **2** (spécialité) field, domain; **dans le ~ financier/philosophique** in the field of finance/philosophy; **la mécanique, ce n'est pas mon ~** mechanics is not my field; **dans tous les ~s** in every field ou domain; **3**○ (territoire) **l'atelier/le grenier c'est mon ~ (réservé)** the workshop/the attic is my territory; **4** Admin **le Domaine** state(-owned) property; **appartenir au Domaine** to be owned by the State.

II Domaines *nmpl*: *government department which manages state-owned land and property.*

■ **~ public** public domain; **tomber dans le ~ public** Jur [*œuvres d'art, invention*] to be in the public domain; [*œuvre littéraire*] to be out of copyright; **~ réservé** Pol, Jur reserved domain.

domanial, **~e**, *mpl* **-iaux** /dɔmanjal, o/ *adj* [*forêt, terrain, biens*] state-owned (*épith*).

dôme /dom/ *nm* dome; **une tente ~** a dome tent.

domestication /dɔmɛstikasjɔ̃/ *nf* **1** (d'un animal) domestication; **2** (d'une énergie) harnessing.

domesticité /dɔmɛstisite/ *nf* **1** (ensemble des domestiques) (household) staff; **2** (condition de domestique) domestic service.

domestique /dɔmɛstik/ **I** *adj* **1** (qui concerne la maison) [*soucis, vie, économie, tâche*] domestic; **le personnel ~** domestic staff; **les travaux ~s** housework; **les accidents ~s** accidents in the home; **2** (domestiqué) [*animal*] domestic; **3** Écon, Ind (concernant un pays) [*marché, consommation*] domestic, home.

II *nmf* servant, domestic; **je ne suis pas ton ~** I'm not your slave ou skivvy○ GB.

domestiquer /dɔmɛstike/ [1] *vtr* **1** (apprivoiser) to domesticate [*animal, espèce*]; **2** (maîtriser) to harness [*électricité, atome, marée*]; **3** (assujettir) to subjugate [*peuple*].

domicile /dɔmisil/ **I** *nm* (d'une personne) place of residence, domicile; (d'une société) registered address; **ils ont regagné leur ~** they went back home; **changer de ~** to move (house); **dernier ~ connu** last known address; **avoir un hôpital à proximité de son ~** to live near ou within easy reach of a hospital; **élire ~ quelque part** lit, fig to take up residence somewhere; ▶**sans**.

II à domicile *loc adj* **travail à ~** working at ou from home; **donner des soins à ~** to give home care; **victoire de Bordeaux à ~** Sport home win for Bordeaux; **'livraisons à ~'** 'home deliveries'.

III à domicile *loc adv* **livrer à ~** to do home deliveries; **masser/coiffer à ~** to do home visits GB ou to make house calls US for massage/hairdressing; **travailler à ~** to work at home.

■ **~ conjugal** marital home; **~ légal** permanent residence; **~ fiscal** *address for tax purposes.*

domiciliaire /dɔmisiljɛʀ/ *adj* Jur **visite ~** domiciliary visit; **perquisition ~** house search.

domiciliation /dɔmisiljasjɔ̃/ *nf* Fin domiciliation.

domicilié, **~e** /dɔmisilje/ **I** *pp* ▶**domicilier**.

II *pp adj* **être ~ à Arras** to live in Arras; Admin to be resident in Arras; **M. Pons, ~ 17 rue Roland**... Mr Pons, currently residing at 17 rue Roland...; **j'habite à Paris, mais je suis ~e à Rennes** I live in Paris, but my official address is in Rennes.

domicilier /dɔmisilje/ [2] *vtr* (**faire**) **~ ses factures** to have one's bills paid by banker's order; **faire ~ ses effets de commerce** to have one bills of exchange domiciled.

dominance /dɔminɑ̃s/ *nf* dominance.

dominant, **~e** /dɔminɑ̃, ɑ̃t/ **I** *adj* **1** (principal) [*couleur, ton, idéologie, rôle*] dominant; [*thème*] main; [*courant, vent, tendance, opinion*] prevailing; [*trait, idée, impression*] main; **2** (au pouvoir) [*classe*] ruling; **3** Biol [*caractère, gène*] dominant.

II dominante *nf* **1** (trait caractéristique) dominant feature; **2** (couleur) main colour[GB]; **à ~e bleue** mainly blue; **3** Mus dominant (note); **septième de ~e** dominant seventh (chord); **4** Univ main subject, major US; **j'ai pris l'anglais en ~e** I took English as my main subject, I majored in English US; **faire des études à ~e littéraire** to study mainly arts subjects.

dominateur, **-trice** /dɔminatœʀ, tʀis/ **I** *adj* [*personne*] domineering; [*caractère, manières, attitude*] overbearing; [*geste, ton, voix*] imperious.

II *nm,f* ruler.

domination /dɔminasjɔ̃/ *nf* domination; **être sous la ~ de** to be dominated by; **pays sous ~ étrangère** (influence) country dominated by a foreign power; (autorité) country under foreign rule; **la ~ de l'Europe par les Romains** the Romans' domination of Europe; **le pays était autrefois sous (la) ~ turque** the country was formerly under Turkish rule; **il est sous la ~ de sa femme** he's completely under his wife's thumb.

dominer /dɔmine/ [1] **I** *vtr* **1** (surplomber) [*maison, montagne*] to dominate [*ville, vallée*]; (dépasser) [*gratte-ciel, sommet*] to tower above [*quartier, montagnes*]; **de là, on domine toute la vallée** from there you get a view of the whole valley; **du haut de la tour, on domine toute la ville** from the top of the tower, you get a view of the whole town; **il est tellement grand qu'il domine tout le monde** he's so tall that he towers over everyone; **2** (s'imposer dans, contre) to dominate [*match, sport, débat*]; to overshadow [*adversaire, équipe*]; **il a dominé le cyclisme mondial pendant dix ans** he dominated world cycling for ten years; **il domine de loin les autres concurrents** he completely overshadows the other competitors; **ils ont été dominés pendant la première mi-temps** they were outplayed in the first half; **3** (prévaloir dans) [*idée, thème, problème*] to dominate [*œuvre, débat*]; **les questions monétaires ont dominé le débat** monetary issues dominated the debate; **4** (maîtriser) to master [*langue, technique, sujet, émotion*]; to overcome [*peur, timidité*]; to control [*colère*]; **~ la situation** to be in control of the situation; **il se laisse ~ par ses passions** his heart rules his head; **5** (avoir la haute main sur) to dominate [*marché, secteur*]; **~ l'économie mondiale** to dominate the world economy; **il est dominé par son frère** he's dominated by his brother; **il se laisse ~ par sa femme** he's hen-pecked; **6** Pol (gouverner) to rule [*pays*]; **leur rêve était de ~ le monde** their dream was to rule the world.

II *vi* **1** (exercer son pouvoir) [*pays, peuple*] to rule, to hold sway; **2** (être en tête) [*équipe, sportif, concurrent*] to be in the lead; **il a dominé pendant toute la course** he was in the lead throughout the race; **elle a dominé pendant les deux premiers sets** she led during the first two sets; **3** (prévaloir) [*impression, idée*] to prevail; [*couleur, goût, parfum*] to stand out; **tel est le sentiment qui domine dans l'opinion publique** this is the prevailing public mood; **c'est le cassis qui domine** the flavour[GB] is mainly blackcurrant; **c'est la persévérance qui domine chez lui** his chief characteristic is perseverance.

III se dominer *vpr* [*personne*] to control oneself.

dominicain, **~e** /dɔminikɛ̃, ɛn/ *adj* **1**

▶ 537 Dominican; **République ~e** Dominican Republic; **2** Relig Dominican.

Dominicain, **~e** /dɔminikɛ̃, ɛn/ *nm,f* **1** ▶ 537 Géog Dominican; **2** Relig Dominican.

dominical, **~e**, *mpl* **-aux** /dɔminikal, o/ *adj* [*repos, promenade, messe*] Sunday (*épith*).

dominion /dɔminjɔ̃/ *nm* Dominion.

Dominique /dɔminik/ ▶ 416, 321 *nprf* Dominica.

domino /dɔmino/ *nm* **1** ▶ 449 Jeux domino; **jouer aux ~s** to play dominoes; **2** (déguisement) domino.

dommage /dɔmaʒ/ *nm* **1** (chose regrettable) (**quel**) **~!** what a shame ou pity!; **c'est ~** it's a shame ou pity (**de faire** to do; **que** that); **c'est très** ou **vraiment ~** it's a great shame ou pity; **il serait ~ que** it would be a shame ou pity if; **c'est pas ~**○! iron great! iron; **2** (dégât) damage ¢; **~s importants** severe damage; **subir des ~s** to suffer damage; **causer des ~s à** to damage; **3** Jur (préjudice) tort; **~ causé à un tiers** third-party damage.

■ **~s corporels** personal injury ¢; **~s immatériels** special damage ¢; **~s matériels** material damage; **~s et intérêts** Jur damages; **il a touché 10 000 francs de ~s et intérêts** he was awarded 10,000 francs in damages ou damages of 10,000 francs; **~s de guerre** Jur war damage ¢.

dommageable /dɔmaʒabl/ *adj* harmful (**pour** to).

dommages-intérêts /dɔmaʒɛ̃teʀɛ/ *nmpl* damages; **10 000 francs de ~** 10,000 francs in damages.

domotique /dɔmɔtik/ *nf* home automation.

domptable /dɔ̃tabl/ *adj* tamable.

domptage /dɔ̃taʒ/ *nm* taming (**de** of).

dompter /dɔ̃te/ [1] *vtr* to tame [*fauve, nature, eaux*]; to bring [sb] to heel [*indiscipliné*]; to crush, to put down [*insurgés, insurrection*]; to overcome, to master [*orgueil, passion*].

dompteur, **-euse** /dɔ̃tœʀ, øz/ ▶ 510 *nm,f* tamer; **~ de lions** lion tamer.

DOM-TOM /dɔmtɔm/ *nmpl* (*abbr* = **départements et territoires d'outre-mer**) *French overseas administrative departments and territories.*

don /dɔ̃/ *nm* **1** (donation) donation; **~s en argent** cash donations; **~s pour la recherche** donations for research; **~s des particuliers** private donations; **faire ~ de** to give [*amour, corps, œuvre*] (**à** to); **~ de soi** self-sacrifice; **2** (talent) gift; **avoir le ~ des langues** to have a gift for ou the gift of languages; **avoir le ~ de faire** to have a talent for doing; **il a le ~ de m'énerver** he has a special talent for getting on my nerves.

■ **~ du sang** blood donation.

DON /deoɛn/ *nm*: *abbr* ▶ **disque**.

donataire /dɔnatɛʀ/ *nmf* donee.

donateur, **-trice** /dɔnatœʀ, tʀis/ *nm,f* donor.

donation /dɔnasjɔ̃/ *nf* **1** (cadeau) donation; **2** Jur gift.

donation-partage, *pl* **donations-partages** /dɔnasjɔ̃paʀtaʒ/ *nf* settlement (by deed).

donc /dɔ̃k/ *conj* **1** (indiquant une conséquence) so; (plus soutenu) therefore; (dans une déduction logique, un syllogisme) therefore; **il n'y avait pas de trains, ils sont ~ partis en voiture** there were no trains, so they left by car; **il avait une réunion, il n'a ~ pas pu venir** he had a meeting, so ou therefore he was unable to come; **nous ne disposons que de très peu de temps, il est ~ important de faire vite** we've got very little time, so ou therefore we've got to act quickly; **l'entreprise perdait de l'argent, il a ~ décidé de vendre** the company was losing money, so ou therefore he decided to sell up; **je pense ~ je suis** I think, therefore I am; **si ce n'est (pas) toi, c'est ~ ton frère** if it wasn't you, then it must have been your brother; **2** (marquant la surprise) so; **c'est ~ pour ça qu'il n'est pas venu!** so that's why he didn't come!; **3** (après interruption, digression) so; **nous disions ~?** so, where were we?; **j'étais ~ en train de lire, lorsque**... so I was reading, when...; **~, pour en revenir au sujet qui nous intéresse,**... so, to come back to the subject we're dealing with,...; **je disais ~ que**... as I was saying...; **4** (pour renforcer une affirmation, un ordre, une question) **laissez-moi ~ tranquille!** leave me alone, won't you?; **tais-toi ~!** be quiet ou shut up○, will you?; **enlève ~ cette casquette ridicule!** come on, take off that ridiculous cap!; **entrez ~!** do come in!; **ne dis ~ pas de bêtises!** don't be silly!; **mais où est-il ~ passé?** where on earth has he gone? ; **c'est ~ là que tu habites!** so, that's where you live then!; **allons ~!** come on!; **tiens ~!** fancy that!; **quoi ~?** what was that?, come again○?; **non mais dis ~, où est-ce que tu te crois?** hey! ou say! US where do you think you are?; **dis ~, où as-tu mis le dossier?** hey! ou say! US, where did you put the file?; **eh bien dites ~!** just fancy!

dondon○ /dɔ̃dɔ̃/ *nf* **une grosse ~** péj a big fat woman.

donjon /dɔ̃ʒɔ̃/ *nm* keep, donjon.

don Juan, *pl* **dons Juans** /dɔ̃ʒɥɑ̃/ *nm* (séducteur) **c'est un vrai ~** he's a real Casanova; **jouer les dons Juans** to be a Casanova.

Don Juan /dɔ̃ʒɥɑ̃/ *npr* **1** Littérat Don Juan; **2** Mus Don Giovanni.

donjuanesque /dɔ̃ʒɥanɛsk/ *adj* [*manœuvre*] Casanova (*épith*).

donjuanisme /dɔ̃ʒɥanism/ *nm* womanizing.

donne /dɔn/ *nf* **1** (aux cartes) deal; **mauvaise** or **fausse ~** misdeal; **2** (rapport de forces) order; **nouvelle ~ économique/internationale** new economic/international order.

donné, **~e** /dɔne/ **I** *pp* ▶ **donner**.

II *pp adj* **1** (possible) **il n'est pas ~ à tout le monde de faire** not everyone can do ou is capable of doing; **il m'a été ~ de travailler avec lui** I had the chance to work with him; **2** (déterminé) [*quantité, durée, endroit, situation*] given; **à un moment ~** gén at one point; (soudain) all at once, all of a sudden; **3** (bon marché) cheap; **c'est ~!** it's a gift ou bargain!; **ce n'est pas ~!** they're not exactly giving it away!; **à ce prix-là, c'est ~!** they're practically giving it away, at that price!

III étant donné *loc adj* given; **étant ~** or **~es les circonstances** given the circumstances; **étant ~** or **~e la nature du phénomène** given the nature of the phenomenon.

IV étant donné que *loc conj* given that; **étant ~ que tout le monde est d'accord** given that everybody agrees; **étant ~ qu'il y a d'autres possibilités** given that there are other possibilities.

V donnée *nf* **1** (élément d'information) fact, element; **c'est une ~e parmi tant d'autres du problème** this is one element of the problem among many; **cette révélation va bouleverser les ~es politiques** this revelation is going to change the whole political picture; **nous n'avons aucune ~e sur cette question** we have no information on this issue; **les ~es de la psychologie/de l'embryologie** data on psychology/embryology; **2** (élément défini) data (+ *v pl* ou *sg*); **les ~es démographiques/informatiques/statistiques** demographic/computer/statistical data; **en ~es brutes** in raw data; **en ~es corrigées des variations saisonnières** Écon according to the seasonally adjusted figures; **après correction des ~es saisonnières** Écon with seasonally adjusted figures.

donner /dɔne/ [1] **I** *vtr* **1** (mettre en la possession de) to give [*livre, jouet, argent, salaire*]; **~ qch à qn** to give sth to sb, to give sb sth; **~ pour les œuvres** to give to charity; **j'ai déjà donné!** I've already made a donation!; **je donnerais beaucoup** or **cher pour savoir qui/comment** I'd give a lot to know who/how; ▶ **chat**; **2** (attribuer) to give [*nom, titre*] (**à** to); **~ un sens particulier à un mot** to give a word a particular meaning; **je lui donne 40 ans** I'd say he/she was 40; **on ne lui donne pas d'âge** you can't tell how old he is; **il me donnait du 'Maître'** he was calling me 'Maître'; **3** (faire avoir) to give [*migraine, appétit, courage, cauchemars*] (**à** to); **~ froid/faim à qn** to make sb feel cold/hungry; **4** (procurer) to give [*objet, emploi, nourriture, réponse, conseil*] (**à** to); Jeux to deal [*cartes*] (**à** to); **~ le bras/la main à qn** to give sb one's arm/hand; **~ à boire à qn** to give sb something to drink; **c'est à toi de ~** Jeux it's your deal; **~ à croire** or **penser** or **comprendre que**... to suggest that...; **~ à qn à penser/croire que**... to make sb think/believe that...; **donne-moi ton genou que j'examine cette blessure** let me see your knee so that I can look at that wound; ▶ **main**; **5** (transmettre, communiquer) to give [*renseignement*] (**à** to); **je vais vous ~ mon adresse** I'll give you my address; **elle m'a donné son rhume** she' s given me her cold; **~ l'heure à qn** to tell sb the time; **6** (confier) to give [*objet, tâche*] (**à faire** to do); **il m'a donné son chat/ses livres à garder** he gave me his cat/his books to look after; **elle donne sa fille à garder à mes parents** she has my parents look after her daughter; **j'ai donné ma voiture à réparer** I've taken my car in to be repaired; **7** (accorder) to give [*temps, moyens, autorisation*]; **je ne te donne pas deux mois pour te faire renvoyer** I'd give you less than two months before you're sacked; **~ tout son temps au club** to devote all one's time to the club; **8** (présenter) [*salle, cinéma*] to show [*film*]; [*théâtre*] to put on [*pièce*]; [*troupe*] to give [*spectacle, représentation*] ; **qu'est-ce qu'on donne au Marignan?** Cin what's showing ou on at the Marignan?; Théât what's playing at the Marignan?; **cette pièce a été donnée pour la première fois en 1951** this play was first performed in 1951; **9** (organiser) to give [*dîner, réception, gala*] (**pour qn** for sb); **10** (assurer) to give [*cours, exposé*] (**à, devant** to); **11** (considérer) to give [*personne, œuvre*] (**comme, pour** as); **les sondages le donnent en tête** the polls put him in the lead; **on donne ce texte pour authentique** this text is given as authentic; **les spécialistes le donnent comme futur champion** the experts point to him as the future champion; **12** (produire) [*aspect*] to give [*sentiment, impression*]; [*plante*] to give [*ombre*]; to produce, to yield [*fruits, jus, substance*]; [*expérience, méthode*] to produce [*résultats*]; [*procédé, éclairage, maquillage*] to give [*aspect, teinte*]; **leur intervention n'a rien donné** their intervention didn't have any effect; **elle lui a donné trois fils** she gave him three sons; **mange des carottes, ça te donnera bonne mine** eat carrots, they're good for your complexion; **13** (manifester) to show [*signes*] (**à** to); **~ des signes de faiblesse** to show signs of weakness; **14**○ (dénoncer) to grass on○ GB, to fink on○ US, to inform on [*complice*] (**à** to); **15** (entreprendre) [*troupe, infanterie, police*] **~ l'assaut à qn** to attack sb; **~ la charge contre qn** to charge at sb.

II *vi* **1** (produire) [*plante*] to produce a crop GB, to yield a crop; **le poirier va bien ~ cette année** the pear tree will produce GB ou yield a good crop this year; **2** (émettre un son) [*radio, hi-fi*] to be playing; **leur téléviseur donne à fond** their television is on full blast; **~ du cor** Chasse to sound the horn; **3** (heurter) **~ sur** ou **contre** [*personne, animal*] to run into; [*tête*] to hit; [*véhicule*] to hit, to run into; **~ de la tête** or **du front contre qch** to hit one's head against sth; **ne plus savoir où ~ de la tête** fig not to know which way to turn; **4** (être orienté) **~ sur** or **dans** [*porte, chambre, fenêtre*] (d'une hauteur) to overlook, to look out over;

(de plain-pied) to look onto [*mer, cour, rue*]; **~ au nord/sud** [*façade, pièce*] to face ou look north/south; **la cuisine donne dans le salon** the kitchen leads into the living-room; **la fenêtre donne sur la mer** the window overlooks the sea; **5** (avoir tendance à) **~ dans** to tend toward(s); **~ dans le masochisme** [*roman, film*] to tend toward(s) masochism; [*personne*] to have masochistic tendencies; **en ce moment, il donne dans la musique baroque** at the moment, he's into○ baroque music; **6** (se lancer) **~ dans une embuscade/un piège** to fall into an ambush/a trap; **7** (consacrer) **~ de soi-même** or **de sa personne** to give of oneself; **~ de soi-même pour faire/pour qch** to devote oneself to doing/to sth; **8** (attaquer) [*troupe, chars*] to attack, to go into action; **faire ~ la troupe** to send the troops into action.

III se donner *vpr* **1** (se livrer) **se ~ à** to devote oneself to [*travail, cause, peinture*]; **se ~ à fond dans qch** to give one's all to sth; **se ~ à un homme** to give oneself to a man; **2** (s'octroyer) **se ~ le temps de faire** to give oneself time to do; **se ~ les moyens de faire** to find the means to do; **pays qui se donne un nouveau président** country which is getting a new president; **il se donnait le nom de Brutus/le titre de docteur** he called himself Brutus/gave himself the title of doctor; ▶**joie**, **temps**; **3** (s'imposer) **se ~ pour** or **comme but/mission de faire** to make it one's aim/mission to do; **il se donne le détachement comme objectif** he makes it his aim to be detached; **il se donne comme objectif de perdre 15 kilos** he has set himself the target of losing 15 kilos; **se ~ pour tâche de faire** to set oneself the task of doing; **je me donne trois jours pour finir** I'll give myself three days to finish; **4** (affecter) **se ~ pour intelligent/pacifiste** to make oneself out to be intelligent/a pacifist; **il se donne pour plus compétent qu'il n'est** he makes himself out to be more competent than he really is; **elle se donne des airs de Marilyn Monroe** she walks around as if she's Marylin Monroe; **se ~ de grands airs** to give oneself airs; **un prétentieux qui se donne des airs de savant** a pretentious man who acts as if he is a scholar; **se ~ bonne conscience** to affect a clear conscience; **se ~ une nouvelle image** to give oneself a new image; **il se donne une importance qu'il n'a pas** he acts as if he's important when he isn't; **5** (échanger) **se ~ des coups** to exchange blows; **se ~ des baisers** to kiss one another; **se ~ rendez-vous** to arrange to meet; **se ~ le mot** to pass the word on; **6** (être joué) [*film*] to be showing (**à** at); [*spectacle*] to be put on (**à** at); [*pièce*] to be playing (**à** at).

IDIOMES **donnant donnant**: **je garde ton chat à Noël, tu gardes le mien à Pâques** fair's fair: I keep your cat at Christmas, you keep mine at Easter; **avec lui, c'est donnant donnant** he never does anything for nothing; **je te le donne en mille**○ you'll never guess.

donneur, **-euse** /dɔnœʀ, øz/ *nm,f* **1** Méd donor; **2** Jeux dealer; **3**○ (dénonciateur) grass○ GB, informer; **4** (personne qui aime donner) **les ~s de bons conseils/d'avis** people who like to give advice/their opinion.

■ **~ d'ordre** Fin principal; **~ d'organe** Méd organ donor; **~ d'ouvrage** Entr employer; **~ de sang** Méd blood donor; **~ de sperme** Méd sperm donor; **~ universel** Méd universal donor.

don Quichotte /dɔ̃kiʃɔt/ *npr* Don Quixote; **jouer les dons Quichottes** to be a righter of wrongs.

donquichottisme /dɔ̃kiʃɔtism/ *nm* pej quixotism péj.

dont /dɔ̃/ *pron rel*

■ **Note** Lorsque la traduction de *dont* fait intervenir une préposition en anglais, deux tournures sont possibles: *c'est un enfant dont je suis fier* = he's a child I'm proud of; = he's a child of whom I am proud. La première traduction est utilisée dans la langue courante, parlée ou écrite; la seconde traduction relève de la langue soutenue, surtout écrite, et n'est pas toujours acceptable: *le livre dont tu m'as parlé* = the book you told me about.

1 (en fonction d'objet indirect) **la jeune fille ~ on nous disait qu'elle avait 20 ans** the girl who they said was 20 ou who was said to be 20; **Sylvaine est quelqu'un ~ on se souvient** Sylvaine is somebody (that) you remember; **l'époque ~ je vous parle** the time I'm talking about; **l'argent ~ je dispose** the money (that) I have available, the money that is available to me; **la maladie ~ il souffre** the illness which he's suffering from; **2** (en fonction de complément d'un adjectif) **des élèves ~ je suis satisfait** pupils I'm satisfied with, pupils with whom I am satisfied; **des renseignements ~ nous ne sommes pas certains** information which we are not sure about ou about which we are not sure; **dans le café ~ il est voisin** in the neighbouring[GB] café; **les vieux journaux ~ leur salon est plein** the old newspapers which their living room is full of ou of which their living room is full; **3** (en fonction de complément circonstanciel) **une voix ~ elle sait admirablement se servir** a voice which she uses to wonderful effect ou she really knows how to use; **les méthodes ~ ils ont usé** the methods (that ou which) they used; **la façon** or **manière ~ elle s'habille** the way (in which) she dresses; **il s'est senti offensé par la façon ~ il avait été traité** he was offended by the way (that) he had been treated; **elle fait des recherches sur la manière ~ les affaires sont traitées** she is doing research on the way in which business is conducted; **j'avais oublié la façon ~ il m'avait traité** I had forgotten the way he ou how he had treated me; **il rentra dans la chambre ~ il était sorti cinq minutes auparavant** he came back into the room (which) he had left five minutes before; **l'arbre ~ on extrait le caoutchouc** the tree from which rubber is extracted; **la famille ~ il descend** the family from which he is descended; **4** (en fonction de complément de nom) **un document ~ l'importance n'échappe à personne** a document the importance of which ou whose importance is clear to everyone; **un canapé ~ les housses sont amovibles** a sofa the covers of which ou whose covers are removable; **un concours ~ le lauréat gagnera...** a competition the winner of which will receive...; **une ville ~ la splendeur vous coupe le souffle** a town whose splendour takes your breath away; **une personne ~ il prétend être l'ami** a person whose friend he claims to be; **une ville ~ 50% des habitants ont plus de 55 ans** a town 50% of whose inhabitants are over 55; **5** (parmi lesquels) **il y a eu plusieurs victimes ~ mon père** there were several victims, one of whom was my father; **des jeunes gens ~ plusieurs avaient les cheveux longs** young men, several of whom had long hair; **l'organisation propose diverses activités ~ le cheval, la natation et le tricot** the organization offers various activities including horse riding , swimming and knitting; **il a sélectionné quelques bouteilles ~ une pour toi** he selected a few bottles including one for you; **elle a écrit plusieurs pièces ~ la meilleure est la dernière** she has written several plays the best of which is ou the best being her latest one; **des boîtes ~ la plupart sont vides** boxes, most of which are empty.

donzelle○ /dɔ̃zɛl/ *nf* pej pretentious young woman; **qu'est-ce que c'est que cette ~?** who does she think she is?

dopage /dɔpaʒ/ *nm* (de chevaux) doping; (d'athlète) illegal drug-taking ou drug use.

dopant /dɔpɑ̃/ *nm* drug.

dope○ /dɔp/ *nf* dope○.

doper /dɔpe/ [1] **I** *vtr* **1** (administrer un dopant) to dope [*cheval, sportif*]; **je prends des vitamines pour me ~**○ **un peu** hum I take vitamins to give me a bit of a boost; **2** Fin to boost, to give [sth] a boost [*monnaie, marché, entreprise*].

II se doper○ *vpr* (se droguer) to take drugs; **se ~ aux amphétamines** to take amphetamines.

Doppler /dɔplɛʀ/ **I** *adj* **effet ~** Doppler effect.

II *nm* Méd Doppler ultrasound examination.

dorade /dɔʀad/ *nf* sea bream.

■ **~ commune** sea bream; **~ grise** black sea bream; **~ rose** red sea bream; **~ royale** gilt-head bream.

Dordogne /dɔʀdɔɲ/ ▶**357**, **692** *nprf* (rivière, département) **la ~** the Dordogne.

doré, **~e** /dɔʀe/ **I** *pp* ▶ **dorer**.

II ▶**193** *pp adj* **1** (qui rappelle l'or) [*chaussures, peinture, papier*] gold (*épith*); [*bronze*] gold-coloured[GB]; [*cadre, chaise*] gilt (*épith*); **à bout ~** gold-tipped (*épith*); **2** (avec de l'or) [*coupole*] gilded; **~ à la feuille** gilded with gold leaf; **~ à l'or fin** gilded; **~ sur tranche** [*livre*] gilt-edged (*épith*); **3** (blond cuivré) [*cheveux, lumière*] golden; [*peau*] bronzed, tanned; [*pain, poulet*] golden brown; **4** (dans la richesse) [*exil*] luxurious; **jeunesse ~e** gilded youth.

III *nm* gilt.

dorénavant /dɔʀenavɑ̃/ *adv* **1** (au présent) from now on, henceforth; **2** (au passé) from then on, henceforth.

dorer /dɔʀe/ [1] **I** *vtr* **1** (couvrir d'or) to gild [*cadre*]; **~ qch à l'or fin** to gild sth with gold leaf; **2** Culin to glaze [*tourte, pâte*]; **~ qch au jaune d'œuf** to glaze sth with beaten egg; **3** (changer la couleur de) [*soleil*] to turn [sth] to gold [*feuillage, blés*]; **sa peau est dorée par le soleil** her/his skin has turned golden brown in the sun.

II *vi* **1** Culin [*poulet*] to brown; **faire ~ qch** to brown sth; **laissez ~** cook until golden brown; **2** liter [*moissons, raisins*] to turn golden.

III se dorer *vpr* **se ~ au soleil** to sunbathe.

IDIOMES **~ la pilule à qn**○ to sugar GB ou sugarcoat US the pill for sb.

doreur, **-euse** /dɔʀœʀ, øz/ ▶**510** *nm,f* gilder.

dorien, **-ienne** /dɔʀjɛ̃, ɛn/ **I** *adj* Géog, Antiq, Mus dorian.

II *nm* Ling Doric (dialect).

dorique /dɔʀik/ *adj* [*colonne, style*] Doric.

dorloter /dɔʀlɔte/ [1] **I** *vtr* to pamper; **se faire ~** to be pampered (**par** by).

II se dorloter *vpr* to pamper oneself.

dormant, **~e** /dɔʀmɑ̃, ɑ̃t/ **I** *adj* **eaux ~es** still waters; **bâti ~** Constr fixed frame.

II *nm* Constr frame; **~ de porte/de fenêtre** door/window frame.

dormeur, **-euse** /dɔʀmœʀ, øz/ **I** *adj* [*ours, poupée*] sleeping (*épith*).

II *nm,f* (personne) sleeper; **c'est un gros ~** he sleeps a lot.

III *nm* Zool **1** (tourteau) edible crab; **2** (requin) nurse shark.

■ **~ du Groenland** Greenland shark.

dormir /dɔʀmiʀ/ [30] *vi* **1** Physiol to sleep; **il dort** he's sleeping, he's asleep; **~ profondément** to sleep soundly; **~ d'un sommeil léger/lourd** to be in a light/deep sleep; **je n'ai pas dormi de la nuit** I didn't sleep (a wink) all night; **~ en chien de fusil** to sleep curled up; **~ tout habillé** to sleep in one's clothes; **avoir envie de ~** to be sleepy; **je dormirais bien un peu** I feel like a nap; **~ debout** [*animal*] to sleep standing up; [*personne*] to be asleep on one's feet; fig (être épuisé) to be dead on one's feet; **le bruit/le café m'empêche de ~** noise/coffee keeps me awake; **il n'en dort plus** he's losing sleep over it; **que ça ne t'em-**

pêche pas de ~! don't lose any sleep over it!; **élève qui dort en classe** fig pupil who pays no attention in class; ▸**sommeil**; **2** (être au repos) to sleep; **en hiver, toute la nature dort** in winter, the whole of nature is dormant ou sleeps; **la ville dormait sous les étoiles** the town slumbered ou lay asleep under the stars; **les manuscrits dormaient dans un tiroir** the manuscripts were gathering dust in a drawer; **des toiles de maîtres dormaient dans le grenier** old masters were gathering dust in the attic; **3** Fin [*argent*] to lie idle.

IDIOMES **ne ~ que d'un œil** to sleep with one eye open; **~ sur ses deux oreilles, ~ tranquille** to rest easy; **~ comme un loir** or **une marmotte** or **une souche** or **un bienheureux** to sleep like a log; **~ à poings fermés** to be fast asleep; **la fortune vient en dormant** Prov good luck comes when you're not looking for it.

dormitif, -ive /dɔʀmitif, iv/ *adj* lit, fig soporific.

dorsal, *mpl* **-aux** /dɔʀsal, o/ **I** *adj* **1** (du dos) [*douleur, muscle*] back; [*vertèbre, nageoire*] dorsal; **2** Phon dorsal.
II dorsale *nf* **1** Géog ridge; **~e océanique** ocean ridge; **2** Météo **~e barométrique** ridge of high pressure; **3** Phon dorsal consonant.

Dorset ▸**692** *nprm* **le ~** Dorset.

dortoir /dɔʀtwaʀ/ **I** *nm* dormitory.
II (-)dortoir (*in compounds*) **banlieue-/ville-~** dormitory suburb/town.

dorure /dɔʀyʀ/ *nf* **1** (revêtement) gilt ₵; **un cadre plein de ~s** a heavily gilded frame; **2** (technique) gilding; **~ à la feuille** gilding with gold leaf.

doryphore /dɔʀifɔʀ/ *nm* Colorado beetle.

dos /do/ ▸**188** *nm* gén (d'homme, animal, de main, vêtement, siège, page) back; (de livre) spine; (de lame) blunt edge; **être sur le ~** to be (lying) on one's back; **avoir le ~ rond** or **voûté** to stoop, to have round shoulders; **mal de ~** backache; **dormir/nager sur le ~** to sleep/swim on one's back; **être à plat ~** to be flat on one's back; **voir qn de ~** to see sb from behind; **au ~ de** (chèque, carte, photo, enveloppe) on the back of; **robe décolletée dans le ~** dress with a low back; **voyager à ~ d'âne/de chameau** to travel riding on a donkey/camel; **tout le matériel a été transporté à ~ d'homme/de mulet** all the equipment was carried by people/mules; **faire qch dans** or **derrière le ~ de qn** to do sth when sb's back is turned; **ils sont arrivés, sac au ~** they arrived, with their rucksacks on their backs; **il n'a rien sur le ~**○ he's wearing hardly anything; **dès que j'ai le ~ tourné** as soon as my back is turned; **~ à ~** lit back to back; **renvoyer deux parties ~ à ~** fig to refuse to come out in favour[GB] of either party; **tourner le ~ à qn** (position) to have one's back to sb; (mouvement) to turn one's back to sb; (par mépris) to turn one's back on sb; **tourner le ~ à qch, avoir le ~ tourné à qch** (position) to have one's back to sth; **depuis son licenciement, tous ses anciens collègues lui tournent le ~** fig since he/she was made redundant, all his/her former colleagues have turned their backs on him/her; **tourner le ~ au progrès/à l'avenir** to turn one's back on progress/the future; **faire le gros ~** [*chat*] to arch its back; [*personne*] to keep one's head down; ▸**cuillère, laine, plein, sucre**.

■ **~ crawlé** back stroke; **~ nageur** Mode racer back.

IDIOMES **tomber sur le ~ de qn**○ to come down on sb like a ton of bricks○; **être sur le ~ de qn**○ to be on sb's back○; **avoir qn sur le ~**○ to have sb on one's back; **courber le ~** to bow and scrape; **mettre qch sur le ~ de qch/qn**○ to blame sth on sth/sb; **il a bon ~ le réveil/train**○! it's easy to blame it on the alarm-clock/train!; **j'ai bon ~** it's always me; **se mettre qn à ~**○ to get on the wrong side of sb; **je l'ai dans le ~**○! I'm stuck○! ; **s'enrichir sur le ~ de qn**○ to get rich at sb's expense; **passer la main dans le ~ de qn**○ to flatter sb; **faire un enfant dans le ~ à qn**○ to play a dirty trick on sb; **faire la bête à deux ~**○ to make love.

dosage /dozaʒ/ *nm* **1** Chimie, Pharm (quantité) amount, proportion; (mesure) measurement; **2** (combinaison) mix; (action de mélanger) mixing; **3** fig (contrôle) controlled use; **~ de l'ironie** controlled use of irony; **4** (proportions) proportions (*pl*); **juste ~** correct proportions.

dos-d'âne /dodan/ *nm inv* Aut, Transp hump; **pont en ~** humpback bridge.

dose /doz/ *nf* **1** Pharm, fig dose; **~ mortelle** lethal dose; **augmenter les ~s** to increase the dose; **à petites ~s** in small doses; **à ~ homéopathique** in tiny doses; **ne pas dépasser la ~ prescrite** do not exceed the stated dose; **en avoir sa ~**○ fig to have one's fill○; **2** (quantité) amount; **avoir une bonne ~ de bêtise/d'égoïsme** not to be short on stupidity/selfishness; **forcer la ~**○ to go a bit far○; **3** (mesure) measure; **deux ~s par litre** two measures per litre[GB].

IDIOMES **en tenir une bonne ~**○ to be thick as two short planks.

doser /doze/ [1] *vtr* **1** Chimie, Culin, Pharm (déterminer la quantité) to measure; (introduire une quantité) to measure out; **dosé à 100 mg** containing 100 mg (**par** per); **2** (contrôler) to use [sth] in a controlled way; **~ sa force** to use one's strength in a controlled way; **~ ses efforts** to pace oneself.

doseur, -euse /dozœʀ, øz/ **I** *adj* measuring; **verre ~** measuring glass.
II *nm* measuring glass.

dossard /dosaʀ/ *nm* number (worn by an athlete); **le ~ numéro 7** number 7.

dossier /dosje/ *nm* **1** gén file, dossier; **~ personnel** personal file; **constituer** or **établir un ~ sur qn/qch** [*détective, policier*] to draw up a file on sb/sth; [*écolier, étudiant*] to do a project on sb/sth; **faire un ~ de demande de prêt/bourse** to make an application for a loan/grant; **~ médical/scolaire** medical/school records (*pl*); **~ d'inscription** Scol, Univ registration form; **sélection sur ~** selection by written application; **2** Jur (documents) file; (affaire) case; **l'avocat connaît parfaitement son ~** the lawyer is well versed in the details of the case; **verser une pièce au ~** to add information to the file; **le ~ a été confié à Agnès** the file has been handed over to Agnès; **fermer** or **classer le ~** to close the file ou case; **3** (sujet) **le ~ brûlant/épineux de la pollution** the controversial/thorny problem of pollution; **délégué chargé du ~ agricole** delegate responsible for agricultural affairs; **notre ~ sur l'alcoolisme** Presse our (special) feature on alcoholism; **4** (classeur) file, folder; **5** (de chaise, fauteuil) back.

■ **~ de presse** press pack.

Dostoïevski /dɔstɔjɛvski/ *npr* Dostoyevsky.

dot /dɔt/ *nf* **1** (de jeune fille, religieuse) dowry; **en ~** as a dowry; **2** (contribution) contribution.

dotation /dɔtasjɔ̃/ *nf* **1** Fin, Admin (somme allouée) allocation; (matériel) endowment; **~ de fonctionnement** allocation for running costs; **~ en capital** capital endowment; **2** (revenu) (de chef d'État) salary; (de famille royale) annuities (*pl*).

doté, ~e /dɔte/ **I** *pp* ▸**doter**.
II *pp adj* **1** fig (riche) **fondation richement ~e** richly endowed foundation; **pays mal ~** poor country; **2** lit **une fille richement ~e** a girl with a large dowry.

doter /dote/ [1] **I** *vtr* **1** (accorder une somme à) **~ qn de qch** to allocate sth to sb; **le projet est doté de deux millions de francs** the project has been allocated two million francs; **2** (fournir en équipement) **~ qn/qch de** to equip sb/sth with; **l'ordinateur est doté d'un nouveau système** the computer is equipped with a new system; **3** fig (accorder) **~ qn/qch de** to endow sb/sth with; **~ qn d'un fort pouvoir** to endow sb with great power; **elle est dotée d'un grand talent** she's endowed with great talent; **la CEE est dotée d'un président** the EEC has a president.
II se doter *vpr* **se ~ de** to acquire [*revenu*]; to create, set up [*service*].

douaire /dwɛʀ/ *nm* dower.

douairière /dwɛʀjɛʀ/ *nf* dowager.

douane /dwan/ *nf* **1** (service) customs (+ *v sg* ou *pl*); **agent des ~s** customs officer; **des marchandises saisies par la ~** goods seized ou confiscated by (the) customs; **visite** or **contrôle de la ~** customs check; **zone/port sous ~** zone/port under the authority of the Customs and Excise; **2** (à la frontière) **bureau de ~** customs, customs house; **déclaration de ~** customs declaration; **attendre/se faire arrêter à la ~** to wait/to be arrested at customs; **passer (à) la ~** to go through customs; **passer des marchandises en ~** to clear goods through customs; **marchandises (entreposées) en ~** bonded goods; **3** (taxe) duty; **payer la ~, payer les droits de ~** to pay (customs) duty ou customs dues; **exempt de ~** duty- free; **soumis aux droits de ~** dutiable.

douanier, -ière /dwanje, ɛʀ/ **I** *adj* [*formalités, barrières*] customs (*épith*).
II ▸**510** *nm* customs officer.

doublage /dublaʒ/ *nm* **1** (de film, d'acteur) dubbing; **~ en français** dubbing in French; **2** (de revêtement, fil) doubling; **3** (de vêtement, cloison) lining; (de bateau) sheathing.

double /dubl/ **I** *adj* [*quantité, somme, dose, épaisseur*] double; [*consonne, étoile*] double; **une ~ vodka** a double vodka; **mener une ~ vie** to lead a double life; **à ~ effet** dual ou double action (*épith*); **évaluer le ~ effet de** to evaluate the combined effect of; **outil à ~ usage** dual-purpose tool; **voiture à ~ commande** car with dual controls; **cassette ~ durée** double-play cassette; **l'avantage est ~** the advantage is twofold; **phrase à ~ sens** sentence with a double meaning; **rue à ~ sens** two-way street; **valise à ~ fond** suitcase with a false bottom; **mouchoirs ~ épaisseur** two-ply tissues GB ou Kleenex®; **~ nationalité** dual citizenship, dual nationality; **avoir le don de ~ vue** to have second sight; **faire qch en ~ exemplaire** to make a duplicate of sth, to do sth in duplicate.
II *adv* **compter ~** to count double; **voir ~** to see double, to have double vision.
III *nm* **1** (deux fois plus) double; **c'est le ~ de ce que j'ai payé!** that's double ou twice what I paid!; **il gagne le ~ de moi** he earns twice as much as I do, he earns double what I do; **je l'ai payé le ~ du prix normal** I paid twice the usual price for it; **30 est le ~ de 15** 30 is twice 15; **leur piscine fait le ~ de la nôtre** their swimming-pool is twice as big as ours ou is twice the size of ours; **il a mis le ~ de temps pour rentrer** he took twice as long ou double the time to come home; **2** (exemplaire supplémentaire) (de facture, document, contrat) copy; (de personne) double; **je lui ai donné un ~ des clés** I gave him a spare set of keys; **faire faire un ~ des clés** to have a spare set of keys cut; **prends ce livre, je l'ai en ~** take this book, I've got two copies of it; **j'ai échangé les images que j'avais en ~** I swapped the pictures of which I had copies ou duplicates; **c'était vraiment ton ~!** he/she really was your double!; **3** Sport (au tennis) doubles (*pl*); **faire un ~** to play a doubles match; **~ dames** ladies' doubles; **~ messieurs** men's doubles; **~ mixte** mixed doubles.

doublé, ~e /duble/ **I** *pp* ▸**doubler**.
II *pp adj* **1** [*vêtement*] lined (**de** with); **2** Cin

[*film*] dubbed; **3** (en plus de) **c'est un imbécile ~ d'un lâche** he's a coward as well as a fool.

III *nm* **1** Sport (deux victoires successives) double; **réussir un beau ~** to pull off a fine double; **2** Équit **faire un ~** to change rein; **3** Mus double; **4** (en orfèvrerie) rolled gold, filled gold US.

double-blanc, *pl* **doubles-blancs** /dublǝblɑ̃/ *nm* (aux dominos) double-blank.

double-crème, *pl* **doubles-crèmes** /dublǝkʀɛm/ *nm* cream cheese.

double-fenêtre, *pl* **doubles-fenêtres** /dublǝfǝnɛtʀ/ *nf* double window.

doublement /dublǝmɑ̃/ **I** *adv* (à double titre) in two ways; **il est ~ coupable** he's doubly guilty, he's guilty on two counts.

II *nm* (de quantité, chiffres, d'effectifs) doubling.

doubler /duble/ [1] **I** *vtr* **1** (multiplier par deux) to double [*effectifs, montant, prix, capacité*]; **~ le pas** to quicken one's pace; **~ la mise** Jeux to double the stakes; fig to up the stakes; **il a doublé sa fortune en cinq ans** he doubled his fortune in five years; **2** Cout, Constr to line [*vêtement, rideau, cloison*] (**de** with); **3** (plier en deux) to fold [sth] in two [*feuille de papier, couverture*]; to double [*ficelle, fil*]; **4** Cin to dub [*film, acteur*]; **le film a été doublé en trois langues** the film has been dubbed into three languages; **5** Cin, Théât (pour remplacement) (dans une scène périlleuse, un plan secondaire) to stand in for [*acteur*]; (pour indisponibilité) to understudy [*acteur*]; **6** (dépasser) to overtake GB, to pass US [*véhicule*]; **il est dangereux de ~ dans les virages** it's dangerous to overtake GB ou pass US on bends; **'défense de ~'** 'no overtaking' GB, 'no passing' US; **~ un véhicule à droite/gauche** to overtake GB ou pass US a vehicle on the right/left; **7** Naut to double [*cap*]; **8** Mus to double; **~ une partie** to double a part; **9**○ (trahir) to double-cross [*personne*].

II *vi* **1** gén [*quantité, chiffre*] to double, to increase twofold; **le terrain a doublé de valeur en dix ans** the land doubled in value within ten years; **2** B Scol (redoubler) to repeat a year.

III se doubler *vpr* **se ~ de qch** to be coupled with sth; **son avarice se double de malhonnêteté** his/her meanness is coupled with dishonesty, he/she is dishonest as well as being mean.

doublet /dublɛ/ *nm* doublet.

doublon /dublɔ̃/ *nm* **1** (monnaie) doubloon; **2** Imprim double, doublet; **3** (faisant double emploi) duplication.

doublure /dublyʀ/ *nf* **1** Cout lining; **une ~ de soie** a silk lining; **2** Théât understudy; Cin (dans une scène périlleuse) double; (dans un plan secondaire) stand-in.

Doubs /du/ ▶357, 692 *nprm* (rivière, département) **le ~** the Doubs.

douce ▶ **doux**.

douce-amère ▶ **doux-amer**.

douceâtre /dusɑtʀ/ *adj* **1** (sucré) [*goût*] sickly sweet; **2** (fade) [*musique*] sickly, schmaltzy○; [*air*] vapid, insipid; [*paroles*] mawkish.

doucement /dusmɑ̃/ *adv* **1** (avec mesure) [*démarrer, freiner*] gently; [*caresser, se peigner*] gently, smoothly; [*faire chauffer*] gently; **il marchait ~ pour ne pas faire craquer le plancher** he walked softly so that the floorboards wouldn't creak; **holà! ~ avec le vin!** hey! go easy on the wine!; **~! je n'ai pas dit ça!** hang on a minute! I never said that!; **~, les enfants!** (calmez-vous) calm down, children!; (faites attention) careful, children!; **ça va ~, sans plus** things are so-so○; **2** (sans bruit) quietly; **ouvrir/fermer ~ une porte** to open/shut a door quietly; **il parlait si ~ qu'on l'entendait à peine** he spoke so quietly that he could scarcely be heard; **3** (lentement) [*avancer, approcher, marcher, conduire*] slowly, quietly; **il se remet (tout) ~ de son opération** he's slowly recovering from his operation; **nous nous habituons ~ à notre nouvelle maison** we're slowly ou gradually getting used to our new house; **4**○ (discrètement) **ça me fait ~ rigoler** it makes me want to laugh; **un regard ~ ironique** a mildly ironic look; **5** (progressivement) gently; **la colline descend ~ vers la rivière** the hill slopes gently down to the river; **la route monte ~ vers le village** the road climbs gently toward(s) the village; **il glisse ~ vers la dépression** he's slowly sinking into depression.

IDIOMES **~ les basses**○! calm down!

doucereux, -euse /dusʀø, øz/ *adj* pej [*manières*] smooth, unctuous; [*personne*] smooth, unctuous; [*paroles*] sugary; [*sourire*] sickly, unctuous.

doucette /dusɛt/ *nf* lamb's lettuce, corn salad.

doucettement○ /dusɛtmɑ̃/ *adv* quietly, gently; **tout ~** very quietly.

douceur /dusœʀ/ **I** *nf* **1** (de matière, tissu, cheveux, peau) softness, smoothness; (de saveur, odeur) mildness; (de fruit, vin) mellowness; (de liqueur, alcool) smoothness; (de lumière, couleur) mellowness, softness; (de musique, son) softness; **la ~ de l'amour** love's sweetness; **2** (de climat, temps, soleil) mildness; **~ de vivre** relaxed rhythm of life; **3** (de visage, traits, ton, voix, gestes, paroles) gentleness; **il est d'une grande ~ avec les enfants** he's very gentle with children; **employer la ~ avec** to use the gentle approach with, to be gentle with; **prendre qn par la ~** to deal gently with sb; **avec ~** [*parler, répondre, agir*] gently; **traiter qn avec ~** to treat sb gently; **4** (de relief, paysage) softness; (de freinage) softness, smoothness; **5** (friandise) sweet GB, candy US; **6** (mot d'amour) **dire des ~s à qn** to whisper sweet nothings to sb.

II en douceur *loc adv* [*freiner, démarrer, conduire, s'arrêter*] gently, smoothly; [*décoller, atterrir*] smoothly; **le problème/malentendu a été réglé en ~** the problem/misunderstanding was sorted out smoothly; **les négociations se sont déroulées en ~** the negotiations went smoothly; **lessive/shampooing qui lave en ~** mild ou gentle washing powder/shampoo; **la transition s'est faite en ~** it was a smooth transition.

IDIOMES **plus fait ~ que violence** Prov gentleness works better than violence.

Douchanbé /duʃambe/ ▶857 *npr* Dushanbe.

douche /duʃ/ **I** *nf* **1** (pour se laver) shower; **prendre une ~** to have GB ou take US a shower; **être sous la ~** to be in the shower; **2**○ (déception) letdown○; **la nouvelle a été pour moi une ~ froide** the news came as a terrible letdown to me; **3**○ (averse) **on a pris une de ces ~s!** we got a real soaking!

II douches *nfpl* (local) showers.

■ **~ écossaise** lit alternating hot and cold shower; fig bucket of cold water; **~ vaginale** douche.

doucher /duʃe/ [1] **I** *vtr* **1** (laver) to give [sb] a shower [*personne*]; **2**○ (calmer) to dampen [*enthousiasme*]; to cool off [*personne*]; **3**○ (mouiller) [*pluie*] to soak [*personne*]; **se faire ~** to get a soaking.

II se doucher *vpr* to take a shower.

douchette /duʃɛt/ *nf* shower head.

doudou○ /dudu/ *nm* baby talk security blanket.

doudoune○ /dudun/ **I** *nf* down jacket.

II doudounes *nfpl* boobs○, breasts.

doué, ~e /dwe/ *adj* **1** (talentueux) gifted, talented (**en** in, at); **être ~ pour** to have a gift for [*théâtre, études*]; **être ~ pour les chiffres** to have a good head for figures; **il n'est pas très ~ pour la finance** he hasn't got much of a flair for finance; **2** (pourvu) **~ de** endowed ou gifted with [*qualité*]; **il est ~ d'une bonne mémoire** he's endowed with a good memory.

douille /duj/ *nf* **1** (de cartouche) cartridge (case); **2** Électrotech socket; **~ volante** light-socket adaptor.

douillet, -ette /dujɛ, ɛt/ *adj* **1** (sensible) pej [*personne*] oversensitive to pain (*jamais épith*); **2** (confortable) [*lit, existence*] cosy GB ou cozy US, comfortable; [*intérieur, appartement*] cosy GB ou cozy US, snug.

douillettement /dujɛtmɑ̃/ *adv* [*installé, blotti*] cosily GB, cozily US, snugly.

douleur /dulœʀ/ ▶271 *nf* **1** (physique) pain; **une ~ aiguë/sourde** a sharp/dull pain; **se tordre de ~** to writhe in pain; **j'ai des ~s/une ~ dans la jambe** I've got pains/a pain in my leg, my leg hurts; **avoir des ~s dans le dos/l'oreille** to have backache/earache; **un médicament contre la ~** a painkiller; **avoir les premières ~s** to go into labour[GB]; **2** (morale) pain; (causée par un deuil) grief; **être accablé de ~** to be grief-stricken; **raviver une ancienne ~** to open an old wound; **nous avons la ~ de vous faire part du décès de** it is with great sorrow that we have to inform you of the death of.

IDIOMES **comprendre sa ~** to understand the meaning of suffering.

douloureusement /duluʀøzmɑ̃/ *adv* **1** (avec douleur morale) [*choquer, bouleverser*] terribly; [*insulter*] grievously; **ressentir ~ les conséquences de qch** fig to feel the painful effects of sth; **les pauvres ressentent plus ~ la crise** the poor have been hit harder by the recession; **2** (avec douleur physique) painfully.

douloureux, -euse /duluʀø, øz/ **I** *adj* **1** (sur l'instant) [*opération, plaie*] painful; **2** (de façon continue) [*dent, tête, ventre, vieille blessure*] aching; **de temps en temps mon bras est ~** my arm aches now and again, I get a pain in my arm now and again; **redevenir ~** to start hurting ou to hurt again; **3** (moralement) [*spectacle, événement, problème*] distressing; [*attente, décision, question*] painful; **s'attaquer au ~ problème du chômage** to tackle the painful issue of unemployment; **4** (exprimant la douleur) [*expression, sourire*] sorrowful.

II douloureuse○ *nf* bill.

doute /dut/ **I** *nm* **1** (incertitude) doubt; **laisser qn dans le ~** to leave sb in a state of uncertainty; **cela est hors de ~** it's beyond doubt; **être en prise au ~** to be beset by doubt; **le ~ m'envahit** I'm overcome by doubt; **jeter le ~ sur** to cast doubt on; **mettre qch en ~** to call sth into question [*propos, honnêteté, compétence*]; **être dans le ~** to be doubtful, to have misgivings (**au sujet de** about); **dans le ~, j'ai préféré ne rien dire** not being sure I didn't say anything; ▶ **abstenir**; **2** (soupçon) doubt; **avoir des ~s** to have doubts ou misgivings (**sur, au sujet de** about); **j'ai des ~s!** I have my doubts!; **un ~ subsiste** or **demeure à ce sujet** there is still some doubt about it; **il a exprimé** or **émis des ~s à propos de** he expressed some doubt about; **il fait peu de ~ que, il ne fait guère de ~ que** there's little doubt that; **il ne fait aucun ~ que, nul ~ que** there's no doubt ou question that; **sa culpabilité ne fait aucun ~** there's no doubt as to his/her guilt; **leur supériorité ne laisse aucun ~ sur l'issue du combat** their superiority leaves no doubt as to the outcome of the fight; **3** Philos, Relig doubt.

II sans doute *loc adv* probably; **il viendra sans ~ demain, sans ~ viendra-t-il demain** he'll probably come tomorrow, no doubt he'll come tomorrow; **vous trouvez sans ~ que j'exagère** you probably think I'm exaggerating; **sans aucun ~, sans nul ~** without any doubt.

douter /dute/ [1] **I** *vtr* **~ que** to doubt that ou whether; **je doute qu'elle vienne ce soir** I doubt (whether) she'll come tonight; **je**

Les douleurs et les maladies

Où est-ce que ça vous fait mal?

où avez-vous mal? = where does it hurt?

Pour traduire avoir mal à, *l'anglais utilise un possessif devant le nom de la partie du corps (alors que le français a un article défini), et un verbe qui peut être* hurt *ou* ache *(faire mal).* hurt *est toujours possible:*

il a mal à la jambe = his leg hurts
sa jambe lui fait mal = his leg hurts
il a mal au dos = his back hurts
il a mal aux yeux = his eyes hurt
il a mal aux oreilles = his ears hurt

ache *est utilisé avec les membres, les articulations, la tête, les dents et les oreilles:*

il a mal au bras = his arm aches

On peut aussi traduire par have a pain in:

il a mal à la jambe = he has a pain in his leg

Pour quelques parties du corps, l'anglais utilise un composé avec -ache:

avoir mal aux dents = to have toothache
avoir mal au dos = to have backache
avoir mal aux oreilles = to have earache
avoir mal au ventre = to have stomachache
avoir mal à la tête = to have a headache (*noter l'article indéfini*)

Attention à:

il a mal au cœur = he feels sick
il a mal aux reins = he has backache

qui n'affectent pas la partie du corps désignée en français.

Les accidents

Là où le français a des formes pronominales (se faire mal à *etc.*) *avec l'article défini, l'anglais utilise des verbes transitifs, avec des adjectifs possessifs:*

il s'est cassé la jambe = he broke his leg
il s'est fait mal au pied = he hurt his foot

Noter:

il a eu la jambe cassée = his leg was broken

Les faiblesses chroniques

Le français avoir le X fragile *peut se traduire par* to have something wrong with one's X *ou* to have X trouble:

avoir le cœur fragile = to have something wrong with one's heart *ou* to have heart trouble
avoir les reins fragiles = to have something wrong with one's kidneys *ou* to have kidney trouble

Pour certaines parties du corps (le cœur, les chevilles), on peut aussi utiliser l'adjectif weak:

avoir le cœur fragile = to have a weak heart

Noter que l'anglais utilise l'article indéfini dans cette tournure.

Les maladies

L'anglais utilise tous les noms de maladie sans article:

avoir la grippe = to have flu
avoir un cancer = to have cancer
avoir une hépatite = to have hepatitis
avoir de l'asthme = to have asthma
avoir les oreillons = to have mumps
être au lit avec la grippe = to be in bed with flu
guérir de la grippe = to recover from flu
mourir du choléra = to die of cholera

Même les noms de maladies suivies d'un complément ne prennent pas toujours d'article:

avoir un cancer du foie = to have cancer of the liver

Mais:

avoir un ulcère à l'estomac = to have a stomach ulcer

Et attention à a cold *(un rhume), qui n'est pas vraiment une maladie:*

avoir un rhume = to have a cold

L'anglais utilise moins volontiers les adjectifs dérivés des noms de maladies, si bien qu'on peut avoir:

être asthmatique = to have asthma *ou* to be asthmatic
être épileptique = to have epilepsy *ou* to be epileptic
être rachitique = to have rickets

Noter:

quelqu'un qui a la malaria = someone with malaria
quelqu'un qui a un cancer = someone with cancer
les gens qui ont le Sida = people with Aids

Les gens qui se font soigner pour une maladie sont désignés par a X patient:

quelqu'un qui se fait soigner pour un cancer = a cancer patient

Les attaques de la maladie

Le français attraper *se traduit par* to get *ou* to catch.

attraper la grippe = to get flu *ou* to catch flu
attraper une bronchite = to get bronchitis *ou* to catch bronchitis

Mais get *est utilisable aussi pour ce qui n'est pas infectieux:*

développer un ulcère à l'estomac = to get a stomach ulcer

Avoir *peut se traduire par* develop *lorsqu'il s'agit de l'apparition progressive d'une maladie:*

avoir un cancer = to develop cancer
avoir un début d'ulcère = to develop an ulcer

Pour une crise passagère, et qui peut se reproduire, on traduira avoir un/une ... *par to* have an attack of ... *ou* a bout of ...:

avoir une crise d'asthme = to have an asthma attack
avoir une bronchite = to have an attack of bronchitis
avoir une crise de malaria = to have a bout of malaria

Noter aussi:

avoir une crise d'épilepsie = to have an epileptic fit

Les traitements

Le français contre *ne se traduit pas toujours par* against.

prendre quelque chose contre le rhume des foins = to take something for hay fever
prendre un médicament contre la toux = to be taking something for a cough
prescrire un médicament contre la toux = to prescribe something for a cough
des cachets contre la malaria = malaria tablets
se faire vacciner contre la grippe = to have a flu injection
vacciner qn contre le tétanos = to give sb a tetanus injection
se faire vacciner contre le choléra = to have a cholera vaccination
un vaccin contre la grippe = a flu vaccine *ou* an anti-flu vaccine

Mais noter:

prendre des médicaments contre la grippe = to take something for flu

Noter l'utilisation de la préposition anglaise on *avec le verbe* operate:

se faire opérer d'un cancer = to be operated on for cancer
le chirurgien l'a opéré d'un cancer = the surgeon operated on him for cancer

---

doute qu'il ait pu avoir son train I doubt (whether) he'll have been able to catch his train; **je ne doute pas qu'il fera de son mieux** I don't doubt (but) that he'll do his best.
II douter de *vtr ind* to have doubts about; **~ de l'honnêteté/la sincérité de qn** to have doubts about sb's honesty/sincerity; **~ de l'innocence de qn** to have doubts about sb's innocence; **~ de soi-même** to have feelings of self-doubt; **je n'ai jamais douté de toi/ton talent** I never doubted you/your talent; **elle l'affirme mais j'en doute** she says it's true but I have my doubts; **il doute de tout, même de l'évidence** he doubts everything, even what's obviously true; **à n'en pas ~** undoubtedly, without a doubt; **elle ne doute de rien**○! iron she's so sure of herself!
III *vi* Philos, Relig to doubt.
IV se douter *vpr* **se ~ de qch** to suspect sth; **se ~ que** to suspect that; **je m'en doutais!** I thought so!, I suspected as much!; **je m'en doute, je m'en serais douté!** iron (c'est évident) obviously! iron; **comme on pouvait s'en ~** as might have been expected; **qui se serait douté que...?** who would have thought that...?; **je me doute (bien) qu'il devait être furieux** I can (well) imagine that he was furious; **nous étions loin de nous ~ que** we didn't have the least idea that, we never dreamed that; **je ne me doutais pas que ça se terminerait comme ça** I never thought ou it never occurred to me that it would end up like that; **il aurait dû se ~ que...** he should have known that...

douteux, -euse /dutø, øz/ *adj* **1** (peu certain) [*résultat, issue, succès*] uncertain; **il est ~ qu'il ait pu s'échapper** it is unlikely that he was able to escape; **2** (ambigu) [*sens, réponse*] ambiguous; **3** (sujet à caution) [*honnêteté, innocence, renseignements*] dubious; [*sincérité, authenticité*] dubious, doubtful; **4** (suspect) [*affaire, individu, transactions, profits*] shady; [*propreté, hygiène, fraîcheur*] dubious, questionable; [*plat, viande*] dubious, suspect; **cravate d'un goût ~** tie in dubious taste; **plaisanterie d'un goût ~** joke in dubious taste.

douve /duv/ *nf* **1** (fossé) (de château) moat; Agric drainage ditch; Équit water jump; **2** (de tonneau) stave; **3** Vét fluke; **~ du foie** liver fluke.

Douvres /duvʀ/ ▶ 857 *npr* Dover.

doux, douce /du, dus/ **I** *adj* **1** (aux sens) [*tissu, matière, cheveux, peau*] soft; [*lumière, musique, voix, sonorité*] soft; [*liqueur, alcool, vin, cidre*] sweet; [*fromage, piment, tabac*] mild; [*shampooing*] mild; **2** (pas froid) [*climat, temps, température*] mild; **il fait ~ aujourd'hui** it's mild today; **on a eu un hiver très ~** we've had a very mild winter; **3** (pas abrupt) [*formes, relief, pente*] gentle; **la route descend en pente douce** the road slopes gently; **4** (léger) [*punition, châtiment*] mild; **5** (gentil) [*personne, animal, regard, geste, tempérament, visage, traits*] gentle; **6** liter (agréable) [*sommeil, surprise, pensée, souvenir, rêve, parfum*] pleasant; [*baisers, caresses*] sweet, gentle; **qu'il est ~ d'aller se coucher!** it's lovely to get into bed!; **qu'il**

est ~ d'être aimé! how sweet it is to be loved!; **7** Écol [*technologie, énergie*] environmentally friendly.

II douce *nf* **ma douce** sweetheart.

■ **~ dingue**○ eccentric, oddball○; **~ rêveur** dreamer.

IDIOMES **filer ~**○ to keep a low profile; **se la couler douce**○ to take it easy; **faire qch en douce**○ to do sth on the sly; **holà! tout ~! tout ~!** steady! steady!; ▶ **œil**.

doux-amer, **douce-amère**, *mpl* **~s**, *fpl* **douces-amères** /duzamɛʀ, dusamɛʀ/ I *adj* fig [*propos*] bitter-sweet, barbed.

II douce-amère *nf* bittersweet, woody nightshade.

douzaine /duzɛn/ *nf* **1** (douze) dozen (*inv*); **deux ~s d'œufs/de verres** two dozen eggs/glasses; **à la ~** by the dozen; **2** (environ douze) about twelve, a dozen or so; **une ~ de jours** a couple of weeks; **il y en a à la ~** there are dozens ou masses of them.

douze /duz/ ▶**545**, **407**, **212** *adj inv, pron* gén twelve.

douzième /duzjɛm/ ▶**545**, **212** *adj* twelfth.

Down ▶**692** *nprm* **le comté de ~** County Down.

doyen, **-enne** /dwajɛ̃, ɛn/ *nm,f* **1** (en âge) **~ (d'âge)** oldest person; **le ~ du pays** the country's oldest citizen; **2** (en ancienneté) the (most) senior member; **3** Relig, Univ dean.

doyenné /dwajɛne/ I *nm* (dignité) deanship; (lieu) deanery.

II *nf* Bot comice (pear).

DPLG /depeɛlʒe/ *adj* (*abbr* = **diplômé par le gouvernement**) **architecte ~** ≈ chartered architect GB, certified architect US.

Dr (*written abbr* = **docteur**) Dr.

drachme /dʀakm/ ▶**46** *nf* drachma.

draconien, **-ienne** /dʀakɔnjɛ̃, ɛn/ *adj* [*loi, attitude*] draconian; [*mesure, punition*] draconian, drastic; [*régime, traitement*] very strict.

dragage /dʀagaʒ/ *nm* (nettoyage) dredging; (fouille) dragging; **~ de mines** minesweeping.

dragée /dʀaʒe/ *nf* **1** (bonbon) sugared almond, dragée; **2** (pilule) sugar-coated pill, dragée spéc; **3** Agric mixed provender.

IDIOMES **la ~ est amère** it's a bitter pill to swallow; **tenir la ~ haute à qn** to hold out on sb.

dragéifier /dʀaʒeifje/ [2] *vtr* **~ qch** to coat sth with sugar; **une pilule dragéifiée** a sugar-coated pill.

dragon /dʀagɔ̃/ *nm* **1** (créature fabuleuse) dragon; **2** Mil, Hist dragoon; **3** (femme acariâtre) dragon; **un ~ de vertu** a dragon of virtue.

dragonnade /dʀagɔnad/ *nf* dragonnade.

dragonne /dʀagɔn/ *nf* gén wrist-strap; (de sabre) sabre[GB]-knot.

dragonnier /dʀagɔnje/ *nm* dragon tree.

drague /dʀag/ *nf* **1** Tech (machine) dredge; (chaland) dredger; **2** Pêche (filet) dragnet; **3**○ **la ~** chatting people up○, coming on to people○ US; (d'homosexuels) cruising○.

■ **~ télématique** *Minitel dating service.*

draguer /dʀage/ [1] *vtr* **1**○ to chat [sb] up○ GB, to come on to○; **elle s'est fait ~ par un drôle de gars** a strange guy tried to pick her up; **aller ~ en boîte**○ [*hétérosexuel*] to go to nightclubs to pick somebody up; [*homosexuel*] to go cruising to nightclubs; **on va ~ ce soir** hum we'll go out on the make tonight○; **il ne peut pas s'empêcher de ~** he can't help being flirtatious; **2** Tech (pour nettoyer) to dredge; (pour fouiller) to drag; **~ le canal pour retrouver un corps** to drag the canal for a body; **3** Pêche to catch [sth] with a dragnet; **~ au chalut** to trawl; **4** Mil to sweep [*mines*]; Naut **l'ancre drague le fond** the ship is dragging its anchor.

dragueur, **-euse** /dʀagœʀ, øz/ I○ *nm,f* **c'est un drôle de ~**○ he's a terrible flirt; **elle est assez dragueuse** she's a bit of a flirt.

II *nm* (pêcheur) dragnet fisherman; (ouvrier) dredge-man; (chaland) dredger.

■ **~ de mines** Mil minesweeper.

drain /dʀɛ̃/ *nm* **1** Tech (underground) drain; **2** Méd drain, drainage tube.

drainage /dʀɛnaʒ/ *nm* **1** Tech, Agric drainage; **2** Méd draining (off); **3** fig drain; **le ~ des cerveaux vers les États-Unis** the brain drain to the United States.

■ **~ lymphatique** lymphatic drainage; **faire un ~ lymphatique à qn** to give sb lymphatic drainage massage.

draine /dʀɛn/ *nf* mistle thrush.

drainer /dʀɛne/ [1] *vtr* **1** Agric to drain [*sol*]; **2** Méd to drain [*cellules, sécrétions*]; **3** (attirer) fig [*spectacle, annonce*] to attract [*public, curieux*] (**vers** to); to siphon off [*capitaux*] (**vers** to).

draisienne /dʀɛzjɛn/ *nf* dandy-horse.

draisine /dʀɛzin/ *nf* Rail track inspection (rail)car.

dramatique /dʀamatik/ I *adj* **1** (tragique) [*problème, situation*] tragic; **ce n'est pas ~ si tu ne viens pas** it's not the end of the world if you don't come; **2** Théât, Littérat [*création, effet*] dramatic; **art ~** drama; **auteur ~** playwright; **critique/centre ~** drama critic/centre.

II *nf* TV, Radio play, drama.

dramatiquement /dʀamatikmɑ̃/ *adv* tragically.

dramatisation /dʀamatizasjɔ̃/ *nf* dramatization.

dramatiser /dʀamatize/ [1] *vtr* to dramatize; **tu dramatises toujours tout** you always dramatize everything.

dramaturge /dʀamatyʀʒ/ ▶**510** *nmf* playwright.

dramaturgie /dʀamatyʀʒi/ *nf* (art) dramatic art; (traité) treatise on dramatic art.

drame /dʀam/ *nm* **1** (événement tragique) tragedy; **un ~ de famille** a family tragedy; **se terminer par un ~** to end in tragedy; **'~ de la jalousie'** 'crime of passion'; **tourner au ~** to take a tragic turn; **s'il part ce n'est pas un ~** if he goes it's not the end of the world; **tu ne vas pas en faire un ~!** don't make a scene about it!; **2** Théât, Cin, Littérat (genre) drama; (pièce) play; **~ en trois actes** three-act play.

■ **~ lyrique** Mus opera; **~ psychologique** psychological drama.

drap /dʀa/ *nm* **1** (de lit) sheet; **~ de coton/soie** cotton/silk sheet; **~ de couleur** coloured[GB] sheet; **~ de dessus/dessous** top/bottom sheet; **2** Tex (tissu) woollen[GB] fabric; **un manteau en ~** a wool coat.

■ **~ de bain** bath sheet; **~ funéraire** pall; **~ de plage** beach towel.

IDIOMES **se mettre** or **fourrer**○ **dans de beaux ~s** to land oneself in a fine mess; **tu nous a mis dans de beaux ~s** a fine mess you've landed us in!

drapé, **~e** /dʀape/ I *pp* ▶ **draper**.

II *pp adj* [*tissu*] draped.

III *nm* Tex, Cout drape; **le ~ d'une robe** the drape of a dress.

drapeau, *pl* **~x** /dʀapo/ *nm* flag; **le ~ européen** the European flag; **être sous les ~x** to be doing military service; **être appelé sous les ~x** to be called up.

■ **~ blanc** white flag; **~ noir** gén black flag; (de pirates) Jolly Roger; **~ tricolore** (drapeau français) tricolour[GB].

draper /dʀape/ [1] I *vtr* (arranger) to drape [*tissu, rideau*]; (envelopper) to drape [*personne, statue*]; **un châle lui drapait les épaules** a shawl was draped around his/her shoulders; **être drapé dans son manteau** to be wrapped in one's coat.

II se draper *vpr* **1** lit **se ~ dans** to wrap oneself in [*manteau, châle*]; **2** fig **se ~ dans sa dignité** to stand on one's dignity; **se ~ dans sa vertu** to pride oneself on one's virtue.

draperie /dʀapʀi/ I *nf* **1** Art drapery; **2** Tex (fabrication) cloth manufacturing; (commerce) cloth trade.

II draperies *nfpl* (de fenêtre) draperies; (de mur) wall-hangings.

drap-housse, *pl* **draps-housses** /dʀaus/ *nm* fitted sheet.

drapier, **-ière** /dʀapje, ɛʀ/ ▶**510** *nm,f* (fabricant) cloth manufacturer; (marchand) (au détail) draper; (en gros) cloth merchant.

drastique /dʀastik/ *adj* fml [*mesure, condition, réduction*] drastic.

dravidien, **-ienne** /dʀavidjɛ̃, ɛn/ *adj* Dravidian.

dressage /dʀɛsaʒ/ *nm* **1** (d'animal) training; **2** Équit (de jeune cheval) breaking in; (entraînement) schooling; (compétition) dressage; **3** (de tente) pitching; (de chapiteau, d'échafaudage) erection.

dresser /dʀese/ [1] I *vtr* **1** (faire obéir) to train [*animal*]; to break in [*cheval*]; **~ qn** to teach sb how to behave; **les enfants, on les dresse**○! children must be taught how to behave!; **2** (ériger) to put up, to pitch [*tente*]; to put up [*chapiteau*]; to put up, to erect [*échafaudage, monument, statue*]; **3** (lever) to raise [*tête, queue*]; **animal qui dresse les oreilles** or **l'oreille** animal that pricks up its ears; **~ l'oreille** fig to prick up one's ears; **4** (établir) to draw up [*plan, liste, bilan, contrat*]; to write out [*procès-verbal*]; **5** (installer) to lay, to set [*table, piège*]; to lay out [*buffet*]; **6** (préparer) Culin to garnish [*plat*]; **7** (influencer) to set (**contre** against).

II se dresser *vpr* **1** (se mettre droit) **le chien se dressa sur ses pattes de derrière** the dog stood up on its hind legs; **se ~ sur la pointe des pieds** to stand on tiptoe; ▶ **ergot**; **2** (s'insurger) **se ~ contre** to rebel against [*injustice*]; **3** (s'élever) [*statue, estrade, obstacle*] to stand; (dominer) [*tour, clocher*] to tower up; **la montagne se dresse à l'horizon** the mountain towers up on the horizon.

dresseur, **-euse** /dʀɛsœʀ, øz/ ▶**510** *nm,f* (d'animal) trainer.

dressoir /dʀɛswaʀ/ *nm* dresser.

dreyfusard, **~e** /dʀɛfyzaʀ, aʀd/ *adj, nm,f* Dreyfusard.

DRH /deɛʀaʃ/ I *nmf* ▶ **directeur**.

II *nf* ▶ **direction**.

dribbler /dʀible/ [1] I *vtr* to dribble around [*joueur*].

II *vi* to dribble.

dribbleur, **-euse** /dʀiblœʀ, øz/ *nm,f* dribbler.

drille /dʀij/ I○ *nm* **joyeux ~** jolly fellow.

II *nf* (outil) drill.

dring /dʀiŋ/ *nm* also onomat dring; **elle entendit le ~ de la sonnette** she heard the bell ring.

drisse /dʀis/ *nf* halyard.

drive /dʀajv/ *nm* drive.

driver¹ /dʀivœʀ/ *nm* (jockey, club) driver.

driver² /dʀive/ [1] I *vtr* to drive [*balle, cheval*].

II *vi* (en tennis) to drive; (en golf) to drive off.

drogue /dʀɔg/ *nf* **1** (stupéfiant) drug; **la ~** drugs; **~ douce/dure** soft/hard drug; **la lutte contre la ~** the fight against drugs; **c'est devenu une ~** fig it has become an addiction; **2**† (remède) drug; (de charlatan) quack remedy.

drogué, **~e** /dʀɔge/ I *pp* ▶ **droguer**.

II *pp adj* [*personne*] on drugs (*après n*); **il a l'air complètement ~** he seems to be doped up to the eyeballs○.

III *nm,f* drug-addict, junkie○.

droguer /dʀɔge/ [1] I *vtr* **1** péj [*médecin*] (avec sédatif) to dope; (en prescrivant) to dish out○ drugs to; **2** (illégalement) to dope [*animal, sportif*]; to drug [*victime*]; to doctor [*boisson*].

II se droguer *vpr* **1** péj (avec des médicaments) to dope oneself (**à, de** with); **2** (avec des stupéfiants) to take drugs, be on drugs; **se ~ à l'héroïne** to be on heroin.

droguerie /dʀɔgʀi/ ▶510| *nf* (magasin) hardware shop GB ou store US; (commerce) hardware trade.

droguet /dʀɔgɛ/ *nm* drugget.

droguiste /dʀɔgist/ ▶510| *nmf* (propriétaire) owner of a hardware shop GB ou store US; (gérant) manager/manageress of a hardware shop GB ou store US.

droit, **~e** /dʀwa, at/ ▶445| I *adj* **1** (pas courbe, pas tordu) [*ligne, route, barre, cheveux, mur, tour, nez*] straight; (pas penché) [*cône, cylindre, prisme*] right; [*écriture*] up-and-down; **le tableau n'est pas ~** the picture isn't straight; **se tenir ~** (debout) to stand up straight; (assis) to sit up straight; **tenir qch ~** to hold sth straight; **le ~ chemin** fig the straight and narrow; **s'écarter du ~ chemin** to stray from the straight and narrow; **descendre en ~e ligne de** to be a direct descendant of; **2** (contraire de gauche) right; **le côté ~** the right side; **du côté ~** on the right(-hand) side; **3** (honnête) [*personne*] straight, upright; [*vie*] blameless; **4** (sensé) [*jugement*] sound; **5** Mode [*jupe*] straight; [*veste*] single-breasted; **6** Math right.
II *adv* [*aller, rouler*] straight; **~ devant** straight ahead; **se diriger ~ vers** to make straight for, to make a beeline for○; **la voiture venait ~ sur nous** the car was coming straight at us; **continuez tout ~** carry straight on; **file tout ~ à la maison** go straight home; **aller ~ au but** or **fait** fig to go straight to the point; **aller ~ à la catastrophe** to be heading straight for disaster; **ça m'est allé ~ au cœur** fig it really touched me; **marcher ~** lit to walk straight; **marcher** or **filer**○ **~** to toe the line; **regarder qn ~ dans les yeux** to look sb straight in the eye; **venir tout ~ de** [*expression, citation*] to come straight out of [*auteur, œuvre*]; **je reviens tout ~ de chez elle/de l'exposition** I've come straight from her place/the exhibition.
III *nm* **1** (prérogative) right; **connaître/faire valoir ses ~s** to know/assert one's rights; **avoir des ~s sur qn/qch** to have rights over sb/sth; **de quel ~ est-ce que tu me juges?** what gives you the right to judge me?; **être dans son (bon) ~, avoir le ~ pour soi** or **de son côté** to be within one's rights; **de (plein) ~** by right(s); **de ~ divin** [*monarque, monarchie*] by divine right; **cela leur revient de ~** it's theirs by right; **c'est tout à fait ton ~** you have every right to do so, you're perfectly entitled to do so; **avoir ~ à** to have the right to [*liberté, nationalité*]; to be entitled to, to be eligible for [*bourse, indemnité*]; **vous avez ~ à une boisson chacun** you're allowed one drink each; **les spectateurs ont eu ~ à un beau match** the spectators were treated to a fine game; **on a eu ~ à ses souvenirs de régiment** iron he treated us to stories about his army days; **il a eu ~ à une amende** iron he got a fine; **avoir le ~ de faire** (la permission) to be allowed to do; (selon la morale, la justice) to have the right to do; **elle n'a pas le ~ de sortir le soir** she isn't allowed to go out at night; **j'ai quand même le ~ de poser une question!** iron I suppose I am allowed to ask a question?; **j'ai le ~ de savoir** I've got a right to know; **elle n'a pas le ~ de me juger/d'exiger ça de moi** she has no right to judge me/to demand that of me; **avoir le ~ de vie ou de mort sur qn** to have (the) power of life and death over sb; **il s'imagine qu'il a tous les ~s** he thinks he can do whatever he likes; **être en ~ de** to be entitled to; **on est en ~ de se demander si**... we are entitled ou we have every right to wonder if...; **ça te donne ~ à**... it entitles you to...; **à bon ~** [*se plaindre, protester*] with good reason; **'à qui de ~'** 'to whom it may concern'; **j'en parlerai à qui de ~**○ I'll speak to the appropriate person; **faire ~ à** to grant [*demande, requête*]; **2** Jur (ensemble de lois) law; **le ~ français/anglais** French/English law; **faire son ~** to study law; **étudiant en ~** law student; **3** (redevance) fee; **acquitter/percevoir un ~** to pay/receive a fee; **~ d'inscription** registration fee; **passible de ~** dutiable; **4** (en boxe) right; **direct du ~** straight right; **crochet/uppercut du ~** right hook/uppercut.
IV **droite** *nf* **1** (opposé à gauche) **la ~e** the right; **la porte de ~e** the door on the right; **être/rouler à ~e** to be/to drive on the right; **tourner à ~e** to turn right; **tenir sa ~e** Aut to keep (to the) right; **à ta ~e, sur ta ~e** on your right; **à ~e de** to the right of; **deuxième couloir à ~e** second corridor on the right; **il ne connaît pas sa ~e de sa gauche** he can't tell (his) right from (his) left; **demander à ~e et à gauche** (partout) to ask everywhere ou all over the place; (à tous) to ask everybody; **être critiqué de ~e et de gauche** to be criticized from all sides ou by everybody; **2** Pol right; **voter à ~e** to vote for the right; **de ~e** [*parti, personne, gouvernement*] right-wing; **être à** or **de ~e** to be right-wing; **3** Math straight line.
■ **~ administratif** administrative law; **~ aérien** Jur air law; **~ des affaires** Jur company law GB, corporate law US; **~ d'aînesse** Jur birthright, primogeniture; **~ d'antenne** broadcasting right; **~ d'asile** Pol right of asylum; **~ au bail** right to the lease; **~ canon** Jur canon law; **~ de cité** Jur (right of) citizenship; fig acceptance; **acquérir ~ de cité** fig to gain acceptance; **avoir ~ de cité** to be accepted; **donner ~ de cité à** to accept; **~ civil** Jur civil law; **~ commercial** commercial law; **~ commun** (prisonnier) nonpolitical; **de ~ commun** [*prisonnier*] nonpolitical, ordinary; [*taux, régime*] ordinary; **~ constitutionnel** Jur constitutional law; **~ coutumier** Jur common law; **~ écrit** Jur statute law; **~ d'entrée** Comm, Fisc import duty; (pour une personne) entrance fee; **~ d'étalage** Comm, Fisc stallage; **~ fil** Cout straight grain; fig main line; **dans le ~ fil de** fig in line with; **~ fiscal** Jur tax law; **~ de grâce** Jur right of reprieve; **~ de grève** Pol right to strike; **~ immobilier** Jur property law; **~ international** Jur international law; **~ maritime** Jur maritime law; **~ de passage** Jur right of way GB, easement US; **~ pénal** Jur criminal law; **~ de port** Fisc port dues; **~ de poursuite** Jur right of action; **~ de préemption** right of preemption; **~ privé** Jur private law; **~ de propriété** right of possession; **~ public** Jur public law; **~ de recours** Jur right of appeal; **~ de regard** Fin right of inspection; gén **avoir ~ de regard sur** to have a say in; **~ de réponse** right of reply; **~ de rétention** lien; **~ du sang** right to citizenship by virtue of kinship; **~ social** Jur labour[GB] law; **~ du sol** right to citizenship by virtue of birth in a country; **~ de timbre** Fisc stamp duty; **~ du travail** Jur labour[GB] law; **~ d'usage** Jur customary right; **~ de veto** right of veto; **~ de visite** Jur right of access; **~ de vote** Pol right to vote; **~s d'auteur** Édition royalties; **~s civiques** Pol civil rights; **~s de douane** Comm, Fisc customs duties; **les ~s de l'homme** human rights; **~s de quai** Fisc wharfage; **~s de reproduction** reproduction rights; **tous ~s de reproduction réservés** all rights reserved; **~s de succession** Fisc inheritance tax; **~s de tirage spéciaux**, **DTS** Fisc special drawing rights, SDR.
IDIOMES **se tenir ~ comme un i** or **un piquet** to hold oneself very erect ou upright.

droitement† /dʀwatmɑ̃/ *adv* [*agir, parler, répondre*] honestly; [*juger*] soundly.

droitier, **-ière** /dʀwatje, ɛʀ/ I *adj* **1** (qui se sert de la main droite) right-handed; **2**○ Pol right-wing.
II *nm,f* **1** (qui se sert de la main droite) right-hander; **des ciseaux pour ~s** right-handed scissors; **2**○ Pol right-winger.

droiture /dʀwatyʀ/ *nf* honesty, uprightness.

drolatique /dʀɔlatik/ *adj* liter comical.

drôle /dʀol/ I *adj* **1** (bizarre) funny, odd; **c'est ~ comme les gens changent** it's funny how people change; **c'est un ~ de type** he's odd; **il avait un ~ d'air** he had an odd expression; **de ~s d'histoires** odd sorts of stories; **c'est ~ de faire/que** it's odd to do/that; **c'est ~ qu'elle n'ait pas téléphoné** it's odd that she hasn't phoned; **ce qui est** or **ce qu'il y a de ~ c'est que** the funny thing is that; **avoir l'air/se sentir (tout) ~** to look/to feel a bit funny○; **faire (tout) ~ à qn** to give sb a funny feeling; **faire une ~ de tête** to make a bit of a face; **vous êtes ~, vous!** iron don't make me laugh!; **~ de remerciement/consolation!** some thanks/consolation!; **2** (amusant) [*histoire, spectacle, comédien*] funny, amusing; [*vie*] fun; **ça n'a rien de ~** there is nothing funny about that; **ce n'est pas ~ de faire** it's no joke doing; **3**○ (grand) **un ~ de courage/travail** a lot of courage/work; **j'ai eu** or **reçu une ~ d'engueulade**○! I got a real telling-off!
II† *nm* old rascal†; **mauvais ~** scoundrel†.
■ **~ de guerre** Hist phoney war.
IDIOMES **j'en ai entendu de ~s** I heard some funny things; **en faire voir de ~s à qn** to lead sb a merry dance.

drôlement /dʀolmɑ̃/ *adv* **1**○ (très, beaucoup) really; **il est ~ énervant** he's really irritating; **c'est ~ bon** it's really good; **les prix ont ~ augmenté** the prices have really gone up; **2** (bizarrement) oddly; **s'habiller ~** to dress oddly; **regarder/sourire ~** to give an odd look/smile.

drôlerie /dʀolʀi/ *nf* **avec ~** amusingly; **être d'une incroyable ~, être incroyable de ~** to be incredibly funny ou amusing; **régal/chef d'œuvre de ~** feast/masterpiece of comedy.

drôlesse† /dʀolɛs/ *nf* pej hussy† péj.

dromadaire /dʀɔmadɛʀ/ *nm* dromedary.

Drôme /dʀom/ ▶357|, 692| *nprf* (rivière, département) **la ~** the Drôme.

drop-goal, *pl* **~s** /dʀɔpgol/ *nm* (coup de pied) drop kick; (but) dropgoal.

drosophile /dʀɔzɔfil/ *nf* fruit fly, drosophila spéc.

dru, **~e** /dʀy/ I *adj* [*cheveux, blés*] thick; [*averse*] heavy.
II *adv* [*pousser*] thickly; [*tomber*] heavily.

drugstore /dʀœgstɔʀ/ *nm* drugstore.

druide /dʀɥid/ *nm* druid.

druidesse /dʀɥidɛs/ *nf* druidess.

druidique /dʀɥidik/ *adj* druidic.

druidisme /dʀɥidism/ *nm* druidism.

drupe /dʀyp/ *nf* drupe.

dryade /dʀijad/ *nf* dryad.

DS /deɛs/ *nf*: *Citroen car of the 1950s*.

DST /deɛste/ *nf* (*abbr* = **Direction de la surveillance du territoire**) French counterintelligence agency.

DTS /deteɛs/ *nmpl*: *abbr* ▶ **droit**.

du /dy/ ▶ **de**.

dû, **due**, *mpl* **dus** /dy/ I *pp* ▶ **devoir**.
II *pp adj* **1** (à payer) owed (*après n*), owing (*après n*), due (*après n*) (**à** to); (exigible) due (*après n*); **l'argent qui m'est ~ par les clients** the money owed to me by customers; **les primes échues dues par l'assuré** the outstanding premiums due or owing by the insured; **les intérêts dus** the interest due; **2** (attribuable à) **~ à** due to; **cet accident est ~ à l'imprudence** this accident is due to carelessness; **mon retard est ~ aux embouteillages** I'm late due to traffic jams; **3** (qui convient à) due (**à** to); **respect ~ à qn/qch** respect due to sb/sth; **4** Admin **en bonne et due forme** in due form.
III *nm* **1** due; (cotisation) dues; **réclamer son ~** to claim one's due; **payer son ~** to pay one's dues; **2** Compta **200 francs**

payés, ~ 30 francs 200 francs paid, 30 francs owing ou outstanding.
IDIOMES **chose promise chose due** a promise is a promise; **à chacun son ~** credit where credit is due.

dual, **~e**, *mpl* **duaux** /dɥal, dɥo/ *adj* [*société*] two-tier (*épith*).

dualisme /dɥalism/ *nm* **1** Philos dualism; **2** Pol **le ~ des partis** the two-party system.

dualiste /dɥalist/ **I** *adj* dualistic.
II *nmf* dualist.

dualité /dɥalite/ *nf* duality.

dubitatif, **-ive** /dybitatif, iv/ *adj* sceptical GB, skeptical US; **d'un air ~** sceptically GB, skeptically US.

dubitativement /dybitativmɑ̃/ *adv* sceptically GB, skeptically US.

Dublin /dyblɛ̃/ ▶ 857 *npr* Dublin.

dublinois, **~e** /dyblinwa, az/ ▶ 857 *adj* of Dublin.

Dublinois, **~e** /dyblinwa, az/ ▶ 857 *nm,f* Dubliner.

duc /dyk/ ▶ 813 *nm* (titre) duke; ▶ **grand**.

duché /dyʃe/ *nm* (seigneurie) dukedom; (domaine) duchy.

duchesse /dyʃɛs/ *nf* **1** (titre) duchess; **la ~ de Bretagne** the Duchess of Brittany; **2** Bot (**poire**) **~** Duchess pear.
IDIOMES **faire sa ~**○ pej to put on airs and graces.

ductile /dyktil/ *adj* ductile.

ductilité /dyktilite/ *nf* ductility.

duègne /dɥɛɲ/ *nf* duenna.

duel /dɥɛl/ *nm* **1** (avec des armes) duel (**à** with); **se battre en ~** to fight a duel; **provoquer qn en ~** to challenge sb to a duel; **2** (en paroles) battle; **3** Ling dual.

duelliste /dɥelist/ *nm* duellist[GB].

duettiste /dɥetist/ *nmf* duettist.

duffel-coat, *pl* **~s** /dœfœlkot/ *nm* duffel coat.

dulcinée /dylsine/ *nf* hum lady-love.

Dulcinée /dylsine/ *npr* Dulcinea.

dum-dum /dumdum/ *nf inv* (**balle**) **~** dumdum (bullet).

dûment /dymɑ̃/ *adv* duly; **je vous ai ~ averti** I gave you due warning.

Dumfries ▶ 692 *nprm* **le ~ and Galloway** Dumfries and Galloway.

dumping /dœmpiŋ/ *nm* dumping; **faire du ~** to dump goods; **faire du ~ social** to practise[GB] social dumping.

dune /dyn/ *nf* dune.

dunette /dynɛt/ *nf* poop.

Dunkerque /dœ̃kɛʀk/ ▶ 857 *npr* Dunkirk.

dunkerquois, **~e** /dœ̃kɛʀkwa, az/ ▶ 857 *adj* of Dunkirk.

Dunkerquois, **~e** /dœ̃kɛʀkwa, az/ ▶ 857 *nm,f* (natif) native of Dunkirk; (habitant) inhabitant of Dunkirk.

duo /dyo, dɥo/ *nm* **1** (œuvre) duet; **un ~ pour violon** a violin duet; **2** (formation) duo; **un ~ de guitaristes** a guitar duo; **chanter en ~** to sing as a duo; **3** Théât double act GB, duo US; **4**○ (couple) pair.

duodécimal, **~e**, *mpl* **-aux** /dɥodesimal, o/ *adj* duodecimal.

duodénal, **~e**, *mpl* **-aux** /dɥɔdenal, o/ *adj* duodenal.

duodénum /dɥɔdenɔm/ *nm* duodenum.

dupe /dyp/ **I** *adj* **être ~** to be taken in ou fooled (**de** by); **je ne suis pas ~** I'm not fooled by that.
II *nf* dupe; **un marché de ~s** a fool's bargain.

duper /dype/ [1] *vtr* to fool, to dupe; **il est facile à ~** he's very gullible.

duperie /dypʀi/ *nf* trickery ¢.

duplex /dyplɛks/ *nm* **1** (appartement) maisonette GB, duplex apartment US; **2** Télécom, TV, Radio duplex.

duplicata /dyplikata/ *nm inv* duplicate.

duplicateur /dyplikatœʀ/ *nm* duplicator.

duplication /dyplikasjɔ̃/ *nf* Tech duplication; Biol replication.

duplicité /dyplisite/ *nf* duplicity; **avec ~** duplicitously.

dupliquer /dyplike/ [1] *vtr* to duplicate.

duquel ▶ **lequel**.

dur, **~e** /dyʀ/ **I** *adj* **1** (difficile à entamer) [*matériau, sol, crème glacée, mine de crayon*] hard; ▶ **dent, détente**; **2** (difficile à mâcher) [*pain, légume*] hard; [*viande*] tough; **3** (rigide) [*pinceau, poil, cuir, carton*] stiff; [*brosse à dents*] hard; [*plastique*] rigid; [*ressort*] hard; **4** (sans confort) [*banquette, siège, matelas*] hard; **5** (malaisé à manipuler) [*fermeture, poignée, pédale*] stiff; [*direction, volant*] heavy; **~ à ouvrir/tourner** hard to open/to turn; **6** (résistant) [*personne*] **~ au mal** tough; **elle est ~e à la fatigue** she doesn't tire easily; **elle est ~e à la tâche** or **au travail** she's a hard worker; **elle est ~e à la douleur** she can stand a lot of pain; **7** (anguleux) [*profil, traits*] hard; [*dessin*] angular; **8** (blessant) [*son, voix, ton, parole, lumière, couleur*] harsh; **il n'y a pas de mots assez ~s pour condamner...** there are no words harsh enough to condemn...; **9** (hostile) [*visage, expression*] severe; **elle lui a jeté un regard ~** she gave him/her a severe look; **10** (intransigeant) [*parents, patron*] (en général) hard; (à l'occasion) harsh; [*régime*] hard; [*faction, politique*] hardline (*épith*); **il est très ~ avec ses élèves** (comme défaut) he's very hard on his pupils; **il est ~ mais juste** (comme qualité) he's tough but fair; **la droite/gauche ~e** the hard Right/Left; ▶ **noyau**; **11** (contraignant) [*loi naturelle, conditions de vie*] harsh; [*conditions de crédit, termes de sécurité*] tough; **12** (éprouvant) [*métier*] gén hard (physiquement) tough; [*climat, nécessité*] harsh; [*concurrence, sport, ascension*] hard, tough; **cela a été une ~e épreuve** it was quite an ordeal; **l'hiver a été très ~ cette année** it's been a very hard winter this year; **le plus ~ sera de faire** the hardest thing will be to do; **le plus ~ est passé/reste à faire** the hardest part is over/is still to come; **il a fait le plus ~ du travail hier** he did the hardest part of the work yesterday; **c'est ~ de se lever si tôt** it's hard to get up so early; **ce fut très ~ pour lui de faire** it was very hard for him to do; **c'est la dure réalité** it's the grim reality; **les temps sont ~s** times are hard; **~, ~○!** it's tough!; **13** (difficile) [*examen, problème*] hard; **pour moi, le plus ~ c'est la syntaxe** for me, the hardest thing is syntax; **~ à** hard to; **~ à résoudre/admettre** hard to solve/admit; **il est ~ à supporter** he's heavy going; **14** (sans fard) [*film, récit, reportage*] hard-hitting (*épith*); **15** (calcaire) [*eau*] hard; **16** Phys [*rayons X*] hard; **les rayons ~s** hard radiation; **17** Phon [*consonne*] (non palatalisée) hard; (tendue) fortis spéc; **18** Naut [*mer*] choppy.
II *nm,f* **1** (personne solide) tough nut○, tough cookie○; **jouer les ~s** to act tough; **c'est un ~ de ~s** he's a real tough nut○; **2** Pol (partisan) hardliner.
III *adv* [*travailler, frapper*] hard; **ça tape ~ aujourd'hui**○ [*soleil*] it's boiling hot today; **ça grimpe**○ **~!** it's a hell○ of a climb!; ▶ **fer**.
IV *nm* permanent structure; **construire en ~** to build a permanent structure; **construction en ~** permanent structure.
V à la dure *loc adv* **j'ai élevé mes enfants à la ~e** my children were brought up the hard way.
VI dures *nfpl* **en faire voir de ~es à ses parents** to give one's parents a hard time; **en dire de ~es à qn** to say cruel things to sb.
■ **~ à cuire** tough nut○ ou cookie○.
IDIOMES **~ comme (de la) pierre** [*objet*] rock-hard (*épith*); [*cœur, personne*] as hard as nails; **être ~ d'oreille** or **de la feuille**◑ to be hard of hearing; **avoir la tête ~e** (obstiné) to be stubborn; (obtus) to be dense; **avoir la vie ~e** [*insectes*] to be difficult to get rid of; [*habitude, préjugé*] to die hard; **elle a la vie ~e** (pas facile) she has a hard life; (résistante) she keeps hanging on; **mener la vie ~e à qn** to give sb a hard time; **la vie est ~e** it's a hard life.

durabilité /dyʀabilite/ *nf* durability.

durable /dyʀabl/ *adj* **1** (stable) [*amélioration, amitié, impression, hausse, victoire*] lasting; [*fascination, attrait, intérêt*] enduring; [*déséquilibre, situation*] long-standing; [*matériau*] durable; **2** Écon [*bien, marchandise*] durable.

durablement /dyʀabləmɑ̃/ *adv* [*s'installer*] on a permanent basis; [*ternir, être à l'abri*] permanently; **nuire ~ à qch** to do lasting damage to sth.

duralumin® /dyʀalymɛ̃/ *nm* Duralumin®.

durant /dyʀɑ̃/ *prép* **1** (exprimant une durée) for; **~ des heures/années** for hours/years; **~ ces trois dernières années** for the past three years; **~ longtemps** for a long time; **des heures/semaines ~** for hours and hours/weeks and weeks, for hours/weeks on end; **deux jours ~** for two whole days; **l'été ~** the whole summer; **plus d'une heure ~** for over an hour; **sa vie ~** throughout his/her life; **l'assistance applaudit cinq minutes ~** the audience clapped for five minutes; **il a subi, plusieurs mois ~, un traitement contre l'acné** he followed a course of treatment for acne for several months; **2** (au cours de) during; **~ l'année 1993/cette période** during the year 1993/that period; **~ la cérémonie/le match** during the ceremony/the match; **~ les trois derniers mois** during the last three months; **trois heures ~ lesquelles il n'a pas arrêté de pleuvoir** three hours during which it rained solidly.

duratif, **-ive** /dyʀatif/ *adj* durative.

Durban /dyʀbɑ̃/ *npr* Durban.

durcir /dyʀsiʀ/ [3] **I** *vtr* **1** (rendre dur) [*sécheresse, froid*] to harden [*sol, pâte*]; **2** (rendre sévère) [*maquillage*] to harden [*traits*]; **3** (radicaliser) to harden [*position*]; to intensify [*mouvement de grève*]; **~ sa politique en matière de** to take a harder line on.
II *vi* [*argile*] to harden; [*ciment, colle*] to set; [*pain*] to go hard; [*artères*] to harden; **~ à l'air** [*colle*] to set in (the) air; **ciment qui durcit vite** quick-setting cement.
III se durcir *vpr* **1** [*argile, artères*] to harden; **à ces mots, son visage se durcit** at these words, his/her face hardened; **2** (se radicaliser) [*ton, attitude*] to become harsher; [*régime*] to become harsher; [*mouvement, conflit*] to intensify.

durcissement /dyʀsismɑ̃/ *nm* **1** (d'argile, artère) hardening; (de ciment, colle) setting; **2** (d'attitude, de position) hardening; (de mouvement, grève) intensification.

durcisseur /dyʀsisœʀ/ *nm* hardener.

durée /dyʀe/ *nf* **1** (période) (de spectacle, séjour, règne, d'études) length; (de contrat) term; (de disque, cassette) playing time; **pour** or **pendant** (**toute**) **la ~ de** for the duration of; **~ de travail/hebdomadaire de travail** working time/week; **~ de la semaine scolaire** school week; **séjour/contrat d'une ~ de trois mois** three-month stay/contract; **d'une ~ de trois mois, le séjour comprend un cours intensif** lasting three months, the stay includes an intensive course; **ils n'ont pas précisé la ~ du projet** they didn't specify how long the project would last; **pour/pendant une ~ limitée/déterminée/fixée** for/over a limited/specified/set period; **pour une ~ indéterminée** [*suspendu, employé*] for an unlimited period; [*fermé*] until further notice; **dépôt/contrat à ~ déterminée** fixed-term deposit/contract; **de courte ~** [*amitié, paix, reprise économique*] short-lived; [*orage, absence*] brief; [*bail, prêt*] short-term; **de longue ~** [*bail, prêt, chômage, contrat*] long-term; [*absence*] long; **2** (longévité) **~**

(de vie) life; ~ **d'utilisation** useful life; **pile/ampoule longue** ~ long-life battery/ bulb; **3** Mus (de note) value; **4** Philos duration.

durement /dyʀmɑ̃/ *adv* **1** (de façon éprouvante) **être** ~ **touché** (affectivement) to be deeply affected; (économiquement) to be badly hit; **gagner** ~ **sa vie** to earn one's living the hard way; **2** (sans aménité) [*punir, critiquer, traiter, parler, reprocher*] harshly; [*regarder*] severely; **3** (fortement) [*frapper, se cogner*] hard.

dure-mère, *pl* **dures-mères** /dyʀmɛʀ/ *nf* dura mater.

durer /dyʀe/ [1] *vi* **1** (avoir une durée de) to last; ~ **dix jours** to last ten days; **ne** ~ **qu'un instant** only to last a moment; **la guerre a duré trois ans** the war lasted three years; **2** (aller) to last (**jusque** until); ~ **jusque vers 1930/jusqu'à lundi/leur mort** to last until about 1930/until Monday/ their death; **3** (se prolonger) to go on; ~ **toute la nuit** to go on all night; ~ **indéfiniment** to go on forever; ~ **des semaines entières** to go on for weeks on end; **la grève dure depuis trois semaines** the strike has been going on for three weeks; **cela fait un an que cela dure** it's already been going on for a year; **4** (se passer) [*conférence, festival*] to run; ~ **du six au dix mai** to run from the sixth to the tenth of May; **5** (être durable) to last; **le président/ma voiture/leur bonheur n'a pas duré** the president/my car/their happiness did not last; **faire** ~ **ses vêtements** to make one's clothes last; **pourvu que ça dure** long may it last; **ça durera ce que ça durera** it may or may not last; **6** (se prolonger longtemps) to go on for long; **la pluie ne va pas** ~ the rain will not go on for long; **ça ne peut plus** ~ it can't go on any longer; **faire** ~ to prolong [*réunion*]; to keep [sb] alive [*patient*]; **faire** ~ **le plaisir** iron to prolong the agony; ▶ **cent**.

dureté /dyʀte/ *nf* **1** (fermeté) (de matériau) hardness; (de viande) toughness; **d'une grande** ~ very hard; **2** (de carton, poils, pinceau, brosse) stiffness; **3** (de siège, matelas) hardness; **4** (de traits, visage) hardness; (de dessin) sharpness; **5** (d'expression, de ton, punition, paroles, métier, climat) harshness; (de regard) severity; (de tâche) hardness; **avec** ~ harshly; [*regarder*] severely; [*punir, juger, traiter, répondre*] harshly; **6** (d'eau) hardness.

Durham ▶ **692** *npr* **le comté de** ~ County Durham.

durillon /dyʀijɔ̃/ *nm* callus.

durite /dyʀit/ *nf* radiator hose.

DUT /deyte/ *nm* (*abbr* = **diplôme universitaire de technologie**) two-year diploma from a university institute of technology.

duvet /dyvɛ/ *nm* **1** (plumes, poils) down; **le** ~ **d'oie** goosedown; **2** (sac de couchage) sleeping bag.

duveté, ~**e** /dyvte/ *adj* downy.

duveteux, **-euse** /dyvtø, øz/ *adj* [*joue, oiseau*] downy; [*étoffe, pelage*] fluffy; [*fruit*] downy GB, fuzzy US.

dyarchie /diaʀʃi/ *nf* diarchy.

Dyfed ▶ **692** *nprm* **le** ~ Dyfed.

dynamique /dinamik/ **I** *adj* **1** gén dynamic; [*match*] lively; **2** Phys dynamic. **II** *nf* **1** Psych dynamics (+ *v sg*); ~ **de groupe** group dynamics; **2** (processus) process; ~ **de paix/de développement** peace/development process; ~ **de rassemblement** process of bringing about consensus; **3** Phys dynamics (+ *v sg*).

dynamiquement /dinamikmɑ̃/ *adv* dynamically.

dynamisation /dinamizasjɔ̃/ *nf* revitalization.

dynamiser /dinamize/ [1] *vtr* to make [sb/ sth] more dynamic; (de nouveau) to revitalize.

dynamisme /dinamism/ *nm* **1** (puissance d'action) dynamism; **être plein de** ~ to be very dynamic; **2** Philos dynamism.

dynamitage /dinamitaʒ/ *nm* **1** lit dynamiting; **2** fig destruction.

dynamite /dinamit/ *nf* lit, fig dynamite; **bâton de** ~ stick of dynamite; **à la** ~ with dynamite.

dynamiter /dinamite/ [1] *vtr* **1** lit to dynamite [*pont*]; **2** fig to destroy [*système*].

dynamiteur, **-euse** /dinamitœʀ, øz/ *nm,f* dynamiter.

dynamo /dinamo/ *nf* dynamo.

dynamo-électrique, *pl* ~**s** /dinamo elɛktʀik/ *adj* dynamoelectric.

dynamographe /dinamɔgʀaf/ *nm* dynamograph.

dynamomètre /dinamɔmɛtʀ/ *nm* dynamometer.

dynamométrique /dinamɔmetʀik/ *adj* dynamometric.

dynastie /dinasti/ *nf* dynasty.

dynastique /dinastik/ *adj* dynastic.

dyne /din/ *nf* dyne.

dysenterie /disɑ̃tʀi/ ▶ **271** *nf* dysentery.

dysentérique /disɑ̃teʀik/ **I** *adj* dysenteric. **II** *nmf* dysentery case.

dysfonctionnement /disfɔ̃ksjɔnmɑ̃/ *nm* **1** Méd dysfunction; **2** (de système) malfunctioning.

dysgraphie /disgʀafi/ *nf* dysgraphia.

dyslexie /dislɛksi/ *nf* dyslexia.

dyslexique /dislɛksik/ *adj, nmf* dyslexic.

dysménorrhée /dismenɔʀe/ *nf* dysmenorrhoea.

dyspepsie /dispɛpsi/ *nf* dyspepsia.

dyspepsique /dispɛpsik/, **dyspeptique** /dispɛptik/ *adj, nmf* dyspeptic.

dyspnée /dispne/ *nf* dyspnoea.

dystrophie /distʀɔfi/ *nf* dystrophy.

Ee

e, E /ə/ *nm inv* e, E; **e dans l'a** a and e joined together.

EAO /əao/ *nm*: *abbr* ▶ **enseignement**.

eau, *pl* **~x** /o/ **I** *nf* **1** Chimie, gén water; **verre d'~** glass of water; **l'~ de source/du robinet** spring/tap water; **~ de pluie** rainwater ¢; **pastis/ouzo sans ~** neat pastis/ouzo; ▶ **bébé, bec, boudin, clair, goutte, moulin, pont**; **2** (masse) water; **au bord de l'~** by the water; **à la surface de l' ~** on the surface of the water; **l'~ est chaude** the water is warm; **une ~ boueuse/jaunâtre** muddy/yellowish water; **avoir la tête hors de l'~** lit to have one's head out of the water; fig to keep one's head above water; **l'~ de la rivière/du lac** the water in the river/the lake; **prendre l'~** [*chaussure*] to let in water; **aller sur l'~** to float; **faire ~** to leak; **être à l'~** lit [*barque, canot*] to be launched; fig [*projet, plan*] to have gone down the drain; **être en ~** lit [*piscine, réservoir*] to be full of water; fig [*personne*] to be dripping with sweat; **mettre à l'~** to launch [*bateau*]; to push [sb] into the water [*personne*]; **mettre en ~** lit to fill with water [*piscine, réservoir*]; fig to make [sb] sweat [*personne*]; **se mettre à l'~** to get into the water; **se jeter à l'~** lit to throw oneself into the water; fig to take the plunge; **tomber à l'~** lit [*personne, objet*] to fall into the water; fig [*projet, plan*] to fall through; **nettoyer le sol à grande ~** to sluice the floor down; **3** (approvisionnement) water; **avoir l'~ et l'électricité** to have water and electricity laid on GB, to be hooked up for water and electricity US; **~ courante** running water; **avoir l'~ (courante)** to have running water; **avoir l'~ froide et l'~ chaude** to have hot and cold water; **couper l'~** to turn the water off at the mains; **consommation d'~** water consumption; **4** (pluie) rain; **trois centimètres d'~** three centimetres[GB] of rain; **5** Minér (transparence) water; **émeraude de la plus belle ~** emerald of the first water.

II eaux *nfpl* **1** Géog, Géol (niveau) water (*sg*); (masse) waters; **les ~x ont baissé** the water has gone down; **les ~x ont reculé** the waters have receded; **~x troubles** lit muddy waters; fig troubled waters; **2** Physiol (liquide amniotique) waters; **elle perd** or **a perdu ses ~x** her waters have broken; **3†** Méd waters; **prendre les ~x** to take the waters; ▶ **bas, grand**.

■ **~ bénite** holy water; **~ capsulée** bottled water; **~ céleste** *fungicidal spray used in vineyards*; **~ de chaux** limewater; **~ de Cologne** (eau de) cologne; **~ dentifrice** mouthwash; **~ distillée** distilled water; **~ douce** fresh water; **~ de fleur d'oranger** orange-flower water; **~ de Javel** ≈ chloride bleach; **~ de lavande** lavender water; **~ lourde** heavy water; **~ de mer** seawater; **~ minérale** mineral water; **~ minérale gazeuse** sparkling mineral water; **~ minérale naturelle** still mineral water; **~ oxygénée** hydrogen peroxide; **~ de parfum** eau de parfum; **~ de parfum** eau de parfum; **~ piquante**○ fizzy water; **~ plate** (du robinet) plain water; (minérale) still mineral water; **~ de rose** rose water; **à l'~ de rose** [*roman, film*] sentimental, schmaltzy○ US; **~ savonneuse** soapy water; **~ de Seltz** seltzer water; **~ sucrée** sugared water; **~ de toilette** eau de toilette; **~ tonique** tonic water; **~ de vaisselle** lit washing-up water GB, dishwater; fig dishwater; **~ vive** white-water; **kayak en ~ vive** white-water canoeing; **~x de crue** floodwaters ¢; **~x de fonte** meltwater ¢; **~x et forêts** Admin forestry authority; **ingénieur des ~x et forêts** forestry officer; **~x grasses** slops; **~x internationales** international waters; **~x ménagères** domestic sewage ¢, grey water GB; **~x minérales** mineral water ¢; **~x de ruissellement** runoff ¢; **~x souterraines** underground water ¢; **~x territoriales** territorial waters; **~x thermales** thermal waters; **~x usées** wastewater ¢.

IDIOMES **mettre l'~ à la bouche de qn** to make sb's mouth water; **j'en ai l'~ à la bouche** my mouth is watering; **c 'est l'~ et le feu** they are like chalk and cheese; **être de la même ~** to be of the same kidney; **ou dans ces ~x-là**○ or thereabouts; **vivre d'amour et d'~ fraîche** to live on love alone.

EAU *written abbr* = **Émirats**.

eau-de-vie, *pl* **eaux-de-vie** /odvi/ *nf* brandy, eau de vie; **pruneaux à l'~** prunes in brandy; **~ de prune/de framboise/de poire** plum/raspberry/pear brandy.

eau-forte, *pl* **eaux-fortes** /ofɔʀt/ *nf* etching.

eaux-vannes /ovan/ *nfpl* black water ¢.

ébahi, ~e /ebai/ **I** *pp* ▶ **ébahir**.

II *pp adj* dumbfounded, astounded (**de voir** to see).

ébahir /ebaiʀ/ [3] **I** *vtr* to dumbfound, astound; **elle m'ébahit par son audace** her audacity dumbfounds me.

II s'ébahir *vpr* to be dumbfounded, astounded (**de, devant** by).

ébahissement /ebaismɑ̃/ *nm* astonishment.

ébarbage /ebaʀbaʒ/ *nm* trimming.

ébarber /ebaʀbe/ [1] *vtr* to trim [*métal, papier, orge*].

ébats /eba/ *nmpl* **1** (d'enfants) frolics; (de sportifs) movements; **2** euph (jeux de l'amour) (amorous) frolics.

ébattre: **s'ébattre** /ebatʀ/ [61] *vpr* [*enfants*] to frolic (about); [*animaux*] to frisk about; (en éclaboussant) to splash about.

ébaubi, ~e /ebobi/ **I** *pp* ▶ **ébaubir**.

II *pp adj* (**tout**) **~** (stupéfait) flabbergasted; (admiratif) bowled over (**devant qch** by sth).

ébaubir†: **s'ébaubir** /ebobiʀ/ [2] *vpr* to be astounded (**devant qch** by sth; **de faire** to do).

ébauche /eboʃ/ *nf* **1** (objet, sculpture) rough shape; (dessin) preliminary sketch; (roman, réforme) preliminary draft; **être encore à l'état d'~** to be still at a ou the rough stage; **2** fig (début) **l'~ d'une amitié** the beginnings of a friendship; **l'~ d'un sourire** a hint of a smile; **l'~ d'un geste** a half-gesture; **l'~ d'un rapprochement** the first moves towards a reconciliation; **3** (action) (de dessin) sketching out; (de sculpture) rough-hewing; (de roman, réforme) drafting.

ébaucher /eboʃe/ [1] **I** *vtr* to sketch out [*tableau, solution*]; to draft [*programme, roman, projet*]; to rough-hew [*statue*]; to begin [*conversation*]; **~ un sourire** to give a glimmer of a smile; **~ un geste** to half make a gesture; **il ébaucha un salut** he half saluted; **un sourire à peine ébauché** the merest hint of a smile; **une solution à peine ébauchée** the merest outline of a solution.

II s'ébaucher *vpr* [*stratégie, solution, roman*] to begin to take shape; [*amitié*] to begin to develop; [*conversation, négociations*] to start; [*image*] to begin to form; **la reprise de l'économie s'ébauche** there are signs of a coming economic revival.

ébaudir†: **s'ébaudir** /ebodiʀ/ [3] *vpr* to rejoice (**de** over).

ébène /ebɛn/ *nf* ebony; **des cheveux d'~** fig jet-black hair; ▶ **faux**.

■ **~ fossile** jet; **~ verte** green ebony.

ébénier /ebenje/ *nm* ebony tree; ▶ **faux**.

ébéniste /ebenist/ ▶ **510** *nmf* cabinet-maker.

ébénisterie /ebenistəʀi/ ▶ **510** *nf* cabinet-making.

éberluer /ebɛʀlɥe/ [1] *vtr* [*nouvelle*] to dumbfound; [*personne*] **~ qn** to take sb aback.

éblouir /ebluiʀ/ [3] *vtr* lit, fig to dazzle (**de** with); **se laisser ~ par** to be dazzled by.

éblouissant, ~e /ebluisɑ̃, ɑ̃t/ *adj* lit, fig dazzling; **~e de beauté** dazzlingly beautiful.

éblouissement /ebluismɑ̃/ *nm* **1** (par une lumière vive) dazzle ¢; **2** fig dazzling experience; **le spectacle fut un ~** it was a dazzling sight; **3** (vertige) dizzy spell.

ébonite /ebɔnit/ *nf* ebonite.

éborgner /ebɔʀɲe/ [1] **I** *vtr* **1** (blesser) **~ qn** to blind sb in one eye; hum to poke sb's eye out; **2** Agric to disbud [*arbre*].

II s'éborgner *vpr* to poke one's eye out.

éboueur /ebuœʀ/ ▶ **510** *nm* dustman GB, garbageman US, refuse collector GB Admin, sanitation worker US Admin.

ébouillanter /ebujɑ̃te/ [1] **I** *vtr* to scald [*personne, ustensile, volaille*]; to warm [*théière*]; to blanch [*légumes*].

II s'ébouillanter *vpr* to scald oneself.

éboulement /ebulmɑ̃/ *nm* **1** (de mur, falaise) collapse; (de matériaux) fall; **~ (de rochers)** rockfall; **~ (de terrain)** mudslide; **2** (rochers) fallen rocks; (terre) earth from a landslide.

ébouler: **s'ébouler** /ebule/ [1] *vpr* [*mur, falaise*] to collapse; [*rochers*] to fall; **faire (s')~ un mur** to cause a wall to collapse; **le terrain va s'~** there is going to be a mudslide; **les pluies torrentielles ont fait ~ le terrain** torrential rains caused a mudslide.

éboulis /ebuli/ *nm* (rochers) mass of fallen rocks; (terre) heap of fallen earth.

■ **~ de gravité** scree ¢.

ébouriffant○, **~e** /ebuʀifɑ̃, ɑ̃t/ *adj* (outré) outrageous; (extraordinaire) incredible.

ébouriffer /ebuʀife/ [1] *vtr* **1** [*vent*] to tousle [*cheveux*]; to ruffle [*plumes, poils*]; [*personne*] to ruffle [*cheveux*]; **tu es tout ébouriffé** your hair is all tousled; **2**○ [*nouvelle, spectacle*] to astound.

ébranchage /ebʀɑ̃ʃaʒ/, **ébranchement** /ebʀɑ̃ʃmɑ̃/ *nm* lopping.

ébrancher /ebʀɑ̃ʃe/ [1] *vtr* to lop.

ébranchoir /ebʀɑ̃ʃwaʀ/ *nm* billhook.

ébranlement /ebʀɑ̃lmɑ̃/ *nm* **1** (vibration) (de vitres) rattling; (de sol, maison) shaking; **2** (choc) shock; (affaiblissement) (de santé, fortune) deterioration; (de régime, ministère) weakening; **3** (départ) departure.

ébranler /ebʀɑ̃le/ [1] **I** *vtr* **1** lit (faire vibrer) to rattle [*vitre*]; to shake [*maison*]; (rendre chancelant) to weaken [*construction*]; **2** (émouvoir) to shake [*personne, pays*]; (affaiblir) to weaken, undermine [*santé, régime*]; to undermine [*confiance, autorité, fortune*]; to disturb [*esprit*]; to shake [*nerfs*]; **fortement ébranlé par les critiques** badly shaken by criticism; **se laisser ~ par des larmes/prières** to let oneself be swayed by tears/entreaties; **3** (mettre en mouvement) **~ une cloche** to set a bell swinging.

II s'ébranler *vpr* [*convoi, train*] to move off; [*cloche*] to start swinging.

ébrécher /ebʀeʃe/ [14] **I** *vtr* **1** to chip [*vaisselle, dent*]; to make a nick in [*lame*]; to damage [*scie*]; fig to tarnish [*réputation*]; **la lame est ébréchée** the blade is nicked; **2** (entamer) to make a hole in [*économies, patrimoine*]; **mes économies sont bien ébréchées** there's quite a dent in my savings.

II s'ébrécher *vpr* [*vaisselle, dent*] to get chipped; [*lame*] to become nicked.

ébréchure /ebʀeʃyʀ/ *nf* (de vaisselle) chip; (de lame) nick.

ébriété /ebʀijete/ *nf* fml Admin intoxication; **en état d'~** in a state of intoxication, under the influence of (alcohol).

ébrouement /ebʀumɑ̃/ *nm* (de cheval) snort.

ébrouer: **s'ébrouer** /ebʀue/ [1] *vpr* **1** [*cheval*] to snort; **2** [*personne, chien*] to shake oneself; [*gros oiseau*] to flap its wings; [*petit oiseau*] to flutter its wings.

ébruitement /ebʀɥitmɑ̃/ *nm* disclosure.

ébruiter /ebʀɥite/ [1] **I** *vtr* to divulge.

II s'ébruiter *vpr* [*nouvelle*] to get out; **il ne faut pas que ça s'ébruite** no word of this must get out.

ébullition /ebylisjɔ̃/ *nf* (de liquide) boiling; **point d'~** boiling point; **au moment de l'~** when boiling point is reached; **entrer en ~** to begin to boil; **arriver/porter à ~** to come/bring to the boil GB ou a boil US.

IDIOMES **être en ~** [*maisonnée, foule*] to be in a fever of excitement; [*pays, cerveau*] to be in a ferment.

écaillage /ekajaʒ/ *nm* **1** (de poisson) scaling; (d'huître) opening; **2** (de peinture, vernis) flaking.

écaille /ekaj/ *nf* **1** (de poisson, reptile, papillon) scale; (d'huître) shell; **2** (pour peignes) tortoiseshell; (pour lunettes) **lunettes/montures en ~** horn-rimmed glasses/frames; **3** (parcelle) flake; **s'en aller en ~s** to flake off; **4** Bot (de bourgeon, cône, d'oignon) scale.

IDIOMES **les ~s lui sont tombées des yeux** the scales fell from his/her eyes.

écailler, **-ère** /ekaje, ɛʀ/ [1] **I** ▶ **510** *nm,f* oyster seller.

II *vtr* **1** Culin to scale [*poisson*]; to open [*huître*]; **2** (endommager) **~ qch** [*intempéries*] to cause [sth] to flake; [*personne*] to chip [sth] off.

III s'écailler *vpr* [*vernis, plâtre*] to flake away.

écailleux, **-euse** /ekajø, øz/ *adj* **1** [*peau, poisson*] scaly; **2** [*plâtre, vernis*] (tombant) flaking; (aspect) flaky.

écaillure /ekajyʀ/ *nf* **1** Zool (agencement) scaling; (ensemble) scales; **2** (de plâtre) flake.

écale /ekal/ *nf* (de noix) husk.

écaler /ekale/ [1] *vtr* to husk [*noix*].

écarlate /ekaʀlat/ ▶ **193** **I** *adj* scarlet; **il devint ~ de rage/honte** he turned scarlet with rage/shame.

II *nf* scarlet.

écarquiller /ekaʀkije/ [1] *vtr* **~ les yeux** to open one's eyes wide (**devant** at); **elle me regardait les yeux écarquillés** she stared at me wide-eyed; **il écarquillait les yeux pour mieux voir** he strained his eyes to see better.

écart /ekaʀ/ **I** *nm* **1** (distance) (entre des objets) distance (**entre** between), gap (**entre** between); (entre des dates, événements) interval (**entre** between); (entre des concepts, attitudes) gap (**entre** between); (entre des versions) difference (**entre** between); **~ inflationniste/technologique** inflationary/technological gap; **un ~ d'un mètre** a one-metre[GB] gap, a gap of one metre[GB]; **~ de six mois** six-month interval, interval of six months; **creuser/réduire l'~** to widen/narrow the gap; **il y a trop d'~ entre eux (en âge)** there's too much of an age gap between them; ▶ **grand**; **2** (variation) difference; **~s de température** differences in temperature; **~s de prix** price differences, differences in prices; **~ des salaires** pay differential; **~ de dix francs/degrés** ten-franc/-degree difference, difference of ten francs/degrees; **~ par rapport à la normale/moyenne** deviation from the norm/mean; **3** (mouvement brusque) (de cheval) shy; (de voiture) swerve; **faire un ~** [*cheval*] to shy; [*voiture*] to swerve; [*piéton*] to leap aside; **4** fig (faute) lapse; **il fait des ~s de régime** he doesn't stick to his diet; **~s de langage** bad language ¢; **5** (aux cartes) discard.

II à l'écart *loc adv* **être à l'~** to be isolated; **ils bavardaient dans le jardin, à l'~** they were talking in the garden GB ou yard US, off by themselves; **elle vit à l'~** she keeps herself to herself; **se tenir à l'~** (éloigné) to stand apart; (refuser de se mêler) to keep oneself to oneself; (ne pas participer) not to join in; **mettre qn à l'~** (éloigner) to push sb aside; (mettre au ban) to ostracize sb; **il ne supporte pas cette mise à l'~** he cannot bear the way he is being ostracized ou ignored; **prendre** or **entraîner qn à l'~** to take sb aside.

III à l'écart de *loc prép* **à l'~ de la ville/route** away from the town/road; **laisser** or **tenir qn à l'~ de** to keep sb away from [*lieu*]; to keep sb out of [*activité*]; **se tenir à l'~ des autres** (dans l'espace) to stand apart from the others; (socialement) to refuse to join in; **rester** or **se tenir à l'~ du conflit/des négociations** to keep out of the conflict/the negotiations.

■ **~ de conduite** lapse in behaviour[GB]; **faire des ~s de conduite** to have occasional lapses; **~ de jeunesse** youthful indiscretion; **~ à la moyenne** Stat deviation from the mean.

écarté, **~e** /ekaʀte/ **I** *pp* ▶ **écarter**.

II *pp adj* **1** (espacé) [*doigts*] spread (*épith, après n*); [*bras*] wide apart (*épith, après n*); [*genoux, jambes*] apart (*épith, après n*); [*yeux*] widely set; **avoir les dents ~es** to have widely spaced teeth; **2** (isolé) [*lieu, village*] isolated, out of the way (*jamais épith*); [*sentier*] out of the way (*jamais épith*).

III ▶ **449** *nm* Jeux écarté.

écartèlement /ekaʀtɛlmɑ̃/ *nm* **1** fig (déchirement) **ressentir un ~ entre** to feel torn between; **2** (supplice) quartering; **condamné à l'~** condemned to be quartered; **3** Hérald quartering.

écarteler /ekaʀtəle/ [17] *vtr* **1** fig (déchirer) to tear [sb] apart; **être écartelé** to be torn (**entre** between); **2** (supplicier) to quarter; **3** Hérald to quarter.

écartement /ekaʀtəmɑ̃/ *nm* (distance) distance, space; **les rangées ont un ~ de 2 mètres** the rows are (set) 2 metres[GB] apart; **~ des rails** Rail gauge; **~ des essieux** Aut wheelbase.

écarter /ekaʀte/ [1] **I** *vtr* **1** (séparer) to move [sth] further apart [*objets*]; to open [*rideaux*]; to open, to spread [*bras, jambes*]; to spread [*doigts*]; to part [*lèvres, feuillage, buissons*]; **~ la foule pour passer** to push one's way through the crowd; **2** (éloigner) to move [sth] aside [*chaise*]; to brush [sth] aside [*mèche*]; to remove [*obstacle*]; to push [sb] aside [*personne*]; to move [sb] on [*badauds*]; **~ qch/qn de qch** lit to move sth/sb away from sth; **~ les obstacles de sa route** to remove the obstacles from one's path; **~ une branche qui gêne** to push a branch out of the way; **ce chemin nous écarte trop** this path takes us too far out of our way; **ce chemin nous écarte de la ferme** this path takes us too far from the farm; **3** fig (détourner) **~ qn de son devoir** to distract sb from his duty; **~ qn de la tentation** to keep sb out of reach of temptation; **cela nous écarte du sujet** we're getting off the point; **4** (éliminer) to dispel [*danger, soupçon*]; to remove [*tentation*]; to eliminate [*risque*]; to eliminate, to push [sb] aside fig [*concurrent*]; **tout danger est écarté** the danger is over; **5** (rejeter) to dismiss, to reject [*idée, argument, solution, candidature*]; to rule out [*possibilité*]; **~ qch des débats** to keep sth out of the discussion; **~ qn de** to exclude sb from [*groupe*]; to remove sb from [*comité, discussion*]; **~ qn du pouvoir/de la scène politique** to remove sb from power/from the political scene.

II s'écarter *vpr* **1** (se séparer) [*foule, nuages*] to part; [*volets*] to open; **2** (s'éloigner) to move away (**de** from); **s'~ discrètement** to withdraw discreetly; **s'~ d'un bond** to leap aside; **écartez-vous, voilà l'ambulance** move out of the way, here's the ambulance; **écartez-vous les uns des autres** spread out a bit; **s'~ l'un de l'autre** [*chemins*] to diverge; **depuis le scandale, on s'écarte d'elle** since the scandal, nobody will have anything to do with her; **3** (dévier) lit, fig **s'~ de** to move away from [*trajectoire, direction, norme*]; to stray from [*chemin*]; to wander off, to stray from [*sujet*]; to diverge from [*vérité*]; **s'~ de la verticale** [*mur*] to be out of plumb; **s'~ de son devoir** to fail in one's duty.

écarteur /ekaʀtœʀ/ *nm* Méd retractor.

écart-type, *pl* **écarts-types** /ekaʀtip/ *nm* Stat standard deviation.

ecchymose /ekimoz/ *nf* bruise, ecchymosis spéc; **couvert d'~s** badly bruised.

Ecclésiaste /eklezjast/ *nprm* **(le livre de) l'~** (the Book of) Ecclesiastes.

ecclésiastique /eklezjastik/ **I** *adj* (du clergé) ecclesiastical; [*ordres, état*] holy.

II *nm* cleric, ecclesiastic†.

écervelé, **~e** /esɛʀvəle/ **I** *adj* featherbrained, birdbrained US.

II *nm,f* featherbrain, birdbrain US.

ECG /œseʒe/ *nm* Méd ECG, electrocardiogram.

échafaud /eʃafo/ *nm* **1** (lieu) scaffold; **monter à l'~** to mount the scaffold; **finir sur l'~** to end up on the scaffold; **2** (peine capitale) guillotine; **il risque l'~** he faces the guillotine; **condamné à l'~** condemned to be guillotined.

échafaudage /eʃafodaʒ/ *nm* **1** Constr scaffolding ¢; **monter un ~** or **des ~s** to put up scaffolding; **2** (tas) stack; **3** fig (montage) edifice.

échafauder /eʃafode/ [1] **I** *vtr* **1** (élaborer) to put [sth] together [*plan, théorie*]; to build up [*fortune*]; **2** (empiler) to stack [sth] up.

II *vi* Constr to put up scaffolding.

échalas /eʃala/ *nm* **1** (pieu) cane; **2**○ (personne) beanpole○.

IDIOMES **raide comme un ~** as stiff as a post.

échalier /eʃalje/ *nm* (échelle) ladder, stile; (clôture) hurdle GB.

échalote /eʃalɔt/ *nf* shallot.

échancré, ~e /eʃɑ̃kʀe/ **I** *pp* ▸ **échancrer.**

II *pp adj* **1** Cout [*robe*] low-cut; [*culotte, maillot*] cut high on the thigh (*après n*); **trop/pas assez ~** [*emmanchure*] cut too wide/too tight (*après n*); **2** (ouvert) [*chemise*] open-necked; **3** [*côte*] indented; [*feuille*] jagged.

échancrer /eʃɑ̃kʀe/ [1] *vtr* **1** Cout (découper) cut away [*encolure, emmanchure*]; **~ une robe sur le devant/sous les bras** to cut a dress low at the front/under the arms; **2** (creuser) [*mer*] to indent [*côte*].

échancrure /eʃɑ̃kʀyʀ/ *nf* **1** Cout **l'~ est trop grande** (d'encolure) it's cut too low at the neck; (d'emmanchure) it's cut too wide under the arms; (de jambe) it's cut too high on the thighs; **2** (de côte) indentation; **3** Anat (d'os) notch.

échange /eʃɑ̃ʒ/ **I** *nm* **1** gén exchange (**entre** between; **contre** for); **~ d'idées/de coups** exchange of ideas/of blows; **vifs ~s sur** heated exchanges on; **il y a eu un ~ de coups entre les supporters** blows were exchanged between the (rival) fans; **ils ne font pas l'~ dans cette boutique** they don't exchange goods in this shop; **les deux pays ont fait un ~ d'experts/de prisonniers** the two countries have exchanged experts/prisoners; **elles ont fait l'~ de leurs manteaux** they've swapped coats; **mon casque est trop petit, on fait l'~?** my helmet is too small, shall we swap?; **les philatélistes font souvent des ~s** stamp collectors often exchange stamps; **~ de partenaires** partner-swapping; **2** Écon, Comm trade ¢; **~s commerciaux** trade; **~s extérieurs** foreign trade; **3** (relations) exchange; **les ~s culturels/universitaires** cultural/university exchanges; **4** (pour un séjour linguistique) exchange; **mon fils fait/va faire un ~ en Italie** my son is/will be on an exchange in Italy; **5** Biol, Phys exchange; **~ gazeux** gaseous exchange; **6** (au tennis, tennis de table) rally; **ils ont fait un long ~** they played a long rally; **faire des ~s pour s'échauffer** to play some warm-up rallies, to warm up; **7** (aux échecs) exchange; **faire un ~** to exchange pieces.

II en échange *loc adv* in exchange, in return; **en ~, le ministre a accordé une aide financière** in return, the minister has granted financial aid; **nous devons en ~ entretenir la maison** in return we must see to the upkeep of the house.

III en échange de *loc prép* in exchange for, in return for; **en ~ de quoi** in exchange for which.

■ **~ de bons procédés** quid pro quo; **~ de créances** Fin debt swap; **~ de créances contre actifs** Fin debt equity swap; **~ de devises dues** Fin currency swap; **~ financier** Fin swap; **~ standard** replacement by a reconditioned part; **'il faut faire un ~ standard'** 'we'll have to replace it with a reconditioned part'.

échangeable /eʃɑ̃ʒabl/ *adj* exchangeable.

échanger /eʃɑ̃ʒe/ [13] **I** *vtr* **1** gén to exchange (**contre** for); **~ des coups** to exchange blows; **nous avons échangé nos adresses** we exchanged addresses; **~ des insultes** to trade insults; **~ des remerciements** to thank each other; **elle et sa sœur échangent souvent leurs vêtements** she often swaps clothes with her sister; **'les articles ne sont ni repris ni échangés'** 'no exchanges or returns'; **2** (au tennis, ping-pong) **~ des balles** to rally.

II s'échanger *vpr* to be exchanged.

échangeur /eʃɑ̃ʒœʀ/ *nm* **1** Aut (intersection) interchange GB, grade separation US; **2** Tech exchanger.

■ **~ de chaleur** heat exhanger; **~ d'ions** ion exchanger.

échangisme /eʃɑ̃ʒism/ *nm* practice of swapping sexual partners, partner-swapping.

échangiste /eʃɑ̃ʒist/ *nmf* swapper of sexual partner, partner-swapper.

échanson /eʃɑ̃sɔ̃/ *nm* cupbearer.

échantillon /eʃɑ̃tijɔ̃/ *nm* (tous contextes) sample.

échantillonnage /eʃɑ̃tijɔnaʒ/ *nm* **1** (prélèvement) sampling; (ensemble) selection; **2** Mus sampling.

échantillonner /eʃɑ̃tijɔne/ [1] *vtr* Sci, Tech, Stat to take a sample of; Ordinat, Télécom to sample.

échappatoire /eʃapatwaʀ/ *nf* way out (**à** of); **répondre par une ~** to answer evasively.

échappée /eʃape/ *nf* **1** Sport break; **2** (escapade) **faire une ~ au bord de la mer** to go for a short break to the seaside; **3** (court instant) spell; **~ de beau temps** bright spell; **4** (vue) **une ~ sur la baie** a glimpse of the bay.

échappement /eʃapmɑ̃/ *nm* **1** (de gaz) (dispositif) exhaust; (expulsion) release; **tuyau d'~** exhaust pipe; **rouler avec l'** or **en ~ libre** to drive without a silencer GB ou muffler US; **2** (d'horlogerie) escapement.

échapper /eʃape/ [1] **I échapper à** *vtr ind* **1** (se dérober) **~ à** (par la fuite) to get away from [*poursuivant, prédateur*]; (par la ruse) to elude [*enquêteur, chasseur*]; **2** (éviter) **~ à** to escape [*mort, destruction, destin, faillite*]; (to manage) to avoid [*accident, châtiment, danger, contraintes*]; **~ à tout contrôle** not to be subject to any control; **~ à une taxation** (légalement) to be exempt from tax; (illégalement) to evade a tax; **personne n'échappe à leurs commentaires acides** no-one is spared their cutting remarks; **~ aux réunions de famille** to get out of family gatherings; **~ à l'obligation de faire** to get out of having to do; **ils s'attendent à ta visite, tu n'y échapperas pas** they're expecting you, you won't be able to get out of it; **3** (se libérer de) **~ à** to escape from [*milieu social*]; to shake off [*angoisse, désespoir*]; **pour ~ aux railleries** to escape being teased; **il n'échappe pas à l'influence de sa mère** he is still under his mother's influence; **c'est l'âge où les enfants commencent à vous ~** it's the age when your children begin to grow away from you; **je sens qu'il m'échappe** [*mari, amant*] I feel that he is drifting away from me; **4** (tomber) **~ à qn** [*objet*] to slip out of sb's hands; **la bouteille a failli m'~** the bottle nearly slipped out of my hands; **~ des mains de qn** [*objet*] to slip out of sb's hands; **5** (être produit involontairement) **un soupir/grognement m'a échappé** I let out a sigh/groan; **une parole cynique m'a échappé** I let slip a cynical comment; **cela m'a échappé** it just slipped out; **6** (intellectuellement) **~ à** to escape; **le titre m'échappe pour le moment** the title escapes me for the moment; **cela m'échappe** (trop compliqué) it's beyond me; **l'ironie de ta remarque ne m'a pas échappé** the irony of your remark did not escape me; **la gravité de la situation n'échappe à personne** the seriousness of the situation is obvious to everybody; **ces disparités n'ont pas échappé au ministre** the minister is fully aware of these disparities; **l'erreur nous a échappé** we did not spot the mistake; **rien ne t'échappe!** you don't miss a thing!; **7** (défier) **~ à** to defy [*classification, logique*]; **~ à la règle** to be an exception to the rule.

II s'échapper *vpr* **1** (s'enfuir) [*personne, animal*] to run away (**de** from); [*oiseau*] to fly away (**de** from); (d'un lieu clos) to escape (**de** from); (ne pas être pris) to get away; **faire ~ qn** to help [sb] escape [*personne*]; **faire ~ un animal** to let an animal out; **laisser ~** [*personne*] to let [sb] get away [*personne, animal*]; to let [sth] slip between one's fingers [*victoire*]; to let [sth] slip [*occasion*]; **2** (se répandre) [*gaz, fumée*] to escape (**de, par** from); [*eau*] to leak (**de, par** from); **laisser ~** [*récipient, fissure, dispositif*] to let [sth] out [*vapeur, fumée*]; **laisser ~ de l'huile/du gaz/de l'eau** [*récipient*] to have an oil/a gas/a water leak; **3** (partir) to get away; **s'~ pour quelques jours** to get away for a few days; **s'~ d'une pièce/réunion** to slip out of a room/meeting; **4** (être produit) **laisser ~** to let [sth] fall [*larmes*]; to let out [*parole, juron, soupir, secret*]; **un faible gémissement s'échappa de ses lèvres** he/she gave a faint groan; **5** Sport to break away.

IDIOMES **l'~ belle** to have a narrow escape.

écharde /eʃaʀd/ *nf* splinter.

écharpe /eʃaʀp/ *nf* (cache-col) scarf; (d'officiel) sash; (bandage) sling; **en ~** (bras) in a sling; **prendre une voiture en ~** to hit a car sideways on GB, to sideswipe a car US.

écharper /eʃaʀpe/ [1] *vtr* **~ qn/qch** to tear sb/sth to pieces; **se faire ~** to get torn to pieces.

échasse /eʃɑs/ *nf* **1** (de berger) stilt; **2** (oiseau) stilt.

IDIOMES **il est monté sur des ~s**○ he's got great long legs.

échassier /eʃasje/ *nm* wading bird.

échauder /eʃode/ [1] *vtr* **1** (décourager) to put [sb] off; **échaudé par sa première expérience, il décide de...** having had his fingers burned by his first experience, he decides...; **2** (ébouillanter) to scald.

IDIOMES **chat échaudé craint l'eau froide** Prov once bitten, twice shy Prov.

échauffement /eʃofmɑ̃/ *nm* **1** Sport warm-up; **exercices/séance d'~** warm-up exercises/session; **2** fig (excitation) heat (**de** of); **3** Tech (de moteur, pneu) overheating; (de sol, d'eau) warming; **4** Bot (de foin, grain, bois) fermentation.

échauffer /eʃofe/ [1] **I** *vtr* **1** Sport to warm up; **2** fig (animer) to stir [*imagination, esprit*]; to stir up [*personne, débat*]; **3** (rendre chaud) to overheat [*corps, liquide, pièce*]; to warm [*sol*]; **4** (produire une fermentation) to start [sth] fermenting.

II s'échauffer *vpr* **1** Sport to warm up; **2** (s'animer) [*imagination, esprit*] to be stirred; [*personne, discussion*] to become heated; **3** (devenir chaud, rouge) [*visage*] to get hot; **4** (fermenter) to begin to ferment.

IDIOMES **~ les oreilles** or **la bile de qn** to vex sb.

échauffourée /eʃofuʀe/ *nf* brawl; Mil skirmish; **une ~ avec qn** a clash with sb.

échauguette /eʃogɛt/ *nf* bartizan.

èche /ɛʃ/ *nf* bait.

échéance /eʃeɑ̃s/ *nf* **1** Fin, Comm (date d'exigibilité) (de dette, facture, loyer, quittance, traite) due date; (d'action, assurance, de bon) maturity date; (d'emprunt) redemption date; **payer avant l'~** to pay before the due date; **payable à (l')~** payable when due; **il attend toujours l'~ pour payer son loyer** he never pays his rent until it is due; **~ fin courant** due at the end of the month; **arriver** or **venir à ~** [*loyer, traite, emprunt*] to fall due; [*assurance, placement*] to mature; **2** (date d'expiration) expiry date; **arriver** or **venir à ~** to expire; **3** (délai) currency; **d'une ~ de 2 mois** with a currency of 2 months; **à longue/brève ~** [*bon, prévision*] long-/short-term; [*renforcer, changer*] in the long/short term; **la loi devrait être votée à brève ~** the law should be passed shortly; **à plus ou moins brève ~** sooner or later; **4** (somme due) (de facture, loyer) payment; (d'emprunt, de dette) repayment; **l'~ est de 800 F** the payment due is 800 F; **payer ses ~s** to make one's payments; **faire face à de lourdes ~** to have a lot of payments to make; **l'~ de fin de trimestre** the end of term payment; **5** (d'événement, de changement) date; (date limite) deadline; **l'~ de la mort** the advent of death; **l'~ électorale** polling GB ou election day; **~ européenne/présidentielle** European/presidential elections.

échéancier /eʃeɑ̃sje/ *nm* Compta schedule of due dates; (calendrier d'échéances) schedule of repayments.

échéant: **le cas échéant** /ləkazeʃeɑ̃/ *loc adv* if need be; (sur un formulaire) **cocher le cas ~** tick GB ou check US where appropriate.

échec /eʃɛk/ **I** *nm* **1** Scol, Univ failure (**à** in GB, on US); **c'est son second ~** it's the second time he's failed; **après trois ~s** after three unsuccessful attempts; **2** (fait de ne pas atteindre son but) failure; (rémédiable) setback; **~ personnel/commercial/scolaire** personal/commercial/academic failure; **malgré les ~s du début** despite the initial setbacks; **~ sentimental** failed love affair; **subir un ~** to fail; (temporairement) to suffer a setback; **courir à l'~** to be heading for failure; **se solder par un ~** to end in failure; **voué à l'~** doomed to failure; **faire ~ à qn/aux projets de qn** to thwart sb/sb's plans; **tenir l'ennemi en ~** to hold the enemy in check; **le virus tient toujours les chercheurs en ~** the virus continues to defy scientists; **3** (défaite) Pol, Sport defeat; Mil reverse; **essuyer** or **subir un ~** to suffer a defeat ou a reverse; **4** Jeux **~ au roi** check; **faire ~ au roi** to check the king; **~ et mat** checkmate; **faire ~ et mat** to checkmate.

II ▶449 **échecs** *nmpl* **les ~s** (jeu) chess; (échiquier et pièces) chess set; (pièces) chessmen; **jouer aux ~s** to play chess; **faire une partie d'~s** to play a game of chess.

échelle /eʃɛl/ *nf* **1** (pour monter, descendre) ladder; **monter à une ~** to climb a ladder; **~ de corde** rope ladder; **~ coulissante** extending ladder GB, extension ladder US; **~ double** double sided ladder; **~ de pompier** firemen's ladder; **faire la courte ~ à qn** to give sb a leg up; **2** (de plan, maquette) scale; **plan à l'~** scale plan; **carte à l'~ de 1/10 000ᵉ** map on a 1:10,000 scale; **la carte est à l'~ de 1/10 000ᵉ** the map has a scale of 1:10,000; **carte à grande ~** large-scale map; **carte à ~ réduite** small-scale map; **3** (système de gradation) scale; **~ de dureté** hardness scale; **~ de Beaufort/Richter** Beaufort/Richter scale; **tremblement de terre de force 5 sur l'~ de Richter** earthquake measuring 5 on the Richter scale; **à l'~ humaine/nationale/mondiale** on a human/national/worldwide scale; **sur une large ~** on a large scale; **4** fig (dans un milieu social) scale, ladder; (dans une entreprise) hierarchy, ladder; **s'élever dans l'~ sociale** to rise up the social scale; **~ des valeurs/de difficulté** scale of values/difficulty; **~ des prix** scale of prices; **~ des salaires** pay scale; **~ mobile des salaires** sliding pay-scale; **5** Mus scale; **6**○ (accroc à un collant) ladder.

■ **~ de bibliothèque** library step; **~ de coupée** accommodation ladder; **~ de meunier** open staircase; **~ de passerelle** companion ladder; **~ de pilote** jacob's ladder; **~ de poissons** fish ladder.

échelon /eʃlɔ̃/ *nm* **1** (d'échelle) rung; **2** Admin (rang) grade; **fonctionnaire au 4ᵉ ~** grade 4 official; **monter/descendre d'un ~** to go up/down a grade; **sauter les ~s** to get accelerated promotion; **3** (niveau) level; **à l'~ ministériel/ de la division** at ministerial/divisional level; **4** Mil (unité) echelon.

échelonnement /eʃlɔnmɑ̃/ *nm* **1** (d'objets) spacing out; **2** (de paiements) spreading out; (de congés, départs) staggering; **3** (gradation) (d'exercices) grading; (de difficultés) gradual introduction; **4** Mil deployment in echelon.

échelonner /eʃlɔne/ [1] **I** *vtr* **1** (espacer) to space [sth] out [*balises*]; **les poteaux sont échelonnés à 30 m d'intervalle** the posts are set 30 metres apart ou at 30 metre intervals; **2** (répartir) to spread [*paiements, travail*] (**sur** over); to stagger [*congés, départs*] (**sur** over); **3** (graduer) to grade [*exercices*]; to build up [*arguments*]; **4** Mil to deploy [sth] in echelon [*troupes*].

II s'échelonner *vpr* **1** [*objets, personnes*] to be positioned at intervals (**sur** over); **2** [*paiements, travaux*] to be spread (**sur** over); [*congés, départs*] to be staggered (**sur** over).

écheveau, *pl* **~x** /eʃvo/ *nm* **1** (de laine, coton) hank, skein; (de fil à broder) skein; **vendu en ~x** sold by the hank; **2** (enchevêtrement) tangle.

échevelé, **~e** /eʃəvle/ **I** *pp* ▶ **écheveler**.

II *pp adj* **1** (décoiffé) tousled; **2** fig [*rythme*] frenzied; [*romantisme*] unbridled; [*course*] mad.

écheveler /eʃəvle/ [19] *vtr* **~ qn** to ruffle sb's hair; **le vent nous échevelait** the wind was ruffling our hair.

échevin /eʃ(ə)vɛ̃/ *nm* **1** Hist municipal magistrate; **2** (en Belgique) deputy burgomaster.

échine /eʃin/ *nf* **1** (colonne vertébrale) spine; **2** (de porc) Culin ≈ spare rib.

IDIOMES **courber l'~ devant** to submit to; **avoir l'~ souple** to be a toady.

échiner: **s'échiner** /eʃine/ [1] *vpr* **s'~ à faire** to make a great effort to do; **il s'échine au travail** he works like a dog; **je m'échine à lui dire/à le convaincre** I'm worn out telling him/trying to persuade him.

échiquier /eʃikje/ *nm* **1** (aux échecs) chessboard; **2** fig (terrain) arena; **3** (motif) chequered GB ou checkered US pattern; **planter en ~** to plant in a chequered GB ou checkered US pattern.

Échiquier /eʃikje/ *nprm* **l'~** the Exchequer, the Treasury.

écho /eko/ *nm* **1** (de son) aussi Ordinat, Tech, TV echo; **~ simple/multiple/radar** single/multiple/radar echo; **effet d'~** echo effect; **il y a de l'~** there is an echo; **divulguer/répéter qch à tous les ~s** to divulge/repeat sth to all and sundry; **faire ~ à qch** to echo sth; **se faire l'~ de qch** to echo sth; **2** (réaction) response; **en ~** in response (**à** to); **avoir/recevoir un ~** to get/receive a response (**de** from); **trouver un ~** or **des ~s** to meet with a response (**à qch** to sth; **auprès de qn, chez qn** from sb; **dans** in); **trouver un large/faible ~** to meet with a great/faint response; **ne trouver aucun ~** to fail to elicit any response; **3** (information) **nous n'avons eu aucun ~ des pourparlers** we have heard nothing about the talks; **4** Presse (anecdote) piece of gossip.

■ **~ flottant** echo flutter.

échographie /ekɔgʀafi/ *nf* scan; **passer une ~** to have a scan, ultrasound scan spéc.

échographier /ekɔgʀafje/ [2] *vtr* to scan.

échographique /ekɔgʀafik/ *adj* ultrasonic.

échoir /eʃwaʀ/ [51] **I** *vi* (loyer) to fall due; (traite) to be payable.

II échoir à *vtr ind* **~ à qn** to fall to sb's share.

échoppe /eʃɔp/ *nf* stall.

échotier, **-ière** /ekɔtje, ɛʀ/ *nm,f* local news reporter.

échouage /eʃwaʒ/ *nm* **1** (processus) beaching; **2** (situation) state of being beached; **3** (endroit) **chercher un ~ pour l'hiver** to look for a suitable place to beach the boat for the winter.

échouement /eʃumɑ̃/ *nm* Naut (échouage involontaire) (processus) stranding; (situation) state of being stranded.

échouer /eʃwe/ [1] **I** *vtr* Naut to beach [*bateau, embarcation*].

II échouer à *vtr ind* [*personne*] to fail [*examen, épreuve*].

III *vi* **1** (ne pas réussir) [*personne, tentative*] to fail; **~ dans une tentative/devant un obstacle** to fail in an attempt/in the face of an obstacle; **~ face à un adversaire** to lose to an opponent; **notre équipe avait échoué en demi-finale** our team had lost in the semifinal; **faire ~** to cause [sth] to fail [*négociations, projet, proposition*]; **2** (se retrouver) [*personne*] to end up; [*objet, dossier*] to end up; **3** Naut [*bateau*] to run aground; **un pétrolier échoué sur les récifs** an oil tanker stranded on the reef.

IV s'échouer *vpr* [*bateau*] to run aground (**sur** on); [*baleine*] to be beached; **la baleine s'est échouée sur la plage** the whale was stranded on the beach.

échu, **~e** /eʃy/ **I** *pp* ▶ **échoir**.

II *pp adj* expired; **payer son loyer à terme ~** to pay one's rent in arrears.

écimage /esimaʒ/ *nm* (d'arbre) pollarding; (de vigne) topping.

écimer /esime/ [1] *vtr* to pollard [*arbre*]; to top [*vigne*].

éclaboussement /eklabusmɑ̃/ *nm* splash.

éclabousser /eklabuse/ [1] *vtr* **1** (mouiller) to splash (**avec** with); (salir) to spatter (**de** with); **~ une page d'encre** to spatter a page with ink, to spatter ink over a page; **~ qn de son luxe** fig to crush sb with a display of wealth; **mur (tout) éclaboussé de sang** blood-spattered wall; **2** (infliger un dommage à) **il a été éclaboussé par ces rumeurs** his good name has been tarnished ou sullied by these rumours[GB].

éclaboussure /eklabusyʀ/ *nf* **1** (d'eau, de boue) splash; (d'encre, de sang) spatter; **2** (sur une réputation) blot, blemish; **sa réputation a reçu quelques ~s** his reputation has been tarnished.

éclair /eklɛʀ/ **I** *adj inv* **rencontre ~** brief meeting; **visite ~** flying visit; **attaque ~** lightning strike; **guerre ~** blitzkrieg; **repas ~** quick meal; **il n'a fait que des passages ~** his visits were brief.

II *nm* **1** Météo flash of lightning; **il y a des ~s** there's lightning; **à** or **avec la vitesse de l'~** with lightning speed; **en un ~** in a flash; **passer comme un ~** to flash past; **traverser l'esprit comme un ~** to flash through one's mind; **en un ~** in the twinkling of an eye; **2** (éclat) (d'explosion, de flash) Phot flash; (de bijou) liter flash; (de regard) glint; **un ~ malicieux dans les yeux des enfants** a mischievous glint in the children's eyes; **leurs yeux lançaient des ~s de colère** their eyes were flashing with anger; **3** (de lucidité, triomphe) moment; **il a eu un ~ de génie** he had a brainwave GB ou brainstorm US; **4** Culin éclair.

■ **~ de chaleur** sheet lightning ₵.

éclairage /eklɛʀaʒ/ *nm* (manière d'éclairer) lighting; (lumière) light; **~ direct/indirect** direct/indirect lighting; **~ électrique** electric light; **~ au gaz** gaslight; **faible ~** dim light; **sous cet ~** fig in that light.

■ **~ zénithal** *natural lighting from above*.

éclairagiste /eklɛʀaʒist/ ▶510 *nm* Théât, Cin electrician; **chef ~** gaffer.

éclairant, **~e** /eklɛʀɑ̃, ɑ̃t/ *adj* [*fusée, bombe*] flare.

éclaircie /eklɛʀsi/ *nf* **1** Météo (espace clair) sunny spell; (embellie) break in the weather; **'temps variable avec de belles ~s dans l'après-midi'** 'the weather will be rather unsettled with some bright intervals in the afternoon'; **2** fml fig (de situation, conflit) respite sout; **prévoir une ~ dans le climat social** to predict some respite in the social climate.

éclaircir /eklɛʀsiʀ/ [3] **I** *vtr* **1** (rendre moins sombre) to lighten [*couleur*]; to lighten the colour[GB] of [*peinture, cheveux*]; to clear [*teint*]; **2** (clarifier) to clarify [*situation, problème, idée*]; (élucider) to shed light on [*énigme, mystère*]; **certains points sont encore à ~** some points still need clarifying; **3** Culin to thin [*sauce*]; **4** (rendre moins épais) [*sylviculteur*] to thin [*futaie*]; [*coiffeur*] to thin [*cheveux*].

II s'éclaircir *vpr* **1** Météo [*ciel, temps, brouillard*] to clear; **l'horizon s'éclaircit** lit the horizon is clearing; fig the outlook is getting brighter; **2** (pâlir) [*couleur, tissu*] to fade; [*teint*] to clear; [*cheveux*] to get lighter; **3** (s'élucider) [*situation, problème, mystère*] to become clearer; **4** (se clairsemer) [*foule, public*] to thin out; [*forêt, jungle*] to thin out; [*cheveux, barbe*] to thin out; **5** (rendre clair) **s'~ les cheveux avec de la camomille** to lighten one's hair with camomile;

s'~ la voix or **la gorge** to clear one's throat.

éclaircissant /eklɛʀsisɑ̃/ **I** *adj m* Cosmét **produit ~** hair lightener.
II *nm* Cosmét (hair) lightener.

éclaircissement /eklɛʀsismɑ̃/ *nm* (explication) explanation; (clarification) clarification ¢; **demander des ~s sur qch** to ask for an explanation of sth; **il a été suspendu de ses fonctions jusqu'à ~ de l'affaire** he was suspended from office till the matter was cleared up; **l'enquête n'a apporté aucun ~ sur l'affaire** the inquiry shed no light on the matter.

éclairé, **~e** /ekleʀe/ **I** *pp* ▶ **éclairer**.
II *pp adj* **1** [*tableau, pièce*] lit; **bien/mal ~** well-/badly-lit; **2** fig [*homme, conseil*] enlightened; [*amateur*] well-informed.

éclairement /eklɛʀmɑ̃/ *nm* **1** Phys illumination; **2** Bot light.

éclairer /ekleʀe/ [1] **I** *vtr* **1** (donner de la lumière à) [*lampe, flamme, fenêtre*] to light [*rue, pièce*]; [*soleil, phare*] to light up [*lieu, objet*]; fig [*yeux*] to light up [*visage*]; [*bijou, col, foulard*] to set off [*vêtement*]; **le soleil n'éclaire jamais ce recoin** the sun never reaches this dark corner; **la joie/un sourire éclaira son visage** his face lit up with joy/a smile; **2** (avec une lampe, bougie etc) to give [sb] some light; (pour montrer le chemin) to light the way for; **3** (expliquer) [*remarque, commentaire*] to throw light on, clarify [*texte, pensée, situation*]; **4** (instruire) to enlighten [*personne*] (**sur** as to); **5** Mil to reconnoitre[GB] [*route, terrain*]; to reconnoitre[GB] for [*convoi, troupe*].
II *vi* [*lampe, bougie*] to give light; **bien/mal ~** to give a good/poor light; **ça éclaire peu** it doesn't give much light.
III s'éclairer *vpr* **1** (s'illuminer) [*écran*] to light up; fig [*visage*] to light up (**de** with); **les rues s'éclairent à 8 h** the street lights go on at 8 o'clock; **2** (se donner de la lumière) **s'~ à l'électricité** to have electric lighting; **nous nous éclairons à la bougie** we use candles for lighting; **j'ai pris une lampe de poche pour m'~** I took a torch GB ou flashlight US to see my way; **3** (s'éclaircir) [*situation*] to become clearer; [*question*] to be cleared up.

éclaireur, **-euse** /eklɛʀœʀ, øz/ *nm,f* **1** (en scoutisme) scout/guide GB, girl scout US; **2** Mil scout; **marcher en ~** to scout ahead; **envoyer qn en ~** to send someone on ahead; **partir en ~** to go on ahead.

éclampsie /eklɑ̃psi/ ▶ **271** *nf* eclampsia.

éclat /ekla/ *nm* **1** (de bois, métal, roche) splinter; **des ~s de verre** splinters of glass; **un ~ d'obus** a piece of shrapnel; **des ~s d'obus** shrapnel ¢; **voler en ~s** lit, fig to shatter; **faire voler qch en ~s** lit, fig to shatter sth; **2** (de lumière, d'astre) brightness; (de phare, projecteur) glare; (de neige, diamant) sparkle; **une lumière d'un ~ insoutenable** an unbearably bright light; **briller de tout son ~** to shine brightly; **3** (de couleur, tissu) brilliance; (de fleur) brightness; (de cheveux, plumes) shine, sheen; (de métal) lustre[GB]; (du teint) radiance; (de chaussure, meuble, vernis) shine; **redonner de l'~ à** to make [sth] look like new [*tissu*]; to put the shine back into [*meuble, cheveux*]; **perdre son ~** [*couleur, tissu*] to fade; [*chevelure*] to lose its shine ou sheen; [*métal*] to go dull; [*teint*] to lose its glow; **4** (de visage, sourire) radiance; (de regard) sparkle; **retrouver l'~ de sa jeunesse** to recover the bloom of youth; **sans ~** [*regard*] dull; [*beauté*] lifeless; **5** (grandeur) splendour[GB]; **avec ~** [*annoncer*] dramatically; [*célébrer, fêter*] with great pomp; **manquer d'~** [*cérémonie, discours*] to lack sparkle; **sans ~** [*personnage, cérémonie, soirée*] dull; **action** or **coup d'~** (admirable) remarkable feat; (qui attire l'attention) grand gesture; **6** (esclandre) scene; **faire un ~** to make a scene; **cela s'est passé sans ~s** there was no scene, it passed off quietly.
■ **~ de colère** fit of anger; **~ de rire** roar of laughter; **ce fut l'~ de rire général** everybody roared with laughter; **partir d'un ~ de rire** to burst out laughing; **être réveillé par des ~s de voix** to be woken up by raised voices.
IDIOMES **rire aux ~s** to roar with laughter.

éclatant, **~e** /eklatɑ̃, ɑ̃t/ *adj* **1** (très brillant) [*lumière*] brilliant; [*soleil*] blazing; **un ciel ~ de lumière** a dazzlingly bright sky; **2** (vif) [*couleur, teinte, plumage*] bright; **des tissus d'un rouge/bleu ~** bright red/blue fabrics; **un drap d'un blanc ~** or **d'une blancheur ~e** a dazzlingly white sheet; **dents d'une blancheur ~e** sparkling white teeth; **~ de blancheur** dazzling white; **avoir une mine ~e** to be glowing with health; **3** (admirable) [*beauté, sourire*] radiant; [*gloire*] shining; [*victoire, réussite*] stunning; [*santé*] radiant; **~ de santé** glowing with health; **~ de beauté**, **d'une beauté ~e** radiantly beautiful; **4** (manifeste) [*preuve, démonstration, illustration*] striking; **être la manifestation ~e de** to be a striking example of; **5** (très bruyant) [*bruit, son*] deafening; [*rire, voix*] ringing.

éclaté, **~e** /eklate/ **I** *pp* ▶ **éclater**.
II *pp adj* **1** (fragmenté) gén fragmented; [*famille*] divided; **2** Art [*dessin, vue*] exploded.

éclatement /eklatmɑ̃/ *nm* **1** (rupture) (de tuyau, veine) bursting; (de rate, foie) rupture; **souffrir d'un ~ de la rate** to have a ruptured spleen; **provoquer l'~ des tuyaux** to cause the pipes to burst; **2** (explosion) (d'obus, de grenade) explosion; (de pneu) blow-out; **3** (de famille, parti, communauté) break-up (**en** into); **4** (d'émeute, incident) outbreak.

éclater /eklate/ [1] **I** *vi* **1** (exploser) [*pneu, bulle, chaudière*] to burst; [*obus, pétard*] to explode; [*tuyau*] to burst; [*bouteille*] to shatter; **~ en mille morceaux** [*bouteille, verre*] to shatter into a thousand pieces; **faire ~** [*personne*] to burst [*bulle, ballon*]; to detonate [*bombe, grenade*]; to let off [*pétard*]; **2** (se rompre) [*canalisation, veine, abcès*] to burst; [*organe*] to rupture; **faire ~** [*gel*] to burst [*tuyau*]; **3** (retentir) [*applaudissement, rire, fusillade*] to break out; [*coup de feu*] to ring out; **un coup de tonnerre a éclaté** there was a sudden clap of thunder; **4** (être révélé) [*scandale, affaire, nouvelle*] to break; [*vérité*] to come out; [*polémique*] to break out; **faire ~ qch au grand jour** to bring sth to light; **ce groupe a éclaté sur la scène internationale en 1974** the group burst onto the international scene in 1974; **5** (survenir) [*guerre, dispute, grève, épidémie*] to break out; [*orage*] to break; [*crise*] to erupt; **6** (être exprimé) [*joie, bonheur*] to manifest itself; [*colère*] to erupt; **laisser ~ sa joie/son bonheur** to give free rein to one's joy/one's happiness; **laisser ~ sa colère/son ressentiment** to give vent to one's anger/one's resentment; **7** (se fragmenter) [*coalition, royaume*] to break up; **~ en** to break up into [*provinces*]; to split into [*tendances*]; **faire ~ un parti** to split a party; **8** (se mettre en colère) [*personne*] to lose one's temper, to blow up○; **~ en reproches contre qn** to heap reproaches on sb; **~ de rire** to burst out laughing; **~ en sanglots** to burst into tears.
II s'éclater◐ *vpr* **s'~ (comme une bête)** to have a really good time.

éclateur /eklatœʀ/ *nm* spark gap.
■ **~ de protection** surge arrester.

éclectique /eklɛktik/ *adj* eclectic.

éclectisme /eklɛktism/ *nm* eclecticism; **il fait preuve d'~ dans ses lectures** his tastes in reading are eclectic.

éclipse /eklips/ *nf* **1** Astron eclipse; **~ de soleil/de lune** solar/lunar eclipse; **2** (interruption) eclipse; **après une longue ~** after a long period of eclipse; **sa popularité connaît une ~** his/her popularity has waned.

éclipser /eklipse/ [1] **I** *vtr* **1** Astron to eclipse; (occulter) to obscure; **2** (surpasser) to outshine; **elle l'éclipse complètement** he is completely eclipsed by her.
II s'éclipser○ *vpr* to slip out ou away.

écliptique /ekliptik/ *adj, nm* ecliptic.

éclisse /eklis/ *nf* **1** Rail fishplate; **2** Méd plate.

éclisser /eklise/ [1] *vtr* Rail to fishplate.

éclopé, **~e** /eklɔpe/ **I** *adj* injured.
II *nm,f* **les ~s** the walking wounded (+ *v pl*); **le match a fait quelques ~s** there were a few bumps and bruises as a result of the match.

éclore /eklɔʀ/ [79] *vi* **1** [*poussin, œuf*] to hatch; [*fleur*] to open (out), to bloom; **faire ~ un œuf** to incubate an egg; **2** liter [*idée*] to dawn; **le XVIIe siècle a vu ~ de grands talents** the 17th century saw the birth of some great talents.

éclosion /eklozjɔ̃/ *nf* **1** (d'œuf) hatching; (de fleur) opening, blooming; **2** liter (de talents) birth.

écluse /eklyz/ *nf* lock.

éclusée /eklyze/ *nf* lockage water.

écluser /eklyze/ [1] *vtr* **1** Naut to lock [sth] through [*péniche*]; (munir d'écluses) to provide [sth] with locks [*rivière*]; **2**◐ fig (boire) to knock back○ [*bouteille*].

éclusier, **-ière** /eklyzje, ɛʀ/ ▶ **510** *nm,f* lock keeper.

écobuage /ekɔbɥaʒ/ *nm* burning over.

écobuer /ekɔbɥe/ [1] *vtr* to burn off [*champ*].

écœurant, **~e** /ekœʀɑ̃, ɑ̃t/ *adj* **1** (physiquement) [*gâteau, odeur, liqueur*] sickly; [*plat*] over-rich; **2** (révoltant) nauseating, revolting; **~ de sentimentalité** nauseatingly sentimental; **3** (trop doué) sickening; **tu es vraiment ~** you make me sick.

écœurement /ekœʀmɑ̃/ *nm* nausea; **répéter jusqu'à l'~** to repeat [sth] ad nauseam.

écœurer /ekœʀe/ [1] *vtr* **1** (physiquement) [*nourriture, odeur*] to make [sb] feel sick; **avoir une mine écœurée** to look sick; **2** (moralement) to sicken.

école /ekɔl/ *nf* **1** Scol (établissement) school; **être à l'~** to be at GB ou in US school; **aller à l'~** to go to school; **le directeur a réuni toute l'~** the headteacher assembled the whole school; **~ de garçons/filles** boys'/girls' school; **enfants des ~s** schoolchildren; **la grande/petite ~** primary/nursery school; **2** (enseignement) school; **l'~ est finie** school is over; **avoir ~** to have school; **mettre un enfant à l'~** to send a child to school; **dès l'~** from the very first days at school; **quitter l'~ à 16 ans** to leave school at 16; **3** (système) education system; **réformer l'~** to reform the education system; **4** Univ (**grande**) **~** *higher education institution with competitive entrance examination*; **une ~ d'ingénieurs** a Grande École of Engineering; **une ~ de commerce** a business school; **5** (source de formation) training (**de** in); **la lexicographie est une ~ de patience** lexicography is a training in patience; **être à bonne ~** to be in good hands; **être de la vieille ~** to be of the old school; **l'~ de la vie** the university of life; **6** (mouvement) school; **~ flamande/romantique** Flemish/Romantic school; **~ de pensée** school of thought; **faire ~** to gain a following.
■ **~ communale** local school; **~ de conduite** driving school; **~ de danse** dancing school; **~ élémentaire** primary school; **~ de gestion** Univ business school, school of business and management GB; **~ hôtelière** hotel management school; **~ d'infirmières** nursing college; **~ de journalisme** school of journalism; **~ de langues** language school; **~ libre** (système) independent education; (établissement) independent school; **~ maternelle** nursery school; **~ militaire** military acad-

emy; **~ de musique** music school; **~ normale**, **EN** primary teacher training college; **~ obligatoire** compulsory schooling; **~ parallèle** progressive school GB, alternative school; **~ de pilotage** flying school; **~ de police** police college GB, police academy US; **~ primaire** primary school; **~ privée** private school; **~ professionnelle** training college; **~ publique** (établissement) state school GB, public school US; (système) state education GB, public education US; **~ de secrétariat** secretarial college; **École centrale des arts et manufactures**, **Centrale**○ *Grande École of Engineering*; **École des chartes**, **les Chartes**○ *School of Palaeography and Archival Studies*; **École des Mines**, **les Mines**○ *Grande École of Mining Studies*; **École Nationale d'administration**, **ENA** *Grande École of Public Management*; **École nationale des ponts et chaussées**, **les Ponts et chaussées**○, **les Ponts**○ *Grande École of Civil Engineering*; **École nationale supérieure des arts et métiers**, **les Arts et métiers**○, **les Arts**○, **ENSAM** *Grande École of Engineering*; **École normale supérieure**, **ENS** *Grande École preparing teachers for higher education*.

écolier, **-ière** /ekɔlje, ɛʀ/ *nm,f* schoolchild, schoolboy/schoolgirl.

écolo○ /ekɔlo/ *nm,f* environmentalist.

écologie /ekɔlɔʒi/ *nf* **1** (doctrine) environmentalism; **2** (science) ecology.

écologique /ekɔlɔʒik/ *adj* **1** [*discours, équilibre, catastrophe*] environmental, ecological; **2** [*impact, intérêt, conscience*] environmental; **3** [*produit*] environment-friendly; **ce n'est pas très ~ (de faire)** it's not environmentally sound (to do).

écologiste /ekɔlɔʒist/ **I** *adj* **1** [*candidat*] Green; **2** [*mesure*] ecological.
II *nmf* **1** (partisan) environmentalist; (candidat) Green; **2** (chercheur) ecologist.

écomusée /ekomyze/ *nm* ≈ open air museum.

éconduire /ekɔ̃dɥiʀ/ [69] *vtr* fml to turn [sb] away.

économat /ekɔnoma/ *nm* **1** (local) bursar's office; **2** (charge) office of bursar.

économe /ekɔnɔm/ **I** *adj* thrifty; **~ de son temps/ses paroles** sparing with his time/words; **il est ~ de ses mouvements** he doesn't waste energy.
II ▶**510** *nmf* bursar.
III *nm* Culin potato peeler.

économétricien, **-ienne** /ekɔnɔmetʀisjɛ̃, ɛn/ ▶**510** *nm,f* econometrician.

économétrie /ekɔnɔmetʀi/ *nf* econometrics (+ *v sg*).

économétrique /ekɔnɔmetʀik/ *adj* econometric.

économie /ekɔnɔmi/ **I** *nf* **1** (de pays, région) economy; **2** (discipline) economics (+ *v sg*); **étudiant en ~** economics student; **3** (somme économisée) saving; **réaliser une ~ de 20 francs sur qch** to save 20 francs on sth; **faire l'~ de** to save the cost of [*repas, voyage*]; **l'~ de temps/de fatigue est minime** the time/energy saved is minimal; **4** (action d'économiser) economy; **par ~ elle ne sort pas** to save money she doesn't go out; **avoir le sens de l'~** to be careful with money; **5** (sobriété) economy; **s'exprimer avec une grande ~ de paroles** to express oneself succinctly; **enseigner aux acteurs une ~ de geste** to teach actors to be economical in their movements.
II économies *nfpl* savings; **avoir des ~s** to have savings; **prendre sur ses ~s** to break ou to dip into one's savings; **faire des ~s** to save up; **faire des ~s d'électricité/de chauffage/de papier** to save on electricity/heating/paper; ▶**chandelle**.
■ **~ dirigée** controlled economy; **~ domestique** home economics; **~ d'entreprise** managerial economics; **~ libérale** = **~ de marché**; **~ de marché** free market (economy), (free) market economy; **~ de marché contrôlée** controlled market economy; **~ mixte** mixed economy; **~ parallèle** black economy; **~ planifiée** planned economy; **~ politique** political economy; **~ d'échelle** economy of scale; **~s d'énergie** energy savings; **inciter les gens à faire des ~s d'énergie** to encourage people to save energy.
IDIOMES **il n'y a pas de petites ~s** every little (bit) helps, every penny counts GB.

économique /ekɔnɔmik/ *adj* **1** Écon [*politique, crise*] economic; **2** (peu coûteux) economical; **~ à l'achat/à l'entretien** cheap to buy/to maintain.

économiquement /ekɔnɔmikmɑ̃/ *adv* **1** Écon economically; **un projet ~ viable** an economically viable project; **2** (pas cher) [*vivre, voyager*] cheaply.

économiser /ekɔnɔmize/ [1] *vtr* **1** (épargner) to save (up) [*argent, somme*]; **~ 10 000 francs** to save up 10,000 francs; **~ ses forces** or **ses efforts** to pace oneself; **2** (réduire la consommation de) to save [*essence, eau, énergie*]; to save on [*chauffage*]; **3** (réduire ses dépenses) to economize; **~ sur qch** to economize on [*chauffage, nourriture*].

économiseur /ekɔnɔmizœʀ/ *nm* fuel-saving device.

économiste /ekɔnɔmist/ ▶**510** *nmf* economist.

écope /ekɔp/ *nf* bailer.

écoper /ekɔpe/ [1] **I** *vtr* Naut to bail out.
II écoper○ **de** *vtr ind* to get, to cop○ [*punition, amende*].
III *vi* to take the rap○; **je ne veux pas ~ pour les autres** I don't want to take the rap for the others.

écoproduit /ekopʀɔdɥi/ *nm* environment-friendly product.

écorce /ekɔʀs/ *nf* (d'arbre) bark; (de fruit) peel; (de châtaigne) skin; **enlever l'~ d'un fruit** to peel a fruit; ▶**arbre**.
■ **l'~ terrestre** the earth's crust.

écorcer /ekɔʀse/ [12] *vtr* to strip the bark from [*arbre*]; to peel [*fruit*].

écorché, **~e** /ekɔʀʃe/ **I** *pp* ▶**écorcher**.
II *pp adj* **~ (vif)** hypersensitive.
III *nm,f* **c'est un ~ (vif)** he's hypersensitive.
IV *nm* Anat écorché; Tech cutaway (diagram).

écorchement /ekɔʀʃəmɑ̃/ *nm* (d'animal) skinning.

écorcher /ekɔʀʃe/ [1] **I** *vtr* **1** (dépecer) to skin [*animal*]; to flay [*victime*]; **2** (blesser) (en éraflant) to graze [*visage, jambe*]; (par frottement) to chafe [*jambe*]; to gall [*cheval*]; **sa voix m'écorche les oreilles** fig her voice grates on my ears; **3** (estropier) to mispronounce [*mot*]; to murder [*chanson, langue*]; **4**○ (tromper) to fleece○ [*client*].
II s'écorcher *vpr* [*personne*] to graze oneself; **s'~ le genou** to graze one's knee.

écorcheur, **-euse** /ekɔʀʃœʀ, øz/ *nm,f* **1** (d'animal) skinner; **2**○ (de client) extortionist.

écorchure /ekɔʀʃyʀ/ *nf* graze.

écorner /ekɔʀne/ [1] *vtr* **1** (entamer) to take the edge off [*gloire, réputation*]; to cut down, make a hole in [*capital, somme*]; **2** (abîmer) to make [sth] dog-eared GB, to dogear US [*livre*]; to chip [*pierre, meuble*]; **3** Vét to poll [*animal*].

écornifler○† /ekɔʀnifle/ [1] *vtr* to scrounge.

écossais, **~e** /ekɔsɛ, ɛz/ ▶**462** **I** *adj* [*caractère, personne, paysage*] Scottish; [*whisky*] Scotch; [*langue*] Scots; [*jupe*] tartan.
II *nm* **1** Ling (dialecte anglais) Scots; (dialecte gaélique) (Scottish) Gaelic; **2** (tissu) tartan (cloth).

Écossais, **~e** /ekɔsɛ, ɛz/ *nm,f* Scotsman/Scotswoman, Scot; **les ~** the Scots.

Écosse /ekɔs/ ▶**692** *nprf* Scotland.

écosser /ekɔse/ [1] *vtr* to shell.

écosystème /ekosistɛm/ *nm* ecosystem.

écot /eko/ *nm* share; **payer son ~ (à qn)** to pay one's share (to sb).

écoulé, **~e** /ekule/ **I** *pp* ▶**écouler**.
II *pp adj* **1** (précédent) past (*épith*); **la semaine/saison ~e** the past week/season; **2** (qui a passé) **délai** or **temps ~** time which has elapsed; **3** Comm (épuisé) exhausted (*jamais épith*); **les stocks sont ~s** the stocks are exhausted; **4** Comm (vendu) sold (*après n*); **la viande ~e était contaminée** the meat sold was contaminated.

écoulement /ekulmɑ̃/ *nm* **1** (d'eau, air, de circulation) flow; (de temps) passing; **2** Méd discharge; **~ nasal** nasal discharge; **~ de sang** bleeding; **3** Comm distribution and sale; **4** (de billets, drogue) circulation (**de** of).

écouler /ekule/ [1] **I** *vtr* **1** Comm to sell [*produit, stock*]; **2** (trafiquer) to pass [*billet, chèque, drogue*]; to fence [*butin*].
II s'écouler *vpr* **1** (passer) [*temps, vie*] to pass; **2** (circuler) [*eau, rivière, sang*] to flow; **3** (sortir accidentellement) [*pétrole, eau*] to escape (**de** from; **dans** into); **4** (être évacué) [*eau*] to drain away; [*air*] to flow; **s'~ de/dans qch** [*eau*] to drain out of/into sth; **5** Comm [*produit*] to move; **s'~ lentement** to move slowly.

écourter /ekuʀte/ [1] *vtr* (abréger) to cut short [*visite, séjour*] (**de dix jours** by ten days); to shorten, to cut down [*discours, texte*] (**de moitié** by half).

écoute /ekut/ *nf* **1** (fait d'écouter) **l'~ de** listening to [*poème, cassette, personne*]; **être à l'~ de qch/qn** lit to be listening to sth/sb; (être attentif à) to be (always) ready to listen to sth/sb; **vous êtes à l'~ de radio X** you're listening to radio X; **restez à l'~ (de nos programmes)** stay tuned; **être à l'~ de l'autre** to be willing to listen to other people; **à la première écoute le disque est décevant** when you first listen to the record it's disappointing; **la qualité d'~** (de réception d'un émetteur) reception; (du son) sound quality; **2** (audience) audience; **avoir une grande/faible ~** to have a large/small audience; **un taux d'~ de 15%** audience ratings of 15%; **heure de grande ~** Radio peak listening time; TV peak viewing time, prime time; **le temps moyen d'~ est de deux heures par jour** Radio the average listening time is two hours a day; TV the average viewing time is two hours a day; **3** Tech **un appareil d'~** a listening device; **un centre d'~(s)** monitoring centre[GB]; **~s téléphoniques** phone-tapping ¢; **je suis sur ~(s)** my phone is being tapped; **mettre qn sur ~(s)** to tap sb's phone; **4** Naut sheet; **5** (de sanglier) ear.

écouter /ekute/ [1] **I** *vtr* **1** (s'appliquer à entendre) to listen to [*conversation, cassette, musique, message*]; **je n'écoutais pas** I wasn't listening; **je vous écoute** I'm listening; **écoutez, j'en ai assez** listen, I've had enough; **~ qn chanter/parler** to listen to sb singing/talking; **écoute comme elle chante bien** just listen—doesn't she sing well?; **écoute, ne sois pas ridicule!** come on, don't be ridiculous!; **~ aux portes** to eavesdrop; **allô oui, j'écoute!** hello!; **2** (accepter d'entendre) to listen to [*explications, témoignage, témoin*]; **3** (être attentif à) to pay attention to [*personne*]; **écoute(-moi)!** pay attention to what I am saying!; **écoute ce qu'elle dit!** pay attention to what she's saying !; **il sait ~ les gens** he's a good listener; **4** (tenir compte de) to listen to [*conseil, rumeur, personne*]; **écoute ton père!** do as your father says!; **5** (se laisser guider par) **~ son cœur** to follow one's own inclination; **~ sa conscience** to be guided by one's conscience; **~ son devoir** to be guided by a sense of duty; **n'écoutant que son courage, il sauta** with no thought of danger, he jumped.
II s'écouter *vpr* **1 s'~ parler** to like the sound of one's own voice; **2** (se dorloter) to

cosset oneself; **3** (faire à sa guise) **si je m'écoutais** if it was up to me.

écouteur /ekutœʀ/ *nm* **1** (de téléphone) earpiece; **2** (de radio, stéréo) earphones (*pl*); (plus grand) headphones (*pl*).

écoutille /ekutij/ *nf* hatch.

écouvillon /ekuvijɔ̃/ *nm* (à bouteilles) bottle-brush; (à fusil) pullthrough GB, swab US; Méd swab.

écouvillonnage /ekuvijɔnaʒ/ *nm* (de fusil, de bouteille) cleaning; Méd swabbing.

écouvillonner /ekuvijɔne/ [1] *vtr* to clean out [*bouteille, fusil*]; Méd to swab.

écrabouiller○ /ekʀabuje/ [1] *vtr* **1** (aplatir) to squash [*fruit, animal*]; to flatten [*fleurs*]; **aïe, tu m'écrabouilles les pieds!** ouch, you're treading on my feet!; **se faire ~** to be squashed○ (**par** by); **2** (vaincre) to crush○, to beat.

écran /ekʀɑ̃/ *nm* **1** Cin (surface) screen; (salle) cinema GB, movie theater US; (art) cinema; **~ (de projection)** screen; **~ géant/panoramique** giant/panoramic screen; **~ perlé** beaded screen; **le grand ~** the big screen; **projection vidéo sur grand ~** video shown on the big screen; **apparaître/montrer à l'~** to appear/show on (the) screen; **porter une œuvre à l'~** to adapt a work for the cinema; **crever l'~** to have a great screen presence; **'bientôt sur vos ~s'** 'coming soon to a cinema GB ou theater US near you'; **le film sortira sur les ~s parisiens en mai** the film will open in Paris in May; **2** Ordinat, TV screen; Électron display; **~ de téléviseur** TV screen; **le petit ~** the small screen; **une vedette du petit ~** a TV star; **3** (pour masquer) lit, fig screen; **la haie fait ~ entre les jardins** the hedge forms a screen between the gardens GB ou yards US; **crème qui fait ~ aux ultraviolets** cream that screens out ultraviolet rays; **crème ~ total** sun block; ▶ **société**; **4** (pour protéger) screen; Nucl shielding; **~ de protection** protective screen; **elle me faisait ~ de son corps contre le vent** her body screened me from the wind.

■ **~ antibruit** soundproofing; **~ cathodique** fluorescent screen; **~ de cheminée** firescreen; **~ de contrôle** monitor; **~ à cristaux liquides** liquid crystal display, LCD; **~ à fenêtres** split screen; **~ fluorescent** = **~ cathodique**; **~ de fumée** lit screen of smoke; fig, Mil smokescreen; **~ (à) haute définition** high-resolution screen; **~ plat** flat screen; **~ pleine page** full page-display; **~ radar** radar screen; **~ solaire** Cosmét sunscreen; **~ tactile** touch screen; **~ thermique** Astronaut heat shield; **~ total** Cosmét sun block; **~ vidéo** video screen; **~ de visualisation** VDU screen.

écrasant, **~e** /ekʀazɑ̃, ɑ̃t/ *adj* **1** lit [*charge, poids*] enormous; **2** fig [*chaleur*] sweltering; [*rôle, défaite, dette*] crushing; [*victoire*] resounding; [*majorité, responsabilité, supériorité*] overwhelming.

écrasé, **~e** /ekʀaze/ **I** *pp* ▶ **écraser**.

II *pp adj* **1** (abîmé, aplati) squashed; **2** (blessé) [*doigt, pied*] crushed; **3** (accablé) **~ de fatigue/douleur/remords** [*personne*] weighed down by exhaustion/grief/remorse; **~ de chaleur** [*village*] sweltering in the heat; **~ par le travail** overwhelmed by work.

écrasement /ekʀazmɑ̃/ *nm* **1** (de mouvement, rébellion) crushing; **2** (réduction) **l'~ des salaires** the reduction in the level of earnings; **3** (fait d'écraser) (de personne) crushing; (de légumes) (par accident) squashing; (pour purée) mashing; **4** fig **avoir un sentiment d'~** to feel overwhelmed.

écrase-merde◐ /ekʀazmɛʀd/ *nm inv* clodhopper○.

écraser /ekʀaze/ [1] **I** *vtr* **1** (blesser, tuer) [*machine, porte, pierre*] to crush [*doigt, personne*]; [*personne*] to squash [*mouche, araignée, coccinelle*]; (avec un véhicule) to run over [*piéton, chien, hérisson*]; **se faire ~** to get run over; **il a failli se faire ~** he nearly got run over; **il est mort écrasé par un rocher** he was crushed to death by a rock; **il écraserait tout le monde pour réussir** fig he would be prepared to trample everyone underfoot to succeed; **2** (endommager) [*personne*] to squash [*boite, chapeau, fruit*]; (plus endommagé) to crush; [*éléphant, tank*] to flatten [*végétation, relief*]; **3** Culin [*personne*] to mash [*légumes, fraises*]; (faire un coulis de) to puree [*tomates, fraises*]; to crush [*grain de poivre, gousse d'ail*]; **de la banane écrasée** mashed banana; **4** (aplatir délibérément) gén to squash; **~ sa cigarette** to stub one's cigarette; **~ une larme** to wipe away a tear; **5** (presser) [*personne*] to press [*nez, visage*] (**contre** against); **~ la pédale d'accélérateur** to put one's foot down; **6** (anéantir) to crush [*révolte, complot, mouvement, adversaire*]; to thrash○ [*équipe, joueur*]; **7** (en étant meilleur, supérieur) [*personne*] to outshine; **8** (humilier) to put down [*personne*]; **9** (accabler) [*chagrin, douleur, remords, responsabilité*] to overwhelm [*personne*]; [*fatigue, sommeil, chaleur*] to overcome [*personne*]; **~ qn de travail/responsabilités** to overwhelm sb with work/responsibilities; **~ les entreprises d'impôts** to overburden firms with taxation.

II s'écraser *vpr* **1** (avoir un accident) [*voiture, train*] to crash; [*automobiliste, motocycliste*] to have a crash; **s'~ contre un mur/arbre** to crash into a wall/tree; **s'~ (au sol)** [*avion, hélicoptère*] to crash (to the ground); **les insectes s'écrasent contre le pare-brise** insects splatter on the windscreen; **2** (être endommagé) [*fruit*] to get squashed; **s'~ au sol** [*bibelot*] to fall and break; **3**○ (se taire) to shut up○; **écrase(-toi)!** shut up!; **4**○ (se soumettre) to keep one's head down; **s'~ devant qn** to keep one 's head down when sb is around.

écrémage /ekʀemaʒ/ *nm* **1** (de lait) skimming; **2** fig creaming off.

écrémer /ekʀeme/ [14] *vtr* **1** (ôter la crème de) to skim [*lait*]; **du lait écrémé** skimmed milk; **2** (sélectionner) to cream off [*candidats*]; **~ une collection d'art** to sell the finest works in a collection.

écrémeuse /ekʀemøz/ *nf* Tech separator.

écrêtage /ekʀetaʒ/ *nm* Électron peak limiting.

écrêter /ekʀete/ [1] *vtr* Électron to limit peaks; Tech to level [*chaussée*].

écrevisse /ekʀəvis/ *nf* crayfish GB, crawfish US.

IDIOMES **rouge comme une ~** as red as a beetroot GB, as red as a beet US.

écrier: **s'écrier** /ekʀije/ [2] *vpr* to exclaim; **s'~ que** to cry that.

écrin /ekʀɛ̃/ *nm* **1** (boîte) case; **2** liter (environnement) setting.

écrire /ekʀiʀ/ [67] **I** *vtr* **1** (tracer, rédiger, communiquer) to write (**à** to; **que** that); **2** (orthographier) to spell; **savoir comment ~ un mot** to know how to spell a word.

II *vi* **1** gén to write; **~ à l'encre** to write in ink; **essaie de mieux ~** try to improve your writing; **tu écris bien/mal** you've got nice/bad writing; **2** (être écrivain) **vivre en écrivant** to make a living by writing; **il écrit** he's a writer.

III s'écrire *vpr* **1** (être tracé, rédigé, communiqué) to be written; **ça ne s'écrit jamais** this is never written; **2** (être orthographié) to be spelled; **Hachette s'écrit avec deux t** Hachette is spelled with two t's; **ça s'écrit comme ça se prononce** it's spelled the way it sounds.

écrit, **~e** /ekʀi, it/ **I** *pp* ▶ **écrire**.

II *pp adj* written; **langue ~e** written language; **épreuve ~e** written test; **règle non ~e** unwritten rule; **c'était ~** it was bound to happen; **il est ~ que je passerai mon temps dans les avions** I am doomed to spend all my time on board planes; **c'est ~ sur ton visage** it's written all over your face.

III *nm* **1** (œuvre) writings (*pl*); **un ~** a piece of writing; **2** (document) document; **par ~** in writing; **3** Scol, Univ (examen) written examination; (travail) written work.

IDIOMES **les paroles s'envolent, les ~s restent** (il ne faut pas s'engager par écrit) never put anything in writing; (faites promettre par écrit) get it in writing.

écriteau, *pl* **~x** /ekʀito/ *nm* sign.

écritoire /ekʀitwaʀ/ *nf* writing case.

écriture /ekʀityʀ/ **I** *nf* **1** (manière) handwriting; **elle a une belle ~** she's got beautiful handwriting; **2** (type) hand; **~ anglaise/bâtarde/moulée** running/bastard/copperplate hand; **3** (texte) writing; **pages couvertes d'~** pages covered with writing; **4** Ling script; **~ hiéroglyphique/phonétique** hieroglyphic/phonetic script; **5** Littérat (activité) writing; **l'~ est ma vie** writing is my whole life; **~ automatique** automatic writing; **l'~ dramatique/littéraire** the writing of plays/literature; **6** (style) style; **une ~ classique** a classical style; **7** Compta (inscription) entry; **passer une ~** to make an entry.

II écritures *nfpl* Compta accounts; **tenir les ~s** to keep the accounts.

Écriture /ekʀityʀ/ *nf* Relig Scripture; **les (saintes) ~s** the Scriptures; **l'~ sainte** Holy Writ.

écrivailler○ /ekʀivɑje/ [1] *vi* pej to be a hack writer, to scribble.

écrivailleur○, **-euse** /ekʀivɑjœʀ, øz/ *nm,f* pej hack, scribbler†.

écrivaillon○ /ekʀivɑjɔ̃/ *nm* pej hack, scribbler†.

écrivain /ekʀivɛ̃/ ▶ **510** *nm* writer.

■ **~ public** letter-writer.

écrivassier○, **-ière** /ekʀivasje, ɛʀ/ *nm,f* hack, scribbler†.

écrou /ekʀu/ *nm* Tech nut.

écrouelles /ekʀuɛl/ *nfpl* scrofula.

écrouer /ekʀue/ [1] *vtr* Jur to commit [sb] to prison.

écroulé, **~e** /ekʀule/ **I** *pp* ▶ **écrouler**.

II *pp adj* **1** [*personne*] overwhelmed; **~ de fatigue** overcome with exhaustion; **~ de rire** doubled up with laughter; **2** [*maison, mur, pont*] in a state of collapse; **un mur à demi ~** a wall half in ruins.

écroulement /ekʀulmɑ̃/ *nm* gén collapse; (de rêves, d'illusions) crumbling.

écrouler: **s'écrouler** /ekʀule/ [1] *vpr* [*mur, personne, régime, fortune, théorie*] to collapse; [*espoir, espérance*] to founder; [*rêve, illusion*] to crumble; **faire ~ qch** to make sth collapse; **tout s'écroule autour d'eux** everything is collapsing around them; **tout à coup leur univers s'écroula** all of a sudden the bottom fell out of their world○, all of a sudden their world collapsed around them; **s'~ de fatigue** to collapse with exhaustion; **il était écroulé**○ **sur son lit** he was slumped on his bed; **s'~**○ **de rire** to be doubled up with laughter.

écru, **~e** /ekʀy/ *adj* **1** (brut) [*toile*] unbleached; [*laine*] undyed; [*soie*] raw; **2** ▶ **193** (couleur) ecru.

ectomorphe /ɛktɔmɔʀf/ *nmf* ectomorph.

ectoplasme /ɛktɔplasm/ *nm* ectoplasm.

ECU /eky/ *nm* CEE, Fin ECU.

écu /eky/ *nm* **1** ▶ **46** Fin (unité monétaire de la CEE) ecu; **2** (en numismatique) ≈ crown; **3** (bouclier) shield; **4** Hérald escutcheon.

écubier /ekybje/ *nm* hawsehole.

écueil /ekœj/ *nm* **1** Naut reef; **2** fig (danger) pitfall.

écuelle /ekɥɛl/ *nf* **1** (récipient) bowl; **2** (contenu) bowlful.

éculé, **~e** /ekyle/ *adj* **1** lit **chaussure ~e** shoe with a worn-down heel; **2** fig [*plaisanterie, théorie*] hackneyed, well-worn (*épith*).

écumage /ekymaʒ/ *nm* (de bouillon, confiture) skimming; (de métal) skimming, scumming.

écumant, **~e** /ekymɑ̃, ɑ̃t/ *adj* foaming; **avoir la bouche ~e** to be foaming at the mouth; **être ~ de rage** to be foaming with rage.

écume /ekym/ *nf* **1** (sur la mer, un torrent) foam; (de bouillon, confiture) scum; (de bière, d'eau savonneuse) froth; (de métal) dross; **2** (bave) foam, froth; **avoir l'~ à la bouche** to be foaming at the mouth (with rage).
■ **~ de mer** Minér meerschaum.

écumer /ekyme/ [1] **I** *vtr* **1** (enlever l'écume) to skim [*bouillon, confiture*]; to skim, deslag [*métal*]; **2** fig (parcourir) to scour; **des pirates qui écument les mers** pirates who scour the seas in search of ships to plunder.
II *vi* **1** (se couvrir d'écume) [*mer, lac*] to foam; [*vin*] to froth; **2** (baver) to foam, froth; **~ de rage** to be foaming with rage.

écumeux, **-euse** /ekymø, øz/ *adj* liter [*lac, vague*] foamy; [*bière*] frothy.

écumoire /ekymwaʀ/ *nf* skimming ladle, skimmer.

écureuil /ekyʀœj/ *nm* squirrel.
■ **~ volant** flying squirrel.

écurie /ekyʀi/ *nf* **1** Équit stable; **~ de course** racing stable; **mener un cheval à l'~** to lead a horse to the stable; **mettre un cheval à l'~** to stable a horse; **2** Sport stable; **l'~ Ferrari** the Ferrari stable; **3** (lieu sale) pigsty.
IDIOMES **sentir l'~** to know one is nearly there.

écusson /ekysɔ̃/ *nm* **1** Mil flash GB; **2** (d'école) crest, badge; (de club, mouvement) badge; (de voiture) insignia; **3** Hérald coat of arms; **~ aux armes de la ville/famille** coat of arms of the city/family; **4** Agric (greffon) scion; **greffe en ~** shield-bud.

écuyer, **-ère** /ekɥije, ɛʀ/ **I** ▶510 *nm,f* **1** Équit (cavalier) horseman/horsewoman; (instructeur) riding instructor; **2** (dans un cirque) horserider.
II *nm* Hist (gentilhomme) squire; (responsable des écuries) equerry.

eczéma /egzema/ ▶271 *nm* eczema ¢; **~ du nourrisson** infantile eczema.

eczémateux, **-euse** /egzematø, øz/ **I** *adj* **1** [*affection, éruption*] eczematous, of eczema (*après n*); **2** [*personne*] suffering from eczema.
II *nm,f* eczema sufferer.

edam /edam/ *nm* Culin Edam.

edelweiss /edɛlvɛs/ *nm inv* Bot edelweiss.

éden /edɛn/ *nm* fig paradise.

Éden /edɛn/ *nprm* Relig Eden; **le jardin d'~** the Garden of Eden.

édénique /edenik/ *adj* **1** lit edenic; **2** fig heavenly.

édenté, **~e** /edɑ̃te/ **I** *pp* ▶ **édenter**.
II *pp adj* [*personne*] (sans dents) toothless; (avec des dents en moins) with teeth missing (*épith, après n*); [*peigne*] with missing teeth (*épith, après n*).
III édentés *nmpl* Zool **les ~s** the edentates.

édenter /edɑ̃te/ [1] *vtr* to break the teeth of [*peigne, scie*].

EDF /ədeɛf/ *nf* (*abbr* = **Électricité de France**) *French Electricity Company*.

édicter /edikte/ [1] *vtr* to enact [*loi, statut, norme*]; to decree [*peine, règle, intention*].

édicule /edikyl/ *nm* **1** (kiosque) kiosk; **2** (toilettes) public convenience.

édifiant, **~e** /edifjɑ̃, ɑ̃t/ *adj* **1** fml (exemplaire) edifying; **2** (instructif) enlightening.

édification /edifikasjɔ̃/ *nf* **1** (de bâtiment, pays) building, construction; **2** fig (d'œuvre, de théorie) building; **3** (instruction) enlightenment; **pour votre ~** for your edification.

édifice /edifis/ *nm* **1** (bâtiment) building; **~ public** public building; **2** fml fig (vaste ensemble organisé) structure, edifice; **l'~ social/politique** the social/political structure.

édifier /edifje/ [2] *vtr* **1** lit to build, to construct [*bâtiment, ville*]; **2** fig to build [*empire, œuvre, théorie*]; **3** (porter à la vertu) to edify; **4** fml (renseigner) to enlighten; **cet incident nous a édifiés sur leurs véritables intentions** this incident enlightened us about ou on their true intentions; **je ne voulais pas y croire mais maintenant je suis édifiée** I didn't want to believe it but now I've had my eyes opened.

édile /edil/ *nm* **1** (conseiller municipal) town councillor[GB]; **2** Antiq aedile.

Édimbourg /edɛ̃buʀ/ ▶857 *npr* Edinburgh.

édit /edi/ *nm* edict.

éditer /edite/ [1] **I** *vtr* **1** (publier) to publish [*œuvre, livre, auteur*]; to release [*cassette, disque*]; **2** (présenter et annoter) to edit; **3** Ordinat to edit.
II s'éditer *vpr* [*livre*] to be published; **il s'édite plus de livres qu'il y a 20 ans** more books are published now than 20 years ago.

éditeur, **-trice** /editœʀ, tʀis/ ▶510 **I** *adj* [*maison, société*] publishing.
II *nm,f* (qui présente et annote des textes) editor.
III *nm* **1** (de livre, photo, musique) publisher; **2** Ordinat editor; **~ de liens/de textes** link/text editor.

édition /edisjɔ̃/ **I** *nf* **1** (action de publier et de diffuser) (de livre) publication; (de disque, cassette) release; (de gravure) edition; **2** (texte, livre, gravure) edition; (disque, cassette) release; **une nouvelle ~ revue et augmentée** a new revised and enlarged edition; **~ critique/originale** critical/first edition; **~ de luxe** deluxe edition; **3** (de livres, revues) publishing (**de** of); (de disque, film) release (**de** of); **être chargé de l'~ d'un livre** to be responsible for publishing a book; **société d'~** publishing firm; **je travaille dans l'~** I work in publishing; **4** Presse, TV, Radio (opération de publication) editing; (tirage) edition; **~ du soir** evening edition; **l'~ de 20 heures du journal télévisé** the eight o'clock (edition of the) news; **5** Art, Sport **la troisième ~ du festival de Cannes** the third Cannes (film) festival; **l'~ 1992 des jeux Olympiques** the 1992 Olympic Games.
II éditions *nfpl* **les ~s Hachette** Hachette (+ *v sg*).

éditique /editik/ *nf* electronic publishing.

édito○ /edito/ *nm* Presse editorial, leader.

éditorial, **~e**, *mpl* **-iaux** /editɔʀjal, o/ **I** *adj* [*politique, service*] editorial.
II *nm* Presse editorial, leader.

éditorialiste /editɔʀjalist/ *nmf* Presse leader writer GB, editorialist US.

édredon /edʀədɔ̃/ *nm* eiderdown.

éducateur, **-trice** /edykatœʀ, tʀis/ ▶510 **I** *adj* educative.
II *nm,f* **~ (spécialisé)** youth worker.

éducatif, **-ive** /edykatif, iv/ *adj* educational.

éducation /edykasjɔ̃/ *nf* **1** (enseignement) education; **~ artistique/musicale/permanente/sexuelle** art/music/continuing/sex education; **ici, les enfants reçoivent une très bonne ~** here, children get a very good education; **2** (formation de personne) education; **faire l'~ de qn** to educate sb; **3** (entraînement) training; **~ de la mémoire** memory training; **~ de la voix** vocal ou voice training; **~ de la volonté** development of willpower; **4** (bonnes manières) manners (*pl*); **manquer d'~** to show a lack of manners; **avoir de l'~** to have good manners; **être sans ~** to be ill-mannered.
■ **Éducation Nationale**, **EN** (ministère) ministry of Education; (système) state education; **~ physique** physical education, PE GB, phys ed US; **~ surveillée** Admin state education system for young offenders.

édulcorant, **~e** /edylkɔʀɑ̃, ɑ̃t/ **I** *adj* sweetening (*épith*).
II *nm* sweetener.

édulcorer /edylkɔʀe/ [1] *vtr* **1** lit to sweeten [*boisson, mets*]; **2** fig (atténuer) fml to tone down [*lettre, propos*].

éduqué, **~e** /edyke/ **I** *pp* ▶ **éduquer**.
II *pp adj* (**bien**) **~** well brought up; **mal ~** badly brought up.

éduquer /edyke/ [1] **I** *vtr* **1** (former) to educate [*personne, peuple*]; to train [*chien*]; **2** (enseigner les usages à) to bring up [*enfant*]; **~ un enfant à s'exprimer poliment** to bring up a child to speak politely; **3** (développer) to train [*oreille*]; to educate [*palais*]; **~ sa volonté** to develop one's willpower; **~ ses sens** to train one's senses.
II s'éduquer *vpr* [*personne*] to get an education; **il s'est éduqué tout seul** he is self-educated.

EEG /əəʒe/ *nm* Méd EEG, electroencephalogram.

effaçable /efasabl/ *adj* [*cassette*] erasable; [*tache*] removable.

effaceur○ /efas/ *nf* C (gomme à effacer) eraser, rubber GB.

effacé, **~e** /efase/ **I** *pp* ▶ **effacer**.
II *pp adj* [*personne*] retiring; **il a une personnalité ~e** he's quite retiring.

effacement /efasmɑ̃/ *nm* **1** (de texte, mots) deletion; **touche/commande d'~** delete key/command; **2** (de cassette, bande magnétique) erasure; **3** (d'une personne) (en général) self-effacement; (devant un rival) withdrawal.

effacer /efase/ [12] **I** *vtr* **1** (faire disparaître) (avec une gomme) to rub out, to erase [*mot, phrase, chiffre, dessin*]; (avec un effaceur) to remove [*mot, phrase*]; (avec un chiffon) to rub out [*mot, dessin*]; (sur un traitement de texte) to delete [*mot, paragraphe*]; to erase [*chanson, texte, film*]; **~ un nom d'une liste** to remove a name from a list; **~ toute trace de son passage** to remove every trace of one's presence; **2** (rendre propre) to erase [*bande magnétique, cassette*]; to clear [*écran, fichier*]; to wipe, to clean [*tableau noir*]; **3** (rendre moins visible) [*soleil*] to fade [*couleur*]; [*pluie*] to erase [*traces, pas*]; [*neige*] to cover (up) [*traces, pas*]; [*crème*] to remove [*rides*]; **l'usure** or **le temps a effacé l'inscription** the inscription has worn away with time; **4** (faire oublier) to blot out [*souvenir, image*]; to dispel [*doute, regret, méfiance*]; to remove [*différence, distinctions*]; **~ une image de sa mémoire** to blot out an image from one's mind; **rien n'efface le passé** nothing can erase the past; **le temps efface la douleur** or **le chagrin** time heals all wounds; **on efface tout et on recommence** lit let's rub it all out and start again; fig let's wipe the slate clean and start all over again; **5** (surpasser) to outshine; **6** (dissimuler) [*personne*] to throw back [*épaules*]; to hold in [*estomac*]; **~ le corps** to stand sideways; **7** Fin to write off [*dette, pertes*].
II s'effacer *vpr* **1** (avec une gomme) **ça s'efface** you can rub it out; **2** (avec le temps) [*inscription, couleur, dessin*] to fade; **mon dessin à la craie s'est effacé** my chalk drawing has got GB ou gotten US rubbed out; **3** (cesser) [*souvenir, image, méfiance, haine*] to fade; [*impression*] to wear off; [*doute, crainte*] to disappear; **son sourire s'effaça** her smile faded; **4** (se tourner sur le côté) [*personne*] to step ou move aside; **s'~ pour laisser passer qn** to step aside to let sb by; **5** (rester discret) [*personne*] to stay in the background; **s'~ devant un rival** to give way to a rival.

effaceur /efasœʀ/ *nm* **~ (d'encre)** correction pen.

effarant, **~e** /efaʀɑ̃, ɑ̃t/ *adj* astounding; **il est d'une bêtise ~e** he's astoundingly stupid.

effarement /efaʀmɑ̃/ *nm* alarm; **à son grand ~** to his great alarm.

effarer /efaʀe/ [1] *vtr* to alarm; **être effaré à l'idée que** to be alarmed at the idea that; **effaré de faire** alarmed to do; **effaré de/par qch** alarmed at/by sth.

effaroucher /efaʀuʃe/ [1] **I** *vtr* **1** (faire fuir) to frighten [sb] away ou off [*personne, animal*] (**en faisant** by doing; **par** with); **2** fml (inquiéter) to alarm (**en faisant** by doing; **par** with); **regard effarouché** alarmed look.

II s'effaroucher *vpr* to take fright (**de, à** at).

effarvatte /efaʀvat/ *nf* (**rousserolle**) **~** reed warbler.

effectif, -ive /efɛktif, iv/ **I** *adj* (réel) [*aide, contrôle*] real; **durée effective du travail** actual time worked; **devenir ~** [*mesure, cessez-le-feu*] to come into effect; **être en recherche effective d'emploi** to be actively looking for a job.

II *nm* (d'école, de classe) number of pupils, enrollment US; (d'université) number of students, enrollment US; (d'entreprise) workforce; (d'une armée) strength; **accroître/réduire les ~s d'une entreprise** to increase/reduce a company's workforce; **un ~ de 200 élèves** 200 pupils on the roll GB, an enrollment of 200 pupils US.

effectivement /efɛktivmɑ̃/ *adv* **1** (en effet) indeed; **le problème est ~ complexe** the problem is indeed complex; **la police est ~ intervenue trop tard** the police did indeed intervene too late; **'vous n'étiez pas chez vous hier soir?'—'non, ~'** 'so you weren't in last night?'—'no, we weren't'; **'tu n'es pas obligé d'y aller'—'non, ~'** 'you don't have to go'—'no, you're right'; **2** (réellement) actually, really; **le cessez-le-feu n'a jamais été ~ respecté** the ceasefire was never actually observed.

effectuer /efɛktɥe/ [1] **I** *vtr* to do [*calcul, réparations, travail, service militaire*]; to make [*paiement, placement, changement, choix, évaluation, saut, atterrissage*]; to carry out [*transaction*]; to conduct [*sondage*]; to serve [*peine*]; **il vient d'~ une visite en Iran** he's just completed a visit to Iran; **~ le contrôle des véhicules** to check the vehicles; **~ une analyse de l'air** to analyse[GB] the air; **~ une inspection du bâtiment** to inspect the building; **~ son apprentissage** to serve an apprenticeship; **~ sa formation en Allemagne** to be trained in Germany.

II s'effectuer *vpr* [*travail*] to be done; [*investissement, intervention*] to be made; [*transaction*] to be carried out; [*reprise économique*] to take place; **l'achèvement du projet pourrait s'~ l'an prochain** the project may be completed next year; **le ramassage des ordures s'effectuera le jeudi** the rubbish will be collected on Thursdays; **la circulation s'effectuera dans un seul sens** traffic will be one-way.

efféminé, ~e /efemine/ **I** *pp* ▶ **efféminer**.

II *pp adj* effeminate.

efféminer /efemine/ [1] **I** *vtr* to emasculate [*art, peuple*].

II s'efféminer *vpr* to become effeminate.

efférent, ~e /efeʀɑ̃, ɑ̃t/ *adj* efferent.

effervescence /efɛʀvesɑ̃s/ *nf* **1** (bouillonnement) effervescence; **2** (émoi) turmoil; **être en ~** to be in turmoil; **la nouvelle a mis la ville en ~** the news threw the whole city into turmoil; **il avait l'esprit en ~** his mind was in a ferment.

effervescent, ~e /efɛʀvesɑ̃, ɑ̃t/ *adj* **1** lit [*comprimé*] effervescent; **2** fig [*foule*] seething; [*caractère*] effervescent.

effet /efɛ/ **I** *nm* **1** (conséquence) effect; **il y a un rapport de cause à ~ entre les deux phénomènes** there is a relation of cause and effect between the two phenomena; **~s négatifs de qch sur qch/qn** adverse ou ill effects of sth on sth/sb; **~s positifs de qch sur qch/qn** beneficial effects of sth on sth/sb; **subir/ressentir les ~s de qch** to suffer from/feel the effects of sth; **avoir un ~ positif/négatif/catastrophique** to have a positive/negative/disastrous effect (**sur** on); **ma remarque a eu l'~ inverse de celui que je voulais** my remark had the opposite effect from the one I intended; **n'avoir aucun ~** [*critique, suggestion, campagne*] to have no effect; [*médicament*] not to work; **leurs remarques n'ont eu aucun ~ sur moi** their remarks didn't affect me; **faire de l'~** [*médicament, traitement*] to work; [*article, commentaire*] to have some effect; **le café/l'alcool me fait beaucoup d'~** coffee/alcohol has a very strong effect on me; **avoir pour ~ de faire** to have the effect of doing; **prendre ~** [*mesure, loi*] to take effect; **sous l'~ de l'alcool** under the influence of alcohol; **sous l'~ de la dévaluation** under the impact of devaluation; **sous l'~ de la passion** in a fit of passion; **sous l'~ de la colère** in a rage; **2** (impression) impression; **faire bon/mauvais ~** [*personne, comportement*] to make a good/bad impression; **être du meilleur ~** [*vêtement*] to look extremely nice; **être du plus mauvais ~** [*vêtement, remarque*] to be in the worst possible taste; **quel ~ cela te fait d'être père?** how does it feel to be a father?; **faire un drôle d'~** [*vitesse, alcool, rencontre*] to make one feel strange; **ça fait de l'~ d'arriver avec une jambe dans le plâtre** arriving with one's leg in plaster makes an impression; **faire son (petit) ~** [*bijou, décoration*] to make quite an impression; **il me fait l'~ d'un homme honnête/d'une crapule** he looks like an honest man/a crook to me; **leur réponse m'a fait l'~ d'une douche froide** their answer came as a real shock to me; **un ~ de surprise** an element of surprise; ▶ **bœuf**; **3** (procédé) effect; **~ comique/de style** comic/stylistic effect; **rechercher l'~** to strive for effect; **ma blague n'a fait rire personne, j'ai raté mon ~** my joke fell flat and no-one laughed; **il ne réussit jamais ses ~s** he tries but it never comes off; **couper tous ses ~s à qn** to steal sb's thunder; **faire des ~s de jambes**○ to show a bit of leg○; **faire des ~s de manches** to wave one' s arms about theatrically; **4** (but) **à cet ~** for that purpose; **5** (phénomène) **l'~ Joule/Doppler** the Joule/Doppler effect; **l'~ Maastricht** the Maastricht effect; **6** Sport spin; **donner de l'~ à une balle** to put spin on a ball.

II en effet *loc adv* **soyez prudent, les routes sont en ~ très glissantes** do be careful because the roads are very slippery indeed; **les résultats sont en ~ excellents** the results are indeed excellent; **'tu n'étais pas chez toi hier soir?'—'en ~'** 'you weren't home yesterday evening?'—'no, I wasn't'; **en ~, tu avais raison** actually, you were right.

III effets *nmpl* (vêtements) things; **rassemblez vos ~s** pack your things.

■ **~ de champ** field effect; **~ de commerce** commercial bill; **~ de filé** *blur that gives an impression of movement*; **~ de levier** leverage; **~ de serre** greenhouse effect; **~ spécial** special effect; **~s publics** government securities; **~s secondaires** side effects.

effeuillage /efœjaʒ/ *nm* **1** Agric thinning out of leaves; **2** hum striptease.

effeuiller /efœje/ [1] **I** *vtr* [*personne*] to thin out the leaves of [*arbre*]; to strip the leaves off [*légume*]; [*vent*] to blow the leaves off [*arbre*].

II s'effeuiller *vpr* [*arbre*] to shed its leaves; [*fleur*] to shed its petals.

IDIOMES **~ la marguerite** to play 'he loves me, he loves me not'.

effeuilleuse○ /efœjøz/ *nf* stripper.

efficace /efikas/ *adj* [*action, méthode, mesure*] effective; [*remède*] effective, efficacious○; [*personne, machine, dispositif*] efficient.

efficacement /efikasmɑ̃/ *adv* [*travailler, fonctionner*] efficiently; [*intervenir, soigner*] effectively.

efficacité /efikasite/ *nf* (d'action, de méthode, mesure) effectiveness; (de remède) effectiveness, efficacy sout; (de personne, machine, dispositif) efficiency.

efficience /efisjɑ̃s/ *nf* efficiency.

efficient, ~e /efisjɑ̃, ɑ̃t/ *adj* efficient.

effigie /efiʒi/ *nf* **1** (représentation) effigy; **en ~** in effigy; **à l'~ de** (maillot, pancarte) emblazoned with the image of; (médaille, timbre, monnaie) bearing the image of; **un billet à l'~ de Saint-Exupéry** a banknote bearing the image of Saint-Exupéry; **2** (symbole) logo.

effilé, ~e /efile/ **I** *pp* ▶ **effiler**.

II *pp adj* **1** [*rasoir, lame*] finely sharpened; **2** [*amandes*] flaked; **3** [*volaille*] oven-ready; **4** [*visage, silhouette, nez, forme*] slender; **5** [*linge, toile*] frayed.

III *nm* Tex fringe.

effiler /efile/ [1] **I** *vtr* **1** to sharpen [*lame, pointe*]; **2** to thin out, taper [*cheveux*]; **3** to string [*haricots verts*]; **4** Tex to unravel [*laine*]; to fray [*coton, lin*].

II s'effiler *vpr* Tex to fray.

effilochage /efilɔʃaʒ/ *nm* fraying.

effilocher /efilɔʃe/ [1] **I** *vtr* Tex, Tech to shred.

II s'effilocher *vpr* **1** [*tissu, vêtement*] to fray; **2** [*confiance, amour*] to dwindle (away); [*relation*] to fizzle out.

efflanqué, ~e /eflɑ̃ke/ *adj* [*animal, personne*] emaciated, raw-boned.

effleurage /eflœʀaʒ/ *nm* light massage.

effleurement /eflœʀmɑ̃/ *nm* light touch.

effleurer /eflœʀe/ [1] *vtr* **1** (frôler) to touch lightly, to brush (against); (égratigner) to graze; **l'idée ne m'a même pas effleuré l'esprit** fig the idea didn't even cross my mind ou occur to me; **le livre ne fait qu'~ la question** fig the book only skims over ou touches on the subject; **2** Tech (en peausserie) to buff.

efflorescence /eflɔʀesɑ̃s/ *nf* **1** Chimie, Méd efflorescence; **2** Bot bloom.

efflorescent, ~e /eflɔʀesɑ̃, ɑ̃t/ *adj* **1** Chimie efflorescent; **2** Bot covered in bloom (*après n*); **3** liter [*végétation, nature*] efflorescent; [*style, mode*] flourishing.

effluent /eflyɑ̃/ *nm* (eaux usées) effluent; **~s radioactifs** radioactive discharge ¢.

effluve /eflyv/ *nm* (nauséabond) unpleasant smell, effluvium; (agréable) fragrance ¢, aroma.

effondré, ~e /efɔ̃dʀe/ **I** *pp* ▶ **effondrer**.

II *pp adj* **1** lit [*toit, mur, canapé*] collapsed (*épith*); **2** fig [*personne*] distraught (**par** at; **de** with).

effondrement /efɔ̃dʀəmɑ̃/ *nm* **1** lit (de toit, pont) collapse; **2** Géol (de terrain) subsidence; **3** fig (de régime, projet, prix, d'économie) collapse; **l'~ des marchés se poursuit** the collapse in the market is continuing.

effondrer: **s'effondrer** /efɔ̃dʀe/ [1] *vpr* **1** (s'écrouler) [*toit, personne, régime, prix, monnaie*] to collapse; [*rêve, illusion*] to crumble; [*espoir, espérance*] to flounder; [*popularité*] to fall drastically; **s'~ dans un fauteuil** to collapse into an armchair; **2** (nerveusement) to collapse; **s'~ en larmes** to dissolve into tears; **s'~ de chagrin** to be distraught with grief.

efforcer: **s'efforcer** /efɔʀse/ [12] *vpr* to try hard (**de faire** to do), to endeavour[GB] (**de faire** to do) sout; **s'~ de comprendre** to try hard to understand.

effort /efɔʀ/ *nm* **1** (physique, intellectuel) effort; **malgré les ~s des sauveteurs** despite all the efforts of the rescue party; **après bien des ~s** after a great deal of effort; **un bel ~** a fine effort; **un ~ de mémoire** an effort to remember; **faire un ~ d'adaptation** to make an effort to adapt, to try to adapt; **faire tous ses ~s pour faire** to make every effort to do; **fais un petit ~ d'imagination!** use a bit of imagination!; **avec mon dos, je ne peux pas faire d'~** with this back of mine, I can't do anything strenuous; **faire ~ sur soi-même** to force oneself to stay calm, to make an effort to stay calm; **après deux heures d'~s, le feu a été maîtrisé** after a two-hour struggle, the fire was brought under control; **allons, encore un petit ~!** (après échec) come on, one more try!, come on, have another go! GB;

(près du bout) come on, you're almost there!; **il transpirait sous l'~ intellectuel** he was sweating as he tried to think; **triompher sans ~** to succeed effortlessly; **on n'a rien sans ~** you never get anywhere unless you try; **2** (subvention, aide) financial aid; (mise de fonds) investment, (financial) outlay; **faire un ~ en faveur des déshérités** to give financial aid to those in need; **consentir un ~ financier pour les écoles** to agree to financial aid for schools; **représenter un gros ~ financier** to represent a substantial outlay; **3** Phys (force exercée) stress; (force subie) strain.

■ **~ de cisaillement** Phys (exercé) shear stress; (subi) shear strain; **~ de guerre** Mil war effort; **~ de torsion** Phys torsional stress; **~ de traction** Phys tensile stress.

effraction /efʀaksjɔ̃/ *nf* Jur breaking and entering; **un vol avec ~** a burglary with forced entry; **ils sont entrés dans la maison par ~** they broke into the house; **il y a eu ~** the premises have been broken into.

■ **~ informatique** computer hacking.

effraie /efʀɛ/ *nf* Zool barn owl.

effranger /efʀɑ̃ʒe/ [13] **I** *vtr* to fray [sth] out.

II s'effranger *vpr* [*vêtement, manches*] to fray.

effrayant, ~e /efʀɛjɑ̃, ɑ̃t/ *adj* **1** (qui fait peur) [*vision, laideur*] frightening; [*maigreur, pâleur*] dreadful; **il a une mine ~e** he looks dreadful; **2**○ (excessif) [*chaleur, prix*] terrible; **il est ~ d'égoïsme** he is frightfully selfish; **3**○ (extraordinaire) terrific○.

effrayer /efʀeje/ [21] **I** *vtr* **1** (faire peur à) to frighten, to scare; (alarmer) to alarm; **son insouciance m'effraie** his carelessness alarms me; **2** (rebuter) to put [sb] off; **les difficultés/prix l'effraient** the difficulties/prices put her off.

II s'effrayer *vpr* to be frightened, to be scared (**de** by).

effréné, ~e /efʀene/ *adj* [*course, rythme, concurrence, spéculation*] frantic, frenetic; [*ambition, luxe, gaspillage*] unbridled.

effritement /efʀitmɑ̃/ *nm* lit crumbling; fig crumbling away.

effriter /efʀite/ [1] **I** *vtr* to crumble [*gâteau*]; to break up [*motte de terre*].

II s'effriter *vpr* **1** (partir en morceaux) [*pierre, plâtre*] to crumble (away); **2** (diminuer) [*majorité, soutien*] to crumble, to collapse; [*fréquentation, popularité*] to dwindle (away); [*monnaie*] to decline (in value), to fall.

effroi /efʀwa/ *nm* liter dread, terror.

effronté, ~e /efʀɔ̃te/ **I** *adj* [*enfant*] cheeky; [*regard, mine, remarque*] cheeky; [*adulte*] (éhonté) shameless; (hardi) cheeky.

II *nm,f* cheeky boy/girl.

effrontément /efʀɔ̃temɑ̃/ *adv* [*sourire, répondre*] cheekily; [*mentir, flatter*] shamelessly.

effronterie /efʀɔ̃tʀi/ *nf* (caractère) cheekiness, effrontery sout; (acte) cheek, effrontery sout; **avec ~** [*sourire, répondre*] cheekily; [*mentir, flatter*] shamelessly.

effroyable /efʀwajabl/ *adj* [*cri, spectacle*] dreadful, horrifying; [*misère, douleur, vacarme*] dreadful, awful.

effroyablement /efʀwajabləmɑ̃/ *adv* **1** (de manière horrible) horribly; **2**○ (excessivement) terribly.

effusion /efyzjɔ̃/ *nf* effusion; **avec ~** [*remercier, parler*] effusively; **sans ~** [*parler, réagir*] unemotionally.

■ **~ de sang** bloodshed.

égailler: s'égailler /egaje/ [1] *vpr* to disperse.

égal, ~e, *mpl* **-aux** /egal, o/ **I** *adj* **1** (identique) equal (**à** to); **plantés à intervalles égaux** planted at an equal distance from each other; **de force/d'intelligence ~e** of equal strength/intelligence, equally strong/intelligent; **à travail ~, salaire ~** equal pay for equal work; **découper un gâteau en parts ~es** to cut a cake into equal portions; **toutes choses ~es d'ailleurs** all things being equal; **à distance ~e de** equidistant from, at the same distance from; **à prix ~, je préfère celui-là** if the price is the same, I'd rather have that one; **augmentation/baisse ~e ou inférieure à 2%** rise/drop of 2% or less; **~ à lui-même, il...** true to form, he...; **2** (régulier) [*terrain, allée*] level; [*lumière*] even; [*teinte*] uniform; [*temps*] settled; [*pouls, respiration*] steady; **d'un pas ~** at an even pace; **avoir un tempérament ~** to be even-tempered; **3** (indifférent) **ça m'est ~** (je n'ai pas de préférence) I don't mind either way; (je m'en moque) I don't care, it makes no difference to me; **les privations leur sont ~es** they don't mind putting up with hardship; **il lui est complètement ~ d'être critiqué** or **qu'on le critique** he couldn't care less about being criticized; **c'est ~, tu aurais pu m'avertir**○ all the same, you could have warned me; **4** (équitable) **la partie n'est pas ~e (entre eux)** they are not evenly matched.

II *nm,f* equal; **être l'~ de qn en mérite/talent** to be sb's equal in terms of merit/talent; **traiter d'~ à ~ avec qn** to deal with sb as an equal; **n'avoir point d'~, ne pas avoir son ~** to have no equal, to be the best there is; **adresse/beauté sans ~e** unrivalled[GB] ou unparalleled skill/beauty; **être d'une beauté sans ~e** to be supremely beautiful; **être d'une bêtise/maladresse sans ~e** to be unbelievably stupid/clumsy; **leur talent n'a d'~ que leur modestie** their talent is only equalled[GB] by their modesty; **il aime/admire l'un à l'~ de l'autre** he loves/admires them both equally; **il fera un piètre ministre, à l'~ de son prédécesseur** he'll make a poor minister, just like his predecessor.

IDIOMES **rester ~ à soi-même** to be one's usual self; **combattre à armes ~s** to be on an equal footing.

égalable /egalabl/ *adj* **difficilement ~** [*beauté, bêtise*] unparalleled; [*technique*] incomparably superior.

également /egalmɑ̃/ *adv* **1** (aussi) also, too; **il enseigne ~ l'histoire** he also teaches history, he teaches history too; **2** (au même degré) [*éligible, fertile*] equally; [*partager, aimer*] equally.

égaler /egale/ [1] *vtr* **1** (atteindre) to equal [*record, vitesse*]; to be as good as [*personne*]; to be as high as [*prix*]; **~ les meilleurs** to rank with the best; **précision/technique jamais encore égalée** hitherto unequalled[GB] precision/technique; **2** (valoir) **rien n'égale un coucher de soleil** nothing can compare with a sunset; **leur intelligence égale leur charme** they're as clever as they're charming; **3** Math **trois plus trois égalent six** three plus three equals six ou is six.

égalisateur, -trice /egalizatœʀ, tʀis/ *adj* [*société, loi*] equalizing; **la mesure a eu sur les prix une action égalisatrice** the move has had the effect of levelling[GB] out prices; **but ~** Sport equalizer.

égalisation /egalizasjɔ̃/ *nf* **1** (des revenus) levelling[GB] out; **l'~ des chances** bringing about equality of opportunity; **2** (de surface, sol) levelling[GB] out; **3** Sport **le penalty a permis l'~** the penalty evened GB ou tied US the score; **rater l'~** to fail to score the equalizer.

égaliser /egalize/ [1] **I** *vtr* **1** (en nivelant) to level [*terrain*]; to level out [*prix, revenus, impôt*]; **~ les droits/chances** to give people equal rights/opportunities; **~ le développement économique dans les deux régions** to balance economic development in the two regions; **2** (en taillant) to even up the ends of [*cheveux*]; to make [sth] the same size [*planches*].

II *vi* Sport to equalize GB, to tie US.

III s'égaliser *vpr* [*impôt*] to become more evenly distributed; [*chances*] to become more equal.

égaliseur /egalizœʀ/ *nm* **~ graphique** Audio graphic equalizer; **~ de potentiel** Électrotech equalizer.

égalitaire /egalitɛʀ/ *adj, nmf* egalitarian.

égalitarisme /egalitaʀism/ *nm* egalitarianism.

égalitariste /egalitaʀist/ *adj, nmf* egalitarian.

égalité /egalite/ *nf* **1** (parité) gén, Pol equality; **garantir/réclamer l'~ des droits/chances** to guarantee/demand equal rights/opportunities; **~ des salaires** or **devant le salaire** equal pay; **il faut les traiter à ~ avec les autres pays** they must be treated on an equal footing with other countries; **les sondages mettent les deux partis à ~** the polls put the two parties neck and neck; **2** Sport **être à ~** to be level GB, to be tied US; **être à ~ de points** to be level on points; **~!** (au tennis) deuce!; **3** (uniformité) (de terrain) flatness; (de climat) temperate nature; (d'humeur) evenness; **4** Math equality.

■ **~ d'âme** equanimity.

égard /egaʀ/ **I** *nm* **1** fml (considération) consideration ¢; **sans ~ pour** without regard for, without considering; **sans aucun/le moindre ~ pour** without any/the slightest regard for; **par ~ pour qn** out of consideration for sb; **avoir quelque ~ pour l'âge de qn** to have some consideration for sb's age; **avoir ~ aux souhaits/à l'âge de qn** to take sb's wishes/age into account; **2** (rapport) **à l'~ de qn** toward(s) sb; **à l'~ de qch** regarding, with regard to sth; **à cet ~** in this respect; **à aucun ~** in no respect; **à plus d'un ~** in several respects; **à tous les ~s** in all respects; **à différents** or **divers ~s** in various respects; **à quelques** or **certains ~s** in some respects; **à beaucoup d'~s** in many respects; **à bien des** or **maints ~s** in many respects; **eu ~ à qch** in view of sth.

II égards *nmpl* (marques d'estime) **avec des ~s** with respect; **manquer d'~s envers qn** to be disrespectful toward(s) sb; **être plein d'~s envers qn** to be attentive to sb's every need.

égaré, ~e /egaʀe/ **I** *pp* ▶ **égarer**.

II *pp adj* **1** [*voyageur, promeneur*] lost; [*animal*] stray (*épith*); [*lettre, colis*] lost, missing; **2** [*air, regard, yeux*] wild, disturbed.

égarement /egaʀmɑ̃/ *nm* **1** (trouble) distraction; **2** (dérèglement) **il est revenu de ses ~s** he has seen the error of his ways; **les ~s du cœur** the caprices of the heart.

égarer /egaʀe/ [1] **I** *vtr* **1** (faire perdre) to lead [sb] astray [*voyageur, groupe, promeneur*]; **une fausse piste destinée à ~ les enquêteurs** a false lead intended to put the investigators off the track; **2** (perdre) to mislay [*objet*]; **3** (dévier) **ne vous laissez pas ~ par ces agitateurs** don't let these agitators lead you astray; **la colère/jalousie vous égare** you're letting your anger/jealousy get the better of you.

II s'égarer *vpr* **1** (se perdre) [*personne, animal*] to get lost, to lose one's way; **des promeneurs égarés dans la forêt** walkers lost in the forest; **2** (être perdu) [*lettre, colis*] to get lost, to go missing; **3** (errer) [*esprit*] to wander; [*personne*] to ramble; **l'auteur s'égare dans des digressions interminables** the author loses his way in endless digressions.

égayer /egeje/ [21] **I** *vtr* to enliven [*conversation, soirée*]; to cheer [sb] up [*malade*]; to amuse [*convives, assemblée*]; to brighten [sth] up [*maison, robe*]; to lighten [*ouvrage, style*]; to brighten [*journée, vie*].

II s'égayer *vpr* [*malade*] to cheer up; [*convives*] to liven up; **s'~ aux dépens de qn** to amuse oneself at sb's expense; **s'~ à voir qch** to be amused at the sight of sth.

Égée /eʒe/ ▶ 555 *npr* Aegeus; **mer ~** Aegean Sea.

égérie /eʒeʀi/ *nf* muse.
Égérie /eʒeʀi/ *npr* Egeria.
égide /eʒid/ *nf* aegis; **sous l'~ de qn/qch** under the aegis of sb/sth.
églantier /eglɑ̃tje/ *nm* wild rose, dog-rose.
églantine /eglɑ̃tin/ *nf* wild rose, dog-rose.
églefin /egləfɛ̃/ *nm* haddock.
église /egliz/ *nf* church; **~ paroissiale/abbatiale** parish/abbey church; **aller à l'~** to go to church; **se marier à l'~** to get married in church; **elle est à l'~** she is in ou at church; **en l'~ de Vinay/Saint-Pierre** in the church at Vinay/of St. Peter.
Église /egliz/ *nf* Church; **l'~ catholique (romaine)** the (Roman) Catholic Church; **l'~ orthodoxe** the Orthodox Church; **les ~s réformées/protestantes** the Reformed/Protestant Churches; **homme d'~** cleric; **gens d'~** clerics.
églogue /eglɔg/ *nf* eclogue.
ego /ego/ *nm inv* ego.
égocentrique /egosɑ̃tʀik/ *adj, nmf* egocentric.
égocentrisme /egosɑ̃tʀism/ *nm* self-centredness[GB], egocentricity spéc.
égocentriste /egosɑ̃tʀist/ *adj, nmf* egocentric.
égoïne /egɔin/ I *adj f* **scie ~** handsaw.
II *nf* handsaw.
égoïsme /egɔism/ *nm* selfishness.
égoïste /egɔist/ I *adj* selfish.
II *nmf* selfish man/woman.
égoïstement /egɔistəmɑ̃/ *adv* selfishly.
égorger /egɔʀʒe/ [13] *vtr* **~ un animal/qn** to cut an animal's throat/sb's throat.
égorgeur, -euse /egɔʀʒœʀ, øz/ *nm,f* cutthroat.
égosiller: s'égosiller /egozije/ [1] *vpr* **1** (se fatiguer la voix) to shout oneself hoarse; **s'~ à faire** to make oneself hoarse doing; **2** (chanter fort) to sing at the top of one's voice; (crier) to yell.
égotisme /egɔtism/ *nm* egotism.
égotiste /egɔtist/ I *adj* egotistical.
II *nmf* egotist.
égout /egu/ *nm* sewer; **eaux d'~** sewage; **système d'~** sewage system.
égoutier, -ière /egutje, ɛʀ/ ▶510 *nm,f* sewage worker.
égouttage /egutaʒ/, **égouttement** /egutmɑ̃/ *nm* (de vaisselle, riz, légumes) draining ¢; (de fromage) straining ¢; (de linge) drip-drying ¢.
égoutter /egute/ [1] I *vtr* to drain [*vaisselle, riz, légumes, frites*]; to strain [*fromage*]; to hang up [sth] to drip [*linge*].
II *vi* [*vaisselle, riz, fromage*] to drain; [*linge*] to drip.
III **s'égoutter** *vpr* [*vaisselle, riz, légumes, fromage*] to drain; [*linge*] to drip dry.
égouttoir /egutwaʀ/ *nm* draining rack GB, (dish) drainer US.
égratigner /egʀatiɲe/ [1] I *vtr* **1** (physiquement) (sur des ronces, un objet pointu) to scratch [*jambe, visage*]; (en tombant) to graze [*jambe, genou*]; to scratch [*meuble, voiture*]; **2** (moralement) to hurt [*personne*].
II **s'égratigner** *vpr* (sur des ronces, un objet pointu) to scratch oneself; (par frottement) to graze oneself.
égratignure /egʀatiɲyʀ/ *nf* **1** (sur la peau) (avec un objet pointu) scratch; (par frottement) graze; **se sortir de qch sans une ~** lit to come out of sth without a scratch; fig to come out of sth with one's reputation unscathed; **2** (de meuble, voiture) scratch.
égrènement /egʀɛnmɑ̃/ *nm* **1** Agric, Bot (de céréale, pois, épis) shelling; (de coton, lin) ginning; (de raisin, cassis, groseilles) picking off; **2** fig (de notes) succession; (d'heures) passing; **~ du chapelet** telling one's beads.
égrener /egʀəne/ [16] *vtr* **1** gén, Culin to shell [*pois, épis*]; to remove the seeds from [*tomate, melon*]; **~ une grappe de raisin** to strip the grapes off the bunch; **2** Tex [*machine*] to gin [*coton*]; **3** fig to chime out [*notes, heures*]; to drone out [*chiffres, chanson*]; **la pendule égrena les douze coups de minuit** the clock chimed out the twelve strokes of midnight; **~ son chapelet** to tell one's beads; **4** Tech to smooth [sth] off [*mur, plâtre, fer*].
égreneuse /egʀənøz/ *nf* **1** Agric sheller; **2** Tex (pour coton) cotton gin; (pour lin) flax gin.
égrillard, ~e /egʀijaʀ, aʀd/ *adj* [*personne*] dirty-minded; [*air, histoire*] bawdy.
Égypte /eʒipt/ ▶321 *nprf* Egypt.
égyptien, -ienne /eʒipsjɛ̃, ɛn/ ▶462, 537
I *adj* Egyptian.
II *nm* Ling Egyptian.
III **égyptienne** *nf* Imprim Egyptian (typeface).
Égyptien, -ienne /eʒipsjɛ̃, ɛn/ ▶537 *nm,f* Egyptian.
égyptologie /eʒiptɔlɔʒi/ *nf* Egyptology.
égyptologue /eʒiptɔlɔg/ ▶510 *nmf* Egyptologist.
eh /e/ *excl* (pour attirer l'attention) hey; **~, tu me fais mal** hey, you're hurting me; **~ bien, que faites-vous?** well, what are you up to?; **~ oui** (ton résigné) so there we are; (pour insister) I'm afraid so.
éhonté, ~e /eɔ̃te/ *adj* [*menteur, mensonge*] brazen; [*demande*] shameless.
eider /edɛʀ/ *nm* eider.
eidétique /edetik/ *adj* eidetic.
einsteinium /ɛnstɛnjɔm/ *nm* einsteinium.
Éire /ɛʀ/ *npr* Éire, Republic of Ireland.
éjaculation /eʒakylasjɔ̃/ *nf* ejaculation; **~ précoce** premature ejaculation.
éjaculer /eʒakyle/ [1] *vi* to ejaculate.
éjectable /eʒɛktabl/ *adj* **siège ~** ejector seat GB, ejection seat US.
éjecter /eʒɛkte/ [1] *vtr* **1** (dans un accident) to throw [sb/sth] out, to eject; **2**○ (expulser) to chuck○ [sb] out [*personne*] (**de** of); **se faire ~** to get chucked○ ou thrown out (**de** of); **3** Tech to eject.
éjection /eʒɛksjɔ̃/ *nf* **1** (de pilote, fluide, cartouche) ejection; **2**○ (expulsion) expulsion; **après son ~ du comité** after being kicked off○ the committee; **après son ~ du club** after being thrown out of the club.
élaboration /elabɔʀasjɔ̃/ *nf* **1** (de projet, stratégie) development; (de solution) working out; (de document) drafting; (de journal, brochure) putting together; **2** Bot, Physiol elaboration.
élaboré, ~e /elabɔʀe/ I *pp* ▶ **élaborer**.
II *pp adj* [*cuisine, traitement*] sophisticated; péj elaborate.
élaborer /elabɔʀe/ [1] *vtr* **1** (préparer) to work [sth] out, to develop [*stratégie*]; to work [sth] out, to devise [*solution, plan*]; to draw up [*document*]; to put [sth] together [*brochure*]; **2** Bot, Physiol to elaborate.
élagage /elagaʒ/ *nm* **1** Agric lopping; **2** (de texte) pruning.
élaguer /elage/ [1] *vtr* **1** Agric to lop [*arbre, branche*]; **2** fig to prune [*texte*].
élagueur, -euse /elagœʀ, øz/ I *nm,f* ▶510 (ouvrier) pruner.
II *nm* (outil) pruning hook.
élan /elɑ̃/ *nm* **1** Sport (pour sauter) run up; **prendre son ~** to take a run up; **saut avec/sans ~** running/standing jump; **2** (force) lit, fig momentum; **prendre de l'~** fig [*parti, entreprise, réforme*] to gather momentum; **casser** or **couper l'~** to stop the momentum; **emportés par leur ~** carried away by their own momentum; **continuer sur son ~** to continue at the same pace; **3** (impulsion) impetus; **donner de l'~/un nouvel ~ à** to give impetus/fresh impetus to [*parti, entreprise, réforme*]; **4** (enthousiasme) enthusiasm; **emporté par son ~** carried along by his own enthusiasm; **dans un bel ~** with great enthusiasm; **avec ~** [*parler*] with passion; **~ patriotique** patriotic fervour[GB]; **5** (mouvement affectif) impulse; **~s passionnés/de générosité** passionate/generous impulses; **contenir ses ~s** to control one's impulses; **~ de tendresse/colère** rush ou surge of tenderness/anger; **~ de patriotisme** surge of patriotism; **6** Zool elk; **~ du Canada** Canadian elk.
élancé, ~e /elɑ̃se/ *adj* [*personne, taille, édifice*] slender.
élancement /elɑ̃smɑ̃/ *nm* **1** (douleur) shooting pain; **~s au bras** shooting pains in one's arm; **2** (aspiration) yearning.
élancer /elɑ̃se/ [12] I *vi* (faire mal à) **mon doigt m'élance** I've got a throbbing pain in my finger; **cela risque de vous ~ toute la nuit** it may continue to give you pain during the night.
II **s'élancer** *vpr* **1** (bondir) [*personne*] to dash forward; **s'~ vers/hors de** to dash toward(s)/out of; **s'~ à l'assaut** to launch an assault (**de** on); **2** (partir) [*coureur, voiture*] to shoot off; [*personne*] to take off; **s'~ à la conquête de l'espace** to take off to conquer space; **3** liter (se dresser) **s'~ vers le ciel** [*arbre, cathédrale*] to soar up towards the sky.
élargi, ~e /elaʀʒi/ I *pp* ▶ **élargir**.
II *pp adj* [*chaussée, rue*] widened; [*format*] enlarged; [*majorité*] increased; [*accord, coopération*] extended; [*gouvernement*] expanded; **la nécessité d'une concertation ~e** the need for broader discussions.
élargir /elaʀʒiʀ/ [3] I *vtr* **1** (rendre plus large) to widen [*chaussée*]; to let [sth] out [*vêtement*]; **cette coiffure lui élargit le visage** this hairstyle makes her face look fuller; **le miroir élargit la pièce** the mirror makes the room look bigger; **2** (déformer) [*personne*] to stretch [*chaussures, pull, veste*]; **3** fig (étendre) to widen [*débat*]; to extend [*contacts, audience, droit*]; to broaden [*connaissances, idées, activités*]; to increase [*majorité, électorat*]; to expand [*moyens, secteur*]; **~ son champ d'action** to widen one's field of action; **4** Jur (libérer) to discharge, release [*détenu*].
II **s'élargir** *vpr* [*famille, groupe*] to expand; [*marge, écart*] to increase; [*débat, route, fleuve*] to widen; [*personne*] to fill out; [*épaules, hanches*] to become broader; [*vêtement*] to stretch; **le fossé entre eux s'élargit** the gap is widening between them.
élargissement /elaʀʒismɑ̃/ *nm* **1** lit (de route) widening; **travaux d'~** carriageway widening GB, widening of the roadway US; **2** fig (de réforme) extension; (de budget, d'activités) expansion; **l'~ de la CEE à d'autres pays** the enlargement of the EEC to include other countries; **3** Jur discharge, release.
élasticité /elastisite/ *nf* (de gaz, siège, peau, vêtement) elasticity; (de démarche) springiness; (de règlement) flexibility.
élastine /elastin/ *nf* Biol elastin.
élastique /elastik/ I *adj* **1** Mode [*dos, bretelle, taille*] elasticated GB, elasticized US; **2** Phys [*gaz, métal, fibre*] elastic; **une démarche ~** a springy walk; **3** [*règlement, horaire*] flexible; [*budget*] elastic; **avoir la conscience ~** to have an elastic conscience, not to be overscrupulous.
II *nm* **1** (lien circulaire) rubber band; (en mercerie) elastic; **le dos est en ~** the back is elasticated GB ou elasticized US; **2** ▶449 (jeu d'enfant) **jouer à l'~** to play elastics ou French-skipping GB; **3** ▶449 Sport (pour sauter) bungee cord; **(faire du) saut à l'~** (to go) bungee jumping; **sauter à l'~** to do a bungee jump.
IDIOMES **les lâcher avec un ~**○ to be tight-fisted.
élastiqué, ~e /elastike/ *adj* Mode elasticated GB, elasticized US.
élastomère /elastɔmɛʀ/ *nm* elastomer.
électeur, -trice /elɛktœʀ, tʀis/ *nm,f* voter, elector; **les ~s de l'Ain** the electorate ou voters of the Ain; **carte d'~** polling card GB, voter registration card US; ▶ **grand**.

électif, -ive /elɛktif, iv/ *adj* [*mandat, système*] elective.

élection /elɛksjɔ̃/ *nf* **1** Pol election (**à** to); **se présenter aux ~s** to stand in the elections GB, to run for office US, to run in the elections; **des ~s libres** free elections; **~ présidentielle** presidential election; **~s primaires/législatives/locales** primary/legislative/local elections; **~s générales** general election; **~ partielle** by-election GB, off-year election US; **le premier tour des ~s** the first ballot; **après son ~** after being elected; **2** (choix) choice; **mon pays d'~** my chosen country.

électoral, ~e, *mpl* **-aux** /elɛktɔʀal, o/ *adj* [*programme, réforme, calendrier, promesse*] electoral; [*affiche, dépense, période*] election (*épith*); [*victoire, défaite, campagne*] election (*épith*), electoral; **la carte ~e du pays** the electoral map of the country.

électoralisme /elɛktɔʀalism/ *nm* electioneering; **faire de l'~** to engage in electioneering.

électoraliste /elɛktɔʀalist/ *adj* [*opération, mesure*] electioneering.

électorat /elɛktɔʀa/ *nm* (d'un pays) electorate, voters; (d'une circonscription) electorate; (groupe social, politique) voters; **l'~ traditionnel** traditional voters; **l'~ du parti** the party voters.

Électre /elɛktʀ/ *npr* Electra.

électricien, -ienne /elɛktʀisjɛ̃, ɛn/ **▶510** *nm,f* (artisan) electrician; **ingénieur ~** electrical engineer.

électricité /elɛktʀisite/ *nf* **1** Électrotech, Phys electricity; **facture d'~** electricity bill; **coupure d'~** power cut; **marcher** or **fonctionner à l'~** to run on electricity; **2** (excitation) tension; **il y a de l'~ dans l'air** there's tension in the air; **l'atmosphère était chargée d'~** the atmosphere was very tense.

électrification /elɛktʀifikasjɔ̃/ *nf* electrification.

électrifier /elɛktʀifje/ [2] *vtr* to bring electricity to [*village, maison*]; to electrify [*voie ferrée*].

électrique /elɛktʀik/ *adj* **1** Tech [*appareil, moteur, four*] electric; [*installation*] electrical; [*alimentation, réseau*] electricity (*épith*); **centrale ~** power station; **2** [*atmosphère*] electric.

électriquement /elɛktʀikmɑ̃/ *adv* electrically.

électrisant, ~e /elɛktʀizɑ̃, ɑ̃t/ *adj* fig electrifying.

électrisation /elɛktʀizasjɔ̃/ *nf* Phys electrification.

électriser /elɛktʀize/ [1] *vtr* **1** Phys to charge [sth] with electricity [*tissu, surface, poil*]; **2** (exalter) to electrify.

électroacoustique /elɛktʀoakustik/ **I** *adj* electroacoustic.
II *nf* electroacoustics (+ *v sg*).

électro-aimant, *pl* **~s** /elɛktʀoɛmɑ̃/ *nm* electromagnet.

électrobiologie /elɛktʀobjɔlɔʒi/ *nf* electrobiology.

électrocardiogramme /elɛktʀokaʀdjɔgʀam/ *nm* electrocardiogram; **faire un ~ à qn** to do an electrocardiogram on sb.

électrocardiographe /elɛktʀokaʀdjɔgʀaf/ *nm* electrocardiograph.

électrocardiographie /elɛktʀokaʀdjɔgʀafi/ *nf* electrocardiography.

électrochimique /elɛktʀoʃimik/ *adj* electrochemical.

électrochirurgie /elɛktʀoʃiʀyʀʒi/ *nf* electrosurgery.

électrochoc /elɛktʀoʃɔk/ *nm* **1** Méd (technique) **~s** electroshock therapy (*sg*), EST; **faire des ~s à qn** to give sb EST; **2** fig (traitement de choc) shock treatment ₵.

électroconvulsivothérapie /elɛktʀokɔ̃vylsivoteʀapi/ *nf* electroconvulsive therapy, ECT.

électrocuter /elɛktʀɔkyte/ [1] **I** *vtr* to electrocute.
II s'électrocuter *vpr* (accidentellement) to be electrocuted.

électrocution /elɛktʀɔkysjɔ̃/ *nf* electrocution.

électrode /elɛktʀɔd/ *nf* electrode.

électrodynamique /elɛktʀodinamik/ **I** *adj* electrodynamic.
II *nf* electrodynamics (+ *v sg*).

électroencéphalogramme /elɛktʀoɑ̃sefalɔgʀam/ *nm* electroencephalogram; **faire un ~ à qn** to do an electroencephalogram on sb.

électrogène /elɛktʀɔʒɛn/ *adj* **groupe ~** (electricity) generator.

électroluminescent, ~e /elɛktʀolyminɛsɑ̃, ɑ̃t/ *adj* electroluminescent.

électrolyse /elɛktʀɔliz/ *nf* electrolysis.

électrolyser /elɛktʀɔlize/ [1] *vtr* to electrolyze.

électrolyte /elɛktʀɔlit/ *nm* electrolyte.

électrolytique /elɛktʀɔlitik/ *adj* electrolytic.

électromagnétique /elɛktʀomaɲetik/ *adj* electromagnetic.

électromagnétisme /elɛktʀomaɲetism/ *nm* electromagnetism.

électromécanicien, -ienne /elɛktʀomekanisjɛ̃, ɛn/ **▶510** *nm,f* electrical engineer.

électromécanique /elɛktʀomekanik/ **I** *adj* electromechanical.
II *nf* electromechanical engineering.

électroménager, -ère /elɛktʀomenaʒe, ɛʀ/ **I** *adj* **appareil ~** electrical domestic ou household appliance.
II *nm* **1** (appareils) electrical domestic ou household appliances (*pl*); **2** (industrie) electrical goods industry.

électrométallurgie /elɛktʀometalyʀʒi/ *nf* electrometallurgy.

électromètre /elɛktʀɔmɛtʀ/ *nm* electrometer.

électromoteur, -trice /elɛktʀomɔtœʀ, tʀis/ *adj* electromotive; **force ~** electromotive force.

électron /elɛktʀɔ̃/ *nm* electron.

électronégatif, -ive /elɛktʀonegatif, iv/ *adj* electronegative.

électronicien, -ienne /elɛktʀɔnisjɛ̃, ɛn/ **▶510** *nm,f* electronics engineer.

électronique /elɛktʀɔnik/ **I** *adj* **1** Électron [*circuit, composant*] electronic; **2** Phys [*microscope, télescope*] electron.
II *nf* electronics (+ *v sg*); **~ grand public** consumer electronics.

électroniquement /elɛktʀɔnikmɑ̃/ *adv* electronically.

électro-optique, *pl* **~s** /elɛktʀoɔptik/ **I** *adj* electro-optic.
II *nf* electron optics (+ *v sg*).

électrophone /elɛktʀɔfɔn/ *nm* record player.

électropositif, -ive /elɛktʀopozitif, iv/ *adj* electropositive.

électroradiologie /elɛktʀoʀadjɔlɔʒi/ *nf* electroradiology.

électroscope /elɛktʀɔskɔp/ *nm* electroscope.

électrostatique /elɛktʀostatik/ **I** *adj* [*décharge, champ*] electrostatic.
II *nf* electrostatics (+ *v sg*).

électrotechnicien, -ienne /elɛktʀotɛknisjɛ̃, ɛn/ **▶510** *nm,f* electrical engineer.

électrotechnique /elɛktʀotɛknik/ *nf* electrical engineering; (discipline) electrotechnology.

électrothérapie /elɛktʀoteʀapi/ *nf* electrotherapy.

électrothermie /elɛktʀotɛʀmi/ *nf* electrothermics (+ *v sg*).

électrovanne /elɛktʀovan/ *nf* (solenoid-operated) control valve.

électrum /elɛktʀɔm/ *nm* electrum.

élégamment /elegamɑ̃/ *adv* [*s'habiller*] elegantly; [*se conduire*] courteously.

élégance /elegɑ̃s/ *nf* **1** (qualité) elegance; **d'une grande ~** [*personne, vêtement*] extremely elegant; **avec ~** [*s'habiller*] elegantly; [*perdre*] gracefully; [*se conduire*] honourably[GB]; [*résoudre un problème*] neatly; **manquer d'~** (dans l'habillement) to lack elegance; (dans la conduite) to behave shabbily; **2** (détail raffiné) touch of elegance; **faire des ~s** to make a show of elegance.

élégant, ~e /elegɑ̃, ɑ̃t/ **I** *adj* **1** (bien habillé) [*personne*] gén smart; (très habillé) elegant; **tu es ~ aujourd'hui** you're looking smart today; **2** (distingué) [*écriture, style*] elegant, polished; [*vêtement*] elegant, stylish; **un comportement peu ~** uncivilized behaviour[GB]; **ce n'est pas très ~ de ta part** it's not very decent of you; **3** (ingénieux) [*solution*] neat, elegant; [*manière*] ingenious.
II *nm,f* dandy/elegant lady.

élégiaque /eleʒjak/ *adj* elegiac.

élégie /eleʒi/ *nf* elegy.

élément /elemɑ̃/ **I** *nm* **1** (constituant) (de structure, d'ensemble) element; (d'appareil) component; (de mélange) ingredient; (de problème) element; (facteur) factor, element; **~ constitutif** essential element; **~ de surprise** element of surprise; **un ~ important de leur philosophie** an important element in their philosophy; **~ décisif** deciding factor; **l'~-clé de leur succès** the key element ou factor in their success; **l'~ humain** the human element ou factor; **l'~ violent du public** the violent element in the public; **~ moteur** (personne) driving force; **2** (de mobilier) unit; **~s de cuisine/rangement** kitchen/storage units; **3** (fait) fact; **disposer de tous les ~s** to have all the facts ou information; **il n'y a aucun ~ nouveau** nothing new has emerged; **4** (individu) **être un bon ~** [*élève*] to be a good pupil; [*travailleur*] to be a good worker; [*joueur*] to be a good player; **~s indésirables/rebelles** undesirable/rebel elements; **5** Tech (de pile) cell; **6** Chimie, Math, Astrol element.
II éléments *nmpl* **1** (rudiments) **(premiers) ~s** basics; (dans un titre) elements; **2** Météo elements; **lutter contre les ~s** to struggle against the elements.
IDIOMES **être** or **se sentir dans son ~** to be ou feel in one's element.

élémentaire /elemɑ̃tɛʀ/ *adj* (de base) [*principe, besoin*] basic; Scol [*niveau*] elementary; (pas compliqué) elementary; **c'est ~!** it's elementary!; **c'est la politesse la plus ~** it's basic ou elementary courtesy.

éléphant /elefɑ̃/ *nm* elephant; **~ d'Asie/d'Afrique** Indian/African elephant.
■ **~ de mer** sea elephant, elephant seal.
IDIOMES **être comme un ~ dans un magasin de porcelaine** to be like a bull in a china shop; **avoir une mémoire d'~** never to forget a thing.

éléphante /elefɑ̃t/ *nf* cow elephant.

éléphanteau, *pl* **~x** /elefɑ̃to/ *nm* (elephant) calf.

éléphantesque /elefɑ̃tɛsk/ *adj* elephantine, enormous.

éléphantiasis /elefɑ̃tjazis/ **▶271** *nm* elephantiasis.

éléphantin, ~e /elefɑ̃tɛ̃, in/ *adj* Zool elephantine.

élevage /elvaʒ/ *nm* **1** (de bétail) livestock farming; **un pays d'~** a livestock farming area; **~ intensif/extensif** intensive/extensive livestock farming; **faire de l'~** to breed GB ou raise US livestock; **produits de l'~** meat and dairy products; **2** (d'animaux spécifiés) **~ de moutons/saumons/poulets** sheep/salmon/chicken farming; **faire de l'~ de bétail/chevaux/porcs** to breed cattle/horses/pigs; **faire l'~ de moutons** to farm GB ou raise US sheep; **d'~** [*huîtres, poisson*] farmed; [*caille, faisan*] captive-bred; **3** (installation) farm; **un ~ de poulets/visons** a poultry/mink farm; **4** (ensemble des animaux) stock; **un ~ de taureaux/porcs** a stock of bulls/ pigs; **un ~ de visons/saumons** a stock of mink/salmon; **5** Vin **~ des vins** wine maturation.

■ **~ hors-sol** battery farming.

élévateur, **-trice** /elevatœʀ, tʀis/ **I** *adj* **1** Tech [*dispositif*] lifting; **2** Anat [*muscle*] elevator.

II *nm* **1** Tech (en manutention) elevator; **2** Anat (muscle) elevator.

élévation /elevasjɔ̃/ *nf* **1** (augmentation) rise (**de** in); **l'~ du niveau de vie/du niveau des eaux** the rise in the standard of living/ in the water level; **2** (noblesse) **l'~ de leurs sentiments** their fine feelings (*pl*); **l'~ de leurs idéaux** their lofty ideals (*pl*); **3** (mouvement) **l'~ de l'âme** the uplifting of the soul; **4** (promotion) elevation; **5** Archit (plan) elevation; **6** Géog **~ de terrain** rise in the ground; **7** Danse elevation; **8** Relig Elevation (of the Host).

■ **Élévation de la Croix** Art Raising of the Cross.

élève /elɛv/ *nmf* gén student; Scol pupil.

■ **~ infirmière** student nurse; **~ officier** trainee officer.

élevé, **~e** /elve/ **I** *pp* ▶ **élever**.

II *pp adj* (éduqué) **enfant bien/mal ~** well brought up/badly brought up child; **ce n'est pas bien ~, c'est mal ~** it's bad manners (**de faire** to do).

III *adj* **1** Écon [*taux, niveau, prix*] high; **plus ~** higher; **moins ~** lower; **le plus ~** the highest; **le moins ~** the lowest; **coût peu ~** low cost; **2** Géog [*plateau*] high; **habiter un étage ~** to live on an upper floor; **3** (important) [*grade, rang*] high; **poste ~ dans la hiérarchie** high-level position; **4** (noble) [*sentiment*] fine; [*principes*] high; [*idéal*] lofty; [*langage*] elevated; [*conversation*] at a very high level.

élever /elve/ [16] **I** *vtr* **1** (construire) to put up [*barrière, barricade, mur*]; to erect [*statue*]; **~ des obstacles** fig to make things difficult; **2** (porter à un degré supérieur) to raise [*température, taux, niveau*]; to extend [*durée*]; **~ le débat** to raise the level of the debate; **~ qn/qch au rang de** to raise sb/ sth to the rank of; **~ un nombre au carré/au cube** to square/to cube a number; **~ un nombre à la puissance deux** Math to raise a number to the power of two; **3** (lever) to raise [*étendard, bras*]; (soulever) to raise, to lift [*chargement*]; **4** (ennoblir) **la poésie élève l'âme** or **l'esprit** poetry is elevating; **5** (amplifier) **~ la voix** or **le ton** lit to raise one's voice; **~ la voix pour défendre qn/qch** fig to speak out on sb's behalf/in favour[GB] of sth; **~ la voix contre qch/qn** to speak out against sth/sb; **6** (formuler) to raise [*objection*]; to voice [*doutes*]; **7** (éduquer) to bring up [*enfant*]; **~ un enfant selon des principes stricts** to bring up a child according to strict principles; **~ un enfant libéralement** to give a child a liberal upbringing; **il a été mal élevé** he has been badly brought up; ▶ **coton**; **8** Agric to keep, to breed [*lapins*]; to rear [*bétail*]; to keep [*volaille, abeilles*]; **9** Vin to mature [*vin*].

II s'élever *vpr* **1** (augmenter) [*température, niveau, taux*] to rise; **s'~ de trois degrés** to rise (by) three degrees; **2** (atteindre) **s'~ à** [*bénéfices, investissements*] to come to; [*chiffre d'affaires*] to stand at; **les réparations se sont élevées à 2000 francs** the repairs came to 2,000 francs; **le nombre des victimes s'élève à 112** the casualty figures stand at 112; **s'~ à 30 mètres de haut** to be 30 metres[GB] high; **3** (se hausser) to rise; **s'~ dans les airs** or **le ciel** [*fumée, montgolfière*] to rise up into the air; [*oiseau*] to soar into the air; **s'~ au-dessus de la barre** [*athlète*] to clear the bar; **s'~ dans la hiérarchie** to rise in the hierarchy; **s'~ au rang des grands cinéastes** to join the ranks of great film-makers; **s'~ au-dessus des intérêts particuliers** to set aside personal considerations; **4** (s'ennoblir) [*âme, esprit*] to be uplifted; **5** (se faire entendre) [*protestations, critiques, voix*] to be heard; **des doutes s'élèvent dans mon esprit** I begin to have doubts; **6** (prendre parti) **s'~ contre qch** to protest against sth; **7** (se dresser) [*clocher, statue*] to stand; **s'~ au-dessus de qch** [*clocher, falaise*] to rise above sth; **8** Agric **s'~ facilement** [*lapins*] to be easy to breed ou keep; [*bétail*] to be easy to rear; [*abeilles, volaille*] to be easy to keep.

éleveur, **-euse** /elvœʀ, øz/ ▶**510** **I** *nm,f* (personne) breeder; **~ de bovins/porcs/chevaux/chiens** cattle/pig/horse/dog breeder.

II éleveuse *nf* (couveuse) brooder.

elfe /ɛlf/ *nm* elf.

élider /elide/ [1] **I** *vtr* to elide.

II s'élider *vpr* [*voyelle*] to elide.

Élie /eli/ *npr* Elijah.

éligibilité /eliʒibilite/ *nf* eligibility (**à** for election to).

éligible /eliʒibl/ *adj* eligible for office.

élimé, **~e** /elime/ **I** *pp* ▶ **élimer**.

II *pp adj* threadbare.

élimer /elime/ [1] **I** *vtr* to wear [sth] thin [*tissu*].

II s'élimer *vpr* to wear thin.

élimination /eliminasjɔ̃/ *nf* **1** (suppression) (d'idéologie, de possibilité) elimination; (d'adversaire) defeat; **procéder par ~s successives** to use a process of elimination; **2** Physiol elimination; **3** (de tache, produit) removal; **4** (meurtre) elimination.

éliminatoire /eliminatwaʀ/ **I** *adj* [*question, match*] qualifying (*épith*); [*note*] eliminatory.

II *nf* qualifier.

éliminer /elimine/ [1] **I** *vtr* **1** (écarter) to get rid of [*substance*] (**de** from); to eliminate [*candidat, équipe*]; to wipe out [*idéologie*] (**de** from); to eradicate [*maladie*] (**de** from); Scol to fail [*élève*] (**à** in); to rule out [*possibilité*]; to eliminate [*erreurs*]; **2** Physiol to eliminate [*toxines*]; **3** (ôter) to remove [*déchet, résidu*]; **4** (tuer) to eliminate, to kill [*personne*]; to get rid of [*insectes*].

II s'éliminer *vpr* [*produit, tache*] to come out.

élingue /elɛ̃g/ *nf* sling.

élire /eliʀ/ [66] *vtr* to elect [*président, maire, représentant*]; **être élu à l'unanimité** to be elected unanimously; **~ un candidat sénateur** to elect a candidate to the Senate; **~ qn à la présidence/au poste de trésorier/à l'Académie française** to elect sb to the presidency/to the position of treasurer/to the French Academy; **elle a été élue maire** she was elected mayor; **se faire ~** to be elected; **être élue Miss Monde** to be voted Miss World; **~ domicile** gén to take up residence; Jur to elect domicile.

élisabéthain, **~e** /elizabetɛ̃, ɛn/ *adj* Elizabethan.

élision /elizjɔ̃/ *nf* elision.

élitaire /elitɛʀ/ *adj* elitist.

élite /elit/ **I** *nf* **1** (meilleure partie) elite; **d'~** [*troupes, unité*] elite (*épith*), crack; [*athlète, étudiant*] high-flying (*épith*); **sujet d'~** high-flier; **2** Imprim elite.

II élites *nfpl* elite (+ *v pl*) (**de** of).

élitisme /elitism/ *nm* elitism.

élitiste /elitist/ *adj* elitist.

élixir /eliksiʀ/ *nm* elixir.

elle /ɛl/ *pron pers f* **1** (sujet) (personne, animal familier) she; (objet, concept, animal) it; **~s** they; **~ a épousé mon frère** she married my brother; **~ a deux enfants** she's got two children; **~ est ingénieur** she's an engineer; **laisse entrer la chatte, ~ miaule** let the cat in, she's miaowing; **~s sont toutes pareilles** they are all the same; **ta mère est-~ arrivée?** has your mother arrived?; **j'aime le jazz, ~ aussi** I like jazz, so does she; **~ qui aime tant le ballet, quel dommage qu'~ ne soit pas là** she loves ballet so much, it's a pity she isn't here; **c'est ~s** (à la porte) they're here; **est-ce ~ qui a renversé du vin?** was she the one who spilled the wine?, was it her that spilled the wine?; **ses collègues et ~ étaient enchantés** she and her colleagues were delighted; **~, ~ ne dit rien** she never says a word, she doesn't say anything; **'je n'aime pas ça!'—'~ non plus'** 'I don't like that!'—'she doesn't either', 'neither does she'; **ta suggestion est excellente, ~ va beaucoup nous aider** your suggestion is excellent, it will help us a lot; **la maison est superbe mais ~ est un peu isolée** the house is superb but it's a bit isolated; **j'ai vu une lionne, ~ était avec ses petits** I saw a lioness, she was with her cubs; **ne prends pas cette assiette, ~ est ébréchée** don't take that plate, it's chipped; **ton idée? ~ est excellente** your idea? it's excellent; **la pie vole tout ce qu'~ trouve** the magpie steals everything it finds; **l'heure a-t-~ sonné?** has the clock struck the hour?; **l'Allemagne a annoncé qu'~ participerait à la réunion** Germany announced that it would be taking part in the meeting; **le Portugal a signé, l'Espagne, ~, n'a pas encore donné son accord** Portugal has signed while Spain has not yet agreed; **2** (dans une comparaison) her; **il travaille plus qu'~** he works more than she does ou than her; **je suis plus jeune qu'~** I'm younger than she is ou than her; **je les vois plus souvent qu'~** (qu'elle ne les voit) I see them more often than she does; (que je ne la vois) I see them more often than her; **3** (après une préposition) (personne, animal familier) her; (animal) it; **à cause d'/autour d'/après ~** because of/around/after her; **un cadeau pour ~** a present for her; **pour ~, c'est un fou** she thinks he's mad, in her eyes he's mad; **je ne pense plus à ~** I don't think about her any more; **sans ~ je n'aurais pas survécu** I wouldn't have survived without her; **à ~** (dans une séquence) it's her turn; **c'est à ~ de choisir** (son tour) it's her turn to choose; (sa responsabilité) it's up to her to choose; **des amis à ~** friends of hers; **elle n'a pas de coin à ~ dans la maison** she doesn't have a room of her own in the house; **à ~, tu as raconté une histoire très différente** you have told her a completely different story; **le bol bleu est à ~** the blue bowl is hers.

ellébore /elebɔʀ/ *nm* hellebore.

elle-même, *pl* **elles-mêmes** /ɛlmɛm/ *pron pers f* **1** (personne) herself; **elles-mêmes** themselves; **elle me l'a dit ~** she told me herself; **elle a décidé ~** she decided herself, she made the decision herself; **elle exclut pour ~ un déplacement à l'étranger** she rules out any trip abroad for herself; **en ~ elle se disait que** she told herself that; (au téléphone) **'Madame Dubois?'—'~'** 'Mrs Dubois?'—'speaking'; **2** (objet, idée, concept) itself; **elles-mêmes** themselves; **ma bague n'a pas de valeur en ~** my ring has no value in itself; **l'œuvre constitue en ~ une introduction à la grammaire** the work in itself is an introduction to grammar; **les taches sont parties d'elles-mêmes** the stains came out by themselves; **en ~ l'idée est simple** the idea in itself is simple, the idea is simple enough in itself.

elles *pron pers fpl* ▶ **elle**.

ellipse /elips/ *nf* **1** Math ellipse; **2** Ling ellipsis.

ellipsoïdal, **~e**, *mpl* **-aux** /elipsɔidal, o/ *adj* ellipsoidal.

ellipsoïde /elipsɔid/ **I** *adj* elliptic.

II *nm* ellipsoid.

elliptique /eliptik/ *adj* **1** Math [*orbite, forme*] elliptic; **2** Ling [*tournure, style*] elliptical.

elliptiquement /eliptikmɑ̃/ *adv* elliptically.

élocution /elɔkysjɔ̃/ *nf* diction; **avoir une ~ lente** to speak slowly; **professeur d'~** elocution teacher; **défaut d'~** speech impediment.

éloge /elɔʒ/ *nm* **1** (louange) praise; **faire l'~ de qn/qch** to sing the praises of sb/sth, to sing sb/sth's praises; **faire l'~ du crime/de la drogue** to extol[GB] crime/drugs; **être digne d'~s** [*personne*] to deserve praise; [*action*] to be praiseworthy; **ne pas tarir d'~s (sur qn/qch)** to be full of praise (for sb/sth); **il a été couvert d'~s par** he was showered with praise by; **leur action ne leur a valu que des ~s** their action was nothing but praiseworthy; **leur action ne leur a pas valu que des ~s** not everybody thought their action praiseworthy; **décerner des ~s à qn** to commend sb; **être tout à l'~ de qn** to do sb great credit; **2** Littérat (discours) eulogy; **écrire l'~ de qn** to write a piece in praise of sb, to write a eulogy to sb sout; **prononcer l'~ de qn** to deliver a eulogy for sb sout; **l'~ de qch** a eulogy to sth.

■ **~ funèbre** funeral oration.

élogieusement /elɔʒjøzmɑ̃/ *adv* enthusiastically.

élogieux, -ieuse /elɔʒjø, øz/ *adj* **1** (qui fait des éloges) [*personne*] full of praise; **2** (qui contient des éloges) [*article, critique, rapport*] laudatory; **parler de qch/qn en termes ~** to talk about sth/sb in glowing terms.

éloigné, ~e /elwaɲe/ **I** *pp* ▶ **éloigner**.

II *pp adj* **1** (dans l'espace) distant; **dans un village ~ de tout** in a remote village; **dans un hameau ~ de 5 kilomètres** in a hamlet 5 kilometres[GB] away; **deux usines ~es de 5 kilomètres** two factories 5 kilometres[GB] apart; **c'est trop ~ pour y aller ce soir** it's too far away to go there this evening; **les maisons ~es du centre** houses far ou a long way from the centre[GB]; **ils vivent ~s les uns des autres** they live far apart; **2** (dans le temps) [*souvenirs*] distant; [*événement*] remote (*jamais épith*); **~ dans le temps** distant (in time); **cela remonte à une époque bien ~e** this goes back to a time long past; **dans un futur peu ~** in the not too distant future; **dans un passé peu ~** not (so) long ago; **deux périodes ~es l'une de l'autre** two periods far apart in time; **3** (dans la famille) [*cousin, parent*] distant; **4** (différent) [*positions, opinions*] poles apart; **très ~ de la réalité** [*déclaration, reportage, estimation*] far removed from reality; **les babouins sont biologiquement plus ~s de l'homme que les chimpanzés** baboons are biologically further removed from man than chimpanzees; **leurs points de vue sont plus ~s que je ne croyais** their points of view are further apart than I thought; **5** (absent) away; **le torero s'est tenu** or **est resté ~ de l'arène pendant deux ans** the bullfighter stayed away from the arena for two years.

éloignement /elwaɲmɑ̃/ *nm* **1** (dans l'espace) distance; **en raison de leur ~, ils ne viennent pas souvent nous voir** because they live so far away, they don't come to see us very often; **elle souffrait de l'~ de ses enfants** being apart from her children was painful to her; **2** (dans le temps) remoteness; **avec l'~, l'événement prend tout son sens** in retrospect, the full significance of the event becomes apparent; **3** (rejet, écart) **l'~ des personnes suspectes** the removal of suspect individuals; **son ~ des milieux littéraires** his lack of contact with literary circles.

éloigner /elwaɲe/ [1] **I** *vtr* **1** lit to move [sb/sth] away (**de** from); **éloignez les enfants/vos chaises du feu** move the children/your chairs away from the fire; **~ les badauds** to move onlookers on; **il vaut mieux les ~ pour qu'ils ne se battent pas** better to separate them so (that) they won't fight; **notre déménagement nous éloigne du village** we're further away from the village now that we've moved; **vos remarques nous éloignent du sujet** your remarks have taken us off the point; **2** fig **ils font tout pour l'~ de moi** they are doing everything to drive us apart; **la nouvelle politique du parti a éloigné plusieurs de ses membres** the party's new policy has alienated several of its members; **elle a éloigné l'éventualité d'une dévaluation** she has dismissed the possibility of a devaluation; **~ une menace/un danger** to remove a threat/a danger; **maintenant que le danger est éloigné** now that the danger has been removed ou has passed.

II s'éloigner *vpr* **1** lit to move away (**de** from); **l'orage s'éloigne** the storm is moving away; **à mesure qu'ils s'éloignaient des côtes** as they moved away from the coast; **ne t'éloigne pas d'ici** don't move from here; **ne t'éloigne pas trop** don't go too far away; **il s'éloigne à pas lents/en courant** he walks away slowly/runs away; **2** fig **s'~ de** [*personne*] to move away from [*idéologie, ligne politique*]; to wander from, to stray from [*sujet*]; **le texte s'éloigne du schéma de base sur deux points** the text differs from the basic pattern on two points; **nos chances de réussite s'éloignent chaque jour un peu plus** our chances of success are becoming more remote by the day; **nous nous éloignons chaque année davantage de notre objectif** every year we are getting further away from our objective; **ne vous éloignez pas du sujet** keep to the point; **3** (s'estomper) [*image, souvenir*] to become blurred.

élongation /elɔ̃gasjɔ̃/ *nf* **1** Méd (accidentelle) pulled muscle; (thérapeutique) traction; **se faire une ~ au mollet** to pull a calf muscle; **2** Astron elongation; **3** Phys displacement.

éloquemment /elɔkamɑ̃/ *adv* eloquently.

éloquence /elɔkɑ̃s/ *nf* eloquence ¢; **un beau morceau d'~** a wonderful bit of eloquence; **avec ~** eloquently; **un regard plein d'~** an eloquent look.

éloquent, ~e /elɔkɑ̃, ɑ̃t/ *adj* [*personne, paroles*] eloquent; **le score est ~** the score speaks for itself.

élu, ~e /ely/ *nm,f* **1** Pol elected representative; **~ local/régional/national** local/regional/national representative; **un ~ de droite** a right-wing representative; **l'~ de Grenoble/de la Drôme** the representative for Grenoble/the Drôme; **les ~s du second tour** the winners of the second round; **2** (personne aimée) beloved; (vainqueur) winner; **l'~ de mon cœur** the one I love; ▶ **heureux**; **3** (choisi par Dieu) elect; **les ~s** the elect (+ *v pl*).

élucidation /elysidasjɔ̃/ *nf* clarification, elucidation sout.

élucider /elyside/ [1] *vtr* to solve [*crime, problème*]; to clarify [*circonstances, conditions*]; **un crime non élucidé** an unsolved crime; **dans des circonstances mal élucidées** in circumstances that remain unclear.

élucubrations /elykybʀasjɔ̃/ *nfpl* rantings.

élucubrer /elykybʀe/ [1] *vtr* pej to dream up [*théorie, plan*].

éluder /elyde/ [1] *vtr* to evade.

Élysée /elize/ *nprm* **1** Pol (**palais de l'**)~ Élysée Palace (*the official residence of the French President*); **course à l'~** race for the French presidency; **2** Mythol Elysium.

élyséen, -éenne /elizeɛ̃, ɛn/ *adj* **1** Pol (du président) [*conseiller*] presidential; (du palais) [*salon*] of the Élysée; **2** Mythol Elysian.

élytre /elitʀ/ *nm* elytron.

elzévir /ɛlzeviʀ/ *nm* **1** Édition (livre) Elzevir; **2** Imprim (caractère) elzevir.

émaciation /emasjasjɔ̃/ *nf* emaciation.

émacié, ~e /emasje/ **I** *pp* ▶ **émacier**.

II *pp adj* emaciated.

émacier /emasje/ [2] **I** *vtr* to emaciate.

II s'émacier *vpr* to become emaciated.

émail, *pl* **-aux** ou **~s** /emaj, o/ *nm* **1** (matière) (*pl* **-aux**) enamel; **en ~, d'~** enamel (*épith*); **2** (objet) (*pl* **-aux**) enamel; **3** Hérald (*pl* **-aux**) tincture; **4** Dent (*pl* **~s**) enamel.

émaillage /emajaʒ/ *nm* enamelling[GB].

émaillé, ~e /emaje/ **I** *pp* ▶ **émailler**.

II *pp adj* [*casserole, cuvette*] enamel (*épith*); [*tôle, fonte*] enamelled.

émailler /emaje/ [1] *vtr* **1** (recouvrir d'émail) to enamel; **2** (marquer) [*erreur, incident*] to punctuate; **une descente émaillée de chutes** a descent punctuated by falls; **3** (emplir) **un discours émaillé d'allusions** a speech sprinkled with allusions; **un match émaillé de fautes** a match full of fouls.

émanation /emanasjɔ̃/ *nf* **1** (effluve) emanation; **~s de gaz** gas fumes; **2** Phys emanation; **3** (organisme dérivé) offshoot; **une ~ du ministère** an offshoot of the ministry; **4** (manifestation) expression, result; **5** Relig emanation.

émancipateur, -trice /emɑ̃sipatœʀ, tʀis/ **I** *adj* [*théorie, influence*] liberating, emancipatory sout.

II *nm,f* liberator, emancipator sout.

émancipation /emɑ̃sipasjɔ̃/ *nf* emancipation.

émancipé, ~e /emɑ̃sipe/ **I** *pp* ▶ **émanciper**.

II *pp adj* (sans préjugés) liberated.

émanciper /emɑ̃sipe/ [1] **I** *vtr* **1** (affranchir) to emancipate [*peuple, personne*]; to liberate [*colonie, pays*] (**de** from); **2** Jur to emancipate [*mineurs, enfant*].

II s'émanciper *vpr* **1** [*pays, colonie*] to gain its independence; **2** [*personne*] to become emancipated.

émaner /emane/ [1] **I** *vi* (s'exhaler) [*chaleur, odeur*] to emanate (**de** from).

II *v impers* **il émane d'elle un charme fou** she exudes charm.

émargement /emaʀʒəmɑ̃/ *nm* signing ¢; **feuille d'~** attendance sheet.

émarger /emaʀʒe/ [13] **I** *vtr* **1** Imprim to trim [*page*]; **2** Admin to sign [*document, circulaire*].

II *vi* **~ à l'université** to be on the payroll of the university; **~ à 20 000 francs** to draw 20,000 francs.

émasculation /emaskylasjɔ̃/ *nf* emasculation.

émasculer /emaskyle/ [1] *vtr* lit, fig to emasculate.

émaux ▶ **émail**.

emballage /ɑ̃balaʒ/ *nm* **1** (dans du carton, plastique dur) packaging; (dans une feuille de papier, de plastique) wrapping; (dans une caisse) packing; **sous ~** [*livre, produit*] wrapped; [*vaisselle*] packed; **2** (feuille de papier, plastique) wrapping; (carton, plastique dur) packaging; **~ perdu/consigné** throw-away/refundable packaging; **3** (secteur industriel) **l'~** packaging.

■ **~ sous vide** vacuum packing.

emballant○, **~e** /ɑ̃balɑ̃, ɑ̃t/ *adj* exciting.

emballement /ɑ̃balmɑ̃/ *nm* **1** (enthousiasme) fad (**pour** for); **2** (colère) outburst of anger; **3** Équit (de cheval) bolting; **4** (de prix, d'inflation) rapid rise; **5** Aut, Tech (de moteur) racing.

emballer /ɑ̃bale/ [1] **I** *vtr* **1** (dans une caisse, boîte) to pack; (envelopper) to wrap; **2**○ (enthousiasmer) **cette idée/ce voyage m'emballe** I am really taken with this idea/trip; **être emballé par** to be taken with; **3**○ (arrêter) [*police*] to take [sb] in; **4**○ (séduire) to score with○; **5** Aut, Tech to race [*moteur*].

II s'emballer *vpr* **1** Équit [*cheval*] to bolt; **2**○ (se passionner) to get carried away (**pour** by); **ça ne m'emballe pas d'aller à Londres** I'm not too keen on going to London; **3** (s'énerver) to get worked up○; **ils ne peuvent pas parler de politique sans s'~** they can't talk politics without getting all worked up○; **4**○ Aut, Tech [*moteur*] to race; **5** (augmenter rapidement) [*prix, inflation*] to shoot up; **le dollar s'est emballé** the dollar has shot up in value.

emballeur, **-euse** /ɑ̃balœʀ, øz/ ▶ 510 *nm,f* packer.

embarbouillé, **~e** /ɑ̃baʀbuje/ *adj* muddled.

embarcadère /ɑ̃baʀkadɛʀ/ *nm* (de passagers) pier; (de marchandises) wharf.

embarcation /ɑ̃baʀkasjɔ̃/ *nf* boat.

embardée /ɑ̃baʀde/ *nf* (d'auto) swerve; (de bateau) yaw; **faire une ~** [*auto*] to swerve; [*bateau*] to yaw.

embargo /ɑ̃baʀgo/ *nm* embargo (**contre, sur** on); **~ aérien/pétrolier** air/oil embargo; **lever l'~** to lift the embargo.

embarqué, **~e** /ɑ̃baʀke/ I *pp* ▶ **embarquer**.
II *pp adj* [*équipement, système*] on-board.

embarquement /ɑ̃baʀkəmɑ̃/ *nm* (montée à bord) boarding (**pour** for); (prise à bord) embarkation; (départ) departure (**pour** for); **formalités d'~** boarding procedures; **l'~ aura lieu dans une heure** boarding will take place in an hour; **l'~ des véhicules sera retardé** the embarkation of vehicles will be delayed; **port d'~** port of embarkation.

embarquer /ɑ̃baʀke/ [1] I *vtr* **1** Aviat, Naut (charger) [*personne*] to load [*marchandises*]; [*passager*] to take [*bagages*]; [*équipage*] to take on board [*passager*]; [*bateau, avion, compagnie*] to carry [*passager, armement*]; [*bateau, équipage*] to pick up [*naufragé*]; **valise embarquée dans la soute** suitcase loaded into the hold; **matériel embarqué à bord d'un avion/sous-marin** equipment loaded on to a plane/submarine; **l'équipage sera embarqué demain** the crew will go aboard tomorrow; **2**○ (emmener) to take [*objet, document*]; [*police*] to pick up [*malfaiteur, manifestant*]; **si tu ne veux plus de ta radio, je l'embarque** if you don't want your radio any more, I'll have it; **allez, viens, je t'embarque!** you come with me!; **n'embarque pas mon briquet!** don't take my lighter!; **~ qn dans sa voiture** to get sb into one's car; **3**○ (engager) **~ qn dans un projet** to get sb involved in a project.
II *vi* (monter à bord) to board; Naut (partir en voyage) to sail (**pour** for); **à quelle heure embarques-tu?** what time do you board?; **quel jour embarques-tu?** when do you sail?; **~ à bord d'un yacht/avion** to board a yacht/plane.
III **s'embarquer** *vpr* **1** Naut (monter à bord) to board; (partir en voyage) to sail (**pour** for) ; **s'~ à bord d'un bateau** to board a ship; **2**○ (se lancer) **s'~ dans des explications/des détails** to launch into an explanation/details; **s'~ dans un projet/une réforme** to embark on a project/a reform; ▶ **biscuit**.

embarras /ɑ̃baʀa/ *nm* **1** (trouble) embarrassment; **dissimuler son ~** to hide one's embarrassment; **l'incident cause à la France un vif ~** the incident is highly embarrassing for France; **2** (gêne financière) **~ d'argent** ou **financiers** financial difficulties; **être/se trouver dans l'~** to be/find oneself in financial difficulties; **tirer qn d'~** to help sb out financially; **ton chèque m'a tiré d'~** your cheque GB ou check US helped me out; **3** (situation délicate) awkward position; **mettre** or **jeter qn dans l'~** to put sb in an awkward position; **tirer qn/se tirer d'~** to get sb/to get oneself out of a difficult situation; **4** (incertitude) **être dans l'~** to be in a quandary; **je conçois votre ~** I understand your dilemma; **éprouver de l'~ pour répondre/devant un problème difficile** to be at a loss for an answer/when faced with a tricky problem; **n'avoir que** or **avoir l'~ du choix** to be spoiled for choice GB, to have too much to choose from; **5**† (obstacle) **il craint d'être un ~ pour vous** he's afraid of being a nuisance (to you); **les ~ de la circulation** road congestion ¢, traffic jams.
■ **~ gastrique** Méd stomach upset.

embarrassant, **~e** /ɑ̃baʀasɑ̃, ɑ̃t/ *adj* **1** (gênant) [*problème, silence, choix, question*] awkward; [*situation*] embarrassing; **2** (encombrant) [*bagages*] cumbersome.

embarrassé, **~e** /ɑ̃baʀase/ I *pp* ▶ **embarrasser**.
II *pp adj* **1** (gêné) [*personne, toux, silence*] embarrassed; **être bien ~ pour répondre/expliquer** to be at a loss for an answer/explanation; **2** (confus) [*discours, explication*] confused; **3** (encombré) [*pièce, bureau*] cluttered (**de** with); **personne ~e d'une grosse valise** person weighed down with a large suitcase; **4** Méd [*estomac*] upset.

embarrasser /ɑ̃baʀase/ [1] I *vtr* **1** (mettre mal à l'aise) [*affaire, question*] to embarrass [*personne*]; **~ le gouvernement** to embarrass the government; **~ qn par des questions indiscrètes** to embarrass sb by asking tactless questions; **leur conduite/générosité m'embarrasse** I find their behaviour[GB]/generosity embarrassing; **je ne voudrais pas vous ~** I don't want to bother you; **ça m'embarrasse de te le rappeler, mais tu me dois 100 francs** I'm sorry to have to remind you, but you owe me 100 francs; **2** (encombrer) [*objets*] to clutter (up) [*pièce, table*] (**de** with); **cette armoire m'embarrasse plutôt qu'autre chose** this wardrobe is more of a nuisance than anything else; **ces paquets t'embarrassent, donne-les moi** those parcels are awkward for you, let me take them.
II **s'embarrasser** *vpr* **1** (s'encombrer) **s'~ de** to burden oneself with [*paquet, personne*]; **je ne veux pas m'~ d'un chien/jardin** I can't be bothered with a dog/garden; **pourquoi t'~ d'un dictionnaire?** why burden yourself with a dictionary?; **2** (se préoccuper) to worry about [*détails*]; **il ne s'embarrasse pas de scrupules** he's not the most scrupulous of people; **s'~ de scrupules inutiles** to be overscrupulous.

embarrer /ɑ̃baʀe/ [1] C I *vtr* (enfermer) to lock.
II **s'embarrer** *vpr* (s'enfermer) to shut oneself away.

embastiller /ɑ̃bastije/ [1] *vtr* Hist to imprison.

embauche /ɑ̃boʃ/ *nf* appointment GB, hiring ¢ US; **~ à l'essai** appointment GB ou hiring US on a trial basis; **salaire d'~** starting salary; **aides à l'~** employment incentives; **société recherche pour ~...** company seeks to recruit...; **l'~ d'un premier salarié** the taking on of ou the appointment of a first employee.

embaucher /ɑ̃boʃe/ [1] I *vtr* **1** (engager) to take on GB, to hire [*jeune, ouvrier*] (**comme** as); (après un stage, intérim) to take on [sb] permanently; **2**○ (pour corvée) to recruit (**pour faire** to do).
II *vi* **1** (recruter) to recruit people; **2**○ (commencer son travail) to start work (**à** at).

embauchoir /ɑ̃boʃwaʀ/ *nm* shoe-tree.

embaumement /ɑ̃bommɑ̃/ *nm* embalming.

embaumer /ɑ̃bome/ [1] I *vtr* **1** (parfumer) [*odeur*] to fill [*lieu*]; **2** (sentir) to smell of [*lavande, cire*]; **3** (conserver) to embalm [*cadavre*].
II *vi* (sentir bon) [*air, jardin, fleurs*] to be fragrant; **ça embaume!** what a pleasant smell!

embaumeur, **-euse** /ɑ̃bomœʀ, øz/ ▶ 510 *nm,f* embalmer.

embellie /ɑ̃beli/ *nf* **1** Naut lull; Météo bright spell; **2** (amélioration) upturn.

embellir /ɑ̃beliʀ/ [3] I *vtr* **1** (réellement) to embellish [*lieu*]; to make [sb/sth] more attractive [*personne*]; **2** (en mentant) to embellish [*récit*]; to embroider [*vérité*].
II *vi* to become more attractive.

embellissement /ɑ̃belismɑ̃/ *nm* **1** (de pièce, maison) refurbishing; **faire des travaux d'~** to carry out improvements; **l'~ du quartier a coûté très cher** smartening the area up was very expensive; **2** (élément amélioré) improvement, embellishment; **3** (inexactitude) embellishment.

emberlificoté○, **~e** /ɑ̃bɛʀlifikɔte/ I *pp* ▶ **emberlificoter**.
II *pp adj* [*texte*] muddled; [*situation*] confused.

emberlificoter○ /ɑ̃bɛʀlifikɔte/ [1] I *vtr* **1** (embrouiller) to entangle [*fil*]; **2** (duper) to take [sb] in○ [*personne*]; **se laisser ~** to be duped ou taken in○.
II **s'emberlificoter** *vpr* **1** lit to get entangled (**dans** in); **2** fig to get mixed up (**dans** in); **s'~ dans des explications** to get tangled in one's explanation.

embêtant, **~e** /ɑ̃bɛtɑ̃, ɑ̃t/ *adj* **1** (fâcheux) tiresome, annoying; **il m'arrive un truc ~** I've got a bit of a problem; **c'est ~ ça!** that's a real nuisance ou drag○!; **être dans une situation ~e** to be in an awkward position; **2** (agaçant) annoying; **3** (lassant) boring.

embêté, **~e** /ɑ̃bete/ I *pp* ▶ **embêter**.
II *pp adj* **1** (embarrassé) embarrassed; **il avait l'air bien ~** he looked quite embarrassed; **2** (dans une situation difficile) **être très ~** to be in real trouble ou in a real mess.

embêtement /ɑ̃bɛtmɑ̃/ *nm* problem.

embêter /ɑ̃bete/ [1] I *vtr* **1** (contrarier) to bother; **ça m'embête de devoir faire** it's a nuisance that I have to do; **si ça ne vous embête pas** if it's not too much trouble; **ça m'embêterait de rater ça** I wouldn't like to miss that; **2** (agacer) to annoy; (importuner) to pester; **il commence à m'~ celui-là** that guy is getting on my nerves; **arrête de m'~** stop annoying me, don't bug○ me; **3** (lasser) to bore.
II **s'embêter** *vpr* **1** (s'ennuyer) to get bored; **2** (s'inquiéter) to worry (**pour** about); **ne t'embête pas pour si peu** don't worry about such trifles; **3** (se compliquer la vie) **s'~ à faire** to go to all the trouble or bother of doing; **je n'ai pas envie de m'~ avec un chien/une voiture** I don't want all the trouble ou hassle○ of a dog/car; **ne t'embête pas avec ça** don't bother with that!; **un hôtel quatre étoiles! tu ne t'embêtes pas!** a four-star hotel! you're doing all right for yourself!; **tu as fouillé ses tiroirs! tu ne t'embêtes pas!** you went through his drawers! you've got a nerve!; **tu appelles ça laver la voiture! tu ne t'embêtes pas!** that's what you call washing the car! you're not exactly straining yourself, are you?

emblaver /ɑ̃blave/ [1] *vtr* **~ un champ** to sow a field with cereals.

emblavure /ɑ̃blavyʀ/ *nf* grainfield.

emblée: **d'emblée** /dɑ̃ble/ *loc adv* **1** (aussitôt) [*accepter, réussir*] straightaway; [*refuser, condamner*] out of hand; [*détester*] at first sight; **2** (dès le début) from the outset.

emblématique /ɑ̃blematik/ *adj* [*dessin, décoration*] emblematic; [*personnage, figure*] symbolic.

emblème /ɑ̃blɛm/ *nm* emblem.

embobiner /ɑ̃bɔbine/ [1] *vtr* **1**○ (tromper) to bamboozle○; **se laisser ~** to be hoodwinked ou bamboozled○; **2** (enrouler) to wind.

emboîtable /ɑ̃bwatabl/ *adj* which fit together (*épith, après n*).

emboîtage /ɑ̃bwataʒ/ *nm* **1** Tech fitting-together; **2** (mise en boîte) packing (*in boxes*); **3** Édition slipcase; **sous ~** in a slipcase.

emboîtement /ɑ̃bwatmɑ̃/ *nm* **1** Tech fitting; **ardoise/tuyau à ~** interlocking slate/pipe; **2** Ling embedding.

emboîter /ɑ̃bwate/ [1] I *vtr* to fit together [*pièces*]; **~ qch dans qch** to fit sth into sth.
II **s'emboîter** *vpr* to fit (**dans** into); **les deux pièces s'emboîtent parfaitement** the two parts fit together perfectly.

IDIOMES **~ le pas à qn** lit, fig to fall in behind sb.

embolie /ɑ̃bɔli/ **▶271** *nf* embolism; **~ pulmonaire/gazeuze** pulmonary/air embolism.

embonpoint /ɑ̃bɔ̃pwɛ̃/ *nm* **1** (état) stoutness; **2** (ventre) bulge; **avoir de l'~** to be stout.

embossage /ɑ̃bɔsaʒ/ *nm* mooring broadside on.

embosser /ɑ̃bɔse/ [1] *vtr* **~ un navire** to moor a ship fore and aft.

embouché, **~e** /ɑ̃buʃe/ *adj* **mal ~** (grossier) coarse; (de mauvaise humeur) in a foul mood.

emboucher /ɑ̃buʃe/ [1] *vtr* Mus to raise [sth] to one's lips [*instrument*].

embouchure /ɑ̃buʃyʀ/ *nf* **1** (de rivière) mouth, embouchure spéc; **2** (d'instrument) mouthpiece, embouchure; **3** (de mors) mouthpiece; **4** (de vase, tuyau) opening.

embourber /ɑ̃buʀbe/ [1] **I** *vtr* to get [sth] stuck in the mud.
II s'embourber *vpr* **1** (dans la boue) to get stuck in the mud; **2** (dans des difficultés) to get bogged down (**dans** in).

embourgeoisement /ɑ̃buʀʒwazmɑ̃/ *nm* embourgeoisement.

embourgeoiser: **s'embourgeoiser** /ɑ̃buʀʒwaze/ [1] *vpr* [*personne*] to become middle-class; [*quartier*] to become gentrified.

embout /ɑ̃bu/ *nm* (de canne, cigare) tip; (de tuyau, d'aspirateur) nozzle; (de pipe) mouthpiece.
■ **~ applicateur** nozzle.

embouteillage /ɑ̃butɛjaʒ/ *nm* **1** (en ville) traffic jam; (sur autoroute) tailback; **il y a dix kilomètres d'~s** there's a ten-kilometre[GB] tailback; **l'~ du ciel** air traffic congestion; **2** (de système) bottleneck; **3** (mise en bouteilles) bottling; **usine d'~ de bière** beer-bottling factory.

embouteiller /ɑ̃buteje/ [1] *vtr* **1** Transp (encombrer) to clog [*route, ciel*]; (boucher) to block [*rue*]; **2** (surcharger) to clog up [*administration, système*]; to jam [*lignes téléphoniques*]; **3** (mettre en bouteilles) to bottle.

emboutir /ɑ̃butiʀ/ [3] *vtr* **1** Mécan to stamp, press [*pièce, tôle*]; **tôle emboutie** stamped sheet metal; **presse à ~** stamping press; **2**○ [*personne, véhicule*] to crash into [*véhicule, obstacle*]; **l'avant est complètement embouti** the front is completely smashed in.

emboutissage /ɑ̃butisaʒ/ *nm* Mécan stamping.

emboutisseur, **-euse** /ɑ̃butisœʀ, øz/ **I ▶510** *nm,f* (ouvrier) stamper.
II emboutisseuse *nf* (machine) stamping press.

embranchement /ɑ̃bʀɑ̃ʃmɑ̃/ *nm* **1** (point de jonction) junction; **2** (voie) (routière) side road; (ferrée) branch line; **3** Bot, Zool branch.
■ **~ particulier** Rail private line ou track.

embrancher /ɑ̃bʀɑ̃ʃe/ [1] **I** *vtr* to link [sth] up (**à, sur** with).
II s'embrancher *vpr* [*route, dérivation*] to link up (**sur** with).

embrasé, **~e** /ɑ̃bʀaze/ **I** *pp* **▶ embraser**.
II *pp adj* **1** (en feu) burning; **2** (illuminé) glowing.

embrasement /ɑ̃bʀazmɑ̃/ *nm* **1** (incendie) blaze; **2** (illumination) dazzling illumination; **3** (agitation sociale) unrest ¢; **4** (élan) **~(s) du corps** passionate arousal; **5** (augmentation) **l'~ des prix** a surge in prices.

embraser /ɑ̃bʀaze/ [1] **I** *vtr* **1** (mettre le feu) to set [sth] ablaze [*bâtiment*]; **2** (agiter) to set [sth] alight [*ville, pays*]; **3** (illuminer) to set [sth] ablaze [*ciel, ville*]; **4** (emplir de passion) to set [sb] on fire [*personne*].
II s'embraser *vpr* **1** (prendre feu) to catch fire; **2** fig [*pays, ville*] to erupt into violence; **3** (devenir illuminé) to be set ablaze; **4** (s'emplir de passion) to burn with desire.

embrassade /ɑ̃bʀasad/ *nf* kissing ¢; **leurs ~s n'en finissaient plus** they hugged and kissed for ages.

embrasse /ɑ̃bʀas/ *nf* tieback.

embrassement /ɑ̃bʀasmɑ̃/ *nm* liter embrace.

embrasser /ɑ̃bʀase/ [1] **I** *vtr* **1** (donner un baiser à) to kiss [*personne*] (**sur** on); to kiss [*joues, front*]; **~ qn à pleine bouche** to kiss sb (full) on the lips; **je t'embrasse** (en fin de lettre) lots of love; (au téléphone) lots of love, take care; **embrasse ta mère pour moi** give my love to your mother; **2** (étreindre) (entre personnalités) to embrace; (entre amis) to hug; **3** fml (choisir) to take up, to pursue [*carrière, profession*]; to embrace [*cause, religion*]; **à 20 ans il décida d'~ la carrière politique** at the age of 20 he decided to pursue a political career; **4** fml (saisir) [*recherche, étude*] to take in [*période, question*]; [*œil, regard, caméra*] to take in [*paysage*]; [*personne, auteur*] to cover [*sujet, domaine*].
II s'embrasser *vpr* (avec des baisers) to kiss (each other) (**sur** on); (s'étreindre) (entre personnalités) to embrace; (entre amis) to hug.
IDIOMES **~ qn comme du bon pain** to hug sb warmly.

embrasure /ɑ̃bʀazyʀ/ *nf* **1** Constr opening; **2** Mil embrasure.
■ **~ de fenêtre** window; **~ de porte** doorway.

embrayage /ɑ̃bʀɛjaʒ/ *nm* **1** (dispositif) clutch; **~ automatique/électromagnétique/hydraulique** automatic/electromagnetic/hydraulic clutch; **sélecteur d'~ automatique** gear lever, gearshift US; **faire patiner l'~** to slip the clutch; **voiture à ~ mécanique** car equipped with a manual gearbox; **2** (communication entre 2 pièces) engaging; (par l'automobiliste) letting out the clutch; **3** (pédale) clutch pedal.

embrayer /ɑ̃bʀeje/ [21] *vi* **1** Aut to engage the clutch, to let out the clutch; Tech to engage; **2**○ (commencer à travailler) to get cracking○; **3**○ (se lancer) **~ sur** or **avec** to launch into [*discours, chanson, sujet*].

embrigadement /ɑ̃bʀigadmɑ̃/ *nm* **1** (enrôlement) recruitment; **2** Mil brigading.

embrigader /ɑ̃bʀigade/ [1] *vtr* **1** (enrôler) to recruit (**dans** into; **comme** as); **2** Mil to brigade.

embringuer○ /ɑ̃bʀɛ̃ge/ [1] **I** *vtr* (dans une affaire, histoire) to drag (**dans** into); (dans un groupe, organisation) to get [sb] involved (**dans** in); **se laisser ~** to get mixed up (**dans** in).
II s'embringuer *vpr* (dans une affaire, situation) to get involved (**dans** in).

embrocation /ɑ̃bʀɔkasjɔ̃/ *nf* embrocation.

embrocher /ɑ̃bʀɔʃe/ [1] **I** *vtr* **1** Culin to put [sth] on a spit [*animal*]; to skewer [*morceau, gigot*]; **2**○ (transpercer) to run [sb] through [*adversaire*].
II s'embrocher○ *vpr* to impale oneself (**sur** on).

embrouillamini○ /ɑ̃bʀujamini/ *nm* muddle.

embrouille○ /ɑ̃bʀuj/ *nf* shady goings-on○ (*pl*); **je n'aime pas ces ~s** I don't like these shady goings-on.

embrouillement /ɑ̃bʀujmɑ̃/ *nm* **1** (enchevêtrement) (action) tangling; (résultat) tangle; **2** (confusion) **l'~ des idées** muddled thinking.

embrouiller /ɑ̃bʀuje/ [1] **I** *vtr* **1** (enchevêtrer) to tangle [*fils, laine*]; **2** (rendre confus) to confuse [*affaire, personne*]; **l'histoire est assez embrouillée** the story is rather confused; **tu m'embrouilles avec tes explications** you're confusing me with your explanations.
II s'embrouiller *vpr* **1** (s'enchevêtrer) [*fils, cheveux*] to become tangled; **2** (devenir confus) [*idées, affaire, personne*] to become confused; **s'~ dans** to get into a muddle with [*comptes*]; to get tangled up in [*explications*].

embroussaillé, **~e** /ɑ̃bʀusaje/ *adj* [*chemin, allée, jardin*] overgrown; [*cheveux, sourcils*] bushy; [*barbe*] shaggy.

embrumé, **~e** /ɑ̃bʀyme/ *adj* **1** (couvert de brume) [*temps*] misty; [*ciel, paysage*] hazy; **avoir les yeux ~s** to have misty eyes; **2** (troublé) [*esprit*] befuddled; [*regard*] glazed; [*voix*] hoarse.

embruns /ɑ̃bʀœ̃/ *nmpl* spray ¢.

embryologie /ɑ̃bʀijɔlɔʒi/ *nf* Méd embryology.

embryologique /ɑ̃bʀijɔlɔʒik/ *adj* embryological.

embryologiste /ɑ̃bʀijɔlɔʒist/, **embryologue** /ɑ̃bʀijɔlɔg/ **▶510** *nmf* embryologist.

embryon /ɑ̃bʀijɔ̃/ *nm* **1** Physiol, Méd embryo; **~ congelé** frozen embryo; **2** fig **l'~ d'une idée/d'un projet** an embryonic idea/project; **projet à l'état d'~** project (still) in its embryonic stages.

embryonnaire /ɑ̃bʀijɔnɛʀ/ *adj* lit, fig embryonic; **projet à l'état ~** project (still) in its embryonic stages.

embûche /ɑ̃byʃ/ *nf* **1** (machination) trap; **dresser des ~s** to set traps; **2** (danger) hazard; (difficulté) pitfall; **semé** or **plein d'~s** lit hazardous; fig fraught with pitfalls.

embuer /ɑ̃bɥe/ [1] **I** *vtr* **1** (couvrir de buée) to mist up, to fog up US; **une vitre embuée** misted-up ou fogged-up US window; **2** (voiler) to mist; **yeux embués de larmes** eyes misty with tears.
II s'embuer *vpr* [*vitre, écran*] to mist up, to fog up US; [*regard, yeux*] to mist over.

embuscade /ɑ̃byskad/ *nf* ambush; **être en ~** to lie in ambush; **dresser** or **tendre une ~ à qn** to set up an ambush for sb; **tomber dans une ~** to be caught in an ambush.

embusqué, **~e** /ɑ̃byske/ **I** *pp* **▶ embusquer**.
II *pp adj* (en embuscade) [*soldats, rebelles*] lying in ambush; [*assassin*] lying in wait.
III *nm* pej (soldat de l'arrière) soldier on a cushy○ posting.

embusquer /ɑ̃byske/ [1] *vtr* to place [sb] in ambush.

éméché○, **~e** /emeʃe/ *adj* **être ~** to be tipsy; **être passablement ~** to be quite ou rather tipsy.

émeraude /emʀod/ **▶193** **I** *adj inv* (couleur) emerald green.
II *nm* (couleur) emerald green.
III *nf* Minér emerald; **un collier d'~s** an emerald necklace.

émergence /emɛʀʒɑ̃s/ *nf* (tous contextes) emergence.

émergent, **~e** /emɛʀʒɑ̃, ɑ̃t/ *adj* emergent.

émerger /emɛʀʒe/ [13] *vi* **1** (apparaître) to emerge; **2**○ (se réveiller) to surface.

émeri /emʀi/ *nm* Minér emery; **être bouché à l'~** lit to have a ground glass stopper; fig to be as thick as two short planks GB, to be dumb.

émerillon /emʀijɔ̃/ *nm* **1** Zool merlin; **2** Tech swivel.

émérite /emeʀit/ *adj* **1** [*joueur, acteur*] outstanding; **2** Univ (titre) **professeur ~** emeritus professor.

émerveillement /emɛʀvɛjmɑ̃/ *nm* wonder (**devant** at; **à la vue de** at the sight of); **pousser un cri d'~** to utter a cry of wonder; **il fait l'~ de ses professeurs** his teachers are greatly impressed by him; **la nature est un ~ perpétuel** nature is an eternal source of wonder.

émerveiller /emɛʀveje/ [1] **I** *vtr* **~ qn** to fill sb with wonder; **être émerveillé par** to marvel at, to be filled with wonder by; **il ouvrait de grands yeux émerveillés** his eyes were round with wonder.
II s'émerveiller *vpr* **s'~ de** or **devant qch** to marvel at sth; **s'~ que qn fasse** to be amazed ou impressed that sb does; **il s'émerveillait qu'elle ait pu faire cela aussi vite** he was amazed ou impressed that she had been able to do it so quickly; **s'~ de tant de génie** to be amazed at ou by such

genius; **s'~ de peu (de chose)** to be easily impressed.

émétique /emetik/ *adj, nm* emetic.

émetteur, -trice /emetœʀ, tʀis/ **I** *adj* **1** Radio, TV broadcasting; **2** Fin, Postes issuing; **banque émettrice** issuing bank.
II *nm* **1** Radio, TV transmitter; **2** Fin (de chèque) drawer; (d'emprunt, de carte) issuer; **3** Ling sender.

émetteur-récepteur, *pl* **émetteurs-récepteurs** /emetœʀʀesɛptœʀ/ *nm* transceiver.

émettre /emɛtʀ/ [60] **I** *vtr* **1** (exprimer) to express [*avis, réserve, vœu*]; to put forward [*hypothèse, recommandation, proposition*]; to raise [*objection*]; **2** (produire) to utter [*cri*]; to produce [*son, chaleur, lumière, vibration*]; to give off [*odeur*]; **3** Admin, Postes to issue [*document, emprunt, timbre, billet de banque*]; **4** Fin to draw [*chèque*]; to float [*emprunt*]; **5** Radio, TV to broadcast [*programme*]; **6** [*avion, bateau*] to send out [*message de détresse*]; **7** Phys to emit [*chaleur, radiation*].
II *vi* Radio, TV to broadcast; **~ à partir de Moscou/sur modulation de fréquence** to broadcast from Moscow/on FM.

émeu /emø/ *nm* Zool emu.

émeute /emøt/ *nf* riot; **tourner à l'~** to turn into a riot; **provoquer des ~s** to cause riots ou rioting; **~s raciales** race riots; **c'est l'~** all hell is breaking loose.

émeutier, -ière /emøtje, ɛʀ/ *nm,f* rioter.

émiettement /emjɛtmɑ̃/ *nm* **1** lit (action de réduire en miettes) crumbling; **2** fig (désagrégation) (de domaine, fortune) splitting up; (de forces, énergie) dissipation; (de temps) frittering away.

émietter /emjete/ [1] **I** *vtr* **1** (réduire en miettes) to crumble [*pain, biscuit, motte de terre*]; **2** (morceler) to split [sth] up [*domaine, territoire, fortune*]; **3** fml (disperser) to dissipate [*forces, activités*]; to fritter away [*temps*].
II s'émietter *vpr* **1** (tomber en miettes) [*pain, roche*] to crumble; **2** (perdre son unité) [*parti, pouvoir*] to crumble; **3** (se morceler) [*héritage*] to be split up.

émigrant, ~e /emigʀɑ̃, ɑ̃t/ *nm,f* emigrant; **population d'~s** emigrant population.

émigration /emigʀasjɔ̃/ *nf* (de personne) emigration; **pays à forte ~** country with a high level of emigration.

émigré, ~e /emigʀe/ **I** *pp* ▶ **émigrer**.
II *pp adj* emigrant; **travailleur ~** emigrant worker.
III *nm,f* gén emigrant; Hist émigré.

émigrer /emigʀe/ [1] *vi* **1** (quitter son pays) [*personne*] to emigrate (**de** from; **en, vers, à** to); **2** (quitter une région) [*personne*] to migrate (**en, vers** to); **3** Zool to migrate (**en, vers, dans** to).

émincé /emɛ̃se/ *nm* Culin émincé, thin slices (*pl*).

émincer /emɛ̃se/ [12] *vtr* to slice [sth] thinly, to cut [sth] into thin slices [*aliment*].

éminemment /eminamɑ̃/ *adv* eminently.

éminence /eminɑ̃s/ *nf* **1** (monticule) hillock littér; **2** Anat protuberance.

Éminence /eminɑ̃s/ *nf* Relig Eminence; **votre/son ~** Your/His Eminence.
■ **~ grise** éminence grise, grey GB ou gray US eminence.

éminent, ~e /eminɑ̃, ɑ̃t/ *adj* eminent, distinguished; **mon ~ confrère** my distinguished colleague.

éminentissime /eminɑ̃tisim/ *adj* **1** Relig most eminent; **2** hum most distinguished ou eminent.

émir /emiʀ/ ▶ 813 *nm* emir.

émirat /emiʀa/ *nm* emirate.

Émirats /emiʀa/ ▶ 321 *nprmpl* **~ arabes unis, EAU** United Arab Emirates.

émissaire /emisɛʀ/ *nm* emissary.

émissif, -ive /emisif, iv/ *adj* emissive.

émission /emisjɔ̃/ *nf* **1** Radio, TV programme[GB]; **~ de radio/de télévision** radio/TV programme[GB]; **~ éducative/littéraire** educational/book programme[GB]; **~ grand public** programme[GB] with universal appeal; **~ sur la France** programme[GB] about France; **2** Admin, Fin, Postes (de document, monnaie, timbre) issue; **3** Sci, Télécom emission; **4** Ling **~ de voix** phonation.

emmagasiner /ɑ̃magazine/ [1] *vtr* **1** Ind, Comm (mettre en magasin) to store; **2** (accumuler) to stockpile [*marchandises, vivres*]; to store [*chaleur, énergie*]; to store up [*connaissances, souvenirs*].

emmailloter /ɑ̃majɔte/ [1] *vtr* to swaddle [*bébé*]; to bandage [*doigt, bras*].

emmancher /ɑ̃mɑ̃ʃe/ [1] **I** *vtr* **1** (mettre un manche à) to fit a handle to; **2**○ (mettre en train) to set [sth] up [*affaire, négociation*].
II s'emmancher○ *vpr* [*affaire*] to start up; [*négociations*] to start; **s'~ bien/mal** to get off to a good/bad start.

emmanchure /ɑ̃mɑ̃ʃyʀ/ *nf* armhole.

emmêler /ɑ̃mɛle/ [1] **I** *vtr* **1** (enchevêtrer) to tangle [*cheveux, fils*]; **2** (embrouiller) to confuse [*affaire*].
II s'emmêler *vpr* **1** (s'enchevêtrer) to get tangled up; **2** (se prendre) **s'~ les pieds dans qch** to get one's feet caught in sth; **s'~ les crayons**○ or **les pédales**○ or **les pinceaux**○ (trébucher) to trip over; (s'égarer) to get into a muddle; **3** (s'embrouiller) to get tangled up (**dans** in); **s'~ dans des explications/un raisonnement** to get tangled up in one's explanations/an argument.

emménagement /ɑ̃menaʒmɑ̃/ *nm* moving in.

emménager /ɑ̃menaʒe/ [13] *vi* to move in; **~ dans** to move into.

emmener /ɑ̃mne/ [16] *vtr* **1** (mener) to take [*personne*] (**à, jusqu'à** to); **~ les enfants à l'école** to take the children to school; **~ promener un enfant** to take a child for a walk; **j'ai emmené ma mère chercher Anne à la gare** I took my mother to pick Anne up from the station; **je vous emmène faire des courses** I'm taking you shopping; **je vous emmène dîner au restaurant** I'm taking you to a restaurant for dinner; **~ les enfants se baigner** to take the children swimming; **~ qn voir qn** to take sb to see sb; **emmène-moi chez toi!** take me home with you!; **veux-tu que je t'emmène en voiture?** do you want a lift GB ou a ride US?; **2**○ (emporter) controv to take; **est-ce que tu as emmené un imperméable/de la lecture?** did you take a raincoat/something to read?; **3** (transporter) [*avion, véhicule*] to carry [*passagers*]; **le car qui les emmenait au bord de la mer** the coach that was taking ou carrying them to the seaside; **4** (arrêter) [*police*] to take [sb] away [*personne*]; **5** (entraîner) [*chef, capitaine*] to lead [*équipe, troupe*].

emmenthal /emɛ̃tal, emɑ̃tal/ *nm* Emmenthal.

emmerdant◑, **~e** /ɑ̃mɛʀdɑ̃, ɑ̃t/ *adj* **1** (ennuyeux) [*livre, orateur*] bloody◑ GB ou damned○ boring; **2** (importun) [*personne, situation*] bloody◑ GB ou damned○ annoying; **l'~ c'est que je suis fauché**○ the annoying thing is that I'm broke○.

emmerde◑ /ɑ̃mɛʀd/ *nm* ou *f* ▶ **emmerdement**.

emmerdé◑, **~e** /ɑ̃mɛʀde/ **I** *pp* ▶ **emmerder**.
II *pp adj* **1** (gêné) embarrassed; **2** (dans une situation difficile) in a mess○.

emmerdement◑ /ɑ̃mɛʀdəmɑ̃/ *nm* problem; **n'avoir que des ~s** to be really in the shit◑; **s'attirer des ~s** to get into trouble, to get oneself in the shit◑; **faire des ~s à qn** to cause trouble for sb.

emmerder◑ /ɑ̃mɛʀde/ [1] **I** *vtr* **1** (importuner) to annoy, to hassle○; **m'emmerdez pas** don't hassle me; **tu m'emmerdes** you're a pain○, you're a pain in the arse● GB ou ass◑ US; **il ne se laisse pas ~** he doesn't let other people bug○ him; **~ le monde** to annoy everybody, to be a pain○; **se faire ~** to get hassled○; **je les emmerde** to hell○ with them, fuck them●; **2** (ennuyer) to bore [sb] to death, to bore [sb] stiff○.
II s'emmerder *vpr* **1** (s'ennuyer) to be bored, to be bored stiff○; **2** (se compliquer la vie) **s'~ à faire** to go to the trouble ou bother of doing; **qu'est ce que j'ai pu m'~ avec cette voiture!** the trouble ou hassle○ I've had with that car!; **je n'ai pas envie de m'~ avec un chien/une voiture** I don't want all the trouble ou hassle○ of a dog/a car; **t'emmerdes pas avec ça!** (avec la finition) don't bother with that!; (avec ce que les gens vont penser) don't waste your time worrying about that!; **un hôtel cinq étoiles, tu t'emmerdes pas!** a 5-star hotel! you're doing all right for yourself!; **tu as fouillé dans mes tiroirs, tu t'emmerdes pas!** you went through my drawers, you've got a nerve ou a bloody cheek○! GB; **tu appelles ça laver la voiture, tu t'emmerdes pas!** that's what you call washing the car, you're not exactly straining yourself, are you?

emmerdeur◑, **-euse** /ɑ̃mɛʀdœʀ, øz/ *nm,f* (qui dérange les autres) troublemaker; (qui agace) pain in the arse● GB ou ass◑ US.

emmieller○ /ɑ̃mjele/ [1] *vtr* **~ qn** to get on sb's nerves.

emmitoufler /ɑ̃mitufle/ [1] **I** *vtr* to wrap [sb/sth] up warmly [*personne, partie du corps*]; **il était emmitouflé dans son manteau** he was wrapped up snugly in his coat.
II s'emmitoufler *vpr* to wrap (oneself) up warmly.

emmouscailler○ /ɑ̃muskaje/ [1] *vtr* to bug○, to annoy.

emmurer /ɑ̃myʀe/ [1] *vtr* to wall [sb/sth] in [*personne, objet*], to immure sout.

émoi /emwa/ *nm* littér agitation, turmoil; **la nouvelle a mis toute la ville en ~** the news threw the whole city into turmoil; **l'arrivée du jeune homme l'avait mise en ~** the young man's arrival had thrown her into a state of confusion.

émollient, ~e /emɔljɑ̃, ɑ̃t/ **I** *adj* emollient.
II *nm* emollient.

émoluments /emolymɑ̃/ *nmpl* **1** (salaire) remuneration, emoluments sout; **2** (de notaire, d'huissier, avocat) fees, emoluments sout.

émondage /emɔ̃daʒ/ *nm* pruning.

émonder /emɔ̃de/ [1] *vtr* **1** lit to prune, to trim [*arbre*]; **2** fig to prune [*texte, article*].

émondoir /emɔ̃dwaʀ/ *nm* pruner, pruning hook.

émotif, -ive /emɔtif, iv/ **I** *adj* [*choc, réaction, caractère, personne*] emotional.
II *nm,f* emotional person.

émotion /emosjɔ̃/ *nf* **1** (réaction affective) emotion; (peur) fright; **rougir/trembler d'~** to blush/tremble with emotion; **la voix chargée d'~** in a choked voice; **donner des ~s à qn**○ to give sb a fright; **tu es remis de tes ~s**○? have you recovered from the shock?; **dans la salle d'audience, l'~ était à son comble** the atmosphere in the courtroom was extremely emotional; **2** (sensibilité) emotion.

émotionné○, **~e** /emosjɔne/ *adj* controv upset; **il en est tout ~** he's all upset about it.

émotionnel, -elle /emosjɔnɛl/ *adj* emotional.

émotivité /emɔtivite/ *nf* **enfant d'une grande ~** highly emotional child.

émoulu, ~e /emuly/ *adj* **frais ~ de** fresh from.

émoussé, ~e /emuse/ **I** *pp* ▶ **émousser**.
II *pp adj* **1** lit [*couteau, lame*] blunt; **2** fig [*curiosité, sensibilité*] blunted, dulled.

émousser /emuse/ [1] **I** *vtr* **1** lit to blunt

[*couteau, lame*]; **2** fig to blunt, to dull [*curiosité, sensibilité*].

II **s'émousser** *vpr* **1** lit [*lame, couteau*] to become ou get blunt; **2** fig [*curiosité, sensibilité*] to become dulled.

émoustillant, ~e /emustijɑ̃, ɑ̃t/ *adj* titillating.

émoustiller /emustije/ [1] *vtr* **1** (égayer) to exhilarate; **2** (exciter) to titillate.

émouvant, ~e /emuvɑ̃, ɑ̃t/ *adj* moving.

émouvoir /emuvwaʀ/ [43] I *vtr* (attendrir) to move; (toucher) to touch; **~ qn (jusqu')aux larmes** to move sb to tears; **votre sollicitude m'émeut** I am touched by your concern; **se laisser ~ par les larmes/prières de qn** to be swayed by sb's tears/pleas; **~ l'opinion** to cause a stir.

II **s'émouvoir** *vpr* **1** (être touché) [*personne*] to be touched; **s'~ à la vue/au souvenir de** to be touched by the sight/memory of; **2** (s'inquiéter) **le gouvernement s'émeut des troubles paysans** the government is becoming concerned about the farmers' unrest; **il ne s'émeut nullement de leur retard** he's not at all worried by the fact that they are late; **il ne s'est pas ému de mes remarques** my remarks didn't bother him; **il n'y a pas de quoi s'~** there's nothing to get excited about; **l'opinion publique fut lente à s'~** there was no public outcry for quite some time; **répondre sans s'~** to reply calmly.

empaillage /ɑ̃pɑjaʒ/ *nm* (de chaise) straw stuffing; (d'animal) stuffing.

empailler /ɑ̃pɑje/ [1] *vtr* **1** to seat [sth] (with straw) [*chaise*]; **2** (naturaliser) to stuff [*animal*]; **3** Agric (protéger avec de la paille) to protect [sth] with straw.

empailleur, -euse /ɑ̃pɑjœʀ, øz/ **▶510** *nm* **1** (d'animaux) taxidermist; **2** (de chaise, fauteuil) chair seater.

empalement /ɑ̃palmɑ̃/ *nm* impalement.

empaler /ɑ̃pale/ [1] I *vtr* to impale [*personne*].

II **s'empaler** *vpr* to be impaled.

empan /ɑ̃pɑ̃/ *nm* span.

empanaché, ~e /ɑ̃panaʃe/ *adj* littér plumed.

empanner /ɑ̃pane/ [1] *vi* Naut to gybe GB, to jibe US.

empaquetage /ɑ̃paktaʒ/ *nm* (dans une boîte) packaging; (dans du papier, tissu etc) wrapping.

empaqueter /ɑ̃pakte/ [20] *vtr* (dans une boîte) to package; (dans du papier, tissu etc) to wrap [sth] up [*objet*].

emparer: **s'emparer** /ɑ̃paʀe/ [1] *vpr* **1** (prendre) **s'~ de** [*personne, groupe*] to take over [*ville, pays, entreprise, record*]; to get hold of [*arme, camion*]; to seize [*pouvoir, personne, prétexte*]; to gain possession of [*ballon*]; to get hold of [*scandale, rumeur, micro, volant*]; **2** (envahir) **s'~ de** [*torpeur, sentiment*] to take hold of [*personne, entreprise, pays*]; **la folie s'est emparée du village** madness has taken hold of the village.

empâtement /ɑ̃pɑtmɑ̃/ *nm* **1** (de corps, visage) bloatedness; **2** (de la langue) furriness; **3** Tech (en peinture) impasto.

empâter /ɑ̃pɑte/ [1] I *vtr* **1** (rendre pâteux) to fur up [*langue*]; **2** (faire grossir) to thicken out [*corps*]; to make puffy [*visage*].

II **s'empâter** *vpr* [*visage*] to become puffy; [*personne*] to put on weight; [*corps*] to thicken out; **il s'est empâté avec l'âge** he has put on weight as he has got GB ou gotten US older.

empathie /ɑ̃pati/ *nf* empathy.

empathique /ɑ̃patik/ *adj* empathic.

empattement /ɑ̃patmɑ̃/ *nm* **1** Tech, Aut wheelbase; **2** Constr footing; **3** Imprim serif.

empêché, ~e /ɑ̃peʃe/ I *pp* ▶ **empêcher**.

II *pp adj* **1** (retenu) **le Président, ~, a dû se décommander** the President has been detained and has had to cancel; **2** fml (incapable) **je serais bien ~ de vous répondre** I would be very hard-pressed to give you an answer; **l'électeur ~ d'aller voter** the voter unable to go and vote.

empêchement /ɑ̃pɛʃmɑ̃/ *nm* unforeseen difficulty; **en cas d'~** if anything should crop up, in case of unforeseen difficulties; **j'ai un ~, peux-tu reporter notre rendez-vous?** something's cropped up, can you make it another time?; **il n'a pas pu venir à cause d'un ~ de dernière minute** he couldn't come because he was unavoidably detained at the last minute.

empêcher /ɑ̃peʃe/ [1] I *vtr* to prevent, to stop; **~ un crime** to prevent a crime; **~ que la vérité ne soit révélée** to prevent ou stop the truth (from) being revealed; **~ qn de faire** to prevent sb from doing, to stop sb from doing; **rien ne m'empêche de partir** there's nothing to stop me (from) leaving; **rien ne vous empêche de le signaler** there's nothing to stop you pointing it out; **rien n'empêche d'imaginer une autre solution** there's no reason why we can't think of another solution; **si tu veux partir, personne ne t'en empêche** if you want to leave, no-one's stopping you; **la pauvreté n'empêche pas la générosité** poverty does not preclude generosity; **l'un n'empêche pas l'autre** the one doesn't necessarily preclude the other; **une disposition qui empêche les fonctionnaires de faire grève** a clause that prevents civil servants from striking; **une absence de vent qui empêche le nuage toxique de se disperser** a lack of wind that keeps the toxic cloud from dispersing; **il a décidé de mettre fin à ses jours, on l'en empêche** he decided to kill himself, he was stopped; **notre handicap ne nous empêche pas de plaisanter** our disability doesn't stop us from making jokes ou doesn't mean we can't make jokes; **un homme empêché de rêver devient fou** a man prevented from dreaming goes mad; **l'attentat a empêché la libération des otages** the attack meant that the hostages couldn't be freed; **pour ~ toute tentative d'OPA** to stave off ou ward off any takeover attempt.

II **s'empêcher** *vpr* **je n'ai pu m'~ de rire** I couldn't help laughing; **je n'ai pas pu m'en ~** I couldn't help it.

III *v impers* **(il) n'empêche** all the same; **il n'empêche que** nonetheless, the fact remains that; **n'empêche que**° for all that, all the same; **il est riche, ça n'empêche pas qu'il est idiot** he's rich, but he's an idiot all the same.

empêcheur, -euse /ɑ̃pɛʃœʀ, øz/ *nm,f* **~ de tourner** or **danser en rond** spoilsport, killjoy.

empeigne /ɑ̃pɛɲ/ *nf* upper.

empennage /ɑ̃pɛnaʒ/ *nm* **1** Aviat empennage, tail; **2** (d'une flèche) flighting, fledging.

empenner /ɑ̃pene/ [1] *vtr* to flight, to fledge.

empereur /ɑ̃pʀœʀ/ **▶813** *nm* emperor.

empesage /ɑ̃pəzaʒ/ *nm* starching.

empesé, ~e /ɑ̃pəze/ I *pp* ▶ **empeser**.

II *pp adj* [*air, style, personne*] starchy; **avoir l'air ~** to look starchy.

empeser /ɑ̃pəze/ [16] *vtr* to starch; **col empesé** starched collar.

empester /ɑ̃pɛste/ [16] I *vtr* **1** (faire sentir mauvais) to stink [sth] out GB ou stink up US [*endroit*]; **2** (gâter) to poison [*ambiance, atmosphère*].

II *vi* to stink, to reek; **ça empeste ici!** it stinks in here!; **ça empeste le parfum** it stinks ou reeks of perfume.

empêtrer /ɑ̃petʀe/ [1] I *vtr* to get [sb] mixed up (**dans** in).

II **s'empêtrer** *vpr* **1** (dans des ronces, cordages) to get entangled (**dans** in); **2** (dans des contradictions, mensonges, raisonnements, discours) to get tangled up (**dans** in); (dans des intrigues, trafics) to get mixed up (**dans** in); **je suis empêtré dans mes comptes/un problème de maths** I'm bogged down in my accounts/a maths GB ou math US problem.

emphase /ɑ̃fɑz/ *nf* **1** (exagération) grandiloquence; **parler avec ~** to speak grandiloquently; **discours plein d'~** grandiloquent speech; **parler sans ~** to speak without affectation; **2** Ling (accent) emphasis.

emphatique /ɑ̃fatik/ *adj* **1** (pompeux) grandiloquent; **2** Ling emphatic.

emphatiquement /ɑ̃fatikmɑ̃/ *adv* grandiloquently.

emphysème /ɑ̃fizɛm/ **▶271** *nm* emphysema.

emphytéotique /ɑ̃fiteɔtik/ *adj* **bail ~** long lease (*from 18 to 99 years*).

empiècement /ɑ̃pjɛsmɑ̃/ *nm* Cout, Mode yoke.

empierrement /ɑ̃pjɛʀmɑ̃/ *nm* **1** (de route, chemin) metalling; (de voie ferrée) ballasting; **2** (couche de pierres) road metal, roadbed.

empierrer /ɑ̃pjeʀe/ [1] *vtr* to metal [*chemin, route*]; to ballast [*voie ferrée*].

empiètement /ɑ̃pjɛtmɑ̃/ *nm* encroachment (**sur** on).

empiéter /ɑ̃pjete/ [14] *vtr ind* **~ sur** lit, fig to encroach upon.

empiffrer°: **s'empiffrer** /ɑ̃pifʀe/ [1] *vpr* to stuff oneself (**de** with).

empilage /ɑ̃pilaʒ/ *nm* **1** (action d'empiler) stacking up; **2** (pile) stack.

empile /ɑ̃pil/ *nf* Pêche trace GB, leader US.

empilement /ɑ̃pilmɑ̃/ *nm* = **empilage**.

empiler /ɑ̃pile/ [1] I *vtr* **1** (mettre en pile) to pile [sth] (up), to stack [sth] (up); **2**° (escroquer) to rip [sb] off°, to fleece°.

II **s'empiler** *vpr* **1** (s'accumuler) [*vaisselle, livres*] to pile up; **2** (s'entasser) [*personnes*] to pile (**dans** into), to crowd (**dans** into).

empileur, -euse /ɑ̃pilœʀ, øz/ *nm,f* **1** (ouvrier) stacker; **2**° (escroc) con man°, swindler.

empire /ɑ̃piʀ/ *nm* **1** Pol empire; **pas pour un ~!** not for the world!; **2** (très grande entreprise) empire; **un ~ financier** a financial empire; **3** fml (ascendant) influence; **avoir de l'~ sur qn** to have influence over sb; **sous l'~ de l'alcool** under the influence of drink; **agir sous l'~ de la colère/jalousie** to act in a fit of anger/jealousy.

Empire /ɑ̃piʀ/ *nm* (règne de Napoléon Ier) **l'~** the Empire; **mobilier/style ~** Empire furniture/style.

■ **l'~ céleste** the Celestial Empire; **l'~ du Milieu** the Middle Kingdom; **l'~ d'Orient** the Byzantine Empire; **l'~ (romain) d'Occident** the Western (Roman) Empire; **l'~ du Soleil Levant** Hist the land of the Rising Sun.

empirer /ɑ̃piʀe/ [1] *vi* to get worse (**avec** with), to worsen (**avec** with); **son état a empiré** his condition has got worse ou has worsened; **mon état/la situation va en empirant** my condition/the situation continues to get worse; **faire ~** to make [sth] worse, to worsen.

empirique /ɑ̃piʀik/ *adj* gén empirical; **de façon ~** by empirical means.

empiriquement /ɑ̃piʀikmɑ̃/ *adv* empirically.

empirisme /ɑ̃piʀism/ *nm* empiricism.

empiriste /ɑ̃piʀist/ *adj, nmf* empiricist.

emplacement /ɑ̃plasmɑ̃/ *nm* **1** (site) site; **l'~ où s'élèvera un bâtiment** the site of a future building; **ils ont trouvé un bon ~ pour leur tente** they found a good site for their tent; **2** (parking) parking space; **'~ réservé aux livraisons'** 'space reserved for delivery vehicles'.

■ **~ publicitaire** Pub advertising space.

emplafonner° /ɑ̃plafɔne/ [1] *vtr* to smash into.

emplâtre /ɑ̃plɑtʀ/ *nm* **1** Méd, Pharm medicated plaster; **2**° (personne) good-for-nothing°;

espèce d'~! you good-for-nothing○!; **3** Tech, Aut patch.

emplette /ɑ̃plɛt/ *nf* (achat) purchase; **faire quelques ~s** to make a few purchases; **faire l'~ de qch** to purchase sth.

emplir /ɑ̃pliʀ/ [3] *vtr*, **s'emplir** *vpr* to fill (**de** with).

emploi /ɑ̃plwɑ/ *nm* **1** (poste de travail) job; **trouver un ~** to find a job; **retrouver un ~** to find a new job; **changer d'~** to change jobs; **créer des ~s** to create jobs; **un ~ de chauffeur** a job as a driver; **sans ~** unemployed, out of work; **2** (embauche) employment; **~ des femmes/jeunes** employment of women/young people; **favoriser/stimuler l'~** to promote/to stimulate employment; **3** (utilisation) use; **~ d'armes chimiques/de fonds** use of chemical weapons/of funds; **ne m'achète pas de gants, avec mes mouffles ça va faire double ~** don't buy me any gloves, my mittens do the job already; **TV couleur à vendre, cause double ~** colour[GB] TV for sale, surplus to requirements; **4** Ling usage; **~ critiqué** controversial usage.
■ **~ d'insertion** job placement; **~ du temps** timetable.
IDIOMES **avoir la tête** or **gueule◑ de l'~** to look the part.

employé, **~e** /ɑ̃plwaje/ ▶**510** *nm,f* **1** (travailleur) employee; **les ~s des banques sont en grève** bank workers ou employees are on strike; **2** (vu par la clientèle) member of staff; **un ~ m'a dit que** a member of staff told me that; **l'~ du gaz passera lundi** the gasman will call on Monday.
■ **~ de banque** bank clerk; **~ de bureau** clerk; **~ aux écritures** ledger clerk; **~ de maison** domestic employee; **~ municipal** local authority employee.

employer /ɑ̃plwaje/ [23] **I** *vtr* **1** (avoir à son service) [*personne, entreprise*] to employ [*personne*] (**comme** as); **elle emploie quinze personnes** she employs fifteen people; **2** (embaucher) [*personne, entreprise*] to hire [*personne*] (**comme** as); **elle compte ~ une secrétaire** she plans to hire a secretary; **3** (utiliser) to use [*mot, méthode, arme, produit*]; **~ la force** to use force; **~ les grands moyens** to use drastic means; **~ son temps à faire** to spend one's time doing.
II s'employer *vpr* **1** (être utilisé) to be used; **mot/produit qui ne s'emploie plus** word/product which is no longer used; **2** (se consacrer) **s'~ à faire** to apply oneself to doing.

employeur, **-euse** /ɑ̃plwajœʀ, øz/ *nm,f* employer.

emplumé, **~e** /ɑ̃plyme/ *adj* feathered, plumed.

empocher /ɑ̃pɔʃe/ [1] *vtr* to pocket.

empoignade○ /ɑ̃pwaɲad/ *nf* **1** (bagarre) scrap○, fight; **2** (dispute) row.

empoigne /ɑ̃pwaɲ/ *nf* **c'était la foire d'~** it was a free-for-all.

empoigner /ɑ̃pwaɲe/ [1] **I** *vtr* to grab (hold of), to seize (**par, au** by).
II s'empoigner *vpr* **1** (se battre) **s'~ avec qn** to grapple with sb; **2** (se quereller) to clash.

empois /ɑ̃pwa/ *nm* starch.

empoisonnant○, **~e** /ɑ̃pwazɔnɑ̃, ɑ̃t/ *adj* [*personne*] (fatigant) wearing; (énervant) [*problème*] annoying.

empoisonné, **~e** /ɑ̃pwazɔne/ **I** *pp* ▶ **empoisonner**.
II *pp adj* [*aliment, flèche*] poisoned (**à** with); [*atmosphère*] sour; [*relations*] sour; [*querelle*] venomous; [*mot*] barbed.

empoisonnement /ɑ̃pwazɔnmɑ̃/ *nm* **1** (intoxication) poisoning ¢; **~ au gaz** gas poisoning; **les ~s sont rares** cases of poisoning are rare; **2** (crime) poisoning; **~ à l'arsenic** poisoning with arsenic; **3** (ennui) trouble ¢; **des tas d'~s** a lot of trouble.

empoisonner /ɑ̃pwazɔne/ [1] **I** *vtr* **1** (pour tuer) to poison [*personne, animal*]; **2** (intoxiquer) to give [sb] food poisoning [*personne*]; to poison [*sang*]; **être empoisonné par des champignons** to get food poisoning from mushrooms; **3** (polluer) to poison [*rivière, air*]; **4** fig to poison [*relation, atmosphère*]; **arrête de m'~!** stop bugging me!; **il m'empoisonne avec ses questions** he gets on my nerves with his questions; **ça m'empoisonne de devoir y aller** it bothers ou bugs me having to go there; **~ la vie de qn** to make sb's life a misery.
II s'empoisonner *vpr* **1** (volontairement) to poison oneself (**à** with); (accidentellement) **il s'est empoisonné avec une huître pas fraîche** he got food poisoning from eating a bad oyster; **2**○ (se rendre malheureux) **s'~ la vie** or **l'existence** to make one's life a misery (**avec** with; **à faire** by doing).

empoisonneur, **-euse** /ɑ̃pwazɔnœʀ, øz/ *nm,f* **1** (criminel) poisoner; **2**○ (importun) nuisance; **quel ~!** he's such a nuisance ou pain○!

empoissonner /ɑ̃pwasɔne/ [1] *vtr* to stock [sth] with fish [*étang, mare*].

emporté, **~e** /ɑ̃pɔʀte/ **I** *pp* ▶ **emporter**.
II *pp adj* **être ~**, **avoir un caractère ~** to be quick-tempered.

emportement /ɑ̃pɔʀtəmɑ̃/ *nm* fit of anger; **dans mon ~ je l'ai frappé** I hit him in a fit of anger; **avec ~** angrily.

emporte-pièce /ɑ̃pɔʀtəpjɛs/ *nm inv* **1** Tech punch; **découper qch à l'~** to punch sth; **jugement/déclaration à l'~** fig rash judgment/declaration; **faire qch à l'~** fig to do sth too hastily; **2** Culin pastry cutter.

emporter /ɑ̃pɔʀte/ [1] **I** *vtr* **1** (prendre avec soi) [*personne*] to take [*objet, vêtement, vivres, document*]; [*vent*] to sweep away [*feuilles mortes*]; **n'oublie pas d'~ un parapluie/à manger** don't forget to take an umbrella/something to eat; **~ qch avec soi** controv to take sth with one [*objet, vêtement, vivres, document*]; **pizzas à ~** takeaway pizzas; **2** (transporter) lit [*ambulance, sauveteurs*] to take [sb] away [*blessé, cadavre*]; [*bateau, train, avion*] to carry away [*passager, fret*]; **se laisser ~ par son élan** fig to get carried away; **se laisser ~ par la colère** to let one's anger get the better of one; **se laisser ~ par son imagination** to let one's imagination run riot; **3** (arracher) [*vent, rivière*] to sweep away [*personne, maison, embarcation, arbre, pont*]; [*obus, balle*] to take [sth] off [*oreille, bras*]; **emporté par le courant** swept away by the current; **4** (causer la mort) **une leucémie l'a emporté** he died of leukaemia; **5** (conquérir) to take [*position*]; **~ l'accord de qn** to get sb's agreement; **~ l'adhésion de qn** to win sb over; **6** (voler) [*personne*] to steal [*bijoux, argenterie, tableau*]; **il est parti en emportant la caisse** he ran off with all the money; **7** (triompher) **l'~** [*équipe, candidat*] to win; [*idée, bon sens*] to prevail; **l'~ sur qn** [*équipe, candidat*] to beat sb; **l'~ sur qch** to overcome sth; **le bon sens l'a emporté** common sense prevailed; **l'~ avec 38% des suffrages/par 2 buts à 1/de 4 points** to win with 38% of the votes/by 2 goals to 1/by 4 points; **l'~ sur son adversaire avec 57% des voix** to defeat one's opponent by getting 57% of the votes; ▶ **paradis**, **tombe**.
II s'emporter *vpr* (s'énerver) [*personne*] to lose one's temper; **il s'emporte facilement** he loses his temper easily.
IDIOMES **~ la bouche**○ or **gueule◑** [*épices, plat, alcool*] to take the roof off one's mouth○.

empoté○, **~e** /ɑ̃pɔte/ **I** *adj* clumsy, awkward.
II *nm,f* clumsy oaf○.

empoter /ɑ̃pɔte/ [1] *vtr* to pot.

empourprer /ɑ̃puʀpʀe/ [1] **I** *vtr* to turn [sth] crimson [*ciel, horizon*].
II s'empourprer *vpr* [*horizon, ciel*] to turn crimson; [*visage, joue*] to flush (**de** with).

empoussiérer /ɑ̃pusjeʀe/ [14] *vtr* to cover [sth] with dust [*route, pièce*].

empreindre /ɑ̃pʀɛ̃dʀ/ [55] **I** *vtr* **1** (marquer) to imprint; **2** (remplir de) to imbue sout (**de** with).
II s'empreindre *vpr* to become marked (**de** by), become imbued (**de** with); **empreint de tristesse** [*personnalité*] imbued with sadness; [*visage*] marked by sadness.

empreinte /ɑ̃pʀɛ̃t/ *nf* **1** (de pas) footprint; (d'animal) track; **2** (de cachet, médaille, monnaie) impression, imprint; **~ d'une serrure** impression of a key; **3** Dent impression; **4** (marque) stamp, mark; **recevoir l'~ de son milieu social** to be stamped ou marked by one's social background.
■ **~s digitales** fingerprints; **~s génétiques** genetic fingerprints.

empressé, **~e** /ɑ̃pʀese/ **I** *pp* ▶ **empresser**.
II *pp adj* **1** (marquant la hâte) [*soins, secours*] prompt; **2** (prévenant) [*admirateur, fiancé*] attentive; **faire l'~** to ingratiate oneself (**auprès de** with).

empressement /ɑ̃pʀɛsmɑ̃/ *nm* **1** (hâte) eagerness; **montrer de l'~**, **faire preuve d'~** to show eagerness (**à faire** to do); **manifester (bien) peu d'~ à faire qch** to show (very) little eagerness to do sth; **avec ~** eagerly; **2** (prévenance) attentiveness; **manifester** or **montrer de l'~** to be attentive (**auprès de**, **à l'égard de** to, toward, towards GB).

empresser: **s'empresser** /ɑ̃pʀese/ [1] *vpr* **s'~ de faire** to hasten to do; **s'~ autour** or **auprès de qn** (pour voir, écouter) to gather attentively around sb; (en témoignant des prévenances) to fuss over sb.

emprise /ɑ̃pʀiz/ *nf* hold, influence; **avoir de l'~ sur qn** to have a hold over sb.

emprisonnement /ɑ̃pʀizɔnmɑ̃/ *nm* imprisonment; **peine d'emprisonnement** prison sentence; **une peine d'~ de 20 ans** a twenty-year prison sentence; **prononcer une peine d'~ contre qn** to sentence sb to imprisonment; **être condamné à l'~ à vie** or **à perpétuité** to be sentenced to life imprisonment.
■ **~ cellulaire** solitary confinement.

emprisonner /ɑ̃pʀizɔne/ [1] *vtr* **1** (mettre en prison) to imprison (**à, dans** in); fig **être emprisonné dans** to be the prisoner of; **2** (retenir) to keep [sb] prisoner (**à, dans** in); **3** (enfermer) to clasp [*personne, main*]; [*vêtement*] to squeeze [*personne, taille*].

emprunt /ɑ̃pʀœ̃/ *nm* **1** (somme) loan; **faire un ~ auprès d'une banque** to take out a bank loan; **contracter** or **faire un ~ de 10 000 francs** to take out a 10,000-franc loan; **souscrire à/émettre/lancer un ~** to subscribe to/issue/float a loan; **~ à court/moyen/long terme** short-/medium-/long-term loan; **un ~ à 10% sur 15 ans** a loan at 10% (repayable) over 15 years; **accorder un ~ à** to grant a loan to; **l'~ a permis à l'État de faire** the loan has enabled the state to do; **~ public** public sector loan; **un ~ d'État** a government loan; **un ~ forcé** or **obligatoire** mandatory loan; **le remboursement d'un ~** repayments on a loan; **2** (action) borrowing; **financé par l'~** financed by borrowing; **d'~** [*voiture*] borrowed; [*nom*] borrowed; **3** (objet) loan; **c'est un ~ fait à un musée/une bibliothèque** it's a loan from a museum/a library; **4** (d'idée, de style, de genre) borrowing; **un ~ fait à un auteur** a borrowing from an author; **5** Ling (processus) borrowing; (élément) borrowing, loan word; **~ à** or **de** borrowing from.

emprunté, **~e** /ɑ̃pʀœ̃te/ **I** *pp* ▶ **emprunter**.
II *pp adj* **1**○ (embarrassé) [*air, geste, personne*] awkward; **2** (prétendu) [*gloire*] reflected.

emprunter /ɑ̃pʀœ̃te/ [1] *vtr* **1** gén, Fin to borrow [*argent, objet, coutume, formule, idée*] (**à qn** from sb); **~ à 10%** to borrow at 10%; **je vais être obligé d'~** I'll have to take out a loan; **~ sur 15 ans à 10%** to take out a loan over 15 years at 10%; **2** (imiter) to

en

Généralités

en, préposition et pronom, est présenté ici dans ses grandes lignes. Les expressions courantes du genre *en vitrine*, *être en colère*, *ne pas s'en faire*, *s'en aller* sont traitées respectivement dans les articles ***vitrine***, ***colère***, ***faire***, ***aller***; de même on trouvera les expressions avec *il y en a* sous **avoir** et les expressions avec *en être à* sous **être**.

Pour les traductions de *en*, préposition, associée à des noms de couleurs, pays, régions, et de *en*, pronom, quand il sert à exprimer des quantités, on consultera aussi les notes d'usage pertinentes. Voir la liste ▶ **1920**

La préposition

en + *gérondif*

La traduction sera différente selon les nuances exprimées.

La simultanéité

L'action est brève

en ouvrant la porte, je me suis souvenue que = as I opened the door, I remembered that
je l'ai croisé en sortant = I met him as I was leaving

L'action dure

prends un café en attendant = have a cup of coffee while you're waiting
elle travaille en chantant = she sings while she works
il sifflait en lavant sa voiture = he was whistling while he was cleaning his car

L'antériorité

en arrivant chez moi, je leur ai téléphoné = when I got back home (*ou* on getting back home), I telephoned them
en la voyant, il rougit = when he saw (*ou* on seeing) her, he blushed

Le déroulement d'une action 'cadre'

en faisant les courses, peux-tu acheter le journal? = while you're doing the shopping, can you buy the paper?
en rangeant, j'ai retrouvé la lettre = while (*ou* as) I was tidying up, I found the letter

La manière

il n'y a pas de traduction systématique:

l'enfant se réveilla en hurlant = the child woke up screaming
il marchait en bombant le torse = he was walking with his chest stuck out

Avec les verbes de mouvement, on optera pour un verbe à particule:

partir/entrer/monter/descendre en courant = to run off/in/up/down

Le moyen

je m'en suis sorti en racontant un mensonge = I got out of it by telling a lie
ouvrez cette caisse en soulevant le couvercle = open this box by lifting the lid
endormir un enfant en lui chantant une berceuse = to sing a child to sleep with a lullaby

Une explication

Dans ce cas, la traduction dépendra de la construction générée par ce qui précède:

elle a fait une erreur en acceptant ce poste = she made a mistake in accepting the job
il a gâché sa vie en l'épousant = he ruined his life by marrying her
il mentait en disant que c'était moi = he was lying when he said it was me

La cause

la cause donnera lieu également à des traductions variées:

il s'est tordu le pied en tombant = he twisted his foot when (*ou* as) he fell
il s'est étranglé en avalant = he choked on his food
elle s'est enrouée en chantant = she made herself hoarse with singing

La condition

tu aurais moins chaud en enlevant ta veste = you'd be cooler (*ou* less hot) if you took your jacket off
en prenant des vitamines, tu serais plus en forme = if you took vitamins you'd feel fitter

Le pronom

en = de lui/d'elle/d'eux/d'elles

en représente un être humain ou un animal familier:

j'en suis content = I am pleased with him/her/them
ils aiment leurs enfants et ils en sont aimés = they love their children and they are loved by them
j'en suis fier (de mes enfants) = I'm proud of them
je connais un bon coiffeur, je t'en donnerai l'adresse = I know a good hairdresser, I'll give you his (*ou* the) address

en représente un animal, un concept, un objet:

j'en suis content = I am pleased with it/them
je m'en souviens = I remember it
deux ans après, on en parlait encore = two years later, we were still talking about it
nous en sommes très peinés = we're very upset about it
j'en suis fier = I'm proud of it
regarde cette robe, j'en aime beaucoup la forme = look at that dress, I like its shape (*ou* the shape of it) a lot

Mais attention, le nom ne se traduit pas toujours littéralement en anglais:

j'ai reçu la facture de téléphone; ça t'intéresserait d'en connaître le montant? = I got the phone bill; would you like to know how much it was for?

Les locutions telles que *en voilà*, *de … en*, *en sorte que*, *en tant que* sont traitées sous ***voilà***, ***de***, ***sorte***, ***tant*** etc.

en représente le lieu d'où l'on vient:

'tu as été voir ta mère?' 'oui, j'en viens' = 'have you been to see your mother?' 'yes, I've just come from there'
il entra dans le café comme j'en sortais = he entered the café as I was coming out

Expression de quantité

en, pronom, peut remplacer des noms dénombrables ou non-dénombrables:

'veux-tu des oranges?' = 'would you like some oranges?'
'oui, j'en veux' = 'yes, I'd like some'
'non, je n'en veux pas' = 'no, I don't want any'
'veux-tu du vin?' = 'would you like some wine?'
'oui, j'en veux' = 'yes, I'd like some'
'non, je n'en veux pas' = 'no, I don't want any'
il en reste encore (des oranges) = there are some left
(du vin) = there is some left
il n'en reste pas beaucoup (des oranges) = there aren't many (of them) left
(du vin) = there isn't much (of it) left
il n'en reste plus (des oranges) = there aren't any left
(du vin) = there isn't any left
prends-en plusieurs = take several *ou* take a few
prends-en un peu = take some
tu as emporté des livres? = have you brought any books?
oui, j'en ai un passionnant = yes, I've got one which is really good
oui, j'en ai deux = yes, I've got two
oui, j'en ai même trop = yes, too many in fact
il n'en a pas lu la moitié (du roman) = he didn't even read half of it
(des articles) = he didn't even read half of them

imitate [*voix, manière*]; **cela emprunte toutes les apparences de la vérité** it has all the appearances of being true; **3** (prendre) to take [*route, chemin, voiture, métro*]; **~ la voix de qn** to speak through sb.

emprunteur, **-euse** /ɑ̃pʀœ̃tœʀ, øz/ **I** *adj* [*organisme, agent*] borrowing the money (*après n*).
II *nm,f* borrower.

empuantir /ɑ̃pɥɑ̃tiʀ/ [3] *vtr* to stink out GB, to stink up US.

empyème /ɑ̃pjɛm/ *nm* empyema.

ému, **~e** /emy/ **I** *pp* ▶ **émouvoir**.
II *pp adj* [*personne*] (attendri) moved; (reconnaissant) touched; (intimidé) nervous; **~ par leur détresse** moved by their plight; **~ par leur générosité** touched by their generosity; **il se sent toujours un peu ~ avant d'entrer en scène** he's always a bit nervous before going on stage; **trop ~s pour exprimer leur gratitude** too overcome to express their gratitude; **une foule ~e et recueillie** a hushed emotional crowd.
III *adj* [*paroles, regard*] full of emotion (*après n*); [*hommage*] warm; [*souvenir*] fond; **il garde un souvenir ~ des gâteaux de sa mère** he has fond memories of his mother's cakes; **d'une voix ~e** with a catch in his/her voice; **regrets/remerciements ~s** heartfelt regrets/thanks.

émulateur /emylatœʀ/ *nm* Ordinat emulator.

émulation /emylasjɔ̃/ *nf* **1** competitiveness, emulation sout; **encourager l'esprit d'~ chez** to encourage a competitive spirit in; **2** Ordinat emulation.

émule /emyl/ *nmf* imitator, emulator; **être l'~ d'un grand maître** to model oneself on ou emulate a great master; **il a fait de nombreux ~s** many people modelled themselves on him.

émuler /emyle/ [1] *vtr* Ordinat to emulate.

émulsifiant, **~e** /emylsifjɑ̃, ɑ̃t/ **I** *adj* emulsifying.
II *nm* emulsifier.

émulsion /emylsjɔ̃/ *nf* emulsion.

émulsionner /emylsjɔne/ [1] *vtr* **1** to emulsify [*liquide*]; **2** Phot to coat [sth] with an emulsion.

en /ɑ̃/ **I** *prép* **1** (lieu) (où l'on est) in; (où l'on va) to; (mouvement vers l'intérieur) into; **vivre ~ France/province/ville** to live in France/the provinces/town; **voyager ~ Chine** to travel in China; **aller ~ Allemagne** to go to Germany; **monter ~ voiture** to get into a car; **aller ~ ville** to go into town; **le train va entrer ~ gare** the train is about to enter the station; **se promener ~ ville** to stroll around town; **2** (temps) (époque) in; (moment déterminé) in; (en l'espace de) in; **~ hiver/1991** in winter/1991; **je prendrai mes vacances ~ septembre** I'm taking my vacation in September; **il a fait ce travail ~ dix jours** he completed the work in ten days; **~ semaine, il mange à la cantine** during the week he eats in the canteen; **3** (moyens de transport) by; **voyager ~ train/avion/voiture/bateau** to travel by train ou rail/plane ou air/car/boat; **je suis venu ~ taxi** I came by taxi; **aller à Marseille ~ avion/voiture** to fly/to drive to Marseilles; **nous avons fait un tour ~ barque** we went out in a rowing-boat; **descendre la rivière ~ aviron** to row down the river; **4** (manière, état) **elle était tout ~ vert/blanc** she was all in green/white; **il est toujours ~ manteau/cravate** he always wears a coat/tie; **un ouvrage ~ vers/français/trois volumes** a work in verse/French/three volumes; **elle était très ~ forme/beauté** she was looking very fit/beautiful; **5** (comme) (en qualité de) as; (de la même manière que) like; **je vous parle ~ ami/connaisseur** I'm speaking (to you) as a friend/connoisseur; **j'ai eu ce livre ~ cadeau/récompense/souvenir** I was given this book as a present/prize/souvenir; **il nous considèrent ~ ennemis** they see us as enemies; **il me traite ~ ennemie** he treats me like an enemy; **agir ~ traître/dictateur** to act like a traitor/dictator, to act in a treacherous/dictatorial way; **6** (transformation) into; **ils se séparèrent ~ plusieurs groupes** they broke up into several groups; **traduire ~ anglais** to translate into English; **changer des francs ~ dollars** to change francs into dollars; **7** (matière) made of; **c'est ~ quoi?** what is it made of?; **c'est ~ or/plastique** it's (made of) gold/plastic; **c'est ~ bois** it's made of wood, it's wooden; **une montre ~ or** a gold watch ; **une veste ~ laine** a woollen[GB] jacket; **le cadre est ~ alliage** the frame is alloy, it's an alloy frame; **8** (pour indiquer une variante) **son fils, c'est lui ~ miniature** his son is just like him only smaller, his son is a smaller version of him; **je voudrais le même ~ plus grand** I'd like the same only bigger; **je voudrais la même ~ bleu** I'd like the same in blue; **9** (indique le domaine, la discipline) in; **~ politique/affaires il faut être rusé** in politics/business you have to be clever; **idée fondamentale ~ droit français** fundamental idea in French law; **~ théorie, c'est exact** in theory, it's correct; **licencié ~ droit** bachelor of law; **docteur ~ médecine** doctor of medicine; **être bon ~ histoire** to be good at history; **10** (mesures, dimensions) in; **compter ~ secondes/années** to count in seconds/years; **les draps se font ~ 90 et ~ 140** the sheets are available in single and double; **le mur fait trois mètres ~ hauteur et six ~ longueur** the wall is three metres[GB] high and six metres[GB] long; **~ profondeur, il y a assez d'espace pour la bibliothèque mais pas ~ hauteur** the space is deep enough for the bookshelves but not high enough; **~ largeur, il y a la place pour une piscine mais pas ~ longueur** widthwise, there's (enough) room for a swimming pool but not lengthwise.

II *pron* **1** (le moyen) **si les abricots sont abîmés, fais-~ de la confiture** if the apricots are bruised make jam with them; **prends cette couverture et couvre-t'~** take this blanket and cover yourself with it; **il sortit son épée et l'~ transperça** he took out his sword and ran him through; **2** (la cause) **ça l'a tellement bouleversé qu'il ~ est tombé malade** it distressed him so much that he fell ill GB ou became sick US; **il a eu un cancer et il ~ est mort** he got cancer and died; **elle a eu un accident de voiture et elle ~ est restée paralysée/infirme** she had a car accident which left her paralysed[GB]/disabled; **3**○ (emphatique) **tu ~ as un beau chapeau!** what a nice hat you've got!; **eh bien! on s'~ souviendra de ce dimanche!** well, we won't forget this Sunday in a hurry!; **je n'~ veux pas de tes excuses**○! I'm not interested in your excuses; **et moi, je n'~ ai pas des soucis, peut-être!** do you think I haven't got worries too!; **j'~ connais qui seraient contents** I know some who would be pleased.

EN /œn/ *nf* **1** *abbr* ▶ **école**; **2** *abbr* ▶ **éducation**.

ENA /ena/ *nf*: *abbr* ▶ **école**.

enamouré, **~e** /ɑ̃namuʀe/ **I** *pp* ▶ **enamourer**.
II *pp adj* [*regard*] amorous; [*mots, air*] loving.

enamourer: **s'enamourer** /ɑ̃namuʀe/ [1] *vpr* to fall in love (**de** with), to become enamoured[GB] littér (**de** of).

énarque /enaʀk/ *nmf* graduate of the ENA.

énarthrose /enaʀtʀoz/ *nf* ball-and-socket joint, enarthrosis spéc.

en-avant /ɑ̃navɑ̃/ *nm inv* (au rugby) knock-on.

encablure /ɑ̃kɑblyʀ/ *nf* Naut cable; **à quelques ~s de là** a few hundred yards away.

encadré, **~e** /ɑ̃kɑdʀe/ **I** *pp* ▶ **encadrer**.
II *pp adj* (supervisé) supervised; **bien/mal ~** poorly/well supervised.
III *nm* Imprim, Presse box; **voir (l')** ~ see (the) box; **~ publicitaire** Pub display ad.

encadrement /ɑ̃kɑdʀəmɑ̃/ *nm* **1** (supervision) supervision; **2** (personnel de supervision) supervisory staff; Entr **(personnel d')~** managerial staff; Mil (officiers) officers (*pl*); **3** Mil (de tir) straddling; **4** Écon control; **~ du crédit/des prix** credit/price control; **5** Art (mise en cadre) framing; (cadre) frame; (tableau) framed picture; **6** Archit framework.

encadrer /ɑ̃kɑdʀe/ [1] **I** *vtr* **1** (superviser) to supervise [*personnel, jeunes, stage, équipe*]; to train [*soldat*]; to contain [*manifestation*]; **2** (entourer) to flank [*personne*]; to frame [*visage, fenêtre, meuble*]; to surround [*vallée*]; **~ de rouge** to outline [sth] in red; **3** Écon (contrôler) to restrict [*crédit*]; to control [*prix*]; **4** Art to frame [*tableau*]; **être à ~**○ hum to be priceless○; **5**○ (percuter) [*voiture*] to crash ou smash○ into [*voiture, portail*]; **se faire ~** to be hit; **6**○ (supporter) to stand; **je ne peux pas l'~** I can't stand him.
II s'encadrer *vpr* **1** (apparaître) to be framed; **s'~ dans une fenêtre** to be framed against a window; **2**○ (percuter sa voiture) to crash one's car (**dans** into).

encadreur /ɑ̃kɑdʀœʀ/ ▶**510** *nm* picture framer.

encager /ɑ̃kaʒe/ [13] *vtr* to cage [*animal*]; to put [sb] behind bars [*personne*].

encagoulé, **~e** /ɑ̃kagule/ *adj* hooded.

encaissable /ɑ̃kɛsabl/ *adj* cashable.

encaisse /ɑ̃kɛs/ *nf* cash in hand.

encaissé, **~e** /ɑ̃kese/ **I** *pp* ▶ **encaisser**.
II *pp adj* [*vallée, rivière*] steep-sided; [*chemin*] cut deep into the hillside (*après n*).

encaissement /ɑ̃kɛsmɑ̃/ *nm* **1** Fin (de cotisation) collection; (de chèque) cashing; (de dividende) receipt; **frais d'~** transaction costs; **2** Géog steeply sided setting.

encaisser /ɑ̃kese/ [1] **I** *vtr* **1** Fin to cash [*somme, chèque*]; to clear [*facture*]; **2**○ (endurer) to take [*but, coups, défaite, situation*]; **je ne peux pas ~ ton frère** I can't stand your brother.
II○ *vi* (résister) to take it; **il sait ~** he can take it.
IDIOMES **~ le coup** to take it all in one's stride.

encaisseur, **-euse** /ɑ̃kɛsœʀ/ *nm,f* collector.

encalminé, **~e** /ɑ̃kalmine/ *adj* becalmed.

encan: **à l'encan** /alɑ̃kɑ̃/ *loc adv* Comm **être à l'~** to be up for auction; **mettre qch à l'~** to put sth up for auction; **vendre qch à l'~** to sell sth to the highest bidder.

encanaillement /ɑ̃kanajmɑ̃/ *nm* slumming ₵.

encanailler: **s'encanailler** /ɑ̃kanaje/ [1] *vpr* [*personne*] to slum it; [*style, ton*] to become vulgar.

encapuchonné, **~e** /ɑ̃kapyʃɔne/ *adj* **des enfants ~s** children with their hoods pulled up.

encart /ɑ̃kaʀ/ *nm* insert.
■ **~ publicitaire** promotional insert.

encarter /ɑ̃kaʀte/ [1] *vtr* to insert.

en-cas /ɑ̃kɑ/ *nm inv* snack.

encastrable /ɑ̃kastʀabl/ *adj* [*four, réfrigérateur*] that can be built in (*épith, après n*); [*lavabo, table de cuisson*] that can be fitted GB ou fit US (*épith, après n*).

encastrement /ɑ̃kastʀəmɑ̃/ *nm* **1** Tech (de four) building in (**de** of); (de lavabo) fitting (**de** of); (dans le sol) sinking (**de** of); **2** Jeux **un puzzle d'~** a lift-out jigsaw puzzle.

encastrer /ɑ̃kastʀe/ [1] **I** *vtr* (entre éléments) to build in [*four, réfrigérateur*]; (sur un plan) to fit [*table de cuisson, lavabo*]; (en retrait) to recess; (dans sol) to sink; **four encastré** built-in oven; **une baignoire encastrée (dans le sol)** a sunken bath; **route encastrée dans la montagne** road set into the mountain; **maison encastrée entre deux immeubles** house hemmed in by ou between two blocks of flats GB ou apartment blocks US.
II s'encastrer *vpr* [*élément*] to fit (**dans** into); **la voiture est venue s'~ sous le camion** the car crashed into the truck ou lorry GB.

encaustique /ɑ̃kɔstik/ *nf* **1** (cire) wax polish; **passer une table à l'~** to wax-polish a table GB, to wax a table; **2** Art (procédé) encaustic painting.

encaustiquer /ɑ̃kɔstike/ [1] *vtr* to wax-polish GB, to wax.

enceindre /ɑ̃sɛ̃dʀ/ [55] *vtr* to encircle (**de** with); **enceint de** encircled by.

enceinte /ɑ̃sɛ̃t/ **I** *adj f* [*femme*] pregnant; **être ~ de trois mois** to be three months pregnant; **être ~ de jumeaux** to be pregnant with twins; **vêtements pour femmes ~s** maternity clothes.
II *nf* **1** (mur) surrounding wall; **~ de fossés/haies** surrounding ditches/hedges; **mur d'~** surrounding wall; **entourer d'une ~** to surround with a wall; **2** (espace) (de prison, ambassade, palais) compound; (de tribunal, d'église) interior; (dans cérémonie, fête) enclosure; **dans l'~ même de l'aéroport** within the airport compound; **l'~ réservée aux personnages officiels** the enclosure reserved for officials; **3** Tech **~ (acoustique)** speaker.
IDIOMES **être ~ jusqu'aux yeux** or **dents** hum to be heavily pregnant.

encens /ɑ̃sɑ̃/ *nm* incense ₵.

encensement /ɑ̃sɑ̃smɑ̃/ *nm* fig showering ₵ of praise (**de** on).

encenser /ɑ̃sɑ̃se/ [1] *vtr* **1** Relig to cense; **2** (flatter) to sing the praises of [*personne*]; to acclaim [*œuvre*]; **le film a été encensé par la critique** the film was acclaimed by the critics.

encenseur, **-euse** /ɑ̃sɑ̃sœʀ, øz/ *nm,f* **1** Relig censer-bearer; **2** (flatteur) flatterer.

encensoir /ɑ̃sɑ̃swaʀ/ *nm* Relig censer.
IDIOMES **donner des coups d'~ à qn** to flatter sb; **savoir manier l'~** to be good at flattery.

encéphale /ɑ̃sefal/ *nm* encephalon.

encéphalique /ɑ̃sefalik/ *adj* brain, encephalic spéc.

encéphalite /ɑ̃sefalit/ ▶**271** *nf* Méd encephalitis.

encéphalogramme /ɑ̃sefalɔgʀam/ *nm* encephalogram; **faire un ~ à qn** to do an encephalogram on sb.

encéphalomyélite /ɑ̃sefalɔmjelit/ ▶**271**

nf **~ myalgique** myalgic encephalomyelitis, ME.

encéphalopathie /ɑ̃sefalɔpati/ *nf* encephalopathy; Vét **~ spongiforme bovine, ESB** Bovine Spongiform Encephalopathy.

encerclement /ɑ̃sɛʀkləmɑ̃/ *nm* surrounding, encirclement; **manœuvre d'~** encircling manoeuvre GB ou maneuver US.

encercler /ɑ̃sɛʀkle/ [1] *vtr* **1** Mil to surround, to encircle [*ville, ennemi*]; **2** (être autour) to be gathered around; **3** (avec un trait) to circle [*chiffre, réponse*].

enchaînement /ɑ̃ʃɛnmɑ̃/ *nm* **1** (d'événements liés entre eux) chain; **~ des idées/erreurs** chain of ideas/mistakes; **~ des causes et des effets** chain of cause and effect; **déclencher un ~ de** to set off a chain of; **2** (suite) sequence; **~ de réponses/de tâches** sequence of answers/of tasks; **~ de scènes/d'arias et de récitatifs** sequence of scenes/of arias and recitatives; **3** (coordination) coordination (**entre** between); **4** Danse, Mus, Sport transition; **travailler ses ~s** to work on smooth transitions.

enchaîner /ɑ̃ʃene/ [1] **I** *vtr* **1** (attacher) to chain up [*personne, animal*]; **~ à** to chain to; **enchaîné à la grille** chained to the railings; **2** (coordonner) to put [sth] together [*idées, mots*]; **3** Danse, Sport to link [*mouvements*]; **4** (soumettre) to enslave [*humanité, peuple*]; to shackle [*presse*].

II *vi* (poursuivre) to go on; **'alors,' enchaîna-t-il** 'so,' he went on; **~ sur l'économie/avec une nouvelle chanson** to move on to the economy/on to a new song.

III s'enchaîner *vpr* **1** (s'attacher) to chain oneself (**à** to); **2** (être coordonné) [*plans, séquences, chapitres*] to follow on; **les plans s'enchaînent mal** the shots do not follow on very well; **à partir de là tout s'est enchaîné** everything followed on from there.

enchanté, ~e /ɑ̃ʃɑ̃te/ **I** *pp* ▶ **enchanter**.

II *pp adj* **1** (heureux) delighted (**de** with; **de faire** to do; **que** that); **~ (de faire votre connaissance)** delighted to meet you, how do you do?; **je suis ~e que tu puisses venir** I am delighted that you can come; **2** (ensorcelé) [*château, forêt*] enchanted.

enchantement /ɑ̃ʃɑ̃tmɑ̃/ *nm* **1** (expérience agréable) delight; **notre séjour a été un ~** our stay was a delight; **2** (état d'âme) delight, rapture; **être dans l'~** to be delighted, to be in raptures; **3** (sortilège) enchantment, spell; **comme par ~** as if by magic.

enchanter /ɑ̃ʃɑ̃te/ [1] *vtr* **1** (faire plaisir à) to delight; **la musique les enchantait** the music was a delight to their ears; **l'idée de te voir m'enchante** I'm delighted at the thought of seeing you; **leur proposition ne m'enchante guère** their offer doesn't exactly thrill me; **2** (ensorceler) to enchant, to put a spell on.

enchanteur, -teresse /ɑ̃ʃɑ̃tœʀ, tʀɛs/ **I** *adj* [*voix*] charming; [*lieu*] magic (*épith*); [*beauté*] enchanting, bewitching.

II *nm,f* **1** (magicien) enchanter/enchantress; **2** (personne charmante) charmer.

enchâssement /ɑ̃ʃasmɑ̃/ *nm* **1** (de pierre précieuse) setting, mounting; **2** Ling embedding.

enchâsser /ɑ̃ʃase/ [1] *vtr* **1** Relig to enshrine [*reliques*]; **2** (dans une monture) to set, mount [*pierre précieuse*]; **3** Ling to embed [*proposition*].

enchère /ɑ̃ʃɛʀ/ **I** *nf* Comm, Jeux (offre) bid; (activité) bidding; **faire une ~** to bid, to make a bid; **pousser l'~ jusqu'à trois millions** to raise the bidding to three million; **pousser les ~s jusqu'à trois millions** to push the bidding up to three million; **les ~s sont ouvertes** the bidding is open; **faire monter les ~s** lit, fig to push up the bidding.

II enchères *nfpl* (vente) auction; **vente aux ~s** auction; **vendre qch aux ~s** to sell sth by auction.

enchérir /ɑ̃ʃeʀiʀ/ [3] *vi* **1** Comm, Jeux to bid; **~ sur qn** to bid more than sb; **~ sur une offre** or **un prix** to make a higher bid; **~ de 50 francs** to raise the bid by 50 francs; **2** (devenir plus cher) to go up in price, to get dearer.

enchérissement /ɑ̃ʃeʀismɑ̃/ *nm* **~ de la vie/du pétrole** rise in the cost of living/in oil prices; **~ des loyers** rent increases (*pl*).

enchérisseur, -euse /ɑ̃ʃeʀisœʀ, øz/ *nm,f* bidder.

enchevêtrement /ɑ̃ʃ(ə)vɛtʀəmɑ̃/ *nm* **1** (de fils, branches, ronces) tangle; (de couloirs, ruelles, souterrains) labyrinth; **2** (de raisonnement, d'idées) muddle; **l'~ d'une intrigue** the twists and turns of a plot.

enchevêtrer /ɑ̃ʃ(ə)vetʀe/ [1] **I** *vtr* **1** lit to tangle [sth] up [*fils, brins de laine, pelotes*] (**dans** in); **2** fig **~ des intrigues** to weave elaborate plots; **être enchevêtré** [*phrases, intrigue*] to be muddled; [*problèmes, affaire*] to be tangled.

II s'enchevêtrer *vpr* **1** [*branches, fils*] to tangle, to get tangled (**dans** in); **2** [*phrases, intrigue, idées*] to become muddled; **3** [*personne*] **s'~ dans** to get tangled up in.

enclave /ɑ̃klav/ *nf* (tous contextes) enclave.

enclavement /ɑ̃klavmɑ̃/ *nm* (situation) enclosure; (processus) enclosing ₵.

enclaver /ɑ̃klave/ [1] *vtr* **1** (enclore) **une région enclavée dans les montagnes** a region enclosed by mountains; **un pays enclavé** a landlocked country; **2** (insérer) to insert.

enclenchement /ɑ̃klɑ̃ʃmɑ̃/ *nm* (de mécanisme) engagement.

enclencher /ɑ̃klɑ̃ʃe/ [1] **I** *vtr* **1** (mettre en train) to launch, to set [sth] in motion; **le processus est maintenant enclenché** the process is now under way; **2** Mécan to set [*minuterie*]; to engage [*mécanisme*]; **laisser une vitesse enclenchée** to leave the car in gear.

II s'enclencher *vpr* **1** (commencer) [*processus, cycle*] to get under way; **2** lit [*mécanisme*] to engage.

enclin, ~e /ɑ̃klɛ̃, in/ *adj* inclined (**à** to; **à faire** to do).

enclitique /ɑ̃klitik/ *adj* enclitic.

enclore /ɑ̃klɔʀ/ [79] *vtr* [*personne, mur, clôture*] to enclose.

enclos /ɑ̃klo/ *nm* gén enclosure; (pour animaux) pen.

enclume /ɑ̃klym/ *nf* Tech, Anat anvil.

IDIOMES **être entre l'~ et le marteau** to be between the devil and the deep blue sea.

encoche /ɑ̃kɔʃ/ *nf* (entaille) notch; (de flèche) nock; **faire une ~ dans** or **sur qch** to make a notch in sth.

encocher /ɑ̃kɔʃe/ [1] *vtr* to make a notch in [*bâton*]; to nock [*flèche*].

encodage /ɑ̃kɔdaʒ/ *nm* (tous contextes) encoding.

encoder /ɑ̃kɔde/ [1] *vtr* (tous contextes) to encode.

encodeur /ɑ̃kɔdœʀ/ *nm* Ordinat encoder.

encoignure /ɑ̃kwaɲyʀ/ *nf* **1** (angle) corner; **2** (placard) corner cupboard; (étagère) set of corner shelves.

encollage /ɑ̃kɔlaʒ/ *nm* (de papier peint) pasting; Imprim gumming.

encoller /ɑ̃kɔle/ [1] *vtr* to paste [*papier peint*]; Imprim to gum.

encolure /ɑ̃kɔlyʀ/ *nf* **1** ▶ **793** (de vêtement) (partie échancrée) neckline; (dimension) collar size; **2** (d'animal) neck; **gagner d'une ~** Turf to win by a neck.

■ **~ américaine** Mode envelope neck.

encombrant, ~e /ɑ̃kɔ̃bʀɑ̃, ɑ̃t/ *adj* **1** [*meuble*] bulky; [*paquet, marchandise, valise*] cumbersome; **2** [*personne, affaire, événement*] troublesome.

encombre: **sans encombre** /sɑ̃zɑ̃kɔ̃bʀ/ *loc adv* without a hitch.

> **encore**
>
> Lorsqu'il signifie *toujours*, *encore* se traduit généralement par *still* dans une phrase affirmative ou interrogative:
>
> *il était encore étudiant quand il s'est marié* = he was still a student when he got married
>
> *habite-t-elle encore ici?* = does she still live here?
>
> *pas encore* se traduit par *not yet*:
>
> *elle n'était pas encore mariée quand elle a eu son premier bébé* = she wasn't yet married when she had her first baby *ou* she was still unmarried when she had her first baby
>
> *il n'est pas encore rentré* = he hasn't come home yet *ou* he still hasn't come home
>
> Dans ce dernier cas, *still* marque l'étonnement ou l'exaspération, alors que *yet* indique un énoncé neutre des faits.
>
> Des exceptions aux traductions fournies ci-dessus et les autres sens de *encore* sont traités ci-dessous.

encombré, ~e /ɑ̃kɔ̃bʀe/ **I** *pp* ▶ **encombrer**.

II *pp adj* **1** [*route, croisement, trottoir, ciel*] congested (**de** with); [*place, pièce, meuble*] cluttered (**de** with); **2** Méd [*organe, voie respiratoire*] obstructed; **3** [*lignes téléphoniques*] blocked; [*standard*] jammed; **4** [*marché*] saturated (**de** with); [*profession*] overcrowded.

encombrement /ɑ̃kɔ̃bʀəmɑ̃/ *nm* **1** (de la circulation) (ralentissement) traffic congestion ₵; (embouteillage) traffic jam; **2** (de standard, fréquences) jamming; **en raison de l'~ des lignes je n'ai pas pu l'avoir** because the telephone lines were blocked I could not reach him; **3** (de voies respiratoires, d'intestin) obstruction; **4** (de pièce, meuble) cluttering; (de couloir, d'escalier, allée) obstruction; (de tribunal, gare) congestion; **5** (de profession) overcrowding; (de marché) saturation; **6** (volume) bulk; **être d'un ~ réduit** to be compact.

encombrer /ɑ̃kɔ̃bʀe/ [1] **I** *vtr* **1** (embarrasser) [*objet, personne*] to clutter up [*pièce, meuble*]; (obstruer) [*objet, personne*] to obstruct [*route, passage, entrée, trottoir*]; **si les enfants vous encombrent** if the children are in your way; **tu m'encombres plus que tu ne me rends service** you are more of a hindrance than a help; **2** [*préoccupation, détails*] to clutter up; **~ de** to clutter up [sth] with [*mémoire, esprit*]; **3** (saturer) to jam [*standard, fréquences*]; to block [*lignes*]; to overcrowd [*profession, activité, université*]; to saturate [*marché*].

II s'encombrer *vpr* lit, fig to burden oneself (**de** with).

encontre: **à l'encontre de** /alɑ̃kɔ̃tʀədə/ *loc prép* **1** (contrairement à) contrary to; **à l'~ des idées reçues, le chinois n'est pas difficile** contrary to general belief, Chinese is not a difficult language; **2** (en opposition à) counter to; **aller à l'~ des principes républicains** to run counter to republican principles; **3** (activement contre) against; **aller à l'~ de la politique gouvernementale** to go against government policy; **imposer des sanctions à l'~ d'un pays** to impose sanctions against a country; **4** (envers) toward(s).

encor‡ = **encore**.

encorbellement /ɑ̃kɔʀbɛlmɑ̃/ *nm* (de fenêtre) corbel; **voûte en ~** corbelled[GB] vault; **maison à ~s** corbelled[GB] house.

encorder: **s'encorder** /ɑ̃kɔʀde/ [1] *vpr* to rope up.

encore /ɑ̃kɔʀ/ **I** *adv* **1** (toujours) still; **je m'en souviens ~** I still remember; **il n'est ~ que midi** it's only midday; **tu en es ~ là?** fig haven't you got GB ou gotten US beyond that by now?; **il se plaignait, ~ et toujours** he was complaining as usual; **hier**

soir ~ elle allait bien only yesterday evening she was fine; **qu'il soit impoli passe ~, mais je n'accepte pas sa méchanceté** the fact that he's rude is one thing, but I won't tolerate his nastiness; **~ heureux** ou **une chance que je m'en sois aperçu** it's lucky that I realized; **2** (toujours pas) **pas ~** not yet; **tu n'as ~ rien vu** you haven't seen anything yet; **cela ne s'est ~ jamais vu/fait** it has never been seen/done before; **je n'ai ~ jamais pu être tranquille ici** up to now, I've never had any peace here; **les abricots ne sont pas ~ mûrs** the apricots aren't ripe yet; **les abricots ne sont pas ~ assez mûrs** the apricots aren't ripe enough yet; **il n'était pas ~ célèbre à cette époque** at that time he wasn't yet famous; **le nom de son remplaçant n'est pas ~ connu** the name of his replacement is still not known; **ce n'est pas ~ de leur âge** they're not old enough yet; **on n'en est pas ~ là** we haven't got to that stage yet; **ce n'est pas ~ sûr** it still isn't definite, it's not definite yet; **3** (de nouveau) again; **les prix ont ~ augmenté** prices have gone up again; **~ toi!** you again!; **elle a ~ gagné/perdu** she has won/lost again; **~ de la purée!** not mashed potatoes again!; **~!** (à un spectacle) encore!; **~ une fois** ou **un coup** once again, one more time; **c'est ~ une histoire d'amour** it's another love story; **qu 'est-ce que j'ai ~ fait?** what have I done now?; **il m'en reste ~ autant à faire** I've still got as much to do again; **j'ai ~ cassé une assiette** I've broken another plate; **elle s'est ~ acheté une nouvelle robe** she has bought herself yet another new dress; **son dernier livre est ~ un roman policier** his/her last book is also a ou is another detective novel; **là ~, fais attention** (à cet endroit aussi) be careful there too ou as well; **là ~, tu dois utiliser le subjonctif** there again, you must use the subjunctive; **ici ~ on retrouve le thème de la mort** here again we find the theme of death; **4** (davantage) more; **j'en veux ~** I want some more; **mange ~ un peu** have some more to eat; **mange ~ un peu d'agneau** have some more lamb; **je vais travailler ~ un peu** I'm going to do a little more work; **tu devrais ~ raccourcir ta robe** you should take your dress up a little more; **cela va ~ aggraver les choses** it's going to make things even worse; **c'est ~ mieux/pire** it's even better/worse; **~ moins/plus** even less/more; **il fait ~ plus froid que d'habitude** it's even colder than usual; **elle est ~ plus grande que moi** she's even taller than me; **5** (en plus) **veux-tu ~ un gâteau?** would you like another cake?; **pendant ~ trois jours** for another three days; **tu as ~ 10 minutes** you've still got 10 minutes, you've got another 10 minutes; **on a ~ 100 km à faire** we (still) have another 100 km to do; **il me reste ~ 500 francs** I've still got 500 francs left; **que dois-je prendre ~?** what else shall I take?; **qu'est-ce qu'il te faut ~?** fig what more do you need ou want?; **et puis quoi ~**○! what next○! ; **quoi ~!** what now!; **qui ~!** who is it now!; **mais ~?** which is to say?; **que dire ~?** what else can be said?; **ou ~** or else; **vous pouvez pratiquer la natation, la plongée sous-marine ou ~ vous initier à la voile** you can swim, go scuba diving, or else learn to sail; **6** (toutefois) **il ne suffit pas d'avoir de bonnes idées, ~ faut-il savoir les exprimer** it's not enough to have good ideas, one must be able to articulate them; **~ faut-il qu'elle accepte** but she still has to accept; **~, s'il voulait travailler, ce serait déjà bien** if he were at least prepared to work, it would be something; **si ~ il était généreux, cela compenserait** if he were at least generous, that would make up for a lot; **7** (seulement) only, just; **il était pratiquement inconnu il y a ~ trois mois** he was practically unknown only ou just three months ago.

II et encore *loc adv* if that; **c'est tout au plus mangeable, et ~!** it's only just edible, if that!; **en voyage, elle n'emporte que sa brosse à dents, et ~!** when she travels, she only takes her toothbrush with her, if that!

III encore que *loc conj* (bien que) even though; **~ qu'il soit jeune, il a déjà beaucoup de talent** even though he's young, he's already very talented; **ce n'est pas mal, ~ que cela pourrait être mieux** it's not bad, but it could still be better.

encorner /ɑ̃kɔʀne/ [1] *vtr* to gore.

encornet /ɑ̃kɔʀnɛ/ *nm* squid.

encoubler /ɑ̃kuble/ [1] H **I** *vtr* (gêner) **tu m'encoubles** you're getting under my feet.

II s'encoubler *vpr* (se prendre les pieds) **s'~ dans qch** to catch one's feet in sth.

encourageant, **~e** /ɑ̃kuʀaʒɑ̃, ɑ̃t/ *adj* encouraging.

encouragement /ɑ̃kuʀaʒmɑ̃/ *nm* encouragement ¢ (**à qch** to sth; **à faire** to do); **d'~** [*parole, cris, sourire*] of encouragement; [*geste*] encouraging; **prodiguer des ~s** to dispense encouragement.

encourager /ɑ̃kuʀaʒe/ [13] *vtr* **1** (pousser) to encourage (**à faire** to do); **2** (de la voix) to cheer [sb] on [*équipe, sportif*].

encourir /ɑ̃kuʀiʀ/ [26] *vtr* fml to incur.

encrage /ɑ̃kʀaʒ/ *nm* inking.

encrassement /ɑ̃kʀasmɑ̃/ *nm* **1** (de filtre, moteur, d'artère) clogging (up); Aut (de bougie) fouling up; **2** (de vêtement, baignoire) dirtying.

encrasser /ɑ̃kʀase/ [1] **I** *vtr* **1** (en obstruant) to clog [sth] (up) [*filtre, moteur, artère*]; to make [sth] sooty [*cheminée*]; **2** (salir) to dirty [*vêtement, baignoire*]; Aut to foul up [*bougie*].

II s'encrasser *vpr* **1** (s'obstruer) [*filtre, moteur, artère*] to clog up; [*cheminée*] to get sooty; **2** (se salir) to get dirty; [*bougie*] to foul up.

encre /ɑ̃kʀ/ *nf* ink; **~ indélébile/invisible** indelible/invisible ink; **~ d'imprimerie** printer's ink; **écrire à l'~** to write in ink.

■ **~ de Chine** Indian ink GB, India ink US; **~ sympathique** invisible ink.

IDIOMES **cela a fait couler beaucoup d'~** a lot of ink has been spilled over this; **c'est écrit de la même ~** this clearly comes from the same pen; **se faire un sang d'~** to be worried stiff; **il faisait une nuit d'~** it was pitch black; **c'est la bouteille à l'~**○ it's as clear as mud○.

encrer /ɑ̃kʀe/ [1] *vtr* to ink.

encreur /ɑ̃kʀœʀ/ *adj m* inking.

encrier /ɑ̃kʀije/ *nm* (encastré) inkwell; (pot) ink pot; (plus décoratif) inkstand.

encroûter○: **s'encroûter** /ɑ̃kʀute/ [1] *vpr* [*personne*] to get in a rut; **il est complètement encroûté dans ses habitudes** he's very set in his ways.

enculé●, **~e** /ɑ̃kyle/ *nm,f* offensive arsehole● GB injur; asshole● US injur.

enculer● /ɑ̃kyle/ [1] *vtr* to bugger●; **allez-vous faire ~** offensive fuck off● injur.

IDIOMES **~ les mouches**● to split hairs.

encuver /ɑ̃kyve/ [1] *vtr* to vat.

encyclique /ɑ̃siklik/ *adj, nf* encyclical.

encyclopédie /ɑ̃siklɔpedi/ *nf* encyclopedia.

encyclopédique /ɑ̃siklɔpedik/ *adj* encyclopedic.

encyclopédiste /ɑ̃siklɔpedist/ *nmf* encyclopedist.

endémie /ɑ̃demi/ *nf* endemic.

endémique /ɑ̃demik/ *adj* [*maladie*] endemic; [*chômage*] endemic, rampant.

endetté, **~e** /ɑ̃dete/ **I** *pp* ▶ **endetter**.

II *pp adj* [*association, hôpital, personne*] in debt (*jamais épith*); [*pays, entreprise*] in debt (*jamais épith*), debtor (*épith*); **être très ~** to be heavily in debt; **être ~ de 10 millions de francs** to be 10 million francs in debt; **être ~ auprès d'une banque** to owe money to a bank.

endettement /ɑ̃dɛtmɑ̃/ *nm* debt; **~ public/extérieur/du tiers-monde** national/foreign/Third World debt; **entraîner l'~ de qn** to put sb in debt; **10 millions de francs d'~** debts of 10 million francs; **le niveau d'~ d'une société** the level of a company's debts.

endetter /ɑ̃dete/ [1] **I** *vtr* to put [sb] into debt.

II s'endetter *vpr* to get into debt (**auprès de** with).

endeuiller /ɑ̃dœje/ [1] *vtr* to plunge [sb] into mourning [*famille, amis*]; to cast a shadow over [*cérémonie, réunion sportive*]; **village/pays endeuillé** griefstricken village/country; **ongles endeuillés** hum dirty fingernails.

endiablé, **~e** /ɑ̃djɑble/ *adj* **1** [*rythme, valse, poursuite*] furious; **2** [*enfant*] boisterous.

endiguement /ɑ̃digmɑ̃/ *nm* **1** (de cours d'eau) confinement; **2** (de manifestants) containment; **3** (de spéculation, révolte, mécontentement) curbing.

endiguer /ɑ̃dige/ [1] *vtr* **1** to confine [*cours d'eau*]; **2** to contain [*manifestants, groupe*]; **3** to curb [*spéculation, mécontentement*].

endimanché, **~e** /ɑ̃dimɑ̃ʃe/ *adj* in one's Sunday best (*après n*).

endive /ɑ̃div/ *nf* chicory ¢ GB, endive US; **~s au jambon** chicory wrapped in ham with a white sauce; **deux ~s** two heads of chicory; **avoir un teint d'~** hum to be as pale as a ghost.

endocarde /ɑ̃dɔkaʀd/ *nm* endocardium.

endocardite /ɑ̃dɔkaʀdit/ **▶271** *nf* endocarditis.

endocarpe /ɑ̃dɔkaʀp/ *nm* endocarp.

endocrine /ɑ̃dɔkʀin/ *adj* endocrine.

endocrinien, -ienne /ɑ̃dɔkʀinjɛ̃, ɛn/ *adj* endocrinal.

endocrinologie /ɑ̃dɔkʀinɔlɔʒi/ *nf* endocrinology.

endocrinologue /ɑ̃dɔkʀinɔlɔg/, **endocrinologiste** /ɑ̃dɔkʀinɔlɔʒist/ **▶510** *nmf* endocrinologist.

endoctrinement /ɑ̃dɔktʀinmɑ̃/ *nm* indoctrination.

endoctriner /ɑ̃dɔktʀine/ [1] *vtr* to indoctrinate.

endoderme /ɑ̃dɔdɛʀm/ *nm* **1** Anat endoderm; **2** Bot endodermis.

endogame /ɑ̃dɔgam/ *adj* endogamous.

endogamie /ɑ̃dɔgami/ *nf* endogamy.

endogène /ɑ̃dɔʒɛn/ *adj* endogenous.

endolori, **~e** /ɑ̃dɔlɔʀi/ **I** *pp* ▶ **endolorir**.

II *pp adj* aching.

endolorir /ɑ̃dɔlɔʀiʀ/ [3] *vtr* to make [sb/sth] ache.

endolymphe /ɑ̃dɔlɛ̃f/ *nf* endolymph.

endomètre /ɑ̃dɔmɛtʀ/ *nm* endometrium.

endométriose /ɑ̃dometʀijoz/ **▶271** *nf* endometriosis.

endommagement /ɑ̃dɔmaʒmɑ̃/ *nm* (action) damaging; (résultat) damage.

endommager /ɑ̃dɔmaʒe/ [13] *vtr* to damage; **le bâtiment a été endommagé à 50%** 50% of the building was damaged.

endomorphe /ɑ̃domɔʀf/ *nmf* endomorph.

endormant, **~e** /ɑ̃dɔʀmɑ̃, ɑ̃t/ *adj* [*travail, film*] mind-numbing.

endormi, **~e** /ɑ̃dɔʀmi/ **I** *pp* ▶ **endormir**.

II *pp adj* **1** Physiol [*personne, animal*] sleeping (*épith*), asleep (*jamais épith*); **enfant ~** sleeping child; **elle paraissait ~e** she seemed to be asleep; **être à moitié ~** to be half asleep; **2** fig [*village, campagne, yeux, cerveau, élève*] sleepy; [*économie, marché*] sluggish; [*public*] lethargic.

III *nm,f* sleepyhead○; **bande d'~s!** you sleepyheads!

endormir /ɑ̃dɔʀmiʀ/ [30] **I** *vtr* **1** (naturellement) [*personne*] to send [sb] to sleep [*enfant*]; (chimiquement) [*personne, substance*] to put [sb] to sleep [*patient*]; **~ un enfant en lui chantant une berceuse** to sing a child to sleep with a lullaby; **~ un enfant**

en le berçant to lull ou rock a child to sleep; **le médecin/l'éther l'a endormie** the doctor/the ether put her to sleep; **2** (donner envie de dormir) [*personne, spectacle, discours*] to send [sb] to sleep [*personne*] (**avec** with); **il va nous ~ avec ses histoires** he is going to send us to sleep with his stories; **3** (tromper) to dupe [*personne, opinion, ennemi*] (**avec** with); **~ l'opposition par des promesses** to dupe the opposition with promises; **se laisser ~ dans une sécurité trompeuse** to be lulled into a false sense of security; **4** (atténuer) to lessen [*vigilance*]; to allay [*soupçon*]; to numb [*faculté*].

II **s'endormir** *vpr* **1** (s'assoupir) to fall asleep; (trouver le sommeil) to get to sleep; **s'~ instantanément/à son bureau/sur un livre** to fall asleep instantly/at one's desk/over a book; **je n'arrivais pas à m'~** I couldn't get to sleep; **2** (se laisser aller) to sit back; **ce n'est pas le moment de nous ~** we shouldn't sit back now; **3** (décéder) fml to pass away.

endormissement /ɑ̃dɔʀmismɑ̃/ *nm* **assurer un ~ rapide** to induce sleep rapidly.

endorphine /ɑ̃dɔʀfin/ *nf* endorphin.

endos /ɑ̃do/ *nm* Fin endorsement.

endoscope /ɑ̃dɔskɔp/ *nm* Méd endoscope.

endoscopie /ɑ̃dɔskɔpi/ *nf* endoscopy.

endoscopique /ɑ̃dɔskɔpik/ *adj* endoscopic.

endosmose /ɑ̃dɔsmoz/ *nf* endosmosis.

endosquelette /ɑ̃doskəlɛt/ *nm* endoskeleton.

endossable /ɑ̃dosabl/ *adj* [*chèque*] endorsable; **non ~** non-endorsable.

endossataire /ɑ̃dosatɛʀ/ *nmf* endorsee.

endossement /ɑ̃dosmɑ̃/ *nm* Fin endorsement.

endosser /ɑ̃dose/ [1] *vtr* **1** (mettre) to put on; **~ l'uniforme/la soutane** to go into the army/the church; **2** (assumer) to take on, shoulder [*responsabilité, risque*]; to shoulder [*conséquence*]; to take on [*rôle*]; to take responsibility for [*erreur, paternité*]; **3** Fin to endorse [*chèque*]; **4** (en reliure) to back [*livre*].

endosseur /ɑ̃dosœʀ/ *nm* Fin endorser.

endossure /ɑ̃dosyʀ/ *nf* (en reliure) backing.

endothermique /ɑ̃dɔtɛʀmik/ *adj* endothermic.

endroit /ɑ̃dʀwa/ I *nm* **1** (lieu) place; **~ calme/idéal** quiet/ideal place; **au bon/mauvais ~** in the right/wrong place; **par ~s** in places; **à quel ~?** where?; **coiffeur/maire de l'~** local hairdresser/mayor; **2** (de tissu, pull) right side; **à l'~** (verticalement) the right way up; (d'un vêtement) the right way round GB ou around US.

II **à l'endroit de** *loc prép* toward(s); **préjugé à l'~ de qn** prejudice toward(s) sb.

enduire /ɑ̃dɥiʀ/ [69] I *vtr* [*personne, machine*] to coat [*surface, objet*] (**de** with).

II **s'enduire** *vpr* **s'~ de** to put [sth] on [*crème*]; **s'~ les mains de crème** to put cream on one's hands.

enduit /ɑ̃dɥi/ *nm* (pour couvrir) coating; (pour boucher) filler.

■ **~ de lissage** surface filler; **~ de rebouchage** filler GB, Spackle® US.

endurable /ɑ̃dyʀabl/ *adj* endurable.

endurance /ɑ̃dyʀɑ̃s/ *nf* **1** (de personne, sportif) stamina; **~ à** resistance to; **2** (de véhicule, moteur, mécanisme) endurance; **épreuve d'~** Aut, Équit endurance race; (pour moto) endurance event; **essai d'~** endurance test.

endurant, **~e** /ɑ̃dyʀɑ̃, ɑ̃t/ *adj* [*personne, sportif*] tough, with stamina (*épith, après n*); [*moteur, véhicule*] hard-wearing.

endurci, **~e** /ɑ̃dyʀsi/ I *pp* ▶ **endurcir**.

II *pp adj* **1** (dur) tough; **assez ~ pour supporter qch** tough enough to endure sth; **2** (invétéré) [*fumeur, joueur, buveur*] inveterate; [*célibataire*] confirmed; [*criminel*] hardened.

endurcir /ɑ̃dyʀsiʀ/ [3] I *vtr* **1** (rendre plus robuste) [*travail, sport*] to strengthen [*corps, caractère*]; **~ qn contre** to build up sb's resistance to; **2** (rendre insensible) [*épreuve, égoïsme*] to harden.

II **s'endurcir** *vpr* **1** (devenir plus robuste) [*corps, caractère*] to become stronger; **2** (devenir insensible) [*cœur, âme*] to become hardened; **s'~ contre** to become inured to.

endurcissement /ɑ̃dyʀsismɑ̃/ *nm* **1** (résistance physique) resistance (**à** to); **2** liter (insensibilité) hardening.

endurer /ɑ̃dyʀe/ [1] *vtr* **1** (supporter physiquement) to endure; **faire ~ qch à qn** to put sb through sth; **2** (tolérer, accepter) to put up with; **~ que qn fasse** to put up with sb doing; **c'est plus que je ne peux ~** it's more than I can bear.

enduro /ɑ̃dyʀo/ I *nm* (épreuve) enduro.

II *nf* (moto) trail bike GB, dirt bike US.

Énée /ene/ *npr* Aeneas.

Énéide /eneid/ *nprf* **l'~** the Aeneid.

énergétique /enɛʀʒetik/ I *adj* **1** Écon energy (*épith*); **besoins/ressources ~s** energy requirements/resources; **politique ~** energy policy; **2** Physiol [*aliment, produit*] high-calorie (*épith*); **aliment peu ~** low-calorie food; **3** Phys energy; **bilan ~** energetics (+ *v sg*).

II *nf* Sci energetics (+ *v sg*).

énergie /enɛʀʒi/ *nf* **1** Écon energy; **consommation/production d'~** energy consumption/production; **faire des économies d'~** to save energy; **encourager les économies d'~** to encourage energy efficiency; **consommer/stocker de l'~** to consume/store energy; **crise de l'~** energy crisis; **2** Phys energy; Tech energy, power; **~ solaire** solar energy; **~ nucléaire** nuclear power ou energy; **~ éolienne** windpower; **~s nouvelles/renouvables** new/renewable energy sources; **3** (force) energy; **plein d'~** full of energy; **dépenser son ~ à faire** to use up one's energy doing; **avec l'~ de la jeunesse** with the energy of youth; **~ créatrice/psychique** creative/psychic energy; **avoir/trouver l'~ de faire** to have/find the energy to do; **mettre toute son ~ à faire qch** to put all one's energy ou energies into doing sth; **avec l'~ du désespoir** driven on by despair; **avec ~** [*travailler*] energetically; [*agir*] forcefully; [*protester*] strongly; **mobiliser toutes les ~s** to mobilize all resources.

énergique /enɛʀʒik/ *adj* **1** (physiquement) [*personne, danse, geste*] energetic; [*poignée de main*] vigorous; [*visage, silhouette*] resolute; **2** fig [*politique, mesure, action*] tough; [*objection, protestation*] strong; [*refus*] firm; [*intervention, tentative*] forceful; [*style*] lively.

énergiquement /enɛʀʒikmɑ̃/ *adv* [*lutter, agir*] forcefully; [*condamner, nier*] emphatically.

énergisant, **~e** /enɛʀʒizɑ̃, ɑ̃t/ I *adj* [*médicament, effet, activité*] energizing; **boisson ~e** energy drink.

II *nm* (stimulant) stimulant.

énergumène /enɛʀgymɛn/ *nmf* **1** (personne exaltée) oddball; **2** (personne inquiétante) suspicious character.

énervant, **~e** /enɛʀvɑ̃, ɑ̃t/ *adj* irritating.

énervé, **~e** /enɛʀve/ I *pp* ▶ **énerver**.

II *pp adj* **1** (irrité) irritated; **2** (agité) nervous, edgy○; **les bêtes sont ~es par l'orage** the thunderstorm makes the animals restless; **cet enfant est ~, il faut qu'il dorme** this child is overexcited, he needs to sleep.

énervement /enɛʀvəmɑ̃/ *nm* **1** (irritation) irritation; **dans un moment d'~** in a moment of exasperation; **2** (agitation) agitation; **elle pleura d'~** she was so on edge that she cried; **il était dans un état d'~ indescriptible** (tendu) his nerves were in shreds; (en colère) he was beside himself with rage.

énerver /enɛʀve/ [1] I *vtr* **1** (agiter) to put [sb] on edge, to make [sb] nervy GB ou nervous; **2** (irriter) **~ qn** to get on sb's nerves, to irritate sb; **tu commences à m'~** you're beginning to get on my nerves.

II **s'énerver** *vpr* to get worked up (**de qch** about sth); **ne nous énervons pas!** let's not get too worked up!; **il s'énerve pour un rien** he gets worked up over nothing.

enfance /ɑ̃fɑ̃s/ *nf* **1** (période) childhood; (de garçon) boyhood; (de fille) girlhood; **la petite ~** early childhood; **2** (enfants) children (*pl*); **3** (début) dawn.

IDIOMES **retomber en ~** to lapse into second childhood; **c'est l'~ de l'art** it's child's play.

enfant /ɑ̃fɑ̃/ *nmf* **1** (jeune être humain) child; (très jeune) Admin, Transp infant; **c'est une ~ terrible** lit she's an unruly child; **l'~ terrible du cinéma français** the enfant terrible of French cinema; **lorsque j'étais ~** when I was a child; **tout ~, je me suis rendu compte**... while still a child, I realized...; **c'est un grand ~** he's such a child; **faire l'~** to act like a child; **un sourire d'~** lit a child's smile; fig a childlike smile; **mes rêves d'~** my childhood dreams; **elle est restée très ~** she is still very childlike; **ce n'est pas une ~ de Marie** she's no angel; **il n'y a plus d'~s!** fig they grow up fast nowadays!; ▶ **vérité**; **2** (fils, fille) child; **~ adoptif/légitime/illégitime** adopted/legitimate/illegitimate child; **être ~ unique** to be an only child; **couple sans ~** childless couple; **c'est un couple sans ~** they have no children; **faire un ~**○ (avoir) to have a child; **faire un ~ à qn**○ to make sb pregnant; **ce roman, c'est son ~** that novel is her baby; **3** (terme d'affection) **mon ~** my child; **bonjour les ~s!** hello children!; **4** (marquant l'origine) child; **un ~ de l'aristocatie/du peuple/de la guerre froide** a child of the aristocracy/of the people/of the Cold War; **c'est une ~ de Nice/de la campagne** she was born and bred in Nice/in the country.

■ **~ de l'amour** love child; **~ bleu** blue baby; **~ de chœur** altar boy; **ce n'est pas un ~ de chœur** fig he's no angel; **~ naturel** natural child; **~ prodige** child prodigy; **~ trouvé** foundling.

enfantement /ɑ̃fɑ̃tmɑ̃/ *nm* liter **1** lit childbirth; **2** fig giving birth (**de** to), bringing to fruition (**de** of).

enfanter /ɑ̃fɑ̃te/ [1] *vtr* lit, fig to give birth to; **tu enfanteras dans la douleur** in sorrow thou shalt bring forth children.

enfantillage /ɑ̃fɑ̃tijaʒ/ *nm* **1** (caprice) **cesse tes ~s!** stop being childish!; **encore un ~!** he's/she's being childish again; **2** (défaut) childishness.

enfantin, **~e** /ɑ̃fɑ̃tɛ̃, in/ *adj* **1** (simple) simple, easy; **c'est d'une simplicité ~e** it's child's play; **2** (d'un enfant) [*geste*] childish; **les émotions/amitiés ~es** children's emotions/friendships; **3** (pour enfant) [*classe*] infant GB, for young children; **mode ~e** children's fashion; **4** (digne d'un enfant) [*homme, sourire, style*] childish péj, childlike.

enfarger: **s'enfarger** /ɑ̃faʀʒe/ [13] *vpr* C (trébucher) **s'~ dans qch** to catch one's foot in sth; **s'~ dans sa phrase** to get one's words mixed up.

enfariné, **~e** /ɑ̃faʀine/ *adj* **1** (saupoudré de farine) covered with flour; **2** (poudré) [*visage*] powdered; **un Pierrot au visage ~** a white-faced Pierrot.

IDIOMES **arriver la gueule ~e**◐ to come in looking like the cat that got the cream.

enfer /ɑ̃fɛʀ/ *nm* **1** Relig Hell; Mythol **les ~s** Hell, the Underworld; **croire à l'~** to believe in Hell; **aller en ~** to go to Hell; **la descente aux ~s** the descent into Hell ou the Underworld; **~ et damnation!** hell and damnation!; **2** fig hell (**de** of); **un ~ de souffrance** a living hell; **il vit un véritable ~** his life is sheer hell; **l'~ des villes** the hell of urban life; **l'~ de la guerre/drogue** the hell of war/drug addiction; **c'est l'~**○ **ce travail!** this work is hell○!; **vision d'~**

vision of hell, hellish sight; **vitesse d'~** hellish pace; **aller/conduire à un train d'~** to go/drive hell for leather○; **il fait une chaleur d'~** it's as hot as hell○; **voiture/soirée d'~**○ hell of a○ car/party; **3**† (section de bibliothèque) private case collection. IDIOMES **croix de bois croix de fer, si je mens je vais en ~** ≈ cross my heart and hope to die; ▶ **paver**.

enfermement /ɑ̃fɛʀməmɑ̃/ *nm* imprisonment, detention.

enfermer /ɑ̃fɛʀme/ [1] **I** *vtr* **1** (dans un lieu) to shut [sth] in [*animal*]; (à clé) to lock [sth] up [*argent, bijou*] (**dans** in); to lock [sb] up, to put [sb] away○ [*criminel, aliéné*] (**dans** in); **garder son sac enfermé dans un tiroir** to keep one's bag locked in a drawer; **elle est bonne à ~**○ she's stark raving mad○, she ought to be locked up; **2** (bloquer) **~ qn dans un rôle** to confine sb to a role; **~ qn dans une situation** to trap sb in a situation; **~ qn dans un dilemme** to put sb in a dilemma; **se laisser ~ dans une position** to get oneself into a corner; **se laisser ~ dans un piège** to get trapped; **être enfermé dans une image** to be a prisoner of one's image; **être enfermé dans le cycle du chômage** to be locked into a pattern of unemployment; **3** (contenir) **~ une théorie en une seule formule** to encapsulate a theory in a single formula; **~ une notion dans un cadre contraignant** to impose a restrictive framework on an idea; **4** Mil, Sport to box [sb] in [*adversaire*]; **se laisser ~** to get boxed in.

II s'enfermer *vpr* **1** gén to lock oneself in; (pour s'isoler) to shut oneself away; (accidentellement) to get locked in; **il s'enferme dans sa chambre pour travailler** he shuts himself in his room to work; **j'ai failli m'~ dans la cave** I nearly got locked in the cellar; **tu ne vas pas t'~ tout l'été!** I hope you're not going to spend the whole summer cooped up indoors!; **ne reste pas enfermé toute la journée!** don't stay cooped up indoors all day!; **ça fait deux heures qu'ils sont enfermés dans le bureau à discuter** they've been closeted in the study for two hours; **2** (se confiner) **s'~ dans** to retreat into; **s'~ dans le cynisme** to retreat into cynicism; **s'~ dans le mutisme** to remain obstinately silent; **s'~ dans ses préjugés** to be stubbornly prejudiced; **s'~ dans ses positions** to be completely intransigent; **être enfermé dans ses pensées** to be wrapped up in one's own thoughts.

enferrer: **s'enferrer** /ɑ̃feʀe/ [1] *vpr* **1** fig to tie oneself up in knots; **s'~ dans des mensonges/une déposition** to get tangled up in lies/a statement; **2** lit [*personne*] to impale oneself (**sur, à** on); [*poisson*] to swallow the hook.

enfiévré, ~e /ɑ̃fjevʀe/ **I** *pp* ▶ **enfiévrer**.
II *pp adj* [*imagination*] fevered (*épith*); [*atmosphère*] feverish; [*discours*] fiery.

enfiévrer /ɑ̃fjevʀe/ [14] *vtr* to excite, to stir up [*population, esprits*].

enfilade /ɑ̃filad/ *nf* **1** (de pièces) succession; (de maisons, tables) row; **six pièces en ~** six rooms leading into each other; **appartement en ~** interconnecting flat GB, railroad apartment US; **maison en ~** interconnecting house GB, shotgun house US; **prendre en ~** Mil to rake, to enfilade spéc; **2** Archit enfilade.

enfiler /ɑ̃file/ [1] **I** *vtr* **1** (mettre) to slip on; **~ un pull à qn** to slip a pullover on sb; **~ des bracelets** to slip on some bracelets; **2** to thread [*fil, aiguille*]; **~ qch sur** to thread sth onto; **3** (entrer dans) to take [*couloir, rue*]; **4** péj (dire) to spout [*phrases*]; **5**● (forniquer avec) to screw●.
II s'enfiler *vpr* **1**○ (avaler) to guzzle down○ [*apéritifs, gâteaux*]; fig to devour [*roman policier*]; **2**○ (faire) to get landed○ with [*corvée*]; **3** (entrer) **s'~ dans** [*couloir, rue*] to take.

enfin /ɑ̃fɛ̃/ *adv* **1** (en dernier lieu) (dans un développement, un discours) finally; (dans une énumération) lastly; **je montrerai, ~, que ces deux systèmes sont compatibles** I will show, finally, that these two systems are compatible; **~ et surtout** last but not least; **2** (marquant le soulagement) at last; **~ seuls!** alone at last!; **j'ai ~ terminé mon travail** I've finished my work at last; **3** (marquant la résignation) (oh) well; **~, puisque tu y tiens** oh well, as you insist; **c'est triste, mais ~, on n'y peut rien** it's sad but, well, we can't do anything about it; **il n'a pas décoléré de la journée, ~ passons, ça ira mieux demain** he's been in a temper all day, anyway, things will be better tomorrow; **4** (marquant l'impatience) for heaven's sake; **vas-tu te taire, ~!** for heaven's sake, can't you be quiet!; **mais ~, cessez de vous disputer!** for heaven's sake, stop arguing!; **5** (en d'autres termes) in short, in other words; **il est intelligent, travailleur, ~ il a tout pour réussir** he's intelligent, hard-working, in short he's got what it takes to succeed; **il y avait mes parents, mes frères et mes cousins, ~ toute la famille** my parents were there, my brothers and cousins, the whole family in fact; **6** (introduit un correctif) well, at least; **il pleut tous les jours, ~ presque** it rains every day, well almost; **elle n'est pas mariée, ~ je crois** she is not married, at least I don't think so; **7** (tout bien considéré) **car ~, mais ~** after all; **8** (marquant la perplexité) **(mais) ~, que signifie toute cette histoire?** what on earth does it all mean?; **(mais) ~, pourquoi n'est-il pas encore arrivé?** why on earth isn't he here yet?; **(mais) ~, c'est incroyable une aventure pareille!** well ou why, I've never heard anything like it!

enflammé, ~e /ɑ̃flame/ **I** *pp* ▶ **enflammer**.
II *pp adj* **1** lit [*forêt, objet, maison*] burning; **2** fig [*personne, déclaration, regard, baiser*] passionate; [*discours*] impassioned, fiery; **~ de** burning with; **3** Méd [*gorge, blessure*] inflamed; [*front, joues*] burning (**par** with); **4** liter (rouge) [*joues, visage*] burning (**de** with); [*ciel*] ablaze (*jamais épith*), blazing.

enflammer /ɑ̃flame/ [1] **I** *vtr* **1** (mettre le feu à) to set fire to [*objet, matériau*]; **2** (exciter) to inflame [*opinion publique, esprit, cœur*]; to fire [*imagination*]; to fuel [*colère*]; (faire rougir) **la fièvre enflammait ses joues** her cheeks were burning with fever; liter **le soleil couchant enflammait le ciel** the sunset set the sky ablaze.
II s'enflammer *vpr* **1** (prendre feu) [*maison, voiture, papier*] to go up in flames; [*essence, bois*] to catch fire; **cela s'enflamme très facilement** it catches fire very quickly; **2** (s'exciter) [*regard*] to blaze; [*esprit, imagination, cœur*] to be fired (**de** with; **à la vue de** by); [*pays, peuple*] to explode; **s'~ pour qn** to become passionate about sb; **s'~ pour qch** to get carried away by sth; **M. Martin s'enflamme, expliquant que...** Mr Martin gets carried away, explaining that...

enflé, ~e /ɑ̃fle/ **I** *pp* ▶ **enfler**.
II *pp adj* **1** lit [*poignet, jambe*] swollen; **2** [*style*] bombastic.
III◑ *nm* bastard◑.

enfler /ɑ̃fle/ [1] **I** *vtr* **1** fig to exaggerate [*récit, événements*]; **~ la voix** to raise one's voice; **2** lit [*vent*] to swell [*voiles*]; [*crues, dégel*] to swell [*eaux, rivière*].
II *vi* **1** lit [*partie du corps*] to swell (up); [*rivière, mer*] to swell; **ma cheville a beaucoup enflé** my ankle has swollen (up) a lot; **2** fig [*rumeur, colère*] to spread.
III s'enfler *vpr* [*colère*] to mount; [*voix, son*] to rise; [*rumeur*] to grow.
IDIOMES **avoir les chevilles qui enflent**○ to be swollen headed○.

enflure /ɑ̃flyʀ/ *nf* **1** Méd swelling; **2**◑ bastard◑.

enfoiré●, ~e /ɑ̃fwaʀe/ *nm,f* arsehole● GB, asshole● US.

enfoncé, ~e /ɑ̃fɔ̃se/ **I** *pp* ▶ **enfoncer**.
II *pp adj* **1** (défoncé) [*siège, lit*] sagging; **2** (rentré) [*yeux*] deep-set; **avoir les yeux ~s (dans les orbites)** to have deep-set eyes; **avoir la tête ~e dans les épaules** to have one's shoulders hunched up.

enfoncement /ɑ̃fɔ̃smɑ̃/ *nm* **1** (creux) (dans un mur) recess; (sur un terrain) dip; **2** Méd crushing **¢**; **~ de la cage thoracique** crushing of the rib cage; **3** Mil (déroute) collapse; **4** (enlisement) **l'~ du pays dans la récession** the country's slide into recession.

enfoncer /ɑ̃fɔ̃se/ [12] **I** *vtr* **1** (faire entrer sans outil) to push in [*piquet, bouchon, pièce de machine*]; **~ un bouchon dans une bouteille** to push a cork into a bottle; **enfonce bien le bouchon** push the cork in tight; **n'enfonce pas trop le piquet** don't push the peg in too far; **enfonce bien la punaise** push the drawing pin in hard; **~ un poignard dans le ventre de qn** to plunge a dagger into sb's stomach; **~ ses mains dans ses poches** to dig one's hands into one's pockets; **~ son mouchoir dans sa poche** to stuff one's handkerchief into one's pocket; **~ son chapeau jusqu'aux yeux/oreilles** to pull one's hat down over one's eyes/ears; **~ une épingle dans une poupée** to stick a pin into a doll; **~ son doigt** to stick one's finger (**dans** into); **~ le coude dans les côtes de qn** to elbow sb in the ribs; **~ sa tête dans un coussin** to bury one's head in a cushion; **2** (faire entrer avec un outil) to knock [sth] in [*clou, piquet*]; **~ un clou/un piquet dans qch** to knock a nail/a post into sth; **n'enfonce pas trop le piquet** don't knock the peg in too far; **enfonce bien les clous** knock the nails in well; **3** (faire céder) to break down [*porte, barrière*]; to break through [*lignes adverses*]; (accidentellement) to crash through [*obstacle*]; to break [*cage thoracique*]; to smash in [*aile de voiture*]; **l'avant du camion est enfoncé** the front of the truck ou lorry GB is smashed in; **~ des portes ouvertes** fig to state the obvious; **4** (vaincre) to defeat [*armée, bataillon*]; to beat [*concurrent, concurrence*]; **5** (abaisser) **ne m'enfonce pas davantage** don't rub it in; **6** (pousser) **~ qn dans la dépression** to make sb even more depressed.
II *vi* (s'enliser) to sink; **~ dans le sable** to sink into the sand.
III s'enfoncer *vpr* **1** (s'enliser) **s'~ dans la neige/le sable** [*personne, véhicule*] to sink in the snow/the sand; **on s'enfonce dans ces fauteuils!** you sink right into these armchairs!; **il s'enfonça dans son fauteuil** he sank back into his armchair; **être enfoncé dans un fauteuil** (confortablement) to be settled cosily GB ou cozily US in an armchair; **s'~ dans la récession** to sink deeper and deeper into recession; **s'~ dans ses pensées** to become lost in thought; **s'~ dans l'erreur** to make error after error; **2** (couler) **s'~ dans l'eau** [*navire, objet*] to sink; **3** (pénétrer) **les piquets s'enfoncent facilement** the posts go in easily; **le poignard s'enfonça dans sa chair** the dagger went deep into the flesh; **4** (se mettre) **s'~ une épine dans le doigt** to get a thorn in one's finger; **5** (aller) **s'~ dans la forêt** to go into the forest; (plus loin) to go further into the forest; **s'~ dans la campagne/le désert** to go right out into the country/the desert; **s'~ dans le brouillard** to disappear into the fog; **s'~ dans le lointain** to disappear into the distance; **s'~ dans les** or **à l'intérieur des terres** to go inland; **6** (se creuser) [*chaussée, terre*] to give way; **7**○ (aggraver son cas) to make things worse for oneself.
IDIOMES **~ qch dans le crâne**○ or **la tête de qn** to get sth into sb's head; **enfonce-toi bien ça dans le crâne**○ or **la tête** get that into your head once and for all.

enfouir /ɑ̃fwiʀ/ [3] **I** *vtr* **1** (enterrer) to bury [*trésor, déchets*]; **2** (dissimuler) **~ son visage dans les coussins** to bury one's face in the cushions; **~ qch dans un sac/tiroir** (sans soin) to shove sth into a bag/drawer;

(avec soin) to tuck sth away in a bag/drawer; **~ ses mains dans ses poches** to shove one's hands into one's pockets; **village enfoui dans la forêt** village buried in the forest.

II s'enfouir *vpr* **1** (se blottir) **s'~ sous les couvertures** to burrow under the blankets; **2** (s'enterrer) to bury oneself (**dans** in).

enfouissement /ɑ̃fwismɑ̃/ *nm* burying (**de** of).

enfourcher /ɑ̃fuʀʃe/ [1] *vtr* to mount [*cheval*]; to get on [*moto, bicyclette*].

enfourner /ɑ̃fuʀne/ [1] **I** *vtr* **1** (pour cuire) Culin to put [sth] in the oven [*pain, rôti*]; Tech to put [sth] in the kiln [*émaux, poterie*]; **2**○ (manger) to stuff down; **3**○ (introduire) **~ qch dans** to stuff sth into.

II s'enfourner○ *vpr* **s'~ dans/sous** to dive into/under.

enfreindre /ɑ̃fʀɛ̃dʀ/ [55] *vtr* to infringe, to break.

enfuir: **s'enfuir** /ɑ̃fɥiʀ/ [9] *vpr* **1** lit [*animal, écolier*] to run away (**de** from); [*oiseau*] to fly away; (d'un lieu clos) to escape (**de** from); **s'~ à Paris** to run off to Paris; **s'~ dans sa chambre** to rush off to one's bedroom; **s'~ vers la frontière** to make off toward(s) the border; **s'~ par les toits/par la porte de derrière** to escape over the rooftops/through the back door; **s'~ à toutes jambes** to run away as fast as one can; **2** fig [*temps, jeunesse*] to fly.

enfumer /ɑ̃fyme/ [1] *vtr* **1** to fill [sth] with smoke [*pièce*]; **tu nous enfumes avec tes cigares!** you're smoking us out with your cigars!; **une pièce enfumée** a smoke-filled room; **2** Chasse to smoke [sth] out [*animal, terrier*].

engagé, **~e** /ɑ̃gaʒe/ **I** *pp* ▶ **engager**.

II *pp adj* [*écrivain, littérature*] (politically) committed.

III *nm,f* enlisted man/woman.

■ **~ volontaire** Mil volunteer.

engageant, **~e** /ɑ̃gaʒɑ̃, ɑ̃t/ *adj* [*personne, manières*] welcoming; [*offre*] attractive; [*plat*] inviting, tempting; **ce n'est pas très ~ comme endroit** it's not a very inviting spot.

engagement /ɑ̃gaʒmɑ̃/ *nm* **1** (promesse) commitment; **~ moral/solennel** moral/solemn commitment; **~s financiers** financial commitments; **prendre un ~** to make a commitment; **prendre l'~ de faire** to undertake to do; **l'~ pris par la direction de faire** the management's undertaking to do; **remplir ses ~s** to honour[GB] one's commitments; **ne pas honorer** or **respecter** or **tenir ses ~s** to fail to honour[GB] one's commitments; **sans ~ de votre part** Jur with no obligation on your part; **2** (participation) involvement; **mon ~ dans la politique/le projet** my involvement in politics/the project; **3** Mil (fait de s'engager) enlistment; (durée) enlistment; (combat) engagement; **un ~ de trois ans** a three-year enlistment; **4** (contrat) engagement; **avoir plusieurs ~s** [*acteur, chanteur*] to have several engagements; **5** (pendant l'accouchement) engagement.

■ **~ contractuel** contractual obligation; **~ à l'essai** employment on a trial basis; **~ politique** political commitment; **~ volontaire** volunteering.

engager /ɑ̃gaʒe/ [13] **I** *vtr* **1** (recruter) to hire [*personnel*]; to enlist [*soldat*]; to engage [*orchestre, danseur*]; **~ qn comme secrétaire** to hire sb as secretary; **2** (commencer) to begin [*politique de réforme, processus*]; **~ des négociations** gén to begin negotiations; (commencer à participer à) to enter into negotiations; **c'est lui qui a engagé la conversation** he started the conversation; **nous avons engagé la conversation** we struck up a conversation; **savoir ~ la conversation avec des gens que l'on ne connaît pas** knowing how to strike up a conversation with strangers; **~ le combat** to go into combat; **~ la partie** (au football) to kick off; **~ une action judiciaire** to take legal action; **3** (obliger) to commit [*personne*]; **cela ne t'engage à rien** this doesn't commit you to anything; **le fait de venir ne t'engage pas** you're not committing yourself by coming; **votre signature vous engage** your signature is binding; **4** (mettre en jeu) to stake [*réputation, honneur*]; **~ sa parole** to give one's word; **5** (introduire) **~ qch dans** to put sth in; **~ la clé dans la serrure** to put the key in the lock; **la clé est mal engagée** the key has gone in askew; **6** (amener) **~ une voiture dans une petite route** to take a car into a country road; **~ un bateau dans un chenal** to take a boat up a channel; **la voiture était déjà engagée dans le carrefour/sur le pont** the car was already in the middle of the intersection/on the bridge; **~ son pays dans une voie difficile** to take one's country along a difficult road; **~ son pays sur la voie des réformes** to commit one's country to a programme[GB] of reform; **7** Écon to lay out [*capitaux*]; **~ des dépenses** to undertake expenditure; **8** (exhorter) **~ qn à faire** to urge sb to do; (conseiller) **~ qn à faire** to advise sb to do; **9** Mil, Sport **~ qn dans une compétition** to enter sb for a competition; **~ des troupes dans une bataille** to commit troops to battle; **10** (donner en gage) to pawn [*objet précieux*].

II s'engager *vpr* **1** (promettre) to promise (**à faire** to do); **elle s'est engagée à fond** she is fully committed; **avant de m'~ plus avant** before committing myself further; **s'~ à financer qch** to undertake to finance sth; **s'~ solennellement à faire** to undertake solemnly to do; **s'~ sur l'honneur à faire** to undertake on one's word of honour[GB] to do; **s'~ vis-à-vis de qn** to take on a commitment to sb; **2** (entreprendre) **s'~ dans des négociations/des études/un projet** to embark on negotiations/studies/a project; **s'~ dans une lutte contre la dictature** to take up the fight against dictatorship; **s'~ dans la bataille** to go into action; **s'~ dans des dépenses** to incur expenses; **3** (s'impliquer) to get involved; **s'~ dans diverses organisations politiques** to get involved in various political organizations; **4** (pénétrer) **s'~ sur une route/dans un tunnel** to go into a road/a tunnel; **s'~ sur un pont** to go onto a bridge; **s'~ dans la forêt** to enter the forest; **avant de s'~ dans un carrefour** before going across an intersection; **une fois que la voiture s'est engagée sur un pont** once the car is on a bridge; **5** (être amorcé) [*action judiciaire, processus, négociations*] to begin; **le combat s'engagea à l'aube** combat began at dawn; **la conversation s'engagea** we/they struck up a conversation; **6** (se faire recruter) **s'~ dans l'armée/la police** to join the army/the police; **il s'est engagé** he has joined up; **s'~ comme secrétaire** to get a job as a secretary; **'engagez-vous'** Mil 'enlist today'; **s'~ dans une compétition** to enter a competition.

engazonner /ɑ̃gazɔne/ [1] *vtr* to turf [*terrain, stade*].

engeance† /ɑ̃ʒɑ̃s/ *nf* pej breed; **ils sont tous de la même ~** they're all of the same breed.

engelure /ɑ̃ʒlyʀ/ *nf* chilblain (**à** on); **avoir des ~s aux pieds** to have chilblains on one's feet.

engendrement /ɑ̃ʒɑ̃dʀəmɑ̃/ *nm* procreation.

engendrer /ɑ̃ʒɑ̃dʀe/ [1] *vtr* **1** (provoquer) to engender [*malaise, mépris*]; **2** Ling, Math to generate; **3** fml (mettre au monde) to beget‡ [*fils, enfant*].

engin /ɑ̃ʒɛ̃/ *nm* **1** (machine, objet, instrument) device; **~ de chasse/pêche** hunting/fishing device; **qu'est-ce que c'est que cet ~**○**?** what's that contraption?; **2** Constr, Transp (véhicule) vehicle; (grosse machine) piece of equipment; **~s de levage/manutention** lifting/handling equipment; **~ de terrassement** earth-moving vehicle; **3** Mil (missile) missile; (bombe) device; (véhicule) vehicle; (matériel du génie) equipment ¢; **~s de guerre** weapons of war.

englober /ɑ̃glɔbe/ [1] *vtr* to include.

engloutir /ɑ̃glutiʀ/ [3] *vtr* **1** (faire disparaître) [*mer, séisme, tempête, nuit, brouillard*] to engulf, to swallow up; **2**○ (dévorer) to gulp [sth] down, to wolf [sth] (down); **3** (dépenser) [*personne, pays*] to squander [*argent, somme*]; (coûter) [*projet, affaire*] to swallow up [*argent, somme*]; **~ sa fortune dans un projet** to sink one's fortune into a project.

engloutissement /ɑ̃glutismɑ̃/ *nm* swallowing up; **ils n'ont rien pu faire contre l'~ du pétrolier** they could do nothing to prevent the tanker from being swallowed up.

engluer /ɑ̃glye/ [1] **I** *vtr* (pour attraper) to lime [*branche, oiseau*].

II s'engluer *vpr* **s'~ dans qch** [*personne*] to become bogged down in sth [*détails*].

engoncé, **~e** /ɑ̃gɔ̃se/ *adj* **je me sens ~ dans cette veste** I feel really restricted in this jacket; **il était ~ dans une veste trop étroite** he was squeezed into a tight jacket.

engorgement /ɑ̃gɔʀʒəmɑ̃/ *nm* **1** (de canalisation) blocking (**de** of); (de route) congestion (**de** of), blocking (up) (**de** of); **un ~ du marché** a glut of products on the market; **2** Méd (d'organe) congestion (**de** of).

engorger /ɑ̃gɔʀʒe/ [13] **I** *vtr* **1** (boucher) to block (up), to clog (up) [*canalisation, tuyauterie*]; **2** (bloquer) to clog up [*routes*]; **un réseau de transports engorgé** an overloaded transport system; **3** Comm to glut [*marché*]; **4** Méd to congest [*organe*].

II s'engorger *vpr* [*canalisation*] to be blocked (up), to be clogged (up); [*route*] to be blocked (up); [*ville, carrefour*] to be blocked (up).

engouement /ɑ̃gumɑ̃/ *nm* **ton ~ pour** your passion for [*musique rock, cinéma fantastique*]; **un ~ pour qn** an infatuation for sb; **l'~ du public pour** the general craze for.

engouer: **s'engouer** /ɑ̃guwe/ [1] *vpr* **s'~ de qn/qch** to become infatuated with [*personne*]; to develop a passion for [*artiste, peinture, musique*].

engouffrer /ɑ̃gufʀe/ [1] **I** *vtr* **1**○ (manger) to gobble up [*plat, nourriture*]; **2** (dépenser) [*personne, pays*] to sink; (coûter) [*projet, affaire*] to swallow up; **~ une fortune dans qch** to sink a fortune into sth; **3** (mettre) to stuff (**dans** into); **4** (faire disparaître) [*mer, nuit*] to engulf.

II s'engouffrer *vpr* **1** lit (dans pièce, passage) [*vent, eau, personne*] to rush (**dans** in; **sous** under; **entre** between); (dans taxi, métro) [*personne*] to dive (**dans** into); **2** fig **s'~ dans** (pour en profiter) to rush to take advantage of; (pour combler un vide) to rush into; **s'~ dans une brèche** to take advantage of a loophole.

engoulevent /ɑ̃gulvɑ̃/ *nm* nightjar.

engourdi, **~e** /ɑ̃guʀdi/ **I** *pp* ▶ **engourdir**.

II *pp adj* (ankylosé, transi) [*membre, doigt*] numb (**par, de** with); (somnolent) [*personne, abeille*] drowsy; fig [*campagne, ville*] sleepy, drowsy; (hébété) [*cerveau, esprit*] dull(ed) (**par** with); **j'ai la jambe ~e** my leg has gone numb ou has gone to sleep.

engourdir /ɑ̃guʀdiʀ/ [3] **I** *vtr* **1** (rendre gourd) to make [sb/sth] numb [*personne, membre*]; **2** (endormir) to make [sb/sth] drowsy [*personne, esprit, abeille*]; to deaden [*douleur*]; **3** (hébéter) to dull [*esprit*]; **le confort/l'oisiveté engourdit** comfort/idleness makes you soft○.

II s'engourdir *vpr* [*membre*] to go numb, to go to sleep; [*corps*] to go numb; [*cerveau, intelligence*] to grow ou become dull.

engourdissement /ɑ̃guʀdismɑ̃/ *nm* **1** (état) (physique) numbness; (mental) (torpeur) drowsiness; (affaiblissement) dullness; **se**

laisser gagner par l'~ to be overcome by drowsiness; **2** (action) (du corps) numbing; (de l'esprit) dulling.

engrais /ɑ̃gʀɛ/ *nm* (animal) manure; (chimique) fertilizer; **~ naturel** natural fertilizer; **mettre un animal à l'~** to fatten an animal.

engraissage /ɑ̃gʀɛsaʒ/ *nm*, **engraissement** /ɑ̃gʀɛsmɑ̃/ *nm* (de bétail) fattening.

engraisser /ɑ̃gʀese/ [1] **I** *vtr* **1** (en élevage) to fatten [*bétail*]; **2** (amender) to fertilize [*sol*]; **3**○ fig (enrichir) to make [sb] rich.
II *vi* (grossir) to get fat.
III s'engraisser○ *vpr* (s'enrichir) to grow fat○; **s'~ de qch** to grow fat on sth; **s'~ sur le dos de qn** to grow fat off sb's back; **s'~ aux dépens de qn** to grow fat at sb's expense.

engramme /ɑ̃gʀam/ *nm* engram.

engrangement /ɑ̃gʀɑ̃ʒmɑ̃/ *nm* (de récolte) gathering in (**de** of).

engranger /ɑ̃gʀɑ̃ʒe/ [13] *vtr* **1** Agric to gather in, to garner sout [*récolte*]; **2** (garder en réserve) to store [*données, information*]; to store up [*souvenirs, expérience*]; to store up [*argent*].

engrenage /ɑ̃gʀənaʒ/ *nm* **1** Mécan gears (*pl*); **l'~ ne fonctionne plus** the gears aren't working any more; **~ cylindrique/hélicoïdal/conique/à vis sans fin** epicyclic/helical/bevel/worm gear; **l'étude des ~s** the study of gearing; **2** fig (de violence, difficultés) spiral; **mettre le doigt dans l'~ (de qch)**, **être pris dans l'~ (de qch)** to get caught up in a spiral (of sth).

engrener /ɑ̃gʀəne/ [16] **I** *vtr* Agric to feed grain into [*machine*].
II *vi* Mécan **~ avec** to engage with.
III s'engrener *vpr* Mécan to engage with each other.

engrosser◑ /ɑ̃gʀose/ [1] *vtr* pej to get [sb] pregnant; **se faire ~** to get oneself pregnant.

engueulade◑ /ɑ̃gœlad/ *nf* **1** (dispute) row (**avec** with; **entre** between); **2** (réprimande) **une ~** a telling off; **après trois ~s** after having been told off three times.

engueuler◑ /ɑ̃gœle/ [1] **I** *vtr* to tell [sb] off [*enfant*]; to give [sb] an earful○ [*adulte*]; **se faire ~** to get told off (**par** by), to get an earful○ (**par** from).
II s'engueuler *vpr* to have a row (**avec qn** with sb).
IDIOMES **~ qn comme du poisson pourri** to tear sb off a strip○; **se faire ~ comme du poisson pourri** to be torn off a strip○.

enguirlander○ /ɑ̃giʀlɑ̃de/ [1] **I** *vtr* to tell [sb] off [*enfant*]; to give sb an earful○ [*adulte*]; **se faire ~** to get told off (**par** by), to get an earful○ (**par** from).
II s'enguirlander *vpr* to have a row (**avec qn** with sb).

enhardir /ɑ̃aʀdiʀ/ [3] **I** *vtr* [*expérience, succès*] to embolden [*personne*]; **enhardi par un premier succès/un sourire** emboldened by an initial success/a smile.
II s'enhardir *vpr* to become bolder.

enharmonique /ɑ̃naʀmɔnik/ *adj* enharmonic.

énième /ɛnjɛm/ *adj* umpteenth; **pour la ~ fois** for the umpteenth time.

énigmatique /enigmatik/ *adj* enigmatic; **d'un air ~** enigmatically.

énigme /enigm/ *nf* **1** (mystère) enigma, mystery; **c'est une ~** it's an enigma ou a mystery; **découvrir la clé** or **le mot de l'~** fig to discover the key ou the answer to the mystery; **2** (devinette) riddle; **parler par ~s** to speak in riddles; **l'~ du Sphinx** the riddle of the Sphinx.

enivrant, **~e** /ɑ̃nivʀɑ̃, ɑ̃t/ *adj* (tous contextes) intoxicating.

enivrement /ɑ̃nivʀəmɑ̃/ *nm* intoxication.

enivrer /ɑ̃nivʀe/ [1] **I** *vtr* **1** [*alcool*] to intoxicate sout, make [sb] drunk; [*air, altitude, mer*] to intoxicate sout; **2** [*succès*] **~ qn** to go to sb's head; **enivré par son succès** intoxicated by his success; **se laisser ~** to get carried away.
II s'enivrer *vpr* **1** lit (se soûler) to get intoxicated sout; **2** fig to become intoxicated with.

enjambée /ɑ̃ʒɑ̃be/ *nf* stride; **avancer à grandes ~s** to stride forward; **s'éloigner à grandes ~s** to stride off; **parcourir la pièce à grandes ~s** to stride across the room; **elle a monté l'escalier en trois ~s** she bounded up the stairs in three strides.

enjambement /ɑ̃ʒɑ̃bmɑ̃/ *nm* enjambement.

enjamber /ɑ̃ʒɑ̃be/ [1] *vtr* **1** [*personne*] to step over [*obstacle*]; **2** [*pont*] to span [*rivière*].

enjeu, *pl* **~x** /ɑ̃ʒø/ *nm* **1** Jeux stake; **2** (ce qui est en jeu) what is at stake; **ces programmes seront l'~ de la prochaine bataille** these programmes[GB] will be the focus of the coming battle ou will be what is at stake in the coming battle; **l'~ dépasse maintenant le sort d'une seule personne** what is at stake now is much more than the fate of a single person; **le journaliste analyse les ~x des élections** the journalist analyses[GB] what is at stake in the elections; **3** (problème) issue; **un ~ économique/politique/commercial** an economic/a political/a commercial issue; **livre consacré aux ~x de l'intelligence artificielle** book devoted to the issues of artificial intelligence.

enjoindre /ɑ̃ʒwɛ̃dʀ/ [56] *vtr* to enjoin [*prudence, silence*] (**à qn** on sb); **~ à qn de faire (qch)** to enjoin sb to do (sth).

enjôler /ɑ̃ʒole/ [1] *vtr* to beguile [*client, homme*]; **se laisser ~ par** to be taken in ou beguiled (**par** by).

enjôleur, **-euse** /ɑ̃ʒolœʀ, øz/ **I** *adj* [*sourire*] bewitching.
II *nm,f* charmer.

enjolivement /ɑ̃ʒɔlivmɑ̃/ *nm* fml embellishment.

enjoliver /ɑ̃ʒɔlive/ [1] *vtr* to embellish.

enjoliveur /ɑ̃ʒɔlivœʀ/ *nm* hubcap.

enjolivure /ɑ̃ʒɔlivyʀ/ *nf* embellishment.

enjoué, **~e** /ɑ̃ʒwe/ *adj* [*personne, caractère*] cheerful, jovial; [*conversation, ton*] light-hearted.

enjouement /ɑ̃ʒumɑ̃/ *nm* fml gaiety, cheerfulness.

enkysté, **~e** /ɑ̃kiste/ *adj* Méd encysted.

enlacé, **~e** /ɑ̃lɑse/ **I** *pp* ▸ **enlacer**.
II *pp adj* **1** [*corps, amants*] entwined (*jamais épith*); **ils se promenaient, ~s** they were walking with their arms around each other; **2** [*fils, initiales*] interlacing.

enlacement /ɑ̃lasmɑ̃/ *nm* **1** (action d'entremêler) intertwining; **un ~ de lanières** intertwined straps; **2** (fait de s'enlacer) embracing; (étreinte) embrace.

enlacer /ɑ̃lɑse/ [12] **I** *vtr* [*personne*] to embrace [*personne*]; [*serpent*] to wrap itself around [*proie*].
II s'enlacer *vpr* [*personnes*] to embrace; [*corps*] to intertwine.

enlaidir /ɑ̃lediʀ/ [3] **I** *vtr* to spoil, to ruin [*paysage, côte*]; to make [sb] look ugly [*personne*].
II *vi* to become ugly.
III s'enlaidir *vpr* [*personne*] to make oneself (look) ugly.

enlevé, **~e** /ɑ̃lve/ **I** *pp* ▸ **enlever**.
II *pp adj* [*morceau, rythme*] lively; **joué à un rythme ~** played at a brisk ou lively tempo.

enlèvement /ɑ̃lɛvmɑ̃/ *nm* **1** (délit) kidnapping[GB], abduction; **l'~ d'un journaliste** the kidnapping[GB] ou abduction of a journalist; **quelques heures après leur ~** a few hours after they were kidnapped ou after their abduction; **2** (de meuble, colis) removal; (d'ordures ménagères) collection.
■ **l'~ des Sabines** Art, Hist the rape of the Sabine women; **l'Enlèvement au sérail** Mus The Abduction from the Seraglio.

enlever /ɑ̃lve/ [16] **I** *vtr* **1** (ôter) to take [sth] away, to remove [*meuble, livre, vase*]; to take [sth] down, to remove [*rideaux, tableau, tuiles*]; to take [sth] off [*vêtement, chapeau, bijou*]; to move, to remove [*véhicule*] (**de** from); **enlève tes affaires de là/les mains de tes poches/tes pieds du fauteuil** get your things out of here/your hands out of your pockets/your feet off the armchair; **2** (supprimer) to remove [*tache, vernis, peinture*] (**de** from); to remove [*pépins, tumeur, amygdales*]; **3** (priver de) to take [sb/sth] away [*personnes, objet, avantage, souci*] (**à** from); **~ à qn l'envie de faire** to put sb off doing; **~ toute signification à qch** to make sth totally meaningless; **cela n'enlève rien à leurs qualités** it doesn't take away from their good qualities in any way; **cela n'enlève rien à l'estime que j'ai pour elle** it doesn't make me think any the less of her; **la tuberculose nous l'a enlevé à 20 ans** euph tuberculosis took him from us at 20; ▸ **pain**; **4** (ravir) [*criminel*] to kidnap, to abduct [*otage*]; liter [*amant*] to carry [sb] off [*bien-aimée*]; **5** (gagner) to carry [sth] off [*coupe, prix, titre*]; to capture [*marché, place forte*]; **6** (avec brio) to give a brilliant rendering of [*morceau de musique*].
II s'enlever *vpr* **1** (disparaître) [*vernis, papier peint*] to come off; [*tache*] to come out; **les taches s'enlèvent plus facilement à l'eau tiède/avec du savon** stains come out more easily with warm water/with soap; **2** (être séparable) [*pièce*] to be detachable; **le miroir peut s'~** the mirror can be removed; **les pépins s'enlèvent?** do you take out ou remove the pips?; **la peau s'enlève?** do you peel it?; **ça s'enlève comment?** [*vêtements, parure*] how do you take ou get it off?; **3** (partir) **enlève-toi de là**○ get off○.

enlisement /ɑ̃lizmɑ̃/ *nm* **1** (lit) sinking; **2** (de négociations, conflit, débat) stalemate; (de mouvement) collapse; **l'~ d'un pays dans la guerre** a country's slide into war.

enliser /ɑ̃lize/ [1] **I** *vtr* to get [sth] stuck [*bateau, véhicule*] (**dans** in).
II s'enliser *vpr* **1** [*bateau, véhicule*] to get stuck, get bogged down (**dans** in); **2** [*enquête, négociations, conflit*] to drag on; **3 s'~ dans** to get bogged down in, sink into; **le pays s'enlise dans la guerre civile** the country is sinking ou being sucked into civil war; **être enlisé dans** (conflit, difficultés) to be embroiled in.

enluminer /ɑ̃lymine/ [1] *vtr* Art to illuminate.

enlumineur, **-euse** /ɑ̃lyminœʀ, øz/ ▸ **510** *nm,f* illuminator.

enluminure /ɑ̃lyminyʀ/ *nf* Art illumination.

enneigé, **~e** /ɑ̃neʒe/ *adj* [*sommet, montagne*] snowy (*épith*); [*route*] covered in snow (*après n*).

enneigement /ɑ̃nɛʒmɑ̃/ *nm* snow coverage; **bulletin d'~** snow report; **l'~ des pistes est insuffisant** there isn't enough snow on the slopes.

ennemi, **~e** /ɛnmi/ **I** *adj* **1** Mil enemy (*épith*); **en terre ~e** in enemy territory; **pays ~s depuis des siècles** countries which have been enemies for centuries; **2** (hostile) hostile; **être ~ de qch** to be opposed to sth.
II *nm,f* **1** (de personne, groupe) enemy; **~ héréditaire** traditional enemy; **se faire des ~s** to make enemies; **se faire un ~ de qn** to make an enemy of sb; **passer à l'~** to go over to the enemy; **tomber entre les mains de l'~** to fall into enemy hands; **c'est l'~ public numéro un** he is public enemy number one; **2** (de principe, d'idée) opponent; **3** (élément nocif) **la censure est l'~e de la liberté** censorship is the enemy of a free society; **l'alcool est l'~ de votre foie/santé** alcohol damages your liver/health.

IDIOMES **le mieux est l'~ du bien** perfectionism can be counter-productive.

ennoblir /ɑ̃nɔbliʀ/ [3] *vtr* to ennoble; **l'âge a ennobli ses traits** age has made him look more distinguished.

ennui /ɑ̃nɥi/ *nm* **1** (sentiment) boredom; **tromper l'~** to escape from boredom; **c'est à mourir d'~** it's enough to bore you stiff ou to death; **quel ~!** what a bore!; **2** (problème) problem; **parler de ses ~s** to discuss one's problems ou troubles; **~s familiaux** family problems ou troubles; **avoir des ~s** to have problems; **j'ai des ~s avec la police** I'm in trouble with the police; **créer des ~s à qn** to make trouble for sb; **le seul ~ c'est que** the only trouble is that; **s'attirer des ~s** to run into trouble (**avec** with); **~s d'argent** money worries ou problems; **~s de santé** health problems; **il m'a cherché des ~s** he tried to create problems for me; **~s pulmonaires** lung problems ou trouble; **~s mécaniques** mechanical problems.

IDIOMES **un ~ ne vient jamais seul** it never rains but it pours.

ennuyé, ~e /ɑ̃nɥije/ **I** *pp* ▶ **ennuyer**.

II *pp adj* **1** (las) [*air, assistance, spectateur*] bored; **~ de tout** bored with everything; **2** (embarrassé) embarrassed; **il avait l'air bien ~** he looked quite embarrassed; **j'étais très ~ de laisser les enfants seuls** I felt awful ou terrible about leaving the children on their own; **3** (dans une situation difficile) **j'aurais été très ~ si je n'avais pas eu la clé** I would have been in real trouble if I hadn't had the key; **4** (à court d'argent) short (of money); **elle est un peu ~e en ce moment** she's a bit short at the moment.

ennuyer /ɑ̃nɥije/ [22] **I** *vtr* **1** (lasser) to bore; **mon travail/mari m'ennuie** my job/husband bores me; **ça m'ennuie à mourir** it bores me to death; **voyager m'ennuie** I find travelling[GB] boring; **2** (déranger) to bother; **est-ce que ça vous ennuierait si j'ouvrais la fenêtre?** would it bother you if I opened a window?; **excusez-moi de vous ~** I'm sorry to disturb you; **ce qui m'ennuie avec lui c'est que** what bothers me about him is that; **est-ce que ça vous ennuierait de m'accompagner?** would you mind coming with me?; **si ça ne vous ennuie pas trop** if you don't mind; **3** (irriter) to annoy; **ça m'ennuie que tu cries sans arrêt** it annoys me the way you shout all the time; **4** (harceler) to hassle○; **arrête de m'~** stop hassling me.

II s'ennuyer *vpr* **1** (être las) to be bored; **elle s'ennuie chez elle** she is bored at home; **s'~ mortellement** to be bored stiff; **avoir l'air de s'~** to look bored; **2** (se lasser) to get bored; **je me suis franchement ennuyée** I got really bored; **s'~ à faire** to get bored doing; ▶ **rat, sou**; **3** (languir) **s'~ de** to miss; **elle s'ennuie de lui** she misses him.

ennuyeux, -euse /ɑ̃nɥijø, øz/ *adj* **1** (lassant) boring; **livre/spectacle/homme ~** boring book/show/man; **c'est ~ de toujours faire la même chose** it's boring doing the same thing all the time; **~ à mourir, mortellement ~** deadly boring; **2** (pénible) tedious; **corvées/invitations ennuyeuses** tedious chores/social gatherings; **3** (agaçant) annoying; **l'~ c'est que** the annoying thing is that; **vous me mettez dans une situation ennuyeuse** you're putting me in an awkward position.

IDIOMES **être ~ comme la pluie** to be as dull as ditchwater.

énoncé /enɔ̃se/ *nm* **1** (de problème, sujet) wording (**de** of); **je n'ai pas compris l'~ de la question** I didn't understand the wording of the question; **l'~ d'une théorie** the exposition of a theory; **2** (de fait) statement (**de** of); **peu après l'~ des premiers résultats** shortly after the first results were declared; **3** Jur pronouncement (**de** of); **à l'~ du verdict, l'accusé s'est effondré** when the verdict was pronounced, the defendant broke down; **4** Ling utterance.

énoncer /enɔ̃se/ [12] **I** *vtr* to pronounce [*jugement*]; to set out, to state [*faits, principes*]; to expound [*théorie*].

II s'énoncer *vpr* **ce que l'on conçoit bien s'énonce clairement** what is well thought out can be clearly expressed.

énonciatif, -ive /enɔ̃sjatif, iv/ *adj* Ling enunciative; **proposition énonciative** enunciative clause.

énonciation /enɔ̃sjasjɔ̃/ *nf* Ling utterance.

enorgueillir /ɑ̃nɔʀgœjiʀ/ [3] **I** *vtr* to make [sb] proud [*personne*].

II s'enorgueillir *vpr* to pride oneself (**de qch** on sth), to take pride (**de qch** in sth); **s'~ de faire qch** to pride oneself on doing sth, to take pride in doing sth; **la ville s'enorgueillit de magnifiques fontaines** fig the town boasts several magnificent fountains.

énorme /enɔʀm/ *adj* **1** (par la taille, la quantité) [*objet, personne, somme*] huge, enormous; [*dépense*] huge, vast; **2** (par l'intensité, l'ampleur) [*scandale, succès, effort*] tremendous; [*erreur, sottise, gaffe*] terrible; [*mensonge, histoire, prétexte*] outrageous; [*rire*] hearty; **mensonge ~** outrageous lie, real whopper○; **il a d'~s possibilités** he is terribly ou tremendously talented; **la différence est ~** there's a world of difference; **ça vous ferait un bien ~** it would do you a power of good; **c'est déjà ~ qu'il les voie** for him to even see them is quite something; **faire un travail ~** [*personne*] to do a tremendous amount of work.

énormément /enɔʀmemɑ̃/ *adv* [*manger, boire*] a tremendous ou an incredible amount; [*parler, changer, apprendre*] a great deal; **il a ~ grossi/maigri** he's put on/he's lost a tremendous ou an incredible amount of weight; **ça s'est ~ construit** there's been a tremendous amount of building; **~ de temps/travail** a tremendous amount of time/work; **~ de gens/cigares** a tremendous number of people/cigars; **il y a ~ à faire/manger** there's a tremendous amount to do/to eat, there's loads○ to do/to eat; **il y a ~ à gagner** there's a lot ou a great deal to be gained; **ça compte ~** it's tremendously important; **ça m'a ~ plu** I liked it immensely; **ça l'a ~ fatigué** it made him tremendously tired; **ça a ~ progressé** it's come on a lot; **il travaille ~** he works very hard, he does a tremendous amount of work; **il gagne ~** he earns a fortune.

énormité /enɔʀmite/ *nf* **1** (de chiffre, taille) hugeness; (de faute, mensonge, requête) enormity; **te rends-tu compte de l'~ de tes paroles?** fig do you realize the enormity of what you're saying?; **2** (propos aberrant) outrageous remark.

enquérir: s'enquérir /ɑ̃keʀiʀ/ [35] *vpr* fml **s'~ de** to inquire about sth; **s'~ de ce que qn fait** to inquire what sb is doing; **s'~ de la santé de qn** to inquire ou ask after sb.

enquête /ɑ̃kɛt/ *nf* **1** Admin, Jur inquiry, investigation (**sur** into); (pour déterminer les causes d'une mort) inquest (**sur** into); **~ de police** police investigation; **~ judiciaire** judicial inquiry; **ouvrir une ~** to open ou set up an investigation ou inquiry; **mener une ~** to lead an investigation ou inquiry; **l'~ suit son cours** the investigation is continuing; **2** Presse, Sociol (reportage) investigation (**sur** into); (sondage) survey (**sur** about); **~ pour sondage** sample survey; **mener une ~ auprès de la population** to carry out a survey among the population; **une ~ par téléphone** a telephone survey.

■ **~ administrative** public inquiry; **~ d'opinion** gén survey; (pour des élections) opinion poll; **~ parlementaire** parliamentary inquiry GB, legislative inquiry US; **~ préliminaire** preliminary investigation; **~ sociale** *investigation allowing a judge to decide on custody rights in a divorce case*.

enquêter /ɑ̃kete/ [1] *vi* [*policier, gendarme*] to carry out an investigation (**sur** into), to investigate; [*expert, technicien, commission*] to hold an inquiry (**sur** into); **la police enquête sur le crime** the police are carrying out an investigation into the crime ou are investigating the crime.

enquêteur, -trice /ɑ̃ketœʀ, tʀis/ ▶ **510** *nm,f* **1** (de police) investigating officer; **2** (pour sondage politique) pollster; (pour sondage commercial) (market research) interviewer.

enquiquinant○, **~e** /ɑ̃kikinɑ̃, ɑ̃t/ *adj* **1** (agaçant) [*bruit, changement*] annoying, irritating; **elle est ~e, celle-là!** she's a real pain○!; **2** (ennuyeux) [*travail*] boring.

enquiquinement○ /ɑ̃kikinmɑ̃/ *nm* **tu parles d'un ~!** what a pain○!; **je n'ai eu que des ~s depuis mon arrivée** I've had nothing but trouble ou hassles since I arrived.

enquiquiner○ /ɑ̃kikine/ [1] **I** *vtr* **~ qn** (agacer) to get on sb's nerves, to irritate sb; (importuner) to pester sb; **ça m'enquiquine d'y aller** it's a real pain○ having to go there; **tu serais bien enquiquiné si tu perdais ta clé** you would be in a real mess if you lost your key.

II s'enquiquiner *vpr* **1** (s'ennuyer) to be bored, to be bored stiff○; **2** (se donner du mal) **s'~ à faire** to go to the trouble ou bother of doing; **je me suis enquiquiné à réparer ce vélo** I went to (a heck○ of) a lot of trouble to mend this bike; **tu ne vas pas t'~ à tout refaire?** you're not going to waste your time doing everything again?

enquiquineur○, **-euse** /ɑ̃kikinœʀ, øz/ *nm,f* pain○, nuisance; **quel ~, alors!** he's such a pain!

enracinement /ɑ̃ʀasinmɑ̃/ *nm* **1** Agric, Bot taking root, rooting; **2** (de colon, peuple) settling; **3** (d'habitude, idée, de principe, parti) (processus) taking root; (situation) deep-rootedness; **cette victoire marque le début de l'~ local du parti** this victory is the sign that the party is beginning to take root locally.

enraciner /ɑ̃ʀasine/ [1] **I** *vtr* **1** Agric, Bot to root; **profondément/solidement enraciné** deeply/firmly rooted; **2** (installer) to establish [*colons, peuple*]; **3** (fixer dans l'esprit) to implant, entrench [*idées, préjugés, principe*].

II s'enraciner *vpr* **1** Agric, Bot to take root; **2** (dans lieu, pays) [*personne*] to put down roots; [*coutume, idée, préjugé, principe*] to take root; **3** (rester trop longtemps) to outstay one's welcome.

enragé, ~e /ɑ̃ʀaʒe/ **I** *pp* ▶ **enrager**.

II *pp adj* **1** (passionné) [*chasseur, collectionneur*] fanatical; **être ~ de** to be mad about; **2** (furieux) enraged; **3** Méd, Vét rabid.

III *nm,f* (passionné, révolté) fanatic.

IDIOMES **manger de la vache ~e** to go through hard times.

enrageant, ~e /ɑ̃ʀaʒɑ̃, ɑ̃t/ *adj* infuriating.

enrager /ɑ̃ʀaʒe/ [13] *vi* to be furious; **~ de devoir faire** to be furious at having to do; **j'enrage de voir** I'm furious to see; **faire ~ qn** (taquiner) to tease sb; (ennuyer) to annoy sb.

enrayer /ɑ̃ʀeje/ [21] **I** *vtr* **1** (maîtriser) to check, to stem [*épidémie, progression*]; to curb [*inflation, chômage*]; to check, to stop [*baisse, développement*]; to stop [sth] escalating [*crise, violence*]; **2** (bloquer) to jam [*revolver*]; **~ le mécanisme** lit to jam the mechanism (**de qch** of sth); fig to put a spanner GB ou wrench US in the works.

II s'enrayer *vpr* lit, fig to get jammed.

enrégimenter /ɑ̃ʀeʒimɑ̃te/ [1] *vtr* Mil, fig to regiment.

enregistrable /ɑ̃ʀəʒistʀabl/ *adj* recordable.

enregistrement /ɑ̃ʀəʒistʀəmɑ̃/ *nm* **1** Audio, Vidéo recording; **l'~ ne rend pas bien les**

graves the low notes don't come out well in the recording; **l'appareil a des problèmes d'~** the machine has problems recording; **2** (de fait, plainte, données) recording; (de nouveaux membres, livres) registration; (de commande) taking down; **3** Jur, Fisc registration; **procéder à l'~ d'une société** to register a company; **4** Transp (de bagages) check-in; **on a perdu beaucoup de temps pour l'~** we wasted a lot of time checking in; **on se retrouvera à l'~** we'll meet at the check-in desk; **5** Ordinat record.

enregistrer /ɑ̃ʀəʒistʀe/ [1] **I** *vtr* **1** Audio, Vidéo to record [*disque, cassette*]; **ils enregistrent (un disque) à Londres** they're recording (an album) in London; **~ qch sur bande magnétique/vidéo** to tape/to videotape sth; **2** (constater) to note [*progrès, échec, signe, phénomène*]; to record [*chute, hausse, baisse*]; **3** (consigner) to make a record of [*dépenses, recettes*]; to take [*commande*]; to record [*données, température*]; to set [*record*]; **les dépenses enregistrées cette année** the expenses on record this year; **4** Admin, Jur, Fisc to register; **5** Transp to check in [*bagages*]; **faire ~ ses bagages** to have one's luggage checked in, to check one's luggage US; **6** (mémoriser) to take in; **il lit beaucoup mais enregistre peu** he reads a lot but doesn't take very much in; **très bien, c'est enregistré** or **j'enregistre**° fine, I've made a mental note of it.

II s'enregistrer *vpr* **1** (au magnétophone) [*personne*] to record ou tape oneself; **2** (à l'aéroport) to check in.

enregistreur, -euse /ɑ̃ʀəʒistʀœʀ, øz/ **I** *adj* recording (*épith*).

II *nm* (appareil) recorder.

■ **~ de vol** flight recorder.

enrhumer /ɑ̃ʀyme/ [1] **I** *vtr* to give [sb] a cold [*personne*].

II s'enrhumer *vpr* to catch a cold; **s'~ facilement** to catch colds easily; **être enrhumé** to have a cold.

enrichi, ~e /ɑ̃ʀiʃi/ **I** *pp* ▸ **enrichir**.

II *pp adj* [*aliment, substance*] enriched (**en** with); **lessive formule ~e** improved formula washing-powder.

enrichir /ɑ̃ʀiʃiʀ/ [3] **I** *vtr* **1** (financièrement) to make [sb] rich [*personne*]; to bring wealth to [*pays*]; **2** (augmenter) to enrich, enhance [*collection, connaissances, ouvrage*] (**de** with); **le musée a enrichi sa collection de nouvelles toiles** the museum's collection has been enhanced by new paintings; **3** Tech to enrich [*aliment, uranium*].

II s'enrichir *vpr* **1** [*personne*] to become ou grow rich; **2** [*collection, langue, expérience, connaissances*] to be enriched (**de** with); **la nouvelle édition s'enrichit d'illustrations** illustrations have been added to the new edition.

IDIOMES **qui paie ses dettes s'enrichit** Prov he who pays his debts gets richer.

enrichissant, ~e /ɑ̃ʀiʃisɑ̃, ɑ̃t/ *adj* [*expérience, conversation, lecture*] rewarding; [*relation*] fulfilling.

enrichissement /ɑ̃ʀiʃismɑ̃/ *nm* **1** (en argent) (de pays) enrichment; (de personne) accumulation of wealth; **2** Tech enrichment.

enrobage /ɑ̃ʀɔbaʒ/ *nm*, **enrobement** /ɑ̃ʀɔbmɑ̃/ *nm* Tech coating (**de** of).

enrober /ɑ̃ʀɔbe/ [1] *vtr* **1** lit (recouvrir) to coat (**de** with); **des amandes enrobées de sucre** sugar-coated almonds; **2** fig (présenter avec ménagements) to wrap up [*nouvelle*] (**de** in).

enrochement /ɑ̃ʀɔʃmɑ̃/ *nm* rip-rap.

enrôlé /ɑ̃ʀole/ *nm* recruit; **un ~ volontaire** a volunteer.

enrôlement /ɑ̃ʀolmɑ̃/ *nm* (dans l'armée, la marine) enlistment (**dans** in); (dans un parti) enrolment[GB] (**dans** in); **~ forcé** impressment.

enrôler /ɑ̃ʀole/ [1] **I** *vtr* gén to recruit; Mil to enlist, to recruit.

II s'enrôler *vpr* **s'~ dans la marine/l'armée de terre** to enrol[GB] ou enlist in the navy/army.

enroué, ~e /ɑ̃ʀwe/ *adj* [*voix*] hoarse, husky; **je suis ~** I am hoarse, my voice is hoarse ou husky; **d'une voix ~e** hoarsely, huskily.

enrouement /ɑ̃ʀumɑ̃/ *nm* hoarseness.

enrouer /ɑ̃ʀwe/ [1] **I** *vtr* to make [sb] hoarse [*personne*].

II s'enrouer *vpr* [*voix*] to go hoarse; [*chanteur, orateur*] to make oneself hoarse; **s'~ à force de crier/parler** to shout/talk oneself hoarse.

enroulement /ɑ̃ʀulmɑ̃/ *nm* **1** (action de s'enrouler) winding, rolling up; **2** (disposition) curling (up); **3** Art Archit scroll, whorl; **4** Électrotech coil.

enrouler /ɑ̃ʀule/ [1] **I** *vtr* **1** (autour d'un axe) to wind (**autour de** round GB, around); **2** (envelopper) to wrap.

II s'enrouler *vpr* **1** [*bande, fil*] to wind (**sur** onto; **autour de** round GB, around); **2** [*personne, animal*] to curl up.

enrouleur /ɑ̃ʀulœʀ/ *nm* drum; **ceinture de sécurité à ~** inertia-reel safety belt.

enrubanner /ɑ̃ʀybane/ [1] *vtr* **1** (pour décorer) to decorate ou trim [sth] with ribbon [*chapeau*]; **2** (pour attacher) to tie ou do [sth] up with ribbons [*paquet*].

ENS /əɛnɛs/ *nf*: *abbr* ▸ **école**.

ensablement /ɑ̃sɑbləmɑ̃/ *nm* (de port, terres) silting-up; (de véhicule) sinking in the sand; (de bateau) stranding (*on a sandbank*).

ensabler /ɑ̃sɑble/ [1] **I** *vtr* **1** to get [sth] stuck in the sand [*véhicule*]; to strand [sth] on a sandbank [*bateau, embarcation*]; **2** to silt up [*port, canal, cours d'eau*]; to cover [sth] with sand [*rue, terres*].

II s'ensabler *vpr* **1** [*véhicule*] to get stuck in the sand; [*bateau*] to get stranded (*on a sandbank*); **2** [*cours d'eau, port*] to silt up, get sanded up; ▸ **portugais**.

ensacher /ɑ̃saʃe/ [1] *vtr* to bag, to pack [sth] into bags [*marchandises*].

ENSAM /ensam/ *nf*: *abbr* ▸ **école**.

ensanglanté, ~e /ɑ̃sɑ̃glɑ̃te/ **I** *pp* ▸ **ensanglanter**.

II *pp adj* [*visage, main, corps, couteau*] bloodstained, bloody; [*blessure*] bloody; [*vêtements*] covered in blood (*jamais épith*), bloodstained.

ensanglanter /ɑ̃sɑ̃glɑ̃te/ [1] *vtr* **1** (couvrir de sang) to cover [sth] with blood, to bloody [*visage, chemise*]; **2** (ravager) to bring bloodshed to [*pays, époque*]; **les émeutes qui ont ensanglanté le pays** the riots that steeped the country in blood; **une violente bagarre a ensanglanté le match** a violent scuffle brought bloodshed to the match.

enseignant, ~e /ɑ̃sɛɲɑ̃, ɑ̃t/ ▸ **510** **I** *adj* **corps/personnel ~** teaching profession/staff; **syndicat ~** teachers' trade union; **syndicalisme/militantisme ~** trade-unionism/militancy amongst teachers.

II *nm,f* Scol teacher; Univ lecturer.

enseigne /ɑ̃sɛɲ/ **I** *nf* **1** Comm (sur magasin) (shop) sign; **~ d'un bar** cf pub-sign GB, bar ou tavern sign US; **~ lumineuse** neon sign; **2** Comm (nom déposé) trade name; **3** Mil, Naut (drapeau) ensign.

II à telle enseigne que *loc conj* so much so that.

■ **~ de vaisseau** ▸ **390** (de 1ère classe) ≈ sub-lieutenant GB, ≈ lieutenant junior grade US; (de 2e classe) ≈ acting sub-lieutenant GB, ≈ ensign US.

IDIOMES **nous sommes logés à la même ~** we are in the same boat.

enseignement /ɑ̃sɛɲmɑ̃/ *nm* **1** (institution) education; **l'~ primaire/secondaire/supérieur** primary/secondary/higher education; **l'~ public/privé/universitaire** state GB ou public US/private/university education; **politique/secteur de l'~** education policy/sector; **réforme de l'~** educational reform; **2** (activité) teaching; **se consacrer à l'~** to devote oneself to teaching; **l'~ des langues vivantes** modern language teaching; **programmes/méthodes/matériaux d'~** teaching programmes[GB]/methods/materials; **carrière de l'~** teaching career; **entrer dans l'~** to enter the teaching profession; **activités/équipements d'~** educational activities/facilities; **3** (formation) instruction; **l'~ théorique/pratique** theoretical/practical instruction; **4** (cours) tuition; **l'~ individuel** individual tuition; **dispenser/recevoir un ~** to give/receive tuition; **5** (leçon) lesson; **~s d'un échec/de l'expérience** lessons drawn from failure/experience; **plein** or **riche d'~s** full of lessons to be learned; **tirer les ~s de** to draw a lesson from.

■ **~ artistique** art education; **~ assisté par ordinateur, EAO** computer-aided learning, CAL; **~ audiovisuel** audiovisual teaching; **~ par correspondance** distance learning; **~ à distance** distance learning; **~ général** mainstream education; **~ libre** denominational education; **~ ménager** Scol domestic science; **~ mixte** coeducation; **~ professionnel** vocational training ou education; **~ religieux** religious instruction; **~ technique** technical education.

enseigner /ɑ̃seɲe/ [1] **I** *vtr* **1** (faire apprendre) to teach; **~ qch à qn** to teach sth to sb, to teach sb sth; **~ la philosophie** to teach philosophy; **bien/mal enseigné** well/poorly taught; **les matières enseignées à l'école** subjects taught in school; **2** (faire comprendre) [*expérience, science, livre, personne*] to teach; **l'expérience nous enseigne que** experience teaches us that.

II *vi* to teach; **~ à qn** to teach sb; **~ à Paris** to teach in Paris; **elle enseigne à des détenus** she teaches prisoners.

III s'enseigner *vpr* to be taught; **le journalisme s'enseigne dans des écoles spéciales** journalism is taught in specialist schools.

ensemble /ɑ̃sɑ̃bl/ **I** *adv* **1** (l'un avec l'autre) together; **aller ~ au cinéma** to go to the cinema GB ou movies US together; **mettre ~ des objets/personnes** to put objects/people together; **chantons tous ~!** let's sing all together!; **ils vont ~/bien ~** they go together/well together; **ils iraient bien ~ ces deux-là!** they'd make a fine pair, those two!; **2** (simultanément) at the same time; **ne parlez pas tous ~!** don't all speak at the same time!; **3** (à la fois) liter **tout ~** at once; **il pratique tout ~ la peinture, la gravure et la sculpture** he's a painter, engraver and sculpter at once.

II *nm* **1** (éléments regroupés) group; **un ~ de personnes/dessins/faits** a group of people/drawings/facts; **l'~ des élèves de la classe** all the pupils in the class; **l'~ de l'œuvre d'un écrivain** the whole of a writer's work; **une vue/idée/politique d'~** an overall view/idea/policy; **plan d'~ d'une ville** general plan of a town; **dans l'~** by and large; **dans l'~ de** throughout; **dans son** or **leur ~** as a whole; **conçu comme un ~** conceived as a whole; **2** (éléments assortis) set; **un ~ de mesures** a set of measures; **un ~ de sacs de voyages** a set of travel bags; **3** (cohésion) unity, cohesion; **tableau sans ~** painting lacking cohesion; **former un bel ~** to form a harmonious whole; **4** (synchronisation) (de gestes) coordination; (de sons) unison; **sans ~** without coordination; **l'orchestre a attaqué avec un ~ parfait** the orchestra began playing in perfect unison; **avec un ~ presque parfait, tous les invités se sont rués sur le buffet** almost as one, all the guests rushed to the buffet; **un mouvement d'~** a coordinated movement; **5** Math set; **~ fini/dérivé** finite/derived set; **théorie des ~s** set theory; **6** (formation musicale) ensemble; **un ~ instrumental/vocal/à cordes** an instrumental/a vocal/a string ensemble; **7** Constr (de bureaux) complex; **~ résidentiel/hôtelier** residential/hotel complex; **~ industriel** industrial estate GB ou park US; **un ~ scolaire** a school building; ▶ **grand**; **8** Mode (avec deux pièces ou plus) outfit; (tailleur) suit; **un ~ (veste) pantalon** a trouser suit GB, a pant suit US.

ensemblier /ɑ̃sɑ̃blije/ ▶ **510** *nm* **1** (décorateur) interior designer; **2** Cin assistant set designer.

ensemencement /ɑ̃smɑ̃smɑ̃/ *nm* Agric sowing (**de** of).

ensemencer /ɑ̃smɑ̃se/ [12] *vtr* **1** Agric to sow; **~ un champ en blé** to sow a field with corn; **2** Pêche **~ une rivière** to stock a river with young fish.

enserrer /ɑ̃seʀe/ [1] *vtr* **1** (mouler) [*vêtement*] to fit tightly round [*taille, hanches, poignet*]; **une bande lui enserrait le poignet** his wrist was tightly bound in a bandage; **2** (serrer fortement) **il lui enserra la taille** he clasped her around the waist; **la pieuvre enserra sa proie** the octopus gripped its prey tightly.

ensevelir /ɑ̃səvəliʀ/ [3] *vtr* **1** fml (enterrer) to bury, to inter sout; **2** (recouvrir) [*volcan, cendres, neige*] to bury; **3** (cacher) liter [*personne*] to hide; [*temps*] to enshroud sout; **faire renaître des querelles ensevelies** to revive long-buried feuds.

ensevelissement /ɑ̃səvəlismɑ̃/ *nm* **1** fml (enterrement) burial; **2** (recouvrement) liter burying.

ENSI /ɛnsi/ *nf* (*abbr* = **École nationale supérieure d'ingénieurs**) *Grande École of engineering.*

ensilage /ɑ̃silaʒ/ *nm* **1** (fourrage) silage; **2** (processus) ensilage.

ensiler /ɑ̃sile/ [1] *vtr* to ensile [*fourrage*]; to store [sth] in a silo [*grain*].

ensileuse /ɑ̃siløz/ *nf* cutter-blower.

ensoleillé, ~e /ɑ̃sɔleje/ *adj* sunny.

ensoleillement /ɑ̃sɔlɛjmɑ̃/ *nm* **1** (exposition au soleil) **la pièce jouit d'un bon ~** the room gets a lot of sun; **2** Météo **l'~ moyen de la région est de 2 000 heures par an** on average the region gets 2,000 hours of sunshine a year.

ensommeillé, ~e /ɑ̃sɔmeje/ *adj* [*personne, voix*] sleepy, drowsy; **il a les yeux tout ~s** he's all sleepy-eyed, his eyes are heavy with sleep.

ensorcelé, ~e /ɑ̃sɔʀsəle/ **I** *pp* ▶ **ensorceler**.

II *pp adj* [*maison, forêt*] enchanted.

ensorceler /ɑ̃sɔʀsəle/ [19] *vtr* **1** (jeter un sort) to cast ou to put a spell on [*ennemi, rival*]; **2** (captiver) [*beauté, esprit, personne*] to bewitch, to enchant [*personne*]; **il a ensorcelé son auditoire** he held his audience spellbound; **il écoutait, ensorcelé** he listened, bewitched ou spellbound.

ensorceleur, -euse /ɑ̃sɔʀsəlœʀ, øz/ **I** *adj* **1** (séduisant) [*personne, sourire*] bewitching, enchanting; **2** (magique) [*formule, philtre*] magic.

II *nm,f* (personne séduisante) charmer.

ensorcellement /ɑ̃sɔʀsɛlmɑ̃/ *nm* **1** (en jetant un sort) bewitchment; **2** (en séduisant) charm, enchantment.

ensuite /ɑ̃sɥit/ *adv* **1** (après) then; (ultérieurement) later, subsequently; **lave-les, ~ essuie-les** wash them, then dry them; **très bien, mais ~?** fine, but then what?; **il ne me l'a dit qu'~** he only told me later ou subsequently; **2** (en second lieu) secondly; **d'abord c'est trop cher, ~ ça ne me plaît pas** firstly, it's too expensive, and secondly I don't even like it.

ensuivre: **s'ensuivre** /ɑ̃sɥivʀ/ [19] *vpr* to follow, to ensue; **ils ont connu la guerre, et tout ce qui s'ensuit** they have lived through war and all that it entails; **jusqu'à ce que mort s'ensuive** until one is dead.

entablement /ɑ̃tabləmɑ̃/ *nm* entablature.

entaché, ~e /ɑ̃taʃe/ **I** *pp* ▶ **entacher**.

II *pp adj* Jur **acte ~ d'un vice de forme** act vitiated by a formal flaw; **~ de nullité** Jur null and void.

entacher /ɑ̃taʃe/ [1] *vtr* fml to sully littér, to besmirch littér [*réputation, honneur*]; to mar [*relations, rapports*]; **l'image du parti est entachée de querelles internes** the party image is marred by internal quarrels.

entaille /ɑ̃taj/ *nf* **1** (blessure) cut; (profonde) gash; **se faire une ~ au bras** to cut ou gash one's arm; **2** (sur objet) gash; (sur un angle) notch.

entailler /ɑ̃taje/ [1] **I** *vtr* to cut into [*bois*]; (profondément) to make a gash in [sth]; **le ciseau entaille le bois** the chisel cuts into the wood.

II s'entailler *vpr* **s'~ le doigt** to cut one's finger; (légèrement) to nick one's finger; (profondément) to gash one's finger.

entame /ɑ̃tam/ *nf* **1** Culin (première tranche) first slice; **2** Sport (début) start; **3** Jeux (première carte) lead.

entamé, ~e /ɑ̃tame/ **I** *pp* ▶ **entamer**.

II *pp adj* **1** (avancé) under way; **la journée/soirée était bien ~e** the day/evening was well under way; **2** (commencé) **le sandwich était à peine ~** the sandwich had hardly been touched; **il y avait un biscuit ~ sur la table** a half-eaten biscuit GB ou cookie US was on the table.

entamer /ɑ̃tame/ [1] **I** *vtr* **1** (démarrer) to start [*activité, journée, grève*]; to initiate [*procédure, poursuites, démocratisation*]; to enter into [*collaboration, bataille, entretien*]; to open [*dialogue, réunion, négociation*]; **j'entamais ma lecture quand il a téléphoné** I was just starting to read when he phoned; **on vient juste d'~ le dessert** we've just started eating dessert; **2** (affaiblir) to undermine [*crédibilité, moral, santé*]; to shake [*détermination*]; to test [*patience*]; **~ la réputation de qn** to undermine sb's reputation; **3** (rogner) to eat into [*économies, capital*]; **4** (commencer à consommer) to cut into [*pain, rôti*]; to open [*bouteille, pot*]; **5** (entailler) to cut into [*bois, peau, os, verre*]; **6** (ronger) to eat into [*métal*].

II s'entamer *vpr* **je me suis entamé la joue** I've cut my cheek.

entartrage /ɑ̃taʀtʀaʒ/ *nm* (de bouilloire) furring-up GB, scaling (**de** of).

entartrer /ɑ̃taʀtʀe/ [1] **I** *vtr* to fur up GB, to scale up [*chaudière, tuyau*].

II s'entartrer *vpr* [*tuyau*] to fur up GB, to scale; [*dents*] to be covered in tartar.

entassement /ɑ̃tasmɑ̃/ *nm* **1** (action) (de choses) piling up, heaping up; (de personnes) cramming together; **2** (résultat) (d'objets) pile; (plus gros) heap.

entasser /ɑ̃tase/ [1] **I** *vtr* **1** (empiler) to pile [*livres, vêtements*] (**dans** into; **sur** onto); **2** (amasser) to hoard [*argent, vieilleries*]; **3** (serrer) to pack, to cram [*personnes, objets*] (**dans** into); **les gens sont entassés sur les gradins** the people are tightly packed ou crammed on the terraces.

II s'entasser *vpr* [*objets*] to pile up; [*personnes*] to crowd, to squeeze (**dans** into); **s'~ sur la place** to crowd into the square; **s'~ sur le quai/la plage** to crowd onto the platform/beach; **on peut s'y ~ à six** you can squeeze six in; **on s'y est entassés à six** six of us squeezed in.

entendement /ɑ̃tɑ̃dmɑ̃/ *nm* understanding; **cela dépasse l'~** it's beyond belief.

entendeur /ɑ̃tɑ̃dœʀ/ *nm* **à bon ~, salut!** you've been warned!

entendre /ɑ̃tɑ̃dʀ/ [6] **I** *vtr* **1** (percevoir par l'ouïe) to hear [*bruit, mot*]; **~ qn pleurer, ~ qn qui pleure** to hear sb crying; **il pleure—oui, je l'entends** he is crying—yes, I can hear him; **tu n'entends pas? c'est pourtant net** can't you hear it? it's quite clear; **réussir à se faire ~** to manage to make oneself heard; **tu as entendu?** did you hear that?; **j'ai mal entendu** I didn't hear properly; **si j'ai bien entendu** if I heard correctly; **une expression qu'on entend à la campagne** an expression you hear in the country; **~ qch de ses propres oreilles** to hear sth with one's own ears; **qu'est-ce que j'entends? tu nous quittes?** what's this I hear? you're leaving (us)?; **elle entend mal** she's hard of hearing; **faire ~ un cri/gémissement** to give a cry/groan; **une explosion se fit ~** there was the sound of an explosion; **j'ai entendu dire que** I've heard (say) that; **je n'en ai jamais entendu parler** I've never heard of it; **je ne veux plus en ~ parler** I don't want to hear another word about it; **vous entendrez parler de moi!** (menace) you haven't heard the last of it!; **on n'entend plus parler de ce projet** nothing more has been heard about the project; **on n'entend plus parler de lui** his name is never mentioned any more; ▶ **mouche**; **2** (prêter attention à) [*juge, police*] to hear [*témoin, témoignage*]; [*dieu*] to hear [*prières, croyant*]; **~ la messe** to attend mass; **à t'~, tout va bien** according to you, everything is fine; **raconter qch à qui veut l'~** to tell sth to anyone who'll listen; **qu'est- ce qu'il ne faut pas ~!** I've never heard such nonsense!; **elle ne veut rien ~** she won't listen; **(que) le ciel vous entende!** let's hope that's how it turns out!; **3** fml (comprendre) to understand [*concept, expression*]; **je n'y entends pas grand-chose** I don't understand much about it; **'c'est confidentiel'—'j'entends bien'** 'it's confidential'—'I quite understand'; **il agit comme il l'entend** he does as he likes; **fais-le comme tu l'entends** do as you think best; **ne pas arriver à se faire ~** not to be able to make oneself understood; **ne pas arriver à se faire ~ de qn** not to be able to get through to sb; **elle m'a laissé** or **donné à** or **fait ~ que** she gave me to understand that; **elle a laissé ~ que** she intimated that; **ils ne l'entendent pas de la sorte** or **de cette oreille** they don't see it that way; **4** (signifier) to mean; **qu'entends-tu par là?** what do you mean by that? ; **ce n'est pas douloureux, j'entends, pas plus qu'une piqûre** it isn't painful, I mean, no more than an injection; **le marxisme entendu comme une philosophie** marxism as a philosophy; **5** fml (avoir l'intention de) **~ faire** to intend doing, to have the intention of doing; **j'entends bien rester ici** I have every intention of staying here; **j'entends qu'on fasse ce que je dis** I expect people to do what I say.

II s'entendre *vpr* **1** (sympathiser) to get on ou along (**avec** with); **ils s'entendent très bien** they get on ou along really well; **ils ne s'entendent pas** they don't get on ou along; ▶ **chat**, **larron**; **2** (se mettre d'accord) to agree (**sur** on); **s'~ sur une heure** to agree on a time; **on leur dit la vérité ou pas? il faudrait s'~** shall we tell them the truth or not? let's get it straight; **entendons-nous bien, personne ne doit leur dire la vérité** it goes without saying, nobody must tell them the truth; **3** (être perçu par l'oreille) [*bruit*] to be heard; (soi-même) to hear oneself; (les uns les autres) to hear each other; **cela s'entendait à l'autre bout de la ville** you could hear it on the other side of town; **4** (être compris) **phrase qui peut s'~ de plusieurs façons** sentence which can be taken in several different ways; **après paiement, s'entend!** after payment, of course!; **cela** or **il s'entend** fml (c'est évident) of course; **ce n'est pas tout à fait ça mais je m'entends** it's not exactly that, but I know what I mean; **5** (être compétent) **s'y ~ en meubles anciens** to know about antiques; **s'~** or **s'y ~ à peindre des portraits** to be good at portraits; **pour te faire culpabiliser, elle s'y entend!** hum when it comes to making you feel guilty, she's an expert (at it) ou she's got it down to a fine art.

entendu, ~e /ɑ̃tɑ̃dy/ **I** *pp* ▶ **entendre**.

II *pp adj* (décidé) **c'est une affaire ~e** it's settled; **'tu viens demain?'—'~!'** 'will you come tomorrow?'—'OK!'; **je fais ceci étant**

~ que I'm doing this on the understanding that.

III *adj* (de connivence) [*clin d'œil, air*] knowing; **d'un air ~** with a knowing look; **avec un clin d'œil/sourire ~** with a knowing wink/smile.

IV **bien entendu** *loc adv* of course; **elle a oublié, (comme de) bien ~** she's forgotten, of course; **bien ~, personne n'a rien vu?** iron naturally, nobody saw anything?; **il est bien ~ qu'elle ne sait rien** of course, she knows nothing.

entente /ɑ̃tɑ̃t/ *nf* **1** (bon rapport) harmony; **~ sexuelle** sexual harmony; **l'~ au sein d'une famille** family harmony; **une famille où il n'y a pas d'~** a family where people don't get on; **une bonne/mauvaise ~ entre deux frères** a good/bad relationship between two brothers; **la bonne ~ de nos deux pays** the friendly relationship between our two countries; **vivre en bonne ~ avec qn** to be on good terms with sb; **2** (alliance) gén, also Jur, Pol understanding; **~ tacite** tacit understanding; **arriver** or **parvenir à une ~** to come to an understanding; **l'~ franco-allemande** the understanding between France and Germany, the Franco-German entente Pol; **3** Comm, Écon (accord) arrangement; **~ commerciale** trade arrangement; **4** (association) **~ sportive** sports club.
■ **l'Entente cordiale** Hist, Pol the entente cordiale; **~ préalable** interim agreement.

enter /ɑ̃te/ [1] *vtr* Agric to graft [*prunier*].

entérinement /ɑ̃teʀinmɑ̃/ *nm* ratification (**de** of).

entériner /ɑ̃teʀine/ [1] *vtr* **1** (ratifier) to ratify; **la loi/réforme entérine un état de faits** the law/reform legalizes a preexisting state of affairs; **2** (admettre) to confirm.

entérique /ɑ̃teʀik/ *adj* enteric.

entérite /ɑ̃teʀit/ **▶271** *nf* Méd enteritis.
■ **~ des chats** feline enteritis.

entérostomie /ɑ̃teʀɔstɔmi/ *nf* enterostomy.

enterré, ~e /ɑ̃teʀe/ I *pp* ▶ **enterrer**.
II *pp adj* **1** (sous terre) [*défunt, conduit, trésor*] buried; **mort et ~** lit, fig dead and buried; **2** (oublié) [*querelle, histoire*] **~ (depuis longtemps)** long-forgotten (*épith*); **cette querelle/histoire est ~e depuis longtemps** this is a long-forgotten quarrel/story, this quarrel/story has been long forgotten.

enterrement /ɑ̃tɛʀmɑ̃/ *nm* **1** (inhumation) burial (**de** of); **2** (obsèques) funeral; **bel ~** nice funeral; **messe d'~** funeral mass; **faire une tête d'~** to look gloomy; **3** (mise à l'écart) shelving; **l'~ du rapport Grunard** the shelving of the Grunard report; **4** (fin) death; **l'~ d'une illusion** the death of an illusion.

enterrer /ɑ̃teʀe/ [1] I *vtr* **1** (inhumer) to bury [*défunt*]; **être enterré vivant** to be buried alive; **être enterré dans l'intimité** to be given a quiet family funeral; **2** (mettre sous terre) to bury [*canalisation, trésor, racine*]; **3** (renoncer à) to say goodbye to [*jeunesse, ambition, idéologie*]; **4** (mettre à l'écart) to shelve [*rapport, projet*].
II **s'enterrer**○ *vpr* to go and hole up○; **ils sont allés s'~ dans un trou perdu** they went and holed up○ in the middle of nowhere.
IDIOMES **~ sa vie de garçon** to have a stag party; ▶ **hache**.

entêtant, ~e /ɑ̃tetɑ̃, ɑ̃t/ *adj* [*odeur, parfum*] heady; [*musique*] insistent.

en-tête, *pl* **en-têtes** /ɑ̃tɛt/ *nm* **1** (de papier) heading; **papier à lettres à ~** headed writing paper; **papier à lettres à ~ de l'hôtel** hotel writing paper; **2** Ordinat header-block.

entêté /ɑ̃tete/ I *pp* ▶ **entêter**.
II *pp adj* [*enfant, mutisme*] stubborn, obstinate.

entêtement /ɑ̃tɛtmɑ̃/ *nm* stubbornness, obstinacy; **mettre de l'~ à réussir** to be determined to succeed; **ton ~ à faire** your insistence on doing.

entêter: **s'entêter** /ɑ̃tete/ [1] *vpr* (se buter) to be stubborn, to dig one's heels in○; (persister) to persist (**dans qch** in sth; **à faire** in doing).

enthousiasmant, ~e /ɑ̃tuzjasmɑ̃, ɑ̃t/ *adj* exciting.

enthousiasme /ɑ̃tuzjasm/ *nm* enthusiasm ¢ (**pour** for); **susciter l'~** to arouse enthusiasm; **refroidir les ~s** to dampen enthusiasm; **le manque d'~ de qn** sb's lack of enthusiasm; **avec ~** enthusiastically; **avec peu d'~** with little enthusiasm; **sans ~** unenthusiastically; **sans grand ~** without much enthusiasm; **il travaille sans grand ~** he hasn't got much enthusiasm for his work; **sans aucun ~** with no enthusiasm at all.

enthousiasmé, ~e /ɑ̃tuzjasme/ I *pp* ▶ **enthousiasmer**.
II *pp adj* enthusiastic (**par/pour** about/over).

enthousiasmer /ɑ̃tuzjasme/ [1] I *vtr* to fill [sb] with enthusiasm; **rien ne l'enthousiasme** he's not a very enthusiastic sort of person; **j'ai été enthousiasmé par le concert** I found the concert exciting.
II **s'enthousiasmer** *vpr* to get enthusiastic (**pour** about).

enthousiaste /ɑ̃tuzjast/ I *adj* enthusiastic.
II *nmf* enthusiast.

enticher: **s'enticher** /ɑ̃tiʃe/ [1] *vpr* **s'~ de** to become infatuated ou besotted GB with [*personne*]; to become passionate about [*objet, idée, activité*]; **être entiché de** to be infatuated ou besotted GB with [*personne*]; to have a passion for [*objet, activité*].

entier, -ière /ɑ̃tje, ɛʀ/ I *adj* **1** (dans sa totalité) whole; **manger un pain ~** to eat a whole ou an entire loaf; **le comité/pays (tout) ~** the whole ou entire committee/country; **la France/l'Europe (tout) entière** the whole of France/Europe; **une heure/année tout entière** one whole hour/year; **il l'a avalé/fait cuire tout ~** he swallowed/cooked it whole; **(pendant) des heures entières** for hours on end; **dans le monde ~** (partout dans le monde) all over the world; (au monde) in the whole world; **il n'y a dans le monde ~ que dix tableaux de lui** there are only ten paintings by him in the whole world; **les travailleurs du monde ~** working people all over the world; **marchandises (venues** or **en provenance) du monde ~** goods from all over the world; **ils arrivent par trains/cars ~s** they arrive by the trainload/coachload GB ou busload; **acheter le champagne par caisses entières** to buy champagne by the crate; **lait ~** full-fat milk; **2** (complet) complete; **c'est une réussite pleine et entière** it's a complete success; **donner entière satisfaction** to give complete satisfaction; **avoir l'entière responsabilité de qch** to have full responsibility for sth; **avoir une entière confiance en qn** to have every confidence in sb; **3** (inaltéré) [*objet, réputation*] intact; **le risque de guerre demeure ~** there is still a very real risk of war; **le problème de l'information reste ~** we have not even begun to address the information problem; **les accords laissent entières deux questions** the agreements fail to address two questions; **le mystère reste ~** the mystery remains unsolved; **4** (sans réserve) **être tout ~ à son travail** to be completely absorbed in one's work; **se donner** or **dévouer tout ~ à une cause** to devote oneself wholeheartedly to a cause; **avoir un caractère ~, être ~** to be thoroughgoing; **5** Vét (non castré) [*chat*] unneutered; [*cheval, bovin*] uncastrated, entire.
II *nm* **1** Math (nombre) integer; **2** (totalité) **en ~, dans son ~** in its entirety; **citer un passage en ~** or **dans son ~** to quote a passage in its entirety, to quote an entire passage; **traiter un problème en ~** to deal with a problem as a whole; **écrit en ~ de ma main** (manuscrit) written entirely in my hand; (non manuscrit) written entirely by me; **en ~ recouvert de tableaux** completely covered with paintings; **tu l'as mangé en ~?** have you eaten all of it ou the whole thing?; **le pays dans son ~** the whole ou entire country.

entièrement /ɑ̃tjɛʀmɑ̃/ *adv* [*refaire, se consacrer*] entirely, completely; [*fini, détruit, désintéressé, gratuit, dominé*] completely, entirely; [*automatisé, équipé*] fully; **avion ~ français** completely French-made plane; **je suis ~ d'accord avec vous** I entirely agree with you; **jouer ~ un morceau** to play a piece of music all the way through; **je partage ~ vos sentiments** I feel exactly the same as you; **je partage ~ votre indignation/vos doutes** I share your indignation/doubts wholeheartedly; **volume ~ inédit** hitherto unpublished volume.

entité /ɑ̃tite/ *nf* (tous contextes) entity.

entoilage /ɑ̃twalaʒ/ *nm* Cout (procédé, toile) interfacing.

entoiler /ɑ̃twale/ [1] *vtr* **1** Cout to put interfacing in [*vêtement*]; **2** (fixer sur une toile) to mount [sth] on canvas; **3** (relier en toile) to bind [sth] in canvas [*livre*].

entôler○ /ɑ̃tole/ [1] *vtr* to rip [sb] off○, to swindle; **se faire ~** to get ripped off○ ou swindled; **~ qn de 50 francs** to swindle sb out of 50 francs.

entomologie /ɑ̃tɔmɔlɔʒi/ *nf* entomology.

entomologique /ɑ̃tɔmɔlɔʒik/ *adj* entomological.

entomologiste /ɑ̃tɔmɔlɔʒist/ **▶510** *nmf* entomologist.

entonner /ɑ̃tɔne/ [1] *vtr* to start singing [*chanson, air*]; to launch into [*thème, discours*]; **~ les louanges de qn** to start singing sb's praises.

entonnoir /ɑ̃tɔnwaʀ/ *nm* **1** (ustensile) funnel; **en ~** funnel-shaped; **2** (cavité) crater.

entorse /ɑ̃tɔʀs/ *nf* **1** Méd sprain; **se faire une ~ à la cheville/au genou** to sprain one's ankle/knee; **avoir une ~ au poignet** to have a sprained wrist; **2** fig (manquement) **~ à la vérité** distortion of the truth; **~ au règlement/à la loi/à un principe** infringement of the rule/of the law/of a principle; **faire une ~ au règlement** to bend ou stretch the rules; **il fait de nombreuses ~s à son régime** he is always breaking his diet.

entortillement /ɑ̃tɔʀtijmɑ̃/ *nm* **1** (de fils) (processus) tangling; (résultat) tangle; **2** (de phrases, style) muddle.

entortiller /ɑ̃tɔʀtije/ [1] I *vtr* **1** (pour entourer) to wind [*ficelle, bande*] (**autour de qch** round[GB] sth); **2** (emmêler) to tangle up [*fils*]; **les fils étaient tout entortillés** the wires were all tangled up; **3**○ fig (embrouiller) to muddle up [*phrases, explications*]; **il nous a donné une version plutôt entortillée de l'affaire** he gave us a rather muddled account of the affair; **4**○ fig (embobiner) to get round[GB] [sb], to win [sb] over GB; **se faire ~** to let oneself be won over.
II **s'entortiller** *vpr* **1** (s'emmêler) [*fils, laine*] to get entangled (**dans** in); **2** (s'enrouler) [*plante*] to twist (**autour de** round[GB]); **3**○ fig (s'embrouiller) to get caught up (**dans** in).

entour /ɑ̃tuʀ/ I **à l'entour de** *loc prép* around; **à l'~ de la ville/la place** around the town/square.
II **entours** *nmpl* (environs) surroundings; **les ~s de la ville/de la ferme** the town's/farm's surroundings.

entourage /ɑ̃tuʀaʒ/ *nm* (famille) family circle; (amis) circle (of friends); (conseillers, courtisans) entourage; **l'~ familial** the family circle; **l'~ présidentiel** the president's entourage; **on dit dans son ~ que** people close to him/her say that.

entouré, ~e /ɑ̃tuʀe/ I *pp* ▶ **entourer**.
II *pp adj* **1** (ceint) **~ de** [*lieu*] surrounded

by ou with; **avoir le poignet/cou ~ d'un mouchoir** to have a handkerchief around one's wrist/neck; **paquet ~ d'un ruban** parcel tied up with a ribbon; **2** (populaire) [*président, femme*] popular; **3** (soutenu) **nos patients sont très ~s** our patients are well looked after; **elle a été très entourée au moment de son veuvage** everybody rallied round GB ou around US her when she lost her husband.

entourer /ɑ̃tuʀe/ [1] **I** *vtr* **1** (être autour) [*bâtiments, clôture, personnes*] to surround; **des collines entourent la ville** the town is surrounded by hills; **des dangers/tentations les entouraient** they were surrounded by danger/temptations; **un châle entourait ses épaules** she had a shawl around her shoulders; **les gens/objets qui nous entourent** the people/things around us; **le monde qui nous entoure** the world around us; **2** (placer autour) **~ qch de qch** to put sth around sth; **~ qn/la taille de qn de son bras** to put one's arm around sb/sb's waist; **~ qch de mystère** to shroud sth in mystery; **~ qn d'affection** to surround sb with love; **~ qn de sollicitude/soins** to lavish attention / care on sb; **~ un mot d'un cercle** to circle a word; **3** (soutenir) to rally round GB ou around US [*malade, veuve*]; **sa famille l'a bien entouré** his family rallied round GB ou around US him.

II s'entourer *vpr* **1** (réunir autour de soi) **s'~ d'amis/objets/de mystère** to surround oneself with friends/things/mystery; **s'~ de précautions** to take every possible precaution; **s'~ de garanties** to make sure that one has every possible guarantee; **2** (se mettre) **s'~ d'une pèlerine/d'un châle** to wrap oneself (up) in a cape/shawl; **s'~ les épaules d'un châle** to put ou wrap a shawl around one's shoulders.

entourloupe○ /ɑ̃tuʀlup/ *nf*, **entourloupette**○ /ɑ̃tuʀlupɛt/ *nf* dirty trick.

entournure /ɑ̃tuʀnyʀ/ *nf* Cout armhole; **être** or **se sentir gêné aux ~s** fig (être mal à l'aise) to be in an awkward position; (être gêné financièrement) to feel the pinch○.

entracte /ɑ̃tʀakt/ *nm* **1** (au théâtre, concert) interval GB, intermission; (au cinéma) intermission; **2** (divertissement) interlude.
■ **~ musical** musical interlude.

entraide /ɑ̃tʀɛd/ *nf* mutual aid (**entre** between); **programme d'~** mutual aid programme[GB]; **groupe d'~** self-help group.
■ **~ judiciaire** international judicial cooperation.

entraider: **s'entraider** /ɑ̃tʀede/ [1] *vpr* to help each other ou one another.

entrailles /ɑ̃tʀɑj/ *nfpl* **1** (d'animal) innards, entrails; **2** (de mère) liter womb; **3** fig, liter (profondeurs) bowels; **découvrir les ~ d'un pays** to discover the very heart of a country.

entrain /ɑ̃tʀɛ̃/ *nm* **1** (de personne) spirit, go○ GB, get-up-and-go○; **quel ~!** what spirit ou go!; **montrer de l'~ à faire qch** to show a lot of energy in doing sth; **il a de l'~** he's got spirit ou go; **elle est pleine d'~** she's full of go ou life; **manquer d'~** to have no go; **travailler/discuter avec ~** to work/talk with gusto; **parler/danser sans ~** to talk/dance half-heartedly; **retrouver son ~** to cheer up; **2** (de soirée, musique, discussion) liveliness; **être plein/manquer d'~** to be/not to be very lively; **une campagne électorale sans ~** a half-hearted electoral campaign, a lack-lustre[GB] electoral campaign.

entraînant, ~e /ɑ̃tʀɛnɑ̃, ɑ̃t/ *adj* lively.

entraînement /ɑ̃tʀɛnmɑ̃/ *nm* **1** (formation) (par soi-même) training; (par un maître) (de sportif, d'équipe) training, coaching; (de cheval) training; (de soldat) training; **d'~** [*match, terrain, jours, horaires*] training (*épith*); **2** (habitude) practice[GB]; **avec un peu d'~, votre travail ne vous semblera plus si difficile** with a little practice[GB], your work won't seem so difficult; **avoir de l'~** to be highly trained; **un ~ à la gestion de document** training in file management; **l'~ à la lecture** reading practice[GB]; **manquer d'~** (être inexpérimenté) to lack practice[GB]; (avoir perdu l'habitude) to be out of practice[GB]; **3** (séance) training session; **4** Tech drive; **~ par courroie/chaîne** belt/chain drive.

entraîner /ɑ̃tʀene/ [1] **I** *vtr* **1** (provoquer) [*cause, problème, erreur*] to lead to [*expansion, mécontentement, dépenses, perturbations*]; **la récession entraîne le chômage** recession leads to unemployment; **une panne a entraîné l'arrêt de la production** a breakdown brought production to a standstill; **2** (emporter) [*courant, rivière*] to carry [sth] away [*barque, épave, nageur*]; **l'avalanche a tout entraîné sur son passage** the avalanche swept away everything in its path; **il a entraîné qn/qch dans sa chute** lit, fig he dragged sb/sth down with him; **3** (conduire) to take [*personne*]; **~ qn sur la piste de danse** to take sb onto the dance floor; **~ Paul à l'écart pour lui parler** to take Paul aside to speak to him; **~ ses invités vers le buffet** to usher one's guests to the buffet; **il a entraîné son amie dans sa fugue** he took his girlfriend with him when he ran away; **~ qn à faire qch** [*personne*] to make sb do sth; [*circonstances*] to lead sb to do sth; **ce sont ses camarades qui l'ont entraîné** his friends dragged him into it; **4** fig (stimuler) to carry [sb] away [*personne, groupe*]; **ses idées novatrices ont entraîné les foules** the masses were carried away by his innovative ideas; **5** (former) to train, to coach [*athlète, équipe, sportif*]; to train [*cheval, soldat*]; **~ qn au combat/au saut en hauteur** to train sb for combat/for the high jump; **un cheval/joueur bien entraîné** a well-trained horse/player; **6** (actionner) [*mécanisme, moteur, piston*] to drive [*machine, roue, turbine*].

II s'entraîner *vpr* **1** (se former) [*sportif, équipe, soldats*] to train; **il s'entraîne tous les jours à la piscine** he trains every day at the swimming pool; **s'~ au javelot/au saut en longueur** to train for the javelin/the longjump; **s'~ au maniement des armes/tir** to practise[GB] handling weapons/shooting; **2** (s'exercer) to prepare oneself (**à qch** for sth); to train oneself (**à faire** to do); **il s'entraîne au débat télévisé** he's preparing himself for televised debates; **un acteur qui s'entraîne à mimer qn** an actor who is training himself to mimic sb; **il s'entraîne devant son miroir** he practises[GB] in front of his mirror; **3** (s'encourager) [*adolescents, délinquants*] to encourage each other; **des enfants qui s'entraînent à faire des bêtises** children encouraging each other to do ou egging each other on to do stupid things.

entraîneur, -euse /ɑ̃tʀɛnœʀ, øz/ **▶510** **I** *nm,f* Sport (de sportif, d'équipe) coach, trainer; (de cheval) trainer.
II entraîneuse *nf* (dans un bar) hostess.

entrapercevoir, entr'apercevoir /ɑ̃tʀapɛʀsəvwaʀ/ [5] *vtr* to catch a glimpse of [*personne, ami, phénomène*]; to glimpse [*solution, possibilité*].

entrave /ɑ̃tʀav/ **I** *nf* fig (gêne) hindrance (**à** to); (à la liberté) restriction (**à** of); **toute ~ à la liberté d'expression** any restriction ou curb on the freedom of speech; **s'exprimer sans ~** to speak freely; **plaisir/liberté sans ~** unbounded pleasure/freedom; **circulation sans ~** free-flowing traffic; **pour ~ à la liberté du culte/travail** Jur for failing to respect freedom of worship/the right to work.
II entraves *nfpl* (d'animal) hobble (*sg*); (de forçat) shackles, fetters littér.

entraver /ɑ̃tʀave/ [1] *vtr* **1** (gêner) to hinder, to impede [*action, cours, projet, circulation*]; **~ la carrière de qn** to hinder sb in his/her career; **2** (attacher) to hobble [*animal*]; to shackle, to fetter [*forçat*]; **3**○ (comprendre) **j'entrave rien** or **que dalle**○ I can understand bugger all◑; **4** Ling **voyelle entravée** checked vowel.

entre /ɑ̃tʀ/ *prép*

■ **Note** *entre* se traduit par *between* sauf lorsqu'il signifie *parmi* (▶ 4) auquel cas il se traduit généralement par *among*.
– Exemples et exceptions sont présentés dans l'article ci-dessous.
– Les expressions telles que *entre parenthèses, entre deux portes, lire entre les lignes* sont traitées respectivement sous ***parenthèse***, ***porte***, ***lire***; de même *entre ciel et terre* se trouve sous ***ciel***, *entre la vie et la mort* sous ***vie*** etc.

1 (dans l'espace, le temps) between; **nous serons absents ~ le 10 et le 15 mai** we'll be away between 10 and 15 May ou from the 10th to the 15th of May; **~ midi et deux** at lunchtime; **quelque part entre Grenoble et Valence** somewhere between Grenoble and Valence; **2** (pour désigner un état intermédiaire) between; **'doux ou très épicé?'—'~ les deux'** 'mild or very spicy?'—'in between'; ▶ **quatre**; **3** (à travers) between; **passer la main ~ les barreaux** to slip one's hand between ou through the bars; **le lézard s'est faufilé ~ les pierres** the lizard threaded its way through the stones; **4** (parmi) among; **~ autres** among others; **~ autres choses** among other things; **choisir ~ plusieurs solutions** to choose between ou from among several solutions; **c'est un exemple ~ mille** it's one example in ou among a thousand; **~ tous ces romans, lequel préfères-tu?** out of all these novels, which one do you like best?; **la chambre 13? pourquoi celle-ci ~ toutes?** room 13? why that one of all rooms GB ou the rooms US? ; **beaucoup/la première/chacune d'~ elles** many/the first/each of them; **cette question est délicate ~ toutes!** this is a highly delicate matter!; **oiseau sauvage ~ tous, le lagopède...** as wild a bird as any, the grouse...; **5** (pour désigner un groupe de personnes) **organiser une soirée ~ amis** to organize a party among friends; **ils discutent ~ hommes** they talk as one man to another; **(soit dit) ~ nous** between you and me (and the gatepost), between ourselves; **nous sommes ~ nous, tu peux parler** (deux personnes) there's just the two of us, you can speak; (plus de deux) we're among friends, you can speak; **venez ce soir, nous en parlerons ~ nous** come this evening, we'll talk about it alone together ou we'll have a quiet talk together; **ceci doit rester ~ nous** this is strictly between the two of us , this mustn't go any further; **6** (pour marquer la distribution) between; **partagez le bénéfice ~ vous** share the profit between you; **~ son travail et l'informatique, il n'a pas le temps de sortir** what with work and his computer he doesn't have time to go out; **7** (pour exprimer une relation) between; **les enfants sont souvent cruels ~ eux** children are often cruel to each other; **ces motifs peuvent se combiner ~ eux** these patterns can be combined (with each other); **deux d'~ eux sont cassés** two of them are broken; **la ressemblance ~ elles est frappante** the resemblance between them is striking; **un accord a été conclu ~ deux maisons d'édition** an agreement was made between two publishing houses.

entrebâillement /ɑ̃tʀəbɑjmɑ̃/ *nm* (de porte, volet, fenêtre) gap (**de** in); (de rideaux) chink (**de** in); **dans** or **par l'~ de** through the gap in.

entrebâiller /ɑ̃tʀəbɑje/ [1] *vtr* to half-open [*porte, fenêtre, volet, rideaux*]; **par la fenêtre entrebâillée** through the half-open window; **la porte était entrebâillée** the door was ajar.

entrebâilleur /ɑ̃tʀəbɑjœʀ/ *nm* door-chain.

entrechat /ɑ̃tʀəʃa/ *nm* Danse entrechat; hum skip; **faire des ~s** hum to skip ou hop about.

entrechoquement /ɑ̃tʀəʃɔkmɑ̃/ *nm* **1** (de casseroles, vaisselle) clattering; (de verres) clinking; (de cymbales) crashing; (de cailloux, cuillères) knocking together; (de lances) clash; **2** (d'idées) clash.

entrechoquer /ɑ̃tʀəʃɔke/ [1] **I** *vtr* to clatter [*casseroles, vaisselle*]; to clink, to chink [*verres*]; to crash [*cymbales*]; to knock ou bang [sth] together [*cailloux, cuillères*].

II s'entrechoquer *vpr* **1** [*verres*] to clink, to chink; [*dents*] to chatter; [*casseroles*] to clatter; **2** [*projets, idées, passions*] to clash.

entrecôte /ɑ̃tʀəkot/ *nf* **1** (portion) entrecôte (steak); **2** (pièce de boucherie) rib steak.

entrecouper /ɑ̃tʀəkupe/ [1] **I** *vtr* to punctuate (**de** by); **film entrecoupé de publicité** film interrupted by adverts; **voix entrecoupée de sanglots** voice broken with sobs; **il dit cela d'une voix entrecoupée** he spoke in a broken voice.

II s'entrecouper *vpr* [*lignes, routes*] to intersect.

entrecroisement /ɑ̃tʀəkʀwazmɑ̃/ *nm* **1** (de traits) criss-crossing, intersecting; (de fils, branches) intertwining, interlacing; **2** (motif) crisscross (pattern).

entrecroiser /ɑ̃tʀəkʀwaze/ [1] **I** *vtr* to intertwine, to interlace [*fils, branches*].

II s'entrecroiser *vpr* (tous contextes) to intertwine.

entre-déchirer: **s'entre-déchirer** /ɑ̃tʀə deʃiʀe/ [1] *vpr* littér lit to tear each other to pieces; fig to tear each other apart.

entre-deux /ɑ̃tʀədø/ *nm inv* **1** Cout insert; **2** (intervalle) intervening period; **3** Sport jump ball.

entre-deux-guerres /ɑ̃tʀədøgɛʀ/ *nm* ou *f inv* interwar period; **la génération de l'~** the interwar generation.

entre-dévorer: **s'entre-dévorer** /ɑ̃tʀə devɔʀe/ [1] *vpr* fig to tear each other to pieces.

entrée /ɑ̃tʀe/ *nf* **1** (point d'accès) entrance (**de** to); **à l'~** at the entrance; **l'~ du bâtiment/de la gare/du tunnel** the entrance to the building/to the station/to the tunnel; **l'hôtel a trois ~s** the hotel has three entrances; **'~'** (sur panneau de boutique, d'hôtel) 'entrance'; (sur panneau de gare, grand magasin, parking) 'way in' GB, 'entrance'; **à l'~ de la ville** on the outskirts of the town; **les ~s de Paris sont encombrées** the roads into Paris are busy; **il y a une pharmacie à l'~ de la rue** there's a chemist's where you turn into the street; **se retrouver à l'~ du bureau** to meet outside the office; **être arrêté à l'~ du territoire** to be arrested at the border; **2** (d'autoroute) (entry) slip road GB, on-ramp US; **avoir un accident à l'~ de l'autoroute** to have an accident at the motorway junction GB ou freeway junction US; **3** (vestibule) gén hall; (d'hôtel, de lieu public) lobby; (porte, grille) entry; **laisse ton manteau dans l'~** leave your coat in the hall; **4** (moment initial) **trois mois après mon ~ à l'université** three months after I got to university; **depuis leur ~ dans notre entreprise** since they joined the company; **l'~ dans la récession ne date pas d'hier** the beginning of the recession was some time ago; **5** (admission) **l'~ d'un pays dans une organisation** (accueil) the admission of a country to an organization; (adhésion) the entry of a country into an organization; **'~ libre'** (gratuite) 'free admission'; (publique) (dans un magasin) 'browsers welcome'; (dans un monument) 'visitors welcome'; **l'~ est gratuite** admission is free; **l'~ est payante** there's an admission charge; **refuser l'~ à qn** to refuse sb entry; **se voir refuser l'~** to be refused entry; **'~ interdite'** 'no admittance', 'no entry'; **6** (place) ticket; **deux ~s gratuites** two free tickets; **nous avons fait 300 ~s** (d'exposition) we had 300 visitors; (de théâtre, ballet) we sold 300 tickets; **spectacle qui fait le plein d'~s** show that's a sell-out; **c'est 30 francs l'~** admission is 30 francs; **ticket** or **billet d'~** ticket; **7** (arriv ée) (de personne) gén, Théât entrance; (de véhicule, marchandises) entry; **faire une ~ remarquée** to make a spectacular entrance; **faire/rater son ~** [*acteur*] to make/to miss one's entrance; **réussir son ~** [*acteur*] to enter on cue; **faire son ~ dans le monde/dans la vie professionnelle** to enter society/professional life; **à l'~ du professeur dans la classe** as ou when the teacher entered the classroom; **juste à l'~ de la voiture dans le virage** just as the car went into the bend; **faire une ~ discrète** to enter discreetly; **8** (commencement) **à l'~ de l'hiver** at the beginning of winter; **d'~ (de jeu)** from the outset, from the very start; **dès l'~** from the outset; **d'~ de jeu, il m'a proposé un marché** he offered me a deal straight off ou right off; **9** Culin (plat) starter; **10** Électron, Électrotech, Ordinat (de donnée) input **₵**; **11** Ling (de dictionnaire) entry; **12** Comm (marchandises) **~s** incoming goods (*in a given period*); **13** Fin (de capitaux) inflow; **14** Compta (recettes) **~s** receipts.

■ **~ d'air** Aviat air intake; Mines intake; **~ des artistes** Théât stage door; **~ des fournisseurs** (d'hôtel, de restaurant) service ou trade entrance; (d'usine, entrepôt) goods entrance; **~ en matière** introduction; **ton ~ en matière a surpris** the way you began surprised people; **~ du personnel** staff entrance; **~ de service** tradesmen's entrance GB, service entrance.

IDIOMES **avoir ses ~s au gouvernement/chez le ministre** to be an intimate in government circles/of the minister.

entrée-sortie, *pl* **entrées-sorties** /ɑ̃tʀesɔʀti/ *nf* Ordinat input-output; **canal d'~** input-output channel.

entrefaites: **sur ces entrefaites** /syʀ sezɑ̃tʀəfɛt/ *loc adv* at that moment, just then.

entrefer /ɑ̃tʀəfɛʀ/ *nm* air-gap.

entrefilet /ɑ̃tʀəfilɛ/ *nm* Presse brief article.

entregent /ɑ̃tʀəʒɑ̃/ *nm* savoir-faire sout.

entr'égorger: **s'entr'égorger** /ɑ̃tʀe gɔʀʒe/ [13] *vpr* lit to tear at each other's throats; fig to be at each other's throats.

entrejambes /ɑ̃tʀəʒɑ̃b/ *nm inv* **1** Cout (fond) crotch; (longueur de pantalon) inside leg GB, inseam US; **2** euph (partie du corps) crotch.

entrelacement /ɑ̃tʀəlasmɑ̃/ *nm* **1** (processus) intertwining, interlacing; **2** (motif) crisscross; **un ~ de sentiers** a crisscross of paths.

entrelacer /ɑ̃tʀəlase/ [12] *vtr*, **s'entrelacer** *vpr* to intertwine, to interlace.

entrelacs /ɑ̃tʀəlɑ/ *nm inv* tracery.

entrelardé, **~e** /ɑ̃tʀəlaʀde/ *adj* **1** Culin streaked with fat; **2** fig larded (**de** with).

entrelarder /ɑ̃tʀəlaʀde/ [1] *vtr* lit, fig **~ qch de qch** to lard sth with sth.

entremêler /ɑ̃tʀəmele/ [1] **I** *vtr* to mix [*objets*]; to interweave [*fils*].

II s'entremêler *vpr* gén to be mixed; [*cheveux*] to get tangled; **une histoire où le vrai et le faux s'entremêlaient** a story in which truth and fiction were mixed; **branches entremêlées** tangled branches.

entremets /ɑ̃tʀəmɛ/ *nm* dessert.

entremetteur, **-euse** /ɑ̃tʀəmɛtœʀ, øz/ *nm,f* **1** (marieur) matchmaker; (proxénète) procurer/procuress; **2** (intermédiaire) go-between.

entremettre: **s'entremettre** /ɑ̃tʀəmɛtʀ/ [60] *vpr* (intervenir) to act as mediator, to mediate (**dans** in; **entre** between).

entremise /ɑ̃tʀəmiz/ *nf* intervention (**auprès de** with); **sans son ~** without his intervention; **proposer son ~ dans une affaire** to offer to act as mediator in a dispute; **il l'a su par mon ~** he heard of it through me.

entrepont /ɑ̃tʀəpɔ̃/ *nm* tween deck.

entreposage /ɑ̃tʀəpozaʒ/ *nm* storage, storing.

entreposer /ɑ̃tʀəpoze/ [1] *vtr* **1** (dans un entrepôt) to store, to put [sth] into storage; (en douane) to bond, to store [sth] in bond; **2** (chez quelqu'un) to store (**chez** at).

entrepôt /ɑ̃tʀəpo/ *nm* **1** (bâtiment) warehouse; **2** (arrière-boutique) stockroom.

■ **~ de douane** bonded warehouse; **~ frigorifique** cold storage plant.

entreprenant, **~e** /ɑ̃tʀəpʀənɑ̃, ɑ̃t/ *adj* (hardi) enterprising; (avec les femmes) **être ~** to come on strong○, to be forward with the ladies.

entreprendre /ɑ̃tʀəpʀɑ̃dʀ/ [52] *vtr* **1** (commencer) to start, to set about [*tâche*]; to start [*travaux, démarches*]; to start, to set out on [*voyage*]; to undertake, embark on [*recherches, ascension, rénovation*]; **~ de faire** (se mettre à) to set about doing; (se donner pour tâche de) to undertake to do; **~ une action en justice** Jur to institute legal proceedings; **~ la réparation/le nettoyage de qch** to set about repairing/cleaning sth; **ce diplôme permet d'~ des études supérieures** this diploma opens the way to higher education; **~ en vain de faire** to try in vain to do; **2** (adresser la parole à) **~ qn** (pour séduire) to set about seducing sb; (pour bavarder) to engage sb in conversation (**au sujet de/sur qch** about sth).

entrepreneur, **-euse** /ɑ̃tʀəpʀənœʀ, øz/ ▶ 510 *nm,f* **1** Constr builder; **2** (de travaux) contractor; **~ en bâtiment** building contractor; **~ de déménagement** removal contractor GB, mover US; **~ de pompes funèbres** undertaker, mortician US; **~ de transports** haulage contractor GB, hauler US; **~ de travaux agricoles** agricultural contractor; **~ de travaux publics** civil engineering contractor; **3** (chef d'entreprise) *boss of a small firm*.

entrepreneurial, **~e**, *mpl* **-iaux** /ɑ̃tʀə pʀənœʀjal, o/ *adj* entrepreneurial.

entrepreneuriat /ɑ̃tʀəpʀənœʀja/ *nm* enterprise.

entreprise /ɑ̃tʀəpʀiz/ *nf* **1** (société) firm, business; **~ privée/publique** private/government-owned firm; **diriger une ~** to run a business; **petites et moyennes ~s** small and medium enterprises; **~ de conseil** firm of consultants GB, consulting firm US; **~ de construction/déménagement/fabrication** building/removal GB ou moving US/manufacturing firm; **~ de travaux publics** civil engineering firm; **~ de pompes funèbres** undertaker's GB, funeral home US; **~ de transports routiers** haulage contractor GB, trucking company US; **~ de franchisage** franchising operation; **~ de service public** public utility company; **création d'~s** business start-ups, creation of new businesses; **la culture d'~** corporate culture; **2** (secteur) business, industry; **réhabiliter l'~** to give business a new credibility; **ce que l'~ attend de l'école** what industry hopes the schools will provide; **3** (projet) undertaking, enterprise; (risqué) venture; **se lancer dans une ~** to undertake a venture; **se livrer à une ~ de déstabilisation du gouvernement** to set out to destabilize the government; **la libre ~** free enterprise; **4** Jur **donner/mettre qch à l'~** to put sth out to tender/to invite tenders for sth.

■ **~ unipersonnelle à responsabilité limitée**, **EURL** company owned by a sole proprietor.

entrer /ɑ̃tʀe/ [1] **I** *vtr* (+ *v avoir*) **1** (transporter) (vu de l'intérieur) to bring [sth] in [*objet, marchandise*]; (vu de l'extérieur) to take [sth] in [*objet, marchandise*]; **~ qch en fraude dans un pays** to smuggle sth into a country; **2** (enfoncer) to stick [*ongles, épée*] (**dans** into); **3** Ordinat to enter [*donnée, instruction*]; **~ qch en mémoire** to enter sth into the memory; **4** Sport to score [*but*].

II *vi* (+ *v être*) **1** (pénétrer) gén to get in, to enter; (en allant) to go in; (en venant) to come in; (en roulant) to drive in; **je l'ai vu ~ dans la maison par la fenêtre/par la porte de**

derrière I saw him get into ou enter the house through the window/by the back door; **la balle est entrée au-dessus de l'oreille** the bullet entered above the ear; **l'eau est entrée par une fissure** the water came in ou got in through a crack; **ils sont entrés en France par l' Italie** they came into France via Italy; **je suis entré dans Paris par le sud** (en voiture) I drove into Paris from the south; **ils sont entrés sur le court/notre territoire/la scène politique** they came onto the court/our territory/the political scene; **nous sommes entrés dans l'eau/la boue jusqu'aux chevilles** we sank up to our ankles in water/mud; **les marchandises entrent et sortent sans aucun contrôle** goods come and go without being checked at all; **entrez!** come in!; **'défense d'~'** (sur une porte) 'no entry'; (sur une barrière) 'no trespassing'; **je ne fais qu'~ et sortir** I can only stay a minute; **laisse-moi ~!** let me in!; **ne laisse pas/j'ai laissé le chat ~ dans la cuisine** don't let/I let the cat into the kitchen; **fais ~ le chat dans la cuisine** let the cat into the kitchen; **je vous ferai ~ par la cuisine** I'll let you in through the kitchen; **faire ~ la table par la fenêtre** (vu de l'intérieur) to bring the table in through the window; (vu de l'extérieur) to take the table in through the window; **fais-la ~** show her in; **faites ~** show him/her/them etc in; **2** (tenir, s'adapter) **c'est trop gros, ça n'entrera jamais** it's too big, it'll never fit; **ça n'entre pas dans la valise** it doesn't fit in the suitcase; **la clé n'entre pas dans la serrure** the key doesn't fit ou won't go in the lock; **faire ~ qch dans une valise** to fit ou get sth into a suitcase; **je n'arrive pas à faire ~ la pièce dans la fente** I can't get the coin into the slot; **on peut faire ~ trente personnes dans la pièce** you can fit ou get thirty people in the room; **nous sommes entrés à dix dans la voiture** we got ten of us into the car; **3** (s'intégrer, commencer) **~ dans** to enter [*débat, période*]; to join [*opposition, entreprise*]; **~ à** to enter [*école, hit-parade*]; to join [*gouvernement, parti, armée*]; to get into [*université*]; **~ en** to enter into [*pourparlers, négociations*]; **il entre en deuxième année** he's going into his second year; **il entre dans sa quarantième année** he's turned thirty-nine; **il entre dans la quarantaine** he's pushing forty; **~ dans la vie de qn** to come into sb's life; **le doute est entré dans mon esprit** I'm beginning to have doubts; **~ dans l'hiver** to enter the winter; **~ en convalescence** to start to convalesce; **n'entrons pas dans ces considérations/les détails** let's not go into those matters/the details; **faire ~ qn dans une organisation/qch dans un système** to get sb into an organization/sth into a system; **il m'a fait ~ au ministère** he got me into the ministry; **je ne sais pas comment cette idée lui est entrée dans la tête** I don't know how he/she got that idea into his/her head; **il entre dans la catégorie des...** he comes into the category of...; **expression entrée dans l'usage** expression which has come into use; **~ dans l'histoire** to go down in history; **~ dans la légende** [*personne*] to become a legend; [*fait*] to become legendary; **~ dans le capital de...** Fin to take a stake in...; **acteur qui entre dans son personnage** actor who gets into his/her character; **mesure qui entre mal dans le cadre d'une politique libérale** measure which does not fit the framework of a liberal policy; **faire ~ un mot nouveau dans le dictionnaire** to put a new word in the dictionary; **cela n'entre pas dans mes attributions** it's not part of my duties; **la question n'entre pour rien dans ma décision** the question has no bearing on my decision; **j'ai fait ~ tes dépenses dans les frais généraux** I've included your expenses in the overheads; **~ en mouvement/fusion** to begin to move/to melt; **~ dans une colère noire** or **une rage folle** to fly into a blind rage; **4** (être un élément de) **les ingrédients qui entrent dans la recette** the ingredients which go into ou make up the recipe; **le carbone entre pour moitié dans ce composé** carbon makes up half (of) this compound; **leurs parts entrent pour 20% dans le capital** their shares make up 20% of the capital.

III *v impers* **il entre une part de chance dans tout** a certain amount of luck goes into everything; **il n'entre pas dans mes intentions de faire** I have no intention of doing; **il n'entre pas dans mes habitudes de faire** I am not in the habit of doing.

entre-rail, *pl* **~s** /ɑ̃tʀəʀɑj/ *nm* gauge.

entresol /ɑ̃tʀəsɔl/ *nm* mezzanine, entresol; **à l'~** on the mezzanine.

entre-temps /ɑ̃tʀətɑ̃/ *adv* meanwhile, in the meantime.

entretenir /ɑ̃tʀətniʀ/ [36] **I** *vtr* **1** (garder en bon état) to look after [*tapis, intérieur, santé, vêtement*]; to maintain [*route, machine, édifice*]; **facile/difficile à ~** [*voiture*] easy/difficult to maintain; [*plante*] easy/difficult to look after; **les mots croisés entretiennent la mémoire** crosswords keep the mind active; **~ sa forme** to keep in shape; **2** (faire vivre) to support, to maintain [*famille, indigent*]; to keep [*maîtresse*]; to maintain, to keep [*armée*]; **se faire ~ par qn** (par un amant) to be kept by sb; (par des amis, parents) to live off sb; **3** (maintenir) to maintain [*équilibre, humidité*]; to keep up [*correspondance, connaissances*]; **~ les inégalités** to maintain inequality; **~ la fraîcheur dans une pièce** to keep a room cool; **~ des liens étroits avec un pays** to have close ties with a country; **~ qn dans l'erreur** to fail to put sb straight; **4** (alimenter) to keep [sth] going [*feu, conversation, rivalités*]; to keep [sth] alive [*amitié, souvenir*]; to sustain [*intérêt*]; (nourrir en soi) to cherish [*espoir, illusion*]; (chez les autres) to foster [*espoir, illusion*]; to feed [*inquiétude, manque d'assurance*]; to fuel [*tensions*]; **5** (informer) **~ qn de qch** to speak to sb about sth; **je dois vous ~ d'une affaire délicate** I must speak to you about a delicate matter.

II s'entretenir *vpr* **1** (converser) **s'~ de qch avec qn** to discuss sth with sb, to converse about sth with sb; **ils se sont entretenus en secret** they had secret talks; **2** (être gardé en bon état) **le marbre, ça s'entretient comment?** how do you look after marble?; **s'~ facilement** [*intérieur, tissu, plante*] to be easy to look after; [*voiture, bâtiment*] to be easy to maintain.

entretenu, **~e** /ɑ̃tʀətny/ **I** *pp* ▶ **entretenir**.

II *pp adj* [*personne*] kept (*épith*); **bien/mal ~** [*intérieur, plante*] well-/badly-kept; [*voiture, bâtiment*] well-/badly-maintained.

entretien /ɑ̃tʀətjɛ̃/ *nm* **1** (soins) (de maison, jardin) upkeep; (de voiture, route, d'immeuble) maintenance; (de vêtement, plante, peau) care; **frais/travaux d'~** maintenance costs/work; **assurer l'~ de** to look after [*intérieur*]; to maintain [*voiture, route, bâtiment*]; **demander beaucoup/peu d'~** [*plante, jardin, tapis*] to need a lot of/little looking after; **être d'un ~ facile** [*intérieur, jardin*] to be easy to look after; [*bâtiment, voiture*] to be easy to maintain; **et pour l'~, que me conseillez-vous?** how should I look after it?; **produit pour l'~ des fours** oven cleaner; **d'~ facile** [*tissu*] easy-care (*épith*); [*intérieur*] easy to look after; [*voiture*] easy to maintain; **2** (nettoyage) cleaning; **3** (conversation) gén discussion; Entr, Presse interview; Pol talks (*pl*), meeting; **demander un ~** to request an interview; **accorder un ~ à qn** to give sb an interview; **j'aimerais avoir un ~ avec vos parents** I'd like to speak ou talk to your parents; **4** (soutien financier) **assurer l'~ d'un enfant/d'une famille** to support a child/a family; **assurer l'~ d'une armée** to maintain an army; **frais d'~** living expenses; **cette somme devrait suffire à ton ~** that should be enough for your living expenses.

■ **~ d'embauche** job interview; **faire passer un ~ d'embauche à un candidat** to interview a candidate; **~ d'appréciation** job appraisal; **~ de carrière** = **~ d'appréciation**.

entre-tuer: **s'entre-tuer** /ɑ̃tʀətɥe/ [1] *vpr* to kill each other.

entrevoir /ɑ̃tʀəvwaʀ/ [46] *vtr* **1** (voir) (brièvement) to catch a glimpse of [*objet, scène, décor*]; (indistinctement) to make out [*objet, silhouette*]; **on entrevoit l'ombre de la dictature/du fascisme** fig the shadow of dictatorship/fascism lurks in the background; **2** (discerner, deviner) to glimpse [*vérité, solution, possibilité, avenir*]; (présager) to foresee, to anticipate [*difficulté, objection, aggravation, amélioration*]; **~ un espoir de paix/de redressement** to see a glimmer of hope for peace/of recovery; **commencer à ~ qch/que...** to begin to see sth/that...; **laisser ~ que** [*signe, résultat*] to indicate that, to suggest that; **laisser ~ qch** [*signe, résultat*] to point to sth.

entrevue /ɑ̃tʀəvy/ *nf* (entretien) meeting; (discussion) Pol talks *pl*; **ménager une ~** to arrange a meeting (**entre** between).

entrisme /ɑ̃tʀism/ *nm* infiltration.

entropie /ɑ̃tʀɔpi/ *nf* entropy.

entrouvert, **~e** /ɑ̃tʀuvɛʀ/ **I** *pp* ▶ **entrouvrir**.

II *pp adj* [*porte*] ajar (*jamais épith*), half open; [*lèvres*] parted; [*abîme*] littér gaping.

entrouvrir /ɑ̃tʀuvʀiʀ/ [32] **I** *vtr* [*personne*] to open [sth] a little ou a crack [*porte, fenêtre*]; [*musée*] to give limited access to [*collection, bibliothèque*].

II s'entrouvrir *vpr* gén [*porte, pays*] to half-open; [*lèvres*] to part.

entuber◐ /ɑ̃tybe/ [1] *vtr* to rip [sb] off○, to swindle [*personne*]; **se faire ~** to get ripped off○ ou swindled; **~ qn de 50 francs** to swindle sb out of 50 francs.

enturbanné, **~e** /ɑ̃tyʀbane/ *adj* [*tête*] turbaned.

énucléation /enykleasjɔ̃/ *nf* enucleation.

énucléer /enyklee/ [11] *vtr* to enucleate.

énumératif, **-ive** /enymeʀatif, iv/ *adj* enumerative.

énumération /enymeʀasjɔ̃/ *nf* **1** (action) enumeration, listing; **2** (liste) catalogue[GB].

énumérer /enymeʀe/ [14] *vtr* to enumerate, to list.

énurésie /enyʀezi/ *nf* enuresis.

énurétique /enyʀetik/ *adj, nm,f* enuretic.

envahir /ɑ̃vaiʀ/ [3] *vtr* **1** (pénétrer dans) [*troupes, foule*] to invade; [*animal, plante*] to overrun; [*sentiment*] to assail; [*douleur, sommeil*] to overcome; [*publicité*] to pervade; [*marchandise*] to flood [*marché*]; **envahi par les fourmis** overrun with ants; **envahi par la jalousie** assailed by envy; **envahi par le sommeil** overcome by sleep; **2** (accaparer) [*personne*] to monopolize; **se laisser ~** to allow oneself to be taken over (**par** by).

envahissant, **~e** /ɑ̃vaisɑ̃, ɑ̃t/ *adj* **1** (gênant) [*personne*] intrusive; **2** (omniprésent) [*doctrine, sentiment*] pervasive; [*musique, odeur, plante*] invasive.

envahissement /ɑ̃vaismɑ̃/ *nm* invasion (**de** of).

envahisseur /ɑ̃vaisœʀ/ *nm* invader; **l'~** the invader.

envasement /ɑ̃vɑzmɑ̃/ *nm* silting up.

envaser /ɑ̃vɑze/ [1] **I** *vtr* to silt up [*estuaire, port*].

II s'envaser *vpr* [*estuaire, port*] to silt up; [*barque*] to get stuck in the mud.

enveloppant, **~e** /ɑ̃vlɔpɑ̃, ɑ̃t/ *adj* **1** (couvrant) [*membrane*] enveloping; [*chaussure*] high-cut; [*manteau*] big and loose; **2** (enjôleur) [*manière*] ingratiating; [*voix*] wheedling.

enveloppe /ɑ̃vlɔp/ *nf* **1** (de lettre) envelope; **sous ~** in an envelope; **~ timbrée pour**

la réponse stamped self-addressed envelope; **2** (emballage) wrapping; (gaine) sheath; (revêtement) (souple) cover; (rigide) casing; Bot (tégument) husk; (cosse) pod; Anat (d'organe) membrane; (peau) skin; Zool (coquille, carapace) shell; **~ charnelle** or **mortelle** mortal coil; **3** (extérieur) exterior; **sous une ~ rude/de cynisme** beneath a rough/cynical exterior; **4** (budget) budget; **l'~ de la défense** the defence[GB] budget; **5** (commission) commission; (gratification) bonus; (indemnité de départ) golden handshake; (pot-de-vin) bribe; **6** Math envelope.

■ **~ autocollante** self-seal envelope; **~ par avion** Poste airmail envelope; **~ budgétaire** Écon budget; **~ électronique** Phys electron cloud; **~ à fenêtre** window envelope; **~ financière globale** Écon overall budget; **~ gommée** gummed envelope; **~ matelassée** padded envelope; **~ de pneu** Aut tyre GB ou tire US casing; **~ premier jour** Postes first day cover; **~ de réexpédition** Postes *envelope provided by the Post Office for forwarding mail.*

enveloppé, **~e** /ɑ̃vlɔpe/ *adj* (gros) [*personne*] plump.

enveloppement /ɑ̃vlɔpmɑ̃/ *nm* **1** Méd pack; **2** Mil envelopment.

envelopper /ɑ̃vlɔpe/ [1] **I** *vtr* **1** (recouvrir) [*personne*] to wrap [sb/sth] (up) [*personne, objet*] (**dans** in); [*housse, revêtement*] to cover [*objet*]; **enveloppe-lui le bras dans un linge humide** wrap a damp cloth around his/her arm; **je vous l'enveloppe?** Comm shall I wrap it for you?; **un manteau l'enveloppait** he/she was wrapped (up) in a coat; **le papier qui enveloppait le vase était rose** the paper around the vase was pink; **2** (encercler) [*brouillard, silence, nuit*] to envelop; [*brume*] to veil; [*mystère, secret*] to surround; **sommets enveloppés de brume** peaks shrouded in mist; **maison enveloppée par les flammes** house engulfed by flames; **3** (entourer) **~ qn de soins/tendresse** to surround sb with care/affection; **~ la baie du regard** to gaze around at the bay; **~ son offre de conditions** to hedge one's proposal around with various conditions; **meurtre enveloppé de mystère** murder shrouded in mystery.

II s'envelopper *vpr* to wrap oneself (up); **s'~ la tête d'un turban** (le mettre) to wrap one's head in a turban; (le porter) to wear a turban; **s'~ de mystère** to shroud oneself in ou to surround oneself with mystery.

enveloppe-réponse, *pl* **enveloppes-réponse** /ɑ̃vlɔpʀepɔ̃s/ *nf* freepost envelope GB, postpaid envelope US.

envenimé, **~e** /ɑ̃vnime/ **I** *pp* ▶ **envenimer**.

II *pp adj* **1** fig [*plume, paroles*] poisoned; [*dispute*] bitter; **2** (infecté) [*plaie*] septic.

envenimer /ɑ̃vnime/ [1] **I** *vtr* **1** (aviver) to inflame [*débat, dispute*]; to fan the flames of [*colère*]; to aggravate [*situation*]; **il n'a fait qu'~ les choses** he only made matters worse; **2** (infecter) **~ une plaie** to make a wound go septic.

II s'envenimer *vpr* **1** fig [*dispute*] to worsen; [*situation*] to turn ugly; **2** [*plaie*] to go septic.

envergure /ɑ̃vɛʀgyʀ/ *nf* **1** (d'ailes) wingspan; **oiseau/avion de X mètres d'~** bird/plane with a wingspan of X metres[GB]; **2** fig (de personne) stature; (de projet, d'entreprise) scale; **un politicien d'~/de son ~** a politician of stature/of his stature; **un architecte de grande ~/d'~ internationale** an architect of considerable stature/of international stature; **un projet/une entreprise de grande/petite ~** a large-/small-scale project/enterprise; **un projet d'~** a substantial project; **un projet/une œuvre d'~ internationale** a project/work of international scope; **prendre une ~ telle que...** to swell to such proportions that...; **sans ~** [*projet, débat*] limited; [*personne*] of no account.

envers[1] /ɑ̃vɛʀ/ *prép* **attitude/cruauté/mansuétude ~ qn** attitude/cruelty/clemency towards GB ou to sb; **méfiant/méprisant ~ qn** mistrustful/scornful of sb; **exigeant/honnête/impatient ~ qn** demanding/honest/impatient with sb; **reconnaissance/fidélité ~ qn** gratitude/loyalty to sb; **méchant/cruel/clément ~ qn** spiteful/cruel/merciful to sb; **avoir des engagements ~** to have obligations towards GB ou to.

IDIOMES **~ et contre tous/tout** in spite of everyone/everything.

envers[2] /ɑ̃vɛʀ/ **I** *nm* (de papier, tableau) back; (de tissu, tricot) wrong side; (de vêtement) inside; (de monnaie) reverse; **l'~ des choses** or **du décor** fig the other side (of the picture).

II à l'envers *loc adv* **1** (inadéquatement) the wrong way; **prendre un problème à l'~** to go about a problem the wrong way; **faire tout à l'~** to do everything backward(s) ou the wrong way; **tout marche à l'~ de nos jours** everything's upside down nowadays; **2** (le haut en bas) upside down; **poser un interrupteur à l'~** to install a switch upside down; **3** (l'intérieur à l'extérieur) inside out; **mettre sa chemise à l'~** to put one's shirt on inside out; **4** (le devant derrière) back to front; **tenir des jumelles à l'~** to hold binoculars back to front; **5** (la droite à gauche) the wrong way round GB ou around US; **mettre ses chaussures à l'~** to put one's shoes on the wrong feet; **6** (à rebours) **passer un film à l'~** to run a film backward(s); ▶ **monde**.

envi: **à l'envi** /alɑ̃vi/ *loc adv* [*répéter, souligner, rappeler*] at every possible opportunity.

enviable /ɑ̃vjabl/ *adj* [*situation, sort*] enviable; **l'économie progresse à un rythme ~** the economy is improving at an enviable rate; **être dans une situation peu ~** to be in an unenviable position.

envie /ɑ̃vi/ *nf* **1** gén urge (**de faire** to do); (de choses à manger) craving (**de** for); **~ folle/subite** insane/sudden urge; **l'~ m'a prise de te téléphoner** I got the urge to phone you; **des ~s de femme enceinte** the cravings of a pregnant woman; **avoir une ~ de chocolat** to have a craving for chocolate; **et s'il lui prenait l'~ de venir?** and what if he suddenly decided to come?; **avoir des ~s de meurtre** to feel like killing somebody; **'change de travail!'—'ce n'est pas l'~ qui me manque'** 'change jobs!'—'don't think I haven't thought of it!'; **avoir ~ de qch** to feel like sth; **avoir ~ de faire** (fortement) to want to do; (passagèrement) to feel like doing; **avoir ~ de vendre la maison** to want to sell the house; **avoir ~ de dormir/de faire pipi**° to want to go to bed/to go to the loo GB ou the bathroom US; **il n'a qu'une ~, (c'est de) partir** all he wants is to leave; **avoir ~ de rire/pleurer/hurler** to feel like laughing/crying/screaming; **je n'ai pas du tout ~ de le rencontrer** I have absolutely no desire to meet him; **avoir ~ de vomir** to feel sick, to have a feeling of nausea; **arrête! tu me donnes ~ de vomir!** stop! you're making me feel sick!; **elle a bien ~ de faire** she would really like to do; **il a ~ que je parte** he wants me to leave; **il a ~ que les choses soient claires** he wants it to be quite clear; **mourir** or **crever**° **d'~ de faire** fig to be dying° to do; **avoir ~ de qn** (sexuellement) to want sb; **donner (l')~ à qn de faire** to make sb want to do; **le livre m'a donné ~ de voir le film** the book made me want to see the film; **2** (convoitise) envy; **regarder qch/écouter qn avec ~** to look at sth/listen to sb enviously ou with envy; **leur piscine fait ~ à tous leurs amis** their swimming pool is the envy of all their friends; **il te fait ~ ce jouet?** would you like that toy?; **ils me font ~ tous ces gens bronzés** all these tanned people make me envious; **3** (angiome) birthmark; (petite peau) hangnail; ▶ **pitié**, **pisser**.

IDIOMES **avoir une ~ pressante** to need to go to the toilet.

envier /ɑ̃vje/ [2] *vtr* to envy; **j'envie ta façon de voir** I envy you your outlook; **comme je t'envie!** how I envy you!; **elle m'envie d'être ton ami** she envies me your friendship; **des musées que le monde entier nous envie** our museums that are the envy of the world; **tu n'as rien à leur ~!** iron you're every bit as bad!

envieusement /ɑ̃vjøzmɑ̃/ *adv* enviously.

envieux, **-ieuse** /ɑ̃vjø, øz/ **I** *adj* envious.

II *nm,f* envious person; **faire des ~** to make people jealous.

environ /ɑ̃viʀɔ̃/ **I** *adv* about; **deux ans ~** about two years; **à ~ dix mètres** about ten metres[GB] away; **~ tous les cinq ans** about every five years.

II environs *nmpl* **une villa des ~s de Paris** a villa on the outskirts of Paris; **être des ~s** to be from the area; **les enfants des ~s** the children from this area.

III aux environs de *loc prép* **1** (lieu) in the vicinity of; **elle habite aux ~s de Moscou** she lives in the vicinity of Moscow; **2** (moment) around; **aux ~s du 15 mai** around May 15th; **3** (quantité) in the region of; **aux ~s de mille francs** in the region of one thousand francs.

environnant, **~e** /ɑ̃viʀɔnɑ̃, ɑ̃t/ *adj* surrounding.

environnement /ɑ̃viʀɔnmɑ̃/ *nm* environment; **Ministère de l'~** Ministry of the Environment; **protection de l'~** protection of the environment; **un produit avec un label ~** or **qui respecte l'~** an environment-friendly product.

environnemental, **~e**, *mpl* **-aux** /ɑ̃viʀɔnmɑ̃tal, o/ *adj* environmental.

environnementaliste /ɑ̃viʀɔnmɑ̃talist/ *nmf* environmentalist.

environner /ɑ̃viʀɔne/ [1] **I** *vtr* to surround.

II s'environner *vpr* **s'~ de** to surround oneself with.

envisageable /ɑ̃vizaʒabl/ *adj* possible; **le projet n'est pas ~ avant deux ans** the project cannot be envisaged for two years.

envisager /ɑ̃vizaʒe/ [13] *vtr* **1** (projeter) to plan (**de faire** to do); **2** (imaginer) to envisage [*hypothèse, situation*]; to foresee [*problème, possibilité*]; **~ l'avenir avec sérénité** to view the future with confidence; **~ le pire** to imagine the worst; **3** (considérer) to consider; **la gestion envisagée comme un art** management as an art.

envoi /ɑ̃vwa/ *nm* **1** Postes (expédition) **tous les ~s de colis sont suspendus** parcel post is suspended; **date d'~** dispatch date GB, mailing date US; **faire un ~ de** to send [*fleurs, livres*]; **date limite d'~ des dossiers d'inscription** deadline for posting GB ou mailing US registration forms; **frais d'~** postage; **2** (ce qui est expédié) **recevoir un ~ postal** to receive something through the post GB ou mail US; **nous attendons un ~ important** we're expecting a large consignment; **quelle est la nature de l'~?** what are you sending?; **nous n'acceptons pas les ~s de plus de deux kilos** we cannot accept parcels over two kilos; **3** (déplacement de personnes, matériel, nourriture) **demander l'~ de troupes/d'une délégation/d'une force de paix** to ask for troops/a delegation/a peace keeping force to be dispatched; **décider l'~ immédiat de vivres/d'hélicoptères** to decide to dispatch food supplies/helicopters immediately; **4** (lancement) **l'~ de la fusée sera reporté** the rocket launch will be postponed; **coup d'~** Sport kick-off; **donner le coup d'~ de** to kick off [*match, campagne*]; to open [*festival, fête*]; **5** Littérat (strophe dédicatoire) envoi; (dédicace manuscrite) inscription.

■ **~ de fonds** remittance of cash; **faire un ~ de fonds** to dispatch cash; **~ en nombre** bulk dispatch GB, bulk mailing US;

~ recommandé registered post ¢ GB, registered mail ¢ US; **faire un ~ recommandé** to send something by registered post GB ou mail US; **~ contre remboursement** cash on delivery, COD; **faire un ~ contre remboursement** to send something COD; **~ en touche** (au football) throw.

envol /ɑ̃vɔl/ *nm* **1** (d'oiseau) flight; (d'avion) takeoff; (d'imagination) flight; (de pensée) soaring; **prendre son ~** [*oiseau, pensée*] to take flight; [*avion*] to take off; [*adolescent*] to leave the nest; **2** (de tarifs) escalation; (de devise) rise; **3** (de région) development.

envolée /ɑ̃vɔle/ *nf* **1** (discours) flight of fancy; **~ artistique/lyrique** artistic/lyrical flight of fancy; **les ~s des avocats** lawyers' oratory; **2** Fin (de monnaie, de Bourse) surge; (des prix) surge (**de** in); **3** (de parti) rise.

envoler: **s'envoler** /ɑ̃vɔle/ [1] *vpr* **1** (partir) [*oiseau*] to fly off (**pour** to); [*avion*] to take off (**pour** for); [*passager*] to take off (**pour** for); **2** (par accident) [*papier, parapluie, chapeau*] to be blown away; **le vent a fait ~ mon chapeau** the wind blew my hat off; **mon portefeuille ne s'est tout de même pas envolé**○ my wallet didn't just disappear; **3** (augmenter) [*prix, loyers, cours, monnaie*] to soar; **4** (disparaître) [*sentiment, rêve*] to vanish; **5**○ (s'enfuir) [*prisonnier*] to do a runner○, to escape.

envoûtant, **~e** /ɑ̃vutɑ̃, ɑ̃t/ *adj* [*film, livre*] spellbinding; [*atmosphère, musique*] enchanting; [*sourire, beauté, charme*] bewitching.

envoûtement /ɑ̃vutmɑ̃/ *nm* (action) bewitchment; (sortilège) spell.

envoûter /ɑ̃vute/ [1] *vtr* to bewitch, to cast a spell over; **être envoûté** lit, fig to be bewitched; **il envoûtait son auditoire** fig he held the audience spellbound.

envoûteur, **-euse** /ɑ̃vutœʀ, øz/ *nm,f* sorcerer/sorceress.

envoyé, **~e** /ɑ̃vwaje/ **I** *pp* ▶ **envoyer**.
II *pp adj* **ça c'est (bien) ~**○! well said!
III *nm,f* (représentant) envoy; **~ du pape/extraordinaire** papal/special envoy; **être l'~ du ciel** or **du Seigneur** fig to be sent from God.
■ **~ spécial** Presse special correspondent.

envoyer /ɑ̃vwaje/ [24] **I** *vtr* **1** (expédier) to send [*lettre, marchandises, cadeau, argent, félicitations, aide*] (**à** to); **Yann vous envoie ses amitiés** Yann sends (you) his regards; **2** (faire déplacer) to send [*ambulance, personne, police, troupes*]; **qui vous envoie?** who sent you?; **je vous envoie un technicien** I will send you an engineer; **~ un reporter à l'étranger/un homme en prison** to send a reporter abroad/a man to jail; **on l'a envoyé étudier à Genève** he was sent off to study in Geneva; **je l'ai envoyé chercher le journal** I sent him out to get the paper; **3** (lancer) to throw [*balle, caillou*]; to fire [*missile, roquette*] (**sur** at); **envoie-moi le savon** throw me the soap; **il m'a envoyé un caillou** he threw a stone at me; **~ qch dans l'œil/les jambes de qn** to hit sb in the eye/the legs with sth; **~ le ballon dans les buts** to put the ball in the net; **4** (asséner) **~ un coup de coude à qn** (amicalement) to give sb a dig in the ribs; (agressivement) to jab sb in the ribs; **~ un coup de pied à qn** to kick sb; **~ une gifle à qn** to slap sb in the face; **il m'a envoyé son poing dans la figure** he punched me in the face; **5** (transmettre) to send [*message, signal*]; **~ des signaux de fumée** to send smoke signals; **6** Naut **envoyez!** about ship!
II s'envoyer *vpr* **1** (échanger) to exchange [*lettres, cadeaux, regards*] ; **s'~ des baisers** (par gestes) to blow each other kisses; **s'~ des clins d'œil** to wink at each other; **2**○ (avaler) to guzzle○ [*alcool, eau*]; to wolf down○ [*repas*]; **il s'est envoyé toute la bouteille** he guzzled down the entire bottle; **3**◑ (posséder sexuellement) to have it off with◑ GB, to get off with◑ US.

IDIOMES **~ qn au diable**○ to tell sb to go to hell○; **~ qn promener**○ or **se faire voir**◑ to send sb packing○; **tout ~ promener**○ to drop the lot○; **il ne me l'a pas envoyé dire**○ and he told me in no uncertain terms; **je ne te l'envoie pas dire**○! tell me about it○!; **s'~ des compliments**○ (à soi-même) to pat oneself on the back; **s'~ en l'air**◑ (forniquer) to get laid◑; (avoir un accident) to crash.

envoyeur /ɑ̃vwajœʀ/ *nm* **retour à l'~** return to sender.

enzyme /ɑ̃zim/ *nm* ou *f* enzyme.

Éole /eɔl/ *npr* Aeolus.

éolien, **-ienne** /eɔljɛ̃, ɛn/ **I** *adj* [*érosion, générateur*] wind; Géol [*dépôts*] aeolian.
II éolienne *nf* (aeolian) windmill.

Éoliennes /eɔljɛn/ ▶416 *adj fpl* **les îles ~** the Eolian Islands.

éosine /eɔzin/ *nf* eosin.

épagneul /epaɲœl/ *nm* spaniel.

épagneule /epaɲœl/ *nf* spaniel bitch.

épais, **épaisse** /epɛ, ɛs/ **I** ▶477 *adj* **1** (pas mince) [*tranche, couche, tissu, tapis*] thick; [*lèvres, taille, chevilles, peau d'animal*] thick; **un mur ~ de deux mètres** a wall two metres[GB] thick; **il n'est pas bien ~ ce petit**○! he's a skinny little fellow!; **2** (pas subtil) [*esprit, intelligence*] dull; [*jeu de mots, plaisanterie*] heavy-handed; [*ruse, procédé*] clumsy; **3** (pâteux) [*sirop, crème, sauce*] thick; **4** (dense) [*feuillage, buisson, chevelure*] thick; [*brume, fumée*] thick; [*ombre*] deep; **5** (profond) [*nuit, silence*] deep.
II *adv* a lot, much; **tu en as mis trop ~** (du beurre, de la peinture) you've put too much on; **il n'y en a pas ~**○! there isn't much (of it)!
III au plus épais de *loc prép* in the midst of [*foule, mêlée*]; in the depths of [*nuit, forêt*].

épaisseur /epɛsœʀ/ *nf* **1** ▶477 (dimension) thickness; **existe en plusieurs ~s** available in several thicknesses; **aérer le sol sur 10 cm d'~** to air the soil to a depth of 10 cm; **niches creusées dans l'~ du mur** niches set in the wall; **couper qch dans (le sens de) l'~** to cut sth sideways; **un mur de deux mètres d'~** a wall two metres[GB] thick; **une cloison de faible ~** a thin partition; **2** (densité) thickness; **dans l'~ des fourrés** in the dense thickets; **3** (de liquide) thickness; **4** (profondeur) depths (*pl*); **dans l'~ de la nuit** in the depths of night; **5** fig (de personnage, projet, d'intrigue) substance; **ses personnages manquent d'~** his characters lack substance; **un politicien sans ~** a dull ou colourless[GB] politician; **6** (couche) layer; **en trois ~s** in three layers.

épaissir /epesiʀ/ [3] **I** *vtr* **1** (rendre consistant) [*farine*] to thicken [*sauce*]; **2** (déformer) [*âge, graisse*] to thicken [*traits, taille*]; [*vêtement*] to broaden [*silhouette*]; **3** (obscurcir) to deepen [*mystère, incertitude*].
II *vi* **1** (devenir consistant) [*sauce*] to thicken; [*gelée*] to set; **faire ~ à feu doux** leave to thicken over a gentle heat; **2** (grossir) [*personne*] to put on weight.
III s'épaissir *vpr* **1** [*sauce, liquide*] to thicken; **2** [*brume*] to thicken; **3** [*mystère*] to deepen; **4** [*taille, silhouette*] to thicken.

épaississant, **~e** /epɛsisɑ̃, ɑ̃t/ **I** *adj* [*substance*] thickening.
II *nm* (produit) thickener.

épaississement /epesismɑ̃/ *nm* thickening.

épanchement /epɑ̃ʃmɑ̃/ **I** *nm* Méd (de sang) effusion; **avoir un ~ de synovie** to have water on the knee.
II épanchements *nmpl* (confidences) outpourings (*pl*).

épancher /epɑ̃ʃe/ [1] **I** *vtr* to give vent to [*colère, amertume*]; to pour out [*chagrin, cœur*].
II s'épancher *vpr* **1** [*personne*] to open one's heart (**auprès de** to), to pour out one's feelings (**auprès de** to); **2** [*sang*] to pour out.

épandage /epɑ̃daʒ/ *nm* **1** Agric (action) spreading; **~ de fumier** manure spreading, manuring; **2** Tech sewage farming; **~ par irrigation** sewage irrigation.

épandre /epɑ̃dʀ/ [6] *vtr* to spread [*engrais, fumier*].

épanoui, **~e** /epanwi/ **I** *pp* ▶ **épanouir**.
II *pp adj* **1** [*fleur*] in full bloom (*après n*); **2** [*sourire, visage*] beaming; **3** [*personne, personnalité*] well-adjusted; [*corps*] ample.

épanouir /epanwiʀ/ [3] **I** *vtr* liter **1** [*soleil*] to open (out) [*fleur*]; [*joie*] to light up [*visage*]; **2** (développer) to make [sb/sth] blossom; **la maternité l'a épanouie** motherhood made her blossom.
II s'épanouir *vpr* **1** (s'ouvrir) [*fleur*] to bloom; **2** (s'éclairer) [*visage*] to light up; **3** (se développer) [*personne, amitié*] to blossom; [*affaires*] to flourish; **permettre aux gens de s'~** to enable people to fulfil[GB] their potential.

épanouissant, **~e** /epanwisɑ̃, ɑ̃t/ *adj* fulfilling.

épanouissement /epanwismɑ̃/ *nm* **1** (de fleur) blooming; **2** (développement) gén development; (de talent) flowering; **favoriser/défavoriser l'~ de qn/qch** to foster/to hamper the development of sb/sth.

épargnant, **~e** /epaʀɲɑ̃, ɑ̃t/ *nm,f* saver; **petit ~** small saver; **en bon ~** as a careful saver.

épargne /epaʀɲ/ *nf* (personnelle) savings (*pl*); **un compte (d') ~** a savings account.

épargner /epaʀɲe/ [1] **I** *vtr* **1** (mettre de côté) to save [*argent*]; **~ 300 francs par semaine** to save 300 francs a week; **2** (ne pas affecter) to spare [*lieu, personne, institution*]; **quartier épargné par les bombardements** neighbourhood[GB] spared by the bombing; **les banques ne sont pas épargnées par l'inflation** banks are not spared by inflation; **3** (éviter) **~ qch à qn** to spare sb sth; **épargnez-leur vos réflexions** spare them your comments; **~ le pire à ses enfants** to spare one's children the worst; **4** (préserver) to save [*force, vêtement*]; **~ ses larmes** to save one's tears.
II *vi* Écon, Fin to save; **ne pas assez ~** not to save enough.
III s'épargner *vpr* to save oneself [*attente, effort*]; **il s'est épargné le désagrément d'une attente** he saved himself the trouble of having to wait.

éparpillement /epaʀpijmɑ̃/ *nm* scattering; **l'~ des services administratifs** the distance between administrative departments; **l'~ de ses activités l'empêche d'accomplir quoi que ce soit** his activities are scattered over such a wide front that he gets nothing done.

éparpiller /epaʀpije/ [1] **I** *vtr* **1** lit to scatter [*personnes, feuilles*]; **famille éparpillée aux quatre coins du monde** family scattered all over the world; **2** fig to fail to concentrate [*forces, attention*].
II s'éparpiller *vpr* **1** [*cendres, foule*] to scatter; **2** [*personne*] to take on too much; [*conversation*] to wander.

épars, **~e** /epaʀ, aʀs/ *adj* scattered.

épatant○, **~e** /epatɑ̃, ɑ̃t/ *adj* marvellous[GB]; **c'est ~!** that's marvellous[GB]!; **elle est ~e dans ce rôle** she's marvellous[GB] in the role.

épate○ /epat/ *nf* showing off; **à l'~** by showing off; **y aller à l'~** to get on by showing off; **faire de l'~** to show off.

épaté, **~e** /epate/ *adj* **1 il a le nez ~** he has a pug nose ou a flat nose; **au nez ~** flat-nosed; **2**○ (surpris) amazed (**de** by).

épatement /epatmɑ̃/ *nm* **1** (de nez) pug shape; **2**○ (surprise) amazement.

épater○ /epate/ [1] **I** *vtr* **1** (impressionner) to impress; **il cherche à ~ ses voisins** he's trying to impress the neighbours[GB]; **ça t'épate, hein?** surprised, aren't you?; **2** (étonner) to amaze; **ça m'épate que**

personne n'ait rien entendu I'm amazed no-one heard anything.

II **s'épater** *vpr* (s'étonner) to marvel (**de** at); **il ne s'épate de rien** nothing surprises him.

épaulard /epolaʀ/ *nm* killer whale.

épaule /epol/ *nf* **1** ▶188 Anat shoulder; **large d'~s** broad-shouldered; **~ contre ~** shoulder to shoulder; **rentrer la tête dans les ~s** to hunch one's shoulders; **enfoncer une porte à coups d'~** to shoulder-charge a door; **2** Culin shoulder; **~ d'agneau** shoulder of lamb.

IDIOMES **changer son fusil d'~** to change one's tactics; **avoir la tête sur les ~s** to have one's head screwed on (tight)○.

épaulé, ~e /epole/ I *pp* ▶ **épauler**.

II *pp adj* [*vêtement*] with padded shoulders.

épaulé-jeté, *pl* **épaulés-jetés** /epole ʒəte/ *nm* clean-and-jerk.

épaulement /epolmɑ̃/ *nm* **1** Archit, Constr shouldering wall; **2** Mil breastworks; **3** Géol escarpment.

épauler /epole/ [1] I *vtr* **1** (aider) to help, to support [*personne*]; **je ne suis pas épaulé** I don't get any support; **2** Chasse, Mil (mettre à l'épaule) to take aim with, to raise [*fusil*]; **3** Cout (rembourrer) to pad the shoulders of [*veste*]; **4** Constr to shoulder.

II *vi* Chasse, Mil to take aim.

épaulette /epolɛt/ *nf* **1** Cout (rembourrage) shoulder-pad; (bretelle) (shoulder-)strap; **2** Mil epaulette.

épave /epav/ *nf* **1** Naut (navire entier) wreck; **2** (voiture) gén wreck; (après un accident) write-off○; (débris) bit of wreckage; **3** (personne) wreck; **4** Jur derelict.

épée /epe/ *nf* **1** (arme) sword; **se battre à l'~** to fight with swords; **tirer l'~** to draw one's sword; **c'est un coup d'~ dans l'eau** fig it was a complete waste of effort; **passer qn au fil de l'~** to put sb to the sword; **2** (personne) swordsman/woman; **excellente ~** excellent swordsman/woman; **3** (sport) épée fencing.

■ **l'~ de Damoclès** the sword of Damocles.

épéiste /epeist/ *nmf* swordsman/woman, épéeist spéc.

épeler /eple/ [19] *vtr* to spell [*mot*].

épépiner /epepine/ [1] *vtr* to seed.

éperdu, ~e /epɛʀdy/ *adj* [*besoin, désir*] overwhelming; [*cri*] frantic; [*regard*] desperate; [*fuite*] headlong (*épith*); [*amour, reconnaissance*] boundless; **~ de** overcome with.

éperdument /epɛʀdymɑ̃/ *adv* [*crier*] frantically; [*amoureux*] madly; **un pays ~ en quête de stabilité politique** a country desperately in search of political stability; **je me moque** or **me fiche**○ **~ de ce qu'il pense** I couldn't care less about what he thinks.

éperlan /epɛʀlɑ̃/ *nm* smelt.

éperon /epʀɔ̃/ *nm* **1** spur; **donner** ou **piquer des ~s** to spur on a horse; **2** (aiguillon) spur; **sous l'~ de la nécessité** under the spur of necessity; **3** (ergot) spur; **4** (ouvrage en saillie) spur; **5** (de bateau) ram.

éperonner /epʀɔne/ [1] *vtr* **1** Équit to spur on [*cheval*]; **2** (aiguillonner) to spur on [*personne*]; **éperonné par la terreur** spurred on by terror; **3** Naut to ram.

épervier /epɛʀvje/ *nm* **1** (oiseau) sparrowhawk; **2** (filet de pêche) cast net.

éphèbe /efɛb/ *nm* **1** hum Adonis; **2** Hist ephebe.

éphédrine /efedʀin/ *nf* ephedrine.

éphémère /efemɛʀ/ I *adj* [*bonheur, amour*] fleeting, ephemeral; [*délice, utopie*] ephemeral; [*succès, gloire*] short-lived, ephemeral; [*produit, insecte*] short-lived; **de manière ~** fleetingly.

II *nm* mayfly, ephemera spéc.

éphéméride /efemeʀid/ I *nf* (calendrier) block calendar, tear-off calendar.

II **éphémérides** *nfpl* Astron ephemerides.

Éphèse /efɛz/ *npr* Ephesus.

éphésien, -ienne /efezjɛ̃, ɛn/ *adj* Ephesian.

épi /epi/ *nm* **1** Bot (de blé, d'avoine) ear; (de fleur) spike; **2** (mèche) (unmanageable) tuft of hair GB, cow-lick US; **3** Tech (jetée) groyne GB, groin US; **se garer en ~** to park at an angle to the kerb GB ou curb US.

■ **~ de faîtage** Constr finial; **~ de maïs** corn cob; **~ du vent** Naut eye of the wind.

épicarpe /epikaʀp/ *nm* epicarp.

épice /epis/ *nf* spice.

épicé, ~e /epise/ I *pp* ▶ **épicer**.

II *pp adj* **1** Culin (parfumé) spicy; (fort) [*curry*] hot; **très ~** highly spiced, very spicy; **2** (grivois) [*anecdote*] spicy, racy.

épicéa /episea/ *nm* spruce.

épicène /episɛn/ *adj* epicene.

épicentre /episɑ̃tʀ/ *nm* (tous contextes) epicentre.

épicer /epise/ [12] *vtr* **1** Culin to spice [*plat*]; **2** fig to add spice to [*conversation*].

épicerie /episʀi/ ▶510 *nf* **1** (boutique) grocer's (shop) GB, grocery (store) US; **à l'~** at the grocer's; **2** (commerce) grocery trade; **3** (produits) groceries.

■ **~ fine** delicatessen.

épicier, -ière /episje, ɛʀ/ ▶510 *nm,f* grocer; **chez l'~** at the grocer's.

■ **~ en gros** wholesale grocer.

Épicure /epikyʀ/ *npr* Epicurus.

épicurien, -ienne /epikyʀjɛ̃, ɛn/ *adj* **1** Philos Epicurean; **2** (bon vivant) epicurean.

épicurisme /epikyʀism/ *nm* Epicureanism.

épidémie /epidemi/ *nf* Méd, fig epidemic.

épidémiologie /epidemjɔlɔʒi/ *nf* epidemiology.

épidémiologique /epidemjɔlɔʒik/ *adj* epidemiological.

épidémiologiste /epidemjɔlɔʒist/ *nmf* epidemiologist.

épidémique /epidemik/ *adj* Méd epidemic.

épiderme /epidɛʀm/ *nm* Anat skin, epidermis spéc; Bot epidermis; **avoir l'~ chatouilleux** fig to be touchy.

épidermique /epidɛʀmik/ *adj* **1** (de l'épiderme) skin (*épith*), epidermal spéc, epidermic spéc; [*blessure*] skin-deep; [*lésion, greffe*] skin; **2** fig [*sensibilité*] extreme; **une réaction ~** a gut reaction.

épididyme /epididim/ *nm* epididymis.

épier /epje/ [2] *vtr* **1** (observer) to spy on [*personne, comportement*]; **il épie tous mes faits et gestes** he watches my every move; **2** (attendre) to be on the lookout for.

épieu, *pl* **~x** /epjø/ *nm* Chasse spear.

épigastre /epigastʀ/ *nm* epigastrium.

épiglotte /epiglɔt/ *nf* epiglottis.

épigone /epigɔn/ *nm* epigone.

épigramme /epigʀam/ *nf* epigram.

épigraphe /epigʀaf/ *nf* epigraph.

épigraphique /epigʀafik/ *adj* epigraphical.

épilation /epilasjɔ̃/ *nf* removal of unwanted hair; (à la cire) waxing.

épilatoire /epilatwaʀ/ *adj* hair-removing, depilatory.

épilepsie /epilɛpsi/ ▶271 *nf* epilepsy; **crise d'~** epileptic fit.

épileptique /epilɛptik/ *adj, nmf* epileptic.

épiler /epile/ [1] I *vtr* to remove unwanted hair from, to depilate; (à la cire) to wax [*jambe, visage*]; to pluck [*sourcils*]; **se faire ~ les jambes** to have one's legs waxed; **crème à ~** hair-removing cream; **pince à ~** tweezers (*pl*).

II **s'épiler** *vpr* **s'~ les sourcils** to pluck one's eyebrows; **s'~ le menton** to remove the hairs from one's chin.

épilobe /epilɔb/ *nf* rosebay willowherb.

épilogue /epilɔg/ *nm* **1** Littérat epilogue[GB]; **2** fig outcome.

épiloguer /epilɔge/ [1] *vi* to go on and on (**sur** about); **inutile d'~** there's no good going on and on about it; **on a beaucoup épilogué sur...** a lot has been said about...

épinard /epinaʀ/ *nm* **1** Bot spinach ¢; **2** Culin **les ~s** spinach ¢.

IDIOMES **ça met du beurre dans les ~s** it makes life that little bit easier.

épine /epin/ *nf* thorn, prickle; **sans ~s** [*mûres*] thornless.

■ **~ blanche** Bot hawthorn; **~ dorsale** Anat spine, backbone; fig backbone; **~ noire** Bot blackthorn.

IDIOMES **ôter** or **enlever** or **retirer à qn une ~ du pied** to take a weight off sb's shoulders.

épinette /epinɛt/ *nf* **1** Mus spinet; **2** Bot spruce; **3** C (boisson) (**bière d'**)**~** spruce beer.

■ **~ blanche** Bot white spruce; **~ noire** Bot black spruce.

épineux, -euse /epinø, øz/ *adj* [*tige*] prickly, thorny; [*problème*] thorny, tricky; [*question*] vexed; [*situation*] tricky; [*caractère*] prickly, touchy.

épinglage /epɛ̃glaʒ/ *nm* pinning.

épingle /epɛ̃gl/ *nf* pin.

■ **~ à chapeau** hatpin; **~ à cheveux** hairpin; **virage en ~** (**à cheveux**) hairpin bend; **~ de cravate** tiepin; **~ neige** very fine hairpin; **~ de** or **à nourrice**, **~ de sûreté** safety pin.

IDIOMES **monter qch en ~** to blow sth up out of proportion; **être tiré à quatre ~s** to be immaculately dressed; **tirer son ~ du jeu** to get out while the going is good.

épingler /epɛ̃gle/ [1] *vtr* **1** (fixer) to pin; **~ une affiche au mur/sur une porte** to pin a poster up on the wall/on a door; **~ ses cheveux** to pin up one's hair; **~ sa cravate** to put in a tiepin; **~ des billets** to pin banknotes GB ou bills US together; **2** Cout to pin; **3** (collectionner) to chalk up [*succès*]; **~ qn/qch à son palmarès** to add sb/sth to one's list of triumphs; **4**○ (prendre à parti) to take [sb] to task [*personne, groupe*]; to single out [sth] for criticism [*propos, défauts*]; **5**○ (arrêter) [*police*] to collar○; **se faire ~** to be collared.

épinglette /epɛ̃glɛt/ *nf* lapel pin.

épinière /epinjɛʀ/ *adj f* **moelle ~** spinal cord.

épinoche /epinɔʃ/ *nf* (three-spined) stickleback.

Épiphanie /epifani/ *nprf* **l'~** Epiphany, Twelfth Night; **à l'~** on Twelfth Night.

épiphénomène /epifenɔmɛn/ *nm* epiphenomenon.

épiphyse /epifiz/ *nf* epiphysis.

épiphyte /epifit/ *adj* epiphytic.

épique /epik/ *adj* epic; **poème ~** epic; **crois-moi, c'était ~**○ hum believe me, it was quite something○.

épiscopal, ~e, *mpl* **-aux** /episkɔpal, o/ *adj* episcopal.

épiscopat /episkɔpa/ *nm* episcopate, episcopacy.

épiscope /episkɔp/ *nm* **1** (appareil optique) episcope GB, opaque projector US; **2** Mil periscope.

épisiotomie /epizjɔtɔmi/ *nf* episiotomy.

épisode /epizɔd/ *nm* episode; **un ~ peu glorieux** a sordid episode; **roman à ~s** serialized novel.

épisodique /epizɔdik/ *adj* **1** (secondaire) [*incident, rôle*] minor; **2** (intermittent) [*crises, relations*] sporadic, episodic sout; [*rôle*] occasional; **plusieurs personnages ~s traversent le roman** several characters flit in and out of the novel.

épisodiquement /epizɔdikmɑ̃/ *adv* sporadically.

épisser /epise/ [1] *vtr* to splice.

épissoir /episwaʀ/ *nm* fid, marline spike.

épissure /episyʀ/ *nf* splice.

épistémologie /epistemɔlɔʒi/ *nf* epistemology.

épistémologique /epistemɔlɔʒik/ *adj* epistemological.

épistolaire /epistɔlɛʀ/ *adj* [*genre*] epistolary; **ils ont des relations ~s** they correspond.

épistolier, **-ière** /epistɔlje, ɛʀ/ *nm,f* letter-writer.

épitaphe /epitaf/ *nf* epitaph; **en ~** as an epitaph.

épithélial, **~e**, *mpl* **-iaux** /epiteljal, o/ *adj* epithelial.

épithélium /epiteljɔm/ *nm* epithelium.

épithète /epitɛt/ *nf* **1** Ling attributive adjective; **2** (qualificatif) epithet.

épitoge /epitɔʒ/ *nf* (d'avocat, de professeur) hood.

épître /epitʀ/ *nf* **1** Littér epistle; **2** Relig Epistle; **les ~s de saint Paul** the Epistles of Saint Paul.

épizootie /epizɔɔti/ *nf* epizootic.

éploré, **~e** /eplɔʀe/ *adj* (affligé) grief-stricken; (en pleurs) tearful, weeping.

éployé, **~e** /eplwaje/ *adj* spread (out).

épluchage /eplyʃaʒ/ *nm* **1** (de fruit, carotte) peeling; **2** Tex (de laine) picking; **3** fig (de texte) dissection.

épluche-légume, *pl* **~s** /eplyʃlegym/ *nm* potato peeler.

éplucher /eplyʃe/ [1] *vtr* **1** lit to peel [*fruit, légume*]; to pick [*laine*]; **2** fig to go through [sth] with a fine-tooth comb [*article, comptes*].

éplucheur /eplyʃœʀ/ *nm* Culin potato peeler.

épluchure /eplyʃyʀ/ *nf* **~ de pomme/d'orange etc** piece of apple/orange etc peel; **~s** peelings.

épointer /epwɛ̃te/ [1] *vtr* to blunt.

éponge /epɔ̃ʒ/ *nf* **1** (pour nettoyer) sponge; **donner un coup d'~ à qch** to sponge sth (down); **2** (tissu) terry-towelling[GB]; **3** Zool sponge.

■ **~ métallique** (pan) scourer.

IDIOMES **passer l'~** to forget the past; **passer l'~ sur qch** to forget all about sth; **boire comme une ~** to drink like a fish; **jeter l'~** to throw in the towel GB ou sponge.

éponger /epɔ̃ʒe/ [13] **I** *vtr* **1** to mop up [*liquide*]; to mop [*sueur, front, surface*]; **2** to absorb [*déficit*]; to soak up [*excédent*]; to pay off [*dettes*]; **~ un retard** to make up for lost time.

II s'éponger *vpr* **s'~ le front/visage** to mop one's brow/face.

éponyme /epɔnim/ **I** *adj* eponymous.

II *nm* eponym.

épopée /epɔpe/ *nf* **1** Littérat epic; **2** (suite d'événements) saga.

époque /epɔk/ *nf* **1** (période quelconque) time; **à l'~, à cette ~** at that time; **à l'~ où** at the time when; **à cette ~ de l'année** (présente) at this time of the year; (passée, future) at that time of the year; **l'an passé/prochain à la même ~** at the same time last/next year; **de l'~** [*objet, mode, esprit*] of the time; **un témoin/souvenir de l'~ où** a witness/memory from the time when; **d'une autre ~** from another time; **il est d'une autre ~** he belongs to another time; **c'est l'~ qui veut ça** it's a sign of the times; **il faut vivre avec son ~** one must move with the times; **l'~ est au pragmatisme** pragmatism is the order of the day; **quelle ~!** what's the world coming to!; **nous vivons une ~ moderne/formidable** iron it's a modern/an amazing world iron; **à mon/leur etc ~** in my/their etc day; **à notre ~** (aujourd'hui) these days; **la pensée/psychiatrie de notre ~** contemporary thought/psychiatry; **les grands artistes/chefs d'œuvre de notre ~** the great artists/masterpieces of our time; **2** (période historique) era; **l'~ féodale/stalinienne** the feudal/Stalinist era; **l'~ victorienne** the Victorian age; **3** (période stylistique) period; **de l'~ surréaliste** from the surrealist period; **un costume/décor d'~** (authentique) a costume from the period/an authentic setting; (imité) a period costume/setting; **d'~ Renaissance/Louis-Philippe** from the Renaissance/Louis-Philippe period; **des meubles d'~** antique furniture; **joué sur instruments d'~** played on period instruments; **4** Astron, Géol epoch.

épouiller /epuje/ [1] *vtr* to delouse.

époumoner: **s'époumoner**○ /epumɔne/ [1] *vpr* lit, fig to shout oneself hoarse, to shout one's head off○; (en chantant) to sing oneself hoarse.

épousailles† /epuzɑj/ *nfpl* nuptials sout.

épouse /epuz/ *nf* wife, spouse.

épousée† /epuze/ *nf* bride.

épouser /epuze/ [1] *vtr* **1** to marry, to wed [*personne*]; **~ un beau parti** to marry into money; **2** to adopt, to espouse [*cause, idée*]; **3** [*chemin*] to follow (closely) [*relief, contours*]; **une robe qui épouse les formes** a figure-hugging dress.

époussetage /epustaʒ/ *nm* dusting.

épousseter /epuste/ [20] *vtr* to dust.

époustouflant○, **~e** /epustuflɑ̃, ɑ̃t/ *adj* amazing, incredible; [*talent*] breathtaking; **~ de courage** amazingly ou incredibly brave.

époustoufler○ /epustufle/ [1] *vtr* to amaze, to astound; **être époustouflé de/par qch** to be flabbergasted ou astounded at/by sth.

épouvantable /epuvɑ̃tabl/ *adj* gén dreadful, terrible; (atroce) appalling.

épouvantablement /epuvɑ̃tabləmɑ̃/ *adv* terribly, dreadfully.

épouvantail /epuvɑ̃taj/ *nm* **1** (à oiseaux) scarecrow; **2**○ (personne laide) fright; **3** (menace) spectre[GB]; **brandir l'~ du protectionnisme** to brandish the spectre[GB] of protectionism.

épouvante /epuvɑ̃t/ *nf* (terreur) terror; (horreur) horror; **glacé d'~** paralysed[GB] with terror; **frappé d'~** terror- ou horror-stricken; **roman/film d'~** horror story/film; **vision d'~** terrifying vision.

épouvanter /epuvɑ̃te/ [1] **I** *vtr* **1** (terrifier) to terrify; **2** (horrifier) to horrify, appal[GB].

II s'épouvanter *vpr* to get frightened (**de** at).

époux /epu/ **I** *nm* husband, spouse.

II *nmpl* **les ~** the (married) couple, the husband and wife; **les jeunes ~** the newly weds; **les ~ Martin** Mr and Mrs Martin.

époxy /epɔksi/ **I** *adj inv* epoxy; **résines ~** epoxy resins.

II *nf* epoxy.

éprendre: **s'éprendre de** /epʀɑ̃dʀ/ [52] *vpr* to become enamoured of, to fall in love with [*personne*]; to develop a passion for [*aventure*].

épreuve /epʀœv/ *nf* **1** (moment pénible) ordeal; **une suite d'~s** a succession of ordeals; **subir de dures ~s** to go through terrible ordeals; **surmonter une ~** to get over an ordeal; **la crise économique et les ~s qu'elle a entraînées** the economic crisis and the suffering it brought with it; **2** (testant valeur, résistance) test; **mettre qch/qn à l'~** to put sth/sb to the test; **mettre à rude ~** to put [sb] to a severe test [*personne*]; to be very hard on [*voiture, chaussures*]; to tax [*patience, nerfs*]; to put a strain on [*amitié, relation*]; **soumettre qch à l'~ de qch** to subject sth to the test of sth; **l'~ de force entre** the test of strength between; **procéder à l'~ d'un appareil** to test a device; **à toute ~** [*patience, solidité*] unfailing (*épith*); **résister à l'~ du temps** to stand the test of time; **l'~ du feu** ordeal by fire; **à l'~ du feu/des balles** [*cloison, vêtement*] fire-/bullet-proof; **3** (partie d'examen) gén (part of an) examination; **~ orale** oral examination; **~ écrite** paper, written examination; **~ d'histoire/de chimie** history/chemistry examination; **une ~ obligatoire/facultative** a compulsory/an optional part of the examination; **la deuxième ~ du concours de piano** the second part of the piano competition; **~ anticipée de français** baccalaureate French paper (*taken one year before the other subjects chosen for the baccalaureate*); **4** Sport **~ d'athlétisme** athletics event; **~s sur terrain/piste** field/track events; **~s éliminatoires** heats; **~s de sélection** trials; **5** Édition, Imprim proof; **premières ~s** galley proofs; **corriger des ~s** to proof-read; **6** Cin **~s de tournage** rushes; **7** Phot proof; (estampe) proof.

■ **~ de vérité** acid test.

épris, **~e** /epʀi, iz/ **I** *pp* ▶ **éprendre**.

II *pp adj* **1** (amoureux) in love (**de** with), smitten†○ (**de** with); **2** (passionné) **~ d'aventure/de voyages** with a great love of adventure/of travelling[GB]; **être ~ de qch** to have a great love of sth.

éprouvant, **~e** /epʀuvɑ̃, ɑ̃t/ *adj* [*attente, période, travail*] gruelling[GB]; [*bruit, climat, situation*] trying.

éprouvé, **~e** /epʀuve/ **I** *pp* ▶ **éprouver**.

II *pp adj* [*méthode, technique*] tried and tested; [*technicien*] dependable.

éprouver /epʀuve/ [1] *vtr* **1** (ressentir) to feel [*regret, désir, amour*]; to have [*sensation, doute, difficulté*]; **~ une gêne à faire** to feel embarrassed to do; **~ le besoin/désir de faire** to feel the need/a desire to do; **~ de la colère contre qn** to feel angry with sb; **~ des difficultés à faire** to have difficulties in doing; **je n'éprouve aucune sympathie pour lui** I thoroughly dislike him; **~ de la jalousie** to be jealous; **~ une sensation de froid** to feel cold; **~ un sentiment d'abandon/d'impuissance** to feel abandoned/powerless; **~ du plaisir** (sexuellement) to experience pleasure; **~ du plaisir à faire** to get pleasure out of doing; **j'éprouve toujours autant de plaisir à t'écrire** I still enjoy writing to you; **2** (mettre à l'épreuve) to test [*personne, sentiment, matériel, théorie, méthode*]; **avoir recours à une technique éprouvée** to resort to a tried and tested technique; **3** (toucher) [*décès, événement*] to distress [*personne*]; [*épidémie, tempête, crise*] to hit [*population, région*]; **le sud du pays a été sévèrement éprouvé par les incendies/la crise** the south of the country has been badly hit ou affected by fires/the crisis; **l'enfant a été très éprouvé par ce qu'il a vu** the child was very distressed by what he saw.

éprouvette /epʀuvɛt/ *nf* (tube) test tube; (échantillon) sample; **bébé ~** test-tube baby.

EPS /œpeɛs/ *nf* (*abbr* = **éducation physique et sportive**) Scol PE.

epsilon /ɛpsilɔn/ *nm inv* epsilon.

épuisant, **~e** /epɥizɑ̃, ɑ̃t/ *adj* [*activité, enfant*] exhausting; [*adulte*] wearing.

épuisé, **~e** /epɥize/ **I** *pp* ▶ **épuiser**.

II *pp adj* **1** (fatigué) [*personne, animal*] exhausted; **être ~ nerveusement** to be emotionally drained; **2** (appauvri) [*sol*] impoverished; **3** (non disponible) [*publication, livre*] out of print; [*article*] out of stock; **notre stock est ~** we're sold out; **4** (consommé) [*stock, vivres*] exhausted.

épuisement /epɥizmɑ̃/ *nm* **1** (fatigue) exhaustion; **tomber d'~** to collapse from exhaustion; **le matériel commence à donner des signes d'~** the equipment is starting to show signs of wearing out; **2** (amenuisement) exhaustion; **~ des vivres/ressources** exhaustion of supplies/resources; **jusqu'à ~ des stocks** Comm while stocks last.

■ **~ des sols** Agric soil impoverishment.

épuiser /epɥize/ [1] **I** *vtr* **1** (fatiguer) [*activité*] to exhaust, wear [sb] out; [*souci, personne*] to wear [sb] out; **2** (finir) to exhaust [*sujet, filon, mine*]; **3** (appauvrir) to impoverish [*sol*].

II s'épuiser *vpr* **1** (se fatiguer) [*personne*] to exhaust oneself; **s'~ à faire qch** to wear oneself out doing sth; **2** (s'amenuiser) [*réserves, ressources*] to become exhausted.

épuisette /epɥizɛt/ *nf* **1** Pêche landing net; (à crevettes) shrimp net; **2** (écope) scoop.

épurateur /epyʀatœʀ/ *nm* purifier.

épuration /epyʀasjɔ̃/ *nf* **1** (de gaz, liquide) purification; (de pétrole) refining; (d'eaux usées) treatment; **2** (de groupe, parti) purge; **3** (de texte) expurgation; (de langue) refining; (de mœurs) cleaning up.
■ **~ extrarénale** Méd haemodialysis.

épure /epyʀ/ *nf* Archit, Tech working drawing; Math diagram.

épurer /epyʀe/ [1] *vtr* **1** Chimie to purify [*eau, gaz*]; **2** to purge [*parti*]; to clean up [*mœurs*]; to refine [*style, goût*]; to expurgate [*texte*].

équanimité /ekwanimite/ *nf* equanimity.

équarrir /ekaʀiʀ/ [3] *vtr* **1** (tailler) to square (off) [*pierre, bois*]; **mal équarri** lit, fig rough-hewn; **2** (découper) to quarter [*animal*].

équarrissage /ekaʀisaʒ/ *nm* **1** (de bois, pierre) squaring (off); **2** (d'animal) quartering; **cheval tout juste bon pour l'~** horse only fit for the knacker's yard GB, horse ready for the glue factory US.

équarrisseur /ekaʀisœʀ/ *nm* slaughterman GB, renderer US; (de chevaux) knacker GB.

équateur /ekwatœʀ/ *nm* Equator.

Équateur /ekwatœʀ/ ▶ **321** *nprm* **(la République de) l'~** Ecuador.

équation /ekwasjɔ̃/ *nf* equation; **~ du premier/second degré** simple/quadratic equation; **mettre en ~** to put into an equation.

équatorial, **~e**, *mpl* **-iaux** /ekwatɔʀjal, o/ *adj* equatorial.

équatorien, **-ienne** /ekwatɔʀjɛ̃, ɛn/ ▶ **537** *adj* Ecuadorian, Ecuadoran.

Équatorien, **-ienne** /ekwatɔʀjɛ̃, ɛn/ ▶ **537** *nm,f* Ecuadorian, Ecuadoran.

équerre /ekɛʀ/ *nf* **1** (à dessin) set square; **en** or **d'~** at right angles; **double ~** T-square; **~ à coulisse** sliding callipers[GB]; **2** (support) (en T) flat T-bracket; (en L) flat angle bracket.

équestre /ekɛstʀ/ *adj* equestrian; **centre ~** riding school.

équeuter /ekøte/ [1] *vtr* to remove the stalk from GB, to stem US [*cerise*]; to hull GB, to stem US [*fraise*].

équidé /ekide/ *nm* equid; **les ~s** Equidae.

équidistance /ekɥidistɑ̃s/ *nf* equidistance; **à ~ de** equidistant from.

équidistant, **~e** /ekɥidistɑ̃, ɑ̃t/ *adj* equidistant (**de** from).

équilatéral, **~e**, *mpl* **-aux** /ekɥilateʀal, o/ *adj* equilateral.

équilibrage /ekilibʀaʒ/ *nm* Mécan balancing.

équilibrant, **~e** /ekilibʀɑ̃, ɑ̃t/ *adj* **régime ~** healthy diet; **shampooing ~** shampoo that restores the hair's natural pH balance.

équilibre /ekilibʀ/ *nm* **1** (fait de ne pas tomber) balance; **garder/perdre l'~** to keep/to lose one's balance; **l'oreille interne est le centre de l'~** the inner ear controls balance; **être en ~ sur qch** [*objet*] to be balanced on sth; [*personne*] to balance on sth; **tenir qch en ~ (sur qch)** to balance sth (on sth); **se tenir en ~ sur un pied** to balance on one leg; **être en ~ instable sur qch** to be precariously balanced on sth; **numéro d'~** balancing act; **2** (entre deux éléments, poids) balance (**entre** between); (stabilité) stability; **l'~ des forces** Pol the balance of power; **l'~ politique/économique** political/economic stability; **l'~ de la terreur** the balance of terror; **l'~ naturel** the natural balance; **trouver un ~** [*pays, couple*] to find a balance; **être en ~** [*objets*] to be balanced; **assurer l'~ budgétaire** to balance the budget; **la préservation des grands ~s naturels** the preservation of the great ecosystems; **3** (bien-être, santé mentale) equilibrium; **manquer d'~** to be unstable; **retrouver son ~** to get back to normal; **4** (bonne combinaison) (de formes, phrase, d'alimentation) balance; **5** Chimie, Phys, Mécan equilibrium.

équilibré, **~e** /ekilibʀe/ **I** *pp* ▶ **équilibrer**.
II *pp adj* **1** [*emploi du temps, alimentation*] balanced; Fin, Mécan balanced; **le chargement est mal ~** the load is unevenly distributed; **2** [*personne, esprit*] well-balanced.

équilibrer /ekilibʀe/ [1] **I** *vtr* (tous contextes) to balance; **donne-moi l'autre sac, ça va m'~** give me the other bag, it'll balance out the first one; **il faut ~ son alimentation/son emploi du temps** one must have a balanced diet/schedule; **~ une façade** (en elle-même) to give balance to a façade; (avec nouvel élément) to balance a façade.
II s'équilibrer *vpr* [*facteurs, coûts*] to balance each other.

équilibriste /ekilibʀist/ *nmf* lit, fig acrobat.

équille /ekij/ *nf* sand eel, (sand) lance.

équin, **~e** /ekɛ̃, in/ *adj* equine; **le patrimoine ~** the national bloodstock.

équinoxe /ekinɔks/ *nm* equinox; **~ de printemps/d'automne** spring/autumn GB ou fall US equinox; **marée d'~** equinoctial spring tide.

équipage /ekipaʒ/ *nm* **1** Astronaut, Aviat, Naut crew; **2** Chasse hunt; **3** Hist (attelage) horse and carriage; **en grand ~** in state; **4** (habillement)† liter accoutrements[GB].

équipe /ekip/ *nf* **1** Sport gén team; (de rameurs) crew; **l'~ de France/d'Irlande** the French/Irish team; **former les ~s** to draw up the teams; **2** (groupe de travail) team; **une ~ de dix personnes** a team of ten people; **travailler en ~** to work as a team; **~ de secours/surveillance** rescue/surveillance team; **~ de dépannage** breakdown crew; **~ pédagogique** teaching staff; **~ de télévision** television crew; **~ de tournage** Cin film unit; **faire ~ avec qn** to team up with sb (**pour faire** to do); **l'~ dirigeante** the management team; **~ de tueurs** band of killers; **3** (de travail posté) shift; **~s successives** (successsive) shifts; **l'~ de nuit** the night shift; **travailler en ~s** to work in shifts; **4** (d'amis) team; pej bunch; **une fine ~** a fine bunch; **à eux deux/trois, ils forment une belle ~!** they make quite a pair, these two/quite a bunch, these three!

équipé, **~e** /ekipe/ **I** *pp* ▶ **équiper**.
II *pp adj* **1** (aménagé) [*appartement, véhicule*] **entièrement ~** fully equipped; **salle de bains/cuisine ~e** fitted bathroom/kitchen; **2** (pourvu) equipped (**de, en qch** with sth; **pour qch** for sth; **pour faire** to do); **bien/mal ~** well-/ill-equipped.
III équipée *nf* **1** (aventure) escapade; **une folle ~e** a wild escapade; **2** (promenade) jaunt.

équipement /ekipmɑ̃/ *nm* **1** (matériel) (d'usine, de cuisine, laboratoire) equipment; (de sportif) kit, gear; **2** (installation) **~s** facilities (*pl*); **~ portuaire** port facilities; **~s scolaires/sociaux/sportifs** school/social/sports facilities; **~ hôtelier d'une station** accommodation facilities of a resort; **3** (processus) (d'armée) equipping; (de soldat, sportif) kitting out; **l'~ de la région a coûté trois millions de francs** improving the region's facilities cost three million francs.
■ **~ automobile** car accessories; **~ de bord** on-board equipment; **~ électrique** (de véhicule) electrics (*pl*); (de maison) electrical fittings (*pl*); **~s collectifs** public facilities; **~s spéciaux** Aut bad weather equipment.

équipementier /ekipmɑ̃tje/ *nm* equipment manufacturer.

équiper /ekipe/ [1] **I** *vtr* to equip [*hôpital, bureau, véhicule*] (**de** with, to); to provide, to equip [*pays, ville*] (**de** with); to kit out GB, to fit out [*personne*] (**de** with).
II s'équiper *vpr* to equip oneself (**de** or **en qch** with sth; **pour qch** for sth; **pour faire** to do).

équipier, **-ière** /ekipje, ɛʀ/ *nm,f* gén team member; (rameur, marin) crew member.

équitable /ekitabl/ *adj* [*personne*] fair-minded, just; [*partage, décision*] fair, equitable.

équitablement /ekitabləmɑ̃/ *adv* equitably, fairly.

équitation /ekitasjɔ̃/ ▶ **449** *nf* (horse-)riding, equitation; **faire de l'~** to go (horse)-riding GB, to go horseback riding US.

équité /ekite/ *nf* equity; **en toute ~** in all fairness.

équivalence /ekivalɑ̃s/ *nf* **1** (valeur identique) equivalence; **à ~ de prix** for the same ou equivalent price; **2** Univ **demander/obtenir une ~** to ask for/obtain recognition of one's qualifications GB, to ask for/obtain advanced standing US; **titre admis en ~** recognized qualification; **obtenir un diplôme par ~** to obtain a diploma by transfer of credits; **3** Fin **mise en ~** equity accounting.

équivalent, **~e** /ekivalɑ̃, ɑ̃t/ **I** *adj* (égal) equivalent (**à** to); (identique) identical (**à** to); **à salaire ~** for the equivalent or same salary.
II *nm* equivalent; **c'est l'~ d'une augmentation de salaire** it's the equivalent of ou it amounts to an increase in salary; **l'~ en eau de la neige** the water equivalent of snow.

équivaloir /ekivalwaʀ/ [45] **I équivaloir à** *vtr ind* to be equivalent to [*quantité*]; to amount to [*effet*]; to be tantamount to [*effet négatif*]; **ça équivaut à un refus/à refuser** it's tantamount to a refusal/to refusing.
II s'équivaloir○ *vpr* **les deux solutions s'équivalent** there isn't much to choose between the two solutions; **ça s'équivaut!** it's six of one and half a dozen of the other.

équivoque /ekivɔk/ **I** *adj* (ambigu) ambiguous, equivocal; (suspect) [*réputation*] dubious; [*conduite*] questionable; (licencieux) [*geste*] indecent; [*regard*] suggestive.
II *nf* (ambiguïté) ambiguity; (faux-fuyant) equivocation; (malentendu) misunderstanding; **sans ~** [*réponse, condamnation, choix, soutien*] unequivocal; [*répondre, condamner, soutenir*] unequivocally; **réponse sans ~** unequivocal reply; **prêter à l'~** to be ambiguous; **lever l'~** to remove any doubt; **user d'~s** to equivocate.

érable /eʀabl/ *nm* **1** (arbre) maple(-tree); **feuille/sirop d'~** maple leaf/syrup GB ou sirup US; **2** (bois) maple(-wood).

érablière /eʀablijɛʀ/ *nf* maple plantation.

éradication /eʀadikasjɔ̃/ *nf* eradication.

éradiquer /eʀadike/ [1] *vtr* to eradicate [*mal, maladie*].

érafler /eʀafle/ [1] **I** *vtr* to scratch, to graze [*peau*]; to scratch [*surface*].
II s'érafler *vpr* to scratch ou graze oneself.

éraflure /eʀaflyʀ/ *nf* (au bras) scratch, graze; (sur une surface) scratch.

éraillé, **~e** /eʀɑje/ *adj* [*voix*] rasping, croaking (*épith*).

érailler /eʀɑje/ [1] **I** *vtr* to scratch [*surface*].
II s'érailler *vpr* [*voix*] to become hoarse.

Érasme /eʀasm/ *npr* Erasmus.

Érato /eʀato/ *npr* Erato.

erbium /ɛʀbjɔm/ *nm* erbium.

ère /ɛʀ/ *nf* **1** Hist, Géol era; **l'~ chrétienne** the Christian era; **100 ans avant notre ~** 100 years BC; **en l'an 1000 de notre ~** in the year 1000 AD; **2** (époque novatrice) age; **à l'~ industrielle/atomique** in the industrial/nuclear age.

érectile /eʀɛktil/ *adj* erectile.

érection /eʀɛksjɔ̃/ *nf* **1** (de statue) erection; fig setting-up, establishment; **2** Physiol erection.

éreintant○, **~e** /eʀɛ̃tɑ̃, ɑ̃t/ *adj* exhausting, killing○.

éreintement○ /eʀɛ̃tmɑ̃/ *nm* **1** (épuisement)

exhaustion; **2** (critique) slating○ GB, panning○.

éreinter○ /eʀɛ̃te/ [1] **I** *vtr* **1** (fatiguer) to exhaust, to tire out; **être éreinté** to be exhausted ou whacked○; **2**○ (critiquer) to slate○ GB, to pan○ [*œuvre, auteur*]; **éreinté par la critique** slated by the critics.
II s'éreinter *vpr* to wear ou tire oneself out; **s'~ à faire qch** to wear oneself out ou kill oneself○ doing sth.

érésipèle† /eʀezipɛl/ *nm* = **érysipèle**.

Érevan /eʀevan/ **▶857** *npr* Yerevan, Erevan.

erg /ɛʀg/ *nm* Géog, Phys erg.

ergatif, -ive /ɛʀgatif, iv/ **I** *adj* ergative.
II *nm* ergative (case).

ergométrie /ɛʀgɔmetʀi/ *nf* measurement of muscular effort.

ergonome /ɛʀgɔnɔm/ **▶510** *nmf* ergonomist.

ergonomie /ɛʀgɔnɔmi/ *nf* ergonomics (+ *v sg*).

ergonomique /ɛʀgɔnɔmik/ *adj* ergonomic.

ergot /ɛʀgo/ *nm* **1** Zool (de coq) spur; (de chien) dewclaw; **2** Bot (de seigle) ergot; **3** Électrotech, Ordinat pin; Tech lug.
IDIOMES **elle s'est dressée sur ses ~s**○ her hackles rose○.

ergotage /ɛʀgɔtaʒ/ *nm* péj hair-splitting, quibbling.

ergoter /ɛʀgɔte/ [1] *vi* péj to split hairs, to quibble (**sur, à propos de** about).

ergoteur, -euse /ɛʀgɔtœʀ, øz/ *nm,f* quibbler.

ergothérapeute /ɛʀgoteʀapøt/ **▶510** *nmf* occupational therapist.

ergotine /ɛʀgɔtin/ *nf* ergot.

ergotisme /ɛʀgɔtism/ *nm* ergotism.

Érié /eʀje/ **▶459** *npr* **le lac ~** Lake Erie.

ériger /eʀiʒe/ [13] **I** *vtr* **1** to erect [*statue, bâtiment*]; **2** to establish, to set up [*tribunal, société*]; **~ la paresse en vertu** to elevate laziness to a virtue; **~ qn en héros** to set sb up as a hero.
II s'ériger *vpr* **1 s'~ en** to set oneself up as; **2** [*bâtiment*] to be erected.

ermitage /ɛʀmitaʒ/ *nm* **1** lit hermitage; **2** fig retreat.

ermite /ɛʀmit/ *nm* **1** lit hermit; **2** fig recluse; **vivre en ~** fig to live the life of a recluse.

éroder /eʀɔde/ [1] **I** *vtr* lit, fig to erode; to erode the value of [*monnaie*]; to undermine [*argument*].
II s'éroder *vpr* fig to become eroded.

érogène /eʀɔʒɛn/ *adj* erogenous.

Eros /eʀos/ *npr* Eros.

érosif, -ive /eʀozif, iv/ *adj* erosive.

érosion /eʀozjɔ̃/ *nf* (tous contextes) erosion; **~ monétaire** depreciation of the currency.

érotique /eʀɔtik/ *adj* erotic.

érotiquement /eʀɔtikmɑ̃/ *adv* erotically.

érotisation /eʀɔtizasjɔ̃/ *nf* eroticization.

érotiser /eʀɔtize/ [1] *vtr* to eroticize.

érotisme /eʀɔtism/ *nm* eroticism.

érotomane /eʀɔtɔman/ *nmf* erotomaniac.

errance /ɛʀɑ̃s/ *nf* restless wandering.

errant, ~e /ɛʀɑ̃, ɑ̃t/ *adj* (par nécessité) wandering; (par choix) rootless; **chien ~** stray dog.

errata /ɛʀata/ *nm inv* errata.

erratique /ɛʀatik/ *adj* **1** Méd [*douleur, grosseur*] erratic; [*fièvre*] intermittent; **2** Géol erratic.

erratum /ɛʀatɔm/ *nm* erratum.

errements /ɛʀmɑ̃/ *nmpl* fml transgressions; **retomber dans ses ~** to go back to one's bad old ways.

errer /ɛʀe/ [1] *vi* [*personne*] to wander (**par** about); [*regard, imagination*] to wander (**sur** over); [*animal*] to roam.

erreur /ɛʀœʀ/ *nf* **1** (inexactitude, idée fausse) mistake; **une grave ~** a serious mistake; **faire** or **commettre des ~s** to make mistakes; **~ de date/de dosage** mistake about the date/the amount; **~ de jugement/d'analyse/de méthode** error of judgment/of analysis/of method; **~ de calcul/de fait/de stratégie** calculation/factual/strategic error; **~ de traduction** translation error, mistranslation; **faire une ~ de diagnostic** to make the wrong diagnosis; **je le croyais riche mais c'était une ~** I thought he was rich but I was mistaken; **ce serait une ~ de croire**... it would be a mistake to think...; **sauf ~ ou omission** errors and omissions excepted; **2** (acte regrettable) mistake; **une ~ de jeunesse** a youthful mistake; **faire** or **commettre l'~ de refuser** to make the mistake of refusing; **faire** or **commettre une ~ en refusant** to make a mistake in refusing; **3** (confusion, fait de se tromper) **par ~** by mistake; **induire qn en ~** to mislead sb; **sauf ~ de ma part** if I'm not mistaken; **être dans l'~** to be mistaken; **vous faites ~** you are mistaken; **il y a ~** there has been a mistake; **il n'y a pas d'~ possible** there's no mistake; **'elle arrive'—'~! c'est lui'** 'here she is'—'no, you're wrong! it's him'; **il y a ~ sur la personne** fml it's a case of mistaken identity sout; **on a tous le droit à l'~** we're all entitled to make mistakes; **cette fois-ci vous n'avez plus droit à l'~** this time you've got to get it right; **le droit à l'~** the right to make mistakes; (des scientifiques) the right to error; **4** Jur error; **~ judiciaire** judicial error; **~ de droit** error of law.
■ **~ de syntaxe** Ordinat syntax error.

erroné, ~e /ɛʀɔne/ *adj* erroneous sout, incorrect; **'code ~'** 'code not valid'.

ersatz /ɛʀzats/ *nm* lit, fig ersatz, substitute; **~ de café** ersatz coffee, coffee substitute.

erse /ɛʀs/ **I ▶462** *nm* Ling Erse.
II *nf* Naut grommet.

éructation /eʀyktasjɔ̃/ *nf* eructation.

éructer /eʀykte/ [1] **I** *vtr* to bawl [*injures*].
II *vi* to eructate.

érudit, ~e /eʀydi, it/ **I** *adj* erudite, scholarly.
II *nm,f* scholar, erudite person.

érudition /eʀydisjɔ̃/ *nf* erudition, scholarship; **avec ~** eruditely.

éruptif, -ive /eʀyptif, iv/ *adj* eruptive.

éruption /eʀypsjɔ̃/ *nf* eruption; **entrer en ~** to erupt.

érysipèle /eʀizipɛl/ **▶271** *nm* erysipelas.

érythème /eʀitɛm/ *nm* erythema.
■ **~ fessier** nappy rash GB, diaper rash US.

Érythrée /eʀitʀe/ **▶692** *nprf* Eritrea.

érythréen, -éenne /eʀitʀeɛ̃, ɛn/ *adj* Eritrean.

Érythréen, -éenne /eʀitʀeɛ̃, ɛn/ *nm,f* Eritrean.

érythrocyte /eʀitʀɔsit/ *nm* erythrocyte.

ès /ɛs/ *prép* **licence ~ lettres** ≈ arts degree, B.A. (degree); **~ qualités** Jur ex officio; **docteur ~ sciences** Doctor of Science, DSc.

Ésaü /ezay/ *npr* Esau.

ESB /œɛsbe/ *nf*: *abbr* ▶ **encéphalopathie**.

esbigner○: **s'esbigner** /ɛzbiɲe/ [1] *vpr* to scarper○ GB, to clear off○.

esbroufe○ /ɛzbʀuf/ *nf* **c'est de l'~** it's all a lot of swank○; **faire de l'~** to swank, to show off; **sans ~** discreetly, without ostentation.

esbroufeur○ /ɛzbʀufœʀ/ *nm* swaggerer, swank.

escabeau, *pl* **~x** /ɛskabo/ *nm* **1** (tabouret) stool; (avec marches) kitchen steps; **2** (échelle) stepladder.

escadre /ɛskadʀ/ *nf* squadron.

escadrille /ɛskadʀij/ *nf* squadron.

escadron /ɛskadʀɔ̃/ *nm* **1** Mil company; **~ de la mort** death squad; **2** (groupe) crowd.

escalade /ɛskalad/ **▶449** *nf* **1** Sport (activité) climbing; (de montagne) ascent; **~ libre/artificielle** free/artificial climbing; **mur/tour d'~** climbing wall/tower; **faire de l'~** to go climbing; **2** (de mur, clôture) climbing; **3** Mil escalation; **4** (aggravation) escalation (**dans, de** of); **5** (augmentation) escalation (**de** in).

escalader /ɛskalade/ [1] *vtr* to scale [*mur, clôture*]; to climb [*montagne*].

escalator /ɛskalatɔʀ/ *nm* escalator®.

escale /ɛskal/ *nf* **1** (arrêt) gén stopover; **je les ai rencontrés à l'~ de Rio** I met them during the stopover in Rio; **faire ~ à Rio** Naut [*navire*] to call at Rio; [*passager*] to stop off in Rio; Aviat [*avion, passager*] to stop over in Rio; **faire une ~ imprévue à Rio** Naut [*navire, passager*] to make an unscheduled stop in Rio; Aviat [*avion, passager*] to have an unscheduled stopover in Rio; **faire Londres-Rio sans ~** [*navire*] to sail London-Rio direct; [*avion*] to fly London-Rio nonstop; **2** (durée) gén stopover; **six jours d'~, une ~ de six jours** a six-day stopover; **3** (lieu) Naut port of call; Aviat stopover.
■ **~ technique** Aviat refuelling[GB] stop; Naut overhaul.

escalier /ɛskalje/ *nm* **1** (ensemble architectural) staircase; **un ~ monumental** a monumental staircase; **2** (ensemble de marches) stairs (*pl*); **il a monté/descendu l'~** or **les ~s en courant** he ran up/down the stairs; **il s'est tué en tombant dans un ~** he fell down the stairs and killed himself; **nous nous sommes croisés dans l'~** we bumped into each other on the stairs.
■ **~ dérobé** concealed staircase; **~ en colimaçon** spiral staircase; **~ d'honneur** grand staircase; **~ mécanique** or **roulant** escalator; **~ de secours** emergency staircase; **~ de service** backstairs (*pl*), service stairs (*pl*).
IDIOMES **avoir l'esprit de l'~** always to think of the perfect retort too late.

escalope /ɛskalɔp/ *nf* escalope; **~ de veau/dinde** veal/turkey escalope.

escamotable /ɛskamɔtabl/ *adj* **1** Aviat retractable; **2** [*meuble, échelle*] foldaway (*épith*).

escamotage /ɛskamɔtaʒ/ *nm* **1** (par illusionniste) **il a réussi l'~ du lapin** he succeeded in making the rabbit disappear; **2** (de roues) retraction; (de meuble) folding away; **3** (dissimulation) (de fait, preuve) cover-up; (de personne) spiriting away; **4**† (vol) pilfering.

escamoter /ɛskamɔte/ [1] **I** *vtr* **1** (faire disparaître à la vue) [*illusionniste*] to make [sth] disappear; **2** (replier) to retract [*roues, aérofreins*]; **~ un lit** to fold a bed away; **3** (dissimuler) to cover up [sth]; **4** (éluder) to evade [*problème, débat*]; **5** (sauter) to skip [*mot, note, repas*]; **6**† (voler) to pilfer.
II s'escamoter *vpr* [*roues, aérofreins*] to retract; [*lit, siège*] to fold away.

escampette /ɛskɑ̃pɛt/ *nf* **prendre la poudre d'~**○ to scarper○ GB, to skedaddle○.

escapade /ɛskapad/ *nf* escapade; (balade) jaunt; **faire une ~** (fugue) to run away; (balade) to go on a jaunt.

escarbille /ɛskaʀbij/ *nf* speck of soot.

escarboucle /ɛskaʀbukl/ *nf* Minér carbuncle.

escarcelle‡ /ɛskaʀsɛl/ *nf* purse.

escargot /ɛskaʀgo/ *nm* Zool, Culin snail; **quel ~**○**!** fig what a slow-coach○!; **avancer comme un ~** to go at a snail's pace.
■ **~ de mer** winkle, periwinkle.

escargotière /ɛskaʀgɔtjɛʀ/ *nf* **1** (parc) snail-farm; **2** (plat) snail (serving) dish.

escarmouche /ɛskaʀmuʃ/ *nf* lit, fig skirmish.

escarpé, ~e /ɛskaʀpe/ *adj* [*chemin, pente*] steep; [*rocher*] craggy.

escarpement /ɛskaʀpəmɑ̃/ *nm* (versant) steep slope, escarpment spéc; (raideur) steepness; **faille d'~** Géol fault scarp.

escarpin /ɛskaʀpɛ̃/ *nm* court shoe GB, pump US.

escarpolette† /ɛskaʀpɔlɛt/ *nf* (garden) swing.

escarre /ɛskaʀ/ *nf* bedsore.

Escaut /ɛsko/ **▶ 357** *nprm* **l'~** the Scheldt.

eschatologie /ɛskatɔlɔʒi/ *nf* eschatology.

esche = **èche**.

Eschyle /ɛʃil/ *npr* Aeschylus.

escient /ɛsjɑ̃/ *nm* **à bon ~** [*agir*] wittingly, advisedly; **à mauvais ~** [*agir, parler*] ill-advisedly.

esclaffer: **s'esclaffer** fml /ɛsklafe/ [1] *vpr* to guffaw, to burst out laughing.

esclandre /ɛsklɑ̃dʀ/ *nm* scene, (public) outburst; **faire un ~** to make a scene.

esclavage /ɛsklavaʒ/ *nm* **1** (système) slavery; (condition) slavery, bondage littér; **réduire qn en ~** to enslave sb [*individu*]; to reduce sb to slavery [*groupe*]; **tenir un peuple dans l'~** to keep a people in bondage; **2** (contrainte) tyranny (**de** of).

esclavagisme /ɛsklavaʒism/ *nm* (doctrine) pro-slavery doctrine; (système) slavery.

esclavagiste /ɛsklavaʒist/ **I** *adj* [*politique*] pro-slavery (*épith*); [*État*] slave (*épith*).
II *nmf* pro-slaver, person in favour[GB] of slavery.

esclave /ɛsklav/ **I** *adj* (asservi) enslaved; (servile) servile; **être ~ de la mode/l'argent/devoir** to be a slave to fashion/money/duty; **être ~ de sa parole** to be a prisoner of one's word.
II *nmf* slave; **mener une vie d'~** to lead a slave's life or a life of slavery; **se rendre l'~ de qn** gén to make oneself into sb's slave; (par amour) to become enslaved to sb.

escogriffe /ɛskɔgʀif/ *nm* **(grand) ~** (tall) lanky ou gangling individual, beanpole○.

escomptable /ɛskɔ̃tabl/ *adj* discountable.

escompte /ɛskɔ̃t/ *nm* discount; **~ de 3%** 3% discount; **~ de caisse/facture** cash/trade discount.

escompter /ɛskɔ̃te/ [1] *vtr* **1** Fin to discount [*effet, traite*]; **2** (espérer) to anticipate, to hope for; **~ que** to expect ou anticipate that; **~ faire** to count on doing, to hope to do.

escopette† /ɛskɔpɛt/ *nf* blunderbuss.

escorte /ɛskɔʀt/ *nf* Mil, Naut escort; (suite) retinue, train; fig accompaniment; **faire ~ à qn** to escort sb; **sous bonne ~** under escort.

escorter /ɛskɔʀte/ [1] *vtr* to escort.

escorteur /ɛskɔʀtœʀ/ *nm* escort vessel.

escouade /ɛskwad/ *nf* **1** Mil squad; **2** (groupe) gang, band.

escrime /ɛskʀim/ **▶ 449** *nf* fencing; **faire de l'~** to fence, to do fencing.

escrimer○: **s'escrimer** /ɛskʀime/ [1] *vpr* **s'~ à faire** to knock○ ou wear oneself out trying to do; **s'~ sur qch** to work ou plug○ away at sth.

escrimeur, **-euse** /ɛskʀimœʀ, øz/ *nm,f* fencer.

escroc /ɛskʀo/ *nm* swindler, crook.

escroquer /ɛskʀɔke/ [1] *vtr* to swindle, to rip [sb] off○; **~ qch à qn**, **~ qn de qch** to swindle sb out of sth; **se faire ~** to be swindled ou ripped off○.

escroquerie /ɛskʀɔkʀi/ *nf* **1** (action) fraud, swindling; **tentative d'~** attempted fraud; **c'est de l'~!** it's a rip-off○, it's daylight robbery; **2** (résultat) swindle.

escudo /ɛskudo/ **▶ 46** *nm* escudo.

Esculape /ɛskylap/ *npr* Aesculapius.

esgourde◑ /ɛzguʀd/ *nf* lug◑ GB, ear.

Ésope /ezɔp/ *npr* Aesop.

ésotérique /ezɔteʀik/ *adj* [*propos*] esoteric; [*cercle*] closed.

ésotérisme /ezɔteʀism/ *nm* esotericism.

espace /ɛspas/ **I** *nm* **1** (place) space; **il manque d'~ dans son bureau** he hasn't got enough space in his office; **le canapé occupe beaucoup d'~** the sofa takes up a lot of space; **2** (lieu réservé à une activité) **~ de loisirs/culturel** leisure/arts complex; **~ d'accueil** reception area; **notre émission est un ~ de liberté** our programme[GB] provides a forum for free expression; **3** (sphère) arena; **~ politique/international** political/international arena; **4** (zone) area; **~ économique/naturel/urbain** economic/natural/urban area; **▶ grand**; **5** (intervalle) gap; **un ~ de 5 cm** a gap of 5 cm; **6** (laps de temps) **en l'~ de** in the space of; **en l'~ de quelques minutes** in the space of a few minutes; **l'~ d'un instant** for a moment; **ils se sont aimés l'~ d'une nuit** they were lovers for a night; **7** Astron space; **la conquête de l'~** the conquest of space; **~ interstellaire** interstellar space; **8** Math space.
II *nf* Imprim space.
■ **~ aérien** Jur airspace; **~ commercial** Comm commercial space **₵**; **~ publicitaire** Pub advertising space **₵**; **~ vert** Écol open space; **~ vital** living space.

espacement /ɛspasmɑ̃/ *nm* **1** gén (processus) spacing out; (situation) growing infrequency; **l'~ des crises** the growing infrequency of the attacks; **2** Imprim spacing; **barre d'~** space bar.

espacer /ɛspase/ [12] **I** *vtr* to space [sth] out [*objets, visites, appels téléphoniques*].
II s'espacer *vpr* to become less frequent.

espace-temps, *pl* **espaces-temps** /ɛspastɑ̃/ *nm* space-time (continuum).

espadon /ɛspadɔ̃/ *nm* swordfish.

espadrille /ɛspadʀij/ *nf* espadrille.

Espagne /ɛspaɲ/ **▶ 321** *nprf* Spain.
IDIOMES **bâtir des châteaux en ~** to build castles in the air.

espagnol, **~e** /ɛspaɲɔl/ **▶ 537** **I** *adj* Spanish.
II ▶ 462 *nm* Ling Spanish.

Espagnol, **~e** /ɛspaɲɔl/ **▶ 537** *nm,f* Spaniard; **les ~s** the Spanish, the Spaniards.

espagnolette /ɛspaɲɔlɛt/ *nf* continental window catch.

espalier /ɛspalje/ *nm* (treillis) espalier; (mur) fruit-wall; (méthode) espalier cultivation; **arbre en ~** espalier (tree).

espar /ɛspaʀ/ *nm* Naut spar.

espèce /ɛspɛs/ **I** *nf* **1** Biol species; **une ~ rare** a rare species; **~s animales/végétales** animal/plant species; **l'~ humaine** mankind; **2** (type) kind, sort; **des ~s de** kinds of, sorts of; **de toute ~** of every kind; **un menteur de la pire** or **de la plus belle ~** a liar of the worst sort; **les individus de ton ~** people of your sort; **en l'~** fml in this instance; **3** (dans description approximative) sort, kind; **il y avait des ~s de colonnes dans l'entrée** there were sort of column things in the entrance; **une ~ de tasse** a sort of cup; **cela n'a aucune ~ d'intérêt/d'importance** that is of absolutely no interest/importance; **~ d'idiot/d'imbécile!** you idiot/fool!; **cette ~ d'idiot n'a même pas...** that stupid idiot didn't even...
II espèces *nfpl* **1** Fin **en ~s** [*payer, règlements*] in cash; **▶ sonnant**; **2** Relig **~s (eucharistiques)** species.

espérance /ɛspeʀɑ̃s/ **I** *nf* aussi Relig hope (**de qch** of sth); **contre toute ~** against all hope; **dans l'~ de trouver une réponse**, **dans l'~ que je trouverai une réponse** in the hope of finding an answer.
II espérances *nfpl* **1** (aspirations) expectations; **un résultat à la hauteur de ses ~s** a result equal to her expectations; **cela va au-delà de toutes mes ~s** it's beyond my wildest dreams; **2**† (héritage attendu) euph expectations.
■ **~ de vie** life expectancy.

espérantiste /ɛspeʀɑ̃tist/ *adj, nmf* Esperanto speaker, Esperantist.

espéranto /ɛspeʀɑ̃to/ **▶ 462** *nm* Esperanto.

espérer /ɛspeʀe/ [14] **I** *vtr* **1** (appeler de ses vœux) **~ qch** to hope for sth; **il n'y a plus rien/grand-chose à ~** there's nothing left/not much left to hope for; **~ faire** to hope to do; **j'espère avoir fait** I hope (that) I have done; **~ que** to hope (that); **ceci, je l'espère, te conviendra** this, I hope, will suit you; **il comprendra, j'espère?** he will understand, I hope?; **'il comprendra?'—'je l'espère/j'espère bien'** 'will he understand?'—'I hope so/I should hope so'; **j'espère que oui/que non** I hope so/not; **que peut-on ~ de plus?** what more can you hope for?; **laisser ~ que** to raise hopes that; **laisser ~ une guérison rapide** to raise hopes of a rapid recovery; **2** (escompter) to expect (**de** from); **je n' en espérais pas tant** it's more than I expected; **laisser ~ qch à qn** to lead sb to expect sth; **je ne t'espérais plus** I had given up on you.
II *vi* to hope; **on peut toujours ~!** iron one can always hope!; **~ en Dieu** to trust in God.

esperluette /ɛspɛʀlɥɛt/ *nf* ampersand.

espiègle /ɛspjɛgl/ **I** *adj* [*enfant, humour*] mischievous, impish (*épith*); [*air, regard*] mischievous; **d'un air ~** mischievously.
II *nmf* imp, little monkey○.

espièglerie /ɛspjɛgləʀi/ *nf* **1** (caractère) mischievousness, impishness; **par ~** out of mischievousness; **2** (action, mot) prank, monkey trick.

espion, **-ionne** /ɛspjɔ̃, ɔn/ **I ▶ 510** *nm,f* spy.
II (miroir) security mirror.

espionnage /ɛspjɔnaʒ/ *nm* espionage, spying; **film/roman d'~** spy film/story.
■ **~ industriel** industrial espionage.

espionner /ɛspjɔne/ [1] *vtr* to spy on [*personne, peuple*]; **~ pour le compte de qn** to spy for sb.

espionnite /ɛspjɔnit/ *nf* hum spy mania.

esplanade /ɛsplanad/ *nf* esplanade.

espoir /ɛspwaʀ/ *nm* **1** (fait d'espérer, sentiment) hope (**de** of); **perdre/rendre ~** to lose/rekindle hope; **reprendre ~** to feel hopeful again; **être plein d'~** to be hopeful ou full of hope; **une (faible) lueur d'~** a (faint) glimmer of hope; **avec l'~ de faire qch** with the hope of doing sth; **dans l'~ de faire qch/de qch** in the hope of doing sth/of sth; **dans l'~ de trouver une solution** or **que je trouverai une solution** in the hope of finding a solution; **dans l'~ de te lire bientôt** hoping to hear from you soon; **avoir l'~ de faire qch** to hope to do sth; **avoir bon ~ de faire qch/que** to have high hopes of doing sth/that; **avec ~** [*dire, regarder*] hopefully, in a hopeful way; **c'est sans ~** (d'une situation) it's hopeless; **je garde ~** I am still hopeful; **2** (raison d' espérer) hope; **de grands/nouveaux ~s** great/new hopes; **tu es notre seul/plus grand ~** you are our only/greatest hope; **reste-t-il un ~?** is there still hope?; **il n'y a plus d'~** there's no hope left; **il y a un ~ d'aboutir** there is some hope of success; **3** (artiste, sportif) **un grand ~ de la musique** a promising young musician; **les jeunes ~s de la musique** the young hopefuls of the music world.
IDIOMES **l'~ fait vivre** we all live in hope; **tant qu'il y a de la vie il y a de l'~** where there's life there's hope.

esprit /ɛspʀi/ *nm* **1** (caractère) mind; **avoir l'~ logique/vif** to have a logical/quick mind; **avoir l'~ mal placé** or **tourné** to have a dirty mind; **avoir l'~ d'aventure** to be adventurous; **avoir un ~ de synthèse** to be good at synthesizing; **avoir l'~ d'à-propos** to have a ready wit; **avoir l'~ de contradiction** to be contrary; **avoir l'~ de système** to systematize things; **avoir l'~ de sacrifice** to be willing to make sacrifices; **2** (cerveau) mind; **garder l'~ libre** to keep an open mind; **l'idée m'a traversé l'~** the idea crossed my mind; **mettre un doute dans l'~ de qn** to sow the seeds of doubt in sb's mind; **cela m'était totalement sorti de l'~** it completely slipped my mind;

avoir/garder qch à l'~ to have/keep sth in mind; **mettre qch dans l'~ de qn** to get sb to bear sth in mind; **mets-toi bien ça dans l'~** bear that in mind; **dans mon/leur ~ c'était facile** the way I/they saw it, it was easy; **paresse d'~** intellectual laziness; **cela m'occupe l'~** it gives me something to think about; **cela me repose l'~** I find it relaxing for the mind; **cela ne t'est jamais venu à l'~?** didn't it ever occur to you?; **se transporter en ~ en 1789** to go back mentally to 1789; **avoir l'~ dérangé** to be disturbed; **avoir l'~ ailleurs** to be miles away; ▶ **simple**; **3** (humour) wit; **pétiller d'~** to sparkle with wit; **avoir de l'~** to be witty; **une réponse pleine d'~** a witty reply; **avec ~** wittily; **femme d'~** witty woman; **faire de l'~** to try to be witty; **tous deux rivalisent d'~** they're each trying to be wittier than the other; **4** (humeur) mood; (disposition) spirit; (ambiance) atmosphere; **avoir l'~ chagrin** to be in a despondent mood; **je n'ai pas l'~ à rire** I'm in no mood for laughing; **dans un ~ de vengeance/confrontation/compromis** in a spirit of revenge/confrontation/compromise; **il y a un meilleur ~** the atmosphere has improved; **5** (personne) individual; **un ~ prudent/rebelle/faible** a cautious/rebellious/spineless individual; **l'un des plus grands ~s de son temps** one of the greatest minds of his/her time; **~ fort** freethinker; **être un ~ libre** to be a free spirit; **calmer les ~s** to calm people down; **les ~s sont échauffés** feeling is running high; **6** (caractéristique) spirit; **conserver l'~ de l'émission** to try to preserve the spirit of the programme[GB]; **dans l'~ de l'époque** or **du temps** in the spirit of the age; **conforme à/contraire à l'~ de l'entreprise** in accordance with/contrary to the company ethic; **7** Philos, Relig spirit; **les choses de l'~** spiritual matters; **8** Mythol spirit; **des ~s maléfiques** evil spirits; **un ~ bienfaisant** a kindly spirit; **croire aux ~s** to believe in ghosts; **'~ es-tu là?'** 'is there anybody there?'; **9** Ling **~ doux/rude** smooth/rough breathing.

■ **~ d'à-propos** ready wit; **~ de caste** class consciousness; **avoir l'~ de caste** to be class conscious; **~ de club** club spirit; **avoir l'~ de club** to be clubbable; **~ de corps** solidarity, esprit de corps sout; **avoir l'~ de corps** to show solidarity; **~ d'équipe** team spirit; **avoir l'~ d'équipe** to have team spirit; **~ de famille** family solidarity; **ils ont l'~ de famille** they're a very close family; **je n'ai pas l'~ de famille** I'm not very family-oriented; **~ frappeur** poltergeist; **Esprit saint** Relig Holy Spirit ou Ghost; **~ de sel**† spirits of salt†; **~ de vin**† spirit of wine†.

IDIOMES **perdre ses ~s** (s'évanouir) to faint; (être très troublé) to take leave of one's senses; **retrouver** or **reprendre ses ~s** (après un malaise) to regain consciousness; (après une émotion) to collect one's wits; **ne pas être un pur ~** to be only flesh and blood; **les grands ~s se rencontrent** great minds think alike.

esquif /ɛskif/ *nm* craft; **frêle ~** frail craft.

esquille /ɛskij/ *nf* splinter (of bone).

esquimau, -aude, *mpl* **~x** /ɛskimo, od/ **I** *adj* Eskimo; **chien ~** husky.
II *nm* **1** Ling Eskimo; **2** ®(glace) chocolate-covered ice lolly GB, ice-cream bar US.

Esquimau, -aude, *mpl* **~x** /ɛskimo, od/ *nm,f* Eskimo.

esquintant○, **~e** /ɛskɛ̃tɑ̃, ɑ̃t/ *adj* exhausting.

esquinter○ /ɛskɛ̃te/ [1] **I** *vtr* **1** (endommager) to damage; **c'est tout esquinté** it's badly damaged; **2** (blesser) to hurt; (fatiguer) to wear [sb] out; **se faire ~** (dans bagarre) to get beaten up; (dans accident) to get hurt; **3** (critiquer) to slate○ GB, to pan○ US [*spectacle*]; to slate○ GB, to trash○ US [*romancier*].
II s'esquinter○ *vpr* (se blesser) to hurt oneself; (se fatiguer) to wear oneself out (**à faire** doing); **s'~ le dos/les yeux** to strain one's back/one's eyes; **s'~ la santé** to ruin one's health.

esquisse /ɛskis/ *nf* **1** (de dessin) sketch; **2** (de programme) outline; **3** (de sourire) hint; **l'~ d'un sourire** a hint of a smile, a suggestion of a smile.

esquisser /ɛskise/ [1] **I** *vtr* to sketch [*portrait*]; to outline, to sketch out [*programme*]; **~ un sourire/une révérence** to half-smile/-curtsey; **~ un geste** to make a vague gesture.
II s'esquisser *vpr* **une solution commence à s'~** a solution is beginning to emerge ou is gradually taking shape.

esquive /ɛskiv/ *nf* **1** Sport (mouvement) dodge; (tactique) dodging; **2** fig dodging, evasion.

esquiver /ɛskive/ [1] **I** *vtr* to duck, to dodge [*coup*]; to sidestep, to dodge [*question*]; to sidestep [*attaque*]; to dodge, to evade [*responsabilité*]; to dodge, to evade [*difficulté*].
II s'esquiver *vpr* **1** (partir) to slip away; **2** (se dérober) to shy away.

essai /esɛ/ **I** *nm* **1** Tech (expérimentation) trial; **faire des ~s** to run trials; **le nouveau modèle est à l'~** the new model is undergoing trials; **prendre une voiture à l'~** to take a car for a run; **vol d'~** test flight; **~ en vol/au sol** flight/ground test; **~ sur route** road test; **2** Tech (analyse, expérience) test; **faire des ~s** to do tests; **le médicament est à l'~** the drug is being tested; **~ de laboratoire** laboratory test; **~ nucléaire** nuclear test; **3** (tentative) try; **un coup d'~** a try; **ce n'est pas son premier coup d'~** it's not his first try; **faire un ~** to have a try; **prendre qn à l'~** to give sb a try-out; **je serai à l'~ pendant un mois** I'll work a month on a trial basis, I'll do a month's try-out; **période d'~** try-out; **4** Littérat essay (**sur** on); **~ philosophique/politique** philosophical/political essay; **5** Sport (en athlétisme) attempt; (au rugby) try; **marquer un ~** to score a try; **transformer un ~** to convert (a try); **6** Minér (analyse) assay.
II essais *nmpl* Courses Aut qualifying round (*sg*); **faire le meilleur temps aux ~s** to clock up the fastest time in the qualifying session.

essaim /esɛ̃/ *nm* lit, fig swarm.

essaimage /esɛmaʒ/ *nm* **1** lit swarming; **2** fig spreading.

essaimer /eseme/ [1] *vi* **1** [*abeilles*] to swarm; **2** [*peuple*] to spread; [*entreprise*] to spread out.

essayage /esɛjaʒ/ *nm* fitting; **cabine/salon d'~** changing cubicle/room.

essayer /eseje/ [21] **I** *vtr* **1** (tenter) to try [*sport, produit, fournisseur, restaurant*]; to try [*méthode, remède, menaces, pleurs*]; **tu devrais ~ ce shampooing** you should try this shampoo; **as-tu essayé la mairie?** have you tried the Town Hall?; **tu devrais ~ l'homéopathie** you should try homeopathy; **avec lui j'ai tout essayé** I've tried everything with him; **~ une voiture** (pour le plaisir) to try a car; (avant d'acheter) to test-drive a car; **~ sa force/son talent** to test one's strength/one's skill; **2** Tech (soumettre à des tests) [*technicien*] to test [*arme, avion, mécanisme, matériau, produit*]; [*technicien*] to run trials on [*voiture, machine*]; [*client*] to try out [*voiture, arme*]; **3** Cout, Mode to try on [*vêtement, chapeau, chaussures*]; to try [*taille, couleur*]; **acheter sans ~** to buy without trying on; **essaie la pointure au-dessous** try the next size down; **4** Minér to assay [*argent, or*].
II *vi* (tenter) to try; **on peut toujours ~** we can always try; **essaie un peu et tu vas voir!** just try it and you'll see!; **~ avec du savon/de l'alcool** to try using soap/alcohol; **~ à la poste/banque** to try the post office/bank; **~ de faire** to try to do; **n'essaie pas de tricher/m'attendrir** don't try to cheat/soften me up; **j'essaierai que tout se passe bien** I'll try to make sure everything goes all right.
III s'essayer *vpr* **s'~ à qch** to have a go at [*sport*]; to try one's hand at [*art, littérature*] ; **il s'essaie au théâtre depuis deux ans** he's been trying his hand at acting for the past two years; **s'~ à faire** to try to do; **à ta place je ne m'y essaierais pas** I wouldn't try it if I were you.

essayeur, -euse /esɛjœʀ, øz/ ▶ **510** *nm,f* **1** Cout fitter; **2** (de monnaie) assayer.

essayiste /esejist/ ▶ **510** *nmf* Littérat essayist.

esse /ɛs/ *nf* **1** Tech (crochet) (S-shaped) hook; (goupille) linchpin; **2** (de violon) f-hole.

essence /esɑ̃s/ *nf* **1** Aut petrol GB, gasoline US, gas○ US; **2** Pharm (extrait) essential oil; **~ de bergamote/d'eucalyptus** bergamot/eucalyptus (essential) oil; **3** Bot (espèce d'arbre) tree species; **~s rares** rare tree species; **4** (caractère essentiel) essence; **par ~** in essence; **5** Philos essence.
■ **~ à briquet** lighter fuel GB, lighter fluid US; **~ ordinaire** ≈ 2-star petrol GB, regular gasoline US; **~ de rose** attar of roses; **~ sans plomb** unleaded (petrol) GB ou gasoline US; **~ super** ≈ 4-star petrol GB, premium gasoline US.

essentiel, -ielle /esɑ̃sjɛl/ **I** *adj* **1** (très important) essential; **cause/différence/tâche essentielle** essential cause/difference/task; **il est ~ de faire/qu'il soit là** it is essential to do/that he (should) be here; **2** (central) key (*épith*), essential; **document/point/rôle ~** key document/point/role; **3** Philos **être ~** to be an essential attribute (**à** of).
II *nm* **1** (chose principale) **c'est l'~** that's the main thing; **l'~ (c')est de faire/que tu sois avec nous** the main thing is to do/that you are with us; **oublier l'~** to forget the most important thing; **aller à l'~** to get to the heart of the matter; **2** (partie la plus importante) bulk; **l'~ de l'effort/du revenu/des voix** the bulk of the effort/income/vote; **pour l'~** mainly; **3** (objets indispensables) basics (*pl*); **n'acheter que l'~** to buy only the basics; **en voyage je n'emporte que l'~** when travelling[GB] I only ever take the bare minimum.

essentiellement /esɑ̃sjɛlmɑ̃/ *adv* **1** (pour la plus grande partie) principally, mainly; **chômage ~ causé par la récession** unemployment principally ou mainly caused by recession; **2** (dans ses aspects les plus importants) essentially; **politique ~ conservatrice** essentially conservative policy.

esseulé, ~e /esœle/ *adj* forlorn.

essieu, *pl* **~x** /esjø/ *nm* axle.

Essonne /esɔn/ ▶ **692** *nprf* (départment) **l'~** Essonne.

essor /esɔʀ/ *nm* **1** (de commerce, technologie, tourisme, région) development; (de mode, tendance, sport) increasing popularity; **prendre son ~** [*entreprise, industrie, région*] to take off; [*personne*] fml to spread one's wings; **prendre un ~ considérable** to be undergoing quite a boom; **être en plein ~** to be booming; **connaître un nouvel ~** [*industrie, entreprise*] to be booming again; [*mode, tendance*] to make a comeback; **donner de l'~ à un projet** to give a boost to a project; **2** fml (d'oiseau) soaring; **l'oiseau/l'avion prend son ~** the bird/the plane soars into the sky; **3** (d'imagination) flight.

essorage /esɔʀaʒ/ *nm* (à la main) wringing; (en machine) spin-drying; **mettre sur '~'** to put on 'spin'.

essorer /esɔʀe/ [1] *vtr* (en tordant) to wring; (par centrifugation) to spin-dry [*linge*]; to spin [*salade*].

essoreuse /esɔʀøz/ *nf* (à tambour) spin-drier GB, spin-dryer US; (à rouleaux) mangle GB, wringer US.
■ **~ à salade** salad spinner.

essoufflement /esufləmɑ̃/ *nm* **1** lit breathlessness; **2** fig loss of impetus.

essouffler /esufle/ [1] **I** *vtr* lit to leave [sb] breathless; **~ ses concurrents** fig to leave one's competitors behind; **être essoufflé** to be out of breath.
II s'essouffler *vpr* lit to get breathless; fig [*économie, projet*] to run out of steam; [*auteur*] to go stale.

essuie /esɥi/ *nm* B **1** (serviette) **~ (de bain)** towel; **2** (torchon) **~ (de vaisselle)** tea towel GB, dish towel US.

essuie-glace, *pl* **~s** /esɥiglas/ *nm* windscreen wiper GB, windshield wiper US.

essuie-mains /esɥimɛ̃/ *nm inv* hand towel.

essuie-phares /esɥifaʀ/ *nm inv* headlight wiper.

essuie-pieds /esɥipje/ *nm inv* doormat.

essuie-tout /esɥitu/ *nm inv* (en rouleau) kitchen roll; (en feuilles) kitchen paper.

essuie-verres /esɥivɛʀ/ *nm inv* glass cloth.

essuie-vitres /esɥivitʀ/ *nm inv* = **essuie-glace**.

essuyage /esɥijaʒ/ *nm* **1** (d'objet mouillé) drying, wiping; **2** (d'objet sale) wiping.

essuyer /esɥije/ [22] **I** *vtr* **1** (rendre sec) to dry, to wipe [*verre, mains*]; to wipe [*table*]; to dry [*enfant, chien*]; **c'est mal essuyé** it hasn't been dried properly; **~ la vaisselle** to dry up, to wipe up, to do the drying up GB; **2** (pour nettoyer) to wipe [*objet, bouche, poussière*]; **3** (éponger) to wipe up, to mop up [*liquide*]; **~ ses larmes** to wipe away one's tears; **4** (subir) to run into [*orage*]; to suffer [*défaite, pertes, affront*]; to endure [*quolibets*]; to meet with [*refus, échec, critiques*]; **pertes essuyées** losses suffered; **~ le feu de l'ennemi** to come under enemy fire; **~ un coup de feu** to be shot at.
II s'essuyer *vpr* **1** (tout le corps) to dry oneself, to towel off US; **2** (partie du corps) (sécher) to dry; (nettoyer) to wipe; **s'~ les mains** to dry or to wipe one's hands.

est /ɛst/ **▶621** **I** *adj inv* [*façade, versant, côté*] east; [*frontière, zone*] eastern.
II *nm* **1** (point cardinal) east; **à l'~ de Paris** [*être, habiter*] east of Paris; **vers l'~** [*aller, naviguer*] east, eastward; **un vent d'~** an easterly wind; **exposé à l'~** east-facing (*épith*); **2** (région) east; **dans l'~ de la France** [*se situer, avoir lieu, habiter, voyager*] in the east of France; [*aller, se rendre*] to the east of France; **l'~ du Japon** eastern Japan; **3** Géog, Pol **l'Est** the East; **vivre dans l'Est** to live in the East; **venir de l'Est** to come from the East; **de l'Est** [*ville, accent*] eastern.

estacade /ɛstakad/ *nf* Naut (brise-lames) breakwater; (appontement) landing stage; Mil Naut boom.

estafette /ɛstafɛt/ *nf* **1** ®Aut van; **2** Mil dispatch rider.

estafilade /ɛstafilad/ *nf* gash.

est-allemand, **~e**, *mpl* **~s** /ɛstalmɑ̃, ɑ̃d/ *adj* East German.

estaminet† /ɛstaminɛ/ *nm* (small) inn.

estampage /ɛstɑ̃paʒ/ *nm* **faire un ~ de qch** to take an impression of sth.

estampe /ɛstɑ̃p/ *nf* **1** Art (sur planche gravée) engraving; (par lithographie) print; **viens voir mes ~s japonaises!** hum come up and see my etchings! hum; **2** Tech stamp.

estamper /ɛstɑ̃pe/ [1] *vtr* **1** Tech to stamp [*métal, monnaie*]; to emboss [*cuir*]; **2**○ (escroquer) to rip [sb] off○, to swindle; **se faire ~** to get ripped off○; **~ qn de 50 francs** to swindle sb out of 50 francs.

estampeur, **-euse** /ɛstɑ̃pœʀ, øz/ *nm,f* **1** **▶510** (ouvrier) stamper; **2**○ (escroc) swindler, shark○.

estampillage /ɛstɑ̃pijaʒ/ *nm* stamping.

estampille /ɛstɑ̃pij/ *nf* lit (cachet, signature) stamp; (label) trademark; fig mark.

estampiller /ɛstɑ̃pije/ [1] *vtr* to stamp [*document*]; to mark [*marchandise*].

est-ce ▶ **être**[1].

este /ɛst/ *adj, nm* = **estonien**.

ester[1] /ɛstɛʀ/ *nm* Chimie ester.

ester[2] /ɛste/ [1] *vi* **~ en justice** to go to court.

esthète /ɛstɛt/ *nmf* aesthete.

esthéticienne /ɛstetisjɛn/ **▶510** *nf* beautician.

esthétique /ɛstetik/ **I** *adj* [*qualité, sens*] aesthetic; [*monument, décor*] aesthetically pleasing; [*pose, geste*] graceful.
II *nf* (théorie) aesthetics (+ *v sg*); (de décor) aesthetic quality; (de geste) grace.
■ **~ industrielle** industrial design.

esthétiquement /ɛstetikmɑ̃/ *adv* aesthetically.

esthétisme /ɛstetism/ *nm* aestheticism.

estimable /ɛstimabl/ *adj* **1** (honorable) [*personne*] worthy, estimable sout; **2** (admirable) [*travail, résultat, effort*] laudable; **3** [*fortune*] **difficilement ~** hard to estimate.

estimatif, **-ive** /ɛstimatif, iv/ *adj* [*coût*] estimated; **un devis ~** an estimate, a quote.

estimation /ɛstimasjɔ̃/ *nf* **1** (de coût) estimate (**de** of); (valeur) valuation (**de** of); (de dégâts) assessment (**de** of); **2** (de distance, temps, d'efficacité) estimate (**de** of); **une ~ de croissance de 3%** an estimated growth of 3%; **3** Stat estimate (**de** of).

estime /ɛstim/ **I** *nf* respect, esteem; **avoir de l'~ pour qn** to have great respect ou esteem for sb; **il a baissé/monté dans mon ~** he has gone down/risen in my estimation ou esteem; **tenir qn en piètre/haute ~** to hold sb in low/high esteem; **son courage a forcé l'~ de tous** her courage has earned her everybody's respect.
II à l'estime *loc adv* **1** Naut, Aviat [*naviguer, piloter*] by dead reckoning; **2** fig **j'ai calculé à l'~** it was guesswork, it was just an estimate.

estimer /ɛstime/ [1] **I** *vtr* **1** (penser) to feel (**que** that); **elle a estimé indispensable/prématuré de faire** she felt it essential/too early to do; **j'estime de mon devoir de faire** I feel ou consider it my duty to do; **~ nécessaire de faire** to consider ou deem sout it necessary to do; **ces mesures, estime l'opposition, sont insuffisantes** the opposition considers these measures to be inadequate; **2** (respecter) to think highly of [*ami, artiste*]; **3** (chiffrer) [*expert*] to value [*tableau, propriété*]; to assess [*dégâts*]; **faire ~ qch** to have sth valued; **~ qch au-dessus/au-dessous de sa valeur** to overvalue/undervalue sth; **~ qch à 500 francs** to value sth at 500 francs [*objet*]; **~ qn à sa juste valeur** to recognize sb's real worth; **~ qch à son juste prix/à sa valeur** fig to recognize the real price/the value of sth; **4** (calculer approximativement) to estimate [*distance, position, temps, nombre, coût*] (**à** at); **une vitesse estimée à 150 km/h** an estimated speed of 150 km/h; **5** (deviner) to reckon; **je l'estime beaucoup moins naïf qu'il n'en a l'air** I reckon he is far less naïve than he looks.
II s'estimer *vpr* **estimez-vous heureux** think ou consider yourself lucky (**que** that); **je ne m'estime pas vraiment récompensé de mes efforts** I don't feel ou consider myself fairly rewarded for my efforts; **je m'estime satisfait de** I am satisfied with.

estivage /ɛstivaʒ/ *nm* summer pasturing (*on high mountain slopes*).

estival, **~e**, *mpl* **-aux** /ɛstival, o/ *adj* (d'été) summer (*épith*); (évoquant l'été) summery.

estivant, **~e** /ɛstivɑ̃, ɑ̃t/ *nm,f* summer visitor.

estiver /ɛstive/ [1] *vtr* **~ des troupeaux** to pasture herds for the summer (*on high slopes*).

estoc /ɛstɔk/ *nm* rapier.
IDIOMES **frapper d'~ et de taille** to cut and thrust.

estocade /ɛstɔkad/ *nf* lit fatal sword thrust; fig final blow; **donner l'~** (dans une corrida) to deliver the death blow (**à** to).

estomac /ɛstɔma/ *nm* **1** Anat stomach; **avoir mal à l'~** to have stomach ache GB ou a stomachache US; **avoir l'~ bien rempli/vide** to have a full/an empty stomach; **il a été touché à l'~** he was hit in the stomach; **j'ai un poids sur l'~** my stomach feels heavy; **avoir l'~ bien accroché** to have a strong stomach; **le repas d'hier m'est resté sur l'~** yesterday's meal is lying heavy on my stomach; **son refus/ce qu'il m'a fait m'est resté sur l'~** his refusal/what he did to me left a nasty taste in my mouth; **prendre/avoir de l'~** to develop/have a paunch; **2**○ fig (courage) guts○ (*pl*); (culot) nerve, cheek; **il faut de l'~ pour faire ça** it takes guts to do that.
IDIOMES **avoir l'~ dans les talons**○ to be famished.

estomaquer○ /ɛstɔmake/ [1] *vtr* to flabbergast, to astound; **être estomaqué** to be flabbergasted ou astounded.

estompe /ɛstɔ̃p/ *nf* **1** (rouleau) stump; **2** (dessin) stumped drawing.

estomper /ɛstɔ̃pe/ [1] **I** *vtr* **1** lit to shade off, to stump spéc [*dessin*]; to shade off [*couleur, fard*]; **2** fig to blur [*paysage, formes*]; to gloss over [*détails*]; **le temps estompe les souvenirs/passions** memories/passions fade with time.
II s'estomper *vpr* [*paysage*] to become blurred; [*couleur, haine, souvenirs*] to fade.

Estonie /ɛstɔni/ **▶321** *nprf* Estonia.

estonien, **-ienne** /ɛstɔnjɛ̃, ɛn/ **▶537**, **462**
I *adj* Estonian.
II *nm* Ling Estonian.

Estonien, **-ienne** /ɛstɔnjɛ̃, ɛn/ **▶537** *nm,f* Estonian.

est-ouest /ɛstwɛst/ *adj inv* east-west; **les relations Est-Ouest** East-West relations.

estouffade /ɛstufad/ *nf* estouffade, braised beef cooked with wine; **canard à l'~** braised duck.

estourbir○ /ɛstuʀbiʀ/ [3] *vtr* **1** (assommer) to knock [sb] out; **2** (étonner) to stun.

estrade /ɛstʀad/ *nf* platform.

estragon /ɛstʀagɔ̃/ *nm* tarragon; **sauce à l'~** tarragon sauce.

estrapade /ɛstʀapad/ *nf* strappado.

estropié, **~e** /ɛstʀɔpje/ **I** *pp* ▶ **estropier**.
II *pp adj* crippled.
III *nm,f* cripple.

estropier /ɛstʀɔpje/ [2] **I** *vtr* **1** lit to maim; **2**○ fig (en prononçant) to mispronounce; (en écrivant) to misspell; (en jouant) to mangle [*sonate*].
II s'estropier *vpr* to maim oneself.

estuaire /ɛstɥɛʀ/ *nm* estuary; **l'~ de la Loire** the Loire estuary.

estudiantin, **~e** /ɛstydjɑ̃tɛ̃, in/ *adj* student (*épith*).

esturgeon /ɛstyʀʒɔ̃/ *nm* sturgeon.

et /e/ *conj* **1** gén and; **mon père ~ ma mère** my father and mother; **~ lui ~ son frère sont alcooliques** both he and his brother are alcoholics; **une écharpe rouge et blanche** a red and white scarf; **il est grand ~ fort** he's tall and strong; **un homme grand ~ fort** a tall strong man; **une vieille femme laide ~ acariâtre** an ugly cantankerous old woman; **elle sait lire ~ écrire** she can read and write; **trois ~ deux (font) cinq** three and two makes five; **il est tombé ~ s'est cassé la jambe** he fell and broke his leg; **il n'est pas venu, ~ c'est aussi bien** he didn't come, and it's just as well; **allez chercher un docteur, ~ faites vite** go and get a doctor, and be quick about it; **~ voilà qu'il sort un couteau de sa poche!** and next thing he whips a knife out of his pocket!; **il y a expert ~ expert** (ils ne se valent pas tous) there are experts and experts; **et tu en es fier?** (exprimant la désapprobation) and you're proud of it?; **~ les enfants de rire!** liter and the children laughed; **~ moi de répondre...** liter so I replied...; **~ le pourboire (alors)?** what about the tip?; **~ si on allait au cinéma?**

how ou what about going to the cinema?; **~ moi alors?** what about me, then?; **je ne les connais pas, ~ toi?** I don't know them, do you?; **moi j'y vais, ~ toi?** I'm going, are you? ou what about you?; **~ alors?, ~ après?** so what?; **je ne l'aime pas; il est laid ~ d'un, il est avare ~ de deux** I don't like him: for one thing he's ugly and for another he's stingy; **elle riait et lui pleurait** she was laughing and he was crying; **2** (dans les nombres) **vingt ~ un/trente ~ un** twenty-one/thirty-one; **trois heures ~ quart** (a) quarter past three GB, three fifteen; **huit heures ~ demie** half-past eight GB, eight thirty.

ETA /œtea/ *nm* (*abbr* = **Euzkadi Ta Askatasuna**) ETA (*Basque separatist movement*).

êta /ɛta/ *nm* eta.

étable /etabl/ *nf* cowshed.

établi, ~e /etabli/ **I** *pp* ▶ **établir**.

II *pp adj* **1** (solide) [*réputation, prestige*] established; **une réputation bien ~e d'humoriste** a well-established reputation as a humorist; **2** (ancré) [*usage, principe*] established; **c'est un rite désormais ~** by now it's an established custom; **il est/a été ~ que**... it has been/was established that...; **des modes de pensée fermement ~s** rigid attitudes; **3** (en place) [*pouvoir, régime*] ruling; [*ordre, autorité*] established.

III *nm* **1** (table de travail) workbench; **2** Hist *Maoist intellectual working in a factory.*

établir /etabliʀ/ [3] **I** *vtr* **1** (fixer) to set up [*résidence, siège social*]; **~ son domicile à Londres** to set up home in London; **~ le prix (de vente) de** to price [*article*]; **2** (instituer) to establish [*règlement, hiérarchie, régime, lien, contact*]; to introduce [*impôt, sanction, discipline*]; to set up [*gouvernement*]; to set [*record, limite, norme*]; **~ une hiérarchie entre ses besoins** to put one's needs in order of priority, to prioritize one's needs; **3** (mettre en forme) to draw up [*liste, plan, bilan, budget, dossier*]; to make out [*compte, facture*]; to prepare, to draw up [*devis*]; to set up [*fiches*]; to make [*diagnostic*]; to draw [*parallèle*]; to edit [*texte, édition*]; to issue [*document*]; **~ un chèque** to make out a cheque GB ou check US (**à l'ordre de** to); **texte établi et annoté par**... text edited and annotated by...; **faire ~ un passeport au nom de**... to issue a passport in the name of...; **4** (assurer) to establish [*réputation, fortune, domination, influence*]; **droit établi sur la base de l'ancienneté** right based on seniority; **5** (prouver) to establish [*fait, identité, culpabilité, innocence*]; **~ que** to establish that; **6**† (pourvoir d'une situation) to settle [*enfant*].

II s'établir *vpr* **1** (se fixer) [*personne*] to settle (**à, en** in); [*organisme*] to set up; **s'~ (comme)** to set up (in business) as; **elle s'est établie (comme) antiquaire** she has set up (in business) as an antique dealer; **s'~ à son compte** to set up one's own business; **2** [*indice, taux, hausse*] to be set (**à** at); **3** (s'instituer) [*relations, liens*] to develop (**sur** out of); [*domination, pouvoir, préjugé*] to become established (**sur** on); **leur collaboration s'est établie sur des besoins communs** their collaboration has developed out of a common need; **le consensus s'établira sur cette question** a consensus will be established on this question.

établissement /etablismɑ̃/ *nm* **1** (entreprise, organisme) gén organization, establishment; (institué) institution; (bâtiments) premises (*pl*); **il est interdit de fumer dans l'~** no smoking on the premises; **'l'~ décline toute responsabilité en matière de vol'** 'the management does not accept responsibility for theft'; **2** (ville, village) settlement; **3** (mise en place) (de relations, contacts, hiérarchie, régime) establishment; (de norme, limite) setting; (de gouvernement) formation; (de campagne) setting up; (de personne, famille, population) settlement; (d'impôt, de taxe, sanction) introduction; **4** (mise en forme) (de liste, plan, dossier) drawing up; (de texte, d'édition) editing; **5** (démonstration) **l'~ de leur culpabilité/innocence** proving they are guilty/innocent; **l'~ de leur identité** establishing their identity.

■ **~ de bains** bathhouse; **~ bancaire** banking institution; **~ commercial** commercial establishment; **~ de crédit** finance company; **~s dangereux, insalubres ou incommodes** Jur premises in such a state as to be prejudicial to health or constituting a nuisance; **~ d'enseignement** educational establishment; **~ d'enseignement supérieur** higher education institution; **~ financier** financial institution; **~ hospitalier** hospital; **~ industriel** plant; **~ pénitentiaire** penal institution; **~ privé** Scol private school; **~ du prix de revient** costing; **~ du prix de vente** pricing; **~ public** Admin public corporation; **~ sanitaire** = **~ de soins**; **~ scolaire** school; **~ de soins** medical establishment; **~ spécialisé** institution; **~ supérieur** = **~ d'enseignement supérieur**; **~ thermal** Méd hydrotherapy centre[GB]; **~ d'utilité publique** Admin public service corporation.

étage /etaʒ/ *nm* **1** (d'immeuble) floor, storey GB, story US; **le premier ~** the first floor GB, the second floor US; **le dernier ~** the top floor; **à tous les ~s** on every floor; **à l'~ au-dessus/au-dessous** on the floor above/below; **dans les ~s** on (one of) the floors above; **grimper deux ~s** to climb two floors; **habiter/se trouver en ~** to live/be above street-level, to live/be above the ground GB ou first US floor; **à l'~** upstairs; **une maison sans ~** a single-storey(ed) house GB, a single-story house US; **une tour de vingt ~s** a twenty-storey tower GB, a twenty-story tower US; **2** (division) (de tour) level; (d'aqueduc, de gâteau, coiffure) tier; (de fusée) stage; **une fusée à trois ~s** a three-stage rocket; **3** (de terrain) terrace; **terrain en ~s** terraced land; **4** Bot (zone) level; **~s de végétation** levels of vegetation; **5** Géol age; **6** Minér level; **7** Électron, Tech stage.

étager /etaʒe/ [13] **I** *vtr* **1** lit to plant [sth] in tiers [*fleurs*]; **~ des maisons sur une pente** to build houses on terraces; **2** fig to graduate [*prix*]; to stagger [*augmentations*]; to introduce [sth] gradually [*réformes*]; **~ des réformes sur deux ans** to introduce reforms gradually over a two-year period.

II s'étager *vpr* **1** lit [*cultures, jardins*] to rise in terraces; [*habitations*] to rise in tiers; **les rizières/maisons s'étagent jusqu'à la mer** (the) ricefields/houses slope down in terraces to the sea; **2** fig [*augmentations, réformes*] to be staggered.

étagère /etaʒɛʀ/ *nf* shelf; **des ~s** (planches) shelves; (meuble) shelf unit(s).

étai /etɛ/ *nm* Constr prop; Mines strut; Naut stay.

étain /etɛ̃/ *nm* **1** (métal) tin; **2** (matière) pewter; **en** or **d'~** pewter (*épith*); **3** (objet) piece of pewter ware; **les ~s** pewter ware.

étal /etal/ *nm* **1** (de marché) stall; **2** (de boucher) butcher's block.

étalage /etalaʒ/ *nm* **1** Comm (de magasin) window display; (de marché) stall; **composer un ~** (vitrine) to dress a window; (étal) to dress a stall; **2** (exhibition) display; **cet ~ de luxe est indécent** this display of luxury is indecent; **faire ~ de** to make a display of; **faire ~ de son érudition/sa richesse** to make a display of one's erudition/wealth.

étalagiste /etalaʒist/ ▶**510** *nmf* (décorateur) window dresser.

étale /etal/ *adj* **1** [*mer, marée, vent*] slack; **2** Naut **navire ~** ship making no headway; **3** (stable) [*situation*] stable.

étalement /etalmɑ̃/ *nm* **1** (dans le temps) staggering; **l'~ des horaires** the staggering of schedules; **j'ai opté pour l'~ des remboursements de ma dette** I opted to pay off my debt by instalments[GB]; **2** (dans l'espace) **~ géographique** geographical dispersion.

étaler /etale/ [1] **I** *vtr* **1** (déployer) to spread out [*carte, document, drap*]; to lay [*nappe, moquette*]; to spread [*tapis*]; Culin to roll [sth] out [*pâte*]; Jeux to lay down [*cartes*]; **2** (éparpiller) to scatter [*papiers, affaires, livres*]; **3** (répandre) to spread [*beurre, pâté, colle*]; to apply [*peinture, maquillage, pommade*]; **4** (échelonner) to spread [*travaux, réformes, remboursements*] (**sur** over); to stagger [*départs, horaires, vacances*] (**sur** over); **5** (exhiber) to flaunt [*richesse, pouvoir, succès*]; to show off [*savoir, charmes*]; to parade [*misère*]; **~ au grand jour** to bring [sth] out into the open [*divergences, vie privée*]; **6** Comm (montrer) to display [*articles, marchandise*]; **7**○ (faire tomber) to lay [sb] out○ [*personne*].

II s'étaler *vpr* **1** (se répandre) [*beurre, peinture*] to spread; **peinture qui s'étale difficilement** paint which does not spread very well; **2** (s'échelonner) [*programme, paiement, embouteillage*] to be spread (**sur** over); [*horaires, départs*] to be staggered (**sur** over); **3** (s'exhiber) [*richesse*] to be flaunted; **s'~ (au grand jour)** [*corruption, lâcheté*] to be plain for all to see; **une photo/un titre qui s'étale en première page d'un journal** a photo/a headline that is splashed all over the front page of a newspaper; **une affiche qui s'étale sur tous les murs de la ville** a poster that is splashed all over the walls in town; **4** (s'étendre) [*paysage*] to spread out; [*ville*] to spread out, to sprawl; **s'~ jusqu'à la mer** to spread out as far as the sea; **5** (se vautrer) [*personne*] to sprawl; (prendre de la place) [*personne*] to spread out; **s'~ sur le divan** to sprawl on the couch; **6**○ (tomber) to go sprawling○; **s'~ de tout son long** to fall flat on one's face; **7**○ (échouer) to fail; **s'~** or **se faire ~ à un examen** to fail ou flunk○ an exam.

étalon /etalɔ̃/ **I** *nm* **1** (cheval) stallion; **conduire un ~ à la jument** to take a stallion to serve a mare; **2**○ (homme) stud○; **3** (modèle) Fin, Mes standard; fig yardstick; **~ de longueur** standard of length; **~ monétaire** monetary standard; **servir d'~ à qn** to be a role model to sb.

II (-)étalon (*in compounds*) **âne(-)~** Zool stud donkey; **arbre(-)~** Hort mother-tree; **groupe(-)~** Sociol standard group; **kilogramme(-)~** Mes standard kilogram; **métal(-)~** Fin standard metal; **mètre(-)~** Mes standard metre[GB].

■ **~ de change or** gold exchange standard; **~ lingot d'or** gold bullion standard.

étalonnage /etalɔnaʒ/, **étalonnement** /etalɔnmɑ̃/ *nm* **1** Mes calibration; Cin, Phot calibration; **2** Psych (de test) standardization.

étalonner /etalɔne/ [1] *vtr* **1** Mes (vérifier) to test; (graduer) to calibrate; Cin, Phot to calibrate; **2** Psych to standardize [*test*].

étalon-or /etalɔ̃ɔʀ/ *nm inv* gold standard.

étamage /etamaʒ/ *nm* (de casserole) tinning; (de métal) tin-plating; (de glace) silvering.

étambot /etɑ̃bo/ *nm* sternpost.

étamer /etame/ [1] *vtr* to tin [*casserole*]; to tin-plate [*métal*]; to silver [*glace*].

étameur /etamœʀ/ ▶**510** *nm* tinsmith.

étamine /etamin/ *nf* **1** Bot stamen; **2** (étoffe, filtre) muslin; **passer qch à l'~** to strain sth (through muslin); **3** Cout (pour broder) aida fabric.

étanche /etɑ̃ʃ/ *adj* **1** lit **~ (à l'eau)** [*montre, combinaison*] waterproof; [*tonneau, embarcation*] watertight; **~ (à l'air)** airtight; **2** fig impenetrable.

étanchéité /etɑ̃ʃeite/ *nf* **~ (à l'eau)** (de montre) waterproof quality; (de citerne) watertightness; **~ (à l'air)** airtightness.

étancher /etɑ̃ʃe/ [1] *vtr* **1** to staunch [*sang*]; to quench lit, fig [*soif*]; to stop up [*voie d'eau*]; **2** Tech to make [sth] watertight [*citerne*].

étançon /etɑ̃sɔ̃/ *nm* shore, prop.

étançonner /etɑ̃sɔne/ [1] *vtr* to shore (up), to prop (up).

étang /etɑ̃/ *nm* pond.

étant /etɑ̃/ *p prés* ▶ **être**[1], **donné** III, IV, **entendu**.

étape /etap/ *nf* **1** (lieu d'arrêt) stop, stopping place; **faire ~ à** to stop off in; **2** (section de trajet) stage; (dans une course) leg; **nous avons fait une ~ de 300 km** we travelled[GB] a distance of 300 km; **3** fig (phase) stage; (palier) step.
IDIOMES **brûler les ~s** to go too far too fast.

état /eta/ ▶321 I *nm* **1** (condition physique) condition; **l'~ du malade s'améliore** the patient's condition is improving; **être dans un ~ stationnaire** to be in a stable condition; **en bon ~ général** in good overall condition; **être en ~ de faire qch** to be in a fit state to do sth; **ne pas être en ~ de faire**, **être hors d'~ de faire** to be in no condition ou in no fit state to do; **mettre qn hors d'~ de faire qch** to render sb incapable of doing sth; **mettre qn hors d'~ de nuire** (légalement) to put sb out of harm's way; (physiquement) to incapacitate sb; **leur ~ de santé est excellent** their (state of) health is excellent; **être dans un triste ~**○**/en piteux ~**○ to be in a sorry/pitiful state; **tu es dans un bel ~!** iron you're in a fine state!; **2** (condition psychique) state; **être dans un ~ d'inquiétude terrible** to be in a terrible state of anxiety; **être dans un ~ d'énervement extrême** to be in a state of extreme irritation; **elle n'est pas en ~ de le revoir** she's in no state to see him again; **je suis hors d'~ de réfléchir** I'm incapable of thinking, I'm in no state to think; **être dans un drôle d'~**○ to be in a hell of a state○; **ne pas être dans son ~ normal** not to be oneself; **ne te mets pas dans des ~s pareils!** don't get into such a state!, don't get so worked up○!; **être dans un ~ second** to be in a trance; **3** (de voiture, livre, tapis) condition; **l'~ de conservation d'un livre** the condition of a book; **l'~ des routes** (conditions climatiques) road conditions; (qualité) the state of the roads; **en bon/mauvais ~** [*maison, cœur, foie*] in good/poor condition; **avoir les dents en mauvais ~** to have bad teeth; **l'~ de délabrement d'une maison** the dilapidated state of a house; **l'~ de conservation d'une momie égyptienne** the state of preservation of an Egyptian mummy; **vérifier l'~ de qch** to check sth; **mettre/maintenir qch en ~** to put/keep sth in working order; **hors d'~ de marche** [*voiture*] off the road, not running; [*appareil*] out of order; **remettre qch en ~** to mend ou repair sth; **remettre une maison en ~** to do up a house; **la remise en ~ d'un réseau routier/de voiture** the repair of a road network/car; **vous devez rendre la maison en l'~ lors de votre départ** you must leave the house as you found it; **les choses sont restées en l'~ depuis leur départ** nothing has been changed since they left; **j'ai laissé les choses en l'~** I left everything as it was; **à l'~ brut** [*huile, pétrole*] in its raw state; [*action, idée*] in its initial stages; **un temple à l'~ de ruines** a temple in a state of ruin; **voiture/bicyclette/ordinateur à l'~ neuf** car/bicycle/computer as good as new; **beauté à l'~ pur** unadulterated beauty; **une voiture en ~ de rouler** a roadworthy car; **un bateau en ~ de naviguer** a seaworthy ship; **4** (d'affaires, économie, de finances, pays) state; **l'~ de l'environnement/d'une entreprise** the state of the environment/a company; **le pays est dans un ~ critique** the country is in a critical state; **cet ~ de choses ne peut plus durer** this state of affairs can't go on; **dans l'~ actuel des choses** in the present state of affairs; **dans l'~ actuel de la recherche médicale** in the present state of medical research; **l'~ de tension entre le gouvernement et l'opposition** the state of tension in relations between the government and the opposition; **ce n'est encore qu'à l'~ de projet** it's still only at the planning stage; **5** Sci (de corps) state; **les ~s de la matière** the states of matter; **l'~ solide/liquide/gazeux** the solid/liquid/gaseous state; **un corps à l'~ liquide/de vapeur** a body in the liquid/vapour[GB] state; **à l'~ naissant** [*gaz*] nascent; **à l'~ pur** [*élément, héroïne*] in its pure state; **6** (situation sociale) state; (métier)† trade; **être boulanger de son ~** to be a baker by trade; **ruiné, il se rappelle son ancien ~** now that he is bankrupt, he remembers how things used to be; **choisir l'~ ecclésiastique** to choose holy orders; **être satisfait/mécontent de son ~** to be satisfied/unhappy with one's lot; **7** Sociol **l'~ civilisé** the civilized state; **naissance d'un nouvel ~ social** birth of a new social order; **des tribus qui vivent encore à l'~ sauvage** tribes still living in a primitive state; **8** Compta statement; **~ de frais** statement of expenses; **~ des comptes** financial statements; **~ financier** financial statement; **~ des ventes d'un magasin** a shop's GB ou store's US sales statement; **9** Jur (statut) status; **~ d'épouse/d'enfant légitime/de parent** status of a spouse/legitimate child/parent; **10** Hist (catégorie sociale) estate; **la notion de classe a remplacé celle d'~** the concept of class replaced that of estate.

II **faire ~ de** *loc verbale* **1** (arguer) to cite [*document, texte, théorie, loi*]; **faire ~ du témoignage/de l'opinion de qn pour étayer une thèse** to cite sb's testimony/opinion in support of a thesis; **2** (mentionner) to mention [*conversation, entretien, découverte*]; **ne faites pas ~ de cette conversation** don't mention this conversation; **la presse a fait ~ de leur conversation** the press reported their conversation; **3** (exposer) to state [*préférences, privilèges, bénéfices*]; to air [*soupçon, idée*]; **4** (se prévaloir de) to make a point of mentioning [*succès, courage*]; **j'ai fait ~ de mes diplômes pour obtenir le travail** I made a point of mentioning my diplomas to get the job; **ils ont fait ~ des services qu'ils nous ont rendus** they made a point of mentioning the things they had done for us in the past.

■ **~ d'alerte** Mil state of alert; **en ~ d'alerte** on the alert; **~ d'âme** (scrupule) qualm; (sentiment) feeling; **ne pas avoir d'~s d'âme** to have no qualms; **~ de choc** Méd, Psych state of shock; **en ~ de choc** in a state of shock; **~ de choses** state of affairs; **~ civil** Admin registry office GB; (de personne) civil status; **~ de conscience** Psych state of consciousness; **~ de crise** Pol, Sociol state of crisis; **~ d'esprit** state ou frame of mind; **~ de fait** fact; **les ~s généraux** Hist the Estates General; **~ de grâce** Relig state of grace; **en ~ de grâce** lit in a state of grace; fig inspired; **~ de guerre** state of war; **~ des lieux** Jur inventory and statement of state of repair; fig appraisal; **faire l'~ des lieux** to draw up an inventory and statement of state of repair; **~ de nature** Sociol the state of nature; **à l'~ de nature** in the state of nature; **~ de rêve** dream state; **~ de santé** state of health; **~ de siège** state of siege; **~s de service** service record; **~ d'urgence** state of emergency; **~ de veille** waking state; ▶ **tiers**.

IDIOMES **être/se mettre dans tous ses ~s**○ to be in/to get into a state○; **il se met dans tous ses ~s pour un rien** he gets all worked up○ ou he gets into a state over nothing; **être réduit à l'~ de loque/d'esclave** to be reduced to a wreck/treated as a slave.

État /eta/ *nm* **1** (nation) state, State; **~ démocratique/totalitaire** democratic/totalitarian state; **servir l'~** to serve the State; **les ~s baltes** the Baltic States; **la souveraineté de l'~** State sovereignty; **être** or **former un ~ dans l'~** to be a state within a state; **coup d'~** coup d'état; **2** (gouvernement) state, government; **le budget de l'~** the state budget; **demander une aide de l'~** to apply for state aid; **réduire les dépenses de l'~** to reduce public ou state spending; **un emprunt d'~** a government loan; **responsabilité de l'~** state ou government liability; **3** (territoire autonome) state; **les ~s fédéraux** the federal states; **les ~s Pontificaux** the Papal States; **les ~s Européens** the European States.
■ **~ de droit** Pol legally constituted state; **~s barbaresques** Hist Barbary States.

étatique /etatik/ *adj* [*contrôle, financement, gestion*] state; **le système ~ d'enseignement** the state education system; **un système d'économie ~** a state-controlled economic system.

étatisation /etatizasjɔ̃/ *nf* state control; **on assiste à une ~ de l'économie** we're seeing the economy being brought under state control.

étatiser /etatize/ [1] *vtr* to bring [sth] under state control [*entreprise, économie, secteur*]; **l'industrie étatisée** state-controlled ou state-run industry.

étatisme /etatism/ *nm* state control, statism.

étatiste /etatist/ I *adj* [*politique, système*] of state control (*épith, après n*), statist.
II *nmf* supporter of state control, statist.

état-major, *pl* **états-majors** /etamaʒɔʀ/ *nm* **1** Mil (officiers) staff (+ *v pl*); **~ de l'armée de terre/de l'air** general staff GB, army staff US/air staff; (lieu) headquarters (+ *v sg* ou *pl*); **2** Pol administrative staff.

États-Unis /etazyni/ ▶321 *nprmpl* **~ (d'Amérique)** United States (of America); **aller aux ~** to go to the (United) States.

étau, *pl* **~x** /eto/ *nm* Tech vice GB, vise US; fig stranglehold (**autour de** on); **être pris en ~** to be caught in a vice-like GB ou vise-like US grip; **l'~ se resserre** the net is tightening (**autour de** around).

étayage /etɛjaʒ/ *nm* Constr shoring up, propping up (**de** of).

étayer /eteje/ [21] *vtr* **1** Constr to shore up, to prop up [*mur, plafond*]; **2** fig to support [*théorie, démonstration*] (**de, par** with); **raisonnement bien étayé** well-sustained argument.

etc (*written abbr* = **et cætera**) etc.

et cætera, **et cetera** /ɛtseteʀa/ *loc adv* et cetera.

été /ete/ ▶738 *nm* summer; **vacances d'~** summer holidays GB ou vacation US; **heure d'~** summertime GB, daylight-saving time US; **~ comme hiver** summer and winter alike, all year round.
■ **~ indien** Indian summer; **~ de la Saint-Martin** Indian summer.

éteignoir /etɛɲwaʀ/ *nm* (de bougie) snuffer.

éteindre /etɛ̃dʀ/ [55] I *vtr* **1** (faire cesser de brûler) to put out, to extinguish [*feu, cigare*]; to put out [*poêle*]; (en soufflant) to blow out [*bougie*]; (avec un éteignoir) to extinguish [*bougie*]; **2** (faire cesser d'éclairer) to switch off, to turn off [*lampe, phare*]; **~ la cuisine** to switch off the kitchen light; **le couloir est éteint** the light is (switched) off in the corridor; **éteins (la lumière)!** switch off the light!; **c'est éteint chez elle** her lights are off; **tous feux éteints** [*rouler, conduire*] without lights; **3** (faire cesser de fonctionner) to switch off, to turn off [*four, téléviseur, chauffage*]; to turn off [*gaz*]; **4** (calmer) to subdue [*colère, désir, passion*]; to quell [*ardeur*]; to dull [*éclat du regard*]; **cela l'a éteint** it has crushed him; **5** (rembourser) to extinguish [*dette*].
II **s'éteindre** *vpr* **1** [*cigare, feu*] to go out; **2** [*phare, radio*] to be turned ou switched off; (par accident) [*lumière*] to go out; [*radio*] to go off; **où s'éteint la lampe?** where do you turn the light off?; **s'~ automatiquement** to go off automatically; **3** [*pièce, fenêtre*] to

Les États, les pays et les continents

Les adjectifs comme anglais peuvent aussi qualifier des personnes (par ex. un touriste anglais, ▶ 537) *et des langues (par ex.* un mot anglais ▶ 462).

Les noms de pays

L'anglais n'utilise pas d'article défini devant les noms de pays et de continents, sauf pour les noms qui ont une forme de pluriel (the United States, the Netherlands, the Philippines *etc.*) *et quelques rares exceptions* (the Congo, the Gambia). *En cas de doute, consulter l'article dans le dictionnaire.*

la France = France
le Brésil = Brazil
Cuba = Cuba
l'Afrique = Africa
aimer la France = to like France
aimer l'Afrique = to like Africa

Attention: les noms qui ont une forme de pluriel se comportent en général comme des noms singuliers.

les États-Unis sont un pays riche = the United States is a rich country

Noter que les noms de continents et de pays qui utilisent les points cardinaux ne prennent pas d'article défini non plus:

l'Amérique du Nord = North America
la Corée du Sud = South Korea

À, au, aux, en

À, au, aux *et* en *se traduisent par* to *avec les verbes de mouvement (par ex.* aller, se rendre *etc) et par* in *avec les autres verbes (par ex.* être, habiter *etc.*).

aller au Brésil = to go to Brazil
aller en Afrique = to go to Africa
vivre au Brésil = to live in Brazil
vivre en Afrique = to live in Africa

De avec les noms de pays et de continents

Les expressions françaises avec de *se traduisent en général en anglais par l'emploi de l'adjectif. Mais voir ci-dessous quelques exceptions.*

Attention: l'anglais emploie toujours la majuscule pour les adjectifs ethniques.

l'ambassade de France = the French embassy
les campagnes de la France = the French countryside
le climat de la France = the French climate
l'équipe de France = the French team
les fleuves et rivières de France = French rivers
l'histoire de France = French history

Mais noter:

l'ambassadeur de France = the French ambassador *ou* the ambassador of France
la capitale de la France = the capital of France
les peuples de l'Afrique = the peoples of Africa
une carte de France = a map of France

Traduction des adjectifs

l'argent français = French money
l'armée française = the French army
l'aviation française = the French air force
la cuisine française = French cooking
la douane française = the French Customs
le gouvernement français = the French government
la langue française = the French language
la littérature française = French literature
la marine française = the French navy
le peuple français = the French nation
la politique française = French politics
les traditions françaises = French traditions
la vie politique française = French politics
une ville française = a French town

En anglais, dans quelques rares cas, on trouve aussi le nom du pays ou du continent utilisé en position d'adjectif: the England team, the Africa question *etc. Il est préférable de ne pas imiter ces tournures.*

go dark; **4** euph (mourir) to pass away ou on; **5** [*famille, nom*] to die out; **6** [*son*] to die away; [*conversation*] to tail off; [*voix*] to become lifeless; [*désir, passion, couleur*] to fade; [*colère, douleur*] to subside; **son regard s'est éteint depuis que** the light in his eyes has gone out since.

éteint, ~e /etɛ̃, ɛ̃t/ **I** *pp* ▶ **éteindre**.
II *pp adj* **1** [*voix*] lifeless; [*regard*] dull; [*couleur*] faded; **il est ~** he is crushed; (moins grave) he has lost his sparkle; **2** [*volcan*] extinct; [*astre*] extinct, dead.

étendard /etɑ̃daʀ/ *nm* standard, flag; **lever l'~ de la révolte** fig to raise the flag of rebellion; **se ranger sous l'~ de** to rally to the cause of.

étendre /etɑ̃dʀ/ [6] **I** *vtr* **1** (allonger) to stretch [*bras, jambe*]; **il a étendu les bras/jambes** he stretched his arms/legs; **2** (déployer) to spread (out) [*bâche, nappe*]; **~ du linge** (dehors) to hang out washing; (dedans) to hang up washing; **3** (coucher) to lay [sb] down [*malade, blessé*]; **~ qn (sur le carreau)**○ (blesser) to lay sb out cold○, to floor[GB] sb; (tuer) to kill sb; **~ qn d'un coup de poing**○ to knock sb out; **se faire ~ à un examen**○ to flunk○ an exam; **ils se sont fait ~ par l'équipe adverse**○ they got thrashed○ by the opposing team; **4** (diluer) to dilute, to water down [*vin, solution*]; **5** (étaler) to spread [*enduit, peinture, beurre*]; Culin to roll out [*pâte*]; **6** (accroître) to extend [*emprise, pouvoir*] (**sur** over); to extend [*mesure, allocation, aide, embargo*] (**à** to); **il faut ~ le champ de nos connaissances** we must extend our range of knowledge; **la société a étendu ses activités à de nouveaux secteurs** the company branched out into new fields.
II s'étendre *vpr* **1** (occuper un espace) to stretch (**sur** over); **s'~ à perte de vue** to extend ou stretch as far as the eye can see; **la forêt s'étend sur 10 000 km²** the forest stretches over 10,000 square kilometres[GB]; **2** (augmenter) [*grève, épidémie, sécheresse, récession*] to spread (**à** to); [*ville*] to expand, to grow; **3** (s'appliquer) [*loi, mesure*] **s'~ à** to apply to; **4** (durer) to stretch (**sur** over), last; **la Renaissance s'étend de la fin du XVe siècle au milieu du XVIe siècle** the Renaissance stretched from the end of the 15th century to the the middle of the 16th century; **les travaux s'étendront sur trois ans** the work will last three years; **5** (s'allonger) to lie down; **6** (s'apesantir) **s'~ sur** to dwell on [*sujet, point*].

étendu, ~e /etɑ̃dy/ **I** *pp* ▶ **étendre**.
II *pp adj* [*ville*] sprawling; [*région, plaine*] vast; [*vocabulaire, connaissances, dégâts*] extensive.
III étendue *nf* **1** (surface) (de terrain) expanse, area; (de sable, d'eau) expanse; **de vastes ~es désertiques** large areas ou expanses of desert; **sur toute l'~e du pays** throughout the country; **2** (de pays, collection) size; **3** (de catastrophe, dégâts) scale, extent; (de connaissances, vocabulaire) range; (d'ignorance) depth; Mus range, compass; **4** (durée) span, length.
■ **~e territoriale** Assur (de contrat) territorial limits (*pl*).

éternel, -elle /etɛʀnɛl/ **I** *adj* **1** (immuable) [*débat, problème*] endless; [*amour, vérité*] eternal; [*enfant, adolescent, optimiste*] eternal; (permanent) [*cravate, sourire*] inevitable; **2** Relig [*damnation, Dieu, salut*] eternal.
II *nm* eternal; **l'homme aspire à l'~** man aspires to the eternal; **l'~ féminin** the eternal feminine.

Éternel /etɛʀnɛl/ *nm* Eternal; **l'~** the Lord; **grand buveur/menteur devant l'~** hum inveterate drinker/liar.

éternellement /etɛʀnɛlmɑ̃/ *adv* **1** (jusqu'à la fin des temps) forever; **nous n'attendrons pas ~** we won't wait forever; **2** (continûment) permanently; **~ instable** permanently unstable; **3** (de manière répétée) perpetually, continually; **~ en retard** perpetually ou continually late; **4** Relig eternally; **~ vrai** eternally true.

éterniser /etɛʀnize/ [1] **I** *vtr* **1** (prolonger) to prolong [*discussion, conflit*]; **2** (rendre immortel) to perpetuate [*réputation*]; to immortalize [*nom*].
II s'éterniser *vpr* **1** (se prolonger) [*processus, débat, situation*] to drag on, to go on forever; **2**○ (s'attarder) to stay for ages.

éternité /etɛʀnite/ *nf* **1** (durée) eternity; **pour l'~** for all eternity; **de toute ~** from time immemorial; **2**○ **cela fait une ~ que je t'attends** I've been waiting for you for ages.

éternuement /etɛʀnymɑ̃/ *nm* sneeze; **le poivre provoque des ~s** pepper makes you sneeze.

éternuer /etɛʀnɥe/ [1] *vi* to sneeze.

êtêtage /etɛtaʒ/ *nm* topping, pollarding.

êtêter /etete/ [1] *vtr* **1** to top, to pollard [*arbre*]; **2** to remove the head of [*clou, sardine*].

éthane /etan/ *nm* ethane.

éthanol /etanɔl/ *nm* ethanol.

éther /etɛʀ/ *nm* **1** Chimie ether; **2** liter (ciel) **l'~** the ether.

éthéré, ~e /eteʀe/ *adj* ethereal.

éthéromane /eteʀɔman/ *nmf* ether addict.

éthéromanie /eteʀɔmani/ *nf* ether addiction.

Éthiopie /etjɔpi/ ▶ 321 *nprf* Ethiopia.

éthiopien, -ienne /etjɔpjɛ̃, ɛn/ ▶ 537 *adj* Ethiopian.

Éthiopien, -ienne /etjɔpjɛ̃, ɛn/ ▶ 537 *nm,f* Ethiopian.

éthique /etik/ **I** *adj* ethical.
II *nf* Philos ethics (+ *v sg*); (conception morale) code of ethics; **l'~ capitaliste** the capitalist ethic.

ethmoïde /ɛtmɔid/ *nm* ethmoid.

ethnie /ɛtni/ *nf* ethnic group.

ethnique /ɛtnik/ *adj* ethnic.

ethnographe /ɛtnɔgʀaf/ ▶ 510 *nmf* ethnographer.

ethnographie /ɛtnɔgʀafi/ *nf* ethnography.

ethnographique /ɛtnɔgʀafik/ *adj* ethnographic.

ethnolinguistique /ɛtnɔlɛ̃gɥistik/ **I** *adj* ethnolinguistic.
II *nf* ethnolinguistics (+ *v sg*).

ethnologie /ɛtnɔlɔʒi/ *nf* ethnology.

ethnologique /ɛtnɔlɔʒik/ *adj* ethnological.

ethnologue /ɛtnɔlɔg/ ▶ 510 *nmf* ethnologist.

éthologie /etɔlɔʒi/ *nf* ethology.

éthologique /etɔlɔʒik/ *adj* ethological.

éthyle /etil/ *nm* ethyl.

éthylène /etilɛn/ *nm* ethylene, ethene spéc.

éthylénique /etilenik/ *adj* ethylenic.

éthylique /etilik/ **I** *adj* **1** (alcoolique) alcoholic; **coma ~** alcoholic coma; **2** Chimie **alcool ~** ethyl alcohol.

II *nmf* alcoholic.

éthylisme /etilism/ ▶ **271** *nm* alcoholism.

étiage /etjaʒ/ *nm* low-water level.

étincelant, **~e** /etɛ̃slɑ̃, ɑ̃t/ *adj* **1** (lumineux) [*soleil*] blazing; [*étoile*] twinkling; [*pierreries, verre*] sparkling; [*plumage, couleur*] brilliant; **~ de propreté** sparkling clean; **2** (remarquable) [*style, esprit, conversation*] scintillating; [*personne*] brilliant; **journaliste ~ d'intelligence** brilliant journalist.

étinceler /etɛ̃sle/ [19] *vi* [*astre*] to twinkle; [*soleil, pierre précieuse, métal, mer, sable*] to sparkle (**de** with); [*yeux, regard*] (de colère) to flash (**de** with); (de joie) to sparkle (**de** with); [*conversation, esprit, beauté*] to sparkle; **~ de mille feux** to sparkle with a myriad lights; **~ de gaieté/d'intelligence/d'esprit** to sparkle with merriment/intelligence/wit.

étincelle /etɛ̃sɛl/ *nf* **1** (incandescence) spark; **le feu lance des ~s** the fire is throwing out sparks; **une gerbe d'~s** a shower of sparks; **~ électrique** electric spark; **2** (lueur) (sur une lame) flash; (sur un diamant) sparkle; (dans le regard) (d'humour) twinkle; (de colère) glint; **jeter des ~s** [*lame, regard, bijou*] to glitter; **3** (manifestation fugitive) **~ d'intelligence/de courage/génie** flash of intelligence/courage/genius.

IDIOMES **ça va faire des ~s**○ fig that will make sparks fly; **faire des ~s** (dans une conversation) to sparkle; (dans l'action) to do brilliantly; **ne pas faire d'~s** to fail to shine; **c'est l'~ qui a mis le feu aux poudres** fig it's what sparked off the crisis.

étincellement /etɛ̃sɛlmɑ̃/ *nm* (d'étoile) twinkling ₵; (de métal) flashing ₵; (de mer, pierreries, soleil) sparkling ₵.

étiolement /etjɔlmɑ̃/ *nm* **1** Bot blanching, etiolation spéc; **2** fig, liter (d'enfant) weakening; (d'esprit) failing.

étioler /etjɔle/ [1] **I** *vtr* **1** Bot to blanch, to etiolate spéc [*plante*]; **2** fig (affaiblir) **la vie urbaine étiole les enfants** town life makes children sickly.

II s'étioler *vpr* **1** Bot to blanch, to etiolate spéc; **2** fig (faiblir) [*enfant*] to become sickly; [*esprit, mémoire*] to fail.

étiologie /etjɔlɔʒi/ *nf* etiology.

étique /etik/ *adj* liter **1** lit [*animal*] emaciated; [*corps*] wasted; **2** fig [*budget*] shrunken.

étiquetage /etiktaʒ/ *nm* lit, fig labelling[GB].

■ **~ génétique** gene tagging.

étiqueter /etikte/ [20] *vtr* **1** (mettre une étiquette à) to label; **2** (cataloguer) to label (**comme** as).

étiquette /etikɛt/ *nf* **1** (à coller) label; (à attacher) tag; **porter une ~** to be labelled[GB]; **coller** or **mettre des ~s sur les gens** fig to label people; **candidat sans ~** fig independent candidate; **2** (protocole) etiquette; **3** Ordinat tag.

étirage /etiʀaʒ/ *nm* (de métal, de verre) drawing.

étirement /etiʀmɑ̃/ *nm* Sport stretching exercise.

étirer /etiʀe/ [1] **I** *vtr* **1** Tech to draw [*métal, verre*]; to pull [sth] into shape [*linge*]; **2** (pour détendre) to stretch; **~ les jambes** to stretch one's legs out.

II s'étirer *vpr* **1** (pour se détendre) [*personne*] to stretch; **2** (se déformer) [*chandail*] to stretch; **3** fig [*procession, chemin*] to stretch out; [*journée*] to seem endless.

Etna /ɛtna/ *nprm* **l'~** Mount Etna.

étoffe /etɔf/ *nf* **1** (tissu) fabric; **2** fig substance; **le scénario manque d'~** the screenplay is lacking in substance; **avoir de l'~** to have what it takes; **avoir l'~ d'un grand homme** to have the makings of a great man; **il a l'~ des héros** he's of the stuff heroes are made of.

étoffer /etɔfe/ [1] **I** *vtr* to expand [*récit, développement*]; to flesh out [*personnage*]; **un récit bien étoffé** a well-developed story.

II s'étoffer *vpr* **1** [*personne*] to put on weight; **2** [*personnage*] to flesh out.

étoile /etwal/ *nf* **1** (astre) star; **ciel sans ~s** starless sky; **à la lueur des ~s** by starlight; **2** (forme) star; **en ~** [*découpage, motif*] star-shaped; **~ à cinq branches** five-pointed star; **carrefour en ~** *roundabout with more than four roads*; **3** (artiste) star; **les ~s du cinéma** film GB ou movie US stars; **4** Tourisme star; **hôtel quatre ~s** four-star hotel.

■ **l'~ du berger** the evening star; **~ de David** Relig star of David; **~ filante** shooting star; **~ jaune** Hist yellow star; **~ de mer** starfish; **~ polaire** Pole Star.

IDIOMES **être né sous une bonne/mauvaise ~** to be born under a lucky/an unlucky star; **coucher** or **dormir à la belle ~** to sleep out in the open.

étoilé, **~e** /etwale/ *adj* **1** [*nuit, ciel*] starry; **2** [*verre, pare-brise*] crazed.

étole /etɔl/ *nf* stole.

étonnamment /etɔnamɑ̃/ *adv* surprisingly.

étonnant, **~e** /etɔnɑ̃, ɑ̃t/ *adj* **1** (inattendu) surprising; **cela n'a rien d'~** there's nothing surprising about that; **et, chose ~e** and, surprisingly enough; **pas ~ qu'il soit malade**○ no wonder he's ill; **2** (extraordinaire) amazing; **être d'une beauté ~e** to be amazingly beautiful.

étonnement /etɔnmɑ̃/ *nm* surprise; **à mon grand ~, elle a accepté** to my amazement ou astonishment, she accepted; **j'ai appris avec ~** I was surprised to find out.

étonner /etɔne/ [1] **I** *vtr* to surprise; **ta réaction m'étonne** I'm surprised by your reaction; **'il viendra?'—'ça m'étonnerait (fort)'** 'will he come?'—'I'd be (very) surprised if he did'; **ça m'étonnerait qu'elle refuse** I'd be surprised if she refused; **tu m'étonneras toujours** you never cease to amaze me; **'tu vas accepter?'—'tu m'étonnes**○**!'** (évidemment) 'are you going to accept?'—'of course I am!'

II s'étonner *vpr* to be surprised (**que** that; **de qch** at sth); **il ne faut pas s'~ que** it should come as no surprise that; **pourquoi s'~ de voir** why should it come as a surprise to see.

étouffant, **~e** /etufɑ̃, ɑ̃t/ *adj* **1** (suffocant) [*chaleur, air, été*] stifling; [*temps*] oppressive; [*pièce*] stuffy; **2** (pesant) [*régime, vie*] oppressive; **il a une mère ~e** he has an overbearing mother.

étouffé, **~e** /etufe/ **I** *pp* ▶ **étouffer**.

II *pp adj* **1** (asphyxié) suffocated; **mourir ~** (par accident) to die of suffocation; (dans la foule) to die in the crush; (par suffocation) to choke to death (**par** on); (lors d'un crime) to have been suffocated; **2** (assourdi) [*son, voix*] muffled (**par** by); **3** (retenu) [*voix, sanglot*] choked; [*rire, cri, bâillement*] suppressed; [*soupir*] discreet.

III étouffée *nf* **à l'étouffée** [*légume, viande*] braised; **cuire à l'~e** to braise.

étouffe-chrétien○ /etufkʀetjɛ̃/ **I** *adj inv* stodgy.

II *nm inv* stodge○ ₵; **un/des ~** stodge.

étouffement /etufmɑ̃/ *nm* **1** (répression) suppression; **2** (de concurrence, d'investissement) curbing; **3** (dissimulation) (de scandale) hushing-up; (de rapport) concealment; **4** (poids) oppression; **~ familial** family oppression; **5** (asphyxie) asphyxiation; **6** Méd (difficulté respiratoire) breathlessness; **il a été pris d'un ~** he had an attack of breathlessness.

étouffer /etufe/ [1] **I** *vtr* **1** (entraver) to stifle [*économie, carrière, création*]; to suppress [*protestation*]; **~ une révolte** to nip a revolt in the bud; **2** (dissimuler) to hush up [*affaire, scandale, crime*]; **3** (asphyxier) [*personne*] to suffocate [*victime*]; [*aliment*] to choke [*personne*]; [*chaleur, bâillon*] to stifle [*personne*]; [*plante, mauvaises herbes*] to choke [*plante*]; **les sanglots l'étouffaient** he/she was choked with tears; **~ qn de caresses/baisers** to smother sb with caresses/kisses; **la générosité ne les étouffe pas** they won't die of generosity; **4** (arrêter) to smother [*feu, incendie*]; to quell [*bagarre*]; **5** (retenir) to stifle [*bâillement*]; to hold back [*soupir, juron, cri*]; **6** (atténuer) [*tapis, porte, double vitrage*] to deaden [*son, voix*] (**sous, par** by).

II *vi* **1** (être mal à l'aise) to feel stifled; **2** (avoir chaud) to be unable to breathe; **on étouffe ici!** it's stifling here!; **~ de chaleur** to feel stifled in the heat; **3** (suffoquer) [*personne, ville*] to suffocate; **4** (mourir asphyxié) to suffocate.

III s'étouffer *vpr* **1** (suffoquer) to choke; **s'~ en mangeant du pain/en avalant une arête** to choke on bread/a fishbone; **s'~ de rage/rire** to choke with rage/laughter; **2** (mourir asphyxié) to suffocate.

étouffoir /etufwaʀ/ *nm* Mus damper.

étoupe /etup/ *nf* (de chanvre) tow; Naut oakum.

étourderie /etuʀdəʀi/ *nf* **1** (caractère irréfléchi) absent-mindedness; **faire qch par ~** to do sth through absent-mindedness; **faute d'~** careless mistake; **2** (erreur) careless mistake.

étourdi, **~e** /etuʀdi/ **I** *pp* ▶ **étourdir**.

II *pp adj* **1** [*personne*] absent-minded; **il est ~** he's absent-minded; **2** [*réponse, paroles*] unthinking.

III *nm,f* scatterbrain.

étourdiment /etuʀdimɑ̃/ *adv* absent-mindedly.

étourdir /etuʀdiʀ/ [3] **I** *vtr* **1** (assommer) to stun, to daze; **le coup de poing m'a étourdi** the punch stunned me; **je me sens étourdi** I feel stunned; **2** (fatiguer) **~ qn** [*vacarme, circulation*] to make sb's head spin; **tu m'étourdis avec ton bavardage** your constant chatter is making my head spin.

II s'étourdir *vpr* **éprouver le besoin de s'~** to feel the need to escape; **s'~ de paroles** to become intoxicated with words.

étourdissant, **~e** /etuʀdisɑ̃, ɑ̃t/ *adj* **1** [*bruit*] deafening; **2** [*réussite, talent*] stunning; **d'une beauté ~e** stunningly beautiful; **à une vitesse ~** at a dizzying speed.

étourdissement /etuʀdismɑ̃/ *nm* **avoir un ~** (vertige) to feel dizzy; (s'évanouir) to have a blackout; **être sujet à des ~s** to suffer from dizzy spells.

étourneau, *pl* **~x** /etuʀno/ *nm* **1** (oiseau) starling; **2**○ (étourdi) scatterbrain○.

étrange /etʀɑ̃ʒ/ **I** *adj* strange; **il est ~ que** it is strange that; **trouver ~ que** to find it strange that; **il se passe des choses ~s** strange things are happening; **coïncidence ~, nous nous sommes rencontrés là** by a strange coincidence we met there; **la vie n'a rien d'~** there is nothing strange about life; **aussi ~ que cela puisse paraître** strange as it may seem; **d'autant plus ~ que** all the more strange in that; **quoi d'~ à ce que** what could possibly be strange about the fact that; **le plus ~ c'est que** the strangest part is that; **chose ~ elle n'a pas répondu** strangely enough she didn't answer.

II *nm* **1** (caractère surprenant) strangeness; **l'~ est que** the strange thing is that; **2** (bizarrerie) bizarre; **penchant pour l'~** penchant for the bizarre.

étrangement /etʀɑ̃ʒmɑ̃/ *adv* **1** (fort curieusement) curiously; **être ~ silencieux** to be curiously silent; **votre composition ressemble ~ à celle de mademoiselle Grunard** your essay is curiously like Miss Grunard's; **rappeler ~ qn/qch** [*livre, objet*] to be curiously reminiscent of sb/sth; **vous me rappelez ~ un ami** it's strange ou uncanny but you remind me of a friend;

~ le ministre reste invisible curiously enough the minister is nowhere to be seen; **2** (remarquablement) surprisingly; **le cri des dauphins ressemble ~ à celui des bébés** the cry of dolphins is surprisingly like that of babies.

étranger, **-ère** /etʀɑ̃ʒe, ɛʀ/ I *adj* **1** (d'un autre pays) [*personne, lieu, langue, capitaux, journal*] foreign; **2** (extérieur) **~ à** [*personne*] not involved in (*après n*) [*affaire, activité*]; outside (*après n*) [*groupe*]; [*fait*] with no bearing on (*après n*) [*problème*]; [*comportement*] unrelated to (*après n*) [*éthique*]; **se sentir ~** to feel like an outsider; **'entrée interdite à toute personne étrangère au service'** 'staff only'; **ta sœur n'est pas étrangère à l'affaire** your sister is not uninvolved in the matter; **3** (inconnu) [*personne, voix, théorie*] unfamiliar (**à** to); **votre visage ne m'est pas ~** I know your face; **le domaine ne m'est pas ~** I am quite familiar with the field; **la peur leur est étrangère** they know no fear.

II *nm,f* **1** (d'un autre pays) foreigner; **les ~s ont besoin d'un visa** foreigners need a visa; **2** (d'un autre groupe) outsider; **on me traite en ~** I am treated as an outsider; **3** (inconnu) stranger; **un ~ rôde dehors** a stranger is prowling outside.

III *nm* **1** (autres pays) **l'~** foreign countries (*pl*); **à l'~** [*aller, séjourner*] abroad; **investissements à l'~** investments abroad; **s'ouvrir sur l'~** to open up to the outside world; **2** (gens d'ailleurs) foreigners (*pl*); **l'exclusion de l'~** the exclusion of foreigners; **3** (marchandises) **acheter ~** to buy foreign goods.

étrangeté /etʀɑ̃ʒte/ *nf* strangeness; **inquiétante ~** uncanniness.

étranglé, **~e** /etʀɑ̃gle/ I *pp* ▶ **étrangler**.

II *pp adj* **1** [*voix*] choked; [*son*] muffled; **d'une voix ~e** in a choked voice; **2** [*rue, vallée*] narrow.

étranglement /etʀɑ̃gləmɑ̃/ *nm* **1** (strangulation) strangling; Méd strangulation; **2** (de voix) tightness; **3** (de vallée, route) (fait) narrowing; (endroit) narrow section; **causer un ~** to narrow; **4** (de petites entreprises, vie économique, presse) stifling.

étrangler /etʀɑ̃gle/ [1] I *vtr* **1** lit to strangle [*victime*]; **j'ai envie de les ~!** fig I feel like throttling them!; **2** (gêner) [*col, cravate*] to choke, to throttle; **3** (comprimer) to pinch in [*taille*]; **4** [*colère, émotion*] to choke [*personne*]; **étranglé par l'émotion/la colère** choked with emotion/anger; **5** (écraser) to cripple [*entreprise, économie*]; **6** (museler) to stifle [*groupe politique, presse*].

II **s'étrangler** *vpr* **1** (avec une corde, un foulard) to strangle oneself; **2** (ne pas pouvoir parler, respirer) to choke; **s'~ de rage/de rire** to choke with rage/laughter; **3** [*cri*] to die in one's throat; **sa voix s'étrangla** his voice caught in his throat; **4** [*vallée, route*] to narrow.

étrangleur, **-euse** /etʀɑ̃glœʀ, øz/ *nm,f* strangler.

étrave /etʀav/ *nf* stem.

être[1] /ɛtʀ/ [7] *vi* (+ *v avoir*) **▶ 324** **1 il n'est pas jusqu'à l'Antarctique qui ne soit pollué** even the Antarctic is polluted; **il en est de Pierre comme de Paul** it is the same with Pierre as with Paul; **voilà ce qu'il en est** (présentation) this is how it is; (conclusion) that's how it is; **il n'en est rien** this isn't at all the case; **il en sera toujours ainsi** it will always be so; **il en a été de même** it was the same; **qu'en est-il de...?** what's the news on...?; **2 je suis à vous tout de suite/dans un instant** I'll be with you right away/in a minute; **je suis à vous** I'm all yours; **être à ce qu'on fait** to have one's mind on what one is doing; **elle est toujours à se plaindre** she's always complaining; **3 il n'est plus** euph he's no longer with us; **ce temps n'est plus** those days are gone; **ces traditions ne sont plus** these traditions are things of the past; **fût-il duc/en cristal** even if he were a duke/it were made of crystal, even were he a duke/were it made of crystal; **n'était leur grand âge** were it not for their advanced age, if it were not for their advanced age; **ne serait-ce qu'en faisant** if only by doing; **ne fût-ce que pour la soulager/qu'un instant** if only to relieve her/for a moment; **fût-ce pour des raisons humanitaires** if only on humanitarian grounds.

IDIOMES **on ne peut pas ~ et avoir été** Prov you can't stay young forever.

être[2] /ɛtʀ/ *nm* **1** (organisme vivant) being; **~ humain/vivant/surnaturel** human/living/supernatural being; **les ~s animés et inanimés** animate and inanimate things; **les ~s et les choses** living things and objects; **un ~ sans défense** a defenceless[GB] creature; **ces plantes sont des ~s inférieurs** these plants are inferior life-forms; **2** (personne) person; **un ~ d'exception** an exceptional person; **un ~ faible et timoré** a weak and timorous person; **les ~s qui doutent** people who doubt; **l'amitié entre deux ~s** friendship between two people; **un ~ cher** or **aimé** a loved one; **ce sont des ~s simples** they're simple beings ou souls; **son mari est un ~ sensible** her husband is a sensitive soul; **3** (nature intime) being; **de tout son ~** [*détester, souhaiter*] with one's whole being; **au fond de son ~, elle savait que** in the core of her being, she knew that; **blessé au plus profond de son ~** hurt to the core; **les ~s contradictoires qui vous habitent** the conflicting selves within you; **4** Philos **l'~** being.

étreindre /etʀɛ̃dʀ/ [55] I *vtr* **1** (serrer) to embrace, to hug [*ami*]; to clasp [*adversaire*]; to clutch [*objet*]; **2** fig (oppresser) to constrain; **la peur/douleur l'étreignait** he was constrained by fear/pain.

II **s'étreindre** *vpr* [*amis, amants*] to embrace (each other).

IDIOMES **qui trop embrasse mal étreint** ≈ grasp all, lose all.

étreinte /etʀɛ̃t/ *nf* **1** (affectueuse, amoureuse) embrace; (violente) grip; **2** fig grip; **l'ennemi resserrait son ~** the army was tightening its grip.

■ **~ fatale** Ordinat deadly embrace.

étrenner /etʀene/ [1] *vtr* (porter) to wear [sth] for the first time, to christen [*vêtement*]; (utiliser) to use [sth] for the first time [*objet, voiture*].

étrennes /etʀɛn/ *nfpl* (cadeau) gift; (argent) money; (gratification) ≈ Christmas box GB, Christmas present.

étrier /etʀije/ *nm* Équit, Anat, Méd stirrup; (de ski) front binding; (d'alpiniste) etrier.

■ **~ de frein** Aut calliper.

IDIOMES **boire le coup de l'~**○ to have one for the road○; **mettre à qn le pied à l'~** to get sb started.

étrille /etʀij/ *nf* **1** (brosse) currycomb; **2** (crabe) velvet swimming crab.

étriller /etʀije/ [1] *vtr* **1** (nettoyer) to curry [*cheval*]; **2** fig (critiquer) to tear to pieces; **3**○ Sport to thrash○; **4**○ (faire trop payer) to fleece○, to overcharge; **se faire ~** to be fleeced.

étripage /etʀipaʒ/ *nm* **1**○ (tuerie) bloodbath; **2** (de bêtes de boucherie) gutting.

étriper /etʀipe/ [1] I *vtr* **1**○ fig (tuer) to slaughter [*adversaire*]; **si je l'attrape, je l'étripe!** hum if I catch him I'll skin him alive!; **se faire ~** to get one's throat cut; **2** (ôter les tripes à) to gut [*veau, porc*].

II **s'étriper**○ *vpr* to murder each other.

étriqué, **~e** /etʀike/ *adj* [*veste*] skimpy; [*vie*] restricted; [*appartement*] cramped; **elle a l'air ~ dans sa robe** her dress looks skimpy; **les esprits ~s** narrow-minded people.

étrivière /etʀivjɛʀ/ *nf* stirrup leather.

étroit, **~e** /etʀwa, at/ I *adj* **1** (pas large) narrow; **c'est trop ~** it is too narrow; **il est ~ d'épaules** he has narrow shoulders; **2** (restreint) [*idée, conception*] narrow; [*domaine professionnel, cercle d'amis*] narrow; **avoir l'esprit ~** to be narrow-minded; **3** (intime) [*amitié, liens familiaux*] close (*épith*); **il y a un rapport ~ entre** there is a close link between; **être en liaison ~e avec** to be in close contact with; **travailler en ~e collaboration avec** to work closely with; **4** (rigoureux) **sous ~e surveillance** (de la police) under close surveillance; **au sens ~ du terme** in the narrow sense of the word; **l'~e observance du carême** the strict observance of Lent.

II **à l'étroit** *loc adv* **nous sommes un peu à l'~** (dans un appartement, une voiture) we're a bit cramped; **être logé à l'~** to live in cramped conditions; **se sentir à l'~** (financièrement) to feel the pinch; **je me sens un peu à l'~ dans ce pantalon/ces chaussures** these trousers GB ou pants US/these shoes feel a bit too tight.

étroitement /etʀwatmɑ̃/ *adv* [*surveiller*] closely; **les deux questions sont ~ liées** the two questions are closely linked; **il observe ~ la consigne** he keeps strictly to the rules.

étroitesse /etʀwatɛs/ *nf* lit, fig narrowness; **~ d'esprit** narrow-mindedness.

étron /etʀɔ̃/ *nm* excreta (*pl*), turd○.

Étrurie /etʀyʀi/ *nprf* Etruria.

étrusque /etʀysk/ *adj, nm* Etruscan.

Étrusque /etʀysk/ *nmf* Etruscan.

étude /etyd/ I *nf* **1** (recherche) study; (enquête) survey; **~ de la CEE** study by the EEC (**sur** of); **~ portant sur** study on; **~ des** or **sur les pesticides** study of pesticides; **~ comparative/préliminaire** comparative/preliminary study; **~ réalisée par** study carried out by; **~ de V. Rossignol** study by V. Rossignol; **l'~ a porté sur mille personnes/deux régions** the survey involved one thousand people/two regions; **2** (observation) study (**de** of); **~ attentive du phénomène/de quatre cas** close study of the phenomenon/of four cases; **3** (prise en considération) (**mise à l'**)**~** consideration; **être/rester à l'~** to be/to be still under consideration; **4** (apprentissage) study; **l'~ des langues étrangères** the study of foreign languages; **5** (d'avoué, de notaire) (bureau) office; (charge) practice; **6** Mus étude; **~s de Chopin** Chopin's études; **~ pour piano** étude for piano; **7** Art study; **~ de mains** study of hands; **8** Scol (salle) study room GB, study hall US; (période) study period; **j'ai deux heures d'~** I've got a two-hour study period.

II **études** *nfpl* Scol, Univ studies; **~s bibliques/théoriques/de droit** biblical/theoretical/law studies; **faire des ~s** to be a student; **continuer/abandonner ses ~s** to continue/abandon one's studies; **elle a fait de brillantes ~s** she was very successful in her studies; **faire** or **poursuivre des ~s de médecine/au Canada** to study medicine/in Canada; **je n'ai pas fait d'~s** (**supérieures**) I didn't go to university ou college; **~s primaires/secondaires/supérieures** primary/secondary/higher education **₵**.

■ **~ de cas** Sociol case study; **~ épidémiologique** Méd epidemiological study; **~ de faisabilité** Écon feasibility study; **~ d'impact** Écol environmental impact assessment; **~ de marché** Entr market research **₵**; **faire** or **réaliser une ~ de marché** to do market research (**sur** on); **~ préparatoire** Art cartoon.

étudiant, **~e** /etydjɑ̃, ɑ̃t/ I *adj* student; **population/colère ~e** student population/anger.

II *nm,f* student; **c'est une** or **elle est ~e** she is a student; **~ en droit/lettres classiques/sciences politiques** law/classics/political science student; **~ de troisième cycle** ≈ postgraduate GB ou graduate US student.

étudié, **~e** /etydje/ I *pp* ▶ **étudier**.

II *pp adj* **1** (méticuleux) [*coupe*] original; [*ligne*] carefully designed; [*discours*] care-

être[1]

Généralités

Dans la plupart des situations exprimant l'existence, l'identité, la localisation, la qualité, *être* sera traduit par *to be*:

je pense donc je suis = I think therefore I am
le soleil est une étoile = the sun is a star
j'étais chez moi = I was at home
l'eau est froide = the water is cold

Les locutions figées contenant *être* sont traitées sous l'entrée appropriée. Ainsi *être en train de/sur le point de/hors de soi* etc. sont respectivement sous ***train***, ***point***, ***hors*** etc.; *comme si de rien n'était* et *quoi qu'il en soit* sous ***comme*** et ***quoi***. Selon le même principe, l'emploi facultatif de *étant* après *considérer comme* et *présenter comme* est traité sous ces verbes; *étant donné (que)* et *étant entendu que* sont sous ***donné*** et ***entendu***.
La plupart des autres emplois de *étant* se traduisent par *being*:

cela (ou *ceci*) *étant* = this being so

En revanche, *c'est-à-dire*, *n'est-ce pas*, *peut-être* et *soit* sont des entrées à part entière, traitées à leur place dans le dictionnaire.

Par ailleurs, on consultera utilement les notes d'usage répertoriées
▶ 1920].

être = verbe auxiliaire

De la voix passive

être auxiliaire de la voix passive se traduit par *to be*. On notera l'emploi des divers temps en anglais.

Au présent

où sont les épreuves?
elles sont révisées par le traducteur = where are the proofs? they are being revised by the translator
votre voiture est réparée = your car has been repaired
les portes sont repeintes chaque année = the doors are repainted every year

Au passé

les épreuves ont été révisées en juin = the proofs were revised in June
les épreuves ont été révisées plusieurs fois = the proofs have been revised several times
les épreuves ont été révisées bien avant ma démission = the proofs had been revised long before I resigned

Du passé dans les temps composés

être se traduit par *to have* si le temps est également composé en anglais – ce qui est beaucoup moins fréquent qu'en français (voir ci-dessus) – sauf avec *naître*. Dans certains contextes, on peut avoir:

elles sont tombées = they have fallen
ils se sont enfuis = they have escaped
elle s'était vengée = she had taken her revenge

Les verbes traduits par une construction passive ou attributive en anglais suivent les mêmes règles au passé:

se vendre = to be sold
tous les livres se sont vendus = all the books have been sold
s'indigner = to be indignant
elle se serait indignée = she would have been indignant

Noter que la forme pronominale à valeur passive est souvent mieux rendue en anglais par une forme intransitive:

les livres se sont bien vendus = the books have sold well

être = aller

Lorsqu'il signifie *aller*, *être* se traduit par *to be* en anglais, mais seulement s'il est directement suivi d'un complément de lieu:

je n'ai jamais été en Chine = I've never been to China

Suivi d'un infinitif, il se rend par *to go to*:

il a été voir son ami = he's gone to see his friend
j'ai été manger au restaurant = I went to eat in a restaurant

Dans le sens de *s'en aller*, on notera les tournures recherchées:

ils s'en furent au théâtre = they went to the theatre
ils s'en furent (déçus) = they left (disappointed)

c'est

Interrogation

est-ce, ou sa variante plus familière *c'est*, se traduit généralement par *is it*:

est-ce leur voiture? = is it their car?
c'est grave? = is it serious?
c'est toi ou ton frère? = is it you or your brother?

Quand *ce* garde sa valeur démonstrative, l'anglais précise la référence:

est-ce clair? = is that clear?
qui est-ce? = who is he/she?
(en montrant une personne) = who is that?

(mais, en parlant de quelqu'un qui vous appelle au téléphone, ou à quelqu'un qui frappe à la porte).

qui est-ce? = who is it?

est-ce n'est généralement pas traduit dans les tournures emphatiques ou permettant d'éviter l'inversion du sujet en français:

est-ce que tu parles russe? = do you speak Russian?
est-ce leur fils, ce garçon? = is this boy their son?
qui est-ce qui l'a fait? = who did it?
qui est-ce que tu as rencontré? = who did you meet?
quand est-ce que tu manges? = when do you eat?
qu'est-ce que c'est? = what is it?
(ou comme vu plus haut) = what is this/that? (selon qu'on montre un objet proche ou éloigné)

Néanmoins, la tournure emphatique est également possible en anglais dans certaines expressions:

qu'est-ce que j'entends? = what's this I hear?
est-ce bien ce qu'il a voulu dire? = is that what he really meant?

Affirmation

c'est se traduit, selon les contextes, *it is* (*it's*), *this is*, *that is* (*that's*):

c'est facile (de critiquer) = it's easy
(ce que tu me demandes, ce travail) = that's easy
c'est moi (réponse à 'qui est-ce?') = it's me
(réponse à 'qui le fait?') = I do
(réponse à 'qui l'a fait?') = I did
(pour me désigner sur une photo, ou comme étant le personnage dont il est question) = that's me (*traduit également* ça, c'est moi)
c'est eux, ce sont eux
(qui sont là-bas, que je montre) = it's them
(qui le font) = they do
(qui l'ont fait) = they did
(qui arrivent) = here they are
ce sont mes enfants (que je vous présente) = these are my children
(qui sont là-bas) = they are my children
c'est cela = that's right
c'est ça! tu crois que je vais faire le travail tout seul? = what's this! do you think I'm going to do the work all by myself?

Lorsqu'il reprend un nom, un infinitif ou une proposition qui le précède *c'est* se traduit seulement par *is*:

réussir, c'est une question de volonté = succeeding is a question of will-power
sortir par ce temps, c'est de la folie = going out in this weather is sheer madness
eux, ce sont mes amis = they are my friends

De même, lorsque *c'est que* reprend un groupe nominal ou une proposition, il se traduit simplement par *is that*:

le comique, c'est que … = the funny thing is that …

On se reportera à l'entrée appropriée, comme ***comique***, ***fort*** etc.

Lorsque *c'est que* sert à donner une explication il se rend généralement, et selon le temps, par *it is that*, *it was that*, mais aussi, pour insister sur l'explication, par *it is/was because*:

si j'ai fait ça, c'est que je ne pouvais pas faire autrement = if I did that, it was because I couldn't do otherwise

ce n'est pas que se traduit la plupart du temps par *it is/was not that* (la contraction est *it's not* plutôt que *it isn't*):

ce n'est pas qu'il soit bête, mais … = it's not that he is stupid, but …

En corrélation avec un pronom relatif, *c'est* peut soit garder sa valeur de présentatif (voir plus haut) et se rendre par *that's*:

c'est le journaliste qui m'a interviewé = that's the journalist who interviewed me
c'est le journaliste dont je te parlais = that's the journalist I was telling you about
c'est le château où je suis né = that's the castle where I was born
c'est ce qui me fait croire que … = that's what makes me think that …
c'est justement ce que je disais = that's exactly what I was saying

soit constituer une tournure emphatique qui se rend en anglais selon la nuance:

c'est de la même femme que nous parlons = we're talking about the same woman
c'était d'en parler devant elle qui me gênait = talking about it in front of her was what made me feel uneasy *ou* what made me feel uneasy was talking about it in front of her
c'est lui/Paul qui l'a cassé
(je le dénonce) = **he/Paul** broke it
(je l'accuse) = **he/Paul** is the one who broke it
c'est mon frère qui l'a écrit = it was my brother who wrote it *ou* my brother's the one who wrote it
c'est de ta sœur que je parlais, pas de toi = it was your sister I was talking about, not you
c'est cette voiture qui m'intéresse = this is the car (that) I am interested in
c'est lui le coupable = **he** is the culprit
ce sont eux les meurtriers = **they** are the murderers

☛ Voir page suivante

être[1]

c'est à suivi d'un infinitif se traduit parfois par *it is* suivi de l'adjectif correspondant si cette même transformation est possible en français:

c'est à désespérer ou *c'est désespérant* = it's hopeless

mais c'est rare, et il est conseillé de se reporter à l'infinitif en question ou à l'un des autres termes obtenus à partir de transformations semblables.

c'est à … de faire (ou parfois *à faire*) se traduira de deux manières:

c'est à Pierre/lui de choisir
(c'est son tour) = it's Pierre's/his turn to choose
(c'est sa responsabilité) = it's up to Pierre/to him to choose

La notion de rivalité contenue dans *c'est à qui* suivi du futur doit être rendue explicite en anglais:

c'est à qui proposera le plus de réformes = each is trying to suggest more reforms than the other
c'était à qui des deux aurait le dernier mot = they were each trying to get in the last word
c'était à qui trouverait le plus d'erreurs dans le texte = they were vying with each other to find the most mistakes in the text

c'est, équivalent de *ça fait* dans le compte d'une somme, se rend par *it is*:

c'est 200 francs = it's 200 francs
c'est combien? = how much is it?

ce sera avec valeur modale de *ce doit être* se traduit *it must be*:

ce sera mon professeur de piano = it must be my piano teacher

être = verbe impersonnel

il est facile de critiquer = it is easy to criticize
il serait nécessaire de faire = it would be necessary to do
il est des gens bizarres = there are some strange people
il n'est pas de jour/d'heure sans qu'il se plaigne = not a day/an hour goes by without him complaining

On se référera par ailleurs aux notes d'usage concernant l'heure et la date; voir aussi les entrées ***temps*** et ***fois***.

il est à suivi d'un infinitif se rend différemment, selon les nuances qu'impose le contexte, par *it must be*, *it has to be*, *it should be*, *it can be* suivis du participe passé. Pour plus de sûreté, on se reportera à l'infinitif en question, où cette construction est généralement traitée.

il est de suivi d'un substantif ou d'un groupe nominal se rend souvent par *it is* suivi directement d'un adjectif ou d'un substantif précédé d'un déterminant (article, pronom):

il est de coutume de faire ou *qu'on fasse* = it is customary (*ou* the custom) to do
il est de notre responsabilité de faire = it is our responsibility to do

Mais ce n'est pas une règle absolue, et il est préférable de consulter des entrées telles que ***goût***, ***règle***, ***notoriété*** etc. pour avoir des traductions adéquates. Voir également **1** ci-dessous pour des exemples supplémentaires.

Emplois avec en

en être

Certains cas sont traités sous la rubrique 'être = verbe impersonnel'; d'autres, expressions figées, le sont sous l'entrée appropriée; voir par exemple ***poche*** et ***frais*** pour *en être de sa poche/pour ses frais*. Enfin, quand l'antécédent de *en* est exprimé dans la phrase, l'expression est traitée plus bas sous *être de*:

où en étais-je? = where was I?
je ne sais plus où j'en suis = I'm lost
'où en es-tu de tes recherches?' 'j'en suis à mi-chemin/au début' = 'how far have you got in your research?' 'I'm halfway through/at the beginning'
elle a eu plusieurs amants/accidents: elle en est à son quatrième = she has had several lovers/accidents: this is her fourth
j'en suis à me demander si … = I'm beginning to wonder whether …
j'en étais à ne pouvoir distinguer le vrai du faux = I'd got to the point where I couldn't distinguish between truth and falsehood

être en

Suivie d'un substantif représentant un vêtement, l'expression peut être traduite *to be in*, mais on consultera l'entrée appropriée pour s'en assurer. Si l'on dit *to be in uniform* ou éventuellement *to be wearing a uniform* pour *être en uniforme*, l'anglais préfère généralement *to be wearing a suit* à *to be in a suit* pour *être en costume* (de même pour *robe*, *tailleur* etc.). Dans le cas d'un déguisement, on a *to be dressed up as*:

être en pirate = to be dressed up as a pirate.

emplois avec y

j'y suis (je vous comprends) = I'm with you
(plus général mais un peu familier) = I get it
je n'y suis pas (je ne comprends pas) = I don't get it
vous y êtes? (vous comprenez?) = are you with me?
(vous êtes prêt(e)?) = are you ready?
20 000 francs? vous n'y êtes pas! = 20,000 francs? you're a long way out!
tu n'y es pas, c'est plus compliqué que ça = you don't realize, it's a lot more complicated than that

Voir aussi les entrées ***y***, adverbe de lieu, et ***pour***.

être + prépositions

La plupart des cas (*être dans*, *sur*, *devant*, *pour*, *après*, *avec* etc.) sont traités sous la préposition correspondante. Ne sont retenus ici que les cas particuliers de *être à* et *être de*.

être à

Les cas où l'on peut faire l'ellipse de *être* ou le remplacer par un autre verbe sont traités sous la préposition *à*; ceux de *en être à* sous la rubrique 'en être', et ceux de *c'est à* sous la rubrique 'c'est'.

Les emplois de *être à* suivi d'un groupe nominal et signifiant 'tendre vers' sont généralement traités sous le substantif approprié, comme ***temps***, ***hausse***, ***agonie*** etc. dans les expressions *le temps est à la pluie*, *être à la hausse*, *être à l'agonie*. De même, quand *être à* signifie un état, c'est sous le substantif ou l'adjectif approprié, comme ***bout***, ***disposition***, ***quai***, ***vif*** etc., qu'on trouvera la ou les traductions de l'expression correspondante.

Suivi d'un infinitif et signifiant *devoir être*, *être à* peut généralement se traduire, en observant les mêmes nuances qu'avec *devoir*, par *must be*, *have to be* ou *should be* suivi du participe passé du verbe anglais. Il reste conseillé de consulter l'infinitif en question, comme ***plaindre***, ***prendre*** etc. On en trouve également un traitement succinct sous les rubriques 'être = verbe impersonnel' et 'c'est'.

Au sens de *appartenir à*, l'anglais utilise *to be* suivi du cas possessif quand le possesseur est un être animé ou d'un pronom possessif si celui-ci est représenté par un pronom objet. Si le cas possessif n'est pas d'usage, on utilise de préférence *to belong to*:

ce livre est à moi = this book is mine
ce livre est à mon frère = this book is my brother's
ces dictionnaires sont au service de traduction = these dictionaries belong to the translation department
à qui est ce chien? = who does this dog belong to? *ou* whose dog is this?

Voir **2** ci-dessous pour des exemples supplémentaires.

être de

Quand elle exprime un état ou une situation, la tournure *être de* suivie d'un substantif sans déterminant est traduite sous le substantif en question, notamment ***avis***, ***garde***, ***service*** etc. De même, certaines expressions où la présence de déterminant est variable, comme dans *être de mauvaise foi/d'une incroyable mauvaise foi* sont traitées sous l'entrée appropriée, en l'occurrence, ***foi***; voir aussi ***humeur***, ***poil*** etc.

La construction *être d'un/d'une* suivie d'un adjectif substantivé ou d'un substantif exprimant une qualité ou un défaut peut généralement être rendue par *to be so* suivi de l'adjectif correspondant en anglais, si le substantif est seul:

elle est d'un ridicule! = she's so ridiculous!
elle est d'une prétention! = she's so pretentious!

Si le substantif est qualifié, l'adjectif devient généralement un adverbe en anglais:

il est d'une exquise courtoisie = he's exquisitely courteous
il est d'une incompétence rare = he's exceptionally incompetent

Mais il n'est pas inutile de vérifier les traductions des adjectifs et substantifs à leur entrée avant de rendre cette construction.

Au sens de *participer à*, *faire partie de*, la tournure *être de* se traduit de façon très variable (voir aussi ***partie***):

il est des nôtres (il vient avec nous) = he's with us
(il est de notre clan, agit et pense comme nous) = he's one of us
serez-vous des nôtres? = will you be (coming) with us?
êtes-vous des nôtres? = are you coming with us? (ici, *coming* est nécessaire, pour éviter l'ambiguïté de *are you with us?*)
les journalistes ne sont pas du voyage = the journalists aren't coming on the trip
les journalistes ne seront pas du voyage = the journalists won't be coming on the trip
ils ont organisé une expédition mais je n'en étais pas = they organized an expedition but I wasn't part of it
il y avait un congrès mais il n'en était pas = there was a congress but he didn't take part

Suivi d'un infinitif et précédé de noms abstraits avec l'article défini (*l'idéal*, *l'essentiel* etc.) ou de superlatifs (*le plus simple*), *être de* se traduit généralement par *to be* suivi de l'infinitif avec *to*:

le plus simple serait de tout recommencer = the simplest thing to do would be to start all over again

fully prepared; **2** (non spontané) [*rire, gestes, démarche*] studied.

étudier /etydje/ [2] **I** *vtr* **1** (se pencher sur) to examine [*dossier, situation, projet de loi*]; to study [*dessin, carte, plan*]; **2** (prendre en considération) to consider [*création, aide, généralisation*]; **~ la vente d'armements** to consider selling weapons; **3** (faire une recherche sur) [*personne*] to study [*animal, système, corps célestes, époque*]; [*science*] to deal with [*problème*]; **4** (apprendre) to study [*langue, violon*]; to learn [*leçon*]; **~ le russe/le chant** to study Russian/singing; **5** (observer) to study [*personne, réaction*]; **~ son adversaire** to study one's opponent; **6** (calculer) to calculate [*geste , effet*]; **7** (concevoir) to design [*nouveau moteur*].
II *vi* **1** (faire des études) **~ à l'école internationale/à Varsovie** to be a student at the international school/in Warsaw; **2** (apprendre) to be studying.

étui /etɥi/ *nm* gén case; **~ à jumelles/lunettes** binocular/spectacle-case; **~ à revolver** holster.

étuve /etyv/ *nf* **1** (bain de vapeur) steam room; fig **le grenier est une ~** the attic is like an oven; **2** (de désinfection) autoclave; (en microbiologie) incubator.

étuvée /etyve/ *nf* **à l'~** braised; **faire cuire à l'~** to braise.

étymologie /etimɔlɔʒi/ *nf* etymology.

étymologique /etimɔlɔʒik/ *adj* etymological.

étymologiquement /etimɔlɔʒikmɑ̃/ *adv* etymologically.

étymologiste /etymɔlɔʒist/ *nmf* etymologist.

étymon /etimɔ̃/ *nm* etymon.

eucalyptus /økaliptys/ *nm* eucalyptus.

eucharistie /økaʀisti/ *nf* (sacrifice) Eucharist; (pain, vin) the Sacrament.

eucharistique /økaʀistik/ *adj* Eucharistic.

Euclide /øklid/ *npr* Euclid.

euclidien, -ienne /øklidjɛ̃, ɛn/ *adj* Euclidean.

eudiomètre /ødjɔmɛtʀ/ *nm* eudiometer.

eugénique /øʒenik/ **I** *adj* eugenic.
II *nf* eugenics (+ *v sg*).

eugénisme /øʒenism/ *nm* eugenics (+ *v sg*).

euh○ /œ/ *excl* (embarras, hésitation) er...

eunuque /ønyk/ *nm* eunuch.

euphémique /øfemik/ *adj* euphemistic.

euphémiquement /øfemikmɑ̃/ *adv* euphemistically.

euphémisme /øfemism/ *nm* euphemism; **par ~** euphemistically.

euphonie /øfɔni/ *nf* euphony.

euphonique /øfɔnik/ *adj* euphonious; **loi ~** rule of euphony.

euphoniquement /øfɔnikmɑ̃/ *adv* euphoniously.

euphonium /øfɔnjɔm/ *nm* euphonium.

euphorbe /øfɔʀb/ *nf* euphorbia.

euphorie /øfɔʀi/ *nf* euphoria.

euphorique /øfɔʀik/ *adj* [*personne*] euphoric; [*marché, Bourse*] bullish.

euphorisant, ~e /øfɔʀizɑ̃, ɑ̃t/ **I** *adj* [*boisson*] stimulating; [*vertu, qualité, atmosphère*] uplifting; [*substance, drogue*] euphoriant.
II *nm* Méd stimulant.

euphoriser /øfɔʀize/ [1] *vtr* **1** [*substance*] **~ qn** to induce euphoria in sb; **2** [*nouvelle, expérience*] to elate.

Euphrate /øfʀat/ ▶**357** *nprm* **l'~** the Euphrates.

eurafricain, ~e /øʀafʀikɛ̃, ɛn/ *adj* [*personne*] Eurafrican; [*entreprise*] Euro-African.

Eurafricain, ~e /øʀafʀikɛ̃, ɛn/ *nm,f* Eurafrican.

eurasiatique /øʀazjatik/ *adj* Eurasian.

Eurasiatique /øʀazjatik/ *nmf* Eurasian.

Eurasie /øʀazi/ *nprf* Eurasia.

eurasien, -ienne /øʀazjɛ̃, ɛn/ *adj* Eurasian.

Eurasien, -ienne /øʀazjɛ̃, ɛn/ *nm,f* Eurasian.

Euratom /øʀatɔm/ *nf* (*abbr* = **European atomic energy commission**) Euratom.

Eure /œʀ/ ▶**692** **I** *nprm* (département) **l'~** Evre.
II ▶**357** *nprf* (rivière) **l'~** the Evre.

Eure-et-Loir /œʀelwaʀ/ ▶**692** *nprm* (département) **l'~** Eure-et-Loir.

eurêka /øʀeka/ *excl* eureka!

Euripide /øʀipid/ *npr* Euripides.

euristique = **heuristique**.

EURL /œyɛʀɛl/ *nf*: *abbr* ▶ **entreprise**.

eurobanque /øʀobɑ̃k/ *nf* Eurobank.

eurochèque /øʀoʃɛk/ *nm* Eurocheque.

eurocommunisme /øʀokɔmynism/ *nm* Eurocommunism.

euroconnecteur /øʀokɔnɛktœʀ/ *nm* (femelle) scart socket; (mâle) scart plug.

eurocrate /øʀokʀat/ *nmf* Eurocrat.

eurodollar /øʀodɔlaʀ/ *nm* Eurodollar.

euro-émission, *pl* **~s** /øʀoemisjɔ̃/ *nf* Euro-issue.

eurofranc /øʀofʀɑ̃/ *nm* Eurofranc.

euromarché /øʀomaʀʃe/ *nm* Euromarket.

euromissile /øʀomisil/ *nm* Euromissile.

euro-obligation, *pl* **~s** /øʀoɔbligasjɔ̃/ *nf* Eurobond.

Europe /øʀɔp/ ▶**321** *nprf* **1** Géog Europe; **l'~ de l'Est** Eastern Europe; **2** Pol CEE **l'~ communautaire** the European community; **l'~ des douze** the twelve, the twelve members of the EC; **l'~ de 1993** Europe in 1993; **l'~ verte** Agricultural Europe; **l'~ de l'espace** the joint European space venture; **l'~ sociale** social aspects in Europe; **faire l'~** to build (the new) Europe.

européanisation /øʀɔpeanizasjɔ̃/ *nf* Europeanization.

européaniser /øʀɔpeanize/ [1] **I** *vtr* to europeanize [*pays*]; **~ un débat** to broaden a debate to a European level.
II s'européaniser *vpr* [*pays*] to become europeanized; [*économie*] to become adapted to a European framework.

européen, -éenne /øʀɔpeɛ̃, ɛn/ **I** *adj* European.
II européennes *nfpl* **les ~s** the European elections.

Européen, -éenne /øʀɔpeɛ̃, ɛn/ *nm,f* **1** Géog (habitant) European; **2** Pol (partisan) pro-European.

eurostratégie /øʀostʀateʒi/ *nf* Eurostrategy.

Eurotunnel /øʀotynɛl/ *nm* Eurotunnel.

Eurovision /øʀovizjɔ̃/ *nf* Eurovision; **en ~** through Eurovision.

Eurydice /øʀidis/ *npr* Eurydice.

eurythmie /øʀitmi/ *nf* eurhythmy.

eustatique /østatik/ *adj* eustatic.

Euterpe /øtɛʀp/ *npr* Euterpe.

euthanasie /øtanazi/ *nf* euthanasia.

eutrophisation /øtʀɔfizasjɔ̃/ *nf* eutrophication.

eux /ø/ *pron pers* **1** (sujet) they; **~ regardent la télévision, nous, nous lisons** they watch television, we read; **~ seuls ont le droit de parler** they alone have the right to speak; **~, ils ne disent jamais ce qu'ils pensent** they never say what they think; **ce sont ~, je les reconnais** it's them, I recognize them; **je sais que ce n'est pas ~ qui ont fait ça** I know they weren't the ones who did it, I know it wasn't them who did it; **2** (dans une comparaison) them; **je travaille plus qu'~** I work more than they do ou than them; **je le vois plus souvent qu'~** (qu'ils ne le voient) I see him more often than they do; (que je ne le vois) I see him more often than them ou than I see them; **3** (objet) **les inviter, ~, quelle idée!** invite THEM, what an idea!; **~, il faut les enfermer** they should be locked up; **4** (après une préposition) them; **à cause d'/autour d'/auprès ~** because of/around/after them; **un cadeau pour ~** a present for them; **pour ~ c'est important?** is it important to them?; **elle ne pense pas à ~** she doesn't think of them; **je n'écris à personne sauf ~** I don't write to anyone but them, I only write to them; **sans ~ nous n'aurions pas pu réussir** we could never have managed without them; **à ~, je peux dire la vérité** I can tell THEM the truth; **ce sont des amis à ~** they're friends of theirs; **ils n'ont pas encore de voiture à ~** they don't have their own car yet; **les journaux sont-ils à ~?** are the newspapers theirs?, do the newspapers belong to them?; **c'est à ~** (appartenance) it's theirs, it belongs to them; **c'est à ~ de faire la vaisselle** it's their turn to do the dishes; **c'est à ~ de choisir** (leur tour) it's their turn to choose; (leur responsabilité) it's up to them to choose; **les verres sont sur la table, certains d'entre ~ sont sales** the glasses are on the table, some of them are dirty.

eux-mêmes /ømɛm/ *pron pers* themselves; **ils me l'ont dit ~** they told me themselves; **ils ont décidé ~** they decided themselves, they made the decision themselves; **après les motos et les voitures les camions ~ commencent à montrer des signes de faiblesse** after the motorbikes and the cars even the lorries are beginning to show signs of weakness; **les chiffres de 1990 enregistrent ~ une forte progression** the figures for 1990 show a marked increase as well; **les experts ~ reconnaissent que...** even the experts admit that...; **ils me l'ont dit d'~** they volunteered the information, they told me themselves; **les meubles n'ont pas de valeur en ~** the furniture has no value in itself.

évacuateur, -trice /evakɥatœʀ, tʀis/ **I** *adj* [*canal*] discharge.
II *nm* sluice.

évacuation /evakɥasjɔ̃/ *nf* **1** (de liquide) discharge; **il y a un problème d'~ de l'eau** the water doesn't drain away; **2** (de lieu, personnes) evacuation.
■ **~ sanitaire** medical evacuation.

évacué, ~e /evakɥe/ *nm,f* evacuee.

évacuer /evakɥe/ [1] *vtr* **1** (faire sortir) to evacuate [*personne*]; (vider) to evacuate [*lieu*]; to drain off [*eaux usées*]; **faire ~ une pièce** to evacuate a room; **2** fig to shrug off [*problème*]; **3** Méd to evacuate [*excréments*]; to eliminate [*toxines*].

évadé, ~e /evade/ *nm,f* escapee.

évader: **s'évader** /evade/ [1] *vpr* **1** (s'enfuir) to escape (**de** from); **faire ~ qn** to help sb to escape; **un prisonnier évadé** an escaped prisoner; **2** fig to get away (**de** from).

évaluable /evalɥabl/ *adj* assessable.

évaluation /evalɥasjɔ̃/ *nf* **1** (de collection, bijou, maison) valuation; **faire l'~ de** to value [*bijou, maison*]; **2** (de coûts, dégâts, besoins, soins) (action) assessment; (résultat) estimate, appraisal US; **~ de l'impôt** tax assessment; **3** Entr (de personnel, employé) appraisal.

évaluer /evalɥe/ [1] *vtr* **1** (estimer approximativement) to estimate [*grandeur, durée*] (**à** at); to assess [*risques, importance, coût*]; to assess [*dégâts, besoins*]; **j'évalue son chiffre d'affaires à moins de** I would put his turnover at less than; **il est difficile d'~ le montant de la dette** it is difficult to assess the total debt; **on évalue à 2 500 le nombre de victimes de l'épidémie** the epidemic has claimed an estimated 2,500 victims; **2** (déterminer la valeur de) to value, to appraise US [*meuble, patrimoine*]; **~ qch à 100 francs** to value sth at 100 francs; **faire ~ un tableau** to have a painting valued ou appraised US; **3** (juger) to assess [*employé, élève*].

évanescent, **~e** /evanesɑ̃, ɑ̃t/ *adj* (tous contextes) evanescent.

évangélique /evɑ̃ʒelik/ *adj* **1** (conforme à l'Évangile) [*charité, vie*] Christian; **2** (de l'église réformée) Evangelical.

évangélisateur, **-trice** /evɑ̃ʒelizatœʀ, tʀis/ **I** *adj* evangelical.
II *nm,f* evangelist; (catholique) missionary.

évangélisation /evɑ̃ʒelizasjɔ̃/ *nf* evangelization.

évangéliser /evɑ̃ʒelize/ [1] *vtr* evangelize.

évangélisme /evɑ̃ʒelism/ *nm* **1** (de l'Évangile) evangelism; **2** (de l'église réformée) Evangelicalism.

évangéliste /evɑ̃ʒelist/ *nm* **1** (apôtre) Evangelist; **2** (de l'église réformée) evangelist.

Évangile /evɑ̃ʒil/ *nm* (message, livre) Gospel; **les quatre ~s** the Four Gospels; **l'~ selon St Marc** the Gospel according to St Mark GB, the Gospel according to Mark; **c'est/ce n'est pas parole d'~** it's/it's not gospel (truth).

évanouir: **s'évanouir** /evanwiʀ/ [3] *vpr* **1** (perdre conscience) to faint (**de** with); **évanoui** unconscious; **2** fig (disparaître) to fade.

évanouissement /evanwismɑ̃/ *nm* **1** Méd (perte de conscience) blackout, fainting fit; **2** fig (disparition) fading; **3** Télécom fading.

évaporation /evapɔʀasjɔ̃/ *nf* evaporation.

évaporé, **~e** /evapɔʀe/ **I** *pp* ▶ **évaporer**.
II *adj* [*personne*] pej giddy.
III *nm,f* pej birdbrain○ péj.

évaporer: **s'évaporer** /evapɔʀe/ [1] *vpr* **1** Chimie, Phys [*liquide*] to evaporate; **faire ~** to evaporate; **2**○ fig (disparaître) to vanish; **il s'est évaporé dans la nature** he vanished into thin air.

évasé, **~e** /evaze/ **I** *pp* ▶ **évaser**.
II *pp adj* [*tuyau*] flared; [*verre*] bell-shaped; [*jupe, manches*] flared; **un vase de forme ~e** a widemouthed vase.

évasement /evazmɑ̃/ *nm* widening out.

évaser /evaze/ [1] **I** *vtr* to widen [sth] at the mouth [*conduit, trou*]; Cout to flare [*vêtement*].
II s'évaser *vpr* [*conduit*] to open out; [*jupe*] to be flared.

évasif, **-ive** /evazif, iv/ *adj* evasive; **d'un air ~** evasively.

évasion /evazjɔ̃/ *nf* **1** (de détenu) escape; **tentative d'~** escape attempt; **2** fig (changement) escape; **la lecture permet l'~** reading is a chance to escape.
■ **~ des capitaux** flight of capital; **~ fiscale** tax avoidance.

évasivement /evazivmɑ̃/ *adv* evasively.

Ève /ɛv/ *nprf* Eve; **en tenue d'~** in one's birthday suit hum.
IDIOMES **elle ne le connaît ni d'~ ni d'Adam** she doesn't know him from Adam.

évêché /eveʃe/ *nm* **1** (territoire) diocese; **2** (résidence) bishop's palace.

éveil /evɛj/ *nm* **1** (de nature, dormeur) awakening; (de vocation, d'intelligence) awakening; (d'amour) dawning; **donner l'~ (à qn)** (mettre en alerte) to arouse (sb's) suspicions; **mettre en ~** to arouse [*curiosité, méfiance*]; **être en ~** [*soupçons, jalousie*] to be aroused; **cela me tenait en ~** [*bruit, soupçons*] it kept me on the alert; **tenir les sens de qn en ~** to thrill sb's senses; **l'~ de l'adolescent à l'amour** the dawning awareness of love in an adolescent; **2** Scol **~, activités d'~** non basic subjects.
■ **~ musical** introduction to music.

éveillé, **~e** /eveje/ **I** *pp* ▶ **éveiller**.
II *pp adj* (alerte, intelligent) [*enfant*] bright; **elle a l'esprit ~** she's bright.

éveiller /eveje/ [1] **I** *vtr* **1** to arouse [*intérêt, curiosité, méfiance*]; to stimulate [*intelligence, imagination*]; **~ la conscience/le goût de qn** to awaken sb's conscience/taste; **sans ~ l'attention** without attracting attention; **qu'est-ce qui a éveillé votre vocation de médecin?** what made you want to become a doctor?; **~ un enfant à la poésie/musique** to introduce a child to poetry/music; **2** (du sommeil) to wake [*dormeur*]; **être éveillé** to be awake.
II s'éveiller *vpr* liter **1** lit [*personne, ville*] to awake; **2** fig [*imagination, intelligence*] to start to develop; **s'~ à l'amour/à d'autres cultures** to discover love/other cultures.

événement /evɛnmɑ̃/ *nm* **1** (incident) event; (occasion) event, occasion; **pour donner de l'éclat à l'~** to give prestige to the event; **je veux assister à l'~** I'd like to be at the event; **être dépassé par les ~s** to be overwhelmed; **riche en ~s** eventful; **2** (fait marquant) event; **c'est tout un ~ quand**... it's quite an event when...; **couvrir l'~** to give coverage to the event; **l'~ de l'année** the big event of the year; **faire** or **créer l'~** to make the news; **3** Math, Stat outcome.

événementiel, **-ielle** /evenmɑ̃sjɛl/ *adj* factual.

évent /evɑ̃/ *nm* **1** (de circuit, réservoir) vent; **2** (de cétacé) blowhole, spiracle spéc.

éventail /evɑ̃taj/ *nm* **1** (objet) fan; **disposer qch en ~** to fan sth out [*cartes, photos, magasines*]; **2** (série) range; **tout un ~ de possibilités** a whole range of possibilities; **~ des prix/salaires** price/salary range.
IDIOMES **avoir les doigts de pied en ~**○ to laze about.

éventaire /evɑ̃tɛʀ/ *nm* (devanture) stall; (de marchand ambulant) tray.

éventé ~e /evɑ̃te/ **I** *pp* ▶ **éventer**.
II *pp adj* [*bière, limonade*] flat; [*parfum, café, thé, moutarde*] stale; [*vin*] past its best (*jamais épith*).

éventer /evɑ̃te/ [1] **I** *vtr* **1** (deviner) to discover [*secret, complot*]; (révéler) to give away [*secret*]; **le secret est éventé** the secret has come out; **2** (avec un éventail) to fan [*personne*]; **3** (aérer) to air [*drap, habits*].
II s'éventer *vpr* **1** (pour se rafraîchir) to fan oneself; **2** [*parfum, café, thé, moutarde*] to go stale; [*vin*] to pass its best; [*bière, limonade*] to go flat.

éventration /evɑ̃tʀasjɔ̃/ *nf* (hernie) rupture.

éventré, **~e** /evɑ̃tʀe/ **I** *pp* ▶ **éventrer**.
II *pp adj* **1** [*personne*] disembowelled[GB]; [*animal*] gutted; **2** fig [*fauteuil*] burst; [*bateau*] smashed up; [*maison*] shattered.

éventrer /evɑ̃tʀe/ [1] **I** *vtr* **1** (blesser) [*personne*] to disembowel; [*taureau*] to gore; **2** (ouvrir) to rip [sth] open [*matelas, sac*]; to burst [sth] open [*malle*]; to force [sth] open [*coffre*]; to shatter [sth] [*mur*].
II s'éventrer *vpr* **1** (se blesser) [*personne*] (dans un accident) to cut one's stomach open; **2** (s'ouvrir) [*sac*] to burst open.

éventreur /evɑ̃tʀœʀ/ *nm* **Jack l'~** Jack the Ripper.

éventualité /evɑ̃tɥalite/ *nf* **1** (événement possible) eventuality; **parer à toute ~** to be prepared for all eventualities; **2** (hypothèse) possibility; **l'~ que** the possibility that; **dans l'~ de qch** in the event of sth.

éventuel, **-elle** /evɑ̃tɥɛl/ *adj* **1** (possible) possible; **2** Jur conditional.

éventuellement /evɑ̃tɥɛlmɑ̃/ *adv* possibly; **il y aura Paul et ~ Nicole** Paul will be there and possibly Nicole; **cela pourrait ~ servir** that might be useful; **~ nous prendrons le train** we could take the train; **'tu viendras?'—'~'** 'will you come?'—'I might'; **je relis et ~ je corrige** I reread and if necessary I correct.

évêque /evɛk/ **▶ 813** *nm* bishop (**de** of).
IDIOMES **un chien regarde bien un ~** a cat may look at a king.

évertuer: **s'évertuer** /evɛʀtɥe/ [1] *vpr* to try one's best (**à faire** to do), to strive (**à faire** to do).

éviction /eviksjɔ̃/ *nf* **1** (expulsion) ousting (**de** from); **2** Jur (dépossession) eviction; **indemnité d'~** compensation for disturbance of business tenancy.
■ **~ scolaire** mandatory absence due to notifiable illness.

évidage /evidaʒ/, **évidement** /evidmɑ̃/ *nm* hollowing-out.

évidemment /evidamɑ̃/ *adv* of course.

évidence /evidɑ̃s/ **I** *nf* (fait d'être évident) obviousness; (vérité évidente) obvious fact; **c'est d'une ~** it's so obvious; **c'est l'~ même** it's glaringly obvious; **nier l'~** to deny the obvious; **se rendre à l'~** to face the facts; **dire une ~** to state the obvious; **de toute ~** or **à l'~, il a oublié** obviously he has forgotten; **nier qch contre toute ~** to deny sth despite all proof to the contrary.
II en évidence *loc* **laisser/mettre qch en ~** lit (pour être vu) to leave/put sth in an obvious ou a prominent place; **j'avais laissé le dossier en ~** (volontairement) I had left the file in a prominent place; (par inadvertance) I had left the file lying around; **les clés sont en ~ sur le bureau** the keys are right in the middle of the desk; **mettre en ~** fig to highlight [*importance, faiblesse, utilité*]; **l'enquête a permis de mettre en ~ le lien entre** the investigation highlighted the link between; **mets-toi (bien) en ~ près de l'entrée** stand by the entrance where you can be seen easily.

évident, **~e** /evidɑ̃, ɑ̃t/ *adj* **1** gén obvious; [*progrès, aggravation*] marked (*épith*); [*preuves*] clear (*épith*); **il est ~ que** it is obvious that; **il ment, c'est ~** he's obviously lying, it is obvious that he is lying; **2**○ **ce n'est pas ~**○ (ce n'est pas si sûr) not necessarily; (ce n'est pas si facile) it's not so easy; **ce n'est pas ~ à faire**○ it's not easy to do.

évider /evide/ [1] *vtr* (creuser) to hollow out [*tronc, tige*]; Culin to scoop out [*légume, fruit*].

évier /evje/ *nm* sink; **~ à un bac/deux bacs** single/double sink.

évincer /evɛ̃se/ [12] *vtr* **1** (écarter) to oust [*candidat, rival*]; **2** Jur (déposséder) to evict.

évitable /evitabl/ *adj* [*erreur*] avoidable; **c'était difficilement ~** it couldn't have been avoided.

évitage /evitaʒ/ *nm* (déplacement) swinging; (espace) room to swing.

évitement /evitmɑ̃/ *nm* **1** Tech **gare/voie d'~** siding; **2 réaction d'~** Biol avoidance reaction; Psych avoidant response.

éviter /evite/ [1] **I** *vtr* **1** (esquiver) to avoid [*obstacle, piéton*]; to dodge [*balle, coup*]; **je n'ai pas pu ~ l'arbre** I couldn't avoid the tree; **2** (s'efforcer de ne pas rencontrer) to avoid [*personne*]; **depuis, elle m'évite** since then, she's been avoiding me; **3** (se soustraire à) to avoid [*problème, crise, erreur, dérapage*]; **pour ~ la contagion** to avoid being infected; **4** (s'abstenir de) **~ qch/de faire** to avoid sth/doing; **évitez le sucre** or **de manger du sucre** avoid sugar ou eating sugar; **il faut ~ que cela (ne) se reproduise** we must make sure it doesn't happen again; **5** (épargner) **~ qch à qn** to save sb sth; **pour leur ~ des ennuis** to save them trouble; **je voulais t'~ une dépense** I wanted to spare you the expense; **~ à qn de faire** to save sb (from) doing; **cela m'évitera d'y aller/de leur téléphoner** it'll save me from going there/from phoning them; **je lis, cela m'évite de penser à eux/m'ennuyer** I read, it keeps me from thinking about them/getting bored.
II *vi* Naut [*navire*] to swing at anchor.
III s'éviter *vpr* [*personnes*] to avoid one another.

évocateur, **-trice** /evɔkatœʀ, tʀis/ *adj* **1** (suggestif) [*thème, image, sensation, nom*] evocative; **un parfum ~ de souvenirs** a scent that brings back memories; **2** (significatif) [*geste, chiffre*] significant.

évocation /evɔkasjɔ̃/ *nf* **1** (remémoration) (action) evocation; (résultat) reminiscence; **~ de souvenirs** bringing back memories; **2** (mention) mention (**de** of); **3** Jur *right of a higher court to summon for review a case pending before a lower court.*

évolué, **~e** /evɔlɥe/ **I** *pp* ▶ **évoluer**.

II *pp adj* **1** (éclairé) [*individu, population*] enlightened; **il n'est pas très ~**○! he's not very bright!; **2** (avancé) [*pays, peuple*] civilized; **3** Ordinat [*langage*] high-level (*épith*); **4** Biol [*espèces*] evolved.

évoluer /evɔlɥe/ [1] *vi* **1** (progresser) [*groupe, individu, goûts*] to evolve, to change; [*idée*] to evolve; [*technique, science*] to advance, to evolve; [*situation*] to develop; **la société évolue** society is changing; **en dix ans il a beaucoup évolué** he's changed a lot in ten years; **on évolue vers une solution** we're moving toward(s) a solution; **faire ~ la situation** to bring about some change in the situation; **maladie qui évolue** progressive illness; **2** (se déplacer gracieusement) [*patineurs, danseurs, nageurs*] to glide; [*deltaplane, avion*] to wheel; **~ sur une piste de danse** to glide about on a dance floor; **ils n'évoluent pas dans le même monde** fig they don't move in the same circles; **3** Mil to manoeuvre GB, to maneuver US.

évolutif, -ive /evɔlytif, iv/ *adj* gén, Méd progressive; **une situation évolutive** a changing situation; **un appareil téléphonique ~** telephone with potential for additional facilities.

évolution /evɔlysjɔ̃/ I *nf* **1** Biol evolution; **l'~ des espèces** the evolution of species; **2** (progrès) (de pays, personne) evolution (**de** of); (de langue) development (**de** of); (de la science) advancement (**de** of); (des goûts, mœurs, mentalités) evolution (**de** of); (d'enquête, étude) progress (**de** of); **~ technologique/sociale** technological/social advancement; **~ politique** political evolution; **~ démographique** demographical change; **l'~ d'une situation** the development of a situation; **~ de carrière** career advancement; **être en pleine ~** to be undergoing rapid change; **l'~ d'une maladie** the progression of an illness; **3** (changement) change (**de** in), variation; **l'~ du pouvoir d'achat** the fluctuations in buying power; **4** Météo **situation générale et ~** general synopsis.

II **évolutions** *nfpl* **1** (mouvements gracieux) **les ~s des patineurs** the skaters' gliding movements; **suivre les ~s de l'avion dans le ciel** to watch the plane wheeling overhead.

évolutionnisme /evɔlysjɔnism/ *nm* evolutionism.

évolutionniste /evɔlysjɔnist/ I *adj* evolutionary.

II *nmf* evolutionist.

évoquer /evɔke/ [1] *vtr* **1** (se remémorer) [*personne*] to recall [*passé, amis, souvenirs*]; **2** (mentionner) to mention [*problème, question*]; **le problème de la retraite sera évoqué à la réunion** the retirement issue will be brought up at the meeting; **il s'est contenté d'~ les grands thèmes du roman** he simply touched on the main themes of the novel; **3** (faire penser à) [*objet, son, image*] to bring back [*souvenir*]; to conjure up [*image*]; to be reminiscent of [*printemps, enfance*]; **cela évoque pour moi l'Asie** it makes me think of Asia; **4** (raconter) [*auteur, musicien*] to evoke [*lieu, moment*]; **5** (par magie) to invoke; **6** Jur **~ une affaire** *to summon for review a case pending before a lower court.*

evzone /ɛvzɔn/ *nm* evzone.

ex[1] /ɛks/ *préf* **~-actrice/champion/maire/premier ministre** former actress/champion/mayor/prime minister; **le Zaïre, ~-Congo belge** Zaïre, the former Belgian Congo.

ex[2] /ɛks/ I○ *nmf inv* (ancien conjoint, concubin, compagnon) ex; (ancien membre) ex-member; **un ~ du Parti** an ex-member of the Communist Party.

II *nm* **1** (*written abbr* = **exemple**) eg; **2** (*written abbr* = **exemplaire**) copy; **25 ~** 25 copies.

exacerbation /ɛgzasɛʀbasjɔ̃/ *nf* exacerbation.

exacerber /ɛgzasɛʀbe/ [1] *vtr* to exacerbate; **exacerbé par** exacerbated by; **une sensibilité exacerbée** an exaggerated sensitivity.

exact, ~e /ɛgza(kt), akt/ *adj* **1** (juste) [*réponse, calcul*] correct; [*prévision*] accurate, correct; **est-il ~ que** is it correct ou true that; **'tu y étais!'—'(c'est) ~'** 'you were there!'—'that's right'; **2** (précis) [*dimension, nombre*] exact; [*circonstances, limites, conditions*] exact, precise; [*identité*] true, exact; [*reproduction*] exact; **indiquez le montant ~** give the exact amount; **tu as l'heure ~e?** do you have the exact ou right time?; **mesurer l'~e ampleur de la catastrophe** to assess the exact ou precise extent of the disaster; **pour être plus ~** to be more precise; **3** (ponctuel) punctual.

exactement /ɛgzaktəmɑ̃/ *adv* gén exactly; **mesurer qch ~** to measure sth accurately; **cela m'a coûté très ~ 203 francs** it cost me exactly 203 francs.

exaction /ɛgzaksjɔ̃/ I *nf* exaction.

II **exactions** *nfpl* gén barbaric acts, acts of violence; (en temps de guerre) atrocities; **~s policières** police brutalities.

exactitude /ɛgzaktityd/ *nf* **1** (justesse) (de réponse, calcul) correctness; (de prévision) accuracy; **2** (précision) (de définition, description, renseignement, dimension) accuracy; (de reproduction) exactness; (de montre) accuracy; **contester l'~ des faits** to deny that the facts are accurate; **avec ~** [*mesurer, raconter*] accurately; **on ne connaît pas avec ~ les circonstances de leur mort** we don't yet know the exact circumstances surrounding their death; **3** (ponctualité) punctuality; ▶ **politesse**.

ex æquo /ɛgzeko/ I *adj inv* (tous contextes) equally placed.

II *adv* **ils ont terminé la course ~** they finished the race joint winners; **ils sont premiers/deuxièmes ~** Sport they've tied for first/second place.

III *nmf inv* Scol equally ranked candidates; Sport equally placed contestants.

exagération /ɛgzaʒeʀasjɔ̃/ *nf* exaggeration; **tomber dans l'~** to start exaggerating; **il est méthodique mais sans ~** he's methodical but not excessively so.

exagéré, ~e /ɛgzaʒeʀe/ I *pp* ▶ **exagérer**.

II *pp adj* **1** (outré) [*détail, récit, estimation*] exaggerated; [*forme, contour*] overdone; **2** (démesuré) [*chiffre, hausse*] excessive; [*louanges, politesse*] exaggerated; [*empressement, pessimisme, sévérité, importance*] excessive; **être d'une sensibilité ~e** to be oversensitive; **il n'est pas ~ de dire que**... it is no exaggeration to say that...; **deux heures de retard, c'est un peu ~!** two hours late, that's a bit much!

exagérément /ɛgzaʒeʀemɑ̃/ *adv* [*insister, augmenter*] excessively; [*optimiste, bruyant*] unduly, excessively.

exagérer /ɛgzaʒeʀe/ [14] I *vtr* (outrer) to exaggerate; **ils ont exagéré l'importance des dégâts** they exaggerated the extent of the damage; **n'exagérons rien** let's not exaggerate; **tu exagères toujours!** you're always exaggerating; **sans ~ nous étions au moins 100** without exaggeration there were at least 100 of us.

II *vi* (abuser) to go too far, to push one's luck.

III **s'exagérer** *vpr* [*personne*] to overestimate; **s'~ l'importance de qch** to overestimate the importance of sth.

exaltant, ~e /ɛgzaltɑ̃, ɑ̃t/ *adj* [*aventure, lecture*] thrilling; [*projet, travail, musique*] inspiring.

exaltation /ɛgzaltasjɔ̃/ *nf* **1** (vive excitation) elation; **parler avec ~** to speak elatedly; **2** (intensification) (d'imagination) stimulation; (de différence, passion) heightening; **3** (glorification) liter glorification.

exalté, ~e /ɛgzalte/ I *pp* ▶ **exalter**.

II *pp adj* (surexcité) [*personne, foule*] elated; [*discours, esprit*] impassioned; (intensifié) [*patriotisme, sentiment*] heightened.

III *nm,f* fanatic.

exalter /ɛgzalte/ [1] I *vtr* **1** (transporter) to elate, to thrill [*personne, foule*]; **2** (intensifier) to heighten [*qualité, nationalisme*]; **3** (glorifier) liter to glorify [*personne, qualité*].

II **s'exalter** *vpr* (s'enthousiasmer) [*personne*] to enthuse.

examen /ɛgzamɛ̃/ *nm* **1** Scol, Univ examination, exam○; **se présenter à** or **passer un ~** to take ou to sit (for) GB an exam; **~ d'entrée/de passage/final** entrance/end-of-year/final exam○; **~ de rattrapage** retake, resit GB; **2** Méd examination; **~ médical/clinique** medical/clinical examination; **~ médical complet** full medical; **~ biologique** biological test(s); **passer des ~s** to have some tests done; **~ de la vue** eye test; **3** (de cas, document, dossier) examination; (de demande, question) consideration; (de situation) gén examination; (avant un changement) review; **à l'~** on examination; **être à l'~** or **en cours d'~** [*dossier, budget*] to be under review; [*question, demande*] to be under consideration; [*cas*] to be under investigation; **se livrer à l'~ de** to examine [*cas, dossier, budget, loi*]; to consider [*question, demande*]; to review [*situation*]; **sans ~** out of hand; **ne pas résister à l'~** not to stand up to scrutiny; **4** (inspection) (de lieu) inspection; (d'objet) examination; **à l'~** on examination; **5** Jur **mettre qn en ~** ≈ to interview sb under caution.

■ **~ blanc** mock (exam)○; **~ de conscience** gén self-examination; Relig examination of one's conscience; **faire son ~ de conscience** to examine one's conscience; **~ partiel** *university term-end exam*; **~ prénuptial** premarital health check; **~ de rattrapage** Scol, Univ resit; **~ spécial d'entrée à l'université**, **ESEU** *university entrance exam for students not having the baccalaureate.*

examinateur, -trice /ɛgzaminatœʀ, tʀis/ *nm,f* examiner.

examiner /ɛgzamine/ [1] I *vtr* **1** (étudier) gén to examine; (pour faire des changements) to review [*situation*]; **rejeter une demande sans l'~** to dismiss a request out of hand; **~ qch de près** to have a close look at sth; **il faut ~ la situation de plus près** the situation must be looked at more closely; **~ qn de la tête aux pieds** to look sb up and down; **2** (observer) to examine [*marchandise, personne, visage*]; **~ le ciel** to scan the sky; **3** Méd to examine [*malade, blessure*]; **4** Scol, Univ to examine (**sur** on).

II **s'examiner** *vpr* to examine oneself.

exanthème /ɛgzɑ̃tɛm/ *nm* exanthema.

exarque /ɛgzaʀk/ *nm* Hist, Relig exarch.

exaspérant, ~e /ɛgzaspeʀɑ̃, ɑ̃t/ *adj* infuriating, exasperating.

exaspération /ɛgzaspeʀasjɔ̃/ *nf* **1** (d'humeur) exasperation; **2** (de besoin, douleur) intensification.

exaspérer /ɛgzaspeʀe/ [14] *vtr* **1** (irriter) to exasperate, to infuriate [*personne*]; **2** (exacerber) to exacerbate [*sentiment, douleur*]; **être exaspéré** to be exasperated (**par** by).

exaucement /ɛgzosmɑ̃/ *nm* (de prière, requête) granting; (de rêve, vœu) fulfilment[GB].

exaucer /ɛgzose/ [12] *vtr* [*Dieu, le ciel*] to grant, to answer [*prière*]; [*personnes*] to fulfil[GB], to satisfy [*désir, requête*].

ex cathedra /ɛkskatedʀa/ *adv* **1** Relig ex cathedra; **2** liter, hum dogmatically.

excavateur /ɛkskavatœʀ/ *nm* Tech excavator.

excavation /ɛkskavasjɔ̃/ *nf* excavation.

■ **~ pelvienne** Anat pelvic cavity.

excavatrice /ɛkskavatʀis/ *nf* Tech excavator.

excaver /ɛkskave/ [1] *vtr* to excavate.

excédant, ~e /ɛksedɑ̃, ɑ̃t/ *adj* exasperating, infuriating.

excédé, ~e /ɛksede/ I *pp* ▶ **excéder**.

II *pp adj* [*air, ton, personne*] infuriated.

excédent /ɛksedɑ̃/ *nm* surplus (**sur** over);

les ~s agricoles agricultural surpluses; **l'~ des dépenses sur les recettes** excess of expenditure over receipts; **~ de bagages/poids** excess baggage/weight.
■ **~ de la balance commerciale** surplus on the trade balance; **~ de la balance des paiements** balance of payments surplus; **~ brut d'exploitation** Compta gross operating surplus; **~ budgétaire** budget surplus.

excédentaire /ɛksedɑ̃tɛʀ/ *adj* [*production*] surplus (*épith*), excess (*épith*); [*personnel, demande, balance commerciale*] surplus (*épith*).

excéder /eksede/ [14] *vtr* **1** (dépasser) to exceed [*quantité, durée*] (**de** by); **le coût du projet a excédé les chiffres prévus de 13%** the cost of the project exceeded the predicted figure by 13%; **2** (agacer) to infuriate.

excellemment /ɛkselamɑ̃/ *adv* fml splendidly, excellently.

excellence /ɛkselɑ̃s/ *nf* excellence; **par ~** par excellence.

Excellence /ɛkselɑ̃s/ *nf* (titre) Excellency; **Son ~, l'ambassadeur de France** His/Her Excellency, the French Ambassador.

excellent, **~e** /ɛkselɑ̃, ɑ̃t/ *adj* excellent (**pour qch** for sth), very good (**pour qn** for sb); **~!** great!

exceller /ɛksele/ [1] *vi* to excel (**dans** in; **à faire** in doing).

excentré, **~e** /ɛksɑ̃tʀe/ *adj* **1** (loin du centre-ville) [*quartier*] outlying (*épith*); **l'école est (très) ~e** the school is (quite) some distance from the town centre[GB]; **2** Mécan **être ~** [*axe*] to be off-centre[GB].

excentricité /ɛksɑ̃tʀisite/ *nf* **1** (de personne, comportement) eccentricity; **2** (de lieu) remoteness; **3** Sci eccentricity.

excentrique /ɛksɑ̃tʀik/ **I** *adj* **1** [*personne, comportement, idée*] eccentric; **2** [*quartier*] outlying; **3** [*courbe*] eccentric.
II *nmf* eccentric.

excentriquement /ɛksɑ̃tʀikmɑ̃/ *adv* eccentrically.

excepté, **~e** /ɛksɛpte/ **I** *pp* ▶ **excepter**.
II *pp adj* (sauf) except; **tous les jours, vendredis et samedis ~s** every day except Fridays and Saturdays; **il n'y a personne, elle ~e** there's nobody except her.
III *prép* (sauf) except; **il l'a dit à tout le monde ~ à moi** he told everybody except me; **tous les enfants sont ici ~ Olga** all the children are here except Olga; **tous les jours, ~ le jeudi** every day except Thursday; **la voiture a très bien marché ~ une petite panne** the car ran very well except for ou apart from one small breakdown.
IV excepté que *loc conj* except that; **la journée s'est bien passée ~ qu'il a plu** the day went very well except that it rained.

excepter /ɛksɛpte/ [1] *vtr* **si l'on excepte** except for, apart from; **sans ~ Paul** not forgetting Paul; **sans ~ personne** without exception.

exception /ɛksɛpsjɔ̃/ *nf* **1** gén exception; **sans ~** without exception; **faire une ~** to make an exception (**pour** for); **faire ~** to be an exception; **~ à la règle** exception to the rule; **à l'~ de, ~ faite de** except for, with the exception of; **à quelques ~s près** with a few exceptions; **sauf ~** with the occasional exception; **d'~** [*personne, destin*] exceptional; [*loi, régime, tribunal*] emergency; **des mesures d'~ ont été prises** emergency measures have been taken; **c'est l'~ qui confirme la règle** it's the exception that proves the rule; **2** Jur demurrer.
■ **~ culturelle** *exclusion of cultural products from the Free Trade provisions of GATT*; **~ d'incompétence** Jur declinatory plea; **~ de nullité** Jur plea of voidance.

exceptionnel, **-elle** /ɛksɛpsjɔnɛl/ *adj* **1** (qui constitue une exception) [*congé, faveur, subvention*] exceptional; [*autorisation, dérogation*] special (*épith*); [*prix*] bargain (*épith*); [*réunion*] extraordinary (*épith*); **à titre ~** exceptionally; **2** (hors du commun) [*circonstances, intelligence, personne*] exceptional; **une année exceptionnelle** a bumper year (**pour** for); **on va parfois au restaurant, mais c'est ~** sometimes we eat at a restaurant, but very rarely.

exceptionnellement /ɛksɛpsjɔnɛlmɑ̃/ *adv* **1** (à titre d'exception) exceptionally; **~, le magasin restera ouvert jusqu'à 21 heures/sera fermé cet après-midi** today only the shop GB ou store US will stay open until 9 o'clock/will be closed in the afternoon; **2** (remarquablement) exceptionally; **~ riche** exceptionally rich.

excès /ɛksɛ/ *nm inv* **1** (surplus) excess; **ôtez l'~ de colle** remove the excess glue; **l'~ de la demande sur l'offre** excess of demand over supply; **~ de cholestérol** excess of cholesterol; **en ~** [*objets, substance*] excess (*épith*); **2** (abus) excess; **commettre des ~** to go too far; **tes ~ de boisson** your excessive drinking; **~ de table** overeating; **faire des ~ de boisson/de table** to drink/eat excessively, to overindulge in drink/food; **des ~ de langage** bad language ¢; **à l'~, avec ~** to excess, excessively; **3** (extrême) **tomber dans l'~** to go too far; **tomber dans l'~ inverse** to go to the opposite extreme; **~ de confiance/d'optimisme/de zèle** overconfidence/overoptimism/overzealousness; **~ de prudence** excessive caution.
■ **~ de pouvoir** Jur ultra vires action; **commettre un ~ de pouvoir** to act ultra vires; **~ de vitesse** Jur speeding; **faire un ~ de vitesse** to break the speed limit; **on lui a retiré son permis après plusieurs ~ de vitesse** he lost his licence[GB] after being caught several times for speeding.

excessif, **-ive** /ɛksesif, iv/ *adj* **1** (qui dépasse la mesure) [*enthousiasme, lenteur, retard, tarifs*] excessive; **cette boutique pratique des prix ~s** the goods in this shop GB ou store US are overpriced; **être d'un optimisme ~** to be overoptimistic; **sans enthousiasme ~** without too much enthusiasm; **sans générosité excessive** without being overgenerous ou unduly generous; **2** (qui manque de modération) [*personne, caractère, tempérament*] extreme; **il est ~** (dans ses opinions, sentiments) he is a man of extremes; (dans ses actes) he does everything to excess.

excessivement /ɛksesivmɑ̃/ *adv* **1** (trop) excessively; **2**° (extrêmement) controv extremely.

exciper /ɛksipe/ [1] *vtr ind* **~ de** to plead [*bonne foi, jeunesse*]; **~ de la chose jugée** Jur to plead res judicata.

excipient /ɛksipjɑ̃/ *nm* excipient.

exciser /ɛksize/ [1] *vtr* **1** Méd to excise; **2** Anthrop to circumcise, remove the clitoris of.

excision /ɛksizjɔ̃/ *nf* **1** Méd excision; **2** Anthrop female circumcision.

excitabilité /ɛksitabilite/ *nf* Physiol excitability; **~ neuro-musculaire** neuromuscular excitability.

excitable /ɛksitabl/ *adj* **1** (irritable) edgy; **2** Physiol excitable.

excitant, **~e** /ɛksitɑ̃, ɑ̃t/ **I** *adj* **1** (stimulant) [*substance*] stimulating (*épith*); **le café est ~** coffee is a stimulant; **2** (palpitant) [*perspective, époque*] exciting; [*découverte, roman, aventure*] thrilling; **une perspective qui n'a rien d'~** a completely unexciting prospect; **3** (érotique) [*personne, vêtement, scène*] sexy.
II *nm* Pharm stimulant; **prendre des ~s** to take stimulants.

excitation /ɛksitasjɔ̃/ *nf* **1** (enthousiasme) excitement; **~ générale** general excitement; **2** (sexuelle) arousal; (stimulation) stimulation; **~ manuelle** manual stimulation; **3** (état) (neuronale) excitation; **4** Électron, Électrotech, Phys excitation; **5** Jur (incitation) incitement; **~ à la débauche/violence** incitement to vice/violence.
■ **~ psychomotrice** Psych psychomotor excitation.

excité, **~e** /ɛksite/ **I** *pp* ▶ **exciter**.
II *pp adj* **1** (déchaîné) [*foule, presse*] frenzied (*épith*), in a frenzy (*jamais épith*); [*atmosphère*] frenzied; [*personne*] (enervé) annoyed; (agité) agitated; **2** (enthousiaste) [*personne*] thrilled, excited; **~ à l'idée de partir** thrilled at the idea of leaving; **~ comme un gosse** as excited as a child; **tu n'as pas l'air très ~** you don't seem very thrilled; **3** (émoustillé) (sexuellement) [*personne, sens*] aroused; (par l'alcool) elated.
III *nm,f* pej **1** (fauteur de troubles) rowdy; **une bande d'~s dans la rue** a bunch of rowdies in the street; **2** (fanatique) fanatic; **3** (nerveux) neurotic.
IDIOMES **être ~ comme une puce** to be like a cat on a hot tin roof.

exciter /ɛksite/ [1] **I** *vtr* **1** (attiser) to stir up [*colère, haine*]; to kindle [*convoitise, désir*]; to inflame [*passions, imagination*]; to whet [*appétit*]; **2** (enthousiasmer) to thrill [*personne*]; **le jazz/la physique ne m'excite pas** jazz/physics doesn't do a lot for me; **3** (émoustiller) [*stimulus*] to arouse [*personne*]; [*alcool*] to work [sb] up [*personne, groupe*]; **4** (énerver) [*personne*] to tease [*animal*]; to get [sb] excited [*enfant*]; to provoke [*adulte*]; [*café*] to make [sb] nervy [*personne*]; [*alcool*] to excite [*personne*]; **~ qn contre** to set sb against; **5** Physiol (stimuler) to stimulate [*zone érogène, palais*]; to excite [*nerf, tissu*].
II s'exciter *vpr* **1** (s'enthousiasmer) to get excited; **s'~ à propos de** to rave about° [*œuvre, personne*]; **2** (s'énerver) to get worked up (**contre qch** about sth); to get angry (**contre qn** with sb).

exclamatif, **-ive** /ɛksklamatif, iv/ *adj* exclamatory.

exclamation /ɛksklamasjɔ̃/ *nf* cry, exclamation.

exclamer: **s'exclamer** /ɛksklame/ [1] *vpr* **1** (s'écrier) to exclaim, to cry (**de** with); **2** (avec admiration) **s'~ sur** to exclaim over.

exclu, **~e** /ɛkskly/ **I** *pp* ▶ **exclure**.
II *pp adj* (non admis) [*personne*] excluded (**de** from); [*hypothèse*] ruled out; **il est tout à fait exclu que tu viennes** it's absolutely out of the question that you should come; **il n'est pas ~ que** it's not impossible that; **il n'est pas complètement ~ que je prenne l'avion** I haven't completely ruled out (the idea of) taking the plane; **se sentir ~** to feel left out.
III *nm,f* **1** (paria) outcast; **les ~s de la croissance/du système** those excluded from economic growth/from the system; **2** (ex-membre) **les ~s du parti** those expelled from the Party.

exclure /ɛksklyʀ/ [78] *vtr* **1** (ne pas inclure) to exclude [*personne*] (**de** from); to rule out [*hypothèse, possibilité*]; **nous n'excluons pas le recours à la force** we are not ruling out resorting to force; **le règlement exclut que les mineurs participent au vote** the regulations prohibit minors from participating in the vote; **2** (rejeter) to expel [*membre de groupe*] (**de** from); to oust [*dirigeant, chef*]; to send [sb] down [*étudiant*]; to cut out [*aliment*]; **~ un élève** (définitivement) to expel a pupil; (temporairement) to suspend a pupil.

exclusif, **-ive** /ɛksklyzif, iv/ **I** *adj* **1** Presse [*interview, document*] exclusive; **2** Comm [*agent, concessionnaire*] sole; [*produit, procédé, modèle*] exclusive; **3** (d'un seul) [*droit, propriété, privilège*] exclusive (**de qch** of sth; **de faire** to do); **4** (absolu) [*personne, tempérament*] intractable; **il est ~ dans ses opinions/idées/goûts** he's very set in his opinions/ideas/tastes; **5** Philos, Math, Ling exclusive.
II exclusive *nf* Pol (mise à l'écart) debar-

ment; **frapper qn d'exclusive** to debar sb; **jeter** or **prononcer l'exclusive** to blackball.

exclusion /ɛksklyzjɔ̃/ **I** *nf* **1** (non-admission) exclusion (**de** from); **2** (expulsion) (définitive) expulsion; (temporaire) suspension; **3** Assur exclusion.

II à l'exclusion de *loc prép* with the exception of.

exclusive ▶ **exclusif**.

exclusivement /ɛksklyzivmɑ̃/ *adv* exclusively; **piscine ~ réservée aux enfants** swimming pool reserved exclusively for children; **ils auront ~ un rôle d'observateurs** they will have an exclusively observational role.

exclusivité /ɛksklyzivite/ *nf* **1** (droits) Comm, Cin, Presse exclusive rights (*pl*); **acheter l'~ d'une marque** to buy the exclusive rights to a brand; **avoir l'~ de la vente/distribution de qch** to have the exclusive sales/distribution rights to sth; **obtenir l'~ de la production et de la commercialisation de qch** to obtain exclusive rights to produce and market sth; **en ~** [*montrer, vendre, publier, projeter*] exclusively; [*produit, interview, document*] exclusive; **tu n'as pas l'~ du bon goût** hum you don't have a monopoly on good taste; **2** (objet, produit) **c'est une ~ de notre entreprise** it's exclusive to our company.

excommunication /ɛkskɔmynikasjɔ̃/ *nf* excommunication.

excommunier /ɛkskɔmynje/ [2] *vtr* to excommunicate.

excrément /ɛkskʀemɑ̃/ *nm* excrement ¢.

excrémentiel, **-ielle** /ɛkskʀemɑ̃sjɛl/ *adj* excremental, fecal.

excréter /ɛkskʀete/ [14] *vtr* to excrete, to eliminate.

excréteur, **-trice** /ɛkskʀetœʀ, tʀis/ *adj* excretory.

excrétion /ɛkskʀesjɔ̃/ **I** *nf* (évacuation) excretion.

II excrétions *nfpl* excrement ¢.

excroissance /ɛkskʀwasɑ̃s/ *nf* **1** Méd growth, excrescence spéc; **2** Bot outgrowth; **3** fig (de groupe) offshoot; (de quartier) outgrowth.

excursion /ɛkskyʀsjɔ̃/ *nf* gén excursion, trip (**dans** in; **à** to); (en car) coach trip (**dans** in; **à** to); **une ~ de trois jours** a three-day excursion; **partir en ~, faire une ~** to go on an excursion ou a trip.

excursionner /ɛkskyʀsjɔne/ [1] *vi* to go on an excursion; (en car) to go on a coach GB ou bus trip.

excursionniste /ɛkskyʀsjɔnist/ *nmf* tourist.

excusable /ɛkskyzabl/ *adj* excusable, forgivable.

excuse /ɛkskyz/ *nf* **1** (justification) excuse; **ce n'est pas une ~ pour faire** it's no excuse for doing; **chercher une ~/des ~s** to look for an excuse/excuses; **il trouve toujours de bonnes ~s pour ne pas venir** he always manages to find an excuse for not coming; **en guise** or **manière d'~** by way of an excuse; **avoir [qch] pour ~** to have [sth] as an excuse; **trouver des ~s à qn** to find excuses for sb; **une ~ à qch** an excuse for sth; **sans ~** inexcusable; **2** (regret) apology; **faire** or **présenter des ~s à qn** to offer one's apologies to sb, to apologize to sb; **attendre/exiger des ~s (de la part de qn)** to expect/demand an apology from sb; **se confondre en ~s** to apologize profusely; **faire un geste d'~** to make an apologetic gesture; **avoir un sourire d'~** to smile apologetically, to give an apologetic smile; **une lettre d'~** a letter of apology; **mille ~s** I'm terribly sorry; **faites ~**○ controv forgive me.

■ **~ légale** lawful excuse.

excuser /ɛkskyze/ [1] **I** *vtr* **1** (pardonner) to forgive [*erreur, absence*]; to pardon [*faute*]; **excusez-le!** forgive him!; **excusez-moi** excuse me, I'm sorry; **veuillez m'~, je vous prie de m'~** I'm so sorry, I do beg your pardon; **vous m'excuserez si** you will forgive me if; **je vous prie de m'~** please forgive me, I apologize; **excusez mon retard** excuse me for being late; **excusez ce désordre** I'm sorry about the mess; **excusez-moi de vous déranger** I'm sorry to disturb you; **vous êtes tout excusé** it's all right; **sa gentillesse fait ~ sa maladresse** he's so nice you forgive him for being clumsy; **2** (justifier) to excuse; **rien n'excuse la cruauté** there is no excuse for cruelty; **3** (dispenser) to excuse [*personne*] ; **demander à être excusé** to ask to be excused; **'étaient excusés'** 'apologies received from the following'; **'excusés'** (sur rapport) 'apologies'; **~ qn de qch** to excuse sb from sth.

II s'excuser *vpr* to apologize (**auprès de** to; **de** for; **d'avoir fait** for doing); **je m'excuse d'être en retard** I'm sorry I'm late; **je m'excuse de vous déranger** I'm sorry to disturb you; **j'ai dû aller m'~ auprès du directeur** I had to go and apologize to the manager.

exécrable /ɛgzekʀabl/ *adj* **1** fml (odieux) [*crime*] heinous sout; [*action, cause*] detestable; **2** (épouvantable) [*caractère, personne*] loathsome; [*humeur*] dreadful; [*journée, nourriture, temps*] dreadful, awful.

exécrablement /ɛgzekʀabləmɑ̃/ *adv* fml execrably.

exécration /ɛgzekʀasjɔ̃/ *nf* fml execration; **avoir qn/qch en ~** to find sb/sth abhorrent sout.

exécrer /ɛgzekʀe/ [14] *vtr* fml to loathe [*personne, chose*]; to abhor sout [*chose*].

exécutable /ɛgzekytabl/ *adj* **1** (faisable) [*plan, projet, ordre*] practicable; [*tâche*] manageable; **2** Jur executable; **contrat non ~** naked ou nude contract.

exécutant, **~e** /ɛgzekytɑ̃, ɑ̃t/ *nm,f* **1** Mus performer; **orchestre de 60 ~s** 60-piece orchestra; **2** (agent) **il dit n'avoir été qu'un ~** he claims he was only obeying orders; **les ~s du meurtre** those who carried out the murder.

exécuter /ɛgzekyte/ [1] **I** *vtr* **1** (faire) to carry out, to accomplish [*tâche, mission*]; to carry out [*travaux, projet*]; to do [*exercice, travail, dessin, plongeon*]; to execute [*saut*]; **faire ~ des travaux** to have work done; **2** (appliquer) to carry out [*consigne, ordre, dessein, menace*]; to fulfil[GB] [*promesse*]; Comm to fill [*commande*]; Jur to fulfil[GB] [*contrat, obligation*]; to enforce [*loi, jugement*]; to implement [*traité*]; Pharm to make up [*ordonnance*]; **3** (tuer) to execute [*condamné, otage*]; to kill [*victime*]; fig to polish off○ [*adversaire*]; to slate GB, to pan○ [*auteur, acteur, politicien*]; to demolish [*œuvre*]; **se faire ~ par les critiques** to be slated GB ou panned○ by the critics; **4** Mus to perform, to play [*morceau*]; **5** Ordinat to run [*programme*]; to execute [*instruction*]; **6** Jur (saisir) to distrain upon [*débiteur*].

II s'exécuter *vpr* (obéir) to comply; **il a fini par s'~** he eventually complied.

exécuteur, **-trice** /ɛgzekytœʀ, tʀis/ **I** *nm,f* (de décision, décret) enforcer.

II *nm* Hist (bourreau) **~ (des hautes œuvres)** executioner.

■ **~ testamentaire** Jur executor.

exécutif, **-ive** /ɛgzekytif, iv/ **I** *adj* Pol executive.

II *nm* executive.

exécution /ɛgzekysjɔ̃/ *nf* **1** (application) (d'ordre) execution; (de menace) carrying out ¢; (de décision, plan, budget) implementation; Jur (de loi, jugement) enforcement; (d'obligation, contrat) fulfilment[GB]; Pharm (d'ordonnance) making up ¢; Fin (d'ordre) carrying out ¢; **mettre à ~** to carry out [*menace*]; to implement [*programme*]; **assez délibéré, passons à l'~** that's enough discussion, let's get on with it! **en ~ de l'article I** Jur pursuant to section I; **en ~ de la loi** Jur in compliance with the law; **2** (réalisation) (de manœuvre, mouvement, travaux) execution; (de projet, programme) implementation; Art (de tableau) painting ¢, execution; Mus (de morceau) performance, execution; **l'~ du programme demandera deux ans** it will take two years to implement the programme[GB]; **confier l'~ des travaux de construction à une entreprise** to give the construction work to a firm; **travaux en cours d'~** work in progress; **veiller à la bonne ~ d'une tâche/commande** to see that a job is done well/an order is filled properly; **d'~ facile** [*plat*] easy to make; [*mouvement*] easy to do; [*morceau*] easy to play; **3** (mise à mort) execution; **4** Ordinat execution; **5** Jur **~ d'un débiteur** distraint of property; **faire l'objet d'une ~ forcée** to be subjected to distraints.

■ **~ capitale** Jur capital punishment; **~ pas à pas** Ordinat single step operation; **~ de travail** Ordinat run.

exécutoire /ɛgzekytwaʀ/ *adj* Jur [*loi, jugement*] enforceable; [*organe, pouvoir*] executory; [*protocole, accord*] binding (**à l'égard de** on); **les décisions forment titre ~** the decisions shall be enforceable.

exécutrice *nf* ▶ **exécuteur I**.

exégèse /ɛgzeʒɛz/ *nf* (tous contextes) exegesis; **faire l'~ d'un texte** to make a detailed analysis of a text.

exégète /ɛgzeʒɛt/ *nmf* gén interpreter; Antiq exegete.

exemplaire /ɛgzɑ̃plɛʀ/ **I** *adj* **1** (modèle) [*conduite, courage*] exemplary; [*élève, mère, république*] model (*épith*); [*atterrissage*] textbook (*épith*); **de façon ~** in exemplary fashion; **avec une discrétion ~** with perfect discretion; **c'est un enfant d'une sagesse ~** he's a model child; **il a été d'une sagesse ~** he's been absolutely perfect; **la gestion de l'entreprise est ~** the firm is a model of good management; **2** (pour l'exemple) [*châtiment, peine*] intended as a warning to others (*après n*), exemplary sout; **il a été puni de façon ~** his punishment was intended as a warning to others; **infliger une peine ~ à qn** to make an example of sb.

II *nm* **1** (de livre, document, journal) copy; (de gravure) print; **~ sur vélin** copy printed on vellum; **tirer un livre à 300 ~s** to print 300 copies of a book; **photocopier qch en dix ~s** to make ten photocopies of sth; **en deux/trois ~s** in duplicate/triplicate; **2** (spécimen) specimen (**de** of), example (**de** of).

■ **~ avec envoi** inscribed copy; **~ gratuit** complimentary copy; **~ justificatif** voucher copy; **~ de presse** review copy; **~ témoin** Édition advance copy.

exemplairement /ɛgzɑ̃plɛʀmɑ̃/ *adv* **vivre ~** to lead an exemplary life; **être puni ~** to be singled out for exemplary punishment.

exemplarité /ɛgzɑ̃plaʀite/ *nf* (de peine) deterrent nature (**de** of).

exemple /ɛgzɑ̃pl/ **I** *nm* **1** (cas) example; **prendre un ~ au hasard** to take a random example; **le seul ~ connu** the only known example; **~ grammatical** grammatical example; **prenez l'~ du Japon** take the case of Japan, take Japan for example; **on connaît peu d'~s de ce phénomène** there are few precedents for this phenomenon; **sans ~** [*situation*] unprecedented; **2** (leçon) warning (**pour** to); **votre renvoi sera un ~ pour les autres** your dismissal will be a warning to the others; **pour l'~** as a warning to others; **en le condamnant à mort, on a voulu faire un ~** the intention in passing the death sentence was to make an example of him; **3** (image) example (**de** of); **donner l'~ du courage à qn** to set sb an example of courage; **donner le bon/mauvais ~** to set a good/bad example; **suivre l'~ de qn** to follow sb's example; **prendre ~ sur qn, prendre qn en ~** to take sb as a model; **à l'~ de qn** following in sb's footsteps; **elle est enseignante, à l'~ de sa mère** she's a teacher, like her mother; **4**

(idéal) model (**de** of); **être l'~ même/l'~ de la gentillesse** to be the very model/a model of kindness; **donner** or **citer qn en ~** to hold sb up as an example; **se donner en ~** to set oneself up as an example.
II **par exemple** *loc adv* **1** (pour illustrer) for example; **les grandes villes, par ~ Paris** large cities, Paris for example; **2** (marquant l'étonnement) (**ça**) **par ~!** how amazing!; **3** (marquant l'indignation) **ça par ~!** well, honestly!

exemplification /ɛgzɑ̃plifikasjɔ̃/ *nf* exemplification.

exemplifier /ɛgzɑ̃plifje/ [2] *vtr* to exemplify.

exempt, **~e** /ɛgzɑ̃, ɑ̃t/ I *adj* **1** (dispensé) exempt (**de** from); **aucun soldat n'est ~ de corvées** no soldier is exempt from duties; **~ d'impôt** tax-free; **~ de droits de douane** duty-free; **2** (dépourvu) free (**de** from); **mon texte n'est pas ~ d'erreurs** my text is not free from mistakes; **des compliments qui n'étaient pas ~s d'ironie/de sous-entendus** compliments which were not without irony/innuendo; **3** (à l'abri) immune (**de** to); **il n'est pas ~ de ce genre de problèmes** he's not immune to this type of problem.
II *nm* Hist, Mil, Relig exempt.

exempté, **~e** /ɛgzɑ̃te/ *nm,f: person exempt from military service.*

exempter /ɛgzɑ̃te/ [1] *vtr* **1** (dispenser) to exempt (**de** from; **de faire** from doing); **être exempté d'impôts/du premier tour** to be exempt from paying tax/playing in the first round; **2** (mettre à l'abri) to preserve (**de** from); **~ des infirmités de l'âge** to preserve from the infirmities of old age.

exemption /ɛgzɑ̃psjɔ̃/ *nf* exemption.

exercé, **~e** /ɛgzɛʀse/ I *pp* ▶ **exercer**.
II *pp adj* [*main*] deft, skilled; [*oreille*] trained; [*œil*] expert, practised[GB]; [*personne*] experienced.

exercer /ɛgzɛʀse/ [12] I *vtr* **1** (appliquer) to exercise [*autorité, droit, responsabilité*] (**sur** over); to exert [*pression, force, influence, contrôle, autorité*] (**sur** on); to have [*effet*] (**sur** on); **~ un chantage sur qn** to blackmail sb; **dans les pays où la guerre/le paludisme exerce ses ravages** in countries devastated by war/malaria; **toute discrimination exercée en raison de la nationalité** any discrimination on grounds of nationality; **~ son talent d'écrivain contre qn** to bring one's skill as a writer to bear against sb; **2** (pratiquer) to exercise [*profession*]; to practise[GB] [*métier, médecine, culte, art*]; **~ le métier de viticulteur/professeur** to work as a wine grower/teacher; **~ la profession de médecin/juriste/d'architecte** to practise[GB] as ou to be a doctor/lawyer/architect; **exerce-t-il un métier** or **une activité?** does he have a job?; **il exerce les fonctions de conseiller technique** he works as a technical adviser; **~ des fonctions consultatives** to act in an advisory capacity; **~ une activité rémunérée** to do paid work; **le voleur qui exerçait son activité sur la côte** the thief who operated on the coast; **3** (entraîner) to train, to exercise [*corps, mémoire, esprit*]; (donner de l'exercice à) to exercise [*corps, muscle*]; **~ qn au tir** or **à tirer** to give sb some shooting practice.
II *vi* (travailler) [*travailleur, employé*] to work; [*médecin, juriste, architecte*] to practise[GB]; **il exerce en tant que conseiller** he works as an adviser.
III **s'exercer** *vpr* **1** (s'entraîner) [*athlète*] to train; [*musicien*] to practise[GB]; **s'~ à la plongée** or **à plonger** to practise[GB] diving; **s'~ au calme/à la patience** to make an effort to stay calm/be patient; **2** (se manifester) [*qualité*] to come out; **leur ingéniosité s'exerce dans tous les domaines** their ingenuity comes out in everything they do; **3** (agir) [*influence, force*] to be exerted (**sur** on); **cette violence s'exerce contre moi** the violence is directed against me.

exercice /ɛgzɛʀsis/ *nm* **1** (d'entraînement) exercise; **faire un ~** to do an exercise; **~ de grammaire/pour violon** grammar/violin exercise; **~s de rééducation** physiotherapy exercises; **~ de prononciation/d'orthographe** pronunciation/spelling drill; **c'est un ~ de démocratie** it's an exercise in democracy; **ça ne s'apprend qu'après un long ~** it takes years of practice; **2** (activité physique) exercise; **faire de l'~** to get some exercise; **se donner de l'~** to take exercise; **3** (activité professionnelle) **avoir dix ans d'~** [*fonctionnaire*] to have been working for 10 years; [*professeur*] to have been teaching for 10 years; [*médecin, avocat*] to have been practising[GB] ou in practice for 10 years; **poursuivi pour ~ illégal de la médecine** prosecuted for practising[GB] medicine illegally GB ou without a license US; **dans l'~ de ses fonctions** [*soldat, policier*] while on duty; [*travailleur*] while at work; **on leur interdit l'~ de toute activité politique/commerciale** they are forbidden to participate in any political/business activity; **être en ~** [*fonctionnaire*] to be in office; [*médecin*] to be in practice; **en ~** [*ministre, président*] incumbent; **entrer en ~** to take up one's duties; **4** (usage) exercise (**de** of); **renoncer à l'~ du droit de réponse** to give up one's right of reply; **5** Mil (instruction) drill; **être à l'~** to be at drill; **faire faire l'~ à des recrues** to drill recruits; **6** Fin (période) **~** (**financier**) financial year; **~ en cours** current year; **7** Fisc (contrôle) tax assessment by an excise officer.
■ **~ d'application** practical exercise; **~ budgétaire** Admin, Compta financial year; **~ comptable** Compta financial year; **~ du culte** worship; **~ d'évacuation** gén emergency evacuation exercise; (en cas d'incendie) fire drill; **~ de tir** shooting practice ¢ GB, target practice ¢; **~s structuraux** Ling structure drills.

exerciseur /ɛgzɛʀsizœʀ/ *nm* (appareil) exerciser.

exergue /ɛgzɛʀg/ *nm* **1** (inscription sur ouvrage) epigraph; **en ~** as an epigraph; **mettre une citation en ~ à un texte** to head a text with a quotation; **mettre une idée/un aspect en ~** to highlight an idea/an aspect; **2** (sur une médaille, une pièce de monnaie) inscription.

exfoliant, **~e** /ɛksfɔljɑ̃, ɑ̃t/ I *adj* [*crème, produit*] exfoliant.
II *nm* exfoliant cream.

exfoliation /ɛksfɔljasjɔ̃/ *nf* exfoliation.

exhalaison /ɛgzalɛzɔ̃/ *nf* fml exhalation.

exhalation /ɛgzalasjɔ̃/ *nf* fml (expiration) exhalation; (transpiration) perspiration.

exhaler /ɛgzale/ [1] fml I *vtr* **1** (expirer) to exhale; **2** (dégager) to exhale [*parfum*]; to give off [*relent*]; to exhale [*tristesse*]; **3** (exprimer) to give vent to [*douleur, colère*].
II **s'exhaler** *vpr* [*parfum*] to waft (**de** from).

exhaussement /ɛgzosmɑ̃/ *nm* raising.

exhausser /ɛgzose/ [1] *vtr* to raise.

exhaustif, **-ive** /ɛgzostif, iv/ *adj* [*liste, guide, synthèse*] exhaustive.

exhaustivement /ɛgzostivmɑ̃/ *adv* exhaustively.

exhaustivité /ɛgzostivite/ *nf* exhaustiveness.

exhiber /ɛgzibe/ [1] I *vtr* to flaunt [*toilettes, richesse, objet*]; to show [*animal*]; to expose [*partie du corps*]; Jur to produce [*lettre, mandat*].
II **s'exhiber** *vpr* **1** [*exhibitionniste*] to expose oneself; **2** pej (se montrer) to flaunt oneself.

exhibition /ɛgzibisjɔ̃/ *nf* **1** (d'animaux) display; **2** Sport demonstration; **match ~** exhibition-match; **3** (étalage) (de richesse, toilettes) parade; (de sentiment) display; **4** (présentation) (de contrat) presentation, production.

exhibitionnisme /ɛgzibisjɔnism/ *nm* lit, fig exhibitionism.

exhibitionniste /ɛgzibisjɔnist/ I *adj* lit, fig exhibitionist.
II *nmf* exhibitionist, flasher○.

exhortation /ɛgzɔʀtasjɔ̃/ *nf* exhortation (**à faire** to do); **~ au calme** call for calm.

exhorter /ɛgzɔʀte/ [1] *vtr* to motivate [*troupes*]; **~ qn à faire** [*personne*] to urge ou to exhort sb to do; [*devoir, incident*] to prompt sb to do; **~ qn au calme/à la patience** to ask sb to remain calm/patient.

exhumation /ɛgzymasjɔ̃/ *nf* **1** (de cadavre) exhumation; (de ruines) excavation; **2** (de document) unearthing; (du passé) resurrection.

exhumer /ɛgzyme/ [1] *vtr* **1** (déterrer) to exhume [*cadavre*]; to excavate [*ruines*]; **2** (tirer de l'oubli) to unearth [*document*] (**de** from); to resurrect [*souvenir, rancunes*].

exigeant, **~e** /ɛgziʒɑ̃, ɑ̃t/ *adj* [*chef, client, patron, public*] demanding; [*parents, professeur*] strict (**sur qch** about sth); [*malade, enfant, plante*] demanding, difficult; [*tâche, métier*] demanding, exacting; [*morale*] demanding, strict; **être ~ avec** or **envers qn/soi-même** to demand a lot of sb/oneself; **un importateur très ~ sur la qualité** an importer with very strict standards as to ou on quality.

exigence /ɛgziʒɑ̃s/ *nf* **1** (demande) demand (**de qch** for sth); **~ de démocratie/justice** demand for democracy/justice; **se soumettre aux ~s de** to yield to the demands of; **2** (obligation) demand, requirement Admin; **les ~s du métier** the demands of the job; **installation qui ne répond pas aux ~s de sécurité/d'hygiène** installation which does not meet security/hygiene requirements; **'sans ~ de diplôme'** 'no formal qualifications are required'; **3** (trait de caractère) **le chef est d'une telle ~** the boss is so demanding; **elle est d'une telle ~ avec ses enfants** she demands such a lot of her children.

exiger /ɛgziʒe/ [13] *vtr* **1** (demander impérativement) [*personne*] to demand [*réponse, réformes, excuses*]; **~ l'abandon du projet/la libération d'un prisonnier** to demand that the project be abandoned/that a prisoner be released; **~ qch de qn** to demand sth of sb; **~ de qn qu'il fasse** to demand that sb do; **elle a exigé qu'il la rembourse immédiatement** she demanded that he repay her immediately; **~ que qch soit fait** or **se fasse** to demand that sth be done; **~ d'être payé/reconnu** to insist on being paid/recognized; **vous exigez trop d'eux** you're too demanding of them; **2** (rendre nécessaire) to require; **un projet exigeant de lourds investissements** a project requiring heavy investment; **~ des soins constants** [*malade, bébé, plante*] to require constant care; **3** (rendre obligatoire) to require; **être exigé** to be required; **comme l'exige la loi/le règlement** as required by law/the rules; **la politesse exige que vous y alliez** politeness requires you to go; **'expérience exigée'** 'experience required'; **'anglais/permis de conduire exigé'** 'English/driver's licence[GB] essential'; **'qualités exigées: sérieux, dynamisme'** 'candidates should be committed and dynamic'; **'tenue de soirée exigée'** 'black tie'.

exigibilité /ɛgziʒibilite/ *nf* (d'impôt, de traite) payability; (de dette) repayability; **la date d'~ de l'impôt** the due date for tax payments.

exigible /ɛgziʒibl/ *adj* [*impôt, traite, dette*] due (*après n*); **le paiement est ~ le 15 mai** payment is due on 15 May.

exigu, **-uë** /ɛgzigy/ *adj* [*pièce, logement, dimensions*] cramped; [*entrée*] narrow; [*espace*] confined; [*place de parking*] tight; [*marché financier*] restricted.

exiguïté /ɛgzigɥite/ *nf* smallness, pokiness péj.

exil /ɛgzil/ *nm* exile; **en ~** in exile.

exilé, **~e** /ɛgzile/ *nm,f* exile.

exiler /ɛgzile/ [1] **I** *vtr* **1** (bannir) to exile; **2** (isoler) to exile; **ils se sentent exilés dans leur petite ville** they feel exiled in their small town; **3** (reléguer) to relegate; **tous mes bibelots ont été exilés au grenier** all my knick-knacks were relegated to the attic.
II s'exiler *vpr* **1** (s'expatrier) to go into exile; **il s'est exilé à Jersey** he went into exile on Jersey; **2** (se retirer) to bury oneself; **s'~ loin du monde** to cut oneself off from the world.

exinscrit /ɛgzɛ̃skʀi/ *adj m* escribed.

existant, **~e** /ɛgzistɑ̃, ɑ̃t/ *adj* [*tarif, pratique, législation, installations*] existing; [*besoins, produits*] current; [*capital*] actual; **non ~** nonexistent.

existence /ɛgzistɑ̃s/ *nf* **1** (réalité) existence; **nier l'~ de Dieu/d'un document** to deny the existence of God/of a document; **je doute de leur ~** I doubt they exist; **l'essence et l'~** Philos essence and being; **2** (vie) life; **las de l'~** tired of life; **le parti a dix ans d'~** the party is ten years old, the party has been in existence for ten years; **assurer l'~ de qn** to provide for sb; **ne te complique pas l'~**○ don't make life difficult for yourself; **3** (mode de vie) lifestyle; **une ~ de fou** a frantic lifestyle; **changer d'~** to change one's lifestyle.

existentialisme /ɛgzistɑ̃sjalism/ *nm* existentialism.

existentialiste /ɛgzistɑ̃sjalist/ *adj, nmf* existentialist.

existentiel, **-ielle** /ɛgzistɑ̃sjɛl/ *adj* existential.

exister /ɛgziste/ [1] **I** *vi* to exist; **la route existe-t-elle vraiment?** does the road really exist?; **les fantômes, ça existe?** do ghosts really exist?; **les mammouths, ça existe encore?** do mammoths still exist?; **dans ces banlieues, on existe sans vivre** in those suburbs, it's a question of existing rather than living; **je n'existe pas pour lui** or **à ses yeux** as far as he's concerned, I don't even exist; **ce risque existe** this is a very real risk; **le savon/la courtoisie, ça existe!** iron there's such a thing as soap/manners, you know!; **si le paradis/la justice existe** if there is such a place as heaven/such a thing as justice; **pour lui, le danger n'existe pas** for him, there's no such word as danger; **la maison existe encore/n'existe plus** the house is still standing/is no longer standing; **autrefois, l'électricité n'existait pas** in the old days, there was no such thing as electricity; **la loi existe depuis dix ans** the law has been in existence for ten years; **cette situation existe depuis six mois** this has been the situation for six months; **c'est une loi/situation qui existe depuis peu** it's a relatively new law/situation; **~ en trois tailles** [*article, produit*] to be available in three sizes; **ces plantes n'existent que dans les Alpes** these plants are found only in the Alps; **la pollution existe partout** pollution is everywhere; **les enfants me donnent une raison d'~** the children give me a reason for living.
II *v impers* to be; **il existe un lieu/des lieux où**... there is a place/there are places where...; **il n'existe pas de plus belle fleur que la rose** there is no more beautiful flower than a rose; **il n'en existe pas de plus grand** it's the biggest in the world; **il n'en existe pas de meilleur** it's the best there is.

ex nihilo /ɛksniilo/ *adv* ex nihilo.

exobiologie /ɛgzobjɔlɔʒi/ *nf* astrobiology, exobiology spéc.

exobiologiste /ɛgzobjɔlɔʒist/ *nmf* astrobiologist, exobiologist spéc.

exocet /ɛgzɔsɛ/ *nm* Zool flying fish.

Exocet /ɛgzɔsɛt/ *nm* Exocet (missile).

exocrine /ɛgzɔkʀin/ *adj* exocrine.

exode /ɛgzɔd/ *nm* exodus (**vers** to); **l'Exode** Bible the Exodus; **l'~** Hist *the exodus from French cities in 1940*.
■ **~ des capitaux** flight of capital; **~ des cerveaux** brain drain; **~ rural** rural depopulation.

exogène /ɛgzɔʒɛn/ *adj* **1** (de l'extérieur) exogenous; **2** Géol exogenetic.

exonération /ɛgzɔneʀasjɔ̃/ *nf* exemption (**de** from); **~ fiscale** or **d'impôt** tax exemption.

exonérer /ɛgzɔneʀe/ [14] *vtr* to exempt [*personne, marchandise, plus-value*] (**de** from); **être exonéré d'impôt** [*personne, somme*] to be exempt from tax; **intérêts exonérés d'impôt** tax-exempt interest; **marchandises exonérées des droits de douane** duty-free goods.

exorbitant, **~e** /ɛgzɔʀbitɑ̃, ɑ̃t/ *adj* **1** (exagéré) [*prix, agios*] exorbitant; [*exigence, privilège*] outrageous; [*pouvoir*] inordinate (*épith*); **2** Jur **~ de** departing from.

exorbité, **~e** /ɛgzɔʀbite/ *adj* bulging (**de** with).

exorcisation /ɛgzɔʀsizasjɔ̃/ *nf* exorcizing.

exorciser /ɛgzɔʀsize/ [1] *vtr* (tous contextes) to exorcize.

exorcisme /ɛgzɔʀsism/ *nm* exorcism (**à** of).

exorciste /ɛgzɔʀsist/ *nm* exorcist.

exorde /ɛgzɔʀd/ *nm* introduction, exordium spéc.

exosmose /ɛgzɔsmoz/ *nf* exosmosis.

exosquelette /ɛgzoskəlɛt/ *nm* exoskeleton.

exothermique /ɛgzotɛʀmik/ *adj* exothermic.

exotique /ɛgzɔtik/ *adj* [*fruit, charme, coutume*] exotic; **avoir le goût de l'~** to have exotic tastes.

exotisme /ɛgzɔtism/ *nm* exoticism.

expansé, **~e** /ɛkspɑ̃se/ *adj* expanded.

expansibilité /ɛkspɑ̃sibilite/ *nf* expansibility.

expansible /ɛkspɑ̃sibl/ *adj* expansive.

expansif, **-ive** /ɛkspɑ̃sif, iv/ *adj* **1** [*personne*] communicative, outgoing; **il est d'un naturel peu ~** he's not very communicative ou outgoing; **2** Tech expansive.

expansion /ɛkspɑ̃sjɔ̃/ *nf* **1** (d'économie, de région) growth; **~ démographique** population growth; **en (pleine) ~** [*organisme, filiale, marché*] (rapidly) growing; [*activité, monnaie*] (rapidly) increasing; **secteurs en ~** growth sectors; **la ville a connu une forte ~ économique** the town has experienced marked economic growth; **2** (de corps, pays) expansion; **~ coloniale** colonial expansion; **3** (d'idées, épidémie) spread.

expansionnisme /ɛkspɑ̃sjɔnism/ *nm* expansionism.

expansionniste /ɛkspɑ̃sjɔnist/ *adj, nmf* expansionist.

expansivité /ɛkspɑ̃sivite/ *nf* expansiveness.

expatriation /ɛkspatʀijasjɔ̃/ *nf* (de personne) expatriation; **l'~ de capitaux** the transfer of capital abroad.

expatrié, **~e** /ɛkspatʀije/ **I** *pp* ▶ **expatrier**.
II *pp adj, nm,f* expatriate.

expatrier /ɛkspatʀije/ [2] **I** *vtr* to deport [*personne*]; to transfer [sth] abroad [*capitaux*].
II s'expatrier *vpr* to emigrate (**en, à** to).

expectative /ɛkspɛktativ/ *nf* **1** (attente prudente) prudent approach; **rester dans l'~** to wait and see; **nous sommes dans l'~** we'll have to wait and see; **2** (espérance) hope; **vivre dans l'~ de qch** to live in hope of sth.

expectorant, **~e** /ɛkspɛktɔʀɑ̃, ɑ̃t/ **I** *adj* expectorant.
II *nm* expectorant.

expectoration /ɛkspɛktɔʀasjɔ̃/ *nf* (action) expectoration; (crachat) sputum ¢.

expectorer /ɛkspɛktɔʀe/ [1] *vtr* to expectorate.

expédient /ɛkspedjɑ̃/ **I** *adj m* **il est ~ de faire** it is expedient to do.
II *nm* expedient; **user d'~s** to resort to expedients; **vivre d'~s** to live by one's wits.

expédier /ɛkspedje/ [2] *vtr* **1** gén to send; (par la poste) to post GB, to mail US [*lettres, colis*]; (faire partir) to dispatch [*marchandises, commande*]; **~ qch à qn** to send sb sth, to send sth to sb; **~ qch par avion/par bateau** to send sth by air mail/by surface mail [*lettre, colis*]; **~ des marchandises par bateau** to ship goods; **~ des marchandises par train** to send goods by rail; **2** (envoyer) to send, dispatch [*personne, estafette, messager*] (**à** to); **on l'a expédié**○ **en prison pour cinq ans** he was sent to jail for five years; **ils ont expédié**○ **leurs trois enfants en colonie de vacances** they packed○ their three children off to a holiday GB ou summer US camp; **~**○ **qn dans l'au-delà** or **au cimetière** to do sb in○, to kill sb; **3** (se débarrasser de)○ to get rid of [*client, importun*]; (bâcler)○ to polish off [*travail, repas*]; **~ un procès/entretien en une heure** pej to get a trial/interview over within one hour; **4** (régler) to deal with; **~ les affaires courantes** to deal with ou dispatch daily business.

expéditeur, **-trice** /ɛkspeditœʀ, tʀis/ **I** *adj* [*bureau, gare*] of dispatch (*après n*).
II *nm,f* sender; **retour à l'~** return to sender.

expéditif, **-ive** /ɛkspeditif, iv/ *adj* [*personne*] brisk, efficient; [*méthode, procédé*] cursory, expeditious sout; **un jugement ~** a hasty verdict; **une justice expéditive** summary justice.

expédition /ɛkspedisjɔ̃/ *nf* **1** (action d'expédier) (de lettre, marchandises) dispatching, sending; (de renforts) sending; (par bateau) shipping; **2** (chose expédiée) gén consignment, shipment US; (par bateau) shipment; **3** Mil, Sport, Sci expedition; **~ punitive** punitive strike; **partir en ~** to set out on an expedition; **4** Jur (de jugement, d'acte notarié) authenticated copy.

expéditionnaire /ɛkspedisjɔnɛʀ/ **I** *adj* [*corps, armée, forces*] expeditionary.
II ▶ **510** *nmf* **1** Comm forwarding agent; **2** Admin copyist.

expéditivement /ɛkspeditivmɑ̃/ *adv* cursorily, quickly, expeditiously sout.

expérience /ɛkspeʀjɑ̃s/ *nf* **1** (pratique) experience; **je le sais par ~** I know from experience; **faire une ~ malheureuse** to have an unfortunate experience; **manquer d'~** to lack experience; **~ professionnelle** work experience; **mon ~ de pilote** my experience as a pilot; **c'est une ~ que je ne renouvellerai pas** that's an experience I wouldn't want to repeat; **l'~ montre que** experience shows that; **j'ai l'~ des enfants** I've experience with children; **avoir de l'~** to be experienced; **ne pas avoir d'~** to be inexperienced; **sans ~** inexperienced; **faire l'~ de qch** to experience sth; **j'en ai fait l'~ à mes dépens** I learned that lesson at my own expense; **je le sais pour en avoir fait l'~** I know it from experience; **2** Sci (essai) experiment (**de** in); **~ réussie** successful experiment; **~ pédagogique** educational experiment; **~ en laboratoire** laboratory experiment; **~s sur les animaux** animal testing ou experiments; **faire une ~** to carry out an experiment.

expérimental, **~e**, *mpl* **-aux** /ɛkspeʀimɑ̃tal, o/ *adj* experimental.

expérimentalement /ɛkspeʀimɑ̃talmɑ̃/ *adv* experimentally.

expérimentateur, **-trice** /ɛkspeʀimɑ̃tatœʀ, tʀis/ *nm,f* experimenter.

expérimentation /ɛkspeʀimɑ̃tasjɔ̃/ *nf* **1** Sci (processus) testing ¢; **dix ans d'~** ten years of testing; **2** Sci (test) test; **effectuer des ~s** to carry out tests; **3** (essai) experimentation; **période d'~** period of experimentation.

expérimenté, **~e** /ɛkspeʀimɑ̃te/ **I** *pp* ▶ **expérimenter**.
II *adj* [*amant, traducteur*] experienced; **'recherchons personnes ~es pour gérer un restaurant'** 'we're looking for experienced people to run a restaurant'.

expérimenter /ɛkspeʀimɑ̃te/ [1] **I** *vtr* **1** (tester) to test [*médicament*] (**sur** on); to try out [*méthode, procédé*]; **2** (éprouver) to experience [*situation*]; **je le sais pour l'avoir expérimenté** I know it from experience.
II *vi* to experiment.

expert, **~e** /ɛkspɛʀ, ɛʀt/ **I** *adj* expert (**à faire** at doing); **d'un œil ~** with an expert eye; **elle n'est pas très ~e en la matière** she's not a great expert on the subject.
II ▶ **510** *nm* **1** (spécialiste) expert (**en** on); **~ en informatique** computer expert; **médecin ~** Jur medical expert; **l'avis d'un ~** expert advice; **2** Assur adjuster.
■ **~ en assurance** loss adjuster; **~ immobilier** chartered surveyor GB, appraiser US; **~ judiciaire** expert witness; **~ maritime** average adjuster.

expert-comptable, *pl* **experts-comptables** /ɛkspɛʀkɔ̃tabl/ ▶ **510** *nm* ≈ chartered accountant GB, certified public accountant US.

expertement /ɛkspɛʀtəmɑ̃/ *adv* expertly.

expertise /ɛkspɛʀtiz/ *nf* **1** (estimation) (de bijou) valuation GB, appraisal US; (de dégâts) assessment; **rapport d'~** expert's report; **2** (compétence) expertise.
■ **~ judiciaire** Jur expert evidence; **~ médico-légale** expert medical evidence.

expertiser /ɛkspɛʀtize/ [1] *vtr* **1** (évaluer) to value GB, appraise US [*bijou*]; to assess [*dégâts*]; **faire ~ une bague** to have a ring valued GB ou appraised US; **2** (authentifier) to authenticate [*tableau*].

expiable /ɛkspjabl/ *adj* expiable.

expiation /ɛkspjasjɔ̃/ *nf* atonement (**de** for), expiation (**de** of).

expiatoire /ɛkspjatwaʀ/ *adj* expiatory.

expier /ɛkspje/ [2] *vtr* **1** (réparer) to atone for, expiate [*crime, faute*] (**par** with); **2** (être puni de) to pay for [*erreur*] (**par** with).

expirant, **~e** /ɛkspiʀɑ̃, ɑ̃t/ *adj* liter [*personne, flamme*] dying; [*voix*] faint.

expiration /ɛkspiʀasjɔ̃/ *nf* **1** Physiol exhalation; **2** (échéance) expiry GB, expiration US; **à l'~ du contrat** when the contract expires; **venir** or **arriver à ~** to expire.

expirer /ɛkspiʀe/ [1] **I** *vtr* to exhale [*air*].
II *vi* **1** (arriver à son terme) to expire; **le contrat a expiré** the contract has expired; **2** (souffler) to breathe out; **inspirez, expirez!** breathe in, breathe out!; **3** (mourir) liter [*personne*] to expire; [*lueur*] to fade.

explétif, **-ive** /ɛkspletif, iv/ **I** *adj* expletive.
II *nm* expletive.

explicable /ɛksplikabl/ *adj* explicable; **peu ~** hard to explain.

explicatif, **-ive** /ɛksplikatif, iv/ *adj* **1** [*note, lettre*] explanatory; **2** Ling [*proposition*] nonrestrictive.

explication /ɛksplikasjɔ̃/ *nf* **1** (éclaircissement) explanation ¢ (**à, de** of); **si tu veux des ~s supplémentaires** if you need any further explanation; **demander/vouloir des ~s** to seek/demand an explanation; **je n'ai pas d'~s à vous donner** I don't have to explain; **document/lettre d'~** explanatory document/letter; **campagne d'~ sur** information campaign about; **nous avons eu une bonne ~** we've talked things through; **2** (cause) (de phénomène) explanation (**de** for); (d'attitude, de décision, panne) reason (**de** for); **3** (altercation) argument; **4** Scol (de passage) commentary; **faire l'~ d'un passage** to analyze a passage.
■ **~ de texte** Scol textual analysis.

explicite /ɛksplisit/ *adj* [*texte, requête, mention*] specific; [*réponse*] definite; [*titre*] self-explanatory; [*film*] explicit; **être ~** [*personne*] to be forthcoming; **être peu ~** [*personne*] not to be very forthcoming; **peu** or **pas très ~** [*texte, chiffres, manière*] ambiguous; **accord plus ou moins ~** more or less tacit agreement.

explicitement /ɛksplisitmɑ̃/ *adv* [*dire, mentionner, rejeter, condamner*] explicitly, unequivocally; [*demander, inciter, citer, autoriser*] specifically; **demander on ne peut plus ~ qch** to ask quite specifically for sth; **faire ~ référence à qch** to make specific reference to sth.

expliciter /ɛksplisite/ [1] *vtr* to clarify, to explain [*propos, objectif, grandes lignes, choix, raison*].

expliquer /ɛksplike/ [1] **I** *vtr* **1** (enseigner) to explain; **explique-leur comment marche le chauffage** explain to them how the heating works; **2** (donner la raison) to explain; **je vais tout t'~** I'll explain everything; **3** (être la raison) to account for; **le hasard n'explique pas tout** chance doesn't account for everything; **4** Scol to comment on, to analyze [*passage*].
II s'expliquer *vpr* **1** (comprendre) **s'~ qch** to understand sth; **je m'explique/ne m'explique pas pourquoi il a menti** I understand ou see/I can't understand ou see why he lied; **je m'explique qu'elle veuille rester** I can quite see that she might want to stay; **2** (être compréhensible) to be understandable; **leur amertume s'explique** their bitterness is understandable; **tout s'explique par le fait que les habitudes ont changé** it's understandable, because times have changed; **tout finira par s'~** everything will become clear; **la chose s'explique d'elle-même** it is self-explanatory; **3** (exposer sa pensée) **je m'explique** let me explain; **elle s'explique bien/mal** she expresses herself well/badly; **sans doute me suis-je mal expliqué** perhaps I didn't make myself clear; **expliquez-vous sur ce point** what do you mean exactly?; **4** (se justifier) to explain (oneself) (**auprès de, devant** to); **le secrétaire devra s'~ auprès du comité** the secretary will have to explain himself to the committee; **s'~ sur son retard** to explain one's late arrival; **5** (résoudre un conflit) **ils se sont expliqués** they talked things through; **allez vous ~ ailleurs** go and sort it out somewhere else; **s'~ à coups de poings** to fight it out; **s'~ à coups de revolver** to shoot it out.

exploit /ɛksplwa/ *nm* **1** gén exploit, feat; (de sportif) feat, achievement; (de guerrier) exploit; **ses ~s amoureux** or **galants** his amorous exploits; **il est arrivé à l'heure? quel ~!** iron he arrived on time? what an achievement!; **2** Jur **~ (d'huissier de justice)** writ.

exploitable /ɛksplwatabl/ *adj* exploitable.

exploitant, **~e** /ɛksplwatɑ̃, ɑ̃t/ *nm,f* **1** Agric farmer; **2** Cin cinema owner GB, exhibitor US; **3** Comm manager.
■ **~ agricole** Agric farmer.

exploitation /ɛksplwatasjɔ̃/ *nf* **1** (traitement injuste) exploitation; **2** (ferme) **~ (agricole)** farm; **petite ~ familiale** small family farm; **3** (entreprise) **~ commerciale/industrielle** business/industrial concern; **4** (mise en valeur) (de mine) working; (de gisement de charbon, de fer) mining; (de gisement, de forêt) exploitation; (de ferme, entreprise) running; (de réseau, liaison aérienne, maritime) operation; (de brevet) using; **coûts d'~** running or operating costs; **autorisation d'~** licence[GB] to operate; **5** (utilisation) **l'~ d'un don** making the most of a talent.

exploité, **~e** /ɛksplwate/ *nm,f* exploited person; **les ~s** the exploited.

exploiter /ɛksplwate/ [1] *vtr* **1** (abuser de) to exploit [*personne*]; **2** (faire valoir) to work [*mine*]; to mine [*gisement de charbon, fer*]; to exploit [*gisement, forêt, source thermale*]; to run [*entreprise*]; to operate [*réseau, liaison aérienne*]; to use [*brevet*]; **il exploite 17 hectares** he farms 17 hectares; **3** (utiliser) to make the most of [*don, renseignement, connaissances*]; péj to exploit [*crédulité, rivalités*]; **~ une situation** to capitalize on a situation.

exploiteur, **-euse** /ɛksplwatœʀ, øz/ *nm,f* exploiter.

explorateur, **-trice** /ɛksplɔʀatœʀ, tʀis/ **I** *adj* [*regard*] searching.
II ▶ **510** *nm,f* (personne) explorer.
III *nm* Méd endoscope.

exploration /ɛksplɔʀasjɔ̃/ *nf* **1** (de continent, mer, terrain) exploration; **~ spatiale** space exploration; **faire un voyage d'~** to go on a voyage of exploration ou discovery; **partir en ~** to go exploring; **l'~ de l'inconscient** fig the exploration of the subconscious; **2** Mines (de gisement, fonds sous-marin) exploration; **3** (de problème, question) investigation, examination; **4** Méd (d'organe) exploration.

exploratoire /ɛksplɔʀatwaʀ/ *adj* exploratory.

explorer /ɛksplɔʀe/ [1] *vtr* **1** (visiter) to explore [*pays, forêt*]; **2** (examiner) to explore [*thème, marché, options, domaine, inconscient*]; to investigate, to examine [*question, cause*]; (du regard) to scan [*horizon, lieu*]; (de la main) to explore [*tiroir, sac*]; **3** Méd to explore [*organe*].

exploser /ɛksploze/ [1] *vi* **1** lit [*bombe, mine, appareil*] to explode; [*véhicule, immeuble*] to blow up; **faire ~** [*personne, dispositif*] to blow up [*avion, voiture*]; to explode [*bombe, mine*]; [*gaz, court-circuit*] to cause [sth] to blow up [*immeuble*]; **2** fig [*colère, jalousie*] to explode; [*joie*] to burst forth; [*acclamations*] to ring out; **laisser ~ sa colère/joie** to give vent to one's anger/joy; **faire ~ qn**○ to make sb blow up○; **le pays va ~** the country is going to explode; **3** (augmenter) [*prix*] to soar, to rocket○; [*ventes*] to boom, to rocket○; [*marché*] to boom; [*demande*] to soar.

exploseur /ɛksplozœʀ/ *nm* blasting machine, exploder.

explosible /ɛksplozibl/ *adj* explosive.

explosif, **-ive** /ɛksplozif, iv/ **I** *adj* (tous contextes) explosive.
II *nm* explosive; **un attentat à l'~** an attack using explosives.
III explosive *nf* Ling plosive, explosive.

explosion /ɛksplozjɔ̃/ *nf* **1** lit explosion; **~ nucléaire** nuclear explosion; **faire ~** to explode; **2** (de haine, colère, violence, rires) outburst, explosion; (de cris) outburst; **une ~ sociale** a social outcry; **3** (de population, fraudes, revendications) explosion (**de** of); **~ démographique** population explosion; **4** (d'art, investissement, de marché) boom (**de** in); **l'~ des prix** price explosion; **l'~ artistique/technologique** the art/technology boom.

exponentiel, **-ielle** /ɛkspɔnɑ̃sjɛl/ *adj* exponential.

exponentiellement /ɛkspɔnɑ̃sjɛlmɑ̃/ *adv* exponentially.

export /ɛkspɔʀ/ *nm* export.

exportable /ɛkspɔʀtabl/ *adj* exportable.

exportateur, **-trice** /ɛkspɔʀtatœʀ, tʀis/ **I** *adj* [*pays*] exporting; [*marché, capacité, industrie, société*] export (*épith*); **les pays ~s de pétrole** oil-exporting countries.
II ▶ **510** *nm,f* exporter.

exportation /ɛkspɔʀtasjɔ̃/ *nf* **1** (activité) export (**de** of); **faire l'~ de qch** to export sth; **encourager l'~** to encourage exports; **la diminution des commandes à l'~** the falling demand for exports; **une politique d'~** an export policy; **2** (marchandises) export; **les ~s de pétrole/matériel** oil/equipment exports.

exporter /ɛkspɔʀte/ [1] **I** *vtr* to export [*marchandises, capitaux, culture*].
II s'exporter *vpr* [*produit, mode*] to be exported; **s'~ bien/mal** to be easy/difficult to export.

exposant, **~e** /ɛkspozɑ̃, ɑ̃t/ **I** *nm,f* exhibitor.

II *nm* Math exponent.

exposé, **~e** /ɛkspoze/ **I** *pp* ▸ **exposer**.

II *pp adj* **1** (situé) [*maison, endroit*] exposed; **côte ~e au vent/à l'ennemi** coast exposed to the wind/to the enemy; **maison ~e au sud** south-facing house; **maison bien ~e** house with a good aspect; **2** (montré) [*tableau*] on show (*après n*); [*denrée*] on display (*après n*); **liste des œuvres ~es** list of exhibits; **3** (vulnérable) **c'est un homme très ~** he's (a man) in a very vulnerable position.

III *nm* **1** (compte-rendu) **~ de** account of, report on [*situation*]; **faire un** or **l'~ des faits** to give a statement of the facts; **2** (conférence) talk (**sur** on); exposé (**sur** on); **faire un ~** to give a talk.

■ **~ des motifs** Jur preamble.

exposer /ɛkspoze/ [1] **I** *vtr* **1** (montrer) to exhibit [*œuvre d'art*]; to display, to put [sth] on display [*marchandise*]; to expose [*condamné*]; **~ qch aux regards** or **à la vue de tous** to put sth on public view ou display; **2** (décrire) to state [*faits*]; to outline [*idée, plan*]; to list [*griefs*]; to explain [*situation*]; to expound [*argument*]; Littérat to set out [*sujet*]; Mus to introduce [*thème*]; **~ sa thèse à qn** to outline one's theory to sb; **~ ses observations sur qch** to give one's comments on sth; **3** Phot to expose; **4** (mettre en danger) to risk [*vie, réputation*]; to stake [*fortune*]; **~ un enfant** Antiq to expose a child; Jur to abandon a child; **5** (soumettre à) to expose (**à** to); **ne reste pas exposé au soleil** (conseil général) stay out of the sun; (mets-toi à l'ombre) don't stay in the sun; **'ne pas ~ à la chaleur'** 'keep away from direct heat'; **être exposé à une maladie** to be exposed to a disease.

II s'exposer *vpr* **1** (se rendre vulnérable) to put oneself at risk; **s'~ à** to risk [*colère, rechute, mort*]; to lay oneself open to, to run the risk of [*poursuites, critiques, représailles*]; **s'~ à tout perdre** to run the risk of losing everything; **il s'est trop exposé dans cette affaire** he has been incautious in his involvement in that business, he's stuck his neck out○ too far in that business; **2** (se placer) **s'~ au soleil** to go out in the sun.

exposition /ɛkspozisjɔ̃/ *nf* **1** (salon, foire) (de tableaux, photos, d'objets d'art) exhibition; (d'animaux, de plantes, marchandises) show; (d'objets à vendre) fair; **~ agricole/florale** agricultural/flower show; **~ universelle** world fair; **2** Comm (dans un magasin, centre commercial) display; **~ de blanc** household linen display; **3** (présentation) (de thèse, situation, faits) exposition; Littérat, Mus exposition; **scène d'~** expository ou introductory scene; **4** (orientation) aspect; **pièce avec une double ~** room with a dual aspect; **la terrasse jouit d'une bonne ~** the terrace has a pleasant aspect; **5** (soumission à un effet) also Phot exposure; **l'~ aux radiations/au soleil** exposure to radiation/to sunlight; **6** Jur (de condamné) exposure; **~ d'enfant** abandonment of a child.

exprès[1] /ɛkspʀɛ/ *adv* **1** (délibérément) deliberately; **je ne l'ai pas fait ~** I didn't do it on purpose, I didn't mean to do it; **c'est fait ~** it's deliberate; **'la porte se referme toute seule'—'c'est fait ~'** 'the door shuts itself'—'that's what it's designed to do!'; **il le fait ~ pour m'embêter** he does it deliberately or on purpose to annoy me; **comme par un fait ~, il a plu ce jour-là** as ill-luck would have it ou as if on purpose, it rained that day; **comme par un fait ~ il était là aussi** as ill-luck would have it, he was there too; **2** (spécialement) specially; **elle est venue (tout) ~ pour faire** she came specially to do.

exprès[2], **-esse** /ɛkspʀɛs/ **I** *adj* [*ordre, condition, clause*] express; **défense expresse d'en parler** all mention of it is expressly forbidden.

II exprès *adj inv* Postes special delivery; **envoyer qch en** or **par ~** to send sth special delivery.

express /ɛkspʀɛs/ **I** *adj inv* **1** Transp [*train, liaison, transports*] express; **2** (rapide) [*nettoyage*] express; [*déjeuner*] quick; **une visite ~** a flying visit.

II *nm inv* **1** Rail express; **2** (café) espresso.

expressément /ɛkspʀɛsemɑ̃/ *adv* expressly.

expressif, **-ive** /ɛkspʀɛsif, iv/ *adj* expressive.

expression /ɛkspʀɛsjɔ̃/ *nf* **1** gén expression; **plein d'~** [*yeux, visage*] expressive; [*chant*] full of expression; **sans ~** expressionless; **avec ~** [*réciter, chanter*] with feeling; **réduire qch à sa plus simple ~** fig to reduce sth to a minimum; **2** (groupe de mots) expression; **~ imagée** or **figurée** figurative expression; **~ idiomatique** idiom, idiomatic expression; **~ figée** set phrase; **~ toute faite** set phrase; péj cliché; **passez-moi l'~!** if you'll pardon the expression!; **bête au-delà de toute ~** too stupid for words; **d'~ française/anglaise** French-speaking/English-speaking.

■ **~ corporelle** self-expression through movement.

expressionnisme /ɛkspʀɛsjɔnism/ *nm* expressionism.

expressionniste /ɛkspʀɛsjɔnist/ *adj, nmf* expressionist.

expressivité /ɛkspʀɛsivite/ *nf* expressiveness.

exprimable /ɛkspʀimabl/ *adj* possible to express; **difficilement ~** [*sentiment, impression*] hard to express.

exprimer /ɛkspʀime/ [1] **I** *vtr* **1** (énoncer) to express [*avis, idée*]; (sans paroles) to show [*désaccord, attitude*]; (donner libre cours à) to express [*personnalité, sentiment*]; **~ qch en français** to say sth in French; **2** (dénoter) [*couleur, mot, poème*] to express; **son visage exprimait la surprise/cruauté** there was an expression of surprise/cruelty on his face; **3** (traduire) to express (**en** in); **~ un prix en dollars/francs** to give a price in dollars/francs; **~ qch en pourcentage** to give sth as a percentage; **4** (extraire) to squeeze [*liquide*] (**de** out of).

II s'exprimer *vpr* **1** (parler, montrer sa personnalité) to express oneself; (donner son avis) to give one's opinion (**sur** on ou about); **si j'ose m'~ ainsi** if I can put it this way; **je me suis mal exprimé** I haven't made myself clear; **s'~ en français** to speak in French; **s'~ par gestes** (sans parler) to use sign language; (emphatiquement) to use gestures to express oneself; **2** (être indiqué) to be represented; **s'~ par un symbole** to be represented by a symbol; **3** (se montrer) [*sentiment, état d'esprit*] to be expressed.

expropriation /ɛkspʀɔpʀijasjɔ̃/ *nf* (de maison, d'immeuble) compulsory purchase, compulsory acquisition; (de terrain) expropriation, compulsory purchase; (de personne) expropriation.

exproprié, **~e** /ɛkspʀɔpʀije/ *nm,f* person whose property has been expropriated.

exproprier /ɛkspʀɔpʀije/ [2] *vtr* **~ qn** to put a compulsory purchase order on sb's property; **~ une maison/un terrain** to put a compulsory purchase order on a house/a piece of land.

expulser /ɛkspylse/ [1] *vtr* **1** (renvoyer) to evict [*locataire*] (**de** from); to deport [*immigré*] (**de** from; **en/vers** to); to expel [*élève, diplomate, dissident, membre*] (**de** from); **2** Sport to send [sb] off [*joueur*]; **3** Physiol to expel [*calcul*]; to excrete [*déchets*].

expulsion /ɛkspylsjɔ̃/ *nf* **1** (de locataire) eviction (**de** from); (d'immigré) deportation (**de** from); (d'élève, de diplomate, dissident) expulsion (**de** from); **ordre** or **arrêté d'~** (d'immigré) deportation order; (de locataire) eviction order; **2** Sport sending-off (**de** from); **3** Physiol (de déchets) excretion (**de** from); (lors d'un accouchement) delivery.

expurger /ɛkspyʀʒe/ [13] *vtr* **1** Édition, Cin to expurgate, to bowdlerize [*texte, scénario*]; **2** Pol to purge [*parti, organisation*] (**de** of).

exquis, **~e** /ɛkski, iz/ *adj* [*parfum, nourriture, œuvre, goût*] exquisite; [*temps*] delightful; [*sourire, personne, geste*] charming; [*moue*] adorable; [*enfant*] delightful, adorable; **être d'une politesse ~e** to be exquisitely polite.

exsangue /ɛgzɑ̃g/ *adj* **1** lit [*personne, blessé*] who has lost a lot of blood (*après n*); [*cadavre, organe*] bloodless; **2** (pâle) [*lèvres*] bloodless; [*mains*] white; [*visage*] ashen; **3** fig [*pays, économie*] drained; [*société, art, littérature*] lifeless; **la guerre a laissé le pays ~** the war has bled the country dry.

exsudation /ɛksydasjɔ̃/ *nf* Méd, Bot exudation.

exsuder /ɛksyde/ [1] **I** *vtr* lit, fig to exude.

II *vi* lit, fig to ooze (**de** from).

extase /ɛkstɑz/ *nf* lit, fig ecstasy; **être/tomber en ~ devant** to be in/go into ecstasy ou raptures over.

extasier: **s'extasier** /ɛkstazje/ [2] *vpr* to go into ecstasies ou raptures (**devant, sur** over); **'magnifique,' s'extasia-t-elle** 'marvellous[GB]', she enthused; **regarder qn d'un air extasié** to look at sb ecstatically.

extatique /ɛkstatik/ *adj* ecstatic.

extenseur /ɛkstɑ̃sœʀ/ **I** *adj m* Anat [*muscle*] extensor.

II *nm* **1** Sport chest-expander; **2** Anat extensor.

extensibilité /ɛkstɑ̃sibilite/ *nf* extensibility.

extensible /ɛkstɑ̃sibl/ *adj* **1** lit [*métal, tissu, matière*] extensible; **2** fig [*liste*] extendable.

extensif, **-ive** /ɛkstɑ̃sif, iv/ *adj* **1** [*culture*] extensive; **2** [*sens*] wider; [*signification, usage*] extended.

extension /ɛkstɑ̃sjɔ̃/ *nf* **1** (de bras, jambe) stretching, extension; (de muscle, cou) stretching; **faire des mouvements d'~ et de flexion** to stretch and bend; **quand votre jambe est en ~** when your leg is extended; **2** Méd extension; **3** (d'industrie) expansion; (de grève, zone, pouvoirs, loi) extension (**à** to); **prendre de l'~** [*industrie*] to expand; [*grève*] to spread ou extend; **et par ~, le mot signifie**... and by extension the word means...; **4** (de ressort, métal) stretching.

exténuant, **~e** /ɛkstenɥɑ̃, ɑ̃t/ *adj* exhausting.

exténuer /ɛkstenɥe/ [1] **I** *vtr* to exhaust; **avoir l'air exténué** to look exhausted.

II s'exténuer *vpr* to wear oneself out (**à faire** doing).

extérieur, **~e** /ɛksteʀjœʀ/ **I** *adj* **1** (hors d'un lieu) [*mur, escalier, température*] outside; [*crépi, menuiserie*] external; [*surface, poche*] outer; [*intérêts, activités*] outside; [*angle*] external; (périphérique) [*mur, boulevard*] outer; **le côté ~, la partie ~e** the outside; **échelle destinée à l'usage ~** ladder for outdoor use; **les abords ~s** the surrounding area; **les quartiers ~s** the outlying districts; **2** (hors de l'être) [*réalité*] external; [*monde*] external, outside; **3** (étranger) Écon, Pol [*commerce, déficit, relations*] external, foreign; [*politique*] foreign; **4** (d'ailleurs) [*personne, organisme, fonds*] outside, from outside (*après n*); [*cause, contrôle, pression*] external, outside; [*intervention, recrutement*] outside; **faire appel à des compétences ~es** to call in outside help; **personne ~e à un groupe** (d'ailleurs) person from outside a group; (étrangère à) person who does not belong to a group; **les pays ~s à la CEE** non-EEC countries; **5** (apparent) [*signe*] outward; [*joie, calme*] apparent, outward; **signe ~ de réussite** outward sign of success; **afficher un calme ~** to be outwardly calm; **leur indifférence est tout ~e** their indifference is only a front; **aspect ~** (de personne) outward appearance; (de bâtiment) outside; **6** (sans rapport avec) **~ à qch** unrelated to sth, outside sth; **question ~e au sujet** question not related to the subject; **7** Sport [*match, victoire*] away (*épith*).

II *nm* **1** (de boîte, maison, ville, pays) outside; **peindre l'~** to paint the outside; **de l'~** [*fermé, vu, juger, observer*] from the outside; **les gens de l'~** (loin du lieu dit) people from other places; (hors d'un organisme) outsiders; **à l'~** outside, outdoors; **rouge à l'~** red on the outside; **à l'~ de la maison** outside the house; **rester à l'~ d'un conflit** to remain outside a conflict; **jeu/plante d'~** outdoor game/plant; **2** (étranger) **relations/échanges avec l'~** foreign ou external relations/trade; **notre image à l'~** our image abroad; **3** (monde autour de soi) outside world; **s'ouvrir sur** or **vers l'~** to open up to the outside world; **nouvelles de l'~** news from the outside world; **4** (apparence) exterior, appearance; **un ~ rude** a gruff exterior; **de l'~, elle n'est pas avenante** at first sight, she doesn't seem very friendly; **5** Cin outdoor location shots; **en ~** on location; **6** Sport **match joué à l'~** away match; **jouer/gagner à l'~** to play/win an away match, to play/win away; **7** (qui ne fait pas partie d'un groupe) outsider; (d'un club) nonmember.

extérieurement /ɛksteʀjœʀmɑ̃/ *adv* **1** (vu du dehors) on the outside, externally; **2** (en apparence) outwardly.

extériorisation /ɛksteʀjɔʀizasjɔ̃/ *nf* (d'émotion) outward expression; Psych (de sensibilité) externalization.

extérioriser /ɛksteʀjɔʀize/ [1] **I** *vtr* to express [*pensée*]; to show [*sentiment*]; Psych to externalize.

II s'extérioriser *vpr* [*personne*] to express oneself; [*émotion*] to be expressed.

extériorité /ɛksteʀjɔʀite/ *nf* exteriority.

exterminateur, **-trice** /ɛkstɛʀminatœʀ, tʀis/ **I** *adj* [*puissance, glaive*] exterminating.

II *nm,f* exterminator (**de** of).

extermination /ɛkstɛʀminasjɔ̃/ *nf* extermination (**de** of); **jusqu'à l'~ de l'ennemi** until the enemy has been wiped out; **camp d'~** death camp.

exterminer /ɛkstɛʀmine/ [1] *vtr* to exterminate [*peuple, animaux*]; to wipe out [*armée, rebelles*].

externat /ɛkstɛʀna/ *nm* **1** Scol (école) day school; **elle préfère l'~** she prefers to be a day pupil ou a non-boarder; **2** Méd, Univ **préparer l'~** to prepare for medical school entrance exams; **faire son ~** to be a non-resident student doctor (in a hospital) GB, to be an extern US.

externe /ɛkstɛʀn/ **I** *adj* **1** (extérieur) [*cause, problème, croissance*] external; [*face*] outside; [*partie*] exterior; **recrutement ~** outside recruitment, recruitment from outside; **2** Méd [*hémorragie, mal*] external; **à usage ~** for external application ou use only; **3** Math external; [*angle*] exterior.

II *nmf* **1** Scol day pupil; **2** Méd, Univ **~ (des hôpitaux)** non-residential medical student GB, extern US.

exterritorialité /ɛkstɛʀitɔʀjalite/ *nf* extraterritoriality.

extincteur /ɛkstɛ̃ktœʀ/ *nm* fire extinguisher.

extinction /ɛkstɛ̃ksjɔ̃/ *nf* **1** Méd **avoir une ~ de voix** to have lost one's voice; **mon ~ de voix a duré trois jours** I lost my voice for three days; **2** (d'espèce, de race) extinction; **une espèce en voie d'~** an endangered species; **3** (action d'éteindre) **après l'~ de l'incendie** after the fire was put out ou extinguished; **après l'~ des feux** after lights out; **4** Jur extinguishment.

extirper /ɛkstiʀpe/ [1] **I** *vtr* **1**○ (faire sortir) to drag [*personne*] (**de** out of, from); **2** liter (faire disparaître) to eradicate, to root out [*vice, mal*] (**de** from); **3** (arracher) to pull out [*plantes, racines, herbes*].

II s'extirper○ *vpr* [*personne*] to drag oneself (**de** out of, from).

extorquer /ɛkstɔʀke/ [1] *vtr* to extort [*argent, aveu, promesse*] (**à qn** from sb).

extorqueur, **-euse** /ɛkstɔʀkœʀ, øz/ *nm,f* **~ (de fonds)** extortionist.

extorsion /ɛkstɔʀsjɔ̃/ *nf* extortion ¢; **~ de fonds** extortion (of money); **être accusé d'~ de fonds** to be accused of extorting money.

extra /ɛkstʀa/ **I** *adj inv* **1**○ [*film, moment etc*] fabulous○; **il est ~ ce type** he's a great guy○; **2** Comm **confiture ~** extra jam; **huile d'olive ~ vierge** extra virgin olive oil.

II *nm inv* **1** (dépense imprévue) extra; **se payer un petit ~** to have a little treat; **faire un** or **des ~** to splash out○; **2** (travail) **faire des ~** (petits travaux) to do bits and pieces; (travail supplémentaire) to do a few extra jobs; **3** (personne) extra person.

extra-atmosphérique, *pl* **~s** /ɛkstʀa atmɔsfeʀik/ *adj* **espace ~** outer space.

extrabudgétaire /ɛkstʀabydʒetɛʀ/ *adj* extrabudgetary, out-of-budget (*épith*).

extracellulaire /ɛkstʀaselylɛʀ/ *adj* extracellular.

extracommunautaire, *pl* **~s** /ɛkstʀa kɔmynotɛʀ/ *adj* non-EEC (*épith*).

extraconjugal, **~e**, *mpl* **-aux** /ɛkstʀa kɔ̃ʒygal, o/ *adj* extramarital.

extra-court, **~e**, *pl* **~s**, **~es** /ɛkstʀa kuʀ, uʀt/ *adj* [*vêtement*] ultra-short; [*texte, film*] very short.

extracteur /ɛkstʀaktœʀ/ *nm* extractor.

extractible /ɛkstʀaktibl/ *adj* removable.

extractif, **-ive** /ɛkstʀaktif, iv/ *adj* [*machine*] extraction (*épith*); [*industries, substances*] extractive.

extraction /ɛkstʀaksjɔ̃/ *nf* **1** Mines (de minerai, pétrole, gaz) extraction; (de charbon, diamants) mining; (d'ardoise, de marbre) quarrying; **2** Méd (de balle, dent) extraction (**de** from); **3** Math extraction; **4** Chimie (d'huile, essences, hydrocarbures, de sucre) extraction; **~ par solvant** extraction using a solvent; **5** (origine) extraction sout; **être de basse/haute ~** to be of low/high birth; **être d'~ bourgeoise** to be from a middle-class background.

extrader /ɛkstʀade/ [1] *vtr* to extradite [*criminel*] (**de** from; **vers** to).

extradition /ɛkstʀadisjɔ̃/ *nf* extradition; **une demande d'~** a request for extradition.

extrados /ɛkstʀado(s)/ *nm* extrados.

extra-fin, **~e**, *mpl* **~s** /ɛkstʀafɛ̃, in/ *adj* [*collants*] ultra-fine; **petits pois ~s** petits pois; **haricots verts ~s** extra-fine French beans.

extrafort, **~e** /ɛkstʀafɔʀ, ɔʀt/ **I** *adj* [*carton, moutarde*] extra-strong.

II *nm* Cout binding tape.

extraire /ɛkstʀɛʀ/ [58] **I** *vtr* **1** (exploiter) to extract [*minerai*]; to mine [*or, houille*]; to quarry [*ardoise, marbre*]; **2** (enlever) to extract, to pull out [*dent*]; to remove [*balle, épine*] (**de** from); to extract [*substance, élément*] (**de** from); **~ un blessé d'une voiture accidentée** to free an injured man from a wrecked car; **passage extrait d'un roman** excerpt from a novel; **3** Math to extract.

II s'extraire *vpr* **s'~ de** to climb out of [*fauteuil, cabine de pilotage*]; hum to struggle out of [*vêtement*].

extrait /ɛkstʀɛ/ *nm* **1** (de livre, film) extract, excerpt; (de discours) extract; **2** (substance) essence, extract; **~ de viande/de légumes** meat/vegetable extract; **3** Compta **~ de compte** abstract of accounts.

■ **~ (d'acte) de naissance** birth certificate; **~ (d'acte) de mariage** marriage certificate; **~ de casier judiciaire (de qn)** copy of (sb's) criminal record.

extra-large, *pl* **~s** /ɛkstʀalaʀʒ/ *adj* Mode extra-large.

extra-léger, **-ère**, *mpl* **~s** /ɛkstʀaleʒe, ɛʀ/ *adj* [*tissu, repas*] extra-light.

extralinguistique /ɛkstʀalɛ̃gɥistik/ *adj* extralinguistic.

extra-long, **-longue**, *mpl* **~s** /ɛkstʀalɔ̃, ɔ̃g/ *adj* [*cigarette*] king-size; [*vêtement*] extra-long.

extralucide /ɛkstʀalysid/ *adj* clairvoyant; **être ~** to be clairvoyant, to have second sight; **voyante ~** clairvoyant.

extra-muros /ɛkstʀamyʀos/ *loc adv* fml outside town.

extranéité /ɛkstʀaneite/ *nf* **1** (qualité) foreignness; **2** (statut) alien status.

extraordinaire /ɛkstʀaɔʀdinɛʀ/ *adj* **1** (qui surprend) [*question, phénomène*] extraordinary; (qui plaît et surprend) [*sensation, paysage, personne*] amazing; (admirable) [*personne, film*] remarkable; (qui plaît beaucoup) [*personne, film*] fantastic○; **d'une intelligence/laideur ~** amazingly intelligent/ugly; **avoir un talent ~** to be remarkably talented; **le film n'avait rien d'~** it wasn't a particularly stunning film; **une quantité ~ de gâteaux** a huge ou enormous number of cakes; **l'~ est que** the extraordinary thing is that; **et si par ~...** and if by some extraordinary twist of fate...; **c'est quand même ~! vous étiez dans la maison et vous n'avez rien entendu?** it's incredible! you were in the house and you heard nothing at all?; **2** (non prévu) [*dépenses, mesure, assemblée*] extraordinary.

extraordinairement /ɛkstʀaɔʀdinɛʀmɑ̃/ *adv* amazingly, extraordinarily.

extraparlementaire /ɛkstʀapaʀləmɑ̃tɛʀ/ *adj* extraparliamentary.

extra-plat, **~e**, *pl* **~s**, **~es** /ɛkstʀapla, at/ *adj* [*briquet, calculatrice, montre*] slimline.

extrapolation /ɛkstʀapɔlasjɔ̃/ *nf* extrapolation.

extrapoler /ɛkstʀapɔle/ [1] **I** *vtr* to extrapolate.

II *vi* **1** (généraliser) to extrapolate (**sur** about); **~ en se basant sur qch** or **à partir de qch** to extrapolate from sth; **2** Math to extrapolate.

extrascolaire /ɛkstʀaskɔlɛʀ/ *adj* [*activités*] extracurricular.

extrasensoriel, **-ielle** /ɛkstʀasɑ̃sɔʀjɛl/ *adj* extrasensory.

extraterrestre /ɛkstʀatɛʀɛstʀ/ **I** *adj* [*invasion*] extraterrestrial; **espace ~** outer space.

II *nmf* extraterrestrial, alien.

extra-utérin, **~e**, *mpl* **~s** /ɛkstʀa yteʀɛ̃, in/ *adj* **grossesse ~e** ectopic pregnancy.

extravagance /ɛkstʀavagɑ̃s/ *nf* **1** (de personne) eccentricity; **2** (de projet, comportement, mode, d'idées) extravagance; **tomber dans l'~** to be excessive, to go over the top○; **3** (de prix) exorbitant nature; **4** (acte) extravagance; **faire/dire des ~s** to do/say extravagant things.

extravagant, **~e** /ɛkstʀavagɑ̃, ɑ̃t/ **I** *adj* **1** [*personne, comportement*] eccentric; **2** [*idée, projet, mode*] extravagant; **3** [*prix*] exorbitant; [*récompense, budget*] extravagant.

II *nm,f* eccentric.

extraversion /ɛkstʀavɛʀsjɔ̃/ *nf* extroversion.

extraverti, **~e** /ɛkstʀavɛʀti/ *adj, nm,f* extrovert.

extrême /ɛkstʀɛm/ **I** *adj* **1** (le plus distant) [*bord, limite*] very; [*bout*] very, far; [*sud, nord*] far; [*partie*] furthest; [*date*] very last; **dans l'~ nord/sud du pays** in the far north/south of the country, in the northernmost/southernmost part of the country; **2** (très grand) [*précision, simplicité, courage, prudence*] extreme; [*pureté*] very great; **l'~ jeunesse du candidat** the candidate's extreme youth; **leur ~ vieillesse** their very great age; **avec une prudence ~** with extreme caution, extremely cautiously;

avec une courtoisie/un plaisir ~ with the greatest courtesy/pleasure; **d'une pureté/complexité ~** extremely pure/complex; **il fait un froid ~** it's extremely cold; **3** (immodéré) [*climat*, *opinion, exemple, situation, comportement*] extreme; [*décision, proposition, remède*] drastic; [*passion*] intense; **il est ~ en tout, c'est quelqu'un d'~** he always goes to extremes; **4** Pol [*parti*] extremist; [*droite, gauche*] far, extreme.

II *nm* **1** (ce qui est excessif) extreme; **cet exemple fait figure d'~** this is an extreme example; **ville de tous les ~s** town of extremes; **c'est pousser la probité/logique à l'~** that's taking honesty/logic to extremes; **inquiet/courageux à l'~** extremely worried/brave; **événement médiatisé à l'~** event which was given a lot of media hype○; **limiter ses dépenses à l'~** to keep one's expenses to a bare minimum; **2** (opposé) extreme; **passer d'un ~ à l'autre** to go from one extreme to the other; **à l'~ opposé** or **inverse** at the other extreme; **les ~s se rejoignent** extremes meet; **3** Météo extreme; **les ~s saisonniers** seasonal extremes.

III extrêmes *nmpl* **1** Pol **les ~s** (d'un parti) the extremists; (au Parlement) the far ou extreme right and left; **2** Math extremes.

extrêmement /ɛkstʀɛmmɑ̃/ *adv* extremely.

extrême-onction, *pl* **extrêmes-onctions** /ɛkstʀɛmɔ̃ksjɔ̃/ *nf* extreme unction; **donner l'~** to give extreme unction (à to).

Extrême-Orient /ɛkstʀɛmɔʀjɑ̃/ **▶ 692** *nprm* **l'~** the Far East.

extrême-oriental, **~e**, *mpl* **-aux** /ɛkstʀɛmɔʀjɑ̃tal, o/ *adj* far eastern; **la concurrence ~e** competition from the Far East.

extrémisme /ɛkstʀemism/ *nm* extremism; **le danger des ~s** the danger of extremism; **l'~ de droite/gauche** right/left extremism.

extrémiste /ɛkstʀemist/ *adj, nmf* extremist.

extrémité /ɛkstʀemite/ *nf* **1** (bout) gén end; (de tube, ligne, rue) end; (de doigt, tige, baguette) tip, end; (d'aiguille) point, end; (de mât, clocher) top; (de surface, champ, ville) edge; fig (de vie) end; **à l'~ de** at the end of [*rue*]; at the top of [*mât*]; at the edge of [*ville*]; **à l'autre ~ de l'Europe** at the other end of Europe; **aux deux ~s** at both ends; **2** (mort) **résister jusqu'à la dernière ~** [*combattant*] to fight to the last drop of blood; [*malade*] to hold out to the last; **(en) être à la dernière ~** to be on the point of death, to be close to death; **3** fig (acte désespéré) extreme; **pousser qn jusqu'à la dernière ~** to push sb to the brink; **pousser qn à une fâcheuse ~** to drive sb to extremes; **se livrer à des ~s** gén to do something extreme; (être violent) to resort to violence; **je crains qu'il ne se livre à quelque regrettable ~** I'm afraid he might do something silly; **4** Anat extremity; **avoir de petites ~s** to have small hands and feet.

extrudeuse /ɛkstʀydøz/ *nf* extruder.

extrusion /ɛkstʀyzjɔ̃/ *nf* Ind, Tech (procédé) extrusion.

exubérance /ɛgzybeʀɑ̃s/ *nf* **1** (de personne, style) exuberance; **avec ~** [*parler*] with exuberance; [*agir*] exuberantly; **2** (de forêt, végétation) luxuriance.

exubérant, **~e** /ɛgzybeʀɑ̃, ɑ̃t/ *adj* **1** [*personne, gestes, joie, œuvre, style*] exuberant; [*imagination*] vivid; **2** [*forêt, végétation, nature*] luxuriant.

exultation /ɛgzyltasjɔ̃/ *nf* exultation.

exulter /ɛgzylte/ [1] *vi* to be exultant (**de qch** with sth), to exult (**de faire** at doing); **après sa victoire, il exultait** after his victory, he was exultant.

exutoire /ɛgzytwaʀ/ *nm* **1** fig outlet; **servir d'~ à qch** to be an outlet for sth; **trouver dans le sport un ~ à son agressivité** to find an outlet for one's agressiveness in sport; **2** Tech outlet.

ex-voto /ɛksvoto/ *nm inv* thanksgiving plaque.

eye-liner, *pl* **~s** /ajlajnœʀ/ *nm* eyeliner.

Ézéchiel /ezekjɛl/ *npr* Ezekiel.

Ff

f, F /ɛf/ *nm inv* **1** (lettre) f, F; **2** (appartement) **F3** 2-bedroom flat GB ou apartment; **3** (*written abbr* = **franc**) **50 F** 50 F.

fa /fa/ *nm inv* (note) F, fa; (en solfiant) fa; **~ dièse** F sharp.

FAB /fab/ *adv*: *abbr* ▶ **franco**.

fable /fɑbl/ *nf* **1** (récit) tale; **~ morale/sociale/politique** moral/social/political tale; **2** Littérat fable; **3** (mensonge) tall story; **il ne cesse d'inventer des ~s** he's always telling tall stories; **je ne te raconte pas une ~** I'm not making it up.
IDIOMES **être la ~ de la ville** (le sujet de conversation) to be the talk of the town; (la risée) to be a laughing stock.

fabliau, *pl* **~x** /fɑblijo/ *nm* fabliau.

fablier /fablije/ *nm* book of fables.

fabricant /fabʀikɑ̃/ *nm* manufacturer.

fabrication /fabʀikasjɔ̃/ *nf* **1** (action de produire) gén making; (pour le commerce) manufacture; **procédé de ~** manufacturing process; **c'est un secret de ~** Ind it's an industrial secret; (de boisson, plat) it's a secret recipe; **il y a un défaut de ~** [*tissu*] it's imperfect; [*machine*] it's faulty; **de ~ française** French-made; **de ~ artisanale** [*banc, potiche*] hand-crafted; [*chocolat*] handmade; [*jambon*] home-cured; [*saucisse*] home-produced; **moutarde de ~ artisanale** ≈ traditional mustard; **~ en série** mass production; **pull/confiture de ma ~** sweater/jam which I made myself; **c'est de ~ maison** it's home-made; **2** pej (de fausses nouvelles) fabrication péj.
■ **~ assistée par ordinateur, FAO** computer-aided manufacturing, CAM.

fabrique /fabʀik/ *nf* **1** (usine) factory; **une ~ de carrelage/pipes** a tile/pipe factory; **2** Hist Relig **la ~, le conseil de ~** *council responsible for the maintenance of a church.*

fabriquer /fabʀike/ [1] **I** *vtr* **1** (produire) gén to make; (industriellement) to manufacture; **produits fabriqués** manufactured goods; **'fabriqué en France'** 'made in France'; **fabriqué en usine/à la main** factory-/handmade; **fabriqué en série** mass-produced; **fabriqué selon des méthodes artisanales** [*objet*] hand-crafted; [*moutarde*] traditional; **2** (pour tromper) to forge [*faux papiers, fausse monnaie*]; to invent [*alibi*]; **c'est une histoire fabriquée** it's a made-up story; **c'est fabriqué de toutes pièces** it's a complete fabrication; **3**○ (faire) **qu'est-ce que tu fabriques?** what are you up to?; **qu'est-ce que tu fabriques ici?** what are you doing here?
II se fabriquer *vpr* **1** (pour soi) **se ~** to make [sth] for oneself [*meuble, appareil*]; **se ~ un personnage** to create a persona for oneself; **2** Comm, Ind to be manufactured; **cela se fabrique au Japon** it's manufactured in Japan.

fabulateur, -trice /fabylatœʀ, tʀis/ *nm,f* compulsive liar.

fabulation /fabylasjɔ̃/ *nf* **1** (fable) lie, tale; **2** (mythomanie) compulsive lying.

fabuler /fabyle/ [1] *vi* **1** (inventer) to make things up; **2** Psych to confabulate.

fabuleusement /fabyløzmɑ̃/ *adv* fabulously.

fabuleux, -euse /fabylø, øz/ *adj* **1** (extraordinaire) [*beauté, temps, richesse*] fabulous; [*somme*] fantastic; **j'ai eu une chance fabuleuse** I had a fantastic stroke of luck; **2** (de légende) [*animal, monstre, être*] mythical.

fabuliste /fabylist/ *nmf* fabulist.

fac○ /fak/ *nf* **1** (faculté) faculty; **2** (université) university; **être en ~** to be at university GB, to be in college US.

façade /fasad/ *nf* **1** Archit, Constr front, façade; **avec deux chambres en ~** with two front bedrooms; **la ~ arrière** the back; **~ nord/est** north/east side; **2** (apparence) façade; **ce n'est qu'une ~** it's all a façade; **tout pour la ~!** it's all for show!
IDIOMES **se refaire la ~**◑ to put one's face on◑.

face /fas/ **I** *nf* **1** (visage) face; **~ à face** face to face; **(étendu) ~ contre terre** lying face downward(s); **à la ~ de qn** [*proclamer, jeter*] in sb's face; **les muscles/os de la ~** the facial muscles/bones; **le côté ~ d'une pièce** the heads side of a coin; **le côté ~ d'une médaille** the face of a medal; ▶ **pile**; **2** (côté) side; **la ~ nord/antérieure/cachée** the north/front/hidden side; **3** (aspect) side; **examiner un problème sous toutes ses ~s** to examine a problem from all sides; **la ~ changeante du monde** the changing face of the world; **une question à plusieurs ~s** a multifaceted question; **la nouvelle gare change la ~ du quartier** the new station changes the look of the district; **la ~ cachée de la politique** the underside of politics; **4** (front) **faire ~** (résister) to face up to things; **se faire ~** (être vis-à-vis) [*personnes*] to face each other; [*objets, maisons*] to be opposite one another; (s'affronter) to confront each other; **faire ~ à** [*maison, chambre*] to face [*lieu*]; [*personne*] to face [*adversaire, défi, accusation*]; to cope with [*exigences, dépenses*]; to meet [*demande, besoin, dette*]; to measure up to [*concurrence*]; **faire ~ à l'inflation/à la sécheresse** to tackle inflation/the drought; **5** Imprim (de caractère) typeface; **6** Dent (de dent) surface.
II de face *loc* [*photo*] fullface (*épith*); [*éclairage*] frontal; **il ne peint/photographie jamais de ~** he never paints people/takes pictures fullface; **elle est plus jolie de ~** she's prettier from the front; **je n'ai pas pu le voir de ~** I couldn't see him from the front; **les cyclistes avaient le vent de ~** the cyclists were riding into the wind; **les deux voitures se sont heurtées de ~** the two cars collided head-on; **aborder un problème de ~** to tackle a problem head-on; **prendre une loge de ~** Théât to take a box facing the stage; **je préfère être assis de ~ au cinéma** I prefer to sit in the centre seats at the cinema.
III en face *loc* **il habite en ~** he lives opposite; **les gens d'en ~** the people opposite; **en ~, on peut voir une tapisserie** opposite, you see a tapestry; **en ~, les joueurs étaient mieux entraînés** the other team was better trained; **avoir le soleil en ~** to have the sun in one's eyes; **regarder la mort en ~** to look death in the face; **voir les choses en ~** to see things as they are; **je leur ai dit la vérité en ~** I told them the truth straight out; **elle n'a pas osé te le dire en ~** she didn't dare tell you to your face; **les partis/l'équipe d'en ~** the opposing parties/team; **le camp d'en ~** gén the opposite side; Pol the opposite camp.
IV en face de *loc prép* **1** (devant) **en ~ de l'église** opposite the church GB, across from the church; **le couple en ~ de moi** the couple opposite me; **ils étaient assis l'un en ~ de l'autre** or **en ~ l'un de l'autre** they were sitting opposite ou facing each other; **2** (en présence de) **ne dis pas ça en ~ des enfants** don't say that in front of the children; **en ~ de lui, elle ne rit jamais** she never laughs in his presence; **en ~ de difficultés imprévues** faced with unexpected difficulties; **3** (comparé à) compared with; **en ~ de ton frère, il paraît timide** compared with your brother, he seems shy.
V face à *loc prép* **1** (devant) **parler ~ aux caméras** to speak facing the cameras; **mon lit est ~ à la fenêtre** my bed faces the window; **2** (confronté à) **~ à cette situation/à l'insuffisance de crédits** in view of this situation/of the shortage of funds.
■ **~ de carême** sourpuss○; **~ de rat**○ rat face○.
IDIOMES **perdre/sauver la ~** to lose/save face; **se voiler** or **couvrir** or **cacher la ~** not to face facts.

face-à-face /fasafas/ *nm inv* (débat) one-to-one debate GB, one-on-one debate US; (confrontation) encounter.

face-à-main, *pl* **faces-à-main** /fasamɛ̃/ *nm* lorgnette.

facétie /fasesi/ *nf* **1** (plaisanterie) facetious remark; **dire des ~s** to make facetious remarks; **2** (farce) practical joke; **faire des ~s** to play tricks.

facétieusement /fasesjøzmɑ̃/ *adv* mischievously.

facétieux, -ieuse /fasesjø, øz/ *adj* [*personne, esprit, nature*] mischievous.

facette /fasɛt/ *nf* lit, fig facet; **à plusieurs ~s** multifaceted; **les multiples ~s de** the many facets of.

fâché, ~e /fɑʃe/ **I** *pp* ▶ **fâcher**.
II *pp adj* **1** (en colère) angry (**contre** with); **2** (brouillé) **être ~ avec qn** to have fallen out with sb; **être ~ avec le latin**○ hum to be no good at Latin; **3** (désolé) sorry (**de qch** about sth); **je ne suis pas ~ de son échec/de les voir partir/qu'ils partent** I'm not sorry he failed/to see them go/that they are leaving; **je suis ~ de leur départ/de vous voir triste** I'm sorry that they are leaving/to see you so sad.

fâcher /fɑʃe/ [1] **I** *vtr* **1** (mettre en colère) to make [sb] angry (**en faisant** by doing); (contrarier, chagriner) to upset [sb] (**en faisant** by doing); **2** (brouiller) **~ qn avec qn** to make sb fall out with sb; **~ deux amis** to make two friends fall out.
II se fâcher *vpr* **1** (se mettre en colère) to get angry (**contre qn** with sb; **à propos de qch, pour qch** about sth); (en perdant le contrôle de soi-même) to lose one's temper (**contre qn** with sb; **à propos de qch, pour qch** over sth); **arrête, ou je vais me ~** stop doing

that, or I'll be cross; **2** (se brouiller) to fall out (**avec qn** with sb; **à propos de qch, pour qch** over sth).
IDIOMES **se ~ tout rouge**○ to be hopping mad○.

fâcherie○ /fɑʃʀi/ *nf* falling out ¢.

fâcheusement /fɑʃøzmɑ̃/ *adv* (regrettablement) unfortunately; (désagréablement) disagreeably.

fâcheux, **-euse** /fɑʃø, øz/ liter **I** *adj* **1** (néfaste) [*influence, exemple*] detrimental; **2** (malencontreux) [*retard, initiative*] unfortunate; **il est ~ qu'il soit** it is unfortunate that he is; **3** (disgracieux) [*effet*] unpleasing; **4** (affligeant) [*nouvelle, événement*] distressing.
II *nm,f* irritating person.

facho○ /faʃo/ *adj, nmf* fascist.

facial, **~e**, *mpl* **-iaux** /fasjal, o/ *adj* Anat facial; ▸ **valeur**.

faciès /fasjɛs/ *nm* **1** Anthrop, Méd facies; **2** (expression) face; **~ énergique/repoussant** strong/repulsive face; **3** Bot, Géol facies; **~ marin/sableux** marine/sandy facies; **4** Archéol culture.

facile /fasil/ **I** *adj* **1** (sans difficulté) easy; **travail/examen/argent ~** easy job/examination/money; **rien de plus ~ (que)** nothing could be easier (than); **c'est tout ce qu'il y a de ~** it's the easiest thing in the world; **assez ~** easy enough; **~ comme tout** as easy as pie; **avoir une** or **la vie ~** to have an easy life; **un travail ~ à faire** an easy job to do; **une erreur/comparaison ~ à faire** an easy mistake/comparison to make; **une personne ~ à vivre** an easy-going person; **il n'est pas ~ à vivre** he's not very easy-going; **~ à casser/définir/éviter** easy to break/define/avoid; **il est** or **c'est ~ de faire** it is easy to do; **ce n'est pas ~ de la croire** it is not easy to believe her; **c'est ~ à comprendre** it's easy to understand; **il m'est/leur est ~ de faire** it is easy for me/them to do; **il ne m'a pas été ~ de les rencontrer** it was not easy for me to meet them; **c'est ~ à dire** it's easy for you/her etc to say; **c'est plus ~ à dire qu'à faire** that's easier said than done; **2** (spontané) **avoir le rire/le verbe/la larme ~** to be quick to laugh/talk/cry; **3** (docile) [*personne, enfant, caractère*] easy-going; [*victime, bouc émissaire*] easy; **femme ~** péj loose woman; **4** (médiocre) [*idéologie, style, musique*] facile; **une plaisanterie un peu ~** a facile joke.
II○ *adv* (facilement) easily; **il a soixante ans ~** he's easily sixty; **je peux y aller ~** I can go there easily.

facilement /fasilmɑ̃/ *adv* **1** (sans difficultés) easily; **on ne rentre pas ~ dans le bâtiment** it's not very easy to get into the building; **elle pleure/rit très ~** she's very quick to cry/laugh; **être ~ adaptable/manipulable** [*machine, dispositif*] to be easy to adapt/manipulate; **2**○ (largement) **j'ai mis ~ deux heures pour venir/faire l'exercice** it took me a good two hours to get here/do the exercise.

facilité /fasilite/ **I** *nf* **1** (absence de difficulté) (de travail, jeu) easiness; (d'acte, utilisation, entretien) ease; **la ~ avec laquelle** the ease with which; **avec ~** with ease; **d'une ~ déconcertante** surprisingly easy; **avec plus de ~ que** more easily than; **d'une grande ~ (d'utilisation)** very easy (to use); **~ d'accès** easy access; **2** (d'expression, de style) fluency; **j'envie ta ~** I envy your fluency; **avec ~** fluently; **3** (médiocrité) **tomber dans/éviter la ~** to tend to take/not to take the easy way out; **je n'aime pas la ~** I don't like the easy option; **4** (docilité) placidness; **5** (disposition) **avoir de la ~ pour qch/pour** or **à faire** to have a gift for sth/for doing.
II facilités *nfpl* **1** (possibilités) **~s commerciales/d'importation** commercial/import opportunities; **donner/avoir toutes ~s pour faire** to afford/have every opportunity to do; **2** Fin **~s (de paiement)** easy terms; **~s de caisse/prêt** overdraft/loan facility (*sg*).

faciliter /fasilite/ [1] *vtr* to make [sth] easier (**à** for); **votre aide m'a facilité la tâche** your help made the job easier for me; **~ les choses** to make things easier.

FACOB /fakɔb/ *nm* (*abbr* = **facultatif obligatoire**) open-cover.

façon /fasɔ̃/ **I** *nf* **1** (manière) way; **la seule/meilleure ~ de faire** the only/best way to do; **la bonne ~ de s'y prendre** the right way to go about it; **la ~ dont tu manges, ta ~ de manger** the way you eat; **de cette ~** that way; **de plusieurs/différentes ~s** in several/various ways; **d'une autre ~** in another way, differently; **d'une ~ ou d'une autre** one way or another; **c'est une ~ comme une autre de faire** it's one way of doing; **d'une certaine ~** in a way; **de toute ~, de toutes les ~s** anyway; **de toutes les ~s possibles** in every possible way; **de la même ~** in the same way (**que** as); **à peu près de la même ~** in much the same way (**que** as); **agir de la même ~** to do the same; **de la ~ suivante** in the following way; **il a une ~ bien à lui** he's got his own particular way of doing things; **il a une drôle de ~ de voir/faire les choses** he has a funny way of looking at/doing things; **en voilà une ~ de travailler!** what a way to work!; **de telle ~ que personne n'a compris** so that nobody understood; **en aucune ~** in no way; **de ~ décisive** in a decisive way, decisively; **de ~ inattendue** in an unexpected way, unexpectedly; **à ma/ta/leur ~** my/your/their (own) way; **à la ~ de** like; **vivre à la ~ des Espagnols** to live as they do in Spain; **fabriqué de ~ artisanale** made by craftsmen; **de ~ à faire** (en vue de) in order to do; (de telle manière que) in such a way as to do; **de ~ (à ce) qu'elle fasse** so (that) she does; **de ~ qu'on puisse arriver à l'heure** so (that) we can arrive on time; **elle nous a joué un tour de sa ~** she played a trick of her own on us; **elle nous a préparé une salade de sa ~** she made us one of her special salads; **je vais leur dire ma ~ de penser** I'll tell them exactly what I think; **cette ~ de faire ne te/leur ressemble pas** that's not like you/them; **~ de parler** so to speak; **de quelle ~ est-il tombé/a-t-il procédé?** how did he fall/proceed?; ▸ **général I 2**; **2** (imitation) **un peigne ~ ivoire** an imitation ivory comb; **sac ~ sellier** saddle-stitched bag; **doublure ~ soie** silk-look lining; **3** (style) style; **spectacle ~ années 70** a 70's-style show; **~ Einstein/Hollywood** Einstein-/Hollywood-style; **4** (main-d'œuvre) **on m'a donné le tissu et j'ai payé la ~** the cloth was a present and I paid for the making-up; **c'est du tissu de bonne qualité mais la ~ est médiocre** the material is good but the garment is badly made; **travailler à ~** [*personne, atelier*] to work to order (*with supplied materials*); **'travaux à ~'** (vêtements féminins) 'dressmaking'; (vêtements masculins) 'tailoring'.
II façons *nfpl* **1** (attitude) **tes ~s me déplaisent** I don't like the way you behave; **en voilà des ~s!** what a way to behave!; **2** (excès de politesse) **faire des ~s** to stand on ceremony; **ne faites pas tant de ~s** don't stand on ceremony; **sans ~(s)** [*repas*] informal; [*personne*] unpretentious; **il a accepté sans ~s** he accepted with alacrity; **non merci, sans ~s** no thank you, really.

faconde /fakɔ̃d/ *nf* fml loquacity; **avoir de la ~** to be loquacious; **quelle ~!** what a talker!

façonnage /fasɔnaʒ/ *nm* **1** Ind (du bois) hewing; (de la pierre) cutting; (du cuir) sleeking; (du papier) converting; (du pétrole) processing; **contrat de ~** (industrie pétrolière) contractual processing ¢ of crude oil; **2** Imprim forwarding.

façonner /fasɔne/ [1] *vtr* **1** (fabriquer) to manufacture [*outil, pièce*]; to make [*chapeau, objet artisanal*]; **2** Ind to hew [*bois*]; to cut [*pierre*]; to fashion [*argile*]; to sleek [*cuir*]; **3** (former) (par l'éducation) to shape [*personne, caractère*]; (par les épreuves) to mould GB ou mold US [*personne, caractère*]; **~ qn à l'obéissance** to train sb to obey.

fac-similé, *pl* **~s** /faksimile/ *nm* **1** (reproduction) facsimile; **le ~ d'une lettre** a facsimile letter; **une édition en ~** a facsimile edition; **2** Télécom facsimile, fax.

facteur, **-trice** /faktœʀ, tʀis/ ▸ **510** **I** *nm,f* postman/postwoman, mailman/mailwoman US.
II *nm* **1** (élément) factor; **~ de risque/décisif/technique/humain** risk/decisive/technical/human factor; **le ~ chance** the element of chance; **2** Math factor; **~ commun/premier** common/prime factor; **mise en ~s** factorization; **mettre en ~s** to factorize, to factor US; **3** Mus **~ d'orgues** organ builder; **~ de pianos/de cornemuses/de harpes** piano/bagpipe/harp maker.
■ **~ Rhésus** Rhesus factor.

factice /faktis/ *adj* **1** (forcé) [*gaieté, sourire, amabilité*] forced; [*style*] contrived; **2** (imité) [*bijoux*] imitation (*épith*); [*fleur, matière, beauté*] artificial; [*bouteille, étalage*] dummy (*épith*).

facticement /faktismɑ̃/ *adv* artificially.

factieux, **-ieuse** /faksjø, øz/ **I** *adj* [*personne, organisation, journal*] seditious.
II *nm,f* dissident.

faction /faksjɔ̃/ *nf* **1** Pol (ligue factieuse) faction; **2** Mil guard duty; **tour de ~** watch; **être de** or **en ~** Mil to be on guard duty; gén to keep watch; **3** Entr shift.

factionnaire /faksjɔnɛʀ/ *nm* **1** (sentinelle) sentry; **2** (ouvrier) shift worker.

factitif, **-ive** /faktitif, iv/ *adj* factitive.

factoriel, **-ielle** /faktɔʀjɛl/ **I** *adj* factorial; **analyse factorielle** factor analysis.
II factorielle *nf* factorial.

factorisation /faktɔʀizasjɔ̃/ *nf* factorization.

factoriser /faktɔʀize/ [1] *vtr* to factorize, to factor US.

factotum /faktɔtɔm/ *nm* general handyman, factotum hum.

factrice ▸ **facteur I.**

factuel, **-elle** /faktɥɛl/ *adj* factual.

factum /faktum/ *nm* pej lampoon.

facturation /faktyʀasjɔ̃/ *nf* **1** (opération) invoicing; **2** (service) invoicing department.

facture /faktyʀ/ *nf* **1** gén bill; (détaillée) invoice; **faire** or **établir une ~** to make out a bill ou an invoice; **~ de téléphone/d'électricité** telephone/electricity bill; **une fausse ~** a forged ou bogus invoice; **2** (dépense) bill; **~ pétrolière** oil bill; **3** (technique) (d'artisan) craftsmanship; (d'artiste) technique; **un fauteuil d'une belle ~** a finely crafted armchair; **4** Mus (fabrication) (d'orgues) building; (d'instruments) making; **la ~ d'une harpe/d'un piano** the making of a harp/of a piano.
■ **~ détaillée** Comm itemized invoice; **~ pro forma** Comm pro forma invoice.

facturer /faktyʀe/ [1] *vtr* **1** (dresser une facture pour) to invoice [*marchandises*]; **2** (faire payer) to charge for; **je ne vous ai pas facturé la main-d'œuvre/le rétroviseur** I didn't charge you for the labour[GB]/for the rearview mirror.

facturette /faktyʀɛt/ *nf* credit card slip.

facturier, **-ière** /faktyʀje, ɛʀ/ ▸ **510** **I** *nm,f* (employé) invoice clerk.
II *nm* (registre) invoice book.
III facturière *nf* (machine) invoicing machine.

facultatif, **-ive** /fakyltatif, iv/ *adj* optional; **épreuve facultative** optional test; **arrêt ~** Transp request stop; **le vaccin est ~ mais recommandé pour les personnes âgées** the vaccine is not compulsory but is recommended for old people.

facultativement /fakyltativmɑ̃/ *adv* optionally.

faculté /fakylte/ *nf* **1** (aptitude) (sensorielle, intellectuelle) faculty; (physique) ability; **la ~ de parler** the faculty of speech; **~s mentales/intellectuelles** mental/intellectual faculties; **conserver l'usage de ses ~s jusqu'au bout** to keep one's faculties right to the end; **la ~ de marcher** the ability to walk; **avoir une grande ~ d'adaptation** to be very adaptable; **je commençais à douter de mes ~s** I was beginning to doubt the evidence of my senses; **2** (liberté) option (**de faire** of doing); **la ~ de choisir** freedom of choice; **3** Univ faculty; **4** Jur (droit) right (**de faire** to do); **5†** (corps médical) **la Faculté** doctors (*pl*).

fada○ /fada/ **I** *adj* crazy○ (**de** about), nuts○ (**de** about).
II *nmf* nutcase○.

fadaises /fadɛz/ *nfpl* twaddle○ ₵, silly chatter ₵; **raconter des ~** to talk twaddle○.

fadasse○ /fadas/ *adj* [*aliment, goût*] tasteless; [*couleur*] drab; [*cheveux*] dull; [*film, livre, personne*] dull.

fade /fad/ *adj* [*aliment, goût*] tasteless; [*couleur*] drab; [*blondeur*] dull; [*odeur*] sickly; [*spectacle, œuvre, personne*] dull.

fadeur /fadœʀ/ **I** *nf* **1** (de goût) blandness; **2** (de style, conversation) dreariness.
II† fadeurs *nfpl* empty compliments.

fading /fadiŋ/ *nm* fading.

fafiot● /fafjo/ *nm* banknote GB, bill US; **des ~s** dough●, money.

fagot /fago/ *nm* bundle of firewood.
IDIOMES **de derrière les ~s**○ very special; **il nous a sorti une bouteille de derrière les ~s**○ he brought out an old bottle of wine that he'd been saving for a special occasion; **il nous a sorti un projet de derrière les ~s**○ he produced a plan that he had been keeping up his sleeve; **sentir le ~** fml to smack of heresy.

fagoter○ /fagɔte/ [1] **I** *vtr* (habiller) to do [sb] up○.
II se fagoter *vpr* to do oneself up○; (**être**) **mal fagoté** (to be) badly dressed; ▶ **as**.

Fahrenheit /faʀɛnajt/ *nm inv* Fahrenheit; **70 degrés ~** 70 degrees Fahrenheit.

faiblard○, **~e** /fɛblaʀ, aʀd/ *adj* pej [*personne, organisme*] weak; [*rendement, spectacle*] (pretty) poor.

faible /fɛbl/ **I** *adj* **1** (sans force) [*malade, organe, pouls*] weak; [*structure, poutre*] weak; [*résistance, défense*] weak; [*monnaie, économie, marché*] weak; [*vue*] poor; **un enfant ~ de constitution** or **de ~ constitution** a child with a frail constitution; **elle est ~ des poumons** she has weak lungs; **2** (sans fermeté) [*parents, gouvernement*] weak; **il est ~ de caractère** he's got a weak character; **la chair est ~** the flesh is weak; **être ~ avec qn** to be soft with sb, to be too soft on sb; **3** (peu considérable) [*proportion, quantité, différence, progression*] small; [*coût, taux, rendement, revenu*] low; [*moyens, portée*] limited; [*avantage*] slight; [*chance*] slim; **c'était une période de ~ natalité** that was a period when the birthrate was low; **la ~ activité du secteur** the low level of activity in the sector; **à ~ vitesse** [*rouler, percuter*] at a low speed; **substance de ~ toxicité** substance with a low toxic content; **à ~ profondeur** [*être, pousser*] at a shallow depth; **de ~ profondeur** [*étang, récipient*] shallow; **il n'a qu'une ~ idée de ce qui l'attend** he has only a vague idea of what's awaiting him; **4** (sans intensité) [*bruit, voix, lueur, vibrations*] faint; [*éclairage*] dim; [*vent, pluie*] light; **une ~ lueur d'espoir** a faint glimmer of hope; **5** (de peu de valeur) [*résultat*] poor; [*score*] low; [*argument*] feeble; [*production*] weak; **un ~ niveau de qualification/formation** poor qualifications/training; **le scénario est bien ~** the script is very weak; **résultats ~s en langues** poor results in languages; **de ~ importance** [*événement, détail*] of little importance; **c'est une ~ consolation** it's small ou little consolation; **6** (manquant de capacités) [*élève, classe*] slow; **j'ai une classe très ~** I've got a very slow class; **elle est ~ en anglais** she's weak in English; **~ d'esprit** feeble-minded; **7** (peu évocateur) [*mot, expression*] inadequate; **c'est un imbécile et le mot est ~!** he's a fool and that's putting it mildly!; **8** Ling weak.
II *nmf* (personne veule) weak-willed person; **c'est un ~** he's weak-willed.
III *nm* (penchant) weakness; **avoir un ~ pour** to have a weakness for [*aliment, objet*]; to have a soft spot for [*personne*].
IV faibles *nmpl* **les ~s** the weak (+ *v pl*); **les économiquement ~s** the economically disadvantaged.

faiblement /fɛbləmɑ̃/ *adv* **1** (mollement) [*se défendre, protester, sourire*] weakly; **2** (doucement) [*frapper*] gently; [*éclairer*] dimly; [*influencer*] slightly; **3** (peu) [*développé, qualifié*] poorly; [*fréquenté*] barely; [*augmenter*] slightly.

faiblesse /fɛblɛs/ *nf* **1** (manque de force) (de personne, structure) weakness; (d'infirme, de vieillard) frailty; **la ~ de l'homme face aux cataclysmes** man's weakness in the face of cataclysms; **ta ~ de constitution** your frail constitution; **la ~ de ma vue** my poor eyesight; **ses jambes tremblaient de ~** his/her legs were so weak they trembled; **le moteur donne des signes de ~** the engine shows signs of being faulty; **2** (manque de fermeté) weakness (**envers** toward, towards GB); **sans ~** [*réprimer*] ruthlessly; [*répression*] ruthless; **avoir la ~ de faire** to be weak enough to do; **mettre qn/être en position de ~** to put sb/to be in a weak position; **3** (insuffisance) inadequacy; **la ~ de nos revenus** our low level of income; **la ~ de la population dans certaines régions** the low population levels in some areas; **4** (manque d'intensité) (de voix) faintness; (d'éclairage) dimness; (de précipitations) lightness; **5** (défaut) weakness; **les ~s de sa théorie/son raisonnement** the weaknesses in his theory/his reasoning; **6** (médiocrité) weakness; **ta ~ en latin** your weakness in Latin; **la ~ de sa mémoire/pensée** the weakness of his memory/reasoning; **7** (défaillance) **avoir une ~** or **des ~s** to feel faint; **être pris de ~(s)** to feel faint; **8** (acte réprouvé) moment of weakness.

faiblir /fɛbliʀ/ [3] *vi* **1** (perdre de sa force) [*personne, pouls*] to get weaker; **ma vue faiblit** my eyesight is failing; **2** (perdre de sa fermeté) [*personne, mouvement, monnaie*] to weaken; **devant tes pleurs il se sentit ~** he weakened ou felt himself weaken at the sight of your tears; **3** (baisser de niveau) [*sportif*] to flag; [*roman, intrigue, jeu*] to decline; [*mémoire*] to fail; [*attention, intérêt, envie*] to wane; [*espoir*] to fade; [*rendement, taux*] to dwindle; [*vitesse*] to slacken; **il a encore faibli en grec** his standard in Greek has declined; **quel humour, ma parole, tu faiblis!** that wasn't very funny, I think you're losing your touch!; **4** (diminuer d'intensité) [*orage, pluie, vent*] to abate; [*bruit, voix*] to grow faint; [*éclairage, ampoule*] to grow dim.

faïence /fajɑ̃s/ *nf* **1** (matière) earthenware; **de** or **en ~** earthenware (*épith*); **l'assiette est en ~** the plate is made of earthenware; **2** (objet) piece of earthenware; **il a acheté de vieilles ~s** he bought some old earthenware.
IDIOMES **se regarder en chiens de ~** to look daggers at each other.

faïencerie /fajɑ̃sʀi/ **▶510** *nf* **1** (usine) pottery; **2** (objets) glazed earthenware ou pottery; **3** (magasin) china shop.

faille /faj/ *nf* **1** Géol (cassure) fault; **ligne de ~** fault line; **2** (lacune) flaw; **sans ~** unfailing; **fidélité sans ~** unfailing loyalty; **3** (rupture) rift; **~s au sein d'un mouvement** rifts within a movement.

faillibilité /fajibilite/ *nf* fallibility.

faillible /fajibl/ *adj* fallible.

faillir /fajiʀ/ [28] *vi* **1** (avec un infinitif) **elle a failli mourir** she almost ou (very) nearly died; **j'ai failli le gifler** I almost ou (very) nearly slapped him; **ils ont failli rater l'avion** they almost ou (very) nearly missed the plane; **il a failli nous voir** he almost ou (very) nearly saw us; **il a failli gagner** he almost ou (very) nearly won; **2** liter **une vieille recette qui n'a jamais failli** an old recipe which has always been reliable; **sans ~** unfailingly; **~ à ses obligations/engagements** to fail in one's obligations/commitments; **~ à sa réputation** to fall short of one's reputation; **ne pas ~ à la tradition** to live up to the tradition; **le courage/la mémoire lui faillit** his courage/memory failed him.

faillite /fajit/ *nf* **1** Comm, Jur bankruptcy; **se mettre en ~** to file for bankruptcy; **être en ~** to be bankrupt; **faire ~** to go bankrupt; **mettre qn en ~** to declare sb bankrupt; **2** (échec) failure; **la ~ d'une politique/d'un système** the failure of a policy/of a system.
■ **~ frauduleuse** fraudulent bankruptcy.

faim /fɛ̃/ *nf* hunger (**de** for); **grève de la ~** hunger strike; **avoir ~** to be hungry; **avoir ~ de** fig to hunger for; **avoir ~ de liberté** to hunger for freedom; **avoir une ~ de loup** to be ravenous; **donner ~ à qn** to give sb an appetite; **ils ont souffert de la ~ pendant la guerre** they went hungry during the war; **manger à sa ~** to have enough to eat; **tromper sa ~** to stave off (one's) hunger; **mourir de ~** (avoir de l'appétit) to be starving; (par manque de nourriture) to die of starvation; **il est mort de ~** he died of starvation, he starved to death; **le spectacle m'a laissé sur ma ~** the show didn't live up to my expectations; **j'attendais des révélations mais je suis resté sur ma ~** I was expecting some big news but I was disappointed.

faine /fɛn/ *nf* (sur l'arbre) beechnut; (tombée) **des ~s** beechmast ₵.

fainéant, **~e** /feneɑ̃, ɑ̃t/ **I** *adj* lazy.
II *nm,f* layabout○ GB, lazybones (*sg*); ▶ **roi**.

fainéanter /feneɑ̃te/ [1] *vi* to laze about.

fainéantise /feneɑ̃tiz/ *nf* laziness.

faire /fɛʀ/ [10] **I** *vtr* **1** (donner, émettre, produire) to make; **le raisin fera un vin excellent** the grapes will make ou produce (an) excellent wine; **cet arbre fait des fleurs/baies** this tree produces flowers/berries; **le garage ferait une belle pièce** the garage would make a nice room; **ils font un beau couple** they make a handsome couple; **il fera un bon médecin** he'll make a good doctor; **les qualités qui font un champion** the qualities which make a champion; **trois et deux font cinq** three and two make five; **ça fait deux chacun** that makes two each; **combien font 13 fois 13?** what's 13 times 13?; **œil fait yeux au pluriel** œil is yeux in the plural; **2** fig (façonner) to shape [*période*]; **les événements qui font l'histoire** events which shape history; **3** (étudier) to do [*licence, diplôme*]; **on a fait la Chine en géographie** we did China in geography; **~ du violon** to study ou play the violin; **tu as fait ton piano?** have you practised your piano?; **~ une école de commerce/les Beaux-Arts** to go to business school/art college; **4** (préparer) to make [*sauce, soupe, thé*]; to prepare [*salade*]; **~ du poulet** to do ou cook a chicken; **qu'est-ce que je fais pour le déjeuner?** what shall I cook ou prepare for lunch?; **5** (nettoyer) to do, to clean [*vitres*]; to clean, to polish [*chaussures*]; **6** (proposer) Comm to do [*service, marque*]; (vendre) to do, to sell [*article*]; **ils ne font pas le petit déjeuner/les réparations** they don't do breakfast/repairs; **je fais beaucoup ce modèle**

faire

Un très grand nombre de tournures et locutions contenant ce verbe sont traitées ailleurs, généralement sous le terme qui suit *faire*, en particulier:

– les expressions décrivant les tâches domestiques, agricoles (*faire la cuisine/moisson*), les occupations manuelles (*faire du tricot/bricolage*), les activités professionnelles ou de loisir (*faire du théâtre, de la photo*), les types d'études (*faire médecine*). Pour ce qui est des jeux, sports et loisirs, voir également la note d'usage correspondante
– les locutions décrivant un mouvement, l'expression, un comportement (*faire un geste/une grimace/le pitre*)
– les expressions dans lesquelles *faire* signifie 'formuler' (*faire une promesse/offre* etc.)
– les expressions décrivant la qualité de la lumière (*il fait jour/sombre*) ou l'état du temps
– les expressions contenant une mesure (*faire 20 mètres de long/15 kilos/20°/15 kilomètres à l'heure* etc.) pour lesquelles on consultera les notes d'usage
– les expressions décrivant une démarche de l'esprit (*se faire une opinion/du souci* etc.)
– les expressions indiquant l'effet produit (*faire peur/mal/plaisir/du tort* etc., *faire cuire/sécher/tomber* etc.)
– *faire* + *venir/entrer/sortir* etc.
– les locutions telles que *faire semblant/exprès, se faire avoir* etc.
– les expressions familières (*faire un enfant* etc.)

Par ailleurs pour les expressions décrivant:
– une activité sportive (*faire du tennis/de la marche/du parapente*)
– une durée (*ça fait 15 ans*)
la consultation des notes d'usage vous fournira des traductions utiles. Voir la liste ▶ 1920. En outre, certaines entrées telles que ***combien***, ***ce***, ***que***, ***comment***, ***laisser***, ***rien***, ***mieux***, ***bien*** etc. fourniront également des traductions utiles.

***To make* ou *to do*?**

Les principales traductions de *faire* sont *to make* et *to do* mais elles ne sont pas interchangeables.

to make traduit *faire* + objet dénotant ce qui est créé, confectionné, composé, réalisé, obtenu; l'objet est le résultat de l'action:

faire son lit = to make one's bed
faire des confitures = to make jam
faire un discours = to make a speech
faire une faute = to make a mistake
faire un bénéfice = to make a profit
je me suis fait un café = I made myself a coffee

to do a le sens plus vague de se livrer à une activité, s'occuper à quelque chose; l'objet peut préciser la nature de l'activité:

faire de la recherche = to do research
faire un exercice = to do an exercise
faire son devoir = to do one's duty

ou bien la nature de l'activité reste indéterminée:

que fait-il (dans la vie)? = what does he do (for a living)?
qu'est-ce que tu fais ce soir? = what are you doing tonight?
la science peut tout faire = science can do anything
j'ai à faire = I have things to do

ou encore le contexte suggère la nature de l'activité:

faire une pièce = to do a room

peut vouloir dire la nettoyer, la ranger, la peindre.

Si *faire* remplace un verbe plus précis, on traduira fréquemment par celui-ci:

faire une maison = to build a house
faire un nid = to build a nest
faire une lettre = to write a letter
faire une visite = to pay a visit
faire un numéro de téléphone = to dial a number

Les périphrases verbales sont parfois rendues par un seul verbe:

faire voir (= montrer) = to show
faire du tissage (= tisser) = to weave

Mais:

faire un peu de tissage = to do a bit of weaving

Faire + infinitif + qn

faire + infinitive + qn, c'est-à-dire obtenir de quelqu'un qu'il agisse d'une certaine manière, se traduit selon le sens de *faire*, par:

to make sb do sth (forcer, être cause que):

fais-la lever = make her get up
ça m'a fait rire = it made me laugh
ça fait dormir = it makes you sleep

to get sb to do sth (inciter):

fais-leur prendre un rendez-vous = get them to make an appointment

to help sb to do sth (aider):

faire traverser la rue à un vieillard = to help an old man across the street

Mais:

faire manger un bébé = to feed a child

Dans l'exemple *ça fait dormir* on notera qu'en anglais le sujet du verbe est toujours exprimé, ce qui n'est pas le cas en français.

(se) faire faire qch (par qn) se traduit par *to have sth done* ou *made (by sb)*, ou, dans une langue plus familière, *to get sth done* ou *made (by sb)*:

(se) faire construire une maison = to have a house built
(se) faire réparer sa voiture = to have *ou* get one's car repaired
c'est la table qu'il a fait faire = it's the table he had made
elle fait exécuter les travaux par un ami = she's having the work done by a friend

Ne faire que

exprime soit la continuité:

il ne fait que pleuvoir = it never stops raining *ou* it rains all the time

soit la restriction:

je ne fais qu'obéir aux ordres = I'm only obeying orders

Faire reprend un autre verbe

Dans ce cas il sera généralement traduit par *to do*:

'je peux regarder?' 'faites ou faites je vous en prie' = 'may I look?' 'please do'
il souffla, comme il l'avait vu faire à son père = he blew, as he had seen his father do
on veut que je parte, mais je n'en ferai rien = they want me to leave, but I'll do nothing of the sort

Vous trouverez d'autres exemples ci-dessous.

en ce moment I'm selling a lot of this particular model at the moment; **l'hôtel fait-il restaurant?** does the hotel do meals, does the hotel have a restaurant?; **7** (cultiver, produire) Agric **~ des céréales** [*personne*] to grow ou do cereals; [*région*] to produce cereals; **8** (se fournir en) **~ de l'eau** Naut, Rail to take on water; **~ (de) l'essence**○ Aut to get petrol GB ou gas US; **~ du bois dans la forêt** to gather wood in the forest; **~ de l'herbe pour les bêtes** to cut grass for the animals; **9** (parcourir) to do [*distance, trajet*]; to go round [*magasins, agences*]; (visiter) to do○ [*région, ville, musées*]; **~ 200 kilomètres** to do 200 kilometres[GB]; **~ Rome-Nice en avion** to do the Rome-Nice journey by plane; **représentant qui fait**○ **la région parisienne** rep○ who does the Paris area; **j'ai dû ~ toute la ville/toutes les boutiques pour trouver ça** I had to go all over town/round GB ou around US all the shops to find this; **~ la vallée de la Loire** to do○ the Loire Valley; **~ l'Écosse** to visit Scotland; **j'ai fait tous les tiroirs mais je ne l'ai pas trouvé** I went through all the drawers but I couldn't find it; **10** (dans le domaine de la santé) to have [*diabète, tension, complexe*]; **~ une crise cardiaque** to have a heart attack; **~ de la fièvre**○ to have ou run a temperature; **~ de l'angine de poitrine** to get angina; **elle m'a encore fait une otite**○! she's had another ear-infection!; **11** (demander un prix) **~ qch à 30 francs** to sell sth for 30 francs, to charge 30 francs for sth; **il me l'a fait à 500 francs** he charged me ou sold it to me for 500 francs; **12** (servir de) to serve as; **ce coin fera bureau** this corner will serve as a study; **13** (user, disposer de) to do; **que vais-je ~ des bagages/enfants?** what am I going to do with the luggage/children?; **qu'as-tu fait du billet?** what have you done with the ticket?; **pour ce qu'elle en fait!** for all she does with it/them!; **pour quoi ~?** what for?; **je n'ai que ~ de** I have no need for; **je n'en ai rien à ~** it's nothing to do with me; **14** (avoir un effet) **~ plus de mal que de bien** to do more harm than good; **qu'as-tu fait à ta sœur?** what have you done to your sister?; **que veux-tu que j'y fasse?** what do you want me to do about it?, what am I supposed to do about it?; **le cachet ne m'a rien fait** the tablet didn't do anything, the tablet had no effect; **ça y fait** it has an effect; **leur départ ne m'a rien fait** their departure didn't affect me at all, their departure left me cold; **ça me fait quelque chose de la voir dans cet état** it upsets me to see her in that state; **ça fait quelque chose pour la grippe?** is it any good for flu?; **pour ce que ça fait!** for all the good it does!; **ça ne vous fait rien que je fume?** do you mind ou does it bother you if I smoke?; **ça ne fait rien à la chose** it doesn't alter ou change anything, it makes no difference; **qu'est-ce que ça peut bien te ~?** what is it to you?; **15** (entraîner, causer) **~ des jaloux** to make some people jealous; **ça a fait leur fortune** it made them rich; **l'explosion a fait 12 morts** the explosion killed 12 people, the explosion left 12 people dead; **ne t'inquiète pas, ça ne fait rien!** don't worry, it doesn't matter!; **ça fait** ou **ce qui fait que j'ai oublié**○ as a result I forgot; **'qu'est-ce que j'ai fait?'—'tu as fait que tu as menti**○ 'what have I done?'—'you lied, that's what you've done'; **faites que tout se passe bien** make sure that all goes well; **16** (transformer) to make; **l'armée en a fait un homme** the army made a man of him; **ils veulent en ~ un avocat** they want to make a lawyer of him; **elle en a fait sa confidente** she's made her her confidante; **ça a fait de lui un révolté** it turned him into a rebel, it made him a rebel; **j'en ai fait un principe** I made it a principle; **~ d'un garage un atelier** to make ou turn a garage into a workshop; **~ sien qch** to make sth one's own; **17** (proclamer) **~ qn duc/général** to make sb a duke/general; **la presse l'a fait diplomate** (à tort) the press made him out to be a diplomat; **ne le fais pas pire qu'il n'est!** don't make him out to be worse than he is!, don't paint him blacker than he is!; **18** (imiter) **~ le malade/le courageux** to pretend to be ill/brave; **~ l'ignorant** or **celui qui ne sait rien** to pretend not to know; **~ le dictateur** to act the dictator; **19** (tenir le rôle de) to be; **quel plaisantin vous faites!** what a joker you are!; **vous ferez les voleurs!** Jeux you be the robbers!; **l'acteur qui fait le roi**○ Cin, Théât the actor who plays the part of the king, the actor who is the king; **20** (dans un souhait) **mon Dieu, faites qu'il réussisse!** God, please let him succeed!; **Dieu** or **le ciel fasse qu'il ne leur arrive rien!** may God ou Heaven protect them!; **21**○ (tromper) **il me l'a fait au baratin/chantage** he talked/blackmailed me into it; **on ne me la fait pas!** I'm not a fool!, I wasn't born yesterday!

II *vi* **1** (agir, procéder) to do, to act; **je n'ai pas pu ~ autrement** I couldn't do otherwise; **fais comme tu veux** do as you like; **elle peut ~ mieux** she can do better; **dans ces situations, il faut ~ vite** in that sort of situation, one must act quickly; **vas-y, mais fais vite!** go, but be quick about it!; **fais comme chez toi** lit, iron make yourself at home; **2** (paraître) to look; **~ jeune/son âge** to look young/one's age; **ça fait bien avec du bleu** it looks nice with blue; **tes lunettes font très distingué** your glasses make you look very distinguished; **il croit que ça fait chic de dire ça** he thinks it's chic to say that; **3** (être) to be; **il veut ~ pompier** he wants to be a fireman; **4** (dire) to say; **'bien sûr,' fit-elle** 'of course,' she said; **le canard fait 'coin-coin'** the duck says ou goes 'quack'; **~ plouf/aïe etc** to go plop/ouch etc; **5** (durer) to last; **sa robe lui a fait deux ans** her dress lasted her two years; **6** (+ *adv de quantité*) **ça fait cher/grand/trop etc** it is expensive/big/too much etc; **7** (pour les besoins naturels) to go; **tu as fait?** have you been?; **~ dans sa culotte** (déféquer) to dirty one's pants; (uriner) to wet one's pants; fig to wet oneself; **8**○ **~ avec** (se contenter de) to make do with [*personne, objet, quantité*]; (supporter) to put up with [*personne, situation*]; **elle est là, et il faudra ~ avec** she's here, and we'll have to put up with her.

III se faire *vpr* **1** (confectionner, exécuter, obtenir pour soi) **se ~ un café** to make oneself a coffee; **se ~ de l'argent/des amis** to make money/friends; **se ~ ses vêtements** to make one's own clothes; **se ~ la cuisine soi-même** to do one's own cooking; **combien se fait-il par mois?** how much does he make a month? ; **se ~ un mec**◑ to have◑ a man; **2** (devenir) (+ *adj attribut*) to get, to become; (+ *n attribut*) to become; **il se fait vieux** he's getting old; **il se fait tard** it's getting late; **sa voix se fit dure** his/her voice hardened ou became hard; **se ~ avocat** to become a lawyer; **3** (se rendre) **se ~ belle/tout petit** to make oneself beautiful/very small; **4** (s'inquiéter) **s'en ~** to worry; **il ne s'en fait pas!** (sans inquiétude) he's not the sort of person to worry about things!; (pas gêné) he's got a nerve!; **5** (s'habituer) **se ~ à** to get used to [*lieu, situation, idée*]; **je ne m'y fais pas** I can't get used to it; **6** (être d'usage) **ça se fait encore ici** it's still done here; **ça ne se fait pas de manger avec les doigts** it's not the done thing ou it's not polite to eat with one's fingers; **7** (être à la mode) [*couleur, style*] to be in (fashion); **le tweed se fait beaucoup cette année** tweed is very much in this year; **ça ne se fait plus** it's no longer fashionable, it's out of fashion; **8** (être produit ou accompli) **c'est ce qui se fait de mieux** it's the best there is; **le mariage s'est fait à Paris** the wedding took place in Paris; **le pont se fera bien un jour** the bridge will be built one day; **souhaitons que la paix se fasse** let's hope there'll be peace; **9** (emploi impersonnel) **il se fit que** it (so) happened that; **il se fit un grand silence** there was complete silence; **il s'est fait un déclic dans mon esprit** something clicked in my mind; **il pourrait se ~ que je parte** I might leave; **comment se fait-il que...?** how is it that...?; **10** (mûrir) [*fromage*] to ripen; [*vin*] to mature; **11**○ (supporter) to put up with, to endure [*importun*]; **il faut se le ~, son copain!** his/her mate is a real pain○!; **12** (avec infinitif) **se ~ couler un bain** to run oneself a bath; **se ~ comprendre** to make oneself understood; **se ~ agresser** to get mugged; **tu vas te ~ écraser!** you'll get run over!

faire-part /fɛʀpaʀ/ *nm inv* announcement; **~ de naissance** birth announcement; **~ de mariage/décès** marriage/death announcement (*posted to individual*); **'cet avis tient lieu de ~'** 'individual announcements will not be posted'.

faire-valoir /fɛʀvalwaʀ/ *nm inv* **1** Cin, Théât foil; **être le ~ de** to be a foil for; **2** Agric farming; **le ~ direct** farming by the owner.

fair-play /fɛʀplɛ/ controv **I** *adj inv* [*personne*] sporting; **ce n'est pas très ~ de leur part** it's not very sporting of them.

II *nm* **le ~** (en sport) sportsmanship, fair play; (en affaires, relations) sense of fair play; **faire preuve de ~** (en sport) to demonstrate one's sportsmanship; (en affaires) to demonstrate one's sense of fair play.

faisabilité /fəzabilite/ *nf* feasibility; **étude de ~** feasability study.

faisable /fəzabl/ *adj* **c'est/ce n'est pas ~** it can/can't be done.

faisan /fəzɑ̃/ *nm* Zool (cock) pheasant.

faisandé, **~e** /fəzɑ̃de/ *adj* **1** Culin gamey, high; (avarié) bad; **2** (corrompu) [*système, milieu*] tainted, corrupt.

faisandeau, *pl* **~x** /fəzɑ̃do/ *nm* young pheasant.

faisander /fəzɑ̃de/ [1] **I** *vtr* to hang [*gibier*].

II se faisander *vpr* **laisser du gibier se ~** to let game hang.

faisane /fəzan/ *nf* (**poule**) **~** hen pheasant.

faisceau, *pl* **~x** /fɛso/ *nm* **1** (de rayon) beam; **~ lumineux** beam of light; **2** (gerbe) bundle; **3** (ensemble) (de preuves, d'habitudes) body; (d'indices, de raisons, soupçons) array; **4** Anat fasciculus; **~ musculaire/nerveux** fasciculus of muscle/nerve fibres[GB]; **5** Mil (d'armes) stack; **formez les ~x!** stack arms!; **6** Antiq, Hist fasces.

■ **~ électronique** or **d'électrons** electron beam; **~ hertzien** radio link; **~ laser** laser beam; **~ de lignes** Télécom trunk group.

faiseur, **-euse** /fəzœʀ, øz/ *nm,f* **1** (producteur) **~ de miracles** miracle-worker; **~ de rimes** rhymester péj; **c'est un ~ d'histoires** he's a fusspot; **~ de bons mots** pej punster, wag; **~ d'intrigues** pej schemer; **2**† (tailleur) tailor.

■ **~ de tours** conjuror; **faiseuse d'anges**† euph backstreet GB ou back-alley US abortionist.

faisselle /fɛsɛl/ *nf* (récipient) strainer (*to drain the whey from curd cheese*); **du fromage en** or **à la ~** ≈ curd cheese.

fait, **~e** /fɛ, fɛt/ **I** *pp* ▶ **faire**.

II *pp adj* **1** (réalisé, accompli) [*tâche*] done; **ce qui est ~ est ~** what's done is done; **bien/mal ~** well/badly done; **il aime le travail bien ~** he likes work that is well done; **c'en est ~ de** that's the end of; **c'est bien ~**○ **(pour toi/lui/elle)!** it serves you/him/her right!; **bien ~ pour lui**○! serves him right!; **bien ~ pour ta gueule**◑! serves you bloody◑ GB ou damn◑ well right!; **2** (constitué) **~ de/en** (d'un élément) made of; (composite) made up of; **mur ~ en pierre** wall made of stone; **une foule ~e de collectionneurs et d'amateurs** a crowd made up of collectors and enthusiasts; **idée/réponse toute ~e** ready-made idea/answer; **formules toutes ~es** clichés; **elle est bien ~e** she's good-looking; **elle a la taille bien ~e** she has a shapely waist; **un corps merveilleusement/mal ~** a marvellous[GB]/an ugly body; **je suis ainsi ~** that's how I am; **la vie est ainsi ~e!** life's like that!; **la vie/société est mal ~e** life/society is unfair; **3** (adapté) **~ pour qch/pour faire** meant for sth/to do; **ils ne sont pas ~s l'un pour l'autre** they're not meant for each other; **ces ciseaux ne sont pas ~s pour couper de la viande** these scissors are not meant for cutting ou to cut meat; **il n'est pas ~ pour travailler** hum he's not cut out for work hum; **ta remarque n'était pas ~e pour arranger les choses** your comment certainly didn't help matters; **4** (conçu) [*programme, dispositif*] designed; **bien/mal ~** well-/badly-designed; **5**○ (pris) done for; **la maison est cernée, nous sommes ~s!** the house is surrounded, we're done for!; **6** (mûr) **un fromage bien ~** a ripe cheese.

III *nm* **1** (élément de réalité, acte) fact; **le ~ d'avoir** the fact of having; **le ~ de faire/d'avoir fait** (the fact of) doing/of having done; **le ~ d'être heureux** being happy; **le ~ d'être parti/tombé** (the fact of) having left/fallen; **le ~ est là** that's the fact of the matter; **le ~ est là** ou **les ~s sont là, il t'a trompé** the fact (of the matter) is that he cheated you; **le ~ est que tu avais raison/que cela n'a pas marché** the fact is that you were right/that it didn't work; **le ~ même que/de faire** the very fact that/of doing; **le simple ~ de faire** the simple fact of doing, simply doing; **le ~ qu'il est** or **soit possible de faire** the fact that it is possible to do; **il a réussi, c'est un ~, mais...** he has succeeded, certainly, but...; **c'est un ~ que** it's a fact that; **s'appuyer sur des ~s** to rely on facts; **reconnaître les ~s** to acknowledge the facts; **s'incliner devant les ~s** to bow to the facts; **au moment des ~s** at the time of the events; **les ~s et gestes de qn** sb's movements; **les menus ~s de la vie quotidienne** the tiny details of everyday life; **2** (ce qui est la cause) **de ce ~** because of this ou that; **du ~ de qch** due to sth; **du ~ même que/de faire** due to the very fact that/of doing; **du ~ que** due to the fact that; **être le ~ de qn** to be due to sb; **cette rencontre n'est pas le ~ du hasard** this encounter isn't due to chance; **par le ~ du hasard** due to chance; **3** (événement) event; **c'est un ~ unique dans l'histoire** it's an event that's unique in history; **le film part de ~s réels** the film is based on real-life events; **4** (sujet) point; **venons-en au ~** let's get to the point; **au ~, je te prie!** get to the point, please!; **aller droit au ~** to go straight to the point; **5** (ce qui caractérise) **le mensonge** or **mentir n'est pas son ~** it isn't like him to lie; **la patience n'est pas son ~** patience isn't his strong point; **elle lui a dit son ~** she told him straight; **6** (exploit) feat, exploit; **les hauts ~s** heroic deeds.

IV au fait /ofɛt/ *excl* by the way.

V de fait *loc* [*situation, pouvoir, gouverneur*] de facto (*épith*); [*exister, supprimer, entraîner*] effectively; (en effet) indeed.

VI en fait *loc adv* in fact, actually; **il s'agit en ~ de son cousin/de faire** it's actually his cousin/a question of doing; **ce poste lui servait en ~ de couverture** this position actually served as a cover for him.

VII en fait de *loc prép* as regards; **en ~ de réforme/philosophie, il s'agit plutôt d'une...** it isn't so much a reform/a philosophy as a...; **en ~ de rénovation du système, ils (en) ont seulement changé quelques éléments** they haven't so much renovated the system as tinkered about at the edges.

■ **~ accompli** fait accompli; **mettre qn devant le ~ accompli** to present sb with a fait accompli; **~ d'actualité** news item; **~ d'armes** feat of arms; **~ divers** Presse (short) news item; **la rubrique (des) '~s divers'** the 'news in brief' column; **~ de guerre** exploit of war; **~ du prince** fiat; **~ de société** fact of life.

IDIOMES **être au ~ de** fml to be informed about; **mettre qn au ~** fml to inform sb; **être sûr de son ~** to be sure of one's facts; **prendre qn sur le ~** to catch sb in the act; ▸**cause**.

faîtage /fɛtaʒ/ *nm* **1** (pièce de charpente) ridgepole; **2** (couverture) roofing.

faîte /fɛt/ *nm* **1** (sommet) (de montagne) summit; (de maison) rooftop; (d'arbre) top; **2** Constr (faîtage) ridgepole; **3** fig (apogée) pinnacle.

faîtière /fɛtjɛʀ/ *adj f* **tuile ~** ridge tile; **lucarne ~** skylight.

faitout /fɛtu/ *nm* stockpot.

faix† /fɛ/ *nm* burden.

fakir /fakiʀ/ *nm* fakir.

falaise /falɛz/ *nf* cliff.

falbalas /falbala/ *nmpl* pej **1** Mode frills and flounces péj; **2** fig frills.

fallacieux, **-ieuse** /falasjø, øz/ *adj* [*argument*] fallacious; [*promesse, prétexte*] false; [*ressemblance*] deceptive; [*espoir*] illusory; **il est ~ de penser que** it's a fallacy to think that.

falloir /falwaʀ/ [50] **I** *v impers* **1 il faut qch/qn** gén we need sth/sb (**pour faire** to do); (sans bénéficiaire) sth/sb is needed ou necessary (**pour faire** to do); **il faudrait trois voitures/trois hommes** we would need three cars/three men; **ce qu'il faut** what is needed; **ce n'est pas ce qu'il faut** this isn't what is needed ou what we need; **ce n'est pas l'outil qu'il faut** that's not the right tool ou the tool we need; **il va ~ plusieurs personnes** it will take several people; **il faut au moins deux jours/dix ans** it takes at least two days/ten years; **il faut de la patience/du courage** it takes patience/courage (**pour faire** to do); **il en faut pour qu'il se fâche** it takes a lot to make him angry; **il en faudrait plus pour m'énerver** it would take more than that to get me annoyed; **il n'en faut pas beaucoup pour te faire rire** it doesn't take much to make you laugh; **c'est plus qu'il n'en faut** it's more than enough; **2 il me/te/leur faut qch** I/you/they need sth; **il me/te/leur faut faire** I/you/they have to do ou must do; **il leur faut 20 000 F et trois ouvriers** they need 20,000 francs and three workmen; **il m'a fallu trois heures pour finir** it took me three hours to finish; **il me faut (absolument) ce livre!** I've got to have that book!; **il vous faudra partir à 8 heures** you'll have to leave at 8 o'clock; **il m'a fallu refuser** I had to refuse; **il ne leur a pas fallu longtemps pour comprendre/finir** they soon understood/finished; **pas assez grand? qu'est-ce qu'il te faut?** not big enough? what more do you want?; **3 il faut faire** (nécessité) we've/you've etc got to do, we/you etc have to do; (autorité, supposition) we/you etc must do; (conseil, suggestion) we/you etc should do; (convenance, reproche) we/you etc ought to do; **il ne faut pas faire** (autorité) we/you etc mustn't do; (conseil) we/you etc shouldn't do; **il faut trouver une solution** we've got to ou we must find a solution; **il faut être fou/idiot pour faire** you'd have to be mad/stupid to do; **il va ~ payer** we'll have to pay up; **il faut manger des fruits** you should eat fruit; **'tu vas payer?'—'il faut bien!'** 'are you going to pay?'—'I have to!'; **il faut faire quelque chose pour elle** something has to ou must be done for her; **il ne faut pas la déranger** she mustn't be disturbed; **il fallait venir me voir!** you should have come to see me!; **faudrait pas me prendre pour un imbécile**○! do you think I'm a fool?; **'tu crois que ça marchera?'—'sais pas, faut voir**○**'** 'do you think it'll work?'—'don't know, we'll have to see'; **il faut l'entendre raconter ses histoires** you should hear him/her tell his/her stories; **qu'est-ce qu'il ne faut pas entendre!** what a lot of nonsense!; **s'il fallait croire tout ce qu'on raconte!** you can't believe everything people say!; **il faut souhaiter que tout ira bien** we'll just have to hope that everything goes well; **il faut dire que** I/you/we etc have to ou must say that; **il faut vous dire que** you should know that; **fallait le dire plus tôt**○! why didn't you say so before?; **nous ne savions pas encore, faut-il le rappeler, qu'il serait élu** it must be remembered that we didn't know then that he would be elected; **il faut le voir pour le croire** it has to be seen to be believed; **il fallait le faire** it had to be done; **faut/fallait le faire**○! (c'est remarquable) it takes/took a bit of doing!; (c'est stupide) would you believe it?; **puisqu'il le faut** since it has to be done; **on va opérer, il le faut** they're going to operate, they've no choice; **s'il le faut** (nécessité) if necessary; (obligation) if I/we/they etc have to; **elle n'en fait pas plus qu'il ne faut** she doesn't do any more than she has to; **il ne fallait pas!** (politesse) you shouldn't have!; **comme il faut** [*agir, se tenir*] properly; **elle est très comme il faut** she's very proper; **encore faudra-t-il trouver de l'argent** we/you/they etc will still have to find the money; **encore faut-il préciser que** it should be added that; **4 il faut que tu fasses** (obligation) you must do, you've got to do, you have to do; (conseil) you should do; (convenance, reproche) you ought to do; **il faut absolument qu'on trouve une solution** we've got to find a solution; **il fallait que ce soit fait** it had to be done; **pourquoi fallait-il que ce soit moi?** why did it have to be me?; **pourquoi fallait-il qu'elle arrive à ce moment-là?** why did she have to turn up just then?; **il faut qu'ils aient été retardés** there must have been some delay; **faut-il qu'elle l'aime pour le croire!** she must love him to believe him!; **je n'ai pas de nouvelles, il faut croire que tout va bien** I haven't heard anything, I just have to suppose everything's all right; **il fallait que cette sacrée**○ **voiture tombe en panne maintenant!** the damn○ car would have to (go and) break down now!; **encore faut-il qu'elle accepte** she's still got to agree; **encore fallait-il qu'elle accepte** she hadn't agreed yet; **encore faudra-t-il qu'elle accepte** she'll still have to agree; **encore faudrait-il qu'elle accepte** she'd still have to agree.

II s'en falloir *vpr* **loin** or **tant s'en faut** far from it; **peu s'en faut** very nearly; **il s'en faut de beaucoup** very far from it; **elle a perdu, mais il s'en est fallu de peu** she lost, but only just; **il s'en est fallu de peu qu'il gagne** he nearly won, he came very close to winning; **il s'en est fallu de 15 secondes qu'elle gagne** she nearly won, there was only 15 seconds in it; **il s'en est fallu d'un rien** or **de presque rien** there was almost nothing in it.

IDIOMES **il faut ce qu'il faut!** there's no point in skimping!; **en moins de temps qu'il ne faut pour le dire** before you could say Jack Robinson.

falot, **~e** /falo, ɔt/ **I** *adj* [*personne*] insignificant.

II *nm* lantern.

falsificateur, **-trice** /falsifikatœʀ, tʀis/ *nm,f* falsifier.

falsification /falsifikasjɔ̃/ *nf* **1** (altération) (de document, comptes) falsification; (de faits, vérité) distortion, falsification; **2** (imitation) forging.

falsifier /falsifje/ [2] *vtr* **1** (altérer) to falsify, to tamper with [*document, comptes, chèque*]; to distort, to falsify [*faits, histoire*]; **2** (contrefaire) to forge [*signature, monnaie*].

faluche /falyʃ/ *nf* B (pain) soda bread.

falzar◐ /falzaʀ/ *nm* trousers (*pl*) GB, pants (*pl*) US.

famé, **~e** /fame/ *adj* **un quartier mal ~** a disreputable ou seedy area; **des cafés mal ~s** disreputable ou shady cafés; **une rue pas très bien ~e** a street of rather ill repute, a rather seedy street.

famélique /famelik/ *adj* [*personne*] emaciated; [*animal*] scrawny.

fameusement /famøzmɑ̃/ *adv* (rudement) remarkably; **~ bien rédigé** remarkably well edited.

fameux, **-euse** /famø, øz/ *adj* **1** (dont on a parlé) much talked-about; **la fameuse conférence de paix** the much talked-about peace conference; **2** (connu de tous) famous; **les ~ bus londoniens à deux étages** the famous London double-deckers; **c'est le ~ soir où** it was the famous night when; **3** (véritable) real, right; **une fameuse bande de fainéants** a real bunch of lazybones; **4** (excellent) excellent; **le repas était ~** the meal was excellent; **pas ~** not great; **ma note n'est pas fameuse** my mark is not great.

familial, **~e**, *mpl* **-iaux** /familjal, o/ **I** *adj* **1** (de famille) [*repas, équilibre, budget*] family (*épith*); **la cellule ~e** the family unit; **la vie ~e** family life; **une entreprise ~e** a family business; **pour des raisons ~es** for family reasons; **2** Aut **berline ~e** estate car GB, station wagon US.

II familiale *nf* Aut estate car GB, station wagon US.

familiariser /familjaʀize/ [1] **I** *vtr* (habituer) to familiarize (**avec** with); (initier) to introduce [sb] to [*politique, langue, science*]; **~ les enfants avec les ordinateurs** to familiarize children with computers; **~ un employé avec l'informatique** to introduce an employee to computing.

II se familiariser *vpr* (s'habituer) to familiarize oneself (**avec** with); (s'initier) to gain knowledge (**avec** of); **se ~ avec son travail/environnement** to familiarize oneself with one's job/environment.

familiarité /familjaʀite/ *nf* **1** (connaissance) familiarity (**avec** with); **~ avec l'art japonais/la région** familiarity with Japanese art/the area; **2** (intimité) familiarity ¢; **~ excessive** undue familiarity; **pas de ~s** don't be too familiar; **il s'est permis des ~s avec moi** he was too familiar with me.

familier, **-ière** /familje, ɛʀ/ **I** *adj* **1** (connu) [*visage, paysage, nom*] familiar (**à** to); **l'auteur ne m'est pas ~** the author is not familiar to me; **2** Ling [*mot, tournure, style*] informal, colloquial; **3** (sans façon) [*entretien, attitude*] informal; [*personne, geste*] familiar; **être ~ avec son personnel** to be familiar with one's staff; **4** (sans gêne) pej [*personne, manières*] familiar; **5** (domestique) **animal ~** pet; **6** (informé) familiar (**de** with); **un expert ~ du projet** an expert familiar with the project; **elle est familière de la littérature russe** she is familiar with Russian literature.

II *nm* **1** (ami proche) close friend (**de** of); **2** (habitué) regular; **les ~s du bar/du quartier** the regulars at the bar/in the neighbourhood[GB].

familièrement /familjɛʀmɑ̃/ *adv* **1** (communément) [*appeler, désigner*] commonly; **on l'appelait ~ Toto** he was commonly called Toto; **2** (sans façon) [*parler, se comporter*] informally; **3** (de manière inconvenante) [*parler, se comporter*] with undue familiarity.

famille /famij/ *nf* **1** Sociol family; **la ~ Pons** the Pons family; **~ monoparentale/nucléaire** one-parent/nuclear family; **une ~ de musiciens** a musical family; **air de ~** family resemblance; **c'est de ~** it runs in the family; **faire partie de la ~** to be one of the family; **je pars en ~** I'm going with my family; **nous partons en ~** we're going as a family; **de ~** [*photo, album, histoire, arrangement*] family (*épith*); **ne pas avoir de ~** to have no relatives; **avoir beaucoup de ~ dans la région** to have lots of relatives in the area; **ma seule ~**

est un vieil oncle my only relative is an old uncle; **rentrer dans sa ~ tous les samedis** to go back home every Saturday; **comment va la petite ~**○? how's the family?; **un petit vin des ~s**○ a nice little wine; **être de bonne ~** to come from a good family; ▶**sept**, **linge**; **2** Art, Pol, Relig (communauté) body; **la ~ socialiste/surréaliste** the socialist/surrealist body; **une ~ politique** a political persuasion; **3** Biol, Bot, Zool family; **4** Ling family; **~ de langues/mots** language/word family.
■ **~ d'accueil** host family; **~ adoptive** adoptive family; **~ naturelle** natural family; **~ nombreuse** family with more than two children; **~ de placement** foster family.

famine /famin/ *nf* famine; **salaire de ~** starvation wages (*pl*); **crier ~** to be starving.

fan /fan/ *nmf* (admirateur) fan.

fana○ /fana/ **I** *adj* mad keen○ GB, crazy○ (**de** about).
II *nmf* fanatic; **c'est un ~ d'informatique** he's a computer fanatic ou freak○; **un ~ de cinéma** a film buff.

fanage /fanaʒ/ *nm* tossing, tedding spéc.

fanal, *pl* **-aux** /fanal, o/ *nm* gén lamp; Naut lantern, (navigation) light; Rail headlamp, headlight.

fanatique /fanatik/ **I** *adj* [*religieux, militant, mouvement*] fanatical; [*admiration, amour*] ardent, unbridled.
II *nmf* **1** (extrémiste religieux) fanatic, fundamentalist; **2** (extrémiste politique) fanatic, extremist; **3**○ (enthousiaste) enthusiast, freak○; **c'est un ~ d'informatique** he's a computer enthusiast ou freak○.

fanatiquement /fanatikmɑ̃/ *adv* fanatically.

fanatiser /fanatize/ [1] *vtr* to fanaticize, to inflame [*peuple, masses*]; **les militants fanatisés criaient des slogans vengeurs** the fanatical militants shouted vengeful slogans.

fanatisme /fanatism/ *nm* fanaticism.

faner /fane/ [1] **I** *vtr* **1** (faire perdre sa fraîcheur à) [*soleil, chaleur*] to wither [*plante*]; **2** (altérer l'éclat de) [*temps, lumière*] to fade [*couleur*]; **le temps a fané son visage** time has taken the bloom from her face; **3** Agric (faire sécher) to toss, to ted spéc [*herbe*].
II *vi* **1** (se flétrir) [*fleurs, plantes*] to wither, to wilt; **2** Agric (faire les foins) to make hay.
III se faner *vpr* **1** [*fleurs, plantes*] to wither, to wilt; **2** [*beauté, couleur*] to fade.

faneur, **-euse** /fanœʀ, øz/ ▶**510** **I** *nm,f* (personne) haymaker.
II faneuse *nf* (machine) tedder.

fanfare /fɑ̃faʀ/ *nf* **1** (orchestre) brass band; **la ~ municipale** the town brass band; **annoncer qch en ~** fig to trumpet sth, to give sth great publicity; **la création de nouveaux emplois a été annoncée en ~ par le gouvernement** the creation of new jobs was loudly trumpeted ou widely publicized by the government; **faire une entrée en ~** to make a spectacular entry; **faire une arrivée en ~** to arrive in spectacular fashion; **tous les matins les enfants nous réveillent en ~** every morning the children wake us up with a great commotion; **2** (air) fanfare.

fanfaron, **-onne** /fɑ̃faʀɔ̃, ɔn/ **I** *adj* [*personne, air, comportement*] boastful, cocky○; [*politique*] arrogant.
II *nm,f* boaster, swaggerer; **faire le ~** to boast, to talk big○.

fanfaronnade /fɑ̃faʀɔnad/ *nf* boasting ¢.

fanfaronner /fɑ̃faʀɔne/ [1] *vi* to boast.

fanfreluches /fɑ̃fʀəlyʃ/ *nfpl* Mode frills and flounces.

fange /fɑ̃ʒ/ *nf* mud, mire; **se complaire dans la ~** fig to wallow in the mire; **son nom a été traîné dans la ~** his name was dragged through the mud.

fangeux, **-euse** /fɑ̃ʒø, øz/ *adj* **1** (boueux) muddy; **2** fig (dépravé) depraved.

fanion /fanjɔ̃/ *nm* gén pennant.

fanon /fanɔ̃/ *nm* **1** (de baleine) baleen plate; **les ~s** whalebone ¢; **2** (repli cutané) (de reptile, dindon) wattle; (de bovin, chien) dewlap; **3** (de cheval) fetlock.

fantaisie /fɑ̃tezi/ *nf* **1** (qualité) imaginativeness; **être plein de ~** [*personne*] to be full of marvellous[GB] ideas; [*roman*] to be highly imaginative; [*logement*] to be unconventional; **manquer de ~** [*personne*] to be staid; [*logement*] to be conventional; [*vie*] to be dull; **2** (preuve d'originalité) **ne pouvoir se permettre aucune ~** to have to behave in a conventional way; **3** (envie soudaine) whim, fancy; **4** (humeur) fancy; **vivre selon sa ~** to do as one pleases; **5** (de peu de valeur) **s'offrir une petite ~** (objet) to buy oneself a little something; (sortie, petit voyage) to spoil oneself; **un bijou ~** a piece of costume jewellery GB ou jewelry US; **accessoires ~** fun accessories; **verres ~** novelty glasses; **alcool ~** *liqueur comprising spirit base and artificial flavouring*[GB]; **6** Mus fantasia, fantasy; Littérat fantasy.

fantaisiste /fɑ̃tezist/ **I** *adj* **1** (peu fiable) [*personne, renseignement, horaires, procédé*] unreliable; [*chiffres, interprétation*] doubtful; **2** (excentrique) [*idée*] far-fetched; [*procédé*] odd; [*personne*] eccentric.
II *nmf* mildly eccentric person.

fantasmagorie /fɑ̃tasmagɔʀi/ *nf* phantasmagoria.

fantasmagorique /fɑ̃tasmagɔʀik/ *adj* phantasmagoric, fantastical.

fantasmatique /fɑ̃tasmatik/ *adj* fantastical.

fantasme /fɑ̃tasm/ *nm* fantasy.

fantasmer /fɑ̃tasme/ [1] *vi* to fantasize (**sur** about).

fantasque /fɑ̃task/ *adj* [*personnage, comportement*] unpredictable; [*image, récit*] fanciful.

fantassin /fɑ̃tasɛ̃/ *nm* infantryman, footsoldier; **les ~s** the infantry.

fantastique /fɑ̃tastik/ **I** *adj* **1** (qui paraît surnaturel) [*spectacle, beauté*] fantastic; **2** (imaginaire) [*créature, personnage*] fantastic; **3**○ (formidable) fantastic○; **4** Art, Cin, Littérat [*film, récit, roman*] fantasy; **le cinéma ~** fantasy films.
II *nm* Art, Cin, Littérat (genre) **le ~** fantasy.

fantastiquement○ /fɑ̃tastikmɑ̃/ *adv* fantastically○.

fantoche /fɑ̃tɔʃ/ **I** *adj* [*gouvernement, organisation*] puppet.
II *nm* **1** (marionnette) puppet; **2** (individu sans personnalité) puppet, cypher GB ou cipher US.

fantomatique /fɑ̃tɔmatik/ *adj* ghostly.

fantôme /fɑ̃tom/ **I** *nm* **1** (spectre) ghost; **2** (souvenir obsédant) ghost, haunting memory.
II (-)fantôme (*in compounds*) **cabinet-~** Pol shadow cabinet GB, ≈ minority leadership US; **image(-)~** Électron, TV ghost; **membre(-)~** Méd phantom limb; **société(-)~** Jur dummy company; **train(-)~** ghost train; **ville(-)~** ghost town.

FAO /ɛfao/ *nf* **1** Écon, Pol (*abbr* = **Food and Agriculture Organization**) FAO; **2** Ordinat *abbr* ▶**fabrication**.

faon /fɑ̃/ *nm* fawn.

faquin‡ /fakɛ̃/ *nm* wretch, scoundrel.

faramineux○, **-euse** /faʀaminø, øz/ *adj* [*prix, somme*] colossal, staggering; [*bêtise*] incredible.

farandole /faʀɑ̃dɔl/ *nf* (danse traditionnelle) farandole; (à la fin d'une soirée) ≈ conga; **faire la ~** (traditionnelle) to dance the farandole; (à la fin d'une soirée) to dance ou do the conga.

faraud†, **~e** /faʀo, od/ **I** *adj* smug, full of oneself (*jamais épith*).
II *nm,f* braggart; **faire le ~** to throw one's weight around.

farce /faʀs/ *nf* **1** (tour) practical joke; **faire une ~ à qn** to play a practical joke on sb; **magasin de ~s et attrapes** joke shop GB, novelty store US; **2** (plaisanterie) joke; **ne te fâche pas, ce n'était qu'une ~** don't be cross, it was only a joke; ▶**dindon**; **3** (bouffonnerie) farce; **la réunion n'a servi à rien, c'était une vaste ~** the meeting was useless, it was a total farce; **4** Théât (pièce) farce; (genre) farce; **5** Culin stuffing, forcemeat.

farceur, **-euse** /faʀsœʀ, øz/ **I** *adj* [*sourire, air*] mischievous; **être ~** [*adulte*] to be a joker○; [*enfant*] to be mischievous.
II *nm,f* **1** (plaisantin) practical joker; **2** (personne peu sérieuse) joker○.

farcir /faʀsiʀ/ [3] **I** *vtr* **1** Culin to stuff (**de** with); **2**○ (surcharger) to cram (**de** with); **~ un discours de citations** to cram a speech with quotations.
II se farcir *vpr* **1**○ (accomplir) to get stuck with○; **c'est toujours les mêmes qui se farcissent tout le travail** it's always the same people who get stuck with all the work; **2**◑ (supporter) to put up with; **je me suis farci mes beaux-parents pendant tout le week-end** I had to put up with my in-laws for the whole weekend; **ce qu'il est bavard, il faut se le ~!** he never stops talking, he's a real pain in the neck○!; **3**○ (surcharger) to cram (**de** with); **elle se farcit la tête de détails inutiles** she crams her head with useless facts; **4**○ (ingurgiter) to polish off○ [*repas, plat, bouteille*]; **5**◑ (posséder sexuellement) to have it off with◑ GB, to ball◑ US.

fard /faʀ/ *nm* make-up; **sans ~** (beauté) natural; (vérité) simple; (avouer) openly.
■ **~ à joues** blusher; **~ à paupières** eye-shadow.
IDIOMES **piquer un ~**○ to go as red as a beetroot GB, to turn as red as a beet US.

farde /faʀd/ *nf* B (dossier) folder.

fardeau, *pl* **~x** /faʀdo/ *nm* lit, fig burden; **plier sous le ~ des responsabilités** to be weighed down with the burden of responsibility.

farder /faʀde/ [1] **I** *vtr* **1** fig to disguise [*vérité*]; **2** lit to put make-up on [*visage*]; **visage outrageusement fardé** face caked in make-up.
II se farder *vpr* [*acteur*] to make up; [*femme*] (tous les jours) to use make-up; (un jour) to put on make-up; **elle s'est fardé les joues** she's put blusher on her cheeks; **tu te fardes trop** you wear too much make-up.

farfadet /faʀfadɛ/ *nm* elf; **des ~s** elves.

farfelu○, **~e** /faʀfəly/ **I** *adj* [*projet, idée*] harebrained○; [*histoire*] far-fetched; [*personne*] scatty○ GB, ditsy○ US, scatterbrained○; [*spectacle*] bizarre.
II *nm,f* (personne) scatterbrain○.
III *nm* (style) scattiness○ GB, flightiness US.

farfouiller○ /faʀfuje/ [1] *vi* to rummage around ou about (**dans** in).

faribole† /faʀibɔl/ *nf* piece of nonsense; **des ~s** nonsense ¢, poppycock○† ¢; **raconter des ~s** to talk poppycock○† ou nonsense.

farine /faʀin/ *nf* flour; (aliment de nourrisson) baby cereal.
■ **~ d'avoine** oatmeal; **~ de blé dur** durum wheat flour; **~ complète** wholemeal flour GB, wholewheat flour; **~ de froment** wheat flour; **~ lactée** ≈ baby cereal; **~ de lin** linseed meal; **~ de maïs** cornflour GB, cornstarch US; **~ de moutarde** Méd mustard powder; **~ d'orge** barley meal; **~ d'os** Agric bone meal; **~ de poisson** Agric fish meal; **~ premier âge** baby cereal (*for babies up to six months*); **~ de seigle** rye flour.
IDIOMES **de la même ~** as bad as each other; **rouler qn dans la ~**○ to pull a fast one on sb○; **se faire rouler dans la ~**○ to be had○.

fariner /faʀine/ [1] *vtr* to flour.

farineux, **-euse** /faʀinø, øz/ **I** *adj* **1** (féculent) [*aliment*] starchy; **2** (rappelant la farine) [*aspect, goût, pommes de terre*] floury; [*fruit*] mealy; [*peau*] peeling; **3** (couvert de farine) [*pain*] floury.

II *nm* starchy food ¢, farinaceous food ¢ spéc.

farniente /faʀnjɛnte/ *nm* lazing about, lazing around; **faire du ~** to laze ou lounge about.

farouche /faʀuʃ/ *adj* **1** (timide) [*enfant, animal*] timid, shy; (insociable) [*personne*] unsociable; **elle est peu ~** iron she's anything but shy; **2** (effrayant) [*regard, mine, aspect*] fierce; [*guerrier*] savage; **3** (acharné) [*ennemi, haine*] bitter; [*adversaire, résolution, opposition*] fierce; [*partisan, loyaliste*] staunch; [*ambition*] driving; [*volonté*] iron (*épith*); **4** (rude) liter [*paysage, côte*] wild.

farouchement /faʀuʃmɑ̃/ *adv* [*opposé, jaloux, indépendant*] fiercely; [*défendre*] fiercely; [*refuser, s'accrocher*] doggedly; **~ anti/pro** violently anti/pro.

fart /faʀt/ *nm* (ski-)wax.

fartage /faʀtaʒ/ *nm* (de skis) waxing.

farter /faʀte/ [1] *vtr* to wax [*skis*].

Far West /faʀwɛst/ *nprm* **le ~** the Far West.

fascicule /fasikyl/ *nm* **1** (brochure) booklet; **2** (partie d'un ouvrage) fascicule; **une encyclopédie de jardinage qui paraît en ~s** a gardening encyclopaedia which comes out in parts.

fascinant, **~e** /fasinɑ̃, ɑ̃t/ *adj* [*personne, film*] fascinating; [*charme, musique*] spellbinding; [*beauté*] bewitching.

fascination /fasinasjɔ̃/ *nf* fascination (**pour qch** with sth); **sa ~ pour les bateaux** his/her fascination with boats; **exercer une ~ sur qn** [*personne, musique*] to hold sb in one's ou its spell; [*télévision, mer*] to hold a fascination for sb; **éprouver une ~ pour qn/qch** to be fascinated by sb/sth.

fasciner /fasine/ [1] *vtr* **1** (captiver) to fascinate; **tout ce qui touche à la mort fascine** everything about death holds a certain fascination; **il regardait, fasciné** he watched in fascination; **2** (envoûter) [*orateur, musique*] to hold [sb] spellbound; [*mer, personne*] to fascinate; **~ l'auditoire par son éloquence** to hold the audience spellbound with one's eloquence; **il restait immobile, comme fasciné** he stood still, spellbound; **se laisser ~ par l'argent/des promesses** to allow oneself to be seduced by money/promises; **3** (hypnotiser) [*regard, spectacle*] to mesmerize; [*serpent*] to hypnotize.

fascisant, **~e** /faʃizɑ̃, ɑ̃t/ *adj* fascistic.

fascisme /faʃism/ *nm* fascism.

fasciste /faʃist/ *adj, nmf* fascist.

faste /fast/ I *adj* (heureux) auspicious; (prospère) [*jour, année*] prosperous, fruitful.

II *nm* splendour[GB], pomp; **avec ~** with pomp.

fast-food /fastfud/ *nm* **1** (établissement) fast food restaurant; **2** (alimentation) fast food.

fastidieux, **-ieuse** /fastidjø, øz/ *adj* tedious, tiresome.

fastoche○ /fastɔʃ/ *adj* dead easy○.

fastueusement /fastɥøzmɑ̃/ *adv* sumptuously, luxuriously; **il vivait ~** he lived in great luxury.

fastueux, **-euse** /fastɥø, øz/ *adj* [*fête, costume, décor*] sumptuous; **leur mode de vie était des plus ~** they led a life of the greatest luxury.

fat, **~e** /fa, at/ I *adj* [*homme, air, manières*] conceited.

II *nm* conceited man.

fatal, **~e** /fatal/ *adj* **1** (inévitable) inevitable; **il était ~ que cela se produise** it was bound to happen; **2** (désastreux) fatal (**à qn/qch** to sb/sth), disastrous (**à qn/qch** for sb/sth); **3** (mortel) fatal; **le voyage lui a été/pourrait lui être ~** the journey proved/could be fatal; **4** (fatidique) [*moment, jour*] fateful; ▶ **femme**.

fatalement /fatalmɑ̃/ *adv* inevitably; **~, les ventes vont chuter** sales will inevitably fall; **ça devait ~ échouer** it was bound to fail.

fatalisme /fatalism/ *nm* fatalism.

fataliste /fatalist/ I *adj* fatalistic.

II *nmf* fatalist.

fatalité /fatalite/ *nf* **1** (sort) **la ~** fate; **déjouer la ~** to cheat fate; **2** (malchance) mischance; **accident dû à la ~** accident caused by bad luck; **par quelle ~ se trouvait-il à Paris?** what twist of fate had brought him to Paris?; **3** (caractère inévitable) inevitability; **il n'y a pas de ~ de l'échec/l'affrontement** failure/confrontation is not inevitable.

fatidique /fatidik/ *adj* fateful.

fatigant, **~e** /fatigɑ̃, ɑ̃t/ *adj* **1** (physiquement) [*sport, voyage*] tiring; [*climat*] wearing; **mon travail est ~ pour les yeux** my job is a strain on the eyes; **2** (intellectuellement) [*travail, recherche*] arduous; **3** (ennuyeux) [*personne, conférence*] tiresome; [*film, conversation*] tedious; **tu es ~e!** you're tiresome!; **c'est ~ de t'écouter** it's tedious listening to you.

fatigue /fatig/ *nf* **1** gén tiredness; **j'ai accumulé de la ~** I've become overtired; **excès de ~** overtiredness; **être mort de ~, tomber de ~** to be dead tired○; **2** Méd fatigue ¢; **~ générale/musculaire/nerveuse** general/muscular/nervous fatigue; **état/source de ~** state/source of fatigue; **trouble dû à la ~** ailment caused by fatigue; **~ visuelle** eyestrain; **3** Tech (de matériau) fatigue; (mécanique) wear and tear.

fatigué, **~e** /fatige/ I *pp* ▶ **fatiguer**.

II *pp adj* **1** (atteint de fatigue) [*personne, animal, jambes, yeux*] tired; **être/sembler/avoir l'air ~** to be/seem/look tired; **être ~ de naissance** hum to be born tired; **j'ai les bras/yeux ~s** my arms/eyes are tired; **2** Méd (souffrant de fatigue) [*personne*] suffering from fatigue (*après n*); [*cœur, foie*] weak; **elle a le cœur ~** she has a weak heart; **3** (las) tired (**de qch** of sth; **de faire** of doing); **elle était ~e de lui/de vivre avec lui** she was tired of him/of living with him.

III *adj* **1** (montrant la fatigue) [*voix*] strained; [*visage, yeux, sourire*] weary; **2** (usé) [*vêtement, chaussure*] worn; [*moteur, voiture*] suffering from wear and tear (*après n*); [*couleur*] faded.

fatiguer /fatige/ [1] I *vtr* **1** (physiquement) to make [sb] tired [*personne*]; to strain [*yeux*]; to make [sth] tired [*jambes*]; to weaken [*estomac, cœur*]; to tire [*cheval*]; **2** (intellectuellement) [*études, travail*] to tire [sb] out [*personne*]; **3** (ennuyer) to wear [sb] out [*personne*]; **tu me fatigues avec tes questions** you wear me out with all your questions; **4** (mécaniquement) to wear out [*moteur, voiture*]; to put a strain on [*matériau, structure*]; **5** Culin to toss [*salade*]; **6** Agric to exhaust [*terre*].

II *vi* **1**○ (physiquement) [*personne*] to get tired; [*jambes, yeux*] to get tired; **depuis son opération il fatigue vite** since his operation he tires easily; **2**○ (intellectuellement) to get tired; **3** (mécaniquement) [*moteur, voiture*] to be labouring[GB]; [*matériau, structure*] to show signs of strain.

III **se fatiguer** *vpr* **1** (devenir fatigué) [*personne*] to get tired (**de** of); **mes yeux se fatiguent vite** my eyes get tired easily; **je me suis fatigué d'elle/de leurs manières/de l'art moderne** I got tired of her/of their manners/of modern art; **2** (se rendre fatigué) [*personne*] to tire oneself out; **ne te fatigue pas trop** lit, hum don't wear yourself out; **se ~ en recherches/en démarches** to wear oneself out doing research/dealing with red tape; **3** (rendre fatigué) **se ~ les yeux** to strain one's eyes; **se ~ les jambes/le cœur** to tire one's legs/heart; **4** (se donner de la peine) **se ~ à faire** to bother doing; **ne te fatigue pas à ranger, je le ferai** don't bother tidying up, I'll do it.

fatras /fatʀa/ *nm* jumble.

fatuité /fatɥite/ *nf* self-conceit; **air de ~** conceited air; **avec ~** conceitedly.

faubourg /fobuʀ/ *nm* **1** (banlieue ouvrière) working class area (*on the outskirts*); **gamin des ~s** working-class kid○; **2** Hist *part of a town outside its walls or former walls.*

faubourien, **-ienne** /fobuʀjɛ̃, ɛn/ *adj* [*accent*] working-class Parisian (*épith*).

fauchage /foʃaʒ/ *nm* (avec une faucheuse) mowing, cutting; (à la faux) scything.

fauchaison /foʃɛzɔ̃/ *nf* **1** (coupe) (avec une faucheuse) mowing, cutting; (à la faux) scything; **2** (saison) haymaking (time).

fauche /foʃ/ *nf* **1**○ (vol) petty thieving; **2** (coupe) (avec une faucheuse) mowing, cutting; (à la faux) scything.

fauché, **~e** /foʃe/ I *pp* ▶ **faucher**.

II○ *adj* (sans argent) broke○ (*jamais épith*), penniless.

III○ *nm,f* **c'est un ~** he's always broke○.

IDIOMES **être ~ comme les blés** to be flat broke○.

faucher /foʃe/ [1] *vtr* **1** (couper) (avec une faucheuse) to mow, to cut; (à la faux) to scythe; **2** (abattre) [*cyclone, pluie, explosion*] to flatten [*arbres, bâtiment*]; [*véhicule, tir*] to mow down [*piéton*]; **la mort l'a fauché en pleine jeunesse** death cut him down in the prime of youth; **3**○ (voler) to pinch○ GB, to steal [*argent, place*]; **on m'a fauché mon vélo** my bike's been pinched○.

faucheur, **-euse** /foʃœʀ, øz/ I *nm,f* **1** (moissonneur) reaper; **2**○ (voleur) petty thief.

II *nm* (araignée) harvestman.

III **faucheuse** *nf* (machine) mowing machine.

faucheux /foʃø/ *nm* (araignée) harvestman.

faucille /fosij/ *nf* sickle; **la ~ et le marteau** the hammer and sickle.

faucon /fokɔ̃/ *nm* **1** Zool falcon, hawk US; **chasser au ~** to hawk; **2** Pol hawk.

■ **~ crécerelle** kestrel; **~ hobereau** hobby; **~ pèlerin** peregrine falcon.

fauconneau, *pl* **~x** /fokɔno/ *nm* young falcon ou hawk US.

fauconnerie /fokɔnʀi/ *nf* **1** (dressage) falconry; (chasse) hawking, falconry; **2** (lieu) hawk house.

fauconnier /fokɔnje/ *nm* falconer.

faudra /fodʀa/ ▶ **falloir**.

faufil /fofil/ *nm* basting thread.

faufilage /fofilaʒ/ *nm* basting.

faufiler /fofile/ [1] I *vtr* Cout to baste.

II **se faufiler** *vpr* **1** (se frayer un chemin) **se ~ à l'intérieur** to worm one's way ou squeeze in; **se ~ à l'extérieur** to slip out; **se ~ entre deux voitures/personnes** [*piéton*] to squeeze between two cars/people; **les cyclistes se faufilaient entre les voitures** the cyclists were weaving in and out of the cars; **se ~ à travers** [*personne*] to thread one's way through [*foule*]; [*voiture, moto*] to thread its way through [*circulation*]; **se ~ par une ouverture étroite** to squeeze through a narrow opening; **2** (s'ajouter) [*élément, question*] to creep into; **3** (sinuer) [*route*] to snake in and out (**entre** between).

faufilure /fofilyʀ/ *nf* basting.

faune /fon/ I *nm* faun.

II *nf* **1** Zool wildlife, fauna; **la ~ du désert** desert wildlife ou fauna; **la ~ marine** marine life; **2** péj (personnes) set, crowd.

faussaire /fosɛʀ/ *nmf* forger.

fausse ▶ **faux I**.

faussement /fosmɑ̃/ *adv* **1** (à tort) [*accuser*] falsely, wrongfully; [*appeler, penser*] wrongly; **2** (hypocritement) [*fragile, naïf*] deceptively; **un air ~ jovial** a deceptively jovial look; **attitude ~ soumise** attitude of feigned submission; **attitude ~ amicale** assumed air of friendliness.

fausser /fose/ [1] *vtr* **1** (déformer) to distort [*résultat, raisonnement, réalité*]; to warp [*esprit*]; **l'amour fausse le jugement** you don't see straight when you're in love; **2**

(abîmer) to distort [*mécanisme*]; to damage [*serrure*]; to bend [*clé, axe*]; to buckle [*lame*].
IDIOMES **~ compagnie à qn** to give sb the slip.

fausset /fosɛ/ *nm* **1** Mus falsetto; **d'une voix de ~** in a falsetto; **2** (de tonneau) spigot.

fausseté /foste/ *nf* (d'argument, de nouvelle) falseness; (de personne) duplicity, insincerity; (de sentiment) insincerity.

faut /fo/ ▶ **falloir**.

faute /fot/ *nf* **1** (erreur) mistake, error; **faire une ~** to make a mistake ou an error; **~ de grammaire/d'orthographe/de ponctuation** grammatical/spelling/punctuation mistake; **~ d'étourderie** or **d'inattention** careless mistake; **~ d'accord/de français** mistake in the agreement/in French; **~ de frappe/de style** keying/stylistic error; **~ d'impression** misprint; **~ de calcul** miscalculation; **~ de jugement** error of judgment; **il a fait un (parcours) sans ~** Équit he had a clear round; fig he's never put a foot wrong; ▶ **double**, **pardonner**; **2** (action coupable) gén misdemeanour[GB]; Jur civil wrong; Relig sin; **commettre une ~** gén to do something wrong; Jur to commit a civil wrong; Relig to sin; **reconnaître sa ~** or **ses ~s** to admit one has done wrong; **être en ~** to be at fault; **prendre qn en ~** to catch sb out; **3** (responsabilité) fault; **c'est (de) ma ~** it's my fault, I'm to blame; **à qui la ~?** whose fault is it, who's to blame?; **c'est la ~ de** or **à**◑ **son frère s'il est en retard** it's his brother's fault if he's late; **par la ~ de qn** because of sb; **rejeter la ~ sur qn** to lay the blame on sb; **4** (manque) **~ de** through ou for lack of, for want of; **~ de temps** through lack of time; **~ de preuves** for lack of evidence; **~ de garanties** in the absence of any guarantees; **~ de mieux** for want of anything better; **ce n'est pourtant pas ~ d'essayer** it's not for want of trying; **mourir ~ de soins** to die of neglect; **~ de quoi** otherwise, failing which; **~ d'avoir pu me déplacer** because I was unable to travel; **sans ~** without fail; **il ne se fait pas ~ de le leur dire** fml he has no qualms about telling them, he's not shy about telling them; ▶ **grive**; **5** Sport gén foul; (au tennis) fault; **faire une ~** to commit a foul; **siffler une ~** to blow the whistle for a foul; **faire une ~ de pied** to make a foot fault; **faire une ~ de main** to handle the ball; **faire une ~ de filet** (au volley-ball) to hit the net.
■ **~ contractuelle** breach of contract; **~ délictuelle** tort; **~ grave** gross misconduct; **~ lourde** gross misconduct (*leading to instant dismissal and loss of financial compensation*); **~ professionnelle** professional misconduct ₵; **commettre une ~ professionnelle** to be guilty of professional misconduct ₵; **~ de service** Admin act of negligence.

fauter† /fote/ [1] *vi* to sin (**avec** with).

fauteuil /fotœj/ *nm* **1** (siège) chair; (bas, rembourré) armchair; **2** Cin, Théât (place) seat; **~ de balcon** seat in the circle; **~ d'orchestre** seat in the stalls GB, orchestra seat US; **3** fig (position, siège) seat; (présidence d'une assemblée) **le ~** the chair; **~ parlementaire** or **de député** seat in parliament; **~ d'académicien** seat in the French Academy; **occuper le ~ présidentiel** to be in the chair; **céder son ~ de leader** to resign as leader.
■ **~ à bascule** rocking chair; **~ club** (big) leather armchair; **~ crapaud** chunky armchair; **~ dentaire** dentist's chair; **~ de jardin** garden chair GB, lawn chair US; **~ de metteur en scène** director's chair; **~ relax** recliner; **~ en rotin** wicker chair; **~ roulant** wheelchair; **~ tournant** swivel chair.
IDIOMES **arriver (comme) dans un ~** to romp home.

fauteur, -trice /fotœʀ, tʀis/ *nm* pej **~ de troubles** troublemaker; **~ de guerre** warmonger.

fautif, -ive /fotif, iv/ **I** *adj* **1** (coupable) [*personne*] guilty, at fault (*après n*); [*véhicule*] at fault (*après n*), in the wrong (*après n*); [*action*] culpable; **être ~** to be guilty ou at fault; **2** (erroné) [*mémoire, raisonnement, édition*] faulty; [*référence*] inaccurate; [*tournure*] incorrect.
II *nm,f* culprit.

fauve /fov/ **I** *adj* **1** ▶ **193** [*couleur*] tawny; **2** [*odeur*] musky; **3** (Art) [*période*] Fauve.
II *nm* **1** (animal féroce) wild animal; (félin) big cat; **les ~s** big cats; **ça sent le ~ dans sa chambre**○ his bedroom stinks○; **2** [*couleur*] fawn; **3** Art Fauvist, Fauve.

fauverie /fovʀi/ *nf* lion house.

fauvette /fovɛt/ *nf* warbler.
■ **~ grisette** whitethroat; **~ des jardins** garden warbler; **~ à tête noire** blackcap.

faux[1], **fausse** /fo, fos/ **I** *adj* **1** (inexact) [*résultat, numéro, interprétation, idée*] wrong; [*impression*] false; [*raisonnement*] false; [*balance*] inaccurate; **c'est (complètement) ~** (erroné) that's (completely) wrong; (non vrai) it's (simply) not true; **il est ~ de croire** it's a mistake to think; **il est ~ de dire** it's not true to say; **2** (postiche) [*nez, barbe, dent, cils*] false; **3** (imité) [*bois, marbre, diamant*] imitation (*épith*); (pour tromper) fake (*épith*); [*porte, tiroir, cloison*] false; **c'est du ~ Louis XV** it's reproduction Louis Quinze; **4** (contrefait) [*billet*] counterfeit (*épith*), forged; [*document*] forged; [*passeport, papiers d'identité*] forged, false; **un ~ Cézanne** a fake Cézanne; **5** (non authentique) (*before n*) [*science, savoir*] pseudo (*épith*); [*liberté, démocratie*] false, illusory; [*besoin*] false; [*policier, évêque*] bogus (*épith*); [*candeur, humilité*] feigned; **c'est un ~ problème/une fausse solution** it's not really a problem/solution at all; **les ~ étudiants** people falsely claiming student status; **afficher une fausse indifférence** to assume an air of indifference; **6** (sans fondement) [*espoir*] false; [*certitude*] mistaken; [*soupçon, crainte*] groundless; [*réputation*] quite unfounded; **7** (mensonger) [*prétexte, déclaration, promesse, accusation*] false; **8** (fourbe) [*personne*] deceitful, false; [*air, regard*] deceitful, shifty; **9** (ambigu) [*situation, position*] false.
II *adv* **1** Mus [*jouer, chanter*] out of tune; fig **sonner ~** [*rire, gaieté, parole*] to have a hollow ring; [*discours*] to sound false; **2** (incorrectement) [*raisonner*] wrongly.
III à faux *loc adv* **1** (à tort) [*accuser*] falsely, wrongly; **2** (de travers) **porter à ~** [*poutre*] to be off balance.
IV *nm* **1** (contraire du vrai) **le ~** what is false; **le vrai et le ~** truth and falsehood; **être dans le ~** fml to be wrong ou mistaken; ▶ **prêcher**; **2** (objet, tableau) fake; (document) forgery; **~ et usage de ~** Jur forgery and use of false documents.
■ **fausse alerte** false alarm; **fausse blonde** dyed blonde; **fausse côte** Anat false rib; **fausse couche** Méd miscarriage; **faire une fausse couche** to have a miscarriage, to miscarry; **fausse dent** false tooth; **fausse ébène** laburnum wood; **fausse facture** Compta bogus invoice; **fausse fenêtre** blind window; **fausse joie** ill-founded joy; **faire une fausse joie à qn** to raise sb's hopes in vain; **fausse manœuvre** lit, fig false move; **fausse modestie** false modesty; **fausse monnaie** forged ou counterfeit currency; **fausse note** Mus wrong note; fig jarring note; **jeter une fausse note** to strike a jarring note; **se dérouler sans une seule fausse note** to go perfectly; **fausse nouvelle** false report; **fausse oronge** fly agaric; **fausse perle** fake ou artificial pearl; **fausse pierre** paste ou artificial stone; **fausse piste** lit, fig wrong track; **fausse pudeur** false modesty; **fausse sortie** Théât false exit; **faire une fausse sortie** to make a stage exit; **~ acacia** false acacia, locust tree; **~ ami** Ling faux ami (*foreign word which looks deceptively like a word in one's own language*); **~ bruit** false rumour[GB]; **~ buis** shrubby milkwort; **~ col** (de chemise) detachable collar; (de bière) head; **~ contact** Électrotech faulty connection; **~ cul**◑ two-faced bastard◑; **~ débutant** false beginner; **~ départ** lit, fig false start; **~ derche**◑ = **~ cul**; **~ ébénier** laburnum; **~ en écriture(s)** Compta, Jur falsification ₵ of accounts; **~ frais** Compta extras, incidental expenses; **~ frère** hum false friend; **~ jeton**○ two-faced person; **c'est un ~ jeton** he's/she's two-faced; **~ jour** lit deceptive light; fig **sous un ~ jour** in a false light; **~ mouvement** false move; **~ nom** false ou assumed name; **~ ourlet** Cout false hem; **~ pas** lit slip; fig (erreur) mistake; (gaffe) faux pas; **faire un ~ pas** lit to trip, stumble; **commettre un ~ pas** (erreur) to make a mistake; (gaffe) to make a faux pas; **il n'a pas commis un seul ~ pas** fig he hasn't put a foot wrong; **~ plafond** false ceiling; **~ pli** crease; **~ prophète** false prophet; **~ seins** falsies○; **~ serments** false declarations of love; **~ sycomore** Norway maple; **~ témoignage** Jur (déposition) false ou perjured evidence; (délit) perjury ₵; **faire un ~ témoignage** to bear false witness, to commit perjury; **~ témoin** Jur lying witness, perjurer; **~ titre** Édition, Imprim half-title.

faux[2] /fo/ *nf* Agric scythe.

faux-bourdon, *pl* **~s** /fobuʀdɔ̃/ *nm* **1** Zool drone; **2** Mus faux bourdon.

faux-filet, *pl* **~s** /fofilɛ/ *nm* sirloin.

faux-fuyant, *pl* **~s** /fofɥijɑ̃/ *nm* **chercher un ~** to try to evade the issue; **user de ~s** to evade the issue, to prevaricate; **après des mois de ~s** after months of prevarication; **répondre sans ~s** to give a straight answer.

faux-monnayeur, *pl* **~s** /fomɔnɛjœʀ/ *nm* forger, counterfeiter.

faux-semblant, *pl* **~s** /fosɑ̃blɑ̃/ *nm* **les ~s** pretence[GB] (*sg*); **entretenir les ~s** to keep up the pretence[GB]; **user de ~s** to put up a pretence[GB], to put on an act.

faux-sens /fosɑ̃s/ *nm inv* mistranslation.

faveur /favœʀ/ **I** *nf* **1** (bienfait) favour[GB]; **faire/demander une ~ à qn** to do/ask sb a favour[GB]; **solliciter une ~ auprès de qn** fml to beg a favour[GB] of sb; **combler qn de (ses) ~s** to pile favours[GB] on sb; **il nous a fait la ~ d'une visite** he honoured[GB] us with a visit; **elle lui a accordé ses ~s** euph she bestowed her favours[GB] upon him; **avoir les ~s de qn, être en ~ auprès de qn** to be in favour[GB] with sb; **s'attirer les ~s de qn** to find favour[GB] with sb; **personnalité qui a la ~ du public** celebrity who is popular with the public; **obtenir qch par ~** to obtain sth as a favour[GB]; **régime** or **traitement de ~** preferential treatment; **2** (ruban) favour[GB], ribbon.
II en faveur de *loc prép* **1** (à l'avantage de) **le jugement a été rendu en sa ~** the court decided in his/her favour[GB]; **la caissière s'est trompée en ma ~** the cashier gave me too much change; **les votes en ~ du candidat de l'opposition** the votes for the opposition candidate; **2** (pour aider) **des mesures en ~ des handicapés** measures to help the disabled; **les mesures en ~ de l'emploi** measures to promote employment; **intervenir en ~ de qn** to intervene on sb's behalf; **3** (partisan de) **être en ~ de qch** to be in favour[GB] of sth; **être en ~ de qn** to be for sb; **4** (en considération de) on account of; **ses torts ont été oubliés en ~ de sa compétence** his/her failings were overlooked on account of his/her efficiency.
III à la faveur de *loc prép* thanks to; **il est arrivé au pouvoir à la ~ d'un coup d'État** he came to power thanks to a coup d'état; **ils se sont enfuis à la ~ de la nuit** they fled under cover of darkness.

favorable /favɔʀabl/ *adj* [*circonstances,*

conditions, occasion] favourable[GB]; **les conditions sont peu ~s à une victoire de la gauche** conditions are not favourable[GB] for a left-wing victory; **les propositions ont reçu un accueil ~** the proposals met with a favourable[GB] reception; **se montrer** or **se présenter sous un jour ~** to show oneself in a favourable[GB] light; **voir qch d'un œil ~** to look favourably[GB] on sth; **être ~ à** (partisan de) to be in favour[GB] of; (propice à) to be favourable[GB] to; **j'ai de lui une opinion ~** I have a good opinion of him; **avoir un préjugé ~ à l'égard de qch** to be favourably[GB] disposed toward(s) sth.

favorablement /favɔʀabləmɑ̃/ *adv* favourably[GB].

favori, **-ite** /favɔʀi, it/ **I** *adj* (tous contextes) favourite[GB].

II *nm,f* favourite[GB]; **c'est le ~ du professeur** he's the teacher's pet.

III *nm* Turf, Sport favourite[GB]; **partir ~** to be the favourite[GB].

IV favoris *nmpl* sideburns, whiskers†.

favoriser /favɔʀize/ [1] *vtr* **1** (avantager) [*personne, groupe*] to favour[GB] [*personne, groupe*] **(par rapport à** over); **l'examinateur a favorisé un candidat** the examiner favoured[GB] one candidate over the others; **les circonstances l'ont favorisé** circumstances were in his favour[GB]; **les milieux favorisés** the privileged classes; **2** (encourager) to encourage; (activement) to promote; **des mesures pour ~ l'emploi** measures to promote ou encourage employment.

favorite ▶ **favori I, II.**

favoritisme /favɔʀitism/ *nm* favouritism[GB].

fax /faks/ *nm* (document) fax; (machine) fax machine; **envoyer qch en ~** to send sth by fax, to fax sth.

faxer /fakse/ [1] *vtr* to fax.

fayot○ /fajo/ *nm* **1** (haricot) bean; **2** (personne) creep○, crawler○.

fayot(t)age◑ /fajɔtaʒ/ *nm* crawling○; **c'est du ~!** that's crawling!

fayot(t)er◑ /fajɔte/ [1] *vi* pej to creep○, to crawl○.

FB (*written abbr* = **franc belge**) BFr.

féal, **~e**, *mpl* **-aux** /feal, o/ *nm,f* liter loyal supporter.

fébrifuge /febʀifyʒ/ *adj, nm* febrifuge, antipyretic.

fébrile /febʀil/ *adj* **1** (nerveux) [*sentiment, geste, moment, œuvre*] feverish; [*personne, équipe*] nervous; **2** Méd (de fièvre) [*malade, état*] feverish.

fébrilement /febʀilmɑ̃/ *adv* feverishly.

fébrilité /febʀilite/ *nf* **1** (agitation) agitation; **après la ~ des dernières heures** after the agitation of the last few hours; **avec ~** agitatedly; **2** (nervosité) nervousness; **~ du marché** nervousness of the market.

fécal, **~e**, *mpl* **-aux** /fekal, o/ *adj* faecal.

fèces /fɛs/ *nfpl* faeces.

fécond, **~e** /fekɔ̃, ɔ̃d/ *adj* **1** (non stérile) [*période, femme*] fertile; **2** (fertile) [*sol*] fertile; [*esprit, imagination*] fertile; **année ~e en incidents** or **rebondissements** eventful year; **3** (prolifique) lit, fig prolific; **4** (fructueux) [*période, effort, travail, idée*] fruitful.

fécondable /fekɔ̃dabl/ *adj* [*femelle*] fertile; [*ovule*] fertilizable.

fécondateur, **-trice** /fekɔ̃datœʀ, tʀis/ *adj* fertilizing.

fécondation /fekɔ̃dasjɔ̃/ *nf* (de femme, femelle) impregnation; (de plante) pollination; (d'œuf, ovule, oosphère) fertilization.

■ **~ artificielle** artificial insemination; **~ croisée** cross-fertilization; **~ in vitro, FIV** in vitro fertilization, IVF.

féconder /fekɔ̃de/ [1] *vtr* **1** (causer la reproduction) to impregnate [*femme, femelle*]; (par insémination) to inseminate [*animal*]; to pollinate [*plante*]; to fertilize [*œuf, ovule, oosphère*]; fig, liter [*semence*] to make [sth] fruitful [*terre*]; **2** (rendre fertile) [*fleuve*] to make [sth] fertile [*terre*]; **3** fig (enrichir) to enrich [*esprit*].

fécondité /fekɔ̃dite/ *nf* **1** (de femme, femelle) fertility; **2** (de sol) fertility; **3** fig (d'idée) potential; (d'auteur) productivity; **la ~ de son esprit** the creative capacity of his/her mind.

fécule /fekyl/ *nf* starch ¢; **~ de pomme de terre** potato starch.

féculent, **~e** /fekylɑ̃, ɑ̃t/ **I** *adj* starchy.

II *nm* starch **C**, starchy food ¢; **les ~s** starches.

FED /ɛfəde/ *nm*: *abbr* ▶ **fonds**.

fédéral, **~e**, *mpl* **-aux** /fedeʀal, o/ *adj* **1** Pol [*république, police, budget*] federal; **2** Comm, Entr, Sport [*association*] federated; **le bureau ~** the association's offices.

fédéraliser /fedeʀalize/ [1] *vtr* to federalize.

fédéralisme /fedeʀalism/ *nm* federalism.

fédéraliste /fedeʀalist/ *adj, nmf* federalist.

fédérateur, **-trice** /fedeʀatœʀ, tʀis/ **I** *adj* federal.

II *nm,f* unifier.

fédératif, **-ive** /fedeʀatif, iv/ *adj* federal.

fédération /fedeʀasjɔ̃/ *nf* federation.

■ **Fédération internationale d'athlétisme amateur**, **FIAA** International Amateur Athletic Federation, IAAF; **Fédération de Russie** Russian Federation.

fédéré, **~e** /fedeʀe/ **I** *pp* ▶ **fédérer**.

II *adj* [*état, club*] federated.

fédérer /fedeʀe/ [14] **I** *vtr* to federate [*États*].

II se fédérer *vpr* [*États*] to federate; [*comités, entreprises*] to form an association.

fée /fe/ *nf* fairy; **bonne/méchante ~** good/wicked fairy.

■ **~ du logis** perfect housewife.

IDIOMES **avoir des doigts** or **mains de ~** to have nimble fingers.

feed-back /fidbak/ *nm inv* feedback.

feeling○ /filiŋ/ *nm* feeling; **y aller au ~** to follow one's feeling.

féerie /fe(e)ʀi/ *nf* **1** (spectacle merveilleux) **une ~ de couleurs** an enchanting display of colours[GB]; **c'est une vraie ~** it's magical; **2** Cin, Théât extravaganza.

féerique /fe(e)ʀik/ *adj* [*beauté, vision*] enchanting; [*monde, paysage, moment*] enchanted.

feignant, **~e** /fɛɲɑ̃, ɑ̃t/ = **fainéant**.

feindre /fɛ̃dʀ/ [55] **I** *vtr* to feign [*émotion, sentiment, état, qualité, maladie*]; **~ la colère/l'ignorance** to feign anger/ignorance; **~ de faire/d'être** to pretend to do/to be; **~ une panne** Aut to pretend to have broken down.

II *vi* to pretend; **inutile de ~** it's no use pretending.

feint, **~e** /fɛ̃, ɛ̃t/ **I** *pp* ▶ **feindre**.

II *pp adj* **1** [*émotion, état*] feigned, put on (*jamais épith*); [*sourire*] false; **avec une gaieté ~e** with feigned cheerfulness; **sa colère/surprise était ~e** his anger/surprise was put on; **son inquiétude n'est pas ~e** his anxiety is genuine; **non ~** genuine; **2** Archit [*fenêtre, arcade*] false.

III feinte *nf* **1** (manœuvre) gén, Mil, Sport feint; (au football, rugby) dummy GB, fake US; **faire une ~e** (au football, rugby) to dummy GB, to fake US; **faire une ~e de passe** to make a dummy pass GB, to fake a pass US; **2**○ (attrape) trick, ruse; **faire une ~e à qn** to trick ou con○ sb; **3†** (dissimulation) pretence[GB] ¢; **sans ~e** openly.

feinter /fɛ̃te/ [1] **I** *vtr* **1** Sport **~ l'adversaire** (en boxe, escrime) to feint at one's opponent; (au football, rugby) to sell one's opponent a dummy GB, to fake out one's opponent US; **~ la passe** to make a dummy pass GB, to fake a pass US; **2**○ (tromper) to con○ [*personne*]; **on l'a feinté/il s'est fait ~** he's been conned○ ou had○.

II *vi* Sport (en escrime) to make a feint; (en boxe) to feint; (au football, rugby) to dummy GB, to fake US.

feldspath /fɛldspat/ *nm* feldspar.

fêlé, **~e** /fɛle/ **I** *pp* ▶ **fêler**.

II○ *adj* (fou) cracked○ (*jamais épith*), off one's rocker○ (*jamais épith*).

III○ *nm,f* loony○; **un ~ du ski/jazz** a ski/jazz freak○.

fêler /fɛle/ [1] **I** *vtr* lit to crack [*tasse, os*]; fig to damage [*amitié*].

II se fêler *vpr* lit [*tasse, os*] to crack; fig [*amitié*] to be damaged; **d'une voix fêlée** in a cracked voice.

félicitations /felisitasjɔ̃/ *nfpl* congratulations (**pour** on; **à** to); **je leur ai adressé mes ~** (de vive voix) I congratulated them; (par lettre, indirectement) I sent them my congratulations; **recevoir des ~** to be congratulated; **être reçu avec les ~ du jury** Scol, Univ to pass with distinction.

félicité /felisite/ **I** *nf* bliss.

II félicités *nfpl* liter joys.

féliciter /felisite/ [1] **I** *vtr* to congratulate [*personne*] (**pour qch** on sth; **à l'occasion de qch** on sth); **~ qn d'avoir fait qch** to congratulate sb on doing sth; **je te félicite!** congratulations!; **je ne te félicite pas!** iron it's nothing to be proud of!

II se féliciter *vpr* (se réjouir) **se ~ de qch** to be very pleased about sth; **je me félicite d'avoir été présent** I'm very pleased I was there; **je me félicite de vous l'entendre dire** I'm very pleased to hear you say it; **il se félicite que l'accord soit conclu** he is very pleased that the agreement has been made; **il a accepté et je m'en félicite** he has agreed, and I am very pleased.

félidé /felide/ *nm* Zool felid; **les ~s** felidae.

félin, **~e** /felɛ̃, in/ **I** *adj* **1** Zool [*race*] feline; [*exposition, fichier, sida*] cat (*épith*); **2** fig [*grâce*] feline; [*yeux*] catlike.

II *nm* feline; **les ~s** felines, the cat family.

fellation /felasjɔ̃/ *nf* fellatio.

félon, **-onne** /felɔ̃, ɔn/ fml **I** *adj* perfidious.

II *nm,f* traitor/traitress.

félonie /felɔni/ *nf* fml **1** (caractère) perfidy sout, treachery; **2** (acte) act of treachery.

felouque /fəluk/ *nf* felucca.

fêlure /fɛlyʀ/ *nf* crack.

femelle /fəmɛl/ **I** *adj* **1** Biol [*hormone*] female; **2** Bot [*plante, fleur*] female; **3** Zool gén female; [*baleine, éléphant*] cow; [*moineau, perroquet*] hen; **cygne ~** pen; **homard ~** hen lobster; **4** Electrotech [*prise*] female; **5** Ling [*trait*] feminine.

II *nf* Zool **1** (animal du sexe fécondé) female; **2** (partenaire sexuel) mate.

féminin, **~e** /feminɛ̃, in/ **I** *adj* **1** (de la femme) [*corps, sexualité, physiologie, hormone*] female; **le sexe ~** the female sex; **un enfant de sexe ~** a female child; **2** (pour femmes) [*activité, magazine*] women's; [*prêt-à-porter, lingerie*] women's, ladies'; [*contraception, préservatif, emploi*] female; **le seul rôle ~** the only female part ou role; **3** (composé de femmes) [*population, collègues, chœur*] female; Sport [*équipe, club*] ladies'; [*sport, judo, record*] women's; **4** (plein de féminité) [*visage, allure*] feminine; **5** Ling [*nom, rime*] feminine.

II *nm* Ling feminine; **au ~** in the feminine.

féminisant, **~e** /feminizɑ̃, ɑ̃t/ *adj* feminizing.

féminisation /feminizasjɔ̃/ *nf* feminization.

féminiser /feminize/ [1] **I** *vtr* **1** to open [sth] up to women [*profession, organisation*]; **2** to make [sth] more feminine [*vêtement*]; **3** to make [sb] more feminine [*personne*]; **4** Biol to feminize.

II se féminiser *vpr* [*profession*] (s'ouvrir aux femmes) to become more open to women; (avoir moins d'hommes) to become predominantly female.

féminisme /feminism/ *nm* feminism.

féministe /feminist/ *adj, nmf* feminist.

féminité /feminite/ *nf* femininity.

femme /fam/ **I** *nf* **1** (adulte de sexe féminin) woman; **~ mariée** married woman; **une voix de ~** a woman's voice; **vêtements pour ~s** women's ou ladies' clothes; **c'est**

la ~ de sa vie she's the love of his life; **c'est la ~ de mes rêves** she's the woman of my dreams; **2** (comme archétype) woman; **métier de ~** woman's job; **la ~ des années 90** the woman of the '90s; **le fait d'être ~** the fact of being a woman; **devenir ~** to become a woman; **un métier de ~** a woman's job; **elle fait très ~** [*jeune fille*] she looks quite grown-up; **elle est très ~** [*femme*] she's very feminine; **elle n'est pas ~ à mentir** she's not a woman to lie; **3** (épouse) wife; **la ~ du directeur** the manager's wife; **c'est sa ~** she's his wife; **prendre ~**† to take a wife†; **prendre qn pour ~** to take sb to wife‡.

II **femme(-)** (*in compounds*) **~-écrivain** woman writer; **~ médecin** woman ou lady† doctor; **~ cadre** executive woman; **~-prêtre** woman priest; **~-soldat** woman soldier; **~ enfant** little-girlish woman; **~-objet** sex object; **femme-femme**○ very feminine woman.

■ **~ d'action** woman of action; **~ active** working woman; **~ d'affaires** businesswoman; **~ à barbe** (au cirque) bearded lady; **~ battue** battered wife; **~ de chambre** (employée d'hôtel, de maison) chambermaid; (attachée au service d'une dame) lady's maid, personal maid; **~ de charge** housekeeper; **~ de cœur** caring person; **~ entretenue** kept woman; **~ facile** pej loose woman; **~ fatale** femme fatale; **~ au foyer** housewife; **~ galante** courtesan; **~ d'intérieur** homemaker; **être très ~ d'intérieur** to care very much about one's home; **~ de journée** = **~ de ménage**; **~ de lettres** woman of letters; **~ de mauvaise vie** loose woman; **~ de ménage** cleaner, cleaning woman ou lady; **~ du monde** well-bred lady; **~ de petite vertu** woman of easy virtue; **~ de service** (dans une collectivité) cleaner, cleaning lady; **~ de tête** assertive woman.

IDIOMES **ce que ~ veut, Dieu le veut** Prov what a woman wants, a woman gets; **souvent ~ varie (bien fol est celui qui s'y fie)** Prov woman is fickle.

femmelette /famlɛt/ *nf* wimp○, weakling.

fémoral, **~e**, *mpl* **-aux** /femɔʀal, o/ *adj* femoral.

fémur /femyʀ/ *nm* thighbone, femur spéc; **se casser le col du ~** to break one's hip.

FEN /fɛn/ *nf* (*abbr* = **Fédération de l'éducation nationale**) FEN (*French teachers' union*).

fenaison /fənɛzɔ̃/ *nf* (saison) haymaking time; (action) haymaking.

fendant, **~e** /fɑ̃dɑ̃, ɑ̃t/ I○ *adj* hilarious.

II *nm* Vin fendant (*Swiss dry white wine*).

fendard◐ /fɑ̃daʀ/ I *adj m* hilarious.

II *nm* (pantalon) trousers (*pl*), pants (*pl*) US.

fendiller /fɑ̃dije/ [1] I *vtr* to chap [*peau, lèvres*]; to craze [*terre*]; to crack [*bois, meuble*].

II **se fendiller** *vpr* [*peau, lèvres*] to chap; [*terre*] to craze over; [*bois, meuble*] to crack; **se ~ à la chaleur** to crack in the heat.

fendre /fɑ̃dʀ/ [6] I *vtr* **1** (couper) to chop [*bois*]; to split [*pierre*]; to slit [*tissu*]; **bûche fendue en deux** split log; **jupe fendue sur le côté** skirt slit up one side; **2** (ouvrir) (légèrement) to chap [*lèvre*]; to crack [*mur, pierre, vase*]; (profondément) to split [*lèvre*]; to split [sth] open [*crâne*]; **crâne fendu** skull split open; **3** fig (déchirer) **~ l'âme** or **le cœur** to be heartbreaking; **~ le cœur à qn** to break sb's heart; **récit à ~ l'âme** heartbreaking story; **4**○ (traverser) **~ l'air** to slice through the air; **~ la foule** to push one's way through the crowd.

II **se fendre** *vpr* **1** (se craqueler) to crack; **2** fig (se déchirer) [*cœur*] to break; **3**○ (faire un effort financier) to cough up○, to shell out○; **tu ne t'es pas fendu!** that didn't break the bank!; **se ~ de** to manage [*sourire, discours*]; to come up with [*cadeau, brochure*]; to cough up○ [*somme d'argent*]; **4** Sport (en escrime) to lunge.

IDIOMES **~ la bise** to run like lightning; **se ~ la pêche**○ or **poire**○ or **gueule**◐ to split one's sides○; **avoir la bouche fendue jusqu'aux oreilles** to be grinning from ear to ear.

fenestrage /fənɛstʀaʒ/ *nm* = **fenêtrage**.

fenestration /fənɛstʀasjɔ̃/ *nf* **1** Archit opening; **2** Méd fenestration.

fenestron /fənɛstʀɔ̃/ *nm* small window.

fenêtrage /fənɛtʀaʒ/ *nm* Archit **1** (fenêtres) windows; **2** (disposition) fenestration; **3** (ornement) arcading.

fenêtre /fənɛtʀ/ *nf* **1** Archit window; **place côté ~** Rail window seat; **regarder/se pencher par la ~** to look/lean out of the window; **être à sa ~** to be at one's window; ▶ **faux**; **2** (d'enveloppe) window; **3** (dans un document) space; **4** Ordinat window; **5** Anat fenestra.

■ **~ basculante** Archit tilt-and-turn window; **~ à battants** Archit casement window; **~ coulissante** Archit sliding window; **~ à croisillons** Archit lattice window; **~ dormante** Archit sash frame window; **~ à guillotine** Archit sash window; **~ de lancement** Astronaut launch window; **~ mansardée** Archit dormer window; **~ à meneaux** Archit mullioned window; **~ de projection** Cin projection window; **~ en saillie** Archit bay window; (arrondie) bow window; **~ à tabatière** Archit skylight; **~ de toit** roof light.

IDIOMES **jeter l'argent par les ~s** to throw money away.

fenêtrer /fənɛtʀe/ [1] *vtr* Archit to make windows in [*façade*].

fenil /fənil/ *nm* hayloft.

fennec /fenɛk/ *nm* fennec.

fenouil /fənuj/ *nm* fennel.

fente /fɑ̃t/ *nf* **1** (ouverture) gén slit; (pour insérer une pièce, carte, lettre) slot; (dans une vis) groove; **2** Cout gén slit; (dans un dos de veste) vent; **veste avec une ~/deux ~s dans le dos** single-vented/double-vented jacket; **3** (fissure) gén crack; (dans du bois) split; (dans une falaise) crevice; **4**◐ (vulve) slit◐, vulva.

■ **~ palpébrale** Anat palpebral fissure.

fenugrec /fənygʀɛk/ *nm* fenugreek.

féodal, **~e**, *mpl* **-aux** /feɔdal, o/ I *adj* feudal.

II *nm* feudal landowner.

féodalisme /feɔdalism/ *nm* feudalism.

féodalité /feɔdalite/ *nf* **1** Hist (caractère) feudalism; (système) feudal system; **2** Écon, Pol (fief) fiefdom.

fer /fɛʀ/ I *nm* **1** Chimie iron; **objet en ~** iron object, object made of iron; **mine/minerai de ~** iron mine/ore; **2** (métal quelconque) metal; **3** fig **de ~** [*discipline, poigne, volonté*] iron; **diriger d'une main de ~** to rule with a rod of iron; **avoir une santé de ~** to have an iron constitution; **4** (objet) (de chaussure) steel tip; (pour marquer) branding iron; (de relieur) blocking tool; **marquer un animal au ~ (rouge)** to brand an animal; **5** (arme) (épée) sword; (lame) blade; **croiser le ~ avec** lit, fig to cross swords with; **6** (train) rail transport; **par ~** by rail.

II **fers**† *nmpl* **1** Méd forceps; **2** (de prisonnier) irons; **mettre un prisonnier aux ~s** to clap a prisoner in irons; **être dans les ~s** lit to be in irons; fig to be in chains.

■ **~ (à cheval)** horseshoe; **mettre un ~ à un cheval** to shoe a horse; **en ~ à cheval** horseshoe-shaped; **~ forgé** wrought iron; **~ à friser** curling iron; **~ à gaufrer** hair crimper; **~ de lance** lit, fig spearhead; **le ~ de lance de l'industrie française** the spearhead of French industry; **~ à repasser** (domestique) iron; (pour carte de paiement) manual imprinter (*for credit card transactions*); **donner un (petit) coup de ~ à qch** to run the iron over sth; **~ (à repasser) à vapeur** steam iron; **~ à souder** soldering iron; **~ à tuyauter** goffering iron.

IDIOMES **s'imposer par le ~ et le feu** to conquer by fire and the sword; **croire dur comme ~** to believe wholeheartedly; **il faut battre le ~ pendant** or **tant qu'il est chaud** Prov strike while the iron is hot; **tomber les quatre ~s en l'air** to fall flat on one's back.

fer-blanc, *pl* **fers-blancs** /fɛʀblɑ̃/ *nm* tinplate.

ferblanterie /fɛʀblɑ̃tʀi/ ▶ **510** *nf* **1** (ustensiles) tinware; **2** (secteur) tin trade; **3** (boutique) ironmonger's GB, hardware store US.

ferblantier /fɛʀblɑ̃tje/ ▶ **510** *nm* **1** (fabricant) tinsmith; **ouvrier ~** tinplate worker; **2** (marchand) ironmonger GB, hardware dealer US.

feria /fɛʀja/ *nf* feria (*annual festival with bullfighting in southern France*).

férié, **~e** /feʀje/ *adj* **jour ~** public holiday GB, holiday US; **c'est ~ demain** tomorrow is a public holiday GB ou a holiday US.

férir /feʀiʀ/ *vtr* **sans coup ~** meeting no resistance.

ferler /fɛʀle/ [1] *vtr* Naut to furl.

fermage /fɛʀmaʒ/ *nm* (mode) tenant farming; (bail) farm tenancy; (redevance) farm rent.

Fermanagh ▶ **692** *npr* **le comté de ~** Fermanagh.

ferme /fɛʀm/ I *adj* **1** (résistant) [*chair, sol*] firm; [*blanc d'œuf, crème*] stiff; **2** (stable) [*personne*] steady; **être ~ sur ses jambes** to be steady on one's legs; **3** (assuré) [*pas, voix, attitude, écriture*] firm; [*geste, exécution, style*] confident; **avoir la ~ intention de faire** to have the firm intention of doing; **d'une main ~** [*diriger, saisir, retenir*] with a firm hand; [*écrire*] in a firm hand; **rester ~ dans l'adversité/dans ses résolutions** to be steadfast in adversity/in one's resolutions; **4** (inflexible) firm; **être** or **se montrer ~ avec les enfants** to be firm with the children; **5** Fin (bien orienté) [*marché, valeur, monnaie*] firm; **6** Comm, Fin (définitif) [*commande, engagement, prix, vente*] firm; **7** Jur (sans sursis) **peine de prison ~** custodial sentence; **cinq ans de prison ~**, **cinq ans ~**○ a five-year sentence with no remission.

II *adv* **1** (sans faiblir) [*discuter, batailler*] vigorously; [*croire*] firmly; **tenir ~** to stand one's ground; **s'ennuyer ~** to be bored stiff; **2** (de façon définitive) **commander ~** to put in a firm order for [*avion, voiture*].

III *nf* **1** Agric (exploitation) farm; (maison) farmhouse; **~ collective/marine/d'élevage** collective/marine/cattle farm; **retaper une vieille ~** to do up an old farmhouse; **à la ~** [*travailler, vie, vente*] on the farm; **2** Comm, Jur (contrat) **(bail à) ~** farming lease; (domaine affermé) leasehold; **donner qch à ~** to lease sth; **3** Constr truss.

■ **~ école** Agric *farm attached to an agricultural college*.

IDIOMES **attendre de pied ~** to be ready and waiting; **je les attends de pied ~** I'm ready for them.

fermé, **~e** /fɛʀme/ I *pp* ▶ **fermer**.

II *pp adj* **1** (hermétique) **être ~ à l'art moderne** to be totally uninterested in modern art; **être ~ à la pitié** [*personne*] to have become callous; **visage ~** inscrutable face; **2** (élitiste) **cercle** or **club ~** exclusive club; **monde très ~** exclusive world; **3** Math [*ensemble*] closed.

fermement /fɛʀməmɑ̃/ *adv* firmly.

ferment /fɛʀmɑ̃/ *nm* lit, fig ferment.

fermentation /fɛʀmɑ̃tasjɔ̃/ *nf* **1** Biol fermentation; **2** (agitation) ferment; **en ~** in ferment.

fermenter /fɛʀmɑ̃te/ [1] *vi* **1** Biol to ferment; **2** (être en effervescence) to be in ferment.

fermentescible /fɛʀmɑ̃tɛsibl/ *adj* fermentable.

fermer /fɛʀme/ [1] **I** *vtr* **1** gén to close, to shut [*porte, fenêtre, boîte, valise, tiroir, livre, parapluie*]; to close, to shut [*yeux, bouche*]; to clench [*poing*]; to draw [*rideau*]; to seal [*lettre*]; to turn off [*robinet, gaz, eau, radio*]; to switch off [*électricité*]; to do up [*vêtement, chaussure*]; to close off [*conduit, passage*]; **la porte est bien/mal fermée** the door is/is not shut properly; **~ sa chemise jusqu'au cou** to button one's shirt right up to the neck; **~ à clé** to lock up [*maison, appartement*]; to lock [*voiture, valise, tiroir*]; **~ à double tour** lit to double-lock [*maison*]; fig to lock securely [*voiture, valise*]; **~ le jeu** Sport to play a defensive game; **~ son cœur** to steel one's heart (**à** against); **une chaîne de montagnes fermait l'horizon** the horizon was bounded by a range of mountains; **2** Admin, Comm, Entr (temporairement) to close [*magasin, aéroport, accès, route, frontière*]; (définitivement) to close down [*entreprise, succursale, centrale*]; to close [*mine, compte bancaire*]; **'on ferme'** 'we're closing'; **fermé le lundi/au public** closed on Mondays/to the public; **région fermée aux étrangers** area not open to foreigners; **3** (terminer) to bring [sth] to a close [*débat, audience*].

II *vi* [*magasin, usine, théâtre*] (temporairement) to close; (définitivement) to close down; **~ bien/mal** [*porte, valise*] to close/not to close properly; **armoire qui ferme à clé** wardrobe that can be locked; **le musée ferme en août** the museum is closed in August.

III se fermer *vpr* **1** lit [*porte*] to shut; [*fleur*] to close up; [*manteau, bracelet*] to fasten; **ma jupe se ferme sur le côté** my skirt fastens at the side; **2** fig [*personne*] to clam up; [*visage*] to harden.

IDIOMES **la ~◑** to shut up○; **la ferme◑!, ferme-la◑!** shut up!; **~ les yeux sur** to turn a blind eye to.

fermeté /fɛʀməte/ *nf* **1** (morale) firmness; **avec ~** firmly; **faire preuve de ~ à l'égard de qn** to take a firm line with sb; **2** (physique) firmness; **3** Fin (de monnaie, valeur) firmness.

fermette /fɛʀmɛt/ *nf* **1** (maisonnette) farmhouse-style cottage; **2** Gén Civ (de barrage) flashboard.

fermeture /fɛʀmətyʀ/ *nf* **1** gén (de magasin, bibliothèque, d'usine) (brève) closing; (longue) closure; (définitive) closing down; (de compte en banque) closing; **jour/heure de ~** closing day/time; **~ annuelle** annual closure; **~ en août/pour travaux** closed in August/for repair work; **depuis la ~ de l'usine** since the factory closed down; **'~ provisoire du pont'** 'bridge temporarily closed'; **la ~ du pont a provoqué des embouteillages** the closing of the bridge caused traffic jams; **nous sommes arrivés juste avant la ~** we arrived just before closing time; **'attention à la ~ des portes'** 'mind the doors'; **la ~ des portes est automatique** the doors close automatically; **2** Tech (dispositif) (de porte) latch; (de fenêtre, meuble) catch; (de sac à main) clasp; (de vêtement) fastening; **~ automatique** automatic locking system; **à ~ automatique** [*portes*] automatic; **3** Phon closure.

■ **~ à baïonnette** bayonet clutch; **~ éclair®** = **~ à glissière**; **tirer** or **remonter la ~ éclair de qch** to zip sth up; **~ à glissière** Cout zip GB, zipper US; **~ magnétique** Tech magnetic lock.

fermier, **-ière** /fɛʀmje, ɛʀ/ **I** *adj* [*beurre, fromage*] farm (*épith*); [*poulet, œufs*] free-range (*épith*); **exploitation fermière** (activité) farming; (ferme) farm.

II ▶ 510 *nm,f* (agriculteur) farmer.

III *nm* Comm, Jur leaseholder.

IV fermière *nf* (femme du fermier) farmer's wife.

■ **~ général** Hist farmer general.

fermoir /fɛʀmwaʀ/ *nm* (de bijou, sac, reliure) clasp.

féroce /feʀɔs/ *adj* **1** (cruel) [*animal*] ferocious; [*rire, humour, portrait, joie, répression, réquisitoire*] savage; [*personne, air*] fierce; **2** (acharné) [*bataille, concurrence*] fierce; **3** (violent) [*appétit*] voracious; [*envie, désir*] violent; ▶ **bête**.

férocement /feʀɔsmɑ̃/ *adv* **1** (avec cruauté) savagely; **2** (violemment) fiercely.

férocité /feʀɔsite/ *nf* **1** (d'animal) ferociousness; **avec ~** ferociously; **2** (de portrait, réplique, rire) savagery; **avec ~** savagely; **3** (de personne, regard, paroles) fierceness; **avec ~** fiercely.

Féroé /feʀɔe/ ▶ 416 *nprfpl* **les (îles) ~** the Faroe Islands, the Faroes.

ferrage /feʀaʒ/ *nm* **1** (d'animal) shoeing; **2** (pour renforcer) reinforcing ¢ with metal.

ferraillage /feʀɑjaʒ/ *nm* steel framework.

ferraille /feʀɑj/ *nf* **1** (morceaux de fer) scrap iron; (morceaux de métal) scrap metal; **2** (dépôt) scrapheap; **être bon pour la ~** to be fit for the scrapheap; **mettre qch à la ~** to scrap sth; **3**○ (monnaie) small change.

ferrailler /feʀɑje/ [1] *vi* **1** (se battre à l'épée) to clash swords; **2** (faire un bruit de ferraille) to clank.

ferrailleur /feʀɑjœʀ/ ▶ 510 *nm* **1** (récupérateur de ferraille) scrap (metal) dealer; **2** (batailleur) swashbuckler.

ferrate /feʀat/ *nm* ferrate.

ferré, **~e** /feʀe/ **I** *pp* ▶ **ferrer**.

II *pp adj* **1** (muni de ferrures) [*animal*] shoed; [*chaussure, bâton*] steel-tipped; [*roue*] rimmed with steel; [*lacet*] tagged; [*coffre*] ironbound; **2** Pêche hooked, struck spéc; **3**○ (instruit) **être ~ en** or **sur qch**○ to be well up on sth○; ▶ **voie**.

ferrement /fɛʀmɑ̃/ *nm* (garniture) iron trim; **~ de cuivre** copper trim.

ferrer /feʀe/ [1] *vtr* **1** to shoe [*cheval, mulet*]; (munir de ferrures) to fit steel tips to [*chaussure*]; to rim [sth] with steel [*roue*]; to tip [sth] with steel [*bâton*]; to tag [*lacet*]; to reinforce [sth] with steel [*porte*]; **2** Pêche to strike [*poisson*].

ferret /feʀɛ/ *nm* (de lacet) (metal) tag (*on shoelace*).

■ **~ d'Espagne** Minér red haematite.

ferreux, **-euse** /feʀø, øz/ *adj* ferrous; **métaux non ~** nonferrous metals.

ferrique /feʀik/ *adj* ferric.

ferrite /feʀit/ *nf* ferrite.

ferro-alliage, *pl* **~s** /feʀoaljaʒ/ *nm* ferroalloy.

ferromagnétique /feʀomaɲetik/ *adj* ferromagnetic.

ferronnerie /feʀɔnʀi/ *nf* **1** (lieu) ironworks (+ *v sg* ou *pl*); **atelier de ~** wrought iron workshop; **2** (travail) (du fer forgé) wrought iron work; (du fer) ironwork; **~ d'art** wrought iron work; **apprendre la ~** to learn to work in iron; **3** (ouvrage) wrought iron work ¢; **une ~** a piece of wrought iron.

ferronnier /feʀɔnje/ ▶ 510 *nm* **1** (fabricant) iron craftsman; **~ d'art** wrought-iron craftsman; **ouvrier ~** ironworker; **2** (commerçant) iron work merchant.

ferronnière /feʀɔnjɛʀ/ *nf* frontlet.

ferroutage /fɛʀutaʒ/ *nm* Transp, Rail piggyback.

ferroviaire /feʀɔvjɛʀ/ *adj* [*transport, collision, trafic*] rail; [*gare, tunnel, compagnie*] railway GB, railroad US.

ferrugineux, **-euse** /feʀyʒinø, øz/ *adj* ferruginous.

ferrure /feʀyʀ/ *nf* **1** (garniture métallique) (de porte, fenêtre) metal fittings (*pl*); (de meuble, coffre) metal band; **2** Équit (fers) shoes (*pl*).

ferry, *pl* **ferries** /feʀi/ *nm* Transp ferry.

ferry-boat, *pl* **~s** /feʀibot/ *nm* gén ferry; (pour véhicules) (car) ferry.

fertile /fɛʀtil/ *adj* **1** Agric [*sol, plaine*] fertile; **2** (riche) [*cerveau, imagination*] fertile; [*année*] productive; **année ~ en événements** eventful year; **journée ~ en émotions** day filled with emotion; **pièce ~ en surprises/bons mots** play full of surprises/witticisms; **affaire ~ en rebondissements** affair with many repercussions; **nation ~ en poètes** nation that produces many poets.

fertilisable /fɛʀtilizabl/ *adj* fertilizable.

fertilisant, **~e** /fɛʀtilizɑ̃, ɑ̃t/ **I** *adj* fertilizing.

II *nm* (engrais) fertilizer.

fertilisation /fɛʀtilizasjɔ̃/ *nf* fertilization.

fertiliser /fɛʀtilize/ [1] *vtr* to fertilize.

fertilité /fɛʀtilite/ *nf* fertility; **d'une grande ~** highly fertile.

féru, **~e** /feʀy/ *adj* **être ~ de qch** to be very keen on sth.

férule /feʀyl/ *nf* **être sous la ~ de qn** to be under sb's iron rule.

fervent, **~e** /fɛʀvɑ̃, ɑ̃t/ **I** *adj* [*croyant, prière*] fervent; [*admirateur, amour*] ardent.

II *nm,f* **~ de tennis** tennis enthusiast GB, tennis buff US; **~ de musique/théâtre** music/theatre[GB] lover.

ferveur /fɛʀvœʀ/ *nf* (de prière) fervour[GB]; (d'amour) ardour[GB]; **avec ~** [*prier*] fervently; [*aimer*] passionately.

fesse /fɛs/ *nf* **1** Anat buttock; **les ~s** the buttocks, the bottom GB ou butt○ US; **un coup de pied aux ~s**○ a kick up the backside; **poser ses ~s**○ to park oneself○; **2**◑ (sexe) **la ~** tits and bums◑; **il y a de la ~◑ ici!** there's some sexy stuff○ here!

IDIOMES **attention à tes ~s**○ watch your step; **avoir la police aux ~s**○ to have the police hot on one's trail; **avoir chaud aux ~s**○ to have a narrow escape○; **coûter la peau des ~s**○ to cost an arm and a leg○; **pousse tes ~s**○! shove over○! GB, scoot over○! US; **montrer ses ~s**○ to strip naked; **serrer les ~s**○ to be scared stiff; **s'occuper de ses ~s**○ to mind one's own business.

fessée /fese/ *nf* smack on the bottom, spanking; **si tu n'es pas sage, tu auras une ~** if you don't behave you'll get your bottom smacked.

fesser /fese/ [1] *vtr* to spank.

fessier, **-ière** /fesje, ɛʀ/ **I** *adj* buttock, gluteal spéc; **muscles ~s** gluteal muscles.

II *nm* **1**○ (fesses) backside○, behind○; **2** Anat (muscle) gluteus; **grand/moyen/petit ~** gluteus maximus/medius/minimus.

fessu○, **~e** /fesy/ *adj* big-bottomed, broad in the beam○ (*jamais épith*).

festif, **-ive** /fɛstif, iv/ *adj* festive.

festin /fɛstɛ̃/ *nm* feast; **faire un ~** to have a feast.

festival /fɛstival/ *nm* Danse, Mus, Théât, Cin festival; **pièce hors ~** play on the fringe; **~ de rock/du film fantastique** rock/fantasy film festival; **~ de bons mots** fig display of brilliant wit.

festivalier, **-ière** /fɛstivalje, ɛʀ/ *nm,f* festival-goer.

festivités /fɛstivite/ *nfpl* festivities.

fest-noz, *pl* **festoù-nos** /fɛstnoz, fɛstunɔz/ *nm* fest-noz, Breton festival.

festoiement /fɛstwamɑ̃/ *nm* feasting.

feston /fɛstɔ̃/ *nm* **1** (guirlande) festoon; **2** Archit festoon; **3** Cout scallop; **col à ~s** Cout scalloped collar.

festonner /fɛstɔne/ [1] *vtr* Cout to scallop [*col*].

festoyer /fɛstwaje/ [23] *vi* to feast.

fêtard○, **~e** /fɛtaʀ, aʀd/ *nm,f* party animal○.

fête /fɛt/ *nf* **1** (jour chômé) public holiday GB, holiday US; **le vendredi saint, c'est ~?** is Good Friday a public holiday GB ou a holiday US?; **sauf dimanches et ~s** except Sundays and public holidays GB ou holidays US; **où passes-tu les ~s de Pâques/fin d'année?** where are you going for Easter/

Christmas?; **2** (jour du saint patron) **c'est ma ~** it's my (saint's) name-day; **bonne ~!** happy name-day!; **ça va être ma ~**○! iron I'm going to cop it○!; **aujourd'hui, c'est la ~ des pompiers** today is the festival of the patron saint of firemen; **3** (solennité religieuse) festival; **~ païenne/chrétienne** pagan/Christian festival; **la ~ des morts** All Souls' Day; **4** (célébration) (day of) celebration; **les ~s du bicentenaire** the bicentenary celebrations; **5** (réjouissances privées) party; **donner** or **faire une ~** to give ou have a party; **faire la ~** to live it up○; **être de la ~** lit to be one of the party; **compte sur moi, je serai de la ~!** fig I'll be there!; **~ de famille** family gathering; **ambiance/air de ~** festive atmosphere/look; **l'ambiance est à la ~** the mood is festive; **toute la ville était en ~** the whole town was in holiday mood; **avoir le cœur en ~** to feel incredibly happy, to be bubbling over with joy; **c'est une ~ pour les yeux** it's a feast for the eyes; **être à la ~** fig to have a field day; **ne pas être à la ~** to be having a bad time; **6** (réjouissances publiques) (foire) fair; (kermesse) fête, fair; (manifestation culturelle) festival; (réjouissances officielles) celebrations (*pl*); **~ de la musique/bière** music/beer festival; **il y a la ~ au village** there's a fair in the village; **que la ~ commence!** let the festivities begin!; **~ paroissiale** parish fête; **les ~s de Carnaval** the carnival festivities; **la ~ de la moisson** the harvest festival.

■ **~ de bienfaisance** charity bazaar; **~ fixe** fixed feast; **~ foraine** funfair; **~ légale** public holiday GB, legal holiday US; **~ des Mères** Mothers' Day, Mothering Sunday GB; **~ mobile** movable feast; **~ des Pères** Fathers' Day; **~ des Rois (Mages)** Twelfth Night, Epiphany; **~ du travail** Labour Day, 1 May; **Fête Nationale** national holiday; (en France) Bastille Day.

IDIOMES **le chien me fait ~ quand je rentre** the dog makes a great fuss of me when I get in; **faire sa ~ à qn**○ to give sb a working over○; **ce n'est pas tous les jours la ~** Prov you have to take the rough with the smooth, life is not a bed of roses.

Fête-Dieu /fɛtdjø/ *nf* Corpus Christi.

fêter /fete/ [1] *vtr* to celebrate [*Noël, anniversaire, succès*]; to fete [*champion, héros, diva*]; **~s ses 20 ans** to celebrate one's twentieth birthday.

fétiche /fetiʃ/ **I** *adj* lucky; **jour/chiffre ~** lucky day/number.

II *nm* **1** (mascotte) mascot; **2** Psych, Relig fetish.

fétichisme /fetiʃism/ *nm* fetishism; **avoir le ~ de qch**○ to have a thing○ about sth.

fétichiste /fetiʃist/ **I** *adj* fetishistic.

II *nmf* fetishist.

fétide /fetid/ *adj* **1** (malodorant) [*odeur*] foul; [*lieu*] foul-smelling; **2** (répugnant) [*personne*] repulsive.

fétidité /fetidite/ *nf* (d'odeur) foulness.

fétu /fety/ *nm* **~ (de paille)** wisp of straw.

IDIOMES **être emporté comme un ~** to be carried off like a straw in the wind.

feu[1], **~e** /fø/ *adj* fml late; **~ la reine, la ~e reine** the late queen.

feu[2], *pl* **~x** /fø/ **I** ▶ **193** *adj inv* **(de couleur) ~** flame-coloured[GB]; **rouge ~** fiery red.

II *nm* **1** (combustion, incendie) fire; **~ de bois/brousse/forêt** wood/bush/forest fire; **~ de braises** glowing embers (*pl*); **en ~** on fire; **au ~!** fire!; **j'ai entendu (quelqu'un) crier au ~** I heard someone shout 'fire!'; **il y a le ~ à l'étable** the cowshed is on fire; **il y a eu le ~ chez elle** she's had a fire; **allumer un ~** to light a fire; **faire un** or **du ~** to make a fire; **prendre ~** to catch fire; **le feu a pris au sous-sol** the fire started in the basement; **le ~ a pris/ne prend pas** the fire is lit/won't light; **mettre le ~ à** to set fire to; **mettre** or **jeter qch au ~** to throw sth on the fire; **mise à ~** (de fusée) blast-off; **au coin du ~** [*s'asseoir, bavarder*] by the fire; [*causerie, rêverie*] fireside (*épith*); **2** (lumière) light; **les ~x de la ville** the lights of the city; **les ~x de la rampe** the footlights; **sous le ~ des projecteurs** lit under the glare of the spotlights; fig in the spotlight; **pleins ~x sur**... the spotlight is on...; **3** (éclat) **briller de mille ~x** [*chandelier, diamant*] to sparkle brilliantly; **les ~x du couchant** the fiery glow of the setting sun; **4** Aut, Aviat, Gén Civ, Naut (signal, indicateur) light; **tous ~x éteints** without lights; **5** (à un carrefour) traffic light; **~ vert/rouge** green/red light; **~ orange** amber GB ou yellow US light; **prenez à droite au ~ (rouge)** turn right at the (traffic) lights; **le ~ est au vert** the lights are green; **avoir/recevoir le ~ vert de qn** fig to have/get the green light ou the go-ahead from sb; **donner son ~ vert à qn** fig to give sb the go-ahead; **6** Culin (de cuisinière) ring GB, burner US; (chaleur) heat; **faire cuire à ~ vif/moyen** cook over a high/medium heat; **faire cuire à petit ~** or **à ~ doux** cook over a gentle heat; **retirez du ~ au bout de 15 minutes** remove from the heat after 15 minutes; **j'ai oublié la soupe sur le ~** I've left the soup on the stove; **attends, j'ai quelque chose sur le ~** just a minute, I've got something cooking; **7** (allumette) **avez-vous du ~?** have you got a light?; **8** (sensation de brûlure) **épice qui met la bouche en ~** spice that burns your mouth; **elle avait les joues en ~** her cheeks were burning ou on fire; **pour apaiser le ~ du rasoir** to soothe shaving burn; **9** (enthousiasme) passion; **avec ~** [*parler, défendre*] with passion; **être plein de ~** [*personne*] to be full of fire; **avoir un tempérament de ~** to have a fiery temperament; **dans le ~ de la discussion/de l'action** in the heat of the discussion/of the moment; ▶ **action**; **10** (tir) **~!** Mil fire!; **~ nourri** sustained fire; **faire ~** to fire (**sur** at); **ouvrir le ~** to open fire (**sur** on); **sous le ~ de l'ennemi** under enemy fire; **coup de ~** shot; **des coups de ~ ont été tirés** shots were fired; **essuyer des coups de ~** to be shot at; **tirer un coup de ~** to shoot into the air; **échange de coups de ~** shooting incident; **le coup de ~ de midi** fig (dans un restaurant) the lunchtime rush; **être pris entre deux ~x** lit, fig to be caught in the crossfire; **sous les ~x croisés de X et de Y** lit, fig under the crossfire of X and Y; **un ~ roulant de critiques** a torrent of criticism; **11** (combat) action; **aller au ~** to go into action ; **envoyer qn au ~** to send sb into action; **baptême du ~** baptism of fire; **12**† (foyer) **un village de 30 ~x** a village of some 30 dwellings; **13**○ (pistolet) shooter○, piece○ US, gun.

■ **~ arrière** rear light GB, tail light US; **~ d'artifice** (spectacle) fireworks display; (un seul) firework; **tirer un ~ d'artifice** (un seul) to let off a firework; (plusieurs) to have fireworks; **~ bactérien** fire blight; **~ de Bengale** Bengal light; **~ de brouillard** fog-light; **~ de camp** campfire; **~ de cheminée** chimney fire; **~ clignotant** indicator GB, blinker US; **~ de croisement** dipped GB ou dimmed US headlight; **~ d'encombrement** marker lamp ou light; **~ follet** will-o'-the-wisp; **~ de gabarit** = **~ d'encombrement**; **~ de joie** bonfire; **~ de marche arrière** = **~ de recul**; **~ de paille** flash in the pan; **~ de recul** reversing GB ou backup US light; **~ de route** main-beam headlight; **passer** or **se mettre en ~x de route** to switch on to full beam GB, to put the high beams on; **~ de signalisation** traffic light; **~ de stationnement** sidelight GB, parking light US; **~ stop** Aut brake light, stop lamp ; **~ tricolore** = **~ de signalisation**; **~x de détresse** warning lights, hazard lamps; **~x de position** Aut sidelights GB, parking lights US; Aviat, Naut navigation lights.

IDIOMES **il n'y a pas le ~**○**!** there's no rush!; **jouer avec le ~** to play with fire; **faire long ~** [*projectile, projet*] to misfire; **ne pas faire long ~**○ not to last long; **il n'y a vu que du ~** he fell for it; **mourir à petit ~** to die a slow death; **faire mourir qn à petit ~** to make sb die a slow death; **avoir le ~ au derrière**○ or **aux fesses**○ or **au cul**◑ (être pressé) to be in a rush; (être salace) to be randy○; ▶ **main**, **lieu**.

feuillage /fœjaʒ/ **I** *nm* **1** Bot foliage ¢, leaves (*pl*); **le ~ persistant** evergreen foliage; **2** (décor) leafage ¢; (branches coupées) cut branches (*pl*).

II feuillages *nmpl* leaves; **le vent dans les ~s** the wind in the leaves.

feuillaison /fœjɛzɔ̃/ *nf* Bot foliation.

feuillard /fœjaʀ/ *nm* **1** (de cerclage) (de colis, malle) strap; (de tonneau) hoop; **2** (en métallurgie) metal strip.

feuille /fœj/ *nf* **1** (d'arbre) leaf; **~s d'eucalyptus/de peuplier/d'érable** eucalyptus/poplar/maple leaves; **~ morte** dead leaf; **descendre en ~ morte** Aviat to do a falling leaf; **être en ~s** [*arbre*] to be in leaf; **arbre à ~s persistantes** evergreen; **arbre à ~s caduques** deciduous tree; **arbre à grandes ~s** broad-leaved tree; **2** (de papier, carton) sheet; **~ de papier** sheet of paper; **~ à dessin/quadrillée** sheet of drawing/squared paper; **~ de brouillon** sheet of scrap paper GB, sheet of scratch paper US; **~ double/simple** double/single sheet (of paper); **~ de timbres** sheet of stamps; ▶ **bon**; **3** (de métal, plastique) (plaque mince) sheet; (pellicule) foil ¢; **~ d'acier/de plomb/de zinc** steel/lead/zinc sheet; **~ d'aluminium/de plastique** aluminium GB ou aluminum US/plastic foil; **~ d'étain** tinfoil ¢; **4** (de placage) veneer ¢; **~ d'acajou** mahogany veneer; **5** (de dorure) **~ d'or, or en ~s** gold leaf ¢; **dorer à la ~** to gild; **~ d'argent** silver leaf ¢; **6** (formulaire) form; **il y plusieurs ~s à remplir** there are several forms to fill out; **7**○ (journal) paper.

■ **~ blanche** blank sheet; **rendre ~ blanche à un examen** to hand in a blank exam paper; **~ de centrage** Aviat balance chart; **~ de chêne** Culin oak-leaf lettuce; **~ de chou**○ (journal) rag○, newspaper; **~ de chou farcie** Culin stuffed cabbage roll; **avoir les oreilles en ~ de chou** to have cauliflower ears; **~ à cigarette** cigarette paper; **~ composée** Bot compound leaf; **~ d'errata** errata sheet; **~ d'impôts** Fisc (déclaration) tax return; (avis de débit) tax demand GB, tax statement US; **~ de maladie** Prot Soc *a form for reclaiming medical expenses from the social security office*; **~ de notes** school report; **~ de paie** payslip GB, pay stub US; **~ de présence** attendance sheet; **~ de programmation** Ordinat worksheet; **~ de route** Mil movement order; **~ de soins** = **~ de maladie**; **~ de température** temperature chart; **~ de vigne** vine leaf; Art fig leaf; **~ de vigne farcie** Culin stuffed vine leaf; **~ volante** loose sheet; **~s de passe** Imprim overs.

IDIOMES **trembler comme une ~** to shake like a leaf.

feuillet /fœjɛ/ *nm* **1** (feuille) leaf; (page) page; **2** Zool (poche d'estomac) omasum.

■ **~ détachable** tear sheet; **bloc à ~s détachables** tear-off pad; **~ embryonnaire** Biol germ layer; **~ d'errata** errata slip; **~ de garde** flyleaf; **~ intercalaire** interleaf; **~ mobile** loose leaf.

feuilleté, **~e** /fœjte/ **I** *pp* ▶ **feuilleter**.

II *pp adj* **1** Géol [*roche*] foliated; **2** Ind [*verre*] laminated; **3** Culin **pâte ~e** puff pastry.

III *nm* Culin savoury[GB] pasty (*made with puff pastry*); **~s au jambon/fromage** ham/cheese pasties.

feuilleter /fœjte/ [20] *vtr* **1** (passer en revue) to leaf through [*dossier, livre, album*]; **2** Culin to turn and roll [*pâte*]; **3** Ind to laminate [*verre*].

feuilleton /fœjtɔ̃/ *nm* **1** Presse, Radio, TV serial; **~ télévisé** gén TV serial; (à rebondissements) soap (opera); **publié en ~** serialized; **c'est un vrai ~** fig it's a real saga; **2** Presse (chronique) column; **3** Littérat (roman-feuilleton) serial.

feuilletoniste /fœjtɔnist/ *nmf* **1** Presse columnist; **2** Littérat serial writer.

feuillette /fœjɛt/ *nf* barrel (*holding 112–144 litres*).

feuillu, **~e** /fœjy/ **I** *adj* **1** (touffu) leafy; **2** Bot [*arbre*] broad-leaved (*épith*).
II *nm* Bot broad-leaved tree.

feuillure /fœjyʀ/ *nf* (rainure) rabbet.

feulement /følmɑ̃/ *nm* growl (*of a tiger*).

feuler /føle/ [1] *vi* [*tigre*] to growl.

feutrage /føtʀaʒ/ *nm* **1** (fabrication) felt-making; **2** (détérioration) felting.

feutre /føtʀ/ *nm* **1** (matière) felt ¢; **2** (chapeau) felt hat; **3** (stylo) felt-tip (pen).

feutré, **~e** /føtʀe/ **I** *pp* ▶ **feutrer**.
II *pp adj* **1** [*étoffe*] (par traitement) felt (*épith*); (par détérioration) felted; **2** (étouffé) [*ambiance, lieu*] hushed; [*son*] muffled; **marcher à pas ~s** to pad along; **3** (garni de feutre) [*bureau*] felt-topped.

feutrer /føtʀe/ [1] **I** *vtr* **1** to felt [*poils, laine*]; **2** (détériorer) to felt [*étoffe*]; **3** (garnir) to felt [*selle*].
II *vi* [*lainage*] to become felted.
III se feutrer *vpr* [*lainage*] to become felted.

feutrine /føtʀin/ *nf* (pour vêtements) fine felt fabric; (pour ameublement, table de billard) baize.

fève /fɛv/ *nf* **1** Bot, Culin broad bean; **2** C (haricot) bean; **~s au lard** baked beans; **3** (figurine) lucky charm (*hidden in Twelfth Night cake*).

féverole /fevʀɔl/ *nf* horse bean.

févier /fevje/ *nm* Bot honey locust.

février /fevʀije/ **▶ 521** *nm* February.

fez /fɛz/ *nm* Mode fez.

FF (*written abbr* = **franc français**) FFr.

FFI /ɛfɛfi/ *nfpl*: *abbr* ▶ **force**.

FFL /ɛfɛfɛl/ *nfpl*: *abbr* ▶ **force**.

fg *written abbr* = **faubourg 2**.

fi† /fi/ *excl* pooh!
IDIOMES **faire ~ de qch** to treat sth with disdain.

FIAA /ɛfiaa/ *nf*: *abbr* ▶ **fédération**.

fiabilité /fjabilite/ *nf* reliability.

fiable /fjabl/ *adj* [*machine, compagnie*] reliable; [*personne*] (sérieuse) reliable; (de confiance) trustworthy.

fiacre /fjakʀ/ *nm* fiacre.

fiançailles /fjɑ̃saj/ *nfpl* engagement (*sg*); **bague de ~** engagement ring.

fiancé, **~e** /fjɑ̃se/ *nm,f* fiancé/fiancée.

fiancer /fjɑ̃se/ [12] **I** *vtr* (promettre)† to betroth† [*fils, fille*] (**à** to).
II se fiancer *vpr* to get engaged (**à** or **avec** to); **êtes-vous fiancé?** are you engaged?

fiasco /fjasko/ *nm* **1** (échec) fiasco; **faire ~** to fail completely; **2** (défaillance sexuelle) sexual failure.

fiasque /fjask/ *nf* straw-sheathed flask.

fibranne® /fibʀan/ *nf* spun viscose.

fibre /fibʀ/ *nf* **1** lit fibre[GB]; **~ musculaire/nerveuse/végétale** muscle/nerve/vegetable fibre[GB]; **aliments riches en ~** high-fibre[GB] food; **~ synthétique** synthetic fibre[GB]; **~ de carbone/d'acier** carbon/steel fibre[GB]; **2** fig (sensibilité) streak; **avoir la ~ patriotique/maternelle** to have a strong patriotic/maternal streak; **jouer sur la ~ nationaliste des électeurs** to play on nationalist feeling among the voters; **il l'aimait de toutes ses ~s** he loved her with all his being.
■ **~ optique** fibre[GB] optics (+ *v sg*); **~ polaire** Tex fleece; **~ de verre** fibreglass[GB].

fibreux, **-euse** /fibʀø, øz/ *adj* (texture) fibrous; (consistance) sinewy.

fibrillation /fibʀijasjɔ̃/ *nf* fibrillation.

fibrille /fibʀij/ *nf* fibril.

fibrine /fibʀin/ *nf* fibrin.

fibrinogène /fibʀinɔʒɛn/ *nm* fibrinogen.

fibrociment® /fibʀɔsimɑ̃/ *nm* fibrocement GB, asbestos cement US.

fibrome /fibʀom/ **▶ 271** *nm* fibroid.

fibroscope /fibʀɔskɔp/ *nm* fibrescope[GB].

fibroscopie /fibʀɔskɔpi/ *nf*: *endoscopy by fibrescope*.

ficelage /fislaʒ/ *nm* **1** (action) (de paquet) tying up; (de mains, pieds) tying; **2** (attaches) string; **le ~ n'a pas tenu** the string didn't hold.

ficelé, **~e** /fisle/ **I** *pp* ▶ **ficeler**.
II *pp adj* [*spectacle, roman*] put together; [*budget, enquête*] organized.

ficeler /fisle/ [19] *vtr* to tie up [*paquet*]; to tie [*mains, pieds*]; **bien/mal ficelé** fig [*intrigue, roman*] well/badly put together; [*projet, enquête*] badly organized.
IDIOMES **~ qn comme un saucisson** to truss sb up like a chicken GB, to hogtie sb US.

ficelle /fisɛl/ *nf* **1** (matière) string, twine; **un morceau de ~** a piece of string; **as-tu de la ~?** have you got any string?; **réparé avec des ~s** repaired with bits of string; **2** (astuce) trick; **les ~s du métier** the tricks of the trade; **la ~ est un peu grosse** it's a bit obvious; **3** Culin (baguette mince) thin baguette.
IDIOMES **tirer sur la ~** to push one's luck; **tirer les ~s** (diriger) to pull the strings.

fichage /fiʃaʒ/ *nm* **~ d'un groupe de personnes** establishing files on a group of people.

fiche /fiʃ/ **I** *nf* **1** (à classer) (en carton) index card; (en papier) (petit) slip; (grand) sheet; **~ médicale** medical card; **~ pratique** card with practical hints; **~ bricolage** card with DIY hints; **~ cuisine** recipe card; **mettre qch sur ~** to put sth on file; **mettre qn sur ~** to put sb on one's files; **2** (formulaire) form; **~ d'inscription** enrolment[GB] form; **3** Électrotech (prise) plug; (broche) pin; **prise à trois ~s** three-pin plug; **4** Télécom, Ordinat plug.
II○ *vtr*, **se fiche** *vpr* = **ficher I 3, 4, 5; II 2, 3, 4.**
■ **~ banane** Électrotech banana plug; **~ (individuelle) d'état civil** Admin *record of personal details for administrative purposes*; **~ de lecture** notes (*from a book*); **faire des ~s de lecture** to take notes; **~ de paie** payslip GB, pay stub US; **~ technique** Tech technical data sheet.

ficher /fiʃe/ [1] **I** *vtr* **1** (répertorier) to put [sth] on a file [*œuvre*]; to open a file on [*personne*]; **être fiché à la police** to be on police files; **avec lui je n'ai aucune chance, je suis fiché** fig, hum I haven't got a chance with him, I'm in his bad books; **2** (enfoncer) to drive [*piquet, pieu, clou*] (**dans** into); **3**○ (faire) to do; **qu'est-ce que tu fiches?** what the heck are you doing○?; **ne rien ~** to do nothing; **je n'ai rien fichu ce matin** I didn't do a thing this morning; **n'en avoir rien à ~** not to give a damn○; **4**○ (donner) **~ un coup à qn** lit to wallop sb; fig to be a real blow to sb; **~ une fessée à qn** to smack sb's bottom; **~ une gifle à qn** to clout○ sb; **~ la trouille à qn** to scare the hell out of sb○; **ça fiche mal au dents** that gives you toothache GB ou a toothache; **'il est rentré?'—'je t'en fiche, je ne l'ai pas revu!'** 'did he come back?'—'you must be joking, I haven't seen him since!'; **je croyais le rencontrer, mais je t'en fiche!** I thought I would meet him but nothing of the sort!; **5**○ (mettre) **~ qch quelque part** to chuck○ sth somewhere; **où est-ce qu'il a bien pu ~ mon journal?** where the hell○ has he put my newspaper?; **~ le feu à qch** to set sth on fire; **~ qch par terre** to knock sth over; **en courant il a fichu le vase par terre** he knocked the vase over as he ran past; **son arrivée a fichu la soirée par terre** or **en l'air** his arrival ruined the party; **~ qn dehors** or **à la porte** (congédier) to give sb the boot○, to can sb US; (faire sortir) to kick sb out○; **~ qn dedans** (induire en erreur) to make sb screw up○ ou mess up; **~ la paix à qn** to leave sb alone.
II se ficher *vpr* **1** (se planter) [*flèche, couteau*] to stick (**dans qch** in sth); **2**○ (se mettre) **se ~ en colère** to fly off the handle○; **se ~ dedans** to screw up○; **il croyait bien faire mais il s'est fiché** or **fichu dedans** he thought he was doing the right thing but he screwed up○; **3** (ridiculiser) **se ~ de qn** (se moquer) to make fun of sb; (manquer de respect) to mess sb about○; **tu ne vois pas qu'il se fiche de toi?** can't you see he's messing you about○?; **le repas était excellent, ils ne se sont pas fichus de nous** the meal was excellent, they did us proud; **se ~ du monde** [*personne, autorité*] to have a hell of a nerve○; **4**○ (être indifférent) **se ~ de ce que qn fait** not to give a damn (about) what sb does○; **je me fiche de ce qu'il dit** I don't give a damn○ (about) what he says; **elle s'en fiche pas mal** she really couldn't give a damn○; ▶ **camp**.

fichier /fiʃje/ *nm* **1** (liste) file; (plusieurs listes) files (*pl*); (dans une bibliothèque) index; **le ~ national de qch** the national file on sth; **~ central** central filing system; **2** (meuble) filing cabinet; (boîte) card index file; **3** Ordinat file.

fichtre○ /fiʃtʀ/ *excl* goodness me!

fichtrement○† /fiʃtʀəmɑ̃/ *adv* jolly○ GB, darned○.

fichu /fiʃy/ **I**○ *pp* ▶ **ficher I 3, 4, 5, II 2, 3, 4.**
II○ *pp adj* **1** (détestable) (*before n*) [*temps*] rotten○; [*pluie*] dreadful; [*voiture, télévision*] flaming GB, damned○, blasted○ (*épith*); [*caractère*] nasty; [*métier*] rotten○; **ce ~ gamin ne veut rien apprendre** this damn○ kid just doesn't want to learn; **c'est à cause de ma ~e maladresse!** it's because I'm so damned○ clumsy!; **2** (condamné) [*personne, chaussures, vêtements, véhicule, machine*] done for; **s'il m'interroge je suis ~e** if he asks me any questions, I'm done for ou sunk○; **c'est ~ maintenant, c'est trop tard!** it's no good now, it's too late!; **s'il pleut c'est ~** if it rains that's the end of that; **c'est la troisième ampoule de ~e** that's the third bulb that's gone ou blown out US; **3** (fait) **comment c'est ~ ce truc?** how's this thing put together ou made?; **être bien ~** [*femme*] to be shapely; [*homme*] to be well built; [*mécanisme, dispositif*] to be well designed; [*appartement*] to be well laid out; [*vêtement*] to be well made; [*atlas, dictionnaire*] to be well laid out; **être mal ~** (malade) [*personne*] to feel lousy○; (mal conçu) [*mécanisme, dispositif*] to be badly designed; [*appartement*] to be badly laid out; [*vêtement*] to be badly cut; [*atlas, dictionnaire*] to be badly laid out; **ce logiciel est très mal ~** this software is really badly designed; **4** (considérable) **une ~e différence** a heck○ of a difference; **5** (capable) **être ~ de faire** to be quite capable of doing; **elle est ~e de réussir ses examens** she's quite capable of passing her exams; **il n'est pas ~ d'écrire une lettre** he can't even write a letter.
III *nm* shawl; **avoir un ~ sur les épaules** to have a shawl around one's shoulders.

fictif, **-ive** /fiktif, iv/ *adj* **1** (inventé) [*personnage, récit*] fictitious, imaginary; [*promesse, identité*] false; **2** Écon, Fin [*actif, dividende*] fictitious; [*valeur*] conventional.

fiction /fiksjɔ̃/ *nf* **1** Littérat fiction; **une œuvre de ~** a work of fiction; **la réalité dépasse la ~** truth is stranger than fiction; **2** TV (genre) drama; (émission) (TV) drama; **3** (invention) fiction; **c'est encore du domaine de la ~** it still belongs to the

realm of fiction; **c'est de la pure ~!** pej it's pure fiction; **4** Jur fiction.
■ **~ de droit** fiction of law; **~ légale** legal fiction.

fictivement /fiktivmɑ̃/ *adv* [*reconstituer, représenter*] fictitiously.

ficus /fikys/ *nm* ficus.

fidèle /fidɛl/ **I** *adj* **1** (constant) [*personne, chien*] faithful (**à** to); **être/rester ~ à son mari/maître** to be/remain faithful to one's husband/master; **être ~ au poste** to be always there; **2** (loyal) loyal (**à** to); **rester ~ à son entreprise** to remain loyal to one's company; **3** (identique) true (**à** to); **être/rester ~ à soi-même/sa parole** to be/to remain true to oneself/one's word; **4** (conforme) [*traduction, récit*] faithful (**à** to); **5** Mes, Sci reliable.
II *nmf* **1** (compagnon) loyal supporter; **les ~s du président** the president's loyal supporters; **2** (personne constante) faithful friend; **3** Relig **les ~s** the faithful (+ *v pl*); **quelques ~s** some of the faithful.

fidèlement /fidɛlmɑ̃/ *adv* **1** (avec exactitude) faithfully; **traduire/reproduire/suivre ~** to translate/reproduce/follow faithfully; **2** (avec loyauté) loyally.

fidélisation /fidelizasjɔ̃/ *nf* **~ de la clientèle** or **des clients/des lecteurs** securing of loyal customers/a loyal readership.

fidéliser /fidelize/ [1] *vtr* to secure the loyalty of [*clients, adhérents*].

fidélité /fidelite/ *nf* **1** (dans un couple) fidelity (**à** to); **~ conjugale** marital fidelity; **2** (d'ami, allié, électeur, de client) loyalty (**à** to); **~ à sa famille/au communisme** loyalty to one's family/to communism; **3** (de celui qui promet) faithfulness (**à** to); **~ à sa parole** faithfulness to one's word; **4** (de traduction, récit) accuracy; **5** Mes, Sci (de mesure) reliability.

Fidji /fidʒi/ ▶**321**, **416** *nprfpl* Fiji; **les (îles) ~** the Fiji Islands.

fidjien, -ienne /fidʒjɛ̃, ɛn/ ▶**537** *adj* Fijian.

Fidjien, -ienne /fidʒjɛ̃, ɛn/ ▶**537** *nm,f* Fijian.

fiduciaire /fidysjɛʀ/ **I** *adj* [*émission, circulation*] fiduciary; **monnaie ~** fiduciary currency, paper money; **société ~** trust company.
II *nmf* trustee.

fief /fjɛf/ *nm* **1** Hist fief; **2** (espace) territory; (de parti) stronghold.

fieffé, ~e /fjefe/ *adj* incorrigible; **~ menteur** incorrigible liar.

fiel /fjɛl/ *nm* **1** (hargne) venom; **déverser son ~ sur qn** to vent one's spleen on sb; **2** Méd bile.

fielleux, -euse /fjɛlø, øz/ *adj* venomous.

fiente /fjɑ̃t/ *nf* droppings (*pl*).

fier[1], **fière** /fjɛʀ/ *adj* **1** (satisfait) proud (**de qn/qch** of sb/sth; **de faire** to do); **tu peux être ~ de toi** lit you have every right to be proud; iron you must be very proud of yourself; **il n'y a pas de quoi être ~!** iron that's nothing to be proud of!; **je suis corse et j'en suis ~, je suis corse et ~ de l'être** I'm a Corsican and proud of it; **je suis fière qu'il ait réussi ses examens** I'm proud of the fact that he passed his exams; **je n'en suis pas peu ~** I'm quite proud of it; **2** (hautain) proud, haughty; (prétentieux) stuck-up○; **il est pas ~ (pour deux sous)**○ he's not (a bit) stuck-up○; **il est devenu ~ depuis sa promotion** he's got GB ou gotten US ou become very stuck-up○ since he was promoted; **il n'était pas si ~ à l'examen!** he wasn't so cocky○ in the exam!; **3** (noble) [*cœur, caractère, démarche, ville*] proud; **avoir fière allure** to cut a fine figure; **4**○ (remarquable) (*before n*) **~ imbécile** an incredible fool; **~ menteur** a terrible liar; **avoir un ~ culot**○ to have an incredible ou a fantastic nerve○; **5** (fougueux) (*before n*) [*monture*] mettlesome; ▶**chandelle**.
IDIOMES **~ comme Artaban** or **un coq** or **un paon** proud as a peacock; **faire le ~** to be haughty.

fier[2]: **se fier** /fje/ [2] *vpr* **1** (placer sa confiance en) **se ~ à** to trust [*personne, promesse*]; to go by, to trust [*apparences*]; **à qui peut-on se ~?** who can one ou you trust?; **ne te fie pas à ce qu'il dit** you can't go by what he says; **2** (compter sur) **se ~ à** to trust, to rely on [*personne, mémoire, instinct, instrument, calculs*]; to trust to [*chance, destin, bonne étoile*]; **le réveil marche mal, ne t'y fie pas** the alarm clock doesn't work properly, you can't rely on it.

fier-à-bras, *pl* **fiers-à-bras** /fjɛʀabʀa/ *nm* braggart.

fièrement /fjɛʀmɑ̃/ *adv* proudly.

fiérot○, **~e** /fjeʀo, ɔt/ *adj* (prétentieux) cocky.

fierté /fjɛʀte/ *nf* pride; **avoir sa ~** to have one's pride; **elle a toujours eu beaucoup de ~** she's always been very proud; **tirer ~ de qch** to take pride in sth; **ce musée fait** or **est la ~ de la ville** this museum is the town's pride and joy; **non sans ~** with a certain amount of pride; **avec ~** [*dire, montrer, recevoir*] proudly.

fiesta○ /fjɛsta/ *nf* party; **faire la ~** to rave it up○.

fièvre /fjɛvʀ/ *nf* **1** Méd (high) temperature; **avoir de la ~** to have a (high) temperature; **2** (agitation) frenzy; **~ d'achats** buying frenzy; **~ intellectuelle/médiatique/populaire** intellectual/media/popular frenzy; **dans la ~** in a frenzy; **pris de ~** caught up in a frenzy; **3** (ardeur) fervour[GB]; **~ nationaliste/patriotique** nationalist/patriotic fervour[GB]; **4** (passion) fever; **~ électorale/politique** election/political fever; **la ~ monte/tombe** the temperature is rising/is dropping.
■ **~ de cheval**○ raging fever; **~ jaune** yellow fever.

fiévreusement /fjevʀøzmɑ̃/ *adv* [*chercher, préparer*] frantically; [*parler*] feverishly.

fiévreux, -euse /fjevʀø, øz/ *adj* **1** Méd feverish; **2** (agité) frantic; **3** (passionné) feverish.

FIFA /fifa/ *nf* (*abbr* = **Fédération internationale de football association**) FIFA.

fifille○ /fifij/ *nf* little girl; **c'est la ~ à son papa** pej she's daddy's little girl.

fifre /fifʀ/ ▶**534** *nm* **1** (instrument) fife; **jouer du ~** to play the fife; **2** (personne) fife player.

fifrelin† /fifʀəlɛ̃/ *nm* **~s** money ¢; **ça ne vaut pas un ~** it's not worth a brass farthing.

figaro† /figaʀo/ *nm* hum barber.

figé, ~e /fiʒe/ **I** *pp* ▶**figer**.
II *pp adj* **1** (immobile) [*attitude, traits, personne*] frozen; [*situation, sourire*] fixed; **~ dans un rôle** locked into a role; **être/rester ~ sur place** to be/stand frozen to the spot; **2** (rigide) [*société, système politique*] fossilized; [*situation*] deadlocked; **être ~ dans ses habitudes** to be set in one's ways; **3** Ling [*expression, locution*] set.

figer /fiʒe/ [13] **I** *vtr* **1** (immobiliser) **la peur figeait leurs visages/traits** their faces/features were frozen with fear; **2** (solidifier) to congeal [*graisse*]; to thicken [*sauce*]; to clot [*sang*].
II se figer *vpr* **1** [*attitude, sourire, personne*] to freeze (**de** with); **se ~ comme une statue, se ~ sur place** to freeze; **2** (se scléroser) [*idéologie, société, personne*] to become fossilized; **se ~ dans ses habitudes** to become set in one's ways; **3** (se solidifier) [*graisse, sauce*] to congeal; [*sang*] to clot; **mon sang se figea dans mes veines** fig the blood froze in my veins.

fignolage /fiɲɔlaʒ/ *nm* **c'est du ~** péj it's just fiddling about; **il ne reste plus que du ~** all we need now are a few finishing touches.

fignoler /fiɲɔle/ [1] **I** *vtr* **1** (terminer) to put the finishing touches to; **2** (soigner) to take great pains over.
II *vi* to fiddle about.

fignoleur, -euse /fiɲɔlœʀ, øz/ *nm,f* perfectionist.

figue /fig/ *nf* fig.
■ **~ de Barbarie** prickly pear.

figuier /figje/ *nm* fig tree.
■ **~ de Barbarie** prickly pear.

figurant, ~e /figyʀɑ̃, ɑ̃t/ *nm,f* **1** (acteur) Cin extra; Théât bit player; **être ~** Cin to be an extra; Théât to have a walk-on part, to be a bit player; **2** (personne secondaire) **n'être qu'un ~** to have a token role.

figuratif, -ive /figyʀatif, iv/ *adj* [*dessin, artiste, art, peinture*] figurative, representational; **un artiste non ~** an abstract artist; **poésie figurative** emblematic ou figured verse.

figuration /figyʀasjɔ̃/ *nf* **faire de la ~** Théât to do bit parts; Cin to be an extra; fig to have a token role.

figurativement /figyʀativmɑ̃/ *adv* Art figuratively.

figure /figyʀ/ *nf* **1** (visage, mine) face; **ma ~ s'allongea** my face fell; **elle changea de ~** her face fell; **jeter à la ~ de qn** to throw [sth] in sb's face [*objet, vérité, défi*]; **ils s'envoient sans cesse des injures à la ~** they're always at each other's throats; **qu'est-ce qu'il a pris dans la ~!** fig he got a real going-over○; **2** (apparence) **faire ~ d'amateur** to look like an amateur; **ne plus avoir ~ humaine** to be unrecognizable; **reprendre ~ humaine** hum to look half-human again; **3** (personnalité) figure; **les grandes ~s de l'Histoire** great historical figures; **4** (schéma, photo, dessin) figure; **~ géométrique** diagram, geometric figure; **5** Art figure; **~ équestre** equestrian figure; **6** Jeux (carte) court card.
■ **~ imposée** compulsory figure; **~ de proue** lit figurehead; fig key figure; **~ de rhétorique** gén figure of speech; Hist Littérat rhetorical figure; **~ de style** stylistic device; **~s libres** freestyle ¢.
IDIOMES **prendre ~** to take shape; **faire bonne ~** (faire bonne impression) to make the right impression; (réussir) to do well; **faire piètre** or **triste ~** (avoir l'air misérable) to look ou cut a sorry figure; (faire mauvaise impression) to give a bad impression.

figuré, ~e /figyʀe/ **I** *adj* **sens ~** figurative sense.
II *nm* Ling figurative sense; **au ~, cela signifie...** in the figurative sense ou figuratively, this means...; **au propre comme au ~** both literally and figuratively.

figurément /figyʀemɑ̃/ *adv* figuratively, metaphorically.

figurer /figyʀe/ [1] **I** *vtr* to represent.
II *vi* [*nom, chose*] to appear; **ne pas ~ dans un rapport** not to appear in a report; **faire ~ dans un rapport** to include [sth] in a report; **un pompier figure parmi les victimes** a fireman is among the casualties; **ce plat ne figure plus au menu** this dish is no longer (included) on the menu; **cette mention ne figure plus dans le contrat** this clause is no longer in the contract.
III se figurer *vpr* to imagine; **je me figure le travail que cela présente** I can well imagine the amount of work it involves; **s'il se figure que...** if he thinks that...; **figure-toi que j'allais justement t'appeler** as it happens ou funnily enough I was just about to call you; **j'avais compris, figurez-vous!** I had actually got the point!; **figure-toi que je l'ai revu dix ans après!** I saw him again ten years later, can you imagine!

figurine /figyʀin/ *nf* figurine.

fil /fil/ **I** *nm* **1** Cout thread, cotton ¢ GB; **du ~ et une aiguille** a needle and thread; **~ d'or/d'argent** gold/silver thread; **avoir des ~s d'argent dans les cheveux** fig to have silver strands in one's hair; ▶**avril**, **coudre**, **retordre**; **2** (fibre naturelle) yarn;

(fibre artificielle, synthétique) filament; **~ cordé/mercerisé/peigné** corded/mercerized/combed yarn; **~ de polyamide** polyamide filament; **3** (câble, corde) (en fibre) string; (métallique) wire; (de pêche) line; (d'arrivée) Sport tape; **4** Électrotech, Télécom (ligne) wire; (de micro, d'appareil électrique) flex GB, cord US; (de téléphone) lead; (de combiné) flex GB, cord US; **sans ~** [*micro, téléphone*] cordless; **coup de ~**○ (phone) call; **j'ai passé/reçu dix coups de ~** I made/got ten phone calls; **passe-moi un coup de ~**○ give me a ring GB ou call; **il y a eu des coups de ~**○ **toute la matinée** the phone's been ringing all morning; **au bout du ~**○ on the phone; ▶ **coiffer**, **inventer**, **patte**; **5** (lin) linen ₵; **6** (enchaînement de texte, conversation) thread; **perdre le ~** to lose the thread; **perdre le ~ des événements** to lose track of events; **~ de la pensée** train of thought; **7** Culin (de haricot, céleri) string; **haricots sans ~s** stringless beans; **haricots pleins de ~s** stringy beans; **8** (d'araignée) thread; **9** (de bois) grain; **dans le ~** [*couper, graver*] with the grain; **10** (tranchant) edge; **11** (défaut dans la pierre) fissure.

II au fil de *loc prép* **au ~ des ans/des siècles** over the years/the centuries; **une tendance qui s'est confirmée au ~ des jours/mois** a tendency which became established as the days/months went by; **au ~ des minutes qui ont suivi l'accident** in the first few minutes following the accident; **au ~ de l'enquête/de la conversation/des réunions** in the course of the investigation/of the conversation/of the meetings; **au ~ des kilomètres, le paysage change** the scenery changes as you travel along; **aller au ~ de l'eau** lit, fig to go with the flow.

■ **~ à âme** Tex core yarn; **~ d'Ariane** Mythol Ariadne's thread; fig vital clue; **~ à bâtir** Cout tacking thread; **~ chirurgical** Méd surgical thread; **~ conducteur** Électrotech conductor; (de roman, intrigue) thread; (d'enquête) lead; **~ de contact** Rail overhead cable; **~ continu** Tex filament yarn; **~ à coudre** Cout sewing thread; **~ à couper le beurre** Culin cheese wire; **il n'a pas inventé le ~ à couper le beurre** fig he's not very bright; **~ dentaire** Dent dental floss; **~ directeur** guiding principle; **~ discontinu** Tex staple yarn; **~ d'Écosse** Tex lisle; **~ électrique** Électrotech electric wire; **~ de fer** wire; **~ de fer barbelé** barbed wire; **~ à plomb** plumb line; **~ à repriser** darning thread; **~ de terre** earth wire GB, ground wire US; **~ à tricoter** Cout knitting yarn; **~ de la Vierge** gossamer thread.

IDIOMES **ne tenir qu'à un ~** to hang by a thread; **être mince comme un ~** to be as thin as a rake; **être sur le ~ du rasoir** to be on a knife edge; **ne plus avoir un ~ de sec**○ to be soaked to the skin○.

fil-à-fil /filafil/ *nm inv* Tex pinstripe.

filage /filaʒ/ *nm* **1** Tex spinning; **2** Tech extrusion; **3** Théât run through.

filaire /filɛʀ/ **I** *adj* Ordinat wire; **représentation ~** wire drawing.

II *nf* Zool filaria.

filament /filamɑ̃/ *nm* **1** gén, Tex filament; **viande pleine de ~s** stringy meat; **2** Électrotech filament; **ampoule à ~** filament bulb.

filamenteux, **-euse** /filamɑ̃tø, øz/ *adj* [*tissu, écorce*] filamentous.

filandreux, **-euse** /filɑ̃dʀø, øz/ *adj* **1** (plein de fils) [*légume, viande*] stringy; **2** (confus) [*exposé, style, explication*] rambling; [*écrivain, orateur*] who rambles (*épith, après n*).

filant, **~e** /filɑ̃, ɑ̃t/ *adj* **1** Culin [*sauce, sirop*] runny; **2** Méd [*pouls*] thready; **3** Astron [*étoile*] shooting.

filariose /filaʀjoz/ ▶ **271** *nf* filariasis.

filasse /filas/ **I** *adj inv* **cheveux** (**blond**) **~** dirty yellow hair.

II *nf* (de lin, chanvre) tow.

filature /filatyʀ/ *nf* **1** (usine) textile mill; **~ de coton/soie** cotton/silk mill; **2** (transformation de textiles) spinning; **la ~ de la laine** the spinning of wool; **3** (surveillance) tailing ₵; **prendre qn en ~** to shadow sb, to tail○ sb.

fildeferiste /fildəfeʀist/ ▶ **510** *nmf* tightrope walker.

file /fil/ *nf* **1** (queue) queue GB, line US; **prenez la ~!** get in the queue! GB, join the line! US; **2** (alignement) line; **se mettre en ~** to get into line; **marcher en ~** to walk in line; **sortir/entrer en ~** to file out/in; **à la ~** (sans s'arrêter) in a row; **3** (sur la chaussée) lane; **reste dans ta ~** keep in lane; **prends la ~ de gauche** take the left-hand lane; **être (garé) en double ~** to be double-parked; **se garer en double ~** to double-park.

■ **~ d'attente** queue GB, line US; **~ indienne** single file; **en ~ indienne** in single file.

filé /file/ *nm* **1** Cin swish pan; **2** Tex spun yarn.

fil-électrode, *pl* **fils-électrodes** /filelɛktʀɔd/ *nm* wire electrode.

filer /file/ [1] **I** *vtr* **1** (transformer en fil) Tex to spin [*laine, coton*]; Ind to draw [*métal*]; ▶ **coton**, **parfait**; **2** Zool [*araignée, chenille*] to spin [*toile, cocon*]; **3** (démailler) to get a run in, to ladder GB [*bas, collant*]; **4** Naut, Pêche (dérouler) to play out [*amarre, ancre, ligne*]; **~ 20 nœuds** [*navire*] to do 20 knots; **5** Mus to hold [*note*]; Théât to run straight through [*scène, pièce*]; Littérat to extend [*métaphore*]; **6** (suivre) to shadow, to tail○ [*suspect*]; **~ le train à qn**○ to be on sb's tail○; **7**○ (donner) to give [*objet, argent*]; **~ un coup à qn** to hit sb.

II *vi* **1** Culin (couler) [*sirop*] to thread; [*fromage fondu*] to go stringy; **2** (se démailler) [*bas, collant*] to ladder GB, to run US; **3** Naut, Pêche (se dérouler) [*cordage*] to unwind; **laisser ~ un câble/une ligne** to play out a cable/line; **4**○ (s'éloigner) [*véhicule, animal*] to go off; [*personne*] to leave; **~ à toute allure** [*véhicule*] to speed off; [*animal*] to run off; [*personne*] to dash off; **je file, je suis en retard** I'll have to dash, I'm late; **file, et que je ne te revoie plus!** clear off○, and don't come back!; ▶ **anglais**; **5**○ (aller) to rush; **il a filé au bar/dans la maison** he rushed to the bar/into the house; **nous avons filé sur Paris** we rushed to Paris; **6**○ (disparaître) [*temps, journée*] to fly past; [*prisonnier*] to get away; **~ entre les mains** [*personne, argent, occasion*] to slip through one's fingers; **laisser ~ une occasion** to let an opportunity slip through one's fingers; **l'argent file** money doesn't last long; **les chocolats ont filé en un rien de temps** the chocolates didn't last long; ▶ **doigt**.

IDIOMES **~ comme le vent** or **une flèche** to go like the wind; **~ des jours heureux** to lead a happy life.

filerie /filʀi/ *nf* wiring.

filet /filɛ/ *nm* **1** Chasse, Pêche, Sport net; **monter au ~** to go up to the net; **envoyer le ballon au fond des ~s** to put the ball in the back of the net; **attirer** or **prendre qn dans ses ~s** fig to get sb in one's clutches; **coup de ~** (par la police) raid; **réussir un beau coup de ~** to carry out a very successful raid; **travailler sans ~** lit to perform without a safety net; fig to throw away the safety net, to take risks; **2** Cout, Tech, Tex (matériau) (textile) netting ₵; (métallique) mesh ₵; **~ de coton** cotton netting; **3** Culin (de viande, poisson) fillet; **~s d'anchois** anchovy fillets; **rôti de porc dans le ~** fillet of pork for roasting; **4** (flux) (d'eau) trickle; (de gaz) (léger) breath; (de fumée) wisp; **un ~ de fumée s'élevait à l'horizon** a wisp of smoke rose up on the horizon; **~ de citron/cognac** Culin dash of lemon juice/brandy; **un ~ de voix** a faint voice; **5** (trait fin) Imprim rule; Édition (sur une couverture, reliure) fillet; Art thin line; **assiette décorée d'un ~ doré** plate decorated with a thin gold line; **6** Presse (article) snippet; **7** Bot (d'étamine) filament; **8** Tech (de vis, d'écrou) thread; **9** Équit (harnais) bridle.

■ **~ à bagages** luggage rack; **~ de camouflage** camouflage net; **~ à cheveux** hairnet; **~ à crevettes** shrimping net; **~ de la langue** frenulum linguae; **~ mignon** Culin filet mignon; **~ à papillons** butterfly net; **~ de pêche** fishing net; **~ de protection** safety net; **~ à provisions** string bag; **~ de la verge** frenulum preputii.

filetage /filtaʒ/ *nm* **1** Tech (processus) threading; **2** Tech (filet) thread; **~ mâle/femelle** external/internal thread; **~ à droite/gauche** right-/left-hand thread; **3** (de poissons) filleting; **4** (en reliure) feathering.

fileté, **~e** /filte/ **I** *pp* ▶ **fileter**.

II *pp adj* Tech [*tige, embout*] threaded.

fileter /filte/ [18] *vtr* **1** Tech to thread [*vis, écrou, tige*]; **2** Ind to fillet [*poisson*].

fileur, **-euse** /filœʀ, øz/ ▶ **510** *nm,f* (de laine, lin) spinner.

filial, **~e**, *mpl* **-iaux** /filjal, o/ **I** *adj* filial.

II filiale *nf* subsidiary; **~e commune** joint subsidiary.

filiation /filjasjɔ̃/ *nf* Sociol filiation; (d'auteur, artiste) filiation; **descendre de qn par ~ directe** to be a direct descendant of sb.

filière /filjɛʀ/ *nf* **1** Scol, Univ (domaine d'études) course of study; **choisir une ~ prestigieuse** to choose a highly regarded course of study; **~s générales/techniques** general/technical courses of study; **nouvelles ~s** new fields; **suivre une ~ scientifique/littéraire** to study science/arts; **2** Écon, Entr, Ind (domaine d'activité) field; (système de production) chain; **la ~ électronique** the electronics field; **créer de nouvelles ~s** to create new fields of activity; **3** (étapes de carrière) **suivre la ~ habituelle** to climb up the usual career ladder; **4** (suite de formalités) official channels (*pl*); **la ~ administrative** the official administrative channels; **5** (de la drogue) **~ (clandestine)** ring; **démanteler une ~** to smash a ring; **remonter une ~** to trace the leaders of a ring; **6** Tech (d'usinage) die; (de tréfilage) draw die; **7** Nucl reactor system; **8** Zool (d'araignée, de chenille) spinneret; **9** Géol, Mines lode; **10** Ordinat card throat.

filiforme /filifɔʀm/ *adj* **1** (mince) [*personne, jambes*] spindly; [*insecte, pattes*] threadlike, filiform spéc; [*construction, sculpture*] spindly; **2** Méd [*pouls*] thready.

filigrane /filigʀan/ *nm* **1** (de papier) watermark; **couronne en ~** watermarked crown; **lire en ~** fig to read between the lines; **être en ~ dans** fig to be implicit in; **apparaissent en ~ des doutes sur le verdict** one can discern doubts about the verdict; **2** (en orfèvrerie, verrerie) filigree; **à décor de ~s** [*verre, vase*] filigree.

filigrané, **~e** /filigʀane/ *adj* [*papier*] watermarked.

filin /filɛ̃/ *nm* Naut rope.

fille /fij/ *nf* **1** (descendante) daughter; **~ adoptive** adopted daughter; **la ~ des Dupont** the Duponts' daughter; **~ de paysans/d'immigrés** daughter of peasants/of immigrants; **de mère en ~** from mother to daughter; **elle a eu une petite ~** she's had a little girl; **ma ~** gén my girl; Relig my child; ▶ **superstition**; **2** (jeune femme) girl; **une petite/grande ~** a little/big girl; **elle fait encore très petite ~** she's still very much a little girl; **faire ~** to look girlish; **être habillé en ~** to be dressed like a girl; **vêtements/jeux pour ~s** girls' clothes/games; **école de ~s** girls' school; **elle n'est pas ~ à s'en faire** she isn't one to worry; **elle est restée ~**† (célibataire) she remained a spinster; ▶ **jeune**, **vieux**; **3**† (prostituée) prostitute.

■ **~ de (bonne) famille** girl from a good family; **~ d'Ève** daughter of Eve; **~ de ferme** farm girl; **~ de joie**† prostitute; **~ à matelots**† sailors' moll; **~ mère**

unmarried mother; **~ perdue**† fallen woman†; **~ publique**†, **~ des rues**† streetwalker; **~ à soldats**† soldiers' moll; **~ soumise**† prostitute; **~ spirituelle** spiritual heir.
IDIOMES **jouer les ~s de l'air**○ to vanish into thin air; **c'est bien la ~ de son père/sa mère** she's very much her father's/her mother's daughter; **la plus belle ~ du monde ne peut donner que ce qu'elle a** with the best will in the world one can only go so far.

fillette /fijɛt/ *nf* **1** (petite fille) little girl; **rayon ~** Comm girlswear department; **2**○ (bouteille) half bottle.
IDIOMES **chausser du 45 ~**○ to have feet like boats○.

filleul /fijœl/ *nm* godson, godchild.

filleule /fijœl/ *nf* goddaughter, godchild.

film /film/ *nm* **1** (œuvre) film, movie US (**sur** about); **un ~ à succès** a box-office success; **tourner/réaliser un ~** to shoot/direct a film; **~ parlant** talking film, talkie○; **~ muet** silent film; **2** (déroulement d'événements) course, sequence; **le ~ des événements de l'été dernier** the course of last summer's events; **3** Cin (pellicule) film; **4** (mince couche) film; **~ protecteur** protective film.
■ **~ d'animation** cartoon; **~ d'aventures** adventure film; **~ catastrophe** disaster film; **~ d'épouvante** ou **d'horreur** horror film; **~ noir** film noir; **~ policier** detective film; **~ publicitaire** publicity film.

filmé, **~e** /filme/ **I** *pp* ▶**filmer**.
II *pp adj* on film; **la version ~e de Hamlet** the film version of Hamlet.

filmer /filme/ [1] *vtr* to film.

filmique /filmik/ *adj* film (*épith*).

filmographie /filmɔgʀafi/ *nf* filmography.

filmologie /filmɔlɔʒi/ *nf* film studies (*pl*).

filon /filɔ̃/ *nm* **1** Minér vein, seam, lode; **un ~ de cuivre/d'or** a vein of copper/of gold; **exploiter un ~** lit, fig to mine a seam; **2**○ (pactole) bonanza; (travail lucratif) cushy number○; **un bon ~ pour se procurer des faux papiers** a good way of getting hold of forged papers; **avoir trouvé le bon** or **un ~** to be on to a good thing.

filou /filu/ **I** *adj* **il est ~** (escroc) he's a crook; (tricheur) he's a cheat; (enfant malin) he's a rascal.
II *nm* (escroc) crook; (tricheur) cheat; (enfant malin) rascal.

filouter /filute/ [1] *vtr* (voler) to diddle○; (au jeu) to cheat; **~ qn de 100 francs** to diddle○ sb out of 100 francs.

filouterie /filutʀi/ *nf* (acte d'escroc) fiddle○, swindle.

fils /fis/ *nm* son; **~ indigne** unworthy son; **le ~ des Dupont** the Duponts' son; **de père en ~** from father to son; **Alexandre Dumas ~** Alexandre Dumas the younger; **Dupont ~** Entr Dupont Junior; **Dupont et ~** Entr Dupont and Son(s); **mon ~** gén my boy; Relig my son.
■ **~ de (bonne) famille** boy from a good family; **Fils de Dieu** Relig Son of God; **Fils prodigue** Bible Prodigal Son; **~ de pute**● son-of-a-bitch◑, SOB◑ US; **~ spirituel** spiritual heir.
IDIOMES **tel père, tel ~** Prov like father, like son Prov; **c'est bien le ~ de son père/sa mère** he's very much his father's/his mother's son.

filtrage /filtʀaʒ/ *nm* **1** (d'appels téléphoniques, informations) screening; **2** (de liquide) filtering.

filtrant, **~e** /filtʀɑ̃, ɑ̃t/ *adj* [*papier, corps, couche*] filter (*épith*); **produit solaire ~** sun screen; **barrage ~** selective blockade.

filtrat /filtʀa/ *nm* filtrate.

filtration /filtʀasjɔ̃/ *nf* Chimie filtration.

filtre /filtʀ/ *nm* (tous contextes) filter; **~ coloré** colour[GB] filter; **cigarette avec ~** filter-tip cigarette; **cigarette sans ~** untipped cigarette.
■ **~ à air** Aut air filter; **~ à café** Culin coffee filter; **~ à café perpétuel** permanent coffee filter; **~ à huile** Aut oil filter; **~ solaire** Cosmét sun screen.

filtrer /filtʀe/ [1] **I** *vtr* **1** (purifier) to filter; **2** (tamiser) to filter [*bruit, lumière*]; **3** (sélectionner) to screen [*visiteurs, appels téléphoniques, informations*].
II *vi* **1** (émerger) [*informations*] (lentement) to filter through; (malgré des précautions) to leak out; [*idée*] to filter through; **la nouvelle a filtré jusqu'aux journalistes/journaux** the news leaked out to the journalists/newspapers; **2** (s'écouler) [*liquide*] to filter through; **3** (passer) [*son, lumière*] to filter.

fin[1], **fine** /fɛ̃, fin/ **I** *adj* **1** (constitué d'éléments très petits) [*sable, poudre, pluie*] fine; **2** (très mince) [*gouttelette, fil, trait de crayon, écriture*] fine; [*tranche, plaque, couche, feuille, verre*] thin; **3** (effilé) [*pinceau, aiguille, plume, pointe*] fine; **4** Comm, Culin [*petits pois, haricots verts*] quality (*épith*); **très ~s** top-quality (*épith*); **5** (délicat) [*cheville, poignet, cou, taille*] slender; [*traits*] fine; **il est très ~ de visage** he's got very fine features; **6** (ouvragé) [*orfèvrerie, broderie, bijou, dentelle*] delicate, fine; **7** (de grande qualité) [*vins, aliments, lingerie*] fine; [*plat, mets, morceau*] delicate; **8** (subtil) [*personne*] perceptive; [*esprit*] shrewd; [*allusion, interprétation*] subtle; [*plaisanterie, humour*] subtle; [*goût*] delicate, subtle; **vraiment c'est ~!** iron that's really clever! iron; **jouer au plus ~ avec qn** to try to outsmart sb; **avoir l'air ~**○ to look a fool; **tu as l'air ~**○ **avec ce chapeau!** you look a sight○ in that hat!; **9** (sensible) **avoir l'ouïe** or **l'oreille ~e** to have a keen sense of hearing; **avoir l'odorat** or **le nez ~** to have a keen sense of smell; **10** (remarquable) (*before n*) excellent; **c'est une ~e cuisinière** she's an excellent cook; **~ gourmet** gourmet; **~ connaisseur** connoisseur; **~ tireur** crack shot; **la ~e fleur des économistes/joueurs d'échecs** the top ou best economists/chess players; ▶**bouche**; **11** (ultime) (*before n*) **au ~ fond de** in the remotest part of [*pays, région*]; at the very bottom of [*tiroir, armoire*]; **ils habitent au ~ fond du Massif central** they live in the remotest part of the Massif Central; **le ~ mot de l'histoire** the truth of the matter.
II *adv* **1** (complètement) **être ~ prêt** to be all set; **~ soûl**○ completely drunk, sloshed○; **2** (finement) [*écrire, moudre*] finely; [*couper*] thinly.
III *nm* **le ~ du ~** the ultimate (**de** in).
IV fine *nf* (boisson) brandy.
■ **~ limier** super-sleuth; **~ renard** sly customer○; **~e gueule**○ gourmet; **~e lame** expert swordsman; **~e mouche** = **~ renard**; **~es herbes** mixed herbs, fines herbes.

fin[2] /fɛ̃/ *nf* **1** (terme) end; (de séance, réunion, période) close, end; (façon dont se termine quelque chose) ending; **à la ~ de** at the end of; **~ août/septembre** at the end of August/September; **en ~ de journée/semaine/mois** at the end of the day/week/month; **à la ~ des années 70** in the late '70s; **en ~ de matinée/d'après-midi** late in the morning/afternoon; **vers** or **sur la ~** toward(s) the end; **en ~ de séance** (à la Bourse) at the close; **jusqu'à la ~** to the (very) end; **jusqu'à la ~ des temps** until the end of time; **toucher** or **tirer à sa ~** to be coming ou drawing to an end; **tout a une ~** everything comes to an end; **prendre ~** to come to an end; **mettre ~ à** to put an end to; **mettre ~ à ses jours** to take one's own life, to put an end to one's life; **'fin'** (dans un film, roman) 'the end'; **la ~ du monde** lit, fig the end of the world; **c'est la ~ de leurs espoirs** it's the end of their hopes; **avoir des ~s de mois difficiles** to find it hard to make ends meet at the end of the month; **la quatrième en partant de la ~** the fourth from the bottom ou end; **la table des matières est à la ~ du livre** the table of contents is at the back of the book; **payable ~ janvier/courant/prochain** payable at the end of January/of this month/of next month; **c'est la ~ de tout** it's the last straw; **mener qch à bonne ~** to carry sth off, to bring sth to a successful conclusion; **c'est un bon film mais je n'ai pas aimé la ~** it's a good film but I didn't like the ending; **sans ~** [*combats, discussions, guerre*] endless, never-ending; [*discuter, épiloguer, se disputer*] endlessly; **à la ~** in the end; **tu vas te taire à la ~**○**!** for God's sake, be quiet!, be quiet already○ US!; **tu m'ennuies à la ~**○**!** you're really getting on my nerves!; **chômeur en ~ de droits** *unemployed person who is no longer entitled to unemployment benefit*; **~ de siècle** pej decadent, fin-de-siècle; **2** (mort) end, death; **une ~ tragique/prématurée** a tragic/premature end ou death; **il ne vous entend plus, c'est la ~** he can no longer hear you, he's dying; **3** (but) end, aim, purpose; **à cette ~** to this end; **à toutes ~s utiles** for whatever purpose it may serve; **arriver** or **parvenir à ses ~s** to achieve one's aims; **à seule ~ de** for the sole purpose of; **ce n'est pas une ~ en soi** it's not an end in itself.
■ **~ de l'exercice** end of the financial year; **~ de semaine** weekend; **~ de série** Comm oddment.
IDIOMES **la ~ justifie les moyens, qui veut la ~ veut les moyens** the end justifies the means.

final, **~e**[1], *mpl* **-aux** /final, o/ **I** *adj* final; **proposition ~e** final clause.
II finale *nf* **1** Sport final; **quart de ~e** quarterfinal; **arriver en ~e** to reach the final(s); **2** Ling final; **en ~e** in final position.

finale[2] /final/ *nm* Mus finale.

finalement /finalmɑ̃/ *adv* **1** (à la fin) in the end, finally; **~, ils sont arrivés avec une heure de retard** in the end they arrived an hour late; **~ nous sommes restés à la maison** in the end we stayed at home; **ils ont ~ réussi à se mettre d'accord** they eventually managed to reach an agreement; **alors, qu'est-ce que vous avez décidé ~?** so what have you decided then?; **2** (en définitive) in fact, after all; **~ on a tout à y gagner** after all, we have everything to gain by it; **~ j'aurais dû refuser/ce n'était pas une bonne solution** as it turned out I should have refused/it wasn't a good solution.

finalisation /finalizasjɔ̃/ *nf* finalization.

finaliser /finalize/ [1] *vtr* to finalize [*accords*]; to complete [*transaction*].

finalisme /finalism/ *nm* Philos finalism.

finaliste /finalist/ *adj, nmf* finalist.

finalité /finalite/ *nf* **1** gén purpose, aim; **2** Philos finality.

finançable /finɑ̃sabl/ *adj* **ce projet est/n'est pas ~** the project can/can't be financed.

finance /finɑ̃s/ **I** *nf* **1** (activité) **la ~** finance; **la haute ~ internationale** international high finance; **la ~ new-yorkaise** New York finance; **le monde/vocabulaire de la ~** the financial world/vocabulary; **c'est un homme de ~** he's a financier; **2** (milieu) financiers (*pl*).
II finances *nfpl* **1** (d'État, entreprise, de ville, foyer) **les ~s** finances; **les ~s locales/publiques/privées** local/public/private finances; **gérer les ~s du pays** to manage the country's finances; **moyennant ~s** for a consideration; **les ~s sont à sec**○ funds are exhausted; **mes ~s sont à sec**○ I'm broke○; **2**○ (ministère) **les Finances** the Ministry (*sg*) of Finance.

financement /finɑ̃smɑ̃/ *nm* financing ₵; **grâce à des ~s privés** thanks to private financing; **le ~ du projet ne sera pas facile** financing the project won't be easy.

financer /finɑ̃se/ [12] **I** *vtr* to finance [*dépenses, projet, personne*].

II○ *vi* (payer) to fork out○.

financier, **-ière** /finɑ̃sje, ɛʀ/ **I** *adj* financial; **directeur/analyste ~** financial director/analyst; **crise économique et financière** economic and financial crisis; **compagnie financière** finance company.

II *nm* **1** Fin financier; **2** Culin small cake (*made with ground almonds and egg whites*).

financièrement /finɑ̃sjɛʀmɑ̃/ *adv* financially.

finasser○ /finase/ [1] *vi* to scheme, to use trickery.

finasserie○ /finasʀi/ *nf* **1** (caractère) scheming; **2** (ruse) trick.

finaud, **~e** /fino, od/ **I** *adj* cunning, wily.

II *nm,f* (homme) wily bird○; (femme) crafty minx.

finauderie /finodʀi/ *nf* **1** (caractère) wiliness, craftiness; **2** (acte) crafty trick.

finement /finmɑ̃/ *adv* **1** (de façon délicate) [*ouvragé, ciselé, tissé*] finely, delicately; **2** (avec subtilité) [*faire remarquer, noter*] cleverly; **c'est ~ joué!** that's a smart ou shrewd move!; **3** (en petits éléments) [*hacher, couper*] finely; **4** (avec précision) [*mesurer*] accurately, precisely.

finesse /finɛs/ *nf* **1** (minceur) (d'aiguille, écriture, de fil, pointe, cheveux, poudre) fineness; (de couche, papier, plaque) thinness; (de lame) keenness, sharpness; **2** (délicatesse) (d'étoffe, de broderie, bijou) delicacy; (de parfum, saveur, aliment) delicacy; (de visage, traits) fineness, delicacy; (de chevilles, poignets, taille, cou) slenderness; **3** (perspicacité) (de personne) perceptiveness; (d'analyse, de remarque) shrewdness, perceptiveness; (d'acteur, interprétation) sensitivity, finesse; **4** (acuité de vue, goût, d'ouïe, odorat) keenness, sharpness; **5** (subtilité) **les ~s d'une langue/discipline** the finer points ou the subtleties of a language/discipline.

finette /finɛt/ *nf* brushed cotton.

fini, **~e** /fini/ **I** *pp* ▶ **finir**.

II *pp adj* **1** (terminé) **être ~** to be over, to be finished; **les vacances sont ~es** the vacation is over; **~ de rire** or **~e la rigolade**○, **il faut travailler maintenant!** the party's over, it's time to get down to work!; **leurs problèmes sont loin d'être ~s** their troubles are far from over; **c'en est ~ de leur domination/leurs espoirs** it's the end of their rule/their hopes; **tout est ~ entre eux** it's all over ou finished between them; **2** (ouvragé) finished; **un vêtement bien/mal ~** a well-/badly-finished garment; **produits ~s** finished products; **3**○ (invétéré) [*menteur, canaille, alcoolique*] out-and-out, complete; **4**○ (usé) [*artiste, politicien*] finished; **en tant qu'homme politique, il est ~** he's finished as a politician; **5** Math [*ensemble, univers*] finite.

III *nm* finish; **ouvrage qui manque de ~** work that lacks finish.

finir /finiʀ/ [3] **I** *vtr* **1** (achever) to finish (off), to complete [*travail, tâche*]; (conclure) to end [*journée, nuit, discours*] (**avec** with); **~ de faire** to finish doing; **finis tes devoirs avant d'aller jouer** finish your homework before you go off to play; **ne l'interromps pas, laisse-le ~ (son histoire)** don't interrupt him, let him finish (his story); **j'ai fini le roman** I have finished the novel; **il a fini la soirée au poste de police/dans une boîte de nuit** he ended the evening at the police station/in a night club; **~ sa vie** or **ses jours en prison/dans la misère** to end one's life ou days in prison/in poverty; **de grâce, finissez vos querelles!** please, put a stop to your quarrelling[GB]!; **pour ~, je dirai que** in conclusion I'll say that; **vous n'avez pas fini de vous disputer?** for goodness sake stop arguing!; **tu n'as pas fini de m'embêter/de te plaindre?** have you quite finished annoying me/complaining?; **elle n'a pas fini de s'inquiéter/d'avoir des problèmes** her worries/troubles are only just beginning; **tu n'as pas fini d'en entendre parler!** you haven't heard the last of it!; **2** (consommer jusqu'au bout) to use up [*provisions, produit, shampooing, détergent*]; to finish [*plat, dessert*]; **j'ai fini le sucre, j'en rachèterai** I've used up all the sugar, I'll buy some more; **qui veut ~ le gâteau/vin?** who wants to finish the cake/wine?, who wants the last of the cake/wine?; **il finit toutes les affaires de son grand frère**○ he gets all his big brother's hand-me-downs.

II *vi* **1** gén to finish, to end; Admin [*contrat, bail*] to run out, to expire; **le spectacle finit dans 20 minutes** the show ends ou finishes in 20 minutes; **tout est bien qui finit bien** all's well that ends well; **le film finit bien/mal** the film has a happy/an unhappy ending; **tu as fini avec le dictionnaire/l'agrafeuse?** have you finished with the dictionary/the stapler?; **ça va mal ~!** it'll end in tears!; **il finira mal ce garçon** that boy will come to a bad end; **le roman finit sur une note optimiste** the novel ends on an optimistic note; **le spectacle a fini par un feu d'artifice** the show ended in ou with a firework display; **la réunion a fini en bagarre** or **par une bagarre** the meeting ended in a brawl; **la route finit en piste** the road ends in a dirt track; **sa barbe finit en pointe** his beard tapers to a point; **les verbes finissant en 'er'** verbs ending in 'er'; **il finira en prison/dans l'armée/à l'hospice/dans la misère** he'll end up in prison/in the army/in the poorhouse/in poverty; **il a fini alcoolique** he ended up an alcoholic; **il a fini directeur de la société** he ended up (as) company director; **2 ~ par faire** to end up doing; **tu vas ~ par te blesser/la vexer/être en retard** you'll end up hurting yourself/offending her/being late; **ils finiront bien par céder** they're bound to give in in the end; **il a fini par se décider/accepter/avouer** he eventually made up his mind/accepted/confessed; **il a fini par s'apercevoir de son erreur** he eventually realized that he'd made a mistake; **elle finira par lui pardonner/l'oublier** she'll forgive him/her/forget him/her in the end; **elle a fini par obtenir satisfaction** she eventually got what she wanted; **3 en ~ avec qch/qn** to have done with sth/sb; **on n'en finira donc jamais avec ce type**○? will we never have done with this guy○?; **finissons-en!** let's get it over and done with!, let's have done with it!; **fais ce qu'il te dit et qu'on en finisse** do as he says and have done with it; **il faut en ~ avec cette situation/violence** we must put an end to this situation/violence; **il veut en ~ avec la vie** he wants to end his life; **le film/l'hiver/la route n'en finit pas** the film/winter/the road seems endless ou never-ending; **il n'en finit pas ce feu rouge!** is this red light ever going to change?; **elle a des jambes qui n'en finissent pas** she's all legs, she's very leggy; **elle n'en finit pas de se préparer** she takes ages○ to get ready; **il n'en finit pas de rabâcher les mêmes histoires** he's forever telling the same stories; **des discussions/problèmes à n'en plus ~** endless discussions/problems; ▶ **queue**.

finish /finiʃ/ *nm* Sport finish; **il l'a emporté au ~** he won at the finishing-line ou -post.

finissage /finisaʒ/ *nm* finishing.

finissant, **~e** /finisɑ̃, ɑ̃t/ *adj* **une civilisation/une époque ~e** a civilization/an era which is drawing to an end; **à l'été ~** in the last days of the summer; **au jour ~** at twilight, as the day was drawing to a close.

finisseur, **-euse** /finisœʀ, øz/ ▶ **510** *nm,f* finisher.

Finistère /finistɛʀ/ ▶ **692** *nprm* (département) **le ~** Finistère.

finition /finisjɔ̃/ *nf* (processus) finishing; (résultat) finish; **faire les ~s** to put the finishing touches (**de** to); **travaux de ~** finishing; **il faut compter deux semaines de plus pour les travaux de ~** allow two weeks extra for finishing; **un meuble aux ~s soignées** a beautifully finished piece of furniture.

finlandais, **~e** /fɛ̃lɑ̃dɛ, ɛz/ ▶ **537** *adj* Finnish.

Finlandais, **~e** /fɛ̃lɑ̃dɛ, ɛz/ ▶ **537** *nm,f* Finn.

Finlande /fɛ̃lɑ̃d/ ▶ **321** *nprf* Finland.

finlandisation /fɛ̃lɑ̃dizasjɔ̃/ *nf* Finlandization.

finnois, **~e** /finwa, az/ ▶ **462** **I** *adj* Finnish.

II *nm* Ling Finnish.

finno-ougrien, **-ienne** /finougʀijɛ̃, ɛn/ **I** *adj* Finno-Ugric.

II *nm* Ling Finno-Ugric.

FINUL /finyl/ *nf* (*abbr* = **Force intérimaire des Nations unies au Liban**) UNIFIL.

fiole /fjɔl/ *nf* **1** (flacon) phial; **2**○ (tête) bonce○; **il s'est payé ma ~** he made fun at my expense.

fion○ /fjɔ̃/ *nm* H (mot blessant) cutting remark.

fioriture /fjɔʀityʀ/ *nf* **1** (ornement) embellishment; **sans ~s** [*meuble, pièce*] unadorned; [*écriture*] plain; [*parler, écrire*] plainly; **faire des ~s** (en écrivant, parlant) to use a flowery style; **2** Mus ornamentation, fioritura spéc.

fioul /fjul/ *nm* fuel oil.

■ **~ domestique** heating oil.

firmament /fiʀmamɑ̃/ *nm* **1** (ciel) firmament; **au ~** in the firmament; **2** fig **au ~ du succès** at the pinnacle of success.

firme /fiʀm/ *nf* firm.

fisc /fisk/ *nm* tax office.

fiscal, **~e**, *mpl* **-aux** /fiskal, o/ *adj* fiscal, tax (*épith*); **l'appareil ~** the fiscal ou tax structure.

fiscalement /fiskalmɑ̃/ *adv* fiscally.

fiscalisation /fiskalizasjɔ̃/ *nf* **1** (imposition) taxation; **2** (financement par l'impôt) funding by taxation.

fiscaliser /fiskalize/ [1] *vtr* **1** (imposer) to tax; **2** (financer par l'impôt) to fund [sth] by taxation.

fiscaliste /fiskalist/ ▶ **510** *nmf* tax specialist.

fiscalité /fiskalite/ *nf* **1** (fait d'imposer) taxation; **la ~ directe** direct taxation; **le poids de la ~** the tax burden; **2** (système) tax system; **~ allemande** German tax system.

fish-eye, *pl* **~s** /fiʃaj/ *nm* fish-eye lens.

fissa○ /fisa/ *adv* **faire ~** to get a move on○.

fissibilité /fisibilite/ *nf* fissionability, fissility.

fissible /fisibl/ *adj* fissionable, fissile.

fissile /fisil/ *adj* Phys, Nucl fissile, fissionable; Minér fissile.

fission /fisjɔ̃/ *nf* fission; **~ nucléaire** nuclear fission.

fissionner /fisjɔne/ [1] *vtr, vi* to split.

fissuration /fisyʀasjɔ̃/ *nf* **1** Tech cracking ¢, fissuring ¢; **2** Méd cracking ¢.

fissure /fisyʀ/ *nf* **1** (petite fente) crack, fissure spéc; **les ~s d'un mur** the cracks in a wall; **2** Anat fissure; **3** fig rift, division.

fissurer /fisyʀe/ [1] **I** *vtr* **1** (fendiller) to crack, to fissure spéc; **2** (diviser) to cause a rift in [*amitié, union*].

II se fissurer *vpr* **1** [*mur, sol*]; to crack, to fissure spéc; **2** [*union*] to break up.

fiston○ /fistɔ̃/ *nm* (tous contextes) sonny○, son.

fistulaire /fistylɛʀ/ *adj* fistular.

fistule /fistyl/ *nf* fistula; **~ anale** anal fistula.

fistuleux, **-euse** /fistylø, øz/ *adj* fistulous.

FIV /fiv/ *nf*: *abbr* ▶ **fécondation**.

fivete /fivɛt/ *nf* ZIFT, zygote intra-fallopian transfer.

fixage /fiksaʒ/ *nm* Phot, Fin fixing; Art (en restauration) consolidation; Tex setting.

fixateur, **-trice** /fiksatœʀ, tʀis/ **I** *adj* [*produit, liquide, bain*] fixative.

II *nm* **1** Art, Phot (produit) fixative; (appareil) (à main) fixative sprayer; (à bouche) fixative mouth blower; **2** Cosmét (après une permanente) neutralizing solution; (laque) fixative; (de parfum) fixative; **3** Biol (pour analyse) fixative.

fixatif /fiksatif/ *nm* fixative.

fixation /fiksasjɔ̃/ *nf* **1** (mise en place) fixing; (attache) fastening; **la ~ des étagères se fait avec des vis** the shelves are fixed with screws; **2** (détermination) setting; **~ de la peine** Jur determination of penalty; **~ des cours** Fin fixing; **3** Sport (de ski) binding; **~ avant/arrière/de sécurité** front/rear/safety binding; **4** Physiol (d'azote, oxygène) fixation; **5** Bot, Zool (processus) attachment; (attache) (de plante) stem; (de mollusque) foot; **6** Art, Phot (de pastel, photo) fixing; **7** Ling fossilization; **8** (de population) settling; **9** Psych fixation; **faire une ~ à la mère** to have a mother fixation; **faire une ~ sur qch/qn** to be fixated on sth/sb.

fixe /fiks/ **I** *adj* **1** (immobile) [*élément, caméra, point*] fixed; **avoir le regard** or **l'œil ~** to have a fixed stare; **il t'observait d'un œil ~** he was staring intently at you; **2** (invariable) [*revenu, prix, taux*] fixed; [*poste, personnel, résidence, couleur*] permanent; **manger à heures ~s** to eat at set times; **il recevait à heure ~** he would receive visitors at a set time; **chaque année/mois à date ~** on the same date every year/month; **poésie à forme ~** poetry in a set form.

II *nm* (salaire) basic salary GB, base pay US.

III *excl* Mil attention!

fixé, **~e** /fikse/ **I** *pp* ▶ **fixer**.

II *pp adj* **1** (renseigné) **me voilà ~ sur ton compte** now I'm wise to you; **tu es ~ maintenant!** you've got the picture now○!; **nous ne sommes pas encore ~s sur le sort des otages** we are still uncertain about the hostages' fate; **2** (certain) **nous ne sommes pas encore très ~s sur ce que nous allons faire** we haven't really decided yet on what we're going to do; **3** (orienté) **le monde entier a les yeux ~s sur vous** the whole world is watching you; **tous les regards étaient ~s sur moi** everyone was watching me; **il avait le regard ~ sur elle** he gazed intently at her; **4** (installé) [*population, famille*] settled; **leur famille est ~e à Paris depuis trois générations** their family has been settled in Paris for three generations.

III *nm* Art glass-picture.

fixe-chaussette, *pl* **~s** /fiksʃosɛt/ *nm* suspender GB, garter US.

fixement /fiksəmɑ̃/ *adv* [*regarder*] fixedly.

fixer /fikse/ [1] **I** *vtr* **1** (attacher) to fix [*objet*] (**à** to; **sur** on); **~ un miroir au mur** to fix a mirror to the wall; **~ avec des boulons/des vis/de la colle** to bolt/to screw/to stick (**sur** to); **2** (décider) to set [*date, prix, taux, conditions, itinéraire*]; **~ son choix sur qch/qn** to decide on sth/sb; **au jour fixé** on the appointed day; **3** (établir) **~ son domicile en France** to make one's home in France; **~ le siège de l'organisation à Paris** to base the organization's headquarters in Paris; **4** (stabiliser) to fix [*couleur, émulsion*]; to establish [*frontières, forme littéraire*]; to regulate [*orthographe, langue*]; **~ ses idées sur le papier/par écrit** to set one's ideas down on paper/in writing; **~ des dunes avec des oyats** to stabilize sand dunes with marram grass; **substance qui fixe l'azote** nitrogen-fixing substance; **5** (concentrer) to focus; **~ son attention/son regard sur qn/qch** to focus one's attention/one's gaze on sb/sth; **6** (observer) to stare at [*personne, objet, point*]; **~ qn d'un regard idiot** to stare at sb stupidly; **qu'est-ce qu'il a à me ~, celui-là?** what's he staring at me like that for?

II se fixer *vpr* **1** Tech (s'attacher) [*équipement, pièce*] to be attached (**à** to); **mon porte-serviettes se fixe au mur avec des ventouses/vis** my towel rail is fixed to the wall with suction cups/screws; **2** (décider) to set oneself [*but, conduite, limite, budget*]; **la tâche qu'il s'est fixée** the task that he set himself; **se ~ comme** or **pour but de faire** to set oneself the goal of doing; **3** (s'installer) [*personne, population*] to settle; (se ranger) [*personne*] to settle down; **se ~ à l'étranger** to settle abroad; **un marginal qui n'a jamais voulu se ~** a dropout who never wanted to settle down; **4** (se figer) **se ~ dans l'esprit/la mémoire de qn** to stick in sb's mind/memory; **les soupçons se sont fixés sur moi** suspicion fell on me; **leur système d'écriture s'est fixé dès l'antiquité** their system of writing was established in ancient times; **5** Zool [*coquillage, moule*] to attach itself (**à, sur** to).

fjord /fjɔʀd/ *nm* fjord.

flac /flak/ *excl* plop!, splash!

flaccidité /flaksidite/ *nf* flaccidity.

flacon /flakɔ̃/ *nm* (bouteille) (small) bottle; (carafe) decanter; Chimie, Pharm flask.

IDIOMES **qu'importe le ~ pourvu qu'on ait l'ivresse** it's the contents that count, not the packaging.

flagada○ /flagada/ *adj inv* whacked○, exhausted.

flagellateur, **-trice** /flaʒɛlatœʀ, tʀis/ *nm,f* flagellator, scourger.

flagellation /flaʒɛlasjɔ̃/ *nf* gén flogging, scourging; Relig flagellation.

flagelle /flaʒɛl/ *nf* flagellum.

flagellé, **~e** /flaʒɛle/ *adj, nm,f* flagellate.

flageller /flaʒɛle/ [1] *vtr* **1** lit (châtier) to flog, to scourge; Relig to flagellate; **2** fig to castigate [*vice, abus*].

flageolant, **~e** /flaʒɔlɑ̃, ɑ̃t/ *adj* **1** [*jambe*] wobbly, trembling; **il était ~ de fatigue** he was weak at the knees with tiredness; **2** [*amitié, entente*] crumbling.

flageoler /flaʒɔle/ [1] *vi* **1** [*personne*] **~ de fatigue** to feel wobbly; **avoir les jambes qui flageolent de fatigue** to be unsteady on one's legs; **~ de peur** to be shaking in one's shoes; **~ d'émotion** to be weak at the knees; **2** [*amitié, entente*] to crumble.

flageolet /flaʒɔlɛ/ *nm* **1** (haricot) flageolet; **2** ▶ **534** (flûte) flageolet.

flagorner /flagɔʀne/ [1] *vtr* to fawn on, to toady to [*personne*]; to curry favour[GB] with [*groupe, public*].

flagornerie /flagɔʀnəʀi/ *nf* toadying ¢, sycophantic behaviour[GB] ¢.

flagorneur, **-euse** /flagɔʀnœʀ, øz/ **I** *adj* [*personne*] toadying, sycophantic; [*discours, article*] fulsome.

II *nm,f* toady, sycophant.

flagrant, **~e** /flagʀɑ̃, ɑ̃t/ *adj* [*échec, déséquilibre, différence, preuve*] obvious; [*injustice, malhonnêteté, violation*] flagrant; [*mensonge, contradiction, discrimination*] blatant; [*erreur, exemple*] glaring; **il ment, c'est ~** it's blatantly obvious that he's lying.

■ **~ délit** Jur *case requiring no further collection of evidence*; **en ~ délit** in flagrante delicto; **prendre qn en ~ délit** to catch sb red-handed; **en ~ délit de vol** in the act of stealing; **en ~ délit de meurtre/d'adultère** in the act of committing murder/adultery; **prendre qn en ~ délit de mensonge** to catch sb out in a lie.

flair /flɛʀ/ *nm* **1** (odorat) nose; **avoir du ~** to have a good nose; **2** (intuition) intuition; **avoir du ~** to have intuition; **ton mari manque de ~** your husband is not intuitive; **nous avons manqué de ~ en vendant la maison** we miscalculated when we sold the house.

flairer /fleʀe/ [1] *vtr* **1** (renifler) to sniff [*objet, vêtement*]; **le chien a flairé une piste** the dog has picked up a scent; **2** (sentir) [*animal*] to scent [*gibier, personne, nourriture*]; [*personne*] to smell [*odeur*]; **3** (discerner) to sniff out [*escroquerie*]; to smell [*piège, mensonge, danger*]; **~ que** to sense that; **~ quelque chose de louche** to smell a rat.

IDIOMES **~ le vent** to see which way the wind is blowing, to read the wind US.

flamand, **~e** /flamɑ̃, ɑ̃d/ ▶ **462** **I** *adj* Flemish.

II *nm* Ling Flemish.

Flamand, **~e** /flamɑ̃, ɑ̃d/ *nm,f* **un ~** a Flemish man; **une ~e** a Flemish woman; **les ~s** the Flemish (+ *v pl*).

flamant /flamɑ̃/ *nm* flamingo.

■ **~ rose** pink flamingo.

flambage /flɑ̃baʒ/ *nm* **1** Culin (de volaille) singeing; (de dessert) flambéing; **2** Tex singeing; **3** Tech buckling.

flambant /flɑ̃bɑ̃/ *adv* **~ neuf/neuve** brand new; **une voiture ~ neuve** a brand new car.

flambard○ /flɑ̃baʀ/ *nm* show-off○, swank; **faire le** or **son ~** to show off, to swank.

flambé, **~e** /flɑ̃be/ **I** *pp* ▶ **flamber**.

II○ *pp adj* (ruiné) [*personne*] done for○ (*jamais épith*).

III flambée *nf* **1** (feu) fire; **faire une ~e** to light a fire; **2** (de violence, haine) flare-up; (des prix, cours) explosion; **la ~e des prix** the explosion in prices.

flambeau, *pl* **~x** /flɑ̃bo/ *nm* **1** (torche) torch; **à la lueur des ~x** by torchlight; **retraite aux ~x** torchlight procession; **2** fig torch (**de** of); **le ~ de la tradition/liberté** the torch of tradition/liberty; **reprendre le ~** to take up the torch; **3** (chandelier) candlestick.

flambement /flɑ̃bmɑ̃/ *nm* Tech buckling.

flamber /flɑ̃be/ [1] **I** *vtr* **1** Culin (à la flamme) to singe [*volaille*]; (avec de l'alcool) to flame, to flambé [*banane, crêpe, omelette*]; **~ qch à l'alcool** to flambé sth in alcohol; **2** Méd to sterilize [sth] in a flame [*aiguille, instrument chirurgical*]; **3**○ (dépenser beaucoup) to squander, to blow○ [*argent, économies*].

II *vi* **1** lit [*combustible*] to burn; [*maison*] to burn down, to go up in flames; **un feu flambait dans la cheminée** a fire was blazing in the hearth; **2** (augmenter) [*prix*] to rocket; [*cours*] to soar; **3** Constr, Tech to buckle.

flambeur○, **-euse** /flɑ̃bœʀ, øz/ *nm,f* **1** (dépensier) big spender; **2** (joueur) big-time gambler.

flamboiement /flɑ̃bwamɑ̃/ *nm* (de feu) blaze; **le ~ des arbres en automne** fig the flaming colours[GB] of the trees in autumn GB ou the fall US.

flamboyance /flɑ̃bwajɑ̃s/ *nf* flamboyance.

flamboyant, **~e** /flɑ̃bwajɑ̃, ɑ̃t/ **I** *adj* **1** gén [*feu, lumière, soleil*] blazing; [*couleur*] flaming; [*ciel, coucher de soleil*] fiery; [*armure*] gleaming; **chevelure ~e** flaming red hair; **2** Archit **gothique ~** Flamboyant Gothic.

II *nm* **1** Bot flame tree; **2** Archit Flamboyant (Gothic) style.

flamboyer /flɑ̃bwaje/ [23] *vi* [*incendie, soleil, ciel, couleur*] to blaze; [*yeux*] gén to flash; (de colère) to blaze (**de** with); [*armure, épée*] to gleam.

flamenco /flamɛnko/ *nm* gén **le ~** the flamenco; (danse) flamenco dancing.

flamingant, **~e** /flamɛ̃gɑ̃, ɑ̃t/ **I** *adj* Ling [*population, région*] Flemish-speaking.

II *nm,f* **1** Ling Flemish speaker; **2** Pol Flemish nationalist.

flamme /flɑm/ **I** *nf* **1** (feu) flame; **la ~ s'est éteinte** the flame went out; **passer une volaille à la ~** to singe a fowl; **2** (passion amoureuse) love; **déclarer sa ~ à qn** to declare one's love to sb; **3** (ardeur) **parler avec ~** to speak passionately; **discours plein de ~** fiery speech; **la ~ de son regard** his/her flashing eyes; **ranimer la ~ d'une tradition** to rekindle a tradition; **4** Postes postmark caption; **5** Mil (drapeau) pennant; Mil Naut (pavillon) pennon.

II flammes *nfpl* (feu) fire ¢; **en ~s** on fire; **être la proie des ~s** to be on fire; **être dévoré par les ~s** to be consumed by the flames; **l'avion est tombé en ~s** the plane went down in flames; **les ~s de l'enfer** Relig the fires of hell.

■ **~ olympique** Sport Olympic flame; **~ du soldat inconnu** eternal flame on the tomb of the unknown soldier.

IDIOMES **descendre qn/qch en ~s** to shoot sb/sth down; **jeter feu et ~** [*personne*] to be raging; **être tout feu tout ~** [*personne*] to be wildly enthusiastic.

flammé, **~e** /flɑme/ *adj* Tech [*céramique*] flambé.

flammèche /flamɛʃ/ *nf* spark.

flan /flɑ̃/ *nm* **1** Culin (crème) ≈ custard; (tarte) custard tart GB, custard flan US; **~ aux pruneaux** custard and prune tart GB ou flan US; **2** Imprim (carton) flong; (empreinte) mould GB, mold US; **3** Tech (de monnaie, médaille, disque) blank.

IDIOMES **faire qch au ~**○ to do sth brazenly; **y aller au ~** to bluff; **en rester comme deux ronds de ~**○ to be dumbfounded.

flanc /flɑ̃/ *nm* **1** Anat (de personne) side; (d'animal) flank, side; **se coucher sur le ~** to lie on one's side; **le cheval battait des ~s** the horse was panting; **être sur le ~**○ to be exhausted, to be deadbeat○; **2** liter (entrailles) **une lance lui perça le ~** a lance pierced his/her entrails; **porter un enfant dans son ~** to carry a child in one's womb; **3** (de montagne, colline, coteau) side; **à ~ de colline/montagne** on the hillside/mountainside; **4** (de navire) side, beam end; **5** Mil flank; **attaquer de ~** to attack on the flank.

IDIOMES **se battre les ~s**○ to strive in vain; **tirer au ~**○ to shirk, to skive○; **prêter le ~ à la critique** to lay oneself open to criticism.

flancher○ /flɑ̃ʃe/ [1] *vi* **1** (manquer de courage) to lose one's nerve; (ne plus faire face) to crack up; **il est en train de ~** (devant une décision) he's coming round GB ou around US; (dans une crise) he's cracking up; **ce n'est pas le moment de ~** this is no time to lose one's nerve; **2** (faiblir) [*cœur, moteur*] to give out; [*mémoire*] to let [sb] down; **j'ai la mémoire qui flanche** my memory lets me down ou is going; **j'ai les jambes qui flanchent** my legs have gone wobbly.

flanchet /flɑ̃ʃɛ/ *nm* Culin flank; **un morceau dans le ~** a piece of flank.

flanc-mou○, *pl* **flancs-mous** /flɑ̃mu/ *nmf* C waster○ GB, lazy bum○ US.

Flandre /flɑ̃dʀ/ ▶ **692** *nprf* **la ~, les ~s** Flanders (+ *v sg*).

Flandre-Occidentale /flɑ̃dʀɔksidɑ̃tal/ ▶ **692** *nprf* West Flanders (+ *v sg*).

Flandre-Orientale /flɑ̃dʀɔʀjɑ̃tal/ ▶ **692** *nprf* East Flanders (+ *v sg*).

flanelle /flanɛl/ *nf* flannel; **jupe de ~** flannel skirt.

■ **~ de coton** flannelette; **avoir les jambes en ~ de coton** to feel weak at the knees.

flâner /flɑne/ [1] *vi* **1** (se promener) to stroll; **~ dans les rues/magasins** to stroll around the streets/shops GB ou stores US; **~ sur les quais** to have a leisurely stroll along the embankment; **ils sont en retard, ils ont dû ~ en route** they're late, they must have been dawdling; **2** (paresser) to loaf○ around; **il flâne toute la journée à la maison** he loafs○ around the house all day long; **il ne faut pas ~ sinon le projet sera en retard** there must be no slacking GB ou idling US or we'll fall behind with the project.

flânerie /flɑnʀi/ *nf* **1** (promenade) stroll; **2** (inaction) lazing around; **la chaleur invite à la ~** the heat makes you lazy.

flâneur, **-euse** /flɑnœʀ, øz/ *nm,f* **1** (promeneur) stroller; **il y avait quelques ~s** there were a few people strolling by; **2** (paresseux) loafer○, idler US.

flanquer /flɑ̃ke/ [1] **I** *vtr* **1** (garnir) to flank; **être flanqué de** [*personne, construction, meuble*] to be flanked by; **il est toujours flanqué de son adjoint** his assistant never leaves his side; **2** Mil to protect the flank of [*unité*]; **3**○ (mettre) to give [*coup, gifle, amende*]; **~ qch par terre** (jeter) to throw sth to the ground; (laisser tomber) to drop sth; (faire tomber) to knock sth to the ground; **~ la frousse**○ or **la trouille**○ **à qn** to give sb a fright, to scare sb; **~ qn dehors** or **à la porte** (d'un travail) to fire sb; (d'un lieu) to chuck○ sb out.

II se flanquer◐ *vpr* **se ~ dans qch** [*véhicule, personne*] to run into sth; **on va se ~ dans un mur si tu continues à conduire à cette vitesse** we're going to run into a wall if you keep driving at this speed; **il s'est flanqué sous le train/par la fenêtre** he threw himself under the train/out of the window; **se ~ par terre** to fall flat on one's face.

flapi○, **~e** /flapi/ *adj* fagged out○ GB, shot○ US, worn out.

flaque /flak/ *nf* **~ (d'eau)** puddle; **~ d'huile/de sang** pool of oil/of blood; **ne marche pas dans les ~s** don't walk in the puddles.

flash, *pl* **~es** /flaʃ/ *nm* **1** Phot flash; **prendre une photo au ~** to take a photo with a flash; **photographie au ~** flash photography; **2** Radio, TV **~ (d'information)** (programmé) news headlines (*pl*); (exceptionnel) news flash; **~ spécial** special news flash; **le ~ de 12 heures** the 12 o'clock news summary; **3** (impact de drogue) flash.

■ **~ automatique** Phot automatic flash; **~ électronique** Phot electronic flash; **~ publicitaire** Pub advert GB, commercial US.

flash-back, *pl* **~s** /flaʃbak/ *nm* Cin, Littérat flashback.

flasher○ /flaʃe/ [1] *vi* **~ sur qch/qn** to fall in love with sth/sb.

flashmètre /flaʃmɛtʀ/ *nm* flash meter.

flasque /flask/ **I** *adj* [*peau, chair, joues*] flabby, flaccid; [*traits*] slack.

II *nm* **1** Aut flange; **~ de moyeu** hub flange; **2** Audio (de bande magnétique) flange; **3** Électrotech (de stator) end shield; **4** Mil (de canon) cheek.

III *nf* (flacon) flask.

flatté, **~e** /flate/ **I** *pp* ▶ **flatter**.

II *pp adj* (honoré) [*personne*] flattered; **je suis très ~ de votre présence/que vous ayez pensé à moi** I'm very flattered by your presence/that you thought of me; **il se sentait ~ dans son orgueil** his ego was flattered.

flatter /flate/ [1] **I** *vtr* **1** (complimenter) to flatter [*personne*]; **je ne dis pas cela pour vous ~** I'm not saying it just to flatter you; **vous me flattez, je n'en mérite pas autant** you flatter me, I don't deserve it; **~ bassement qn** to toady to sb; **sans vouloir vous ~** I say this without flattery; **il aime qu'on le flatte** he likes flattery; **2** (honorer) **leur visite a flatté tout le village** the whole village felt honoured[GB] by their visit; **3** (encourager) to encourage [*sentiment, vice*]; **~ qn dans son amour-propre** to boost sb's ego; **4** (caresser) to pat [*animal*]; **5** (être agréable) to delight [*narines, palais, regard, oreilles*]; **6** (avantager) [*photo, vêtement, éclairage*] to flatter [*personne*].

II se flatter *vpr* **1** (prétendre) **je me flatte de m'exprimer au moins de façon claire** I flatter myself that I'm at least articulate; **2** (tirer vanité) to pride oneself (**de** on; **de faire** on doing); **je me flatte d'avoir une maison très accueillante** I pride myself on having a very welcoming house.

flatterie /flatʀi/ *nf* flattery ¢; **être sensible à la ~** or **aux ~s** to be susceptible to flattery; **de basses ~s** toadying ¢.

flatteur, **-euse** /flatœʀ, øz/ **I** *adj* **1** (avantageux) [*portrait, éclairage*] flattering; [*distinction, récompense*] gratifying; **peu ~** unflattering; **l'article ne le montre pas sous un jour ~** he doesn't appear in a favourable[GB] light in the article; **2** (obséquieux) [*personne, paroles*] sycophantic; **il est très ~** he's a real toady ou sycophant.

II *nm,f* toady, sycophant.

flatulence /flatylɑ̃s/ *nf* wind ¢, flatulence ¢ spéc; **avoir des ~s** to suffer from wind ou flatulence.

flatulent, **~e** /flatylɑ̃, ɑ̃t/ *adj* flatulent.

fléau, *pl* **~x** /fleo/ *nm* **1** (calamité) blight; **~ social** blight on society; **bienfait ou ~?** a blessing or a curse?; **le ~ de Dieu** the scourge of God; **2** (personne) pest; **3** Agric flail; **battre le blé au ~** to flail wheat; **4** Tech (de balance) beam.

■ **~ d'armes** Hist flail.

fléchage /fleʃaʒ/ *nm* signposting; **le ~ d'un itinéraire** the signposting of a route.

flèche /flɛʃ/ *nf* **1** (arme) arrow; **pointe de ~** arrowhead; **atteint/transpercé par une ~** hit/pierced by an arrow; **~ empoisonnée** poisoned arrow; **les ~s de l'Amour/de Cupidon** Love's/Cupid's darts; **partir/passer en** or **comme une ~** to shoot off/to shoot past; **monter en ~** [*fusée*] to shoot upward(s); [*prix*] to soar; ▶ **Parthe**; **2** (signe) arrow; **suivez la ~** follow the arrow; **3** (raillerie) barbed remark; **décocher une ~ contre qn/qch** to make a barbed remark about sb/sth; **4** (d'église) spire; (de grue) jib; (de charrue, charrette) beam; ▶ **avion**; **5** Tech (de dalle, poutre) deflection.

IDIOMES **il fait ~ de tout bois** it's all grist to his mill.

flécher /fleʃe/ [14] *vtr* to signpost.

fléchette /fleʃɛt/ ▶ **449** *nf* **1** (objet) dart; **2** (activité) darts (+ *v sg*); **une partie de ~s** a game of darts.

fléchi, **~e** /fleʃi/ **I** *pp* ▶ **fléchir**.

II *pp adj* Ling **forme ~e** inflected form.

fléchir /fleʃiʀ/ [3] **I** *vtr* **1** (plier) to bend; **2** (ébranler) to sway [*personne, opinion*]; to weaken [*volonté, résistance*].

II *vi* **1** (ployer) [*poutre*] to sag, to bend; [*genoux*] to bend; [*jambes*] to give way; **2** (faiblir) [*attention*] to flag, to falter; [*courage*] to waver; [*volonté, résistance*] to weaken; [*production, demande*] to fall off; [*cours, franc*] to weaken, to fall; [*prix*] to fall, to come down; **~ de 2%** to fall by 2%; **3** (céder) [*personne, armée*] to yield; (s'adoucir) [*personne*] to relent; **se laisser ~** to relent, to let oneself be swayed; **sans ~** (stoïquement) unflinchingly; (obstinément) stubbornly.

fléchissement /fleʃismɑ̃/ *nm* **1** (de bras, corps, genou) bending; **2** (de volonté, courage) weakening; **3** (fait de céder) yielding; **4** (de production, taux, croissance) fall, drop (**de** in).

fléchisseur /fleʃisœʀ/ *adj m* (**muscle**) **~** flexor (muscle).

flegmatique /flɛgmatik/ *adj* phlegmatic.

flegmatiquement /flɛgmatikmɑ̃/ *adv* phlegmatically.

flegme /flɛgm/ *nm* **1** (placidité) phlegm, composure; **perdre son ~ habituel** to lose one's usual composure; **prendre une nouvelle avec ~** to take a piece of news phlegmatically; **2**† Méd phlegm.

flémingite○ /flemɛ̃ʒit/ *nf* hum bone idleness; **il a une ~ aiguë** he's suffering from acute bone idleness.

flemmard○, **~e** /flemaʀ, aʀd/ **I** *adj* bone idle (*jamais épith*).

II *nm,f* lazybones○ (*sg*), lazy devil○.

flemmarder○ /flemaʀde/ [1] *vi* to loaf○ around; **~ au lit** to lie in.

flemmardise○ /flemaʀdiz/ *nf* laziness.

flemme○ /flɛm/ *nf* laziness; **j'ai la ~ de faire** I can't be bothered to do○, I'm too lazy to do; **j'ai la ~ aujourd'hui** I just can't be bothered○ today; **tirer sa ~** to laze around.

fléole /fleɔl/ *nf* timothy.

flet /flɛ/ *nm* flounder.

flétan /fletɑ̃/ *nm* halibut.

■ **~ noir** black halibut.

flétri, **~e** /fletʀi/ **I** *pp* ▶ **flétrir**.

II *pp adj* **1** [*fleur*] faded; [*fruit*] shrivelled[GB]; **2** [*beauté*] faded.

flétrir /fletʀiʀ/ [3] **I** *vtr* **1** (faner) **le temps a**

flétri sa beauté her beauty has faded with time; **2** (stigmatiser) to blacken [*nom, mémoire, réputation*]; **3** (souiller) to corrupt [*enfant, innocence*]; **4** Hist (marquer au fer) to brand [*criminel*].

II se flétrir *vpr* **1** [*plante*] to wither; [*fleur*] to fade; [*fruit*] to shrivel; **2** [*beauté, visage, peau*] to fade.

flétrissement /fletʀismɑ̃/ *nm* **1** liter (de peau, visage) withering; **2** Bot wilt.

flétrissure /fletʀisyʀ/ *nf* (de réputation, mémoire) blot, stain (**de** on).

fleur /flœʀ/ *nf* **1** Bot gén flower; Hort bloom; **être en ~s** [*jardin*] to be full of flowers; [*camélia*] to be in bloom ou flowering; [*poirier, lilas*] to be in blossom; **jeune fille en ~** liter girl in the first flower of womanhood littér; **à ~s** [*tissu*] floral, flowery; [*papier peint, chemise*] flower-patterned, flowery; **chapeau à ~s** flowery hat; **prés parsemés de ~s** flowery meadows; **'ni ~s ni couronnes'** 'no flowers by request'; **2** liter (le meilleur) **la (fine) ~ de la chevalerie/des arts** the flower of chivalry/of the art world; **être/mourir dans la ~ de l'âge** to be/die in the prime of life; **3** liter (niveau) **à ~ d'eau** [*écueil, rocher*] just above the water; **4** (de cuir) grain; **côté ~** grain layer.

■ **~ artificielle** artificial flower; **~ des champs** wild flower; **~ composée** composite flower; **~ de farine** superfine white flour; **~ de lys** fleur-de-lis, heraldic lily; **~ d'oranger** (fleurs) orange blossom; (arôme) orange flower water; **~ de soufre** flower of sulphur[GB].

IDIOMES **être ~ bleue** to be starry-eyed ou romantic; **être belle comme une ~** to be as pretty as a picture; **avoir une sensibilité à ~ de peau** to be hypersensitive; **avoir les nerfs à ~ de peau** to be a bundle of nerves; **couvrir qn de ~s** to shower sb with compliments; **envoyer des ~s à qn**○ to pat sb on the back; **faire une ~ à qn**○ to do sb a favour[GB]; **vous ne lui avez pas fait de ~ en le nommant à ce poste**○ you haven't done him any favours[GB] in giving him that job; **arriver** or **s'amener**○ **comme une ~** to turn up just like that.

fleurdelisé, ~e /flœʀdəlize/ *adj* **1** gén [*drapeau, étoffe, manteau*] decorated with fleurs-de-lis (*après n*); **2** Hérald flory; **contre ~** counter flory.

fleurer /flœʀe/ [1] *vtr* **1** (embaumer) to be fragrant with; **~ la lavande** to be fragrant with lavender; **2** (évoquer) **~ le scandale** to smack of scandal.

fleuret /flœʀɛ/ **▶ 449** *nm* **1** Sport (épée) foil; (discipline) foil; **pratiquer le ~** to practise[GB] foil-play; **2** Tech (de perforatrice) drill rod.

■ **~ électrique** electric foil; **~ moucheté** buttoned foil; **se battre à ~ moucheté** to fence with buttoned foils.

fleurette /flœʀɛt/ *nf* **1** (fleur) little flower; **2** Culin **crème ~** whipping cream.

IDIOMES **conter ~† à qn** to woo† sb.

fleurettiste /flœʀɛtist/ *nmf* Sport foil fencer.

fleuri, ~e /flœʀi/ **I** *pp* ▶ **fleurir**.

II *pp adj* **1** [*champs, jardin, chemin*] full of flowers; [*arbre, buisson*] (de petites fleurs) in blossom; (de grosses fleurs) in bloom; **2** (décoré) [*table*] decorated with flowers; **leur maison est toujours très ~e** their house is always full of flowers; **les maisons ~es** houses covered in flowers; **sa tombe n'est jamais ~e** there are never any flowers on his grave; **à la boutonnière ~e** with a flower in his buttonhole; **gagnant du concours des villes ~es de France** first in the France in bloom competition; **3** (à fleurs) [*papier, robe, tissu*] flowery; **4** [*teint*] florid, ruddy; [*nez*] spotty GB, pimply; **barbe ~e** hoary beard; **5** (très orné) [*style, termes*] flowery péj.

fleurir /flœʀiʀ/ [3] **I** *vtr* to decorate [sth] with flowers [*balcon, maison, table*]; to put flowers on [*tombe*]; to put a flower in [*boutonnière*].

Les fleuves et les rivières

L'anglais ne distingue pas entre fleuve *et* rivière*; dans les deux cas, c'est le mot* river *qui est utilisé, avec ou sans majuscule.*

Les noms de fleuves et de rivières

L'anglais utilise toujours l'article défini devant les noms de fleuves et de rivières.

le Nil	=	the Nile
l'Amazone	=	the Amazon
la Saône	=	the Saône

Le mot river *est parfois utilisé, mais n'est jamais obligatoire. En anglais britannique, il est avant le nom propre, en anglais américain il est après.*

la Tamise	=	the River Thames (*GB*) *ou* the river Thames
le Potomac	=	the Potomac River (*US*) *ou* the Potomac river

***De* avec les noms de fleuves et de rivières**

Les expressions françaises avec de *se traduisent en général par l'emploi des noms de fleuves et de rivières en position d'adjectifs.*

un affluent de la Tamise	=	a Thames tributary
l'eau de la Seine	=	Seine water
l'estuaire de la Tamise	=	the Thames estuary
les industries de la Tamise	=	Thames industries
les péniches de la Tamise	=	Thames barges

Mais:

l'embouchure de la Tamise	=	the mouth of the Thames
la source de la Tamise	=	the source of the Thames

II *vi* **1** [*rosier, camelia*] to flower, to bloom; [*cerisier, lilas*] to blossom; **2** (apparaître) [*supermarchés, pavillons*] to spring up; [*affiches, graffiti*] to appear; **3** (prospérer) to thrive, to flourish; **4** (se couvrir de boutons) [*visage, menton*] to come ou break out in spots GB ou pimples.

fleuriste /flœʀist/ **▶ 510** **I** *nmf* (commerçant) florist.

II *nm* (magasin) flower shop, florist's.

fleuron /flœʀɔ̃/ *nm* **1** (joyau) jewel (in the crown); **le ~ de la parfumerie française** the jewel of the French perfume industry; **2** Imprim fleuron; (en fin de chapitre) tailpiece; **3** Archit gén fleuron; (de pignon) finial; **4** Bot floret; **5** Culin fleuron.

fleuve /flœv/ **I** *nm* **1** Géog river; **au bord d'un ~** by a river; **2** (flot de boue, lave, sang) river (**de** of); **~ de larmes** flood of tears; **~(s) humain(s)** stream of humanity.

II (-)fleuve (*in compounds*) **discours/procès/conférence(-)~** interminable speech/trial/meeting.

■ **~ Bleu** Yangtze, Chang Jiang; **~ Jaune** Yellow River, Huang He; **~ Rouge** Red River, Song Koi.

flexibilité /flɛksibilite/ *nf* **1** (de branche) pliability; (de lame) flexibility; (de corps) suppleness; **2** (d'économie, horaire, de personne) flexibility; **~ de l'emploi** Écon flexibility of labour[GB]; **3** Tech (de matériau, tuyau, suspension) flexibility.

flexible /flɛksibl/ **I** *adj* **1** (souple) [*branche*] pliable; [*lame*] flexible; [*corps*] supple; **2** (adaptable) [*personne, horaire, budget*] flexible; **3** Tech [*matériau, tuyau, suspension*] flexible; **4** (docile) [*personne, caractère*] malleable.

II *nm* (tuyau souple) **~ de douche** shower hose; **~ de gaz** rubber gas pipe; **~ de robinet** nozzle; **~ de cimentation** Tech cementing hose.

flexion /flɛksjɔ̃/ *nf* **1** (d'objet) bending; (de bras, jambe) flexing; **ressort qui résiste à la ~** spring that doesn't bend; **muscles qui participent à la ~ de la main** muscles used for flexing the hand; **2** Ling inflection.

flexionnel, -elle /flɛksjɔnɛl/ *adj* [*langue*] inflected; [*forme, marque*] inflectional.

flexure /flɛksyʀ/ *nf* Géol fold, flexure.

flibustier /flibystje/ *nm* **1** Hist (pirate) freebooter; **2** (escroc) swindler.

flic○ /flik/ **I** *nm* pej cop○, policeman; **les ~s** the cops, the police (+ *v pl*).

II flic flac *nm* (*also onomat*) splash; **faire ~ flac** to go splish splash.

flicage○ /flikaʒ/ *nm* (d'une ville, d'un quartier) heavy policing (**de** of); (d'élèves, employés) strict discipline (**de** of).

flicaille◑ /flikaj/ *nf* pej **la ~** the pigs○ (*pl*) péj, the police (+ *v pl*).

flingue◑ /flɛ̃g/ *nm* gun, piece○.

flinguer◑ /flɛ̃ge/ [1] **I** *vtr* to blow [sb] away○, to shoot; **se faire ~** to get shot.

II se flinguer *vpr* to blow one's brains out○, to shoot oneself; **il n'y a pas de quoi se ~**○ it's not the end of the world; **il y a de quoi se ~** it's enough to make you blow your brains out○.

flint /flint/ *nm* flint glass, optical flint spéc.

flip /flip/ *nm* **1**○ (dépression) **être (vraiment) le ~** [*film, roman*] to be a real downer○; [*lieu*] to be creepy○; **être en plein ~, avoir un ~** [*drogué*] to freak out○; **2** Culin **porto ~** egg flip (*with port*).

flippant◑, **~e** /flipɑ̃, ɑ̃t/ *adj* (déprimant) [*situation, lieu, maison*] spooky○, creepy○; **tu es vraiment ~** you really freak me out○ ou give me the creeps○.

flipper[1] /flipœʀ/ **▶ 449** *nm* Jeux (billard électrique) pinball machine; (pièce mobile) flipper; (jeu) pinball; **jouer au ~** to play pinball.

flipper[2]○ /flipe/ [1] *vi* (être perturbé) to freak out○; (être déprimé) to be depressed ou down○; **il est complètement flippé**○ he's off his head○; **ta maison me fait ~** your house gives me the creeps○.

fliquer◑ /flike/ [1] *vtr* to plant police in [*quartier, manifestation*]; to keep [sb] under surveillance [*personne*]; **un quartier très fliqué** a heavily policed district.

flirt /flœʀt/ *nm* **1** (activité) flirting (**avec** with); **2** (relation) flirtation, brief romance; **un ~ d'été** a summer romance; **le ~ entre Cuba et la Chine** fig the flirtation between Cuba and China; **3** (personne) boyfriend/girlfriend; **un de mes anciens ~s** one of my old flames.

flirter /flœʀte/ [1] *vi* to flirt (**avec** with).

FLN /ɛfɛlɛn/ *nm*: *abbr* ▶ **front**.

FLNC /ɛfɛlɛnse/ *nm* (*abbr* = **Front de libération nationale corse**) *former Corsican independence movement.*

FLNKS /ɛfɛlɛnkaɛs/ *nm* (*abbr* = **Front de libération nationale kanak socialiste**) *Kanak independence movement in New Caledonia.*

floc /flɔk/ **I** *nm* Tech flock.

II *excl* plop!; (plus fort) splash!

flocage /flɔkaʒ/ *nm* (uni) flocking; (avec motifs) flock printing.

floche /flɔʃ/ *nf* B (pompon) tassel.

flocon /flɔkɔ̃/ *nm* (de neige, savon) flake; (de poussière) speck; (de laine) bit; (de fumée) wisp; **la neige tombe à gros ~s** the snow is falling in big flakes.

■ **~ de neige** Météo snowflake; **~s d'avoine** Culin oat flakes GB, oatmeal ¢ US; **~s de pomme de terre** Culin instant mashed potato mix (*sg*).

floconneux, -euse /flɔkɔnø, øz/ *adj* **1** gén [*laine, nuage*] fleecy; [*neige*] powdery; **2** Chimie [*précipité*] flocculent.

floculation /flɔkylasjɔ̃/ *nf* flocculation.

floculer /flɔkyle/ [1] *vi* to flocculate.

flonflons /flɔ̃flɔ̃/ *nmpl* **1** Mus brass band music ¢; **2** fig **il a été accueilli sous les ~** they put out the red carpet for him; **il a été**

reçu sans ~ there was no red carpet to greet him.

flop○ /flɔp/ *nm* (échec) flop; **faire un ~** to flop.

flopée○ /flɔpe/ *nf* **(toute) une ~ de gamins/livres** a whole load○ GB ou slew○ US of kids/books, masses (*pl*) of kids/books .

floqué, **~e** /flɔke/ *adj* [*papier, tissu*] flocked.

floraison /flɔʀɛzɔ̃/ *nf* **1** (de fleurs) flowering, blooming; **2** (développement) (de talents, d'idées) flowering; (de commerce, d'activités) growth, upsurge; (d'entreprises) rash.

floral, **~e**, *mpl* **-aux** /flɔʀal, o/ *adj* [*exposition, composition*] flower (*épith*); [*art, feuille, organe*] floral; **parc ~** flower garden.

floralies /flɔʀali/ *nfpl* flower show.

flore /flɔʀ/ *nf* **1** (végétation) flora; **2** (ouvrage) flora, botanical handbook.
■ **~ intestinale** intestinal flora.

floréal /flɔʀeal/ *nm* Floréal (*eighth month of the French revolutionary calendar, ≈ May*).

Florence /flɔʀɑ̃s/ ▶**857** *npr* Florence.

florentin, **~e** /flɔʀɑ̃tɛ̃, in/ **I** ▶**857** *adj* Florentine.
II *nm* Culin Florentine.

Florentin, **~e** /flɔʀɑ̃tɛ̃, in/ ▶**857** *nm,f* (natif) native of Florence; (habitant) inhabitant of Florence.

florès /flɔʀɛs/ *nm* **faire ~** [*mot, technique, personne*] to be thriving.

Floride /flɔʀid/ ▶**692** *nprf* Florida.

florilège /flɔʀilɛʒ/ *nm* anthology.

florin /flɔʀɛ̃/ ▶**46** *nm* **1** (monnaie des Pays-Bas) guilder; **2** Hist (ancienne monnaie) florin.

florissant, **~e** /flɔʀisɑ̃, ɑ̃t/ *adj* **1** [*activité, économie, industrie, art*] flourishing, thriving; [*ville, pays*] thriving; [*théorie*] fashionable; **2** [*teint*] ruddy; **il est d'une santé ~e** he's blooming.

flot /flo/ **I** *nm* **1** (grande quantité) (de courrier, documents, réfugiés) flood; (de circulation, questions, visiteurs, lave) stream; (de critique) torrent; **le ~ de sa chevelure cachait ses épaules** his/her hair flowed over his/her shoulders; **2** (marée) liter tide; **3** Équit rosette; **4**◑ **C** (enfant) kid○, child.
II à flot *loc adv* **couler à ~(s)** lit, fig to flow; **être à ~** lit, fig to be buoyant; **remettre un navire à ~** to refloat a boat; **remettre qch à ~** fig to put sth back on its feet; **remettre qn à ~** fig to put sb back on their feet.
III flots *nmpl* liter **les ~s** the billows littér, the deep (*sg*) littér.

flottable /flɔtabl/ *adj* [*bois, rivière*] floatable.

flottage /flɔtaʒ/ *nm* (du bois) drive.

flottaison /flɔtɛzɔ̃/ *nf* Naut **~ en charge** load line; **ligne de ~** waterline.

flottant, **~e** /flɔtɑ̃, ɑ̃t/ *adj* **1** [*bois, ligne, mine*] floating; [*brume, nuage*] drifting; **2** [*vêtements, cheveux*] flowing.

flottation /flɔtasjɔ̃/ *nf* flotation.

flotte /flɔt/ *nf* **1** Aviat, Naut, Transp fleet; **une ~ de vingt bateaux/autocars** a fleet of twenty boats/coaches; **2**○ (pluie) rain; **3**○ (eau) water; **ta soupe, c'est de la ~** your soup is like dishwater; **4** (flotteur) float.
■ **~ aérienne** air fleet; **~ de commerce** Naut merchant navy fleet GB, merchant marine US; **~ de guerre** Mil naval fleet; **~ marchande** = **~ de commerce**.

flottement /flɔtmɑ̃/ *nm* **1** (indécision) wavering **¢**; **il y eut un ~ dans l'assemblée** there was some wavering in the assembly; **après beaucoup de pressions, d'incertitudes et de ~s** after much pressure, uncertainty and wavering; **2** Fin (de monnaie) floating; **3** (de drapeau, vêtement) fluttering.

flotter /flɔte/ [1] **I** *vtr* to float [*bois, troncs*].
II *vi* **1** (sur un liquide) to float (**sur** on; **dans** in); **~ à la dérive** to drift; **2** (dans l'air) [*brume, vapeur*] to drift; [*drapeau*] to fly; **un parfum entêtant flottait dans la pièce** a heady perfume drifted through the air; **un sourire flottait sur ses lèvres** a smile hovered on his/her lips; **~ au vent** [*drapeau, fanion*] to flutter in the wind; [*cheveux*] to stream in the wind; **elle flotte dans ses vêtements** her clothes are hanging off her; **3** Fin [*monnaie*] to float.
III○ *v impers* (pleuvoir) to rain; **il flotte** it's raining; **qu'est-ce qu'il flotte!** what a downpour!

flotteur /flɔtœʀ/ *nm* (de ligne, filet, d'hydravion) float; (de chasse d'eau) ballcock.
■ **~ de carburateur** Aut floating valve.

flottille /flɔtij/ *nf* flotilla.
■ **~ de pêche** fishing fleet.

flou, **~e** /flu/ **I** *adj* **1** lit [*contour, photo, image*] blurred; [*coiffure, cheveux*] soft; [*vêtement, voile*] loose; **2** fig [*concept, statut, style*] vague, woolly péj; [*texte, souvenir, personnage*] vague; [*passé*] hazy.
II *nm* **1** lit (de photo, contour) fuzziness; **2** fig vagueness, woolliness péj; **il règne en ce domaine un certain/le plus grand ~ juridique** the law is rather/extremely vague in this area.
■ **~ artistique** Cin, Phot soft focus; fig artistry.

flouer /flue/ [1] *vtr* to cheat [*personne*]; **se faire ~** to be had○.

flouze◑ /fluz/ *nm* dough○, money.

fluctuant, **~e** /flyktɥɑ̃, ɑ̃t/ *adj* [*prix, cours, opinion*] fluctuating; [*personne, temps*] fickle; **les goûts sont ~s** tastes change.

fluctuation /flyktɥasjɔ̃/ *nf* fluctuation (**de** in).

fluctuer /flyktɥe/ [1] *vi* to fluctuate.

fluet, **-ette** /flyɛ, ɛt/ *adj* [*corps, personne*] slight; [*bras, jambe*] frail; [*voix*] thin.

fluide /flɥid/ **I** *adj* **1** (coulant) [*huile, peinture*] fluid; **rendre une peinture plus ~** to thin a paint; **2** (aisé) [*style*] fluent; [*circulation*] moving freely (*jamais épith*); [*situation*] fluid; **la circulation redevient ~** the traffic is moving freely again.
II *nm* **1** Phys fluid; **2** (de médium) (psychic) powers (*pl*).

fluidifier /flɥidifje/ [2] *vtr* to thin [*sang*]; to loosen [*mucosité*].

fluidité /flɥidite/ *nf* **1** Phys fluidity; **2** (de style, diction) fluency; (de vêtement) flowing lines (*pl*).

fluo○ /flyo/ **I** ▶**193** *adj inv* [*couleur, vêtement*] fluorescent.
II *nm* **la mode du ~** the fashion for Day-glo®.

fluor /flyɔʀ/ *nm* fluorine; **dentifrice au ~** fluoride toothpaste.

fluoration /flyɔʀasjɔ̃/ *nf* fluoridation.

fluoré, **~e** /flyɔʀe/ *adj* fluoride (*épith*); **dentifrice ~** fluoride toothpaste.

fluorescéine /flyɔʀesein/ *nf* fluorescein.

fluorescence /flyɔʀesɑ̃s/ *nf* fluorescence.

fluorescent, **~e** /flyɔʀesɑ̃, ɑ̃t/ *adj* fluorescent.

fluorine /flyɔʀin/ *nf* fluorspar, fluorite US.

fluorose /flyɔʀoz/ ▶**271** *nf* fluorosis.

fluorure /flyɔʀyʀ/ *nm* fluoride; **~ de sodium** sodium fluoride.

flush /flœʃ/ *nm* flush; **~ royal** royal flush.

flûte /flyt/ ▶**534** **I** *nf* **1** Mus flute; **petite ~** piccolo; **jouer de/aimer la ~** to play/to like the flute; **2** (verre) (champagne) flute; **3** (pain) *French loaf*; **4**○ (jambe) leg.
II○ *excl* damn○!, darn it○!
■ **~ à bec** recorder; **~ de Pan** panpipes (*pl*); **~ traversière** (transverse) flute.

flûté, **~e** /flyte/ *adj* [*voix, son*] piping (*épith*).

flûtiau, *pl* **~x** /flytjo/ ▶**534** *nm* **1** (flûte champêtre) pipe; **2** (flûte d'enfant) penny whistle.

flûtiste /flytist/ ▶**510** *nmf* flautist, flutist US.

fluvial, **~e**, *mpl* **-iaux** /flyvjal, o/ *adj* [*érosion, plaine*] fluvial; [*port, bassin, embarcation, transport*] river (*épith*).

fluviomètre /flyvjɔmɛtʀ/ *nm* water level gauge.

flux /fly/ *nm* **1** Physiol flow; **~ menstruel** menstrual flow; **2** Phys flux; **~ lumineux/magnétique** luminous/magnetic flux; **~ énergétique** energy flux; **3** Écon flow; **~ de capitaux** capital flow; **4** (marée) flood tide; **le ~ et le reflux** lit flood tide and ebb tide; fig (de foule, d'opinion) the ebb and flow; **5** (mouvement) influx; **~ migratoire/touristique** influx of immigrants/tourists; **6** Entr **production en ~ tendus** just-in-time production; **distribution en ~ tendus** just-in-time distribution; **gestion à ~ tendus** management system with posts of different contractual status.
■ **~ monétaires** financial flows; **~ physiques** flows of goods and services.

fluxion /flyksjɔ̃/ ▶**271** *nf* **~ dentaire** Dent swelling; **~ de poitrine** Méd pleuropneumonia.

FM /ɛfɛm/ **I** *nm* Mil (*abbr* = **fusil-mitrailleur**) MG.
II *nf* Radio (*abbr* = **frequency modulation**) FM; **en ~** on FM.

FMI /ɛfɛmi/ *nm*: *abbr* ▶**fonds**.

FO /ɛfo/ *nf*: *abbr* ▶**force**.

FOB /ɛfobe/ *adj inv* (*abbr* = **free on board**) FOB.

foc /fɔk/ *nm* jib; ▶**grand**.
■ **~ en l'air** jib topsail; **~ d'artimon** mizzen staysail.

focal, **~e**, *mpl* **-aux** /fɔkal, o/ **I** *adj* [*axe, distance, plan*] focal.
II focale *nf* **1** (distance) focal length; **2**○ (objectif) **une ~e de 50 mm** a 50 mm lens.

focalisation /fɔkalizasjɔ̃/ *nf* **1** Électron (de particules) focusing; **2** (concentration) focus; **la ~ des médias sur un événement** media focus on an event.

focaliser /fɔkalize/ [1] **I** *vtr* **1** Phys to focus [*rayons*]; to focalize [*faisceau d'électrons*]; **2** (concentrer) to focus [*espoirs, attention*] (**sur** on); to concentrate [*efforts*] (**sur** on); **un parti qui focalise tous les espoirs** a party on which everybody's hopes are pinned.
II se focaliser *vpr* (se concentrer) [*aspirations, espoirs*] to be focused (**sur** on).

fœhn /føn/ *nm* föhn.

foène, **foëne** /fwɛn/ *nf* **1** Pêche (pour petits poissons) fish-gig; (pour gros poissons) spear; **2** Ind alligator grab.
■ **~ de repêchage** Ind fishing grab.

fœtal, **~e**, *mpl* **-aux** /fetal, o/ *adj* [*développement, position*] foetal.

fœtus /fetys/ *nm* foetus.

fofolle ▶**foufou**.

foi /fwa/ *nf* **1** Relig faith; **la ~ chrétienne** the Christian faith; **avoir la ~** to be a believer; ▶**montagne**; **2** (confiance) faith; **avoir ~ en qn/qch** to have faith in sb/sth; **perdre ~ en** to lose one's faith in; **ajouter ~ à qch** to put faith in sth; **3** (sincérité) **ma ~** upon my word; **ma ~ oui** well yes; **~ d'honnête homme**† on my word as a gentleman; **faire qch de bonne ~** or **en toute bonne ~** to do sth with the best intentions; **en toute bonne ~ je crois que** in all sincerity, I believe that; **je crois qu'il est de bonne ~** I think he is genuine; **bonne/mauvaise ~** Philos good/bad faith; **de bonne ~** Jur [*acquéreur, détenteur*] bona fide (*épith*); **il répondait avec une mauvaise ~ évidente** (manière) he answered with patent insincerity; **je suis stupéfait de sa mauvaise ~** (caractère) I am amazed at his insincerity; **elle est d'une incroyable mauvaise ~** she's so insincere; **il est de mauvaise ~** (en parlant) he doesn't mean a word of it; **tu es de mauvaise ~!** you know that isn't true!; **il faut vraiment être de mauvaise ~ pour nier que** you have to be pretty hypocritical to deny that; **4** (assurance) **sur la ~ de témoins** on the evidence of witnesses; **sur la ~ de documents/de ce rapport** on the strength of documents/of this report; **en ~**

de quoi in witness whereof; **qui fait** or **faisant ~** [*texte, signature*] authentic; **l'original fait ~** the original shall be deemed authentic; **sous la ~ du serment** under oath.

IDIOMES **voir avec les yeux de la ~** to see only what one wants to see; **sans ~ ni loi** fearing neither God nor man; **n'avoir ni ~ ni loi** to fear neither God nor man.

foie /fwa/ *nm* **1** Anat liver; **avoir mal au ~** ≈ to have an upset stomach; **crise de ~** indigestion; **2** Culin liver.

■ **~ d'agneau** lamb's liver; **~ de génisse** beef liver; **~ gras** foie gras; **~ de porc** pig's liver; **~ de veau** calf's liver; **~s de volaille** chicken livers.

IDIOMES **se ronger les ~s**○ to worry; **avoir les ~s**◑ to have the jitters○.

foie-de-bœuf, *pl* **foies-de-bœuf** /fwadbœf/ *nm* Bot beefsteak fungus.

foin /fwɛ̃/ **I** *nm* **1** Agric (herbe séchée) hay ₵; **tas de ~** haystack; **faire les ~s** to make hay; **la saison des ~s** the haymaking season; ▶ **bête**; **2**○ (tabac sans goût) old socks○ (*pl*).

II‡ *excl* **~ de vos conseils/richesses!** I pour scorn on your advice/wealth!

■ **~ d'artichaut** choke.

IDIOMES **avoir** or **mettre du ~ dans ses bottes** to be well-to-do; **faire du ~**○ (faire du bruit) to make a hell○ of a racket ou noise; (faire du scandale) to cause a scandal.

foire /fwaʀ/ *nf* **1** Comm fair; **~ du livre** book fair; **~ aux olives/aux bestiaux** olive/cattle fair; **2** (fête foraine) fun fair; **3**○ pej (bruit, confusion) bedlam; **ce bureau est une vraie ~** it's bedlam in this office; **faire la ~**○ to live it up○; **il passe son temps à faire la ~** he spends all his time raving it up.

foirer◑ /fwaʀe/ [1] *vi* **1** (échouer) [*plan, entreprise*] to be a complete disaster ou balls-up◑ GB ou ball-up◑ US; **faire ~ qch** to bungle sth; **2** (ne pas exploser) [*pétard, fusée*] to fail to go off.

foireux◑, **-euse** /fwaʀø, øz/ **I** *adj* **1** (voué à l'échec) [*coup, projet*] half-baked; **2** (raté) [*coup*] bungled; **3** (sans valeur) [*chèque, explosif*] dud; **4** (bancal) [*raisonnement*] shaky.

II *nm,f* **1** (peureux) coward, chicken○; **2** (incapable) bungler.

fois /fwa/ **I** *nf* **1** (avec numéral) **une ~** once; **deux ~** twice; **trois/quatre/plusieurs ~** three/four/several times; **une/deux ~ et demie** one/two and a half times; **quatre ~ trois font douze** four times three is twelve; **une seule ~** only once; **je ne l'ai vue qu'une ou deux ~/que deux ou trois ~** I only saw her once or twice/two or three times; **une nouvelle ~, une ~ de plus** once again; **une autre ~** (encore) once more; (si ça se répète) next time; (à un autre moment) another time; **l'autre ~** (à la dernière occasion) last time; (à la seconde occasion) the second time; **d'autres ~** at other times; **bien des ~, maintes ~** liter many times; **la plupart des ~** most of the time, more often than not; **tant de ~** so many times; **autant de ~ qu'il le faudra** as many times as necessary; **une (bonne) ~ pour toutes** once and for all; **il faudrait qu'il neige une bonne ~** what we need is one good fall of snow; **une à deux ~ par jour** once or twice a day; **deux ~ par an** twice a year; **deux ou trois ~ par mois** two or three times a month; **plus/moins de cinq ~ par semaine** more/less than five times a week; **plus d'une ~** more than once; **une ~ sur deux** half the time, every other time; **une ~ sur trois** every third time; **deux/trois ~ sur cinq** two/three times out of five; **neuf ~ sur dix** fig nine times out of ten; **une ~ tous les trois jours** once every three days; **pour une ~** for once; **tu l'as vexé, pour une ~ qu'il était de bonne humeur** you upset him when he was in a good mood for once; **une ~ encore** once more; **encore une ~, je ne suis pas d'accord** once again, I don't agree; **c'est la seule ~ que** it's the only time (that); **la seule ~ où je l'ai vu** the only time we met; **toutes les ~ que** every time (that); **cette ~(-ci), je réussirai** this time I'll succeed; **cette ~(-là), ça n'a pas marché** that time it didn't work; **ça va pour cette ~, mais ne recommencez pas!** it's all right this once but don't do it again!; **chaque ~** each ou every time; **c'est à chaque ~ la même chose!** it's the same thing every time!; **comme (à) chaque ~** as usual; **deux ~ plus petit** half as big, half the size; **deux ~ plus cher** twice as expensive; **deux ~ moins lourd** half the weight; **deux ~ moins cher** half as expensive, half the price; **par deux ~** [*frapper, tomber, essayer*] twice; **il vaut mieux le dire deux ~ plutôt qu'une** it needs saying twice; **y regarder** or **réfléchir à deux ~ avant de faire** to think twice before doing; **c'est dix ~ trop lourd/cher!** it's far too heavy/expensive!; **c'est trois ~ rien!** it's nothing at all!; **vous pouvez régler en trois/plusieurs ~** you can pay in three/several instalments[GB]; **2** (avec ordinal) time; **une deuxième ~** a second time; **je l'ai vue une première ~** I saw her for the first time; **une dernière ~** one last time; **(à) la première/deuxième ~** the first/second time; **la prochaine ~** next time; **c'est la dernière ~** it's the last time; **les deux premières/dernières ~** the first/last two times; **les premières ~ c'est amusant** the first few times it's fun; **ce n'est pas la première ~ que** it's not the first time (that); **pour la troisième ~ de l'année** for the third time this year; **pour la énième ~** for the hundredth time; **la première/dernière ~ que je vous ai parlé** when I first/last talked to you; **la dernière ~ que je lui ai parlé** (jusqu'à ce jour) last time I spoke to him; (avant sa mort) the last time I spoke to him; **quand l'avez-vous vue pour la première ~?** when did you first see her?, when was the first time you saw her?

II à la fois *loc* **deux à la ~** [*prendre des objets, monter des marches*] two at a time; **porter trois valises à la ~** to carry three suitcases at the same time; **elle est à la ~ intelligente et travailleuse** she's both clever and hardworking; **il veut toujours tout faire à la ~** he always wants to do everything at the same time; **pour des raisons à la ~ culturelles, sociales et religieuses** for cultural, social and religious reasons; **ne répondez pas tous à la ~!** lit, iron don't all answer at once! lit, iron; **tout à la ~ écrivain, metteur en scène et acteur** (he's) a writer, director and actor all rolled into one.

III des fois○ *loc* (parfois) sometimes; **y a des ~ où** there are times○ when; **tu n'as pas vu mon chien, des ~?** you wouldn't have seen my dog, by any chance?; **des ~ que** in case; **je ne veux pas y aller, des ~ qu'on rencontre mon patron!** I don't want to go (there), in case we run into my boss!; **non mais des ~!** (indignation) well really!

IDIOMES **il était** or **il y avait une ~** once upon a time there was; **je t'ai déjà dit cent** or **trente-six ~ de ne pas faire ça!** I've already told you a hundred ou a thousand times not to do that!

foison: **à foison** /afwazɔ̃/ *loc adv* aplenty; **il y a des pommes à ~** there are plenty of apples, there are apples aplenty; **il a des idées à ~** he's full of ideas.

foisonnant, **~e** /fwazɔnɑ̃, ɑ̃t/ *adj* [*imagination*] teeming; [*vie*] crowded; [*activité*] hectic; [*œuvre, production*] rich in detail (*après n*); **~ de** rich in.

foisonnement /fwazɔnmɑ̃/ *nm* **1** (prolifération) proliferation; (profusion) profusion; (de personnes) crowds; **un ~ de couleurs** a riot of colours[GB]; **2** (d'une substance) expansion.

foisonner /fwazɔne/ [1] *vi* **1** (abonder) [*idées, erreurs*] to abound; **le gibier foisonne dans le parc** the estate is teeming with game; **les erreurs foisonnent dans le texte** the text is bristling with errors; **2** (regorger) **~ de** or **en** to have an abundance of; **le pays foisonne de richesses/talents** the country has an abundance of riches/talent; **le jardin foisonne de fleurs** the garden is full of flowers; **le livre foisonne d'idées/d'erreurs** the book is teeming with ideas/bristling with errors; **3** (augmenter de volume) [*substance*] to expand.

fol ▶ **fou I.**

folasse○ /fɔlas/ **I** *adj f* pej batty○, dotty○.

II *nf* ninny○.

folâtre /fɔlɑtʀ/ *adj* [*personne, caractère, humeur*] playful; **être d'humeur ~** to be in a playful mood.

folâtrer /fɔlɑtʀe/ [1] *vi* [*personne*] to romp about; [*jeune animal*] to frisk, to frolic.

foliacé, **~e** /fɔljase/ *adj* **1** Bot foliaceous; **2** Minér foliated.

foliation /fɔljasjɔ̃/ *nf* (époque de l'année) foliation, leafing; (disposition) leaf arrangement.

folichon○, **-onne** /fɔliʃɔ̃, ɔn/ *adj* **ne pas être ~** (médiocre) [*œuvre, résultats, santé*] to be far from brilliant; (sinistre) [*époux, vie, vacances*] not to be much fun.

folie /fɔli/ *nf* **1** (démence) madness; **crise** or **coup de ~** brainstorm; **basculer dans la ~ meurtrière** to become a homicidal maniac; **2** (déraison) madness; **c'est de la ~ pure** it's sheer madness; **être pris de ~** to go mad GB ou crazy; **aimer qn/qch à la ~** to be mad GB ou crazy about sb/sth, to love sb/sth to distraction sout; **des spectateurs/une salle en ~** an ecstatic crowd/audience; **3** (acte déraisonnable) act of folly; **cette ~ leur a coûté la vie** it was an act of folly which cost them their lives; **mes ~s de jeunesse** my youthful follies; **elle a fait une ~ en acceptant** she was mad to accept; **4** (passion) **avoir la ~ du marbre/des antiquités** to be mad GB ou crazy about marble/about antiques; **5** (dépense inconsidérée) extravagance; **faire une ~, faire des ~s** to be extravagant.

■ **~ à deux** Méd folie à deux; **~ douce** sheer madness; **c'est de la ~ douce** it's sheer madness; **~ furieuse** stark raving madness; **être pris de ~ furieuse** to go berserk; **~ des grandeurs** delusions (*pl*) of grandeur; **avoir la ~ des grandeurs** to have delusions of grandeur.

folié, **~e** /fɔlje/ *adj* Bot foliate.

folingue○ /fɔlɛ̃g/ *adj* nuts○, mad.

folio /fɔljo/ *nm* folio.

foliole /fɔljɔl/ *nf* Bot leaflet.

folioter /fɔljɔte/ [1] *vtr* to foliate.

folique /fɔlik/ *adj* **acide ~** folic acid.

folk /fɔlk/ **I** *adj inv* [*festival, musique*] folk.

II *nm* **le ~** folk music; **chanteur de ~** folk singer.

folklo○ /fɔlklo/ *adj* [*personne*] eccentric; [*soirée*] crazy○; **ça va être ~** it'll be some laugh○!

folklore /fɔlklɔʀ/ *nm* **1** (traditions) folklore; **2**○ (rituel) razzmatazz○; **ça fait partie du ~** it's part of the usual razzmatazz.

folklorique /fɔlklɔʀik/ *adj* **1** (traditionnel) [*musique, coutume*] folk (*épith*); [*costume*] traditional; **2**○ (loufoque) [*personnage*] eccentric; [*voiture, soirée*] crazy○.

folle ▶ **fou I, II, IV.**

follement /fɔlmɑ̃/ *adv* **s'amuser ~** to have a terrific ou brilliant○ GB time; **un spectacle ~ drôle** a terribly funny show; **~ amoureux** or **épris** infatuated, madly in love○.

follet /fɔlɛ/ *adj m* **feu ~** will-o'-the-wisp; **esprit ~** flighty creature.

folliculaire /fɔlikylɛʀ/ *adj* Méd [*trouble, rupture*] follicular.

follicule /fɔlikyl/ *nm* Anat, Bot follicle.

■ **~ de De Graaf** Graafian follicle; **~ tuberculeux** Méd miliary tuberculosis.

folliculine /fɔlikylin/ *nf* œstrone.

folliculite /fɔlikylit/ ▶ **271** *nf* folliculitis.

folliculostimuline, *pl* **~s** /fɔlikylostimylin/ *nf* follicle-stimulating hormone, FSH.

fomentateur, **-trice** /fɔmɑ̃tatœʀ, tʀis/ *nm,f* **~ de troubles** agitator.

fomentation /fɔmɑ̃tasjɔ̃/ *nf* fomenting, fomentation.

fomenter /fɔmɑ̃te/ [1] *vtr* to stir up, to foment sout [*discorde, troubles*]; to instigate [*révolte, coup d'État*].

fonçage /fɔ̃saʒ/ *nm* **1** (de moule) lining; **2** (de puits) sinking; **3** (de tonneau) bottoming.

foncé, **~e** /fɔ̃se/ **I** *pp* ▶ **foncer**.
II ▶ **193** *pp adj* [*couleur*] gén dark; [*rose, mauve*] deep; **robes vert ~** dark green dresses; **avoir la peau ~e/les cheveux ~s** to be dark-skinned/dark-haired.

foncer /fɔ̃se/ [12] **I** *vtr* **1** (assombrir) to make [sth] darker [*couleur*]; to make [sth] deeper [*rose, mauve*]; **2** Culin to line [*moule, plat*] (**avec** with); **3** Tech to sink [*puits*]; to bottom [*tonneau*].
II *vi* **1**○ (aller très vite) [*chauffeur, voiture, coureur*] to tear along○ (**vers** toward, towards GB); **fonce!** get a move on○!, put your foot down!; **il va falloir ~ pour terminer à temps** we'll have to rush to finish in time; **2**○ (se précipiter) **~ vers/dans/à travers** to rush ou dash toward(s)/into/through; **~ sur qch/vers la sortie** to make a dash for sth/for the exit; **~ sur qn** (en attaquant) to charge at sb; **le taureau m'a foncé dessus** the bull came charging at me; **~ tête baissée dans la bagarre** to rush headlong into the fray; **~ à New York/Londres** to dash over to New York/London; **il n'est pas du genre à ~** (prudent) he's not the type to rush into things; (pas décisif) he's not the type to go for it○; **fonce!** (n'hésite pas) go for it○!; **3** (s'assombrir) [*couleur*] to darken; [*rose, mauve*] to deepen; [*tissu*] to go darker; **~ au soleil** [*lunettes*] to go darker in the sun.

fonceur○, **-euse** /fɔ̃sœʀ, øz/ **I** *adj* [*personne*] go-getting○ (*épith*), dynamic.
II *nm,f* go-getter○.

foncier, **-ière** /fɔ̃sje, ɛʀ/ **I** *adj* **1** [*impôt*] land; [*revenu*] from land (*après n*); [*politique, loi*] on land (*après n*); [*propriété, noblesse*] landed; **propriétaire ~** landowner; **2** (inhérent) intrinsic.
II *nm* real estate.

foncièrement /fɔ̃sjɛʀmɑ̃/ *adv* fundamentally.

fonction /fɔ̃ksjɔ̃/ *nf* **1** Admin, Entr (poste) post; (activité) duties (*pl*); **prendre ses ~s, entrer en ~s** to take up one's post; **depuis votre prise de** or **entrée en ~s** since you took up your post; **se démettre/être démis de ses ~s** gén to resign/to be dismissed from one's post; [*membre du gouvernement*] to resign/to be dismissed from office; **dans le cadre de mes ~s** as part of my duties; **dans l'exercice de leurs ~s** while carrying out their duties; **la formation n'entre pas dans leurs ~s** training is not part of their duties; **occuper la ~ de secrétaire** to hold the position of secretary; **quitter ses ~s** to leave one's job; **être/rester en ~(s)** to be/stay in office; **logement de ~** accommodation provided with the job; **voiture de ~** company car; **occuper d'importantes ~s** to hold important office; **être appelé à de hautes ~s** to be called to high office; **2** (dépendance) **en ~ de** according to; **être ~ de** to vary according to; **réagir en ~ de cinq paramètres** to react according to five parameters; **le salaire est ~ des diplômes** the salary varies according to qualifications; **3** (rôle) function; **~ d'une machine/un produit** function of a machine/a product; **avoir pour ~ de faire** to be designed to do; **faire ~ de** to serve as; **faire ~ de dessert/levier** to serve as dessert/a lever; **4** Biol function; **les ~s hépatiques** liver functions; **la ~ crée l'organe** the organ is shaped by its function; **5** Math, Ordinat function; **~ du deuxième degré** second degree function; **~ continue/dérivée/exponentielle/périodique** continuous/derived/exponential/periodic function; **6** (secteur) profession; **~ enseignante/médicale** teaching/medical profession; **7** Tech function; **la ~ avance rapide est en panne** the fast forward function does not work; **8** Chimie function; **~ acide/base** acid/base function; **9** Ling function; **~ sujet/complément** subject/complement function; **~ connotative/dénotative** connotative/denotative function.
■ **~ de ~s** Math functional; **~ primitive** Ordinat primitive; **~ publique** Admin civil service; **entrer dans la ~ publique** to join the civil service.

fonctionnaire /fɔ̃ksjɔnɛʀ/ ▶ **510** *nmf* **1** (petit, moyen) civil servant; **2** (haut) government official; **haut ~** senior civil servant.
■ **~ international** international official.

fonctionnalisme /fɔ̃ksjɔnalism/ *nm* functionalism.

fonctionnalité /fɔ̃ksjɔnalite/ *nf* Ordinat functionality ₵.

fonctionnariat /fɔ̃ksjɔnaʀja/ *nm* civil service.

fonctionnariser /fɔ̃ksjɔnaʀize/ [1] *vtr* to make [sb/sth] work for the state [*paysans, médecine*].

fonctionnel, **-elle** /fɔ̃ksjɔnɛl/ *adj* (tous contextes) functional.

fonctionnellement /fɔ̃ksjɔnɛlmɑ̃/ *adv* functionally.

fonctionnement /fɔ̃ksjɔnmɑ̃/ *nm* **1** (d'institution, organe, du marché) functioning; **~ d'une entreprise/de la démocratie/du cerveau** functioning of a company/of democracy/of the brain; **~ quotidien/interne** everyday/internal functioning; **bon ~** smooth functioning; **problème de ~** functioning problem; **2** (d'équipement) working; **gêner le ~ du moteur** to impede the working of the engine; **mauvais ~** malfunction; **en ~** in service; **entrer en ~** to come into service; **après l'entrée/la remise en ~ de la chaudière** after the boiler was put/was put back into service; **être en état de ~** to be in working order.

fonctionner /fɔ̃ksjɔne/ [1] *vi* to work; **~ à merveille** to work perfectly; **mal ~** not to work very well; **~ à l'essence/l'électricité** [*machine*] to run on petrol GB ou gas US/electricity; **~ comme un alibi** to be used as an excuse; **~ comme une société anonyme** to operate as a public company; **~ comme un système d'alarme** to serve as an alarm signal; **~ à la vodka** hum [*personne*] to live on vodka.

fond /fɔ̃/ **I** *nm* **1** (partie inférieure) bottom; **dans le** or **au ~ du verre/de mon sac** in the bottom of the glass/of my bag; **au ~ du tiroir/de la vallée/de la mer** at the bottom of the drawer/of the valley/of the sea; **tout au ~ du canal** at the very bottom of the canal; **puits sans ~** fig bottomless pit; **vider les ~s de bouteilles** to empty out all the old bottles; **faire les ~s de poubelles** to go through the rubbish GB ou garbage US; **toucher le ~** (dans l'eau) to touch the bottom; fig to hit rock bottom; **envoyer un navire par le ~** to sink a ship; **descendre au ~ d'un puits/de la mine** to go down a well/the mine; **travailler au ~** [*mineur*] to work down the mine; **avoir dix ans de ~** [*mineur*] to have spent ten years down the mine; ▶ **tiroir**; **2** Géog, Tech (paroi) (horizontale) bottom; (verticale) back; **le ~ de la casserole est en cuivre** the bottom of the saucepan is copper; **le ~ du placard se démonte** the back of the cupboard comes out; **valise à double ~** suitcase with a false bottom; **~ de la mer** seabed; **~ de l'océan** ocean floor; ▶ **grand**; **3** (partie reculée) (de cour, magasin) back; (de couloir, pièce) far end; **au ~ de l'armoire** in the back of the wardrobe; **être assis tout au ~** to be sitting right at the back; **la chambre/l'étagère du ~** the back bedroom/shelf; **au ~ des bois** deep in the woods; **j'ai une arête coincée au ~ de la gorge** there's a fishbone stuck in my throat; **avancer dans le ~** (dans un bus) to move up the bus; **de ~ en comble** [*fouiller, nettoyer, refaire*] from top to bottom; **4** (essence) **quel est le ~ de ta pensée?** what do you really think?; **quel est le ~ du problème?** what is the problem exactly?; **poser des questions de ~** to ask some fundamental questions; **faire des critiques de ~ sur qch** to find fundamental flaws in sth; **les problèmes de ~ sont résolus** the basic problems have been solved; **aller au ~ des choses** to sort it all out; **atteindre** or **toucher le ~ du désespoir** to be in the depths of despair; **un ~ de vérité** an element of truth; **un débat de ~** an in-depth debate; **au ~** or **dans le ~, le problème est simple** the problem is simple, in fact; **dans le ~, tu as raison** you're right, really; **5** Littérat (contenu) content; **le ~ et la forme** form and content; **être d'accord sur le ~** to agree on the content; **6** (intérieur) **regarder qn au ~ des yeux** (avec amour) to look deep into sb's eyes; (avec suspicion) to give sb a searching look; **je vous remercie du ~ du cœur** thank you from the bottom of my heart; **au ~ de son cœur** or **d'elle-même, elle le sait** deep down she knows it; **tout au ~ de lui-même il regrette ses actes** deep in his heart he regrets what he did; **elle a un bon ~** she's very good at heart; **il a un mauvais ~** he's got a nasty streak; **7** (arrière-plan) background; **sur ~ noir** on a black background; **sur ~ de soleil couchant** with a sunset in the background; **sur ~ de récession** against a background of recession; **~ musical** background music; **sur ~ de musique** with music playing in the background; **8** (petite quantité) **donne-moi juste un ~ de porto** give me just a drop of port; **laisser un ~ de verre/de bouteille** to leave a drop in one's glass/the bottle; **9** Naut (hauteur d'eau) **il n'y a pas assez de ~ pour plonger/mouiller** the water is not deep enough to dive/anchor; **il y a vingt mètres de ~** the water is twenty metres[GB] deep; **l'épave gisait par trente mètres de ~** the wreck lay thirty metres[GB] down; **10** Sport **épreuve de ~** long-distance event; **11** Cout (de pantalon) seat.
II à fond *loc adv* **1** (complètement) **connaître son domaine à ~** [*spécialiste*] to be an expert in one's field; **s'engager à ~** to commit oneself totally; **soutenir qn/qch à ~, être à ~ pour**○ **qn/qch** to support sb/sth wholeheartedly; **nettoyer la maison à ~** to give the house a thorough cleaning; **respirer à ~** to breathe deeply; **mettre la radio/le chauffage à ~** to turn the radio/the heating right up; **2**○ (vite) **rouler à ~** to drive at top speed; **il est arrivé à ~** he came rushing in.
■ **~ d'artichaut** Culin artichoke bottom; **~ blanc** Culin white stock; **~ brun** Culin brown stock; **~ d'œil** Anat back of the eye, fundus of the eye spéc; Méd (examen) ophthalmoscopic examination; **~ de robe** Mode slip; **~ de tarte** Culin pastry case; **~ de teint** Cosmét foundation GB, make-up base US; **~s marins** Géog depths of the sea.
IDIOMES **user ses ~s de culotte sur le même banc** fig to be at school together.

fondamental, **~e**, *mpl* **-aux** /fɔ̃damɑ̃tal, o/ *adj* **1** (essentiel) [*droit, question, différence, élément, principe*] basic, fundamental; [*objectif, besoin, idée, raison*] basic; [*cause, changement, conflit, importance, rôle*] fundamental; [*atout*] crucial; **libertés ~es** basic liberties, fundamental freedoms; **ce qui est ~ c'est que** the essential is that; **2** Mus [*note*] fundamental; **3** Ling (vocabulaire) basic; **français/anglais ~** basic French/English.

fondamentalement /fɔ̃damɑ̃talmɑ̃/ *adv* **1** (au fond) fundamentally; **être ~ optimiste/modéré/différent** to be fundamentally optimistic/moderate/different; **2** (totalement) [*s'opposer, changer*] radically; **être ~ modifié** to be radically changed.

fondamentalisme /fɔ̃damɑ̃talism/ *nm* fundamentalism.

fondamentaliste /fɔ̃damɑ̃talist/ **I** *adj* fundamentalist.

II *nmf* **1** Relig fundamentalist; **2** Sci (chercheur) scientist engaged in basic research.

fondant, **~e** /fɔ̃dɑ̃, ɑ̃t/ **I** *adj* [*neige, glace*] melting; [*poire, biscuit*] which melts in the mouth (*épith, après n*); [*viande*] tender; **bonbon ~** fondant.

II *nm* **1** Culin fondant icing; (bonbon) fondant; **2** Tech flux.

fondateur, **-trice** /fɔ̃datœʀ, tʀis/ *nm,f* gén founder; **groupe ~** founding group; **membre ~** founder member; **principe ~** founding principle; **mécanismes/mythes ~s** fundamental mechanisms/myths; **les pères ~s** the founding fathers; **l'acte ~ de la République** the act that founded the Republic.

fondation /fɔ̃dasjɔ̃/ **I** *nf* (action) foundation; Jur (organisme) foundation.

II fondations *nfpl* lit, fig foundations; **creuser les ~s de qch** to lay the foundations of sth.

fondé, **~e** /fɔ̃de/ **I** *pp* ▶ **fonder**.

II *pp adj* (légitime) [*réclamation, reproche*] justifiable; [*crainte*] well-founded; [*demande*] legitimate; **vos reproches ne sont pas ~s** your criticisms are unfounded; **mes craintes étaient tout à fait ~es** my fears were well founded; **ce que tu dis n'est pas ~** what you say has no justification; **non ~, mal ~** [*accusation*] groundless; [*confiance*] misplaced; **être ~ à faire** (moralement) to be justified in doing.

■ **~ de pouvoir** Jur (de personne) proxy; (de société) authorized representative; (de banque) manager.

fondement /fɔ̃dmɑ̃/ *nm* **1** (bases) foundation; **jeter/saper les ~s de** to lay/undermine the foundations of; **être sans** or **dénué de ~** [*allégations, craintes*] to be unfounded, to be without foundation; **2**○ (fesses) hum posterior hum.

fonder /fɔ̃de/ [1] **I** *vtr* **1** (créer) to found [*ville, parti, journal*]; **~ une famille** or **un foyer** to get married; **le prix Nobel a été fondé en 1901** the Nobel prize was established in 1901; **'maison fondée en 1920'** 'established 1920'; **2** (baser) to base (**sur** on); **il a fondé sa théorie sur Hegel** he based his theory on Hegel; **ma réflexion est fondée sur des faits** my observation is based on fact; **~ ses espoirs sur qch/qn** to place one's hopes in sth/sb.

II se fonder *vpr* **se ~ sur** [*théorie, méthode, stratégie*] to be based on; [*personne*] to go on; **je me fonde sur ce que je sais** I'm going on what I know; **sur quoi te fondes-tu?** what have you got to go on?

fonderie /fɔ̃dʀi/ *nf* **1** (atelier de moulage) foundry; **2** (moulage) casting.

fondeur, **-euse** /fɔ̃dœʀ, øz/ **I** *nm,f* Sport cross-country skier.

II *nm* ▶ **510** (patron) foundry owner; (ouvrier) foundry worker, caster.

fondre /fɔ̃dʀ/ [6] **I** *vtr* **1** Ind (liquéfier) to melt down [*métal*]; to smelt [*minerai*]; **2** Art, Imprim, Ind (fabriquer) to cast [*statue, caractère, lingot*]; **3** (combiner) to combine [*paragraphes, groupes*] (**dans, en** into); to blend [*couleurs*].

II *vi* **1** (se liquéfier) [*neige, métal, beurre*] to melt; **viande qui fond dans la bouche** meat which melts in your mouth; **faire ~** to melt; **2** (se dissoudre) [*sucre*] to dissolve; **faire ~ dans un peu d'eau** to dissolve in a little water; **3** (baisser) [*réserve, économies*] to melt away; [*action*] to drop sharply (**de** by); ▶ **neige**; **4** (maigrir) [*personne*] to waste away; **avoir fondu de dix kilos** to have lost ten kilos; **faire ~** to help the weight come off; **5** (s'attendrir) to soften; **il fond devant sa petite-fille** his heart melts when he sees his granddaughter; **~ en larmes** or **pleurs** to dissolve into tears; **6** (s'abattre) fml **~ sur** [*troupe, oiseau*] to swoop down on [*lieu, troupeau*]; [*malheur*] to overwhelm [*personne, peuple*]; [*calamité*] to ravage [*lieu*].

III se fondre *vpr* **se ~ dans** [*personne, silhouette*] to blend in with [*obscurité, foule, peuple*].

fondrière /fɔ̃dʀijɛʀ/ *nf* pothole.

fonds /fɔ̃/ **I** *nm* (collection) collection.

II *nmpl* Comm, Écon, Fin (capital) funds, capital ¢; **recueillir des ~** to raise money; **manquer de ~** to be short of funds; **être en ~** to be in funds; **gérer des ~** to manage funds; **affecter des ~** to earmark funds; **mise de ~** capital outlay; **rentrer dans ses ~** to recover outlay; **disposer des ~ nécessaires** to have (available) the necessary funds; **à ~ perdus** without recovering outlay, at a loss.

■ **~ d'amortissement** sinking fund; **~ de bienfaisance** charity fund; **~ bloqués** frozen assets; **~ de commerce** Comm, Jur business, good will; **~ commun de placement** unit trust GB, mutual fund US; **~ d'État** government securities; **~ de garantie** guarantee fund; **~ de placement** investment fund; **~ de prévoyance** provident fund; **~ propres** equity capital; **~ publics** public funds; **~ de roulement** working capital; **~ secrets** secret funds; **~ de solidarité** mutual aid fund; **~ spéciaux** special funds; **~ de terre** Jur land, tenement; **Fonds européen de développement, FED** European Development Fund; **Fonds européen de la jeunesse** European Youth Federation; **Fonds monétaire international, FMI** International Monetary Fund, IMF; **Fonds social européen, FSE** European Social Fund.

fondu, **~e** /fɔ̃dy/ **I** *pp* ▶ **fondre**.

II *pp adj* [*beurre*] melted; [*métal*] molten; [*sucre*] dissolved.

III *nm* **1** Cin dissolve; **ouverture/fermeture en ~** fade in/out; **2** Radio fading.

IV fondue *nf* Culin gén fondue; (au fromage) (cheese) fondue.

■ **~ enchaîné** Cin cross fading; **~e bourguignonne** fondue bourguignonne (*meat dipped in hot oil*), meat fondue US; **~e chinoise** Chinese fondue; **~e savoyarde** cheese fondue.

fongible /fɔ̃ʒibl/ *adj* fungible.

fongicide /fɔ̃ʒisid/ **I** *adj* fungicidal.

II *nm* fungicide.

fontaine /fɔ̃tɛn/ *nf* gén fountain; (pour boire) drinking fountain; (source) spring; **aller chercher de l'eau/boire à la ~** to fetch water/ to drink from the fountain.

IDIOMES **c'est une vraie ~**○ what a crybaby○; **il ne faut jamais dire: ~ je ne boirai pas de ton eau** Prov never say never.

Fontainebleau /fɔ̃tɛnblo/ ▶ **857** *npr* Fontainebleau.

fontanelle /fɔ̃tanɛl/ *nf* fontanelle GB, fontanel US.

fonte /fɔ̃t/ *nf* **1** (métal) cast iron; **~ émaillée** enamelled[GB] cast iron; **de** or **en ~** cast-iron (*épith*); **fourneau en ~** cast-iron stove; **2** (liquéfaction) (de métal) melting down; (de minerai) smelting; (de glace, neige) melting; **3** Météo (de cours d'eau, glace, neige) thawing; **4** (fabrication de cloche, statue) casting; (objet fabriqué) cast; **5** Imprim (fabrication de caractères) casting; (police de caractères) font; **6** (sacoche) (saddle) holster, saddle bag.

■ **~ d'aluminium** aluminium GB ou aluminum US cast; **~ des neiges** thaw; **à la ~ des neiges** when the snow thaws; **~ des semis** damping-off, seedling blight.

fonts /fɔ̃/ *nmpl* **~ baptismaux** font (*sg*).

foot○ /fut/ *nm*: *abbr* = **football**.

football /futbol/ ▶ **449** *nm* football GB, soccer.

■ **~ américain** american football GB, football US.

footballeur, **-euse** /futbolœʀ, øz/ ▶ **510** *nm,f* footballer GB, football GB ou soccer player.

footing /futiŋ/ ▶ **449** *nm* **1** (activité) jogging; **2** (trajet) jog; **faire un ~** to go for a jog.

for /fɔʀ/ *nm* **dans** or **en son ~ intérieur** in one's heart of hearts, deep down.

forage /fɔʀaʒ/ *nm* **1** (de métal, roche) drilling; (de puits) sinking; **effectuer** or **faire des ~s** to drill; **2** Méd (d'os) drilling.

forain, **-aine** /fɔʀɛ̃, ɛn/ **I** *adj* fairground, carnival (*épith*) US; **marchand ~** (itinerant) stallkeeper.

II *nm* **1** (marchand) stallkeeper, stallholder; **2** (amuseur) travelling[GB] showman; **les ~s** fairground people, carnies○ US.

forban /fɔʀbɑ̃/ *nm* Hist (pirate) pirate; fig (escroc) rogue.

forçage /fɔʀsaʒ/ *nm* forcing.

forçat /fɔʀsa/ *nm* (bagnard) convict; (galérien) galley slave; **vie de ~** fig life of drudgery; **c'est un travail de ~** fig it's slave labour[GB].

IDIOMES **travailler comme un ~** to work like a slave ou Trojan.

force /fɔʀs/ **I** *nf* **1** (de personne) (robustesse) strength ¢; (capacités physiques) **~s** strength; **~ musculaire/morale** muscular/ moral strength; **~ de caractère** strength of character; **avoir de la ~** to be strong; **ne plus avoir de ~** to have no strength left; **avoir de la ~ dans les jambes** to have strength in one's legs; **avoir/trouver/ donner la ~ de faire** to have/find/give the strength to do; **je n'ai plus la ~ de marcher** I no longer have the strength to walk; **mes ~s m'abandonnent** I'm getting weak; **reprendre des ~s** to regain one's strength; **ça te donnera des ~s** it will build up your strength; **être à bout de ~s** to feel drained; **c'est au-dessus de mes ~s** it's too much for me; **de toutes ses ~s** [*lancer*] with all one's might; [*désirer*] with all one's heart; **dans la ~ de l'âge** in the prime of life; **avec ~** [*nier*] strongly; [*affirmer*] firmly; **faire ~ de rames** to pull hard on the oars; **faire ~ de voiles** to crowd on sail; **2** (contrainte) force; **~ armée** armed force; **recourir à la ~** to resort to force; **être converti/emmené de ~** to be converted/taken away by force; **être marié de ~** to be forced into marriage; **faire faire qch à qn de ~** to force sb to do sth; **entrer de ~ dans un lieu** to force one's way into a place; **jouer en ~** Sport to play flat out; **par la ~ des choses** through force of circumstance; **vouloir à toute ~** to want at all costs; **~ est/ m'est de faire** there is/I have no choice but to do; **coup de ~** Mil strike; **3** (puissance) (de pays, groupe, secteur) strength; fig (d'expression) force; (de personne) strength; **la ~ militaire/économique du pays** the country's military/economic strength; **c'est ce qui fait leur ~** that's where their strength lies; **ils sont de même ~** or **de ~ égale aux échecs** they are evenly matched at chess; **être de ~ à faire** to be up to doing; **tu n'es pas de ~ à t'attaquer à lui** you're no match for him; **joueur/traducteur de première ~** top-flight ou top-quality player/translator; **revenir en ~, faire un retour en ~** to make a strong comeback; **4** (poids) (d'argument, accusation, de conviction) force; **la ~ de l'habitude** force of habit; **avoir ~ de loi** to have the force of law; **5** Phys, fig force; **~ d'attraction** force of attraction; **~ centrifuge** centrifugal force; **~s naturelles/occultes** natural/occult forces; **les ~s de marché** Écon market forces; **les ~s du mal** the forces of evil; **6** (intensité) (de choc, séisme, vent) force; (de désir, sentiment) strength; **vent de ~ 1 à 3** breeze blowing at force 1 to 3; **vent de ~ 4 à 7** wind force 4 to 7; **vent de ~ 8 à 10** force 8 to 10 gale; **7** (ensemble humain) force; **~ de vente** sales force; **~ d'alternance** alternative force; **~s productives** productive forces; **~s d'opposition** opposition forces;

être/arriver en ~ to be present/to arrive in force; **8** Mil (corps) force; (effectifs) **~s** forces; **~ multinationale** multinational force; **~s aériennes** air force; **~s navales** navy; **~s terrestres** army; **~s armées/intégrées/d'occupation** armed/integrated/occupying forces; **d'importantes ~s de police** large numbers of police.

II† *adv* **donner ~ exemples** to give many an example; **avec ~ excuses/remerciements** with profuse apologies/thanks.

III à force de *loc prép* **réussir à ~ de patience/travail** to succeed by dint of patience/hard work; **à ~ d'économies** or **d'économiser, elle a pu l'acheter** by saving very hard, she was able to buy it; **il est aphone à ~ de crier** he shouted so much (that) he lost his voice; **à ~ de frotter, tu vas le déchirer** if you keep on rubbing it, you'll tear it; **à ~**○**, elle l'a cassé** she ended up breaking it.

■ **~ d'action rapide** Mil rapid reaction force; **~ d'âme** fortitude; **~ de dissuasion** Mil deterrent force; fig deterrent; **~ de frappe** (arme nucléaire) nuclear weapons (*pl*); (groupe) strike force; **~ d'interposition** Mil peacekeeping force; **~ d'intervention** Mil task force; **~ de la nature** (real) Goliath; **~ de pénétration** Tech penetration; **~ publique** police force; **~s de l'ordre** forces of law and order; **~s vives** life blood ¢; **Force ouvrière, FO** Pol *French trade union*; **Forces françaises de l'intérieur, FFI** Hist *Resistance forces operating in France during the Second World War*; **Forces françaises libres, FFL** Hist Free French Forces.

forcé, **~e** /fɔʀse/ **I** *pp* ▶ **forcer**.
II *pp adj* **1** (contraint) [*démission, mariage, exil*] forced; (accidentel) [*baignade, douche*] unintentional; **2** (artificiel) [*gaieté, sourire, comparaison*] forced; **cours ~** Fin forced price; **3** Hort forced; **la culture ~e** forcing; **4**○ (inéluctable) **c'est ~!** there's no way around it○!; **c'est ~ qu'il/elle fasse** he's/she's bound to do.

forcement /fɔʀsəmɑ̃/ *nm* forcing.

forcément /fɔʀsemɑ̃/ *adv* **entraîner/devenir ~** to lead to/to become; **être ~** to be bound to be; **elle viendra ~ tôt ou tard** she is bound to come sooner or later; **pas ~** not necessarily; **j'ai été ~ surpris** obviously I was surprised; **'j'ai faim'—'~, tu n'as pas déjeuné!'** 'I'm hungry'—'well, it's hardly surprising, you had no lunch!'

forcené, **~e** /fɔʀsəne/ **I** *adj* (acharné) [*optimisme, égoïsme*] insane; [*rythme*] furious; [*activité*] frenzied; [*individualiste*] crazed; **c'est une travailleuse ~e** she's a workaholic.
II *nm,f* (enragé) maniac; (armé) crazed gunman; **crier/travailler comme un ~** to scream/work like a maniac ou mad thing.

forceps /fɔʀsɛps/ *nm* forceps (*pl*); **accouchement par ~** forceps delivery.

forcer /fɔʀse/ [12] **I** *vtr* **1** (contraindre) to force; **nous ne voulons ~ personne** we don't want to force anybody; **~ qn à faire** to force sb to do; **~ l'ennemi à négocier** to force the enemy to negotiate; **~ qn à qch** to force sb into sth; **être forcé à l'exil** to be forced into exile; **être forcé de faire** to be forced to do; **2** (faire céder) to force [*porte, serrure*]; **le tiroir a été forcé** the drawer has been forced; **~ la porte de qn** fig to force one's way into sb's house; **3** (passer au travers) to break through [*barrière, enceinte, défense*]; to break [*blocus*]; **~ le passage** to force one's way through; **~ l'entrée** to force one's way in; **4** (imposer) to force [*négociation, décision*]; **~ l'admiration** to command admiration; **~ la victoire** to secure victory; **~ la paix** to impose a peace settlement; **5** (pousser) to force [*allure, rythme, cadence*]; to stretch [*sens*]; to contrive [*métaphore*]; to push [sth] to the limits [*talent*]; **~ la dose** or **note** to overdo it; **~ le ton** to raise one's voice; **~ le trait** to exaggerate; **6** (traquer) Chasse to run down [*lièvre*]; Mil to track down [*ennemi*]; **7** Agric, Hort to force [*plante*].
II forcer sur *vtr ind* **1** (abuser) **~ sur** to overdo [*vin, sel, couleur*]; **j'ai un peu forcé sur le rouge hier soir** I overdid the red wine a bit last night; **2** Naut **~ sur les avirons** to pull on the oars; **3** Tech **~ sur** to overtighten [*vis*]; to force [*mécanisme*].
III *vi* **1** (faire trop d'efforts) to overdo it; **j'ai trop forcé** I overdid it; **gagner sans ~** to win easily; **2** (exercer une pression) to force it; **ne force pas, tu vas le casser** don't force it or you'll break it; **appuyez/serrez sans ~** do not press/tighten too much; **3** (résister) **la porte/charnière force** the door/hinge is sticking.
IV se forcer *vpr* **1** (se contraindre) to force oneself (**à faire** to do); **il se força à sourire** he forced himself to smile; **2** (faire des efforts) **il se force pour manger** it's a real effort for him to eat.
IDIOMES **~ la main à qn** to force sb's hand.

forcing /fɔʀsiŋ/ *nm* pressure; **faire le ~** to put on the pressure (**pour faire** to do).

forcir /fɔʀsiʀ/ [3] *vi* **1** [*vent*] to become stronger; **2** [*personne*] to put on weight.

forclore /fɔʀklɔʀ/ [79] *vtr* Jur **se laisser ~** to fail to make one's claim within the statutory time-limit.

forclusion /fɔʀklyzjɔ̃/ *nf* Jur failure to make a claim within the statutory time-limit.

forer /fɔʀe/ [1] *vtr* to drill, to bore [*métal, bois, roche*]; to sink [*puits*].

forestier, **-ière** /fɔʀɛstje, ɛʀ/ **I** *adj* **1** [*région, massif*] forested; [*espèce, chemin, paysage, ressources*] forest (*épith*); **maison forestière** forestry worker's house; **exploitation forestière** (travail) forestry; (site) forestry plantation; **industrie forestière** timber industry; **2** Culin [*escalope*] with mushrooms.
II ▶ **510** *nm* forestry worker, forester.

foret /fɔʀɛ/ *nm* drill.

forêt /fɔʀɛ/ *nf* **1** lit forest; **~ vierge/équatoriale** virgin/equatorial forest; **la ~ de Fontainebleau** the forest of Fontainebleau; **~ tropicale** rain forest; **2** fig forest; **~ d'antennes/de drapeaux** forest of aerials/of flags.
IDIOMES **c'est l'arbre qui cache la ~** you can't see the wood for the trees.

forêt-galerie, *pl* **forêts-galeries** /fɔʀɛgalʀi/ *nf* gallery forest.

Forêt-Noire /fɔʀɛnwaʀ/ *nprf* **1** ▶ **692** (région) **la ~** the Black Forest; **2** (gâteau) Black Forest gâteau GB ou cake.

foreuse /fɔʀøz/ *nf* drill.

forfaire /fɔʀfɛʀ/ [10] *vi* fml **~ à** to be false to [*promesse, honneur*]; to fail in [*devoir*].

forfait /fɔʀfɛ/ *nm* **1** Comm, Entr (prix global) fixed rate; **travailler/être payé au ~** to work for/to be paid a fixed rate; **~ hebdomadaire** weekly rate; **un ~ de 15 francs** a fixed price of 15 francs; **un ~ de 160 francs pour trois concerts/pour le festival** a 160 franc flat-rate ticket covering three concerts/for the festival; **2** Tourisme (séjour) package; **~ avion-auto** fly-drive package; **le ~ comprend le voyage et 5 nuits d'hôtel** the all-in package covers travel and 5 nights' hotel accommodation; **3** Tourisme, Transp (carte d'accès) pass; **~ skieur** ski pass; **~ ferroviaire** rail pass; **4** Sport (d'un joueur, une équipe) withdrawal; **gagner par ~** to win by default; **déclarer ~** gén to give up; Sport to withdraw; **5** Turf forfeit; **6** Fisc **être au ~** to be taxed at a rate calculated according to estimated turnover; **7** (crime) hideous crime.
■ **~ journalier** Prot Soc *individual contribution to cost of state hospital care*.

forfaitaire /fɔʀfɛtɛʀ/ *adj* **prix ~** contract ou all-inclusive price; **coût ~** inclusive cost; **tarif ~** flat fare ou fee; **taxe/perception ~** flat-rate tax/collection; **somme ~** lump sum; **indemnité ~** basic allowance; **amende ~** standard fine.

forfaiture /fɔʀfɛtyʀ/ *nf* **1** Jur malfeasance; **2** Hist felony.

forfanterie /fɔʀfɑ̃tʀi/ *nf* **1** (caractère) boastfulness; **par ~** to show off; **2** (action) swaggering ¢; (propos) bragging ¢.

forge /fɔʀʒ/ *nf* (atelier) forge, smithy; (feu) forge; (aciérie) ironworks (+ *v sg* ou *pl*).

forgé, **~e** /fɔʀʒe/ **I** *pp* ▶ **forger**.
II *pp adj* [*objet, métal*] wrought; **~ à la main** hand-wrought (*épith*); **fer ~** wrought iron; **grille en fer ~** wrought-iron gate.

forger /fɔʀʒe/ [13] **I** *vtr* **1** Ind to forge [*fer, fer à cheval, instrument, pièce mécanique*]; **2** (élaborer) to build [*amitié*]; to build up [*unité, entente*]; to forge [*liens, alliances*]; to form [*caractère*]; **3** (créer) to coin [*mot*]; to invent [*théorie*]; to create [*métaphore*]; **une histoire forgée de toutes pièces** a complete fabrication.
II se forger *vpr* **se ~ des excuses/un alibi** to invent excuses/an alibi (for oneself); **se ~ un idéal** to create an ideal for oneself; **se ~ une réputation de meneur/d'incorruptible** to build up a reputation as a leader/for scrupulous honesty.

forgeron /fɔʀʒəʀɔ̃/ ▶ **510** *nm* blacksmith, smith; **chez le ~** at the blacksmith's ou smithy.
IDIOMES **c'est en forgeant qu'on devient ~** Prov practice makes perfect Prov.

formage /fɔʀmaʒ/ *nm* forming; **~ des métaux** metal forming.
■ **~ à chaud** thermoforming; **~ hydraulique** hydroforming.

formalisation /fɔʀmalizasjɔ̃/ *nf* formalization.

formaliser /fɔʀmalize/ [1] **I** *vtr* Math to formalize.
II se formaliser *vpr* to take offence[GB], to take exception (**de** to); **se ~ d'un rien** to be easily offended.

formalisme /fɔʀmalism/ *nm* **1** (excessif) péj formality; **il est d'un ~ excessif** he is a stickler for form; **2** Art, Philos formalism.

formaliste /fɔʀmalist/ **I** *adj* **1** péj [*personne*] formal; [*religion, droit*] formalistic; **il est très ~** he's a stickler for form; **2** Art, Philos formalist.
II *nmf* formalist.

formalité /fɔʀmalite/ *nf* Admin formality; **les ~s de douane** customs formalities; **remplir une ~** to comply with a formality; **les ~s à accomplir pour obtenir un visa** the necessary procedure to obtain a visa; **simplifier les ~s** to simplify procedure; **ce n'est qu'une ~** it's a mere formality; **par pure ~** as a matter of form; **sans autre ~** fig without further ado.

formant /fɔʀmɑ̃/ *nm* Ling formant.

format /fɔʀma/ *nm* **1** (taille) (de journal, disquette) format; (de papier, livre, photo, d'objet) size; **de grand/très grand ~** [*article, livre, cadre*] large/extra large; **2** Ordinat, Vidéo (mode d'enregistrement) format; **3** Cin gauge.

formatage /fɔʀmataʒ/ *nm* Ordinat formatting; **faire un ~** to format.

formater /fɔʀmate/ [1] *vtr* Ordinat to format.

formateur, **-trice** /fɔʀmatœʀ, tʀis/ **I** *adj* [*influence, élément, rôle*] formative.
II ▶ **510** *nm,f* training officer.

formatif, **-ive** /fɔʀmatif, iv/ *adj* formative.

formation /fɔʀmasjɔ̃/ *nf* **1** (instruction) (scolaire) education; (professionnelle) training (**en** in); **~ militaire** military training; **il est ingénieur de ~** he's an engineer by training; **il a reçu une ~ d'ingénieur** he was trained as an engineer; **avoir une ~ littéraire** to have an arts background; **la ~ des jeunes/maîtres** youth/teacher education; **il n'a aucune ~** he has no training; **en ~** [*stagiaire, technicien*] undergoing training (*après n*); **'~ assurée'** 'training provided'; **quelle est votre ~?** what education and training have you had?; **2** (cours) training course; **3** (de gouvernement, parti, d'équipe) forming; **il a été chargé de la ~ du gouvernement** he was asked to form the government; **la ~ de leur parti a pris deux mois** it took two months to form their party; **4** (apparition) formation; **on observe la ~ de rougeurs/d'escarres** red blotches/bedsores appear; **ils s'interrogent encore sur la ~ des planètes** they're still wondering how the planets were formed; **au moment de la ~ des glaciers** at the time when the glaciers were (being) formed; **'trous en formation'** 'uneven carriageway'; **5** (puberté) puberty; **6** (ensemble) formation; **une ~ végétale/granitique** a formation of vegetation/of granite; **une ~ nuageuse** a cloud formation; **7** (groupe) group; **~ politique/musicale/syndicale** political/musical/trade union group; **8** Mil (détachement) detachment; (disposition) formation; **~ aérienne/de combat/en carré** aerial/combat/square formation; **~ en ligne** Aviat line formation.

■ **~ continue** adult continuing education; **~ de mots** Ling word-formation; **~ permanente** = **~ continue**; **~ professionnelle** professional training; **~ sur le tas** on-the-job training.

forme /fɔʀm/ **I** *nf* **1** (concrète) shape; (abstraite) form; **une ~ de vie/d'intelligence** a form of life/of intelligence; **prendre ~** to take shape; **prendre la ~ de** (concrètement) to take the shape of; (abstraitement) to take the form of; **de ~ ronde** round; **une racine en ~ de corps humain** a root in the shape of a human body; **un titre en ~ de slogan** a title in the form of a slogan; **une critique en ~ de compliment** a criticism in the form ou guise of a compliment; **mettre qch en ~** to shape sth; **remettre qch en ~** to put sth back into shape; **donner ~ à qch** to give shape to sth; **donner une ~ légale à un texte** to give a legal form to a text; **sous ~ de** in the form of; **sous une ~ réduite** in a reduced form; **sous une autre ~** in another form; **sous des ~s différentes** in different forms; **sous ~ de tableau** in tabular form; **sous ~ d'exportations** in exports; **sous quelle ~...?** in what form...?; **juger sur la ~** to judge on form; **sans ~** shapeless; **2** (modalité) (de gouvernement, contrat, violence) form; (de paiement, recrutement) method; **dans sa ~ actuelle** in its present form; **une nouvelle ~ de pensée** a new way of thinking; **3** (procédé, condition) form; **en bonne et due ~** in due form; **pour la ~** [*protester, critiquer*] as a matter of form; **pour la bonne ~** to formalize things; **de pure ~** purely formal; **sans autre ~ de procès** fig without further ou more ado; **4** Ling, Littérat form; **à la ~ négative** in the negative form; **la ~ du féminin** the feminine form; **poème à ~ fixe** fixed-form poem; **5** (état général) form; **en ~** on form; **en bonne/grande ~** in good/peak form; **perdre/ne plus avoir la ~** to go off/to be off form; **très en ~** in tip-top form; **au mieux de sa ~** on top form; **être en pleine ~**, **tenir la ~** to be in great shape; **mettre qn en ~** to get sb fit; **remettre qn en ~** to get sb fit again; **se remettre en ~** to get fit again; **une séance de remise en ~** a fitness session; **6** Tech (de cordonnier, bottier) last; (de chapelier, modiste) block; **7** Imprim forme GB, form US.

II formes *nfpl* **1** (corps humain) figure (*sg*); **elle a des ~s rondes/anguleuses/plantureuses** she has a rounded/angular/full figure; **femme aux ~s élancées** slender woman; **pull qui moule les ~s** figure-hugging sweater; **prendre des ~s** to fill out; **2** (d'objet, de bâtiment) lines; **monument aux ~s pures/modernes** monument with clean/modern lines; **3** (règles) **faire qch dans les ~s** to do sth in the correct manner; **y mettre les ~s** to be tactful; **respecter les ~s** to respect convention.

formé, **~e** /fɔʀme/ **I** *pp* ▶ **former**.

II *pp adj* **1** (composé) made up (**de** of); (dessiné) formed (**de** from); **équipe ~e de chercheurs et d'étudiants** team made up of researchers and students; **le triangle ~ par les trois villes** the triangle formed by the three towns; **2** (instruit) educated; (professionnellement) trained (**à faire** to do); **3** (façonné) [*écriture, lettre, phrase*] formed; **bien ~** well-formed; **mal ~** badly-formed; **4** (mûr) [*adolescent*] who has reached sexual maturity (*épith, après n*); [*épi, fruit*] formed; [*caractère, goût*] formed.

formel, **-elle** /fɔʀmɛl/ *adj* **1** [*intention*] express (*épith*); [*refus, démenti*] categorical, flat; [*promesse*] definite; [*ordre, interdiction*] strict; [*personne*] categorical; **donner un démenti ~ à qch** to deny sth categorically; **être ~ sur qch** [*personne*] to be definite about sth; [*loi*] to be clear ou explicit on sth; **il a dit 20 heures, je suis ~** he said 8 pm, I'm quite positive about it; **2** Art, Ling, Philos formal; **3** (superficiel) [*politesse*] formal; **une question purement formelle** a token question; **c'est purement ~** it's just a formality.

formellement /fɔʀmɛlmɑ̃/ *adv* **1** (expressément) [*démentir*] categorically; [*interdire*] strictly; **il est ~ interdit/illégal de faire** it is strictly forbidden/illegal to do; **2** (de façon officielle) [*condamner, inculper, décider*] officially; **il a ~ mis en cause son frère** he officially implicated his brother; **l'homme a été ~ identifié** the man has been clearly identified; **3** Art, Ling, Philos formally.

former /fɔʀme/ [1] **I** *vtr* **1** (prendre l'aspect de) to form [*cercle, rectangle*]; **la rivière forme un coude** the river forms a bend; **2** (constituer) to form, constitute; **les personnes formant le comité** the people forming the committee; **ils forment un couple très uni** they are a very close couple; **il forme avec son partenaire une brillante équipe** he and his partner make a brilliant team; **formez des groupes de cinq** get into groups of five; **3** (réunir les éléments de, réaliser) to form; **~ un gouvernement** to form a government; **~ un train** to form a train; **~ une équipe/une commission/une association** to form a team/a commission/an association; **4** (donner une formation à) to train [*personnel*] (**à faire** to do); (éduquer) to educate [*personne, goût*]; to develop, form [*personnalité, caractère, esprit*]; to develop [*intelligence*]; to form [*opinion*]; **~ qn au traitement de texte** to train sb in word processing; **enseignement qui permet de ~ des individus responsables** teaching which produces responsible people; ▶ **jeunesse**; **5** (produire) to form [*abcès, pellicule*]; **6** (mettre en forme) to form [*lettres, phrases*]; **7** (concevoir) fml to conceive [*projet*]; **je forme le vœu que tout se passe bien** I hope that everything goes well.

II se former *vpr* **1** (se créer) to form; **un caillot s'est formé dans l'artère** a clot has formed in the artery; **l'image qui se forme sur la rétine** the image that forms on the retina; **il se forme de la buée** condensation forms; **2** (être créé) to be formed; **le gouvernement s'est formé autour d'une politique commune** the government was formed around a common policy; **3** (acquérir une formation) to train, to be trained (**à** in); **se ~ à la vente/au marketing** to train in sales/in marketing; **il est allé se ~ au Japon** he went to train in Japan; **4** (s'éduquer) [*caractère, personnalité, style*] to develop; [*personne*] to educate oneself; **son style s'est formé peu à peu** his style developed gradually; **il s'est formé à l'école de la vie** he was educated in the university of life; **5** (concevoir) to form.

formica® /fɔʀmika/ *nm* Formica®; **table en ~** Formica®(-topped) table.

formidable /fɔʀmidabl/ *adj* **1** (considérable) [*force, puissance, croissance*] tremendous; [*recul*] considerable; [*explosion, chahut*] enormous; **2**○ (épatant) [*soirée, spectacle, livre*] great, fantastic○; [*personne*] marvellous[GB]; **être ~ de patience/gentillesse avec qn** to be wonderfully patient with sb/kind to sb; **être ~**○ **avec qn** (généreux) to be wonderful to sb; (patient) to be wonderful with sb; **3**○ (incroyable) incredible; **c'est quand même ~ qu'elle n'ait pas téléphoné!** it's incredible she hasn't phoned!; **c'est ~, il ne nous a même pas présentés!** iron terrific, he didn't even introduce us!

formidablement /fɔʀmidabləmɑ̃/ *adj* awfully; **il a ~ grossi** he's got GB ou gotten US awfully fat; **ça s'est ~ amélioré** there's been a tremendous improvement; **il joue ~ bien** he plays tremendously well.

formique /fɔʀmik/ *adj* formic.

formol /fɔʀmɔl/ *nm* formalin.

Formose /fɔʀmoz/ ▶ **416** *nprf* Hist Formosa.

formulable /fɔʀmylabl/ *adj* that can be formulated (*après n*).

formulaire /fɔʀmylɛʀ/ *nm* **1** (imprimé) form; **~ de demande d'emploi** job application form; **~ de déclaration des revenus** tax return form; **2** (de notaire, pharmacien) formulary.

formulation /fɔʀmylasjɔ̃/ *nf* (action) formulation; (chose formulée) wording, formulation; **la ~ de cette idée est difficile** it's not easy to express that idea; **je ne suis pas d'accord avec la ~** I disagree with the way it's worded ou formulated.

formule /fɔʀmyl/ *nf* **1** (expression) expression; **la ~ est heureuse** that's well put; **~ toute faite** set phrase; **une ~ creuse** an empty formula; **2** Comm (option) option; **la ~ train-bateau n'est pas économique** the boat-train option isn't economical; **nous proposons plusieurs ~s d'hébergement** we offer several accommodation options; **3** (méthode) method; **~ de paiement** method of payment; **il a trouvé la bonne ~ pour s'enrichir** he hit on a good way of making money; **4** (conception) concept; **nouvelles ~s de vie familiale** new concepts of family life; **5** Sci formula; **6** (formulaire) form; **7** Sport Aut **~ un/deux/trois** Formula One/Two/Three; **un Grand prix de ~ un** a Formula One Grand Prix; **8** (présentation) (d'émission, de magazine) format; **l'émission a changé de ~** the programme[GB] has got a new format.

■ **~ dentaire** Dent dental formula; **~ développée** Phys structural formula; **~ exécutoire** Jur order for enforcement; **~ incantatoire** incantation; **~ magique** (en magie) magic words; fig magic formula; **~ de politesse** gén polite phrase; (à la fin d'une lettre) letter ending.

formuler /fɔʀmyle/ [1] *vtr* **1** gén to express [*sentiment, souhait, réserves, pensée*]; to put [sth] into words [*idée*]; to set out, to state [*grief, plainte*]; to draw up [*plan, contrat, acte notarié*]; to write out [*ordonnance*]; **~ une réponse** to give an answer; **2** Chimie, Math to formulate.

fornication /fɔʀnikasjɔ̃/ *nf* fornication.

forniquer /fɔʀnike/ [1] *vi* to fornicate.

fors‡ /fɔʀ/ *prép* liter save, except.

forsythia /fɔʀsisja/ *nm* forsythia.

fort, **~e**[1] /fɔʀ, fɔʀt/ **I** *adj* **1** (puissant) [*personne, pays, monnaie, économie, lunettes, médicament*] strong; **armée ~e de 10 000 hommes** 10,000-strong army; **notre compagnie est ~e de 30 appareils** Aviat our airline can boast 30 aircraft; **~ d'un chiffre d'affaires en hausse/de trois joueurs internationaux**... boasting an increased turnover/three international players...; **~s de leur approbation/expérience**... boosted ou fortified by their approval/experience...; **le roi est plus ~ que la dame** Jeux a king is worth more than a queen; **trouver plus ~ que soi** to meet one's match; **s'attaquer** or **s'en prendre à plus ~ que soi** to take on someone bigger than oneself; ▶ **partie**; **2** (résistant) [*carton, papier, colle*] strong; **3** (intense) [*bruit*] loud; [*lumière*] bright; [*cha-*

leur, activité, pression] intense; [*crampe, douleur*] bad; [*fièvre*] high; [*sentiment, soupçon*] strong; [*crainte, colère, mécontentement*] deep; **une ~e grippe** a bad attack of flu; **avoir une ~e envie de faire** to feel a strong desire to do; **4** (violent) [*coup, poussée, secousse*] hard; [*pluie*] heavy; [*vent*] strong; **5** (concentré) [*café, cigarette, alcool, moutarde*] strong; [*épice, piment, curry*] hot; **un vin ~** a strong wine, a wine with a high degree of alcohol; **au sens ~ du mot** fig in the fullest sense of the word; **6** (accusé) [*accent, personnalité, odeur, tendance, impression*] strong; [*pente*] steep; **7** (ample) [*somme, majorité, réduction*] large; [*concentration, taux, inflation*] high; [*demande, consommation*] high, heavy; [*expansion, pénurie*] great; [*baisse, augmentation*] sharp; [*croissance*] strong; [*différence*] big; [*délégation, contingent, dose*] strong; **~e émigration/abstention** high level of emigration/abstention; **de ~e puissance** very powerful; **8** (doué) good (**en, à** at; **pour faire** to do); **ceux qui sont ~s en latin** those who are good at Latin; **il est ~ pour ne rien faire** iron he's good at doing nothing; **9** (ferme) [*personne*] strong; **rester ~ dans le malheur** to remain strong in adversity; **je me fais ~ de la convaincre** I feel confident ou I am sure that I can convince her; **10** (gros) [*personne*] stout; [*hanches*] broad; [*poitrine*] large; [*cuisses*] big; **être ~e de poitrine** to have a large bust; **11**○ (exagéré) **c'est un peu ~!** that's a bit much○!; (prix) that's a bit steep○!; **le plus ~, c'est que**... (surprenant) the most amazing thing is that...; (absurde) the most ridiculous thing is that...

II *adv* **1** (très) [*bon, déçu, émouvant, mécontent*] extremely; [*bien, logiquement, vite*] very; **~ recherché/demandé** very much sought after/in demand; **c'est ~ dommage** it's a great pity, it's extremely regrettable; **2** (beaucoup) [*douter, soupçonner*] very much; **avoir ~ à faire**○ to have a lot to do; **j'ai eu ~ à faire**○ **pour le convaincre** I had a hard job convincing him; **3** (avec force) [*frapper, tirer, pousser, frotter*] hard; [*serrer*] tight; [*respirer*] deeply; [*parler, crier*] loudly; [*sentir*] strongly; [*coller*] firmly; **souffle ~!** blow hard!; **le vent souffle ~** there's a strong wind; **parler de plus en plus ~** to speak louder and louder; **mon cœur bat trop ~** my heart is beating too fast; **le chauffage marche trop ~** the heating is turned up too high; **dire haut et ~** to say loud and clear; **y aller un peu ~**○ to go a bit too far; **y aller un peu ~ sur la moutarde/le sel** to overdo the mustard/the salt; **revenir très ~** [*coureur, équipe*] to make a strong comeback; **4** (bien) well; **il ne va pas très ~** he's not very well; **(moi) ça ne va pas très ~** I'm not all that well○; **chez eux ça ne va pas très ~** things aren't going so well for them; **marcher ~** [*entreprise*] to do well; **faire** or **frapper (très) ~**○ to do (really) well; **attaquer** or **commencer très ~**○ to start off really well.

III *nm* **1** Archit, Mil (ouvrage fortifié) fort; **2** (personne puissante) **les ~s et les faibles** the strong and the weak; ▶**raison**; **3** (domaine d'excellence) strong point; **les échecs ne sont pas mon ~** chess is not my strong point; **la générosité n'est pas ton ~** generosity is not your strong point.

IV au plus fort de *loc prép* **au plus ~ de l'été/de l'incendie** at the height of summer/of the fire; **au plus ~ de l'hiver** in the depths of winter; **au plus ~ de la bataille** in the thick of the fighting; **au plus ~ de la pluie** in the middle of the downpour.

■ **~ des halles** market porter; fig Goliath; **~ en thème**○ Scol swot○ GB, grind○ US; **~e tête** rebel.

IDIOMES **~ comme un bœuf** or **Turc** strong as an ox; **c'est plus ~ que moi/qu'elle** (incontrôlable) I/she just can't help it; **c'est plus ~ que l'as de pique**○ or **que de jouer au bouchon** that beats it all, that takes the biscuit○.

forte[2] /fɔʀte/ **I** *adv* forte.

II *nm inv* forte; **jouer un ~** to play forte.

fortement /fɔʀtəmɑ̃/ *adv* (avec force) [*attirer, encourager, critiquer, croire*] strongly; (de façon très marquée) [*augmenter, baisser, accélérer, se détériorer*] sharply; (à un haut niveau) [*centralisé, industrialisé*] highly; (profondément) [*ébranlé, impressionné, ancré*] deeply; [*endommagé, pollué*] badly; [*déplaire, handicaper*] severely; (lourdement) [*armé, investir*] heavily; **il est ~ question de démolir l'usine** demolition of the factory is being seriously considered ou is on the cards.

forteresse /fɔʀtəʀɛs/ *nf* lit fortress, stronghold; fig stronghold.

■ **~ volante** Aviat flying fortress.

fortiche○ /fɔʀtiʃ/ **I** *adj* smart, clever (**en** at).

II *nmf* brain○.

fortifiant, ~e /fɔʀtifjɑ̃, ɑt/ **I** *adj* **1** [*boisson, médicament*] fortifying; [*air*] bracing; [*séjour*] restorative; **2** liter [*lecture*] uplifting.

II *nm* Méd tonic.

fortification /fɔʀtifikasjɔ̃/ *nf* fortification.

fortifié, ~e /fɔʀtifje/ **I** *pp* ▶ **fortifier**.

II *pp adj* **1** Mil [*site, enceinte*] fortified; **église ~e** fortified church; **2** Vin [*vin*] fortified.

fortifier /fɔʀtifje/ [2] **I** *vtr* **1** (donner de la robustesse) to strengthen [*ongles, cheveux*]; **2** (donner des forces) [*repas*] to fortify; [*sport*] to make [sb] strong; [*vacances, vitamines*] to do [sb] good; **3** (consolider) to reinforce [*construction*]; to strengthen [*foi, régime*]; **4** Mil (défendre) to fortify [*accès, ville*].

II se fortifier *vpr* **1** (se donner des forces) (en mangeant) to build oneself up; (en s'exerçant) to build up one's strength; **2** (se consolider) [*régime*] to get stronger; [*foi*] to grow stronger.

fortin /fɔʀtɛ̃/ *nm* (small) fort.

fortiori ▶ **a fortiori**.

fortissimo /fɔʀtisimo/ **I** *adv* fortissimo.

II *nm inv* (signe) fortissimo; (passage) fortissimo passage.

Fortran /fɔʀtʀɑ̃/ *nm* Fortran.

fortuit, ~e /fɔʀtɥi, it/ *adj* [*rencontre*] accidental, chance (*épith*); [*incident, circonstance*] fortuitous; [*remarque, découverte*] fortuitous, chance (*épith*); [*occasion*] unexpected; **rien n'est ~** nothing happens by chance; **'toute ressemblance serait purement ~e'** 'any similarity is purely accidental'.

fortuitement /fɔʀtɥitmɑ̃/ *adv* by chance, fortuitously sout.

fortune /fɔʀtyn/ *nf* **1** (richesse) fortune; **~ personnelle/considérable** personal/considerable fortune; **véritable/petite ~** real/small fortune; **grandes ~s** large fortunes; **~ estimée à plus de dix millions** fortune estimated at more than ten million; **valoir une ~** to be worth a fortune; **dépenser une ~** to spend a fortune (**à faire** doing; **pour, en** on); **faire ~** to make a fortune (**dans** in; **en faisant** doing); **faire ~ en Amérique** to make one's fortune in America; **chercher ~** to seek one's fortune; **une des plus grosses ~s du Venezuela** one of Venezuela's wealthiest people; **2** (chance) **(bonne) ~** good fortune; **avoir la (bonne) ~ de faire/d'avoir fait** to have the good fortune to do/to have done; **profiter de sa bonne ~** to make the most of one's good fortune; **mauvaise ~** bad luck; ▶**audacieux**; **3** (destinée) fortunes (*pl*); **~ d'un parti/club** fortunes of a party/club; **avec une ~ diverse, avec des ~s diverses** with varying fortunes; **~ d'un mot/d'un film/d'un artiste** fortunes of a word/of a film/of an artist; **4** (improvisé) **de ~** makeshift; **abri de ~** makeshift shelter; ▶**pot**.

IDIOMES **faire contre mauvaise ~ bon cœur** to put on a brave face.

fortuné, ~e /fɔʀtyne/ *adj* **1** (riche) wealthy, well-off; **2** liter (favorisé) fortunate.

forum /fɔʀɔm/ *nm* (lieu, débat) forum.

■ **~ de discussion** Ordinat newsgroup.

fosse /fos/ *nf* **1** (cavité) pit; **2** (tombe) grave; **3** Mines (puits) pit; **4** Sport (pour le saut) sandpit; (pour le plongeon) diving pool; **5** Aut (de garage) inspection pit; **6** Chasse pitfall; **7** Anat fossa.

■ **~ d'aisances** Constr earth closet; **~ d'ascenseur** Constr lift shaft GB, elevator shaft US; **~ commune** communal grave; **~ aux lions** lions' den; **~ océanique** Géog oceanic trench; **~ d'orchestre** orchestra pit; **~ de plongée** Sport diving pool; **~ à purin** Agric slurry pit; **~ septique** Constr septic tank; **~ de visite** Aut, Rail inspection pit; **~s nasales** Anat nasal passages.

fossé /fose/ *nm* **1** gén ditch; (de château) moat; **aller dans le** or **au ~** to go into the ditch; **2** fig (écart) gap (**entre** between); (désaccord) rift (**entre** between); **le ~ qui sépare les riches et les pauvres s'agrandit** the gap between the rich and the poor is widening; **ça a creusé un ~ entre eux** it caused a rift between them.

■ **~ antichar** Mil anti-tank ditch; **~ d'effondrement** Géol rift valley; **le ~ des générations** the generation gap.

fossette /fosɛt/ *nf* dimple; **avoir une ~ au menton** to have a dimple in one's chin.

fossile /fosil/ **I** *adj* fossil (*épith*).

II *nm* lit, fig fossil.

fossilifère /fosilifɛʀ/ *adj* fossil-bearing, fossiliferous spéc.

fossilisation /fosilizasjɔ̃/ *nf* (de plante etc) fossilization; **couche favorable à la ~** fossilizing layer ou stratum.

fossiliser /fosilize/ [1] **I** *vtr* to fossilize.

II se fossiliser *vpr* to fossilize.

fossoyeur /foswajœʀ/ *nm* lit gravedigger; fig destroyer (**de** of).

fou (**fol** *before vowel or mute h*), **folle** /fu, fɔl/ **I** *adj* **1** (dément) [*personne, chien*] mad; **être/devenir ~** to be/go mad; **un tueur ~** a crazed killer; **2** (insensé) [*personne, idée*] mad GB, crazy; [*regard*] wild; [*soirée, spectacle, livre, histoire*] crazy; **tu n'es pas un peu ~?** are you mad ou crazy?; **il y a de quoi devenir ~, c'est à vous rendre ~!** it's enough to drive you mad GB ou crazy!; **un fol espoir** a wild hope; **réaliser ses rêves les plus ~s** to see one's wildest dreams come true; **les rumeurs les plus folles ont circulé** the craziest rumours[GB] were going around; **il faut être ~ pour faire ça!** you'd have to be mad ou crazy to do that!; **être ~ furieux**○ to be raving mad; **être ~ à lier**○ to be stark raving mad○; **entre eux c'est l'amour ~** they're madly in love; **~ de colère** mad with rage; **~ de joie** wild with joy; **~ (amoureux) de qn, ~ d'amour pour qn** madly in love with sb, crazy about sb; **être ~ de musique/peinture** to be mad about music/painting; **3** (considérable) [*gaieté, enthousiasme*] mad; [*monde, succès*] huge; **il y avait un monde ~** there was a huge crowd; **conduire à une vitesse folle** to drive at a crazy speed; **avoir un mal ~ à faire** to find it incredibly difficult to do; **mettre un temps ~ pour faire** to take an incredibly long time to do; **ça m'a coûté un prix ~** it cost me a fortune; **dépenser/gagner un argent ~** to spend/to earn a fortune; **c'est ~ ce que le temps passe vite!** it's amazing how time flies!; **4** (incontrôlable) [*véhicule, cheval*] runaway; [*terreur*] mad; [*mèche*] stray; [*cheveux*] straggly· [*course*] headlong; **avoir** or **prendre le ~ rire** to have a fit of the giggles.

II *nm,f* **1** (personne démente) madman/madwoman; **envoyer qn chez les ~s**○ to send sb to the nuthouse○; **courir/travailler comme un ~/une folle** to run/work like mad; **rire comme un ~**○ to laugh one's head off; **2** (personne insensée) madman/madwoman; **une folle m'a coupé la route!** some madwoman cut in in front of me!; **c'est un ~ d'art contemporain** he's mad about contemporary art; **un ~ du volant**○ a car freak○; **quelle bande de ~s!** what a bunch of lunatics!

III *nm* **1** Hist (à la cour) fool, court jester; **2** Jeux (aux échecs) bishop.

IV **folle**◑ *nf* (homosexuel) **(grande) folle** fairy○ GB injur, queen◑.

■ **folle avoine** Bot wild oat; **~ de Bassan** gannet; **~ de Dieu** Relig religious extremist.

IDIOMES **faire les ~s**○ to fool about; **plus on est de ~s plus on rit**○ the more the merrier; ▶ **amuser**, **guêpe**.

foucade /fukad/ *nf* liter (caprice) whim, passing fancy.

Foucault /fuko/ *npr* **courants de ~** Phys eddy currents; **pendule de ~** Phys Foucault's pendulum.

foudre /fudʀ/ I *nm* **1** (tonneau) cask; **2**† hum **~ de guerre** true warrior; **il n'a rien d'un ~ de guerre** he's not exactly a great warrior.

II *nf* Météo lightning; **la ~ est tombée sur le bâtiment** the building was struck by lightning; **la ~ a mis le feu aux installations** the installations were set on fire by lightning; **frappé par la ~** struck by lightning.

III **foudres** fml *nfpl* wrath ¢; **s'attirer/affronter les ~s de qn** to incur/to face sb's wrath.

IDIOMES **coup de ~** love at first sight; **entre elle et lui ce fut un coup de ~ réciproque** it was love at first sight for both of them; **se marier sur un coup de ~** to rush into marriage; **avoir le coup de ~ pour qn/qch** to be really taken with sb/sth.

foudroyant, **~e** /fudʀwajɑ̃, ɑ̃t/ *adj* [*attaque, riposte, progrès*] lightning (*épith*), sudden; [*succès, révélation*] meteoric; [*regard*] thundering; [*mort*] sudden; **il a été victime d'une leucémie/crise ~e** he was struck down by leukemia/a heart attack.

foudroyer /fudʀwaje/ [23] *vtr* **1** (frapper) [*orage*] to strike down [*arbre*]; **il est mort foudroyé** he was struck dead by lightning; **elle le foudroya du regard** she looked daggers at him○; **2** (abattre) [*maladie*] to strike down; [*nouvelle, malheur*] to cut [sb] to the quick.

fouet /fwɛ/ *nm* **1** (à lanières) whip; **faire claquer son ~** to crack one's whip; **donner dix coups de ~ à qn** to give sb ten lashes of the whip; **donner le ~ à qn** to flog sb; **coup de ~** lit whip lash; fig boost; **donner un coup de ~ à l'économie** to give the economy a boost; **le grand air m'a donné un coup de ~** the fresh air invigorated me; **la crise économique a frappé l'industrie de plein ~** the economic crisis has hit the industry full-force; **la balle l'a heurté de plein ~** the bullet struck him full-force; **les deux véhicules se sont heurtés de plein ~** the two vehicles collided head-on; **2** Culin whisk; **~ mécanique** hand whisk; **3** Naut hoisting rope.

fouettard /fwɛtaʀ/ *adj m* **le père ~** ≈ the bogeyman.

fouetté /fwɛte/ *nm* fouetté.

fouetter /fwɛte/ [1] I *vtr* **1** (frapper avec un fouet) to flog [*personne*]; to whip [*animal*]; **il a été fouetté jusqu'au sang** he was flogged until the blood ran; **2** (frapper) **la pluie/un vent froid leur fouettait le visage** rain/a cold wind lashed their faces; **~ le sang** to make one's blood tingle; **3** Culin to whisk GB, to beat US; **crème fouettée** whipped cream.

II *vi* **1** (battre) **la pluie fouettait contre les vitres** the rain lashed against the windows; **2**◑ (sentir mauvais) to stink○; **3**◑ (avoir peur) to be scared stiff○.

IDIOMES **il n'y a pas de quoi ~ un chat** it's no big deal○; **avoir d'autres chats à ~** to have other fish to fry.

foufou○, **fofolle** /fufu, fɔfɔl/ I *adj* scatter-brained.

II *nm,f* scatterbrain.

fougasse /fugas/ *nf*: *flat loaf*.

fougère /fuʒɛʀ/ *nf* (plante) fern; (végétation) bracken ¢; **ma ~ a besoin d'être arrosée** my fern needs watering; **le sentier se perd dans les ~s** the path disappears into the bracken.

fougue /fug/ *nf* enthusiasm.

fougueusement /fugøzmɑ̃/ *adv* enthusiastically.

fougueux, **-euse** /fugø, øz/ *adj* [*cheval*] spirited; [*personne, élan, déclaration*] enthusiastic.

fouille /fuj/ *nf* **1** (de lieu, personne, bagages) search; **~ corporelle** body search; **~ systématique** thorough search; **2** Archéol excavation; **~ à ciel ouvert** daylight excavation; **chantier** or **champ de ~s** archaeological site; **3**◑ (poche) pocket.

fouillé, **~e** /fuje/ I *pp* ▶ **fouiller**.

II *pp adj* [*travail, étude, portrait*] detailed; [*style*] elaborate.

fouille-merde◑ /fujmɛʀd/ *nmf inv* shit-stirrer◑, muckraker.

fouiller /fuje/ [1] I *vtr* **1** (explorer) to search [*maison, bagage, vêtement*]; to rifle through, to search [*poches*]; to search, to rummage through [*pièce*]; (en palpant) to frisk [*personne*]; (de manière approfondie) to search [*personne*]; **2** Archéol to dig [*site*]; **3** (approfondir) to examine [sth] closely [*sujet, question*].

II *vi* (chercher) **~ dans** to rummage through [*poches, tiroir, armoire*]; to search [*mémoire*]; to sift through [*souvenirs*]; to delve into [*passé*].

III **se fouiller**◑ *vpr* **tu peux toujours te ~** you can go and take a running jump○ GB, you can go jump○ US.

fouillis /fuji/ *nm* **1** (désordre) mess; **si tu voyais le ~ dans ma cuisine** if you could see the mess in my kitchen; **2** (ensemble désordonné) jumble; **~ d'idées/de souvenirs/de papiers** jumble of ideas/of memories/of papers; **~ de verdure** tangle of greenery.

fouine /fwin/ *nf* **1** Zool stone marten; **visage** or **tête de ~** weasel face; **2** (curieux) snooper.

fouiner /fwine/ [1] *vi* **1** (sans but) to forage about; **2 ~ dans** to rummage through [*objets, papiers*]; to poke one's nose into [*affaires, vie, passé*].

fouineur, **-euse** /fwinœʀ, øz/ I *adj* **1** (curieux) inquisitive; **2** (indiscret) pej nosey[GB] péj.

II *nm,f* **1** (curieux) bargain hunter; **2** (indiscret) snooper.

fouir /fwiʀ/ [3] *vtr* to root about in (**de** with).

fouisseur, **-euse** /fwisœʀ, øz/ *adj* [*animal*] burrowing; [*pattes*] adapted for burrowing (*après n*).

foulage /fulaʒ/ *nm* **1** Vin (du raisin) treading; **2** Tex (du tissu) milling GB, fulling US; (du cuir) tumbling; **3** Ordinat embossment.

foulant○, **~e** /fulɑ̃, ɑ̃t/ *adj* tiring.

foulard /fulaʀ/ *nm* scarf, headscarf.

■ **~ islamique** Muslim headscarf.

foule /ful/ *nf* **1** (multitude de personnes) gén crowd; (menaçante) mob; **tirer dans la ~** to fire into the crowd; **se frayer un chemin dans la ~** to make one's way through the crowd; **mettre la ~ en délire** to send the crowd into a frenzy; **la ~ hostile** the hostile mob; **la ~ des acheteurs/manifestants** the crowds of shoppers/demonstrators; **il n'y a pas ~ aujourd'hui** there isn't exactly a crowd today; **il y avait ~ à la réunion** there were masses of people at the meeting; **ce groupe n'attire** or **ne déplace pas les ~s** this band isn't exactly a crowd-puller; **les admirateurs de l'écrivain sont venus en ~ à la conférence** the writer's admirers flocked to the conference; **2** (grand nombre) mass; **une ~ de détails/d'indices/de questions** a mass of details/of clues/of questions; **une ~ de gens** a crowd of people; **des ~s de piétons** crowds of pedestrians; **3**† (peuple) **la ~** pej the masses (*pl*); **chercher à plaire à la ~** to seek to please the masses.

foulée /fule/ *nf* (enjambée) stride; **rester** or **courir dans la ~ de qn** Sport to tail sb; **dans la ~ de leurs prédécesseurs/la mode punk** fig in the wake of their predecessors/punk fashion; **dans la ~ d'un événement** in the aftermath of an event; **dans la ~ il a ajouté/dit...** in the same breath, he added/said...; **dans la ~ il a...** while he was at it, he...

fouler /fule/ [1] I *vtr* **1** Vin to tread [*raisin*]; **2** Tex to mill GB, full US [*tissu*]; to tumble [*cuir*]; **3** (marcher sur) **~ le sol de Mars** to set foot on Mars; **~ qch aux pieds** lit to trample sth underfoot; **~ aux pieds les usages/la loi** fig to ride roughshod over customs/the law.

II **se fouler** *vpr* **1** Méd **se ~ le poignet/la cheville** to twist ou sprain one's wrist/ankle; **avoir la cheville foulée** to have a sprained ankle; **2**○ (se fatiguer) to strain oneself; **tu ne t'es pas foulé** you didn't kill yourself○.

fouloir /fulwaʀ/ *nm* **1** (à raisin) winepress; **2** Dent plugger; **3** Ind (en métallurgie) rammer.

foulon /fulɔ̃/ *nm* **terre à ~** fuller's earth.

foulque /fulk/ *nf* coot.

foultitude○ /fultityd/ *nf* multitude.

foulure /fulyʀ/ *nf* sprain; **avoir une ~ du poignet** to have a sprained wrist.

four /fuʀ/ *nm* **1** Culin (de boulanger, cuisine) oven; **mettre qch au ~** to put sth in the oven; **mettre à ~ moyen** to put in a medium oven; **cuire au ~** (viande) to roast; (gâteau, poisson) to bake; **poulet au ~** roast chicken; **2** Ind furnace; (à céramique) kiln; **3**○ Théât (échec) flop○; **faire un ~** to flop○; ▶ **moulin**, **petit**.

■ **~ à catalyse** oven with self-clean linings; **~ à chaleur tournante** fan(-assisted) oven; **~ à chaux** lime kiln; **~ crématoire** crematory (furnace); **~ électrique** electric oven; **~ à gaz** gas oven; **~ à induction** induction furnace; **~ Martin** open-hearth furnace; **~ à micro-ondes** microwave oven; **~ à pain** bread oven; **~ à pyrolyse** self-cleaning oven; **~ à réverbère** reverberatory furnace; **~ solaire** solar furnace.

IDIOMES **il fait noir comme dans un ~** it's pitch dark in here.

fourbe /fuʀb/ I *adj* [*caractère, individu*] deceitful.

II *nmf* deceitful person.

fourberie /fuʀbəʀi/ *nf* (de caractère) deceitfulness; (acte) deceit.

fourbi○ /fuʀbi/ *nm* **1** (objets personnels) gear○; (de soldat) kit; **2** (désordre) shambles○ (+ *v sg*).

fourbir /fuʀbiʀ/ [3] *vtr* to burnish [*casseroles*]; **~ ses armes** lit to burnish one's weapons; fig to prepare for battle.

fourbu, **~e** /fuʀby/ *adj* (épuisé) exhausted; **la randonnée m'a ~** the hike has exhausted me.

fourbure /fuʀbyʀ/ *nf* Vét laminitis.

fourche /fuʀʃ/ *nf* **1** (outil) (à foin) pitchfork; (de jardinier) fork; **2** (division) fork; **faire une ~** to fork; **3** (de vélo, moto) fork; **4** B (temps libre) spare time; ▶ **caudines**.

fourcher /fuʀʃe/ [1] *vi* **1** (se diviser) [*branche, route*] to fork; [*cheveu*] to split; **2**○ (faire un lapsus) **ma/sa etc langue a fourché** it was a slip of the tongue; **3** B (avoir du temps libre) to have some spare time.

fourchette /fuʀʃɛt/ *nf* **1** (de table) fork; **~ à gâteau/poisson** cake/fish fork; ▶ **manier**; **2** (gamme) (de prix, température, fluctuation) range; (de revenus, d'âge) bracket; **dans une ~ comprise entre 1000 et 1 800 francs** in a price range of 1,000 to 1,800 francs; **la ~ des 25–34 ans** the 25–34 age bracket; **~ supérieure d'imposition** higher tax bracket; **~ horaire** period; **3** Zool (d'oiseau) wishbone; (de cheval) frog;

4 Aut, Mécan selector fork; **5** Jeux (aux échecs) fork; **faire une ~** to fork two pieces.

■ **~ du sternum** Anat suprasternal notch; **~ vulvaire** Anat fourchette.

IDIOMES **avoir un bon coup de ~**○ to have a hearty appetite.

fourchu, ~e /fuʀʃy/ *adj* [*langue, branche*] forked; [*sabot, pied*] cloven; [*menton*] cleft; **cheveux ~s** hair with split ends.

fourgon /fuʀgɔ̃/ *nm* **1** (camion) van; **2** Rail goods wagon GB, freight car US; **~ de tête** leading wagon GB, first car US; **~ de queue** last wagon GB, caboose US; **3** (de pompiers) (à pompe) fire engine; (à réservoir) water tender; **4** (pique-feu) poker.

■ **~ à bagages** luggage van GB, baggage car US; **~ à bestiaux** cattle truck; **~ cellulaire** police van GB, patrol wagon US; **~ de déménagement** removal van GB, moving van US; **~ mortuaire** hearse; **~ postal** mail van GB, mail truck US.

fourgonner /fuʀgɔne/ [1] I *vtr* to poke [*feu, poêle, four*].

II○ *vi* to rummage (**dans** in).

fourgonnette /fuʀgɔnɛt/ *nf* (small) van.

fourguer◑ /fuʀge/ [1] *vtr* to flog○ (**à** to) GB, to sell [sth] off (**à** to).

fouriérisme /fuʀjeʀism/ *nm* Fourierism.

fourme /fuʀm/ *nf*: *mild blue cheese.*

fourmi /fuʀmi/ *nf* **1** Zool ant; **~ ailée** or **volante** winged ou flying ant; **c'est un travail de ~** it's a laborious task; **faire un travail de ~** to go through it with a fine-tooth comb; **2** (personne travailleuse) beaver; **3** (revendeur de drogue) small-time dealer.

IDIOMES **avoir des ~s dans les jambes** (avoir des picotements) to have pins and needles in one's legs; (être impatient) to have itchy feet; **travailler comme une ~** to be as busy as a bee.

fourmilier /fuʀmilje/ *nm* anteater.

fourmilière /fuʀmiljɛʀ/ *nf* **1** Zool ant hill; **2** fig hive of activity.

IDIOMES **donner un coup de pied dans la ~** to stir up a hornets' nest.

fourmillement /fuʀmijmɑ̃/ *nm* **1** (mouvement) hustle and bustle; **2** (abondance) **un ~ de gens/voitures** a mass of people/cars; **un ~ d'idées** a host of ideas; **3** (picotement) tingling sensation; **ressentir des ~s dans le bras** to have a tingling sensation in one's arm.

fourmiller /fuʀmije/ [1] I **fourmiller de** *vtr ind* [*texte, traduction*] to be chock-full of [*erreurs*]; [*musée, ville*] to be swarming with [*touristes, visiteurs*]; [*forêt, région*] to be teeming with [*animaux*]; [*ville*] to be bustling with [*activités*].

II *vi* **1** (abonder) to abound (**dans** in); **les rats fourmillent dans le quartier** the neighbourhood[GB] is swarming with rats; **livre où fourmillent les exemples** book bursting with examples; **2** (picoter) **j'ai les jambes qui fourmillent** I've got pins and needles in my legs.

fournaise /fuʀnɛz/ *nf* **1** (endroit chaud) blaze; **le bureau est une vraie ~!** the office is like an oven!; **la ville est une ~ en été** the town is baking hot in summer; **2** C (chaudière) boiler GB, furnace US.

fourneau, *pl* **~x** /fuʀno/ *nm* **1** Tech furnace; **2** (de pipe) bowl; **3** (cuisinière) stove; **être/retourner à ses ~x** to be doing/to go back to the cooking; ▶ **haut**.

fournée /fuʀne/ *nf* (tous contextes) batch.

fourni, ~e /fuʀni/ I *pp* ▶ **fournir**.

II *pp adj* (approvisionné) **bien/mal ~** [*magasin, usine*] well-/ill-stocked (**en** with); [*table*] sparsely/lavishly provided (**en** with).

III *adj* (dense) [*barbe*] bushy; [*chevelure*] thick; [*herbe*] lush; [*groupe*] large; [*emploi du temps*] busy.

fournil /fuʀni(l)/ *nm* bakehouse; **faire le ~** to work in the bakehouse.

fourniment○ /fuʀnimɑ̃/ *nm* clutter.

fournir /fuʀniʀ/ [3] I *vtr* **1** (donner) to supply [*dossier, équipement, secours, information, argent*]; to give [*exemple, travail*]; to provide [*excuse, énergie, service*]; to make [*contribution, paiement*]; to contribute [*effort*]; to produce [*preuve, alibi*]; **~ à qn** to supply sb with [*biens, données*]; to give [sth] to sb [*exemple*]; to provide sb with [*occasion, moyen*]; to make [sth] to sb [*contribution*]; **~ qn en** to supply sb with [*biens*]; **2** Jeux to deal [*cartes*]; to play [*as*].

II **se fournir** *vpr* (s'approvisionner) **se ~ chez** or **auprès de** [*personne*] to buy from; [*entreprise*] to get supplies from; **je me fournis en café chez eux** I buy my coffee from them; **la société se fournit en papeterie auprès d'un grossiste** the company gets its stationery supplies from a wholesaler.

fournisseur, -euse /fuʀnisœʀ, øz/ I *adj* **pays ~** exporting country; **pays ~s d'armes** arms-exporting countries.

II *nm* supplier; **premier/deuxième ~ de** largest/second-largest supplier of; **chez votre ~** from your supplier; **~ attitré** official supplier; **~s du quartier** local retailers; **~ de drogue/cocaïne** drug/cocaine dealer; **~ de la famille impériale** purveyor to the Imperial family.

fourniture /fuʀnityʀ/ *nf* **1** Comm (vente) supply ¢; **embargo sur la ~ d'armes** embargo on the supply of arms; **accord pour la ~ de** agreement for the supply of; **~s** sales; **~s chinoises de coton** Chinese sales of cotton; **2** (équipement) equipment ¢.

■ **~s de bureau** office stationery ¢; **~s de laboratoire** Sci, Ind laboratory equipment; **~s scolaires** Scol school stationery.

fourrage /fuʀaʒ/ *nm* forage.

■ **~ sec** fodder; **~ ensilé** silage.

fourrager, -ère [13] /fuʀaʒe, ɛʀ/ I *adj* [*betterave, plante*] fodder.

II *vi* **~ dans** to rummage through [*papiers, dossiers*]; to rummage in [*tiroirs, placards*].

III **fourragère** *nf* Mil shoulder lanyard; **porter la fourragère** to wear a lanyard.

fourre /fuʀ/ *nf* H (couverture protectrice) cover.

fourré, ~e /fuʀe/ I *pp* ▶ **fourrer**.

II *pp adj* **1** Culin [*bonbon, gâteau*] filled (**à** with); **~ au chocolat** with chocolate filling (*après n*); **2** Mode (de fourrure) fur-lined; (d'étoffe, de peau, foin) lined (**de, en** with); **col ~ de renard/vison** fox-/mink-lined collar; **3**○ (installé) **toujours ~ à l'église/au café** always hanging about the church/at the café; **où étais-tu ~?** where have you been hiding?

III *nm* (buisson) thicket.

fourreau, *pl* **~x** /fuʀo/ *nm* **1** (d'épée) scabbard; (de parapluie) cover; **mettre l'épée au ~** to sheathe one's sword; **tirer l'épée du ~** to unsheathe one's sword; **2** (robe) sheath dress; **3** (de cheval) sheath.

fourrer /fuʀe/ [1] I *vtr* **1**○ (mettre) to stick○; **~ ses mains au fond de ses poches** to stick○ one's hands deep in one's pockets; **~ son arme dans son étui** to stick○ one's weapon into its holster; **~ sa valise sous son lit** to stick○ one's suitcase under one's bed; **~ qch dans la tête de qn** to put sth into sb's head; **2** Culin to fill [*gâteau*] (**avec, de** with); **~ une génoise avec de la crème** to fill a sponge cake with cream; **3** Mode to line [*vêtement*] (**avec, de** with).

II **se fourrer**○ *vpr* (se mettre) **se ~ dans un coin/sous une couverture** [*personne*] to get into a corner/under a blanket; **aller se ~ dans/sous** [*objet*] to get itself stuck in/under; **se ~ dans les jambes de qn** to get under sb's feet; **se ~ une idée dans la tête** to get an idea into one's head; **ne plus savoir où se ~** not to know where to put oneself; **se ~ dans une sale affaire** or **histoire** to get mixed up in a bad business.

fourre-tout /fuʀtu/ I *adj inv* **1** pej [*groupe*] ragbag; [*solution*] coverall; **2** [*pièce, placard*] storage; **sac ~** holdall GB, carryall US.

II *nm inv* **1** (trousse) pencil case; (pièce) storage room; (sac) holdall GB, carryall US; **2** (ramassis) pej hotchpotch GB, hodgepodge US.

fourreur /fuʀœʀ/ ▶ **510** *nm* furrier.

fourrier /fuʀje/ *nm* **1** Hist Mil (du logement) harbinger; (de l'approvisionnement) quartermaster; **2** Naut purser.

fourrière /fuʀjɛʀ/ *nf* (pour animaux, véhicules) pound; **mettre un chien à la ~** to put a dog in the pound; **mettre une voiture à la** or **en ~** to impound a car.

fourrure /fuʀyʀ/ *nf* **1** Mode fur; **manteau de ~** fur coat; **fausse ~** imitation fur; **2** Zool coat; **~ du tigre** coat of the tiger.

■ **~ polaire** Mode fleece.

fourvoiement /fuʀvwamɑ̃/ *nm* liter **1** (tromperie) deception; **2** (erreur) mistake; (méprise) blunder.

fourvoyer /fuʀvwaje/ [23] I *vtr* liter (perdre) to get [sb] lost (**dans** in); (tromper) to mislead; (par mauvais exemple) to lead [sb] astray (**dans** into).

II **se fourvoyer** *vpr* liter **1** (se perdre) to lose one's way (**dans** in); **2** (se tromper) to make a mistake; **il s'est fourvoyé dans un trafic de contrebande** he's got himself mixed up in a smuggling racket.

foutaise◑ /futɛz/ *nf* (**c'est de la**) **~!** crap◑!

foutoir◑ /futwaʀ/ *nm* (désordre) shambles○ (*sg*); (agitation) complete chaos; **comment peux-tu vivre dans ce ~?** how can you live in such a shambles○?; **c'est le ~ dans cette classe!** it's complete chaos in this classroom!

foutre /futʀ/ [6] I● *nm* (sécrétion) come●, sperm.

II◑ †*excl* bugger me◑! GB, fuck●!; **~ non!** no bloody way◑! GB, no fucking way●!; **je n'en sais ~ rien!** I know fuck all about it●.

III *vtr* **1**◑ (faire) to do; **qu'est-ce qu'il fout?** what the hell's he doing◑?; **ne rien ~** to do bugger all◑ GB, to do fuck all●; **qu'est-ce que ça peut ~?** what the hell does it matter◑?; **qu'est-ce que tu veux que ça me foute?** why should I give a shit about it◑?; **qu'est-ce que ça peut te/leur ~?** what the hell has it got to do with you/them○?; **n'en avoir rien à ~** not to give a damn○ ou shit◑; **2**◑ (donner) **~ un coup à qn** lit to wallop sb○; fig to be a real blow to sb; **sa mort nous a foutu un coup** his death was a terrible blow to us; **~ une gifle à qn** to clout○ sb; **~ un coup de pied à qn** to kick sb; **~ la trouille à qn** to scare the hell○ ou shit◑ out of sb; **'il t'a remercié?'—'je t'en fous oui!'** 'did he thank you?'—'you must be bloody joking◑!', 'no fucking way●!'; **je leur en foutrais moi des augmentations!** they can shove◑ their pay rise GB ou their raise US up their backsides●!; **3**◑ (mettre) **~ qch quelque part** to stick○ sth somewhere; **où t'as foutu les clés?** what the hell have you done with the keys○?; **~ son nez partout** to stick one's nose into everything; **~ la pagaille** or **la merde**◑ or **le bordel**● (déranger) to make a bloody mess◑ GB, to make a fucking mess●; (semer la zizanie) to stir things up; **~ son pied au cul de qn**● to kick sb up the arse● GB ou ass○ US; **~ son poing dans la gueule**◑ **de qn** to sock○ sb in the mouth; **~ qn dehors** or **à la porte** to give [sb] the boot○ [*employé, élève*]; to kick [sb] out○ [*visiteur, immigré*]; **~ qn en colère** or **rogne** to make sb as mad as hell○; **~ le camp** [*personne*] to be off○ GB, to split○ US; [*choses*] to fall apart; **fous(-moi) le camp d'ici!** get lost○!; **tout fout le camp** everything's falling apart; **ça la fout mal** it makes a lousy○ impression; **4**● †(posséder sexuellement) to fuck●; **aller se faire ~** to go to hell○; **envoyer qn se faire ~** to tell sb to go to hell○.

IV● †*vi* (forniquer) to fuck●.

V **se foutre**◑ *vpr* **1** (se mettre) **se ~ en colère** to fly off the handle○; **se ~ dedans** to screw up◑; **il s'est foutu dedans avec ses calculs** he screwed up in his calculations; **s'en ~ plein les poches** to rake it in○; **se ~ en l'air** (en voiture) to have an accident; (se suicider) to top oneself○; **2** (se donner) **je me foutrais des claques!** sometimes I could kick myself!; **3** (se battre) **se ~ dessus** or **sur la gueule**◑ to beat (the) shit◑ out of each other; **4** (ridiculiser) **se ~ de (la gueule de) qn** to take the piss out of sb◑; **il ne s'est pas foutu de toi** he really did you proud!; **se ~ du monde** [*personne, institution*] to have a bloody GB ou hell of a◑ US nerve; **5** (être indifférent) not to give a shit◑ (**de** about); **je me fous de ce qu'il pense** I don't give a damn○ ou shit◑ about what he thinks; **je m'en fous** I don't give a damn○ ou shit◑.

foutrement◑ /futʀəmɑ̃/ *adv* [*bon, intéressant*] bloody◑ GB, fucking●.

foutriquet○ /futʀikɛ/ *nm* pej whippersnapper†.

foutu◑, **~e** /futy/ **I** *pp* ▶ **foutre**.
II *pp adj* **1** (mauvais) (*before n*) [*temps*] bloody awful◑ GB, fucking●; [*idée*] bloody stupid◑ GB, fucking●; [*caractère*] bloody awful◑ GB; **~e voiture** bloody◑ car GB, fucking● car; **2** (condamné) **être ~** [*personne, chaussures, vêtement*] to have had it○; [*machine, mécanisme*] to be knackered◑ GB, to be screwed up◑ US; **s'il me trouve, je suis ~** if he finds me I've had it○; **tout n'est pas ~** it's not a complete cock-up◑ GB ou screw-up○ US; **ça fait un an de ~** that's a whole year wasted; **3** (fait) **il est ~ comment leur appartement?** what's their apartment like?; **être bien ~** [*personne*] to have a good body; [*appartement, dictionnaire*] to be well laid out; [*vêtement*] to be well made; **être mal ~** (laid) [*personne*] to be unattractive; (malade) [*personne*] to feel lousy○; (mal conçu) [*appartement, dictionnaire*] to be badly laid out; [*vêtement*] to be badly made; **4** (capable) **être ~ de faire** to be bloody GB ou totally capable of doing; **il n'est même pas ~ de répondre** he can't even bloody◑ GB ou fucking● answer, he can't be bothered○ to answer.
IDIOMES **café bouillu café ~**○ boiled coffee is ruined coffee.

fox /fɔks/ *nm inv* = **fox-terrier**.

fox-hound, *pl* **~s** /fɔksawnd/ *nm* foxhound.

fox-terrier, *pl* **~s** /fɔkstɛʀje/ *nm* fox terrier.

foyer /fwaje/ *nm* **1** (domicile) home; **quitter/regagner le ~ conjugal** to leave/return to the conjugal home; **rester au ~** to stay at home; **fonder un ~** to get married; **rentrer dans ses ~s** to go home; **renvoyer qn dans ses ~s** Mil (exempter) to exempt sb from national service; (démobiliser) to demobilize sb; **2** Sociol (famille) household; **3** (résidence) hostel (**de, pour** for); **un ~ de travailleurs/d'étudiants** a workers'/students' hostel; **4** (club) club; **~ pour personnes âgées** senior citizens' club; **5** Cin, Théât (point de rencontre) foyer; **6** (de cheminée) hearth; **7** (centre actif) (d'incendie) fire; (de résistance) pocket†; (d'intrigue) hot bed; **il reste trois ~s à éteindre** three fires are still burning; **8** (centre de propagation) (d'incendie) heart; (d'épidémie) source; (de rébellion) seat; **9** Phys (point de convergence) focus; **lunettes à double/triple ~** bifocals/trifocals; **10** Math (de conique) focus.
■ **~ fiscal** Fisc household for tax purposes; **~ infectieux** Méd focus; **~ de placement** Prot Soc foster home; **~ réel** Phys real focus; **~ virtuel** Phys virtual focus.

frac /fʀak/ *nm* morning coat.

fracas /fʀaka/ *nm* (de chute) crash; (de vagues) roar; (de ville, bataille) din; **le ~ du tonnerre** burst(s) of thunder; **tomber avec ~** to fall with a crash; **lancer un produit à grand ~** fig to launch a product in a blaze of publicity; **renvoyé avec perte(s) et ~** summarily dismissed.

fracassant, **~e** /fʀakasɑ̃, ɑ̃t/ *adj* **1** (violent) [*bruit*] deafening; **2** (sensationnel) [*entrée, déclaration, nouvelle*] sensational; [*succès, débuts*] stunning.

fracasser /fʀakase/ [1] **I** *vtr* to smash [*vitrine, crâne, mâchoire*].
II se fracasser *vpr* [*objet, véhicule*] to smash, crash (**contre** against); [*vagues*] to crash (**contre, sur** against).

fraction /fʀaksjɔ̃/ *nf* **1** Math fraction; **2** (partie) (de terrain, somme, jour) part; (de société, jeunesse) section; (de produits, des électeurs) proportion of [*produits, électeurs*]; **en une ~ de seconde** in a split second, in a fraction of a second; **la ~ conservatrice du parti** the conservative faction of the party; **une petite/importante ~ d'électeurs** a small/sizable minority of voters; **par ~ de 5 jours** for every 5-day period; **3** Relig (du pain) breaking.

fractionnaire /fʀaksjɔnɛʀ/ *adj* Math fractional.

fractionnel, **-elle** /fʀaksjɔnɛl/ *adj* [*activités*] divisive.

fractionnement /fʀaksjɔnmɑ̃/ *nm* **1** (division) division; (morcellement) fragmentation; **~ d'actions** Fin share split GB, stock split US; **2** (échelonnement) (d'envois) staggering; (de paiements) spreading; **autoriser le ~ sur trois ans du remboursement** to allow the repayments to be spread over three years; **3** Chimie, Biol, Méd fractionation.

fractionner /fʀaksjɔne/ [1] **I** *vtr* **1** (diviser) to divide up [*travail, groupe, total*]; (fragmenter) to split [*parti, opposition*]; **200 km fractionnés en 6 étapes** 200 km divided up into 6 stages; **entraînement fractionné** Sport interval training; **2** (échelonner) to stagger [*envois*]; to spread [*paiements*].
II se fractionner *vpr* [*parti*] to split.

fractionniste /fʀaksjɔnist/ **I** *adj* [*activités*] divisive.
II *nmf* factionalist.

fracture /fʀaktyʀ/ *nf* Géol, Méd fracture; **~ du poignet** fractured wrist; **~ ouverte** compound fracture; **~ de fatigue** stress fracture.

fracturer /fʀaktyʀe/ [1] **I** *vtr* **1** Méd to fracture [*os*]; **2** (pour pénétrer) to break [*vitrine, porte*]; to force [*serrure, coffre*].
II se fracturer *vpr* **se ~ la cheville** to fracture one's ankle.

fragile /fʀaʒil/ *adj* **1** (cassable) fragile; **attention, c'est ~!** careful, it's fragile!; **'~'** 'fragile'; **2** (faible) [*personne, constitution*] frail; [*peau, œil*] sensitive; [*estomac, foie*] delicate; [*cœur*] weak; **avoir une santé ~** to have poor health; **avoir les poumons ~** to have weak lungs; **il est ~ du foie, il a le foie ~** he has a delicate liver; **3** (instable) [*esprit, personne*] fragile.
IDIOMES **~ comme du cristal** or **du verre** as fragile as china.

fragiliser /fʀaʒilize/ [1] *vtr* lit, fig to weaken.

fragilité /fʀaʒilite/ *nf* **1** (aptitude à se briser) fragility; **2** (de personne, constitution, santé) frailty; (de peau, d'œil) sensitivity; (d'estomac, de foie) delicateness; (de cœur) weakness; (de cheveux) brittleness; **3** (instabilité) fragility.

fragment /fʀagmɑ̃/ *nm* **1** (morceau isolé) (de tasse, d'os) fragment; (de cheveu) piece; (de tissu) bit; **des ~s de conversation/chanson** snatches of conversation/song; **2** (passage d'une œuvre) passage; **~ de vie/d'histoire** slice of life/of history.

fragmentaire /fʀagmɑ̃tɛʀ/ *adj* [*informations, connaissance*] patchy, fragmentary; [*vue, exposé*] sketchy; [*action, effort*] sporadic.

fragmentation /fʀagmɑ̃tasjɔ̃/ *nf* **1** fig (division) division; (morcellement) splitting up; **2** lit (de pierre) fragmentation.

fragmenter /fʀagmɑ̃te/ [1] **I** *vtr* (casser) to break up [*substance*]; (morceler) to split up [*domaine, parti*]; to divide up [*travail*]; to break up [*vacances, texte*]; **~ une œuvre** to divide a work into sections; **avoir une vue fragmentée d'une question** to have a fragmented view of an issue.
II se fragmenter *vpr* [*pierre*] to break (**en** into); [*parti*] to split (**en** into).

fragrance /fʀagʀɑ̃s/ *nf* liter fragrance.

frai /fʀɛ/ *nm* Zool **1** (fécondation) fertilization; (ponte) spawning; (période) spawning season; **2** (œufs) (de poisson) eggs (*pl*); (de batracien) spawn; **3** (alevins) fry.

fraîche ▶ **frais I, V.**

fraîchement /fʀɛʃmɑ̃/ *adv* **1** (récemment) [*creusé, repeint*] freshly; [*débarqué, nommé*] newly; **fleurs ~ cueillies** freshly cut flowers; **2** (sans empressement) [*recevoir*] coldly; **elle a été ~ accueillie** she was given a cool welcome; **3**○ **'comment allez-vous?'—'~'** 'how are you?'—'cold'.

fraîcheur /fʀɛʃœʀ/ *nf* **1** (température) (agréable) coolness; (plus froide) coldness; **dans la ~ d'une chambre** in the coolness of a bedroom; **donner une sensation de ~** to make [sb] feel cool; **attention à la ~ du soir!** watch out for the cold evening air!; **2** Comm, Culin (d'aliment) freshness; **perdre de sa ~** to lose its freshness; **~ garantie** guaranteed fresh; **3** (jeunesse) freshness; **pour redonner de la ~ à votre teint/au linge blanc** to put some freshness back into your skin/into your whites; **son œuvre est d'une grande ~** his work has a great freshness about it; **le spectacle manque de ~** the show is stale.

fraîchir /fʀɛʃiʀ/ [3] *vi* **1** (devenir moins chaud) [*temps*] to get cooler; **2** (devenir plus froid) [*temps*] to become colder; **3** Météo [*vent*] to freshen.

frais, **fraîche** /fʀɛ, fʀɛʃ/ **I** *adj* **1** (légèrement froid) [*temps, eau, nuit, endroit*] cool; (trop froid) [*nuit, eau, vent, boisson*] cold; **les soirées sont fraîches** the evenings are cold ou chilly; **'servir ~'** 'serve chilled'; **il fait ~ ce matin** (c'est agréable) it's cool this morning; (il fait froid) it's rather chilly this morning; **le fond de l'air est ~** there's a chill in the air; **2** (récent) [*nouvelles, souvenir, traces, neige*] fresh; [*peinture, colle, encre*] wet; **c'est encore très ~ dans ma mémoire** it's still very fresh in my memory; **de fraîche date** [*lettre, membre*] recent; **3** Comm, Culin [*produit, pain, poisson, œuf, lait, légumes*] fresh; **4** (jeune) [*teint, visage, peau*] fresh; [*voix*] young; **une fraîche jeune fille** a fresh-faced young girl; **5** (nouveau) [*troupes, chevaux, équipe*] fresh; **apporter un peu d'air ~ à qch** to bring a breath of fresh air to sth; **de l'argent ~** more money; ▶ **dispos**; **6** (léger) [*senteur, parfum, décor, couleur*] fresh; **se sentir tout ~** to feel very fresh; **7** (sans chaleur) [*accueil, ambiance*] cool.
II *adv* **1** (depuis peu) **~ rasé** freshly shaved; **des fleurs fraîches cueillies** freshly-picked flowers; **du foin ~ coupé** freshly-cut hay; **un livre tout ~ paru** a newly-published book; **~ débarqués de leur village** fresh from their village; **2** (froid) **il fait ~** it's cool.
III *nm* **1** (fraîcheur) **se tenir au ~** to stay in the cool; **prendre le ~** to get some fresh air; **mettre qch au ~** (pour le conserver) to put sth in a cool place; (pour le refroidir) to put sth to cool; **j'ai mis le champagne au ~** I've put the champagne to cool; **'à conserver au ~'** 'store in a cool place'; **mettre qn au ~**○ (en prison) to put sb inside○; **2** Météo, Naut **grand ~** moderate gale.
IV *nmpl* **1** gén (dépenses) expenses; **~ d'hospitalisation** hospital expenses; **~ annexes** fringe expenses; **~ d'habillement/médicaux/de justice** clothing/medical/legal expenses; **avoir de gros ~** to have some big expenses; **à peu de/grands ~** at little/great expense; **à moindres ~** at very little cost; **tous ~ payés** all expenses paid; **le voyage est aux ~ de l'entreprise** the trip is being paid for by the company; **le voyage est à vos ~** you'll have to pay for the trip yourself; **vivre aux ~ de la société** to live off society; **aux ~**

de qn fig at sb's expense; **partager les ~** to share the cost; **faire des ~** [*personne*] to spend a lot of money; [*événement, achat*] to cost a lot; **cela fait des ~ de partir en vacances** going on vacation costs a lot; **rentrer dans ses ~** to cover one's expenses; **se mettre en ~ pour qn** to put oneself out for sb; **en être pour ses ~**○ lit to have to pay; fig to get nothing for one's pains; **faire les ~ de qch** to bear the brunt of sth; **les petites entreprises font les ~ de la récession** the small companies are bearing the brunt of the recession; **arrêter les ~** fig to stop wasting one's time; ▶**faux**; **2** (coûts d'un service professionnel) fees; **~ d'agence/d'expertise** agency/consultancy fees; **3** Comm (coûts d'un service commercial) charges; **~ de location/transport** hire/transport charges; **4** Fin (commission) charges; **~ de courtage/change** brokerage/exchange charges; **5** Compta (coûts) costs; **~ de publicité/trésorerie** advertising/finance costs; **~ fixes/variables** fixed/variable costs; **6** Fisc (dépenses) expenses.

V à la fraîche *loc adv* (le matin) in the cool of the morning; (le soir) in the cool of the evening.

■ **~ d'annulation** Tourisme cancellation fees; **~ bancaires** Fin bank charges; **~ déductibles** Fisc allowable expenses; **~ de déplacement** (d'employé) travel expenses; (de réparateur) call-out charge (*sg*); **~ divers** Compta miscellaneous costs; **~ d'expédition** Postes postage and packing; Transp freight; **~ d'exploitation** Compta operating costs; **~ de fonctionnement** Entr running costs; **~ de garde** Fin (de titres en dépôt) management charges; (d'enfant) (à payer) childminding fees; Fisc childminding expenses; **~ généraux** Compta overheads; **~ de gestion** Compta management costs; Fin management charges; **~ d'inscription** gén registration fees; Scol school fees GB, tuition fees US; Univ tuition fees, academic fees GB; **~ de port** Comm, Postes postage ¢; **~ professionnels** Fisc professional expenses; **~ réels** Fisc allowable expenses; **~ de représentation** Admin, Entr (encourus) entertainment expenses; (alloués) entertainment allowance (*sg*); **~ de scolarité** Scol tuition fees, school fees GB.

IDIOMES **être ~ comme une rose** or **un gardon** to be as fresh as a daisy; **nous voilà ~**○! now we're in a fix○!

fraisage /fʀɛzaʒ/ *nm* milling (process).

fraise /fʀɛz/ **I** **▶193** *adj inv* strawberry-pink.

II *nf* **1** (fruit) strawberry; **2** (en boucherie) **~ de veau** calf's caul; **3** (angiome) strawberry mark; **4** Mode (collerette) ruff; **5** (outil) (pour aléser) reamer; (pour percer) countersink(-bit); (machine) (pour couper) milling-cutter; (pour forage, de dentiste) drill; **6** Zool (de dindon) wattle.

■ **~ des bois** wild strawberry.

IDIOMES **ramener sa ~**○ to stick one's nose in○.

fraiser /fʀeze/ [1] *vtr* Tech (évaser) to ream [*cylindre*]; to mill [*pièce*]; **vis à tête fraisée** countersink screw.

fraiseur, -euse /fʀɛzœʀ, øz/ **▶510** **I** *nm,f* (ouvrier) cutter.

II fraiseuse *nf* (machine) milling machine.

fraisier /fʀɛzje/ *nm* **1** Bot strawberry plant; **2** Culin (gâteau) strawberry gateau.

fraisure /fʀɛzyʀ/ *nf* countersink.

framboise /fʀɑ̃bwaz/ **I** **▶193** *adj inv* (couleur) raspberry-coloured[GB].

II *nf* **1** (fruit) raspberry; (liqueur) raspberry liqueur; **2** (angiome) strawberry mark.

framboisier /fʀɑ̃bwazje/ *nm* (cultivé) raspberry cane; (sauvage) raspberry bush.

franc[1], **franche** /fʀɑ̃, fʀɑ̃ʃ/ **I** *adj* **1** (honnête) [*personne*] frank, straight; [*réponse*] straight, candid; [*regard*] frank, candid; [*rire*] open, honest; [*discussion*] frank; **pour être ~** to be frank, to be perfectly honest; **je vais être ~ avec vous** I'm going to be straight with you, I'm going to give it to you straight; **il n'est pas ~** he doesn't play straight, there's something shifty about him; **jouer ~ jeu** to play fair; **2** (sans ambiguïté) (*before n*) [*victoire*] absolute, out-and-out; [*répulsion, aversion*] absolute, sheer; [*gaieté*] open, uninhibited; **il est d'une franche sottise** he's downright ou plain stupid; **c'est un spectacle d'une franche grossièreté** it's a downright rude show; **3** (sans mélange) [*goût, vin, couleur*] pure; **4** Comm, Jur (exempt de taxe) [*marchandises, boutique*] duty-free; **~ de port** postage paid.

II *adv* **parler ~** to be perfectly frank.

III **▶46** *nm* Fin (monnaie) franc; **en ~s constants/courants** in constant/current francs; **un ~ symbolique de dommages et intérêts** Jur ≈ nominal damages; **une radio à trois ~s six sous**○ a cheap radio.

■ **~ belge** Belgian franc; **~ français** French franc; **~ lourd** new franc; **~ suisse** Swiss franc.

IDIOMES **être ~ du collier** to be bold; **~ comme l'or** as straight as a die, absolutely honest.

franc[2], **franque** /fʀɑ̃, fʀɑ̃k/ *adj* Frankish.

Franc, **Franque** /fʀɑ̃, fʀɑ̃k/ *nm,f* Frank.

français, **~e** /fʀɑ̃sɛ, ɛz/ **▶537**, **462** **I** *adj* French; **à la ~e** [*modernisme, libéralisme*] French-style (*épith*).

II *nm* Ling French.

Français, **~e** /fʀɑ̃sɛ, ɛz/ **▶537** *nm,f* Frenchman/Frenchwoman; **le ~ moyen** gén the average Frenchman; pej the typical Frenchman.

franc-bord, *pl* **francs-bords** /fʀɑ̃bɔʀ/ *nm* Naut free board.

franc-comtois, **~e**, *pl* **francs-comtois**, **franc-comtoises** /fʀɑ̃kɔ̃twa, az/ **▶692** *adj* from Franche-Comté.

Franc-comtois, **~e**, *pl* **Francs-comtois**, **Franc-comtoises** /fʀɑ̃kɔ̃twa, az/ **▶692** *nprm,f* (natif) native of Franche-Comté; (habitant) inhabitant of Franche-Comté; **les ~** the people of Franche-Comté.

France /fʀɑ̃s/ **▶321** *nprf* France; Hist **la ~ libre** Free France.

Francfort /fʀɑ̃kfɔʀ/ **▶857** *npr* Frankfurt.

franche ▶**franc I.**

Franche-Comté /fʀɑ̃ʃkɔ̃te/ **▶692** *nprf* **la ~** Franche-Comté.

franchement /fʀɑ̃ʃmɑ̃/ *adv* **1** (honnêtement) [*parler, s'exprimer*] openly, frankly; [*demander*] straight out; [*répondre*] candidly; [*dire*] frankly; **je lui ai demandé ~ ce qu'il comptait faire** I asked him straight out what he intended to do; **je vais vous dire ~ ce que j'en pense** I'll tell you exactly what I think; **~ non, je n'ai pas beaucoup aimé** to be frank ou honest I didn't like it very much; **tu avoueras ~ que tu es allé trop loin!** you must admit that you went too far!; **2** (sans hésiter) [*appuyer*] firmly; [*entrer*] boldly; **tape ~, sinon le clou ne s'enfoncera jamais** hammer hard, otherwise the nail will never go in; **servez-vous ~, il y en a assez pour tout le monde** help yourself to as much as you like, there's enough for everybody; **allez-y ~** go right ahead; **allez-y, versez ~!** go ahead, don't be afraid of pouring in too much!; **3** (complètement) really; **il m'a ~ déçu/agacé/impressionné** he really disappointed/annoyed/impressed me; **le film était ~ nul** the film was really awful; **on a ~ bien rigolé**● we had a really good laugh; **elle est ~ bête** she is downright ou plain stupid; **4** (exclamatif) really, honestly; **~! tu ne trouves pas qu'il exagère?** really ou honestly! don't you think he's going a bit far?

franchir /fʀɑ̃ʃiʀ/ [3] *vtr* to cross [*fossé, ligne d'arrivée, seuil, montagne, océan*]; to get over [*mur, barrière, clôture*]; to cover [*distance*]; **~ un obstacle** lit to clear an obstacle; fig to overcome an obstacle; **le perchiste a franchi les six mètres** the pole vaulter cleared six metres[GB]; **~ la barre des 10%** to pass the 10% mark; **~ un cap difficile** to get through a difficult period; **l'équipe a franchi le cap des quarts de finale** the team got past the quarterfinals; **~ le cap de la cinquantaine** to turn fifty; **l'entreprise a franchi un cap décisif en rachetant sa rivale** buying up its rival was an important turning point for the company.

IDIOMES **~ le pas** to take the plunge.

franchisage /fʀɑ̃ʃizaʒ/ *nm* Comm franchising.

franchise /fʀɑ̃ʃiz/ *nf* **1** (qualité) (de personne, aveu) frankness; (de ton) sincerity; (de regard) honesty; **en toute ~** quite frankly; **avoir le mérite de la ~** to have the merit of being frank; **manquer de ~** to lack sincerity; **2** (exemption) exemption; **3** Assur excess GB, deductible US; **4** Comm franchise; **accorder une ~** to grant a franchise; **mettre en ~** to franchise; **magasin en ~** franchised shop; **5** Hist (de ville) charter.

■ **~ de bagages** Aviat baggage allowance; **~ douanière** Admin exemption from customs duties; **en ~ douanière** duty-free; **~ fiscale** Fisc tax exemption; **~ postale** (sur une enveloppe) 'postage paid'; **envoyer qch en ~ postale** to send sth post free.

franchisé, **~e** /fʀɑ̃ʃize/ Comm **I** *adj* franchised.

II *nm,f* franchisee.

franchiser /fʀɑ̃ʃize/ [1] *vtr* to franchise.

franchiseur /fʀɑ̃ʃizœʀ/ *nm* Comm franchiser.

franchissable /fʀɑ̃ʃisabl/ *adj* [*obstacle*] surmountable; [*col*] passable; **la rivière n'est pas ~ à cette période de l'année** the river can't be crossed at this time of year.

franchissement /fʀɑ̃ʃismɑ̃/ *nm* (de col, rivière, ravin, seuil) crossing ¢; (d'obstacle, de haie) clearing ¢; **~ de la ligne continue** Aut crossing the white line.

franchouillard○, **~e** /fʀɑ̃ʃujaʀ, aʀd/ *adj* pej typically French.

francilien, -ienne /fʀɑ̃siljɛ̃, ɛn/ *adj* [*personne*] from the Île-de-France; [*industrie, habitant, population*] of the Île-de-France.

francisation /fʀɑ̃sizasjɔ̃/ *nf* **1** (de mot) gallicization; (de mode de vie) Frenchification; **2** Jur, Naut **~ d'un navire** registering a ship as French.

franciscain, **~e** /fʀɑ̃siskɛ̃, ɛn/ *adj, nm,f* Franciscan.

franciser /fʀɑ̃size/ [1] **I** *vtr* **1** to Frenchify [*mode de vie*]; Ling to gallicize [*mot*]; **2** Jur, Naut to register [sth] as French [*navire*].

II se franciser *vpr* [*mot*] to become gallicized; [*manières, personne*] to become Frenchified.

francité /fʀɑ̃site/ *nf* Frenchness.

franc-jeu, *pl* **francs-jeux** /fʀɑ̃ʒø/ *nm* fair play; **faire preuve de ~** to play fair, to show one's sense of fair play.

franc-maçon, **-onne**, *pl* **francs-maçons**, **franc-maçonnes** /fʀɑ̃masɔ̃, ɔn/ **I** *adj* Masonic.

II *nm,f* Freemason.

franc-maçonnerie, *pl* **~s** /fʀɑ̃masɔnʀi/ *nf* **1** (association) **la ~** Freemasonry, the order of Freemasons; **2** (entente) pej freemasonry.

franc-maçonnique, *pl* **~s** /fʀɑ̃masɔnik/ *adj* Masonic.

franco /fʀɑ̃ko/ *adv* **1** Comm **~ de port** [*lettre, colis*] postage paid; [*livraisons*] carriage paid; **2**○ (sans hésiter) **y aller ~** (explication) to go straight to the point; (action) to go right ahead.

■ **~ à bord, FAB** free on board, FOB.

franco-canadien, **-ienne** /fʀɑ̃kokanadjɛ̃, ɛn/ **I** *adj* French-Canadian.

II *nm* Ling Canadian French.

franco-français, **~e** /fʀɑ̃kofʀɑ̃sɛ, ɛz/ *adj* Presse ou hum specifically French.

François /fʀɑ̃swa/ *npr* Francis; **Saint ~ d'Assise** Saint Francis of Assisi.
IDIOMES **faire à qn le coup du père ~** to hit sb over the head.

francophile /fʀɑ̃kɔfil/ *adj, nmf* Francophile.

francophilie /fʀɑ̃kɔfili/ *nf* Francophilia sout, love of all things French.

francophobe /fʀɑ̃kɔfɔb/ *adj, nmf* Francophobe.

francophobie /fʀɑ̃kɔfɔbi/ *nf* Francophobia.

francophone /fʀɑ̃kɔfɔn/ **I** *adj* [*pays, personne*] French-speaking; **littérature ~** literature in the French language.
II *nmf* French speaker.

francophonie /fʀɑ̃kɔfɔni/ *nf* **1** (ensemble des francophones) French-speaking world; **2** (phénomène culturel) French as a world language.

franco-québécois /fʀɑ̃kokebekwa/ *nm* Ling French Canadian.

franc-parler /fʀɑ̃paʀle/ *nm* frankness; **avoir son ~** to speak one's mind.

franc-tireur, *pl* **francs-tireurs** /fʀɑ̃tiʀœʀ/ *nm* **1** (combattant) sniper; **2** (personne indépendante) maverick.

frange /fʀɑ̃ʒ/ *nf* **1** (en tissu, laine) fringe; **2** (de cheveux) fringe GB, bangs (*pl*) US; **3** fig (bord) fringe; **à la ~** on the fringe; **4** (minorité) fringe group; **une ~ de** a minority of; **5** (en optique) fringe; **~s d'interférence** interference fringes.

franger /fʀɑ̃ʒe/ [13] *vtr* to fringe (**de** with).

frangin○ /fʀɑ̃ʒɛ̃/ *nm* brother.

frangine○ /fʀɑ̃ʒin/ *nf* sister.

frangipane /fʀɑ̃ʒipan/ *nf* Culin (crème) frangipane; (gâteau) frangipane cake.

franglais /fʀɑ̃glɛ/ *nm* Franglais.

franque ▶ **franc²**.

franquette○: **à la bonne franquette** /alabɔnfʀɑ̃kɛt/ *loc adv* **recevoir qn à la bonne ~** to have sb round GB ou over for an informal meal; **c'est à la bonne ~** it's just an informal meal.

franquisme /fʀɑ̃kism/ *nm* Francoism.

franquiste /fʀɑ̃kist/ *adj, nmf* Francoist.

frappant, **~e** /fʀapɑ̃, ɑ̃t/ *adj* striking.

frappe /fʀap/ *nf* **1** (de monnaie, médaille) (action) striking; (empreinte) stamp, impression; **2** (de texte) typing; **le texte est à la ~** the text is being typed out; **3** Sport (de footballeur) kick; (de boxeur) punch; **ce boxeur a une ~ redoutable** this boxer packs a mean punch○; **4**◑ (voyou) (**petite**) **~** hoodlum○.

frappé, **~e** /fʀape/ **I** *pp* ▶ **frapper**.
II *pp adj* **1** (rafraîchi) [*champagne, vin blanc*] chilled; [*cocktail*] frappé, mixed with crushed ice; [*café*] iced; **2**○ (fou) crazy○, nuts○.

frapper /fʀape/ [1] **I** *vtr* **1** (taper sur) gén to hit, to strike; **~ à la tête** lit to hit [sb] on the head [*personne*]; fig to strike at the leadership of [*mouvement, organisation*]; **le marteau vient ~ la corde du piano** the hammer strikes the piano string; **le ballon l'a frappé en plein visage** the ball hit ou struck him right in the face; **~ le sol du pied** to stamp one's foot; **~ qn à coups de matraque** to club sb; **~ qn/qch à coups de pied** to kick sb/sth; **~ qn/qch à coups de poing** to punch sb/sth; **~ les trois coups** Théât *to give three knocks to signal that the curtain is about to rise*; **2** (asséner) to strike; **~ un coup** (à la porte) to knock (once); (dans une bagarre) to strike a blow; **~ fort** or **un grand coup** lit to hit hard; (à la porte) to knock hard; fig to pull out all the stops; **l'horloge venait de ~ les 12 coups de minuit** the clock had just struck midnight; **3** Tech to strike [*monnaie, médaille*]; **4** (affecter) [*chômage, épidémie, impôt*] to hit; **les cadres frappés par le chômage** the executives hit by unemployment; **les régions frappées par la crise/sécheresse** areas hit by the recession/drought; **le nouvel impôt frappe durement les classes les plus défavorisées** the new tax hits the poor very hard; **le malheur qui les frappe** the misfortune which has befallen them; **être frappé par le malheur** to be stricken by misfortune; **être frappé d'apoplexie/de paralysie** to be struck down ou stricken by apoplexy/by paralysis; **la maladie l'a frappé dans la force de l'âge** he was struck down by illness in the prime of life; **être frappé de mutisme** to be dumbstruck ou dumbfounded; **les taxes qui frappent les produits français/de luxe** duties imposed on French/luxury goods; **5** (marquer) to strike; **ce qui m'a frappé c'est leur arrogance** what struck me was their arrogance; **être frappé par** to be struck by; **j'ai été frappé par leur ressemblance** I was struck by how alike they were; **ce qui me frappe le plus c'est...** what strikes me the most is...; **j'ai été frappé de voir/d'entendre que...** I was amazed to see/hear that...; **~ l'imagination de qn** to catch sb's imagination; **6** (rafraîchir) to chill [*champagne, vin*].
II *vi* **1** gén to hit, to strike; **~ du poing sur la table** to bang one's fist on the table; **~ du pied** to stamp one's foot; **~ sur une casserole/un tambour** to bang on a saucepan/a drum; **~ dans ses mains** to clap one's hands; **~ à** to knock on ou at [*porte, fenêtre, carreau*]; **'entrez sans ~'** 'come straight in'; **on a frappé** there was a knock at the door; **2** (sévir) to strike; **les gangsters ont encore frappé**○ the gangsters have struck again.
III se frapper○ *vpr* (s'inquiéter) to get worked up○; ▶ **estoc**.

frappeur /fʀapœʀ/ *adj m* **esprit ~** poltergeist.

frasque /fʀask/ *nf* escapade; **faire des ~s** to get up to mischief; **ses ~s de jeunesse** his youthful indiscretions.

fraternel, **-elle** /fʀatɛʀnɛl/ *adj* **1** (entre amis) [*accueil, sourire*] fraternal; [*amitié, tendresse*] brotherly; **il est très ~ avec lui** he treats him just like a brother; **2** (entre frères) [*amour*] brotherly; [*relations*] between siblings (*après n*).

fraternellement /fʀatɛʀnɛlmɑ̃/ *adv* in a brotherly fashion.

fraternisation /fʀatɛʀnizasjɔ̃/ *nf* fraternizing (**avec** with).

fraterniser /fʀatɛʀnize/ [1] *vi* to fraternize (**avec** with).

fraternité /fʀatɛʀnite/ *nf* fraternity, brotherhood.

fratricide /fʀatʀisid/ **I** *adj* fratricidal.
II *nmf* (personne) fratricide.
III *nm* (crime) fratricide.

fratrie /fʀatʀi/ *nf* siblings (*pl*).

fraude /fʀod/ *nf* **1** Jur fraud ¢; **~ électorale/fiscale** electoral/tax fraud; **passer qch/qn en ~** to smuggle sth/sb in; **sortir qch en ~** to smuggle sth out; **entrer** or **passer en ~** (au cinéma) to slip in without paying; (dans un pays) to enter illegally; **2** Scol, Univ cheating ¢.

frauder /fʀode/ [1] **I** *vtr* to defraud [*douane, créancier*] (**de** of).
II *vi* (dans le métro) to travel without a ticket; (au cinéma) to slip in without paying; (à un examen) to cheat (**sur** over).

fraudeur, **-euse** /fʀodœʀ, øz/ *nm,f* gén swindler; (du fisc) defrauder; (à un examen) cheat.

frauduleusement /fʀodyløzmɑ̃/ *adv* fraudulently.

frauduleux, **-euse** /fʀodylø, øz/ *adj* fraudulent.

frayer /fʀeje/ [21] **I** *vtr* **~ un passage à qn à travers la foule/un bois** to clear a path for sb through the crowd/the woods; fig **~ le chemin** or **la voie à qch** to pave the way for sth; Zool [*cerf*] to fray.
II *vi* **1** (entretenir des relations) **~ avec** to be friendly with; **il ne fraye pas avec ces gens-là** he doesn't mix with that sort of person; **2** Zool [*femelle*] to spawn; [*mâle*] to fertilize the eggs.
III se frayer *vpr* lit (s'ouvrir) **se ~ un chemin dans** or **à travers un champ/une salle** to make one's way across a field/a room; **se ~ un chemin dans** or **à travers la foule/forêt** to make one's way through the crowd/forest; **se ~ une voie à travers les pièges de la vie** to make one's way through life's pitfalls.

frayeur /fʀɛjœʀ/ *nf* **1** (état de peur intense) fear; **il poussait des cris de ~** he was screaming in fear; **j'ai eu un moment de ~** I had a fright; **2** (une peur) fright; **donner** or **faire des ~s à qn** to give sb a fright; **j'ai eu une de ces ~s!** I got such a fright!

fredaine /fʀədɛn/ *nf* **faire des ~s** to have amorous adventures.

fredonnement /fʀədɔnmɑ̃/ *nm* humming ¢.

fredonner /fʀədɔne/ [1] *vtr* to hum.

free-lance /fʀilɑ̃s/ *nmf* freelance, freelancer; **travailler en ~** to work freelance ou as a freelancer.

freesia /fʀezja/ *nm* freesia.

freezer /fʀizœʀ/ *nm* freezer compartment GB, icebox.

frégate /fʀegat/ *nf* **1** Naut frigate; **2** Zool frigate bird.

frein /fʀɛ̃/ *nm* **1** (de véhicule) brake; **avoir de bons ~s** to have good brakes; **la voiture n'a plus de ~s** the car's brakes are not working; **les ~s du véhicule ont lâché** the vehicle's brakes failed; **donner un coup de ~** to brake hard; **des traces de coups de ~s** skid marks; **un violent coup de ~ a projeté le passager contre le pare-brise** the driver braked hard throwing the passenger against the windscreen; **2** (entrave) restraints (*pl*); (**être**) **un ~ à** (to be) a brake ou curb on; **mettre un ~ à** to curb [*expansion, immigration, optimisme*]; **donner un coup de ~ à** to act as a sharp brake ou curb on; **mettre un coup de ~** (**brutal**) **à** to put a (sharp) brake ou curb on; **sans ~** [*faire, gouverner*] without restraint; [*imagination, ambition*] unbridled; [*échange, commerce*] unrestrained; **3**† (pour cheval) bit; **4** Mil muzzle brake.
■ **~ à main** hand brake; **serrer/desserrer le ~ à main** to put on/to take off the hand brake; **~ moteur** engine brake; **utiliser le ~ moteur** to use one's gears (to slow down); **~ de parcage** parking brake; **~ à pied** foot brake; **~ de service** service break; **~ de stationnement** = **~ de parcage**; **~s à disques** disc brakes; **~s pneumatiques** air brakes; **~s à tambour** drum brakes.
IDIOMES **ronger son ~** to champ at the bit.

freinage /fʀɛnaʒ/ *nm* **1** (de véhicule) braking; **dispositif de ~** braking system; **la distance de ~** stopping distance; **traces de ~** skid marks; **2** (de développement, d'inflation, augmentation) slowing down.

freiner /fʀene/ [1] **I** *vtr* **1** (faire ralentir) to slow down [*véhicule, parachute, chute*]; **2** (gêner) to impede [*personne, avance, ennemi*]; **3** (modérer) to curb [*inflation, consommation*]; to restrain [*personne*]; **~ l'ambition/l'enthousiasme de qn** to curb sb's ambition/enthusiasm.
II *vi* **1** (en voiture, moto, vélo) to brake; **la voiture a freiné trop tard** the car braked too late; **cette voiture freine bien** this car has good brakes; **~ à bloc** or **à fond** to slam on the brakes; **2** (à ski, sur patins) to slow down.

frelaté, **~e** /fʀəlate/ *adj* **1** [*alcool*] adulterated; [*goût*] unnatural; **2** [*milieu, plaisirs*] dubious.

frêle /fʀɛl/ *adj* [*personne, embarcation, apparence*] frail; [*jambe, bras, cou*] weak; [*structure*] flimsy; [*voix*] thin; [*son*] faint.

frelon /fʀəlɔ̃/ *nm* hornet.

freluquet† /fʀəlykɛ/ *nm* little squirt○, whippersnapper†.

frémir /fʀemiʀ/ [3] *vi* **1** (trembler) [*voile, feuille, aile, violon*] to quiver; [*lac*] to ripple; [*vitre*] to rattle (gently); **le vent frémit dans le feuillage** the wind is fluttering through the leaves; **le vent faisait ~ les eaux du port** the wind rippled the waters of the harbour[GB]; **2** (sous l'effet d'une émotion) [*lèvre, narine, main*] to tremble; [*personne*] (d'indignation, impatience, de colère, joie, plaisir) to quiver (**de** with); (de dégoût, d'horreur, effroi) to shudder (**de** with); **frémissant de rage/d'enthousiasme** quivering with rage/with enthusiasm; **je frémis à cette idée** I shudder at the thought; **tout mon être frémit** (d'horreur) my whole being shuddered; (de plaisir) my whole being thrilled; **ça fait ~ de penser que**... it makes you shudder to think that...; **poésie/sensibilité frémissante** vibrant poetry/sensitivity; **3** Culin [*liquide*] to start to come to the boil; **laisser ~ 10 minutes** simmer for 10 minutes; **faire cuire dans l'eau frémissante** simmer gently in water.

frémissement /fʀemismɑ̃/ *nm* **1** (vibration) quiver, tremor; **le ~ du vent dans les arbres** the rustle of the wind in the trees; **2** (sous l'effet d'une émotion) (de narine, lèvre, main) trembling ₵; (de personne, corps) (dû à la joie, la colère, à l'impatience, au plaisir) quiver; (dû à l'horreur, l'effroi, au dégoût) shudder; **un ~ de terreur/joie parcourut la foule** a ripple of terror/joy ran through the crowd; **il ressentit un ~ de tout son être** (de plaisir) his whole being thrilled; (de terreur) his whole being shuddered.

frênaie /fʀenɛ/ *nf* ash-grove.

frêne /fʀɛn/ *nm* **1** (arbre) ash (tree); **2** (bois) ash (wood).

frénésie /fʀenezi/ *nf* frenzy; **avec ~** [*lutter*] frantically; [*danser*] frenziedly; [*applaudir*] wildly.

frénétique /fʀenetik/ *adj* [*applaudissements*] wild; [*lutte, activité*] frenzied; [*joueur*] frenetic.

frénétiquement /fʀenetikmɑ̃/ *adv* [*lutter*] frantically; [*secouer*] frenetically; [*danser*] frenziedly; [*applaudir*] wildly.

fréon® /fʀeɔ̃/ *nm* Freon®.

fréquemment /fʀekamɑ̃/ *adv* frequently.

fréquence /fʀekɑ̃s/ *nf* **1** Phys frequency; **à ~ vocale** Télécom tone dialling; **la nuit la ~ des bus diminue** at night the buses are less frequent; **2** fig (caractère répandu) high incidence, frequency.

fréquent, **~e** /fʀekɑ̃, ɑ̃t/ *adj* **1** (dans le temps) [*train, événement*] frequent; **faire un usage ~ de qch** to use sth frequently; **il est ~ que cela arrive** it happens frequently; **2** (répandu) [*maladie, attitude*] common.

fréquentable /fʀekɑ̃tabl/ *adj* **1** (de bonne réputation) [*personne, club*] respectable; **pas ~** [*personne*] not respectable; [*club*] disreputable; **2** (jugé digne de soi) [*personne*] whom one can associate with (*épith, après n*); [*club*] in which one can be seen (*épith, après n*); **ce ne sont pas des gens ~s** they are not the sort of people one should associate with; **ce club n'est pas ~** it's not the sort of club in which to be seen.

fréquentatif, **-ive** /fʀekɑ̃tatif, iv/ *adj* Ling frequentative.

fréquentation /fʀekɑ̃tasjɔ̃/ *nf* **1** (amis) company ₵; **avoir de bonnes/mauvaises ~s** to keep good/bad company; **je surveille les ~s de mes enfants** I keep an eye on the sort of people my children mix with; **c'est une mauvaise ~ pour toi** that's not the sort of person you should associate with; **2** (action) **la ~ de ces gens** associating with these people; **la ~ des grands auteurs** fml habitual reading of great authors; **la ~ des cafés/clubs** frequenting cafés/clubs; **la ~ de l'église/de l'école/des cours** attending church/school/classes; **3** (présence) **bonne ~ des cours** regular attendance at classes; **baisse de la ~ scolaire** drop in school attendance; **~ de l'église/des théâtres** churchgoing/theatregoing[GB]; **record de ~ des théâtres** record theatre[GB] audiences (*pl*); **la ~ des théâtres est en baisse/hausse** fewer/more people are going to the theatre[GB].

fréquenté, **~e** /fʀekɑ̃te/ **I** *pp* ▶**fréquenter**.

II *pp adj* [*café, plage, théâtre*] popular; [*rue, carrefour*] busy; **lieu bien/mal ~** place that attracts the right/wrong sort of people; **la plage/cantine est peu ~e** not many people go to the beach/canteen.

fréquenter /fʀekɑ̃te/ [1] **I** *vtr* **1** (côtoyer) to associate with [*genre de personne, connaissance*]; to see [sb] frequently [*amis, famille*]; to move in [*milieu*]; **ce ne sont pas des gens à ~** they are not the sort of people one should associate with; **nous les fréquentons peu** we don't have much to do with them; **je ne veux pas que tu les fréquentes** I don't want you to have anything to do with them; **elle ne fréquente pas n'importe qui** (par sagesse) she chooses her friends carefully; (par snobisme) she doesn't go around with just anybody; **~ les grands auteurs** fml to read the works of great writers; **2** (sortir) to go out with [*jeune homme/jeune fille*]; **3** (aller à) to attend [*école, église, cours*]; to visit [*musée, site*]; to go to [*restaurant, plage*]; to frequent sout [*clubs, salons*]; **il fréquente les bars** he hangs about○ in bars; **si tu fréquentais moins les cafés** if you spent less time in cafés.

II se fréquenter *vpr* **1** (se voir) [*amis*] to see one another; **nous nous fréquentons peu** we don't see a great deal of each other; **2** (sortir ensemble) [*jeune couple*] to go out together.

frère /fʀɛʀ/ *nm* **1** (dans la famille) brother; **c'est mon grand/petit ~** he's my big/little brother; **Dupont et ~s** (enseigne) Dupont Brothers; **aimer qn comme un ~** to love sb like a brother; **tu es un ~ pour moi** you're like a brother to me; **~s ennemis** rivals within the same camp; **2** (relation) brother; **tous les hommes sont ~s** all men are brothers; **mes biens chers ~s** Relig my dear brethren; **nos ~s travailleurs/marins** our fellow workers/sailors; **vieux ~** old pal; **peuple** or **pays ~** fellow nation; ▶**faux**; **3** Relig brother; **~ Jacques** Brother Jacques; **être élevé chez les ~s** to be educated by the brothers (*in a Catholic school*).

■ **~ d'armes** brother-in-arms; **~ jumeau** twin brother; **~ lai** lay brother; **~ de lait** foster brother; **~s maçons** brother Masons.

frérot○ /fʀeʀo/ *nm* kid○ brother.

fresque /fʀɛsk/ *nf* **1** Art fresco; **2** fig panorama.

fret /fʀɛt/ *nm* freight; **~ aérien** air freight; **avion de ~** cargo plane; **compagnie de ~** freight company.

fréter /fʀete/ [14] *vtr* **1** (donner en location) to charter out; **2** (prendre en location) to charter.

fréteur /fʀetœʀ/ *nm* **1** (armateur) owner; **2** (bénéficiaire) charterer.

frétillant, **~e** /fʀetijɑ̃, ɑ̃t/ *adj* **1** (qui s'agite) [*poisson*] wriggling; [*queue de chien*] wagging; **2** (gai) vivacious, frisky.

frétillement /fʀetijmɑ̃/ *nm* **1** (de poisson) wriggling ₵; (de queue de chien) wagging ₵; **2** fig **avoir des ~s d'impatience** to be quivering with impatience.

frétiller /fʀetije/ [1] *vi* **1** [*poisson*] to wriggle; **~ de la queue** [*chien*] to wag its tail; **2** fig **~ d'aise/d'impatience** to be quivering with pleasure/impatience.

fretin /fʀətɛ̃/ *nm* lit, fig **(menu) ~** small fry.

frette /fʀɛt/ *nf* Tech gén binder; (qui se pose à chaud) shrink ring.

freudien, **-ienne** /fʀødjɛ̃, ɛn/ *adj, nm,f* Freudian.

freudisme /fʀødism/ *nm* Freudianism.

freux /fʀø/ *nm* Zool rook.

friabilité /fʀijabilite/ *nf* friability.

friable /fʀijabl/ *adj* [*roche, pâte*] crumbly; [*terre*] friable.

friand, **~e** /fʀijɑ̃, ɑ̃d/ **I** *adj* **être ~ de qch** to be very fond of sth.

II *nm* Culin puff; **~ au fromage/à la viande** cheese/meat puff.

friandise /fʀijɑ̃diz/ *nf* gén delicacy; (bonbon) sweet GB, candy US.

Fribourg /fʀibuʀ/ *npr* **1** ▶**857** (ville) Fribourg; **2** ▶**692** (région) **le canton de ~** the canton of Fribourg.

fric○ /fʀik/ *nm* dough○, money; **être bourré de ~** to be loaded○.

fricandeau, *pl* **~x** /fʀikɑ̃do/ *nm* braised veal ₵.

fricassée /fʀikase/ *nf* fricassee.

fricative /fʀikativ/ *adj f, nf* fricative.

fric-frac○, *pl* **~s** /fʀikfʀak/ *nm* break-in.

friche /fʀiʃ/ *nf* Agric waste land; **en ~** [*terre*] uncultivated, waste (*épith*).

frichti○ /fʀiʃti/ *nm* grub○.

fricoter○ /fʀikɔte/ [1] **I** *vtr* **1** (cuisiner) to cook up [*plat*]; **2** (manigancer) to cook up○ [*mauvais coup*].

II *vi* (flirter) **il fricote avec sa voisine** he's got something going with his neighbour[GB]; (s'acoquiner) **ils fricotent avec des gens bizarres** they hang around○ with some weird people.

friction /fʀiksjɔ̃/ *nf* **1** Méd rub; **2** (désaccord) friction ₵; **il y a des ~s entre eux** there is friction between them; **entre eux tout devient cause de ~** they turn everything into an issue; **3** Phys, Mécan friction; **force/galet de ~** frictional force/roller; **jouet à ~** friction-driven toy.

frictionner /fʀiksjɔne/ [1] **I** *vtr* to give a rub to [*personne*]; to rub [*pieds, tête*].

II se frictionner *vpr* to rub oneself down.

frigidaire® /fʀiʒidɛʀ/ *nm* refrigerator.

frigide /fʀiʒid/ *adj* frigid.

frigidité /fʀiʒidite/ *nf* frigidity.

frigo○ /fʀigo/ *nm* fridge○.

frigorifié, **~e** /fʀigɔʀifje/ **I** *pp* ▶**frigorifier**.

II *pp adj* **1** [*viandes*] frozen; **2** [*personne*] frozen.

frigorifier /fʀigɔʀifje/ [2] *vtr* to freeze.

frigorifique /fʀigɔʀifik/ *adj* [*vitrine, camion*] refrigerated; **machine ~** refrigeration system.

frigoriste /fʀigɔʀist/ ▶**510** *nmf* refrigeration specialist.

frileusement /fʀiløzmɑ̃/ *adv* **relever son col ~** to pull up one's collar against the cold; **se serrer ~ l'un contre l'autre** to huddle close together against the cold; **être emmitouflé ~** to be muffled up against the cold.

frileux, **-euse** /fʀilø, øz/ *adj* **1** (sensible au froid) sensitive to the cold; **être (très) ~** [*personne*] to feel the cold; **relever son col d'un geste ~** to pull up one's collar against the cold; **2** (timoré) [*attitude, politique*] cautious.

frilosité /fʀilozite/ *nf* **être d'une grande ~** to feel the cold a lot.

frimaire /fʀimɛʀ/ *nm* Frimaire (*third month of the French revolutionary calendar*, ≈ *December*).

frimas /fʀima/ *nmpl* liter fig cold weather ₵.

frime○ /fʀim/ *nf* **1** (pour l'épate) **pour la ~** for show; **arrête ta ~!** stop showing off; **2** (simulation) pretence[GB]; **c'est de la ~** it's all pretence[GB].

frimer○ /fʀime/ [1] *vi* to show off○.

frimeur○, **-euse** /fʀimœʀ, øz/ *nm,f* show-off○.

frimousse○ /fʀimus/ *nf* little face.

fringale○ /fʀɛ̃gal/ *nf* **j'ai la ~** I'm absolutely starving○; fig **avoir une ~ de livres** to have an insatiable desire for books.

fringant, **~e** /fʀɛ̃gɑ̃, ɑ̃t/ *adj* [*cheval*] spirited; [*personne*] dashing; [*allure*] brisk.

fringué◑, **~e** /fʀɛ̃ge/ **I** *pp* ▶ **fringuer**.
II *pp adj* **bien/mal ~** well/badly turned out○.

fringuer◑: **se fringuer** /fʀɛ̃ge/ [1] *vpr* to dress.

fringues◑ /fʀɛ̃g/ *nfpl* gear ¢.

fripe○ /fʀip/ *nf* secondhand clothes (*pl*).

fripé, **~e** /fʀipe/ **I** *pp* ▶ **friper**.
II *pp adj* [*tissu*] crumpled; [*visage, bébé*] wrinkled.

friper /fʀipe/ [1] *vtr*, **se friper** *vpr* to crease, to crumple.

friperie /fʀipʀi/ *nf* secondhand clothes shop GB ou store US.

fripier, **-ière** /fʀipje, ɛʀ/ ▶**510**⌋ *nm,f* secondhand clothes dealer.

fripon○, **-onne** /fʀipɔ̃, ɔn/ **I** *adj* [*air, yeux*] mischievous.
II *nm,f* rascal.

fripouille○ /fʀipuj/ *nf* **1** (escroc) crook○; **2** (affectueusement) (**petite**) **~!** (little) monkey!

friqué◑, **~e** /fʀike/ *adj* loaded○, very rich.

frire /fʀiʀ/ [64] **I** *vtr* to fry; **du poisson frit** fried fish.
II *vi* to fry; **faire ~ du poisson** to deep-fry fish.

frisant, **~e** /fʀizɑ̃, ɑ̃t/ *adj* [*lumière*] slanting.

frisbee® /fʀizbi/ *nm* frisbee®.

frise /fʀiz/ *nf* Archit frieze.

frisé, **~e** /fʀize/ **I** *pp* ▶ **friser**.
II *pp adj* [*cheveux*] curly; [*personne*] curly-haired; **être très ~** to have very curly hair.
III frisée *nf* (salade) curly endive, frisée.
IDIOMES **être ~ comme un mouton** to have frizzy hair.

friselis /fʀizli/ *nm* (de feuillage) gentle rustling; (de source) babbling.

friser /fʀize/ [1] **I** *vtr* **1** (boucler) to curl [*cheveux, moustache*]; **~ qn** to curl sb's hair; **se faire ~** to have one's hair curled; **la pluie me frise les cheveux** the rain makes my hair go curly ou frizzy; **2** (frôler) [*remarque, attitude*] to border on [*insolence, grossièreté*]; [*personne*] to be on the brink of [*catastrophe*]; **il frise les quarante ans** he's getting on for forty; **cela frise les 10%** it's approaching 10%.
II *vi* [*cheveux. moustache*] to curl; [*personne*] to have curly hair.
III se friser *vpr* **se ~ les cheveux** to curl one's hair.

frisette○ /fʀizɛt/ *nf* little curl.

frison, **-onne** /fʀizɔ̃, ɔn/ **I** *adj* Géog Frisian.
II *nm,f* Zool Friesian.
III ▶**462**⌋ *nm* Ling Frisian.

Frison, **-onne** /fʀizɔ̃, ɔn/ *nm,f* Frisian.

frisotter /fʀizɔte/ [1] **I** *vtr* to twiddle [*barbe*]; to twist [*foulard*].
II *vi* (naturellement) to be curly; (temporairement) to go curly; **la pluie fait ~ ses cheveux** the rain makes her hair go curly.

frisquet○, **-ette** /fʀiskɛ, ɛt/ *adj* [*vent*] biting; [*air*] chilly; **il fait ~** it's nippy○.

frisson /fʀisɔ̃/ *nm* **1** (de froid, fièvre, désir, plaisir) shiver (**de** of); (de peur, d'horreur) shudder; **avoir un ~ de** (de froid, fièvre) to shiver with; (de désir, plaisir) to tremble with; (de peur, d'horreur) to shudder with; **j'ai des ~s** I keep shivering; **être saisi de ~s** to be seized by a fit of shivering; **fièvre accompagnée de ~s** fever accompanied by shivering; **grand ~** great thrill; **2** (de feuillage) rustling; (de lac) rippling.

frissonnement /fʀisɔnmɑ̃/ *nm* **1** (de feuillage) rustling; (de lac) rippling; **2** (de froid, fièvre, plaisir, désir) shivering (**de** of); (de peur, d'horreur) shuddering (**de** of).

frissonner /fʀisɔne/ [1] *vi* **1** (de fièvre, froid) to shiver (**de** with); (de peur, d'horreur) to shudder (**de** with); (de désir, plaisir, d'orgueil) to tremble (**de** with); **2** liter [*feuillage, lac*] to tremble; **3** (commencer à bouillir) [*eau, lait*] to simmer.

frisure /fʀizyʀ/ *nf* curls (*pl*); **cheveux rebelles à toute ~** hair which is impossible to curl.

frite /fʀit/ *nf* **1** Culin chip GB, French fry US; **manger des ~s tous les jours** to eat chips GB ou fries US every day; **2**◑ (forme) **avoir la ~** to be feeling great; **ne pas avoir la ~** (physiquement) to be off colour[GB]; (moralement) to be feeling low.

friterie /fʀitʀi/ *nf* chip shop GB, French-fries stall US.

friteuse /fʀitøz/ *nf* chip pan GB, French fryer US.
■ **~ électrique** deep fryer.

friture /fʀityʀ/ *nf* **1** Culin (méthode) frying (**à** in); (graisse) fat; (huile) oil; (aliment) fried food; (poissons) ≈ whitebait (*pl*); **ça sent la ~** there's a smell of frying; **2** (parasites) crackling.

Fritz◑† /fʀits/ *nm* offensive Jerry◑† GB injur, kraut◑ injur.

frivole /fʀivɔl/ *adj* [*existence, personne, propos*] frivolous; [*esprit*] shallow; [*querelle*] trivial.

frivolement /fʀivɔlmɑ̃/ *adv* frivolously.

frivolité /fʀivɔlite/ **I** *nf* **1** (caractère) frivolousness; **2** (chose sans importance) frivolity; **3** (dentelle) tatting.
II frivolités† *nfpl* fancy goods.

froc /fʀɔk/ *nm* **1**◑ (pantalon) trousers (*pl*) GB, pants (*pl*) US; **2** Relig habit.
IDIOMES **faire dans son ~**◑ to be shitting◑ oneself, to be scared shitless◑; **baisser son ~**◑ to eat humble pie; **jeter son ~ aux orties** to give up one's vocation.

froid, **~e** /fʀwɑ, fʀwad/ **I** *adj* **1** (à basse température) cold; **eau/nuit/région ~e** cold water/night/region; ▶ **vengeance**; **2** (sans chaleur) [*personne, lumière, beauté, couleur, voix, objectivité*] cold; [*accueil, manières, réponse*] cool; [*ton, rapport, mots, observateur, œil*] dispassionate; [*haine*] callous; [*monstre*] cold-blooded; [*humour*] deadpan; [*rage, colère*] controlled; **être ~ avec qn** to be cool toward(s) sb; **laisser ~** to leave [sb] cold; **rester ~ devant** to remain unmoved by.
II *adv* **il fait ~** it's cold.
III *nm* **1** (basse température) cold; **il fait un de ces ~s** it's freezing cold; **~ vif** biting cold; **à l'abri du ~** sheltered from the cold; **engourdi par le ~** numb with cold; **sortir dans le ~** to go out in the cold; **se protéger contre le ~** to protect oneself against the cold; **avoir ~** to be cold; **avoir ~ aux pieds** to have cold feet; **attraper** or **prendre ~** to catch a cold; **mourir de ~** lit (dehors) to die of exposure; (sous un toit) to die of cold; fig to be freezing to death; **venir du ~** to come in from the cold; **coup de ~** Méd chill; Météo cold snap; **être/rester au ~** to be/to stay in the cold; **conserver au ~** keep in a cool place; ▶ **grand**, **souffler**; **2** (distance) coldness; **le ~ de ton regard** the coldness of your stare; **il y a un certain ~ dans nos relations** there's a certain coolness in our relationship; **ils sont en ~ avec moi/la France** relations between them and me/France are strained; **jeter un ~** to cast a chill (**dans, sur** over); **il y a eu comme un ~** it was as if a chill had been cast over everything.
IV à froid *loc adv* **1** Tech **coulée/vulcanisation/étirage/laminage/démarrage à ~** cold casting/vulcanization/drawing/rolling/start; **2** (sans préparation) spontaneous; **plaisanterie/provocation à ~** spontaneous joke/provocation; **3** (sans passion) **analyse/sondage/discussion à ~** impartial analysis/poll/discussion; **4** Méd **opérer à ~** to perform non-critical surgery.
■ **~ industriel** Ind refrigeration.
IDIOMES **battre ~ à qn** to cold-shoulder sb; **il fait un ~ de canard** or **de loup** it is bitterly cold; **faire ~ dans le cœur** to sadden one's heart; **avoir/faire** or **donner ~ dans le dos** to feel/send a shiver down the spine; **ne pas avoir ~ aux yeux** to be fearless; **garder la tête ~e** to keep a cool head.

froidement /fʀwadmɑ̃/ *adv* **1** (sans émotion) coolly; **répondre/recevoir ~** to answer/greet [sb] coolly; **abattre ~** to shoot [sb] down in cold blood [*personne, animal*]; **2** (calmement) with a cool head; **regarder les choses ~** to look at things coolly.

froideur /fʀwadœʀ/ *nf* (d'œuvre, de sentiment, parole) coldness; (d'accueil) coolness; **avec ~** coolly.

froidure /fʀwadyʀ/ *nf* **1** (froid) cold; **2** Méd (gelure) frostbite.

froissement /fʀwasmɑ̃/ *nm* **1** (de tissu, papier, feuille) (action) crumpling; (bruit) rustling; **2** Méd strain.

froisser /fʀwase/ [1] **I** *vtr* **1** lit (chiffonner) to crease, to crumple [*tissu, vêtement*]; to crumple [*papier*]; **2**○ Aut **il n'y a que de la tôle froissée** it was the car that took the knocks; **3** (blesser) to hurt [*personne, sensibilité*]; **~ l'amour-propre de qn** to hurt sb's pride; **4** Méd to strain [*muscle, nerf*].
II se froisser *vpr* **1** (se chiffonner) [*tissu, vêtement, papier*] to crease; **ma robe s'est froissée** my dress is creased; **2** (s'offusquer) to be hurt (**de** by); **3** Méd to strain.

frôlement /fʀolmɑ̃/ *nm* **1** (contact) brushing ¢; **un ~ suffit pour déclencher le système** you only need to go near the system to set it off; **2** (bruit) (de feuille, papier, tissu) rustling; (d'ailes) fluttering.

frôler /fʀole/ [1] **I** *vtr* **1** (toucher) [*personne, main, genou*] to brush; [*ballon, balle, pierre*] to graze; [*voiture, conducteur*] to scrape; **2** (passer près) [*balle, ballon, pierre, voiture*] to miss narrowly; [*personne*] to brush past [*personne*]; to brush against [*objet, mur*]; to come close to [*succès*]; to approach [*somme, taux*]; **il a frôlé la mort** he came within a hair's breadth of dying, he had a brush with death; **ses blagues frôlent le mauvais goût** his jokes border on bad taste; **l'automobiliste a frôlé les 200 km/h** the driver almost reached a speed of 200 km per hour; **il frôlait les 200 kg** it weighed close to 200 kg.
II se frôler *vpr* **1** (se toucher) [*personne, main, genou*] to brush against each other; **2** (sans se toucher) [*objet, voiture, conducteur*] to just miss each other; [*personne*] to brush past each other; **ils se sont frôlés sans se voir** they brushed past (each other) without seeing each other.

fromage /fʀɔmaʒ/ *nm* **1** cheese; **manger du ~** to eat cheese; **trois ~s** three cheeses; **~ rapé** grated cheese; **~ fondu** melted cheese; **soufflé au ~** cheese soufflé; **~ (au lait) de vache/chèvre/brebis** cow's/goat's/ewe's milk cheese; **~ à pâte molle** soft cheese; **~ à pâte cuite** hard cheese; **~ à pâte persillée** blue cheese; **~ fait/pas fait** ripe/unripe cheese; **2**○ (situation rentable) little earner○ GB; **il a trouvé un bon ~** he's found a nice little earner GB, he's hit pay dirt US; **se partager le ~** to split the profits.
■ **~ blanc** or **frais** fromage frais; **~ maigre** low-fat cheese; **~ à tartiner** cheese spread; **~ de tête** brawn GB, head cheese US.
IDIOMES **faire un ~ de qch**○ to make a big deal○ out of sth.

fromager, **-ère** /fʀɔmaʒe, ɛʀ/ **I** *adj* [*production*] cheese; **associations fromagères** cheese producers' associations.
II ▶**510**⌋ *nm* **1** (fabricant) cheesemaker; (commerçant) cheese seller; **aller chez le ~** to go to the cheese shop; **2** Bot kapok tree.

fromagerie /fʀɔmaʒʀi/ ▶**510**⌋ *nf* (fabrique) dairy; (magasin) cheese shop; (**rayon**) **~** cheese counter.

fromegi◑ /fʀɔmʒi/ *nm* cheese.

froment /fʀɔmɑ̃/ *nm* wheat; **farine de ~** wheat flour.

frometon◐ /fʀɔmtɔ̃/ *nm* cheese.

fronce /fʀɔ̃s/ *nf* gather; **jupe à ~s** gathered skirt.

froncement /fʀɔ̃smɑ̃/ *nm* **avoir un léger ~ de sourcils** to frown slightly.

froncer /fʀɔ̃se/ [12] **I** *vtr* **1** Cout to gather; **2 ~ les sourcils** to frown; **~ le nez** lit to wrinkle one's nose; fig not to be very keen.

II se froncer *vpr* **ses sourcils se froncèrent** he/she frowned; **son nez s'est froncé** lit he/she wrinkled his/her nose; fig he/she was not very keen.

fronceur /fʀɔ̃sœʀ/ *adj* **ruban ~** curtain tape.

frondaison /fʀɔ̃dɛzɔ̃/ *nf* **1** liter (feuillage) foliage ₵; **2** Bot foliation.

fronde /fʀɔ̃d/ *nf* **1** (arme) sling; (jouet) catapult GB, slingshot US; **2** (révolte) revolt; **vent/esprit de ~** mood/spirit of revolt; **3** Bot frond.

Fronde /fʀɔ̃d/ *nprf* **la ~** the Fronde.

fronder /fʀɔ̃de/ [1] *vtr* to satirize.

frondeur, **-euse** /fʀɔ̃dœʀ, øz/ **I** *adj* [*personne, esprit*] rebellious; [*propos*] anti-authoritarian.

II *nm* troublemaker.

front /fʀɔ̃/ **I** *nm* **1** Anat forehead, brow littér; **avoir le ~ haut** to have a high forehead; **s'essuyer le ~** to wipe one's brow; **elle a une cicatrice sur le** or **au ~** she has a scar on her forehead; **relever le ~** fig to stand up for oneself; **c'est lui le coupable, c'est écrit sur son ~** he's the culprit, it's written all over his face; **2** Mil front; **être envoyé au ~** to be sent to the front; **le ~ ennemi** the enemy front; **sur le ~ social/de l'emploi** fig on the social/job front; **faire ~ commun contre l'ennemi** to stand together against the enemy; **faire ~ à qn/qch** to stand up to sb/sth; **3** (façade) façade; **4** Météo front; **~ chaud/froid** warm/cold front; **5** Pol front.

II de front *loc adv* **aborder un problème de ~** to tackle a problem head-on; **les voitures se sont heurtées de ~** the cars collided head-on; **ils marchaient à quatre de ~** they were walking four abreast; **mener plusieurs tâches de ~** to have several tasks on the go.

■ **Front de libération nationale**, **FLN** Hist National Liberation Front, FLN; **~ de mer** seafront; **Front populaire** Hist Popular Front; **~ de taille** Mines coalface.

IDIOMES **avoir le ~ de faire qch** to have the face ou effrontery to do sth; ▶ **sueur**.

frontal, **~e**, *mpl* **-aux** /fʀɔ̃tal, o/ **I** *adj* **1** [*attaque*] frontal; [*choc, collision*] head-on (*épith*); **lave-linge à chargement ~** front-loading washing machine; **2** Anat frontal.

II *nm* **1** Anat frontal bone; **2** (en équitation) browband.

frontalier, **-ière** /fʀɔ̃talje, ɛʀ/ **I** *adj* [*zone, querelle, conflit*] border (*épith*); [*travail*] cross-border (*épith*); **travailleur ~** person who works across the border.

II *nm,f* person living near the border.

frontière /fʀɔ̃tjɛʀ/ *nf* **1** Géog, Pol frontier, border; **tracer/réviser les ~s** to draw/redraw the frontiers; **ouvrir/fermer/passer la ~** to open/close/cross the border; **à l'intérieur de nos ~s** at home; **hors de nos ~s** abroad; **leur renommée passe les ~s** they're internationally famous; **2** (limite) **~s entre les disciplines** boundaries between disciplines; **faire reculer les ~s de la connaissance** to push back the frontiers of knowledge; **au-delà des ~s du possible** beyond the realms of possibility; **ça l'a conduit aux ~s de la mort** it led him to the very brink of death.

■ **~ naturelle** Géog natural boundary.

frontispice /fʀɔ̃tispis/ *nm* (titre) title page; (illustration) frontispiece.

fronton /fʀɔ̃tɔ̃/ *nm* **1** Archit pediment; **2** (à la pelote basque) (mur) front wall; (terrain) pelota court.

frottement /fʀɔtmɑ̃/ *nm* **1** (mouvement) rubbing ₵; **2** (bruit) **j'entends des ~s** I can hear something rubbing; **3** Mécan, Phys friction ₵; **réduire le ~** or **les ~s** to reduce friction; **coefficient/force de ~** friction coefficient/force; **résistance de ~** frictional resistance; **usure par ~** frictional wear; **4**○ (désaccord) friction ₵; **il y a du ~ entre eux** there's friction between them.

■ **~ pleural** Méd pleural fremitus.

frotter /fʀɔte/ [1] **I** *vtr* **1** (masser) to rub; **frotte-moi le dos** rub my back; **n'ayez pas peur de ~** don't be afraid to rub hard; **~ une allumette** to strike a match; **2** (nettoyer) to scrub [*peau, parquet, linge, tapis*]; to polish [*argenterie*].

II *vi* to rub (**sur** on; **contre** on, against); **mes chaussures frottent** my shoes are rubbing; **le bas de la porte frotte** the bottom of the door is scraping against the floor.

III se frotter *vpr* **1** (se frictionner) **se ~ les yeux** to rub one's eyes; **se ~ les mains** lit, fig to rub one's hands; **2** (se nettoyer) to scrub oneself; **se ~ les mains** to scrub one's hands; **3** (se mesurer) **se ~ à** lit, fig to take on; **se ~ à plus fort que soi** to take on someone bigger than oneself.

IDIOMES **se faire ~ les oreilles**○ to have one's ears boxed; **qui s'y frotte s'y pique** if you go looking for trouble, you'll find it.

frottis /fʀɔti/ *nm* **1** Biol smear; **se faire faire un ~ vaginal** to have a cervical smear; **2** Art scumble.

frottoir /fʀɔtwaʀ/ *nm* **1** (pour allumettes) friction strip; **2** (pour parquet) scrubbing brush.

froufrou /fʀufʀu/ *nm* **1** (bruissement) swishing sound; **faire du ~** to swish; **2** (ornement) frill; **une robe à ~s** a frilly dress.

froufroutant, **~e** /fʀufʀutɑ̃, ɑ̃t/ *adj* **1** (bruissant) swishing; **2** (avec volants) frilly.

Frounzé /fʀunze/ ▶ **857** *npr* Hist Frunze.

froussard○, **~e** /fʀusaʀ, aʀd/ **I** *adj* chicken-livered○, cowardly.

II *nm,f* chicken○, coward.

frousse○ /fʀus/ *nf* fright; **avoir la ~** to be scared (**de** of); **j'ai eu une de ces ~s** I had a terrible fright; **il m'a flanqué** or **fichu la ~** he gave me a fright.

fructidor /fʀyktidɔʀ/ *nm* Fructidor (*twelfth month of the French revolutionary calendar, ≈ September*).

fructification /fʀyktifikasjɔ̃/ *nf* (formation des fruits) fruit formation; (ensemble des fruits) yield.

fructifier /fʀyktifje/ [2] *vi* **1** [*capital*] to yield a profit; [*affaire*] to flourish; [*théorie*] to bear fruit; **faire ~ son argent** to make one's money grow; **2** [*arbre*] to bear fruit; [*terre*] to be productive.

fructose /fʀyktoz/ *nm* fructose.

fructueusement /fʀyktɥøzmɑ̃/ *adv* profitably.

fructueux, **-euse** /fʀyktɥø, øz/ *adj* (fécond) [*relation, réunion*] fruitful; [*essai, carrière*] successful; [*travail*] productive; (lucratif) profitable.

frugal, **~e**, *mpl* **-aux** /fʀygal, o/ *adj* [*personne, repas*] frugal.

frugalement /fʀygalmɑ̃/ *adv* frugally.

frugalité /fʀygalite/ *nf* frugality; **avec ~** frugally.

frugivore /fʀyʒivɔʀ/ **I** *adj* frugivorous.

II *nm* fruit-eating animal.

fruit /fʀɥi/ *nm* **1** gén, Culin fruit ₵; **voulez-vous un ~?** would you like some fruit?; **aimer les ~s** to like fruit; **acheter des ~s** to buy fruit; **2** Bot fruit; **la tomate est un ~** the tomato is a fruit; **3** (résultat) fruit; **récolter les ~s de ses efforts/de la victoire** to reap the fruits of one's efforts/of victory; **c'est le ~ de l'expérience** that's the fruit of experience; **le ~ de mes entrailles** the fruit of my womb; **porter ses ~s** to bear fruit; **le ~ de l'adultère** the offspring of an adulterous liaison; **4** Constr, Gén Civ (de mur, barrage, canal) batter.

■ **~ confit** Culin candied ou glacé fruit; **~ défendu** Bible forbidden fruit; **~ déguisé** Culin (avec glaçage) sugar-coated fruit; (à la pâte d'amande) marzipan fruit; **~ de la passion** Bot, Culin passion fruit; **~ sec** Culin dried fruit; (personne) disappointment; **~ tombé** Agric windfall; **~s de mer** Culin seafood ₵; **~s rafraîchis** Culin fruit salad ₵; **~s rouges** Culin soft fruit ₵ GB, berries US; **~s au sirop** Culin fruit ₵ in syrup GB ou sirup US; **~s de la terre** fruits of the earth.

fruité, **~e** /fʀɥite/ *adj* [*alcool, parfum*] fruity.

fruiterie /fʀɥitʀi/ *nf* (magasin) greengrocer's GB, fruit seller's; (entrepôt) fruit warehouse.

fruitier, **-ière** /fʀɥitje, ɛʀ/ **I** *adj* [*arbre, cargo*] fruit (*épith*).

II ▶ **510** *nm,f* fruiterer GB, fruit seller US.

III *nm* **1** (verger) orchard; (planté d'agrumes) grove; **2** (arbre) fruit tree; **3** (pièce) storeroom for fruit; (entrepôt) fruit warehouse; **4** (fromager) cheese maker.

IV fruitière *nf* (fromagerie) cheese dairy.

frusques○ /fʀysk/ *nfpl* gear○ ₵, clothes (*pl*); **de vieilles ~** old clothes.

fruste /fʀyst/ *adj* **1** [*personne, manières, apparence*] uncouth; [*langage, expression*] crude; [*art, style*] unsophisticated; **2** Tech [*médaille*] worn; [*sculpture*] weatherbeaten.

frustrant, **~e** /fʀystʀɑ̃, ɑ̃t/ *adj* **1** [*situation, travail*] frustrating; [*attitude, réponse*] unsatisfactory; **2** Psych [*parent, éducateur*] repressive, frustrating spéc.

frustration /fʀystʀasjɔ̃/ *nf* **1** gén, Psych frustration; **un sentiment de ~** a feeling of frustration; **2** Jur deprivation.

frustré, **~e** /fʀystʀe/ **I** *adj* frustrated.

II *nm,f* dissatisfied person.

frustrer /fʀystʀe/ [1] *vtr* **1** (décevoir) **~ qn/les efforts de qn** to thwart sb/sb's efforts; **~ qn dans son attente** to disappoint sb's hopes; **2** (priver) **~ qn de qch** to deprive sb of sth; (malhonnêtement) to cheat sb (out) of sth; **3** (léser) to defraud [*créanciers*]; **4** Psych to frustrate.

FS (*written abbr* = **franc suisse**) SFr.

FSE /ɛfɛsə/ *nm*: *abbr* ▶ **fonds**.

fuchsia /fyʃja/ **I** ▶ **193** *adj inv* fuchsia (*épith*).

II *nm* fuchsia.

fuchsine /fyksin/ *nf* fuchsin.

fucus /fykys/ *nm* fucus.

fuel = **fioul**.

fufute○ /fyfyt/ *adj inv* sharp; **ce n'est pas ~ de ta part** that isn't very clever of you.

fugace /fygas/ *adj* [*sensation, souvenir, reflet, instant, odeur*] fleeting; [*symptôme*] elusive.

fugacité /fygasite/ *nf* liter (de sensation, reflet) fleetingness; (de souvenir) elusiveness; (d'odeur) evanescence; (de beauté) transience.

fugitif, **-ive** /fyʒitif, iv/ **I** *adj* **1** (échappé) [*prisonnier*] escaped; [*esclave*] runaway (*épith*); **un criminel ~** a fugitive from justice; **2** (bref) [*sensation, pensée, ombre, espoir*] fleeting; [*plaisir, joie*] elusive; **le bonheur est ~** happiness is elusive.

II *nm,f* (malfaiteur) fugitive; (prisonnier) escapee; (enfant, esclave) runaway.

fugitivement /fyʒitivmɑ̃/ *adv* fleetingly.

fugue /fyg/ *nf* **1** (escapade) **faire une ~** (enfant) to run away; (animal) to run off; **un enfant en ~** a runaway child; **c'est sa première ~** it's the first time he/she has run away; **elle est en ~** she has run away (**de** from); **2** Mus fugue.

fuguer /fyge/ [1] *vi* [*enfant*] to run away (**de** from); [*animal*] to run off.

fugueur, **-euse** /fygœʀ, øz/ **I** *adj* **c'est un enfant ~** this child is always running away.

II *nm,f* runaway (child).

fuir /fɥiʀ/ [29] **I** *vtr* **1** (quitter) to flee [*pays, ville, oppression*]; to flee from [*combats, amour*]; **2** (éviter) to escape [*hiver*]; to avoid [*responsabilité, discussion, personne*]; to steer clear of [*problème, journalistes, foule*]; to stay out of [*soleil*]; **~ les médias** to shun publicity.

II *vi* **1** (partir) [*personne, soldat, capitaux*] to flee; [*animal*] to run away; **~ en Chine/à l'étranger/devant l'ennemi** to flee to China/abroad/in the face of the enemy; **~ à toutes jambes** to run for it; **faire ~** to scare [sb] off [*personne*]; **faire ~ les clients/spectateurs/investisseurs** to scare customers/spectators/investors off; **laid à faire ~** ugly as sin; **2** (suinter) [*robinet, gaz, toit, stylo*] to leak; **3** (se dérober) [*personne, regard*] to be evasive; **~ devant ses responsabilités** not to face up to one's responsibilities; **4** liter (défiler et disparaître) [*nuages*] to sail by; [*arbres*] to flash past; [*navire*] to sail into the distance; [*temps*] to fly by; [*bonheur*] to fade.

III **se fuir** *vpr* (s'éviter) to avoid each other; **les deux familles se fuient** the two families avoid each other.

fuite /fɥit/ *nf* **1** (mouvement) gén flight; (de fugitif) escape; **~ précipitée/éperdue** hurried/headlong flight; **protéger sa ~** to cover one's escape; **mettre qn en ~** to put sb to flight; **en ~** runaway (*épith*), on the run (*jamais épith*); **prendre la ~** [*personne*] to flee; [*fugitif*] to escape; [*voiture*] to speed off; **la ~ des cerveaux aux États-Unis** the brain drain to the US; **~ de capitaux** Fin flight of capital; **la ~ des capitaux en Suisse/hors de France** the flight of capital to Switzerland/from France; **~ en Égypte** Bible Flight into Egypt; **2** (attitude) escape (**devant** from; **dans** into); **~ devant la vie/dans le travail** escape from life/in work; **~ en avant** headlong rush (**vers** into); **3** (d'information) leak; **~s avant l'examen** leaks before the examination; **~s publiées dans la presse** leaks published in the press; **4** Tech (suintement) leak; **~ d'eau/d'huile** water/oil leak; **~ dans un tuyau** leak in a pipe; **5** liter (d'années) swift passage; (de temps) passing; (de nuages) drift.

fulgurant, **~e** /fylgyʀɑ̃, ɑ̃t/ *adj* [*réflexes, attaque*] lightning (*épith*); [*réponse, ascension, progression*] dazzling; [*imagination*] brilliant; [*douleur*] searing (*épith*); **ses progrès ont été ~s** he/she has made terrific progress; **une lueur ~e** a blinding flash; **elle lui lança des regards ~s** she looked at him/her with blazing eyes.

fuligineux, **-euse** /fyliʒinø, øz/ *adj* **1** [*flamme, teinte*] sooty; **2** [*propos, raisonnement*] obscure.

full /ful/ *nm* full house; **un ~ aux as par les dames** three aces and two queens.

fulmar /fylmaʀ/ *nm* fulmar.

fulminant, **~e** /fylminɑ̃, ɑ̃t/ *adj* **1** (furieux) furious; **2** Chimie fulminating, detonating; **poudre ~e** fulminating powder.

fulminate /fylminat/ *nm* fulminate; **~ de mercure** mercury fulminate.

fulmination /fylminasjɔ̃/ *nf* **1** (imprécation) fulmination; **lancer des ~s contre qn/qch** to rail against sb/sth; **2** Chimie detonation; **3** Relig fulmination.

fulminer /fylmine/ [1] **I** *vtr* **1** (prononcer) to hurl [*insultes*] (**contre** at); to fling [*menaces*] (**contre** at); **2** Relig to fulminate (**qch contre qn** sth against sb).

II *vi* **1** (enrager) to fulminate (**contre** against); **il fulminait intérieurement** he was seething; **2** Chimie to detonate.

fulminique /fylminik/ *adj* fulminic.

fumage /fymaʒ/ *nm* **1** Culin smoking; **2** Agric manuring.

fumant, **~e** /fymɑ̃, ɑ̃t/ *adj* **1** (dégageant de la fumée) smoking; (dégageant de la vapeur) steaming; **2** Chimie fuming; **3**○ (sensationnel) terrific○; **faire un coup ~** to pull off a real coup (**à qn** on sb); **préparer un coup ~ contre** or **à qn** to have a nasty surprise in store for sb.

fumasse◑ /fymas/ *adj* **être ~** to be fuming.

fumé, **~e** /fyme/ **I** *pp* ▶ **fumer**.

II *pp adj* **1** Culin [*viande, poisson*] smoked; **2** (teinté) [*vitre, lunettes*] tinted; [*verre*] smoked; **des lunettes à verres ~s** tinted glasses.

III *nm* Culin smoked food; **un goût de ~** a smoky taste.

IV **fumée** *nf* **1** (de feu) smoke; (d'usine, de pot d'échappement) **~es** fumes; **~e de cigare** cigar smoke; **les ~es des toits de la ville** smoke from the chimneys of the town; **partir** or **s'évanouir en ~e** fig to go up in smoke; **la ~e vous dérange?** do you mind my smoking?; **2** (vapeur) steam; **dans les ~es de l'alcool** or **de l'ivresse** fig in an alcoholic stupor.

IDIOMES **il n'y a pas de ~e sans feu** Prov there's no smoke without fire Prov.

fume-cigarette /fymsigaʀɛt/ *nm inv* cigarette holder.

fumée ▶ **fumé II, IV.**

fumer /fyme/ [1] **I** *vtr* **1** [*fumeur*] to smoke; **~ la cigarette/la pipe** to smoke cigarettes/a pipe; **2** Culin to smoke [*viande, poisson*]; **3** Agric to manure [*sol*].

II *vi* **1** [*fumeur*] to smoke; **2** [*volcan, cheminée*] to smoke; [*étang, grog*] to steam; [*acide*] to give off fumes; **3**○ (être en colère) to fume○.

IDIOMES **~ comme un pompier** or **sapeur** to smoke like a chimney.

fumerie /fymʀi/ *nf* **~ (d'opium)** opium den.

fumerolle /fymʀɔl/ *nf* fumarolic gas ¢.

fumet /fymɛ/ *nm* **1** Culin (de viande) aroma; (de vin) bouquet; (sauce) fumet; **2** (forte odeur) smell, odour[GB]; **3** Chasse (de gibier) scent.

fumeur, **-euse**[1] /fymœʀ, øz/ *nm,f* smoker; **un grand ~** a heavy smoker; **zone ~s/non ~s** smoking/non-smoking area; **compartiment non ~** non-smoking compartment.

fumeux, **-euse**[2] /fymø, øz/ *adj* **1** (vague) [*théorie, propos*] woolly GB, wooly US; [*personne*] woolly-minded; **2** (produisant de la fumée) smoky; (brumeux) misty.

fumier /fymje/ *nm* **1** Agric manure; **tas de ~** dunghill; **2**◑ (salaud) offensive (**espèce de**) **~!** you shit◑! injur; **c'est un beau ~** he's a real shit◑.

fumigateur /fymigatœʀ/ *nm* fumigator.

fumigation /fymigasjɔ̃/ *nf* fumigation.

fumigatoire /fymigatwaʀ/ *adj* fumigating.

fumigène /fymiʒɛn/ **I** *adj* Mil [*grenade, pot*] smoke; Agric [*appareil, poudre*] fumigating.

II *nm* Mil smoke device; Agric fumigator.

fumiste /fymist/ **I**○ *adj* pej **être un peu ~** (peu sérieux) to be a bit of a joker○; (charlatan) to be a bit of a phoney○; (paresseux) to be a bit of a skiver○ GB ou laggard US.

II *nm,f* **1**○ (fantaisiste) joker○; (charlatan) phoney○; (paresseux) skiver○ GB, laggard US; **2** ▶ **510** (technicien) (pour cheminée) chimney specialist; (pour appareil de chauffage) stove fitter.

fumisterie /fymistəʀi/ *nf* **1**○ (action peu sérieuse) joke; **c'est une/de la ~** it's a joke; **2** (profession) (pour les cheminées) chimney engineering; (pour les appareils de chauffage) stove fitting.

fumivore /fymivɔʀ/ *adj* [*bougie, appareil*] smoke-absorbing; [*foyer*] smokeless.

fumoir /fymwaʀ/ *nm* **1** (pour fumeurs) smoking-room; **2** (pour viandes, poissons) smokehouse.

fumure /fymyʀ/ *nf* **1** (avec de l'engrais) fertilization; (avec du fumier) manuring; **2** (engrais) fertilizer; (fumier) manure.

fun /fœn/ *nm* **1** (planche) funboard; **2** (sport) funboard sailing.

funambule /fynɑ̃byl/ ▶ **510** *nmf* tightrope walker; **un numéro de ~s** a tightrope act.

funambulesque /fynɑ̃bylɛsk/ *adj* **1** (de funambule) [*art, technique*] of tightrope walking; [*souplesse, exploit*] of a tightrope walker; **2** (excentrique) [*projet, idée*] outlandish.

funambulisme /fynɑ̃bylism/ *nm* tightrope walking.

funèbre /fynɛbʀ/ *adj* **1** (funéraire) funeral (*épith*); **convoi/service ~** funeral procession/service; **éloge ~** funeral oration; **2** (lugubre) funereal, gloomy.

funérailles /fyneʀɑj/ *nfpl* funeral; **des ~ nationales** a state funeral.

funéraire /fyneʀɛʀ/ *adj* [*cérémonie, frais*] funeral; [*objet, monument*] funerary; **dalle** or **stèle ~** tombstone, gravestone GB.

funérarium /fyneʀaʀjɔm/ *nm* funeral parlour[GB].

funeste /fynɛst/ *adj* **1** (qui est source de malheur) [*erreur, conseil*] fatal; [*décision, jour*] fateful; [*conséquence*] dire; **être ~ à qn/qch** to be fatal for sb/sth; **2** (de mort) fml [*pressentiment, signe*] of death (*épith, après n*).

funiculaire /fynikylɛʀ/ *nm* funicular.

funk(y) /fœnk(i)/ *adj, nm* funk.

fur: **au fur et à mesure** /ofyʀeaməzyʀ/ **I** *loc adv* (régulièrement) as one goes along; **je préfère les informer au ~ et à mesure** I prefer to inform them as I go along; **au ~ et à mesure leur technique s'est améliorée** their technique improved as they went along; **passe-moi les livres, je les rangerai au ~ et à mesure** pass me the books, I'll put them away as I go along; **il inventait des explications au ~ et à mesure** he was making up explanations as he went along.

II **au fur et à mesure de** *loc prép* **au ~ et à mesure de leurs besoins** as and when they need it; **vous serez payés au ~ et à mesure de l'avancement des travaux** you'll be paid as the work progresses; **la championne joue de mieux en mieux au ~ et à mesure des matchs** the champion is playing better and better with each match; **placer les gens au ~ et à mesure de leur arrivée** to seat people as and when they arrive.

III **au fur et à mesure que** *loc conj* **le chemin se rétrécissait au ~ et à mesure qu'on avançait** the path grew progressively narrower as we went along; **au ~ et à mesure que les gens arrivaient** as people arrived; **au ~ et à mesure que la soirée avançait, il devenait de plus en plus animé** as the evening went on, he became more and more animated.

furax○ /fyʀaks/ *adj inv* mad○, hopping mad○ (*jamais épith*); **être ~ de devoir faire qch** to be mad○ at having to do sth; **je suis ~ d'avoir dit ça** I could kick myself for saying that○.

furet /fyʀɛ/ *nm* **1** Zool ferret; **2** (jeu) *children's game where one tries to find a hidden object being passed around*; **3** (de plombier) snake.

furetage /fyʀtaʒ/ *nm* **1** (d'enfant, de curieux) rummaging, ferreting around; **2** Chasse ferreting.

fureter /fyʀte/ [18] *vi* to rummage, to ferret around (**dans** in).

fureteur, **-euse** /fuʀtœʀ, øz/ *adj* [*personne, air, humeur, regard*] inquisitive; [*yeux*] prying.

fureur /fyʀœʀ/ *nf* **1** (colère) rage, fury; **~ aveugle/noire** blind/unholy rage; **accès/crise de ~** bout/fit of rage; **être en ~ contre qn/qch** to be in a rage with sb/about sth; **se mettre en ~ contre qn/qch** to fly into a rage with sb/sth; **exciter la ~ de qn**, **mettre qn en ~** to make sb furious; **2** (passion) frenzy; **avec ~** frenziedly; **s'adonner au jeu avec ~** to gamble frenziedly; **~ de vivre** lust for life; **avoir la ~ du jeu/de lire/d'écrire** to be addicted to gambling/to reading/to writing; **faire ~** to be all the rage; **ce sport fait ~ en ce moment** this sport is all the rage at the moment.

furia /fyʀja/ *nf* (d'admirateurs, de manifestants) frenzy; (de joueurs, d'équipe) zeal.

furibard○, **~e** /fyʀibaʀ, aʀd/ *adj* hopping mad○ (*jamais épith*).

furibond, **~e** /fyʀibɔ̃, ɔ̃d/ *adj* [*air*] incensed; [*voix, regard, yeux*] wrathful; **être ~** to be furious; **rouler des yeux ~s** to roll one's eyes in rage.

furie /fyʀi/ *nf* **1** (rage) rage, fury; **mettre qn en ~** to make sb furious; **entrer en ~** to become furious, to fly into a rage; **2** (violence) fury; **taureau/vent en ~** raging bull/wind; **3** (harpie) fury.

Furie /fyʀi/ *nprf* Mythol Fury; **les ~s** the Furies.

furieusement /fyʀjøzmɑ̃/ *adv* **1** (violemment) [*attaquer, cogner*] furiously; [*injurier*] violently; [*répondre*] angrily; **2**○ (extrêmement) [*beau*] fantastically; [*bon, long, drôle*] incredibly; **j'ai ~ envie de dormir** I'm dying to go to sleep; **elle ressemble ~ à son père** she's incredibly like her father.

furieux, **-ieuse** /fyʀjø, øz/ *adj* **1** (irrité) [*personne, geste, air, ton*] furious; [*foule, animal, cris*] angry; **jeter un regard ~ à qn** to cast a furious look at sb; **rendre qn ~** to make sb furious; **être ~ contre qn** to be furious with sb; **être ~ de qn/qch** to be infuriated by sb/sth; **être ~ de faire** to be furious at doing; **être ~ que** to be furious that; **il est ~ que je ne sois pas venu** he's furious that I didn't come; **parler sur un ton ~** to speak angrily; **2**○ (intense) [*envie*] terrible; **3** (violent) [*combats*] intense; [*tempête, vent, torrent*] raging.

furioso /fyʀjozo/ *adj* furioso.

furoncle /fyʀɔ̃kl/ *nm* boil, furuncle spéc.

furonculose /fyʀɔ̃kyloz/ ▶**271** *nf* furunculosis.

furtif, **-ive** /fyʀtif, iv/ *adj* **1** (discret, rapide) furtive; **marcher d'un pas ~** to tread furtively; **2** (passager) [*soupçon, joie, émotion*] fleeting; **3** Mil (indétectable) **avion ~** stealth bomber.

furtivement /fyʀtivmɑ̃/ *adv* furtively.

fusain /fyzɛ̃/ *nm* **1** (arbuste) spindle tree; **2** Art (matière) charcoal, fusain spéc; (crayon) charcoal crayon; (dessin) charcoal drawing; **au ~** (dessiner) in charcoal; (dessin) charcoal (*épith*).

fuseau, *pl* **~x** /fyzo/ *nm* **1** (pour filer) spindle; **en ~** [*jambe de pantalon, muscle*] tapering; [*colonne, arbre*] spindle-shaped; **arbre taillé en ~** tree trimmed in a spindle shape; **2** (pour dentelle) lace bobbin; **dentelle au ~** bobbin-lace; **3** (pantalon) **~(x) (de ski)** ski pants (*pl*); **4** Zool spindle-shell; **5**○ (jambe) pin○, leg.
■ **~ horaire** time zone; **changer de ~ horaire** to change time zones.

fusée /fyze/ *nf* **1** (en astronautique, pyrotechnie) rocket; **~ interplanétaire** interplanetary rocket; **2** Mil (missile) rocket, missile; (détonateur) fuse; **3** Aut stub axle.
■ **~ air-air** air-to-air missile; **~ antichar** antitank rocket ou missile; **~ asphyxiante** gas bomb; **~ de détresse** distress rocket; **~ éclairante** flare; **~ gigogne** or **à étages** multistage rocket; **~ intercontinentale** intercontinental (ballistic) missile; **~ mer-air** sea-to-air missile; **~ mer-mer** ship-to-ship missile; **~ porteuse** Astronaut carrier rocket; **~ de signalisation** signal rocket; **~ sol-air** surface-to-air missile.
IDIOMES **partir comme une ~** to set off like a rocket.

fusée-sonde, *pl* **fusées-sondes** /fyzesɔ̃d/ *nf* Astronaut probe (rocket).

fuselage /fyzlaʒ/ *nm* fuselage.

fuselé, **~e** /fyzle/ *adj* [*muscle, doigt*] tapering; [*arbre, colonne, structure*] spindle-shaped.

fuséologie /fyzeɔlɔʒi/ *nf* rocketry, rocket technology.

fuser /fyze/ [1] *vi* **1** (retentir) to ring out; **cris qui fusent de tous côtés** shouts ringing out on every side; **les rires/insultes/critiques fusaient** laughter/insults/criticism came from all sides; **laisser ~ des injures** to call out insults; **2** (jaillir) [*objet*] to rocket; [*liquide*] to spurt out; [*lumière*] to pour; [*lueur, malice, colère*] to flash (**sur** across); **3** Tech [*cire, bougie*] to melt, to fuse; [*poudre*] to burn out.

fusette /fyzɛt/ *nf* reel (of thread).

fusibilité /fyzibilite/ *nf* fusibility.

fusible /fyzibl/ **I** *adj* fusible.
II *nm* (fil, cartouche) fuse.

fusiforme /fyzifɔʀm/ *adj* fusiform.

fusil /fyzi/ *nm* **1** (arme) gun, shotgun; Mil rifle; **un coup de ~** lit a rifle ou gun shot; **dans ce restaurant c'est le coup de ~**○ fig they really sting you in that restaurant; **à portée de ~** within range; **2** (chasseur) gun; (soldat) rifle; **être un bon/mauvais ~** to be a good/bad shot; **3** (pour aiguiser) sharpening steel; **4** (allume-gaz) gas igniter.
■ **~ antichar** antitank gun; **~ d'assaut** assault rifle ou gun; **~ à canon scié** sawn-off shotgun; **~ de chasse** hunting rifle; **~ à deux coups** double-barrelled[GB] gun ou rifle; **~ de guerre** army rifle; **~ à harpon** harpoon gun; **~ lance-grenade** grenade rifle ou gun; **~ à lunette** rifle ou gun with telescopic sight; **~ à pompe** pump gun; **~ à répétition** repeater; **~ sous marin** speargun.
IDIOMES **partir la fleur au ~** to set off without a care in the world; ▶ **chien**, **épaule**.

fusilier /fyzi(l)je/ *nm* rifleman, fusilier; Hist fusilier.
■ **~ (commando) de l'air** airforce commando; **~ marin** marine; **~ mitrailleur** machinegunner.

fusillade /fyzijad/ *nf* **1** (bruit) gunfire ¢; (bataille) shoot-out; **un bruit de ~** a noise of gunfire; **2** (exécution) shooting.

fusiller /fyzije/ [1] *vtr* **1** (exécuter) to shoot; **~ qn pour trahison** to shoot sb for treason; **faire ~ qn** to have sb shot; **2**○ (abîmer) to wreck; **3**○ (avec un appareil photo) **~ qn** to click away at sb.
IDIOMES **~ qn du regard** to give sb a withering look.

fusil-mitrailleur, *pl* **fusils-mitrailleurs** /fyzimitʀajœʀ/ *nm* light machine gun.

fusion /fyzjɔ̃/ *nf* **1** (liquéfaction) (de métal) melting, fusion spéc; (de glace) melting; **roche/métal en ~** molten rock/metal; **2** Biol, Nucl, Phys fusion; **~ (thermo)nucléaire** nuclear fusion; **3** Ling fusion; **4** (union) (d'entreprises, de partis, listes, professions) merger (**entre** between); (de systèmes, cultures, théories) fusion (**entre** of); (de peuples, races) mixing (**entre** of).

fusion-absorption, *pl* **fusions-absorptions** /fyzjɔ̃apsɔʀpsjɔ̃/ *nf* absorption.

fusionnement /fyzjɔnmɑ̃/ *nm* amalgamation.

fusionner /fyzjɔne/ [1] *vtr, vi* to merge.

fustanelle /fystanɛl/ *nf* fustanella.

fustigation /fystigasjɔ̃/ *nf* **1** (condamnation) castigation; **2** (action de battre) thrashing.

fustiger /fystiʒe/ [13] *vtr* **1** (condamner) to castigate, to lambast; **2** (battre) to thrash.

fût /fy/ *nm* **1** (tonneau) cask, barrel; **mettre du vin en ~** to cask wine; (pour produits chimiques) drum; **2** (d'arbre) trunk; **3** (de colonne) shaft; **4** (de fusil) barrel casing.

futaie /fytɛ/ *nf* (forêt) forest of tall trees; (bosquet) group of tall trees; (plantation) plantation of tall trees.

futaille /fytɑj/ *nf* cask, barrel.

futaine /fytɛn/ *nf* fustian; **vêtement de** or **en ~** fustian garment.

futal◐ /fytal/, **fute**◐ /fyt/ *nm* trousers (*pl*) GB, pants (*pl*) US.

futé, **~e** /fyte/ **I** *adj* [*personne, animal*] wily, crafty péj; [*sourire, réponse*] crafty; **ce n'est pas très ~** that isn't very clever.
II *nm,f* **petit ~** cunning little devil.

fute-fute○ /fytfyt/ = **fufute**.

futile /fytil/ *adj* [*projet, prétexte, distraction*] trivial; [*personne, existence, propos*] superficial; [*cadeau*] trifling; [*tentative*] weak.

futilité /fytilite/ **I** *nf* (insignifiance) superficiality.
II futilités *nfpl* (paroles) banalities; (objets) trifles; (actions) trivial activities; (détails) trivial details; **s'attacher à des ~s** to attach importance to trivial details.

futur, **~e** /fytyʀ/ **I** *adj* [*besoin, dirigeant, étudiant, client, construction*] future; **les générations ~es** future generations; **son ~ mari** her future husband; **mon ~ mari** my husband-to-be, my future husband; **les ~s époux** the engaged couple (*sg*); **les ~es mères** expectant mothers; **cet enfant, c'est un ~ artiste/champion** that child has the makings of an artist/a champion.
II† *nm,f* (fiancé) intended.
III *nm* **1** (avenir) future; **le téléviseur/train du ~** the television/train of the future; **2** Ling future; **au ~** in the future (tense).
■ **~ antérieur** Ling future perfect; **~ proche** Ling periphrastic future; **~ simple** Ling future tense.

futurisme /fytyʀism/ *nm* futurism.

futuriste /fytyʀist/ **I** *adj* **1** (ultramoderne) [*architecture, décor, voiture, vision*] futuristic; **2** Art, Littérat futurist.
II *nmf* futurist.

futurologie /fytyʀɔlɔʒi/ *nf* futurology.

futurologue /fytyʀɔlɔg/ ▶**510** *nmf* futurologist.

fuyant, **~e** /fɥijɑ̃, ɑ̃t/ *adj* [*personne, électeur, public*] fickle; [*regard*] shifty; [*caractère*] slippery○; [*point, horizon*] receding; [*bonheur*] elusive; **front/profil ~** receding forehead/profile.

fuyard, **~e** /fɥijaʀ, aʀd/ *nm,f* **1** (fugitif) runaway; **2** (déserteur) deserter.

g, **G** /ʒe/ *nm inv* **1** (lettre) g, G; **2** (*written abbr* = **gramme**) **250 g** 250 g; **3 G7** *abbr* ▶ **groupe**.

gabardine /gabaʀdin/ *nf* **1** Tex gabardine; **2** (imperméable) gabardine; **un homme en ~** a man in a gabardine.

gabarit /gabaʀi/ *nm* **1** (de véhicule) size; **véhicule hors ~** oversize vehicle; **2**° (de personne) (corpulence) build; (aptitudes) calibre[GB]; **l'équipe possède un bon nombre de grands ~s** the team has quite a few hefty players; **3** Tech (modèle) template; (appareil) gauge[GB].
■ **~ de chargement** Rail loading gauge.

gabegie /gabʒi/ *nf* (gaspillage) waste (due to mismanagement); (désordre) muddle.

gabelle /gabɛl/ *nf* gabelle, salt tax.

gabelou /gablu/ *nm* **1** pej (douanier) customs officer; **2** Hist gabeller.

gabier /gabje/ *nm* (sur un voilier) topman.

Gabon /gabɔ̃/ **▶ 321** *nprm* Gabon.

gabonais, **~e** /gabɔnɛ, ɛz/ **▶ 537** *adj* Gabonese.

Gabonais, **~e** /gabɔnɛ, ɛz/ **▶ 537** *nm,f* Gabonese.

gâchage /gɑʃaʒ/ *nm* Constr (de plâtre, mortier) mixing.

gâche /gɑʃ/ *nf* **1** (de serrure) strike, keep; **2** (de maçon) (plasterer's) trowel.

gâcher /gɑʃe/ [1] *vtr* **1** (gaspiller) to waste [*temps, occasion, nourriture*]; to throw away [*vie, talent*]; **2** (dégrader) to spoil [*réception, spectacle, plaisir*]; to ruin [*affaire*]; **3** Constr to mix [*plâtre, mortier*].
IDIOMES **~ le métier** to ruin the trade (*by undercutting prices*).

gâchette /gɑʃɛt/ *nf* **1** (d'arme) tumbler; controv (détente) trigger; **appuyer sur la ~** to pull the trigger; **avoir la ~ facile** to be trigger-happy; **2** (tireur) shot; **une fine ~** a good shot; **la meilleure ~ de l'Ouest** the fastest gun in the West; **3** (de serrure) tumbler.

gâcheur, **-euse** /gɑʃœʀ, øz/ *nm,f* **1** (gaspilleur) wasteful person; (trouble-fête) spoilsport; **2** (plâtrier) plasterer's ou bricklayer's mate.

gâchis /gɑʃi/ *nm* (gaspillage) waste **¢**; (pagaille) mess; **faire du ~** (gaspiller) to be wasteful; (mettre la pagaille) to create havoc.

gadget /gadʒɛt/ *nm* **1** (objet inutile) gadget; **un magasin de ~s** a gadget shop; **civilisation du ~** gadget-ridden society; **2** (dispositif ingénieux) gadget; péj gimmick; **tenir du ~**, **n'être qu'un ~** to be just a gimmick.

gadin° /gadɛ̃/ *nm* **ramasser** or **prendre un ~** to fall flat on one's face.

gadoue /gadu/ *nf* **1**° (boue) mud; **patauger dans la ~** to flounder through the mud; **2**† Agric manure.

GAEC /gaɛk/ *nm* (*abbr* = **groupement agricole d'exploitation en commun**) *farm run as a non-trading partnership by between two and ten farmers*.

gaélique /gaelik/ **▶ 462** *adj, nm* Gaelic.

gaffe /gaf/ *nf* **1**° (acte) boob° GB, blooper° US, blunder; (parole) clanger° GB, blooper° US; **faire une ~** (acte) to blunder; (parole) to drop a clanger GB, to make a blooper° US; **faire ~** to watch out; **fais ~, tu vas tomber!** watch out, you're going to fall!; **il faut faire ~** you must watch out; **j'ai pas fait ~** I wasn't paying attention; **faire ~ à** to watch out for; **fais ~ aux voitures** watch out for the cars; **fais ~ à ce que tu dis** watch what you say; **fais ~ à toi!** (menace) watch it!; (conseil) take care; **faire ~ que** to be careful that; **2** Naut boathook; **3** Pêche gaff.

gaffer /gafe/ [1] **I** *vtr* Pêche to gaff.
II° *vi* (en actions) to make a boob° GB, to make a blooper° US, to blunder; (en paroles) to drop a clanger° GB, to make a blooper° US.

gaffeur°, **-euse** /gafœʀ, øz/ **I** *adj* [*personne*] blundering (*épith*); **il est ~** he's a blunderer.
II *nm,f* blunderer.

gag /gag/ *nm* **1** gag; **2** (incident drôle) joke; **c'était le ~!** it was hysterical!

gaga° /gaga/ **I** *adj inv* (gâteux) gaga°; (débile) daft° GB, silly; **devenir ~** to go gaga.
II *nmf* dodderer°.

gage /gaʒ/ **I** *nm* **1** (garantie) security **¢**, surety **¢**; **laisser sa montre en ~** to leave one's watch as security ou surety; **prêter sur ~s** to lend against surety; **mettre en ~** to pawn [sth]; **2** Jeux (pénitence) forfeit; **faire son ~** to pay one's forfeit; **3** (d'amour, de fidélité, bonne foi) pledge; **donner des ~s d'amitié à qn** to pledge friendship to sb; **ta ténacité est le ~ de ta réussite future** your tenacity is a guarantee of your future success.
II gages† *nmpl* (salaire) wages; **être aux ~s de qn**† [*domestique*] to be in sb's service; **tueur à ~s** hired killer.

gager /gaʒe/ [13] *vtr* **1** fml (supposer) **~ que** to suppose that, to wager† that; **gageons que cette mode passera très vite** it's a safe bet that the fashion won't last; **2** (mettre en gage) to pawn; **3**† Fin (garantir) to secure [*emprunt*] (**sur qch** on sth).

gageure /gaʒyʀ/ *nf* challenge; **cela relève de la ~** it's a bit of a challenge.

gagnable /gaɲabl/ *adj* winnable.

gagnant, **~e** /gaɲɑ̃, ɑ̃t/ **I** *adj* [*billet, numéro, équipe, cheval*] winning (*épith*); **j'ai misé sur le cheval ~** I bet on the winning horse; **donner un cheval/qn ~** to tip a horse/sb to win; **faire des coups ~s** (au tennis) to hit winners; (aux échecs) to make winning moves; **jouer** or **partir ~** to be on to a winner; **être** or **sortir ~** to come out on top (**de** in).
II *nm,f* (personne) winner (**de qch** in sth); (cheval) winner, winning horse; (billet) winning ticket; **jouer le ~** Turf to back the winner; **le grand ~** the real winner.

gagne-pain /gaɲpɛ̃/ *nm inv* (ce qui fait vivre) livelihood; **mes jambes sont mon ~** my legs are my livelihood.

gagne-petit /gaɲpəti/ **I** *adj inv* pej **être ~** to be after every last penny.
II *nmf inv* low-wage earner; **c'est un/une ~** he/she doesn't earn much.

gagner /gaɲe/ [1] **I** *vtr* **1** (remporter) to win [*compétition, prix, guerre, procès, voix*]; **~ une voiture à un concours** to win a car in a competition; **le numéro 123 gagne 500 francs** number 123 wins 500 francs; **~ aux points** to win on points; **~ d'une longueur/d'une tête** to win by a length/by a head; **pour lui, rien n'est encore gagné** fig he's not there yet, he's still got a long way to go; **c'est gagné!** lit we've done it!; iron well done!; **à tous les coups l'on gagne!** every one a winner!; **2** (percevoir, mériter) to earn; **~ 10 000 francs par mois** to earn 10,000 francs a month; **~ tout juste de quoi vivre** to earn just enough to live on; **~ sa vie en faisant** to earn one's living (by) doing; **il gagne bien/très largement sa vie** he makes a good/a very good living; **ta prime, tu l'as bien gagnée** you've certainly earned your bonus; **tu as bien gagné ton repos** you've certainly earned your rest; **un repos bien gagné** a well-earned rest; **il a gagné 500 francs/une fortune sur la vente du tableau** he made 500 francs/a fortune from the sale of the picture; **les sommes gagnées au jeu** gambling gains; **c'est toujours ça de gagné!** well, that's something anyway!; **3** (acquérir) to gain [*réputation, avantage*]; **~ deux points en Bourse** to gain two points on the stock market; **il a perdu une collègue mais gagné une amie** he's lost a colleague but gained a friend; **nous avons tout à ~ de cette réforme** we have everything to gain from this reform; **tu ne gagneras rien à t'obstiner** you'll gain nothing by being stubborn; **~ du temps** (atermoyer) to gain time; **~ du terrain** [*personne, armée, voiture, idées*] to gain ground (**sur** on); [*incendie*] to spread; **~ de la vitesse** to gather speed; **il a gagné de l'assurance** he has gained ou grown in self-confidence; **elle a gagné 5 cm en un an** she's grown 5 cm in a year; **il a gagné 9 kilos** he's put on 9 kilos; **l'équipe a gagné trois places** the team has moved up three places; **4** (économiser) to save [*temps*]; **par l'autoroute on gagne une heure** going by the motorway GB ou freeway US saves an hour; **~ de la place en faisant** to make more room by doing; **5** (attirer) to win [sb] over (**à** to); **~ qn à sa cause** to win sb over to one's cause; **il a su ~ quelques opposants** he managed to win a few dissenters over; **~ l'estime/l'amitié/le cœur de qn** to win sb's esteem/friendship/heart; **6** (atteindre) [*voyageur, véhicule*] to reach, to get to [*lieu*]; **7** (se propager) [*incendie, maladie, troubles, chômage*] to spread to [*lieu*]; **8** (s'emparer de) [*peur, angoisse, émotion, découragement*] to overcome [*personne*]; **le rire/la fatigue me gagnait peu à peu** I was gradually overcome with laughter/fatigue; **le sommeil la gagna** sleep overcame her; **je sentais le froid me ~** I started to feel cold; **9** (battre) to beat [*personne*] (**à** at); **gagner qn aux échecs** to beat sb at chess; **~ qn de vitesse** to outstrip sb.
II *vi* **1** (réussir) to win (**à** at); **tu ne gagneras pas à ce petit jeu** you won't win at this little game; **bon, tu as gagné, on reste à la maison** all right, you win, we'll stay at home; **~ aux courses/à la roulette** to win

at the races/at roulette; **le candidat qui a gagné aux élections** the candidate who won the election; **il a gagné sur ce point, mais...** he won on this point, but...; **2** (tirer avantage) **ce vin gagne à être bu un peu frais** this wine is best drunk ou is at its best when drunk slightly chilled; **le film gagne à être vu en version originale** the film is best seen in the original version; **vous gagneriez à diversifier vos produits** it would be to your advantage to diversify; **elle gagne à être connue** she improves on acquaintance; **3** (acquérir plus) to gain (**en** in); **les entreprises ont gagné en productivité** firms have improved their productivity; **vin qui gagne en arôme avec l'âge** wine whose aroma improves with age; **4** (être bénéficiaire) **y ~** to come off better; **y ~ en** to gain in; **5** (recouvrir) [*mer*] to encroach (**sur** on).

gagneur, **-euse** /gaɲœʀ, øz/ *nm,f* winner; **avoir un tempérament de ~** to be a born winner.

gai, **~e** /gɛ/ **I** *adj* **1** (joyeux) [*personne, humour*] happy, gay; [*caractère, regard*] cheerful; [*visage*] happy; [*réunion, conversation, œuvre*] light-hearted; [*couleur, papier peint*] bright, cheerful; **j'ai repeint la pièce en rose, ça fait plus ~** I've repainted the room in pink, it makes it more cheerful; **2** iron (plaisant) **c'est ~** great!; **il pleut, c'est ~** great! it's raining; **ils viennent à huit pendant cinq jours, ça va être** or **ça promet d'être ~!** eight of them are coming for five days, that's going to be great fun!; **ça promet d'être ~** that promises to be great fun; **3** (éméché) merry; **4**○ (homosexuel) controv gay.

II○ *nm* (homosexuel) controv gay.

■ **~ luron** cheery fellow GB, gay blade US.

gaïac /gajak/ *nm* Bot lignum vitae, guaiacum.

gaiement /gemɑ̃/ *adv* **1** [*marcher, partir, chanter*] cheerfully, merrily; [*décoré*] cheerfully; **2** iron happily; **allons-y ~** iron let's get on with it.

gaieté /gete/ *nf* (de personne, caractère, lieu, spectacle, d'histoire) gaiety, cheerfulness; **mettre qn en ~** to cheer sb up; **livre/histoire d'une grande ~** very cheerful book/story; **il ne l'a pas fait de ~ de cœur** he wasn't very happy about doing it; **ne crois pas que j'y vais de ~ de cœur** don't think I'm happy about going; **avec ~** gaily, cheerfully.

gaillard, **~e** /gajaʀ, aʀd/ **I** *adj* **1** (vigoureux) [*homme*] strapping; [*air*] energetic; [*pas*] lively; **être d'humeur ~e** to be in a chirpy mood; **2** (grivois) [*chanson*] ribald.

II *nm,f* strapping lad/girl; **un grand/beau ~** a tall/handsome strapping man; **viens ici, mon ~**○**!** come here, lad○ GB ou buddy○ US!

III *nm* **1** (lascar) sly customer○; **un drôle de ~** a crafty devil○; **2** (fils) boy.

IV gaillarde *nf* **1** Danse galliard; **2** Bot gaillardia.

■ **~ d'arrière** Naut poop; **~ d'avant** Naut (en marine ancienne) forecastle; (en marine moderne) forward superstructure.

gaillardement /gajaʀdəmɑ̃/ *adv* (avec vigueur) [*avancer, suivre*] cheerfully; (avec courage) [*s'engager, foncer*] bravely.

gaillardise† /gajaʀdiz/ *nf* **1** (grivoiserie) ribald remark; **2** (bonne humeur) high spirits (*pl*).

gain /gɛ̃/ *nm* **1** (argent) earnings (*pl*); **tirer un ~ médiocre de ses efforts** to get a meagre[GB] return for one's efforts; **cette maison représente les ~s de toute une vie de labeur** this house represents the fruits of a lifetime's hard work; **mes ~s au jeu** my gambling gains; **2** Fin (profit en Bourse) gain; **être en ~** [*société, action*] to be gaining (in value); **clôturer sur un ~ de 3 points** to close 3 points up; **3** (économie) saving; **c'est un ~ de temps considérable** it saves a considerable amount of time; **4** Électron, Télécom gain.

■ **~ de productivité** Écon productivity gains (*pl*).

gainage /gɛnaʒ/ *nm* (de fil électrique) insulation; (de tuyau) casing.

gaine /gɛn/ *nf* **1** (de poignard) sheath; **2** Mode girdle; **3** Tech (de fil électrique) insulation ¢; (de tuyau) casing; **4** Bot sheath; **5** Art (socle) plinth.

■ **~ d'ascenseur** lift shaft GB, elevator shaft US; **~ de fumée** flue; **~ à ordures** waste disposal chute GB, garbage chute US; **~ de ventilation** ventilation duct.

gainé, **~e** /gene/ **I** *pp* ▶ **gainer**.

II *pp adj* [*jambes, poitrine*] sheathed (**de** in); [*objet*] covered; [*fil électrique*] sheathed.

gaine-culotte, *pl* **gaines-culottes** /gɛnkylɔt/ *nf* panty girdle.

gainer /gene/ [1] *vtr* **1** (mouler) [*robe*] to sheathe [*corps*]; **2** Tech to sheathe [*fil électrique*].

gainier /genje/ *nm* Bot Judas tree.

gala /gala/ *nm* gala; **soirée/dîner de ~** gala evening/dinner; **tenue de ~** evening dress ¢.

Galaad /galaad/ *npr* **1** Bible Gilead; **2** Littérat Galahad.

galactique /galaktik/ *adj* galactic.

galactogène /galaktɔʒɛn/ *adj, nm* galactagogue.

galactomètre /galaktɔmɛtʀ/ *nm* galactometer.

galactophore /galaktɔfɔʀ/ *adj* **canal ~** lactiferous duct.

galactose /galaktoz/ *nm* galactose.

galalithe® /galalit/ *nf* Galalith®.

galamment /galamɑ̃/ *adv* gallantly.

galandage /galɑ̃daʒ/ *nm* thin brick partition.

galant, **~e** /galɑ̃, ɑ̃t/ **I** *adj* **1** (délicat envers les femmes) gallant, gentlemanly; **il est très ~** he's very gentlemanly; **2** (obligeant) **soyez ~** be a gentleman; **3** (amoureux) **elle était en ~e compagnie** she was in the company of a gentleman; **rendez-vous ~** tryst; **4** Art, Mus [*style*] galant.

II† *nm* (fiancé) beau†.

galanterie /galɑ̃tʀi/ *nf* **1** (courtoisie) gallantry; **2**† (liaison amoureuse) amorous intrigue†; **3**† (propos flatteur) flattering remark.

galantine /galɑ̃tin/ *nf* galantine.

Galapagos /galapagos/ **▶416** *nprfpl* **les (îles) ~** the Galapagos (Islands).

galapiat○† /galapja/ *nm* rapscallion†.

Galatée /galate/ *npr* Galatea.

galaxie /galaksi/ *nf* galaxy.

galbe /galb/ *nm* curve.

galbé, **~e** /galbe/ **I** *pp* ▶ **galber**.

II *pp adj* [*colonne*] with entasis (*épith, après n*); [*pied de meuble*] curved; **épaule bien ~e** shapely shoulder.

galber /galbe/ [1] *vtr* to shape.

gale /gal/ **▶271** *nf* **1** Méd scabies ¢; **tu peux t'asseoir près de moi, je n'ai pas la ~**○ hum you can sit next to me, you won't catch anything; **2** Vét (du chien, chat) mange; (du mouton) scab; **3** Bot scab.

IDIOMES **il est mauvais** or **méchant comme la ~** he's a nasty customer○ ou a nasty piece of work○ GB.

galéjade /galeʒad/ *nf* tall story.

galéjer /galeʒe/ [14] *vi* to spin a yarn; **tu ne vois pas qu'il galèje?** can't you see he's having you on○ GB ou putting you on○ US?

galène /galɛn/ *nf* galena, galenite.

galère /galɛʀ/ *nf* **1** Hist (vaisseau) galley; **condamné aux ~s** (à ramer) sentenced to the galleys; (aux travaux forcés) sentenced to hard labour[GB]; **2**○ (situation pénible) hell○; **c'est la** or **une ~ pour trouver un boulot**○ it's hell trying to find a job; **vie de ~** dog's life; **c'est ~!** it's a real pain○!; **3**○ (situation embrouillée) mess○; **que diable est-il allé faire dans cette ~?** why on earth did he get involved in that mess?; **elle s'est embarquée dans une drôle de ~** she's got GB ou gotten US herself into a fine mess; **être dans la même ~** fig to be in the same boat.

galérer○ /galeʀe/ [14] *vi* **1** (peiner) to have a hard time (**pour faire** doing); **2** (travailler) to slave away, to slog away○.

galerie /galʀi/ *nf* **1** Archit (de maison, musée) gallery; **2** Art (magasin) gallery; (collection) collection; **~ d'art** or **de peinture** art gallery; **une ~ de peintures du XIX**ᵉ a collection of 19th century paintings; **3** (de mine, grotte) gallery; (de taupe) tunnel; **4** Aut (pour bagages) **~ (de toit)** roof rack; **5** (de théâtre) gallery; **amuser la ~**○ to play to the gallery; **pour épater la ~**○ (in order) to impress the crowd.

■ **~ marchande** shopping arcade; **Galerie des Glaces** Hall of mirrors.

galérien /galeʀjɛ̃/ *nm* Hist (sur une galère) galley slave; (au bagne) convict; fig **vie de ~** dog's life; **travailler comme un ~** to slave away.

galeriste /gal(ə)ʀist/ *nmf* Art gallery owner.

galet /galɛ/ *nm* **1** (caillou) pebble; **2** Tech roller.

galetas /galta/ *nm* **1** (taudis) hovel; **2** (mansarde) garret; **3**○ (grenier) attic.

galette /galɛt/ *nf* **1** Culin (gâteau) plain round flat cake; (crêpe) pancake; **2**○ (argent) money, dough○.

■ **~ des Rois** Twelfth Night cake (*containing bean or lucky charm*).

IDIOMES **plat comme une ~** flat as a pancake.

galeux, **-euse** /galø, øz/ **I** *adj* **1** (atteint de gale) [*personne*] with scabies (*épith, après n*); [*éruption*] scabby; [*chien*] mangy; [*mouton*] scabby; [*arbre*] covered with scab (*après n*); **2** (décrépit) [*mur*] peeling; [*bâtiment, quartier*] slummy.

II *nm,f* **1** lit person with scabies; **2**○ fig scum○ ¢; **ils le traitent de ~** they call him scum○.

galhauban /galobɑ̃/ *nm* backstays (*pl*).

Galice /galis/ **▶692** *nprf* Galicia.

Galicie /galisi/ *nprf* Galicia.

Galien /galjɛ̃/ *npr* Galen.

Galilée /galile/ **I** *npr* Galileo.

II **▶692** *nprf* Galilee; **mer de ~** Sea of Galilee.

Galiléen, **-éenne** /galileɛ̃, ɛn/ *nm,f* Galilean.

galimatias /galimatja/ *nm* (parlé) gibberish; (écrit) rubbish.

galion /galjɔ̃/ *nm* galleon.

galipette○ /galipɛt/ *nf* **1** (cabriole) somersault; **faire des ~s** to turn somersaults; **2** (ébat érotique) **faire des ~s avec qn** to fool around with sb.

galle /gal/ *nf* **1** Bot gall; **~ du chêne** oak apple, oak gall; **2** Zool gall wasp.

Galles /gal/ **▶692** *nprfpl* **le pays de ~** Wales (*sg*).

gallican, **~e** /galikɑ̃, an/ *adj, nm,f* Gallican.

gallicanisme /galikanism/ *nm* Gallicanism.

gallicisme /galisism/ *nm* (dans une langue étrangère) gallicism; (en français) French idiom.

gallinacé, **~e** /galinase/ **I** *adj* gallinaceous.

II *nm* gallinacean; **les ~s** Galliformes.

gallique /galik/ *adj* **1** Hist Gallic; **2** Chimie gallic.

gallium /galjɔm/ *nm* gallium.

gallois, **~e** /galwa, az/ **▶462** **I** *adj* Welsh.

II *nm* Welsh.

Gallois, **~e** /galwa, az/ *nm,f* Welshman/Welshwoman; **les ~** the Welsh.

gallon /galɔ̃/ **▶117** *nm* gallon; **~ améri-**

cain (3,785 l) US gallon; **~ canadien** or **impérial** (4,54 l) imperial gallon.

gallo-romain, **~e** /galɔʀɔmɛ̃, ɛn/ *adj* Gallo-Roman.

Galloway ▶ 692 *nprm* ▶ **Dumfries**.

galoche /galɔʃ/ *nf* (sabot, godillot) clog; **menton en ~** protruding chin.

galon /galɔ̃/ *nm* **1** Cout braid ¢; **bordé d'un ~** trimmed with braid; **2** Mil stripe; **gagner ses ~s** [*personne*] to win promotion; [*système, théorie, méthode*] to gain acceptance; **prendre du ~** [*soldat, civil*] to be promoted.

galonné, **~e** /galɔne/ **I** *pp* ▶ **galonner**.
II *pp adj* **1** Cout [*veste*] trimmed with braid; **2** Mil [*militaire*] of officer class (*épith, après n*); [*manche*] displaying the insignia of rank (*épith, après n*).
III○ *nm* slang brass hat○.

galonner /galɔne/ [1] *vtr* Cout to trim with braid; **galonné d'argent** trimmed with silver braid.

galop /galo/ *nm* **1** Équit gallop; **petit ~** canter; **grand ~** full gallop; **un cheval au ~** a galloping horse; **le cheval est parti au ~** the horse set off at a gallop; **se mettre au ~** to break into a gallop; **faire du ~** to gallop; **au ~!** gallop!; **s'enfuir au (triple) ~**○ [*personne*] to run off double-quick; **vas-y au ~**○! hurry up about it○!; **2** Danse, Mus galop.
■ **~ d'essai** trial run; **~ à faux** counter canter; **~ juste** true canter.
IDIOMES **chassez le naturel il revient au ~** Prov what's bred in the bone will come out in the flesh Prov.

galopade /galɔpad/ *nf* **1** Équit gallop; **2**○ fig (course précipitée) stampede; **3**○ (précipitation) nonstop rush; **hier ça a été la ~** yesterday was a nonstop rush; **4** (course) stampede.

galopant, **~e** /galɔpɑ̃, ɑ̃t/ *adj* [*inflation*] galloping; [*prolifération, démographie*] soaring.

galoper /galɔpe/ [1] *vi* **1** Équit [*cheval, cavalier*] to gallop; **ne laisse pas ~ ton imagination** fig don't let your imagination run away with you; **2**○ (en faisant du bruit) [*enfant*] to charge (around); **3** (se dépêcher) [*adulte*] to dash (around); **j'ai dû ~ toute la journée** I've had to dash around all day.

galopeur, **-euse** /galɔpœʀ, øz/ *nm,f* galloper.

galopin /galɔpɛ̃/ *nm* **1** (enfant) rascal; **petit ~!** you little rascal!; **2** (verre) *small glass of beer*.

galure○ /galyʀ/, **galurin**○ /galyʀɛ̃/ *nm* hat.

galvanique /galvanik/ *adj* [*courant*] galvanic.

galvanisant, **~e** /galvanizɑ̃, ɑ̃t/ *adj* fig galvanizing.

galvanisation /galvanizasjɔ̃/ *nf* **1** Tech galvanizing; **2** Physiol, fig galvanization.

galvaniser /galvanize/ [1] *vtr* lit, fig to galvanize.

galvanisme /galvanism/ *nm* galvanism.

galvanomètre /galvanɔmɛtʀ/ *nm* galvanometer.

galvanoplastie /galvanɔplasti/ *nf* (pour protéger) electroplating; (pour reproduire) electrotyping.

galvanoplastique /galvanɔplastik/ *adj* galvanoplastic.

galvanotype /galvanɔtip/ *nm* electrotype.

galvanotypie /galvanɔtipi/ *nf* electrotyping.

galvaudage /galvodaʒ/ *nm* **1** (de talent) abuse, waste; (de réputation) sullying; **2**† (musardage) loafing around.

galvauder /galvode/ [1] **I** *vtr* to sully [*réputation*]; to dull [*gloire*]; to abuse, to waste [*don, talent*]; to overwork [*idée, théorie, expression*]; to squander [*fortune*]; **expression galvaudée** overused ou hackneyed expression.
II† *vi* (muser) to loaf around.
III se galvauder *vpr* [*personne*] to cheapen oneself.

gamba /gɑ̃ba, *pl* as/ *nf* large (Mediterranean) prawn.

gambade /gɑ̃bad/ *nf* skip; **faire des ~s** to gambol.

gambader /gɑ̃bade/ [1] *vi* **1** [*animal, enfant*] to gambol; **2** [*imagination*] to wander; **ma pensée gambadait** my mind flitted from one thing to another.

gambe /gɑ̃b/ ▶ 534 *nf* **viole de ~** viola da gamba.

gamberge○ /gɑ̃bɛʀʒ/ *nf* hard thought.

gamberger○ /gɑ̃bɛʀʒe/ [13] **I** *vtr* to cook up○ [*plan*].
II *vi* to think hard.

gambette○ /gɑ̃bɛt/ *nf* gam○, leg.

Gambie /gɑ̃bi/ ▶ 321 *nprf* **la ~** the Gambia.

gambien, **-ienne** /gɑ̃bjɛ̃, ɛn/ ▶ 537 *adj* Gambian.

Gambien, **-ienne** /gɑ̃bjɛ̃, ɛn/ ▶ 537 *nm,f* Gambian.

gambiller○ /gɑ̃bije/ [1] *vi* to jig.

gambit /gɑ̃bi/ *nm* gambit.

gamelle /gamɛl/ *nf* (de soldat) dixie GB, mess kit; (de campeur) billycan GB, tin dish; (d'ouvrier) lunchbox; (d'animal) dish.
IDIOMES **prendre** or **ramasser une ~**○ (tomber, échouer) to fall flat on one's face○.

gamète /gamɛt/ *nm* gamete.

gamin, **~e** /gamɛ̃, in/ **I** *adj* [*air, allure*] youthful; [*caractère, attitude*] childish.
II *nm,f* kid○; **un grand ~** a big kid; **ces sales ~s** those nasty kids; **souvenir de ~** childhood memory; **~ des rues** street urchin; **quand il était tout ~** when he was still a kid.

gaminerie /gaminʀi/ *nf* **1** (caractère) (d'homme) boyishness; (de femme) girlishness; **2** (action, propos) childish behaviour[GB], fooling about ¢; **je n'aime pas tes ~s** I don't like your fooling about.

gamma /gama/ *nm inv* gamma.

gammaglobuline /gamaglɔbylin/ *nf* gammaglobulin.

gamme /gam/ *nf* **1** Mus scale; **~ ascendante/descendante** rising/falling scale; **faire ses ~s** Mus to practise[GB] (one's) scales; **monter/descendre la ~** to go up/ to go down the scale; **2** (série) range; **haut/bas/milieu de ~** top/bottom/middle of the range; **produit (de) bas de ~** (en qualité) low quality product; (en prix) cheap product; **modèle/service/projet (de) haut de ~** upmarket model/service/project; **viser le haut/bas de ~** to aim at the top/lower end of the market; **passer par toute la ~ des émotions** to experience the whole gamut of emotions.

gammée /game/ *adj f* **croix ~** swastika.

ganache /ganaʃ/ *nf* **1** Culin chocolate cream filling; **2** Zool (de cheval) lower jaw; **3**† (idiot) **vieille ~** old fool.

Gand /gɑ̃/ ▶ 857 *npr* Ghent.

gandin† /gɑ̃dɛ̃/ *nm* pej dandy.

gang○ /gɑ̃g/ *nm* gang.

Gange /gɑ̃ʒ/ ▶ 357 *nprm* **le ~** the Ganges.

ganglion /gɑ̃glijɔ̃/ *nm* ganglion; **avoir des ~s**○ to have swollen glands.
■ **~ lymphatique** lymph node.

ganglionnaire /gɑ̃glijɔnɛʀ/ *adj* ganglionic.

gangrène /gɑ̃gʀɛn/ ▶ 271 *nf* **1** Méd, Vét gangrene; **2** fig (corruption) canker.

gangrener /gɑ̃gʀəne/ [16] **I** *vtr* fig to corrupt; **milieu gangrené** corrupt environment.
II se gangrener *vpr* **1** Méd, Vét to become gangrenous; **pied gangrené** gangrenous foot; **2** fig to become corrupt.

gangreneux, **-euse** /gɑ̃gʀɛnø, øz/ *adj* gangrenous.

gangster○ /gɑ̃gstɛʀ/ *nm* **1** (bandit) gangster; **2** (escroc) swindler.

gangstérisme○ /gɑ̃gsteʀism/ *nm* organized crime.

gangue /gɑ̃g/ *nf* **1** Minér, Mines gangue; **~ de boue/cendres** coating of mud/ashes; **2** fig **extraire les idées de leur ~** to pick out the good ideas and discard the dross.

ganse /gɑ̃s/ *nf* Cout braid.

ganser /gɑ̃se/ [1] *vtr* to trim [sth] with braid; **gansé de blanc** trimmed with white braid.

gant /gɑ̃/ *nm* glove; **~s de cuir/laine** leather/woollen[GB] gloves; **~s fourrés** fur-lined gloves.
■ **~ de boxe** boxing glove; **~ de caoutchouc** rubber glove; **~ de crin** massage glove; **~ de ménage** rubber glove; **~ de toilette** ≈ (face) flannel GB, wash cloth US.
IDIOMES **son tailleur lui va comme un ~** her suit fits her like a glove; **tes nouvelles fonctions te vont comme un ~** your new duties suit you down to the ground; **mettre** or **prendre des ~s avec qn** to handle sb with kid gloves; **elle n'a pas pris de ~s pour m'annoncer mon renvoi** she didn't pull any punches when telling me I was fired; **jeter/relever le ~** to throw down/to take up the gauntlet.

ganté, **~e** /gɑ̃te/ **I** *pp* ▶ **ganter**.
II *pp adj* [*main*] gloved; [*personne*] wearing gloves (*après n*); **~ de satin** [*main*] satin-gloved (*épith*); [*personne*] wearing satin gloves (*après n*).

gantelet /gɑ̃tlɛ/ *nm* **1** Hist Mil gauntlet; **2** (en fauconnerie) hawking glove.

ganter /gɑ̃te/ [1] **I** *vtr* to put gloves on [*main, personne*].
II se ganter *vpr* to put one's gloves on.

ganterie /gɑ̃tʀi/ ▶ 510 *nf* (fabrique) glove factory; (industrie) glove-making industry; (commerce) glove trade; (boutique) glove shop.

gantier, **-ière** /gɑ̃tje, ɛʀ/ ▶ 510 *nm,f* glover.

Gap /gap/ ▶ 857 *npr* Gap.

gapençais, **~e** /gapɑ̃sɛ, ɛz/ ▶ 857 *adj* of Gap.

Gapençais, **~e** /gapɑ̃sɛ, ɛz/ ▶ 857 *nm,f* (natif) native of Gap; (habitant) inhabitant of Gap.

garage /gaʀaʒ/ *nm* **1** (pour se garer) garage; **rentrer sa voiture au ~** to put one's car in the garage; **2** ▶ 510 (station-service) garage.
■ **~ d'autobus** bus depot; **~ à canots** boathouse; **~ à vélos** bicycle shed; (dans un bâtiment) bicycle storage area.

garagiste /gaʀaʒist/ ▶ 510 *nmf* (propriétaire) garage owner; (ouvrier) car mechanic.

garance /gaʀɑ̃s/ ▶ 193 **I** *adj inv* bright red.
II *nf* (plante, teinture) madder.

garant, **~e** /gaʀɑ̃, ɑ̃t/ **I** *adj* **être** or **se porter ~ de qch/qn** to vouch for sth/sb; **je me porte ~ de leur discrétion** I can vouch for their discretion.
II *nm,f* Fin, Jur, Pol guarantor; **le ~ des institutions** the guarantor of the institutions; **être le ~ d'un prêt** to stand guarantor for a loan.
III *nm* (assurance) guarantee; **être le ~ de** to guarantee; **ta détermination est le ~ de ta popularité** your determination guarantees your popularity.

garanti, **~e** /gaʀɑ̃ti/ **I** *pp* ▶ **garantir**.
II *pp adj* **1** (protégé) with a guarantee (*épith, après n*); **ma voiture d'occasion est ~e six mois** my secondhand car has a six-month guarantee; **2** (certifié) guaranteed; **fromage ~ pur chèvre** guaranteed pure goat's milk cheese; **3** Écon (promis) guaranteed; **prix/salaire ~** guaranteed price/ wage; **4**○ (certain) guaranteed; **échec ~** guaranteed failure.
III garantie *nf* **1** Comm guarantee, warranty; **~e du fabricant** manufacturer's guarantee; **sous ~e** under guarantee; **bon de ~e** guarantee; **2** Fin (négociable) security ¢; (fiduciaire) guarantee; **en ~e** as security; **~e de la Banque de France** guarantee from the Bank of France; **3** Assur cover ¢; **~e responsabilité civile** third-party

cover; **montant des ~es** sum insured; **4** (certitude) guarantee (**de** of); **~e de succès** guarantee of success; **~e contre** guarantee against; **je ne vous donne aucune ~e** I can't give you any guarantee; **offrir toutes les ~es** to give every guarantee; **donner la ~e que** to guarantee that; **5** Jur guarantee; **~es légales** legal guarantees.

garantir /gaʀɑ̃tiʀ/ [3] *vtr* **1** (promettre) to guarantee; **~ à qn qch/que** to guarantee sb sth/that; **je ne vous garantis rien** I can't guarantee you anything; **je ne garantis pas qu'elle soit là** I can't guarantee that she's there; **2** (protéger) to guarantee [*sécurité, indépendance, droit*]; **~ la sécurité et la paix** to guarantee peace and security; **3** (assurer) **~ qch à qn** to guarantee sth to sb; **~ un emploi aux diplômés** to guarantee jobs to graduates; **4** Fin to guarantee [*emprunt, investissement, paiement*]; **5** Comm to guarantee [*produit*].

garbure /gaʀbyʀ/ *nf* soup (*made with cabbage and confit of goose*).

garce◑ /gaʀs/ *nf* bitch◑, cow◑.

garçon /gaʀsɔ̃/ ▶**510** *nm* **1** (enfant, adolescent, fils) boy; **petit ~** little boy; **tu es un grand ~ maintenant** you're a big boy now; **2** (jeune homme) young man, (young) fellow GB, (young) guy; **un brave** or **gentil ~** a nice lad GB ou guy US; **être beau** or **joli ~** to be good-looking, to be a handsome fellow GB ou guy US; ▶**mauvais**; **3** (célibataire) bachelor; **rester ~** to remain single ou a bachelor; **vieux ~** old bachelor; ▶**enterrer**; **4** (serveur) waiter; **5** (employé de magasin) (shop) assistant GB, salesclerk US.

■ **~ d'ascenseur** lift GB ou elevator US attendant; **~ boucher** butcher's assistant; **~ de bureau** office boy; **~ de cabine** Naut cabin steward; **~ de café** waiter; **~ coiffeur** hairdresser's assistant; **~ de courses** messenger; **~ d'écurie** stable lad GB, stableboy; **~ d'étage** floor housekeeper; **~ de ferme** farmhand; **~ d'honneur** best man; **~ de laboratoire** laboratory assistant; **~ livreur** delivery man; **~ manqué** tomboy; **~ de recettes** bank messenger.

garçonne /gaʀsɔn/ *nf* **avoir les cheveux taillés** or **être coiffée à la ~** to have an urchin cut.

garçonnet /gaʀsɔnɛ/ *nm* little boy; **taille/rayon ~** Comm boys' size/department.

garçonnière /gaʀsɔnjɛʀ/ *nf* bachelor flat GB, bachelor apartment US.

Gard /gaʀ/ ▶**357**, **692** *nprm* (rivière, département) **le ~** the Gard.

garde /gaʀd/ ▶**510** **I** *nm* **1** (soldat, policier) guard; **2** (de malade) carer; (de prison) warder.

II *nf* **1** (infirmière) nurse; **2** (groupe) guard; **la vieille ~** fig the old guard; **à moi, la ~!** help! guards!; **3** (surveillance, protection) **monter la ~** [*soldat*] to mount guard; **monter la ~ auprès de** to keep watch over [*prisonnier, malade*]; to stand guard over [*enfant, homme politique*]; **placer/mettre qn sous bonne ~** to put sb under guard [*suspect, prisonnier*]; **être sous la ~ de qn** [*prisonnier*] to be guarded by sb; [*enfant, objet de valeur*] to be looked after by sb; Jur to be in sb's custody; **elle a obtenu la ~ de ses enfants** Jur she was granted custody of her children; **laisser qch/un animal en ~ chez qn** to leave sth/an animal to be looked after by sb; **confier qch/qn à la ~ de X** to leave X to look after sth/sb; **assurer la ~ d'une villa** to be in charge of the security of a villa; **4** (continuité de service) **être de ~** [*docteur, infirmière*] to be on call; [*soldat, sentinelle*] to be on guard duty; **la pharmacie de ~** the duty chemist's GB, the emergency drugstore US; **5** Sport (position de défense) guard, on-guard position; **en ~!** on guard!; **il a une excellente ~** he has an excellent on-guard position; **se mettre en ~** to square up; **baisser sa ~** lit, fig to lower one's guard; **être/se tenir sur ses ~s** to be/to remain on one's guard; **mettre qn en ~** to warn sb (**à propos de** about; **contre** against); **mise en ~** warning; **prendre ~** (se méfier) to watch out (**à** for); (se soucier) to be careful (**de faire** to do); **sans y prendre ~** inadvertently; **n'avoir ~ de faire** fml to be careful not to do; **6** (d'épée) hilt; **jusqu'à la ~** [*plonger, enfoncer*] up to the hilt; **7** Édition (**page de**) **~** endpaper.

■ **~ champêtre** ≈ local policeman (*appointed by the municipality*); **~ du corps** bodyguard; **~ descendante** Mil outgoing guard; **~ d'enfant** childminder GB, day-care lady US; **~ forestier** forest warden, forest ranger; **~ d'honneur** guard of honour^GB; **~ impérial** Hist soldier of the Imperial Guard; **~ impériale** Hist Imperial Guard; **~ montante** Mil new guard, relieving guard; **~ pontifical** member of the papal guard; **~ pontificale** papal guard; **~ républicain** member of the Republican Guard; **~ républicaine** Republican Guard; **~ rouge** Red Guard; **~ des Sceaux** French Minister of Justice; **~ au sol** Aut road clearance; **~ suisse** Swiss Guard; **~ à vue** Jur ≈ police custody; **placer qn en ~ à vue** to hold sb for questioning.

Garde /gaʀd/ ▶**459** *npr* **le lac de ~** Lake Garda.

garde-à-vous /gaʀdavu/ *nm inv* (action) standing to attention; (ordre) **~** (**fixe**)! attention!; **se mettre au ~** to stand to attention.

garde-barrière, *pl* **~s** /gaʀdbaʀjɛʀ/ ▶**510** *nmf* level-crossing keeper GB, gateman (*at grade crossing*) US.

garde-boue /gaʀdəbu/ *nm inv* mudguard.

garde-chasse, *pl* **gardes-chasse(s)** /gaʀdəʃas/ ▶**510** *nm* (de domaine public) game warden; (de domaine privé) gamekeeper.

garde-chiourme /gaʀdəʃjuʀm/ *nm inv* **1** Hist overseer; **2** (surveillant) prison warder.

garde-corps /gaʀdəkɔʀ/ *nm inv* gén guardrail; Naut handrail.

garde-côte, *pl* **~s** /gaʀdəkot/ *nm* (bateau) coastguard ship.

garde-feu /gaʀdəfø/ *nm inv* fire screen.

garde-fou, *pl* **~s** /gaʀdəfu/ *nm* **1** (parapet) parapet; **2** fig safeguard; **ériger** or **dresser un ~ contre** to provide a safeguard against.

garde-frontière, *pl* **gardes-frontières** /gaʀdfʀɔ̃tjɛʀ/ ▶**510** *nm* (personne) border guard.

garde-malade, *pl* **gardes-malades** /gaʀdmalad/ ▶**510** *nmf* home nurse.

garde-manger /gaʀdmɑ̃ʒe/ *nm inv* **1** (armoire grillagée) meat safe; **2** (placard) pantry, larder.

garde-meubles /gaʀdəmœbl/ *nm inv* furniture storage warehouse; **mettre qch au ~** to put sth in store ou storage.

gardénal® /gaʀdenal/ *nm* phenobarbitone GB, phenobarbital US.

gardénia /gaʀdenja/ *nm* gardenia.

garde-pêche /gaʀdəpɛʃ/ ▶**510** *nm inv* (garde) water bailiff GB, game and fish warden US; (bateau) patrol boat.

garder /gaʀde/ [1] **I** *vtr* **1** (conserver, préserver) to keep [*argent, objet*]; to keep [sth] on [*chapeau, vêtement*]; to keep [sb] on [*employé, domestique*]; **~ qch pour soi** to keep sth to oneself [*secret, critiques*]; **il me garde toujours une de ses meilleures bouteilles** he always keeps one of his best bottles for me; **la formule a gardé tout son sens** the phrase has kept all its meaning; **elle m'a gardé une heure dans son bureau/au téléphone** she kept me in her office/on the phone for an hour; **elle a gardé ses enfants auprès d'elle** she kept her children with her; **gardez à votre teint toute sa fraîcheur** keep your complexion fresh (**en faisant** by doing); **pour ~ à votre collection toute sa qualité** to keep your collection in good condition; **un secret bien gardé** a well-kept secret; **ils gardent la suprématie en matière d'électronique** they retain the lead in electronics; **ils nous ont gentiment gardés pour la nuit/à dîner** they kindly asked us to stay overnight/on for dinner; **~ le meilleur pour la fin** to keep the best until last; **~ le lit** to stay in bed; **~ la chambre** to stay indoors; **2** (surveiller, protéger) gén [*soldat, policier, gardien*] to guard; [*personne*] to look after [*maison, enfant, animal, objet*]; **qui garde votre maison/chat/fille?** who's looking after your house/cat/daughter?; **faire ~ ses enfants par qn** to have one's children looked after by sb; **parking gardé** supervised or attended car park; **l'entrepôt est/n'est pas gardé** there's a/there's no security guard at the warehouse.

II se garder *vpr* **1** (éviter) **se ~ de faire** to be careful not to do; **il faut se ~ de conclure trop vite** one should be careful not to jump to conclusions; **il se garde bien de dire ce qu'il pense vraiment** he's careful not to say what he really thinks; **elle s'est bien gardée de répondre directement** she was careful not to answer directly; **ils se sont gardés de tout commentaire/d'un optimisme exagéré** they were wary of making any comment/of being over-optimistic; **je me garde de toute interprétation hâtive** I'm wary of making any hasty interpretation; **2** (se conserver) [*aliment*] to keep; **se ~ un mois** to keep for a month.

garderie /gaʀdəʀi/ *nf* **1** (local) day nursery; **2** (service) after-school child-minding facility.

garde-robe, *pl* **~s** /gaʀdəʀɔb/ *nf* **1** (vêtements, armoire) wardrobe; **2**† (toilettes) water closet†.

garde-voie, *pl* **gardes-voie** /gaʀdəvwa/ ▶**510** *nm* railway line guard GB, railroad guard US.

gardian /gaʀdjɑ̃/ ▶**510** *nm* herdsman (*in the Camargue*).

gardien, **-ienne** /gaʀdjɛ̃, ɛn/ ▶**510** **I** *nm,f* **1** (d'usine, entreprise, de locaux) security guard; (d'hôtel, de château) caretaker; (d'immeuble) caretaker GB, janitor US; (de parc, zoo, square) keeper; (de prison) warder; **2** Sport keeper; **3** (personne qui préserve) fml guardian; **l'Académie, gardienne de la langue** the Academy, guardian of the language; **se faire le ~ des traditions** to set oneself up as a guardian of tradition.

II gardienne *nf* **gardienne** (**d'enfant**) fml childminder GB, day-care lady US.

■ **~ de but** goalkeeper; **~ de musée** museum attendant; **~ de nuit** night watchman; **~ de la paix** police officer; **~ de parking** car park attendant; **~ de phare** lighthouse keeper.

gardiennage /gaʀdjenaʒ/ *nm* (d'immeuble) caretaking; (de bureaux, magasins, d'usines) security; (d'enfant) childminding GB, day care US; **société de ~** security firm; **faire du ~** [*vigile*] to be a security guard.

gardon /gaʀdɔ̃/ *nm* roach.

IDIOMES **être frais comme un ~** to be as fresh as a daisy.

gare /gaʀ/ **I** *nf* (railway) station; **~ d'Oxford** Oxford station; **~ de banlieue** suburban station; **être en ~** [*train*] to be in the station; **entrer en ~** [*train*] to arrive.

II *excl* **1** (pour prévenir) **~** (**à toi**)! watch out!; **~ à ton portefeuille/aux kilos!** watch your wallet/your weight!; **~ aux voleurs!** watch out for thieves!; **~ à l'avenir!** watch what happens in the future!; **~ à ta réputation!** mind your reputation!; **~ de ne pas te faire voler!** mind you don't get robbed!; **~ à qui ferait une erreur!** mind you don't make a mistake!; **mais ~! elle n'est pas bête** be careful! she's no fool; **2** (pour menacer) **~ à toi!** careful!, watch it◑!; **~ aux tricheurs!** anyone who cheats will be in trouble!

■ **~ de marchandises** goods station GB,

freight station US; **~ maritime** harbour[GB] station; **~ routière** (cars) coach station GB, bus station US; (camions) truck depot; **~ de triage** marshalling[GB] yard; **~ de voyageurs** passenger station.
IDIOMES **sans crier ~** without any warning.

garenne /gaʀɛn/ **I** *nm* (lapin) wild rabbit.
II *nf* Chasse private hunting ground; Pêche private fishing area.

garer /gaʀe/ [1] **I** *vtr* **1** Transp to park [*voiture, bus, avion*]; **2** (abriter) to store [*blé, moisson*].
II se garer *vpr* **1** (stationner) to park; **2** (s'écarter) [*véhicule, bateau*] to pull over; [*piéton*] to move out of the way; **3**○ (se protéger) **se ~ de** to avoid [*danger, gens indiscrets, coups*].

Gargantua /gaʀgɑ̃tɥa/ *npr* Gargantua; **un appétit de ~** a gargantuan appetite.

gargantuesque /gaʀgɑ̃tɥɛsk/ *adj* gargantuan.

gargariser: se gargariser /gaʀgaʀize/ [1] *vpr* **1** Méd to gargle; **2**○ fig **se ~ de** to revel in.

gargarisme /gaʀgaʀism/ *nm* (action) gargling; (solution) gargle, mouthwash; **faire des ~s d'eau salée** to gargle with salt water.

gargote /gaʀgɔt/ *nf* cheap eating place, greasy spoon○.

gargotier, -ière /gaʀgɔtje, ɛʀ/ *nm,f* owner of a cheap eating place.

gargouille /gaʀguj/ *nf* (décoratif) gargoyle; (pour la pluie) waterspout.

gargouillement /gaʀgujmɑ̃/ *nm* (d'eau) gurgling ¢; (intestinal) rumbling ¢; **j'ai des ~s** my stomach is rumbling ou growling US.

gargouiller /gaʀguje/ [1] *vi* [*eau, fontaine*] to gurgle; [*ventre*] to rumble, to growl US.

gargouillis /gaʀguji/ *nm inv* = **gargouillement**.

gargoulette /gaʀgulɛt/ *nf* (earthenware) water jug GB, water pitcher US; **boire à la ~** to drink from a jug without letting one's lips touch the spout.

garnement /gaʀnəmɑ̃/ *nm* tearaway GB, brat○.

garni, ~e /gaʀni/ **I** *pp* ▶ **garnir**.
II *pp adj* **1** (rempli) **bien ~** [*portefeuille*] full; [*réfrigérateur*] well-stocked (*épith*); [*buffet*] copious; **une assiette bien ~e** a plateful; **2**† (meublé) [*chambre*] furnished.
III *nm* (chambre) bedsit GB, furnished room; (hôtel) boarding house.

garnir /gaʀniʀ/ [3] **I** *vtr* **1** (remplir) [*personnes, livres, objets, meubles*] to fill [*pièce*]; [*personne*] to stock [*rayons, congélateur, placards*] (**de** with); **une boîte garnie de bonbons** a box filled with sweets GB ou candy US; **2** (rembourrer) to stuff [*coussin, fauteuil*] (**de** with); **3** (couvrir) to line [*coffret, tiroir*] (**de qch** with sth); to cover [*siège*] (**de** with); **des sièges garnis de cuir** seats with leather upholstery; **4** Mode (orner) to trim [*robe, tissu*] (**de** with); (doubler) to line [*vêtement*] (**de** with); **5** Culin (décorer) to decorate [*dessert, gâteau, table*] (**de** with); to garnish [*viande, poisson*] (**de** with); **~ de fraises/fleurs** to decorate with strawberries/flowers; **garnissez la viande de légumes** serve the meat with vegetables.
II se garnir *vpr* [*salle, stade*] to fill up (**de** with).

garnison /gaʀnizɔ̃/ *nf* Mil garrison; **ville de ~** garrison town; **être en ~ à Metz** to be garrisoned at Metz.

garniture /gaʀnityʀ/ *nf* **1** Culin (accompagnement) side dish; (décoration) (de dessert) decoration; (de viande, poisson) garnish; **servir avec une ~ de légumes** serve with vegetables as a side dish; **pour la ~ mettez des fraises et des framboises** decorate with strawberries and raspberries; **~ de persil** garnish of parsley; **2** Mode (sur un chapeau, une robe) trimming; **3** (dans un coffret, tiroir) lining; **une belle ~ rouge** a nice red lining; **4** Aut (sellerie) upholstery.
■ **~ de bureau** desk accessories (*pl*); **~ de cheminée** mantelpiece ornaments (*pl*); **~ d'embrayage** Aut clutch lining; **~ de feu** or **foyer** fire irons (*pl*); **~ de frein** Aut brake lining; **~ hygiénique** sanitary towel.

Garonne /gaʀɔn/ ▶ **357**, **692** *nprf* **la ~** the Garonne.

garrigue /gaʀig/ *nf* garrigue, scrubland (*in southern France*).

garrot /gaʀo/ *nm* **1** Méd tourniquet; **poser un ~ à qn** to put a tourniquet on sb; **2** Zool (de quadrupède) withers (*pl*); **le cheval mesure 1,50 m au ~** ≈ the horse is 15 hands; **3** Tech (de corde) tightening peg; **4** (instrument de supplice) garrotte.

garrotter /gaʀɔte/ [1] *vtr* **1** (lier) to tie up [*prisonnier*]; to bind [*bras, jambes*]; **2** fig (bâillonner) to muzzle, to gag [*peuple*]; to stifle [*opposition, liberté*]; **3** (supplicier) to garrotte.

gars○ /ga/ *nm* (garçon, jeune homme) lad GB, boy; (type) guy○, bloke○ GB; **salut les ~!** hi lads GB ou guys○!

Gascogne /gaskɔɲ/ ▶ **692** *nprf* **la ~** Gascony; **le golfe de ~** the Bay of Biscay.

gascon, -onne /gaskɔ̃, ɔn/ **I** *adj* Gascon.
II ▶ **462** *nm* Ling Gascon.

Gascon, -onne /gaskɔ̃, ɔn/ *nm,f* Gascon.
IDIOMES **faire une offre de ~** to raise false hopes.

gasconnade /gaskɔnad/ *nf* (histoire) boast, boastful story; (vantardise) bragging ¢; **dire des ~s** to brag.

gas-oil /gazwal/ *nm* diesel (oil).

gaspacho /gaspatʃo/ *nm* gazpacho.

Gaspésie /gaspezi/ ▶ **692** *nprf* Gaspé Peninsula.

gaspillage /gaspijaʒ/ *nm* (par négligence) (action) wasting; (conséquence) waste; **quel ~!** what a waste!; **c'est du ~** it's wasteful; (par prodigalité) squandering.

gaspiller /gaspije/ [1] *vtr* **1** (gâcher) to waste [*temps, argent, nourriture*]; **c'est de l'argent gaspillé** it's a waste of money; **ne gaspille pas tant** don't be so wasteful; **2** (dissiper) to squander [*forces, talent, ressources*].

gaspilleur, -euse /gaspijœʀ, øz/ **I** *adj* wasteful.
II *nm,f* gén waster; (dilapidateur) squanderer; **quel ~ tu fais!** how wasteful you are!

gastéropode /gasteʀɔpɔd/ *nm* gastropod; **les ~s** Gastropoda.

gastralgie /gastʀalʒi/ *nf* gastralgia.

gastralgique /gastʀalʒik/ *adj* gastralgic.

gastrique /gastʀik/ *adj* gastric.

gastrite /gastʀit/ ▶ **271** *nf* gastritis ¢.

gastro-entérite, *pl* **~s** /gastʀoɑ̃teʀit/ ▶ **271** *nf* gastroenteritis ¢.

gastro-entérologie /gastʀoɑ̃teʀɔlɔʒi/ *nf* gastroenterology.

gastro-entérologue, *pl* **~s** /gastʀo ɑ̃teʀɔlɔg/ ▶ **510** *nmf* gastroenterologist.

gastro-intestinal, **~e**, *mpl* **-aux** /gastʀoɛ̃tɛstinal, o/ *adj* gastrointestinal.

gastronome /gastʀɔnɔm/ *nmf* gourmet, gastronome.

gastronomie /gastʀɔnɔmi/ *nf* gastronomy.

gastronomique /gastʀɔnɔmik/ *adj* gourmet (*épith*), gastronomic.

gastropode /gastʀɔpɔd/ *nm* = **gastéropode**.

gastroscopie /gastʀɔskɔpi/ *nf* gastroscopy.

gâteau, *pl* **~x** /gɑto/ **I** *adj inv* [*papa, mamie*] doting.
II *nm* **1** Culin cake; **~ d'anniversaire** birthday cake; **2**○ fig (butin) spoils (*pl*); **se tailler une part du ~** to take one's share of the spoils; **se partager le ~** to divide the spoils; **obtenir 5% du ~ électoral** to obtain 5% of the votes; **3** Tech (masse compacte) cake.
■ **~ apéritif** cocktail biscuit; **~ au chocolat** chocolate cake; **~ de cire** honeycomb; **~ marbré** marble cake; **~ de miel** = **~ de cire**; **~ de riz** rice pudding; **~ salé** = **~ apéritif**; **~ sec** biscuit GB, cookie US; **~ de semoule** semolina pudding.
IDIOMES **c'est du ~**○! it's a piece of cake○!; **c'est pas du ~**○! it's no picnic!

gâter /gɑte/ [1] **I** *vtr* **1** (choyer) to spoil [*enfant, personne*]; **un enfant gâté** a spoiled child; **on a été gâtés côté temps** we've been very lucky with the weather; **il n'a pas été gâté par la nature** iron he hasn't been blessed by Nature; **2** (abîmer) to ruin, to spoil [*fruit*]; to ruin [*dent*]; to spoil [*paysage*]; **3** (gâcher) to spoil [*plaisir*]; **il est intelligent et beau, ce qui ne gâte rien** he's intelligent, and handsome into the bargain.
II se gâter *vpr* **1** (s'abîmer) [*viande*] to go bad, to go off GB; [*fruit, dent*] to rot; **avoir les dents gâtées** to have bad teeth; **2** (se détériorer) [*situation*] to take a turn for the worse; [*temps*] to change for the worse; **ça se gâte!** fig there's going to be trouble!

gâterie /gɑtʀi/ *nf* little treat.

gâteux, -euse /gɑtø, øz/ **I** *adj* (avec l'âge) senile; fig **il est ~ avec sa fille** fig he's dotty about his daughter○.
II *nm,f* (personne sénile) senile person; **vieux ~**○ old dodderer○.

gâtifier○ /gɑtifje/ [2] *vi* to go all soppy○ (**avec qn** with sb).

gâtisme /gɑtism/ ▶ **271** *nm* (sénilité) senility; **être atteint de ~** to be senile.

GATT /gat/ *nm* (*abbr* = **General Agreement on Tariffs and Trade**) GATT.

gauche /goʃ/ ▶ **445** **I** *adj* **1** gén [*œil, main etc*] left; **la partie/le côté ~ de qch** the left-hand part/side of sth; **2** (maladroit) [*personne, manières*] awkward; [*style*] clumsy; **d'un air ~** [*demander, s'excuser*] awkwardly; **3** (déformé) [*objet en bois*] warped; [*objet en métal*] bent; **4** Math [*courbe*] skew.
II *nm* (en boxe) left-hander.
III *nf* **1** (côté) **la ~** the left; **de ~ à droite** from left to right; **à ~** [*être, rouler*] on the left; [*rester, aller, regarder*] to the left; [*tourner*] left; **tenir sa ~** to keep to the left; **à ~ de** to the left of; **à ma/votre ~** on my/your left; **en bas/haut à ~** in the bottom/top left-hand corner; **de ~** [*page, mur, trottoir, file*] left-hand; **2** Pol Left; **victoire pour la ~** victory for the Left; **voter à ~** to vote for the Left; **de ~** [*gouvernement, idée, journaliste*] left-wing; **être de** or **à ~** to be left-wing; **la ~ du parti libéral** the left wing of the liberal party.
IDIOMES **passer l'arme à ~**○ to kick the bucket○; **se lever du pied ~**○ to get out of bed on the wrong side GB, to get up on the wrong side of the bed US; **jusqu'à la ~**○ completely, thoroughly; **avoir de l'argent à ~** to have money stashed away; **mettre de l'argent à ~**○ to put money aside.

gauchement /goʃmɑ̃/ *adv* awkwardly.

gaucher, -ère /goʃe, ɛʀ/ **I** *adj* left-handed.
II *nm,f* left-handed person; **~ contrarié** naturally left-handed person (*forced to write with their right hand*).

gaucherie /goʃʀi/ *nf* awkwardness; **leur ~ est telle que** they are so awkward that.

gauchir /goʃiʀ/ [3] **I** *vtr* to warp [*objet en bois*]; to bend [*objet en métal*].
II *vi* [*objet en bois*] to become warped; [*objet en métal*] to become bent.

gauchisant, ~e /goʃizɑ̃, ɑ̃t/ *adj* [*journal, groupe*] leftish (*épith*); **être ~** to have leftish tendencies.

gauchisme /goʃism/ *nm* leftism.

gauchiste /goʃist/ *adj, nmf* leftist.

gaudriole /godʀijɔl/ *nf* **1** (propos) broad joke; **2**○ (débauche) debauchery.

gaufrage /gofʀaʒ/ *nm* (de cuir, tissu, papier) (en relief) embossing; (pour donner un aspect froissé) crinkling.

gaufre /gofʀ/ *nf* **1** Culin waffle; **2** Zool honeycomb.

gaufrer /gofʀe/ [1] *vtr* (imprimer en relief) to emboss [*velours, cuir, papier*]; (donner un aspect froissé) to crinkle [*coton, papier, cuir*]; ▶ **fer**.

gaufrette /gofʀɛt/ *nf* wafer.

gaufrier /gofʀije/ *nm* waffle iron US.

gaufrure /gofʀyʀ/ *nf* embossing ¢.

gaulage /golaʒ/ *nm* **le ~ des noix** knocking walnuts out of the tree with a pole.

gaule /gol/ *nf* **1** (pour récolter les noix) long thin pole; (de bouvier, vacher) switch; **2** (de pêcheur) fishing rod.

Gaule /gol/ *nprf* Gaul.

gauler /gole/ [1] *vtr* **1** Agric **~ un noyer** to knock the nuts out of a walnut tree; **2**○ to catch; **se faire ~** to get caught; (par la police) to get nicked○ GB ou nabbed○.

gaullien, **-ienne** /goljɛ̃, ɛn/ *adj* **le style ~** the de Gaulle style.

gaullisme /golism/ *nm* Gaullism.

gaulliste /golist/ *adj, nmf* Gaullist.

gaulois, **~e** /golwa, az/ **I** *adj* **1** Hist Gallic; **2** (paillard) [*histoire, propos*] bawdy.
II ▶ **462** *nm* Ling Gaulish.

Gaulois, **~e** /golwa, az/ *nm,f* Gaul.

gauloisement /golwazmɑ̃/ *adv* bawdily.

gauloiserie /golwazʀi/ *nf* **1** (plaisanterie) bawdy joke; **2** (caractère paillard) bawdiness.

gausser: **se gausser** /gose/ [1] *vpr* liter (railler) to mock; (plaisanter) **vous vous gaussez!** you are joking!; **se ~ de** to laugh at, to mock.

gavage /gavaʒ/ *nm* (des oies) force-feeding.

gave /gav/ *nm* mountain stream.

gaver /gave/ [1] **I** *vtr* **1** (nourrir) to force-feed [*oies*]; to stuff [sb] with food [*personne*]; **~ qn de gâteaux** to stuff sb with cakes; **être gavé** to be full up; **2** fig **~ qn d'âneries** to cram sb's head with silly ideas; **~ qn de publicité** to bombard sb with advertising.
II se gaver *vpr* **1** (se nourrir) to stuff oneself (**de** with); **2** fig **se ~ de** to devour [*romans, émissions*].

gavotte /gavɔt/ *nf* gavotte.

gavroche /gavʀɔʃ/ **I** *adj inv* [*air*] cheeky, sassy○ US.
II *nm* street urchin.

gay /gɛ/ *adj inv, nm* gay, homosexual.

gaz /gaz/ **I** *nm inv* **1** Ind, Minér (domestique) gas; **baisser le ~** to turn down the gas; **cuisiner au ~** to cook with gas; **avoir le ~** to have gas; **se chauffer au ~** to have gas heating; **chaudière/compteur à ~** gas boiler/meter; **cuisinière à ~** gas stove, gas cooker GB; **2** Chimie gas; **à l'état de ~** [*corps*] in its gaseous state; **3**○ Sport (en alpinisme) **il y a du ~** there's a lot of space there.
II *nmpl* **1** Mécan air-fuel mixture (*sg*); **mettre les ~**○ fig to step on the gas○; **rouler à pleins ~**○ to go at full throttle; **le projet marche (à) pleins ~**○ the project is firing on all cylinders○; **2** Physiol wind (*sg*); **avoir des ~** to have wind.
■ **~ asphyxiant** asphyxiating gas ¢; **~ butane** butane gas; **~ carbonique** carbon dioxide; **~ de combat** poison gas ¢; **~ d'échappement** Aut exhaust fumes (*pl*); **~ hilarant** laughing gas; **~ lacrymogène** teargas; **~ des marais** marsh gas; **~ moutarde** mustard gas; **~ naturel** natural gas; **~ parfait** ideal gas; **~ rare** rare gas; **~ sulfureux** sulphur[GB] dioxide; **~ de ville** mains gas.
IDIOMES **il y a de l'eau dans le ~**○ there's trouble brewing.

Gaza /gaza/ ▶ **857** *npr* Gaza; **la bande de ~** the Gaza Strip.

gazage /gazaʒ/ *nm* gassing ¢.

gaze /gɑz/ *nf* gauze; **une compresse/bande de ~** a gauze compress/bandage.

gazé, **~e** /gaze/ **I** *pp* ▶ **gazer**.
II *pp adj* **soldat ~** soldier who was gassed.
III *nm,f* Mil gas victim.

gazéification /gazeifikasjɔ̃/ *nf* **1** (de boisson) carbonation; **2** (de produit carboné) gasification.

gazéifier /gazeifje/ [2] *vtr* **1** (rendre pétillant) to carbonate [*boisson*]; **2** (transformer en gaz) to gasify.

gazelle /gazɛl/ *nf* gazelle; **des yeux de ~** doe eyes.

gazer /gaze/ [1] **I** *vtr* (asphyxier) to gas.
II○ *vi* **ça gaze?** how's things○?; **oui, ça gaze** things are fine.

gazetier, **-ière** /gaztje, ɛʀ/ *nm,f* journalist.

gazette /gazɛt/ *nf* **1** (journal) newspaper; hum rag; **2** (personne) gossip; **la ~ du quartier** the local gossip; **faire la ~ de** or **sur**○ to give the info on○.

gazeux, **-euse** /gazø, øz/ *adj* **1** [*boisson*] fizzy; **eau gazeuse** (naturelle) sparkling mineral water; (gazéifiée) carbonated water; **2** Chimie, Phys gaseous.

gazier, **-ière** /gazje, ɛʀ/ **I** *adj* gas (*épith*); **industrie gazière** gas industry.
II ▶ **510** *nm* (ouvrier) gas worker; (agent) gasman.

gazinière /gazinjɛʀ/ *nf* gas cooker GB, gas stove.

gazoduc /gazɔdyk/ *nm* gas pipeline.

gazogène /gazɔʒɛn/ *nm* (générateur) gas generator.

gazole /gazɔl/ *nm* diesel (oil) GB, fuel oil US.

gazoline /gazɔlin/ *nf* gasoline.

gazomètre /gazɔmɛtʀ/ *nm* gasometer.

gazon /gazɔ̃/ *nm* **1** (herbe) grass, turf; (en plaque) turf; **une plaque de ~** a piece of turf; **2** (pelouse) lawn; **tennis sur ~** lawn tennis; **jouer sur ~** to play on grass courts.

gazonner /gazɔne/ [1] *vtr* to turf, to grass.

gazouillement /gazujmɑ̃/ *nm* (d'oiseau) twittering ¢; (de bébé, source) babbling ¢.

gazouiller /gazuje/ [1] *vi* [*oiseau*] to twitter; [*bébé, source*] to babble.

gazouilleur, **-euse** /gazujœʀ, øz/ *adj* [*oiseau*] twittering; [*bébé, source*] babbling.

gazouillis /gazuji/ *nm inv* = **gazouillement**.

GB (*written abbr* = **Grande-Bretagne**) GB.

gdb○ /ʒedebe/ *nf*: *abbr* ▶ **gueule**.

GDF /ʒedeɛf/ (*abbr* = **Gaz de France**) French Gas Board.

geai /ʒɛ/ *nm* jay.

géant, **~e** /ʒeɑ̃, ɑ̃t/ **I** *adj* **1** (démesuré) huge, enormous; **2** (de grande taille) giant; **raie ~e** giant ray; **3** Comm, Pub [*paquet*] jumbo; **4**○ (extraordinaire) **c'est ~!** it's brilliant GB ou great!
II *nm* lit, fig giant; **~ de l'industrie** industrial giant.
III géante *nf* giantess.

gecko /ʒeko/ *nm* gecko.

géhenne /ʒeɛn/ *nf* **la ~** Gehenna.

Geiger /ʒeʒɛʀ/ *npr* **compteur ~** Geiger counter.

geignard, **~e** /ʒɛɲaʀ, aʀd/ **I** *adj* [*personne*] moaning; [*enfant*] whining; [*ton, musique*] wailing.
II *nm,f* moaner, whiner.

geignement /ʒɛɲəmɑ̃/ *nm* (plainte) moan, groan.

geindre /ʒɛ̃dʀ/ [55] *vi* [*malade*] to moan, to groan; (faiblement) to whimper; [*pleurnichard*] to whine; [*mécontent*] to moan; [*violon*] to wail; [*meuble*] to creak.

geisha /gɛʃa/ *nf* geisha (girl).

gel /ʒɛl/ *nm* **1** Météo frost; **protection contre le ~** protection from frost; **résistant au ~** frost-resistant; **2** Écon (blocage au niveau atteint) **~ de** freeze on; **~ des subventions** freeze on subsidies; **~ des prix/salaires** price/wage freeze; **~ des terres** set-aside; **3** Fin (immobilisation) freezing; **~ des avoirs** freezing of assets; **4** (suspension) putting on ice; **après le ~ du projet, il a fallu faire** after the project had been put on ice it became necessary to do; **5** Chimie, Cosmét, Pharm gel; **~ contraceptif** contraceptive gel; **~ coiffant** hair gel; **~ de silice** silica gel; **6** Tech freezing; **~ des tuyauteries** freezing of pipes.

gélatine /ʒelatin/ *nf* gelatine GB, gelatin US; **~ en poudre/en feuilles** gelatine GB ou gelatin US powder/leaves.

gélatineux, **-euse** /ʒelatinø, øz/ *adj* gelatinous.

gelé, **~e** /ʒəle/ **I** *pp* ▶ **geler**.
II *pp adj* **1** (durci par le froid) [*eau, sol, personne, pied*] frozen; **2** (très froid) **j'ai les oreilles ~es** my ears are frozen; **3** Méd [*orteil, phalange*] frost-bitten; **4** Écon, Fin, Pol [*prix, avoirs, négociation*] frozen.
III gelée *nf* **1** Culin (de fruit) jelly; (de viande, poisson) (suc naturel) gelatinous stock; (préparation) aspic; **~e de cassis** blackcurrant jelly; **ma ~e n'a pas pris** my jelly has not set; **œuf/poulet en ~e** egg/chicken in aspic; **2** Cosmét gel; **~e hydratante** moisturizing gel; **3** Météo frost; **~es matinales** early morning frosts.
■ **~e blanche** Météo hoarfrost; **~e royale** Pharm royal jelly.

geler /ʒəle/ [17] **I** *vtr* **1** (durcir) to freeze [*eau, sol*]; **2** (endommager) to freeze [*doigt, pied*]; to nip [*plante*]; **3** (bloquer) to freeze [*salaire, prix*]; **4** (suspendre) to suspend [*projet, production, processus*]; **5** Fin (immobiliser) to freeze [*compte, avoirs*].
II *vi* **1** (se solidifier) [*eau, sol*] to freeze; **2** (être endommagé) [*doigt, pied*] to freeze; [*plante*] to be frosted; **3**○ (avoir froid) to be freezing; **on gèle** it's freezing; **4** Jeux (être loin, à cache-tampon) **tu gèles!** you're freezing!
III se geler *vpr* **1**○ (avoir froid) to freeze; **se ~ les fesses**○ or **le cul**● to freeze to death; **on se les gèle**● it's bloody◑ GB ou damn○ US freezing; **2** Méd **il s'est gelé un orteil** he got frostbite in one toe.
IV *v impers* to freeze; **il** or **ça gèle** it's freezing; **il gèle à pierre fendre** it's absolutely freezing.

gélifiant /ʒelifjɑ̃/ *nm* gelling agent.

gélifier /ʒelifje/ [2] **I** *vtr* to gel.
II se gélifier *vpr* to gel.

gélinotte /ʒelinɔt/ *nf* hazel grouse.

gélose /ʒeloz/ *nf* agar-agar.

gélule /ʒelyl/ *nf* capsule.

Gémeaux /ʒemo/ ▶ **874** *nprmpl* Gemini.

gémellaire /ʒemɛl(l)ɛʀ/ *adj* **grossesse ~** twin pregnancy.

gémellité /ʒemelite/ *nf* (de grossesse) twinbirth; (de frères, sœurs) twinhood.

gémination /ʒeminasjɔ̃/ *nf* gemination.

géminé, **~e** /ʒemine/ **I** *adj* **1** Biol, Bot, Ling geminate; **2** Archit gemelled[GB].
II géminée *nf* Ling geminate.

gémir /ʒemiʀ/ [3] *vi* [*malade*] to moan, to groan (**de** with); (faiblement) to whimper; [*pleurnichard*] to moan; [*plancher, meuble*] to creak; (sous un poids) to groan; [*vent*] to moan; **d'une voix gémissante** in a whining voice.

gémissement /ʒemismɑ̃/ *nm* (de personne) moan; (plus fort) groan (**de** of); (prolongé) moaning ¢, groaning ¢; (de plancher) creak; (prolongé) creaking ¢; (du vent) moan.

gemme /ʒɛm/ *nf* **1** (pierre) gem, gemstone; **2** (résine) resin.

gemmer /ʒɛme/ [1] *vtr* to tap [sth] for resin [*pin*].

gémonies /ʒemɔni/ *nfpl* **vouer qn aux ~** to expose sb to public contempt.

gênant, **~e** /ʒɛnɑ̃, ɑ̃t/ *adj* **1** (incommode) [*meuble, jouet, carton*] cumbersome; [*problème, bruit*] annoying; [*odeur*] unpleasant; **j'irai à pied, ce n'est pas ~** I'll walk, it's no problem; **c'est ~ ce bureau au milieu de la pièce** this desk in the middle of the room is a nuisance; **2** (qui met mal à l'aise) [*question, commentaire, témoin, situation*] embarrassing; **tous ces cadeaux, c'est ~!** all these presents, it's embarrassing!; **ce qui est ~ c'est que** the embarrassing thing is that.

gencive /ʒɑ̃siv/ *nf* gum; ▶ **plein**.

IDIOMES **prendre un coup dans les ~s**○ to be kicked in the teeth○.

gendarme /ʒɑ̃daʀm/ **▶ 510** *nm* **1** Mil gendarme, French policeman; **jouer aux ~s et aux voleurs** to play cops and robbers; **la peur du ~** fig the fear of authority; **jouer les ~s du monde** fig to act the role of world policeman; **2** (personne autoritaire) **quel ~!** what a bossy person!; **je n'ai pas envie de faire le ~** I don't want to have to lay down the law; **3** (organe de surveillance) watchdog; **4** Zool (punaise) stinkbug; **5** Culin (saucisson) dried sausage.

■ **~ couché** road hump, sleeping policeman GB; **~ mobile** Mil member of mobile police unit.

gendarmer: **se gendarmer** /ʒɑ̃daʀme/ [1] *vpr* to protest (**contre** about).

gendarmerie /ʒɑ̃daʀm(ə)ʀi/ *nf* **1** (bureaux) police station; **2** (logement) police quarters (*pl*); **3** (corps) **~ (nationale)** gendarmerie, French police force.

■ **~ mobile** Mil mobile police unit.

gendre /ʒɑ̃dʀ/ *nm* son-in-law.

gène /ʒɛn/ *nm* gene.

gêne /ʒɛn/ *nf* **1** (embarras) embarrassment; **j'ai senti une ~ dans l'assistance** I could sense that the audience was embarrassed; **éprouver de la ~** to feel embarrassed; **sans aucune** or **la moindre ~** without the least hint of embarrassment; **il n'y a pas de ~ à avoir** there's nothing to be embarrassed about; **2** (physique) discomfort; **sensation** or **impression de ~** feeling of discomfort; **ressentir une ~ à l'articulation du genou** to feel some discomfort in one's knee joint; **ressentir** or **éprouver une ~ en avalant/respirant** to have difficulty swallowing/breathing; **~ respiratoire** breathing difficulties (*pl*); **3** (nuisance) inconvenience; **la ~ occasionnée par la grève** the inconvenience caused by the strike; **~ visuelle/phonique** visual/sound disturbance; **4** (pauvreté) poverty; **vivre dans la ~** to live in poverty.

IDIOMES **là où il y a de la ~ il n'y a pas de plaisir** it's a pity to spoil somebody's pleasure.

gêné, **~e** /ʒene/ **I** *pp* ▶ **gêner**.

II *pp adj* **1** (mal à l'aise) [*personne, regard, silence*] embarrassed; **avoir l'air/se sentir un peu ~** to seem/to feel somewhat embarrassed; **pas ~e, elle m'est passée devant** she pushed in front of me, not in the least bit embarrassed; **il n'est pas ~ celui-là**○**!** he's got a hell of a○ nerve!; **2** (engoncé) **il est ~ dans sa veste** his jacket is too tight for him; **3** (désargenté) short of money; **je suis un peu ~ ce mois-ci** I'm a bit short of money this month.

généalogie /ʒenealɔʒi/ *nf* genealogy.

généalogique /ʒenealɔʒik/ *adj* genealogical; **livres ~s** Biol genealogy books; **arbre ~** family tree.

généalogiste /ʒenealɔʒist/ **▶ 510** *nmf* genealogist.

génépi /ʒenepi/ *nm* Bot genépi; (alcool) genépi liqueur.

gêner /ʒene/ [1] **I** *vtr* **1** (déranger sérieusement) [*personne*] to disturb [*personne*]; (déranger par sa présence, sa conversation) [*personne*] to bother [*personne*]; **tu gênes tout le monde avec ta musique!** you're disturbing everyone with your music!; **si je te gêne je peux m'en aller** if I'm bothering you, I'll go away; **ça te gêne si j'allume?** do you mind if I switch the light on?; **cela ne me gêne pas** I don't mind (**de faire** doing); **tu crois que ça le gênerait de dire pardon?** iron do you think it'd hurt him to say sorry?; **oui je fume, et alors, ça te gêne?** yes I smoke, so what?; **2** (incommoder) [*fumée, bruit, lumière*] to bother; **baisse le store, le soleil me gêne** lower the blind, the sun is bothering me; **3** (mettre mal à l'aise) [*question, regard, personne*] to embarrass [*personne*]; **ne dis pas ça, tu me gênes!** don't say that, you're embarrassing me!; **ça me gêne d'accepter** I don't really like to accept; **si cela te gêne de les appeler, je le ferai** if you don't like to call them, I'll do it; **cela me gêne d'avoir à te le rappeler mais...** I hate to have to remind you, but...; **4** (entraver) [*pluie, tempête*] to disrupt [*événement*]; [*voiture*] to block [*circulation*]; [*ceinture*] to restrict [*respiration*]; [*personne*] to be in the way of [*discussion, progrès*]; [*obstacle*] to hamper [*progrès, procession*]; **la neige gênait la progression des marcheurs** the snow hampered the walkers' progress; **tu gênes la circulation garé de cette façon** you're blocking the traffic by parking like that; **~ le passage** to be in the way; **rien n'est venu ~ les négociations** nothing got in the way of the negotiations; **pousse-toi, tu me gênes** get out of my way; **les chiffres gênent la compréhension du texte** the figures make the text difficult to understand; **5** (faire mal) [*caillou, ceinture*] to hurt [*personne*]; **quelque chose dans ma chaussure me gêne** something in my shoe is hurting me.

II se gêner *vpr* **1** (se bousculer) [*personnes*] to get in each other's way; **à trois dans la cuisine on se gêne** three people in the kitchen only get in each other's way; **on tient à quatre sans se ~** it can hold four people comfortably; **2** (faire des façons) **pourquoi se ~?** why hesitate?; **je ne me suis pas gênée pour le leur rappeler**○ I made a point of reminding them; **je vais me ~ tiens**○ iron see if I don't; **ne vous gênez pas pour moi, continuez** iron don't mind me, carry on GB ou continue.

général, **~e**, *mpl* **-aux** /ʒeneʀal, o/ **I** *adj* **1** (collectif) general; **accord/sentiment/mouvement ~** general agreement/feeling/movement; **de l'avis ~** in most people's opinion; **dans l'intérêt ~** in the public interest; **à la surprise/satisfaction ~e** to everyone's surprise/satisfaction; **2** (d'ensemble) general; **situation/caractéristique/réforme ~e** general situation/feature/reform; **en ~, de façon** or **d'une manière ~e** generally, in general; **la réunion a lieu en ~ le soir** the meeting generally takes place in the evening; **en Chine et en ~ en Asie** in China and more generally in Asia; **parler en ~** to speak in general terms; **l'humanité en ~** humankind in general; **en règle ~e** as a rule; **en règle ~e les soins sont gratuits** as a rule medical care is free.

II ▶ 390 *nm* **1** Mil general; **mon ~!** general!; **le ~ Grunard** General Grunard; **2** Relig (supérieur) general; **3** Philos general; **le ~ et le particulier** the general and the particular.

III générale *nf* **1** Théât dress rehearsal; **2** (épouse de général) general's wife.

■ **~ d'armée** Mil general; **~ d'armée aérienne** Mil ≈ air chief marshal GB, ≈ general US; **~ de brigade** Mil ≈ brigadier GB, ≈ brigadier general US; **~ de brigade aérienne** Mil ≈ air commodore GB, ≈ brigadier general US; **~ de corps aérien** Mil ≈ air marshal GB, ≈ lieutenant general US; **~ de corps d'armée** Mil ≈ lieutenant general; **~ de division** Mil ≈ major general; **~ de division aérienne** Mil ≈ air vice marshal GB, ≈ major general US.

généralement /ʒeneʀalmɑ̃/ *adv* generally; **plus ~** more generally; **elle se lève tôt ~** she generally gets up early; **octobre est ~ doux** October is generally mild.

généralisable /ʒeneʀalizabl/ *adj* which can be generalized (*épith, après n*) (**à** to apply to); **l'expérience est ~ à d'autres domaines** the experiment can be generalized to apply to other fields.

généralisateur, **-trice** /ʒeneʀalizatœʀ, tʀis/ *adj* **propos ~s** generalizations; **principe ~** generalized principle; **avoir l'esprit ~** to tend to generalize.

généralisation /ʒeneʀalizasjɔ̃/ *nf* **1** (systématisation) (de politique, d'impôt) general implementation; (de vaccination) widespread administration; (de langue) general use; **2** (déduction) generalization; **~ grossière** gross generalization; **3** (de maladie, grève) spread.

généralisé, **~e** /ʒeneʀalize/ **I** *pp* ▶ **généraliser**.

II *pp adj* [*conflit, pessimisme, corruption*] widespread; [*processus, surproduction*] general; [*cancer*] generalized.

généraliser /ʒeneʀalize/ [1] **I** *vtr* to make [sth] general [*impôt, vaccination, examen*]; to put [sth] into general use [*méthode*].

II *vi* to generalize; **ne généralisez pas** do not generalize.

III se généraliser *vpr* [*technique*] to become standard; [*impôt*] to become widely applicable; [*phénomène, grève, maladie*] to spread (**à** to).

généralissime /ʒeneʀalisim/ *nm* generalissimo.

généraliste /ʒeneʀalist/ **I** *adj* [*chaîne, revue, ingénieur*] non-specialized; [*conception*] broad; **médecin ~** general practitioner.

II ▶ 510 *nmf* general practitioner, GP GB.

généralité /ʒeneʀalite/ *nf* **1** (notion générale) generality; **se perdre dans les ~s** to get lost in generalities; **2** (règle générale) **devenir ~** to become general.

générateur, **-trice** /ʒeneʀatœʀ, tʀis/ **I** *adj* **1** (créateur) **~ de** which generates; **être ~ de** to generate; **2** (servant à engendrer) generative; **élément ~** Math generator.

II *nm* Ordinat, Tech generator.

III génératrice *nf* Électrotech generator; Math generatrix.

■ **~ d'états** Ordinat report program generator; **~ isotopique** Nucl radio isotope power generator; **~ d'ozone** ozonator; **~ de vapeur** steam boiler.

génératif, **-ive** /ʒeneʀatif, iv/ *adj* Ling generative.

génération /ʒeneʀasjɔ̃/ *nf* **1** (dans une famille) generation; **de ~ en ~** from generation to generation, through the generations; **ils sont en France depuis deux ~s** they've been in France for two generations; **immigré de première/seconde ~** first-/second-generation immigrant; **la ~ de ma grand-mère** my grandmother's generation; **le fossé des ~s** the generation gap; **2** (personnes du même âge) generation; **la nouvelle ~** the new generation; **la jeune ~** the younger generation; **les peintres de leur ~** painters of their generation; **la ~ romantique/politique** the romantic/political generation; **3** (stade du progrès technique) generation; **une nouvelle ~ d'avions/d'ordinateurs** a new generation of aircraft/of computers; **ordinateur de la cinquième ~** fifth-generation computer; **4** (production d'énergie, électricité) generation; **5** Biol generation.

■ **~ spontanée** spontaneous generation.

générer /ʒeneʀe/ [14] *vtr* (tous contextes) to generate.

généreusement /ʒeneʀøzmɑ̃/ *adv* (noblement) generously; (libéralement) liberally.

généreux, **-euse** /ʒeneʀø, øz/ *adj* **1** (plein de largesse) generous (**envers** to); **2** (plein de grandeur d'âme) [*personne, caractère*] generous; [*idée, geste, sacrifice*] noble; **3** (copieux) [*portion*] generous; **poitrine généreuse** large bust; **une femme aux formes généreuses** a well-rounded woman; **4** (fertile) liter [*terre, sève*] fruitful; [*plaine*] bountiful littér.

générique /ʒeneʀik/ **I** *adj* [*nom, terme, caractère, médicament*] generic.

II *nm* Cin, Radio, TV **1** (liste) credits (*pl*); **le ~ de début/fin** opening/closing credits; **il n'était pas au ~** his name was not on the credits; **2** (présentation) titles (*pl*).

générosité /ʒeneʀozite/ *nf* **1** (largesse) generosity (**envers** to, towards); **un don/une personne d'une grande ~** a very generous gift/person; **2** (grandeur d'âme) generosity of spirit; **agir avec ~** to show generosity of spirit.

Gênes /ʒɛn/ **▶ 857** *npr* Genoa.

genèse /ʒənɛz/ *nf* **1** (d'œuvre d'art, de projet, style, mythe) genesis; (d'État) birth; **2** Bible **la Genèse** Genesis.

genêt /ʒənɛ/ *nm* Bot broom.
■ **~ à balai** broom; **~ commun** common broom; **~ d'Espagne** Spanish broom; **~ des teinturiers** dyer's greenweed.

généticien, **-ienne** /ʒenetisjɛ̃, ɛn/ ▶ 510 *nm,f* geneticist.

génétique /ʒenetik/ **I** *adj* [*code, génie, manipulation*] genetic.
II *nf* genetics (+ *v sg*).

génétiquement /ʒenetikmɑ̃/ *adv* genetically.

gêneur, **-euse** /ʒɛnœʀ, øz/ *nm,f* troublemaker.

Genève /ʒənɛv/ *npr* **1** ▶ 857 (ville) Geneva; **2** ▶ 692 (région) **le canton de ~** the canton of Geneva.

genevois, **~e** /ʒənvwa, az/ ▶ 857 *adj* of Geneva.

Genevois, **~e** /ʒənvwa, az/ ▶ 857 *nm,f* (natif) native of Geneva; (habitant) inhabitant of Geneva.

genévrier /ʒənevʀije/ *nm* juniper.

génial, **~e**, *mpl* **-iaux** /ʒenjal, o/ *adj* **1** (ayant du génie) brilliant; **2** (inspiré par le génie) [*plan, idée, conception, réalisation*] brilliant, inspired; [*invention, découverte*] brilliant; **3**○ (fantastique) [*spectacle, coupe de cheveux, livre*] brilliant GB, fantastic○, great; [*personne*] great; [*idée*] brilliant; **~!** brilliant! GB, great!; **c'est un type ~** he's a great bloke GB ou guy.

génialement /ʒenjalmɑ̃/ *adv* brilliantly.

génie /ʒeni/ *nm* **1** (aptitude) genius; **peintre/écrivain de ~** painter/writer of genius; **avoir du ~** to be a genius; **le ~ de qn** the genius of sb; **un coup de ~** a stroke of genius; **avoir un coup de ~** to have a flash of inspiration; **idée de ~** brainwave; **2** (personne) genius; **ce n'est pas un ~, leur fils** their son isn't exactly a genius; **~ du mal** evil genius; **petit ~** little genius; **3** (talent) genius; **le ~ architectural** architectural genius; **avoir le ~ du commerce** to have a great gift for business; **il a le ~ de tout embrouiller** he's a real genius at making a mess of things; **4** Mythol (esprit) spirit; (dans les contes) genie; **le ~ de la forêt** the spirit of the forest; **Aladin et le ~ de la lampe** Aladdin and the Genie of the lamp; **être le bon/mauvais ~ de qn** to be sb's guiding/evil spirit; **5** (ingénierie) engineering; **6** Mil (activité) military engineering; (personnel) **le ~** the Engineers (*pl*); **soldat/officier du ~** soldier/officer in the Engineers.
■ **~ chimique** chemical engineering; **~ civil** (activité) civil engineering; (personnel) civil engineers (*pl*); **~ climatique** climatic engineering; **~ cognitif** knowledge engineering; **~ génétique** genetic engineering; **~ industriel** industrial engineering; **~ rural** agricultural engineering.

genièvre /ʒənjɛvʀ/ *nm* (arbuste) juniper; (baie) juniper berry; (eau-de-vie) Dutch gin.

génique /ʒenik/ *adj* [*thérapie*] gene.

génisse /ʒenis/ *nf* heifer; **foie de ~** beef liver.

génital, **~e**, *mpl* **-aux** /ʒenital, o/ *adj* [*appareil, organes*] genital.

géniteur, **-trice** /ʒenitœʀ, tʀis/ **I** *nm,f* hum (parent) parent, pater/mater hum.
II *nm* Zool (reproducteur) sire.

génitif /ʒenitif/ *nm* Ling genitive; **au ~** in the genitive.

génito-urinaire, *pl* **~s** /ʒenitoyʀinɛʀ/ *adj* genito-urinary.

génocide /ʒenɔsid/ *nm* genocide.

génois, **~e** /ʒenwa, az/ ▶ 462 **I** *adj* Genoese.
II *nm* **1** Ling Genoese; **2** Naut genoa (jib).
III génoise *nf* Culin ≈ sponge cake.

Génois, **~e** /ʒenwa, az/ *nm,f* Genoese.

génome /ʒenom/ *nm* genome; **~ humain** human genome.

génothèque /ʒenɔtɛk/ *nf* gene library, gene bank.

génotype /ʒenɔtip/ *nm* genotype.

genou, *pl* **~x** /ʒ(ə)nu/ ▶ 188 **I** *nm* **1** (d'homme, animal) knee; **assieds-toi sur mes ~x** sit on my knee ou lap; **prends-la sur tes ~x** put her on your knee ou lap; **être dans l'eau jusqu'aux ~x**, **avoir de l'eau jusqu'aux ~x** to be knee-deep in water; **jupe en dessous/au-dessus du ~** skirt below/above the knee; **arriver au ~** [*jupe*] to be knee-length; [*botte*] to come up to the knee; [*pull, veste*] to come down to one's knees; **donner un coup de ~ à qn** to knee sb; **mettre (un) ~ à terre devant qn** lit to kneel down in front of sb; fig to pay homage to sb; **2** (de pantalon, collant) knee; **3** Naut, Tech knee.
II à genoux *loc adv* **être à ~x** to be kneeling, to be on one's knees; **se mettre à ~x** gén to kneel down; (pour implorer) to go down on one's knees; **tomber à ~x** to fall to one's knees; **à ~x!** down on your knees!; **je vous le demande à ~x!** fig I'm begging you!; **être à ~x devant qn** fig to worship sb.
IDIOMES **faire du ~ à qn**○ to play footsie○ with sb; **être sur les ~x**○ [*personne*] to be on one's last legs; **mettre qn sur les ~x**○ to wear sb out.

genouillère /ʒənujɛʀ/ *nf* Sport knee pad; Méd knee support ou bandage; Vét knee boot.

genre /ʒɑ̃ʀ/ *nm* **1** (sorte) sort, kind, type (**de** of); **réparations en tout ~** or **tous ~s** all types of repairs; **c'est ce qu'on fait de mieux dans le ~** it's the best of its kind; **c'est le ~ macho**○ he's the macho type○; **c'est le ~ rabat-joie** he/she's a killjoy; **c'est le** or **elle est du ~ à arriver sans prévenir** she's the sort ou type who turns up without warning; **tu vois le ~!** you know the type!; **les barbus, ce n'est pas mon ~** men with beards are not my type; **les descriptions du ~ magazine féminin** women's magazine-type descriptions; **~ de vie** lifestyle; **elle n'est pas mal dans son ~** she's quite pretty in her way; **quelque chose dans ce ~** something like that; **un peu dans le ~ de mon frère/de ta robe** a bit like my brother/your dress; **Marianne, ce n'est pas le même ~ que sa sœur** Marianne is not at all like her sister; **2** (comportement) **ce n'est pas mon ~ de tricher** cheating is not my style, cheating is not the sort of thing I do; **c'est bien son ~** it's just like him/her; **3** (allure) **avoir mauvais ~** to look disreputable; **avoir le ~ bohème** to look the bohemian type; **elle n'est pas vraiment jolie, mais elle a un ~** she's not really pretty, but there's something about her; **pour se donner un ~** (in order) to make oneself look different; **4** Ling gender; **s'accorder en ~** to agree in gender; **5** Art, Littérat genre; **le ~ picaresque/épistolaire** the picaresque/epistolary genre; **peinture de ~** genre painting; **6** Bot, Zool genus.
■ **le ~ humain** mankind.

gens[1] /ʒɑ̃/ *nmpl* **1** (personnes) people; **il y a des ~ qui**... there are (some) people who...; **que pensent les ~?** what do people think?; **les ~ de la ville** town ou city dwellers; **les ~ de la campagne** country people ou folk; **les ~ du coin** the local people, the locals péj; **les ~ sans histoires** ordinary people; **des tas**○ **de ~** loads of○ people; **la plupart des ~** most people; **les ~ heureux** happy people; **les vieilles ~** old people; **tous les braves ~** all good people; **toutes les mauvaises ~** all bad people; **écoutez bonnes ~**‡ hark ye here, good people‡; **2** (domestiques) servants, household; (escorte) retinue (*sg*).
■ **~ d'affaires** business people; **~ d'armes** men at arms; **~ de cour** courtiers; **~ d'église** clergymen; **~ d'épée** soldiers; **~ de lettres** writers; **~ de loi** lawyers; **~ de maison** servants; **~ du monde** polite society; **~ de robe** lawyers; **~ de théâtre** actors; **~ du voyage** travelling people.

■ Note When used with *gens*, the adjectives *bon, mauvais, petit, vieux, vilain* are placed before *gens* and in the feminine: (*toutes*) *les vieilles gens*. But the gender of *gens* itself does not change: *les bonnes gens sont heureux*. All other adjectives behave normally: (*tous*) *les braves gens*.

gens[2], *pl* **gentes** /ʒɛ̃s, ʒɛ̃tɛs/ *nf* Antiq gens.

gent /ʒɑ̃/ *nf*† **1** (personnes) **la ~ masculine/féminine** mankind/womankind, men (*pl*)/women (*pl*); **2** (animaux) race.

gentiane /ʒɑ̃sjan/ *nf* **1** (fleur) gentian; **2** (liqueur) gentian liqueur.

gentil, **-ille** /ʒɑ̃ti, ij/ **I** *adj* **1** (agréable) kind, nice (**avec** to); **aide-moi, tu seras ~** give me a hand, will you?; **c'est ~, je vous remercie** that's very kind of you, thank you; **sois ~, réponds au téléphone** do me a favour[GB], answer the phone; **vous êtes trop ~** you are too kind; **avoir un mot ~ pour qn** to have a nice ou kind word for sb; **ce n'est pas ~ ce que tu viens de faire** what you've just done wasn't very nice; **vous seriez ~ de faire moins de bruit** would you mind making a bit less noise?; **c'est ~ de sa part** that's kind ou nice of him/her; **2** (obéissant) good; **3** péj **le spectacle/film était ~** the show/film was harmless enough; **c'est bien ~ tout ça, mais**... that's all very well, but...; **il est (bien) ~** he's nice enough; **4** (non négligeable) [*somme, récompense*] fair.
II *nm* Hist Relig gentile.

gentilhomme, *pl* **gentilshommes** /ʒɑ̃tijɔm, ʒɑ̃tizɔm/ *nm* Hist gentleman; **~ campagnard** country gentleman.

gentilhommière /ʒɑ̃tijɔmjɛʀ/ *nf* country house.

gentille ▶ **gentil I.**

gentillesse /ʒɑ̃tijɛs/ *nf* **1** (bonté) kindness (**envers** to); **avoir la ~ de faire** to be kind enough to do; **ayez la ~ de** be kind enough to; **être d'une grande ~ avec** or **envers qn** to be very kind to sb; **faites-moi la ~ de**... would you do me the favour[GB] of...?; **2** (action, paroles désagréables) **ils ont échangé quelques ~s** iron they exchanged insults; **dire des ~s sur qn** iron to say unpleasant things about sb.

gentillet, **-ette** /ʒɑ̃tijɛ, ɛt/ *adj* **1** (agréable) **être ~** [*enfant*] to be a sweetie; **2** péj [*personne, livre, film*] nice enough.

gentiment /ʒɑ̃timɑ̃/ *adv* **1** (aimablement) kindly; **se moquer ~ de qn** to tease sb playfully; **je leur ai fait ~ comprendre** in the nicest possible way I made them understand; **2** (sagement) [*travailler, jouer*] quietly.

génuflexion /ʒenyflɛksjɔ̃/ *nf* genuflection; **faire une ~** to genuflect.

géocentrique /ʒeosɑ̃tʀik/ *adj* geocentric.

géocentrisme /ʒeosɑ̃tʀism/ *nm* geocentric theory.

géochimie /ʒeoʃimi/ *nf* geochemistry.

géode /ʒeɔd/ *nf* geode.

géodésie /ʒeɔdezi/ *nf* geodesy.

géodésique /ʒeɔdezik/ *adj, nf* geodesic.

géodynamique /ʒeɔdinamik/ **I** *adj* geodynamic.
II *nf* geodynamics (+ *v sg*).

géographe /ʒeɔgʀaf/ ▶ 510 *nmf* geographer.

géographie /ʒeɔgʀafi/ *nf* geography; **~ économique/humaine/physique** economic/human/physical geography.

géographique /ʒeɔgʀafik/ *adj* geographical.

géographiquement /ʒeɔgʀafikmɑ̃/ *adv* geographically.

geôle /ʒol/ *nf* liter jail.

geôlier, **-ière** /ʒolje, ɛʀ/ *nm,f* liter jailer.

géologie /ʒeɔlɔʒi/ *nf* geology.

géologique /ʒeɔlɔʒik/ *adj* geological.

géologiquement /ʒeɔlɔʒikmɑ̃/ *adv* geologically.
géologue /ʒeɔlɔg/ ▶ 510 *nmf* geologist.
géomagnétique /ʒeomaɲetik/ *adj* geomagnetic.
géomagnétisme /ʒeomaɲetism/ *nm* geomagnetism.
géomancie /ʒeomɑ̃si/ *nf* geomancy.
géomètre /ʒeɔmɛtʀ/ I ▶ 510 *nmf* **1** Tech land surveyor; **~ expert** ≈ chartered surveyor; **2**† Math geometrician.
II *nm* Zool geometrid.
géométrie /ʒeɔmetʀi/ *nf* geometry; **~ analytique/descriptive/plane** analytical/descriptive/plane geometry; **~ dans l'espace** solid geometry; **à ~ variable** fig [*discours, doctrine, traitement*] infinitely variable (*épith*).
géométrique /ʒeɔmetʀik/ *adj* [*espace, forme, construction*] geometric; [*méthode, démonstration, précision*] geometrical.
géométriquement /ʒeɔmetʀikmɑ̃/ *adv* geometrically.
géomorphologie /ʒeomɔʀfɔlɔʒi/ *nf* geomorphology.
géophysicien, -ienne /ʒeofizisjɛ̃, ɛn/ ▶ 510 *nm,f* geophysicist.
géophysique /ʒeofizik/ I *adj* [*études, prospection*] geophysical.
II *nf* geophysics (+ *v sg*).
géopolitique /ʒeɔpɔlitik/ I *adj* geopolitical.
II *nf* geopolitics (+ *v sg*).
Géorgie /ʒeɔʀʒi/ *nprf* **1** ▶ 692 (État américain) Georgia; **2** ▶ 321 (État indépendant) Georgia.
■ **~ du Sud** (île) South Georgia.
géorgien, -ienne /ʒeɔʀʒjɛ̃, ɛn/ ▶ 537, 462 I *adj* Georgian.
II *nm* Ling Georgian.
Géorgien, -ienne /ʒeɔʀʒjɛ̃, ɛn/ ▶ 537 *nm,f* Georgian.
géorgique /ʒeɔʀʒik/ *adj* georgic.
géostationnaire /ʒeostasjɔnɛʀ/ *adj* geostationary.
géosynchrone /ʒeosɛ̃kʀon/ *adj* geosynchronous.
géosynclinal, *pl* **-aux** /ʒeosɛ̃klinal, o/ *nm* geosyncline.
géothermie /ʒeotɛʀmi/ *nf* (énergie) geothermal power.
géothermique /ʒeotɛʀmik/ *adj* geothermal; **gradient ~** geothermal gradient.
géotropisme /ʒeotʀɔpism/ *nm* geotropism.
gérable /ʒeʀabl/ *adj* manageable; **situation difficilement ~** a situation which is hard to handle ou manage.
gérance /ʒeʀɑ̃s/ *nf* (fonction, exploitation, administration) management; **mettre en ~** to appoint a manager for [*magasin, société*]; to appoint a managing agent ou an agent for [*immeuble*]; **prendre en ~** to take over the management of [*magasin, société*]; to become managing agent of [*immeuble*]; **assurer la ~ de qch** to manage sth; **pendant leur ~** under their management.
■ **~ libre** Comm, Entr contract management; **~ salariée** Comm, Entr salaried management.
géranium /ʒeʀanjɔm/ *nm* geranium.
gérant, ~e /ʒeʀɑ̃, ɑ̃t/ *nm,f* **1** (de magasin, commerce, d'usine) manager; (d'immeubles) (managing) agent; **'nouveau ~'** 'under new management'; **2** Presse editor.
■ **~ d'affaires** Jur business ou financial manager; **~ libre** Comm contract manager; **~ de portefeuille**† Fin portfolio manager; **~ salarié** Comm salaried manager.
gerbage /ʒɛʀbaʒ/ *nm* **1** (mise en gerbes) binding; **2** (mise en piles) stacking.
gerbe /ʒɛʀb/ *nf* **1** (bouquet) bouquet; (mortuaire) wreath; **une ~ de glaïeuls** a bunch of gladioli; **déposer une ~ au monument aux morts** to lay a wreath on the war memorial; **2** (d'étincelles, écume, eau) spray; **3** Agric (de blé) sheaf.
gerber /ʒɛʀbe/ [1] I *vtr* **1** (lier en gerbes) to bind [*blé*]; **2** (empiler) to stack [*fûts*].
II◐ *vi* (vomir) to puke◐, to vomit.
gerbera /ʒɛʀbeʀa/ *nm* gerbera.
gerbille /ʒɛʀbij/ *nf* gerbil.
gerboise /ʒɛʀbwaz/ *nf* jerboa.
gercer /ʒɛʀse/ [12] I *vtr* [*froid, vent*] to chap [*main, lèvres, peau*]; **avoir les mains/lèvres gercées** to have chapped hands/lips.
II *vi* [*lèvres, mains*] to become chapped; **une crème qui empêche les mains de ~** a cream which prevents the hands from becoming chapped.
gerçure /ʒɛʀsyʀ/ *nf* crack; **avoir les mains pleines de ~s** to have badly chapped hands; **mettez des gants pour éviter les ~s** wear gloves to prevent chapping.
gérer /ʒeʀe/ [14] *vtr* **1** (administrer) to manage [*production, temps*]; to manage, to run [*commerce, propriété*]; to run [*pays*]; **un portefeuille géré par une banque privée** a portfolio managed by a private bank; **il gère bien ses affaires** he manages his business well; **une entreprise bien gérée** a well-managed ou well-run company; **une entreprise mal gérée** a badly run ou poorly managed company; **~ une tutelle** Jur to supervise a guardianship; **2** fig (traiter) to handle [*situation, information, problème, crise*]; **mal ~ qch** to handle sth badly; **3** Ordinat to manage [*fichiers, bases de données*].
gerfaut /ʒɛʀfo/ *nm* gyrfalcon.
gériatre /ʒeʀjatʀ/ ▶ 510 *nmf* geriatrician.
gériatrie /ʒeʀjatʀi/ *nf* **1** (discipline) geriatrics (+ *v sg*); **service de ~** geriatric ward; **2** (service) geriatric ward.
gériatrique /ʒeʀjatʀik/ *adj* geriatric.
germain, ~e /ʒɛʀmɛ̃, ɛn/ *adj* **1** (dans la famille) **cousin ~** first cousin; **2** Hist Germanic.
Germain, ~e /ʒɛʀmɛ̃, ɛn/ *nm,f* Hist German.
germanique /ʒɛʀmanik/ *adj, nm* Germanic.
germanisant, ~e /ʒɛʀmanizɑ̃, ɑ̃t/ *nm,f* Germanist.
germaniser /ʒɛʀmanize/ [1] I *vtr* to germanize.
II **se germaniser** *vpr* to become germanized.
germanisme /ʒɛʀmanism/ *nm* Ling Germanism.
germaniste /ʒɛʀmanist/ *nmf* Germanist.
germanophone /ʒɛʀmanɔfɔn/ I *adj* German-speaking (*épith*); **être ~** to speak German.
II *nmf* German speaker.
germe /ʒɛʀm/ *nm* **1** (d'embryon, de graine) germ; (d'œuf) germinal disc; (de pomme de terre) sprout; **~ de blé** wheat germ; **~s de soja** bean sprouts; **2** (début) seed (**de** of); **contenir une crise en ~** to contain the seeds of a crisis; **on trouve cette idée/théorie en ~ dans...** we find this idea/theory in embryonic form in...
■ **~ dentaire** Dent tooth bud.
germen /ʒɛʀmɛn/ *nm* germ cells (*pl*).
germer /ʒɛʀme/ [1] *vi* **1** fig (naître) [*idée, soupçon*] to form; **2** Bot [*blé*] to germinate; [*pomme de terre*] to sprout; **pommes de terre germées** sprouting potatoes.
germicide /ʒɛʀmisid/ I *adj* germicidal.
II *nm* germicide.
germinal, ~e, *mpl* **-aux** /ʒɛʀminal, o/ I *adj* Biol germinal.
II *nm* Germinal (*seventh month of the French revolutionary calendar*, ≈ *April*).
germinateur, -trice /ʒɛʀminatœʀ, tʀis/ *adj* germinative.
germinatif, -ive /ʒɛʀminatif, iv/ *adj* germinal.
germination /ʒɛʀminasjɔ̃/ *nf* germination.
germoir /ʒɛʀmwaʀ/ *nm* **1** (récipient) seed tray; (chauffé) propagator; **2** (de brasserie) malt-house.
germon /ʒɛʀmɔ̃/ *nm* albacore, longfin tuna.
gérondif /ʒeʀɔ̃dif/ *nm* (nom verbal latin, anglais) gerund; (adjectif verbal latin) gerundive; (forme verbale en français) gerund.
gérontocratie /ʒeʀɔ̃tɔkʀasi/ *nf* gerontocracy.
gérontologie /ʒeʀɔ̃tɔlɔʒi/ *nf* gerontology.
gérontologique /ʒeʀɔ̃tɔlɔʒik/ *adj* gerontological.
gérontologue /ʒeʀɔ̃tɔlɔg/ ▶ 510 *nmf* gerontologist.
Gers /ʒɛʀ/ ▶ 357, 692 *nprm* (rivière, département) **le ~** the Gers.
gésier /ʒezje/ *nm* gizzard.
gésir /ʒeziʀ/ [37] *vi* fml **1** (être couché) [*personne*] to be lying; **elle gît/gisait sur son lit** she is/was lying on her bed; **2** (être abandonné) [*feuilles, vêtements*] to be lying about ou around; **3** fig (se trouver) [*difficulté, solution, problème*] to lie.
gestaltisme /gɛstaltism/ *nm* Psych, Philos Gestalt psychology.
gestation /ʒɛstasjɔ̃/ *nf* **1** Physiol gestation; **période de ~** gestation period; **2** fig (d'œuvre, de roman, crise) gestation; **un livre en ~** a book in gestation.
geste /ʒɛst/ I *nm* **1** (mouvement) movement; (mouvement expressif) gesture; **un ~ brusque** a sudden movement; **il sortit un couteau de sa poche d'un ~ rapide** he whipped a knife out of his pocket; **des ~s répétitifs/désordonnés** repetitive/uncoordinated movements; **~ malheureux/maladroit** unfortunate/clumsy movement; **il nous a fait signe d'avancer d'un ~ de la main/de la tête** he waved/nodded to us to come forward; **un ~ de découragement/protestation/refus** a gesture of despondency/protest/refusal; **des ~s obscènes** obscene or rude gestures; **d'un ~ de la tête, il m'indiqua le balai** he indicated the broom to me with a nod of his head; **il approuva d'un ~ de la tête** he nodded his approval; **il fait beaucoup de ~s quand il parle** he waves his hands ou he gesticulates a lot when he speaks; **pas un ~ ou je tire!** don't move or I'll shoot!; **il n'a pas fait un ~ pour m'aider** fig he didn't make a move ou intervene to help me; **elle n'a qu'un ~ à faire pour le faire réintégrer** fig she only has to say the word to have him reinstated; **il pourrait faire un ~ quand même!** fig he could at least show that he cares; **joindre le ~ à la parole** to suit the action to the word; **2** (acte) gesture, act; **un ~ de bonne volonté/d'apaisement** a gesture of good will/of appeasement; **un ~ attentionné** a thoughtful gesture; **un ~ désespéré** a desperate act; **un ~ symbolique** a token gesture; **un beau ~** a noble gesture.
II *nf* Hist Littérat *set of French epic poems of the Middle Ages.*
gesticulation /ʒɛstikylasjɔ̃/ *nf* **1** (geste) gesticulation; **2** fig (affectation) posturing ¢.
gesticuler /ʒɛstikyle/ [1] *vtr* **1** (en parlant) to gesticulate; **2** (s'agiter) to fidget.
gestion /ʒɛstjɔ̃/ *nf* **1** (administration) management; **l'entreprise souffre d'une mauvaise ~** the company suffers from poor management; **une ~ saine** sound management; **durant leur ~** under their management; **~ informatisée/du temps** computerized/time management; **la ~ de son temps de travail** the management of one's working time; **la ~ de la production** production control; **2** (de situation, crise, d'information) handling; **3** (discipline) management; **faire de la ~** to do business studies, to study management; **avoir un diplôme de ~** to have a business studies ou a management diploma; **4** Ordinat (de fichiers, base de données) management.
■ **~ administrative** administration; **~ budgétaire** budgetary control; **~ contrô-**

lée Jur receivership; **être mis sous ~ contrôlée** [*société*] to go into receivership; **~ financière** financial management; **~ du personnel** personnel management; **~ de portefeuille** Fin portfolio management; **~ prévisionnelle** (forward) planning; **~ de la production assistée par ordinateur**, **GPAO** computer-aided production management; **~ des ressources humaines** human resource management; **~ des risques** risk management; **~ sociale** Admin, Pol social management; Entr industrial relations (+ *v sg*); **~ des stocks** stock control GB, inventory control US; **~ de trésorerie** corporate cash management.

gestionnaire /ʒɛstjɔnɛʀ/ **I** *adj* Écon [*technique, organisme*] administrative.
II *nmf* administrator; **avoir des qualités de ~** to be a good administrator; **un poste de ~** an administrative position (**chez** with).
III *nm* Mil administrative commandant.
■ **~ de fichiers** Ordinat file-management system; **~ de portefeuille** Fin portfolio manager.

gestuel, **-elle** /ʒɛstɥɛl/ **I** *adj* gestural; **peinture gestuelle** action painting.
II gestuelle *nf* body language.

geyser /ʒezɛʀ/ *nm* geyser.

Ghana /gana/ ▶ **321** *nprm* Ghana.

ghanéen, **-éenne** /ganeɛ̃, ɛn/ ▶ **537** *adj* Ghanaian.

Ghanéen, **-éenne** /ganeɛ̃, ɛn/ ▶ **537** *nm,f* Ghanaian.

ghetto /geto/ *nm* lit, fig ghetto.

gibbeux, **-euse** /ʒibø, øz/ *adj* **1** [*forme*] liter bulging; [*dos*] humped; **2** Astron gibbous.

gibbon /ʒibɔ̃/ *nm* gibbon.

gibbosité /ʒibozite/ *nf* Méd kyphosis.

gibecière /ʒibsjɛʀ/ *nf* Chasse gamebag; Scol satchel.

gibelotte /ʒiblɔt/ *nf* gibelotte, rabbit stewed in wine.

giberne /ʒibɛʀn/ *nf* Mil cartridge pouch.

gibet /ʒibɛ/ *nm* gallows (*sg*); **condamner qn au ~** to sentence sb to the gallows.

gibier /ʒibje/ *nm* Chasse, Culin game; **petit ~** small game; **manger du ~** to eat game; **gros ~** lit big game; fig big time criminals (*pl*); **être un ~ facile pour les escrocs** fig to be an easy target for conmen; **c'est du ~ de potence** he'll/they'll come to a bad end.
■ **~ d'eau** water fowl (+ *v pl*); **~ à plumes** game birds (*pl*); **~ à poil** game animals (*pl*).

giboulée /ʒibule/ *nf* shower; **les ~s de mars** ≈ April showers GB.

giboyeux, **-euse** /ʒibwajø, øz/ *adj* [*région, plaine, réserve*] full of game (*après n*).

Gibraltar /ʒibʀaltaʀ/ *nprm* Gibraltar.

gibus /ʒibys/ *nm* opera hat.

GIC /ʒeise/ *nm*: *abbr* ▶ **grand**.

giclée /ʒikle/ *nf* (d'eau, de sang, lait) spurt; (d'encre) squirt.

gicler /ʒikle/ [1] *vi* **1** (jaillir) [*sang, eau*] to spurt (**de** from); [*jus*] to squirt (**sur** onto); **l'eau giclait du tuyau percé** water was spurting from the hole in the pipe; **le champagne m'a giclé à la figure** the champagne sprayed in my face; **la voiture a fait ~ de la boue** the car sprayed up mud; **2**● (partir) to split○, to piss off●.

gicleur /ʒiklœʀ/ *nm* **1** (de carburateur) jet; **2** (de lave-vaisselle) spray.
■ **~ de ralenti** Aut idling jet.

GIE /ʒeiə/ *nm*: *abbr* ▶ **groupement**.

gifle /ʒifl/ *nf* **1** (claque) slap in the face; **donner** or **coller**○ **une ~ à qn** to slap sb in the face; **donner une bonne gifle à qn** to whack sb; **flanquer**○ **une paire de ~s à qn** to clip sb around the ears○; **recevoir** or **prendre**○ **une paire de ~s** to get a clip around the ears○; **2** (affront) slap in the face (**pour** for).

gifler /ʒifle/ [1] *vtr* **1** (frapper) to slap [*personne*]; **~ qn du revers de la main** to slap sb with the back of one's hand; **2** (cingler) [*pluie, vent*] to lash; **la pluie me giflait le visage** the rain was lashing my face.

GIG /ʒeiʒe/ *nm*: *abbr* ▶ **grand**.

gigantesque /ʒigɑ̃tɛsk/ *adj* huge, gigantic; **de taille ~** huge, gigantic.

gigantisme /ʒigɑ̃tism/ *nm* **1** (de bâtiment, ville, statue) colossal size; (de projet, spectacle, congrès) giant scale; **2** Bot, Méd gigantism.

GIGN /ʒeiʒeɛn/ *nm* (*abbr* = **groupe d'intervention de la gendarmerie nationale**) *branch of the police specialized in cases of armed robbery, terrorism etc.*

gigogne /ʒigɔɲ/ *adj* **lit ~** hideaway bed; **tables ~s** nest of tables.

gigolo /ʒigɔlo/ *nm* gigolo; **faire le ~** to be a gigolo.

gigot /ʒigo/ *nm* (d'agneau) leg of lamb; **tranche de ~** slice of lamb; **~ de mouton** leg of mutton; **~ de chevreuil** haunch of venison.

gigoter /ʒigɔte/ [1] *vi* gén to wriggle; (nerveusement) to fidget.

gigue /ʒig/ *nf* **1** Culin haunch; **une ~ de chevreuil** a haunch of venison; **2**○ (fille) **une grande ~** a great beanpole○ of a girl; **3** (air) gigue; (danse) jig; **danser la ~** to dance a jig.

gilet /ʒilɛ/ *nm* **1** (en tricot) cardigan; **~ sans manches** sleeveless cardigan; **2** (en tissu, cuir) waistcoat GB, vest US.
■ **~ pare-balles** bulletproof vest; **~ de sauvetage** lifejacket.

gin /dʒin/ *nm* gin; **~ tonic** gin and tonic.

gingembre /ʒɛ̃ʒɑ̃bʀ/ *nm* ginger.

gingival, **~e**, *mpl* **-aux** /ʒɛ̃ʒival, o/ *adj* gingival.

gingivite /ʒɛ̃ʒivit/ ▶ **271** *nf* gingivitis.

ginkgo /ʒinko/ *nm* ginkgo, maidenhair tree.

ginseng /ʒinsɑ̃g/ *nm* ginseng.

girafe /ʒiʀaf/ *nf* **1** Zool giraffe; **avoir un cou de ~** to have a long neck; **2**○ hum (personne) beanpole○; **3**○ Cin (perche) boom.
IDIOMES **peigner la ~**○ to waste one's time doing a pointless task.

girafon /ʒiʀafɔ̃/ *nm* baby giraffe.

girandole /ʒiʀɑ̃dɔl/ *nf* **1** (guirlande) fairy lights (*pl*); **2** (feu d'artifice, jet d'eau) girandole; **3** (chandelier) girandole.

giration /ʒiʀasjɔ̃/ *nf* gyration.

giratoire /ʒiʀatwaʀ/ *adj* [*mouvement*] gyratory; **carrefour** or **sens ~** roundabout GB, traffic circle US.

girofle /ʒiʀɔfl/ *nm* clove; **un clou de ~** a clove.

giroflée /ʒiʀɔfle/ *nf* wallflower.

giroflier /ʒiʀɔflije/ *nm* clove (tree).

girolle /ʒiʀɔl/ *nf* chanterelle.

giron /ʒiʀɔ̃/ *nm* **1** (genoux) lap; **elle tenait l'enfant dans son ~** she was holding the child on her lap; **2** fig (environnement) bosom; **retourner dans le ~ familial** to return to the bosom of one's family; **3** Hérald gyron.

gironde○ /ʒiʀɔ̃d/ *adj f* [*femme*] well-rounded.

Gironde /ʒiʀɔ̃d/ ▶ **692** *nprf* (estuaire, département) **la ~** the Gironde.

girondin, **~e** /ʒiʀɔ̃dɛ̃, in/ *adj* **1** Géog [*économie, vignoble, population*] of the Gironde (*après n*); **2** Hist [*parti, politique*] Girondist.

Girondin /ʒiʀɔ̃dɛ̃/ *nm* Hist Girondist.

girouette /ʒiʀwɛt/ *nf* **1** windvane; **2** fig (personne) weathercock.

gisant /ʒizɑ̃/ *nm* recumbent effigy.

gisement /ʒizmɑ̃/ *nm* **1** Géol, Mines deposit; **~ de pétrole exploitable** oil deposit; **2** Naut bearing.

gît ▶ **gésir**.

gitan, **~e** /ʒitɑ̃, an/ *adj, nm,f* Gypsy.

gîte /ʒit/ **I** *nm* **1** (refuge) shelter; (demeure) home; **le ~ et le couvert** board and lodging GB, room and lodging US; **2** Culin (en boucherie) **~ (à la noix)** ≈ top rump; **3** (de lièvre) form.
II *nf* Naut list.
■ **~ rural** self-catering cottage.

gîter /ʒite/ [1] *vi* Naut (pencher) to list; (être échoué) to be beached.

givrage /ʒivʀaʒ/ *nm* Aviat icing; Aut freezing up.

givrant /ʒivʀɑ̃/ *adj m* **brouillard ~** freezing fog.

givre /ʒivʀ/ *nm* Météo (sur sol, plante) frost; (sur pare-brise, hélice) ice.

givré, **~e** /ʒivʀe/ **I** *pp* ▶ **givrer**.
II *pp adj* (couvert de givre) [*vitre*] frosty; [*branche*] covered in frost; [*neige*] frozen.
III *adj* **1**○ (fou) crazy; **il est ~** he's crazy ou bonkers○; **2** (avec du sucre) [*verre*] frosted; ▶ **citron**, **orange**.

givrer /ʒivʀe/ [1] *vi*, **se givrer** *vpr* to frost over.

glabre /glabʀ/ *adj* **1** (imberbe) beardless; (rasé) clean-shaven, smooth-shaven; **2** Bot glabrous.

glaçage /glasaʒ/ *nm* **1** Imprim, Phot (de papier, photo) glazing; **2** Culin (de poisson, viande, légume) glazing; (au sucre) icing; (au blanc d'œuf) glazing.

glace /glas/ **I** *nf* **1** (eau congelée) ice; **de ~** [*accueil*] icy; [*visage*] stony; **rompre** or **briser la ~** fig to break the ice; **2** (dessert) ice cream; **~ à l'eau** water ice; **au dessert il y a de la ~** there is ice cream for dessert; **~ à la fraise/à la pistache** strawberry/pistachio ice cream; **une ~ en cornet**, **un cornet de ~** an ice-cream cone; **~ (à l')italienne** Italian-style ice cream; **une ~ en pot**, **un petit pot de ~** a tub of ice cream; **3** (de viande, volaille, poisson) glaze; **4** (miroir) mirror; **~ à main/en pied** hand/full-length mirror; **se regarder dans une ~** to look (at oneself) in a mirror; **tu ferais mieux de te regarder dans une ~** fig you'd better take a long hard look at yourself; **~ sans tain** two-way mirror; **5** (panneau de verre) (plaque) sheet of glass; (de vitrine) glass; (de voiture) window.
II glaces *nfpl* (de montagne) ice field (*sg*); (des pôles) ice sheet (*sg*); **quand les ~s fondent** when the ice melts; **navire pris dans les ~s** icebound ship; **le navire est resté pris dans les ~s** the ship remained icebound.
IDIOMES **rester de ~** to remain unmoved.

glacé, **~e** /glase/ **I** *pp* ▶ **glacer**.
II *pp adj* **1** (très froid) [*pluie, vent, boisson*] ice-cold, icy; [*douche*] ice-cold; [*air*] icy; **j'ai les mains ~es** my hands are frozen; **je suis ~** I'm freezing; **thé/café ~** iced tea/coffee; **2** Culin (recouvert de glaçage) [*gâteau*] iced; [*fruit*] glacé (*épith*); **3** (intimidant) [*accueil, atmosphère*] frosty, icy; [*sourire*] chilly; [*voix*] cold; **4** Tech [*photo, papier*] glossy; **5** (gelé) [*fontaine, fleuve, sol*] frozen.

glacer /glase/ [12] **I** *vtr* **1** (transir) to freeze [*corps, partie du corps*]; to chill [sb] to the bone [*personne*]; **~ le sang de qn** fig to make sb's blood run cold; **2** (rafraîchir) to chill [*boisson, liquide, melon, fruit*]; **3** (intimider) [*personne, regard*] to intimidate; **~ qn d'effroi** to make sb's blood run cold; **~ qn de peur** to fill sb with fear; **4** Tech to glaze [*papier, photo, poterie, peinture*]; **5** Culin to glaze [*fruit, viande, légume*]; to ice [*gâteau*]; **6** (durcir) to freeze [*eau, flaque*].
II se glacer *vpr* [*sourire, expression*] to freeze; **son expression se glaça en une grimace** his/her expression became fixed in a grimace; **mon sang se glaça dans mes veines** fig my blood froze.

glaciaire /glasjɛʀ/ **I** *adj* glacial; **calotte ~** icecap.
II *nm* glacial period.

glacial, **~e**, *mpl* **~s** or **-iaux** /glasjal, o/ *adj* **1** (froid) [*froid, temps, fluide*] icy; [*pluie, journée, vent*] icy, freezing cold; **2** fig (hostile) [*personne, accueil*] frosty; [*silence*] stony; [*regard*] icy; **elle est d'un abord ~** she comes over as very cold.

glaciation /glasjasjɔ̃/ *nf* glaciation.

glacier /glasje/ *nm* **1** Géog glacier; **2** ▶510 (pâtissier) ice-cream maker; **3** (établissement) ice-cream parlour[GB].

glacière /glasjɛʀ/ *nf* coolbox GB, cooler, ice chest US; **c'est une vraie ~ ici** it's like a fridge in here.

glaciologie /glasjɔlɔʒi/ *nf* glaciology.

glaciologique /glasjɔlɔʒik/ *adj* glaciological.

glaciologue /glasjɔlɔg/ ▶510 *nmf* glaciologist.

glacis /glasi/ *nm* **1** Géol, Mil glacis; **2** Pol block; **3** Archit glacis; **4** Art glaze.

glaçon /glasɔ̃/ *nm* **1** ice cube; **vodka/jus d'orange avec des ~s** vodka/orange juice with ice; **un jus de pomme sans ~s** an apple juice with no ice ou without ice; **2** (dans une rivière) block of ice; (sur un toit, arbre) icicle; **3**○ pej (personne) iceberg.

gladiateur /gladjatœʀ/ *nm* gladiator; **un combat de ~s** gladiatorial combat.

glaïeul /glajœl/ *nm* gladiolus; **un bouquet de ~s** a bunch of gladioli.

glaire /glɛʀ/ *nf* **1** Physiol mucus; **avoir des ~s** to have catarrh; **2** (blanc d'œuf) albumen.

■ **~ cervicale** cervical mucus.

glaireux, -euse /glɛʀø, øz/ *adj* Physiol mucous.

glaise /glɛz/ *nf* clay.

glaiseux, -euse /glɛzø, øz/ *adj* clayey.

glaive /glɛv/ *nm* double-edged sword; **le ~ et la balance** fig the sword and the scales of justice.

Glamorgan ▶692 *nprm* **le Mid/South/West ~** Mid/South/West Glamorgan.

gland /glɑ̃/ *nm* **1** Bot (de chêne) acorn; **2** Anat glans; **3** (décoration) tassel.

glande /glɑ̃d/ *nf* Anat gland; **~s salivaires/mammaires** salivary/mammary glands; **~ thyroïde** thyroid gland.

IDIOMES **avoir les ~s**◑ (être irrité) to be pissed off◑; (être angoissé) to be worried sick○; **foutre les ~s à qn**◑ (irriter) to piss sb off◑; (angoisser) to worry sb sick○.

glander◑ /glɑ̃de/ [1] *vi* to bum around○, to piss around◑ GB; **qu'est-ce que tu glandes◑?** what are you up to?; **il glande rien ce mec**◑ that guy does bugger◑ all GB ou bums around○ all day US.

glandeur◑**, -euse** /glɑ̃dœʀ, øz/ *nm,f* pej lazy sod○ GB, bum○ US.

glandouiller◑ /glɑ̃duje/ [1] *vi* = **glander**.

glandulaire /glɑ̃dylɛʀ/ *adj* Méd glandular.

glaner /glane/ [1] *vtr* to glean [*renseignements, grains, champ*].

glaneur, -euse /glanœʀ, øz/ *nm,f* gleaner.

glapir /glapiʀ/ [3] **I** *vtr* [*personne*] to screech [*injures, protestations*].

II *vi* **1** Zool [*chiot*] to yap; [*renard*] to bark; [*grue*] to whoop; **2**○ (hurler) [*personne*] to shriek; [*haut-parleur, radio*] to blare.

glapissement /glapismɑ̃/ *nm* **1** (de chiot) yapping ¢; (de renard) barking ¢; (de grue) whooping ¢; **2** (de personne) shrieking ¢; (de radio) blaring ¢.

Glaris /glaʀis/ *npr* **1** ▶857 (ville) Glarus; **2** ▶692 (région) **le canton de ~** the canton of Glarus.

glas /glɑ/ *nm* toll, knell; **sonner le ~** lit [*personne*] to toll the bell; [*cloche*] to toll; fig to sound the death knell (**de** for).

glaucome /glokom/ ▶271 *nm* glaucoma.

glauque /glok/ *adj* [*eaux, mare, lumière*] murky; [*atmosphère, rue*] squalid.

glaviot◑ /glavjo/ *nm* gob of spit○.

glavioter◑ /glavjɔte/ [1] *vi* to spit.

glèbe /glɛb/ *nf* liter glebe.

glissade /glisad/ *nf* **1** lit (jeu) slide; (dérapage) skid; **il aurait pu se casser la jambe pendant sa ~** he could have broken his leg when he slipped; **faire une ~** [*enfant*] to slide; [*joueur*] to slip; [*véhicule*] to skid; **2** fig (de prix, monnaie, cote électorale) slide; **arrêter la ~ des prix** to stop prices sliding GB ou from sliding.

glissando /glisɑ̃do/ *nm* glissando.

glissant, ~e /glisɑ̃, ɑ̃t/ *adj* **1** (où l'on dérape) slippery; **terrain ~** fig dangerous ground; **2** Fin **sur 7 jours ~s** over a 7-day period.

glisse /glis/ *nf* **1** (de ski, skieur) gliding; **2**○ (ski) skiing.

glissé, ~e /glise/ **I** *pp* ▶ **glisser**.

II *pp adj* (en tricot) **maille ~e** slip stitch.

III *nm* Danse sliding step.

glissement /glismɑ̃/ *nm* **1** (déplacement) sliding; **les deux pièces se superposent par ~** the two parts slide over each other; **2** (évolution) (de sens) shift; (d'électorat, opinion) swing; (de prix) fall; **un ~ à droite** a swing to the right.

■ **~ de terrain** Géol landslide.

glisser /glise/ [1] **I** *vtr* **1** (mettre) to slip [*objet*] (**dans** into); **j'ai glissé la lettre dans ma poche/sous la porte** I slipped the letter into my pocket/under the door; **il a glissé l'anneau à mon doigt** he slipped the ring onto my finger; **~ un oreiller sous la tête d'un malade** to slide a pillow under a patient's head; **elle a glissé la main dans mes cheveux** she ran her fingers through my hair; **2** (introduire) to slip in [*remarque, commentaire, critique*]; **~ une anecdote dans la conversation** to slip an anecdote into the conversation; **3** (dire furtivement) **~ qch à l'oreille de qn** to whisper sth in sb's ear; **4** (en tricot) to slip [*maille*].

II *vi* **1** (être glissant) [*route, trottoir, savon*] to be slippery; **ça glisse** it's slippery; **2** (être déstabilisé) [*personne*] to slip; [*chapeau, robe, écharpe*] to slip (down); [*outil, couteau*] to slip; [*véhicule*] to skid; **~ de** to slip out of; **~ des mains de qn** [*savon, bouteille*] to slip out of sb's hands; **une tuile/le ramoneur a glissé du toit** a tile/the chimney sweep fell off the roof; **3** (se déplacer) gén to slide; (avec grâce) to glide; **descendre les escaliers en glissant sur la rampe** to slide down the bannisters; **se laisser ~ le long d'une corde/d'un mur** to slide down a rope/a wall; **un cygne/canoë glissait sur le lac** a swan/canoe was gliding over the lake; **4** (ne pas accrocher) [*piston, ski, tiroir, cloison*] to slide; **mes skis ne glissent pas** my skis are sticking; **la neige glisse bien/ne glisse pas** the snow is nice and smooth/is sticking; **leur regard glissait d'un tableau à l'autre** their gaze wandered from one picture to another; **leur regard glissait sur l'assistance** they surveyed the people present; **5** (passer insensiblement) **~ dans l'ennui** to become bored; **~ dans le pessimisme** to sink into gloom; **l'électorat glisse à droite** there's a swing to the right among the electorate; **le parti a glissé vers le terrorisme** there has been a swing toward(s) terrorism in the party; **le roman glisse de la comédie au drame** the novel moves imperceptibly from comedy to drama; **6** (ne pas affecter) **~ sur** [*injure, critique*] to have no effect on; **7** (ne pas approfondir) **~ sur** to skate over [*sujet, question, passé*].

III se glisser *vpr* **1** (pénétrer) **se ~ dans** gén to slip into; (furtivement) to sneak into; **se ~ dans son lit** to slip into bed; **se ~ dans les draps** to slip between the sheets; **le voleur s'est glissé dans la chambre** the thief sneaked into the room; **2** (se faufiler) to slip; **se ~ derrière un rideau** to slip behind a curtain; **se ~ dans la foule** to slip through the crowd; **se ~ parmi les invités** to slip in among the guests; **se ~ parmi les badauds** to edge through the onlookers; **je me suis glissé vers la sortie/au premier rang** I slid toward(s) the exit/into the front row; **le chat s'est glissé sous la voiture** the cat crept under the car; **3** (s'insinuer) [*sentiment, erreur*] to creep into [*personne, texte*]; **l'ennui se glissa entre nous** boredom crept into our relationship.

IDIOMES **~ entre les mains** or **doigts de qn** [*criminel*] to slip through sb's fingers.

glissière /glisjɛʀ/ *nf* Tech slide; (d'autoroute) crash barrier; **à ~** [*porte, fenêtre*] sliding (*épith*); **fermeture à ~** zip GB, zipper US.

■ **~ de sécurité** crash barrier.

global, ~e, *mpl* **-aux** /glɔbal, o/ *adj* [*revenu, somme, effectif*] total; [*croissance, résultat, coût, vision*] overall; [*accord, plan, solution, village*] global; [*étude*] comprehensive; ▶ **méthode**.

globalement /glɔbalmɑ̃/ *adv* on the whole; **un bilan ~ positif** an assessment that is, on the whole, positive.

globalisation /glɔbalizasjɔ̃/ *nf* globalization.

globalité /glɔbalite/ *nf* **considérer qch dans sa ~** to consider sth in its entirety.

globe /glɔb/ *nm* **1** Géog (Terre) earth, globe; **stratégie à l'échelle du ~** global strategy; **parcourir le ~** to globe-trot; **il a voyagé aux quatre coins du ~** he's been to all four corners of the earth; **2** (sphère en verre) (de lampe) lamp globe; (de protection) glass case; **mettre qch sous ~** to put sth in a glass case; **3** Archit dome.

■ **~ impérial** orb; **~ oculaire** Anat eyeball; **~ terrestre** (mappemonde) globe; (Terre) earth.

globe-trotter /glɔbtʀɔtɛʀ/ *nm* globe-trotter.

globulaire /glɔbylɛʀ/ *adj* **1** Méd corpuscular; **numération ~** blood count; **2** (sphérique) [*corps*] spherical; [*masse*] globular.

globule /glɔbyl/ *nm* Biol, gén globule, corpuscle; (du sang) blood cell.

■ **~ blanc** white cell; **~ polaire** polar body; **~ rouge** red cell.

globuleux, -euse /glɔbylø, øz/ *adj* [*œil*] protruding.

globuline /glɔbylin/ *nf* globulin.

glockenspiel /glɔkɛnʃpil/ ▶534 *nm* glockenspiel.

gloire /glwaʀ/ *nf* **1** (renom) glory, fame; **la ~ militaire** military glory; **la ~ littéraire** literary fame; **la ~ et la fortune** fame and fortune; **se couvrir de ~** to cover oneself with glory; **chercher la ~** to seek fame; **c'est ce qui a fait leur ~** that's what made them famous; **avoir** or **connaître son heure de ~** to have one's hour of glory; **2** (mérite) credit; **s'attribuer la ~ de qch** to take the credit for sth; **faire qch pour la ~** to do sth (just) for the sake of it; **3** (hommage) glory, praise; **~ à Dieu!** glory be to God, praise the Lord!; **monument à la ~ de qn** monument to the glory of sb; **rendre ~ à qn/au courage de qn** to pay tribute to sb/to sb's courage, to praise sb/sb's courage; **4** (sujet de fierté) **tirer ~ de qch/de faire qch** to pride oneself on sth/on doing sth; **5** (personne) celebrity; (dans le monde du spectacle) star; **les ~s locales** hum the local worthies○; **6** (splendeur) glory; **la ~ de la Grèce** the glory of Greece; **dans toute leur ~** in all their glory; **7** Art (auréole) **le Christ en ~** Christ in majesty.

gloria /glɔʀja/ *nm inv* Relig Gloria.

gloriette /glɔʀjɛt/ *nf* **1** Archit (pavillon) gazebo; **2** (tonnelle) arbour[GB]; **3** (volière) domed bird-cage.

glorieusement /glɔʀjøzmɑ̃/ *adv* [*combattre*] with glory; **tomber ~ au champ d'honneur** to fall gloriously on the field of battle; **triompher ~** to have a great triumph.

glorieux, -ieuse /glɔʀjø, øz/ *adj* **1** (illustre) [*temps, ancêtre, destin, exploit*] glorious; **un passé peu ~** a far from glorious past; **2** liter (suffisant) [*air, ton*] self-satisfied.

glorification /glɔʀifikasjɔ̃/ *nf* glorification.

glorifier /glɔʀifje/ [2] **I** *vtr* to glorify [*personne, Dieu, travail*].

II se glorifier *vpr* to glory (**de qch** in sth; **d'avoir fait** in having done), to boast (**de qch** about sth; **d'avoir fait** about having done); **il n'y a pas de quoi se ~** that's nothing to be proud of.

gloriole /glɔʀjɔl/ *nf* péj misplaced pride, vainglory littér.

glose /gloz/ *nf* (annotation, développement) gloss; (note explicative) note.

gloser /gloze/ [1] **I** *vtr* to annotate [*texte*].
II *vi* (discourir) to ramble on (**sur** about).

glossaire /glɔsɛʀ/ *nm* glossary.

glossématique /glɔsematik/ *nf* glossematics (+ *v sg*).

glossine /glɔsin/ *nf* glossina, tsetse fly.

glossolalie /glɔsolali/ *nf* glossolalia.

glottal, **~e**, *mpl* **-aux** /glɔtal, o/ *adj* glottal.

glotte /glɔt/ *nf* glottis; **coup de ~** Ling glottal stop.

Gloucestershire ▶ 692 *nprm* **le ~** Gloucestershire.

glouglou /gluglu/ *nm* **1**○ (de liquide) gurgling sound; **faire des ~s** to make a gurgling sound; **2** Zool (cri du dindon) gobbling sound; **le dindon fait ~**○ the turkey goes gobble-gobble○.

glouglouter /gluglute/ [1] *vi* **1**○ [*liquide*] to gurgle; **2** [*dindon*] to gobble.

gloussement /glusmɑ̃/ *nm* (de poule) clucking ¢; (de personne) chuckle; **avec des ~s de satisfaction** with a satisfied chuckle.

glousser /gluse/ [1] *vi* [*poule*] to cluck; [*personne*] to chuckle.

glouton, **-onne** /glutɔ̃, ɔn/ **I** *adj* [*personne*] gluttonous; [*appétit*] voracious.
II *nm,f* glutton.
III *nm* Zool wolverine.

gloutonnement /glutɔnmɑ̃/ *adv* [*manger*] greedily; [*lire*] voraciously; **avaler ~ un bol de soupe** to wolf down a bowl of soup.

gloutonnerie /glutɔnʀi/ *nf* gluttony; **manger avec ~** to wolf down one's food.

gloxinia /glɔksinja/ *nm* gloxinia.

glu /gly/ *nf* **1** Chasse bird lime; **prendre des oiseaux à la ~** to lime birds; **2** (colle) glue.

gluant, **~e** /glyɑ̃, ɑ̃t/ *adj* **1** (collant) [*main, pâtes*] sticky; [*poisson, mur, boue*] slimy; **2**○ (obséquieux) [*personne*] slimy; **il est ~!** he's a creep○!

glucide /glysid/ *nm* carbohydrate; **trop de ~s** too much carbohydrate; **riche/pauvre en ~s** high/low in carbohydrates.

glucose /glykoz/ *nm* glucose.

glutamate /glytamat/ *nm* glutamate; **~ de sodium** monosodium glutamate, MSG.

gluten /glytɛn/ *nm* gluten; **pain au ~** gluten bread.

glutineux, **-euse** /glytinø, øz/ *adj* glutinous.

glycémie /glisemi/ *nf* **taux de ~** blood sugar level.

glycérine /gliseʀin/ *nf* glycerin; **savon à la ~** glycerin soap.

glycériner /gliseʀine/ [1] *vtr* to coat [sth] with glycerin.

glycérol /gliseʀɔl/ *nm* glycerol.

glycérophtalique /gliseʀɔftalik/ *adj* [*résine*] alkyd; **peinture ~** oil-based paint.

glycine /glisin/ *nf* Bot wisteria.

glycogène /glikɔʒɛn/ *nm* glycogen.

glycol /glikɔl/ *nm* glycol.

gnangnan○ /ɲɑ̃ɲɑ̃/ *adj inv* [*personne, film, histoire*] silly.

gneiss /gnɛs/ *nm* gneiss.

gnocchi /ɲɔki/ *nm* gnocchi (+ *v sg* ou *pl*).

gnognotte○ /ɲɔɲɔt/ *nf* **c'est de la ~!** (c'est facile) it's dead easy○; **c'est pas de la ~!** (de bonne qualité) it's not your common or garden variety○; (difficile) it's quite a business○.

gnôle○ /ɲol/ *nf* hooch○, spirits (*pl*); **un petit verre de ~** a drop of the hard stuff○ GB, a snort○ US.

gnome /gnom/ *nm* gnome.

gnomique /gnɔmik/ *adj* Littérat gnomic.

gnon○ /ɲɔ̃/ *nm* (bosse sur une voiture) dent; (ecchymose) bruise; **il m'a flanqué un ~** he socked me; **prendre un ~** [*personne, voiture*] to get hit.

gnose /gnoz/ *nf* gnosis.

gnosticisme /gnɔstisism/ *nm* gnosticism.

gnostique /gnɔstik/ *adj, nmf* gnostic.

gnou /gnu/ *nm* gnu.

gnouf◐ /ɲuf/ *nm* prison, nick○ GB.

go /go/ ▶ 449 **I** *nm* Jeux go.
II tout de go *loc adv* [*annoncer, dire*] straight out; **elle est entrée tout de ~** she came straight in.

GO /ʒeo/ **I** *nm* (*abbr* = **gentil organisateur**) (animateur) organizer.
II *nfpl* Radio (*written abbr* = **grandes ondes**) LW.

goal○ /gol/ *nm* Sport goalkeeper, goalie○.

gobelet /gɔblɛ/ *nm* **1** (en plastique, carton) cup; (en verre) tumbler; (en métal) beaker; **~ en carton** paper cup; **2** Jeux shaker.

gobe-mouche, *pl* **~s** /gɔbmuʃ/ *nm* **1** Zool flycatcher; **2** (personne naïve)○† sucker○.

gober /gɔbe/ [1] *vtr* **1** (avaler) to suck [*œuf*]; to swallow [sth] whole [*huître*]; **2**○ (croire) to swallow, to fall for○ [*mensonge*]; **~ le morceau** to fall for it, hook, line and sinker; **3**○ (supporter) **je ne peux pas le ~** I can't stand him.

goberger○: **se goberger** /gɔbɛʀʒe/ [13] *vpr* (se choyer) to pamper oneself; (bien manger) to indulge oneself.

Gobi /gɔbi/ *nprm* **(désert de) ~** Gobi (desert).

godailler○ /gɔdaje/ [1] *vi* to ruck.

godasse○ /gɔdas/ *nf* shoe.

godelureau†, *pl* **~x** /gɔdlyʀo/ *nm* (dandy) popinjay†.

godemiché /gɔdmiʃe/ *nm* dildo.

goder /gɔde/ [1] *vi* (vêtement) to ruck; (papier peint) to wrinkle.

godet /gɔdɛ/ *nm* **1** (gobelet) goblet; (petit récipient) pot; **on va prendre un ~**○**?** let's go and have a drink; **2** Cout (faux pli) ruck; (pan de jupe) gore; **jupe à ~s** gored skirt; **3** Gén Civ bucket; **4** Jeux (à dés) shaker.

godiche○ /gɔdiʃ/ **I** *adj* silly; **avoir un air ~** to look silly.
II *nf* ninny.

godille /gɔdij/ **I** *nf* **1** Naut (aviron) steering oar; **2** Sport (à ski) wedeln; **faire (de) la ~** to wedeln.
II○ **à la ~** *loc adj* péj [*système*] crummy○.

godiller /gɔdije/ [1] *vi* Sport (à skis) to wedeln.

godillot /gɔdijo/ *nm* **1**○ (soulier) clodhopper○; **2**† Mil (brodequin) combat boot; **3** (inconditionnel) pej yes-man, unquestioning supporter (**de** of).

goéland /gɔelɑ̃/ *nm* gull.
■ **~ argenté** herring gull; **~ cendré** common gull.

goélette /gɔelɛt/ *nf* schooner.

goémon /gɔemɔ̃/ *nm* (algues) wrack; Agric (engrais) seaweed fertilizer.

gogo○ /gogo/ **I** *nm* (dupe) sucker○.
II à gogo *loc adv* **vin à ~** wine galore; **de l'argent, il en a à ~** he's got loads of money.

goguenard, **~e** /gɔgnaʀ, aʀd/ *adj* quietly ironic; **avoir l'air ~** to have a quietly ironic air.

goguenardise /gɔgnaʀdiz/ *nf* (attitude) ironic mockery ¢.

gogues◐ /gɔg/ *nmpl* (toilettes) bog◐ (*sg*) GB, can○ (*sg*) US.

goguette○: **en goguette** /ɑ̃gɔgɛt/ **I** *loc adj* (ivre) tipsy.
II *loc adv* **partir en ~** to go on a spree.

goinfre /gwɛ̃fʀ/ **I** *adj* **être ~** to be a greedy pig○.
II *nmf* greedy pig○.

goinfrer○: **se goinfrer** /gwɛ̃fʀe/ [1] *vpr* to stuff oneself○ (**de** with).

goinfrerie○ /gwɛ̃fʀəʀi/ *nf* piggishness○, greed.

goître /gwatʀ/ *nm* goitre[GB].

goîtreux, **-euse** /gwatʀø, øz/ **I** *adj* goitrous.
II *nm,f* goitre[GB] sufferer.

golden /gɔldɛn/ *nf inv* Golden Delicious (apple).

golf /gɔlf/ ▶ 449 *nm* **1** (sport) golf; **champion de ~** golf champion; **une leçon de ~** a golfing lesson; **jouer au ~** to play golf; **2** (terrain) golf course.
■ **~ miniature** miniature golf.

golfe /gɔlf/ *nm* (grand) gulf; (petit) bay; **le ~ de Guinée/du Mexique** the Gulf of Guinea/of Mexico; **le ~ de Gascogne/du Bengale** the Bay of Biscay/of Bengal; **le ~ Persique** the Persian Gulf.

Golfe /gɔlf/ ▶ 692 *nprm* **le ~**, **la région du ~** the Gulf; **la crise du ~** the Gulf crisis.

golfeur, **-euse** /gɔlfœʀ, øz/ ▶ 510 *nm,f* golfer.

Golgotha /gɔlgɔta/ *nprm* **le ~** Golgotha.

Goliath /gɔljat/ *npr* Goliath.

gombo /gɔ̃bo/ *nm* **1** (plante) okra; **2** (soupe) gombo.

gomina® /gɔmina/ *nf* hair cream.

gominer: **se gominer** /gɔmine/ [1] *vpr* to slick one's hair back; **cheveux gominés** slicked-back hair.

gommage /gɔmaʒ/ *nm* **1** (action d'effacer) rubbing-out, erasing; **2** (action d'enduire) gumming; **3** Cosmét scrub; **se faire faire un ~ du corps/du visage** to have a body/facial scrub.

gomme /gɔm/ **I** *nf* **1** (pour effacer) eraser, rubber GB; **2** (substance) gum; **3** (bonbon) gum drop; **4** C (chewing-gum) **~ (à mâcher)** chewing gum; **5** Méd gumma.
II à la gomme○ *loc adj* péj [*idée, personne*] pathetic, useless; [*renseignement, machine, invention*] useless; [*projet*] hopeless.
■ **~ adhésive** blu-tack®; **~ arabique** gum arabic; **~ à encre** ink eraser.
IDIOMES **mettre (toute) la ~**○ (en voiture, à moto) to step on it○; (en avion, bateau) to give it full throttle○; (avec une radio) to turn it up full blast.

gomme-gutte, *pl* **gommes-guttes** /gɔmgyt/ *nf* gamboge.

gommer /gɔme/ [1] *vtr* **1** (effacer) to erase, to rub [sth] out [*mot*]; **2** (faire disparaître) to smooth out [*ride*]; to erase [*passé, frontière*]; to iron out [*différence*]; to soothe away [*fatigue*]; **3** (enduire) to gum; **papier gommé** gummed paper; **4** Cosmét to scrub [*peau*].

gomme-résine, *pl* **gommes-résines** /gɔmʀezin/ *nf* gum resin.

gommeux, **-euse** /gɔmø, øz/ **I** *adj* **1** gén [*arbre*] gum-yielding; [*substance*] gummy, sticky; **2** Méd gummatous.
II○ *nm* dandy.

gommier /gɔmje/ *nm* gum tree.

Gomorrhe /gɔmɔʀ/ ▶ 857 *npr* Gomorrha.

gonade /gɔnad/ *nf* gonade.

gonadotrope /gɔnadɔtʀɔp/ *adj* gonadotrophic.

gonadotrophine /gɔnadɔtʀɔfin/ *nf* gonadotrophin.

gond /gɔ̃/ *nm* hinge; **sortir de ses ~s** [*porte*] to come off its hinges; fig [*personne*] to fly off the handle○; **faire sortir qn de ses ~s** to make sb fly off the handle○.

gondolage /gɔ̃dɔlaʒ/ *nm* (de papier) crinkling ¢; (de bois) warping ¢; (de métal) buckling ¢.

gondolant○, **~e** /gɔ̃dɔlɑ̃, ɑ̃t/ *adj* (drôle) hilarious○.

gondole /gɔ̃dɔl/ *nf* **1** Naut gondola; **en ~** in a gondola; **2** Comm (de supermarché) sales shelf, gondola spéc.

gondolement /gɔ̃dɔlmɑ̃/ *nm* = **gondolage**.

gondoler /gɔ̃dɔle/ [1] **I** *vi* [*papier*] to crinkle; [*bois*] to warp; [*métal*] to buckle.
II se gondoler *vpr* **1** [*papier*] to crinkle;

[*bois*] to warp; [*métal*] to buckle; **2**○ (rire) to laugh.

gondolier, **-ière** /gɔ̃dɔlje, ɛʀ/ ▶**510** *nm,f* gondolier.

gonfalon /gɔ̃falɔ̃/ *nm* gonfalon.

gonfalonnier /gɔ̃falɔnje/ *nm* gonfalonier.

gonflable /gɔ̃flabl/ *adj* inflatable.

gonflage /gɔ̃flaʒ/ *nm* **1** (de pneu, ballon) inflation; **station de ~** Aut air point (for pumping up tyres); **2** Cin (de film) enlarging, blowing up.

gonflant, **~e** /gɔ̃flɑ̃, ɑ̃t/ *adj* **1** [*shampooing*] extra-body; **2**◑ (ennuyeux) boring; (agaçant) irritating.

gonflé, **~e** /gɔ̃fle/ **I** *pp* ▶ **gonfler**.
II *pp adj* **1** (plein d'air) [*pneu, ballon*] inflated; [*joue*] puffed out; **2** (enflé) [*bourgeon, veine, sein*] swollen (**de** with); [*ventre*] (après un repas) bloated; (de malade) swollen, distended; [*yeux, visage*] puffy, swollen; [*muscle*] bulging, flexed; [*sac*] bulging (**de** with); **yeux ~s de sommeil/de larmes** eyes heavy with sleep/swollen with tears; **éponge ~e d'eau** sponge saturated with water; **3** Aut [*moteur*] souped-up (*épith*); **voiture au moteur ~** hot rod GB, muscle car US.
III *adj* **1**○ (courageux) gutsy○; **être ~** to have guts○; **c'est ~** it takes guts○; **2**○ (impudent) cheeky; **être ~** to have a nerve○; **(il est) ~, le mec**○! the guy's got a nerve!

gonflement /gɔ̃fləmɑ̃/ *nm* **1** (enflure) (de pied, paupière) swelling; (de ventre) distension; **2** (augmentation) (de budget, nombres) increase (**de** in); (de résultats) inflation (**de** of); **3** (de pneu) inflation; (d'éponge) saturation.

gonfler /gɔ̃fle/ [1] **I** *vtr* **1** (remplir d'air) (avec la bouche) to blow up [*ballon, pneu*]; to fill [*poumon*] (**de** with); to puff out [*joue*]; (avec une pompe) to inflate, to pump up [*ballon, pneu*]; **être gonflé à bloc** [*pneu*] to be fully inflated; fig [*personne*] to be raring○ to go; **le vent gonfle la voile** the wind swells ou fills the sail; **le vent gonfle ma chemise** the wind makes my shirt billow; **2** (faire augmenter) [*personne*] to tense, to flex [*muscle*]; [*objet*] to make [sth] bulge [*poche, sac*]; [*eau*] to saturate [*éponge*]; [*pluie*] to make [sth] swollen [*rivière*]; [*sève*] to swell [*bourgeon*]; **la limonade gonfle l'estomac** lemonade makes you feel bloated; **3** fig **la joie gonflait mon cœur** my heart was bursting with joy; **leur victoire les a gonflés d'orgueil** their victory has gone to their heads; **4** (augmenter) to increase [*bénéfices, effectifs*]; to bump up○, to push up [*prix*]; to inflate [*statistiques*]; to exaggerate [*importance*]; **5**◑ (énerver) **~ qn** to get on sb's nerves; **tu me gonfles!** you're getting on my nerves!; **6** Cin to enlarge, to blow [sth] up [*film*]; **7** Aut to soup up [*moteur, voiture*].
II *vi* **1** (enfler) [*pied, sein*] to swell (up), to get swollen; [*visage, paupière*] to swell (up), to become puffy; [*riz, bois, éponge*] to swell; [*gâteau, pâte*] Culin to rise; **laisser ~ le riz** leave the rice to swell; **2** (augmenter) [*somme, effectifs*] to increase; **faire ~ les prix** to push prices up.
III se gonfler *vpr* **1** (enfler) [*voile*] to swell, to fill; [*rivière*] to become swollen; **l'éponge se gonfle (d'eau)** the sponge becomes saturated with water; **se ~ d'orgueil** fig to be full of one's own importance; **2** (augmenter) [*recette, budget, effectifs*] to increase (**de** by).

gonflette○ /gɔ̃flɛt/ *nf* pej **faire de la ~** to pump iron○, to go body-building.

gonfleur /gɔ̃flœʀ/ *nm* gén, Aut (air) pump.

gong /gɔ̃g/ *nm* **1** ▶**534** Mus gong; **2** Sport (en boxe) bell.

goniomètre /gɔnjɔmɛtʀ/ *nm* goniometer.

goniométrie /gɔnjɔmetʀi/ *nf* goniometry.

goniométrique /gɔnjɔmetʀik/ *adj* goniometric.

gonococcie /gɔnɔkɔksi/ *nf* gonorrhea.

gonocoque /gɔnɔkɔk/ *nm* gonococcus.

gonorrhée† /gɔnɔʀe/ ▶**271** *nf* gonorrhea.

gonze◑ /gɔ̃z/ *nm* guy○, bloke○ GB.

gonzesse◑ /gɔ̃zɛs/ *nf* **1** (femme) bird○ GB, chick○ US; **2** (homme) sissy○.

gordien /gɔʀdjɛ̃/ *adj m* **trancher le nœud ~** to cut the Gordian knot.

goret /gɔʀɛ/ *nm* **1** Zool piglet; **2**○ (enfant sale) little pig○.

gorge /gɔʀʒ/ *nf* **1** ▶**188** Anat throat; **avoir mal à la ~** to have a sore throat; **couper la ~ à qn** to cut ou slit sb's throat; **le chien m'a sauté à la ~** the dog leaped at my throat; **rire/voix de ~** throaty laughter/voice; **l'odeur/la fumée nous a pris à la ~** the smell/the smoke got to our throats; **je suis pris à la ~, je n'ai plus un sou et je dois payer mon loyer** I'm in a fix○, I haven't got a penny and I've got to pay my rent; **tenir qn à la ~** lit to have sb by the throat; fig to have a stranglehold over sb; **des sanglots me montèrent à la ~** sobs rose in my throat; **avoir la ~ sèche** to have a dry throat; **avoir la ~ serrée** or **nouée** (d'émotion) to have a lump in one's throat; (de peur, trac) to have one's heart in one's mouth; **à ~ déployée, à pleine ~** [*chanter*] at the top of one's voice; [*rire*] uproariously; **je te ferai rentrer tes mots** or **paroles dans la ~**! I'll make you eat your words!; **ta remarque m'est restée en travers de la ~** I found your comment hard to swallow ou very hard to take; **ma question m'est restée dans la ~** I couldn't get the question out; ▶ **couteau**; **2** (poitrine) bosom, breast; **3** Géog gorge; **les ~s du Tarn/du Verdon** the gorge of the Tarn/of the Verdon; **4** Tech (de poulie) groove; (de serrure) tumbler; **5** Archit groove.
IDIOMES **faire des ~s chaudes de qn/qch** to laugh sb/sth to scorn; **rendre ~** to return ill-gotten gains.

gorgé, **~e** /gɔʀʒe/ **I** *pp* ▶ **gorger**.
II *pp adj* **~ de nourriture** glutted with food; **~ d'eau** [*terre*] waterlogged; [*éponge*] saturated with water (*jamais épith*); **fruit ~ de soleil** fruit bursting with sunshine.

gorge-de-pigeon /gɔʀʒdəpiʒɔ̃/ *adj inv* iridescent; **soie ~** shot silk.

gorgée /gɔʀʒe/ *nf* gén (petite) sip; (grande) gulp; **avaler une ou deux ~s** to take a couple of swallows; **boire à petites ~s** to take little sips; **boire à grandes ~s** to drink in gulps; **boire son café à grandes/petites ~s** to gulp down/to sip one's coffee; **il a vidé son verre d'une seule ~** he emptied his glass in one gulp.

gorger /gɔʀʒe/ [13] **I** *vtr* to force-feed [*volaille*]; **~ qn de nourriture** to stuff○ sb with food.
II se gorger *vpr* **se ~ de nourriture** to gorge oneself; **la terre se gorge d'eau** the soil soaks up water.

gorgone /gɔʀgɔn/ *nf* **1** Archit (tête décorative) Gorgon's head; **2** Zool (poisson) gorgonian.

Gorgone /gɔʀgɔn/ *npr* Mythol Gorgon; **les trois ~s** the three Gorgons.

gorille /gɔʀij/ *nm* **1** Zool gorilla; **2**○ (garde du corps) bodyguard, heavy○.

gosier /gozje/ *nm* throat, gullet; **ce vin (m')écorche le ~**○ hum this wine is like paint stripper; **ça m'est resté en travers du ~** it stuck in my throat.
IDIOMES **s'humecter le ~** to wet one's whistle; **chanter à plein ~** to sing at the top of one's voice.

gospel /gɔspɛl/ *nm* **1** (style) gospel music; **2** (chant) gospel song.

gosse○ /gɔs/ **I** *adj* **rester ~** to be still a kid at heart; **tu fais très ~ dans cette robe** you look like a little girl in that dress.
II *nmf* (enfant) kid○, child; **sale ~** brat○; **c'est un grand ~** he is still a kid at heart; **il est beau ~** he's a good-looking fellow.

Goth /go/ *nmf* Goth.

gotha /gɔta/ *nm* (noblesse) aristocracy; (haute société) high society; **fréquenter le ~ politique/financier** to move in high political/financial circles; **le ~ des publicitaires** the top advertising agents (*pl*); **le ~ économique** the economic elite.

gothique /gɔtik/ **I** *adj* Gothic.
II *nm* Gothic; **le ~ flamboyant** flamboyant Gothic.

gouache /gwaʃ/ *nf* **1** (peinture) gouache, poster paint; **peindre à la ~** to paint in gouache; **2** (tableau) gouache.

gouaille /gwɑj/ *nf* (esprit moqueur) cheek.

gouailleur, **-euse** /gwɑjœʀ, øz/ *adj* [*personne, sourire, humeur*] cheeky.

goualante† /gwalɑ̃t/ *nf* (plaintive) song.

gouape○ /gwap/ *nf* lout.

goudron /gudʀɔ̃/ *nm* **1** (pour revêtement) tar, tarmac® GB; **2** Chimie tar; **'~s 12 mg'** '12 mg tar'.

goudronnage /gudʀɔnaʒ/ *nm* tarring ¢.

goudronné, **~e** /gudʀɔne/ **I** *pp* ▶ **goudronner**.
II *pp adj* tarmac.

goudronner /gudʀɔne/ [1] *vtr* to tarmac.

goudronneux, **-euse** /gudʀɔnø, øz/ **I** *adj* tarry.
II goudronneuse *nf* (machine) tarring machine.

gouffre /gufʀ/ *nm* **1** (fosse) chasm, abyss; **le ~ de Padirac** the caves (*pl*) of Padirac; **2** fig **le ~ de l'oubli** the pit of oblivion; **le pays est au bord du ~** the country is on the brink of the abyss; **leur maison est un ~** their house is a real drain on their finances.

gouge /guʒ/ *nf* gouge; **tailler à la ~** to gouge out.

gougère /guʒɛʀ/ *nf* gougère (*choux pastry with added cheese*).

gougnafier○ /guɲafje/ *nm* pej knucklehead○.

gouille /guj/ *nf* H (flaque) puddle.

gouine◑ /gwin/ *nf* offensive dyke◑ injur, lesbian.

goujat /guʒa/ *nm* boor; **en ~, comme un ~** boorishly.

goujaterie /guʒatʀi/ *nf* boorishness; **il est d'une ~ incroyable** he's incredibly boorish.

goujon /guʒɔ̃/ *nm* **1** Zool gudgeon; **2** Tech (cheville) gén pin; (en bois) dowel.
IDIOMES **taquiner le ~**○ to do the odd bit of fishing.

goulag /gulag/ *nm* Gulag.

goulasch /gulaʃ/ *nm* ou *f* goulash ¢.

goule /gul/ *nf* ghoul.

goulée○ /gule/ *nf* (de liquide) gulp; (de nourriture) mouthful; (d'air) gulp; **d'une ~** in one gulp.

goulet /gulɛ/ *nm* (de port) narrows (*pl*); (en montagne) gully.
■ **~ d'étranglement** bottleneck.

gouleyant, **~e** /gulɛjɑ̃, ɑ̃t/ *adj* [*vin*] light.

goulot /gulo/ *nm* (de bouteille) neck; **boire au ~** to drink from the bottle.
■ **~ d'étranglement** bottleneck.

goulotte /gulɔt/ *nf* Tech chute.

goulu, **~e** /guly/ **I** *adj* greedy.
II *nm,f* glutton.

goulûment /gulymɑ̃/ *adv* greedily.

goupil‡ /gupi(l)/ *nm* fox.

goupille /gupij/ *nf* Tech pin.

goupillé○, **~e** /gupije/ **I** *pp* ▶ **goupiller**.
II *pp adj* set up, thought up; **c'est ~ comment, ce moteur?** how does this engine work?; **bien/mal ~** [*appareil, installation*] well-/badly-designed; [*procédé*] well-/badly-thought out; **pas mal ~, cet engin!** it's pretty clever this thing!

goupiller /gupije/ [1] **I** *vtr* **1**○ (combiner) to fix○; **2** Tech to pin.
II se goupiller○ *vpr* **comment ça se goupille ton projet?** how is your plan shaping up○ or working out?; **ça s'est bien/mal goupillé** it turned out well/badly.

goupillon /gupijɔ̃/ *nm* **1** (brosse) bottle

brush; **2** Relig holy water sprinkler, aspergillum.

gourance◑ /guʀɑ̃s/ *nf* mistake, boob○.

gourbi /guʀbi/ *nm* **1** (hutte) hut; **2**○ (logement) hovel.

gourd, **~e**[1] /guʀ, guʀd/ *adj* (engourdi) [*doigt, membre*] numb.

gourde[2] /guʀd/ **I** *adj*○ (niais) [*personne*] dumb○, gormless○ GB.

II *nf* **1** (pour liquide) (en cuir ou écorce) gourd; (bidon, flacon) flask; **2** Bot gourd; **3**○ (sot) dope○.

gourdin /guʀdɛ̃/ *nm* bludgeon, cudgel; **frapper qn à coups de ~** to bludgeon sb.

gourer◑: **se gourer** /guʀe/ [1] *vpr* (dans un calcul) to make a mistake; (dans une supposition) to be mistaken; **se ~ d'adresse/de jour** to get the address/the day wrong.

gourgandine† /guʀgɑ̃din/ *nf* hussy†, loose woman†.

gourmand, **~e** /guʀmɑ̃, ɑ̃d/ **I** *adj* **1** (amateur) (de sucreries) fond of sweet things (*jamais épith*); (de nourriture) fond of good food (*jamais épith*); (glouton) greedy; **il est ~** he loves his food GB, he's into food US; **je ne suis pas ~e** I'm not that interested in food; **il est ~ (de sucreries)** he has a sweet tooth; **il est ~ de fromage/gâteaux** he can't resist cheese/cakes; **ma voiture est ~e** my car is heavy on petrol GB, my car is a gas hog○ US; **2** (gastronomique) **repas ~** gourmet meal; **étape ~e** good eating place; **3** (avide d'argent) grasping; **un courtier ~** a grasping broker; **4** (sensuel) [*lèvres*] sensuous; **il la regardait d'un air ~** he looked at her hungrily.

II *nm,f* (amateur de nourriture) **c'est un ~** (pour les sucreries) he has a sweet tooth; (pour la nourriture) he loves his food GB, he's into food US; **petit ~!** you greedy little thing!

IDIOMES **être ~ comme une chatte** to be a real gourmet.

gourmander /guʀmɑ̃de/ [1] *vtr* to berate sout, to scold; **se faire ~** to be rebuked or scolded.

gourmandise /guʀmɑ̃diz/ **I** *nf* (pour les sucreries) weakness for sweet things; (pour la nourriture) weakness for good food; (défaut) greed; (péché) gluttony; **la ~ est un péché capital** gluttony is a deadly sin; **j'en reprends par ~** I shouldn't, but I can't resist it; **avec ~** [*manger, regarder*] greedily.

II gourmandises *nfpl* (friandises) sweets GB, candies US.

gourme /guʀm/ *nf* Vét strangles (+ *v sg*).

IDIOMES **jeter sa ~** to sow one's wild oats.

gourmet /guʀmɛ/ *nm* gourmet; **un régal pour les ~s** a feast for the gourmet.

gourmette /guʀmɛt/ *nf* **1** (de poignet) chain bracelet; **2** Équit curb chain.

gourou /guʀu/ *nm* guru.

gousse /gus/ *nf* Bot pod; **~ de vanille** vanilla pod; **~ d'ail** clove of garlic.

gousset /gusɛ/ *nm* **1** (poche) fob; **2** (de collant) gusset; **3** Tech gusset; **4** Hérald gusset.

goût /gu/ *nm* **1** Physiol (sens) taste; (appréciation) palate; **agréable/désagréable au ~** pleasant-/unpleasant-tasting; **avoir le ~ exercé** to have a keen palate; **stimuler/émousser le ~** to stimulate/to dull one's sense of taste; **éduquer le ~ des enfants** to teach children to appreciate food; **2** (saveur) taste; **avoir un ~ sucré/désagréable** to have a sweet/an unpleasant taste; **avoir un ~ de brûlé/de pêche** to taste burned/of peaches; **avoir un petit ~ de miel** to taste slightly of honey; **avoir bon/mauvais ~** to taste nice/unpleasant; **avoir un petit ~** to taste a bit strange; **laisser un (mauvais) ~ dans la bouche** to leave a nasty taste in one's mouth; **le vin a un léger ~ de bouchon** the wine tastes slightly corked; **donner du ~ à qch** to give sth flavour[GB]; **n'avoir aucun ~** to be tasteless; **3** (discernement) taste; **avoir du ~** to have taste; **se fier à son ~** to trust to one's own taste; **avoir un ~ très sûr** to have unfailingly good taste; **avoir bon/mauvais ~** to have good/bad taste; **de bon/mauvais ~** [*décor, vêtement, plaisanterie*] in good/bad taste (*après n*); **d'un ~ douteux** [*décor, plaisanterie, scène*] in dubious taste (*après n*); **les gens de ~** people with good taste; **c'étaient des personnes de ~** they had good taste; **avec/sans ~** [*décorer*] tastefully/tastelessly; **s'habiller avec/sans ~** to be well-/badly-dressed; **sans ~ ni grâce** [*personne, visage*] plain and ordinary; **il serait de mauvais ~ de faire** it would be in bad taste to do; **avoir le bon ~ de faire** to have the decency to do; **avoir le bon ~ de ne pas faire** to have the good taste not to do; **avoir le mauvais ~ de faire** to be tactless enough to do; **4** (gré) liking; **trop chaud à mon ~** too hot for my liking; **avoir du ~ pour la peinture** to have a liking for painting; **ne pas être du ~ de tout le monde** [*situation, réforme, proposition*] not to be to everyone's liking; [*décor, site, aliment, forme d'art*] not to be everyone's cup of tea; **je n'ai rien trouvé à mon ~ chez l'antiquaire** I didn't find anything I liked in the antique shop; **elle ne trouve pas mon fils à son ~** she doesn't like my son; **mon choix n'était pas au ~ de mon père** my father didn't approve of my choice; **je n'ai aucun ~ pour la politique** I have absolutely no interest in politics; **je n'ai plus ~ à rien** I've lost interest in things; **elle reprend ~ à la vie** she's starting to enjoy life again; **avoir le ~ du risque** to like taking risks; **avoir le ~ du détail** [*peintre, écrivain*] to like detail; [*décorateur, designer*] to pay attention to detail; **être au ~ du jour** to be trendy; to be 'in'; **se mettre au ~ du jour** to update one's image; **remettre qch au ~ du jour** to bring sth back into fashion; **il a pris ~ à la pêche/aux échecs** he got to like fishing/chess; **il semble prendre ~ à la politique** he seems to be developing a taste for politics; **faire qch par ~** to do sth for pleasure; **dans le ~ classique** in the classical style; **dans le ~ de Picasso** in the style of Picasso; **quelque chose dans** or **de ce ~-là**○ something a bit like that○; **je vais te faire passer le ~ de me critiquer en public**○ I'll teach you to criticize me in public; **5** (préférence) taste; **je ne connais pas tes ~s** I don't know your tastes; **avoir des ~s simples/de luxe** to have simple/expensive tastes; **mes ~s littéraires/artistiques** my taste in literature/art; **il y en a pour tous les ~s** there's something to suit all tastes; **'c'est joli?'—'ça dépend des ~s!'** 'is it pretty?'—'that's a matter of taste!'; **chacun ses ~s** to each his own, there's no accounting for taste.

IDIOMES **avoir un ~ de revenez-y** [*dessert, plat*] to be moreish GB, to make you want seconds US; **avoir un ~ de trop peu** or **pas assez** to be on the stingy side; **tous les ~s sont dans la nature** Prov it takes all sorts to make a world Prov; **des ~s et des couleurs on ne discute pas** Prov there's no accounting for taste.

goûter /gute/ [1] **I** *nm* **1** (collation, nourriture) snack (*eaten by children mid-morning or mid-afternoon*); **2** (réunion d'enfants) children's party; **~ d'anniversaire** children's birthday party.

II *vtr* **1** (essayer) to taste, to try; **goûtez-moi ça!** have a taste of this!; **je peux ~?** may I taste it?; **2** (apprécier) to enjoy [*plaisir, paix, silence, solitude*]; to appreciate [*spectacle, discours, plaisanterie*]; **je goûte fort peu ce genre de plaisanterie** I don't really appreciate that kind of joke.

III goûter à *vtr ind* **1** (essayer) **~ à** to try [*aliment, boisson*]; **il n'a pas voulu ~ à mon soufflé** he wouldn't try my soufflé; **mais tu y as à peine goûté!** but you've hardly touched it!; **2** (faire l'expérience de) **~ à** to have a taste of [*liberté, indépendance, pouvoir, plaisir*]; **~ aux joies/charmes de la campagne** to sample the joys/pleasures of the countryside.

IV goûter de *vtr ind* to have a taste of; **avoir goûté de la prison** to have had a taste of life in prison; **il va ~ de mon fouet!** he's going to get a taste of my whip!

V *vi* [*enfant*] to have one's mid-afternoon snack.

goûteur, **-euse**[1] /gutœʀ, øz/ ▶**510** *nm,f* taster; **~ d'eau** water taster.

goûteux, **-euse**[2] /gutø, øz/ *adj* tasty.

goutte /gut/ **I** *nf* **1** (de liquide) drop; **~ d'eau/de sang** drop of water/of blood; **~ de pluie** raindrop; **~ de rosée** dewdrop; **~ à ~** drop by drop; **tomber ~ à ~** to drip; **pas une ~ de sang n'a été versée** not a drop of blood was spilled; **à grosses ~s** [*pleuvoir*] heavily; [*transpirer*] profusely; **hier il est tombé quelques ~s** there were a few spots of rain yesterday; **'de la vodka?'—'juste une ~!'** 'some vodka?'—'just a drop!'; **il n'y a plus une ~ de vin dans la maison** there isn't a drop of wine left in the house; **passer entre les ~s** fig to manage to avoid trouble; **boire qch jusqu'à la dernière ~** lit, fig to drink sth to the (very) last drop; **~ de sueur** bead of sweat; **2**○ (eau-de-vie) brandy; **3** Archit gutta; **4** ▶**271** Méd gout.

II gouttes *nfpl* Méd, Pharm drops; **~s pour le nez/pour les yeux** nose/eye drops.

■ **~ d'eau** (bijou) drop.

IDIOMES **se ressembler comme deux ~s d'eau** to be as alike as two peas in a pod; **c'est une ~ d'eau dans la mer** or **l'océan** it's a drop in the ocean; **avoir la ~ au nez** to have a runny nose; **on n'y voit ~** you can't see a thing; ▶**vase**.

goutte-à-goutte /gutagut/ *nm inv* Méd drip; **être nourri au ~** to be drip-fed; **il est au ~** he has been put on a drip.

gouttelette /gutlɛt/ *nf* droplet.

goutter /gute/ [1] *vi* to drip (**de** from).

goutteux, **-euse** /gutø, øz/ *adj* gouty.

gouttière /gutjɛʀ/ *nf* **1** (de toit) gutter; (de descente) drainpipe; **2** Méd (d'immobilisation) splint.

■ **~ sagittale** Anat sagittal suture; **~ vertébrale** Anat vertebral groove.

gouvernable /guvɛʀnabl/ *adj* **facilement/difficilement ~** easy/difficult to govern.

gouvernail /guvɛʀnaj/ *nm* **1** Naut rudder; **2** fig helm; **tenir le ~** to be at the helm; **tenir le ~ d'une main ferme** to have a firm hand on the tiller; **abandonner le ~** to step down.

gouvernant, **~e** /guvɛʀnɑ̃, ɑ̃t/ **I** *adj* [*classe, parti*] ruling, governing.

II gouvernants *nmpl* **les ~s** (gouvernement) the government; **~s et gouvernés** those who govern and those who are governed; **nos ~s** our rulers.

III gouvernante *nf* **1** (institutrice) governess; **2** (domestique) housekeeper.

gouverne /guvɛʀn/ *nf* **1** (information) **pour votre ~** for your information; **2** Aviat control surface.

■ **~ de direction** rudder; **~ latérale** aileron; **~ de profondeur** elevator.

gouvernement /guvɛʀnəmɑ̃/ *nm* government; **faire partie du** or **être au ~** to be a member of the government; **le ~ Chirac** the Chirac Government; **sous un autre ~** under a different regime ou government.

gouvernemental, **~e**, *mpl* **-aux** /guvɛʀnəmɑ̃tal, o/ *adj* **1** (du gouvernement) [*arrêté, décision, politique*] government (*épith*); [*responsabilité*] governmental; **l'équipe ~e** the government; **non ~** non-governmental; **2** (au pouvoir) [*majorité, parti*] ruling; **3** (favorable au gouvernement) [*journal*] pro-government.

gouverner /guvɛʀne/ [1] **I** *vtr* **1** Pol to govern, to rule [*pays, peuple*]; **le parti qui gouverne** the ruling party, the party in

power, the governing party; **2** (dominer) [*personne*] to control [*désir, émotion, passion, vie*]; [*argent, intérêt*] to rule [*monde, hommes*]; **3** Naut to steer [*ship*]; **4** Ling to govern.
II **se gouverner** *vpr* **le droit des peuples à se ~** the right of peoples to self-government.

gouvernés /guvɛʀne/ *nmpl* Pol **les ~** those who are governed.

gouverneur /guvɛʀnœʀ/ *nm* governor; **~ militaire** military governor.

goy, *pl* **goyim** /gɔj, gɔjim/ *nmf* goy○, gentile.

goyave /gɔjav/ *nf* guava.

goyavier /gɔjavje/ *nm* guava (tree).

GPAO /ʒepeao/ *nf*: *abbr* ▶ **gestion**.

GPL /ʒepeɛl/ *nm* (*abbr* = **gaz de pétrole liquéfié**) LPG.

GQG /ʒekyʒe/ *nm*: *abbr* ▶ **grand**.

GR /ʒeɛʀ/ *nm* long-distance footpath.

Graal /gʀɑl/ *nm* Grail.

grabat /gʀaba/ *nm* pallet.

grabataire /gʀabatɛʀ/ I *adj* bedridden.
II *nmf* bedridden invalid; **les ~s** the bedridden.

grabuge○ /gʀabyʒ/ *nm* **il va y avoir du ~** (dispute) there'll be ructions GB, there'll be a ruckus○ US; (violence) there's going to be fisticuffs; **faire du ~** to raise hell○.

grâce /gʀɑs/ I *nf* **1** (beauté) (de geste, personne) grace; (de paysage) charm; (de style) elegance; **sans ~** [*geste*] ungraceful; [*visage*] plain; [*personne*] lacking in charm (*jamais épith*); [*paysage*] nondescript; [*style*] inelegant; **se mouvoir avec/sans ~** to move gracefully/awkwardly; **2** (volonté) **bonne/mauvaise ~** good/bad grace; **de bonne/mauvaise ~** with (a) good/bad grace, willingly/grudgingly; **avoir la bonne ~ d'admettre que** to have the good grace to admit that; **il aurait mauvaise ~ à refuser** it would be ungracious of him to refuse; **3** (faveur) favour[GB]; **accorder une ~ à qn** to grant sb a favour[GB]; **chercher/gagner les bonnes ~s de qn** to seek/win sb's favour[GB]; **trouver ~ auprès de qn/aux yeux de qn** to find favour[GB] with sb/in sb's eyes; **faire à qn la ~ d'accepter** fml to do sb the honour[GB] of accepting; **il nous a fait la ~ d'assister à la réunion** he honoured[GB] us with his presence at the meeting; **fais-nous la ~ de te taire!** do us a favour[GB], be quiet!, please, be quiet!; **à la ~ de Dieu!** it's in God's hands!; **de ~** fml please; (avec impatience) for pity's sake; **donner le coup de ~ à qn** lit, fig to deal sb the death blow; **ce fut le coup de ~ pour lui** that was the final stroke for him; **4** (pardon) mercy; Jur (free) pardon; **demander/crier ~** to beg/cry for mercy; **solliciter/obtenir sa ~** Jur to seek/receive a pardon; **~ présidentielle/royale** Jur presidential/royal pardon; **~!** (have) mercy!; **je vous fais ~ des détails** I'll spare you the details; **5** (remerciement) liter thanks; **rendre ~(s) à qn de qch** to give thanks to sb for sth; **~ à Dieu!** thank God!; **6** Relig (bonté divine) grace; **être touché par la ~** Relig to be touched by God's grace.
II **grâces** *nfpl* **1** (prière) **dire les ~s** to say grace (after a meal); **2**† (gracieusetés) hum **avec mille ~s** very graciously; **elle lui fit mille ~s pour essayer de le fléchir** she used all her charm to get round him.
III **grâce à** *loc prép* **~ à** thanks to; **il s'en est tiré ~ à Dieu** fig by some miracle he was all right.

Grâce /gʀɑs/ I *nf* (titre) Grace; **votre ~** your Grace.
II *nprf* Mythol **les trois ~s** the three Graces.

gracier /gʀasje/ [2] *vtr* to pardon, to reprieve.

gracieusement /gʀasjøzmɑ̃/ *adv* **1** (gratuitement) free of charge; **un billet/cadeau vous sera ~ offert** you will be given a free ticket/gift; **2** (élégamment) [*danser*] gracefully; **3** (aimablement) [*recevoir*] graciously.

gracieuseté /gʀasjøzte/ *nf* liter **1** (amabilité) graciousness; **2** (geste aimable) kindness, courtesy; (mot aimable) kind word.

gracieux, -ieuse /gʀasjø, øz/ *adj* **1** (beau) [*geste, personne*] graceful; **sa gracieuse Majesté** fml his/her gracious Majesty; **2** (généreux) fml [*concours, aide*] kind, generous; **3** (avenant) [*personne, sourire*] gracious; **4** Jur [*juridiction*] inherent; [*décision*] made by exercise of the inherent jurisdiction of the court (*après n*); **recours ~** application for review.

gracile /gʀasil/ *adj* slender.

gracilité /gʀasilite/ *nf* slenderness.

Gracques /gʀak/ *nprmpl* **les ~** the Gracchi.

gradation /gʀadasjɔ̃/ *nf* **1** gén, Art, Phot gradation; **2** Ling (en rhétorique) climax; **~ descendante** anticlimax.

grade /gʀad/ ▶ **390** *nm* **1** (niveau hiérarchique) rank; **nommé au ~ de** appointed to the rank of; **de ~ élevé** high-ranking (*épith*); **monter en ~** to be promoted; **casser un officer de son ~** to demote an officer to the ranks; **2** Univ (titre) degree; **~ de docteur** doctor's degree; **3** Math (en géométrie) grade; **4** Ind (viscosité de lubrifiant) grade.
IDIOMES **en prendre pour son ~**○ to be hauled over the coals, to get a good dressing-down.

gradé, ~e /gʀade/ *nm,f* Mil noncommissioned officer.

gradient /gʀadjɑ̃/ *nm* Math, Phys gradient.

gradin /gʀadɛ̃/ *nm* (de salle) tier; (d'arène) terrace; (de stade) **les ~s** the terraces GB, the bleachers US; **en ~s** [*terrain*] terraced.

graduation /gʀadɥasjɔ̃/ *nf* (d'instrument de mesure) graduation.

gradué, ~e /gʀadɥe/ *adj* **règle ~e** ruler; **verre ~** measuring cup; (avec bec verseur) measuring jug.

graduel, -elle /gʀadɥɛl/ I *adj* gradual.
II *nm* Relig gradual.

graduellement /gʀadɥɛlmɑ̃/ *adv* gradually.

graduer /gʀadɥe/ [1] *vtr* **1** gén to increase [*difficulté*]; to grade GB, to graduate US [*exercices*]; **2** Tech to graduate [*instrument*].

graffiteur, -euse /gʀafitœʀ, øz/ *nm,f* graffiti artist.

graffiti /gʀafiti/ *nmpl* graffiti.

graille◑ /gʀɑj/ *nf* grub○ ¢, chow○ ¢ US; **à la ~!** grub's up○!

grailler /gʀɑje/ [1] I◑ *vtr* (manger) to eat.
II *vi* Zool [*corneille*] to caw.

graillon /gʀɑjɔ̃/ *nm* **1**○ (graisse frite) **ça sent le ~** it smells of stale fat; **2**◑ (crachat) gob of spit.

grain /gʀɛ̃/ *nm* **1** (céréales) grain; **donner du ~ aux poules** to feed corn GB ou grain to the hens; **poulet nourri au ~** corn-fed GB ou grain-fed chicken; **2** (graine) grain; **~ de poivre** peppercorn; **poivre en ~s** Culin (whole) peppercorns (*pl*); **~ de café** coffee bean; **café en ~s** Comm coffee beans (*pl*); **~ de moutarde** mustard seed; **3** (baie) berry; **~ de cassis** blackcurrant; **~ de genièvre** juniper berry; **~ de raisin** grape; **4** (de collier, chapelet) bead (**de** of); **5** (de pollen, sel, sable) grain (**de** of); (de poussière) speck (**de** of); (de semoule, sucre) grain; **6** fig (brin) **un ~ de fantaisie/folie** a touch of fantasy/madness; **un ~ de bon sens** a scrap ou an ounce of common sense; **7** (texture) **le ~** the grain (**de** of); **à gros ~** coarse grained; **d'un ~ très fin** very fine-grained; **8** Météo, Naut (bourrasque) gust (of wind); (averse) squally shower; Naut squall.
■ **~ de beauté** beauty spot, mole.
IDIOMES **avoir un (petit) ~**○ to be a bit loony○; **mettre son ~ de sel**○ to put ou stick one's oar in○; ▶ **ivraie**.

graine /gʀɛn/ *nf* seed; **~s** (grosses ou individuelles) seeds; (petites pour semence) seed ¢; (pour oiseaux) birdseed ¢; **monter en ~** [*légume*] to run to seed; hum [*enfant*] to shoot up; **ton fils, c'est de la mauvaise ~** your son is a bad lot○; **c'est de la ~ de voyou** they'll come to a bad end.
IDIOMES **casser la ~**○ to have a bite to eat; **prends-en de la ~**○ let that be an example to you.

graineterie /gʀɛnt(ə)ʀi/ ▶ **510** *nf* **1** (activité) seed trade; **2** (magasin) seedsman's shop GB, feedstore US.

grainetier /gʀɛntje/ ▶ **510** *nm* seedsman GB; **il est ~** he runs a feedstore US.

graissage /gʀɛsaʒ/ *nm* Tech greasing, lubricating; **à ~ automatique** self-lubricating.

graisse /gʀɛs/ *nf* **1** (tissu adipeux) fat; (de baleine, phoque) blubber; **2** Culin fat; **~ animale/végétale** animal/vegetable fat; **mangez moins de ~s** eat less fat; **3** (lubrifiant) grease.
■ **~ de porc** Culin lard; **~ de rôti** Culin dripping GB, drippings (*pl*) US.
IDIOMES **secouer sa ~** to get a move on○.

graisser /gʀɛse/ [1] *vtr* **1** (enduire) to grease [*poêle*]; to grease, to lubricate [*rouage*]; **2** (salir) to leave greasy marks on, to make [sth] greasy; **'ne graisse pas'** 'nongreasy'.
IDIOMES **~ la patte à qn**○ to grease sb's palm.

graisseur, -euse[1] /gʀɛsœʀ, øz/ I *adj* greasing, lubricating (*épith*).
II *nm* (ouvrier, dispositif) lubricator.

graisseux, -euse[2] /gʀɛsø, øz/ *adj* gén greasy; Méd [*tissu, tumeur, bourrelet*] fatty.

graminacées /gʀaminase/ *nfpl* **les ~** grasses, Graminaceae spéc.

graminée /gʀamine/ I *adj f* [*plante*] grass (*épith*), graminaceous spéc.
II *nf* **une ~** a grass; **les ~s** grasses, Graminaceae spéc.

grammage /gʀamaʒ/ *nm* (de papier) weight.

grammaire /gʀamɛʀ/ *nf* **1** Ling (science) grammar; **la ~ du japonais** Japanese grammar; **livre/cours de ~** grammar book/lesson; **faute de ~** grammatical mistake; **~ descriptive/générative/structurale** descriptive/generative/structural grammar; **2** (manuel) grammar; **une ~ latine** a Latin grammar; **une ~ du chinois** a Chinese grammar.

grammairien, -ienne /gʀamɛʀjɛ̃, ɛn/ ▶ **510** *nm,f* grammarian.

grammatical, ~e, *mpl* **-aux** /gʀamatikal, o/ *adj* grammatical.

grammaticalement /gʀamatikalmɑ̃/ *adv* grammatically.

grammaticalité /gʀamatikalite/ *nf* grammaticality.

gramme /gʀam/ ▶ **620** *nm* gram; **il n'a pas un ~ de bon sens** he hasn't an ounce of common sense.

gramophone® /gʀamɔfɔn/ *nm* gramophone.

grand, ~e /gʀɑ̃, gʀɑ̃d/ I *adj* **1** (de dimensions importantes) (en hauteur) [*personne, arbre, tour, cierge*] tall; (en longueur, durée) [*bras, enjambée, promenade, voyage*] long; (en largeur) [*angle, marge*] wide; (en étendue, volume) [*lac, ville, salle, trou, édifice, paquet*] large, big; [*tas, feu*] big; (démesuré) [*pied, nez, bouche*] big; **un homme (très) ~** a (very) tall man; **un ~ homme brun, un homme ~ et brun** a tall dark man; **plus ~ que nature** larger than life; **ouvrir de ~s yeux** to open one's eyes wide; **2** (nombreux, abondant) [*famille, foule*] large, big; [*fortune*] large; **~e braderie** big sale; **pas ~ monde** not many people; **faire de ~es dépenses** to spend a lot of money; **il fait ~ jour** it's broad daylight; **laver à ~e eau** to wash [sth] in plenty of running water [*légumes*]; to wash [sth] down [*sol*]; **à ~ renfort de publicité** with much publicity; **3** (à un degré élevé) [*rêveur, collectionneur, travailleur, ami, ennemi, pécheur*] great; [*tricheur, joueur, lâcheur, idiot*] big; [*buveur, fumeur*] heavy; **~ amateur de ballet** great ballet lover; **c'est un ~ timide** he's very

Les grades

La liste suivante regroupe les grades des trois armes, armée de terre, marine et aviation du Royaume-Uni et des États-Unis. Pour les traductions, consulter les articles dans le dictionnaire.

En anglais comme en français, l'armée de terre et l'armée de l'air distinguent deux catégories: les officiers, commissioned officers (*GB*) *ou* warrant officers (*US*), *à partir du grade de* Second Lieutenant/Pilot Officer, *et tous les autres, à l'exception de* Private/Aircraftman/Airman, non-commissioned officers (the NCOs, *dire* [ðɪ ensiːəʊz]:

L'armée de terre

Royaume-Uni	**États-Unis**
the British Army	the United States Army
Field Marshal (FM)*	General of the Army (GEN)
General (Gen)	General (GEN)
Lieutenant†-General (Lt-Gen)	Lieutenant† General (LTG)
Major-General (Maj-Gen)	Major General (MG)
Brigadier (Brig)	Brigadier General (BG)
Colonel (Col)	Colonel (COL)
Lieutenant†-Colonel (Lt-Col)	Lieutenant† Colonel (LTC)
Major (Maj)	Major (MAJ)
Captain (Capt)	Captain (CAPT)
Lieutenant† (Lieut)	First Lieutenant† (1LT)
Second Lieutenant† (2nd Lt)	Second Lieutenant† (2Lt)
—	Chief Warrant Officer (CWO)
	Warrant Officer (WO)
Regimental Sergeant Major (RSM)	Command Sergeant Major (CSM)
Company Sergeant Major (CSM)	Staff Sergeant Major (SSM)
	1st Sergeant (1 SG)
—	Master Sergeant (MSG)
—	Sergeant 1st Class (SFC)
Staff Sergeant‡ (S/Sgt)	Staff Sergeant (SSG)
ou Colour Sergeant‡ (C/Sgt)‡	
Sergeant (Sgt)	Sergeant (SGT)
Corporal (Cpl)	Corporal (CPL)
Lance Corporal (L/Cpl)	Private First Class (P1C)
Private (Pte) *ou* Rifleman (Rfm)	Private (PVT)
ou Guardsman (Gdm)‡	

La marine

Royaume-Uni	**États-Unis**
the Royal Navy (RN)§	the United States Navy (USN)§
Admiral of the Fleet	Fleet Admiral
Admiral (Adm)*	Admiral (ADM)
Vice-Admiral (V-Adm)	Vice Admiral (VADM)
Rear-Admiral (Rear-Adm)	Rear Admiral (RADM)
Commodore (Cdre)	Commodore (CDRE)
Captain (Capt)	Captain (CAPT)
Commander (Cdr)	Commander (CDR)
Lieutenant†-Commander (Lt-Cdr)	Lieutenant† Commander (LCDR)
Lieutenant† (Lt)	Lieutenant† (LT)
Sub-Lieutenant† (Sub-Lt)	Lieutenant† Junior Grade (LTJG)
Acting Sub-Lieutenant† (Act Sub-Lt)	Ensign (ENS)
	Chief Warrant Officer (CWO)
Midshipman	Midshipman
Fleet Chief Petty Officer (FCPO)	—
—	Master Chief Petty Officer (MCPO)
	Senior Chief Petty Officer (SCPO)
Chief Petty Officer (CPO)	Chief Petty Officer (CPO)
—	Petty Officer 1st Class (PO1)
	Petty Officer 2nd Class (PO2)
Petty Officer (PO)	Petty Officer 3rd Class (PO3)
Leading Seaman (LS)	Seaman (SN)
Able Seaman (AB)	—
Ordinary Seaman (OD)	
Junior Seaman (JS)	Seaman Apprentice (SA)
	Seaman Recruit (SR)

L'armée de l'air

Royaume-Uni	**États-Unis**
the Royal Air Force (RAF)¶	the United States Air Force (USAF)‖
Marshal of the Royal Air Force	General of the Air Force
Air Chief Marshal (ACM)*	General (GEN)
Air Marshal (AM)	Lieutenant† General (LTG)
Air Vice-Marshal (AVM)	Major General (MG)
Air Commodore (Air Cdre)	Brigadier General (BG)
Group Captain (Gp Capt)	Colonel (COL)
Wing Commander (Wing Cdr)	Lieutenant† Colonel (LTC)
Squadron Leader (Sqn Ldr)	Major (MAJ)
Flight Lieutenant† (Flt Lt)	Captain (CAPT)
Flying Officer (FO)	First Lieutenant† (1LT)
Pilot Officer (PO)	Second Lieutenant† (2LT)
Warrant Officer (WO)	—
Flight Sergeant (FS)	Chief Master Sergeant (CMSGT)
—	Senior Master Sergeant (SMSGT)
—	Master Sergeant (MSGT)
Chief Technician (Chf Tech)	Technical Sergeant (TSGT)
Sergeant (Sgt)	Staff Sergeant (SSGT)
Corporal (Cpl)	Sergeant (SGT)
Junior Technician (Jnr Tech)	—
Senior Aircraftman (SAC)	—
ou Senior Aircraftwoman	
Leading Aircraftman (LAC)	Airman First Class (A1C)
ou Leading Aircraftwoman	*ou* Airwoman First Class
Aircraftman	Airman Basic (AB)
ou Aircraftwoman	

Comment parler des militaires

L'anglais emploie l'article indéfini pour les noms de grades utilisés avec les verbes to be (*être*), to become (*devenir*), to make (*faire*) *etc.*

Dans les expressions suivantes, colonel *est pris comme exemple; les autres noms de grades s'utilisent de la même façon.*

il est colonel = he is a colonel
il est colonel dans l'armée de terre = he is a colonel in the army
devenir colonel = to become a colonel
on l'a nommé colonel = he was made a colonel

Mais avec le verbe to promote *ou dans l'expression* the rank of ..., *l'anglais n'emploie pas l'article indéfini:*

être promu colonel = to be promoted colonel
ou to be promoted to colonel
il a le grade de colonel = he has the rank of colonel

L'anglais n'emploie pas non plus l'article défini lorsque le grade est suivi du nom propre:

le colonel Jones est arrivé = Colonel Jones has arrived

Comparer:

le colonel est arrivé = the colonel has arrived

Noter que le mot Colonel *prend une majuscule en anglais devant le nom propre, mais rarement dans les autres cas.*

Comment s'adresser aux militaires

D'un militaire à son supérieur:

oui, mon colonel = yes, sir
oui, colonel = yes, ma'am

D'un militaire à son inférieur en grade:

oui, sergent = yes, sergeant

* *Les abréviations sont utilisées uniquement par écrit et avec les noms propres, par ex.:* Capt. Jones.
† *Noter la prononciation (GB):* [lefˈtenənt], *(US):* [luːˈtenənt].
‡ *Le nom varie selon le régiment.*
§ *Les abréviations* RN *et* USN *ne sont utilisées que par écrit.*
¶ *Pour* the RAF, *dire* [ðɪɑːreɪef].
‖ *L'abréviation* USAF *n'est utilisée que par écrit. Dire* the US Air Force.

shy; **les ~s malades** very sick people; **c'est un ~ cardiaque** he has a serious heart condition; **4** (important) [*découverte, migration, expédition, événement, nouvelle, honneur*] great; [*date*] important; [*rôle*] major; [*problème, décision*] big; (principal) main; **c'est un ~ jour pour elle** it's a big day for her; **une ~e partie de la maison** a large part of the house; **une ~e partie des habitants** many of the inhabitants; **la ~e majorité** the great ou vast majority; ▶**scène**; **5** (principal) main; **le ~ escalier** the main staircase; **le ~ problème/obstacle** the main ou major problem/obstacle; **les ~s axes routiers** the main ou trunk GB roads; **les ~s points du discours** the main points of the speech; **les ~es lignes d'une politique** the broad lines of a policy; **6** (de premier plan) Écon, Pol [*pays, société, industriel, marque*] leading; **les ~es industries** the big industries; **7** (brillant, remarquable) [*peintre, œuvre, civilisation, vin, cause*] great; [*cœur, âme*] noble; **c'est un ~ homme** he's a great man; **les ~s écrivains** great authors; **un ~ nom de la musique** a great musician; **un ~ monsieur du théâtre** a great gentleman of the stage; **Louis/Pierre le Grand** Louis/Peter the Great; **les ~s noms du cinéma/de la littérature indienne** the big names of the cinema/of Indian literature; **de ~e classe** [*produit*] high-class; [*exploit*] admirable; ▶**esprit**; **8** (âgé) [*frère, sœur*] elder; [*élève*] senior GB, older; (adulte) grown-up; **mon ~ frère** my elder brother; **les ~es classes** Scol the senior forms GB, the upper classes US; **quand il sera ~** when he grows up; **mes enfants sont ~s** my children are quite old; **une ~e fille comme toi!** a big girl like you!; **12 ans! tu es assez ~ pour te débrouiller** 12 years old! you're old enough to cope; **9** (qualifiant une mesure) [*hauteur, longueur, distance, poids, valeur, âge*] great; [*dimensions, taille, pointure, quantité, nombre, étendue*] large; [*vitesse*] high; [*kilomètre, mois, heure*] good; **il est ~ temps que tu partes** it's high time you were off ou you went; **10** (intense, extrême, fort) [*bonté, lâcheté, pauvreté, amitié, chagrin, faim, danger, différence, intérêt*] great; [*bruit*] great, loud; [*froid*] severe; [*chaleur*] intense; [*vent*] strong, high; [*tempête*] big, violent; **avec ~ plaisir** with great ou much pleasure; **dans le plus ~ secret** in great secrecy; **d'une ~e bêtise/timidité** very ou extremely stupid/shy; **à ma ~e honte/surprise** much to my shame/surprise; **sans ~ espoir/enthousiasme** without much hope/enthusiasm; **sans ~e importance** not very important; **il n'y a pas ~ mal à cela/à faire** there isn't much harm in that/in doing; **avoir ~ faim/soif** to be very hungry/thirsty; **avoir ~ besoin de** to be badly in need of; **ça te ferait le plus ~ bien** it would do you a world of good; **à ~s cris** loudly; ▶ **cas, remède**; **11** (de rang social élevé) [*famille, nom*] great; **~e dame** great lady; **la ~e bourgeoisie** the upper middle class; **12** (grandiose) [*réception*] grand; **~s projets** grand designs; **avoir ~e allure, avoir ~ air** to look very impressive; **13** (emphatique) [*mot*] big; [*phrase*] high-sounding; **un ~ merci** a big thank you; **faire de ~s gestes** to wave one's arms about; **et voilà, tout de suite les ~s mots** there you go, straight off the deep end.

II *nm,f* **1** (enfant) big boy/girl; Scol senior GB ou older pupil; **il a fait ça tout seul comme un ~** he did it all by himself like a big boy; **il fait le ménage comme un ~** he does the housework like a grown-up; **pour les ~s et les petits** for old and young alike; **2** (terme d'affection) **mon ~, ma ~e** my darling.

III *adv* wide; **ouvrir ~ la bouche** to open one's mouth wide; **ouvrir tout ~ les bras** to throw one's arms open; **les fenêtres sont ~(es) ouvertes** the windows are wide open; **ouvrir la porte toute ~e** to open the door wide; **ouvrir ~ ses oreilles** fig to prick up one's ears; **ouvrir tout ~ son cœur** fig to open one's heart; **les bottes chaussent ~** the boots are large-fitting; **leurs vêtements taillent ~** their clothes are cut on the large side; **voir ~** fig to think big.

IV *nm* (pays) big power; (entreprise) leader, big name; **les ~s de ce monde** the great and the good; Pol the world's leaders; **les cinq ~s** Pol the Big Five; **les ~s de l'automobile** the top car manufacturers; **c'est un ~ de la publicité** he's big in advertising.

V en grand *loc adv* [*ouvrir*] wide, completely; **faire de l'élevage en ~** to breed animals on a large scale; **quand ils reçoivent, ils font les choses en ~** when they entertain they do things on the grand scale or they really go to town○.

■ **~ argentier** Hist royal treasurer; hum keeper of the nation's purse, Finance minister; **le ~ art** alchemy; **~ banditisme** organized crime; **~ bassin** (de piscine) main pool; Anat upper pelvis; **~ cacatois** main royal sail; **~ caniche** standard poodle; **le ~ capital** Écon big money, big investors *pl*; **~ commis de l'État** top civil servant; **~ coq de bruyère** capercaillie; **~ corbeau** raven; **~ couturier** couturier; **~ débutant** absolute beginner; **~ duc** Zool eagle owl; **~ écart** Danse, Sport splits (*sg*); **faire le ~ écart** to do the splits; **le ~ écran** the big screen; **~ électeur** (en France) *elector who votes in the elections for the French Senate*; (aux États-Unis) presidential elector; **~ ensemble** high-density housing complex; **la vie dans les ~s ensembles** high-rise living; **~ d'Espagne** Spanish grandee; **~ foc** outer jib; **~ frais** Météo moderate gale; **~ hunier** main topsail; **~ hunier fixe** lower main topsail; **~ hunier volant** upper main topsail; **~ invalide civil, GIC** *civilian who is registered severely disabled*; **~ invalide de guerre, GIG** Prot Soc *ex-serviceman who is registered severely disabled*; **le ~ large** Naut the high seas (*pl*); **~ magasin** Comm department store; **~ maître** (aux échecs) grand master; **~ maître de l'ordre des Templiers** Hist Grand Master of the Knights Templar; **~ mât** Naut mainmast; **le ~ monde** high society; **le Grand Nord** Géog the Far North; **Grand Œuvre** Great Work; **~ officier de la Légion d'Honneur** *high-ranking officer of the Legion of Honour*[GB]; **le Grand Orient** the Grand Lodge of France; **~ panda** giant panda; **Grand Pardon** Day of Atonement; **~ patron** Méd senior consultant GB, head doctor US; **~ perroquet** Naut main topgallant sail; **~ prêtre** Relig, fig high priest; **~ prix** Courses Aut, Sport grand prix; **le ~ public** the general public; Comm **produit ~ public** consumer product; **~ quart** Naut six-hour watch; **Grand quartier général, GQG** Mil General Headquarters, GHQ; **~ quotidien** Presse big national daily; **~ roque** Jeux (aux échecs) castling long; **le Grand Siècle** Hist the 17th century (*in France*); **~ teint** colourfast[GB]; **~ tétras** capercaillie; **~ tourisme** Courses Aut, Aut GT, gran turismo; **le Grand Turc** the Sultan; **~ veneur** Chasse master of the hounds; **~e Armée** Hist Grande Armée (*Napoleon's army*); **~e Baie Australienne** Géog Great Australian Bight; **la ~e banlieue** the outer suburbs (*pl*); **Grande Barrière (de Corail)** Géog Great Barrier Reef; **la ~e bleue** the sea; **la ~e cuisine** Culin haute cuisine; **~e distribution** Écon volume retailing; **la Grande Guerre** Hist the First World War; **~e gueule**○ loud mouth○; **~e hune** Naut maintop; **la ~e muette** the army; **la ~e muraille de Chine** Géog the Great Wall of China; **~e personne** grown-up, adult; **la ~e presse** the popular dailies (*pl*); **~e puissance** Pol superpower; **~e roue** (de foire) big wheel GB, Ferris wheel US; **~e série** Comm mass production; **fabriqué en ~e série** mass-produced; **~e surface** Comm supermarket; **~es eaux** fountains; fig (pleurs) waterworks; **dès qu'on la gronde, ce sont les ~es eaux** the minute you tell her off, she turns on the waterworks; **~es lignes** Rail main train routes; **~es marées** spring tides; **~es ondes** Radio long wave (*sg*); **Grandes Plaines** Géog Great Plains; **les ~s blessés** the seriously injured; **~s corps de l'État** Admin senior branches of the civil service; **~s espaces** École open spaces; **~s fauves** Zool big cats; **~s fonds** Naut ocean depths; **les ~s froids** the cold of winter; **Grands Lacs** Géog Great Lakes; **~s singes** Zool great apes; ▶ **école, voyage**.

grand-angle, *pl* **grands-angles** /gʀɑ̃tɑ̃gl, gʀɑ̃zɑ̃gl/, **grand-angulaire**, *pl* **grands-angulaires** /gʀɑ̃tɑ̃gylɛʀ, gʀɑ̃zɑ̃gylɛʀ/ **I** *adj* wide-angle.
II *nm* wide-angle lens.

grand-chantre, *pl* **grands-chantres** /gʀɑ̃ʃɑ̃tʀ/ *nm* precentor.

grand-chose /gʀɑ̃ʃoz/ **I** *pron indéf* **pas ~** not much, not a lot; **ça ne vaut pas ~** it isn't worth much ou a lot; **ça ne sert pas à ~** it's not much use; **je n'ai pas vu ~ d'intéressant** I didn't see anything much of interest; **il n'y a plus ~ à faire** there isn't much ou a lot left to do; **'tu t'es fait mal?'—'ce n'est pas ~'** 'have you hurt yourself?'—'it's nothing much'; **on l'a puni pour pas ~** he was punished for something very minor.
II *nmf inv* péj **un pas ~** a worthless individual, a useless○ character.

grand-croix, *pl* **grands-croix** /gʀɑ̃kʀwa/ **I** *nm* (personne) holder of the grand cross.
II *nf inv* (décoration) grand cross.

grand-duc, *pl* **grands-ducs** /gʀɑ̃dyk/ ▶ **813** *nm* grand duke.
IDIOMES **faire la tournée des grands-ducs** to have a night on the town.

grand-duché, *pl* **grands-duchés** /gʀɑ̃dyʃe/ *nm* grand duchy.

Grande-Bretagne /gʀɑ̃dbʀətaɲ/ ▶ **416** *nprf* Great Britain.

grande-duchesse, *pl* **grandes-duchesses** /gʀɑ̃ddyʃɛs/ ▶ **813** *nf* grand duchess.

grandement /gʀɑ̃dmɑ̃/ *adv* **1** (largement) [*faciliter, intéresser*] greatly; [*aider, contribuer*] a great deal; [*reconnaissant*] extremely; **2** (avec faste) in style; **faire ~ les choses** to do things in style.

grandeur /gʀɑ̃dœʀ/ *nf* **1** (taille) size; **être de la ~ d'un mouchoir** to be the size of a handkerchief; **être de la même ~** to be the same size; **~ nature, en vraie ~** [*maquette, reproduction*] full-scale (*épith*); [*peinture, portrait, statue*] life-size; **2** (énormité) scale; **3** (élévation) greatness; **la ~ de leur sacrifice** their great sacrifice; **ce fut une finale sans ~** Sport it wasn't a great ou memorable final; **4** (gloire, puissance) greatness; **politique de ~** politics of national greatness; **5** Astron, Math magnitude; **de première ~** Astron, fig of the first magnitude; **~ de base** Math base quantity.
■ **~ d'âme** generosity of spirit; **par ~ d'âme** out of generosity of spirit.

Grand-Guignol /gʀɑ̃giɲɔl/ *nm* **c'est du ~** fig it's farcical; Théât **le ~** Grand Guignol theatre[GB].

grand-guignolesque, *pl* **~s** /gʀɑ̃giɲɔlɛsk/ *adj* **1** fig farcical; **2** Théât [*spectacle*] blood-and-thunder (*épith*).

grandiloquence /gʀɑ̃dilɔkɑ̃s/ *nf* pomposity, grandiloquence sout.

grandiloquent, **~e** /gʀɑ̃dilɔkɑ̃, ɑ̃t/ *adj* pompous, grandiloquent sout.

grandiose /gʀɑ̃djoz/ *adj* [*ruines, site, édifice, décor*] grandiose; [*proportions*] imposing; [*réussite, fête*] spectacular; [*geste, personnage*] grand.

grandir /gʀɑ̃diʀ/ [3] **I** *vtr* **1** (rendre plus grand) [*loupe*] to magnify; [*talons*] to make [sb] look taller; **2** (exagérer) to exaggerate [*danger, importance*]; **3** (ennoblir) **sortir grandi d'une épreuve** to come out of an ordeal with increased stature; **sa promotion ne l'a pas grandi à mes yeux** I don't think any more highly of him because he's been promoted.
II *vi* **1** (en taille) [*plante, enfant*] to grow; (en âge) [*enfant*] to grow up; **~ de 20 cms** to grow 20 cms; **je te trouve bien grandi** haven't you grown; **devenir raisonnable en grandissant** to become sensible as one grows up; **~ dans l'estime de qn** fig to go up ou rise in sb's esteem; **2** (en nombre, importance, intensité) [*société, entreprise*] to expand; [*rumeur, inquiétude, danger, réputation, foule*] to grow; [*obscurité*] to increase; **les jours grandissent** the days are getting longer; **aller grandissant** liter [*inquiétude*] to become greater and greater; [*bruit*] to become louder and louder.
III se grandir *vpr* lit to make oneself (look) taller.

grandissant, **~e** /gʀɑ̃disɑ̃, ɑ̃t/ *adj* growing; **influence sans cesse ~e** ever-increasing influence.

grandissement /gʀɑ̃dismɑ̃/ *nm* fml (de loupe) magnification.

grandissime /gʀɑ̃disim/ *adj* hum tremendous.

grand-livre, *pl* **grands-livres** /gʀɑ̃livʀ/ *nm* Compta ledger.
■ **~ de la dette publique** Fin national debt register.

grand-maman, *pl* **grands-mamans** /gʀɑ̃mamɑ̃/ *nf* grandma.

grand-mère, *pl* **grands-mères** /gʀɑ̃mɛʀ/ *nf* **1** (aïeule) grandmother; **2** (vieille femme) old granny○.

grand-messe, *pl* **~s** /gʀɑ̃mɛs/ *nf* **1** Relig High Mass; **2** fig ritual gathering.

grand-oncle, *pl* **grands-oncles** /gʀɑ̃tɔ̃kl, gʀɑ̃zɔ̃kl/ *nm* great-uncle.

grand-papa, *pl* **grands-papas** /gʀɑ̃papa/ *nm* grandpa○, granddad○.

grand-peine /gʀɑ̃pɛn/ **I** *nf* **avoir ~ à faire** to have great difficulty doing.
II à grand-peine *loc adv* fml with great difficulty.

grand-père, *pl* **grands-pères** /gʀɑ̃pɛʀ/ *nm* **1** (aïeul) grandfather; **2**○ (vieillard) old man, granddad○.

grand-route, *pl* **~s** /gʀɑ̃ʀut/ *nf* main road, highroad GB.

grand-rue, *pl* **~s** /gʀɑ̃ʀy/ *nf* High Street GB, Main Street US.

grands-parents /gʀɑ̃paʀɑ̃/ *nmpl* grandparents.

grand-tante, *pl* **grand(s)-tantes** /gʀɑ̃tɑ̃t/ *nf* great-aunt.

grand-vergue, *pl* **grand(s)-vergues** /gʀɑ̃vɛʀg/ *nf* Naut main yard.

grand-voile, *pl* **grand(s)-voiles** /gʀɑ̃vwal/ *nf* mainsail.

grange /gʀɑ̃ʒ/ *nf* barn.

granit(e) /gʀanit/ *nm* granite; **dalle de ~** granite slab.

granité, **~e** /gʀanite/ **I** *adj* **1** (à petits grains) [*surface, cuir, papier*] grained; **2** (à gros grains) [*coton, lin*] slubbed; [*laine*] bouclé.
II *nm* **1** Culin granita; **2** Tex (en coton) slubbed cotton; (en lin) slubbed linen; (en laine) bouclé wool.

graniteux, **-euse** /gʀanitø, øz/ *adj* Minér granite (*épith*).

granitique /gʀanitik/ *adj* **1** Minér granite (*épith*), granitic; **2** fig [*conviction*] rock-solid.

granito /gʀanito/ *nm* Constr terrazzo ₵.

granivore /gʀanivɔʀ/ **I** *adj* granivorous.
II *nm* granivorous animal.

granulaire /gʀanylɛʀ/ *adj* granular.

granulat /gʀanyla/ *nm* Constr ballast ₵.

granulation /gʀanylasjɔ̃/ *nf* **1** (texture) granulation; **surface qui présente des ~s** surface that is grainy ou granular; **2** Phot graininess; **3** Tech (processus) granulation.

granule /gʀanyl/ **I** *nm* Géol, Ind granule; Pharm granule, pellet.
II *nf* Astron granule.

granulé, **~e** /gʀanyle/ **I** *adj* [*surface*] granular.
II *nm* granule.

granuleux, **-euse** /gʀanylø, øz/ *adj* **1** (en granules) [*roche, neige*] granular; **2** (à petits grains) [*papier*] grained; [*peau, cuir*] grainy.

graphe /gʀaf/ *nm* graph; **la théorie des ~s** graph theory.

graphème /gʀafɛm/ *nm* grapheme.

graphie /gʀafi/ *nf* Ling **1** (écriture) written form; **2** (orthographe) spelling; **~ fautive** misspelling; **~ étymologique** etymological spelling.

graphique /gʀafik/ **I** *adj* **1** Art, Math [*forme, représentation, art, œuvre*] graphic; **2** Ordinat [*écran, tablette*] graphic; [*mode, mémoire, logiciel*] graphics (*épith*); **informatique ~** computer graphics (*pl*).
II *nm* graph; **~ à bandes** or **en colonnes** bar chart ou graph.

graphiquement /gʀafikmɑ̃/ *adv* graphically.

graphisme /gʀafism/ *nm* **1** (d'un artiste, d'une époque) style of drawing; **2** (écriture) handwriting; **3** Art, Pub (design) graphic design; (dessins, images) graphics (*pl*); (art) graphic arts (*pl*).

graphiste /gʀafist/ **▶510** *nmf* graphic designer or artist.

graphite /gʀafit/ *nm* graphite.

graphiter /gʀafite/ [1] *vtr* to graphitize; **huile/graisse graphitée** graphite oil/grease.

graphiteux, **-euse** /gʀafitø, øz/ *adj* graphitic.

graphologie /gʀafɔlɔʒi/ *nf* graphology.

graphologique /gʀafɔlɔʒik/ *adj* graphological.

graphologue /gʀafɔlɔg/ **▶510** *nmf* graphologist, handwriting expert.

grappe /gʀap/ *nf* **1** (de fruits) bunch; (de fleurs) cluster; **~ de raisin/de groseilles** bunch of grapes/of redcurrants; **~s humaines** fig clusters of people; **2** (assemblage) **~ de ballons** bunch of balloons; **~s de saucissons/d'ail** strings of sausages/of garlic.
IDIOMES **lâcher la ~ à qn**° to get off sb's back°, to let sb alone.

grappillage /gʀapijaʒ/ *nm* gleaning ₵; **faire du ~** (se renseigner) to glean information; (économiser) to make petty economies.

grappiller /gʀapije/ [1] **I** *vtr* to pick up [*fruits, fleurs*]; to glean [*renseignements*]; **~ quelques sous à droite à gauche** to scrape together some money.
II° *vi* (prendre du raisin grain par grain) to pick at the grapes.

grappin /gʀapɛ̃/ *nm* **1** Naut (petite ancre) grapnel; (crochet d'abordage) grappling irons (*pl*); **2** Tech (de grue) grab.
IDIOMES **mettre le ~ sur qn** to get sb into one's clutches.

gras, **grasse** /gʀɑ, gʀɑs/ **I** *adj* **1** (contenant de la graisse) [*substance, bouillon*] fatty; [*poisson*] oily; [*fromage*] full fat; **2** (huileux) [*papier, peau, cheveux*] greasy; [*boue*] sticky, slimy; [*charbon, houille*] bituminous[GB]; **3** (dodu) plump; (gros) fat; **▶veau**; **4** (vulgaire) [*plaisanterie*] crude, coarse; [*rire*] coarse; **5** (abondant) liter [*salaire*] fat; [*récolte*] bumper (*épith*); **ce n'est pas ~** it's rather meagre[GB]; **6** (riche) [*prairie*] lush; **7** Imprim [*caractère*] bold; **en (caractères) ~** in bold (type); **8** Méd [*toux*] loose, phlegmy.
II *adv* **1** Culin **cuisiner ~** to use a lot of fat in cooking; **manger ~** to eat fatty foods; **2** Relig **faire ~** to eat meat; **3**° (beaucoup) **pas ~** not a lot; **il y en a pas ~ dans l'assiette**° there isn't a lot to eat; **4** Méd **tousser ~** to have a loose ou phlegmy cough; **5** (vulgairement) [*rire*] coarsely.
III *nm* **1** (de viande) fat; **▶discuter**; **2** (corps huileux) grease; **taché de ~** grease-stained; **une tache de ~** a grease stain; **3** (partie charnue) (de bras, mollet) the fleshy part (**de** of); **le ~ du pouce** the cushion of the thumb.

gras-double /gʀadubl/ *nm* tripe.

grassement /gʀasmɑ̃/ *adv* **1** (généreusement) [*payer, entretenir*] handsomely; [*noter*] generously; [*nourrir*] lavishly; **2** (richement) [*vivre*] off the fat of the land; **3** (vulgairement) [*rire*] coarsely.

grasseyement /gʀasɛjmɑ̃/ *nm* gén guttural pronunciation; Phon uvular trill.

grasseyer /gʀaseje/ [1] *vi* Phon to speak with an uvular R.

grassouillet, **-ette** /gʀasujɛ, ɛt/ *adj* chubby, plump.

grata /gʀata/ *adj* **▶persona**.

gratifiant, **~e** /gʀatifjɑ̃, ɑ̃t/ *adj* gratifying; **il est ~ de voir que** it is gratifying to note that; **travail ~** rewarding job.

gratification /gʀatifikasjɔ̃/ *nf* **1** (satisfaction) gratification; **~ personnelle** personal gratification; **2** Entr (prime) bonus.

gratifier /gʀatifje/ [2] *vtr* **1** (faire bénéficier) **~ qn de qch** to give sb sth; **il a gratifié le serveur d'un pourboire princier** he gave the waiter a princely tip; **il l'a gratifié d'un bon coup de pied** he gave him a good kick; **sa voisine l'a gratifié d'un beau sourire** the girl next door favoured[GB] him with a lovely smile ou bestowed a lovely smile on him; **2** (satisfaire) to gratify; **se sentir gratifié** to feel gratified.

gratin /gʀatɛ̃/ *nm* **1** (croûte) gratin (*topping of breadcrumbs and cheese*); **au ~** au gratin; **sole au ~** sole au gratin; **macaroni au ~** macaroni cheese GB, macaroni and cheese US; **2** (plat) gratin (*dish with a topping of breadcrumbs and cheese*); **~ de pommes de terre** potatoes au gratin; **~ dauphinois** gratin Dauphinois (*sliced potatoes baked with cream*); **3**° (élite) **le ~** the upper crust.

gratiné, **~e** /gʀatine/ **I** *adj* **1** Culin au gratin (*après n*); **2**° (spécial) [*personne, vêtement, style*] weird; [*problème, examen*] mind-bending°.
II gratinée *nf* Culin onion soup au gratin.

gratiner /gʀatine/ [1] **I** *vtr* to brown [*plat*].
II *vi* **faire ~ un plat** to brown a dish.

gratis /gʀatis/ **I** *adj inv* free; **le concert est ~** the concert is free.
II *adv* free GB, for free US; **on est entrés ~ au musée** we got into the museum free GB ou for free US.

gratitude /gʀatityd/ *nf* gratitude; **manifester** or **exprimer sa ~ à qn** to show one's gratitude to sb; **avoir de la ~ pour qn** to be grateful to sb.

gratouiller° /gʀatuje/ [1] *vtr* **1** (démanger) to make [sb] itch [*personne*]; **ça me gratouille** it makes me itch; **j'ai la gorge qui me gratouille** I've got an itch in my throat; **2** (gratter) to scratch [sth] lightly [*objet*]; **3** (jouer) to strum [*guitare*].

grattage /gʀataʒ/ *nm* **1** (pour modifier) (de papier, carton) scratching; (de mur, métal, bois) scraping; **obtenir un motif par ~** to scrape a pattern; **2** (pour enlever) (sur papier) scratching out; (sur mur, métal, bois) scraping off; (de case sur un coupon) scratching; **effacer un mot par ~** to scratch out a word.

gratte° /gʀat/ *nf* **1** (petit profit) **faire de la ~** to make a bit on the side; **2** (guitare) guitar.

gratte-ciel /gʀatsjɛl/ *nm inv* sky-scraper.

gratte-cul°, *pl* **~s** /gʀatky/ *nm* rosehip.

gratte-dos /gʀatdo/ *nm inv* back-scratcher.

grattement /gʀatmɑ̃/ *nm* scratching ₵.

gratte-papier /gʀatpapje/ *nm inv* pen-pusher GB, pencil-pusher US.

gratter /gʀate/ [1] **I** *vtr* **1** (frotter) (légèrement) to scratch; (pour nettoyer) to scrape; (pour enlever) to scrape off [*peinture, boue*]; (pour soulager) to scratch; **peux-tu me ~ le dos?** can you scratch my back?; **ne gratte pas, ça va saigner** don't scratch, it'll bleed; **2** (démanger) [*bouton, cicatrice*] to make [sb] itch [*personne*]; **ce pull en laine me gratte** this woollen[GB] sweater itches ou makes me itch; **ça me gratte partout** I'm itching all over; **3**° (gagner) **il a gratté quelques francs sur l'argent des courses** he fiddled a few francs from the shopping money; **il gratte régulièrement un quart d'heure sur son temps de travail** he regularly works a quarter of an hour less than he's supposed to; **4**° (dépasser) to manage to get ahead of; **il a gratté tous ses concurrents** he managed to get ahead of all his fellow competitors.
II° **gratter de** *vtr ind* **~ de la guitare** to strum the guitar.
III *vi* **1** (faire un bruit) **~ à la porte** to scratch at the door; **on entendait ~ timidement au volet** there was a timid scratching at the shutter; **2**° (écrire) to scribble.
IV se gratter *vpr* [*personne, animal*] to scratch; **se ~ la tête** [*personne*] to scratch one's head.
IDIOMES **il peut (toujours) se ~**° he can go and jump in the lake.

grattoir /gʀatwaʀ/ *nm* **1** (de cordonnier, menuisier, boulanger) scraper; **2** (pour semelles) shoe-scraper; **3** (de boîte d'allumettes) striking strip.

grattons /gʀatɔ̃/ *nmpl* pork scratchings.

gratuit, **~e** /gʀatɥi, it/ *adj* **1** (non payant) [*place, échantillon, service*] free; [*logement*] rent-free; **numéro d'appel gratuit** Freefone number GB, toll-free number US; **entrée ~e** admission free GB, free admission; **à titre ~** free of charge; **le concert était ~** the concert was free; **2** (injustifié) [*violence, méchanceté, meurtre*] gratuitous; [*accusation*] spurious; [*exercice*] pointless; [*remarque*] uninvited; **3** (désintéressé) disinterested; **leurs compliments ne sont jamais ~s** their compliments are never entirely disinterested.

gratuité /gʀatɥite/ *nf* **1** (caractère non payant) **la ~ de l'enseignement** free education; **2** (caractère injustifié) unwarranted nature, gratuitous nature; **3** (caractère désintéressé) disinterested nature.

gratuitement /gʀatɥitmɑ̃/ *adv* **1** (gratis) free GB, for free US; **2** (sans rétribution) [*travailler, réparer*] for nothing; **3** (sans motif) gratuitously.

gravats /gʀava/ *nmpl* rubble ₵.

grave /gʀav/ **I** *adj* **1** (préoccupant) [*problème, erreur, blessure, maladie, accident*] serious;

l'heure est ~ the situation is serious; **un blessé ~** a seriously injured person; **l'accident a fait un mort et deux blessés ~s** the accident left one dead and two seriously injured; **remets-toi, ce n'est pas bien ~!** cheer up, it doesn't matter!; **2** (digne) [*air, ton, visage*] grave, solemn; **3** (de basse fréquence) [*voix*] deep; [*note, registre*] low; [*son*] low-pitched.

II graves *nmpl* (d'amplificateur) **les ~s** the bass (*sg*); **baisse les ~s et monte les aigus** reduce the bass and increase the treble.

graveleux, -euse /gʀavlø, øz/ *adj* **1** (obscène) [*plaisanterie, histoire*] smutty; [*propos, conversation*] indecent; **2** (qui contient du gravier) [*terre*] gravelly; **3** (qui contient des corps durs) [*poire*] gritty.

gravelot /gʀavlo/ *nm* plover; **grand ~** ringed plover.

gravement /gʀavmɑ̃/ *adv* **1** (avec solennité) [*parler, demander, regarder*] gravely, solemnly; **2** (de façon importante) [*offenser, se tromper, blesser, endommager*] seriously; **il est ~ malade** he's seriously ill.

graver /gʀave/ [1] *vtr* **1** (sur la pierre, le métal etc) to engrave [*inscription, motif*] (**sur** on); (sur bois) **il a gravé son nom sur l'arbre** he carved his name on the tree; **~ à l'eau-forte** to etch; **être gravé sur le front de qn** fig to be written all over sb's face; **2** fig **l'épisode est gravé à jamais dans leur mémoire** the episode is engraved on their memory forever; **3** Audio (produire) **~ un disque** to make a record.

graveur, -euse /gʀavœʀ, øz/ ▶510 *nm,f* Art, Tech engraver; **~ sur bois/marbre** wood/marble engraver.

gravide /gʀavid/ *adj* gravid.

gravier /gʀavje/ *nm* **1** gén, Constr, Gén Civ **du ~** gravel; **ratisser le ~** to rake the gravel; **des ~s** gravel ¢; **2** Géol pebbles (*pl*).

gravière /gʀavjɛʀ/ *nf* gravel pit.

gravillon /gʀavijɔ̃/ *nm* **1** Constr, Gén Civ (pierres concassées) **du ~** chippings (*pl*); **2** (petits cailloux) grit ¢; **un ~** a bit of grit.

gravillonner /gʀavijɔne/ [1] *vtr* to gravel [*route*].

gravillonneuse /gʀavijɔnøz/ *nf* grit spreader.

gravimétrie /gʀavimetʀi/ *nf* **1** Phys gravimetry; **2** Chimie gravimetric analysis.

gravir /gʀaviʀ/ [3] *vtr* to climb up [*côte, colline*]; (avec peine) to struggle up [*escaliers, étages*]; **~ les échelons de la hiérarchie** to move up through the hierarchy.

gravissime /gʀavisim/ *adj* extremely serious.

gravitation /gʀavitasjɔ̃/ *nf* gravitation.

■ **~ universelle** Phys Newton's law of gravitation.

gravitationnel, -elle /gʀavitasjɔnɛl/ *adj* gravitational.

gravité /gʀavite/ *nf* **1** (caractère préoccupant) (de problème, situation) seriousness, gravity; (de blessure, maladie) seriousness; **une blessure/un accident sans ~** a minor injury/accident; **2** (caractère solennel) solemnity; **3** Phys gravity; **centre de ~** centre[GB] of gravity.

graviter /gʀavite/ [1] *vi* **1** Astron, Phys [*astre*] to orbit (**autour de** around); **2** fig (évoluer) **il gravite dans les cercles de la finance** he moves in financial circles; **il gravite dans l'orbite des grands de ce monde** he mixes with the rich and famous.

gravure /gʀavyʀ/ *nf* **1** (procédé) **la ~** engraving; **la ~ sur bois/verre/pierre/cuivre** wood/glass/stone/copperplate engraving; **2** Art (estampe) engraving; **les ~s de Callot** Callot's engravings; **3** (reproduction) print; **4** Édition plate; **5** Audio (de disque) making.

■ **~ sur bois** Art (en creux) wood engraving; (en relief) woodcut; **~ en creux** intaglio; **~ sur cuivre** Art copperplate; **~ à l'eau-forte** Art etching; **~ de mode** lit fashion plate; **c'est une vraie** or **elle a l'air d'une ~ de mode** fig she looks like she's just stepped out of a fashion magazine.

gré /gʀe/ *nm* **1** (convenance) **être au ~ de qn** [*qualité, objet*] to be to sb's liking; **si la chambre n'est pas à votre ~** if the room isn't to your liking; **trop fort/violent à mon ~** too strong/violent for my liking; **vous pouvez modifier le décor à votre ~** you can modify the decoration as you wish; **contre le ~ de qn** against sb's will; **nous sommes retenus contre notre ~** we're being held against our will; **de plein ~** willingly; **de mon/ton etc plein ~** of my/your etc own free will; **de bon ~** gladly; **de mauvais ~** reluctantly; **bon ~ mal ~** willy-nilly; **de ~ ou de force** one way or another; **de ~ à ~** [*transaction, vendre*] by mutual agreement; **2** fml (gratitude) **savoir ~ à qn de qch** to be grateful to sb for sth; **je lui sais ~ de ce qu'il a fait** I'm grateful to him for what he's done; **3** (hasard) **j'ai flâné au ~ de mon humeur** I strolled where the mood took me; **au ~ des circonstances** as circumstances dictate.

grèbe /gʀɛb/ *nm* grebe.

grec, grecque /gʀɛk/ **I** ▶537 *adj* **1** [*île, antiquité, mythologie, art, langue*] Greek; **2** [*nez, profil*] Grecian; ▶ **calendes**.

II ▶462 *nm* Ling Greek; **le ~ ancien/moderne** Ancient/Modern Greek.

III grecque *nf* **1** Art Greek key; **2** Culin **à la grecque** à la grecque.

Grec, Grecque /gʀɛk/ ▶537 *nm,f* Greek.

Grèce /gʀɛs/ ▶321 *nprf* Greece; **~ antique** Ancient Greece; **en ~** in Greece.

gréco-latin, ~e, *mpl* **~s** /gʀekolatɛ̃, in/ *adj* Graeco-Latin.

gréco-romain, ~e, *mpl* **~s** /gʀekoʀomɛ̃, ɛn/ *adj* Graeco-Roman; **lutte ~e** Graeco-Roman.

grecque ▶ **grec**.

gredin, ~e /gʀədɛ̃, in/ *nm,f* **1** hum rascal; **2**† (crapule) knave‡, scoundrel†.

gréement /gʀemɑ̃/ *nm* Naut rigging ¢.

gréer /gʀee/ [11] *vtr* to rig; **navire gréé en goélette** ship rigged as a schooner.

greffage /gʀɛfaʒ/ *nm* grafting ¢.

greffe /gʀɛf/ **I** *nm* Jur office of the Clerk of the Court.

II *nf* **1** Méd (d'organe) transplant; (de peau) graft; **~ du cœur/des poumons** heart/lung transplant; **~ de moelle osseuse** bone-marrow transplant; **2** Agric (opération) grafting ¢; (résultat) graft; **la ~ a bien pris** the graft has taken well.

greffer /gʀefe/ [1] **I** *vtr* **1** Méd to transplant [*organe*]; to graft [*tissu*]; **on lui a greffé un rein** he's had a kidney transplant; **2** Agric to graft [*rosier, arbre*].

II se greffer *vpr* **se ~ sur qch** [*événement, affaire, problème*] to come along on top of sth.

greffier, -ière /gʀefje, ɛʀ/ ▶510 *nm,f* clerk of the court GB, court clerk US.

greffon /gʀɛfɔ̃/ *nm* **1** Agric graft, scion; **2** Méd (organe à greffer) transplant organ; (organe greffé) transplanted organ; (tissu greffé) graft.

grégaire /gʀegɛʀ/ *adj* [*animal*] gregarious; **esprit** or **instinct ~** herd instinct.

grégarisme /gʀegaʀism/ *nm* gregariousness.

grège /gʀɛʒ/ ▶193 *adj, nm* oatmeal.

grégeois /gʀeʒwa/ *adj m* **feu ~** Greek fire.

grégorien, -ienne /gʀegɔʀjɛ̃, ɛn/ *adj* Gregorian; **calendrier ~** Gregorian calendar; **chant ~** Gregorian chant, plainsong.

grêle /gʀɛl/ **I** *adj* **1** (mince) [*silhouette*] skinny; [*jambes, arbre*] spindly; **2** (aigu) [*voix*] reedy; [*son*] thin.

II *nf* **1** Météo hail ¢; **orage de ~** hailstorm; **il tombe de la ~** it's hailing; **2** (volée) **une ~ de balles/pierres** a hail of bullets/stones; **recevoir une ~ de coups** to be showered with blows.

grêlé, ~e /gʀele/ *adj* [*visage, peau*] pockmarked.

grêler /gʀele/ [1] *v impers* to hail; **il grêle** it's hailing; **il a grêlé sur les vignes** the vines were hit by hail.

grêlon /gʀɛlɔ̃/ *nm* hailstone.

grelot /gʀəlo/ *nm* small (spherical) bell; **coup de ~**○ (appel téléphonique) phone call; **donner un coup de ~ à qn** to give sb a ring GB ou call.

IDIOMES **avoir les ~s**◐ to have got the willies○, to be scared.

grelottement /gʀəlɔtmɑ̃/ *nm* **1** (frissonnement) shivering; **2** (bruit) ringing.

grelotter /gʀəlɔte/ [1] *vi* **1** (trembler) to shiver (**de** with); **fermez la fenêtre, on grelotte ici**○! shut the window, we're freezing in here!; **2** (sonner) to tinkle.

greluche◐ /gʀəlyʃ/ *nf* pej woman, bint◐ GB.

grenade /gʀənad/ *nf* **1** Mil (engin) grenade; **lancer une ~** to throw a grenade; **attentat à la ~** grenade attack; **2** Mil (ornement d'uniforme) badge; **3** Bot, Culin pomegranate.

■ **~ défensive** fragmentation grenade; **~ fumigène** smoke grenade; **~ à fusil** rifle grenade; **~ lacrymogène** tear gas grenade; **~ à main** hand grenade; **~ à manche** stick hand grenade.

Grenade /gʀənad/ **I** ▶857 *npr* (ville d'Espagne) Granada.

II ▶321 *nprf* (État) **la ~** Grenada.

grenadier /gʀənadje/ *nm* **1** Bot pomegranate tree; **2** Mil grenadier.

grenadine /gʀənadin/ *nf* (sirop) **(sirop de) ~** grenadine; **une ~ à l'eau** water with grenadine.

Grenadines /gʀənadin/ ▶416 *nprfpl* **les ~** the Grenadines.

grenaille /gʀənaj/ *nf* Tech (de métal) **~ d'acier** steel filings (*pl*); **~ de plomb** lead shot.

grenat /gʀəna/ ▶193 **I** *adj inv* dark red.

II *nm* **1** Minér garnet; **2** (couleur) dark red.

grené, ~e /gʀəne/ *adj* [*dessin*] stippled; [*cuir*] grainy.

grenier /gʀənje/ *nm* **1** Constr attic, loft; (grange) loft; **~ à foin** hay loft; **~ à grain** granary; **2** fig (région) **~ (à blé)** breadbasket, granary (**de** of).

Grenoble /gʀənɔbl/ ▶857 *npr* Grenoble.

grenoblois, ~e /gʀənɔblwa, az/ ▶857 *adj* of Grenoble.

Grenoblois, ~e /gʀənɔblwa, az/ ▶857 *nm,f* (natif) native of Grenoble; (habitant) inhabitant of Grenoble.

grenouillage○ /gʀənujaʒ/ *nm* shady manoeuvres (*pl*) GB ou maneuvers (*pl*) US.

grenouille /gʀənuj/ *nf* frog; **cuisses de ~** frogs' legs; **les ~s coassent** frogs croak.

■ **~ de bénitier**○ holy Joe○; **~ rousse** Zool common frog; **~ taureau** Zool bullfrog; **~ verte** Zool edible frog.

IDIOMES **manger la ~**○ to abscond with the cash.

grenouillère /gʀənujɛʀ/ *nf* Mode stretch suit GB, Babygro® GB, creepers (*pl*) US.

grenu, ~e /gʀəny/ *adj* [*papier, tissu, peau*] grained; [*roche*] granular.

grès /gʀɛ/ *nm inv* **1** (roche) sandstone; **2** (céramique) stoneware; **un plat de** or **en ~** a stoneware dish; **3** (objet) piece of stoneware; **de beaux ~** beautiful stoneware ¢.

gréseux, -euse /gʀezø, øz/ *adj* sandstone (*épith*).

grésil /gʀezil/ *nm* hail.

grésillement /gʀezijmɑ̃/ *nm* **1** (dans un téléphone, à la radio) crackling ¢ (**dans** on); **2** (de beurre, huile) sizzling ¢ (**dans** in).

grésiller /gʀezije/ [1] **I** *vi* **1** [*radio, téléphone*] to crackle; **ça grésille dans l'écouteur** the line is crackling; **2** [*beurre, huile*] to sizzle.

II *v impers* to hail.

gressin /gʀesɛ̃/ *nm* breadstick.

grève /gʀɛv/ *nf* **1** (cessation du travail) strike; **faire** or **être en ~** to be on strike; **se mettre en ~** to go ou come out on strike; **lancer un mot d'ordre de** or **un appel à la ~** to call a strike; **la ~ des infirmières/des trains continue** the nurses'/rail strike continues; **mouvement de ~** industrial action; **déclencher un mouvement de ~** to take industrial action; **faire ~ par solidarité** to come out in sympathy GB, to strike in sympathy US; **2** (rivage) shore; **sur la ~** on the shore.
■ **~ d'avertissement** token strike; **~ de la faim** hunger strike; **entamer une ~ de la faim** to go on hunger strike; **~ générale** general strike; **~ illimitée** indefinite strike; **~ de l'impôt** refusal to pay taxes; **~ perlée** selective strike; **~ sauvage** wildcat strike; **~ de solidarité** sympathy strike; **~ surprise** lightning strike; **~ sur le tas** sit-down strike; **~ tournante** staggered strike; **~ des urnes** refusal to vote; **~ du zèle** work-to-rule; **faire une ~ du zèle** to go on a work-to-rule.

grever /gʀəve/ [16] *vtr* to be a burden on [*pays, contribuable, individu*]; to put a strain on [*budget, économie*]; **l'entreprise est grevée de charges** the company has crippling overheads; **la maison est grevée d'hypothèques** the house is mortgaged to the hilt.

gréviste /gʀevist/ *nmf* striker; **les mineurs/étudiants ~s** the striking miners/students.
■ **~ de la faim** hunger striker.

gribiche /gʀibiʃ/ *adj* **sauce ~** *mayonnaise made of a chopped hard-boiled egg, capers and herbs.*

gribouillage○ /gʀibujaʒ/ *nm* **1** (dessin confus) scribble; **faire du ~** or **des ~s** to doodle; **2** (écriture confuse) scrawl; **ta signature est un ~** your signature is a scrawl.

gribouiller /gʀibuje/ [1] **I** *vtr* to scribble [*nom, adresse, notes*] (**sur** on); to scribble in [*album, cahier*]; **~ un plan** to draw a rough map.
II *vi* to doodle (**sur** on).

gribouilleur, **-euse** /gʀibujœʀ, øz/ *nm,f* (peintre) dauber péj; (écrivain) scribbler péj.

gribouillis /gʀibuji/ *nm inv* = **gribouillage**.

grief /gʀijɛf/ *nm* grievance; **exposer ses ~s** to air one's grievances; **avoir un ~** or **des ~s contre qn** to have a grievance against sb; **je ne t'en fais pas ~** I don't hold it against you; **il nous a fait ~ de ne pas avoir agi à temps** he held it against us that we hadn't acted in time.

grièvement /gʀijɛvmɑ̃/ *adv* [*blessé*] seriously; [*brûlé*] badly; [*atteint*] severely; **être ~ blessé à la jambe/tête** to sustain serious leg/head injuries; **il a ~ blessé trois personnes** he seriously injured three people.

griffe /gʀif/ *nf* **1** Zool claw; **sortir/rentrer ses ~s** lit [*félin*] to show/sheathe its claws; fig [*personne*] to show/sheathe one's claws; **se faire les ~s** or **faire ses ~s** lit [*félin*] to sharpen its claws (**sur** on); fig [*personne*] to sharpen one's claws; **coup de ~** scratch; **donner un coup de ~ à qn** to scratch sb; **toutes ~s dehors** lit, fig ready to pounce; **entre les ~s du chat** in the cat's clutches; **tomber entre les ~s de qn** fig to fall into sb's clutches; **sortir des ~s de qn** to escape from sb's clutches; **2** Comm (marque) label; **~ d'un grand couturier** designer label; **3** (signature) signature stamp; **apposer sa ~ sur** to stamp one's signature on; **4** fig (marque distinctive) **on reconnaît la ~ du maître** you can recognize the master's touch; **5** (en bijouterie) claw; **6** Bot (d'asperge) crown; **7** Phot **~ (de flash)** hot shoe.

griffé, **~e** /gʀife/ **I** *pp* ▶ **griffer**.
II *pp adj* [*vêtements, cravate, stylo, article*] designer (*épith*); **tous mes vêtements sont ~s** I only wear designer clothes.

griffer /gʀife/ [1] **I** *vtr* **1** (égratigner) [*animal, personne*] to scratch [*personne, bras, jambe*]; **tu m'as griffé le doigt!** you've scratched my finger!; **~ qn au visage/à la joue** to scratch sb on the face/on the cheek; **se faire ~** to get scratched (**par** by); **2** Comm to put one's name to [*foulard, stylo*].
II se griffer *vpr* [*personne*] to scratch oneself; **se ~ au visage** to scratch one's face.

griffon /gʀifɔ̃/ *nm* **1** (chien) griffon; **2** (vautour) griffon (vulture); **3** Mythol griffin; **4** (de source thermale) spring.

griffonnage /gʀifɔnaʒ/ *nm* (texte mal écrit) scribble; (dessin rapide) quick sketch.

griffonner /gʀifɔne/ [1] *vtr* **1** (écrire) to scrawl [*nom, adresse, lettre*]; **~ un plan** to draw a rough map; **2** (dessiner) to sketch [*caricature, portrait*] (**sur** on).

griffu, **~e** /gʀify/ *adj* [*doigt, main*] clawed (*épith*).

griffure /gʀifyʀ/ *nf* scratch (**sur** on).

grignotage /gʀiɲɔtaʒ/ *nm* **1** (fait de manger) nibbling ¢; **2** (diminution) (de libertés, salaire, capital) erosion (**de** of); (de terres, secteur) encroachment (**de** on).

grignotement /gʀiɲɔtmɑ̃/ *nm* gnawing ¢, nibbling ¢.

grignoter /gʀiɲɔte/ [1] **I** *vtr* **1** (manger un peu) [*personne, animal*] to nibble [*sandwich, noisette, biscuit*]; **tu n'as pas quelque chose à ~?** have you got anything to nibble? GB, do you have anything to snack on? US; **2** (empiéter) to encroach on [*terres, secteur*]; to conquer [*part de marché*]; **3** (entamer) to fritter away [*fortune, héritage*]; [*activité*] to encroach on [*temps libre*]; to erode [*droit*]; **4** (gagner) [*coureur, concurrent*] to gain [*secondes, avance, mètres*]; **elle a grignoté trois places au championnat** she crept up three places in the championships.
II *vi* **1** Zool [*rongeur*] to gnaw, to nibble; **2** [*personne, animal*] to nibble; **il est toujours en train de ~** he's always nibbling; **elle ne mange pas, elle grignote!** she doesn't eat, she just nibbles!

grigou○ /gʀigu/ *nm* skinflint○ GB, tightwad○ US.

gri-gri, *pl* **gris-gris** /gʀigʀi/ *nm* lucky charm, talisman.

gril /gʀil/ *nm* **1** (de cuisinière) grill GB, broiler US; (plaque) grill pan GB, broiler US; **viande cuite au ~** grilled meat; **2** (torture) **subir le supplice du ~** to be roasted alive; **mettre qn/être sur le ~** fig to put sb/to be on tenterhooks.

grill /gʀil/ *nm* (restaurant) grillroom.

grillade /gʀijad/ *nf* **manger des ~s** to eat grilled meat.
■ **~ de porc** Culin shoulder chop.

grillage /gʀijaʒ/ *nm* **1** (treillis) (pour clôture) wire netting; (à gros trous hexagonaux) chicken wire; (à trous fins) wire mesh; **2** (de café, noisettes) roasting; **3** Tech (de minerai) roasting.

grillagé, **~e** /gʀijaʒe/ **I** *pp* ▶ **grillager**.
II *pp adj* [*enclos*] fenced with wire (*après n*); [*fenêtre, porte*] covered with wire mesh (*après n*).

grillager /gʀijaʒe/ [13] *vtr* to fit a screen to [*soupirail, fenêtre*]; to put chicken wire around [*poulailler*]; to put wire netting around [*jardin, enclos*].

grille /gʀij/ *nf* **1** (clôture) railings (*pl*); (porte) (iron) gate; (de prison) bars (*pl*); (d'évier, égout) drain; (de râpe, bouche d'aération, confessionnal) grille; (de four, réfrigérateur) shelf; (de poêle, cheminée) grate; **il y a des ~s en fer forgé à toutes les fenêtres** there are wrought iron bars on all the windows; **2** (de mots croisés, d'horaires) grid; **une ~ de 10 cases** a grid of 10 squares; **3** Radio, TV (de programmes) programme[GB]; **4** (système d'interprétation) model; **5** Admin scale; **~ des salaires** salary scale; **6** Électron grid.
■ **~ d'analyse** analytical grid; **~ de départ** Courses Aut starting grid; **~ de loto** lottery card.

grillé, **~e** /gʀije/ **I** *pp* ▶ **griller**.
II *pp adj* **1** (cuit) [*viande, poisson, maïs*] grilled; [*tartine, pain*] toasted; [*amandes, marrons*] roasted; **2** (croustillant) [*peau, croûte*] crispy, well-browned (*épith*); **un gratin bien ~** a well-browned gratin; **3** (hors d'usage) [*moteur, résistance*] burned out; **l'ampoule est ~e** the bulb has gone ou blown; **4**○ (révélé) [*espion, affaire*] exposed; **je suis ~** my cover is blown.

grille-pain /gʀijpɛ̃/ *nm inv* toaster.

griller /gʀije/ [1] **I** *vtr* **1** Culin to grill [*viande, poisson, maïs*]; to toast [*pain*]; to roast [*amandes, marrons*]; **2**○ (fumer) to smoke [*cigarette, paquet*]; **3** (mettre hors d'usage) to burn out [*appareil électrique*]; to blow [*ampoule*]; **4**○ (ne pas respecter) to jump○, to go through [*feu rouge*]; to ignore [*stop, priorité*]; to go past [sth] without stopping [*station, gare*]; **5**○ (révéler) to give the game away about [*personne*] (**auprès de qn** to sb); **se faire ~** [*espion, indicateur*] to blow one's cover; **6**○ (dépasser) **~ un adversaire** to manage to get ahead of one's opponent.
II *vi* **1** Culin to grill; **faire ~** to grill [*viande, poisson, maïs*]; to toast [*pain*]; to roast [*amandes, marrons*]; **ne rajoute pas de charbon pendant que la viande grille** don't add charcoal while the meat is grilling; **2** (être désireux) **~ de faire** to be itching to do; **~ d'impatience** to be burning with impatience; **3** [*ampoule*] to go; **l'ampoule a grillé** the bulb has gone ou blown.

grilloir /gʀijwaʀ/ *nm* grill GB, broiler US.

grillon /gʀijɔ̃/ *nm* cricket.

grimaçant, **~e** /gʀimasɑ̃, ɑ̃t/ *adj* grimacing.

grimace /gʀimas/ *nf* **1** (expression) (de douleur, dégoût) grimace; (comique) funny face; **faire des ~s** lit to make faces; fig to be fussy; **faire une ~ à qn** to make ou pull a face at sb; **des ~s pour amuser les enfants** funny faces to amuse the children; **faire la ~** (devant un prix élevé) to wince; (de réticence) to make ou pull a face; **faire une ~ de douleur** to grimace in pain; **les ~s du beau monde parisien** the posturings of Parisian high society; ▶ **singe**, **soupe**; **2** Cout (faux pli) **la couture fait une ~** the stitching is puckering up the material; **3** Archéol, Archit grotesque.

grimacer /gʀimase/ [12] **I** *vtr* **~ un sourire** to force a smile.
II *vi* **1** gén to grimace; **~ de dégoût/de dépit/de douleur/sous l'effort** to grimace in disgust/in disappointment/with pain/under the strain; **le soleil le faisait ~** he screwed up his eyes in the sun; **2** Cout [*vêtement, encolure*] to pucker up.

grimacier, **-ière** /gʀimasje, ɛʀ/ *adj* **1** (qui fait des grimaces) [*enfant, comique*] who pulls faces a lot (*épith*) (*après n*); **2** (affecté) [*acteur, chanteur*] affected.

grimage /gʀimaʒ/ *nm* **1** (action) making-up ¢; **2** (résultat) make-up.

grimer /gʀime/ [1] **I** *vtr* to make [sb] up [*personne*] (**en** as); **~ qn en clown** to make sb up as a clown; **être grimé en vieillard** to be made up to look old.
II se grimer *vpr* to make oneself up; **se ~ en clown** to make oneself up as a clown.

grimoire /gʀimwaʀ/ *nm* **1** (livre de sorcellerie) book of magic; **2** (écrit obscur) arcane text.

grimpant, **~e** /gʀɛ̃pɑ̃, ɑ̃t/ *adj* [*plante, rosier*] climbing.

grimpe○ /gʀɛ̃p/ *nf* rock climbing.

grimpée /gʀɛ̃pe/ *nf* climb.

grimper /gʀɛ̃pe/ [1] **I** *nm* Sport **~ (à la corde)** rope-climbing ¢.
II *vtr* (gravir) to climb [*escaliers, étages, côte*]; **j'ai dû ~ six étages!** I had to climb six floors!
III *vi* **1** (escalader) **~ aux arbres** to climb

up trees; **~ sur** or **dans un arbre** to climb a tree; **~ jusqu'à la cime de l'arbre** to climb up to the top of the tree; **~ à la corde** to climb the rope; **~ sur le mur/la scène/les genoux de qn** to climb up onto the wall/the stage/sb's knees; **grimpe sur mon dos** get on my back; **grimpe dans ton lit** get into bed; **allez! grimpe** (dans une voiture) come on! get in; **2**○ (suivre une pente raide) [*route, sentier*] to be a steep climb; **qu'est-ce que ça grimpe!** it's a steep climb!; **le chemin grimpe à travers les sapins** the path climbs up through the fir trees; **3**○ (augmenter) [*température, prix*] to climb; **~ de 13°C/30%** to climb by 13°C/30%; **la nouvelle a fait ~ les cours de l'or** the news pushed up the price of gold; **4**○ (progresser) to move up; **~ de sept places/de deux points/en première division** to go up seven places/two points/into the first division; **5**○ Sport (faire de l'escalade) to go climbing.

grimpereau, *pl* **~x** /gʀɛ̃pʀo/ *nm* creeper.
■ **~ des bois** tree creeper; **~ des jardins** short-toed tree creeper.

grimpette○ /gʀɛ̃pɛt/ *nf* **1** (ascension raide) climb; **deux heures de ~** a two-hour climb; **2** (varappe) rock-climbing.

grimpeur, **-euse** /gʀɛ̃pœʀ, øz/ *nm,f* (varappeur) rock-climber; (cycliste) climber.

grinçant, **~e** /gʀɛ̃sɑ̃, ɑ̃t/ *adj* **1** (bruyant) [*porte, serrure*] creaking; [*son, musique*] grating; **2** (acerbe) [*ton, humour, propos*] scathing; [*plaisanterie, personne*] caustic; [*rire*] nasty.

grincement /gʀɛ̃smɑ̃/ *nm* **1** (type de bruit) (de porte, plancher, charnière) creaking ¢; (de craie) squeaking ¢; (de violon) screeching ¢; **2** (bruit) (de porte) creak; (de craie) squeak; (de violon) screech; **tes ~s de dents m'ont réveillée** the sound of you grinding your teeth woke me up; **provoquer des ~s de dents** fig to cause much gnashing of teeth.

grincer /gʀɛ̃se/ [12] *vi* [*porte, charnière, branche*] to creak; [*violon*] to screech; [*craie*] to squeak; **~ des dents** lit to grind one's teeth; fig to gnash one's teeth; **faire ~ les dents à qn** [*craie, bruit*] to set sb's teeth on edge; [*décision, action*] to cause much gnashing of teeth.

grincheux, **-euse** /gʀɛ̃ʃø, øz/ **I** *adj* grumpy GB, grouchy.
II *nm,f* (old) misery GB, grouch.

gringalet /gʀɛ̃galɛ/ **I** *adj m* [*garçon, homme*] puny.
II *nm* runt.

gringue○ /gʀɛ̃g/ *nm* **faire du ~ à qn** to chat sb up○ GB, to come on to sb○.

griot /gʀijo/ *nm*: *travelling*GB *black African poet and musician*.

griotte /gʀijɔt/ *nf* Bot, Culin morello cherry; **~s au chocolat** (morello) cherry liqueur chocolates.

grippage /gʀipaʒ/ *nm* **1** (de mécanisme) seizing (up); **2** fig **provoquer un ~ de l'économie** to cause the economy to grind to a halt.

grippal, **~e**, *mpl* **-aux** /gʀipal, o/ *adj* **affection ~e**, **état ~** flu.

grippe /gʀip/ ▶**271** *nf* flu ¢, influenza ¢ spéc; **avoir la ~** to have flu GB, to have the flu; **vaccin contre la ~** flu vaccine.
■ **~ asiatique** Méd Asian flu; **~ espagnole** Méd Spanish flu; **~ intestinale** Méd gastric flu GB, intestinal flu US.
IDIOMES **prendre qn/qch en ~**○ to take a sudden dislike to sb/sth.

grippé, **~e** /gʀipe/ *adj* Méd **être ~** to have flu GB, to have the flu.

gripper /gʀipe/ [1] **I** *vtr* Tech [*manque d'huile, rouille*] to make [sth] seize up [*piston, moteur*].
II *vi* lit [*moteur, engrenages*] to seize up; fig [*négociations, processus*] to grind to a halt; **le moteur est grippé** the engine has seized up.
III se gripper *vpr* **1** lit [*moteur, mécanisme*] to seize up; **2** fig [*négociations, processus*] to grind to a halt.

grippe-sou○, *pl* **~s** /gʀipsu/ *nm* skinflint○ GB, tightwad US.

gris, **~e** /gʀi, iz/ ▶**193** **I** *adj* **1** (couleur) grey GB, gray US; **~ bleu** blue-grey GB, blue-gray US; **~ métallisé** metallic grey GB ou gray US; **2** (morne) [*temps*] grey GB, gray US; [*banlieue, rue*] dreary; [*existence*] dull; [*pensées*] gloomy; **tout est ~ dans ma vie** I lead a dull life; **il fait ~**, **le temps est ~** it's a grey GB ou gray US day; **3** (ivre) tipsy.
II *nm* **1** (couleur) grey GB, gray US; **s'habiller en ~** to wear grey GB ou gray US; **2** (tabac gris) cheap tobacco.
■ **~ acier** steel grey GB ou gray US; **~ anthracite** charcoal grey GB ou gray US; **~ ardoise** slate grey GB ou gray US; **~ perle** pearl grey GB ou gray US; **~ souris** mid-grey GB, mid-gray US; **~ tourterelle** dove grey GB ou gray US.
IDIOMES **faire ~e mine** to be none too pleased; **la nuit tous les chats sont ~** Prov all cats are grey GB ou gray US in the dark.

grisaille /gʀizaj/ *nf* **1** (ennui) dullness; **sortir de la ~ quotidienne** to escape the daily grind; **2** (temps gris) greyness GB, grayness US; **dans la ~ de l'hiver** in the greyness GB ou grayness US of winter; **3** (couleur grisâtre) dinginess; **4** Art grisaille; **revers peint en ~** reverse painted in grisaille.

grisant, **~e** /gʀizɑ̃, ɑ̃t/ *adj* **1** (exaltant) [*vitesse, vent, valse, plaisir*] exhilarating; [*succès, pouvoir, danger*] intoxicating; **2** (enivrant) [*parfum, odeur*] heady.

grisâtre /gʀizɑtʀ/ ▶**193** *adj* [*couleur, ciel*] greyish GB, grayish US; [*drap, linge*] dingy; [*matin, existence*] dull.

grisbi◐ /gʀizbi/ *nm* dough○, money.

grisé /gʀize/ ▶**193** *nm* grey GB ou gray US tint.

griser /gʀize/ [1] **I** *vtr* **1** (exalter) [*vent, vitesse, valse, plaisir, aventure*] to exhilarate; [*succès, pouvoir, danger*] to intoxicate; **être grisé par la vitesse** to be exhilarated by speed; **se laisser ~ par le pouvoir** to let power go to one's head; **2** (enivrer) [*odeur, parfum*] to intoxicate; **être grisé par un parfum** to be intoxicated by a scent; **le vin m'a grisé** the wine has gone to my head.
II se griser *vpr* **se ~ de** to get drunk on [*succès, pouvoir*].

griserie /gʀizʀi/ *nf* (exaltation) exhilaration; **la ~ du succès** the exhilaration of success.

grisonnant, **~e** /gʀizɔnɑ̃, ɑ̃t/ *adj* [*cheveux, moustache*] greying GB, graying US; **il a les tempes ~es** he's greying GB ou graying US at the temples.

grisonnement /gʀizɔnmɑ̃/ *nm* greying GB, graying US.

grisonner /gʀizɔne/ [1] *vi* [*personne, chevelure, barbe*] to go grey GB, to gray US.

Grisons /gʀizɔ̃/ ▶**692** *nprmpl* Géog **le canton des ~**, **les ~** the canton of Graubünden; **viande des ~** dried beef (*served in thin slices*).

grisou /gʀizu/ *nm* firedamp; **coup de ~** firedamp explosion.

grisoumètre /gʀizumɛtʀ/ *nm* firedamp detector.

grive /gʀiv/ *nf* thrush.
■ **~ draine** mistle thrush; **~ musicienne** song thrush.
IDIOMES **faute de ~s on mange des merles** Prov half a loaf is better than no bread Prov.

grivèlerie /gʀivɛlʀi/ *nf*: *nonpayment of a restaurant bill*.

grivois, **~e** /gʀivwa, az/ *adj* [*chanson*] bawdy; [*allusion, plaisanterie*] coarse; **être d'humeur ~e** to be in a saucy mood.

grivoiserie /gʀivwazʀi/ *nf* (caractère grivois) suggestiveness; (propos grivois) suggestive remark.

grizzli, **grizzly** /gʀizli/ *nm* grizzly bear.

groenendael /gʀɔnɛndal/ *nm* Belgian sheepdog, Groenendael.

Groenland /gʀɔɛnlɑ̃d/ *nprm* Greenland.

groenlandais, **~e** /gʀɔɛnlɑ̃dɛ, ɛz/ *adj* Greenland (*épith*).

Groenlandais, **~e** /gʀɔɛnlɑ̃dɛ, ɛz/ *nm,f* Greenlander.

grog /gʀɔg/ *nm* ≈ hot toddy.

groggy /gʀɔgi/ *adj* **1** Sport (en boxe) groggy; **2**○ (drogué, fatigué) groggy; **3**○ (abasourdi) dazed.

grognard /gʀɔɲaʀ/ *nm*: *soldier of the Old Guard of Napoleon I*.

grognasse◐ /gʀɔɲas/ *nf* offensive cow◐ injur, old bag○ injur.

grogne○ /gʀɔɲ/ *nf* discontent; **la ~ monte chez les commerçants** discontent is on the increase among retailers; **c'est la ~ chez les mineurs** the miners are discontented.

grognement /gʀɔɲəmɑ̃/ *nm* **1** (son) (de personne) grunt; (de chien, lion) growl; **émettre un ~ de colère/mécontentement** to growl with anger/displeasure; **pousser des ~s de satisfaction/plaisir** to grunt with satisfaction/pleasure; **2** Zool (cri du cochon) grunt; (cri de l'ours) growl.

grogner /gʀɔɲe/ [1] **I** *vtr* to mutter [*insultes, reproches*].
II *vi* **1** (émettre un son, protester) [*personne*] lit, fig to grumble; **~ de douleur** to groan with pain; **~ de satisfaction/plaisir** to grunt with satisfaction/pleasure; **2** Zool [*cochon*] to grunt; [*ours, chien, lion*] to growl.

grognon /gʀɔɲɔ̃/ **I** *adj m* [*adolescent, adulte*] grumpy GB, grouchy US; [*bébé*] fretful, fractious.
II *nm* moaner GB, grouch US.

groin /gʀwɛ̃/ *nm* snout.

grolle◐ /gʀɔl/ *nf* shoe.

grommeler /gʀɔmle/ [19] **I** *vtr* to mutter [*insultes, reproches*]; to murmur [*compliment*].
II *vi* **1** [*personne*] to grumble; **il a grommelé pendant tout le repas** he grumbled throughout the whole meal; **~ après** or **contre qch/qn** to grumble about sth/sb; **2** Zool [*sanglier*] to snort.

grommellement /gʀɔmɛlmɑ̃/ *nm* (de personne) groan; (de sanglier) snort.

grondement /gʀɔ̃dmɑ̃/ *nm* (d'avalanche, de tonnerre, canon) rumble; (de torrent, vagues, machine) roar; (de chien, d'ours) growl; (de foule, d'émeutiers) angry murmur; **les ~s du moteur** the roar of the engine.

gronder /gʀɔ̃de/ [1] **I** *vtr* (réprimander) to tell [sb] off [*élève, enfant*]; **ses parents l'ont grondé** his parents told him off; **se faire ~ par qn** to get told off by sb.
II *vi* **1** (grogner) [*chien, ours, félin*] to growl (**contre, après** at); **2** (tonner) [*tonnerre, avalanche, canons, volcan, fleuve*] to rumble; [*machine, vent*] to roar; **3** (être menaçant) [*colère, mécontentement, révolte*] to be brewing (**au sein de, chez** among).

grondin /gʀɔ̃dɛ̃/ *nm* gurnard.

groom /gʀum/ *nm* **1** (valet) bellboy GB, bellhop US; **2** Tech door closer ou check.

gros, **grosse** /gʀo, gʀos/ **I** *adj* (*before n*) **1** (volumineux) gén big, large; [*tête, cœur*] lit large; [*cigare*] big, fat; **2** (épais) [*lèvres, genoux, chevilles*] thick; [*couverture, pull, rideau*] thick; **3** (gras) [*homme, femme, enfant*] fat; [*bébé*] big; [*ventre*] fat, big; **un ~ bonhomme** a fat lump; **4** (important) [*entreprise, exploitation*] big, large; [*commerçant, producteur, industriel, actionnaire, client*] big; [*contrat, investissement, marché*] big; [*dégâts*] considerable; [*dépense, héritage, somme*] big; [*récolte, cueillette*] big; **un de nos plus ~ clients/actionnaires** one of our major customers/shareholders; **5** (grave) [*problème, erreur*] serious, big; [*difficulté, déception, défaut*] big, major; **6** (fort) [*mensonge, surprise*] big; [*rhume*] bad; [*sanglots*] loud; [*soupir, voix*] deep; [*câlin, larmes, appétit*] big; [*pluie, chute de neige*] heavy; [*orage*] big; [*temps, mer*] rough; [*buveur, fumeur*] heavy; [*mangeur*] big; **par ~ temps** in rough weather; **avoir une grosse fièvre** to have a very high temperature; **avoir une grosse faim** to be very hungry; **d'une grosse voix** in a very serious voice; **pendant les grosses chaleurs** when the weather is at its hottest; **~ malin!** you silly fool○!; **un ~ fainéant/porc** a real lazybones/dirty pig; **7** (rude) [*traits*] coarse, heavy; [*rire*] coarse; [*drap, laine*] coarse.

II *nm,f* fat man/woman; **un petit ~** a small fat man; **une bonne grosse** a plump old dear; **mon ~** my old thing; **les petits payent pour les ~** fig the rich live off the backs of the poor.

III *adv* **1** (en gros caractères) [*écrire*] big ou in big letters; **essaie d'écrire moins/plus ~** try to write smaller/bigger; **2** (beaucoup) [*miser, risquer, gagner, perdre*] lit a lot of money; fig a lot; **jouer ~** lit, fig to play for high stakes; **il y a ~ à parier que**... it's a good bet that...

IV *nm* **1** (plupart) **le ~ de** the majority ou bulk of [*spectateurs, lecteurs, passagers*]; the main body of [*manifestants, troupes, armée, expédition*]; the bulk of [*travail*]; the main part of [*effort, dépenses, revenus*]; most of [*été, hiver, saison*]; most of [*déficit*]; **le ~ de la troupe a suivi** the main body of the group followed; **2** Comm wholesale trade; **de ~** [*magasin, commerce, prix*] wholesale; **3** Pêche game fish; **la pêche au ~** game fishing.

V en ~ *loc* **1** (dans les grandes lignes) [*expliquer, raconter*] roughly; **en ~, voilà ce qui s'est passé** that's roughly what happened; **il s'agit, en ~, de savoir si**... what's roughly involved is finding out if...; **en ~ je suis d'accord avec toi** basically, I agree with you; **2** Comm [*acheter, vendre*] wholesale, in bulk; [*achat, vente*] wholesale (*épith*), bulk (*épith*); **3** (en gros caractères) [*écrit, imprimé*] in big letters.

VI grosse *nf* **1** (copie d'acte) engrossment; **2** (douze douzaines) gross.

■ **~ bétail** Agric large livestock; **~ bonnet**○ big wig○ GB, big shot○; **~ bras**○ strong man; **~ coup**○ a big deal; **réussir un ~ coup** to pull off a big deal; **~ cube**○ Aut, Transp big bike○ ou motorbike, big hog○ US; **~ cul**○ big truck; **~ gibier** Chasse big game; fig big time criminals (*pl*); **~ lard**○ fat slob○; **~ linge** heavy washing; **~ lot** Jeux first prize, jackpot; **gagner** or **décrocher le ~ lot** lit, fig to hit the jackpot ; **~ morceau**○ (travail) big job; **s'attaquer à un ~ morceau** to tackle a big job; **~ mot** swearword; **dire des ~ mots** to use bad language, to swear; **~ œuvre** Constr shell (of a building); **nous avons fini le ~ œuvre** we've finished the shell (of the building); **~ plan** Cin close-up; **en ~ plan** in close-up; **faire un ~ plan sur** to do a close-up of; **~ plein de soupe**○ fatso○; **~ rouge**○ red plonk○ GB, cheap red wine; **~ sel** Culin coarse salt; **~ titre** Presse headline; **être en ~ titres dans les journaux** to hit the (newspaper) headlines; **grosse caisse** Mus bass drum; **grosse légume**○ = **~ bonnet**; **grosse tête**○ brain box○ GB, brain○.

IDIOMES **faire une grosse tête à qn**◐ to give sb a thick ear○ GB, to beat sb upside the head○ US; **avoir le cœur ~** to have a heavy heart; **en avoir ~ sur le cœur** or **la patate**○ to be very upset; **~ comme le poing** as big as my fist; **~ comme une tête d'épingle** no bigger than a pinhead; **c'est un peu ~ comme histoire!** that's a bit of a tall story!; **il dit des bêtises grosses comme lui** he says ridiculous foolish things.

groseille /gʀozɛj/ **▶ 193** **I** *adj inv* red.

II *nf* redcurrant.

■ **~ blanche** white currant; **~ à maquereau** gooseberry; **~ rouge** redcurrant.

groseillier /gʀozeje/ *nm* redcurrant bush.

■ **~ à maquereau** gooseberry bush.

gros-grain, *pl* **~s** /gʀogʀɛ̃/ *nm* grosgrain.

Gros-Jean /gʀoʒɑ̃/ *nm* **être ~ comme devant** to be left feeling a real mug○.

gros-porteur, *pl* **~s** /gʀopɔʀtœʀ/ *nm* Aviat jumbo aircraft.

grossesse /gʀosɛs/ *nf* pregnancy; **pendant la ~** during pregnancy; **au neuvième mois de sa ~** in the ninth month of her pregnancy; **~ à risques** risk pregnancy; **robe de ~** maternity dress.

■ **~ nerveuse** (chez une femme) phantom pregnancy GB, false pregnancy US; (chez un homme) sympathetic pregnancy; **~ extra-utérine** ectopic pregnancy.

grosseur /gʀosœʀ/ *nf* **1** (volume) size; **des grêlons/un kyste de la ~ d'une orange** hailstones/a cyst the size of an orange; **2** (épaisseur) (d'aiguille) size; (de fil) thickness; **3** (bosse, kyste) lump; **avoir une ~ au sein** to have a lump in one's breast.

grossier, **-ière** /gʀosje, ɛʀ/ *adj* **1** (impoli) [*personne, geste, plaisanterie*] rude; [*langage*] bad; **un ~ personnage** an uncouth individual; **2** (sans finesse) [*esprit, être, rire, traits, visage*] coarse; [*plaisirs*] low; [*formes*] crude; **3** (médiocre) [*copie, imitation*] crude; [*étoffe, chevelure*] coarse; [*mobilier*] basic; [*vêtements*] crudely fashioned; **nourriture grossière** coarse fare ¢; **4** (rudimentaire) [*nettoyage*] cursory; [*ébauche, idée, estimation*] rough; [*travail*] crude; **5** (flagrant) [*ignorance*] crass; [*erreur*] glaring; [*procédé, manœuvre, provocation*] crude.

grossièrement /gʀosjɛʀmɑ̃/ *adv* **1** (de façon sommaire) [*évaluer, calculer*] roughly; **2** (sans soin particulier) [*réparer, construire*] crudely; **elle a ~ recollé les morceaux** she stuck the pieces crudely back together; **une pierre ~ taillée** a rough-hewn stone; **3** (avec impolitesse) [*parler, répondre*] rudely; **4** (lourdement) **se tromper ~** to be utterly mistaken.

grossièreté /gʀosjɛʀte/ *nf* **1** (inconvenance) rudeness; **ils sont d'une ~!** they're so rude!; **2** (mot grossier) rude word GB, dirty word US; **dire des ~s** to use bad language GB, to talk dirty US; **3** (manque de finesse) (de jugement, d'interprétation) crudeness; (de personne, visage, traits) coarseness; **4** (caractère rudimentaire) coarseness; **travail/finition d'une grande ~** very crude work/finish.

grossir /gʀosiʀ/ [3] **I** *vtr* **1** (agrandir) [*lunettes, verre, microscope*] to enlarge [*image*]; **2** (faire augmenter) to increase [*effectifs*]; to boost [*nombre, liste*]; to increase, to boost [*profits*]; to add to [*troupeau*]; **~ les rangs** or **la foule** to swell the ranks; **dix personnes sont venues ~ la liste des adhérents** ten people came and boosted the membership list; **pour ~ nos effectifs de 50 personnes** to increase our workforce by fifty people; **3** (exagérer) to exaggerate [*incident, affaire*]; **4** (faire paraître plus gros) [*vêtement, motif*] to make [sb] look fat; **5** (rendre plus large) [*pluie, neige*] to swell [*fleuve, torrent*].

II *vi* **1** (prendre du poids) [*personne, animal*] to put on weight; **il a beaucoup grossi** he's put on a lot of weight; **~ de cinq kilos** to put on five kilos; **elle n'en mange pas, ça fait ~** she doesn't eat that, it's fattening; **2** (devenir plus grand) [*soleil, vague*] to grow; [*bosse, tumeur*] to grow; [*fleuve, torrent*] to swell; [*entreprise, groupe, cagnotte*] to grow; **3** (augmenter) [*troupeau, chiffre, effectifs*] to grow; **4** (s'intensifier) [*tempête, orage*] to get worse; [*rumeur, crise*] to grow.

grossissant, **~e** /gʀosisɑ̃, ɑ̃t/ *adj* **1** (en optique) [*verre*] magnifying; **2** (qui augmente) [*flot, foule*] swelling.

grossissement /gʀosismɑ̃/ *nm* **1** (fait de grossir) enlargement; **un ~ anormal du foie** an abnormally enlarged liver; **2** (exagération) exaggeration; **le ~ des faits par la presse** distortion of the facts in the press; **3** (en optique) magnification.

grossiste /gʀosist/ *nmf* wholesaler; **~ en matériel électrique** electrical appliances wholesaler.

grosso modo /gʀosomodo/ *adv* [*représenter, coïncider, aller, être*] roughly; **~, je suis satisfaite** broadly speaking I am satisfied.

grotesque /gʀɔtɛsk/ **I** *adj* **1** (risible) [*personne, accoutrement, coiffure*] ridiculous; [*idée, histoire*] ridiculous, grotesque; [*histoire, remarque, commentaires*] preposterous; **tout ceci est ~!** all this is preposterous!; **2** Art, Littérat grotesque; **style ~** grotesque style.

II *nm* **1** (caractère risible) (d'accoutrement) ridiculous aspect; (de personne) ludicrous aspect; (d'histoire) silly nature; **être d'un ~ absolu** [*histoire, situation*] to be utterly ridiculous; [*personne*] to be absolutely ludicrous; **2** Art, Littérat **le ~** the grotesque.

III grotesques *nfpl* Art (motifs) grotesques.

grotte /gʀɔt/ *nf* **1** Géog cave; **2** Archit grotto.

grouillant, **~e** /gʀujɑ̃, ɑ̃t/ *adj* [*lieu*] swarming (**de** with); **foule ~e** swarming crowd.

grouillement /gʀujmɑ̃/ *nm* (d'insectes, de vers) swarming ¢; **le ~ de la foule m'étourdissait** the swarming crowds made my head spin.

grouiller /gʀuje/ [1] **I** *vi* [*vers, insectes*] to swarm about; [*gens*] to mill about; **~ de** to be swarming with; **la plage grouille de monde** the beach is swarming with people; **le fromage grouille d'asticots** the cheese is crawling with maggots.

II○ **se grouiller** *vpr* to get a move on○; **grouille-toi!** get a move on○!

grouillot /gʀujo/ *nm* runner.

groupage /gʀupaʒ/ *nm* **1** Transp bulking; **~ de marchandises** bulking of merchandise; **envoi en ~** collective shipment; **2** Méd blood grouping.

groupe /gʀup/ *nm* **1** (ensemble de personnes) group (**de** of); **un ~ de touristes/d'écoliers** a group ou party of tourists/of schoolchildren; **un ~ de musiciens** a group ou band of musicians; **travailler/voyager en ~** to work/travel in a group; **par ~s de deux** in pairs, in twos; **former un ~ autour de qn** [*badauds*] to form a group ou to cluster around sb; [*disciples*] to form a group around sb; **2** (ensemble d'objets) group; (plus petit) cluster (**de** of); **un ~ d'arbres** a cluster ou clump of trees; **3** Écon, Fin, Ind, Presse group; **~ financier** financial group.

■ **~ abélien** Math Abelian group; **~ d'autodéfense** vigilance committee; **~ de chasse** hunting party, hunt; **~ de choc** Mil fighter group; **~ de combat** combat unit; **~ électrogène** (electricity) generator; **~ ethnique** ethnic group; **~ de mots** word group; **~ de niveau** Scol attainment-level group; **~ parlementaire** parliamentary group; **~ politique** political group; **~ de presse** newspaper group; **~ de pression** pressure group; **~ de recherches** research group; **~ de réflexion** discussion group; **~ à risque** at-risk group; **~ sanguin** blood group; **~ scolaire** school; **~ des Sept, G7** group of Seven, G7 countries (*pl*); **~ social** Sociol social group; **~ témoin** Sci control group; **~ de travail** working party.

groupement /gʀupmɑ̃/ *nm* **1** (association) association, group; **un ~ de consommateurs** a consumers' group; **un ~ politique** a political grouping; **2** (classification) grouping; **le ~ d'animaux par famille** the grouping of animals by family.

■ **~ d'achat** ≈ buyers' cooperative; **~ agricole d'exploitation en commun** ≈ farming cooperative; **~ forestier** forest community; **~ de gendarmerie** ≈ police unit; **~ d'intérêt économique, GIE** association for developing commercial interests.

grouper /gʀupe/ [1] **I** *vtr* to put [sth]

together [*factures, chèques*]; **~ ses achats** (dans un même magasin) to make all one's purchases in the same store; (à plusieurs acheteurs) to make a group purchase; **sauter en groupant les genoux** to jump with one's knees held against one's chest.

II se grouper *vpr* **1** (physiquement) [*personnes*] to gather (**autour de** around); **groupez-vous par classes** get into your class groups; **se ~ par trois** to form groups of three; **2** (s'organiser) to form a group (**autour de** around); **groupez-vous sur les marches/dans le salon pour la photo** form a group on the stairs/in the lounge for the picture; **restez groupés** keep together, stay in a group; **en cas de fusillade, ne restez pas groupés** if there's any firing, scatter; **courir/avancer groupés** to run/march in a group.

groupie /ɡʀupi/ *nf* groupie.

groupuscule /ɡʀupyskyl/ *nm* (very) small group.

grouse /ɡʀuz/ *nf* grouse.

GRS /ʒeɛʀɛs/ *nf*: *abbr* ▶ **gymnastique**.

gruau, *pl* **~x** /ɡʀyo/ *nm* **1** Culin (bouillie) gruel; **2** (fleur de froment) fine wheat flour; **3** (avoine décortiquée) groats (*pl*); (céréale décortiquée) grits (*pl*).

grue /ɡʀy/ *nf* **1** Tech crane; **manœuvrer une ~** to operate a crane; **~ hydraulique/flottante** hydraulic/floating crane; **2** Zool crane; **3**○ (prostituée) slut○ péj, prostitute.

■ **~ cendrée** Zool common crane; **~ couronnée** Zool crowned crane.

IDIOMES **faire le pied de ~**○ to hang around.

gruger /ɡʀyʒe/ [13] *vtr* to dupe [*personne, associé*]; **se faire** or **se laisser ~** to be duped.

grume /ɡʀym/ *nf* **1** Ind (unbarked) log; **bois en ~** (unbarked) log; **2** Vin (grain de raisin) grape.

grumeau, *pl* **~x** /ɡʀymo/ *nm* lump; **la pâte est pleine de ~x** the batter is all lumpy; **faire des ~x** [*personne*] to make lumps; [*sauce, mélange*] to go lumpy.

grumeleux, -euse /ɡʀymlø, øz/ *adj* Culin [*sauce, mélange, pâte*] lumpy.

grutier, -ière /ɡʀytje, ɛʀ/ ▶ **510** *nm,f* crane operator, crane driver.

gruyère /ɡʀyjɛʀ/ *nm* Gruyère, Swiss cheese.

Guadeloupe /ɡwadlup/ ▶ **692**, **416** *nprf* **la ~** Guadeloupe.

guadeloupéen, -éenne /ɡwadlupeɛ̃, ɛn/ *adj* Guadeloupian.

Guadeloupéen, -éenne /ɡwadlupeɛ̃, ɛn/ *nm,f* (natif) native of Guadeloupe; (habitant) inhabitant of Guadeloupe.

guano /ɡwano/ *nm* guano.

Guatémala /ɡwatemala/ ▶ **321** *nprm* Guatemala.

guatémaltèque /ɡwatemaltɛk/ ▶ **537** *adj* Guatemalan.

Guatémaltèque /ɡwatemaltɛk/ ▶ **537** *nmf* Guatemalan.

gué /ɡe/ *nm* ford; **franchir un ~** to cross a ford; **passer un ruisseau à ~** to ford a stream.

IDIOMES **on ne change pas de chevaux au milieu du ~** Prov you can't swap horses in midstream.

guéable /ɡeabl/ *adj* [*rivière*] fordable.

guède /ɡɛd/ *nf* woad.

guéguerre○ /ɡeɡɛʀ/ *nf* gén squabble **C**; **c'est la ~ au bureau** at the office there's a lot of squabbling; **la ~ entre les partis continue** the parties are still squabbling.

guelfe /ɡɛlf/ **I** *adj* Guelphic.

II *nmf* Guelph.

guelte /ɡɛlt/ *nf* commission, percentage on sales; **être payé à la ~** to be paid on commission.

guenille /ɡənij/ *nf* rag; **en ~s** in rags.

guenon /ɡənɔ̃/ *nf* **1** Zool female monkey; **2**○ (femme) ugly woman.

guépard /ɡepaʀ/ *nm* cheetah.

guêpe /ɡɛp/ *nf* wasp.

IDIOMES **pas folle la ~**○! I'm/you're etc not just a pretty face○!

guêpier /ɡepje/ *nm* **1** (nid de guêpes) wasps' nest; **2** (situation difficile) tight corner; **se fourrer**○ **dans/se sortir d'un ~** to get oneself into/out of a tight corner; **dans quel ~ es-tu allé te fourrer**○**?** what kind of mess have you got GB ou gotten US yourself into?; **3** (oiseau) bee-eater.

guêpière /ɡepjɛʀ/ *nf* basque, bodyshaper with suspenders GB ou garters US.

guère /ɡɛʀ/ *adv* **1** (modifiant un adjectif) **les résultats n'étaient ~ probants/différents/meilleurs le mois suivant** the results were hardly convincing/any different/any better the following month; **les étudiants ne sont ~ optimistes/préparés** the students aren't very optimistic/really prepared; **2** (modifiant un adverbe) **et le mois suivant ça n'a ~ été mieux** and the following month it was hardly any better; **l'appareil ne coûte ~ plus de 10 000 francs** the appliance doesn't cost much more than 10,000 francs; **il ne faut ~ plus de dix minutes pour faire** it won't take much more than ten minutes to do; **3** (modifiant un verbe) **il n'a ~ mangé** he hardly ate, he ate hardly anything; **ne ~ manifester d'enthousiasme** to show hardly any enthusiasm; **la situation n'a ~ évolué** the situation has hardly changed; **on ne remarque ~ la différence** you can hardly tell the difference; **je n'ai ~ eu de mal à les convaincre** I didn't have much trouble convincing them, I hardly had any trouble convincing them; **je n'ai ~ les moyens de faire** I can barely ou hardly afford to do; **aujourd'hui la question n'a ~ d'importance** today the question hardly matters ou is hardly important; **il n'apprécie ~ ta décontraction** he doesn't much care for your casual attitude; **on ne voit ~ comment elle pourra s'en sortir** it is hard to see how she'll be able to manage; **il n'avait ~ le choix** he didn't really have a choice, he had little choice; **je n'ai ~ l'habitude de faire** I'm not really in the habit of doing; **ils ne se font ~ d'illusions sur leur avenir** they don't hold out much hope for their future; **elle n'a ~ de chances de retrouver du travail** she has little chance of finding another job; **hors contexte les chiffres n'ont ~ de sens** out of context the figures are practically meaningless; **il ne fait ~ de doute que** there is little doubt that.

guéret /ɡeʀɛ/ *nm* (jachère) fallow land **¢**.

guéridon /ɡeʀidɔ̃/ *nm* pedestal table.

guérilla /ɡeʀija/ *nf* **1** (forme de combat) guerilla warfare; **~ urbaine** urban guerilla warfare; **2** (groupe) guerillas (*pl*); **~ armée** armed guerillas; **mouvement de ~** guerilla movement.

guérillero /ɡeʀijeʀo/ *nm* guerilla.

guérir /ɡeʀiʀ/ [3] **I** *vtr* **1** Méd [*médecin, traitement, cure*] to cure [*personne, maladie, fièvre*] (**de** of; **avec** with; **par** by); to heal [*blessure*]; **cela soulage mais ne guérit pas** it brings relief but it does not act as a cure; **2** fig **~ qn de** to cure sb of [*habitude, vice, timidité*].

II *vi* Méd [*personne, animal*] to recover, to get well; [*blessure*] to heal; [*entorse*] to get better; [*rhume*] to get better, to clear up; **~ de qch** to recover from sth; **je suis guéri** (de rhume, maladie bénigne) I'm better; (de maladie grave) I've made a complete recovery; fig never again!

III se guérir *vpr* **1** Méd [*personne*] to cure oneself; [*maladie*] to be cured; **2** fig **se ~ de** to overcome [*timidité, préjugés*]; to get rid of [*habitude*].

guérison /ɡeʀizɔ̃/ *nf* **1** (de malade) recovery; **2** (de fracture, blessure) healing.

guérissable /ɡeʀisabl/ *adj* [*malade, maladie*] curable.

guérisseur, -euse /ɡeʀisœʀ, øz/ ▶ **510** *nm,f* healer.

guérite /ɡeʀit/ *nf* (de sentinelle) sentry box; (de douanier, chantier) hut; (de garage, péage) booth.

Guernesey /ɡɛʀnəzɛ/ ▶ **416** *nprf* Guernsey.

guerre /ɡɛʀ/ *nf* (conflit) war; (technique) warfare; **entrer en ~** to go to war (**contre** against); **l'entrée en ~ d'un pays** a country's entry into the war; **être en ~** to be at war (**avec** with); **état de ~** state of war; **faire la ~** to wage war (**à** against, on); **mon grand-père a fait la ~** my grandfather was ou fought in the war; **mourir à la ~** to die in the war; **les pays en ~** the warring nations; **entre elle et lui, c'est la ~!** it's war between those two!; **c'est la ~ ouverte entre les deux compagnies** it's open warfare between the two firms; **les deux candidats se livrent une ~ sans merci** it's out-and-out war between the two candidates, it's no holds barred between the two candidates; **faire la ~ aux retardataires/fautes d'orthographe** to wage war on latecomers/spelling mistakes; **elle lui fait la ~ pour qu'il range sa chambre** she's fighting a running battle with him to try and get him to tidy his room; **partir en ~ contre le gaspillage/les préjugés/les fraudeurs** to wage war on waste/prejudice/fare dodgers; **les enfants jouent à la ~** the children are playing at GB ou playing soldiers; ▶ **grand**.

■ **~ de Cent Ans** Hundred Years' War; **~ chimique** (conflit) chemical war; (technique) chemical warfare; **~ civile** civil war; **~ éclair** blitzkrieg, lightning war; **~ économique** economic warfare; **~ d'Espagne** Spanish Civil War; **~ des étoiles** Star Wars; **~ froide** Cold War; **~ du Golfe** Gulf War; **~ mondiale** world war; **Première/Deuxième** or **Seconde Guerre mondiale** World War I/II, First/Second World War; **troisième ~ mondiale** third world war; **~ de mouvement** war of movement; **~ des nerfs** war of nerves; **~ nucléaire** (conflit) nuclear war; (technique) nuclear warfare; **~ de positions** war of position; **~ psychologique** psychological warfare; **~ de 14** 1914–18 war; **~ de religion** war of religion; **~ sainte** holy war; **~ de Sécession** American Civil War; **~ totale** total war, all-out war; **~ de tranchée** trench warfare; **~ de Troie** Trojan War; **~ d'usure** war of attrition; **~ du Vietnam** Vietnam War; **~s puniques** Hist the Punic Wars.

IDIOMES **à la ~ comme à la ~** in time of hardship you have to make the best of things; **c'est de bonne ~** it's only fair, it's fair enough; **être sur le pied de ~** to be on a war footing; **de ~ lasse, elle renonça à le convaincre** realizing that she was fighting a losing battle, she gave up trying to convince him.

guerrier, -ière /ɡɛʀje, ɛʀ/ **I** *adj* [*peuple, âme, air*] warlike; [*chant, exploit*] war (*épith*).

II *nm,f* warrior.

guerroyer /ɡɛʀwaje/ [23] *vi* to wage war (**contre** against, on).

guet /ɡɛ/ *nm* **1** gén lookout; **faire le ~** to be on the lookout; **2** Mil watch.

guet-apens, *pl* **guets-apens** /ɡɛtapɑ̃/ *nm* lit ambush; fig trap; **tomber dans un ~** lit to be caught in an ambush; fig to fall into a trap.

guêtre /ɡɛtʀ/ *nf* **1** Sport leggings (*pl*); **2** Mode gaiter; ▶ **traîner**; **3** Équit boot.

guetter /ɡete/ [1] *vtr* **1** (surveiller) to watch [*proie, malfaiteur, réaction*]; to watch out for [*signe*]; to listen for [*téléphone*]; to look out for [*facteur, ami*]; to keep an eye out for [*faute*]; **je guettais le moindre bruit** I was alert for the slightest noise; **~ la parution du journal** to be waiting for the newspaper to come out; **~ l'arrivée de l'ennemi** to lie in wait for the enemy; **2** (menacer) [*déclin,* *appauvrissement, danger*] to threaten [*personne, entreprise*]; **la folie le guette** he is on the brink of madness; **la fatigue guette les conducteurs** tiredness is a threat for drivers.

guetteur, **-euse** /gɛtœʀ, øz/ **I** *nm,f* lookout.

II *nm* Hist watchman.

gueulante◑ /gœlɑ̃t/ *nf* **pousser sa** or **une ~** to kick up a real fuss○.

gueulard, **~e** /gœlaʀ, aʀd/ **I**◑ *adj* [*bébé, supporter*] yelling (*épith*); [*musique, radio*] blaring; **qu'est-ce que tu es ~!** you never stop yelling!

II◑ *nm,f* loudmouth.

III *nm* Tech (de haut-fourneau, poêle) mouth; (de chaudière) throat.

gueule /gœl/ *nf* **1**◑ (visage) face; **casser la ~ à qn** to beat sb up; **balancer son poing dans la ~ de qn** to punch sb in the face; **prendre un coup en plein dans la ~** to get punched in the face; **c'est bien fait pour leur ~** (it) serves them right; **il en fait une ~** (mélancolique) he looks really down; (furieux) he looks pretty pissed off◑; **il a la ~ de l'emploi** he really looks the part; **se cogner sur la ~** to have a punch-up; ▶ **plein**; **2**◑ (bouche humaine) mouth; **(ferme) ta ~!** shut your face○ GB ou mouth○ US!; **vos ~s là-dedans** shut up in there; **coup de ~** outburst; **pousser un coup de ~** to kick up a real fuss○; **être** or **avoir une grande ~** to be a bigmouth○; **ramener sa grande ~** to put one's oar in; ▶ **fin**[1]; **3**◑ (aspect) look; **le gâteau a une drôle de ~** the cake looks weird; **avoir de la ~** to look great ou terrific; **4** Zool (bouche d'animal) mouth; **5** (de tunnel, four, canon) mouth; **être bourré jusqu'à la ~** [*canon*] to be loaded to the muzzle.

■ **~ d'amour** heart-throb○; **~ de bois**, **gdb**○ hangover; **avoir la ~ de bois** to have a hangover, to be hung over; **~ cassée** war veteran with severe facial injuries; **~ noire** miner, coal-face worker.

IDIOMES **faire** or **tirer la ~**◑ to be sulking; **il leur fait la ~** he's not talking to them; **s'en mettre plein la ~**◑ to stuff oneself ou one's face; **se bourrer** or **soûler la ~**◑ to get blind drunk; ▶ **loup**.

gueule-de-loup, *pl* **gueules-de-loup** /gœldəlu/ *nf* snapdragon.

gueulement◑ /gœlmɑ̃/ *nm* yell; (plus fort) bellow.

gueuler◑ /gœle/ [1] **I** *vtr* (crier) to yell [*insultes*]; to bawl out [*réponse*]; (chanter) to bellow out.

II *vi* **1** [*personne*] (crier) to yell, to bawl; (chanter) to bawl, to howl; (protester) to kick up a real fuss; **~ de douleur** to scream with pain; **~ contre** or **après qn/qch** to carp ou bang on against sb/sth; **ça va ~** all hell will break loose◑; **2** [*animal*] to make a racket○; **3** [*radio, télévision*] to blare out; **faire ~ qch** to have sth blaring out; **4** [*couleur*] to clash.

IDIOMES **~ comme un âne** or **putois** or **perdu** to scream blue GB ou bloody US murder○.

gueules /gœl/ *nm inv* Hérald gules.

gueuleton○ /gœltɔ̃/ *nm* blowout○, big meal.

gueuletonner○ /gœltɔne/ [1] *vi* to have a blowout○, to have a big meal.

gueux, **gueuse** /gø, gøz/ **I**† *nm,f* (pauvre) beggar; (personne vile) rogue.

II gueuse *nf* Ind, Tech pig.

IDIOMES **courir la gueuse**○ to go looking for a bit of skirt○.

gueuze /gøz/ *nf* gueuse beer.

gugusse○ /gygys/ *nm* fool, twit○; **faire le ~** to play the fool, to act the goat○ GB.

gui /gi/ *nm* **1** Bot mistletoe; **2** Naut boom.

IDIOMES **au ~ l'an neuf!** Happy New Year!

guibolle○ /gibɔl/ *nf* pin○, leg.

guiches† /giʃ/ *nfpl* kiss curls.

guichet /giʃɛ/ *nm* **1** (comptoir vitré) window; (comptoir ouvert) (de banque) counter; (de stade, musée, gare) ticket office; (de théâtre, cinéma) box office, ticket office; **la pièce se jouera à ~s fermés** the play is sold out; **2** (dans mur, porte) grille; **3** Archit portico.

■ **~ automatique** automatic teller machine, ATM.

guichetier, **-ière** /giʃtje, ɛʀ/ ▶ **510** *nm,f* ticket clerk.

guidage /gidaʒ/ *nm* **1** Aviat guidance; **2** Mécan, Mines guide.

guide /gid/ **I** *nm* **1** (accompagnateur) guide; **~ de haute montagne** mountain guide; **2** (ouvrage) guide; **un ~ des restaurants/des étudiants** a restaurant/student guide; **~ pratique** practical guide; **3** (conseiller) guide; **4** Mécan, Tech guide.

II *nf* (Catholic) guide GB, (Catholic) girl scout US.

III guides *nfpl* Équit reins; **petites ~s** lead reins.

guide-âne, *pl* **~s** /gidɑn/ *nm* **1** (pour écrire) ruled guide sheet; **2** (manuel) handbook.

guide-interprète, *pl* **guides-interprètes** /gidɛ̃tɛʀpʀɛt, gidzɛ̃tɛʀpʀɛt/ ▶ **510** *nmf* tour guide and interpreter.

guider /gide/ [1] **I** *vtr* **1** (montrer le chemin) to show [sb] the way (**vers** to); **~ jusque** to take [sb] to, to lead [sb] to; **~ dans** or **à travers** to take [sb] around; **il m'a guidé dans les couloirs** he showed me the way through the corridors; **il a guidé les policiers (jusque) sur les lieux de l'accident** he took ou led the policemen to the scene of the accident; **le chien guide l'aveugle** the dog guides the blind man; **2** (orienter) [*étoile*] to guide; [*flair, trace*] to lead; [*panneau indicateur*] to direct; **3** (diriger) to guide [*cheval, avion, missile*]; **4** (conseiller) to guide; **~ un enfant dans ses études** to guide a child in his studies; **se laisser ~ par son instinct** to let oneself be guided by instinct.

II se guider *vpr* **se ~ sur** to set one's course by [*soleil*]; **se ~ sur l'exemple de qn** to take sb as a model.

guidon /gidɔ̃/ *nm* **1** (de bicyclette, moto) handlebars (*pl*); **2** (de pistolet) front sight; **3** (drapeau) guidon.

guigne /giɲ/ *nf* (malchance) bad luck; **avoir la ~** to be dogged by bad luck.

IDIOMES **se soucier** or **se moquer de qch/qn comme d'une ~** not to give a fig○ ou a toss○ about sth/sb.

guigner /giɲe/ [1] *vtr* **1** (convoiter) to have one's eye on [*place, héritage*]; **2**○ (lorgner) to eye [*personne, chose*].

guignol /giɲɔl/ *nm* **1** (spectacle de marionnettes) puppet show, ≈ Punch and Judy show; **c'est du ~** fig it's farcical, it's a complete farce; **2** péj (personne peu sérieuse) clown, joker; **faire le ~** to clown around.

guignon† /giɲɔ̃/ *nm* bad luck; **avoir du ~** to be dogged by bad luck.

guilde /gild/ *nf* guild.

guili-guili○, *pl* **~s** /giligili/ *nm* tickle, tickle; **faire ~ à qn** to tickle sb.

guillaume /gijom/ *nm* rabbet plane.

Guillaume /gijom/ *npr* **~ le Conquérant** William the Conqueror; **~ d'Orange** William of Orange; **~ Tell** William Tell.

guilledou /gijdu/ *nm* **courir le ~** to go gallivanting.

guillemets /gijmɛ/ *nmpl* inverted commas GB, quotation marks; **ouvrir/fermer les ~** to open/close inverted commas; **mettre qch entre ~** to put sth in inverted commas; **ton fidèle ami, entre ~** iron your, in inverted commas, faithful friend.

guillemot /gijmo/ *nm* guillemot.

guilleret, **-ette** /gijʀɛ, ɛt/ *adj* [*personne, air*] perky, jaunty.

guillocher /gijɔʃe/ [1] *vtr* to ornament [sth] with guilloche.

guillotine /gijɔtin/ *nf* guillotine.

guillotiner /gijɔtine/ [1] *vtr* to guillotine.

guimauve /gimov/ *nf* **1** Bot, Méd (marsh) mallow; Culin marshmallow; **2** (mièvrerie) slush, schmaltz○ US; **c'est de la ~** it's pure slush ou schmaltz; **film à la ~** slushy ou schmaltzy film.

guimbarde /gɛ̃baʀd/ *nf* **1**○ (vieille voiture) banger GB, crate○ US; **2** Mus Jew's harp.

guimpe /gɛ̃p/ *nf* **1** (chemisette) high-necked sleeveless blouse; **2** (de religieuse) wimple; **3**† (plastron) tucker.

guincher○ /gɛ̃ʃe/ [1] *vi* to dance.

guindé, **~e** /gɛ̃de/ *adj* [*personne, air*] stiff, formal; [*atmosphère*] formal; [*style*] stilted, formal.

guindeau, *pl* **~x** /gɛ̃do/ *nm* gypsy; **poupée de ~** gypsy head.

guinder /gɛ̃de/ [1] *vtr* **1** (rendre peu naturel) to make [sb] look stiff [*personne*]; to make [sth] (rather) awkward [*démarche, allure*]; to make [sth] stilted [*style*]; **2** Naut (hisser) to raise, to hoist.

guinée /gine/ *nf* guinea.

Guinée /gine/ ▶ **321** *nprf* Guinea; **golfe de ~** Gulf of Guinea; **~ équatoriale** Equatorial Guinea.

Guinée-Bissao /ginebisao/ ▶ **321** *nprf* Guinea-Bissau.

guinéen, **-éenne** /gineɛ̃, ɛn/ ▶ **537** *adj* Guinean.

Guinéen, **-éenne** /gineɛ̃, ɛn/ ▶ **537** *nm,f* Guinean.

guingois: **de guingois** /degɛ̃gwa/ *loc adv* **être de ~** [*meuble, maison*] to be lopsided; **aller de ~** to go askew.

guinguette /gɛ̃gɛt/ *nf*: *small restaurant with music and dancing.*

guipure /gipyʀ/ *nf* guipure (lace).

guirlande /giʀlɑ̃d/ *nf* (de fleurs, feuillage) garland; (de Noël) tinsel; (de papier) paper chain; (en plein air) bunting ¢.

■ **~ électrique** set ou string of fairy lights; **~ de marguerites** daisy chain.

guise /giz/ *nf* **1 à ma/ta etc ~** just as I/you etc wish ou please; **n'en faire qu'à sa ~** to do exactly as one pleases ou likes; **laissez-les vivre à leur ~!** let them live their own lives!; **2 en ~ de** by way of; **recevoir un cadeau en ~ de remerciement** to receive a present by way of thanks.

guitare /gitaʀ/ ▶ **534** *nf* guitar.

■ **~ classique** classical guitar; **~ électrique** electric guitar; **~ folk** folk guitar; **~ hawaïenne** Hawaiian guitar; **~ rythmique** rhythm guitar.

guitariste /gitaʀist/ ▶ **510** *nmf* guitarist; **~ classique/de jazz** classical/jazz guitarist.

guitoune○ /gitun/ *nf* tent.

Gulf Stream /gœlfstʀim/ *nm* Gulf Stream.

gus○ /gys/ *nm* guy○, bloke○ GB.

gustatif, **-ive** /gystatif, iv/ *adj* [*sens, organe*] of taste; **perdre ses qualités gustatives** [*aliment*] to lose its taste.

guttural, **~e**, *mpl* **-aux** /gytyʀal, o/ **I** *adj* [*voix, langue, consonne*] guttural.

II gutturale *nf* guttural.

Guyana /gɥijana/ ▶ **321** *nprf* Guyana; **République de ~** Republic of Guyana.

guyanais, **~e** /gɥijanɛ, ɛz/ ▶ **537** *adj* Guyanese.

Guyanais, **~e** /gɥijanɛ, ɛz/ ▶ **537** *nm,f* Guyanese.

Guyane /gɥijan/ ▶ **692** *nprf* Guyana; **~ française** French Guyana; **~ hollandaise** Hist Dutch Guiana.

Gwent ▶ **692** *nprm* **le ~** Gwent.

Gwynedd ▶ **692** *nprm* **le ~** Gwynedd.

gym○ /ʒim/ ▶ **449** *nf* **1** Scol (éducation physique) physical education, PE, phys ed○ US; **le prof de ~** the PE teacher; **2** Sport (gymnastique) gymnastics.

gymkhana /ʒimkana/ *nm* **1** (en voiture, à moto) rally; **se livrer à un ~ dans les rues de la ville** fig to go roaring through the town; **2** (à pied) lit obstacle race; fig obstacle course.

gymnase /ʒimnɑz/ *nm* gymnasium.

gymnaste /ʒimnast/ *nmf* gymnast.

gymnastique /ʒimnastik/ ▶ **449** *nf* (discipline) gymnastics (+ *v sg*); (exercices) exercises (*pl*); **~ féminine/masculine** (en compétition) women's/men's gymnastics; (en amateur) gymnastics for women/men; **~ respiratoire/abdominale** breathing/stomach exercises; **je fais 20 minutes de ~ tous les matins** I exercise for 20 minutes every morning; **~ intellectuelle** or **de l'esprit** fig mental exercise; **faire** or **se livrer à toute une ~ pour attraper les verres/faire un emploi du temps** to tie oneself in knots to reach the glasses/make a timetable. ■ **~ aquatique** aquagym; **~ corrective** ≈ physiotherapy exercises (*pl*); **~ d'entretien** keep fit; **~ rythmique et sportive**, **GRS** eurythmics (+ *v sg*); **~ suédoise** callisthenics (+ *v sg*).

gymnique /ʒimnik/ *adj* [*exercice*] gymnastic.

gynécée /ʒinese/ *nm* gynaeceum.

gynécologie /ʒinekɔlɔʒi/ *nf* gynaecology.

gynécologique /ʒinekɔlɔʒik/ *adj* gynaecological.

gynécologue /ʒinekɔlɔg/ ▶ **510** *nmf* gynaecologist.

gypaète /ʒipaɛt/ *nm* bearded vulture, lammergeyer.

gypse /ʒips/ *nm* gypsum.

gypseux, **-euse** /ʒipsø, øz/ *adj* gypseous.

gypsophile /ʒipsɔfil/ *nf* gypsophila.

gyrocompas /ʒiʀokɔ̃pa/ *nm* gyrocompass.

gyrophare /ʒiʀɔfaʀ/ *nm* flashing light, emergency rotating light.

gyroscope /ʒiʀɔskɔp/ *nm* gyroscope.

gyroscopique /ʒiʀɔskɔpik/ *adj* gyroscopic.

gyrostat /ʒiʀɔsta/ *nm* gyrostat.

h, **H** /aʃ/ *nm inv* **1** (lettre) h, H; **h aspiré** aspirate, aspirated h; **h muet** mute h, silent h; **2** (heure) **9 h 10** 9.10; **l'heure h** zero hour.

ha /'a/ **1** = **ah I**; **2** (*written abbr* = **hectare**) hectare.

habile /abil/ *adj* **1** (adroit) [*bricoleur, examinateur, policier, écrivain*] clever; [*avocat, diplomate, orateur*] skilful[GB]; [*politicien*] smart; [*vendeuse*] clever, skilful[GB]; **~ à qch/à faire** good at sth/at doing; **être ~ aux échecs** to be a good chess player; **être ~ de ses mains** or **de ses doigts** to be clever with one's hands; **2** (fait avec adresse) [*film, contrefaçon, discours, formule, accord*] clever; [*manœuvre, décision*] clever, smart; **ce n'était pas très ~ de votre part** that wasn't very clever of you; **3** Jur **être ~ à faire** to have legal capacity to do.

habilement /abilmɑ̃/ *adv* (adroitement) skilfully[GB]; (intelligemment) cleverly.

habileté /abilte/ *nf* **1** (adresse) (de personne) skill (**à faire** at doing); **~ à** skill at; **avec ~** skilfully[GB]; **2** (de discours, manœuvre) skilfulness[GB].

habilitation /abilitasjɔ̃/ *nf* authorization (**à faire** to do); **clause d'~** enabling clause.

habiliter /abilite/ [1] *vtr* to authorize (**à faire** to do); **être habilité à faire** to be authorized to do.

habillage /abijaʒ/ *nm* **1** (revêtement) (de siège, mur) covering; (d'appareil, de radiateur, tuyauterie) casing; **2** (présentation) packaging; **servir d'~** to serve as an image (**pour qch** for sth; **pour faire** to do); **3** (fait d'habiller) dressing.

habillé, **~e** /abije/ **I** *pp* ▶ **habiller**.

II *pp adj* **1** (élégant, cérémonieux) [*robe*] smart; [*dîner, soirée*] formal; **les invités étaient tous très ~s** the guests were all very dressed up; **2** (vêtu) dressed; **~ de noir** dressed in black; **~ comme un clochard** dressed like a tramp; **3** (déguisé) **~ en pirate/prêtre** dressed up as a pirate/priest.

habillement /abijmɑ̃/ *nm* **1** (activité) clothing; **2** (vêtements) clothing.

habiller /abije/ [1] **I** *vtr* **1** (mettre des vêtements à) to dress [*personne*] (**de qch** in sth); **2** (déguiser) to dress [sb] up (**en** as); **~ un enfant en pirate** to dress a child up as a pirate; **3** (fournir en vêtements) to clothe [*enfant*]; to provide [sb] with clothing [*recrue, acteur, personnel*]; **4** (faire des vêtements pour) to clothe [*enfant, famille*]; to dress [*acteur, personnel*]; **5** (convenir) [*vêtements*] to suit [*personne*]; **un rien l'habille** she looks good in anything; **6** (revêtir) to cover [*mur, siège*] (**de** with); to encase [*appareil, radiateur, tuyauterie*]; **7** (préparer) to dress [*viande, volaille*].

II s'habiller *vpr* **1** (mettre ses vêtements) to get dressed, to dress; **il en met du temps à s'~!** he certainly takes his time getting dressed!; **2** (choisir son style) to dress; **s'~ jeune/vieux** to dress young/old; **s'~ à la dernière mode** to dress in the latest fashion; **s'~ long/court** to wear long/short clothes; **s'~ comme un mannequin** to dress like a model; **3** (se vêtir élégamment) to dress up; **s'~ pour un cocktail** to dress up for a cocktail party; **4** (se fournir en vêtements) to get one's clothes; **s'~ chez un grand couturier** to get one's clothes from a couturier; **s'~ sur mesure** to have one's clothes made to measure; **s'~ en prêt-à-porter** to buy one's clothes off the peg GB ou off the rack US; **5** (se travestir) to dress up (**en** as); **~ en femme/pirate** to dress up as a woman/pirate.

habilleur, **-euse** /abijœʀ, øz/ **▶510** *nm,f* dresser.

habit /abi/ **I** *nm* **1** (de marié) (queue-de-pie) tails (*pl*), morning coat; (tenue) morning dress; **il s'est marié en ~** he got married in morning dress; **2** (déguisement) (de professionnel) outfit; (de personnage) costume; **~ de cow-boy/de pirate** cowboy/pirate outfit; **~ de Pierrot/d'Arlequin** Pierrot/Harlequin costume; **3** Relig (de moine, nonne) habit; **prendre l'~** to take the cloth; **quitter l'~** to leave the priesthood; ▶ **moine**.

II habits *nmpl* (vêtements) clothes; **~s neufs** lit new clothes; fig new look.

■ **~ de chasse** Chasse hunting clothes; **~ de cheval** Équit riding clothes, riding habit; **~ de cour** Hist court dress; **~ ecclésiastique** Relig clerical dress; **~ de lumière** matador's costume; **~ vert** green coat (*of a member of the Académie française*); **~s du dimanche** Sunday best.

habitabilité /abitabilite/ *nf* **1** (d'habitation) habitability, fitness (for habitation); **2** (de véhicule, d'ascenseur) capacity.

habitable /abitabl/ *adj* **1** (pouvant être habité) habitable; **logement ~ immédiatement** accommodation ready to move into; **2** (servant à l'habitation) **surface** or **espace ~** living space; **150 m² ~s** 150 m² of living space.

habitacle /abitakl/ *nm* **1** Aviat cockpit; Astronaut cabin; **2** Aut interior, passenger compartment; **3** Naut binnacle.

habitant, **~e** /abitɑ̃, ɑ̃t/ *nm,f* **1** (personne) (de ville, pays, région) inhabitant; (de quartier, d'immeuble) resident; **nombre d'~s au km²** number of inhabitants per square kilometre[GB]; **les habitants du quartier** the local residents; **par ~** per head ou person; **pour 1000 ~s** for every 1,000 people; **loger chez l'~** Tourisme to stay as a paying guest; Mil to be billetted with a local family; **2** liter (personne) dweller; (animal) beast; **les ~s de l'air/de la forêt/des mers** the denizens of the air/of the forest/of the seas.

habitat /abita/ *nm* **1** (milieu) habitat; **2** (mode de peuplement) settlement; **~ urbain/groupé/sédentaire** urban/grouped/fixed settlement; **3** (mode de logement) housing; **~ collectif/individuel** communal/individual housing.

habitation /abitasjɔ̃/ *nf* **1** (construction) house, dwelling; **on distinguait au loin quelques ~s** we could make out a few houses ou dwellings in the distance; **un groupe d'~s** a group of dwellings; **2** (résidence) home; **une ~ bien située** a well-sited property; **3** (fait d'habiter) living; **immeuble d'~** block of flats GB, apartment building US.

■ **~ à loyer modéré, HLM** (appartement) ≈ council flat GB, low-rent apartment US; (immeuble) ≈ block of council flats GB, low-rent apartment building US; (maison) ≈ council house GB, low rent house US.

habité, **~e** /abite/ **I** *pp* ▶ **habiter**.

II *pp adj* **1** [*planète, zone, territoire*] inhabited; **2** Astronaut [*vol, navette*] manned; **un vol non ~** an unmanned flight.

habiter /abite/ [1] **I** *vtr* **1** (résider à) [*personne, animal*] to live in; **il habite une maison/Paris/la campagne** he lives in a house/in Paris/in the country; **~ une planète** to live on a planet; **2** fml [*sentiment*] to dwell in [*personne, cœur, âme*].

II *vi* **1** (résider) [*personne*] **~ à** or **en** to live in; **~ à Paris/à l'hôtel** to live in Paris/in a hotel; **~ en banlieue** to live in the suburbs; **~ rue Cardinet** to live in the rue Cardinet; **~ à l'étranger** to live abroad; **~ au 6 rue de la Paix** to live at 6 rue de la Paix; **~ chez ses parents** to live with one's parents; **2** fml **être habité par** to be filled with.

habitude /abityd/ **I** *nf* **1** (manière d'agir) habit; **faire qch par ~** to do sth out of habit; **prendre/avoir de mauvaises ~s** to pick up/have bad habits; **je vais lui faire perdre l'~ d'entrer sans frapper** I'm going to get him out of the habit of entering without knocking; **avoir pour ~ de faire** to be in the habit of doing; **il avait pour ~ d'arriver sans prévenir** it was his habit to arrive unannounced; **ce n'est pas dans ses ~s d'être impoli** he is not usually impolite; **il n'est pas encore ici, ce n'est pas dans ses ~s d'être en retard** he is not here yet, it's not like him to be late; **ils ont l'~ de se coucher tôt** they usually go to bed early; **avoir ses ~s** to have got GB or gotten US into a routine; **avoir ses petites ~s** to have one's own way of doing things; **ne perdons pas les bonnes ~s** let's stick to what we usually do; **comme à leur ~, suivant leur ~** as they usually do; **2** (fait d'être accoutumé) habit; **c'est une question d'~** it's a matter of habit ou of getting used to it; **avoir l'~ de qch** to be used to sth; **avoir une grande ~ de qch** to be very used to sth; **avoir l'~ de faire** to be used to doing; **l'~ de la conduite la nuit lui est venue facilement** he easily got used to night driving; **t'inquiète pas, j'ai l'~** don't worry, I'm used to it; **3** (coutume) (de pays, région) custom; (de personne, population) habit; **~s alimentaires** eating habits.

II d'habitude *loc adv* usually.

habitué, **~e** /abitɥe/ *nm,f* (de café, restaurant) regular (customer); (de stade, piscine, musée) regular; (ami) regular (visitor).

habituel, **-elle** /abitɥɛl/ *adj* [*heure, endroit*] usual; [*geste, réaction, défaut*] usual, customary.

habituellement /abitɥɛlmɑ̃/ *adv* usually, generally.

habituer /abitɥe/ [1] **I** *vtr* **1** (accoutumer) to get [sb/sth] used (**à qn/qch** to sb/sth; **à faire** to doing); **~ son chien à coucher dehors** to get one's dog used to sleeping outside; **2** (former) to teach (**à faire** to do; **à ne pas**

faire not to do); **~ un enfant à ne jamais mentir** to teach a child never to lie.

II **s'habituer** *vpr* to get used ou accustomed (**à qn/qch** to sb/sth; **à faire** to doing).

hâbleur, **-euse** /ˈɑblœʀ, øz/ I *adj* boastful.
II *nm,f* boaster; **c'est un ~** he's always boasting.

hachage /ˈaʃaʒ/ *nm* gén chopping; (de viande) mincing; (plus grossièrement) chopping.

hache /ˈaʃ/ *nf* axe GB, ax US; **une ~ de pierre** a stone axe GB ou ax US; **abattre un arbre à la ~** to fell a tree with an axe GB ou ax US; **donner un coup de ~ à qch** to give sth a blow with an axe GB ou ax US; **d'un coup de ~** with a blow of the axe GB ou ax US; **il a démoli la porte à coups de ~** he broke down the door with an axe GB ou ax US; **visage taillé à la ~** angular face; **la ~ du bourreau** the executioner's axe GB ou ax US.
■ **~ d'abordage** poleaxe; **~ d'armes** battle-axe lit; **~ de bûcheron** woodcutter's axe GB ou ax US; **~ de guerre** gén battle axe GB ou ax US; (d'indien) tomahawk.
IDIOMES **enterrer la ~ de guerre** to bury the hatchet; **déterrer la ~ de guerre** to go on the warpath.

haché, **~e** /ˈaʃe/ I *pp* ▶ **hacher**.
II *pp adj* **1** Culin [*viande*] minced; [*oignon, persil*] chopped; **ajouter les oignons finement ~s** add the finely-chopped onion; **bifteck ~** hamburger; **viande ~e** mince meat; **2** (saccadé) [*style, phrase, discours*] disjointed.
III *nm* Culin mince.

hache-légumes /ˈaʃlegym/ *nm inv* vegetable cutter.

hache-paille /ˈaʃpaj/ *nm inv* chaff cutter.

hacher /ˈaʃe/ [1] *vtr* **1** (couper) to mince [*viande*]; (plus grossièrement) to chop [*viande*]; to chop [*oignon, persil*]; **~ au couteau** to chop [sth] up with a knife; **~ finement** or **menu** to chop finely; **hachez menu** or **finement les oignons** finely chop the onions; **2** (broyer) to crush [*récolte, feuille*]; to cut [sb/sth] to pieces [*personne, chair, main*]; **ils se sont fait ~ par la mitrailleuse** they were cut to pieces by the machine gun fire.

hachette /ˈaʃɛt/ *nf* hatchet; **donner un coup de ~ à qch** to give sth a blow with a hatchet; **d'un coup de ~** with a blow of the hatchet.

hache-viande /ˈaʃvjɑ̃d/ *nm inv* mincer.

hachis /ˈaʃi/ *nm* Culin **~ de viande** mince(d) meat; **~ de mouton/de porc** minced mutton/pork; **~ d'échalottes/de persil** chopped shallots/parsley.
■ **~ Parmentier** ≈ shepherd's pie.

hachisch /ˈaʃiʃ/ *nm* hashish; **fumer du ~** to smoke hashish.

hachoir /ˈaʃwaʀ/ *nm* **1** (appareil) mincer; **~ électrique** electric mincer; **~ à main** hand-operated mincer; **2** (couteau) (food) chopper, mincing knife; **3** (planche) chopping board.

hachure /ˈaʃyʀ/ *nf* hatching ₵.

hachurer /ˈaʃyʀe/ [1] *vtr* to hatch; **partie hachurée** hatched area.

haddock /ˈadɔk/ *nm* smoked haddock.

Hadrien /adʀijɛ̃/ *npr* Hadrian.

hagard, **~e** /ˈagaʀ, aʀd/ *adj* [*visage, air, personne*] dazed; [*yeux*] wild.

hagiographie /aʒjogʀafi/ *nf* hagiography.

haie /ˈɛ/ *nf* **1** Bot hedge; **une ~ de cyprès** a cypress hedge; **2** Sport (en athlétisme) hurdle; Équit fence; **course de ~s** (en athlétisme) hurdle race, hurdles; Équit steeple chase; **le 110 mètres ~s** the 110 metre[GB] hurdles; **3** (rangée) (de personnes, policiers, manifestants) line; (d'objets) row; **une ~ de pieux** a row of poles; **former une ~** to make a line; **une double ~ de soldats** a double line of soldiers.
■ **~ vive** hedge.
IDIOMES **faire la ~**, **former** or **faire une ~ d'honneur** to form a guard of honour[GB].

haillon /ˈɑjɔ̃/ *nm* rag; **vêtu de ~s** dressed in rags; **en ~s** in rags.

Hainaut /ˈɛno/ ▶ **692** *nprm* Hainaut.

haine /ˈɛn/ *nf* hatred (**de qn** of sb; **de qch** of sth); **~ religieuse/politique** political/religious hatred; **incitation à la ~ raciale** incitement to racial hatred; **la ~ de l'envahisseur/du mensonge** hatred of the invader/of lies; **sans ~** without hatred; **s'attirer la ~ de qn** to earn oneself sb's hatred; **avoir** or **éprouver de la ~ pour qn** to feel hatred toward(s) sb, to hate sb; **avoir de la ~ pour qch**, **avoir la ~ de qch** to hate sth; **concevoir de la ~ pour qch/qn** to harbour[GB] hatred for sth/sb; **par ~ de qch** out of hatred for sth.

haineusement /ˈɛnøzmɑ̃/ *adv* [*regarder, répondre, parler*] with hatred; [*saisir, jeter, frapper*] in hatred.

haineux, **-euse** /ˈɛnø, øz/ *adj* full of hatred (*après n*).

haïr /ˈaiʀ/ [25] I *vtr* to hate [*personne, chose*]; **se faire ~** to make oneself hated (**de** by); **~ le mensonge/la malhonnêteté** to hate lies/dishonesty; **il nous hait d'avoir choisi qn d'autre** he hates us for choosing sb else; **~ que** to hate it when; **elle hait qu'on se moque d'elle** she hates it when people make fun of her.
II **se haïr** *vpr* **1** [*personnes, ennemis*] to hate each other; **2 je me hais de ma lâcheté/d'avoir été lâche** I hate myself for my cowardice/for being a coward.

haire /ˈɛʀ/ *nf* hair shirt.

haïssable /ˈaisabl/ *adj* detestable, hateful.

Haïti /aiti/ ▶ **321**, **416** *nprm* Haiti; **la République d'~** the Republic of Haiti; **en ~** in Haiti.

haïtien, **-ienne** /aisjɛ̃, ɛn/ ▶ **537**, **462** I *adj* Haitian.
II *nm* Ling Haitian.

Haïtien, **-ienne** /aisjɛ̃, ɛn/ ▶ **537** *nm,f* Haitian.

halage /ˈalaʒ/ *nm* (canal barge) towing; **chemin de ~** towpath; **chevaux de ~** towhorses.

hâle /ˈɑl/ *nm* (sun)tan; **mon ~ n'a pas tenu** my (sun)tan didn't last.

hâlé, **~e** /ˈɑle/ I *pp* ▶ **hâler**.
II *pp adj* (par le soleil) suntanned; (par l'air, une lampe) tanned.

haleine /alɛn/ *nf* **1** (air expiré) breath; **avoir mauvaise ~** to have bad breath; **2** (respiration) breathing; **~ régulière/saccadée** regular/uneven breathing; **avoir l'~ courte** to be short of breath; **retenir son ~** to hold one's breath; **être hors d'~** to be out of breath; **à perdre ~** until one is out of breath; **courir à perdre ~** to run until one is gasping for breath; **rire à perdre ~** to laugh until one's sides ache; **reprendre ~** lit to get one's breath back; fig to have a rest; **tenir qn en ~** to hold ou keep sb spellbound; **un travail de longue ~** a long-drawn-out job; **3** liter (de vent) breath; (de fleur, jardin) scent.

haler /ˈale/ [1] *vtr* to tow [*bateau*]; to haul in [*corde, chaîne*].

hâler /ˈɑle/ [1] *vtr* to tan.

haletant, **~e** /ˈaltɑ̃, ɑ̃t/ *adj* [*personne*] panting, breathless; [*animal*] panting; [*voix*] breathless; **avoir une respiration ~e** to be gasping for breath.

halètement /ˈalɛtmɑ̃/ *nm* **1** (après un effort) panting ₵; (d'émotion) breathlessness ₵; **2** (de machine) puffing ₵.

haleter /ˈalte/ [18] *vi* **1** [*personne*] to gasp for breath; [*animal*] to pant; **~ de** [*personne*] to be breathless with; [*animal*] to pant with; **2** [*machine*] to puff; [*poitrine*] to heave.

haleur, **-euse** /ˈalœʀ, øz/ *nm,f* boat hauler.

hall /ˈol/ *nm* entrance hall GB, lobby US; **le ~ de l'hôtel** the hotel foyer GB, the hotel lobby; **~ (de gare)** lit concourse; **on dirait un ~ de gare** pej it looks like the inside of a railway station.
■ **~ d'accueil** reception; **~ d'exposition** exhibition hall; **~ de montage** assembly shop.

hallali /ˈalali/ *nm* Chasse mort; **sonner l'~** to blow ou sound the mort.

halle /ˈal/ I *nf* market hall.
II **halles** *nfpl* covered market.
■ **~ aux grains** corn exchange; **~ à marchandises** goods depot; **~ aux vins** wine market.

hallebarde /ˈaləbaʀd/ *nf* halberd.
IDIOMES **il pleut** or **tombe des ~s** it's raining cats and dogs.

hallebardier /ˈalbaʀdje/ *nm* halberdier.

hallucinant○, **~e** /alysinɑ̃, ɑ̃t/ *adj* astounding.

hallucination /alysinasjɔ̃/ *nf* hallucination; **avoir des ~s** lit to hallucinate; fig to be seeing things.

hallucinatoire /alysinatwaʀ/ *adj* hallucinatory.

halluciné, **~e** /alysine/ I *adj* **1** (hagard) [*regard, air*] wild; **2** [*malade*] suffering from hallucinations (*après n*).
II *nm,f* **1**○ (illuminé) crank; **2** person suffering from hallucinations.

hallucinogène /alysinɔʒɛn/ I *adj* hallucinogenic.
II *nm* hallucinogen.

halo /ˈalo/ *nm* **1** (de phares, lampe) **~ de lumière** circle of light; **entouré d'un ~ de mystère** shrouded in mystery; **2** Astron halo; **3** Phot flare ₵, halation ₵ spéc; **des ~s** points of flare.

halogène /alɔʒɛn/ I *adj* **1** Chimie halogenous; **2** [*lampe, éclairage*] halogen (*épith*).
II *nm* (tous contextes) halogen.

halte /ˈalt/ I *nf* **1** (temps d'arrêt) stop; **faire une ~** to stop somewhere; **faire une courte ~** to stop somewhere for a little while; **2** (lieu d'arrêt) stop.
II *excl* gén stop!; Mil halt!; **~-là, ça suffit comme ça!** stop it, that's enough!; **~ à la vivisection!** stop vivisection!; **nous disons ~ au terrorisme/aux spéculateurs** we are calling for an end to terrorism/to speculation.

halte-garderie, *pl* **haltes-garderies** /ˈaltəgaʀdəʀi/ *nf* ≈ playgroup.

haltère /altɛʀ/ *nm* (pour une main) dumbbell; (à deux mains) barbell; **faire des ~s** to do weightlifting.

haltérophile /alteʀɔfil/ *nmf* weightlifter.

haltérophilie /alteʀɔfili/ ▶ **449** *nf* weightlifting.

hamac /ˈamak/ *nm* hammock.

hamamélis /amamelis/ *nm* hamamelis.

Hambourg /ɑ̃buʀ/ ▶ **857** *npr* Hamburg.

hambourgeois /ɑ̃buʀʒwa/ *nm* C (hamburger) hamburger.

hamburger /ˈɑ̃buʀgɛʀ/ *nm* hamburger.
■ **~ à cheval** hamburger topped with an egg.

hameau, *pl* **~x** /ˈamo/ *nm* hamlet.

hameçon /amsɔ̃/ *nm* hook.
IDIOMES **mordre à l'~** to take the bait.

hammam /ˈamam/ *nm* hammam, Turkish bath.

hampe /ˈɑ̃p/ *nf* **1** (de drapeau, parasol) pole; (d'arme) shaft; **2** Bot scape; **3** (de lettre) vertical stroke; **4** (de bœuf) flank.

Hampshire ▶ **692** *nprm* **le ~** Hampshire.

hamster /ˈamstɛʀ/ *nm* hamster.

han /ˈɑ̃/ I *nm inv* grunt.
II *excl* hrumpf!

hanap /ˈanap/ *nm* hanap.

hanche /ˈɑ̃ʃ/ ▶ **188**, **793** *nf* **1** Anat hip; **le pistolet sur la ~** a pistol at one's hip; **avoir les mains sur les ~s** to stand with one's hands on one's hips, to stand with arms akimbo; **prothèse de la ~** hip replacement; **2** Équit haunch.

hand○ /ˈɑ̃d/ *nm*: *abbr* = **handball**.

handball /ˈɑ̃dbal, ˈɑ̃dbol/ ▶449 *nm* handball.

handballeur, **-euse** /ˈɑ̃dbalœʀ, øz/ *nm,f* handball player.

handicap /ˈɑ̃dikap/ *nm* **1** (infirmité) disability, handicap; **2** (désavantage) handicap; **c'est un ~ pour ta carrière** it's a handicap in your career; **3** Sport (de joueur) handicap; (course) handicap (race).

handicapant, **~e** /ˈɑ̃dikapɑ̃, ɑ̃t/ *adj* disabling.

handicapé, **~e** /ˈɑ̃dikape/ **I** *pp* ▶ **handicaper**.

II *pp adj* **1** (infirme) disabled, handicapped; **~ à vie** permanently disabled; **2** (désavantagé) **être ~** to be at a disadvantage; **3** Sport, Turf handicapped; **cheval lourdement ~** horse carrying a big handicap.

III *nm,f* disabled person; **les ~s** the disabled; **~ moteur** person with motor disability.

handicaper /ˈɑ̃dikape/ [1] *vtr* (tous contextes) to handicap.

handisport /ɑ̃dispɔʀ/ *adj* wheelchair (*épith*); **équipe ~** team of wheelchair athletes.

hangar /ˈɑ̃gaʀ/ *nm* gén (large) shed; (entrepôt) warehouse.

■ **~ d'aviation** hangar; **~ à bateaux** boathouse.

hanneton /ˈantɔ̃/ *nm* cockchafer GB, June bug US; ▶ **piquer**.

Hannibal /anibal/ *npr* Hannibal.

Hanoi /anɔj/ ▶857 *npr* Hanoi.

Hanovre /ˈanɔvʀ/ ▶857 *npr* Hanover.

hanse /ˈɑ̃s/ *nf* Hist hansa; **la Hanse (teutonique)** the Hanseatic League.

hanséatique /ˈɑ̃seatik/ *adj* Hanseatic.

hanter /ˈɑ̃te/ [1] *vtr* (tous contextes) to haunt; **lieu hanté** haunted place; ▶ **dire**.

hantise /ˈɑ̃tiz/ *nf* dread; **avoir la ~ de qch** to dread sth; **être seul, c'est une ~ chez moi** being alone is something I dread.

happer /ˈape/ [1] *vtr* **1** (saisir) to catch [*nourriture, insecte*]; to seize [*animal, bras*]; **~ qch au vol** to catch sth in mid-air; **2** (faucher) **être happé par** to be caught up in [*machine*]; to be hit by [*voiture, train*]; **3** (engloutir) **être happé par** to be swallowed up by [*bouche de métro, foule*].

haquenée‡ /ˈakne/ *nf* palfrey‡.

hara-kiri, *pl* **~s** /ˈaʀakiʀi/ *nm* hara-kiri; **(se) faire ~** to commit hara-kiri.

harangue /ˈaʀɑ̃g/ *nf* harangue.

haranguer /ˈaʀɑ̃ge/ [1] *vtr* to harangue.

haras /ˈaʀa/ *nm* stud farm.

harassant, **~e** /ˈaʀasɑ̃, ɑ̃t/ *adj* exhausting.

harassement /ˈaʀasmɑ̃/ *nm* fml exhaustion.

harasser /ˈaʀase/ [1] *vtr* to exhaust.

harcèlement /ˈaʀsɛlmɑ̃/ *nm* harassment.

■ **~ sexuel** sexual harassment.

harceler /ˈaʀsəle/ [17] *vtr* **1** (importuner) [*démarcheur, mendiant, journaliste*] to pester; **~ qn de questions** to pester sb with questions; **~ qn pour obtenir qch** to pester sb for sth; **harcelé par les moustiques** plagued by mosquitoes; **les remords le harcèlent** he's plagued by remorse; **2** (poursuivre) to harass [*ennemi*].

hard○ /ˈaʀd/ **I** *adj inv* (pornographique) hardcore (*épith*).

II *nm inv* **1** Mus hard rock; **2** (pornographie) hard porn○; **3** Ordinat *abbr* = **hardware**.

harde /ˈaʀd/ **I** *nf* **1** (d'animaux sauvages) herd; **2** Chasse pack.

II hardes *nfpl* liter rags.

hardi, **~e** /ˈaʀdi/ **I** *adj* **1** (intrépide, osé) bold; **2** (impudent) risqué.

II *excl* **~ les gars!** go for it, lads GB ou guys!

hardiesse /ˈaʀdjɛs/ *nf* **1** (intrépidité, originalité) boldness; **avoir la ~ de faire** to be bold enough to do; **2** liter (impudence) brazenness; **3** (parole, action impudente) **se permettre des ~s avec qn** to take liberties with sb.

hardiment /ˈaʀdimɑ̃/ *adv* **1** (avec intrépidité) boldly; **2** (impudemment) brazenly.

hardware /ˈaʀdwɛʀ/ *nm* controv hardware.

harem /ˈaʀɛm/ *nm* harem.

hareng /ˈaʀɑ̃/ *nm* herring.

■ **~ saur** smoked herring.

IDIOMES **sec comme un ~ saur** as thin as a reed; ▶ **caque**.

hargne /ˈaʀɲ/ *nf* aggression; **avec ~** aggressively; **plein de ~** very aggressive.

hargneusement /ˈaʀɲøzmɑ̃/ *adv* aggressively.

hargneux, **-euse** /ˈaʀɲø, øz/ *adj* aggressive.

haricot /ˈaʀiko/ *nm* **1** (plante, graine) bean; **2** Méd kidney bowl.

■ **~ beurre** wax bean; **~ blanc** haricot bean; **~ à écosser** broad bean; **~ de Lima** butterbean; **~ mange-tout** French bean; **~ rouge** red kidney bean; **~ sec** dried bean; **~ vert** French bean.

IDIOMES **c'est la fin des ~s**○ we've had it; **il me court sur le ~**◑ he gets on my nerves ou on my wick○ GB, he bugs me○.

haridelle /ˈaʀidɛl/ *nf* (cheval) pej nag.

harissa /ˈaʀisa/ *nf* harissa.

harki /ˈaʀki/ *nm*: *Algerian soldier who fought on the French side in the war of independence.*

harmonica /aʀmɔnika/ ▶534 *nm* mouth organ, harmonica.

harmoniciste /aʀmɔnisist/ ▶534, 510 *nmf* harmonica player.

harmonie /aʀmɔni/ *nf* **1** (d'entente) harmony; **en ~ avec** gén in harmony with; **mobilier en ~ avec le style des années 50** furniture in keeping with the style of the 50s; **vivre en parfaite ~ avec la nature/ses voisins** to live in perfect harmony with nature/one's neighbours[GB]; **2** Mus (connaissance des accords) harmony; (orchestre) wind band.

■ **~ imitative** Littérat onomatopoeia; **~ vocalique** Ling vowel harmony.

harmonieusement /aʀmɔnjøzmɑ̃/ *adv* harmoniously.

harmonieux, **-ieuse** /aʀmɔnjø, øz/ *adj* **1** (agréable) [*musique, voix, style*] harmonious; **2** (en accord) [*couleurs, architecture, courbes*] harmonious; [*gestes*] graceful; [*vie, équilibre, mélange*] harmonious, happy; **former un ensemble ~** to blend harmoniously; **ils forment un couple ~** they are very well suited.

harmonique /aʀmɔnik/ *adj, nm* harmonic.

harmoniquement /aʀmɔnikmɑ̃/ *adv* harmonically.

harmonisation /aʀmɔnizasjɔ̃/ *nf* gén harmonization; Ling vowel harmony.

harmoniser /aʀmɔnize/ [1] **I** *vtr* **1** (rendre harmonieux) to coordinate [*couleurs*]; **2** (rendre cohérents) to harmonize, to make [sth] consistent [*règles, positions*]; **3** Mus to harmonize.

II s'harmoniser *vpr* **bien s'~** [*couleurs, caractères*] to go together well.

harmonium /aʀmɔnjɔm/ *nm* harmonium.

harnachement /ˈaʀnaʃmɑ̃/ *nm* **1** (de cheval) (pièces) harness; (processus) harnessing; **2**○ (de personne) get-up○.

harnacher /ˈaʀnaʃe/ [1] *vtr* **1** Équit to harness [*cheval*]; **2**○ (équiper) to rig out○ [*personne*].

harnais /ˈaʀnɛ/ *nm* **1** (d'animal) harness; **2** (d'alpiniste, de parachutiste etc) harness; **~ de sécurité** safety harness.

■ **~ d'engrenages** Mécan train of gears.

IDIOMES **blanchir sous le ~** to spend one's whole life in harness.

haro† /ˈaʀo/ *excl* **~ sur qn/qch** a plague† on sb/sth; **crier ~ sur qn/qch** to inveigh sb/sth, to rail against sb/sth.

harpagon /aʀpagɔ̃/ *nm* liter miser, Scrooge.

harpe /ˈaʀp/ ▶534 *nf* harp.

■ **~ éolienne** aeolian harp.

harpie /ˈaʀpi/ *nf* **1** Mythol harpy; **les Harpies** the Harpies; **2** (femme acariâtre) harpy; **3** (aigle) harpy eagle.

harpiste /ˈaʀpist/ ▶534, 510 *nmf* harpist.

harpon /ˈaʀpɔ̃/ *nm* harpoon; **pêcher la baleine au ~** to go whaling with harpoons.

harponnage /ˈaʀpɔnaʒ/ *nm* harpooning.

harponner /ˈaʀpɔne/ [1] *vtr* **1** Pêche to harpoon [*baleine*]; **2** (arrêter)○ to waylay [*badaud*]; to nab○ [*malfaiteur*].

harponneur /ˈaʀpɔnœʀ/ *nm* harpoonist.

hasard /ˈazaʀ/ *nm* **1** (cause imprévisible) chance; **leur théorie n'admet pas le ~** their theory does not admit of chance; **le ~ nous a fait découvrir que...** we discovered by chance that...; **c'est le ~ qui nous a réunis** we were brought together by chance; **c'est dû au ~** it's due to chance; **rien n'a été laissé au ~** nothing was left to chance; **ce n'est pas l'effet** or **le fait** or **le fruit du ~ si...** it is no accident that...; **ce n'est pas un ~ si...** it's no accident that...; **s'en remettre au ~, compter sur le ~** to trust to luck (**pour** as regards; **pour faire** to do); **le ~ a voulu que...** as luck would have it,...; **au ~** [*choisir, marcher, tirer, désigner*] at random; **prenons un exemple au ~** let's take an example at random; **répondre au ~** to answer off the top of one's head; **j'ai dit cela au ~, sans réfléchir** I said it off the top of my head, I wasn't thinking; **au ~ de nos rencontres/discussions, j'ai découvert que** it emerged by chance from our meetings/discussions that; **au ~ de mes promenades** on my walks; **par ~** [*découvrir, rencontrer, trouver, voir*] by chance; **vous n'auriez pas vu mon stylo, par ~?** you wouldn't by any chance have seen my pen?; **si par ~** if by any chance; **tout à fait par ~** quite by chance; **par le plus grand des ~s** by sheer chance; **par un malencontreux ~** by an unfortunate accident; **par un curieux ~** by a curious coincidence; **par un heureux ~** by a stroke of luck; **quel heureux ~!** what a stroke of luck!; **c'est un ~ malheureux** it's bad luck; **je m'en suis souvenu par ~** I happened to remember it; **comme par ~, il a oublié son argent** iron surprise, surprise, he's forgotten his money; **à tout ~** (par précaution) just in case; (pour une tentative) on the off chance; **les ~s de la vie** the fortunes of life; **2**† (péril) hazard; **les ~s de la guerre** the hazards of war.

IDIOMES **le ~ fait bien les choses** fate is a great provider.

hasarder /ˈazaʀde/ [1] **I** *vtr* **1** (avancer) to venture [*conseil, explication, idée*]; **2** (risquer) to risk [*vie, réputation, honneur*].

II se hasarder *vpr* to venture (**à faire** to do); **se ~ dans la forêt** to venture into the forest.

hasardeux, **-euse** /ˈazaʀdø, øz/ *adj* (peu sûr) risky; (dangereux) hazardous.

hasch○ /ˈaʃ/ *nm* drug users' slang (*abbr* = **haschisch**) hash○.

haschi(s)ch ▶ **hachisch**.

hase /ˈaz/ *nf* doe-hare.

hâte /ˈɑt/ *nf* **1** (précipitation) haste; **montrer peu de ~ à faire** to show very little haste in doing; **en toute ~** in great haste; **sans ~** without haste; **à la ~** hastily; **un rapport rédigé à la ~** a hastily drawn up report; **dans ta ~** in your haste; **2** (impatience) **avoir ~ de faire qch** to be impatient to do sth; **j'ai ~ de partir** I'm impatient to leave; **j'ai ~ qu'elle vienne** I can't wait for her to come; **il n'a qu'une ~, c'est de partir** he has only one wish, and that's to leave.

hâter /ˈɑte/ [1] **I** *vtr* to hasten; **le soulèvement a hâté la chute du dictateur** the uprising hastened the dictator's fall; **~ le pas** to quicken one's step ou pace.

II se hâter *vpr* to hurry, to rush; **se ~ de faire** to rush to do, to hasten to do.

IDIOMES **hâte-toi lentement** more haste, less speed.

hâtif, -ive /ˈɑtif, iv/ *adj* **1** (rapide) [*jugement, recrutement*] hasty, hurried; **une lecture hâtive du journal** a skim through the newspaper; **2** Agric [*variété, plante*] early.

hâtivement /ˈɑtivmɑ̃/ *adv* hurriedly, hastily.

hauban /ˈobɑ̃/ *nm* **1** Naut shroud; **2** Tech (souple) stay; (rigide) brace.

haubaner /ˈobane/ [1] *vtr* Naut, Tech to stay, brace; **pont haubané** stayed-girder bridge.

hausse /ˈos/ *nf* **1** (augmentation) (de prix, salaires, loyer, demande) increase (**de** in); (de coût, dépenses, taux, chômage, température) rise (**de** in); **forte/légère ~ des prix** sharp/slight increase in prices; **~ saisonnière** seasonal increase; **il y a eu 10% de ~** there was a 10% increase; **une ~ de 10%/10F** a 10%/10F increase (**sur** in); **une ~ moyenne de 10%** an average increase of 10%; **être en ~** [*prix, baromètre, température*] to be rising; [*marchandise*] to be going up in price; **subir une forte ~** to rocket, to shoot up; **en ~ de 10% par rapport à 1990** up 10% compared with 1990; **revoir** or **réviser à la ~** to revise upward(s); **2** (en Bourse) (de monnaie, cours, valeur) rise (**de** in); **jouer à la ~** to speculate on a rise; **valeur en ~** lit, fig rising security; **la Bourse a ouvert en ~** the Stock exchange opened on the up; **pousser les valeurs à la ~** to push securities up; **être à la ~** [*devise*] to be rising; [*tendance*] to be upward(s); [*marché*] to be on the uptrend; **la tendance/le marché à la ~** the bullish trend/market; **en ~ de 10 points** up 10 points; **3** (d'arme à feu) rear sights (*pl*).

haussement /ˈosmɑ̃/ *nm* (d'épaules) shrug; **elle eut un ~ d'épaules** she shrugged her shoulders; **il marqua son intérêt par un ~ de sourcils** he raised his eyebrows in an interested way.

hausser /ˈose/ [1] **I** *vtr* **1** (élever) to shrug [*épaules*]; to raise [*sourcils*]; **~ le ton** or **la voix** lit to raise one's voice; fig to adopt an aggressive tone; **2** (augmenter) to raise [*prix*]; to increase [*exigences, prétentions*]; **3** (surélever) to raise [*mur, maison*].

II se hausser *vpr* **se ~ au niveau de** to rise up to the level of; **se ~ sur la pointe des pieds** to stand on tiptoe.

IDIOMES **se ~ du col** to pull oneself up.

haussier, -ière /ˈosje, ɛʀ/ Fin **I** *adj* [*marché*] bullish.

II *nm,f* bull.

haut, ~e /ˈo, ˈot/ **I** *adj* **1** ▶ 477 (étendu verticalement) [*montagne, mur, talon*] high; [*arbre, monument, bâtiment*] tall; [*herbe*] long, tall; **homme de ~e taille** tall man; **un objet plus ~ que large** an object that is higher than it is wide; **un bâtiment ~ de 20 étages** a building 20 storeys GB ou stories US high, a 20-storey GB ou 20-story US building; **un mât ~ de 10 mètres** a mast ten metres[GB] high, a ten-metre[GB] mast; **plus ~/moins ~ que** higher/lower than; **l'immeuble dans lequel il habite est très ~** he lives in a block of high-rise flats GB ou a high-rise apartment block US; **attention, la première marche est ~e** be careful, the first step is steep; **2** (situé en altitude) high; **une ~e branche** a high branch; **la partie ~e d'un bâtiment/mur/arbre** the top part of a building/wall/tree; **l'étagère la plus ~e** the top shelf; **une robe à taille ~e** a high-waisted dress; **3** (dans une échelle de valeurs) [*fréquence, pression, température, prix, capacité, précision*] high; [*note, ton*] high, high-pitched; **les ~s salaires/revenus** high salaries/incomes; **parler à ~e voix** to speak loudly; **dire/lire qch à ~e voix** to say/read sth out loud; **jouer une carte plus ~e** to play a higher card; **être à ~ risque** to be very risky; **être du plus ~ ridicule** to be highly ridiculous; **au plus ~ point** immensely, intensely; **aimer qch au plus ~ point** to like sth immensely; **produit de ~e qualité** high-quality product; **avoir une ~e opinion de qn/soi-même** to have a high opinion of sb/oneself; **tenir qn en ~e estime** to hold sb in high esteem ou regard; **4** (dans une hiérarchie) (*before n*) [*personnage, situation, poste*] high-ranking; [*clergé, magistrat*] senior; [*société, rang*] high; [*responsabilités*] big; [*dirigeant, responsable*] senior, high-ranking; **les plus ~es instances** the highest authorities; **bénéficier de ~es protections** to have friends in high places; **le ~ Comité/Conseil pour** the National Committee/Council for; **~e surveillance** close supervision; **5** Géog upper; **la ~e Égypte** Upper Egypt; **le ~ Nil** the Upper Nile; **6** Hist **dater de la plus ~e antiquité** to date from earliest antiquity; **le ~ Moyen Âge** the early Middle Ages.

II *adv* **1** (à un niveau élevé) [*monter, s'élever, voler, sauter*] high; **voler très ~ dans le ciel** to fly high in the sky; **un personnage ~ placé** a person in a high position; **viser trop ~** to aim too high; **la lune est ~ dans le ciel** the moon is high up in the sky; **~ perché sur** perched high on; **le plus ~** the highest; **sauter le plus ~** to jump the highest; **de ~** from above; **2** (dans le temps) far back; **aussi ~ qu'on remonte dans l'antiquité** however far back in history we go; **3** (dans un texte) **plus ~** above; **comme indiqué plus ~** as noted above; **colle-le plus ~ sur la page** stick it higher up on the page; **voir plus ~** see above; **4** (fort) loudly; **parler ~** to talk loudly; **parlez moins ~!** keep your voice down!; **parlez plus ~!** speak up!; **dire qch bien ~** to say sth loud(ly); **mettre la radio plus ~** to turn the radio up; **tout ~** out loud; **parler ~ et clair** fig to speak unambiguously; **ne dire** or **n'avoir jamais un mot plus ~ que l'autre** never to raise one's voice.

III *nm* **1** (partie élevée) top; **le ~ du mur** the top of the wall; **le ~ du visage** the top part of the face; **le ~ du corps** the top half of the body; **dans le ~ (de)** at the top (of); **l'appartement/l'étagère du ~** the top flat/shelf; **les pièces du ~** the upstairs rooms; **sur le ~ de la colline/côte** at the top of the hill/slope; **commencer par le ~** to start at the top; **prendre qch par le ~** to get hold of the top of sth; **du ~ de** from the top of; **de** or **du ~ en bas** from top to bottom; **parler du ~ d'un balcon/d'une tribune** to speak from a balcony/a platform; **le ~ de son maillot de bain** the top of her swimsuit; **2** (hauteur) **mesurer** or **faire 50 mètres de ~** to be 50 metres[GB] high; **une tour de 35 m de ~** a 35 m tower; **être à son plus ~** to be at its highest level.

IV en haut *loc* (à l'étage supérieur) upstairs; (à un étage supérieur) on an upper floor; (de rideau, mur, page) at the top; (le ciel, le paradis) above; **le bruit vient d'en ~** the noise is coming from above; **tout en ~** right at the top; **jusqu'en ~** up to the top, right to the top; **passer par en ~** (par la route) to take the top road; **les voleurs sont entrés par en ~** (par l'étage) the thieves got in upstairs; **ordre qui vient d'en ~** order from the top; **mettez la date en ~ de la page à droite** put the date in the top right-hand corner of the page.

V hauts *nmpl* Géog heights; **les ~s de Meuse** the heights of the Meuse.

VI haute○ *nf* upper crust○; **fréquenter les gens de la ~e** to rub shoulders with the upper crust.

■ **~ en couleur** [*personnage, tableau, texte*] colourful[GB]; **~ fait** heroic deed; **~ fonctionnaire** senior civil servant; **~ lieu de** centre[GB] of ou for; **en ~ lieu** in high places; **une décision prise en ~ lieu** a decision taken at a high level; **~ plateau** high plateau; **~e définition** TV high definition; **télévision (à) ~e définition** high definition TV; **écran à ~e définition graphique** Ordinat screen with high resolution graphics; **~e école** lit, Équit haute école, classical equitation; **c'est un exercice de ~e école** fig it's a very advanced exercise; **~e mer** Naut open sea; **Haute Cour (de Justice)** High Court of Justice; **~es eaux** high water (*sg*); **~es sphères** high social circles; **~es terres** Géog highlands; **~es voiles** Naut upper sails; **~s fourneaux** blast furnace.

IDIOMES **marcher la tête ~e** to walk with one's head held high; **prendre** or **regarder** or **voir les choses de ~** (sans s'arrêter aux détails) to see things in broad terms; (avec sérénité) to have a detached view of things; **tomber de ~** to be dumbfounded; **regarder qn de ~ en bas** to look sb up and down; **avoir** or **connaître des ~s et des bas** to have one's ups and downs; **~ les mains!** hands up!; **l'emporter** or **gagner** or **vaincre ~ la main** to win hands down; **prendre qn/qch de ~** to look down one's nose at sb/sth; ▶ **cri**, **pavé**.

hautain, ~e /ˈotɛ̃, ɛn/ *adj* haughty.

hautainement /ˈotɛnmɑ̃/ *adv* littér haughtily.

hautbois /ˈobwɑ/ ▶ 534 *nm* **1** (instrument) oboe; **2** (instrumentiste) oboist.

hautboïste /ˈobɔist/ ▶ 534, 510 *nmf* oboist.

haut-commissaire, *pl* **hauts-commissaires** /ˈokɔmisɛʀ/ *nm* Admin high commissioner.

haut-commissariat, *pl* **hauts-commissariats** /ˈokɔmisaʀja/ *nm* Admin **1** (fonction) post of high commissioner; **2** (service) high commission.

haut-de-chausse(s), *pl* **hauts-de-chausses** /ˈodʃos/ *nm* (knee) breeches.

haut-de-forme, *pl* **hauts-de-formes** /ˈodfɔʀm/ *nm* top hat.

haute-contre, *pl* **hautes-contre** /ˈotkɔ̃tʀ/ ▶ 134 *nf* Art, Mus counter tenor.

Haute-Corse /ˈotkɔʀs/ ▶ 692 *nprf* (département) **la ~** Haute-Corse.

haute(-)fidélité, *pl* **hautes(-)fidélités** /ˈotfidelite/ *nf* Électrotech **1** (qualité) **chaîne ~** hi-fi system; **2** (technique) ¢ **la ~** hi-fi, high fidelity.

Haute-Garonne /ˈotgaʀɔn/ ▶ 692 *nprf* (département) **la ~** the Haute-Garonne.

Haute-Loire /ˈotlwaʀ/ ▶ 692 *nprf* (département) **la ~** the Haute-Loire.

Haute-Marne /ˈotmaʀn/ ▶ 692 *nprf* (département) **la ~** the Haute-Marne.

hautement /ˈotmɑ̃/ *adv* **1** (à un haut degré) highly; **2** (ouvertement) openly.

Haute-Normandie /ˈotnɔʀmɑ̃di/ ▶ 692 *nprf* **la ~** Haute-Normandie.

Hautes-Alpes /ˈotzalp/ ▶ 692 *nprfpl* (département) **les ~** the Hautes-Alpes.

Haute-Saône /ˈotson/ ▶ 692 *nprf* (département) **la ~** the Haute-Saône.

Haute-Savoie /ˈotsavwa/ ▶ 692 *nprf* (département) **la ~** Haute-Savoie.

Hautes-Pyrénées /ˈotpiʀene/ ▶ 692 *nprfpl* (département) **les ~** the Hautes-Pyrénées.

hauteur /ˈotœʀ/ **I** *nf* **1** ▶ 477 (dimension verticale) height; **une tour d'une ~ de 30 m** a tower 30 metres[GB] high; **le bâtiment a 15 m de ~** the building is 15 m high; **un mur de 3 m de ~** a 3 m wall; **tableaux suspendus à des ~s différentes** pictures hung at different heights ou levels; **perdre de la ~** to lose height; **prendre de la ~** lit [*avion, oiseau*] to climb, to gain height; **~ libre** or **maximum 5 m** Aut max headroom 5 m; **à ~ d'homme** at about the height of a person; **à ~ d'yeux** or **des yeux** at eye level; **2** (profondeur) (d'eau, de rivière) depth; **~ d'eau** Naut depth of water; **d'une ~ d'eau de 10 m** 10 m deep; **3** Sport **la ~, le saut en ~** the high jump; **il est bon en ~** he's good at the high jump; **4** Cout (de robe, jupe) length; **acheter 2 ~s de tissu pour faire une robe** to buy 2 dress lengths of material; **dans le sens de la ~** lengthwise; **5** (éminence) hill; **chapelle située sur une ~** chapel on a hill; **gagner les ~s** to reach high ground; **il y a encore de la neige sur les ~s** there is still some snow on the mountain tops; **habiter sur les ~s de la ville** to live in the upper part of the town; **6** Math (de triangle) altitude; (de trapèze, cylindre) height; **7** (qualité morale) nobility; **~ d'âme** nobility of spirit; **~ de conception/d'idées** lofty conception/ideas; **8** péj (arrogance) haughtiness; **parler/répondre avec ~** to speak/reply haughtily; **regard/refus plein de ~** haughty look/refusal; **9** (en acoustique) pitch; **10** Astron altitude; **prendre la ~ d'une étoile** to measure the altitude of a star.

II à la hauteur *loc* **1** (au niveau) **suspendre un tableau à la ~ des autres** to hang a picture level with ou at the same height as the others; **arriver à la ~ de** to come up to; **raccourcir une jupe à la ~ des genoux** to shorten a dress to knee-level; **2** (à côté) **arriver à la ~ de** to draw level with; **quand son bateau est arrivé à la ~ du nôtre** when his boat drew level with ours; **un déraillement s'est produit à la ~ de Rouen** there was a derailment near Rouen; **3** fig **être à la ~** to measure up; **être à la ~ de qn** to match up to sb; **être à la ~ de sa tâche/ses responsabilités** to be up to ou equal to one's job/one's responsibilities; **être à la ~ des espérances/attentes de qn** to live up to sb's hopes/expectations; **être à la ~ du talent de qn** [*scénario, sujet*] to do justice to sb's talent; **l'interprétation n'était pas à la ~ de la qualité du texte** the acting didn't do justice to the quality of the text; **être à la ~ de la situation/des circonstances** to be equal to the situation/the circumstances; **4** (en valeur, quantité) **à (la) ~ de 5000 F/10%** up to 5,000 F/10%; **contribuer à qch à ~ de 10%** to take a stake of up to 10% in sth.

■ **~ d'appui** Constr, Archit chest height; **à ~ d'appui** at chest height (*épith*); **~ sous plafond** height from floor to ceiling.

IDIOMES **tomber de toute sa ~** to fall headlong; **se dresser de toute sa ~** [*personne*] to draw oneself up to one's full height; [*animal*] to stand on its hind legs.

Haute-Volta /ʹotvɔlta/ *nprf* Hist Upper Volta.

haut-fond, *pl* **hauts-fonds** /ʹofɔ̃/ *nm* Naut shallows (*pl*).

haut(-)fourneau, *pl* **hauts(-) fourneaux** /ʹofuʀno/ *nm* Ind blast furnace.

haut-le-cœur /ʹolkœʀ/ *nm inv* retching ©, heaving ©, gagging ©; **avoir des ~** to retch ou heave, to gag; **en voyant les images nous avons eu un ~** fig the pictures turned our stomachs.

haut-le-corps /ʹolkɔʀ/ *nm inv* start, jump; **avoir un ~** to start, to jump.

haut-parleur, *pl* **~s** /ʹopaʀlœʀ/ *nm* Électrotech loudspeaker.

■ **~ d'aigus** tweeter; **~ de graves** boomer.

haut-relief, *pl* **hauts-reliefs** /ʹoʀəljɛf/ *nm* Archit, Art high relief.

Haut-Rhin /ʹoʀɛ̃/ **▶692** *nprm* (département) **le ~** the Haut-Rhin.

Hauts-de-Seine /ʹodsɛn/ **▶692** *nprmpl* (département) **les ~** Hauts-de-Seine.

hauturier, **-ière** /ʹotyʀje, ɛʀ/ *adj* [*pêche*] deep-sea; [*navire*] ocean-going.

havage /ʹavaʒ/ *nm* Mines cutting.

havane /ʹavan/ **I ▶193** *adj inv* tobacco-brown.

II *nm* **1** (tabac) Havana tobacco; **2** (cigare) Havana cigar.

Havane /ʹavan/ **▶857** *npr* **la ~** Havana.

hâve /ʹɑv/ *adj* fml [*visage*] haggard, gaunt.

haver /ʹave/ [1] *vtr* Mines, Tech to cut.

haveuse /ʹavøz/ *nf* Mines, Tech cutting machine.

havrais, **~e** /ʹɑvʀɛ, ɛz/ **▶857** *adj* of Le Havre.

Havrais, **~e** /ʹɑvʀɛ, ɛz/ **▶857** *nm,f* (natif) native of Le Havre; (habitant) inhabitant of Le Havre.

havre /ʹɑvʀ/ *nm* **1** fig haven; **~ de paix** haven of peace; **2†** (port) small port, haven.

Havre /ʹɑvʀ/ **▶857** *npr* **le ~** le Havre.

havresac /ʹavʀəsak/ *nm* haversack.

Hawaï /awaj/ **▶692**, **416** *nprf* Hawaii.

hawaïen, **-ïenne** /awajɛ̃, ɛn/ *adj* Hawaiian; **éruption de type ~** Hawaiian eruption.

Haye /ʹɛ/ **▶857** *npr* **la ~** the Hague.

hayon /ʹajɔ̃/ *nm* (de voiture) hatchback; (de charrette) grill.

■ **~ élévateur** lifting tailboard ou tailgate.

hé /ʹe/ *excl* **~! vous là-bas!** hey, you!; **~! ~! ~! il m'a cru!** ha-ha! he believed me!

heaume /ʹom/ *nm* helmet.

hebdomadaire /ɛbdɔmadɛʀ/ **I** *adj* [*fermeture, visite, départ*] weekly; **quatre heures ~s** four hours weekly, four hours a week.

II *nm* weekly (magazine).

hébergement /ebɛʀʒəmɑ̃/ *nm* **1** (commercial) accommodation; **il faut augmenter la capacité d'~ touristique** we have to increase the amount of tourist accommodation; **2** (social) housing; **~ d'urgence** emergency housing; **les conditions d'~ des personnes âgées** housing conditions for the elderly.

héberger /ebɛʀʒe/ [13] *vtr* **1** (loger) [*personne*] to put [sb] up [*amis*]; to accommodate [*touristes*]; **2** (donner asile) [*pays*] to take in [*réfugiés*]; **3** (abriter) [*bâtiment*] to accommodate, to provide accommodation for [*touristes*]; [*refuge*] to provide shelter for [*montagnards, sans-abri*].

hébété, **~e** /ebete/ *adj* [*regard*] stupid; **il la regardait d'un air ~** he stared at her stupidly; **être ~ par qch** to be stupefied by [*alcool, travail*]; **~ de fatigue/douleur** numb with fatigue/grief.

hébétement /ebɛtmɑ̃/ *nm* stupor.

hébétude /ebetyd/ *nf* hebetude sout, stupor.

hébraïque /ebʀaik/ *adj* [*études*] Hebrew.

hébraïsant, **-ante** /ebʀaizɑ̃, ɑ̃t/ *nm,f* Hebraist.

hébraïser /ebʀaize/ [1] *vtr* to Hebraize.

hébraïsme /ebʀaism/ *nm* Hebraism.

hébraïste /ebʀaist/ *nmf* Hebraist.

hébreu, *pl* **~x** /ebʀø/ **▶462** **I** *adj m* Hebrew; **l'État ~** the State of Israel.

II *nm* Ling Hebrew.

IDIOMES **pour moi, c'est de l'~** it's all Greek to me.

Hébreu, *pl* **~x** /ebʀø/ *nm* Hebrew; **les ~x** the Hebrews.

Hébrides /ebʀid/ **▶416** *nprfpl* **les (îles) ~** the Hebrides.

HEC /aʃəse/ *nf* (*abbr* = **Hautes études commerciales**) *major business school.*

hécatombe /ekatɔ̃b/ *nf* **1** (massacre) massacre, slaughter; **l'examen a été une ~** fig lots of people failed the exam; **2** Antiq hecatomb.

hectare /ɛktaʀ/ **▶783** *nm* hectare.

hecto /ɛkto/ **I** *nm* (*abbr* = **hectogramme**) hectogram.

II hecto(-) (*in compounds*) hecto.

hectogramme /ɛktɔgʀam/ **▶620** *nm* hectogram.

hectolitre /ɛktɔlitʀ/ **▶117** *nm* hectolitre[GB].

hectomètre /ɛktɔmɛtʀ/ **▶477** *nm* hectometre[GB].

hectométrique /ɛktɔmetʀik/ *adj* **borne ~** hectometre[GB]-marker (*on a road*).

hectopascal /ɛktɔpaskal/ *nm* milibar.

hédonisme /edɔnism/ *nm* hedonism.

hédoniste /edɔnist/ **I** *adj* hedonistic.

II *nmf* hedonist.

hégélianisme /egeljanism/ *nm* Hegelianism.

hégélien, **-ienne** /egeljɛ̃, ɛn/ *adj, nm,f* Hegelian.

hégémonie /eʒemɔni/ *nf* hegemony.

hégire /eʒiʀ/ *nf* **l'~** the Hegira.

hein○ /ʹɛ̃/ *excl* (pour faire répéter) what○?, sorry?, pardon me? US; **ça t'étonne, ~?** (pour savoir) that's surprised you, has it?; (pour insister) that's surprised you, hasn't it?; **tu ne m'en veux pas, ~?** you're not angry with me, are you?

hélas /ʹelas/ *excl* alas; **~! il ne me reste plus rien** sadly, I have nothing left; **j'ai, ~, perdu toute ma famille** sadly, I have lost all my family; **'va-t-elle mieux?'—'~ non!'** 'is she any better?'—'unfortunately not!'

Hélène /elɛn/ *npr* Helen; **~ de Troie** Helen of Troy.

héler /ʹele/ [14] **I** *vtr* to hail [*taxi*]; to hail sout, to call [*personne*].

II se héler *vpr* to call out to one another.

hélianthe /eljɑ̃t/ *nm* helianthus.

hélianthine /eljɑ̃tin/ *nf* methyl orange, helianthine spéc.

hélice /elis/ *nf* **1** Naut, Aviat (screw) propeller; **2** Archit, Math, Biol helix; **3** Tech (de moulin à café) blade; (de ventilateur) blades (*pl*).

hélico○ /eliko/ *nm* chopper○, helicopter.

hélicoïdal, **~e**, *mpl* **-aux** /elikɔidal, o/ *adj* **1** Math, Mécan, Tech [*mouvement, axe*] helical; [*escalier*] spiral; **2** Bot helicoid.

hélicoïde /elikɔid/ *nm* helicoid.

hélicon /elikɔ̃/ **▶534** *nm* Mus helicon.

hélicoptère /elikɔptɛʀ/ *nm* helicopter; **en ~** in a helicopter.

■ **~ armé** armed helicopter; **~ de combat** attack helicopter.

héliographe /eljɔgʀaf/ *nm* heliograph.

héliographie /eljɔgʀafi/ *nf* heliography.

héliogravure /eljɔgʀavyʀ/ *nf* **1** (procédé) gravure printing; **2** (image) gravure.

héliomarin, **~e** /eljɔmaʀɛ̃, in/ *adj* [*cure*] sun-and-seawater.

héliotrope /eljɔtʀɔp/ *nm* Bot, Minér heliotrope.

héliport /elipɔʀ/ *nm* heliport.

héliporté, **~e** /elipɔʀte/ *adj* [*troupes, unité*] helicopter-borne.

hélitreuiller /elitʀœje/ [1] *vtr* to winch [sb] to safety (*by helicopter*).

hélium /eljɔm/ *nm* helium.

hélix /eliks/ *nm* helix.

hellène /ellɛn/ *adj* [*peuple, voilier*] Hellenic.

Hellène /ellɛn/ *nm* Hellene.

hellénique /ellenik/ *adj* Hellenic.

helléniser /ellenize/ [1] *vtr* to hellenize.

hellénisme /ellenism/ *nm* Hellenism.

helléniste /ellenist/ *nmf* Hellenist.

Helsinki /ɛlsinki/ **▶857** *npr* Helsinki.

helvète /ɛlvɛt/ *adj* Helvetian.

Helvète /ɛlvɛt/ *nmf* Helvetian.

Helvétie /ɛlvesi/ *nprf* Helvetia.

helvétique /ɛlvetik/ *adj* Helvetic, Swiss; **la Confédération ~** Switzerland.

helvétisme /ɛlvetism/ *nm* Swiss French expression.

hématie /emati, emasi/ *nf* red blood cell, erythrocyte spéc.

hématologie /ematɔlɔʒi/ *nf* haematology.

hématologique /ematɔlɔʒik/ *adj* haematological.

hématologue /ematɔlɔg/ **▶510** *nmf* haematologist.

hématome /ematom/ *nm* bruise, haematoma spéc.

hémicycle /emisikl/ *nm* (de théâtre) semicircular auditorium; (salle quelconque) semicircular room; **l'~ (de l'Assemblée nationale)** the benches of the French National Assembly.

hémiplégie /emipleʒi/ *nf* paralysis of one side of the body, hemiplegia spéc.

hémiplégique /emipleʒik/ I *adj* hemiplegic; **être ~** to be paralysed[GB] down one side, to be a hemiplegic.
II *nmf* hemiplegic.

hémisphère /emisfɛʀ/ *nm* Anat, Géog hemisphere; **~ cérébral** cerebral hemisphere; **l'~ Nord/Sud** Géog the northern/southern hemisphere.

hémisphérique /emisfeʀik/ *adj* hemispherical.

hémistiche /emistiʃ/ *nm* (moitié de vers) hemistich; **coupe à l'~** caesura.

hémoglobine /emɔglɔbin/ *nf* **1** Physiol haemoglobin; **2**○ (sang) blood.

hémophile /emɔfil/ I *adj* haemophilic; **être ~** to be a haemophiliac.
II *nmf* haemophiliac.

hémophilie /emɔfili/ *nf* haemophilia.

hémorragie /emɔʀaʒi/ *nf* **1** Méd haemorrhage, bleeding ¢; **~ cérébrale** cerebral haemorrhage; **~ interne** internal bleeding; **pour arrêter l'~** to stop the bleeding; **2** (fuite) (de capitaux, devises) massive outflow; (de partisans, populations, clients) exodus; **3** (pertes humaines) massive loss of (human) life; **l'~ due à la guerre** the massive loss of life due to the war.

hémorragique /emɔʀaʒik/ *adj* haemorrhagic.

hémorroïdal, **~e**, *mpl* **-aux** /emɔʀɔidal, o/ *adj* **1** Méd haemorrhoidal; **2** Anat [*artère, nerf*] anorectal.

hémorroïdes /emɔʀɔid/ ▶271 *nfpl* piles, haemorrhoids; **avoir des ~** to have piles.

hémostatique /emɔstatik/ I *adj* haemostatic.
II *nm* haemostat.

henné /'ene/ *nm* henna; **se teindre les cheveux au ~** to henna one's hair.

hennin /'enɛ̃/ *nm* Hist hennin.

hennir /'eniʀ/ [3] *vi* [*cheval*] to neigh, to whinny.

hennissement /'enismɑ̃/ *nm* neigh, whinnying ¢.

hep /(h)ɛp/ *excl* hey!

héparine /epaʀin/ *nf* heparin.

hépatique /epatik/ I *adj* hepatic; **insuffisance ~** liver failure, hepatic insufficiency spéc.
II *nmf* person with a liver complaint.
III *nf* Bot **1** (lichen) liverwort; **les ~s** Hepaticae; **2** (fleur) hepatica.

hépatite /epatit/ ▶271 *nf* hepatitis; **~ B** hepatitis B; **~ virale** viral hepatitis.

hépatologie /epatɔlɔʒi/ *nf* hepatology.

heptaèdre /ɛptaɛdʀ/ *nm* heptahedron.

heptagonal, **~e**, *mpl* **-aux** /ɛptagɔnal, o/ *adj* heptagonal.

heptagone /ɛptagɔn/ *nm* heptagon.

heptasyllabe /ɛptasilab/ I *adj* heptasyllabic.
II *nm* heptasyllable.

heptathlon /ɛptatlɔ̃/ *nm* heptathlon.

Héra /eʀa/ *npr* Hera.

Héraclès /eʀaklɛs/ *npr* Heracles.

Héraclite /eʀaklit/ *npr* Heraclitus.

héraldique /eʀaldik/ I *adj* heraldic.
II *nf* heraldry.

héraldiste /eʀaldist/ *nmf* heraldist.

Hérault /'eʀo/ ▶357, 692 (fleuve, département) *nprm* **l'~** the Hérault.

héraut /'eʀo/ *nm* **1** (annonciateur) liter harbinger; **2** Hist (officier) **~ d'armes** herald.

herbacé, **~e** /ɛʀbase/ *adj* herbaceous.

herbage /ɛʀbaʒ/ *nm* pasture.

herbager, **-ère** /ɛʀbaʒe, ɛʀ/ *adj* **1** [*région*] with extensive pastureland (*épith, après n*); **2** [*élevage*] on pastureland (*épith, après n*).

herbe /ɛʀb/ I *nf* **1** (revêtement végétal) grass; **un brin d'~** a blade of grass; **une touffe d'~** a tuft of grass; **marcher/s'étendre sur l'~** to walk/lie on the grass; **'défense de marcher sur l'~'** 'keep off the grass'; **2** Bot (plante) **un talus de hautes ~s** a bank of tall grass; **mauvaise ~** weed; **3** Bot, Culin aromatic herb; **fines ~s** gén mixed herbs, fines herbes; (ciboulette) chives; **4**○ (marijuana) grass○, marijuana.
II **en herbe** *loc adj* **1** (encore vert) [*blé, avoine*] in the blade (*après n*); **2** (jeune) [*musicien, footballeur*] budding.
■ **~s folles** wild grass.
IDIOMES **couper l'~ sous les pieds de qn** to beat sb to it.

herbeux, **-euse** /ɛʀbø, øz/ *adj* grassy.

herbicide /ɛʀbisid/ I *adj* [*produit*] herbicidal.
II *nm* weed killer, herbicide.

herbier /ɛʀbje/ *nm* **1** (de plantes séchées) herbarium; **faire un ~** to build up a herbarium; **2** (de planches illustrées) set of plant illustrations.

herbivore /ɛʀbivɔʀ/ I *adj* herbivorous.
II *nm* herbivore.

herborisation /ɛʀbɔʀizasjɔ̃/ *nf* **1** (cueillette) plant collecting, botanizing spéc; **2** (excursion) plant-collecting trip, botanizing trip spéc.

herboriser /ɛʀbɔʀize/ [1] *vi* to collect plants, to botanize spéc.

herboriste /ɛʀbɔʀist/ ▶510 *nmf* herbalist.

herboristerie /ɛʀbɔʀistəʀi/ ▶510 *nf* **1** (vente) herb trade; **2** (boutique) herbalist's shop GB ou store US.

herbu, **~e** /ɛʀby/ *adj* grassy.

hercule /ɛʀkyl/ *nm* **c'est un ~** he's a big strong guy○; **~ de foire** strongman.

Hercule /ɛʀkyl/ *npr* Hercules; **les travaux d'~** Mythol the Labours of Hercules; **c'est un travail d'~** fig it's a Herculean task.

herculéen, **-éenne** /ɛʀkyleɛ̃, ɛn/ *adj* Herculean.

hercynien, **-ienne** /ɛʀsinjɛ̃, ɛn/ *adj* Hercynian.

hère /'ɛʀ/ *nm* liter **un pauvre ~** a poor wretch.

héréditaire /eʀeditɛʀ/ *adj* Biol, Jur, Méd hereditary; **l'ennemi ~** fig the traditional enemy.

héréditairement /eʀeditɛʀmɑ̃/ *adv* hereditarily.

hérédité /eʀedite/ *nf* **1** Biol heredity; **2** (origines) background; **il a une ~ chargée**○ his family history is very bad; **3** Jur (de possession, charge, titre) hereditary nature; (biens)† fml estate.

Hereford ▶692 *nprm* **le ~ and Worcester** Hereford and Worcester.

hérésie /eʀezi/ *nf* **1** Relig heresy; **tomber en ~** to become a heretic; **2** (opinion, théorie) heresy; hum (action) sacrilege; **une ~ scientifique** a scientific heresy; **du vin blanc avec du gibier, quelle ~!** white wine with game, that's sacrilege!

hérétique /eʀetik/ I *adj* heretical.
II *nmf* heretic.

hérissé, **~e** /'eʀise/ I *pp* ▶ **hérisser**.
II *pp adj* [*plumes*] ruffled; **il a les cheveux ~s** (volontairement) he's got spiky hair; (involontairement) he's got hair that sticks up.

hérisser /'eʀise/ [1] I *vtr* **1** (dresser) [*oiseau*] to ruffle (up) [*plumes*]; [*hérisson, porc-épic*] to raise [*piquants*]; **le chat a hérissé ses poils** the cat's fur bristled; **le froid hérisse les poils** the cold gives you goose pimples; **fou de terreur, les cheveux hérissés sur la tête** mad with terror, his hair standing on end; **2** (garnir) **~ qch de** to spike sth with; **~ une fosse de pieux** to spike a pit with stakes; **le haut du mur est hérissé de tessons de bouteilles** the top of the wall is spiked with broken glass; **question hérissée de difficultés** fig question fraught with difficulties; **3**○ (irriter) [*situation*] to set sb's teeth on edge○; [*personne*] to make sb cringe.
II **se hérisser** *vpr* **1** (se dresser) [*poils, cheveux*] to stand on end; [*animal*] to bristle; **2**○ (s'irriter) to bristle○; **il se hérisse à la moindre remarque** he bristles at the slightest remark.

hérisson /'eʀisɔ̃/ *nm* **1** Zool hedgehog; **2** (de ramoneur) (chimney sweep's) brush; **3** (égouttoir à bouteilles) bottle-drainer; **4** Mil (défense) hedgehog; **5** Agric toothed roller; **6** Tex porcupine roller.
■ **~ de mer** sea urchin.

héritage /eʀitaʒ/ *nm* **1** (biens légués) inheritance; **faire un ~** to come into an inheritance; **il a laissé un gros ~ à ses enfants** he left his children a big inheritance; **une tante à ~** a wealthy aunt; **laisser qch en ~** to bequeath sth (**à qn** to sb); **recevoir qch en ~** to inherit sth; **il l'a eu par ~** he inherited it; **mes grosses mains sont un ~ de mon grand-père** I inherited my coarse hands from my grandfather; **2** (survivance du passé) (concret) inheritance; (abstrait) heritage, legacy; **nous sommes fiers de notre ~ culturel** we are proud of our cultural heritage; **l'~ du dictateur se fait encore sentir** the dictator's legacy can still be felt.

hériter /eʀite/ [1] I *vtr* to inherit; **~ la couronne** to inherit the throne; **~ qch de qn** to inherit sth from sb.
II **hériter de** *vtr ind* **1** Jur to inherit [*argent, bien*]; **la maison dont il a hérité** the house he inherited; **ce peintre a largement hérité de l'impressionnisme** this painter has inherited a great deal from Impressionism; **nous héritons de la pagaille laissée par nos prédécesseurs** we have inherited the mess left by our predecessors; **lois/coutumes héritées du XVe siècle** laws/customs which have come down from the 15th century; **2**○ (se retrouver encombré de) to be landed with.
III *vi* (être légataire) to inherit; (faire un héritage) to come into an inheritance; **qui héritera?** who will inherit?; **quand il aura hérité** when he comes into his inheritance; **~ de qn** to receive an inheritance from sb.

héritier, **-ière** /eʀitje, ɛʀ/ *nm,f* Jur heir/heiress (**de** to); **mourir sans ~** to die without an heir; **être l'~ d'une grande fortune/longue tradition** to be the heir to a large fortune/long tradition; **l'~ spirituel de qn** sb's spiritual heir.
■ **~ testamentaire** Jur legatee.

hermaphrodisme /ɛʀmafʀɔdism/ *nm* hermaphroditism.

hermaphrodite /ɛʀmafʀɔdit/ I *adj* (tous contextes) hermaphroditic.
II *nm* hermaphrodite.

herméneutique /ɛʀmenøtik/ I *adj* hermeneutic.
II *nf* hermeneutics (*+ v sg*).

Hermès /ɛʀmɛs/ *npr* Hermes.

hermétique /ɛʀmetik/ *adj* **1** lit (étanche) [*joint, récipient*] hermetic; [*fermeture*] (aux gaz) airtight; (aux liquides) watertight; **assurer la fermeture ~ de qch** to ensure that sth is hermetically sealed; **2** (impénétrable) [*frontière*] closed, sealed-off (*jamais épith*); [*milieu, société*] impenetrable; [*blocus, embargo*] solid; **3** (indéchiffrable) [*poésie, auteur*] abstruse; [*visage, expression*] inscrutable; **il est ~ à l'astrologie/au cricket** astrology/cricket is a closed book to him; **4** (ésotérique) [*livres, philosophie*] Hermetic.

hermétiquement /ɛʀmetikmɑ̃/ *adv* **1** [*fermé, clos, scellé*] hermetically; **fermer ses frontières ~** to seal off one's borders; **2** [*s'exprimer*] abstrusely.

hermétisme /ɛʀmetism/ *nm* **1** (caractère indéchiffrable) abstruseness; **2** (occultisme) hermeticism; **3** Littérat hermeticism.

hermine /ɛʀmin/ *nf* **1** (animal) stoat; **2** (fourrure) ermine; **3** Hérald ermine.

herminette /ɛʀminɛt/ *nf* adze GB, adz US.

herniaire /'ɛʀnjɛʀ/ *adj* hernial.

hernie /'ɛʀni/ *nf* **1** Méd hernia; **~ étran-**

glée strangulated hernia; **~ hiatale** hiatus hernia; **2** (de pneu) bulge.

Hérode /eʀɔd/ *npr* Herod.

Hérodote /eʀɔdɔt/ *npr* Herodotus.

héroï-comique, *pl* **~s** /eʀɔikɔmik/ *adj* mock-heroic.

héroïne /eʀɔin/ *nf* **1** (personnage) heroine; **2** (stupéfiant) heroin.

héroïnomane /eʀɔinɔman/ *nmf* heroin addict.

héroïque /eʀɔik/ *adj* [*personne, fait*] heroic; [*poème*] epic; **aux débuts ~s de l'aviation** in the pioneering days of aviation, in the heroic early days of aviation.

héroïquement /eʀɔikmɑ̃/ *adv* heroically.

héroïsme /eʀɔism/ *nm* heroism; **sortir par ce temps, c'est de l'~!** hum to go out in weather like this is nothing short of heroic!; **avec ~** [*lutter, supporter*] heroically.

héron /'eʀɔ̃/ *nm* heron.
■ **~ cendré** grey GB ou gray US heron.

héros /'eʀo/ *nm* hero; **c'est un vrai ~ de roman** he's like something out of a book; **mourir en ~** to die a hero's death; **être accueilli en ~** to be given a hero's welcome.

herpès /ɛʀpɛs/ **▶271** *nm* herpes; **~ de la lèvre** cold sore, herpes labialis spéc; **~ génital** genital herpes.
■ **~ circiné** ringworm.

herpétique /ɛʀpetik/ *adj* herpetic.

hersage /'ɛʀsaʒ/ *nm* harrowing ¢.

herse /'ɛʀs/ *nf* **1** Agric harrow; **2** (grille d'entrée) portcullis; **3** Théât (éclairage) batten GB, bank of floodlights US; **4** Mil (barrage routier) caltrop barrier; **5** (sur un cours d'eau) trap.

Hertfordshire **▶692** *nprm* **le ~** Hertfordshire.

hertz /(')ɛʀts/ *nm inv* hertz.

hertzien, **-ienne** /ɛʀtzjɛ̃, ɛn/ *adj* [*onde*] Hertzian; [*station, système, liaison*] radio-relay.

hésitant, **~e** /ezitɑ̃, ɑ̃t/ **I** *adj* [*geste, dessin, défense*] hesitant; [*démarche, pas, réponse, voix*] hesitant, faltering; [*victoire*] undecided; [*démarrage*] shaky; **elle s'exprime dans un anglais ~** she speaks in faltering English.
II hésitants *nmpl* (d'un sondage) **les ~s** the don't knows.

hésitation /ezitasjɔ̃/ *nf* **1** (indécision) indecision, hesitancy; **il a eu une seconde d'~** he hesitated for a second; **répondre sans (la moindre) ~** to reply without (the slightest) hesitation; **2** (signe d'incertitude) hesitation ¢; **se décider après bien des ~s** to make up one's mind after much hesitation; **elle a marqué une ~ avant de poursuivre (son discours)** she hesitated before continuing (her speech); **lever les dernières ~s de qn** to overcome sb's final doubts.

hésiter /ezite/ [1] *vi* to hesitate (**sur** over; **devant** before); **ne pas ~ à** not to hesitate to; **elle n'a pas hésité une seconde** she didn't hesitate for a second; **elle n'a pas donné de réponse, elle hésite encore** she hasn't given an answer yet, she's still undecided; **il n'y a pas à ~** it's got to be done; **j'hésite entre deux solutions** I'm not sure which solution is the best; **'alors, tu viens?'—'j'hésite'** 'are you coming?'—'I can't make up my mind'; **j'hésite sur le chemin/la décision à prendre** I'm not sure which path/decision to take; **il hésitait sur ce qu'il convenait de faire** he was not sure what to do for the best; **j'hésite entre deux films/plusieurs possibilités** I can't decide between two films/several possibilities; **~ à venir** to be unsure whether to come (or not); **j'hésite à interrompre leur conversation** I don't like to interrupt their conversation; **les docteurs hésitent à l'opérer** the doctors are reluctant to operate on him/her; **j'ai hésité longtemps à vous écrire** I hesitated for a long time before writing to you.

Hespérides /ɛspeʀid/ *nprfpl* Mythol **1** (îles) **les ~** the Hesperides; **2** (gardiennes du jardin) **les ~** the Hesperides; **le jardin des ~** the Hesperides (+ *v sg*).

hétaïre /etaiʀ/ *nf* **1** Antiq hetaera; **2†** (prostituée) prostitute.

hétéro○ /eteʀo/ *adj, nmf* heterosexual.

hétéroclite /eteʀɔklit/ *adj* [*population, clientèle*] heterogeneous; [*œuvre*] eclectic; [*objets, matériaux*] miscellaneous.

hétérodoxe /eteʀɔdɔks/ *adj* heterodox.

hétérodoxie /eteʀɔdɔksi/ *nf* heterodoxy.

hétérogène /eteʀɔʒɛn/ *adj* [*groupe, ensemble*] mixed, heterogeneous sout; [*nombre*] mixed; **une classe très ~** a very mixed class.

hétérogénéité /eteʀɔʒeneite/ *nf* heterogeneity.

hétérosexualité /eteʀɔsɛksɥalite/ *nf* heterosexuality.

hétérosexuel, **-elle** /eteʀɔsɛksɥɛl/ *adj, nm,f* heterosexual.

hétérozygote /eteʀɔzigɔt/ **I** *adj* heterozygous.
II *nmf* heterozygote.

hêtraie /'ɛtʀɛ/ *nf* beech wood.

hêtre /'ɛtʀ/ *nm* **1** (arbre) beech (tree); **2** (bois) beechwood.

heu /'ø/ *excl* er...

heur† /œʀ/ *nm* good fortune; **ne pas avoir l'~ de plaire à qn** not to have the good fortune to please sb.

heure /œʀ/ **▶407**, **801**, **860** *nf* **1** (soixante minutes) hour; **une ~ avant** or **plus tôt** an hour before; **deux ~s après** or **plus tard** two hours later; **en une ~** in an hour; **24 ~s sur 24** lit, fig twenty four hours a day, round the clock; **dans l'~ qui a suivi** within the hour; **dans les 24 ~s** within 24 hours; **d'~ en ~** [*augmenter, empirer*] by the hour; **suivre qch ~ par ~** to follow sth hour by hour; **deux ~s de repos/d'attente** a two-hour rest/wait; **toutes les deux ~s** every two hours; **il y a un train toutes les ~s** there's a train every hour; **après trois ~s d'avion** after three hours on the plane, after a three-hour flight; **être à trois ~s de train/d'avion de Paris** to be three hours away from Paris by train/plane; **être à trois ~s de marche de Paris** to be a three-hour walk from Paris; **faire trois ~s de bateau/d'avion** to be on the boat/plane for three hours; **faire du 60 à l'~**○, **faire 60 km à l'~** to do 60 km per hour; **être payé à l'~** to be paid by the hour; **gagner 200 francs de l'~** to earn 200 francs an hour; **la semaine de 35 ~s** the 35-hour week; **avoir deux ~s de chimie par semaine** to have two hours of chemistry per week; **une petite ~** an hour at the most; **une bonne ~** a good hour; **ça fait une ~ que je t'attends!** (par exagération) I've been waiting for an hour!; **nous avons parlé du projet pendant des ~s** we talked about the project for hours on end; **2** (indication) time; **l'~ exacte** or **juste** the exact ou right time; **quelle ~ est-il?** what time is it, what's the time?; **tu as l'~?** have you got the time? ; **à quelle ~...?** (at) what time...?; **à 11 ~s, ~ de Paris** at 11, Paris time; **il ne sait pas lire l'~** he can't tell the time; **se tromper d'~** to get the time wrong; **il est 10 ~s** it's 10 (o'clock); **il est 10 ~s 20** it's 20 past 10; **il est 10 ~s moins 20** it's 20 to 10; **à 5 ~s du matin/de l'après-midi** at 5 in the morning/in the afternoon, at 5 am/pm; **à 4 ~s pile** or **tapantes**○ at 4 o'clock sharp ou on the dot; **mettre/remettre sa montre à l'~** to set/reset one's watch; **l'~ tourne** time is passing; **3** (point dans le temps) time; **l'~ d'un rendez-vous/de la prière** the time of an appointment/for prayer; **il est** or **c'est l'~ de faire** it's time to do; **c'est l'~, il faut que j'y aille** it's time, I must go; **l'~ d'arrivée/de départ** the arrival/departure time; **~s d'ouverture/de fermeture** opening/closing times; **arriver/être à l'~** to arrive/be on time; **à l'~ convenue** at the agreed time; **'sandwiches à toute ~'** 'sandwiches available at any time'; **à une ~ indue** at an unearthly hour; **à une ~ avancée (de la nuit)** late at night; **de bonne ~** [*se lever, partir*] early; **il doit être loin à l'~ qu'il est** he must be a long way off by now; **c'est son ~** it's his/her usual time; **il ne viendra pas à l'~ qu'il est** he won't come this late; **mourir avant l'~** to die before one's time; **ton ~ viendra** your time will come; **son ~ est venue** his/her time has come; **à l'~ où je te parle** while I'm speaking to you, at this very moment; **de la première ~** [*résistant, militant*] from the very beginning; **à la première ~** at first light; **de dernière ~** [*manœuvre, décision*] last-minute; **un résistant de la dernière ~** a late convert to the resistance; **ta dernière ~ est arrivée** your time has come; **4** (période, époque) time; **à l'~ actuelle, pour l'~** at the present time; **à l'~ où...** at a time when...; **à l'~ de la restructuration/détente** at a time of restructuring/détente; **à l'~ de la pause** during the break; **l'~ du déjeuner/thé/dîner** lunchtime/teatime/dinnertime; **aux ~s des repas** at mealtimes; **pendant les ~s de bureau/de classe** during office/school hours; **l'~ est à l'entreprise individuelle** the current trend is for private enterprise; **l'~ n'est pas à la polémique/l'optimisme** this is no time for controversy/optimism; **l'~ est grave** the situation is serious; **il est peintre/poète à ses ~s** he paints/writes poetry in his spare time; **c'est la bonne/la mauvaise ~** it's the right/a bad time; **à la bonne ~!** well done!; **5** (ère) era; **vivre à l'~ des satellites/de l'audiovisuel** to live in the satellite/audiovisual era.
■ **~ d'affluence** Transp peak hour; **aux ~s d'affluence** during peak hours; **~ d'été** Admin summer time GB, daylight saving(s) time US; **~ H** Mil, fig zero hour; **~ d'hiver** Admin winter time GB, daylight saving(s) time US; **~ légale** Admin standard time; **~ locale** Admin local time; **~ de pointe** Transp rush hour; **aux ~s de pointe** during (the) rush hour; **~s canoniales** Relig canonical hours; **~s supplémentaires** Entr overtime; **faire des ~s supplémentaires** to do ou work overtime; ▶ **quatorze**.
IDIOMES **avant l'~, c'est pas l'~, après l'~, c'est plus l'~**○ there's no time but the right time; **vivre à cent à l'~**○ fig to be always on the go○.

heureusement /œʀøzmɑ̃/ *adv* **1** (par chance) fortunately (**pour** for); **~, il ne pleuvait pas** fortunately, it wasn't raining; **fort ~, on en est resté là** very fortunately, that was the end of it; **~ pour nous qu'elle ne t'a pas vu** fortunately for us she didn't see you; **~ que tu es là!** it's a good job you're here!; **~ que tu as pris ton parapluie** it's a good job you've got your umbrella; **2** (avec bonheur) fml [*réparti*] successfully; [*terminé, conclu*] nicely; **~ situé** well-situated; **des exemples ~ choisis** well-chosen examples.

heureux, **-euse** /œʀø, øz/ *adj* **1** (satisfait) [*personne, visage, enfance*] happy (**de faire** to do); **être ~ de vivre** to be happy with life; **elle a tout pour être heureuse** she has everything she needs to be happy; **je serais trop ~ de vous aider** I should ou would be only too happy to help you; **être ~ en ménage** to be happily married; **je suis ~ qu'il soit guéri** I am pleased (that) he is better; **très ~ de faire votre connaissance** (very) pleased to meet you; **Monsieur et Madame Bon sont ~ de vous faire part de...** Mr and Mrs Bon are pleased to announce...; **2** (satisfaisant) [*issue, fin*] happy; [*surprise*] pleasant; **3** (optimiste) [*nature, caractère*] happy; **4** (chanceux) lucky; **l'~ gagnant** the lucky winner; **je m'estime ~ d'être encore en vie** I consider myself lucky to be still alive;

L'heure

Quelle heure est-il?

En anglais, on donne l'heure en utilisant les prépositions past *et* to *(ou* after *et* of *aux États-Unis). Par ex., pour 4 h 05,* five past four, five after four *(US), pour 4 h 50,* ten to five, ten of five *(US) etc. Dans un style plus officiel, on juxtapose les chiffres des heures et des minutes: par ex., pour 4 h 10,* four ten. *Dans les horaires de trains etc, on utilise aussi l'horloge de vingt-quatre heures: par ex, pour 16 h 23,* sixteen twenty-three. *Dans le tableau suivant,* past *peut être remplacé par* after *(US) et* to *peut être remplacé par* of *(US).*

il est ...	it is ...	dire
4 h	4 o'clock	four o'clock *ou* four
4 h du matin	4 am	four o'clock* *ou* four [eɪ em] *ou* four o'clock in the morning
4 h de l'après-midi	4 pm	four o'clock *ou* four [piː em] *ou* four o'clock in the afternoon
4 h 02	4.02	two minutes past four† *ou* four oh two
4 h 05	4.05	five past four† *ou* four oh five
4 h 10	4.10	ten past four *ou* four ten
quatre heures et quart	4.15	a quarter past four
4 h 15	4.15	four fifteen
4 h 20	4.20	twenty past four *ou* four twenty
4 h 23	4.23	twenty-three minutes past four *ou* four twenty-three
4 h 25	4.25	twenty-five past four *ou* four twenty-five
quatre heures et demie	4.30	half past four
4 h 30	4.30	four thirty
4 h 37	4.37	four thirty-seven
cinq heures moins vingt	4.40	twenty to five
4 h 40	4.40	four forty
cinq heures moins le quart	4.45	a quarter to five
4 h 45	4.45	four forty-five
cinq heures moins dix	4.50	ten to five
4 h 50	4.50	four fifty
cinq heures moins cinq	4.55	five to five
4 h 55	4.55	four fifty-five
17 h 00	5 pm	five o'clock in the afternoon*
17 h 15	5.15 pm	a quarter past five *ou* five fifteen
17 h 23	5.23 pm	twenty-three minutes past five *ou* five twenty-three
18 h 00	6 pm	six o'clock *ou* six [piː em]
12 h	12.00	twelve o'clock
midi	12.00	noon *ou* twelve noon
minuit	12.00	midnight *ou* twelve midnight
zéro heure *ou* 00 h 00	00.00	midnight

quelle heure est-il?	=	what time is it?
il est quatre heures à ma montre	=	my watch says four o'clock
pouvez-vous me donner l'heure?	=	could you tell me the time?
il est quatre heures juste	=	it's exactly four o'clock
il est environ quatre heures	=	it's about four o'clock *ou* it's about four‡
il va être quatre heures	=	it's nearly four o'clock
il est presque quatre heures	=	it's almost four o'clock
il est à peine plus de quatre heures	=	it's just after four o'clock
il est quatre heures passées	=	it's gone four*

Quand?

à quelle heure cela est-il arrivé?	=	what time did it happen? *ou* what time did it happen at?
à quelle heure va-t-il venir?	=	what time will he come? *ou* what time will he come at?
c'est arrivé à quatre heures	=	it happened at four o'clock
il viendra à quatre heures	=	he's coming at four o'clock
à quatre heures dix	=	at ten past four
à quatre heures et demie	=	at half past four (*GB*), at half after four (*US*)
à quatre heures précises	=	at four o'clock exactly
soyez là à quatre heures pile	=	be there at four o'clock on the dot
aux environs de quatre heures	=	at about four o'clock
à quatre heures au plus tard	=	at four o'clock at the latest
un peu après quatre heures	=	shortly after four o'clock
il faut que ce soit prêt avant quatre heures	=	it must be ready by four
je serai là jusqu'à quatre heures	=	I'll be there until four
je ne serai pas là avant quatre heures	=	I won't be there until four
de 7 h à 9 h	=	from seven till nine
ouvert de 9 h à 5 h	=	open from nine to five
fermé entre treize et quatorze heures	=	closed from 1 to 2 pm
toutes les heures à l'heure juste	=	every hour on the hour
toutes les heures à dix	=	at ten past every hour

* *Lorsqu'il s'agit d'horaires de trains, d'avions etc, on peut écrire* 0400, *qui est prononcé* oh four hundred hours, *de même* sixteen hundred hours, twenty-four hundred hours *etc.*

† *Le mot* minutes *ne peut être omis qu'avec les multiples de 5.*

‡ *Dans la conversation,* o'clock *est souvent omis.*

encore ~ que tu sois en vie! at least you're alive!; **c'est** or **il est ~ qu'il soit venu** it's lucky he came; **'il a réussi!'—'encore ~!'** 'he succeeded!'—'just as well!'; **être l'~ propriétaire de...** to be the proud owner of...; **5** (réussi) [*combinaison, idée*] happy; [*proportions*] pleasing; [*formulation*] happy, felicitous sout; **rouge et orange, ce n'est pas très ~** red with orange, that's not a very happy combination; **ce n'est pas très ~ comme choix de mots** it's an unfortunate ou unhappy choice of words.

■ **l'heureuse élue** (en amour) the lucky lady; (à un jeu) the lucky winner; **l'~ élu** (en amour) the lucky man; (à un jeu) the lucky winner; **les ~ élus** the happy ou chosen few; **~ événement** happy event; **attendre un ~ événement** to be expecting a baby.

IDIOMES **être ~ comme un roi** or **un pape** to be happy as a lark ou as Larry; **tu vas faire un ~/des ~** you will make somebody happy/some people happy; **~ au jeu, malheureux en amour** Prov lucky at cards, unlucky in love Prov; **pour vivre ~, vivons cachés** Prov happy are they who value their privacy.

heuristique /øʀistik/ **I** *adj* [*approche, méthode, solution*] heuristic.

II *nf* **1** (ensemble de règles) heuristics (+ *v sg*); **2** (procédure) heuristic.

heurt /ˈœʀ/ *nm* **1** (friction) (différend) conflict; (accrochage) clash; **faire qch sans ~** to do sth smoothly; **leur relation ne va pas sans ~s** their relationship has its ups and downs; **2** (contraste) clash.

heurté, ~e /ˈœʀte/ **I** *pp* ▶ **heurter**.

II *pp adj* [*style, rythme*] jerky, uneven; [*sons, couleurs, tons*] clashing.

heurter /ˈœʀte/ [1] **I** *vtr* **1** (cogner contre) [*objet*] to hit, strike; [*personne*] to collide with [*personne, véhicule*]; to bump into [*objet, personne à l'arrêt*]; **la voiture a heurté un piéton** the car hit ou struck a pedestrian; **la bicyclette a heurté le bord du trottoir** the bicycle hit the kerb GB ou curb US; **sa tête heurta le mur** his head hit ou struck the wall; **~ qn avec qch** to knock sb with sth; **~ qch avec qch** to knock against sth with sth; **il a heurté la table avec sa valise** he knocked against the table with his suitcase; **2** (cogner) **~ qch avec** or **contre qch** to knock sth against sth; **3** (offenser) to offend [*personne, nation, bonne conscience*]; to go against [*convenances*]; to hurt [*sentiment*]; **~ l'opinion publique** [*action*] to run counter to public opinion; [*personne*] to conflict with public opinion; **~ qn de front** to clash with sb head-on.

II *vi* **~ contre** to strike; **sa tête heurta contre le mur** his head struck the wall.

III se heurter *vpr* **1** (se cogner) [*véhicules, personnes*] to collide; [*verres, tasses*] to bang ou knock against each other; **les idées se heurtaient dans sa tête** ideas were jostling ou whirling about in his head; **se ~ contre** or **à qn/qch** to bump into sb/sth; **2** (rencontrer) **se ~ à** to come up against [*préjugé, crainte, problème*]; **se ~ à un refus** to come up against a refusal; **3** (s'affronter) [*idées, couleurs*] to clash ou conflict (**à** with); [*personne*] to clash (**à** with).

heurtoir /ˈœʀtwaʀ/ *nm* **1** (marteau de porte) (door) knocker; **2** Rail buffers.

hévéa /evea/ *nm* rubber tree, hevea spéc.

hexadécimal, ~e, *mpl* **-aux** /ɛgzadesimal, o/ **I** *adj* hexadecimal.

II *nm* Ordinat hexadecimal code.

hexaèdre /ɛgzaɛdʀ/ **I** *adj* hexahedral.

II *nm* hexahedron.

hexaédrique /ɛgzaedʀik/ *adj* hexahedral.

hexagonal, ~e, *mpl* **-aux** /ɛgzagɔnal, o/ *adj* **1** Math hexagonal; **2**° (français) journ French.

hexagone /ɛgzagɔn/ *nm* **1** Math hexagon; **2**° (France métropolitaine) journ **l'Hexagone** France.

hexamètre /ɛgzamɛtʀ/ **I** *adj* hexametric.

II *nm* hexameter.

hiatale /ˈjatal/ *adj f* Méd **hernie ~** hiatus hernia.

hiatus /ˈjatys/ *nm* **1** Anat, Phon hiatus; **2** (décalage) discrepancy (**entre** between).

hibernal, ~e, *mpl* **-aux** /ibɛʀnal, o/ *adj* **1** Zool [*sommeil*] winter (*épith*); **2** Bot [*floraison, germination*] winter (*épith*), hibernal spéc.

hibernation /ibɛʀnasjɔ̃/ *nf* Biol, Zool hibernation; **être en ~** to be in hibernation.

■ **~ artificielle** Méd induced hypothermia.

hiberner /ibɛʀne/ [1] *vi* to hibernate.

hibiscus /ibiskys/ *nm* hibiscus.

hibou, *pl* **~x** /ˈibu/ *nm* owl.

hic° /ˈik/ *nm* snag; **voilà le ~, c'est bien là le ~** there's the snag.

hic et nunc /ˈikɛtnunk/ *loc adv* immediately.

hickory /ˈikɔʀi/ *nm* hickory.

hideur /ˈidœʀ/ *nf* hideousness.

hideusement /ˈidøzmɑ̃/ *adv* hideously.

hideux, -euse /ˈidø, øz/ *adj* hideous.

hier /jɛʀ/ *adv* yesterday; **~ après-midi/matin** yesterday afternoon/morning; **~ (au) soir** last night, yesterday evening; **toute la journée d'~** all day yesterday; **~ encore, il me disait** only yesterday, he

was saying to me; **il y a eu une semaine ~** a week ago yesterday; **je m'en souviens comme si c'était ~** I remember it as if it was yesterday; **l'ennemi d'~ est devenu l'allié d'aujourd'hui** yesterday's enemy has become the ally of today; **le Paris d'~** the Paris of yesterday; **chansons d'~ et d'aujourd'hui** songs of yesterday and today; **ce problème ne date pas d'~** this problem is nothing new.
IDIOMES **je ne suis pas né d'~** I wasn't born yesterday.

hiérarchie /ˈjeʀaʀʃi/ *nf* hierarchy.

hiérarchique /ˈjeʀaʀʃik/ *adj* [*organisation, système*] hierarchical; **mon supérieur ~** my immediate superior; **mes supérieurs ~s** my superiors; **par la voie ~** through the correct channels.

hiérarchiquement /ˈjeʀaʀʃikmɑ̃/ *adv* hierarchically.

hiérarchisation /ˈjeʀaʀʃizasjɔ̃/ *nf* (action) organization into a hierarchy; (système) hierarchical system.

hiérarchiser /ˈjeʀaʀʃize/ [1] *vtr* to organize [sth] into a hierarchy [*structure, système*]; to prioritize [*tâches*]; **~ les salaires** to establish a wages hierarchy.

hiératique /jeʀatik/ *adj* hieratic.

hiéroglyphe /ˈjeʀɔglif/ *nm* **1** (caractère) hieroglyph; **2** (système) **les ~s** hieroglyphics (+ *v sg*).

hiéroglyphique /ˈjeʀɔglifik/ *adj* hieroglyphic.

hi-fi /ˈifi/ **I** *adj inv* hi-fi; **une chaîne ~** a hi-fi system.
II *nf inv* **la ~** hi-fi equipment.

Highlands ▶ **692** *nprm* **les ~** the Highlands.

hi-han /ˈiɑ̃/ *nm* (*also onomat*) heehaw.

hi-hi /ˈii/ *excl* **1** (rire) tee-hee!; **2** (pleurs) boohoo!

hilarant, **~e** /ilaʀɑ̃, ɑ̃t/ *adj* hilarious; **gaz ~** laughing gas.

hilare /ilaʀ/ *adj* **être ~** to be laughing; **un visage ~** a merry face.

hilarité /ilaʀite/ *nf* mirth, hilarity; **déchaîner** or **déclencher l'~ générale** to cause great mirth.

hile /ˈil/ *nm* **1** Bot hilum; **2** Anat hilus.

Himalaya /imalaja/ ▶ **692** *nm* **l'~** the Himalayas (*pl*); **dans l'~** in the Himalayas; **les forêts/montagnes de l'~** the Himalayan forests/mountains.

himalayen, **-enne** /imalajɛ̃, ɛn/ *adj* Himalayan.

hindi /ˈindi/ ▶ **462** *adj, nm* Hindi.

hindou, **~e** /ɛ̃du/ *adj, nm,f* Hindu.

hindouisme /ɛ̃duism/ *nm* Hinduism.

hindouiste /ɛ̃duist/ *adj, nmf* Hindu.

hindoustani /ɛ̃dustani/ ▶ **462** *nm* Hindustani.

hip /ip/ ▶ **hourra**.

hippie /ˈipi/ *adj, nmf* hippie.

hippique /ipik/ *adj* [*manifestation, centre, sport*] equestrian; **concours ~** showjumping event GB, horse show US; **club** or **cercle ~** riding school; **journaliste ~** racing journalist.

hippisme /ipism/ *nm* equestrianism.

hippocampe /ipɔkɑ̃p/ *nm* **1** Zool sea horse, hippocampus spéc; **2** Anat, Mythol hippocampus.

Hippocrate /ipɔkʀat/ *npr* Hippocrates; **le serment d'~** the Hippocratic oath.

hippodrome /ipɔdʀom/ *nm* **1** gén racecourse GB, racetrack US; **2** Antiq hippodrome.

hippogriffe /ipɔgʀif/ *nm* hippogriff.

hippomobile /ipɔmɔbil/ *adj* horse-drawn.

hippophagique /ipɔfaʒik/ *adj* **boucherie ~** horsemeat butcher's.

hippopotame /ipɔpɔtam/ *nm* hippopotamus.

hippy, *pl* **hippies** /ˈipi/ *adj, nmf* hippie.

hirondelle /iʀɔ̃dɛl/ *nf* **1** Zool swallow; **2**○ (agent de police) policeman on a bicycle.
■ **~ de cheminée** common swallow GB, barn swallow US; **~ de fenêtre** house martin; **~ de mer** (common) tern; **~ de rivage** sand martin.
IDIOMES **une ~ ne fait pas le printemps** Prov one swallow doesn't make a summer.

hirsute /ˈiʀsyt/ *adj* **1** (peu soigné) [*personne, apparence*] dishevelled[GB], tousled; [*cheveux*] unkempt, tousled; [*barbe*] unkempt, shaggy; **2** Bot, Zool [*animaux, plantes*] hirsute.

hispanique /ispanik/ ▶ **462** *adj, nmf* Hispanic.

hispanisant, **~e** /ispanizɑ̃, ɑ̃t/ *nm,f* Hispanicist.

hispanisme /ispanism/ *nm* Hispanicism.

hispaniste /ispanist/ *nmf* Hispanicist.

hispano-américain, **~e**, *mpl* **~s** /ispanoameʀikɛ̃, ɛn/ ▶ **462** *adj* Hispanic-American, Spanish-American.

hispano-arabe, *pl* **~s** /ispanoaʀab/ *adj* Hispano-Arab.

hispanophone /ispanofɔn/ **I** *adj* [*pays, groupe, personne*] Spanish-speaking.
II *nmf* Spanish speaker.

hisse /ˈis/ *excl* **oh ~!** heave-ho!

hisser /ˈise/ [1] **I** *vtr* **1** (faire monter) to hoist [*charge, piano*]; to hoist [sb] (up) [*personne*]; to hoist, to run up [*voile, drapeau*]; **2** fig **~ qn à la tête/au rang/au niveau de** to push sb to the head/to the rank/to the level of.
II se hisser *vpr* **1** (monter avec effort) to heave oneself up, to haul oneself up; **se ~ sur un mur** to heave or haul oneself up onto a wall; **2** fig (parvenir) to pull oneself up (**jusqu'à** to (the level of)).

histamine /istamin/ *nf* histamine.

histaminique /istaminik/ *adj* histaminic.

histoire /istwaʀ/ *nf* **1** (discipline) history; **aimer/enseigner/étudier l'~** to like/teach/study history; **élève qui n'est pas bon en ~** pupil who is bad at history; **l'~ de France/Chine** French/Chinese history; **l'~ de l'art/de la littérature** the history of art/of literature; **entrer dans** or **marquer l'~** to go down in history; **un lieu chargé d'~** a place steeped in history; **l'~ jugera** or **se fera juge** posterity will be the judge; **c'est de l'~ ancienne** (c'est sans intérêt) that's ancient history; (mieux vaut l'oublier) that was a long time ago; **la petite ~ veut que**... it is said that...; **pour la petite ~**... history has it that...; **2** (récit) story; **raconter une ~ de fantômes à qn** to tell sb a ghost story; **c'est l'~ d'une grande découverte** it's the story of a great discovery; **c'est toujours la même ~** fig it's always the same old story; **c'est une autre/une tout autre ~** it's another/quite another story; **tout ça, c'est des ~s**○! that's all fiction!; **une ~ à dormir debout** a tall story; **raconter des ~s** to tell fibs; **ne me raconte pas d'~s!** you're making it up!; **c'est une ~ de fous** (c'est incroyable) it's/it was absolutely crazy!; (sur les fous) it's a joke about mad people; ▶ **coudre**; **3** (aventure, affaire) **~ d'amour** love affair; **c'est sûrement une ~ d'argent/de fesses**○ there must be money/sex involved; **se disputer pour une ~ d'argent/de voiture/d'héritage** to fight over money/a car/an inheritance; **~ de famille** family matter; **le plus beau/drôle de l'~, c'est que**... the best/funniest part of it is that...; **il m'est arrivé une drôle d'~** a funny thing happened to me; **4** (difficulté, problème) **en voilà des ~s!** what a to-do!, what a fuss!; **elle fait toujours des ~s** she's always making a fuss; **il n'y a pas de quoi en faire une ~** there's no need to get worked up about it; **il nous a fait toute une ~ pour un carreau cassé** he went on○ at us in the most ridiculous way about a broken window; **c'est une femme à ~s** she's a troublemaker; **un locataire/voisin sans ~s** a perfectly good tenant/neighbour[GB]; **un brave type sans ~s** a nice straightforward chap GB, a regular guy US; **une vie sans ~s** an uneventful life; **je ne veux pas d'~s avec le propriétaire** I don't want any trouble with the landlord; **il faut toujours qu'il s'attire des ~s** he's always getting into trouble; **ça va faire des ~s avec elle si**... she'll be upset if...; **ça a été toute une ~ pour faire** it was a terrible job doing; **chercher des ~s à qn** to go on at sb; **au travail, et pas d'~s**○! get on with it, no messing about○!; **5**○ **~ de faire** just to do; **prends quelques jours de repos, ~ de te changer les idées** take a few days' rest, just to have a break from everything; **si je l'ai critiquée, c'était ~ de voir sa réaction** I only criticized her to see how she would take it; **~ de rire** or **s'amuser** just for fun.
■ **~ naturelle** Sci natural history; **~s de brigands** cock and bull stories.

histologie /istɔlɔʒi/ *nf* histology.

histologique /istɔlɔʒik/ *adj* histological.

historié, **~e** /istɔʀje/ *adj* Art historiated.

historien, **-ienne** /istɔʀjɛ̃, ɛn/ ▶ **510** *nm,f* historian; **~ d'art** art historian; **se faire l'~ de qch** to give a historical account of sth.

historiette /istɔʀjɛt/ *nf* little story.

historiographe /istɔʀjɔgʀaf/ *nmf* historiographer.

historiographie /istɔʀjɔgʀafi/ *nf* historiography.

historique /istɔʀik/ **I** *adj* **1** (relatif au passé) historical; **2** (important) [*fait, accord, discours, personnage, journée*] historic; **3** Ling **passé ~** past historic; **présent ~** historic present.
II *nm* **faire l'~ du cinéma/d'un mot** to trace the history of the cinema/of a word; **faire l'~ d'une institution** to tell the story of an institution.

historiquement /istɔʀikmɑ̃/ *adv* historically.

histrion /istʀijɔ̃/ *nm* **1** (mauvais acteur) ham actor; **2** Antiq (acteur comique) comic actor, histrion sout.

hitlérien, **-ienne** /itleʀjɛ̃, ɛn/ **I** *adj* Hitlerian.
II *nm,f* Hitlerite.

hitlérisme /itleʀism/ *nm* Hitlerism.

hit-parade, *pl* **~s** /ˈitpaʀad/ *nm* charts (*pl*); **premier au ~** top of the charts.

hittite /ˈitit/ ▶ **462** *adj, nm* Hittite.

Hittite /ˈitit/ *nmf* Hittite.

hiver /ivɛʀ/ ▶ **738** *nm* **1** (saison) winter; **en ~** in winter, in the wintertime; **~ rude/précoce** hard/early winter; **les longues soirées d'~** the long winter evenings; **au cœur de l'~, au plus fort de l'~** in the depths of winter; **été comme ~** in summer and winter alike, all year round; **il ne passera pas l'~** he won't last through the winter; **2** (année) liter winter; **il a eu 60 ~s** he has seen sixty winters littér.

hivernage /ivɛʀnaʒ/ *nm* **1** (de bétail) wintering; **2** (de navires) over wintering; **3** (saison des pluies) rainy season.

hivernal, **~e**, *mpl* **-aux** /ivɛʀnal, o/ **I** *adj* **1** (d'hiver) winter (*épith*), hibernal spéc; **2** (comme en hiver) [*jour, température*] wintry.
II hivernale *nf* (course de montagne) winter race, winter ascent.

hiverner /ivɛʀne/ [1] **I** *vtr* Agric to winter [*bétail*].
II *vi* (passer l'hiver) [*animaux, bateaux*] to winter; [*personnes*] to spend the winter.

HLM /aʃɛlɛm/ *nm* ou *f*: *abbr* ▶ **habitation**.

ho /ˈo/ *excl* hey (there)!

hobereau, *pl* **~x** /ˈɔbʀo/ *nm* **1** (gentilhomme) country squire; **2** (faucon) hobby.

hochement /ˈɔʃmɑ̃/ *nm* **~ (de tête)** (de haut en bas) nod; (de droite à gauche) shake of the head.

hochequeue /ˈɔʃkø/ *nm* wagtail.

hocher /ˈɔʃe/ [1] *vtr* **~ la tête** (de haut en

bas) to nod; (de droite à gauche) to shake one's head.

hochet /ˈɔʃɛ/ *nm* rattle.

hockey /ˈɔkɛ/ ▶449 *nm* **~ (sur glace)** ice hockey; **~ sur gazon** hockey GB, field hockey US; **jouer au ~** to play hockey.

hockeyeur, **-euse** /ˈɔkɛjœʀ, øz/ *nm,f* hockey player.

hoirie /waʀi/ *nf* **avancement d'~** Jur advancement.

holà /ˈɔla/ *excl* **1** (pour appeler) hey (there)!; **2** (pour arrêter un animal) whoa!

IDIOMES **mettre le ~ à qch** to put an end ou a stop to sth.

holding /ˈɔldiŋ/ *nm ou f* holding company.

hold-up, *pl* **~** ou **~s** /ˈɔldœp/ *nm* hold-up **(de qch** at sth); **commettre un ~** to stage a hold-up.

holistique /ɔlistik/ *adj* holistic.

hollandais, **~e** /ˈɔlɑ̃dɛ, ɛz/ ▶462 I *adj* Dutch.

II *nm* Ling Dutch.

III **hollandaise** *nf* Agric Friesian (cow).

Hollandais, **~e** /ˈɔlɑ̃dɛ, ɛz/ *nm,f* Dutchman/Dutchwoman; **les ~** the Dutch.

hollande /ˈɔlɑ̃d/ *nm* Culin Dutch cheese.

Hollande /ˈɔlɑ̃d/ ▶692 *nprf* Holland.

hollywoodien, **-ienne** /ˈɔliwudjɛ̃, ɛn/ *adj* Hollywood (*épith*); **un film dans le style ~** a Hollywood-style film.

holocauste /ɔlɔkost/ *nm* **1** Relig holocaust, burned offering; **2** fig (total) sacrifice; **3** (massacre) holocaust.

hologramme /ɔlɔgʀam/ *nm* hologram.

holographie /ɔlɔgʀafi/ *nf* holography.

holophrastique /ɔlɔfʀastik/ *adj* holophrastic.

homard /ˈɔmaʀ/ *nm* lobster.

IDIOMES **rouge comme un ~** as red as a beetroot.

homélie /ɔmeli/ *nf* homily.

homéopathe /ɔmeɔpat/ ▶510 *nmf* homeopath; **médecin ~** homeopath.

homéopathie /ɔmeɔpati/ *nf* homeopathy.

homéopathique /ɔmeɔpatik/ *adj* [*traitement, préparation, pharmacie*] homeopathic; **à doses ~s** fig in small doses.

Homère /ɔmɛʀ/ *npr* Homer.

homérique /ɔmeʀik/ *adj* **1** Littérat Homeric, Homerian; **2** (épique) epic, Homeric.

homicide /ɔmisid/ I *adj* [*folie, geste*] homicidal; [*intentions*] homicidal, murderous.

II *nmf* (personne) homicide.

III *nm* (crime) homicide.

■ **~ par imprudence** Jur unintentional manslaughter; **~ involontaire** = **~ par imprudence**; **~ avec préméditation** Jur murder with malice aforethought, premeditated murder; **~ volontaire** Jur intentional manslaughter.

hominidé /ɔminide/ *nm* hominid; **les ~s** Hominidae.

hominien /ɔminjɛ̃/ *nm* hominoid; **les ~s** Hominoidae.

hommage /ɔmaʒ/ I *nm* **1** (témoignage de respect) homage, tribute; **en ~ à qn** in homage ou tribute to sb; **rendre ~ à qn/qch** to pay tribute to sb/sth; **rendre ~ à Dieu** to pay homage to God; **c'est lui faire trop d'~ que de faire** it's making too much of him to do; **2** (don) **faire ~ de qch à qn** to present sb with sth; **'~ de l'auteur'** 'with the author's compliments'; **3** Hist homage.

II **hommages** *nmpl* **1** (salutations) respects; **présenter ses ~s** to pay one's respects (**à** to); **'mes ~s, Madame'** 'my respects'; **'mes ~s à votre femme'** 'give my regards to your wife'; **2** (compliments) compliments; **elle est sensible aux ~s** she is sensitive to compliments.

hommasse /ɔmas/ *adj* mannish.

homme /ɔm/ *nm* **1** Anthrop **l'~** man; **l'~ primitif/de Néanderthal** primitive/Neanderthal man; ▶**Dieu**; **2** (genre humain) **l'~** mankind; **l'avenir de l'~** the future of mankind; **3** (être humain) human being; **digne du nom d'~** fit to be called human; **la santé/les maladies de l'~** human health/diseases; **la société des ~s** human society; **trop d'~s sur la Terre** too many people on Earth; **un ~ à la mer!** Naut man overboard!; **comme un seul ~** as one; **4** (adulte de sexe masculin) man; **sois un ~** be a man; **un ~ fait** a grown man; **vélo/métier d'~** man's bicycle/job; **parler d'~ à ~** to speak man to man; **5** (sorte d'individu) **vieil/brave ~** old/good man; **~ de talent** man of talent; **~ de génie** (man of) genius; **l'~ de la réunification** the man who achieved reunification; **l'~ de la situation** the right man for the job; **c'est un ~ à fuir** he's a man to be avoided; **voilà ton ~** (que tu cherchais) that's your man; (qui convient) he's the man for you; **être l'~ de confiance de qn** to be sb's right-hand man; **il n'est pas ~ à se venger** he's not the type of man to want revenge; **l'~ du jour** the man of the moment; **6**○ (mari, amant) man○; **c'est mon ~** he's my man○.

■ **~ d'action** man of action; **~ d'affaires** businessman; **~ d'armes** man-at-arms; **~ de l'art** gén expert; (médecin) doctor; **~ de barre** Naut helmsman; **~ de bien** philanthropist; **~ des bois** Anthrop wild man; Zool† orang-utang; **~ des cavernes** caveman; **l'~ des cavernes était un chasseur** the cavemen were hunters; **~ d'Église** man of the cloth; **~ d'épée** Mil soldier; **~ d'équipage** Naut crewman; **avec 10 ~s d'équipage** with a crew of 10; **~ d'esprit** wit; **~ d'État** Pol statesman; **~ d'expérience** man of experience; **~ à femmes** womanizer; **~ fort** Pol key man; **~ au foyer** Sociol house-husband; **~ d'honneur** man of honour[GB]; **~ de journée** Sociol day labourer[GB]; **~ de lettres** man of letters; **~ de loi** lawyer; **~ de main** hired hand; **~ de ménage** (male) cleaner; **~ de mer** seaman; **~ du monde** gentleman; **~ de l'ombre** behind-the-scenes operator; **~ de paille** front, straw man US; **~ de parole** man of his word; **~ de peine** labourer[GB]; **~ de peu** contemptible individual; **~ du peuple** man of the people; **~ de plume** writer; **~ politique** Pol politician; **~ de presse** Presse pressman; **~ de qualité**† gentleman; **~ de robe** lawyer; **l'~ de la rue** the man in the street; **~ de science** scientist; **~ de terrain** man with practical experience; Pol grass-roots politician; **~ à tout faire** handyman; **~ de troupe** Mil private; **~s en blanc** journ surgeons.

IDIOMES **un ~ averti en vaut deux** Prov forewarned is forearmed.

homme-grenouille, *pl* **hommes-grenouilles** /ɔmgʀənuj/ *nm* frogman.

homme-orchestre, *pl* **hommes-orchestres** /ɔmɔʀkɛstʀ/ *nm* lit, fig one-man band.

homme-sandwich, *pl* **hommes-sandwichs** /ɔmsɑ̃dwitʃ/ *nm* sandwich man.

homo○ /omo/ *adj, nmf* homosexual.

homogène /ɔmɔʒɛn/ *adj* **1** (uniforme) [*groupe, ensemble, mélange*] homogeneous; **2** (cohérent) [*équipe, gouvernement*] united, harmonious; [*base*] consistent.

homogénéisation /ɔmɔʒeneizasjɔ̃/ *nf* homogenization.

homogénéiser /ɔmɔʒeneize/ [1] *vtr* to homogenize [*substance, société, ensemble*].

homogénéité /ɔmɔʒeneite/ *nf* (de substance) homogeneity; (de gouvernement, d'équipe) unity, homogeneity.

homographe /ɔmɔgʀaf/ I *adj* [*mots*] homographic.

II *nm* homograph.

homologation /ɔmɔlɔgasjɔ̃/ *nf* **1** Admin (de produit, d'appareil) approval; **2** Sport (de performance, record) ratification, official recognition; **3** Jur homologation fml, approval; **~ de testament** Jur probate of will.

homologie /ɔmɔlɔʒi/ *nf* **1** gén similarity, homology; **2** Chimie, Math homology.

homologue /ɔmɔlɔg/ I *adj* **1** gén [*grades, titres*] equivalent, homologous; **2** Sci, Math [*éléments, angles, membres*] homologous.

II *nmf* **1** (personne) counterpart, opposite number; **le ministre français et son ~ britannique** the French minister and his/her British counterpart ou his/her opposite number in Britain; **2** Chimie (composé) homologue[GB].

homologuer /ɔmɔlɔge/ [1] *vtr* **1** Admin (déclarer conforme) to approve, to homologate sout [*produit, appareil*]; **2** Sport (enregistrer) to ratify, recognize officially [*record, performance*]; **3** Jur (valider) to confirm [*acte, contrat*]; to grant probate of [*testament*]; to approve, to authorize [*tarif*].

homonyme /ɔmɔnim/ I *adj* Ling homonymous; **dans le film ~** in the film of the same name.

II *nm* **1** Ling homonym; **2** (personne) namesake.

homonymie /ɔmɔnimi/ *nf* Ling homonymy.

homonymique /ɔmɔnimik/ *adj* homonymic.

homophone /ɔmɔfɔn/ I *adj* **1** Ling homophonous; **2** Mus homophonic.

II *nm* Ling homophone.

homophonie /ɔmɔfɔni/ *nf* Ling, Mus homophony.

homosexualité /omɔsɛksɥalite/ *nf* homosexuality.

homosexuel, **~elle** /omɔsɛksɥɛl/ *adj, nm,f* homosexual.

homozygote /omɔzigɔt/ I *adj* homozygous.

II *nmf* homozygote.

homuncule /ɔmɔ̃kyl/ *nm* homunculus.

Honduras /ˈɔ̃dyʀas/ ▶321 *nprm* Honduras; **le ~ britannique** Hist British Honduras.

hondurien, **-ienne** /ˈɔ̃dyʀjɛ̃, ɛn/ ▶537 *adj* Honduran.

Hondurien, **-ienne** /ˈɔ̃dyʀjɛ̃, ɛn/ ▶537 *nm,f* Honduran.

Hongkong /ˈɔ̃ŋkɔ̃ŋ/ *npr* Hong Kong.

hongre /ˈɔ̃gʀ/ I *adj* gelded.

II *nm* gelding.

Hongrie /ˈɔ̃gʀi/ ▶321 *nprf* Hungary.

hongrois, **~e** /ˈɔ̃gʀwa, az/ I ▶537 *adj* Hungarian.

II ▶462 *nm* Ling Hungarian.

Hongrois, **~e** /ˈɔ̃gʀwa, az/ ▶537 *nm,f* Hungarian.

honnête /ɔnɛt/ *adj* **1** (intègre) [*personne*] honest; [*produit, portrait, réponse*] honest; [*élections*] fair; **2** (honorable) [*personne*] decent; [*vie*] respectable; [*intentions, moyens*] honest; [*intention*] honourable[GB]; **les ~s gens** decent people; **il s'agit d'une affaire ~** it's all above board; **c'est une proposition ~** it's a genuine offer; **3** (juste) [*arbitre, prix, marché*] fair; **4** (moyen) [*travail, salaire, repas*] reasonable; [*résultat*] fair; **5**† (poli) [*personne*] civil; [*manière*] courteous.

■ **~ femme**† respectable woman; **~ homme**† gentleman.

honnêtement /ɔnɛtmɑ̃/ *adv* **1** (avec probité) [*gérer, dire*] honestly; [*répondre*] frankly; [*agir, se conduire*] properly, honourably[GB]; [*juger*] fairly; [*reconnaître*] freely; **gagner sa vie ~** to earn an honest living; **~, tu as tort** to be quite frank, you are wrong; **réponds-moi ~** will you give me a straight answer?; **~, tu les crois?** do you really believe them?; **2** (convenablement) [*rétribuer*] fairly; **gagner ~ sa vie** to earn a decent living; **s'acquitter ~ d'une tâche** to do a decent job; **travail ~ payé** reasonably well-paid job; **3** (avec courtoisie) courteously.

honnêteté /ɔnɛtte/ *nf* **1** (probité, franchise) honesty; **avec ~** honestly; **être d'une parfaite ~** to be scrupulously honest;

avoir l'~ de faire to be honest enough to do; **2†** (vertu) virtue; (décence, pudeur) decency.

honneur /ɔnœʀ/ **I** *nm* **1** (fierté) honour[GB] ¢; **sens de l'~** sense of honour[GB]; **homme d'~** man of honour[GB]; **l'~ est sauf** my/our etc honour[GB] is safe; **porter atteinte à/laver l'~ de qn** to cast a slur on/to avenge sb's honour[GB]; **mettre son ~ en jeu** to put one's honour[GB] at stake; **mettre** or **se faire un point d'~ à faire** to make it a point of honour[GB] to do; **promettre sur l'~** to promise on one's honour[GB]; **s'être engagé sur l'~ à faire** to be honour[GB] bound to do; **sauver l'~ de qn** to uphold the honour[GB] of sb; **l'~ national** national pride; **sauver l'~** to save face; **faire appel à l'~ de qn** to appeal to sb's sense of honour[GB]; **faire ~ à sa parole/ses engagements** to honour[GB] one's word/one's commitments; **avec ~** [*servir*] honourably[GB]; **dans l'~** [*capituler, se réconcilier*] honourably[GB]; **jouer pour l'~** to play for the love of it; **combattre pour l'~** to fight as a matter of honour[GB]; **être l'~ de sa famille/son école** [*personne*] to be a credit to one's family/one's school; **2** (mérite) credit; **votre honnêteté vous fait ~** your honesty does you credit; **ces mots sont l'~ de leur auteur** these words do credit to their author; **c'est l'~ de qn d'avoir fait** it's to sb's credit that he/she etc did; **ce fut tout à leur ~ d'avoir fait** it was all credit to them that they did; **l'~ de la victoire revient à** credit for the victory is due to; **3** (privilège) honour[GB]; **avoir l'~ de faire** to have the honour[GB] of doing; **accorder/faire à qn l'~ de faire** to give/do sb the honour[GB] of doing ; **laisser à qn l'~ de faire** to let sb have the honour[GB] of doing; **c'est un ~ de faire** it's an honour[GB] to do; **c'est un grand ~ pour qn de faire** it's a great honour[GB] for sb to do; **se disputer l'~ de qch/de faire** to fight over the honour[GB] of sth/of doing; **à qui ai-je l'~?** fml to whom do I have the honour[GB] of speaking? sout; **~ au perdant!** loser goes first!; **à toi l'~!** you do the honours[GB]!; **vous me faites trop d'~** you flatter me; **j'ai l'~ de vous informer du fait que** I beg to inform you that; **j'ai l'~ de solliciter de votre bienveillance l'autorisation de faire** I would respectfully request permission to do; **d'~** [*escalier, cour*] main; ▸**seigneur**; **4** (célébration) **être (mis) à l'~** [*personne*] to be honoured[GB]; **mettre qn à l'~** to honour[GB] sb; **être à l'** or **en ~** [*chose*] to be in favour[GB]; **être remis à l'~** [*tradition, usage, discipline*] to regain favour[GB]; **remise à l'~** (de tradition, mot) renewed popularity; **faire** or **rendre ~ à qn** to honour[GB] sb; **faire ~ à un repas** to do justice to a meal; **~ à celui/ceux qui** all praise to him/those who; **en l'~ de qn** in sb's honour[GB]; **en l'~ de qch** in honour[GB] of sth; **en quel ~○?** iron any particular reason why?; **en quel ~ êtes-vous en retard?** any particular reason why you're late?; **5** Jeux (carte haute) honour[GB].

II honneurs *nmpl* (distinction) honours[GB]; **rechercher/refuser les ~s** to seek/shun honours[GB]; **avec les ~s (de la guerre)** [*s'en sortir, être éliminé, partir*] honourably[GB]; **avec (tous) les ~s dus à leur rang** with all the honour[GB] due to their rank; **être accueilli avec les ~s réservés aux chefs d'État** to be received with the ceremony reserved for heads of State; **rendre les ~s à** Mil (funèbres) to pay the last honours[GB] to; (militaires) to honour[GB]; **la richesse et les ~s** wealth and glory; **faire les ~s de la maison à qn** to show sb around the house, to do sb the honours[GB] of the house†; **avoir les ~s de la presse** [*personne, événement*] to be mentioned in the press.

■ **~s funèbres** Mil last honours[GB]; **~s militaires** Mil military honours[GB].

IDIOMES **en tout bien tout ~** (sans arrière-pensées) with no hidden motive; **il l'a invitée à dîner en tout bien tout ~** he invited her out to dinner with no ulterior motive; **il est venu prendre un verre, mais c'était en tout bien tout ~** he came round for a drink but that's all there was to it.

honnir /ˈɔniʀ/ [3] *vtr* liter to execrate; **être honni de qn** to be execrated by sb.

IDIOMES **honni soit qui mal y pense** (devise) honi soit qui mal y pense; gén evil unto him who evil thinks.

honorabilité /ɔnɔʀabilite/ *nf* integrity; **d'une parfaite ~** entirely honourable[GB].

honorable /ɔnɔʀabl/ *adj* **1** (respectable) [*personne, métier, reddition*] honourable[GB]; [*compagnie, marque*] venerable; **notre très ~ président** our most honourable[GB] president; **sortie ~** honourable[GB] way out; **2** (suffisant) [*classement, score*] creditable; [*moyens financiers, nombre, proportion*] sizable; [*salaire*] decent; **une très ~ douzième place** a very creditable twelfth place; **une contribution très ~** a very sizable contribution.

■ **~ correspondant** (agent secret) man; **notre ~ correspondant à la Havane** our man in Havana.

honorablement /ɔnɔʀabləmɑ̃/ *adv* **1** (de façon respectable) [*négocier, se retirer*] honourably[GB]; **se comporter très ~** to behave wholly honourably; **~ connu** [*famille*] highly respected; [*compagnie*] venerable; **2** (suffisamment) decently; **gagner ~ sa vie** to earn a decent living.

honoraire /ɔnɔʀɛʀ/ **I** *adj* [*membre, président*] honorary; **professeur ~** emeritus professor; **doyen ~** dean emeritus.

II honoraires *nmpl* (rétributions) fee (*sg*); **recevoir des ~s de mille francs** to be paid a fee of one thousand francs; **leurs ~s sont élevés** their fees are high; **note d'~s** bill.

honorer /ɔnɔʀe/ [1] **I** *vtr* **1** (rendre hommage) to honour[GB] [*Dieu, personne, équipe, mémoire*] (**de** with; **de faire** to do; **que** that); **~ qn de sa confiance** to honour[GB] sb with one's trust; **je suis très honoré d'être parmi vous** I feel very honoured[GB] to be among you; **(je suis) très honoré** I am most honoured[GB]; **je serais honoré de vous recevoir** I would be honoured[GB] by your visit; **2** (acquitter) to honour[GB] [*promesse, engagement, dette, échéance*]; **~ sa signature** to honour[GB] one's signature; **3** (procurer de la fierté à) [*personne*] to be a credit to [*pays, profession, parents*]; **vous honorez votre pays** you are a credit to your country; **4** (donner du mérite à) [*qualité*] to do [sb] credit [*personne*]; **votre courage vous honore** your bravery does you credit; **5†** fml, euph (posséder sexuellement) to be intimate with euph [*femme*].

II s'honorer *vpr* **1** (être fier) to be proud (**de qch** of sth; **de faire** of doing); **2** (s'attirer de la considération) to bring credit on oneself; **vous vous êtes honoré par votre choix** you brought credit on yourself by your choice.

honorifique /ɔnɔʀifik/ *adj* [*poste, distinction, présidence, diplôme*] honorary; **être nommé président à titre ~** to be appointed honorary president; **être nommé à titre ~** to be appointed on an honorary basis.

honoris causa /ɔnɔʀiskoza/ *loc adj* [*docteur*] honorary; **il est docteur ~ de l'université d'Oxford** he's an honorary doctor of the university of Oxford; **être nommé docteur ~** to be awarded an honorary doctorate.

honte /ˈɔ̃t/ *nf* **1** (gêne) shame; **rougir de ~** to blush with shame; **couvrir qn de ~** to cover sb with shame; **se couvrir de ~** to be mortified; **éprouver de la ~** to feel ashamed; **avoir ~ de ce qu'on a fait/d'avoir mal agi** to be ashamed of what one has done/of having acted badly; **avoir ~ de qn/qch** to be ashamed of sb/sth; **il n'y a pas de ~ à faire** there's nothing to be ashamed of in doing; **il devrait avoir ~ de son incompétence/d'exploiter les touristes** he ought to be ashamed of his incompetence/of exploiting tourists; **faire ~ à qn** to make sb ashamed; **tu me fais ~ avec ton chapeau** I'm ashamed to be seen with you wearing that hat; **sans ~, toute ~ bue** fml shamelessly; **à ma (grande) ~** to my (great) embarrassment; **j'ai cru mourir de ~!** I could have died of embarrassment!; **n'ayez pas ~ de poser des questions** don't be embarrassed about asking questions; **avouer qch sans ~** to acknowledge sth openly; **sans fausse ~** quite openly; **2** (discrédit) disgrace; **être** or **faire la ~ de qn/d'un métier** to be a disgrace to sb/to a profession; **jeter la ~ sur qn/qch** to bring disgrace upon sb/sth; **quelle ~!** what a disgrace!; **c'est une ~ de voir ça** it's disgraceful to see things like that; **~ à celui/ceux qui**... shame on him/those who...; **3** (scandale) disgrace.

honteusement /ˈɔ̃tøzmɑ̃/ *adv* (ignoblement) [*traiter, trahir*] shamefully; (sans honte) [*plagier, tricher*] shamelessly.

honteux, -euse /ˈɔ̃tø, øz/ *adj* **1** (déshonorant) [*conduite, secret*] disgraceful (**de faire** to do); **de honteuses manipulations électorales** disgraceful electoral manipulations; **il est ~ que le gouvernement se comporte ainsi** it's disgraceful that the government should behave in this way; **qu'y a-t-il de ~ à voter pour X?** what is there to be ashamed of in voting for X?; **2** (gêné) [*personne*] ashamed (**de qn/qch** of sb/sth).

hop /ˈɔp/ *excl* **1** (pour stimuler) **allez ~, saute!** come on, jump!; **allez ~, on y va!** come on then, let's go!; **allez ~, dehors!** off you go out of here!; **2** (pour action rapide) presto; **c'est facile, tu appuies là et ~, c'est fait!** it's easy, just press here and presto, it's done!

hôpital, *pl* **-aux** /ɔpital, o/ *nm* hospital; **~ de campagne** field hospital; **j'ai passé une semaine à l'~** I spent a week in hospital GB ou in the hospital US; **aller à l'~** [*patient*] to go to hospital; [*visiteur*] to go to the hospital.

■ **~ de jour** outpatient clinic.

IDIOMES **c'est l'~ qui se moque de la charité** it's the pot calling the kettle black.

hoquet /ˈɔkɛ/ *nm* hiccup; **avoir le ~** to have hiccups; **avoir un ~ de frayeur** to gulp with fright; **le moteur eut quelques ~s puis s'arrêta** the engine sputtered then stopped.

hoqueter /ˈɔkte/ [20] *vi* [*personne*] to hiccup; [*moteur*] to sputter; **~ de frayeur** to gulp with fright; **dit-elle en hoquetant** she hiccuped.

Horace /ˈɔʀas/ *npr* **1** (auteur) Horace; **2** (héros) Horatius; **les ~s et les Curiaces** the Horatii and the Curiatii.

horaire /ɔʀɛʀ/ **I** *adj* [*salaire, rendement, débit, tarif*] per hour; **une augmentation ~ de trois francs** a pay rise of three francs per hour; **tranche** or **plage ~** timeslot.

II *nm* **1** Transp (de train, bus) timetable GB, schedule US; (d'avion, de vols) schedule; **~ d'été/d'hiver** summer/winter timetable; **être en avance sur l'~** [*train, bus, car, avion*] to be ahead of schedule; **être en retard sur l'~** [*train, bus, car, avion*] to be running late; **obtenir les ~s de train par téléphone** to find out the train times by phone; **2** (emploi du temps) timetable, schedule; **les ~s de travail** working hours; **les ~s des cours** timetable of classes ou lessons; **avoir un ~ chargé** to have a busy timetable ou schedule; **les ~s libres** or **à la carte** flexitime.

horde /ˈɔʀd/ *nf* (de barbares, touristes) horde; (de chiens, loups) pack.

■ **~ primitive** Psych primal horde.

horion† /ˈɔʀjɔ̃/ *nm* blow; **distribuer des ~s** to hit out.

horizon /ɔʀizɔ̃/ *nm* **1** Astron horizon; **scruter l'~** to scan the horizon; **à l'~** [*être, apparaître*] on the horizon; [*disparaître,* *sombrer*] below the horizon; **l'~ est bouché** lit there are clouds on the horizon; fig the road ahead is not clear; **2** fig (avenir) outlook; **l'~ politique/économique est sombre** the political/economic outlook is gloomy; **des dangers/réformes se profilent à l'~** dangers/reforms are appearing on the horizon; **cet emploi m'ouvre de nouveaux ~s** this job opens up new perspectives for me; **à l'~ 2000** by the year 2000; **3** fig (univers) horizons (*pl*); **élargir son ~** to widen one's horizons; **son ~ intellectuel est limité** he has limited intellectual horizons; **changer d'~** to have a change of scene; **ils viennent d'~s très divers** they come from very varied backgrounds.

■ **~ artificiel** Aviat artificial horizon.

horizontal, **~e**, *mpl* **-aux** /ɔʀizɔ̃tal, o/ **I** *adj* horizontal.

II horizontale *nf* **1** Math(ligne) horizontal; **à l'~e** in a horizontal position; **2**○ (prostituée) prostitute.

horizontalement /ɔʀizɔ̃talmɑ̃/ *adv* horizontally.

horizontalité /ɔʀizɔ̃talite/ *nf* horizontality.

horloge /ɔʀlɔʒ/ *nf* clock; **avec la précision d'une ~** with the accuracy of a clock; **avoir la régularité d'une ~, être réglé comme une ~** to be as regular as clockwork.

■ **~ astronomique** Astron astronomical clock; **~ atomique** Phys atomic clock; **~ biologique** Biol biological clock; **~ interne** Biol internal clock; **~ murale** wall clock; **~ parlante** Télécom speaking clock GB, timeline US; **téléphoner à l'~ parlante** to ring the speaking clock GB, to call the time US.

horloger, **-ère** /ɔʀlɔʒe, ɛʀ/ **I** *adj* watchmaking (*épith*).

II ▶ **510**, *nm,f* watchmaker.

■ **~ bijoutier** jeweller[GB].

horlogerie /ɔʀlɔʒʀi/ ▶ **510** *nf* (industrie) watchmaking; (boutique) watchmaker's (shop); (produits) clocks and watches (*pl*); **pièce d'~** watch component.

■ **~ bijouterie** jeweller's shop GB, jewelry store US.

hormis /'ɔʀmi/ *prép* fml save sout, except (for).

hormonal, **~e**, *mpl* **-aux** /ɔʀmɔnal, o/ *adj* [*problème, activité, cycle*] hormonal; [*insuffisance, traitement*] hormone (*épith*); **mécanisme ~** endocrine system.

hormone /ɔʀmɔn/ *nf* hormone; **~ de croissance** growth hormone.

horodateur, **-trice** /ɔʀɔdatœʀ, tʀis/ **I** *adj* **horloge horodatrice** parking ticket machine.

II *nm* (de stationnement) parking ticket machine.

horoscope /ɔʀɔskɔp/ *nm* horoscope; **faire l'~ de qn** to cast sb's horoscope; **lire son ~** to read one's horoscope.

horreur /ɔʀœʀ/ *nf* **1** (atrocité) horror; **dans toute son ~** in all its horror; **les ~s de la guerre/commises dans les camps de concentration** the horrors of war/committed in concentration camps; **2** (parole méchante) awful thing; **dire des ~s de** or **sur qn** to say awful things about sb; **3** (épouvante) horror; **remplir qn d'~** to fill sb with horror; **éprouver de l'~ à la vue de** to feel horror at the sight of; **faire qch/se détourner avec ~** to do sth/to turn away in horror; **être glacé/muet d'~** to be frozen/dumb with horror; **être saisi d'~** to be horror-struck; **être une ~** [*personne, chose, œuvre*] to be horrible; **quelle ~!** how horrible!; **4** (aversion) loathing; **inspirer de l'~ à qn** to inspire loathing in sb; **avoir ~ de qn/qch, avoir qn/qch en ~** to loathe sb/sth; **avoir ~ de faire** to hate doing; **il a une sainte ~ du travail/de parler en public** he absolutely loathes work/speaking in public; **les chats ont ~ de l'eau** cats hate water; **j'ai ~ qu'on me dérange** I hate being disturbed; **la nature a ~ du vide** nature abhors a vacuum; **prendre qn en ~** to begin to loathe sb; **ton attitude me fait ~** your attitude horrifies me; **le poisson cru me fait ~** I find raw fish disgusting.

IDIOMES **c'est (vraiment) l'~**○ it's (really) the pits○.

horrible /ɔʀibl/ *adj* **1** (abominable) [*cri, spectacle, mort, maladie*] horrible; [*temps*] filthy; [*moment, séjour*] dreadful; [*meurtre, scène, vision*] horrific; [*douleur, bruit, tâche*] terrible; [*dessein, soupçon, pensée*] horrible; [*lettre, paroles, personne*] nasty; **il fait un froid ~** it's terribly cold; **2** (répugnant) [*goût, odeur, mélange*] revolting; [*créature, sorcière*] horrid; [*nourriture*] dreadful; **3** (laid) [*visage, objet, cicatrice*] hideous.

horriblement /ɔʀibləmɑ̃/ *adv* **1** (effroyablement) [*brûlé, mutilé, abîmé*] horribly; **2** (terriblement) [*dangereux, froid*] terribly.

horrifiant, **~e** /ɔʀifjɑ̃, ɑ̃t/ *adj* horrifying.

horrifier /ɔʀifje/ [2] *vtr* to horrify; **être horrifié** to be horrified (**par** by; **de faire** at doing).

horripilant, **~e** /ɔʀipilɑ̃, ɑ̃t/ *adj* exasperating; **il est d'une lenteur ~e** he's exasperatingly slow.

horripiler /ɔʀipile/ [1] *vtr* to exasperate, to drive [sb] up the wall○.

hors /'ɔʀ/

■ **Note** Lorsque *hors* et *hors de* sont suivis d'un nom sans article reportez-vous à ce nom. Ainsi *hors catégorie* est traité sous ***catégorie*** et *hors d'atteinte* sous ***atteinte***. Une expression telle que *se mettre hors la loi* figure sous ***loi***. *hors-la-loi* est une entrée à part.

– Les autres emplois de *hors* sont présentés dans l'article ci-dessous.

I *prép* liter apart from, save sout.

II hors de *loc prép* (dans l'espace) (position fixe) outside; (avec mouvement) out of; fig outside; **~ d'Allemagne/de la CEE** outside Germany/the EC; **il sauta ~ de son bain** he jumped out of his bath; **~ de l'histoire/des divisions politiques traditionnelles** outside History/the traditional political divide; **elle passe le plus de temps possible ~ de chez elle** she spends as much time as possible out of the house; **~ d'ici!** get out of here!; **~ de chez soi** away from home.

■ **~ tout** overall; **longueur ~ tout d'un édifice/wagon** overall length of a building/carriage.

IDIOMES **être ~ de soi** to be beside oneself; **il est arrivé en criant, ~ de lui** he arrived shouting, beside himself; **cela m'a mis ~ de moi** it infuriated me.

hors-bord /'ɔʀbɔʀ/ **I** *adj* [*moteur*] outboard.

II *nm inv* powerboat, speedboat; **faire du ~** to go powerboating ou speedboating.

hors-d'œuvre /'ɔʀdœvʀ/ *nm inv* **1** Culin starter, hors d'oeuvre; **en ~ nous avons des escargots, du pâté** as a starter we have snails, pâté; **'~ variés'** 'assorted hors d'oeuvres'; **2**○ fig foretaste; **la gifle n'était qu'un ~** the slap was just a foretaste ou just for starters○.

hors-jeu /'ɔʀʒø/ *nm inv* (**pour**) ~ for offside; **la règle du ~** the offside rule; **les Marseillais ont totalisé trois ~** Marseilles was offside three times.

hors-la-loi /'ɔʀlalwa/ *nm inv* outlaw.

hors-piste /'ɔʀpist/ *nm inv* off-piste skiing; **faire du ~** to go off-piste skiing.

hors-texte /'ɔʀtɛkst/ *nm inv* plate.

hortensia /ɔʀtɑ̃sja/ *nm* hydrangea.

horticole /ɔʀtikɔl/ *adj* horticultural.

horticulteur, **-trice** /ɔʀtikyltœʀ, tʀis/ ▶ **510** *nm,f* horticulturist.

horticulture /ɔʀtikyltyʀ/ *nf* horticulture.

hosanna /'ɔzana/ *nm* hosanna; **~ au plus haut des cieux** hosanna in the highest.

hospice /ɔspis/ *nm* **1** (asile) home; **finir à l'~** to end up in the poorhouse; **2**† Relig hospice†.

■ **~ de vieillards** old people's home.

hospitalier, **-ière** /ɔspitalje, ɛʀ/ **I** *adj* **1** Méd [*personnel, secteur*] hospital (*épith*); **centre ~** hospital; **2** (accueillant) [*atmosphère, lieu*] hospitable; **3** Relig [*ordre*] charitable; **sœur hospitalière** sister of mercy.

II *nm,f* Relig member of a charitable order; (de l'ordre de St Jean) hospitaller[GB].

hospitalisation /ɔspitalizasjɔ̃/ *nf* hospitalization.

■ **~ à domicile** Méd, Prot Soc home (medical) care.

hospitaliser /ɔspitalize/ [1] *vtr* to hospitalize; **se faire ~** to be hospitalized, to go into hospital GB ou into the hospital US; **être hospitalisé d'urgence** to be rushed to the hospital.

hospitalité /ɔspitalite/ *nf* hospitality; **offrir l'~** to offer hospitality (**à** to); **être connu pour son ~** to have a reputation for hospitality; **avoir le sens de l'~** to know how to treat one's guests; **demander l'~ à qn** to ask sb for shelter.

hospitalo-universitaire, *pl* **~s** /ɔspitaloynivɛʀsitɛʀ/ *adj* **centre ~** teaching hospital.

hostellerie /ɔstɛlʀi/ *nf* (country) inn.

hostie /ɔsti/ **I** *nf* Relig Host.

II○ *excl* C damn○!

hostile /ɔstil/ *adj* hostile (**à** to).

hostilement /ɔstilmɑ̃/ *adv* with hostility.

hostilité /ɔstilite/ *nf* hostility (**à** to; **à l'égard de, envers** to, toward, towards GB); **les ~s** Mil hostilities; **ouvrir/cesser/reprendre les ~s** to start/cease/resume hostilities.

hosto◑ /ɔsto/ *nm* hospital.

hôte /ot/ **I** *nm* **1** (personne qui invite) host; **2** (résident) (personne) occupant; (animal) inhabitant; **3** Biol host.

II *nmf* **1** (personne invitée) guest; **2** (d'appartement) occupant; (d'hôtel) guest.

■ **~ de marque** distinguished guest; **~ de passage** temporary guest; **~ payant** Tourisme paying guest.

hôtel /otɛl/ *nm* hotel; **~ de luxe/4 étoiles** luxury/4 star hotel; **~ borgne** seedy hotel; **descendre à l'~** to stay at a hotel; **vivre à l'~** to live in a hotel; **passer une nuit à l'~** to spend a night in a hotel.

■ **~ des impôts** tax office; **~ de la Monnaie** Admin (French) Mint; **~ particulier** Archit townhouse; **~ de passe** hotel used by prostitutes; **~ de tourisme** Tourisme tourist hotel; **~ des ventes** Comm saleroom; **~ de ville** Admin ≈ town hall.

hôtel-club, *pl* **hôtels-clubs** /otɛlklœb/ *nm* (hotel-based) holiday club.

hôtel-Dieu, *pl* **hôtels-Dieu** /otɛldjø/ *nm* main hospital.

hôtelier, **-ière** /otalje, ɛʀ/ ▶ **510** **I** *adj* [*groupe, industrie, chaîne*] hotel (*épith*); [*école, formation*] in hotel-management (*épith, après n*); **capacité hôtelière d'une région** total amount of hotel accommodation in an area.

II *nm,f* hotelkeeper.

hôtellerie /otɛlʀi/ *nf* **1** (profession) hotel business; **2** (établissement) (country) inn.

hôtel-restaurant, *pl* **hôtels-restaurants** /otɛlʀɛstɔʀɑ̃/ *nm* hotel-restaurant.

hôtesse /otɛs/ ▶ **510** *nf* **1** (professionnelle) (de société, magasin) receptionist; (d'exposition) hostess; (de train, bateau) stewardess; **2** (personne qui invite) hostess.

■ **~ d'accueil** receptionist; **~ de l'air** Aviat stewardess, flight attendant spéc; **~ au sol** Aviat ground attendant, ground hostess.

hotte /'ɔt/ *nf* **1** (de vendangeur) basket (*carried on the back*); **2** (de cheminée) hood; **3** (de cuisinière) hood GB, range hood US.

■ **~ aspirante** extractor hood GB, ventilator US; **la ~ du Père Noël** Father Christmas's sack GB, Santa Claus's sack US.

hottentot, **~e** /ˈɔtɑ̃to, ɔt/ *adj* Hottentot.

Hottentot, **~e** /ˈɔtɑ̃to, ɔt/ *nm,f* Hottentot.

hou /ˈu/ *excl* **1** (pour effrayer) boo!; **2** (pour appeler) hey!; **~, ~! tu viens?** hey! are you coming?; **3** (pour faire honte) tut-tut; **~, la vilaine!** oh, you/the naughty girl!

houblon /ˈublɔ̃/ *nm* hop **C**.

houblonnière /ˈublɔnjɛʀ/ *nf* hopfield.

houe /ˈu/ *nf* hoe.

houille /ˈuj/ *nf* (charbon) coal; **~ maigre/grasse** lean/bituminous coal.

■ **~ blanche** hydroelectric power; **~ bleue** tidal power; **~ incolore** wind power; **~ d'or** solar power; **~ rouge** geothermal power.

houiller, **-ère** /ˈuje, ɛʀ/ **I** *adj* [*gisement, industrie*] coal (*épith*); [*terrain*] coal-bearing; [*région*] coalmining.

II houillère *nf* **1** (dépôt) coalmine; **2** (exploitation) colliery.

houle /ˈul/ *nf* swell; **il y a de la ~** there's a swell; **la ~ est forte** there's a heavy swell.

houlette /ˈulɛt/ *nf* **1** (de berger) crook; **sous la ~ de** fig under the leadership of; **2** (de jardinier) trowel; **3†** (d'évêque) crozier.

houleux, **-euse** /ˈulø, øz/ *adj* **1** [*mer*] rough; **2** [*réunion, débat*] stormy.

houmous /ˈumus/ *nm* Culin houmous GB, hummus US.

houppe /ˈup/ *nf* **1** (de cheveux) tuft; (de fils) tassel; **2** (à poudrer) powder puff.

houppelande /ˈuplɑ̃d/ *nf* greatcoat.

houppette /ˈupɛt/ *nf* **1** (à poudrer) powder puff; **2** (de cheveux) little tuft (of hair).

hourra /ˈuʀa/ **I** *nm* (acclamation) cheer; **accueilli sous les ~s de la foule** greeted by the cheers of the crowd; **pousser des ~s** to cheer; **pousser un ~ de joie** to give a shout of joy.

II *excl* hurrah!; **hip hip hip ~!** hip hip hurrah!

houspiller /ˈuspije/ [1] *vtr* to scold; **se faire ~** to be scolded.

housse /ˈus/ *nf* gén cover; (de chaise, sofa) slipcover; (de siège de voiture) seat cover; (de vêtements) garment bag; (de machine à écrire) dust cover; **mettre qch sous (une) ~** to cover sth up; **mettre une ~ à** to slipcover [*chaise, sofa*].

■ **~ de couette** duvet cover, quilt cover.

houx /ˈu/ *nm* holly.

HS○ /ˈaʃɛs/ *adj* (*abbr* = **hors service**) [*machine, voiture*] on the blink○; [*personne*] knackered○ GB, shot○ US; **son travail l'a mis ~** his job has really knackered him GB, his job has tuckered○ him US.

HT 1 (*written abbr* = **hors taxes**) exclusive of tax; **2** (*written abbr* = **haute tension**) HV.

huard, **huart** /yaʀ/ *nm* C (palmipède) loon.

hublot /ˈyblo/ *nm* (de bateau) porthole; (d'avion) window; (de machine à laver) door.

huche /ˈyʃ/ *nf* (coffre) chest.

■ **~ à pain** bread bin.

hue /ˈy/ *excl* (pour cheval) gee up!; ▶ **dia**.

huées /ˈɥe/ *nfpl* booing **¢**; **partir sous les ~** to be booed off; **discours interrompu par des ~** speech interrupted by booing; **sous les ~ des spectateurs/de la foule** booed by the audience/the crowd.

huer /ˈɥe/ [1] **I** *vtr* to boo [*auteur, discours*]; **se faire ~** to be booed.

II *vi* [*hibou*] to hoot.

hugolien, **-ienne** /ˈygoljɛ̃, ɛn/ *adj*: *of (or in the manner of) Victor Hugo.*

huguenot, **~e** /ˈygno, ɔt/ *adj, nm,f* Huguenot.

huilage /ɥilaʒ/ *nm* Tech oiling, lubrication.

huile /ɥil/ *nf* **1** (substance) oil; **~ vierge/végétale** virgin/vegetable oil; **~ de première pression à froid** oil of the first pressing; **sardines à l'~** sardines in vegetable oil; **pommes à l'~** potato salad; **2** Art (tableau) oil painting; **ses ~s sont plus célèbres que ses aquarelles** his oil paintings ou oils are more famous than his watercolours[GB]; **3**○ (personnage important) big shot○, bigwig○.

■ **~ d'arachide** groundnut oil GB, peanut oil; **~ de cade** oil of cade; **~ de colza** rapeseed oil; **~ de coude** hum elbow grease; **~ essentielle** essential oil; **~ de foie de morue** cod liver oil; **~ de graissage** lubricating oil; **~ de lin** linseed oil; **~ de maïs** corn oil; **~ pour moteur** motor oil;**~ de noix** walnut oil; **~ d'olive** olive oil; **~ de palme** palm oil; **~ de paraffine** liquid paraffin; **~ de ricin** castor oil; **~ solaire** Cosmét suntan oil; **~ de table** cooking oil; **~ de tournesol** sunflower oil.

IDIOMES **tout/ça baigne dans l'~**○ everything/it is going smoothly; **jeter** or **verser de l'~ sur le feu** to add fuel to the fire; **mettre de l'~ dans les rouages** to oil the wheels.

huiler /ɥile/ [1] *vtr* to oil [*peau, mécanisme, poêle*]; **bien huilé** [*mécanisme, machine*] lit, fig well-oiled; [*reportage, scénario*] fig slick.

huilerie /ɥilʀi/ *nf* **1** (usine) oil mill; **2** (commerce) oil trade.

huileux, **-euse** /ɥilø, øz/ *adj* oily.

huilier /ɥilje/ *nm* (oil and vinegar) cruet.

huis /ˈɥi/ *nm* **1‡** door; **2** Jur **~ clos** closed hearing, hearing held in camera; **ordonner un ~ clos** (avant un procès) to order a hearing in camera; (pendant un procès) to clear the court; **demander/obtenir le ~ clos** to request/obtain a hearing in camera; **à ~ clos** Jur in camera; fig behind closed doors.

huisserie /ɥisʀi/ *nf* (de porte) doorframe; (de fenêtre) window frame; **les ~s de la maison** the door and window frames of the house.

huissier /ɥisje/ ▶ **510** *nm* **1** Jur **~ (de justice)** bailiff; **2** (portier) porter; (de tribunal) usher.

huit /ˈɥit, but before consonant ˈɥi/ ▶ **545**, **407**, **212** **I** *adj inv* eight; **~ jours** (semaine) a week; (précisément) eight days; **téléphone-moi dans ~ jours** phone GB ou call me in a week ou in a week's time; **je pars mardi en ~** I'm leaving a week on Tuesday; **donner ses ~ jours à qn** lit, fig to give sb a week's notice.

II *pron* eight.

III *nm inv* **1** (numéro) eight; **2** (trajectoire) **décrire un ~** to do a figure of eight.

huitain /ˈɥitɛ̃/ *nm* Littérat octave.

huitaine /ˈɥitɛn/ *nf* **1** (semaine) about a week; **dans une ~ (de jours)** in about a week; **sous ~** within a week; **remettre qch à ~** to postpone sth for a week; **2** (environ huit) about eight.

huitante /ˈɥitɑ̃t/ ▶ **545** *adj inv, pron* H eighty.

huitième /ˈɥitjɛm/ ▶ **545**, **212** **I** *adj* eighth.

II *nf* Scol *fourth year of primary school, age 9–10.*

■ **le ~ art** television; **~ de finale** Sport *round before the quarter finals.*

huître /ɥitʀ/ *nf* oyster.

■ **~ perlière** pearl oyster; **~ plate** flat oyster.

IDIOMES **se fermer comme une ~** to clam up.

huîtrier, **-ière** /ɥitʀije, ɛʀ/ **I** *adj* oyster (*épith*).

II *nm* (oiseau) oystercatcher.

III huîtrière *nf* (banc) oyster bed; (parc) oyster farm.

hulotte /ˈylɔt/ *nf* tawny owl.

hululement /ˈylylmɑ̃/ *nm* hooting **¢**.

hululer /ˈylyle/ [1] *vi* to hoot.

hum /ˈœm/ *excl* hm.

humain, **~e** /ymɛ̃, ɛn/ **I** *adj* **1** gén human; **c'est ~!** it's only human!; **sauver des vies ~es** to save lives; **pertes ~es** loss of life **¢**; **marée ~e** tide of humanity; **2** (clément) [*solution, régime*] humane; [*personne*] human, understanding.

II *nm* **1** (personne) human being; **2** (être terrestre) human; **3** Philos **l'~ et le divin** the human and the divine; **perdre le sens de l'~** to lose the human element.

IDIOMES **l'erreur est ~e** to err is human.

humainement /ymɛnmɑ̃/ *adv* **1** (pour l'être humain) [*possible, impossible*] humanly; **2** (sans cruauté) [*traiter, se comporter*] humanely.

humanisation /ymanizasjɔ̃/ *nf* (de prison, conditions de vie) humanization; (de politique, régime politique) softening.

humaniser /ymanize/ [1] **I** *vtr* to humanize [*prison, conditions de vie, régime politique*]; to make [sb/sth] more human [*personne, ville, procédure, politique*].

II s'humaniser *vpr* [*prison, procédure, personne*] to become more human.

humanisme /ymanism/ *nm* humanism.

humaniste /ymanist/ *adj, nmf* humanist.

humanitaire /ymanitɛʀ/ *adj* humanitarian.

humanitarisme /ymanitaʀism/ *nm* humanitarianism.

humanitariste /ymanitaʀist/ *adj, nmf* humanitarian.

humanité /ymanite/ **I** *nf* **1** (genre humain) humanity; **crimes contre l'~** crimes against humanity; **2** (altruisme) humanity, humaneness; **avec ~** [*traiter*] humanely; **3** Philos, Relig humanity.

II humanités† *nfpl* classics; **faire ses ~s** to study classics, to read classics GB.

humanoïde /ymanɔid/ *adj, nm* humanoid.

Humberside ▶ **692** *nprm* **le ~** Humberside.

humble /œbl/ **I** *adj* [*personne*] (par soi-même) unassuming; (vis-à-vis d'autres) humble; [*ton, manières*] unassuming; [*condition, travail, origine*] humble; [*maison, demeure*] modest; **votre ~ serviteur** your humble servant; **à mon ~ avis** in my humble opinion; **se faire ~ devant qn** to humble oneself before sb.

II humbles *nmpl* **les ~s** the common people.

humblement /œbləmɑ̃/ *adv* humbly.

humecter /ymɛkte/ [1] **I** *vtr* to moisten (**de, avec** with).

II s'humecter *vpr* **s'~ les lèvres** to moisten one's lips; **s'~ le gosier**◑ to wet one's whistle○.

humer /ˈyme/ [1] *vtr* **1** (inspirer) to sniff [*air*]; **2** (sentir) liter to smell [*fleur, potage*].

huméral, **~e**, *mpl* **-aux** /ymeʀal, o/ *adj* humeral; **artère ~e** brachial artery.

humérus /ymeʀys/ *nm* humerus.

humeur /ymœʀ/ *nf* **1** (disposition passagère) mood; **être de bonne/mauvaise ~** to be in a good/bad mood; **être d'une ~ de chien** to be in a foul mood; **être d'~ à faire qch** to be in the mood to do sth; **je ne suis pas d'~ à écouter tes histoires** I'm in no mood to listen to your stories; **être d'~ massacrante** to be in a hell of a mood; **2** (disposition dominante) temper; **être d'~ égale** to be even-tempered; **être d'~ inégale** to be moody; **un jeune homme à l'~ chagrine** a sulky young man; **un spectacle plein de bonne ~** a very happy show; **des crises de mauvaise ~** bad moods; **elle est connue pour sa bonne ~** she's known for her good humour[GB] ou for being good-humoured[GB]; **3** (mauvaise disposition) **geste/mouvement d'~** bad-tempered gesture/movement; **dans un mouvement d'~** with a bad-tempered gesture; **il m'a répondu avec ~** he answered me bad-temperedly; **4‡** Méd humour†[GB]; **les ~s** the humours[GB]

■ **~ aqueuse** Physiol aqueous humour[GB]; **~ vitrée** Physiol vitreous humour[GB].

humide /ymid/ *adj* **1** (imprégné de liquide) [*linge, cheveux, maison, draps*] damp; **il avait le regard ~** his eyes were moist with tears; **2** Géog, Météo [*climat, région, air*] humid; [*saison*] rainy; **il fait froid et ~** it's cold and damp; **il fait chaud et ~, il fait une chaleur ~** it's muggy.

humidificateur /ymidifikatœʀ/ *nm* humidifier.

humidification /ymidifikasjɔ̃/ *nf* humidification.

humidifier /ymidifje/ [2] *vtr* to dampen [*linge, papier*]; to spray [sth] (with water) [*peau, plante*]; to humidify [*air*].

humidité /ymidite/ *nf* **1** (état) dampness; **je n'aime pas l'~** I don't like dampness; **produit craignant l'~** product which should be stored in a dry place; **le livre est resté à l'~** the book has been left in a damp place; **2** (résultat) damp; **il y a de l'~ sur les murs** there's damp on the walls; **problème d'~** damp problem; **des traces d'~** damp marks; **prendre l'~** to be affected by damp; **3** Météo (d'air, de climat, de région) humidity.

humiliant, ~e /ymiljɑ̃, ɑ̃t/ *adj* humiliating; **cela n'a rien d'~** there's no shame in it.

humiliation /ymiljasjɔ̃/ *nf* humiliation; **essuyer une ~** to suffer a humiliation.

humilier /ymilje/ [2] *vtr* to humiliate; **se sentir humilié** to feel humiliated (**par** by; **de faire** about doing).

humilité /ymilite/ *nf* **1** (de personne) humility; **en toute/avec ~** in all/with humility; **2** (de condition, tâche) humble nature.

humoral, ~e, *pl* **-aux** /ymɔʀal, o/ *adj* humoral†.

humoriste /ymɔʀist/ **▶510** *nmf* **1** (auteur) humorist; **2** (farceur) joker.

humoristique /ymɔʀistik/ *adj* humorous; **dessin ~** cartoon; **dessinateur ~** cartoonist.

humour /ymuʀ/ *nm* (de personne, situation) humour[GB]; **~ noir** black humour[GB]; **être plein d'~** [*film, histoire*] to be full of humour[GB]; [*personne*] to have a good sense of humour[GB]; **avoir (le sens) de l'~** to have a sense of humour[GB]; **ne pas avoir** or **manquer d'~** to have no sense of humour[GB]; **avec ~** humorously; **savoir faire preuve d'~** to take things well; **prendre les choses avec ~** to see the humorous side of things; **il n'a pas su apprécier l'~ de la situation** he couldn't see the funny side of it; **faire de l'~** to make jokes.

humus /ymys/ *nm* humus.

Hun /'œ̃/ *nm* Hun.

hune /'yn/ *nf* Naut top; **grande ~** maintop.
■ **~ de misaine** foretop.

hunier /'ynje/ *nm* Naut topsail; **grand ~** main topsail; **grand ~ fixe/volant** lower/upper main topsail; **petit ~** fore topsail.

huppe /'yp/ *nf* **1** Zool hoopoe; **2** (crête) crest.

huppé, ~e /'ype/ *adj* **1**○ (mondain) upper-crust (*épith*); **2** [*oiseau*] crested.

hure /'yʀ/ *nf* **1** (tête, trophée) head; **2** Culin brawn GB, headcheese US.

hurlement /'yʀləmɑ̃/ *nm* (d'animal) howl, howling **¢**; (de personne) yell, howl; (de sirène) wailing **¢**, blaring **¢**; **pousser un ~ de douleur** to howl with pain.

hurler /'yʀle/ [1] **I** *vtr* **1** (crier) to yell [*propos, remarques*]; **'ça suffit!' hurla-t-il** 'that's enough!' he yelled; **~ des injures à qn** to shout abuse at sb; **~ à qn de faire** to yell at sb to do; **~ à qn que** to yell at sb that; **~ sa souffrance/colère** to give vent to one's misery/anger; **2** (diffuser très fort) [*télévision, radio, magnétophone*] to blare out [*chansons, discours*].
II *vi* **1** (pousser des cris) [*animaux, personnes*] to howl; **~ de rage/douleur/frayeur** to howl with rage/pain/terror; **~ de rire** to roar with laughter; **c'est à ~ de rire** it's enough to make you roar with laughter; **les gens hurlaient au scandale** people were outraged by the scandal; **quand je vois ça, ça me fait ~** it makes me want to scream when I see that; **2** (parler fort) to yell; **3** (faire du bruit) [*sirène*] to wail; [*vent, tempête*] to roar; [*télévision, radio*] to blare, to be going full blast; [*haut-parleur*] to blare, to be on full blast.
IDIOMES **~ avec les loups** to follow the crowd; **~ à la mort** to bay at the moon.

hurluberlu, ~e /yʀlybɛʀly/ *nm,f* oddball○.

huron, -onne /'yʀɔ̃, ɔn/ **▶462** **I** *adj* Huron.
II *nm* Ling Huron.

Huron, -onne /'yʀɔ̃, ɔn/ **I** *nm,f* Huron.
II **▶459** *npr* **le lac ~** Lake Huron.

husky, *pl* **huskies** /əski/ *nm* husky.

hussard /'ysaʀ/ *nm* hussar.

hussarde /'ysaʀd/ *nf* **à la ~** roughly.

hutte /'yt/ *nf* hut.

hybridation /ibʀidasjɔ̃/ *nf* hybridization.

hybride /ibʀid/ **I** *adj* **1** Biol hybrid; **2** [*création, construction*] hybrid; **c'est une situation ~** it's not a clear-cut situation.
II *nm* hybrid.

hybrider /ibʀide/ [1] *vtr* to cross, to hybridize spéc.

hybridisme /ibʀidism/ *nm* hybridism.

hydracide /idʀasid/ *nm* hydracid.

hydratant, ~e /idʀatɑ̃, ɑ̃t/ **I** *adj* moisturizing.
II *nm* moisturizer.

hydratation /idʀatasjɔ̃/ *nf* **1** Cosmét moisturizing; **2** Physiol hydration; **3** Chimie hydration.

hydrate /idʀat/ *nm* hydrate.
■ **~ de carbone** carbohydrate.

hydrater /idʀate/ [1] **I** *vtr* **1** Cosmét to moisturize [*peau*]; **2** Physiol to hydrate [*tissu, organisme*]; **3** Chimie to hydrate.
II s'hydrater *vpr* **1** Physiol [*personne*] **bien s'~** to take plenty of fluids; **2** Chimie (devenir un hydrate) to undergo hydration.

hydraulique /idʀolik/ **I** *adj* hydraulic.
II *nf* hydraulics (+ *v sg*).

hydravion /idʀavjɔ̃/ *nm* seaplane, hydroplane.

hydre /idʀ/ *nf* **1** Mythol Hydra; **2** fig hydra-headed monster.

hydrocarbure /idʀokaʀbyʀ/ *nm* hydrocarbon.

hydrocéphale /idʀosefal/ *adj, nmf* hydrocephalic.

hydrocéphalie /idʀosefali/ **▶271** *nf* hydrocephalus.

hydrocortisone /idʀokɔʀtizɔn/ *nf* hydrocortisone.

hydrocution /idʀokysjɔ̃/ *nf* immersion hypothermia.

hydrodynamique /idʀodinamik/ **I** *adj* hydrodynamic.
II *nf* hydrodynamics (+ *v sg*).

hydroélectricité /idʀoelɛktʀisite/ *nf* hydroelectricity.

hydroélectrique /idʀoelɛktʀik/ *adj* hydroelectric.

hydrofuge /idʀɔfyʒ/ *adj* [*mastic, vernis*] water-repellent.

hydrogénation /idʀɔʒenasjɔ̃/ *nf* hydrogenation.

hydrogène /idʀɔʒɛn/ *nm* hydrogen.
■ **~ lourd** Chimie deuterium.

hydrogéner /idʀɔʒene/ [14] *vtr* to hydrogenate.

hydroglisseur /idʀoglisœʀ/ *nm* hydroplane.

hydrographe /idʀɔgʀaf/ **▶510** *nmf* hydrographer.

hydrographie /idʀɔgʀafi/ *nf* hydrography.

hydrographique /idʀɔgʀafik/ *adj* hydrographic.

hydrologie /idʀɔlɔʒi/ *nf* hydrology.

hydrologique /idʀɔlɔʒik/ *adj* hydrologic.

hydrologiste /idʀɔlɔʒist/, **hydrologue** /idʀɔlɔg/ **▶510** *nmf* hydrologist.

hydrolyse /idʀoliz/ *nf* hydrolysis.

hydrolyser /idʀolize/ [1] *vtr* to hydrolyse[GB].

hydromel /idʀɔmɛl/ *nm* mead.

hydromètre /idʀɔmɛtʀ/ *nm* hydrometer.

hydrométrie /idʀɔmetʀi/ *nf* hydrometry.

hydrométrique /idʀɔmetʀik/ *adj* hydrometric.

hydrophile /idʀɔfil/ *adj* [*tissu, matière*] absorbent.

hydrophobe /idʀɔfɔb/ *adj* hydrophobic.

hydrophobie /idʀɔfɔbi/ *nf* hydrophobia.

hydrophone /idʀɔfɔn/ *nm* hydrophone.

hydropisie† /idʀɔpizi/ **▶271** *nf* dropsy†.

hydropneumatique /idʀɔpnømatik/ *adj* hydropneumatic.

hydroptère /idʀɔptɛʀ/ *nm* hydrofoil.

hydrorésistant, ~e /idʀoʀezistɑ̃, ɑ̃t/ *adj* water resistant.

hydrosphère /idʀɔsfɛʀ/ *nf* hydrosphere.

hydrostatique /idʀɔstatik/ **I** *adj* hydrostatic.
II *nf* hydrostatics (+ *v sg*).

hydrothérapie /idʀɔteʀapi/ *nf* hydrotherapy.

hydroxyde /idʀɔksid/ *nm* hydroxide.

hyène /'jɛn/ *nf* hyena.

hygiaphone® /iʒjafɔn/ *nm* grill (*perforated communication panel*).

hygiène /iʒjɛn/ *nf* **1** (pour la propreté) hygiene; **contraire à l'~** unhygienic; **par mesure d'~** for (the sake of) hygiene; **pour l'~ des cheveux** (in order) to keep hair clean; **~ scolaire/sportive** health guidelines for schools/sportspeople; **2** (comme science) hygiene; **veillez à une bonne ~ alimentaire** eat sensibly, have a healthy diet; **avoir une bonne/mauvaise ~ de vie** to have a healthy/an unhealthy lifestyle.
■ **~ corporelle** personal hygiene; **~ dentaire** dental hygiene; **~ féminine** feminine hygiene; **~ mentale** mental health; **~ publique** public hygiene.

hygiénique /iʒjenik/ *adj* **1** (concernant la propreté) hygienic; **2** (sain) [*boisson, mode de vie*] healthy; **promenade ~** constitutional.

hygiéniste /iʒjenist/ **▶510** *nmf* hygienist.

hygromètre /igʀɔmɛtʀ/ *nm* hygrometer.

hygrométrie /igʀɔmetʀi/ *nf* hygrometry.

hygrométrique /igʀɔmetʀik/ *adj* hygrometric.

hygroscope /igʀɔskɔp/ *nm* hygroscope.

hymen /imɛn/ *nm* **1** Anat hymen; **2** (mariage) liter nuptial bond.

hyménée /imene/ *nm* liter nuptial bond.

hyménoptère /imenɔptɛʀ/ *nm* hymenopteran; **les ~s** Hymenoptera.

hymne /imn/ *nm* Littérat, Mus, fig hymn; **~ à la vie** fig hymn to life.
■ **~ national** national anthem.

hypallage /ipalaʒ/ *nm* hypallage.

hyperacidité /ipɛʀasidite/ *nf* **~ gastrique** hyperacidity.

hyperactif, -ive /ipɛʀaktif, iv/ *adj* hyperactive.

hyperbare /ipɛʀbaʀ/ *adj* **caisson ~** decompression chamber.

hyperbole /ipɛʀbɔl/ *nf* **1** Math hyperbola; **2** Littérat hyperbole.

hyperbolique /ipɛʀbɔlik/ *adj* Littérat, Math hyperbolic.

hypercalorique /ipɛʀkalɔʀik/ *adj* high in calories (*jamais épith*), high-calorie (*épith*).

hypercholestérolémie /ipɛʀkɔlɛsteʀɔlemi/ **▶271** *nf* hypercholesterolemia.

hyperclassique /ipɛʀklasik/ *adj* [*situation, réaction*] absolutely classic; **roman** or **pièce** or **film ~** great classic.

hyperconnu, ~e /ipɛʀkɔny/ *adj* extremely famous.

hypercorrection /ipɛʀkɔʀɛksjɔ̃/ *nf* Ling hypercorrection.

hypercultivé, ~e /ipɛʀkyltive/ *adj* extremely learned.

hyperdoué, **~e** /ipɛʀdwe/ *adj* exceptionally gifted.

hyperémotif, **-ive** /ipɛʀemɔtif, iv/ *adj* hyperemotional.

hyperglycémie /ipɛʀglisemi/ *nf* hyperglycaemia.

hyperinflation /ipɛʀɛ̃flasjɔ̃/ *nf* hyperinflation.

hyperinformé, **~e** /ipɛʀɛ̃fɔʀme/ *adj* very well informed.

hyperlien /ipɛʀljɛ̃/ *nm* hyperlink.

hyperlipidémie /ipɛʀlipidemi/ *nf* hyperlipaemia.

hyperluxueux, **-euse** /ipɛʀlyksyø, øz/ *adj* [*appartement*] superluxurious; [*voiture*] ultraluxurious.

hypermarché /ipɛʀmaʀʃe/ *nm* hypermarket GB, large supermarket.

hypermétrope /ipɛʀmetʀɔp/ *adj* longsighted, hyperopic spéc.

hypermétropie /ipɛʀmetʀɔpi/ *nf* longsightedness, hyperopia spéc.

hypernerveux, **-euse** /ipɛʀnɛʀvø, øz/ **I** *adj* highly strung.
II *nm,f* **c'est un ~** he's highly strung.

hyperonyme /ipɛʀɔnim/ *nm* hyperonym.

hyperpuissant, **~e** /ipɛʀpɥisɑ̃, ɑ̃t/ *adj* [*voiture, moteur*] extremely powerful.

hyperrapide /ipɛʀʀapid/ *adj* [*véhicule*] ultra-high speed; **faire un travail ~**○ to work at top speed.

hyperréalisme /ipɛʀʀealism/ *nm* hyperrealism.

hypersensibilité /ipɛʀsɑ̃sibilite/ *nf* hypersensitivity (**à** to).

hypersensible /ipɛʀsɑ̃sibl/ **I** *adj* hypersensitive.
II *nmf* hypersensitive person.

hypersophistiqué, **~e** /ipɛʀsɔfistike/ *adj* [*personne, vêtement*] ultrasophisticated; [*théorie*] highly sophisticated.

hyperspécialisé, **~e** /ipɛʀspesjalize/ *adj* highly specialized.

hypertendu, **~e** /ipɛʀtɑ̃dy/ **I** *adj* **1**○ extremely tense; **2** Méd suffering from high blood pressure ou hypertension spéc.
II *nm,f* **1**○ very tense person; **2** Méd person suffering from high blood pressure ou hypertension spéc.

hypertension /ipɛʀtɑ̃sjɔ̃/ *nf* **~ (artérielle)** high blood pressure, hypertension spéc; **avoir de l'~** to have high blood pressure.

hypertexte /ipɛʀtɛkst/ *nm* hypertext.

hyperthyroïdie /ipɛʀtiʀɔidi/ **▶271** *nf* hyperthyroidism.

hypertrophie /ipɛʀtʀɔfi/ *nf* **1** Méd enlargement, hypertrophy spéc; **2** (de ville, d'administration) overdevelopment.

hypertrophié, **~e** /ipɛʀtʀɔfje/ **I** *pp* **▶ hypertrophier**.
II *pp adj* **1** Méd enlarged, hypertrophic spéc; **2** [*administration, ville, sentiment*] overdeveloped.

hypertrophier /ipɛʀtʀɔfje/ [2] **I** *vtr* Méd to hypertrophy.
II s'hypertrophier *vpr* **1** Méd to hypertrophy; **2** [*administration, ville, sentiment*] to become overdeveloped.

hypertrophique /ipɛʀtʀɔfik/ *adj* Méd hypertrophic.

hypnose /ipnoz/ *nf* hypnosis; **être en état d'~** lit to be under hypnosis, to be in a hypnotic trance; fig to be in a hypnotic trance.

hypnotique /ipnɔtik/ *adj, nm* hypnotic.

hypnotiser /ipnɔtize/ [1] **I** *vtr* **1** lit to hypnotize; **2** fig to hypnotize, mesmerize; **hypnotisé par cet étrange spectacle** mesmerized by this strange sight.
II s'hypnotiser *vpr* **s'~ sur** to become obsessed by [*détail, problème*].

hypnotiseur, **-euse** /ipnɔtizœʀ, øz/ **▶510** *nm,f* hypnotist.

hypnotisme /ipnɔtism/ *nm* hypnotism.

hypoallergénique /ipɔalɛʀʒenik/ *adj* hypoallergenic.

hypocagne = **hypokhâgne**.

hypocalorique /ipɔkalɔʀik/ *adj* low-calorie (*épith*), low in calories (*jamais épith*).

hypocondriaque /ipɔkɔ̃dʀijak/ *adj, nmf* hypochondriac.

hypocondrie /ipɔkɔ̃dʀi/ *nf* hypochondria.

hypocoristique /ipɔkɔʀistik/ **I** *adj* hypocoristic.
II *nm* hypocorism.

hypocrisie /ipɔkʀizi/ *nf* hypocrisy; **être d'une grande ~** to be very hypocritical.

hypocrite /ipɔkʀit/ **I** *adj* hypocritical.
II *nmf* hypocrite.

hypocritement /ipɔkʀitmɑ̃/ *adv* hypocritically.

hypodermique /ipɔdɛʀmik/ *adj* hypodermic.

hypoglucidique /ipɔglysidik/ *adj* [*aliment*] low-carbohydrate (*épith*).

hypoglycémie /ipɔglisemi/ *nf* hypoglycaemia.

hypokhâgne /ipɔkaɲ/ *nf* students' slang *first year preparatory class in humanities for entrance to École normale supérieure*.

hyponyme /ipɔnim/ *nm* hyponym.

hypophyse /ipɔfiz/ *nf* pituitary gland, hypophysis spéc.

hyposodé, **~e** /ipɔsɔde/ *adj* low-salt (*épith*).

hypostyle /ipɔstil/ *adj* hypostyle.

hypotaupe /ipɔtop/ *nf* students' slang *first year preparatory class in mathematics and science for entrance to Grandes Écoles*.

hypotendu, **~e** /ipɔtɑ̃dy/ *adj* suffering from low blood pressure ou hypotension spéc.

hypotension /ipɔtɑ̃sjɔ̃/ *nf* **~ (artérielle)** low blood pressure, hypotension spéc.

hypoténuse /ipɔtenyz/ *nf* hypotenuse.

hypothalamus /ipɔtalamys/ *nm* hypothalamus.

hypothécable /ipɔtekabl/ *adj* mortgageable.

hypothécaire /ipɔtekɛʀ/ *adj* mortgage (*épith*); **prêt/contrat ~** mortgage loan/ deed; **inscription ~** registration of mortgage; **créancier/débiteur ~** mortgagee/ mortgager.

hypothèque /ipɔtɛk/ *nf* **1** mortgage; **prendre/rembourser une ~** to take out/pay off a mortgage; **prendre une ~ sur l'avenir** fig to mortgage one's future; **2** fig (doute) doubt; (danger) threat, danger; **lever l'~** (doute) to remove the doubt; (danger) to remove the threat.

hypothéquer /ipɔteke/ [14] *vtr* to mortgage; fig to endanger, put [sth] at risk [*chances, objectifs*]; **~ l'avenir** fig to mortgage one's future.

hypothermie /ipɔtɛʀmi/ *nf* hypothermia.

hypothèse /ipɔtɛz/ *nf* hypothesis; **~ de travail** working hypothesis; **émettre l'~ que** to put forward the hypothesis that; **faire des ~s** to speculate (**sur** about); **se refuser à la moindre ~** to refuse to speculate; **dans l'~ où il serait élu** should he be elected, in the event of his being elected; **dans la pire des ~s** in the worst scenario imaginable; **écarter/retenir l'~ de l'accident** to rule out/accept the possibility of an accident.

hypothétique /ipɔtetik/ *adj* hypothetical.

hypothétiquement /ipotetikmɑ̃/ *adv* hypothetically.

hypotonie /ipɔtɔni/ *nf* hypotonicity.

hysope /izɔp/ *nf* hyssop.

hystérectomie /isteʀɛktɔmi/ *nf* hysterectomy.

hystérie /isteʀi/ *nf* hysteria; **~ collective** mass hysteria.

hystérique /isteʀik/ **I** *adj* hysterical.
II *nmf* **1** (nerveux) pej bundle of nerves; **2** Méd, Psych hysteric.

hystérographie /isteʀɔgʀafi/ *nf* uterography; **passer une ~** to have a uterography.

i, I /i/ *nm inv* i, I.
IDIOMES **mettre les points sur les i** to dot the i's and cross the t's.

IA /ia/ *nf* ▶ **intelligence**.

iambe /jɑ̃b/ *nm* (pied, genre) iamb, iambus; (vers, poème) iambic poem.

iambique /jɑ̃bik/ *adj* iambic.

IAO /iao/ *nf*: *abbr* ▶ **ingénierie**.

Ibadan /ibadɑ̃/ ▶ **857** *npr* Ibadan.

Ibère /ibɛʀ/ *nprmf* Iberian.

ibérique /ibeʀik/ *adj* Iberian; **la péninsule ~** the Iberian peninsula.

ibidem /ibidɛm/ *adv* ibidem.

ibis /ibis/ *nm* ibis.

Icare /ikaʀ/ *npr* Icarus.

iceberg /ajsbɛʀg, isbɛʀg/ *nm* iceberg; **la partie visible de l'~** fig the tip of the iceberg; **la partie cachée de l'~** fig what lies below the tip of the iceberg.

ichtyologie /iktjɔlɔʒi/ *nf* ichthyology.

ichtyologique /iktjɔlɔʒik/ *adj* ichthyological.

ichtyologiste /iktjɔlɔʒist/ ▶ **510** *nmf* ichthyologist.

ichtyose /iktjoz/ ▶ **271** *nf* ichthyosis.

ici /isi/ *adv* **1** (dans l'espace) here; **d'~ à là-bas** from here to there; **~ et là** here and there; **~ (tout de suite)!** (à un chien) come here!, heel!; **il faut une voiture pour venir jusqu'~** you need a car to get here; **'~ la tour de contrôle'** 'Control Tower here'; **c'est ~ que la balle a traversé la tôle** this is where the bullet came through the metal; **c'est ~ que nous descendons** this is where we get off; **c'est ~ même que les accords furent signés** it was in this very place that the agreements were signed; **par ~ la sortie** this way out; **par ~ les bonnes affaires!** good bargains this way!; **par ~! j'ai trouvé quelque chose!** come here! I've found something!; **les gens sont plutôt méfiants par ~** the people around here are a bit wary; **il y a une belle église par ~** there is a fine church near here; **les gens d'~** the locals; **allô? bonjour, ~ Grovagnard** hello? this is Grovagnard speaking; **~ Luc Pichon à Washington, à vous Paris** this is Luc Pichon in Washington, back to you in Paris; **je vois ça d'~!** I can just picture it!; **vous êtes ~ chez vous!** make yourself at home!; **2** (dans le temps) **arrêtons ~ notre conversation** let's stop the conversation (right) there; **jusqu'~** (au présent) until now; (dans le passé) until then; **d'~ peu** shortly; **d'~ demain/à l'an 2000** by tomorrow/by the year 2000; **d'~ cinq minutes/deux jours** five minutes/two days from now; **je te téléphone ce soir, d'~ là, tâche de te reposer** I'll phone you tonight, in the meantime try and rest; **d '~ là, on sera tous morts** by then, we'll all be dead; **d'~ à ce qu'il démissionne/change d'avis, il n'y a pas loin** it won't be long before he hands in his notice/changes his mind; **il l'aime bien, mais d'~ à ce qu'il l'épouse**... he likes her, but as for marrying her...

ici-bas /isiba/ *adv* here below; **les choses d'~** the things of this world.

icône /ikon/ *nf* (tous contextes) icon.

iconoclasme /ikɔnɔklasm/ *nm* iconoclasm.

iconoclaste /ikɔnɔklast/ **I** *adj* iconoclastic.
II *nmf* iconoclast.

iconographe /ikɔnɔgʀaf/ ▶ **510** *nmf* Édition art editor.

iconographie /ikɔnɔgʀafi/ *nf* (sur un thème) iconography; (illustrations) illustrations (*pl*).

iconographique /ikɔnɔgʀafik/ *adj* iconographic.

ictère /iktɛʀ/ ▶ **271** *nm* icterus.

id. *written abbr* = **idem**.

Idaho /idao/ ▶ **692** *nprm* Idaho.

idéal, ~e, *mpl* **-aux** /ideal, o/ **I** *adj* (parfait, imaginaire) ideal.
II *nm* **1** (modèle de perfection) ideal; **avoir un ~** to have ideals; **2** (ce qui convient) **ce n'est pas l'~** it's not ideal; **l'~ serait de partir en mai** the ideal thing would be to leave in May; **dans l'~** ideally.

idéalement /idealmɑ̃/ *adv* ideally.

idéalisation /idealizasjɔ̃/ *nf* idealization.

idéaliser /idealize/ [1] *vtr* to idealize.

idéalisme /idealism/ *nm* idealism.

idéaliste /idealist/ **I** *adj* gén idealistic; Philos idealist.
II *nmf* idealist.

idée /ide/ *nf* **1** (inspiration, projet) idea (**de qch** of sth; **de faire** of doing); **quelle ~!** what an idea!; **être plein d'~s** to be full of ideas; **donner des ~s à qn** to give sb ideas; **ne jamais être à court d'~s** never to be short of ideas; **une ~ de cadeau pour qn** an idea for a present for sb; **avoir une ~** to have an idea; **être fou de joie à l'~ de/que** to be over the moon at the idea of/that; **il y a de l'~ dans ce projet** there are some good ideas in the project; **avoir de l'~** to be inventive; **avoir une ~ derrière la tête** to have something in mind; **il n'a qu'une ~ en tête, apprendre à piloter** all he can think about is learning to fly; **sortir sans manteau en hiver, quelle ~!** how stupid to go out without a coat in winter!; **2** (opinion) idea (**sur** about); (réflexion) thought; **avoir son ~ sur** to have one's own idea about; **l'histoire des ~s** the history of ideas; **j'ai ma petite ~ sur le sujet** I have my own theory about that; **avoir ~ que** to think that; **se faire une haute ~ de** to think a lot of; **se faire des ~s** to imagine things; **mettre de l'ordre dans ses ~s** (dans l'immédiat) to gather one's thoughts; (à long terme) to order one's thoughts; **avoir les ~s larges** to be broad-minded; **ça te changera les ~s** it'll take your mind off things; **changer d'~** to change one's mind; **avoir des ~s de gauche** to have left-wing tendencies; **avoir de la suite dans les ~s** (savoir ce que l'on veut) to be single-minded; iron (être entêté) not to be easily deterred; **manquer de suite dans les ~s** to lack tenacity; **faire à son ~** to do as one thinks best; **3** (aper çu) idea; **donner à qn une ~ de l'étendue de** to give sb an idea of the extent of; **as-tu une ~ du temps qu'il faut pour faire** do you have any idea how long it takes to do; **4** (esprit) **avoir dans l'~ que** to have an idea that; **avoir dans l'~ de faire** to plan to do; **il n'est venu à l'~ de personne de faire** nobody has thought of doing; **il ne leur viendrait jamais à l'~ de faire** it would never occur to them to do; **tu ne m'ôteras pas de l'~ qu'on aurait dû tourner à droite** I still think that we should have turned right; **il s'est mis dans l'~ de faire** he's taken it into his head to do; **mets-toi bien dans l'~ qu'il ne partira jamais** get it into your head that he'll never leave; **5** (représentation abstraite) idea; **l'~ de justice/du beau** the idea of justice/beauty.
■ **~ cadeau** gift idea; **~ fixe** idée fixe, obsession; **c'est une ~ fixe chez lui** he's got a fixation about it; **~ force** key idea; **~ de génie** brainwave○; **~ noire** dark thought; **~ reçue** idée reçue; **~ toute faite** second-hand idea.

idem /idɛm/ *adv* ditto; **tu seras puni et lui ~** you'll be punished and so will he.

identifiable /idɑ̃tifjabl/ *adj* identifiable.

identificateur /idɑ̃tifikatœʀ/ *nm* Ordinat identifier.

identification /idɑ̃tifikasjɔ̃/ *nf* identification (**à, avec** with).

identifier /idɑ̃tifje/ [2] **I** *vtr* **1** (reconnaître) to identify; **être identifié comme principal suspect** to be identified as the main suspect; **non identifié** unidentified; **2** (assimiler) to identify (**à** with; **avec** with; **et** with).
II s'identifier *vpr* (être comparable) to become identified (**à** with); (vouloir ressembler) to identify (**à** with).

identique /idɑ̃tik/ *adj* **1** (pareil) identical (**à** to); **2** (constant) unchanged.

identiquement /idɑ̃tikmɑ̃/ *adv* identically.

identité /idɑ̃tite/ *nf* **1** Philos identity; **~ culturelle** cultural identity; **2** (état civil) identity; **fausse ~** false identity; **~ d'emprunt** assumed identity; **(les services de) l'~ judiciaire** the French criminal records office; ▶ **relevé**; **3** (similarité) similarity; **ils se sont découvert une ~ de vues/goûts** they discovered that they had similar views/tastes; **4** Math, Psych identity.

idéogramme /ideɔgʀam/ *nm* ideogram.

idéographie /ideɔgʀafi/ *nf* ideography.

idéographique /ideɔgʀafik/ *adj* ideographic.

idéologie /ideɔlɔʒi/ *nf* ideology.

idéologique /ideɔlɔʒik/ *adj* ideological.

idéologue /ideɔlɔg/ *nmf* ideologist.

ides /id/ *nfpl* Antiq ides; **les ~ de mars** the ides of March.

IDHEC /idɛk/ *nm* (*abbr* = **Institut des hautes études cinématographiques**) *institute for advanced film studies*.

idiolecte /idjɔlɛkt/ *nm* idiolect.

idiomatique /idjɔmatik/ *adj* idiomatic.

idiome /idjom/ *nm* idiom.

idiosyncrasie /idjɔsɛ̃krazi/ *nf* idiosyncrasy.

idiosyncratique /idjɔsɛ̃kʀatik/ *adj* idiosyncratic.

idiot, ~e /idjo, ɔt/ **I** *adj* **1** gén stupid; **2**† Méd idiot† (*épith*).
II *nm* **1** gén idiot; **l'~ du village** the

Les îles

Article ou pas article?

En anglais, les noms d'îles se comportent comme les noms de pays: seuls les noms pluriels prennent un article (pour les îles qui sont aussi des pays, **▶ 321**).

Chypre	=	Cyprus
aimer Chypre	=	to like Cyprus
la Corse	=	Corsica
aimer la Corse	=	to like Corsica
les Baléares	=	the Balearics
aimer les Baléares	=	to like the Balearics

Noter que certains noms d'îles sont pluriels en français mais singuliers en anglais, et ne prennent donc pas d'article.

les îles Fidji	=	Fiji
j'aime les îles Fidji	=	I like Fiji
les Samoas occidentales	=	Western Samoa

En, à, aux

En, à *et* aux *se traduisent par* to *avec les verbes de mouvement (par ex.* aller, se rendre *etc.*):

aller à Chypre	=	to go to Cyprus
aller à Sainte-Hélène	=	to go to St Helena
aller en Corse	=	to go to Corsica
aller aux Baléares	=	to go to the Balearics

Avec les autres verbes (par ex. être, habiter, *etc.*), en, à *et* aux *se traduisent normalement par* in. *Cependant, pour les toutes petites îles, on traduira par* on.

vivre en Corse	=	to live in Corsica
vivre à Chypre	=	to live in Cyprus
vivre aux Baléares	=	to live in the Balearics
vivre à Naxos	=	to live on Naxos

Pour la traduction des expressions avec de, **▶ 321**.

Avec ou sans island

L'anglais utilise toujours les mots island *ou* islands *dans les cas où le français utilise* île *ou* îles.

l'île de Guernesey	=	the island of Guernsey
les îles Baléares	=	the Balearic Islands
les Baléares	=	the Balearics

Noter que isle *n'est plus utilisé que dans quelques noms d'îles, comme the* Isle of Man, the Isle of Wight, the Orkney Isles, *etc.*

village idiot; **faire l'~** (sans simuler) to behave like an idiot; (en simulant) to act innocent GB, to act dumb; **2†** Méd idiot†.

idiotie /idjɔsi/ *nf* **1** (parole) stupid thing; **2** (ânerie) rubbish ¢ GB, garbage ¢ US; **toutes ces ~s à la radio** all this rubbish on the radio; **3** (caractère) gén stupidity; **4†** Méd idiocy†.

idiotisme /idjɔtism/ *nm* Ling idiom.

idoine /idwan/ *adj* suitable.

idolâtre /idɔlɑtʀ/ **I** *adj* idolatrous.

II *nmf* idolator.

idolâtrer /idɔlɑtʀe/ [1] *vtr* to idolize.

idolâtrie /idɔlɑtʀi/ *nf* idolatry.

idole /idɔl/ *nf* idol.

IDS /ideɛs/ *nf*: *abbr* **▶ initiative**.

idylle /idil/ *nf* **1** (liaison) love affair (**entre** between); **vivre/nouer une ~** to live through/start a love affair; **l'~ entre les deux partis** the love affair between the two parties; **2** (poème) idyll.

idyllique /idilik/ *adj* (tous contextes) idyllic.

if /if/ *nm* **1** (arbre) yew; **2** (bois) yew.

IFOP /ifɔp/ *nm* (*abbr* = **Institut français d'opinion publique**) French institute for opinion polls.

IGF /iʒeɛf/ *nm*: *abbr* **▶ impôt**.

igloo /iglu/ *nm* igloo.

IGN /iʒeɛn/ *nm* (*abbr* = **Institut géographique national**) organization responsible for producing maps of France; **une carte de l'IGN** ≈ an OS map.

Ignace /iɲas/ *npr* Ignatius; **saint ~ de Loyola** St Ignatius Loyola.

igname /iɲam/ *nf* yam.

ignare /iɲaʀ/ **I** *adj* ignorant.

II *nmf* ignoramus.

ignifugation /iɲifygasjɔ̃/ *nf* fireproofing.

ignifuge /iɲifyʒ/ *adj* [*substance, produit*] fireproofing (*épith*).

ignifugeant, **~e** /iɲifyʒɑ̃, ɑ̃t/ **I** *adj* [*substance, produit*] fireproofing (*épith*).

II *nm* fireproofing agent.

ignifuger /iɲifyʒe/ [13] *vtr* to fireproof; **un mur ignifugé** a fireproof wall.

ignoble /iɲɔbl/ *adj* **1** (condamnable) [*personne, conduite, acte, procédé*] vile; **c'est un ~ individu** he's a disgusting individual; **une ~ trahison** a vile betrayal; **de façon ~** in a vile way; **être ~ avec qn** to be vile to sb; **2** (infect) [*lieu, quartier*] squalid; [*nourriture, tableau, roman*] revolting.

ignoblement /iɲɔbləmɑ̃/ *adv* vilely.

ignominie /iɲɔmini/ *nf* **1** (déshonneur) ignominy; **l'~ de l'exil** the ignominy of exile; **se couvrir d'~** to bring dishonour[GB] upon oneself; **2** (caractère ignoble) **l'~ de cette accusation** this ignominious accusation; **traiter qn avec ~** to treat sb abominably; **3** (acte honteux) dreadful thing; **elle a commis des ~s** she did some dreadful things; **c'est une ~!** it's an outrage!

ignominieusement /iɲɔminjøzmɑ̃/ *adv* ignominiously.

ignominieux, **-ieuse** /iɲɔminjø, øz/ *adj* fml ignominious sout.

ignorance /iɲɔʀɑ̃s/ *nf* **1** (état) ignorance (**en** of); **~ totale** total ignorance; **être d'une ~ crasse** to be totally ignorant; **par ~** out of ignorance; **dans l'~ de** ignorant of; **être dans l'~** to be in the dark (**de** about); **tenir qn dans l'~** to keep sb in the dark (**de** about); **2** (lacune) gap in (one's) knowledge; **▶ superstition**.

ignorant, **~e** /iɲɔʀɑ̃, ɑ̃t/ **I** *adj* ignorant (**de** of; **en, dans** in); **être ~ de tout** to know nothing about anything.

II *nm,f* ignoramus; **faire l'~** to feign ignorance.

ignoré, **~e** /iɲɔʀe/ **I** *pp* **▶ ignorer**.

II *pp adj* (inconnu) unknown (**de qn** to sb); (méprisé) ignored (**de** by); **vivre ~** to live in obscurity.

ignorer /iɲɔʀe/ [1] **I** *vtr* **1** (ne pas savoir) not to know; **j'ignore les détails** I don't know the details; **j'ignore comment/où/si** I don't know how/when/if; **~ tout de qch** to know nothing of ou about sth; **ne rien ~ de qch** to know everything about sth; **2** (ne pas connaître l'existence de) not to have heard of; **il ignore le savon** iron he's never heard of soap; **~ l'existence de** to be unaware of the existence of; **3** (ne pas tenir compte de) to ignore [*personne, règle, recherches*]; **il ignore les règles du jeu** he ignores ou disregards the rules of the game; **le chercheur a ignoré les récentes découvertes** the researcher has ignored recent developments; **quand il me voit il m'ignore** when he sees me he ignores me; **tu n'as qu'à l'~** just ignore him; **4** (ne pas éprouver) not to feel [*émotion, sentiment*]; **il ignorait la peur** he didn't know what fear was.

II s'ignorer *vpr* (ne pas se connaître) **vous êtes un poète qui s'ignore** you are a poet without knowing it; **c'est un génie qui s'ignore** he's a genius but he does not know it; **un amour qui s'ignore** an unconscious love.

IGS /iʒeɛs/ *nf*: *abbr* **▶ inspection**.

iguane /igwan/ *nm* iguana.

iguanodon /igwanɔdɔ̃/ *nm* iguanodon.

il /il/

■ **Note** *il* pronom personnel masculin représentant une personne du sexe masculin ou un animal familier mâle se traduit par *he* (1); lorsqu'il représente un objet, un concept, un animal non familier, *il* se traduit par *it*; *il* peut également se traduire par *she* lorsqu'il représente un navire.

– *il* pronom personnel neutre sujet d'un verbe impersonnel se traduit généralement par *it*. On se reportera au verbe.

I *pron pers m* **1** (personne, animal familier) he; **~s** they; **~ a épousé ma sœur** he married my sister; **~s sont heureux** they're happy; **as-tu vu le chat? ~ n'est pas dans sa corbeille** have you seen the cat? he's not in his basket; **sera-t-~ à la réunion?** will he be at the meeting?; **Pierre a-t-~ téléphoné?** has Pierre phoned?; **2** (objet, concept, animal) it; **~s** they; **prends le livre, ~ est sur la table** take the book, it's on the table; **regarde ce cheval, ~ est magnifique** look at this horse, it's lovely; **le Japon a annoncé qu'~ participerait à la réunion** Japan announced that it would be taking part in the meeting.

II *pron pers neutre* it; **~ pleut** it's raining; **~ va pleuvoir** it's going to rain.

île /il/ *nf* island.

■ **~ artificielle** (pour forage) artificial island; **l'~ de Beauté** Tourisme Corsica; **~ flottante** Culin floating island; **~ de glace** Sci ice island.

Île-de-France /ildəfʀɑ̃s/ **▶ 692** *nprf* **l'~** Ile-de-France.

Île-du-Prince-Édouard /ildypʀɛ̃sedwaʀ/ **▶ 692** *nprf* Prince Edward Island.

iléon /ileɔ̃/ *nm* ileum.

Iliade /iljad/ *nprf* **l'~** the Iliad.

iliaque /iljak/ *adj* iliac; **os ~** hip bone.

îlien, **-ienne** /iljɛ̃, ɛn/ *nm,f* islander.

ilion /iljɔ̃/ *nm* ilium.

Ille-et-Vilaine /ilevilɛn/ **▶ 692** *nprf* (département) **l'~** Ille-et-Vilaine.

illégal, **~e**, *mpl* **-aux** /ilegal, o/ *adj* (tous contextes) illegal.

illégalement /ilegalmɑ̃/ *adv* illegally.

illégalité /ilegalite/ *nf* **1** (caractère) illegality ¢; **agir/travailler dans l'~** to act/work illegally; **être dans l'~** to be in breach of the law, to do something illegal; **entrer dans l'~** to start acting illegally; **2** (acte illégal) breach of the law; **des ~s répétées** repeated breaches of the law.

illégitime /ileʒitim/ *adj* **1** (hors mariage) [*union, amour*] illicit; [*enfant*] illegitimate; **2** (illégal) [*décision, mesure, pouvoir*] illegal; **3** (injustifié) [*revendication*] unfounded.

illégitimement /ileʒitimmɑ̃/ *adv* illegitimately; **prétendre ~ à un héritage** to lay illegitimate claim to a legacy.

illégitimité /ileʒitimite/ *nf* gén illegitimacy; (d'amour) illicitness; **un enfant né dans l'~** an illegitimate child.

illettré, **~e** /iletʀe/ *adj, nm,f* illiterate.

illettrisme /iletʀism/ *nm* illiteracy.

illicite /ilisit/ *adj* [*vente, gain, amour, plaisir*] illicit; [*pratique, contrat, trafic*] unlawful.

illicitement /ilisitmɑ̃/ *adv* illicitly.

illico○ /iliko/ *adv* straightaway, sharpish○; **~ presto**○ pronto○.

illimité, **~e** /ilimite/ *adj* unlimited; **disposer de crédits/pouvoirs ~s** to have unlimited funds/powers.

Illinois /ilinwa/ **▶ 692** *nprm* Illinois.

illisibilité /ilizibilite/ *nf* illegibility.

illisible /ilizibl/ *adj* **1** [*écriture, mot, document*] illegible; **2** [*œuvre, auteur*] unreadable.

illisiblement /iliziblәmɑ̃/ *adv* [*écrire*] illegibly.

illogique /ilɔʒik/ *adj* illogical.

illogiquement /ilɔʒikmɑ̃/ *adv* illogically.

illogisme /ilɔʒism/ *nm* illogicality.

illumination /ilyminasjɔ̃/ **I** *nf* **1** (action d'éclairer) floodlighting; **l'~ du bâtiment a coûté très cher** it cost a great deal to floodlight the building; **2** (inspiration) gén flash of inspiration; Relig spiritual enlightenment ¢; **ce matin j'ai eu une ~** I had a brainwave ou flash of inspiration this morning.

II illuminations *nfpl* (de ville, rue, bâtiment) illuminations; (de sapin, fête) lights.

illuminé, **~e** /ilymine/ **I** *pp* ▶ **illuminer**.
II *pp adj* **1** (éclairé) [*monument, site*] floodlit; **une place ~e par des projecteurs** a floodlit square; **2** (brillant) [*regard, visage*] radiant (**par**, **de** with); **3** (inspiré) [*poète, prédicateur*] inspired.
III *nm,f* gén visionary; péj crank.

illuminer /ilymine/ [1] **I** *vtr* **1** (éclairer) gén to illuminate; (avec projecteurs) to floodlight; **2** (donner de l'éclat) [*sourire*] to light up [*visage*]; [*foi, passion*] to illuminate [*vie*]; [*décor, couleur*] to cheer up [*façade, site*]; **la passion illuminait leur regard** their eyes shone with passion.
II s'illuminer *vpr* **1** (s'éclairer) [*ville, rue*] to light up; **le ciel s'illumine de feux d'artifices** the sky is lit up with fireworks; **2** (prendre de l'éclat) [*visage*] to light up (**de** with).

illusion /ilyzjɔ̃/ *nf* **1** (croyance) illusions (*pl*) (**sur** about); **elle n'a pas la moindre ~ là-dessus** she has absolutely no illusions about it; **sans ~ aucune** with no illusions at all; **être sans ~(s)** to have no illusions; **ne pas se faire d'~s** to have no illusions; **je ne me fais guère** or **pas trop d'~s** I don't hold out much hope; **entretenir les ~s de qn** to encourage sb in their illusions; **se faire des ~s** to delude oneself (**sur** about); **il se donne l'~ de dominer la situation** he likes to think that he's in control of the situation; **entretenir qn dans l'~ que**... to allow sb to continue in the mistaken belief that...; **2** (apparence trompeuse) illusion; **le prestidigitateur crée des ~s** the conjurer creates illusions; **donner l'~ de la vie/de l'amour** to give the illusion of life/of love; **ses promesses ne font pas ~** his promises don't fool anyone; **il ne fera pas ~ longtemps** he won't fool people for long, people will soon see through him.
■ **~ d'optique** Phys optical illusion.

illusionner: **s'illusionner** /ilyzjɔne/ [1] *vpr* to delude oneself (**sur qch/qn** about sth/sb).

illusionnisme /ilyzjɔnism/ *nm* **1** (art du prestidigitateur) conjuring; **2** Art, Pol (effet) illusionism.

illusionniste /ilyzjɔnist/ **▶510** *nmf* **1** (prestidigitateur) conjurer, illusionist; **2** (politicien) illusionist.

illusoire /ilyzwaʀ/ *adj* [*solution, remède, promesse, bonheur*] illusory; **il serait ~ de croire que**... it would be an illusion to believe that...

illustrateur, **-trice** /ilystʀatœʀ, tʀis/ **▶510** *nm,f* illustrator.

illustratif, **-ive** /ilystʀatif, iv/ *adj* illustrative.

illustration /ilystʀasjɔ̃/ *nf* **1** (exemple) illustration; **2** (image) illustration; **3** (iconographie) illustration; **un texte original enrichi par une ~ remarquable** an original text strikingly illustrated; **elle se chargera de l'~ de l'album** she will illustrate the album.

illustre /ilystʀ/ *adj* (tous contextes) illustrious; **l'~ M. Guicharel** the illustrious Mr Guicharel; **un ~ inconnu** a perfect nobody.
■ **Illustre Compagnie** French Academy.

illustré, **~e** /ilystʀe/ **I** *pp* ▶ **illustrer**.
II *pp adj* illustrated (**de** with).
III *nm* (journal) comic.

illustrer /ilystʀe/ [1] **I** *vtr* to illustrate (**de** with).
II s'illustrer *vpr* [*personne*] to distinguish oneself.

illustrissime† /ilystʀisim/ *adj* most illustrious.

îlot /ilo/ *nm* **1** Géog (petite île) islet; **2** (espace réduit) **désert parsemé d'~s de végétation** desert scattered with isolated patches of vegetation; **un ~ de paix** a haven of peace; **3** (groupe d'habitations) block.
■ **~ directionnel** traffic island; **~s de Langerhans** islets of Langerhans; **~ de vente** display stand.

îlotage /ilɔtaʒ/ *nm* Admin division into neighbourhoods[GB] (*for policing*).

ilote /ilɔt/ *nmf* Antiq Helot.

îlotier /ilɔtje/ *nm* Admin community policeman.

ils *pron pers mpl* ▶ **il**.

image /imaʒ/ *nf* **1** (reproduction) picture; **il ne sait pas lire mais il aime bien regarder les ~s** he can't read but he likes looking at the pictures; **2** Cin, TV (sur une pellicule) frame; (qualité de réglage) picture; (qualité artistique) photography; **24 ~s par seconde** 24 frames per second; **l'~ est trop sombre** the picture is too dark; **le scénario n'est pas formidable mais il y a de très belles ~** the storyline isn't great but there is some very beautiful photography; **le film contient des ~s choquantes** the film contains some shocking scenes; **nous vous présenterons quelques ~s de ce film** we'll show you an excerpt ou extract from the film; **l'industrie de l'~** Vidéo the video industry; Phot the photography industry; **3** (reflet) reflection, image; Phys image; **4** (représentation) picture; **leur livre donne une ~ totalement fausse de la situation/du pays** their book gives a totally false picture of the situation/country; **ils sont l'~ même du bonheur parfait** they are the picture of perfect happiness; **à l'~ de ses prédécesseurs, c'est un bureaucrate sans imagination** just like his predecessors, he's an unimaginative bureaucrat; **5** Littérat image; **il s'exprime par ~s** he expresses himself in images ou metaphors; **étudier les ~s d'un poème** to study the imagery of a poem; **6** Scol *reward given to pupils in the form of a small picture*.
■ **~ d'Épinal** lit *simplistic 19th century print of traditional French life*; fig clichéd image; **~ de marque** (de produit) brand image; (de société) corporate image; (de politicien, personnalité) (public) image; **~ pieuse** holy picture; **~ réelle** Phys real image; **~ virtuelle** Phys virtual image.

imagé, **~e** /imaʒe/ *adj* [*langage, style*] colourful[GB]; **il s'exprime de façon très ~e** he speaks in a very colourful[GB] way.

imagerie /imaʒʀi/ *nf* **1** (thématique) imagery; **~ populaire/romantique** popular/romantic imagery; **2** (industrie) print trade; **3** Ordinat imaging; **~ médicale** medical imaging.

imagier, **-ière** /imaʒje, ɛʀ/ *nm,f* **1** (marchand d'images) print-seller; (fabricant) print-manufacturer; **2** (sculpteur) figurine carver.

imaginable /imaʒinabl/ *adj* conceivable, imaginable.

imaginaire /imaʒinɛʀ/ **I** *adj* **1** (inventé) [*personnage, héros*] fictitious, imaginary; [*monde, univers*] imaginary, fictional; [*problème, ennemi*] imaginary; **2** Math [*nombre, partie*] imaginary.
II *nm* **1** (imagination) imagination; **l'~ collectif** the collective imagination; **être du domaine de l'~** to belong to the realms of the imagination; **2** (monde imaginé) **l'~ d'un auteur** the imaginative world of an author; **l'histoire bascule brusquement dans l'~** the story suddenly veers into make-believe.

imaginatif, **-ive** /imaʒinatif, iv/ *adj* imaginative.

imagination /imaʒinasjɔ̃/ *nf* imagination; **avoir de l'~** to have imagination, be imaginative; **manquer d'~** to lack imagination; **il a une ~ débordante** he has a very vivid ou fertile imagination; **cela a frappé mon ~** this caught my imagination; **faire preuve d'~** to show imagination; **un enfant plein d'~** a very imaginative child; **des chiffres qui dépassent** or **défient l'~** mind-boggling figures°.

imaginer /imaʒine/ [1] **I** *vtr* **1** (se représenter) to imagine, picture [*personne, chose, scène*]; **je l'imaginais plus grand** I imagined him to be taller; **je l'imaginais comme un héros** I imagined him as a hero; **tu n'imagines pas comme c'est douloureux/beau** you can't imagine how painful/beautiful it is; **imagine sa tête quand on lui a annoncé qu'il allait être père!** just picture his face when he was told he was going to be a father!; **on imagine difficilement qu'il puisse être élu** it's hard to believe that he will be elected; **j'imagine mal comment il pourrait gagner maintenant** I can't see how he could win now; **2** (supposer) to suppose; **imagine qu'il ne soit pas d'accord**... suppose he doesn't agree...; **3** (inventer) to devise, think up [*méthode, moyen*]; **il avait imaginé un moyen de s'enrichir rapidement** he had devised ou thought up a way of getting rich quickly; **que vas-tu ~?** how can you think such a thing?
II s'imaginer *vpr* **1** (se représenter) to imagine, picture [*chose, personne*]; **elle s'imaginait une plage bordée de cocotiers** she imagined ou pictured a beach bordered with coconut palms; **imaginez-vous qu'il est resté trois jours sans manger!** just imagine, he didn't eat for three days!; **2** (se voir) to picture oneself; **s'~ à 60 ans/au volant d'une superbe voiture** to picture oneself at 60/at the wheel of a superb car; **3** (croire) to think (**que** that); **elle s'imagine qu'elle peut réussir sans travailler** she thinks that she can succeed without doing any work.

imago /imago/ **I** *nm* Zool imago.
II *nf* Psych imago.

imam /imam/ **▶813** *nm* imam.

IMAO /imao/ *nm* (*abbr* = **inhibiteur de la monoamine-oxydase**) monoamine oxidase inhibitor.

imbattable /ɛ̃batabl/ *adj* (tous contextes) unbeatable (**à** at; **en** at).

imbécile /ɛ̃besil/ **I** *adj* [*personne, régime, remarque, mesure*] idiotic.
II *nmf* fool; **passer pour un ~** to look a fool; **faire l'~** to play the fool; **prendre qn pour un ~** to take sb for a fool; **~!**, **espèce d'~!** silly fool!; **faut quand même pas prendre les gens pour des ~s!** do they think people are stupid?; **jouer les ~s** to play dumb; **un ~ heureux** a happy simpleton; **pauvre ~!** poor fool!

imbécillité /ɛ̃besilite/ *nf* **1** (manque d'intelligence) stupidity; **avoir l'~ de faire** to be stupid enough to do; **il est d'une ~ rare** he's exceptionally stupid; **2** (manifestation de bêtise) **cesse de faire des ~s!** stop acting like an idiot!; **cesse de dire des ~s!** don't talk such nonsense!; **quelle ~!** (œuvre) what rubbish! GB, what garbage! US; (acte) what a stupid thing to do!; (propos) what nonsense!

imberbe /ɛ̃bɛʀb/ *adj* beardless.

imbiber /ɛ̃bibe/ [1] **I** *vtr* (imprégner) [*personne*] to soak [*chiffon, compresse, pâtisserie*] (**de** in); [*liquide*] to soak [*tissu, papier, sol*]; **imbibé d'eau** soaked in water.
II s'imbiber *vpr* **1** (s'imprégner) [*tissu, papier, sol*] to become soaked (**de** with); **laisser un tissu s'~ d'encre** to let a fabric soak up ink; **2**° fig (boire) to get tanked up°.

imbrication /ɛ̃bʀikasjɔ̃/ *nf* **1** (enchevêtrement) (d'objets) interlocking **¢**; (de rêves, souvenirs) intermingling **¢**; **2** Archit, Constr (de tuiles) overlapping **¢**, imbrication spéc; **3** Ordinat interleaving.

imbriqué, **~e** /ɛ̃bʀike/ **I** *pp* ▶ **imbriquer**.
II *pp adj* **1** Archit, Constr [*tuiles, ardoises, écailles*] overlapping, imbricate spéc; **2** fig [*problèmes, questions*] interlinked.

imbriquer /ɛ̃bʀike/ [1] **I** *vtr* **1** (faire se chevaucher) to overlap; **2** (faire s'enchevêtrer) to interlock [*objets*]; **3** Ordinat to interleave.
II s'imbriquer *vpr* **1** Archit, Constr [*tuiles, écailles, toits*] to overlap; **2** (s'enchevêtrer) [*chapitres, parties de récit*] to be interwoven; [*problèmes, questions*] to be interlinked; [*pièces*] to interlock; **tous ces problèmes**

s'imbriquent les uns dans les autres these problems are all interlinked.

imbroglio /ɛ̃bʀɔglijo/ *nm* **1** (situation compliquée) mess, imbroglio sout; **2** Théât (theatrical) imbroglio.

imbu, **~e** /ɛ̃by/ *adj* full (**de** of); **être ~ de soi-même** or **de sa personne** to be full of oneself.

imbuvable /ɛ̃byvabl/ *adj* **1** [*liquide*] undrinkable; **2**○ [*personne, discours, spectacle*] unbearable.

imitable /imitabl/ *adj* **facilement/difficilement ~** easy/difficult to imitate (*jamais épith*).

imitateur, **-trice** /imitatœʀ, tʀis/ ▶ **510** *nm,f* **1** (comédien) impressionist; **2** Art imitator.

imitatif, **-ive** /imitatif, iv/ *adj* imitative.

imitation /imitasjɔ̃/ *nf* **1** (action d'imiter) gén imitation; (de personne) impression; **l'~ de la nature/d'un son** the imitation of nature/of a sound; **faire un numéro d'~** to do impressions; **2** Comm imitation; **une pâle ~** a pale imitation; **c'est de l'~** it's imitation; **~ or/cuir/lézard** imitation gold/leather/lizardskin; **un sac ~ crocodile** an imitation crocodile handbag; **un manteau en ~ vison** a fake mink coat; **des bijoux ~** imitation jewels.

imiter /imite/ [1] *vtr* **1** (copier) to imitate [*geste, comportement, cri*]; to imitate, to copy [*maître, héros*]; to forge [*signature*]; **les enfants imitent leurs parents** children imitate their parents; **un revêtement de sol qui imite le bois** an imitation parquet flooring; **2** Théât [*personne*] to do an impression of [*acteur, personnalité*]; **3** (faire pareil) to do the same; **il part, je vais l'~** he's leaving and I'm going to do the same.

immaculé, **~e** /imakyle/ *adj* immaculate. ■ **l'Immaculée Conception** Relig the Immaculate Conception.

immanence /imanɑ̃s/ *nf* immanence.

immanent, **~e** /imanɑ̃, ɑ̃t/ *adj* [*justice, donnée*] immanent.

immangeable /ɛ̃mɑ̃ʒabl/ *adj* inedible.

immanquable /ɛ̃mɑ̃kabl/ *adj* [*panneau, cible*] impossible to miss; [*succès*] guaranteed.

immanquablement /ɛ̃mɑ̃kabləmɑ̃/ *adv* inevitably.

immatérialité /imateʀjalite/ *nf* immateriality.

immatériel, **-ielle** /imateʀjɛl/ *adj* **1** gén, Philos immaterial; **2** Jur intangible; **biens ~s** intangible assets.

immatriculation /imatʀikylasjɔ̃/ *nf* gén, Admin registration; **d'~** [*numéro, plaque*] registration GB, license US.

immatriculer /imatʀikyle/ [1] *vtr* gén, Admin to register [*personne, société*]; to register GB ou license US [*véhicule*]; **se faire ~ au consulat** to register with the consulate; **faire ~ un véhicule** to have a vehicle registered GB ou licensed US; **le propriétaire de la voiture immatriculée 8235 NG 69** the owner of the car, registration number GB ou license number US 8235 NG 69.

immature /imatyʀ/ *adj* immature.

immaturité /imatyʀite/ *nf* immaturity.

immédiat, **~e** /imedja, at/ **I** *adj* **1** (instantané) [*conséquence, effet, action, réaction*] immediate; **demander le retrait ~ des troupes** to ask for immediate withdrawal of troops; **décider l'envoi ~ de qn** to decide to send sb immediately; **embarquement ~** Aviat now boarding; **2** (le plus proche) [*voisin, environnement*] immediate; [*successeur*] direct; **en contact ~ avec la peau** in direct contact with the skin.
II *nm* **l'~** the present; **pour l'~** for the moment; **dans l'~** for the time being.

immédiatement /imedjatmɑ̃/ *adv* [*intervenir, partir, installer*] immediately; **~ consommable** ready to eat.

immédiateté /imedjat(ə)te/ *nf* immediacy.

immémorial, **~e**, *mpl* **-iaux** /imemɔʀjal, o/ *adj* immemorial; **depuis des temps immémoriaux** since time immemorial.

immense /imɑ̃s/ *adj* [*lieu, personne, objet, main, arbre, foule, succès, difficulté, ressources*] huge; [*chagrin, douleur, regret*] immense; [*joie, plaisir, courage*] great; **l'~ majorité des gens** the vast majority of people.

immensément /imɑ̃semɑ̃/ *adv* immensely.

immensité /imɑ̃site/ *nf* **1** (de lieu) immensity; (de connaissances) breadth; **2** (vaste étendue) expanse; **les ~s montagneuses** the mountainous expanses.

immergé, **~e** /imɛʀʒe/ **I** *pp* ▶ **immerger**.
II *pp adj* [*corps, objet*] submerged; [*terres, récifs*] sunken; [*sous-marin*] submerged; **la partie ~e de l'iceberg** lit the invisible part of the iceberg.

immerger /imɛʀʒe/ [13] **I** *vtr* (jeter à l'eau) to immerse [*objet*]; to bury [sth] at sea [*cadavre*]; to dump [sth] in the sea [*déchets*].
II s'immerger *vpr* **1** lit [*sous-marin*] to dive; **2** fig [*personne*] to immerse oneself (**dans** in).

immérité, **~e** /imeʀite/ *adj* undeserved.

immersion /imɛʀsjɔ̃/ *nf* **1** (de corps, d'objet) immersion; (de cadavre) burial at sea; (de déchets) dumping; **baptême par ~** (baptism by) immersion; **2** Géog (de terres) flooding; **3** Scol immersion (**dans** in).
■ **~ totale** Scol total immersion.

immettable○ /ɛ̃metabl/ *adj* [*vêtement*] unwearable.

immeuble /imœbl/ **I** *adj* **biens ~s** Jur (propriétés) real property (*sg*) GB, real estate (*sg*) US; Compta (actifs) real assets.
II *nm* **1** (bâtiment) building; **un ~ de dix étages** a ten-floor building; **2** Jur real asset.
■ **~ de bureaux** Constr office block GB, office building; **~ d'habitation** Constr residential block GB, apartment building US; **~ intelligent** Constr smart building; **~ de rapport** rented property GB, rental building US.

immigrant, **~e** /imigʀɑ̃, ɑ̃t/ *adj, nm,f* immigrant.

immigration /imigʀasjɔ̃/ *nf* immigration; **lois sur l'~** immigration laws; **le débat sur l'~** the debate on immigration.

immigré, **~e** /imigʀe/ **I** *adj* immigrant (*épith*); **travailleur ~** immigrant worker.
II *nm,f* immigrant; **~ clandestin** illegal immigrant GB, illegal alien US.

immigrer /imigʀe/ [1] *vi* to immigrate.

imminence /iminɑ̃s/ *nf* imminence (**de** of); **devant l'~ de** in view of the imminence of.

imminent, **~e** /iminɑ̃, ɑ̃t/ *adj* [*arrivée, libération, chute, accouchement*] imminent.

immiscer: **s'immiscer** /imise/ [12] *vpr* to interfere (**dans** in).

immixtion /imiksjɔ̃/ *nf* interference.

immobile /imɔbil/ *adj* **1** lit [*personne, animal, corps*] motionless; [*véhicule, barque*] stationary; [*feuillage, mer*] motionless; [*regard*] unwavering; **se tenir** or **rester ~** to keep still; **2** fig [*dogme*] fixed.

immobilier, **-ière** /imɔbilje, ɛʀ/ **I** *adj* [*secteur, agent, crédit, investissement, annonce*] property GB, real-estate US; ▶ **bien**.
II *nm* **l'~** property GB, real estate US; **la flambée de l'~** the steep rise in property prices GB ou real estate US; **l'~ de loisirs** leisure property GB, vacation property US.

immobilisation /imɔbilizasjɔ̃/ **I** *nf* **1** lit (action) immobilization; (résultat) immobility; **la fracture exige l'~ totale du bras** the fracture requires complete immobilization of the arm; **le tribunal peut ordonner l'~ d'un véhicule** the court can order that a vehicle be immobilized; **attendre l'~ de la machine** wait until the machine has stopped; **après ~ complète du train** after the train has come to a complete stop; **2** Fin (de capital) locking up (**de** of); **3** Jur conversion into immovables.
II immobilisations *nfpl* Fin fixed assets.

immobiliser /imɔbilize/ [1] **I** *vtr* **1** (arrêter) to bring [sth] to a standstill [*véhicule*]; to stop [*machine, cheval*]; to immobilize [*armée*]; **2** (maintenir immobile) to immobilize [*personne, membre, avion, adversaire*]; **elle a été immobilisée pendant un mois** she was laid up○ ou immobilized for a month; **l'avion est immobilisé en bout de piste** the plane is immobilized at the end of the runway; **3** (paralyser) [*grève, crise*] to bring [sth] to a halt [*économie, situation, pays*]; **4** Fin to tie up [*capitaux*]; **5** Jur to convert [sth] into immovables [*biens*].
II s'immobiliser *vpr* (volontairement) [*conducteur, piéton, foule*] to stop; (involontairement) [*véhicule, personne*] to come to a halt; **la voiture s'est immobilisée sur le côté** the car came to a halt on the side of the road.

immobilisme /imɔbilism/ *nm* opposition to change.

immobiliste /imɔbilist/ **I** *adj* [*politique, discours*] which opposes change (*épith, après n*); [*personne*] who opposes change (*épith, après n*).
II *nmf* opponent of change.

immobilité /imɔbilite/ *nf* gén (de personne, d'animal) immobility; (d'eau, air, de paysage, feuillage) stillness.

immodéré, **~e** /imɔdeʀe/ *adj* [*besoin, goût, amour, dépenses*] excessive; [*propos, attitude*] immoderate; **faire un usage ~ de l'alcool** to abuse alcohol.

immodérément /imɔdeʀemɑ̃/ *adv* immoderately.

immodeste /imɔdɛst/ *adj* immodest.

immolateur /imɔlatœʀ/ *nm* immolator.

immolation /imɔlasjɔ̃/ *nf* immolation; **~ par le feu** immolation by fire.

immoler /imɔle/ [1] **I** *vtr* Relig to sacrifice, immolate sout [*victime, animal*] (**sur** on; **à** to); **~ une victime aux dieux** to sacrifice a victim to the gods.
II s'immoler *vpr* to commit suicide as a public protest; **s'~ par le feu** to set fire to oneself.

immonde /imɔ̃d/ *adj* **1** (sale) [*lieu*] filthy; [*bête*] foul; **2** (révoltant) [*personne, nourriture*] revolting.

immondices /imɔ̃dis/ *nfpl* refuse ¢ GB, trash ¢ US.

immoral, **~e**, *mpl* **-aux** /imɔʀal, o/ *adj* immoral.

immoralement /imɔʀalmɑ̃/ *adv* immorally.

immoralisme /imɔʀalism/ *nm* immoralism.

immoraliste /imɔʀalist/ *adj, nmf* immoralist.

immoralité /imɔʀalite/ *nf* immorality; **d'une ~ totale** totally immoral.

immortaliser /imɔʀtalize/ [1] **I** *vtr* to immortalize [*moment, souvenir, personne*].
II s'immortaliser *vpr* to achieve immortality.

immortalité /imɔʀtalite/ *nf* immortality.

immortel, **-elle** /imɔʀtɛl/ **I** *adj* [*âme, dieu, œuvre, beauté, symbole*] immortal.
II *nm,f* **1**○ (académicien) *member of the Académie française*; **2** Mythol Immortal.
III immortelle *nf* Bot everlasting (flower).
■ **immortelle blanche** Bot pearly everlasting; **immortelle des sables** Bot strawflower, helichrysum.

immotivé, **~e** /imɔtive/ *adj* [*colère, action*] unmotivated; [*réclamation, crainte*] groundless.

immuabilité /imɥabilite/ *nf* immutability.

immuable /imɥabl/ *adj* [*loi, cycle, geste*] immutable; [*rituel, tradition, paysage*] unchanging; [*légende*] enduring; [*bonheur*] perpetual.

immuablement /imɥabləmɑ̃/ *adv* immutably.

immunisation /imynizasjɔ̃/ *nf* immunization.

immuniser /imynize/ [1] *vtr* **1** Méd to immunize (**contre** against); **2** (protéger) **~ qn contre** to make sb immune to [*peur, critique*]; **être immunisé contre qch** to be immune to sth; **~ qn contre l'envie de faire qch** to cure sb of wanting to do sth.

immunitaire /imynitɛʀ/ *adj* Méd immune.

immunité /imynite/ *nf* immunity; **~ diplomatique/fiscale** diplomatic/tax immunity.

immunodéficitaire /imynodefisitɛʀ/ *adj* immunodeficient.

immunodépresseur /imynodepʀesœʀ/ **I** *adj* immunosuppressive.

II *nm* immunosuppressant.

immunogène /imynoʒɛn/ *adj* immunogenic.

immunoglobuline /imynoglɔbylin/ *nf* immunoglobulin.

immunologie /imynolɔʒi/ *nf* immunology.

immunologique /imynolɔʒik/ *adj* immunological.

immunologiste /imynolɔʒist/ ▶**510**| *nmf* immunologist.

immunothérapie /imynoteʀapi/ *nf* immunotherapy.

immutabilité /imytabilite/ *nf* immutability.

impact /ɛ̃pakt/ *nm* **1** (choc) impact; (trace) mark; **des traces d'~** marks of impact; **des ~s de balles** bullet holes; **2** (effet) impact; **avoir de l'~ sur** to have an impact on; **avoir un ~ considérable** to have a considerable impact; **sous l'~ de qch** under the impact of sth.

impair, ~e /ɛ̃pɛʀ/ **I** *adj* **1** Math [*nombre, numéro*] odd; [*jour, année*] odd-numbered; **2** Anat unpaired.

II *nm* **1** (gaffe) indiscretion, faux pas; **commettre un ~** to make a faux pas; **2** Jeux odd numbers (*pl*); **jouer l'~** to play the odd numbers.

impalpable /ɛ̃palpabl/ *adj* impalpable; [*poudre*] very fine to the touch (*jamais épith*).

imparable /ɛ̃paʀabl/ *adj* [*coup, tir, botte*] unstoppable; [*riposte*] unanswerable; [*argument, raisonnement*] irrefutable.

impardonnable /ɛ̃paʀdɔnabl/ *adj* unforgivable, unpardonable; **vous êtes ~ d'avoir fait** it was unforgivable of you to do.

imparfait, ~e /ɛ̃paʀfɛ, ɛt/ **I** *adj* **1** (ayant des défauts) [*image, représentation, homme*] imperfect; **2** (incomplet) [*connaissance, guérison*] partial; [*travail*] unfinished; **3** Ling [*prétérit, subjonctif*] imperfect.

II *nm* Ling imperfect; **l'~ de l'indicatif/du subjonctif** the imperfect indicative/subjunctive.

imparfaitement /ɛ̃paʀfɛtmɑ̃/ *adv* imperfectly.

impartial, ~e, *mpl* **-iaux** /ɛ̃paʀsjal, o/ *adj* impartial.

impartialement /ɛ̃paʀsjalmɑ̃/ *adv* impartially.

impartialité /ɛ̃paʀsjalite/ *nf* impartiality; **en toute ~ voici ce que j'en pense** from a completely impartial standpoint, this is what I think.

impartir /ɛ̃paʀtiʀ/ [3] *vtr* **~ qch à qn** to allow sb sth [*temps*]; to grant sb sth [*dons, pouvoirs*]; **~ un délai à qn pour faire** to give sb a set time to do; **faire qch dans les temps impartis** to do sth within the given time; **le délai imparti à qn pour faire** the time given to sb to do.

impasse /ɛ̃pas/ *nf* **1** (cul-de-sac) dead end, cul-de-sac GB; **2** (situation sans issue) deadlock; **conduire dans une ~** to lead to a deadlock; **conduire qn dans une ~** to lead sb into deadlock; **être dans l'~** or **dans une ~** to have reached (a) deadlock; **sortir de l'~** to break ou end the deadlock; **~ constitutionnelle/diplomatique** constitutional/diplomatic deadlock; **3** Scol, Univ **faire une ~** to skip parts of one's revision GB ou review US; **faire une ~ en histoire** to skip parts of one's history revision; **4** Jeux finesse.

impassibilité /ɛ̃pasibilite/ *nf* impassivity.

impassible /ɛ̃pasibl/ *adj* impassive.

impassiblement /ɛ̃pasibləmɑ̃/ *adv* impassively.

impatiemment /ɛ̃pasjamɑ̃/ *adv* impatiently.

impatience /ɛ̃pasjɑ̃s/ *nf* impatience; **montrer des signes d'~** to show signs of impatience; **piétiner d'~** to seethe with impatience; **avec ~** impatiently; **mourir** or **brûler d'~ de faire** to be dying to do.

impatiens /ɛ̃pasjɑ̃s/ *nf inv* Bot busy lizzie.

impatient, ~e /ɛ̃pasjɑ̃, ɑ̃t/ **I** *adj* impatient.

II *nm,f* impatient person; **quel ~ tu fais!** you are so impatient!

III impatiente *nf* Bot busy lizzie.

impatienter /ɛ̃pasjɑ̃te/ [1] **I** *vtr* to irritate (**avec** with; **en faisant** by doing).

II s'impatienter *vpr* to get impatient, to lose patience; **s'~ devant qch** to get impatient with sth; **s'~ de qch** to lose patience over sth; **s'~ contre qn/qch** to get impatient with sb/about sth.

impavide /ɛ̃pavid/ *adj* unperturbed; **~ devant le danger** unperturbed by the danger.

impayable○ /ɛ̃pɛjabl/ *adj* [*histoire, personne*] priceless○; **elle est ~!** she's a scream○!, she's priceless○!

impayé, ~e /ɛ̃pɛje/ **I** *adj* unpaid.

II *nm* **les ~s** unpaid debts, outstanding debts.

impeccable /ɛ̃pɛkabl/ *adj* **1** (soigné) [*travail, style*] perfect, faultless; [*hygiène*] impeccable; **s'exprimer dans un français ~** to speak perfect ou faultless French; **2** (propre) [*vêtement, tenue*] impeccable; [*appartement, maison*] spotless; [*rue, plage*] spotlessly clean; [*papiers, tapis*] in perfect condition; **il est toujours ~** he's always impeccably dressed; **3**○ (parfait) great○, perfect.

impeccablement /ɛ̃pɛkabləmɑ̃/ *adv* [*repassé, vêtu*] impeccably; [*enveloppé, posé*] beautifully; **~ nettoyé/tenu** spotlessly clean/kept; **travail ~ fait** perfect ou faultless job; **il parle ~ le français** he speaks perfect ou faultless French.

impécunieux, -ieuse /ɛ̃pekynjø, øz/ *adj* fml impecunious.

impécuniosité /ɛ̃pekynjozite/ *nf* fml impecuniosity.

impédance /ɛ̃pedɑ̃s/ *nf* impedance.

impedimenta /ɛ̃pedimɛnta, ɛ̃pedimɛ̃ta/ *nmpl* impedimenta.

impénétrabilité /ɛ̃penetʀabilite/ *nf* (de végétation, forteresse, texte, mystère) impenetrability; (de personne, visage, caractère) inscrutability.

impénétrable /ɛ̃penetʀabl/ *adj* **1** [*végétation, forteresse, texte, mystère*] impenetrable (**à** to); **2** [*personne, caractère, visage*] inscrutable.

IDIOMES **les voies du Seigneur sont ~s** God moves in mysterious ways.

impénitence /ɛ̃penitɑ̃s/ *nf* impenitence.

impénitent, ~e /ɛ̃penitɑ̃, ɑ̃t/ *adj* **1** [*buveur, fumeur*] inveterate; [*célibataire*] confirmed; **2** Relig impenitent sout, unrepentant.

impensable /ɛ̃pɑ̃sabl/ *adj* unthinkable, unimaginable.

imper○ /ɛ̃pɛʀ/ *nm* raincoat, mac○ GB.

impératif, -ive /ɛ̃peʀatif, iv/ **I** *adj* imperative; **il est ~ de faire qch** it is imperative that sth should be done.

II *nm* **1** (contrainte) imperative; **~s économiques/budgétaires/sociaux** economic/budgetary/social imperatives; (de la mode) demand; (de qualité, solidarité, prévision) necessity (**de** for); (de situation) imperative (**de** of); (d'emploi du temps) constraints (**de** of); **les ~s de la concurrence/modernité** the need to be competitive/up to date; **2** Ling imperative; **~ présent/passé** present/past imperative.

impérativement /ɛ̃peʀativmɑ̃/ *adv* **il faut ~ faire** it is imperative ou absolutely necessary to do; **répondre ~ avant le 31 janvier** replies must be received before January 31; **nous faire parvenir ~ le formulaire avant lundi** the form must reach us before Monday.

impératrice /ɛ̃peʀatʀis/ *nf* empress; **l'~ Joséphine** the Empress Josephine.

imperceptibilité /ɛ̃pɛʀsɛptibilite/ *nf* imperceptibility.

imperceptible /ɛ̃pɛʀsɛptibl/ *adj* imperceptible (**à** to).

imperceptiblement /ɛ̃pɛʀsɛptibləmɑ̃/ *adv* imperceptibly.

imperfectible /ɛ̃pɛʀfɛktibl/ *adj* that cannot be perfected (*épith, après n*).

imperfectif, -ive /ɛ̃pɛʀfɛktif, iv/ **I** *adj* imperfective.

II *nm* imperfective.

imperfection /ɛ̃pɛʀfɛksjɔ̃/ *nf* **1** (manque de perfection) imperfection; **2** (défaut) (de personne, travail, d'objet) imperfection, defect; (de mécanisme, machine) defect; (de caractère, personnalité, méthode) shortcoming.

impérial, ~e, *mpl* **-iaux** /ɛ̃peʀjal, o/ **I** *adj* imperial; **la Chine/Rome ~e** Imperial China/Rome.

II impériale *nf* **1** Transp upper deck; **autobus à ~e** double-decker bus; **2** (barbe) imperial.

impérialement /ɛ̃peʀjalmɑ̃/ *adv* imperially.

impérialisme /ɛ̃peʀjalism/ *nm* imperialism.

impérialiste /ɛ̃peʀjalist/ *adj, nmf* imperialist.

impérieusement /ɛ̃peʀjøzmɑ̃/ *adv* **1** (autoritairement) imperiously; **2** (de façon urgente) urgently.

impérieux, -ieuse /ɛ̃peʀjø, øz/ *adj* **1** (autoritaire) [*personne, ton, allure, voix, air*] imperious; **d'un ton ~** imperiously; **2** (urgent) [*besoin, nécessité, désir*] pressing.

impérissable /ɛ̃peʀisabl/ *adj* [*denrées, œuvre, gloire*] imperishable; **le spectacle ne m'a pas laissé un souvenir ~** iron the show was not what you'd call an unforgettable experience.

impéritie /ɛ̃peʀisi/ *nf* fml incompetence.

imperméabilisation /ɛ̃pɛʀmeabilizasjɔ̃/ *nf* waterproofing.

imperméabiliser /ɛ̃pɛʀmeabilize/ [1] *vtr* to waterproof.

imperméabilité /ɛ̃pɛʀmeabilite/ *nf* **1** (de tissu, vêtement, bâche, peinture) waterproof qualities; (de sol, matière) impermeability; **2** (de personne) imperviousness (**à** to).

imperméable /ɛ̃pɛʀmeabl/ **I** *adj* **1** [*tissu, vêtement, bâche, peinture*] waterproof; [*sol, matière*] impermeable; **2** (insensible) impervious (**à** to); **être ~ à un argument** to be deaf ou impervious to an argument.

II *nm* raincoat.

impersonnalité /ɛ̃pɛʀsɔnalite/ *nf* **1** (caractère impersonnel) impersonality; **2** Ling impersonal form.

impersonnel, -elle /ɛ̃pɛʀsɔnɛl/ *adj* (tous contextes) impersonal; **de façon impersonnelle** impersonally.

impersonnellement /ɛ̃pɛʀsɔnɛlmɑ̃/ *adv* impersonally, dispassionately.

impertinence /ɛ̃pɛʀtinɑ̃s/ *nf* **1** (caractère) impertinence; **avec ~** impertinently; **2** (parole) impertinent remark, impertinence sout.

impertinent, ~e /ɛ̃pɛʀtinɑ̃, ɑ̃t/ **I** *adj* impertinent (**envers qn** to sb).

II *nm,f* impertinent person; **vous n'êtes qu'une ~e!** you're extremely impertinent!

imperturbabilité /ɛ̃pɛʀtyʀbabilite/ *nf* imperturbability.

imperturbable /ɛ̃pɛʀtyʀbabl/ *adj* imperturbable, unruffled; **~, José continua son histoire** quite unperturbed, José continued with the story; **rester ~** to remain unruffled (**face à, devant** in the face of).

imperturbablement /ɛ̃pɛʀtyʀbabləmɑ̃/ *adv* [*continuer, écouter*] unperturbed; [*sérieux, aimable*] invariably.

impétigo /ɛ̃petigo/ ▶271 *nm* impetigo.

impétrant, **~e** /ɛ̃petʀɑ̃, ɑ̃t/ *nm,f* **1** (récipiendaire) *person receiving a qualification*; **2** (candidat) controv applicant.

impétueusement /ɛ̃petɥøzmɑ̃/ *adv* impetuously.

impétueux, **-euse** /ɛ̃petɥø, øz/ *adj* **1** (fougueux) [*orateur*] impassioned; [*personne, caractère, jeunesse*] impetuous, hot-headed; **2** (violent) [*vent, torrent*] raging.

impétuosité /ɛ̃petɥozite/ *nf* (de personnes) impetuousness; (de vent, torrent) fury.

impie /ɛ̃pi/ **I** *adj* [*paroles, actes*] impious.
II *nmf* impious person.

impiété /ɛ̃pjete/ *nf* impiousness.

impitoyable /ɛ̃pitwajabl/ *adj* [*personne, juge, tribunal*] merciless, pitiless (**avec** with; **envers** towards GB, to US); [*lutte, guerre, loi*] relentless; [*sélection, analyse, châtiment*] ruthless; **les critiques ont été ~s avec lui** the critics have shown him no mercy; **l'univers ~ qu'il décrit** the pitiless world that he describes.

impitoyablement /ɛ̃pitwajabləmɑ̃/ *adv* mercilessly.

implacabilité /ɛ̃plakabilite/ *nf* implacability, relentlessness.

implacable /ɛ̃plakabl/ *adj* [*logique*] implacable; [*répression, réquisitoire, verdict*] harsh; [*négociateur, critique*] implacable.

implacablement /ɛ̃plakabləmɑ̃/ *adv* [*progresser, continuer*] relentlessly; [*réprimer*] ruthlessly.

implant /ɛ̃plɑ̃/ *nm* implant; **~ dentaire** dental implant.

implantable /ɛ̃plɑ̃tabl/ *adj* implantable.

implantation /ɛ̃plɑ̃tasjɔ̃/ *nf* **1** (mise en place) (de secte, parti, d'industrie) establishment; (d'usine, entreprise) setting up, construction; (d'appareils, équipement) installation; (de cheveux) implantation; (de personnes, groupes) settlement; **~ massive/locale/industrielle/internationale** massive/local/industrial/international development; **2** (entreprise) site; **les ~s de la firme à l'étranger** the firm's sites abroad; **3** (disposition) (de bâtiments, machines) layout; (de dents) implantation; **4** Méd implantation.

implanté, **~e** /ɛ̃plɑ̃te/ **I** *pp* ▶ **implanter**.
II *pp adj* **1** (établi) [*usine, parti, personne*] established; [*population*] settled; **l'entreprise est bien ~e en France** the firm is well established in France; **un préjugé solidement ~ chez** or **parmi**... a deeply rooted prejudice among...; **2** (fixé) [*racines*] established; **dents bien/mal ~es** straight/crooked teeth.

implanter /ɛ̃plɑ̃te/ [1] **I** *vtr* **1** (établir) to establish [*usine, entreprise, représentant*]; to build [*hypermarché, cinéma*]; to open [*agence, cafétéria*]; to install [*équipements, machines*]; to introduce [*produit, système, mode*]; to instil[GB] [*idées, préjugés*]; **2** Méd to implant [*prothèse, cheveux*].
II s'implanter *vpr* [*entreprise, régime*] to establish itself; [*usine*] to be built; [*parti, produit, système, mode*] to establish itself; [*personne*] to settle; [*parti, doctrine*] to gain a following; **s'~ sur un marché** to gain a foothold in a market.

implication /ɛ̃plikasjɔ̃/ *nf* **1** (participation) involvement (**dans** in); **il nie toute ~ dans l'attentat à la bombe** he denies any involvement in the bombing; **2** (conséquence) implication (**sur** for); **3** (engagement personnel) commitment; **4** Math implication.

implicite /ɛ̃plisit/ *adj* **1** (non formulé) implicit; **le consensus ~** the tacit consensus; **2** Ordinat default (*épith*); **affectation/option ~** default assignment/option.

implicitement /ɛ̃plisitmɑ̃/ *adv* **1** (non explicitement) implicitly; **il lui a ~ apporté son soutien** he supported him tacitly; **2** Ordinat by default.

impliquer /ɛ̃plike/ [1] **I** *vtr* **1** (mêler) to implicate [*personne*] (**dans** in); **il a été directement impliqué dans le scandale** he was directly implicated in the scandal; **2** (faire participer) to involve [*personnel, employé*] (**dans** in); **se sentir impliqué dans un projet** to feel involved in a project; **3** (mettre en jeu) to involve [*mesure*]; **cela implique de faire** that involves doing; **cela implique qu'elle fasse** that involves her doing; **un tel projet implique de gros moyens** such a project involves a lot of money; **4** (signifier) to mean; **cela implique qu'elle le fera** this means she'll do it.
II s'impliquer *vpr* to get involved (**dans** in).

implorant, **~e** /ɛ̃plɔʀɑ̃, ɑ̃t/ *adj* [*personne, yeux, voix*] imploring, beseeching; **d'un air ~** imploringly.

imploration /ɛ̃plɔʀasjɔ̃/ *nf* liter entreaty.

implorer /ɛ̃plɔʀe/ [1] *vtr* **1** (supplier) to beseech, implore [*personne, juge, dieux*] (**de faire** to do); **2** (demander) to beg for [*délai, faveur*]; **~ la clémence/le pardon de qn** to beg for sb's clemency/forgiveness; **~ l'aide de qn** to beg sb for help.

imploser /ɛ̃ploze/ [1] *vi* to implode.

implosif, **-ive** /ɛ̃plozif, iv/ **I** *adj* implosive.
II implosive *nf* Phon implosive.

implosion /ɛ̃plozjɔ̃/ *nf* **1** Tech implosion; **2** (de système, parti, groupe) collapse.

impoli, **~e** /ɛ̃pɔli/ **I** *adj* [*personne, geste*] rude (**envers** to), impolite (**envers** to).
II *nm,f* rude ou impolite person.

impoliment /ɛ̃pɔlimɑ̃/ *adv* rudely, impolitely.

impolitesse /ɛ̃pɔlitɛs/ *nf* **1** (conduite) rudeness, impoliteness; **avec ~** rudely; **2** (acte) **commettre de graves ~s** to behave very rudely.

impondérabilité /ɛ̃pɔ̃deʀabilite/ *nf* imponderability.

impondérable /ɛ̃pɔ̃deʀabl/ **I** *adj* imponderable.
II *nm* imponderable; **il reste beaucoup d'~s** there are still many imponderables; **sauf ~s, nous partirons à 10 h** barring unforeseen cicumstances, we shall leave at 10 o'clock.

impopulaire /ɛ̃pɔpylɛʀ/ *adj* unpopular.

impopularité /ɛ̃pɔpylaʀite/ *nf* unpopularity.

importable /ɛ̃pɔʀtabl/ *adj* **1** Écon [*marchandise*] importable; **2** (qu'on ne peut pas porter) [*vêtement*] unwearable; [*valise, fardeau*] (encombrant) too awkward to carry; (trop lourd) too heavy to carry.

importance /ɛ̃pɔʀtɑ̃s/ *nf* **1** (gravité) importance; **c'est de la plus haute** or **première ~** it's of the highest ou of the utmost importance; **c'est d'une ~ capitale/vitale** it's of immense/vital importance; **d'~ relative** of relative importance; **donner** or **accorder de l'~ à qch** to attach importance to sth; **attacher beaucoup/très peu d'~ à qch** to attach great/very little importance to sth; **prendre de l'~** [*événement, affaire*] to gain in importance; **sans ~** [*élément, fait, détail*] unimportant; **cela est sans ~** it's not important; **avoir de l'~** to be important; **avoir son ~** to have importance; **n'avoir aucune ~** (pas grave) to be unimportant; (pas essentiel) to make no difference; **d'~** [*fait, événement, problème*] important; **quelle ~?** what does it matter?, so what○!; **2** (taille) (de réduction, société) size; (de travail, d'effort) amount; (de massacres, dégâts) extent; **prendre de l'~** [*société, ville*] to increase in size; **ville d'~ moyenne** medium-sized town; **d'une certaine ~** sizable; **battre** or **rosser**○ **qn d'~** to beat sb soundly; **3** (influence) importance; **prendre de l'~** [*personne*] to become more important; **pour se donner de l'~** to make oneself look important.

important, **~e** /ɛ̃pɔʀtɑ̃, ɑ̃t/ **I** *adj* **1** (essentiel) [*rôle, discours, événement, problème*] important; **il est ~ qu'elle sache** it is important that she should know; **l'~ est de faire** what's important is to do; **peu ~** not very important; **2** (considérable) [*réduction, hausse, baisse*] significant; [*nombre, effort, écart*] considerable; [*communauté, colonie, héritage*] sizable; [*ville, société*] large; [*retard*] lengthy; [*actionnaire*] major; **3** (influent) [*personne, poste, œuvre*] important; **avoir/prendre un air ~** to have/adopt a self-important manner.
II *nm,f* **faire l'~, jouer les ~s** to act important○.

importateur, **-trice** /ɛ̃pɔʀtatœʀ, tʀis/ **I** *adj* [*pays*] importing (*épith*); [*société*] import (*épith*); **pays ~s de pétrole/d'armes** oil-/arms-importing countries.
II *nm,f* importer.

importation /ɛ̃pɔʀtasjɔ̃/ *nf* **1** (introduction) importation; **d'~** [*coûts, compagnie, quotas*] import (*épith*); [*produit, article*] imported; **2** (produit) import; **~s de luxe** luxury imports.

importer /ɛ̃pɔʀte/ [1] **I** *vtr* to import [*marchandise, main-d'œuvre, mode*] (**de** from); to introduce [*espèce végétale*] (**de** from).
II *v impers* **1** (être important) **cela importe peu** it doesn't much matter; **ce qui importe c'est qu'elle comprenne** what matters is that she (should) understand; **peu importe** or **qu'importe qu'elle ne comprenne pas** it doesn't matter ou what does it matter if she doesn't understand; **'il pleut!'—'peu importe!'** 'it's raining!'—'never mind!'; **lequel?—n'importe** which one?—it doesn't matter; **2** (dans locutions) **n'importe quel enfant** any child; **à n'importe quel moment** at any time; **n'importe qui** anybody, anyone; **n'importe lequel** any; **n'importe où** anywhere; **viens n'importe quand** come anytime; **prends n'importe quoi** take anything; **n'importe quoi de tranchant** any sharp object; **elle dit n'importe quoi** she talks nonsense; **c'est (du) n'importe quoi** it's rubbish; **c'est fait n'importe comment** it's done any old how○; **mon père, ce n'est pas n'importe qui** my father's not just anybody.

import-export /ɛ̃pɔʀɛkspɔʀ/ *nm inv* import-export trade; **faire de l'~, être dans l'~** [*personne, société*] to be in the import-export trade; **d'~** [*société*] import-export (*épith*).

importun, **~e** /ɛ̃pɔʀtœ̃, yn/ **I** *adj* **1** [*personne*] (gênant) troublesome; (irritant) tiresome; (indésirable) unwelcome; **un visiteur ~** an unwelcome visitor; **je ne voudrais pas être ~** I don't wish to intrude; **2** [*visite, intervention*] ill-timed; [*remarque*] ill-chosen; [*question*] awkward.
II *nm,f* (visiteur) unwelcome visitor; (gêneur) tiresome individual.

importuner /ɛ̃pɔʀtyne/ [1] *vtr* **1** (ennuyer) to bother (**de** with); **2** (déranger) to disturb.

importunité /ɛ̃pɔʀtynite/ *nf* importunity.

imposable /ɛ̃pozabl/ *adj* [*personne*] liable to tax (*après n*); [*revenu, bénéfice*] taxable; **non ~** [*personne*] not liable to tax (*après n*); [*revenu, bénéfice*] non-taxable.

imposant, **~e** /ɛ̃pozɑ̃, ɑ̃t/ *adj* [*stature, monument*] imposing; [*cérémonie, œuvre*] impressive.

imposé, **~e** /ɛ̃poze/ **I** *pp* ▶ **imposer**.
II *pp adj* **1** (fixé) [*tarif, délai*] fixed; **2** (obligatoire) [*thème, travail*] set; **3** Sport [*mouvement, figure*] set.

imposer /ɛ̃poze/ [1] I *vtr* **1** (rendre obligatoire) [*personne*] to impose [*sanctions, délai*] (**à qn** on sb); to lay down [*règlement*]; [*situation*] to require [*mesures, changement*]; **~ ses amis à ses parents** to impose one's friends on one's parents; **~ que** to rule that; **on leur a imposé de faire** they were obliged ou forced to do; **~ le port de lunettes protectrices aux ouvriers** to make it obligatory for workers to wear protective goggles; **cela impose qu'on réfléchisse au problème** this demands that we think about the problem; **il nous a imposé sa présence** he forced his presence on us; **elle nous a imposé le silence** she made us be quiet; **2** (faire admettre) to impose [*idée, volonté, point de vue*]; to set [*style, mode*]; **cela l'a imposé comme un des meilleurs chirurgiens** this has established him as one of the best surgeons; **3** (inspirer) to command [*respect, admiration*]; **4** Fisc to tax [*personne, produit, revenu*]; **5** Imprim to impose.
II **en imposer** *vtr ind* to be impressive; **elle en impose!** she's impressive!; **elle en impose par son calme/intelligence** her calm/intelligence is impressive; **elle en impose à ses élèves** she inspires respect in her pupils; **ne t'en laisse pas ~** don't let yourself be overawed (**par** by).
III **s'imposer** *vpr* **1** (être évident) [*choix, solution*] to be obvious (**à** to); (être requis) [*prudence, mesure, changement*] to be called for; **une visite au Louvre s'impose** a visit to the Louvre is a must; **s'~ comme évident** to be obvious; **2** (s'astreindre à) to impose [sth] on oneself [*horaires, habitudes alimentaires, discipline*]; **s'~ un sacrifice/des efforts démesurés** to force oneself to make a sacrifice/a huge effort; **s'~ de travailler le soir** to make it a rule to work in the evening; **3** (déranger) to impose oneself (**à qn** on sb); **je ne voudrais pas m'~** I wouldn't like to impose; **4** (se faire admettre) **il s'est imposé comme leader** he established himself as the leader; **la ville s'est imposée comme capitale culturelle** the city established itself as the cultural capital; **s'~ comme langue officielle** to come in as the official language; **s'~ dans un domaine** [*personne*] to make a name for oneself in a field; **s'~ sur un marché** [*produit, firme*] to establish itself in a market; **s'~ par son intelligence** to stand out because of one's intelligence; **s'~ comme le plus grand architecte contemporain** to be universally acknowledged as the greatest contemporary architect; **5** (pour dominer) [*personne*] to make one's presence felt; [*volonté*] to impose itself.

imposition /ɛ̃pozisjɔ̃/ *nf* **1** Fisc taxation; **double ~** double taxation; **de nouvelles ~s** new forms of taxation; **2** Imprim imposition.
■ **~ des mains** laying on of hands.

impossibilité /ɛ̃pɔsibilite/ *nf* impossibility (**de faire** of doing); **être dans l'~ de faire, se voir dans l'~ de faire** to be unable to do, to find it impossible to do; **mettre qn dans l'~ de faire** to make it impossible for sb to do; **l'~ dans laquelle il se trouvait de faire** the fact that he was unable to do; **l'~ d'une telle rencontre** the impossibility of such a meeting taking place.

impossible /ɛ̃pɔsibl/ I *adj* **1** (impensable, infaisable) impossible; **~ à faire** impossible to do; **problème ~ à résoudre** problem that is impossible to solve; **il est ~ que** it is impossible ou not possible that; **il est ~ qu'il soit déjà arrivé** he cannot possibly have arrived yet; **il n'est pas ~ que** it is not impossible that; **il n'est pas ~ qu'il démissionne** it is not impossible that he will resign; **être ~ (à qn) de faire** to be impossible (for sb) to do; **il m'est ~ de faire** it is impossible for me to do, I cannot possibly do; **cela m'est ~** I really can't; **2**○ (insupportable) [*enfant, personne*] impossible, insufferable; (extravagant) [*goût, heure, habitude, nom*] impossible; **rendre la vie ~ à qn** to make life impossible for sb.
II *nm* **l'~** the impossible; **demander l'~ (à qn)** to ask the impossible ou the earth (of sb); **faire** or **tenter l'~** to do everything one can; **les médecins ont tenté l'~ pour le sauver** the doctors did everything they could to save him; **si, par ~** if, by some remote chance ou by some miracle.
III *excl* out of the question!
IDIOMES **à l'~ nul n'est tenu** Prov nobody can be expected to do the impossible; **~ n'est pas français** there's no such word as 'can't'.

imposte /ɛ̃pɔst/ *nf* **1** (pierre) impost; **2** (de fenêtre) transom.

imposteur /ɛ̃pɔstœʀ/ *nm* impostor.

imposture /ɛ̃pɔstyʀ/ *nf* **1** (action de tromper) deception, imposture sout; **2** (acte de tromperie) fraud.

impôt /ɛ̃po/ I *nm* **1** (prélèvement) tax; **payer ses ~s** to pay one's taxes; **payer 20 000 F d'~s** to pay 20,000 F in tax; **avant/après ~** before/after tax; **~ direct/indirect** direct/indirect tax; **~ progressif/proportionnel** progressive/proportional tax; **2** (fiscalité) **l'~** taxation.
II **impôts** *nmpl* (institution) **les ~s** tax (*sg*); **réduire les ~s** to reduce tax; **payer des ~s** to pay tax.
■ **~ additionnel** surtax; **~ sur les bénéfices** corporation tax; **~ sur le capital** tax on capital; **~ foncier** property tax; **~ sur la fortune** wealth tax; **~ sur les grandes fortunes**, **IGF** ≈ wealth tax; **~ indiciaire** wealth-related tax; **~s locaux** local taxes; **~ sur le patrimoine** inheritance tax; **~ sur les plus-values** capital gains tax; **~ de quotité** proportional tax; **~ sur le revenu** income tax; **~ sur le revenu des personnes physiques**, **IRPP** personal income tax; **~ sur les sociétés** corporate tax, company tax; **~ de solidarité sur la fortune**, **ISF** ≈ wealth tax.

impotence /ɛ̃pɔtɑ̃s/ *nf* lack of mobility; **~ fonctionnelle** impaired mobility.

impotent, **~e** /ɛ̃pɔtɑ̃, ɑ̃t/ I *adj* [*vieillard*] infirm.
II *nm,f* person with impaired mobility.

impraticable /ɛ̃pʀatikabl/ *adj* **1** [*chemin, route*] impassable; **2** [*projet*] unworkable, impracticable.

imprécation /ɛ̃pʀekasjɔ̃/ *nf* imprecation.

imprécatoire /ɛ̃pʀekatwaʀ/ *adj* imprecatory.

imprécis, **~e** /ɛ̃pʀesi, iz/ *adj* [*contour, forme*] vague; [*idée, concept*] hazy; [*souvenir, renseignement, date*] vague; [*tir, coup*] inaccurate; [*résultats, statistiques, mot, information*] imprecise; [*personne*] vague (**à propos de** about); **la loi est ~e à ce sujet** the law is vague on that point; **être ~ dans son raisonnement/ses attaques** to be imprecise in one's reasoning/attacks.

imprécision /ɛ̃pʀesizjɔ̃/ *nf* (de connaissances) imprecision; (de données, résultats, renseignement, document, carte) vagueness; (de tir, coup) inaccuracy.

imprégnation /ɛ̃pʀeɲasjɔ̃/ *nf* **1** Tech (dans du bois, tissu) impregnation; **2** Méd **~ alcoolique dans l'organisme** alcohol level in the blood; **~ en œstrogènes** oestrogen levels; **3** fig **apprendre une langue par ~** to learn a language by immersing oneself in it.

imprégner /ɛ̃pʀeɲe/ [14] I *vtr* **1** (saturer) Tech to impregnate [*tissu, bois*] (**de** with); to dye [*cuir*]; **l'humidité imprègne les murs** there is damp in the walls; **une forte odeur de tabac imprégnait leurs vêtements** their clothes smelled strongly of tobacco; **2** fig **son éducation l'a imprégné de préjugés** his upbringing riddled him with prejudices; **une doctrine imprégnée de christianisme** a doctrine heavily influenced by Christian thinking.
II **s'imprégner** *vpr* [*étudiant*] to immerse oneself (**de** in).

imprenable /ɛ̃pʀənabl/ *adj* [*citadelle*] impregnable; [*vue*] magnificent and protected.

impréparation /ɛ̃pʀepaʀasjɔ̃/ *nf* lack of preparation.

imprésario /ɛ̃pʀesaʀjo/ ▸ **510** *nm* agent, impresario.

imprescriptibilité /ɛ̃pʀɛskʀiptibilite/ *nf* imprescriptibility.

imprescriptible /ɛ̃pʀɛskʀiptibl/ *adj* imprescriptible.

impression /ɛ̃pʀesjɔ̃/ *nf* **1** (sentiment immédiat) impression; **quelles sont vos ~s?** what are your impressions?; **ma première ~ a été que...** my first impression was that...; **échangez vos ~s** tell each other your impressions; **se fier à ses ~s** to trust one's first impressions; **2** (marque morale) impression; **faire peu/beaucoup d'~** to make little/a great impression; **faire ~** [*personne, exploit*] to make an impression; **faire bonne/mauvaise ~** to make a good/bad impression (**sur qn** on sb); **faire forte ~** to make a strong impression; **il ne m'a fait aucune ~** he didn't make any impression on me; **3** (sensation) impression; **avoir l'~ de faire** to feel one is doing; **j'ai l'~ de planer/d'étouffer/d'être surveillé** I feel I am gliding/suffocating/being watched; **j'ai comme l'~ d'avoir**○**...** iron I somehow feel I have...; **avoir l'~ que** to have a feeling that; **j'ai comme l'~ que**○**...** iron I have a vague feeling that...; **donner une ~ d'immensité/de chaleur/de satiété** to give an impression of vastness/of warmth/of satiety; **donner l'~ de faire/d'être** to give the impression of doing/being; **donner l'~ que...** to give the impression that...; **il veut donner l'~ qu'il écoute/participe** he wants to give the impression that he is listening/participating; **le film laisse une ~ de malaise** this film leaves one feeling uneasy; **ça m'a fait une drôle d'~ de les revoir** it was a strange feeling seeing them again; **4** Imprim, Tech (de textes, tissus, billets, d'affiches) printing; **faire de l'~ sur tissu** to print on fabric; **technique d'~** printing process; **défaut d'~** printing error; **~ en couleurs** colour[GB] printing; **~ typographique/offset** letterpress/offset printing; **l'ouvrage est à l'~** the book is with the printers; **faute d'~** misprint; **5** (motif imprimé) pattern; **6** Phot exposure; **temps d'~** exposure time; **7** Art, Constr primer.

impressionnable /ɛ̃pʀesjɔnabl/ *adj* **1** (sensible) sensitive; (influençable) impressionable; **il est peu ~** he's not easily shocked; **2** Phot [*papier, plaque*] sensitized.

impressionnant, **~e** /ɛ̃pʀesjɔnɑ̃, ɑ̃t/ *adj* **1** (remarquable) [*résultat, nombre, collection, spectacle, joueur*] impressive; [*arsenal, défi*] formidable; **être ~ de bêtise** to be amazingly stupid; **un film ~ de vérité** an amazingly realistic film; **2** (choquant) [*spectacle, image*] disturbing.

impressionner /ɛ̃pʀesjɔne/ [1] *vtr* **1** (faire de l'effet) [*personne, qualité, spectacle*] to impress [*personne*]; **j'ai été très impressionné par ton travail** I was very impressed by your work; **se laisser facilement ~** to be easily impressed; **ne te laisse pas ~ par les examinateurs** don't let the examiners upset you; **le dernier candidat m'a favorablement impressionné** I was favourably[GB] impressed by the last candidate; **2** (choquer) [*spectacle, image*] to disturb [*personne*]; **3** Physiol to act on [*rétine, oreille*]; **4** Phot to expose [*pellicule*].

impressionnisme /ɛ̃pʀesjɔnism/ *nm* Impressionism.

impressionniste /ɛ̃pʀesjɔnist/ I *adj* **1** Art Impressionist; **2** Littérat, Mus impressionistic.
II *nmf* Impressionist.

imprévisibilité /ɛ̃pʀevizibilite/ *nf* unpredictability.

imprévisible /ɛ̃pʀevizibl/ **I** *adj* unpredictable.
II *nm* **un ~** an unexpected event; **l'~** the unexpected.

imprévoyance /ɛ̃pʀevwajɑ̃s/ *nf* lack of foresight.

imprévoyant, **~e** /ɛ̃pʀevwajɑ̃, ɑ̃t/ **I** *adj* improvident.
II *nm,f* improvident person.

imprévu, **~e** /ɛ̃pʀevy/ **I** *adj* **1** (non prévu) unforeseen; **dépenses ~es** unforeseen expenses; **2** (non prévisible) unexpected; **réaction ~e** unexpected reaction.
II *nm* **1** (incident) hitch; **~ de dernière minute** last-minute hitch; **sauf ~** barring accidents; **2** (choses inattendues) **l'~** the unexpected; **faire face à l'~** to cope with the unexpected; **plein d'~** [*personne, film*] quirky; [*vacances, voyage*] with a few surprises (*épith, après n*); [*métier*] never dull (*jamais épith*), which is never dull (*épith, après n*); **3** (dépense exceptionnelle) unforeseen expense.

imprimable /ɛ̃pʀimabl/ *adj* printable.

imprimante /ɛ̃pʀimɑ̃t/ *nf* printer.
■ **~ à bulle d'encre** bubble-jet printer; **~ à jet d'encre** ink-jet printer; **~ (à) laser** laser printer; **~ à marguerite** daisywheel printer; **~ matricielle** dot matrix printer.

imprimatur /ɛ̃pʀimatyʀ/ *nm inv* Relig, fig imprimatur.

imprimé, **~e** /ɛ̃pʀime/ **I** *pp* ▶ **imprimer**.
II *pp adj* Imprim, Tex [*image, papier, tissu*] printed.
III *nm* **1** (formulaire) form; **~ fiscal** tax form; **2** (papier imprimé) printed matter ¢; **envoyer qch au tarif ~s** to send sth at printed paper rate; **3** (tissu) print; **un ~ à fleurs/noir et blanc** a floral/black and white print; **l'~ et l'uni** printed and plain fabrics; **de très beaux ~s** beautiful prints.

imprimer /ɛ̃pʀime/ [1] *vtr* **1** Imprim to print [*texte, journaux, étiquettes, billets*]; Tex to print a design on [*tissu*]; **~ sur aluminium/papier recyclé** to print on aluminium GB ou aluminum US/recycled paper; **un tissu imprimé de motifs géométriques** fabric with a geometric pattern; **2** (publier) to publish [*texte, ouvrage, auteur*]; **3** (reproduire) to stamp [*cachet, sceau*] (**sur** on); to print [*initiales*] (**sur** on); **4** (transmettre) [*personne*] to give [*style, direction, orientation, cadence*] (**à qch/qn** to sth/sb); to transmit [*impulsion, oscillation*] (**à qch** to sth); **il a imprimé un nouveau style au débat** he gave a new style to the debate; **~ un mouvement de rotation à une roue** to start a wheel turning; **5** (laisser une empreinte) [*personne*] to leave an imprint of [*forme, dents, pied*] (**dans** in; **sur** in); **des traces de pneus imprimées dans la boue** wheel tracks imprinted in the mud; **6** (graver) [*temps, vieillesse*] to etch [*rides*]; **être imprimé dans la mémoire de qn** [*souvenir, images*] to be engraved in sb's memory; **être imprimé sur le visage de qn** [*tristesse, joie*] to be written all over sb's face.

imprimerie /ɛ̃pʀimʀi/ *nf* **1** (technique) printing; **la découverte de l'~** the discovery of printing; **atelier d'~** printing shop; **2** (entreprise) printing works (+ *v sg*); (personnel) printers (*pl*), print workers (*pl*); **une ~ d'étiquettes** label-printing company; **une ~ clandestine** an underground printing press.
■ **~ industrielle** (secteur) trade printing; (entreprise) trade printing company; **~ de labeur** (secteur) book printing; (entreprise) book printer's (+ *v sg ou pl*); **Imprimerie nationale** government publications office.

imprimeur /ɛ̃pʀimœʀ/ ▶ **510** *nm* **1** (directeur) printer; **~ éditeur** printer and publisher; **2** (ouvrier) (**ouvrier**) **~** print worker, printer.

improbabilité /ɛ̃pʀɔbabilite/ *nf* improbability.

improbable /ɛ̃pʀɔbabl/ *adj* [*rencontre, score, hypothèse, risque*] unlikely, improbable; **le score avancé est hautement ~** the results announced are highly unlikely; **il est ~ qu'il puisse venir** it is unlikely that he will be able to come.

improductif, **-ive** /ɛ̃pʀɔdyktif, iv/ **I** *adj* **1** (qui ne produit rien) gén unproductive; Fin **capitaux ~s** idle capital; **2** Entr **le personnel ~** ancillary staff.
II *nm,f* **les ~s** ancillary staff ¢.

improductivité /ɛ̃pʀɔdyktivite/ *nf* unproductiveness.

impromptu, **~e** /ɛ̃pʀɔ̃pty/ **I** *adj* impromptu.
II *adv* impromptu; **arriver ~ chez un ami** to arrive at a friend's unexpectedly.
III *nm* Littérat, Mus impromptu.

imprononçable /ɛ̃pʀɔnɔ̃sabl/ *adj* unpronounceable.

impropre /ɛ̃pʀɔpʀ/ *adj* **1** (incorrect) [*terme, tournure, usage*] incorrect; **2** (inadapté) **~ à** [*eau, produit*] unfit for [*consommation*]; [*plage*] unsafe for [*baignade*].

improprement /ɛ̃pʀɔpʀəmɑ̃/ *adv* incorrectly.

impropriété /ɛ̃pʀɔpʀijete/ *nf* **1** (caractère impropre) incorrectness; **2** (mot impropre) incorrect usage.

improvisateur, **-trice** /ɛ̃pʀɔvizatœʀ, tʀis/ *nm,f* improviser; **talent d'~** talent for improvisation.

improvisation /ɛ̃pʀɔvizasjɔ̃/ *nf* **1** (prestation) improvisation; **mon discours était une ~** my speech was improvised; **2** (genre) **l'~** improvisation; **~ libre** free improvisation; **tout laisser à l'~** to improvise at the last minute.

improvisé, **~e** /ɛ̃pʀɔvize/ **I** *pp* ▶ **improviser**.
II *pp adj* **1** (non préparé) [*discours, poème, chanson*] improvised; **2** (de fortune) [*civière, pont, table*] improvised; [*repas, rencontre*] impromptu (*épith*); [*moyens, réforme*] makeshift (*épith*); [*solution*] ad hoc; [*chauffeur, cuisinier*] stand-in.

improviser /ɛ̃pʀɔvize/ [1] **I** *vtr* to improvise, extemporize [*poème, sonate*]; to improvise [*chapeau, tableau, repas, discours*]; to concoct [*excuse, alibi*]; **~ un hôpital/une école** to set up a makeshift hospital/school; **~ une rencontre** to set up an impromptu meeting.
II *vi* to improvise; **~ à l'orgue** to improvise on the organ; **savoir ~** to know how to improvise.
III s'improviser *vpr* **1** (se faire) [*personne*] **s'~ cuisinier/avocat** to act as a cook/lawyer; **2** (se créer) **un camp pour réfugiés ne s'improvise pas** you can't create a refugee camp just like that.

improviste: **à l'improviste** /alɛ̃pʀɔvist/ *loc adv* unexpectedly.

imprudemment /ɛ̃pʀydamɑ̃/ *adv* [*parler, traverser*] carelessly; [*agir, montrer, annoncer, s'attaquer*] unwisely; [*conduire*] recklessly.

imprudence /ɛ̃pʀydɑ̃s/ *nf* **1** (témérité) carelessness; **l'~ de l'automobiliste** the driver's carelessness; **avoir l'~ de faire** to be foolish enough to do; **être d'une grande ~** to be very careless; **2** (acte) **commettre une ~/des ~s** to do something foolish/foolish things; **pas d'~s surtout** make sure you don't do anything foolish.

imprudent, **~e** /ɛ̃pʀydɑ̃, ɑ̃t/ **I** *adj* [*personne, automobiliste, parole*] careless; [*action, comportement*] rash; **il est ~ de la part de qn de faire** it is rash of sb to do.
II *nm,f* foolhardy person; **les ~s** the foolhardy.

impubère /ɛ̃pybɛʀ/ *adj* [*fille, garçon*] prepubescent; [*corps*] pre-pubescent.

impubliable /ɛ̃pybljjabl/ *adj* unpublishable.

impudemment /ɛ̃pydamɑ̃/ *adv* impudently.

impudence /ɛ̃pydɑ̃s/ *nf* **1** (effronterie) impudence; **avoir l'~ de faire** to have the impudence to do; **l'~ de ton attitude/de tes paroles** the impudence of your attitude/of your language; **2** (acte) impudent behaviour[GB] ¢; (parole) impudent remark.

impudent, **~e** /ɛ̃pydɑ̃, ɑ̃t/ **I** *adj* impudent.
II *nm,f* impudent person.

impudeur /ɛ̃pydœʀ/ *nf* (physique) immodesty; (de sentiments) shamelessness.

impudicité /ɛ̃pydisite/ *nf* indecency.

impudique /ɛ̃pydik/ *adj* [*geste, parole*] obscene; [*vêtement*] indecent; [*personne*] shameless.

impudiquement /ɛ̃pydikmɑ̃/ *adv* shamelessly, brazenly.

impuissance /ɛ̃pɥisɑ̃s/ *nf* **1** (incapacité) (de personne, gouvernement) impotence; **l'~ de qn face à qch** the helplessness of sb in the face of sth; **~ à faire** inability to do; **réduire qn à l'~** to render sb powerless; **2** Physiol impotence; **l'~ sexuelle** sexual impotence.

impuissant, **~e** /ɛ̃pɥisɑ̃, ɑ̃t/ **I** *adj* **1** (inefficace) [*personne, gouvernement, police*] powerless; [*effort*] vain; **~ à faire** powerless to do; **assister ~ à qch** to watch sth helplessly; **2** Physiol impotent; **~ sexuellement** sexually impotent.
II *nm* Méd impotent man.

impulsif, **-ive** /ɛ̃pylsif, iv/ **I** *adj* impulsive.
II *nm,f* impulsive person.

impulsion /ɛ̃pylsjɔ̃/ *nf* **1** (force) impetus; **donner une (nouvelle) ~ à** to give fresh impetus to; **donner une ~ considérable à** to give considerable impetus to; **sous l'~ de qn** at sb's instigation; **sous l'~ de l'Allemagne/du parti/du maire** at the instigation of Germany/the party/the mayor; **sous l'~ de la psychanalyse** thanks to psychoanalysis; **2** (désir) impulse; **~ brusque** sudden impulse; **3** Psych drive; **~ morbide** morbid drive; **4** Phys (en dynamique) impulse; **5** Électron, Électrotech, Phys, Télécom pulse.

impulsivité /ɛ̃pylsivite/ *nf* impulsiveness; **avec ~** impulsively.

impunément /ɛ̃pynemɑ̃/ *adv* [*voler, souiller, régner, bafouer*] with impunity; **on ne joue pas ~ avec sa santé** you don't play fast and loose with your health and get away with it.

impuni, **~e** /ɛ̃pyni/ *adj* [*crime, coupable*] unpunished; **rester ~** to go unpunished.

impunité /ɛ̃pynite/ *nf* impunity; **bénéficier/être assuré d'une totale ~** to be granted/guaranteed immunity from prosecution; **faire qch en toute ~** to do sth with complete impunity.

impur, **~e** /ɛ̃pyʀ/ *adj* **1** (immoral) [*cœur, pensées*] impure; **2** (souillé) [*eau, air*] dirty; [*sang*] tainted; **3** (mélangé) [*minerai*] impure; **4** Relig [*animal, personne*] unclean.

impureté /ɛ̃pyʀte/ *nf* Cosmét impurity; **débarrasser la peau de ses ~s** to cleanse the skin of impurities.

imputabilité /ɛ̃pytabilite/ *nf* Jur imputability.

imputable /ɛ̃pytabl/ *adj* **1** gén [*erreur, accident, échec*] attributable (**à** to); **2** Compta [*somme, financement*] chargeable (**sur** to).

imputation /ɛ̃pytasjɔ̃/ *nf* **1** (accusation) accusation, imputation sout; **répondre à des ~s calomnieuses** to answer slanderous accusations; **2** Compta charging (**à** to).

imputer /ɛ̃pyte/ [1] *vtr* **1** (attribuer) to attribute (**à** to), to impute sout (**à** to); **plusieurs crimes lui ont été imputés** several crimes were imputed to him; **2** Compta to charge (**sur** to).

imputrescibilité /ɛ̃pytʀesibilite/ *nf* rotproof quality.

imputrescible /ɛ̃pytʀesibl/ *adj* rotproof.

INA /ina/ *nm* (*abbr* = **Institut national de l'audiovisuel**) *French national institute for audiovisual archives, training and research.*

inabordable /inabɔʀdabl/ *adj* **1** (impossible à atteindre) [*côte, sommet*] inaccessible; [*personne, milieu*] unapproachable; **2** (très cher) [*produit, service*] prohibitively priced; [*prix, tarif*] prohibitive; **les loyers deviennent ~s** rents are becoming prohibitive; **cet hôtel est ~ pour nous/eux** this hotel is beyond our/their means.

inabouti, **~e** /inabuti/ *adj* [*projet*] unfinished; [*rêve, désir*] unfulfilled.

in absentia /inabsɑ̃sja/ *loc adv* in absentia.

inaccentué, **~e** /inaksɑ̃tɥe/ *adj* Phon unstressed.

inacceptable /inaksɛptabl/ *adj* unacceptable (**pour** to).

inaccessibilité /inaksesibilite/ *nf* inaccessibility.

inaccessible /inaksesibl/ *adj* **1** (hors d'atteinte) [*lieu*] inaccessible (**à qn** to sb); [*personne*] unapproachable; **une région ~ par la route** a region that is inaccessible by road; **2** (hors de portée) [*vérité*] unattainable (**à qn** by sb); [*rêve*] impossible; **ce livre est ~ pour lui** this book is beyond him; **3** (insensible) **il est ~ à la pitié** he's incapable of pity.

inaccompli, **~e** /inakɔ̃pli/ I *adj* **1** gén [*travail, projet*] unfinished; [*désir, souhait*] unfulfilled; **2** Ling imperfective.
II *nm* Ling imperfective

inaccomplissement /inakɔ̃plismɑ̃/ *nm* (de désir, souhait) non-fulfilment[GB]; (de clause) nonobservance; **l'~ d'une promesse** failure to keep a promise.

inaccoutumé, **~e** /inakutyme/ *adj* unusual.

inachevé, **~e** /inaʃve/ *adj* unfinished.

inachèvement /inaʃɛvmɑ̃/ *nm* incompleteness.

inactif, **-ive** /inaktif, iv/ I *adj* **1** gén [*personne, cerveau, journée*] idle; **rester ~** to remain idle; **2** Sociol [*personne*] inactive; [*population*] non-working; **3** Fin [*capital*] idle; [*marché*] slow; [*compte*] dormant; **4** Géol [*volcan*] inactive; **5** [*substance, composé*] inactive.
II *nm,f* Sociol non-worker; **les ~s** the non-working population ¢.

inaction /inaksjɔ̃/ *nf* (absence d'activité) inactivity.

inactivité /inaktivite/ *nf* **1** (manque d'activité) inactivity; **~ forcée** enforced inactivity; **2** Admin, Mil inactivity; **être en ~** to be out of active service.

inadaptation /inadaptasjɔ̃/ *nf* **1** gén (de loi, d'équipement) inappropriateness (**à** for); **2** Psych, Sociol maladjustment (**à** to); **~ sociale/affective** social/emotional maladjustment.

inadapté, **~e** /inadapte/ I *adj* **1** Psych, Sociol [*enfant, enfance*] maladjusted; **2** (qui ne convient pas) [*méthode, moyen*] inappropriate (**à** for); [*outil*] unsuitable (**à** for); [*système, loi*] ill-adapted (**à** to); **avoir un comportement ~ à la situation** to behave inappropriately; **3** (mal préparé) [*personne*] ill-equipped (**à** for).
II *nm,f* Psych, Sociol (personne) maladjusted person; (enfant) maladjusted child; **les ~s** maladjusted people.

inadéquat, **~e** /inadekwa, at/ *adj* [*système, moyen, réponse*] inadequate; [*structure, bâtiment*] unsuitable.

inadéquation /inadekwasjɔ̃/ *nf* (inadaptation) unsuitability; (décalage) disparity; **l'~ entre l'offre et la demande** the discrepancy between supply and demand.

inadmissibilité /inadmisibilite/ *nf* Jur (de preuve) inadmissibility.

inadmissible /inadmisibl/ *adj* **1** (intolérable) [*comportement, erreur, situation*] intolerable; **2** (inacceptable) [*proposition*] unacceptable; **3** Jur [*preuve*] inadmissible.

inadvertance: **par inadvertance** /paʀinadvɛʀtɑ̃s/ *loc adv* inadvertently.

inaliénabilité /inaljenabilite/ *nf* Jur inalienability.

inaliénable /inaljenabl/ *adj* Jur inalienable.

inaltérabilité /inalteʀabilite/ *nf* **1** Tech (résistance) (de matière, substance) unalterability, resistance; (de couleur) fastness; **~ d'un matériau à l'air/à l'humidité** resistance of a material to the effects of air/damp; **2** (permanence) permanence; **l'~ de nos principes** the immutability of our principles.

inaltérable /inalteʀabl/ *adj* **1** Tech (résistant) [*matériau, substance*] unalterable, non-corroding; [*couleur*] fade-resistant; **~ à** resistant to the effects of; **2** (immuable) [*ciel, air*] unchanging; [*caractère*] constant; [*principe*] immutable; [*espoir, règle, attachement*] steadfast; [*sentiment, humour*] unfailing.

inaltéré, **~e** /inalteʀe/ *adj* [*métal, substance*] unaltered; [*air, ciel*] pure.

inamical, **~e**, *mpl* **-aux** /inamikal, o/ *adj* unfriendly.

inamovibilité /inamɔvibilite/ *nf* Admin (de personne) irremovability; (de fonction, charge) permanence.

inamovible /inamɔvibl/ *adj* **1** [*fonctionnaire, magistrat*] irremovable; [*poste, charge*] for life (*après n*); **être ~** hum [*personne*] to be a permanent fixture; **2** (qu'on ne peut retirer) [*panneau, élément*] fixed; **3** (qu'on ne peut modifier) [*règle*] immutable.

inanimé, **~e** /inanime/ *adj* [*matière*] inanimate; [*personne, corps*] (inconscient) unconscious; (sans vie) lifeless.

inanité /inanite/ *nf* **1** (manque d'intérêt) inanity; **2** (inutilité) futility, pointlessness.

inanition /inanisjɔ̃/ *nf* starvation; **mourir d'~** to die of starvation; **tomber d'~** to feel faint with hunger.

inaperçu, **~e** /inapɛʀsy/ *adj* **passer ~** to go unnoticed; **ta remarque n'est pas passée ~e** your remark didn't go unnoticed.

inappétence /inapetɑ̃s/ *nf* Méd, Psych inappetence.

inapplicable /inaplikabl/ *adj* [*théorie, réforme*] unworkable; [*clause, traité*] unenforceable.

inapplication /inaplikasjɔ̃/ *nf* **1** (d'élève) lack of application; **2** (de loi, réglementation) **~ de** failure to enforce GB, nonenforcement of US.

inappliqué, **~e** /inaplike/ *adj* **1** [*élève*] lacking application (*après n*); **2** [*loi, réglementation*] unenforced.

inappréciable /inapʀesjabl/ *adj* **1** (exceptionnel) [*service, soutien*] invaluable; [*avantage*] inestimable; **2** (indéfinissable) [*quantité, différence*] imperceptible.

inapte /inapt/ I *adj* **1** gén unfit (**à** for; **à faire** to do); **2** Mil **~ (au service militaire)** unfit (for military service).
II *nmf* Mil man/woman unfit for military service; **les ~s (au service militaire)** those declared unfit for military service.

inaptitude /inaptityd/ *nf* **1** gén unfitness (**à qch** for sth; **à faire** for doing); **~ à vivre en société** unfitness for living in society; **2** Mil **~ (au service militaire)** unfitness (for military service).

inarticulé, **~e** /inaʀtikyle/ *adj* inarticulate.

inassimilable /inasimilabl/ *adj* **1** [*aliment*] indigestible; **2** [*personnes, groupe*] that cannot be integrated (*épith, après n*).

inassouvi, **~e** /inasuvi/ *adj* [*appétit*] insatiable; [*soif*] fig unquenchable (*épith*); [*personne, corps, chair*] unsatisfied; [*ambition, âme*] unfulfilled; [*haine*] enduring.

inassouvissable /inasuvisabl/ *adj* insatiable.

inassouvissement /inasuvismɑ̃/ *nm* **~ de qch** failure to satisfy sth.

inattaquable /inatakabl/ *adj* **1** Mil [*forteresse, position*] unassailable; **2** (qui échappe aux critiques) [*personne, conduite, réputation*] irreproachable; **3** (irréfutable) [*argumentation, jugement*] irrefutable; [*droit*] unchallengeable; [*honnêteté*] indisputable; **4** Tech (inaltérable) [*matériau, substance*] (par la rouille) rust-proof; (par les vers) woodworm-proof; (par le temps) weatherproof.

inattendu, **~e** /inatɑ̃dy/ I *adj* unexpected.
II *nm* **1** (ce qui est imprévu) **l'~** the unexpected; **2** (caractère imprévisible) unexpectedness.

inattentif, **-ive** /inatɑ̃tif, iv/ *adj* **1** (distrait) [*enfant*] inattentive; [*air*] distracted; **2** (indifférent) [*personne*] heedless (**à** of).

inattention /inatɑ̃sjɔ̃/ *nf* **1** (manque d'attention) inattention; **moment d'~ (de qn)** lapse of concentration (on the part of sb); **2** Scol (erreur) careless mistake; **faute** or **erreur d'~** careless mistake.

inaudible /inodibl/ *adj* **1** (trop faible) inaudible; **2** (insupportable) unbearable.

inaugural, **~e**, *mpl* **-aux** /inogyʀal, o/ *adj* **1** (d'ouverture) [*cérémonie*] inauguration; [*discours, séance*] inaugural; **2** (tout premier) [*vol, voyage*] maiden.

inauguration /inogyʀasjɔ̃/ *nf* **1** (cérémonie) (de plaque, statue) unveiling; (de route, musée, bâtiment) inauguration; **cérémonie d'~** inauguration ceremony; **discours d'~** inaugural speech; **2** (ouverture) (de congrès, pont, d'exposition) opening; **3** (commencement) (de politique) launching.

inaugurer /inogyʀe/ [1] *vtr* **1** (par une cérémonie) to unveil [*statue, plaque*]; to open [*autoroute, musée, école*]; **2** (ouvrir) [*personne*] to open [*congrès, débat, exposition*]; to inaugurate [*série d'articles*]; to launch [*politique*]; **3** (marquer le début) [*événement, politique*] to mark the start of [*période*]; **4**○ (utiliser pour la première fois) to christen○ [*vêtement, voiture*].

inauthentique /inotɑ̃tik/ *adj* **1** (faux) [*œuvre*] not genuine (*jamais épith*); **2** (factice) [*personne, vie*] unauthentic.

inavouable /inavwabl/ *adj* shameful.

inavoué, **~e** /inavwe/ *adj* [*acte, crime, vice*] unconfessed; [*objectif, raison, but*] undisclosed; [*crainte, peur*] hidden; [*amour*] undeclared.

INC /iɛnse/ *nm* (*abbr* = **Institut national de la consommation**) French national consumer council.

inca /ɛ̃ka/ *adj inv* Inca.

Inca /ɛ̃ka/ *nmf* Inca.

incalculable /ɛ̃kalkylabl/ *adj* **1** (impossible à compter) innumerable; **un nombre ~ de fois** innumerable times; **2** (considérable) [*conséquences, risques*] incalculable.

incandescence /ɛ̃kɑ̃dɛsɑ̃s/ *nf* incandescence; **porter qch à ~** to heat sth until it's red hot.

incandescent, **~e** /ɛ̃kɑ̃dɛsɑ̃, ɑ̃t/ *adj* [*filament*] incandescent; [*métal*] white-hot; [*braises, lave, magma*] glowing.

incantation /ɛ̃kɑ̃tasjɔ̃/ *nf* incantation.

incantatoire /ɛ̃kɑ̃tatwaʀ/ *adj* incantatory.

incapable /ɛ̃kapabl/ I *adj* **1** (qui ne peut pas) (par nature) incapable (**de faire** of doing; **de qch** of sth); (temporairement) unable (**de faire** to do); **elle est ~ de méchanceté/de se concentrer** she's incapable of meanness/of concentrating; **il a été ~ de répondre à ma question** he was unable to answer my question; **2** (incompétent) incompetent; **un chef ~** an incompetent boss.
II *nmf* **c'est un ~!** he's useless!; **nous sommes gouvernés par des ~s** we are governed by incompetents.
■ **~ majeur** Jur person under disability; **~ mineur** Jur person legally incapable because a minor.

incapacitant, **~e** /ɛ̃kapasitɑ̃, ɑ̃t/ *adj* incapacitating.

incapacité /ɛ̃kapasite/ *nf* **1** (impossibilité) inability (**à faire** to do); **être dans l'~ de faire** to be unable to do; **2** (incompétence) incompetence (**en matière de** as regards);

3 (invalidité) disability; **~ partielle/totale** partial/total disability; **~ temporaire/permanente** temporary/permanent disability; **4** Jur incapacity; **~ civile** or **juridique** legal incapacity; **~s électorales** *cases leading to disenfranchisement*.

■ **~ d'exercice** Jur *incapacity to exercise a right*; **~ de jouissance** Jur *incapacity to enjoy a right*; **~ de travail** Jur, Prot Soc unfitness for work.

incarcération /ɛ̃kaʀseʀasjɔ̃/ *nf* imprisonment.

incarcérer /ɛ̃kaʀseʀe/ [14] *vtr* to imprison, jail; **il est incarcéré depuis trois ans** he has been in prison for three years.

incarnat, **~e** /ɛ̃kaʀna, at/ ▶**193** I *adj* incarnadine; ▶**trèfle**.
II *nm* incarnadine.

incarnation /ɛ̃kaʀnasjɔ̃/ *nf* **1** (personnification) incarnation, embodiment; **être l'~ du mal/de la bêtise** to be evil/stupidity incarnate sout ou personified; **2** Mythol, Relig incarnation.

incarné, **~e** /ɛ̃kaʀne/ I *pp* ▶**incarner**.
II *pp adj* **1** (personnifié) incarnate (*après n*); **cet homme, c'est la bêtise/la bonté ~e** that man is stupidity/kindness itself ou incarnate sout; **2** Relig incarnate (*après n*); **3** [*ongle*] ingrowing.

incarner /ɛ̃kaʀne/ [1] I *vtr* **1** (représenter) [*personne*] to embody, represent; **il incarne le conservatisme/l'espoir** he represents conservatism/hope; **2** (interpréter) [*acteur*] to play, portray [*personnage*]; **3** Relig to incarnate.
II **s'incarner** *vpr* **1** (être représenté) to be embodied (**dans** in); **les idéaux qui s'incarnent dans la révolution** the ideals embodied in the revolution; **toutes leurs aspirations s'incarnent dans leur nouveau président** their new president is the embodiment of ou embodies all their aspirations; **2** Relig to become incarnate (**dans** in); **3** lit **j'ai un ongle qui s'incarne** I have an ingrowing toenail.

incartade /ɛ̃kaʀtad/ *nf* **1** (écart de conduite) misdemeanour[GB]; **il a encore fait des ~s** he's been up to mischief again; **2** Équit shy; **faire une ~** to shy.

incassable /ɛ̃kasabl/ *adj* unbreakable.

incendiaire /ɛ̃sɑ̃djɛʀ/ I *adj* **1** [*matières, bombe, engin*] incendiary; **2** [*déclaration, discours, éditorial*] inflammatory; **3** [*sourire*] provocative.
II *nmf* arsonist.

incendie /ɛ̃sɑ̃di/ *nm* fire; **un ~ s'est déclaré au premier étage** a fire broke out on the first GB ou second US floor; **~ de forêt** forest fire; **borne d'~** fire hydrant; **lutte contre l'~** firefighting.

■ **~ criminel** arson.

incendié, **~e** /ɛ̃sɑ̃dje/ I *pp* ▶**incendier**.
II *pp adj* [*bâtiment*] burned-out; [*forêt*] burned; [*habitant*] made homeless by the fire (*après n*).
III *nm,f* Assur person affected by the fire.

incendier /ɛ̃sɑ̃dje/ [2] *vtr* **1** (brûler) to burn down, to torch [*bâtiment*]; to burn, to torch [*véhicule, ville, forêt, récolte*]; **trois maisons ont été incendiées pendant l'émeute** three houses were burned down during the riot; **2** (mettre le feu à) to set fire to; **3**○ (réprimander) to give [sb] a rocket○ GB, to lay into○; **se faire ~** to get a rocket○ GB; **~ qn du regard** to glower at sb; **4** fig (illuminer) to set [sth] ablaze, to make [sth] blaze with light [*vitres, paysage*].

incertain, **~e** /ɛ̃sɛʀtɛ̃, ɛn/ *adj* **1** (indéterminé) [*date, durée, origine*] uncertain; [*effet*] unknown; [*contours*] blurred; [*couleur*] indeterminate; [*sourire, sentiment*] vague; **être d'une humeur ~e** to be moody; **2** (aléatoire) [*résultat, entreprise, profit*] uncertain; [*temps*] unsettled; **leur guérison demeure ~e** their recovery is not guaranteed; **période ~e** period of uncertainty; **3** (hésitant) [*personne*] uncertain; [*électeur*] undecided; [*pas, voix*] hesitant; **être ~ de qch** not to be sure about sth; **mes sentiments sont ~s** I'm not sure of my feelings.

incertitude /ɛ̃sɛʀtityd/ *nf* **1** (d'avenir, de résultat, témoignage, prévision) uncertainty; **période de d'~** period of uncertainty; **~ économique** economic uncertainty; **les ~s d'une situation** the uncertainties of a situation; **2** (de personne) uncertainty; **laisser qn à ses ~s** to keep sb guessing; **être/vivre dans l'~** to be/live in a state of uncertainty; **mon ~ est totale** I'm completely in the dark; **vivre dans l'~ du lendemain** to live from day to day; **être dans l'~ sur ce que l'on doit faire** not to be sure what to do.

incessamment /ɛ̃sesamɑ̃/ *adv* very shortly; **~ sous peu** hum in next to no time.

incessant, **~e** /ɛ̃sɛsɑ̃, ɑ̃t/ *adj* [*bruit, pluie, appels, querelles*] incessant; [*effort, activité*] unceasing; [*critiques*] unremitting; [*changements*] constant.

incessible /ɛ̃sesibl/ Jur *adj* untransferable.

inceste /ɛ̃sɛst/ *nm* incest; **commettre un ~** to commit incest.

incestueux, **-euse** /ɛ̃sɛstɥø, øz/ *adj* (coupable d'inceste) incestuous; (né d'un inceste) born of an incestuous liaison; (constituant un inceste) incestuous; **amour ~** incestuous love.

inchangé, **~e** /ɛ̃ʃɑ̃ʒe/ *adj* unchanged; **le cours est ~** Fin the price is unchanged.

inchangeable /ɛ̃ʃɑ̃ʒabl/ *adj* unchangeable.

inchantable /ɛ̃ʃɑ̃tabl/ *adj* unsingable.

inchauffable /ɛ̃ʃofabl/ *adj* impossible to heat.

inchavirable /ɛ̃ʃaviʀabl/ *adj* uncapsizable.

inchoatif, **-ive** /ɛ̃kɔatif, iv/ *adj* Ling inchoative, inceptive.

incidemment /ɛ̃sidamɑ̃/ *adv* **1** (au passage) in passing; **2** (par hasard) by chance.

incidence /ɛ̃sidɑ̃s/ *nf* **1** (effet) impact (**sur** on); **avoir une ~ sur qch** to have an impact on sth; **2** Phys incidence; **point d'~** point of incidence; **3** Méd incidence.

incident, **~e** /ɛ̃sidɑ̃, ɑ̃t/ I *adj* **1** (peu important) incidental; **2** Ling [*proposition*] parenthetical; **3** Phys [*lumière*] incident.
II *nm* **1** (événement fortuit) incident; **~ diplomatique/nucléaire/de frontière** diplomatic/nuclear/border incident; **en cas d'~** if anything should happen; **2** (perturbation) **~ (de parcours)** hitch; **~ technique** technical hitch; **~ de séance** procedural hitch; **l'~ est clos** the matter is closed; **3** Jur incidental plea; **soulever un ~** to raise a point of law.
III **incidente** *nf* Ling parenthetical clause.

incinérateur /ɛ̃sineʀatœʀ/ *nm* **1** (pour déchets) incinerator; **2** (crématoire) crematorium GB, crematory US.

incinération /ɛ̃sineʀasjɔ̃/ *nf* (de déchets) incineration; (de corps) cremation.

incinérer /ɛ̃sineʀe/ [14] *vtr* to burn [*bois*]; to incinerate [*déchets*]; to cremate [*corps*]; **choisir de se faire ~** to choose to be cremated.

incise /ɛ̃siz/ *nf* **1** Mus phrase; **2** Ling comment clause.

inciser /ɛ̃size/ [1] *vtr* to make an incision in, to incise spéc [*bois, peau*]; to lance [*abcès*].

incisif, **-ive** /ɛ̃sizif, iv/ I *adj* **1** (perçant) [*écrit, discours, critique*] incisive; [*portrait*] telling; [*regard*] piercing; **2** (coupant) [*instrument*] sharp.
II **incisive** *nf* Anat, Dent incisor.

incision /ɛ̃sizjɔ̃/ *nf* **1** (action) (de peau, d'écorce) incision; (d'abcès) lancing ₵; **2** (coupure) incision; **faire** or **pratiquer une ~ dans** to make an incision in [*peau, écorce*]; to lance [*abcès*].

incitatif, **-ive** /ɛ̃sitatif, iv/ *adj* incentive (*épith*); **être ~** to act as an incentive; **mesure incitative**, **facteur ~** incentive.

incitation /ɛ̃sitasjɔ̃/ *nf* **1** (encouragement) incentive (**à** to); **2** Jur (excitation) incitement (**à** to).

■ **~ fiscale** Fin tax incentive; **~ à la débauche** incitement to moral corruption; **~ à la haine raciale** Jur incitement to racial hatred.

inciter /ɛ̃site/ [1] *vtr* [*personne, situation, attitude*] to encourage (**à faire** to do); [*événement, décision*] to prompt (**à faire** to do); **la croissance incite à investir/incite les particuliers à investir** growth encourages investment/encourages people to invest; **la campagne de presse a incité le président à intervenir** the press campaign prompted the president to intervene; **la récession incite à la prudence** the recession is making people cautious; **~ à l'espoir/au découragement** to be hopeful/discouraging; **~ vivement** to urge; **~ qn à la haine raciale** to incite sb to racial hatred; **~ à la haine raciale** to stir up racial hatred.

incivilité /ɛ̃sivilite/ *nf* fml incivility sout (**à l'égard de** to, toward, towards GB).

inclassable /ɛ̃klasabl/ *adj* unclassifiable.

inclément, **~e** /ɛ̃klemɑ̃, ɑ̃t/ *adj* fml inclement sout.

inclinable /ɛ̃klinabl/ *adj* [*dossier, tablette*] adjustable; [*parasol*] with tilt action (*épith, après n*); **fauteuil (à dossier) ~** reclining chair GB, recliner US.

inclinaison /ɛ̃klinɛzɔ̃/ *nf* **1** (de route, pente) incline; (de mur, siège) angle; (de toit) slope; **l'~ de ton écriture** the way your writing slopes; **2** Math angle.

inclination /ɛ̃klinasjɔ̃/ *nf* **1** (disposition naturelle) inclination (**à faire** to do); **avoir une ~ à faire** to be inclined to do; **suivre son ~** to follow one's natural inclinations; **2** (de la tête) nod; (du buste) bow; **3** liter (amour) inclination; **mariage d'~** love match.

incliné, **~e** /ɛ̃kline/ *adj* **1** (pas horizontal) [*plateau, fonds marins*] sloping; [*toit*] steep; **le plancher est ~** the floor slopes; **2** (pas vertical) [*mur, tour*] leaning; **tenir qch ~** to hold sth at an angle.

incliner /ɛ̃kline/ [1] I *vtr* **1** (pencher) to tilt [*parasol*]; to tip up [*flacon*]; **~ le buste** to lean forward; **~ la tête** to move one's head; **~ la tête sur le côté** to put one's head on one side; **saluer qn en inclinant la tête** to greet sb with a nod; **2** fml (inciter) **cela m'incline à la confiance** this inclines me to be trusting; **ceci m'incline à penser que** this leads me to think that.
II *vi* fml to be inclined (**à faire** to do); **~ à penser que** to be inclined to think that; **~ à la prudence** or **à être prudent** to be inclined to be cautious.
III **s'incliner** *vpr* **1** (se pencher) to lean forward; (par politesse, respect) to bow; **s'~ devant qn/très bas** to bow to sb/very low; **2** (ne pas contester) **s'~ devant qch** to bow to sth, to accept sth; **s'~ devant les décisions de qn/les faits** to accept sb's decisions/the facts; **s'~ devant le règlement** to obey the rules; **je m'incline** I have to agree; **3** (s'avouer vaincu) to give in○ (**devant** to); **le gouvernement va devoir s'~** the government will have to give in○ ou to concede defeat; **s'~ devant une armée plus nombreuse** to give in○ to an army of superior strength, concede defeat in the face of an army of superior strength; **en finale, X s'incline devant Y** Sport in the final, X lost to Y; **4** (témoigner du respect) **s'~ devant l'érudition/le courage de qn** to admire sb's learning/courage; **5** (devenir oblique) [*moto*] to lean over.

inclure /ɛ̃klyʀ/ [78] *vtr* **1** (intégrer) to include [*nom, personne*]; **nous ne pouvons vous ~ sur la liste/dans notre groupe** we can't include you on the list/in our group; **2** (comprendre) [*liste, programme, prix, forfait, réforme*] to include; **3** (joindre) to enclose [*document, argent*]; **4** (ajouter) to insert [*correction, modification, clause*]; **5** Math to include; **A inclut B** A includes B.

inclus, **~e** /ɛ̃kly, yz/ I *pp* ▶**inclure**.

II *pp adj* **1** (compris) **il y avait 20 personnes, enfants ~** there were 20 people, including children; **jusqu'au second chapitre ~** up to and including chapter two; **jusqu'à jeudi ~** up to and including Thursday GB, through Thursday US; **les taxes sont ~es dans le prix** taxes are included in the price; **2** (joint) enclosed; **3** Math **B est ~ dans A** B is a subset of A.

inclusif, **-ive** /ɛ̃klyzif, iv/ *adj* Ling, Philos inclusive.

inclusion /ɛ̃klyzjɔ̃/ *nf* **1** gén, Ling, Math, Philos inclusion; **2** Biol (élément hétérogène) inclusion body; (technique) **~ dans la paraffine** embedding in paraffin.

inclusivement /ɛ̃klyzivmɑ̃/ *adv* **jusqu'au 4 mai ~** up to and including May 4 GB, through May 4 US.

incoagulable /ɛ̃koagylabl/ *adj* incoagulable.

incoercible /ɛ̃kɔɛʀsibl/ *adj* [*rire*] irrepressible; [*angoisse, envie*] uncontrollable; **vomissements ~s du matin** morning sickness ¢.

incognito /ɛ̃kɔɲito/ **I** *adv* incognito.

II *nm* **garder l'~** to remain incognito.

incohérence /ɛ̃kɔeʀɑ̃s/ *nf* **1** (manque de logique) incoherence ¢; **avec ~** incoherently; **2** (contradiction) discrepancy; **présenter des ~s** to show discrepancies.

incohérent, **~e** /ɛ̃kɔeʀɑ̃, ɑ̃t/ *adj* [*propos, comportement, personne*] incoherent; [*attitude, raisonnement*] illogical; **il se montre plutôt ~ dans ses décisions** he tends to be inconsistent in his decisions.

incollable /ɛ̃kɔlabl/ *adj* **1**○ (qui a réponse à tout) [*personne*] impossible to catch out (*jamais épith*); **un candidat ~** a candidate who can't be caught out; **elle est ~ en latin** you can't catch her out in Latin; **2** Culin **riz ~** easy-cook rice.

incolore /ɛ̃kɔlɔʀ/ *adj* **1** (sans couleur) [*liquide, gaz, crème*] colourless[GB]; [*vernis, verre*] clear; **2** (sans originalité) colourless[GB].

incomber /ɛ̃kɔ̃be/ [1] **I** *vtr ind* **~ à** [*devoir, tâche, mission, dépense*] to fall to; [*responsabilité, faute*] to lie with; **la faute en incombe à...** the fault lies with...

II *v impers* **il incombe à qn de faire** (par obligation) it is incumbent upon sb to do; (par rôle) the onus is on sb to do; Jur it rests with sb to do.

incombustible /ɛ̃kɔ̃bystibl/ *adj* incombustible.

incommensurabilité /ɛ̃kɔmɑ̃syʀabilite/ *nf* incommensurability.

incommensurable /ɛ̃kɔmɑ̃syʀabl/ *adj* **1** (immense) [*bêtise, ignorance*] boundless; [*océan*] boundless; [*profondeur*] infinite; **2** Math incommensurable.

incommensurablement /ɛ̃kɔmɑ̃syʀabləmɑ̃/ *adv* fml incommensurably

incommodant, **~e** /ɛ̃kɔmɔdɑ̃, ɑ̃t/ *adj* unpleasant.

incommode /ɛ̃kɔmɔd/ *adj* **1** (peu pratique) [*équipement*] inconvenient; [*installation*] awkward; [*horaire*] unsatisfactory; **2** (inconfortable) [*siège, logement, position*] uncomfortable.

incommodé, **~e** /ɛ̃kɔmɔde/ **I** *pp* ▶ **incommoder**.

II *pp adj* **1** (souffrant) unwell, indisposed fml; **2** (intoxiqué) **personnes ~es** people affected.

incommoder /ɛ̃kɔmɔde/ [1] *vtr* [*chaleur, bruit, fumée*] to bother; [*interruption*] to disturb; **être incommodé par des émanations de gaz** to be overcome by gas fumes.

incommunicabilité /ɛ̃kɔmynikabilite/ *nf* incommunicability.

incommunicable /ɛ̃kɔmynikabl/ *adj* incommunicable.

incomparable /ɛ̃kɔ̃paʀabl/ *adj* [*site, mérite, artiste*] incomparable; **d'un charme ~** extremely charming.

incomparablement /ɛ̃kɔ̃paʀabləmɑ̃/ *adv* **~ meilleur marché/plus agréable/moins difficile** far cheaper/more pleasant/less difficult.

incompatibilité /ɛ̃kɔ̃patibilite/ *nf* gén, Sci incompatibility (**de qch et qch** of sth with sth); **il y a ~ entre leur politique et la nôtre** our policies are incompatible.

■ **~ de fonctions** Jur incompatibility of offices; **~ d'humeur** Jur incompatibility of temper; gén personality conflict.

incompatible /ɛ̃kɔ̃patibl/ *adj* incompatible (**avec** with).

incompétence /ɛ̃kɔ̃petɑ̃s/ *nf* gén incompetence; Jur incompetency; **un employé d'une rare ~** an exceptionally incompetent employee.

■ **~ territoriale** Jur incompetency ratione loci.

incompétent, **~e** /ɛ̃kɔ̃petɑ̃, ɑ̃t/ **I** *adj* incompetent; **je suis ~ en la matière** or **en ce domaine** it's not my province.

II *nm,f* incompetent person.

incomplet, **-ète** /ɛ̃kɔ̃plɛ, ɛt/ *adj* incomplete.

incomplètement /ɛ̃kɔ̃plɛtmɑ̃/ *adv* [*guéri, résolu, utilisé*] not fully, incompletely.

incomplétude /ɛ̃kɔ̃pletyd/ *nf* lack of fulfilment[GB]; **éprouver un sentiment d'~** to feel unfulfilled[GB].

incompréhensible /ɛ̃kɔ̃pʀeɑ̃sibl/ *adj* incomprehensible (**à**, **pour** to).

incompréhensif, **-ive** /ɛ̃kɔ̃pʀeɑ̃sif, iv/ *adj* unsympathetic.

incompréhension /ɛ̃kɔ̃pʀeɑ̃sjɔ̃/ *nf* (intellectuelle) incomprehension; (affective) lack of understanding.

incompressibilité /ɛ̃kɔ̃pʀɛsibilite/ *nf* **1** Phys (de matière) incompressibility; **2** Écon (de dépenses) irreducibility.

incompressible /ɛ̃kɔ̃pʀɛsibl/ *adj* **1** Phys [*matière*] incompressible; **2** Compta, Écon [*dépenses, charges*] fixed; **3** Jur **peine ~** sentence without possibility of remittance.

incompris, **~e** /ɛ̃kɔ̃pʀi, iz/ **I** *adj* **un artiste ~** an artist whose work is not understood; **il a été totalement ~ de ses contemporains** his contemporaries totally failed to understand his work.

II *nm,f* misunderstood person; **c'est un ~** he has always been misunderstood.

inconcevable /ɛ̃kɔ̃svabl/ *adj* inconceivable; **il est ~ que** it is inconceivable that.

inconciliable /ɛ̃kɔ̃siljabl/ *adj* irreconcilable.

inconditionnel, **-elle** /ɛ̃kɔ̃disjɔnɛl/ **I** *adj* **1** (sans conditions) [*cessez-le-feu, reddition, évacuation*] unconditional; **2** (absolu) [*soutien, appui*] unqualified; [*obéissance, soumission, responsabilité*] absolute; [*adhésion*] wholehearted; **3** (sans réserve) [*partisan, militant, amateur*] dedicated.

II *nm,f* (admirateur) devoted admirer; (fanatique) fan; **je suis un ~ de Mozart** I'm absolutely mad○ about Mozart.

inconditionnellement /ɛ̃kɔ̃disjɔnɛlmɑ̃/ *adv* [*soutenir, s'engager, admirer*] wholeheartedly.

inconduite /ɛ̃kɔ̃dɥit/ *nf* gén misbehaviour[GB]; Jur misconduct.

inconfort /ɛ̃kɔ̃fɔʀ/ *nm* **1** (matériel) lack of comfort; **vivre dans l'~** to live without one's creature comforts; **2** (intellectuel) awkwardness.

inconfortable /ɛ̃kɔ̃fɔʀtabl/ *adj* **1** (sans confort) [*lieu, siège*] uncomfortable; **2** (désagréable) [*situation, position*] awkward.

incongru, **~e** /ɛ̃kɔ̃gʀy/ *adj* [*comportement*] out of place (*jamais épith*); [*bruit*] odd; [*objet, situation, parole*] incongruous.

incongruité /ɛ̃kɔ̃gʀɥite/ *nf* **1** (étrangeté) incongruity; **2** (acte) faux-pas; (parole) incongruous remark.

inconnu, **~e** /ɛ̃kɔny/ **I** *adj* [*personne, causes, destination*] unknown (**de** to); [*territoires*] unexplored; **mers ~es** uncharted waters; **il est ~ des services de police** he's unknown to the police; **enfant né de père ~** child by father unknown; **~ à cette adresse** not known at this address; **votre visage ne m'est pas ~** your face is familiar; **ressentir une émotion ~e** to experience a strange feeling.

II *nm,f* **1** (personne non célèbre) unknown (person); **c'est un ~ qui a reçu le prix Nobel de littérature** an unknown writer won the Nobel prize; **2** (étranger) stranger; **ne parle pas aux ~s** don't talk to strangers; **il s'est épris d'une ~e** he fell in love with a complete stranger.

III *nm* **l'~** the unknown.

IV **inconnue** *nf* **1** Math unknown; **2** (facteur d'incertitude) unknown; **beaucoup trop d'~es** far too many unknowns.

inconsciemment /ɛ̃kɔ̃sjamɑ̃/ *adv* (sans le savoir) subconsciously; (sans le vouloir) unintentionally, unconsciously.

inconscience /ɛ̃kɔ̃sjɑ̃s/ *nf* **1** (absence de jugement) lack of thought; (devant un danger) foolhardiness; **rentrer seule à 2 h du matin, c'est de l'~** walking home alone at 2 o'clock in the morning is foolhardy; **2** Méd unconsciousness.

inconscient, **~e** /ɛ̃kɔ̃sjɑ̃, ɑ̃t/ **I** *adj* **1** (sans jugement) unthinking; (devant un danger) foolhardy; **être ~ de** (par ignorance) to be unaware of; (par incompréhension) not to realize; **il faut être ~ pour rouler à cette vitesse** you have to be mad○ ou crazy○ to drive at that speed; **2** Méd (sans connaissance) unconscious; **3** Psych [*acte, geste*] unconscious, automatic; [*sentiment*] subconscious; [*réaction*] unconscious.

II *nm,f* **c'est un ~** he's totally irresponsible.

III *nm* Psych **l'~** the unconscious.

■ **l'~ collectif** the collective unconscious.

inconséquence /ɛ̃kɔ̃sekɑ̃s/ *nf* (de raisonnement) inconsistency; (de conduite) fecklessness.

inconséquent, **~e** /ɛ̃kɔ̃sekɑ̃, ɑ̃t/ *adj* [*personne, comportement, raisonnement*] inconsistent.

inconsidéré, **~e** /ɛ̃kɔ̃sideʀe/ *adj* **1** (irréfléchi) [*propos, geste, action*] ill-considered; [*prêt*] ill-advised; **2** (excessif) [*usage, consommation*] excessive.

inconsidérément /ɛ̃kɔ̃sideʀemɑ̃/ *adv* **1** (imprudemment) [*dire, promettre*] rashly; [*prêter*] ill-advisedly; **2** (excessivement) [*boire*] to excess; [*dépenser*] wildly.

inconsistance /ɛ̃kɔ̃sistɑ̃s/ *nf* **1** (d'œuvre) lack of substance; (de personne) lack of character; **2** (de substance) thin consistency.

inconsistant, **~e** /ɛ̃kɔ̃sistɑ̃, ɑ̃t/ *adj* **1** [*raisonnement, argumentation, scénario*] flimsy; [*programme*] lacking in substance (*épith*); [*personne*] characterless; **2** [*substance, mélange*] thin.

inconsolable /ɛ̃kɔ̃sɔlabl/ *adj* inconsolable.

inconsommable /ɛ̃kɔ̃sɔmabl/ *adj* unfit for consumption (*jamais épith*).

inconstance /ɛ̃kɔ̃stɑ̃s/ *nf* fickleness.

inconstant, **~e** /ɛ̃kɔ̃stɑ̃, ɑ̃t/ *adj* fickle; **elle est ~e (en amour)** she's fickle.

inconstitutionnel, **-elle** /ɛ̃kɔ̃stitysjɔnɛl/ *adj* unconstitutional.

inconstructible /ɛ̃kɔ̃stʀyktibl/ *adj* [*terrain, zone*] where building is not permitted (*épith, après n*).

incontestabilité /ɛ̃kɔ̃tɛstabilite/ *nf* incontestability; **clause d'~** incontestability clause.

incontestable /ɛ̃kɔ̃tɛstabl/ *adj* [*fait, preuve, valeur*] unquestionable, indisputable, incontestable; [*victoire*] outright (*épith*); **il est ~ que** it is indisputable that; **c'est ~!** it's indisputable!

incontestablement /ɛ̃kɔ̃tɛstabləmɑ̃/ *adv* unquestionably, indisputably.

incontesté, **~e** /ɛ̃kɔ̃tɛste/ *adj* [*maître, champion*] undisputed; [*principe, droit, auto-*

rité, fait] uncontested; [*victoire*] undisputed, outright (*épith*).

incontinence /ɛ̃kɔ̃tinɑ̃s/ *nf* Méd incontinence; **~ nocturne** bed-wetting; **~ verbale** incontrollable talkativeness, verbal diarrhoea, prolixity sout.

incontinent, **~e** /ɛ̃kɔ̃tinɑ̃, ɑ̃t/ I *adj* Méd incontinent.

II *nm,f* Méd incontinent person.

III† *adv* forthwith.

incontournable /ɛ̃kɔ̃tuʀnabl/ *adj* [*question, problème*] that must be addressed (*épith, après n*); [*auteur, livre*] considered to be essential reading (*après n*); [*personne, figure*] to be reckoned with (*après n*); [*statistiques, chiffres*] that cannot be ignored (*épith, après n*).

incontrôlable /ɛ̃kɔ̃tʀolabl/ *adj* **1** (invérifiable) unverifiable; **2** (que l'on ne peut maîtriser) uncontrollable; **l'incendie est vite devenu ~** the fire quickly got out of control.

incontrôlé, **~e** /ɛ̃kɔ̃tʀole/ *adj* **1** (non vérifié) [*information, affirmation*] unverified, unchecked; **2** (non maîtrisé) [*individus, actes, violence*] uncontrolled.

inconvenance /ɛ̃kɔ̃vnɑ̃s/ *nf* **1** (de discours, démarche, proposition) impropriety, unseemliness; **2** (acte) impropriety.

inconvenant, **~e** /ɛ̃kɔ̃vnɑ̃, ɑ̃t/ *adj* [*terme*] unsuitable; [*attitude, propos, discours*] improper, unseemly; **il serait ~ de refuser leur invitation** it would be unseemly ou impolite to refuse their invitation.

inconvénient /ɛ̃kɔ̃venjɑ̃/ *nm* drawback, disadvantage; **les avantages et les ~s de la vie à la campagne** the advantages and the drawbacks ou disadvantages of living in the country; **cette situation n'est pas sans ~s** this situation is not without its drawbacks; **le seul ~ c'est que cette voiture coûte cher** the only snag about this car is that it's expensive; **si vous n'y voyez pas d'~** if you have no objection; **je ne vois pas d'~ à ce qu'il reste dîner** I see no reason why he should not stay for dinner; **y a-t-il un ~ à reporter la réunion?** is there any objection to postponing the meeting?; **il n'y a aucun ~ à reporter la réunion** the meeting can easily be postponed.

inconvertibilité /ɛ̃kɔ̃vɛʀtibilite/ *nf* inconvertibility.

inconvertible /ɛ̃kɔ̃vɛʀtibl/ *adj* inconvertible.

incoordination /ɛ̃koɔʀdinasjɔ̃/ *nf* lack of coordination.

incorporable /ɛ̃kɔʀpɔʀabl/ *adj* **1** [*objet, substance*] incorporable; **2** [*recrue*] recruitable.

incorporalité /ɛ̃kɔʀpɔʀalite/ *nf* liter incorporeality.

incorporation /ɛ̃kɔʀpɔʀasjɔ̃/ *nf* **1** Mil enlistment GB, induction US; **2** Culin blending.

incorporé, **~e** /ɛ̃kɔʀpɔʀe/ I *pp* ▸ **incorporer**.

II *pp adj* [*micro, antenne, cellule*] built-in.

incorporel, **-elle** /ɛ̃kɔʀpɔʀɛl/ *adj* **1** Jur [*droits, biens*] intangible; **2** (immatériel) incorporeal.

incorporer /ɛ̃kɔʀpɔʀe/ [1] *vtr* **1** Culin to blend (**à** into; **dans** with); **~ les œufs au mélange** blend ou fold the eggs into the mixture; **2** (faire entrer dans un ensemble) to incorporate [*chapitre, article, paragraphe*]; **3** Mil to enlist GB, induct US [*recrue*].

incorrect, **~e** /ɛ̃kɔʀɛkt/ *adj* **1** (comportant des fautes) [*terme, langue, style*] incorrect; [*montage, réglage*] faulty, incorrect; [*prévisions*] inaccurate; [*interprétation, raisonnement*] incorrect; **2** (inconvenant) [*conduite*] improper; [*terme*] unsuitable; [*personne*] impolite; **être ~ avec qn** to be rude ou impolite to sb; **3** (déloyal) [*personne, procédé*] unfair; **il a été très ~ avec son associé** he treated his associate very shabbily ou unfairly.

incorrectement /ɛ̃kɔʀɛktəmɑ̃/ *adv* **1** (de façon défectueuse) [*écrire, s'exprimer, assembler*] incorrectly; **2** (de façon déloyale) [*se conduire, agir*] shabbily.

incorrection /ɛ̃kɔʀɛksjɔ̃/ *nf* **1** (de style, langue) incorrectness; (de conduite, comportement) impropriety; **2** (faute) inaccuracy.

incorrigible /ɛ̃kɔʀiʒibl/ *adj* incorrigible.

incorruptibilité /ɛ̃kɔʀyptibilite/ *nf* incorruptibility.

incorruptible /ɛ̃kɔʀyptibl/ I *adj* incorruptible.

II *nmf* incorruptible person.

incrédibilité /ɛ̃kʀedibilite/ *nf* incredibility.

incrédule /ɛ̃kʀedyl/ I *adj* **1** (sceptique) [*personne*] incredulous; [*expression, air*] of disbelief (*après n*), incredulous; **2** (en matière religieuse) unbelieving (*épith*).

II *nmf* unbeliever, nonbeliever.

incrédulité /ɛ̃kʀedylite/ *nf* **1** gén incredulity; **faire preuve d'~** to be incredulous; **avec ~** with disbelief; **un sourire d'~** an incredulous smile; **2** Relig lack of belief.

incrément /ɛ̃kʀemɑ̃/ *nm* increment.

incrémentation /ɛ̃kʀemɑ̃tasjɔ̃/ *nf* incrementation.

incrémenter /ɛ̃kʀemɑ̃te/ [1] *vtr* to increment.

incrémentiel, **-ielle** /ɛ̃kʀemɑ̃sjɛl/ *adj* incremental.

increvable /ɛ̃kʀəvabl/ *adj* **1**○ (inépuisable) [*personne*] tireless, indefatigable; [*appareil, voiture, moteur*] that goes on forever (*épith, après n*); **2** (qui ne peut être crevé) [*pneu*] puncture-proof.

incriminer /ɛ̃kʀimine/ [1] *vtr* [*personne*] to accuse [*personne*]; [*preuve, indice*] to incriminate [*personne*]; **le journaliste/l'article incriminé** the offending journalist/article, the journalist/article in question.

incrochetable /ɛ̃kʀɔʃtabl/ *adj* [*serrure*] burglar-proof.

incroyable /ɛ̃kʀwajabl/ *adj* **1** (impossible ou difficile à croire) [*récit, nouvelle, information, événement, coïncidence*] incredible, unbelievable; **c'est ~ ce qu'il a grandi!** it's incredible how he's grown!; **~ mais vrai** strange but true; **2** (hors du commun) [*chance, courage, vitesse, beauté*] incredible, amazing; [*cruauté, paresse, bêtise*] incredible; **il est d'une intelligence/ignorance ~** he's incredibly intelligent/ignorant; **cette fille est ~, elle est toujours en retard!** that girl is incredible, she's always late!

incroyablement /ɛ̃kʀwajabləmɑ̃/ *adv* incredibly, unbelievably.

incroyance /ɛ̃kʀwajɑ̃s/ *nf* unbelief.

incroyant, **~e** /ɛ̃kʀwajɑ̃, ɑ̃t/ I *adj* unbelieving (*épith*).

II *nm,f* unbeliever, nonbeliever.

incrustation /ɛ̃kʀystasjɔ̃/ *nf* **1** Art (procédé) inlaying; (résultat) inlay; **un objet orné d'~s** an object decorated with inlay; **~s d'or** gold inlay; **un meuble à ~s de nacre** a piece of furniture inlaid with mother-of-pearl; **2** Géol (dépôt) encrustation; **3** Tech (dans chauffage) scale, fur GB; **4** Cout panel.
■ **~s de dentelle** Cout lace panels.

incruster /ɛ̃kʀyste/ [1] I *vtr* **1** Art to inlay [*objet*] (**de** with); **incrusté de qch** inlaid with sth; **2** (couvrir d'un dépôt) [*eau, calcaire*] to scale [sth] up, to fur [sth] up [*chaudière, tuyauterie*]; **3** Cout **robe incrustée de diamants** dress encrusted with diamonds; **incrusté de dentelles** with lace panels.

II **s'incruster** *vpr* **1** (s'agglomérer) [*caillou, coquillage*] to become embedded ou encrusted (**dans** in); **2**○ (s'imposer) [*personne*] to install oneself; **3** Tech [*chaudière, tuyauterie*] to get scaled up.

incubateur, **-trice** /ɛ̃kybatœʀ, tʀis/ I *adj* incubating.

II *nm* Méd incubator.

incubation /ɛ̃kybasjɔ̃/ *nf* **1** (de maladie, d'œuf) incubation; **période d'~** incubation period; **2** (de révolution, d'insurrection) hatching.

incube /ɛ̃kyb/ *nm* incubus.

incuber /ɛ̃kybe/ [1] *vtr* to incubate, hatch.

inculpation /ɛ̃kylpasjɔ̃/ *nf* Jur charge (**de, pour** of); **être sous le coup d'une ~** to be facing charges; **procéder à une ~** to bring a charge; **notifier son ~ à qn** to notify sb of the charge brought against them.

inculpé, **~e** /ɛ̃kylpe/ *nm,f* ≈ accused; **faites entrer les ~s** have the accused brought in.

inculper /ɛ̃kylpe/ [1] *vtr* to charge (**de, pour** with); **être inculpé de** or **pour** to be charged with.

inculquer /ɛ̃kylke/ [1] *vtr* to inculcate (**à** in), to instil[GB] (**à** in).

inculte /ɛ̃kylt/ *adj* **1** [*personne*] uncultivated; **2** [*terres, étendues*] uncultivated.

incultivable /ɛ̃kyltivabl/ *adj* unworkable, unfarmable.

inculture /ɛ̃kyltyʀ/ *nf* lack of culture.

incunable /ɛ̃kynabl/ I *adj* [*ouvrage, édition*] incunabular.

II *nm* incunabulum.

incurabilité /ɛ̃kyʀabilite/ *nf* incurability.

incurable /ɛ̃kyʀabl/ I *adj* **1** Méd [*maladie, malade*] incurable; **2** fig [*sottise, ivrogne*] incurable, hopeless; [*personne*] incurable; **il est d'une ~ bêtise** he is incurably stupid.

II *nmf* incurable.

incurablement /ɛ̃kyʀabləmɑ̃/ *adv* incurably.

incurie /ɛ̃kyʀi/ *nf* negligence, carelessness.

incursion /ɛ̃kyʀsjɔ̃/ *nf* (tous contextes) incursion, foray; **faire une ~ dans** to make an incursion ou a foray into.

incurvé, **~e** /ɛ̃kyʀve/ I *pp* ▸ **incurver**.

II *pp adj* curved.

incurver /ɛ̃kyʀve/ [1] I *vtr* to curve, bend.

II **s'incurver** *vpr* to curve, bend.

indatable /ɛ̃databl/ *adj* undatable.

Inde /ɛ̃d/ ▸ **321** *nprf* India.

indécelable /ɛ̃deslabl/ *adj* undetectable.

indécemment /ɛ̃desamɑ̃/ *adv* indecently.

indécence /ɛ̃desɑ̃s/ *nf* **1** (manque de décence) (de tenue, attitude) indecency; (de propos) impropriety; **ce luxe, quelle ~!** such luxury is quite obscene; **2** (acte) act of indecency; (parole) obscenity.

indécent, **~e** /ɛ̃desɑ̃, ɑ̃t/ *adj* **1** [*joie*] improper, indecent; **2** [*tenue, geste, propos, spectacle*] indecent; **3** [*chance, succès, luxe*] obscene, indecent; **avoir une chance ~e** to be disgustingly lucky.

indéchiffrable /ɛ̃deʃifʀabl/ *adj* **1** (indécryptable) [*code, message, écriture, document*] indecipherable; **2** (énigmatique) [*regard, personnage*] inscrutable; [*mystère*] incomprehensible.

indéchirable /ɛ̃deʃiʀabl/ *adj* tear-proof.

indécis, **~e** /ɛ̃desi, iz/ I *adj* **1** (ponctuellement) **il est encore ~** he hasn't decided yet; **il est ~ sur l'attitude à avoir** he's undecided as to what attitude he should take; **2** (de nature) [*personne, caractère, esprit*] indecisive; **3** (incertain) [*résultats, victoire, bataille*] uncertain; **4** (peu concluant) [*résultats, victoire, bataille*] inconclusive; **5** (imprécis) [*sourire*] uncertain; [*pensées, termes*] undefined, vague; [*temps*] unsettled, uncertain.

II *nm,f* indecisive person; (électeur) floating voter.

indécision /ɛ̃desizjɔ̃/ *nf* **1** (hésitation) indecision, uncertainty; **2** (trait de caractère) indecisiveness (**sur, quant à** about); **être dans l'~** to be undecided.

indéclinable /ɛ̃deklinabl/ *adj* indeclinable.

indécrottable○ /ɛ̃dekʀɔtabl/ *adj* (incorrigible) hopeless.

indéfectible /ɛ̃defɛktibl/ *adj* [*attachement, amitié, lien*] indissoluble, indefectible; [*haine*] enduring; [*soutien*] unfailing.

indéfectiblement /ɛ̃defɛktibləmɑ̃/ *adv* [*attaché*] indefectibly; [*soutenir*] unfailingly.

indéfendable /ɛ̃defɑ̃dabl/ *adj* indefensible.

indéfini, **~e** /ɛ̃defini/ *adj* **1** (sans limites) [*espace, nombre, temps*] indeterminate; **2** (vague) [*tristesse, mélancolie*] undefined; [*malaise*] vague; [*durée*] indeterminate, indefinite; **3** Ling [*article, mot, adjectif*] indefinite.

indéfiniment /ɛ̃definimɑ̃/ *adv* indefinitely.

indéfinissable /ɛ̃definisabl/ *adj* undefinable.

indéformable /ɛ̃defɔʀmabl/ *adj* that will not lose its shape (*épith, après n*).

indéfrisable† /ɛ̃defʀizabl/ *nf* perm, permanent wave†.

indélébile /ɛ̃delebil/ *adj* indelible.

indélicat, **~e** /ɛ̃delika, at/ *adj* **1** (impoli) [*personne, propos, comportement*] indelicate, tactless; **2** (malhonnête) [*invité, employé, procédé*] dishonest.

indélicatesse /ɛ̃delikatɛs/ *nf* **1** (impolitesse) indelicacy, tactlessness; **2** (malhonnêteté) dishonesty; **3** (acte malhonnête) act of dishonesty.

indémaillable /ɛ̃demajabl/ **I** *adj* [*tissu, jersey, tricot*] run-resistant; [*bas*] run-resistant, ladderproof GB.
II *nm* (tissu) run-resistant material.

indémêlable /ɛ̃demɛlabl/ *adj* [*affaire, intrigue*] that cannot be untangled (*épith, après n*).

indemne /ɛ̃dɛmn/ *adj* unscathed, unharmed; **sortir ~ d'un accident** to escape uninjured ou unharmed after an accident.

indemnisable /ɛ̃dɛmnizabl/ *adj* [*victime*] entitled to compensation (*après n*); [*dommage*] indemnifiable.

indemnisation /ɛ̃dɛmnizasjɔ̃/ *nf* **1** (paiement) indemnification; **2** (somme versée) indemnity, compensation ¢; **recevoir une ~** to receive compensation; **100 000 francs d'~** 100,000 francs compensation.

indemniser /ɛ̃dɛmnize/ [1] *vtr* to indemnify (**de** for), to compensate (**de** for); **se faire ~** to receive compensation.

indemnité /ɛ̃dɛmnite/ *nf* **1** Jur (dédommagement) indemnity, compensation ¢; **verser des ~s** to pay compensation; **2** Prot Soc (élément de rémunération) allowance.
■ **~ de chômage** unemployment benefit; **~ de déménagement** relocation expenses (+ *v pl*); **~ de déplacement** travel allowance; **~ journalière** sick pay; **~ de licenciement** severance pay ¢, redundancy payment GB; **~ de logement** housing allowance; **~ parlementaire** French deputy's allowances (*pl*); **~ de résidence** weighting allowance; **~s de guerre** war indemnities.

indémodable /ɛ̃demɔdabl/ *adj* **choisir un modèle ~** to choose a style that won't date.

indémontrable /ɛ̃demɔ̃tʀabl/ *adj* undemonstrable.

indéniable /ɛ̃denjabl/ *adj* undeniable, unquestionable.

indéniablement /ɛ̃denjabləmɑ̃/ *adv* undeniably, unquestionably.

indentation /ɛ̃dɑ̃tasjɔ̃/ *nf* (de littoral, feuille) indentation.

indépendamment /ɛ̃depɑ̃damɑ̃/ **I** *adv* independently.
II indépendamment de *loc prép* **1** (en faisant abstraction de) regardless of; **~ de ce qui s'est passé, vous avez des devoirs à remplir** regardless of what has happened, you have obligations to fulfil; **2** (outre) in addition to.

indépendance /ɛ̃depɑ̃dɑ̃s/ *nf* independence; **elle tient à son ~** she likes her independence; **se battre pour l'/son ~** to fight for independence/one's independence; **~ d'esprit** independence of mind; **~ matérielle** financial independence.

indépendant, **~e** /ɛ̃depɑ̃dɑ̃, ɑ̃t/ **I** *adj* **1** [*personne*] independent (**de** of); **2** [*chambre, entrée*] separate; **maison ~e** detached house.
II *nm,f* **1** (travailleur) freelance, self-employed person; **travailler en ~** to work freelance, to be self-employed; **2** (candidat) independent.

indépendantiste /ɛ̃depɑ̃dɑ̃tist/ **I** *adj* [*revendications*] independence (*épith*); [*mouvement, organisation*] (pro-)independence (*épith*); **être ~** to favour[GB] independence.
II *nmf* **1** (combattant) freedom fighter; **2** (militant) member of an independence movement.

indéracinable /ɛ̃deʀasinabl/ *adj* [*préjugés, sentiment*] ineradicable.

indéréglable /ɛ̃deʀeglabl/ *adj* [*mécanisme*] totally reliable.

Indes† /ɛ̃d/ *nprfpl* Hist **les ~** the Indies.
■ **~ occidentales** Hist West Indies; **~ orientales** Hist East Indies.

indescriptible /ɛ̃dɛskʀiptibl/ *adj* indescribable.

indésirable /ɛ̃deziʀabl/ **I** *adj* [*personne*] undesirable; Méd **effets ~s** adverse reactions.
II *nmf* undesirable.

indestructibilité /ɛ̃dɛstʀyktibilite/ *nf* indestructibility.

indestructible /ɛ̃dɛstʀyktibl/ *adj* **1** [*matériau, construction*] indestructible; **2** [*personne, défense*] indestructible; [*solidarité, union, amitié*] enduring.

indétectable /ɛ̃detɛktabl/ *adj* undetectable.

indéterminable /ɛ̃detɛʀminabl/ *adj* indeterminable.

indétermination /ɛ̃detɛʀminasjɔ̃/ *nf* **1** (indécision) indecision; **être dans l'~** to be undecided; **2** (imprécision) vagueness; **3** Math indetermination.

indéterminé, **~e** /ɛ̃detɛʀmine/ *adj* **1** (non établi) [*nombre, quantité*] indeterminate; [*raison, cause*] uncertain; **l'origine de l'incendie reste ~e** the cause of the fire has not yet been identified; **pour une période** or **durée ~e** for an indeterminate period; **la réunion est remise à une date ~e** the meeting has been postponed until a date yet to be fixed; **un nombre ~ de qch** an unspecified number of sth; **2** (hésitant) (de caractère) indecisive; (ponctuellement) undecided; **rester ~ sur** to remain undecided about; **3** Math indeterminate.

index /ɛ̃dɛks/ *nm inv* **1** (table alphabétique) index; **l'Index** Hist the Index; **mettre qch/qn à l'~** to blacklist sth/sb; **2** Ordinat index; **3** ▶188 Anat index finger, forefinger; **porter une bague à l'~** to wear a ring on one's index finger; **tenir qch entre le pouce et l'~** to hold sth between thumb and forefinger; **4** Tech pointer.

indexation /ɛ̃dɛksasjɔ̃/ *nf* **1** Écon indexation, index-linking; **l'~ des salaires sur les prix** the index-linking of salaries to the inflation rate; **2** (pour classer) indexing.

indexer /ɛ̃dɛkse/ [1] *vtr* **1** Écon to index-link [*salaire, pension, taux*]; **~ qch sur qch** to index sth to sth; **les salaires sont indexés sur le taux d'inflation** salaries are indexed to the inflation rate; **2** (pour classer) to index [*livre, document*]; **3** Ordinat to index.

Indiana /ɛ̃djana/ ▶692 *nprm* Indiana.

indic○ /ɛ̃dik/ *nm* stool pigeon○, grass○ GB, informer.

indicateur, **-trice** /ɛ̃dikatœʀ, tʀis/ **I** *adj* **panneau** or **poteau ~** signpost.
II *nm* **1** (délateur) informer; **2** (indice) indicator; **les principaux ~s économiques** key economic indicators; **~ de tendance** market indicator; **3** (brochure) (de rues) directory; (d'horaires) timetable; **4** Tech gauge, indicator; **~ de pression** pressure gauge; **~ de niveau d'huile** oil gauge; **~ lumineux** (warning) light; **~ de vitesse** speed indicator; **~ (de changement) de direction** Aut (direction) indicator.
■ **~ coloré** Chimie indicator.

indicatif, **-ive** /ɛ̃dikatif, iv/ **I** *adj* **1** [*prix*] indicative; **à titre ~** as a rough guide; **2** Ling [*mode, forme*] indicative.
II *nm* **1** Ling indicative; **à l'~** in the indicative; **le futur de l'~** the future indicative; **2** Télécom **~ (téléphonique)** dialling[GB] code; **~ de département/pays** area/country code; **3** Radio, TV (d'émission) theme tune.
■ **~ d'appel** Radio call sign.

indication /ɛ̃dikasjɔ̃/ *nf* **1** (action d'indiquer) indication; **il n'y a pas d'~ d'origine** the place of origin is not indicated; **il n'y a pas d'~ de date/lieu** no date/place is specified; **sur l'~ de qn** on sb's recommendation; **2** (renseignement) information ¢; **n'avoir aucune ~ sur qch** to have no information about sth; **fournir des ~s précises/utiles** to give precise/useful information; **ses ~s n'ont servi à rien/ont été précieuses** his information was useless/valuable; **sauf ~ contraire** unless otherwise indicated; **quelle est l'~ donnée par le cadran?** what's the reading on the dial?; **3** (instruction) instruction; **se conformer aux** or **suivre les ~s données** to follow the instructions provided; **4** (indice) indication; **5** (d'un médicament) **~s (thérapeutiques)** indications.
■ **~ scénique** stage direction.

indice /ɛ̃dis/ *nm* **1** (signe apparent) sign, indication; **être l'~ de qch** to be a sign of sth; **2** (dans une enquête) clue; **les enquêteurs n'ont aucun ~** the police have no clues; **recueillir/découvrir plusieurs ~s** to collect/discover several clues; **3** Écon, Fin index; **l'~ CAC 40/Dow Jones** the CAC/Dow Jones index; **4** (évaluation) **~ de popularité** popularity rating; **l'~ d'écoute** audience ratings (*pl*); **5** Phys, Math index.
■ **~ composite** composite index; **~ du coût de la vie** cost of living index; **~ général** general index; **~ des matières premières** raw materials index; **~ des prix à la consommation** retail price index GB, consumer price index US; **~ de traitement** Admin salary grading.

indiciaire /ɛ̃disjɛʀ/ *adj* **grille ~** salary structure; **impôt ~** wealth-related tax.

indicible /ɛ̃disibl/ *adj* unspeakable.

indiciblement /ɛ̃disibləmɑ̃/ *adv* unspeakably.

indien, **-ienne** /ɛ̃djɛ̃, ɛn/ ▶537 **I** *adj* (d'Inde) Indian; (d'Amérique) (North American) Indian, Native American; **chef ~** Indian chief.
II indienne *nf* **1** (tissu) (printed) calico; **2** (nage) sidestroke.

Indien, **-ienne** /ɛ̃djɛ̃, ɛn/ **I** ▶555 *adj* **l'océan ~** the Indian Ocean.
II ▶537 *nm,f* **1** (d'Inde) Indian; **2** (d'Amérique du Nord) (North American) Indian, Native American; **les ~s Comanche/Cheyenne** the Comanche/Cheyenne Indians.

indifféremment /ɛ̃difeʀamɑ̃/ *adv* **1** (sans distinction) equally; **frapper ~ tous les travailleurs** to affect all the workers equally; **2** (sans préférence) **il fume ~ la pipe ou le cigare** he is equally happy to smoke a pipe or cigars; **3** (selon les cas) **servir ~ de salon, de salle à manger ou de bureau** to be used either as a living-room, a dining-room or an office.

indifférence /ɛ̃difeʀɑ̃s/ *nf* indifference (**à** to; **à l'égard de** to; **devant** to); **dans l'~ générale/quasi-générale** amidst total/more or less total indifference.

indifférencié, **~e** /ɛ̃difeʀɑ̃sje/ *adj* **1** (indistinct) indistinct; **2** Biol undifferentiated.

indifférent, **~e** /ɛ̃difeʀɑ̃, ɑ̃t/ **I** *adj* **1** (impassible) [*air, regard*] indifferent; [*personne, public*] indifferent (**à** to); **rester ~** to remain indifferent; **laisser ~** to be uninspiring; **ne pas laisser ~** to provoke strong reactions; **laisser qn ~** [*œuvre, événement, politique*] to leave sb cold; [*personne*] to make no impression on sb; **ça m'est tout à fait ~** it makes absolutely no difference to me; **2** (sans importance) [*âge, sexe*] irrelevant; **il est ~ que** it is immaterial whether.
II *nm,f* **1** (impassible) detached person; **2** (personne sans opinion) apathetic person.

indifférer /ɛ̃difeʀe/ [14] *vtr* **1** [*problème,

politique, situation] not to be of any concern to; **ne pas ~ qn** to be of concern to sb; **2** [*personne, œuvre*] to leave [sb] indifferent.

indigence /ɛ̃diʒɑ̃s/ *nf* destitution, extreme poverty; **vivre/tomber dans l'~** to be/become destitute; **~ intellectuelle** intellectual poverty.

indigène /ɛ̃diʒɛn/ **I** *adj* **1** Bot, Zool [*faune, flore*] indigenous; **2** [*population, coutume, langue*] (du pays) local; (d'une colonie) native.
II *nmf* (natif du pays) local, native hum; (d'une colonie) native.

indigéniste /ɛ̃diʒenist/ *nmf* indigenist.

indigent, **~e** /ɛ̃diʒɑ̃, ɑ̃t/ **I** *adj* **1** (sans moyens) [*personne, famille, peuple*] destitute; **2** (insuffisant) [*imagination*] weak; [*éclairage*] poor; [*végétation*] sparse.
II *nm,f* pauper; **les ~s** the destitute, the poor.

indigeste /ɛ̃diʒɛst/ *adj* [*aliment, roman*] indigestible.

indigestion /ɛ̃diʒɛstjɔ̃/ *nf* **1** Méd indigestion ¢; **avoir une ~** to have (an attack of) indigestion; **j'ai eu une ~ de fraises** I made myself sick eating strawberries; **2** fig **avoir une ~ de qch** to be fed up° with sth; **j'ai tellement regardé la télévision que j'en ai une ~** I've watched so much television that I'm sick of it.

indignation /ɛ̃diɲasjɔ̃/ *nf* indignation (**devant** at); **avec ~** indignantly.

indigne /ɛ̃diɲ/ *adj* **1** (méprisable) [*conduite, procédé, attitude*] disgraceful; [*mère, fils*] bad; **c'est un père ~** he's not fit to be a father, he's a bad father; **2** (pas digne) **~ de qn** [*propos, acte*] unworthy of sb; **ce travail est ~ de lui** he's too good for that job; **il trouve le travail ~ de lui** he thinks the job is beneath him; **elle est ~ de ton amitié** she is unworthy of your friendship, she doesn't deserve your friendship; **il est ~ de représenter son pays** he's unfit to represent his country; **ce film est ~ de figurer au palmarès** this film doesn't deserve to win a prize; **3** Jur [*personne*] excluded from inheritance (*après n*).

indigné, **~e** /ɛ̃diɲe/ **I** *pp* ▶ **indigner**.
II *pp adj* indignant (**de** at).

indigner /ɛ̃diɲe/ [1] **I** *vtr* to make [sb] indignant, to outrage [*personne*].
II **s'indigner** *vpr* to be indignant (**de** about); **elle s'indigne de la situation** she's indignant about ou outraged by the situation; **il s'indigne de voir les injustices se perpétuer** he is outraged by the continuing injustices; **'c'est intolérable,' s'indigna-t-il** 'it's intolerable,' he exclaimed indignantly.

indignité /ɛ̃diɲite/ *nf* **1** (caractère) despicableness; **2** (action) despicable act, disgraceful act.
■ **~ nationale** national unworthiness (*sentence passed on French collaborators involving the loss of civil liberties*); **~ successorale** Jur exclusion of an heir from the succession.

indigo /ɛ̃digo/ ▶ **193** *adj inv, nm* indigo.

indigotier /ɛ̃digɔtje/ *nm* Bot indigo.

indiqué, **~e** /ɛ̃dike/ **I** *pp* ▶ **indiquer**.
II *pp adj* **1** (recommandé) [*traitement*] recommended; **ça n'est pas très ~** [*aliment, trajet*] it's better avoided; **le moyen tout ~ d'échouer** the sure way to fail; **2** (convenu) **à l'heure ~e** at the specified time; **au lieu ~** at the specified place.

indiquer /ɛ̃dike/ [1] *vtr* **1** (montrer où se trouve) [*personne*] to point out, to point to [*objet, lieu*]; [*pancarte*] to show the way to [*ville, magasin*]; **il indiqua l'endroit du doigt** he pointed out the place; **le panneau indique (la direction de) Mâcon** the signpost shows which direction to take for Mâcon; **~ qch à qn** to tell sb where sth is; **pouvez-vous m'~ la banque la plus proche?** can you tell me where the nearest bank is?; **je lui ai indiqué le chemin à prendre** I told him which way to go; **~ sa place à qn** to show sb to his/her seat; **2** (être un indice de) to indicate (**que** that); **Is-sur-Tille, comme son nom l'indique, est au bord de la Tille** Is-sur-Tille, as its name indicates, is on the banks of the Tille; **rien n'indique que les deux affaires soient liées** there is nothing to indicate ou suggest that the two matters are connected; **les chiffres indiquent une légère reprise** the figures show a slight recovery; **tout indique qu'il sera élu** all the signs are that he will be elected; **3** (conseiller) **~ qn à qn** to give sb's name to sb; **je peux t'~ un bon médecin** I can give you the name of a good doctor; **4** (signaler, dire) to give [*heure, date*]; **'indiquez vos nom et adresse'** 'give your name and address'; **indique-moi ton heure d'arrivée** tell me what time you are arriving; **l'heure indiquée sur le programme est fausse** the time given on the programme[GB] is wrong; **l'auteur a omis d'~ la date de parution** the writer has not given the date of publication; **comme il l'indique dans son introduction...** as he says in his introduction...; **~ que** [*personne, communiqué*] to indicate that; **~ à qn comment faire** [*personne, notice*] to tell sb how to do; **on m'a indiqué la marche à suivre** I've been told the procedure; **5** (afficher) [*horloge, compteur, baromètre, panneau*] to show; **la carte n'indique que les grandes routes** the map only shows the main roads; **le montant exact n'est pas indiqué** the exact total isn't shown; **le restaurant/théâtre n'est pas indiqué** there are no signs to the restaurant/theatre; **le village est très mal/bien indiqué** the village is very badly/well signposted; **au carrefour, tu verras, c'est indiqué** at the crossroads you'll see it's signposted.

indirect, **~e** /ɛ̃diʀɛkt/ *adj* [*publicité, aide, rapport, conséquence*] indirect; Jur [*héritier, ligne*] collateral; **de manière ~e** indirectly, in a roundabout way.

indirectement /ɛ̃diʀɛktəmɑ̃/ *adv* indirectly; (de façon détournée) in a roundabout way, indirectly.

indiscernable /ɛ̃disɛʀnabl/ *adj* imperceptible.

indiscipline /ɛ̃disiplin/ *nf* lack of discipline; **faire preuve d'~** to behave in an undisciplined way.

indiscipliné, **~e** /ɛ̃disipline/ *adj* undisciplined, unruly.

indiscret, **-ète** /ɛ̃diskʀɛ, ɛt/ **I** *adj* **1** (trop curieux) [*question*] indiscreet; [*personne*] inquisitive; **combien gagnez-vous, si ce n'est pas ~?** how much do you earn, if you don't mind my asking?; **il y a des oreilles ~s ici** there are eavesdroppers about; **à l'abri des regards ~s** away from prying eyes; **2** (qui ne sait pas garder un secret) [*propos, personne*] indiscreet.
II *nm,f* (bavard) indiscreet person; (curieux) inquisitive person, nosy parker°.

indiscrètement /ɛ̃diskʀɛtmɑ̃/ *adv* [*révéler*] indiscreetly; [*demander*] inquisitively.

indiscrétion /ɛ̃diskʀesjɔ̃/ *nf* **1** (curiosité) inquisitiveness; **il est d'une grande ~** he's very inquisitive; **sans ~, combien gagnez-vous?** if you don't mind my asking, how much do you earn?; **2** (tendance à trop parler) lack of discretion; **elle est d'une grande ~** she's very indiscreet; **3** (parole indiscrète) indiscreet remark; **une ~ a permis d'apprendre que** it came out that.

indiscutable /ɛ̃diskytabl/ *adj* indisputable, unquestionable.

indiscutablement /ɛ̃diskytabləmɑ̃/ *adv* indisputably, unquestionably.

indiscuté, **~e** /ɛ̃diskyte/ *adj* undisputed.

indispensable /ɛ̃dispɑ̃sabl/ **I** *adj* [*équipement, employé, activité*] essential (**à** to; **pour** for); [*argent*] necessary (*épith*), essential (*jamais épith*); [*aide, élément*] essential (**à** to; **pour** for), vital (**à** to; **pour** for); [*précaution*] necessary; **un objet ~ à la survie dans le désert** an object essential for survival in the desert; **être ~ à qn** to be indispensable to sb; **se croire ~** to consider oneself indispensable; **se rendre ~** to make oneself indispensable; **c'est ~** it's essential; **il est ~ de faire** it's essential to do; **rénover le réseau routier est ~** it is essential for the road network to be renovated; **il est ~ que qn fasse** it is essential for sb to do.
II *nm* **l'~** essentials (*pl*); **n'emporte que l'~** only take the essentials with you; **faire l'~** to do what is necessary.

indisponibilité /ɛ̃dispɔnibilite/ *nf* unavailability.

indisponible /ɛ̃dispɔnibl/ *adj* unavailable, not available (*jamais épith*).

indisposé, **~e** /ɛ̃dispoze/ **I** *adj* unwell, indisposed.
II **indisposée** *adj f* euph **elle est ~e en ce moment** it's her time of the month.

indisposer /ɛ̃dispoze/ [1] *vtr* **1** (agacer) to annoy; **~ les autorités/le pouvoir** to upset the authorities/the government; **2** (rendre légèrement malade) to upset, to make [sb] feel ill [*personne*].

indisposition /ɛ̃dispozisjɔ̃/ *nf* indisposition; **souffrir d'une légère ~** to be slightly indisposed.

indissociable /ɛ̃disɔsjabl/ *adj* inseparable (**de** from).

indissolubilité /ɛ̃disɔlybilite/ *nf* indissolubility.

indissoluble /ɛ̃disɔlybl/ *adj* indissoluble.

indissolublement /ɛ̃disɔlybləmɑ̃/ *adv* indissolubly.

indistinct, **~e** /ɛ̃distɛ̃, ɛ̃kt/ *adj* indistinct.

indistinctement /ɛ̃distɛ̃ktəmɑ̃/ *adv* indistinctly.

indium /indjɔm/ *nm* indium.

individu /ɛ̃dividy/ *nm* **1** (personne privée) individual; **la société écrase l'~** society crushes the individual; **il s'est attaqué à l'~ plutôt qu'au parti qu'il représente** he attacked the person rather than the party he represents; **il se soucie avant tout de son ~** he's very self-centred[GB]; **2** (personne physique) human being, person; **dans l'organisme d'un ~** in the human body, in a person's body; **3** (homme suspect) individual; **un sinistre/dangereux ~** a sinister/dangerous individual ou character; **un ~ armé** an armed man; **l'~ l'a braqué** the man pointed a gun at him; **4** Sci (unité) subject; **l'étude a été réalisé sur une population de cent ~s** the study covered a group of one hundred subjects.

individualisation /ɛ̃dividɥalizasjɔ̃/ *nf* individualization, adapting to individual needs; **~ de salaires** wage negotiation on an individual basis; **~ de la peine** Jur individualization of sentencing.

individualisé, **~e** /ɛ̃dividɥalize/ *adj* [*enseignement, formation*] tailored to individual needs (*après n*), individualized US; [*salaire*] negotiated on an individual basis (*après n*).

individualiser /ɛ̃dividɥalize/ [1] **I** *vtr* **1** (adapter) to tailor [sth] to individual needs, individualize US [*enseignement, horaire*]; to negotiate [sth] on an individual basis [*salaire*]; **~ une peine** Jur to make a sentence fit the individual offender; **2** (distinguer) [*caractère*] to individualize [*personne, être vivant*].
II **s'individualiser** *vpr* to become more individual.

individualisme /ɛ̃dividɥalism/ *nm* individualism.

individualiste /ɛ̃dividɥalist/ **I** *adj* individualistic.
II *nmf* individualist.

individualité /ɛ̃dividɥalite/ *nf* **1** (indentité) individuality; **2** (originalité) individuality; **3** (personnalité) personality.

individuel, **-elle** /ɛ̃dividɥɛl/ **I** *adj* **1** (pour une personne) [*portion, sachet, sport, cours, convocation*] individual; [*entretien, douche*] private; [*chauffe-eau*] separate, private; [*voi-

ture] personal, private; [*chambre, cellule*] single (*épith*); **maison individuelle** (detached) house; **épreuve individuelle** Sport individual event; **assurance individuelle** Assur private insurance plan ou scheme GB; **2** (d'une seule personne) [*initiative, réussite*] individual; **nous n'aborderons pas les cas ~s** we won't discuss individual cases; **à titre ~** on an individual basis; **un problème d'ordre ~** a personal problem, a problem of a personal nature; **touriste ~** tourist not travelling[GB] in a group; **3** (qui concerne l'individu) [*propriété*] private; [*responsabilité*] personal.
II *nm* **1** Philos **l'~** individual matters (*pl*); **2** Sport **il a obtenu de bons résultats en ~** he did well in the individual events; **3** Tourisme **voyage en groupe ou en ~** group or individual travel.

individuellement /ɛ̃dividɥɛlmɑ̃/ *adv* individually.

indivis, **~e** /ɛ̃divi, iz/ *adj* [*héritiers, propriétaires*] joint (*épith*); [*biens*] (communs) jointly-held; (non partagés) undivided; **posséder une maison en** or **par ~** to own a house jointly.

indivisaire /ɛ̃divizɛʀ/ *nmf* joint owner.

indivisément /ɛ̃divizemɑ̃/ *adv* jointly, in joint names.

indivisibilité /ɛ̃divizibilite/ *nf* indivisibility.

indivisible /ɛ̃divizibl/ *adj* indivisible; **une et ~** one and indivisible.

indivisiblement /ɛ̃divizibləmɑ̃/ *adv* indivisibly.

indivision /ɛ̃divizjɔ̃/ *nf* Jur joint ownership; **posséder qch en ~** to own sth jointly; **ils sont encore dans l'~** they have still not divided up the estate.

Indochine /ɛ̃dɔʃin/ *nprf* Indochina.

indochinois, **~e** /ɛ̃dɔʃinwa, az/ *adj* Indochinese.

Indochinois, **~e** /ɛ̃dɔʃinwa, az/ *nm,f* Indochinese; **les ~s** the Indochinese.

indocile /ɛ̃dɔsil/ *adj* [*personne*] intractable; [*enfant*] unruly.

indocilité /ɛ̃dɔsilite/ *nf* (d'enfant) unruliness.

indo-européen, **-éenne**, *mpl* **~s** /ɛ̃doøʀɔpeɛ̃, ɛn/ **I** *adj* Indo-European.
II *nm* Ling Indo-European.

Indo-Européen, **-éenne**, *mpl* **~s** /ɛ̃doøʀɔpeɛ̃, ɛn/ *nm,f* **les ~s** Indo-Europeans.

indolence /ɛ̃dɔlɑ̃s/ *nf* (de personne) laziness, indolence sout; (d'administration) apathy, indifference.

indolent, **~e** /ɛ̃dɔlɑ̃, ɑ̃t/ *adj* lazy, indolent.

indolore /ɛ̃dɔlɔʀ/ *adj* painless.

indomptable /ɛ̃dɔ̃tabl/ *adj* [*tempérament, peuple, courage*] indomitable; [*colère, passion*] uncontrollable, ungovernable; [*personnes*] uncontrollable; [*animaux*] untamable; **avec une énergie ~** with tireless energy.

indompté, **~e** /ɛ̃dɔ̃te/ *adj* [*nation, peuple*] unsubdued, untamed; [*orgueil, tempérament*] fierce; [*courage*] dauntless.

Indonésie /ɛ̃dɔnezi/ **▶321** *nprf* Indonesia.

indonésien, **-ienne** /ɛ̃dɔnezjɛ̃, ɛn/ **▶462**, **537** **I** *adj* Indonesian.
II *nm* Ling Indonesian.

Indonésien, **-ienne** /ɛ̃dɔnezjɛ̃, ɛn/ **▶537** *nm,f* Indonesian.

Indre /ɛ̃dʀ/ **I** **▶692** *nprm* (département) **l'~** Indre.
II **▶357** *nprf* (rivière) **l'~** the Indre.

Indre-et-Loire /ɛ̃dʀelwaʀ/ **▶692** *nprm* (département) **l'~** Indre-et-Loire.

indu, **~e** /ɛ̃dy/ **I** *adj* **1** (inconvenant) [*heure*] ungodly, unearthly; [*propos, réaction*] inappropriate, unseemly; **2** (sans fondement) [*somme, profit*] unwarranted, unjustified.
II *nm* payment made in error.

indubitable /ɛ̃dybitabl/ *adj* indubitable; **il nous cache quelque chose, c'est ~** he's hiding something from us, there's no doubt about it; **il est ~ que** there is no doubt that.

indubitablement /ɛ̃dybitabləmɑ̃/ *adv* undoubtedly, indubitably sout; **prouver ~** to prove beyond doubt.

inducteur, **-trice** /ɛ̃dyktœʀ, tʀis/ **I** *adj* inductive.
II *nm* inductor, inductance.

inductif, **-ive** /ɛ̃dyktif, iv/ *adj* inductive.

induction /ɛ̃dyksjɔ̃/ *nf* (tous contextes) induction; **par ~** by induction.

induire /ɛ̃dɥiʀ/ [69] *vtr* **1** (entraîner) [*événement, mesures, phénomène*] to lead to, bring about; **dans les entreprises locales, les emplois induits se chiffrent à une centaine** jobs created by local firms number about a hundred; **2** (conclure) to infer, conclude (**de qch** from sth); **j'en induis que** I infer from this that; **3** (inciter) to induce (**à faire** to do); **~ qn à mal faire** to induce sb to do wrong, to lead sb astray; **~ qn en erreur** to mislead sb; **4** Électrotech to induce [*courant*].

induit /ɛ̃dɥi/ *nm* inductor.

indulgence /ɛ̃dylʒɑ̃s/ *nf* **1** (de parent, public) indulgence (**envers** to, toward, towards GB); **plein d'~** indulgent; **sans ~** [*regard*] stern; [*regarder, parler*] sternly; **2** (de jury, d'examinateur) leniency (**envers** to, toward, towards GB); **avec ~** leniently.

indulgent, **~e** /ɛ̃dylʒɑ̃, ɑ̃t/ *adj* [*parent, public*] indulgent (**avec** with); [*sourire, critique*] indulgent; [*jury, examinateur*] lenient (**envers** to, toward, towards GB); **se montrer ~** [*juge*] to show leniency; [*examinateur*] to be lenient.

indûment /ɛ̃dymɑ̃/ *adv* unduly, unjustifiably.

induration /ɛ̃dyʀasjɔ̃/ *nf* induration.

induré, **~e** /ɛ̃dyʀe/ *adj* indurate.

indurer /ɛ̃dyʀe/ [1] *vtr*, **s'indurer** *vpr* Méd to indurate.

Indus /ɛ̃dys/ **▶357** *nprm* **l'~** the Indus.

industrialisation /ɛ̃dystʀializasjɔ̃/ *nf* industrialization.

industrialisé, **~e** /ɛ̃dystʀijalize/ **I** *pp* ▶ **industrialiser**.
II *pp adj* **pays ~s** industrialized countries.

industrialiser /ɛ̃dystʀialize/ [1] **I** *vtr* to industrialize.
II s'industrialiser *vpr* to become industrialized.

industrie /ɛ̃dystʀi/ *nf* **1** (activité) industry; **développer/relancer l'~** to develop/boost industry; **2** (secteur) industry; **~ automobile/chimique/textile/d'armement** car/chemical/textile/arms industry; **l'~ du cinéma** the film industry; **l'~ hôtelière** the hotel trade; **l'~ légère/lourde/de pointe** light/heavy/high-tech industry; **l'~ du spectacle** the entertainment industry ou business; **les ~s de transformation** the processing ou manufacturing industries; **3** (entreprise) industrial concern ou firm; **4†** (ingéniosité) ingenuity; **5†** (métier) trade; **exercer sa coupable ~** hum to ply one's evil trade.

industriel, **-ielle** /ɛ̃dystʀijɛl/ **I** *adj* industrial; [*pain*] factory-made, factory-baked; **en quantité industrielle** in vast ou huge amounts.
II *nm,f* industrialist, manufacturer; **les ~s de l'agro-alimentaire/armement/aéronautique** food/arms/aircraft manufacturers.

industriellement /ɛ̃dystʀijɛlmɑ̃/ *adv* [*fabriquer, produire*] industrially; [*gérer*] on an industrial basis.

industrieux, **-ieuse** /ɛ̃dystʀijø, øz/ *adj* liter industrious.

inébranlable /inebʀɑ̃labl/ *adj* **1** [*personne, conviction, résolution*] unshakeable, unwavering; **rester/demeurer ~** to be/remain unshakeable ou unwavering; **rester ~ dans ses convictions** to stick firmly to one's convictions; **rester ~ dans l'épreuve** to stand firm in adversity; **2** [*roc, construction*] immovable, solid.

inébranlablement /inebʀɑ̃lablǝmɑ̃/ *adv* unshakeably, unwaveringly.

inéchangeable /ineʃɑ̃ʒabl/ *adj* [*marchandise, article*] that cannot be exchanged (*après n*).

inécoutable○ /inekutabl/ *adj* [*disque*] unbearable, unendurable.

inédit, **~e** /inedi, it/ **I** *adj* **1** (jamais publié) [*livre, pièce, traduction*] (previously) unpublished; [*disque, film*] (previously) unreleased; **2** (original) [*procédé, information, spectacle, situation*] (totally) new.
II *nm* **1** (ouvrage) (previously) unpublished work ou article; **un ~ de Diderot** a previously unpublished work by Diderot; **2** (le nouveau) **voilà de l'~** that's something completely new.

inéducable /inedykabl/ *adj* **1** (impossible à éduquer) ineducable; **2** (incorrigible) incorrigible.

ineffable /inefabl/ *adj* **1** (inexprimable) [*joie, bonheur, sensation*] ineffable, unutterable; **l'~ Dupont est de retour** hum the ineffable Dupont is back; **2** (ridicule) [*cravate, chapeau*] ludicrous, outrageous.

ineffablement /inefabləmɑ̃/ *adv* ineffably, unutterably.

ineffaçable /inefasabl/ *adj* lit, fig indelible.

inefficace /inefikas/ *adj* [*traitement, médicament, mesure*] ineffective; (totalement) ineffectual; [*méthode, système, service, appareil*] inefficient; (totalement) ineffectual; [*travailleur*] (improductif) inefficient.

inefficacement /inefikasmɑ̃/ *adv* **1** (sans grand succès) ineffectively; (sans aucun succès) ineffectually; **2** (de manière incompétente) inefficiently.

inefficacité /inefikasite/ *nf* **1** (absence de résultats) ineffectiveness, inefficacy sout; **2** (rendement insuffisant) inefficiency.

inégal, **~e**, *mpl* **-aux** /inegal, o/ *adj* **1** (dissemblable) unequal; **couper un gâteau en trois parts ~es** to cut a cake into three unequal parts; **de taille/force ~e** of unequal size/strength; **des événements d'importance ~e** events of varying importance; **2** (déséquilibré) [*lutte, partage, chances*] unequal; [*partie*] uneven; **3** (irrégulier) [*pouls, rythme*] irregular, uneven; [*production, travail*] irregular; [*chemin, surface*] uneven; **4** (variable) [*humeur, caractère*] changeable, erratic; [*auteur, œuvre, style*] uneven; **il a un jeu ~** he is an inconsistent player; **avec un bonheur ~** with mixed success.

inégalable /inegalabl/ *adj* incomparable, matchless; **une danseuse ~** an incomparable dancer, a dancer without equal.

inégalé, **~e** /inegale/ *adj* unequalled[GB], unrivalled[GB].

inégalement /inegalmɑ̃/ *adv* (de manière dissemblable) unequally; (de manière irrégulière) unevenly; **une œuvre ~ appréciée** a work which received a mixed reception.

inégalité /inegalite/ *nf* **1** (disproportion) disparity (**entre** between; **de** in); **~ d'âge** disparity in age; **l'~ des ressources/moyens** the disparity in resources/means; **2** (iniquité) inequality (**devant** as regards); **les ~s sociales** social inequalities; **réduire les ~s** to reduce inequalities; **s'attaquer aux ~s** to attack ou fight inequality; **3** (irrégularité) (d'humeur) changeability; (de terrain, surface) unevenness; **4** Math inequality.

inélégamment /inelegamɑ̃/ *adv* inelegantly.

inélégance /inelegɑ̃s/ *nf* inelegance.

inélégant, **~e** /inelegɑ̃, ɑ̃t/ *adj* **1** (mal habillé) inelegant; **2** (mesquin) [*procédé, comportement*] shabby.

inéligibilité /ineliʒibilite/ *nf* ineligibility.

inéligible /ineliʒibl/ *adj* ineligible.

inéluctabilité /inelyktabilite/ *nf* inevitability, ineluctability sout.

inéluctable /inelyktabl/ *adj, nm* inevitable, ineluctable sout.

inéluctablement /inelyktabləmɑ̃/ *adv* inevitably.

inemployable /inɑ̃plwajabl/ *adj* unusable.

inemployé, **~e** /inɑ̃plwaje/ *adj* [*intelligence, capacité*] unused; [*énergie, ressources*] untapped.

inénarrable /inenaʀabl/ *adj* hilarious.

inentamé, **~e** /inɑ̃tame/ *adj* [*réserves, pécule*] untouched; [*énergie, confiance*] unaffected.

inenvisageable /inɑ̃vizaʒabl/ *adj* inconceivable.

inepte /inɛpt/ *adj* [*personne, gouvernement*] inept; [*jugement*] inane; [*film, remarque*] idiotic.

ineptie /inɛpsi/ *nf* **1** (caractère inepte) inanity; **des propos d'une ~ totale** totally idiotic remarks; **2** (parole stupide) idiotic remark; (acte stupide) stupid thing.

inépuisable /inepɥizabl/ *adj* **1** (très abondant) [*ressources, richesse, patience*] inexhaustible; **2** (intarissable) **il est ~ sur qch** he can talk for hours about sth.

inéquation /inekwasjɔ̃/ *nf* inequation.

inéquitable /inekitabl/ *adj* unfair, inequitable sout.

inerte /inɛʀt/ *adj* **1** (sans réaction) [*corps, membre, personne*] inert; **2** Phys, Chimie inert; **3** (apathique) [*personne, groupe*] apathetic.

inertie /inɛʀsi/ *nf* **1** Phys, Chimie inertia; **2** (passivité) apathy, inertia; **arracher qn à son ~** to force sb out of their apathy; **lutter contre l'~ administrative** to fight against administrative inertia; **l'organisation fonctionne par ~** the organization relies on its own momentum.

inertiel, **-ielle** /inɛʀsjɛl/ *adj* inertial; **à guidage ~** with inertial guidance.

inespéré, **~e** /inɛspeʀe/ *adj* [*victoire, score, gains*] unhoped for; **c'est une occasion ~e de faire** this is a heaven-sent opportunity to do.

inesthétique /inɛstetik/ *adj* (laid) unsightly; (au niveau artistique) unaesthetic.

inestimable /inɛstimabl/ *adj* [*fortune, valeur*] inestimable; [*dommages*] incalculable; [*tableau, cadeau*] priceless; [*aide, service*] invaluable.

inévitable /inevitabl/ **I** *adj* **1** (certain) inevitable; **rendre qch ~** to make sth inevitable; **il est ~ que** it is inevitable that; **2** hum (incontournable) (*before n*) [*personne*] inevitable; **l'~ Paul était là** Paul was there, as always; **il y avait l'~ clown** there was the inevitable clown.
II *nm* **l'~** the inevitable.

inévitablement /inevitabləmɑ̃/ *adv* inevitably.

inexact, **~e** /inegza, akt/ *adj* (pas juste) [*chiffre, analyse, information*] inaccurate; **il est ~ de dire que** it is inaccurate to say that; **c'est ~!** that's not accurate!

inexactement /inegzaktəmɑ̃/ *adv* inaccurately.

inexactitude /inegzaktityd/ *nf* **1** (caractère inexact) inaccuracy; **2** (erreur) inaccuracy; **le texte contient plusieurs ~s** the text contains several inaccuracies; **3** (manque de ponctualité) unpunctuality.

inexaucé, **~e** /inɛgzose/ *adj* [*souhait, vœu*] unfulfilled; [*prière*] unanswered.

inexcusable /inɛkskyzabl/ *adj* [*faute, action, conduite*] inexcusable; **tu es ~** there's no excuse for it!

inexécutable /inɛgzekytabl/ *adj* [*plan, projet, programme*] impracticable, unworkable; [*ordre*] which cannot be carried out (*épith, après n*).

inexécution /inɛgzekysjɔ̃/ *nf* (de travaux, d'une tâche) non-performance; (de contrat, d'obligation) non-fulfilment[GB]; **l'~ d'un ordre peut entraîner des sanctions** failure to carry out an order can lead to sanctions.

inexercé, **~e** /inegzɛʀse/ *adj* [*personne, groupe, oreille*] untrained; [*main*] unpractised[GB].

inexistant, **~e** /inegzistɑ̃, ɑ̃t/ *adj* **1** (absent) [*contrôle, moyens, aide*] nonexistent; **les risques ne sont pas ~s** there are certain risks; **2** pej (sans intérêt) **c'est un type complètement ~**[○] that guy is a complete nonentity.

inexistence /inegzistɑ̃s/ *nf* **1** (de preuves, faits, contrat) nonexistence; **2** (de personne) worthlessness; **3** (d'acte juridique) quality of being void ab initio.

inexorabilité /inɛgzɔʀabilite/ *nf* inexorability.

inexorable /inɛgzɔʀabl/ *adj* **1** (inévitable) inexorable; **diminuer de façon ~** to be declining inexorably; **2** fml (impitoyable) [*personne, volonté*] relentless.

inexorablement /inɛgzɔʀabləmɑ̃/ *adv* inexorably.

inexpérience /inɛkspeʀjɑ̃s/ *nf* inexperience.

inexpérimenté, **~e** /inɛkspeʀimɑ̃te/ *adj* **1** (sans expérience) [*personne, personnel*] inexperienced; **2** (non testé) [*méthode, procédé*] untried, untested.

inexpiable /inɛkspijabl/ *adj* inexpiable.

inexpié, **~e** /inɛkspje/ *adj* [*crime*] unexpiated.

inexplicable /inɛksplikabl/ *adj* inexplicable.

inexplicablement /inɛksplikabləmɑ̃/ *adv* inexplicably.

inexpliqué, **~e** /inɛksplike/ *adj* unexplained; **rester** or **demeurer ~** to remain unexplained.

inexploitable /inɛksplwatabl/ *adj* [*mine, gisement*] unworkable; [*richesses*] unexploitable; [*renseignements, documents, découverte*] unusable.

inexploité, **~e** /inɛksplwate/ *adj* [*richesses, sol*] unexploited; [*ressources, marché, créneau*] untapped, unexploited; [*documents*] unused; [*talent, potentiel*] untapped.

inexplorable /inɛksplɔʀabl/ *adj* unexplorable.

inexploré, **~e** /inɛksplɔʀe/ *adj* unexplored.

inexplosible /inɛksplozibl/ *adj* inexplosive.

inexpressif, **-ive** /inɛkspʀesif, iv/ *adj* inexpressive.

inexpressivité /inɛkspʀesivite/ *nf* inexpressiveness.

inexprimable /inɛkspʀimabl/ *adj* inexpressible.

inexprimé, **~e** /inɛkspʀime/ *adj* unspoken.

inexpugnable /inɛkspyɲabl/ *adj* impregnable.

inextensible /inɛkstɑ̃sibl/ *adj* non-stretch.

in extenso /inɛkstɛ̃so/ **I** *loc adj* [*texte, discours, compte-rendu*] full, complete.
II *loc adv* [*publier, lire*] in full, in extenso sout.

inextinguible /inɛkstɛ̃gibl/ *adj* **1** [*feu, incendie*] inextinguishable; **2** [*passion, ardeur*] inextinguishable; [*soif*] unquenchable; [*fou rire*] uncontrollable.

in extremis /inɛkstʀemis/ **I** *loc adj* **1** (de dernière minute) [*sauvetage, accord*] last-minute; **2** (avant la mort) [*mariage, baptême*] deathbed.
II *loc adv* **1** (au dernier moment) at the last minute; **on l'a sauvée ~** she was rescued at the last minute; **2** (avant la mort) on one's deathbed, in extremis sout.

inextricable /inɛkstʀikabl/ *adj* inextricable.

inextricablement /inɛkstʀikabləmɑ̃/ *adv* inextricably.

infaillibilité /ɛ̃fajibilite/ *nf* infallibility.

infaillible /ɛ̃fajibl/ *adj* infallible.

infailliblement /ɛ̃fajibləmɑ̃/ *adv* infallibly.

infaisable /ɛ̃fəzabl/ *adj* unfeasible, impossible; **c'est difficile mais pas ~** it's difficult but not impossible.

infamant, **~e** /ɛ̃famɑ̃, ɑ̃t/ *adj* **1** [*accusation, propos*] defamatory sout; **2** [*acte, conduite*] infamous, dishonourable[GB]; **il est ~ de faire** it's dishonourable[GB] to do; **3** Jur **peine ~e** judicial sentence involving loss of civil rights.

infâme /ɛ̃fɑm/ *adj* **1** (répugnant) [*nourriture, odeur, boisson*] revolting, disgusting; **2** (ignoble) [*individu*] despicable; [*trahison*] base; [*crime*] odious.

infamie /ɛ̃fami/ *nf* **1** (caractère) infamy; **2** (acte vil) act of infamy; (calomnie) slanderous remark.

infant, **~e** /ɛ̃fɑ̃, ɑ̃t/ *nm,f* infante/infanta.

infanterie /ɛ̃fɑ̃tʀi/ *nf* infantry; **dans l'~** in the infantry.
■ **~ de marine** *army corps serving alongside French Navy in overseas operations.*

infanticide /ɛ̃fɑ̃tisid/ **I** *adj* [*mère, père*] infanticidal.
II *nmf* (meurtrier) child killer.
III *nm* (meurtre) infanticide; **commettre un ~** to commit infanticide.

infantile /ɛ̃fɑ̃til/ *adj* **1** (relatif aux enfants) [*maladie*] childhood; [*mortalité*] infant; [*psychologie, protection*] child; **2** (puéril) [*personne, comportement, caprice*] infantile, childish.

infantilisant, **~e** /ɛ̃fɑ̃tilizɑ̃, ɑ̃t/ *adj* infantilizing.

infantilisation /ɛ̃fɑ̃tilizasjɔ̃/ *nf* infantilization.

infantiliser /ɛ̃fɑ̃tilize/ [1] *vtr* to encourage [sb] to behave like a child, to infantilize.

infantilisme /ɛ̃fɑ̃tilism/ *nm* **1** pej childishness, infantile behaviour[GB]; **faire preuve d'~** to behave childishly; **2** Méd infantilism.

infarctus /ɛ̃faʀktys/ *nm* **▶271** Méd (du myocarde) heart attack, myocardial infarction spéc; **faire**[○] or **avoir un ~** to have a coronary, to have a heart attack; **tu as failli me donner un ~** you nearly gave me a heart attack.

infatigable /ɛ̃fatigabl/ *adj* [*personne, esprit*] tireless.

infatigablement /ɛ̃fatigabləmɑ̃/ *adv* tirelessly.

infatuation /ɛ̃fatɥasjɔ̃/ fml *nf* conceit, self-satisfaction.

infatué, **~e** /ɛ̃fatɥe/ *adj* **être ~ de sa personne** or **soi-même** to be full of oneself.

infatuer: **s'infatuer** /ɛ̃fatɥe/ [1] *vpr* fml to become infatuated (**de qn** with sb).

infécond, **~e** /ɛ̃fekɔ̃, ɔ̃d/ *adj* [*œuf, animal, personne*] infertile; [*terre, esprit, pensée*] barren.

infécondité /ɛ̃fekɔ̃dite/ *nf* infertility.

infect, **~e** /ɛ̃fɛkt/ *adj* [*temps, odeur, humeur*] foul; [*plat*] revolting; [*personne, attitude, lieu*] horrible; **être ~ avec qn** to be horrible to sb.

infecter /ɛ̃fɛkte/ [1] **I** *vtr* **1** Méd to infect; **2** fig to poison.
II **s'infecter** *vpr* to become infected, to go septic.

infectieux, **-ieuse** /ɛ̃fɛksjø, øz/ *adj* infectious.

infection /ɛ̃fɛksjɔ̃/ *nf* **1** Méd infection; **2** fig **être une ~** (sentir mauvais) to stink; (être répugnant) to be disgusting.

inféodation /ɛ̃feɔdasjɔ̃/ *nf* **1** fig dependence (**à** on); **2** Hist infeudation.

inféoder /ɛ̃feɔde/ [1] **I** *vtr* **1** (soumettre) to pledge [*personne, groupe*] (**à** to); **être inféodé à** to be the vassal of; **2** Hist to enfeoff.
II **s'inféoder** *vpr* **s'~ à** to pledge oneself to.

inférence /ɛ̃feʀɑ̃s/ *nf* inference.

inférer /ɛ̃feʀe/ [14] *vtr* **~ de qch que** to

infer from sth that; **~ qch de qch** to infer sth from sth.

inférieur, **~e** /ɛ̃feʀjœʀ/ I *adj* **1** (situé en bas dans l'espace) [*mâchoire, membres, paupière, lèvre*] lower; [*niveaux, étages*] lower, bottom; **dans le coin ~ gauche** in the bottom left-hand corner; **2** (situé en bas dans une hiérarchie) [*grades, classes sociales*] lower; **les échelons ~s d'une hiérarchie** the lower echelons of a hierarchy; **on l'a rétrogradé au rang ~** he was demoted to the next rank down; **il t'est hiérarchiquement ~** he's below you in the hierarchy; **3** (en valeur) [*température, vitesse, coût, salaire, nombre*] lower (**à** than); [*taille, dimensions*] smaller (**à** than); [*durée*] shorter (**à** than); **mes notes sont ~es à la moyenne** my marks GB ou grades US are below average; **des coûts de production ~s à la moyenne** lower than average production costs; **le niveau de vie est très ~ à celui des pays occidentaux** the standard of living is much lower than in Western countries; **taux d'intérêt ~s à 10%** interest rates lower than 10%; **les chiffres sont ~s de 20% aux prévisions** the figures are 20% lower than predicted; **être en nombre ~** to be fewer in number; **4** (de qualité moindre) [*travail, ouvrage, qualité*] inferior (**à** to); **un objet/ouvrage de qualité ~e** an object/a work of inferior quality; **leur flotte/aviation est ~e à celle de l'ennemi** their fleet/air force is inferior to that of the enemy; **il ne t'est ~ en rien** he's in no way inferior to you; **ton adversaire t'était ~** your opponent was not as good as you; **5** Math **si a est ~ à b** if a is less than b; **x est ~ ou égal à y** x is less than or equal to y; **6** Astron inferior; **7** Biol, Bot, Géol, Zool lower.

II *nm,f* inferior; **traiter qn en ~** to treat sb as an inferior.

infériorité /ɛ̃feʀjɔʀite/ *nf* inferiority; **l'~ de l'aviation ennemie** the inferiority of the enemy aircraft; **leur ~ en nombre** their numerical inferiority; **complexe d'~** inferiority complex; **sentiment d'~** feeling of inferiority; **être en position d'~** to be in an inferior position.

infermentescible /ɛ̃fɛʀmɑ̃tesibl/ *adj* which will not ferment (*épith, après n*).

infernal, **~e**, *mpl* **-aux** /ɛ̃fɛʀnal, o/ *adj* **1** (insupportable) [*bruit, cadence, chaleur*] infernal; **cycle ~** unstoppable chain of events; **2** [*situation, circulation*] diabolical; **ce gosse est ~**° that child is a monster; **3** Mythol infernal.

infertile /ɛ̃fɛʀtil/ *adj* barren, infertile.

infertilité /ɛ̃fɛʀtilite/ *nf* barrenness, infertility.

infestation /ɛ̃fɛstasjɔ̃/ *nf* infestation.

infester /ɛ̃fɛste/ [1] *vtr* **1** gén to infest, overrun; **infesté de rats/requins** rat-/shark-infested; **infesté de puces** flea-ridden; **jardin infesté d'orties** garden overrun with nettles; **zone infestée de mines** area littered with mines; **zone infestée de pirates** area overrun with pirates; **les vices qui infestent la société** the vices that plague society; **2** Méd, Vét to infest.

infibulation /ɛ̃fibylasjɔ̃/ *nf* infibulation.

infidèle /ɛ̃fidɛl/ I *adj* **1** (inconstant) [*mari, maîtresse*] unfaithful (**à qn** to sb); [*ami*] disloyal; [*électeur*] fickle; **~ à sa parole/ses promesses** untrue to one's word/one's promise; **2** (non conforme) [*traduction, récit*] inaccurate; [*photo, témoignage*] unreliable; **3** Relig infidel.

II *nmf* **1** (inconstant) unfaithful man/woman; **2** Relig infidel.

infidélité /ɛ̃fidelite/ *nf* **1** (dans un couple) infidelity (**à** to); **~ conjugale** marital infidelity; **~s du mari** husband's infidelities; **faire des ~s à** to be unfaithful to; **2** (d'ami, allié, électeur, de client) (comportement) disloyalty (**à** to); (acte) act of disloyalty; **~ à une promesse** failure to fulfil[GB] a promise; **faire des ~s à qn** to be disloyal to sb; **3** (de traduction) inaccuracy.

infiltration /ɛ̃filtʀasjɔ̃/ *nf* **1** (de liquide) seepage ¢; **~s d'eau** water seepage; **il y a des ~s dans la pièce** water is seeping into the room; **2** (d'espions) infiltration (**dans** into); **3** Méd injection (**dans** into); **se faire faire des ~s de cortisone** to have cortisone injections.

infiltrer /ɛ̃filtʀe/ [1] I *vtr* to infiltrate [*organisation*].

II **s'infiltrer** *vpr* **1** [*liquide*] to seep through; [*lumière, froid*] to filter in; **le doute s'infiltra dans son esprit** he began to have doubts; **2** [*personne*] **s'~ dans** to infiltrate [*groupe, lieu*].

infime /ɛ̃fim/ *adj* (petit) tiny, minute; **chance ~** very remote chance.

infini, **~e** /ɛ̃fini/ I *adj* infinite; **avec d'~es précautions** with infinite care.

II *nm* Math, Phot infinity; **plus/moins l'~** plus/minus infinity; **à l'~** [*répéter, varier*] ad infinitum.

infiniment /ɛ̃finimɑ̃/ *adv* **1** (énormément) immensely; **~ reconnaissant** immensely grateful; **~ plus** infinitely more; **2** Math infinitely; **~ grand** infinitely great.

infinité /ɛ̃finite/ *nf* infinity; **une ~ de** an endless number of.

infinitésimal, **~e**, *mpl* **-aux** /ɛ̃finitezimal, o/ *adj* infinitesimal.

infinitif, **-ive** /ɛ̃finitif, iv/ I *adj* infinitive.

II *nm* infinitive; **à l'~** in the infinitive; **~ de narration** historic infinitive.

infirmatif, **-ive** /ɛ̃fiʀmatif, iv/ *adj* Jur invalidating; **~ de qch** invalidating sth.

infirmation /ɛ̃fiʀmasjɔ̃/ *nf* quashing, invalidation.

infirme /ɛ̃fiʀm/ I *adj* gén disabled; (par l'âge) infirm; **devenir ~ à la suite d'un accident** to be disabled after an accident.

II *nmf* disabled person; **les ~s** the disabled; **~ moteur** physically disabled person.

infirmer /ɛ̃fiʀme/ [1] *vtr* gén, Jur to invalidate; **ni confirmé, ni infirmé** neither confirmed nor denied.

infirmerie /ɛ̃fiʀməʀi/ *nf* gén infirmary; (d'école) sick room; (de bateau) sick bay.

infirmier /ɛ̃fiʀmje/ **▶510** *nm* male nurse.

■ **~ en chef** Méd charge nurse GB, head nurse US; **~ major** Mil senior nursing officer.

infirmière /ɛ̃fiʀmjɛʀ/ **▶510** *nf* nurse; **~ diplômée d'État** state registered nurse.

■ **~ à domicile** Méd ≈ visiting nurse; **~ en chef** Méd (nursing) sister GB, head nurse US; **~ major** Mil senior nursing officer.

infirmité /ɛ̃fiʀmite/ *nf* **1** gén disability; (de vieillesse) infirmity; **2** (imperfection) weakness.

infixe /ɛ̃fiks/ *nm* Ling infix.

inflammable /ɛ̃flamabl/ *adj* **1** Chimie flammable; **~ à l'air/la chaleur** flammable in air/on heating; **2** fig [*tempérament*] inflammable.

inflammation /ɛ̃flamasjɔ̃/ *nf* **1** Méd inflammation; **2** Chimie ignition.

inflammatoire /ɛ̃flamatwaʀ/ *adj* Méd inflammatory.

inflation /ɛ̃flasjɔ̃/ *nf* **1** Écon inflation ¢; **taux d'~ de 3%** 3% inflation rate; **l'~ est de 3%** inflation is at 3%; **forte/faible ~** high/low inflation; **~ annuelle** annual inflation; **~ galopante/rampante** galloping/rampant inflation; **réduire/limiter l'~** to cut/curb inflation; **~ des salaires/prix** wage/price inflation; **~ du crédit/des coûts médicaux** credit/medical-costs inflation; **2** (profusion) flood; **~ des diplômes/de l'information** flood of diplomas/of information; **~ verbale** flood of words.

■ **~ par les coûts** Écon cost-push inflation; **~ par la demande** Écon demand-pull inflation.

inflationniste /ɛ̃flasjɔnist/ *adj* [*menace, spirale, poussée*] inflationary; **tensions ~s** inflationary pressures.

infléchi, **~e** /ɛ̃fleʃi/ I *pp* ▶ **infléchir**.

II *pp adj* Phon [*voix, voyelle*] inflected; Bot [*branche*] inflexed.

infléchir /ɛ̃fleʃiʀ/ [3] I *vtr* **1** (assouplir) to soften [*position, politique*]; **se laisser ~** to let oneself be swayed; **2** (faire dévier) to deflect [*trajectoire*]; **3** (faire baisser) **~ la courbe des dépenses** to curb spending; **4** Phon to inflect [*voix*].

II **s'infléchir** *vpr* **1** (s'assouplir) [*position, politique*] to soften; **2** (se courber) [*tige, route*] to bend; [*poutre*] to sag; **~ à gauche** to bend to the left; **3** (dévier) [*trajectoire*] to deflect; **4** (commencer à baisser) [*courbe*] to level off; **5** Math [*courbe*] to inflect.

infléchissement /ɛ̃fleʃismɑ̃/ *nm* **1** (assouplissement) softening; **2** (baisse) slight drop; **~ de 3%** slight drop of 3 %; **3** (modification) shift (**de** in); **~ du marché** shift in the market.

inflexibilité /ɛ̃flɛksibilite/ *nf* inflexibility.

inflexible /ɛ̃flɛksibl/ *adj* inflexible.

inflexiblement /ɛ̃flɛksibləmɑ̃/ *adv* inflexibly.

inflexion /ɛ̃flɛksjɔ̃/ *nf* **1** (changement) change (**de, dans** in); **~ de la politique économique** change in the economic policy; **2** (baisse) slight drop (**de** in); **~ des résultats** slight drop in the results; **3** (mouvement) **~ du corps** bow; **~ de la tête** bow; **4** (vocale) inflection; **5** Math (de courbe) inflection.

■ **~ vocalique** Phon vowel inflection.

infliger /ɛ̃fliʒe/ [13] *vtr* **1** (faire subir) to inflict [*désagrément, défaite, mauvais traitements*] (**à** on); to deliver [*affront*] (**à** to); **~ une leçon à qn** to teach sb a lesson; **~ un camouflet à qn** to insult sb; **~ une humiliation à qn** to humiliate sb; **~ un démenti à qn** [*personne*] to refute sb; [*événement*] to prove sb wrong; **2** Jur to impose [*amende, condamnation, punition*] (**à** on); to give [*avertissement*] (**à** to).

inflorescence /ɛ̃flɔʀɛsɑ̃s/ *nf* inflorescence.

influençable /ɛ̃flyɑ̃sabl/ *adj* impressionable.

influence /ɛ̃flyɑ̃s/ *nf* **1** (effet) influence (**sur** on); **il exerce** or **a une bonne/mauvaise ~ sur son frère** he's a good/bad influence on his brother; **sous l'~ de** under the influence of; **avoir une ~ bénéfique/néfaste** [*facteur, phénomène*] to have a beneficial/detrimental effect (**sur** on); **sous l'~ de la colère/peur** [*être*] full of anger/fear; [*agir*] out of anger/fear; **2** (pouvoir) influence ¢; **avoir beaucoup d'~** to have a lot of influence; **3** Art, Littérat influence (**sur** on); **l'~ de Locke sur Rousseau** the influence of Locke on Rousseau; **4** Pol (rôle) influence ¢.

influencer /ɛ̃flyɑ̃se/ [12] *vtr* to influence [*enfant, électeur, artiste, commission*]; to affect [*économie, situation*]; **leur conduite nous a favorablement influencés** we were favourably[GB] impressed by their behaviour[GB].

influent, **~e** /ɛ̃flyɑ̃, ɑ̃t/ *adj* influential.

influenza /ɛ̃flyɛnza/ **▶271** *nf* influenza.

influer /ɛ̃flye/ [1] *vtr ind* **~ sur** to have an influence on; **~ négativement sur** to have a negative influence on.

influx /ɛ̃fly/ *nm* **1** Physiol **~ nerveux** nerve impulse; **2** Astrol influence; **~ bénéfique** favourable[GB] influence.

infographie /ɛ̃fogʀafi/ *nf* computer graphics; **~ par coordonnées/quadrillage** coordinate/roster graphics.

in-folio /infɔljo/ *adj inv, nm inv* folio.

informateur, **-trice** /ɛ̃fɔʀmatœʀ, tʀis/ *nm,f* **1** gén, Ling informant; **2** (indicateur de police) informer, stool pigeon°, grass° GB.

informaticien, **-ienne** /ɛ̃fɔʀmatisjɛ̃, ɛn/ I *adj* [*ingénieur, technicien*] computer (*épith*).

II *nm,f* **▶510** computer scientist.

informatif, **-ive** /ɛ̃fɔʀmatif, iv/ *adj* informative.

information /ɛ̃fɔʀmasjɔ̃/ *nf* **1** (renseignement) information ¢; **une ~** a piece of information; **diffuser l'~ sur qch** to spread information about sth; **avoir accès à l'~** to have access to information; **ces ~s sont confidentielles** this is confidential information; **pour votre ~** for your information; **prendre des ~s sur qn/qch** to find out about sb/sth; **un voyage d'~** a fact-finding trip; **l'~ du public est insuffisante** the public is ill-informed; **réunion d'~** briefing; **2** Presse, Radio, TV (nouvelle) piece of news, news item; **les ~s** the news ¢; **les ~s politiques/sportives** the political/sports news; **écouter/regarder les ~s** to listen to/watch the news; **les ~s télévisées** the television news; **nous venons de recevoir une ~ de dernière minute** there's some news just in; **3** Presse, Radio, TV (activité) reporting; (résultat) information; (médias) media; **de meilleurs journalistes pour une meilleure ~** better journalists for a better standard of reporting; **défendre le droit à l'~** to defend freedom of information; **les métiers de l'~** careers in the media; **contrôler l'~** to control the media; **hebdomadaire d'~** weekly newspaper; **presse d'~** newspapers; **4** Ordinat information; **théorie de l'~** information theory; **le traitement de l'~** data ou information processing; **unité d'~** unit of information; **5** Jur inquiry; **~ judiciaire** judicial inquiry; **ouvrir une ~** to open a judicial inquiry; **~ judiciaire contre X** judicial inquiry against person or persons unknown.

■ **~ génétique** Biol genetic information.

informatique /ɛ̃fɔʀmatik/ **I** *adj* [*système, équipement*] computer.

II *nf* (science) computer science, computing; (techniques) information technology, IT.

informatiquement /ɛ̃fɔʀmatikmɑ̃/ *adv* **traiter ~ des données** to process data on a computer.

informatisation /ɛ̃fɔʀmatizasjɔ̃/ *nf* computerization.

informatiser /ɛ̃fɔʀmatize/ [1] **I** *vtr* to computerize.

II s'informatiser *vpr* to become computerized.

informe /ɛ̃fɔʀm/ *adj* [*masse, vêtement, silhouette*] shapeless; [*projet, brouillon*] rough.

informé /ɛ̃fɔʀme/ *nm* Jur **pour plus ample ~** for further information; **jusqu'à plus ample ~** pending further information.

informel, -elle /ɛ̃fɔʀmɛl/ *adj* informal.

informer /ɛ̃fɔʀme/ [1] **I** *vtr* **1** (mettre au courant) to inform [*personne, groupe*] (**de** about; **que** that); **s'il y a du nouveau, soyez gentil de m'en ~** please keep me informed if there's any news; **je vous en informerai en temps voulu** I'll inform you in due course; **le rôle de la presse est d'~** the role of the media is to inform; **il est mieux informé que moi sur le sujet** he is better informed about the subject than I am; **nous informons notre aimable clientèle que le magasin restera ouvert jusqu'à 20 heures** we wish to inform our customers that the store will stay open till 8pm; **les milieux bien informés** well-informed circles; **de source bien informée** from a reliable source; **2** Philos to inform.

II *vi* Jur to hold an inquiry ou investigation; **~ sur un crime** to hold an inquiry into a crime; **~ contre X** to proceed against person or persons unknown.

III s'informer *vpr* **1** (suivre l'actualité) to keep oneself informed; **avec cette station de radio, on peut s'~ vingt-quatre heures sur vingt-quatre** on this radio station, you can get news right round the clock; **2** (se mettre au courant) **s'~ de qch** to inquire about sth; **ils se sont informés de ta santé** they inquired about your health; **informez-vous des prix avant d'acheter** check the prices before you buy; **s'~ si** to check whether; **s'~ si le train est arrivé** to check whether the train has arrived; **3** (prendre des renseignements) **s'~ sur qn** to make inquiries about sb; **je me suis informé à votre sujet** I made inquiries about you.

informulé, ~e /ɛ̃fɔʀmyle/ *adj* unformulated.

inforoute/ɛ̃fɔʀut/*nf* info highway.

infortune /ɛ̃fɔʀtyn/ *nf* misfortune; **compagnon d'~** companion in adversity.

infortuné, ~e /ɛ̃fɔʀtyne/ **I** *adj* ill-fated.

II *nm,f* unfortunate.

infra /ɛ̃fʀa/ *adv* below; **voir ~** see below.

infraction /ɛ̃fʀaksjɔ̃/ *nf* Jur offence[GB]; **commettre une ~** to commit an offence[GB]; **~ à** breach of; **c'est une ~ à la loi/au règlement** it's a breach of the law/the regulations; **être en ~ avec la loi** [*personne*] to break the law; [*accord*] to be in breach of the law; **votre voiture stationne en ~** your car is illegally parked.

infranchissable /ɛ̃fʀɑ̃ʃisabl/ *adj* [*obstacle*] insurmountable; [*frontière*] impassable.

infrangible /ɛ̃fʀɑ̃ʒibl/ *adj* fml infrangible sout, unbreakable.

infrarouge /ɛ̃fʀaʀuʒ/ *adj, nm* infrared; **missile guidé par ~** heat-seeking missile.

infrason /ɛ̃fʀasɔ̃/ *nm* infrasound.

infrastructure /ɛ̃fʀastʀyktyʀ/ *nf* **1** (équipements) facilities (*pl*); **~ hôtelière/médicale** hotel/medical facilities; **~s de transport/sportives** transport/sports facilities; **~s routières** road infrastructure (*sg*); **2** Écon infrastructure; **3** Constr, Gén Civ substructure.

infréquentable /ɛ̃fʀekɑ̃tabl/ *adj* [*lieu, personne*] unsavoury.

infroissable /ɛ̃fʀwasabl/ *adj* crease-resistant.

infructueux, -euse /ɛ̃fʀyktɥø, øz/ *adj* fruitless.

infumable /ɛ̃fymabl/ *adj* unsmokable.

infus, ~e /ɛ̃fy, yz/ *adj* **il croit qu'il a la science ~e** he thinks he knows everything.

infuser /ɛ̃fyze/ [1] **I** *vtr* **1** Culin to brew, to infuse [*thé*]; to infuse [*tisane*]; **2** (introduire) to infuse [*culture*] (**à** into).

II *vi* [*thé*] to brew, to infuse; [*tisane*] to infuse.

infusion /ɛ̃fyzjɔ̃/ *nf* **1** (tisane) herbal tea; **~ de camomille** camomile tea; **boîte de 20 ~s** box of 20 herbal tea bags; **2** (processus) infusion.

ingambe /ɛ̃gɑ̃b/ *adj* sprightly.

ingénier: **s'ingénier** /ɛ̃ʒenje/ [2] *vpr* to do one's utmost (**à faire** to do); **il s'ingénie à me rendre la vie impossible** he does his utmost to make my life unbearable.

ingénierie /ɛ̃ʒeniʀi/ *nf* engineering; **société d'~** engineering company.

■ **~ assistée par ordinateur**, **IAO** computer-aided engineering, CAE.

ingénieur /ɛ̃ʒenjœʀ/ ▶ **510** *nm* engineer; **~ agronome/chimiste/électricien/du son/système** agricultural/chemical/electrical/sound/systems engineer; **~ des travaux publics** civil engineer; **~ en chef/général** chief/senior engineer; **école d'~s** engineering course.

ingénieur-conseil, *pl* **ingénieurs-conseils** /ɛ̃ʒenjœʀkɔ̃sɛj/ *nm* consulting engineer.

ingénieusement /ɛ̃ʒenjøzmɑ̃/ *adv* ingeniously.

ingénieux, -ieuse /ɛ̃ʒenjø, øz/ *adj* ingenious.

ingéniosité /ɛ̃ʒenjozite/ *nf* ingenuity.

ingénu, ~e /ɛ̃ʒeny/ **I** *adj* ingenuous.

II *nm,f* **un ~** an ingenuous man; **une ~e** an ingénue.

ingénuité /ɛ̃ʒenɥite/ *nf* ingenuousness; **avec ~** ingenuously; **en toute ~** in all innocence.

ingénument /ɛ̃ʒenymɑ̃/ *adv* ingenuously.

ingérable /ɛ̃ʒeʀabl/ *adj* unmanageable.

ingérence /ɛ̃ʒeʀɑ̃s/ *nf* interference ¢ (**dans** in); **devoir/droit d'~** duty/right to interfere.

ingérer /ɛ̃ʒeʀe/ [14] **I** *vtr* Physiol to ingest.

II s'ingérer *vpr* to interfere (**dans** in).

ingestion /ɛ̃ʒɛstjɔ̃/ *nf* ingestion.

ingouvernable /ɛ̃guvɛʀnabl/ *adj* [*pays*] ungovernable.

ingrat, ~e /ɛ̃gʀa, at/ **I** *adj* **1** (sans reconnaissance) [*personne, public, pays, mémoire*] ungrateful; **2** (sans agrément) [*œuvre*] arid; [*lieu, paysage*] unwelcoming; [*visage, physique*] unattractive; **3** (sans récompense) [*vie, métier, tâche, rôle*] unrewarding; [*terre*] unproductive.

II *nm,f* ungrateful person.

ingratitude /ɛ̃gʀatityd/ *nf* **1** (manque de reconnaissance) ingratitude (**envers** to; **de la part de qn** on sb's part); **faire preuve d'~** to show ingratitude, to be ungrateful; **2** (manque d'agrément) (de visage) unattractiveness; (de terre) aridity.

ingrédient /ɛ̃gʀedjɑ̃/ *nm* ingredient.

inguérissable /ɛ̃geʀisabl/ *adj* incurable.

inguinal, ~e, *pl* **-aux** /ɛ̃gɥinal, o/ *adj* inguinal.

ingurgitation /ɛ̃gyʀʒitasjɔ̃/ *nf* ingurgitation.

ingurgiter /ɛ̃gyʀʒite/ [1] *vtr* **1** (avaler) to gulp down [*boisson, aliment*]; to swallow [*médicament*]; **2** (assimiler) to take in [*donnée*]; to devour [*livre*]; to learn [*programme*].

inhabitable /inabitabl/ *adj* uninhabitable.

inhabité, ~e /inabite/ *adj* **1** (sans habitants) [*maison, région*] uninhabited; **2** Astronaut [*engin, vol*] unmanned.

inhabituel, -elle /inabitɥɛl/ *adj* unusual (**de la part de** for); **très ~ de leur part** very unusual for them.

inhabituellement /inabitɥɛlmɑ̃/ *adv* unusually.

inhalateur /inalatœʀ/ *nm* inhaler.

inhalation /inalasjɔ̃/ *nf* inhalation; **faire des ~s** to have inhalations.

inhaler /inale/ [1] *vtr* to inhale.

inhérence /ineʀɑ̃s/ *nf* inherence.

inhérent, ~e /ineʀɑ̃, ɑ̃t/ *adj* inherent (**à** in).

inhiber /inibe/ [1] *vtr* to inhibit; **être inhibé** to be inhibited.

inhibiteur, -trice /inibitœʀ, tʀis/ **I** *adj* [*médicament*] inhibitive; [*réaction*] inhibitory; [*facteur*] inhibiting.

II *nm* inhibitor, suppressant.

inhibition /inibisjɔ̃/ *nf* inhibition.

inhospitalier, -ière /inɔspitalje, ɛʀ/ *adj* inhospitable.

inhumain, ~e /inymɛ̃, ɛn/ *adj* inhuman.

inhumanité /inymanite/ *nf* inhumanity.

inhumation /inymasjɔ̃/ *nf* **1** (mise en terre) burial; **2** (cérémonie) funeral.

inhumer /inyme/ [1] *vtr* to bury.

inimaginable /inimaʒinabl/ *adj* **1** (impossible à imaginer) unimaginable; **2** (impossible à concevoir) unthinkable.

inimitable /inimitabl/ *adj* inimitable.

inimitié /inimitje/ *nf* enmity sout, animosity; **~s** feelings of animosity; **leurs choix leur ont valu des ~s** their decisions generated feelings of animosity toward(s) them.

ininflammable /inɛ̃flamabl/ *adj* non-flammable.

inintelligent, ~e /inɛ̃teliʒɑ̃, ɑ̃t/ *adj* unintelligent.

inintelligible /inɛ̃teliʒibl/ *adj* unintelligible.

inintéressant, ~e /inɛ̃teʀesɑ̃, ɑ̃t/ *adj* uninteresting; **pas ~** not without interest.

ininterrompu, ~e /inɛ̃tɛʀɔ̃py/ *adj* **1** (continu dans le temps) [*processus*] uninterrupted; [*chute, hausse*] continuous; [*bruit, circulation*] endless; **2** (continu dans l'espace) [*procession*] unbroken.

inique /inik/ *adj* iniquitous.

iniquité /inikite/ *nf* iniquity.

initial, **~e**, *mpl* **-iaux** /inisjal, o/ I *adj* initial.
II **initiale** *nf* initial; **à l'~e** in initial position (*après n*).

initialement /inisjalmɑ̃/ *adv* initially.

initialisation /inisjalizasjɔ̃/ *nf* initialization.

initialiser /inisjalize/ [1] *vtr* to initialize.

initiateur, **-trice** /inisjatœʀ, tʀis/ *nm,f* **1** (de projet, mode) originator; (de publication, mobilisation) instigator; **2** (de personne) instructor.

initiation /inisjasjɔ̃/ *nf* **1** (formation) introduction (**à** to); **~ à l'anglais/la gestion** introduction to English/management; **~ musicale** introduction to music; **~ sexuelle** sexual initiation; **d'~** [*cours, semaine, stage*] introductory; **2** (admission à la connaissance) initiation; **rites d'~** initiation rites.

initiatique /inisjatik/ *adj* initiatory.

initiative /inisjativ/ *nf* initiative; **~ de paix** peace initiative; **à l'~ de qn** on sb's initiative; **prendre l'~** to take the initiative (**de** for; **de faire** in doing); **plusieurs ~s ont été prises** several initiatives have been made; **une de leurs ~s en ce domaine a été de faire** one of their initiatives in this field was to do; **faire preuve d'~** to show initiative; **avoir de l'~**, **avoir l'esprit d'~** to have initiative.
■ **~ de défense stratégique**, **IDS** Strategic Defense Initiative, SDI.

initié, **~e** /inisje/ *nm,f* **1** (formé et admis) initiate; **2** Fin insider trader.

initier /inisje/ [2] I *vtr* **1** (former) to introduce (**à** to); **2** (admettre à la connaissance) to initiate (**à** into); **3** (être à l'origine de) to initiate [*projet, réforme*].
II **s'initier** *vpr* **s'~ à l'escrime/au parachutisme** (to start) to learn fencing/skydiving; **s'~ à une langue** to start to learn a language; **s'~ à la photo** to learn about photography.

injectable /ɛ̃ʒɛktabl/ *adj* injectable.

injecter /ɛ̃ʒɛkte/ [2] I *vtr* to inject (**dans** into); **~ qch à qn** to inject sb with sth.
II **s'injecter** *vpr* **1** [*personne*] to inject oneself with; [*médicament*] to be injected; **2** [*œil*] to become bloodshot; **avoir les yeux injectés de sang** to have bloodshot eyes.

injecteur /ɛ̃ʒɛktœʀ/ *nm* injector.

injection /ɛ̃ʒɛksjɔ̃/ *nf* injection; **en ~(s)** by injection; **par ~ de** by the injection of; **~ de capitaux** or **crédits** injection of funds; **se faire une ~ de** to inject oneself with.

injoignable /ɛ̃ʒwaɲabl/ *adj* incommunicado.

injonction /ɛ̃ʒɔ̃ksjɔ̃/ *nf* injunction; **obéir aux ~s de** to comply with the injunctions of.
■ **~ thérapeutique** *probation order with a condition of attendance on a drug rehabilitation programme.*

injouable /ɛ̃ʒwabl/ *adj* [*pièce*] unperformable; [*morceau*] unplayable.

injure /ɛ̃ʒyʀ/ *nf* **1** (insulte) abuse **¢**; **couvrir qn d'~s** to heap abuse on sb; **proférer des ~s** to pour out abuse; **2** (offense) injury (**à** to); **faire ~ à qn** to insult sb; **3** Jur **être inculpé d'~ à qn** to be charged with abusing sb; **4** (ravage) fml ravages (*pl*); **l'~ des ans** the ravages of time.

injurier /ɛ̃ʒyʀje/ [1] I *vtr* to swear at; **se faire ~** to be sworn at (**par** by).
II **s'injurier** *vpr* to swear at one another.

injurieux, **-ieuse** /ɛ̃ʒyʀjø, øz/ *adj* [*parole, écrit*] abusive, offensive; [*attitude*] insulting.

injuste /ɛ̃ʒyst/ *adj* unfair (**envers** to); **il est ~ qu'on l'ait choisi plutôt que moi** it is unfair that he should have been chosen rather than me.

injustement /ɛ̃ʒystəmɑ̃/ *adv* [*accusé, condamné*] unjustly; [*méconnu, négligé*] unfairly.

injustice /ɛ̃ʒystis/ *nf* **1** (caractère injuste) (d'impôt, de société) injustice; (de personne) unfairness; **2** (absence de justice) injustice; **combattre l'~** to fight injustice; **3** (acte injuste) injustice; **réparer une ~** to right a wrong; **quelle ~!** how unfair!

injustifiable /ɛ̃ʒystifjabl/ *adj* unjustifiable.

injustifié, **~e** /ɛ̃ʒystifje/ *adj* unjustified.

inlassable /ɛ̃lasabl/ *adj* [*personne*] tireless; [*activité*] unrelenting.

inlassablement /ɛ̃lasabləmɑ̃/ *adv* tirelessly.

inné, **~e** /inne/ I *adj* innate.
II *nm* innate.

innervant, **~e** /innɛʀvɑ̃, ɑ̃t/ *adj* **gaz ~** nerve gas.

innervation /innɛʀvasjɔ̃/ *nf* innervation.

innerver /innɛʀve/ [1] *vtr* Physiol to innervate.

innocemment /inɔsamɑ̃/ *adv* innocently; **pas ~** disingenuously.

innocence /inɔsɑ̃s/ *nf* innocence; **en toute ~** in all innocence.

innocent, **~e** /inɔsɑ̃, ɑ̃t/ I *adj* innocent (**de** of); **la question n'est pas ~e** the question is not entirely innocent; **on demande une main ~e** somebody impartial is required.
II *nm,f* **1** (être pur) innocent; **2** (personne non coupable) innocent person; **une ~e** an innocent woman; **faire l'~**, **jouer les ~s** to play the innocent.
IDIOMES **aux ~s les mains pleines** fortune favours[GB] fools.

innocenter /inɔsɑ̃te/ [1] *vtr* **1** Jur to prove [sb] innocent (**de** of); **être innocenté** to be proved innocent; **2** (excuser) to clear (**de** of).

innocuité /inɔkɥite/ *nf* harmlessness; **en toute ~** without any risks.

innombrable /innɔ̃bʀabl/ *adj* **1** (multiple) countless; **2** (immense) [*foule, armée*] vast.

innommable /innɔmabl/ *adj* **1** (ignoble) [*comportement, saleté, terreur*] unspeakable; [*plat, boisson*] revolting; **2** (indicible) [*mystère*] indefinable.

innommé, **~e** /innɔme/ *adj* fml undefined.

innovant, **~e** /inɔvɑ̃, ɑ̃t/ *adj* innovative.

innovateur, **-trice** /inɔvatœʀ, tʀis/ I *adj* innovative.
II *nm,f* innovator.

innovation /inɔvasjɔ̃/ *nf* innovation (**dans**, **en matière de** in); **~s technologiques** technological innovations; **capacité d'~** ability to innovate.

innover /inɔve/ [1] *vi* [*personne, entreprise*] to innovate (**en matière de** in); [*équipement*] to break new ground.

inobservable /inɔbsɛʀvabl/ *adj* unobservable.

inoccupation /inɔkypasjɔ̃/ *nf* (de personne) inactivity; (de lieu) non-occupation.

inoccupé, **~e** /inɔkype/ *adj* unoccupied.

in-octavo /inɔktavo/ *adj inv*, *nm inv* octavo.

inoculable /inɔkylabl/ *adj* inoculable.

inoculation /inɔkylasjɔ̃/ *nf* inoculation.

inoculer /inɔkyle/ [1] *vtr* **1** (vacciner) to inoculate (**contre** against); **~ qch à qn** to inoculate sb with sth; **2** (contaminer) **~ qch à qn** to infect sb with sth [*virus, maladie, idée*].

inodore /inɔdɔʀ/ *adj* [*substance*] odourless[GB]; [*fleur*] scentless.

inoffensif, **-ive** /inɔfɑ̃sif, iv/ *adj* harmless.

inondable /inɔ̃dabl/ *adj* [*région*] liable to flooding (*après n*).

inondation /inɔ̃dasjɔ̃/ *nf* **1** (situation) flood; **les ~s de l'an dernier** last year's floods; **2** (processus) flooding.

inonder /inɔ̃de/ [1] I *vtr* **1** (submerger) [*pluie, fleuve*] to flood [*lieu*]; [*personne*] to flood [*lieu*] (**de** with); **zone inondée** flooded area; **j'ai inondé les voisins** I flooded the neighbours[GB]; **la piste est inondée d'huile** the track is flooded with oil; **2** (baigner) [*soleil, lumière*] to flood [*lieu*]; **inondé de sueur/sang** bathed in sweat/blood; **inondé de lumière** flooded with light; **les larmes lui inondaient le visage**, **il avait le visage inondé de larmes** his face was bathed in tears; **3** (envahir) [*commerçants, marque*] to flood [*marché*] (**de** with); to inundate [*clients*] (**de** with); [*produit*] to flood [*marché*]; [*joie*] to flood [*cœur*]; [*visiteurs*] to flood into [*lieu*].
II **s'inonder** *vpr* (s'asperger) **s'~ de** to douse oneself with [*parfum*].

inopérable /inɔpeʀabl/ *adj* inoperable.

inopérant, **~e** /inɔpeʀɑ̃, ɑ̃t/ *adj* ineffective; **caractère ~** ineffectiveness.

inopiné, **~e** /inɔpine/ *adj* unexpected.

inopinément /inɔpinemɑ̃/ *adv* unexpectedly.

inopportun, **~e** /inɔpɔʀtœ̃, yn/ *adj* **1** (non souhaitable) inappropriate; **2** (mal à propos) ill-timed.

inopposabilité /inɔpozabilite/ *nf* non-invocability.

inopposable /inɔpozabl/ *adj* non-invocable.

inorganique /inɔʀganik/ *adj* **1** Chimie inorganic; **2** Méd functional.

inorganisé, **~e** /inɔʀganize/ *adj* disorganized.

inoubliable /inublijabl/ *adj* unforgettable.

inouï, **~e** /inwi/ *adj* [*événement, succès, violence*] unprecedented; [*personne*] incredible, unbelievable péj; **c'est ~** that's unheard-of; **chose ~e** something unheard of.

inox /inɔks/ *nm* stainless steel; **casserole en ~** stainless steel pan.

inoxydable /inɔksidabl/ I *adj* [*métal*] non-oxidizing; **acier ~** stainless steel.
II *nm* stainless steel.

inqualifiable /ɛ̃kalifjabl/ *adj* unspeakable.

in-quarto /inkwaʀto/ *adj inv*, *nm inv* quarto.

inquiet, **-iète** /ɛ̃kjɛ, ɛt/ I *adj* **1** (de nature) [*caractère, personne*] anxious; **2** (alarmé) worried; **elle commence à être inquiète** she's starting to get worried; **il est ~ de ne pas avoir de leurs nouvelles** he's worried that he hasn't heard from them; **il est ~ d'avoir trouvé la porte fermée** he's worried because he found the door locked; **~ pour** worried about; **3** (empli de crainte) [*air, voix, regard, propos*] anxious, worried.
II *nm,f* worrier; **c'est un (éternel) ~** he's a (perpetual) worrier.

inquiétant, **~e** /ɛ̃kjetɑ̃, ɑ̃t/ *adj* [*situation, nouvelle, silence*] worrying, disturbing; [*visage, regard, yeux, personnage*] frightening; **l'état du malade est ~** the state of the patient is worrying.

inquiéter /ɛ̃kjete/ [14] I *vtr* **1** (soucier) to worry; **ce que vous venez de me dire m'inquiète un peu** I find what you've just told me rather worrying; **le phénomène commence à ~ les spécialistes** specialists are beginning to be concerned about the phenomenon; **2** (demander des comptes à) [*police, douanier*] to bother, to trouble; **les douaniers ne l'ont pas inquiété** the customs officers didn't bother him; **faire qch sans être inquiété** (pour une action courte) to do sth without being disturbed; (pour une action longue) to do sth without interference; **ils ont eu deux heures pour vider le coffre sans être inquiétés** they had two hours to empty the safe without being disturbed; **pendant la guerre il a pu continuer ses activités sans être inquiété** during the war he was able to continue his activities undisturbed; **il a pu quitter le pays sans être inquiété** he was able to leave the country without any trouble; **3** (harceler) fml to harass [*pays, région*]; **4**○ (mettre en difficulté) to worry, to threaten [*équipe, adversaire*]; to threaten [*hiérarchie, chef, influence*].
II **s'inquiéter** *vpr* **1** (s'alarmer) to worry, to

get worried; **ne t'inquiète pas il a dû être retardé** don't worry, he must have been delayed; **téléphone à tes parents sinon ils vont s'~** telephone your parents otherwise they'll get ou be worried; **il n'est que midi, je ne m'inquiète pas** I'm not worried, it's only twelve o'clock; **je commence à m'~** I'm beginning to get worried; **il ne s'est pas inquiété** he didn't get worried; **il s'inquiète** he's worried; **s'~ de qch** to be worried about sth, to get worried about sth; **il n'y a pas de quoi s'~** there's nothing to get worried about, there's nothing to worry about; **je m'inquiète de ne pas l'avoir vu aujourd'hui** I'm worried that I haven't seen him today; **s'~ des conséquences/du danger de** to worry about the consequences/danger of; **s'~ pour** to worry about; **ne t'inquiète pas pour elle** don't worry about her; **c'est surtout pour lui que je m'inquiète** it's him in particular I'm worried about; **2** (s'enquérir) **s'~ de qch** to inquire about sth; **s'~ de savoir si/combien** to inquire (as to) whether/how much.

inquiétude /ɛ̃kjetyd/ *nf* **1** (état) anxiety, concern; **être un sujet d'~** to give cause for concern ou anxiety; **avec ~** with concern; **être fou d'~** to be beside oneself with worry; **soyez sans ~** don't worry; **2** (trouble) worry; **avoir** or **éprouver des ~s au sujet de** to be worried ou concerned about; **j'ai beaucoup d'~s à ton sujet** I'm very worried ou concerned about you; **il n'y a pas d'~ à avoir** there's nothing to worry ou be concerned about; **ma seule ~** my only worry ou concern; **provoquer de vives ~s parmi la population** to cause real concern among the population.

inquisiteur, **-trice** /ɛ̃kizitœʀ, tʀis/ **I** *adj* inquisitive.

II *nm,f* inquisitor; **grand ~** Grand Inquisitor.

inquisition /ɛ̃kizisjɔ̃/ *nf* inquisition.

Inquisition /ɛ̃kizisjɔ̃/ *nf* Inquisition.

inquisitorial, **~e**, *pl* **-iaux** /ɛ̃kizitɔʀjal, o/ *adj* inquisitorial.

inracontable /ɛ̃ʀakɔ̃tabl/ *adj* (trop compliqué) too difficult to explain (*après n*); (trop osé) unrepeatable.

insaisissabilité /ɛ̃sɛzisabilite/ *nf* Jur privilege from seizure.

insaisissable /ɛ̃sɛzisabl/ *adj* **1** [*voleur, animal, caractère, personnage*] elusive; [*nuance, image*] imperceptible; **2** Jur privileged from seizure.

insalissable /ɛ̃salisabl/ *adj* [*tissu, surface*] stain-resistant.

insalubre /ɛ̃salybʀ/ *adj* **1** gén [*local, lieu*] unhealthy, prejudicial to health; [*travail*] potentially health-damaging (*épith*); [*logement*] unfit for habitation (*jamais épith*); **2** Jur which constitutes a health hazard (*épith, après n*).

insalubrité /ɛ̃salybʀite/ *nf* (d'immeuble, ville) insalubrity sout; (de climat) unhealthiness, insalubrity sout.

insanité /ɛ̃sanite/ *nf* **1** (propos insensé) rubbish ₵; **c'est une ~** it's rubbish; **proférer** or **débiter des ~s** to come out with a lot of rubbish (**sur** about); **2** (déraison) insanity.

insatiabilité /ɛ̃sasjabilite/ *nf* insatiability.

insatiable /ɛ̃sasjabl/ *adj* [*appétit, demande, curiosité, personne*] insatiable.

insatiablement /ɛ̃sasjabləmɑ̃/ *adv* insatiably.

insatisfaction /ɛ̃satisfaksjɔ̃/ *nf* dissatisfaction ₵ (**quant à** with).

insatisfait, **~e** /ɛ̃satisfɛ, ɛt/ **I** *adj* [*personne*] dissatisfied (**de** with); [*désir, ambition, requête*] unsatisfied.

II *nm,f* **c'est un ~** he's never satisfied.

inscription /ɛ̃skʀipsjɔ̃/ *nf* **1** Scol enrolment[GB]; Univ registration; **l'~ d'un enfant à l'école** the enrolment of a child at school; **ils ont refusé leur ~ à l'école** they refused to enrol[GB] them at the school; **les ~s seront closes le 15 novembre** the closing-date for registration is 15 November; **~ à un concours** entrance for a competitive exam; **il y a mille nouvelles ~s par an** a thousand new students register ou matriculate every year; **2** (enregistrement) (de personne, nom, données) entering; (de société) registration; **~ au registre du commerce** business registration; **~ à un tournoi** entering for a tournament; **l'~ au club coûte 200 francs** the membership fee for the club costs 200 francs; **~ électorale/sur les listes électorales** registration as a voter/on the electoral roll; **~ à la cote** (stock exchange) listing; **demande d'~ à Wall Street** application to be listed on Wall Street; **3** (écriture) (élaborée) inscription; (hâtive) graffiti; **~s cunéiformes** cuneiform inscriptions; **~s racistes sur un mur** racist graffiti on a wall; **~ en lettres d'or** inscription in gold lettering; **panneau portant l'~ 'sortie'** sign saying 'exit'.

■ **~ comptable** Compta accounting entry; **~ de faux** Jur plea of forgery; **~ hypothécaire** Jur registration of mortgage; **~s administratives** Univ admissions.

inscrire /ɛ̃skʀiʀ/ [67] **I** *vtr* **1** (enregistrer) [*institution, enseignant*] to enrol[GB] [*élève*]; to register [*étudiant*]; **je l'ai inscrite à l'école du quartier/à un cours de violon** I enrolled her at the local primary school/for violin lessons; **~ qn sur une liste** to enter sb's name on a list; **~ une question à l'ordre du jour** to place an item on the agenda; **se faire ~ à** to join; **se faire ~ sur les listes électorales** to get oneself put on the electoral roll; **faites-vous ~ à la mairie pour le tournoi** put your name down at the Town Hall for the tournament; **2** (écrire) to write down [*nom, rendez-vous*].

II s'inscrire *vpr* **1** (faire enregistrer) Scol to enrol[GB]; Univ to register, to matriculate; **s'~ à l'université** to register at the university; **s'~ à un parti/club** to join a party/club; **s'~ à un examen** to enter for an exam; **s'~ à un tournoi** to enter (one's name) for a tournament; **s'~ au chômage** to register as unemployed; **s'~ sur les listes électorales** to get oneself put on the electoral roll; **2** (faire partie de) **s'~ dans le cadre de** to be in line with; **s'~ dans la logique de** to fit into the scheme of; **s'~ dans une stratégie/un plan de restructuration** to be part of a strategy/a restructuring programme[GB]; **s'~ dans une volonté de réforme** to be part and parcel of a desire for reform; **le nouveau bâtiment s'inscrit mal dans l'architecture du quartier** the new building does not fit in well with the architecture of the area; **3 s'~ en faux contre qch** to dispute the validity of sth.

inscrit, **~e** /ɛ̃skʀi, it/ **I** *pp* ▸ **inscrire**.

II *pp adj* **1** lit Scol enrolled; Univ registered; **ceux qui sont ~s à l'université** those registered at the university; **les personnes ~es sur la liste d'attente** those on the waiting list; **mon nom n'est pas ~ sur la liste** my name isn't on the list; **cette œuvre n'était pas ~e au programme** this work wasn't on the programme[GB]; **le débat ~ à l'ordre du jour** the debate on the agenda; **les personnes non ~es à l'association/au club** nonmembers of the association/of the club; **60% des électeurs ~s** 60% of registered voters; **les députés non ~s** *independent members of the French Parliament*; **2** fig **~ dans la mémoire/le cœur de qn** engraved in ou on sb's memory/heart.

III *nm,f* (élève) registered student; (électeur) registered voter.

insécable /ɛ̃sekabl/ *adj* indivisible.

insecte /ɛ̃sɛkt/ *nm* insect.

insecticide /ɛ̃sɛktisid/ **I** *adj* insecticidal.

II *nm* insecticide.

insectivore /ɛ̃sɛktivɔʀ/ **I** *adj* insectivorous.

II *nm* insectivore.

insécurité /ɛ̃sekyʀite/ *nf* insecurity ₵.

INSEE /inse/ *nm* (*abbr* = **Institut national de la statistique et des études économiques**) French national institute of statistics and economic studies.

inséminateur, **-trice** /ɛ̃seminatœʀ, tʀis/ **I** *adj* insemination (*épith*).

II ▶ **510** *nm,f* inseminator.

insémination /ɛ̃seminasjɔ̃/ *nf* insemination; **~ artificielle** artificial insemination.

inséminer /ɛ̃semine/ [1] *vtr* to inseminate.

insensé, **~e** /ɛ̃sɑ̃se/ **I** *adj* **1** (extravagant) [*pari, histoire, projet*] insane; **c'est ~!** that's insane!; **tenir des discours ~s** to talk complete nonsense; **2**° (excessif) [*cohue, embouteillage, gains*] phenomenal; **j'ai un travail ~** I've got a phenomenal amount of work.

II *nm,f* madman/madwoman.

insensibilisation /ɛ̃sɑ̃sibilizasjɔ̃/ *nf* anaesthetization.

insensibiliser /ɛ̃sɑ̃sibilize/ [1] *vtr* Méd to anaesthetize.

insensibilité /ɛ̃sɑ̃sibilite/ *nf* **1** (absence de réaction) imperviousness, insensibility (**à** to); **~ à la douleur/au bruit/à la poésie** imperviousness to pain/to noise/to poetry; **2** (indifférence) insensitivity (**à** to); **~ aux malheurs d'autrui** insensitivity to the misfortunes of others.

insensible /ɛ̃sɑ̃sibl/ *adj* **1** (sans réaction) impervious, insensible (**à** to); **~ à la douleur/au froid** impervious to pain/to the cold; **Picasso me laisse ~** Picasso leaves me cold°; **2** (indifférent) insensitive (**à** to); **elle n'est pas restée ~ à tes avances/souffrances** she wasn't insensitive to your advances/suffering; **3** (imperceptible) [*changement*] imperceptible.

insensiblement /ɛ̃sɑ̃sibləmɑ̃/ *adv* imperceptibly.

inséparable /ɛ̃sepaʀabl/ **I** *adj*, *nmf* [*phénomènes, personnes*] inseparable (**de** from); **ce sont des ~s** they're inseparable; **Paul et son ~ parapluie** hum Paul and his inevitable umbrella; **voilà les ~s!** hum here come the terrible twins!

II *nm* Zool (perruche) lovebird; **un couple d'~s** a pair of lovebirds.

inséparablement /ɛ̃sepaʀabləmɑ̃/ *adv* inseparably.

insérer /ɛ̃seʀe/ [14] **I** *vtr* to insert [*encart, annonce, disquette, clé, aiguille*] (**dans** in); to incorporate [*sujet*] (**dans** into); to include [*œuvre, chapitre*] (**dans** in); to integrate [*personne, élément, institution*] (**dans** into); **bien inséré dans la société** well integrated into society; **inséré professionnellement** integrated into the workforce.

II s'insérer *vpr* **1** gén [*encart, disquette*] to be inserted; [*personne*] to fit in; **s'~ dans** [*personne*] to fit into; **cette mesure s'insère dans un contexte de rigueur** this measure is to be seen in the context of austerity; **s'~ entre le volant et le siège** to squeeze in between the wheel and the seat; **2** [*muscle*] to be attached (**sur** to).

INSERM /insɛʀm/ *nm* (*abbr* = **Institut national de la santé et de la recherche médicale**) French national health and medical research institute.

insert /ɛ̃sɛʀ/ *nm* **1** Cin insert (shot); **2** Radio, TV news flash.

insertion /ɛ̃sɛʀsjɔ̃/ *nf* **1** (d'objet, d'annonce, de clause) insertion; **2** (intégration) integration; **faciliter l'~ des immigrés/des jeunes** to facilitate the integration of immigrants/of the young; **~ professionnelle/sociale** professional/social integration; **3** Anat, Bot (de ligament, feuille) insertion; **4** Jur **~ légale** publication of a legal judgment in the press.

insidieusement /ɛ̃sidjøzmɑ̃/ *adv* insidiously.

insidieux, **-ieuse** /ɛ̃sidjø, øz/ *adj* insidious.

insigne /ɛ̃siɲ/ **I** *adj* fml [*honneur, faveur, privilège*] great, signal sout (*épith*); [*service*] distinguished; [*maladresse*] remarkable iron;

avoir l'~ honneur de faire to have the great honour[GB] of doing.

II *nm* (signe distinctif) badge; **arborer un ~** to sport a badge.

III **insignes** *nmpl* (emblème) insignia (*pl*); **les ~s de la royauté** the insignia of royalty.

insignifiance /ɛ̃siɲifjɑ̃s/ *nf* (de personne) insignificance; (de conversation, grief) triviality.

insignifiant, ~e /ɛ̃siɲifjɑ̃, ɑ̃t/ *adj* **1** (sans intérêt) [*personne, personnage, détail*] insignificant; [*traits*] nondescript; **2** (infime) [*somme, cadeau, hausse*] insignificant.

insinuant, ~e /ɛ̃sinɥɑ̃, ɑ̃t/ *adj* [*manière, ton*] insinuating (*épith*); **propos ~s** insinuations.

insinuation /ɛ̃sinɥasjɔ̃/ *nf* insinuation.

insinuer /ɛ̃sinɥe/ [1] I *vtr* **1** (suggérer) to insinuate (**que** that); **2** (introduire) to slip (**dans** into).

II **s'insinuer** *vpr* [*personne*] (physiquement) to slip (**dans** into); (socialement) to ingratiate oneself (**auprès de qn** with sb); [*sentiment, idée*] to creep (**dans** into); [*liquide, odeur*] to seep (**dans** into); **le doute s'insinuait en eux** or **dans leur esprit** doubt crept into their minds; **s'~ dans les bonnes grâces de qn** to curry favour[GB] with sb.

insipide /ɛ̃sipid/ *adj* **1** (sans saveur) [*nourriture, cuisine*] insipid, tasteless; **2** (fade) [*livre, existence, bavardage*] dull; [*personne, personnage*] insipid.

insipidité /ɛ̃sipidite/ *nf* insipidity.

insistance /ɛ̃sistɑ̃s/ *nf* insistence; **l'~ de qn à faire** sb's insistence on doing; **avec ~** insistently; **accent d'~** emphatic accent.

insistant, ~e /ɛ̃sistɑ̃, ɑ̃t/ *adj* [*ton, regard, appel, rumeur, demande*] insistent; **se montrer ~** to be insistent; **de façon ~e** insistently, in an insistent manner.

insister /ɛ̃siste/ [1] *vi* **1** (persévérer) (auprès d'une personne) to be insistent (**auprès de** with), to insist; (au téléphone, à une porte, avec machine) to keep trying; **il ne voulait pas venir avec nous, j'ai dû ~** he didn't want to come with us, I had to insist; **entendu je n'insiste pas!** OK I won't insist!; **je n'insiste pas puisque vous conduisez** I won't insist since you're driving; **~ pour parler à qn** to insist on speaking to sb; **j'ai dû ~ pour qu'il vienne** I had to press him to come; **il insiste pour être reçu** he insists on being seen; **'ça ne répond pas'—'insiste, il est peut-être dans le jardin'** 'there's no reply!'—'keep on trying, he may be in the garden GB ou yard US'; **inutile d'~, ils doivent être sortis** it's pointless to keep on trying, they must be out; **inutile d'~, il est têtu** there's no point in insisting, he's stubborn; **il est parti sans ~** he left without further ado; **2** (mettre l'accent) **~ sur** to stress, to lay stress on [*résultat, événement, danger, besoin*]; to put the emphasis on [*orthographe, présentation, attitude*]; **n'insistons pas sur cette question délicate** let's not dwell on this delicate question; **~ sur la nécessité de faire** to stress the need to do; **3** (repasser plusieurs fois) **~ sur** to pay particular attention to [*tache, défaut, aspérité*].

insolation /ɛ̃sɔlasjɔ̃/ ▶271 *nf* **1** (coup de soleil) sunstroke ¢; **attraper une ~** to get sunstroke; **il a eu deux ~s cet été** he's had sunstroke twice this summer; **2** (exposition) exposure to the sun, insolation spéc; Phot (de plaque, film) exposure; **une trop longue ~ est néfaste pour l'organisme** overexposure to the sun is harmful to the body; **3** Météo (ensoleillement) sunny period; **région qui jouit d'une belle ~** region which enjoys beautiful sunny weather.

insolemment /ɛ̃sɔlamɑ̃/ *adv* **1** (sans respect) insolently; **2** (de façon provocante) unashamedly.

insolence /ɛ̃sɔlɑ̃s/ *nf* **1** (irrespect) insolence; **une fille/réponse d'une rare ~** an exceptionally insolent girl/answer; **2** (parole) insolent remark; **3** (arrogance) arrogance.

insolent, ~e /ɛ̃sɔlɑ̃, ɑ̃t/ I *adj* **1** (irrespectueux) [*enfant, ton, attitude*] insolent, cheeky○; **2** (arrogant) [*rival, vainqueur*] arrogant; **3** (provocant) [*personne, jeunesse*] brazen; [*luxe, succès, fortune, joie*] unashamed.

II *nm,f* insolent person; **l'~ m'a tiré la langue** the cheeky thing stuck his tongue out at me; **petite ~e!** cheeky girl!

insolite /ɛ̃sɔlit/ *adj, nm* unusual; **goût de l'~** taste for the unusual.

insolubilité /ɛ̃sɔlybilite/ *nf* insolubility.

insoluble /ɛ̃sɔlybl/ *adj* [*matière*] insoluble; [*problème, question*] insoluble.

insolvabilité /ɛ̃sɔlvabilite/ *nf* insolvency.

insolvable /ɛ̃sɔlvabl/ *adj* insolvent.

insomniaque /ɛ̃sɔmnjak/ *adj, nmf* insomniac.

insomnie /ɛ̃sɔmni/ ▶271 *nf* **1** (maladie) insomnia ¢; **avoir des ~s** to have insomnia; **2** (nuit sans sommeil) sleepless night.

insondable /ɛ̃sɔ̃dabl/ *adj* [*abîme, mystère*] unfathomable; [*tristesse, désespoir, bêtise*] immense.

insonore /ɛ̃sɔnɔʀ/ *adj* **1** (qui amortit les sons) [*matériau, mur*] soundproof; **2** (qui ne produit pas de son) soundless.

insonorisation /ɛ̃sɔnɔʀizasjɔ̃/ *nf* soundproofing.

insonoriser /ɛ̃sɔnɔʀize/ [1] *vtr* to soundproof; **mal insonorisé** poorly soundproofed.

insouciance /ɛ̃susjɑ̃s/ *nf* **1** (absence de souci) carefreeness, insouciance sout; **vivre dans l'~** to lead a carefree life; **2** (absence d'inquiétude) lack of concern (**de** for); **son ~ de l'avenir/du danger** his lack of concern for the future/for danger.

insouciant, ~e /ɛ̃susjɑ̃, ɑ̃t/ I *adj* [*personne, humeur, rire*] carefree; **il mène une existence ~e** he leads a carefree life; **~ du lendemain** without a thought for the future (*épith, après n*).

II *nm,f* happy-go-lucky person; **c'est un ~** he's happy-go-lucky.

insoucieux, -ieuse /ɛ̃susjø, øz/ *adj* fml unconcerned (**de** by).

insoumis, ~e /ɛ̃sumi, iz/ I *adj* (rebelle) [*contrée, peuple*] unsubdued; **soldat ~** draft dodger.

II *nm,f* Mil draft dodger.

insoumission /ɛ̃sumisjɔ̃/ *nf* **1** (rébellion) insubordination; **2** Mil avoidance of the draft.

insoupçonnable /ɛ̃supsɔnabl/ *adj* beyond suspicion (*après n*).

insoupçonné, ~e /ɛ̃supsɔne/ *adj* [*ressources, force, menace, difficultés*] unsuspected; [*richesses, perspectives, horizons*] undreamed of.

insoutenable /ɛ̃sutnabl/ *adj* **1** (intolérable) [*violence, douleur, scène, cris*] unbearable; **un film d'une violence ~** an unbearably violent film; **2** (impossible à suivre) [*cadence, allure, concurrence*] impossible; **3** (indéfendable) [*cause, opinion, théorie*] untenable.

inspecter /ɛ̃spɛkte/ [1] *vtr* to inspect.

inspecteur, -trice /ɛ̃spɛktœʀ, tʀis/ ▶813 *nm,f* inspector.

■ **~ d'académie** Scol ≈ local schools inspector; **~ en chef** head supervisor; **~ des contributions** Fisc tax inspector; **~ départemental de l'Éducation nationale** Scol ≈ regional schools inspector; **~ des finances** Fin ≈ inspector of public finances; **~ général de l'Éducation nationale** Scol ≈ national schools inspector; **~ des impôts** Fisc tax inspector; **~ de police** ≈ detective constable GB; **~ de police divisionnaire** ≈ detective chief inspector GB; **~ de police principal** ≈ detective inspector GB; **~ du travail** Admin government inspector (*concerned with health and safety and respect of labour laws*) ; **~ des travaux finis** hum skiver○ GB, shrinker○ US; **~ des ventes** Comm sales supervisor.

inspection /ɛ̃spɛksjɔ̃/ *nf* **1** (contrôle) inspection; **ronde** or **tournée d'~** tour of inspection GB, inspection tour US; **~ de routine** routine inspection; **j'ai subi une ~ en règle à la douane** I was thoroughly searched by customs; **le professeur a eu trois ~s en cinq ans** the teacher has been inspected three times in five years; **faire l'~ de qch** to inspect sth; **2** (ensemble d'inspecteurs) inspectorate.

■ **~ académique** ≈ local schools inspectorate; **~ générale des finances** ≈ inspectorate of public finances; **~ du travail** ≈ labour[GB] inspectorate; **Inspection générale des services, IGS** French police complaints authority.

inspectorat /ɛ̃spɛktɔʀa/ *nm* inspectorship.

inspirateur, -trice /ɛ̃spiʀatœʀ, tʀis/ I *adj* **1** (qui donne l'inspiration) inspiring; **2** Anat [*muscles*] inspiratory.

II *nm,f* **1** (d'idée, de théorie) initiator; (de complot) instigator; **2** (d'artiste, œuvre) inspiration; **elle a été ton inspiratrice** she was your inspiration, she inspired you.

inspiration /ɛ̃spiʀasjɔ̃/ *nf* **1** (souffle créateur) inspiration ¢; **attendre/chercher l'~** to wait for/look for inspiration; **avoir de l'~** to have inspiration; **manquer d'~** to lack inspiration; **auteur sans ~** uninspired author; **2** (influence) inspiration; **source d'~** source of inspiration; **œuvre d'~ romantique** work of romantic inspiration; **3** (idée) inspiration; **soudain, il eut une ~** he had a sudden inspiration, he had a brainwave○; **4** Physiol inspiration; **5** Relig inspiration; **~ divine/céleste** divine/heavenly inspiration.

inspiré, ~e /ɛ̃spiʀe/ I *pp* ▶ **inspirer**.

II *pp adj* [*auteur, artiste, œuvre*] inspired; **il prit un air ~ et se mit à jouer** he assumed the air of one inspired, and began to play; **être bien/mal ~ de faire** to be well-advised/ill-advised to do; **il a été mal ~ d'accepter leur invitation** he was ill-advised to accept their invitation; **~ de** based on; **un roman ~ des vieux contes populaires** a novel based on old folk tales.

inspirer /ɛ̃spiʀe/ [1] I *vtr* **1** (donner de l'inspiration à) to inspire [*personne, mouvement*]; **les paysages maritimes ont inspiré le poète** the poet was inspired by seascapes; **c'est un sujet qui ne m'inspire pas du tout** it's a subject which doesn't inspire me at all; **2** (donner envie à) to appeal to; **ça ne m'inspire pas** that doesn't appeal to me; **3** (susciter) to inspire; **~ la méfiance/le dégoût à qn** to inspire distrust/disgust in sb; **il ne m'inspire pas confiance** I don't have much confidence in him; **ce poème lui a inspiré sa plus célèbre œuvre musicale** this poem inspired his most famous piece of music; **vos remarques m'ont inspiré plusieurs réflexions** your remarks made me think of several things ou brought several thoughts to my mind.

II *vi* (inhaler) to breathe in, to inhale sout.

III **s'inspirer** *vpr* **1** (prendre son inspiration) **s'~ de** to draw one's inspiration from; **il s'est inspiré d'une légende populaire** he drew his inspiration from a popular legend; **la révolution s'est inspirée de ces idéaux** the revolution was inspired by these ideals; **2** (prendre exemple) **s'~ de qn** to follow sb's example, to take a leaf out of sb's book; **inspirez-vous d'elle!** follow her example!

instabilité /ɛ̃stabilite/ *nf* **1** (de situation, pays, prix) instability; (de temps) changeability; (de population) unsettled lifestyle; **2** (de personne) (emotional) instability; **~ mentale** mental instability; **3** Chimie, Phys instability.

instable /ɛ̃stabl/ I *adj* **1** [*monnaie, économie, construction*] unstable; [*temps*] unsettled; **2** [*personne, caractère*] unstable; **3** Chimie, Phys unstable.

II *nmf* unstable character.

installateur, **-trice** /ɛ̃stalatœʀ, tʀis/ *nm,f* **~ de gaz** gas fitter; **~ de chauffage central** heating engineer.

installation /ɛ̃stalasjɔ̃/ **I** *nf* **1** (mise en place) (de téléphone, chauffage, gaz, lave-vaisselle) installation, putting in; (de toilettes publiques, douches, canalisations) putting in; (de système de sécurité, d'équipement informatique) installation; (de table pliante, chevalet) putting up; **l'~ du bureau près de la fenêtre** putting the desk near the window; **~ gratuite** 'free installation'; **2** (appareils) system; **3** (déménagement) move; **depuis mon ~ à Paris** since I moved to Paris; **l'~ de réfugiés dans de nouveaux territoires** the settlement of refugees in new territories; **l'~ des forains sur la place** the setting up of the fair in the square; **4** (manière d'être installé) **notre ~ est rudimentaire/temporaire** we're not properly/permanently settled; **5** (implantation) (d'usine) installation; **l'~ d'entreprises étrangères dans la région** foreign companies setting up in the area; **6** (usine) plant; **7** (professionnellement) **ton ~ à ton compte** your setting up on your own; **8** (arrivée) **dès leur ~ au pouvoir, les insurgés...** as soon as they came to power, the rebels...; **quelques jours après l'~ du nouveau gouvernement** a few days after the new government took office.

II installations *nfpl* gén facilities.

■ **~ de chauffage** heating system; **~ électrique** electric wiring; **~ téléphonique** telephone system; **~s militaires** military installations; **~s nucléaires** nuclear sites; **~s pétrolières** oil production facilities; **~s sanitaires** sanitation ₵; **~s sidérurgiques** steelworks (+ *v sg* ou *pl*), steelyard (*sg*); **~s sportives** sports facilities.

installé, **~e** /ɛ̃stale/ **I** *pp* ▶ **installer**.

II *pp adj* (établi) [*personne*] living (**à** in); [*organisme, société*] based (**à** in); **être bien ~ dans un fauteuil** to be ensconced ou comfortably installed in an armchair; **c'est un homme ~** fig he's very nicely set up.

installer /ɛ̃stale/ [1] **I** *vtr* **1** (mettre en place) to install, to put in [*lave-vaisselle, évier, chauffage central*]; to put up [*table pliante, chevalet, sculptures, étagère*]; to set out [*marchandise*]; to set up [*infrastructure militaire*]; (raccorder) to connect [*gaz, téléphone, électricité*]; **faire ~ une antenne parabolique** to have a satellite dish put up ou installed; **~ le bureau près de la fenêtre** to put the desk near the window; **~ un chapiteau sur la place** to put up the big top on the square; **2** (aménager) to do up [*maison, local, cuisine*]; **~ une chambre dans le grenier** to make a bedroom in the attic; **3** (implanter) to set up [*usine*]; **~ son siège à Paris** to set up their headquarters in Paris; **4** (loger) to put [*invité*] (**dans** in); **~ qn dans un fauteuil** to sit sb in an armchair; **5** Admin to install [*magistrat*]; **il a été installé dans ses fonctions** he took up his duties; **~ qn à un poste** to appoint sb to a post; **~ qn au pouvoir** to put sb into power.

II s'installer *vpr* **1** (devenir durable) [*régime*] to become established; [*atmosphère, morosité, récession*] to set in; **le doute s'installe dans leur esprit** they're beginning to have doubts; **2** (professionnellement) to set oneself up in business; **s'~ à son compte** to set up one's own business; **3** (pour vivre) to settle; **partir s'~ à l'étranger/en province** to go and live abroad/in the provinces; **s'~ dans une routine** to become fixed in a routine; **s'~ temporairement chez des amis** to move in temporarily with friends; **je viendrai te voir quand tu seras installé** I'll come and see you when you're settled in; **4** (se mettre à l'aise) **s'~ dans un fauteuil** to settle into an armchair; **s'~ au soleil/près de la fenêtre** to sit in the sun/by the window; **s'~ pour travailler/à son bureau** to settle down to work/at one's desk; **être bien installé dans un fauteuil** to be sitting comfortably in an armchair; **tu es bien installé?** are you sitting comfortably?; **installe-toi, j'arrive!** make yourself at home, I'm coming!; **dès qu'il est invité quelque part, il s'installe** when he is invited somewhere, he really makes himself at home; **on est mal installé sur ces chaises** these chairs are uncomfortable; **5** (être mis en place) **l'appareil s'installe facilement** the appliance is easy to install; **6** (s'implanter) **des usines étrangères vont s'~ dans la région** foreign companies are going to open factories in the area; **le musée devrait s'~ en banlieue** the museum will probably be situated in the suburbs.

instamment /ɛ̃stamɑ̃/ *adv* [*prier, demander*] insistently.

instance /ɛ̃stɑ̃s/ *nf* **1** Pol (autorité) authority; **les ~s internationales** international authorities; **l'~ supérieure** the higher authority; **l'~ suprême** the highest authority; **en dernière ~** in the final analysis; **les ~s d'un parti politique** the leaders of a political party; **2** (demande) entreaty; **il a accepté sur les ~s de ses amis** he accepted on the entreaties of his friends; **il m'a demandé avec ~ de venir** he pleaded with me to come; **3** Jur (action) legal proceedings (*pl*); (juridiction) level of jurisdiction; **introduire une ~** to start legal proceedings, to institute an action; **être en ~ de divorce** to be engaged in divorce proceedings; **~ supérieure** higher level; **en seconde ~** on appeal; **4** (attente) **l'affaire est en ~** the matter is pending; **courrier en ~** mail pending attention; **train en ~ de départ** train about to depart.

instant, **~e** /ɛ̃stɑ̃, ɑ̃t/ **I** *adj* [*demande, prière, supplication*] insistent; [*besoin*] pressing.

II *nm* **1** (durée brève) moment, instant; **je ne peux rester que quelques ~s** I can only stay for a moment; **un ~ de faiblesse/répit** a moment of weakness/respite; **un ~!** just a minute!; **il y a un ~** a moment ago; **je n'en ai pas douté un seul ~** I didn't doubt it for one moment; **en un ~** in an instant, in no time at all; **l'~ propice** the right moment; **à tout** or **chaque ~** all the time; **dans un ~** in a moment; **l'~ d'avant il était en bonne santé** a moment before he had been in perfect health; **l'~ d'après il était mort** a moment later ou the next minute he was dead; **ne pas perdre un ~** not to waste any time; **d'~ en ~** every minute; **par ~s** at times; **pour l'~** for the moment, for the time being; **il devrait arriver d'un ~ à l'autre** he should arrive any minute now; **2** (le présent) moment; **vivre dans l'~** to live for the present ou the moment; **à l'~ (même)** this instant ou minute; **à l'~ même où** just when; **au même ~** at that very moment ou minute; **de tous les ~s** [*attention, concentration*] constant.

instantané, **~e** /ɛ̃stɑ̃tane/ **I** *adj* [*réponse, riposte, effet*] instantaneous, instant (*épith*); [*explosion, mouvement, mort*] instantaneous; [*boisson, potage, plat*] instant; [*vision, lueur, éclair*] momentary.

II *nm* Phot snapshot.

instantanément /ɛ̃stɑ̃tanemɑ̃/ *adv* instantly.

instar: **à l'instar de** /alɛ̃staʀdə/ *loc prép* following the example of.

instauration /ɛ̃stɔʀasjɔ̃/ *nf* (d'impôts, de règles, débat, système) institution; (de régime, gouvernement) establishment.

instaurer /ɛ̃stɔʀe/ [1] **I** *vtr* to institute [*loi, taxe, contrôle, usage*]; to establish [*régime, gouvernement, dialogue, quota*]; to impose [*couvre-feu*]; **~ un climat de confiance** to create a climate of confidence.

II s'instaurer *vpr* (tous contextes) to be established.

instigateur, **-trice** /ɛ̃stigatœʀ, tʀis/ *nm,f* (de troubles) instigator; (de mouvement) originator.

instigation /ɛ̃stigasjɔ̃/ *nf* **à l'~ de qn** at sb's instigation.

instillation /ɛ̃stilasjɔ̃/ *nf* instillation.

instiller /ɛ̃stile/ [1] *vtr* to instil[GB] (**dans** into; **à** into).

instinct /ɛ̃stɛ̃/ *nm* instinct; **agir à l'~** to act instinctively; **d'~** instinctively; **l'~ de conservation** the instinct of self-preservation; **~ grégaire/maternel** herd/maternal instinct.

instinctif, **-ive** /ɛ̃stɛ̃ktif, iv/ *adj* [*réaction, mouvement*] instinctive; **c'est quelqu'un d'~** he/she's someone who relies on instinct.

instinctivement /ɛ̃stɛ̃ktivmɑ̃/ *adv* instinctively.

instituer /ɛ̃stitɥe/ [1] *vtr* **1** (créer) [*personne, gouvernement, organisme*] to institute [*organisation, politique, usage, législation*]; **2** (nommer) Relig to institute [*cardinal*]; Jur to appoint [*légataire*]; **~ qn son héritier** to appoint sb one's heir.

institut /ɛ̃stity/ *nm* institute.

■ **~ de beauté** beauty salon ou parlour[GB]; **~ de crédit** Fin lending organization; **~ d'émission** Fin central bank; **Institut de France** *body representing the five French academies*; **~ médico-légal** forensic science laboratory; **~ médico-pédagogique** special school; **~ de sondage** polling organization.

instituteur, **-trice** /ɛ̃stitytœʀ, tʀis/ **▶510** *nm,f* (d'école primaire) (primary school) teacher; (d'école maternelle) (nursery school) teacher.

institution /ɛ̃stitysjɔ̃/ **I** *nf* **1** (administration) institution; **2** (établissement d'enseignement) private school; **~ de jeunes filles** private school for girls; **~ religieuse** (de jeunes filles) convent school; (de jeunes gens) school for boys (*run by a religious order*); **3** (action) institution (**de** of); **4** (établissement pour enfants, vieillards, malades) institution; **5** Jur **~ d'héritier** appointment of an heir.

II institutions *nfpl* Pol institutions.

■ **l'~ hospitalière** hospitals (*pl*); **l'~ judiciaire** the judiciary; **l'~ militaire** the military; **l'~ policière** the police (+ *v pl*); **l'~ scolaire** schools (*pl*).

institutionnalisation /ɛ̃stitysjɔnalizasjɔ̃/ *nf* institutionalization.

institutionnaliser /ɛ̃stitysjɔnalize/ [1] **I** *vtr* to institutionalize [*usage, organisme, droit*].

II s'institutionnaliser *vpr* [*organisation, pratique*] to become institutionalized.

institutionnel, **-elle** /ɛ̃stitysjɔnɛl/ *adj* [*système, réforme, crise*] institutional; **des investisseurs/clients ~s** institutional investors/clients; **la droite/gauche institutionnelle** the parliamentary right/left.

institutrice ▶ **instituteur**.

instructeur /ɛ̃stʀyktœʀ/ **I** *adj* **1** Jur [*magistrat, juge*] examining; **2** Mil [*sous-officier, capitaine*] drill.

II *nm* gén, Mil instructor.

instructif, **-ive** /ɛ̃stʀyktif, iv/ *adj* [*rencontre, histoire*] instructive; [*voyage, livre*] informative; [*expérience*] enlightening.

instruction /ɛ̃stʀyksjɔ̃/ **I** *nf* **1** (formation) education ₵; Mil training; **l'~ de la jeunesse** the education of the young; **~ des recrues** Mil training of recruits; **2** (connaissances) education ₵; **niveau d'~ insuffisant** poor level of education; **homme sans ~** uneducated man; **manquer d'~** to be uneducated; **avoir de l'~** to be well-educated; **3** Admin (circulaire) directive; **~ ministérielle** ministerial directive; **4** Jur *preparation of a case for eventual judgment*; **5** Ordinat (énoncé) instruction; (pas de séquence) statement.

II instructions *nfpl* (directives) instructions; **donner des ~s à ses employés** to give instructions to one's employees; **~s de lavage** washing instructions.

■ **~ civique** civics (+ *v sg*); **~ publique** Hist state education GB, public education US; **~ religieuse** religious instruction.

instruire /ɛ̃stʀɥiʀ/ [69] **I** *vtr* **1** (former) [*personne*] to teach [*enfant, jeunesse*]; [*personne*] to train [*soldats*]; **ce film ne vise pas à ~** this film is not intended to be educational; **2** Jur **~ une affaire** to prepare a case for judgment; **le juge chargé d'~ l'affaire** the judge in charge of preparing the case for judgment; **~ contre qn** to make a case against sb; **3** fml (informer) **~ qn de qch** to inform sb of sth; **il nous a instruits de ses intentions** he informed us of his intentions.
II s'instruire *vpr* **1** (apprendre) to learn; **on s'instruit à tout âge** it's never too late to learn; **2** fml (s'informer) **s'~ de qch** to find out about sth; **il s'est instruit des intentions de ton collègue** he found out what your colleague's intentions were.

instruit, **~e** /ɛ̃stʀɥi, it/ **I** *pp* ▸ **instruire**.
II *pp adj* [*personne*] educated.

instrument /ɛ̃stʀymɑ̃/ *nm* **1** (objet) instrument; **~s de chirurgie/d'optique** surgical/optical instruments; **voler/piloter aux ~s** Aviat to fly on instruments; **2** Mus instrument; **~ à cordes/à percussion/à vent** string/percussion/wind instrument; **jouer d'un ~** to play an instrument; **3** (agent) tool; (moyen) instrument; **être l'~ de qn** to be sb's tool; **être l'~ de la vengeance de qn** to be the instrument of sb's revenge; **ce rapport est un ~ de réflexion** the report is a discussion document; **des ~s idéologiques/pédagogiques/financiers** ideological/educational/financial tools; **~ de gestion** management tool.
■ **~ ancien** Mus period instrument; **~ de musique** musical instrument; **~s aratoires** Agric ploughing GB ou plowing US implements; **~s de bord** Aviat, Naut controls.

instrumental, **~e**, *mpl* **-aux** /ɛ̃stʀymɑ̃tal, o/ **I** *adj* Mus, Ling instrumental.
II *nm* Ling instrumental; **à l'~** in the instrumental.

instrumentation /ɛ̃stʀymɑ̃tasjɔ̃/ *nf* Mus, Tech instrumentation.

instrumenter /ɛ̃stʀymɑ̃te/ [1] *vi* **1** Jur to draw up a formal document; **2** Mus to instrument, to orchestrate.

instrumentiste /ɛ̃stʀymɑ̃tist/ *nmf* **1** Mus instrumentalist; **2** Méd theatre nurse GB, scrub nurse GB, operating-room nurse US; **3** Ind instrumentation engineer.

insu: **à l'insu de** /alɛ̃sydə/ *loc prép* **1** (sans le dire) **je suis parti à leur ~** I left without their knowing; **à l'~ de sa femme** without his wife ou wife's knowing it; **2** (sans en avoir conscience) without knowing it, without realizing it; **je me suis trahi à mon ~** I gave myself away without realizing or knowing it; **ils ont été filmés à leur ~** they were filmed without (their) knowing it.

insubmersible /ɛ̃sybmɛʀsibl/ *adj* unsinkable.

insubordination /ɛ̃sybɔʀdinasjɔ̃/ *nf* insubordination.

insubordonné, **~e** /ɛ̃sybɔʀdɔne/ *adj* gén rebellious, insubordinate sout; Mil insubordinate.

insuccès /ɛ̃syksɛ/ *nm* failure.

insuffisamment /ɛ̃syfizamɑ̃/ *adv* **1** (pas assez) insufficiently; **2** (mal) inadequately.

insuffisance /ɛ̃syfizɑ̃s/ *nf* **1** (pénurie) insufficiency, shortage; **~ des ressources** insufficiency of resources; **2** (médiocrité) poor standard; **l'~ de ton travail** the poor standard of your work; **3** (déficit) shortfall; **l'~ de la production/de la demande** the shortfall in production/demand; **4** (lacune) shortcoming; **ce n'est pas à moi de pallier tes ~s** it's not for me to make up for your shortcomings; **5** Méd insufficiency; **~ cardiaque/rénale/respiratoire** cardiac/renal/respiratory insufficiency.

insuffisant, **~e** /ɛ̃syfizɑ̃, ɑ̃t/ **I** *adj* **1** (quantitativement) [*nombre, rendement*] insufficient; **personnel ~** insufficient staff; **renforts en nombre ~** insufficient reinforcements; **2** (qualitativement) [*mesures, connaissances*] inadequate; **préparation ~e** inadequate preparation; **tes résultats en histoire sont ~s** your results in history are not good enough.
II *nm,f* Méd **~ rénal/cardiaque** person suffering from renal/cardiac insufficiency.

insufflation /ɛ̃syflasjɔ̃/ *nf* insufflation.

insuffler /ɛ̃syfle/ [1] *vtr* **1** to instil[GB] [*espoir, dynamisme*] (**à** into); **~ la vie à qn** to breathe life into sb; **2** Méd to insufflate [*oxygène*] (**dans** into; **à** into).

insulaire /ɛ̃sylɛʀ/ **I** *adj* [*population, traditions*] island (*épith*); [*mentalité*] insular péj.
II *nmf* islander.

insularité /ɛ̃sylaʀite/ *nf* insularity.

insuline /ɛ̃sylin/ *nf* insulin.

insulino-dépendant, **~e** /ɛ̃sylinodepɑ̃dɑ̃, ɑ̃t/ *adj* insulin-dependent.

insultant, **~e** /ɛ̃syltɑ̃, ɑ̃t/ *adj* [*propos, comportement*] insulting (**pour** to); **ton attitude était ~e pour moi** I found your behaviour[GB] insulting.

insulte /ɛ̃sylt/ *nf* insult; **c'est une ~ à leur mémoire/intelligence** it is an insult to their memory/intelligence; **écrire une lettre d'~s** to write an insulting letter; **des ~s racistes** racist insults, racist abuse; **dire des ~s à qn** to insult sb; **faire à qn l'~ de refuser** fml to insult sb by refusing.

insulter /ɛ̃sylte/ [1] **I** *vtr* **1** (injurier) to insult [*personne*]; **se faire ~** to be shouted at insultingly (**par** by); **2** (offenser) [*méfiance, attitude*] to be an insult to [*personne*].
II s'insulter *vpr* to exchange insults.

insupportable /ɛ̃sypɔʀtabl/ *adj* unbearable.

insupportablement /ɛ̃sypɔʀtabləmɑ̃/ *adv* unbearably.

insupporter /ɛ̃sypɔʀte/ [1] *vtr* **elle nous/m'insupporte** we/I can't stand her.

insurgé, **~e** /ɛ̃syʀʒe/ **I** *pp* ▸ **s'insurger**.
II *pp adj, nm,f* insurgent, rebel.

insurger: **s'insurger** /ɛ̃syʀʒe/ [13] *vpr* **1** (se soulever) [*population, ville*] to rise up (**contre** against); **2** (protester) [*personne, groupe*] to be up in arms (**contre** against).

insurmontable /ɛ̃syʀmɔ̃tabl/ *adj* [*problème, tâche, dette*] insurmountable; [*désaccord*] insuperable; [*timidité, aversion*] unconquerable.

insurpassable /ɛ̃syʀpasabl/ *adj* unsurpassable.

insurrection /ɛ̃syʀɛksjɔ̃/ *nf* **1** (de population) insurrection, uprising; **le foyer d'~** the centre[GB] of the uprising; **mouvements d'~** rebel movements; **des scènes d'~** scenes of revolt; **2** fig revolt (**contre** against).

insurrectionnel, **-elle** /ɛ̃syʀɛksjɔnɛl/ *adj* insurrectionary.

intact, **~e** /ɛ̃takt/ *adj* intact (*jamais épith*); **maintenir qch ~** to keep sth intact; **rester ~** to remain intact; **leur gloire pour l'instant ~e** their glory that remains intact for the moment.

intangibilité /ɛ̃tɑ̃ʒibilite/ *nf* inviolability.

intangible /ɛ̃tɑ̃ʒibl/ *adj* **1** (inviolable) [*lois, principes*] inviolable; **2** (impalpable) sout [*gaz, fluides, présence*] intangible.

intarissable /ɛ̃taʀisabl/ *adj* [*imagination, inspiration, bavard*] inexhaustible; [*bavardage, larmes*] endless; [*source*] neverending; **elle est ~** she can go on forever (**sur** about).

intarissablement /ɛ̃taʀisabləmɑ̃/ *adv* endlessly.

intégrable /ɛ̃tegʀabl/ *adj* **fonction ~** integrable function.

intégral, **~e**, *mpl* **-aux** /ɛ̃tegʀal, o/ **I** *adj* **1** [*paiement, remboursement*] full, in full (*après n*); [*bronzage*] all-over (*épith*); **2** [*édition, texte, discours*] complete, unabridged; **voir un film en version ~e** to see the uncut version of a film.
II intégrale *nf* **1** Mus **l'~e des concertos pour piano** the complete collection of piano concertos; **jouer l'~e des concertos pour piano** to perform all the piano concertos; **l'~e de Brassens** the complete Brassens collection; **2** Math integral.

intégralement /ɛ̃tegʀalmɑ̃/ *adv* [*payer, citer, publier*] in full; [*refuser, rejeter*] completely.

intégralité /ɛ̃tegʀalite/ *nf* **l'~ de leur salaire** their entire salary; **payer une dette dans son ~** to pay a debt in full; **payer l'~ d'une peine** to serve a full sentence; **diffuser un opéra dans son ~** to broadcast an opera in its entirety.

intégrante /ɛ̃tegʀɑ̃t/ *adj f* **partie ~** integral part; **faire partie ~ de qch** to be an integral part of sth.

intégration /ɛ̃tegʀasjɔ̃/ *nf* **1** gén integration (**à**, **dans** into); **~ sociale** integration into society; **2**○ (entrée) **il fête son ~ à Harvard** he's celebrating getting into Harvard.

intègre /ɛ̃tɛgʀ/ *adj* [*personne, caractère, vie*] honest; **c'est un homme ~** he's a man of integrity.

intégrer /ɛ̃tegʀe/ [14] **I** *vtr* **1** (insérer) to insert, to include [*chapitres, articles*] (**à**, **dans** into); **2** (assimiler) to integrate [*communauté, population*] (**à**, **dans** into); **une architecture bien intégrée dans l'environnement** a piece of architecture which fits in well with its environment; **3**○ (entrer dans) **après sa formation, il a intégré la garde présidentielle** after his training, he joined the presidential guard; **il vient d'~ Harvard** he has just got into Harvard; **4** (inclure) [*solution, budget*] to include [*mesure, dépenses*]; **5** Math to integrate [*fonction*].
II s'intégrer *vpr* **1** [*population, communauté*] to integrate (**à**, **dans** with); **2** [*architecture, immeuble*] to fit in (**à**, **dans** with).

intégrisme /ɛ̃tegʀism/ *nm* fundamentalism.

intégriste /ɛ̃tegʀist/ *adj, nmf* fundamentalist.

intégrité /ɛ̃tegʀite/ *nf* integrity.

intellect /ɛ̃telɛkt/ *nm* intellect.

intellectualisation /ɛ̃telɛktɥalizasjɔ̃/ *nf* intellectualization.

intellectualiser /ɛ̃telɛktɥalize/ [1] *vtr* to intellectualize.

intellectualisme /ɛ̃telɛktɥalism/ *nm* intellectualism.

intellectuel, **-elle** /ɛ̃telɛktɥɛl/ **I** *adj* [*travail, facultés, activité, supériorité*] intellectual; [*fatigue, effort*] mental; [*milieu, œuvre*] intellectual; [*goût, musique*] highbrow.
II *nm,f* intellectual; **c'est un ~ de gauche** he's a left-wing intellectual.

intellectuellement /ɛ̃telɛktɥɛlmɑ̃/ *adv* [*supérieur, médiocre*] intellectually; [*se fatiguer*] mentally.

intelligemment /ɛ̃teliʒamɑ̃/ *adv* intelligently.

intelligence /ɛ̃teliʒɑ̃s/ **I** *nf* **1** (aptitude, faculté) intelligence; **faire preuve d'~** to show intelligence; **~ pratique** practical intelligence; **son ~ est vive, il est d'une ~ vive** he has a sharp mind; **avec ~** intelligently; **2** (compréhension) understanding; **nécessaire à la bonne ~ du texte** necessary for a complete understanding of the text; **3** (entente) agreement; **agir d'~ avec qn** to act in agreement with sb; **être d'~ avec qn** to have a secret understanding ou agreement with sb; **faire des signes d'~ à qn** to make signs of complicity to sb; **être en bonne/mauvaise ~ avec qn** to be on good/bad terms with sb; **4** (personne intelligente) great intellect.
II intelligences *nfpl* (complicité) secret relations ou dealings; **avoir des ~s dans la place** to have inside contacts.
■ **~ artificielle**, **IA** Ordinat artificial intelligence, AI.

intelligent, **~e** /ɛ̃teliʒɑ̃, ɑ̃t/ *adj* [*personne*] intelligent, clever; [*choix, réponse, regard, comportement*] intelligent; **un être ~** an intelligent being; **ce n'est pas ~ de ta part d'avoir fait** it wasn't very clever of you to do; **c'est ~!** iron that's clever!

intelligentsia /ɛ̃teliʒɛntsja/ *nf* intelligentsia.

intelligibilité /ɛ̃teliʒibilite/ *nf* intelligibility.

intelligible /ɛ̃teliʒibl/ *adj* intelligible (**à** to); **de manière ~** in an intelligible way, intelligibly; **parler à haute et ~ voix** to speak loudly and clearly.

intelligiblement /ɛ̃teliʒibləmɑ̃/ *adv* intelligibly.

intempérance /ɛ̃tɑ̃peʀɑ̃s/ *nf* intemperance.

intempérant, **~e** /ɛ̃tɑ̃peʀɑ̃, ɑ̃t/ *adj* intemperate.

intempéries /ɛ̃tɑ̃peʀi/ *nfpl* bad weather ¢.

intempestif, **-ive** /ɛ̃tɑ̃pɛstif, iv/ *adj* [*démarche, demande, arrivée*] untimely; [*curiosité, joie, zèle*] misplaced.

intempestivement /ɛ̃tɑ̃pɛstivmɑ̃/ *adv* at an inopportune moment.

intemporalité /ɛ̃tɑ̃pɔʀalite/ *nf* timelessness.

intemporel, **-elle** /ɛ̃tɑ̃pɔʀɛl/ *adj* (immuable) [*vérités, principes, art*] timeless.

intenable /ɛ̃t(ə)nabl/ *adj* **1** (insupportable) [*odeur, chaleur, situation*] unbearable; **2** (indiscipliné) [*personne, enfant*] difficult; **3** (indéfendable) [*théorie, raisonnement*] untenable.

intendance /ɛ̃tɑ̃dɑ̃s/ *nf* **1** Scol (service) administration; (bureau, personnel) administrative offices; **il faut que l'~ suive** backup is necessary; **l'~ ne suit pas** the backup is not forthcoming; **2** Hist (charge d'intendant) intendancy.

intendant, **~e** /ɛ̃tɑ̃dɑ̃, ɑ̃t/ **I** *nm,f* Scol bursar.
II *nm* **1** Mil (général) quartermaster; (financier) paymaster; **2** (de domaine) steward; **3** Hist intendant.
III intendante *nf* Relig Mother Superior.

intense /ɛ̃tɑ̃s/ *adj* intense.

intensément /ɛ̃tɑ̃semɑ̃/ *adv* intensely.

intensif, **-ive** /ɛ̃tɑ̃sif, iv/ **I** *adj* intensive.
II *nm* intensive.

intensification /ɛ̃tɑ̃sifikasjɔ̃/ *nf* intensification.

intensifier /ɛ̃tɑ̃sifje/ [2] **I** *vtr* to intensify [*sensation, sentiment*]; to intensify, to step up [*échanges, production*].
II s'intensifier *vpr* to intensify.

intensité /ɛ̃tɑ̃site/ *nf* **1** (force) intensity; **la tempête diminue d'~** the storm is dying down; **2** Phys (électrique) current.

intensivement /ɛ̃tɑ̃sivmɑ̃/ *adv* intensively.

intenter /ɛ̃tɑ̃te/ [1] *vtr* **~ un procès à qn** to sue sb; **~ une action contre qn** to bring an action against sb.

intention /ɛ̃tɑ̃sjɔ̃/ *nf* intention; **agir avec les meilleures ~s du monde** to act with the best of intentions; **il n'est pas dans ses ~s de faire** he has no intention of doing; **avoir l'~ de faire** to intend to do; **c'est l'~ qui compte** it's the thought that counts; **dans l'~ de faire** with the intention of doing; **à l'~ de qn** [*déclaration, geste*] aimed at sb; [*œuvre*] intended for sb; [*fête*] in sb's honour[GB]; ▶ **paver**.

intentionné, **~e** /ɛ̃tɑ̃sjɔne/ *adj* **bien/mal ~** well-/ill-intentioned.

intentionnel, **-elle** /ɛ̃tɑ̃sjɔnɛl/ *adj* intentional.

intentionnellement /ɛ̃tɑ̃sjɔnɛlmɑ̃/ *adv* intentionally.

interactif, **-ive** /ɛ̃tɛʀaktif, iv/ *adj* interactive.

interaction /ɛ̃tɛʀaksjɔ̃/ *nf* interaction.
■ **~ faible** Phys weak interaction; **~ forte** Phys strong interaction.

interactivement /ɛ̃tɛʀaktivmɑ̃/ *adv* interactively.

interallemand, **~e** /ɛ̃tɛʀalmɑ̃, ɑ̃d/ *adj* between the two Germanies (*après n*).

interallié, **~e** /ɛ̃tɛʀalje/ *adj* [*état-major, force*] joint allied.

interarabe /ɛ̃tɛʀaʀab/ *adj* between Arab nations (*après n*).

interarmées /ɛ̃tɛʀaʀme/ *adj inv* [*force, état-major*] joint.

interarmes /ɛ̃tɛʀaʀm/ *adj inv* [*opération*] combined; [*école*] interservices (*épith*).

interbancaire /ɛ̃tɛʀbɑ̃kɛʀ/ *adj* interbank (*épith*).

interbibliothèques /ɛ̃tɛʀbiblijɔtɛk/ *adj inv* **prêt ~** interlibrary loan.

intercalaire /ɛ̃tɛʀkalɛʀ/ **I** *adj* **feuille** or **feuillet ~** insert; **jour/mois ~** intercalary day/month.
II *nm* (de séparation) divider.

intercaler /ɛ̃tɛʀkale/ [1] **I** *vtr* **1** (insérer) to insert (**dans** into; **entre** between); **2** (ajouter) to intercalate [*jour, mois*].
II s'intercaler *vpr* [*rendez-vous*] to fit (**entre** in between); [*feuillet, exemple*] to be inserted (**entre** between); [*personne, véhicule*] to come (**entre** in between).

intercéder /ɛ̃tɛʀsede/ [14] *vi* to intercede (**auprès de qn** with sb; **en faveur de qn** on sb's behalf).

intercellulaire /ɛ̃tɛʀselylɛʀ/ *adj* intercellular.

intercepter /ɛ̃tɛʀsɛpte/ [1] *vtr* to intercept.

interception /ɛ̃tɛʀsɛpsjɔ̃/ *nf* interception; **chasseur d'~** Mil Aviat interceptor.

intercesseur /ɛ̃tɛʀsesœʀ/ *nm* intercessor.

intercession /ɛ̃tɛʀsesjɔ̃/ *nf* intercession.

interchangeabilité /ɛ̃tɛʀʃɑ̃ʒabilite/ *nf* interchangeability.

interchangeable /ɛ̃tɛʀʃɑ̃ʒabl/ *adj* interchangeable.

interchrétien, **-ienne** /ɛ̃tɛʀkʀetjɛ̃, ɛn/ *adj* [*affrontements*] between opposing Christian factions (*après n*).

interclasse /ɛ̃tɛʀklas/ *nm* break (between classes).

interclubs /ɛ̃tɛʀklœb/ *adj inv* interclub.

intercommunal, **~e**, *mpl* **-aux** /ɛ̃tɛʀkɔmynal, o/ *adj* [*coopération*] between local councils (*épith, après n*); [*équipement*] district (*épith*).

intercommunautaire /ɛ̃tɛʀkɔmynotɛʀ/ *adj* CEE within the EC (*après n*).

intercommunication /ɛ̃tɛʀkɔmynikasjɔ̃/ *nf* intercommunication.

interconnecter /ɛ̃tɛʀkɔnɛkte/ [1] *vtr* to interconnect.

interconnexion /ɛ̃tɛʀkɔnɛksjɔ̃/ *nf* interconnection.

intercontinental, **~e**, *mpl* **-aux** /ɛ̃tɛʀkɔ̃tinɑ̃tal, o/ *adj* [*vol, missile*] intercontinental.

intercostal, **~e**, *mpl* **-aux** /ɛ̃tɛʀkɔstal, o/ *adj* [*nerf*] intercostal; [*douleur*] in the ribs (*après n*).

interdépartemental, **~e**, *mpl* **-aux** /ɛ̃tɛʀdepaʀtəmɑ̃tal, o/ *adj* **1** Entr, Univ interdepartmental; **2** Admin *involving several departments*.

interdépendance /ɛ̃tɛʀdepɑ̃dɑ̃s/ *nf* interdependence.

interdépendant, **~e** /ɛ̃tɛʀdepɑ̃dɑ̃, ɑ̃t/ *adj* interdependent.

interdiction /ɛ̃tɛʀdiksjɔ̃/ *nf* **1** (action d'interdire) banning; **demander l'~ de qch** to ask for sth to be banned; **'~ de fumer'** 'no smoking'; **'~ de dépasser'** 'no overtaking' GB, 'no passing' US; **'~ de stationner'** 'no parking'; **il a été condamné avec ~ d'exercer sa profession** he was found guilty and banned from practising[GB]; **la décision est en contradiction avec l'~ du travail des mineurs** the decision contravenes the ban on child labour[GB]; **2** (chose interdite) ban; **maintenir/lever une ~** to maintain/lift a ban; **toutes les ~s d'importer de la viande...** all bans on meat imports...; **trois mois d'~ de sortie du territoire** a three-month ban on leaving the country; **3** (de fonctionnaire) barring from office; **fonctionnaire frappé d'~** civil servant who has been barred from holding office; **4** Jur **~ (judiciaire)** declaration of legal incompetence.
■ **~ de séjour** prohibition on residence.

interdigital, **~e**, *mpl* **-aux** /ɛ̃tɛʀdiʒital, o/ *adj* interdigital.

interdire /ɛ̃tɛʀdiʀ/ [65] **I** *vtr* **1** (ne pas autoriser) to ban, to prohibit [*film, ouvrage, meeting, commerce, publicité, vente*]; to ban [*alcool, tabac*]; **~ la vente de qch** to ban the sale of sth; **la loi qui interdit le travail de nuit des femmes** the law banning nightwork for women; **~ à qn l'entrée de sa maison** to refuse sb entry to one's house; **le médecin m'a interdit les bains de soleil/l'alcool** the doctor has told me not to sunbathe/not to drink alcohol; **~ qn de parole** to forbid sb to talk; **X est interdit d'antenne/d'enseignement** X is banned from broadcasting/teaching; **~ à qn de faire**, **~ que qn fasse** to forbid sb to do; **on lui a interdit de parler** he was forbidden to talk; **la loi interdit qu'on fume dans les lieux publics** the law forbids smoking in public places; **il est interdit de parler au chauffeur/prendre des photos** it is forbidden to talk to the driver/take photos; **c'est interdit par la loi** it is forbidden by law; **il est interdit de fumer/mendier/cracher** no smoking/begging/spitting; **2** (rendre impossible) **mon état de santé m'interdit le sport/l'alcool** I can't play sports/drink alcohol on account of my health; **son manque de qualifications lui interdit tout espoir de promotion** he has no hope of promotion because he lacks qualifications; **~ à qn de faire** to prevent sb from doing; **la discrétion m'interdit d'en dire plus** discretion prevents me from saying more; **les circonstances nous interdisent tout commentaire** the circumstances prevent us from commenting; **3** (suspendre) to ban [sb] from holding office [*fonctionnaire*].
II s'interdire *vpr* **s'~ le chocolat** to keep off chocolate; **s'~ les sorties** to refrain from going out; **s'~ de penser** to stop oneself from thinking.

interdisciplinaire /ɛ̃tɛʀdisiplinɛʀ/ *adj* **1** Scol [*cours, activité*] cross-curricular; **2** Univ interdisciplinary.

interdisciplinarité /ɛ̃tɛʀdisiplinaʀite/ *nf* Univ interdisciplinarity.

interdit, **~e** /ɛ̃tɛʀdi, it/ **I** *pp* ▶ **interdire**.
II *pp adj* **1** (défendu) prohibited, forbidden; **baignade/pêche/chasse ~e** swimming/fishing/hunting prohibited; **stationnement ~** no parking; **entrée ~e** no entry ou admittance; **dépassement ~** no overtaking GB, no passing US; **film ~ aux moins de 13 ans** film unsuitable for children under 13; **film ~ aux moins de 18 ans** film for adults over 18 only; **être ~ de séjour** Jur to be subject to a prohibition on residence; fig to be banned (**dans** from).
III *adj* (stupéfait) dumbfounded; **être** or **rester ~** to be dumbfounded; **la nouvelle l'a laissé tout ~** he was really dumbfounded by the news; **Paul, tout ~, me regardait** Paul was staring at me, dumbfounded.
IV *nm* **1** (chose interdite) (par les lois) proscription; (par les conventions) taboo; **lever un ~** to remove a proscription; **la transgression de l'~** or **des ~s** breaking taboos; **braver tous les ~s** to defy all taboos; **2** (condamnation) bar; **jeter** or **lancer** or **prononcer l'~ sur qn** to debar ou bar sb.
■ **~ alimentaire** Relig dietary restrictions (*pl*).

interentreprises /ɛ̃tɛʀɑ̃tʀəpʀiz/ *adj inv* [*rivalité*] inter-company; [*coopération*] within the business community (*après n*).

intéressant, **~e** /ɛ̃teʀesɑ̃, ɑ̃t/ **I** *adj* **1** (qui retient l'attention) interesting (**de faire** to do;

pour qn for sb); **il est ~ de noter que** it's interesting to note that; **2** (qui offre des ressources) interesting; **3** (avantageux) [*prix, offre, conditions, opérations*] attractive; [*affaire*] favourable[GB]; **il est plus ~ de payer au comptant qu'à crédit** it's better to pay in cash rather than by credit; **il est ~ d'acheter dans l'immobilier** property is a good buy.
II *nm,f* **faire l'~** or **son ~** to show off.
IDIOMES **être dans une situation ~e**○ to be pregnant.

intéressé, **~e** /ɛ̃teʀese/ I *pp* ▶ **intéresser**.
II *pp adj* **1** (attiré) interested (**par** in); **il est très ~ par notre proposition** he's very interested in our proposal; **il est peu ~ par l'affaire** he has little interest in the matter; **se dire** or **déclarer ~ par qch** to express an interest in sth; **2** (captivé) [*public, auditoire*] attentive; **la salle semblait peu ~e** the audience didn't seem very attentive; **3** (concerné) **les parties ~es** those concerned; **toute personne ~e** all those interested (+ *v pl*); **les personnes ~es aux bénéfices** people with a share in the profits; **4** (qui vise un profit) [*personne, avis , point de vue, démarche*] self-interested (*épith*); **il est ~** he acts out of self-interest; **ses conseils étaient ~s** his advice was given out of self-interest.
III *nm,f* person concerned; **les ~s** people concerned; **le principal ~** the person most directly concerned; **les principaux ~s** those most directly concerned.

intéressement /ɛ̃teʀɛsmɑ̃/ *nm* Entr (système) profit-sharing; (revenu) share in the profits; **fixe plus ~** basic salary plus share in the profits; **~ des salariés** profit-sharing scheme.

intéresser /ɛ̃teʀese/ [1] I *vtr* **1** (retenir l'attention) to interest; **personne/rien ne les intéresse** they're not interested in anybody/anything; **votre projet m'intéresse** I'm interested in your project; **ça ne m'intéresse pas** I'm not interested (**de faire** in doing); **votre émission n'intéresse plus personne** nobody finds your programme[GB] interesting any more; **aujourd'hui l'environnement intéresse les gens** today people take an interest in the environment; **2** (concerner) [*problème, décision, mesures*] to concern; **l'accord intéresse une vingtaine de personnes** the agreement concerns twenty-odd people; **la protection du site intéresse tout le monde** the protection of the site is of concern to all; **3** Entr **~ les salariés aux bénéfices** to offer a profit-sharing scheme to employees.
II **s'intéresser** *vpr* **s'~ à** gén to be interested in; (en s'engageant) to take an interest in; **il ne s'intéresse qu'aux femmes/insectes** he's only interested in women/insects; **de plus en plus de gens s'intéressent à l'environnement** more and more people are taking an interest in the environment.

intérêt /ɛ̃teʀɛ/ *nm* **1** (attention) interest (**pour** in); **susciter** or **éveiller l'~ de qn** to arouse sb's interest; **porter un grand ~ à qch** to take a great interest in sth; **manifester** or **marquer son ~ pour qch** to express one's interest in sth; **trouver** or **prendre un certain ~ à faire** to find it interesting to do; **avec ~** [*lire, observer, attendre*] with interest; **2** (attrait) interest; **votre livre est d'un grand ~** or **présente un grand ~** your book is of great interest; **recherche digne d'~** worthwhile research; **livre plein d'~** book of exceptional interest; **sans ~** uninteresting; **n'avoir pas grand ~** not to have much to recommend it; **3** (avantage, utilité) interest; **d'~ général/public/commun** of general/public/common interest; **dans l'~ de qn/de tous** in sb's/everyone's interest; **l'~ supérieur de la nation** the supreme interest of the nation; **c'est dans votre ~ de faire** it's in your interest to do; **elle a tout ~ à faire/à ce que qch se fasse** it is in her best interest to do/that sth be done; **contraire aux ~s de qn** against sb's interests; **c'est dans ton ~** it's for your own good; **être du plus grand ~ pour qn** to concern sb in particular; **tu as ~ à faire**○ you'd be well advised to do; **quel ~ auraient-ils à faire?** what would be the point in their doing?; **y a ~**○**!** you bet○!; **je ne vois pas l'~ de cette réforme/de faire** I don't see the point of this reform/of doing; **par ~** [*agir*] out of self-interest; [*se marier*] for money; **4** Fin (de crédit) interest ₵; **prêt sans ~s** interest-free loan; **porter ~** [*compte*] to bear interest; **porteur d'~** interest-bearing (*épith*); **payer des ~s** to pay interest; **~s simples/composés** simple/compound interest; **5** Fin (part) interest; **avoir/détenir des ~s dans une société** to have/to hold interests in a company; **des ~s dans le sucre/nickel** interests in sugar/nickel.

inter-États /ɛ̃teʀeta/ *adj inv* [*relations*] inter-state.

interethnique /ɛ̃teʀɛtnik/ *adj* [*relations*] between ethnic communities (*après n*); [*violence, affrontements*] (entre tribus) intertribal; (entre communautés) racial.

interface /ɛ̃tɛʀfas/ *nf* Ordinat, Tech interface.
■ **~ de raccordement** Ordinat attachment unit interface, AUI.

interférence /ɛ̃tɛʀfeʀɑ̃s/ *nf* gén, Phys interference.

interférent, **~e** /ɛ̃tɛʀfeʀɑ̃, ɑ̃t/ *adj* interferential.

interférer /ɛ̃tɛʀfeʀe/ [14] *vi* **1** fig to interfere (**avec** with); **les deux projets risquent d'~** the two projects might interfere with each other; **2** Phys to interfere.

interféron /ɛ̃tɛʀfeʀɔ̃/ *nm* interferon.

intergouvernemental, **~e**, *mpl* **-aux** /ɛ̃tɛʀguvɛʀnəmɑ̃tal, o/ *adj* intergovernmental.

intérieur, **~e** /ɛ̃teʀjœʀ/ I *adj* **1** (au-dedans) [*mur, escalier, température*] internal, interior; [*cour*] inner; [*mer*] inland; [*poche*] inside; [*frontière*] internal; **côté ~** inside; **pour l'aménagement ~ de votre maison** for the interior decoration of your house; **lire notre article en pages ~es** read our article inside; **2** (d'un pays) [*politique, marché, consommation, conflit*] domestic; [*ligne, vol, réseau*] domestic; **sur le plan ~** on the domestic front; **3** (d'une organisation) [*règlement, organisation*] internal; **4** (intime) [*vie, sentiment, nécessité, voix*] inner.
II *nm* **1** (de boîte, journal, d'enveloppe, armoire) inside; (de voiture) interior; **fermé de l'~** locked from the inside; **à l'~** inside, indoors; **les enfants jouent à l'~** the children are playing inside; **à l'~ de** inside; **à l'~ des frontières/de la ville/du périmètre** inside the borders/town/perimeter; **à l'~ du régime/parti** inside the regime/party; **à l'~ des terres** inland; **2** (habitation) interior; **fière de son ~** proud of her home; **d'~** [*jeu*] indoor; **plante d'~** houseplant, indoor plant; **3** (de pays) interior; **sur la côte et à l'~ du pays** on the coast and inland; **les villes de l'~** the inland towns; **4** Sport **~ gauche/droit** inside-left/right.

intérieurement /ɛ̃teʀjœʀmɑ̃/ *adv* **1** (en soi-même) [*rire, rager*] inwardly; **2** (au-dedans) **verrouillé/doublé ~** bolted from the/lined on the inside.

intérim /ɛ̃teʀim/ *nm* **1** (période) interim (period); **dans** or **pendant l'~** in the interim; **par ~** on an interim basis; **président par ~** acting president; **2** (fonction) interim duties; **assurer l'~ de** to stand in for; **3** (travail temporaire) temporary work; **société** or **agence d'~** gén temporary employment agency; (de secrétariat) temping agency; **travailler en ~** to do temporary work, to temp○.

intérimaire /ɛ̃teʀimɛʀ/ I *adj* [*fonction, comité*] interim; [*ministre*] acting, interim; [*emploi, personnel, secrétaire*] temporary.
II *nmf* gén worker from a temporary employment agency; (secrétaire) temporary secretary, temp○; (médecin, prêtre) locum GB, stand-in US.

interindividuel, **-elle** /ɛ̃tɛʀɛ̃dividɥɛl/ *adj* interpersonal.

intériorisation /ɛ̃teʀjɔʀizasjɔ̃/ *nf* internalization.

intérioriser /ɛ̃teʀjɔʀize/ [1] *vtr* **1** (garder en soi) to internalize [*colère, peur, sentiment*]; **2** (intégrer) to internalize [*valeurs, règlement*].

intériorité /ɛ̃teʀjɔʀite/ *nf* interiority.

interjectif, **-ive** /ɛ̃tɛʀʒɛktif, iv/ *adj* interjectional.

interjection /ɛ̃tɛʀʒɛksjɔ̃/ *nf* **1** Ling interjection; **2** Jur lodging.

interjeter /ɛ̃tɛʀʒəte/ [20] *vtr* Jur **~ appel** to lodge an appeal.

interlignage /ɛ̃tɛʀliɲaʒ/ *nm* spacing.

interligne /ɛ̃tɛʀliɲ/ I *nm* Imprim (espace) line space; **ajouter un mot dans l'~** to add a word between the lines; **double ~** double spacing.
II *nf* Imprim lead.

interligner /ɛ̃tɛʀliɲe/ [1] *vtr* (séparer) to space [*texte*].

interlocuteur, **-trice** /ɛ̃tɛʀlɔkytœʀ, tʀis/ *nm,f* **1** (dans une conversation) interlocutor sout; **se faire comprendre de son ~** to make oneself understood by the person one is talking to; **un ~ anonyme affirmant parler au nom de...** an anonymous caller, claiming to speak on behalf of...; **la confrontation de ses idées à celles d'un ~** debating one's ideas with someone else; **2** (dans une négociation) representative, spokesperson; **reconnaître qn comme un ~ valable** to acknowledge sb as a recognized spokesperson; **les insurgés ne peuvent être un ~ dans les négociations** the insurgents will not be allowed any representation in the negotiations; **3** (contact) **X est le seul ~** X is the only contact; **le client n'a qu'un seul ~ dans la société** the client only deals with one person in the company; **l'~ privilégié du gouvernement** the person the government prefers to deal with.

interlope /ɛ̃tɛʀlɔp/ *adj* **1** (louche) [*milieu, personne*] shady; **2** (illégal) illegal.

interloquer /ɛ̃tɛʀlɔke/ [1] *vtr* to take [sb] aback; **rester interloqué** to be taken aback.

interlude /ɛ̃tɛʀlyd/ *nm* TV, Mus interlude.

intermariage /ɛ̃tɛʀmaʀjaʒ/ *nm* intermarriage.

intermède /ɛ̃tɛʀmɛd/ *nm* interlude.

intermédiaire /ɛ̃tɛʀmedjɛʀ/ I *adj* [*entreprises, taux, étape, situation*] intermediate; **il n'existe pas de structure ~ entre la prison et l'hôpital psychiatrique** there's no alternative between prison and a psychiatric hospital; **avez-vous la taille/une couleur ~?** do you have a size/colour[GB] in between?
II *nmf* **1** (dans des négociations, un débat) go-between, intermediary; **jouer un rôle** or **servir d'~** to act as go-between (**entre** between); **2** Écon middleman.
III *nm* **sans ~** [*faire, agir*] without any intermediary; [*traiter, vendre*] direct, without a middleman; **faire qch sans l'~ de qn/qch** to do sth without (the intermediary of) sb/sth; **par l'~ de** through.
IV **intermédiaires** *nmpl* Chimie intermediates.

intermédiation /ɛ̃tɛʀmedjasjɔ̃/ *nf* intermediation.

intermezzo /ɛ̃tɛʀmedzo/ *nm* intermezzo.

interminable /ɛ̃tɛʀminabl/ *adj* **1** (qui dure longtemps) [*procès, guerre, spectacle, attente*] interminable, never-ending; **2** (qui est long) [*file, lettre, plage*] endless.

interminablement /ɛ̃tɛʀminabləmɑ̃/ *adv* endlessly, interminably.

interministériel, **-ielle** /ɛ̃tɛʀministeʀjɛl/ *adj* [*comité, commission, réunion*] interdepartmental.

intermittence /ɛ̃tɛʀmitɑ̃s/ *nf* **1** **par ~** [*pleuvoir*] on and off, intermittently; [*travailler*] intermittently; **2** Méd (rémission) remission; (de cœur, pouls) irregularity.

intermittent, **~e** /ɛ̃tɛʀmitɑ̃, ɑ̃t/ **I** *adj* [*pluie, efforts, fièvre*] intermittent; [*bruit*] sporadic; [*travail*] periodic; **les travailleurs ~s** contract workers.
II *nm,f* contract worker; **les ~s du spectacle** contract workers in showbusiness.

intermoléculaire /ɛ̃tɛʀmɔlekylɛʀ/ *adj* intermolecular.

intermusculaire /ɛ̃tɛʀmyskylɛʀ/ *adj* intermuscular.

internat /ɛ̃tɛʀna/ *nm* **1** Scol (école) boarding school; (dortoirs) dormitories (*pl*); (élèves) boarders; **être en ~** to be at a boarding school; **2** Univ Méd (fonction) appointment as a house officer; (concours) examination for appointment as a house officer; **pendant mon ~** during my period as a house officer.

international, **~e**, *mpl* **-aux** /ɛ̃tɛʀnasjɔnal, o/ **I** *adj* (tous contextes) international.
II *nm,f* (athlète) international.
III internationaux *nmpl* Sport (de tennis, golf, d'athlétisme) internationals.

Internationale /ɛ̃tɛʀnasjɔnal/ *nf* **1** (groupement) International; **2** (hymne) Internationale.

internationalement /ɛ̃tɛʀnasjɔnalmɑ̃/ *adv* internationally.

internationalisation /ɛ̃tɛʀnasjɔnalizasjɔ̃/ *nf* internationalization.

internationaliser /ɛ̃tɛʀnasjɔnalize/ [1] **I** *vtr* (tous contextes) to internationalize.
II s'internationaliser *vpr* to become international.

internationalisme /ɛ̃tɛʀnasjɔnalism/ *nm* internationalism.

internationaliste /ɛ̃tɛʀnasjɔnalist/ *adj, nmf* internationalist.

internationalité /ɛ̃tɛʀnasjɔnalite/ *nf* internationality.

internaute /ɛ̃tɛʀnot/ *nmf* Netsurfer.

interne /ɛ̃tɛʀn/ **I** *adj* **1** (à l'intérieur) [*crise, règlement, document, concours*] internal; [*cours, formation*] in-house (*épith*); **~ à** within; **la crise ~ au parti** the crisis within the party; **2** Méd (dans le corps) [*paroi, organe, hémorragie*] internal; Anat [*oreille*] inner; **médecine ~** internal medicine; **à usage ~** for internal use; **3** Math, Phys internal; [*angle*] interior.
II *nmf* **1** Scol boarder; **je suis ~** I'm a boarder; **2** Univ Méd house officer GB, intern US; **~ en médecine/chirurgie** house physician/surgeon.

internement /ɛ̃tɛʀnəmɑ̃/ *nm* (de prisonnier, dissident) internment; (de malade mental) committal (to a psychiatric institution); **demander l'~ de qn** to request that sb be committed; **être victime d'un ~ abusif** to be wrongfully committed (to a psychiatric institution).

interner /ɛ̃tɛʀne/ [1] *vtr* Jur to intern [*prisonnier politique*]; to commit [*malade, aliéné*]; **faire ~ qn** to have sb committed; **il est bon à ~** hum he ought to be locked away in a loony bin○.

Internet /ɛ̃tɛʀnɛt/ *nm* Internet.

interocéanique /ɛ̃tɛʀɔseanik/ *adj* interoceanic.

interosseux, **-euse** /ɛ̃tɛʀɔsø, øz/ *adj* interosseous.

interparlementaire /ɛ̃tɛʀpaʀləmɑ̃tɛʀ/ *adj* [*comité*] interparliamentary GB, joint (*épith*).

interpellateur, **-trice** /ɛ̃tɛʀpelatœʀ, tʀis/ *nm,f* gén questioner; Pol interpellator.

interpellation /ɛ̃tɛʀpelasjɔ̃/ *nf* **1** (action policière) questioning ⊄; **lors de la manifestation, il y a eu quinze ~s** at the demonstration, fifteen people were questioned by the police; **procéder à des ~s** to take people in for questioning; **2** (adresse) calling out (**de** to); **l'~ de X par Y** Y's calling out to X; **3** Pol interpellation.

interpeller /ɛ̃tɛʀpɔle/ [1] **I** *vtr* **1** (appeler) to call out to; (apostropher) to shout at; **2** (interroger sur place) to question; (emmener au poste) to take [sb] in for questioning; **3** Pol to interpellate.
II s'interpeller *vpr* [*personnes*] (amicalement) to shout to one another; (agressivement) to shout at one another.

interpénétration /ɛ̃tɛʀpenetʀasjɔ̃/ *nf* interpenetration.

interpénétrer: **s'interpénétrer** /ɛ̃tɛʀpenetʀe/ [14] *vpr* [*théories, cultures, idées*] to interpenetrate.

interphone® /ɛ̃tɛʀfɔn/ *nm* **1** (dans un bureau) intercom; **parler à qn par l'~** to speak to sb over the intercom; **2** (dans un immeuble) entry phone.

interplanétaire /ɛ̃tɛʀplanetɛʀ/ *adj* interplanetary.

Interpol /ɛ̃tɛʀpɔl/ *nm* Interpol.

interpolation /ɛ̃tɛʀpɔlasjɔ̃/ *nf* interpolation.

interpoler /ɛ̃tɛʀpɔle/ [1] *vtr* to interpolate.

interposer /ɛ̃tɛʀpoze/ [1] **I** *vtr* to interpose sout (**entre** between); **par qn/qch interposé** through the intermediary of; **il vit par personne interposée** he leads a vicarious existence.
II s'interposer *vpr* to intervene (**dans** in; **pour faire** to do; **entre** between).

interposition /ɛ̃tɛʀpozisjɔ̃/ *nf* interposition; **force d'~** peacekeeping force.

interprétable /ɛ̃tɛʀpʀetabl/ *adj* interpretable.

interprétariat /ɛ̃tɛʀpʀetaʀja/ *nm* interpreting; **école d'~** interpreting school.

interprétation /ɛ̃tɛʀpʀetasjɔ̃/ *nf* **1** (explication) interpretation (**de** of); **~ marxiste/psychanalytique** marxist/psychoanalytical interpretation; **erreur d'~** error of interpretation; **fausse** or **mauvaise ~** misinterpretation; **on peut donner plusieurs ~s à ce phénomène** this phenomenon can be interpreted in several ways; **2** Mus, Théât (exécution) performance; (façon de comprendre) interpretation; **3** (métier) interpreting.

interprète /ɛ̃tɛʀpʀɛt/ **▶510** *nmf* **1** (traducteur) interpreter; **~ consécutif/simultané** consecutive/simultaneous interpreter; **servir d'~ à qn, faire l'~ pour qn** to act as an interpreter for sb; **2** Mus (exécutant) performer; (soliste) soloist; **3** Cin, Théât performer; **les ~s d'une pièce** the cast of a play; **4** (porte-parole) spokesperson; **se faire l'~ de qn** to act as sb's spokesperson; **soyez mon ~ auprès de lui** speak to him on my behalf; **5** (de texte) exponent; (de présage, rêve) interpreter.

interpréter /ɛ̃tɛʀpʀete/ [14] **I** *vtr* **1** Cin, Mus, Théât to play [*rôle, personnage*]; to sing [*chanson*]; to perform [*sonate, morceau*]; **2** (tirer une signification de) to interpret [*texte, paroles, événement, conduite*] (**comme** as); **~ le silence de qn comme un aveu** to interpret sb's silence as an admission of guilt; **ne pas savoir comment ~ qch** not to know what to make of sth; **mal ~ qch** to misinterpret sth; **~ qch en mal/en bien** to take sth the wrong/right way.
II s'interpréter *vpr* to be interpreted; **l'événement/le texte peut s'~ de plusieurs façons** the event/the text can be interpreted in several ways.

interpréteur /ɛ̃tɛʀpʀetœʀ/ *nm* interpreter.

interprofessionnel, **-elle** /ɛ̃tɛʀpʀɔfɛsjɔnɛl/ *adj* interprofessional.

interrègne /ɛ̃tɛʀʀɛɲ/ *nm* interregnum.

interrogateur, **-trice** /ɛ̃tɛʀɔgatœʀ, tʀis/ **I** *adj* [*regard, ton*] inquiring; **elle les a regardés d'un air ~** she looked at them inquiringly.
II *nm,f* (de candidat) examiner; (de suspect) interrogator.

interrogatif, **-ive** /ɛ̃tɛʀɔgatif, iv/ *adj* Ling [*pronom, phrase, forme*] interrogative.

interrogation /ɛ̃tɛʀɔgasjɔ̃/ *nf* **1** (de témoin, soi-même) questioning (**sur** about); **2** Ling question; **~ directe/indirecte** direct/indirect question; **3** Scol test; **~ écrite/orale** written/oral test; **4** Ordinat query.
■ **~ à distance** Télécom remote access.

interrogatoire /ɛ̃tɛʀɔgatwaʀ/ *nm* Pol, Jur (de témoin, d'accusé) cross-examination; (d'espion, otage) interrogation; **subir un ~** to undergo cross-examination; **après six heures d'~ il a avoué son crime** after six hours' interrogation, he confessed to the crime.

interrogeable /ɛ̃tɛʀɔʒabl/ *adj* which can be interrogated; **répondeur ~ à distance** remote-access answering machine.

interroger /ɛ̃tɛʀɔʒe/ [13] **I** *vtr* **1** (questionner) [*juge, procureur*] to cross-examine [*témoin, accusé*]; [*police*] to question [*témoin*] (**sur** about); to interrogate [*espion*]; [*journaliste*] to put questions to [*personnage, politicien*] (**sur** on); **interrogé sur l'Europe, le président a déclaré...** when questioned about Europe, the president declared...; **50% des personnes interrogées** 50% of those questioned; **être interrogé comme témoin** to be called as a witness; **2** (consulter) to query [*ordinateur*]; **~ son répondeur** to check one's calls; **3** Scol [*professeur*] to test [*élève*] (**sur** on).
II s'interroger *vpr* **s'~ sur qn/qch** to wonder about sb /sth; **on s'interroge devant l'ampleur des réformes annoncées** the scope of the reforms which have been announced makes one wonder.

interrompre /ɛ̃tɛʀɔ̃pʀ/ [53] **I** *vtr* **1** (momentanément) [*événement, personne*] to interrupt [*émission, repas, conversation*]; to break off [*relations, dialogue*]; to disrupt [*circulation*]; to cut off [*distribution d'eau*]; [*personne*] to cease [*activité*]; **~ son repas/sa lecture pour répondre au téléphone** to stop eating/reading to answer the phone; **elle a interrompu son discours** she stopped ou broke off in the middle of her speech; **les employés ont interrompu le travail en signe de protestation** the employees stopped work in protest; **2** (définitivement) [*maladie, événement*] to put an end to [*carrière, études, vacances*]; Méd to stop [*traitement*]; to terminate [*grossesse*]; **3** (couper la parole à) to interrupt [*interlocuteur*]; **ne m'interromps pas tout le temps!** stop interrupting all the time!
II s'interrompre *vpr* **1** (soi-même) **s'~ dans son travail/sa lecture** to stop working/reading (**pour faire** to do); **2** (l'un l'autre) to interrupt each other; **3** (s'arrêter) [*pluie, conversation, fête*] to stop.

interrupteur /ɛ̃tɛʀyptœʀ/ *nm* switch.
■ **~ à bascule** toggle switch; **~ à lames** knife switch; **~ va-et-vient** two-way switch.

interruption /ɛ̃tɛʀypsjɔ̃/ *nf* **1** (arrêt) break (**de** in); **après une ~ de trois mois** after a three-month break; **après l'~ des vacances d'été** after the summer break; **une ~ momentanée de l'image** TV a momentary loss of picture; **une ~ momentanée du programme** TV a break in transmission; **sans ~** [*ouvert, habité, bombardé*] continuously; **j'ai travaillé/joué sans ~ jusqu'à minuit** I worked/played nonstop until midnight; **2** (fin) ending (**de** of); **l'~ du dialogue entre** the breaking off of the dialogue[GB] between.
■ **~ de prescription** Jur interruption of prescription; **~ volontaire de grossesse**, **IVG** Méd termination of pregnancy.

interscolaire /ɛ̃tɛʀskɔlɛʀ/ *adj* inter-school.

intersection /ɛ̃tɛʀsɛksjɔ̃/ *nf* intersection.

intersidéral, **~e**, *mpl* **-aux** /ɛ̃tɛʀsideʀal, o/ *adj* interstellar.

interstellaire /ɛ̃tɛʀstelɛʀ/ *adj* [*espace, milieu*] interstellar.

interstice /ɛ̃tɛʀstis/ *nm* (de plancher) crack; (de volets, stores) chink; **à travers les ~s des volets** through the chinks in the shutters.

intersyndical, **~e**, *mpl* **-aux** /ɛ̃tɛʀ sɛ̃dikal, o/ *adj* inter-union.

intersyndicale /ɛ̃tɛʀsɛ̃dikal/ *nf* group of several unions.

intertitre /ɛ̃tɛʀtitʀ/ *nm* Cin insert title.

intertropical, **~e**, *mpl* **-aux** /ɛ̃tɛʀ tʀɔpikal, o/ *adj* intertropical.

interurbain, **~e** /ɛ̃tɛʀyʀbɛ̃, ɛn/ **I** *adj* **1** [*liaisons, transports*] interurban; **2** Télécom [*communications*] trunk; [*appel*] trunk, long distance.
II *nm* **l'~** long distance telephone service.

intervalle /ɛ̃tɛʀval/ *nm* **1** (dans l'espace) space; **planter des arbres à ~s réguliers** to plant trees at regular intervals; **2** (dans le temps) interval; **dans l'~** meanwhile, in the meantime; **3** Mus interval.

intervenant, **~e** /ɛ̃tɛʀvənɑ̃, ɑ̃t/ **I** *nm,f* (invité) gén speaker; Radio, TV panel member; (participant) contributor.
II *nm* **1** Fin (en Bourse) dealer; **2** Jur intervenor; **3** Comm acceptor.
■ **~ bénévole** Jur amicus curiae, friend of the court.

intervenir /ɛ̃tɛʀvəniʀ/ [36] *vi* (+ *v être*) **1** (se produire) [*changements*] to take place; [*accord*] to be reached; [*augmentation*] to occur; **2** (prendre part) [*orateur*] to speak (**dans** in); **~ sur le marché** Fin to intervene in the market; **3** (agir en urgence) [*armée, police, pompiers*] to intervene; **le chirurgien a décidé d'~** the surgeon decided to operate; **4** (intercéder) to intercede; **~ auprès de qn pour qn** to intercede with sb on sb's behalf; **~ auprès de qn pour qch** to intercede with sb to try to obtain sth; **~ comme médiateur** to play the role of mediator.

intervention /ɛ̃tɛʀvɑ̃sjɔ̃/ *nf* **1** (engagement) intervention (**en faveur de** on behalf of; **auprès de** with); **~ de l'armée/la police** military/police intervention; **2** (participation) (d'orateur) speech; (de conférencier) lecture; **l'~ du ministre à la télévision** the speech made by the minister on television; **~ sur le marché** intervention in the market; **3** Méd (opération) operation; **~ chirurgicale** (surgical) operation (**sur qn** on sb); **elle vient de subir une petite ~** she has just had a minor operation.
■ **~ en appel** Jur appeal proceedings (*pl*).

interventionnisme /ɛ̃tɛʀvɑ̃sjɔnism/ *nm* interventionism.

interventionniste /ɛ̃tɛʀvɑ̃sjɔnist/ **I** *adj* interventionist; **non ~** noninterventionist.
II *nmf* interventionist.

interversion /ɛ̃tɛʀvɛʀsjɔ̃/ *nf* (de mots, d'objets) inversion; (de rôles) reversal.

intervertir /ɛ̃tɛʀvɛʀtiʀ/ [3] *vtr* to invert [*objets*]; to reverse [*rôles*].

interview /ɛ̃tɛʀvju/ *nf* interview; **dans une ~ exclusive à un magazine anglais** in an exclusive interview in an English magazine.

interviewé, **~e** /ɛ̃tɛʀvjuve/ *nm,f* interviewee.

interviewer /ɛ̃tɛʀvjuve/ [1] *vtr* to interview.

intervieweur, **-euse** /ɛ̃tɛʀvjuvœʀ, øz/ *nm, f* interviewer.

intervocalique /ɛ̃tɛʀvɔkalik/ *adj* intervocalic.

intestat /ɛ̃tɛsta/ *adj, nmf* intestate.

intestin /ɛ̃tɛstɛ̃/ *nm* bowel, intestine; **~ grêle** small intestine; **gros ~** large intestine.

intestinal, **~e**, *mpl* **-aux** /ɛ̃tɛstinal, o/ *adj* [*paroi, perforation*] intestinal; **avoir des problèmes intestinaux** to have bowel problems.

intimation /ɛ̃timasjɔ̃/ *nf* summons (*sg*).

intime /ɛ̃tim/ **I** *adj* **1** (personnel) [*vie, carnet, journal*] private; [*ami, rapports, secrets*] intimate; [*hygiène, toilette*] personal; **avoir des relations ~s avec qn** to be on intimate terms with sb; **2** (entre proches) [*fête, dîner*] intimate; [*conversation*] private; [*cérémonie, mariage*] quiet; **3** (douillet) [*pièce*] cosy GB ou cozy US, intimate; **4** (profond) [*structure, sens*] innermost; [*connaissance*] intimate; [*conviction*] deep; **j'ai la conviction ~** or **l'~ conviction que...** I firmly believe that..., it is my firm conviction that...
II *nmf* close friend, intimate; **un ~ de qn** an intimate of sb; **c'est Jojo pour les ~s** my friends call me Jojo.

intimé, **~e** /ɛ̃time/ *nm,f* Jur respondent.

intimement /ɛ̃timmɑ̃/ *adv* intimately; **les deux problèmes sont ~ liés** the two problems are intimately connected; **je suis ~ convaincu que...** I'm absolutely convinced that...

intimer /ɛ̃time/ [1] *vtr* **~ à qn l'ordre de faire** to order sb to do.

intimidable /ɛ̃timidabl/ *adj* **être ~** to be easily intimidated.

intimidant, **~e** /ɛ̃timidɑ̃, ɑ̃t/ *adj* [*situation, regard, professeur*] intimidating.

intimidateur, **-trice** /ɛ̃timidatœʀ, tʀis/ *adj* intimidating.

intimidation /ɛ̃timidasjɔ̃/ *nf* intimidation; **céder à des mesures d'~** to allow oneself to be intimidated; **d'~** [*manœuvre, geste, parole*] intimidatory.

intimider /ɛ̃timide/ [1] *vtr* to intimidate; **se laisser ~ par qn/qch** to be intimidated by sb/sth.

intimisme /ɛ̃timism/ *nm* Art intimism.

intimiste /ɛ̃timist/ *adj, nmf* intimist.

intimité /ɛ̃timite/ *nf* **1** (lien) intimacy; **il y avait entre eux une parfaite ~** they were on very intimate terms; **2** (privé) privacy; **dans l'~ de leur chambre** in the privacy of their bedroom; **dans la plus stricte ~** in the strictest privacy; **ils ont fêté Noël dans l'~** they had a quiet Christmas; **dans l'~ il est beaucoup plus chaleureux** in private he is much warmer; **3** (vie privée) private life; **l'~ de l'artiste** the artist's private life; **4** (de maison, pièce, cadre) cosiness; **5** (fond) depths (*pl*); **dans l'~ de votre conscience** in the depths of your conscience.

intitulé /ɛ̃tityle/ *nm* title, heading.
■ **~ de compte** Fin account holder's name.

intituler /ɛ̃tityle/ [1] **I** *vtr* to call; **j'ai intitulé mon livre...** I called my book...; **livre intitulé...** book called ou entitled...
II s'intituler *vpr* [*livre, émission*] to be called, entitled.

intolérable /ɛ̃tɔleʀabl/ *adj* [*souffrance, vacarme, chaleur*] intolerable, unbearable; [*attitude*] intolerable; [*images*] deeply shocking; **de façon ~** intolerably; **pousser qch jusqu'à l'~** to push sth beyond acceptable limits; **il est ~ que** it is intolerable that.

intolérance /ɛ̃tɔleʀɑ̃s/ *nf* **1** (sectarisme) intolerance; **2** Méd allergy (**à** to); **~ solaire** allergy to the sun ou to sunshine.

intolérant, **~e** /ɛ̃tɔleʀɑ̃, ɑ̃t/ *adj* intolerant.

intonation /ɛ̃tɔnasjɔ̃/ *nf* Phon, Mus intonation; **faire une faute d'~** to get the intonation wrong; **l'~ moqueuse de ta voix** your mocking tone.

intouchable /ɛ̃tuʃabl/ **I** *adj* [*personnage*] irreproachable.
II *nmf* Relig untouchable.

intox(e)○ /ɛ̃tɔks/ *nf* Pol disinformation; **faire de l'~** to spread disinformation.

intoxication /ɛ̃tɔksikasjɔ̃/ *nf* **1** Méd poisoning; **~ par le plomb** lead poisoning; **~ par les champignons** poisoning caused by eating fungi; **17 ~s mortelles** 17 deaths due to poisoning; **2** (propagande) disinformation.
■ **~ alimentaire** Méd food poisoning.

intoxiquer /ɛ̃tɔksike/ [1] **I** *vtr* **1** (empoisonner) to poison; **2** fig (abrutir) to brainwash; **être intoxiqué par la télévision** to be turned into a zombie by television.
II s'intoxiquer *vpr* to poison oneself (**en faisant** by doing).

intracellulaire /ɛ̃tʀaselylɛʀ/ *adj* intracellular.

intra-conjugal, **~e**, *mpl* **-aux** /ɛ̃tʀakɔ̃ʒygal, o/ *adj* **insémination intra-conjugale** artificial insemination (*using the husband's sperm*).

intradermique /ɛ̃tʀadɛʀmik/ *adj* [*injection*] intradermal.

intrados /ɛ̃tʀado(s)/ *nm* intrados.

intraduisible /ɛ̃tʀadɥizibl/ *adj* **1** (qu'on ne peut traduire) [*expression, auteur*] untranslatable; **2** (inexprimable) [*émotion*] inexpressible.

intraitable /ɛ̃tʀɛtabl/ *adj* [*concurrent, patron*] inflexible; **je serai ~ là-dessus** I will not budge on this.

intra-muros /ɛ̃tʀamyʀos/ **I** *loc adj* **de Paris ~ à la grande banlieue** from the very heart of Paris to the outermost suburbs.
II *loc adv* [*construire, habiter*] in ou within the town itself.

intramusculaire /ɛ̃tʀamyskylɛʀ/ *adj* [*injection*] intramuscular.

intransigeance /ɛ̃tʀɑ̃ziʒɑ̃s/ *nf* intransigence; **être d'une ~ absolue** to be absolutely uncompromising ou intransigent.

intransigeant, **~e** /ɛ̃tʀɑ̃ziʒɑ̃, ɑ̃t/ *adj* [*attitude, discours, principe*] uncompromising; [*personne*] intransigent (**sur** on); [*patriote, partisan*] staunch.

intransitif, **-ive** /ɛ̃tʀɑ̃zitif, iv/ **I** *adj* intransitive.
II *nm* intransitive verb.

intransitivement /ɛ̃tʀɑ̃zitivmɑ̃/ *adv* intransitively.

intransitivité /ɛ̃tʀɑ̃zitivite/ *nf* intransitivity.

intransmissibilité /ɛ̃tʀɑ̃smisibilite/ *nf* Biol untransferability.

intransmissible /ɛ̃tʀɑ̃smisibl/ *adj* [*maladie*] non-infectious; [*savoir*] incommunicable.

intransportable /ɛ̃tʀɑ̃spɔʀtabl/ *adj* [*marchandises*] untransportable; [*blessé*] who should not be moved (*épith, après n*).

intrant /ɛ̃tʀɑ̃/ *nm* Écon input.

intra-utérin, **~e**, *mpl* **~s** /ɛ̃tʀayteʀɛ̃, in/ *adj* intra-uterine.

intraveineux, **-euse** /ɛ̃tʀavenø, øz/ **I** *adj* intravenous.
II intraveineuse *nf* intravenous injection.

intrépide /ɛ̃tʀepid/ *adj* [*aventurier, regard, pas*] intrepid, bold; [*menteur*] barefaced (*épith*).

intrépidité /ɛ̃tʀepidite/ *nf* boldness, intrepidity; **avec ~** boldly, fearlessly.

intrigant, **~e** /ɛ̃tʀigɑ̃, ɑ̃t/ **I** *adj* **1** (retors) scheming (*épith*); **2** (curieux) intriguing.
II *nm,f* schemer.

intrigue /ɛ̃tʀig/ *nf* **1** (machination) intrigue; **2** Littérat plot; **une ~ policière/amoureuse** a detective/love story.

intriguer /ɛ̃tʀige/ [1] *vtr* **1** (susciter la curiosité) to intrigue; **elle m'intrigue** I find her intriguing; **2** (manœuvrer) to intrigue, scheme.

intrinsèque /ɛ̃tʀɛ̃sɛk/ *adj* [*valeur, contenu*] intrinsic.

intrinsèquement /ɛ̃tʀɛ̃sɛkmɑ̃/ *adv* intrinsically; **un texte/projet jugé ~ mauvais** a text/project seen as intrinsically flawed.

introducteur, **-trice** /ɛ̃tʀɔdyktœʀ, tʀis/ *nm,f* **1** (personne qui présente) **servir d'~ à qn** to introduce sb (**auprès de** to); **2** (personne qui introduit) **l'~ du tabac en France** the man who introduced tobacco to France.

introduction /ɛ̃tʀɔdyksjɔ̃/ *nf* **1** (d'objet, sonde, clé) insertion (**dans** into); **2** (de visiteur) ushering (**dans** into); **~ des visi-**

teurs ushering in of the guests; **3** (présentation) **il s'est chargé de mon ~ auprès du grand patron** he got me introduced to the big boss; **une lettre d'~ auprès de qn** a letter of introduction to sb; **4** (de mode, sport, produit, mesure, technique) introduction; **5** (importation) **~ de substances illicites** smuggling of illegal substances; **6** Littérat, Mus (préliminaire) introduction (**à**, **de** to); **l'~ d'un livre** the introduction to a book; **7** (initiation) introduction; **~ à la physique nucléaire** introduction to nuclear physics.

■ **~ en Bourse** Fin listing; **~ d'instance** Jur institution of legal proceedings.

introduire /ɛ̃tʀɔdɥiʀ/ [69] **I** *vtr* **1** (insérer) to insert [*objet*] (**dans** into); **~ une clé dans une serrure** to insert a key into a lock; **2** (faire entrer) (en grande pompe) to usher [sb] in [*invité, visiteur*]; (clandestinement) to smuggle [*personne*] (**dans** into); **3** (présenter) to introduce [*personne*]; **il m'a promis qu'il m'introduirait auprès du ministre** he promised me that he would introduce me to the minister; **4** (faire adopter) to introduce [*mesures, coutume, produit, idée*] (**dans** into); **~ une nouvelle législation** to introduce new legislation; **5** (importer illicitement) to smuggle [*produits, drogue*] (**dans** into); **6** Fin **~ (en Bourse)** to float [*titre*].

II s'introduire *vpr* **1** (pénétrer) [*personne, eau, fumée*] to get (**dans** into); **les cambrioleurs se sont introduits dans la maison par la lucarne** the burglars got into the house through the skylight; **s'~ dans une maison/pièce par effraction** to break into a house/room; **2** (se faire admettre) [*personne*] to gain admittance (**dans** to); **3** (être adopté) [*mode, mot, idée*] to be introduced (**dans** into).

introduit, **~e** /ɛ̃tʀɔdɥi, it/ **I** *pp* ▶**introduire**.

II *pp adj* **être ~ dans les milieux bancaires** to know a lot of people in banking circles; **être bien ~ auprès de qn** to have access to sb.

intromission /ɛ̃tʀɔmisjɔ̃/ *nf* intromission (**dans** into).

intronisation /ɛ̃tʀɔnizasjɔ̃/ *nf* **1** (de souverain, d'évêque) enthronement; **2** (de mode, doctrine) fml establishment.

introniser /ɛ̃tʀɔnize/ [1] *vtr* **1** to enthrone [*souverain, évêque*]; **2** fig, hum to establish [*personne*] (**comme** as); **3** fig, fml to establish [*mode, doctrine*].

introspectif, **-ive** /ɛ̃tʀɔspɛktif, iv/ *adj* introspective.

introspection /ɛ̃tʀɔspɛksjɔ̃/ *nf* introspection.

introuvable /ɛ̃tʀuvabl/ *adj* **1** (qu'on ne peut trouver) [*personne, endroit, adresse*] untraceable; [*objet*] which cannot be found (*épith, après n*); [*équilibre, compromis*] unattainable; **le voleur reste ~** the thief has still not been found; **mon portefeuille est ~** my wallet has disappeared without a trace, I can't find my wallet anywhere; **2** (rare) [*collaborateur, spécialiste*] that cannot be found (*épith, après n*); [*livre, antiquité*] unobtainable.

introversion /ɛ̃tʀɔvɛʀsjɔ̃/ *nf* introversion.

introverti, **~e** /ɛ̃tʀɔvɛʀti/ **I** *adj* introverted.

II *nm,f* introvert.

intrus, **~e** /ɛ̃tʀy, yz/ *nm,f* intruder; **'cherchez l'~'** Jeux 'spot the odd one out' GB, 'pick the one that doesn't fit' US.

intrusion /ɛ̃tʀyzjɔ̃/ *nf* **1** (irruption) intrusion (**dans** into); **2** (ingérence) (de personne, pays) interference (**dans** in); (d'objet, idée) intrusion; **3** Géol intrusion; **d'~** [*roches, nappes*] intrusive.

intubation /ɛ̃tybasjɔ̃/ *nf* intubation.

intuber /ɛ̃tybe/ [1] *vtr* to intubate.

intuitif, **~ive** /ɛ̃tɥitif, iv/ *adj* [*personne, esprit*] intuitive; **avoir une connaissance intuitive de qch** to have an intuitive understanding of sth.

intuition /ɛ̃tɥisjɔ̃/ *nf* intuition; **avoir l'~ de/que** to have an intuition about/that; **avoir de l'~** to have intuition.

intuitivement /ɛ̃tɥitivmɑ̃/ *adv* intuitively.

intumescence /ɛ̃tymɛsɑ̃s/ *nf* intumescence.

intumescent, **~e** /ɛ̃tymɛsɑ̃, ɑ̃t/ *adj* intumescent.

inuit, **~e** /inɥit/ *adj* Inuit.

Inuit, **~e** /inɥit/ *nm,f* Inuit.

inusable /inyzabl/ *adj* [*pneus, chaussures*] hardwearing.

inusité, **~e** /inyzite/ *adj* **1** Ling (inexistant) not used (*jamais épith*); (rare) uncommon, not in common use (*jamais épith*); **les formes du passé sont ~es** the past tense forms are not used; **2** (inhabituel) [*bruit, chaleur, démarche*] unusual.

inutile /inytil/ *adj* **1** [*objet, développement*] useless; [*fatigue, travail, démarche, discussion*] pointless; [*crainte, prescriptions*] needless; **(il est) ~ de faire** there's no point in doing; **il est ~ que vous partiez** there's no point in your leaving; **~ de dire que** needless to say; **~ de me demander si** it's no use asking me whether; **~ de rincer** no need to rinse; **sans risques/frais ~s** without unnecessary risks/expenditure; **mes efforts sont restés ~s** my efforts were in vain; **2** [*personne, employé*] useless; **se sentir ~** to feel useless.

inutilement /inytilmɑ̃/ *adv* [*se fatiguer, dramatiser, se déranger*] unnecessarily; [*s'inquiéter, souffrir*] needlessly; [*attendre, chercher, discuter, mourir*] in vain.

inutilisable /inytilizabl/ *adj* unusable.

inutilisé, **~e** /inytilize/ *adj* unused.

inutilité /inytilite/ *nf* (d'objet, effort, de personne) uselessness; (de démarche, dépense) pointlessness.

invaincu, **~e** /ɛ̃vɛ̃ky/ *adj* [*guerrier, équipe, pays*] undefeated; [*sportif, joueur*] unbeaten; [*maladie*] unconquered.

invalidant, **~e** /ɛ̃validɑ̃, ɑ̃t/ *adj* disabling.

invalidation /ɛ̃validasjɔ̃/ *nf* invalidation; **l'~ d'un député** the invalidation of the election of a deputy.

invalide /ɛ̃valid/ **I** *adj* **1** Méd disabled; **un accident l'a rendu ~ à vie** an accident left him disabled for life; ▶**grand**; **2** Jur [*contrat, acte*] invalid.

II *nmf* disabled person; **les ~s** the disabled.

III *nm* Mil disabled ex-serviceman.

■ **~ civil** Prot Soc registered disabled civilian; **~ de guerre** Prot Soc registered disabled ex-serviceman; **~ du travail** Prot Soc victim of an industrial injury.

invalider /ɛ̃valide/ [1] *vtr* Jur to invalidate [*contrat, testament, élections*].

invalidité /ɛ̃validite/ *nf* **1** Méd disability; **~ permanente** permanent disability; **2** Jur invalidity.

invariabilité /ɛ̃vaʀjabilite/ *nf* invariability.

invariable /ɛ̃vaʀjabl/ *adj* invariable.

invariablement /ɛ̃vaʀjabləmɑ̃/ *adv* invariably.

invariant, **~e** /ɛ̃vaʀjɑ̃, ɑ̃t/ **I** *adj* invariant.

II *nm* invariant.

invasion /ɛ̃vazjɔ̃/ *nf* Mil, fig invasion; **l'~ de capitaux étrangers sur le marché** the invasion of the market by foreign capital.

invective /ɛ̃vɛktiv/ *nf* invective ¢, abuse ¢; **se répandre en ~s** to pour out abuse (**contre** against).

invectiver /ɛ̃vɛktive/ [1] **I** *vtr* to hurl abuse at.

II invectiver contre *vtr ind* fml to rail against sout [*personne, injustice*].

III s'invectiver *vpr* to hurl abuse at each other.

invendable /ɛ̃vɑ̃dabl/ *adj* unsalable.

invendu, **~e** /ɛ̃vɑ̃dy/ **I** *adj* [*articles, marchandises, livres*] unsold.

II *nm* gén unsold item; (livre, journal) unsold copy.

inventaire /ɛ̃vɑ̃tɛʀ/ *nm* **1** Comm (opération) stocktaking GB, inventory US; (liste) stocklist GB, inventory US; **faire l'~** to do the stocktaking GB, to take inventory US; **2** (de valise, garde-robe) list of contents; (de patrimoine, collection) inventory; **faire l'~ de sa valise** (dresser une liste) to make a list of the contents of one's suitcase; (vérifier le contenu) to go through one's suitcase; **faire l'~ d'une collection/d'une succession** to draw up an inventory of a collection/of an inheritance.

inventer /ɛ̃vɑ̃te/ [1] **I** *vtr* to invent [*machine, jeu, technique, remède*]; to devise [*moyen, subterfuge*]; to invent, make up [*excuse, raison*]; **histoire inventée** made-up story; **tu inventes** you're making it up; **je n'invente rien** every word is true; **je ne sais plus quoi ~ pour te faire plaisir**○ I can't think what else to do to make you happy.

II s'inventer *vpr* **1** (pour soi) **il s'est inventé une enfance malheureuse** he's invented an unhappy childhood for himself; **elle s'invente toujours de bonnes raisons/des excuses** she can always find a good reason/an excuse; **2 ça ne s'invente pas** that has to be true.

IDIOMES **il n'a pas inventé la poudre**○ or **l'eau tiède**○ or **le fil à couper le beurre**○ he is not very bright.

inventeur, **-trice** /ɛ̃vɑ̃tœʀ, tʀis/ ▶**510** *nm,f* **1** gén inventor; **2** Jur (découvreur d'un bien) finder.

inventif, **-ive** /ɛ̃vɑ̃tif, iv/ *adj* **1** (novateur) inventive; **2** (débrouillard) resourceful.

invention /ɛ̃vɑ̃sjɔ̃/ *nf* **1** (création) invention; **l'~ de la photographie** the invention of photography; **une ~ langagière/théâtrale** a linguistic/theatrical invention; **elle nous a servi un plat de son ~** she served us a dish she'd invented herself; **2** (mensonge) fabrication; **c'est de l'~ pure** it's a complete fabrication; **ce ne sont que des ~s** it's not true at all; **c'est encore une histoire de ton ~** it's just another one of your stories; **3** (imagination) ¢ inventiveness; **faire preuve d'~** to be inventive.

inventivité /ɛ̃vɑ̃tivite/ *nf* inventiveness.

inventorier /ɛ̃vɑ̃tɔʀje/ [2] *vtr* **1** Comm to make out a stocklist GB ou an inventory US of [*marchandises*]; **2** Jur to draw up an inventory of [*biens, succession*]; **3** (passer en revue) to list the contents of [*garde-robe*]; to catalogue[GB] [*bibliothèque, musée*].

invérifiable /ɛ̃veʀifjabl/ *adj* unverifiable.

inverse /ɛ̃vɛʀs/ **I** *adj* **1** [*position, ordre, situation*] inverse; [*direction, effet, démarche*] opposite; **en raison ~ de** in inverse proportion to; **on s'est retrouvé dans la situation ~** the exact opposite happened to us; **en sens ~** [*aller, repartir*] in the opposite direction; [*venir, arriver*] from the opposite direction; **attention aux voitures qui arrivent en sens ~** beware of oncoming traffic; **une voiture a heurté un camion roulant en sens ~** a car was in collision with a truck coming the opposite way; **2** Math [*élément, fonction*] inverse; **matrice ~** inverse of a matrix.

II *nm* **1** gén **l'~** the opposite, the reverse; **aller à l'~ de** to be the opposite ou reverse of; **à l'~** conversely; **à l'~ de ce qui s'est passé l'an dernier** unlike last year; **à l'~ de ce qu'il croyait** contrary to what he thought; **c'est comme ça qu'il faut faire et non** or **pas l'~** that's how it should be done and not the other way around; **2** Math inverse.

inversement /ɛ̃vɛʀsəmɑ̃/ *adv* **1** gén conversely; **et/ou ~** and/or vice-versa; **2** Math inversely; **~ proportionnel** in inverse proportion (**à** to).

inverser /ɛ̃vɛʀse/ [1] **I** *vtr* **1** (intervertir) to invert [*position, termes, proposition*]; to reverse [*tendance, sens, rôles, ordre*]; **une pyramide inversée** an inverted pyramid; **position inversée** inverted position; **quelques années plus tard, la situation était inversée** several years later, it was the other way around; **image inversée** mirror image; **2** Tech to reverse [*courant électrique, mouvement*].

II s'inverser *vpr* [*tendance, rôles, rapports*] to be reversed.

inverseur /ɛ̃vɛʀsœʀ/ *nm* reverser.

inversion /ɛ̃vɛʀsjɔ̃/ *nf* **1** (d'éléments, de rôles, valeurs) inversion; (de tendance, processus) reversal; **2** Ling, Anat, Psych, Chimie inversion; **3** Électrotech reversal.

■ **~ de commande** Aviat reversal of control; **~ de relief** Géol inverted relief; **~ de température** Météo temperature inversion.

invertase /ɛ̃vɛʀtɑz/ *nf* invertase.

invertébré, ~e /ɛ̃vɛʀtebʀe/ **I** *adj* invertebrate.

II *nm* invertebrate; **les ~s** invertebrates.

inverti, ~e /ɛ̃vɛʀti/ **I** *adj* Chimie [*sucre*] invert.

II *nm,f* invert†, homosexual.

invertir /ɛ̃vɛʀtiʀ/ [3] *vtr* **1** (inverser) to invert [*termes, éléments*]; to reverse [*sens, ordre*]; **2** Électrotech to reverse [*courant*]; **3** Chimie to invert.

investigateur, -trice /ɛ̃vɛstigatœʀ, tʀis/ **I** *adj* [*esprit*] inquiring.

II *nm,f* investigator.

investigation /ɛ̃vɛstigasjɔ̃/ *nf* investigation; **d'~** [*journalisme, méthode*] investigative.

investir /ɛ̃vɛstiʀ/ [3] **I** *vtr* **1** (placer) to invest [*capitaux*] (**dans** in); **~ en Bourse** to invest on the Stock Exchange; **2** (charger) to invest [*personne*] (**de** with); to invest [*ambassadeur, ministre*]; to induct [*juge, magistrat*]; **être investi d'un droit** to be invested with a right; **~ qn de sa confiance** to put one's trust in sb; **3** (se répandre dans) [*policiers*] to go into [*locaux, place*]; [*touristes, manifestants*] to take over [*lieu*]; **4** (dépenser) to invest [*énergie*] (**dans** in); **5** Psych to invest emotionally in [*personne, enfant*]; **6** (encercler) [*armée*] to besiege [*lieu*].

II s'investir *vpr* (énergiquement) to put oneself (**dans** into); (sentimentalement) to invest a lot of emotion (**dans** into).

investissement /ɛ̃vɛstismɑ̃/ *nm* **1** Fin (opération) investment (**dans** in); (somme) investment; **un ~ de 40 millions de francs** an investment of 40 million francs, a 40 million franc investment; **d'~** [*plan, capacité, coût*] investment; [*problème, fonds*] investment; **2** (dépense de travail, temps) investment; **c'est un énorme ~ de temps** it's an enormous investment in terms of time; **3** Psych investment; **4** Mil (encerclement) investing (**de** of).

■ **~ direct** Entr direct investment; **~ de portefeuille** Fin portfolio investment.

investisseur /ɛ̃vɛstisœʀ/ *nm* investor.

investiture /ɛ̃vɛstityʀ/ *nf* (de président, gouvernement) investiture; (de candidat) nomination; **d'~** [*cérémonie, discours*] investiture (*épith*).

invétéré, ~e /ɛ̃veteʀe/ *adj* **1** (impénitent) [*buveur, voleur, tricheur*] inveterate; [*menteur*] compulsive; **2** (enraciné) [*haine, habitude, mal*] deep-rooted, deepseated.

invincibilité /ɛ̃vɛ̃sibilite/ *nf* invincibility; **avoir un sentiment d'~** to feel invincible.

invincible /ɛ̃vɛ̃sibl/ *adj* **1** (qui ne peut être vaincu) [*armée, pays, force, volonté*] invincible; [*joueur, sportif*] invincible, unbeatable; **2** (irréfutable) [*vérité, argumentation*] irrefutable.

inviolabilité /ɛ̃vjɔlabilite/ *nf* **1** (de règle, frontière, territoire) inviolability; **~ du domicile** Jur inviolability of private property; **~ du corps humain** *principle safeguarding the rights of a dead person in relation to organ donation*; **2** (protection de diplomate) inviolability; (privilège de parlementaire) privilege of freedom from arrest; **3** (de forteresse, porte, coffre) impregnability.

inviolable /ɛ̃vjɔlabl/ *adj* **1** (sacré) [*loi, secret, frontière, refuge*] inviolable; **2** (impénétrable) [*coffre, porte*] impregnable.

inviolé, ~e /ɛ̃vjɔle/ *adj* fml inviolate.

invisibilité /ɛ̃vizibilite/ *nf* invisibility.

invisible /ɛ̃vizibl/ **I** *adj* **1** (non perceptible) [*particule, pellicule, réparation, couture*] invisible; **~ à l'œil nu** invisible to the naked eye; **2** (hors de vue) **rester ~** [*personne*] not to put in an appearance; **l'orchestre restait ~** the orchestra was hidden from view; **la route était ~ depuis la maison** the road could not be seen from the house; **l'acteur est resté ~ pendant deux mois** the actor wasn't seen for two months; **3** (non disponible) [*personne*] unavailable; **4** (caché, secret) [*vestiges*] hidden; [*danger, menace*] unseen; [*exportations*] invisible.

II *nm* **l'~** the invisible.

invitation /ɛ̃vitasjɔ̃/ *nf* (prière, exhortation) invitation (**à** to); (document) invitation; **à** or **sur l'~ de qn** at sb's invitation; **recevoir/lancer/décliner une ~** to receive/send/decline an invitation; **accepter l'~ de qn/du gouvernement** to accept sb's/the government's invitation; **entrer sans ~** to enter without an invitation; **carte** or **carton d'~** invitation card; **lettre d'~** letter of invitation; **c'est une ~ à la révolte** it's inviting a revolt.

invite /ɛ̃vit/ *nf* fml invitation (**à** to); **à l'~ de** at the behest of sout.

invité, ~e /ɛ̃vite/ *nm,f* guest.

■ **~ d'honneur** guest of honour[GB]; **~ de marque** distinguished guest.

inviter /ɛ̃vite/ [1] **I** *vtr* **1** (prier de venir) to invite (**à** to); **il m'a invité chez lui pour le week-end/à son mariage** he invited me to his house for the weekend/to his wedding; **2** (payer) **~ qn à déjeuner/à prendre un verre** to take sb out for lunch/for a drink; **3** (engager) to invite [*personne, pays, organisme*] (**à** to; **à faire** to do); (demander) to ask [*personne, gouvernement, parti*] (**à** to; **à faire** to do); **il ne m'a même pas invité à m'asseoir** he didn't even invite ou ask me to sit down; **4** (inciter) [*temps, événements*] to induce [*personne*] (**à** to); [*attitude, explication*] to lead [*personne*] (**à** to) ; **le temps n'invite guère à la promenade** it's not particularly nice weather for a walk; **~ à la réflexion** to be thought-provoking.

II s'inviter *vpr* [*personne*] to invite oneself.

in vitro /invitʀo/ *loc adj, loc adv* in vitro.

invivable /ɛ̃vivabl/ *adj* [*situation, relations, maison*] unbearable; [*personne, enfant*] impossible, unbearable.

in vivo /invivo/ *loc adj, loc adv* in vivo.

invocation /ɛ̃vɔkasjɔ̃/ *nf* invocation (**de** of).

invocatoire /ɛ̃vɔkatwaʀ/ *adj* invocatory.

involontaire /ɛ̃vɔlɔ̃tɛʀ/ *adj* **1** (incontrôlé) [*réaction, geste*] involuntary; [*cri, mensonge, faute*] unintentional; **2** (par hasard) [*intermédiaire, héros, témoin*] unwitting.

involontairement /ɛ̃vɔlɔ̃tɛʀmɑ̃/ *adv* (sans le vouloir) [*soupirer, crier, sourire*] involuntarily; (sans préméditation) [*blesser, casser*] unintentionally; **si je vous ai blessé, c'est bien ~** I didn't mean to hurt you.

invoquer /ɛ̃vɔke/ [1] *vtr* **1** (alléguer) to invoke [*clause, loi, circonstances, prétexte*]; **le motif invoqué** the motive adduced; **~ qn comme exemple** to cite sb as an example; **2** Relig to invoke [*Dieu, saints*]; **3** (solliciter) fml to invoke [*aide, autorité*] (**contre** against).

invraisemblable /ɛ̃vʀɛsɑ̃blabl/ *adj* **1** (non crédible) [*événement, histoire*] unlikely; [*hypothèse, aventure*] improbable; **2**° (inouï) [*vêtement, attitude, nombre*] fantastic, incredible.

invraisemblance /ɛ̃vʀɛsɑ̃blɑ̃s/ *nf* **1** (caractère) unlikelihood; **2** (détail) improbability.

invulnérabilité /ɛ̃vylneʀabilite/ *nf* invulnerability.

invulnérable /ɛ̃vylneʀabl/ *adj* invulnerable.

iode /jɔd/ *nm* iodine.

ioder /jɔde/ [1] *vtr* to iodize; **eau iodée** iodized water.

iodoforme /jɔdɔfɔʀm/ *nm* iodoform.

ion /jɔ̃/ *nm* ion.

Ionie /jɔni/ ▶ 692 *nprf* Ionia.

ionien, -ienne /jɔnjɛ̃, ɛn/ **I** *adj* **1** [*personne, philosophie*] Ionian; **2** [*dialecte*] Ionic.

II *nm* Ling Ionic.

Ionien, -ienne /jɔnjɛ̃, ɛn/ **I** ▶ 416, 555 *adj* **îles Ioniennes** Ionian Islands; **mer Ionienne** Ionian Sea.

II *nm,f* Ionian.

ionique /jɔnik/ **I** *adj* **1** Phys [*charge, liaison, produit*] ionic; **2** Antiq, Géog [*art, philosophie, langue*] Ionic.

II *nm* Archit (ordre) Ionic order.

ionisation /jɔnizasjɔ̃/ *nf* ionization.

ioniser /jɔnize/ [1] *vtr* to ionize; **rayonnements ionisants** ionizing radiation ¢.

ionosphère /jɔnɔsfɛʀ/ *nf* ionosphere.

iota /jɔta/ *nm inv* iota.

IDIOMES **ne pas changer/bouger d'un ~** not to change/move one iota.

Iowa /ajowa/ ▶ 692, 357 *nprm* Iowa.

ipéca /ipeka/ *nm* ipecac.

ipso facto /ipsofakto/ *loc adv* ipso facto.

IRA /iʀa/ *nf* (*abbr* = **Irish Republican Army**) IRA.

Irak /iʀak/ ▶ 321 *nprm* Iraq.

irakien, -ienne /iʀakjɛ̃, ɛn/ ▶ 537 *adj* Iraqi.

Irakien, -ienne /iʀakjɛ̃, ɛn/ ▶ 537 *nm,f* Iraqi.

Iran /iʀɑ̃/ ▶ 321 *nprm* Iran.

iranien, -ienne /iʀanjɛ̃, ɛn/ ▶ 462, 537 **I** *adj* Iranian.

II *nm* Ling Iranian.

Iranien, -ienne /iʀanjɛ̃, ɛn/ ▶ 537 *nm,f* Iranian.

irascibilité /iʀasibilite/ *nf* fml irascibility.

irascible /iʀasibl/ *adj* [*personne*] irascible sout, quick-tempered; **avoir un caractère ~** to be quick-tempered.

IRCAM /iʀkam/ *nm* (*abbr* = **Institut de recherche et de coordination acoustique-musique**) *institute of experimental music.*

ire /iʀ/ *nf* liter ire littér, anger.

iridié, ~e /iʀidje/ *adj* **platine ~** platiniridium.

iridium /iʀidjɔm/ *nm* iridium.

iris /iʀis/ *nm* **1** Bot (fleur) iris; **2** Anat (de l'œil) iris; **3** Phot (diaphragme) iris diaphragm.

■ **~ d'Espagne** Spanish iris; **~ fétide** stinking iris, gladdon; **~ de Florence** Florentine iris; **~ des marais** yellow flag.

irisation /iʀizasjɔ̃/ *nf* iridescence ¢.

irisé, ~e /iʀize/ **I** *pp* ▶ **iriser**.

II *pp adj* [*pierre, verre, plumage*] iridescent.

iriser /iʀize/ [1] **I** *vtr* [*lumière, soleil*] to make [sth] iridescent [*cristal, mer*].

II s'iriser *vpr* [*cristal, mer, plumage*] to become iridescent.

irlandais, ~e /iʀlɑ̃dɛ, ɛz/ ▶ 462, 537 **I** *adj* Irish.

II *nm* Ling Irish.

Irlandais, ~e /iʀlɑ̃dɛ, ɛz/ ▶ 537 *nm,f* Irishman/Irishwoman; **les ~ du Nord** the northern Irish.

Irlande /iʀlɑ̃d/ ▶ 321 *nprf* Ireland; **la République d'~** the Republic of Ireland; **l'~ du Nord** Northern Ireland.

ironie /iʀɔni/ *nf* irony; **l'~ du sort** the irony of fate; **faire de l'~** to be ironic.

ironique /iʀɔnik/ *adj* ironic.

ironiquement /iʀɔnikmɑ̃/ *adv* ironically.

ironiser /iʀɔnize/ [1] *vi* to be ironic (**sur**

about); **'tu es déjà prête!' ironisa-t-il** 'ready so soon!' he said ironically.

iroquois, **~e** /iʀɔkwa, az/ **▶462** I *adj* Iroquois.
II *nm* Ling Iroquois.

Iroquois, **~e** /iʀɔkwa, az/ *nm,f* Iroquois.

IRPP /iɛʀpepe/ *nm*: *abbr* ▶ **impôt**.

irradiation /iʀadjasjɔ̃/ *nf* **1** Nucl radiation; **tué par ~** killed by radiation; **dix morts par ~** ten deaths through ou from radiation; **2** Phys (émission de rayonnement) irradiation; **3** Ind irradiation; **~ alimentaire** food irradiation.

irradier /iʀadje/ [2] I *vtr* (exposer aux radiations) to irradiate [*tumeur, organe, personne*]; **déchets irradiés** radioactive waste.
II *vi* (se propager) to radiate (**dans** through).

irraisonné, **~e** /iʀɛzɔne/ *adj* irrational.

irrationalisme /iʀasjɔnalism/ *nm* irrationalism.

irrationalité /iʀasjɔnalite/ *nf* irrationality.

irrationnel, **-elle** /iʀasjɔnɛl/ I *adj* irrational.
II *nm* irrational.

irrattrapable /iʀatʀapabl/ *adj* irretrievable; **retard ~** irretrievable delay.

irréalisable /iʀealizabl/ *adj* [*entreprise, idée, rêve*] unachievable; [*projet*] unworkable.

irréalisme /iʀealism/ *nm* lack of realism.

irréaliste /iʀealist/ *adj* unrealistic.

irréalité /iʀealite/ *nf* unreality.

irrecevabilité /iʀəsəvabilite/ *nf* Jur inadmissibility.

irrecevable /iʀəsəvabl/ *adj* Jur inadmissible.

irréconciliable /iʀekɔ̃siljabl/ *adj* irreconcilable.

irrécupérable /iʀekypeʀabl/ *adj* **1** [*objets, capital*] irrecoverable; [*meubles, voiture*] irretrievable; **2** [*personne, délinquant*] irretrievable; **3**○ hum beyond redemption (*après n*).

irrécusable /iʀekyzabl/ *adj* **1** gén [*signe, preuve, vérité*] indisputable; **2** Jur [*témoin, juge, témoignage*] unimpeachable.

irréductibilité /iʀedyktibilite/ *nf* littér **1** (d'opposition, de caractère) implacability; **2** Math irreducibility.

irréductible /iʀedyktibl/ I *adj* **1** [*opposition, volonté*] implacable; [*personne, motivation*] indomitable; [*conflit*] relentless; **2** Math, Méd irreducible.
II *nmf* diehard.

irréel, **-elle** /iʀeɛl/ I *adj* unreal.
II *nm* unreal.
■ **~ du passé** Ling past hypothetical condition; **~ du présent** Ling present hypothetical condition.

irréfléchi, **~e** /iʀefleʃi/ *adj* **1** (précipité) [*action, décision, propos*] ill-considered; **2** (étourdi) [*personne*] careless; **3** (irrationnel) [*chagrin, hostilité, peur*] irrational.

irréflexion /iʀeflɛksjɔ̃/ *nf* thoughtlessness; **faire preuve d'~** to show a lack of thought.

irréfutabilité /iʀefytabilite/ *nf* irrefutability.

irréfutable /iʀefytabl/ *adj* irrefutable.

irréfutablement /iʀefytabləmɑ̃/ *adv* irrefutably.

irréfuté, **~e** /iʀefyte/ *adj* unrefuted.

irrégularité /iʀegylaʀite/ *nf* **1** (acte critiquable) irregularity; **des ~s ont été commises au dépouillement** irregularities took place in the counting of votes; **2** (en quantité) irregularity; **l'~ de la production** the irregular production; **3** (en qualité) irregularity, unevenness; **4** (défaut) irregularity; (de surface) unevenness; **les ~s du sol** the uneven ground; **5** Ling irregularity.

irrégulier, **-ière** /iʀegylje, ɛʀ/ *adj* **1** (sans régularité) [*forme, visage, croissance, pouls, respiration*] irregular; [*écriture, résultats, qualité, sol*] uneven; **2** [*procédure, transaction, méthode*] irregular; [*immigré, travailleur, vente*] illegal; **immigré en situation irrégulière** illegal immigrant; **être en situation irrégulière** to be in breach of the regulations; **3** (inégal) [*élève, athlète*] whose performance is uneven (*épith, après n*); **4** Mil [*troupe, combattant*] irregular; **5** Ling [*verbe, pluriel*] irregular.

irrégulièrement /iʀegyljɛʀmɑ̃/ *adv* **1** (illégalement) illegally; **2** (sans régularité) [*découper, se conjuguer*] irregularly; [*répartir*] unevenly; [*travailler*] erratically.

irréligion /iʀʀeliʒjɔ̃/ *nf* irreligion.

irrémédiable /iʀ(ʀ)emedjabl/ I *adj* [*perte, faute*] irretrievable, irreparable; [*déclin*] irremediable sout, irreversible; [*situation*] irremediable sout, beyond remedy (*après n*).
II *nm* **il est tellement désespéré qu'il pourrait commettre l'~** he's so desperate that he might do something foolish.

irrémédiablement /iʀ(ʀ)emedjabləmɑ̃/ *adv* irreparably, irremediably.

irrémissible /iʀʀemisibl/ *adj* fml **1** (impardonnable) unpardonable, irremissible sout; **2** (inexorable) inexorable.

irremplaçable /iʀɑ̃plasabl/ *adj* irreplaceable.

irréparable /iʀʀepaʀabl/ I *adj* [*machine, voiture, appareil*] beyond repair (*après n*); [*dégât, ravage*] irreparable; [*tort, faute, crime, injure*] irreparable; **votre veste/poste de radio est ~** your jacket/radio is beyond repair.
II *nm* **commettre l'~** to go beyond the point of no return, to do what cannot be undone.

irréparablement /iʀʀepaʀabləmɑ̃/ *adv* irreparably, irretrievably.

irrépréhensible /iʀʀepʀeɑ̃sibl/ *adj* fml blameless.

irrépressible /iʀepʀesibl/ *adj* **1** [*sourire, désir*] irrepressible; [*rire, larmes*] uncontrollable; **2** [*évolution, effondrement*] unstoppable.

irréprochable /iʀepʀɔʃabl/ *adj* [*conduite, vie, employé*] irreproachable, beyond reproach (*après n*); [*travail*] perfect, impeccable; [*goût, élégance, manières*] impeccable.

irrésistible /iʀezistibl/ *adj* [*séducteur, charme*] irresistible; [*besoin*] compelling; [*envie, passion*] overpowering; [*essor, ascension, offensive*] irresistible, unstoppable; [*humour, personne, blague*] hilarious.

irrésistiblement /iʀezistibləmɑ̃/ *adv* irresistibly.

irrésolu, **~e** /iʀʀezɔly/ *adj* **1** (indécis) [*personne*] indecisive, irresolute sout; **2** (sans solution) [*problème, question, énigme*] unsolved.

irrésolution /iʀʀezɔlysjɔ̃/ *nf* fml indecisiveness, irresolution sout.

irrespect /iʀɛspɛ/ *nm* lack of respect (**de** for), disrespect (**de** for).

irrespectueusement /iʀɛspɛktɥøzmɑ̃/ *adv* disrespectfully.

irrespectueux, **-euse** /iʀɛspɛktɥø, øz/ *adj* disrespectful (**envers** to, toward, towards GB).

irrespirable /iʀɛspiʀabl/ *adj* **1** [*air, gaz*] unbreathable; **2** [*climat, ambiance, atmosphère*] stifling; **ouvrez les fenêtres, c'est ~ ici** open the windows, it's stifling in here.

irresponsabilité /iʀɛspɔ̃sabilite/ *nf* **1** (manque de sérieux) irresponsibility; **2** Jur non-accountability.

irresponsable /iʀɛspɔ̃sabl/ *adj* **1** (qui agit avec légèreté) [*personne, attitude*] irresponsible; **de façon ~** irresponsibly; **2** Jur non-accountable.

irrétrécissable /iʀetʀesisabl/ *adj* (tissu) nonshrink (*épith*), unshrinkable; [*traitement*] nonshrink (*épith*).

irrévérence /iʀʀeveʀɑ̃s/ *nf* fml **1** (manque de respect) irreverence (**envers, à l'égard de** to, toward, towards GB); **parler/agir avec ~** to speak/act irreverently; **2** (acte) irreverent act; (parole) irreverent remark.

irrévérencieusement /iʀʀeveʀɑ̃sjøzmɑ̃/ *adv* fml irreverently.

irrévérencieux, **-ieuse** /iʀʀeveʀɑ̃sjø, øz/ *adj* irreverent (**envers** to, toward, towards GB).

irréversibilité /iʀevɛʀsibilite/ *nf* irreversibility.

irréversible /iʀevɛʀsibl/ *adj* **1** gén, Chimie, Phys irreversible; **2** Tech [*engrenage, mécanisme*] non-reversible; [*prise de courant, connecteur*] one-way.

irrévocabilité /iʀevɔkabilite/ *nf* gén, Jur irrevocability.

irrévocable /iʀevɔkabl/ *adj* irrevocable.

irrévocablement /iʀevɔkabləmɑ̃/ *adv* irrevocably.

irrigable /iʀigabl/ *adj* irrigable.

irrigateur /iʀigatœʀ/ I *adj m* Méd irrigating.
II *nm* Agric, Méd irrigator.

irrigation /iʀigasjɔ̃/ *nf* **1** Agric irrigation; **2** Méd (de plaie, cavité) irrigation; (en sang) supply of blood; **une mauvaise ~ du cerveau** an insufficient blood supply to the brain.

irriguer /iʀige/ [1] *vtr* **1** Agric to irrigate; **2** Méd to irrigate [*plaie*]; **le sang irrigue les organes** organs are supplied with blood.

irritabilité /iʀitabilite/ *nf* irritability.

irritable /iʀitabl/ *adj* irritable.

irritant, **~e** /iʀitɑ̃, ɑ̃t/ I *adj* **1** (agaçant) irritating, annoying; **2** Méd irritant.
II *nm* Pharm, Méd irritant.

irritation /iʀitasjɔ̃/ *nf* **1** (agacement) irritation, annoyance; **2** Méd (inflammation) irritation.

irriter /iʀite/ [1] I *vtr* **1** (agacer) to irritate, to annoy; **il avait l'air très irrité** he seemed very annoyed; **il est irrité par leurs jérémiades continuelles** he is irritated by their continual moaning; **2** Méd to irritate; **le frottement m'a irrité la peau** the friction irritated my skin.
II **s'irriter** *vpr* **1** (s'énerver) to get annoyed (**de** about, over), to get angry (**de** about, over); **2** Méd [*organe*] to become irritated, to become inflamed.

irruption /iʀypsjɔ̃/ *nf* (apparition) irruption sout; **faire ~ dans** to burst into, to rush into [*pièce, bâtiment, rue*]; **ils ont fait ~ dans le monde du rock il y a dix ans** they burst onto the rock scene ten years ago; **l'~ de l'informatique dans le monde du travail** the sudden emergence of computers in the workplace.

Isaac /izaak/ *npr* Isaac.

isabelle /izabɛl/ **▶193** *adj inv* light buff; **cheval ~** dun horse.

Isaïe /izai/ *npr* Isaiah.

isard /izaʀ/ *nm* izard.

ischion /iskjɔ̃/ *nm* ischium.

Isère /izɛʀ/ **▶357**, **692** *nprf* (rivière, département) **l'~** the Isère.

ISF /iɛsɛf/ *nm* ▶ **impôt**.

Isis /izis/ *npr* Isis.

islam /islam/ *nm* **l'~** Islam.

islamique /islamik/ *adj* Islamic.

islamisation /islamizasjɔ̃/ *nf* Islamization.

islamiser /islamize/ [1] *vtr* to Islamize.

islamisme /islamism/ *nm* Islam.

islamiste /islamist/ I *adj* Islamic.
II *nmf* Islamist.

islandais, **~e** /islɑ̃dɛ, ɛz/ **▶462**, **537** I *adj* Icelandic.
II *nm* Ling Icelandic.

Islandais, **~e** /islɑ̃dɛ, ɛz/ **▶537** *nm,f* Icelander.

Islande /islɑ̃d/ **▶321** *nprf* Iceland.

isobare /izobaʀ/ I *adj* isobaric.
II *nf* isobar.

isocèle /izosɛl/ *adj* isosceles; **triangle ~** isosceles triangle.

isochrone /izokʀon/, **isochronique** /izokʀɔnik/ *adj* isochronal.

isoglosse /izoglɔs/ *nf* isogloss.

isolable /izɔlabl/ *adj* isolable.

isolant, **~e** /izɔlɑ̃, ɑ̃t/ I *adj* 1 Constr, Électrotech [*matériau*] insulating; **la laine de verre est très ~e** fibreglass[GB] is a very good insulator; 2 Ling [*langue*] isolating.

II *nm* insulating material; **~ thermique** thermal insulator.

isolateur /izɔlatœʀ/ *nm* insulator.

isolation /izɔlasjɔ̃/ *nf* 1 Tech insulation; **~ thermique** thermal insulation; **~ acoustique** soundproofing; 2 Psych isolation.

isolationnisme /izɔlasjɔnism/ *nm* isolationism.

isolationniste /izɔlasjɔnist/ *adj, nmf* isolationist.

isolé, **~e** /izɔle/ I *pp* ▸ **isoler**.

II *pp adj* 1 (très éloigné) [*village, région*] remote; 2 (un peu à l'écart) [*maison, arbre*] isolated (**de** from); 3 (détaché d'un ensemble) [*cas, événement, incident*] isolated; **tireur ~** Mil lone gunman, sniper; **des tirs ~s** Mil sniper fire ¢; 4 (seul) isolated, lonely; (sans alliés) [*politicien, pays*] isolated.

III *nm,f* 1 (personne qui agit seule) **attentats commis par des ~s** attacks carried out by individuals acting independently; 2 (personne délaissée) lonely person.

isolement /izɔlmɑ̃/ *nm* 1 (éloignement) (de village, région) remoteness; (de maison) isolated location; 2 (absence de contacts) (de personne âgée, malade, chômeur) isolation, loneliness; (de pays, politicien) isolation; **il faut aider le pays à sortir de son ~ diplomatique** the country must be given help to break out of its diplomatic isolation; 3 (mise à l'écart) (de malade) isolation; (de prisonnier) solitary confinement; 4 (de gène, substance, virus) isolation; 5 Électrotech insulation.

isolément /izɔlemɑ̃/ *adv* [*agir, travailler, considérer*] in isolation.

isoler /izɔle/ [1] I *vtr* 1 (priver de contacts) to isolate [*malade, politicien, dissident*] (**de** from); to put [sb] in solitary confinement [*prisonnier*]; **ses opinions extrémistes l'ont isolé de ses collègues** his radical views isolated him from ou set him apart from his colleagues; 2 (séparer d'un ensemble) to isolate [*gène, substance, élément*]; **~ un problème** to isolate a problem; **~ une citation de son contexte** to take a quote out of context; 3 Constr (contre le bruit) to soundproof [*pièce*]; (contre la chaleur, le froid) to insulate (**contre** against); 4 Électrotech to insulate; 5 Méd to cover [sth] with a dressing [*plaie*].

II **s'isoler** *vpr* [*personne, ermite*] to isolate oneself (**de** from); **il s'est isolé dans un coin pour lire une lettre** he withdrew into a corner to read a letter.

isoloir /izɔlwaʀ/ *nm* voting ou polling GB booth.

isomère /izomɛʀ/ I *adj* isomeric.

II *nm* isomer.

isomérie /izomeʀi/ *nf* isomerism.

isométrie /izometʀi/ *nf* isometry.

isométrique /izometʀik/ *adj* isometric.

isomorphe /izomɔʀf/ *adj* isomorphic.

isomorphisme /izomɔʀfism/ *nm* isomorphism.

isorel® /izɔʀɛl/ *nm* hardboard.

isotherme /izotɛʀm/ I *adj* 1 (maintenant une température constante) [*camion, wagon*] thermally insulated; **boîte/seau ~** ice box/bucket; **bouteille ~** insulated bottle; **sac ~** cool bag; 2 Météo, Sci isothermal.

II *nf* isotherm.

isotope /izotɔp/ I *adj* isotopic.

II *nm* isotope.

isotopique /izotɔpik/ *adj* isotopic.

Israël /isʀaɛl/ ▸ 321 *nprm* Israel; **en ~** in Israel; **l'État d'~** the State of Israel.

israélien, -ienne /isʀaeljɛ̃, ɛn/ ▸ 537 *adj* Israeli.

Israélien, -ienne /isʀaeljɛ̃, ɛn/ ▸ 537 *nm,f* Israeli.

israélite /isʀaelit/ I *adj* Jewish.

II *nmf* 1 Hist Israelite; 2 (juif) Jew.

issu, **~e** /isy/ I *adj* 1 (originaire) **être ~ de** to come from; **il est ~ d'un milieu modeste** he comes from a modest background; **les jeunes ~s de familles pauvres** young people from poor families; 2 (résultant) **être ~ de** to result from; **les problèmes ~s de la décolonisation** problems resulting from decolonization.

II **issue** *nf* 1 (sortie) exit; **toutes les ~es étaient bloquées** all the exits were blocked off; **'sans ~e'** 'no exit'; 2 (solution) solution (**à** to), way out (**à** to); **situation sans ~e** situation with no solution ou way out; **se ménager une ~e** to leave oneself a way out; 3 (dénouement) outcome; **~e tragique d'une affaire** tragic outcome of a case; **l'~e du procès reste incertaine** the outcome of the trial remains uncertain; **à l'~e de** at the end of; **à l'~e de trois jours de pourparlers** at the close ou conclusion of three days of talks.

■ **~e de secours** emergency exit.

Istanbul /istɑ̃bul/ ▸ 857 *npr* Istanbul.

isthme /ism/ *nm* isthmus.

isthmique /ismik/ *adj* isthmian.

Istrie /istʀi/ *nprf* **l'~** Istria.

italianisant, **~e** /italjanizɑ̃, ɑ̃t/ I *adj* [*art*] Italianate.

II *nm,f* Italian scholar.

italianisme /italjanism/ *nm* Italianism, Italicism.

Italie /itali/ ▸ 321 *nprf* Italy.

italien, -ienne /italjɛ̃, ɛn/ ▸ 462, 537 I *adj* Italian.

II *nm* Ling Italian.

Italien, -ienne /italjɛ̃, ɛn/ ▸ 537 *nm,f* Italian.

italique /italik/ I *adj* 1 Imprim italic; 2 Hist, Ling Italic.

II *nm* 1 Imprim italics (*pl*); **mettre qch en ~(s)** to put sth in italics, to italicize sth; 2 Ling Italic.

item /itɛm/ I *adv* ditto.

II *nm* item.

itératif, -ive /iteʀatif, iv/ *adj* 1 Ling, Math, Philos iterative; 2 Jur repeated, reiterated.

itération /iteʀasjɔ̃/ *nf* fml iteration.

Ithaque /itak/ ▸ 416 *nprf* Ithaca.

itinéraire /itineʀɛʀ/ *nm* 1 (de voyage) route; (détaillé) itinerary; 2 fig career; **~ politique/professionnel** political/professional career.

■ **~ bis** Gén Civ, Transp alternative route, holiday GB ou vacation US route; **~ de délestage** relief route; **~ de déviation** Gén Civ diversion.

> **Les itinéraires**
>
> **Comment s'y rendre**
>
> OK, you come out of the station. Go straight across the car park into Main Street. Keep straight on for several hundred yards over the first two sets of traffic lights and turn right at the third set into Grant Street. Take the third street on the left and walk down to the end – you'll find yourself facing the theatre. Go down the alleyway to the left of the theatre and you'll come out in West Street, with a bank on the right-hand corner as you reach the end. Cross over the road, going right towards a piece of open ground. The last shop before the open space is a tailor's with a coffee shop on the first floor. I'll be there with the gold and two single first-class tickets to Bali. Don't be late – I shan't wait!

itinérant, **~e** /itineʀɑ̃, ɑ̃t/ *adj* [*personnel*] travelling[GB]; [*musicien, artiste*] itinerant; [*spectacle, exposition*] touring; [*vie*] peripatetic; [*cirque*] travelling[GB]; **faire un camp ~** to go on a camping tour; **faire du tourisme ~** to go on a touring holiday GB, to go on a driving trip US.

itou○ /itu/ *adv* hum too; **tu t'en vas? moi ~!** you're leaving? me too!

IUP /iype/ *nm* (*abbr* = **Institut universitaire professionnel**) vocational university institute.

IUT /iyte/ *nm* (*abbr* = **Institut universitaire de technologie**) university institute of technology.

Ivan /ivɑ̃/ *npr* Ivan; **~ le Terrible** Ivan the Terrible.

IVG /iveʒe/ *nf* ▸ **interruption**.

ivoire /ivwaʀ/ ▸ 193 I *adj inv* ivory.

II *nm* 1 (d'éléphant) ivory; **en ~**, **d'~** ivory (*épith*); 2 (de dent) dentine GB, dentin US.

ivoirien, -ienne /ivwaʀjɛ̃, ɛn/ ▸ 537 *adj* of the Ivory Coast.

Ivoirien, -ienne /ivwaʀjɛ̃, ɛn/ ▸ 537 *nm,f* (natif) native of the Ivory Coast; (habitant) inhabitant of the Ivory Coast.

ivoirin, **~e** /ivwaʀɛ̃, in/ ▸ 193 *adj* liter ivory (*épith*).

ivraie /ivʀɛ/ *nf* rye-grass.

IDIOMES **séparer le bon grain de l'~** to separate the wheat from the chaff.

ivre /ivʀ/ *adj* 1 (troublé par l'alcool) intoxicated, drunk; **légèrement ~** a bit tipsy GB, slightly drunk; **~ mort** dead ou blind drunk; 2 (transporté) drunk (**de** with); **~ de liberté** exhilarated ou intoxicated by freedom; **~ de bonheur/pouvoir** drunk with happiness/power; **~ de rage/colère** wild with rage/anger.

ivresse /ivʀɛs/ *nf* 1 (ébriété) drunkenness, intoxication; **en état d'~** in a state of intoxication; **conduite en état d'~** Jur driving while intoxicated, drunken driving, DWI US; 2 (exaltation) exhilaration; **~ de la victoire/du pouvoir** the exhilaration of victory/of power; ▸ **flacon**.

■ **~ des profondeurs** decompression sickness.

ivrogne /ivʀɔɲ/ *nmf* drunkard.

ivrognerie /ivʀɔɲ(ə)ʀi/ *nf* drinking.

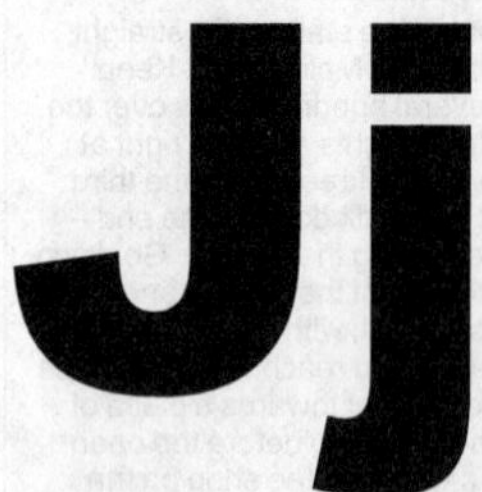

j, J /ʒi/ *nm inv* j, J; **le jour J** D-day; **jour J moins dix** ten days from D-day.

j' ▶**je.**

jabot /ʒabo/ *nm* **1** (d'oiseau, abeille) crop; **2** (ornement) jabot; **chemise à ~** shirt with a jabot.

jacasse /ʒakas/ *nf* **(pie) ~** magpie.

jacassement /ʒakasmɑ̃/ *nm* **1** (bavardage) chattering ₵; **2** (cri de la pie) chattering ₵.

jacasser /ʒakase/ [1] *vi* **1** [*bavard*] to chatter; **2** Zool [*pie*] to chatter.

jacasseur, -euse /ʒakasœʀ, øz/ **I** *adj* [*oiseau*] chattering; [*personne*] chattering.

II *nm,f* **c'est un ~** he's always yapping away○.

jachère /ʒaʃɛʀ/ *nf* (pratique, état) fallow; (terrain) fallow land ₵; **en ~** lying fallow; **laisser un champ en ~** to leave a field lying fallow.

jacinthe /ʒasɛ̃t/ *nf* **1** (fleur) hyacinth; **2†** (pierre précieuse) hyacinth.

■ **~ des bois** bluebell; **~ d'Espagne** Bot common water hyacinth.

jack /(d)ʒak/ *nm* jack plug; **prise ~** (mâle) jack plug; (femelle) jack socket.

jackpot /(d)ʒakpɔt/ *nm* **1** (combinaison gagnante) jackpot; **gagner le ~** to hit the jackpot; **2** (machine) slot machine.

jacobée /ʒakɔbe/ *nf* ragwort.

jacobin, ~e /ʒakɔbɛ̃, in/ *adj, nm,f* **1** Hist Jacobin; **2** Pol radical.

Jacobin, ~e /ʒakɔbɛ̃, in/ *nm,f* Hist Jacobin.

jacobinisme /ʒakɔbinism/ *nm* **1** Hist Jacobinism; **2** Pol radicalism.

jacobite /ʒakɔbit/ *adj, nmf* Jacobite.

jacquard /ʒakaʀ/ **I** *adj inv* Jacquard.

II *nm* **1** (tissu) Jacquard; **tricoter en ~** to knit in Jacquard; **2** (métier) Jacquard loom.

jacquerie /ʒakʀi/ *nf* **1** Hist peasant revolt, jacquerie; **2** (émeute) uprising.

Jacques /ʒak/ **I** *nm* **faire le ~** to play the fool; **jouer à ~ a dit** to have a game of Simon says.

II *npr* Hist James.

jacquet /ʒakɛ/ ▶**449** *nm* **1** (jeu) backgammon; **2** (tablette) backgammon board.

jacquot /ʒako/ *nm* **1** Zool West African grey GB ou gray US parrot; **2**○ baby talk (perroquet) pretty polly.

jactance /ʒaktɑ̃s/ *nf* **1** (suffisance) haughtiness; **un homme plein de ~** a haughty man; **2**● (bavardage) chatter.

jacter● /ʒakte/ [1] *vi* (parler) to jaw○, to talk.

jacuzzi® /ʒakyzi/ *nm* jacuzzi®.

jade /ʒad/ ▶**193** **I** *adj* **(vert) ~** jade-green; **chemise ~** jade-green shirt.

II *nm* **1** (pierre) jade; **collier/statuette de** or **en ~** jade necklace/statuette; **2** (couleur) jade green; **3** (objet) jade; **un ~ chinois** a Chinese jade.

jadis /ʒadis/ **I†** *adj inv* **dans le** or **au temps ~** in bygone days, in days of old; **du temps ~** of bygone days, of days gone by; **les contes du temps ~** tales of days gone by.

II *adv* formerly, in the past; **~, la vie était différente** in the past, life was different; **une tapisserie aux couleurs ~ vives** a tapestry whose colours[GB] were once bright; **les institutions/mœurs de ~** the institutions/customs of long ago.

jaguar /ʒagwaʀ/ *nm* Zool jaguar.

jaillir /ʒajiʀ/ [3] *vi* **1** (sortir impétueusement) [*liquide, source, gaz, air*] to gush out (**de** of); [*larmes*] to well up (**de** from); [*flamme, étincelle*] to shoot up (**de** from); **une lueur jaillit dans l'obscurité** a light pierced the darkness; **2** (apparaître subitement) [*personne, animal*] to spring up (**de** from); (en sortant) to spring out (**de** from); [*voiture*] to shoot out (**de** from); **3** (se produire spontanément) [*rires, cris, plaisanteries*] to burst out (**de** from); **4** (s'élever) [*clocher, immeuble, arbre*] to thrust up, tower up (**au-dessus de** above); **5** (se révéler) [*idée, preuve, vérité*] to emerge (**de** from).

jaillissement /ʒajismɑ̃/ *nm* (de liquide, source) gushing out ₵; (d'idées, de voix) outpouring.

jais /ʒɛ/ *nm* **1** Minér (pierre) jet; **un collier de ~** a jet necklace; **2** ▶**193** (couleur) **(noir) de ~** jet-black (*épith*), jet black (*jamais épith*); **des cheveux/yeux de ~** jet-black hair/eyes.

Jakarta /dʒakaʀta/ ▶**857** *npr* Jakarta.

jalon /ʒalɔ̃/ *nm* **1** (point important) milestone; **être un (important) ~ dans l'histoire de l'Europe** to be a milestone in the history of Europe; **poser les ~s d'une réforme** to take the first steps toward(s) a reform; **2** (piquet) marker.

jalon-mire, *pl* **jalons-mires** /ʒalɔ̃miʀ/ *nm* target rod.

jalonnement /ʒalɔnmɑ̃/ *nm* marking out ₵.

jalonner /ʒalɔne/ [1] *vtr* **1** (marquer) [*événement, succès, échec*] to punctuate [*vie, carrière, histoire*]; **une journée jalonnée de péripéties** a day full of incidents; **2** (border) [*objet, plante*] to line [*route, piste*]; **des platanes jalonnent la route** plane trees line the road; **3** (délimiter avec une marque) [*personne*] to mark out [*route, terrain*].

jalousement /ʒaluzmɑ̃/ *adv* **1** (avec jalousie) jealously; (avec envie) enviously; **2** (avec un soin inquiet) jealously; **garder ~ un secret** to keep a secret jealously; **veiller ~ sur qn/qch** to watch jealously over sb/sth.

jalouser /ʒaluze/ [1] **I** *vtr* to be jealous of [*personnes, qualités, avantages*]; **un homme très jalousé** a much envied man.

II se jalouser *vpr* to be jealous of one another.

jalousie /ʒaluzi/ *nf* **1** (sentiment) jealousy ₵ (**à l'égard de, envers** towards[GB]); **susciter des ~s chez les concurrents** to arouse jealousy among competitors; **tuer par ~** to kill out of jealousy; **2** Constr (treillis) jalousie, slatted blind; (persienne) (à lattes verticales) vertical blind; (à lattes horizontales) Venetian blind; **3** Bot (œillet) sweet william.

jaloux, -ouse /ʒalu, uz/ **I** *adj* jealous (**de** of); **avec un soin ~** jealously, with meticulous care.

II *nm,f* jealous man/woman; **faire des ~** to make people jealous.

IDIOMES **être ~ comme un tigre** to be extremely jealous.

jamaïquain, ~e /ʒamaikɛ̃, ɛn/ ▶**537** *adj* Jamaican.

Jamaïquain, ~e /ʒamaikɛ̃, ɛn/ ▶**537** *nm,f* Jamaican.

Jamaïque /ʒamaik/ ▶**321**, **416** *nprf* Jamaica.

jamais /ʒamɛ/ *adv* **1** (à aucun moment) never; **il n'écrit ~** he never writes; **n'écrit-il ~?** doesn't he ever write?; **je ne pense pas lui avoir ~ écrit** I don't think I have ever written to him; **je n'écrirai ~ plus** or **plus ~** I'll never write again; **ce n'est ~ assez/certain** it's never enough/certain; **~ plus!** never again!; **rien n'est ~ certain** nothing is ever certain; **elle n'est ~ contente** she's never satisfied; **sans ~ comprendre** without ever understanding; **sait-on ~?** you never know; **c'est du ~ vu!** you've never seen anything like it!; **~ de la vie!** never!; **~, au grand ~, je ne reviendrai** I shall never ever return; **c'est le moment ou ~** it's now or never; **c'est pour lui le moment ou ~ de faire** it's a case of now or never if he is to do; ▶**tard**; **2** (à tout autre moment) ever; **plus belle que ~** prettier than ever; **plus/moins que ~** more/less than ever; **elle est heureuse comme ~** she has never been happier; **si ~ tu passes à Oxford, viens me voir** if you are ever in Oxford, come and see me; **on a ce qu'il faut si ~ il pleut** we have everything we need in case it rains; **3** (toujours) **à ~, à tout ~** forever; **4** (seulement) **ce n'est ~ que** it is only; **il ne fait ~ que son devoir** he is only doing his duty; **ça ne fait ~ qu'un problème de plus** iron it's just one more problem.

jambage /ʒɑ̃baʒ/ *nm* **1** (de lettre) downstroke; **2** Constr (support) jamb.

jambe /ʒɑ̃b/ *nf* **1** ▶**188** Anat, Zool leg; **avoir une ~ plus courte que l'autre** to have one leg shorter than the other; **mes ~s ne me portent plus** my legs won't carry me any further; **avoir des ~s bien faites** to have nice ou good legs; **avoir de bonnes ~s** to have strong ou sturdy legs; **avoir des ~s de 20 ans** to have the legs of a 20-year-old; **plier les ~s** (debout) to bend one's knees; (assis) to draw one's legs up; **croiser les ~s** to cross one's legs; **être assis les ~s croisées** to be sitting with one's legs crossed; **il avait les ~s écartées** his legs were wide apart; **aller** or **courir à toutes ~s** to run as fast as one's legs can carry one; **avoir une ~ raide** to have a stiff leg; **j'ai mal aux ~s** my legs are hurting; **j'ai les ~s lourdes** my legs feel heavy; **se retrouver/tomber les ~s en l'air** to land/fall flat on one's back; **j'ai les ~s coupées** or **brisées** my legs feel like lead; **j'ai les ~s comme du coton** I feel weak at the knees; **traîner la ~**○ to trudge along; ▶**plein**; **2** Tech, Cout leg.

■ **~ artificielle** artificial leg; **~ de bois** wooden leg; **c'est comme un emplâtre** or **cataplasme** or **cautère sur une ~ de bois** it's useless; **~ de force** Constr strut.

IDIOMES **cela me fait une belle ~**○ a fat

lot of good○ that does me; **il ne tient plus sur ses ~s** he can hardly stand up; **couper bras et ~s à qn** to leave sb speechless; **les ~s me rentrent dans le corps, je n'ai plus de ~s** I'm on my last legs○, I'm very tired; **prendre ses ~s à son cou** to take to one's heels; **parlez-lui de mariage et il prendra les ~s à son cou** mention marriage and you won't see him for dust○; **donner des ~s à qn** to add wings to sb's heels; **avoir qn dans les ~s** to have sb under one's feet; **tenir la ~ à qn** to keep talking to sb; **faire une partie de ~s en l'air**◑ to have a roll in the hay○; **traiter qn par-dessus** or **par-dessous la ~** to treat sb in an offhand manner; **faire qch par-dessus** or **par-dessous la ~** to do sth in a slipshod manner.

jambier, **-ière** /ʒɑ̃bje, ɛʀ/ I *adj* Méd, Anat **muscle ~ postérieur** posterior tibial muscle spéc.
II **jambière** *nf* **1** (de randonneur) legging; (de joueur de hockey) pad; (de danseur) leg-warmer; **2** (de soldat) greave.

jambon /ʒɑ̃bɔ̃/ *nm* **1** ham; **sandwich/omelette au ~** ham sandwich/omelette; **une tranche de ~** a slice of ham; **acheter du ~** to buy some ham; **acheter un ~** to buy a ham; **2**○ (cuisse) thigh.
■ **~ beurre** (buttered) ham sandwich; **~ blanc** cooked ham; **~ cru** raw ham; **~ cuit** = **~ blanc**; **~ fumé** smoked ham; **~ de Paris** = **~ blanc**; **~ de Parme** Parma ham; **~ de pays** cured ham; **~ salé** salted ham; **~ d'York** York ham.

jambonneau, *pl* **~x** /ʒɑ̃bɔno/ *nm* knuckle of ham.

jamboree /ʒɑ̃bɔʀe/ *nm* jamboree.

janissaire /ʒanisɛʀ/ *nm* janissary.

jansénisme /ʒɑ̃senism/ *nm* Jansenism.

janséniste /ʒɑ̃senist/ *adj, nm,f* Jansenist.

jante /ʒɑ̃t/ *nf* **1** (bord de roue) rim; **2** (roue sans pneu) wheel; **rouler sur la ~**○ to drive on a flat tyre GB ou tire US.

janvier /ʒɑ̃vje/ **▶521** *nm* January; **du premier ~ à la Saint-Sylvestre** from New Year's Day to New Year's Eve.

japon /ʒapɔ̃/ *nm* **1** (papier) Japanese paper; **2** (porcelaine) Japanese porcelain.

Japon /ʒapɔ̃/ **▶321** *nprm* Japan.

japonais, **~e** /ʒapɔnɛ, ɛz/ **▶537**, **462**
I *adj* Japanese.
II *nm* Ling Japanese.

Japonais, **~e** /ʒapɔnɛ, ɛz/ **▶537** *nm,f* Japanese; **les ~** the Japanese.

japonaiserie /ʒapɔnɛzʀi/, **japonerie** /ʒapɔnʀi/ *nf* (bibelot japonais) Japanese curio.

jappement /ʒapmɑ̃/ *nm* yapping ¢; **les ~s du chien** the yapping of the dog.

japper /ʒape/ [1] *vi* to yap.

jaquette /ʒakɛt/ *nf* **1** Mode (de femme) jacket; (d'homme) morning coat; **2** (de livre) dust jacket; **3** Dent crown.
IDIOMES **être de la ~ (flottante)**○ to be limp-wristed○.

jardin /ʒaʀdɛ̃/ *nm* **1** (privé) garden GB, yard US; **faire son ~** to work in one's garden GB ou in the yard US; **chaise/table de ~** garden chair/table GB, patio chair/table US; **2** (parc) gardens (*pl*), park; **aller au ~** to go to the park; **le ~ des Oliviers** the Garden of Gethsemane.
■ **~ d'acclimatation** = **~ zoologique**; **~ d'agrément** ornamental ou pleasure garden; **~ anglais** landscape garden; **~ botanique** Bot botanical gardens (*pl*); **~ d'enfants** kindergarten; **~ à la française** formal garden; **~ d'hiver** winter garden; **~ japonais** Japanese garden; **~ potager** vegetable garden; **~ public** public garden; (plus grand) park; **~ secret** private domain; **~s suspendus** hanging gardens; **~ zoologique** Zool zoological gardens (*pl*).
IDIOMES **jeter une pierre dans le ~ de qn** to make snide remarks about sb, to have a dig at sb○; **c'est une pierre dans ton ~** that was meant for you; **il faut cultiver notre ~** we must tend our patch.

jardinage /ʒaʀdinaʒ/ *nm* gardening; **faire du ~** to do some gardening; **outils de ~** gardening tools.

jardiner /ʒaʀdine/ [1] *vi* to do some gardening; **il aime ~** he enjoys gardening.

jardinerie /ʒaʀdinʀi/ **▶510** *nf* garden centre[GB]

jardinet /ʒaʀdinɛ/ *nm* small garden GB, small yard US.

jardinier, **-ière** /ʒaʀdinje, ɛʀ/ **▶510** I *adj* (de jardin) garden; **plante jardinière** garden plant.
II *nm,f* (personne) gardener; **outils de ~** gardener's tools.
III **jardinière** *nf* **1** (plat) **jardinière (de légumes)** jardinière; **2** (bac à fleurs) jardinière; (sur un rebord de fenêtre) window-box.
■ **~ fleuriste** horticulturalist; **~ paysagiste** landscape gardener; **~ pépiniériste** nurseryman; **jardinière d'enfants** Scol kindergarten teacher.

jargon /ʒaʀgɔ̃/ *nm* **1** (langue de métier) jargon; **~ médical/juridique/publicitaire** medical/legal/advertising jargon; **~ administratif** officialese; **~ journalistique** journalese; **2** (langage incorrect) ungrammatical language; (langue étrangère) foreign language, lingo○; (sabir) patois.

jargonner /ʒaʀgɔne/ [1] *vi* **1** (parler en jargon) [*spécialiste, bureaucrate*] to talk in jargon; **2** (parler de façon inintelligible) to talk gibberish; **3** Zool [*oie*] to honk.

Jarnac /ʒaʀnak/ *nprm* **coup de ~** decisive and unexpected blow; **recevoir un** or **le coup de ~** to be caught off guard.

jarre /ʒaʀ/ *nf* (earthenware) jar.

jarret /ʒaʀɛ/ *nm* **1** Anat (d'humain) ham, hollow of the knee; **avoir des ~s d'acier** to have strong legs; **2** Zool (d'animal) hock; **3** Culin **~ de veau/porc** knuckle of veal/pork.

jarretelle /ʒaʀtɛl/ *nf* suspender GB, garter US.

jarretière /ʒaʀtjɛʀ/ *nf* garter; **l'Ordre de la Jarretière** the Order of the Garter.

jars /ʒaʀ/ *nm* gander.

jaser /ʒaze/ [1] *vi* **1** (médire) to gossip (**sur** about); **on jase sur ses fréquentations** people are gossiping about the company he keeps; **ça fait ~** it sets people talking; **2** (jacasser) [*pie, geai, merle*] to chatter; **3** C (bavarder) [*personne*] to chat.

jaseur, **-euse** /ʒazœʀ, øz/ *nm,f* (personne médisante) gossip.

jasmin /ʒasmɛ̃/ *nm* **1** (arbuste) jasmine; **2** (parfum) jasmine; **thé au ~** jasmine tea.

jaspe /ʒasp/ *nm* **1** (pierre) jasper; **bijou en ~** piece of jasper jewellery GB ou jewelry US; **2** (objet en jaspe) jasper ornament.

jaspé, **~e** /ʒaspe/ *adj* mottled.

jaspiner◑ /ʒaspine/ [1] *vi* to chat.

jatte /ʒat/ *nf* bowl, basin.

jauge /ʒoʒ/ *nf* **1** (pour mesurer) gauge; **~ d'essence** petrol GB ou gas US gauge; **~ d'huile** dipstick; **2** (capacité) capacity; (de navire) tonnage.

jaugeage /ʒoʒaʒ/ *nm* gauging.

jauger /ʒoʒe/ [13] *vtr* **1** (évaluer) to size [sb] up [*personne*]; to get the measure of [*candidat, élève*]; to weigh [sth] up [*idée, avantage*]; to judge [*œuvre*]; **2** Tech to measure [*capacité, volume*]; **~ un réservoir** to measure the capacity of a reservoir; **3** Naut [*navire*] to have a tonnage of.

jaunâtre /ʒonɑtʀ/ **▶193** *adj* [*éclairage, tissu*] yellowish; [*teint, peau*] sallow.

jaune /ʒon/ **▶193** I *adj* **1** (couleur) yellow; **~ orange** orangy[GB] yellow; **elle a les dents ~s** she's got yellow teeth; **il a le teint ~** he's got a sallow complexion; **2** (asiatique) [*race, continent*] Asian.
II *nm* **1** (couleur) yellow; **s'habiller en ~** to wear yellow; **2** Culin **~ (d'œuf)** (egg) yolk; **séparer les blancs des ~s** separate the whites from the yolks; **3** (briseur de grève) pej blackleg GB péj, scab péj.
■ **~ canari** canary yellow; **~ citron** lemon yellow; **~ moutarde** mustard yellow; **~ d'or** golden yellow; **~ paille** straw-coloured[GB]; **~ poussin** bright yellow; **~ safran** saffron yellow.
IDIOMES **rire ~**○ to give a forced laugh.

Jaune /ʒon/ *nmf* (east) Asian.

jauni, **~e** /ʒoni/ I *pp* **▶jaunir**.
II *pp adj* [*papier, herbe*] yellowed; **doigts ~s par la nicotine** nicotine-stained fingers.

jaunir /ʒoniʀ/ [3] I *vtr* [*soleil*] to turn [sth] yellow [*papier, herbe*]; [*thé*] to make [sth] go yellow [*dents*]; [*nicotine*] to stain [*doigts*]; **le temps a jauni les photos** the photos have gone yellow with age.
II *vi* [*papier, tissu*] to go yellow.

jaunisse /ʒonis/ **▶271** *nf* Méd jaundice.
IDIOMES **il va en faire une ~**○! that's going to put his nose out of joint!

jaunissement /ʒonismɑ̃/ *nm* yellowing (**de** of).

java /ʒava/ *nf* **1** (danse) popular dance; **2**◑ (fête) rave-up○; **faire la ~** to rave it up○.

Java /ʒava/ **▶416** *nprf* Java.

javanais, **~e** /ʒavanɛ, ɛz/ **▶462** I *adj* Javanese.
II *nm* **1** Ling Javanese; **2** (jargon) *French spoken slang formed by adding 'av' in the middle of each syllable.*

Javanais, **~e** /ʒavanɛ, ɛz/ **▶537** *nm,f* Javanese.

Javel /ʒavɛl/ *nf* **(eau de) ~** ≈ bleach.

javeline /ʒavlin/ *nf* javelin.

javelle /ʒavɛl/ *nf* Agric swath.

javellisation /ʒavelizasjɔ̃/ *nf* chlorination.

javelliser /ʒavelize/ [1] *vtr* to chlorinate [*eau*]; **très javellisée** heavily chlorinated.

javelot /ʒavlo/ **▶449** *nm* **1** (objet) javelin; **2** Sport (discipline) **(lancer du) ~** javelin.

jazz /dʒaz/ *nm* jazz; **musique de ~** jazz (music).

jazzman, *pl* **jazzmen** /dʒazman, mɛn/ *nm* jazz musician, jazzman.

J.-C. (*written abbr* = **Jésus-Christ**) **avant ~** BC; **après ~** AD.

je[1] (**j'** *before vowel or mute h*) /ʒ(ə)/ *pron pers* I; **j'aimerais bien mais ~ ne peux pas** I'd like to but I can't; **comment dirais-~?** how shall I put it?

je[2] /ʒə/ *nm* Philos **le ~** the I.

jean /dʒin/ *nm* **1** (pantalon) jeans (*pl*); **ton ~ est déchiré** your jeans are ripped; **acheter un ~** to buy a pair of jeans; **2** (tissu) denim; **une chemise/un blouson en ~** a denim shirt/jacket.

Jean /ʒɑ̃/ *npr* John; **saint ~ Baptiste** St John the Baptist; **saint ~ de la Croix** St John of the Cross; **saint ~ l'Évangéliste** St John the Evangelist.
IDIOMES **c'est ~ qui rit et ~ qui pleure** one minute he's laughing, the next he's crying.

jean-foutre◑ /ʒɑ̃futʀ/ *nm inv* waster○, good-for-nothing.

Jeanne d'Arc /ʒandaʀk/ *npr* Joan of Arc.

jeannette /ʒanɛt/ *nf* **1** (pour repasser) sleeve board; **2** (en scoutisme) ≈ Brownie.

jeep /dʒip/ *nf* jeep.

Jéhovah /ʒeɔva/ *nm* Jehovah; **un témoin de ~** a Jehovah's witness.

je-m'en-foutisme○ /ʒ(ə)mɑ̃futism/ *nm inv* couldn't-care-less attitude.

je-m'en-foutiste○, *pl* **~s** /ʒ(ə)mɑ̃futist/ *nmf* person with a couldn't-care-less attitude.

je-ne-sais-quoi /ʒənsɛkwa/ *nm inv* **avoir un ~** to have a certain something.

jérémiades /ʒeʀemjad/ *nfpl* moaning ¢; **cesse tes ~** stop moaning.

Jérémie /ʒeʀemi/ *npr* Jeremiah.

Jéricho /ʒeʀiko/ **▶857** *npr* Jericho.

jéroboam /ʒeʀɔboam/ *nm* jeroboam.

jerrican /ʒeʀikan/ *nm* five-gallon container, jerrycan.

jersey /ʒɛʀzɛ/ *nm* **1** (en tricot) stocking stitch; **au point de ~** in stocking stitch; **2** Ind, Tex jersey; **jupe en ~** jersey skirt.

Jersey /ʒɛʀzɛ/ **▶ 416** *nprf* Jersey.

Jérusalem /ʒeʀyzalɛm/ **▶ 857** *npr* Jerusalem.

jésuite /ʒezɥit/ **I** *adj* **1** Relig [*noviciat, style*] Jesuit; **2** (hypocrite) Jesuitical.
II *nm* Jesuit.

jésuitique /ʒezɥitik/ *adj* Jesuitical.

jésuitisme /ʒezɥitism/ *nm* Jesuitism.

jésus /ʒezy/ *nm* **1** (statue) statue of the infant Jesus; **2** (saucisson) ≈ coarse salami; **3** Imprim (**papier**) **~** ≈ super royal; **4** (terme d'affection) **mon ~** my little angel.

Jésus /ʒezy/ **I** *npr* Jesus; **l'enfant ~** the infant Jesus GB, the Christ child; **le petit ~** baby Jesus.
II○ *excl* **~ (Marie)!** Jesus!; **doux ~!** good God!

Jésus-Christ /ʒezykʀi/ *npr* Jesus Christ.

jet[1] /ʒɛ/ *nm* **1** (lancer) (action) throwing ¢; (distance) throw; **les ~s de pierres peuvent être mortels** stone throwing can be lethal; **un ~ de 30 mètres au disque** Sport a 30-metre[GB] discus-throw; **à un ~ de pierre** a stone's throw away (**de** from); **accueilli par des ~s de pierres/d'injures** greeted with a volley of stones/of insults; **2** (jaillissement) (de liquide, vapeur) jet; (de salive) spurt; (de flammes) burst; (de lumière) flash; **~ d'eau bouillante** jet of boiling water; **~ de sable** Tech sand-blast; **premier ~** fig first sketch ou attempt; **du premier ~** at the first attempt; **passer au ~** to hose down [*voiture, sol*]; **à ~ continu** [*parler, écrire*] nonstop; **3** Tech (coulage) cast(ing); **d'un seul ~** [*couler*] in one piece; [*écrire*] in one go; **4** Bot, Hort (pousse) shoot.
■ **~ d'eau** (fontaine, jaillissement) fountain; (de tuyau) hosepipe; (de fenêtre) weathering.

jet[2] /dʒɛt/ *nm* Aviat jet.

jetable /ʒətabl/ *adj* [*briquet, rasoir, couche*] disposable.

jeté, **~e** /ʒəte/ **I**○ *adj* (fou) crazy; **elle est complètement ~e** she's completely crazy.
II *nm* **1** Danse jeté; **2** Sport (en haltérophilie) jerk; **3** (en tricot) **une maille envers, un ~** purl one, wool round needle (once).
III jetée *nf* **1** (sur l'eau) pier; (plus petite) jetty; **2** (d'aéroport) terminal corridor.
■ **~ de lit** bedspread; **~ de table** runner.

jeter /ʒəte/ [20] **I** *vtr* **1** (lancer) to throw [*caillou, dé*]; (avec force) to hurl, fling [*objet*]; **~ qch à qn** (pour qu'il l'attrape) to throw sth to sb; (pour faire mal, peur) to throw sth at sb; **~ un os à un chien** to throw a dog a bone; **~ une assiette à la tête de qn** to throw a plate at sb; **~ qch par terre/sur la table/en l'air** to throw sth to the ground/on the table/(up) in the air; **~ une bûche dans la cheminée** to throw a log on the fire; **~ les bras autour du cou de qn** to throw ou fling one's arms around sb's neck; **~ le buste en avant/la tête en arrière** to throw one's chest out/one's head back; **2** (placer rapidement) to throw (**dans** into; **sur** over); (étaler) **~ une couverture sur un matelas/un blessé** to throw a blanket over a mattress/an injured person; **~ une lettre à la boîte** to drop a letter into the letter-box; **~ quelques idées sur le papier** fig to jot down a few ideas; **3** (se débarrasser) to throw away ou out [*vieilleries, ordures*]; **~ qch à la poubelle** to throw sth out, to throw sth in the bin GB ou the garbage US; **être bon à ~** to be fit for the bin GB ou the garbage US; **▶ froc**; **4** (expédier) **~ qn dehors/par la fenêtre** to throw sb out/out of the window; **~ qn en prison** to throw sb in jail; **~ bas** to flatten [*adversaire, immeuble*]; **se faire ~**○ to get oneself thrown out; **~ qn**○ to throw sb out; **5** (émettre) to give [*cri*]; to throw [*lumière, ombre*]; to cast [*reflet*]; **~ un vif éclat** to shine brightly; **~ mille feux** to sparkle; **en ~**○ [*personne, voiture*] to be quite something○; **▶ vu VI**; **6** (construire) to build [*pont*]; to forge [*lien*]; to lay [*fondations*]; **~ un pont sur un cours d'eau** to bridge a river, to throw a bridge across a river; **7** (causer) to create [*confusion*] (**dans** in; **parmi** among); to cause [*consternation*]; to sow [*terreur*]; to instil[GB] [*vie*]; **~ l'émoi dans la ville** to throw the town into turmoil; **8** (plonger) **~ qn dans** to throw sb into; **~ qn dans le désespoir** to throw sb into despair; **~ le pays dans le désordre** to throw the country into chaos; **9** (lancer en paroles) to hurl [*insultes*] (**à qn** to sb); **'tu es fou,' jeta-t-elle** 'you must be mad,' she said; **~ quelques commentaires** (dans une discussion) to put in a few comments; **~ qch à la tête** or **au visage de qn** to throw sth in sb's face [*vérité, défi*].
II se jeter *vpr* **1** (se précipiter) [*personne*] to throw oneself; **se ~ du haut d'un pont/par la fenêtre/dans le canal** to throw oneself off a bridge/out of the window/into the canal; **se ~ aux pieds de qn/dans les bras de qn** to throw oneself at sb's feet/into sb's arms; **se ~ sur** to fall upon [*adversaire*]; to pounce on [*proie, nourriture, journal*]; **se ~ au cou de qn** to fling oneself around sb's neck; **se ~ à l'eau** lit to jump into the water; fig to take the plunge; (**aller**) **se ~ contre un arbre** [*conducteur, voiture*] to drive headlong into a tree; **se ~ tête baissée dans qch** to rush headlong into sth; **se ~ à la tête de qn** to throw oneself at sb; **▶ cravate**; **2** (être jetable) to be disposable; **3** (être mis au rebut) to be disposed of; **où est-ce que les bouteilles se jettent?** where do the bottles ou empties○ go?; **4** [*cours d'eau*] to flow (**dans** into).
IDIOMES **n'en jetez plus (la cour est pleine)**○ hold your horses○.

jeteur, **-euse** /ʒətœʀ, øz/ *nm,f* thrower.
■ **~ de sort** sorcerer; **jeteuse de sort** sorceress.

jeton /ʒ(ə)tɔ̃/ **I** *nm* **1** (pour un appareil) token; (pour un jeu de société) counter; (au casino) chip; **▶ faux**[1]; **2**◑ (coup) punch; **prendre un ~**◑ [*personne*] to get punched; [*voiture*] to get dented.
II *nmpl* **avoir les ~s**◑ to be scared stiff; **donner les ~s à qn**◑ to put the wind up sb○, to scare sb shitless◑.
■ **~ de présence** director's fee.

jet-set /dʒɛtsɛt/ *nm* jet-set.

jet-ski /dʒɛtski/ **▶ 449** *nm* Sport **1** (activité) jet-skiing; **2** (embarcation) jet-ski.

jeu, *pl* **~x** /ʒø/ **▶ 449** *nm* **1** Jeux, Sport (activité) **le ~** gén play ¢; (avec de l'argent) gambling ¢; (type) **un ~** a game; **le ~ est nécessaire au développement de l'enfant** play is necessary to a child's development; **apprendre par le ~** to learn through play; **perdre une fortune au ~** to lose a fortune in gambling; **on va faire un ~** let's play a game; **les règles du ~** the rules of the game; **ce n'était qu'un ~** it was only a game; **jouer (un) double ~** fig to play a double game; **à quel ~ joue-t-il?** fig what's his game?; **il y a une part de ~ dans leur attitude** they're never completely serious about things; **il fait ça par ~** he does it for fun; **je lui ai dit ça par ~ mais elle m'a cru** I told her that for fun but she believed me; **ils se livrent déjà au petit ~ de deviner qui le remplacera** they're already having fun trying to guess who will replace him; **ce fut un ~ (d'enfant) pour lui de résoudre cette énigme** it was child's play for him to solve this enigma; **ton avenir est en ~** your future is at stake; **entrer en ~** fig to come into the picture; **d'entrée de ~** right from the start; **se prendre** or **se piquer au ~** to get hooked; **il s'est pris au ~ de la politique** he got hooked on politics; **se laisser prendre au (petit) ~ de qn** to fall for sb's (little) game; **être pris** or **se prendre à son propre ~** to be caught at one's own game; **battre qn à son propre ~** to beat sb at his/her own game; **mettre en ~** to put [sth] into play [*ballon, balle*]; to bring [sth] into play [*éléments, facteurs, données*]; to stake [*somme, objet, titre, honneur*]; **remettre la balle en ~** to put the ball back into play; **remise en ~** (au football, après une touche) throw; (au hockey, après un but) face-off; **mettre tout en ~ pour faire** to go all out to do; **être hors ~** (au football) to be offside; **ils ont beau ~ de me critiquer** it's easy for them to criticize me; **2** Jeux, Sport (manche) game; **il a gagné (par) trois ~x à deux** he won by three games to two; **3** Jeux (main aux cartes) hand; **avoir un bon** or **beau ~** to have a good hand; **avoir du ~** to have a good hand; **cacher son ~** lit to conceal one's hand; fig not to show one's hand; **4** Comm, Jeux (matériel) (d'échecs, de dames) set; (de cartes) deck; (de société) game; **5** (manière de jouer) (d'acteur) acting ¢; (de musicien) playing ¢; (de footballeur, joueur de tennis) game; **~ sobre/brillant** (d'acteur) restrained/brilliant acting; **~ défensif** or **fermé** defensive game; **~ d'attaque** or **ouvert** attacking game; **6** (série) set; **~ de clés/tournevis** set of keys/screwdrivers; **~ d'épreuves** Imprim set of proofs; **7** (interaction, effet) (de reflets, d'ombres) play; (de rapprochements, forces, d'alliances) interplay; **le libre ~ des associations/de l'imagination** the free play of associations/of the imagination; **effet spécial obtenu par un ~ de miroirs** special effect obtained by mirrors; **8** (possibilité de mouvement) Mécan play; Anat free movement; **le ~ des pistons** the play of the pistons; **le ~ des articulations/muscles** the free movement of joints/muscles; **il n'y a pas assez de ~** there's not enough play; **il y a du** or **trop de ~** there's too much play; **donner du ~ à** to loosen; **▶ chandelle**, **épingle**, **heureux**, **quille**, **vieux**, **vilain**.
■ **~ d'adresse** Jeux game of skill; **~ d'argent** Jeux, Turf game played for money; **jouer à des ~ d'argent** to gamble; **~ de caractères** Ordinat character set; **~ codé** Ordinat coded set; **~ de construction** Jeux (activité) construction game; (pièces) construction set; **~ d'écritures** Compta juggling ¢ the books; **grâce à un ~ d'écritures** by juggling the books; **~ éducatif** Jeux educational game; **~ d'équipe** Sport team game; **~ d'éveil** Jeux early-learning game; **~ d'extérieur** Jeux outdoor game; **~ de hasard** Jeux game of chance; **la vie est un ~ de hasard** fig life is a lottery; **~ d'initialisation** Ordinat initialization deck; **~ d'intérieur** Jeux indoor game; **~ de jambes** Sport footwork; **~ de massacre** Jeux ≈ coconut shy GB; fig massacre; **~ de mots** Ling pun; **~ de l'oie** Jeux ≈ snakes and ladders GB; **~ d'orgue** Mus organ stop; **~ de paume** Sport (activité) real tennis; (terrain) real tennis court; **~ de piste** Jeux treasure hunt; **~ radiophonique** Radio radio game show; **~ de rôles** Scol role playing ¢; **~ de scène** Théât stage business; **~ de société** Jeux (échecs, monopoly® etc) board game; (charades etc) party game; **~ télévisé** TV (TV) game show; **~ vidéo** Vidéo video game; **~ à XIII** Sport rugby league; **~x de grattage** Jeux scratchcards; **Jeux Olympiques**, **JO** Sport Olympic Games, Olympics; **Jeux Olympiques d'été/d'hiver** Summer/Winter Olympics.
IDIOMES **jouer le ~** to play the game; **jouer le grand ~** to pull all the stops out○; **c'est pas de** or **du ~**○**!** that's not fair!; **faire le ~ de qn** to play into sb's hands; **'faites vos ~x'** (au casino) 'faites vos jeux'; **'les ~x sont faits'** (au casino) 'les jeux sont faits'; fig 'the die is cast'.

jeu-concours, *pl* **jeux-concours** /ʒøkɔ̃kuʀ/ *nm* competition; **participer à un ~** to enter a competition.

jeudi /ʒødi/ **▶ 750** *nm* Thursday.
■ **~ de l'Ascension** Relig Ascension day;

Les jeux et les sports

Les noms de jeux et de sports

En anglais, tous les noms de jeux et de sports sont singuliers. Ils ne prennent pas d'article défini.

le football = football
j'aime le football = I like football
les échecs = chess
j'aime les échecs = I like chess
les règles des échecs = the rules of chess
jouer aux échecs = to play chess
savez-vous jouer aux échecs? = can you play chess?
faire une partie d'échecs = to play a game of chess
faire un bridge = to have a game of bridge

Certains noms de jeux et de sports ont une forme de pluriel, mais ils se comportent tout de même comme des singuliers: billiards, bowls, checkers, darts, dominoes, draughts *etc.*

les dominos sont un jeu facile = dominoes is easy
le jeu de boules est pratiqué par les dames et les messieurs = bowls is played both by men and women

Les noms des joueurs

Certains noms de sportifs en anglais se forment en ajoutant -er au nom du sport.

un footballeur = a footballer
un golfeur = a golfer
un coureur de 100 mètres = a 100-metre runner
un coureur de haies = a hurdler

Mais ceci n'est pas toujours possible. Par contre, pour les sports d'équipe, on peut toujours utiliser le mot player *précédé du nom du sport.*

un joueur de football = a football player
un joueur de rugby = a rugby player

En cas de doute, consulter l'article dans le dictionnaire.

Pour les noms de personnes qui jouent à des jeux, on utilise la même construction avec player.

un joueur d'échecs = a chess player

Noter que dans les exemples suivants chess *peut être remplacé par presque tous les noms de sports et de jeux. En cas de doute, consulter l'article dans le dictionnaire.*

il joue très bien aux échecs = he's very good at chess *ou* he's a very good chess player
un champion d'échecs = a chess champion
le champion du monde d'échecs = the world chess champion
je ne joue pas aux échecs = I am not a chess player *ou* I don't play chess

Les événements

une partie d'échecs = a game of chess
jouer aux échecs avec qn = to play chess with sb
jouer aux échecs contre qn = to play chess against sb
gagner une partie d'échecs = to win a game of chess
battre qn aux échecs = to beat sb at chess
perdre une partie d'échecs = to lose a game of chess
jouer dans l'équipe d'Angleterre = to play for England
gagner le championnat de Grande-Bretagne = to win the British championship
j'espère que l'Angleterre va gagner = I hope England wins
Douai a perdu 2 à zéro = Douai lost 2 nil
Nantes 2–Lyon 0 = *dire* Nantes two, Douai nil
il est arrivé quatrième = he came fourth

De *avec les noms de jeux et de sports:*

un championnat d'échecs = a chess championship
un club d'échecs = a chess club
l'équipe d'Angleterre d'échecs = the English chess team
un fan d'échecs = a chess enthusiast

L'anglais utilise la même construction dans des cas où le français a un mot différent, par ex.:

un échiquier = a chess board

Mais:

les règles des échecs = the rules of chess
une partie d'échecs = a game of chess (a chess game *est possible, mais moins fréquent*)

En cas de doute, consulter l'article dans le dictionnaire.

Activités sportives

Les jeux:

faire du tennis/rugby = to play tennis/rugby

Les arts martiaux et disciplines:

faire du judo/de la boxe/de la gymnastique = to do judo/boxing/gymnastics

Les activités de plein air:

faire de l'équitation/de l'aviron/du jogging = to go riding/rowing/jogging

Les jeux de cartes

Noter que dans les exemples suivants clubs *pourrait être remplacé par* hearts, spades *ou* diamonds.

le huit de trèfle = the eight of clubs
l'as de trèfle = the ace of clubs
jouer le huit de trèfle = to play the eight of clubs
l'atout est trèfle = clubs are trumps
demander du trèfle = to call clubs
as-tu du trèfle? = do you have clubs?

~ noir Hist Black Thursday; **~ saint** Relig Maundy Thursday.
IDIOMES **ça aura lieu la semaine des quatre ~s**○! never in a month of Sundays!

jeun: **à jeun** /aʒœ̃/ *loc adv* **1** (l'estomac vide) [*partir, boire, fumer*] on an empty stomach; **être à ~ pour une prise de sang/opération** Méd to have had nothing to eat or drink on the day of a blood test/an operation; **soyez à ~** don't eat or drink anything; **2**○ (qui n'a pas bu d'alcool) sober.

jeune /ʒœn/ **I** *adj* **1** (non vieux) [*personne, public, clientèle*] young; [*animal, arbre, montagne*] young; [*pays, vin*] young; [*industrie*] new; [*allure, coiffure, visage*] youthful; **il est tout ~** he's very young; **elle n'est plus très ~** she's not so young anymore; **un ~ garçon/homme** a young boy/man; **une ~ femme/personne** a young woman/person; **les ~s gens** young people; **le ~ Sartre** the young Sartre; **être ~ de caractère** to be young at heart; **être ~ d'esprit** to be young in spirit; **un corps encore ~** a youthful body; **des ~s pousses** young shoots; **les ~s générations** the younger generation (*sg*); **nos ~s années** the years of our youth; **le ~ âge** youth; **2** (cadet) (*avant n*) [*frère, sœur, fils, fille*] younger; **c'est mon ~ frère** he's my younger brother; **leur plus ~ fille** their youngest daughter; **être plus ~ que qn** to be younger than sb; **être moins ~ que qn** to be older than sb; **Pline le Jeune** Pliny the Younger; **3** (nouveau dans son état) (*avant n*) [*médecin, avocat*] newly-qualified; [*chanteur, député, champion, mère, père, équipe*] new; **un ~ diplômé** a new graduate; **être ~ dans le métier** to be new to the trade; **un ~ couple** a young couple; **le ~ marié** the groom; **la ~ mariée** the bride; **les ~s mariés** the newlyweds; **4** (naïf) naïve; **que tu es ~!** how naïve you are!; **5**○ (insuffisant) **un bouteille pour six, c'est un peu ~!** one bottle between six people, that's not much!
II *nmf* young person; **c'est un ~ qui m'a répondu** a young man answered me; **les ~s** young people; **place aux ~s!** make way for the young!; **les ~s comme les vieux** young and old alike.
III *adv* **s'habiller ~** to dress young; **se coiffer ~** to wear one's hair in a young style; **faire ~** [*personne*] to look young; **ça fait ~ de porter un jean** wearing jeans makes you look young.
■ **~ cadre dynamique** dynamic young executive; **~ fille** girl; **~ loup** up and coming executive; **~ premier** Théât, Cin romantic lead.

jeûne /ʒøn/ *nm* **1** (privation) fasting; **pratiquer** or **observer le ~** to fast; **jour de ~** fast day; **2** (période) period of fasting.

jeûner /ʒøne/ [1] *vi* Méd, Relig to fast.

jeunesse /ʒœnɛs/ *nf* **1** (période) youth; **dans ma ~** in my youth; **la première** or **prime ~** early youth; **le charme de la ~** the charms of youth; **une seconde ~** a new lease of life; **il n'a pas eu de ~** he didn't have a proper youth; **un amour de ~** an early girlfriend/boyfriend; **une erreur de ~** a youthful error; **il n'est plus de la première ~** hum he's no longer in the first flush of youth hum; **2** (fait d'être jeune) youth; **la ~ des candidats** the fact that the candidates are young, the youthfulness of the candidates; **quand on a la ~, tout est possible** when you are young, everything is possible; **3** (comme qualité) youthfulness; **la ~ de sa voix** the youthfulness of his/her voice; **avoir un air de ~** to look young; **avoir une grande ~ d'esprit** to be young in spirit; **être plein de ~** to be full of vitality; **4** (les jeunes) young people (*pl*); **la ~ ouvrière** young working people; **l'entrain de la ~** the enthusiasm of the young; **littérature/émissions pour la ~** literature/programmes[GB] for young people; **la ~ étudiante** students (*pl*); ▶ **vieillesse**; **5**○ †(femme) young woman.
■ **~ dorée** bright young things (*pl*), gilded youth; **~s communistes** Communist youth movement (*sg*); **~s hitlériennes** Hist, Pol Hitler Youth; **Jeunesses musicales (de France)** *organization promoting musical activities for young people.*
IDIOMES **il faut que ~ se passe** youth must have its fling; **les voyages forment la ~** travel broadens the mind.

jeunet○, **-ette** /ʒœnɛ, ɛt/ **I** *adj* young.
II *nm,f* (garçon) young lad; (fille) young girl.

jeûneur, **-euse** /ʒønœʀ, øz/ *nm,f* faster.

jeunot○, **-otte** /ʒœno, ɔt/ **I** *adj* young.
II *nm* young lad.

jf *nf*: *written abbr* = **jeune fille** or **femme**.

jh *nm*: *written abbr* = **jeune homme**.

jiu-jitsu /ʒjyʒitsy/ ▶ **449** *nm* jiu-jitsu.

JO /ʒio/ **I** *nm*: *abbr* ▶ **journal**.
II *nmpl*: *abbr* ▶ **jeu**.

joaillerie /ʒoajʀi/ *nf* **1** (technique) jewellery-making GB, jewelry-making US; (métier) jewellery GB ou jewelry US (trade); **2** ▶ **510** (magasin) jeweller's shop GB, jewelry store US; **3** (articles) jewellery GB, jewelry US.

joaillier, **-ière** /ʒɔalje, ɛʀ/ **I** *adj* [*industrie*] jewellery GB, jewelry US.
II ▶510 *nm,f* jeweller.

job○ /dʒɔb/ *nm* (travail) job; (petit boulot) casual job; (pour les vacances) summer job.

Job /ʒɔb/ *npr* Job; **le livre de ~** the Book of Job.
IDIOMES **pauvre comme ~** as poor as a church mouse.

jobard○, **~e** /ʒɔbaʀ, aʀd/ **I** *adj* [*personne*] gullible.
II *nm,f* (naïf) sucker○.

jobardise○ /ʒɔbaʀdiz/ *nf* gullibility.

jockey /ʒɔkɛ/ *nm* jockey.

Joconde /ʒɔkɔ̃d/ *npr* **la ~** the Mona Lisa.

jocrisse† /ʒɔkʀis/ *nm* ninny†.

jodler = **yodler**.

joggeur, **-euse** /dʒɔgœʀ, øz/ *nm,f* jogger.

jogging /dʒɔgiŋ/ *nm* **1** ▶449 (activité) jogging; **chaussures de ~** trainers GB, running shoes; **2** (séance) **faire son ~ quotidien** to go for one's daily jog; **3** (survêtement) track suit.

joie /ʒwa/ **I** *nf* **1** (bonheur) joy; **la ~ éclairait son visage** his/her face glowed with joy; **être au comble de la ~** to be overjoyed; **~ sans mélange** or **sans partage** pure joy; **cette enfant fait la ~ de ses parents** this child is the pride and joy of her parents; **la ~ de faire** the joy ou pleasure of doing; **la ~ de retrouver sa maison** the joy ou pleasure of getting back home; **des cris de ~** cries of joy; **il y a eu des explosions de ~ dans toute la ville** the whole town erupted with joy; **c'est une ~ de le regarder** he's a joy to look at; **quelle ~!** how wonderful!; **être ivre de ~** to be drunk with happiness ou delight; **sauter/pleurer de ~** to jump/cry for joy; **avoir de la ~ au cœur** to have a cheerful disposition; **un enfant plein de ~** a happy ou sunny child; **beaucoup de ~** great happiness; **faire la ~ de qn** to gladden ou delight sb, to make sb happy; **être en ~** to be delighted; **mettre qn en ~** to delight sb; **pour** or **à la plus grande ~ de qn** to sb's great delight; **être tout à la ~ de faire** to be carried away by the thrill of doing; **c'est la ~ dans les rues** happiness reigns in the streets; **'comment ça va au travail?'—'c'est pas la ~**○**!'** 'how are things at work?'—'not great○!'; **2** (plaisir) pleasure; **cela a été une ~ de vous recevoir** it has been a pleasure to have ou having you; **exprimer/dire sa ~ de faire** to express one's pleasure at doing; **avoir la ~ de faire** to have the pleasure of doing; **accepter qch avec ~** to accept sth with pleasure; **se faire une ~ de faire** (envisager avec plaisir) to look forward to doing; (faire avec plaisir) to be delighted to do; ▶**faux**[1]; **3** (source de plaisir) pleasure, joy; **leurs seules ~s** their only pleasures.
II joies *nfpl* (aspects agréables) (du monde, des sens) pleasures; (de l'amour, d'une activité) pleasures, joys; **goûter aux ~s de l'amour** to taste the joys of love; **s'adonner/se livrer aux ~s de qch** to devote oneself to/to give oneself over to the joys of sth.
■ **~ de vivre** joie de vivre, exuberance.
IDIOMES **s'en donner à cœur ~** lit to enjoy oneself to the full; fig to have a field day.

joignable /ʒwaɲabl/ *adj* **il n'est pas ~ en ce moment** he can't be reached (on the phone) at the moment.

joindre /ʒwɛ̃dʀ/ [56] **I** *vtr* **1** (communiquer avec) to reach, to get hold of [*personne*]; **chercher à ~ qn** to try to reach ou get hold of sb; **~ qn au téléphone** to get in touch with sb by telephone; **2** (ajouter) (dans une lettre, un paquet) to enclose [*timbre, chèque*] (**à** with); (en agrafant, fixant) to attach (**à** to); **je joins un cadeau/livre à mon envoi** I am sending a gift/book as well; **les avantages joints à l'emploi** the advantages that come with the job; **~ sa voix au concert de protestations** to add one's voice to the chorus of protest; **3** (relier) [*rue, pont, passage*] to link, to join (**à** with); **~ qch à qch** to link sth with sth; **4** (allier) **~ qch à qch** to combine sth with sth; **~ l'intelligence à la simplicité** to combine intelligence with simplicity; **5** (mettre ensemble) to join, to put [sth] together [*planches, tôles*]; **~ les pieds** to put one's feet together; **~ deux objets bout à bout** to put two things end to end; **~ des plaques de métal par une soudure** to weld sheets of metal together; **6** Jur [*tribunal, juge*] to combine [*procès, course*].
II *vi* (coïncider) [*planche*] to fit properly; [*fenêtre, porte*] to shut ou close properly.
III se joindre *vpr* **1** (se mêler) **se ~ à** to join [*personne, famille, groupe*]; to join with [*mouvement, groupe, parti*]; to mix with [*sentiment, émotion*]; to be added to [*problème, crise, ennui*]; **toute la famille se joint à moi pour vous souhaiter une bonne année** all the family join me in wishing you a happy New Year; **se ~ à la foule** to mix ou mingle with the crowd; **se ~ à la conversation** to join in the conversation; **2** (s'unir) [*lèvres*] to meet; [*mains*] to join.
IDIOMES **~ les deux bouts**○ to make ends meet.

joint /ʒwɛ̃/ *nm* **1** Constr, Tech (de planches, meubles, fenêtres) joint; (de robinet) washer; (de tuyauterie) seal; (de carrelage, briques) joint; **2** Aut joint; **3** Anat joint; **4**○ (cigarette de drogue) joint○.
■ **~ de cardan** Aut cardan joint; **~ de culasse** Aut cylinder head gasket; **~ de dilatation** expansion joint; **~ d'étanchéité** seal.
IDIOMES **peux-tu me prêter un peu d'argent pour faire le ~**○ **(jusqu'en septembre)** could you lend me some money to tide me over (till September); **chercher/trouver le ~**○ to look for/to find the answer.

jointif, **-ive** /ʒwɛ̃tif, iv/ *adj* [*planches*] butt-jointed, edge-to-edge; [*cloison*] abutting, contiguous.

jointoiement /ʒwɛ̃twamɑ̃/ *nm* Constr pointing.

jointoyer /ʒwɛ̃twaje/ [23] *vtr* Constr to point.

jointure /ʒwɛ̃tyʀ/ *nf* Anat, Tech joint; **la ~ du genou** the knee joint.

joint-venture, *pl* **joint-ventures** /dʒɔjntvɛntʃəʀ/ controv *nm* joint venture; **signer un ~** to sign a joint-venture agreement.

jojo○ /ʒoʒo/ **I** *adj inv* (*always neg*) nice; **il n'est pas ~ ton chapeau** your hat isn't very nice; **ce n'est pas ~ ce qu'ils lui ont fait** (moralement) it wasn't very nice what they did to him/her; (physiquement) they made a mess of him/her○.
II *nm* **un affreux ~** (enfant) a horrible brat○; (drôle d'individu) a weirdo○.

joker /ʒɔkɛʀ/ *nm* **1** (aux cartes) joker; **2** fig trump card; **sortir/jouer/utiliser son ~** to bring out/play/use one's trump card; **3** Sport (en sport d'équipe) all-round substitute; **4** Ordinat wild card.

joli, **~e** /ʒɔli/ **I** *adj* **1** (beau) [*fille, femme*] pretty; [*garçon*] handsome, good-looking; [*animal, meuble, objet*] handsome, lovely; [*vêtement, fleur, visage, trait, yeux*] pretty, lovely; [*maison, paysage, jardin, œuvre, mot, tableau*] nice, lovely; [*vase, coup de crayon*] nice, pleasing; **faire ~** to look nice, look good; **ça fait ~ ce meuble dans ta chambre** this piece of furniture looks nice in your room; **ce n'est pas ~ (de faire)** it's not nice (to do); **ce n'était pas ~ à voir** it wasn't a pretty sight; **c'est ~ de dire du mal de ses parents** iron that's a fine thing saying nasty things about one's parents; **c'est ~ de faire cela!** that's a fine thing to do!; **c'est ~ d'avoir fait cela!** that was a fine thing to do!; **2** (non négligeable) [*somme, bénéfice*] nice; [*situation, profession*] good; [*coup de publicité, résultat, réussite*] great; [*coup de pied, but*] great, nice.
II *nm* **1** (ce qui est intéressant) **le plus ~ c'est que** the funny ou funniest thing is (that); **il t'a raconté le plus ~?** did he tell you the best part?; **2** (action répréhensible) iron **c'est du ~ de voler dans les magasins** that's a fine thing to do, stealing from shops GB ou stores US iron.
■ **~ cœur** smooth talker; **faire le ~ cœur** to play Romeo.
IDIOMES **être ~ à croquer** or **comme un cœur** to be as pretty as a picture.

joliesse /ʒɔljɛs/ *nf* prettiness.

joliment /ʒɔlimɑ̃/ *adv* **1** (agréablement) [*meublé, illustré, décoré*] prettily, nicely; [*dire*] nicely; **comme l'a ~ dit X** as X so nicely put it; **2**○ (remarquablement) [*content, battu, bien*] really; [*manœuvrer*] nicely; **nous nous sommes ~ battus** we fought really hard; **il s'est fait ~ recevoir** iron he got a fine reception.

Jonas /ʒɔnas/ *npr* Jonah.

jonc /ʒɔ̃/ *nm* **1** (plante) rush; **2** (en bijouterie) (bague) plain band; (bracelet) plain bangle.

jonchée /ʒɔ̃ʃe/ *nf* liter **une ~ de papiers couvrait le tapis** papers were strewn all over the carpet.

joncher /ʒɔ̃ʃe/ [1] *vtr* [*papiers, vêtements, ordures*] to litter, to be strewn over [*sol, plancher etc*]; [*feuilles, pétales*] to be strewn over [*sol*]; **~ le sol de** to strew the ground with; **être jonché de** to be strewn with.

jonchets /ʒɔ̃ʃɛ/ *nmpl* spillikins (+ *v sg*) GB, jackstraws (+ *v sg*).

jonction /ʒɔ̃ksjɔ̃/ *nf* **1** (point de rencontre) junction; **à la ~** at the junction; **point de ~** meeting point; **2** (action de joindre) link-up; **faire une ~ entre A et B** to link up A and B; **3** Mil link-up; **opérer une ~** [*armée, manifestants*] to link up; **4** Électrotech junction.

joncture /ʒɔ̃ktyʀ/ *nf* juncture.

jonglage /ʒɔ̃glaʒ/ *nm* juggling.

jongler /ʒɔ̃gle/ [1] *vi* to juggle (**avec** with); **~ avec les chiffres/horaires** fig to juggle figures/timetables.

jongleur, **-euse** /ʒɔ̃glœʀ, øz/ ▶510 *nm,f* **1** (de cirque) juggler; **2**† (ménestrel) jongleur.

jonque /ʒɔ̃k/ *nf* Naut junk.

jonquille /ʒɔ̃kij/ ▶193 **I** *adj inv*, *nm* (couleur) daffodil yellow.
II *nf* Bot daffodil.

Jordanie /ʒɔʀdani/ ▶321 *nprf* Jordan.

jordanien, **-ienne** /ʒɔʀdanjɛ̃, ɛn/ ▶537 *adj* Jordanian.

Jordanien, **-ienne** /ʒɔʀdanjɛ̃, ɛn/ ▶537 *nm,f* Jordanian.

Josué /ʒozɥe/ *npr* Joshua.

jouable /ʒwabl/ *adj* **1** (faisable) feasible; **le coup est** or **c'est ~** it's feasible; **la partie n'est pas ~ sans capitaux** it's not feasible without capital; **le pari est ~** the gamble might pay off; **2** (qu'on peut jouer) [*composition, musique, morceau*] playable; **une pièce qui n'est pas ~** a play that's impossible to stage.

joual /ʒual/ ▶462 *nm* joual.

joue /ʒu/ ▶188 *nf* **1** Anat cheek; **avoir de bonnes ~s** to have plump cheeks; **~ contre ~** cheek to cheek; **tendre** or **présenter l'autre ~** Bible to turn the other cheek; **~ de bœuf** Culin ox cheek; **2** Mil **en ~!** aim!; **mettre qn/qch en ~** to take aim at sb/sth; **tenir qn en ~** to train one's gun on sb; **3** Naut bow; **4** (de meuble) side panel.

jouer /ʒwe/ [1] **I** *vtr* **1** Jeux, Sport, Turf to play [*match, jeu, partie*]; to play [*carte, couleur, atout*]; to move [*pièce d'échecs, pion de dames*]; to back [*cheval, favori*]; to stake [*somme, argent, objet*]; to risk [*réputation, vie*]; **partie mal jouée** poorly played game; **~ carreau** to play diamonds; **~ un cheval gagnant/placé** to back a horse to win/for a place; **jouons le dîner à la courte**

paille let's draw straws to see who pays for dinner; **c'est joué d'avance** it's a foregone conclusion; **tout n'est pas encore joué** there's everything to play for; **~ le tout pour le tout** to go for broke○; ▶ **pendable**; **2** Mus to play [*morceau, compositeur, disque*] (**à** on); **~ du Bach à la guitare** to play some Bach on the guitar; **concerto admirablement joué** beautifully played concerto; **3** Cin, Théât [*personne*] to perform [*pièce, auteur*]; [*personne*] to play [*rôle, personnage*]; [*cinéma*] to show [*film*]; [*théâtre*] *to put on* [*pièce*]; **l'auteur le plus joué de France** the most frequently performed playwright in France; **mon rêve est de ~ Figaro** my dream is to play Figaro; **faire ~ une pièce** to stage a play; **quel film joue-t-on au Rex?** what film is showing at the Rex?; **théâtre qui ne joue que de l'avant-garde** theatre[GB] that only puts on avant-garde plays; ▶ **fille**, **scène**; **4** (incarner) **~ les imbéciles** to play dumb; **~ les innocents** or **l'innocent** to play the innocent; **~ le désespoir/la surprise** to pretend to be in despair/surprised; **~ les héros** to take unnecessary risks.

II jouer à *vtr ind* to play [*tennis, échecs, roulette*]; to play with [*poupée*]; to play [*cowboy, Tarzan*]; to bet on [*courses*]; **à quoi jouez-vous?** lit what are you playing?; fig what are you playing at?; **~ à qui perd gagne** to play 'loser takes all'; **~ à la marchande/au docteur** to play shops/doctors and nurses; **~ au con**◐ to play dumb; ▶ **souris**.

III jouer de *vtr ind* **1** Mus **~ de** to play [*instrument*]; **~ du violon/de la flûte** to play the violin/the flute; **2** (se servir de) **~ de** to exploit [*capacité, ascendant, influence, infirmité*] (**pour faire** to do).

IV *vi* **1** (s'amuser) [*enfant, animal*] to play (**avec** with); **allez ~ dehors, les enfants!** go and play outside, children!; **va faire ~ les enfants dans le parc** take the children to play in the park; **chat qui joue avec une souris** cat playing with a mouse; **on n'est pas ici pour ~!** we're not here to play games!; **c'était pour ~, ne le prenez pas mal!** I was only joking, don't be offended!; **2** (pratiquer un jeu) to play; (avec de l'argent) to gamble; **~ pour de l'argent** to play for money; **il joue dans l'équipe de Bordeaux** he plays for Bordeaux; **à toi de ~!** lit your turn!; fig the ball's in your court!; **bien joué!** (au jeu) well played!; fig well done!; **~ gagnant/perdant** to be onto a winner/loser; **j'en ai assez, je ne joue plus!** I've had enough, count me out!; **arrête de ~ avec ton stylo/ta bague!** stop fiddling with your pen/your ring!; **3** (traiter à la légère) **~ avec** to gamble with [*vie, santé*]; to put [sth] on the line [*réputation*]; to play with [*sentiments*]; **ne joue pas avec mon cœur** don't play with my feelings; **4** (spéculer) to gamble; **~ en Bourse** to gamble on the stock exchange; **~ gros/petit** to gamble for high/small stakes; **~ le sterling à la baisse** to sell sterling short; **~ le sterling à la hausse** to take a long position on sterling; **~ sur** to play on [*crédulité, lassitude*]; to speculate in [*valeur boursière*]; **~ sur les dissensions au sein d'un parti** to play on disagreements within a party; ▶ **tableau**; **5** Cin, Mus, Théât [*acteur*] to act; [*musicien, radio, disque, musique*] to play; **~ dans un film** to act in a film; **dans quelle pièce/quel théâtre joue-t-elle?** which play/theatre[GB] is she acting in?; **~ en mesure** to play in time; **le pianiste a joué devant/pour un public réduit** the pianist played to/for a small audience; **6** (produire des effets) [*lumière, flammes, vent*] to play; **une brise légère jouait dans tes cheveux/dans les branchages** a light breeze played with your hair/in the branches; **7** (intervenir) [*argument, clause*] to apply; [*âge, qualification*] to matter; **cet argument ne joue pas dans ce cas** that argument doesn't apply ou mean much in this case; **l'âge ne joue pas dans ce métier** age doesn't matter in this job; **les questions d'argent ne jouent pas entre eux** money is not a problem between them; **les considérations qui ont joué dans ma décision** the considerations that played a part in my decision; **~ en faveur de qn** to work in sb's favour[GB]; **~ comme un déclic** to serve as the trigger; **faire ~ la clé dans la serrure** to jiggle the key in the lock; **faire ~ ses relations** to make use of one's connections; **ses relations n'ont pas joué comme prévu** his/her connections didn't prove as useful as expected; **faire** or **laisser ~ le marché** to allow the free play of market forces; **8** Mécan (être mal ajusté) to be loose; **le contrevent a joué et ne ferme plus** the shutter has worked loose and won't close any more; **l'humidité a fait ~ les boiseries** the damp has made the panelling[GB] warp.

V se jouer *vpr* **1** Cin, Mus, Théât [*musique, air*] to be played; [*film*] to be shown; [*pièce, auteur, compositeur*] to be performed; **2** Jeux, Sport [*jeu, sport*] to be played; [*partie, rencontre*] (amicalement) to be played; (avec enjeu) to be played out; **le match s'est joué sous la pluie** the match was played in the rain; **3** (être en jeu) [*avenir, sort, paix*] to be at stake, to hang in the balance; **c'est l'avenir du pays qui se joue** the future of the country is at stake ou hangs in the balance; **le sort des réfugiés va se ~ à la conférence sur la paix** the fate of the refugees hangs on the peace conference; **le drame qui se joue dans le tiers-monde** the drama which is being played out in the Third World; **il va se ~ une partie décisive entre les deux firmes** a decisive contest is going to be played out between the two firms; **4** (triompher de) **se ~ de** to make light of [*difficulté*]; to defy [*pesanteur, gravité*]; to make light work of [*obstacle, réglementation*]; **il a triomphé de tous ses concurrents/tous les obstacles comme en se jouant** he triumphed over all his competitors/all obstacles without even trying.

jouet /ʒwɛ/ *nm* **1** (objet pour enfant) toy; **2** (victime) plaything; **il n'a été qu'un ~ entre les mains de cet intrigant** he was just a plaything to that schemer; **être le ~ de ses camarades** (à l'école) fml to be bullied by one's schoolmates; **être le ~ d'une illusion** to be the victim of an illusion; **être le ~ d'une hallucination** to be in the grip of hallucination; **être le ~ des vagues/du vent** to be at the mercy of the waves/of the wind.

joueur, -euse /ʒwœʀ, øz/ **I** *adj* **1** (qui aime s'amuser) [*enfant, animal, tempérament*] playful; **2** (qui risque de l'argent) gambling (*épith*); **être ~** to be a gambling man; **être joueuse** to be a gambling woman.

II *nm,f* **1** Sport, Jeux, Mus player; **une joueuse de tennis** a woman tennis player; **un ~ de mandoline** a mandolin player; **un ~ de cornemuse** a piper; **être beau/mauvais ~** to be a good/bad ou poor loser; **il s'est montré beau ~** he proved himself to be a good loser; **ne sois pas si mauvaise joueuse!** don't be such a bad sport!; **2** (personne qui joue de l'argent) gambler.

joufflu, ~e /ʒufly/ *adj* [*personne*] chubby-cheeked; [*visage*] chubby.

joug /ʒu/ *nm* **1** Agric yoke; **2** (sujétion) yoke; **tomber/se trouver sous le ~ de** to come/to be under the yoke of; **secouer le ~** to cast off the shackles; **3** (de balance) beam.

jouir /ʒwiʀ/ [3] **I jouir de** *vtr ind* (bénéficier) [*personne*] to enjoy [*droit, considération, soutien, avantage*]; to enjoy the use of [*bien, concession*]; [*lieu*] to enjoy [*climat, vue*]; **~ de toutes ses facultés** to have the use of all one's faculties.

II *vi* **1** (sexuellement) to have an orgasm; **2**○ (méchamment) **je jouis de les voir échouer** it gives me a kick○ to see them fail; **3**○ (souffrir) to suffer agonies.

jouissance /ʒwisɑ̃s/ *nf* **1** Jur (usage) use; **~ des installations** use of the facilities; **avoir la ~ de qch** to enjoy the use of sth; **2** (plaisir) pleasure; **~ artistique** artistic pleasure; **3** (orgasme) orgasm.

jouisseur, -euse /ʒwisœʀ, øz/ *nm,f* hedonist.

jouissif◐, **-ive** /ʒwisif, iv/ *adj* (tous contextes) really great.

joujou, *pl* **~x** /ʒuʒu/ *nm* baby talk toy; **faire ~** to play (**avec** with).

joule /ʒul/ *nm* joule.

jour /ʒuʀ/ ▶ **801** **I** *nm* **1** (période de vingt-quatre heures) day; **en un ~** in one day; **dans les trois ~s** within three days; **mois de trente ~s** thirty-day month; **barbe de trois ~s** three days' growth of beard; **trois fois par ~** three times a day; **c'est à trois ~s de train** it's three days away by train; **ces derniers ~s** these last few days; **un ~ de plus ou de moins ne changera rien** one day here or there won't make any difference; **les ~s se suivent et ne se ressemblent pas** every day is different; **dans huit ~s** in a week's time, in a week; **quinze ~s** a fortnight GB; **tous les quinze ~s** every fortnight GB ou two weeks US; **d'un ~** [*bonheur, espoir*] fleeting; [*mode*] passing; [*reine*] for a day; **deux poussins d'un ~** two one-day old chicks; **être la vedette d'un ~** to be here today and gone tomorrow; **des ~s et des ~s** for ever and ever; **dès le premier ~** right from the start; **~ après ~** (quotidiennement) day after day; (progressivement) little by little; **vivre au ~ le ~** to live one day at a time; **gagner sa vie au ~ le ~** to scratch a living; **voir les choses au ~ le ~** to take each day as it comes; **noter ses pensées au ~ le ~** to note down one's thoughts every day; ▶ **barbe III 1**; **2** (date) day; **ce ~-là** that day; **quel ~ sommes-nous?** what day is it today?; **elle viendra un ~** she'll come one day; **c'est mon ~ de courses** it's my shopping day; **viens un ~ où il n'y sera pas** come on a day he's out, come one day when he's out; **le ~ où je mourrai** the day I die; **un ~ ou l'autre** some day; **l'autre ~** the other day; **un de ces ~s** one of these days; **un beau ~** one fine day; **tous les ~s** every day; **de tous les ~s** everyday; **~ pour ~** to the day; **de ~ en ~** from day to day; **à ce ~** to date; **à ~** up to date; **mettre à ~** (actualiser) to bring up to date [*courrier, travail*]; to update [*édition*]; (révéler) to expose, to reveal [*mystère, secret, trafic, problème*]; **mise à ~** (actualisation) (d'édition, de données, statistiques, connaissances) updating (**de** of); (découverte) (de secret, trafic) revelation (**de** of); **édition mise à ~** updated edition; **tenir à ~** to keep up to date; **jusqu'à ce ~** (maintenant) until now; (alors) until then; **de nos ~s** nowadays; **d'un ~ à l'autre** [*être attendu*] any day now; [*changer*] from one day to the next; **du ~ au lendemain** overnight; **nouvelle/mode du ~** latest news/fashion; **au ~ d'aujourd'hui**○ today; **3** (du lever au coucher du soleil) day; **les ~s raccourcissent** the days are getting shorter; **pendant le ~** during the day; **nuit et ~** night and day; **tout le ~** all day; **le ~ se lève** it's getting light; **lumière du ~** daylight; **au lever** or **point du ~** at daybreak; **le petit ~** the early morning; **se lever avec le ~** to get up at the crack of dawn; **travailler de ~** to work days; **travail de ~** day work; **4** (clarté) daylight; **il fait ~** it's daylight; **laisser entrer le ~** to let in the daylight; **en plein ~** in broad daylight; **faire qch au grand ~** to do sth for all to see; **se faire ~** [*vérité*] to come to light; **mettre au ~** to unearth [*vestige*]; to bring [sth] to light [*réalité*] ; **jeter un ~ nouveau sur qch**, **éclairer qch d'un ~ nouveau** to shed new light on sth; ▶ **faux**[1]; **5** (aspect) **sous ton meilleur/pire ~** at your best/worst; **je ne te connaissais pas sous ce ~** I knew nothing of that side of you; **je t'ai vu sous ton vrai ~** I saw you in your true colours;

sous un ~ avantageux in a favourable[GB] light; **6** fig **donner le ~ à qn** to bring sb into the world; **donner ~ à qch** to give rise to sth; **voir le ~** [*personne*] to come into the world; [*œuvre, projet*] to see the light of day; [*organisme*] to come into being; **mes ~s sont comptés** my days are numbered; **finir ses ~s à la campagne** to end one's days in the country; **des ~s difficiles** hard times; **attenter à ses ~s** to make a suicide attempt; **avoir encore de beaux ~s devant soi** still to have a future; **les beaux ~s reviennent** spring will soon be here; **7** Constr (ouverture) gap; **~ dans un mur/entre des tuiles** gap in a wall/between tiles; **8** Cout **~s** openwork (embroidery) ¢; **faire des ~s** to do openwork; **une bordure avec des ~s** an openwork border; **~s à fils tirés** drawn thread work; **motif à ~s** (en tricot) lacy pattern.

■ **~ de l'An** New Year's day; **~ d'arrivée** day of arrival; **~ astronomique** astronomical day; **~ calendaire** calendar day; **~ de chance** lucky day; **~ de colère** day of wrath; **~ de départ** day of departure; **~ de deuil** day of mourning; **~ de deuil national** national day of mourning; **~ férié** bank holiday GB, legal holiday US; **~ de fermeture** closing day; **~ de fête** (férié) holiday; **aujourd'hui c'est ~ de fête** fig it's a great day today; **~ franc** clear day; **~ du Grand Pardon** Relig Day of Atonement; **~ J** D day; **~ du Jugement** Relig Judgment Day; **~ maigre** Relig day of abstinence (*without meat*); **~ des morts** Relig All Souls' Day; **~ ouvrable** working day; **~ de paie** payday; **~ de planche** Naut lay day; **~ de relâche** Théât closing day; **~ du Seigneur** Relig Sabbath; **~ sidéral** sidereal day; **~ solaire** solar day; **~ de souffrance** Constr opening looking on to a neighbour[GB]; **~ de travail** working day; **~ utile** lawful day.

IDIOMES **Rome ne s'est pas faite en un ~** Rome wasn't built in a day; **beau comme le ~** very good-looking; **ce n'est pas mon ~!** this isn't my day!; **être dans un bon ~** to be in a good mood; **être dans un mauvais ~** to be having an off day; **il y a des ~s avec et des ~s sans** there are good days and bad days.

Jourdain /ʒuʀdɛ̃/ ▶ 357 *nprm* **le ~** the River Jordan.

journal, *pl* **-aux** /ʒuʀnal, o/ *nm* **1** Presse (quotidien) newspaper, paper; (revue) magazine; (bureaux) newspaper office; **journaux du matin/du soir** morning/evening papers; **2** TV, Radio news bulletin, news ¢; **le ~ de vingt heures** the eight o'clock news; **3** Littérat journal.

■ **~ de bord** Naut, Transp logbook; **~ intime** diary; **~ de mode** Presse fashion magazine; **Journal officiel**, **JO** *government publication listing new acts, laws etc*; **~ télévisé** television news ¢.

journalier, **-ière** /ʒuʀnalje, ɛʀ/ **I** *adj* [*travail, taux, variation*] daily; **main-d'œuvre journalière** day labour[GB].

II *nm* day labourer[GB].

journalisme /ʒuʀnalism/ *nm* journalism; **~ sportif** sports reporting.

journaliste /ʒuʀnalist/ ▶ 510 *nmf* journalist; **~ de la presse écrite** journalist for the written press; **~ de la radio** radio journalist.

■ **~ économique** economic affairs correspondent; **~ sportif** sports correspondent.

journalistique /ʒuʀnalistik/ *adj* journalistic; **en style ~** in journalese.

journée /ʒuʀne/ ▶ 801 *nf* **1** (jour) day; **belles/dures/sombres ~s** beautiful/hard/dark days; **~ de repos** day off; **~ historique** historic day; **dans la ~** during the day; **en milieu de ~** in the middle of the day; **en fin de ~** at the end of the day; **toute la ~** all day; **à longueur de ~** all day long; **tout au long de la ~** throughout the day; **une rude ~ nous attend** we're in for a hard day; **la ~ d'hier** yesterday; **toute la ~ du mardi 5 juin** throughout the day on Tuesday 5 June; **la ~ de mardi/dimanche** Tuesday/Sunday; **2** (période de travail) day; **faire des ~s de huit heures** to work an eight-hour day; **j'ai gagné ma ~!** iron I may as well pack and go home!; **être payé à la ~** to be paid by the day.

■ **~ d'action** day of action; **~ continue** Entr continuous working day; **faire la ~ continue** to work with a short lunch break; **~ d'études** conference; **~ d'information** awareness day; **~ portes ouvertes** Entr, Pub open day GB, open house US; **~ de protestation** Pol day of protest.

journellement /ʒuʀnɛlmɑ̃/ *adv* **1** (tous les jours) every day; **2** (fréquemment) [*se voir, se produire*] all the time.

joute /ʒut/ *nf* **1** fig (duel) jousting ¢, battle; **~ oratoire** or **verbale** sparring match; **2** Sport, Hist joust.

■ **~ lyonnaise** or **nautique** Jeux water tournament (*in which teams joust in boats*).

jouter /ʒute/ [1] *vi* (à cheval) to joust (**contre** against, with); (sur des barques) to joust (*in water tournament*).

jouteur, **-euse** /ʒutœʀ, øz/ *nm,f* (à cheval) jouster; (sur l'eau) jouster (*in water tournament*).

jouvence /ʒuvɑ̃s/ *nf* **bain** or **cure de ~** rejuvenating experience; **fontaine** or **source de ~** Fountain of Youth.

jouvenceau‡, **-elle**, *mpl* **~x** /ʒuvɑ̃so, ɛl/ *nm,f* youth/maiden†.

jouxter /ʒukste/ [1] *vtr* to adjoin [*bâtiment, terrain, frontière*].

jovial, **~e**, *mpl* **~s** or **-iaux** /ʒɔvjal, o/ *adj* [*personne, air, mine*] jovial.

jovialement /ʒɔvjalmɑ̃/ *adv* jovially.

jovialité /ʒɔvjalite/ *nf* joviality.

joyau, *pl* **~x** /ʒwajo/ *nm* lit, fig jewel, gem; **Séville, ~ de l'Andalousie** Seville, the jewel of Andalusia; **incrusté de ~x** bejewelled[GB].

■ **les ~x de la Couronne** the crown jewels.

joyeusement /ʒwajøzmɑ̃/ *adv* **1** [*parler, raconter, crier, s'exclamer*] happily, joyfully; [*rire*] happily, merrily; [*courir*] happily; [*célébrer*] joyfully, merrily; [*sauter, bondir*] for joy; **2** iron happily.

joyeuseté /ʒwajøzte/ *nf* joy; **et autres ~s** and other similar joys.

joyeux, **-euse** /ʒwajø, øz/ **I** *adj* [*personne*] cheerful, cheery; [*groupe*] merry; [*cri, rire*] joyous, merry; [*air, ton, musique*] cheerful, happy; [*regard, geste*] joyful; [*visage*] happy; [*caractère, humeur, ambiance*] cheerful; **avoir l'air ~** to look cheerful; **être tout ~** to be overjoyed; **c'est ~!** iron that's great!; **être en joyeuse compagnie** to be in merry company; **mener joyeuse vie** to live it up○.

II joyeuses● *nfpl* balls●.

jubé /ʒybe/ *nm* rood screen.

jubilaire /ʒybilɛʀ/ *adj* [*année, médaille*] jubilee.

jubilation /ʒybilasjɔ̃/ *nf* joy, jubilation.

jubilé /ʒybile/ *nm* jubilee.

jubiler /ʒybile/ [1] *vi* to be jubilant, to rejoice (**de faire** to do); (avec arrogance) to gloat; **'j'ai réussi mon examen,' jubila-t-il** 'I've passed my exam,' he said jubilantly.

jucher /ʒyʃe/ [1] **I** *vtr* (percher) to perch (**sur** on).

II se jucher *vpr* (se percher) **se ~ sur** to perch on; **être juché sur** to be perched on.

Juda /ʒyda/ *npr* Judah.

judaïcité /ʒydaisite/ *nf* Jewishness.

judaïque /ʒydaik/ *adj* [*loi*] Judaic; [*héritage, rites*] Jewish.

judaïsme /ʒydaism/ *nm* Judaism.

judaïté /ʒydaite/ *nf* Jewishness.

judas /ʒyda/ *nm* **1** (aussi **Judas**) (traître) Judas; **2** (dans une porte) door viewer, peephole.

Judas /ʒyda/ *npr* Bible Judas; **~ Macchabée** Judas Maccabeus.

Judée /ʒyde/ ▶ 692 *nprf* Judaea; **arbre de ~** Judas tree.

judéité /ʒydeite/ *nf* Jewishness.

judéo-chrétien, **-ienne**, *mpl* **~s** /ʒydeo kʀetjɛ̃, ɛn/ *adj* [*tradition*] Judaeo-Christian.

judéo-espagnol, **~e**, *mpl* **~s** /ʒydeo ɛspaɲɔl/ *adj* Judaeo-Spanish.

judiciaire /ʒydisjɛʀ/ *adj* [*acte, conquête, institution, erreur*] judicial; ▶ **casier**, **police**.

judiciairement /ʒydisjɛʀmɑ̃/ *adv* judicially.

judicieusement /ʒydisjøzmɑ̃/ *adv* judiciously.

judicieux, **-ieuse** /ʒydisjø, øz/ *adj* [*personne*] of sound judgment (*épith, après n*); [*conseil, idée*] sound; [*choix*] wise, sound; [*utilisation, critique*] judicious; **il semblerait ~ de faire** it would seem wise to do.

judo /ʒydo/ ▶ 449 *nm* judo; **faire une prise de ~ à qn** to take sb in a judo hold.

judoka /ʒydoka/ *nmf* judoka.

juge /ʒyʒ/ *nm* **1** ▶ 510, 813 Jur judge; **elle est ~** she is a judge; **le ~ Morin** gén Judge Morin; (des juridictions supérieures) Mr ou Mrs Justice Morin; **oui, Monsieur le ~** yes, Your Honour[GB]; **comparaître devant le ~** to appear before the court; **être à la fois ~ et partie** to be both judge and judged; **2** (de jeu, concours) judge; **3** (personne compétente) judge; **être bon/mauvais ~** to be a good/bad judge; **être son propre ~** to be one's own judge; **se faire ~ de qch** to be the judge of sth; **je te laisse ~ de la situation** I'll let you be the judge of the situation; **tu es seul ~** only you can judge.

■ **~ aux affaires matrimoniales** Jur *judge specializing in matrimonial affairs*; **~ de l'application des peines** Jur *judge appointed to oversee conditions of a prisoner's sentence*; **~ de chaise** Sport umpire; **~ des enfants** Jur *judge dealing in cases involving minors*; **~ de filet** Sport net cord judge; **~ d'instruction** Jur examining magistrate; **~ de ligne** Sport lines judge; **~ de paix** ≈ justice of the peace; **~ des référés** Jur judge in chambers; **~ de touche** Sport linesman; **~ des tutelles** Jur *judge administering the property of people under guardianship*.

jugé: **au jugé** /oʒyʒe/ *loc adv* [*évaluer*] by guesswork; **dessiner** or **tracer un plan au ~** to draw a rough map; **avancer au ~** to follow one's nose; **se diriger au ~ vers/dans** to work one's way toward(s)/in; **tirer au ~** to shoot blind.

jugeable /ʒyʒabl/ *adj* Jur [*affaire, personne*] subject to judgment (*après n*).

jugement /ʒyʒmɑ̃/ *nm* **1** (opinion) judgment; **erreur de ~** error of judgment; **le ~ de l'histoire** the judgment of history; **porter un ~ sur qch/qn** to pass judgment on sth/sb; **porter un ~ hâtif/négatif sur qch** to pass a hasty/negative judgment on sth; **avoir peur du** or **redouter le ~ de qn** to be afraid of what sb will think of one; **s'en remettre au ~ de qn** to defer to sb's judgment; **2** (aptitude) judgment; **n'avoir aucun ~** to have no judgment; **fausser le ~ de qn** to distort sb's judgment; **3** Jur (processus) judgment; (décision) (pour un crime) verdict; (pour un délit) judgment, decision; **prononcer un ~** (pour un crime) to give one's verdict; (pour un délit) to pass judgment; **passer en ~** [*affaire*] to go to court.

■ **~ par défaut** judgment by default; **~ de Dieu** Divine Judgment; Hist ordeal; **~ incident** interlocutory judgment; **~ de Salomon** the judgment of Solomon; **~ de valeur** value judgment; **Jugement dernier** Last Judgment.

jugeote○ /ʒyʒɔt/ *nf* common sense;

manquer de ~ to have no common sense; **si tu avais un peu de ~** if you had any (common) sense.

juger /ʒyʒe/ [13] I **au juger** *loc adv* ▶ **jugé**.
II *vtr* **1** (former une opinion sur) to judge; **~ qn sur les apparences** or **la mine** to judge sb by his/her appearance; **~ sur les apparences** to judge by appearances; **jugez-le d'après ses actes** judge him by what he does; **je jugerai par moi-même** I'll judge for myself; **à toi de ~ s'il faut accepter ou pas** it's up to you to judge whether to accept or not; **ce n'est pas à moi de ~** I don't think it's any of my business; **l'histoire jugera** history will judge; **2** (considérer) to consider; **~ qn intelligent** to consider sb intelligent; **~ qch dangereux/difficile** to consider sth dangerous/difficult; **~ que qch est dangereux** to consider sth dangerous ou that sth is dangerous; **~ dangereux que qn fasse** to consider it dangerous for sb to do; **~ bon/nécessaire de faire** to consider it a good idea/necessary to do; **un film jugé médiocre** a film considered (to be) mediocre; **ne le juge pas mal** don't think badly of him; **je t'avais mal jugé** I misjudged you; **3** Jur (examiner) to try [*affaire, personne*]; (décider) to judge [*affaire*]; to arbitrate in [*différend, litige*]; **l'affaire sera jugée demain** the case will be heard ou tried tomorrow; **l'affaire est jugée** Jur the case is closed; **le tribunal jugera** the court will decide; **~ en droit/fait** to make a judgment based on the statutes/facts; **4** (pour un concours) to judge [*candidats, films*].
III **juger de** *vtr ind* **1** (évaluer) **~ de** to assess [*niveau, valeur, capacité*]; **j'en jugerai par moi-même** I'll judge for myself; **pour autant qu'on puisse en ~** as far as one can judge; **à en ~ par tes réponses** judging by ou from your answers; **2** (imaginer) **jugez de ma colère** imagine my anger.
IV **se juger** *vpr* **1** (se considérer) to consider oneself; **2** Jur [*affaire*] to be heard.

jugulaire /ʒygylɛʀ/ I *adj* [*veine*] jugular.
II *nf* **1** (de casque, képi) chin strap; **2** Anat jugular.

juguler /ʒygyle/ [1] *vtr* to stamp out [*épidémie, chômage, fléau*]; to check [*hémorragie*]; to curb [*inflation*].

juif, juive /ʒɥif, ʒɥiv/ I *adj* [*religion, communauté*] Jewish.
II *nm,f* Jew; ▶ **petit**.
■ **le Juif errant** the Wandering Jew.

juillet /ʒɥijɛ/ ▶ **521** *nm* July; **le 14 ~** the Fourteenth of July, Bastille day.

juillettiste○ /ʒɥijetist/ *nmf* July holidaymaker GB, July vacationer US.

juin /ʒɥɛ̃/ ▶ **521** *nm* June.

juive ▶ **juif**.

jujube /ʒyʒyb/ *nm* jujube.

jujubier /ʒyʒybje/ *nm* jujube tree.

juke-box, *pl* **~es** /dʒukbɔks/ *nm* jukebox.

julep /ʒylɛp/ *nm* julep.

jules○ /ʒyl/ *nm* **1** hum (compagnon) boyfriend, man○; **2**† (pot de chambre) chamber pot, jerry○ GB.

julien, -ienne /ʒyljɛ̃, ɛn/ I *adj* [*ère, calendrier*] Julian.
II **julienne** *nf* **1** Culin (potage, garniture) julienne (**de** of); **légumes taillés en julienne** vegetables cut in julienne strips; **2** Zool ling; **3** Bot rocket.

Juliette /ʒyljɛt/ *npr* **Roméo et ~** Romeo and Juliet.

jumeau, -elle, *mpl* **~x** /ʒymo, ɛl/ I *adj* **1** Biol [*frère, sœur*] twin; [*fruits*] double; **2** Constr, Tech [*lits*] twin; **3** Admin [*ville*] twin.
II *nm,f* (personne) twin.
III **jumelle** *nf* binoculars (*pl*); **une paire de jumelles, des jumelles** (a pair of) binoculars; **à la jumelle** through binoculars.
■ **jumelles de théâtre** opera glasses.

jumelage /ʒymlaʒ/ *nm* (de communes, clubs) twinning.

jumelé, ~e /ʒymle/ I *pp* ▶ **jumeler**.
II *pp adj* [*communes, clubs*] twinned; [*billet, pari*] double; [*fenêtres, colonnes*] twin.

jumeler /ʒymle/ [19] *vtr* **1** Admin to twin [*communes, clubs*] (**à** with); to combine [*expositions, événements*]; **2** Tech to double [*poutres, roues*].

jumelle ▶ **jumeau**.

jument /ʒymɑ̃/ *nf* mare.
■ **~ de course** filly.

jumping /dʒœmpiŋ/ *nm* showjumping.

jungle /ʒœ̃gl/ *nf* (tous contextes) jungle; **la loi de la ~** the law of the jungle.

junior /ʒynjɔʀ/ I *adj inv* **1** Sport junior; **2** [*vêtements, magasin*] children's.
II *nmf* junior.

Junon /ʒynɔ̃/ *npr* Juno.

junte /ʒœ̃t/ *nf* junta.

jupe /ʒyp/ *nf* **1** Mode skirt; **~ fendue** slit skirt; **~ droite** straight skirt; **~ plissée** pleated skirt; **2** Tech skirt; **~ de piston** piston skirt.
■ **~ portefeuille** wraparound skirt.
IDIOMES **il est toujours dans les ~s de sa mère** he's tied to his mother's apron strings.

jupe-culotte, *pl* **jupes-culottes** /ʒyp kylɔt/ *nf* culottes (*pl*).

jupette /ʒypɛt/ *nf* short skirt; **~ de tennis** tennis skirt.

Jupiter /ʒypitɛʀ/ I *npr* Mythol Jupiter.
II *nprf* Astron Jupiter.
IDIOMES **il se croit sorti de la cuisse de ~** he thinks he's God's gift to the world○.

jupon /ʒypɔ̃/ *nm* petticoat; ▶ **coureur**.
IDIOMES **courir le ~** to womanize.

Jura /ʒyʀa/ ▶ **692** *nprm* (région, département) **le ~** the Jura; **le ~ suisse** the Swiss Jura.

jurassien, -ienne /ʒyʀasjɛ̃, ɛn/ *adj* of the Jura (Mountains).

jurassique /ʒyʀasik/ *adj, nm* Jurassic.

juré, ~e /ʒyʀe/ I *pp* ▶ **jurer**.
II *pp adj* **1** (assermenté) [*expert*] on oath (*après n*); [*traducteur*] sworn-in (*épith*); **2** (éternel) [*fidélité, ennemi*] sworn.
III *nm* **1** Jur juror; **2** Art, Sport member of the jury.

jurer /ʒyʀe/ [1] I *vtr* **1** (promettre) to swear; (moins fort) to promise; **~ de faire** to swear to do; (moins fort) to promise to do; **~ à qn de faire** to swear to sb to do; (moins fort) to promise sb to do; **jure-moi de ne rien dire** swear you won't say anything; **jure-le!** swear!; **~ que** to swear that; **~ à qn que** to swear to sb that; **on jurerait (que c'est) de la soie** you'd swear it was silk; **faire ~ à qn de faire** to make sb swear to do; **2**○ (affirmer) **je te jure que ça fait mal** I can tell you it hurts; **ah mais je te jure!** honestly○!; **il y en a, je te jure!** honestly, some people!; ▶ **dieu**; **3** (en prêtant serment) to swear, to pledge [*fidélité, obéissance*]; to swear [*amour éternel*]; **on leur a fait ~ le secret** they were sworn to secrecy; **je (te) jure le secret sur cette affaire** I swear I'll keep this a secret; **je le jure** I swear; **~ sur la Bible/l'honneur** to swear on the Bible/one's honour[GB]; **je (le) jure sur la tête de mes enfants** or **de ma mère** I swear on my mother's life; **~ la mort de qn/la ruine de qch** to vow that sb will die/that sth will fail; **~ de tuer qn** to vow to kill sb.
II **jurer de** *vtr ind* to swear to; **j'en jurerais** I would swear to it.
III *vi* **1** (dire des jurons) to swear (**après, contre** at); ▶ **charretier**; **2** (détonner) [*couleurs*] to clash (**avec** with); [*détail, construction*] to look out of place (**avec** in); **3** (être partisan de) **ne ~ que par** to swear by.
IV **se jurer** *vpr* **1** (l'un l'autre) to swear [sth] to one another [*fidélité*]; **2** (à soi-même) to vow (**de faire** to do).
IDIOMES **il ne faut ~ de rien** Prov never say never.

juridiction /ʒyʀidiksjɔ̃/ *nf* **1** (pouvoir) jurisdiction; **hors de/sous ma ~** outside/within my jurisdiction; **2** (tribunaux) courts (*pl*); **~ civile** civil courts; **~ militaire** military courts; **~ de droit commun** courts of common law; **~ judiciaire** courts of justice; **~ de simple police** magistrate's courts GB, police courts US; **~ administrative** administrative tribunals (*pl*).

juridique /ʒyʀidik/ *adj* [*statut, langue, formation*] legal; [*décision*] of the court (*après n*); **il n'y aura pas de conséquences ~s** there will be no legal consequences; **du point de vue ~** from a legal standpoint; **agir sur le plan ~** to take legal action; **vide ~** gap in the law.

juridiquement /ʒyʀidikmɑ̃/ *adv* legally.

jurisconsulte /ʒyʀiskɔ̃sylt/ *nm* legal adviser[GB].

jurisprudence /ʒyʀispʀydɑ̃s/ *nf* case law, precedent; **faire ~** to set a legal precedent.

juriste /ʒyʀist/ ▶ **510** *nmf* **1** (qui étudie le droit) jurist; **2** (qui pratique le droit) lawyer.

juron /ʒyʀɔ̃/ *nm* swearword; **dire** or **pousser des ~s** to swear.

jury /ʒyʀi/ *nm* **1** Jur jury; **président du ~** foreman of the jury; **2** Art, Sport panel of judges; **3** Univ board of examiners.

jus /ʒy/ *nm* **1** (de fruit) juice; **~ de pomme/citron** apple/lemon juice; **2** (de viande) (qui exsude) juices (*pl*); (sauce servie) gravy; **cuire qch au ~** to cook sth in the juices from the meat; **cuire dans son ~**○ fig [*personne*] to be boiling; **laisser qn cuire** or **mijoter dans son ~**○ fig to let sb stew in his own juice; **3**○ (café) coffee; **prendre un ~ au comptoir** to have a coffee at the bar; **4**○ (eau de baignade) drink○, water; **se jeter/tomber au ~** to jump/fall in the water; **tous au ~!** everyone in!; **5**○ (courant électrique) juice○, electricity; **il n'y a plus de ~** the power's off; **prendre le ~** to get a shock.
■ **~ de chaussettes**○ pej dishwater, very weak coffee.
IDIOMES **ça vaut le ~**○ it's worth it; **c'est du 50/30 au ~** soldiers' slang only 50/30 days to demob○.

jusant /ʒyzɑ̃/ *nm* ebb tide.

jusqu'au-boutisme /ʒyskobutism/ *nm* gén hardline attitude; péj extremist attitude.

jusqu'au-boutiste, *pl* **~s** /ʒyskobutist/ I *adj* [*politique, attitude*] gén hardline (*épith*); péj extremist.
II *nmf* gén hardliner; péj extremist.

jusque (jusqu' *before vowel*) /ʒysk/ I *prép* **1** (dans l'espace) **aller jusqu'à Paris/jusqu'en Amérique** (insistant sur la destination atteinte) to go as far as Paris/America; (insistant sur la distance parcourue) to go all the way to Paris/America; **courir jusqu'au bout du jardin** to run right down to the bottom of the garden GB ou the back of the yard US; **suivre qn ~ dans sa chambre** to follow sb right into his/her room; **il a marché jusqu'à moi** he walked right up to me; **la nouvelle n'était pas officiellement arrivée jusqu'à nous** the news hadn't reached us officially; **ils l'ont suivi ~ chez lui** they followed him all the way home ou right up to his front door; **descendre jusqu'à 100 mètres de profondeur** to go down to a depth of 100 metres[GB]; **jusqu' où comptez- vous aller?** lit, fig how far do you intend to go?; **2** (dans le temps) until, till; **je t'ai attendu jusqu'à huit heures** I waited for you until ou till eight o'clock; **~ vers (les) dix heures** until ou till about ten o'clock; **ne bougez pas jusqu'à mon retour** don't move until ou till I get back; **jusqu'alors** until then; **jusqu'à présent** or **maintenant, jusqu'ici** (up) until now; **jusqu'à ce jour tout s'était bien passé** (up) until that day everything had gone well; **jusqu'au dernier moment** up to ou until ou till the last moment; **jusqu'à l'âge de 10 ans il n'a pas fréquenté l'école** until he was 10 (years old) he didn't go to school; **jusqu'à quand restes-tu à Oxford?** how long are you staying in Oxford?; **laisser mijoter jusqu'à évaporation complète de**

l'eau leave to simmer until all the water has evaporated; **3** (limite supérieure) up to; (limite inférieure) down to; **il peut soulever jusqu'à dix kilos** he can lift up to ten kilos; **cela peut coûter jusqu'à 200 francs par personne** it can cost up to 200 francs per person; **transport gratuit jusqu'à 10 ans** free transport up to the age of 10; **avoir de l'eau jusqu'aux chevilles/cuisses** to be up to one's ankles/thighs in water, to be ankle-/thigh-deep in water; **un repli du dollar qui descend jusqu'à 5,41 francs** a fall in the dollar which has gone down to 5.41 francs; **je le suivrai jusqu'au bout** fig I'll follow him to the (very) end; **4** (avec une notion d'exagération) to the point of; **pousser la cruauté jusqu'au sadisme** to carry cruelty to the point of sadism, to be so cruel as to be sadistic; **être poli jusqu'à l'obséquiosité** to be polite to the point of obsequiousness, to be so polite as to be obsequious; **il est bien trop bon, jusqu'à la bêtise** he's too nice for his own good; **jusqu'à faire** to the point ou extent of doing; **aller jusqu'à faire** to go so far as to do; **5** (y compris) even; **l'épidémie s'est répandue ~ dans les régions les plus reculées** the epidemic spread to even the most remote regions; **jusqu'à ses amis ont refusé de lui parler** even his friends refused to speak to him; **il y avait des détritus ~ sous la table/derrière la porte** there was rubbish everywhere, even under the table/behind the door; **ils sont venus, jusqu'au dernier** every last one of them came; **il a repeint toute la pièce, jusqu'aux boutons de porte** he repainted the whole room, right down to the door knobs.

II jusqu'à ce que *loc conj* until; **je reste toujours jusqu'à ce qu'il s'endorme** I always stay until he is asleep; **je reste jusqu'à ce qu'elle soit rétablie** I'll stay until she has recovered; **je suis resté jusqu'à ce qu'elle soit rétablie** I stayed until she had recovered.

jusque-là /ʒyskəla/ *adv* **1** (dans le temps) until then, up to then; **j'attends les résultats, ~ je ne peux rien dire** I'm waiting to hear the results, until then ou in the meantime I have nothing to say; **c'est le plus terrible hiver qu'on ait connu ~** it's the hardest winter we've ever had ou anyone has ever known ou in living memory; **2** (dans l'espace) up to here; (plus loin) up to there; **on avait de l'eau ~** (aux genoux etc) the water was up to here; **l'eau est montée ~** (en pointant vers un objet) the water came up to there.

IDIOMES **en avoir ~ de qch/qn**○ to have had it up to here with sth/sb○, to have had just about enough of sth/sb; **en avoir ~ de faire**○ to be sick-and-tired of doing○; **j'en ai ~**○**!** I've had it up to here○!, I've had enough○!; **s'en mettre ~**○ to stuff one's face○.

jusques liter = **jusque**.

jusquiame /ʒyskjam/ *nf* henbane.

justaucorps /ʒystokɔʀ/ *nm* **1** (pour la danse) leotard; **2** (sous-vêtement) body stocking; **3** Hist doublet.

juste /ʒyst/ **I** *adj* **1** (impartial) [*personne*] fair; **2** (équitable) [*règlement, partage*] fair; [*récompense, sanction, cause*] just; **ce n'est pas ~!** it's not fair!; **il est ~ que/de faire** it is fair that/to do; **il est ~ qu'il ait réussi** it is fair that he succeeded; **il ne serait pas ~ de tout te donner** it wouldn't be fair to give you everything; **~ retour des choses, il a été dédommagé** it was poetic justice that he got compensation; **trouver un ~ milieu** to find a happy medium; **~ ciel**†**!** Good Heavens!; **3** (légitime) [*colère, certitude*] righteous (*épith*); [*revendication*] legitimate; [*raison*] good; [*crainte*] justifiable; [*raisonnement, remarque, comparaison*] valid; **j'ai de ~s raisons de ne pas le croire** I have good reason not to believe him; **à ~ raison** or **titre** quite rightly, with good reason; **ta remarque est très ~** your remark is very valid; **dire des choses ~s** to make some valid points; **4** (adéquat) right; **trouver le mot ~** to find the right word; **c'est (très) ~!** that's (quite) right!; **comme de ~ il était en retard** as one might expect ou as per usual, he was late; **5** (exact) [*calcul, proportion, heure, analyse*] correct; **j'ai tout ~** I've got everything right; **avoir l'heure ~** to have the correct time; **connaître le ~ prix des choses** fig to know the true value of things; **apprécier qn/qch à sa ~ valeur** to appreciate sb fully/the true value of sth; **6** (précis) [*instrument de mesure*] accurate; **ma montre n'est pas très ~** my watch is not very accurate; **7** Mus [*piano, voix*] in tune (*jamais épith*); [*note*] true; **ton piano n'est pas ~** your piano is out of tune; **8** (trop ajusté) [*vêtement, chaussure*] tight; **trop/un peu ~** too/a bit tight; **9** (à la limite) **un poulet pour six c'est un peu ~** one chicken for six people is stretching it a bit; **une heure pour y aller c'est un peu ~** one hour to get there is cutting it a bit fine; **nous sommes un peu ~s en ce moment**○ money is a bit tight○ at the moment; **j'ai réussi à éviter le bus mais ça a été ~**○ I managed to avoid the bus but it was a close shave○.

II *adv* **1** (sans erreur) [*chanter*] in tune; [*sonner*] true; [*deviner*] right; **elle a vu ~ dans ses prévisions** she was right in her forecasts; **viser ~** lit to aim straight; fig to hit the nail on the head; **2** (précisément) just; **~ quand j'arrivais** just as I was arriving; **c'est ~ ce qu'il me faut** that is just or exactly what I need; **c'est ~ avant/après la poste** it's just before/after the post office; **~ après les informations** just ou straight after the news; **j'ai ~ assez (d'argent)** I've got just enough (money); **~ à temps** just in time; **'tu as eu ton train?'—'oui mais tout ~'** 'did you catch your train?'—'yes, but only just'; **3** (seulement) just; **j'en prends ~ un** I'm just taking one; **ils ont ~ eu le temps de manger** they just had time to eat; **4** (depuis peu) **(tout) ~** only just; **j'arrive ~** I've only just arrived; **il vient ~ de partir** he's only just left; **il a tout ~ vingt ans** he's only just twenty; **5** (à peine) hardly; **c'est tout ~ s'il sait lire/tient debout** he can hardly read/stand; **6** (parcimonieusement) **j'ai prévu trop/un peu ~ pour le repas** I didn't prepare enough/quite enough food; **calculer les prix au plus ~** to calculate the prices down to the last penny.

III au juste *loc adv* exactly; **que s'est-il passé au ~?** what happened exactly?; **je ne sais pas au ~ combien nous serons** I don't know exactly how many of us there will be.

IV *nm* righteous man; **les ~s** the righteous; ▶**sommeil**.

justement /ʒystəmɑ̃/ *adv* **1** (précisément) precisely; **c'est ~ ce qu'il ne fallait pas dire** that's precisely what one shouldn't have said; **'pourquoi te fâcher il ne t'a rien dit'—'~!'** 'why are you getting angry he didn't say anything to you'—'precisely!'; **2** (à l'instant) just; **je parlais ~ de toi** I was just talking about you; **elle vient ~ de partir** as a matter of fact she's just left; **~, à ce propos je voulais te dire que** as a matter of fact, while we're on the subject, I wanted to tell you that; **3** (avec justesse) [*dire, répondre*] correctly; **comme l'a fort ~ souligné Nina** as Nina so correctly pointed out; **4** (légitimement) [*se flatter, s'inquiéter*] justifiably.

justesse /ʒystɛs/ **I** *nf* **1** (pertinence) **être convaincu de la ~ d'une décision** to be sure that a decision is correct; **avec ~** [*souligner, remarquer*] correctly; **2** (précision) accuracy; **un tir d'une ~ remarquable** a remarkably accurate shot; **avec ~** [*analyser, prévoir, mesurer*] accurately; **3** Mus **le piano n'est pas d'une ~ fantastique** the piano is rather out of tune; **chanter avec ~** to sing in tune.

II de justesse *loc adv* only just; **on a évité la catastrophe/bagarre de ~** we only just avoided disaster/a fight; **il a eu son avion, mais de ~** he got his plane but only just; **elle a été réélue de ~** she was reelected only by a narrow margin; **j'ai réussi mes examens de ~** I passed my exams but only just, I just scraped○ through my exams; **remporter une victoire de ~** to win a narrow victory, to win by a narrow margin; **s'en sortir de ~** to have a narrow escape.

justice /ʒystis/ *nf* **1** (principe) justice; (équité) fairness; **par souci de ~ sociale** out of concern for social justice; **en toute ~** in all fairness; **il n'y a pas de ~!** there's no justice!; **agir avec ~** to act fairly ou justly; **ce n'est que ~** it is only fair ou right; **2** (application) justice; **la ~ divine** divine justice; **rendre la ~** to dispense justice; **demander/obtenir ~** to demand/obtain justice; **il faut leur rendre** or **faire cette ~ qu'ils sont...** one has to acknowledge that they are...; **se faire ~ (à soi-même)** (se venger) to take the law into one's own hands; (se suicider) to take one's own life; **3** (pouvoir) **la ~** (lois) the law; (institution) the legal system; (tribunaux) the courts (*pl*); **être livré à la ~** to be handed over to the law; **il a des ennuis** or **démêlés avec la ~ de son pays** he's in trouble with the law in his country; **aller en ~** to go to court; **poursuivre qn en ~** to take sb to court; **être traduit en ~** to be brought before the courts; **témoigner en ~** to give evidence in a court of law; **la ~ fonctionne mal** the legal system doesn't work properly; **intenter une action en ~ contre qn** to bring (a) legal action against sb; **passer en ~** to stand trial.

■ **~ militaire** Mil military law.

justiciable /ʒystisjabl/ **I** *adj* **1** Jur answerable (**de** for; **de qch devant qn** to sb for sth); **2** (relevant de) **~ de la psychiatrie** requiring psychiatric treatment (*épith, après n*).

II *nmf* **~ d'un juge/tribunal** person under the jurisdiction of a judge/a court.

justicier, **-ière** /ʒystisje, ɛʀ/ **I** *adj* **un bandit ~** an outlaw who rights wrongs.

II *nm,f* (redresseur de torts) righter of wrongs; **se faire le ~ de qn** to right the wrongs done to sb.

justifiable /ʒystifjabl/ *adj* justifiable.

justificateur, **-trice** /ʒystifikatœʀ, tʀis/ *adj* justificatory.

justificatif, **-ive** /ʒystifikatif, iv/ **I** *adj* [*facture, document*] supporting; **pièce justificative** documentary evidence ₵; **exemplaire ~** Édition voucher copy.

II *nm* **1** gén documentary evidence ₵ (**de** of); **~ de domicile** proof of domicile; **~ de frais** receipt; **2** Édition voucher copy.

justification /ʒystifikasjɔ̃/ *nf* **1** (action) justification; **2** (preuve) (orale) explanation; (écrite) documentary evidence; **3** Imprim justification; **~ à droite/gauche** right/left justification.

justifié, **~e** /ʒystifje/ **I** *pp* ▶**justifier**.

II *pp adj* **1** (légitime) [*impression, inquiétude, choix*] justified; **la méfiance ~e des électeurs** the justified distrust of the electorate; **un choix non ~** an unjustified choice; **2** (expliqué) justified (**par** by).

justifier /ʒystifje/ [2] **I** *vtr* **1** (rendre acceptable) to justify [*méthode, politique, thèse, décision*] (**par** by); **cela justifie qu'il parte demain** this justifies his leaving tomorrow; ▶**moyen**; **2** (confirmer après coup) to vindicate; **les faits ont justifié nos craintes** the facts vindicated our fears; **3** (excuser) to vindicate [*coupable*]; to justify [*comportement, retard, absence*]; to explain [*ignorance*]; **tu essaies toujours de la ~** you are always making excuses for her; ▶**fin²**; **4** Imprim to justify [*texte*]; **~ à droite/à gauche** to justify to the right/left.

II justifier de *vtr ind* to give proof of [*domicile, identité*]; to have [*expérience professionnelle, connaissance*]; **le candidat**

devra ~ de quatre ans d'expérience the successful candidate will have four years' experience.

III se justifier *vpr* **1** (se disculper) (devant un tribunal) to clear oneself; (devant une personne) to make excuses; **n'essaie pas de te ~** don't try to make excuses; **2** (être explicable) to be justified (**par** by); **ta décision peut se ~** your decision can be justified.

jute /ʒyt/ *nm* **1** (fibre) jute; **toile de ~** hessian; **2** (tissu) hessian.

juter /ʒyte/ [1] *vi* [*fruit*] to ooze with juice.

juteux, **-euse** /ʒytø, øz/ **I** *adj* **1** [*fruit*] juicy; **2**○ [*affaire, projet*] profitable, juicy○.
II○ *nm* soldiers' slang adjutant.

Juvénal /ʒyvenal/ *npr* Juvenal.

juvénile /ʒyvenil/ *adj* [*sourire, caractère*] youthful; [*délinquance, mortalité*] juvenile; [*public*] young; [*assemblée*] of young people (*épith, après n*).

juvénilité /ʒyvenilite/ *nf* youthfulness.

juxtalinéaire /ʒykstalineɛʀ/ *adj* [*traduction*] line by line (*épith*).

juxtaposer /ʒykstapoze/ [1] *vtr* to juxtapose [*termes, idées*].

juxtaposition /ʒykstapozisjɔ̃/ *nf* (de termes, d'idées) juxtaposition.

Kk

k, **K** /ka/ *nm inv* k, K.

kabbale /kabal/ *nf* cabala.

Kaboul /kabul/ ▶ 857 *npr* Kabul.

kabyle /kabil/ ▶ 462 *adj*, *nm* Kabyle.

Kabyle /kabil/ *nmf* Kabyle.

Kabylie /kabili/ ▶ 692 *nprf* Kabylia.

kafkaïen, **-ïenne** /kafkajɛ̃, ɛn/ *adj* **1** [*ambiance*] Kafkaesque; **2** [*études*] Kafka (*épith*).

kaiser /kezɛʀ/ *nm* Kaiser.

kakatoès /kakatɔɛs/ *nm* cockatoo.

kaki /kaki/ **I** ▶ 193 *adj inv* khaki.
II *nm* **1** Bot persimmon; **2** (couleur) khaki.

kalachnikov® /kalaʃnikɔf/ *nf* Kalashnikov.

Kalahari /kalaaʀi/ *nprm* **le désert du ~** the Kalahari desert.

kaléidoscope /kaleidɔskɔp/ *nm* kaleidoscope.

kaléidoscopique /kaleidɔskɔpik/ *adj* kaleidoscopic.

kamikaze /kamikaz/ *adj*, *nm* kamikaze.

Kampala /kɑ̃pala/ ▶ 857 *npr* Kampala.

Kampuchéa /kɑ̃putʃea/ *nprm* Hist Kampuchea.

kampuchéen, **-éenne** /kɑ̃putʃeɛ̃, ɛn/ *adj* Kampuchean.

Kampuchéen, **-éenne** /kɑ̃putʃeɛ̃, ɛn/ *nm,f* Kampuchean.

kanak = **canaque**.

kangourou /kɑ̃guʀu/ **I** *adj inv* **poche ~** front pocket; **slip ~** pouch-front briefs (*pl*).
II *nm* **1** Zool kangaroo; **2** ®(sac pour bébé) baby carrier.

Kansas /kɑ̃sas/ ▶ 692 *nprm* Kansas.

kantien, **-ienne** /kɑ̃sjɛ̃, ɛn/ *adj* Kantian.

kantisme /kɑ̃tism/ *nm* Kantianism.

kaolin /kaɔlɛ̃/ *nm* kaolin.

kapok /kapɔk/ *nm* kapok.

kapokier /kapɔkje/ *nm* kapok tree.

kaput○ /kaput/ *adj inv* [*personne*] dog-tired○; [*objet, machine*] kaput○.

karaoké /kaʀaɔke/ *nm* karaoke.

karaté /kaʀate/ ▶ 449 *nm* karate.

karatéka /kaʀateka/ *nmf* karateka.

karcher® /kaʀʃɛʀ/ *nm* pressurized water gun.

karité /kaʀite/ *nm* shea; **beurre de ~** shea butter.

karma /kaʀma/ *nm* karma.

karstique /kaʀstik/ *adj* karstic.

kart /kaʀt/ *nm* go-kart.

karting /kaʀtiŋ/ ▶ 449 *nm* go-karting; **faire du ~** to go karting.

kasbah /kazba/ *nf* kasbah.

kasher /kaʃɛʀ/ *adj inv* kosher.

Katmandou /katmɑ̃du/ ▶ 857 *npr* Kat(h)mandu.

kayak /kajak/ ▶ 449 *nm* kayak; **faire du ~** to go canoeing.

kazakh, **~e** /kazak/ **I** ▶ 537 *adj* Kazak.
II ▶ 462 *nm* Kazak.

Kazakh, **~e** /kazak/ ▶ 537 *nm,f* Kazak.

Kazakhstan /kazakstɑ̃/ ▶ 321 *nprm* Kazakhstan.

keffieh /kefje/ *nm* kaffiyeh.

Kent ▶ 692 *nprm* **le ~** Kent.

Kentucky /kɛntyki/ ▶ 692 *nprm* Kentucky.

Kenya /kenja/ ▶ 321 *nprm* Kenya.

kényan, **~e** /kenjɑ̃, an/ ▶ 537 *adj* Kenyan.

Kényan, **~e** /kenjɑ̃, an/ ▶ 537 *nm,f* Kenyan.

képi /kepi/ *nm* kepi.

kératine /keʀatin/ *nf* keratin.

kermesse /kɛʀmɛs/ *nf* fête GB; **une atmosphère de ~** a jolly atmosphere.

kérosène /keʀozɛn/ *nm* kerosene.

ketch /kɛtʃ/ *nm* ketch.

keynésien, **-ienne** /kenezjɛ̃, ɛn/ *adj* Keynesian.

kF *written abbr* = **kilofranc**.

kg (*written abbr* = **kilogramme**) kg.

KGB /kaʒebe/ *nm* Hist KGB.

khâgne○ /kaɲ/ *nf* students' slang *second year preparatory class in humanities for entrance to École Normale Supérieure*.

khâgneux○, **-euse** /kaɲø, øz/ *nm,f* students' slang *student in khâgne preparatory class*.

khalife /kalif/ *nm* caliph.

Khartoum /kaʀtum/ ▶ 857 *npr* Khartoum.

khi /ki/ *nm inv* chi.

khmer, **khmère** /kmɛʀ/ ▶ 462 **I** *adj* Khmer.
II *nm* Khmer.

Khmer, **Khmère** /kmɛʀ/ *nm,f* Khmer; **les ~s rouges** Khmer Rouge.

khôl /kol/ *nm* kohl.

kibboutz, *pl* **-tzim** /kibuts, kibutsim/ *nm* kibbutz.

kick /kik/ *nm* kick-start.

kidnapper /kidnape/ [1] *vtr* to kidnap; **se faire ~** to be kidnapped[GB].

kidnappeur, **-euse** /kidnapœʀ, øz/ *nm,f* kidnapper[GB].

kidnapping /kidnapiŋ/ *nm* kidnapping[GB].

Kiev /kjɛf/ ▶ 857 *npr* Kiev.

kif /kif/ *nm* **1** (haschich) kif; **2**○ **c'est du ~** it's all the same.

kif-kif○ /kifkif/ *adj inv* **c'est ~ (bourricot)** it's all the same○.

Kigali /kigali/ ▶ 857 *npr* Kigali.

kiki○ /kiki/ *nm* **1** (cou) **serrer le ~ de qn** to strangle sb; **2** (ami) **c'est parti, mon ~!** here we go!

kil◑ /kil/ *nm* bottle.

Kilimandjaro /kilimɑ̃dʒaʀo/ *nprm* **le (mont) ~** Mount Kilimanjaro.

kilo[1] /kilo/ *préf* kilo.

kilo[2] /kilo/ ▶ 620 *nm* (*abbr* = **kilogramme**) kilo; **deux ~s de pommes** two kilos of apples; **prendre des ~s** to put on weight.

kilocalorie /kilɔkalɔʀi/ *nf* kilocalorie.

kilocycle /kilɔsikl/ *nm* kilocycle.

kilofranc /kilɔfʀɑ̃/ *nm* 1,000 French francs.

kilogramme /kilɔgʀam/ ▶ 620 *nm* kilogram.

kilohertz /kilɔɛʀts/ *nm* kilohertz.

kilométrage /kilɔmetʀaʒ/ *nm* (distance) ≈ mileage; **~ illimité** unlimited mileage.

kilomètre /kilɔmɛtʀ/ ▶ 477, 783, 860 *nm* kilometre[GB]; **50 ~s à l'heure** 50 kilometres[GB] per ou an hour; **coût du ~** cost per kilometre[GB]; **marcher des ~s** to walk for miles.

kilomètre-heure *pl* **kilomètres-heure** /kilɔmɛtʀœʀ/ ▶ 860 kilometre[GB] per hour.

kilométrer /kilɔmetʀe/ [14] *vtr* ≈ to measure the mileage of [*trajet*].

kilométrique /kilɔmetʀik/ *adj* [*distance*] in kilometres[GB]; [*prix, coût*] per kilometre[GB].

kilo-octet /kilɔɔktɛ/ *nm* kilobyte.

kilotonne /kilɔtɔn/ *nf* kiloton.

kilovolt /kilɔvɔlt/ *nm* kilovolt.

kilowatt /kilɔwat/ *nm* kilowatt.

kilowattheure /kilɔwatœʀ/ *nm* kilowatt-hour.

kilt /kilt/ *nm* kilt.

kimono /kimɔno/ *nm* **1** Mode kimono; **2** Sport ≈ judo suit.

kinase /kinɑz/ *nf* kinase.

kiné○ /kine/ *nmf* physio○ GB, physical therapist US.

kinésique /kinezik/ *nf* kinesics (+ *v sg*).

kinésithérapeute /kineziteʀapøt/ ▶ 510 *nmf* physiotherapist GB, physical therapist US.

kinésithérapie /kineziteʀapi/ *nf* physiotherapy GB, physical therapy US.

kinesthésie /kinɛstezi/ *nf* kinesthesia.

Kinshasa /kinʃasa/ ▶ 857 *npr* Kinshasa.

kiosque /kjɔsk/ *nm* **1** (à journaux) kiosk; **2** (abri de jardin) pavilion; **3** Naut (de bateau) pilot house; (de sous-marin) conning tower.
■ **~ à musique** bandstand.

kippa /kipa/ *nf* skull cap, kippa.

kir /kiʀ/ *nm* kir.

kirghiz, **~e** /kiʀgiz/ **I** ▶ 537 *adj* Kirghiz.
II ▶ 462 *nm* Kirghiz.

Kirghiz, **~e** /kiʀgiz/ ▶ 537 *nm,f* Kirghiz.

Kirghizie /kiʀgizi/ *nprf* ▶ **Kirghizistan**.

Kirghizistan /kiʀgizistɑ̃/ ▶ 321 *nprm* Kirghizstan, Kirghizia.

Kiribati /kiʀibati/ ▶ 321 *nprm* Kiribati.

kirsch /kiʀʃ/ *nm* kirsch.

kit /kit/ *nm* kit; **vendu en ~** sold in kit form.

kitchenette /kitʃənɛt/ *nf* kitchenette.

kitsch /kitʃ/ *adj inv* kitsch.

kiwi /kiwi/ *nm* **1** (fruit) kiwi; **2** Zool kiwi.

klaxon® /klaksɔn/ *nm* (car) horn; **entendre un coup de ~** to hear a car horn; **donner un coup de ~** to hoot (one's horn) GB, to honk (the horn) US.

klaxonner /klaksɔne/ [1] **I** *vtr* to hoot GB, to honk US.
II *vi* to hoot one's horn GB, to honk the horn US.

klebs○ /klɛps/ *nm* mutt○, dog.

kleenex® /klinɛks/ *nm* tissue GB, Kleenex®.

kleptomane /klɛptɔman/ *adj*, *nmf* kleptomaniac.

kleptomanie /klɛptomani/ *nf* kleptomania.

km (*written abbr* = **kilomètre**) km.

knickers /knikɔʀs/ *nmpl* walking breeches GB, knickers US.

knock-out /nɔkaut/ **I** *adj* **1** [*boxeur*] knocked out; **2**○ (épuisé) shattered○ GB, bushed○ US.
II *nm* knock-out; **gagner par ~** to win by a knock-out.

Ko (*written abbr* = **kilo-octet**) KB.

KO /kao/ **I** *adj* (*abbr* = **knocked out**) **1** Sport KO'd○; **mettre qn ~** to KO○ sb; **2**○ (épuisé) shattered○ GB, bushed○ US.
II *nm* (*abbr* = **knock-out**) KO○.

koala /kɔala/ *nm* koala (bear).

kôhl /kol/ *nm* kohl.

kola = **cola**.

kolkhoze /kɔlkoz/ *nm* kolkhoz.

kolkhozien, **-ienne** /kɔlkozjɛ̃, ɛn/ **I** *adj* kolkhoz.
II *nm,f* kolkhoz worker.

kopeck /kɔpɛk/ **▶46** *nm* kopeck; **ça ne vaut pas un ~** it's not worth a penny.

koran /kɔʀɑ̃/ *nm* Koran.

kouglof /kuglɔf/ *nm* kugelhopf.

Koweït /kɔwet/ **▶321**, **857** *nprm* (pays, ville) Kuwait.

koweïtien, **-ienne** /kɔwetjɛ̃, ɛn/ **▶537** *adj* Kuwaiti.

Koweïtien, **-ienne** /kɔwetjɛ̃, ɛn/ **▶537** *nm,f* Kuwaiti.

krach /kʀak/ *nm* **1** Fin crash; **~ boursier** stock market crash; **2** Écon (faillite) collapse.

kraft /kʀaft/ *nm* brown paper.

Kremlin /kʀɛmlɛ̃/ *nprm* **le ~** the Kremlin.

kremlinologue /kʀɛmlinɔlɔg/ *nmf* Kremlinologist, Kremlin-watcher○.

krill /kʀil/ *nm* krill.

krypton /kʀiptɔ̃/ *nm* krypton.

Kuala Lumpur /kwalalumpuʀ/ **▶857** *npr* Kuala Lumpur.

Ku Klux Klan /kukluksklɑ̃/ *nm* Ku Klux Klan.

kumquat /kumkwat/ *nm* kumquat.

kung-fu /kuŋfu/ **▶449** *nm inv* kung-fu.

kurde /kyʀd/ **▶462** **I** *adj* Kurdish.
II *nm* Kurdish.

Kurde /kyʀd/ *nmf* Kurd.

Kurdistan /kyʀdistɑ̃/ **▶692** *nprm* Kurdistan.

kW (*written abbr* = **kilowatt**) kW.

K-way® /kawe/ *nm* windcheater GB, windbreaker US.

kWh (*written abbr* = **kilowattheure**) kWh.

kyrie eleison /kiʀijeeleisɔn/ *nm* kyrie eleison.

kyrielle /kiʀjɛl/ *nf* **une ~ de qch** a string of sth.

kyste /kist/ *nm* cyst.

kystique /kistik/ *adj* cystic.

l, **L** /ɛl/ *nm inv* **1** (lettre) l, L; **2** (*written abbr* = **litre**) **20 l** 20 l.

l' ▶ **le**.

la[1] *art déf, pron* ▶ **le**.

la[2] /la/ *nm* Mus (note) A; (en solfiant) lah; **concerto en ~ majeur** concerto in A major; **donner le ~** lit to give an A; fig to set the tone.

là /la/

■ **Note** Lorsque *là* est employé par opposition à *ici* il se traduit par (*over*) *there*: *ne le mets pas ici, mets-le là* = don't put it here, put it there; lorsque *là* signifie ici il se traduit par (*over*) *here*: *viens là* = come (over) here.
– Lorsque *là* est utilisé avec un sens temporel il se traduit par *then*: *et là, le téléphone a sonné* = and then the phone rang.
– Pour les autres emplois voir l'article ci-dessous. *celle-là*, *celui-là* etc sont traités en entrée à part entière suivant l'ordre alphabétique.

I *adv* **1** (désignant un lieu) (par opposition à ici) there; (ici) here; **'où es-tu?'—'je suis ~'** 'where are you?'—'I'm here'; **j'ai mal ~** it hurts here; **qui va ~?** who's there?; **il n'est pas ~ pour l'instant** he's not here at the moment; **tu étais ~ quand c'est arrivé?** were you there when it happened?; **pose-le ~** put it there; **rester ~ à ne rien faire** to hang around doing nothing; **et moi je suis ~ à attendre** and here I am, waiting; **ils sont tous ~ à crier/écrire** there they all are screaming/writing away; **2** (à ce moment) then; **tu attends que ça bouille et ~ tu mets les herbes aromatiques** you wait for it to boil and then you put the herbs in; **et ~, tout à coup, quelqu'un a crié** and then, all of a sudden, someone screamed; **à quelque temps de ~** some time later; **il n'en est pas encore ~** he hasn't yet reached that stage; **s'il en est (arrivé) ~, c'est que**... if he's reduced to that, it's because...; **d'ici ~** between now and then; **d'ici ~ j'ai le temps de voir** I've got time to decide between now and then; **3** (pour renforcer l'énoncé) **~ d'accord, j'ai eu tort** OK then, I was wrong; **alors ~ tu exagères!** now you're going too far!; **~ c'est différent** that's a different matter; **c'est ~ votre meilleur rôle** that was your best part; **c'est bien ~ ce qui me chagrine** that's precisely what's bothering me; **4** (dans cela, en cela) **je ne vois ~ rien d'anormal** I don't see anything unusual in that; **il y a ~ une contradiction** there's a contradiction there ou in that; **que vas-tu chercher ~?** what are you thinking of?; **que me dites-vous ~?** what are you telling me?; **5** (à ce point) **je vais m'en tenir ~** I'm going to stay where I am; **j'en étais ~ de mes réflexions, quand**... my thoughts had gone that far, when...; **nous n'en sommes pas ~** (près du but) we haven't gone that far; (ce n'est pas si catastrophique) we haven't reached that point yet; **6** (suivi d'une proposition relative) **c'est ~ que** (à cet endroit) that's where; (à ce moment) that's when; **c'est ~ que réside la difficulté** that's where the difficulty lies; **c'est ~ que j'ai compris** that's when I understood; **~ où** where; **~ où j'habite/il est** where I live/he is; **il veut réussir ~ où personne n'a osé se lancer** he wants to succeed where no-one has dared venture before; **7** (pour renforcer un adjectif démonstratif) **en ce temps-~** in those days; **ce jour-~** that day; **cet homme-~** that man; **ces gens-~** those people; **dans ce cas-~** in that case; **8** (précédé d'une préposition) **de ~** (de cet endroit) from there; (pour cette raison) hence; **de ~ au village** from there to the village; **de ~ mon étonnement** hence my surprise; **de ~ à penser que**... that's no reason to think that...; **elle était un peu pâle mais de ~ à appeler le docteur** she was a bit pale but that's no reason to call the doctor; **par ~** (par cet endroit) here; (dans cette direction) this way; (dans cette zone) around there; **cela se passe dans les Alpes ou quelque part par ~** it's set in the Alps or somewhere around there; **il a fallu en passer par ~** fig we had to go through it; **qu'entendez-vous par ~?** what do you mean by that?; **si tu y vas par ~** fig if you go so far as saying that.

II *excl* there!; **~, tout doux!** there now, calm down!; **~, c'est fini, ne pleure plus** there, it's over, don't cry.

là-bas /labɑ/ *adv* **1** (à l'endroit que l'on indique) over there; (dans un lieu non indiqué mais connu) there; ▶ **voir**; **2** (dans un autre pays) over there.

label /labɛl/ *nm* **1** Comm quality-label; **~ de qualité** quality-label; **2** fig hallmark; **porter le ~ d'un parti politique** to bear the hallmark of a political party; **une émission qui a le ~ (du) service public** a programme[GB] that bears the hallmark of the national broadcasting network; **3** (maison de disques) label.

labeur /labœʀ/ *nm* liter labour[GB]; **les fruits de mon ~** the fruits of my labour[GB]; **le dur ~ de votre prédécesseur** the hard work of your predecessor.

labial, **~e**, *mpl* **-iaux** /labjal, o/ **I** *adj* labial.

II labiale *nf* labial.

labialisation /labjalizasjɔ̃/ *nf* labialization.

labialiser /labjalize/ [1] *vtr* to labialize.

labié, **~e** /labje/ *adj* labiate.

labiodental, **~e**, *mpl* **-aux** /labjodɑ̃tal, o/ **I** *adj* labiodental.

II labiodentale *nf* labiodental.

labo○ /labo/ *nm* (*abbr* = **laboratoire**) lab○.

laborantin, **~e** /labɔʀɑ̃tɛ̃, in/ **▶510** *nm,f* laboratory assistant.

laboratoire /labɔʀatwaʀ/ **I** *nm* **1** Pharm, Ind laboratory; **préparé en ~** prepared in a laboratory; **testé en ~** laboratory-tested; **de ~** [*animal, appareil*] laboratory; **essais en ~** laboratory tests; **2** fig hotbed (**de** of); **une région ~ du marketing** a dynamic marketing region; **3** Comm (de boucherie, pâtisserie) ≈ backshop.

II -laboratoire (*in compounds*) **camion-~** mobile laboratory; **ferme-~** research farm.

■ **~ d'analyses médicales** medical laboratory; **~ cosmétologique** cosmetics company; **~ de langues** language laboratory; **~ orbital** skylab; **~ pharmaceutique** pharmaceutical company; **~ photographique** photo laboratory; **~ de recherches** research laboratory.

laborieusement /labɔʀjøzmɑ̃/ *adv* laboriously.

laborieux, **-ieuse** /labɔʀjø, øz/ *adj* **1** [*travail, tractations, processus*] arduous, laborious; [*accouchement*] difficult; **2** [*style*] laborious; **3** [*classes, couches*] working; [*victoire*] hard-won (*épith*); **4**○ **c'est ~!** it's taking long enough!; **5**† [*personne*] hardworking; **c'est ~ de leur faire faire leurs devoirs!** it's hard work getting them to do their homework!

labour /labuʀ/ *nm* **1** (travail) ploughing ¢ GB, plowing ¢ US; **l'époque des ~s** ploughing GB ou plowing US time; **cheval de ~** plough GB ou plow US horse; **2** (terrain) ploughed GB ou plowed US field.

labourable /labuʀabl/ *adj* arable.

labourage /labuʀaʒ/ *nm* ploughing GB, plowing US.

labourer /labuʀe/ [1] *vtr* **1** Agric to plough GB, to plow US; **champs labourés** ploughed GB ou plowed US fields; **~ à la charrue** to work with a plough GB ou plow US, to plough GB, to plow US; **2** (creuser) to churn up [*sol, route*]; **les chars ont labouré la route** the tanks churned up the road; **les voyous lui ont labouré les côtes** the hooligans gave him/her a beating; **3** (écorcher) to lacerate [*peau*]; **il avait le dos labouré par les éclats d'obus** his back was lacerated by shrapnel; **visage labouré de coups de griffes** face covered in scratches.

laboureur /labuʀœʀ/ **▶510** *nm* **1** liter ploughman GB, plowman US; **2**† (cultivateur) farmer.

labrador /labʀadɔʀ/ *nm* (chien) labrador.

Labrador /labʀadɔʀ/ **▶692** *nprm* Géog Labrador.

labyrinthe /labiʀɛ̃t/ *nm* **1** Archit maze; **2** Mythol labyrinth; **3** fig labyrinth, maze; **4** Anat (de l'oreille interne) labyrinth.

labyrinthique /labiʀɛ̃tik/ *adj* labyrinthine.

lac /lak/ **▶459** *nm* (naturel) lake; (artificiel) reservoir; **les Grands Lacs** the Great Lakes; **le ~ des cygnes** Swan Lake; **le ~ d'Annecy/Érié** Lake Annecy/Erie.

IDIOMES **tomber dans le ~** to fall through.

laçage /lasaʒ/ *nm* lacing (up).

lacanien, **-ienne** /lakanjɛ̃, ɛn/ *adj, nm,f* Lacanian.

Lacédémone /lasedemɔn/ **▶857** *nprf* Lacedaemon.

lacer /lase/ [12] *vtr* to lace up [*chaussures, corset*].

lacération /laseʀasjɔ̃/ *nf* laceration.

lacérer /laseʀe/ [14] *vtr* to lacerate [*peau, chair*]; to slash [*vêtement, tableau, affiche*].

lacet /lasɛ/ *nm* **1** (de soulier, corset) lace; **chaussures à ~s** lace-ups, lace-up shoes; **nouer ses ~s** to do up one's laces; **2** (de route) hairpin bend; **une route en ~s** a twisting road; **3** (de chasseur, braconnier) snare; **tendre un ~** to set a snare.

lâchage /lɑʃaʒ/ *nm* **1** (abandon) desertion; **2** (panne) failure.

lâche /lɑʃ/ I *adj* **1** (sans courage) [*personne, attitude, crime*] cowardly; **2** (distendu) [*liens, ceinture, nœud*] loose; **3** (sans rigueur) [*règlement, fonctionnement*] lax; [*style, scénario, trame*] woolly.
II *nmf* coward.

lâchement /lɑʃmɑ̃/ *adv* **il nous a ~ abandonnés** he abandoned us, the coward; **ils se sont ~ enfuis à notre arrivée** they fled like cowards on our arrival; **il a été ~ assassiné** he was assassinated in a cowardly way.

lâcher /lɑʃe/ [1] I *nm* (de ballons, d'oiseaux) release.
II *vtr* **1** (cesser de tenir) to drop [*objet*]; to let go of [*corde, branche*]; **lâchez vos armes!** drop your guns!; **ne lâche pas la corde!** don't let go of the rope!; **lâchez-moi le bras!** let go of my arm!; **lâche-moi** lit let go of me; fig○ give me a break○, leave me alone; **~ prise** lit to lose one's grip; fig to give up; ▶**proie**; **2** (produire) to come out with [*mot, phrase, juron, gaffe*]; to reveal [*information*]; to let out [*soupir, cri, pet, rot*]; **~ une rafale de mitraillette** to fire a stream of bullets; **il n'a pas lâché un mot de toute la soirée** he didn't utter a word all evening; ▶**bordée**; **3** (laisser partir) to let [sb/sth] go [*personne, animal, chariot*]; **il a lâché ses chiens** he released his dogs; **elle a lâché ses chiens sur lui** she set her dogs on him; **il ne m'a pas lâché une seconde** he didn't leave me to myself for a second; **il ne la lâche pas des yeux** or **du regard** he never takes his eyes off her; **4** (abandonner) to drop [*ami, associé, activité*]; **lâché par ses anciens amis** dropped by his former friends; **la peur ne la lâche plus depuis** she's been in the grip of fear ever since; **5**○ (accepter de donner, de vendre) to let [sth] go [*objet*]; **~ de l'argent** to cough up○; **~ qch à qn** to let sb have sth [*argent, objet*]; **6** Sport (distancer) to break away from [*concurrent*] ; **il a lâché le peloton dans la montée** he broke away from the main field on the slope.
III *vi* (céder) [*corde, lien, nœud*] to give way; [*freins*] to fail; [*nerfs*] to break.

lâcheté /lɑʃte/ *nf* **1** (défaut) cowardice ₡; **par ~** out of cowardice; **2** (acte) cowardly act.

lâcheur○, **-euse** /lɑʃœʀ, øz/ *nm,f* unreliable person; **tu n'es qu'un ~!** you're totally unreliable!

lacis /lasi/ *nm* **un ~ de ruelles** a maze of small streets.

laconique /lakɔnik/ *adj* [*auteur, style*] laconic; [*réponse, langage*] terse.

laconiquement /lakɔnikmɑ̃/ *adv* [*s'exprimer, rédiger*] laconically, concisely; [*répondre*] tersely.

laconisme /lakɔnism/ *nm* (d'auteur, de style) concision; (de réponse, d'annonce) terseness.

lacrymal, **~e**, *mpl* **-aux** /lakʀimal, o/ *adj* lachrymal.

lacrymogène /lakʀimɔʒɛn/ *adj* [*grenade, bombe*] teargas; **gaz ~** teargas.

lacs /la/ *nm inv* (nœud coulant) snare; **~ d'amour** Hérald love knot.

lactaire /laktɛʀ/ *nm* milk cap.
■ **~ délicieux** saffron milk cap; **~ toisonné** woolly milk cap; **~ velouté** fleecy milk cap.

lactalbumine /laktalbymin/ *nf* lactalbumin.

lactarium /laktaʀjɔm/ *nm* milk bank.

lactase /laktɑz/ *nf* lactase.

lactation /laktasjɔ̃/ *nf* lactation.

lacté, **~e** /lakte/ *adj* **1** (qui contient du lait) [*produit, alimentation*] milk (*épith*); **2** (laiteux) [*liquide, blanc*] milky; **la voie ~e** the Milky Way.

lactifère /laktifɛʀ/ *adj* lactiferous.

lactique /laktik/ *adj* lactic.

lactogène /laktɔʒɛn/ *adj* lactogenic.

lactose /laktoz/ *nm* lactose.

lactosérum /laktoseʀɔm/ *nm* whey; **~ en poudre** whey powder.

lacunaire /lakynɛʀ/ *adj* **1** (incomplet) [*texte, connaissances*] incomplete; **2** Biol [*système, tissu*] lacunary; **3** Psych [*amnésie*] lacunar.

lacune /lakyn/ *nf* **1** (d'œuvre, de manuscrit) lacuna; (d'éducation, de connaissances) gap; (de loi) gap; (d'argumentation) hole; **2** Bot lacuna; **3** Géol gap.
■ **~ électronique** electron hole; **~ réticulaire** lattice hole.

lacuneux, **-euse** /lakynø, øz/ *adj* lacunary.

lacustre /lakystʀ/ *adj* **cité ~** lake dwelling.

lad /lad/ *nm* stable-boy.

là-dedans /lad(ə)dɑ̃/ *adv*

■ **Note** De même que *là* se traduit soit par *here* soit par *there*, *là-dedans*, au sens littéral, se traduit par *in here* ou *in there* suivant que l'objet dont on parle se trouve près ou non du locuteur.

(près) in here; (plus loin) in there; **mets ça ~** (près) put this in here; (plus loin) put it in there; **on étouffe ~** (près) it's boiling in here; (plus loin) it's boiling in there!; **il y a ~ tout un symbolisme** there's a lot of symbolism in it; **debout ~**○**!** get up!; **et moi ~ qu'est-ce que je fais**○**?** and where do I come in?; **y en a ~**○**!** I'm/he's etc not just a pretty face!

là-dessous /lad(ə)su/ *adv*

■ **Note** De même que *là* se traduit soit par *here* soit par *there*, *là-dessous* au sens littéral, se traduit par *under here* ou *under there* suivant que l'objet dont on parle se trouve près ou non du locuteur.

1 (sous une surface) (près) under here; (plus loin) under there; **le dossier est ~** (près) the file is under here; (loin) the file is under there; **2** (dans cette histoire) **il y a qch de louche**○ **~** there's something fishy○ about all this.

là-dessus /lad(ə)sy/ *adv*

■ **Note** De même que *là* se traduit soit par *here* soit par *there*, *là-dessus*, au sens littéral, se traduit par *on here* ou *on there* suivant que l'objet dont on parle se trouve près ou non du locuteur.

1 (sur une surface) (près) on here; (plus loin) on there **pose ton livre ~** (près) put your book on here; (plus loin) put your book on there; **2** (sur ce sujet) on it; **il a insisté ~** he insisted on it; **nous sommes d'accord ~** we agree; **qu'as-tu à dire ~?** what have you got to say about it?; **il y a un bon livre ~** there's a good book on it; **j'ai travaillé ~ pendant deux ans** I worked on it for two years; **3** (sur ce) (quelques secondes après) with that; (quelque temps après) after that; **~ il a raccroché** with that he hung up; **~ elle est partie vivre en Italie** after that she went to live in Italy; **4** (sur cette impression) **nous nous sommes quittés ~** we parted at that point.

ladite ▶**ledit**.

ladre /ladʀ/ I *adj* liter [*personne*] miserly.
II *nm* liter (avare) miser.

ladrerie /ladʀəʀi/ *nf* liter miserliness.

lagon /lagɔ̃/ *nm* lagoon.

lagopède /lagɔpɛd/ *nm* grouse.
■ **~ des Alpes** ptarmigan; **~ d'Écosse** red grouse; **~ des saules** willow grouse.

Lagos /lagɔs/ ▶**857** *npr* Lagos.

lagunaire /lagynɛʀ/ *adj* lagoon (*épith*).

lagune /lagyn/ *nf* lagoon.

là-haut /lao/ *adv*

■ **Note** De même que *là* se traduit soit par *here* soit par *there*, *là-haut*, au sens littéral, se traduit par *up here* ou *up there* suivant que l'objet dont on parle se trouve près ou non du locuteur.

> **Les lacs**
>
> **Les noms de lacs**
>
> *L'anglais n'utilise pas l'article défini devant les noms de lacs. Le mot* Lake *prend une majuscule lorsqu'il est utilisé devant le nom propre.*
>
> le lac Supérieur = Lake Superior
> le lac Victoria = Lake Victoria
>
> *Les mots* Loch *et* Lough *s'utilisent de la même façon.*
>
> le loch Ness = Loch Ness
> le lough Erne = Lough Erne
>
> *Le* de *utilisé en français pour les lacs qui portent des noms de villes n'est pas traduit en anglais.*
>
> le lac de Constance = Lake Constance
> le lac d'Annecy = Lake Annecy
>
> *Dans ce cas, l'anglais utilise toujours le mot* Lake. *Dans d'autres cas,* Lake *peut être omis:*
>
> le lac Balaton = Balaton *ou* Lake Balaton
> le lac Titicaca = Titicaca *ou* Lake Titicaca
>
> *En cas de doute, il est toujours préférable d'employer* Lake.

1 (en hauteur) (près) up here; (plus loin) up there; **~ dans le ciel** up in the sky; **il veut grimper ~** he wants to climb up there; **de ~** from up there; **tout ~** (all the) way up there; **2** (à l'étage) upstairs; **3** (au paradis) in heaven.

lai, **~e** /lɛ/ I *adj* (convers) [*frère, sœur*] lay.
II *nm* (poème) lay.
III **laie** *nf* **1** (femelle du sanglier) wild sow; **2** (chemin) forest track; **3** (de tailleur de pierre) bushhammer.

laïc *nm* = **laïque**.

laîche /lɛʃ/ *nf* sedge.

laïcisation /laisizasjɔ̃/ *nf* secularization.

laïciser /laisize/ [1] *vtr* to secularize.

laïcisme /laisism/ *nm* secularism.

laïcité /laisite/ *nf* (concept) secularism; (nature) secularity.

laid, **~e** /lɛ, lɛd/ I *adj* **1** (pas beau) ugly; **2** (choquant) disgusting; **c'est ~ de faire ça** it's rude to do that.
II *nm* ugliness; **c'est d'un ~!** it's hideous!

laideron /lɛdʀɔ̃/ *nm* ugly girl, plain Jane○.

laideur /lɛdœʀ/ *nf* ugliness; **être d'une ~ repoussante** to be hideously ugly; **ton chapeau est d'une ~!** your hat is hideous!; **les ~s de la politique** the ugly side of politics.

laie ▶**lai** I, III.

lainage /lɛnaʒ/ *nm* **1** (étoffe) woollen[GB] material; **une robe de ~** a woollen[GB] dress; **2** (vêtement) woollen[GB] garment, woolly○; **3** Comm, Ind **les ~s** woollens[GB]; **faire le commerce des ~s** to trade in woollens[GB]; **travailler dans les ~s** to work in the woollen[GB] trade.

laine /lɛn/ *nf* **1** (sur animal) wool; **2** (matière) wool; **de** or **en ~** woollen[GB], wool (*épith*); **le manteau est en ~** it's a wool coat; **3**○ (vêtement) **une (petite) ~** a woolly.
■ **~ en suint** unwashed wool; **~ peignée** worsted; **~ polaire** fleece; **~ à repriser** darning wool; **~ à tapisserie** tapestry wool; **~ à tricoter** knitting wool; **~ de verre** glass wool; **~ vierge** new wool GB, virgin wool US; **pure ~ vierge** pure new GB ou virgin US wool.
IDIOMES **elle se laisse tondre** or **manger la ~ sur le dos** she lets people walk all over her ou take advantage of her.

laineux, **-euse** /lɛnø, øz/ *adj* woolly.

lainier, **-ière** /lɛnje, ɛʀ/ I *adj* [*industrie, commerce*] wool (*épith*); [*région*] wool-producing; [*race*] bred for its wool.
II ▶**510** *nm,f* (commerçant) wool trader; (ouvrier) wool worker; (industriel) manufacturer in the wool industry.

laïque /laik/ I *adj* [*école, enseignement*] nondenominational GB, public US; [*vie, loi,*

laisser

Verbe transitif

laisser verbe transitif se traduit généralement par *to leave*. On trouvera la traduction des expressions comme *laisser la parole à qn, laisser qch en suspens, laisser à qn le soin de, laisser qn pour mort etc.* sous le nom ou l'adjectif. Attention, *to leave* verbe transitif ne s'utilise jamais sans complément:

laisse, si tu n'as plus faim!	=	leave it if you've had enough!
laisse, c'est trop lourd pour toi!	=	leave it, it's too heavy for you!
non merci, je laisse, c'est trop cher	=	no thank you, I think I'll leave it, it's too expensive

Voir **I**.

***laisser* + sujet + infinitif**

On trouvera la traduction des expressions comme *laisser voir, laisser courir, laisser à penser* etc. sous le deuxième verbe.

Lorsque *laisser* signifie permettre de ou ne pas empêcher de, on pourra le traduire par *to let*:

vous avez laissé pousser des mauvaises herbes	=	you've let weeds grow
il ne laisse pas ses enfants regarder la télévision	=	he doesn't let his children watch television
laisse-le pleurer/critiquer/dormir	=	let him cry/criticize/sleep
ne laisse pas le chat monter sur le canapé	=	don't let the cat climb on the settee
ne laisse pas brûler la sauce	=	don't let the sauce burn
quand on laisse le repassage s'accumuler	=	if you let the ironing mount up

Voir **II**.

***se laisser* + infinitif**

De façon très générale, le verbe pronominal suivi d'un verbe à l'infinitif peut se traduire par *to let oneself*:

laisse-toi couler jusqu'au fond	=	let yourself sink to the bottom

Quand la structure signifie plus précisément *accepter l'action d'autrui* on traduira par *to let sb do sth*:

il s'est laissé coiffer	=	he let me/her etc. do his hair
il ne se laisse pas caresser	=	he won't let you stroke him

Quand *se laisser* peut être remplacé par *être* on traduira par *to be*:

se laisser envahir par un sentiment de bien-être	=	to be overcome by a feeling of well-being

Voir **III**.

esprit] secular; [*État, république*] secular; [*habit*] (de prêtre) lay; (de religieux) secular.

II *nmf* layman/laywoman; **les ~s** lay people.

III○ *nf* (école) **la ~** ≈ the state primary school system (*in France*).

laisse /lɛs/ *nf* **1** (pour chien) lead, leash; **tenir un chien en ~** to keep a dog on a lead ou on the leash; **2** Géog (partie de rivage) foreshore; (limite) **~ de basse/haute mer** low-/high-water mark; **3** Littérat laisse.

laissé-pour-compte, laissée-pour-compte, *mpl* **laissés-pour-compte** /lesepuʀkɔ̃t/ **I** *adj* **1** [*marchandise*] returned; **2** [*personne*] rejected.

II *nm,f* (personne) outcast.

III *nm* Comm returned goods (*pl*).

laisser /lese/ [1] **I** *vtr* **1** to leave [*parapluie, pourboire, marge, trace*]; **~ qch à qn** gén to leave sb sth; (à sa mort) to leave sb sth; **~ la liberté à qn** to let sb go free; **~ la vie à qn** to spare sb's life; **il laisse une veuve et deux enfants** he leaves a wife and two children; **~ qn quelque part** (déposer) to leave sb ou drop sb (off) somewhere; **je te laisse** (en sortant d'un bâtiment) I must be off ou go; (en sortant d'une pièce, au téléphone) I must go; (en fin de lettre) I'll have to stop; **laisse tes livres et viens te balader** put your books away and come for a stroll; **partez en vacances et laissez vos problèmes** take a vacation and leave your problems behind; **laissons de côté les raisons de son départ** let's not go into why he/she left; **laissez la rue Palassou sur votre gauche** (dépasser) you'll see rue Palassou on your left; **2** (confier) to leave (**à qn** with sb); **~ les clés au gardien** to leave the keys with the caretaker; **jamais je ne lui laisserais les enfants** I would never leave the children with him/her; **3** (accorder) **~ qch à qn** to give sb sth [*temps, chance*]; **~ le choix à qn** to give sb the choice; (choix peu important) to let sb choose; **4** (céder, prêter, ne pas retirer) **~ qch à qn** to let sb have sth; **laisse ce jouet à ton frère** let your brother have the toy; **je vous le laisse pour 100 francs** (céder) I'll let you have it for 100 francs; **je te laisse ma voiture pendant 15 jours** (ne pas prendre avec soi) I'll leave you my car for two weeks; (prêter) I'll let you have my car for two weeks, you can have my car for two weeks; **tu devrais ~ ta place à la vieille dame** you should let the old lady have your seat; **5** (perdre) to lose; **~ une jambe à la guerre** to lose a leg in the war; **tu y laisseras ta santé** you'll ruin your health; **je ne veux pas y ~ ma peau**○ I don't want it to kill me; **6** (ne pas s'occuper de) to leave; **laisse-le, ça lui passera** ignore him, he'll get over it; **'qu'est-ce qui ne va pas?'—'rien, laisse, ce n'est pas grave'** 'what's wrong?'—'nothing really, don't worry'; **non, laisse, je te l'offre!** no, no, it's my treat!; **7** (abandonner) to leave; **je te laisse à tes occupations** I'll let you get on; **laisse-le à ses rêves** let him dream; **8** (maintenir) to leave; **~ un animal en liberté** to leave an animal in the wild; **je ne voulais pas le ~ dans l'ignorance** I wanted him to know; **9** (rendre) to leave; **cela l'a laissé froid/sans voix** it left him cold/speechless; **~ qn perplexe** to puzzle sb; **cela me laisse sceptique** I'm sceptical; **10** liter (cesser) **cela ne laisse pas d'étonner** it is a continual source of amazement.

II *v aux* **~ qn/qch faire** to let sb/sth do; **~ qn parler/pleurer** to let sb speak/cry; **laisse-moi entrer/sortir/passer** let me in/out/through; **laisse-moi faire** (ne m'aide pas) let me do it; (je m'en occupe) leave it to me; **laisse-la faire!** (ne t'en mêle pas) let her get on with it!; **laisse-la faire, elle reviendra toute seule** just leave her, she'll come back of her own accord; **ils s'entretuent et on laisse faire** they're killing each other and we just sit back and do nothing; **laisse faire!** (qu'importe) so what!; **laissons faire le temps** let things run their course.

III se laisser *vpr* **se ~ bercer par les vagues** to be lulled by the waves; **il se laisse insulter** he puts up with insults; **elle n'est pas du genre à se ~ faire** (laisser abuser) she won't be pushed around; **c'est parce que tu te laisses faire** (pas assez autoritaire) it's because you're too easy going; **il ne veut pas se ~ faire** (coiffer, laver etc) he won't let you touch him; **laisse-toi faire, c'est un bon coiffeur** leave it to him, he's a good hairdresser; **s'il veut te l'offrir, laisse-toi faire!** if he wants to buy it for you, let him do it; **se ~ aller** (tous contextes) to let oneself go; **se ~ aller au désespoir** to give in to despair; **ça se laisse manger**○! iron it's quite palatable iron.

IDIOMES **'c'est cher'—'c'est à prendre ou à ~'** 'it's expensive'—'take it or leave it'; **c'est cher mais c'est à prendre ou à ~** it's expensive but that is how it is; **il y a à prendre et à ~ dans ce qu'elle dit** I'd take what she says with a pinch of salt.

laisser-aller /leseale/ *nm inv* **1** (dans la tenue) scruffiness; **2** (dans le travail) sloppiness.

laisser-faire /lesefɛʀ/ *nm inv* laisser-faire, laissez-faire.

laissez-passer /lesepase/ *nm inv* pass.

lait /lɛ/ *nm* **1** (de mammifère) milk; **le ~ s'est sauvé** the milk has boiled over; **le ~ a tourné** the milk has gone sour ou turned; **au ~** with milk, milk (*épith*); **dessert au ~** milk pudding GB, milk dessert; **thé/café au ~** tea/coffee with milk; **frère/sœur de ~** foster brother/sister (*who has had the same wet nurse*); **2** (de végétal) milk; **~ d'amande/de coco/de soja** almond/coconut/soya milk; **3** Cosmét milk; **~ démaquillant** or **de toilette** cleansing milk.

■ **~ caillé** curd; **~ de chaux** Constr whitewash; **~ concentré non sucré** evaporated milk; **~ concentré sucré** sweetened condensed milk; **~ condensé** = **~ concentré**; **~ cru** untreated milk; **~ demi-écrémé** semiskimmed milk GB, low-fat milk US; **~ écrémé** skimmed milk GB, skim milk ou nonfat milk US; **~ entier** whole milk; **~ homogénéisé** homogenized milk; **~ instantané** instant dried milk; **~ longue conservation** longlife milk GB; **~ maternel** breastmilk; **~ maternisé** ≈ formula feed; **~ pasteurisé** pasteurized milk; **~ en poudre** powdered milk; **~ de poule** Culin eggnog; **~ stérilisé** sterilized milk; **~ UHT** UHT milk.

IDIOMES **si on lui pressait le nez il en sortirait du ~** he's/she's still wet behind the ears.

laitage /lɛtaʒ/ *nm* dairy product.

laitance /lɛtɑ̃s/ *nf* Culin, Zool soft roe.

laiterie /lɛtʀi/ *nf* **1** (usine) dairy; **2** (industrie) dairy industry; **3**† (crémerie) dairy.

laiteux, -euse /lɛtø, øz/ *adj* [*liquide, blanc, lueur*] milky; [*teint, peau*] creamy; [*mur, peinture*] milk-white.

laitier, -ière /lɛtje, ɛʀ/ **I** *adj* **1** [*industrie, produit*] dairy; [*production*] milk; **2** [*race, chèvre*] milk-yielding; [*vache*] milk.

II **▶510** *nm,f* **1** (livreur) milkman/milkwoman; **2**† (crémier) dairyman/dairymaid.

III *nm* (de fonderie) slag.

IV laitière *nf* (vache) milk cow; **c'est une bonne laitière** it's a good milker○.

laiton /lɛtɔ̃/ *nm* brass.

laitue /lɛty/ *nf* lettuce.

laïus○ /lajys/ *nm* speech.

laïusser○ /lajyse/ [1] *vi* to hold forth.

lama /lama/ *nm* **1** (animal) llama; **2** (religieux) lama.

lamaïsme /lamaism/ *nm* Lamaism.

lamantin /lamɑ̃tɛ̃/ *nm* manatee.

lamaserie /lamasʀi/ *nf* lamasery.

lambda /lɑ̃bda/ **I**○ *adj inv* [*individu, lecteur*] average.

II *nm inv* lambda.

lambeau, *pl* **~x** /lɑ̃bo/ *nm* **1** (d'étoffe) rag; (de papier, peau, cuir) strip; (de chair) ribbon; **des vêtements en ~x** rags; **une robe en ~x** a ragged dress; **une affiche en ~x** a tattered poster; **mettre qch en ~x** to tear sth to pieces; **tomber/partir en ~x** to fall to pieces; **2** fig (de patrimoine) scraps (*pl*); **fortune qui part en ~x** fortune which is dribbling away; **des ~x de conversation** snatches of conversation.

lambin○, **~e** /lɑ̃bɛ̃, in/ **I** *adj* slow; **elle est encore plus ~e que son frère** she's even more of a slowcoach○ GB ou slowpoke○ US than her brother.

II *nm,f* slowcoach○ GB, slowpoke○ US.

lambiner○ /lɑ̃bine/ [1] *vi* to dawdle; **cesse de ~** stop dawdling.

lambourde /lɑ̃buʀd/ *nf* **1** Constr (support de parquet) floor batten; (support de solives) wall plate; **2** Hort spur.

lambrequin /lɑ̃bʀəkɛ̃/ *nm* (bordure) (en tissu) valance; (en bois, métal) frieze.

lambris /lɑ̃bʀi/ *nm* (en bois) panelling[GB] ¢; (en marbre) marble walls (*pl*); (au plafond) mouldings[GB] (*pl*); **sous les ~** fig in the corridors of power.

lambrisser /lɑ̃bʀise/ [1] *vtr* (avec du bois) to panel; **pièce lambrissée** panelled[GB] room; **~ de marbre** to line with marble.

lame /lam/ *nf* **1** (de couteau, scie, mixer, tournevis) blade; (de bulldozer) blade; **~ à double tranchant** double-edged blade; **visage en ~ de couteau** hatchet face; **2** (couteau) knife; (épée) sword; (personne) **une fine ~** an expert swordsman; **3** (plaque mince) (de métal, bois, etc) strip; (de store, persienne) slat; (de ressort) leaf; (de schiste) layer; (pour microscope) **~ (porte-objet)** slide; **4** (vague) breaker.

■ **~ de fond** lit ground swell; fig upheaval; **~ de parquet** (longue) parquet strip; (courte) parquet block; **~ de rasoir** razor blade; **coupant comme une ~ de rasoir** razor-sharp.

lamé, ~e /lame/ **I** *adj* lamé (*épith*).
II *nm* lamé; **en ~** lamé (*épith*).

lamelle /lamɛl/ *nf* **1** (de bois, métal) small strip; **2** Culin (de truffe, fromage) sliver; **découper en fines ~s** to slice thinly; **3** Bot (de champignon) gill; **4** (de mica) flake; **5** (pour microscope) cover glass.

lamellé, ~e /lamɛl(l)e/ *adj* [*ardoise*] foliated; [*bois*] laminated.

lamellé-collé, *pl* **lamellés-collés** /lamɛlekɔle/ *nm* laminated timber ¢.

lamellibranche /lamellibʀɑ̃ʃ/ *nm* bivalve; **les ~s** the Lamellibranchia.

lamentable /lamɑ̃tabl/ *adj* **1** (minable) [*émission, résultat, jeu*] pathetic; **de façon ~** pathetically; **2** liter (pitoyable) [*spectacle, cri*] pitiful; [*mort, accident*] terrible; [*voix, ton*] plaintive.

lamentablement /lamɑ̃tabləmɑ̃/ *adv* [*échouer*] miserably; [*pleurer*] piteously.

lamentation /lamɑ̃tasjɔ̃/ *nf* **1** (plainte) wailing, lamentation sout; **le livre des Lamentations** the Book of Lamentations; **le Mur des Lamentations** the Wailing Wall; **2** (paroles plaintives) whining○ ¢; **j'en ai assez de ses ~s continuelles** I've had enough of his/her whining.

lamenter: **se lamenter** /lamɑ̃te/ [1] *vpr* to moan (**sur** about); **il ne cesse de se ~** he's always moaning about something; **ça ne sert à rien de se ~** there's no point in moaning; **se ~ sur son propre sort** to feel sorry for oneself; **elle se lamente d'avoir manqué cette occasion** she bemoans sout the fact that she missed that opportunity.

lamento /lamɛnto/ *nm* lament.

laminage /laminaʒ/ *nm* **1** Tech (de métaux) rolling; **~ à chaud/froid** hot/cold rolling; **2** fig (de salaires, bénéfices) erosion; (de parti, personne) annihilation.

laminé /lamine/ *nm* rolled-steel section.

laminer /lamine/ [1] *vtr* **1** Tech to roll; **~ à chaud/froid** to hot-/cold-roll; **2** fig to erode [*bénéfice, salaire*]; to destroy [*politicien*]; to annihilate [*parti*].

lamineur, -euse /laminœʀ, øz/ *nm,f* rolling-mill worker; **cylindre ~** roller.

laminoir /laminwaʀ/ *nm* rolling mill.

lampadaire /lɑ̃padɛʀ/ *nm* (de salon) standard lamp GB, floor lamp US; (de rue) streetlight.

lampant /lɑ̃pɑ̃/ *adj m* **pétrole ~** paraffin GB, kerosene US.

lamparo /lɑ̃paʀo/ *nm* (fishing) lamp; **pêche au ~** lamp-fishing.

lampe /lɑ̃p/ *nf* gén lamp, light; (ampoule) bulb; (tube électronique)† valve GB, electron tube US; **griller une ~** to blow a bulb; **la ~ a grillé** the bulb has gone.

■ **~ à acétylène** acetylene lamp; **~ à alcool** spirit lamp; **~ à arc** arc light ou lamp; **~ à bronzer** sun lamp; **~ de bureau** desk light ou lamp; **~ de chevet** bedside light ou lamp; **~ électrique** torch GB, flashlight US; **~ à essence** paraffin lamp GB, kerosene lamp US; **~ fluorescente** fluorescent light; **~ (à) halogène** halogen lamp; **~ à huile** oil lamp; **~ à incandescence** incandescent lamp; **~ à iode** quartz iodine ou halogen lamp; **~ de lecture** reading light ou lamp; **~ à pétrole** paraffin lamp GB, kerosene lamp US; **~ de poche** pocket torch GB, flashlight US; **~ solaire** = **~ à bronzer**; **~ à souder** blow lamp GB, blow torch; **~ de sûreté** safety lamp; **~ témoin** indicator light; **~ tempête** hurricane lamp; **~ à vapeur de mercure/sodium** mercury-/sodium-vapour[GB] lamp.

IDIOMES **s'en mettre**○ or **foutre**● **plein la ~** to stuff oneself to the gills○.

lampée○ /lɑ̃pe/ *nf* gulp.

lamper /lɑ̃pe/ [1] *vtr* to gulp down [*soupe, vin*].

lampion /lɑ̃pjɔ̃/ *nm* paper lantern.

IDIOMES **réclamer qch sur l'air des ~s** to chant a slogan demanding sth.

lampiste /lɑ̃pist/ *nm* **1** fig subordinate; **2** ▶ 510 lit lamplighter; Rail lampman.

IDIOMES **c'est la faute du ~** the subordinate's to blame.

lampisterie† /lɑ̃pistəʀi/ *nf* lamp store.

lamproie /lɑ̃pʀwa/ *nf* (de mer) sea lamprey; (d'eau douce) river lamprey.

Lancashire ▶ 692 *nprm* **le ~** Lancashire.

lance /lɑ̃s/ *nf* (de chasse, guerre) spear; (de tournoi) lance; **recevoir un coup de ~** to be hit by a spear; **désarçonné par un coup de ~** unseated by a violent thrust from a lance.

■ **~ d'arrosage** garden hose nozzle; **~ d'incendie** fire hose nozzle.

IDIOMES **rompre une ~ avec** or **contre qn** to cross swords with sb.

lancée /lɑ̃se/ *nf* **arrêter un coureur en pleine ~** to stop a runner in his stride; **sur sa ~** lit without slackening one's pace; fig while he/she was at it; (dans le même esprit) in the same vein; **poursuivre** or **continuer sur sa ~** (activité) to continue to forge ahead; (discours) to continue in the same vein.

lance-flammes /lɑ̃sflam/ *nm inv* flame-thrower.

lance-fusées /lɑ̃sfyze/ *nm inv* rocket launcher.

lance-grenades /lɑ̃sgʀənad/ *nm inv* grenade launcher.

lance-harpon /lɑ̃saʀpɔ̃/ *adj inv* **canon ~** harpoon gun.

lancement /lɑ̃smɑ̃/ *nm* **1** (mise en route) (de navire, compagnie, campagne, d'offensive) launching; (de programme, processus) setting up; **le ~ des travaux a eu lieu en 1980** work began in 1980; **2** Comm (mise sur le marché) (de produit, livre, film) launch; (d'emprunt) floating; (d'acteur, écrivain) promotion; **~ publicitaire** publicity launch; **3** Tech (de missile, satellite) (processus) launching; (action) launch; **base de ~** launching site; **~ réussi** successful launch; **le ~ aura lieu à 15 h** the launch will take place at 3 pm; **4** Ind, Entr (de fabrication, travail) scheduling; **5** (action de projeter) throwing; Sport throwing; **~ du disque/javelot/marteau** throwing the discus/javelin/hammer; **~ du poids** putting the shot; **6** Constr, Tech (de pont) building.

lance-missiles /lɑ̃smisil/ *nm inv* missile launcher.

lance-pierres /lɑ̃spjɛʀ/ *nm inv* catapult.

IDIOMES **manger au ~**○ to gobble one's food; **payer qn avec un ~**○ to pay sb peanuts○.

lancer /lɑ̃se/ [12] **I** *nm* **1** Sport (action) throwing; (coup) throw; **aire de ~** throwing area; **le ~ du disque/javelot/marteau** throwing the discus/javelin/hammer; **le ~ du poids** putting the shot; **son troisième ~** his/her third throw; **2** Pêche **le ~, la pêche au ~** rod and reel fishing; **prendre une truite au ~** to catch a trout with a rod and reel.

II *vtr* **1** (jeter) to throw [*ballon, caillou*]; (violemment) to hurl, to fling [*objet*]; Pêche to cast [*ligne*]; Sport to throw [*disque, javelot, marteau*]; **~ le poids** to put the shot; **~ qch par terre/dans l'eau/en l'air** to throw sth to the ground/in the water/(up) in the air; **~ qch à qn** (pour qu'il l 'attrape) to throw sth to sb; (pour faire peur, mal) to throw sth at sb; **lance-moi la balle** throw me the ball, throw the ball to me; **~ une assiette à la tête de qn** to throw ou fling a plate at sb; **il lance à 30 mètres** Sport he can throw 30 metres[GB]; **~ un coup de pied/poing à qn** to kick/punch sb; **~ ses bras en avant** to swing one's arms forward; **2** (envoyer) to launch [*satellite, fusée*]; to fire [*flèche, missile*] (**sur, à** at); to drop [*bombe*] (**sur** on); **~ ses chiens après qn/sur une piste** to set one's dogs on sb/on a trail; **~ son cheval dans la foule** to spur one's horse forward into the crowd; **~ ses troupes à l'assaut** to send one's troops into the attack; **la cathédrale lance ses flèches vers le ciel** the spires of the cathedral soar into the sky; **3** (projeter) to throw out [*fumée, flammes, lave, étincelles*]; **~ des éclairs** [*yeux*] to flash; **~ mille feux** [*bijou*] to sparkle; **4** (émettre) to give [*regard, cri*]; to sing [*note*]; to put out [*rumeur*]; to issue [*avis, ultimatum, mandat d'amener*]; to send out [*SOS, invitation*]; to float [*emprunt, idée*]; **~ une proposition au hasard** to toss out a suggestion; **5** (proférer) to hurl [*insulte*] (**à** at); to make [*menace, accusation*] (**contre** against); to let out [*juron*]; to crack [*plaisanterie*]; **~ une bêtise** to say something silly; **~ une accusation à qn** to level an accusation at sb; **il m'a lancé que** he told me that; **lança-t-il** he said; **'à demain !' lança-t-il** 'see you tomorrow!' he called; **lança-t-il avec désinvolture** he said casually; **6** (mettre en route) to launch [*navire*]; to launch [*offensive, projet, enquête, affaire, campagne publicitaire*]; Comm, Pub to launch [*produit, marque, entreprise, chanteur*]; **~ qn dans une carrière** to launch sb on a career; **c'est le film qui l'a lancé** it's the film which made his name; **~ un pays sur la voie de la démocratisation** to put a country on the road to democracy; **~ qn sur un sujet** to start ou set sb off on a subject; **7** (faire démarrer) to start up [*engine*]; to set [sth] going [*balancier, hélice*]; (faire accélérer) to take [sth] to full speed [*véhicule*]; **~ une voiture à 150 km/h** to take a car up to 150 kph; **une fois le véhicule lancé** once the vehicle has got up speed; **le train était lancé à fond** the train was tearing along; **~ un cheval** to give a horse its head; **~ sa monture au galop** to spur one's mount into a gallop; **8** Gén Civ **~ un pont sur une rivière** to bridge a river, to throw a bridge across a river.

III○ *vi* (élancer) to throb; **mon doigt me lance** my finger is throbbing.

IV se lancer *vpr* **1** (s'engager) **se ~ dans** to launch into [*explication*]; to embark on [*opération, programme, dépenses*]; to take up [*passe-temps, informatique, cuisine*]; **se ~ dans les affaires/le surgelé** to go into business/frozen foods; **se ~ dans la lecture d'un roman** to start reading a novel; **se ~ dans des dépenses** to get involved in expense; **se ~ dans l'inconnu** to venture into the unknown; **2** (sauter) to leap, to jump; (s'élancer) **se ~ dans une course** to set off on a race; **se ~ à la conquête d'un pays/du marché** to set out to conquer a

Les langues

Les adjectifs comme anglais *peuvent aussi qualifier des personnes:* un touriste anglais (▶ 537) *et des choses:* la cuisine anglaise (▶ 321). *Dans les expressions suivantes,* English *est pris comme exemple; les autres noms de langues s'utilisent de la même façon.*

Les noms de langues

L'anglais n'utilise pas l'article défini devant les noms de langues. Noter aussi l'emploi de la majuscule, obligatoire en anglais.

apprendre l'anglais	=	to learn English
étudier l'anglais	=	to study English
l'anglais est facile	=	English is easy
j'aime l'anglais	=	I like English
parler anglais	=	to speak English
parler couramment l'anglais	=	to speak good English *ou* to speak English fluently
je ne parle pas très bien l'anglais	=	I don't speak very good English *ou* my English isn't very good

En avec les noms de langues

Avec un verbe, en anglais *se traduit par* in English:

dis-le en anglais	=	say it in English

Après un nom, en anglais *se traduit par* in English *ou par l'adjectif* English. *Noter l'emploi de la majuscule, obligatoire pour l'adjectif et le nom.*

un livre en anglais	=	a book in English *ou* an English book*
une émission en anglais	=	an English-language broadcast

* *Noter que* an English book *est ambigu, tout comme* un livre français, *qui peut signifier* un livre en français *ou* un livre qui vient de France.

Mais attention:

traduire en anglais	=	to translate into English

De avec les noms de langues

Les expressions françaises avec de *se traduisent en général en utilisant l'adjectif.*

un cours d'anglais	=	an English class
un dictionnaire d'anglais	=	an English dictionary
une leçon d'anglais	=	an English lesson
un manuel d'anglais	=	an English textbook
un professeur d'anglais	=	an English teacher

Noter que ceci peut signifier aussi un professeur anglais. *Pour éviter l'ambiguïté, on peut dire* a teacher of English.

La traduction de l'adjectif français

l'accent anglais	=	an English accent
une expression anglaise	=	an English expression
la langue anglaise	=	the English language
un mot anglais	=	an English word
un proverbe anglais	=	an English proverb

L'anglais a peu d'équivalents simples des adjectifs et des noms français en -phone.

un arabophone	=	an Arabic speaker
il est arabophone	=	he is an Arabic speaker
l'Afrique anglophone	=	English-speaking Africa

country/to get the market; **se ~ dans le vide** to leap ou jump into space; **se ~ du toit** to jump off the roof; **se ~ sur qn** to leap at sb, to fall on sb; **lance-toi!** fig go on (then)!; **j'hésitais mais je me suis quand même lancé** I hesitated but eventually I went ahead; **3** (prendre de l'élan) to get a run-up; **recule pour que je me lance** move back a bit so I can get a run at it ou get up some speed; **4** (s'envoyer) [*personnes*] (pour attraper) to throw [sth] to each other [*ballon, objet*]; (pour faire mal) to throw [sth] at each other [*pierre, projectile*]; to exchange [*injures, insultes*]; **5** (se faire connaître) [*chanteur, acteur*] to make a name for oneself.

■ **~ franc** (au basket) free throw.

lance-roquettes /lɑ̃sʀɔkɛt/ *nm inv* rocket launcher; **~ multiple, LRM** multiple launch rocket system, MLRS.

lance-satellites /lɑ̃ssatelit/ *nm inv* satellite launcher.

lance-torpilles /lɑ̃stɔʀpij/ *nm inv* **tube ~** torpedo tube.

lancette /lɑ̃sɛt/ *nf* **1** Méd lancet; **2** Archit lancet (arch).

lanceur, -euse /lɑ̃sœʀ, øz/ **I** *nmf* **1** Sport thrower; **~ de disque** discus thrower; **2** (en affaires) promoter.

II *nm* Astronaut **~ (spatial)** launcher.

lancier /lɑ̃sje/ *nm* Mil lancer.

lancinant, ~e /lɑ̃sinɑ̃, ɑ̃t/ *adj* [*douleur*] nagging (*épith*), shooting (*épith*); [*musique, rythme*] insistent; [*problème*] nagging (*épith*).

lanciner /lɑ̃sine/ [1] **I** *vtr* fig (tourmenter) [*idée, remords*] to torment [*personne*]; **le doute me lancine** I've got a nagging doubt.

II *vi* lit **une douleur qui lancine** a nagging pain.

lançon /lɑ̃sɔ̃/ *nm* sand eel.

landais, ~e /lɑ̃dɛ, ɛz/ **I** *adj* **poulet/berger ~** Landes chicken/shepherd; **la forêt ~e** the forest of the Landes.

II *nm,f* (natif) native of the Landes region; (habitant) inhabitant of the Landes region.

landau /lɑ̃do/ *nm* **1** (d'enfant) pram GB, baby carriage US; **2** (voiture à cheval) landau.

lande /lɑ̃d/ *nf* moor.

Landes /lɑ̃d/ ▶ 692 *nprfpl* (département) **les ~** the Landes.

langage /lɑ̃gaʒ/ *nm* language; **le ~ des abeilles/fleurs** the language of bees/flowers; **elle m'a tenu un tout autre ~** she said something completely different to me; **faire entendre le ~ de la raison** to speak with the voice of reason.

■ **~ administratif** bureaucratic language, official jargon; **~ d'assemblage** assembler language, assembly language; **~ chiffré** code; **~ journalistique** journalese; **~ machine** machine language (code); **~ procédural** Ordinat procedural language; **~ de programmation** programming[GB] language; **~ des sourds-muets** sign language.

langagier, -ière /lɑ̃gaʒje, ɛʀ/ *adj* [*activité, rapports*] linguistic; [*structure*] language (*épith*); [*habitudes*] speech (*épith*).

lange /lɑ̃ʒ/ *nm* **1** (pour emmailloter) swaddling clothes (*pl*); **2** (couche de change) nappy GB, diaper US.

IDIOMES **être dans les ~s** to be in its infancy.

langer /lɑ̃ʒe/ [13] *vtr* **1** (emmailloter) to wrap [sb] in swaddling clothes [*bébé*]; **2** (mettre une couche) to put a nappy GB ou diaper US on [*bébé*].

langoureusement /lɑ̃guʀøzmɑ̃/ *adv* [*embrasser, s'étirer*] languorously.

langoureux, -euse /lɑ̃guʀø, øz/ *adj* [*yeux, voix, musique*] languorous.

langouste /lɑ̃gust/ *nf* spiny lobster, rock lobster GB, crawfish GB.

langoustier /lɑ̃gustje/ *nm* (filet) lobster pot; (bateau) lobster boat.

langoustine /lɑ̃gustin/ *nf* langoustine, scampi.

langue /lɑ̃g/ *nf* **1** Anat tongue; **avoir la ~ blanche** or **chargée** to have a coated ou furred tongue; **tirer la ~** (comme insulte) to stick out one's tongue (**à qn** at sb); (au médecin) to put out one's tongue; (avoir soif) to be dying of thirst; (avoir des problèmes d'argent) to struggle financially; **donner des coups de ~** to lick; **se passer la ~ sur les lèvres** to lick one's lips; ▶ **chat**, **sept**; **2** Ling (système) language; (discours) speech; **aimer les ~s** to love languages; **~ vivante** gén living language; (comme matière) modern language; **~ morte** dead language; **~ officielle/étrangère** official/foreign language; **~ artificielle/naturelle** artificial/natural language; **~ écrite/parlée** written/spoken language; **en ~ familière/populaire/soutenue** in informal/popular/formal speech; **en ~ vulgaire** in vulgar language; **professeur/centre de ~s** language teacher/centre[GB]; **la ~ de Racine** the language of Racine; **les industries de la ~** language industries; **ne pas parler la même ~** lit, fig not to speak the same language; **en ~ anglaise** in English; **être un écrivain de ~ anglaise** to write in English; **radio/journal de ~ anglaise** English-language radio/newspaper; **les pays de ~ anglaise** English-speaking countries; **3** (personne) **les ~s vont aller bon train** people will talk; **mauvaise** or **méchante ~** malicious gossip; **être mauvaise ~** to be a malicious gossip; **être/avoir une ~ de vipère** to be/have a wicked tongue; **4** (forme allongée) **~ de terre** spit of land; **~ de feu** liter tongue of flame littér.

■ **~ d'apprentissage** foreign language; **~ d'arrivée** target language; **~ de bœuf** ox tongue; **~ de bois** political cant; **~ cible** = **~ d'arrivée**; **~ de départ** source language; **~ maternelle** mother tongue; **~ d'origine** native language; **~ source** = **~ de départ**; **~ verte** slang.

IDIOMES **avoir la ~ bien pendue**○ to be very talkative; **avoir la ~ bien affilée** to have a vicious tongue; **les ~s sont bien affilées aujourd'hui** the knives are out today; **tenir sa ~** to hold one's tongue; **avoir la ~ trop longue** to be unable to keep one's mouth shut; **ça lui brûle la ~** he's dying○ to talk about it; **avoir qch sur le bout de la ~** to have sth on the tip of one's tongue; **prendre ~ avec qn** fml to make contact with sb.

langue-de-chat, *pl* **langues-de-chat** /lɑ̃gdəʃa/ *nf* langue de chat (*long thin finger biscuit*).

Languedoc /lɑ̃gdɔk/ ▶ 692 *nprm* **le ~** the Languedoc.

languedocien, -ienne /lɑ̃gdɔsjɛ̃, ɛn/ ▶ 692 **I** *adj* of the Languedoc.

II *nm,f* (natif) native of the Languedoc; (habitant) inhabitant of the Languedoc.

Languedoc-Roussillon /lɑ̃gdɔkʀusijɔ̃/ ▶ 692 *nprm* **le ~** (the) Languedoc-Roussillon.

languette /lɑ̃gɛt/ *nf* **1** (de soulier) tongue; (de cartable) strap; (de fermoir) flap; (de pain, jambon) long narrow strip; **découpez en ~s** cut in strips; **2** Mus, Tech tongue.

langueur /lɑ̃gœʀ/ *nf* languor; **être pris de ~** [*personne*] to be overcome with languor; [*économie*] to be torpid; **la Bourse est prise de ~** the stock market is sluggish; **des yeux pleins de ~** languid eyes.

languide /lɑ̃gid/ *adj* languid.

languir /lɑ̃giʀ/ [3] **I** *vi* **1** (manquer d'énergie) [*personne, conversation*] to languish; [*économie*] to be sluggish; **dans l'incertitude/d'ennui** to languish in uncertainty/in boredom; **2** (souffrir d'attendre) **~ après qn** to pine for sb; **~ d'amour pour qn** to be pining with love for sb; **je languis de vous revoir** I'm longing to see you; **faire ~ qn** to keep sb in suspense; **ne me fais pas ~**

don't keep me in suspense; **3†** liter (s'étioler) [*personne*] to languish littér; [*plante*] to wither.

II **se languir** *vpr* to pine (**de** for).

languissant, **~e** /lɑ̃gisɑ̃, ɑ̃t/ *adj* **1** (sans entrain) [*personne*] listless; [*économie, commerce*] sluggish; [*conversation, récit*] listless; **2** liter [*regard*] lovesick.

lanière /lanjɛʀ/ *nf* (pour attacher) strap; (de fouet) lash; **découper en ~s** to cut up into strips.

lanoline /lanɔlin/ *nf* lanolin; **savon à la ~** lanolin soap.

lanterne /lɑ̃tɛʀn/ *nf* **1** (lampe) lantern; ▶**vessie**; **2** Aut (feu de position) sidelight GB, parking light US; **3** Archit lantern; **4**○ (personne lente) slowcoach○.

■ **~ magique** magic lantern; **~ sourde** dark lantern; **~ vénitienne** Chinese lantern.

IDIOMES **être la ~ rouge** to bring up the rear; **notre entreprise est la ~ rouge de la région** our company is bringing up the rear in the region; **éclairer la ~ de qn** to enlighten sb (**sur qch** about sth); **à la ~!** hang 'm high!

lanterneau, *pl* **~x** /lɑ̃tɛʀno/ *nm* **1** Archit lantern; **2** (de toit de caravane) skylight.

lanterner○ /lɑ̃tɛʀne/ [1] *vi* to dawdle○.

lanternon /lɑ̃tɛʀnɔ̃/ *nm* Archit lantern.

lanthane /lɑ̃tan/ *nm* lanthanum.

Laos /laɔs/ ▶**321** *nprm* Laos.

laotien, **-ienne** /laɔsjɛ̃, ɛn/ ▶**462**, **537**

I *adj* Géog Laotian.

II *nm* Ling Laotian.

Laotien, **-ienne** /laɔsjɛ̃, ɛn/ ▶**537** *nm,f* Laotian.

Lao-Tseu /laɔtsø/ *npr* Lao-Tzu.

La Palice /lapalis/ *npr* **une vérité de ~** a truism.

lapalissade /lapalisad/ *nf* truism.

laparoscopie /lapaʀɔskɔpi/ *nf* laparoscopy.

laparotomie /lapaʀɔtɔmi/ *nf* laparotomy.

lapement /lapmɑ̃/ *nm* lapping ¢.

laper /lape/ [1] *vtr* to lap (up) [*soupe, lait*].

lapereau, *pl* **~x** /lapʀo/ *nm* young rabbit.

lapidaire /lapidɛʀ/ I *adj* **1** fig [*commentaire, formule*] pithy; [*style*] pithy, lapidary sout; **2** lit [*inscription*] lapidary.

II ▶**510** *nm* (profession) lapidary.

lapidation /lapidasjɔ̃/ *nf* stoning.

lapider /lapide/ [1] *vtr* **1** (tuer) to stone [sb] to death [*personne*]; **être lapidé** to be stoned to death; **2** (attaquer) to throw stones at [*personne*].

lapin /lapɛ̃/ *nm* **1** (animal, viande) rabbit; **faire du ~ à la moutarde/aux olives** to cook rabbit with mustard/with olives; **le coup du ~** (coup asséné) rabbit punch; (choc en voiture) whiplash injury; **cage** or **cabane à ~s** lit rabbit hutch; fig○ (immeuble) tower block; **2** (fourrure) rabbit(skin); **manteau de** or **en ~** rabbit(skin) coat; **3**○ (terme d'affection) dear; **ça va mon (petit) ~?** how are you, dear?; ▶**pet**.

■ **~ angora** angora rabbit; **~ de garenne** wild rabbit; **~ nain** dwarf rabbit.

IDIOMES **se reproduire comme des ~s**○ to breed like rabbits; **poser un ~ à qn**○ to stand sb up; **courir comme un ~** to be in great shape; **tirer qn comme un ~** to take potshots at sb; **se faire tirer comme des ~s**○ to be picked off like flies; **c'est un chaud ~**○ he's a randy devil.

lapine /lapin/ *nf* doe rabbit.

lapis lazuli /lapislazyli/ *nm* lapis lazuli.

lapon, **~e** /lapɔ̃, ɔn/ ▶**462** I *adj* Géog Lapp.

II *nm* Ling Lapp.

Lapon, **~e** /lapɔ̃, ɔn/ *nm,f* Lapp.

Laponie /lapɔni/ ▶**692** *nprf* **la ~** Lapland.

laps /laps/ *nm* **~ de temps** period of time.

lapsus /lapsys/ *nm* slip; **~ révélateur** Freudian slip.

laquage /lakaʒ/ *nm* (application de vernis) lacquering; (application de peinture) application of gloss paint GB ou enamel US; **pour le ~ des portes, choisissez** when choosing gloss paint for your doors, use.

laquais /lakɛ/ *nm* lackey.

laque /lak/ I *nm* Art piece of lacquerware.

II *nf* **1** Cosmét hairspray; **2** (résine, vernis) lacquer; (peinture) gloss paint GB, enamel US.

laqué, **~e** /lake/ I *pp* ▶**laquer**.

II *pp adj* **1** [*cheveux*] lacquered; [*ongles*] lacquered, varnished; **2** [*peinture*] gloss; **les portes sont ~es gris** the doors are painted with grey GB ou gray US gloss paint GB ou enamel US; **3** Culin **canard ~** Peking duck; **porc ~** roast glazed pork.

laquelle /lakɛl/ *pron f, adj* ▶**lequel**.

laquer /lake/ [1] I *vtr* to lacquer [*meuble*]; to paint [sth] in gloss GB ou enamel US [*porte*].

II **se laquer** *vpr* **se ~ les cheveux** to put hairspray on one's hair.

larbin○ /laʀbɛ̃/ *nm* pej **1** (domestique) servant; fig flunkey; **2** (faible) doormat○.

larcin /laʀsɛ̃/ *nm* **1** (vol) petty theft; **2** (produit du vol) spoils (*pl*).

lard /laʀ/ *nm* ≈ fat streaky bacon; **~ maigre/fumé** streaky/smoked bacon; ▶**gros**.

IDIOMES **faire du ~**○ to pile on○ weight GB, to put on weight; **je ne savais pas si c'était du ~ ou du cochon** I didn't know what to think.

larder /laʀde/ [1] *vtr* **1** Culin to lard (**de** with); **un rôti lardé** a larded joint GB ou roast US; **2** fig, pej **~ un texte de citations** to cram a text with quotations.

IDIOMES **~ qn de coups de couteau** to stab sb repeatedly.

lardoire /laʀdwaʀ/ *nf* larding-needle.

lardon /laʀdɔ̃/ *nm* **1** Culin bacon cube; **frisée aux ~s** frisée lettuce with bacon cubes; **2**◐ (enfant) kid○, brat○ péj, child.

lares /laʀ/ *nmpl* lares.

largable /laʀgabl/ *adj* [*capsule*] separable; **réservoir ~** drop tank.

largage /laʀgaʒ/ *nm* **1** Mil (de bombe) dropping; (de parachutistes) drop; **2** Astronaut jettisoning.

large /laʀʒ/ I *adj* **1** ▶**477** (de grande dimension) [*front, épaules, hanches, paumes, nez*] broad; [*couloir, avenue, rivière, lit*] wide; [*sillon*] broad; [*manteau*] loose-fitting; [*pantalon*] loose; [*jupe, cape*] full; [*chandail*] big; [*geste, mouvement*] sweeping; [*sourire*] broad; [*courbe, détour*] long; **une caisse aussi ~ que haute** a box as wide as it is high; **faire de ~s gestes des bras** to make sweeping gestures with one's arms; **former un ~ cercle** to form a big circle; **être ~ d'épaules/de hanches** to have broad shoulders/hips; **être ~ de trois mètres** to be three metres[GB] wide; **2** (important) [*avance, bénéfice*] substantial; [*choix, gamme, public*] wide; [*concertation, coalition*] broad; [*extrait, majorité*] large; **remporter une ~ victoire** to win by a wide margin; **dans une ~ mesure, pour une ~ part** to a large extent; **au sens ~** in a broad sense; **prendre une ~ part dans qch** to take a large part in sth; **bénéficier d'un ~ soutien** to have widespread support; **3** (généreux) [*personne*] generous (**avec** to); **4** (aisé) [*vie*] comfortable; **mener une existence ~** to live very comfortably; **5** (ouvert) **avoir les idées ~s, être ~ d'idées** to be broad-minded, to be liberal; **avoir l'esprit ~, être ~ d'esprit** to be broad-minded.

II *adv* **1** (généreusement) [*prévoir*] on a generous scale; [*calculer, mesurer*] on the generous side; **il vaut mieux prévoir ~** it's better to plan on a generous scale; **et quand je dis dix je suis ~**○! and when I say ten I'm erring on the generous side!; **trois kilos de spaghetti, tu as vu ~**○! three kilos of spaghetti, you don't believe in skimping, do you?; **2** Mode **s'habiller ~** to wear loose-fitting clothes; **un modèle qui chausse ~** a wide-fitting shoe.

III *nm* **1** (largeur) **faire quatre mètres de ~** to be four metres[GB] wide; **un ruban de deux centimètres de ~** a ribbon five centimetres[GB] wide; **être au ~**○ to have plenty of room; **2** Naut open sea; **gagner le ~** to reach the open sea; **au ~** offshore; **au ~ de Marseille/des côtes bretonnes** off Marseilles/the coast of Brittany; **l'air/le vent du ~** the sea air/breeze; **prendre le ~** Naut to sail; fig○ to make oneself scarce○; ▶**grand**.

IDIOMES **ne pas en mener ~**○ to be worried stiff○.

largement /laʀʒəmɑ̃/ *adv* **1** (massivement) [*admis, approuvé, représenté*] widely; [*disperser, irriguer, répandre*] widely; **le rapport a été très ~ approuvé** the report was very widely approved; **opinion/croyance ~ répandue** widely held opinion/belief; **l'auteur le plus ~ connu à l'étranger** the author most widely known abroad; **se prononcer ~ en faveur de/contre qch** to pronounce oneself largely in favour[GB] of/against sth; **un auteur ~ méconnu** a virtually unknown author; **2** (en grande partie) largely, to a large extent; **l'amélioration est ~ due à la restructuration** the improvement is due to a large extent to restructuring; **être ~ responsable de qch** to be largely responsible for sth; **3** (nettement) **l'opposition a ~ remporté les élections** the opposition won the elections by a wide margin; **être ~ vainqueur** to win by a comfortable margin; **être ~ majoritaire** to have a comfortable majority; **arriver ~ en tête** to be a clear winner; **~ en dessous/au-dessus de la limite** well under/over the limit; **~ supérieur à la moyenne** well over the average; **~ périmé** well over the date of expiry; **~ sous-estimé** very underestimated; **~ satisfait** very satisfied; **il dépasse ~ les autres** (en taille) he's much taller than the others; **couvrir ~ le genou** to cover one's knees comfortably; **4** (amplement) **tu as ~ le temps** you've got plenty of time; **'tu crois que j'ai assez d'argent?'—'~!'** 'do you think I've got enough money?'—'plenty!'; **ils ont ~ de quoi vivre** they've got more than enough to live on; **c'est ~ suffisant, cela suffit ~** that's more than enough, that's plenty; **la croissance dépasse ~ nos prévisions** growth is greatly exceeding our forecasts; **5** (au moins) easily; **ma valise pesait ~ 15 kilos** my suitcase easily weighed 15 kilos; **une chaîne en or vaudrait ~ le double** a gold chain would easily be worth double; **6** (généreusement) [*indemniser, subventionner, contribuer*] generously; **être ~ rémunéré** to be very generously paid; **7** (dans l'aisance) [*vivre*] comfortably; **8** (en grand) **~ ouvert** [*fenêtre, porte, tiroir*] wide open; [*col, veste*] open; **ouvrir ~ la fenêtre** to open the window wide; **ouvrir ~ les portes de qch** to throw wide the gates of sth; **notre parti est ~ ouvert aux jeunes** our party welcomes young people.

largesse /laʀʒɛs/ I *nf* generosity, largesse sout; **être d'une grande ~ avec qn** to be very generous with sb.

II **largesses** *nfpl* generous gifts; **répandre ses ~s** to give lavishly.

largeur /laʀʒœʀ/ *nf* **1** ▶**477** (dimension) gén width, breadth; (en géométrie) breadth; **occuper toute la ~ de qch** to take up the full width of sth; **ce tissu existe en différentes ~s** this material comes in different widths; **en petite/grande ~** in a narrow/broad width; **une lame de deux centimètres de ~** a blade two centimetres[GB] wide; **être rayé/déchiré sur toute la ~** to be scratched/torn right across; **dans le sens de la ~** widthwise; **2** (ouverture) **~ d'esprit** or **de vues** broad-mindedness; **faire preuve d'une grande ~ d'esprit** to show considerable broad-mindedness.

IDIOMES **se faire avoir dans les grandes ~s**○ to be taken in hook, line and sinker○.

largo /laʀgo/ *adj, adv* largo.

largué, **~e** /laʀge/ **I** *pp* ▶ **larguer**.
II *pp adj* **1**○ (dépassé) (par un raisonnement) lost; (par les événements) out of touch; **2**○ (marginal) spaced out○.

larguer /laʀge/ [1] *vtr* **1** Mil, Aviat to drop [*bombe, missile*]; to drop [*parachutiste*]; to release [*satellite, navette*]; **2** Naut to launch [*vedette*]; to unfurl [*voile*]; **~ les amarres** lit to cast off; fig to set off; **3**○ (abandonner) to give up [*études, appartement*]; to leave [*travail*]; to chuck○, to leave [*petit ami*]; to drop [*projet*]; **se faire ~** to get chucked (**par qn** by sb); **4**○ (dépasser) to outstrip [*concurrent*].

larme /laʀm/ *nf* **1** Physiol tear; **en ~s** in tears; **avoir les ~s aux yeux** to have tears in one's eyes; **au bord des ~s** close to tears; **le film m'a fait venir les ~s aux yeux** the film brought tears to my eyes; **y aller de sa (petite) ~** to shed a little tear; **tirer des ~s à qn** to move sb to tears; **retenir ses ~s** to hold back one's tears; **il n'a pas versé une ~** he didn't shed a tear; **fondre en ~s** to burst into tears; **elle a ri aux ~s** she laughed till she cried; **pleurer à chaudes ~s** to cry as though one's heart would break; **passer du rire aux ~s** to be laughing one minute and crying the next; **avoir la ~ facile** to cry at the slightest thing; **avoir la ~ à l'œil** to be a bit weepy; **pleurer toutes les ~s de son corps** to cry one's eyes out; **avoir des ~s dans la voix** to speak with a catch in one's voice; **2**○ (petite quantité) drop (**de** of).
■ **~s de crocodile** crocodile tears; **verser des ~s de crocodile** to shed crocodile tears.

larmier /laʀmje/ *nm* dripstone.

larmoiement /laʀmwamɑ̃/ *nm* **1** Physiol watering of the eyes; **2** (pleurnicherie) snivelling[GB].

larmoyant, **~e** /laʀmwajɑ̃, ɑ̃t/ *adj* **1** (qui pleure) [*personne*] tearful; [*yeux*] full of tears (*après n*); **2** (qui veut attendrir) [*ton, voix*] whining; [*discours*] maudlin; [*personne*] snivelling[GB].

larmoyer /laʀmwaje/ [23] *vi* **1** Physiol [*yeux*] to water; **la fumée me fait ~ (les yeux)** smoke makes my eyes water; **2** (pleurnicher) to whine (**sur qch** about sth; **chez qn** to sb).

larron /laʀɔ̃/ *nm* **1** hum scoundrel; **2** thief; **les deux ~s** the two thieves.
IDIOMES **s'entendre comme ~s en foire** to be as thick as thieves; **l'occasion fait le ~** Prov opportunity makes the thief.

larvaire /laʀvɛʀ/ *adj* **1** fig [*état*] embryonic; **2** Zool [*phase, migration*] larval.

larve /laʀv/ *nf* **1** Zool larva; **2** (être humain) péj (sans volonté) wimp○; (sans dignité) worm péj.

larvé, **~e** /laʀve/ *adj* **1** gén latent; **2** Méd atypical.

laryngé, **~e** /laʀɛ̃ʒe/ *adj* laryngeal.

laryngectomie /laʀɛ̃ʒɛktɔmi/ *nf* laryngectomy.

laryngien, **-ienne** /laʀɛ̃ʒjɛ̃, ɛn/ *adj* = **laryngé**.

laryngite /laʀɛ̃ʒit/ ▶ **271** *nf* laryngitis.

laryngologie /laʀɛ̃gɔlɔʒi/ *nf* laryngology.

laryngologiste /laʀɛ̃gɔlɔʒist/ *nmf*, **laryngologue** /laʀɛ̃gɔlɔg/ ▶ **510** *nmf* laryngologist.

laryngoscope /laʀɛ̃gɔskɔp/ *nm* laryngoscope.

laryngoscopie /laʀɛ̃gɔskɔpi/ *nf* laryngoscopy.

laryngotomie /laʀɛ̃gɔtɔmi/ *nf* laryngotomy.

larynx /laʀɛ̃ks/ *nm inv* larynx.

las, **lasse** /lɑ, lɑs/ **I** *adj* weary (**de** of); **~ de la vie/de vivre** weary of life/of living.
II las‡ *excl* alas‡!

lasagnes /lazaɲ/ *nfpl* lasagna ¢; **des ~ délicieuses** a delicious lasagna.

lascar○ /laskaʀ/ *nm* (gaillard) fellow; (débrouillard) crafty devil; (enfant) devil.

lascif, **-ive** /lasif, iv/ *adj* liter [*personne, pose, regard*] lascivious; [*tempérament*] lustful.

lascivement /lasivmɑ̃/ *adv* liter lasciviously.

lascivité /lasivite/ *nf* liter lasciviousness.

laser /lazɛʀ/ *nm* laser; **faisceau ~** laser beam; **imprimante à ~** laser printer.

laserothérapie /lazɛʀoteʀapi/ *nf* laser treatment.

lassant, **~e** /lasɑ̃, ɑ̃t/ *adj* **1** (ennuyeux) [*discours*] tedious; [*reproches*] tiresome; **2** (fatigant) tiring.

lasser /lɑse/ [1] **I** *vtr* (ennuyer) to bore [*personne, audience*]; (excéder) to weary [*personne, audience*]; **elle nous lasse avec ses jérémiades** she wears us out with her moaning; **ces discours commencent à les ~** they are becoming tired of these speeches; **~ la patience/bonne volonté de qn** to exhaust sb's patience/goodwill.
II se lasser *vpr* **1** [*personne*] to grow tired (**de qn/qch** of sb/sth; **de faire** of doing); **sans se ~** (infatigablement) without tiring; (patiemment) tirelessly; **2** [*patience*] to wear thin; [*enthousiasme, attention*] to flag.
IDIOMES **tout passe, tout lasse, tout casse** nothing lasts forever.

lassitude /lasityd/ *nf* weariness; **par ~** from sheer weariness; **avec ~** wearily.

lasso /laso/ *nm* lasso; **prendre au ~** to lasso.

latence /latɑ̃s/ *nf* latency; **période de ~** Méd latent period; Psych latency (period); fig initial period.

latent, **~e** /latɑ̃, ɑ̃t/ *adj* [*danger, maladie, possibilités*] latent; [*angoisse, jalousie*] underlying; **à l'état ~** in a latent state.

latéral, **~e**, *mpl* **-aux** /lateʀal, o/ *adj* **1** (sur le côté) [*porte, sortie*] side (*épith*); (parallèle) [*nef, tunnel*] lateral; **2** fig [*problème, objectif*] parallel; **3** Phon lateral.

latéralement /lateʀalmɑ̃/ *adv* **1** lit (de côté) [*arriver*] from the side; (sur le côté) [*placer, s'agrandir*] sideways, laterally; **2** (indirectement) indirectly.

latérite /lateʀit/ *nf* laterite.

latex /latɛks/ *nm* latex.

latin, **~e** /latɛ̃, in/ **I** *adj* **1** Antiq [*auteurs, textes*] Latin; **2** (méditerranéen) [*tempérament*] Latin; [*culture*] Mediterranean; **3** Ling **langues ~es** Romance languages; **4** Relig [*église, croix, rite*] Latin.
II ▶ **462** *nm* Ling Latin; **~ de cuisine** péj dog Latin; **~ populaire** or **vulgaire** Vulgar Latin; **bas ~** low Latin.
IDIOMES **c'est à y perdre son ~** one can't make head or tail of it.

Latin, **~e** /latɛ̃, in/ *nm,f* Latin; **les ~s** the Latin people.

latinisation /latinizasjɔ̃/ *nf* latinization.

latiniser /latinize/ [1] *vtr* to latinize.

latinisme /latinism/ *nm* Latinism.

latiniste /latinist/ *nmf* Latinist.

latinité /latinite/ *nf* **1** Ling (de style) latinity; **2** (de culture) Latin character; **3** (monde latin) **l'étendue de la ~** the extent of Latin civilization.

latino-américain, **~e**, *mpl* **~s** /latino ameʀikɛ̃, ɛn/ *adj* Latin-American.

Latino-Américain, **~e**, *mpl* **~s** /latino ameʀikɛ̃, ɛn/ *nm,f* Latin American.

latitude /latityd/ **I** *nf* **1** Astron, Géog latitude; **à 35° de ~ nord** at a latitude of 35° north; **par 38° de ~ nord** at latitude 38° north; **2** (liberté) latitude; **disposer d'une grande/d'une certaine ~** to have a great deal of/a certain amount of latitude; **avoir toute ~ de faire qch** to be entirely free to do sth; **donner** or **laisser toute ~ à qn (pour faire qch)** to give sb a free hand (to do sth).
II latitudes *nfpl* (régions, climats) latitudes; **sous nos ~s** in these latitudes; **sous toutes les ~s** in all parts of the world.

latitudinaire /latitydinɛʀ/ *adj, nmf* latitudinarian.

latrines /latʀin/ *nfpl* latrines.

lattage /lataʒ/ *nm* lathing.

latte /lat/ *nf* **1** Constr (de plafond, mur) lath; (de plancher) board; **2** (de sommier, siège) slat; **3**◐ (chaussure) shoe; **coup de ~** boot up the backside○ GB, kick in the butt◐ US; **4**○ (ski) ski.

latter /late/ [1] *vtr* to lath.

lattis /lati/ *nm* lathing.

laudanum /lodanɔm/ *nm* laudanum.

laudateur, **-trice** /lodatœʀ, tʀis/ fml **I** *adj* laudatory sout.
II *nm,f* adulator.

laudatif, **-ive** /lodatif, iv/ *adj* laudatory.

lauréat, **~e** /lɔʀea, at/ *nm,f* **1** (de compétition) winner; **~ d'un prix** prizewinner; **une ~e du prix Nobel** a Nobel prizewinner; **2** Scol, Univ successful candidate.

laurier /lɔʀje/ **I** *nm* **1** Bot laurel; **~ commun** bay (tree); **2** Culin **feuille de ~** bay leaf; **ajouter du ~** add some bay leaves.
II lauriers *nmpl* laurels; **se couvrir de ~s** [*soldat*] to distinguish oneself; [*écrivain*] to win many awards; [*candidat*] to perform outstandingly; **s'endormir** or **se reposer sur ses ~s** to rest on one's laurels.

laurier-cerise, *pl* **lauriers-cerises** /lɔʀjesəʀiz/ *nm* cherry laurel.

laurier-rose, *pl* **lauriers-roses** /lɔʀjeʀoz/ *nm* oleander.

laurier-sauce, *pl* **lauriers-sauce** /lɔʀjesos/ *nm* **1** Bot bay (tree); **2** Culin bay leaf.

laurier-tin, *pl* **lauriers-tins** /lɔʀjetɛ̃/ *nm* viburnum.

lavable /lavabl/ *adj* washable; **~ en machine** machine washable.

lavabo /lavabo/ **I** *nm* (cuvette) washbasin, washbowl.
II lavabos *nmpl* euph lavatory (*sg*).

lavage /lavaʒ/ *nm* **1** (de linge, sol, mains) washing; (de plaie) cleaning; **le ~ des vitres** window cleaning; **2** (cycle de machine à laver) wash; **un ~** a wash; **après trois ~s la tache est partie** after three washes the stain disappeared; **3** Tech washing.
■ **~ de cerveau** brainwashing; **faire du ~ de cerveau à qn** to brainwash sb; **~ d'estomac** or **gastrique** stomach washout; **faire un ~ d'estomac à qn** to pump sb's stomach (out); **on m'a fait un ~ d'estomac** I had my stomach pumped (out).

lavallière /lavaljɛʀ/ *nf* floppy necktie.

lavande /lavɑ̃d/ ▶ **193** **I** *adj inv* lavender; **bleu ~** lavender blue.
II *nf* lavender; **essence de ~** oil of lavender.

lavandière /lavɑ̃djɛʀ/ *nf* **1** (oiseau) wagtail; **2** ▶ **510** (blanchisseuse) washerwoman.

lavasse /lavas/ **I** *adj* [*couleur*] wishy-washy.
II○ *nf* **c'est de la ~** (soupe, café) it tastes like dishwater.

lave /lav/ *nf* lava ¢; **coulée de ~** lava flow.

lavé, **~e** /lave/ *adj* [*couleur*] watery; **dessin ~** wash drawing.

lave-auto, *pl* **~s** /lavoto/ *nm* C (station de lavage) car wash.

lave-glace, *pl* **~s** /lavglas/ *nm* windscreen GB ou windshield US washer.

lave-linge /lavlɛ̃ʒ/ *nm inv* washing machine.

lavement /lavmɑ̃/ *nm* Méd enema; **~ baryté** barium enema; **faire un ~ à qn** to give sb an enema; **on lui a fait un ~** he was given an enema.

laver /lave/ [1] **I** *vtr* **1** (nettoyer) to wash [*vêtement, enfant, voiture*]; **~ qch à l'eau froide** to wash sth in cold water; **~ son linge** to do one's washing; **il lave et je repasse** he does the washing and I do the ironing; **~ la vaisselle** to do the dishes, to do the

le

Article

le, la, les article défini se traduit par *the* (invariable) quand le nom qu'il précède est déterminé par un contexte supposé connu de l'interlocuteur:

passe-moi le sel	=	pass me the salt
le déjeuner d'anniversaire	=	the birthday lunch
le courage de faire	=	the courage to do

Il ne se traduit pas quand ce nom exprime une généralité ou que son contexte est indéterminé:

le sel de mer	=	sea salt
pendant le déjeuner	=	during lunch
le courage seul ne suffit pas	=	courage alone isn't enough

the se prononce /ðə/ devant consonne et h aspiré, /ðɪ/ devant voyelle et h muet (hour, honest, honour, heir), et /ðiː/ quand il est employé de manière emphatique pour indiquer l'excellence (comme **le** en français dans *c'est **le** poète de la liberté*).

Ne sont traités ci-dessous que les cas où l'article se traduit différemment de *the*, ou ne se traduit pas, ou se rend par une structure particulière, à l'exclusion de ceux qui sont développés dans les notes d'usage répertoriées **▶ 1920**, notamment celles concernant ***les jours de la semaine, les douleurs et les maladies, les jeux et les sports, les nationalités, les langues, les pays, les nombres, les titres de politesse*** etc.

Dans la composition du superlatif, l'anglais ne répète pas l'article:

l'homme le plus riche du monde	=	the richest man in the world
l'homme le plus intelligent du monde	=	the most intelligent man in the world

Les noms de plat sur un menu ne prennent pas d'article:

le steak au poivre vert	=	steak with green peppercorns

Il n'y a pas d'article après *whose*:

les enfants dont la mère …	=	the children whose mother …

L'article se traduit avec les noms d'inventions:

la charrue = the plough   *l'ordinateur* = the computer

Noter:

la Terre est ronde	=	the Earth is round
sur la planète Terre	=	on planet Earth
au contraire de la Terre, Mars …	=	unlike Earth, Mars …

Pronom personnel

Le pronom personnel se traduit selon le genre et le nombre de l'antécédent en anglais: *him* pour représenter une personne de sexe masculin, un animal familier mâle; *her* pour une personne de sexe féminin, un animal familier femelle, un bateau, un véhicule qu'on aime bien ou dont on parle avec ironie; *it* pour une chose, un concept, un pays, une institution, un animal; *them* pour un antécédent régissant un verbe au pluriel.

---

washing-up GB; **~ qch à grande eau** to wash sth down; **~ qch au jet** to hose sth down; **~ une surface avec une éponge** to wash a surface with a sponge; **~ qch à la brosse** to scrub sth; **~ ses carreaux** to clean one's windows; **▶ linge**; **2** (désinfecter) to clean [*plaie*]; **~ son organisme** to clean out one's system; **3** liter [*pluie, orage*] to wash [*rue, ciel*]; **4** (innocenter) to clear ; **~ qn d'une accusation/d'un soupçon** to clear sb of an accusation/of a suspicion; **5** (venger) liter to wash away [*humiliation, péché*]; **~ qch dans le sang** [*injure, outrage*] to exact retribution in blood for sth; **6** Art to wash.

II se laver *vpr* **1** (soi-même) to wash; **je vais me ~** I'm going to wash ou to have a wash; **se ~ la tête/les mains** to wash one's hair/one's hands; **se ~ les dents** to brush one's teeth; **se ~ d'un affront** liter to exact retribution for an insult littér; **2** [*tissu, vêtement*] to be washable; **se ~ à l'eau froide** to be washable in cold water; **se ~ facilement** to be easy to wash; **se ~ en machine** to be machine washable.

IDIOMES **se ~ les mains de qch** to wash one's hands of sth; **je m'en lave les mains** I'm washing my hands of it.

laverie /lavʀi/ *nf* **1** (blanchisserie) **~ (automatique)** launderette, laundromat® US; **2** Minér washery.

lavette /lavɛt/ *nf* **1** (pour la vaisselle) dishcloth, dishrag US; **2**○ pej (personne) wimp○ péj; **3** H (de toilette) flannel GB, wash cloth US.

laveur, -euse /lavœʀ, øz/ **▶ 510** *nm,f* gén cleaner; **~ de carreaux/voitures** window/car cleaner.

lave-vaisselle /lavvɛsɛl/ *nm inv* dishwasher.

lavis /lavi/ *nm* **1** (technique) wash; **faire un dessin au ~** to do a wash drawing; **2** (dessin) wash drawing.

lavoir /lavwaʀ/ *nm* **1** (pour la lessive) wash house; **2** Minér washery.

laxatif, -ive /laksatif, iv/ **I** *adj* laxative.

II *nm* laxative.

laxisme /laksism/ *nm* **1** laxity; **faire preuve de ~ à l'égard de qn** to be too lax with sb; **2** Relig Laxism.

laxiste /laksist/ **I** *adj* **1** lax (**à l'égard de, avec** with); **2** Relig Laxist.

II *nmf* **c'est un ~** he is lax.

layette /lɛjɛt/ *nf* baby clothes (*pl*), layette; **rayon ~** babywear department.

layon /lɛjɔ̃/ *nm* track.

Lazare /lazaʀ/ *npr* Lazarus.

lazaret /lazaʀɛ/ *nm* (dans un port) lazaret; (dans un hôpital) isolation ward.

lazulite /lazylit/ *nf* lazulite.

lazzi /ladzi/ *nmpl inv* jeer; **être accueilli par des ~ de la foule** to be greeted by the jeers of the crowd.

le, la[1] (**l'** *before vowel or mute h*), *pl* **les** /lə, la, l, lɛ/ **I** *art déf* **1** (avec complément de nom) **la jupe/fille de ma sœur** my sister's skirt/daughter; **les chapitres du livre** the chapters of the book; **la table de la cuisine** the kitchen table; **2** (en parlant d'une personne) **il est arrivé les mains dans les poches** he came with his hands in his pockets; **elle s'est cogné ~ bras** she banged her arm; **elle m'a pris par ~ bras** she took me by the arm; **elle a reçu une tomate dans l'œil** a tomato hit her in the eye; **3** (avec un nom d'espèce) **l'homme préhistorique/de Cro-Magnon** prehistoric/Cro-Magnon man; **l'araignée n'est pas un insecte** spiders are not insects, the spider isn't an insect; **les droits de l'enfant** children's rights; **elle aime les chevaux** she likes horses; **4** (avec un nom propre) **les Dupont** the Duponts; **les Newton, Einstein et autres génies** the Newtons, Einsteins and other geniuses; **la Marion**○ (femme) Marion; **la Fleurette** (vache, jument) old Fleurette; **Le Caravage** Caravaggio; **la Caballé** Caballé; **la Noël** Christmas; **la Saint-Michel** St. Michael's day; **~ roi Olaf** King Olaf; **j'ai acheté ~ Cézanne/la Volvo**® I bought the Cézanne/the Volvo®; **5** (avec un adjectif) **je prendrai la bleue/la plus foncée** I'll take the blue one/the darkest one; **~ ridicule de cette affaire** what is ridiculous about this matter; **les pauvres** the poor; **Pierre ~ Grand** Peter the Great; **6** (avec préposition et nombre) **arriver sur** or **vers les 11 heures** to arrive about 11 o'clock; **coûter dans les 20 francs** to cost about 20 francs; **il doit avoir dans la cinquantaine** he must be about fifty; **7** (pour donner un prix, une fréquence etc) a, an; **50 francs ~ kilo/la douzaine** 50 francs a kilo/a dozen; **trois fois la semaine/l'an** three times a week/a year; **8** (dans les exclamations) **l'imbécile!** the fool!; **ah, l'imbécile!** what a fool!; **la pauvre!** the poor thing!; **la méchante!** the naughty girl!; **(oh) la jolie robe!** what a pretty dress!

II *pron pers* **je ne ~/la/les comprends pas** I don't understand him/her/them.

III *pron neutre* **1** (complément) **je ~ savais** (je suis au courant) I knew; (j'aurais dû m'en douter) I knew it; **je ne veux pas ~ savoir** I don't want to know (about it); **si je ne ~ fais pas, qui ~ fera?** if I don't do it, who will?; **je ~ croyais aussi, mais...** I thought so too, but...; **si c'est lui qui ~ dit...** if HE says so...; **tu vois, je te l'avais dit!** you see, I told you so!; **je te l'avais bien dit qu'il avait tort** I did tell you that he was wrong; **'ils auront fini demain'—'espérons-~!'** 'they'll have finished tomorrow'—'let's hope so!'; **comme tu peux bien l'imaginer, le train avait du retard** as you can well imagine, the train was late; **2** (attribut) **'est-elle satisfaite?'—'je ne crois pas qu'elle ~ soit'** 'is she satisfied?'—'I don't think she is' ou 'I don't think so'; **le jardin n'était pas entretenu, maintenant il l'est** the garden GB ou yard US wasn't tidy, now it is.

lé /le/ *nm* **1** (de tissu, papier peint) width; **2** (de jupe) panel.

LEA /ɛləa/ *nfpl* (*abbr* = **langues étrangères appliquées**) *university language course with emphasis on business and management.*

leader /lidœʀ/ *nm* Comm, Pol, Presse leader; **région/usine ~** foremost region/factory.

leadership /lidœʀʃip/ *nm* **1** (rôle de leader) leading role; **2** (suprématie) supremacy.

leasing /liziŋ/ *nm* leasing; **en ~** on a leasing basis.

lèche /lɛʃ/ *nf* **1**○ (flatterie) bootlicking○, apple-polishing○ US; **faire de la ~** to be a bootlicker○, to be an apple-polisher○ US; **faire de la ~ à qn** to lick sb's boots○; **2** Art (touche) tiny brush-stroke.

lèche-bottes○ /lɛʃbɔt/ **I** *nmf inv* bootlicker○, apple-polisher○ US.

II *nm* bootlicking○, apple-polishing○ US; **faire du ~** to be a bootlicker○, to be an apple-polisher○ US.

lèche-cul● /lɛʃky/ **I** *nmf inv* arse[GB]-licker●, ass-kisser● US.

II *nm* arse[GB]-licking●, ass-kissing● US; **faire du ~** to be an arse[GB]-licker●, to kiss ass● US.

lèchefrite /lɛʃfʀit/ *nf* dripping pan.

lécher /leʃe/ [1] **I** *vtr* **1** (avec la langue) to lick [*cuillère, assiette*]; **lèche la crème que tu as sur les doigts** lick the cream off your fingers; **il a léché tout ce qui restait dans l'assiette/le bol** he's licked the plate/bowl clean; **2** (effleurer) [*flamme*] to lick; [*mer*] to lap against; **3**○ (peaufiner) to polish [*œuvre*]; **traduction léchée** polished translation; **4**○ **~ les vitrines** to go window-shopping.

II se lécher *vpr* **se ~ les doigts** to lick one's fingers.

IDIOMES **~ les bottes**○ **de qn** to lick sb's boots○, to brown-nose sb◑ US; **~ le cul**● **à qn** to lick sb's arse●[GB], to kiss sb's ass● US.

lécheur○, **-euse** /leʃœʀ, øz/ *nm,f* péj bootlicker○, brown-noser◑ US.

lèche-vitrines /lɛʃvitʀin/ *nm inv* window-shopping; **faire du ~** to go window-shopping.

lécithine /lesitin/ *nf* lecithin.

leçon /ləsɔ̃/ *nf* **1** Scol lesson; **prendre/donner des ~s de piano** to take/give piano lessons; **la voile en 20 ~s** sailing in 20 lessons; **réciter ses ~s** to recite one's lessons; **apprendre sa ~** to learn one's lesson; **lire/expliquer une ~** to read/explain a lesson; **2** (punition, avis) lesson; **donner une (bonne) ~ à qn** to teach sb a lesson; **cela leur servira de ~** that will teach them a lesson; **cela te servira de ~** let that be a lesson to you; **elle m'a fait la ~** she lectured me; **donner des ~s de morale à qn** to preach to sb; **je n'ai de ~s à recevoir de personne** nobody is going to tell me what to do; **elle pourrait nous donner des ~s en matière de courage** she could teach us a thing or two about courage; **3** (conclusion) lesson; **tirer une ~ de qch** to draw a lesson from sth; **la ~ de la fable** the moral of the story.

■ **~ de choses**† nature study; **~ particulière** private lesson.

lecteur, **-trice** /lɛktœʀ, tʀis/ I **▶510** *nm,f* **1** gén, Édition reader; **c'est un grand ~ de Proust** he's an avid reader of Proust; **2** Univ (language) teaching assistant.

II *nm* **1** Ordinat reader; **~ optique** optical scanner ou reader; **~ de disquettes** disk drive; **2** (en hi-fi) player; **~ de cassettes** cassette player; **~ laser** CD player.

lectorat /lɛktɔʀa/ *nm* readership.

lecture /lɛktyʀ/ *nf* **1** (de livre, journal) reading; **la ~ à voix haute** reading aloud; **à la deuxième ~** on the second reading; **organiser des ~s d'œuvres théâtrales/de poésies** to organize play/poetry readings; **livre d'une ~ ardue/agréable** book which is difficult/pleasant to read or a difficult/good read; **faire la ~ à qn** to read to sb; **donner ~ de qch** fml to read out sth; **2** (interprétation) reading, interpretation; **une ~ marxiste/freudienne** a Marxist/Freudian reading; **3** (ce qu'on lit) reading material; **tu as pris de la ~?** have you brought something to read?; **avoir de bonnes/mauvaises ~s** (jugement de valeur) to read good/trashy books; (jugement moral) to read edifying/unsavoury[GB] books; **ce sont mes ~s préférées** it's what I like reading best, it's my favourite[GB] (kind of) reading; **4** (de musique, radiographie, graphique) reading; **~ à vue** sight-reading; **5** Pol reading; **proposition de loi adoptée en première ~** bill passed at its first reading; **6** (en hi-fi) playback; **7** Ordinat reading; **~ optique** optical scanning ou reading.

ledit, **ladite**, *pl* **lesdits**, **lesdites** /lədi, ladit, ledi, ledit/ *adj* the aforementioned.

légal, **~e**, *mpl* **-aux** /legal, o/ *adj* [*âge, définition, formalités, voies*] legal; [*activité, possession*] lawful; **monnaie ~e** legal tender; **domicile ~** official residence; **avoir une existence ~e** to be legally recognized; **dans les formes ~es** according to law; **durée ~e** (permise) period permitted by law; (prescrite) period prescribed by law.

légalement /legalmɑ̃/ *adv* (selon la loi) legally; (sans enfreindre la loi) lawfully.

légalisation /legalizasjɔ̃/ *nf* (pour rendre légal) legalization; (pour certifier) authentication.

légaliser /legalize/ [1] *vtr* (rendre légal) to legalize; (certifier) to authenticate.

légalisme /legalism/ *nm* legalism.

légaliste /legalist/ *adj, nmf* legalist.

légalité /legalite/ *nf* (conformité à la loi) legality; (légitimité) lawfulness; **rester dans/sortir de la ~** to remain within/transgress the law.

légat /lega/ *nm* legate.

légataire /legatɛʀ/ *nmf* legatee; **~ universel** sole legatee.

légation /legasjɔ̃/ *nf* (en diplomatie) legation.

légendaire /leʒɑ̃dɛʀ/ *adj* legendary.

légende /leʒɑ̃d/ *nf* **1** (fable) legend; **entrer dans la ~** to become legendary; **entrer vivant dans la ~** to become a legend in one's own lifetime; **elle reste fidèle à sa ~** she lives up to her legendary reputation; **2** (inscription) (de médaille) legend; (d'illustration) caption; (de carte) key; **3** (mensonge) tall story.

léger, **-ère** /leʒe, ɛʀ/ I *adj* **1** (pesant peu) light; **une valise légère à porter** a suitcase which is light to carry; **se sentir plus ~** fig to have a great weight off one's mind; **être/se sentir plus ~ de 1 000 francs** hum to be/feel 1,000 francs lighter; **2** Culin [*plat, repas, recette, cuisine*] light; **3** (souple) [*personne, danseuse*] light, nimble; [*allure, démarche*] light; [*pas*] springy; [*mouvement*] nimble; [*toucher*] Mus light; **avoir une démarche légère** to have a light step; **marcher d'un pas ~** to walk with a light ou springy step; **4** (faible) [*rire*] gentle; [*coup*] soft, gentle; [*caresse*] light, gentle; [*blessure, modification, progrès, baisse, hausse, faute, retard*] slight; [*douleur, crainte, condamnation*] mild; [*goût, odeur, tremblement, espoir*] faint; [*vent, pluie, brume, vapeur*] light; [*accent, bruit*] faint, slight; [*punition*] mild, lenient; [*couche, étendue, nuage*] thin; [*blessure*] minor; **l'accident a fait trois blessés ~s** three people were slightly injured in the accident; **5** (peu concentré) [*café, thé, chocolat, alcool, bière*] weak; [*parfum, vin*] light; [*tabac*] mild GB, light US; **6** (superficiel) [*action, initiative*] ill-considered; [*jugement, propos*] thoughtless, careless; [*argument, preuve*] weak, flimsy; **il est un peu ~** he doesn't really think about things; **se montrer ~** to act without thought; **7**○ (insuffisant) **c'est un peu ~** it's a bit skimpy; **8** (frivole) [*femme*] loose; [*mœurs*] loose, lax; [*mari, amant, caractère, humeur*] fickle; **9** Mil [*arme, division*] light.

II *adv* [*voyager*] light; **cuisiner/manger ~** to cook/eat light meals; **hier soir nous avons mangé ~** we had a light meal yesterday evening.

III **à la légère** *loc adv* (sans réfléchir) [*parler, agir, répondre*] without thinking; [*accuser*] rashly; **prendre qch à la légère** not to take sth seriously.

légèrement /leʒɛʀmɑ̃/ *adv* **1** (faiblement) [*appuyer, bouger, agiter*] gently; [*masser, frotter, gratter*] gently, lightly; [*habillé, vêtu*] lightly; [*parfumer*] lightly, slightly; [*trembler, sucrer, saler, teinté*] slightly; **il est très ~ blessé** he is very slightly hurt; **il est ~ plus grand que son frère** he is slightly taller than his brother; **être habillé ~** to be dressed for warm weather; **être habillé trop ~** not to be dressed warmly enough; **2** Culin [*manger*] lightly; **3** (avec souplesse) [*marcher, courir*] lightly, nimbly; **4** (avec désinvolture) [*agir, parler, se conduire*] without thinking; **parler ~ d'une chose sérieuse** to speak nonchalantly ou glibly about a serious matter.

légèreté /leʒɛʀte/ *nf* **1** lit lightness; **cette valise est d'une ~ incroyable** this suitcase is incredibly light; **2** Culin lightness; **donner de la ~ à qch** to make sth lighter; **3** (souplesse) (de personne, danseur) lightness, nimbleness; (d'allure, de démarche, mouvement, style) lightness; (de toucher) Mus lightness; **avec ~** lightly; **4** (faiblesse) (de rire, caresse) softness, gentleness; (de coup, voix) softness; (de douleur) mildness; (de bruit) faintness; (de punition, condamnation) leniency; (de faute, d'erreur) triviality; **5** (de café, thé, chocolat) weakness; (de vin, parfum) lightness; (de tabac) mildness GB, lightness US; **6** (superficialité) (de jugement, propos) lack of thought (**de qch** behind sth); **faire preuve de ~ dans qch** to take sth lightly; **j'ai été surpris de la ~ avec laquelle il...** I was surprised by how lightly he...; **7** (frivolité) looseness; (caractère volage) fickleness.

légiférer /leʒifeʀe/ [14] *vi* **1** lit to legislate; **2** fig to lay down the law.

légion /leʒjɔ̃/ *nf* **1** Hist, Mil legion; **2** (multitude) army (**de** of); **ils sont ~** they are legion.

■ **la Légion (étrangère)** the Foreign Legion; **la Légion d'honneur** the Legion of Honour[GB].

légionnaire /leʒjɔnɛʀ/ I *nmf* (qui a la Légion d'honneur) member of the Legion of Honour[GB].

II *nm* (romain) legionary; (de la Légion étrangère) legionnaire.

législateur, **-trice** /leʒislatœʀ, tʀis/ I *nm,f* legislator, law-maker.

II *nm* (assemblée) legislature.

législatif, **-ive** /leʒislatif, iv/ I *adj* legislative; **élections législatives** ≈ general elections.

II *nm* legislature.

législation /leʒislasjɔ̃/ *nf* legislation; **~ du travail** labour[GB] legislation.

législature /leʒislatyʀ/ *nf* **1** (durée) term of office; **2** (assemblée) legislature.

légiste /leʒist/ *nm* jurist.

légitimation /leʒitimasjɔ̃/ *nf* legitimization.

légitime /leʒitim/ I *adj* **1** (selon la loi) [*enfant, droit, pouvoir*] legitimate; [*union, époux, héritier*] lawful; **2** (justifié) [*revendication, action*] legitimate; [*grief, colère*] justifiable; **il est ~ de dire/faire** one can legitimately say/do; **3** (juste) [*salaire*] fair; [*récompense*] just.

II *nf*◑ **ma ~** the missus○.

■ **~ défense** self-defence[GB]; **agir en état de ~ défense** to act in self-defence[GB].

légitimement /leʒitimmɑ̃/ *adv* legitimately.

légitimer /leʒitime/ [1] *vtr* to legitimize.

légitimisme /leʒitimism/ *nm* legitimism.

légitimiste /leʒitimist/ *adj, nmf* legitimist.

légitimité /leʒitimite/ *nf* **1** Jur legitimacy; **2** (d'une action) lawfulness.

Le Greco /ləgʀeko/ *npr* El Greco.

legs /lɛg/ *nm* **1** Jur (de biens mobiliers) legacy; (de terres, biens immobiliers) devise; (d'effets personnels) bequest; (à un musée, une fondation) bequest; **faire un ~ à qn** to leave a legacy to sb; **2** fig legacy.

léguer /lege/ [14] *vtr* **1** (par testament) to leave sth (**à qn** to sb), bequeath (**à qn** to sb) spéc; **~ qch à qn par testament** to bequeath sth to sb; **2** (transmettre) to hand down [*traditions*]; to pass on [*qualité, défaut*]; **la situation économique léguée au gouvernement** the economic situation inherited by the government.

légume /legym/ I *nm* **1** lit vegetable; **~s verts** green vegetables; **~s secs** pulses; **2**○ fig, péj vegetable.

II○ *nf* **grosse ~** big wig○ GB, big shot○ US.

légumier, **-ière** /legymje, ɛʀ/ I *adj* vegetable (*épith*).

II *nm* vegetable dish.

légumineuse /legyminøz/ *nf* leguminous plant.

Leibniz /lajbnitz/ *npr* Leibnitz.

Leicestershire **▶692** *nprm* **le ~** Leicestershire.

leitmotiv /lajtmɔtiv/ *nm* (tous contextes) leitmotiv; **revenir comme un ~ dans qch** to run as a leitmotiv through sth.

Léman /lemɑ̃/ **▶459** *npr* **le lac ~** Lake Geneva.

lemmatisation /lɛmatizasjɔ̃/ *nf* lemmatization.

lemmatiser /lematize/ [1] *vtr* to lemmatize.

lemme /lɛm/ *nm* lemma.

lemming /lemiŋ/ *nm* lemming.

lémure /lemyʀ/ *nm* Mythol shade, ghost.

lémurien /lemyʀjɛ̃/ *nm* lemur; **les ~s** the Lemuridae.

lendemain /lɑ̃dəmɛ̃/ I *nm* **1** (jour suivant) **le ~** the following day; **dès le ~** the (very) next day; **jusqu'au ~** until the next ou following day; **le ~ de l'accident** the day after the accident; **il est venu nous voir le ~ de son arrivée** he came to see us the day after he arrived; **la journée du ~** the following day; **le ~ matin/soir** the following morning/evening; **le ~ dans l'après-midi/la soirée** the next day in the afternoon/the evening; **~ de fête** day after a public holiday GB ou the holiday US; **du jour**

au ~ from one day to the next; **2** (période qui suit) **au ~ de** (in the period) after; **au ~ de la guerre** just after the war; **3** (avenir) **le ~** tomorrow, the future; **songer au ~** to think of the future; **sans ~** [*bonheur, succès*] short-lived.

II **lendemains** *nmpl* **1** (issue) outcome; (conséquences) consequences; **2** (perspectives) future; **cela nous promet de beaux** or **d'heureux ~s** the future looks very promising ou bright for us; **des ~s difficiles** difficult days ahead; **promettre des ~s qui chantent** to promise a brighter future.

IDIOMES **il ne faut jamais remettre au ~ ce qu'on peut faire le jour même** Prov never put off till tomorrow what you can do today.

lénifiant, **~e** /lenifjɑ̃, ɑ̃t/ *adj* [*médicament, remarque*] soothing.

lénifier /lenifje/ [2] *vtr* to soothe.

Lénine /lenin/ *npr* Lenin.

Léningrad /leningʀad/ ▶ 857 *npr* Hist Leningrad.

léninisme /leninism/ *nm* Leninism.

léniniste /leninist/ *adj, nmf* Leninist.

lénitif, **-ive** /lenitif, iv/ I *adj* lenitive.

II *nm* lenitive.

Lens /lɑ̃s/ ▶ 857 *npr* Lens.

lensois, **~e** /lɑ̃swa, az/ ▶ 857 *adj* of Lens.

Lensois, **~e** /lɑ̃swa, az/ ▶ 857 *nm,f* (natif) native of Lens; (habitant) inhabitant of Lens.

lent, **~e** /lɑ̃, ɑ̃t/ I *adj* slow (**dans** in); [*film, véhicule*] slow-moving; [*poison*] slow-acting; **être ~ à faire** to be slow to do ou in doing; **être ~ au travail** to be a slow worker; **avoir l'esprit ~** to be slow-witted.

II **lente** *nf* Zool nit.

lentement /lɑ̃t(ə)mɑ̃/ *adv* slowly; **progresser ~** to make slow progress.

IDIOMES **qui va ~ va sûrement** Prov slowly but surely.

lenteur /lɑ̃tœʀ/ *nf* slowness (**à faire** to do, in doing); **avec ~** slowly; **~ d'esprit** slow-wittedness; **les ~s de l'administration** the slowness of the administration.

lentigo /lɑ̃tigo/ *nm* lentigo.

lentille /lɑ̃tij/ *nf* **1** Bot, Culin lentil; **2** Méd, Tech lens; **~s cornéennes** or **de contact** contact lenses; **~s dures/souples** hard/soft contact lenses; **mettre ses ~s** to put in one's contact lenses.

■ **~ concave** concave lens; **~ convergente** convergent lens; **~ convexe** convex lens; **~ divergente** divergente lens; **~ d'eau** Bot duckweed; **~ réfringente** refractive lens.

léonin, **~e** /leɔnɛ̃, in/ *adj* liter **1** [*aspect, chevelure*] leonine; **2** [*marché, contrat, clause*] one-sided; [*partage*] inequitable; **3** Littérat leonine.

léopard /leɔpaʀ/ *nm* **1** (animal) leopard; **2** (fourrure) leopardskin; **manteau de ~** leopardskin coat.

■ **~ de mer** sea leopard.

LEP /lɛp/ *nm*: *abbr* ▶ **lycée**.

lépidoptère /lepidɔptɛʀ/ *nm* (insecte) Lepidopteran; **les ~s** lepidoptera.

lépiote /lepjɔt/ *nf* parasol mushroom.

lèpre /lɛpʀ/ ▶ 271 *nf* **1** Méd leprosy; **avoir la ~** to have leprosy; **2** (de pierre) leprous mould GB ou mold US.

lépreux, **-euse** /lepʀø, øz/ I *adj* **1** Méd leprous; **2** [*pierre, mur*] flaking.

II *nm,f* leper.

léproserie /lepʀozʀi/ *nf* leper hospital, leprosarium spéc.

lequel /ləkɛl/, **laquelle** /lakɛl/, **lesquels** *mpl*, **lesquelles** *fpl* /lekɛl/, (avec *à*) **auquel**, **auxquels** *mpl*, **auxquelles** *fpl* /okɛl/, (avec *de*) **duquel** /dykɛl/, **desquels** *mpl*, **desquelles** *fpl* /dekɛl/

■ **Note** Lorsque la traduction du verbe de la proposition relative introduite par *lequel, laquelle* etc fait intervenir une préposition en anglais trois traductions sont possibles: *le carton dans lequel tu as mis les bouteilles* = the box you put the bottles in; = the box that *ou* which you put the bottles in; = the box in which you put the bottles. Les deux premières traductions relèvent de la langue courante, parlée ou écrite; la troisième traduction sera préférée dans une langue plus soutenue, surtout écrite.

– La forme interrogative fonctionne de la même façon, avec seulement deux possibilités; la seconde étant préférée dans la langue écrite soutenue: *dans lequel de ces cartons as-tu mis les bouteilles?* = which of these boxes did you put the bottles in?; = in which of these boxes did you put the bottles?

I **lequel**, **laquelle**, **lesquels**, **lesquelles** *adj* (avec personne) who; (autres cas) which; **il m'a présenté son cousin, ~ cousin vit en Allemagne** he introduced me to his cousin, who lives in Germany; **il a acheté une voiture d'occasion, laquelle voiture est déjà en panne** he bought a second-hand car, which has already broken down; **elle a envoyé son dossier au service des inscriptions, ~ dossier a été perdu** she sent her file to the registration office, and it was lost; **auquel cas** in which case; **auquel cas il faudrait nous prévenir** in which case you'd have to contact us.

II *pron rel* **1** (en fonction de sujet) (représentant une personne) who; (dans les autres cas) which; **il a donné le colis au réceptionniste, ~ me l'a remis** he gave the package to the receptionist, who gave it to me; **la voiture a percuté le mur, ~ s'est écroulé** the car hit the wall, which collapsed; **2** (en fonction d'objet) (représentant une personne) whom; (dans les autres cas) which; **l'ami auquel tu as écrit** the friend to whom you wrote, the friend (who) you wrote to; **les gens contre lesquels les mesures ont été prises** the people against whom the measures were taken; **la table sur laquelle tu as posé la tasse** the table on which you put the cup, the table (which) you put the cup on; **les gens chez lesquels nous sommes allés** the people whose house we went to.

III *pron inter* which; **laquelle de ces bagues préfères-tu?** which of these rings do you prefer?; **de tous ces employés, lesquels sont les plus compétents?** of all these employees, which are the most competent?; **parmi tous ses enfants, duquel est-ce qu'elle t'a le plus parlé?** out of all her children, which (one) did she tell you most about?; **auquel de tes amis as-tu écrit?** which of your friends did you write to?, to which of your friends did you write?; **auquel de ces personnages vous identifiez-vous?** with which of these characters do you identify?, which of these characters do you identify with?; **je ne sais pas laquelle de ces deux versions croire** I don't know which of these two versions to believe; **je ne sais pas à laquelle de ces annonces répondre** I don't know which of these ads I should reply to ou to which of these ads I should reply; **parmi ces voitures, je me demande laquelle est la plus fiable** I wonder which of these cars is the most reliable; **'j'ai vu un film de Chaplin hier'—'~?'** 'I saw a Charlie Chaplin film yesterday'—'which one?'; **'j'ai rencontré deux des frères Grovagnard ce matin'—'lesquels?'** 'I met two of the Grovagnard brothers this morning'—'which ones?'

les ▶ **le**.

lesbien, **-ienne** /lɛsbjɛ̃, ɛn/ I *adj* lesbian.

II **lesbienne** *nf* lesbian.

lesdites ▶ **ledit**.

lesdits ▶ **ledit**.

lèse-majesté /lɛzmaʒɛste/ *nf inv* lese-majesty; **crime de ~** crime of lese-majesty.

léser /leze/ [14] *vtr* **1** (causer du tort à) to wrong [*personne*]; to prejudice [*droits, intérêts*]; **la partie lésée** the injured party; **2** fig to hurt [*sentiment*]; **3** (endommager) to damage [*organe*].

lésiner /lezine/ [1] *vi* **~ sur** to skimp on [*argent, moyens, travail, ingrédient*]; to be sparing with [*compliments*]; **ne pas ~ sur** to be liberal with [*ingrédient, argent, compliments*]; **ne pas ~ sur la dépense** to spare no expense.

lésion /lezjɔ̃/ *nf* Méd lesion; **~ pulmonaire** pulmonary lesion.

lésionnel, **-elle** /lezjɔnɛl/ *adj* [*signe, syndrome*] of a lesion; [*maladie*] caused by a lesion.

Lésotho /lezoto/ ▶ 321 *nprm* Lesotho.

lesquels, **lesquelles** /lekɛl/ *pron, adj* ▶ **lequel**.

lessivable /lesivabl/ *adj* washable.

lessivage /lesivaʒ/ *nm* **1** (de surface, mur) washing; **2** Géol leaching.

lessive /lesiv/ *nf* **1** (produit) (en poudre) washing powder; (liquide) washing liquid; **2** (tâche ménagère, linge) washing; **faire la ~** to do the washing; **faire une ~ de blanc** to wash some whites; **faire deux lessives par semaine** to do two washes a week; **3** Chimie lye.

lessiver /lesive/ [1] *vtr* **1** (laver) to wash [*mur, sol*]; **2**° (épuiser) **être lessivé**° hum to be washed out°; **3** Chimie to leach.

lessiveuse /lesivøz/ *nf* boiler, copper GB.

lest /lɛst/ *nm* **1** Naut, Aviat ballast; **jeter** or **lâcher du ~** lit to jettison ballast; **lâcher du ~** fig to make concessions; **2** Pêche (sur un filet) weight.

lestage /lɛstaʒ/ *nm* Naut, Aviat ballasting.

leste /lɛste/ *adj* **1** (souple) [*personne, animal*] agile; [*démarche, pas*] nimble; **marcher d'un pas ~** to walk nimbly; **un vieillard encore ~** a still sprightly old man; **2** (osé) [*propos, plaisanterie, réplique*] risqué.

IDIOMES **avoir la main ~**° to be always ready with a slap.

lestement /lɛstəmɑ̃/ *adv* (avec souplesse) [*marcher, courir, sauter*] nimbly.

lester /lɛste/ [1] *vtr* **1** Naut Aviat to ballast; **2** (charger) to stuff sth (**de** with).

let /lɛt/ *nm* Sport let; **une balle ~** a let.

létal, **~e**, *mpl* **-aux** /letal, o/ *adj* lethal; **dose ~e** lethal dose.

léthargie /letaʀʒi/ *nf* **1** (engourdissement) (de personne) lethargy; (d'économie) sluggishness; **sortir de sa ~** to shake off one's lethargy; **tirer qn de sa ~** to shake sb out of his/her lethargy; **2** Méd lethargy.

léthargique /letaʀʒik/ *adj* **1** [*personne*] lethargic; [*industrie, économie*] sluggish; **2** Méd lethargic.

letton, **-onne** /lɛtɔ̃, ɔn/ I ▶ 537 *adj* Latvian.

II ▶ 462 *nm* Ling **le ~** Latvian.

Letton, **-onne** /lɛtɔ̃, ɔn/ ▶ 537 *nm,f* Latvian ou Lett; **les ~s** the Latvians ou Letts.

Lettonie /lɛtɔni/ ▶ 321 *nprf* Latvia.

lettre /lɛtʀ/ I *nf* **1** (signe graphique) letter; **les ~s de l'alphabet** the letters of the alphabet; **~ minuscule** small letter; **~ majuscule** or **capitale** capital letter; **~ d'imprimerie** block letter; **en ~s majuscules** in capital letters; **un mot de trois ~s** a three-letter word; **en toutes ~s** lit in full; **écrire la date/somme en toutes ~s** write the date/sum out in full; **c'est écrit en toutes ~s dans le rapport** fig it's down in black and white in the report; **c'est écrit en grosses ~s** it's written in big letters; **les Romains furent des urbanistes avant la ~** the Romans were city planners before they were invented; ▶ **cinq**; **2** (écrit adressé) letter; **une ~ de félicitations/remerciements/condoléances** a letter of congratulations /thanks/condolence; **~ d'accompagnement** covering letter; **~ de réclamation** letter of complaint; **~ de rupture** letter ending a relationship; **une ~ de recommandation/candidature/démission**

a letter of recommendation/application/resignation; **~ anonyme/de menaces** anonymous/threatening letter; **une petite ~** a note; **3** (contenu d'un texte) letter; **l'esprit et la ~ d'un texte** the spirit and the letter of a text; **à la ~, au pied de la ~** [*appliquer, suivre*] to the letter; **il prend à la ~ tout ce qu'on lui dit** he takes everything you say literally.

II lettres *nfpl* **1** Univ, Scol (français) French; (plus général) arts GB, humanities US; **étudiant en ~s** (français) student reading French GB, student majoring in French US; (plus général) arts GB ou humanities US student; **faculté de ~s** arts faculty GB, school of the humanities; **être en ~s, faire des études de ~s** to do an arts degree, to study humanities US; **professeur de ~s** teacher of French (for native speakers); **docteur ès ~s** ≈ Doctor of Philosophy; **2** (culture littéraire) letters; **homme/femme de ~s** man/woman of letters; **les gens de ~s** writers; **avoir des ~s** to be well read; **le monde des ~s** the literary world.

■ **~ de cachet** lettre de cachet; **~ capitulaire** Édition decorated initial; **~ de change** bill of exchange; **~ de château** thank you letter, bread and butter letter; **~ circulaire** circular; **~ de crédit** letter of credit; **~ d'intention** letter of intention; **~ ornée** illuminated letter; **~ ouverte** open letter (**à** to); **~ recommandée** registered letter; **~ de voiture** Comm waybill, consignment note; **~s classiques** French and Latin; **~s de créance** credentials; **~s modernes** French language and literature; **~s de noblesse** letters patent of nobility; **avoir ses ~s de noblesse** fig to have an illustrious history; **gagner ses ~s de noblesse** fig to win one's spurs; **~s patentes** letters patent; **~s supérieures** *preparatory class for entrance exam for the École Normale Supérieure*.

IDIOMES **passer comme une ~ à la poste**○ [*décision, réforme*] to go through smoothly ou without a hitch; [*excuse*] to be accepted without any questions; **un événement à graver en ~s d'or** an event to remember; **écrit en ~s de feu** written in letters of fire; **devenir ~ morte** to become a dead letter; **rester ~ morte** to go unheeded.

lettré, ~e /letʀe/ **I** *adj* [*personne, gens*] well-read; [*milieu*] literary.

II *nm,f* man/woman of letters; **une œuvre de ~** a learned work.

lettrine /letʀin/ *nf* initial letter.

leu: **à la queue leu leu** /alakøløle/ *loc adv* in single file.

leucémie /løsemi/ ▶**271** *nf* leukaemia.

leucémique /løsemik/ **I** *adj* [*personne*] suffering from leukaemia; [*cellule*] leukaemic.

II *nmf* leukaemia sufferer.

leucocyte /løkɔsit/ *nm* leucocyte GB, leukocyte US.

leucocytose /løkɔsitoz/ ▶**271** *nf* leucocytosis[GB].

leucorrhée /løkɔʀe/ *nf* leucorrhoea.

leur, (*pl* **leurs**) /lœʀ/

■ **Note** En anglais, on ne répète pas le possessif coordonné: *leur nom et leur adresse* = their names and addresses.

I *pron pers inv* them; **je ~ ai donné ton numéro de téléphone** I gave them your telephone number; **une lettre ~ a été adressée** a letter was sent to them; **promesse ~ a été faite que** they were given a promise that; **il ~ a expliqué le fonctionnement de l'appareil** he told them how the machine worked; **il ~ a fallu faire** they had to do; **on ~ a fait visiter la ville** they were shown around the town.

II *adj poss mf, pl* **~s** their; **elles ressemblent à ~ père** they look like their father; **elles ont pris ~ parapluie** they took their umbrellas; **~ merveille de fille**○ their adorable daughter; **~ fille à eux**○ their daughter; **un de ~s amis** a friend of theirs; **ils sont partis chacun de ~ côté** they went their separate ways, each went his own way; **à ~ arrivée/départ** when they arrived/left; **pendant ~ absence** while they were away; **ils ont fait ~ mon point de vue** they've adopted my point of view.

III le leur, la leur, les leurs *pron poss* theirs; **celui-là, c'est le ~** that's theirs; **je suis parti de mon côté, eux du ~** I went my way and they went theirs; **le ~, de jardin, est plus beau**○ their garden is nicer; **qu'ils aient chacun le ~** let them have one each; **mes idées ne sont pas les ~s** we think differently; **ils pensent d'abord aux ~s** (à leur famille) they put their own ou their families first; **il est des ~s** (de leur groupe) he's one of them; **ils m'ont demandé d'être des ~s** they asked me to come along; **ils vivent loin des ~s** (de leur famille) they live far away from their families; **ils ont encore fait des ~s** they've been up to mischief again!

leurre /lœʀ/ *nm* **1** (tromperie) illusion; **c'est un ~ de croire qu'elle vous aidera** you're deluding yourself if you think she'll help you; **2** Pêche, Chasse lure; **3** Mil decoy.

leurrer /lœʀe/ [1] **I** *vtr* **1** (tromper) to delude (**par** with; **sur** about); **se laisser ~** to let oneself be taken in; **2** (en fauconnerie) to lure [*oiseau*].

II se leurrer *vpr* to delude oneself (**de** with; **au sujet de** about).

levage /ləvaʒ/ *nm* **1** Tech (de charge) lifting; **appareil de ~** lifting apparatus; **puissance/vitesse/treuil de ~** lifting power/speed/winch; **2** Culin (de pâte) raising, leavening.

levain /ləvɛ̃/ *nm* **1** Culin (agent de levage) leaven GB, sourdough US; **pain au/sans ~** leavened/unleavened bread; **2** Biol, Ind (agent de fermentation) starter; **~ lactique** lactic starter; **3** (force) catalyst; **le nationalisme est un ~ de haine** nationalism is a catalyst of hatred.

levant /ləvɑ̃/ **I** *adj m* **soleil ~** rising sun; **au soleil ~** at sunrise; **pays** or **empire du Soleil ~** land of the Rising Sun.

II *nm* east; **au ~** in the east; **du ~ au couchant** from east to west.

Levant /ləvɑ̃/ *nprm* **le ~** the Levant.

levantin†, ~e /ləvɑ̃tɛ̃, in/ *adj* Levantine.

levé, ~e /ləve/ **I** *pp* ▶ **lever**.

II *pp adj* **1** (dressé) **dit-il, les sourcils ~s** he said, with raised eyebrows; **une forêt de drapeaux et de poings ~s** a forest of flags and clenched fists; **voter à main ~e** to vote by a show of hands; **2** (hors du lit) [*personne*] up; **elle n'est pas encore ~e** she's not up yet; **elle est toujours la première ~e** she's always the first up.

III *nm* Géog (relevé) survey; **faire un ~ du terrain** to do a land survey.

IV levée *nf* **1** (suppression) (d'embargo, état de siège, de sanctions, loi martiale, préavis de grève, peine) lifting (**de** of); (de siège) raising; (de mesures, quotas) suspension (**de** of); (d'immunité parlementaire) removal (**de** of); (d'anonymat, de secret, tabou) ending (**de** of); (de séance) close (**de** of); **2** Postes (de courrier) collection; **deux ~es par jours** two collections a day; **'heures des ~es'** 'collections' GB, 'collection time' US; **3** Jeux (aux cartes) trick; **faire une ~e** to take a trick; **4** Géog (remblai) levee; **~e de terre** levee of earth; **un chemin construit sur les ~es du fleuve** a path built on the levees of the river; **5** Mil (recrutement) levying; **procéder à la ~e de troupes** to levy troops.

■ **~e de boucliers** outcry; **provoquer** or **susciter une ~e de boucliers** to cause an outcry; **~e du corps** *solemn transfer of the body*; **~e d'écrou** Jur release; **~e des impôts** Fisc levying of taxes; **~e en masse** Mil mass mobilization; **~e d'option** Fin, Jur exercise of an option; **~e des scellés** Jur breaking of the seals; **procéder à la ~e des scellés** to break the seals.

IDIOMES **faire qch au pied ~** to do sth off the cuff.

lève-glace, *pl* **~s** /lɛvglas/ *nm* Aut **~ électrique** (option) electric windows (*pl*); (mécanisme) electric winder.

lever /ləve/ [16] **I** *nm* **1** (sortie du lit) **au ~, boire un jus de fruit** on getting up, drink some fruit juice; **être là au ~ des enfants** to be there when the children get up; **2** Géog ▶ **levé III**.

II *vtr* **1** (dresser) gén to raise [*main, doigt, bras, poing, sourcil, jambe*]; **~ la main** or **le doigt** (pour parler) to put up one's hand; **~ la main sur qn** (pour frapper) to raise one's hand to sb; **~ les bras au ciel** to throw up one's hands (**de** in); **~ le pied** gén to lift up one's foot; (ralentir) lit, fig to slow down; (partir)○ to clear off○; **lève les pieds quand tu marches!** pick your feet up when you walk!; **~ les yeux** or **la tête** (regarder) to look up (**sur, vers** at); **ne pas ~ les yeux** or **le nez**○ **de qch** not to look up from sth; **sans ~ les yeux** [*dire, répondre*] without looking up; [*travailler, étudier*] without a break; **~ les yeux au ciel** to raise one's eyes to heaven; **~ la patte**○ (uriner) [*chien*] to cock a leg; **il a levé la patte contre l'arbre** it cocked its leg up against the tree; **~ son cul**● to get off one's arse● GB ou ass● US; ▶ **doigt**; **2** (soulever) to lift [*objet*]; to raise [*barrière*]; **~ un chargement de quelques mètres** to lift a load a few metres[GB]; **~ son verre** to raise one's glass (**à** to); **~ le rideau** Théât to raise the curtain; **~ une vitre** Aut to wind up a window; **~ les filets** Pêche to haul in the nets; **3** (sortir du lit) to get [sb] up [*enfants, malade*]; **4** (mettre fin à) to lift [*embargo, sanction, peine, contrôle*]; to raise [*siège*]; to dispel [*doute, malentendu, ambiguïté, mystère*]; to end [*tabou, secret, isolement, audience*]; to remove [*obstacle, difficultés, incertitude*]; to close [*séance*]; **5** (collecter) to raise [*capitaux, fonds*]; to levy [*impôt*]; **6** (recruter) to levy [*troupes*]; **7** Fin to take up [*actions, achat à terme*]; **~ une option** to exercise an option; **8** Chasse (débusquer) to flush out [*gibier, perdrix*]; **~ un lièvre** lit to start a hare; fig to open a can of worms; **9** Géog **~ un plan** to carry out a survey; **10** Culin (découper) **~ un filet (de poisson)** to fillet a fish; **~ une cuisse de poulet** to carve a chicken leg; **11**○ (séduire) to pick up○ [*homme, femme, client*].

III *vi* **1** Culin [*pâte*] to rise; **2** Agric, Hort [*semis, blé*] to come up.

IV se lever *vpr* **1** (sortir du lit) to get up; **se ~ tôt/la nuit** to get up early/in the night; **avoir du mal à se ~** to find it difficult to get up; **il faut se ~ de bonne heure**○ **pour comprendre ce qu'il dit** you need to be pretty clever○ to understand what he says; ▶ **gauche**; **2** (se mettre debout) to stand up; **se ~ de sa chaise** to rise from one's chair; **il l'a aidée à se ~** he helped her to her feet; **se ~ pour applaudir** to rise to one's feet to applaud; **se ~ de table** to get up from the table; **'accusé, levez-vous!'** Jur 'the accused will stand'; **se ~ sur ses étriers** Équit to stand on one's stirrups; **'lève-toi et marche'** 'arise, take up thy bed and walk'; **3** (se dresser) [*partie du corps*] to rise; **des mains se sont levées** some hands went up; **des poings se lèvent** fists are being shaken; **4** (s'insurger) [*personne, peuple*] to rise up (**contre** against); **5** (apparaître) [*soleil, lune*] to rise (**sur** over); **le soleil va se ~** the sun is about to rise; **le jour se lève** it's getting light; **6** Météo (s'agiter) [*vent*] to rise; [*brise*] to get up; (s'éclaircir) [*nuages, brouillard, brume*] to clear; [*temps*] to clear up; **7** Théât **le rideau se lève** the curtain rises (**sur** on).

■ **~ des couleurs** Mil raising of the colours[GB]; **~ du drapeau** raising of the flag; **~ du jour** daybreak; **au ~ du jour** at daybreak; **~ de rideau** (début de la représentation) curtain up; (prélude) curtain raiser; **partir au/manquer le ~ de rideau** to leave at/to miss curtain up; **en ~ de rideau, match Ali–Chang** as a curtain raiser, Ali vs Chang match; **~ du roi** Hist King's levee; **assister au ~ du roi** to be present at the King's levee; **~ du soleil** sunrise; **au ~ du soleil** at sunrise.

lève-tard /lɛvtaʀ/ *nmf inv* late riser.

lève-tôt /lɛvto/ *nmf inv* early riser, early bird○.

lève-vitre, *pl* **~s** /lɛvvitʀ/ *nm* = **lève-glace**.

levier /ləvje/ *nm* **1** Phys, Tech (de levage) lever; **utiliser un bâton comme ~** to use a stick as a lever; **soulever qch avec un ~** to lever sth up; **2** Tech (de commande) lever; **tirer sur le ~** to pull on the lever; **3** fig lever; **le ~ des institutions européennes** the lever of European institutions; **un puissant ~ pour l'industrie** a very effective lever for industry.

■ **~ d'armement** Mil (de fusil) bolt handle; Phot advance lever; **~ de changement de vitesse** Aut gear lever GB, gear shift US; (de bicyclette) gear switch; **~ de commande** Aviat control stick; **être aux ~s de commande** fig to be in the driving seat; **~ de frein à main** Aut hand brake lever; **~ de vitesses** = **~ de changement de vitesse**.

lévitation /levitasjɔ̃/ *nf* levitation; **être en ~** to be in a state of levitation.

lévite /levit/ *nm* Levite.

Lévitique /levitik/ *nm* **le ~** (the Book of) Leviticus.

levraut /ləvʀo/ *nm* leveret.

lèvre /lɛvʀ/ *nf* **1** (sur le visage) lip; **~ supérieure/inférieure** upper/lower lip; **avoir le sourire aux ~s** to have a smile on one's lips; **être sur toutes les ~s** to be on everyone's lips; **du bout des ~s** (rire, manger) half-heartedly; (parler, répondre) grudgingly; ▶ **cœur**; **2** (de la vulve) labium; **les petites/grandes ~s** labia minora/majora; **3** (de faille, plaie) lip, edge.

IDIOMES **être suspendu aux ~s de qn** to hang on sb's every word; **il y a loin de la coupe aux ~s** Prov there's many a slip twixt cup and lip.

levrette /ləvʀɛt/ *nf* **1** (femelle du lévrier) greyhound bitch; **2** (lévrier d'Italie) Italian greyhound; **3**● **en ~** doggy fashion○, from behind.

lévrier /levʀije/ *nm* greyhound.

■ **~ afghan** Afghan hound.

levure /ləvyʀ/ *nf* yeast.

■ **~ de bière** brewer's yeast; **~ de boulanger** baker's yeast; **~ chimique** baking powder.

lexème /lɛksɛm/ *nm* lexeme.

lexical, **~e**, *mpl* **-aux** /lɛksikal, o/ *adj* lexical.

lexicalisation /lɛksikalizasjɔ̃/ *nf* **1** Ling lexicalization; **2** Ordinat lexicographic sort.

lexicaliser /lɛksikalize/ [1] **I** *vtr* **1** Ling to lexicalize; **2** Ordinat to sort.

II se lexicaliser *vpr* Ling to become lexicalized.

lexicographe /lɛksikɔgʀaf/ ▶**510** *nmf* lexicographer.

lexicographie /lɛksikɔgʀafi/ *nf* lexicography.

lexicographique /lɛksikɔgʀafik/ *adj* lexicographical.

lexicologie /lɛksikɔlɔʒi/ *nf* lexicology.

lexicologique /lɛksikɔlɔʒik/ *adj* lexicological.

lexicologue /lɛksikɔlɔg/ ▶**510** *nmf* lexicologist.

lexie /lɛksi/ *nf* lexical item.

lexique /lɛksik/ *nm* **1** (unilingue) glossary; (bilingue) vocabulary (book); **2** Ling lexicon, lexis.

lézard /lezaʀ/ *nm* **1** (animal) lizard; **2** (peau) lizard(skin); **sac en ~** lizard(skin) bag.

■ **~ des murailles** wall lizard; **~ vert** green lizard.

IDIOMES **faire le ~** to bask in the sun.

lézarde /lezaʀd/ *nf* lit, fig crack.

lézarder /lezaʀde/ [1] **I** *vtr* to crack.

II○ *vi* **~ au soleil** to bask in the sun.

III se lézarder *vpr* lit, fig to crack.

liaison /ljɛzɔ̃/ *nf* **1** Transp link; **~ aérienne/ferroviaire/maritime/routière** air/rail/sea/road link; **la ~ Calais–Douvres** the Calais–Dover line ou route; **la compagnie aérienne assure la ~ Paris–Washington** the airline operates flights on the Paris–Washington route; **2** Radio, Télécom **~ radio** radio contact; **établir une ~** to establish contact; **~ satellite/téléphonique** satellite/telephone link; **la ~ est mauvaise, je vous entends mal** the connection is bad, I can't hear you properly; **être en ~ avec qn** to be in contact with sb; **3** (contact) **assurer la ~ entre différents services** to liaise between different services; **il est resté en ~ avec ses anciens collègues** he kept in contact ou in touch with his former colleagues; **travailler/agir en ~ avec** to work/act in collaboration with; **4** (rapport logique) connection; **manque de ~ dans les idées** lack of connection between ideas; **5** (relation amoureuse) affair; **6** Ling, Phon liaison; **faire la ~** to make a liaison; **une ~ fautive** a wrong liaison; **7** Mus slur; **8** Culin thickening; **faire une ~** to thicken a sauce; **9** Ordinat link; **10** Chimie bond; **~ covalente/hydrogène** covalent/hydrogen bond.

liane /ljan/ *nf* creeper, liana.

liant, **~e** /ljɑ̃, ljɑ̃t/ **I** *adj* (sociable) sociable.

II *nm* **1** Tech (souplesse) flexibility; **2** Constr binder; **~ hydraulique** hydraulic binder ou lime.

liasse /ljas/ *nf* (de billets) wad; (de lettres, papiers, documents) bundle; **mettre des billets en ~** to make (up) a wad of notes ou bills US.

Liban /libɑ̃/ ▶**321** *nprm* Lebanon.

libanais, **~e** /libanɛ, ɛz/ ▶**537** *adj* Lebanese.

Libanais, **~e** /libanɛ, ɛz/ ▶**537** *nm,f* Lebanese.

libation /libasjɔ̃/ *nf* libation (**à** to); **faire des ~s** Antiq to offer libations; fig hum to indulge in libations.

libelle /libɛl/ *nm* liter lampoon; **faire** or **répandre des ~s contre qn** to lampoon sb.

libellé /libɛlle/ *nm* (de jugement, lettre) wording; **je ne peux pas lire le ~ du chèque** I can't see who the cheque is made out to.

libeller /libɛlle/ [1] *vtr* **1** Admin to draw up [*acte, contrat*]; **2** fml to word [*lettre, demande, article*]; **3** to make out [*chèque, mandat*]; **~ un chèque à l'ordre de** to make out a cheque GB ou check US to; **un chèque mal libellé** a badly made out cheque GB ou check US.

libellule /libɛllyl/ *nf* dragonfly.

liber /libɛʀ/ *nm* phloem.

libérable /libeʀabl/ *adj* **1** Jur **détenu ~** (à l'issue de sa peine) prisoner due for release; (par remise de peine) prisoner eligible for release; **prévenu ~** defendant to be discharged; **2** Mil [*conscrit, contingent*] to be discharged soon (*après n*).

libéral, **~e**, *mpl* **-aux** /libeʀal, o/ **I** *adj* **1** (tolérant) [*personne, discipline, morale*] liberal; **il est assez ~** he's fairly liberal; **2** (favorable aux libertés) [*personne, idée, régime*] liberal; **3** Pol [*parti, gouvernement, candidat*] Liberal; **4** Écon [*économie, doctrine*] free-market (*épith*); **être partisan de l'économie ~e** to support a free-market economy; ▶ **profession**.

II *nm,f* **1** Pol Liberal; **2** Écon free marketeer.

libéralement /libeʀalmɑ̃/ *adv* (avec générosité) liberally.

libéralisation /libeʀalizasjɔ̃/ *nf* **1** Écon, Fin liberalization; **~ économique/financière** economic/financial liberalization; **~ des échanges/du marché** trade/market liberalization; **~ des transports aériens** or **du ciel** airline deregulation; **2** Pol liberalization; **~ du régime/système politique** liberalization of the regime/political system; **~ des mœurs** relaxation of moral standards.

libéraliser /libeʀalize/ [1] **I** *vtr* to liberalize [*commerce, économie, transports, loi, pays*].

II se libéraliser *vpr* [*pays, mœurs*] to become more liberal.

libéralisme /libeʀalism/ *nm* liberalism.

libéralité /libeʀalite/ **I** *nf* **1** (générosité) liberality; **avec ~** liberally; **2** Jur (donation) gift.

II libéralités *nfpl* liter generosity ¢; **les ~s de l'État** the state's generosity; **vivre des ~s de qn** to live off sb's generosity; **dépenser sa fortune en ~s** to give one's fortune away in gifts.

libérateur, **-trice** /libeʀatœʀ, tʀis/ **I** *adj* [*effet, pouvoir, esprit*] liberating; **dieu ~** redeemer.

II *nm, f* **1** (de pays, ville, personne) liberator; **2** Relig **le Libérateur** the Redeemer.

libération /libeʀasjɔ̃/ *nf* **1** (de prisonnier, d'otage) release; **exiger la ~ de tous les otages** to demand the release of all the hostages; **2** (de pays, ville, peuple) liberation; **armée/front/mouvement de ~** liberation army/front/movement; **3** (affranchissement) liberation; **~ des esclaves** liberation of slaves; **~ sexuelle** sexual liberation; **~ des femmes** or **de la femme** women's liberation; **4** (soulagement) relief; **éprouver un sentiment de ~** to feel a sense of relief; **5** Écon (de prix) deregulation; (d'échanges) freeing; **~ des loyers/tarifs** lifting of rent/tariff controls; **~ des mouvements de capitaux** removal of control on capital flows; **6** Fin (d'actions, de capital) paying up; **7** Mil discharge; **attendre sa ~** to await one's discharge; **8** Phys (d'énergie) release.

Libération /libeʀasjɔ̃/ *nf* Hist (de 1944) Liberation; **à la ~** at the time of the Liberation.

libératoire /libeʀatwaʀ/ *adj* **clause ~** waiver clause; **paiement ~** Fisc payment in full discharge; Comm full payment; **prélèvement ~** tax deduction at standard rate.

libéré, **~e** /libeʀe/ **I** *pp* ▶ **libérer**.

II *pp adj* **1** (émancipé) [*homme, femme*] liberated; **2** (délivré) [*pays, zone, ville*] free; **3** (disponible) [*poste, lieux*] vacant; **les locaux ~s seront modernisés** the vacant premises will be modernized; **4** (affranchi) [*personne, entreprise*] free (**de** from); **~ d'obligations** free from obligations.

libérer /libeʀe/ [14] **I** *vtr* **1** (délivrer) to liberate [*pays, ville*] (**de** from); to free [*compagnon, otage*] (**de** from); **2** (relâcher) to release [*otage, détenu*] (**de** from); to free [*esclave, animal*] (**de** from); **3** (laisser partir) to allow [sb] to go [*employé, élève*]; **~ ses élèves avant l'heure** to let one's pupils go early, to allow one's pupils to go early; **4** (affranchir) (de contraintes) to liberate [*personne, imagination*] (**de** from); (de fonctions) to relieve [*ministre, employé*] (**de** of); (de service militaire) to discharge [*soldat*] (**de** from); **~ un associé de sa parole/ses obligations/ses dettes** to release a partner from his word/his obligations/his debts; **~ qn de l'emprise de qn** to free sb from sb's hold; **5** (ne pas retenir) to release [*émotion, énergie*]; to give free rein to [*instinct, imagination*]; **6** (soulager) to relieve [*esprit, personne*] (**de** of); to unburden [*cœur, conscience*] (**de** of); **7** (débarrasser) to vacate [*appartement, bureau*]; to clear [*passage, trottoir*] (**de** of); **les lieux doivent être libérés avant la fin du mois** the premises must be vacated by the end of the month; **~ la chambre avant midi** (dans un hôtel) to check out before noon; **8** (dégager) to free [*bras, main*] (**de** from); to release [*ressort, cran, mécanisme*]; **9** Écon (libéraliser) to liberalize [*économie, échanges*]; (débloquer) to deregulate [*prix*]; **~ les**

loyers/tarifs to lift rent/tariff controls; **10** Fin to pay up [*actions, capital*]; **11** Chimie, Phys (produire) to release [*gaz, énergie, électrons*].

II se libérer *vpr* **1** (se délivrer) [*personne*] to free oneself (**de** from); [*pays, entreprise*] to free itself (**de** from); **je me suis libéré de mes chaînes/obligations** I have freed myself from my chains/obligations; **se ~ les bras/jambes** to free one's arms/legs; **se ~ d'une dette/d'un impôt** to pay a debt/a tax; **se ~ d'une inhibition** to get rid of an inhibition; **2** (se rendre disponible) **j'essaierai de me ~ mercredi** I'll try and be free on Wednesday.

Liberia /libeʀja/ ▶ 321 *nprm* Liberia.

libérien, **-ienne** /libeʀjɛ̃, ɛn/ ▶ 537 *adj* Liberian.

Libérien, **-ienne** /libeʀjɛ̃, ɛn/ ▶ 537 *nm,f* Liberian.

libériste /libeʀist/ *nmf* glider, gliding enthusiast.

libertaire /libɛʀtɛʀ/ *adj, nmf* libertarian.

liberté /libɛʀte/ *nf* **1** (condition, état) freedom ¢; **choisir la ~** to choose freedom; **recouvrer la ~** to regain one's freedom; **amour de la ~** love of freedom; **vive la ~!** long live freedom!; **lutter pour la ~** to fight for freedom; **Statue de la ~** Statue of Liberty; **~, égalité, fraternité** Liberty, Equality, Fraternity; **élever des animaux en ~** to raise animals in a natural habitat; **espèce vivant en ~** species living wild; **être en ~** to be free; **l'assassin est toujours en ~** the killer is still at large; **2** (latitude) freedom ¢; **peu de/trop de ~** little/too much freedom; **en toute ~** with complete freedom; **~ d'action/de mouvement/de choix** freedom of action/of movement/of choice; **donner à qn la ~ de faire** to give sb freedom to do; **avoir sa ~** to be free; **avoir toute ~ pour faire** to be quite free to do; **n'avoir aucune ~ de manœuvre** to have no room for manoeuvre GB ou maneuver US; **ne pas avoir une grande ~ de choix** not to have much choice; **3** (hardiesse) freedom; **~ de ton** outspokenness; **une ~ qui frise l'impertinence** outspokenness bordering on impertinence; **~ d'esprit** independence of mind; **s'exprimer avec une étonnante ~** to be remarkably outspoken; **prendre la ~ de faire** to take the liberty of doing; **prendre des ~s avec qn/qch** to take liberties with sb/sth; **4** (droit) freedom; **~ de pensée/d'expression/d'opinion/de parole** freedom of thought/of expression/of opinion/of speech; **~s individuelles/fondamentales** individual/fundamental liberties; **porter atteinte aux ~s** to undermine civil liberties.

■ **~ d'association** Jur, Pol freedom of association; **~ civile** Jur civil liberty; **~ conditionnelle** Jur parole; **mettre qn en ~ conditionnelle** Jur to release sb on parole; **~ de conscience** Pol freedom of conscience; **~ de l'enseignement** Jur freedom of choice in education; **~ d'installation** Jur, CEE freedom of establishment; **~ de la presse** Pol freedom of the press; **~ des prix** Comm, Jur free prices (*pl*); **~ provisoire** Jur provisional release (*pending trial*); **en ~ provisoire** provisionally released; **mettre en ~ provisoire** to release provisionally; **mise en ~ provisoire** provisional release; **~ surveillée** Jur probation; **en ~ surveillée** on probation; **mise en ~ surveillée** release on probation; **mettre en ~ surveillée** to release on probation; **~ du travail** Jur freedom of contract; **~s publiques** Jur, Pol civil liberties; **~s syndicales** Jur, Pol trade union rights.

libertin, **~e** /libɛʀtɛ̃, in/ *adj, nm,f* libertine.

libertinage /libɛʀtinaʒ/ *nm* **1** (manière) libertinage; **2** (doctrine) libertinism.

libidinal, **~e**, *mpl* **-aux** /libidinal, o/ *adj* libidinal.

libidineux, **-euse** /libidinø, øz/ *adj* libidinous.

libido /libido/ *nf* libido.

libraire /libʀɛʀ/ ▶ 510 *nmf* bookseller.

librairie /libʀɛʀi/ ▶ 510 *nf* **1** (magasin) bookshop GB, bookstore; **~ d'art/religieuse** art/religious bookshop; **~ de livres anciens** antiquarian bookshop; **en ~** in bookshops; **dans toutes les ~s dès lundi** available in all bookshops from Monday; **2** (activité) bookselling business.

librairie-papeterie, *pl* **librairies-papeteries** /libʀɛʀipapɛtʀi/ ▶ 510 *nf* stationer's and bookshop GB ou bookstore.

libre /libʀ/ *adj* **1** gén [*personne, condition, pays*] free (**de faire** to do); **être ~ de ses décisions/choix** to be free to decide/choose; **~ à toi de faire** it's up to you whether you do; **~ à elle de partir** it's up to her whether she goes or not; **être ~ de ses actes** to do as one wishes; **dans le ~ exercice de leurs fonctions** in the unrestricted discharge of their duties; **2** (dénué) free (**de** from); **~ de préjugés** free from prejudice; **être ~ de soucis** to enjoy peace of mind; **~ d'hypothèque** [*propriété*] free of mortgage; **3** (direct) [*personne*] free and easy; [*manière*] free; [*allure*] easy; [*opinion*] candid; [*morale*] easygoing; **être ~ avec qn** to feel at ease with sb; **avoir une conversation très ~** to talk in a very relaxed way; **être ~ dans ses propos/son comportement** to talk/behave in an uninhibited fashion; **4** (dégagé) [*main, pouce*] free; [*route, voie*] lit, fig clear; **avoir/garder les mains ~s** lit to have/keep one's hands free; fig to be/remain a free agent; **un téléphone avec une option 'main ~'** a telephone with a hands-free facility; **5** (disponible) [*personne, chambre*] available; [*place*] empty; [*siège*] free; **'~ de suite'** (dans une annonce) [*personne, appartement à louer*] 'available immediately'; [*appartement à vendre*] 'with immediate vacant possession'; **6** (non occupé) [*WC*] vacant; **la ligne n'est pas ~** (au téléphone) the number is engaged GB ou busy US.

■ **~ arbitre** Philos free will; **avoir son ~ arbitre** to be possessed of free will; **~ concurrence** Écon free competition; **~ entreprise** Écon free enterprise; **~ à l'importation** Comm, Jur free from import control; **~ jouissance** Jur free enjoyment.

IDIOMES **être ~ comme l'air** to be as free as a bird.

libre-échange /libʀeʃɑ̃ʒ/ *nm* free trade.

libre-échangiste, *pl* **~s** /libʀeʃɑ̃ʒist/ **I** *adj* free trade (*épith*); **politique ~** free trade policy.

II *nmf* (partisan) free-trader.

librement /libʀəmɑ̃/ *adv* freely; **parler/choisir/partir/traduire ~** to speak/choose/leave/translate freely; **~ cité/adapté** loosely quoted/adapted; **parlez-moi ~** feel free to speak to me.

libre(-)pensée, *pl* **libres(-)pensées** /libʀəpɑ̃se/ *nf* **1** (doctrine) free thought; **2** (groupe) freethinkers (*pl*).

libre(-)penseur, *pl* **libres(-)penseurs** /libʀəpɑ̃sœʀ/ *nm* freethinker.

libre-service, *pl* **libres-services** /libʀəsɛʀvis/ **I** *adj inv* [*magasin, restaurant*] self-service (*épith*).

II *nm* **1** (système) **le ~** self-service; **en ~** [*magasin, restaurant*] self-service; **2** (magasin) self-service shop GB ou store US; (restaurant) self-service restaurant.

■ **~ bancaire** automatic teller.

librettiste /libʀɛtist/ *nmf* librettist.

libretto /libʀɛtto/ *nm* libretto.

Libreville /libʀəvil/ ▶ 857 *npr* Libreville.

Libye /libi/ ▶ 321 *nprf* Libya.

libyen, **-enne** /libjɛ̃, ɛn/ ▶ 537 *adj* Libyan.

Libyen, **-enne** /libjɛ̃, ɛn/ ▶ 537 *nm,f* Libyan.

lice /lis/ *nf* lists (*pl*); **entrer en ~** to enter the lists; **depuis leur entrée en ~** since they entered the lists; **être en ~** to have entered the lists.

licence /lisɑ̃s/ *nf* **1** Univ (bachelor's) degree; **~ en droit** law degree; **~ de** or **ès lettres** arts degree, liberal arts degree US, BA; **~ de chimie** chemistry degree, BSc GB ou BS US in chemistry; **préparer une ~ d'anglais** to do a degree in English; **être en ~ d'anglais** to be in the final year of an English degree; **2** Comm, Jur licence[GB]; **~ de fabrication/de vente** manufacturing/distribution licence[GB]; **~ d'importation/d'exportation** import/export licence[GB]; **~ de débit de boissons** licence for the sale of alcoholic drinks GB, liquor license US; **fabriquer qch sous ~ japonaise** to make sth under licence[GB] from a Japanese manufacturer; **produit sous ~** licensed product; **3** Sport membership card (*of a national sports association*); **avoir sa ~ de tennis** to be a member of the national tennis federation; **4** (liberté) licence[GB]; **~ orthographique** licence[GB] with regard to spelling; **~ poétique** poetic licence[GB]; **avoir toute ~ de faire** to have a free hand to do; **5†** (libertinage) licentiousness.

licencié, **~e** /lisɑ̃sje/ **I** *pp* ▶ **licencier**.

II *pp adj* [*étudiant*] graduate (*épith*); **enseignant ~** graduate teacher GB, teacher with a college degree US.

III *nm,f* **1** Univ graduate GB, college graduate US; **un ~ en droit/ès lettres** a law/an arts ou liberal arts US graduate; **2** Sport member (*of a sports federation*); **3** Écon **~ (économique)** person made redundant GB, laid-off worker US.

licenciement /lisɑ̃simɑ̃/ *nm* (pour faute) dismissal; **~ (économique)** redundancy GB, lay-off; **une série de ~s** a round of redundancies GB, a series of lay-offs; **~ collectif** mass redundancy, mass lay-offs; **procéder au ~ de 20 personnes** to make 20 people redundant GB, to lay 20 people off.

■ **~ sec** enforced redundancy (*without compensation*).

licencier /lisɑ̃sje/ [2] *vtr* (pour raisons économiques) to make [sb] redundant GB, to lay [sb] off US; (pour faute) to dismiss GB, to let [sb] go; **les grandes entreprises licencient beaucoup** big companies are making a lot of people redundant GB ou are laying a lot of people off.

licencieux, **-ieuse** /lisɑ̃sjø, øz/ *adj* licentious.

lichen /likɛn/ *nm* lichen.

lichette○ /liʃɛt/ *nf* **1** (de pain, viande, fromage) morsel; **2** (pour œuf à la coque) soldier○ (*for egg*) GB, *finger of buttered bread eaten with a boiled egg*; **3** B (attache) loop.

licite /lisit/ *adj* lawful.

licol /likɔl/ *nm* headcollar GB, halter US.

licorne /likɔʀn/ *nf* Mythol unicorn.

■ **~ de mer** Zool narwhal.

licou† /liku/ *nm* halter.

licteur /liktœʀ/ *nm* lictor.

lie /li/ *nf* **1** Vin dregs (*pl*), lees (*pl*); **~ de vin** wine dregs ou lees; **2** fig dregs (*pl*) (**de** of).

IDIOMES **il faut boire la coupe** or **le calice jusqu'à la ~** you have to see it through to the bitter end.

Liechtenstein /liʃtənʃtɛn/ ▶ 321 *nprm* Liechtenstein.

lied, *pl* **lieder** or **~s** /lid, lidœʀ/ *nm* lied.

lie-de-vin /lidvɛ̃/ ▶ 193 *adj inv* wine, wine-coloured[GB].

liège /ljɛʒ/ *nm* cork; **de** or **en ~** [*revêtement, panneau*] cork (*épith*); **bouchon en ~** cork.

Liège /ljɛʒ/ ▶ 857, 692 *npr* Liège; **la province de ~** Liège (province).

liégeois, **~e** /ljeʒwa, az/ ▶ 857 *adj* of Liège; **café/chocolat ~** *iced coffee/chocolate topped with whipped cream*.

Liégeois, **~e** /ljeʒwa, az/ ▶ 857 *nm,f* (natif) native of Liège; (habitant) inhabitant of Liège.

lien /ljɛ̃/ *nm* **1** (attache) (pour une personne) bond littér, strap; (pour un objet) gén strap; (plus fin) string; fig bond; **se libérer de ses ~s** lit, fig to free oneself of one's bonds; **ses ~s l'avaient blessé aux poignets** his wrists were injured where they had been tied; **2** (rapport) connection, link; **les deux événements n'ont aucun ~ entre eux** there is absolutely no connection ou link between the two events; **3** (relation) gén link, tie; (d'ordre affectif) tie, bond; **~s économiques/diplomatiques** economic/diplomatic links ou ties; **ses ~s avec la pègre sont bien connus** his connections ou links with the underworld are well-known; **~ d'amitié** ties of friendship; **~s affectifs** emotional ties ou bonds; **~s de parenté/du sang** family/blood ties; **il n'a aucun ~ de parenté avec elle** he's not related to her at all; **être uni par les ~s du mariage** to be joined ou united in marriage.

lier /lje/ [1] **I** *vtr* **1** (attacher) to tie [sb/sth] up [*personne, fleurs, paille*]; **~ un paquet** or **un colis avec de la ficelle** to tie up a parcel with string; **~ qn à un lit/arbre** to tie sb to a bed/tree; **il avait les mains liées** lit, fig his hands were tied; **être pieds et poings liés** lit, fig to be bound hand and foot, to be hogtied US; **2** (unir) to bind; **un contrat le lie à son entreprise** a contract binds him to his company; **notre avenir est lié à celui de l'Europe** our future is bound up with that of Europe; **ils sont très liés** they are very close; **être lié avec qn** to be very close to sb, to be very friendly with sb; **3** (établir un rapport) to link [*idées, événements*] (**à** to); **~ l'aide économique à des changements politiques** to link economic aid to political change; **tous ces problèmes sont liés** these problems are all linked ou related; **4** (commencer) **~ amitié avec qn** to strike up a friendship with sb; **~ connaissance avec qn** to make sb's acquaintance; **ils ont lié connaissance** they became acquainted; **~ conversation avec qn** to strike up a conversation with sb; **5** Constr to bind [*pierres, briques*]; **~ des briques avec du ciment** to bind bricks with cement; **6** Culin to thicken [*sauce*]; **7** Mus to slur [*notes*].
II se lier *vpr* [*personnes*] to make friends (**avec qn** with sb); **ils se sont liés d'amitié à l'école** they made friends at school; **il se lie difficilement** he doesn't make friends easily.
IDIOMES **avoir partie liée avec qn** to be in league with sb.

lierre /ljɛʀ/ *nm* ivy.

liesse /ljɛs/ *nf* jubilation (**de** of); **en ~** jubilant.

lieu /ljø/ **I** *nm* **1** (*pl* **~s**) (poisson) **~ (noir)** coley, black pollock; **2** (*pl* **~x**) (endroit) place; **un bon ~ de promenade** a good place for walking; **complément/adverbe de ~** adverbial/adverb of place; **choisir le ~ de la cérémonie** to choose where the ceremony will take place; **mettre qch en ~ sûr** to put sth in a safe place; **~ de rendez-vous** or **de rencontre** meeting place; **~ d'habitation/de naissance** place of residence/of birth; **~ de pèlerinage** place of pilgrimage; **~ de culte** place of worship; **~ de vente** retail outlet, point of sale; **sur le ~ de travail** in the workplace; **~ de passage** thoroughfare; **~ de l'action/du crime** scene of the action/of the crime; **sur le ~ du drame** at the scene of the tragedy; **~ de tournage** (film) set; **en tous ~x** everywhere; **en ~ et place de qn** [*signer, agir*] on behalf of sb; **en premier ~** in the first place, firstly; **en second ~** secondly; **en dernier ~** lastly; **avoir ~** to take place; **tenir ~ de** to serve as [*réfectoire, chambre*]; **cette lettre tient ~ d'invitation** this letter is an invitation; **il y a ~ de s'inquiéter** there is cause for anxiety; **il n'y a pas ~ de s'affoler** there is no cause for panic; **s'il y a ~** if necessary; **cela n'a pas ~ d'être** it shouldn't be so; **tes critiques n'ont pas ~ d'être** there are no grounds for your criticisms; **elle a ~ d'être contente** she has cause to be happy; **donner ~ à** to cause ou give rise to [*scandale*]; ▸ **haut**.
II au lieu de *loc prép* instead of.
III au lieu que *loc conj* rather than.
IV lieux *nmpl* **1** (endroit) parts; **repérer les ~x** to have a scout around; (pour des raisons malhonnêtes) to stake out the place; **sur les ~x** [*être*] at the scene; [*arriver*] on the scene; **notre envoyé spécial est déjà sur les ~x** our special correspondent is already at the scene; **2** (habitation) premises; **visiter/quitter les ~x** to visit/leave the premises; **le maître des ~x** the master of the house.
■ **~ commun** commonplace; **~ géométrique**† locus; **~ jaune** yellow pollock; **~ de plaisir** euph brothel; **~ public** public place; **~ saint** holy place; **~ scénique** stage; **~x d'aisances**† euph toilets.
IDIOMES **n'avoir ni feu** or **être sans feu ni ~** to have neither hearth nor home†.

lieu-dit, *pl* **~s** or **lieux-dits** /ljødi/ *nm* locality.

lieue /ljø/ ▸ **477** *nf* Hist league; **~ marine** league.
IDIOMES **j'étais à cent** or **mille ~s d'imaginer** I never for a moment imagined; **à vingt ~s à la ronde** for miles around.

lieuse /ljøz/ *nf* binder.

lieutenant /ljøtnɑ̃/ ▸ **390** *nm* **1** Mil (armée de terre) ≈ lieutenant GB, ≈ first lieutenant US; (armée de l'air) ≈ flying officer GB, ≈ first lieutenant US; **2** Naut first officer.
■ **~ de vaisseau** lieutenant.

lieutenant-colonel, *pl* **lieutenants-colonels** /ljøtnɑ̃kɔlɔnɛl/ ▸ **390** *nm* (armée de terre) ≈ lieutenant-colonel; (armée de l'air) ≈ wing commander GB, ≈ lieutenant colonel US.

lièvre /ljɛvʀ/ *nm* **1** Zool hare; **2** Sport pacemaker.
IDIOMES **courir plusieurs ~s à la fois** to have several irons in the fire.

lift /lift/ *nm* (au tennis) topspin.

lifter /lifte/ [1] *vtr* to put topspin on [*balle*]; **faire un revers lifté** to do a backhand with topspin.

liftier, -ière /liftje, ɛʀ/ ▸ **510** *nm,f* lift attendant GB, elevator operator US.

lifting /liftiŋ/ *nm* Méd, Cosmét face-lift; **se faire faire un ~** to have a face-lift.

ligament /ligamɑ̃/ *nm* ligament; **se déchirer un ~** to tear a ligament.

ligamenteux, -euse /ligamɑ̃tø, øz/ *adj* ligamentous.

ligature /ligatyʀ/ *nf* **1** Méd (opération) tying; (résultat) ligature; **on lui a fait une ~ des trompes** she had her tubes tied; **2** Mus, Tech, Imprim ligature; **3** Hort tying up.

ligaturer /ligatyʀe/ [1] *vtr* **1** Méd to tie, to ligature spéc; **se faire ~ les trompes** to have one's tubes tied; **2** Hort to tie up.

lige /liʒ/ *adj* **1** Hist liege; **2** fml (dévoué) **être l'homme ~ de qn** to be sb's devoted supporter.

lignage /liɲaʒ/ *nm* **1** (de famille) lineage; **de haut ~** of noble lineage; **2** Imprim linage.

ligne /liɲ/ *nf* **1** (trait) line; **~ blanche/continue/discontinue** Aut white/solid/broken line; **~ de départ/d'arrivée** Sport starting/finishing line; **~s de la main** lines of the hand; **~ de chance** line of fortune; **~ de cœur/vie** heart/life line; **~ de défense** line of defence[GB]; **~ de l'horizon** the line of the horizon; **~ courbe/brisée** curved/broken line; **~ droite** gén straight line; (de route) straight piece of road; Courses Aut straight; **en ~ droite il y a environ 200 mètres** as the crow flies it's about 200 metres[GB]; **la dernière ~ droite avant l'arrivée** the home stretch; **papier à ~s** lined paper; **2** (d'écriture) line; **écrire quelques ~s à qn** to drop sb a line; **je vous écris ces quelques ~s pour vous dire**... this is just a quick note to tell you...; **faire faire des ~s à qn** (punition) to give sb lines; **être payé à la ~** to be paid by the line; **à la ligne!** (dans une dictée) start a new paragraph; **3** Transp (de bus, Aviat, Naut) (service) service; (parcours) route; (de métro, train) line; **la ~ Paris-Rome** Aviat the Paris to Rome route; Rail the Paris to Rome line; **~ de chemin de fer** railway line; **~s secondaires/de banlieue** Rail branch/commuter lines; **~ maritime/aérienne** sea/air route; **paquebot de ~** liner; **~s intérieures** Aviat domestic flights; **4** Électrotech (câble) cable; TV (définition) line; **~ électrique à haute tension** high-tension cable; **~ aérienne/souterraine** overhead/underground cable; **5** Télécom line; **la ~ est mauvaise** it's a bad line; **il y a quelqu'un d'autre sur la ~** we've got a crossed line; **'vous avez madame Pomier en ~'** 'Mrs Pomier is on the line for you'; **'restez en ~'** 'hold the line please'; **la ~ est coupée avec Rome** Rome is unobtainable at present; **avoir** or **obtenir la ~** to get through; **6** (silhouette) figure; **avoir/garder la ~** to be/stay slim; **retrouver la ~** to get back one's figure; **c'est mauvais pour la ~** it's bad for the figure; **7** (contour) **les ~s** (de meuble, voiture) lines; (de corps) contours; (de visage) lines; (de collines) outline (*sg*); **la ~ aérodynamique d'une voiture** the aerodynamic lines of a car; **la ~ bleue des Vosges** the blue line of the Vosges; **les ~s d'un paysage** the rise and fall of a landscape; **8** (allure générale) (de mobilier, style, vêtement) look; **lancer une nouvelle ~** to launch a new look; **9** Comm (gamme) line; **une ~ de produits de beauté** a line of beauty products; **10** (idée, point) outline; **les ~s essentielles de mon programme/projet** the broad outline of my programme[GB]/project; **raconter un événement dans ses grandes ~s** to describe an event in broad outline; **11** (orientation) (de parti politique) line; **les partisans de la ~ dure/modérée du parti** the party hardliners/moderates; **la ~ politique/idéologique** the political/ideological line; **être dans la ~** to follow the party line; **12** Pêche fishing line; **pêche à la ~** angling; **13** (alignement) line; (rangée) row; **une ~ de poteaux/voitures** a line of posts/cars; **derrière les ~s ennemies** Mil behind the enemy lines; **la ~ des avants/arrières** (au rugby) the front/back row; (au football) the forwards/backs; **mettez-vous en ~** line up ou get into line; **ils sont en ~ pour le départ** they are lined up for the start; **hors ~** [*talent, acteur*] outstanding; **être en seconde ~** fig to take second place; **14** Ordinat **en ~** on line; **15** (en généalogie) line; **~ directe** direct line of descent; **héritier en ~ directe** direct heir.
■ **~ de but** Sport goal line; **~ de champ** Phys line of force; **~ de coke**○ line of coke○; **se faire une ~ de coke** to do a line of coke; **~ de conduite** line of conduct; **~ de crédit** Fin line of credit; **~ de crête** Géog crest line; **~ de démarcation** boundary; Mil demarcation line; **~ d'eau** Naut waterline; **~ équinoxiale** Géog equator; **~ de faille** Géol faultline; **~ de faîte** Géog crest line; **~ de feu** line of fire; **~ de flottaison** Naut waterline; **~ de flottaison en charge** load ou Plimsoll line; **~ de force** Phys line of force; **~ de fuite** vanishing line; **~ mélodique** Mus melodic line; **~ de mire** line of sight; **~ de niveau** Géol line level; **~ de partage des eaux** watershed; **~ de tir** line of fire; **~ de touche** Sport gén touchline; (au basket) boundary line; **~ de visée** = **~ de mire**.
IDIOMES **être en première ~** lit, Mil to be in the front line; fig to be in the firing line; **monter en première ~** lit to go up to the front; fig to move into the attack; **entrer en ~ de compte** to be taken into account ou consideration; **il faut faire entrer en ~ de compte le fait que** account should be taken of the fact that; **cela ne devrait pas entrer**

en ~ de compte dans votre prise de décision that shouldn't enter ou come into your decision.

lignée /liɲe/ *nf* **1** (descendants) descendants; (famille) line of descent; **il est le dernier d'une longue ~** he's the last of a long line; **de haute ~** of noble descent; **2** (filiation spirituelle) tradition; **être dans la ~ des romantiques** to be in the Romantic tradition.

ligneux, **-euse** /liɲø, øz/ *adj* woody, ligneous spéc.

lignifier: **se lignifier** /liɲifje/ [2] *vpr* to lignify.

lignite /liɲit/ *nm* brown coal, lignite spéc.

ligoter /ligɔte/ [1] *vtr* **1** lit [*personne*] to truss [sb] up [*personne*] (**avec** with); **~ qn à qch** to tie sb to sth; **2** fig **~ qn** [*accord, règlement*] to bind sb; [*personne*] to tie sb's hand.

ligue /lig/ *nf* league.

liguer /lige/ [1] **I** *vtr* **~ qn contre** to get sb to join forces against.

II se liguer *vpr* [*personnes*] to join forces; **se ~ avec/contre** to join forces with/against; **être ligué avec/contre** to be in league with/against.

Ligurie /ligyʀi/ **▶ 692** *nprf* **la ~** Liguria.

lilas /lila/ **I ▶ 193** *adj inv* lilac.

II *nm* lilac; **un bouquet de ~** a bunch of lilac.

Lille /lil/ **▶ 857** *npr* Lille.

lilliputien, **-ienne** /lilipysjɛ̃, ɛn/ *adj, nm,f* Lilliputian.

lillois, **~e** /lilwa, az/ **▶ 857** *adj* of Lille.

Lillois, **~e** /lilwa, az/ **▶ 857** *nm,f* (natif) native of Lille; (habitant) inhabitant of Lille.

Lima /lima/ **▶ 857** *npr* Lima.

limace /limas/ *nf* **1** Zool slug; **2**◐ (chemise) shirt.

IDIOMES **se traîner comme une ~** to crawl along at a snail's pace.

limaçon /limasɔ̃/ *nm* **1** Zool snail; **2** Anat cochlea.

limage /limaʒ/ *nm* filing.

limaille /limaj/ *nf* filings (*pl*).

limande /limɑ̃d/ *nf* dab; **filet de ~** fillet of dab.

IDIOMES **être plate comme une ~** to be as flat as a board.

limande-sole, *pl* **limandes-soles** /limɑ̃dsɔl/ *nf* lemon sole.

limbe /lɛ̃b/ **I** *nm* Tech Astron Bot limb.

II limbes *nmpl* Relig limbo ¢ (**de** of); **être/rester dans les ~s** to be/remain in limbo.

Limbourg /lɛ̃buʀ/ **▶ 692** *nprm* Limburg.

lime /lim/ *nf* **1** Tech file; **à la ~** with a file; **donner un coup de ~ à qch** to file sth; **2** Bot lime; **3** Zool lima.

■ **~ à bois** Tech wood file; **~ à ongles** Cosmét nail file.

limer /lime/ [1] **I** *vtr* **1** (façonner) to file [*ongle, métal*]; to file down [*clé, aspérité*]; **avoir les ongles ~s** to have filed nails; **2** (couper) to file through [*barreau*].

II se limer *vpr* **se ~ les ongles** to file one's nails.

limier /limje/ *nm* **1** (chien) bloodhound; **2**○ (détective, policier) sleuth; **un fin ~** a super-sleuth.

liminaire /liminɛʀ/ *adj* [*feuilles, texte, déclaration*] prefatory; [*étape, mesure*] preliminary.

limitatif, **-ive** /limitatif, iv/ *adj* limiting, restrictive; **liste limitative/non limitative** closed/open list.

limitation /limitasjɔ̃/ *nf* (de pouvoir, liberté) limitation, restriction; (de prix, taux d'intérêt) control ¢; **~s budgétaires/des prix** budget/price control; **la ~ des armements** arms control, arms limitation; **la ~ des missiles nucléaires à 5 000** the limitation of nuclear missiles to 5,000.

■ **~ de vitesse** Aut speed limit.

limite /limit/ **I**○ *adv* **tes plaisanteries sont ~** your jokes are bordering on the offensive; **ça a été ~ mais j'ai eu mon avion** I managed to catch my plane but it was a close thing.

II *nf* **1** (ligne de séparation) border; **la ligne noire représente la ~ entre les deux États** the black line shows the border between the two states; **2** (partie extrême) (de domaine, terrain) boundary; (de mer, forêt) edge; **les ~s du village** the boundaries of the village; **3** (borne) also Math limit; **aller jusqu'à la ~ de ses forces** to push oneself to the limit; **ma patience a des ~s** there are limits to my patience; **connaître ses ~s** to know one's (own) limitations; **tout de même, il y a des ~s !** there are limits, you know!; **s'imposer des ~s** to set oneself limits; **franchir les ~s de la décence** to go beyond the bounds of decency; **leur générosité/bêtise est sans ~** their generosity/stupidity knows no bounds; **leur énergie semble sans ~** their energy seems boundless; **faire reculer les ~s du possible** to push back the bounds of possibility; **il a montré ses ~s dans cette affaire** his limitations became evident in this affair; **vraiment, il dépasse les ~s!** he's really going too far!; **à la ~, j'ai envie de démissionner** I almost feel like resigning; **à la ~, je préférerais que tu ne viennes pas** I'd sooner you didn't come really; **à la ~, je préférerais qu'il refuse** I'd almost prefer it if he refused; **à la ~ je peux te prêter 100 francs** at a pinch GB ou in a pinch US, I can lend you 100 francs; **à la ~ je pourrais aller le chercher à la gare** if it comes to it, I could go and pick him up at the station; **4** (bord) **à la ~ de** on the verge of; **elle était à la ~ de la crise de nerfs** she was on the verge of a nervous breakdown; **peinture/plaisanterie à la ~ du mauvais goût** painting/joke bordering on bad taste; **activités à la ~ de la légalité** activities bordering on the illegal; **un spectacle à la ~ du supportable** an almost unbearable sight; **5** (cadre) **dans une certaine ~** up to a point, to a certain extent; **dans la ~ de, dans les ~s de** within the limits of; **ils font ce qu'ils peuvent, dans la ~ de leurs ressources** they do what they can, within the limits of their resources; **nous vous aiderons dans la ~ de nos moyens** we will help you in as far as our means allow; **accepter des spectateurs dans la ~ des places disponibles** to accept spectators subject to the availability of seats; **dans la ~ du possible** as far as possible.

III (-)limite (*in compounds*) **âge ~** maximum age; **cas ~** Méd, Psych borderline case; **date ~** (pour une inscription) deadline, closing date; (pour remettre un travail) deadline; **date ~ de vente** sell-by date; **hauteur/largeur/poids ~** Transp maximum height/width/weight; **vitesse ~** maximum speed.

■ **~ d'âge** age limit; **~ d'élasticité** yield point; **~ de rupture** breaking point.

limité, **~e** /limite/ **I** *pp* **▶ limiter**.

II *pp adj* (restreint) [*possibilité, conversation, ressources, intérêt*] limited; **un nombre de places ~** a limited number of places; **il est assez ~** he's rather limited; **le choix est ~** there isn't much to choose from; **devoir en temps ~** question to be answered within a set time limit.

limiter /limite/ [1] **I** *vtr* **1** (restreindre) to limit, to restrict [*pouvoir, dépenses, durée, nombre*] (**à** to); **limite tes recherches à un aspect particulier du problème** confine ou restrict your research to a particular aspect of the problem; **je limiterai mon intervention à une ou deux remarques** I'll restrict my speech to one or two remarks only; **cela limite nos possibilités** that rather limits our scope; **nous sommes limités dans le temps** our time is limited; **la vitesse est limitée à 90 km/h** the speed limit is 90 km/h; **~ les dégâts** to minimize the damage; **2** (border) **la clôture qui limite notre propriété** the enclosure which marks the boundaries of our property; **des champs limités par des haies** fields bordered by hedges.

II se limiter *vpr* **1** (se restreindre) **il ne sait pas se ~** he doesn't know when to stop, he doesn't know when he's had enough; **se ~ à deux verres de bière/dix cigarettes par jour** to limit oneself to two glasses of beer/ten cigarettes a day; **je me limiterai à quelques observations** I'll only make a few observations; **limitez-vous au sujet** confine yourself to the subject; **2** (se résumer) **se ~ à** to be limited to; **l'histoire ne se limite pas à une suite de dates** history is not limited to a series of dates; **la vie ne se limite pas au travail** there's more to life than work.

limitrophe /limitʀɔf/ *adj* [*pays, État, département, province*] bordering; [*ville*] border (*épith*); **les pays ~s de la France** the countries bordering France.

limogeage /limɔʒaʒ/ *nm* (en destituant) dismissal; (en déplaçant) removal.

limoger /limɔʒe/ [13] *vtr* (destituer) to dismiss; (déplacer) to transfer.

limon /limɔ̃/ *nm* **1** Géol silt; **2** (sur une voiture à cheval) shaft; **3** (d'escalier) stringer; **4**† Bot lemon.

limonade /limɔnad/ *nf* (boisson gazeuse) lemonade GB, lemon soda US.

limonadier, **-ière** /limɔnadje, ɛʀ/ **▶ 510** *nm,f* **1** (fabricant) soft drinks manufacturer; (vendeur) soft drinks seller; **2**† (cafetier) café owner.

limoneux, **-euse** /limɔnø, øz/ *adj* [*terre*] silty; [*eau, rivière*] silt-laden.

limousin, **~e** /limuzɛ̃, in/ **▶ 692** **I** *adj* of Limousin.

II limousine *nf* Aut limousine.

Limousin, **~e** /limuzɛ̃, in/ **I** *nm,f* **1** (natif) native of Limousin; **2** (habitant) inhabitant of Limousin.

II ▶ 692 *nprm* **le ~** Limousin.

limpide /lɛ̃pid/ *adj* **1** lit [*eau, ciel, air, cristal*] clear, limpid; **2** fig [*sentiment, souvenir*] pure; [*explication, style*] clear, lucid.

limpidité /lɛ̃pidite/ *nf* **1** lit (d'eau, de ciel, cristal) clarity, limpidity littér; **2** fig (d'explication, de style) clarity, lucidity.

lin /lɛ̃/ *nm* **1** (fibre, plante) flax; **2** (tissu) linen; **chemise/toile de ~** linen shirt/cloth.

linceul /lɛ̃sœl/ *nm* lit, fig shroud.

Lincolnshire **▶ 692** *nprm* **le ~** Lincolnshire.

linéaire /lineɛʀ/ *adj* linear.

linéaments /lineamɑ̃/ *nmpl* **1** (de visage) lineaments; (d'objet) lines; **2** (ébauche) outline (*sg*).

linéarité /lineaʀite/ *nf* (d'écriture) linear quality; (d'événements) linear progression.

linge /lɛ̃ʒ/ *nm* **1** (domestique) linen; **~ sale/de couleur** dirty/coloured[GB] linen; **2** (lessive) washing; **avoir du ~ à laver** to have some washing to do; **corde** or **fil à ~** clothes line; **▶ gros**; **3** (sous-vêtements) underwear; **changer de ~** to change one's underwear; **▶ petit**; **4** (torchon) cloth; **envelopper qch dans un ~** to wrap sth up in a cloth.

■ **~ de corps** underwear; **~ de cuisine** kitchen towels (*pl*); **~ de maison** household linen; **~ de table** table linen; **~ de toilette** bathroom linen.

IDIOMES **être blanc comme un ~** to be as white as a sheet; **on doit laver son ~ sale en famille** people shouldn't wash their dirty linen in public; **déballer son ~ sale** to reveal one's guilty secret.

lingère /lɛ̃ʒɛʀ/ *nf* **1** (personne) laundry woman; **2** (armoire) linen cupboard GB, linen closet US.

lingerie /lɛ̃ʒʀi/ *nf* **1** (local) linen room; **2** (linge de corps) **~ (féminine)** lingerie; **~ fine** fine lingerie; **3** (industrie) lingerie industry.

lingette /lɛ̃ʒɛt/ *nf* ≈ baby wipe.

lingot /lɛ̃go/ *nm* ingot; **~ de métal** metal ingot.
■ **~ d'or** gold ingot (*weighing 1 kg*).

lingual, **~e**, *mpl* **-aux** /lɛ̃gwal, o/ *adj* lingual.

lingue /lɛ̃g/ *nf* ling.

linguiste /lɛ̃gɥist/ ▶510 *nmf* linguist.

linguistique /lɛ̃gɥistik/ **I** *adj* linguistic; **communauté ~** speech community.
II *nf* linguistics (+ *v sg*).

linguistiquement /lɛ̃gɥistikmɑ̃/ *adv* linguistically.

liniment /linimɑ̃/ *nm* liniment.

lino /lino/ *nm* lino GB, linoleum.

linoléum /linɔleɔm/ *nm* linoleum.

linon /linɔ̃/ *nm* Tex lawn.

linotte /linɔt/ *nf* linnet.

linotype® /linɔtip/ *nf* Linotype®.

linteau, *pl* **~x** /lɛ̃to/ *nm* lintel.

lion /ljɔ̃/ *nm* lion; **la part du ~** the lion's share; **se tailler la part du ~** to take the lion's share.
■ **~ de mer** sealion.
IDIOMES **se battre** or **se défendre comme un ~** to fight like a tiger; **avoir mangé du ~** to be full of beans○ GB, to be full of pep○ US; **descendre dans la fosse aux ~s** to enter the lion's den. ▶ **cage**.

Lion /ljɔ̃/ ▶874 *nprm* Leo.

lionceau, *pl* **~x** /ljɔ̃so/ *nm* lion cub.

lionne /ljɔn/ *nf* lioness.

lipase /lipɑz/ *nf* lipase.

lipide /lipid/ *nm* lipid.

liposome /lipɔzom/ *nm* liposome.

liposuccion /liposysjɔ̃/ *nf* liposuction.

lippe† /lip/ *nf* bottom lip.

lippu, **~e** /lipy/ *adj* [*bouche, personne*] full-lipped; [*lèvre*] full.

liquéfaction /likefaksjɔ̃/ *nf* liquefaction.

liquéfiable /likefjabl/ *adj* liquefiable.

liquéfiant, **~e** /likefjɑ̃, ɑ̃t/ *adj* liquefacient.

liquéfier /likefje/ [2] **I** *vtr* to liquefy.
II se liquéfier *vpr* **1** [*cire, glace, gaz*] to liquefy; **2**○ (avoir peur) to turn to jelly; **3**○ (avoir très chaud) to wilt.

liquette○ /likɛt/ *nf* shirt.

liqueur /likœʀ/ *nf* **1** (boisson) liqueur; **~ de poire/framboise** pear/raspberry liqueur; **2** Pharm liquor.

liquidateur, **-trice** /likidatœʀ, tʀis/ *nm,f* Jur liquidator, receiver; **~ judiciaire** official receiver.

liquidatif, **-ive** /likidatif, iv/ *adj* **acte ~** act of bankruptcy; **valeur liquidative** market value.

liquidation /likidasjɔ̃/ *nf* **1** Jur, Comm (d'entreprise, de bien) liquidation; (de dettes, comptes, succession) settlement, selling off; **~ judiciaire** or **forcée** compulsory liquidation; **~ volontaire** voluntary liquidation; **société en ~** company in liquidation; **mettre une société en ~** to put a company into liquidation ou receivership, to liquidate a company; **entrer en ~** to go into receivership ou liquidation; **~ des impôts** payment of taxes; **2** Comm (vente) clearance; **~ totale (du stock)** total clearance; **3** (de soucis, problèmes) settling; **4**○ (meurtre) liquidation○; **5** Fin settlement; **~ de fin de mois** monthly settlement; **jour de ~** settlement day.

liquide /likid/ **I** *adj* liquid; **se présenter sous forme ~** to come in liquid form; **trop ~** [*aliment, colle, sauce*] too thin; **argent ~** cash; **miel ~** clear honey.
II *nm* **1** (substance) liquid; **2** (argent) cash; **payer en ~** to pay cash.
III *nf* Ling liquid.
■ **~ correcteur** correction fluid, white-out (fluid) US; **~ de frein** brake fluid; **~ organique** body fluid; **~ de refroidissement** coolant; **~ séminal** seminal fluid.

liquider /likide/ [1] *vtr* **1** Jur to settle [*comptes*]; to liquidate [*société, commerce*]; to realize [*biens*]; to liquidate, to settle [*dettes*]; **2** Comm (vendre) to clear [*marchandises, stock*]; **3**○ (régler) to settle [*problèmes, querelles*]; **4**○ (se débarrasser de) to liquidate○ [*adversaire, témoin*]; **5**○ (consommer complètement) to demolish [*plat*]; to empty [*verre*]; to clear [*assiette*].

liquidité /likidite/ *nf* **1** (caractère liquide) liquidity; **2** Fin liquidity; **des ~s** liquid assets.

liquoreux, **-euse** /likɔʀø, øz/ *adj* [*vin*] sweet and strong; [*vapeur, odeur*] liqueur-like.

lire /liʀ/ [66] **I** ▶461 *nf* lira; **payer en ~s** to pay in lire ou liras.
II *vtr* **1** (déchiffrer) to read [*mot, journal, auteur, langue*]; **~ qch à qn** to read sth to sb; **apprendre à ~** to learn to read; **elle sait ~** she can read; **~ à voix haute** or **à haute voix** to read aloud; **lis la page 5** gén read page 5; (à voix haute) read out page 5; (en entier) read through page 5; **c'est un livre à ~/qu'il faut ~** it's a book worth reading/one ought to read; **~ Platon dans le texte** to read Plato in the original; **~ qch comme une critique** to interpret sth as a criticism; **un auteur/magazine qui est très lu** a widely read author/magazine; **au lieu de 'il' il fallait ~ 'elle'** for 'he' read 'she'; **'lu et approuvé'** 'read and approved'; **~ qch en diagonale** to skim through sth, scan sth; **~ sur les lèvres de qn** to lip-read what sb is saying; **dans l'espoir de vous ~ bientôt** hoping to hear from you soon; **2** Méd, Mus to read [*radiographie, musique*]; **3** (en hi-fi) aussi Ordinat to read; **4** (discerner) to read [*avenir*]; **~ les cartes/lignes de la main** to read cards/palms; **~ la haine dans les yeux/sur le visage de qn** to see hate written in sb's eyes/on sb's face; **~ dans les pensées de qn** to read sb's mind; **~ dans le cœur de qn** to see into sb's heart.
IDIOMES **~ dans le jeu de qn** to see through sb; **~ entre les lignes** to read between the lines; **~ sur le visage de qn comme dans un livre** to read sb like a book.

lirette /liʀɛt/ *nf* **tapis en ~** rag rug.

lis /lis/ *nm* lily.

Lisbonne /lisbɔn/ ▶857 *npr* Lisbon.

liseré /lizʀe/ *nm*, **liséré** /lizeʀe/ *nm* (raie) edging; (ruban) piping; **un ~ de sable blanc** a strip of white sand.

liseron /lizʀɔ̃/ *nm* bindweed, convolvulus.

liseuse /lizøz/ *nf* **1** (veste) bed jacket; **2** (couvrant un livre) book cover; **3** (lampe) small reading lamp.

lisibilité /lizibilite/ *nf* **1** (d'écriture, de lettre) legibility; **écriture d'une parfaite ~** perfectly legible handwriting; **2** (de roman, document) readability.

lisible /lizibl/ *adj* **1** [*écriture, manuscrit*] legible; **2** [*auteur, roman*] readable.

lisiblement /liziblǝmɑ̃/ *adv* legibly.

lisière /lizjɛʀ/ *nf* **1** (de bois, champ) edge; (de village) outskirts; fig (bord) verge; **2** Tex selvage.

lissage /lisaʒ/ *nm* smoothing.

lisse /lis/ **I** *adj* [*peau, surface, cheveux*] smooth; [*pneu*] worn.
II *nf* Naut (rambarde) handrail; (de coque) ribband.

lisser /lise/ [1] **I** *vtr* to smooth [*cheveux*]; to stroke [*barbe, moustache*]; to smooth (out) [*vêtement, nappe*]; to smooth [*cuir*]; **l'oiseau lisse ses plumes** the bird is preening its feathers ou itself.
II se lisser *vpr* **se ~ la barbe** to stroke one's beard; **le chat se lisse le poil** the cat is licking its fur.

listage /listaʒ/ *nm* Ordinat listing.

liste /list/ *nf* gén list (**de** of); Pol list (of candidates) GB, ticket US; **dresser** or **établir une ~** to draw up a list; **faire la ~ de** to list, to make a list of; **~ de commissions** shopping list; **venir grossir la ~ de** to swell the ranks of [*personnes*]; to add to the list of [*erreurs, problèmes*].
■ **~ d'attente** waiting list; **~ bloquée** Pol fixed list (of candidates); **~ civile** civil list; **~ de contrôle** checklist; **~ électorale** electoral roll; **être inscrit sur les ~s électorales** to be on the electoral roll, to be registered to vote; **~ de mariage** wedding list; **~ panachée** flexible list (*where voters can choose candidates from several lists*).
IDIOMES **être sur (la) ~ rouge** to be ex-directory GB, to have an unlisted number US; **se faire mettre sur (la) ~ rouge** to go ex-directory GB, to get an unlisted number US; **être sur la ~ noire de qn** to be in sb's bad books.

listel /listɛl/ *nm* **1** Archit listel, fillet; **2** (de pièce, médaille) rim; **3** (de livre) fillet.

lister /liste/ [1] *vtr* to list.

listériose /listeʀjoz/ ▶271 *nf* listeriosis, listeria.

listing /listiŋ/ *nm* controv listing.

lit /li/ *nm* **1** (meuble) bed; **~ à une place** or **d'une personne** single bed; **~ à deux places** or **de deux personnes** double bed; **~ dur/moelleux** hard/soft bed; **aller** or **se mettre au ~** to go to bed; **garder le ~** to stay in bed; **être/rester/fumer au ~** to be/stay/smoke in bed; **mettre qn au ~** to put sb to bed; **tirer qn du ~** lit to drag sb out of bed; **le réveil le tira du ~** the alarm got him out of bed; **elle est pas mal au ~**○ she's pretty good in bed○; **il voudrait bien la mettre** or **l'avoir dans son ~**○ he would like to get her into bed; **au ~!** (à un enfant) bedtime!; **2** (structure) bed; **~ métallique/en acajou** metal/mahogany bed; **3** (literie) bed; **faire/défaire un ~** to make/unmake a bed; **le ~ était tout défait** the bedclothes were rumpled; **le ~ n'était pas défait** the bed had not been slept in; **4** (unité d'accueil) bed; **un hôtel/hôpital de 300 ~s** a 300-bed hotel/hospital; **cette station offre 2500 ~s** there are 2,500 beds available in this resort; **5** Jur (mariage) marriage; **enfants (nés) du même/premier ~** children from the same/first marriage; **6** Culin, Géol (couche) bed; **7** Géog (de cours d'eau) bed; **la rivière est sortie de son ~** the river has overflowed its banks; **détourner un fleuve de son ~** to alter the course of a river; **8** (direction du vent) set.
■ **~ à baldaquin** four-poster bed; **~ bateau** sleigh bed; **~ breton** = **~ clos**; **~ de camp** camp bed GB, cot US; **~ clos** box bed; **~ de douleur** liter bed of pain; **~ empilable** stacking bed; **~ d'enfant** cot GB, crib US; **~ fluvial** Géog riverbed; **~ gigogne** hideaway bed; **~ mécanique** adjustable bed GB, hospital bed US; **~ de mort** death-bed; **~ pliant** folding bed; **~ en portefeuille** apple-pie bed; **~ de repos** day-bed; **~s superposés** bunk bed.
IDIOMES **comme on fait son ~ on se couche** Prov as you make your bed so you must lie in it Prov.

litanie /litani/ *nf* lit, fig litany.

lit-cage, *pl* **lits-cages** /likaʒ/ *nm* folding metal cot.

litchi /litʃi/ *nm* lychee, litchi.

liteau, *pl* **~x** /lito/ *nm* **1** (en bois) (de toiture) batten; (d'étagère) bracket; **2** Cout, Tex (de nappe, serviette) coloured stripe.

litée /lite/ *nf* litter.

literie /litʀi/ *nf* bedding.

lithiné, **~e** /litine/ **I** *adj* **sels ~s** lithium salts; **eau ~e** lithia water.
II lithinés *nmpl* lithium tablets.

lithium /litjɔm/ *nm* lithium.

litho○ /lito/ *nf* litho, lithog.

lithographe /litɔgʀaf/ **I** *adj* lithographic.
II *nmf* lithographer.

lithographie /litɔgʀafi/ *nf* **1** (technique) lithography; **2** (estampe) lithograph.

lithographier /litɔgʀafje/ [2] *vtr* to lithograph.

lithographique /litɔgʀafik/ *adj* lithographic.

lithosphère /litɔsfɛʀ/ *nf* lithosphere.

litière /litjɛʀ/ *nf* **1** (de vaches) litter; (de chevaux) bedding; (pour chats) cat litter, kitty litter US; **changer la ~ du chat** to change the cat litter; **changer les ~s** to muck out GB, to clean the stables; **2** (lit portatif) litter.

litige /litiʒ/ *nm* dispute; **statuer sur un ~** Jur to give a ruling on a case; **saisir le tribunal d'un ~** Jur to refer a matter to the court; **point de ~** gén bone of contention; Jur point at issue; **être en ~** Jur to be involved in litigation; **les parties en ~** the litigants.

litigieux, **-ieuse** /litiʒjø, øz/ *adj* [*affaire, point, sujet*] contentious; [*hypothèse, argument*] contentious; [*personne*] litigious.

litorne /litɔʀn/ *nf* fieldfare.

litote /litɔt/ *nf* gén, hum understatement; (en rhétorique) litotes; **dire qu'il n'est pas aimable, c'est une ~** to say that he is not very pleasant is an understatement ou is putting it mildly.

litre /litʀ/ **▶117** *nm* (mesure) litre[GB]; (bouteille) litre[GB] bottle; **être vendu au ~** to be sold by the litre[GB].

litron○ /litʀɔ̃/ *nm* litre[GB] of wine.

littéraire /liteʀɛʀ/ **I** *adj* [*œuvre, critique, prix*] literary; [*études, formation*] arts, liberal arts (*épith*) US; **elle est très ~** she is very literary.

II *nm,f* (par penchant) literary person; (étudiant) arts ou liberal arts US student.

littéral, **~e**, *mpl* **-aux** /liteʀal, o/ *adj* gén literal; **arabe ~** written Arabic.

littéralement /liteʀalmɑ̃/ *adv* [*signifier, traduire*] literally; [*citer*] verbatim.

littérateur /liteʀatœʀ/ *nm* man of letters; péj scribbler.

littérature /liteʀatyʀ/ *nf* **1** (œuvres) literature; **en ~** in literature; **2** (discipline) literature; **cours de ~ comparée** comparative literature course; **3** (métier d'écrivain) **se lancer dans la ~** to take up a writing career; **4** (documentation) literature; **il y a une abondante ~ sur le sujet** there is a wealth of literature on the subject; **5** pej (verbiage) waffle○; **tout cela n'est que ~** it's a lot of waffle○.

■ **~ de gare** pej pulp literature; **~ policière** detective stories; **~ de science-fiction** science-fiction.

littoral, **~e**, *mpl* **-aux** /litɔʀal/ **I** *adj* [*navigation, eaux, ville*] coastal (*épith*); [*faune, flore*] inshore (*épith*); [*colline, topographie*] littoral (*épith*).

II *nm* coastal region, coast, littoral spéc; **~ étroit** narrow coastline; **le ~ breton** the Brittany coast.

Lituanie /litɥani/ **▶321** *nprf* Lithuania.

lituanien, **-ienne** /litɥanjɛ̃, ɛn/ **I** **▶537** *adj* Lithuanian.

II **▶462** *nm* Ling Lithuanian.

Lituanien, **-ienne** /litɥanjɛ̃, ɛn/ **▶537** *nm,f* Lithuanian.

liturgie /lityʀʒi/ *nf* liturgy.

liturgique /lityʀʒik/ *adj* liturgical.

livarde /livaʀd/ *nf* sprit; **voile à ~** spritsail.

livide /livid/ *adj* [*personne, visage*] deathly pale; [*pâleur*] ghastly; liter [*aube, teint, lueur*] livid.

lividité /lividite/ *nf* lividness; **la ~ de l'aube** liter the livid greyness GB ou grayness US of dawn.

living /liviŋ/ *nm* **1** (pièce) living-room; **2** (mobilier) living-room suite.

living-room, *pl* **~s** /liviŋʀum/ *nm* living-room.

Livourne /livuʀn/ *npr* Leghorn, Livorno.

livrable /livʀabl/ *adj* [*article, marchandise, manuscrit*] which can be delivered.

livraison /livʀɛzɔ̃/ *nf* **1** (de marchandise) delivery; **payable à la ~** payable on delivery; **voiture de ~** delivery van; **'~s à domicile'** (sur une annonce publicitaire) 'we do home deliveries'; **'Livraisons'** (espace réservé) 'deliveries only'; **il est venu prendre ~ de la commande** he came to pick up the order; **il faut qu'ils cessent leurs ~s d'armes aux rebelles** they must stop providing the rebels with arms; **2** (marchandises) delivery; **3** Édition, TV (partie) part, instalment.

livre /livʀ/ **I** *nm* **1** (volume publié) book; **~ d'images/d'art** picture/art book; **~ pour enfants** children's book; **ne connaître qch que par les ~s** only to know about sth from books; **à ~ ouvert** [*traduire*] off the cuff; **religions du ~** Bible-based religions; **c'est mon ~ de chevet** lit it's my bedside reading; fig it's my bible; **2** (registre) book; Compta (account) book, ledger; **3** (volume) book; **un ouvrage en 12 ~s** a work in 12 books; **4** (industrie) **l'industrie du ~** the book industry ou trade GB; **les métiers du ~** trades within the book industry.

II *nf* **1** **▶46** (monnaie) pound; **~ sterling** pound sterling; **~ irlandaise** Irish pound, punt; **2** **▶620** (unité de masse) (demi-kilo) half a kilo; (anglo-saxonne) pound.

■ **~ blanc** blue book; **~ de bord** logbook; **~ de caisse** cash book; **~ de classe = ~ scolaire**; **~ de comptes** accounts book; **~ de cuisine** cookery book, cookbook; **~ de l'élève** pupil's workbook; **~ d'heures** Book of Hours; **~ de lecture** reading book, reader; **~ du maître** teacher's book; **~ de messe** missal, mass book; **~ d'or** visitors' book; **~ de poche®** paperback; **~ scolaire** schoolbook, textbook; **~ à succès** bestseller.

IDIOMES **parler comme un ~** to talk like a book; **cela c'est passé comme dans les ~s** it was like something out of a book.

livrée /livʀe/ *nf* (de domestique) livery; **en ~** in livery; **la ~ de la misère** fig the badge of poverty.

livrer /livʀe/ [1] **I** *vtr* **1** Comm to deliver [*marchandises*] (**to** à); **se faire ~ qch** to have sth delivered; **nous livrons à domicile** we do home deliveries; **~ qn** to deliver sb's order; **2** (remettre) to hand [sb] over [*personne, criminel, prisonnier*] (**à** to); (en trahissant) to betray [*complice, secret*] (**to** à); to pass [sth] on [*document, renseignement*] (**à** to); **3** (abandonner) **ils ont livré le meurtrier à la colère de la foule** they abandoned the murderer to the mob; **le pays a été livré au pillage/chaos** the country was given over to plunder/chaos; **être livré à soi-même** to be left to one's own devices; **4** (confier) **il nous livre un peu de lui-même dans ses romans** he reveals something of himself in his novels; **les volcans ne nous ont pas encore livré tous leurs secrets** volcanoes have not yet yielded all their secrets up to us.

II se livrer *vpr* **1** (s'adonner) **se ~ à l'étude** to devote oneself to one's studies; **se ~ à la débauche** to give oneself over to vice; **se ~ à des violences** to commit acts of violence; **se ~ à un trafic de drogue** to engage in drug trafficking; **il s'est livré à des critiques acerbes contre ses ennemis** he criticized his enemies harshly; **2** (se rendre) **se ~ à** [*terroristes, bandits*] to give oneself up to, to surrender to; **3** (se confier) **se ~ à un ami** to confide in a friend; **il ne se livre pas facilement** he doesn't open up easily.

IDIOMES **~ bataille** to do battle (**à** with); **~ passage à qn** to let sb through.

livresque /livʀɛsk/ *adj* **savoir** or **culture ~** book-learning.

livret /livʀɛ/ *nm* **1** (livre) booklet, small book; (registre) record book; **2** (d'opéra) libretto.

■ **~ de caisse d'épargne** ≈ savings book GB, bankbook (*for a savings account*) US; **~ d'épargne logement** ≈ building society passbook GB, bankbook US; **~ de famille** family record book (*of births, marriages and deaths*); **~ militaire** *record given on completion of military service stating obligations in case of mobilization*; **~ scolaire** school report book.

livreur, **-euse** **▶510** /livʀœʀ, øz/ *nm,f* delivery man/delivery woman.

LOA /ɛloa/ *nf*: *abbr* ▶ **location**.

lob /lɔb/ *nm* Sport lob; **il a réussi d'excellents ~s** he lobbed magnificently.

lobby, *pl* **lobbies** /lɔbi/ *nm* lobby.

lobe /lɔb/ *nm* **1** Anat, Bot, Géog, Zool lobe; **~ de l'oreille** ear lobe; **2** Archit foil.

lobé, **~e** /lɔbe/ *adj* **1** Bot lobed, sinuate; **2** Archit foiled, foliated.

lobectomie /lɔbɛktɔmi/ *nf* lobectomy.

lobélie /lɔbeli/ *nf* lobelia.

lober /lɔbe/ [1] *vtr, vi* to lob.

lobotomie /lɔbɔtɔmi/ *nf* lobotomy.

lobule /lɔbyl/ *nm* Anat, Bot lobule.

local, **~e**, *pl* **-aux** /lɔkal, o/ **I** *adj* gén [*journal, industrie, autorités*] local; [*douleur*] localized; [*averses*] localized; **contraceptif ~** *barrier method of contraception including spermicidal creams etc*; **22 heures heure ~e** 22.00 local time.

II *nm* **1** (pièce quelconque) place; **ils ont un ~ pour répéter** they've got a place where they can rehearse; **les scouts ont besoin d'un ~** the scouts need a place to meet; **2** (pièce à usage déterminé) **~ (à usage) commercial** commercial premises (*pl*); **~ professionnel** or **d'activité** business premises (*pl*); **locaux habitables** residential units; **la réunion aura lieu dans les locaux du lycée** the meeting will take place on school premises; **les locaux de l'usine** factory premises; **dans les locaux de la gendarmerie** at the police station; **les locaux du journal/du parti socialiste** the newspaper/Socialist Party's offices.

localement /lɔkalmɑ̃/ *adv* **1** (relativement à un lieu) on a local level; **2** (à certains endroits) locally; **appliquer la crème ~** apply the cream locally.

localisable /lɔkalizabl(ə)/ *adj* **une douleur difficilement ~** a pain that is difficult to locate.

localisation /lɔkalizasjɔ̃/ *nf* **1** (emplacement) location; **la ~ d'un navire en détresse/d'un bruit** locating a ship in distress/a noise; **2** (limitation) **la ~ d'un incendie/d'un conflit** localizing a fire/a conflict.

■ **~ cérébrale** localization of brain function.

localiser /lɔkalize/ [1] **I** *vtr* **1** (repérer) to locate [*personne, bruit*]; to locate [*fuite, panne*]; **2** (circonscrire) to localize [*incendie, maladie, conflit*].

II se localiser *vpr* to become localized.

localité /lɔkalite/ *nf* Géog, Biol locality.

locataire /lɔkatɛʀ/ *nmf* tenant; **être ~** to be renting.

locatif, **-ive** /lɔkatif, iv/ **I** *adj* [*revenu, secteur, valeur*] rental.

II *nm* **1** Ling locative; **au ~** in the locative; **2** (secteur immobilier) rental sector.

location /lɔkasjɔ̃/ *nf* **1** (d'immobilier) (par le propriétaire) renting out; (par le locataire) renting **¢**; **~ de terrains/logements** renting of land/accommodation; **agence de ~** rental agency; **donner** or **mettre en ~** to rent out, to let GB; **maison en ~** rented house; **2** (logement) rented accommodation **¢**; **les ~s se font rares** rented accommodation is becoming scarce; **être en ~** to live in rented accommodation; **3** (loyer) rent; **payer la ~ tous les mois** to pay the rent monthly; **4** (de matériel) hire **¢**; **~ de voitures/d'outils** car/tool hire; **véhicule de ~** hire vehicle; **contrat de ~** rental agreement; **~ de téléviseurs/vidéos** TV/video rental; **coût de ~** cost of hiring; **5** (de spectacle) reservation, booking GB; **faire les ~s** to reserve, to book GB the seats; **la ~ des places sera ouverte à partir du 3 juin**

tickets will be available from 3 June; **guichet de ~** box office.
■ **~ avec option d'achat**, **LOA** leasing.

location-vente, *pl* **locations-ventes** /lɔkasjɔ̃vɑ̃t/ *nf* **1** (d'immobilier) 100% mortgage scheme; **en ~** on a 100% mortgage; **2** (d'équipement) hire purchase; **3** (location avec option d'achat) leasing.

loch /lɔk/ *nm* **1** Naut log; **2** (en Écosse) (lac) loch.

loche /lɔʃ/ *nf* **1** (poisson) (d'eau douce) loach; (de mer) rockling; **2** (limace) grey GB ou gray US slug.

lock-out /lɔkaut/ *nm inv* lock-out; **lever le ~** to end the lock-out.

locomoteur, **-trice** /lɔkɔmɔtœʀ, tʀis/ *adj* locomotive.

locomotion /lɔkɔmosjɔ̃/ *nf* locomotion.

locomotive /lɔkɔmɔtiv/ *nf* **1** Rail engine, locomotive; **~ à vapeur** steam engine; **2** fig (meneur) driving-force; (d'une mode) trendsetter; (personne, région dynamique) powerhouse; Sport pace-setter.
IDIOMES **souffler comme une ~** to puff and pant.

locuste /lɔkyst/ *nf* locust.

locuteur, **-trice** /lɔkytœʀ, tʀis/ *nm,f* speaker; **~ natif** native speaker.

locution /lɔkysjɔ̃/ *nf* (grammaticale) phrase; (expression) idiom; **~ figée/adverbiale** fixed/adverbial phrase; **~ toute faite** set phrase.

loden /lɔdɛn/ *nm* **1** (tissu) loden; **2** (manteau) loden coat.

lœss /løs/ *nm inv* loess.

lof /lɔf/ *nm* luff, windward side; **aller au ~** to luff, to sail into the wind; **virer ~ pour ~** to wear (ship).

lofer /lɔfe/ [1] *vi* to luff, to bring the ship round to windward.

logarithme /lɔgaʀitm/ *nm* logarithm, log; **table de ~s** log table.

logarithmique /lɔgaʀitmik/ *adj* logarithmic.

loge /lɔʒ/ *nf* **1** (de gardien d'immeuble) lodge; **2** Théât (d'artiste) dressing room; (de spectateur) box; **3** (de franc-maçons) (lieu) lodge; (groupe) **Loge** Lodge; **frères de Loge** Lodge brothers; **Grande Loge** Grand Lodge; **4** Archit loggia; **5** Bot loculus; **les ~s** loculi.
IDIOMES **être aux premières ~s** to be in an ideal position.

logé, **~e** /lɔʒe/ **I** *pp* ▶ **loger**.
II *pp adj* housed; **bien/mal ~** well/badly housed; **être ~, nourri, blanchi** to have bed, board and one's laundry done; **de quoi te plains-tu, tu es ~ nourri!** what are you complaining about? you have bed and board ou board and lodging; ▶ **enseigne**.

logeable /lɔʒabl/ *adj* **1** (à grande contenance) roomy; **2** (peu encombrant) that doesn't take up much room.

logement /lɔʒmɑ̃/ *nm* **1** (local d'habitation) accommodation ¢; **chercher un ~** to look for accommodation ou a place to live; **les ~s sont chers** accommodation is very expensive; **nous allons construire 6000 ~s** we are going to build 6,000 houses and flats GB ou apartments US; **l'achat d'un ~** (appartement) buying a flat ou an apartment US; (maison) buying a house; **~ individuel** (appartement) flat GB, apartment US; (maison) house; **2** (fait de loger) housing; **la crise/le marché du ~** the housing crisis/market; **loi sur le ~** housing law; **3** Tech (de bille, rouleau) housing; (de pêne) guides (*pl*).
■ **~ locatif** accommodation for rent; **~ social** local authority housing GB, public housing US.

logement-foyer, *pl* **logements-foyers** /lɔʒmɑ̃fwaje/ *nm* sheltered accommodation.

loger /lɔʒe/ [13] **I** *vtr* **1** (fournir un logement permanent à) [*mairie, service social*] to house [*famille, étudiant, réfugié*]; **2** (héberger temporairement) [*personne*] to put [sb] up [*ami, stagiaire*]; [*mairie, école*] to provide accommodation for [*sinistrés, stagiaires*]; **pourrais-tu me ~ cette semaine?** could you put me up this week?; **les élèves seront logés chez l'habitant** the students will be put up with local families; **~ qn dans** to put sb up in; **on logera le stagiaire dans la petite chambre** we'll put the student in the small room; **3** (contenir) [*hôtel, pensionnat*] to have accommodation for; **4** (placer) **~ qch dans un placard** to put sth in a cupboard [*objet, livres*]; **je n'ai pas pu ~ tous mes meubles dans le salon** I couldn't fit all my furniture in the living room; **~ le ballon dans un coin du filet** to slam the ball into a corner of the net; **5** (faire pénétrer) **~ une balle dans la tête/le bras de qn** to shoot sb in the head/the arm; **~ une idée dans la tête de qn** to put an idea into sb's head.
II *vi* **1** (habiter) to live; **~ à Rennes/en banlieue** to live in Rennes/in the suburbs; **~ chez qn** to live in sb's house; **~ chez un particulier** to have a room in a private house; **2** (résider temporairement) to stay; **elle ne sait pas où ~** she doesn't know where to stay; **~ à l'hôtel/en auberge de jeunesse** to stay at a hotel/at a youth hostel; **~ chez qn** to stay with sb; **~ chez l'habitant** to stay with a family.
III se loger *vpr* **1** (trouver un logement) [*personne*] to find accommodation, to find a place to live; **2** (avoir un lieu d'habitation) **avec cette somme, je dois me nourrir et me ~** with that I have to pay for food and accommodation ou housing; **3** (se placer) **se ~ dans qch** [*ballon*] to land in sth; (en se fixant) to get stuck in sth; [*poussière, saletés*] to collect in sth; **la balle est venue se ~ dans le genou** the bullet lodged in his knee; **c'est une bactérie qui se loge dans les canalisations** it's a bacterium that establishes itself in pipes; **se ~ une balle dans la tête** to shoot oneself in the head.

logeur /lɔʒœʀ/ *nm* lodger.

logeuse /lɔʒøz/ *nf* (female) lodger.

loggia /lɔdʒja/ *nf* loggia.

logiciel, **-ielle** /lɔʒisjɛl/ **I** *adj* software (*épith*); **génie ~** software engineering.
II *nm* **1** (ensemble de programmes) software ¢; **~ intégré/de base** integrated/system(s) software; **~ contributif** shareware; **~ public** freeware; **2** (programme) program, software package; **~ de jeux/d'application** games/application program.

logicien, **-ienne** /lɔʒisjɛ̃, ɛn/ *nm,f* logician; **raisonner en ~** to reason logically.

logique /lɔʒik/ **I** *adj* **1** gén logical; **il n'est pas ~ avec lui-même** he is not consistent; **2**○ (compréhensible) reasonable; **ce serait ~ qu'ils soient partis** it would be reasonable for them to have left.
II *nf* **1** gén logic (**de** of); **manquer de ~** to be illogical; **~ industrielle/financière** industrial/financial logic; **défier toute ~** to defy all logic; **avec ~** logically, in a logical way; **c'est dans la ~ des choses** it's in the nature of things; **~ déductive** deductive reasoning; **cela s'inscrit dans la même ~** it fits into the same scheme; **en toute ~** logically; **~ de guerre** logic of war; **2** Philos, Math, Ordinat logic.

logiquement /lɔʒikmɑ̃/ *adv* logically.

logis /lɔʒi/ *nm* liter home, dwelling; **le maître du ~** the master of the house.

logistique /lɔʒistik/ **I** *adj* logistical; **soutien ~** logistical support.
II *nf* logistics (+ *v sg*) (**de** of).

logithèque /lɔʒitɛk/ *nf* software library.

logo /lɔgo/ *nm* (*abbr* = **logotype**) logo.

logomachie /lɔgɔmaʃi/ *nf* **1** littér logomachy; **2** (verbiage) péj pompous verbosity.

logomachique /lɔgɔmaʃik/ *adj* péj logomachical.

logorrhée /lɔgɔʀe/ *nf* **1** Psych compulsive talking, logorrhea spéc; **2** péj verbal diarrhoea○ GB, diarrhea of the mouth US.

logotype /lɔgɔtip/ *nm* logo.

loi /lwa/ *nf* **1** Jur (règle) law (**sur** on; **contre** against); **adopter/voter/abroger une ~** to adopt/pass/repeal a law; **obéir aux ~s** to obey the law; **être au-dessus des ~s** to be above the law; **se faire une ~ de faire** to make it a rule for oneself to do; **2** (corps de lois) **la ~** the law; **enfreindre la ~** to break the law; **respecter la ~** to respect the law; **appliquer la ~** to administer ou apply the law; **avoir la ~ pour soi** to have the law on one's side; **subir la ~ de qn** to be ruled by sb; **d'après la ~ française** under French law; **c'est la ~ du plus fort qui règne ici** the law of the strongest prevails here; **mettre qn/qch hors la ~** to outlaw sb/sth; **tomber sous le coup de la ~** to be ou constitute an offence[GB]; **faire la ~** fig to lay down the law; **3** (principe) aussi Sci law; **~s physiques/économiques** laws of physics/economics; **les ~s de la nature/gravitation** the laws of nature/gravity; **les ~s du marché** the laws of the free market; **c'est la ~ des séries** things always happen in a row; **4** (convention) rule; **les ~s de l'hospitalité** the rules of hospitality; **la ~ du milieu** the law of the underworld; **la ~ du silence** (règle de conduite) code of silence; (pour protéger) conspiracy of silence.
■ **~ d'amnistie** *act granting amnesty to some offenders*; **~ communautaire** CEE community law; **~ de composition** Math law of composition; **~ constitutionnelle** constitutional law; **~ divine** divine law; **~ électorale** electoral law; **~ de finances** finance act GB ou bill US; **~ de la jungle** law of the jungle; **~ martiale** martial law; **~ de l'offre et de la demande** Écon the law of supply and demand; **~ d'orientation** framework law; **~ sur la presse** *legislation preventing monopoly of the press*; **~ de programme** Fin finance act; **~s d'exception** emergency legislation; ▶ **nécessité**.

loi-cadre, *pl* **lois-cadres** /lwakadʀ/ *nf* outline law.

loin /lwɛ̃/ **I** *adv* **1** (dans l'espace) a long way, far littér; **c'est ~** it's a long way; **c'est très ~** it's a very long way; **c'est assez ~** it's quite a long way; **c'est trop ~** it's too far; **ils doivent être déjà ~ maintenant** they must be a long way ou far away by now; **elle ne peut pas être bien ~** she can't be too far away ou off; **est-ce ~?** is it far (away)?; **ce n'est pas très ~** it's not very far (away); **il habite plus ~** he lives further ou farther away; **ils sont ~ derrière** they're far behind ou a long way behind; **aussi** or **si** or **du plus ~ que l'on regarde, on ne voit que des champs de lavande** however far you look, you can see nothing but lavender fields; **les vignes s'étendaient aussi ~ que l'on pouvait voir** the vineyards stretched as far as you ou the eye could see; **du plus ~ qu'il m'aperçut, il se mit à agiter les bras** as soon as he saw me, he began to wave; **voir plus ~** (dans un texte) see below; ▶ **lèvre**, **monture**, **nez**; **2** (dans le temps) **tout cela est bien ~** that was all a long time ago; **comme c'est ~!** what a long time ago that was!; **aussi** or **du plus ~ que l'on recherche, on n'arrive pas à trouver d'où vient l'erreur** however far back we go, we can't find where the mistake originated; **aussi ~ que je me souvienne** as far back ou as long as I can remember; **d'aussi** or **du plus ~ que me me souvienne** for as long as I can remember; **les vacances sont déjà ~** the vacation is long past now, it's a long time since the vacation now ; **un événement qui remonte ~ dans le passé** an event which dates back a long way; **cela remonte à ~** it's a long time ago; **c'est encore ~ (dans l'avenir)** it's still a long way off (in the future); **l'été n'est plus très ~ maintenant** summer isn't far off now; **le temps n'est pas si ~ où...** it's not so long since...; **il est bien ~**

le temps où... it's a long time since...; **plus ~ dans le roman/film** at a later point in the novel/film; **3** fig **il y a ~ d'une idée à sa réalisation** there's a wide gap between an idea and its fulfilment[GB]; **de là à dire qu'il est incompétent, il y a ~** there's a big difference between that and saying he's incompetent; **de là à dire qu'il est incompétent, il n'y a pas ~** that comes close to saying he's incompetent; **tu sembles si ~** (distant) you seem so distant; (absorbé) you seem miles away; **il n'est pas bête, ~ s'en faut!** he's not stupid, far from it!; **cela peut aller très ~** it can go very far; **ça va beaucoup plus ~** it goes much further; **il est allé trop ~** he went too far; **ce livre/film ne va pas ~** this book/film GB ou movie US is a bit shallow; **la décentralisation n'est pas allée très ~** decentralization didn't get very far; **votre fille est brillante, elle ira ~** your daughter is brilliant, she'll go far; **avec 1500 francs par mois, on ne va pas aller ~** we won't get very far on 1,500 francs a month; **ils veulent aller plus ~ dans leur coopération** they want to extend their cooperation; **il ne peut pas aller plus ~ dans son soutien** he can't increase his support.

II loin de *loc prép* **1** (dans l'espace) far from; **est-ce encore ~ d'ici?** is it much further ou farther from here?; **non ~ de** not far from; **2** (dans le temps) far from; **cette époque n'est pas si ~ de nous** we're not so far from that time; **on est encore ~ d'avoir fini** we're still far from finished, we're still a long way off finishing; **nous sommes encore ~ de la fin des examens** the end of the exams is still a long way off; **il n'est pas ~ de 11 heures** it's not far off 11 o'clock; **cela ne fait pas ~ de quatre ans que je suis ici** I've been here for almost four years now; **3** fig far from, a long way from; **je me sens ~ de tout cela** I feel detached from all that; **c'est très ~ de ce que j'attendais** it's not anywhere near what I expected; **elle n'est pas arrogante, ~ de là!** she's not arrogant, far from it! ; **~ de moi l'idée de vous offenser** far be it from me to offend you; **~ de moi cette idée!** nothing could be further from my mind!; **bien ~ de ces discours de paix** far removed from these peace talks; **avec l'imprimante, ça fait pas ~ de 10000 francs** if you include the printer, you're talking about 10,000 francs or thereabouts.

III de loin *loc adv* **1** (d'un endroit éloigné) from a distance, from afar littér; **je l'ai vu arriver de ~** I saw him coming from a distance; **je ne vois pas très bien de ~** I can't see very well at a distance; **2** fig from a distance; **vu de ~, cela n'a pas l'air très dangereux** seen from a distance, it doesn't seem very dangerous; **il voit les choses de ~** he sees things from a distance; **c'est de ~ ton meilleur roman** it's by far your best novel; **il est de ~ le premier acheteur de films français** he's far and away ou by far the main buyer of French films; **leur férocité a dépassé de ~ celle de**... their ferocity far surpassed that of...

IV au loin *loc adv* (dans le lointain) in the distance; **tout au ~** far away in the distance.

V de loin en loin *loc adv* **1** (séparé dans l'espace) **on pouvait voir des maisons de ~ en ~** you could see houses scattered here and there; **les arbres étaient plantés de ~ en ~** the trees were planted at wide intervals; **2** (de temps en temps) every now and again, every now and then.

IDIOMES **~ des yeux, ~ du cœur** Prov out of sight, out of mind Prov.

lointain, ~e /lwɛ̃tɛ̃, ɛn/ **I** *adj* **1** (dans l'espace) [*terre, expédition, musique, ami*] distant; **2** (dans le temps) [*passé, civilisation, souvenir*] distant; [*avenir, échéance, objectif*] distant; **les jours ~s où**... the far-off days when...; **~e est l'époque où**... the time is far distant when...; **3** (indirect) [*ressemblance, rapport*] remote; [*cause*] indirect; [*parent, héritier*] distant; **4** (détaché) [*personne, air*] distant; **elle écoutait, le regard ~** she was listening with a faraway look in her eyes.

II *nm* background; **dans le ~** [*apercevoir, entendre*] in the distance; **le regard plongé dans le ~** gazing into the distance.

loir /lwaʀ/ *nm* (edible) dormouse.

IDIOMES **être paresseux comme un ~** to be bone idle.

Loire /lwaʀ/ **▶357**, **692** *nprf* (fleuve, département) **la ~** the Loire; **la vallée de la ~** the Loire valley; **les Pays de la ~** the Loire region.

Loire-Atlantique /lwaʀatlɑ̃tik/ **▶692** *nprf* (département) **la ~** the Loire-Atlantique.

Loiret /lwaʀɛ/ **▶357**, **692** *nprm* (affluent, département) **le ~** the Loiret.

Loir-et-Cher /lwaʀeʃɛʀ/ **▶692** *nprm* (département) **le ~** the Loir-et-Cher.

loisible /lwazibl/ *adj* fml permissible; **il nous est ~ de faire** we have a right to do.

loisir /lwaziʀ/ *nm* **1** (temps libre) leisure ¢, spare time ¢; **pendant mes moments de ~, pendant mes ~s** in my leisure time ou spare time; **industrie/civilisation du ~** or **des ~s** leisure industry/society; **(tout) à ~** at (great) leisure; **2** (possibilité) **avoir le ~/tout ~ de faire** to have time/plenty of time to do; **donner/laisser à qn le ~ de faire** to allow/leave sb the time to do; **3** (activité) leisure activity; **~s sportifs/de plein air** sporting/outdoor activities.

lolo /lolo/ *nm* **1**○ baby talk (lait) milk; **2**◐ (sein) boob○, tit◐.

lombaire /lɔ̃bɛʀ/ **I** *adj* lumbar.

II *nf* lumbar vertebra.

lombalgie /lɔ̃balʒi/ *nf* lumbago.

lombard, ~e /lɔ̃baʀ, aʀd/ **I** *adj* gén Lombard; [*architecture, écriture*] Lombardic.

II ▶462 *nm* Ling Lombard dialect.

Lombardie /lɔ̃baʀdi/ **▶692** *nf* Lombardy.

lombes /lɔ̃b/ *nmpl* loins.

lombric /lɔ̃bʀik/ *nm* earthworm.

Lomé /lome/ **▶857** *npr* Lomé.

londonien, -ienne /lɔ̃dɔnjɛ̃, ɛn/ **▶857** *adj* of London.

Londonien, -ienne /lɔ̃dɔnjɛ̃, ɛn/ *nm,f* Londoner.

Londres /lɔ̃dʀ/ **▶857** *npr* London.

long, longue /lɔ̃, lɔ̃g/ **▶477** **I** *adj* **1** (dans l'espace) [*tige, cils, patte, lettre, robe, table, distance*] long; **une chemise à manches longues** a shirt with long sleeves, a long-sleeved shirt; **des femmes en robe longue** women in long dresses; **être ~ de six mètres** to be six metres[GB] long; **un tuyau ~ de trois mètres** a pipe three metres[GB] long, a three-metre[GB] long pipe; **plus/trop ~ de deux mètres** two metres[GB] longer/too long; **au ~ cours** Naut [*voyage, navigation*] ocean; [*capitaine*] fully-licensed; **2** (dans le temps) [*moment, vie, voyage, exil, film, silence*] long; [*amitié*] long-standing; **pendant les longues soirées d'hiver** during the long winter evenings; **ta longue habitude des enfants** your great experience of children; **une traversée/entrevue longue de 40 minutes** a 40 minute crossing/interview; **être ~ à faire** [*personne*] to be slow to do; [*chose*] to take a long time to do; **il est toujours ~ à se décider** he's always slow to make up his mind; **qu'est-ce que tu es ~!** you're so slow!; **aliment ~ à cuire** food that takes a long time to cook; **être en longue maladie** to be on extended sick leave; **je ne serai pas ~** (pour aller quelque part) I won't be long; (pour un discours) I will be brief; **il guérira, mais ce sera ~** he will get better, but it's going to be a long time; **huit mois, c'est ~** eight months is a long time; **être ~ à la détente**○ to be slow on the uptake○; **il trouve le temps ~** time hangs heavy on his hands; **pendant de longues heures/années** for hours/years; **3** Ling (syllabe, voyelle) long.

II *adv* **1** (beaucoup) **en dire ~/trop ~/plus ~** to say a lot/too much/more **(sur qch/qn** about sth/sb**)**; **j'aimerais en savoir plus ~ sur elle** I'd like to know more about her; **je pourrais t'en dire ~ sur lui** I could tell you a thing or two about him; **2** Mode **s'habiller ~** to wear longer skirts.

III *nm* **1** (longueur) **10 mètres de ~** 10 metres[GB] long; **un câble de six mètres de ~** a cable six metres[GB] long, a six-metre[GB] long cable; **mesurer** or **avoir** or **faire deux mètres de ~** to be two metres[GB] long; **en ~** [*découper, fendre*] lengthwise; **de ~ en large** [*marcher*] up and down; **arpenter une pièce de ~ en large** to pace up and down a room; **en ~ et en large** [*raconter*] in great detail; **en ~, en large et en travers** [*raconter*] at great length; **le ~ du mur** (en longueur) along the wall; (en hauteur) up ou down the wall; **tout le ~ de qch** (dans l'espace) all along sth; (dans le temps) all the way through sth; **j'ai couru tout le ~ du chemin, j'ai couru tout du ~** I ran all the way; **elle a pleuré tout le ~ du film** she cried (all the way) through the film; **tomber de tout son ~** to fall flat (on one's face); **2** Mode **le ~** long clothes (*pl*), lower hemlines (*pl*); **la mode est au ~** hemlines are down (this season); **s'habiller en ~** to wear a full-length dress.

IV longue *nf* **1** Ling (syllabe) long syllable; (voyelle) long vowel; **2** Jeux (aux cartes) long suit (**à** in); **3** Sport *game of boules played in the south of France.*

V à la longue *loc adv* in the end, eventually; **à la longue on s'habitue** in the end you get used to it.

■ **~ métrage** Cin feature-length film.

longanimité /lɔ̃ganimite/ *nf* (endurance) long suffering; (tolérance) forbearance.

long-courrier, *pl* **~s** /lɔ̃kuʀje/ *nm* (navire) ocean-going ship; (avion) long-range aircraft.

longe /lɔ̃ʒ/ *nf* **1** (de cheval) (pour attacher) tether; (pour mener) rein; **mener/faire travailler un cheval à la ~** to lead/to lunge[GB] a horse; **2** (de faucon) jess; **3** (en boucherie) loin.

longer /lɔ̃ʒe/ [13] *vtr* **1** (aller le long de) [*personne, voiture, train*] to go along [*forêt, côte, enceinte*]; to follow [*rivière, canal*]; [*bateau*] to sail along [*côte*]; **2** (s'étendre le long de) [*jardin, route, chemin*] to run alongside [*lac, forêt, champ*].

longeron /lɔ̃ʒʀɔ̃/ *nm* **1** (de pont) (central) girder; **2** (de châssis) Rail sideframe; Aut side rail ou member; **3** Aviat (de fuselage) longeron; (d'aile) spar.

longévité /lɔ̃ʒevite/ *nf* **1** (longue vie) lit, fig longevity; **l'extraordinaire ~ de la tortue** the extraordinary longevity of the tortoise; **2** (durée quelconque) (d'objet, de plante) lifespan; (d'animal, humain) life expectancy; **~ maximale** maximum lifespan.

longiligne /lɔ̃ʒiliɲ/ *adj* lanky, rangy.

longitude /lɔ̃ʒityd/ *nf* longitude; **à** or **par 30° de ~ est/ouest** at longitude 30° east/west.

longitudinal, ~e, *mpl* **-aux** /lɔ̃ʒitydinal, o/ *adj* gén longitudinal; [*axe, coupe, fibres, cassure*] longitudinal, lengthwise.

longitudinalement /lɔ̃ʒitydinalmɑ̃/ *adv* longitudinally, lengthwise.

longtemps /lɔ̃tɑ̃/ *adv* **1** [*attendre, dormir etc*] (for) a long time; (avec négation, dans question) (for) long; **j'y ai vécu ~** I lived there for a long time; **il n'a pas mis ~, ça ne lui a pas pris ~** it didn't take him long; **il t'a fallu ~?** did it take you long?; **malade pendant ~** ill for a long time; **(pendant) ~ j'ai cru que** for a long time, I believed (that); **X, ~ détenu/ministre,**... X, who was in prison/a minister for a long time,...; **ils ne se sont pas vus pendant ~** they didn't see each other for a long time; **partir pour ~** to go away for a long time; **tu en as pour ~/encore pour ~?** (à te préparer) will you be long/much longer?; **il n'en a plus pour ~** (à vivre) he won't last much

Les mesures de longueur (1)

Les unités

Le système métrique est de plus en plus utilisé en Grande-Bretagne et aux États-Unis pour les mesures de longueur. Mais les anciennes mesures ont encore cours, et sont quelquefois préférées, notamment pour les distances, exprimées en miles, et non en kilomètres. Les commerçants utilisent en général les deux systèmes.

Équivalences

1 inch	=	2,54 cm		
1 foot	=	12 inches	=	30,48 cm
1 yard	=	3 feet	=	91,44 cm
1 furlong	=	220 yards	=	201,17 m
1 mile	=	1760 yards	=	1,61 km

Pour la prononciation des nombres, voir ***les nombres*** **▶ 545**.

dire			dire
one millimetre	1 mm	0.04 in*	*inches*
one centimetre	1 cm	0.39 in	
one metre	1 m	39.37 ins	
		3.28 ft	*feet*†
		1.09 yds	*yards*
one kilometre‡	1 km	1094 yds	
		0.62 ml	*miles*

* *Le symbole de* inch *est* ": *4 inches = 4".*
† *Le symbole de* foot *et* feet *est* ': *5 feet 4 inches = 5' 4".*
‡ *Deux prononciations possibles:* [kɪ'lɒmɪtə(r)] *ou* ['kɪləmiːtə(r)]

Pour l'écriture, noter:
- *on écrit* -metre *en anglais britannique, mais* -meter *en anglais américain;*
- *pour le système métrique, les abréviations sont les mêmes en anglais qu'en français;*
- *l'anglais utilise un point là où le français a une virgule.*

il y a 100 centimètres dans un mètre	=	there are 100 centimetres in one metre
il y a douze pouces dans un pied	=	there are twelve inches in one foot
il y a trois pieds dans un yard	=	there are three feet in one yard

La distance

quelle distance y a-t-il entre A et B?	=	what's the distance from A to B? *ou* how far is it from A to B?
à quelle distance de l'église se trouve l'école?	=	how far is the school from the church?
il y a 2 km	=	it is 2 kilometres
il y a environ 2 km	=	it is about 2 kilometres
la distance est de 2 km	=	the distance is 2 kilometres
il y a 2 km entre A et B	=	it is 2 kilometres from A to B
A est à 2 km de B	=	A is 2 kilometres from B

(*Noter l'absence d'équivalent anglais de la préposition française* à *avant le chiffre dans le dernier exemple.*)

à peu près 2 km	=	about 2 kilometres
presque 3 km	=	almost 3 kilometres
plus de 2 km	=	more than 2 kilometres *ou* over 2 kilometres
moins de 3 km	=	less than 3 kilometres *ou* under 3 kilometres
A est plus loin de B que C de D	=	it is further from A to B than from C to D *ou* A is further away from B than C is from D
C est plus près de B que A	=	C is nearer to B than A is
A est plus près de B que de C	=	A is nearer to B than to C
A est aussi loin que B	=	A is as far away as B
A et B sont à la même distance	=	A and B are the same distance away

Noter l'ordre des mots dans l'adjectif composé anglais, et l'utilisation du trait d'union. Noter aussi que kilometre, *employé comme adjectif, ne prend pas la marque du pluriel.*

une promenade de 10 kilomètres	=	a 10-kilometre walk

La longueur

combien mesure la corde?	=	how long is the rope?
elle mesure 10 m de long	=	it is 10 metres long
elle fait 10 m de long	=	it is 10 metres in length
une corde d'environ 10 m de long	=	a rope about 10 metres long *ou* 10 metres in length
à peu près 10 m	=	about 10 metres
presque 11 m	=	almost 11 metres
plus de 10 m	=	more than 10 metres
moins de 11 m	=	less than 11 metres
A est plus long que B	=	A is longer than B
B est plus court que A	=	B is shorter than A
A est aussi long que B	=	A is as long as B
A et B ont la même longueur	=	A and B are the same length
A a la même longueur que B	=	A is the same length as B
10 mètres de corde	=	10 metres of rope
6 mètres de soie	=	6 metres of silk
vendu au mètre	=	sold by the metre

Noter l'ordre des mots dans les adjectifs composés anglais, et l'utilisation du trait d'union. Noter aussi que metre *et* foot, *employés comme adjectifs, ne prennent pas la marque du pluriel.*

une corde de 10 mètres	=	a 10-metre rope *ou* a rope 10 metres long
un python de six pieds de long	=	a six-foot-long python *ou* a python six feet long

☛ Voir page suivante

longer; **prévoir qch ~ à l'avance** to plan sth a long time ahead; **~ avant/après** long before/after; **avant ~** (d'ici peu) before long; **pas avant ~** not for a long time; **on ne le saura pas de ~** we won't know for a long time; **j'ai attendu trop ~** I waited too long; **je peux le garder plus ~?** can I keep it a bit longer?; **plus ~ que prévu** longer than anticipated; **durer assez ~** (suffisamment) to last long enough; (une longue période) to last quite a long time; **aussi ~ qu'il le faudra** as long as necessary; **on te revoit dans ~**○**?** will it be long before we see you again?; **une lettre/visite ~ attendue** a long-awaited letter/visit; **2** (avec il y a, depuis, cela fait etc) (marquant la continuité) (for) a long time, (for) long; (quand l'action est terminée) a long time ago, long ago; **il y a** or **cela fait ~ que je le connais, je le connais depuis ~** I've known him for a long time; **il ne travaille pas ici depuis ~, il n'y a pas ~ qu'il travaille ici** he hasn't worked ou been working here (for) long; **ça fait** or **il y a ~ que tu attends?** have you been waiting long?; **il y a** or **voilà** or **ça fait ~ qu'il n'a pas téléphoné** he hasn't phoned for ages ou a long time, it's (been) a long time ou ages since he phoned; **il n'y a plus ~ à attendre** there's not long to wait now, it won't be much longer now; **il est mort depuis ~, cela fait** or **il y a** or **voilà ~ qu'il est mort** he died a long time ago, he's been dead a long time; **il ne conduisait plus depuis ~** he had stopped driving ages ago ou long before then; **il n'y a pas si ~ c'était encore possible** it was still possible until quite recently.

longue ▶ long I, IV, V.

longuement /lɔ̃gmɑ̃/ *adv* (pendant longtemps) [*hésiter, cuire*] for a long time; (en détail) [*expliquer, interroger*] at length; **nous avons ~ bavardé** we talked for a long time; **j'y ai ~ réfléchi** I've given it a lot of thought; **plus ~** (plus longtemps) for longer; (en plus grand détail) at greater length; **projet ~ médité** carefully considered project; **l'éclairage a été ~ travaillé** the lighting has been carefully thought out.

longuet, **-ette** /lɔ̃gɛ, ɛt/ **I**○ *adj* [*film, discours*] rather lengthy; [*orateur*] long-winded.
II *nm* Culin breadstick.

longueur /lɔ̃gœʀ/ **I** *nf* **1** (dimension) length; **dans (le sens de) la ~** lengthways GB, lengthwise US; **être déchiré/fendu sur toute la ~** to be ripped/cracked right (the way) along GB ou along the whole length; **la maison est tout en ~** the house is (very) long and narrow; **un câble de trois mètres de ~** or **d'une ~ de trois mètres** a cable three metres[GB] long, a three-metre[GB] long cable; **en ~ la pièce fait sept mètres** the room is seven metres[GB] long; **d'une ~ impressionnante** incredibly long; **2** (distance entre deux concurrents) length; **gagner d'une ~/de trois ~s** to win by one length/three lengths; **avoir** or **posséder une ~ d'avance sur qn** Sport to be one length ahead of sb; fig to be ahead of sb; **avoir plusieurs ~s d'avance sur qn** Sport to be several lengths ahead of sb; fig to have a clear lead over sb; **3 ▶ 449** Sport (en athlétisme) **la ~, le saut en ~** the long ou broad US jump; (en natation) length; **faire des ~s** to do ou swim lengths; **4** (durée) length; **traîner en ~** [*film, livre*] to go on forever.
II longueurs *nfpl* (dans un film, livre, discours) overlong passages.
III à longueur de *loc prép* **à ~ de journée** all day long; **à ~ d'année** all year round; **à ~ de temps** all the time; **à ~ d'émissions** programme[GB] after programme[GB].
■ **~ d'onde** Phys, fig wavelength; **être sur la même ~ d'onde** to be on the same wavelength.

longue-vue, *pl* **longues-vues** /lɔ̃gvy/ *nf* telescope.

look○ /luk/ *nm* (allure, style) look; (image) image.

looping /lupiŋ/ *nm* loop; **faire** or **exécuter un ~** to loop the loop; **l'avion fait un dernier ~** the plane makes a final loop.

lopin /lɔpɛ̃/ *nm* **~ (de terre)** patch of land, plot (of land).

loquace /lɔkas/ *adj* talkative, loquacious; **ils ne sont pas très ~s là-dessus** they are not very communicative on the subject.

loquacité /lɔkasite/ *nf* talkativeness, loquacity.

loque /lɔk/ **I** *nf* **1** (vieux vêtement) pile of rags; **2** (personne) **~ (humaine)** (human) wreck; **je suis une vraie ~ aujourd'hui** I feel an absolute wreck today; **il est devenu une ~** he is a shadow of his former self.
II loques *nfpl* (guenilles) rags; **vêtu de ~s** (dressed) in rags; **être en ~s** to be in tatters; **tomber en ~s** to fall to pieces.

loquet /lɔkɛ/ *nm* latch.

Les mesures de longueur (2)

La hauteur

La taille des personnes

combien mesure-t-il? = how tall is he?
ou (*si l'on veut obtenir un chiffre précis*) what is his height?

En anglais, la taille des personnes est donnée en pieds (feet) *et en pouces* (inches), *jamais en yards. En gros, 1,50 m = cinq pieds, et 1,80 m = six pieds.*

il mesure 1,80 m = he is 6 feet tall *ou* he is 6 feet *ou* he is 1.80 m
il mesure 1,75 m = he is 5 feet 10 inches *ou* he is 5 feet 10 *ou* he is 1.75 m

Dans la conversation courante, on utilise souvent foot *au lieu de* feet*: on peut donc dire:* he is 5 foot 10 inches *ou* 5 foot 10.

à peu près 1,80 m = about 6 ft
presque 1,80 m = almost 6 ft
plus de 1,75 m = more than 5 ft 10 ins
moins de 1,85 m = less than 6 ft 3 ins
Pierre est plus grand que Paul = Pierre is taller than Paul
Paul est plus petit que Pierre = Paul is smaller than Pierre
ou Paul is shorter than Pierre
Pierre est aussi grand que Paul = Pierre is as tall as Paul
Pierre a la même taille que Paul = Pierre is the same height as Paul
Pierre et Paul ont la même taille = Pierre and Paul are the same height

Noter l'ordre des mots dans l'adjectif composé anglais, et l'utilisation du trait d'union. Noter également que foot*, employé comme adjectif, ne prend pas la marque du pluriel.*

un athlète d'un mètre quatre-vingts = a six-foot athlete

On peut aussi dire an athlete six feet tall. *De même,* a footballer over six feet in height, *etc.*

La hauteur des choses

quelle est la hauteur de la tour? = what is the height of the tower?
combien mesure la tour? = what is the height of the tower?
elle fait 23 mètres de haut = it is 23 metres high
elle mesure 23 mètres de hauteur = it is 23 metres high
ou it is 23 metres in height
elle a une hauteur de 23 m = its height is 23 metres
une tour d'environ 25 m de haut = a tower about 25 metres high
ou about 25 metres in height
à une hauteur de 20 mètres = at a height of 20 metres
A est plus haut que B = A is higher than B
B est moins haut que A = B is lower than A
A est aussi haut que B = A is as high as B
A et B sont de la même hauteur = A and B are the same height
A est de la même hauteur que B = A is the same height as B

Noter l'ordre des mots dans l'adjectif composé anglais, et l'utilisation du trait d'union. Noter aussi que metre*, employé comme adjectif, ne prend pas la marque du pluriel.*

une tour haute de 23 mètres = a 23-metre-high tower

On peut aussi dire: a tower 23 metres high. *De même,* a mountain over 4,000 metres in height, *etc.*

à quelle altitude est l'avion? = how high is the plane?
à quelle altitude vole l'avion? = what height is the plane flying at?
l'avion vole à 5 000 m d'altitude = the plane is flying at 5,000 metres
son altitude est de 5 000 m = its altitude is 5,000 metres
à une altitude de 5 000 m = at an altitude of 5,000 metres

La largeur

L'anglais dispose de deux mots pour la largeur: wide *mesure la distance entre deux limites* (a wide valley; *le nom est* width)*, alors que* broad *décrit ce qui remplit un espace d'une certaine largeur* (a broad avenue; *le nom est* breadth).

Les expressions suivantes utilisent wide *et* width*, mais* broad *et* breadth *s'emploient de la même façon.*

quelle est la largeur de la rivière? = how wide is the river?
ou what width is the river?
elle fait 7 m = it is 7 metres
elle fait 7 m de large = it is 7 metres wide
ou it is 7 metres in width
ou it is 7 metres across
elle fait environ 7 m de large = it is about 7 metres wide
A est plus large que B = A is wider than B
B est plus étroit que A = B is narrower than A
A est aussi large que B = A is as wide as B
A et B sont de la même largeur = A and B are the same width
A est de la même largeur que B = A is the same width as B

Noter l'ordre des mots dans l'adjectif composé anglais, et l'utilisation du trait d'union. Noter aussi que metre*, employé comme adjectif, ne prend pas la marque du pluriel.*

une rivière de 7 m de large = a seven-metre-wide river

On peut aussi dire: a river seven metres wide. *De même,* a ditch two metres wide, a piece of cloth two metres in width, *etc.*

La profondeur

quelle est la profondeur du lac? = how deep is the lake
ou what depth is the lake?
ou what is the depth of the lake?
il fait 4 m = it is 4 metres deep
il fait 4 m de profondeur = it is 4 metres in depth
il fait environ 4 m de profondeur = it is about 4 metres deep
un lac de 4 mètres de profondeur = a lake four metres deep
ou a lake four metres in depth

Noter l'absence d'équivalent anglais de la préposition française de avant *le chiffre dans les expressions de ce genre. Mais:*

à une profondeur de dix mètres = at a depth of ten metres
A est plus profond que B = A is deeper than B
B est moins profond que A = B is shallower* than A
A est aussi profond que B = A is as deep as B
A et B ont la même profondeur = A and B are the same depth
A a la même profondeur que B = A is the same depth as B
un puits de 7 m de profondeur = a well seven metres deep

* *Noter que l'adjectif* shallow (*peu profond*) *n'a pas d'équivalent simple en français.*

loqueteau, *pl* **~x** /lɔkto/ *nm* catch, (small) latch.

loqueteux, -euse /lɔktø, øz/ *adj* fml [*vêtement, livre*] tattered; [*personne*] ragged (*épith*).

lordose /lɔʀdoz/ ▶ 271 *nf* lordosis.

lorgner° /lɔʀɲe/ [1] *vtr* to eye up° GB, to give [sb] the eye° [*femme*]; to cast longing glances at [*bijou, gâteau*]; to have one's eye on [*héritage, titre, poste*]; **~ qch du coin de l'œil** to cast sidelong glances at sth.

lorgnette /lɔʀɲɛt/ *nf* (d'opéra) opera-glasses; (de marine) spy-glass.

IDIOMES **regarder** or **voir qch par le petit bout de la ~** to take a very blinkered or simplistic view of sth.

lorgnon /lɔʀɲɔ̃/ *nm* (face-à-main) lorgnette; (pince-nez) pince-nez.

lori /lɔʀi/ *nm* Zool lory.

loriot /lɔʀjo/ *nm* oriole.

■ **~ jaune** golden oriole.

lorrain, **~e** /lɔʀɛ̃, ɛn/ **I** *adj* [*dialecte, région*] Lorraine (*épith*).

II ▶ 462 *nm* Ling Lorraine dialect.

Lorrain, **~e** /lɔʀɛ̃, ɛn/ **I** *nm,f* inhabitant of Lorraine; **les ~s** the people of Lorraine.

II Lorraine ▶ 692 *nf* **la ~e** Lorraine.

lors /lɔʀ/ **I lors de** *loc prép* **1** (pendant) during; **il a déclaré ~ d'un entretien avec un journaliste que**... he stated during an interview with a journalist that...; **~ d'un discours télévisé d'une demi-heure** during a half-hour televised speech; **2** (au moment de) at the time of; **75% des usagers se disent satisfaits contre 60% ~ de l'enquête précédente** 75% of users were satisfied compared with 60% at the time of the previous survey; **~ de ta venue, nous irons à la campagne** when you come, we'll go to the countryside.

II lors même que *loc conj* even if; **~ même que cela se produirait** even if that were to happen, were this to happen.

lorsque (**lorsqu'** before vowel or mute h) /lɔʀsk(ə)/ *conj* when.

■ **Note** *lorsque* se traduit par *when*: *lorsque je suis allée au Portugal* = when I went to Portugal; *lorsqu'elle travaille, elle n'aime pas être dérangée* = she doesn't like to be disturbed when she's working.
– Attention, on n'utilise jamais le futur après *when*: *lorsqu'il aura terminé* = when he's finished.

losange /lɔzɑ̃ʒ/ *nm* rhomb, lozenge; **en ~** diamond-shaped; **pavage en ~s** diamond paving.

losangé, **~e** /lɔzɑ̃ʒe/ *adj* [*tissu, frise*] with a diamond pattern.

lot /lo/ *nm* **1** (portion) (de succession, partage) share, portion Jur; (d'émotions, de surprises) share; (de terrain) plot; **répartir une somme en cinq ~s** to divide a sum into five shares; **j'ai eu mon ~ d'ennuis aujourd'hui** I've had my share of troubles today; **2** (à la loterie) prize; **~ de consolation** consolation prize; **gagner le gros ~** lit, fig to hit the jackpot; **3** (d'objets en vente) gén batch; (aux enchères) lot; **acheter/vendre qch par ~s** to buy/sell sth by the batch; **le ~ numéro 7** lot 7; **4** (de personnes) group; **être/se maintenir au-dessus du ~** to be/stay above the average; **se détacher du ~** to be a cut above the rest; **5** Ordinat batch; **traitement par ~s** batch processing; **6** (destin) fate, lot; **des mois de préparation pour une seule course, c'est le ~ de tout concurrent** months of preparation for a single race, that's the lot of every competitor; **la souffrance est son ~** he was born to suffer.

Lot /lɔt/ ▶ 357, 692 *nprm* (rivière, département) **le ~** the Lot.

loterie /lɔtʀi/ *nf* (avec lots) raffle; (de fête foraine) tombola GB, raffle US; (à grande échelle) lottery; **jouer/gagner à la ~** to have a go° at/to win on the lottery; **cet examen est une vraie ~** this exam is a real lottery.

Lot-et-Garonne /lɔtegaʀɔn/ *nprm* (département) **le ~** the Lot-et-Garonne.

Loth /lɔt/ *npr* Lot.

Lothian ▶ 692 *nprm* **le ~** Lothian.

loti, **~e** /lɔti/ *adj* **bien/mal ~** well/badly off; **les locataires du dernier étage sont les mieux/plus mal ~s** the top floor tenants are best/worst off; **bien/mal ~ par la nature** blessed/not blessed by nature; **me**

voilà bien ~e avec un patron pareil! iron just my luck to land up with a boss like him!

lotion /losjɔ̃/ *nf* lotion; **~ après/avant rasage** after-/pre-shave (lotion); **~ pour le visage** face lotion; **~ capillaire** or **pour les cheveux** hair lotion.

lotionner /losjɔne/ [1] *vtr* to apply lotion to, to put a lotion on.

lotir /lɔtiʀ/ [3] *vtr* **1** (répartir) to share out [*biens, immeubles*]; to divide [sth] land into plots ou lots US [*terrain*]; **terrain(s) à ~** plots ou lots US for sale; **2** (attribuer) to allot, apportion Jur (**qn de qch** sth to sb).

lotissement /lɔtismɑ̃/ *nm* **1** (ensemble de parcelles) housing estate GB, subdivision US; **2** (parcelle) plot, lot US; **3** (morcellement) dividing up.

loto /lɔto/ **▶449** *nm* lotto; **jouer au ~** to play lotto; **le ~ national** national lottery; **le ~ sportif** ≈ the national sport lottery.

IDIOMES **avoir des yeux en boules de ~** to have goggle eyes.

lotte /lɔt/ *nf* (de mer) monkfish, angler fish; (de rivière) burbot.

lotus /lɔtys/ *nm* lotus.

louable /luabl/ *adj* **1** [*intention, effort*] commendable, praiseworthy; **2** [*logement, bureau*] suitable for letting GB ou renting (*après n*); **difficilement ~** difficult to let GB ou rent.

louage /luaʒ/ *nm* **~ de services** contract of employment; **voiture de ~** rented car GB, rental car US; **contrat de ~** rental agreement.

louange /luɑ̃ʒ/ *nf* praise; **chanter les ~s de qn/de qch** to sing sb's/sth's praises; **à la ~ de** in praise of; **digne de ~** praiseworthy.

louangeur, -euse /lwɑ̃ʒœʀ, øz/ *adj* laudatory.

loubard○ /lubaʀ/ *nm* hooligan, delinquent youth.

louche /luʃ/ **I** *adj* (équivoque) [*individu, affaire, passé*] shady; [*lieu*] seedy; **c'est (plutôt) ~** it's rather fishy; **il y a quelque chose de ~ dans cette affaire** or **histoire** there is something fishy○ about this business; **se livrer à des manœuvres plutôt ~s** to get involved in rather shady business.

II *nf* **1** (ustensile) ladle; (contenu) ladleful; **2**○ (main) hand; **▶serrer**.

loucher /luʃe/ [1] *vi* **1** Méd to squint, to have a squint; **il louche** he has a squint, he's cross-eyed; **2**○ (convoiter) **~ sur les filles/gâteaux** to eye the girls/cakes; **~ sur l'héritage/un titre** to have one's eye on the inheritance/a title.

louer /lue/ [1] **I** *vtr* **1** (donner en location) to let GB, to rent out [*maison, terrain*] (**à** to); to hire [*salle*]; to hire out GB, to rent out [*équipement, véhicule, film*] (**à** to); **'à ~'** 'for rent', 'to let' GB; **la maison est à ~** the house is for rent ou to let GB; **chambre à ~** room for rent, room to let GB; **~ une caravane à la semaine** to rent out a caravan GB ou trailer US by the week; **2** (prendre en location) to rent [*maison, terrain*] (**à** from); to hire [*salle*]; to hire GB, to rent [*équipement, véhicule, film*] (**à** from); **cherche chambre à ~** wanted, room to rent; **~ une caravane pour une semaine** to rent a caravan for a week; **3** (embaucher) to hire [*personnel*]; **~ les services** to hire the services (**de qn** of sb); **4** (réserver) to reserve [*chambre d'hôtel*]; [*théâtre*] to take a booking GB ou reservation for [*place*]; [*spectateur*] to reserve, to book GB [*place*]; **5** (rendre grâce à) to praise (**de, pour** for); **Dieu soit loué** thank God.

II se louer *vpr* **1** (se donner en location) [*maison, terrain*] to be for rent, to be to let GB; (se prendre en location) [*maison*] to be rented out, to be let GB; **2** (se féliciter) liter **se ~ d'avoir fait** to congratulate oneself on doing.

loueur /luœʀ/ *nm* **1** (entreprise) hire company; **~ de voitures** car hire company; **2** (bailleur) lessor.

loufiat◑ /lufja/ *nm* waiter.

loufoque /lufɔk/ *adj* crazy○.

lougre /lugʀ/ *nm* lugger.

louis /lwi/ *nm inv* Hist (monnaie) louis; **~ d'or** (gold) louis.

louise-bonne, *pl* **louises-bonnes** /lwiz bɔn/ *nf* louise-bonne pear.

Louisiane /lwizjan/ **▶692** *nprf* Louisiana.

loukoum /lukum/ *nm* Turkish delight ¢.

loulou /lulu/ *nm* **1** (chien) spitz; **2**○ (voyou) hooligan, delinquent youth; **3**○ (terme d'affection) pet○ GB, honey US.

■ **~ de Poméranie** Pomeranian.

louloutte○ /lulut/ *nf* **1** (fille) girl; **2** (terme d'affection) pet○ GB, honey US.

loup /lu/ *nm* **1** (mammifère) wolf; **le grand méchant ~** the big bad wolf; **avoir une faim de ~** to be ravenous; **à pas de ~** stealthily; **crier au ~** lit, fig to cry wolf; **~ solitaire** lone wolf; **▶jeune**; **2** (poisson) **~ (de mer)** (sea) bass; **3**○ (terme d'affection) **mon petit** or **grand** or **gros ~** my pet○; **4** (masque) domino, mask; **5** Tech (défaut) flaw, defect.

■ **~ à crinière** maned wolf; **~ doré** jackal; **(vieux) ~ de mer** old salt, old tar.

IDIOMES **être connu comme le ~ blanc** to be known to everybody; **hurler avec les ~s** to follow the herd ou crowd; **se jeter dans la gueule du ~** to stick one's head in the lion's mouth; **faire entrer le ~ dans la bergerie** to let the wolf into the fold; **elle a vu le ~** hum she's lost her virginity; **les ~s ne se mangent pas entre eux** Prov (there is) honour[GB] among thieves; **la faim fait sortir le ~ du bois** Prov needs must (when the devil drives); **quand on parle du ~ (on en voit la queue** or **il sort du bois)** Prov speak of the devil; **l'homme est un ~ pour l'homme** Prov dog eat dog.

loup-cervier, *pl* **loups-cerviers** /lusɛʀvje/ *nm* lynx.

loupe /lup/ *nf* **1** (lentille) magnifying glass; **à la ~** lit with a magnifying glass; **examiner qch à la ~** lit to look at sth through a magnifying glass; fig to put sth under the microscope; **2** Bot (grosseur) burr; (bois) **~ de noyer** burr walnut; **~ d'orme** burr elm; **3** Méd (cyste) cyst; **4** (pierre) gemstone with flaws.

■ **~ binoculaire** low-power stereo microscope.

loupé○ /lupe/ *nm* (erreur) blunder; (défaut) defect.

louper○ /lupe/ [1] **I** *vtr* **1** (manquer) to miss [*train, occasion, personne*]; **la prochaine fois, ils ne te louperont pas** next time they'll get you; **il n'en loupe pas une** he's always opening his big mouth; **2** (ne pas réussir) to flunk○ [*examen*]; to screw up○ [*sauce, ouvrage*]; to bungle [*entrée en scène*]; **il a loupé son coup** he botched it; **la soirée est complètement loupée** the evening is a wash-out.

II *vi* **j'avais dit que ça se casserait, ça n'a pas loupé** I said it would break, and sure enough it did; **chaque fois que je m'en sers ça ne loupe pas, ça se casse** without fail, every time I use it, it breaks; **tu vas tout faire ~** you'll mess everything up, you'll screw everything up○.

loup-garou, *pl* **loups-garous** /lugaʀu/ *nm* werewolf.

loupiot○ /lupjo/ *nm* kid○, little boy.

loupiote○ /lupjɔt/ *nf* small lamp.

loupiotte○ /lupjɔt/ *nf* kid○, little girl.

lourd, ~e /luʀ, luʀd/ **I** *adj* **1** (d'un poids élevé) [*personne, objet, métal*] heavy; **plus ~ que l'air** heavier than air; **~ à transporter** heavy to carry; **2** (donnant une sensation de pesanteur) [*estomac, jambe, tête, pas*] heavy; [*geste*] clumsy, ungainly; **j'ai les jambes ~es** my legs feel heavy ou ache; **il a la tête ~e** his head feels heavy; **j'ai les paupières ~es** my eyes feel heavy; **il a les yeux ~s de sommeil** his eyes are heavy with sleep; **avoir le pas ~, marcher d'un pas ~** to walk with a heavy step; **3** (indigeste) [*repas, aliment*] heavy; [*vin*] heady; **~ à digérer** heavy on the stomach; **4** (dense) [*protection*] heavy; [*chevelure*] thick; **5** Ind, Mil [*armement, équipement*] heavy; **6** (onéreux) [*investissement, amende, fiscalité, gestion*] heavy; **7** (grave) [*condamnation, perte, défaite, responsabilité*] heavy; [*présomption, erreur*] serious; **8** (encombrant) [*administration, structure*] unwieldy; [*effectifs*] great; **9** (massif) [*personne, animal*] ungainly; [*corps, objet, architecture, poitrine*] heavy; [*bâtiment*] squat; **10** (sans finesse) [*personne*] oafish; [*voix*] thick; [*plaisanterie*] flat; [*regard*] blunt; [*style*] clumsy, ponderous; [*odeur, parfum*] heavy; **11** (pénible) [*ciel, atmosphère, silence*] heavy; [*temps, chaleur*] muggy, sultry; **12** (chargé) (de danger, conséquences) fraught (**de** with); (de haine, menaces, sous-entendus) charged (**de** with); **ciel ~ de nuages** sky heavy with clouds; **13** (difficilement praticable) [*piste, sol, terrain*] heavy; **14** Fin (médiocre) [*marché, tendance*] sluggish.

II *adv* **1 peser ~** (être d'un poids élevé) to weigh heavy; (compter beaucoup) **peser/ne pas peser ~** to carry a lot of/not to carry very much weight (**sur** with); **2** (pour le temps) **il fait ~** it's close; **3**○ (beaucoup) **pas ~** not a lot, not much; **elle n'en fait/sait pas ~** she doesn't do/know a lot ou much; **trente francs ça ne fait pas ~** thirty francs isn't a lot ou much; **10 personnes, ça ne fait pas ~** 10 people, that's not a lot; **il ne reste pas ~ de beurre** there's not much butter left.

III lourde○ *nf* (porte) door.

IDIOMES **avoir le cœur ~** to have a heavy heart; **être ~ comme du plomb** to be (as) heavy as lead; **avoir la main ~e** (avec taxes, exercices, punitions) to be heavy-handed; **avoir la main ~e avec le sel/son parfum** to overdo the salt/the perfume.

lourdais, ~e /luʀdɛ, ɛz/ **▶857** *adj* of Lourdes.

Lourdais, ~e /luʀdɛ, ɛz/ **▶857** *nm,f* (natif) native of Lourdes; (habitant) inhabitant of Lourdes.

lourdaud, ~e /luʀdo, od/ **I** *adj* [*personne*] oafish; [*esprit*] dull; [*discours*] clumsy.

II *nm,f* oaf.

lourde ▶lourd I, III.

lourdement /luʀdəmɑ̃/ *adv* **1** (fortement) heavily; **se tromper ~** to be gravely mistaken; **2** (sans finesse) **marcher/se déplacer ~** to walk/move clumsily; **insister ~** to labour[GB] the point; **insister ~ sur** to keep going on about; **elle a insisté ~ pour que je l'emmène avec moi** she pestered me to take her with me.

lourder◑ /luʀde/ [1] *vtr* (congédier) to kick [sb] out○; **se faire ~** to get kicked out○.

Lourdes /luʀd/ **▶857** *npr* Lourdes.

lourdeur /luʀdœʀ/ *nf* **1** (d'organisation, de secteur, réseau) complexity ¢; **~s administratives** administrative complexity; **2** (sensation de pesanteur) heaviness; **j'ai des ~s dans les jambes** my legs feel heavy ou ache; **avoir des ~s d'estomac** to feel bloated; **3** (maladresse) clumsiness; **C** clumsy expression; **4** (importance) (d'imposition, investissement) burden; (de condamnation) heaviness, stiffness; **la ~ des subventions/impôts/pertes** the heavy subsidies/taxes/losses; **5** (poids élevé) weight; **6** (manque de raffinement) (de personne) oafishness; (de plaisanterie) poorness; (d'architecture) ungainliness; **7** (de temps) closeness, mugginess; (d'ambiance) heaviness; **8** (de terrain) heaviness; **9** (de marché, tendance boursière) sluggishness.

lourdingue○ /luʀdɛ̃g/ *adj* [*personne*] clumsy; [*film, musique*] heavy-going; [*plaisanterie*] unsubtle; [*style*] ungainly.

loustic○ /lustik/ *nm* pej (individu) chap, guy; (gamin) kid○; (farceur) joker péj; **drôle de ~**

funny chap, weird guy; **faire le ~** to play the fool.

loutre /lutʀ/ *nf* **1** (animal) otter; **2** (fourrure) otterskin; **veste en ~** otterskin jacket.
■ **~ de mer** sealskin.

louve /luv/ *nf* she-wolf.

louveteau, *pl* **~x** /luvto/ *nm* **1** Zool wolf cub; **2** (scout) (wolf) cub GB, cub scout US.

louvoiement /luvwamɑ̃/ *nm* (tergiversation) hedging; (biais) manoeuvre GB, maneuver US, manoeuvring GB, maneuvring US.

louvoyage /luvwajaʒ/ *nm* Naut beating to windward, tacking.

louvoyer /luvwaje/ [23] *vi* **1** Naut to beat to windward, to tack; **2** (biaiser) to manoeuvre GB ou maneuver US; (tergiverser) to hedge.

lover /lɔve/ [1] **I** *vtr* to coil [*câble*].
II se lover *vpr* [*serpent, anguille*] to coil itself up; [*chat, personne*] to curl up.

loyal, **~e**, *mpl* **-aux** /lwajal, o/ *adj* **1** (fidèle) [*ami*] true; [*serviteur*] loyal, faithful; **bons et loyaux services** good and faithful service; **2** (honnête) [*procédé, conduite*] honest; [*concurrence*] fair; **~ en affaires** straight ou honest in business; **à la ~e** fairly; **3** Comm [*qualité*] marketable, merchantable GB; **valeur ~e et marchande** fair market value; **bon et ~ inventaire** true and accurate inventory.
■ **loyaux coûts** (purchaser's) contract costs.

loyalement /lwajalmɑ̃/ *adv* [*servir*] faithfully; [*se battre*] fairly; [*informer*] honestly; **accepter ~ une défaite** to accept a defeat sportingly.

loyalisme /lwajalism/ *nm* loyalty.

loyaliste /lwajalist/ *adj, nmf* loyalist.

loyauté /lwajote/ *nf* **1** (fidelité) loyalty (**envers** to); **2** (honnêteté) (de personne, conduite) honesty; (de procédé) honesty, fairness; **manque de ~** dishonesty.

loyer /lwaje/ *nm* rent; **~ mensuel de 3 000 francs** monthly rent of 3,000 francs; **les ~s sont élevés** rents are high; **hausse des ~s** rent increase.
■ **~ de l'argent** Écon, Fin interest rates (*pl*).

Lozère /lɔzɛʀ/ **▶692** *nprf* (département) **la ~** Lozère.

LSD /ɛlɛsde/ *nm* (*abbr* = **Lyserg Säure Diäthylamid**) LSD.

Luanda /luɑ̃da/ **▶857** *npr* Luanda.

lubie /lybi/ *nf* whim; **avoir des ~s** to have whims.

lubricité /lybʀisite/ *nf* (de personne) lustfulness, lechery; (de propos, conduite, gravure) lewdness.

lubrifiant, **~e** /lybʀifjɑ̃, ɑ̃t/ **I** *adj* lubricating.
II *nm* lubricant.

lubrification /lybʀifikasjɔ̃/ *nf* lubrication.

lubrifier /lybʀifje/ [2] *vtr* to lubricate.

lubrique /lybʀik/ *adj* [*personne*] lecherous; [*œil, danse, image*] lewd.

Luc /lyk/ *npr* Luke.

lucane /lykan/ *nm* stag beetle.

lucarne /lykaʀn/ *nf* **1** (fenêtre) (small) window; (dans un toit) skylight; (en saillie) dormer window; **2** (au football) top corner of the net.
IDIOMES **tu vois ça de ta ~** that's how you see it from your end.

Lucerne /lysɛʀn/ *npr* **1** **▶857** (ville) Lucerne; **2** **▶692** (région) **le canton de ~** the canton of Lucerne.

lucide /lysid/ *adj* [*personne, politique*] clear-sighted; Méd lucid; [*esprit, intelligence*] lucid, clear; [*analyse*] lucid; **être ~ sur soi-même** to have no illusions about oneself.

lucidement /lysidmɑ̃/ *adv* [*envisager, penser, juger*] clearly.

lucidité /lysidite/ *nf* **1** Méd lucidity; **moments de ~** lucid moments; **il a toute sa ~** he has all his wits about him; **2** (perspicacité) (de personne) clear-headedness; (d'esprit) clarity; **raisonner avec ~** to think clearly; **il a agi en toute ~** he knew perfectly well what he was doing; **juger en toute ~** to judge without any illusion.

Lucifer /lysifɛʀ/ *npr* Lucifer.

luciole /lysjɔl/ *nf* firefly.

lucratif, **-ive** /lykʀatif, iv/ *adj* lucrative; **assez ~** [*emploi*] fairly well-paid; [*opération*] fairly profitable.

lucre /lykʀ/ *nm* pej lucre.

Lucrèce /lykʀɛs/ **I** *nprm* Lucretius.
II *nprf* Lucretia.

ludiciel /lydisjɛl/ *nm* computer game.

ludion /lydjɔ̃/ *nm* Cartesian devil ou diver.

ludique /lydik/ *adj* **1** [*activité, espace*] play (*épith*); **c'est très ~** it's highly recreational; **2** Psych [*théorie, activité, fonction*] ludic.

ludothèque /lydɔtɛk/ *nf* toy library.

luette /lyɛt/ *nf* uvula.

lueur /lɥœʀ/ **I** *nf* **1** (faible clarté) (faint) light (**de** of); **les ~s de la ville** the city lights; **les premières ~s de l'aube** the first light of dawn; **pas la moindre ~ d'espoir** fig not the faintest glimmer of hope; **à la ~ des étoiles/d'une bougie/d'une lampe de poche** by starlight/candlelight/torchlight GB, flashlight US; **à la ~ des événements d'hier** fig in the light of yesterday's events; **jeter une faible ~** to cast a poor light; **2** (rougeoiement) glow; **les dernières ~s d'un incendie/du soleil couchant** the dying glow of a fire/of the sunset; **3** (éclat fugitif) lit, fig gleam, flash.
II lueurs *nfpl* (connaissances) (vague) knowledge **¢**; **apporter ses ~s sur qch** to bring one's knowledge to bear on sth; **avez-vous des ~s sur la situation?** can you throw any light on the situation?

luge /lyʒ/ **▶449** *nf* **1** (objet) toboggan GB, sled US; **2** (sport) luge; **faire de la ~** to go tobogganing GB ou sledding US.

lugeur, **-euse** /lyʒœʀ, øz/ *nm,f* luger.

lugubre /lygybʀ/ *adj* [*paysage, pensée, maison, individu*] gloomy; [*son, chant*] mournful, lugubrious.

lui /lɥi/ *pron pers*

■ **Note** Lorsqu'il représente une personne de sexe masculin ou un animal familier mâle, *lui* peut avoir plusieurs fonctions et se traduira différemment selon les cas: *lui, c'est un menteur* = HE'S a liar; *donne-lui à boire* = give him something to drink. Voir I.
– Lorsqu'il représente un objet, un concept, une plante, un animal mâle ou femelle, quel que soit le genre du mot, *lui* se traduira par *it* ou ne se traduira pas. Voir II.
– Lorsqu'il représente une personne de sexe féminin ou un animal familier femelle, *lui* = *à elle* se traduira par *her*: *je ne lui dirai rien* = I won't say anything to her. Voir III.

I *pron pers m* (personne, animal familier) **1** (en fonction sujet) **elle lit, ~ regarde la télévision** she' s reading, HE'S watching TV; **~ et moi avons longuement discuté** he and I had a long chat; **~ seul a le droit de parler** he alone has the right to talk; **ses collègues et ~ étaient ravis** he and his colleagues were delighted; **~, il ne dit jamais ce qu'il pense** HE never says what he thinks; **c'est ~** (à la porte) it's him; **~ c'est ~ et moi c'est moi** he and I are different; **je sais que ce n'est pas ~ qui a fait ça** I know it wasn't he ou him who did it; **~ qui pensait avoir bien répondu à l'examinateur!** and HE was the one who thought he had given the right answer at the exam!; **l'Espagne a signé, le Portugal, ~, n'a pas encore donné son accord** Spain has signed while Portugal hasn't yet agreed; **le toit, ~, n'a pas besoin d'être réparé** the ROOF doesn't need to be repaired; **l'appartement, ~, a été vendu** the apartment was sold; **2** (dans une comparaison) him; **je travaille plus que ~** I work more than him ou than he does; **je les vois plus souvent que ~** (qu'il ne les voit) I see them more often than he does; (que je ne le vois) I see them more often than him ou than I see him; **elle est plus âgée que ~** she's older than him ou than he is; **3** (en fonction d'objet) **le frapper, ~, quelle idée!** hit HIM? what a thought!; **~, il faut l'enfermer** HE should be locked away; **4** (après une préposition) him; **à cause de/autour de/après ~** because of/around/after him; **un cadeau pour ~** a present for him; **pour ~ c'est important?** is it important to him?; **elle ne pense plus à ~** she doesn't think about him anymore; **je n'écris à personne sauf ~** I don't write to anyone but him, I only write to him; **sans ~, nous n'aurions pas pu réussir** we could never have managed without him; **à ~** (en jouant) his turn; **ce sont des amis à ~** they're friends of his ; **il n'a pas encore de voiture à ~** he doesn't have his own car yet; **à ~, je peux dire la vérité** I can tell HIM the truth; **la tasse verte est-elle à ~?** is the green cup his?, does the green cup belong to him?; **c'est à ~** (appartenance) it's his, it belongs to him; (séquence) it's his turn; **c'est à ~ de faire la vaisselle** it's his turn to do the dishes; **c'est à ~ de choisir** (son tour) it's his turn to choose; (sa responsabilité) it's up to him to choose; **5** (lui = à lui) **il ne ~ a pas fait mal** he didn't hurt him; **je le ~ ai donné** I gave it to him; **je ~ en veux** I bear a grudge against him; **rends-~ ses jouets** give him back his toys.
II *pron pers mf* (objet, concept, animal, plante) it; **le parti/l'association lance un appel, apportez-~ votre soutien** the party/the association is launching an appeal—give it your support; **mon article était terminé puis j'ai décidé de ~ ajouter des photos** my article was finished and then I decided to include some photos; **ta plante n'est pas vigoureuse, tu devrais ~ mettre de l'engrais** your plant isn't very healthy, you should feed it ou give it some fertilizer.
III *pron pers f* (personne, animal familier) her; **je l'ai rencontrée hier et ~ ai annoncé la nouvelle** I met her yesterday and told her the news; **rends-~ sa jupe/ses jouets** give her back her skirt/her toys; **je ne le ~ ai pas dit** I didn't tell her.

lui-même /lɥimɛm/ *pron pers* **1** (personne) himself; **il me l'a dit ~** he told me himself; **il a décidé ~** he decided himself, he made the decision himself; **il exclut pour ~ un déplacement à l'étranger** he rules out any trip abroad for himself; **en ~ il se disait que** he told himself that; **'M. Greiner?'—'~'** 'Mr Greiner?'—'speaking'; **2** (objet, idée, concept) itself; **l'objet n'a pas de valeur en ~** the object has no value in itself; **le livre constitue en ~ une introduction à l'apiculture** the book in itself is an introduction to bee-keeping.

luire /lɥiʀ/ [69] *vi* [*soleil, surface polie*] to shine; [*braises*] to glow; **les yeux du loup luisaient dans l'obscurité** the wolf's eyes gleamed in the dark; **~ de sueur/d'humidité** to glisten with sweat/with damp; **leur regard luisait de colère** their eyes shone ou burned with anger.

luisant, **~e** /lɥizɑ̃, ɑ̃t/ **I** *adj* gén [*surface polie*] shining (**de** with); [*surface mouillée*] glistening (**de** with); [*yeux*] gleaming; **yeux ~s de désir/colère** eyes burning with desire/anger; **tissu ~ d'usure** material shiny with wear.
II *nm* sheen (**de** of, on).

lumbago /lœbago/ **▶271** *nm* back pain, lumbago spéc.

lumière /lymjɛʀ/ **I** *nf* **1** gén, Phys light; **~ naturelle/artificielle/électrique** natural/artificial/electric light; **la ~ des étoiles** starlight; **la ~ du soleil** sunlight; **la ~ du jour** daylight; **que la ~ soit!** let there be light!; **il doit être là puisqu'il y a de la ~ chez lui/dans la cuisine** he must be in because the lights are on/there's a light on in the kitchen; **il y a une ~ très parti-**

culière dans cette région there's a very special quality to the light in this region; **le traitement de la ~ chez ce peintre** this painter's use of light; **les ~ de la ville** the city lights; **il a éteint toutes les ~s** he put all the lights out; **il lisait à la ~ d'une chandelle** he was reading by candlelight; **2** fig (éclairage) light; **la ~ de la raison** liter the light of reason; **à la ~ des récents événements** in the light of recent events; **mettre qch en ~** (mettre en évidence) to highlight sth; (révéler) to bring sth to light; **agir en pleine ~** to act openly, to be open in one's dealings; **faire (toute) la ~ sur une affaire** to bring the truth about a matter to light; **3** fig (personne éminente) leading light, luminary sout; **ce n'est pas une ~** he'll never set the world on fire; **4** Tech aperture; (d'arme à feu) touchhole; (d'outil à bois) mouth.

II **lumières** *nfpl* **1** (feux d'un véhicule) lights; **2**○ (connaissances) **j'ai besoin de vos ~s** I need to pick your brains; **aider qn de ses ~s** to give sb the benefit of one's wisdom; **avoir des ~s sur qch** to have some knowledge of a subject.

■ **~ d'admission** intake port; **~ blanche** white light; **~ cendrée** earthshine; **~ d'échappement** exhaust port; **~ froide** cold light; **~ noire** black light.

Lumières /lymjɛʀ/ *nfpl* **les ~** the Enlightenment; **les philosophes des ~** the philosophers of the Enlightenment; **le siècle des ~** the Age of Enlightenment.

lumignon /lymiɲɔ̃/ *nm* **1** (lampe) (dim) lamp; **2**† (bougie) candle-end.

luminaire /lyminɛʀ/ *nm* **1** (lampe) light (fitting); **2** Relig lights (*in a religious ceremony*); **3** Astrol luminary.

luminance /luminɑ̃s/ *nf* luminance.

lumination /lyminasjɔ̃/ *nf* Phot **indice de ~** exposure value.

luminescence /lyminɛsɑ̃s/ *nf* luminescence.

luminescent, **~e** /lyminɛsɑ̃, ɑ̃t/ *adj* luminescent.

lumineusement /lyminøzmɑ̃/ *adv* [*exposer, expliquer*] clearly, lucidly.

lumineux, **-euse** /lyminø, øz/ *adj* **1** (qui émet de la lumière) [*corps, point*] luminous; **cadran ~ d'une montre/d'un réveil** luminous dial of a watch/of an alarm clock; **panneau ~** electronic display (board); **enseigne lumineuse** neon sign; **faisceau ~** beam of light, light beam; **rayon ~** ray of light; **source lumineuse** source of light; **2** (clair) [*exposé, explication*] clear, lucid; **elle est d'une intelligence lumineuse** she's brilliant, she's remarkably intelligent; **une idée lumineuse** a brilliant idea, a brainwave○; **3** (radieux) [*teint, regard*] radiant.

luminosité /lyminozite/ *nf* **1** gén brightness, luminosity liter; **2** Sci luminosity.

lump /lœmp/ *nm* lumpfish; **œufs de ~** lumpfish roe ¢.

lunaire /lynɛʀ/ I *adj* **1** (de lune) lunar; **mois/fusée ~** lunar month/rocket; **paysage ~** lunar landscape; **2** (rêveur) dreamy; **air ~** dreamy look.

II *nf* Bot honesty.

lunaison /lynɛzɔ̃/ *nf* lunar month, synodic month.

luna-park /lynapaʀk/ *nm* luna park.

lunatique /lynatik/ I *adj* moody.

II *nm,f* moody person.

lunch /lœʃ/ *nm* (en journée) buffet (lunch); (en soirée) buffet (supper); **~ de mariage** wedding breakfast.

lundi /lœdi/ **▶750** *nm* Monday; **le ~ de Pâques/de Pentecôte** Easter/Whit Monday; **le ~ noir** Black Monday.

lune /lyn/ *nf* **1** (astre) moon; **pleine ~** full moon; **nuit sans ~** moonless night; **~ nouvelle** new moon; **2** (mois) month; **sept ~s** seven months; **cela fait des ~s que je ne les ai pas vus** I haven't seen them for months and months.

■ **~ de miel** honeymoon; **~ rousse** ≈ April moon.

IDIOMES **avoir une face de ~** to be moon-faced; **être dans la ~** to have one's head in the clouds; **avoir l'air de tomber de la ~** to look blank; **demander la ~** to cry for the moon; **promettre la ~** to promise the earth ou the moon; **décrocher la ~** to do the impossible; **voir la ~ en plein soleil**◑ to have a clear view of sb's arse◑ GB ou ass◑ US.

luné○, **~e** /lyne/ *adj* **bien ~** cheerful; **mal ~** grumpy; **comment était-il ~ ce soir?** what sort of mood was he in this evening?

lunetier, **-ière** /lyntje, ɛʀ/ I *adj* [*industrie*] spectacle-making.

II **▶510** *nm* **1** Comm optician; **2** Ind spectacle-maker.

lunette /lynɛt/ I *nf* **1** Archit lunette; **2** (siège de toilettes) lavatory seat.

II **lunettes** *nfpl* **1** (optiques) glasses; **mettre ses ~s** to put on one's glasses; **porter des ~s** to wear glasses; **une paire de ~s** a pair of glasses; **~s cerclées de métal/d'or** steel-/gold-rimmed glasses; **~s d'écaille** horn-rimmed glasses; **2** (de protection) goggles; **~s de ski/de natation** skiing/swimming goggles.

■ **~ d'approche** Astron telescope; **~ arrière** Aut rear window; **~ marine** nautical telescope; **~ de visée** Mil telescopic sight; **~s noires** dark glasses; **~s de soleil** sunglasses.

lunetterie /lynɛtʀi/ *nf* spectacle trade; **société de ~** optical company.

lunule /lynyl/ *nf* **1** Anat half-moon, lunule spéc; **2** Math lune.

lupanar /lypanaʀ/ *nm* house of ill repute.

lupin /lypɛ̃/ *nm* lupin GB, lupine US.

lupus /lypys/ **▶271** *nm* lupus.

■ **~ érythémateux** lupus erythematosus; **~ vulgaire** lupus vulgaris.

lurette○ /lyʀɛt/ *nf* **il y a** or **cela fait belle ~ qu'elle a tout dépensé** she spent it all ages○ ago; **il y a** or **cela fait belle ~ que je ne l'ai pas vue** it's been ages○ since I last saw her; **il n'a rien publié depuis belle ~** he has not published anything for ages○.

lurex® /lyʀɛx/ *nm* Lurex®; **robe en ~** lurex dress.

luron /lyʀɔ̃/ *nm* fellow; **gai** or **joyeux** or **sacré ~** jolly fellow.

lusitanien, **-ienne** /lyzitanjɛ̃, ɛn/ I *adj* Lusitanian.

II *nm* Ling Lusitanian Portuguese.

Lusitanien, **-ienne** /lyzitanjɛ̃, ɛn/ *nm,f* Lusitanian.

lusophone /lyzɔfɔn/ fml I *adj* Portuguese-speaking.

II *nmf* Portuguese-speaker.

lustrage /lystʀaʒ/ *nm* **1** (processus) (de bois, métal, cuir) buffing; (de textile) lustring; (de voiture) polishing; **2** (résultat) sheen.

lustral, **~e**, *mpl* **-aux** /lystʀal, o/ *adj* **1** (purificateur) lustral; **2** (quinquennal) lustral.

lustre /lystʀ/ I *nm* **1** (au plafond) chandelier; **~ en cristal** crystal chandelier; **2** (éclat) (de surface) sheen; (de cheveux) shine; **redonner du ~ aux cheveux** to restore shine to dull hair; **3** (de lieu, d'institution) prestigious image; **donner un ~ à** to give a prestigious image to; **rendre** or **redonner du ~ à** to restore the prestigious image of; **donner un nouveau ~ à** to give fresh appeal to; **perdre de son ~** to become rather lacklustre; **4** (cinq années) lustrum.

II **lustres** *nmpl* (longue période) a long time, ages○; **ils le savent depuis des ~s** they have known that for a long time; **on ne les a pas vus depuis des ~s** we haven't seen them for ages○.

lustré, **~e** /lystʀe/ I *pp* ▶ **lustrer**.

II *pp adj* **1** (naturellement) glossy; (d'usure) shiny; **2** Tex glazed.

lustrer /lystʀe/ [1] I *vtr* **1** (faire briller) to polish [*chaussure, miroir*]; to make [sth] shine [*cheveux, vêtement*]; **pâte à ~** polish; **2** Tex to glaze.

II **se lustrer** *vpr* [*vêtement*] to become shiny.

lustrerie /lystʀəʀi/ *nf* lighting appliance industry.

lustrine /lystʀin/ *nf* **manchette de ~** cotton oversleeve.

Lutèce /lytɛs/ **▶857** *npr* Lutetia.

lutécien /lytesjɛ̃/ *nm* Géol Lutetian.

luth /lyt/ *nm* **1** **▶534** Mus lute; **2** Littérat lyre; **3** Zool leatherback.

luthéranisme /lyteʀanism/ *nm* lutheranism.

lutherie /lytʀi/ *nf* manufacture of stringed instruments.

luthérien, **-ienne** /lyteʀjɛ̃, ɛn/ *adj, nm,f* Lutheran.

luthier /lytjе/ **▶510** *nm* stringed instrument maker.

luthiste /lytist/ **▶534** *nmf* lutenist.

lutin /lytɛ̃/ *nm* **1** (démon) goblin; **2** (enfant) imp; **petit ~** little imp.

lutiner /lytine/ [1] *vtr* liter to flirt with.

lutrin /lytʀɛ̃/ *nm* (meuble) lectern; (de table) bookstand.

lutte /lyt/ *nf* **1** (opposition entre personnes) conflict (**avec** with; **contre** with); (plus pénible) struggle; **~ sociale/religieuse/politique** social/religious/political conflict; **~ d'influence** power struggle; **être en ~ contre** or **avec qn** to be in conflict with sb; **se livrer à une ~ sans merci contre qn** to engage in a ruthless battle against sb; **2** (action énergique) fight (**pour** for; **contre** against); (plus pénible) struggle; **la ~ contre le cancer** the fight against cancer; **~ antiterroriste/antipollution/antichômage** fight against terrorism/pollution/unemployment; **~ contre le racisme** fight against racism; **être en ~** to be fighting ou struggling (**pour** for; **contre** against); **de haute ~** fml [*gagner, obtenir qch*] after a hard-fought struggle; **3** (antagonisme entre forces) conflict, struggle; **la ~ entre le bien et le mal** the struggle between good and evil; **4** **▶449** Sport wrestling; **prise de ~** wrestling hold; **faire de la ~** to wrestle.

■ **~ armée** armed conflict; **~ biologique** biological control; **~ de classes** class war; **~ d'intérêts** conflict of interest; **~ libre** all-in wrestling; **~ pour la vie** struggle for existence.

lutter /lyte/ [1] *vi* **1** (s'opposer) [*partie, peuple, pays*] to struggle; **le peuple ne doit pas cesser de ~** the people must not give up the fight; (plus pénible) the people must not give up the struggle; **~ contre qn** [*armée, autorité*] to fight against [*oppresseur, rebelles, armée*]; **2** (agir énergiquement) [*personne, groupe*] to fight (**pour qch** for sth; **pour faire** to do); **pour vivre il faut ~** you have to fight to stay alive; **~ contre** to fight [*crime, pollution, chômage*]; to fight against [*violence*]; to contend with [*intempéries, bruit*]; **aider le malade à ~ contre sa maladie** to help the sick person fight back; **~ contre l'abus d'alcool et de tabac** to combat alcohol and drug abuse; **Louis luttait contre le sommeil** Louis was fighting off sleep; **~ pour la démocratie/les droits de qn** to fight for democracy/sb's rights; **~ pour obtenir/sauvegarder qch** to fight to obtain/keep sth; **3** Sport [*adversaires*] to wrestle (**contre** against; **avec** with).

lutteur /lytœʀ/ *nm* **1** gén fighter; **avoir un tempérament de ~** to be a fighter; **2** Sport wrestler.

lutteuse /lytøz/ *nf* **1** gén fighter; **2** Sport wrestler.

lux /lyks/ *nm inv* lux.

luxation /lyksasjɔ̃/ *nf* **1** Méd dislocation; **~ à l'épaule** dislocation of the shoulder; **2** Dent luxation.

■ **~ du cristallin** ectopia lentis.

luxe /lyks/ *nm* luxury; **vivre dans le ~** to live in luxury; **résidence/produits/voitures de ~** luxury home/products/cars; **s'offrir** or **se payer le ~ de faire** (financièrement) to afford the luxury of doing; fig to give oneself the satisfaction of doing; **il peut se payer ce ~** he can afford it; **ce n'est pas du ~** it has to be done; **je l'ai nettoyé et ça n'était pas du ~** I gave it a much needed clean; **avoir des goûts de ~** to have expensive tastes; **industrie du ~** luxury goods industry; **horlogerie de ~** fine watchmaking; **épicerie de ~** delicatessen; **magasin de ~** exclusive shop; **boutique de ~** boutique.

Luxembourg /lyksɑ̃buʀ/ ▶ 857, 321, 692 *nprm* Luxembourg; **grand-duché de ~** Grand Duchy of Luxembourg.

luxembourgeois, **~e** /lyksɑ̃buʀʒwa, az/ I *adj* **1** ▶ 537 (du Luxembourg) of Luxembourg; **2** ▶ 857 (de Luxembourg) Luxembourg.

II ▶ 462 *nm* Ling *German dialect spoken in Luxembourg*.

Luxembourgeois, **~e** /lyksɑ̃buʀʒwa, az/ ▶ 537 *nm,f* (natif) native of Luxembourg; (habitant) inhabitant of Luxembourg.

luxer /lykse/ [1] I *vtr* to dislocate.

II **se luxer** *vpr* to dislocate; **se ~ l'épaule** to dislocate one's shoulder.

luxueusement /lyksɥøzmɑ̃/ *adv* luxuriously.

luxueux, **-euse** /lyksɥø, øz/ *adj* [*appartement, tapis, voiture*] luxurious; [*magazine, brochure*] glossy.

luxure /lyksyʀ/ *nf* lust.

luxuriance /lyksyʀjɑ̃s/ *nf* luxuriance.

luxuriant, **~e** /lyksyʀjɑ̃, ɑ̃t/ *adj* luxuriant.

luxurieux, **-ieuse** /lyksyʀjø, øz/ *adj* liter lustful.

luzerne /lyzɛʀn/ *nf* alfalfa, lucerne GB.

lycée /lise/ *nm* **1** Scol (avant 1975) secondary school; (depuis 1975) *school preparing students aged 15–18 for the baccalaureate*; **~ Carnot/Voltaire** Lycée Carnot/Voltaire; **2** Philos lyceum.

■ **~ agricole** agricultural college; **~ (d'enseignement) professionnel, L(E)P** vocational school.

lycéen, **-éenne** /liseɛ̃, ɛn/ I *adj* secondary school (*épith*); **vie lycéenne** secondary school life.

II *nm,f* secondary school student.

lymphatique /lɛ̃fatik/ *adj* **1** (nonchalant) lethargic, lymphatic sout; **2** Physiol lymphatic; **circulation/système ~** lymphatic circulation/system.

lymphatisme /lɛ̃fatism/ *nm* (nonchalance) lethargy.

lymphe /lɛ̃f/ *nf* lymph.

lymphocyte /lɛ̃fɔsit/ *nm* lymphocyte; **~ T** T-lymphocyte.

lymphoïde /lɛ̃fɔid/ *adj* lymphoid.

lynchage /lɛ̃ʃaʒ/ *nm* lynching ₵.

lyncher /lɛ̃ʃe/ [1] *vtr* to lynch.

lynx /lɛ̃ks/ *nm* lynx.

■ **~ roux** bobcat.

IDIOMES **avoir un œil** or **des yeux de ~** to be lynx-eyed.

Lyon /ljɔ̃/ ▶ 857 *npr* Lyons.

lyonnais, **~e** /ljɔnɛ, ɛz/ I ▶ 857 *adj* of Lyons.

II **lyonnaise** *nf* **1** Culin lyonnaise; **à la ~e** à la lyonnaise; **2** Jeux *regional game of boules*.

Lyonnais, **~e** /ljɔnɛ, ɛz/ *nm,f* (natif) native of Lyons; (habitant) inhabitant of Lyons.

lyophilisation /ljɔfilizasjɔ̃/ *nf* freeze-drying.

lyophiliser /ljɔfilize/ [1] *vtr* to freeze-dry; **café lyophilisé** freeze-dried coffee.

lyre /liʀ/ ▶ 534 *nf* lyre.

lyrique /liʀik/ I *adj* **1** Mus [*chant, compositeur, morceau, représentation, association*] operatic; [*chanteur, saison, monde, enregistrement*] opera; **opéra ~** lyric opera; **2** Littérat [*poésie, poète*] lyric; [*contenu, élan, simplicité*] lyrical; **être** or **se montrer ~** to wax lyrical (**sur** about).

II *nm* **1** Mus operatic works (*pl*); **2** Littérat (poésie) lyric poetry; (contenu) lyricism; (poète) lyric poet.

lyrisme /liʀism/ *nm* **1** (contenu) lyricism; **avec ~** lyrically; **2** (poésie lyrique) lyric poetry.

lys /lis/ *nm* lily.

IDIOMES **blanc comme un ~** lily-white.

lysimaque /lizimak/ *nf* loosestrife.

Mm

m, **M** /ɛm/ *nm inv* **1** (lettre) m, M; **2** (*written abbr* = **mètre**) **30 m** 30 m.

m' ▶ **me**.

M. ▶813 (*written abbr* = **Monsieur**) Mr; **~ Bon** Mr Bon.

ma ▶ **mon**.

MA /ɛma/ *nf* (*abbr* = **maître auxiliaire**) *secondary teacher without tenure*.

maboul◑, **~e** /mabul/ **I** *adj* crazy○, barmy○ GB.
II *nm,f* fool, nutcase○.

mac◑ /mak/ *nm* pimp, ponce◑ GB.

macabre /makabʀ/ *adj* macabre.

macache◑ /makaʃ/ *adv* **~ (bono)** no way.

macadam /makadam/ *nm* tarmac®.

macadamiser /makadamize/ [1] *vtr* to tarmac.

Macao /makao/ ▶857 *npr* Macao.

macaque /makak/ *nm* **1** Zool macaque; **2**○ (homme laid) ugly man.
■ **~ rhésus** rhesus monkey.

macareux /makaʀø/ *nm* puffin.

macaron /makaʀɔ̃/ *nm* **1** (gâteau) macaroon; **2** (insigne) lapel badge; (étiquette autocollante) sticker; **3** (natte) coiled plait GB ou braid US; **4**○ (coup) clout○.

macaroni /makaʀɔni/ *nm* Culin macaroni ¢; **des ~s** macaroni.

macaronique /makaʀɔnik/ *adj* macaronic.

Maccabées /makabe/ *nprmpl* Maccabees.

maccarthysme /makkaʀtism/ *nm* McCarthyism.

macchabée◑ /makabe/ *nm* stiff◑, corpse.

macédoine /masedwan/ *nf* (salade) macedoine, salad of cooked diced vegetables; (jardinière) mixed diced vegetables (*pl*).
■ **~ de fruits** fruit salad.

Macédoine /masedwan/ ▶692 *nprf* **la ~** Macedonia.

macédonien, **-ienne** /masedɔnjɛ̃, ɛn/ *adj* Macedonian.

macération /maseʀasjɔ̃/ *nf* **1** Culin, Vin soaking, steeping; **pendant leur ~, les fruits s'imprègnent de...** while the fruit is soaking it absorbs...; **2** Relig mortification; **s'infliger des ~s** to mortify one's flesh.

macérer /maseʀe/ [14] **I** *vtr* Relig to mortify; **~ son corps/sa chair** to mortify the ou one's body/flesh.
II *vi* **1** Culin, Pharm [*plante, fruit, légume*] to soak, to steep; [*viande*] to marinate; (dans du vinaigre) [*cornichon*] to pickle; **faire ~** to steep, to soak; **laisser ~ les cornichons pendant deux mois** leave gherkins to pickle for two months; **2** fig **~ dans son ignorance** to wallow in one's ignorance; **~ dans les remords** to be racked by ou with remorse.

macfarlane /makfaʀlan/ *nm* Mode Inverness cape.

Mach /mak/ *nm* Mach; **voler à ~ 2** to fly at Mach 2; **nombre de ~** Mach number.

mâche /mɑʃ/ *nf* lamb's lettuce.

mâchefer /mɑʃfɛʀ/ *nm* clinker.

mâcher /mɑʃe/ [1] *vtr* **1** (broyer) to chew [*aliments, objet*]; **mâche avant d'avaler** chew before swallowing; **2** Tech to chew up.
IDIOMES **~ la besogne** or **le travail à qn** to break the back of the work for sb; **il ne mâche pas ses mots** he doesn't mince his words.

machette /maʃɛt/ *nf* machete.

machiavel /makjavɛl/ *nm* Machiavelli; **c'est un ~** he's a real Machiavelli.

Machiavel /makjavɛl/ *npr* Machiavelli.

machiavélique /makjavelik/ *adj* Machiavellian.

machiavélisme /makjavelism/ *nm* Machiavellianism.

mâchicoulis /mɑʃikuli/ *nm* machicolation.

machin○ /maʃɛ̃/ *nm* **1** (objet dont on ne trouve pas le nom) thing, thingummy○, whatsit○; **passe-moi le ~ qui est sur la table** pass me that thingummy that's on the table; **qu'est-ce que c'est que ce ~-là?** what on earth's that?; **2** (chose) thing; **les armes! je me méfie de ces ~s-là** weapons! I steer clear of that sort of stuff; **il vaut mieux ne pas toucher à ces ~s-là** it's best to keep away from that sort of stuff; **ce sont des ~s dangereux** they're dangerous things; **vieux ~s** old things; **le seul que je possède est un vieux ~ des années 30** the only one I've got is an old 1930's job○; **un vieux ~ noir qui me descendait aux chevilles** a long black affair that came down to my ankles; **3** (personne) **vieux ~** old so-and-so○; **le pays est dirigé par de vieux ~s** the country is ruled by old fogeys○.

Machin○, **~e** /maʃɛ̃, in/ **I** *nm,f* (pour remplacer un patronyme) what's-his-name○/what's-her-name○; **tu as vu ~?** have you seen what's-his-name?; **la mère ~e** Mrs whatsit.
II Machin(-) (*in compounds*) **~-chose**○, **~-chouette**○, **~-truc**○ what's-his-name.

machinal, **~e**, *mpl* **-aux** /maʃinal, o/ *adj* [*geste, réaction*] mechanical; **jeter un coup d'œil ~** to glance absent-mindedly.

machinalement /maʃinalmɑ̃/ *adv* mechanically, without thinking.

machination /maʃinasjɔ̃/ *nf* plot; **des ~s** plots, machinations; **il jure qu'il est victime d'une ~** he swears he's the victim of a plot.

machine /maʃin/ *nf* **1** Tech (appareil) machine; **taper une lettre à la ~** to type a letter; **coudre un ourlet à la ~** to machine-sew a hem; **lavable en ~** machine-washable; **langage ~** Ordinat machine language; **je ne suis pas une ~!** I'm not a machine!; **la civilisation de la ~** the age of the machine; **2** (moteur) engine; **salle des ~s** engine room; **faire ~ arrière** Naut to go astern; fig to back-pedal; **3** (système) machine; **la ~ sociale/administrative/économique** the social/administrative/economic machine; **4**○ (lavage) **faire deux ~s (de linge)** to do two loads of washing.
■ **~ agricole** agricultural machine; **~ de bureau** piece of office equipment; **~s de bureau** office equipment ¢; **~ à calculer** calculating machine; **~ composée** compound machine; **~ à coudre** sewing machine; **~ à écrire** typewriter; **~ infernale** (engin explosif) infernal machine; (bombe) time bomb; **~ à laver** washing machine; **~ à laver la vaisselle** dishwasher; **~ à repasser** press, ironing machine; **~ simple** simple machine; **~ à sous** fruit machine GB, slot machine, one-armed bandit; **~ à traire** milking machine; **~ à tricoter** knitting machine; **~ à** or **de traitement de texte** word processor; **~ à vapeur** steam engine; **~ volante** flying machine.

machine-outil, *pl* **machines-outils** /maʃinuti/ *nf* machine tool.

machiner /maʃine/ [1] *vtr* to hatch [*complot*]; to plot [*trahison*].

machinerie /maʃinʀi/ *nf* **1** (ensemble des machines) machinery; **2** (local) gén machine room; Naut engine room; **3** Théât stage machinery.

machinisme /maʃinism/ *nm* mechanization; **~ agricole** agricultural mechanization.

machiniste /maʃinist/ ▶510 *nmf* **1** Théât stagehand; Cin, TV scene shifter; **2** Transp driver.

machisme /ma(t)ʃism/ *nm* (idéologie) male chauvinism; (comportement) machismo.

machiste /ma(t)ʃist/ **I** *adj* male chauvinist.
II *nm* male chauvinist.

macho○ /matʃo/ **I** *adj* macho.
II *nm* macho man.

mâchoire /mɑʃwaʀ/ *nf* jaw; **~ inférieure/supérieure** lower/upper jaw; **serrer les ~s** to clench one's teeth.
■ **~ de frein** Aut brake shoe.
IDIOMES **bâiller/rire à s'en décrocher la ~** to yawn/laugh one's head off.

mâchonnement /mɑʃɔnmɑ̃/ *nm* gén chewing; Méd bruxism.

mâchonner /mɑʃɔne/ [1] *vtr* to chew.

mâchouiller /mɑʃuje/ [1] *vtr* to chew (on).

mâchurer /mɑʃyʀe/ [1] *vtr* **1** (barbouiller) to blotch [*papier*]; to get [sth] dirty [*habit, visage*]; **2** Imprim to blot, to blur [*feuille*]; **3** Tech (endommager) to dent; **4** (mordiller) to chew.

macle /makl/ = **macre**.

maçon, **-onne** /masɔ̃, ɔn/ **I** *adj* Zool [*abeille, guêpe*] mason.
II *nm* **1** ▶510 gén, Constr bricklayer; (entrepreneur) builder; (qui construit en pierre) mason; **2** (franc-maçon) Mason.

Mâcon /makɔ̃/ ▶857 *npr* Mâcon.

maçonnage /masɔnaʒ/ *nm* **1** (travaux) gén building; (pose de briques) bricklaying; **2** (ouvrage) masonry-work, brickwork.

mâconnais, **~e** /makɔnɛ, ɛz/ ▶857 *adj* of Mâcon.

Mâconnais, **~e** /makɔnɛ, ɛz/ **I** ▶857 *nm,f* (natif) native of Mâcon; (habitant) inhabitant of Mâcon.
II ▶692 *nm* **le ~** the Mâcon area.

maçonner /masɔne/ [1] *vtr* **1** (construire) to build; **2** (revêtir) (avec des pierres) (à l'extérieur) to face [sth] with stone; (à l'intérieur) to line [sth] with stone; (avec des briques) (à l'extérieur) to face [sth] with bricks; (à l'intérieur) to line [sth] with bricks.

maçonnerie /masɔnʀi/ *nf* **1** (travaux) building; **travaux de ~** building work; **travailler dans la ~** to be in the building trade; **2**

(ouvrage) masonry-work; **~ de béton** concrete masonry; **grosse ~** superstructure; **petite ~** interior building; **3** (franc-maçonnerie) Masonry.

maçonnique /masɔnik/ *adj* masonic.

macramé /makʀame/ *nm* macramé; **en ~** in macramé (work).

macre /makʀ/ *nf* Bot water chestnut.

macreuse /makʀøz/ *nf* **1** Culin chuck (steak); **2** Zool scoter.

macrobiotique /makʀɔbjɔtik/ **I** *adj* macrobiotic.
II *nf* macrobiotics (+ *v sg*).

macrocéphale /makʀosefal/ *adj, nmf* macrocephalic.

macrocéphalie /makʀosefali/ *nf* macrocephaly.

macrocosme /makʀokɔsm/ *nm* macrocosm.

macroéconomie /makʀoekɔnɔmi/ *nf* macroeconomics (+ *v sg*).

macroéconomique /makʀoekɔnɔmik/ *adj* macroeconomic.

macrographie /makʀɔgʀafi/ *nf* macrography.

macro-instruction /makʀoɛ̃stʀyksjɔ̃/ *nf* macro-instruction.

macromolécule /makʀomɔlekyl/ *nf* macromolecule.

macrophage /makʀofaʒ/ **I** *adj* macrophagic.
II *nm* macrophage.

macrophotographie /makʀofɔtɔgʀafi/ *nf* macrophotography.

macroscopique /makʀɔskɔpik/ *adj* macroscopic.

macrostructure /makʀostʀyktyʀ/ *nf* macrostructure.

maculé, **~e** /makyle/ **I** *pp* ▶ **maculer**.
II *pp adj* gén [*devoir, feuille*] smudged (**de** with); **être ~ de sang/de boue** to be spattered with blood/mud.

maculer /makyle/ [1] *vtr* **~ de boue** to spatter [sth] with mud [*vêtements, chaussures*]; **~ de sang** to spatter [sth] with blood [*vêtements, chaussures*]; to smudge [*devoir, feuille*] (**de** with).

Madagascar /madagaskaʀ/ ▶ **321**, **416** *nprf* Madagascar; **à ~** in Madagascar; **la République démocratique de ~** the Malagasy Republic.

madame, *pl* **mesdames** /madam, medam/ ▶ **813** *nf* **1** (titre donné à une inconnue) **Madame** (dans une lettre) Dear Madam; **Madame, Monsieur** Dear Sir/Madam; **bonsoir ~** good evening!; **pardon ~, pouvez-vous m'indiquer la poste?** excuse me please, could you tell me where the post office is?; **et pour ~ ce sera?** (au restaurant) and for you madam?; **occupez-vous de ~** (dans un magasin) could you attend to this lady, please?; **~! votre parapluie!** excuse me! you've forgotten your umbrella!; **mesdames et messieurs bonsoir** good evening ladies and gentlemen; **2** (titre donné à une femme dont on connaît le nom, pour l'exemple Bon) **bonjour, ~** good morning, Ms Bon ou Mrs Bon; **Chère Madame** (dans une lettre) Dear Ms Bon, Dear Mrs Bon; **Madame Blanc** (sur une enveloppe) Ms Blanc, Mrs Blanc; **Madame le Ministre** (en lui parlant) Minister; (dans une lettre) Dear Minister; **3** (formule de respect utilisée avec une femme dont on connaît le nom) **comment va Madame votre mère?** how is your (dear) mother?; **veuillez m'annoncer à Madame** tell madam that I am here; **Madame est servie!** dinner is served; **j'en parlerai à Madame** I'll speak to Madam about it; **4** Hist Madame.

■ Note L'anglais possède un équivalent féminin de monsieur, *Ms* /miz/, qui permet de faire référence à une femme dont on connaît le nom sans préciser sa situation de famille: *Ms X.*

madeleine /madlɛn/ *nf* madeleine.

Madeleine /madlɛn/ *npr* Madeleine.
IDIOMES **pleurer comme une ~** to cry one's eyes out.

mademoiselle, *pl* **mesdemoiselles** /madmwazɛl, medmwazɛl/ ▶ **813** *nf* **1** (titre donné à une inconnue) **Mademoiselle** (dans une lettre) Dear Madam; **bonjour, ~** good morning; **entrez, mesdemoiselles** do come in; **pardon ~, je cherche la poste** excuse me, I'm looking for the post office; **occupez-vous de ~** (dans un magasin) could you attend to this lady, please?; **et pour ~, comme d'habitude?** (au café, bar etc) will it be the usual, madam?; **mesdames, mesdemoiselles, messieurs** ladies and gentlemen; **2** (titre donné à une jeune fille dont on connaît le nom, pour l'exemple Bon) Ms Bon, Miss Bon; **Chère Mademoiselle** (dans une lettre) Dear Ms ou Miss Bon; **bonjour, ~** good morning Ms ou Miss Bon; **Mademoiselle Brun** (sur une enveloppe) Ms Brun, Miss Brun; **3** (formule de respect) **~ votre fille**† your daughter; **~ boude?** hum madam's sulking, is she? hum.

■ Note L'anglais possède un équivalent féminin de monsieur, *Ms* /miz/, qui permet de faire référence à une femme dont on connaît le nom sans préciser sa situation de famille: *Ms X.*

madère /madɛʀ/ *nm* madeira.

Madère /madɛʀ/ ▶ **416** *nprf* Madeira.

madérisation /madeʀizasjɔ̃/ *nf* maderization.

madériser /madeʀize/ [1] *vtr*, **se madériser** *vpr* to maderize.

madone /madɔn/ *nf* Art madonna; **elle est belle comme une ~** she is serenely beautiful; **un visage de ~** a serenely beautiful face.

Madone /madɔn/ *npr* **la ~** the Madonna.

madras /madʀas/ *nm* **1** (tissu) madras cotton; **2** (foulard) madras headscarf.

Madras /madʀas/ ▶ **857** *npr* Madras.

madré, **~e** /madʀe/ **I** *adj* liter crafty.
II *nm,f* liter crafty one.

madrépore /madʀepɔʀ/ *nm* madrepore.

Madrid /madʀid/ ▶ **857** *npr* Madrid.

madrier /madʀije/ *nm* beam.

madrigal, *pl* **-aux** /madʀigal, o/ *nm* **1** Mus madrigal; **2**† (compliment) compliment.

madrilène /madʀilɛn/ ▶ **857** *adj* of Madrid.

Madrilène /madʀilɛn/ *nmf* (natif) native of Madrid; (habitant) inhabitant of Madrid.

maelström /malstʀɔm/ *nm* Météo, fig maelstrom.

maestria /maɛstʀija/ *nf* brilliance, panache; **avec ~** with great panache.

maestro /maɛstʀo/ *nm* maestro.

maf(f)ia /mafja/ *nf* mafia; **la ~ de la drogue** the drugs mafia; **la Mafia** the Mafia; **un gros bonnet de la Mafia** a big wheel in the Mafia.

maf(f)ieux, **-ieuse** /mafjø, øz/ **I** *adj* mafia (*épith*).
II *nm* mafioso.

maf(f)ioso /mafjozo/ *nm* mafioso.

magasin /magazɛ̃/ *nm* **1** Comm (boutique) shop GB, store US; (plus grand) store; **grand ~** department store; **une chaîne de ~s** a chain of shops GB ou stores US; **en vente dans les ~s spécialisés** available in specialist shops GB ou stores US; **tenir/prendre un ~** to run/to open a shop GB ou store US; **faire les ~s** to go shopping; **~ de chaussures/d'alimentation** shoe/food shop GB ou store US; **~ à succursales multiples** chain of shops, chain store; **avoir qch en ~** to have sth in stock; **2** Ind store, storehouse; **mettre qch en ~** to put sth in stock; **avoir/garder en ~** to have/to keep in stock; **3** Tech (d'arme, appareil photo) magazine.
■ **~ des accessoires** Théât prop room; **~ d'armes** Mil armoury[GB]; Comm gunsmith's; **~ d'aubaines** C discount store; **~ du corps** Mil regimental warehouse; **~ des décors** Théât (scene) dock; **~ diététique** health-food shop GB ou store US; **~ de sport** sports shop GB ou store US.

magasinage /magazinaʒ/ *nm* **1** (action) warehousing; **2** (séjour) stocking period; **droits/frais de ~** warehousing rights/costs.

magasiner /magazine/ [1] *vi* C (faire des achats) **je n'aime pas ~** I don't like shopping; **aller ~** to go shopping.

magasinier, **-ière** /magazinje, ɛʀ/ ▶ **510** *nm,f* **1** (dans une entreprise) stock controller; **2** (gardien de dépôt) warehouse keeper, warehouseman.

magazine /magazin/ *nm* Presse, Radio, TV magazine; **~ hebdomadaire** weekly magazine; **~ des inventeurs/pour les jeunes** magazine for inventors/teenagers; **~ d'information** news magazine; **~s féminins** women's magazines.

magdalénien, **-ienne** /magdalenjɛ̃, ɛn/ **I** *adj* Magdalenian.
II *nm* **le ~** the Magdalenian era.

mage /maʒ/ *nm* magus; **les rois ~s** the Magi, the (Three) Wise Men.

magenta /maʒɛ̃ta/ ▶ **193** *adj, nm* magenta.

Maghreb /magʀɛb/ ▶ **692** *nprm* **le ~** the Maghreb.

maghrébin, **~e** /magʀebɛ̃, in/ *adj* North African, Maghrebi.

Maghrébin, **~e** /magʀebɛ̃, in/ *nm,f* **1** (habitant) inhabitant of the Maghreb; **2** (immigré) North African.

magicien, **-ienne** /maʒisjɛ̃, ɛn/ ▶ **510** *nm,f* **1** (qui pratique la magie) magician/enchantress; **Circé la magicienne** the enchantress Circe; **2** (dans un spectacle) conjuror, magician; **3** (génie) wizard; **un ~ des mots** a wizard with words; **un ~ de l'économie** an economic wizard.

magie /maʒi/ *nf* **1** (science) magic; **~ blanche/noire** white/black magic; **comme par ~** as if by magic; **2** (dans un spectacle) conjuring; **3** (effet puissant) magic (**de** of); **la ~ des mots** the magic of words.

Maginot /maʒino/ *npr* **ligne ~** Maginot line.

magique /maʒik/ *adj* **1** lit magic (*épith*), magical; **baguette/potion ~** magic wand/potion; **pouvoir/formule ~** magic power/words (*pl*); **2** fig [*beauté, décor*] magical.

magiquement /maʒikmɑ̃/ *adv* magically.

magistère /maʒistɛʀ/ *nm* **1** Relig magisterium; **2** Univ *high-level University degree combining academic coursework with work experience in industry*.

magistral, **~e**, *mpl* **-aux** /maʒistʀal, o/ *adj* **1** (remarquable) [*habileté, interprétation*] masterly; [*œuvre, étude, succès*] brilliant; **réussir un coup ~** to bring off a masterstroke; **2** liter [*ton*] magisterial; **cours ~** lecture; **3** hum [*correction, gifle*] tremendous; **4** Pharm [*médicament*] magistral, prescription.

magistralement /maʒistʀalmɑ̃/ *adv* brilliantly.

magistrat /maʒistʀa/ *nm* **1** Jur ≈ magistrate; **~ instructeur** examining magistrate; **les ~s du siège** the judges; **2** Admin magistrate.

magistrature /maʒistʀatyʀ/ *nf* **1** Jur magistracy; **2** Admin (fonction) public office; (durée de cette fonction) term ou tenure of office; **arriver à la ~ suprême** to reach the highest office in the land.
■ **la ~ assise** the judges (*pl*); **la ~ debout** the state ou public prosecutors (*pl*).

magma /magma/ *nm* **1** Chimie, Géol magma; **2** (mélange confus) jumble.

magmatique /magmatik/ *adj* magmatic.

magnanime /maɲanim/ *adj* magnanimous (**avec, envers** with, towards[GB]); **se montrer ~** to be magnanimous.

magnanimement /maɲanimmɑ̃/ *adv* magnanimously.

magnanimité /maɲanimite/ *nf* magnanimity (**avec, envers** with, towards[GB]); **faire preuve de ~** to show magnanimity.

magnat /maɲa/ *nm* magnate, tycoon; **un ~ de la presse/du pétrole** a press/an oil magnate.

magner◑: **se magner** /maɲe/ [1] *vpr* to get a move on○; **magne-toi le train**○ or **cul**● shift your arse● GB ou ass◑ US, get your ass in gear◑ US.

magnésie /maɲezi/ *nf* magnesia.

magnésium /maɲezjɔm/ *nm* magnesium.

magnétique /maɲetik/ *adj* magnetic; **champ ~** magnetic field.

magnétisable /maɲetizabl/ *adj* magnetizable.

magnétisation /maɲetizasjɔ̃/ *nf* magnetization.

magnétiser /maɲetize/ [1] *vtr* **1** Phys to magnetize; **2** (pour soigner) to magnetize; **3** (charmer) to hypnotize, to mesmerize.

magnétiseur, -euse /maɲetizœʀ, øz/ **▶510** *nm,f* (magnetic) healer.

magnétisme /maɲetism/ *nm* gén magnetism; **~ terrestre** terrestrial magnetism; **le ~ de qn** sb's magnetism; **le ~ d'un discours** the magnetic power of a speech; **leur ~ sur les foules** their magnetic effect on crowds.

magnétite /maɲetit/ *nf* magnetite.

magnéto /maɲeto/ **I**○ *nm*: *abbr* = **magnétophone**.
II *nf* Électrotech magneto.

magnétoélectrique /maɲetoelɛktʀik/ *adj* magnetoelectric.

magnétophone /maɲetɔfɔn/ *nm* (à cassette) cassette (tape) recorder; (à bande) tape recorder; **enregistrer qch au ~** to record sth, to tape sth.

magnétoscope /maɲetɔskɔp/ *nm* (à cassette) video (cassette) recorder, VCR; (à bande) video (tape) recorder; **enregistrer qch au ~** to video sth.

magnétoscoper /maɲetɔskɔpe/ [1] *vtr* to video, to record [sth] on video.

magnétoscopique /maɲetɔskɔpik/ *adj* **enregistrement ~** video recording; **bande/image ~** video tape/image.

magnétosphère /maɲetɔsfɛʀ/ *nf* magnetosphere.

magnificat /maɲifikat/ *nm inv* (cantique, musique) Magnificat.

magnificence /maɲifisɑ̃s/ *nf* **1** (splendeur) splendour[GB]; **2** (générosité) munificence; **recevoir qn avec ~** to entertain sb lavishly; **3** fig (de style) grandeur.

magnifier /maɲifje/ [1] *vtr* **1** (élever) to idealize [*souvenir, sentiment*]; **2** (célébrer) to glorify [*héroïsme, exploit*].

magnifique /maɲifik/ *adj* (très beau) splendid; (visant à éblouir) magnificent; **elle a été ~ dans ce rôle** she was splendid in the part; **il a été ~ de courage** he showed magnificent courage.

magnifiquement /maɲifikmɑ̃/ *adv* gén splendidly; [*recevoir*] lavishly; **un rôle ~ interprété** a splendid interpretation of the role.

magnitude /maɲityd/ *nf* **1** Astron magnitude; **2** Géol strength; **séisme de ~ 5,6** earthquake measuring 5.6 (on the Richter scale).

magnolia /maɲɔlja/ *nm* magnolia (tree).

magnum /magnɔm/ *nm* Vin magnum (bottle).

magot /mago/ *nm* **1**○ (somme d'argent) pile○ (of money); **amasser un joli ~** to make a nice pile; **2** Art magot; **3** Zool Barbary ape, magot.

magouillage○ /magujaʒ/ *nm* fiddling○, cheating.

magouille○ /maguj/ *nf* **1** (procédé) fiddling○; **2** (résultat) trick; **de sombres ~s** dirty tricks; **~s politiques** political skulduggery ₵; **~s financières** financial skulduggery ₵, sharp practice ₵; **~s électorales** election rigging ₵.

magouiller○ /maguje/ [1] *vi* to fiddle○, to cheat.

magouilleur, -euse /magujœʀ, øz/ *nm,f* fiddler○, cheat.

magret /magʀɛ/ *nm* **~ de canard** duck breast.

magyar, ~e /magjaʀ/ *adj* Magyar.

Magyar, ~e /magjaʀ/ *nm,f* Magyar.

mahara(d)jah, *pl* **~(s)** /maaʀadʒa/ *nm* maharaja(h).

maharani, *pl* **~(s)** /maaʀani/ *nf* maharani.

mah-jong, *pl* **~s** /maʒɔ̃g/ **▶449** *nm* mahjong.

Mahomet /maɔmɛ/ *npr* Mohammed.

mahométan†, **~e** /maɔmetɑ̃, an/ *adj, nm,f* Mahometan†, Mohammedan.

mai /mɛ/ **▶521** *nm* May; **le premier ~** May Day; **▶ avril**.

maie /mɛ/ *nf* dough trough (*in lidded decorative coffer*).

maïeutique /majøtik/ *nf* maieutics (+ *v sg*).

maigre /mɛgʀ/ **I** *adj* **1** gén thin, skinny, scrawny; Méd [*personne*] thin, underweight; [*animal, bras, jambe*] thin; **2** Culin [*jambon, viande*] lean; [*yaourt, fromage*] low-fat; **3** Relig [*aliment*] non-meat; [*repas, jour*] without meat; **4** (médiocre) [*résultat*] poor; [*talents, repas, économies*] meagre[GB]; [*espoir*] slim; [*consolation*] small, scant; [*applaudissements*] scant; [*texte, devoir*] skimpy; **5** (peu volumineux) [*filet d'eau, paquet*] thin; [*gazon*] sparse; [*chevelure*] sparse, thin; **6** Imprim **caractère ~** light type.
II *nmf* thin man/woman; **c'est une fausse ~** she looks thinner than she is.
III *nm* (de viande) lean.
IDIOMES **~ comme un clou** or **un coucou** as thin as a rake, as skinny as a rail US; **faire** or **manger ~** to abstain from meat.

maigrelet, -ette /mɛgʀəlɛ, ɛt/ *adj* skinny, scrawny.

maigrement /mɛgʀəmɑ̃/ *adv* [*payé, récompensé*] poorly.

maigreur /mɛgʀœʀ/ *nf* **1** (de personne, partie du corps) thinness; **être d'une grande ~** to be very thin; **2** (faible quantité) meagreness[GB], scantiness.

maigrichon, -onne /mɛgʀiʃɔ̃, ɔn/ *adj* skinny, scrawny.

maigrir /mɛgʀiʀ/ [3] **I** *vtr* [*vêtement, couleur*] to make [sb] look thinner; [*maladie, soucis*] to make [sb] lose weight.
II *vi* to lose weight, to slim; **~ de trois kilos** to lose three kilos; **on l'a trouvé maigri** he looked as if he had lost weight; **~ des hanches/des cuisses** to lose weight around one's hips/from one's thighs; **il a maigri du visage** his face has got GB ou gotten US thinner; **faire ~ qn** [*exercice, régime*] to make sb lose weight; **pour ~** [*crème, exercice*] slimming GB, reducing (*épith*) US; [*cachet, pilule*] diet.

mail /maj/ *nm* **1** (allée) mall, avenue; **2** (jeu) pall-mall; **3** (maillet) mallet.

mailing /mɛliŋ/ *nm* **1** (principe) direct mail advertising; **2** (envoi) mail shot; **faire un ~** to do a mail shot; **3** (document) mailing pack.

maillage /majaʒ/ *nm* **1** (de filet) mesh size; **2** (création de réseau) creation of a network; (réseau créé) network.

maille /maj/ *nf* **1** (de tricot) stitch; **à fines/grosses ~s** fine-/loose-knit (*épith*); **une ~ tirée** a pulled stitch; **une ~ qui file** (en tricotant) a dropped stitch; (sur un collant) a ladder; **monter 20 ~s** to cast on 20 stitches; **2** (de filet) mesh; **passer à travers les ~s** [*poisson*] to pass through the net; [*malfaiteur*] to slip through the net; **3** (de grillage, chaînette) link; **4** Tex (tissu) knitted fabric, jersey.
■ **~ (à l')endroit** plain stitch; **faites deux ~s à l'endroit** knit two; **~ (à l')envers** purl stitch; **faites une ~ à l'envers** purl one; **~ glissée** slip stitch; **~ serrée** (au crochet) double crochet.
IDIOMES **avoir ~ à partir avec qn/la justice** to have a brush with sb/the law.

maillechort /majʃɔʀ/ *nm* nickel silver.

maillet /majɛ/ *nm* **1** (marteau) mallet; **~ de croquet** croquet mallet; **2** (arme) mace.

mailloche /majɔʃ/ *nf* **1** (maillet) mallet, beetle; **2** Mus beater.

maillon /majɔ̃/ *nm* link; **le dernier ~ de la chaîne** the last link in the chain.

maillot /majo/ *nm* **1** (sous-vêtement) vest GB, undershirt US; **2** (de sport) (sans manches) singlet; (de football, rugby) shirt; (de cyclisme) jersey.
■ **~ de bain** swimsuit; **un ~ une pièce/deux pièces** a one-piece/two-piece swimsuit; **~ de corps** vest GB, undershirt US; **~ jaune** (vêtement) yellow jersey; (cycliste) leader in the Tour de France.

main /mɛ̃/ **▶188** *nf* **1** Anat hand; **~ droite/gauche** right/left hand; **se laver les ~s** to wash one's hands; **marcher les ~s dans les poches** to walk with one's hands in one's pockets; **saluer qn de la ~** to wave at sb; **d'un signe de la ~ elle indiqua que...** with her hand she indicated that...; **la ~ dans la ~** lit hand in hand; fig close together; **avoir les ~s liées** lit, fig to have one's hands tied; **haut les ~s!** hands up!; **passer de ~ en ~** [*objet, livre*] to pass from hand to hand; **tenir qch à la ~** to hold sth in one's hand; **se tenir la ~** to hold hands; **avoir une brûlure à la ~** to have a burn on one's hand; **donne-moi la ~** (pour être tenue) give me your hand; (pour être serrée) let's shake hands; (pour un soutien moral) hold my hand; **demander la ~ de qn** to ask for sb's hand (in marriage); **prendre qch d'une (seule) ~** to pick sth up with one hand; **prendre qch à deux ~s** to take sth with both hands; **ramasser qch à pleines ~s** to pick up handfuls of sth; **saisir qch à pleines ~s** to take a firm hold of sth; **glisser** or **tomber des ~s de qn** to slip out of sb's hands; **avoir qch bien en ~(s)** lit to hold sth firmly; fig to have sth well in hand; **être adroit de ses ~s** to be good with one's hands; **si tu portes** or **lèves la ~ sur elle** if you lay a finger on her; **faire qch à la ~** to do sth by hand; **faire qch de ses propres ~s** to do sth with one's own hands; **fait ~** [*produit*] handmade; **cousu/tricoté ~** hand-sewn/-knitted; **à la ~** (sans machine) [*contrôler, régler*] manually; **à ~s nues** [*se battre*] with one's bare hands; **jouer du piano à quatre ~s** to play a duet on the piano; **dessiner à ~ levée** to draw freehand; **voter à ~ levée** to vote by a show of hands; **se faire faire les ~s** to have a manicure; **attaque/vol à ~ armée** armed attack/robbery; **avoir besoin d'un coup de ~** to need a hand; **donner un coup de ~ à qn** to give sb a hand; **dix secondes montre** or **chronomètre en ~** ten seconds exactly; **▶ courage, doigt, dos, uni, vilain**; **2** (personne) **une ~ secourable** a helping hand; **une ~ criminelle avait saboté** someone with criminal intentions had sabotaged; **3** (dénotant le contrôle, la possession) hand; **la ~ de Dieu/du destin** the hand of God/fate; **changer de ~s** to change hands; **avoir qch sous la ~** to have sth to hand; **c'est ce que j'avais sous la ~** it's what I had; **je n'ai rien sous la ~ pour recoudre ton bouton** I've got nothing here to sew your button back on; **cela m'est tombé sous la ~** I just happened to come across it; **mettre la ~ sur qch** (retrouver) to lay one's hand on sth; (trouver) to get one's hands on sth; **je n'arrive pas à mettre la ~ dessus** I can't lay my hands on it, I can't find it; **après être passé par les ~s de ma fille** after my daughter had had it; **je l'ai eu entre les ~s mais** I did have it but; **être entre les ~s de qn** [*pouvoir,* *responsabilité, entreprise*] to be in the hands of sb; **avoir/prendre qch en ~s** to have/to take sth in hand [*affaire, tâche*]; **se prendre par la ~** (soi-même) to take oneself in hand; **prendre qn par la ~** lit, fig to take sb by the hand; **être en (de) bonnes/mauvaises ~s** to be in good/not to be in good hands; **avoir la ~ haute sur** to have control over; **avoir les choses en ~** to have things in hand; **avoir qch bien en ~** to have sth well in hand; **à ne pas mettre entre toutes les ~s** [*livre*] not for general reading; **tomber entre les ~s de qn** to fall into sb's hands; **repartir avec un contrat en ~(s)** to leave with a signed contract; **elle est arrivée preuve en ~** she had concrete proof; **avoir/arriver les ~s vides** to be/arrive empty-handed; **je le lui ai remis en ~s propres** I gave it to him/her in person; **de la ~ à la ~** [*vendre, acheter*] privately; **être payé de la ~ à la ~** to be paid cash (in hand); **de seconde ~** secondhand; **de première ~** (dans une annonce) 'one owner'; **avoir des renseignements de première ~** to have first-hand information; ▶**innocent**, **velours**; **4** (origine) **peinture de la ~ de Bosch** original painting by Bosch; **écrit de la ~ du président** written by the president himself; **reconnaître la ~ d'un auteur/d'un artiste** to recognize a writer's/an artist's style; **de ma plus belle ~** (écriture) in my best handwriting; **5** (dénotant l'habileté) **avoir le coup de ~** to have the knack; **il faut d'abord se faire la ~** you have to learn how to do it first; **avoir la ~ légère** to have a light touch; **6** Zool (de primate) hand; **7** (longueur approximative) **une ~** a hand's width; **8** Imprim (de papier) quire; **9** Sport (au football) handball; **il y a ~!** handball!; **10** Jeux (cartes de chacun) hand; (tour de jeu) deal; **bonne/mauvaise ~** strong/weak hand; **perdre la ~** lit to lose the deal; fig to lose one's touch; **garder la ~** lit to keep one's hand; fig to keep one's hand in; **11** (direction) **à ~ droite/gauche** on the right/left.

■ **~ chaude** Jeux hot cockles (+ *v sg*); **~ courante** Constr handrail; Compta daybook.

IDIOMES **j'en mettrais ma ~ au feu** or **à couper** I'd swear to it; **d'une ~ de fer** [*gouverner, diriger*] with an iron rod; **il n'y est pas allé de ~ morte!** he didn't pull his punches!; **avoir la ~ leste** to be always ready with a good hiding; **laisser les ~s libres à qn** to give sb a free hand ou rein; **passer la ~** to step down (**à** in favour[GB] of); **faire ~ basse sur** to help oneself to [*biens*]; to take over [*marché, pays*]; **en venir aux ~s** to come to blows; **avoir la ~ heureuse/malheureuse** to be lucky/unlucky; **mettre la dernière ~ à** to put the finishing touches to; **il y en a autant que sur ma ~**○ there aren't any; **ils peuvent se donner la ~** péj (deux personnes) they're both the same; (plusieurs personnes) they're all the same; **mettre la ~ aux fesses**○ **de qn** to feel sb up○; **que ta ~ gauche ignore ce que fait ta ~ droite** let not thy left hand know what thy right hand doeth.

mainate /mɛnat/ *nm* mynah bird.

main-d'œuvre, *pl* **mains-d'œuvre** /mɛ̃dœvʀ/ *nf* **1** (travailleurs) labour[GB] ₵; **~ bon marché/qualifiée/immigrée** cheap/skilled/immigrant labour[GB]; **~ féminine** female labour[GB]; **2** (travail) labour[GB]; **coût de la ~** labour[GB] costs (*pl*).

Maine /mɛn/ ▶**692** *nprm* Maine.

Maine-et-Loire /mɛnelwaʀ/ ▶**692** *nprm* (département) **le ~** Maine-et-Loire.

main-forte /mɛ̃fɔʀt/ *nf inv* **prêter ~ à qn** to come to sb's aid.

mainlevée /mɛ̃lve/ *nf* **~ de saisie** replevin, restoration of goods taken in distraint; **~ d'hypothèque** release of mortgage; **~ d'opposition** withdrawal of opposition; **accorder ~ d'une saisie** to grant replevin.

mainmise /mɛ̃miz/ *nf* **1** (domination) control (**sur** over); **avoir la ~ sur qch** to have control over sth; **2** Jur seizure.

maint, **~e** /mɛ̃, mɛ̃t/ *adj indéf* many (+ *pl*), many a (+ *sg*); **pour ~ lecteur** for many a reader, for many readers; **on retrouvera le même phénomène dans ~e famille** we come across the same phenomenon in many families; **j'y ai séjourné ~es fois** I've stayed there many a time, many's the time I've stayed there; **~s politiciens** many a politician; **~es et ~es fois** time and (time) again; **à ~es reprises** many times.

maintenance /mɛ̃tnɑ̃s/ *nf* maintenance.

maintenant /mɛ̃t(ə)nɑ̃/ *adv* **1** (à présent) now; **où allons-nous ~?** where shall we go now?; **jusqu'à ~ il venait tous les jours** up until now he came every day; **à partir de ~** from now on; **il y a ~ dix ans qu'il est mort** he's been dead ten years now; **~ que** now that; **il faut commencer dès ~** we must start straightaway; **c'est ~ qu'il faut planter vos rosiers** now is the time to plant your rose bushes; **imaginons ~ que** now let's imagine that; **il doit avoir fini ~** he must have finished by now; **2** (dans le passé) **il devait ~ finir sa thèse et trouver du travail** he now had to finish his thesis and find work; **elle a précisé qu'elle attendait ~ un moment favorable** she explained that she was now waiting for the right moment; **3** (l'époque actuelle) today; **la jeunesse de ~** the youth of today; **les mœurs de ~** today's social mores; **4** (de nos jours) nowadays; **~ les choses se font différemment** nowadays people do things differently; **c'est plus difficile ~** it's more difficult now(adays); **5** (désormais) now; **~ tu pourras utiliser ma voiture** now you can use my car; **~ il était enfin libre de faire ce qu'il voulait** at last he was free to do what he wanted; **6** (cela dit) now; **je t'ai averti, ~ tu fais ce que tu veux** I've warned you, now do what you want.

maintenir /mɛ̃t(ə)niʀ/ [36] **I** *vtr* **1** (faire durer) to maintain [*situation, équilibre, privilège*]; to keep [*paix, cessez-le-feu*]; to keep up [*coutumes*]; **~ l'ordre** to maintain order; **faire ~ l'ordre** to have order maintained; **ils ont maintenu le secret** they kept it secret; **~ les prix** to keep prices stable; **~ un régime** to prop up a regime; **2** (soutenir) to support [*bâtiment, mur, poitrine, cheville*]; **3** (conserver en l'état) to keep; **~ la tête hors de l'eau** to keep one's head above the water; **~ qch en équilibre** to keep ou hold sth balanced; **~ qch droit/debout** to keep ou hold sth straight/upright; **~ un assemblage avec des chevilles** to hold a structure together with pins; **~ qn en vie/sous les verrous** to keep sb alive/under lock and key; **~ la température** to maintain the temperature; **être maintenu dans ses fonctions** to be kept on in one's post; **4** (ne pas retirer) to stand by [*décision, accusation*]; **je maintiens ce que j'ai dit** I stand by what I said; **je l'ai dit et je le maintiens** I said that and I stand by it; **~ que** to maintain that; **~ sa candidature** (pour un emploi) to go through with one's application; Pol not to withdraw one's candidacy.

II se maintenir *vpr* **1** [*prix, pouvoir d'achat*] to remain stable; [*système politique*] to remain in force; [*monnaie*] to hold steady (**à** at); **2** (dans un lieu, état) [*personne*] to remain, to stay; **se ~ au pouvoir** to remain ou stay in power; **se ~ debout** to remain standing; **se ~ en bonne santé** to keep oneself in good health; **3** (ne pas se dégrader) [*malade*] to remain stable; [*personne, vieillard*] to remain in good health; **leur santé se maintient** they remain in good health; **si le temps se maintient (au beau)** if the (fine) weather holds; **4** Pol [*candidat*] **se ~ au second tour** to continue to stand GB ou run US in the second round.

maintien /mɛ̃tjɛ̃/ *nm* **1** (d'état de fait, de privilèges) maintaining; **notre but c'est le ~ des prix** our aim is to keep prices stable; **assurer le ~ de l'ordre** to maintain order; **2** (de branchement, système) maintaining; **3** (de poitrine, chevilles) support; **4** Pol **le ~ de sa candidature est peu probable** it is unlikely that he will continue to stand GB ou run US; **5** (allure) deportment; **cours de ~** deportment lessons.

maire /mɛʀ/ *nm* mayor.

■ **~ adjoint** deputy mayor.

IDIOMES **passer devant Monsieur le ~** hum to get married.

mairie /mɛʀi/ *nf* **1** (administration) gén town council GB ou hall US; (dans une grande ville) city council; **être élu à la ~ de** to be elected mayor of; **2** (bureaux) town hall.

mais[1] /mɛ/ *conj* **1** (introduisant une correction, une opposition) but; **il est intelligent ~ paresseux** he's intelligent but lazy; **elle n'arrive pas lundi ~ mardi** she's not arriving on Monday but on Tuesday, she's arriving on Tuesday, not Monday; **non seulement il est malhonnête, ~ en plus il s'en vante** not only is he dishonest but on top of that he boasts about it; **il est acteur ~ aussi écrivain** he's an actor and a writer as well; **incroyable ~ vrai** strange but true; **~ il avait pourtant dit qu'il viendrait** but he did say he would come; **2** (pour renforcer) **~ c'est de la folie!** but that's madness!; **~ c'est tout naturel!** but it's only natural!; **~ ne t'inquiète donc pas!** don't you worry about it; **~ c'est vrai, je t'assure!** but it's true, I tell you! ; **il est bête, ~ bête!** he's so incredibly stupid!; **il faisait chaud, ~ chaud!** it was so incredibly hot!; **je n'ai rien compris, ~ vraiment rien!** I understood absolutely nothing!; **'est-ce que je peux venir aussi?'—'~ oui!** or **bien sûr!** or **certainement!'** 'can I come too?'—'of course!'; **3** (marquant l'indignation, l'impatience) **~ où est-il passé?** where on earth○ has he got to?; **~ qu'est-ce qui se passe ici?** what on earth○ is going on here?; **~ vas-tu te taire!** can't you just shut up○?; **non ~ (des fois)**○**!** for God's sake!, really!; **non ~ quel culot!** really! what a nerve!; **non ~ des fois**○**! pour qui se prend-il?** really! ou I ask you! who does he think he is?; **(non) ~**◑ **il commence à m'énerver celui-là!** that guy is really beginning to get on my nerves!; **4** (marquant la surprise) **~, vous pleurez!** good heavens, you're crying!; **~ alors, vous m'avez menti!** so you lied to me!; **~ je te croyais parti à l'étranger!** well! I thought you'd gone abroad!; **~ qu'est-ce qui t'a pris?** what on earth○ came over you?; **5** (comme transition) **~ j'y pense** now that I come to think of it; **~, je m'égare** but I digress; **~ dis-moi, tu le connais aussi?** so you know him too?

mais[2] /mɛ/ *nm* **il n'y a pas de ~ (qui tienne)** there are no buts about it.

IDIOMES **il n'en pouvait ~** he couldn't take it any more.

maïs /mais/ *nm* **1** Agric maize GB, corn US; **farine de ~** cornflour; **épi/grain de ~** ear/grain of corn; **2** Culin sweetcorn; **épi de ~** corn on the cob.

maison /mɛzɔ̃/ **I** *adj inv* **1** (fait chez soi, comme chez soi) home-made; (fait sur place) made on the premises; **commentaire/humour ~** iron typical comment/humour[GB]; **2** (d'une entreprise) **notre formation/spécialiste ~** our very own training scheme/specialist; **3**○ (très bon) first class.

II *nf* **1** (bâtisse) house; **~ individuelle** detached house; **2** (domicile familial) home; **rester à la ~** to stay at home; **quitter la ~** to leave home; **la ~ familiale** the family home; **elle tient la ~** she runs the house; **gérer le budget de la ~** to manage the household budget; **il m'a fait les honneurs de la ~** he showed me round the house; **la ~ du Seigneur** the House of the Lord; **3** (personnes habitant ensemble) house, household; (domestiques) household; **la ~ du roi** the royal household; **ami de la ~** friend of the family; **le fils de la ~** the son of the family; **faire la jeune fille de la ~** hum to do the honours[GB]; **employés** or **gens de ~** domestic staff; **c'est une ~**

de fous! it's a madhouse!; **4** (lignée) family; **descendant d'une grande ~** descendant of a great family; **~ d'Orange** House of Orange; **5** (société) firm; **il n'est pas de la ~** he's not with the firm; **avoir 15 ans de ~** to have been with the firm for 15 years; **~ d'édition /de (haute) couture** publishing/fashion house; **~ de production** production company; **la ~ Hachette** Hachette; **~ de confiance** reliable company; **'la ~ ne fait pas crédit'** 'no credit given'; **'la ~ n'accepte pas les chèques'** 'we do not take cheques[GB]'; **'la Maison du livre étranger'** the Foreign Bookshop; **6** Astrol house.

■ **~ d'arrêt** prison (*for offenders with sentences under two years*); **~ de campagne** house in the country; **~ centrale** prison (*for offenders with sentences over two years*); **~ close** brothel; **~ de commerce** (business) firm; **~ communale** community centre[GB]; **~ de convalescence** convalescent home; **~ de correction** institution for young offenders; **~ de la culture** ≈ community arts centre[GB]; **~ de gros** wholesalers (*pl*); **~ des jeunes et de la culture, MJC** ≈ youth club; **~ de jeu** gaming house; **~ de maître** manor; **~ maternelle** home for single mothers; **~ mère** (siège) headquarters (*pl*); (établissement principal) main branch; **~ normande** half-timbered house; **~ de passe** brothel; **~ de poupée** doll's GB ou doll US house; **~ de redressement** institution for young offenders; **~ religieuse** (couvent) convent; **~ de repos** rest home; **~ de retraite** old people's ou retirement home; **~ de santé** nursing home; **~ de tolérance†** brothel; **la Maison Blanche** the White House.

IDIOMES **c'est gros comme une ~** it sticks out a mile; **avoir un pied dans la ~** to have a foot in the door; **c'est la ~ du bon Dieu** it's open house.

maisonnée /mɛzɔne/ *nf* gén household; (famille) family.

maisonnette /mɛzɔnɛt/ *nf* (small) house.

maistrance /mɛstʀɑ̃s/ *nf* ≈ petty officers (*pl*).

maître, -esse /mɛtʀ, ɛs/ **▶390** **I** *adj* **1** (en contrôle) **être ~ de soi** (libre) to be one's own master; (calme) to have self-control; **être ~ de sa vie** to be one's own man/woman; **ne plus être ~ de soi** to have lost all self-control; **être ~ de ses émotions** to keep one's emotions under control; **être ~ chez soi** to be master in one's own house; **être ~ du destin de qn** to have sb's fate in one's hands; **être ~ de son (propre) destin** to be master of one's destiny; **devenir/redevenir ~ de son destin** to take/regain control of one's destiny; **être ~ de la situation** to be in control of the situation; **rester ~ de la décision** to retain control over the decision; **être ~ de son véhicule/la balle** to be in control of one's vehicle/the ball; **se rendre ~ d'une ville/d'un navire** to take over a city/a ship; **▶charbonnier**; **2** (principal) **idée maîtresse** key idea; **~ mot** catchword; **~ ouvrage** or **œuvre maîtresse** magnum opus; **qualité maîtresse** main quality; **maîtresse branche, branche maîtresse** Bot limb; **être passé ~ dans l'art de qch/de faire** to be a past master of sth/at doing; **être ~ dans l'art du récit/de négocier** to be a master of narrative/at negotiating; **maîtresse femme** high-powered woman.

II *nm,f* **1** Scol teacher; **notre maîtresse est dehors** our teacher is outside; **maîtresse!** (pour l'appeler) please, miss!; **2** (de maison) master/mistress; **la maîtresse des lieux** the mistress ou lady of the house; **~s et valets** upstairs and downstairs; **3** (d'animal) owner; (de chien) master; **un chat et sa maîtresse** a cat and its owner; **un chien et son ~** a dog and its master; **sans ~** ownerless.

III *nm* **1** (dirigeant) **être (le) seul ~ à bord** lit, fig to be in sole command; **être le ~ du pays/de la ville** to rule the country/the city; **le ~ du Kremlin/du monde** the ruler of the Kremlin/of the world; **être ~ de faire** to be free to do; **être son propre ~** to be one's own master/mistress; **régner en ~** to reign (**sur** over); **régner en ~ absolu** to reign supreme (**sur** over); **décider en ~** to have the final say; **être le ~ du jeu** to have the upper hand; **avoir l'oreille du ~** to have the boss's ear; **▶serviteur**; **2** (expert) **tu es un ~** you're an expert; **Hitchcock, le ~ du genre/du suspense** Hitchcock, the master of the genre/of suspense; **~ consommé/reconnu** consummate/acknowledged master; **en ~** masterfully; **joué de main de ~** played in a masterly fashion; **coup de ~** masterstroke; **▶grand**; **3** (guide, enseignant) master; **Platon est mon seul ~** Plato is my only master; **4** Art, Littérat master; **les ~s anversois/vénitiens** the Antwerp/Venetian masters; **les ~s de la littérature mondiale** the masters of world literature; **Maître de 1518/de Flémalle** Master of 1518/of Flémalle; **▶petit**; **5** (titre) Maître; **comment allez-vous, cher ~?** how are you, dear Maître?; **6** Mil, Naut (grade) ≈ chief petty officer, CPO; **▶premier**; **7** Jeux **être ~ à carreau/pique** to hold the master card in diamonds/spades.

IV maîtres *nmpl* Scol teachers; **parents et ~s** parents and teachers; **grève des ~s** teachers' strike.

V maîtresse *nf* **1** (amante) mistress; **avoir de nombreuses maîtresses** to have many mistresses; **2†** (bien-aimée) lover†.

■ **~ d'armes** Sport fencing instructor; **~ auxiliaire, MA** Scol *secondary teacher without tenure*; **~ des cérémonies** master/mistress of ceremonies, MC; **~ chanteur** Mus meistersinger; **~ de chapelle** kapellmeister; **~ de chœur** choirmaster/choirmistress; **~ de conférences** Univ ≈ senior lecturer GB, associate professor US; **poste de ~ de conférences** ≈ senior lectureship GB, associate professorship US; **~ d'école†** schoolmaster†; **~ d'équipage** Chasse master of foxhounds, MFH; Naut boatswain; **~ des forges** ironmaster; **~ d'hôtel** maître d'hôtel GB, maître d' US; **~ d'internat** ≈ housemaster; **~ de manège** riding instructor; **~ de musique†** music master†/mistress†; **~ d'œuvre** Constr project manager; **~ d'ouvrage** (privé) employer; (public) contracting authority; **~ à penser** mentor; **~ de recherches** senior researcher; **maîtresse d'école** Scol schoolmistress†; **maîtresse d'internat** Scol ≈ housemistress; **maîtresse de maison** lady of the house.

IDIOMES **trouver son ~** to meet one's match; **nul ne peut servir deux ~s** a man cannot serve two masters.

maître-à-danser, *pl* **maîtres-à-danser** /mɛtʀadɑ̃se/ *nm* Tech inside calliper[GB].

maître-assistant, ~e, *mpl* **maîtres-assistants** /mɛtʀasistɑ̃, ɑ̃t/ *nm,f* Univ ≈ senior lecturer GB, senior instructor US.

maître-autel, *pl* **maîtres-autels** /mɛtʀotɛl/ *nm* high altar.

maître-chanteur, *pl* **maîtres-chanteurs** /mɛtʀəʃɑ̃tœʀ/ *nm* blackmailer.

maître-chien, *pl* **maîtres-chiens** /mɛtʀəʃjɛ̃/ *nm* dog-handler.

maître-cylindre, *pl* **maîtres-cylindres** /mɛtʀəsilɛ̃dʀ/ *nm* Aut master cylinder.

maître-nageur, *pl* **maîtres-nageurs** /mɛtʀənaʒœʀ/ **▶510** *nm* **1** (enseignant) swimming instructor; **2** (surveillant) (de piscine) pool attendant; (de plage) lifeguard.

■ **~ sauveteur** lifeguard.

maîtrisable /mɛtʀizabl/ *adj* [*problème, sentiment*] containable; **coût ~** cost which can be kept down; **effet ~** effect which can be controlled; **non ~** uncontrollable.

maîtrise /mɛtʀiz/ *nf* **1** (virtuosité) mastery ¢; **grande ~** absolute mastery; **admirer la ~ d'un musicien** to admire the mastery of a musician; **avec ~** masterfully; **2** (connaissance approfondie) perfect command; **une ~ de la langue/du domaine** a perfect command of the language/of the field; **3** (calme) **~ (de soi)** self-control ¢; **faire preuve d'une ~ impressionnante** to show admirable self-control; **4** (contrôle) control; **~ de l'inflation/des dépenses publiques** control of inflation/of public expenditure; **conserver la ~ d'une entreprise/des sols** to retain control of a company/of land; **la ~ de la qualité** quality control; **5** (exploitation) harnessing; **~ de l'énergie/l'atome** harnessing of energy/nuclear energy; **6** Mil (domination) supremacy; **avoir la ~ aérienne/navale/terrestre** to have air/sea/land supremacy; **7** Entr (catégorie professionnelle) supervisory management; **8** Univ master's degree; **une ~ d'anglais** a master's in English; **9** Mus (chœur) choir; (école) choir school.

■ **~ de conférences** Univ ≈ senior lectureship GB, associate professorship US; **~ d'œuvre** undertaking of a contract.

maîtriser /mɛtʀize/ [1] **I** *vtr* **1** (contenir) to control [*sentiment, urbanisme, rire, dépenses, manifestation, destin*]; to get [sth] under control [*épidémie*]; to bring [sth] under control [*incendie*]; to overcome [*forcené, adversaire*]; to control [*enfant, animal*]; to hold back [*flots*]; to handle [*panne, problème*]; to stem the tide of [*immigration*]; **2** (connaître parfaitement) to master [*langue, sujet, technique*].

II se maîtriser *vpr* to have self-control; **ne plus se ~** to have lost one's self-control.

maïzena® /maizena/ *nf* cornflour.

majesté /maʒɛste/ *nf* (grandeur) majesty (**de** of); **Christ en ~** Christ in majesty; **un air de ~** an air of dignity; **sa Majesté** His/Her Majesty.

majestueusement /maʒɛstɥøzmɑ̃/ *adv* majestically.

majestueux, -euse /maʒɛstɥø, øz/ *adj* [*bâtiment, avenue*] majestic; [*personne, démarche*] stately.

majeur, ~e /maʒœʀ/ **I** *adj* **1** Jur of age (*jamais épith*) spéc; **être ~** to be over 18 ou of age spéc; **elle sera ~e en mai** she will be 18 in May ou come of age in May spéc; **les étudiants ~s** students (who are) over 18; **2** (le plus important) [*cause, défi*] main, major; (en logique) [*terme, prémisse*] major; **c'est un problème ~** it's a major problem; **c'est le problème ~** it's the main problem; **la ~e partie de ma carrière** most of ou the major part of my career; **en ~e partie** for the most part; **3** Mus major; **en ré ~** in D major; **4** Jeux **tierce/quinte ~e** tierce/quint major; **5** Relig **ordres ~s** major orders.

II *nm,f* (en âge) person over 18, major spéc.

III *nm* (doigt) middle finger.

Majeur /maʒœʀ/ **▶459** *npr* **le lac ~** Lake Maggiore.

major /maʒɔʀ/ *nm* **1** Univ **sortir ~ de sa promotion** to come first in one's year; **2** **▶390** Mil (dans l'armée de terre, de l'air) *French rank above that of warrant officer* GB ou *chief warrant officer* US; (dans la marine) *French rank above that of fleet chief petty officer* GB ou *chief warrant officer* US.

majoration /maʒɔʀasjɔ̃/ *nf* (tous contextes) increase; **une ~ de 2%** an increase of 2%, a 2% increase; **la ~ des cotisations** the increase in contributions.

majordome /maʒɔʀdɔm/ *nm* butler, majordomo.

majorer /maʒɔʀe/ [1] *vtr* to increase; **~ une somme de 10 francs/15%** to increase a sum by 10 francs/15%.

majorette /maʒɔʀɛt/ *nf* majorette.

majoritaire /maʒɔʀitɛʀ/ *adj* [*parti, scrutin, système, actionnaire*] majority (*épith*);

coton/laine ~ cotton/wool blend; **être ~ dans une assemblée/une région** to have the majority in an assembly/a region.

majoritairement /maʒɔʀitɛʀmɑ̃/ *adv* **1** (à la majorité) [*décider, choisir*] by a majority (vote); **2** (en majorité) **province ~ catholique/socialiste** predominantly Catholic/socialist province; **les capitaux ne sont pas ~ européens** the funds are not, for the most part, European.

majorité /maʒɔʀite/ *nf* **1** (dans un vote) majority; **~ absolue** absolute majority; **~ relative** or **simple** simple majority; **avoir la ~** to have a majority; **être élu à une forte/faible ~** to be elected with a large/small majority; **texte adopté à la ~ des deux-tiers** law passed with a two-thirds majority; **approuvé par une ~ de 70% des votants** approved by a majority of 70% of the voters; **la ~ silencieuse** the silent majority; **2** (des gens, choses) majority; **la ~ de la population** most of the population; **la ~ des cas** the majority of cases; **la ~ d'entre eux sont des toxicomanes** most of them are drug-users; **la ~ des députés a voté pour la motion** the majority of deputies voted for the motion; **ils sont en ~** they are in the majority; **ce sont, en ~, des enfants** they are, for the most part, children; **pays à ~ catholique** predominantly Catholic country; **3** (parti majoritaire) **la ~** the government; **dans les rangs de la ~** in government ranks; **un élu de la ~** an elected representative of the party in power.

■ **~ qualifiée** Pol qualified majority.

Majorque /majɔʀk/ ▶ **416** *nprf* Majorca.

majorquin, ~e /majɔʀkɛ̃, in/ *adj* Majorcan.

majuscule /maʒyskyl/ **I** *adj* (en écriture) capital; Imprim upper-case; **A ~** capital A, upper-case A.

II *nf* (en écriture) capital (letter); Imprim upper-case letter; **écrire en ~s** to write in (block) capitals.

mal, *mpl* **maux** /mal, mo/ ▶ **271** **I** *adj inv* **1** (répréhensible) wrong; **qu'a-t-elle fait de ~?** what has she done wrong?; **c'est ~ de faire** it's wrong to do; **2** (mauvais) bad; **ce ne serait pas ~ de déménager** it wouldn't be a bad idea to move out; ▶ **an**; **3**○ **un film pas ~** a rather good film; **elle est pas ~** (physiquement) she's rather good looking; **c'est quelqu'un de pas ~** (sous tous rapports) he's/she's really nice; **'et l'autre robe?'—'pas ~!'** 'and the other dress?'—'it's not bad!'; **pas ~ la robe!** what a great dress!

II *nm* **1** (peine) **sans ~** easily; **sans trop de ~** quite easily; **non sans ~** not without difficulty; **avoir du ~ à faire** to find it difficult to do; **avoir beaucoup/un peu de ~ à faire** to find it very/a bit difficult to do; **avoir un ~ fou**○ or **de chien**○ **à faire** to have a hell of a job○ doing; **se donner du ~ pour faire qch** to go to a lot of trouble to do sth; **se donner beaucoup de ~ pour qn/pour faire qch** to go to a great deal of trouble on sb's account/to do sth; **ne te donne pas ce ~!** don't bother!; **donne-toi un peu de ~!** make some effort!; **2** (douleur) **faire ~** lit, fig to hurt; **se faire ~** to hurt oneself; **ça ne fait pas ~** it doesn't hurt; **ça va faire ~** lit it's going to hurt ou be painful; (nouvel impôt) it's going to hurt; (apprendre la vérité) it's going to be painful; (être remarquable) it's going to be big○; **j'ai ~** it hurts; **avoir ~ partout** to ache all over; **elle avait très ~** she was in pain; **ma jambe me fait ~** my leg hurts; **ces bottes me font ~ aux pieds** these boots hurt my feet; **avoir ~ à la tête/à l'estomac** to have a headache/a stomach-ache; **avoir ~ au dos/aux dents/aux oreilles** to have backache/toothache/earache; **avoir ~ à la gorge** to have a sore throat; **j'ai ~ aux yeux** my eyes are sore; **j'ai ~ au genou/au cou/au doigt** my knee/neck/finger hurts; **j'ai ~ au cœur** I feel sick GB ou nauseous US; **j'ai ~ au ventre** I have a stomach-ache; **ça me fait ~ au ventre** lit it gives me a stomach-ache; fig○ I find it really upsetting; **j 'ai ~ aux articulations** I have aching joints; **souffrir mille maux** to suffer the torments of the damned; **3** (maladie) **~ sans gravité** minor illness; **~ incurable** incurable disease; **le ~ a progressé** the disease has got GB ou gotten US worse; **tu vas attraper du ~**○ you'll catch something; ▶ **remède**, **patience**; **4** (manque) **être en ~ de** (ne pas avoir) to be short of; (ne pas recevoir) to be lacking in; **être en ~ d'inspiration** to be short of inspiration; **être en ~ d'affection** to be lacking in affection; **5** (dommage) **le ~ est fait** the harm is done; **faire du ~ à** (durablement) to harm [*personne, économie*]; (momentanément) to hurt [*personne, économie*]; **il n'y a pas de ~** or **grand ~ à cela** there's no harm in that; **il n'y a pas de ~** (formule de politesse) there's no harm done; **une douche ne te fera pas de ~** hum a shower wouldn't do you any harm; **ne rien faire de ~** not to do anything wrong; **quel ~ y a-t-il à cela?** what harm is there in that?; **mettre à ~ qch** to damage sth; **mettre à ~ qn** to give sb a hard time; **6** (calamité) **qu'elle parte, est-ce vraiment un ~?** is it really a bad thing that she is leaving?; **un ~ à combattre** an evil that must be fought; **7** (méchanceté) **penser à ~** to have evil intentions; **sans songer** or **penser à ~** without meaning any harm; **dire du ~ de qn/qch** to speak ill of sb/sth; **après avoir fait le ~ pendant des années** after years of evil-doing; **8** Philos, Relig evil; **conflit entre le bien et le ~** conflict between good and evil; **forces du ~** forces of evil.

III *adv* **1** (avec incompétence) [*fait, écrit, conçu, lire, conduire*] badly; **elle travaille ~** her work isn't good; **elle joue ~** (maintenant) she's playing badly; (en général) she's not a good player; **s'y prendre ~ avec qn** to deal with sb the wrong way; **pas ~ écrit/conçu** rather well written/designed; **pas trop ~ écrit/conçu** quite well written/designed; ▶ **étreindre**; **2** (de manière défectueuse) **~ fonctionner/ouvrir** not to work/open properly; **fonctionner très ~** not to work properly GB ou right US at all; **enfant ~ élevé** badly brought up child; **c'est un petit ~ élevé** he's a badly brought up little brat; **elle est ~ en point** she's not too good; (très grave) she's in a bad way; **dire quelque chose ~ à propos** to make an inappropriate remark; **3** (difficilement) **ça s'explique ~** it's difficult to explain; **on voit ~ comment** it's difficult to see how; **marcher ~** [*personne*] to walk with difficulty; **4** (insuffisamment) [*éclairé*] poorly, badly; [*payé*] badly; **je t'entends ~** I can't hear you very well; **il entend ~** (permanent) he's slightly deaf, he doesn't hear very well; **ils mangent ~** they don't eat very well; **je les connais ~** I don't know them well; **~ entretenu** neglected; **pas ~ payé/équipé** rather well-paid/-equipped; ▶ **cordonnier**; **5** (sans goût) [*s'habiller, meubler*] badly; **6** (de manière erronée) [*diagnostiqué, adressé*] wrongly; **~ m'a pris de faire ça** I should never have done that; **~ interpréter** to misinterpret; **j'avais ~ compris** I had misunderstood; **~ informé** ill-informed; **7** (défavorablement) **aller ~** [*personne*] not to be well; [*affaires, vie*] to go badly; [*vêtement*] not to fit well; **'comment va-t-elle?'—'~!'** 'how is she?'—'not very well!'; **le vert te va pas ~**○ green rather suits you!; **aller de plus en plus ~** [*personne*] to be getting worse; [*affaires, vie*] to get worse and worse; **se sentir ~** (santé) not to feel well; (mal à l'aise) to feel awkward; **se trouver ~** to faint; **être ~** [*personne*] to feel awful; **être ~** (**assis** or **couché** or **installé**) not to be comfortable; **être au plus ~** to be critically ill; **être ~ remis** not to have fully recovered; **dormir/tourner/commencer ~** to sleep/to turn out/to begin badly; **ne le prenez pas ~** don't take it badly ou the wrong way; **être ~ avec qn** to be on bad terms with sb; **se mettre ~ avec qn** to fall out with sb; **être ~ vu** not to be well thought of; **aller pas ~**○ [*personne, affaires*] to be fine; **8** (de manière critiquable) [*se conduire*] badly; **~ faire** to do wrong; **ils nous traitent ~** (employeurs) they don't treat us well; **traiter ~** (frapper) to ill-treat; **se tenir ~** (grossièrement) to have bad manners; (voûté) to have a bad posture; **elle parle ~** she uses bad language; **tu as ~ agi** you shouldn't have done that; **il serait ~ venu de faire** it would be unseemly to do; ▶ **acquis**.

IV○ **pas mal** *loc adv* (beaucoup) **il a pas ~ bu** he's had quite a lot to drink; **il a bu pas ~ de bière** he's drunk quite a lot of beer; **elle a pas ~ d'amis** she has quite a few friends; **il est pas ~ violent** he's rather violent; **ça a mis pas ~ de temps** it took quite a long time.

■ **~ de l'air** airsickness; **avoir le ~ de l'air** (ponctuellement) to feel airsick; (généralement) to suffer from airsickness; **~ blanc** whitlow; **~ de dents** toothache; **avoir des maux de dents** to have frequent toothache GB ou toothaches US; **~ de dos** backache ₵; **~ d'estomac** stomach-ache; **avoir des maux d'estomac** (ponctuellement) to have a stomach-ache; (souvent) to suffer from stomach-ache GB ou stomach-aches US; **~ de gorge** sore throat; **avoir un ~ de gorge** to have a sore throat; **avoir des maux de gorge** to get sore throats; **~ des grands ensembles** *social problems attendant on high-density housing*; **~ de mer** seasickness; **avoir le ~ de mer** (ponctuellement) to feel seasick; (généralement) to suffer from seasickness; **~ du pays** homesickness; **avoir le ~ du pays** to feel homesick; **~ du siècle** world-weariness; **~ de tête** headache; **avoir des maux de tête** (ponctuellement) to have headaches; (souvent) to suffer from ou get headaches; **~ des transports** motion sickness; **avoir le ~ des transports** to be prone to motion sickness.

IDIOMES **ça me ferait ~ (aux seins)**◑ (d'étonnement) I'd be amazed; (d'écœurement) it would really piss me off◑; **entre** or **de deux maux il faut choisir le moindre** Prov it's a matter of choosing the lesser of two evils.

malabar○ /malabaʀ/ *nm* beefy bloke○ GB ou guy○ US.

Malacca /malaka/ *npr* **presqu'île de ~** Malay peninsula.

Malachie /malaki/ *npr* Bible Malachi.

malachite /malakit/ *nf* malachite.

malade /malad/ **I** *adj* **1** [*personne*] ill (*épith*), sick; [*animal*] sick; [*arbre, plante*] diseased; **tomber ~** [*personne*] to fall ill ou sick, to get sick US; **être ~** to be ill ou sick; **être ~ en voiture/en bateau/en avion** to get carsick/seasick/airsick; **j'en suis ~** fig it makes me sick; **gravement/très gravement ~** seriously/critically ill; **se rendre ~** to make oneself ill ou sick; **ça le rend ~ rien que d'y penser** it makes him sick just to think about it; **~ de peur/jalousie** sick with fear/jealousy; **être ~ d'inquiétude** to be worried sick; **se faire porter ~** to report sick; **2** [*poumons, côlon*] diseased; [*dent*] bad; [*œil, jambe*] (par maladie) diseased; (par accident) injured; [*corps, esprit*] sick; **3**○ (fou) crazy; **être ~ (de la tête)**○ to be crazy; **4** (en mauvais état) **être ~** [*entreprise, institution, pays, objet*] to be in a bad way ou sorry state; **le pays est ~ de l'inflation** the country is suffering from inflation.

II *nmf* gén sick man/woman; (dans un cadre médical ou hospitalier) patient; **les ~s** the sick, the patients; **son mari est un grand ~** her husband is seriously ill.

■ **~ imaginaire** hypochondriac; **~ mental** mentally ill person; **les ~s mentaux** the mentally ill; **c'est un ~ mental** he's mentally ill.

IDIOMES **être ~ comme un chien**○ or **une bête**○ gén to be really ill; (vomir) to be as sick as a dog.

maladie /maladi/ *nf* **1** (d'un malade) illness; (affection) disease; Admin sickness; **allocation ~** sickness benefit; **congé ~** sick leave; **pendant sa longue ~** during his long illness; **~s chroniques/contagieuses** chronic/contagious diseases; **~ des poumons/de peau** lung/skin disease; **~ vénérienne** venereal disease, VD; **une ~ mentale** a mental illness; **~ infantile** lit childhood disease; fig teething troubles (*pl*); **il va en faire une ~**○ **si tu oublies** fig he'll have a fit○ if you forget; **c'est une ~ de l'âme** it's a sickness of the soul; **2** (fléau) disease; **la pauvreté et la ~** poverty and disease; **3** (de végétal, d'animal) disease; **4**○ (manie) mania; **avoir la ~ du rangement** to have a mania for tidiness; **c'est une ~ chez lui** he is obsessive (about it); **c'est une ~ chez lui, il est toujours en retard** he's got a terrible habit of always turning up late.
■ **~ bleue** cyanosis; **~ diplomatique** diplomatic illness; **~ honteuse** Méd† venereal disease; fig shameful disease; **~ du légionnaire** legionnaire's disease; **~ professionnelle** occupational disease; **~ sexuellement transmissible, MST** sexually transmitted disease, STD; **~ du sommeil** sleeping sickness; **~ de la vache folle** mad cow disease.

maladif, **-ive** /maladif, iv/ *adj* **1** [*enfant, air*] sickly; **être d'une pâleur maladive** to be unhealthily pale; **2** [*jalousie, timidité*] pathological; **être d'une jalousie maladive** to be pathologically jealous; **il a un besoin ~ de mentir** he's a pathological liar.

maladresse /maladʀɛs/ *nf* **1** (manque d'adresse) clumsiness; **excusez ma ~** forgive my clumsiness; **il est d'une ~!** he's so clumsy!; **2** (manque de tact) tactlessness; **il a agi avec ~ envers elle** he was tactless to her; **3** (manque d'aisance) awkwardness; **s'exprimer avec ~** to express oneself awkwardly; **4** (erreur) (de personne) mistake; (de traduction, texte) clumsy part; **les ~s du gouvernement ont provoqué le mécontentement** mistakes by the government gave rise to discontent; **il y a des ~s de style dans ta lettre** there are infelicities of style in your letter; **5** (bévue) blunder; **commettre une ~** to make a blunder (**en faisant** by doing); **accumuler les ~s** to make one blunder after another.

maladroit, **~e** /maladʀwa, wat/ **I** *adj* **1** (malhabile) [*personne, geste, œuvre, style, traduction*] clumsy; [*écriture*] faltering; **il est très ~ de ses mains/avec un pinceau** he's very clumsy with his hands/with a brush; **2** (sans tact) [*personne, propos*] tactless; **ce fut très ~ de ta part** it was very tactless of you; **3** (qui manque d'aisance) awkward; **un garçon maigre et ~** a lanky awkward boy; **4** (qui manque de finesse) [*personne, négociations*] inept; **il est trop ~ pour convaincre** he doesn't come over very well.
II *nm,f* (personne gauche) clumsy person; (gaffeur) tactless person; **ce ~ fait tout tomber sur son passage** he's so clumsy, he knocks everything over; **je ne confierais pas cette affaire à un tel ~** I wouldn't trust the deal to such an oaf.

maladroitement /maladʀwatmɑ̃/ *adv* (sans adresse) clumsily; (sans tact) tactlessly; (sans aisance) awkwardly; (sans finesse) ineptly.

malaga /malaga/ *nm* **1** (raisin) Malaga grape; **2** (vin) Malaga.

mal-aimé, **~e**, *mpl* **~s** /malɛme/ **I** *adj* **être ~** to be starved of affection.
II *nm,f* **être le ~ des journalistes** to be unpopular with the press; **les ~s** people who are starved of affection.

malais, **~e**[1] /malɛ, ɛz/ **I** ▶537 *adj* Malay.
II ▶462 *nm* Ling Malay.

Malais, **~e** /malɛ, ɛz/ ▶537 *nm,f* Malay.

malaise[2] /malɛz/ *nm* **1** Méd feeling of faintness; **avoir** or **prendre un ~** to feel faint; **2** (gêne) uneasiness; **il y a (comme) un ~**○ there's a bit of a problem; **3** (état de crise) unrest, malaise sout (**chez** among); **~ politique/des cadres** political/executive unrest; **~ économique** economic malaise.
■ **~ cardiaque** mild heart attack.

malaisé, **~e** /malɛze/ *adj* difficult (**à faire, de faire** to do); **l'entreprise est ~e** it's a difficult undertaking.

Malaisie /malɛzi/ ▶321 *nprf* Malaysia.

malandrin† /malɑ̃dʀɛ̃/ *nm* brigand†.

malappris†, **~e** /malapʀi, iz/ **I** *adj* ill-bred.
II *nm,f* lout.

malaria /malaʀja/ ▶271 *nf* malaria.

malavisé, **~e** /malavize/ *adj* ill-advised, unwise (**de faire** to do).

Malawi /malawi/ ▶321 *nprm* Malawi.

malawien, **-ienne** /malawjɛ̃, ɛn/ ▶537 *adj* Malawian.

Malawien, **-ienne** /malawjɛ̃, ɛn/ ▶537 *nm,f* Malawian.

malaxage /malaksaʒ/ *nm* (de beurre) creaming; (de pâte) kneading; (de béton) mixing.

malaxer /malakse/ [1] *vtr* **1** (pétrir) to cream [*beurre*]; to knead [*pâte*]; **2** (mélanger) **~ qch et** or **avec qch** to mix sth and sth; **~ du ciment** to mix cement.

malaxeur /malaksœʀ/ *nm* mixer.

malchance /malʃɑ̃s/ *nf* bad luck, misfortune; **avoir la ~ de faire** to have the bad luck to do; **jouer de ~** to be dogged by bad luck; **par ~** as ill luck would have it.

malchanceux, **-euse** /malʃɑ̃sø, øz/ **I** *adj* unlucky.
II *nm,f* unlucky person.

malcommode /malkɔmɔd/ *adj* inconvenient.

Maldives /maldiv/ ▶416, 321 *nprfpl* **les (îles) ~** the Maldives, the Maldive Islands.

maldonne /maldɔn/ *nf* (aux cartes) misdeal; (malentendu) misunderstanding; **il y a ~** lit there's been a misdeal; fig there's been a misunderstanding; **faire ~** to misdeal.

mâle /mɑl/ **I** *adj* **1** Biol [*hormone*] male; **2** Bot [*plante, fleur*] male; **3** Zool gén male; [*éléphant, baleine*] bull; [*antilope, lièvre, lapin*] buck; [*moineau, perroquet*] cock; **cygne ~** cob; **canard ~** drake; **homard ~** cock lobster; **4** Électrotech [*fiche, prise*] male; **5** (viril) [*voix, assurance*] manly.
II *nm* **1** Zool (animal du sexe fécondant) male; **2** Zool (partenaire sexuel) mate; **3** hum (homme viril) **(beau) ~** he-man○.

malédiction /malediksjɔ̃/ **I** *nf* curse; **la ~ pèse sur eux** there's a curse on them.
II† *excl* curses!

maléfice /malefis/ *nm* evil spell.

maléfique /malefik/ *adj* [*influence*] evil, baleful littér.

malencontreusement /malɑ̃kɔ̃tʀøzmɑ̃/ *adv* [*survenir*] inopportunely; [*annoncer*] inappropriately; **j'avais ~ oublié mon chéquier** unfortunately, I had forgotten my cheque GB ou check US book.

malencontreux, **-euse** /malɑ̃kɔ̃tʀø, øz/ *adj* [*erreur, remarque*] unfortunate.

malentendant, **~e** /malɑ̃tɑ̃dɑ̃, ɑ̃t/ **I** *adj* **être ~** to be hard of hearing; **elle est ~e** she's hard of hearing.
II *nm,f* person who is hearing-impaired; **les ~s** the hearing-impaired.

malentendu /malɑ̃tɑ̃dy/ *nm* misunderstanding; **dissiper** or **faire cesser un ~** to clear up a misunderstanding.

mal-être /malɛtʀ/ *nm inv* malaise.

malfaçon /malfasɔ̃/ *nf* defect (*caused by bad workmanship*); **il y a eu ~ dans le mur** the wall has been badly done.

malfaisance /malfəzɑ̃s/ *nf* (de personne) evil disposition; (d'idéologie) harmful effect.

malfaisant, **~e** /malfəzɑ̃, ɑ̃t/ *adj* [*personne, génie*] evil; [*influence, idéologie*] harmful.

malfaiteur /malfɛtœʀ/ *nm* criminal, malefactor sout; **association de ~s** criminal conspiracy.

malformation /malfɔʀmasjɔ̃/ *nf* malformation (**de** of).

malfrat○ /malfʀa/ *nm* criminal.

malgache /malgaʃ/ ▶537, 462 *adj, nm* Malagasy.

Malgache /malgaʃ/ ▶537 *nmf* Malagasy.

malgracieux, **-ieuse** /malgʀasjø, øz/ *adj* unpleasant.

malgré /malgʀe/ **I** *prép* in spite of, despite; **~ les efforts de qn** despite sb's efforts; **~ les apparences** in spite of appearances; **~ le froid/le soleil** despite the cold/the sun; **elle l'a épousé ~ son âge** she married him in spite of his age; **elle est toujours belle ~ les années** she's still beautiful despite her years; **leur amitié est toujours solide ~ les années** they are still very close friends in spite of the years; **~ le fait que** in spite of ou despite the fact that; **nous avons acheté la maison ~ son prix** we bought the house in spite of the price; **nous avons acheté la maison ~ son prix élevé** we bought the house although it was expensive; **~ d'incontestables progrès** although there has been clear progress; **~ l'absence de liens diplomatiques entre les deux pays** although the two countries have no diplomatic ties; **~ cela, ~ tout** nevertheless; **~ qn** against sb's wishes; **~ soi** in spite of oneself; **presque ~ soi** [*accorder, signer*] against one's better judgment, reluctantly; [*aller, assister, épouser*] reluctantly.
II malgré que *loc conj* **1** (bien que) controv even though; **2** littér **~ qu'il en ait** in spite of his wishes to the contrary.

malhabile /malabil/ *adj* clumsy.

malhabilement /malabilmɑ̃/ *adv* clumsily.

malheur /malœʀ/ **I** *nm* **1** (adversité) adversity, misfortune; **même dans le ~** even in adversity; **tomber dans le ~** to be struck by misfortune; **avoir sa part de ~** to have one's share of misfortune; **elle fait le ~ de sa famille** she brings her family nothing but unhappiness; ▶**bonheur**; **2** (coup du sort) misfortune; (grave) tragedy; (accident) accident; **une série de ~s** a series of misfortunes; **les ~s qui l'ont frappé** the misfortunes that befell him; **le grand ~ de ma jeunesse** the great tragedy of my youth; **un ~ est si vite arrivé!** accidents can so easily happen!; **il leur arrivera ~!** something terrible will happen to them!; **tous nos petits ~s** all our little troubles; **raconter ses ~s à qn** to tell sb one's troubles; **le grand ~!** so what!; **3** (malchance) misfortune; **jouer de ~** to be dogged by misfortune; **ceux qui ont le ~ de perdre leur emploi** those who are unfortunate enough ou have the misfortune to lose their jobs; **j'ai eu le ~ de le leur dire** I made the mistake of telling them; **pour mon ~** unfortunately for me; **par ~ il y avait grève ce jour-là, le ~ a voulu qu'il y ait grève ce jour-là** as bad luck would have it, there was a strike that day; **si par ~ la guerre éclatait** if war should break out, which God forbid; **porter ~** to be ou bring bad luck; **le ~, c'est que...** the trouble is,...; **son ~, c'est qu'elle est paresseuse** her trouble is that she's lazy; **~ à qui...** woe betide anyone who...; **ce temps de ~**○ this wretched weather.
II *excl* **~! ne dis jamais ça!** for heaven's sake! don't ever say such a thing!; **(oh) ~! il nous a vus!** oh my God○, he's seen us!
IDIOMES **il va faire un ~**○ (avoir du succès) he'll be a sensation; (être violent) he'll do something he'll regret; (faire un éclat) he'll cause a scene; **un ~ n'arrive jamais seul** Prov it never rains but it pours; **à quelque chose ~ est bon** Prov every cloud has a silver lining Prov.

malheureusement /maløʀøzmɑ̃/ *adv* unfortunately.

malheureux, **-euse** /maløʀø, øz/ **I** *adj* **1** (pas heureux) [*personne, visage, vie*] unhappy; (plus fort) miserable; **rendre qn ~** to make sb unhappy; **je suis ~ de ne (pas) pouvoir** I'm really unhappy that I can't; **ne prends pas cet air ~!** don't look so miserable; **si c'est pas ~**○ **de voir/d'entendre** isn't it awful to see/hear; **2** (à plaindre) [*victime*] unfortunate; **3** (marqué par la malchance) [*candidat*] unlucky (**en** in); [*coïncidence*] unfortunate; [*passion*] ill-fated; **~ en affaires** unlucky in business; **être ~ au jeu** to be an unlucky gambler; (aux cartes) to be unlucky at cards; **4** (regrettable) [*mot, geste, choix*] unfortunate; **une initiative malheureuse** an unfortunate move; **c'est bien ~ mais c'est comme ça** it's very unfortunate but that's how it is; **c'est ~ que tu ne puisses pas venir** it's a pity ou shame that you can't come; **'j'ai fini!'—'ce n'est pas ~**○**!'** 'I've finished!'—'about time too!'; **5** (négligeable) [*somme*] paltry, pathetic; **pour trois ~ francs** for a paltry three francs; **seulement dix ~ visiteurs** only a pathetic ten visitors.
II *nm,f* **1** (personne peu chanceuse) **le ~/la malheureuse a cru que**... the poor man/the poor woman thought that...; **il a souffert, le ~!** he really went through it, poor man!; **ne fais pas cela, malheureuse!** don't do that, for heaven's sake; **2** (personne indigente) poor person; **les ~** the needy.
IDIOMES **être ~ comme les pierres** to be as miserable as sin; **heureux au jeu, ~ en amour** Prov lucky at cards, unlucky in love Prov.

malhonnête /malɔnɛt/ **I** *adj* **1** (indélicat) [*commerçant, politicien, conduite*] dishonest; **2**† (inconvenant) improper; **faire des propositions ~s** to make improper suggestions.
II *nmf* **1** (personne indélicate) dishonest person; **2** (personne incivile) rude person.

malhonnêtement /malɔnɛtmɑ̃/ *adv* dishonestly.

malhonnêteté /malɔnɛtte/ *nf* (de personne, projet) dishonesty.

Mali /mali/ **▶321** *nprm* Mali.

malice /malis/ *nf* **1** (taquinerie) mischief; **avec** or **non sans ~** mischievously; **2**† (malveillance) malice; **être sans ~** to be harmless; **ne pas entendre ~ à** (propos émis) to mean no harm by; (propos perçus) to see no harm in.

malicieusement /malisjøzmɑ̃/ *adv* mischievously.

malicieux, **-ieuse** /malisjø, øz/ *adj* [*enfant, esprit, regard*] mischievous.

malien, **-ienne** /maljɛ̃, ɛn/ **▶537** *adj* Malian.

Malien, **-ienne** /maljɛ̃, ɛn/ **▶537** *nm,f* Malian.

maligne ▶ **malin**.

malignité /maliɲite/ *nf* malignancy.

malin, **maligne** /malɛ̃, maliɲ/ **I** *adj* **1** (intelligent) [*personne, air, esprit*] clever; **être ~** to be clever; **il est trop ~ pour se laisser prendre** he's too clever to be taken in; **elle n'est pas bien** or **très maligne** she isn't very bright; **j'ai eu l'air ~!** iron I looked a right fool○ GB, I looked like a total fool!; **c'est ~**○**!** iron very clever!; **ce n'est pas (très) ~**○ **de ta part** that wasn't very clever ou bright of you; **bien ~ celui qui peut me dire** a prize for anyone who can tell me; **2**○ (difficile) **ce n'est pas plus ~ que ça** that's all there is to it; **ce n'est pas bien ~** it's not exactly difficult; **3** (méchant) malicious; **prendre un ~ plaisir à faire** to take malicious pleasure in doing; **l'esprit ~** the Evil One, the Devil; **4** Méd [*tumeur*] malignant.
II *nm,f* **1** (personne rusée) clever person; **un petit ~**○ (enfant) a little devil○; iron smart aleck○; **regardez-moi ce gros ~**○**!** who's the bright spark○ GB ou the smart one US!; **faire le** or **son ~**○ to show off; **jouer au plus ~**○ to play the wise guy○; **2** Littérat **le Malin** Satan, the Devil.
IDIOMES **à ~, ~ et demi** Prov there's always someone who will outwit you.

malingre /malɛ̃gʀ/ *adj* [*personne, arbre*] sickly; [*bras*] wasted.

malintentionné, **~e** /malɛ̃tɑ̃sjɔne/ *adj* malicious.

malle /mal/ *nf* **1** Aut **~ (arrière)** boot GB, trunk US; **2** (coffre, valise) trunk; **faire ses ~s** to pack one's bags; **se faire la ~**◑ to clear off○.

malléabilité /maleabilite/ *nf* malleability.

malléable /maleabl/ *adj* malleable.

malle-poste, *pl* **malles-poste** /malpɔst/ *nf* mail coach.

mallette /malɛt/ *nf* (d'enfant) vanity case; (pour le bureau) briefcase; (pour les voyages) overnight case.
■ **~ pédagogique** information pack.

mal-logé, **~e**, *mpl* **~s** /mallɔʒe/ *nm,f*: *person living in substandard accommodation*.

malmener /malməne/ [16] *vtr* **1** (maltraiter) to manhandle [*personne*]; **2** (mettre en difficulté) to give [sb] a rough ride [*adversaire*]; **3** (critiquer) to slate○ GB, to trash○ US [*auteur, œuvre*]; **4** [*auteur, élève*] to misuse [*langue, grammaire*].

malnutrition /malnytʀisjɔ̃/ *nf* malnutrition.

malodorant, **~e** /malɔdɔʀɑ̃, ɑ̃t/ *adj* foul-smelling (*épith*).

malotru, **~e** /malɔtʀy/ *nm,f* boor.

malouin, **~e** /malwɛ̃, in/ **▶857** *adj* of Saint-Malo.

Malouin, **~e** /malwɛ̃, in/ **I** *nm,f* **1** (natif) native of Saint-Malo; **2** (habitant) inhabitant of Saint-Malo.
II Malouines ▶416 *nprfpl* **les (îles) ~es** the Falklands, the Falkland Islands.

malpoli○, **~e** /malpɔli/ **I** *adj* rude.
II *nm,f* rude person; **c'est un ~/une ~e** he/she has bad manners.

malpropre /malpʀɔpʀ/ **I** *adj* **1** (sale) [*personne, visage, chambre, habit*] dirty; **2** (malhonnête) [*individu, conduite, manœuvres*] unsavoury[GB].
II *nmf* (personne peu recommandable) unsavoury[GB] individual; **se faire renvoyer** or **jeter comme un ~** to be chucked out○.

malproprement /malpʀɔpʀəmɑ̃/ *adv* [*manger*] messily; [*travailler*] sloppily.

malpropreté /malpʀɔpʀəte/ *nf* **1** (saleté) dirtiness; **vivre dans la ~** to live in squalor; **2** (acte malhonnête) dirty trick○.

malsain, **~e** /malsɛ̃, ɛn/ *adj* lit, fig unhealthy.

malséant, **~e** /malseɑ̃, ɑ̃t/ *adj* unseemly.

malsonnant, **~e** /malsɔnɑ̃, ɑ̃t/ *adj* offensive.

malt /malt/ *nm* malt; **de ~** malt (*épith*); **whisky pur ~** pure malt whisky.

maltage /maltaʒ/ *nm* malting.

maltais, **~e** /maltɛ, ɛz/ **I ▶537** *adj* Maltese.
II ▶462 *nm* Ling Maltese.
III maltaise *nf* (orange) Maltese orange.

Maltais, **~e** /maltɛ, ɛz/ **▶537** *nm,f* Maltese.

maltase /maltɑz/ *nf* maltase.

Malte /malt/ **▶416**, **321** *nprf* **(l'île de) ~** Malta.

malté, **~e** /malte/ *adj* [*orge, lait*] malted; [*biscuit*] malt (*épith*); [*goût*] malty.

malthusianisme /maltyzjanism/ *nm* Malthusianism; **~ économique** Malthusian economics (+ *v sg*).

malthusien, **-ienne** /maltyzjɛ̃, ɛn/ *adj* Malthusian.

maltose /maltoz/ *nm* maltose.

maltraiter /maltʀɛte/ [1] *vtr* **1** (rudoyer) to mistreat [*personne, animal*]; **2** (critiquer) to slate○ GB, to trash○ US [*auteur, ouvrage, spectacle*]; **3** [*auteur, élève*] to misuse [*langue, grammaire*].

malus /malys/ *nm inv* Assur loaded premium.

malveillance /malvɛjɑ̃s/ *nf* **1** (antipathie) malice; **2** (intention de nuire) malicious intent; **incendie dû à la ~** malicious arson.

malveillant, **~e** /malvɛjɑ̃, ɑ̃t/ **I** *adj* [*personne*] malicious; [*propos, regard*] malicious.
II *nm,f* malicious person.

malvenu, **~e** /malvəny/ *adj* [*propos, intervention*] out of place (*jamais épith*); **tu es ~ de te plaindre** you're in no position to complain.

malversation /malvɛʀsasjɔ̃/ *nf* gén malpractice **¢**; Fin embezzlement **¢**; **commettre des ~s** to embezzle money.

malvoisie /malvwazi/ *nm* malmsey (wine).

malvoyant, **~e** /malvwajɑ̃, ɑ̃t/ **I** *adj* partially sighted.
II *nm,f* partially sighted person; **les ~s** the partially sighted.

maman /mɑmɑ̃/ *nf* mum○ GB, mom○ US, mummy○ GB, mommy○ US, mother; **les ~s peuvent venir aider** mothers can come and help.

mambo /mɑ̃mbo/ *nm* mambo.

mamelle /mamɛl/ *nf* **1** Zool (pis) udder; (de chat, chien) teat; **2**† or pej (sein) bosom†, tit◑.

mamelon /mamlɔ̃/ *nm* **1** Anat nipple; **2** Géog hillock, mamelon spéc.

mamelouk /mamluk/ *nm* Mameluke.

mamie /mami/ *nf* **1** (grand-mère) granny○, grandma○; **2** (vieille femme) pej old granny○ péj.

mammaire /mamɛʀ/ *adj* mammary.

mammectomie /mamɛktɔmi/ *nf* mastectomy.

mammifère /mamifɛʀ/ **I** *adj* [*animal*] mammiferous.
II *nm* mammal; **un ~ marin** a marine mammal.
III mammifères *nmpl* (classe) mammals, Mammalia spéc.

mammographie /mamɔgʀafi/ *nf* mammography.

mammouth /mamut/ *nm* mammoth.

mammy = **mamie**.

mamours○ /mamuʀ/ *nmpl* display (*sg*) of affection; **faire des ~ à qn** to be affectionate with sb.

mam'selle○, **mam'zelle**○ /mamzɛl/ *nf* miss.

mamy = **mamie**.

manade /manad/ *nf* herd of bulls or horses.

management /manaʒmɑ̃/ *nm* management.

manager[1] /manaʒœʀ/ *nm* = **manageur**.

manager[2] /manaʒe/ [13] *vtr* to manage [*entreprise, équipe, artiste*].

manageur /manaʒœʀ/ **▶510** *nm* manager.

manant† /manɑ̃/ *nm* **1** Hist (paysan) peasant; **2** pej (homme grossier) boor.

manche /mɑ̃ʃ/ **I** *nm* **1** (pour tenir) (d'outil, ustensile) handle; (de violon, guitare) neck; ▶ **cognée**; **2** (os) (de gigot) knuckle; (de côtelette) bone; **3**○ (maladroit) clumsy idiot; **peindre/jouer comme un ~** to be a hopeless painter/player; **il s'y est pris comme un ~** he set about it in a clumsy fashion.
II *nf* **1** Cout sleeve; **~ courte/trois-quarts** short/three-quarter sleeve; **robe à ~s courtes/longues** short-sleeved/long-sleeved dress; **sans ~s** sleeveless; **2** Jeux, Sport round; (aux cartes) hand; (au bridge) game; (au tennis)† set; **3**○ (quête) **faire la ~** [*baladin*] to pass the hat round[GB]; [*mendiant*] to beg.
■ **~ à air** Naut air shaft; Météo wind sock; **~ à balai** lit broomhandle; (de sorcière) broomstick; Aviat joystick; (personne maigre)○ beanpole; **~ ballon** Mode puff sleeve; **~ chauve-souris** Mode batwing sleeve; **~ gigot** Mode leg-of-mutton sleeve; **~ à incendie** fire hose; **~ kimono** kimono

sleeve; **~ montée** set-in sleeve; **~ raglan** raglan sleeve; **~ tailleur** tailored sleeve; **~ à vent** Naut air shaft.
IDIOMES **être** or **se mettre du côté du ~**○ to be on the winning side; **tomber sur un ~**○ to hit a snag; **avoir qn dans la ~** to have sb in one's pocket; **se faire tirer par la ~** to need coaxing; **c'est une autre paire de ~s**○ it's a different ball game○.

Manche /mɑ̃ʃ/ *nprf* **1** ▶**555** **la ~** the (English) Channel; **le tunnel sous la ~** the Channel tunnel; **2** ▶**692** (département) **la ~** the Manche.

manchette /mɑ̃ʃɛt/ *nf* **1** Mode (de chemise) double cuff; (de protection) oversleeve; (en dentelle) cuff; **2** Presse (titre) headline; **faire la ~** to make the headlines; **3** (coup) chop; **4** (note) marginal note; **en ~** in the margin.

manchon /mɑ̃ʃɔ̃/ *nm* **1** Mode muff; **2** Tech (pièce cylindrique) sleeve; **3** Mil (d'arme) jacket; **4** Anat (d'articulation) sleeve.
■ **~ d'accouplement** Tech joint sleeve; **~ à incandescence** incandescent mantle.

manchot, **-otte** /mɑ̃ʃo, ɔt/ **I** *adj* (d'un bras) one-armed; (d'une main) one-handed; **il est ~** (d'un bras) he's only got one arm; **ne pas être ~**○ to be pretty good with one's hands○.
II *nm,f* (personne) (d'un bras) one-armed person; (d'une main) one-handed person.
III *nm* Zool penguin.
■ **~ empereur** Zool emperor penguin; **~ royal** Zool king penguin.

mandale◑ /mɑ̃dal/ *nf* clout○, slap; **filer une ~ à qn** to give sb a clout○.

mandant, **~e** /mɑ̃dɑ̃, ɑ̃t/ *nm* Jur principal; Pol constituent.

mandarin /mɑ̃daʀɛ̃/ *nm* **1** Hist, fig mandarin; **2** ▶**462** Ling Mandarin (Chinese).

mandarinal, **~e**, *mpl* **-aux** /mɑ̃daʀinal, o/ *adj* mandarin (*épith*).

mandarinat /mɑ̃daʀina/ *nm* **1** Hist mandarinate; **2** pej establishment.

mandarine /mɑ̃daʀin/ *nf* mandarin orange.

mandarinier /mɑ̃daʀinje/ *nm* mandarin tree.

mandat /mɑ̃da/ *nm* **1** Postes money order, postal order GB; **toucher un ~** to cash a money order; **2** (fonction, charge) term of office; **~ présidentiel** presidential term of office; **exercer un** or **son ~** to be in office; **3** (pouvoir) mandate, authorization; **donner ~ à qn de faire** to authorize sb to do; **4** (en droit international) mandate; **sous ~** under mandate; **territoire sous ~** mandate, mandated territory; **être placé sous ~** to become a mandate.
■ **~ d'amener** summons (+ *v sg*); **~ d'arrêt** (arrest) warrant; **~ de comparaître** summons (+ *v sg*); **~ de dépôt** committal order; **~ d'expulsion** (hors d'un pays) expulsion order; (hors d'une maison) eviction order; **~ international** Jur mandate; Postes international money order; **~ de perquisition** search warrant; **~ postal** money order, postal order GB; **~ télégraphique** telegraphic money order.

mandataire /mɑ̃datɛʀ/ *nmf* **1** Jur proxy; **2** (représentant) representative; Comm agent.

mandat-carte, *pl* **mandats-cartes** /mɑ̃dakaʀt/ *nm* postal order (*in the form of a postcard*).

mandatement /mɑ̃datmɑ̃/ *nm* (paiement) payment (by money order).

mandater /mɑ̃date/ [1] *vtr* **1** to appoint [sb] as one's representative; (pour une mission) to give a mandate to; **dûment mandaté par ses électeurs** Pol duly elected; **2** Fin (payer) to pay [sth] by money order [*somme*]; (libeller) to write out a money order for [*somme*].

mandat-lettre, *pl* **mandats-lettres** /mɑ̃dalɛtʀ/ *nm* postal order.

mandchou, **~e** /mɑ̃dʃu/ **I** *adj* Manchu.
II ▶**462** *nm* Ling Manchu.

Mandchou, **~e** /mɑ̃dʃu/ *nm,f* Manchu.

Mandchourie /mɑ̃dʃuʀi/ ▶**692** *nprf* Manchuria.

mandement /mɑ̃dmɑ̃/ *nm* **1** Relig pastoral letter; **2** Jur (ordre) executory formula.

mander† /mɑ̃de/ [1] *vtr* **1** (convoquer) to summon [*personne*] (**à** to); **2** (informer par écrit) **~ qch à qn** to send word to sb of sth.

mandibule /mɑ̃dibyl/ *nf* **1** Anat, Zool mandible; **2**○ (mâchoire) jaw.
IDIOMES **jouer des ~s**○ to feed one's face○.

mandoline /mɑ̃dɔlin/ ▶**534** *nf* mandolin.

mandragore /mɑ̃dʀagɔʀ/ *nf* mandrake.

mandrill /mɑ̃dʀil/ *nm* mandrill.

mandrin /mɑ̃dʀɛ̃/ *nm* (de perceuse) chuck; (pour agrandir un trou) drift; (pour emboutir) punch.

manducation /mɑ̃dykasjɔ̃/ *nf* manducation.

manécanterie /manekɑ̃tʀi/ *nf* choir school.

manège /manɛʒ/ *nm* **1** (de fête foraine) roundabout GB, merry-go-round; **faire un tour de ~** to have a ride on the merry-go-round; **2** Équit (centre équestre) riding school; (piste) **~ (couvert)** indoor school ou arena; **travailler en ~** to school a horse in an arena; **exercice/figure de ~** schooling exercise/movement; **3** (piste de cirque) ring; **4** Agric, Tech (pour puiser) treadmill; **5** (manœuvre habile) (little) trick, (little) game; **j'ai bien observé ton ~** I know what you are up to.

mânes /mɑn/ *nmpl* manes.

maneton /mantɔ̃/ *nm* crankpin.

manette /manɛt/ *nf* **1** gén lever; (de jeu) joystick; **~ des gaz** throttle; **à fond les ~s**○ at full throttle ou (at) full blast; **2** fig (commandes) **~s** controls.

manganate /mɑ̃ganat/ *nm* manganate.

manganèse /mɑ̃ganɛz/ *nm* manganese.

mangeable /mɑ̃ʒabl/ *adj* **1** (raisonnablement bon) edible; **à peine ~** barely edible; **très ~** perfectly acceptable; **2** (propre à la consommation) edible.

mangeaille○ /mɑ̃ʒaj/ *nf* food, grub○.

mange-disque, *pl* **~s** /mɑ̃ʒdisk/ *nm* toy record player.

mangeoire /mɑ̃ʒwaʀ/ *nf* (pour chevaux, bovins) manger; (pour porcs) trough; (pour poules) feeding trough; (pour oiseaux) feeding tray.

manger /mɑ̃ʒe/ [13] **I** *nm* (nourriture) food; **apporter son ~** to bring one's own food.
II *vtr* **1** (consommer) to eat [*nourriture*]; **~ du pain/des cerises/un poulet** to eat bread/cherries/a chicken; **il n'y a rien à ~ dans la maison** there's no food in the house; **qu'est-ce qu'on mange à midi?** what's for lunch?; **je ne vais pas te/la ~**○! fig I won't eat you/her○!; **on en mangerait** he/she/it is good enough to eat; ▶**blé**, **enragé**, **grive**, **pain**, **soupe**; **2** (dépenser) [*personne*] to use up [*capital, économies*]; to go through [*fortune, héritage*]; [*inflation*] to eat away at [*profits, économies*]; [*activité*] to take up [*temps, journées*]; **~ l'argent de qn** [*dépenses*] to eat up sb's money; [*personne*] to go through sb's money; **3** (recouvrir) [*barbe*] to hide [*visage*]; **visage mangé par la barbe** face hidden by a beard; **4** (attaquer) [*rouille, pluie, acide*] to eat away [*métal*]; [*mites*] to eat [*laine*]; **être mangé aux rats** to be gnawed by rats; **être mangé** or **se faire ~ par les moustiques** to be eaten alive by mosquitoes; **être mangé par l'inquiétude** to be consumed with anxiety; **se faire ~ par son concurrent** to be devoured by the competition; **5** (mal articuler) **~ ses mots** not to speak clearly, to mumble.
III *vi* (se nourrir) to eat; **~ dans une assiette/dans un bol** to eat from ou off a plate/out of a bowl; **~ dans la main de qn** lit to eat out of sb's hand; **ils viendront te ~ dans la main** fig you'll have them eating out of your hand; **~ à sa faim** to eat one's fill; **donner à ~ à** to feed [*bébé, animal*]; to give [sb] something to eat [*pauvre*]; **donner** or **faire à ~ à** to cook for [*famille*]; **je leur ai donné des légumes à ~** I gave them some vegetables; **~ froid** (un plat refroidi) to eat [sth] cold [*soupe, quiche*]; (un repas froid) to have a cold meal; **inviter qn à ~** to invite sb for a meal; **je vous invite à ~ à midi** let me take you to lunch; **~ chinois/grec** to have a Chinese/Greek meal; **~ au restaurant** to eat out; **on mange mal ici** the food is not good here; **avoir fini de ~** to have finished one's meal.
IV se manger *vpr* **le gaspacho se mange froid** gazpacho is served cold; **le poulet peut se ~ avec les doigts** you can eat chicken with your fingers; ▶**loup**, **vengeance**.
IDIOMES **~ la consigne** or **commission** to forget one's orders.

mange-tout /mɑ̃ʒtu/ *nm inv* **1** (haricot) French bean; **2** (pois) mangetout GB, snow pea US.

mangeur, **-euse** /mɑ̃ʒœʀ, øz/ *nm,f* **bon/gros ~** good/big eater.
■ **~ de grenouilles** (Français) frog○ injur; **mangeuse d'hommes** man-eater.

manglier /mɑ̃glije/ *nm* mangrove (tree).

mangoustan /mɑ̃gustɑ̃/, **mangoustanier** /mɑ̃gustanje/ *nm* (arbre, fruit) mangosteen.

mangouste /mɑ̃gust/ *nf* **1** Zool mongoose; **2** Bot mangosteen.

mangrove /mɑ̃gʀɔv/ *nf* mangrove swamp.

mangue /mɑ̃g/ *nf* mango.

manguier /mɑ̃gje/ *nm* mango (tree).

maniabilité /manjabilite/ *nf* (de véhicule) manoeuvrability GB, maneuverability US; **outil d'une bonne ~** tool which is easy to use; **notre voiture allie la ~ à la puissance** our car is both easy to handle and powerful.

maniable /manjabl/ *adj* [*objet, voiture, bateau*] easy to handle (*jamais épith*); [*format, livre*] manageable in size (*après n*); [*avion*] easy to fly (*jamais épith*); [*enfant, caractère*] amenable; **elle a un caractère peu ~** she has an intractable personality.

maniaco-dépressif, **-ive**, *mpl* **~s** /manjakodepʀesif, iv/ *adj, nm,f* manic-depressive.

maniaque /manjak/ **I** *adj* **1** [*personne*] (tatillon) particular; (exigeant) fussy; (à marottes) cranky; **2** [*souci, besoin*] obsessive; [*soin*] fanatical; **elle a un souci ~ de l'ordre** she is obsessive about tidiness; **3** Méd manic.
II *nmf* **1** (personne excentrique) crank; (personne tatillonne) fusspot GB, fussbudget US; **2** (fanatique) fanatic; **être un ~ de l'orthographe** to be a stickler for spelling; **c'est un ~ de l'ordre** he's obsessive about tidiness; **c'est un ~ du foot**○ he's soccer mad○; **3** (détraqué) maniac; **4** Méd manic.
■ **~ sexuel** sex maniac.

maniaquerie /manjakʀi/ *nf* **1** (caractère) fussiness; **il est d'une ~ insupportable** he's unbearably fussy; **2** (acte) **ses ~s** his/her fussy ways.

manichéen, **-éenne** /manikeɛ̃, ɛn/ **I** *adj* Philos, Relig Manichean; fig dualistic; **il est très ~** fig he sees everything in black and white.
II *nm,f* Manichean, Manichee.

manichéisme /manikeism/ *nm* Philos, Relig Manicheism.

manie /mani/ *nf* **1** (habitude) habit (**de faire** of doing); **la sale ~ de fumer au lit** the awful habit of smoking in bed; **avoir la ~ de tout garder** to be a compulsive hoarder; **c'est une vraie ~** it's an absolute obsession; **2** (marotte) quirk, idiosyncrasy; **chacun a ses (petites) ~s** we all have our little quirks ou funny ways; **avoir la ~ de l'ordre/la propreté** to be fanatical about tidiness/cleanliness; **3** Méd mania; **~ de la persécution** persecution mania.

maniement /manimɑ̃/ *nm* **1** (manipulation)

gén handling; (de machine) operation; (de langue) command; **être d'un ~ aisé** [*outil*] to be easy to handle; [*machine*] to be easy to operate; [*voiture*] to handle well; **2** (gestion) management.

■ **~ d'armes** Mil arms drill.

manier /manje/ [2] I *vtr* **1** (palper) to handle [*objet*]; fig to handle [*sommes, argent*]; to manage [*fonds*]; **2** (utiliser) to handle [*outil*]; to use [*langue*]; **~ l'ironie/le paradoxe** to handle irony/paradox skilfully[GB]; **~ l'aviron** to pull ou ply littér the oars; **~ l'épée** to wield the sword; **~ l'aiguille avec dextérité** to be skilled at needlework; **bien ~ la plume/le pinceau** fig to be a good writer/painter; **3** (diriger) to handle [*cheval, véhicule, personnes*]; **4** (pétrir) to mould GB, to mold US [*argile, cire*].

II **se manier** *vpr* **1 se ~ aisément** [*outil*] to be easy to handle; [*voiture*] to handle well; **2**◐ = **se magner**.

IDIOMES **~ la fourchette avec entrain**○ hum to have a hearty appetite; **il sait ~ la brosse à reluire**○ he's good at buttering people up○.

manière /manjɛʀ/ I *nf* **1** (façon) way; **de cette ~** (comme ceci) this way, like this; (comme cela) that way, like that; **d'une ~ ou d'une autre** in one way or another; **il n'y a pas d'autre ~** there's no other way; **d'une certaine ~** in a way; **la seule/la meilleure ~ de faire** the only/best way to do; **la bonne ~ de s'y prendre** the right way to go about it; **la ~ dont tu danses, ta ~ de danser** the way you dance; **leur ~ de vivre/penser** their way of life/thinking; **leur ~ de voir/faire les choses** their way of seeing/doing things; **leur ~ d'être** the way they are; **de toutes les ~s possibles** in every possible way; **de telle ~ que** in such a way that; **de ~ (à ce) qu'il fasse** so that he does; **de ~ à faire** so as to do; **en aucune ~** in no way; **de la même ~** [*travailler*] in the same way; [*agir*] the same way; **à ma/ta/leur ~** my/your/their (own) way; **à la ~ d'un enfant** like a child; **il nous a joué un tour à sa ~** he played a trick of his own on us; **cette ~ de faire ne te/leur ressemble pas** that's not like you/them; **de ~ décisive** decisively, in a decisive way; **de ~ inattendue** unexpectedly, in an unexpected way; **de quelle ~ peut-on faire?** how can one do?; **il nous regarde d'une drôle de ~** he's looking at us in a funny way; **de toute ~, de toutes ~s** anyway, in any case; **en ~ d'excuse/de remerciement** by way of apology/of thanks; **2** (méthode) **employer la ~ forte** to use strong-arm tactics; **il ne reste plus que la ~ forte** there's no alternative but to use force; **je ne crois pas à la ~ forte pour élever les enfants** I don't believe in the use of force when bringing up children; **utiliser la ~ douce** to use kid gloves; **3** (style) style; **à la ~ de qn/qch** in the style of sb/sth; **à la ~ américaine** in the American style; **vivre à la ~ d'un aristocrate** to live like an aristocrat; **c'est un Picasso dernière ~** this is a late Picasso ou an example of Picasso's later work; **c'est une ~ de savant fou** he's a bit of a mad scientist.

II **manières** *nfpl* **1** (savoir-vivre) manners; **avoir de bonnes/mauvaises ~s** to have good/bad manners; **il n'a pas de ~s** he has no manners; **qu'est-ce que c'est que ces ~s!** what manners!; **je vais t'apprendre les bonnes ~s** I'll teach you some manners; **il connaît les belles ~s** he has exquisite manners; **en voilà des ~s!** what a way to behave!; **2** (excès de politesse) **faire des ~s** to stand on ceremony; **ne faites pas de ~s** don't stand on ceremony, you don't have to be so formal.

maniéré, ~e /manjeʀe/ *adj* **1** pej [*personne, ton, style*] affected, mannered sout; **2** Art [*peintre, écrivain, genre*] mannered.

maniérisme /manjeʀism/ *nm* Art mannerism.

maniériste /manjeʀist/ I *adj* [*style, artiste*] manneristic.

II *nmf* mannerist.

manieur, -ieuse /manjœʀ, øz/ *nm,f* **c'est un grand ~ d'argent/d'hommes** he's very good at handling money/people.

manif○ /manif/ *nf* (*abbr* = **manifestation**) demo○.

manifestant, ~e /manifɛstɑ̃, ɑ̃t/ *nm,f* demonstrator.

manifestation /manifɛstasjɔ̃/ *nf* **1** (pour protester) demonstration (**contre** against; **pour** for); (pour soutenir) rally (**en faveur de** for); **~ pour la paix** peace rally; **2** (réunion, événement) event; **~s sportives/culturelles/estivales** sporting/cultural/summer events; **3** (de maladie, phénomène) appearance; **4** (de solidarité, joie, mauvaise foi) expression; (de problème, réalité) indication; (de sentiment, désir) manifestation.

■ **~ silencieuse** vigil; **~ de soutien** rally (**en faveur de** for).

manifeste /manifɛst/ I *adj* obvious, manifest.

II *nm* Art, Pol manifesto.

manifestement /manifɛstəmɑ̃/ *adv* obviously, manifestly.

manifester /manifɛste/ [1] I *vtr* **1** (faire connaître) to show, to demonstrate [*soutien, opposition, solidarité, volonté*]; to signal, to demonstrate [*inquiétude, humeur*]; to show [*curiosité, sentiment, qualité*]; **~ son désir de faire** to signal one's desire to do; **~ sa présence** to make one's presence known (**par** by; **en faisant** by doing); **2** (indiquer) [*résultats électoraux, décision*] to reveal.

II *vi* to demonstrate (**contre** against; **en faveur de** for); **appeler à ~ le 5 juin** to call a demonstration for 5 June.

III **se manifester** *vpr* **1** (devenir apparent) [*symptôme*] to manifest itself; [*phénomène*] to appear; [*peur, maladie, inquiétude*] to show itself; **une tendance au changement se manifeste** a tendency for change can be seen; **des signes encourageants commencent à se ~** encouraging signs are becoming apparent ou manifest; **2** (faire signe) **il ne s'est pas encore manifesté** (en personne) there is still no sign of him; (par lettre, téléphone) we still haven't heard from him; **l'auteur des lettres anonymes s'est encore manifesté** the anonymous letter writer has been heard from again; **3** (répondre à un appel, une offre) [*candidat, témoin*] to come forward.

manifold /manifɔld/ *nm* duplicate book.

manigance /manigɑ̃s/ *nf* little scheme.

manigancer /manigɑ̃se/ [12] *vtr* to be up to; **qu'est-ce qu'elle manigance encore?** what's she up to now?; **~ un mauvais coup** to hatch up a scheme.

manille /manij/ I *nm* (cigare) Manila cigar.

II *nf* **1** ▶449 Jeux manille; **2** Naut, Tech shackle.

Manille /manij/ ▶857 *npr* Manila.

manioc /manjɔk/ *nm* manioc, cassava.

manipulable /manipylabl/ *adj* [*personne*] easily manipulated.

manipulateur, -trice /manipylatœʀ, tʀis/ I *adj* [*démarche*] manipulative.

II *nm,f* **1** ▶510 (technicien) technician; **2** pej (provocateur) manipulator; **3** (prestidigitateur) conjurer; (de marionnettes) puppeteer.

III *nm* **1** Tech manipulator; **2** Électrotech, Télécom key.

■ **~ de laboratoire** laboratory technician; **~ radio** radiographer.

manipulation /manipylasjɔ̃/ *nf* **1** (d'objet, de produit) handling; **la ~ de produits dangereux** handling of dangerous chemicals; **2** (d'opinion, de personne) manipulation ₵; (de résultats, statistiques) massaging ₵; **~s politiques** political scheming ₵; **~s électorales** electoral rigging ₵; **se livrer à une ~ de la presse** to manipulate the press; **3** Méd manipulation ₵; **~ vertébrale** manipulation of the spine; **~ génétique** genetic manipulation; **4** (sur une substance) operation; Scol, Univ (expérience) experiment; **5** (prestidigitation) sleight of hand; **la ~ de marionnettes** operating puppets; **6** Télécom (de signal) keying.

manipule /manipyl/ *nm* Antiq, Relig maniple.

manipuler /manipyle/ [1] *vtr* **1** (avec les mains) to handle [*objet, substance, véhicule*]; to manipulate [*bouton*]; **~ qch avec délicatesse** to handle sth carefully; **arrête de ~ ce vase** stop playing with that vase; **2** (utiliser) to handle [*chiffres*]; to use [*mots*]; **3** (falsifier) to massage [*données, chiffres*]; **~ les registres** Compta to cook○ GB ou tamper with US the books; **4** (influencer) to manipulate [*opinion, presse, personne*]; **5** Théât to operate [*marionnettes*].

Manitoba /manitɔba/ ▶692 *nprm* Manitoba.

manitou /manitu/ *nm* **1**○ fig big noise○, big wheel○; **un grand ~ de la finance** a big noise in the financial world; **2** Relig manitou.

manivelle /manivɛl/ *nf* **1** (de voiture) (pour démarrer) starting handle; (pour les roues) wheel brace; **2** (de puits, treuil, store) handle; (de pédalier) pedal crank.

IDIOMES **donner le premier tour de ~** Cin to start filming.

manne /man/ *nf* Bot, Relig manna; fig (aubaine) windfall, godsend; **~ céleste** manna from Heaven.

IDIOMES **arriver comme une ~** to be like manna from heaven, to be a godsend.

mannequin /mankɛ̃/ ▶510 *nm* **1** (de mode) model; **elle est ~ chez** she models for; **2** (de vitrine) dummy, mannequin; **3** (de couturière) tailor's dummy, mannequin; **4** (dans un musée, au cinéma) dummy; **5** (de dessinateur) mannequin, lay figure.

IDIOMES **s'habiller comme un ~** to be dressed like a fashion plate.

manœuvrabilité /manøvʀabilite/ *nf* manoeuvrability GB, maneuvrability US.

manœuvrable /manœvʀabl/ *adj* [*véhicule, bateau*] manœuvrable GB, maneuverable US; **la voiture est ~** the car handles well.

manœuvre /manœvʀ/ I ▶510 *nm* unskilled worker.

II *nf* **1** (avec véhicule) (opération) manoeuvre GB, maneuver US; (maniement) manoeuvring GB, maneuvering US; **effectuer** or **faire une ~** to carry out a manoeuvre GB ou maneuver US; **effectuer une ~ de dépassement** to overtake GB, to pass US, to perform the overtaking procedure GB; **il a fait une fausse ~ et a heurté l'arbre** he made a mistake and hit the tree; **~s précédant le décollage** taxiing before take off; **~ d'accostage** landing operation; **~ d'abordage** boarding operation; ▶**faux**; **2** (d'appareil, de dispositif) operation; **3** (pour obtenir quelque chose) tactic, manoeuvre GB, maneuver US; **une ~ destinée à faire** a manoeuvre GB ou maneuver US to do; **~s électorales** electoral tactics; **~s frauduleuses** Jur deception ₵; **4** Mil manoeuvre GB, maneuver US; **faire des/partir en ~s** to be/go on manoeuvres GB ou maneuvers US; **grandes ~s** large-scale manoeuvres GB ou maneuvers US; **~ enveloppante** surrounding manoeuvre GB ou maneuver US; **champ** or **terrain de ~s** military training area; **5** Rail (mouvement) shunting GB, switching US; **6** Naut (cordage) rigging.

manœuvrer /manœvʀe/ [1] I *vtr* **1** (déplacer habilement) to manoeuvre GB, to maneuver US [*véhicule*]; **2** (actionner) to operate [*dispositif, machine*]; **3** (manipuler) to manoeuvre GB, to maneuver US [*personne, groupe*].

II *vi* to manoeuvre GB, to maneuver US; **j'ai dû ~ pour sortir la voiture** I had to carry out a tricky manoeuvre GB ou maneuver US to get the car out.

manœuvrier, -ière /manœvʀije, ɛʀ/ I *adj* [*personne*] tactically skilled; [*qualités*] tactical.

II *nm,f* tactician.

manoir /manwaʀ/ *nm* manor (house).

manomètre /manɔmɛtʀ/ *nm* pressure gauge, manometer.

manométrie /manɔmetʀi/ *nf* manometry.

manométrique /manɔmetʀik/ *adj* manometric.

manouche○ /manuʃ/ *nmf* gypsy.

manquant, ~e /mɑ̃kɑ̃, ɑ̃t/ *adj* missing.

manque /mɑ̃k/ **I** *nm* **1** (insuffisance) (d'eau, imagination, hygiène, argent, de soins) lack (**de** of); (de personnel, main-d'œuvre) shortage (**de** of); **par ~ de résistance/d'intérêt/de ressources** for ou through lack of stamina/ of interest/of resources; **quel ~ de chance** ou **bol**○ ou **pot**○! what bad luck!; **il voulait venir mais, ~ de chance, il est tombé malade** he wanted to come but, just his luck, he fell ill; **2** (lacune) gap; **il n'a pas fait d'études et pour pallier ce ~, il a suivi des cours du soir** he didn't go to university and, to make up for this gap in his education, he went to evening classes; **3** (privation) **ressentir un ~** to feel an emptiness; **être en ~ d'affection** to be in need of affection; **être en (état de) ~** [*drogué*] to be suffering from withdrawal symptoms; **4** Tex (de tissu, tapisserie) defect, missing pick spéc; **5** Jeux (à la roulette) manque.

II à la manque○ *loc adj* **un héros/philosophe à la ~** a would-be hero/philosopher; **tu parles d'une idée à la ~** what a useless idea; **j'en ai marre de cette bagnole**○ **à la ~** I'm fed up with this lousy○ car.

■ **~ à gagner** loss of earnings.

manqué, ~e /mɑ̃ke/ **I** *pp* ▶ **manquer**.

II *pp adj* [*essai, tentative*] failed; [*rendez-vous, occasion*] missed; [*plat, gâteau*] ruined; [*photo*] spoiled; [*roman, film*] disappointing; [*vie*] wasted.

III *adj* **c'est un poète ~** (incapable) he's a failed poet; (il en a les qualités) he should have been a poet.

IV *nm* iced cake; **moule à ~** round cake tin.

manquement /mɑ̃kmɑ̃/ *nm* **~ à la discipline/à la morale** breach of discipline/of morals; **~ au devoir** gén breach of duty; Admin, Jur dereliction of duty; **~ à une promesse** failure to keep a promise; **c'est un ~ à toutes les règles élémentaires de la courtoisie** this violates all the rules of basic courtesy.

manquer /mɑ̃ke/ [1] **I** *vtr* **1** (ne pas atteindre, ne pas voir) to miss [*cible, objectif, spectacle, événement*]; **la balle l'a manqué de peu** the bullet just missed him; **~ une marche** to miss a step; **une grande maison rose à la sortie du village, vous ne pouvez pas la ~** a big pink house as you come out of the village, you can't miss it; **~ l'école** to miss school; **un film à ne pas ~** a film not to be missed; **j'ai manqué le début du film** I missed the beginning of the film; **tu n'as rien manqué, le film est nul** you didn't miss anything, it's an awful film; **il n'en manque pas une**○ you can rely on him to put his foot in it; **2** (être en retard pour) to miss [*train, bus, avion, personne*] (**de** by); **vous l'avez manquée de cinq minutes** you missed her/it by five minutes; **3** (ne pas réussir) to spoil, to ruin [*plat, gâteau, photo*]; to botch○ [*expérience de laboratoire*]; **~ sa vie** to make a mess of one's life; **elle a manqué son solo** she made a mess of her solo; **cet événement nous a fait ~ plusieurs contrats** this incident has lost us several contracts; **~ son coup**○ to fail; **4**○ (ne pas sanctionner) **la prochaine fois je ne le manquerai pas** next time I won't let him get away with it; **elle ne l'a pas manqué** she put him in his place.

II manquer à *vtr ind* **1** (faire éprouver un sentiment d'absence) **~ à qn** to be missed by sb; **ils nous manquent** we miss them; **la Bretagne/ma tante me manque** I miss Brittany/my aunt; **2** (ne pas respecter) **~ à son devoir/honneur** to fail in one's duty/ honour[GB]; **~ à ses promesses** to fail to keep one's promises; **~ à sa parole** to break one's word.

III manquer de *vtr ind* **1** (avoir en quantité insuffisante) **~ de** to lack, to be lacking in [*patience, talent, courage, imagination, ambition*]; to lack, to be short of [*argent, provisions, matériel, personnel, main-d'œuvre*]; to lack [*expérience, pratique*]; **on ne manque de rien ici** we don't want ou lack for anything here; **elle ne manque pas de détracteurs/prétendants** she's not short of critics/suitors, she doesn't lack critics/ suitors; **le roman manque d'humour** the novel lacks humour[GB]; **ma cousine ne manque pas d'humour** my cousin's got a good sense of humour[GB]; **elle ne manque pas de charme** she's not without charm; **il ne manque pas de culot**○! he's got a nerve!; **la soupe manque de sel/poivre** there isn't enough salt/pepper in the soup; **ouvre la fenêtre, on manque d'air ici** open the window, it's stuffy in here; **il manque de magnésium/calcium** he has a magnesium/calcium deficiency; **2** (toujours à la forme négative) **si vous passez dans la région, ne manquez pas de nous rendre visite** if you're in the area, be sure and visit us; **je ne manquerai pas de vous le faire savoir** I'll be sure to let you know; **ne manquez pas de le signaler** be sure and report it; **'remercie-le de ma part'—'je n'y manquerai pas'** 'thank him for me'—'I won't forget ou I most certainly shall'; **je ne manquerai pas de le leur dire** I'll be sure to tell them, I won't forget to tell them; **on ne peut ~ d'être surpris** one can't fail to be surprised; **ça ne pouvait ~ d'arriver** it was bound to happen; **et évidemment, ça n'a pas manqué**○! and sure enough that's what happened!; **3** (faillir) **il a manqué (de) casser un carreau** he almost broke a windowpane; **elle a manqué (de) s'évanouir en le voyant** she almost fainted when she saw him.

IV *vi* **1** (faire défaut) **j'ai fait l'inventaire: rien ne manque** I've done the inventory and nothing is missing; **trois soldats manquaient à l'appel** three soldiers were missing at roll call; **les vivres vinrent à ~** supplies were running out; **ne fais pas cette tête, ce ne sont pas les garçons qui manquent!** don't look so downcast, there are plenty more fish in the sea!; **ce ne sont pas les occasions qui manquent** there's no lack of opportunity; **le moment venu, le courage leur manqua** when the time came, their courage failed them; **je suis tellement outré que les mots me manquent** I'm so outraged that words fail me; **les mots me manquent pour exprimer ma joie/mon dégoût** I can't find the words to express my joy/my disgust; **le temps me manque pour t'expliquer** I don't have enough time to explain to you; **ce n'est pas l'envie qui me manque de faire** it's not that I don't want to do; **le pied lui manqua** liter he/she missed his/her footing; **2** (être absent) [*élève, personne*] to be absent; **cet étudiant manque très souvent** this student is very often absent.

V *v impers* **il manquait deux fourchettes** two forks were missing; **il manque 500 francs dans la caisse** 500 francs are missing from the cash register; **il manque une roue à la voiture** there's a wheel missing from the car; **il lui manque un doigt** he's got a finger missing; **il lui manque un œil/bras** he's only got one eye/arm; **il leur manque 2000 francs pour pouvoir acheter la voiture** they're 2,000 francs short of the amount they need to buy the car; **il nous manque deux joueurs pour former une équipe** we're two players short of a team; **il manque une signature à ce contrat** (il n'est pas signé) the contract isn't signed; (sur plusieurs signatures) there's a signature missing on the contract; **il manque du sel dans cette soupe** there isn't enough salt in the soup; **ça manque d'animation ici!** it's not very lively here!; **il ne manquerait plus que ça!** that would be the last straw!; **il ne manquerait plus qu'il se mette à pleuvoir** all (that) we need now is for it to start raining.

VI se manquer *vpr* **1** (soi-même) to bungle one's suicide attempt; **2** (ne pas se voir) to miss each other.

mansarde /mɑ̃saʀd/ *nf* (pièce) attic room.

mansardé, ~e /mɑ̃saʀde/ *adj* [*pièce*] attic (*épith*).

mansuétude /mɑ̃sɥetyd/ *nf* indulgence.

mante /mɑ̃t/ *nf* **1** Zool (insecte) mantis; **2** Mode mantle.

■ **~ religieuse** Zool praying mantis; fig man-eater.

manteau, *pl* **~x** /mɑ̃to/ *nm* **1** (vêtement) coat; **2** (de brume) blanket; (de neige) blanket, mantle littér; **le ~ de la nuit** the cloak of darkness; **3** fig (masque) cloak; **4** Géol mantle; **5** Zool (de mollusque) mantle; **6** Nucl blanket; **7** Hérald mantling.

■ **~ d'Arlequin** Théât proscenium arch; **~ de cheminée** Constr mantelpiece; **~ de pluie**† raincoat.

IDIOMES **sous le ~** illicitly.

mantelet /mɑ̃tlɛ/ *nm* **1** Naut deadlight; **2** (de femme) mantelet; (de prélat) mantelletta.

mantille /mɑ̃tij/ *nf* mantilla.

mantisse /mɑ̃tis/ *nf* mantissa.

Mantoue /mɑ̃tu/ ▶ **857** *npr* Mantua.

mantra /mɑ̃tʀa/ *nm* mantra.

manucure /manykyʀ/ ▶ **510** **I** *nmf* (personne) manicurist.

II *nf* (soins, technique) manicure; **se faire faire une ~** to have a manicure.

manucurer /manykyʀe/ [1] *vtr* to give [sb] a manicure [*personne*]; **se faire ~** to have a manicure; **ongles manucurés** manicured nails.

manuel, -elle /manɥɛl/ **I** *adj* **1** [*activité, travailleur, habileté*] manual; **2** Tech **passer en (mode) ~, passer en fonction manuelle, passer sur ~** to switch to manual.

II *nm,f* **1** (par métier) manual worker; **2** (par goût) **c'est une manuelle** she likes working with her hands; (par don) she is good with her hands.

III *nm* **1** Scol textbook; **~ de grec** Greek textbook; **2** Sci, Tech, Univ manual; **~ de mathématiques appliquées** manual of applied mathematics.

■ **~ de conversation** phrase book; **~ d'utilisation** instruction manual; **~ scolaire** school textbook.

manuellement /manɥɛlmɑ̃/ *adv* **1** Tech (non automatiquement) [*fonctionner, régler, calculer*] manually; **2** (avec les mains) [*travailler*] with one's hands.

manufacturable /manyfaktyʀabl/ *adj* manufacturable.

manufacture /manyfaktyʀ/ *nf* **1** (établissement) factory; **~ de tabacs/d'armes** tobacco/armaments factory; **2** (fabrication) manufacture.

manufacturer /manyfaktyʀe/ [1] *vtr* to manufacture.

manufacturier, -ière /manyfaktyʀje, ɛʀ/ **I** *adj* manufacturing.

II *nm,f* manufacturer.

manu militari /manymilitaʀi/ *adv* forcibly.

manuscrit, ~e /manyskʀi, it/ **I** *adj* **1** (écrit à la main) [*page, lettre*] handwritten; **2** Édition, Littérat, Mus [*livre, partition*] manuscript (*épith*).

II *nm* manuscript; **~ original/enluminé/ dactylographié** original/illuminated/typed manuscript; **~ sur vélin** manuscript on vellum.

■ **~s de la Mer morte** Dead Sea Scrolls.

manutention /manytɑ̃sjɔ̃/ *nf* **1** (activité) handling; **appareil de ~** handling equipment; **2** (local) warehouse.

manutentionnaire /manytɑ̃sjɔnɛʀ/ ▶ **510** *nm* warehouseman.

manutentionner /manytɑ̃sjɔne/ [1] *vtr* to handle.

maoïsme /maoism/ *nm* Maoism.

maoïste /maoist/ *adj, nmf* Maoist.

maori /maɔʀi/ ▶ 462 *nm* Ling Maori.

maous◑, **-ousse** /maus/ *adj* massive.

mappemonde /mapmɔ̃d/ *nf* **1** (carte) map of the world (in two hemispheres); **2** (globe) controv globe.

Maputo /mapyto/ ▶ 857 *npr* Maputo.

maquer◑: **se maquer** /make/ [1] *vpr* **se ~ avec qn** to shack up◑ with sb; **elle est maquée** she's shacked up◑ with somebody; (prostituée) she's working for a pimp○.

maquereau, *pl* **~x** /makʀo/ *nm* **1** Zool mackerel; ▶ **groseille**; **2**◑ (souteneur) pimp○.

■ **~ espagnol** Spanish mackerel, chub mackerel.

maquerelle◑ /makʀɛl/ *nf* (dans une maison close) madam.

maquette /makɛt/ *nf* **1** (modèle réduit) Archit, Ind, Tech scale model; Cin model; (jouet) **~ d'avion** model aeroplane GB ou airplane US; **2** (grandeur nature) Ind, Tech, Théât mock-up; **3** Art (dessin) sketch; (sculpture) maquette; **4** (de livre) dummy.

■ **~ de couverture** sample cover; **~ de mise en page** paste-up; **~ typographique** page sample.

maquettiste /maketist/ ▶ 510 *nmf* Édition typographic designer.

maquignon /makiɲɔ̃/ *nm* **1** lit horse dealer; **2** péj shady operator.

maquignonnage /makiɲɔnaʒ/ *nm* **1** lit horse dealing; **2** péj sharp practice.

maquignonner /makiɲɔne/ [1] *vtr* **1 ~ une bête** to disguise an animal's faults prior to selling it; **2** to rig [*affaire*].

maquillage /makijaʒ/ *nm* **1** (action) making-up; (résultat) make-up; **2** (fard) make-up; **3** péj (de document, vérité) doctoring.

■ **~ de théâtre** greasepaint.

maquiller /makije/ [1] **I** *vtr* **1** (farder) to make [sb/sth] up [*acteur, visage*]; **peu maquillé** lightly made-up; **2** (déguiser) to doctor [*document, chiffres, vérité*]; **~ une voiture** to change a car's identity; **~ un crime en accident** to disguise a crime as an accident.

II se maquiller *vpr* (mettre du fard) to put make-up on; (porter du fard) to wear make-up.

maquilleur, **-euse** /makijœʀ, øz/ ▶ 510 *nm,f* Théât make-up artist.

maquis /maki/ *nm* **1** Géog maquis; **2** Hist maquis; **prendre le ~** [*résistant*] to join the maquis; [*fuyard*] to go underground; **3** (dédale) labyrinth (**de** of).

maquisard, **~e** /makizaʀ, aʀd/ *nm,f* **1** Hist maquis, member of the Resistance; **2** (guerillero) partisan.

marabout /maʀabu/ *nm* **1** Zool marabou; **2** Relig marabout.

maraîchage /maʀɛʃaʒ/ *nm* market gardening GB, truck farming US.

■ **~ en serre** glasshouse GB ou greenhouse US cultivation; **~ sous châssis** cold-frame cultivation.

maraîcher, **-ère** /maʀɛʃe, ɛʀ/ **I** *adj* **produits ~s** market garden produce ¢ GB, truck ¢ US; **la culture maraîchère** market gardening GB, truck farming US; **jardin ~** market garden GB, truck farm US.

II ▶ 510 *nm,f* market gardener GB, truck farmer US.

marais /maʀɛ/ *nm* **1** Géog marsh; (dans les tropiques) swamp; **2** fig quagmire.

■ **~ salant** saltern.

Marais /maʀɛ/ *nprm* **le ~** the Marais (*district in Paris*).

marasme /maʀasm/ *nm* **1** Écon, Pol stagnation; **~ politique/économique** political/economic stagnation; **le ~ de la construction navale** the slump in the shipbuilding industry; **être dans le ~** or **en plein ~** to be in the doldrums; **2** (abattement) depression; **3** Méd failure to thrive, marasmus spéc.

marasquin /maʀaskɛ̃/ *nm* maraschino.

marathon /maʀatɔ̃/ **I** *nm* (tous contextes) marathon.

II -marathon (*in compounds*) **session/visite-~** marathon session/visit.

marathonien, **-ienne** /maʀatɔnjɛ̃, ɛn/ *nm,f* marathon runner.

marâtre /maʀɑtʀ/ *nf* **1** péj (mère cruelle) cruel mother; (mère dénaturée) unnatural mother; **2**† (belle-mère) stepmother.

maraud, **~e** /maʀo, od/ **I**† *nm,f* péj (homme) rascal; (femme) hussy†.

II maraude *nf* gén pilfering; Jur petty theft (*of fruit, crops*); Mil marauding; **en ~e** [*taxi*] cruising for fares (*après n*); [*voyou*] on the prowl (*jamais épith*).

maraudage /maʀodaʒ/ *nm* gén pilfering; Jur petty theft (*of fruit, crops*).

marauder /maʀode/ [1] *vi* **1** (voler) to pilfer; Mil to maraud; **~ dans les fermes** to pilfer from farms; **2** (être à l'affût) [*taxi*] to cruise for fares; [*voyou*] to prowl around.

maraudeur, **-euse** /maʀodœʀ, øz/ **I** *adj* [*taxi*] cruising for fares (*après n*); [*oiseau*] thieving.

II *nm,f* (voleur) petty thief; (rôdeur) prowler.

marbre /maʀbʀ/ *nm* **1** (roche) marble; **2** (plaque de meuble) marble top; (statue) marble statue; **3** Aut jig; **passer une voiture au ~** to inspect a car for accident damage; **4** Imprim bed; **livre sur le ~** book at press.

IDIOMES **rester de ~** (impassible) to remain stony-faced; (insensible) to remain stonily indifferent; **garder un visage de ~** to remain stony-faced; **la nouvelle les laissa de ~** they were completely unmoved by the news; **froid comme le ~** as cold as marble.

marbrer /maʀbʀe/ [1] *vtr* **1** Tech to marble [*papier, cuir*]; **2** (marquer) **le froid lui marbrait le visage** his/her face was blotchy with the cold; **peau marbrée** mottled skin; **il avait le dos marbré de coups** or **de bleus** his back was mottled with bruises; **pelage roux marbré de noir** red coat mottled with black.

marbrerie /maʀbʀəʀi/ *nf* **1** (industrie) marble industry; (travail du marbre) marble masonry; **~ funéraire** monumental masonry; **ouvrages de ~** marblework ¢; **2** (atelier) marble mason's workshop; **~ funéraire** monumental mason's workshop.

marbrier, **-ière** /maʀbʀije, ɛʀ/ **I** *adj* [*industrie*] marble.

II ▶ 510 *nm* (ouvrier, entrepreneur) marble mason; **~ funéraire** monumental mason; **~ d'art** artist in marble.

III marbrière *nf* marble quarry.

marbrure /maʀbʀyʀ/ *nf* (sur papier, cuir) marbling ¢; (sur la peau) blotchiness ¢; (hématomes) mottling ¢.

marc /maʀ/ *nm* **1** (eau-de-vie) marc; **~ de raisin** grape marc; **2** (résidu de fruits) marc; **3** Jur **partager au ~ le franc** to make a pro rata division of assets.

■ **~ de café** coffee grounds (*pl*); **lire l'avenir dans le ~ de café** to read the future in coffee cups; **~ de pomme** pomace.

marcassin /maʀkasɛ̃/ *nm* young wild boar.

marcassite /maʀkasit/ *nf* marcasite.

marchand, **~e** /maʀʃɑ̃, ɑ̃d/ **I** *adj* Comm [*produit, denrée*] marketable, salable; [*secteur, trafic, économie*] trade; **qualité ~e** marketable quality; **prix ~** market ou ruling price; **valeur ~e** market ou commercial value.

II ▶ 510 *nm,f* **1** (commerçant) trader; (négociant) dealer, merchant; (dans une boutique) shopkeeper; (sur un marché) stallholder; **~ d'armes/de bestiaux** arms/cattle dealer; **~ de soie/vins** silk/wine merchant; **jouer à la ~e** to play shops; **2** Hist merchant; **une nation de ~s** a trading nation.

■ **~ ambulant** hawker; **~ de canons** pej arms dealer; **~ de chapeaux** hatter; **~ de chaussures** shoe retailer; **~ de couleurs** ironmonger GB, hardware merchant; **~ au détail** retailer; **~ de fromage** cheesemonger GB, cheese merchant; **~ de fruits** fruiterer; **~ de glaces** ice cream vendor; **~ en gros** wholesaler, wholesale merchant ou dealer; **~ de journaux** (dans un magasin) newsagent; (dans la rue) newsvendor; **~ de légumes** greengrocer GB; **~ de marrons** chestnut vendor; **~ de meubles** furniture retailer; **~ de poissons** fishmonger; **~ des quatre saisons** costermonger GB, fruit and vegetable merchant; **~ de sable** fig sandman; **le ~ de sable est passé** the sandman has been; **~ à la sauvette** street vendor; **~ de sommeil**○ dosshouse○ GB ou pit US owner; **~ de soupe**○ (restaurateur) second-rate restaurant owner; (profiteur) money-grubber○; **~ de tabac** tobacconist GB, keeper of a smoke shop US; **~ de tableaux** art dealer; **~ de tapis** carpet salesman; **c'est un vrai ~ de tapis**○ pej he's just a petty wrangler; **ce sont des discussions de ~ de tapis**○ pej this is just petty wrangling; **~ de tissus** draper; **~ de vins** wine merchant; **~ de voyages**○ travel agent.

marchandage /maʀʃɑ̃daʒ/ *nm* **1** (sur le prix) haggling (**de** over); **après un long ~** after lengthy haggling; **faire du ~** to haggle; **2** (tractations) bargaining ¢, haggling péj; **des ~s politiques** political bargaining; **se livrer à un féroce ~** to engage in hard political bargaining ou fierce horse-trading; **3** Jur **le gouvernement veut réprimer le ~ de main-d'œuvre** the government wants to put an end to labour[GB]-only subcontracting.

marchander /maʀʃɑ̃de/ [1] *vtr* **1** to haggle over [*marchandise, tableau, prix*]; to haggle for [*rabais*]; **payer sans ~** to pay without haggling; **2** fig, fml **~ son accord** to give one's approval grudgingly; **~ sa peine** not to put oneself out; **il n'a pas marchandé ses éloges** he was not sparing in his praises; **3** Jur to subcontract on a labour[GB]-only basis.

marchandeur, **-euse** /maʀʃɑ̃dœʀ, øz/ *nm,f* **1** (personne qui marchande) haggler; **2** Jur subcontractor supplying labour[GB] only.

marchandisage /maʀʃɑ̃dizaʒ/ *nm* Écon merchandising.

marchandise /maʀʃɑ̃diz/ *nf* **1** (articles) **des ~s** goods, merchandise ¢; **exporter/transporter des ~s** to export/transport goods; **les ~s sont entreposées dans le hangar** the goods are stored in the warehouse; **100 000 francs de ~s** 100,000 francs' worth of goods; **~s en gros/au détail** wholesale/retail goods; **2** (produit) goods (*pl*); **livrer/fournir la ~** to deliver/to provide the goods; **les trafiquants ont essayé d'écouler la ~** the traffickers tried to dispose of the goods; **ce fromager a de la bonne ~** this cheese shop has good produce; **tromper** or **voler qn sur la ~** to swindle sb.

IDIOMES **il a essayé de nous vendre sa ~**○ he tried to win us over; **vanter** or **étaler sa ~**○ to parade one's wares.

marchante /maʀʃɑ̃t/ *adj f* **aile ~** Mil wheeling flank; fig active element.

marche /maʀʃ/ **I** *nf* **1** ▶ 449 (déplacement de personne) (activité) walking; (trajet) walk; Sport walking; **faire de la ~** to go walking; **la ~ à pied** walking; **faire un peu de ~** to do some walking; **faire une petite ~** to take a short walk; **à 10 minutes de ~** 10 minutes' walk away; **ralentir/accélérer la ~** to walk slower/faster; **ta ~ est trop rapide pour les enfants** you're walking too quickly for the children; **10 km ~** Sport 10 km walk; **2** Mil, Pol (déplacement de groupe) march; **~ pour la paix/de protestation** peace/protest march; **soldats en ~** soldiers on the march; **ils ont organisé une ~ devant l'ambassade** they organized a march past the embassy; **faire ~ sur**

[*soldats , manifestants, rebelles*] to march on; **se mettre en ordre de ~** Mil to get in marching formation; **en avant, ~!** Mil forward march!; **fermer la ~** to bring up the rear; **ouvrir la ~** to be at the head of the march; **3** (fonctionnement de véhicule) progress; **la ~ du train a été gênée** the progress of the train was hampered; **en ~** moving (*épith*); **prendre un bus en ~** to climb aboard a moving bus; **dans le sens contraire de la ~** facing backward(s); **dans le sens de la ~** facing forward(s); **4** (fonctionnement de mécanisme) operation; **bonne ~** smooth operation; **en état de ~** in working order; **s'assurer de la bonne ~ d'une machine** to ensure that a machine is in good working order; **mettre en ~** to start [*machine, moteur*]; to start up [*chaudière, réacteur*]; to switch on [*téléviseur, vidéo, ordinateur*]; fig to set [sth] in motion [*réforme, projet, processus*]; **la mise en ~ du lave-vaisselle est très simple** starting the dishwasher is very simple; **la mise en ~ du réacteur a pris plus d'un an** starting up the reactor took over a year; **la remise en ~ de la chaudière** starting the boiler up again; **se mettre en ~** [*appareil, véhicule*] to start up; [*réveil, sonnerie*] to go off; [*projet, réforme, plan*] to get going; **être en ~** [*machine, moteur*] to be running; [*téléviseur, radio*] to be on; **5** (fonctionnement d'organisme) running; **bonne ~ de l'entreprise/expédition** smooth running of the company/expedition; **6** (déroulement) (d'événements) course; (de récit, d'intrigue) unfolding; **la ~ du temps/du progrès/de l'histoire** the march of time/of progress/of history; **~ à suivre** procedure (**pour faire** for doing); **la meilleure ~ à suivre pour qch** the best way of going about sth; **7** Constr (d'escalier, escabeau, de train, bus) step; **attention à la ~!** mind the step! GB, watch the step!; **cirer les ~s (de l'escalier)** to wax the stairs; **8** Mus march; **~ funèbre/nuptiale** funeral/wedding march.

II marches *nfpl* (limites) marches.

■ **~ d'angle** Constr pie stair; **~ arrière** Aut reverse; **passer la ~ arrière** to go into reverse; **sortir en ~ arrière** to reverse out; **faire ~ arrière** fig to backpedal; **~ avant** forward; **~ forcée** Électrotech override; Mil forced march; **mettre en ~ forcée** to override; **modernisation/libéralisation à ~ forcée** fig accelerated modernization/liberalization; **~ palière** Constr landing step.

IDIOMES **prendre le train en ~** (par hasard) to join halfway through; (par intérêt) to climb onto the bandwagon.

marché /maʀʃe/ *nm* **1** Comm market; **~ aux fleurs** flower market; **~ couvert** covered market; **~ en plein air** open-air market; **vendre/acheter ses pommes au ~** to sell/buy one's apples at the market; **les jours de ~** market days; **faire son ~** to do one's shopping at the market; **il fait les ~s de la région pour vendre son miel** he does the rounds of the markets in the area to sell his honey; **mettre qch sur le ~** to put sth on the market; **retirer qch du ~** to withdraw sth from the market; **2** Fin market; **~ boursier** stock market; **~ financier/monétaire/de l'or** financial/money/gold market; **le ~ de l'automobile/de l'art/de l'immobilier** the car/art/property market; **~ baissier/haussier** bearish/bullish market; **~ d'acheteurs/de vendeurs** buyers'/sellers' market; **3** Écon (débouché) market; (lieu) marketplace; **ouvrir un nouveau ~** to open up a new market; **pénétrer un ~** to break into a market; **un des plus grands ~s du monde** one of the largest marketplaces in the world; **~ porteur** buoyant market; **4** (arrangement) deal; **un ~ avantageux** a good deal; **conclure un ~ avec qn** to strike a deal with sb; **~ conclu!** it's a deal!; **c'est un ~ de dupes** it's a bum◑ deal, we've been had○; **bon/meilleur ~** [*produit*] cheap/cheaper; **vendre (à) meilleur ~** to sell cheaper; **par-dessus le ~**○ to top it all.

■ **~ des capitaux** capital market; **~ captif** captive market; **~ des changes** Fin foreign exchange market; **~ au comptant** spot market; **~ de contrats à terme** futures market; **~ de l'emploi** job market; **~ extérieur** foreign market; **~ gris** grey GB ou gray US market; **~ interbancaire** interbank market; **~ d'intérêt national, MIN** *government instituted wholesale food market*; **~ intérieur** (national) domestic ou home market; (de la CEE) internal market; **~ libre** free market; **~ des matières premières** commodity market; **~ noir** black market; **acheter au ~ noir** to buy on the black market; **~ obligataire** bond market; **~ pétrolier** Fin oil market; **~ public** Admin public works contract; **~ aux puces** flea market; **~ à règlement mensuel** forward market; **~ à terme** forward market; **~ du travail** labour[GB] market; **~ unique** single market; **~ des valeurs** stock market; **Marché commun** Common Market.

IDIOMES **faire bon ~ de qch** to set little value on sth.

marchéage /maʀʃeaʒ/ *nm* marketing mix.

marchepied /maʀʃəpje/ *nm* **1** (de véhicule) (marche simple) step; (série de marches) steps (*pl*); **2** (escabeau) steps (*pl*); **3** fig stepping stone; **servir de ~ à qn** to be a stepping stone for sb.

marcher /maʀʃe/ [1] *vi* **1** (utiliser ses pieds) [*personne, animal, robot*] to walk; **il marche vite** he walks fast; **~ à travers champs** to walk across fields; **allons ~ un peu** let's go for a little walk; **~ avec des talons/chaussures plates** to wear high heels/flat shoes; **2** (poser le pied) to tread (**dans** in; **sur** on); **j'ai marché sur mes lunettes** I trod on my spectacles; **~ sur les pieds de qn** to tread on sb's toes; **tu m'as marché sur le pied** you stood on my foot; **se laisser ~ sur les pieds** fig to let oneself be walked over; **à la soirée on se marchait sur les pieds** fig the party was packed; **ne marche pas dans les flaques** don't walk in the puddles; **~ dans une flaque d'eau** to step in a puddle; **l'homme marchera sur Mars** man will walk on Mars; **3** (avancer) to go; **notre train marche vite** our train goes fast; **malgré les embouteillages, nous avons bien marché** despite the traffic jams, we've made good time; **~ vers la gloire** fig to be on the road to fame; **~ sur les mains** [*gymnaste*] to walk on one's hands; **~ en tête de cortège** to march at the head of the procession; **~ sur Paris/le palais présidentiel** to march on Paris/the presidential palace; **4** (fonctionner) [*mécanisme, dispositif*] to work; [*système, réforme, procédé*] to work; **ma radio marche bien/marche mal** my radio works well/doesn't work properly; **insecticide qui ne marche pas pour les fourmis** insecticide that doesn't work on ants; **faire ~ qch** to get sth to work; **ma montre ne marche plus** my watch has stopped working; **la poste marche de mieux en mieux** the postal service is getting better and better; **~ au gaz/à l'électricité** to run on gas/on electricity; **Ivan marche à la vodka** hum Ivan lives on vodka; **les trains/bus ne marchent pas le dimanche** the trains/buses don't run on Sundays; **5**○ (aller) **~ (bien)/~ mal** [*travail, relations, examen*] to go well/not to go well; [*affaires, film, livre, élève*] to do well/not to do well; [*acteur*] to go down well/not to go down well; **comment a marché ton examen?** how did your exam go?; **comment marchent les affaires?** how is business?; **6**○ (être d'accord) to go for it; **je marche** I'll go for it; **c'est trop risqué, je ne marche pas** it's too risky, count me out; **elle marche pour cent francs par jour** she's agreed to one hundred francs a day; **pour cent francs, ça marche** for one hundred francs, you're on; **ça marche!** (marché conclu) it's a deal!; (la commande est prise) coming up!; **7**○ (croire naïvement) to fall for it; **tu verras, elle marchera à tous les coups** you'll see, she falls for it every time; **faire ~ qn** to pull sb's leg; **je te faisais ~** I was just pulling your leg; **elle fait ~ sa mère comme elle veut** she's got her mother wrapped round her little finger; **8**○ (obéir) **faire ~ son monde** or **personnel** to be good at giving orders.

IDIOMES **il ne marche pas, il court**○**!** he's as gullible as they come; **~ sur la tête de qn**○ to walk all over sb.

marcheur, **-euse** /maʀʃœʀ, øz/ *nm, f* walker; **bon/mauvais ~** good/poor walker.

marcottage /maʀkɔtaʒ/ *nm* Agric layering.

marcotte /maʀkɔt/ *nf* Agric layer.

marcotter /maʀkɔte/ [1] *vtr* Agric to layer.

mardi /maʀdi/ ▶**750** *nm* Tuesday; **~ gras** Shrove Tuesday.

mare /maʀ/ *nf* **1** (étang) pond; **~ aux canards** duck pond; **2** (grande quantité) pool (**de** of); **~ de sang** pool of blood.

marécage /maʀekaʒ/ *nm* **1** lit marsh; (sous les tropiques) swamp; **2** fig quagmire.

marécageux, **-euse** /maʀekaʒø, øz/ *adj* **1** lit [*sol*] marshy; (sous les tropiques) swampy; [*faune, flore*] marsh (*épith*); **2** fig [*terrain, situation*] sticky○.

maréchal, *pl* **-aux** /maʀeʃal, o/ ▶**390** *nm* ≈ field marshal GB, general of the army US.

■ **~ de camp** Hist ≈ brigadier; **~ d'Empire** marshal of the (French) Empire; **~ de France** marshal of France; **~ des logis** ≈ sergeant; **~ des logis-chef** ≈ staff sergeant.

maréchalat /maʀeʃala/ *nm* marshalcy, marshalship.

maréchale /maʀeʃal/ *nf* marshal's wife.

maréchalerie /maʀeʃalʀi/ *nf* **1** (profession) farriery, blacksmith's trade; **2** (atelier) blacksmith's workshop.

maréchal-ferrant, *pl* **maréchaux-ferrants** /maʀeʃalfɛʀɑ̃, maʀeʃofɛʀɑ̃/ ▶**510** *nm* farrier, blacksmith.

maréchaussée /maʀeʃose/ *nf* Hist mounted police (+ *v pl*); **voilà la ~!** hum here come the police!

marée /maʀe/ *nf* **1** Géog tide; **la ~ monte/descend** the tide is coming in/is going out; **une ~ d'équinoxe** an equinoctial tide; **les grandes ~s** the spring tides; **à ~ haute/basse** at high/low tide, at high/low water; **la ~ montante/descendante** the rising/ebbing tide; **à ~ montante/descendante** when the tide comes in/goes out; **partir avec la ~** [*bateau, pêcheur*] to leave with the tide; [*temps, nuage*] to disappear as the tide goes out; **l'odeur de la ~** the smell of the sea; **sentir la ~** [*air*] to smell of the sea; **2** fig (de personnes, sentiments, d'émotions) flood; (de voitures) mass, flood; **une ~ humaine** a human tide; **une ~ d'antisémitisme** a tide of antisemitism; **3** (produits pêchés) fresh fish.

■ **~ noire** oil slick.

IDIOMES **contre vents et ~s** (à l'avenir) come hell or high water; (dans le passé) against all odds.

marelle /maʀɛl/ ▶**449** *nf* hopscotch; **jouer à la ~** to play hopscotch.

marémoteur, **-trice** /maʀemɔtœʀ, tʀis/ *adj* tidal; **usine marémotrice** tidal power station.

marengo /maʀɛ̃go/ **I** *adj inv* Culin **veau ~** veal Marengo.

II *nm* Mode dark cloth with white flecks.

marennes /maʀɛn/ *nf inv* Marennes oyster.

mareyeur, **-euse** /maʀɛjœʀ, øz/ ▶**510** *nm,f* fish wholesaler.

margarine /maʀgaʀin/ *nf* margarine.

marge /maʀʒ/ **I** *nf* **1** Imprim (espace) margin; **~ de gauche/droite/du haut/bas** left/right/top/bottom margin; **laisser/tracer une**

~ de 4 cm à gauche to leave/to rule a margin of 4 cm on the left of the page; **annoter un texte dans la** or **en ~** to make notes on a text in the margin; **2** (écart) leeway; **on a 10 minutes de ~ pour changer de train** we've got 10 minutes ou 10 minutes' leeway to change trains; **le train n'est qu'à midi, on a de la ~** the train isn't until midday, we've got plenty of leeway; **tu peux mettre ta valise, il y a de la ~** you can put your suitcase in, there's plenty of room; **se sentir en ~** to feel like an outsider; **3** (latitude) scope; **tu devrais me laisser plus de ~ d'autonomie/plus de ~ de décision** you should give ou allow me more autonomy/more scope for making decisions; **leur ~ d'action est faible** or **étroite** they have very little room for manoeuvre GB ou maneuver US; **ne disposer d'aucune ~ d'initiative** to have no scope to use one's initiative; **4** Comm (profit) (écart) profit margin; (pourcentage) mark-up; **avoir une faible ~** to have a small profit margin.

II **en marge de** *loc prép* **1** (à l'écart) **vivre en ~ de la société** to live on the fringes of society; **vivre en ~ de la loi** to live outside the law; **certains pays craignent de rester en ~ de l'Europe** some countries are afraid they will remain on the periphery of Europe; **2** (parallèlement) **les chefs d'État se sont rencontrés en ~ de la conférence** the heads of state met outside the conference proper; **en ~ de la réunion, le président a déclaré à la presse** outside the meeting, the president told the press; **deux protocoles ont été signés en ~ de l'accord de septembre** two treaties were signed alongside September's agreement; **en ~ des cérémonies officielles** alongside the official celebrations.

■ **~ bénéficiaire** profit margin; **~ brute** gross profit; **~ brute d'autofinancement**, **MBA** cash flow; **~ commerciale** gross profit; **~ continentale** continental shelf; **~ d'erreur** margin of error; **~ de fluctuation** margin of fluctuation, fluctuation band; **~ de garantie** margin; **~ de liberté** degree of freedom; **~ de manœuvre** room for manoeuvre GB ou maneuver US; **~ de sécurité** safety margin; **~ de tolérance** tolerance margin.

margelle /maʀʒɛl/ *nf* edge, rim (**de** of).

marger /maʀʒe/ [13] *vtr* **1** (réserver une marge) to set the margins of [*texte, page*]; **~ à gauche de 4 centimètres** to set the left margin at 4 centimetres[GB]; **2** Imprim to feed [sth] (in) [*feuille*].

margeur /maʀʒœʀ/ *nm* Imprim (de machine à écrire) margin stop; (machine) machine feeder.

marginal, **~e**, *mpl* **-aux** /maʀʒinal, o/ I *adj* **1** (secondaire) [*occupations, rôle*] marginal; **2** (non conformiste) [*artiste, métier*] fringe (*épith*); **3** (en marge de la société) on the margins of society (*après n*); **4** (dans la marge) [*note, commentaire*] in the margin (*après n*); **5** Écon, Stat marginal.

II *nm,f* dropout; **les marginaux** the fringe elements of society.

marginalisation /maʀʒinalizasjɔ̃/ *nf* marginalization.

marginaliser /maʀʒinalize/ [1] I *vtr* to marginalize [*politicien, communauté*].

II **se marginaliser** *vpr* [*communauté*] to put oneself on the fringes of society; [*artiste*] to put oneself on the fringe.

marginalisme /maʀʒinalism/ *nm* Écon marginalism.

marginalité /maʀʒinalite/ *nf* marginality; **vivre dans la ~** to live on the fringes of society; **le parti est sorti de la ~** the party has come in from the cold.

margoulette○ /maʀgulɛt/ *nf* **se casser la ~** to come a cropper○ GB, to fall flat on one's face.

margoulin○ /maʀgulɛ̃/ *nm* crook○, conman.

marguerite /maʀgəʀit/ *nf* **1** (fleur) daisy; **2** (de machine à écrire) daisywheel; **imprimante à ~** daisywheel printer.

IDIOMES **effeuiller la ~** to play he/she loves me, he/she loves me not.

marguillier /maʀgije/ *nm* churchwarden.

mari /maʀi/ *nm* husband.

mariable /maʀjabl/ *adj* marriageable.

mariage /maʀjaʒ/ *nm* **1** (union) marriage; **donner sa fille en ~** to give one's daughter in marriage; **un ~ heureux** a happy marriage; **s'opposer à un ~** to oppose a marriage; **au début de leur ~** in the early days of their marriage; **il ne pense qu'au ~** marriage is all he thinks about; **fêter ses 50 ans de ~** to celebrate fifty years of marriage; **né d'un premier ~** from a previous marriage; **faire un ~ de raison** or **convenance** to make a marriage of convenience; **faire un ~ d'amour/argent** to marry for love/money; **faire un riche ~** to marry into money; **un enfant né hors ~** a child born out of wedlock; **c'est pour quand le ~?** when is the big day?; **2** (cérémonie) wedding; **la cérémonie du ~** the wedding ceremony; **un ~ en blanc** a white wedding; **le ~ a été célébré hier/à la mairie** the wedding took place yesterday/at the Town Hall; **leur ~ a été célébré à l'église** their marriage was followed by a church service; **cadeau de ~** wedding present; **messe de ~** nuptial mass; **3** fig (association) (de couleurs, parfums, goûts) marriage; (d'entreprises, de réseaux) merger; (de partis) alliance; (de techniques) fusion; **4** Jeux (aux cartes) marriage; **faire des ~s** to score marriages; **faire le ~ à pique** to have the King and Queen of spades.

■ **~ blanc** (contrat) marriage in name only, paper marriage; (non consommé) unconsummated marriage; **faire un ~ blanc** (contractuel) to marry in name only; (ne pas le consommer) to have an unconsummated marriage; **~ civil** register office ou civil wedding; **faire un ~ civil** to have a register office ou civil wedding; **~ de la main gauche**† common-law marriage; **c'est un ~ de la main gauche** they're living together; **~ morganatique** morganatic marriage; **~ putatif** putative marriage; **~ religieux** church wedding; **faire un ~ religieux** to have a church wedding.

IDIOMES **c'est le ~ de la carpe et du lapin**○ it's a mismatch.

marial, **~e**, *mpl* **~s** or **-iaux** /maʀjal, o/ *adj* Marian.

Marianne /maʀjan/ *npr* Marianne (*female figure personifying the French Republic*).

Mariannes /maʀjan/ ▶321, 416 *nprfpl* **îles ~** Mariana Islands.

Marie /maʀi/ *npr* Bible Mary.

marié, **~e** /maʀje/ I *pp* ▶ **marier**.

II *pp adj* [*personne, couple*] married (**à, avec** to); **être bien/mal ~** to have made a good/bad marriage.

III *nm,f* **le (jeune) ~** the (bride)groom; **la (jeune) ~e** the bride; **les (jeunes) ~s** the newlyweds; **vive la ~e!** bless the bride!; **vive le ~!** bless the groom!

marie-couche-toi-là◑ /maʀikuʃtwala/ *nf inv* offensive tart○, promiscuous woman.

marie-jeanne○ /maʀiʒan/ *nf* marijuana.

marie-louise, *pl* **maries-louises** /maʀi lwiz/ *nf* (picture) mount.

marier /maʀje/ [2] I *vtr* **1** (unir) [*maire, prêtre*] to marry [*personne*] (**à, avec** to); **ils sont mariés depuis dix ans** they've been married (for) ten years; **avoir des filles à ~** to have daughters to marry off; **on l'a mariée de force à 18 ans** she was forced into marriage when she was 18; **nous avons encore un fils à ~** we still have one unmarried son; **elle marie sa sœur samedi**○ she's going to her sister's wedding on Saturday; **je n'ai pas de compte à te rendre, on n'est pas mariés**○! I don't owe you an explanation, we're not married!; **2**○ (épouser) to marry; **il a marié la fille du boulanger**○ he married the baker's daughter; **3** (associer) to marry [*couleurs, parfums, goûts, styles, sons, langues*]; **l'écossais est facile à ~ avec les couleurs franches** tartan marries ou goes well with plain colours[GB].

II **se marier** *vpr* **1** [*personne*] to get married; **se ~ avec qn** to marry sb, to get married to sb; **ils se sont mariés à l'église** their marriage was followed by a church service; **2** [*tissus, couleurs*] to go well (**avec** with).

marie-salope, *pl* **maries-salopes** /maʀisalɔp/ *nf* **1** Naut hopper barge; **2**◑ (femme malpropre) slut◑.

marieur, **-ieuse** /maʀjœʀ, øz/ *nm,f* matchmaker.

marigot /maʀigo/ *nm* marshland.

marijuana /maʀiʀwana/ *nf* marijuana.

marin, **~e**[1] /maʀɛ̃, in/ I *adj* **1** (de mer) [*courant, faune*] marine (*épith*); [*air, sel, monstre*] sea (*épith*); [*prospection*] offshore (*épith*); [*bateau*] seaworthy; **2** (de marin) **pull ~** seaman's jersey; **costume ~** sailor suit.

II *nm* sailor; **peuple de ~s** seafaring nation.

■ **~ d'eau douce** fair-weather sailor; **~ pêcheur** fisherman.

IDIOMES **avoir le pied ~** to be a good sailor, not to get seasick.

marina /maʀina/ *nf* marina.

marinade /maʀinad/ *nf* marinade.

marine[2] /maʀin/ I ▶193 *adj inv* (couleur) navy (blue).

II *nm* (soldat) marine.

III *nf* **1** Mil Naut, Naut navy; **~ marchande** merchant navy; **~ de guerre** navy; **de ~** [*instrument, expression, signaux*] nautical; **2** Art seascape.

mariner /maʀine/ [1] I *vtr* gén to marinate; **harengs marinés** pickled herrings.

II *vi* **1** Culin to marinate; **2**○ (attendre) to hang about○; (en prison) to stew○; **laisser** or **faire ~ qn** to let sb stew.

maringouin /maʀɛ̃gwɛ̃/ *nm* C mosquito.

marinier /maʀinje/ ▶510 *nm* bargee GB, bargeman US.

marinière /maʀinjɛʀ/ *nf* Mode smock.

mariol(le)◑ /maʀjɔl/ *nm* **c'est un ~** (rusé) he's a crafty bugger◑; (fanfaron incompétent) he thinks he's smart, he's a wise guy○ US; **faire le** or **son ~** to try to be smart.

marionnette /maʀjɔnɛt/ I *nf* lit, fig puppet.

II **marionnettes** *nfpl* puppet show (*sg*).

■ **~ à fils** marionette; **~ à gaine** glove puppet.

marionnettiste /maʀjɔnetist/ ▶510 *nmf* puppeteer.

mariste /maʀist/ *nmf* Marist.

marital, **~e**, *mpl* **-aux** /maʀital, o/ *adj* Jur **sans autorisation ~e** without the husband's permission.

maritalement /maʀitalmɑ̃/ *adv* **vivre ~** to live as man and wife.

maritime /maʀitim/ *adj* **1** (près de la mer) [*climat, plante*] maritime; [*région*] coastal; **2** (utilisant la mer) [*navigation, trafic, fret, nation, commerce*] maritime; [*compagnie, agent*] shipping.

marivaudage /maʀivodaʒ/ *nm* **1** (badinage) gallant sophisticated banter; **2** Littérat refined affectation (*in the style of Marivaux*).

marivauder /maʀivode/ [1] *vi* (badiner) to exchange gallant sophisticated banter.

marjolaine /maʀʒɔlɛn/ *nf* marjoram.

mark /maʀk/ ▶46 *nm* mark; **~ allemand** German mark.

marketing /maʀketiŋ/ *nm* marketing; **~ direct** direct marketing.

marlin /maʀlɛ̃/ *nm* marlin.

marlou◑ /maʀlu/ *nm* ponce◑ GB, pimp.

marmaille○ /maʀmaj/ *nf* rabble of kids○ ou brats○ péj; **taisez-vous, la ~!** shut up, you rabble!

marmelade /maʀməlad/ *nf* **1** Culin stewed

fruit; **~ d'abricots** stewed apricots; **2**○ (aliment trop cuit) mush; **en ~** [*aliments cuits*] cooked to a mush; [*aliments crus*] squashed into a pulp; **réduire qn en ~**○ to beat sb to a pulp○; **j'ai le dos en ~**○ my back is killing○ me.

■ **~ d'oranges** (orange) marmalade.

marmite /maʀmit/ *nf* **1** (pour ragoût) casserole; (pour soupe) pot; **2** (contenu) potful.

■ **~ de géant** Géol pothole; **~ norvégienne** haybox.

IDIOMES **faire bouillir la ~** to bring home the bacon.

marmiton /maʀmitɔ̃/ *nm* chef's assistant.

marmonnement /maʀmɔnmɑ̃/ *nm* (murmure) mumbling ¢; (ronchonnement) muttering ¢.

marmonner /maʀmɔne/ [1] *vtr* to mumble [*prière, excuse*]; to mutter [*injure*]; **qu'est-ce que tu marmonnes?** what are you mumbling about?

marmoréen, -éenne /maʀmɔʀeɛ̃, ɛn/ *adj* **1** Géol [*roche*] marble; **2** littér [*beauté*] marble-like; [*froideur*] marmoreal.

marmot○ /maʀmo/ *nm* kid○, brat○ péj.

IDIOMES **croquer le ~** to hang about.

marmotte /maʀmɔt/ *nf* **1** Zool marmot; **2** fig sleepyhead.

IDIOMES **dormir comme une ~** to sleep like a log.

marmottement /maʀmɔtmɑ̃/ *nm* (murmure) mumbling ¢; (ronchonnement) muttering ¢.

marmotter /maʀmɔte/ [1] *vtr* to mumble [*prière, excuse*]; to mutter [*injure*].

marmouset /maʀmuzɛ/ *nm* **1** (figurine) grotesque figurine; **2**○ †(enfant) nipper GB, shover US.

marnage /maʀnaʒ/ *nm* **1** Agric marling; **2** Géog tidal range.

marne /maʀn/ *nf* marl.

Marne /maʀn/ ▶ 357, 692 *nprf* (rivière, département) **la ~** the Marne.

marner /maʀne/ [1] **I** *vtr* Agric to marl.

II○ *vi* to slog away○; **faire ~ qn** to make sb slog.

marneux, -euse /maʀnø, øz/ *adj* marly.

marnière /maʀnjɛʀ/ *nf* marl pit.

Maroc /maʀɔk/ ▶ 321 *nprm* Morocco.

marocain, ~e /maʀɔkɛ̃, ɛn/ ▶ 537 *adj* Moroccan.

Marocain, ~e /maʀɔkɛ̃, ɛn/ ▶ 537 *nm,f* Moroccan.

maronite /maʀɔnit/ *adj, nmf* Maronite.

maronner○ /maʀɔne/ [1] *vi* to moan and groan; **ça m'a fait ~** it made me cross.

maroquin /maʀɔkɛ̃/ *nm* **1** (cuir) morocco (leather); **2** fig (portefeuille ministériel) **obtenir un ~** to become a minister.

maroquinerie /maʀɔkinʀi/ ▶ 510 *nf* **1** (magasin) leather shop; **2** (art) leather craftsmanship; (industrie) leather industry; (commerce) leather trade; (articles) leather goods (*pl*).

maroquinier /maʀɔkinje/ ▶ 510 *nm* **1** (commerçant) trader in fine leather goods; **2** (artisan) fine leather craftsman; (fabricant) producer of fine leather goods.

marotte /maʀɔt/ *nf* **1** (thème favori) pet subject, hobby horse; (occupation) pet ou favourite[GB] hobby; **il a la ~ des mots croisés** doing crosswords is his pet hobby; **2** (marionnette) puppet; **3** Hist (de bouffon) (fool's) bauble.

marouflage /maʀuflaʒ/ *nm* marouflage.

maroufle /maʀufl/ *nf* strong glue.

maroufler /maʀufle/ [1] *vtr* **1** (coller) to stick, to marouflage spéc; **2** (renforcer) to back; (avec tissu) to line.

marquage /maʀkaʒ/ *nm* **1** (étiquetage) gén marking; (au fer) branding; **le ~ des bêtes d'un troupeau** branding the animals in a herd; **le ~ du linge est obligatoire** clothes must have a name tag; **2** Sport marking; **le ~ d'un adversaire** marking an opponent; **3** Gén Civ (de route) road marking; **4** Ordinat highlighting ¢.

marquant, ~e /maʀkɑ̃, ɑ̃t/ *adj* [*fait, événement, moment*] memorable; [*souvenir*] lasting; [*qualité, rôle, élément*] essential; [*personne, œuvre, spectacle*] outstanding.

marque /maʀk/ *nf* **1** Comm, Ind (dénomination) (de café, lessive, cosmétique) brand; (de machine à laver, matériel hi-fi, voiture, d'ordinateur) make; **quelle ~ de dentifrice me conseilles-tu?** what brand of toothpaste do you advise me to get?; **la première ~ de chaussures de sport** the top name in sport shoes; **des voitures de ~ japonaise** Japanese cars; **produits de ~** branded goods ou articles; **2** (trace) mark; (indice) sign; **faire une ~ sur le mur** to make a mark on the wall; **faire une ~ au couteau** to make a notch with a knife; **les ~s du bétail** the brands on cattle; **~ de pneus** skid mark; **porter les ~s du temps** to show signs of age; **on voit encore les ~s de coups** you can still see the bruises; **~s d'usure/d'érosion/de fatigue** signs of wear/of erosion/of fatigue; **~ de naissance** birthmark; **~ de doigts** fingermarks (*pl*); **~ de pas** footprint; **~ de brûlure** (sur un tissu) scorch mark; (sur la peau, le parquet) burn; **les ~s d'une richesse passée** the signs of past wealth; **3** (preuve) sign; (expression) mark; **c'est la ~ d'une grande confiance en soi** it's a sign of great self-confidence; **il l'a fait en ~ d'estime** he did it as a mark of his esteem; **4** (particularité) mark; **la ~ d'un artiste** an artist's mark; **laisser sa ~** to make one's mark; **5** (haut niveau) **invité de ~** distinguished guest, VIP; **personnage de ~** eminent person; **6** Jeux, Sport (décompte) score; **tenir la ~** to keep (the) score; **la ~ est de 2 à 1** the score is 2 to 1; **mener à la ~** to be in the lead; **prendre ses ~s** (en saut) to plan one's run-up; **à vos ~s, prêts, partez!** (au départ d'une course) on your marks, get set, go!; **7** Ling marker; **~ du pluriel** plural marker.

■ **~ déposée** Comm registered trademark; **~ de fabricant** or **fabrication** manufacturer's brand name; **~ de fabrique** trademark; **~ d'infamie** stigma.

marqué, ~e /maʀke/ **I** *pp* ▶ **marquer**.

II *pp adj* **1** (affecté) **il a le corps ~ de traces de coups** he's bruised all over; **elle est restée ~e par la guerre** the war left its mark on her; **c'est un homme ~** he's been through the mill; **visage ~** worn face; **traits ~s** worn features; **2** (affirmé) definite; **différence ~e** definite difference; **préférence ~e** distinct preference; **elle est trop ~e à gauche** she comes over as too left-wing; **il a des opinions très ~es** he's very opinionated; **être ~ politiquement** to be known for one's political views; **3** (jalonné) marked; **une époque ~e par les conflits sociaux** a period marked by social unrest; **4** Ling marked; **non ~** unmarked.

marquer /maʀke/ [1] **I** *vtr* **1** (étiqueter) to mark [*article*]; to brand [*bétail*]; to mark out [*emplacement, limite*]; **~ des vêtements au nom d'un enfant** to put nametapes on a child's clothes; **~ d'une croix** to mark with a cross; **2** (signaler) to mark, to signal [*début, fin, rupture*]; **~ la reprise des hostilités** to mark ou signal the renewal of hostilities; **3** (laisser une trace sur) [*personne, coup, empreinte*] to mark [*corps, objet*]; **des taches de graisse marquent les pages** the pages are covered in greasy marks; ▶ **blanc**; **4** (influencer) [*événement, drame, œuvre*] to leave its mark on [*personne, esprit*]; **c'est quelqu'un qui m'a beaucoup marqué** he/she was a strong influence on me; **c'est un événement qui m'a beaucoup marqué** it's an event that really left its mark on me; **5** (écrire) to mark [*prix*]; to write [sth] (down), to put [sth] (down) [*renseignement*]; **j'ai oublié de ~ la date dans mon agenda** I forgot to put the date in my diary; **marquez cela sur mon compte** put it on my account; **~ les élèves absents** to mark students absent; **qu'est-ce qu'il y a de marqué?** what does it say?; **6** (indiquer) [*montre*] to say [*heure*]; [*jauge, chiffres*] to show [*pression, température*]; **l'horloge marque dix heures** the clock says ten o'clock; **le thermomètre marque 35°C** the thermometer registers ou says 35°C; **~ le féminin** Ling to indicate the feminine; **l'aiguille marquait 60 km/h** the speedometer was at 60 km/h; **il marquait ses propos d'un hochement de tête** he nodded emphatically as he spoke; **~ la mesure** Mus to beat time; **7** (exprimer) to show [*volonté, désapprobation, sentiment*]; **il faut ~ le coup** (célébrer) let's celebrate; (exprimer le mécontentement) we can't let it go just like that; **quand quelqu'un a mentionné son nom, il a marqué le coup** when he heard the name, it really registered; **8** (souligner) **~ une fête nationale par un défilé** to celebrate a national holiday with a parade; **9** (faire) **~ un temps (d'arrêt)** to pause; **~ un silence** to fall silent; **10** (être caractéristique de) [*idée, discours, attitude*] to be characteristic of [*personne, parti, époque*]; **11** Sport to score [*but, essai, point*]; to mark [*adversaire*].

II *vi* **1** (laisser une trace) to leave a mark (**sur** on); **2** (être important) [*homme politique, artiste*] to leave one's mark; [*événement*] to be significant; **un événement qui a marqué dans l'histoire** a significant historical event; **3** Sport to score; **il a réussi à ~** he managed to score.

marqueté, ~e /maʀkəte/ *adj* inlaid.

marqueterie /maʀkɛtʀi/ *nf* **1** (art) marquetry; (produit) inlay; **en ~** inlaid; **bois de ~** inlay, wood for marquetry; **2** fig (ensemble disparate) mosaic.

marqueur, -euse /maʀkœʀ, øz/ **I** *nm,f* Jeux, Sport (de points, buts) scorer; Agric (de bétail) brander; Comm (de marchandises) marker; Mil (de tir) marker.

II *nm* **1** (stylo) marker (pen); **2** Biol, Ling marker; **3** Jeux, Sport (tableau) scoreboard.

III marqueuse *nf* (machine) labelling[GB] machine.

■ **~ radioactif** Chimie label.

marquis, ~e /maʀki, iz/ **I** *nm,f* (titre) marquis/marchioness.

II marquise *nf* **1** (auvent) glass canopy GB, marquee US; (tente) marquee GB, tent US; **2** (bague) marquise ring; **3** (siège) ≈ Gainsborough chair; **4** Culin **~e (au chocolat)** rich chocolate mousse.

marquisat /maʀkiza/ *nm* (titre, fief) marquisate.

marquise ▶ **marquis** I, II.

Marquises /maʀkiz/ ▶ 416 *nprfpl* **les (îles) ~** the Marquesas Islands.

marraine /maʀɛn/ *nf* **1** Relig (d'enfant) godmother; **être (la) ~ de qn** to be godmother to sb; **2** (d'enfant défavorisé) sponsor; **3** (de fleur) **~ d'une rose** *woman after whom a rose is named*; (de bateau) *woman who ceremonially launches a ship*; **4** (de candidat) sponsor.

■ Note en anglais *godmother* n'est jamais une forme d'adresse.

■ **~ de guerre** *soldier's wartime female penfriend*.

Marrakech /maʀakɛʃ/ ▶ 857 *npr* Marrakesh.

marrant○, **~e** /maʀɑ̃, ɑ̃t/ **I** *adj* **1** (amusant) funny; **ce qu'il est ~!** he's a laugh○; **ce/il n'est pas ~** (ennuyeux) it's/he's not much fun; (austère, déprimant) it's/he's pretty grim○; (pénible) it's/he's a real pain○; **2** (bizarre) funny, odd.

II *nm,f* lit, iron joker.

marre○ /maʀ/ *adv* **en avoir ~** to be fed up○ (**de qch** with sth; **de faire** with doing); **je commence à en avoir plus que ~ de ce boulot** I've had just about enough of this job; **y en a ~** enough's enough; **c'est ~** that's that.

marrer○: **se marrer** /maʀe/ [1] *vpr* (s'amuser) to have a great time; (rire) to have a good laugh; **il n'y a pas de quoi se ~** there's nothing to laugh about; **faire ~ qn** to make sb laugh; **qu'est-ce qui te fait ~?** what are you laughing about?

marri†, **~e** /maʀi/ *adj* saddened, grieved†.

marron, **-onne** /maʀɔ̃, ɔn/ I *adj* **1** (malhonnête) [*notaire, avocat*] bent○, crooked; (non qualifié) [*courtier*] unlicensed; [*docteur*] unqualified; **2** Hist [*esclave*] runaway.
II ▶193 *adj inv* (couleur) brown; **~ clair/foncé** light/dark brown.
III *nm* **1** Bot (non comestible) horse chestnut, conker GB; (châtaigne) chestnut; **2** (couleur) brown; **3**◐ (coup) thump○, clout○; **il m'a filé un ~** he landed me one○.
■ **~ glacé** marron glacé; **~ d'Inde** horse chestnut, conker GB; **~s chauds** roast chestnuts.
IDIOMES **tirer les ~s du feu** fig (faire son profit) to reap the benefits; (être la victime) to be a cat's paw; **je suis ~**◐ (dupé) I've been had○; (coincé) I'm stuck○.

marronnier /maʀɔnje/ *nm* chestnut (tree).
■ **~ d'Inde** horse chestnut (tree).

mars /maʀs/ ▶521 *nm* March.
IDIOMES **arriver comme ~ en carême** to come as sure as night follows day.

Mars /maʀs/ I *npr* Mythol Mars.
II *nprf* Astron Mars.

marseillais, **~e** /maʀsɛjɛ, ɛz/ ▶857 *adj* of Marseilles; **une histoire ~e** ≈ a tall story.

Marseillais, **~e** /maʀsɛjɛ, ɛz/ I *nm,f* (natif) native of Marseilles; (habitant) inhabitant of Marseilles.
II **Marseillaise** *nf* Marseillaise (*French national anthem*).

Marseille /maʀsɛj/ ▶857 *npr* Marseilles.

marsouin /maʀswɛ̃/ *nm* **1** Zool porpoise; **2**† soldiers' slang ≈ marine.

marsupial, **~e**, *mpl* **-iaux** /maʀsypjal, o/ I *adj* marsupial.
II *nm* marsupial.

marte /maʀt/ *nf* = **martre**.

marteau, *pl* **~x** /maʀto/ I○ *adj* cracked○.
II *nm* **1** (de menuisier, commissaire-priseur, médecin, piano) hammer; (de juge, président) gavel; (de porte) knocker; (d'horloge) striker; **un coup de ~** a blow from a hammer; **donner un coup de ~ à qch** to hit sth with a hammer; **enfoncer qch à coups de ~** to hammer sth in; **casser qch à coups de ~** to take a hammer to sth; **passer sous le ~** (aux enchères) to come under the hammer; **2** Anat hammer; **3** ▶449 Sport hammer; **lancer le ~** to throw the hammer.
■ **~ pneumatique** pneumatic drill; ▶ **enclume**.

martel† /maʀtɛl/ *nm* **se mettre ~ en tête** to get worried (**pour** about).

martelage /maʀtəlaʒ/ *nm* (de métal) beating.

martèlement /maʀtɛlmɑ̃/ *nm* **1** (bruit) hammering; (d'obus, de talons, musique) pounding; **2** (de métal) beating; **3** fig (de mots) rapping out.

marteler /maʀtəle/ [17] *vtr* **1** [*forgeron, orfèvre*] to beat, to planish spéc [*métal*]; [*poings, talons, artillerie*] to pound; **cuivre martelé** beaten copper; **~ qn de ses poings** to pound away at sb with one's fists; **leurs bottes martelaient le pavé** their boots pounded on the cobbles; **cette musique me martèle le crâne**○ this music is pounding through my head; **2** (scander) to rap out [*syllabes, phrases*]; **3** (répéter) **~ qch à qn** to hammer sth into sb; **~ à qn que** to drum it into sb that.

martial, **~e**, *mpl* **-iaux** /maʀsjal, o/ *adj* [*art*] martial; [*air, pas*] military.

martien, **-ienne** /maʀsjɛ̃, ɛn/ *adj, nm,f* Martian.

martinet /maʀtinɛ/ *nm* **1** Zool swift; **2** (fouet) ≈ whip; **3** Tech tilt hammer.

martingale /maʀtɛ̃gal/ *nf* **1** Cout half belt; **2** Équit martingale; **3** Jeux (doublement) martingale; (système) winning system.

martiniquais, **~e** /maʀtinikɛ, ɛz/ *adj* Martinique (*épith*).

Martiniquais, **~e** /maʀtinikɛ, ɛz/ *nm,f* (natif) native of Martinique; (habitant) inhabitant of Martinique.

Martinique /maʀtinik/ ▶692, 416 *nprf* **la ~** Martinique.

martin-pêcheur, *pl* **martins-pêcheurs** /maʀtɛ̃pɛʃœʀ/ *nm* kingfisher.

martre /maʀtʀ/ *nf* **1** (animal) marten; **2** (fourrure) sable; **manteau de ~** sable (coat); **pinceau de ~** sable hair brush.

martyr, **~e**[1] /maʀtiʀ/ I *adj* [*héros, nation*] martyred littér; **enfant ~** battered child.
II *nm,f* martyr (**d'une cause** to a cause); **être le ~ de qn** to be tormented by sb; **être le ~ de son ambition** to be a martyr to one's ambition.
IDIOMES **prendre** or **se donner des airs de ~** to put on a martyred look.

martyre[2] /maʀtiʀ/ *nm* (supplice) Relig, fig martyrdom; (souffrance) agony, suffering; **sa vie fut un long ~** his/her life was one of constant suffering; **c'est un ~ pour les parents** it's agonizing for the parents; **pour lui, l'inaction est un ~** for him, inactivity is sheer torture; **souffrir le ~** to suffer agony; **je souffre le ~ dans ces chaussures** these shoes are sheer torture.

martyriser /maʀtiʀize/ [1] *vtr* **1** (torturer) [*personne*] to torment [*victime, animal*]; to batter [*enfant*]; **2** Relig to martyr.

marxien, **-ienne** /maʀksjɛ̃, ɛn/ *adj* Marxian.

marxisant, **~e** /maʀksizɑ̃, ɑ̃t/ *adj* [*discours, livre*] Marxist oriented; **elle est (de tendance) ~e** she has Marxist leanings.

marxisme /maʀksism/ *nm* Marxism.

marxisme-léninisme /maʀksismleninism/ *nm* Marxism-Leninism.

marxiste /maʀksist/ *adj, nm,f* Marxist.

marxiste-léniniste, *pl* **marxistes-léninistes** /maʀksistleninist/ *adj, nmf* Marxist-Leninist.

maryland /maʀilɑ̃d/ *nm* Maryland (tobacco).

Maryland /maʀilɑ̃d/ ▶692 *nprm* Maryland.

mas /mɑ/ *nm* farmhouse (*in Provence*).

mascara /maskaʀa/ *nm* mascara.

mascarade /maskaʀad/ *nf* **1** (pour duper) farce; **~ de justice** travesty of justice; **2** (bal) masquerade; (défilé) fancy dress parade; (accoutrement) pej fancy dress.

mascaret /maskaʀɛ/ *nm* (tidal) bore.

mascotte /maskɔt/ *nf* mascot.
■ **~ de radiateur** Aut radiator badge.

masculin, **~e** /maskylɛ̃, in/ I *adj* **1** Physiol [*corps, sexualité, physiologie, hormone*] male; **le sexe ~** the male sex; **un enfant de sexe ~** a male child; **2** (pour hommes) [*revue, prêt-à-porter, parfum, activité*] men's; [*contraception, préservatif, emploi*] male; **le seul rôle ~** the only male part; **3** (composé d'hommes) [*population, collègues, chœur*] male; Sport [*équipe, club, sport, judo, record*] men's; **4** (viril) [*visage, allure*] masculine; **5** Ling [*nom, rime*] masculine.
II *nm* Ling masculine.

masculiniser /maskylinize/ [1] *vtr* (d'aspect) to make [sb] look masculine; Biol to make [sb] masculine.

masculinité /maskylinite/ *nf* **1** (qualité) masculinity; **2** (en démographie) **rapport de ~** male to female ratio.

maskinongé /maskinɔ̃ʒe/ *nm* Zool muskellunge, musky○.

maso○ /mazo/ (*abbr* = **masochiste**) I *adj inv* masochistic (*épith*); **être complètement ~** to be a real sucker for punishment○.
II *nm,f* masochist.

masochisme /mazɔʃism/ *nm* masochism.

masochiste /mazɔʃist/ I *adj* masochistic.
II *nmf* masochist.

masquage /maskaʒ/ *nm* masking.

masque /mask/ *nm* **1** (sur le visage) mask; **il avait** or **portait un ~ de chien** he was wearing a dog mask; **~ de gaze** surgical mask; **~ protecteur** protective mask; **~ d'arlequin** Harlequin mask; **~ de carnaval** carnival mask; **~ d'escrime** fencing mask; **2** Cosmét face-pack; **~ antirides** anti-wrinkle face-pack; **3** Méd (aspect) look; **le ~ de la maladie** the look of ill-health; **4** (expression) expression; (pour cacher ses sentiments) appearance; **prendre un ~ tragique** to put on a tragic expression; **se couvrir du ~ de la vertu** to hide behind the appearance of virtue; **sous le ~ de qch** under the guise of sth; **5** liter (personne) masquerader, masker; **6** Ordinat mask; **~ de saisie** data capture mask; **~ d'interruptions** interrupt mask; **7** (en graphisme) contact print; **8** Électron mask.
■ **~ d'apiculteur** beekeeper's veil; **~ funéraire** funeral mask; **~ à gaz** gas mask; **~ de grossesse** mask of pregnancy, chloasma spéc; **~ mortuaire** death mask; **~ à oxygène** oxygen mask; **~ de plongée** diving mask; **~ purifiant** Cosmét face-pack; **~ de soudeur** face shield; **le Masque de fer** the Iron Mask; **l'homme au Masque de fer** the Man in the Iron Mask.
IDIOMES **jeter le ~** to show one's true colours[GB]; **bas les ~s!** no more pretending now; **arracher le ~ à qn** to unmask sb.

masqué, **~e** /maske/ I *pp* ▶ **masquer**.
II *pp adj* **1** (avec un masque) masked; **il est apparu le visage ~** he appeared wearing a mask; **2** fig (dissimulé) [*défaut*] concealed; [*voix*] disguised.

masquer /maske/ [1] I *vtr* **1** (cacher) to conceal [*usure, défaut*] (**à** from); to hide [*paysage*] (**à** from); to mask [*sentiment, vérité, problème, phénomène, goût, odeur*]; **2** (couvrir) to block [*orifice, lumière*]; to cover [*lampe*]; **3** Mil to mask [*dispositif*].
II **se masquer** *vpr* (se cacher à soi-même) to hide [sth] from oneself [*vérité, sentiment*].

Massachusetts /masaʃysɛts/ ▶692 *nprm* Massachusetts.

massacrante /masakʀɑ̃t/ *adj f* **être d'humeur ~** to be in a foul mood.

massacre /masakʀ/ *nm* **1** (tuerie) (de personnes) massacre ¢; (d'animaux) slaughter ¢; **2**○ Sport, fig massacre; **3**○ (gâchis) botch(-up); **ne peins pas ça, tu vas faire un ~**○ don't paint it, you'll make a hash○ of it; **4** Chasse (trophée) stag's antlers (*pl*); **5** Hérald attire.
■ **le Massacre des Innocents** Bible the Massacre of the Innocents.
IDIOMES **faire un ~**○ [*acteur, chanteur*] to be a roaring○ success; [*homme d'affaires, joueur*] to make a killing; **arrêtez le ~**○! stop making such a mess of things!

massacrer /masakʀe/ [1] I *vtr* **1** (tuer) to massacre, to slaughter [*personnes*]; to slaughter [*animaux*]; **2**○ (battre à plate couture) to slaughter○, to make mincemeat of○ [*adversaire*]; **se faire ~** to be slaughtered ou thrashed; **3**○ (abîmer) to wreck, to ruin; (en taillant) to hack [sth] about; **4**○ (maltraiter) to make a complete mess of [*poème, musique*]; to botch [*travail, traduction*]; **il massacre le français** his French is atrocious; **5**○ (critiquer) to savage GB, to trash US [*auteur, œuvre*].
II **se massacrer** *vpr* **1** [*ennemis*] lit, fig to slaughter one another; **2**○ (se taillader, s'écorcher) **elle s'est massacré les mains dans les ronces** she cut her hands to ribbons in the brambles.

massage /masaʒ/ *nm* massage; **faire un ~ à qn** to give sb a massage.
■ **~ cardiaque** Méd heart massage; **~ thaïlandais** Thai massage.

masse /mas/ *nf* **1** (ensemble) mass; **~ rocheuse** rocky mass; **~ neigeuse/nua-**

geuse mass of snow/cloud; **~ d'air chaud** mass of warm air; **~ d'eau** body of water; **~ informe** shapeless mass; **une ~ humaine** a mass of humanity; **la ~ croissante des chômeurs** the swelling ranks of the unemployed (*pl*); **statue taillée dans la ~** statue hewn from the block; **homme taillé dans la ~** tall muscular man; **teinté dans la ~** mass-coloured[GB]; **2** (grande quantité) **une ~ de** a lot of; **une ~ de poussière/documents** a lot of dust/documents; **exécutions en ~** mass executions; **faire des recrutements en ~** to embark on a mass recruitment drive; **ils sont venus en ~** they came in droves; **produire qch en ~** to mass-produce sth; **production de ~** mass production; **la population a voté en ~** there was a high turnout at the election; **les manifestants ont envahi le stade en ~** the demonstrators invaded the stadium en masse; **il a des ~s○ d'argent/de copains/de livres** he's got masses ou loads○ of money/of friends/of books; **'tu as aimé ce livre?'—'pas des ~s'○** 'did you like this book?'—'not much ou particularly'; **je ne le connais pas des ~s○** I don't know him that well; **des hommes comme lui, je n'en connais pas des ~s○** he's a rare bird; **3** (majorité) bulk; **la ~ des électeurs demeure indécise** the bulk of the electorate remains undecided; **4** (peuple) **la ~** the masses (*pl*); **~s laborieuses** working classes; **les ~s paysannes** the peasantry (+ *v sg* ou *pl*); **culture de ~** mass culture; **littérature de ~** popular literature; **enseignement/loisirs de ~** education/leisure activities for the masses; **moyens de communication de ~** mass media; **5** Phys mass; **~ atomique/moléculaire** atomic/molecular mass; **6** Électrotech earth GB, ground US; **mettre un fil électrique à la ~** to earth GB ou ground US an electric wire; **7** Art mass; **8** Pharm mass; **9** (maillet) sledgehammer; **enfoncer qch à la ~** or **à coups de ~** to knock sth in with a sledgehammer.

■ **~ d'armes** mace; **~ critique** critical mass; **~ inerte** inertial mass; **~ monétaire** money supply; **~ pesante** gravitational mass; **~ salariale** (total) wage bill; **~ spécifique** or **volumique** density.

IDIOMES **se noyer** or **fondre dans la ~** to get lost in the crowd; **(se laisser) tomber comme une ~** to collapse; **dormir comme une ~** to sleep like a log○; **être à la ~**◑ to be crackers○ GB ou nuts○, to be mad.

masselotte /maslɔt/ *nf* **1** Mécan balance weight; **2** (en fonderie) feeder.

massepain /maspɛ̃/ *nm* marzipan cake.

masser /mase/ [1] **I** *vtr* **1** (assembler) to assemble [*personnes*]; to mass [*troupes*]; **2** (frictionner) to massage [*membre, personne*]; **se faire ~** to have a massage; **3** (au billard) **~ la bille** to play a massé shot.

II se masser *vpr* **1** (s'assembler) [*badauds, troupes*] to mass; **2** (frictionner) **se ~ les jambes** to massage one's legs.

massette /masɛt/ *nf* **1** (de cantonnier) club hammer; (de tailleur de pierre) stonemason's hammer; **~ à embouts plastiques** plastic-tipped hammer; **2** Bot bulrush GB, cattail US.

masseur, **-euse** /masœʀ, øz/ ▶**510** **I** *nm,f* (personne) masseur/masseuse.

II *nm* (appareil) massager.

massicot /masiko/ *nm* **1** Imprim, Tech guillotine; **2** Minér massicot.

massicoter /masikɔte/ [1] *vtr* to guillotine.

massif, **-ive** /masif, iv/ **I** *adj* **1** (d'aspect lourd) [*colonne, porte*] massive, heavy; [*meuble, traits*] heavy; [*personne*] heavily built; [*silhouette*] massive; **2** (par la quantité, le nombre) [*attaque, dose, foule, publicité*] massive; [*licenciements*] mass (*épith*); **des départs ~s** a mass exodus; **3** (pur) **or/argent/noyer ~** solid gold/silver/walnut.

II *nm* **1** Géog massif; **2** Hort (groupe) clump; (parterre) bed.

■ **le Massif central** the Massif Central.

massification /masifikasjɔ̃/ *nf* **1** (banalisation) pej popularization; **2** (expansion) overall expansion.

massifier /masifje/ [2] *vtr* **1** (accroître) to expand massively; **2** péj to standardize [*goûts, besoins*]; **culture massifiée** culture for the masses.

massique /masik/ *adj* specific.

massivement /masivmɑ̃/ *adv* [*embaucher, manifester*] in great numbers; [*injecter*] in massive doses; [*absorber*] in large quantities; [*voter*] overwhelmingly.

mass media /masmedja/ *nmpl* mass media.

massue /masy/ *nf* gén, Sport club; **coup de ~** lit blow with a club; (événement) crushing blow; (somme) staggering sum; **donner un coup de ~ à qn/qch** lit to hit sb/sth with a club; **assommer/tuer qn à coups de ~** to club sb senseless/to death; **en ~** [*antennes*] club-shaped.

mastère /mastɛʀ/ *nm*: *Master's degree in France*.

mastic /mastik/ **I** ▶**193** *adj inv* (couleur) putty-coloured[GB], cream (*épith*).

II *nm* **1** (pour vitres) putty; (pour trous) filler; (pour arbres) grafting wax; **2** (résine) mastic; **3** (erreur) transposition.

masticage /mastikaʒ/ *nm* (de vitre) puttying; (de fente) filling.

masticateur, **-trice** /mastikatœʀ, tʀis/ *adj* masticatory.

mastication /mastikasjɔ̃/ *nf* mastication.

masticatoire /mastikatwaʀ/ *adj, nm* masticatory.

mastiquer /mastike/ [1] *vtr* **1** (mâcher) to chew, to masticate; **2** (boucher) to putty [*vitre*]; to fill in [*fente*]; to plug [*fuite*].

mastite /mastit/ ▶**271** *nf* mastitis.

mastoc○ /mastɔk/ *adj inv* [*personne*] hefty○, bulky; [*objet*] huge.

mastodonte /mastɔdɔ̃t/ *nm* **1** fig (personne) colossus, hulk○; (animal) monster; (objet) huge thing; **2** Zool mastodon.

mastoïde /mastɔid/ *adj, nf* mastoid.

mastoïdite /mastɔidit/ *nf* mastoiditis.

masturbation /mastyʀbasjɔ̃/ *nf* masturbation.

masturber /mastyʀbe/ [1] *vtr*, **se masturber** *vpr* to masturbate.

m'as-tu-vu○ /matyvy/ **I** *adj inv* showy.

II *nmf inv* show-off.

masure /mazyʀ/ *nf* hovel.

mat, **~e** /mat/ **I** *adj* **1** [*peinture, ton, métal, papier*] matt; **2** [*peau, teint*] olive (*épith*); **3** [*son, bruit*] dull; **4** Phon mellow.

II *nm* (aux échecs) **~!** checkmate!; **échec et ~** checkmate; **faire qn ~** to put sb in checkmate; **être ~** to be in checkmate; **j'ai été ~ en sept coups** I was checkmated in seven moves.

mât /mɑ/ *nm* **1** Naut mast; ▶**grand**; **2** (perche, pylône) gén pole; Sport climbing pole; **~ de drapeau** flagpole.

■ **~ d'artimon** Naut mizzenmast; **~ de charge** Naut derrick; **~ de cocagne** greasy pole; **~ de hune** Naut topmast; **~ de misaine** Naut foremast; **~ de pavillon** Naut jackstaff; **~ de perroquet** Naut topgallant mast; **~ de signal** Rail signal post.

matador /matadɔʀ/ ▶**510** *nm* matador.

matamore /matamɔʀ/ *nm* braggart; **faire le ~** to swagger.

match /matʃ/ *nm* **1** Sport (jeux d'équipe) match GB, game US; (de boxe, lutte, tennis) match; **~ nul** draw GB, tie US; **faire ~ nul** to draw GB, to tie US; **2** Écon, Ind competition.

■ **~ aller** first leg; **~ amical** friendly match; **~ avancé** match GB ou game that has been brought forward; **~ de barrage** decider; **~ de classement** league match; **~ à domicile** home match ou game; **~ à l'extérieur** away match ou game; **~ retour** second leg, return match.

maté /mate/ *nm* (plante, infusion) maté.

matelas /matla/ *nm* **1** (de lit) mattress; **~ de laine/de mousse/à ressorts** woollen[GB]/foam-rubber/spring mattress; **2** (de feuilles, neige) (naturel) carpet; (pour s'étendre) bed.

■ **~ d'air** Constr air space; **~ alternant** Méd ripple mattress; **~ d'eau** water bed; **~ à langer** changing mat; **~ de plage** inflatable mattress, Lilo®; **~ pneumatique** air bed.

matelassage /matlasaʒ/ *nm* (de porte) padding; (de siège) upholstering; (de tissu) quilting.

matelassé, **~e** /matlase/ **I** *pp* ▶**matelasser**.

II *pp adj* [*tissu, vêtement*] quilted; **porte ~e** (de cuir) padded door; (de tissu) baize door.

III *nm* quilted material.

matelasser /matlase/ [1] *vtr* **1** (rembourrer) to pad [*porte*]; to upholster [*siège*]; (doubler) to quilt [*tissu, vêtement*]; **2** (recouvrir) to carpet (**de** with).

matelassier, **-ière** /matlasje, ɛʀ/ ▶**510** *nm,f* mattress maker.

matelot /matlo/ ▶**390** *nm* seaman, sailor; Mil Naut ≈ ordinary seaman GB, ≈ seaman apprentice US.

■ **~ breveté** or **qualifié** Naut ≈ able seaman GB, ≈ seaman US.

matelotage /matlɔtaʒ/ *nm* ropework.

matelote /matlɔt/ *nf* **1** Culin matelote, fish stew; **2** (danse) hornpipe.

mater /mate/ [1] *vtr* **1** (soumettre) to put down [*révolte*]; to bring [sb/sth] into line [*rebelles, insurgés*]; to take [sb/sth] in hand [*enfant, cheval*]; to bring [sth] under control [*incendie*]; to overcome [*passion, orgueil*]; **je vous materai, moi○!** I'll show you who's boss here!; **2◑** (épier) to spy on; (lorgner) to ogle; **3** (dépolir) to give a matt finish to [*métal*]; to frost [*verre*]; **argent maté** matt silver; **4** (aux échecs) to checkmate.

mâter /mɑte/ [1] *vtr* to mast.

matérialisation /mateʀjalizasjɔ̃/ *nf* **1** (de projet, d'idée, espoir) realization; **2** (signalisation) marking; **3** (en spiritisme) materialization; **4** Phys materialization.

matérialiser /mateʀjalize/ [1] **I** *vtr* **1** (concrétiser) to realize [*rêve*]; to fulfil[GB] [*espoir*]; to keep [*promesse*]; to make [sth] happen [*projet*]; **des décisions qui seront matérialisées par un traité** decisions that will be embodied in a treaty; **le fleuve matérialise la frontière** the river forms the border; **2** (signaliser) to mark [*route, aire*]; **'chaussée non matérialisée sur 3 km'** 'no road markings for 3 km'.

II se matérialiser *vpr* [*projet, idée*] to materialize; **ne pas se ~** to fail to materialize.

matérialisme /mateʀjalism/ *nm* materialism.

■ **~ dialectique** dialectical materialism; **~ historique** historical materialism.

matérialiste /mateʀjalist/ **I** *adj* **1** Philos materialist; **2** (terre à terre) [*personne, préoccupations*] materialistic; **être bassement ~** to be terribly materialistic.

II *nmf* materialist.

matérialité /mateʀjalite/ *nf* **1** (de fait, preuve, crime) reality; **2** (de l'âme) materiality.

matériau, *pl* **~x** /mateʀjo/ *nm* **1** (documentation) material ₵; **~x de recherche** research material; **2** Constr material; **~x de construction** building materials.

matériel, **-ielle** /mateʀjɛl/ **I** *adj* **1** gén [*conditions, confort, biens, aide, dégât, preuve*] material; [*plaisirs*] worldly; [*sécurité*] financial; [*problème, moyens*] practical; [*obstacle*] tangible, concrete; **sur le plan ~** in practical terms; **je suis dans l'impossibilité matérielle de vous aider** I really cannot help you; **il n'a pas le temps ~ de s'occuper de cela** he simply hasn't got the time to deal with that; **2** (matérialiste) materialistic; **considérations bassement matériel-**

les low, materialistic motives; **3** Philos [*cause, univers, être, vérité, substance*] material.

II *nm* **1** (équipement) equipment; **acheter du ~** to buy equipment; **~ médical/militaire** medical/military equipment; **~ agricole** farm machinery; **~ de jardinage/bricolage** gardening/DIY tools (*pl*); **2** (documentation) material; **~ de propagande** propaganda material.

■ ~ génétique genetic material; **~ de guerre** military hardware; **~ humain** workforce; **~ informatique** hardware; **~ pédagogique** teaching materials (*pl*); **~ de peinture** Art artist's materials (*pl*); Constr paint supplies (*pl*); **~ roulant** rolling stock; **~ scolaire** (de l'école) school equipment; (des élèves) stationery and writing materials (*pl*).

matériellement /materjelmɑ̃/ *adv* **1** (physiquement) **exister ~** really to exist; **cesser ~ d'exister** no longer to have any physical existence; ; **c'est ~ possible** it can be done; **c'est impossible ~** it's a physical impossibility; **ne pas être ~ capable d'avoir fait** to be physically incapable of having done; **2** (financièrement) financially; **aider ~ qn** to give material assistance to sb; **ils sont ~ défavorisés** they're badly off materially speaking; **~, c'est un peu difficile** things are a bit tight○ financially.

maternage /matɛʀnaʒ/ *nm* mothering; (excessif) mollycoddling, babying.

maternel, **-elle** /matɛʀnɛl/ **I** *adj* **1** (d'une mère) [*instinct*] maternal; [*amour*] motherly; (comme d'une mère) [*sollicitude, geste, personne*] motherly; **2** (de la mère) **biens/conseils ~s** mother's property/advice; **3** (de sa propre mère) **dans l'atelier ~ il apprend à...** in his mother's workshop he learns to...; **4** (dans la famille) [*ligne, tante, grand-père*] maternal; **du côté ~** on the mother's ou maternal side.

II maternelle *nf* Scol nursery school.

maternellement /matɛʀnɛlmɑ̃/ *adv* in a motherly way.

materner /matɛʀne/ [1] *vtr* to mother; (à l'excès) to mollycoddle, to baby.

maternité /matɛʀnite/ *nf* **1** (état de mère) motherhood; **désirer la ~** to want children; **2** (grossesse) pregnancy; **de ~** [*allocation, congé*] maternity; **3** (établissement) maternity hospital; (service) maternity ward; **4** Art **une ~ de Raphaël** a Madonna and Child by Raphael.

■ ~ de substitution surrogate motherhood.

math○ /mat/ *nfpl* **1** = **maths**; **2** ▶ **mathématique**.

mathématicien, **-ienne** /matematisjɛ̃, ɛn/ ▶**510** *nm,f* mathematician.

mathématique /matematik/ **I** *adj* **1** Math mathematical; **2** fig **c'est ~** (logique) it follows; (inévitable) it's bound to happen; (certain) it's a dead cert○ GB, it's dead certain.

II mathématiques *nfpl* mathematics (+ *v sg*); **les ~s appliquées** applied maths GB ou mathematics.

■ ~s supérieures/spéciales, **math sup**○/**spé**○ *first/second year of preparation for entry to science Grandes Écoles.*

mathématiquement /matematikmɑ̃/ *adv* **1** Math [*démontrer*] mathematically; **2** fig (logiquement) logically; (inévitablement) **ça devait ~ arriver** it was bound to happen.

matheux○, **-euse** /matø, øz/ *nm,f* (étudiant, spécialiste) mathematician.

maths○ /mat/ *nfpl* (*abbr* = **mathématiques**) maths (+ *v sg*) GB, math○ (*sg*) US.

matière /matjɛʀ/ *nf* **1** (substance) material; **~ inflammable** flammable material; **mes voyages me fournissent la ~ de mes romans** my travels provide me with material for my novels; **2** Biol, Chimie, Philos, Phys matter; **~ organique** organic matter; **la ~ vivante** organic matter; **3** (sujet) matter Ȼ; **je ne suis pas compétent en la ~** it's not my province; **en ~ littéraire/financière/commerciale** as far as literature/finance/business is concerned; **en ~ de cuisine/d'art/d'emploi** as far as cooking/art/employment is concerned; **donner** or **fournir ~ à plaisanterie** to make people smile; **donner ~ à des critiques** to give rise to criticism; **~ à réflexion** food for thought; **il y a là ~ à rire** it's ludicrous; **il n'y a pas là ~ à plaisanter** it's no laughing matter; **il n'y a pas là ~ à se féliciter** there's no call for complacency; **4** Scol, Univ (discipline) subject; **~ obligatoire/à option** compulsory/optional subject; **~s littéraires/scientifiques** arts/science subjects.

■ ~s fécales faeces; **~s grasses** fat Ȼ; **fromage à 25% de ~s grasses** cheese with 25% fat content; **~ grise** grey GB ou gray US matter; **~ interstellaire** cosmic dust; **~ plastique** plastic; **jouets en ~ plastique** plastic toys; **les ~s plastiques** plastics; **~ première** raw material; **~s premières agricoles** agricultural raw materials.

MATIF /matif/ *nm* (*abbr* = **marché à terme d'instruments financiers**) financial futures market.

Matignon /matiɲɔ̃/ *nprm*: *offices of the French Prime Minister.*

matin /matɛ̃/ **I** *adv* [*se lever, partir*] very early.

II *nm* **1** (début de la journée) morning; **la réunion est le ~** the meeting is in the morning; **travailler le ~** to work in the morning, to work mornings; **tous les samedis ~** every Saturday morning; **à demain ~!** see you tomorrow morning; **5 heures du ~** gén 5 (o'clock) in the morning; (pour un horaire) 5 am; **le ~ du 3, le 3 au ~** on the morning of the 3rd; **le ~ des événements** on the morning of the events; **au ~ il avait oublié** by morning he had forgotten; **du ~ au soir** from morning till night; **brume/promenade du ~** morning mist/walk; **de bon ~** early in the morning; **de grand ~** at daybreak; **au petit ~** in the early hours; **à prendre ~, midi et soir** Méd to be taken three times a day; **2** (matinée) morning; **par un beau ~ d'été** on a fine summer morning; **3** fig (origine) **le ~ de la vie** the springtime of life; **aux ~s de la civilisation** at the dawn of civilization.

IDIOMES **être du ~** to be a morning person; **un de ces quatre ~s** one of these days.

matinal, **~e**, *mpl* **-aux** /matinal, o/ *adj* [*toilette, promenade*] morning (*épith*); [*brume, gelée*] Météo (early) morning (*épith*); **heure ~e** early hour; **il est ~** (d'habitude) he is an early riser; (aujourd'hui) he's up early.

mâtiné, **~e** /mɑtine/ *adj* **1** (mélangé) **un anglais ~ de français** a mixture of English and French; **du moderne ~ de rococo** a cross between modern and rococo; **2** (de race croisée) [*animal*] crossbred; **~ de** crossed with.

matinée /matine/ *nf* **1** (période) morning; **dans la ~** in the morning; **(toute) une ~ de travail** a (whole) morning's work; **en début/fin de ~** at the beginning/end of the morning; **2** Cin, Théât matinée; **nous y allons en ~** we're going to a matinée of the show; **le film/spectacle passera en ~** there'll be an afternoon showing/performance.

■ ~ dansante tea dance; **~ enfantine** children's matinée.

IDIOMES **faire la grasse ~** to have a lie-in GB, to sleep in.

matines /matin/ *nfpl* matins.

matois, **~e** /matwa, az/ **I** *adj* wily.

II *nm,f* sly person; **c'est un fin ~** he's a sly one.

maton○, **-onne** /matɔ̃, ɔn/ *nm* screw○ GB, prison warder.

matou /matu/ *nm* tomcat.

matraquage /matʀakaʒ/ *nm* **1** lit bludgeoning, batoning GB; **2** fig **~ publicitaire** (advertising) hype; **~ des prix** slashing of prices; **faire du ~ pour un produit** to plug○ a product.

matraque /matʀak/ *nf* gén club; (de policier) truncheon GB, baton GB, billy US; (de malfaiteur) cosh GB, blackjack US; **recevoir un coup de ~** [*manifestant*] to be hit with a truncheon; **il m'a donné deux coups de ~** he clubbed me twice; **c'est le coup de ~**○ fig it costs a fortune.

matraquer /matʀake/ [1] *vtr* **1** (assommer) [*policier*] to club; [*malfaiteur*] to cosh GB, to blackjack US; **~ l'ennemi** Mil to hammer the enemy; **~ qn avec des médicaments**○ to knock sb out with drugs; **2** (imposer) [*médias*] to bombard [*public*] **(de** with); to plug [*produit, chanson*]; **3** (critiquer) to clobber [*personne, ouvrage*]; **4** (réduire) to slash [*prix*]; **5**○ (escroquer) [*commerçant*] to rip off○ [*touriste*]; **~ les consommateurs** not to give the customer a fair deal.

matriarcal, **~e**, *mpl* **-aux** /matʀijaʀkal, o/ *adj* matriarchal.

matriarcat /matʀijaʀka/ *nm* matriarchy.

matrice /matʀis/ *nf* **1** Math, Ordinat, Stat matrix; **~ réelle/complexe** matrix of real/complex numbers; **2** Tech (moule) die; (pour disque) matrix; **3** Admin register; **4**† Anat (utérus) womb.

■ ~ cadastrale cadastre[GB]; **~ à points** Ordinat dot matrix; **~ du rôle des contributions** original of register of taxes.

matricide /matʀisid/ **I** *adj* matricidal.

II *nmf* (personne) matricide.

III *nm* (crime) matricide.

matriciel, **-ielle** /matʀisjɛl/ *adj* **1** Math matrix (*épith*); **2** Ordinat **imprimante matricielle** dot matrix printer; **3** Fisc *pertaining to the tax register.*

matricule /matʀikyl/ **I** *nm* (numéro) Mil service ou army number; Admin reference ou official number.

II *nf* (registre) roll, register; (extrait) entry on the roll.

IDIOMES **gare à ton ~**○**!** watch out (or you'll catch it)○!

matrimonial, **~e**, *mpl*, **-iaux** /matʀimɔnjal, o/ *adj* marriage (*épith*), matrimonial; **agence ~e** marriage bureau.

matrone /matʀɔn/ *nf* **1** (femme imposante) matronly woman; **2** Antiq matron.

maturation /matyʀasjɔ̃/ *nf* **1** (de fruit, fromage) ripening; (du vin) maturing; (de cellule, d'abcès) maturation; **2** (d'idée) development.

mature /matyʀ/ *adj* fml mature.

mâture /mɑtyʀ/ *nf* masts (*pl*).

maturité /matyʀite/ *nf* gén maturity; **~ d'esprit** (psychological) maturity; **manquer de ~** to be immature; **en pleine ~** [*homme, femme*] of mature years; [*auteur*] at the height of one's powers; [*entreprise*] fully developed; **arriver** or **parvenir à ~** [*fruit, personne*] to reach maturity; [*entreprise*] to realize its full potential.

maudire /modiʀ/ [80] *vtr* to curse.

maudit, **~e** /modi, it/ **I** *pp* ▶ **maudire**.

II *adj* **1**○ (satané) (*before n*) blasted○, damned○; **2** (rejeté) (*after n*) [*écrivain, héros*] accursed sout **(de** by); **~s soient-ils** a curse on them; **(que) ~ soit le jour qui t'a vu naître** a curse on the day you were born.

III *nm,f* damned soul; **les ~s** the damned.

Maudit /modi/ *nprm* **le ~** the Evil one.

maugréer /mogʀee/ [11] *vi* to grumble **(contre** about).

maul /mol/ *nm* maul; **faire un ~** to ruck.

maure /mɔʀ/ *adj* Moorish.

Maure /mɔʀ/ *nmf* Moor.

mauresque /mɔʀɛsk/ *adj* Moorish.

Mauresque /mɔʀɛsk/ *nf* Moorish woman.

Maurice /mɔʀis/ ▶**321**, **416** *nprf* **l'île ~** Mauritius.

mauricien, **-ienne** /mɔʀisjɛ̃, ɛn/ ▶**537** *adj* Mauritian.

Mauricien, -ienne /mɔʀisjɛ̃, ɛn/ ▶ 537 *nm,f* Mauritian.

Mauritanie /mɔʀitani/ ▶ 321 *nprf* Mauritania.

mauritanien, -ienne /mɔʀitanjɛ̃, ɛn/ ▶ 537 *adj* Mauritanian.

Mauritanien, -ienne /mɔʀitanjɛ̃, ɛn/ ▶ 537 *nm,f* Mauritanian.

mausolée /mozɔle/ *nm* mausoleum.

maussade /mosad/ *adj* [*voix, humeur*] sullen; [*temps*] dull; [*paysage, perspective, conjoncture*] bleak; [*Bourse, marché*] sluggish.

maussaderie /mosadʀi/ *nf* sullenness.

mauvais, ~e /mɔvɛ, ɛz/ **I** *adj* **1** (d'un goût désagréable) **être ~** [*nourriture, boisson*] to be horrible; **ne pas être ~** [*nourriture, boisson*] to be quite good; **2** (de qualité inférieure) [*repas, restaurant*] poor; [*tabac, alcool, café*] cheap; [*voiture, œuvre, spectacle*] terrible; [*nourriture, hébergement, livre*] bad; [*dictionnaire, bibliothèque, lycée, enregistrement*] poor; **ne pas être ~** to be all right; **3** (mal fait) [*cuisine, travail, gestion, éducation*] poor; [*prononciation, départ*] bad; **4** (inadéquat) [*conseil, décision, définition, exemple, idée, solution, conditions de travail*] bad; [*projet*] flawed; [*renseignement*] wrong; [*éclairage, vue, mémoire, santé, hygiène, alimentation*] poor; **il ne serait pas ~ de faire** it wouldn't be a bad idea to do; **~ pour la santé** bad for one's health; **5** (inapproprié) wrong; **la ~e méthode/solution/personne/date/clé** the wrong method/solution/person/date/key; **6** (incompétent) [*auteur, équipe*] bad (**en** at); [*élève, nageur, chasseur, amant*] mediocre; [*cuisinier, travailleur, menteur*] bad; [*avocat, médecin*] incompetent; **être ~ en français** [*élève*] to be bad at French; **parler un ~ français** to speak French badly; **7** (déplaisant) [*nuit, rêve, nouvelle, journée, impression*] bad; [*situation*] difficult; [*surprise*] nasty; [*vacances*] terrible; ▶ **fortune**, **sang**; **8** (méchant) [*animal*] vicious; [*personne, sourire, remarque, ton*] nasty; **d'une ~e nature** evil-natured; **~ coup** (mauvaise action) mischief ¢; (méchanceté) dirty trick; (blessure) nasty knock; (revers) terrible blow; **préparer un ~ coup** to be up to mischief; **faire subir un ~ coup au gouvernement** to deal a terrible blow to the government; **de ~e humeur** in a bad mood (*après n*); ▶ **colère**; **9** (grave) [*fièvre, rhume*] nasty; **10** (peu lucratif) [*rendement, terre*] poor; [*salaire, pension*] low; [*récolte, saison*] bad; **11** (peu flatteur) [*cote, résultat, critique, image, opinion*] poor; [*chiffres, critique*] bad; **12** (répréhensible) [*père, fils, citoyen, comportement*] bad; [*chrétien*] poor; [*instinct*] base; [*tendance*] unfortunate; [*génie, intention, pensée*] evil; ▶ **coton**, **pli**; **13** Météo [*vent, pluie*] nasty; [*traversée, mer*] rough; **la météo est ~e** the weather forecast is bad; **14** Jeux **~e main/carte** weak hand/card; ▶ **numéro**, **pas**[2].

II○ *nm,f* **1** (incapable) (en classe) dunce; (en général) useless individual; **2** (méchant) brute.

III *adv* **sentir ~** lit to smell; fig○ to look bad; **sentir très ~** lit, fig to stink; **ouvre la fenêtre, ça sent ~** open the window, there's a nasty smell; **la police est là, ça sent ~** the police are here, things are looking bad; **il fait ~** Météo the weather is bad.

IV *nm* (mauvais côté) **le bon et le ~** the good and the bad; **il y a du bon et du ~ chez chacun** there's good and bad in everyone; **il n'y a pas que du ~ dans le projet** the project isn't all bad.

■ **~ esprit** (personne) scoffing person; (attitude) scoffing attitude; **faire du ~ esprit** to scoff; **~ garçon** tough guy; **~ lieux** fleshpots; **~ plaisant** person with a warped sense of humour[GB]; **~ traitements** ill-treatment ¢; **faire subir des ~ traitements à qn** to ill-treat sb; **~e herbe** weed; **~e querelle** unprovoked argument; **faire une ~e querelle à qn** to pick on sb; **~es rencontres** bad company ¢; **faire de ~es rencontres** to get into bad company.

IDIOMES **la trouver** or **l'avoir ~e**○ to be furious.

mauve /mov/ **I** ▶ 193 *adj, nm* mauve.

II *nf* mallow.

mauviette /movjɛt/ *nf* pej wimp○.

mauvis /movi/ *nm* redwing.

maux ▶ **mal**.

max○ /maks/ **I** *adv* **20 francs ~** 20 francs max○; **à 3 heures ~** by 3 at the latest.

II *nm inv* **coûter un ~** to cost a packet○ GB ou bundle○; **prendre un ~** [*inculpé*] to get a stiff○ sentence; **tirer un ~** (d'argent) to make a bomb○ (**de** out of).

III un max *loc adv* a lot; **travailler un ~** to work flat out; **fumer un ~** to smoke like a trooper○; **s'ennuyer un ~** to be bored stiff○.

maxi[1] /maksi/ *préf* **~-jupe** maxi-skirt; **~-poitrine** extra-large bust; **~ 45 tours** Audio (seven-inch) EP; **~-bouteille** Comm one-and-a-half litre[GB] bottle; **~ salle de conférences**○ extra-large conference room; **il y a un ~-choix**○ there's a huge choice.

maxi[2] /maksi/ **I**○ *adj inv* (maximal) [*vitesse, prix, puissance*] maximum.

II○ *adv* (au maximum) **travailler 15 heures ~** to work a maximum of 15 hours; **j'ai grossi de trois kilos ~** I gained three kilos at the very most.

maxillaire /maksilɛʀ/ **I** *adj* maxillary.

II *nm* jawbone, maxilla spéc; **~ inférieur/supérieur** lower/upper jawbone.

maxima ▶ **a maxima**, **maximum**.

maximal, ~e, *mpl* **-aux** /maksimal, o/ *adj* maximum; **températures ~es** maximum temperatures.

maximaliser /maksimalize/ [1] *vtr* to maximize [*avantage, profits, pertes*].

maximaliste /maksimalist/ **I** *adj* [*revendication, position, discours*] uncompromising; [*attitude, personne*] hard-line (*épith*).

II *nmf* hard-liner.

maxime /maksim/ *nf* maxim.

maximiser /maksimize/ [1] *vtr* = **maximaliser**.

maximum, *pl* **~s** ou **maxima** /maksimɔm, maksima/ **I** *adj* [*température, rendement, vitesse, confort*] maximum; **11 jours, c'est le délai ~** it will take 11 days at (the) most; **cours ~ autorisé du DM** DM's ceiling rate.

II *nm* **1** (limite supérieure) maximum; **contenir un ~ de deux grammes de sel par litre** to contain a maximum of two grams of salt per litre[GB]; **obtenir un prêt jusqu'à un ~ de...** to obtain a loan for a maximum amount of...; **un ~ de 11 jours, 11 jours (au) ~** eleven days at (the) most; **10 francs au grand ~** 10 francs at the very most; **au ~** [*travailler, développer*] to the maximum; [*réduire*] as much as possible; **détenir 20% du capital au ~** to hold no more than 20 per cent of the capital; **rouler au ~**○ to drive flat out○; **obtenir le ~ d'avantages** to get as many advantages as possible; **faire le ~** to do one's utmost; **atteindre son ~** [*bruit, forme, inflation*] to reach its peak; [*douleur*] to be at its worst; **2** Météo **~ (de température)** maximum temperature; **3**○ (grande quantité) **manger le** or **un ~** to stuff○ oneself; **le** or **un ~ de problèmes** a lot of problems; **faire un ~ de bruit** to be as noisy as possible; **gagner/coûter le** or **un ~** to make/cost a packet○ GB ou bundle○; **obtenir le** or **un ~** (dans une transaction) to get the best possible deal; **4** Jur maximum sentence; **requérir le ~** to recommend the maximum sentence.

III un maximum *loc adv* a lot; **travailler un ~** to work flat out○ ou a lot; **fumer un ~** to smoke a lot, to smoke like a trooper○; **s'ennuyer un ~** to be bored stiff○.

maya /maja/ **I** *adj* Mayan.

II ▶ 462 *nm* Ling Maya.

Maya /maja/ *nmf* Maya.

Mayence /majɑ̃s/ ▶ 857 *npr* Mainz.

Mayenne /majɛn/ ▶ 357, 692 *nprf* (rivière, département) **la ~** Mayennne.

mayonnaise /majɔnɛz/ *nf* mayonnaise; **faire de la ~** to make mayonnaise; **quand la ~ prend** when the mayonnaise begins to thicken; **poisson à la ~** fish with mayonnaise.

Mayotte /majɔt/ ▶ 416 *nprf* Mayotte.

mazagran /mazagʀɑ̃/ *nm*: *thick china goblet for coffee*.

mazette† /mazɛt/ *excl* goodness gracious†!

mazout /mazut/ *nm* (fuel) oil; **cuve à ~** oil tank; **poêle à ~** oil stove; **chauffage au ~** oil-fired heating.

mazouter /mazute/ [1] *vtr* to cover with oil; **rivage/oiseau mazouté** shore/bird covered in oil (from a slick).

MBA /ɛmbea/ *nf*: *abbr* ▶ **marge**.

MC /ɛmse/ **I** *nm*: *abbr* ▶ **maître**.

II *nmpl*: *abbr* ▶ **montant**.

MCM /ɛmseɛm/ *nmpl*: *abbr* ▶ **montant**.

me (**m'** *before vowel or mute h*) /m(ə)/ *pron pers* **1** (objet) me; **il ~ déteste** he hates me; **elle a essayé de ~ frapper** she tried to hit me; **si tu m'entends, réponds** if you can hear me, answer; **2** (me = à moi) **tu ne m'as pas fait mal** you didn't hurt me; **ne ~ dis pas que tu l'as perdu** don't tell me you've lost it; **elle ~ l'a offert pour mon anniversaire** she gave it to me for my birthday; **il m'en veut** he bears a grudge against me; **3** (pronom réfléchi) myself; **je ~ déteste** I hate myself; **je ~ soigne** I look after myself; **je ~ lave (les mains)** I wash (my hands); **je vais ~ faire belle** I'm going to get dressed up; **je m'en veux** I'm angry with myself; **on m'a dit de ~ méfier** I was told to be careful.

Me *written abbr* = **maître** III 5.

mea culpa /meakylpa/ *excl* mea culpa!, it's my fault!

méandre /meɑ̃dʀ/ **I** *nm* Géog meander.

II méandres *nmpl* fig **les ~s de l'administration** the maze of officialdom; **les ~s de ta pensée** the rambling development of your ideas.

méat /mea/ *nm* **1** Anat meatus; **2** Biol **~ intercellulaire** intercellular space.

mec○ /mɛk/ *nm* bloke○ GB, guy○; **beau ~** gorgeous guy; **mon ~** my man○ ou bloke○ GB; **un vrai ~** a real man○.

mécanicien, -ienne /mekanisjɛ̃, ɛn/ **I** *adj* mechanical; **ingénieur ~** mechanical engineer.

II ▶ 510 *nm,f* (ouvrier) mechanic.

III *nm* **1** Rail engine driver GB, (locomotive) engineer US; **2** Aviat flight engineer; **3** Naut engineer; **4** Dent dental technician.

■ **~ navigant** Aviat flight engineer.

mécanicien-dentiste, *pl* **mécaniciens-dentistes** /mekanisjɛ̃dɑ̃tist/ ▶ 510 *nmf* dental technician.

mécanicisme /mekanisism/ *nm* Philos mechanism.

mécanique /mekanik/ **I** *adj* **1** (manuel) [*hachoir, tondeuse*] hand (*épith*); [*machine à écrire*] manual; [*montre, petite voiture*] wind-up (*épith*); [*jouet, train*] clockwork (*épith*), wind-up (*épith*); **2** Mécan (doté d'une machine) mechanical; **appareil/excavatrice ~** mechanical equipment/excavator; **3** Agric, Ind (fait à la machine) machine (*épith*); **fil/tissage/séchage ~** machine yarn/weaving/drying; **traite/tonte ~** machine milking/shearing; **4** Mécan (de machine) [*ennui, panne*] mechanical; **défaillance ~** mechanical failure; **se déplacer de façon ~** to move mechanically; **pièce ~** machine part; **construction ~** mechanical engineering; **industrie ~** engineering industry; **5** Phys mechanical; **lois ~s** laws of mechanics; **6** (non chimique) **méthodes ~s de contraception** barrier methods of contraception; **7** (irréfléchi) [*geste*] mechanical, automatic; [*rire*] empty.

II *nf* **1** Mécan (science) mechanics (+ *v sg*); **un génie de la ~** a mechanical genius; **un terme de ~** a mechanical term; **avoir le sens de la ~** to be mechanically-minded; **une merveille de ~** a marvel of engineering; **2** Phys mechanics (+ *v sg*); **3** (fonctionnement) mechanics (*pl*); **la ~ d'une campagne électorale** the mechanics of running a campaign; **la ~ de la gestion** the mechanics of management; **4**○ (machine) machine; **c'est une belle ~ ta moto** your motorbike is a fine machine.

■ **~ des fluides** fluid mechanics (+ *v sg*); **~ ondulatoire** wave mechanics (+ *v sg*); **~ quantique** quantum mechanics (+ *v sg*); **~ des sols** soil mechanics (+ *v sg*).

mécaniquement /mekanikmɑ̃/ *adv* **1** Mécan mechanically; **fabriqué ~** machine-made; **2** (sans réfléchir) [*travailler, répondre*] mechanically.

mécanisation /mekanizasjɔ̃/ *nf* mechanization.

mécaniser /mekanize/ [1] **I** *vtr* to mechanize.

II **se mécaniser** *vpr* to mechanize.

mécanisme /mekanism/ *nm* **1** Mécan (organe moteur) mechanism; **le ~ est cassé/doit être remplacé** the mechanism is broken/has to be replaced; **2** (de machine, d'organe) mechanism; **le ~ de l'oreille** the mechanism of the ear; **3** (fonctionnement) mechanism; **~s financiers/des changes/du marché** financial/exchange/market mechanisms; **~ d'une négociation** mechanism of a negotiation; **le ~ de la pensée** the thought process; **4** Psych mechanism; **5** Philos (doctrine) mechanism.

■ **~ de défense** Psych defence[GB] mechanism; **~ d'entraînement** Mécan driving mechanism.

mécaniste /mekanist/ Philos **I** *adj* mechanistic.

II *nmf* mechanist.

mécano○ /mekano/ *nm* mechanic.

mécanographe /mekanɔgʀaf/ ▶ **510** *nmf* punch card operator.

meccano® /mekano/ *nm* Meccano® GB, erector set US.

mécénat /mesena/ *nm* **1** (artistique) patronage; **~ d'entreprise** corporate patronage; **2** (parrainage) sponsorship.

mécène /mesɛn/ *nm* **1** (des arts) patron of the arts; **2** (parrain) sponsor.

Mécène /mesɛn/ *npr* Maecenas.

méchamment /meʃamɑ̃/ *adv* **1** (avec méchanceté) [*faire, parler, sourire*] spitefully, maliciously; [*frapper, se battre*] viciously; **traiter qn ~** to treat sb badly; **2**○ (extrêmement) [*travailler*] terribly hard; [*abîmer*] dreadfully, badly; [*étonné, bon, bien*] terribly; **ils nous en veulent ~**○ they're terribly angry with us.

méchanceté /meʃɑ̃ste/ *nf* **1** (de personne) nastiness, malice, meanness; **par pure ~** out of pure spite ou malice; **avec ~** spitefully, nastily; **sans ~** without malice; **être d'une incroyable ~** to be vicious ou really nasty; **2** (de geste, propos, regard, d'acte) maliciousness, meanness; (plus fort) viciousness; **3** (acte) malicious act; (propos) malicious remark; **faire/dire des ~s** to do/to say malicious ou nasty things.

méchant, **~e** /meʃɑ̃, ɑ̃t/ **I** *adj* **1** (malveillant) [*personne, regard, propos, action*] nasty, malicious, mean; **ce n'est pas une ~e femme** she's not such a bad woman; **être de ~e humeur** to be in a foul mood; **avoir l'air ~** to look mean; **être ~ avec qn** to be horrible ou mean to sb; **2** (dangereux) [*animal, personne*] vicious; **quand il a bu, il devient ~** he gets ou turns nasty when he's been drinking; **attention chien ~!** beware of the dog!; **3** (mauvais) (*before n*) [*outil, instrument*] poor quality, wretched; [*route*] dreadful; [*roman, poète, écrivain*] mediocre, second-rate; **4** (grave) (*before n*) [*grippe, affaire, blessure*] nasty, bad; **ce n'est pas bien ~** it's not very bad ou serious; **5**○ (extraordinaire) [*allure, voiture, succès*] fantastic○, terrific○; **une ~e tempête** a terrific storm; **une ~e averse** a heavy shower; **une ~e balafre** a nasty scar; **une ~e gueule de bois**○ a bad hangover, a hell○ of a hangover; **une ~e explosion** a hell○ of an explosion.

II *nm,f* **1** (au cinéma) villain, baddy○; **2** (enfant) naughty boy/girl.

mèche /mɛʃ/ *nf* **1** (de cheveux) lock; (teinte) streak; **avoir des ~s blanches** to have white streaks; **se faire faire des ~s** to have streaks put in one's hair, to have one's hair frosted US; **2** (de bougie, lampe, briquet) wick; **3** Méd packing ¢; **changer la ~** to change the packing; **4** (d'explosif, arme, de fusée) fuse; **5** (outil) (drill) bit; **une ~ de 9** a number 9 bit.

■ **~ folle** stray lock; **~ lente** safety fuse; **~ rebelle** wayward lock.

IDIOMES **être de ~ avec qn**○ to be in cahoots○ with sb péj, to be hand in glove with sb; **vendre la ~** to let the cat out of the bag.

mécher /meʃe/ [14] *vtr* **1** Méd to pack; **2** Vin to sulphurize[GB].

méchoui /meʃwi/ *nm* (repas) North African style barbecue, lamb roast US; (viande grillée) spit-roast lamb; **faire un ~** (repas) to organize a North African style barbecue; (plus précis) to spit-roast a lamb.

mécompte /mekɔ̃t/ *nm* setback.

méconnaissable /mekɔnɛsabl/ *adj* (complètement) unrecognizable; (difficile à reconnaître) barely recognizable.

méconnaissance /mekɔnɛsɑ̃s/ *nf* liter **1** (ignorance) (total) ignorance (**de qch** of sth), lack of knowledge (**de qch** about sth); **2** (sous-estimation) (de situation) misreading (**de** of); (de personne, mérite, travail) undervaluing (**de** of); **3** (refus de connaître) disregard (**de** of).

méconnaître /mekɔnɛtʀ/ [73] *vtr* **1** (se méprendre sur) to misread [*situation*]; to misunderstand [*problème*]; to be mistaken about [*cause, intention*]; **~ que** to fail to understand that; **c'est le ~ que de penser qu'il en restera là** it is a mistake to think that he will stop at that; **2** (sous-estimer) to underestimate [*difficulté, portée, gravité*]; to underrate [*œuvre, talent*]; to undervalue [*qualité, importance*]; **toute tentative pour ~ l'importance de cette découverte** any attempt to play down the importance of this discovery; **3** (refuser de connaître) to flout [*loi, règlement*]; to disregard [*devoir*]; **~ les services rendus** to show no appreciation of the help given; **je ne méconnais pas que**... I am not unaware that...

méconnu, **~e** /mekɔny/ **I** *pp* ▶ **méconnaître**.

II *pp adj* [*artiste, œuvre*] neglected; [*mérites, talent*] undervalued; [*valeur*] unrecognized.

III *nm,f* **un grand ~** a neglected genius; **il joue les ~s** he claims to be misunderstood.

mécontent, **~e** /mekɔ̃tɑ̃, ɑ̃t/ **I** *adj* **1** (pas satisfait) [*client, patron*] dissatisfied (**de** with); [*électeur*] discontented (**de** with); **je ne suis pas ~ de lui/d'avoir fini** I'm rather pleased with him/to have finished; **2** (contrarié) displeased (**que** that); (irrité) annoyed (**de** at); **3** (pas heureux) miserable, discontented (**de** with).

II *nm,f* malcontent.

mécontentement /mekɔ̃tɑ̃tmɑ̃/ *nm* **1** (insatisfaction) dissatisfaction; **2** (déception) discontent; **3** (irritation) annoyance; (déplaisir) displeasure.

mécontenter /mekɔ̃tɑ̃te/ [1] *vtr* **1** (irriter) to annoy; **2** (courroucer) [*décision*] to anger [*peuple*].

Mecque /mɛk/ ▶ **857** *nprf* **la ~** Mecca.

mécréant, **~e** /mekʀeɑ̃, ɑ̃t/ *adj, nm,f* heathen.

mecton◑ /mɛktɔ̃/ *nm* pej (little) squirt○ péj.

médaille /medaj/ *nf* **1** (récompense) medal; **~ d'or/d'argent/de bronze** gold/silver/bronze medal; **2** (pièce) coin; **3** (plaque d'identification) name tag; **4** (bijou) medallion.

■ **~ militaire** *decoration awarded for outstanding gallantry in the field*; **~ du travail** long-service medal.

médaillé, **~e** /medaje/ **I** *pp* ▶ **médailler**.

II *pp adj* [*sportif*] medal-winning (*épith*); [*animal, vin*] prize-winning (*épith*); [*soldat*] decorated (*épith*); [*reportage, journaliste*] award-winning (*épith*); **un champion plusieurs fois ~** a champion with several medals to his credit.

III *nm,f* (sportif) medallist[GB]; gén person who has received a medal.

médailler /medaje/ [1] *vtr* **1** Sport to award a medal to [*sportif*]; **2** Mil to decorate [*militaire*]; **se faire ~** to be decorated; **3** to award a prize to [*animal, vin*]; to make an award to [*reportage, journaliste*].

médaillon /medajɔ̃/ *nm* **1** (bijou) locket; **2** (en architecture, art décoratif) medallion; **3** Culin medallion; **4** Presse, TV **en ~** inset.

Mède /mɛd/ *nmf* Mede; **les ~s** the Medes.

médecin /mɛdsɛ̃/ ▶ **510** *nm* doctor; **aller chez le ~** to go to the doctor's; **tu devrais voir ton ~** you should see your doctor ou GP; **~ spécialiste** or **spécialisé** specialist; **~ traitant** GP.

■ **~ de l'âme** or **des âmes** confessor; **~ assermenté** *doctor sworn under oath to administer routine medical certificates required by the civil service*; **~ acupuncteur** acupuncturist; **~ de bord** ship's doctor; **~ de campagne** country doctor; **~ de famille** family doctor; **~ de garde** duty doctor, doctor on duty; **~ homéopathe** homeopath; **~ légiste** forensic surgeon; **~ militaire** army doctor; **~ scolaire** school doctor; **~ du sport** sports doctor; **~ du travail** ≈ company medical officer.

médecin-chef, *pl* **médecins-chefs** /mɛdsɛ̃ʃɛf/ ▶ **510** *nm* Méd senior consultant; Mil chief medical officer.

médecin-conseil, *pl* **médecins-conseils** /mɛdsɛ̃kɔ̃sɛj/ ▶ **510** *nm* ≈ medical adviser.

médecine /mɛdsin/ *nf* **1** (discipline) medicine; **faire des études de ~**, **faire (sa) ~** to study medicine; **~ générale/spécialisée/infantile** general/specialized/paediatric medicine; **étudiant en ~** medical student; **docteur en ~** medical doctor; **faculté de ~** faculty of medicine; **2** (profession) medicine; **exercer la ~** to practise[GB] medicine; **être inculpé d'exercice illégal de la ~** to be charged with practising[GB] medicine illegally ou without a license US.

■ **~ homéopathique** homeopathic medicine; **~ légale** forensic medicine; **~ par les plantes** herbal medicine; **~ préventive** preventive medicine; **~ scolaire** ≈ school health service; **~ sportive** sports medicine; **~ du travail** ≈ occupational medicine; **~ vétérinaire** veterinary medicine; **~s douces** alternative medicine ¢; **~s naturelles** natural medicine ¢; **~s parallèles** alternative medicine ¢.

médecine-ball, *pl* **~s** /medsinbol/ *nm* Sport medicine ball.

Médée /mede/ *npr* Mythol Medea.

média /medja/ **I** *nm* (moyen, procédé de communication) medium.

II **médias** *nmpl* **les ~s** the media.

médial, **~e**, *mpl* **-iaux** /medjal, o/ **I** *adj* medial.

II **médiale** *nf* **1** Stat median; **2** Phon medial.

médian, **~e** /medjɑ̃, an/ **I** *adj* **1** Anat, Math, Phon, Stat median (*épith*); **2** Pol **une solution ~e** a compromise solution.

II médiane *nf* Math, Stat median.
médiante /medjɑ̃t/ *nf* mediant.
médiat, **~e** /medja, at/ *adj* fml mediate sout.
médiateur, **-trice** /medjatœʀ, tʀis/ **I** *adj* mediatory.
II *nm* gén mediator; (entre le public et l'administration) ombudsman.
III médiatrice *nf* Math perpendicular bisector.
médiathèque /medjatɛk/ *nf* multimedia library.
médiation /medjasjɔ̃/ *nf* mediation; **tenter une ~** to make an attempt at mediation.
médiatique /medjatik/ *adj* **1** (par les médias) [*exploitation, amplification*] by the media; **2** (dans les médias) [*succès, retentissement*] media (*épith*); **3** (attirant l'attention des médias) [*événement*] media (*épith*); **geste ~** publicity-grabbing gesture; **vedette ~** media personality; **l'aspect ~ de qch** the way sth attracts media attention; **il n'est pas très ~** he doesn't come over well on television and in the press; **4** (utilisant les médias) [*personne*] media-conscious; [*campagne électorale*] conducted through the media; **5** (des médias) **milieu ~** media (*pl*); **chef-d'œuvre ~** media success.
médiatisation /medjatizasjɔ̃/ *nf* media coverage; **la ~ excessive du sport** over-exposure of sport in the media.
médiatiser /medjatize/ [1] *vtr* **1** Presse, TV to give [sth] publicity in the media; **~ un événement** to make an event the focus of media attention; **2** Hist, Philos to mediatize.
médiator /medjatɔʀ/ *nm* plectrum.
médiatrice ▶ **médiateur** III.
médical, **~e**, *mpl* **-aux** /medikal, o/ *adj* medical.
médicalement /medikalmɑ̃/ *adv* medically.
médicalisation /medikalizasjɔ̃/ *nf* **1** (fait de donner un caractère médical) medicalization; **2** (implantation de structures médicales) provision of health care.
médicaliser /medikalize/ [1] *vtr* **1** (faire relever de la médecine) to medicalize [*délinquance, folie, maternité*]; **2** (doter de structures médicales) to provide [sth] with health care [*pays, région, campagne*].
médicament /medikamɑ̃/ *nm* medicine ¢, drug, remedy (**pour** for; **contre** to prevent); **mes ~s** my medicine; **un ~ très fort** a powerful drug.
■ **~ de confort** ≈ over-the-counter remedy.
médicamenteux, **-euse** /medikamɑ̃tø, øz/ *adj* **1** [*produit*] medicinal; **2** [*traitement*] drug (*épith*); **3** [*eczéma, allergie*] drug-related.
médicastre† /medikastʀ/ *nm* quack○.
médication /medikasjɔ̃/ *nf* treatment ¢, medication ¢.
médicinal, **~e**, *mpl* **-aux** /medisinal, o/ *adj* [*plante, substance*] medicinal.
médico-chirurgical, **~e**, *mpl* **-aux** /medikoʃiʀyʀʒikal, o/ *adj* **centre ~**, **clinique ~e** *treatment centre*[GB] *with surgical facilities*.
médico-légal, **~e**, *mpl* **-aux** /mediko legal, o/ *adj* [*examen, expertise*] forensic; **certificat ~** autopsy report; **institut ~** forensic science laboratory.
médico-pédagogique, *pl* **~s** /mediko pedagɔʒik/ *adj* **institut ~** special school.
médico-social, **~e**, *mpl* **-iaux** /medi kosɔsjal, o/ *adj* **centre ~** ≈ community health centre[GB].
médico-sportif, **-ive**, *pl* **~s** /medikospɔʀtif, iv/ *adj* **centre ~** *injury treatment and fitness centre*[GB] *for athletes*.
médiéval, **~e**, *mpl* **-aux** /medjeval, o/ *adj* medieval.
médiéviste /medjevist/ *nmf* medievalist.
médina /medina/ *nf* medina.
Médine /medin/ ▶ **857** *npr* Medina.
médiocre /medjɔkʀ/ **I** *adj* **1** (aux capacités insuffisantes) [*personne, ouvrier*] mediocre, second-rate; [*élève, enseignant, intelligence, esprit*] below-average, mediocre; **être d'une intelligence ~** to be of mediocre ou below-average intelligence; **2** (de qualité insuffisante) [*travail, études, qualité, résultat*] mediocre; [*terrain, nourriture, temps*] poor; (sans valeur) [*film, œuvre*] mediocre, indifferent; [*intérêt, succès*] limited; [*vie*] humdrum; [*bonheur*] ordinary; [*carrière*] mediocre; **d'un intérêt ~, de ~ intérêt** of limited interest; **3** (en quantité insuffisante) [*revenu, rentabilité*] meagre[GB]; [*rendement, lumière, résultat*] poor; **4** (sans intensité) [*désir, plaisir, attraction, ambition*] limited; [*sentiment*] mediocre.
II *nmf* [*personne*] loser, no-hoper○ GB.
médiocrement /medjɔkʀəmɑ̃/ *adv* (mal) [*travailler, dessiner, payer*] rather badly; **vivre ~** to lead a humdrum life.
médiocrité /medjɔkʀite/ *nf* **1** (de personne, travail, sentiment) mediocrity; **la ~ de ces élèves** the mediocre standard of these pupils; **2** (de revenus, résultats, lumière) meagreness[GB].
médire /mediʀ/ [65] *vtr ind* **~ de** to speak ill of; (injustement) to malign; **réforme/personne dont on a beaucoup médit** much maligned reform/person.
médisance /medizɑ̃s/ *nf* **1** (action) malicious gossip ¢; **2** (propos) **une ~** a malicious rumour[GB]; **des ~s** malicious gossip ¢.
médisant, **~e** /medizɑ̃, ɑ̃t/ **I** *adj* [*personne, propos*] malicious.
II *nm,f* malicious gossip ou person.
méditatif, **-ive** /meditatif, iv/ **I** *adj* meditative.
II *nm,f* meditative person.
méditation /meditasjɔ̃/ *nf* **1** (recueillement) meditation (**sur** on); **entrer en ~** to go into meditation; **2** (pensée) **tes ~s** your thoughts ou meditations; **3** (titre d'un écrit) meditation.
méditer /medite/ [1] **I** *vtr* (projeter) to contemplate (**de faire** doing); (évaluer) to mull over [*paroles, conseil*]; **un projet longuement médité** a carefully considered project.
II *vi* to meditate; **~ sur** to meditate on [*existence, Dieu*]; to ponder on ou over [*problème, conséquences*].
Méditerranée /mediteʀane/ ▶ **555** *nprf* **la (mer) ~** the Mediterranean (Sea).
méditerranéen, **-éenne** /mediteʀaneɛ̃, ɛn/ *adj* Mediterranean.
médium /medjɔm/ *nm* **1** (voyant) medium, psychic; **2** Mus middle register; **3** (en logique) middle term; **4** (pour peinture) binder; **5** (moyen de communication) medium.
médius /medjys/ *nm* middle finger.
médoc /medɔk/ *nm* (vin) Médoc (wine).
Médoc /medɔk/ ▶ **692** *nprm* **le ~** the Médoc.
médullaire /medylɛʀ/ *adj* medullary.
méduse /medyz/ *nf* Zool jellyfish.
Méduse /medyz/ *npr* Mythol Medusa.
méduser /medyze/ [1] *vtr* to dumbfound; **en rester médusé** to be dumbfounded.
meeting /mitiŋ/ *nm* Pol meeting, rally; Sport meeting GB, meet US.
■ **~ aérien** air show.
méfait /mefɛ/ **I** *nm* gén misdemeanour[GB]; (plus grave) crime; (d'enfant) misdeed.
II méfaits *nmpl* (dégâts) (de l'alcool, du tabac) detrimental effect (*sg*); (de la pollution, d'une politique) damaging effects; (de la grêle, du temps) ravages.
méfiance /mefjɑ̃s/ *nf* mistrust, suspicion; **je vous recommande la ~** I suggest that you proceed with caution; **éveiller/apaiser la ~ de qn** to arouse/to allay sb's suspicions; **avoir de la ~ pour** to be wary of; **n'avoir que ~ pour** or **à l'égard de** to be extremely wary of; **avec ~** warily; **s'approcher avec ~** to approach warily; **faire qch sans ~** to do sth unsuspectingly; **être sans ~** (de nature) to be naïve; **~ de qn envers qn/ qch** sb's wariness of sb/sth.
méfiant, **~e** /mefjɑ̃, ɑ̃t/ *adj* [*personne, air, regard, attitude, parole*] suspicious, distrustful; [*police, caractère, personnalité*] wary; **elle est d'un naturel ~** she's always very wary; **regarder qn/qch d'un œil ~** to look at sb/sth suspiciously.
méfier: **se méfier** /mefje/ [2] *vpr* **1** (ne pas faire confiance) **se ~ de qn/qch** not to trust sb/sth; **méfie-toi de ce qu'il dit** don't trust what he says; **il se méfie de toutes les idées modernes** he's wary of modern ideas; **ils ne se sont pas méfiés de lui** they placed too much trust in him; **sans se ~** quite trustingly; **2** (faire attention à) to be careful; **se ~ de qch** to be wary of sth; **ne pas se ~ de** not to watch out for; **tu ne t'es pas méfié et tu es tombé** you fell because you weren't being careful enough; **méfie-toi! la route est glissante** be careful! the road is slippery; **méfie-toi, tu vas recevoir une gifle** watch it! you'll get a slap; **tu aurais dû te ~** you should have been more careful; **3**○ (prendre garde) controv **se ~ que** to make sure (that); **méfiez-vous que la police ne vous retrouve pas** make sure (that) the police don't find you.
méforme /mefɔʀm/ *nf* Sport lack of form.
méga[1] /mega/ *préf* **1** Mes, Sci mega; **mégavolt** megavolt; **2**○ (gigantesque) **~-concert** huge concert; **~-fête** colossal bash○; **~-entreprise** mega-firm.
méga[2]○ /mega/ *adj inv* mega○.
mégacycle /megasikl/ *nm* megacycle.
mégahertz /megaɛʀtz/ *nm* megahertz.
mégalithe /megalit/ *nm* megalith.
mégalithique /megalitik/ *adj* megalithic.
mégalo○ /megalo/ *adj, nmf* megalomaniac.
mégalomane /megalɔman/ *adj, nmf* megalomaniac.
mégalomanie /megalɔmani/ *nf* megalomania.
mégalopole /megalɔpɔl/ *nf* megalopolis.
mégaoctet /megaɔktɛ/ *nm* megabyte.
mégaphone /megafɔn/ *nm* **1** (avec amplificateur) loudhailer; **2** (porte-voix) megaphone.
mégarde: **par mégarde** /paʀmegaʀd/ *loc adv* inadvertently.
mégatonne /megatɔn/ *nf* megaton.
mégawatt /megawat/ *nm* megawatt.
mégère /meʒɛʀ/ *nf* shrew.
mégisserie /meʒisʀi/ *nf* **1** (action) tanning; **2** (lieu) tannery.
mégot /mego/ *nm* (de cigarette) cigarette butt ou end; (de cigare) stub.
mégotage○ /megɔtaʒ/ *nm* cheeseparing, penny-pinching.
mégoter○ /megɔte/ [1] *vi* to skimp (**sur** on); **mais tu mégotes!** you're being stingy○.
méhari /meaʀi/ *nm* dromedary.
méhariste /meaʀist/ *nm* **1** gén camel rider; **2** Mil *soldier of the French Camel corps*.
meilleur, **~e** /mɛjœʀ/ **I** *adj* **1** (comparatif) better (**que** than); **cette radio a un son épouvantable, tu devrais en acheter une ~e** the sound on this radio is very bad, you should buy a better one; **en attendant des jours ~s** hoping for better days; **il n'y a pas (de) ~ berger dans toute la région** there's no better shepherd in the entire region; **jamais il n'avait mangé (de) ~e choucroute** he'd never eaten better sauerkraut; **2** (superlatif) best; **le ~ des deux** the better of the two; **c'est le ~ de l'équipe** he's the best in the team; **il se fournit chez les ~s grossistes** he buys from the best wholesalers; **ce sont les ~s amis du monde** they're the best of friends; **ta plaisanterie n'était pas du ~ goût** your joke wasn't in the best of taste; **c'est le ~ des pères** he's the best of fathers; **c'est sur terre battue qu'il est le ~** [*joueur de tennis*] he's at his best on clay; **tu ne manges pas la croûte? c'est pourtant ce**

qu'il y a de ~! aren't you going to eat the crust? but it's the best bit!; **aubergiste! du vin et du ~!** innkeeper! some wine, and make it your best!; **un petit chapeau du ~ effet** a very stylish little hat; **leur disque a reçu le ~ accueil** their record was very well received; **au ~ prix** [*acheter*] at the lowest price; [*vendre*] at the highest price.

II *nm,f* **le ~, la ~e** the best one; **ce sont toujours les ~s qui s'en vont** it's always the best ones who go first; **que le ~ gagne** may the best man win.

III *adv* better; **ça sent ~ maintenant** it smells better now; **il fait ~ aujourd'hui qu'hier** the weather is better today than it was yesterday.

IV *nm* **mange donc la croûte, c'est le ~!** eat the crust, it's the best bit!; **donner le ~ de soi-même** to give of one's best; **pour le ~ et pour le pire** for better or for worse; **il passe le ~ de son temps à des niaiseries** he spends the best part of his time fooling around; **garder le ~ pour la fin** to keep the best bit until the end; **prendre le ~ sur qn** to get the better of sb; **et le ~ c'est que la dépanneuse est tombée en panne aussi!** and the best bit of it is that the tow truck broke down as well!

V meilleure *nf* **tu connais la ~e?** have you heard the best one yet?; **ça c'est la ~e!** that's the best one yet!; **j'en passe et des ~es!** that's the least of it, I could go on!

IDIOMES **tout est pour le mieux dans le ~ des mondes** all is for the best in the best of all possible worlds.

méiose /mejoz/ *nf* meiosis.

méjuger /meʒyʒe/ [13] **I** *vtr* to misjudge.

II méjuger de *vtr ind* **~ de** to underrate, to underestimate.

III se méjuger *vpr* to underestimate oneself.

Mékong /mekɔ̃g/ ▶ **357** *nprm* Mekong (river).

mélaminé, ~e /melamine/ *adj* laminated.

mélancolie /melɑ̃kɔli/ *nf* melancholy; Méd melancholia.

mélancolique /melɑ̃kɔlik/ **I** *adj* melancholy; Méd melancholic.

II *nmf* Méd melancholic.

mélancoliquement /melɑ̃kɔlikmɑ̃/ *adv* melancholically, in a melancholy fashion.

Mélanésie /melanezi/ *nprf* Melanesia.

mélanésien, -ienne /melanezjɛ̃, ɛn/ **I** *adj* Melanesian.

II *nm* Ling Melanesian.

Mélanésien, -ienne /melanezjɛ̃, ɛn/ *nm,f* Melanesian.

mélange /melɑ̃ʒ/ **I** *nm* **1** (action) (de produits, peintures, couleurs, populations) mixing; (de thés, tabacs) blending; **faire** or **opérer un ~** to make a mixture ou blend; **bonheur/joie sans ~** unadulterated happiness/joy; **2** (résultat) (de thés, tabacs) blend; (de légumes, produits, d'idées) combination; (de peintures, couleurs, céréales, sentiments) mixture; **un ~ explosif** an explosive mixture; **c'est un ~ (coton et synthétique)** it's a mix (of cotton and synthetic fibres[GB]).

II mélanges *nmpl* (recueil) miscellany (*sg*).

mélanger /melɑ̃ʒe/ [13] **I** *vtr* **1** (pour former un tout) to blend [*tabacs, alcools, thés, huiles*]; to mix, to combine [*couleurs, peintures, teintes*]; to mix [*liquides*]; **~ les œufs et le sucre** to mix the eggs and the sugar together; **c'est du coton mélangé** it's a cotton mix; **~ au fouet** to beat [sth] together; **2** (associer) to put together [*styles, personnes, objets*]; **ne pas ~ le linge de couleur et le linge blanc** don't mix the coloureds GB ou colors US with the whites; **3** (mettre en désordre) to mix up, to jumble up; **il a mélangé les lettres et les factures** he mixed ou jumbled up the letters and the invoices; **~ les cartes** to shuffle (the cards); **4** (confondre) to mix up [*dates, faits, personnes, noms*]; **il mélange les prénoms de ses petits-enfants maintenant** he mixes up the names of his grandchildren now; **mais non! tu mélanges tout!** no! you're getting it all mixed up; ▶ **serviette**.

II se mélanger *vpr* **1** (pour former un tout) [*tabacs, alcools, thés, huiles*] to blend; [*céréales*] to mix; [*couleurs, peintures, teintes*] to mix, to blend together; **l'huile se mélange mal avec le vinaigre** oil does not mix well with vinegar; **2** (en créant une confusion) [*idées, faits, chiffres, souvenirs*] to get muddled (up); **les souvenirs se mélangent dans ma tête** the memories are getting muddled (up) in my head.

mélangeur /melɑ̃ʒœʀ/ *nm* Tech **1** (appareil) mixer; **2** (robinet) **(robinet) ~** mixer tap GB, mixer faucet US.

mélanine /melanin/ *nf* melanin.

mélanome /melanom/ *nm* melanoma.

mélasse /melas/ *nf* **1** Culin (noire) black treacle GB, molasses (*pl*); **2**○ (boue) muck; (brouillard) murk; (confusion) shambles○ (*sg*), mess.

IDIOMES **être dans la ~**○ to be in a mess○.

Melba /mɛlba/ *adj inv* **pêche ~** peach melba.

Melbourne /mɛlbuʀn/ ▶ **857** *npr* Melbourne.

mêlé, ~e /mele/ **I** *pp* ▶ **mêler**.

II *pp adj* [*éléments, public, société*] mixed; [*sons, parfums, eaux*] mingled; **~ de** mingled with; **avec une crainte ~e de respect** with mingled fear and respect; **plaisir ~ de regret** pleasure tinged with regret.

III mêlée *nf* **1** (bataille, cohue) mêlée; **~e générale** free-for-all; **la ~e devint générale** it turned into a free-for-all; **se jeter dans la ~e** to fling oneself into the fray; **2** Sport (au rugby) scrum; **plonger dans la ~e** to dive into the scrum; **~e ordonnée** set scrum; **~e ouverte** loose scrum, ruck; **~e tournée** wheeled scrum; **3** fig (contestation) fray; **rester en dehors** or **au-dessus de la ~e** to keep out of the fray.

mêler /mele/ [1] **I** *vtr* **1** (mélanger) to mix [*produits, couleurs*]; to blend [*ingrédients, essences*]; to blend [*cultures, peuples*]; to combine [*thèmes, influences*]; **servis seuls ou mêlés à d'autres fruits** served on their own or mixed with other fruits; **~ le vrai et le faux** to mix truth and falsehood; **~ ses souvenirs de considérations générales** to mix personal memories with general observations; **~ le narratif de brèves descriptions** to intersperse the narrative with short descriptions; **~ ironie et tendresse** to combine irony and tenderness; **2** (allier en soi) **~ l'utile à l'agréable** [*séjour, activité*] to be both useful and pleasurable; **~ l'ironie à la colère** to be ironic and angry at the same time; **elle mêla ses larmes aux miennes** her tears mingled with mine; **3** (impliquer) **~ qn à** (à un scandale) to get sb involved ou mixed up in; (à des négociations) to involve sb in; (à une conversation) to bring sb into; **être mêlé à** (à un scandale) to be mixed up ou involved in; (à des négociations) to be involved in; (à une conversation) to be included in.

II se mêler *vpr* **1** (s'unir) [*ethnies, cultures, religions*] to mix; [*odeurs, parfums, voix, eaux*] to mingle; **jazz et reggae se mêlent dans leur musique** their music is a mixture of jazz and reggae; **intelligence et naïveté se mêlent chez cet acteur** he's both intelligent and naive as an actor; **un magazine où se mêlent littérature et sciences** a magazine that covers both literature and science; **2 se ~ à** (se joindre à) to mingle with; (être sociable) to mix with; (participer à) to join in; **se ~ à la foule** to mingle with the crowd; **ils ne se mêlent pas aux gens du village** they don't mix with the villagers; **se ~ à la conversation** to join in the conversation; **il s'est mêlé à une affaire douteuse** he got mixed up in some shady business; **3** (s'occuper) **se ~ de** to meddle in; **il se mêle de tout** he interferes ou meddles in everything; **mêle-toi de tes affaires**○ or **oignons**◐ mind your own business; **de quoi je me mêle**○**!** what's it got to do with you?; **se ~ de faire** to take it upon oneself to do; **quand il se mêle de préparer le repas** when he takes it upon himself to prepare the meal; **s'il se mêle de pleuvoir** if it goes and rains (now); **il n'avait pas à se ~ de faire ça** he had no business doing that; **quand l'amour s'en mêle!** when love comes into it!

mélèze /melɛz/ *nm* larch.

méli-mélo, *pl* **mélis-mélos** /melimelo/ *nm* (mélange) hotchpotch GB, hodgepodge US; (fouillis) jumble, mess; (imbroglio) muddle.

mélioratif, -ive /meljɔʀatif, iv/ *adj* meliorative.

mélisse /melis/ *nf* lemon balm; **eau de ~** melissa ou balm water.

mellifère /mɛlifɛʀ/ *adj* melliferous.

mélo○ /melo/ **I** *adj* [*film, pièce*] slushy○, schmaltzy○; **feuilleton ~** Radio, TV soap (opera).

II *nm* melodrama; **c'est du pur ~** (film, pièce) it's a real tear-jerker○, it's pure schmaltz○.

mélodie /melɔdi/ *nf* **1** Mus melody; (air) tune; (pièce vocale) song; **2** (de vers, poème) melodiousness.

mélodieusement /melɔdjøzmɑ̃/ *adv* melodiously.

mélodieux, -ieuse /melɔdjø, øz/ *adj* melodious.

mélodique /melɔdik/ *adj* melodic.

mélodramatique /melɔdʀamatik/ *adj* melodramatic.

mélodrame /melɔdʀam/ *nm* melodrama.

mélomane /melɔman/ **I** *adj* music-loving (*épith*); **être ~** to be a music lover.

II *nmf* music lover.

melon /məlɔ̃/ *nm* **1** Bot, Culin melon; **2** Mode **(chapeau) ~** bowler (hat) GB, derby (hat) US.

■ **~ d'eau** watermelon; **~ d'hiver** honeydew melon.

mélopée /melɔpe/ *nf* **1** chant; **2** Hist Mus melopoeia.

Melpomène /mɛlpɔmɛn/ *npr* Melpomene.

MEM /mɛm/ *nf*: *abbr* ▶ **mémoire**.

membrane /mɑ̃bʀan/ *nf* gén membrane; (de haut-parleur) diaphragm.

membraneux, -euse /mɑ̃bʀanø, øz/ *adj* membranous.

membre /mɑ̃bʀ/ *nm* **1** (de club, famille, parti) member; **~ fondateur/actif/honoraire/à vie** founder/active/honorary/life member; **être ~ de** to be a member of; **les ~s du gouvernement/de l'équipage** the members of the government/of the crew; **les ~s du parti/comité** the members of the party/committee, the party/committee members; **devenir ~ d'un parti/club** to join a party/club; **carte/insigne de ~** membership card/badge; **le club compte 400 ~s** the club has 400 members or a membership of 400; **le parti a perdu beaucoup de ~s** the party's membership has fallen considerably; **les pays ~s/non ~s** the member/non-member countries; **2** Anat, Zool limb; **~s supérieurs** upper limbs; **~s inférieurs** lower limbs; **~ antérieur** forelimb; **~ postérieur** hind limb; **3** Math (d'équation, expression) member; **premier/deuxième ~** first ou left/second ou right member.

■ **~ fantôme** Méd phantom limb; **~ de phrase** Ling part of a sentence; **~ viril** Anat male member.

membrure /mɑ̃bʀyʀ/ *nf* **1** Anat limbs (*pl*); **2** Constr rib; **3** Naut rib.

même /mɛm/ **I** *adj* **1** (identique) same; **en ~ temps** at the same time; **être de la ~ grandeur** or **taille** to be the same size; **c'est toujours la ~ chose** it's always the same;

tu dis toujours la ~ chose that's what you always say; **elle porte la ~ robe qu'hier/que sa sœur** she's wearing the same dress as yesterday/as her sister; **j'étais dans la ~ classe que lui** I was in the same class GB ou grade US as him; **être de la ~ valeur (que)** to be worth the same (as); **2** (suprême) [*bonté, dévouement, générosité*] itself; **il est la perfection/la ponctualité ~** he's perfection/punctuality itself; **c'est l'intelligence ~** he's/she's intelligence itself; **3** (exact) **le jour ~ où** the very same day that; **à l'heure ~ où, au moment ~ où** at the very moment when; **c'est l'endroit ~ du meurtre** this is the very place where the murder took place; **les lieux ~s du meurtre/de l'accident** the (actual) scene of the murder/of the accident; **les fondements ~s de la société** the very foundations of society; **par cela ~** by this very fact; **ce sont les termes ~s qu'il a employés** those were his exact ou very words; **quant aux thèmes ~s à traiter** as for the precise subjects for discussion; **c'est cela ~** that's it exactly.

II *adv* **1** (pour renchérir) even; **je ne m'en souviens ~ plus** I can't even remember; **on peut ~ ajouter** one might even add; **2** (précisément) very; **c'est ici ~ que je l'ai rencontré** I met him at this very place; **aujourd'hui ~** this very day; **c'est alors ~ qu'elle arriva** she arrived at that very moment.

III **de même** *loc adv* **vous partez? nous de ~** are you leaving? so are we; **agir** or **faire de ~** to do the same; **il a refusé de venir et sa sœur de ~** he refused to come and so did his sister; **il a de ~ refusé de venir** he also refused to come; **il en est** or **va de ~ pour** the same is true of; **il n'en est plus de ~ depuis 1970** this is no longer the case since 1970; **cette remarque ne s'adresse pas qu'à lui, il en est de ~ pour vous** this comment isn't just aimed at him, the same goes for you; (de la même manière) **de ~ en France l'armée...** similarly in France, the army...

IV **de même que** *loc conj* **de ~ que la première entreprise a fait faillite, la seconde n'a pas duré très longtemps** just as the first business went bankrupt, the second one didn't last very long either; **le prix de l'essence de ~ que celui du tabac a augmenté de 10%** the price of petrol GB ou gas US, as well as that of tobacco, has risen by 10%; **de ~ que son prédecesseur, il a démissionné** he resigned as did his predecessor, like his predecessor he resigned.

V **même si** *loc conj* even if.

VI **même que**◑ *loc conj* **il roulait à toute allure, ~ qu'il a failli avoir un accident** he was going at top speed and he nearly had an accident, and all○.

VII *pron indéf* **le ~, la ~, les ~s** the same; **j'ai le ~** I've got the same one; **ce sont toujours les ~s qui sont punis** it's always the same ones who get punished; **le ~ que** the same as; **le groupe est le ~ qu'en 1980** the group is the same as it was in 1980; **la loi est la ~ qu'en France** the law is the same as it is in France; **ce sont les ~s qui disaient** these are the same people who said; **Smirnov, le ~ que l'on soupçonne aujourd'hui** Smirnov, the same person suspected today; **le système sera le ~ que celui de mon vieil ordinateur** the system will be the same as the one on my old computer ou as that on my old computer; **la qualité sera la ~ que celle de** the quality will be the same as that of; **ce sac est le ~ que celui de Pierre** this bag is the same as Pierre's.

mémé○ /meme/ *nf* **1** (grand-mère) gran○, granny○; ▶**ortie**; **2** (vieille femme) pej old granny○ péj.

mêmement /mɛm(ə)mɑ̃/ *adv* fml likewise.

mémento /memɛ̃to/ *nm* **1** (livre) guide; **2**† (agenda) diary GB, personal calendar US; **3** (prière) **~ des morts/vivants** prayers (*pl*) for the dead/living.

mémère○ /memɛʀ/ *nf* **1** péj old granny○; **le chien-chien à sa ~** Mummy's little doggy; **2** (grand-mère) granny○.

mémo○ /memo/ *nm* note.

Mémo-Appel /memoapɛl/ *nm* Télécom reminder call service (*in France*).

mémoire /memwaʀ/ **I** *nm* **1** Admin (rapport) memo; **2** Univ (exposé) dissertation (**sur** on); **3** Jur statement of case; **4** Compta (pour coûts) memorandum.

II *nf* **1** (faculté) memory; **~ auditive/visuelle** auditive/visual memory; **avoir de la ~** to have a good memory; **si j'ai bonne ~** if I remember rightly; **ne pas avoir de ~** to have a bad memory; **sa ~ la trahit souvent** her memory often lets her down; **avoir la ~ des dates/visages** to have a good memory for dates/faces; **une histoire gravée dans ma ~** a story engraved on my memory; **quand il s'agit de l'argent qu'on te doit, tu retrouves vite la ~!** hum when someone owes you money, you remember fast enough!; **mon grand-père sera toujours présent dans ma ~** I will always remember my grandfather; **des faits qui sont dans toutes les ~s** facts that everyone remembers; **ça m'est soudain revenu en ~** it suddenly came back to me; **je n'ai pas cette affaire en ~** I can't call that matter to mind; **ça m'est resté en ~** I have never forgotten it; **j'ai toujours son visage en ~** I still remember his/her face; **chacun a gardé en ~ cette image** everyone remembers that image; **citer de ~** to quote from memory; **de ~ d'homme** in living memory; **de ~ de journaliste, on n'avait jamais vu cela** no journalist could remember such a thing happening before; **la ~ collective** collective memory; **2** (souvenir) memory (**de** of); (réputation) reputation, good name (**de** of); **honorer la ~ des soldats disparus** to honour[GB] the memory of the fallen soldiers; **venger/réhabiliter la ~ de qn** to avenge/to clear sb's reputation ou good name; **en ~ de** to the memory of, in memory of; **d'illustre/de sinistre ~** [*personnage, fait*] illustrious/sinister; **pour ~** (à titre de rappel) for the record; (pour conserver) for reference; **je mentionne ce dossier pour ~ seulement** I mention this file for the record only; **garder un dossier pour ~** to keep a document for reference; **3** Ordinat (espace adressable) memory; (unité fonctionnelle) storage; **une ~ de 640K** a 640K memory; **la capacité de ~** the memory capacity ou size; **mettre des données en ~** to input data; **calculatrice/téléphone à ~** calculator/telephone with a memory.

III Mémoires *nmpl* Littérat (souvenirs) memoirs.

■ **~ à accès direct** random access memory, RAM; **~ centrale** main storage ou memory; **~ dynamique** dynamic memory, DOM; **~ externe** external storage; **~ immunologique** immunological memory; **~ interne** internal memory ou storage; **~ de maîtrise** Univ dissertation (*which constitutes part of the French master's degree*); **~ morte, MEM** read-only memory, ROM; **~ principale** = **~ centrale**; **~ tampon** buffer memory; **~ vive, MEV** random access memory , RAM.

IDIOMES **avoir la ~ courte** to have a short memory.

Mémophone /memofɔn/ *nm* Télécom public voice mail service.

mémorable /memɔʀabl/ *adj* memorable.

mémorandum /memɔʀɑ̃dɔm/ *nm* **1** (en diplomatie) memorandum; **2** (de choses à faire) note; (carnet) notebook; **3** Comm memo; (imprimé) order form.

mémorial, **~e**, *mpl* **-iaux** /memɔʀjal, o/ *nm* **1** Archit memorial; **2** Littérat memorials (*pl*).

mémorialiste /memɔʀjalist/ *nmf* memorialist.

mémorisation /memɔʀizasjɔ̃/ *nf* **1** (apprentissage) memorization; (faculté de retenir) powers (*pl*) of memory; **2** Ordinat storage.

mémoriser /memɔʀize/ [1] *vtr* **1** (apprendre par cœur) to memorize [*liste*]; (retenir) to remember [*fait, noms*]; **2** Ordinat to store; **données mémorisées** stored data.

menaçant, **~e** /mənasɑ̃, ɑ̃t/ *adj* [*geste, regard, ton, ombre, présence*] menacing, threatening; [*personne*] menacing; **être ~, dire des paroles ~es** [*personne*] to make threats; **se faire ~** [*personne*] to start to make threats; [*temps*] to look threatening; **le temps était ~** the weather looked threatening.

menace /mənas/ *nf* threat; **~s de mort** death threats; **faire peser une ~ sur qn/qch** to pose a threat to sb/sth; **~s en l'air** idle threats; **geste de ~** menacing ou threatening gesture; **céder à/employer la ~** to give in to/to use threats; **obtenir de l'argent par la ~** to obtain money with menaces; **sous la ~** [*avouer, signer*] under duress; **tenir qn sous la ~ d'une révélation/d'un divorce** to threaten sb with a revelation/a divorce; **tenir qn sous la ~ d'une arme** to hold sb at gunpoint; **faire qch sous la ~ d'une arme** to do sth at gunpoint.

menacer /mənase/ [12] *vtr* **1** (terroriser) to threaten [*personne*]; **~ qn d'un couteau** to threaten sb with a knife; **vous a-t-il menacé?** did he threaten you?; **2** (agiter une menace) to threaten (**de faire** to do); **~ qn d'une amende** to threaten sb with a fine; **~ qn de mort** to threaten to kill sb; **la pluie menace** rain is threatening; **3** (mettre en danger) to pose a threat to [*pays, santé*]; **être menacé** [*équilibre, économie*] to be in jeopardy; [*vie*] to be in danger; [*tranquillité*] to be threatened; [*carrière*] to be on the line; **toute la population est menacée** the entire population is at risk; **4** (risquer) **la chaudière menace d'exploser** the boiler could explode at any moment; **le retard menace d'être long** the delay threatens to be long.

ménage /menaʒ/ *nm* **1** Écon, Sociol, Stat household; **une voiture par ~** one car per household; **la consommation des ~s** household consumption; **2** (couple) couple; (rapports) relationship; **vieux/jeune ~** old/young couple; **~ sans enfants** childless couple; **rien ne va plus dans leur ~** their relationship doesn't work any more; **se mettre en ~ avec qn** to set up home with sb; **ils sont** or **vivent en ~ depuis deux ans** they've been living together for two years; **être heureux/malheureux en ~** to get on well/badly with one's partner; **scènes de ~** domestic rows; **il est pour la paix des ~s** he doesn't want to interfere in other people's domestic quarrels; **3** (administration domestique) **tenir** or **conduire son ~** to look after the house; **monter son ~** to buy the household goods; **pain/saucisson de ~** ordinary bread/sausage; **4** (entretien d'intérieur) housework; **faire le ~** lit to do the cleaning; fig (dans un parti politique, une organisation) to do the cleaning up; **le ~ n'a pas été fait dans le salon** the living-room hasn't been cleaned; **faire le ~ à fond** to have a thorough clean; **faire des ~s** to do domestic cleaning work.

■ **~ à trois** ménage à trois.

IDIOMES **faire bon ~** [*personne*] to get on well (**avec** with); [*chose*] to be compatible (**avec** with).

ménagement /menaʒmɑ̃/ *nm* **avec ~s** [*dire, annoncer, parler*] gently; **sans ~s** [*dire, annoncer, parler*] bluntly; [*jeter, pousser*] roughly, unceremoniously; **elle est fragile, traite-la avec ~** she's delicate, be gentle with her; **annoncez-leur la nouvelle avec beaucoup de ~s** break the news to them gently; **il faut le traiter avec ~(s) car il est très puissant** you need to handle him very carefully as he is very powerful; **il traite ses employés sans ~s** he treats his employees shabbily, he shows no consideration for his employees; **la police l'a embarqué sans aucun ~** the police bundled him unceremoniously ou roughly into the van.

ménager[1] /menaʒe/ [13] I *vtr* **1** (traiter avec précaution) to handle [sb] carefully [*collaborateur*]; to deal carefully with [*adversaire*]; to be gentle with, to treat [sb] gently [*personne âgée, malade, convalescent*]; to be careful with, to take care of [*machine, matériel*]; **ils savent ~ leurs alliés** they're careful not to upset their allies, they handle their allies carefully; **essaie de le ~, il est encore fragile** try and be gentle with him, he hasn't totally recovered yet; **~ la susceptibilité de qn** to humour[GB] sb; **tu devrais ~ ton moteur** you should be careful with your engine; **les critiques n'ont pas ménagé le cinéaste** the critics didn't spare the film director; **~ les oreilles de qn** to spare sb's ears; **~ sa santé** to look after one's health; **ménage tes poumons, arrête de fumer** give your lungs a chance: stop smoking; ▶**chèvre**; **2** (employer avec économie) to be careful with [*vêtements, économies, ressources*]; to save [*forces*]; **elle ne nous a pas ménagé les critiques** she wasn't sparing in her criticism of us; **il ne ménage pas ses efforts** or **sa peine** he spares no effort; **il ménage ses paroles** he's a man of few words; **elle n'a pas ménagé ses termes** or **expressions** she didn't mince her words; **3** (installer) **~ un escalier dans un bâtiment** to install a staircase in a building; **~ un passage/une issue de secours** to make an opening/an emergency exit; **~ un espace pour un meuble** to make some space for a piece of furniture; **4** (régler avec soin) to organize, to arrange [*entrevue, rencontre*]; **~ des transitions dans un texte** to make smooth transitions in a text; **~ un temps de pause entre les séquences** to allow for breaks between sequences; **je lui ménage une petite surprise dont il se souviendra** iron I'm arranging a little surprise for him that he won't forget; **l'auteur ménage ses effets** the author saves his/her best effects until the end.

II **se ménager** *vpr* **1** (s'économiser) [*personne*] to take it easy; **vous devriez vous ~ un peu** you should take it easy, you shouldn't overexert ou overtax yourself; **2** (se préparer) **se ~ une issue** or **une porte de sortie** fig to leave oneself a way out.

ménager[2], **-ère** /menaʒe, ɛʀ/ I *adj* **1** (de la maison) [*occupations, tâches*] domestic; [*ustensiles, équipement*] household, domestic; **appareils ~s** domestic appliances; **travaux ~s** housework ¢, domestic chores; **2**† (économe) **être ~ de** to be economical with [*temps, argent*].

II **ménagère** *nf* **1** (personne) housewife; **2** (couverts) canteen of cutlery.

ménagerie /menaʒʀi/ *nf* (de cirque, zoo) menagerie; **cette classe est une vraie ~!** this classroom is a real zoo!

mendélévium /mɛ̃delevjɔm/ *nm* mendelevium.

mendélien, **-ienne** /mɛ̃deljɛ̃, ɛn/ *adj* Mendelian.

mendiant, **~e** /mɑ̃djɑ̃, ɑ̃t/ I *adj* **les ordres ~s** the mendicant orders.

II *nm,f* beggar.

III **mendiants** *nmpl* Culin *mixture of almonds, dried figs, hazelnuts and raisins.*

mendicité /mɑ̃disite/ *nf* begging; **vivre de la ~** to beg for a living; **en être réduit à la ~** to be reduced to begging.

mendier /mɑ̃dje/ [2] I *vtr* to beg for; **~ qch auprès de qn** to beg sb for sth.

II *vi* to beg.

mendigot◐, **~e** /mɑ̃digo, ɔt/ *nm,f* beggar.

mendigoter◐ /mɑ̃digɔte/ [1] *vi* to beg.

meneau, *pl* **~x** /meno/ *nm* (horizontal) transom; (vertical) mullion; **une fenêtre à ~x** a mullioned window.

menées /məne/ *nfpl* plotting ¢; **déjouer les ~ de qn** to foil sb's plotting.

Ménélas /menelas/ *npr* Menelaus.

mener /məne/ [16] I *vtr* **1** (accompagner) gén **~ qn quelque part** to take sb somewhere; (en voiture) to drive sb somewhere; **2** (guider) to lead [*bête, enfant, convoi*]; **~ un animal par une corde** to lead an animal on a rope; **~ qn à l'échafaud** to take sb to the scaffold; **~ paître le troupeau** to lead the flock to pasture; **~ son embarcation parmi les récifs** to guide one's boat through the reef; **3** (commander) to lead [*hommes, équipe, pays, délégation*]; to run [*entreprise, pays*]; **il ne se laisse pas ~ par sa grande sœur** he won't be bossed about○ ou around○ US by his older sister; **l'égoïsme mène le monde** the world is ruled by self-interest; **se laisser ~ par son seul intérêt** to be motivated by pure self-interest; ▶**dur**, **nez**; **4** gén, Sport (avoir l'avantage) to lead; **la France mène le championnat devant l'Allemagne par trois points** France is leading the championship three points ahead of Germany; **5** (aller, faire aller) **~ à Lille/au village** [*route*] to go ou lead to Lille/to the village; **~ qn quelque part** [*route*] to take sb somewhere; **notre promenade nous mena jusqu'au fleuve** our walk took us as far as the river; **la voie qui mène à la démocratie** the road to democracy; ▶**Rome**; **6** (faire aboutir) **~ à** [*baisse, échec, catastrophe, découverte*] to lead to; **~ qn à conclure que** to lead sb to conclude that; **je ne vois pas où cela nous mène** I can't see where this is getting ou leading us; **~ droit à** gén to lead [sb/sth] straight to; **cela le mènera droit en prison** that will land him in jail; **cela mène à tout** it leads to all kinds of things; **cela ne mène à rien** it doesn't lead anywhere; **parler ne mène à rien** talking won't get you anywhere; **cette histoire peut te ~ loin** (avoir des conséquences graves) it could be a very nasty business; **50 francs, cela ne nous mènera pas loin** 50 francs, that won't get us very far; **des indices qui ne mènent nulle part** clues which don't lead anywhere; **~ qch à bien** or **à bonne fin** or **à (son) terme** to complete [sth] successfully [*projet*]; to bring [sth] to a successful conclusion [*négociation, enquête*]; to handle [sth] successfully [*opération délicate*]; **7** (poursuivre) to carry out [*étude, réforme*]; to pursue [*politique*]; to run [*campagne*]; **~ une enquête** gén to hold an investigation ou enquiry GB; (en tant que chef) to head an investigation ou enquiry GB; **~ des discussions oiseuses** to engage in pointless discussion; **~ deux choses de front** to pursue two aims simultaneously; **~ une vie exemplaire/misérable** to lead a blameless/wretched existence; **~ une vie de moine** to live like a hermit; **~ sa vie comme on l'entend** to live as one pleases; **~ des combats violents** to fight furiously; **~ une offensive contre un pays** to conduct an offensive against a country; **~ une guerre sans pitié** to wage a bitter war; **~ une grève de la faim** to be on hunger strike; ▶**bâton**; **8** (tracer) **~ une ligne d'un point à un autre** to draw a line between two points.

II *vi* Sport to be in the lead; **~ par trois buts à un** to lead by three goals to one.

IDIOMES **~ la danse** or **le jeu** to call the tune; **~ grand train** or **la grande vie** to live it up.

ménestrel /menɛstʀɛl/ *nm* minstrel.

ménétrier /menetʀije/ *nm* village fiddler.

meneur, **-euse** /mənœʀ, øz/ *nm,f* leader; **avoir des qualités de ~** to have leadership qualities.

■ **~ d'hommes** leader of men; **~ de jeu** compere GB, master of ceremonies US, emcee US; **meneuse de revue** leading showgirl.

menhir /meniʀ/ *nm* menhir.

méninge /menɛ̃ʒ/ I *nf* Anat meninx.

II **méninges**○ *nfpl* brains○; **se creuser les ~s** to rack one's brains.

méningé, **~e** /menɛ̃ʒe/ *adj* meningeal.

méningite /menɛ̃ʒit/ ▶**271** *nf* meningitis; **tu ne risques pas d'attraper une ~!** hum you're not exactly straining yourself!

ménisque /menisk/ *nm* meniscus.

ménopause /menɔpoz/ *nf* menopause.

ménopausée /menɔpoze/ *adj f* post-menopausal (*épith*).

menotte /mənɔt/ I *nf* (petite main) tiny hand.

II **menottes** *nfpl* handcuffs; **avoir les ~s aux poignets** to be handcuffed; **passer les ~s à qn** to handcuff sb.

menotter /mənɔte/ [1] *vtr* to handcuff.

mensonge /mɑ̃sɔ̃ʒ/ *nm* **1** (assertion fausse) lie; **dire des ~s/un ~ à qn** to tell sb lies/a lie; **un tissu de ~s** a tissue of lies; **un pieux ~** a white lie; **un ~ par omission** a lie by omission; **2** (principe) **le ~** lying; **avoir horreur du ~** to loathe lying.

mensonger, **-ère** /mɑ̃sɔ̃ʒe, ɛʀ/ *adj* [*propos, accusations*] false; [*publicité*] misleading; [*campagne*] dishonest.

menstruation /mɑ̃stʀyasjɔ̃/ *nf* menstruation.

menstruel, **-elle** /mɑ̃stʀyɛl/ *adj* menstrual.

menstrues /mɑ̃stʀy/ *nfpl* menses.

mensualisation /mɑ̃sɥalizasjɔ̃/ *nf* **j'ai demandé la ~ de mes factures** I've arranged to pay my bills on a monthly basis; **la ~ des salaires existe depuis longtemps** salaries have been paid on a monthly basis for a long time.

mensualisé, **~e** /mɑ̃sɥalize/ *adj* **1** [*paiement*] monthly (*épith*); **2** [*salaire, employé*] paid monthly (*jamais épith*); **mon salaire est ~** my salary is paid monthly.

mensualiser /mɑ̃sɥalize/ [1] *vtr* **1** (étaler) **~ des versements** to pay in monthly instalments[GB]; **2** (payer un mois de travail) **les salaires ont été mensualisés** wages are now paid on a monthly basis.

mensualité /mɑ̃sɥalite/ *nf* **1** (versement) monthly instalment[GB]; **payer qch par ~s** to pay for sth in monthly instalments[GB], to make monthly payments for sth; **payer qch en plusieurs ~s** to pay for sth in several monthly instalments[GB]; **2** (salaire) monthly salary.

mensuel, **-elle** /mɑ̃sɥɛl/ I *adj* monthly.

II *nm* Presse monthly magazine.

mensuellement /mɑ̃sɥɛlmɑ̃/ *adv* once a month, monthly.

mensuration /mɑ̃syʀasjɔ̃/ I *nf* mensuration.

II **mensurations** *nfpl* measurements.

mental, **~e**, *mpl* **-aux** /mɑ̃tal, o/ I *adj* [*âge, cruauté*] mental; **handicapé ~** mentally handicapped person; **malade ~** mentally ill person.

II *nm* (esprit) mind.

mentalement /mɑ̃talmɑ̃/ *adv* **1** (par la pensée) [*compter, se représenter, élaborer*] in one's head; **2** (sur le plan mental) mentally.

mentalité /mɑ̃talite/ *nf* mentality; **belle ~!** the mentality of some people!; **la ~ des Français** the French mentality.

menterie† /mɑ̃tʀi/ *nf* lie.

menteur, **-euse** /mɑ̃tœʀ, øz/ I *adj* [*personne*] untruthful; [*propos, écrits*] full of lies (*après n*); **être ~** to be a liar.

II *nm,f* liar, fibber○; **menteuse!** you liar!

menthe /mɑ̃t/ *nf* **1** (plante) mint; **à la ~** [*dentifrice*] mint (*épith*); **2** (infusion) mint tea; **3** (sirop) **~ (à l'eau)** mint cordial.

■ **~ aquatique** water mint; **~ des champs** wild mint; **~ poivrée** peppermint; **~ pouliot** pennyroyal; **~ verte** spearmint.

menthol /mɛ̃tɔl/ *nm* menthol.

mentholé, **~e** /mɛ̃tɔle/ *adj* mentholated; [*bonbon, cigarette, dentifrice*] menthol (*épith*).

mention /mɑ̃sjɔ̃/ *nf* **1** (action de citer) mention; **la ~ d'un accident dans les journaux** the mention of an incident in the newspapers; **être digne de ~** to be worthy of mention; **sans ~ de** with no mention of; **faire ~ de qch** to mention sth; **ne pas faire ~ de qch** to make no mention of sth; **il a été fait ~ de cet événement plusieurs fois** this event was mentioned several times; **il n'est pas fait mention de** no mention is made of; **faire ~ de l'existence de qch** to acknowledge the existence of sth; **2** Scol, Univ **~ passable** *pass with 50 to 60%*; **~ assez bien** *pass with 60 to 70%*; **~ bien** *pass with 70 to 80%*; **~ très bien** *pass with 80% upwards*; **il a obtenu une ~ à son examen** he got a merit in his exam; **~ honorable/très honorable** (à un doctorat) with merit/distinction; **3** (indication) note; **dossier portant la ~ 'secret'** file marked 'secret'; **rayer la ~ inutile** or **les ~s inutiles** delete as appropriate.
■ **~ spéciale** Art, Cin special award (**à, pour** for).

mentionner /mɑ̃sjɔne/ [1] *vtr* to mention; **il n'a pas mentionné qch** he didn't mention sth, he made no mention of sth; **ci-dessus mentionné** mentioned above; **mentionné ci-dessous** mentioned below.

mentir /mɑ̃tiʀ/ [30] **I** *vi* **1** (ne pas dire la vérité) [*personne*] to lie, to tell lies (**sur** about); **~ à qn** to lie to sb, to tell sb lies; **~ par intérêt/par jeu** to lie for personal gain/for fun; **tu mens!** you're lying!; **ne mens pas!** don't tell lies!; **il ment lorsqu'il dit que** he is lying when he says that; **sans ~, le poisson était grand comme ça!** no lie, the fish was this big!; **2** (être trompeur) [*publicité, statistiques, apparences*] to be misleading; **faire ~ des prévisions/le proverbe** to give the lie to forecasts/the proverb.
II se mentir *vpr* **1** (à soi-même) to fool oneself (**sur** about); **2** (l'un l'autre) to lie to one another (**sur** about).
IDIOMES **bon sang ne saurait ~** Prov blood will tell Prov; **il ment comme il respire** he's a born liar; ▶ **arracheur**.

menton /mɑ̃tɔ̃/ *nm* chin; **~ fuyant/en galoche** receding/protruding chin; **double ~** double chin; **relever** or **dresser le ~** to stick out one's jaw.

mentonnière /mɑ̃tɔnjɛʀ/ *nf* **1** (de couvre-chef) chinstrap; **2** (de violon) chin rest; **3** (bandage) chin bandage; **4** (d'armure) chinpiece, beaver.

mentor /mɛ̃tɔʀ/ *nm* mentor.

menu, **~e** /məny/ **I** *adj* **1** (petit) [*personne*] slight; [*pied*] tiny; [*taille*] slender; [*brindille, écriture*] small; [*voix*] thin; **couper en ~s morceaux** to cut into tiny pieces; **à pas ~s** with tiny steps; **2** (sans importance) [*corvées, travaux*] small; [*occupations, obligations*] trifling; [*frais, soucis, dépenses, difficultés*] minor; [*détails*] minute; [*plaisirs*] little.
II *adv* [*écrire*] small; [*hacher*] finely.
III *nm* **1** (liste) menu; **le ~ à 100 F/à prix fixe** the 100 F/set menu; **~ dégustation** special house menu; **le ~ du jour** today's menu; **~ gastronomique/touristique** gourmet/middle-price menu; **au ~** on the menu; **choisir au ~** to choose from the menu; **2** (repas) meal; **planifiez vos ~s** plan your meals; **3** (régime) diet; **4** (programme) programme[GB]; **au ~** on the programme[GB]; **5** Ordinat menu.
IV par le menu *loc adv* [*décrire, raconter*] in (great) detail.
■ **~ déroulant** Ordinat pull-down menu; **~e monnaie** small change; **~ fretin** lit, fig small fry; **~ gibier** small game; **~ peuple** humble folk (+ *v pl*); **~s propos** small talk ¢.

menuet /mənɥɛ/ *nm* minuet.

menuiserie /mənɥizʀi/ *nf* **1** (travail du bois, profession, industrie) joinery; (discipline, passe-temps) woodwork; **un atelier de ~** a joiner's workshop; **2** (atelier) carpenter's shop; **3** (boiseries) woodwork ¢.
■ **~ métallique** metal doors, windows and frames (*pl*).

menuisier /mənɥizje/ ▶**510** *nm* joiner GB, finish carpenter, woodworker.

Méphistophélès /mefistofelɛs/ *npr* Mephistopheles.

méphistophélique /mefistofelik/ *adj* liter Mephistophelian.

méphitique /mefitik/ *adj* fml foul, mephitic sout.

méplat, **~e** /mepla, at/ **I** *adj* flat.
II *nm* plane.

méprendre: **se méprendre** /mepʀɑ̃dʀ/ [52] *vpr* fml to be mistaken (**sur** about), to be wrong (**sur** about); **elles se ressemblent tellement, c'est à s'y ~** they're so much alike, it's hard to tell them apart.

mépris /mepʀi/ *nm* **1** (dédain) contempt, scorn (**de** for); **avoir du ~ pour qn/qch** to despise sb/sth, to scorn sb/sth; **ton/sourire de ~** contemptuous ou scornful tone/smile; **2** (indifférence) **~ de** contempt for [*argent, succès*]; disregard for [*danger, mort, convenances*]; **au ~ de la loi/du danger** regardless of the law/of danger.

méprisable /mepʀizabl/ *adj* [*personne, action*] contemptible; (plus fort) despicable; [*somme, idée*] insignificant.

méprisant, **~e** /mepʀizɑ̃, ɑ̃t/ *adj* [*geste, sourire, attitude*] contemptuous, scornful; [*personne*] disdainful, scornful; **être ~ avec qn** to treat sb with contempt.

méprise /mepʀiz/ *nf* mistake; **par ~** by mistake.

mépriser /mepʀize/ [1] *vtr* to despise [*personne, argent*]; to scorn [*danger, conseils, offre*]; to be scornful of [*convenances, honneurs*]; to disregard [*détails, règles*].

mer /mɛʀ/ ▶**555** *nf* **1** (étendue d'eau) sea; **niveau de la ~** sea level; **une ~ d'huile** a glassy sea; **vent de ~** sea breeze; **la vie en ~** life at sea; **par voie de ~** by sea; **en pleine ~** out at sea; **être en ~** to be at sea; **prendre la ~** [*personne, bateau*] to go to sea, to put to sea; **un homme à la ~!** man overboard!; **en bord de ~** by the sea; **mettre un bateau à la ~** to launch a boat; **eau de ~** seawater; **embarquer de gros paquets de ~** to ship water; **coup de ~** breaker; **~ de sable** sea of sand; **2** (zone côtière) seaside; **aller à la ~** to go to the sea, to go to the ocean US; **la ~ me convient mieux que la montagne** I prefer the seaside to the mountains; **3** (marée) tide; **la ~ monte** the tide is coming in; **la ~ est haute/basse** the tide is high/low.
■ **~ Blanche** White Sea; **~ de Chine** China Sea; **~ d'Irlande** Irish Sea; **~ Morte** Dead Sea; **~ Noire** Black Sea; **~ du Nord** North Sea; **~ Rouge** Red Sea.
IDIOMES **ce n'est pas la ~ à boire** it's not all that difficult.

mer-air /mɛʀɛʀ/ *adj inv* [*engin, missile*] sea-to-air.

mercanti /mɛʀkɑ̃ti/ *nm* pej profiteer.

mercantile /mɛʀkɑ̃til/ *adj* pej mercenary péj.

mercantilisme /mɛʀkɑ̃tilism/ *nm* **1** Écon mercantilism; **2** (mentalité) pej mercenary mentality; **le ~ foncier de notre société** the fundamentally mercenary nature of our society.

mercaticien, **-ienne** /mɛʀkatisjɛ̃, ɛn/ ▶**510** *nm,f* marketing expert.

mercatique /mɛʀkatik/ *nf* marketing.

mercenaire /mɛʀsənɛʀ/ *adj, nmf* mercenary.

mercerie /mɛʀsəʀi/ ▶**510** *nf* **1** (boutique) haberdasher's shop GB, notions store US; **2** (articles) haberdashery GB, notions (*pl*) US; **3** (activité) haberdashery trade GB, notions trade US.

mercerisé, **~e** /mɛʀsəʀize/ *adj* mercerized.

merchandising /mɛʀtʃɑ̃dajsiŋ/ *nm* controv merchandising.

merci /mɛʀsi/ **I** *nm* thank you; **tu leur diras un grand ~ de ma part** give them a big thank you from me; **mille ~s** thank you so much; **un grand ~ à Mia pour son aide** a big thank you to Mia for her help.
II *nf* mercy; **sans ~** [*lutte*] without mercy (*après n*), merciless (*épith*); **à la ~ de qn** at sb's mercy, at the mercy of sb; **à leur ~** at their mercy; **tenir qn à sa ~** to hold sb at one's mercy; **à la ~ du temps** at the mercy of the weather; **on est toujours à la ~ d'un changement de dernière minute** you're always in danger of a last minute change.
III *excl* thank you, thanks○ (**à** to; **de, pour** for; **de faire, d'avoir fait** for doing); **~ beaucoup** thank you very much; **~ d'avance** thank you in advance; **~ à tous d'être venus** thank you all for coming; **~ à vous!** (repartie) thank YOU!; **non ~** no thank you, no thanks○; **y aller seule? ~ bien!** or **non ~!** go alone? no thank you!; **~ pour tout** thanks○ for everything; **~ mille fois** very many thanks; **Dieu ~** thank God; **dire ~** to say thank you; **tu pourrais dire ~!** you might say thank you!; **ils sont partis sans même dire ~** they left without even saying thank you.

mercier, **-ière** /mɛʀsje, ɛʀ/ ▶**510** *nm, f* haberdasher GB, notions seller US.

mercredi /mɛʀkʀədi/ **I** ▶**750** *nm* (jour) Wednesday.
II○ *excl* euph sugar○!
■ **~ des Cendres** Ash Wednesday.

mercure /mɛʀkyʀ/ *nm* mercury; **thermomètre à ~** mercury thermometer.

Mercure /mɛʀkyʀ/ **I** *npr* Mythol Mercury.
II *nprf* Astron Mercury.

mercuriale /mɛʀkyʀjal/ *nf* **1** Bot mercury; **2** Comm (liste) market price list; (tarif) market price; **3** (semonce) liter rebuke.

mercuriel, **-ielle** /mɛʀkyʀjɛl/ *adj* mercurial; **intoxication mercurielle** mercury poisoning.

mercurochrome® /mɛʀkyʀɔkʀɔm/ *nm* Mercurochrome®, antiseptic.

merde /mɛʀd/ **I**● *nf* **1** (matière) shit◑; **j'ai marché dans la ~** I've trodden in some shit◑; **2** (étron) turd○; **une ~ de chien** a dog turd○; **3** (objet de mauvaise qualité) crap◑; **on mange de la ~ dans ce restaurant** that restaurant serves crap◑ food; **chaussures/boulot de ~** crap◑ shoes/job; **il a fait un temps de ~** the weather was bloody◑ awful; **cette voiture de ~** this bloody◑ car; **4** (pagaille) mess○; **être dans la ~** to be in the shit◑; **être dans la ~ jusqu'au cou** to be in deep shit◑; **on n'est pas dans la ~ maintenant** iron we're really in the shit◑ now; **mettre** or **foutre** or **semer la ~** to stir up the shit◑.
II◑ *excl* shit◑!; **dire ~ à qn** to tell sb to piss off◑; **'monsieur, je vous dis ~'** 'balls◑ to you!'; (**et**) **~ pour lui** tough shit◑!; **~ alors** shit◑!; **~ (puissance treize)!** (pour porter chance) good luck!
IDIOMES **ne pas se prendre pour une ~**● to think the sun shines out of one's arse● GB ou ass◑ US; **avoir un œil qui dit ~ à l'autre**◑ to be cross-eyed.

merder● /mɛʀde/ [1] *vi* [*candidat, bricoleur, affaire, projet*] to screw up◑, to fuck up●; **j'ai merdé à l'examen** I screwed up in my exam; **qu'est-ce que tu merdes?** what the fuck● are you doing?

merdeux●, **-euse** /mɛʀdø, øz/ **I** *adj* **se sentir ~** to squirm (with embarrassment).
II *nm,f* arsehole● GB, asshole◑ US, shit◑; **un petit ~** a little shit◑.

merdier● /mɛʀdje/ *nm* (situation) bloody mess◑; (désordre, fouillis) shambles (*sg*).

merdique● /mɛʀdik/ *adj* [*film, livre*] crappy◑; [*voiture, appareil, pays*] crap◑.

mère /mɛʀ/ **I** *nf* **1** (génitrice) mother; **elle est ~ de trois enfants** she is the mother of three (children); **devenir ~** to become a mother; **elle est comme une ~ pour moi** she's like a mother to me; **elles sont sages-femmes de ~ en fille** they have been midwives for generations; **mariée et ~ de deux enfants** married with two children; **retourner chez sa ~** to go home to mother; **les chiots et leur ~** the puppies and their mother; **la Grèce, ~ des arts** fig Greece, mother of the arts; **2**○ (femme) **la ~ Michel** old mother Michel; **comment allez-vous, ~ Colas?** how are you, Mrs Colas?; **3** (dans un couvent) **~ supérieure** Mother Superior; **oui, ma ~** yes, Reverend Mother; **~ abbesse** abbess; **~ Teresa** Mother Teresa; **4** Tech (moule) mould GB, mold US; ▶ **oisiveté**, **prudence**.

II (-)mère (*in compounds*) **cellule ~** Biol parent cell; **maison ~** parent company; **plante ~** Bot parent plant.

■ **~ adoptive** foster mother; **~ biologique** biological mother; **~ célibataire** single mother; **~ donneuse** donor mother; **~ de famille** gén mother; (ménagère) housewife; **~ patrie** motherland, fatherland; **~ porteuse** Méd surrogate mother; **~ poule** hum mother hen; **~ du vinaigre** Chimie mother of vinegar.

IDIOMES **il tuerait père et ~ pour avoir qch** he'd kill to get sth.

mère-grand† /mɛʀgʀɑ̃/ *nf* grandmother.

merguez /mɛʀgɛz/ *nf inv* spicy sausage.

mergule /mɛʀgyl/ *nm* little auk.

méridien, **-ienne** /meʀidjɛ̃, ɛn/ **I** *adj* **1** Astron, Géog meridian; **2** liter [*heure, ombre*] midday, noon.

II *nm* **1** Géog meridian; **~ d'origine/de Greenwich** prime/Greenwich meridian; **2** Astron meridian.

III méridienne *nf* **1** Math meridian line; **2** Astron (en géodésie) line of triangulation points; **3** (sieste) liter siesta; **4** (lit) ≈ day bed.

méridional, **~e**, *mpl* **-aux** /meʀidjɔnal, o/ **I** *adj* **1** (du sud de la France) [*accent, type, exagération*] Southern; **2** Géog [*versant, côte, région*] southern.

II *nm,f* Southerner.

meringue /məʀɛ̃g/ *nf* meringue.

meringué, **~e** /məʀɛ̃ge/ **I** *pp* ▶ **meringuer**.

II *pp adj* meringue-topped (*épith*), covered with meringue (*jamais épith*).

meringuer /məʀɛ̃ge/ [1] *vtr* to cover [sth] with meringue [*gâteau*]; to add a meringue topping to [*dessert*].

mérinos /meʀinos/ *nm inv* **1** (mouton) merino; **2** (étoffe) merino.

IDIOMES **laisser pisser le ~**◐ to let things take their course.

merise /məʀiz/ *nf* wild cherry.

merisier /məʀizje/ *nm* **1** (arbre) wild cherry tree; **2** (bois) cherry wood.

méritant, **~e** /meʀitɑ̃, ɑ̃t/ *adj* deserving.

mérite /meʀit/ *nm* **1** (vertu permanente) merit; (pour un événement ponctuel) credit; **un homme de (grand) ~** a man of (great) merit; **il a au moins le ~ d'être sincère** he has the merit of being sincere, but at least he's sincere; **au ~** according to merit; **il a eu le ~ de permettre le dialogue entre les deux parties** it's to his credit that he got the two sides around the negotiating table; **ne me remerciez pas, tout le ~ revient à mon collaborateur** don't thank me, all the credit should go to my colleague; **avoir du ~ à faire qch** to deserve credit for doing sth; **tu as au moins le ~ d'avoir essayé** at least you tried; **il n'y a aucun ~ à faire** there's no merit in doing; **vous n'en avez que plus de ~** you deserve all the more credit for it; **il a eu grand ~ à faire** it was greatly to his credit that he did; **cette voiture n'est pas très belle mais elle a le ~ de rouler/d'exister** this car isn't very much to look at but at least it goes GB ou runs US/but it's better than nothing; **2** (qualité) merit, quality; **ce livre a ses ~s** the book has its merits; **si nombreux que soient ses ~s, il n'est pas sans défauts** however many qualities he may have, he's not without his faults; **vanter les ~s de qn/qch** to sing the praises of sb/sth; **avoir le double ~ d'être confortable et puissant** to be comfortable and powerful; **3** (décoration) **ordre (national) du Mérite** *French award for distinguished services in a public or private capacity*; **4** Relig **les ~s** the good works.

mériter /meʀite/ [1] **I** *vtr* [*personne, action*] to deserve [*estime, encouragements, récompense, punition*]; **il mériterait qu'on lui fasse subir le même sort** he deserves the same treatment, it would serve him right if somebody did the same to him; **tu n'as que ce que tu mérites** you've got GB ou gotten US what you deserve, it serves you right; **un délit qui mérite une peine très lourde** a crime that warrants ou deserves a very heavy penalty; **~ d'être lu** to be worth reading; **l'endroit mérite le détour** this place is worth the detour; **~ réflexion** to be worth considering; **cette théorie mérite qu'on s'y intéresse** this theory is worth studying; **il a reçu une gifle et il l'a bien méritée** he got a slap round GB ou in the face and it was nothing less than he deserved; **succès/repos (bien) mérité** well-deserved success/rest; **punition/récompense méritée** well-deserved punishment/reward; **sa lettre mérite une réponse** his/her letter merits a reply.

II mériter de *vtr ind* **avoir bien mérité de la patrie** to have earned the recognition of one's countrymen.

III se mériter *vpr* **c'est quelque chose qui se mérite** it's something that has to be earned.

méritocratie /meʀitokʀasi/ *nf* meritocracy.

méritocratique /meʀitokʀatik/ *adj* meritocratic.

méritoire /meʀitwaʀ/ *adj* praiseworthy, commendable.

merlan /mɛʀlɑ̃/ *nm* whiting.

IDIOMES **faire des yeux de ~ frit à qn**○ (de surprise) to goggle at sb; (amoureusement) to look at sb with lovesick eyes.

merle /mɛʀl/ *nm* blackbird; ▶ **grive**.

■ **le ~ blanc** (personne) the one in a million; (chose) the impossible.

merlette /mɛʀlɛt/ *nf* female blackbird.

merlin /mɛʀlɛ̃/ *nm* (de bûcheron) cleaver; (de boucher) poleaxe.

merlu /mɛʀly/ *nm* hake.

merluche /mɛʀlyʃ/ *nf* **1** (merlu) hake; **2** (morue séchée) stockfish.

merluchon /mɛʀlyʃɔ̃/ *nm* small hake.

mer-mer /mɛʀmɛʀ/ *adj inv* [*engin, missile*] sea-to-sea.

mérou /meʀu/ *nm* grouper.

mérovingien, **-ienne** /meʀovɛ̃ʒjɛ̃, ɛn/ *adj* Merovingian.

Mérovingien, **-ienne** /meʀovɛ̃ʒjɛ̃, ɛn/ *nm,f* Merovingian.

Merseyside ▶ **692** *nprm* **le ~** Merseyside.

mer-sol /mɛʀsɔl/ *adj inv* [*engin, missile*] sea-to-surface.

merveille /mɛʀvɛj/ **I** *nf* **1** (chose admirable) marvel, wonder; **ta maison/confiture est une pure ~** your house/jam is marvellous[GB]; **les sept ~s du monde** the seven wonders of the world; **la huitième ~ du monde** the eighth wonder of the world; **il se prend pour la huitième ~ du monde** he thinks he's God's gift to humanity; **et, ~ des ~s**... and wonder of wonders...; **la ~ des ~s** the most wonderful thing in the world; **une ~ de finesse** a marvel ou miracle of delicacy; **faire ~** or **des ~s** to work wonders ou miracles; **2** Culin fritter.

II à merveille *loc adv* [*jouer, cuisiner*] marvellously[GB], wonderfully; **la voiture marche à ~** the car goes like a dream; **notre plan a fonctionné à ~** our plan worked wonderfully ou like a dream; **se porter à ~** to be in excellent health.

merveilleusement /mɛʀvɛjøzmɑ̃/ *adv* marvellously[GB], wonderfully.

merveilleux, **-euse** /mɛʀvɛjø, øz/ **I** *adj* **1** (admirable) marvellous[GB], wonderful; **il est ~ de faire** it is marvellous ou wonderful to do; **2** Littérat [*conte*] fabulous.

II *nm* Littérat **le ~** the fabulous.

mes ▶ **mon**.

mésalliance /mezaljɑ̃s/ *nf* misalliance; **faire une ~** to marry beneath one's station.

mésallier: **se mésallier** /mezalje/ [2] *vpr* to marry beneath one's station.

mésange /mezɑ̃ʒ/ *nf* tit.

■ **~ bleue** blue tit; **~ charbonnière** great tit; **~ huppée** crested tit; **~ nonnette** marsh tit.

mésaventure /mezavɑ̃tyʀ/ *nf* misadventure; **les ~s d'un jeune voyageur** the misadventures of a young traveller; **connaître** or **avoir une ~** to have an unfortunate experience; **par ~** by some misfortune.

mescaline /mɛskalin/ *nf* mescaline.

mesclun /mɛsklœ̃/ *nm* mixed salad (*made of young shoots and leaves of wild plants*).

mesdames ▶ **madame**.

mesdemoiselles ▶ **mademoiselle**.

mésencéphale /mezɑ̃sefal/ *nm* midbrain, mesencephalon spéc.

mésentente /mezɑ̃tɑ̃t/ *nf* dissension; (moins grave) disagreement.

mésentère /mezɑ̃tɛʀ/ *nm* mesentery.

mésestime /mezɛstim/ *nf* liter low regard.

mésestimer /mezɛstime/ [1] *vtr* liter to underrate [*artiste, œuvre*]; to underestimate [*collaborateur, qualité, difficulté*].

mésintelligence /mezɛ̃teliʒɑ̃s/ *nf* liter dissension (**entre** between).

mesmérisme /mɛsmeʀism/ *nm* mesmerism.

mésolithique /mezolitik/ *adj, nm* Mesolithic.

mésomorphe /mezomɔʀf/ *nmf* mesomorph.

méson /mezɔ̃/ *nm* meson.

Mésopotamie /mezɔpɔtami/ *nprf* Mesopotamia.

mésopotamien, **-ienne** /mezɔpɔtamjɛ̃, ɛn/ *adj* Mesopotamian.

Mésopotamien, **-ienne** /mezɔpɔtamjɛ̃, ɛn/ *nm,f* Mesopotamian.

mésosphère /mezɔsfɛʀ/ *nf* mesosphere.

mésozoïque /mezozɔik/ *adj, nm* Mezozoic.

mesquin, **~e** /mɛskɛ̃, in/ *adj* **1** (vil) [*personne*] mean-minded, petty-minded; [*esprit, attitude, procédé*] pretty; **2** (chiche) [*personne*] mean GB, cheap○ US; [*récompense*] stingy.

mesquinement /mɛskinmɑ̃/ *adv* **1** (bassement) meanly; **2** (chichement) stingily.

mesquinerie /mɛskinʀi/ *nf* **1** (caractère) (bassesse) meanness; (avarice) stinginess; **2** (action) mean trick; (remarque) mean remark ou comment.

mess /mɛs/ *nm* Mil mess.

message /mesaʒ/ *nm* gén, Ling, Ordinat, Télécom message; **transmettre/adresser un ~** to give/send a message (**à** to); **je peux laisser un ~?** can I leave a message?; **~ de paix** message of peace; **~ de détresse** SOS message; **film à ~** film with a message; **faire passer un ~** lit to pass a message (**à** to); fig to get a message across (**à** to).

■ **~ publicitaire** commercial.

messager, **-ère** /mesaʒe, ɛʀ/ **I** *nm,f* **1** (qui transmet) messenger; (en diplomatie) envoy; **2** (qui présage) liter herald littér.

II *nm* Télécom **~ de poche** pager.

messagerie /mesaʒʀi/ *nf* **1** Transp freight forwarding; **2** Télécom messaging.

■ **~ électronique** electronic mail; **~**

rose *sex chat-line via Minitel®*; **~ vocale** voice messaging, voice mail; **~s aériennes** air freight service (*sg*); **~s maritimes** sea service (*sg*); **~s de presse** press distribution service (*sg*).

messe /mɛs/ *nf* **1** Relig mass; **aller à la ~** to go to mass; **dire la ~/une ~** to say mass/a mass; **servir la ~** to serve at mass; **2** Mus mass (**en** in).

■ **~ basse** low mass; fig **~s basses**○ whispering; **arrêtez de faire des ~s basses**○! stop whispering together!; **~ de minuit** midnight mass; **~ des morts** mass for the dead; **~ noire** black mass.

Messeigneurs ▶ **Monseigneur**.

messeoir† /meswaʀ/ [41] *vi* fml to be unbecoming.

messianique /mesjanik/ *adj* messianic.

messianisme /mesjanism/ *nm* messianism.

messidor /mesidɔʀ/ *nm* Messidor (*tenth month of the French revolutionary calendar, ≈ July*).

messie /mesi/ *nm* messiah; **le Messie** the Messiah.

IDIOMES **attendre qn comme le Messie**○ to wait anxiously for sb.

messied ▶ **messeoir**.

messieurs ▶ **monsieur**.

messin, **~e** /mɛsɛ̃, in/ **▶857** *adj* of Metz.

Messin, **~e** /mɛsɛ̃, in/ *nm,f* (natif) native of Metz; (habitant) inhabitant of Metz.

messire‡ /mesiʀ/ *nm* my Lord.

mestre /mɛstʀ/ *nm* mainmast.

mesurable /məzyʀabl/ *adj* [*pression, grandeur*] measurable; **non ~** unmeasurable; **ce n'est pas ~** it can't be measured.

mesurage /məzyʀaʒ/ *nm* measuring.

mesure /məzyʀ/ *nf* **1** (initiative) measure; **~ économique/administrative/préventive** economic/administrative/preventive measure; **par ~ d'économie** as an economy measure, to save money; **prendre des ~s** gén to take measures; (autoritairement) to take steps; **par ~ de sécurité** as a safety precaution; **~ de faveur** favour[GB]; **2** (dimension) measurement; **prendre les ~s de qch** lit to take the measurements of sth; **prendre les ~s de qn** [*couturière*] to take sb's measurements; **faire prendre ses ~s** to be measured up (for sth); **prendre la ~ de la tâche qui nous attend** to assess the scale of the task ahead; **prendre la ~ des événements politiques** to make an assessment of political events; **prendre l'exacte ~ de la concurrence** to weigh up the competition; **(fait) sur ~** [*robe, costume, chemise*] made-to-measure, custom-made US; [*chaussures*] handmade; [*maison*] custom-built; **c'est fait sur ~**, **c'est du sur ~** [*vêtement*] it's made to measure ou custom-tailored US; **le sur ~** made-to-measure ou custom-tailored US clothes (*pl*); **tu as un emploi sur ~** the job is tailor-made for you; **à la ~ de l'homme** [*bâtiment, architecture*] on a human scale; **emploi à la ~ de ses ambitions** job which is commensurate with one's ambition; **c'est une adversaire à ta ~** she is a match for you; **des résultats qui donnent la ~ de tes capacités** results which show your true worth; **donner toute sa ~** to show one's worth; **pour faire bonne ~** for good measure; **3** (évaluation) measurement; **unité de ~** unit of measurement; **instrument** or **appareil de ~** measuring device; **permettre la ~ d'une distance au mètre près** [*instrument*] to allow one to measure distances to within a metre[GB]; **4** (unité) measure; **le système des poids et des ~s** the weights and measures system; **une ~ de volume** a measure of volume; ▶ **deux**; **5** (récipient, contenu) measure; **~ de volume** (pour liquides) liquid measure; (pour solides) dry measure; **deux ~s de lait pour une ~ d'eau** two parts milk to one of water; ▶ **deux**; **6** (modération) moderation; **manquer de ~** to lack moderation; **parler avec ~** to weigh one's words; **agir avec ~** to behave in a moderate way; **sans ~** [*dépenser*] wildly; [*boire*] to excess; **une jalousie sans ~** an excessive jealousy; **garder une juste ~ en toute chose** to keep a sense of proportion in all things; **dépasser la ~** to go too far; **7** Mus bar; **barre de ~** bar line GB, bar US; **~ simple** simple ou duple time; **~ composée** compound ou triple time; **c'est une ~ à trois temps** it's in three time; **battre la ~** to beat time; **jouer en ~** to play in time; **danser en ~** to dance in time to the music; **8** (situation) **être en ~ de promettre/rembourser** to be in a position to promise/reimburse; **un individu en ~ de tuer** an individual capable of killing; **le malade n'est pas en ~ de vous parler** the patient cannot talk to you; **le réseau ferroviaire n'est pas en ~ de** the rail network cannot; **9** (limite) **je t'aiderai, dans la ~ où je le pourrai** or **de mes moyens** I'll help you as much as I can; **dans la ~ du possible** as far as possible; **dans une certaine ~** to some extent; **dans quelle ~** to what extent; **dans une large ~** largely, to a large extent; **elle a raison, dans une large ~** she is largely right, to a large extent she is right; **c'est vrai, dans une large ~** it is largely true, to a large extent it is true; **dans une plus ou moins large ~** to a greater or lesser extent; **dans une moindre ~** to a lesser extent; **dans la ~ où existe déjà un tel système** insofar as such a system already exists.

mesuré, **~e** /məzyʀe/ **I** *pp* ▶ **mesurer**.

II *pp adj* [*propos*] measured; [*attitude*] moderate; **être ~ dans ses propos** to weigh one's words; **des pas ~s** measured steps.

mesurer /məzyʀe/ [1] **▶477**, **783**, **793** **I** *vtr* **1** Mes to measure [*longueur, hauteur, quantité, objet, lieu*] (**en** in); (pour prélever une partie) to measure off [*longueur*]; to measure out [*poids, volume*]; (avant travaux) to measure up [*recoin, salle de bains*]; **~ au centimètre près** to measure to the nearest centimetre[GB]; **~ 20 centimètres de tissu** to measure off 20 centimetres[GB] of fabric; **~ 200 grammes de farine** to measure out 200 grammes[GB] of flour; **~ les fenêtres pour faire des rideaux** to measure the windows for curtains; **~ le tour de hanche/de cou de qn** to take sb's hip/neck measurement; **2** (évaluer) to measure [*productivité, écart, séquelles*] ; to assess [*difficultés, risques*]; to consider [*conséquences*]; **~ les effets de qch** to assess ou to measure the effects of sth; **~ sa force contre** or **avec qn** to pit one's strength against sb; **mal ~ la portée de qch** to miscalculate the implications of sth; **~ le succès de qch à qch** to gauge the success of sth by sth; **~ qn du regard** or **des yeux** to weigh sb up; **~ le désarroi de qn** to get an idea of how upset sb is; **faire ~ à qn la gravité de qch** to make sb understand the seriousness of sth; **~ ses paroles** to weigh one's words; **ne pas ~ ses propos** to speak without restraint; **3** (donner sans générosité) **~ la nourriture à qn** to mete out food stingily to sb; **le temps nous est mesuré** our time is limited; **ne pas ~ ses efforts** to try one's utmost.

II *vi* **~ 20 mètres carrés** to be 20 metres[GB] square; **~ 2 mètres de large/de long** to be 2 metres[GB] wide/long; **~ 20 mètres de profondeur** to be 20 metres[GB] deep; **~ 2 mètres de haut** [*mur*] to be 2 metres[GB] high; **elle mesure 1,60 m** [*personne*] she's 1.60 m tall.

III se mesurer *vpr* **1** Mes **se ~ en mètres** to be measured in metres[GB]; **2** (s'affronter) **se ~ des yeux** or **du regard** to weigh one another up; **se ~ à** or **avec qn** to pit one's strength against sb; **se ~ à un problème** to tackle a problem.

mésusage /mezyzaʒ/ *nm* fml misuse (**de** of).

mésuser /mezyze/ [1] *vtr ind* fml **~ de** to misuse [*autorité*].

métabolique /metabɔlik/ *adj* metabolic.

métabolisme /metabɔlism/ *nm* metabolism.

métacarpe /metakaʀp/ *nm* metacarpus.

métacarpien, **-ienne** /metakaʀpjɛ̃, ɛn/ **I** *adj* metacarpal.

II *nm* metacarpal.

métairie /metɛʀi/ *nf* tenanted farm.

métal, *pl* **-aux** /metal, o/ *nm* metal; **métaux précieux** precious metals; **pièce de** or **en ~** metal coin.

■ **~ jaune** journ gold.

métalangage /metalɑ̃gaʒ/ *nm* metalanguage.

métalangue /metalɑ̃g/ *nf* metalanguage.

métalinguistique /metalɛ̃gɥistik/ *adj* metalinguistic.

métallerie /metalʀi/ *nf* metalworking.

métallifère /metalifɛʀ/ *adj* metalliferous.

métallique /metalik/ *adj* **1** lit (en métal) metal (*épith*); (ressemblant au métal) metallic; **c'est ~** it's made of metal; **2** fig [*son, voix, reflet*] metallic; **le bruit ~ des clés/des couverts** the clink of keys/cutlery.

métallisation /metalizasjɔ̃/ *nf* metallization.

métallisé /metalize/ **I** *pp* ▶ **métalliser**.

II *pp adj* [*vert, bleu*] metallic; **peinture ~e** paint with a metallic finish.

métalliser /metalize/ [1] *vtr* to silver [*miroir*].

métallo○ /metalo/ *nm* metalworker.

métallographie /metalɔgʀafi/ *nf* metallography.

métallographique /metalɔgʀafik/ *adj* metallographic.

métalloïde /metalɔid/ *nm* metalloid.

métallurgie /metalyʀʒi/ *nf* (technique) metallurgy; (industrie) metalworking industry.

métallurgique /metalyʀʒik/ *adj* metallurgical.

métallurgiste /metalyʀʒist/ **▶510** *nm* (ouvrier) metalworker; (industriel) metallurgist.

métamorphique /metamɔʀfik/ *adj* metamorphic.

métamorphisme /metamɔʀfism/ *nm* metamorphism.

métamorphose /metamɔʀfoz/ *nf* gén complete transformation; Mythol, Zool metamorphosis (**de qch en qch** of sth into sth).

métamorphoser /metamɔʀfoze/ [1] **I** *vtr* to transform completely; **je l'ai trouvée métamorphosée** I found her completely transformed; **~ qn en qch** to turn sb into sth.

II se métamorphoser *vpr* to be completely transformed; **se ~ en** to metamorphose into.

métaphore /metafɔʀ/ *nf* metaphor; **s'exprimer par ~s** to speak in metaphors.

métaphorique /metafɔʀik/ *adj* [*sens, valeur*] metaphorical.

métaphoriquement /metafɔʀikmɑ̃/ *adv* metaphorically.

métaphysicien, **-ienne** /metafizisjɛ̃, ɛn/ *nm,f* metaphysician.

métaphysique /metafizik/ **I** *adj* metaphysical.

II *nf* **1** Philos metaphysics (+ *v sg*); **2** fig pej philosophizing péj.

métaphysiquement /metafizikmɑ̃/ *adv* metaphysically.

métapsychique /metapsiʃik/ *adj* psychic.

métapsychologie /metapsikɔlɔʒi/ *nf* metapsychology.

métastase /metastɑz/ *nf* metastasis.

métatarse /metataʀs/ *nm* metatarsus.

métatarsien, **-ienne** /metataʀsjɛ̃, ɛn/ **I** *adj* metatarsal.

II *nm* metatarsal.

métathèse /metatɛz/ *nf* metathesis.

métayage /metejaʒ/ *nm* tenant farming GB, sharecropping US.

Les métiers et les professions

Les personnes

que fait-il dans la vie? = what does he do? *ou* what's his job?

Au singulier l'anglais emploie l'article indéfini devant les noms de métiers et de professions utilisés avec les verbes to be (*être*), to become (*devenir*), *etc., ou avec* as.

il est mécanicien	=	he is a mechanic
elle est dentiste	=	she is a dentist
elle est professeur d'histoire	=	she is a history teacher
c'est un bon boucher	=	he is a good butcher
il travaille comme boucher	=	he works as a butcher
il est employé comme mécanicien	=	he works as a mechanic
elle veut devenir architecte	=	she wants to be an architect
ils sont bouchers	=	they are butchers
ce sont de bons bouchers	=	they are good butchers

Les lieux

S'il y a un nom en anglais pour désigner la personne (the butcher, the baker, the chemist *etc.*), *on peut utiliser ce nom pour désigner le lieu où elle travaille.*

aller chez le boucher	=	to go to the butcher's* *ou* to go to the butcher's shop†
travailler dans une boucherie	=	to work at a butcher's *ou* to work at a butcher's shop
acheter quelque chose chez le boucher	=	to buy something at the butcher's *ou* to buy something at the butcher's shop

Dans les cas où le lieu ne s'appelle pas shop *ou* store, *la première de ces deux formes est toujours possible.*

aller chez le coiffeur = to go to the hairdresser's

On peut aussi employer surgery *pour les professions médicales ou* office *pour les architectes, les avocats, les comptables, etc.*

aller chez le médecin	=	to go to the doctor's surgery (*GB*) *ou* office (*US*)
aller chez l'avocat	=	to go to the lawyer's office

On peut, dans certains cas, utiliser le nom particulier du lieu, s'il existe (bakery, grocery *etc.*).

aller à la boulangerie = to go to the bakery

Dans les cas où le français dit chez le marchand de X, *on peut, en général, dire en anglais* at/to the X shop.

aller chez le marchand de poissons	=	to go to the fish shop
acheter quelque chose chez le marchand de fruits	=	to buy something at the fruit shop

De même shoe shop (*chaussures*), toy shop (*jouets*), wine shop (*vin*) *etc.*

* *Au lieu de* to the butcher's, *on peut aussi dire* to the butcher. *Mais la forme avec* 's *est préférable.*

† *Attention: ce qui s'appelle* shop *en anglais britannique s'appelle en général* store *en anglais américain.*

métayer, **-ère** /meteje, ɛʀ/ *nm,f* tenant farmer GB, sharecropper US.

métazoaire /metazɔɛʀ/ *nm* metazoan.

méteil /metɛj/ *nm*: *mixed crop of wheat and rye.*

métempsycose /metɑ̃psikoz/ *nf* metempsychosis.

météo /meteo/ **I** *adj inv* [*bulletin, carte, prévisions*] weather (*épith*).

II *nf* **1** (organisme) Met Office GB, Weather Service US; **les prévisions de la ~** the forecast from the Met Office; **que dit la ~?** what's the forecast?; **2** (prévisions) weather forecast; **dans un instant la ~** coming next, the weather.

■ **~ marine** shipping forecast.

météore /meteɔʀ/ *nm* meteor.

IDIOMES **passer comme un ~** (avoir un bref succès) to be a flash in the pan; (faire une visite éclair) to be gone in a flash.

météorique /meteɔʀik/ *adj* [*impact, poussière*] meteoric; **nuage ~** swarm of meteors.

météorite /meteɔʀit/ *nm* or *nf* meteorite.

météorologie /meteɔʀɔlɔʒi/ *nf* meteorology.

■ **la ~ nationale** the Meteorological Office GB, Weather Service US.

météorologique /meteɔʀɔlɔʒik/ *adj* [*phénomène*] meteorological; **conditions ~s** weather conditions.

météorologiste /meteɔʀɔlɔʒist/, **météorologue** /meteɔʀɔlɔg/ **▶510** *nmf* meteorologist.

métèque /metɛk/ *nm* offensive foreigner, wog◐ GB injur.

méthadone /metadɔn/ *nf* methadon.

méthane /metan/ *nm* methane.

méthanier /metanje/ *nm* LPG tanker.

méthanol /metanɔl/ *nm* methanol.

méthode /metɔd/ *nf* **1** gén, Philos method; **~s terroristes** terrorist methods; **la ~ expérimentale/déductive** the experimental/deductive method; **le Discours de la ~** Discourse on method; **~ de gestion/fabrication** management/production method; **une ~ d'enseignement/de lecture** a teaching/reading method; **~ active** progressive method; **~ audio-visuelle** audiovisual method; **~ directe** (d'enseignement des langues) direct ou natural method; **~ globale** look and say method; **~ syllabique** phonics (+ *v sg*); **2** (qualité logique) **procéder avec calme et ~** to proceed calmly and methodically; **il manque de ~** he's unmethodical, he's not methodical; **avoir de la ~** to be methodical; **3** (livret d'apprentissage) (de musique) method, tutor GB; (de langues) course book GB, textbook US; **une ~ de violon** a violin method ou tutor; **une ~ de russe** a Russian course book ou textbook; **4** (approche) way; **j'ai ma ~ pour le convaincre** I've got a way of convincing him; **il n'y a pas de ~ miracle pour réussir** there is no magic formula for success.

méthodique /metɔdik/ *adj* [*démonstration, vérification*] methodical; [*esprit, personne*] methodical.

méthodiquement /metɔdikmɑ̃/ *adv* methodically; **procédons ~** let's take things step by step.

méthodisme /metɔdism/ *nm* Methodism.

méthodiste /metɔdist/ *adj, nmf* Methodist.

méthodologie /metɔdɔlɔʒi/ *nf* methodology.

méthodologique /metɔdɔlɔʒik/ *adj* methodological.

méthyle /metil/ *nm* methyl.

méthylène /metilɛn/ *nm* **1** (alcool méthylique) methyl alcohol; **2** (dérivé du méthane) methylene; **▶bleu**.

méthylique /metilik/ *adj* **alcool ~** methyl alcohol.

méticuleusement /metikyløzmɑ̃/ *adv* meticulously.

méticuleux, **-euse** /metikylø, øz/ *adj* [*personne, soin*] meticulous; [*travail, choix*] painstaking; **il est d'une propreté méticuleuse** he's scrupulously clean.

méticulosité /metikylozite/ *nf* meticulousness.

métier /metje/ *nm* **1** (activité rémunérée) job; (intellectuel) profession; (manuel) trade; (artisanal) craft; **c'est mon ~ (de faire ça)!** it's my job!; **il a fait tous les ~s** he's tried his hand at everything, he's done all kinds of jobs; **choisir un ~** to decide on a job ou trade ou profession; **apprendre un ~** (manuel) to learn a trade; **ils sortent de l'école sans ~** they come out of college without any practical skills; **entrer dans le ~** (manuel) to enter the trade; **bien connaître son ~** to be good at one's job, to know one's stuff○; **il est cuisinier/coiffeur de son ~** he's a cook/hairdresser by trade; **il est chirurgien/juriste/potier de son ~** he is a surgeon/lawyer/potter by profession; **un maçon de ~** a professional mason; **terme de ~** specialized term; **les gens du ~** the professionals, people in the business; **pour faire une bonne traduction, il faut être du ~** it takes a professional translator to do a good translation; **ne t'inquiète pas, elle est du ~** don't worry, she knows what she's doing; **le ~ des armes** the army; **choisir le ~ des armes** to decide on a military career; **2** (rôle) job; **faire son ~ de reine/mère** to do one's job as queen/a mother; **3** (expérience) **avoir du ~** to be experienced; **manquer de ~** to lack experience; **avoir 20 ans de ~** to have 20 years' experience; **c'est le ~ qui rentre!** you learn by your mistakes!; **le ~ rentre?** are you getting the hang of it?; **4** (objet) loom; **~ à tisser** weaving loom; **remettre qch sur le ~** fig to rework sth.

IDIOMES **faire le plus vieux ~ du monde** euph to practise[GB] the oldest profession.

métis, **-isse** /metis/ **I** *adj* **1** [*famille, enfant*] mixed-race (*épith*); [*animal*] hybrid, crossbred; [*plante*] hybrid; **2** [*toile*] union (*épith*).

II *nm,f* (personne) person of mixed-race.

III *nm* Tex cotton and linen cloth; **en ~** made of cotton and linen.

métissage /metisaʒ/ *nm* (de personnes) interbreeding; (de plantes, d'animaux) crossing; **~ culturel** cultural cross-fertilization.

métisser /metise/ [1] *vtr* to cross [*animal, plante*].

métonymie /metɔnimi/ *nf* metonymy.

métonymique /metɔnimik/ *adj* metonymic.

métrage /metʀaʒ/ *nm* **1** (de tissu) length; **un petit ~** a short length; **2** (de mur, parquet) length in metres[GB]; **3** Cin (de film) length; **court ~** short (film); **long ~** feature-length film; **moyen ~** medium-length film.

mètre /mɛtʀ/ *nm* **1** **▶477**, **783**, **793**, **860**, **866** (mesure) metre[GB]; **ça s'achète/ça se vend au ~** you buy it/it's sold by the metre[GB]; (en sport) **le 60/100/1 500 ~s** the 60/100/1,500 metres[GB]; **faire** or **piquer un cent ~s**○ fig to break into a run; **2** (instrument de mesure) (metre[GB]) rule GB, yardstick US; **3** Littérat metre[GB].

■ **~ carré** square metre[GB]; **~ de couturière** tape measure; **~ cube** cubic metre[GB]; **~ enrouleur** retractable tape measure; **~ étalon** standard metre[GB]; **~ pliant** folding (metre[GB]) rule; **~ ruban** tape measure.

métré /metʀe/ *nm* **1** (de quantités) quantity surveying; **2** (mesure) measurement.

métrer /metʀe/ [14] *vtr* to measure [sth] in metres[GB] [*terrain*].

métreur, **-euse** /metʀœʀ, øz/ **▶510** *nm,f* **~ (vérificateur)** quantity surveyor.

métrique /metʀik/ **I** *adj* Math, Mes metric; **système ~** metric system.

II *nf* **1** Littérat metrics (+ *v sg*); **2** Math metric theory.

métro /metʀo/ *nm* **1** (réseau) underground GB, subway US; **prendre le ~** to take the

underground; **2** (rame) underground train GB, subway US; **j'ai raté le dernier ~** I've missed the last underground train.
■ **~ aérien** elevated railway.
IDIOMES **~, boulot, dodo**○ the daily grind; **avoir toujours un ~ de retard, être toujours en retard d'un ~** to be always the last to hear about things.

métrologie /metʀɔlɔʒi/ *nf* metrology.

métrologique /metʀɔlɔʒik/ *adj* metrological.

métronome /metʀɔnɔm/ *nm* metronome.
IDIOMES **faire qch avec la régularité d'un ~** to do sth as regularly as clockwork.

métropole /metʀɔpɔl/ *nf* **1** (capitale d'un pays) metropolis; (grande ville) major city; **~ d'équilibre** or **régionale** regional capital; **2** (France métropolitaine) Metropolitan France; **travailler en ~** to work in Metropolitan France.

métropolitain, **~e** /metʀɔpɔlitɛ̃, ɛn/ **I** *adj* **1** Transp [*réseau*] underground GB, subway US; **2** Géog [*culture, investisseur*] from Metropolitan France; **3** Relig [*archevêque*] metropolitan.
II *nm,f* Géog person from Metropolitan France.
III† *nm* Transp underground GB, subway US.

métropolite /metʀɔpɔlit/ *nm* metropolitan.

mets /mɛ/ *nm* dish, delicacy.

mettable /mɛtabl/ *adj* [*vêtement*] wearable.

metteur /mɛtœʀ/ *nm* **~ en pages** Imprim make-up man; **~ en scène** Cin, Théât director.

mettre /mɛtʀ/ [60] **I** *vtr* **1** (placer dans un endroit, une position) to put [*chose, partie du corps, personne*]; **~ un vase sur la table/des bûches dans la cheminée/le vin au frais** to put a vase on the table/logs on the fire/the wine in a cool place; **j'ai mis ta voiture au garage** I've put your car in the garage for you; **~ les pieds sur la table/les mains sur la tête** to put one's feet on the table/one's hands on one's head; **~ les mains en l'air/un timbre à l'envers** to put one's hands up/a stamp on upside down; **on m'a mis devant/tout au fond** they put me at the front/right at the back; **je l'ai mise sur ses pieds** I put her on her feet; **je mets les enfants à la crèche** I send the children to a creche; **il m'a mis en bas de chez moi** he dropped me off outside my door; **on m'a mis debout** they stood me up; **nous l'avons mise à l'hôtel** we put her up at the hotel; **2** (projeter involontairement) to drop [*solide*]; to spill [*liquide, poudre*]; **~ de la confiture sur le tapis** to drop jam on the carpet; **~ de la colle/farine partout** to spill glue/flour all over the place; **3** (placer sur le corps) to put on [*vêtement, bijou, maquillage, lunettes, préservatif, serviette*]; **mets ton écharpe** put your scarf on; **je vais ~ du mascara** I'll put some mascara on; **4** (placer dans le corps) to put in [*tampon, suppositoire, plombage*]; **on m'a mis un plombage** I had a filling; **5** (porter habituellement sur le corps) to wear [*lunettes, type de vêtement, parfum*]; **dans mon école les garçons mettent des cravates** in my school boys wear ties; **je ne mets jamais de chapeau** I never wear a hat; **6** (placer dans une situation, un état) **~ qn dans une situation embarrassante** to put sb in an embarrassing situation; **~ qn en colère/en joie** to make sb angry/happy; **~ qn en fureur** to enrage sb; **~ qn au désespoir** to drive sb to despair; **~ qn de bonne/mauvaise humeur** to put sb in a good/bad mood; **tu me mets hors de moi** you infuriate me; **~ qn à la chaîne/à la reliure** to put sb on the assembly line/on binding; **~ qn au travail** to put sb to work; **~ qn au piano/au latin** to start sb on the piano/on Latin; **~ les enfants à regarder la télévision** to put the children in front of the television; **si vous nous quittez, on mettra quelqu'un d'autre** if you leave us, we'll find somebody else; **~ le riz à cuire** to put the rice on; **~ le linge à sécher** to put the washing out to dry; **7** (classer) **~ la famille avant tout le reste** to put one's family first; **~ ses études au-dessus de tout** to put one's studies first; **je le mets au premier rang de tous les écrivains** I rank him the best writer of all; **8** (disposer) **~ les assiettes** to put the plates on the table; **~ les verres/la moutarde/un cendrier** to put out the glasses/the mustard/an ashtray; **~ les chaises/une autre chaise** to bring chairs/another chair; **~ une nappe** to put on a tablecloth; **je t'ai mis des draps propres** I've put clean sheets on for you; **9** (faire fonctionner) **~ la radio/la télévision/le chauffage** to put the radio/the television/the heating on; **~ les nouvelles/la deuxième chaîne** to put the news/channel 2 on; **~ plus fort** to turn up [*appareil*] ; **~ moins fort** to turn down [*appareil*] ; **mets plus/moins fort!** turn it up/down!; **~ les essuie-glaces/les phares** to switch on ou put on the windscreen GB ou windshield US wipers/the headlights; **~ le réveil** to set the alarm; **~ le verrou** to bolt the door; **~ le loquet** to latch the door; **10** (installer) to put in [*chauffage, douche, téléphone, placard*]; to put up [*rideau, lustre, étagère*]; **faire ~ le téléphone** to have a telephone put in; **je t'ai mis une prise** I've put in a socket for you; **~ de la moquette** to lay a carpet; **faire ~ de la moquette** (dans une pièce) to have a carpet laid; (dans plusieurs pièces) to have carpets laid; **~ du carrelage** to lay tiles; **11** (écrire) to put up [*inscription*]; **ils ont mis des graffiti partout/sur la colonne** they've put graffiti everywhere/on the column; **il met que tout va bien** (dans une lettre) he says ou writes that everything's fine; **qu'est-ce que je dois ~?** what shall I put?; **~ au passif/au singulier** to put into the passive/into the singular; **~ en vers** to put into verse; **je t'ai mis un mot** I've left you a note; **est-ce qu'on met un trait d'union à 'multinational'?** is there a hyphen in 'multinational'?; **il faut ~ un trait d'union** you must put a hyphen in; **~ sa signature sur un document** to put one's signature to a document; **mettez votre signature ici** sign here; **mettez le pronom qui convient** (remplacez) replace with the appropriate pronoun; (bouchez les trous) insert the appropriate pronom; **~ en musique** to set to music; **~ en anglais** to put into English; **~ son brouillon au propre** or **au net** to write out ou up one 's notes; **12** (ajouter) to add [*ingrédient*] (**dans** to); to put [*accessoire, élément décoratif*]; **~ du sel dans la soupe** to put some salt in the soup; **~ un peu de piment dans un récit** to add a little spice to a story; **~ une sonnette à son vélo/des pompons à ses pantoufles** to put a bell on one's bicycle/pompoms on one's slippers; **~ une radio à sa voiture/une doublure à sa veste** to put a radio in one's car/a lining in one's jacket; **13** (consacrer) **~ tout son cœur dans son travail** to put one's heart into one's work; **y ~ du sien** to put oneself into it; **~ toute son énergie à essayer de comprendre** to put all one's energy into trying to understand; **~ des moyens importants au service d'une cause** to use all possible means to further a cause; **~ de la rigueur dans sa démarche** to become more thorough in one's approach; **14** (investir, dépenser) to put [*argent*] (**dans, sur** into); **~ tout son argent dans son commerce** to put all one's money into one's business; **j'ai tout mis sur le pétrole** I've put everything into oil; **il a tout mis sur un cheval/une équipe** he's put everything on a horse/a team; **combien pouvez-vous ~?** (pour acheter) how much can you afford?; (pour contribuer) how much can you put in?; **15** (prendre) [*activité*] to take [*heures, jours, années*] (**pour faire** to do); **elle a bien mis une heure** it took her easily an hour; **~ un temps fou**○ to take ages○; **16**○ (vendre) **je vous mets des tomates?** would you like some tomatoes?; **je vous en mets combien? deux, trois?** how many would you like? two, three?; **17**○ (attribuer) **je vous ai mis trois sur vingt** I've given you three out of twenty; **18**○ (battre) **ils nous ont mis trois à zéro** they beat us three nil GB ou three to nothing US; **je lui ai mis une gifle** I gave him/her a slap (across the face); **tu veux que je te mette mon poing sur la figure?** do you want my fist in your face○?; **qu'est-ce qu'il m'a mis!** what a thrashing○ he gave me!; **19**○ (partir) **les ~** to beat it○; **je dois les ~** I'd better beat it; **20**○ (dire) **mettons dix dollars/à dix heures** let's say ten dollars/at ten; **21**○ (supposer) **mettons qu'il vienne, qu'est-ce que vous ferez?** supposing ou say he comes, what will you do?; **22**◑ (ficher) **tu peux te le ~ où je pense** or **quelque part** you know where you can put○ it ou stick◑ it; **va te faire ~** get stuffed◑!
II *vi* Vét, Zool **~ bas** gén to give birth, to drop; [*vache*] to calve; [*brebis*] to lamb; [*jument*] to foal.
III se mettre *vpr* **1** (se placer dans un endroit, une position) **se ~ devant la fenêtre** (debout) to stand in front of the window; (assis) to sit down in front of the window; (couché) to lie (down) in front of the window; **se ~ sur les mains** to stand on one's hands; **se ~ sur le dos** to lie on one's back; **se ~ au lit** to go to bed; **se ~ debout** to stand up; **se ~ sur ses jambes** to get to one's feet; **ne plus savoir où se ~** not to know where to put oneself; **se ~ les mains sur la tête** to put one's hands on one's head; **se ~ les doigts dans le nez** to pick one's nose; **où est-ce que ça se met?** where does this go?; **2** (projeter involontairement sur soi) to spill [sth] on oneself [*liquide, poudre*]; **se ~ de la confiture** to get jam on oneself; **se ~ de la boue sur ses chaussures/de l'encre sur le nez/une poussière dans l'œil** to get mud on one's shoes/ink on one's nose/some grit in one's eye; **s'en ~ partout** to get it all over oneself; **3** (placer sur son corps) to put on [*vêtement, bijou, maquillage*]; **se ~ un foulard/un collier/du rouge à lèvres** to put on a scarf/a necklace/lipstick; **se ~ de la poudre sur le visage** to put some powder on one's face, to powder one's face; **je ne sais pas quoi me ~** I don't know what to put on; **4** (placer dans son corps) to put in [*suppositoire, tampon*]; **5** (commencer) **se ~ à l'anglais/au tennis** to take up English/tennis; **se ~ à prendre des somnifères** to start taking sleeping pills; **ma voiture se met à avoir des problèmes** my car is starting to go wrong; **il va se ~ à pleuvoir** it's going to start raining; **il se met à faire froid/du vent** it's starting to get cold/windy; **6** (tourner) **le temps s'est mis au froid/au beau/à la pluie** the weather has turned cold/fine/to rain; **7** (se lancer) **elle s'est mise à leur recherche** she started looking for them; **je me suis mis sur l'affaire** I started looking into the case; **8** (se placer dans une situation, un état) **se ~ en tort** to put oneself in the wrong; **se ~ dans une situation impossible** to get (oneself) into an impossible situation; **se ~ dans une sale affaire** to get involved in some shady business; **je me mets de ton côté** I'm on your side; **je préfère me ~ bien avec lui** I prefer to get on the right side of him; **se ~ à l'aise** to make oneself comfortable; **se ~ en colère** to get angry; **se ~ nu** to take off one's clothes; **on va se ~ ensemble**○ (sous le même toit) we're going to live together; **il s'est mis avec elle**○ (de son côté) he's on her side; (sous le même toit) he's moved in with her; **9** (s'habiller) **se ~ en tenue d'été** to put on summer clothes; **se ~ en arlequin** to dress up as Harlequin; **se ~ en jaune** to wear yellow; **10** (se grouper) **ce n'est pas la peine de vous (y) ~ à dix** there's no need for ten of you; **ils s'y sont mis à au moins trente** there were at

least thirty of them; **11**○ (manger) **je m'en suis mis un maximum** I really stuffed○ myself; **s'en ~ plein la panse**○ or **lampe**○ or **gueule**● to stuff○ oneself; **qu'est-ce qu'on s'est mis!** we really stuffed○ ourselves!; **12** (se battre) **qu'est-ce qu'on s'est mis!** we really laid○ into each other!

Metz /mɛ(t)s/ ▶**857** *npr* Metz.

meuble /mœbl/ **I** *adj* [*sol*] loose.
II *nm* **1** gén piece of furniture; **un ~** a piece of furniture; **des ~s** furniture; **un ~ de jardin** a piece of garden furniture; **~ hi-fi/vidéo** hi-fi/video unit; **~ de cuisine/salle de bains/rangement** kitchen/bathroom/storage unit; **2** Hérald charge.
■ **~ de toilette** wash stand.
IDIOMES **sauver les ~s** to salvage something; **faire partie des ~s** to be part of the furniture; **être dans ses ~s** to have a home of one's own; **s'installer dans ses ~s** to set up home GB ou house.

meublé, ~e /mœble/ **I** *pp* ▶ **meubler**.
II *pp adj* furnished; **chambre ~e/non ~e** furnished/unfurnished room.
III *nm* furnished flat GB, furnished apartment US.

meubler /mœble/ [1] **I** *vtr* **1** (garnir de meubles) to furnish [*maison, pièce*] (**de, avec** with); **2** (constituer l'ameublement) **un simple lit meuble la chambre** the room is furnished only with a bed; **3** (décorer) **la plante/l'étagère meuble bien la pièce** the plant/the shelf makes the room look more cosy GB ou cozy US; **4** (remplir) to fill [*solitude, silence*]; **dire des banalités pour ~ la conversation** to make small talk to fill the gaps in the conversation.
II se meubler *vpr* to furnish one's home; **ils se sont meublés en moderne/Louis XV** they bought modern/Louis XV furniture.

meuf○ /mœf/ *nf* gén woman; (petite amie) girlfriend.

meuglement /møgləmɑ̃/ *nm* mooing ¢.

meugler /møgle/ [1] *vi* to moo.

meuh /mø/ *nm* (*also onomat*) moo.

meulage /mølaʒ/ *nm* grinding ¢.

meule /møl/ *nf* **1** Tech (de moulin) millstone; (pour aiguiser) grindstone; Dent grinding wheel; **2** (fromage) round; **3** Agric **~ de foin** haystack; **~ de paille** rick of straw; **4**◑ bikers' slang (moto) machine◑ GB, hog◑ US.

meuler /møle/ [1] *vtr* Tech to grind [*pièce métallique*]; Dent to trim [*couronne*].

meuleuse /møløz/ *nf* (electric) grinder.

meulière /møljɛʀ/ *nf* **pierre ~** burrstone.

meunerie /mønʀi/ *nf* **1** (industrie) flour milling (industry); **2** (corporation) millers (*pl*); **3** (profession) milling.

meunier, -ière /mønje, ɛʀ/ **I** *adj* [*industrie*] flour-milling.
II ▶**510** *nm,f* miller.
III meunière *nf* (épouse du meunier) miller's wife; **truite/sole meunière** trout/sole meunière.

Meurthe-et-Moselle /mœʀtemɔzɛl/ ▶**692** *nprf* (département) **la ~** Meurthe-et-Moselle.

meurtre /mœʀtʀ/ *nm* murder.

meurtrier, -ière /mœʀtʀije, ɛʀ/ **I** *adj* [*combats, répression*] bloody; [*explosion, accident*] fatal; [*épidémie*] deadly; [*arme*] lethal; [*folie*] murderous; [*route, carrefour*] very dangerous; **le lundi de Pâques a été très ~ sur la route** Easter Monday was a day of carnage on the roads; **les derniers séismes ont été très ~s** recent earthquakes have claimed many casualties.
II *nm,f* murderer.
III meurtrière *nf* Archit arrow slit, loophole spéc.

meurtrir /mœʀtʀiʀ/ [3] **I** *vtr* **1** (faire mal) to hurt; (contusionner) to bruise; **les menottes lui meurtrissent les poignets** the handcuffs are hurting his/her wrists; **j'avais le visage/corps meurtri par les coups** my face/body was bruised by the blows; **2** (endommager) to bruise [*fruit*]; to spoil [*légume*]; **3** (blesser moralement) to wound.
II se meurtrir *vpr* to hurt oneself.

meurtrissure /mœʀtʀisyʀ/ *nf* lit, fig bruise.

Meuse /møz/ ▶**357**, **692** *nprf* (fleuve, département) **la ~** the Meuse.

meute /møt/ *nf* **1** Chasse pack of hounds; **lâcher la ~ sur** to set the pack on; **2** fig (groupe) pack; **arriver en ~** to come in droves; **la ~ des créanciers** the pack of creditors.

MEV /mɛv/ *nf*: *abbr* ▶ **mémoire**.

mévente /mevɑ̃t/ *nf* Comm drop in sales.

mexicain, ~e /mɛksikɛ̃, ɛn/ ▶**537** *adj* Mexican.

Mexicain, ~e /mɛksikɛ̃, ɛn/ ▶**537** *nm,f* Mexican.

Mexico /meksiko/ ▶**857** *npr* Mexico City.

Mexique /mɛksik/ ▶**321** *nprm* Mexico; **golfe du ~** Gulf of Mexico.

mézigue◑ /mezig/ *pron pers* me, yours truly○, muggins○ GB.

mezzanine /medzanin/ *nf* **1** Constr mezzanine; **2** Cin balcony; Théât circle GB, mezzanine US.

mezza voce /medzavɔtʃe/ *loc adv* **1** Mus [*chanter*] mezza voce; **2** liter [*parler, dire*] in an undertone.

mezzo /mɛdzo/ ▶**134** *nm, nf* mezzo.

mezzo-soprano, *pl* **~s** /medzosɔpʀano/ ▶**134** **I** *nm* (voix) mezzo-soprano.
II *nf* (personne) mezzo-soprano.

mezzo-tinto /mɛdzotinto/ *nm inv* mezzotint.

MF /ɛmɛf/ *nf*: *abbr* ▶ **modulation**.

Mgr ▶**813** (*written abbr* = **Monseigneur**) Mgr.

mi[1] /mi/ *préf* **à la ~-mai/saison** in mid-May/season; **dès la ~-mai** as from mid-May; **~-1994** sometime in the middle of 1994; **à la ~-journée** halfway through the day; **à ~-pente** halfway up the hill; **à ~-combat/carrière/mandat** in mid-fight/career/term; **à ~-parcours** in the middle; **à la ~-séance** (à la Bourse) at mid-session; **~-chinois, ~-français** [*personne*] half Chinese, half French; [*style, objet*] part Chinese, part French; **~-homme, ~-animal** half man, half beast; **~-chrétien, ~-païen** part Christian, part pagan; **~-religieux, ~-littéraire** semireligious, semiliterary; **~-sceptique, ~-amusé** half sceptic, half amused.

mi[2] /mi/ *nm inv* (note) E; (en solfiant) mi, me.

miam-miam○ /mjammjam/ *excl* yum-yum○!, yummy○!

miaou /mjau/ *nm* (*also onomat*) miaow GB, meow; **faire ~** to go miaow GB ou meow.

miasme /mjasm/ *nm* miasma.

miaulement /mjolmɑ̃/ *nm* miaowing GB, meowing, mewing.

miauler /mjole/ [1] *vi* to miaow GB, to meow, to mew.

mi-bas /mibɑ/ *nm inv* knee sock, long sock.

mica /mika/ *nm* **1** (minerai) mica; **2** (utilisé comme vitre) mica, isinglass.

micacé, ~e /mikase/ *adj* **1** Minér micaceous; **2** (ressemblant à du mica) mica-like.

mi-carême /mikaʀɛm/ *nf*: *Thursday of the third week in Lent.*

micaschiste /mikaʃist/ *nm* micaschist.

miche /miʃ/ **I** *nf* Culin round loaf; (petit pain) roll.
II miches● *nfpl* fig (fesses) bum○ (*sg*) GB, butt○ (*sg*) US.

Michel-Ange /mikɛlɑ̃ʒ/ *npr* Michelangelo.

micheline /miʃlin/ *nf* small local train (*running on diesel*).

mi-chemin: **à mi-chemin** /amiʃmɛ̃/ *loc adv* lit halfway; fig halfway through; **à ~ de chez moi** halfway home; **à ~ entre qch et qch** halfway between sth and sth.

micheton○ /miʃtɔ̃/ *nm* **1** (client) trick○ GB, john○ US; **2** (gogo) sucker○.

Michigan /miʃigan/ ▶**459**, **692** *nprm* Michigan; **le lac ~** Lake Michigan.

mi-clos, ~e /miklo, oz/ *adj* half-closed.

micmac○ /mikmak/ *nm* **1** (intrigue) shady○ goings-on (*pl*), scheming; **faire des ~s** to scheme péj, to wheel and deal○; **2** (désordre) muddle, mess○.

mi-corps: **à mi-corps** /amikɔʀ/ *loc adv* up to the waist; **saisir qn à ~** to grab sb round the waist.

mi-côte: **à mi-côte** /amikot/ *loc adv* (en montant) halfway up; (en descendant) halfway down.

mi-course: **à mi-course** /amikuʀs/ *loc adv* Sport halfway through the race; fig halfway through.

micro /mikʀo/ **I** *nm* **1** (microphone) microphone, mike○; **parler dans le ~** to speak into the microphone; **dire qch au ~** to say sth into the microphone; **tenir le ~** to be at the mike○; **une annonce au ~** an announcement over the microphone; **annoncer au ~ de la BBC que** to announce on the BBC that; **mettre des ~s dans une pièce** to bug a room; **2**○ (micro-ordinateur) micro○, microcomputer.
II○ *nf* (micro-informatique) microcomputing.
■ **~ caché** bug.

micro-ampère /mikʀoɑ̃pɛʀ/ *nm* microampere.

microanalyse /mikʀoanaliz/ *nf* microanalysis.

microbalance /mikʀobalɑ̃s/ *nf* microbalance.

microbe /mikʀɔb/ *nm* **1** gén germ, bug○, microbe spéc; **~ de la grippe** flu bug; **attraper un ~** to catch a bug; **avoir un ~ dans le sang** to have a blood infection; **2** (dans la saleté) germ; **3** Biol microbe; **4**○ offensive (petite personne) squirt○.

microbien, -ienne /mikʀɔbjɛ̃, ɛn/ *adj* microbic.

microbiologie /mikʀobjɔlɔʒi/ *nf* microbiology.

microbiologique /mikʀobjɔlɔʒik/ *adj* microbiological.

microbiologiste /mikʀobjɔlɔʒist/ ▶**510** *nmf* microbiologist.

microcéphale /mikʀosefal/ *adj, nmf* microcephalic.

microcéphalie /mikʀosefali/ *nf* microcephaly.

microchirurgie /mikʀoʃiʀyʀʒi/ *nf* microsurgery; **~ des yeux** microsurgery on the eyes.

microcircuit /mikʀosiʀkɥi/ *nm* microcircuit.

microclimat /mikʀoklima/ *nm* microclimate.

microcosme /mikʀɔkɔsm/ *nm* microcosm.

microcosmique /mikʀɔkɔsmik/ *adj* microcosmic.

microcoupure /mikʀokupyʀ/ *nf* (creux de tension) dropout; (coupure de courant) power line disturbance, PLD.

micro-cravate, *pl* **micros-cravates** /mikʀokʀavat/ *nm* lapel-microphone.

microéconomie /mikʀoekɔnɔmi/ *nf* microeconomics (+ *v sg*).

microéconomique /mikʀoekɔnɔmik/ *adj* microeconomic.

micro-édition /mikʀoedisjɔ̃/ *nf* desktop publishing.

microélectronique /mikʀoelɛktʀɔnik/ *nf* microelectronics (+ *v sg*).

microfiche /mikʀɔfiʃ/ *nf* microfiche.

microfilm /mikʀɔfilm/ *nm* microfilm.

microfilmer /mikʀɔfilme/ [1] *vtr* to microfilm.

micrographie /mikʀɔgʀafi/ *nf* micrography.

micrographique /mikʀɔgʀafik/ *adj* micrographic.

micro-informatique /mikʀoɛ̃fɔʀmatik/ *nf* microcomputing.

micromètre /mikʀɔmɛtʀ/ *nm* **1** (instrument) micrometer; **2** ▶**477** (unité) micrometre[GB].

micrométrie /mikʀɔmetʀi/ *nf* micrometry.

micrométrique /mikʀɔmetʀik/ *adj* micrometric.

micron /mikʀɔ̃/ ▶**477** *nm* micron.

Micronésie /mikʀɔnezi/ ▶**321**, **416** *nprf* Micronesia; **États fédérés de ~** Federated States of Micronesia.

micro-onde, *pl* **~s** /mikʀoɔ̃d/ **I** *nf* microwave; **à ~s** microwave (*épith*).
II micro-ondes° *nm inv* (four) microwave°.

micro-ordinateur, *pl* **~s** /mikʀoɔʀdinatœʀ/ *nm* microcomputer.

micro-organisme, *pl* **~s** /mikʀoɔʀganism/ *nm* microorganism.

microphone /mikʀɔfɔn/ *nm* microphone.

microphotographie /mikʀɔfɔtɔgʀafi/ *nf* **1** (technique) microphotography; **2** (image) microphotograph.

microphysique /mikʀofizik/ *nf* microphysics (+ *v sg*).

micropilule /mikʀopilyl/ *nf* mini-pill.

microprocesseur /mikʀopʀɔsesœʀ/ *nm* microprocessor; **carte à ~** smart card.

microscope /mikʀɔskɔp/ *nm* microscope; **examiner qch au ~** lit to examine sth under a microscope; fig to scrutinize sth; **examen au ~** microscopic examination.
■ **~ électronique** electron microscope; **~ binoculaire** compound microscope; **~ monoculaire** simple microscope.

microscopique /mikʀɔskɔpik/ *adj* **1** Sci microscopic; **2** (très petit) tiny, minute.

microseconde /mikʀosəgɔ̃d/ *nf* microsecond.

microsillon /mikʀɔsijɔ̃/ *nm* **(disque) ~** microgroove record.

microstructure /mikʀostʀyktyʀ/ *nf* microstructure.

microtraumatisme /mikʀotʀomatism/ *nm* Méd strain injury; **~s répétés** repetitive strain injury (*sg*).

micro-trottoir /mikʀotʀɔtwaʀ/ *nm inv* Radio **faire un ~** to interview the public.

miction /miksjɔ̃/ *nf* micturition.

mi-cuisse: **à mi-cuisse** /amikɥis/ *loc adv* above one's knees; **il avait de l'eau jusqu'à ~** the water came well above his knees; **sa jupe lui arrivait à ~** her skirt was well above her knees.

mi-cuisson: **à mi-cuisson** /amikɥisɔ̃/ *loc adv* halfway through cooking.

Middle West /midœlwɛst/ = **Midwest**.

midi /midi/ ▶**407** **I** *adj inv* midi; **chaîne ~** midi system.
II *nm* **1** (heure) twelve o'clock, midday, noon; **~ un quart** or **et quart** (a) quarter past twelve; **~ et demi** half past twelve; **~ moins dix** ten to twelve; **il est ~ (pile)** it's (exactly) twelve o'clock, it's twelve on the dot; **la chambre doit être libérée pour ~** the room must be vacated by twelve noon; **je fais mes courses entre ~ et quatorze heures** I go shopping in my lunch hour; **il ne faut pas s'exposer en plein ~** you mustn't sunbathe in the middle of the day; **on partira vers les ~**° we'll leave at around midday ou noon; ▶**quatorze**; **2** (heure du déjeuner) lunchtime; **jeudi/samedi ~** Thursday/Saturday lunchtime; **cachets à prendre ~ et soir** tablets to be taken at lunchtime and in the evening; **on en parlera à ~** we'll talk about it at lunchtime; **on déjeune ensemble à ~?** shall we have lunch together?; **qu'est-ce qu'on mange à ~?** what are we having for lunch?; **3** (point cardinal) south; **ma maison est orientée au ~** or **en plein ~** my house faces south.
IDIOMES **chacun voit ~ à sa porte** everybody has their own way of looking at things.

Midi /midi/ ▶**692** *nprm* **le ~ (de la France)** the South (of France).

midinette /midinɛt/ *nf* feather-brained young girl, bimbo°; **elle a une âme** or **un cœur de ~** she's a romantic schoolgirl at heart; **elle a des goûts de ~** her tastes are those of a romantic schoolgirl; **un roman pour ~s** a sentimental ou slushy novel.

Midi-Pyrénées /midipiʀene/ ▶**692** *nprm* **le ~** the Midi-Pyrénées.

mi-distance: **à mi-distance** /amidistɑ̃s/ *loc adv* halfway; **à ~ de qch et de qch** halfway between sth and sth.

Midlands ▶**692** *nprfpl* **les West ~** the West Midlands.

Midwest /midwɛst/ ▶**692** *nprm* Middle West, Midwest; **du ~** [*accent, État*] Midwestern; **les gens du ~** the Midwesterners.

mie /mi/ *nf* **1** (par opposition à la croûte) bread without the crusts; **de la ~ (de pain)** Culin fresh breadcrumbs (*pl*); **il mange la ~ et laisse toujours la croûte** he eats the bread and always leaves the crusts; **2**† liter **ma ~** my beloved.

miel /mjɛl/ *nm* honey; **~ d'acacias** acacia honey; **les ~s d'importation** imported honey; **au ~** made with honey; **tes paroles sont de ~** fig your words are soothing.
IDIOMES **être tout sucre tout ~** to be as sweet ou nice as pie°; **faire son ~ de qch** to turn sth to one's advantage.

miellé, ~e /mjɛle/ *adj* **1** (contenant du miel) sweetened with honey; **2** (évoquant le miel) honey-like.

mielleusement /mjɛløzmɑ̃/ *adv* unctuously.

mielleux, -euse /mjɛlø, øz/ *adj* [*ton, paroles*] unctuous, honeyed; [*personne*] fawning.

mien, mienne /mjɛ̃, mjɛn/ **I** *adj poss* **ces idées, je les ai faites miennes** I adopted these ideas; **tu seras mienne** (mon épouse) you will be mine.
II le mien, la mienne, les miens, les miennes *pron poss* mine; **prends le ~** take mine; **je préfère la mienne** I prefer my own ou mine; **votre prix sera le ~** name your price; **les ~s** (ma famille) my family (*sg*).

miette /mjɛt/ *nf* crumb; **ramasser les ~s** to sweep up the crumbs; **donne m'en juste une ~** just give me a little bit ou a taste; **ne pas laisser une ~ de qch** not to leave a scrap of sth; **réduire en ~s** to smash [sth] to bits [*vase*]; to shatter [*bonheur, espoirs*]; to reduce [sth] to shreds [*théorie*]; **elle n'en perd pas une ~**° she's taking it all in; **nous n'avons eu que les ~s** we only had the leftovers; **il ne restait que les ~s** there was virtually nothing left.

mieux /mjø/ **I** *adj inv* better; **être ~ que** to be better than; **le ~, la ~, les ~** (de plusieurs) gén the best; (de caractère) the nicest; (d'aspect) the most attractive; **la ~ des deux** gén the better one; (d'aspect) the more attractive one; **elle est ~ en brune/sans lunettes** she looks better as a brunette/without spectacles; **quelque chose de ~** something better; **il n'y a rien de ~** there's nothing like it; **ce qu'il y a de ~** the best.
II *adv* **1** (comparatif) better; **parler ~ l'anglais que ses parents** to speak English better than one's parents; **parler ~ l'anglais que l'espagnol** to speak English better than Spanish; **parler anglais comme les autres, ni ~ ni plus mal** to speak English like the others, no better and no worse; **elle parle anglais un peu/beaucoup ~ qu'avant** she speaks English slightly/much better than she did before; **tu peux faire ~** you can do better; **je ne peux pas te dire ~** that's all I can tell you; **qui dit ~?** gén any other offers?; (aux enchères) any advance on that bid?; **elle n'est pas guérie, mais elle est ~** she's not completely recovered, but she is better than she was; **tu serais ~ au lit** you'd be better off in bed; **elle va** or **se porte ~** she's better; **elle est ~ portante** she's in better health; **j'aime ~ rester ici** I'd rather stay here; **il vaudrait ~ rester/partir** it would be best to stay/leave; **il vaut encore ~ être en retard qu'absent** better be late than not go at all; **tu ferais ~ de partir/de leur parler** you'd better leave/speak to them, it would be best if you left/spoke to them; **~ encore** better still; **~ que jamais** better than ever; **qui ~ est** moreover; **de ~ en ~** gén better and better; **parler anglais de ~ en ~** to get better and better at (speaking) English; **aller de ~ en ~** [*malade*] to be getting stronger all the time; **tu n'as pas d'argent? de ~ en ~** iron you've no money now? that's absolutely great°! iron; **ils criaient à qui ~ ~** they were all shouting each one louder than the other; **on la critiquait à qui ~ ~** each person criticized her more harshly than the last; **c'est ~ que bien, c'est merveilleux** it's not just good, it's marvellous[GB]!; **c'est on ne peut ~** it's perfect; ▶**deux**, **tard**; **2** (superlatif) **le ~, la ~, les ~** (de plusieurs) the best; (de deux) the better; **l'acteur le ~ payé du monde** the best-paid actor in the world; **il est le ~ payé des deux** he's the better paid one ou he earns more; **les ouvriers les ~ formés** the best-trained workers; **la personne la ~ habillée** the best-dressed person; **c'est ici qu'on mange le ~** this is the best place to eat; **cela s'est passé le ~ du monde** it all went fine; **je me porte le ~ du monde** I'm feeling absolutely fine; **nous nous entendons le ~ du monde** we get on famously; **être des ~ payés** to be extremely well paid.
III *nm* **le ~ est d'oublier/d'accepter/de refuser** the best thing ou course is to forget it/to accept/to refuse; **il y a un/du ~** there is an/some improvement; **s'attendre à ~** to expect better; **en attendant ~** till something better comes along; **il y a ~** it's nothing special; **il n'y a pas ~** it's the best there is; **tu ne trouveras pas ~** it's as good as you'll get; **rester ici, je ne demande pas ~** staying here suits me perfectly; **je ne demande pas ~ que de rester ici** I'm perfectly happy staying here; **j'espérais ~** it's not as good as I hoped; **faire de son ~** to do one's best; **fais pour le ~, fais au ~** do whatever is best; **tout va pour le ~** everything's fine; **cela prendra trois semaines, au ~** it'll take at least three weeks; **elle est au ~ avec sa voisine** she is on very good terms with her neighbour[GB]; **elle est au ~ de sa forme** she's on GB ou in US top form; **c'est le même, en ~** it's the same, only better; **changer en ~** to change for the better; ▶**ennemi**.

mieux-être /mjøzɛtʀ/ *nm inv* improved well-being.

mieux-vivre /mjøvivʀ/ *nm inv* improved living standards (*pl*).

mièvre /mjɛvʀ/ *adj* [*personne, charme, remarque*] vapid; [*sourire*] sickly; [*roman, tableau, musique*] soppy.

mièvrerie /mjɛvʀəʀi/ *nf* **1** (de personne, charme, parole, sourire) vapidity; (de roman, tableau, musique) soppiness; (de compliment, d'excuse) feebleness; **2** (parole, action) **tes ~s m'agacent** your simpering ways get on my nerves.

mi-figue /mifig/ *adj inv* **~ mi-raisin** [*sourire*] half-hearted; [*compliment*] ambiguous; [*remarque*] half-humourous[GB]; **dire qch d'un ton ~ mi-raisin** to say sth half in jest half in earnest; **on m'a fait un accueil ~ mi-raisin** I got a mixed reception.

mi-fin, *pl* **~s** /mifɛ̃/ *adj m* [*haricot, petit pois*] medium-sized.

mignard, ~e /miɲaʀ, aʀd/ *adj* also pej [*personne, sourire*] cute°, sweet; [*style*] twee°; [*décor*] dainty, twee°.

mignardise /miɲaʀdiz/ *nf* (de personne, style) affectation; (de décor) daintiness, affectation; (de visage, sourire) sweetness.

mignon, -onne /miɲɔ̃, ɔn/ **I** *adj* **1** (joli) cute; **2** (gentil) sweet, kind; **sois ~, va**

fermer la porte be a dear and close the door.

II° *nm,f* darling, love!

mignonnet, -ette /miɲɔnɛ, ɛt/ **I** *adj* pretty, cute US.

II mignonnette *nf* Culin coarse-ground pepper.

migraine /migʀɛn/ *nf* splitting headache; (plus fort) migraine; **avoir la** or **une ~** to have a headache; **une forte ~** a bad attack of migraine; **donner la ~ à qn** lit to give sb migraine; fig to give sb a headache.

migraineux, -euse /migʀɛnø, øz/ **I** *adj* **il est ~** he suffers from migraine.

II *nm,f* migraine sufferer.

migrant, ~e /migʀɑ̃, ɑ̃t/ *adj, nm,f* migrant.

migrateur, -trice /migʀatœʀ, tʀis/ **I** *adj* migratory; **cellule migratrice** migratory cell.

II *nm* migratory bird, migrant.

migration /migʀasjɔ̃/ *nf* **1** gén, Biol, Méd, Zool (déplacement) migration; **~ saisonnière** (d'ouvriers) seasonal migration; (de vacanciers) seasonal departures (*pl*); **~ journalière** or **quotidienne** commuting; **2** Relig transmigration.

migratoire /migʀatwaʀ/ *adj* migratory.

migrer /migʀe/ [1] *vi* to migrate (**à, en, vers** to).

mi-hauteur: **à mi-hauteur** /amiotœʀ/ *loc adv* (en montant) halfway up; (en descendant) halfway down.

mi-jambe: **à mi-jambe** /amiʒɑ̃b/ *loc adv* (up) to one's knees; **avoir de l'eau jusqu'à ~** to be up to one's knees in water, to be knee-deep in water.

mijaurée /miʒoʀe/ *nf* **ne fais pas ta ~** don't put on such airs; **petite ~!** little madam!

mijoter /miʒɔte/ [1] **I** *vtr* **1** Culin to prepare [*plat*]; **2**° (manigancer) to cook up; **qu'est-ce que tu mijotes encore?** what are you cooking up now?

II *vi* Culin to simmer; **laissez ~ pendant une heure** leave to simmer for one hour; **faire ~** to simmer.

IDIOMES **laisser qn ~ dans son jus** to let sb stew in his/her own juice.

mijoteuse® /miʒɔtøz/ *nf* slow cooker.

mikado /mikado/ ▶449 *nm* spillikins (+ *v sg*).

mil /mil/ **I** *adj* = **mille**[1].

II *nm* millet.

milady /milɛdi/ *nf* milady.

milan /milɑ̃/ *nm* Zool kite.

Milan /milɑ̃/ ▶857 *npr* Milan.

milanais, ~e /milanɛ, ɛz/ ▶857 *adj* Milanese.

Milanais, ~e /milanɛ, ɛz/ *nm,f* Milanese.

mildiou /mildju/ *nm* mildew.

mile /majl, mil/ ▶477 *nm* (1609 m) mile.

milice /milis/ *nf* militia; **une ~ ouvrière** a workers' militia; **~ de quartier** local vigilante group.

Milice /milis/ *nf* **la ~** the Milice (*French wartime paramilitary organization which collaborated with the Germans against the Resistance*).

milicien, -ienne /milisjɛ̃, ɛn/ *nm,f* **1** Mil militiaman/militiawoman; **2** Hist member of the Milice.

milieu, *pl* **~x** /miljø/ **I** *nm* **1** (dans l'espace) middle; **au ~** in the middle; **au ~ de** in the middle of; **au beau** or **en plein ~** right in the middle; **en son ~** [*percé, décoré*] in the middle; **couper qch par le ~** to cut sth down the middle; **la fenêtre du ~** the middle window, the window in the middle; **je préfère celle du ~** I prefer the one in the middle; **avoir une place en ~ de train** to be sitting halfway down the train; ▶ **nez**; **2** (dans le temps) middle; **au ~ de** in the middle of, halfway through; **au ~ de la nuit** in the middle of ou halfway through the night; **en plein** or **au beau ~ du repas** right in the middle of the meal; **vers le ~ de** toward(s) the middle of, about halfway through; **j'en suis au ~** I'm halfway through; **en ~ de matinée** in the middle of the morning, mid-morning; **en ~ d'après-midi** in the middle of the afternoon, mid-afternoon; **en ~ de journée** in the middle of the day; **en ~ de semaine** midweek; **en ~ de trimestre/d'année** in the middle of the term/of the year; **les ~x de journée sont torrides** it gets oppressively hot in the middle of the day; **3** (moyen terme) middle ground; **entre l'amour et la haine, il y a un ~** there is a middle ground between love and hate; **c'est vrai ou faux, il n'y a pas de ~** it's either right or wrong, there's no in-between; **4** (environnement) environment; **~ naturel/marin/tropical** natural/marine/tropical environment; **en ~ stérile** in a sterile environment; **le ~ familial** the home environment; **en ~ rural** in the country; **en ~ urbain** in a town, in towns; **en ~ hospitalier** (dans les hôpitaux) in hospitals; (dans un hôpital) in a hospital; **en ~ scolaire** (dans les écoles) in schools; (dans une école) in a school; **le ~ carcéral** prison life; **5** (origine, appartenance sociale) background, milieu; (groupe) circle; **ils ne sont pas du même ~** they are from different backgrounds; **connaître des gens de tous les ~x** to know people from every walk of life; **les ~x universitaires/d'affaires/officiels** academic/business/official circles; **un ~ professionnel très conservateur** a very conservative sector; **se former en ~ professionnel** to do training in the workplace; **le ~ de l'édition** the world of publishing; **le ~ de la politique** the world of politics; **le ~** (pègre) the underworld; **6** Math (de segment) midpoint.

II au milieu de *loc prép* **1** (parmi) among; **vivre au ~ des singes/de ses ennemis** to live among apes/one's enemies; **au ~ de mes papiers** among my papers; **être au ~ de ses amis** to be with one's own friends; **2** (entouré de) surrounded by; **au ~ des sarcasmes/des soupçons/des odeurs de cuisine** surrounded by sarcastic remarks/suspicious attitudes/cooking smells; **travailler au ~ du bruit** to work surrounded by noise; **rester calme au ~ des difficultés** to remain calm in the midst of difficulties; **au ~ du désastre** in the midst of disaster; **vivre au ~ du désordre** to live in a mess; **au ~ des rires** amid laughter; **au ~ des applaudissements** to applause.

■ **~ de culture** breeding ground; **~ de terrain** (joueur) midfield player; (endroit) midfield.

militaire /militɛʀ/ **I** *adj* **1** lit [*hôpital, autorités, honneurs, véhicule, musique*] military; [*médecin, aumônier*] army (*épith*); **école ~** military academy; **coup d'État ~** military coup; **personnel/ingénieur ~** military staff/engineer; **région ~** area under military command; **vie ~** army life; **camion ~** army truck; **2** fig [*attitude, raideur*] military; [*discipline*] tight; **il est d'une exactitude ~** you could set your watch by him.

II ▶510 *nm* serviceman; **un ~ de carrière** a regular GB, a career soldier US; **être ~** to be in the army; **les ~s ont pris le pouvoir** the army ou military have taken power.

militairement /militɛʀmɑ̃/ *adv* **1** lit by military means; **zone occupée ~** military occupied zone; **2** fig (efficacement) with military efficiency; péj along military lines.

militant, ~e /militɑ̃, ɑ̃t/ **I** *adj* militant.

II *nm,f* (de syndicat, parti) active member, activist; (de cause) campaigner; **les ~s de base** the rank-and-file members.

militantisme /militɑ̃tism/ *nm* political activism.

militarisation /militaʀizasjɔ̃/ *nf* militarization.

militariser /militaʀize/ [1] **I** *vtr* to militarize; **zone militarisée** militarized zone.

II se militariser *vpr* to become militarized.

militarisme /militaʀism/ *nm* militarism.

militariste /militaʀist/ **I** *adj* militaristic.

II *nmf* militarist.

militaro-industriel, -ielle, *pl* **~s** /militaʀoɛ̃dystʀiɛl/ *adj* military-industrial.

militer /milite/ [1] *vi* **1** (agir) to campaign (**pour, en faveur de** for; **contre** against); **2** (être engagé) to be a political activist; **3** (appartenir politiquement) **il milite au Parti communiste/dans un parti de droite** he's an active member of the Communist Party/of a right-wing party; **4** (constituer un argument) **~ pour** or **en faveur de** to argue in favour[GB] of; **~ contre** to militate against.

mille[1] /mil/ ▶545, 212 **I** *adj inv* a thousand, one thousand; **deux/trois ~** two/three thousand; **il y avait deux à trois ~ personnes** there were between two and three thousand people.

II *pron* **je les ai tous les ~** I have all one thousand of them.

III *nm inv* **1** Comm, Math a thousand, one thousand; **vendre qch au ~** to sell sth by the thousand; **2** ▶477, 860 Aviat, Naut **~ (marin)** nautical mile; **3** Sport (cible) bull's eye; **mettre** or **taper dans le ~** lit to hit the bull's-eye; fig to hit the nail on the head; **4** Édition, Presse **le roman en est à son deuxième ~** the novel has sold over one thousand copies.

IV pour mille *loc adj* Stat per thousand.

IDIOMES **tu aurais vu leur tête! ça valait ~**°**!** you should have seen their faces! it was priceless!; **je ne gagne pas des ~ et des cents** I don't earn very much; **je vous le donne en ~** you'll never guess (in a million years).

mille[2] /mil/ ▶477 *nm* **1** Naut **~ (marin** or **nautique)** (nautical) mile; **2** Aviat (air) mile.

millefeuille /milfœj/ *nm* millefeuille (*small layered cake made of puff pastry filled with custard and cream*).

millénaire /milenɛʀ/ **I** *adj* **1** (de mille ans) **un arbre ~** a one thousand year old tree, a tree that is one thousand years old; **deux fois ~** over two thousand years old; **2** (vieux) [*tradition, phénomène*] age-old.

II *nm* **1** (période) millennium; **à l'aube du troisième ~** at the dawn of the third millennium ou the twenty-first century; **pendant des ~s** for thousands of years; **2** (anniversaire) millennium, millenary.

millénarisme /milenaʀism/ *nm* millenarianism.

millénariste /milenaʀist/ *nmf* millenarian.

millénium /milenjɔm/ *nm* **1** Relig millennium; **2** liter golden age.

mille-pattes /milpat/ *nm inv* centipede, millipede.

millepertuis /milpɛʀtɥi/ *nm* St John's wort.

milleraies /milʀɛ/ *nm inv* **(velours) ~** needlecord.

millésime /milezim/ *nm* **1** (de vin) vintage, year; (de monnaie, médaille) date; **un vin d'un excellent ~** a fine vintage wine; **2** Aut year of manufacture; **3** (dans une date) millennial figure.

millésimé, ~e /milezime/ *adj* [*vin*] vintage (*épith*); [*monnaie*] bearing a date (*épith, après n*); **ce vin est ~** this is a vintage wine; **une bouteille ~e** a bottle of vintage wine.

millet /mijɛ/ *nm* millet.

■ **~ des oiseaux** birdseed, millet.

milliampère /miliɑ̃pɛʀ/ *nm* milliamp.

milliard /miljaʀ/ ▶545 *nm* thousand million GB, billion; **six ~s de francs** six billion ou thousand million GB francs; **il y a des ~s d'étoiles** there are billions of stars.

milliardaire /miljaʀdɛʀ/ *nmf* multimillionaire, billionaire; **il est ~** he is a multi-millionaire.

milliardième /miljaʀdjɛm/ **▶545** *adj* thousand millionth GB, billionth.

millibar /milibaʀ/ *nm* millibar.

millième /miljɛm/ **▶545** *adj* thousandth.

millier /milje/ *nm* **1** (mille) thousand; **un ~** a thousand; **2** (environ mille) about a thousand; **un ~ d'étudiants** (about) a thousand students; **des ~s de gens** thousands of people; **il y en avait des ~s, ils étaient des ~s** there were thousands of them; **par ~s** by the thousand.

milligramme /miligʀam/ **▶620** *nm* milligram.

millilitre /mililitʀ/ **▶117** *nm* millilitre[GB].

millimètre /milimɛtʀ/ **▶477** *nm* millimetre[GB].

millimétré, **~e** /milimetʀe/ *adj* graduated in millimetres[GB]; **papier ~** graph paper.

millimétrique /milimetʀik/ *adj* millimetric.

million /miljɔ̃/ **▶545** *nm* million; **trois ~s d'habitants** three million inhabitants; **des ~s de gens** millions of people; **être riche à ~s** to be worth millions; **cela va coûter des ~s** it will cost a fortune.

millionième /miljɔnjɛm/ **▶545** *adj* millionth; **au ~** to the sixth decimal place.

millionnaire /miljɔnɛʀ/ **I** *adj* **être ~** [*entreprise, société*] to be worth millions; [*personne*] to be a millionaire.

II *nmf* millionaire; **un ~ en dollars** a dollar millionaire.

millivolt /milivɔlt/ *nm* millivolt.

milord /milɔʀ/ *nm* (noble anglais) lord; (riche étranger) rich foreigner.

mi-lourd, *pl* **~s** /miluʀ/ *nm* light heavyweight.

mime /mim/ **▶510** *nm* **1** Théât (acteur) mime artist GB, mime; (genre) mime, pantomime US; (pièce) mime; (jeu) miming; **spectacle de ~** mime show; **2** (imitateur) mimic.

mimer /mime/ [1] *vtr* **1** Théât to mime; **2** (imiter) to mimic.

mimétique /mimetik/ *adj* **1** [*animal*] mimetic; **2** [*comportement*] imitative; [*violence*] copycat.

mimétisme /mimetism/ *nm* **1** Zool mimicry; **2** (imitation) **par ~** through unconscious imitation.

mimi○ /mimi/ **I** *adj* (joli) cute; (gentil) sweet, kind.

II *nm* (baiser) little kiss.

mimique /mimik/ **I** *adj* **langage ~** sign language.

II *nf* **1** (expression comique) funny face; **2** (gestes et expressions) expressions and gestures (*pl*); (des sourds-muets) sign language; **avoir des ~s très expressives** to make eloquent use of gestures and facial expressions.

mimodrame /mimɔdʀam/ *nm* mime.

mimosa /mimoza/ *nm* mimosa; ▶ **œuf**.

MIN /ɛmiɛn/ *nm*: *abbr* ▶ **marché**.

minable○ /minabl/ **I** *adj* **1** (médiocre) [*travail, salaire, cadeau, comportement*] pathetic, lousy; [*personne*] pathetic; [*délit*] petty; **2** (misérable) [*personne*] pathetic; [*logement, bar, vêtement*] crummy○; [*existence*] miserable.

II *nmf* pej (médiocre) pathetic○ character; (raté) loser○.

minage /minaʒ/ *nm* Mil mining.

minaret /minaʀɛ/ *nm* minaret.

minauder /minode/ [1] *vi* (dans l'allure) to mince about; (de la voix, du sourire) to simper; (faire une moue séduisante) to pout; **'non,' dit-elle en minaudant** 'no,' she simpered.

minauderies /minodʀi/ *nfpl* affected mannerisms.

minaudier, **-ière** /minodje, ɛʀ/ *adj* liter affected, simpering.

mince /mɛ̃s/ **I** *adj* **1** (fin) [*personne, corps, taille, jambe*] slim, slender; [*doigt, cou, bras*] slender; [*visage, lèvre, bouche, nez*] thin; [*tranche, couche, lame, mur, filet d'eau*] thin; [*livre*] slim; [*bande de terre*] narrow; **2** (faible) [*consolation, succès*] small; [*espoir, chance, majorité*] slim; [*indice, preuve, théorie, intrigue*] tenuous; [*différence*] slight; [*volume d'affaires, revenus, pension, salaire*] meagre; **l'avantage/la distance/la tâche n'est pas ~** it's no small advantage/distance/task; **ce ne serait pas une ~ victoire** it would be no small victory; **ce n'est pas un ~ exploit** that's no mean feat; **ce n'est pas une ~ affaire** (difficile) that' s no small task; (secondaire) that's no trivial matter.

II *excl* **~ (alors)!** (étonnement) wow○!; (dépit) blast○! GB, darn (it)○! US.

minceur /mɛ̃sœʀ/ **I** *adj inv* **cuisine ~** low-calorie dishes (*pl*).

II *nf* **1** (de personne, corps, taille, jambes) slimness, slenderness; (de doigt, cou, bras) slenderness; (de visage, lèvre, bouche, nez) thinness; (de tranche, couche, lame, mur) thinness; **2** (d'indice, intrigue, de preuve) tenuousness; (de volume d'affaires, revenus) meagreness[GB].

mincir /mɛ̃siʀ/ [3] *vi* to lose weight; **beaucoup ~** to lose a lot of weight; **comment ~ sans peine** slimming without tears; **régime pour ~** (slimming) diet; **il a minci de visage** his face has got GB ou gotten US thinner.

mine /min/ **I** *nf* **1** (expression) expression; (aspect) look; **avoir la ~ boudeuse** to have a sulky expression, to look sulky; **faire triste ~** to have a gloomy expression, to look gloomy; **tu en fais une ~!** why are you looking like that?; **ne fais pas cette ~!** don't look like that!; **sous sa ~ aimable, c'est quelqu'un de très dur** beneath his/her pleasant exterior, he/she is very hard; **juger les gens sur leur ~** to judge people by appearances; **faire ~ d'accepter/de ne pas comprendre** to pretend to accept/not to understand; **faire ~ de partir/frapper** to make as if to go/to hit; **elle nous a dit, ~ de rien**○**, que** she told us, casually, that; **il est doué, ~ de rien**○ it may not be obvious, but he's very clever; **~ de rien**○**, elle arrive toujours à ses fins** without being obvious about it, she always gets her way; **elle a raison, ~ de rien**○ she's right, you know; **2** (apparence) **avoir mauvaise ~** to look a bit off-colour[GB]; **avoir une sale**○ or **petite ~** to look a bit off-colour[GB]; **avoir une ~ resplendissante** to be glowing with health; **avoir une ~ de papier mâché** to look washed out; **avoir bonne ~** [*personne*] to look well; [*tarte, rôti*] to look appetizing; **j'aurais bonne ~!** iron I would look really stupid!; **3** (pour dessiner) lead; **crayon à ~ dure/grasse** hard/soft pencil; **4** Mines gén mine; (de charbon) gén colliery GB, mine; (puits) pit GB, mine; **~ à ciel ouvert** opencast mine; **travailler à la ~** to be a miner, to work in a mine; **l 'exploitation des ~s** mining; **une région de ~s** a coal-mining area; **~ d'or** lit, fig gold mine; **5** (source) source; **~ d'informations** fig mine of information; **une ~ d'adresses utiles** a source of useful addresses; **6** Mil mine; **sauter sur une ~** to be blown up by a mine; **~ terrestre** land mine; **~ antichar/antipersonnel** antitank/antipersonnel mine.

II mines *nfpl* **1** (minauderies) simpering ₵; **faire des ~s** to simper; **2** Admin **les Mines** *official body responsible for regulating weights and measures and changes made to motor vehicles*; ▶ **école**.

■ **~ de crayon** lead; **~ de plomb** graphite ₵.

IDIOMES **ne pas payer de ~**○ not to look anything special○.

miner /mine/ [1] *vtr* **1** (affaiblir) to sap [*moral, énergie*]; to undermine [*santé, confiance en soi, gouvernement, parti*]; **cela me mine** it's wearing me down; (plus fort) it's eating me alive; **miné par les soucis** worn down by anxiety; **pays miné par la corruption** country undermined by corruption; **2** (creuser sous) to wear away [*bâtiment, talus*]; **3** Mil to mine; **le terrain est miné** lit the ground is mined; fig it's a minefield; **avancer en terrain miné** fig to enter a minefield.

minerai /minʀɛ/ *nm* ore; **~ de fer/d'étain** iron/tin ore.

minéral, **~e**, *mpl* **-aux** /mineʀal, o/ **I** *adj* **1** [*huile, sel, eau, règne*] mineral; [*chimie*] inorganic; **2** fig [*paysage*] barren.

II *nm* mineral.

minéralier /mineʀalje/ **I** *adj* ore (*épith*); **port/navire ~** ore terminal/carrier.

II *nm* ore carrier.

minéralisation /mineʀalizasjɔ̃/ *nf* mineralization.

minéraliser /mineʀalize/ [1] **I** *vtr* to mineralize; **eau minéralisée** mineral water.

II se minéraliser *vpr* to mineralize.

minéralogie /mineʀalɔʒi/ *nf* mineralogy.

minéralogique /mineʀalɔʒik/ *adj* **1** Géol mineralogical; **2** Admin, Aut **numéro ~** registration number GB, license number US; **plaque ~** number plate GB, license plate US.

minéralogiste /mineʀalɔʒist/ **▶510** *nmf* mineralogist.

minerve /minɛʀv/ *nf* **1** Méd surgical collar GB, neck brace US; **2** ®Imprim small platen printer.

Minerve /minɛʀv/ *npr* Minerva.

minet /minɛ/ *nm* **1** (chat) pussycat; **2**○ (terme d'affection) **mon ~** my sweetie○; **3**○ (jeune dandy) pretty boy○.

minette /minɛt/ *nf* **1** (chatte) pussycat lang enfantin; **2** (jeune fille) cool chick○.

IDIOMES **faire ~ à qn**● to go down on sb●.

mineur, **~e** /minœʀ/ **I** *adj* **1** Jur under 18 (*après n*); **un enfant ~** a child under the age of 18, a minor spéc; **elle est ~e** she's under 18; **2** (peu important) minor; **3** Mus minor; **en ré ~** in D minor; **en mode ~** in a minor key; **4** Relig **ordres ~s** minor orders.

II *nm,f* Jur person under 18, minor spéc.

III *nm* **1** **▶510** (ouvrier) miner; **~ de fond** pit worker; **2** (soldat) soldier who lays mines.

IV mineure *nf* (en logique) minor.

mini[1] /mini/ *préf* mini; **~-sommet** mini-summit; **~-révolution** mini-revolution.

mini[2] /mini/ **I** *adj inv* **1**○ (minuscule) tiny; **c'est ~ comme prêt/piscine** it's a tiny loan/swimming pool; **2** Mode **la mode ~** the fashion for the mini.

II *nm* **1** Mode **la mode du ~** the fashion for the mini; **s'habiller en ~** to wear mini-skirts; **2**○ Ordinat minicomputer, mini○.

miniature /minjatyʀ/ **I** *adj* [*voiture, objet*] miniature (*épith*).

II *nf* **1** gén miniature; **reproduction en ~** miniature replica; **c'est Versailles en ~** it's a miniature version of Versailles; **2** Art miniature; **3**○ (nain) offensive shrimp○.

miniaturisation /minjatyʀizasjɔ̃/ *nf* miniaturization.

miniaturiser /minjatyʀize/ [1] *vtr* to miniaturize.

miniaturiste /minjatyʀist/ *nmf* miniaturist.

mini-boom, *pl* **~s** /minibum/ *nm* mini-boom.

minibus /minibys/ *nm inv* minibus.

minicassette® /minikasɛt/ *nf* minicassette®.

minier, **-ière** /minje, ɛʀ/ *adj* mining.

mini-golf, *pl* **~s** /minigɔlf/ *nm* (terrain, sport) mini-golf.

mini-informatique /miniɛ̃fɔʀmatik/ *nf* minicomputing.

mini-jupe, *pl* **~s** /miniʒyp/ *nf* mini-skirt.

minima ▶ **a minima**, **minimum**.

minimal, **~e**, *mpl* **-aux** /minimal, o/ *adj*

minimal, minimum; **les températures ~es** minimum temperatures.

minimalisme /minimalism/ *nm* minimalism.

minimaliste /minimalist/ *adj, nmf* minimalist.

minime /minim/ **I** *adj* [*dégâts, différence*] trifling, negligible; [*chance*] slim, slender; [*avantage, dépenses*] minimal, negligible; [*rôle*] minor.

II *nmf* **1** Sport junior (*7 to 13 years old*); **il est passé chez les ~s** he has moved up to the juniors; **2** Relig Minim.

minimisation /minimizasjɔ̃/ *nf* minimization, playing down.

minimiser /minimize/ [1] *vtr* to minimize, to play down.

minimum, *pl* **~s** ou **minima** /minimɔm, minima/ **I** *adj* [*température, vitesse*] minimum; **prix/poids/âge ~** minimum price/weight/age; **un an, c'est le délai ~** it will take one year at least.

II *nm* **1** (limite inférieure) minimum; **ils n'ont que le strict ~ pour vivre** they only have the bare minimum to live on; **nous essaierons de vous déranger un ~** we'll try to disturb you as little as possible; **en faire un ~** to do as little as possible; **il faut travailler un ~ si tu veux réussir** you have to do a bit of work if you want to succeed; **un ~ d'égards/de bon sens** a certain amount of respect/of common sense; **un ~ d'hygiène** a basic level of hygiene; **en un ~ de temps** in as short a time as possible; **avec un ~ d'efforts** with a minimum of effort; **prendre le ~ de risques** to take as few risks as possible; **il faut au ~ deux heures pour faire le trajet** it takes at least two hours for that journey; **au ~ 2 000 francs** 2,000 francs minimum, at least 2,000 francs; **2** Jur minimum sentence; **requérir le ~** Jur to recommend the minimum sentence.

■ **~ vital** subsistence level.

mini-ordinateur, *pl* **~s** /miniɔrdinatœr/ *nm* minicomputer.

minipilule /minipilyl/ *nf* low-dose combined pill.

miniski /miniski/ **▶ 449** *nm* miniski.

ministère /ministɛr/ *nm* **1** Pol (service administratif) gén ministry; (au Royaume-Uni, aux États-Unis) department; (bâtiment) ministry; (durée des fonctions d'un ministre) ministry; (charge) ministership; **il travaille dans un ~** he works in a ministry ou a government department; **2** Pol (équipe gouvernementale) cabinet, government; **former un ~** to form a government ou cabinet; **3** Jur **le ~ public** (service) the public prosecutor's office; (magistrat) the prosecuting magistrate, the prosecution; **4** (entremise) fml **offrir** or **proposer son ~ pour faire** to offer to act as mediator to do; **par ~ d'huissier/d'avocat** through a bailiff/a lawyer; **5** Relig ministry.

■ **~ des Affaires étrangères** ministry of Foreign Affairs; **~ de l'Agriculture** ministry of Agriculture; **~ du Commerce** ministry of Trade; **~ de la Culture** ministry of Culture; **~ de la Défense nationale** ministry of Defence[GB]; **~ de l'Économie et des finances** ministry of Finance; **~ de l'Éducation nationale** ministry of Education; **~ de l'Environnement** ministry of the Environment; **~ de l'Intérieur** ministry of the Interior; **~ de la Justice** ministry of Justice; **~ des Postes et télécommunications** Postal and Telecommunications ministry; **~ de la Recherche** ministry of Research; **~ de la Santé** ministry of Health; **~ des Transports** ministry of Transport GB ou Transportation US; **~ du Travail** ministry of Employment.

ministériel, -ielle /ministeʀjɛl/ *adj* ministerial, cabinet (*épith*).

ministrable /ministʀabl/ **I** *adj* [*personne*] likely to be appointed minister.

II *nmf* potential candidate for minister.

ministre /ministʀ/ *nm* **1** Pol gén minister; (au Royaume-Uni) Secretary of State; (aux États-Unis) Secretary; **~ délégué** minister of state GB, under-secretary US (**auprès de** to); **~ sans portefeuille** minister without portfolio; **~ par intérim** acting minister; **les ~s** the cabinet (+ *v sg* ou *pl*); **Madame le ~** Minister GB, Madam Secretary US; **Monsieur le ~** Minister GB, Mr Secretary US; **2** (en diplomatie) (envoyé) envoy; **3** Relig minister; **~ du culte** minister of religion; **▶ premier**.

■ **~ des Affaires étrangères** minister of Foreign Affairs; **~ de l'Agriculture** Agriculture minister; **~ du Commerce** minister of Trade; **~ conseiller** minister counsellor; **~ de la Culture** minister of Culture; **~ de la Défense nationale** Defence minister; **~ de l'Économie et des finances** Finance minister; **~ de l'Éducation nationale** minister for Education; **~ de l'Environnement** minister of the Environment; **~ d'État** (titre) *honorary title conferred on government minister*; (sans portefeuille) minister without portfolio; **~ de l'Intérieur** Interior minister; **~ de la Justice** minister of Justice; **~ plénipotentiaire** minister plenipotentiary; **~ de la Recherche** minister of Research; **~ résident** minister resident; **~ de la Santé** minister of Health; **~ des Transports** Transport GB ou Transportation US minister; **~ du Travail** minister of Employment.

Minitel® /minitɛl/ *nm* Télécom Minitel (*terminal linking phone users to a database*); **sur** or **au ~** on Minitel; **par le ~** by Minitel.

minium /minjɔm/ *nm* **1** (peinture) red lead paint; **2** Chimie minium.

minivague /minivag/ *nf* soft perm; **se faire faire une ~** to have a soft perm.

Minnesota /minezɔta/ **▶ 692** *nprm* Minnesota.

minoen, -enne /minɔɛ̃, ɛn/ *adj* Minoan.

minois /minwɑ/ *nm* fresh young face; **joli petit ~** pretty little face.

minon○ /minɔ̃/ *nm* H (poussière) fluff ₵.

minoration /minɔʀasjɔ̃/ *nf* **1** Comm (sous-estimation) (de bien, marchandise) undervaluation; (de prix) underestimation; **il y a eu ~ de la valeur réelle** the true value was underestimated; **2** (réduction) reduction; **~ de 2%** 2 percent reduction; **~ des prix** cut in prices; **~ des prix de 2%** 2 percent price cut.

minorer /minɔʀe/ [1] *vtr* **1** (réduire) to reduce [*prix, taux*] (**de** by); **2** (sous-estimer) to undervalue [*biens*]; to underestimate [*montant*].

minoritaire /minɔʀitɛʀ/ **I** *adj* [*groupe, tendance, actionnaire*] minority (*épith*); **nous restons ~s** we are still in the minority.

II *nmf* member of a minority group; **les ~s** those in the minority; **une poignée de ~s** a small minority.

minorité /minɔʀite/ *nf* **1** (groupe) minority; **~ agissante/ethnique** active/ethnic minority; **être en ~** to be in the minority; **être mis en ~** to be defeated; **2** (petit nombre) minority (**de** of); **3** (d'âge) minority; **pendant sa ~** during his/her minority; **~ pénale** Jur ≈ legal infancy.

■ **~ de blocage** Fin blocking minority.

Minorque /minɔʀk/ **▶ 416** *nprf* Minorca.

Minotaure /minɔtɔʀ/ *npr* **le ~** the Minotaur.

minoterie /minɔtʀi/ *nf* **1** (usine) flour mill; **2** (industrie) flour-milling (industry).

minotier /minɔtje/ **▶ 510** *nm* miller.

minou /minu/ *nm* **1** (chat) pussycat lang enfantin; (pour appeler un chat) **~ ~!** puss puss○!; **2**○ (terme d'affection) **mon gros ~** my sweetie○.

minoune○ /minun/ *nf* C kiss.

Minsk /minsk/ **▶ 857** *npr* Minsk.

minuit /minɥi/ **▶ 407** *nm* midnight; **à ~** at midnight; **~ et demi** half past twelve, half past midnight; **~ moins le quart** a quarter to twelve, a quarter to midnight; **de ~** [*messe, soleil*] midnight.

minus○ /minys/ *nmf inv* pej moron○; **c'est un ~** he's a moron, he's a dead loss○.

minuscule /minyskyl/ **I** *adj* **1** (tout petit) [*chose, personne*] tiny; [*quantité*] tiny, minute; **2** (en écriture) small; Imprim lower-case; **d ~** small d, lower-case d.

II *nf* (en écriture) small letter; Imprim lower-case letter.

minutage /minytaʒ/ *nm* (precise) timing.

minute /minyt/ **▶ 407**, **801** **I** *nf* **1** (unité de temps) minute; **2** (court moment) minute, moment; **il revient dans cinq ~s** he'll be back in five ou a few minutes; **on ne peut se permettre une ~ d'inattention** you can't let your attention wander for a moment ou second; **hé! ~**○**!, ~ papillon**○**!** hang on a minute○!; **il peut arriver d'une ~ à l'autre** he may arrive any minute now ou at any minute; **j'en ai pour une ~** I won't be a minute; **je suis à toi dans une ~** I'll be with you in a minute; **l'angoisse monte de ~ en ~** fear is mounting by the minute; **il n'y a pas une ~ à perdre** there isn't a moment to lose; **ne pas avoir une ~ à soi** not to have a moment to oneself; **on vient de me l'apporter à la ~** it has just been brought to me this very second; **c'est pas à la ~**○ it's not desperate ou urgent; **à la ~ où je vous parle** just as I'm speaking to you; **3** Jur **~ d'un jugement/acte notarié** record of a decision/notarial deed; **~s d'un procès/d'une rencontre** minutes of a trial/of a meeting; **4** (unité d'angle) minute.

II (-)minute (*in compounds*) **'clés-~'** 'keys cut while you wait'; **'nettoyage-~'** 'same day dry cleaning'.

■ **~ de silence** minute's silence; **la ~ de vérité** the moment of truth.

minuter /minyte/ [1] *vtr* (chronométrer) to time; (prévoir) to work out the timing of; **mon temps est minuté** my time is limited; **l'opération doit être minutée à la seconde** the operation requires split-second timing.

minuterie /minytʀi/ *nf* (d'éclairage) (interrupteur) time-switch; (mécanisme) automatic lighting.

minuteur /minytœʀ/ *nm* (d'appareil électroménager) timer.

minutie /minysi/ *nf* (de personne, travail) meticulousness; **la lexicographie exige une grande ~** lexicography requires meticulous attention to detail; **travail d'une grande ~** (à faire) very detailed work; (fait) meticulous work; **avec ~** with meticulous care.

minutieusement /minysjøzmɑ̃/ *adv* (avec soin) with meticulous care; (dans le détail) in great detail.

minutieux, -ieuse /minysjø, øz/ *adj* [*historien, ouvrier, soin*] meticulous; [*préparation*] careful; [*étude, description*] detailed; **travail ~** (à faire) meticulous work, work requiring meticulous care; (fait) work executed with meticulous care.

miocène /mjɔsɛn/ *adj, nm* Miocene.

mioche○ /mjɔʃ/ *nmf* kid○; **sale ~** horrible brat○.

mirabelle /miʀabɛl/ *nf* **1** (fruit) mirabelle (*small yellow plum*); **2** (eau-de-vie) plum brandy.

miracle /miʀakl/ **I** *adj inv* **un remède/une solution ~** a miracle cure/solution; **un procédé/matériau ~** a miraculous process/material; **un médicament ~** a wonder drug; **une méthode ~** a magic formula.

II *nm* **1** Relig, fig miracle; **il faudrait un ~ pour qu'il guérisse** only a miracle could cure him; **à moins d'un ~ nous ne pourrons pas sauver l'entreprise** nothing short of a miracle will help us save the business;

~ économique economic miracle; **accomplir** or **faire un ~** Relig to work a miracle; fig to work miracles; **tenir du ~** to be a miracle; **croire aux ~s** lit to believe in miracles; fig to live in cloud cuckoo land○; **il n'y a pas de quoi crier au ~** there's nothing miraculous about it; **un ~ de l'architecture/de la littérature** an architectural/a literary wonder; **un ~ de beauté/d'équilibre** a miracle of beauty/balance; **un ~ de la nature** a miracle of nature; **par ~** miraculously; **comme par ~** as if by magic; **2** (drame sacré) miracle play.

miraculé, ~e /miʀakyle/ Relig **I** *adj* [*malade, personne*] miraculously cured.
II *nm,f* person on whom a miracle has been worked; **c'est un ~** he has been saved by a miracle; **les ~s de la route** people who have miraculously survived a road accident.

miraculeusement /miʀakyløzmɑ̃/ *adv* miraculously.

miraculeux, -euse /miʀakylø, øz/ *adj* [*guérison, vision, apparition, grotte*] miraculous; [*progrès, réussite, découverte, intervention*] miraculous; [*remède, traitement*] which works miracles ou wonders (*épith, après n*); [*produit*] which works wonders (*épith, après n*).

mirador /miʀadɔʀ/ *nm* **1** Mil watchtower; **2** Chasse raised hide; **3** Archit belvedere.

mirage /miʀaʒ/ *nm* **1** (vision) lit, fig mirage; **2** Tech (d'œufs) candling.

mi-raisin /miʀɛzɛ̃/ *adj inv* ▶ **mi-figue**.

miraud○, **~e** /miʀo, od/ *adj* shortsighted; **complètement ~** blind as a bat○.

mire /miʀ/ *nf* **1** TV test card GB, test pattern US; **2** (en topographie) levelling[GB] staff.

mire-œufs /miʀø/ *nm inv* candler.

mirer /miʀe/ [1] **I** *vtr* **1** Tech to candle [*œuf*]; **2** (dans un miroir) **~ son visage dans l'eau** to gaze at one's reflection in the water; **la ville mire ses édifices dans les canaux** the town's buildings are mirrored in its canals.
II se mirer *vpr* liter [*personne*] to gaze at one's reflection; [*objet*] to be reflected.

mirettes◑ /miʀɛt/ *nfpl* peepers○, eyes; **en avoir plein les ~** to be dazzled.

mirifique /miʀifik/ *adj* iron fabulous○.

mirliflore† /miʀliflɔʀ/ *nm* (dandy) fop†; (fanfaron) braggart.

mirliton /miʀlitɔ̃/ *nm* Mus reed pipe.

miro○ = **miraud**.

mirobolant○, **~e** /miʀɔbɔlɑ̃, ɑ̃t/ *adj* fabulous○.

miroir /miʀwaʀ/ *nm* lit, fig mirror; **~ déformant/grossissant/de poche** distorting/magnifying/pocket mirror; **~ plan/sphérique** flat/curved mirror.
■ **~ aux alouettes** lit, fig lure; **la publicité, ~ aux alouettes de notre société...** advertising, a snare and a delusion in our society...; **~ de courtoisie** Aut courtesy mirror.

miroitement /miʀwatmɑ̃/ *nm* liter (de vitre) sparkling ¢; (de l'eau) shimmering ¢.

miroiter /miʀwate/ [1] *vi* [*objet*] to sparkle; [*eau*] to shimmer; **faire ~ qch à qn** fig to hold out the prospect of sth to sb.

miroiterie /miʀwatʀi/ ▶ **510** *nf* **1** (industrie) mirror industry; (commerce) mirror business; **2** (atelier) mirror factory.

miroitier, -ière /miʀwatje, ɛʀ/ ▶ **510** *nm,f* (vendeur) mirror dealer; (fabricant) mirror manufacturer.

mironton /miʀɔ̃tɔ̃/, **miroton** /miʀɔtɔ̃/ *nm* (bœuf) **~** beef stew (*with onion sauce*).

mis, ~e /mi, miz/ **I** *pp* ▶ **mettre**.
II *pp adj* **1** (vêtu) **être bien ~** to be well-dressed; **être bizarrement ~** to be oddly dressed; **2** (présentable) **un jeune homme bien ~ (de sa personne)** a presentable young man.
III mise *nf* **1** Jeux, Turf **doubler/récupérer sa ~e** to double/recover one's stake; **une ~e de cinq francs** a five-franc bet; **perdre sa ~e** to lose one's bet; **j'ai joué toute ma ~e sur Lola** I staked everything on Lola; **2** (tenue) **~e soignée/négligée** well-groomed/sloppy appearance; **ta ~e est négligée** you're sloppily dressed.
■ **~e de fonds** Fin investment; **~e en plis** Cosmét set; **se faire faire une ~e en plis** to have one's hair set.
IDIOMES **être de ~e** [*comportement*] to be proper; [*remarque*] to be appropriate; **ne pas être de ~e** [*comportement, remarque*] to be out of place; **je t'ai sauvé la ~e**○ I saved your bacon○.

■ Note Les expressions du type *mise en boîte, mise à feu, mise à mort* sont traitées sous le deuxième élément: on se reportera à *boîte, feu, mort* etc.

misaine /mizɛn/ *nf* **(voile de) ~** foresail.

misanthrope /mizɑ̃tʀɔp/ **I** *adj* misanthropic.
II *nmf* misanthropist, misanthrope.

misanthropie /mizɑ̃tʀɔpi/ *nf* misanthropy.

misanthropique /mizɑ̃tʀɔpik/ *adj* misanthropic.

miscible /misibl/ *adj* miscible (**à** with).

mise-bas, *pl* **mises-bas** /mizbɑ/ *nf* Vét birth; **~ d'un veau** birth of a calf.

miser /mize/ [1] **I** *vtr* to bet [*argent*] (**sur** on).
II *vi* **1** (parier) **~ sur le 2** (au casino) to place a bet on the 2; **~ sur un cheval** Turf to put money on a horse; **~ à dix contre un** to bet ten to one; **il a misé sur le cheval gagnant** he backed the winning horse; **~ sur le mauvais cheval** lit to bet on the wrong horse; fig to make the wrong choice; ▶ **tableau**; **2** (compter) **~ sur la situation/qualité** to bank on the situation/quality; **~ sur un événement/sa chance/ses efforts** to count on an event/one's luck/one's efforts; **~ sur qn** to place all one's hopes in sb.

misérabilisme /mizeʀabilism/ *nm* **1** (d'écrivain) sordid realism; **2** (d'individu) tendency to dwell on the dark side; **faire du ~** to dwell on the dark side.

misérabiliste /mizeʀabilist/ *adj* [*film, spectacle*] which dwells on sordid reality (*épith, après n*); **écrivain ~** writer of sordid realism.

misérable /mizeʀabl/ **I** *adj* **1** (très pauvre) [*personne*] destitute, poor; [*habit*] shabby; [*vie, condition, pays*] poor, wretched; [*maison, pièce*] squalid, dingy; **2** (dérisoire) [*somme, salaire*] meagre[GB]; [*affaire*] pathetic; **se battre pour un ~ croûton** to fight over a miserable piece of bread; **3** (pitoyable) [*fin, existence*] pitiful, miserable.
II *nmf* **1** (indigent) pauper; **il a l'air d'un ~** he looks down and out ou like a pauper; **2**† (personne méprisable) scoundrel.

misérablement /mizeʀabləmɑ̃/ *adv* **1** (pauvrement) wretchedly, miserably; **2** (pitoyablement) miserably, pitifully.

misère /mizɛʀ/ *nf* **1** (pauvreté) (de personne) destitution, extreme poverty; (de lieu) squalor, destitution; **être dans la ~** to be destitute; **s'enfoncer dans la ~** to become totally destitute; **réduire qn à la ~** to reduce sb to poverty; **crier** or **pleurer ~** to bewail one's poverty, to poor-mouth○ US; **2** (détresse) misery, wretchedness; **c'est ~ que de faire** it is distressing ou upsetting to do; **c'est ~ que de voir ça!** it is distressing to see such things; **la ~ des temps** the hardship of the times; **quelle ~!** what a wretched pity!; **~ (de moi**†**)!** woe is me†!; **3** (ennui) trouble, woe; **on a tous nos petites ~s** we all have our little troubles ou problems; **faire des ~s à qn** to give sb a hard time, to be nasty to sb; **4** (somme dérisoire) pittance; **il a acheté ça pour une ~** he bought it for a pittance ou song; **5** Bot wandering Jew, tradescantia.
■ **~ intellectuelle** intellectual poverty; **~ noire** dire poverty; **~ sexuelle** sexual deprivation.

miserere /mizeʀeʀe/ *nm inv* Miserere.

miséreux, -euse /mizeʀø, øz/ **I** *adj* destitute, deprived.
II *nm,f* destitute person; **les ~** the destitute.

miséricorde /mizeʀikɔʀd/ **I** *nf* **1** Relig mercy; **2** Archit misericord.
II† *excl* mercy†!

miséricordieux, -ieuse /mizeʀikɔʀdjø, øz/ *adj* merciful.

misogyne /mizɔʒin/ **I** *adj* [*personne, propos, livre*] misogynous; **il est très ~** he's a real misogynist.
II *nmf* misogynist.

misogynie /mizɔʒini/ *nf* misogyny.

miss /mis/ *nf inv* **1** (reine de beauté) **Miss France** Miss France; **2**○ (jeune fille) **ça va la ~?** how's our young lady?

missel /misɛl/ *nm* missal.

missile /misil/ *nm* missile; **~ tactique/stratégique/nucléaire/balistique** tactical/strategic/nuclear/ballistic missile; **~ de moyenne/courte portée** intermediate-/short-range missile; **~ de croisière** cruise missile; **~ antichars/antiaérien** anti-tank/anti-aircraft missile; **~ embarqué à bord de navire** sea-launched cruise missile, SLCM.

mission /misjɔ̃/ *nf* **1** (tâche) mission, task; **donner à qn la ~ de faire** to give sb the task of doing; **charger qn d'une ~, confier une ~ à qn** to entrust sb with a mission; **charger qn d'une ~ de confiance** to entrust sb with an important task; **remplir sa ~** to complete one's mission; **'~ accomplie!'** 'mission accomplished!'; **il s'est donné pour ~ de faire** he has taken upon himself to do; **j'ai pour ~ de faire** my mission is to do; **2** (fonction temporaire) mission, assignment; **~ officielle/secrète** official/secret mission ou assignment; **~ d'information, ~ d'enquête** special fact-finding mission; **être envoyé en ~ auprès de qn** to be sent to sb on special assignment; **être envoyé en ~ d'étude/de contrôle/d'inspection** to be sent to make a study/a check/an inspection; **3** (groupe) mission, team; **~ d'experts/observateurs** team of experts/observers; **4** Mil (but) mission; **5** Relig (charge, organisation, bâtiment) mission; (groupe) missionary group; **pays de ~** missionary country.
■ **~ de bons offices** mission of mediation; **~ diplomatique** diplomatic mission; **~ de paix** peace mission.

missionnaire /misjɔnɛʀ/ *adj, nmf* missionary.

Mississippi /misisipi/ ▶ **692**, **357** *nprm* Mississippi.

missive /misiv/ *nf* missive.

Missouri /misuʀi/ ▶ **692**, **357** *nprm* Missouri.

mistigri /mistigʀi/ *nm* **1** Jeux (valet de trèfle) mistigris; (jeu) mistigris; **2**○ (chat) pussycat○.

mistoufle† /mistufl/ *nf* **1** (misère) poverty; **être dans la ~** to be hard up; **2** (méchanceté) dirty trick.

mistral /mistʀal/ *nm* mistral.

mitaine /mitɛn/ *nf* fingerless mitt.

mitan† /mitɑ̃/ *nm* middle.

mitard○ /mitaʀ/ *nm* prisoners' slang cooler○.

mite /mit/ *nf* (clothes) moth; **mon pull est mangé par les** or **aux ~s** my jumper is all moth-eaten.
■ **~ du fromage** cheese mite.
IDIOMES **ce n'est pas mangé aux** or **piqué des ~s**○ that's quite something.

mi-temps /mitɑ̃/ **I** *nm inv* **1** (emploi) part-time job; **un poste à ~** a part-time job; **2** (système) part-time work ¢; **elle travaille à ~** she works part-time; **il est serveur à ~** he's a part-time waiter.
II *nf inv* Sport (arrêt) half-time; (moitié de match) half; **à la ~** at half-time; **en**

première/deuxième ~ in the first/second half.

miter: **se miter** /mite/ [1] *vpr* [*vêtement*] to become moth-eaten; **mité** moth-eaten.

miteux, **-euse** /mitø, øz/ **I** *adj* [*quartier, hôtel*] seedy; [*vêtements*] shabby; [*personne*] down-at-heel.

II *nm,f* down-and-out.

Mithridate /mitʀidat/ *npr* Mithridates.

mithridatiser /mitʀidatize/ [1] *vtr* to make [sb] immune to a poison by administering frequent small doses.

mitigation /mitigasjɔ̃/ *nf* mitigation.

mitigé, **~e** /mitiʒe/ *adj* (incertain) [*accueil*] lukewarm; [*succès*] qualified; [*conclusions*] ambivalent; **ils ont réagi de manière ~e à la proposition** their reaction to the proposal was mixed.

mitigeur /mitiʒœʀ/ *nm* mixer tap GB, mixer faucet US.

mitochondrie /mitɔkɔ̃dʀi/ *nf* mitochondrion.

mitonner /mitɔne/ [1] **I** *vtr* to cook [sth] lovingly [*plat, repas*]; to prepare the ground carefully for [*projet, affaire*].

II *vi* Culin [*plat*] to cook slowly.

III se mitonner *vpr* **1** Culin **se ~ un petit plat** to cook a nice little meal for oneself; **2** fig **se ~ un bel avenir** to carve out a nice future for oneself.

mitose /mitoz/ *nf* mitosis.

mitoyen, **-enne** /mitwajɛ̃, ɛn/ *adj* **1** Jur (en commun) [*cloison, haie*] dividing; [*arbre*] jointly owned; **mur ~** party wall; **2** (contigu) controv [*bâtiment*] adjoining; **la maison mitoyenne de la nôtre** the house adjoining ours.

mitoyenneté /mitwajɛnte/ *nf* (copropriété) joint ownership (**de** of).

mitraillade /mitʀajad/ *nf* (coups de feu) machine gun fire; (affrontement) exchange of machine gun fire.

mitraillage /mitʀajaʒ/ *nm* **1** Mil machine-gunning (**de** of); **2** fig **~ (de questions)** quick-fire questioning; **se livrer à un vrai ~** to fire a volley of questions.

■ **~ au sol** strafing.

mitraille /mitʀaj/ *nf* **1** Mil (d'artillerie) hail of bullets; **2**○ (monnaie) small change.

mitrailler /mitʀaje/ [1] *vtr* **1** Mil to machine-gun; **~ au sol** to strafe; **2**○ (bombarder) **~ qn de cailloux**○ to pelt sb with stones; **~ qn de questions** to fire questions at sb; **3**○ (photographier) to take photo after photo of [*tableau, personne*]; **se faire ~ par les photographes** to be besieged by photographers.

mitraillette /mitʀajɛt/ *nf* submachine gun.

mitrailleur /mitʀajœʀ/ *nm* gunner.

mitrailleuse /mitʀajøz/ *nf* machine gun.

mitral, **~e**, *mpl* **-aux** /mitʀal, o/ **I** *adj* [*orifice, insuffisance, valvule*] mitral.

II mitrale *nf* mitral valve.

mitre /mitʀ/ *nf* **1** (coiffure) mitre[GB]; **recevoir** or **coiffer la ~** to be made a bishop; **2** Constr cowl.

mitré, **~e** /mitʀe/ *adj* mitred[GB].

mitron /mitʀɔ̃/ *nm* baker's boy.

mi-voix: **à mi-voix** /amivwa/ *loc adv* [*parler, chanter*] in a low voice.

mixage /miksaʒ/ *nm* sound mixing; **salle** or **studio de ~** sound mixing studio.

mixer[1] /miksɛʀ/ = **mixeur**.

mixer[2] /mikse/ [1] *vtr* Audio to mix.

mixeur /miksœʀ/ *nm* (batteur) mixer; (broyeur) blender.

mixité /miksite/ *nf* gén mixing of sexes; (à l'école) coeducation; **la ~ dans les vestiaires** mixed changing rooms.

mixte /mikst/ *adj* **1** (pour les deux sexes) [*école*] coeducational; [*classe, équipe sportive*] mixed; [*concours*] open to both sexes (*après n*); [*salon de coiffure*] unisex; **enseignement ~** coeducation; **2** (mélangé) [*mariage, couple*] mixed; [*économie, capital*] mixed; [*commission*] joint (*épith*); [*roche*] mixed; [*peau*] combination (*épith*); [*chaudière*] dual-system (*épith*); [*scrutin*] dual; **cuisinière ~** combined gas and electric cooker GB ou stove; **entreprise** or **société ~** joint venture.

mixtion /mikstjɔ̃/ *nf* (mélange) compounding; (médicament) mixture.

mixture /mikstyʀ/ *nf* **1** (plat cuisiné) concoction; **2** Pharm mixture; **3** (mélange) mishmash○ péj.

MJC /ɛmʒise/ *nf*: *abbr* ▶ **maison**.

MLF /ɛmɛlɛf/ *nm* (*abbr* = **mouvement de libération des femmes**) ≈ Women's Lib.

Mlle ▶ **813** (*written abbr* = **Mademoiselle**) Ms, Miss; **~ Lévy** Ms Lévy, Miss Lévy.

Mlles ▶ **813** (*written abbr* = **Mesdemoiselles**) Misses; **~ Huet et Cordelle** Misses Huet and Cordelle, Ms Huet and Ms Cordelle.

mm (*written abbr* = **millimètre**) mm.

MM. ▶ **813** (*written abbr* = **Messieurs**) Messrs; **~ Brun et Rosec** Messrs Brun and Rosec.

Mme ▶ **813** (*written abbr* = **Madame**) Ms, Mrs; **~ Bon** Ms Bon, Mrs Bon.

Mmes ▶ **813** (*written abbr* = **Mesdames**) **~ Huet et Cordelle** Ms Huet and Ms Cordelle, Mrs Huet and Mrs Cordelle.

mnémonique /mnemɔnik/ *adj* mnemonic.

mnémotechnique /mnemɔtɛknik/ **I** *adj* [*moyen, procédé*] mnemonic.

II *nf* mnemonics (+ *v sg*).

Mo (*written abbr* = **mégaoctet**) Mb, MB.

mob○ /mɔb/ *nf* (vélomoteur) moped.

mobile /mɔbil/ **I** *adj* **1** (non fixe) [*pièce, élément*] mobile; [*feuillet*] loose; [*fête*] movable; **échelle ~ des salaires** sliding salary scale; **2** (non sédentaire) [*personnel*] mobile; **3** (motorisé) [*antenne, unité*] mobile; **4** (non figé) [*visage, traits*] mobile.

II *nm* **1** (motif) motive; **le ~ du crime** the motive for the crime; **sans ~ apparent** without any apparent motive; **2** Phys moving body; **3** Art mobile.

mobilier, **-ière** /mɔbilje, ɛʀ/ **I** *adj* **biens ~s** movable property ¢, movables; **valeurs mobilières** securities; **plus-values mobilières** capital gains on the sale of securities.

II *nm* furniture; **~ de bureau** office furniture.

■ **~ national** state furnishings (*pl*); **~ urbain** street furniture.

mobilisable /mɔbilizabl/ *adj* **1** Mil [*militaire, réserviste*] subject to mobilization; [*civil*] subject to call-up, subject to draft US; **2** fig [*ressources*] available; [*personnes, militants*] who can be called upon ou mobilized (*épith, après n*).

mobilisateur, **-trice** /mɔbilizatœʀ, tʀis/ *adj* **1** [*slogan, discours*] rousing; [*projet, activité*] stimulating; [*personne*] inspiring; **2** Mil **centre ~** mobilization centre[GB].

mobilisation /mɔbilizasjɔ̃/ *nf* **1** Mil (de militaire, réserviste) mobilization; (de civil) call-up, draft US; **décréter la ~** to order mobilization; **~ générale** lit mobilization; fig all-out effort; **2** fig (de ressources, d'hommes, esprits) mobilization; **appeler à la ~ contre** to call for mobilization against.

mobiliser /mɔbilize/ [1] **I** *vtr* **1** Mil to mobilize [*militaire, réserviste*]; to call up, to draft US [*civil*]; **être mobilisé** to be put on active service GB ou duty US; **2** (rassembler) to mobilize, to call upon [*militants, amis*] (**pour faire** to do); **~ les travailleurs autour d'un projet/parti** to get the workers to support a project/party; **le projet a mobilisé l'attention des étudiants** the project caught the attention of the students; **3** (faire agir) to rally; **ce problème a mobilisé tous les parents** this issue rallied all the parents; **~ les énergies** to mobilize people to act; **4** fig (mettre en jeu) to mobilize [*forces, volonté*]; to summon up [*courage*]; to call on [*raison*].

II se mobiliser *vpr* [*militants, étudiants*] to rally, to mobilize; **se ~ autour d'un parti** to rally round a party; **se ~ autour d'un projet** to devote one's energies to a project.

mobilité /mɔbilite/ *nf* **1** Sociol mobility; **~ géographique/sociale** geographical/social mobility; **2** Méd (faculté de se déplacer) mobility; **personne à ~ réduite** person with restricted mobility; **3** (caractère changeant) mobility; **4** (vivacité) liveliness, quickness.

mobylette® /mɔbilɛt/ *nf* moped.

mocassin /mɔkasɛ̃/ *nm* **1** (chaussure) moccasin, loafer; **2** (serpent) water moccasin.

moche○ /mɔʃ/ *adj* **1** (laid) [*personne*] ugly; [*vêtement, papier peint*] ghastly; [*couleur*] awful; **le temps est ~ aujourd'hui** the weather is awful today; **2** (triste) dreadful; **3** (mesquin) [*attitude*] nasty (**avec** to); **c'est ~ de dire/faire ça** that's a nasty thing to say/do.

IDIOMES **~ comme un pou** as ugly as sin.

mocheté○ /mɔʃte/ *nf* **1** (caractéristique) ugliness; **il est d'une ~!** he's unbelievably ugly!; **2** (personne laide) horror.

modal, **~e**, *mpl* **-aux** /mɔdal, o/ **I** *adj* modal.

II *nm* modal verb.

modalité /mɔdalite/ **I** *nf* Ling, Mus, Philos modality.

II modalités *nfpl* **1** gén (conditions) terms; (façon de fonctionner) practical details; **les ~s du débat/cessez-le-feu ont été fixées** the terms of the debate/ceasefire have been fixed; **les ~s de l'opération/l'unification** the practical details of the operation/the unification process; **~s de remboursement** terms of repayment; **~s de financement** methods of funding; Scol, Univ **~s d'inscription** enrolment[GB] procedure ¢; **~s de contrôle** methods of assessment; **2** Jur clauses.

modanais, **~e** /mɔdanɛ, ɛz/ ▶ **857** *adj* of Modane.

Modanais, **~e** /mɔdanɛ, ɛz/ *nm,f* (natif) native of Modane; (habitant) inhabitant of Modane.

Modane /mɔdan/ ▶ **857** *npr* Modane.

mode /mɔd/ **I** *nm* **1** (façon) way, mode; **~ de pensée/vie** way of thinking/life; **~ de gouvernement** mode of government; **~ de transport** mode of transport GB ou transportation US; **~ de paiement** method of payment; **le ~ de fonctionnement de qch** the way sth operates; **traiter le sujet sur le ~ comique/poétique** to treat the subject in a comic/poetic vein; **2** Ling mood; **3** Mus, Ordinat, Philos mode.

II *nf* **1** (en matière d'habillement, d'idées) fashion; **c'est la ~** it's the fashion; **c'est une ~** it's a trend; **lancer une ~** to start a trend; **une ~ passagère** a fad; **c'est passé de ~** it's gone out of fashion; **elle suit/ne suit pas la ~** she follows/ignores fashion; **s'habiller à la dernière ~** to wear the latest fashions; **la ~ des cheveux longs/mini-jupes** the fashion for long hair/mini-skirts; **la ~ est aux cheveux courts** short hair is in fashion; **c'était une ~** it was fashionable; **~ masculine/féminine** men's/women's fashion; **coupe/coloris ~** fashionable cut/colour[GB]; **à la ~** (qui fait la mode) [*vêtement, style*] fashionable, in fashion; [*thème, personnage*] in fashion; (qui suit la mode) [*vêtement, personne*] fashionable; [*jeune*] fashionable, trendy; (populaire) [*romancier*] who is in vogue (*épith, après n*); [*chanteur*] popular; **c'est très à la ~ d'être végétarien** it's very fashionable to be a vegetarian; **la ~ est à la cuisine végétarienne** vegetarian cooking is all the rage ou is in fashion; **2** (secteur d'activité) fashion industry; **travailler dans la ~** to work in the fashion industry ou business; **présentation de ~** fashion show.

■ **~ dialogué** Ordinat conversational mode; **~ d'emploi** (de machine) instructions (*pl*) ou directions (*pl*) for use; (de plat cuisiné) cooking instructions (*pl*).

modelage /mɔdlaʒ/ *nm* **1** (activité) modelling; **le ~ de la cire** wax modelling; **faire du ~** to make models; **2** (objet) model; **un ~ en cire** a wax model.

modèle /mɔdɛl/ **I** *adj* [*employé, mari, usine, prison*] model (*épith*); [*conduite*] perfect, exemplary; **fermes ~s** model farms.
II *nm* **1** (exemple) example; **suivre un ~** to follow an example; **offrir un ~ d'intégration** to be an example of integration; **servir de ~ à qn/qch** to serve as an example for sb/sth; **prendre ~ sur qn** to do as sb does/did, to do like sb; **sur le ~ américain** on the American model; **être un ~ de clarté** to be a model of clarity; **~ à suivre** (personne) somebody to look up to; **c'est un ~ à ne pas suivre** (personne) he's/she's not a good role model; **2** Comm, Ind (type) model; (taille) size; **choisir la couleur, la taille et le ~** to select the colour[GB], size and model; **le dernier ~** the latest model; **~ sport/de luxe/standard** sports/de luxe/standard model; **grand/petit ~** large-/small-size (*épith*); **~ familial** family-size (*épith*); **le grand ~ de tente, la tente grand ~** the large-size tent; **le ~ au-dessus** (en taille) the next size up; (en prix) the more expensive version; **construit sur le même ~** built to the same design; **3** Cout, Mode (création) model; (type d'article) style; **essaie ce ~** try this style; **4** (échantillon) **~ de signature** specimen signature; **compléter selon le ~** Scol do the exercise following the example; **5** ▶510 Art, Phot (personne) model; **6** (système) model; **~ éducatif/de société** educational/social model; **sortir du ~ bureaucratique** to break out of the bureaucratic mould GB ou mold US; **7** Sci (structure formalisée) model; **~ économique/transformationnel** economic/transformational model; **8** (reproductible) pattern; **~ de conjugaison/déclinaison** conjugation/declension pattern; **~ de tricot** knitting pattern; **9** Ind, Tech (objet à reproduire) model.
■ **~ déposé** Jur registered pattern; **~ réduit** scale model; **~ réduit d'avion** model plane.

modelé, **~e** /mɔdle/ **I** *pp* ▶ **modeler**.
II *pp adj* **bien ~** [*corps, jambe*] shapely; [*visage*] finely-sculpted.
III *nm* **1** Art, Géog relief; **2** (de visage, corps) contours (*pl*).

modeler /mɔdle/ [17] **I** *vtr* **1** (façonner) to model [*argile, pâte*]; to model [*statue, figurine*] (**dans** in, out of); to style [*chevelure*]; to shape, to mould GB ou mold US [*individu, esprit, caractère*]; **l'érosion a modelé le paysage** the landscape has been shaped by erosion; **2** (copier) **~ sa conduite sur** to model one's behaviour[GB] on.
II se modeler *vpr* to model oneself (**sur** on).

modeleur, **-euse** /mɔdlœʀ, øz/ ▶510 *nm,f* **1** (artiste) model-maker; **2** (ouvrier) pattern maker.

modélisation /mɔdelizasjɔ̃/ *nf* modelling.

modéliser /mɔdelize/ [1] *vtr* to model.

modélisme /mɔdelism/ *nm* modelling, model-making.

modéliste /mɔdelist/ ▶510 *nmf* **1** (de vêtements) (dress) designer; **2** (de maquettes) model-maker.

modem /mɔdɛm/ *nm* modem.

Modène /mɔdɛn/ ▶857 *npr* Modena.

modérateur, **-trice** /mɔdeʀatœʀ, tʀis/ **I** *adj* moderating (*épith*).
II *nm,f* fig (personne) moderating influence; (fonction) moderator.
III *nm* Nucl moderator.

modération /mɔdeʀasjɔ̃/ *nf* **1** (sens de la mesure) moderation; **avec ~** in moderation; **faire preuve de ~ dans** to show moderation in; **plein de ~** very moderate; **2** (de prix, taxe) reduction; **3** (de peine, règle) mitigation.

modéré, **~e** /mɔdeʀe/ **I** *adj* [*personne, parti, candidat*] moderate (**dans** in); [*vent, vitesse, usage, parole*] moderate; [*prix*] reasonable; [*tempérament*] even; [*enthousiasme*] mild.
II *nm,f* moderate.

modérément /mɔdeʀemɑ̃/ *adv* **1** (moyennement) relatively; **2** (avec retenue) in moderation; **3** (légèrement) slightly.

modérer /mɔdeʀe/ [14] **I** *vtr* to curb [*dépenses, ambition, sentiments, désirs*]; to soften [*attitude, politique*]; to moderate [*propos, langage, critiques*]; to reduce [*vitesse*]; to dim [*éclat de lampe*].
II se modérer *vpr* to exercise self-restraint (**dans** in); **modère-toi!** show some self-restraint!

moderne /mɔdɛʀn/ *adj* (tous contextes) modern; **je n'aime pas le (mobilier) ~** I don't like modern furniture.

modernisateur, **-trice** /mɔdɛʀnizatœʀ, tʀis/ *adj, nm,f* progressive.

modernisation /mɔdɛʀnizasjɔ̃/ *nf* modernization.

moderniser /mɔdɛʀnize/ [1] **I** *vtr* to modernize [*institution, secteur, matériel*]; to update [*loi, manuel*].
II se moderniser *vpr* to be modernized, to be brought up to date.

modernisme /mɔdɛʀnism/ *nm* **1** (goût) modernity; **2** (mouvement) modernism.

moderniste /mɔdɛʀnist/ **I** *adj* modernistic.
II *nmf* modernist.

modernité /mɔdɛʀnite/ *nf* modernity.

modern style /mɔdɛʀnstil/ *nm inv* Art Deco style.

modeste /mɔdɛst/ *adj* **1** (peu important) [*investissement, budget, conquête, palmarès*] modest; [*facture, coût*] moderate; [*revenu, somme*] modest; **2** (sans faste) [*appartement, immeuble*] modest; **3** (socialement) [*famille, milieu*] humble; **4** (sans vanité) modest; **un homme ~ et discret** a modest and discreet man; **avoir le triomphe ~** to be modest about one's success.

modestement /mɔdɛstəmɑ̃/ *adv* **1** (sans superflu) modestly, simply; **être ~ logé** to be in cheap accommodation; **être ~ vêtu** to be wearing cheap clothes; **2** (sans orgueil) modestly.

modestie /mɔdɛsti/ *nf* **1** (absence d'orgueil) modesty; **fausse ~** false modesty; **2** (pauvreté) modesty.

modicité /mɔdisite/ *nf* lowness; **la ~ de leurs revenus** their low income; **la ~ des prix** the low prices.

modifiable /mɔdifjabl/ *adj* modifiable.

modificateur, **-trice** /mɔdifikatœʀ, tʀis/ **I** *adj* modifying (*épith*).
II *nm* modifier.
■ **~ de focale** Phot converter lens.

modificatif, **-ive** /mɔdifikatif, iv/ **I** *adj* **1** Ling modifying; **2** Admin **texte ~** amendment.
II *nm* Admin amendment.

modification /mɔdifikasjɔ̃/ *nf* modification; **apporter une ~ à qch** to add a modification to sth; **faire des ~s à** to modify, to make modifications to; **adopter un projet de loi sans ~/avec des ~s** to pass a bill unamended/with amendments.

modifier /mɔdifje/ [2] **I** *vtr* gén to change; Tech to alter, to modify [*moteur, système*]; Pol to amend [*projet de loi*]; Ling to modify.
II se modifier *vpr* to change, to alter.

modique /mɔdik/ *adj* [*somme, ressources*] modest.

modiste /mɔdist/ ▶510 *nf* milliner.

modulable /mɔdylabl/ *adj* [*format, prélèvement*] adjustable; [*salle*] multi-purpose; [*horaire*] flexible.

modulaire /mɔdylɛʀ/ *adj* modular.

modulateur, **-trice** /mɔdylatœʀ, tʀis/ **I** *adj* modulation (*épith*).
II *nm,f* modulator.

modulation /mɔdylasjɔ̃/ *nf* **1** Phys, Radio modulation; **2** (flexibilité) flexibility; **3** (adaptation) adjustment.
■ **~ de fréquence**, **MF** frequency modulation, FM; **être sur ~ de fréquence** to be on FM; **poste à ~ de fréquence** FM radio.

module /mɔdyl/ *nm* **1** (élément d'assemblage) module; (pour cuisine) unit; **2** (véhicule) module; **3** (étalon de mesure) module; **4** Math, Phys modulus; **5** Univ module.

moduler /mɔdyle/ [1] **I** *vtr* **1** to modulate [*voix, son, couleurs*]; **elle modulait une berceuse** she sweetly sang a lullaby; **2** (adapter) to adjust [*prix*]; to adapt [*politique*]; **3** Radio, Télécom to modulate.
II *vi* to modulate.

modus vivendi /mɔdysvivɛ̃di/ *nm inv* modus vivendi.

moelle /mwal/ *nf* **1** Anat marrow; **transi jusqu'à la ~** fig frozen to the marrow; **sucer qn jusqu'à la moelle** fig to suck sb dry; **2** Culin marrow; **3** Bot pith; **4** (quintessence) marrow.
■ **~ épinière** spinal cord; **~ osseuse** bone marrow; **greffe de ~ osseuse** bone marrow transplant.

moelleusement /mwaløzmɑ̃/ *adv* [*installé*] snugly; [*étendu*] luxuriously.

moelleux, **-euse** /mwalø, øz/ **I** *adj* **1** [*tissu, tapis*] thick; [*lit, vêtement*] soft; [*nid*] cosy GB, cozy US; **2** [*vin*] mellow; [*dessert*] smooth; [*viande*] tender; **3** [*voix*] mellifluous; **4** [*ligne, touche*] fluid; [*couleur, ton*] soft; **5**† [*courbe du corps*] soft; [*formes, épaules*] softly rounded.
II *nm* **1** (de tissu, voix, couleur, courbe) softness; **2** (de vin) mellowness; (de viande) tenderness; (de dessert) smoothness; **3** (de voix) mellifluousness.

moellon /mwalɔ̃/ *nm* Constr stone; **~ creux** cavity block, breeze block.

mœurs /mœʀ(s)/ *nfpl* **1** (usages) (d'époque, de pays, peuple) customs, mores sout; (de milieu social) lifestyle (*sg*); **les ~ de la bourgeoisie/des banlieusards** the bourgeois/suburban lifestyle; **entrer dans les ~** [*usage, pratique*] to become part of everyday life; **il faut vivre avec les ~ de son temps** you've got to move with the times; **roman/comédie de ~** Littérat novel/comedy of manners; **l'évolution des ~** the change in attitudes; **les ~ politiques** political practices; **2** (habitudes de conduite) habits; **avoir des ~ austères/simples** to have austere/simple habits, to have an austere/a simple lifestyle; **les ~ des renards** the habits of foxes; **3** (moralité) morals; **des ~ relâchées** or **dissolues** loose morals; **avoir des ~ irréprochables** to have the highest moral standards; **leur conduite est contraire aux bonnes ~** their behaviour[GB] is not in keeping with good moral standards; **la police des ~, les Mœurs**○ the vice squad; **une sordide affaire de ~** a sordid sex case; ▶ **adoucir**.
IDIOMES **autres temps, autres ~** other days, other ways.

mohair /mɔɛʀ/ *nm* mohair; **de** or **en ~** mohair (*épith*); **laine ~** mohair.

moi[1] /mwa/ *pron pers* **1** (sujet) **~ qui aime tant le chocolat, je ne peux plus en manger** I, who love chocolate so much, can't eat it any more; **c'est ~** (au téléphone) it's me; **'j'ai faim'—'~ aussi'** 'I'm hungry'—'me too', 'so am I'; **'qui a cassé le vase?'—'~!/pas ~!'** 'who broke the vase?'—'I did!/I didn't!', 'me!/not me!'; **'est-ce toi qui as mon livre?'—'non, ce n'est pas ~'** 'have you got my book?'—'no, I haven't'; **'qui veut partir à pied?'—'~!'** 'who wants to go on foot?'—'me!', 'I do!'; **c'est ~ qui ai cassé la vitre** I was the one who broke the windowpane; **mes collègues et ~ sommes heureux de faire** my colleagues and I are happy to do; **~, je ne dis rien** I'm not saying anything; **mon amie et ~ avons décidé de nous marier** my girlfriend and I have decided to get married; **'je**

moins[1]

Généralités

La traduction en anglais de *moins* est *less*. Cependant, elle n'est utilisée que dans un nombre de cas assez restreint:

en moins de trois jours = in less than three days

Très souvent, même quand une traduction avec *less* est possible, l'anglais a recours à d'autres moyens. Certains sont réguliers:

ma chambre est moins grande que la tienne = my bedroom isn't as big as yours
j'ai moins d'expérience que toi = I don't have as much experience as you (do) *ou* I have less experience than you (do)
c'est moins compliqué que vous ne le croyez = it's not as complicated as you think *ou* it's less complicated than you think

D'autres ne le sont pas:

j'essaie de moins fumer = I'm trying to cut down on my smoking *ou* I'm trying to smoke less

moins de

Lorsque *moins de*, déterminant indéfini, est suivi d'un nom dénombrable, la règle voudrait que l'on traduise par *fewer* mais dans la langue parlée on utilise également *less*.

Les expressions *le moins possible*, *le moins du monde* sont traitées respectivement sous ***possible*** et ***monde***.

On trouvera ci-dessous exemples et exceptions illustrant les différentes fonctions de *moins*.

On pourra également se reporter aux notes d'usage portant notamment sur ***les quantités***, l'expression de ***l'âge*** etc. Consulter l'index ▶ **1920**.

n'aime pas ça!'—'~ non plus' 'I don't like that!'—'neither do I', 'me neither'; **2** (dans une comparaison) **il travaille plus que ~** he works more than me ou than I do; **elle est plus âgée que ~** she's older than me ou than I am; **il les voit plus souvent que ~** (que je ne les vois) he sees them more often than I do; (qu'il ne me voit) he sees them more often than me ou than he sees me; **3** (objet direct) me; **pince-~, je rêve** pinch me, I'm dreaming; **crois-~, ce n'est pas facile** believe me, it's not easy; **frappe-~ si tu l'oses** hit me if you dare; **4** (après une préposition) me; **à cause de/autour de/après ~** because of/around/after me; **un cadeau pour ~** a present for me; **pour ~ il est fou** personally, I think he's mad; **il ne pense pas à ~** he doesn't think of me; **elle n'écrit à personne sauf à ~** she doesn't write to anyone but me; **sans ~ ils n'auraient jamais terminé** they would never have finished without me; **passe-~ le sel** pass me the salt; **téléphone-~** phone me; **à ~** (à l'aide) help!; (à mon tour) (it's) my turn!; **des amis à ~** friends of mine; **je n'ai pas de coin à ~ dans la maison** I haven't got a room of my own in the house; **à ~, elle a raconté une histoire très différente** she told me quite a different story; **la tasse bleue est à ~** the blue cup is mine; **c'est à ~** (appartenance) it's mine, it belongs to me; (tour) it's my turn; **c'est à ~ de faire la vaisselle** it's my turn to do the dishes; **c'est à ~ de choisir** (mon tour) it's my turn to choose; (ma responsabilité) it's up to me to choose.

moi[2] /mwa/ *nm* **1** Psych **le ~** the self; **2**○ **le vrai ~** the real me.

moignon /mwaɲɔ̃/ *nm* stump.

moi-même /mwamɛm/ *pron pers* myself; **je l'ai fait ~** I did it myself; **j'exclus pour ~ un déplacement à l'étranger** personally I have no intention of going abroad; **en ~ je me disais que ça n'avait pas d'importance** I told myself that it didn't matter; **étant ~ agriculteur** being a farmer myself.

moindre /mwɛ̃dʀ/ *adj* **1** (comparatif) lesser; **événements/sociétés de ~ importance** events/companies of lesser importance; **dans une ~ mesure** to a lesser extent; **considérer qch comme un ~ mal** to consider sth as the lesser of two evils; **à ~ prix** more cheaply; **2** (superlatif) **le ~** the least (**de, des** of); **il n'y a pas le ~ doute là-dessus** there isn't the least ou slightest doubt about it; **c'est le ~ de mes soucis** that's the least of my worries; **la générosité n'est pas la ~ de ses qualités** generosity is not the least of his/her qualities; **c'est la ~ des choses** it's the least I could do; **ce serait la ~ des politesses de répondre à leur lettre** you could at least have the courtesy to reply to their letter; **ils n'ont pas fait la ~ remarque/le ~ effort** they didn't make the slightest remark/the slightest effort; **je n'ai pas la ~ intention de faire** I haven't the slightest intention of doing; **je n'ai pas la ~ idée de l'endroit où j'ai mis mes clés** I haven't the slightest idea where I put my keys; **je n'en ai pas la ~ idée** I haven't got the slightest idea ou a clue○; **de nombreux scientifiques, et non des ~s, ont critiqué l'expérience** many scientists, and highly respected ones at that, have criticized the experiment; **il cumule plusieurs fonctions dont la ~ n'est pas celle de maire** he combines various duties, not least of which is that of mayor; **dernier point à souligner et non des ~s** last but not least.

moine /mwan/ *nm* **1** Relig monk; **2** Zool (phoque) monk seal; (vautour) black vulture; (macareux) puffin; **3** (chauffe-lit) bedwarmer.

IDIOMES **l'habit ne fait pas le ~** Prov you can't judge a book by its cover, appearances can be deceptive.

moineau, *pl* **~x** /mwano/ *nm* **1** (oiseau) sparrow; **2**○ fig (individu) **vilain ~** pej dirty crook.

IDIOMES **il a une tête** or **cervelle de ~** he is a featherbrain.

moinillon /mwanijɔ̃/ *nm* young monk.

moins[1] /mwɛ̃/ **I** *prép* **1** (dans une soustraction) minus; **8 ~ 3 égale 5** 8 minus 3 is ou equals 5; **il a retrouvé sa voiture, ~ les roues** he got his car back without ou minus hum the wheels; **2** (pour dire l'heure) to; **il est huit heures ~ dix** it's ten (minutes) to eight; **il est ~ vingt**○ it's twenty to○, it's twenty minutes to the hour; **il était ~ une**○ or **~ cinq**○ it was a close shave○; **3** (dans une température) minus; **il faisait ~ 15 degrés** it was minus 15 (degrees).

II *adv* **1** (modifiant un verbe) (comparatif) less; (superlatif) **le ~** the least; **je lis ~ ces derniers temps** I read less these days; **ils sortent ~ maintenant qu'ils ont un enfant** they don't go out as much or they go out less often now that they have a child; **il importe ~ de changer le règlement que de le faire appliquer** changing the rule is less important than implementing it; **je gagne ~ qu'elle** I earn less than she does, I don't earn as much as she does; **c'est ~ un artiste qu'un bon artisan** he's not so much an artist as a good craftsman; **c'est ~ une question d'argent qu'une question de principe** it's not so much a question of money as a question of principle; **de ~ en ~** less and less; **~ je sors, ~ j'ai envie de sortir** the less I go out, the less I feel like going out; **~ je le vois, mieux je me porte** the less I see him, the better I feel; **c'est lui qui travaille le ~ de tous** he's the one who works the least of all; **le film qui m'a le ~ plu** the film I liked the least; **ce que j'aime le ~ chez lui** what I like least about him; **2** (modifiant un adjectif) (comparatif) less; (superlatif) **le ~, la ~, les ~** (de deux) the less; (de plus de deux) the least; **il est ~ grand/doué que son père** he's not as tall/gifted as his father; **c'est ~ facile qu'il n'y paraît** it's not as easy as it seems; **il est ~ menteur que sa sœur** he's less of a liar than his sister; **c'est ~ problématique que je ne croyais** it's less problematic ou less of a problem than I thought, it's not as problematic as I thought; **les jeunes et les ~ jeunes** the young and the not so young; **dans le livre il y a du bon et du ~ bon** in the book, there are bits that are good and bits that are not so good; **il n'en est pas ~ vrai que** it's nonetheless true that; **il ressemble à son frère en ~ gros** he looks like his brother, only thinner; **ce sont les employés les ~ compétents de l'entreprise** they're the least competent employees in the company; **un individu des ~ recommandables** a most unsavoury individual; **3** (modifiant un adverbe) (comparatif) less; (superlatif) **le ~** least; **tu devrais rester ~ longtemps dans le sauna** you shouldn't stay so long in the sauna; **elle chante ~ bien qu'avant** she doesn't sing as well as she used to; **il fait ~ beau que l'an dernier** the weather isn't as good as it was last year; **c'est le ~ bien payé des deux** he's the less well-paid of the two; **le ~ souvent** (the) least often.

III moins de *dét indéf* **1** (avec un nom dénombrable) **~ de livres/d'assiettes/d'arguments** fewer books/plates/arguments; **j'ai ~ de livres que toi** I don't have as many books as you ou I have fewer books than you; **mangez ~ de graisses** eat less fat; **il y a ~ de candidats** there are fewer candidates; **ils ont ~ de chances d'être élus** they are less likely to be elected; **les éditeurs publient ~ de livres** publishers are publishing fewer books; **pas ~ de** no fewer than; **2** (avec un nom non dénombrable) **~ de sucre/vin/papier** less sugar/wine/paper; **~ de bruit/lumière** less noise/light; **il a parlé avec ~ de hargne** he spoke less aggressively; **il y a ~ de monde aujourd'hui qu'hier** there are fewer people today than there were yesterday; **pas ~ de** no less than; **c'est lui qui a le ~ d'expérience des trois** of the three he's the one with the least experience; **3** (avec un numéral) **en ~ de trois heures** in less than three hours; **dans ~ de trois heures** in less than three hours; **le voyage a duré un peu ~ de trois heures** the journey took a bit less than ou just under three hours; **il est ~ de 3 heures** it's not quite 3 o'clock; **les enfants de ~ de 6 ans** children under 6; **les ~ de 20 ans** people under 20, the under-twenties; **une planche de ~ de deux m ètres de long** a plank less than two metres[GB] long; **~ de huit candidats** fewer than eight candidates; **tu ne trouveras rien à ~ de 500 francs** you won't find anything for less than 500 francs ou for under 500 francs; **ça m'a coûté ~ de 200 francs** it cost me less than 200 francs ou under 200 francs.

IV à moins *loc adv* **on serait furieux à ~** it's more than enough to make one angry.

V à moins de *loc prép* **à ~ de partir maintenant, il n'arrivera pas à l'heure** unless he leaves now he won't get there on time; **à ~ d'un miracle il va échouer** unless there's a miracle, he's going to fail.

VI à moins que *loc conj* **à ~ qu'il ne veuille venir** unless he wants to come.

VII à tout le moins *loc adv* to say the least.

VIII au moins *loc adv* at least; **tout au**

Les mois de l'année

Les noms des mois

L'anglais emploie la majuscule pour les noms de mois. Les abréviations sont courantes en anglais familier écrit, par ex. dans une lettre à un ami: I'll see you on Mon 17 Sept.

		abréviation anglaise
janvier	January	Jan
février	February	Feb
mars	March	Mar
avril	April	Apr
mai	May	May
juin	June	Jun
juillet	July	Jul
août	August	Aug
septembre	September	Sept
octobre	October	Oct
novembre	November	Nov
décembre	December	Dec

Dans les expressions suivantes, May *est pris comme exemple. Tous les autres noms de mois s'utilisent de la même façon.*

mai a été pluvieux = May was wet

L'anglais peut utiliser les noms de mois même là où le français a recours à l'expression le mois de ...

j'aime le mois de mai = I like May
le mois de mai le plus chaud = the warmest May
nous avons eu un beau mois de mai = we had a lovely May

Quand?

Pour l'expression de la date, **▶ 212**.

nous sommes en mai = it is May

Avec les autres verbes que be *(*être*), en se traduit normalement par* in.

en mai = in May *or* (*littéraire*) in the month of May

je suis né en mai = I was born in May
je te verrai en mai = I'll see you in May
l'an prochain en mai = in May next year

Noter aussi:

cette année-là en mai = that May
en mai prochain = next May
l'année dernière en mai = last May
dans deux ans en mai = the May after next
il y a deux ans en mai = the May before last
tous les ans en mai = every May
tous les deux ans en mai = every other May
presque tous les ans en mai = most Mays

Comparer:

un matin en mai = one morning in May
un matin de mai = one May morning *ou* on a May morning
début mai = in early May
au début de mai = at the beginning of May
fin mai = in late May
à la fin de mai = at the end of May
à la mi-mai = in mid-May
depuis mai = since May
pendant tout le mois de mai = for the whole of May *ou* for the whole month of May
tout au long du mois de mai = all through May *ou* throughout May

De avec les noms de mois

Les expressions françaises avec de *se traduisent par l'emploi du nom de mois en position d'adjectif.*

les fleurs de mai = May flowers
la pluie du mois de mai = the May rain
le soleil du mois de mai = the May sunshine
le temps du mois de mai = May weather
les soldes du mois de mai = the May sales

~ at least; **il y avait au ~ 3 000 personnes** there were at least 3,000 people; **au ~, lui, il a réussi dans la vie** he, at least, succeeded in life; **tu l'as remercié, au ~?** you did thank him, didn't you?

IX de moins *loc adv* **ça m'a pris deux heures de ~** it took me two hours less; **le kilo de pêches valait deux francs de ~ que la veille** a kilo of peaches cost two francs less than it had the day before; **j'ai un an de ~ que lui** I'm a year younger than he is; **il a obtenu 25% de voix de ~ que son adversaire** he got 25% fewer votes than his opponent.

X du moins *loc adv* at least; **c'est du ~ ce qu'il m'a raconté** at least that's what he told me; **si du ~ tu es d'accord** that is if you agree.

XI en moins *loc adv* **il y avait deux fourchettes en ~ dans la boîte** there were two forks missing from the box; **il est revenu du front avec une jambe en ~/avec un doigt en ~** he came back from the front with only one leg/with a finger missing; **c'est tout le portrait de son père, la moustache en ~** he's/she's the spitting image of his/her father without the moustache GB ou mustache US.

XII pour le moins *loc adv* to say the least; **ton attitude est pour le ~ étrange** your attitude is strange to say the least (of it).

moins² /mwɛ̃/ *nm* **1** Math minus; **le signe ~** the minus sign; **2**° (inconvénient) minus.
■ **~ que rien** *nmf* good-for-nothing, nobody.

moins-value, *pl* **~s** /mwɛ̃valy/ *nf* **1** (diminution de valeur) depreciation; **2** (déficit des recettes fiscales) shortfall.

moirage /mwaʀaʒ/ *nm* **1** (activité) (de tissu) moiréing; (de papier, soie) watering; **2** (aspect) (d'un tissu) moiré; (de papier, soie) watered effect.

moire /mwaʀ/ *nf* **1** (étoffe) moire; **2** (procédé) (de tissu) moiréing; (de soie) watering; **3** (aspect) (d'un tissu) moiré; (de la soie) watered effect; **4** (reflet) (de tissu, d'eau) shimmer; (de métal) glisten.

moiré, ~e /mwaʀe/ **I** *adj* [*tissu*] moiré; [*soie, papier*] watered; [*eau, vêtement*] shimmering; [*métal, bijou*] glistening.

II *nm* **1** (de tissu) moiré; (de soie) watered appearance; **2** (de l'eau) shimmer; (de métal) glisten.

moirer /mwaʀe/ [1] **I** *vtr* **1** to moiré [*tissu*]; to water [*soie, papier*]; **2** littér to make [sth] shimmer [*eau*]; to make [sth] glisten [*métal, parquet*] (**de** with).

II se moirer *vpr* littér [*surface mouvante*] to shimmer; [*surface immobile*] to glisten.

moirure /mwaʀyʀ/ *nf* **1** (de tissu) moiré ¢; **2** littér (d'eau) shimmering ¢; (de métal, bijou) glistening ¢.

mois /mwa/ **▶ 17**, **801** *nm inv* **1** (division de l'année) month; **le livre/disque du ~** the book/record of the month; **le ~ dernier/prochain** last/next month; **au ~ de juin** in June; **faire un stage de six ~** to do a six-month training course; **un bébé de trois ~** a three-month-old baby; **il a trois ~** he's three months old; **elle est enceinte de trois ~** she's three months pregnant; **il a mis des ~ à s'en remettre** it took him months to recover; **gagner 8 000 francs par ~** to earn 8,000 francs a month; **il y a cinq ~ de cela** that was five months ago; **il y a un ~ qu'il travaille** he has been working for a month; **c'est dans un ~** it's in a month('s time); **à moins de deux ~ du premier tour** with the first round less than two months away; **louer au ~** to rent by the month; **2** (salaire) monthly salary.
■ **~ civil** calendar month; **~ légal** thirty days; **~ lunaire** lunar month; **~ de Marie** month of Mary; **~ solaire** solar month.
IDIOMES **tous les 36 du ~**° once in a blue moon°.

moïse /mɔiz/ *nm* Moses basket GB, bassinet US.

Moïse /mɔiz/ *npr* Bible Moses.

moisi, ~e /mwazi/ **I** *pp* **▶ moisir**.

II *pp adj* [*aliment*] mouldy GB, moldy US; [*objet, plante*] mildewed; **le pâté est complètement ~** the pâté has gone completely mouldy GB ou moldy US.

III *nm* mould GB, mold US; **odeur/goût de ~** musty smell/taste; **sentir le ~** to smell musty.

moisir /mwaziʀ/ [3] *vi* **1** [*aliment*] to go mouldy GB ou moldy US; [*objet, plante*] to become mildewed; **2**° (stagner) [*personne*] to stagnate; [*argent, objet*] to gather dust; **bon, on va pas ~ ici**° right, we're not going to hang around here all day!

moisissure /mwazisyʀ/ *nf* (sur des aliments, du bois) mould ¢ GB, mold ¢ US; (sur des meubles, tapis, plantes) mildew ¢; **odeur de ~** musty smell; **des murs couverts de ~s** walls covered in patches of mildew.

moisson /mwasɔ̃/ *nf* **1** Agric (activité, produits récoltés) harvest; (époque) harvest time; **faire la ~** or **les ~s** to harvest; **2** fig haul (**de** of); **une ~ de prix** a haul of prizes.

moissonner /mwasɔne/ [1] *vtr* **1** Agric to harvest; **2** fig to gather [*renseignements*]; to amass [*documents*]; to reap [*récompenses*]; to win [*distinctions, médailles*].

moissonneur, -euse /mwasɔnœʀ, øz/ **I** *nm,f* (personne) harvester.

II moissonneuse *nf* (machine) reaper.

moissonneuse-batteuse, *pl* **moissonneuses-batteuses** /mwasɔnøzbatøz/ *nf* combine harvester.

moite /mwat/ *adj* **1** [*climat, chaleur*] muggy; **2** [*mur, objet*] damp; [*peau*] sweaty.

moiteur /mwatœʀ/ *nf* (de l'air) mugginess; (de la peau) sweatiness.

moitié /mwatje/ *nf* **1** gén half; **la ~ de qch** half of sth; **partager qch en deux ~s** to divide sth into two halves; **une ~ rouge et l'autre bleue** one half red and the other blue; **la première ~ du mois** the first half of the month; **il en a mangé plus/moins de la ~** he ate more/less than half of it ou them; **la ~ d'entre eux** half of them; **la peinture, c'est la ~ de ma vie** half of my life is devoted to painting; **à ~ vide/fou/convaincu** half empty/crazy/convinced; **dormir à ~**° to be half asleep; **vivre ~ à Paris, ~ à Nice** to spend half one's time in Paris and half in Nice; **dépenser ~ moins d'argent** to spend half as much money ou half the money; **vendre à ~ prix** to sell at half-price; **articles à ~ prix** half-price goods; **s'arrêter à la ~** to stop halfway through; **à ~ cassé** damaged; **raccourcir de ~** to shorten by half; **trop long de ~** too long by half; **c'est plus large/cher de ~** it's half as wide/expensive again; **je n'y crois qu'à ~** I don't entirely believe it; **il n'était pas qu'à ~ ivre**°! he wasn't half drunk°!; **ne pas faire les choses à ~** not to do things by halves; **il fait toujours les**

choses à ~ he never does anything properly; **être pour ~ dans qch** to be instrumental in sth; **partager les gains par ~** to split the profits; ▶ **pardonner**; **2**○ (époux) **ma ~** my better half○.

moitié-moitié /mwatjemwatje/ *adv* (en proportions égales) half-and-half; **'de l'eau dans votre pastis?'—'oui, ~'** 'do you like water in your pastis?'—'yes please, half-and-half'; **partager ~ avec qn** (dépense, cadeau) to go halves with sb; (gains) to split the profits with sb; **partager son temps ~ entre son travail et sa famille** to split one's time between work and family life.

moka /mɔka/ *nm* **1** (café) mocha; **2** (gâteau) mocha cake.

mol ▶ **mou** I.

molaire /mɔlɛʀ/ **I** *adj* Chimie molar.
II *nf* Dent molar.

molasse /mɔlas/ *nf* Géol molasse.

Moldau /mɔldo/ ▶**357**⌋ *nprf* Vltava.

moldave /mɔldav/ ▶**462**⌋, **537**⌋ **I** *adj* **1** Géog Moldovan; **2** Hist, Ling Moldavian.
II *nm* Ling Moldavian.

Moldave /mɔldav/ *nmf* **1** ▶**537**⌋ Géog Moldovan; **2** Hist Moldavian.

Moldavie /mɔldavi/ *nprf* **1** ▶**321**⌋ (pays) Moldova; **2** Hist Moldavia.

mole /mɔl/ *nf* Chimie mole.

môle /mol/ *nm* **1** (brise-lames) breakwater; **2** (pour s'amarrer) pier, jetty.
■ **~ de débarquement** landing pier ou jetty.

moléculaire /mɔlekylɛʀ/ *adj* molecular.

molécule /mɔlekyl/ *nf* molecule.

moleskine /mɔlɛskin/ *nf* **1** (imitant le cuir) imitation leather, Leatherette®; **2** (pour doublures) moleskin; **3** (de café) wall seat.

molester /mɔlɛste/ [1] *vtr* to manhandle, to rough up○.

moleté, ~e /mɔlte/ *adj* knurled.

molette /mɔlɛt/ *nf* **1** Tech (de clé) adjusting knob; (d'instrument optique) focusing knob; (pour découper) rotary cutter; (pour graver, ciseler) roulette; **2** (de briquet) striker wheel; **3** Équit (d'éperon) rowel.

mollard◑ /mɔlaʀ/ *nm* gob○ (of spit).

mollasse /mɔlas/ **I**○ *adj* pej **1** (physiquement) sluggish; **2** (moralement) soft.
II *nf* Géol molasse.

mollasson○**, -onne** /mɔlasɔ̃, ɔn/ **I** *adj* sluggish.
II *nm,f* **quel ~!** he's so slow!

molle ▶ **mou** I.

mollement /mɔlmɑ̃/ *adv* **1** (paresseusement) idly, nonchalantly; **2** (faiblement) [*travailler, acquiescer*] without much enthusiasm; [*protester, soutenir*] half-heartedly; [*démentir, répondre*] rather unconvincingly; [*frapper*] gently; **3** (doucement) [*tomber*] softly; [*couler*] gently.

mollesse /mɔlɛs/ *nf* **1** (caractère moelleux) softness; **2** (manque de tenue) (de chair) flabbiness; (de cheveux) limpness; (de trait du visage) weakness; **3** (apathie) (de personne, d'élève) listlessness; (de poignée de main) limpness; **~ d'une démarche** languid way of moving; **4** (manque d'autorité) **la ~ d'un père envers ses enfants** a father's soft treatment of his children; **la ~ de qn face à qn** sb's failure to stand up to sb; **il a réagi avec trop de ~ face à la crise** he was too soft in handling the crisis; **5** (manque de conviction) (de personne, réponse) lack of conviction; (d'idéologie) laxness; (d'idée, de style) woolliness; (d'opposition, interprétation, de discours) weakness; (de reprise, croissance) sluggishness.

mollet, -ette /mɔlɛ, ɛt/ **I** *adj* **1** [*lit*] soft; **2** [*œuf*] soft-boiled.
II ▶**188**⌋ *nm* calf; **des ~s de coq** legs like sticks; **avoir des ~s de cycliste** to have muscular calves.

molletière /mɔltjɛʀ/ **I** *adj f* **bande ~** puttee.
II *nf* legging.

molleton /mɔltɔ̃/ *nm* **1** (en laine) flannel; (en coton) flannelette; **2** (pour table) (table) felt; (pour planche à repasser) (ironing board) cover.

molletonner /mɔltɔne/ [1] *vtr* to line with fleece; **un blouson molletonné** a fleece-lined jacket.

mollir /mɔliʀ/ [3] *vi* **1** (céder) [*courage*] to fail; [*autorité*] to diminish; [*enthousiasme*] to cool; [*ténacité*] to flag; [*attention*] to wander; [*résistance*] to grow weaker; [*personne*] to relent, to soften; **2** Météo [*vent*] to die down, to abate; **3** (perdre sa force) [*genou*] to give way; [*bras*] to go weak; **~ de peur/fatigue** [*jambe, genou*] to go weak with fear/fatigue; **~ sous le poids de** [*jambe, genou*] to give way beneath the weight of; [*bras*] to go weak with the weight of.

mollo◑ /molo/ *adv* easy; **vas-y ~!** take it easy!; **vas-y ~ avec le vin!** go easy on the wine!

mollusque /mɔlysk/ *nm* **1** Zool mollusc GB, mollusk US; **2**○ (personne) drip○, wimp○.

molosse /mɔlɔs/ *nm* huge dog.

Molotov /mɔlɔtɔf/ *npr* Molotov; **cocktail ~** Molotov cocktail.

Moluques /mɔlyk/ ▶**416**⌋ *nprfpl* **îles ~** Moluccas.

molybdène /mɔlibdɛn/ *nm* molybdenum.

môme /mom/ **I**○ *nmf* (enfant) kid○; péj brat○.
II◑ *nf* girl; **une jolie ~** a pretty girl.

moment /mɔmɑ̃/ *nm* **1** (instant précis) moment; **au ~ décisif/crucial** at the decisive/crucial moment; **au dernier ~** at the last moment; **jusqu'au dernier ~** till the last moment; **à n'importe quel ~, à tout ~** at any time; **le ~ venu** (dans l'avenir) when the time comes; (dans le passé) when the time came; **il devrait arriver/ça devrait être prêt d'un ~ à l'autre** he should arrive/it should be ready any minute now; **à aucun ~ il n'a abordé le sujet** at no time did he touch on the subject; **cela a été évoqué à un ~ ou à un autre** it was mentioned at some time or other; **à un ~ donné** (quelconque) at some point; (fixé) at a given moment; **à quel ~ a-t-elle dit ça?** at what point did she say that?; **au même ~** at the same time; **sur le ~ j'ai cru qu'il plaisantait** at first ou to start with I thought he was joking; **à ce ~-là j'habitais à l'étranger** at that time I was living abroad; **à ce ~-là le téléphone a sonné** just then the phone rang; **à ce ~-là il vaut mieux que j'aille te chercher** in that case it's better if I come and pick you up; **au ~ de l'accident/de ta naissance** at the time of the accident/of your birth; **au ~ de sortir/poser la question il a changé d'avis** just as he was about to go out/ask the question he changed his mind; **au ~ où** gén at the time (when); **au ~ où il quittait son domicile** as he was leaving his home; **jusqu'au ~ où** until; **du ~ que** (pourvu que) as long as, provided; (puisque) since; **du ~ que tu le dis!** if you say so!; **à partir du ~ où tu es prêt** as soon as you are ready; (pourvu que) provided ou as long as you are ready; (puisque) since you are ready; **2** (temps bref) moment; **dans un ~** in a moment; **un ~, j'ai presque fini!** just a moment, I've nearly finished!; **ça ne prendra qu'un petit ~** it'll only take a moment; **elle n'a pas un ~ à elle** she hasn't got a moment to herself; **elle a parfois des ~s de lucidité** she has moments of lucidity; **j'ai eu un ~ d'affolement** I had a moment of panic; **j'ai eu un ~ d'incertitude** I hesitated for a moment; **3** (temps long) **j'en ai encore pour un ~** it'll take quite a while yet ou a while longer; **pour le ~** for the time being; **tu en as pour un ~ à avoir mal** you'll feel uncomfortable for quite some time; **ça va prendre un ~** it will take a while; **voilà déjà un (bon** or **petit) ~ que je les attends/je n'ai pas de leurs nouvelles** I've been waiting for them/I haven't heard from them for quite a while ou quite some time; **je ne l'ai pas vue depuis un ~** I haven't seen her for a while; **au bout d'un ~, après un ~** after a while; **4** (présent) **du ~** [*ennemi, préoccupations, célébrités*] of the moment; **en ce ~** at the moment; **pour le ~** for the moment; **savoir profiter du ~ présent** to live every moment to the full; **5** (période) **par ~s** at times; **c'est le ~ de la journée où** it's the time of day when; **nous avons vécu de bons ~s/des ~s difficiles ensemble** we've had some good times/difficult times together; **il y a des ~s où j'ai envie de tout laisser tomber** there are times when I want to give everything up; **les ~s forts du film** the film's highlights; **les ~s forts du match** the highlights of the match; **cela a été un ~ fort** (émouvant) it was a moment of intense emotion; **dans ses meilleurs ~s, il fait penser à Orson Welles** at his best, he reminds one of Orson Welles; **à mes ~s perdus** in my spare time; **les derniers ~s de qn** sb's last moments; **6** (instant propice) **pose la question, c'est le ~** go ahead and ask, now's the time!; **ce n'est pas le ~** gén it's not the right moment; (inopportun) now is not the time; **tu aurais dû demander, c'était le ~** you should have asked, the time was right; **~ favorable** or **propice** right moment; **il arrive toujours au bon** iron or **mauvais ~!** he certainly picks his moment to call! iron; **choisir son ~ pour faire** iron to pick one's moment to do iron; **7** Math moment; **8** Phys momentum.
■ **~ psychologique** psychological moment.

momentané, ~e /mɔmɑ̃tane/ *adj* [*affolement, dégoût, désaccord*] momentary; **apporter une aide ~e à qn** to give sb temporary assistance; **interruption ~e du son/de l'image** temporary loss of sound/of picture.

momentanément /mɔmɑ̃tanemɑ̃/ *adv* [*arrêter, hésiter, oublier*] for a moment, momentarily.

mômeries○ /momʀi/ *nfpl* childishness ¢; **arrête avec tes ~!** stop acting like a child!

momie /mɔmi/ *nf* mummy.

momification /mɔmifikasjɔ̃/ *nf* mummification.

momifier /mɔmifje/ [2] **I** *vtr* to mummify.
II se momifier *vpr* to mummify.

mon, ma, *pl* **mes** /mɔ̃, ma, me/ *adj poss*

■ **Note** Au vocatif, on n'emploie généralement pas le possessif en anglais: *ma chérie!* = darling!; *merci, mon Père!* = thank you, Father!; *oui mon général!* yes, sir!; *mes chers amis!* = dear friends! On ne répète pas le possessif coordonné: *mon café et mon cognac* = my coffee and cognac.

my; **mes chaussures** my shoes; **~ imbécile de mari**○ my stupid husband; **ma mère à moi**○ my mother; **un de mes amis** a friend of mine; **j'ai ~ idée** I have my own ideas about that; **j'ai ma migraine** I've got one of my headaches; **à ~ arrivée/départ** when I arrived/left; **pendant ~ absence** while I was away; **j'ai ~ lundi** (cette semaine) I'm off on Monday; (toutes les semaines) I have Mondays off; **je te réserve ~ lundi** I'll keep Monday free for you.

monacal, ~e, *mpl* **-aux** /mɔnakal, o/ *adj* lit, fig monastic.

Monaco /mɔnako/ ▶**321**⌋, **857**⌋ *npr* Monaco.

monade /mɔnad/ *nf* monad.

monarchie /mɔnaʀʃi/ *nf* monarchy; **~ constitutionnelle** constitutional monarchy.

monarchique /mɔnaʀʃik/ *adj* monarchical.

monarchisme /mɔnaʀʃism/ *nm* monarchism.

monarchiste /mɔnaʀʃist/ *adj, nmf* monarchist.

monarque /mɔnaʀk/ *nm* monarch; **~ de droit divin** monarch by divine right.

monastère /mɔnastɛʀ/ *nm* monastery.

monastique /mɔnastik/ *adj* monastic.

monceau, *pl* **~x** /mɔ̃so/ *nm* pile; **un ~ de ruines** a pile of rubble.

mondain, **~e** /mɔ̃dɛ̃, ɛn/ **I** *adj* **1** (dans la haute société) [*réception, vie*] society (*épith*); **conversation ~e** polite conversation; **2** (de la haute société) **il est très ~** he's a socialite.

II *nm,f* socialite.

III mondaine○ *nf* (brigade) vice squad.

mondanités /mɔ̃danite/ *nfpl* **1** (réceptions mondaines) society events; **2** (politesses) **se faire des ~** to stand on ceremony.

monde /mɔ̃d/ *nm* **1** (terre) world; **l'homme le plus grand/le plus riche du ~** the tallest/the wealthiest man in the world; **ce sont les meilleurs amis du ~** they are the best of friends; **expliquer le plus calmement/logiquement du ~ que** to explain quite calmly/logically that; **pas le moins du ~** not in the least ou slightest; **si vous êtes le moins du ~ soucieux** if you are (in) the least bit worried; **s'il souffrait le moins du ~** if he felt any pain at all ou the slightest pain; **se porter le mieux du ~** to be fine; **au ~** gén on earth, in the world; **personne/rien au ~ ne la fera changer d'avis** she won't change her mind for anybody/anything; **pour rien au ~ il ne raterait le match** he wouldn't miss the match for anything; **dans le ~ entier** all over the world; **à travers le ~** throughout the world; **aller** or **voyager de par le ~** liter, **parcourir le ~** to travel the world; **il irait jusqu'au bout du ~ pour la retrouver** he would go to the ends of the earth to find her again; **c'est le bout du ~!**, **c'est au bout du ~!** it's miles from anywhere!, it's in the back of beyond!; **mon père habite à l'autre bout du ~** my father lives halfway around the world; **ce n'est pas le bout du ~!** fig it's not such a big deal!; **comme le ~ est petit!** it's a small world!; ▶**métier**; **2** (société humaine) world; **la faim/paix dans le ~** world famine/peace; **être les premiers au ~ à faire** to be the first in the world to do; **vouloir refaire le ~** to want to change the world ; **être ouvert sur le ~** to be aware of what is going on in the world; **se retirer du ~** to withdraw from the world; **à la face du ~** for all the world to see; **3** (ici-bas) **les biens de ce ~** worldly goods; **en ce bas ~** here below; **l'autre ~** the next world, the world to come; **elle n'est plus de ce ~** euph she's no longer with us euph; **quand je ne serai plus de ce ~** euph when I have departed this world; **la perfection n'est pas de ce ~** there is no such thing as perfection; **le ~ des vivants** the land of the living; **je n'étais pas encore au ~** I wasn't yet born; ▶**grand**; **4** (microcosme, section) world; **le ~ du travail/des idées** the world of work/of ideas; **le ~ arabe/médical** the Arab/medical world; **le ~ libre** the free world; **le ~ moderne** the modern world; **le ~ animal** the animal kingdom; **ils ne sont pas du même ~** (milieu) they are from different social backgrounds; **c'est un ~ à part** it's a completely different world; **cet événement marqua la fin d'un ~** this event marked the end of an era; ▶**ancien**; **5** (gens) people; **il y a du ~** (une foule) there are a lot of people; (des gens) there's someone there; **de plus en plus de ~** more and more people; **il n'y a pas grand ~** there aren't many people; **tout le ~** everybody, everyone; **voir beaucoup de ~** to have a busy social life ; **j'ai du ~ ce soir**○ I'm having people round GB ou over US tonight; **elle se moque** or **se fout**● **du ~!** what does she take us for?; **tout mon petit ~** my family and friends (*pl*); **réunir tout son ~** (entourage) to get everyone together; **6** (bonne société) society; **sortir dans le ~** to go out into society; **le beau** or **grand ~** high society; **7** (écart) **il y a un ~ entre** there's a world of difference between; **un ~ nous sépare, il y a un ~ entre nous** we are worlds apart.

IDIOMES **mettre un enfant au ~** to bring a child into the world; **venir au ~** to come into the world; **se faire (tout) un ~ de qch** to get all worked up about sth; **ainsi va le ~** that's the way it goes; **depuis que le ~ est ~** since the beginning of time; **il faut de tout pour faire un ~** Prov it takes all sorts to make a world Prov; **c'est le ~ à l'envers!** the world's turned upside down!; **c'est un ~**○**!** that's a bit much!

monder /mɔ̃de/ [1] *vtr* to hull, to husk.

mondial, **~e**, *mpl* **-iaux** /mɔ̃djal, o/ *adj* [*tournoi, record, congrès, littérature, économie*] world (*épith*); [*problème, succès*] worldwide; **à l'échelle ~e** on a worldwide scale; **la capitale ~e du cinéma** the cinema capital of the world; **le numéro un ~ de l'édition** the world's top publishing house; **première/seconde guerre ~e** First/Second World War.

mondialement /mɔ̃djalmɑ̃/ *adv* **être ~ connu** to be known all over the world.

mondialisation /mɔ̃djalizasjɔ̃/ *nf* (de marché, sport, phénomène) globalization; **la ~ d'un conflit** the worldwide spread of a conflict.

mondialiser /mɔ̃djalize/ [1] **I** *vtr* to globalize [*marché, échanges*]; to cause [sth] to spread worldwide [*conflit*].

II se mondialiser *vpr* to become globalized.

mondialisme /mɔ̃djalism/ *nm* internationalism.

mondialiste /mɔ̃djalist/ *nmf* internationalist.

mondovision /mɔ̃dɔvizjɔ̃/ *nf* satellite broadcasting; **retransmettre en ~** to broadcast worldwide via satellite.

monégasque /monegask/ ▶**537** *adj* Monegasque.

Monégasque /monegask/ ▶**537** *nmf* Monegasque.

monème /mɔnɛm/ *nm* moneme.

monétaire /mɔnetɛʀ/ *adj* [*valeur, réserve, unité, système, stabilité*] monetary; [*marché, circulation*] money (*épith*).

monétarisme /mɔnetaʀism/ *nm* monetarism.

monétariste /mɔnetaʀist/ *adj, nmf* monetarist.

monétique /monetik/ *nf* electronic banking.

monétiser /mɔnetize/ [1] *vtr* to monetize.

mongol, **~e** /mɔ̃gɔl/ **I** ▶**537** *adj* Géog Mongolian; **l'empire ~** Hist the Mongol Empire.

II ▶**462** *nm* Ling Mongolian.

Mongol, **~e** /mɔ̃gɔl/ *nm,f* ▶**537** Mongolian.

Mongolie /mɔ̃gɔli/ ▶**321** *nprf* Mongolia; **la République populaire de ~** the Mongolian People's Republic.

Mongolie-Intérieure /mɔ̃gɔliɛ̃teʀjœʀ/ ▶**692** *nprf* Inner Mongolia.

mongolien, **-ienne** /mɔ̃gɔljɛ̃, ɛn/ controv **I** *adj* Méd [*traits, enfant*] Down's syndrome (*épith*); **être ~** to have Down's syndrome.

II *nm,f* Méd (enfant) Down's syndrome child.

mongolique /mɔ̃gɔlik/ *adj* Mongolian.

mongolisme /mɔ̃gɔlism/ *nm* controv Méd **le ~** Down's syndrome.

monisme /mɔnism/ *nm* monism.

moniste /mɔnist/ **I** *adj* monistic.

II *nmf* monist.

moniteur, **-trice** /mɔnitœʀ, tʀis/ **I** ▶**510** *nm,f* **1** (de sport, conduite) instructor; **~ de natation/d'aviation** swimming/flying instructor; **un ~ d'auto-école** a driving instructor; **2** (de colonie de vacances, centre aéré) group leader GB, counselor US; **3** Univ teaching assistant.

II *nm* TV monitor; Ordinat monitor system.

■ **~ cardiaque** heart monitor.

monitorage /mɔnitɔʀaʒ/ *nm* monitoring.

monitorat /mɔnitɔʀa/ *nm* Univ (activité) tutoring; (système) tutorial system.

monnaie /mɔnɛ/ *nf* **1** (unité monétaire) currency; **~ forte/faible** strong/weak currency; **ils se servent de jetons comme ~** they use tokens as currency; **fausse ~** forged ou counterfeit currency; ▶**singe**; **2** (pièces et billets de faible valeur) change; **petite** or **menue ~** small change; **faire de la ~** to get some change; **faire de la ~ à qn** to give sb (some) change; **il est allé faire la ~ de 100 francs** he went to get change for 100 francs; **est-ce que vous pouvez me faire la ~ de 10 francs?** can you give me change for 10 francs?; **passez** or **envoyez la ~**○**!** cough up the money○!; **3** (appoint) change; **garder/rendre la ~** to keep/give the change; **elle m'a rendu la ~ sur 100 francs au lieu de 200 francs** she gave me change from 100 francs instead of 200 francs; **4** (pièce) coin; **~ d'or/d'argent** gold/silver coin; **émettre/retirer une ~** to issue/withdraw a coin; **battre ~** to mint ou strike coins; **frapper une ~** to strike coins ou a coinage; **5** (bâtiment) **l'hôtel de la Monnaie, la Monnaie** the Mint; **6** Écon (argent) money.

■ **~ divisionnaire** fractional currency; **~ d'échange** Écon trading currency; fig bargaining chip; **les otages ont servi de ~ d'échange** the hostages were used as a bargaining chip; **~ fiduciaire** fiduciary currency, paper money; **~ légale** legal tender; **~ métallique** coin; **~ de papier** paper money; **~ de réserve** reserve currency.

IDIOMES **rendre à qn la ~ de sa pièce** to give sb a dose of his/her own medicine, to pay sb back in his/her own coin; **c'est ~ courante** it's commonplace.

monnaie-du-pape, *pl* **monnaies-du-pape** /mɔnɛdypap/ *nf* Bot honesty.

monnayable /mɔnɛjabl/ *adj* **1** [*bon, billet*] convertible; **2** [*diplôme, talent*] marketable.

monnayer /mɔnɛje/ [21] *vtr* **1** lit to convert [sth] into cash; **2** fig to capitalize on [*talent, expérience*]; **~ qch contre qch** to exchange sth for sth; **~ son silence/accord** to exact a price for one's silence/agreement; **3** Tech to mint [*or, pièce*].

mono /mono/ **I** *adj inv* (*abbr* = **monophonique**) mono (*épith*).

II○ *nmf*: *abbr* = **moniteur I 2**.

III○ *nm*: *abbr* = **monoski**.

IV *nf* (*abbr* = **monophonie**) mono; **en ~** in mono.

monoacide /monoasid/ *adj* monoacid.

monoatomique /monoatɔmik/ *adj* monatomic.

monobasique /monobazik/ *adj* monobasic.

monobloc /monoblɔk/ *adj inv* cast in one piece (*après n*).

monocaméral, **~e**, *mpl* **-aux** /mono kameʀal, o/ *adj* unicameral.

monocaméralisme /monokameʀalism/, **monocamérisme** /monokameʀism/ *nm* unicameralism.

monocellulaire /monosɛlylɛʀ/ *adj* **famille ~** nuclear family.

monochrome /monokʀom/ *adj, nm* monochrome.

monocle /mɔnɔkl/ *nm* monocle.

monoclonal, **~e**, *mpl* **-aux** /mɔno klonal, o/ *adj* monoclonal; **anticorps ~** monoclonal antibody.

monocolore /mɔnokɔlɔʀ/ *adj* monochrome.

monocoque /mɔnɔkɔk/ **I** *adj* [*bateau*] monohull; [*voiture*] monocoque.

II *nm* (bateau) monohull.

monocorde /mɔnɔkɔʀd/ **I** *adj* [*voix, discours*] monotonous; [*instrument*] single-string (*épith*); **sur** or **d'un ton ~** in a monotone.

II *nm* (instrument) monochord.

monoculaire /monokylɛʀ/ *adj* **microscope ~** simple microscope.

monoculture /mɔnokyltyʀ/ *nf* monoculture.

monocycle /mɔnosikl/ *nm* monocycle.

monocylindrique /mɔnosilɛ̃dʀik/ *adj* single-cylinder (*épith*).

monocyte /mɔnɔsit/ *nm* monocyte.

monodie /mɔnɔdi/ *nf* Mus monophony; Antiq, Théât monody.

monogame /mɔnɔgam/ **I** *adj* monogamous.
II *nmf* monogamist.

monogamie /mɔnɔgami/ *nf* monogamy.

monogamique /mɔnɔgamik/ *adj* monogamistic.

monogramme /mɔnɔgʀam/ *nm* monogram.

monographie /mɔnɔgʀafi/ *nf* monograph (**sur** on).

monographique /mɔnɔgʀafik/ *adj* [*exposition*] one-man (*épith*).

monoï /mɔnɔj/ *nm inv* coconut oil (*used in cosmetics*).

mono-industrie, *pl* **~s** /mɔnoɛ̃dystʀi/ *nf* single industry.

monokini /mɔnɔkini/ *nm* monokini.

monolingue /mɔnɔlɛ̃g/ *adj* monolingual.

monolinguisme /mɔnɔlɛ̃gɥism/ *nm* monolingualism.

monolithe /mɔnɔlit/ **I** *adj* monolithic.
II *nm* monolith.

monolithique /mɔnɔlitik/ *adj* monolithic.

monolithisme /mɔnɔlitism/ *nm* **1** (de parti) monolithic nature; **2** Archit monolithic system.

monologue /mɔnɔlɔg/ *nm* monologue; **le ~ d'Hamlet** Hamlet's soliloquy.
■ **~ intérieur** stream of consciousness.

monologuer /mɔnɔlɔge/ [1] *vi* (parler seul) to deliver a monologue; péj to hold forth.

monomane /mɔnɔman/, **monomaniaque** /mɔnɔmanjak/ *nmf* monomaniac.

monomanie /mɔnɔmani/ *nf* monomania.

monôme /mɔnom/ *nm* **1** Math monomial; **2** (d'étudiants) *single-file, often rowdy street procession at the end of exams.*

monométallisme /mɔnɔmetalism/ *nm* monometallism.

monomoteur, **-trice** /mɔnɔmɔtœʀ, tʀis/ **I** *adj* single-engined.
II *nm* single-engined aircraft.

mononucléaire /mɔnonykleɛʀ/ *adj, nm* mononuclear.

mononucléose /mɔnɔnykleoz/ **▶271** *nf* mononucleosis.
■ **~ infectieuse** glandular fever, infectious mononucleosis spéc.

monoparental, **~e**, *mpl* **-aux** /mɔnɔpaʀɑ̃tal, o/ *adj* **famille ~e** single-parent family.

monopartisme /mɔnopaʀtism/ *nm* one-party system.

monophasé, **~e** /mɔnɔfaze/ **I** *adj* single-phase (*épith*).
II *nm* single-phase current; **en ~** single-phased.

monophonie /mɔnɔfɔni/ *nf* monophony.

monophonique /mɔnɔfɔnik/ *adj* monophonic.

monophtongue /mɔnɔftɔ̃g/ *nf* monophthong.

monoplace /mɔnɔplas/ **I** *nm* Aviat single-seater (aircraft).
II *nf* Aut one-seater (car).

monoplan /mɔnɔplɑ̃/ *nm* monoplane.

monopole /mɔnɔpɔl/ *nm* lit, fig monopoly; **avoir le ~ de** to have a monopoly of; **exercer un ~ sur l'importation des denrées** to have a monopoly in food imports.

monopolisation /mɔnɔpɔlizasjɔ̃/ *nf* monopolization.

monopoliser /mɔnɔpɔlize/ [1] *vtr* (tous contextes) to monopolize.

monopoliste /mɔnɔpɔlist/ *adj* [*système, économie*] monopoly (*épith*).

monopolistique /mɔnɔpɔlistik/ *adj* monopolistic.

monoprix® /mɔnɔpʀi/ *nm* local chain store.

monoprocesseur /mɔnɔpʀɔsesœʀ/ **I** *adj m* single-chip (*épith*).
II *nm* single-chip computer.

monoprogrammation /mɔnɔpʀɔgʀamasjɔ̃/ *nf* monoprogramming.

monorail /mɔnɔʀaj/ **I** *adj inv* monorail.
II *nm* (voie) monorail; (wagon) monorail car.

monorime /mɔnɔʀim/ *nm* monorhyme.

monoski /mɔnɔski/ **▶449** *nm* (ski) monoski; (sport) monoskiing.

monospace /mɔnɔspas/ *nm* Aut people carrier GB, minivan US.

monostandard /mɔnɔstɑ̃daʀ/ *adj inv* TV, Vidéo one-standard (*épith*).

monosyllabe /mɔnɔsil(l)ab/ *nm* monosyllable.

monosyllabique /mɔnɔsil(l)abik/ *adj* monosyllabic.

monosyllabisme /mɔnɔsil(l)abism/ *nm* monosyllabism.

monothéique /mɔnɔteik/ *adj* monotheistic.

monothéisme /mɔnɔteism/ *nm* monotheism.

monothéiste /mɔnɔteist/ **I** *adj* monotheistic.
II *nmf* monotheist.

monotone /mɔnɔtɔn/ *adj* **1** (sans variété) monotonous; **2** Math monotone.

monotonie /mɔnɔtɔni/ *nf* monotony.

monotype /mɔnɔtip/ **I** *adj* Biol, Bot monotypic.
II *nm* **1** Naut one-design boat; **2** Art, Biol monotype.

monovalent, **~e** /mɔnɔvalɑ̃, ɑ̃t/ *adj* monovalent.

monoxyde /mɔnɔksid/ *nm* monoxide; **~ de carbone** carbon monoxide.

monozygote /mɔnɔzigɔt/ *adj* monozygotic.

Monrovia /mɔ̃ʀɔvja/ **▶857** *npr* Monrovia.

Monseigneur, *pl* **Messeigneurs** /mɔ̃sɛɲœʀ, mesɛɲœʀ/ *nm* **1** (forme d'adresse) (à un prince) Your Highness; (à un membre de la famille royale) Your Royal Highness; (à un cardinal) Your Eminence; (à un duc, archevêque) Your Grace; (à un évêque) Your Lordship, My Lord (Bishop); **~ désire-t-il…?** would His Highness like…?; **2** (titre) **~ le duc d'X** His Grace, the duke of X.

monsieur, *pl* **messieurs** /məsjø, mesjø/ **▶813** *nm* **1** (titre donné à un inconnu) **Monsieur** (dans une lettre) Dear Sir; **bonjour, ~** good morning; **pardon ~, je cherche la poste** excuse me, I'm looking for the post office; **~?** (à un guichet) can I help you, sir?; **occupez-vous de ~** (dans un magasin) could you attend to this gentleman, please?; **et pour ~, une vodka comme d'habitude?** will it be the usual, sir?; **mesdames, mesdemoiselles, messieurs, bonsoir** (dans un discours) good evening ladies and gentlemen; **madame, monsieur, bonsoir** (à la radio, télévision) good evening; **2** (titre donné à un homme dont on connaît le nom, pour l'exemple Bon) **bonjour, ~** good morning, Mr Bon; **cher Monsieur** (dans une lettre) Dear Mr Bon; **Monsieur Rosec** (sur une enveloppe) Mr Rosec; **M. Brun est en réunion** Mr Brun is in a meeting; **Monsieur le curé** Father Bon; **Monsieur le ministre** (en lui parlant) Minister; **merci Monsieur le président** (de club, d'association) thank you Mr Chairman; (de la République) thank you Mr President; **moi Monsieur!** (à un enseignant) please sir!; **3** (homme) man; **un vieux ~** an old man; **deux messieurs m'attendaient** two men were waiting for me; **un ~ d'une cinquantaine d'années** a man of about fifty; **'dis bonjour au ~'** 'say hello to the nice man'; **le ~ avec la veste rouge** the man in the red jacket; **le simple/double messieurs** the men's singles/doubles; **c'était un (grand) ~!** he was a (true) gentleman!; **4** (formule de respect utilisée avec un homme dont on connaît le nom) **'Monsieur a sonné?'** 'you rang sir?'; **tu comprends, Monsieur a ses habitudes!** iron His Lordship is rather set in his ways you see!; **5** Hist **Monsieur, frère du roi** Monsieur, the king's brother.
■ **~ Tout-le-Monde** the man in the street.

monstre /mɔ̃stʀ/ **I**○ *adj* [*manifestation, travail, succès, banquet*] huge; [*culot, publicité*] colossal; **'soldes ~s'** 'mammoth sales'; **ils ont fait une publicité ~** they did a colossal advertising campaign (**pour qch** for sth).
II *nm* **1** Mythol (être fantastique) monster; **2** Biol, Zool (être difforme) freak (of nature); **3** (animal, objet gigantesque) monster; **4** (personnage ignoble) monster; **un ~ froid** a cold-blooded monster; **un ~ d'orgueil/de paresse** a monstrously arrogant/lazy person; **un ~ d'ingratitude** an ungrateful wretch; **5** (enfant) monster; **petit ~** little monster.
■ **~ marin** sea monster; **~ sacré** superstar; **un ~ sacré du cinéma** a giant of the cinema.

monstrueusement /mɔ̃stʀyøzmɑ̃/ *adv* lit, fig [*riche, bête, intelligent*] horrendously; **il est ~ gros** he's a monstrous size.

monstrueux, **-euse** /mɔ̃stʀyø, øz/ *adj* **1** (choquant) [*idée, crime, personne, cruauté, ingratitude*] monstrous; **2** (hideux) hideous; **il est d'une laideur monstrueuse** he's hideously ugly; **3** (énorme) [*bruit, erreur*] colossal; **d'une bêtise monstrueuse** incredibly stupid.

monstruosité /mɔ̃stʀyozite/ *nf* **1** (de crime, conduite) monstrousness; **2** (acte) atrocity; (objet) monstrosity; **commettre des ~s** to commit atrocities; **dire des ~s** to say preposterous things; **cette calomnie est une ~** this is a monstrous slander; **3** (difformité) Biol, Zool deformity.

mont /mɔ̃/ *nm* **1** Géog (montagne) mountain; **▶promettre**; **2** Géog (suivi d'un nom propre) Mount; **3** (en chiromancie) mount.
■ **le ~ Blanc** Mont Blanc; **le ~ Everest** Mount Everest; **le ~ des Oliviers** the Mount of Olives; **~ de Vénus** Anat mons veneris.
IDIOMES **être toujours par ~s et par vaux** to be always on the move.

montage /mɔ̃taʒ/ *nm* **1** (organisation) set-up; **2** (assemblage) (de meuble, machine, d'appareil) assembly; (de tente) putting up; Cout (de col) putting on; (de manche) setting in; **atelier/chaîne de ~** assembly shop/line; **3** Cin (de film) editing; **table/salle de ~** cutting table/room; **4** (de pierre précieuse) setting, mounting; **le ~ d'une perle sur une bague** the setting ou mounting of a pearl in a ring; **5** Électrotech connection; **~ en série/en parallèle** connection in series/in parallel; **6** Imprim imposition.
■ **~ financier** Fin financial set-up; **~ photo** photomontage; **faire un ~ photo** to make a (photo)montage; **~ sonore** sound montage.

montagnard, **~e** /mɔ̃taɲaʀ, aʀd/ **I** *adj* [*peuple, plante*] mountain (*épith*); [*coutume*] highland (*épith*); **la vie ~e** life in the mountains.
II *nm,f* **1** (habitant) mountain dweller; **les ~s** mountain people; **2** (en cyclisme) climber.

Montagnard /mɔ̃taɲaʀ/ *nm* Hist member of the Mountain; **les ~s et les Girondins** the Mountain and the Girondists.

montagne /mɔ̃taɲ/ *nf* **1** (élévation) mountain; **pays de ~s** mountainous country; **2** (région montagneuse) **la ~** the mountains (*pl*); **une semaine à la** or **en ~** a week in the mountains; **de ~** [*route, animal*] mountain (*épith*); **il neige en haute/basse ~** it's snowing on the upper/lower slopes; **village situé en haute ~** village high up in the mountains; **village de**

basse ~ village in the foothills of the mountains; **station de ski de moyenne montagne** medium altitude ski resort; **3** (grande quantité) mountain (**de** of); **des ~s de repassage/papiers** mountains of ironing/papers.

■ **les ~s Rocheuses** the Rocky Mountains, the Rockies; **~s russes** big dipper (*sg*) GB, roller coaster (*sg*); **~ à vaches**○ fig easy walks (*pl*); (pour ski) easy slopes (*pl*).

IDIOMES **se faire une ~ de qch** to get really worked up about sth; **faire battre des ~s** to stir up trouble; **la foi déplace** or **soulève les ~s** faith can move mountains; **il n'y a que les ~s qui ne se rencontrent pas** Prov there are none so distant that fate cannot bring them together Prov; **c'est la ~ qui accouche d'une souris** hum a great deal of effort leading to nothing much.

Montagne /mɔ̃taɲ/ *nprf* Hist **la ~** the Mountain.

montagneux, **-euse** /mɔ̃taɲø, øz/ *adj* mountainous.

Montana /mɔ̃tana/ **▶692** *nprm* **le ~** Montana.

montant, **~e** /mɔ̃tɑ̃, ɑ̃t/ **I** *adj* **1** (qui monte) [*cabine, groupe*] going up (*après n*); **la voiture ~e a la priorité** the car going uphill has right of way GB ou the right of way US; **2** Naut (qui va vers l'amont) going upstream (*après n*); **3** (en pente) [*rue, chemin*] uphill; [*courbe*] rising; **4** Mode [*col*] high; [*chaussettes*] long; **chaussures ~es** ankle boots.

II *nm* **1** (somme) sum; **un ~ global** a sum total; **le ~ des pertes/bénéfices** the total losses/profits; **le ~ du budget de la défense** the total defence[GB] budget; **le ~ du contrat** the (total) value of the contract; **d'un** or **pour un ~ de** [*chèque, déficit, épargne*] to the amount of; [*marchandises, propriété*] for a total of, amounting to; **2** (de porte, fenêtre, châssis) upright, jamb; (horizontal) transom; (d'échafaudage) pole; (d'échelle) upright; (de carrosserie) pillar.

■ **~ de barrière** gatepost; **~ de bride** Équit cheekpiece; **~ de but** goalpost; **~ de lit** bedpost; **~s compensatoires (monétaires)**, **MC(M)** (monetary) compensatory amounts.

mont-blanc, *pl* **monts-blancs** /mɔ̃blɑ̃/ *nm*: *chestnut purée dessert topped with whipped cream.*

mont-de-piété, *pl* **monts-de-piété** /mɔ̃dpjete/ *nm* pawnshop, pawnbroker's; **mettre qch au ~** to pawn sth.

monte /mɔ̃t/ *nf* mounting, covering; **mener une jument à la ~** to take a mare to stud.

monté, **~e** /mɔ̃te/ **I** *pp* ▶ **monter**.

II *pp adj* **1**○ (équipé) equipped; **être bien ~ en draps/linge de toilette** to have a good stock of sheets/bathroom towels; **te voilà bien ~e avec un mari comme ça!** iron you're in a bad way with a husband like that!; **être bien ~**◑ [*homme, animal*] to be well-hung◑ ou well-endowed○; **2** (à cheval) mounted.

III montée *nf* **1** (action de grimper) (d'escalier, de route, pente, colline) climb; (de montagne) climb, ascent; **la descente est-elle moins difficile que la ~e?** is the climb down less difficult than the climb up?; **à la ~e les véhicules sont prioritaires** vehicles going uphill have right of way GB ou the right of way US; **'ne pas gêner la ~e des voyageurs'** 'do not obstruct passengers boarding'; **vous gênez la ~e des voyageurs ici** you're in the way of the passengers getting on; **2** (action de s'élever) (pour avion, ballon, fusée) climb, ascent; **~e à la verticale** vertical climb ou ascent; **l'ascenseur s'est bloqué à la ~e** the lift GB ou elevator US got stuck on the way up ou as it was going up; **3** (élévation de niveau) (action) rising (**de** of); (résultat) rise (**de** in); **la ~e des eaux a entraîné des dégâts importants** the rise in the water level caused considerable damage; **la ~e de la sève dans un arbre** the rising of the sap in a tree; **on observe une nette ~e des eaux de l'océan** you can see quite clearly that the sea level has risen; **une brusque ~e d'adrénaline** a surge ou rush of adrenaline; **4** Fin rise (**de** in); (de coûts, frais) increase (**de** in); **la ~e du dollar** the rise in the dollar; **la brusque ~e du prix du pétrole** the surge ou sudden rise in oil prices; **5** (progression) (de chômage) rise (**de** in); (d'opposition, de résistance, phénomène) rise (**de** of); (d'intolérance, de violence) rise, increase (**de** in); (de dangers, risques) increase (**de** in); **la ~e de la présence étrangère** the increased foreign presence; **on observe une ~e de l'inquiétude/de la colère à travers le pays** we note a mounting concern/anger throughout the country; **6** (pente) hill; **il y a une ~e très raide** there's a very steep hill; **une légère ~e** a slight slope; **7** (fait d'emmener plus haut) taking up; **la ~e des matériaux se fait encore à cheval** the materials are still taken up on horseback; **8** Sport **~e de Papin** Papin moves up the field; **9** Physiol **la ~e de lait se produit deux jours après la naissance** the milk comes in two days after birth.

monte-charge /mɔ̃tʃaʀʒ/ *nm inv* goods lift GB ou elevator US.

monte-en-l'air○ /mɔ̃tɑ̃lɛʀ/ *nm inv* cat burglar.

monténégrin, **~e** /mɔ̃teneɡʀɛ̃, in/ **▶692** *adj* Montenegrin.

Monténégrin, **~e** /mɔ̃teneɡʀɛ̃, in/ *nm,f* Montenegrin.

Monténégro /mɔ̃teneɡʀo/ **▶692** *nprm* Montenegro.

monte-plats /mɔ̃tpla/ *nm inv* dumbwaiter, small lift GB ou elevator US.

monter /mɔ̃te/ [1] **I** *vtr* (+ *v avoir*) **1** (transporter) (en haut) gén to take [sb/sth] up [*personne, objet*] (**à** to); (à l'étage) to take [sb/sth] upstairs [*personne, objet*]; (d'en bas) gén to bring [sb/sth] up [*personne, objet*] (**de** from); (de l'étage) to bring [sb/sth] upstairs [*personne, objet*]; **~ les valises au grenier** to take the suitcases up to the attic; **~ les bouteilles de la cave** to bring the bottles up from the cellar; **je peux vous ~ au village** I can take you up to the village; **monte-moi mes pantoufles** bring my slippers up (to me); **je leur ai fait ~ les valises au grenier** I made them take the suitcases up to the attic; **j'ai fait ~ le piano dans la chambre** I had the piano taken up to the bedroom; **faites -moi ~ les dossiers secrets** get the secret files brought up to me; **2** (placer plus haut) to put [sth] up [*objet*]; to raise [*étagère*] (**de** by); **monte le store** put the blind up; **j'ai monté le vase sur l'étagère du haut** I put the vase on the top shelf; **tu peux me ~ cette valise sur l'armoire?** can you put ou get this suitcase up on the wardrobe for me?; **~ l'étagère d'un cran/de 20 centimètres** to raise the shelf by one notch/by 20 centimetres[GB]; **3** (réussir à transporter) to get [sth] up [*objet*]; **impossible de ~ le piano par l'escalier/par la fenêtre** it's impossible to get the piano up the stairs/up through the window; **comment va-t-on ~ le piano?** (à l'étage) how are we going to get the piano upstairs?; (dans le camion) how are we going to get the piano in?; **4** (parcourir) (en allant) to go up [*pente, rue, marches*]; to go up, to climb [*côte, escaliers*]; (en venant) to come up [*pente, rue, marches, escaliers*]; **je l'ai vu ~ les escaliers sur les** or **à genoux** I saw him go ou climb up the stairs on his knees; **~ la colline à bicyclette** to cycle up the hill; **je leur ai fait ~ la colline en courant** I made them run up the hill; **il m'a fait ~ les escaliers trois fois** he made me go upstairs ou up the stairs three times; **5** (en valeur, intensité) to turn up [*volume, thermostat, gaz*]; Mus to raise the pitch of [*instrument*]; Art to intensify [*couleur*]; **monte un peu la radio** turn the radio up a bit; **~ un violon d'un ton** to raise the pitch of a violin by a tone; **6** Culin to beat, to whisk [*blanc d'œuf, mayonnaise*]; **~ les blancs en neige** (dans une recette) beat ou whisk the egg whites until stiff; **~ une sauce** to thicken a sauce; **7** (rendre hostile) **~ qn contre qn** to turn ou set sb against sb; **~ qn contre un projet** to put sb off a plan; **être monté contre qn** to have it in for sb; **8** (chevaucher) to ride [*cheval, âne, éléphant*]; **ce cheval n'a jamais été monté** this horse has never been ridden (before); **9** (couvrir, saillir) to mount, to cover; **10** (assembler) to assemble [*meuble, appareil, machine*]; to put up [*tente, échafaudage*]; to set, to mount [*pierre précieuse*]; to mount [*gravure, estampe, photo*]; Mus to string [*instrument*]; **~ un film** Cin to edit a film; **~ une page** Imprim to set (up) a page; **~ une émission** TV to edit a broadcast; **~ en parallèle** Électrotech to connect in parallel; **11** Cout to put [sth] in [*col*]; to set [sth] in [*manche*]; **~ un manteau/une robe** to make up a coat/a dress; **12** (organiser) to hatch [*complot*]; to mount [*attaque, opération militaire*]; to set up [*société, opération financière*]; Théât to stage, to put on [*pièce*]; **~ un spectacle** to stage ou put on a show; **~ une histoire de toutes pièces** to concoct ou fabricate a story from beginning to end; **13** (fournir) **~ son ménage/sa maison** to set up home/house; **~ sa garde-robe** to build up one's wardrobe.

II *vi* (+ *v être*) **1** (se déplacer) [*personne*] (en allant) gén to go up (**à** to); (à l'étage) to go upstairs; (en venant) gén to come up (**de** from); (à l'étage) to come upstairs; [*train, ascenseur, téléphérique*] (en allant) to go up; (en venant) to come up; [*avion, hélicoptère*] to climb; [*oiseau*] to fly up; [*soleil, brume*] to rise (**sur** over); [*fumée, odeur, bruit*] to come up; **reste-ici, je monte au grenier** stay here, I'm going up to the attic; **peux-tu ~ chercher mon sac?** can you go upstairs and get my bag?; **tu peux ~ m'aider à pousser l'armoire?** can you come upstairs and help me push the wardrobe?; **il est monté s'allonger** he went upstairs to lie down; **te voilà! tu es monté par l'ascenseur?** there you are! did you come up in the lift GB ou elevator US?; **tu es monté à pied?** gén did you walk up?; (plutôt que par l'ascenseur) did you come up on foot?; **je préfère ~ par l'escalier** I prefer to go up by the stairs; **nous sommes montés par le sentier/la route** (à pied) we walked up by the path/the road; (à cheval) we rode up by the path/the road; **il est monté au col à bicyclette/en voiture** he cycled/drove up to the pass; **il est monté vers moi en rampant** he crawled up to me; **où est l'écureuil? il a dû ~ à l'arbre** where's the squirrel? it must have gone up ou climbed the tree; **monte, je te suis** go on up, I'll follow you; **monte ici!** come up here!; **je suis monté en haut de la tour/au sommet de la falaise** I went up to the top of the tower/to the top of the cliff; **~ sur** [*personne*] to step onto, to get onto [*trottoir, marche*]; [*animal*] to get onto [*marche, trottoir*]; [*personne, animal*] to climb onto [*mur, tabouret*]; **il est monté sur le toit** [*enfant, chat*] he's/it's gone up onto the roof; **~ à l'échelle/l'arbre/la corde** to climb (up) the ladder/the tree/the rope; **~ à la verticale** [*ballon, alpiniste*] to climb vertically; **~ au ciel** to ascend into Heaven; **l'air chaud fait ~ les ballons/planeurs** warm air makes balloons/gliders rise; **elle m'a fait/ne m'a pas laissé ~ dans sa chambre** she had me/didn't let me go up to her bedroom; **faites-les ~** (clients, marchandises) send them up; **2** (sur un moyen de transport) **~ dans une voiture** to get in a car; **~ dans un train/bus/avion** to get on a train/bus/plane; **~ dans un canoë/sur un bateau** to get into a canoe/on a boat; **il n'est jamais monté en avion** he's never been on a plane; **il a peur de ~ en avion** he's afraid of flying; **~ à bord** to get on board; **~ sur** to get on [*âne, cheval, bicyclette, tracteur*]; **monté sur son cheval/sur son chameau, il parcourait le pays** he travelled[GB] the country on horseback/on his camel; **3** (s'étendre de bas en haut) [*route, voie ferrée*] to go uphill, to climb; [*terrain*] to rise; [*canalisation, ligne téléphonique*] (en allant) to go up; (en venant) to come up; **~ jusqu'à** [*chemin, muraille, escalier*] (description) to go up to; (emphase) to go up as far as; **~ jusqu'au sommet** [*route, ligne téléphonique*] to go right up to the top; **~ en lacets** [*route*] to wind its way up; **~ en pente douce** [*terrain, route*] to slope up gently; **~ en pente raide** [*terrain, route*] to climb steeply; **~ brusquement sur 200 mètres** [*pente, route*] to climb sharply for 200 metres[GB]; **4** (atteindre) [*vêtement, liquide, neige*] to come up (**jusqu'à** to); **des chaussettes qui montent jusqu'aux genoux** socks that come up to the knees; **il avait des chaussettes qui lui montaient aux genoux** he was wearing knee socks; **l'eau nous montait jusqu'à la taille** the water came up to our waists, we were waist-deep in water; **l'eau montait sur la berge** the water came up onto the bank; **5** (augmenter) [*niveau, baromètre, température, pression, prix, taux*] to rise, to go up (**à** to; **de** by); [*marée*] to come in; Mus [*mélodie*] to rise; **le franc est** or **a monté par rapport à la livre** the franc has risen ou gone up against the pound; **faire ~ les cours de 2%** to push prices up by 2%; **ça va faire ~ le dollar** it'll send ou push the dollar up; **ça fait ~ la température** gén it raises the temperature; Méd it puts one's temperature up; **ça ne fera pas ~ leur niveau de vie** it won't raise their standard of living; **6** (se rendre, séjourner) **~ à** or **sur Paris** (de province) to go up to Paris; **~ à Lyon** (du Midi) to go up to Lyons; **7** (chevaucher) **~ (à cheval)** to ride; **~ à bicyclette/moto** to ride a bicycle/motorbike; **il ne sait pas ~ (à cheval)** he can't ride; **elle monte à cheval deux fois par semaine** she goes riding ou rides twice a week; **8** Mil **~ à l'assaut** or **l'attaque** to mount an attack (**de** on); **~ au front** to move up to the front; **~ en ligne** to move up the line; **~ au combat** to go into battle; **9** Jeux (aux cartes) to play a higher card; **~ à carreau/l'atout** to play a higher diamond/trump; **10** (progresser) (dans une hiérarchie) to rise, to move up; (en notoriété) [*artiste*] to rise; **à force de ~, il deviendra directeur** he'll work his way right up to director; **c'est un jeune peintre qui monte** he's an up-and-coming ou a rising young painter; **~ en puissance** [*parti, politicien*] to rise; **11** (gagner en intensité) [*colère, émotion*] to mount; [*sanglots*] to rise; [*larmes*] to well up; **le ton monta** (animation) the conversation became noisier; (énervement) the discussion became heated; **12** (saisir) **~ à la gorge de qn** [*sanglots, cri*] to rise (up) in sb's throat; **~ à la tête de qn** [*vin, alcool, succès*] to go to sb's head; **le rouge lui est monté au front** he/she went red in the face; **13** Aut, Tech **~ à 250 km/h** [*véhicule*] to go up to ou reach 250 km/h; [*automobiliste*] to go up to 250 km/h; **~ en puissance** [*moteur*] to increase in power.

III se monter *vpr* **1** (s'élever) **se ~ à** [*dépenses, frais, facture*] to come to, to amount to; [*dette*] to amount to; **2** (s'équiper) to get oneself set up (**en** with).

IDIOMES **se ~ la tête**○ to get worked up○.

monteur, **-euse** /mɔ̃tœʀ, øz/ ▶510 *nm,f* **1** Ind fitter; **~ ajusteur** fitter; **~ en chauffage** central heating engineer; **~ en lignes électriques** linesman GB, lineman US; **~ réparateur** assembler engineer; **2** Cin editor; **3** (en typographie) paste-up artist.

monteur-électricien, *pl* **monteurs-électriciens** /mɔ̃tœʀelɛktʀisjɛ̃/ ▶510 *nm* electrical fitter.

monteur-mécanicien, *pl* **monteurs-mécaniciens** /mɔ̃tœʀmekanisjɛ̃/ ▶510 *nm* fitter.

Montevideo /mɔ̃tevideo/ ▶857 *npr* Montevideo.

montgolfière /mɔ̃gɔlfjɛʀ/ *nf* **1** (ballon) hot-air balloon; **2** ▶449 (sport) (hot-air) ballooning; **faire de la ~** to go (hot-air) ballooning.

monticule /mɔ̃tikyl/ *nm* **1** (butte) hillock; **2** (amas) mound (**de** of).

montmartrois, **~e** /mɔ̃maʀtʀwa, az/ *adj* of Montmartre.

montmorency /mɔ̃mɔʀɑ̃si/ *nf inv* (cerise) Montmorency cherry.

Montpellier /mɔ̃pəlje/ ▶857 *npr* Montpellier.

montpelliérain, **~e** /mɔ̃pəljeʀɛ̃, ɛn/ ▶857 *adj* of Montpellier.

Montpelliérain, **~e** /mɔ̃pəljeʀɛ̃, ɛn/ *nm,f* (natif) native of Montpellier; (habitant) inhabitant of Montpellier.

montrable /mɔ̃tʀabl/ *adj* [*personne*] presentable; [*images, film*] suitable for viewing (*après n*); **habillé comme ça, il n'est pas ~!** dressed like that, he's not fit to be seen!; **ces images ne sont pas ~s à des enfants** these pictures are not suitable for children.

montre /mɔ̃tʀ/ *nf* **1** (objet) watch; **~ à affichage numérique** digital display watch; **~ à aiguilles** watch with hands; **~ étanche** waterproof watch; **~ à** or **de gousset** fob watch; **~ marine** seaman's watch; **~ de poche** pocket watch; **~ de précision** precision watch; **~ à quartz** quartz watch; **~ à remontoir** stemwinder ou stemwinding watch; **~ à répétition** repeater watch; **il est 5 heures à ma ~** it's 5 o'clock by my watch; **il a mis trois heures ~ en main** it took him three hours exactly; **étape** or **course** or **épreuve contre la ~** race against the clock; **2** (action de montrer) fml **faire ~ de** to show [*prudence, courage*]; to display [*esprit, habileté*]; **3** (ostentation) liter **pour la ~** (pour la décoration) for show; (pour sauver les apparences) for the sake of appearances; **4** Comm (présentation) display, show; **articles en ~** articles on display ou in the window.

Montréal /mɔ̃ʀeal/ ▶857 *npr* Montreal.

montréalais, **~e** /mɔ̃ʀealɛ, ɛz/ ▶857 *adj* of Montreal.

Montréalais, **~e** /mɔ̃ʀealɛ, ɛz/ *nm,f* Montrealer.

montrer /mɔ̃tʀe/ [1] **I** *vtr* **1** (faire voir) to show [*objet, passeport*]; **~ qch à qn** to show sb sth, to show sth to sb; **je vais vous ~ votre chambre** I'll show you your room; **laissez-moi vous ~ la maison** let me show you around the house; **robe qui montre les épaules** off-the-shoulders dress; ▶**patte**; **2** (faire connaître) to show [*problème, sentiments*]; to show, to reveal [*intentions, connaissances*]; **~ des signes d'impatience/de faiblesse** to show signs of impatience/of weakness; **~ que** to show that; **j'ai essayé de lui ~ qu'il se trompait** I tried to show him that he was wrong; **~ à qn comment faire/comment se servir de qch** to show sb how to do/how to use sth; **attends un peu, je vais te ~**○**!** just you wait, I'll show you○! ; **elle a honte de ses parents, elle n'ose pas les ~** she's ashamed of her parents, she keeps them out of sight; **3** (indiquer) [*personne*] to point out, to show [*trace, lieu, objet*]; [*panneau, boussole*] to point to [*direction*]; [*tableau, graphique, sondage*] to show [*évolution, résultats*]; **~ qch à qn** to point sth out to sb; **~ qch du doigt** or **d'un geste** to point to sth, to point sth out; **~ qn du doigt** lit to point at sb; fig to point the finger at sb; **~ le chemin à qn** lit, fig to show sb the way.

II se montrer *vpr* **1** (se révéler) [*personne*] to show oneself to be; [*choses*] to prove (to be); **le gouvernement s'est montré confiant** the government showed itself to be confident; **mes craintes se sont montrées vaines** my fears proved to be groundless; **elle s'est montrée à la hauteur de la situation** she showed she was up to it; **se ~ d'un pessimisme exagéré** to be overly pessimistic; **il s'est montré serviable** he was very helpful; **il faut se ~ optimiste** we must try to be optimistic; **2** (se faire voir) to show oneself; **après cela, il n'ose plus se ~** after that, he doesn't dare show his face; **elle n'osait pas se ~ avec lui** she didn't dare be seen with him; **on n'est pas obligés de rester mais il faut au moins se ~** we don't have to stay but we should at least put in an appearance; **le président est allé se ~ à Prague** the president has gone to put in an appearance in Prague; **il aime se ~ serrant la main à des gens importants** he likes to be seen shaking hands with important people; **3** (apparaître) to appear; **le soleil s'est montré entre deux averses** the sun came out between two showers.

IDIOMES **~ la porte à qn** to show sb the door; **~ le poing à qn** to shake one's fist at sb; **~ les dents** to bare one's teeth; **~ le bout de son** or **du nez** [*personne*] to show one's face; [*soleil*] to peep through; [*fleurs, plantes*] to poke through.

montreur, **-euse** /mɔ̃tʀœʀ, øz/ ▶510 *nm,f* **~ d'animaux** animal trainer; **~ de marionnettes** puppeteer; **~ d'ours** bear tamer.

monture /mɔ̃tyʀ/ *nf* **1** (animal) mount; **2** Tech mount; (de lunettes) frames (*pl*); (de bague) setting.

IDIOMES **qui veut aller** or **voyager loin ménage sa ~** Prov you have to learn to pace yourself.

monument /mɔnymɑ̃/ *nm* **1** (commémoratif) monument; **un ~ à la mémoire des victimes** a monument in memory of the victims; **2** (édifice) (historic) building; **visiter les ~s de Paris** to see the sights of Paris; **3** fig **être un ~ de bêtise** [*personne*] to be monumentally stupid; **un des ~s de la peinture mondiale** a masterpiece of painting.

■ **~ historique** ancient monument; **classé ~ historique** listed as an ancient monument; **~ aux morts** war memorial.

monumental, **~e**, *mpl* **-aux** /mɔnymɑ̃tal, o/ *adj* **1** Art [*sculpture, escalier*] monumental; **2** (imposant) [*œuvre, biographie*] monumental; **3** (énorme) [*bêtise, gaffe, erreur*] monumental; **il est d'une ignorance/arrogance ~e** he's monumentally ignorant/arrogant.

moquer /mɔke/ [1] **I**† *vtr* (railler) to mock.

II se moquer *vpr* **1** (ridiculiser) to make fun (**de** of), to laugh (**de** at); **arrête de te ~!** stop teasing ou poking fun!; **vous vous moquez (de moi) ou quoi?** are you making fun of me or what?; **de qui se moque-t-on?** they've got a nerve!; **2** (être indifférent) **se ~ de** not to care about; **je me moque de vos histoires** I don't care about your problems; **il se moque bien de ça** he really couldn't care less (about it); **elle s'en moque complètement** she really couldn't care less; **ils se moquent de paraître ridicules** they couldn't care less about looking ridiculous; **se ~ que** not to care if; **je me moque qu'ils viennent ou pas** I don't care if ou whether they come or not; ▶**chemise**, **guigne**; **3** (tromper) **se ~ de qn** to fool sb; **se ~ des gens** to take people for fools; **ils se sont moqués de nous avec leurs promesses** they took us for a ride○.

IDIOMES **je m'en moque comme de l'an quarante**○ I don't give a damn○.

moquerie /mɔkʀi/ *nf* **1** (remarque) mocking remark; **il supporte mal les ~s** he can't tolerate people making fun of him; **être en butte aux ~s** to be the target of mockery; **2** (action) mockery.

moquette /mɔkɛt/ *nf* **1** (tapis) fitted carpet GB, wall-to-wall carpet US; **faire poser une** or **de la ~** to have a fitted carpet laid GB, to have wall-to-wall carpeting fitted; **2** Tex moquette.

moquetter /mɔkete/ [1] *vtr* to carpet [*pièce*].

moqueur, **-euse** /mɔkœʀ, øz/ **I** *adj* **être ~** to be always making fun of people.
II *nm* (oiseau) mockingbird.

moraine /mɔʀɛn/ *nf* moraine.

morainique /mɔʀenik/ *adj* morainic.

moral, **~e**, *mpl* **-aux** /mɔʀal, o/ **I** *adj* **1** (éthique) moral; **n'avoir aucun sens ~** to have no sense of right and wrong; **prendre l'engagement ~ de faire qch** to make a binding commitment to do sth; **sur le plan ~** morally; **2** (mental) [*torture, douleur*] mental; [*courage, soutien*] moral; **douleur ~e** mental anguish; **force ~e** moral fibre^GB^; **3** (conforme aux bonnes mœurs) [*œuvre, personne*] moral; [*conduite*] ethical; **le conseil qu'il t'a donné n'était pas très ~** the advice he gave you was morally dubious; **ce n'est pas très ~ d'avoir fait cela** that was not a very ethical thing to do.
II *nm* **1** (disposition d'esprit) morale; **le ~ des troupes est bon/mauvais** the troops' morale is high/low; **avoir bon ~, avoir le ~** to be in good spirits; **ne pas avoir le ~** to feel down; **pour travailler ici, faut vraiment avoir le ~**○! you have to be crazy to work here!; **avoir le ~ à zéro** to feel very down; **remonter le ~ de qn** to raise sb's spirits ou morale, to cheer sb up; **il a un ~ d'acier** nothing gets him down○; **garder le ~** to keep up one's morale, to keep one's chin up○; **saper le ~ de qn** to undermine sb's morale; **2** (psychique) mind; **le ~ et le physique** mind and body; **au ~ comme au physique** mentally and physically.
III morale *nf* **1** (règles de conduite) morality; **attitude contraire à la ~e** immoral attitude; **leur ~e** their moral code; **obéir à une ~e stricte** to live by a strict moral code, to have strict morals; **2** (enseignement) moral; **la ~e de tout ceci** the moral of all this; **faire la ~e à qn** fig to give sb a lecture; **3** Philos **la ~e** moral philosophy, ethics; **un ouvrage de ~e** a work of moral philosophy ou of ethics.

moralement /mɔʀalmɑ̃/ *adv* **1** (conformément à la morale) morally, ethically; **être ~ responsable** to be morally responsible; **se sentir ~ obligé de faire** to feel morally obliged to do; **2** (psychiquement) psychologically.

moralisant, **~e** /mɔʀalizɑ̃, ɑ̃t/ *adj* [*discours, ton*] moralizing; [*fin*] moral.

moralisateur, **-trice** /mɔʀalizatœʀ, tʀis/ *adj* [*personne, ton, discours*] moralizing, moralistic; [*histoire*] with a moral (*épith, après n*).

moralisation /mɔʀalizasjɔ̃/ *nf* (des masses) moral improvement; (de régime, presse) cleaning up.

moraliser /mɔʀalize/ [1] **I** *vtr* to clean up [*campagne électorale*]; to reform [*vie publique*].
II *vi* to moralize (**sur** about).

moralisme /mɔʀalism/ *nm* moralism.

moraliste /mɔʀalist/ **I** *adj* moralistic.
II *nmf* gén moralist; péj moralizer; Philos moral philosopher.

moralité /mɔʀalite/ *nf* **1** (de personne, société) morals (*pl*), moral standards (*pl*); **un individu d'une ~ douteuse** an individual with dubious morals; **n'avoir aucune ~** to have no sense of right and wrong; **il n'y a plus de ~** there's no sense of right and wrong any more; **quelle ~!** how immoral!; **2** (d'œuvre, action) morality; **la ~ publique** public morality; **3** (leçon) moral; **~, ne faites confiance à personne** the moral is, don't trust anybody.

morasse /mɔʀas/ *nf* Imprim foundry proof.

moratoire /mɔʀatwaʀ/ **I** *adj* **dommages-intérêts ~s** damages for delay (*in fulfilling a legal obligation*); **sentence ~** suspended judgment.
II *nm* moratorium.

moratorium /mɔʀatɔʀjɔm/ *nm* moratorium.

morave /mɔʀav/ **▶692** *adj* Moravian; **frères ~s** Bohemian Brethren.

Morave /mɔʀav/ *nmf* Moravian.

Moravie /mɔʀavi/ **▶692** *nprf* Moravia.

morbide /mɔʀbid/ *adj* morbid.

morbidité /mɔʀbidite/ *nf* morbidity.

morbier /mɔʀbje/ *nm* H (horloge) grandfather clock.

Morbihan /mɔʀbiɑ̃/ **▶692** *nprm* (département) **le ~** the Morbihan.

morbleu‡ /mɔʀblø/ *excl* zounds‡!

morceau, *pl* **~x** /mɔʀso/ *nm* **1** gén (d'aliment) piece, bit; (de verre) piece, fragment; (de bois) piece; (d'étoffe) piece; **être en ~x** Culin [*sucre*] to be in lumps; [*viande*] to be in cubes; (cassé) to be in pieces ou bits; **couper en ~x** to cut in ou into pieces; **casser en mille ~x** to break into a thousand pieces; **mettre qch en ~x** to break [sth] to pieces [*vase*]; to tear [sth] into pieces [*drap*]; to pull [sth] to pieces [*jouet*]; **manger un ~**○ to have a snack; **2** Culin (en boucherie) cut; **bon ~** nice cut; **bas ~** cheap cut; **~ de choix** choice cut; **▶gros**; **3** Mus (œuvre) piece; **~ de piano** piano piece; (partie d'œuvre) section; (partie de concert) item; **4** Littérat (extrait) extract, passage; **recueil de ~x choisis** collection of selected extracts; **le chapitre 8/cette entreprise est un gros** or **sacré ~**○ chapter 8/this firm is quite substantial; **5**◑ (femme) **beau** or **joli ~** nice bit of stuff○ GB, nice piece○.
■ ~ de bravoure Littérat purple passage; fig bravura passage.
IDIOMES emporter le ~○ to get one's way; **lâcher** or **cracher le ~**○ to spill the beans; **recoller les ~x** to patch things up.

morceler /mɔʀsəle/ [19] *vtr* to divide up [*héritage, terrain*] (**en** into); to split up [*pays*].

morcellement /mɔʀsɛlmɑ̃/ *nm* **1** (action) (d'héritage, de terrain) dividing up; (de pays) splitting up; **2** (résultat) division; **le ~ des terres** the division of land into smaller units.

mordant, **~e** /mɔʀdɑ̃, ɑ̃t/ **I** *adj* **1** (caustique) [*ironie, critique, ton*] caustic, scathing; [*personne*] scathing; **être ~** to be scathing (**à l'égard de qn/qch** about sb/sth); **avoir l'esprit ~** to have a biting wit; **2** (saisissant) [*froid*] biting.
II *nm* **1** (causticité) sarcasm; **le ~ de leurs remarques/critiques** the sarcastic ou caustic tone of their remarks/criticisms; **avec ~** sarcastically; **2**○ (énergie de personne, d'équipe) zip○; **retrouver de son ~** to get some of one's zip○ back; **3** Chimie, Tech mordant; **4** Mus mordent.

mordicus○ /mɔʀdikys/ *adv* pigheadedly○, stubbornly.

mordillage /mɔʀdijaʒ/, **mordillement** /mɔʀdijmɑ̃/ *nm* nibbling **₵**.

mordiller /mɔʀdije/ [1] *vtr* to nibble at; (plus fort) to chew.

mordoré, **~e** /mɔʀdɔʀe/ *adj* [*ton, feuillage*] golden brown; [*raisin*] gold-tinged; **d'un brun ~** golden brown.

mordre /mɔʀdʀ/ [6] **I** *vtr* **1** lit [*chien, personne*] to bite [*personne, animal, objet*]; [*serpent*] to bite [*animal, personne*]; **~ qn à la jambe/au bras** to bite sb on the leg/on the arm; **il m'a mordu le mollet/l'oreille** he bit me on the calf/the ear; **~ qn jusqu'au sang** to bite sb and draw blood; **~ qch à pleines dents** to sink one's teeth into sth; **~ son crayon** to chew one's pencil; **se faire ~** to get bitten (**par** by); **2** (entamer) [*lime*] to bite [*métal*]; [*acide, rouille*] to eat into [*métal, plaque*]; **3** (empiéter) [*voiture*] to go over [*ligne jaune*].
II mordre à *vtr ind* (saisir avec la bouche) **~ à l'appât** or **l'hameçon** lit, fig to take the bait; **'ça mord?'** 'are the fish biting?'
III *vi* **1** (planter ses dents) **~ dans une pomme** to bite into an apple; **2** (empiéter) **~ sur la ligne jaune** to go over the yellow line; **~ sur l'électorat de gauche** [*parti*] to encroach on Labour territory; **3**○ (croire naïvement) to fall for it○.
IV se mordre *vpr* **1** (soi-même) [*personne*] to bite oneself; **se ~ la langue** lit, fig to bite one's tongue; **2** (l'un l'autre) to bite each other.
IDIOMES s'en ~ les doigts to kick oneself for sth.

mordu, **~e** /mɔʀdy/ **I**○ *adj* **1** (passionné) [*personne*] **être ~ de qch** to be mad○ about sth; **2** (amoureux) [*personne*] smitten; **cette fois-ci, elle est (bien) ~e!** she's (really) smitten this time!
II○ *nm,f* fan, buff○; **pour les ~s du ski** for skiing fans ou buffs.

more = **maure**.

moresque = **mauresque**.

morfal◑, **~e** /mɔʀfal/ **I** *adj* greedy.
II *nm,f* greedyguts◑ (+ *v sg*) GB, hog○ US.

morfondre: se morfondre /mɔʀfɔ̃dʀ/ [6] *vpr* **1** (attendre) to hang around; **se ~ à attendre** or **en attendant** to wait dejectedly; **2** (languir) to pine; **le pays se morfond dans la crise** fig the country is stagnating in recession.

morganatique /mɔʀganatik/ *adj* **mariage ~** morganatic marriage.

morgue /mɔʀg/ *nf* **1** (lieu) morgue; (dans un hôpital) mortuary; **2** (arrogance) arrogance; **avoir de la ~, être plein de ~** to be arrogant.

moribond, **~e** /mɔʀibɔ̃, ɔ̃d/ **I** *adj* [*personne*] dying; [*industrie, civilisation*] moribund.
II *nm,f* dying man/woman; **les ~s** the dying.

moricaud, **~e** /mɔʀiko, od/ **I**○ *adj* swarthy.
II *nm,f* offensive coloured^GB^ person, wog○ injur.

morigéner /mɔʀiʒene/ [14] *vtr* to reprimand; **se faire ~** to be reprimanded.

morille /mɔʀij/ *nf* morel (mushroom).

morillon /mɔʀijɔ̃/ *nm* tufted duck.

mormon, **~e** /mɔʀmɔ̃, ɔn/ *adj, nm,f* Mormon.

mormonisme /mɔʀmɔnism/ *nm* Mormonism.

morne /mɔʀn/ *adj* **1** [*personne, attitude, silence*] gloomy; [*visage*] glum; [*regard*] doleful; **2** [*paysage, lieu, existence, débat, vacances*] dreary; [*temps, journée*] dismal; **une rue ~** a drab street.

mornifle○ /mɔʀnifl/ *nf* (gifle) smack, clip round the ear GB.

morose /mɔʀoz/ *adj* [*personne, vieillesse, humeur*] morose; [*journée, lieu, ton, atmosphère, bilan, vie*] gloomy; [*Bourse*] bearish.

morosité /mɔʀozite/ *nf* gloom; **la ~ s'est emparée du pays** the country is sunk in gloom; **se complaire dans la ~** to wallow in gloom; **~ de la Bourse** lacklustre trading.

morphe /mɔʀf/ *nm* morph.

Morphée /mɔʀfe/ *npr* Morpheus.
IDIOMES être dans les bras de ~ to be in the arms of Morpheus.

morphématique /mɔʀfematik/ *adj* morphemic.

morphème /mɔʀfɛm/ *nm* morpheme; **~ libre/lié** free/bound morpheme.

morphine /mɔʀfin/ *nf* morphine.

morphine-base /mɔʀfinbɑz/ *nf* morphine base.

morphinisme /mɔʀfinism/ *nm* morphinism.

morphinomane /mɔʀfinɔman/ **I** *adj* addicted to morphine (*après n*).
II *nmf* morphine addict.

morphinomanie /mɔʀfinɔmani/ *nf* morphine addiction.

morphologie /mɔʀfɔlɔʒi/ *nf* morphology.

morphologique /mɔʀfɔlɔʒik/ *adj* morphological.

morphologiquement /mɔʀfɔlɔʒikmɑ̃/ *adv* morphologically.

morphométrie /mɔʀfɔmetʀi/ *nf* morphometry.

morphophonologie /mɔʀfofɔnɔlɔʒi/ *nf* morphophonology.

morphosyntaxe /mɔʀfosɛ̃taks/ *nf* morphosyntax.

morphosyntaxique /mɔʀfosɛ̃taksik/ *adj* morphosyntactic.

morpion /mɔʀpjɔ̃/ *nm* **1** ▶ 449 (jeu) noughts and crosses GB, tick-tack-toe US; **faire un ~** to play (a game of) noughts and crosses GB ou tick-tack-toe US; **2**◑ (enfant) brat○; **3**◑ (pou) crab (louse).

mors /mɔʀ/ *nm inv* **1** Équit bit; **prendre le ~ aux dents** [*cheval*] to take the bit between its teeth; [*personne*] (colère subite) to fly off the handle○; (énergie subite) to take the bit between one's teeth; **2** Tech (d'étau, de pince) jaw; **3** Édition (de reliure) joint; **~ fendus** cracked joints.
■ **~ de bride** curb bit; **~ de filet** snaffle bit.

morse /mɔʀs/ *nm* **1** Zool walrus; **2** Télécom (**alphabet** or **code**) **~** Morse code.

morsure /mɔʀsyʀ/ *nf* **1** (plaie) bite; **~ de chien** bite from a dog; **~ de serpent** snakebite; **2** (action) **la ~ du froid/gel** the biting cold/frost; **la ~ de l'acide** the bite of acid.

mort[1] /mɔʀ/ *nf* **1** (d'être vivant) death; **~ par asphyxie/strangulation** death by asphyxiation/strangulation; **peu avant sa ~** a short time before his/her death; **mourir de ~ naturelle** to die of natural causes; **mourir de sa belle ~** to die peacefully in old age; **mourir de ~ violente** to die a violent death; **il a eu** or **connu une ~ paisible** he died peacefully; **souhaiter** or **vouloir la ~ de qn** to wish sb dead; **porter tout ça! tu veux ma ~?** hum you want me to carry all this! are you trying to kill me, or what?; **il n'y a pas eu ~ d'homme** lit there were no fatalities; **ce n'est pas la ~!** hum it won't kill you!; **avoir une ~ sur la conscience** to have somebody's death on one's conscience; **être à deux doigts de la ~** to be at death's door; **j'ai vu la ~ de près** I saw death close up; **signer son arrêt de ~** to sign one's death warrant; **trouver la ~ dans un accident** to die in an accident; **à la ~ de mon oncle** (à partir de ce moment-là) on the death of my uncle; (peu après) after my uncle died; **se battre** or **lutter jusqu'à la ~** to fight to the death; **jusqu'à ce que ~ s'ensuive** [*battre, torturer*] to death; **trouver la ~** liter to die; **donner la ~** liter to kill; **se donner la ~** liter to kill oneself; **être/mettre en danger de ~** to be/to put [sb] in mortal danger; **mettre qn à ~** to put sb to death; **mise à ~** (de condamné, prisonnier) killing; (de taureau) dispatch; (de système, d'entreprise) rundown; **souffrir mille ~s** to die a thousand deaths; **un engin de ~** (arme) a deadly weapon; (véhicule, invention) a deadly contraption; **à ~ le dictateur!**, **~ au dictateur!** death to the dictator!; **à ~** [*duel, lutte*] to the death; [*guerre*] ruthless; [*freiner, serrer*] like mad○; [*frapper, battre, lutter*] to death; [*blessé*] fatally; **blesser à ~** to inflict a fatal injury; **je leur en veux à ~**○ I'll never forgive them; **on est fâchés à ~**○ we'll never have anything to do with each other again; ▶ **cheval**, **souffle**; **2** (d'activité, étoile) death.
■ **~ cérébrale** brain death; **~ clinique** clinical death; **~ subite** sudden death; **~ subite du nourrisson** cot death GB, crib death US; **un ~ vivant** one of the living dead; **les ~s vivants** the living dead; **tu as l'air d'un ~ vivant** you look like death warmed up GB ou over US.
IDIOMES **être pâle comme la ~** to be as pale as death; **la ~ dans l'âme** with a heavy heart.

mort[2], **~e** /mɔʀ, mɔʀt/ **I** *pp* ▶ **mourir**.
II *pp adj* **1** (sans vie) dead; **être ~ de faim** fig to be starving; **je suis ~e de froid** I'm freezing to death; **il est ~ de sommeil** he's dropping with tiredness; **il était comme ~** he seemed dead; **il est ~ pour la danse** he's lost to the world of dance; **~ ou vif** dead or alive; **plus ~ que vif** half dead with fear; **bouge pas ou t'es un homme ~!** don't move or you're a dead man!; **laisser qn pour ~** to leave sb for dead; ▶ **rat**; **2** (très fatigué) half-dead; **3** (partie du corps) [*dent*] dead; **mes orteils sont comme ~s** my toes have gone numb; **avoir le regard ~** or **les yeux ~s** to have no spark of life in one's eyes; **4** (sans activité) dead; **le quartier est ~ le soir** the area is dead in the evening; **c'est ~ ici!** it's like a graveyard here!; **c'est une période/saison ~e pour le tourisme** it's a slack time/season for tourism; **eaux ~es** stagnant water ¢; **bras ~ d'une rivière** oxbow; **5** (disparu) [*civilisation*] dead; [*ville*] lost; **mon amour pour elle est ~** my love for her is dead; **6**○ (hors d'usage) [*appareil, batterie*] dead.
III *nm,f* (défunt) dead person, dead man/woman; **faire dire une messe pour un ~** to have a mass said for somebody who has died; **les ~s** the dead; **jour** or **fête des ~s** Relig All Souls' Day.
IV *nm* **1** (victime) fatality; **il y a eu 12 ~s** there were 12 dead; **il n'y a pas eu de ~s** there were no fatalities, nobody was killed; **l'attentat n'a fait qu'un ~** the attack claimed only one life○; **2** (cadavre) body; **faire la toilette du ~** to lay out the body; **faire le ~** (être immobile) to play dead; (éviter les contacts) to lie low.
IDIOMES **ne pas y aller de main ~e** not to pull any punches; **être à la place du ~**○ (en voiture) to sit in the front passenger seat.

mortadelle /mɔʀtadɛl/ *nf* mortadella.

mortaise /mɔʀtɛz/ *nf* mortise.

mortaiser /mɔʀteze/ [1] *vtr* to mortise.

mortalité /mɔʀtalite/ *nf* mortality; **(taux de) ~** mortality rate; **la ~ infantile** infant mortality.

mort-aux-rats /mɔʀoʀa/ *nf inv* rat poison.

morte-eau, *pl* **mortes-eaux** /mɔʀto, mɔʀtzo/ *nf* neap(-tide); **marées de ~** neap-tides.

mortel, **-elle** /mɔʀtɛl/ **I** *adj* **1** (qui provoque la mort) [*coup, blessure, accident, chute*] fatal; [*poison, dose, gaz*] lethal; [*venin*] deadly; [*champignon*] deadly poisonous; **c'est une maladie mortelle** it can be fatal; ▶ **plaie**; **2** (intense) [*froid, pâleur, silence*] deathly; [*angoisse, frayeur*] mortal; **3** (implacable) [*ennemi*] mortal; **4** (ennuyeux) [*réunion, spectacle, personne*] deadly boring; [*attente*] deadly; **5** (susceptible de mourir) [*être*] mortal.
II *nm,f* liter mortal; **heureux ~s!** hum o happy mortals!

mortellement /mɔʀtɛlmɑ̃/ *adv* **1** [*blessé, atteint*] fatally; **2** [*ennuyeux*] deadly; [*pâle*] deathly.

morte-saison, *pl* **mortes-saisons** /mɔʀt(ə)sɛzɔ̃/ *nf* off season.

mortier /mɔʀtje/ *nm* **1** Constr mortar; **2** Mil mortar; **obus de ~** mortar shell; **3** (récipient) mortar; **4** (bonnet de magistrat) *small hat worn by French magistrates*; **5** Univ (coiffe) mortarboard.

mortifiant, **~e** /mɔʀtifjɑ̃, ɑ̃t/ *adj* mortifying.

mortification /mɔʀtifikasjɔ̃/ *nf* mortification.

mortifier /mɔʀtifje/ [2] **I** *vtr* to mortify.
II se mortifier *vpr* Relig to mortify oneself.

mortinatalité /mɔʀtinatalite/ *nf* incidence of still births.

mort-né, **~e**, *mpl* **~s** /mɔʀne/ *adj* **1** [*enfant*] stillborn; **2** [*œuvre, projet*] abortive.

mortuaire /mɔʀtɥɛʀ/ *adj* [*cérémonie*] funeral; **veillée ~** wake.

morue /mɔʀy/ *nf* **1** Zool cod; **2**● (prostituée) offensive slut◑ injur.

morutier, **-ière** /mɔʀytje, ɛʀ/ **I** *adj* cod-fishing (*épith*).
II *nm* **1** (navire) cod-fishing boat; **2** ▶ 510 (pêcheur) cod fisherman.

morve /mɔʀv/ *nf* **1** (sécrétion) nasal mucus, snot◑; **avoir la ~ au nez** lit to have a runny ou snotty nose; fig○ to be just a brat○; **2** Vét glanders (+ *v sg*).

morveux, **-euse** /mɔʀvø, øz/ **I** *adj* **1** [*enfant*] snotty-nosed◑ (*épith*); **se sentir ~** to feel embarrassed; **2** Vét [*cheval*] glandered.
II○ *nm,f* **1** (gamin) pej guttersnipe○; **2** (prétentieux) cocky little upstart○.

mosaïque /mɔzaik/ **I** *adj* **1** Art [*pavage, parquet*] mosaic (*épith*); **2** Relig [*loi*] Mosaic (*épith*).
II *nf* **1** (assemblage, art) mosaic; **vus d'avion, les champs formaient une ~** seen from the plane, the fields formed a patchwork; **2** Agric (maladie) mosaic (disease); **~ du tabac** tobacco mosaic.

Moscou /mɔsku/ ▶ 857 *npr* Moscow.

moscovite /mɔskɔvit/ ▶ 857 *adj* of Moscow.

Moscovite /mɔskɔvit/ *nmf* Muscovite.

Moselle /mɔzɛl/ ▶ 357, 692 *nprf* (rivière, département) **la ~** Moselle.

mosquée /mɔske/ *nf* mosque.

mot /mo/ *nm* **1** gén word; **~ de deux syllabes** two-syllable word; **~ mal orthographié** misspelled word; **~ savant/d'argot** learned/slang word; **le poids des ~s** the force of words; **en d'autres ~s** in other words; **en quelques ~s** in a few words; **chercher ses ~s** to grope for words; **il ne parle pas un ~ d'anglais** he doesn't speak a word of English; **peser ses ~s** to weigh one's words; **jouer sur les ~s** to play on words; **~ pour ~** [*répéter, traduire, reprendre*] word for word, verbatim; **faire du ~ à ~** to translate word for word; **au sens fort du ~** in the full sense of the word; **je n'en crois pas un (traître) ~** I don't believe a word of it; **à ~s couverts** [*avouer , accuser*] in veiled terms; **au bas ~** at least; **en un ~** in a word; **explique-moi en deux ~s** tell me briefly; **pour eux, l'amitié n'est pas un vain ~** they take friendship seriously; **il n'y a pas de ~s pour décrire leur bêtise/leur comportement** their stupidity/their behaviour[GB] defies description; **il n'y a pas d'autre ~** that's the only word for it; **il est bête et le ~ est faible!** he's stupid and that's putting it mildly!; **'manger', il n'a que ce ~ à la bouche** all he can talk about is eating; ▶ **gros**; **2** (paroles) word; **dire un ~ à qn** to have a word with sb; **échanger quelques ~s** to exchange a few words; **je ne veux pas entendre un ~!** I don't want to hear a word; **je n'ai pas pu leur tirer un ~** I couldn't get a word out of them; **il faut lui arracher les ~s à celui-là!** getting him to talk is like getting blood out of a stone!; **sans ~ dire**, **sans dire un ~** without saying a word; **ne pas souffler** or **piper**○ **~** not to say a word; **ne pas pouvoir placer un ~** to be unable to get a word in edgeways; **prendre qn au ~** to take sb at his/her word; **avoir le dernier ~** to have the last word; **je n'ai pas dit mon dernier ~** I haven't said my last word; **toucher**○ **un ~ de qch à qn** to have a word with sb about sth; **glisser un ~ à qn** to have a quick word with sb; **des ~s que tout cela!** it's just hot air!; **si tu as besoin de moi tu n'as qu'un ~ à dire** if you need me you've only to say the word; **sur ces ~s il sortit** with that, he left; **il ne dit jamais un ~ plus haut que l'autre** he never raises his voice; **avoir son ~ à dire** to be entitled to one's say; **viens par ici, j'ai deux ~s à te dire!** euph come here, I've got a bone to pick with you!; **pour reprendre les ~s de Marina** as Marina put it; **50 francs pour les deux c'est mon dernier ~** 50 francs the pair but that's my last offer; **avoir toujours le ~ pour rire** to be a born joker; **3** (petite lettre) note; **un ~ d'excuse** Scol an excuse note; **envoyer/écrire/laisser un ~** to send/write/leave a note; **4** Ordinat word.

■ **~ d'auteur** Littérat literary quotation; **~ composé** Ling compound (word); **~ d'enfant** child's saying; **~ d'esprit** witticism, witty remark; **~ de la fin** closing words (*pl*); **avoir le ~ de la fin** to have the last word; **~ grammatical** Ling function word, grammatical word; **~ de liaison** link word; **~ machine** machine word; **~ d'ordre** watchword; **~ d'ordre de grève** call for strike; **~ d'ordre revendicatif** demand, claim; **~ outil** = **~ grammatical**; **~ de passe** password; **~ plein** Ling full word; **~ vide** Ling prop ou empty word; **~s croisés** Jeux crosswords; **~s doux** sweet nothings; **susurrer des ~s doux à qn** to whisper sweet nothings.

IDIOMES **avoir** or **échanger des ~s avec qn** euph to have words with sb; **ne pas avoir peur des ~s** to call a spade a spade; **manger ses ~s** to mumble; **se donner** or **passer le ~** to pass the word around.

motard, **~e** /motaʀ, aʀd/ **I**○ *nm,f* motorcyclist, biker○.
II ▶**510** *nm* (de police) police motorcyclist; (de gendarmerie) *motorcyclist in the gendarmerie*; (d'armée) army motorcyclist.

mot-clé, *pl* **mots-clés** /moklе/ *nm* key word.

motel /motɛl/ *nm* motel.

motet /motɛ/ *nm* motet.

moteur, **-trice** /motœʀ, tʀis/ **I** *adj* **1** (qui entraîne) [*force, principe*] driving (*épith*); **être l'élément ~ de qch** to be the driving force behind sth; **jouer un rôle ~ dans** to play a dynamic role in; **la voiture a quatre roues motrices** the car has four-wheel drive; **les roues motrices sont à l'avant** it's a front-wheel drive (car); **les roues motrices sont ensablées** the traction wheels are stuck in the sand; **2** Méd, Physiol [*trouble, aphasie, fibre*] motor (*épith*).
II *nm* **1** lit (électrique) motor; (autre) engine; **voiture avec ~ (à l')arrière/(à l')avant** car with an engine at the back/in front; **le ~ développe** or **fait 500 cv** the engine is 500 hp; **un ~ (de) 8 cylindres** an 8-cylinder engine; **un véhicule à ~** a motor vehicle; **un ~ (à) 4 temps** a 4-stroke engine; **un ~ (de) 2 litres** a 2-litre[GB] engine; **un ~ poussé** or **gonflé**○ a souped-up engine; **une voiture avec le ~ en marche** a car with the engine running; **2** fig driving force; **être le ~ de qch** [*personne, motif*] to be the driving force behind sth.
III *excl* Cin action!
IV motrice *nf* Rail (locomotive) engine.

■ **~ d'appoint** booster; **~ asynchrone** asynchronous motor; **~ atmosphérique** atmospheric engine; **~ à combustion interne** internal combustion engine; **~ diesel** diesel engine; **~ électrique** electric motor; **~ à explosion** internal combustion engine; **~ hydraulique** hydraulic engine; **~ à injection** fuel injection engine; **~ ionique** ion engine; **~ à réaction** jet engine; **~ rotatif** rotary engine; **~ synchrone** synchronous motor; **~ turbo** turbo engine; **~ à vapeur** steam engine.

moteur-fusée, *pl* **moteurs-fusées** /motœʀfyze/ *nm* rocket engine.

motif /motif/ *nm* **1** (raison) grounds (*pl*) (**de** for); **il y a des ~s d'espérer/de se réjouir** there are grounds for hope/for rejoicing; **pour le même ~** on the same grounds; **être réformé pour ~s médicaux** to be exempt from military service on medical grounds; **pour un ~ d'ordre politique** on politically-related grounds; **~s de divorce** grounds for divorce; **vos récriminations sont sans ~** there are no grounds for your complaint; **2** (cause) reason (**de** for); **~s de notre retard** reasons for our lateness; **avez-vous un ~ valable?** do you have a valid reason?; **3** (motivation) motive; **les ~s sont politiques** the motives are political; **~ profond** real motive; **absence de ~** lack of motive; **sans ~ apparent** for no apparent motive; **avoir pour ~** to have as a motive; **quel que soit leur ~** whatever their motive; **4** (décoration) pattern; **à ~ floral/géométrique** with a floral/geometric pattern; **5** (thème) motif.

motion /mosjɔ̃/ *nf* Jur, Pol motion; **déposer une ~** to table a motion; **faire passer une ~** to have a motion passed; **voter une ~ en faveur de/contre** to pass a motion in favour[GB] of/against.

■ **~ de censure** motion of censure.

motivant, **~e** /motivɑ̃, ɑ̃t/ *adj* [*salaire*] attractive; [*travail*] rewarding; [*raison*] worthwhile.

motivation /motivasjɔ̃/ *nf* **1** Psych motivation; **~ des élèves** pupils' motivation; **absence de ~** lack of motivation; **2** (raison) motive; **~s profondes** deep-seated motives; **3** Ling (caractère non arbitraire) motivation.

motivé, **~e** /motive/ **I** *pp* ▶ **motiver**.
II *pp adj* **1** (enthousiaste) [*personne, équipe*] motivated (**pour** as regards; **pour faire** to do); **un étudiant peu ~** a student lacking motivation; **il est peu ~** he lacks motivation; **2** (légitime) [*exigence, retard, décision, plainte*] justifiable; **3** (avec explications) [*texte*] explanatory; **4** Ling (non arbitraire) motivated.

motiver /motive/ [1] **I** *vtr* **1** (pousser) to motivate [*personne*] (**à faire** to do); **~ un employé par une augmentation de salaire** to give an employee the incentive of a pay rise GB ou a raise US; **2** (causer) [*événement, résultat*] to lead to [*décision, action*]; **motivé par** caused by.
II se motiver *vpr* [*personne*] to motivate oneself.

moto /moto/ *nf* **1** (véhicule) (motor)bike; **à ~** by motorbike; **une course de ~s** a motorcycle race; **2** (activité) motorcycling.

motocross /motokʀɔs/ ▶**449** *nm inv* motocross, scramble GB; **faire du ~** to go scrambling GB.

moto-crottes○ /motokʀɔt/ *nf inv* pooper-scooper○.

motoculteur /motokyltœʀ/ *nm* (motorized) cultivator.

motoculture /motokyltyʀ/ *nf* motorized cultivation.

motocycle /motosikl/ *nm* motorcycle.

motocyclette /motosiklɛt/ *nf* motorcycle.

motocyclisme /motosiklism/ ▶**449** *nm* motorcycle racing; **faire du ~** to do motorcycle racing.

motocycliste /motosiklist/ **I** *adj* [*rallye, brigade*] motorcycle (*épith*); **le sport ~** the sport of motorcycling.
II *nmf* motorcyclist.

motonautique /motonotik/ *adj* speedboat (*épith*).

motonautisme /motonotism/ ▶**449** *nm* speedboat racing; **faire du ~** to go speedboat racing.

motoneige /motonɛʒ/ *nf* snowmobile.

motopompe /motopɔ̃p/ *nf* power-driven pump.

motorisation /motoʀizasjɔ̃/ *nf* motorization; **taux de ~** rate of car ownership.

motoriser /motoʀize/ [1] *vtr* **1** (équiper de véhicules à moteur) to motorize; **troupes motorisées** motorized troops; **être motorisé**○ to have transport GB ou transportation US; **les personnes motorisées/non motorisées**○ people with transport/without transport; **2** (équiper de moteur) to motorize.

motoriste /motoʀist/ ▶**510** *nmf* **1** Ind (constructeur) engine builder; **2** (mécanicien) mechanic.

mot-racine, *pl* **mots-racines** /moʀasin/ *nm* root word.

motrice ▶ **moteur**.

motricité /motʀisite/ *nf* Psych motivity.

motte /mɔt/ *nf* **1** (morceau de terre) (dans un champ) **~ (de terre)** clod (of earth); (dans une pelouse) turf; **~ de gazon** clump of lawn; **2** Hort (ensemble racines et terre) rootball; **plantation en ~** ball planting; **3** (morceau de beurre) **~ (de beurre)** slab of butter; **acheter du beurre en ~** to buy butter by weight; **4**● (pubis féminin) *female pubic region*, pussy◑.

motteux /motø/ *nm* wheatear.

motus /motys/ *excl* **~ (et bouche cousue)** keep it under your hat.

mot-valise, *pl* **mots-valises** /movaliz/ *nm* portmanteau word.

mou (**mol** *before vowel or mute h*), **molle** /mu, mɔl/ **I** *adj* **1** (pas ferme) [*coussin, matière*] soft; [*tige, étoffe*] limp; [*choc*] dull; **2** (sans tenue) [*trait du visage*] weak; [*chair, ventre*] flabby; [*cheveux*] limp; **3** (apathique) [*personne, enfant*] listless; [*poignée de main*] limp; [*croissance, reprise économique*] sluggish; **4** (sans énergie) [*parent, professeur*] soft, overindulgent; **5** (sans conviction) péj [*version, libéralisme*] watered-down; [*discours, résistance*] feeble, weak.
II *nm* **1** (personne) pej wimp○ péj; **2** (en boucherie) lights (*pl*) GB, lungs (*pl*) US; **3** (de corde) slack; **avoir du ~** to be slack; **donner du ~** to let (the rope) out a bit; **donner/laisser du ~ à qn**○ fig to give sb/to let sb have a bit of leeway.

IDIOMES **bourrer le ~ à qn**◑ to have sb on○ GB, to put sb on US.

mouchard, **~e** /muʃaʀ, aʀd/ **I**○ *nm,f* **1** (de police) informer; (en prison) grass○ GB, squealer○ péj; **2** Scol sneak○ péj.
II *nm* **1** Tech (appareil) tachograph; **2** (orifice) spyhole.

mouchardage○ /muʃaʀdaʒ/ *nm* **1** (pour la police) informing; **2** (en prison) grassing○ GB, squealing○; **3** Scol sneaking○.

moucharder○ /muʃaʀde/ [1] *vtr* **1** (pour la police) to inform (**qn** on sb); **2** (en prison) to grass○ GB, to squeal○ (**qn** on sb); **3** Scol to sneak○, to split○ (**qn** on sb).

mouche /muʃ/ *nf* **1** (insecte) fly; **2** Mode patch, beauty spot; **3** (de cible) bull's eye; **faire ~** lit to hit the bull's eye; fig to be right on target; **4** (de fleuret) button.

■ **~ artificielle** Pêche artificial fly; **~ bleue** bluebottle; **~ commune** or **domestique** housefly; **~ à merde**◑ dung fly; **~ à miel** bee; **~ verte** greenbottle; **~ du vinaigre** fruit fly.

IDIOMES **il ne ferait pas de mal à une ~** he wouldn't hurt a fly; **on entendrait une ~ voler** you could hear a pin drop; **quelle ~ les a piqués?** what's got GB ou gotten US into them?; **regarder voler les ~s** to stare into space; **prendre la ~** to fly off the handle; **tomber comme des ~s** to drop like flies.

moucher /muʃe/ [1] **I** *vtr* **1** (dégager) **~ son nez** to blow one's nose; **~ qn** lit to blow sb's nose; fig○ to put sb in his/her place; **se faire ~**○ fig to get put in one's place; **~ du sang** to blow one's nose and find blood; **2** (éteindre) to snuff (out) [*chandelle, mèche*].
II se moucher *vpr* to blow one's nose.

IDIOMES **il ne se mouche pas du pied** or **du coude** (mener grand train) he lives the high life; (être prétentieux) he's full of airs and graces.

moucheron /muʃʀɔ̃/ *nm* **1** (insecte) midge; **2** (personne) midget.

moucheté, **~e** /muʃte/ *adj* **1** [*laine, étoffe*] flecked; [*plumage, œuf, poisson*] speckled; [*pelage*] spotted; [*cheval*] dappled; **un foulard gris ~ de rose** a grey GB ou gray US scarf with pink flecks; **2** [*fleuret*] buttoned.

mouchetis /muʃti/ *nm* (textured ou stippled) rendering.

moucheture /muʃtyʀ/ *nf* (de léopard) spot; (de tissu) fleck; (de peau, plumage) speckle.

mouchoir /muʃwaʀ/ *nm* (en coton) handkerchief; (en papier) tissue GB, Kleenex®;

~ en papier tissue; **agiter son ~** to wave one's handkerchief; **sortir** or **tirer son ~** to get one's handkerchief out; **à la fin du film, on tire son ~** the film's a real tear-jerker at the end.
IDIOMES **faire un nœud à son ~** to tie a knot in one's handkerchief; **grand comme un ~ de poche** [*jardin*] the size of a postage stamp; **arriver dans un ~** [*candidats, concurrents*] to have a close finish.

Moudjahidin /mudʒaidin/ *nmpl* mujaheddin, mujahedeen.

moudre /mudʀ/ [77] *vtr* to grind.

moue /mu/ *nf* pout; **une ~ boudeuse/de dégoût** a sulky/disgusted pout; **une ~ dubitative** a doubtful pout; **faire la ~** (bouder) to pout; (pour exprimer un doute) to pull a face; **faire la ~ devant qch** to pull a face at sth.

mouette /mwɛt/ *nf* (sea) gull.
■ **~ rieuse** black-headed gull; **~ tridactyle** kittiwake.

moufeter = **moufter**.

mouf(f)ette /mufɛt/ *nf* skunk.

moufle /mufl/ *nf* **1** Mode mitten; **2** Tech tackle block.

mouflet○, **-ette** /muflɛ, ɛt/ *nm,f* kid○, child.

mouflon /muflɔ̃/ *nm* mouflon.

moufter◑ /mufte/ [1] *vi* to protest; **partir/accepter sans ~** to leave/to accept without turning a hair ou batting an eyelid; **personne n'a moufté** nobody turned a hair ou batted an eyelid.

mouillage /mujaʒ/ *nm* **1** Naut (manœuvre) anchoring; **~ de mines** Mil minelaying; **être au ~** to lie ou ride at anchor; **2** Naut (emplacement) anchorage; **3** (de vin, lait) watering(-down).

mouillé, **~e** /muje/ **I** *pp* ▶ **mouiller**.
II *pp adj* wet (**de** with).
III *adj* Ling [*consonne*] palatalized.

mouiller /muje/ [1] **I** *vtr* **1** (rendre humide) [*personne, pluie*] to wet [*linge, sol*]; to get [sth] wet [*vêtements, chaussures*]; **mouillez bien vos cheveux** wet your hair thoroughly; **se faire ~** to get wet; **2** (être incontinent) [*personne*] to wet [*drap, culotte*]; **3** Naut, Pêche to drop [*ancre*]; to lay [*mine*]; to cast [*ligne*]; **4**○ (compromettre) to drag [sb] into, to implicate; **5** Culin to moisten; **~ avec du lait/vin** to moisten with milk/wine; **6** Ling to palatalize [*consonne*].
II *vi* **1** Naut to anchor, to drop anchor; **2**◑ (avoir peur) to be scared stiff, to be scared; **3**◑ (être excitée) to be wet.
III se mouiller *vpr* **1** lit (avec de l'eau) to get wet; (en urinant) [*bébé*] to wet oneself; **2**○ (s'impliquer) to stick one's neck out○; **il ne se mouille jamais** he never sticks his neck out.
IV○ *v impers* **ça mouille** it's raining.

mouillette /mujɛt/ *nf* soldier○ GB, finger of bread eaten with a boiled egg.

mouilleur /mujœʀ/ *nm* **1** (de timbres) (stamp) sponge; **2** Naut (dispositif) tumbler.
■ **~ de mines** minelayer.

mouillure /mujyʀ/ *nf* **1** (tache humide) damp patch; **2** (de consonne) palatalization.

mouise○ /mwiz/ *nf* **être dans la ~** to be in dire straits, to be stony broke○.

moujik /muʒik/ *nm* muzhik.

moukère◑ /mukɛʀ/ *nf* woman.

moulage /mulaʒ/ *nm* **1** (fabrication de moule) moulding GB ou molding US (process); (fabrication d'épreuve, reproduction) casting; **faire un ~ de qch** to take a cast of sth; **2** (épreuve, objet reproduit) Art cast; (en métallurgie) casting; **3** (de verre) press moulding GB ou molding US; **4** (de vêtement, chaussure) moulding GB, molding US; **5** (de grains) milling.
■ **~ à cire perdue** lost-wax casting; **~ par injection** injection moulding GB ou molding US; **~ par rotation** rotational moulding GB ou molding US.

moulant, **~e** /mulɑ̃, ɑ̃t/ *adj* [*vêtement*] skin-tight, tight-fitting.

moule /mul/ **I** *nm* **1** Art, Ind mould GB, mold US; fig (modèle imposé) mould GB, mold US; **le ~ de l'école** the school mould GB ou mold US; **ils ont été coulés dans le même ~** fig they were cast in the same mould GB ou mold US; **être fait au ~** (aspect esthétique) to be perfectly shaped; **2** Culin (pour gâteau, pain) tin, pan US; (pour gelées) mould GB, mold US; **~ à fond amovible** loose-bottomed cake tin GB ou pan US.
II *nf* Zool mussel; **~s (à la) marinière** Culin *mussels cooked in wine*.
■ **~ à brioche** brioche tin; **~ à cake** loaf tin; **~ à flan** flan dish; **~ à gaufre** Culin waffle iron; fig○ nitwit○; **~ à gâteaux** cake tin GB, cakepan US; **~ à tarte** flan dish, pie pan US.

moulé, **~e** /mule/ **I** *pp* ▶ **mouler**.
II *pp adj* **1** Ind [*pièce*] moulded GB, molded US; [*verre*] (press) moulded GB ou molded US; [*aluminium*] cast; **statue de plâtre ~** moulded GB ou molded US plaster statue; **2** (serré) **une femme ~e dans une robe de cuir/un pull** a woman in a skin-tight leather dress/a clinging sweater; **3** Culin [*pain, baguette*] baked in a (shaped) tin; **4** (bien formé) [*écriture*] copperplate (*épith*); [*lettre*] well-formed.

mouler /mule/ [1] *vtr* **1** (fabriquer avec un moule) to mould GB, to mold US [*substance*]; to cast [*liquide*]; to mint [*médaille*]; **2** (prendre une empreinte) to take a cast of [*bas-relief, visage, main*]; **3** (coller à) [*vêtement*] to cling (tightly) to, to hug [*corps, buste, hanches*]; **une mini-jupe élastique qui moule les fesses** an elastic mini skirt which hugs the bottom.

mouleur, **-euse** /mulœʀ, øz/ ▶ **510** *nm,f* moulder GB, molder US.

moulin /mulɛ̃/ *nm* **1** (édifice) mill; **2** (machine à moudre) mill; **3**○ (moteur) engine.
■ **~ à café** coffee grinder, coffee mill; **~ à eau** water mill; **~ à légumes** vegetable mill; **~ à paroles** chatterbox; **~ à poivre** pepper mill; **~ à prières** Relig prayer wheel; **~ à vent** windmill.
IDIOMES **apporter de l'eau au ~ de qn** to fuel sb's arguments; **on ne peut être à la fois au four et au ~** one can't be in two places at once; **on y entre comme dans un ~** one can just slip in; **se battre contre des ~s à vent** to tilt at windmills; **jeter son bonnet par-dessus les ~s** to let one's hair down.

mouliné /muline/ *nm* stranded cotton.

mouliner /muline/ [1] *vtr* **1** Culin to purée [*pommes de terre*]; to grind, to mill [*poivre, café*]; **2** Tex to throw; **3** Pêche to reel in.

moulinet /mulinɛ/ *nm* **1** (de canne à pêche) reel; **2** (de travail) winch; **3** (mouvement) **faire des ~s avec les bras** gén to wave one's arms about; Sport to do windmills; **faire des ~s avec un bâton** to twirl a stick.

moulinette® /mulinɛt/ *nf* (small) vegetable mill; **passer qch à la ~** lit to put sth through the mill; **passer qn à la ~** fig to put sb through the mill.

moulinois, **~e** /mulinwa, az/ ▶ **857** *adj* of Moulins.

Moulinois, **~e** /mulinwa, az/ *nm,f* (natif) native of Moulins; (habitant) inhabitant of Moulins.

Moulins /mulɛ̃/ ▶ **857** *npr* Moulins.

moult† /mult/ *adv* many.

moulu, **~e** /muly/ **I** *pp* ▶ **moudre**.
II *pp adj* lit [*café, poivre*] ground.
III○ *adj* fig **~ (de fatigue)** worn out; **~ (de coups)** beaten black and blue.

moulure /mulyʀ/ *nf* (ornement) moulding GB, molding US; (baguette à rainures) casing.

moulurer /mulyʀe/ [1] *vtr* (orner) to decorate [sth] with mouldings GB ou moldings US.

moumoute○ /mumut/ *nf* **1** (perruque) toupee; **2** (vêtement) sheepskin jacket.

mourant, **~e** /muʀɑ̃, ɑ̃t/ **I** *adj* **1** (en train de mourir) [*personne, animal*] dying (**de** of); **2** (en train de disparaître) [*entreprise, politique, système*] moribund; **3** (qui décline) [*lumière*] fading; **d'une voix ~e** fig in a weak tone.
II *nm,f* dying person; **les ~s** the dying (+ *v pl*).

mourir /muʀiʀ/ [34] **I** *vi* (+ *v être*) **1** (cesser de vivre) [*personne, animal, plante*] to die (**de** of; **pour qn/qch** for sb/sth; **pour faire** to do); **~ jeune** to die young; **~ d'un cancer/d'une crise cardiaque** to die of cancer/of a heart attack; **~ de chagrin** to die of grief ou of a broken heart; **~ de faim/vieillesse** lit to die of hunger/old age; **~ de froid** lit (dehors) to die of exposure; (sous un toit) to die of cold; **je meurs de soif** fig I'm dying of thirst; **je meurs de faim** fig I'm starving; **je meurs de froid** fig I'm freezing to death; **je meurs de sommeil** fig I'm dropping with tiredness; **c'était à ~ (de rire)**! it was hilarious!; **plutôt ~ que de lui demander une faveur** I'd rather die than ask him/her a favour[GB]; **tu mourras centenaire!** you'll live to (be) a hundred! ; **~ assassiné** to be murdered; **~ empoisonné** to die of poisoning; **~ étranglé** (par accident) to strangle to death; (par meurtre) to be strangled to death; **~ debout** to be active to the end; **~ au monde** [*moine, ermite*] to die to the world; **elle meurt d'amour pour lui** she's pining for him; **laisser qn ~** to let sb die (**de qch** of sth); **il s'est laissé ~ après la mort de sa femme** he gave up and died after the death of his wife; **se laisser ~ de faim** to starve oneself to death; **faire ~ qn** to kill sb; **l'auteur fait ~ le héros à la troisième page** the author kills the hero off on the third page; ▶ **champ**, **feu**; **2** (cesser d'exister) [*civilisation, tradition, entreprise*] to die; [*sentiment, amitié*] to die; **3** liter (faiblir) [*lueur, jour*] to fade away littér; [*feu, flamme*] to die down; [*son*] to die away; [*conversation*] to die away; [*vagues*] to break and fall back.
II se mourir *vpr* liter or fml [*personne*] to be dying; [*civilisation, tradition*] to be dying; [*flamme, feu, braises*] to die down; [*sentiment, son, chant*] to die away; **elle se meurt d'amour pour lui** she's pining with love for him.
IDIOMES **partir c'est ~ un peu** to say goodbye is to die a little; **je ne veux pas ~ idiot** hum I want to know; **on n'en meurt pas!, tu n'en mourras pas!** hum it won't kill you!; **je veux bien ~ or que je meure si**... I'll eat my hat if...; **plus idiot/paresseux que lui, tu meurs**○! they don't come any dumber/lazier!

mouroir /muʀwaʀ/ *nm* pej old people's home, twilight home péj.

mouron /muʀɔ̃/ *nm* Bot pimpernel.
■ **~ blanc** chickweed; **~ des champs** scarlet pimpernel; **~ des oiseaux** = **~ blanc**.
IDIOMES **se faire du ~**○ to worry.

mouscaille◑ /muskaj/ *nf* **être dans la ~** (avoir des ennuis) to be up the creek○; (être dans la misère) to be flat broke○.

mousquet /muskɛ/ *nm* musket.

mousquetaire /muskətɛʀ/ *nm* musketeer; **bottes à la ~** highwayman's boots; **poignet ~** double cuff.

mousqueton /muskətɔ̃/ *nm* **1** Tech snap clasp; **2** Sport (en alpinisme) carabiner; **3** Mil carbine.

moussaillon○ /musajɔ̃/ *nm* ship's apprentice.

moussaka /musaka/ *nf* moussaka.

moussant, **~e** /musɑ̃, ɑ̃t/ *adj* [*gel*] foaming (*épith*); **non ~** [*savon, lessive*] low-lather; **ce savon est très ~** this soap gives a good lather.

mousse /mus/ **I** *nm* Naut ship's apprentice.
II *nf* **1** Bot moss; **2** (bulles) gén foam; (de savon, lessive) lather; (sur le lait, le café) froth; (sur la bière) head; **il y a de la ~ dans ta barbe** you've got foam in your beard; **il y a**

trop de ~ dans ma bière my beer is too frothy; **3** Culin mousse; **~ au chocolat** chocolate mousse; **~ de saumon** salmon mousse; **~ de foie de canard** duck-liver mousse; **4** (matière) foam rubber; **matelas en ~** foam-rubber mattress; **5** Mode, Tex **bas/chaussettes en ~** stretch stockings/socks; **6**○ (verre de bière) glass of beer.

■ **~ carbonique** fire-fighting foam; **~ de Ceylan** Ceylon moss; **~ de Corse** worm moss; **~ d'Irlande** carrageen; **~ de nylon**® stretch nylon; **~ de platine** platinum sponge; **~ à raser** shaving foam.

IDIOMES **se faire de la ~**○ to get into a tizzy○ ou lather○; **pierre qui roule n'amasse pas ~** Prov a rolling stone gathers no moss Prov.

mousseline /muslin/ *nf* **1** Tex (de coton) muslin; (de soie) chiffon; **2** Tech (en reliure) mull GB, crash US; **3** Culin mousse.

mousser /muse/ [1] *vi* [*champagne*] to bubble; [*bière*] to foam; [*détergent, savon*] to lather; **faire ~** to work [sth] up into a lather [*savon, détergent*].

IDIOMES **faire ~ qn**○ to praise sb; **se faire ~**○ to sing one's own praises.

mousseron /musʀɔ̃/ *nm* St George's mushroom; **(faux) ~** fairy ring mushroom.

mousseux, -euse /musø, øz/ **I** *adj* **1** (contenant des bulles) [*vin*] sparkling; [*bière*] fizzy; **2** (qui évoque la mousse) frothy; **des dentelles mousseuses** frothy lace.

II *nm* Vin sparkling wine.

mousson /musɔ̃/ *nf* monsoon; **~ d'hiver/été** winter/summer monsoon.

moussu, ~e /musy/ *adj* **1** Bot (couvert de mousse) [*sol, pierre, branche*] mossy; **2** (ressemblant à de la mousse) [*cheveux*] woolly.

moustache /mustaʃ/ **I** *nf* moustache GB, mustache US; **porter la ~** or **des ~s** to wear ou have a moustache GB ou mustache US; **commencer à avoir de la ~** to start to get a moustache GB ou mustache US.

II moustaches *nfpl* (de félin, phoque, rongeur) whiskers.

■ **~ en brosse** toothbrush moustache GB ou mustache US; **~ à la gauloise** walrus moustache GB ou mustache US; **~ en guidon de vélo**○ handlebar moustache GB ou mustache US.

moustachu, ~e /mustaʃy/ **I** *adj* [*personne*] with a moustache GB ou mustache (*épith, après n*) US; **il est ~** he has a moustache GB ou mustache US.

II *nm* man with a moustache GB ou mustache US; **c'est un ~** he has a moustache GB ou mustache US.

moustiquaire /mustikɛʀ/ *nf* (en tissu) mosquito net; (en métal) mosquito screen.

moustique /mustik/ *nm* **1** Zool mosquito; **2**○ (enfant) (little) mite○.

moût /mu/ *nm* (de raisin, pomme) must; (de houblon, d'orge) wort.

moutard◐ /mutaʀ/ *nm* (enfant) kid○.

moutarde /mutaʀd/ **I** ▶ **193** *adj inv* mustard.

II *nf* Bot, Culin mustard; **~ forte** English mustard GB, hot mustard US; **~ de Dijon** Dijon mustard.

■ **~ blanche** white mustard; **~ sauvage** charlock.

IDIOMES **la ~ me monte au nez**○! I'm beginning to see red!

moutardier /mutaʀdje/ *nm* (récipient) mustard pot.

IDIOMES **il se prend pour le premier ~ du pape** he thinks he's the cat's whiskers.

mouton /mutɔ̃/ **I** *nm* **1** Zool sheep; **compter les ~s** to count sheep; **2** Culin mutton; **côte de ~** mutton chop; **3** (peau) sheepskin; **veste en ~ retourné** sheepskin jacket; **4** pej (personne soumise) sheep péj; **5**○ (dans une prison) grass○ GB, stool pigeon.

II moutons *nmpl* **1** (nuages) small fleecy clouds; **2** (petites vagues) white horses GB, whitecaps; **3** (poussière) fluff ₵.

■ **~ à cinq pattes** rare bird; **~ de Panurge** pej sheep; **ce sont des ~s de Panurge** they follow one another like sheep.

IDIOMES **il frise comme un ~** his hair goes all frizzy; **fris é comme un ~** frizzy-haired; **revenons à nos ~s**○ let's get back to the subject ou point.

moutonnement /mutɔnmɑ̃/ *nm* **le ~ du ciel** the sky breaking up into fleecy clouds; **regarder le ~ des vagues** to watch the white horses break.

moutonner /mutɔne/ [1] *vi* [*mer*] to be covered with white horses; [*ciel*] to be full of fleecy clouds.

moutonneux, -euse /mutɔnø, øz/ *adj* [*toison*] curly, fluffy; [*chevelure*] frizzy; [*mer*] covered with white horses.

moutonnier, -ière /mutɔnje, ɛʀ/ *adj* **1** [*élevage*] sheep (*épith*); **2** pej [*comportement*] sheeplike péj.

mouture /mutyʀ/ *nf* **1** (produit moulu) grind; **mon moulin à café donne une excellente ~** my coffee grinder produces an excellent grind; **2** (processus) (pour céréales) milling; (pour café) grinding; **3** (version) version; **première ~** first version; **nouvelle ~** new version, rehash péj.

mouvance /muvɑ̃s/ *nf* **1** (sphère d'influence) sphere of influence; **être dans la ~ d'un parti** to be generally affiliated with a party; **2** Hist (d'un fief) subinfeudation.

mouvant, ~e /muvɑ̃, ɑ̃t/ *adj* **1** lit (qui s'enfonce) [*sol*] unstable; **2** (qui bouge) [*groupe*] shifting; [*champ de blé*] undulating; **reflets ~s** shimmering reflections; **3** (qui évolue) [*situation, réalité, opinion*] changing; **électorat ~** floating voters (*pl*).

mouvement /muvmɑ̃/ *nm* **1** (geste) movement; **faire un ~** to move, to make a move; **il fit un ~ pour se dégager** he made a move to break away; **je ne peux pas faire un seul ~** I can't move at all; **tu es libre de tes ~s** you can come and go as you please; **~ de danse** dance movement; **~ de gymnastique** gymnastic exercise; **apprendre les ~s du crawl** to learn stroke for the front crawl; **avoir un ~ d'humeur** to show a flash of annoyance; ▶ **faux**; **2** (déplacement) gén movement; Phys movement, motion; **le ~ des vagues** the movement of the waves; **~s sismiques** seismic movements; **~ de reflux** backward movement; **le ~ des bateaux à l'entrée du port** the movement of ships at the entrance to a port; **le ~ de personnel dans une entreprise** staff changes in a company; **~ de retraite** withdrawal; **accélérer le ~** to speed up; **ralentir le ~** to slow down; **se mettre en ~** to get moving; **~ ondulatoire** or **périodique** wave motion; **~ hélicoïdal/ascendant/absolu/fixe** helical/upward/absolute/relative motion; **~ perpétuel** perpetual motion; **le ~ d'un pendule** the movement ou swing of a pendulum; **la toupie décrit un ~ de rotation** the top describes a rotary motion; **mettre qch en ~, imprimer un ~ à qch** to set sth in motion; **3** (animation) bustle; **il y a du ~ dans la rue** there's a lot of bustle in the street; **toute la maison était en ~** the whole household was bustling about ou bustling with activity; **une rue pleine de ~** a busy street; **suivre le ~** fig to follow the crowd; **4** (élan) impulse, reaction; **mon premier ~ a été de me mettre en colère** my initial reaction ou my first impulse was to get angry; **dans un ~ de générosité** on a generous impulse; **un ~ de colère/pitié** a surge of anger/pity; **un ~ de panique** a panic reaction; **un bon ~** a kind ou nice gesture; **fais un bon ~, donne-moi 100 francs** do me a good turn and give me 100 francs; **agir de son propre ~** to act of one's own accord; **un ~ général de rejet** a generally hostile reaction; **un ~ de masse** a mass movement; **5** (pour contester, revendiquer) action; **le ~ étudiant** the student protest movement; **~ de contestation** protest action; **~ de grève** strike, industrial action ₵; **~ de rébellion** rebel movement; **6** (groupe) movement, group; **~ de jeunesse** youth movement; **~ de protection/défense de** movement for the protection/defence[GB] of; **7** (évolution) **le ~ des idées** the evolution of ideas; **être dans le ~** to move with the times; **vivre dans un milieu en ~** to live in a changing environment; **~ de décentralisation/démocratisation** trend toward(s) decentralization/democratization; **~ de création d'emploi** trend toward(s) job creation; **8** Écon, Fin (fluctuation) fluctuation; (échange) transaction; (tendance) trend; **le ~ du marché** market fluctuations (*pl*); **~ de hausse/de baisse** upward/downward trend (**de** in); **un ~ de reprise** a movement toward(s) recovery; **~s financiers** financial transactions; **~ de capitaux** movement ou flow of capital; **~ d'un compte** turnover on an account; **~ de fonds** movement of funds; **9** Littérat (de récit, poème) movement; **10** Mus (partie d'une œuvre) movement; **11** Mécan (de montre, d'horloge) movement; **~ d'horlogerie commandant un contact électrique** clockwork mechanism controlling an electrical contact.

mouvementé, ~e /muvmɑ̃te/ *adj* **1** [*vie, semaine*] eventful, hectic; [*réunion*] lively; [*récit, voyage*] eventful; **l'histoire ~e d'un pays** a country's turbulent history; **2** [*relief, terrain*] rough.

mouvoir /muvwaʀ/ [43] fml **I** *vtr* **1** (mettre en mouvement) [*personne*] to move; [*énergie, mécanisme*] to drive [*machine*]; **machine mue par l'électricité** machine driven by electricity; **2** (pousser) [*sentiment, désir, impulsion*] to drive; **il était mû par un désir puissant** he was driven by a powerful desire.

II se mouvoir *vpr* [*personne, nuage, véhicule*] to move; **mes jambes ne peuvent plus se ~** I cannot move my legs any more.

moyen, -enne /mwajɛ̃, ɛn/ **I** *adj* **1** (intermédiaire en dimension, poids) [*stature, taille, épaisseur, surface*] medium; [*ville, entreprise, légume*] medium-sized; [*fil*] of medium thickness; **ma chambre est de grandeur moyenne** my room is medium-sized; **de moyenne portée** medium-range; **de ~ calibre** of medium calibre[GB] (*après n*); **le cours ~ d'un fleuve** Géog the middle reaches of a river; **2** (passable) average (**en** in); **tes résultats sont assez ~s** your results are fairly average; **un élève très ~** a very average pupil; **'comment était le repas/l'hôtel?'—'~'** 'how was the meal/the hotel?'—'so-so'; **3** (dans une hiérarchie) [*cadre, revenu*] middle; [*échelon*] intermediate; **les salaires ~s** (personnes) people on middle incomes; **4** (ordinaire) [*citoyen, spectateur, utilisateur, lecteur*] average; **le Français ~** the average Frenchman; **5** (après évaluation, calcul) [*nombre, taux, revenu, température*] average, mean; **6** (de compromis) [*solution, position*] middle-of-the-road; **ils pratiquent des prix ~s** their prices are reasonable; **7** Ling **voyelle moyenne** mid-vowel.

II *nm* **1** (façon de procéder) means (*sg*) (**de faire** of doing), way (**de faire** of doing); **c'est le ~ le plus sûr/le moins coûteux** it's the most reliable/the least expensive means ou way; **c'est un ~ comme un autre** it's as good a way as any; **par tous les ~s** by every possible means; **par n'importe quel ~** by hook or by crook○; **empêcher qn de faire qch par tous les ~s** to stop sb from doing sth by fair means or foul; **consolider son autorité par tous les ~s** to use every possible means to consolidate one's authority; **tous les ~s sont bons** any means will do; **tous les ~s leur sont bons** they'll stop at nothing; **pour lui tous les ~s sont bons pour gagner de l'argent** there's nothing he wouldn't do to make money; **tous les ~s lui sont bons pour ne pas travailler** he'll/she'll do anything not to work; **employer les grands ~s** to resort to drastic measures; **2** (d'action, expression, de production) means; (d'investigation, de paiement) method; **~ de communication** means of communication; **3** (possibilité) way; **il y a ~ de faire** there's a way of doing; **il y a ~ de s'en sortir** there's a way out; **n'y avait-il pas ~ de faire autrement?** was there no other way to go about it?; **(il n'y a) pas ~ d'être tranquille ici** there's no peace around here; **(il n'y a) pas ~ de lui faire comprendre qu'il a tort** it's impossible to make him realize he's wrong; **lui faire admettre qu'il a tort? pas ~!** make him admit he's wrong? no chance!; **4** Ling **complément de ~** adverbial phrase of means.

III au moyen de *loc prép* (d'une action, d'un référendum) by means of; (d'un objet) by means of, by using.

IV par le moyen de *loc prép* by means of, through.

V moyens *nmpl* **1** (ressources financières) means; **manquer de ~s** to lack the resources (**pour faire** to do); **faute de ~s** through lack of money; **vivre au-dessus de ses ~s** to live beyond one's means; **je n'ai pas les ~s de faire** I can't afford to do; **mes ~s ne me permettent pas de partir en vacances** I can't afford to take a vacation; **avoir de petits/grands ~s** not to be/ to be very well off; **avoir les ~s**○ to be well off; **2** (soutien matériel) resources; **la ville a mis d'énormes ~s à notre disposition** the town put vast resources at our disposal; **je n'ai ni le temps ni les ~s de taper ce texte** I have neither the time nor the equipment to type this text; **se donner les ~s de son efficacité** to take the necessary steps to achieve efficiency; **donner à qn les ~s de faire** to give sb the means to do; **j'ai dû y aller par mes propres ~s** I had to go (there) under my own steam○, I had to make my own way there; **se débrouiller par ses propres ~s** to manage on one's own; **3** (compétences) ability; **cet élève a les ~s de réussir** this pupil has the ability to succeed ou do well; **il a de petits ~s** he has limited ability; **être au-dessus des ~s de qn** to be beyond sb's abilities ou capabilities; **être en possession de tous ses ~s** (intellectuellement) to be at the height of one's powers; (physiquement) to be at the peak of one's strength; **ne plus avoir tous ses ~s** to be no longer in full possession of one's faculties; **perdre ses ~s** to go to pieces.

VI moyenne *nf* **1** (norme) average; **être plus riche que la moyenne** to be better off than the average; **il est plus grand que la moyenne des hommes** he is taller than the average man; **être inférieur/supérieur à la moyenne** to be below/above (the) average; **être au-dessous/au-dessus de la moyenne** to be below/above average; **être dans la moyenne** to be average; **des résultats extrêmement faibles par rapport à la moyenne européenne** extremely poor results against ou compared to the European average; **2** Scol (moitié de la note maximale) half marks GB, 50%; **j'ai eu tout juste la moyenne** (à un examen) I barely passed; (à un devoir) I just got half marks GB, I just got 50%; **3** (après calcul) average; **la moyenne d'âge** the average age; **calculer une moyenne** to work out an average; **en moyenne** on average; **4** (vitesse) average speed; **faire une moyenne de 30 km/h** to do an average speed of ou to average 30 kph.

■ **~ français** Ling Middle French; **~ de locomotion** = **~ de transport**; **~ métrage** Cin medium-length film; **~ de trésorerie** financial means; **~ de transport** means of transport GB ou transportation US; **moyenne arithmétique** Math arithmetic mean; **moyenne géométrique** Math geometric mean; **moyenne harmonique** Math harmonic mean; **Moyen Âge** Middle Ages (*pl*); **le bas/haut Moyen Âge** the late/early Middle Ages; **Moyen Empire** Middle Kingdom.

IDIOMES **la fin justifie les ~s** the end justifies the means; **qui veut la fin veut les ~s** Prov he who wills the end wills the means Prov.

moyenâgeux, -euse /mwajɛnɑʒø, øz/ *adj* **1** Hist (médiéval) medieval; **2** péj (dépassé) [*idée, pratique*] antiquated, medieval.

moyen-courrier, *pl* **~s** /mwajɛ̃kuʀje/ *nm* medium-haul airliner.

moyennant /mwajɛnɑ̃/ *prép* for; **~ finances, vous pouvez changer de nom** for a fee ou a consideration, you can get your name changed; **je l'ai eu ~ finances** I paid for it; **il est sorti de prison ~ finances** he bought his way out of prison; **~ 20 francs par personne/un versement initial/rançon** for 20 francs a head/a down payment/a ransom; **~ abonnement** on payment of a subscription; **~ quelques modifications/un effort considérable** with a few adjustments/a tremendous effort; **~ quoi** (en conséquence de quoi) in view of which; (en échange de quoi) in return for which; **il va travailler samedi, ~ quoi il ne viendra pas lundi** he's going to work on Saturday, so he won't come on Monday.

moyennement /mwajɛnmɑ̃/ *adv* [*intelligent, riche, cultivé*] moderately; [*réussir, comprendre*] moderately well; [*aimer, apprécier*] to a certain extent.

Moyen-Orient /mwajɛnɔʀjɑ̃/ ▶692 *nprm* Middle East; **au ~** in the Middle East.

moyeu, *pl* **~x** /mwajø/ *nm* Mécan hub; **~ d'embrayage/de roue** clutch/wheel hub.

mozambicain, -aine /mɔzɑ̃bikɛ̃, ɛn/ ▶537 *adj* Mozambican.

Mozambicain, -aine /mɔzɑ̃bikɛ̃, ɛn/ ▶537 *nm,f* Mozambican.

Mozambique /mɔzɑ̃bik/ ▶321 *nprm* Mozambique.

MST /ɛmɛste/ *nf*: *abbr* ▶**maladie**.

mû, mue[1] ▶**mouvoir**.

mucosité /mykɔzite/ *nf* mucus ¢.

mucoviscidose /mykovisidoz/ ▶271 *nf* cystic fibrosis.

mucus /mykys/ *nm* mucus.

mue[2] /my/ *nf* **1** Zool (renouvellement) (d'insecte) metamorphosis; (de serpent, lézard) sloughing of the skin; (d'oiseau, de mammifère) moulting[GB]; (de cerf) casting; **2** Zool (dépouille) (d'insecte, de serpent) slough, sloughed skin; (d'oiseau) shed feathers (*pl*); (de mammifère) shed fur; (de cerf) shed antlers (*pl*); **3** (de voix) breaking GB, changing US; **pendant sa ~ il n'osait plus chanter** while his voice was breaking GB ou changing US he didn't dare to sing; **4** fig (transformation) transformation.

muer /mɥe/ [1] **I** *vtr* liter to transform (**en** into).

II *vi* **1** Zool [*insecte*] to metamorphose; [*serpent, lézard*] to slough its skin; [*oiseau, mammifère*] to moult[GB]; [*cerf*] to cast its antlers; **2** [*voix*] to break GB, to change US; **adolescent qui mue** teenager whose voice is breaking GB ou changing US.

III se muer *vpr* (être transformé) to be transformed (**en** into); (activement) to transform oneself (**en** into).

müesli /mysli/ *nm* muesli.

muet, -ette /mɥɛ, ɛt/ **I** *adj* **1** Méd [*personne*] dumb; **sourd et ~** deaf and dumb, deaf-mute; **2** (qui refuse de parler) [*témoin, foule, presse, pouvoir*] silent (**sur, à propos de** on); **rester ~** to remain silent; **le rapport est ~ sur cette question** the report remains silent on this point; **3** (incapable de parler) speechless; **sous le choc, elle resta muette** the shock left her speechless; **~ de** (d'admiration, de terreur) speechless with; **rester ~ de** to be struck dumb with; **4** (inexprimé) [*reproche, douleur, serment, colère*] silent; **5** Cin [*cinéma, film*] silent; [*rôle*] non-speaking (*épith*); **6** Phon [*voyelle, consonne*] mute, silent; **7** (sans bruit) [*ville, cloche*] silent; **8** (sans inscription) [*carte de géographie, page*] blank; [*menu*] unpriced.

II *nm,f* Méd mute; **les ~s** the dumb (+ *v pl*).

III *nm* Cin silent screen; **le passage du ~ au parlant** the transition from the silent screen to the talkies.

IV muette *nf* Hist **la grande muette** the army.

muezzin /mɥɛdzin/ *nm* muezzin.

mufle /myfl/ **I** *adj* [*personne*] boorish, loutish.

II *nm* **1** Zool (museau) (de ruminant) muffle; (de carnassier) muzzle; **2** (malotru) boor, lout; **comportement de ~** boorish ou loutish behaviour[GB].

muflerie /myfləʀi/ *nf* boorishness.

muflier /myflije/ *nm* antirrhinum, snapdragon.

mufti /myfti/ *nm* Relig mufti.

muge /myʒ/ *nm* grey GB ou gray US mullet.

mugir /myʒiʀ/ [3] *vi* [*vache*] to low; [*taureau, bœuf*] to bellow; [*vent*] to howl, to roar; [*sirène*] to wail; [*vagues, mer, torrent*] to roar.

mugissement /myʒismɑ̃/ *nm* **1** (de vache) lowing ¢; (de taureau, bœuf) bellowing ¢; **pousser des ~s** (vache) to moo; **2** (de vent) howling ¢, roaring ¢; (de sirène) wailing ¢; (de vagues) roar ¢.

muguet /mygɛ/ *nm* **1** (fleur) lily of the valley; **2** ▶271 (maladie) thrush.

mulâtre /mylɑtʀ/ *adj, nm* mulatto.

mulâtresse /mylɑtʀɛs/ *nf* mulatto.

mule /myl/ *nf* **1** Zool female mule; **2** (pantoufle) mule; **3** (passeur de drogue) mule; **~ aveugle** unwitting drugs carrier.

mulet /mylɛ/ *nm* **1** (équidé) (male) mule; **2** (poisson) grey mullet GB, mullet US; **3** Sport back-up car.

muletier, -ière /myltje, ɛʀ/ **I** *adj* **sentier** or **chemin ~** mule track.

II ▶510 *nm* muleteer, mule skinner○ US.

Mulhouse /myluz/ ▶857 *npr* Mulhouse.

mulhousien, -ienne /myluzjɛ̃, ɛn/ ▶857 *adj* of Mulhouse.

Mulhousien, -ienne /myluzjɛ̃, ɛn/ *nm,f* (natif) native of Mulhouse; (habitant) inhabitant of Mulhouse.

mulot /mylo/ *nm* fieldmouse.

multicarte /myltikaʀt/ *adj inv* **représentant ~** (sales) representative for several firms.

multicellulaire /myltiselylɛʀ/ *adj* multicellular.

multicolore /myltikɔlɔʀ/ *adj* multicoloured[GB].

multicoque /myltikɔk/ *adj, nm* multihull.

multicouche /myltikuʃ/ *adj* multi-layered.

multiculturel, -elle /myltikyltyʀɛl/ *adj* multicultural.

multidimensionnel, -elle /myltidimɑ̃sjɔnɛl/ *adj* multidimensional.

multiethnique /myltiɛtnik/ *adj* multi-ethnic.

multiflore /myltiflɔʀ/ *adj* multiflora.

multifonction /myltifɔ̃ksjɔ̃/ *adj inv* gén multipurpose; Ordinat multifunction.

multiforme /myltifɔʀm/ *adj* [*aspect*] multiform; [*vie, danger*] many-sided; [*réalité*] multifaceted.

multigrade /myltigʀad/ *adj* **huile ~** multigrade oil.

multilatéral, ~e, *mpl* **-aux** /myltilateʀal, o/ *adj* multilateral.

multilingue /myltilɛ̃g/ *adj* multilingual.

multilinguisme /myltilɛ̃gɥism/ *nm* multilingualism.

multimédia /myltimedja/ *adj* multimedia.

multimilliardaire /myltimiljaʀdɛʀ/ *nmf* multimillionaire.

multimillionnaire /myltimiljɔnɛʀ/ *nmf* multimillionaire.

multinational, ~e, *mpl* **-aux** /myltinasjɔnal, o/ **I** *adj* multinational.

II **multinationale** *nf* multinational (company).

multipare /myltipaʀ/ I *adj* multiparous.
II *nf* multipara.

multipartisme /myltipaʀtism/ *nm* multiparty system.

multipartite /myltipaʀtit/ *adj* **1** (multilatéral) [*réunion, traité*] multipartite; **2** (avec plusieurs partis) [*élections*] multi-party (*épith*).

multiple /myltipl/ I *adj* **1** (nombreux) [*raisons, occasions*] numerous, many; [*naissances*] multiple; **après de ~s spéculations/tergiversations** after much speculation/hesitation; **salle/appareil à usages ~s** multipurpose hall/appliance; **à choix ~** multiple-choice (*épith*); **2** (divers) [*buts, causes, facettes*] many, various; **3** Bot, Math, Phys multiple.
II *nm* Art, Math multiple.

multiplex /myltiplɛks/ Télécom I *adj inv* multiplex.
II *nm inv* multiplex system.

multiplexeur /myltiplɛksœʀ/ *nm* Télécom multiplexer.

multipliable /myltiplijabl/ *adj* multipliable.

multiplicande /myltiplikɑ̃d/ *nm* multiplicand.

multiplicateur, **-trice** /myltiplikatœʀ, tʀis/ I *adj* multiplying.
II *nm* multiplier.

multiplicatif, **-ive** /myltiplikatif, iv/ *adj* Ling, Math multiplying.

multiplication /myltiplikasjɔ̃/ *nf* **1** (augmentation) **~ de** increase in the number of; **(le miracle de) la ~ des pains** the miracle of the loaves and fishes; **2** Math (processus) multiplication ¢; (opération) multiplication; **apprendre à faire des ~s** to learn to do multiplication; **il fait des ~s à longueur de journée** he does multiplications all day long; **faire une erreur de ~** to make a mistake in the multiplication; **ta ~ est fausse** your multiplication is wrong; **3** Mécan gear ratio; **4** Biol, Bot multiplication.

multiplicité /myltiplisite/ *nf* multiplicity.

multiplier /myltiplije/ [2] I *vtr* **1** Math to multiply [*chiffre*] **(par** by); **2** (augmenter) to increase [*risques, chances, gains, rendement, fortune*]; to increase the number of [*trains, accidents*]; **~ les bénéfices par cinq/par cent** to increase profits fivefold/a hundredfold; **~ les risques d'accident par trois/dix** to make the risk of accident three/ten times more likely; **3** (faire en grand nombre) **~ les excuses/exemples** to give endless excuses/examples; **~ les visites/erreurs** to make endless visits/mistakes.
II **se multiplier** *vpr* **1** (augmenter) [*succursales, villas*] to grow in number; [*incidents, arrestations*] to be on the increase; [*difficultés, obstacles*] to increase; [*contacts, disputes*] to become more frequent; **2** (se reproduire) [*animaux, microbes*] to multiply.

multipolaire /myltipolɛʀ/ *adj* multipolar.

multiprise /myltipʀiz/ *adj* **pince ~** adjustable pliers (*pl*).

multiprogrammation /myltipʀogʀamasjɔ̃/ *nf* Ordinat multiple programming.

multipropriété /myltipʀopʀijete/ *nf* time-sharing; **acheter un appartement en ~** to buy a time-share in a flat GB ou apartment US.

multiracial, **~e**, *mpl* **-iaux** /myltiʀasjal, o/ *adj* multiracial.

multirisque /myltiʀisk/ *adj* **assurance ~** comprehensive insurance; **(assurance) ~ habitation** comprehensive household insurance.

multisalle /myltisal/ *adj inv* **cinéma ~** cinema complex GB, multiplex US.

multiséculaire /myltisekylɛʀ/ *adj* very ancient.

multistandard /myltistɑ̃daʀ/ *adj inv* [*téléviseur, magnétoscope*] multistandard.

multitâche /myltitaʃ/ *adj* multitask (*épith*).

multitraitement /myltitʀɛtmɑ̃/ *nm* Ordinat multiprocessing.

multitude /myltityd/ *nf* **1** (grand nombre) **une ~ de** (d'objets, de touristes) a mass of; (d'idées, de raisons) a lot of, many; **2** (foule de gens) multitude, throng.

multivitaminé, **~e** /myltivitamine/ *adj* multivitamin (*épith*).

mumuse○ /mymyz/ **faire ~** to play **(avec** with).

Munich /mynik/ ▶857 *npr* Munich.

munichois, **~e** /mynikwa, az/ I ▶857 *adj* [*personne*] from Munich; [*bière, spécialité*] Munich (*épith*).
II *nm* Hist péj *supporter of the policy of appeasement*; **les ~** *those who signed the Munich agreement.*

municipal, **~e**, *mpl* **-aux** /mynisipal, o/ I *adj* Admin [*conseil, conseiller*] (de petite ville) local, town (*épith*); (de grande ville) city (*épith*); [*impôt, élections, arrêté*] local; [*parc, piscine, bibliothèque*] municipal.
II **municipales** *nfpl* local elections.

municipalité /mynisipalite/ *nf* **1** (ville) municipality; **2** (conseil) (de petite ville) town council; (de grande ville) city council.

munificence /mynifisɑ̃s/ *nf* munificence.

munificent, **~e** /mynifisɑ̃, ɑ̃t/ *adj* munificent.

munir /myniʀ/ [3] I *vtr* **1** to provide [*personne*] **(de** with); **~ les passagers de gilets de sauvetage** to provide passengers with lifejackets; **les enfants étaient munis de repas froids** the children had packed lunches; **muni des derniers sacrements** Relig fortified with the last rites; **2** (équiper) **~ un bâtiment d'un escalier de secours** to put a fire escape on a building; **~ une maison d'une chaudière supplémentaire** to put an extra boiler into a house; **appareil photo muni d'un flash** camera fitted with a flash; **porte munie d'un verrou** door with a bolt.
II **se munir** *vpr* **il faut vous ~ de gants** (apporter) you should bring gloves; (emporter) you should take gloves; **manifestants munis de barres de fer** demonstrators carrying iron bars; **se ~ de patience** to summon up one's patience; **se ~ de courage** to pluck up one's courage.

munitions /mynisjɔ̃/ *nfpl* ammunition ¢, munitions; **dépôt de ~** munitions depot.

muqueux, **-euse** /mykø, øz/ I *adj* mucous.
II **muqueuse** *nf* mucous membrane.

mur /myʀ/ I *nm* **1** gén, Archit, Constr wall; **un ~ de pierre/de briques** a stone/brick wall; **il y avait des tableaux aux ~s** there were pictures (hanging) on the walls; **monter** or **élever un ~** to put up a wall; **~ mitoyen/de clôture/d'enceinte** party/boundary/outer wall; **les ~s de la ville** the city walls; **hors des ~s (de la ville)** lit outside the city walls, fig outside the city limits; **coller qn au ~** to put sb up against the wall and shoot him/her; **être le dos au ~** to have one's back to the wall; **rester** or **être entre quatre ~s** to be cooped up; **c'est à se taper** or **cogner la tête contre les ~s** you feel like banging your head against the wall○; **les ~s ont des oreilles** walls have ears; **faire du ~**○ (au tennis) to practise[GB] hitting a ball against the wall; **faire les pieds au ~** lit to do a handstand against the wall; fig to tie oneself up in knots; **2** (obstacle) wall; **se heurter à un ~ de silence** to come up against a wall of silence; **3** (personne froide) cold fish; **parler à un ~** to be talking to a brick wall.
II **murs** *nmpl* (local) (d'entreprise) premises; (d'ambassade, de palais) confines; **le ministre est dans nos ~s aujourd'hui** the minister is with us today; **être dans ses ~s** to own one's own house.
■ **~ d'appui** (de soutènement) retaining wall; (parapet) parapet; **~ de l'Atlantique** Atlantic Wall; **~ de Berlin** Berlin wall; **~ portant** or **porteur** load-bearing wall; **~ du son** sound barrier; **franchir le ~ du son** to break the sound barrier; **~ de soutènement** retaining wall; **Mur des Lamentations** Wailing Wall.
IDIOMES **faire le ~** (s'échapper) to go over the wall; (au football) to make a wall; **mettre qn au pied du ~** to call sb's bluff; **être au pied du ~** to be up against the wall.

mûr, **~e** /myʀ/ I *adj* **1** [*fruit, blé*] ripe; **2** (intellectuellement) mature; **être ~ pour son âge** to be mature for one's age; **être ~ pour faire** to be mature enough to do; **après ~e réflexion** after careful consideration; **3** (psychologiquement) ready **(pour qch** for sth; **pour faire** to do); **il est ~ pour des aveux** he's ready to confess; **être ~ pour la démocratie/pour changer de régime** to be ready for democracy/to change regime; **4** (adulte) mature; **l'âge ~** middle age; **il a attendu l'âge ~ pour écrire** he only started writing in his later years; **5** [*affaire, situation*] at a decisive stage (*jamais épith*); **6** [*abcès, bouton*] **être ~** to have come to a head; **7**○ [*étoffe*] worn; **8**◐ (soûl) tight○.
II **mûre** *nf* blackberry.
IDIOMES **en voir des vertes et des pas ~es**○ to go through a lot ou through some hard times; **en faire voir à qn des vertes et des pas ~es**○ to put sb through hard times; **il en a dit des vertes et des pas ~es**○ (histoires osées) he told some dirty jokes; **il en a dit des vertes et des pas ~es à ton sujet**○ he said a lot of nasty things about you; **en entendre des vertes et des pas ~es**○ to hear some quite outrageous things.

murage /myʀaʒ/ *nm* Archit, Constr (de fenêtre, porte) walling up.

muraille /myʀaj/ *nf* lit, fig great wall; **~ de rochers/brouillard/fumée** great wall of rocks/fog/smoke; **couleur (de) ~**, **gris ~** dirty grey GB ou gray US; **la Grande Muraille de Chine** the Great Wall of China.

mural, **~e**, *mpl* **-aux** /myʀal, o/ *adj* [*panneau, revêtement, carte*] wall (*épith*); [*plante*] climbing; [*four*] wall-mounted; **peinture ~e** Art mural.

mûrement /myʀmɑ̃/ *adv* carefully; **~ réfléchi** [*décision, projet*] carefully thought through; **j'y ai ~ réfléchi** I thought it through very carefully.

murène /myʀɛn/ *nf* moray eel.

murer /myʀe/ [1] I *vtr* to build a wall around [*champ, propriété*]; to brick up [*fenêtre, porte*]; to block off [*galerie, pièce*]; to wall [sb] up [*criminel, personne*].
II **se murer** *vpr* [*personne*] **depuis la mort de sa femme il se mure chez lui** since his wife died, he has shut himself away and stays in all the time; **se ~ dans son obstination** to dig one's heels in; **se ~ dans la solitude** to retreat into isolation.

muret /myʀɛ/ *nm*, **murette** /myʀɛt/ *nf* low wall.

murex /myʀɛks/ *nm* murex.

mûrier /myʀje/ *nm* mulberry tree.
■ **~ blanc** white mulberry tree; **~ noir** black mulberry tree.

mûrir /myʀiʀ/ [3] I *vtr* **1** [*soleil*] to ripen [*fruit*]; **2** [*épreuve, temps*] to mature [*personne*]; **3** [*personne*] to develop [*projet*].
II *vi* **1** [*fruit*] to ripen; **~ au soleil** to ripen in the sun; **faire ~ des bananes** to ripen bananas; **2** [*personne*] to mature; **3** [*projet, idée*] to evolve, to mature; [*talent*] to mature; [*passion*] to develop; **laisser ~ une affaire** to leave a matter to develop; **4** [*abcès, bouton*] to come to a head; **5** [*vin*] to mature.

mûrissage /myʀisaʒ/ *nm* (de fruits) ripening.

mûrissement /myʀismɑ̃/ *nm* (de fruit) ripening; (de projet) evolution, maturing.

mûrisserie /myʀisʀi/ *nf* ripening store.

Les instruments de musique

Les instruments

L'anglais emploie l'article défini devant les noms d'instruments de musique, même avec le verbe to play (*jouer*).

apprendre le piano	=	to learn the piano
étudier le piano	=	to study the piano
jouer du piano	=	to play the piano

Les morceaux de musique

un arrangement pour piano	=	an arrangement for piano *ou* a piano arrangement
une sonate pour violon	=	a violin sonata
un concerto pour piano et orchestre	=	a concerto for piano and orchestra
la partie pour piano	=	the piano part

Les musiciens

Le suffixe anglais -ist *correspond au suffixe français* -iste.

un violoniste	=	a violinist
un pianiste	=	a pianist

Dans les autres cas; on peut toujours dire a — player.

un corniste	=	a horn player

De même, an oboe player, a piccolo player, *etc.*

En anglais comme en français, le nom de l'instrument est parfois utilisé pour parler des musiciens.

les trombones	=	the trombones

***De** avec les noms d'instruments de musique*

un cours de violon	=	a violin class
une leçon de violon	=	a violin lesson
un professeur de violon	=	a violin teacher
un solo de violon	=	a violin solo

murmure /myʀmyʀ/ *nm* **1** (chuchotement) murmur; **~ d'admiration/d'indignation** murmur of admiration/of protest; **2** (plainte sourde) **~s** mutterings; **3** liter (de vent) whisper; (de source) murmur, babbling; **4** (rumeur) rumour[GB]; **des ~s courent dans la ville** rumours[GB] are going around town.

murmurer /myʀmyʀe/ [1] **I** *vtr* **1** (chuchoter) to murmur; **~ qch à qn/à l'oreille de qn** to murmur sth to sb/into sb's ear; **2** (dire) to say; **on murmure qu'il est** he is rumoured[GB] to be; **on murmure que** it is rumoured[GB] that.

II *vi* **1** (chuchoter) [*personne*] to murmur; [*vent*] to whisper; [*ruisseau, source*] to babble; **2** (se plaindre) to mutter; **obéir sans ~** to obey without a murmur; **3** (faire courir des bruits) to spread rumours[GB]; **on murmure à leur sujet** there are rumours[GB] about them.

musaraigne /myzaʀɛɲ/ *nf* shrew.

musarder /myzaʀde/ [1] *vi* to wander around.

musc /mysk/ *nm* musk.

muscade /myskad/ *nf* **1** Bot, Culin nutmeg; **noix ~** nutmeg; **2** (de prestidigitateur) (conjuror's) ball.

IDIOMES **passez ~!** hey presto!

muscadet /myskadɛ/ *nm* (vin) Muscadet; (cépage) Muscadet grape.

muscadier /myskadje/ *nm* nutmeg tree.

muscardin /myskaʀdɛ̃/ *nm* (common) dormouse.

muscari /myskaʀi/ *nm* grape hyacinth.

muscat /myska/ *nm* **1** (raisin) muscat grape; **2** (vin) muscat.

muscle /myskl/ *nm* Anat muscle; **~s striés/lisses** striated/smooth muscles; **c'est du ~**○ it's all muscle; **être tout en ~s**○ to be all muscle; **avoir du ~**○ to be strong; **faire du ~**○ to do bodybuilding.

musclé, **~e** /myskle/ *adj* **1** lit muscular; **2** fig (vigoureux) [*style*] sinewy; [*musique, discours*] powerful; [*réaction*] strong; (dur) [*discours, intervention, politique, match*] tough; **3** Écon [*entreprise, économie, industrie*] competitive.

muscler /myskle/ [1] **I** *vtr* **1** lit **~ les bras/jambes** to develop the arm/leg muscles; **ça muscle** it develops the muscles; **2** fig to strengthen; **~ l'industrie** to make industry more competitive.

II se muscler *vpr* **1** [*personne*] to develop one's muscles; **2** [*entreprise*] to become more competitive.

musculaire /myskylɛʀ/ *adj* [*tissu, fibre*] muscle (*épith*); [*force, faiblesse*] muscular.

musculation /myskylasjɔ̃/ *nf* Sport (**exercices de**) **~** bodybuilding; (après une maladie) exercises to strengthen the muscles; **salle de ~** weights room.

musculature /myskylatyʀ/ *nf* musculature; **avoir une ~ bien développée** to have well developed muscles.

musculeux, **-euse** /myskylø, øz/ *adj* **1** [*bras, personne*] muscular; **2** Anat [*tissu*] muscle (*épith*).

muse /myz/ *nf* **1** Littérat, Mythol Muse; **les neuf ~s** the Muses; **taquiner la ~** hum to dabble in verse; **2** (inspiration) muse.

museau, *pl* **~x** /myzo/ *nm* **1** (de chien, bovin, d'ovin) muzzle; (de porc) snout; (de renard) nose; **2**○ (visage) face; **se frotter le ~** fig to kiss; **3** Culin brawn GB, head cheese US.

musée /myze/ *nm* gén museum; (d'art et de peinture) art gallery GB, art museum US; **leur maison, c'est le ~ des horreurs**○ hum everything in their house is indescribably ugly; **une ville ~** a city of great historical and artistic importance.

■ **~ de cire** waxworks (+ *v sg* ou *pl*), wax museum.

museler /myzəle/ [19] *vtr* lit, fig to muzzle.

muselière /myzəljɛʀ/ *nf* muzzle; **mettre une ~ à un chien** to muzzle a dog.

musellement /myzɛlmɑ̃/ *nm* lit, fig muzzling.

muséologie /myzeɔlɔʒi/ *nf* museology.

muser /myze/ [1] *vi*† to wander around.

musette /myzɛt/ **I** *nm* ou *f* Mus (air, instrument) musette; **orchestre ~** accordion band; **valse ~** waltz (to the accordion).

II *nm* **1** Mus (style) accordion music; **2** (bal) dance (*where accordion music is played*).

III *nf* **1** (sac) (de soldat) haversack; (d'ouvrier) lunchbag; **2** Zool common shrew.

muséum /myzeɔm/ *nm* natural history museum.

musical, **~e**, *mpl* **-aux** /myzikal, o/ *adj* [*événement*] musical; [*revue, critique*] music (*épith*); [*choix*] of music (*épith, après n*).

musicalement /myzikalmɑ̃/ *adv* musically.

musicalité /myzikalite/ *nf* musicality.

music-hall, *pl* **~s** *nm* /mysikol/ music hall; **artiste de ~** music hall ou variety artist; **spectacle de ~** variety show.

musicien, **-ienne** /myzisjɛ̃, ɛn/ **I** *adj* musical.

II ▶ **510** *nm,f* musician.

musicographe /myzikɔgʀaf/ ▶ **510** *nmf* musicographer.

musicographie /myzikɔgʀafi/ *nf* musicography.

musicologie /myzikɔlɔʒi/ *nf* musicology.

musicologue /myzikɔlɔg/ ▶ **510** *nmf* musicologist.

musique /myzik/ *nf* **1** (art, notes) music; **la ~ classique/sacrée/folklorique** classical/sacred/folk music; **la ~ de film** film music; **la ~ de Bach** the music of Bach, Bach's music; **dîner en ~** to dine with soft music playing; **travailler en ~** to work with music in the background; **faire de la gymnastique en ~** to do exercises to music; **mettre en ~** to set [sth] to music [*poème, texte*]; **faire de la ~** (savoir jouer) to play an instrument; (jouer) to play; ▶ **adoucir**; **2** (œuvre) **une ~ triste** a sad piece of music; **une ~ pour piano** a piece of piano music; **une ~ de film** a film score; **sur une ~ de** with music by; **3** (orchestre) band; **4** (de source, mot, vent) music.

■ **~ d'ambiance** gén background music; péj piped music, Muzak®; **~ de chambre** chamber music; **~ de fond** background music.

IDIOMES **c'est toujours la même ~**○ it's always the same old refrain ou story; **connaître la ~**○ to know the score○; **je ne peux pas aller plus vite que la ~** I can't go any faster than I'm already going; **en avant la ~**○! off we go!; **être réglé comme du papier à ~** [*personne*] to be as regular as clockwork; [*voyage, congrès, projet*] to go very smoothly.

musiquette○ /myzikɛt/ *nf* Mus bland music.

musoir /myzwaʀ/ *nm* pierhead.

musqué, **~e** /myske/ *adj* **1** [*parfum*] musky; [*cheveux*] musk-scented; **2** Zool **bœuf ~** musk ox; **rat ~** muskrat.

mussipontain, **~e** /mysipɔ̃tɛ̃, ɛn/ ▶ **857** *adj* of Pont-à-Mousson.

Mussipontain, **~e** /mysipɔ̃tɛ̃, ɛn/ *nm,f* (natif) native of Pont-à-Mousson; (habitant) inhabitant of Pont-à-Mousson.

musulman, **~e** /myzylmɑ̃, an/ *adj, nm,f* Muslim.

mutabilité /mytabilite/ *nf* mutability.

mutant, **~e** /mytɑ̃, ɑ̃t/ *adj, nm,f* Biol, fig mutant.

mutation /mytasjɔ̃/ *nf* **1** Admin, Jur transfer; **2** (transformation) transformation; **en pleine ~** in the process of radical transformation; **une profonde ~** a total transformation; **3** Biol, Ling, Mus mutation.

muter /myte/ [1] **I** *vtr* **1** Admin to transfer [*fonctionnaire*]; **2** Vin to stop the fermentation of [*moût*].

II *vi* Biol to mutate.

mutilateur, **-trice** /mytilatœʀ, tʀis/ *adj* [*arme*] mutilating.

mutilation /mytilasjɔ̃/ *nf* (d'arbre, de membre, texte) mutilation; (de paysage) disfigurement.

■ **~ volontaire** Mil self-inflicted injury.

mutilé, **~e** /mytile/ *nm,f* disabled person.

■ **~ de guerre** disabled war veteran; **~ du travail** *person disabled through an accident at work*.

mutiler /mytile/ [1] **I** *vtr* to mutilate [*être vivant, corps, tableau, texte*]; to disfigure [*paysage*].

II se mutiler *vpr* to inflict an injury on oneself.

mutin, **~e** /mytɛ̃, in/ **I** *adj* mischievous.

II *nm* (soldat, marin) mutineer; (prisonnier) rioter.

mutiné, **~e** /mytine/ **I** *pp* ▶ **mutiner**.

II *pp adj* mutinous.

III *nm,f* (soldat, marin) mutineer; (prisonnier) rioter.

mutiner: **se mutiner** /mytine/ [1] *vpr* [*marins, soldats*] to mutiny; [*prisonniers*] to riot.

mutinerie /mytinʀi/ *nf* (de marins, soldats) mutiny; (de prisonniers) riot.

mutisme /mytism/ *nm* **1** (silence) silence; **s'enfermer dans un ~ complet** to withdraw into total silence; **2** Psych mutism.

mutité /mytite/ *nf* muteness, dumbness.

mutualisme /mytɥalism/ *nm* mutualism.

mutualiste /mytɥalist/ **I** *adj* mutualist.

II *nmf* member of a mutual insurance company.

mutualité /mytɥalite/ *nf* **1** (système) mutual insurance system; **2** (organisme) mutual insurance company.

mutuel, **-elle** /mytɥɛl/ **I** *adj* mutual.

II mutuelle *nf* mutual insurance company.

mutuellement /mytɥɛlmɑ̃/ *adv* mutually; **s'aider ~** to help each other.

myalgique /mjalʒik/ *adj* ▶ **encéphalomyélite.**

mycélium /miseljɔm/ *nm* mycelium.

Mycènes /misɛn/ ▶ 857 *npr* Mycenae.

mycénien, -ienne /misenjɛ̃, ɛn/ I ▶ 857 *adj* Mycenaean.
II *nm* Ling Mycenaean.

mycologie /mikɔlɔʒi/ *nf* mycology.

mycologique /mikɔlɔʒik/ *adj* mycological.

mycologue /mikɔlɔg/ ▶ 510 *nmf* mycologist.

mycose /mikoz/ ▶ 271 *nf* mycosis.
■ **~ du pied** athlete's foot; **~ vaginale** thrush.

myéline /mjelin/ *nf* myelin.

myélite /mjelit/ ▶ 271 *nf* myelitis.

mygale /migal/ *nf* tarantula.

myocarde /mjɔkaʀd/ *nm* myocardium.

myopathie /mjɔpati/ ▶ 271 *nf* myopathy.

myope /mjɔp/ I *adj* short-sighted, myopic spéc.
II *nmf* short-sighted person.
IDIOMES **~ comme une taupe** as blind as a bat.

myopie /mjɔpi/ *nf* **1** lit short-sightedness, myopia spéc; **avoir une légère/forte ~** to be slightly/very short-sighted; **2** fig short-sightedness.

myosotis /mjɔzɔtis/ *nm* forget-me-not.

myriade /miʀjad/ *nf* liter myriad (**de** of).

myriapode /miʀjapɔd/ *nm* myriapod.

myrmidon /miʀmidɔ̃/ *nm* liter pipsqueak○.

myrrhe /miʀ/ *nf* myrrh.

myrte /miʀt/ *nm* myrtle.

myrtille /miʀtij/ *nf* bilberry, blueberry.

mystère /mistɛʀ/ *nm* **1** (énigme) mystery; **ça n'a plus de ~ pour lui** it's no longer a mystery to him; **auteur/diplomate ~** mysterious author/diplomat; **'combien gagne-t-il?'—'~ (et boule de gomme○)!'** 'how much does he earn?'—'nobody knows'; **2** (fait de cacher) secrecy; **entourer qch de ~** to surround sth in secrecy; **je n'en fais pas ~** I make no secret of it; **il n'est un ~ pour personne que** it's an open secret that; **3** Relig mystery; Littérat Mystery play; **4** Antiq (rite) rite; **5** Culin ice cream (*covered with meringue and praliné*).

mystérieusement /misteʀjøzmɑ̃/ *adv* mysteriously.

mystérieux, -ieuse /misteʀjø, øz/ *adj* **1** (inexplicable, étrange) [*maladie, disparition, personnage*] mysterious; **2** (qui fait des mystères) mysterious, secretive; **faire le ~** to assume an air of mystery.

mysticisme /mistisism/ *nm* mysticism.

mystificateur, -trice /mistifikatœʀ, tʀis/ I *adj* [*personne*] who likes playing tricks; [*lettre, coup de fil*] hoax (*épith*); [*attitude*] intended to dupe (*après n*); **faire qch dans un esprit ~** to do sth for a hoax, to do sth to trick people.
II *nm,f* hoaxer.

mystification /mistifikasjɔ̃/ *nf* **1** (canular) hoax; **2** (illusion) myth.

mystifier /mistifje/ [2] *vtr* to hoodwink [*individu*]; to fool, to dupe [*peuple*].

mystique /mistik/ I *adj* mystical.
II *nmf* mystic.
III *nf* **1** (doctrine) mysticism; **2** (mystère) mystique; **3** (passion) blind belief (**de** in); **avoir la ~ révolutionnaire** to have a blind belief in revolution.

mystiquement /mistikmɑ̃/ *adv* mystically.

mythe /mit/ *nm* gén myth; **le ~ d'Orphée** the myth of Orpheus; **le ~ de l'alcool qui fortifie** the myth that alcohol fortifies.

mythique /mitik/ *adj* mythical.

mythologie /mitɔlɔʒi/ *nf* mythology.

mythologique /mitɔlɔʒik/ *adj* mythological.

mythomane /mitɔman/ I *adj* mythomaniac; **être un peu ~** to tend to embroider the facts.
II *nmf* mythomaniac.

mythomanie /mitɔmani/ *nf* mythomania.

myxomatose /miksɔmatoz/ *nf* myxomatosis.

Nn

n, N /ɛn/ **I** *nm inv* **1** n, N; **2 nº** (*written abbr* = **numéro**) no.

II N *nf* Transp (*abbr* = **nationale**) **sur la N7** on the N7.

n' ▶ **ne**.

na /na/ *excl* baby talk so there!

nabab /nabab/ *nm* **1** (homme riche) mogul; **2** (en Inde) nabob.

nabot, **~e** /nabo, ɔt/ *nm,f* offensive dwarf injur.

Nabuchodonosor /nabykɔdɔnɔzɔʀ/ *npr* Nebuchadnezzar.

nacelle /nasɛl/ *nf* **1** (de ballon) gondola; **2** (de landau) carrycot GB, carrier US; **3** (d'ouvrier) cradle.

nacre /nakʀ/ *nf* mother-of-pearl; **de ~** [*bouton*] mother-of-pearl; [*teint, peau*] pearly.

nacré, **~e** /nakʀe/ *adj* [*vernis à ongles, peau, reflet*] pearly.

nacrer /nakʀe/ [1] *vtr* **1** Tech to make [sth] pearly [*substance, surface*]; **2** (iriser) to cast a pearly sheen over.

nadir /nadiʀ/ *nm* nadir.

nævus, *pl* **nævi** /nevys, nevi/ *nm* naevus.

nage /naʒ/ *nf* **1** (natation) swimming; **200/400 mètres quatre ~s** Sport 200/400 metres[GB] medley; **regagner la rive à la ~** to swim back to shore; **traverser un fleuve à la ~** to swim across a river; **s'enfuir à la ~** to escape by swimming away; **2** (sueur) **être en ~** to be in a sweat; **arriver en ~** to arrive dripping with sweat; **mettre qn en ~** to bring sb out in a sweat; **3** Naut rowing; **4** Culin **à la ~** [*homard, écrevisse*] à la nage, cooked in an aromatic court-bouillon.

■ **~ sur le dos** backstroke; **~ indienne** sidestroke; **~ libre** Sport freestyle.

nageoire /naʒwaʀ/ *nf* **1** (de poisson) fin; **~ anale/dorsale** anal/dorsal fin; **~s pectorales/pelviennes** pectoral/pelvic fins; **2** (de mammifère, reptile, d'oiseau) flipper.

nager /naʒe/ [13] **I** *vtr* to swim; **~ le cent mètres** to swim the hundred metres[GB]; **~ le crawl** to do the crawl.

II *vi* **1** (dans l'eau) [*poisson, personne*] to swim; **~ sur le dos** to swim on one's back; **~ bien/mal** to be a good/bad swimmer; **les tomates nagent dans l'huile** the tomatoes are swimming in oil; **2** fig **~ dans le bonheur** to bask in contentment; **~ dans l'opulence** to live a life of luxury; **~ dans ses vêtements** to be lost in one's clothes; **elle nage dans sa robe** her dress is far too big for her; **3**○ (mal comprendre) to be absolutely lost; **je nage complètement en algèbre** I'm absolutely lost in algebra; **4** Naut to row.

IDIOMES **~ comme un poisson** to swim like a fish; **~ à contre-courant** fig to swim against the tide; **~ entre deux eaux** to run with the hare and hunt with the hounds.

nageur, **-euse** /naʒœʀ, øz/ *nm,f* **1** Sport swimmer; **2** (rameur) oarsman/oarswoman.

■ **~ de combat** Mil Naut frogman.

naguère /nagɛʀ/ *adv* **1** (récemment) quite recently; **2** (autrefois) controv formerly.

naïade /najad/ *nf* naiad.

naïf, **naïve** /naif, iv/ **I** *adj* **1** (sans artifice) [*personne*] artless; [*foi*] simple; (crédule) [*réponse, foi*] naïve; [*personne*] naïve, gullible; **2** Art naïve.

II *nm,f* innocent, gullible fool péj.

III *nm* (peintre) naïve painter.

nain, **~e** /nɛ̃, nɛn/ **I** *adj* [*arbre, étoile*] dwarf (*épith*); [*lapin, chien*] miniature.

II *nm,f* (personne) dwarf.

III naine *nf* Astron (étoile) dwarf.

■ **le ~ jaune** Jeux pope Joan; **~e blanche** Astron white dwarf.

Nairobi /nɛʀobi/ ▶**857** *npr* Nairobi.

naissain /nɛsɛ̃/ *nm* spat.

naissance /nɛsɑ̃s/ *nf* **1** (début de la vie) birth; **~ prématurée** premature birth; **date et lieu de ~** date and place of birth; **italien de ~** Italian by birth; **sourd/paralysé de ~** deaf/paralysed[GB] from birth; **c'est de ~ chez lui** he was born like that; **donner ~ à** to give birth to; **à ma/ta ~** when I was/you were born; **dès leur ~ on les pèse** as soon as they are born they're weighed; **2** (enfant qui naît) birth; **16% des ~s** 16% of births; **3** (début) (d'œuvre, de mouvement, courant, sentiment) birth; (de produit) first appearance; (de télévision, technologie) birth; (de rumeur) start; **le mouvement a pris ~ dans le milieu ouvrier** the movement sprang up in the working classes; **l'idée a donné ~ à de multiples œuvres** the idea gave rise to many works; **4** (base) **il a une cicatrice à la ~ du cou** he has a scar at the bottom of his neck.

naissant, **~e** /nɛsɑ̃, ɑ̃t/ *adj* [*barbe, art, pays*] new; [*seins*] budding (*épith*); [*sentiment, succès*] growing.

naître /nɛtʀ/ [74] *vi* **1** (venir au monde) [*personne, animal*] to be born; **elle est née le 5 juin 92** she was born on 5 June 92; **le bébé doit ~ à la fin du mois** the baby is due at the end of the month; **elle vient de ~** she's only just been born; **les bébés qui viennent de ~** newborn babies; **l'enfant à ~** the unborn baby ou child; **voir qn ~** lit to see sb being born; **je l'ai vu ~** fig I have known him since he was born; **être né sourd/cardiaque** to be born deaf/with a heart condition; **être né paresseux/fatigué** to be born lazy/tired; **tous les hommes naissent libres** all men are born free; **être né de père italien/inconnu** to be born of an Italian/unknown father; **être né dans une famille de cinq enfants** to be born into a family of five children; **être né pour faire** to be born to do; **il est né pour enseigner/gouverner** he was born to teach/govern; **être né sous le signe du Lion** to be born under the sign of Leo; **Madame Masson née Roux** Mrs Masson née Roux; **il naît environ six enfants par nuit** about six children are born every night; **il n'est pas encore né celui qui me fera changer d'avis** hum there isn't a person living who could make me change my mind; **2** (commencer d'exister) [*mouvement, projet*] to be born; [*entreprise*] to come into existence; [*amour, amitié*] to spring up; [*jour*] to break; [*soupçon, doute*] to arise; **~ de** to arise out of [*fusion, désir*]; **faire ~** to give rise to [*espoir, jalousie, conflit, sourire*]; **voir ~** to see the birth of [*conflit, désenchantement, journal*]; **3** (commencer à s'intéresser) liter **~ à** to awaken to [*art, religion*]; ▶ **étoile, pluie**.

naïve ▶ **naïf** I, II.

naïvement /naivmɑ̃/ *adv* gén naively; (sans artifice) artlessly.

naïveté /naivte/ *nf* gén naivety; (naturel) artlessness; **avoir la ~ de croire que**... to be naïve enough to believe that...; **il y a quelque ~ à penser que**... it's rather naïve to think that...

naja /naʒa/ *nm* cobra.

Namibie /namibi/ ▶**321** *nprf* Namibia.

namibien, **-ienne** /namibjɛ̃, ɛn/ ▶**537** *adj* Namibian.

Namibien, **-ienne** /namibjɛ̃, ɛn/ ▶**537** *nm,f* Namibian.

Namur /namyʀ/ ▶**857**, **692** *npr* Namur; **la province de ~** Namur (province).

nana○ /nana/ *nf* girl, bird○ GB, chick○ US; **une chouette/super ~** a great/gorgeous girl; **sa ~** his woman○.

nanan† /nanɑ̃/ *nm* **c'est du ~!** (délicieux) it's lovely!; (facile) it's a piece of cake!

nancéien, **-ienne** /nɑ̃sejɛ̃, ɛn/ ▶**857** *adj* of Nancy.

Nancéien, **-ienne** /nɑ̃sejɛ̃, ɛn/ ▶**857** *nm,f* (natif) native of Nancy; (habitant) inhabitant of Nancy.

Nancy /nɑ̃si/ ▶**857** *npr* Nancy.

nanisme /nanism/ *nm* dwarfism, nanism spéc.

nankin /nɑ̃kɛ̃/ **I** ▶**193** *adj inv* light yellow.

II *nm* (tissu) nankeen.

Nankin /nɑ̃kɛ̃/ ▶**857** *npr* Nanking.

nanoseconde /nanɔs(ə)gɔ̃d/ *nf* nanosecond.

nantais, **~e** /nɑ̃tɛ, ɛz/ ▶**857** *adj* of Nantes.

Nantais, **~e** /nɑ̃tɛ, ɛz/ ▶**857** *nm,f* (natif) native of Nantes; (habitant) inhabitant of Nantes.

Nantes /nɑ̃t/ ▶**857** *npr* Nantes.

nanti, **~e** /nɑ̃ti/ **I** *adj* **1** (riche) well-off; **2** Jur [*créancier*] secured.

II *nmpl* **les ~s** pej the well-off, the well-heeled○ (+ *v pl*).

nantir /nɑ̃tiʀ/ [3] **I** *vtr* **1** liter (pourvoir) **~ qn de** to provide sb with [*objet*]; to award [sth] to sb [*titre, pouvoirs*]; **2** Jur to secure [*emprunt*]; to give [sb] security [*créancier*]; to pledge [*bien, valeurs*].

II se nantir *vpr* liter (se munir de) **se ~ de** to provide oneself with [*certificat, autorisation*]; to equip oneself with [*parapluie*]; **bien nanti contre la pluie** hum well protected against the rain.

nantissement /nɑ̃tismɑ̃/ *nm* Jur **1** (action) pledging (**sur** of); **2** (contrat) deed of security for debt, pledge agreement; **3** (gage) collateral (security); **prêter sur ~** to lend GB ou loan US on collateral; **déposé** or **remis en ~** lodged as security ou collateral.

napalm /napalm/ *nm* napalm; **bombe/**

Les nationalités

Les adjectifs ethniques comme anglais *peuvent aussi qualifier des langues* (*par ex.* un mot anglais, ▶ 462) *et des choses* (*par ex.* la cuisine anglaise, ▶ 321).

En anglais, les noms et les adjectifs ethniques se forment de plusieurs manières. On peut distinguer cinq groupes. Noter que l'anglais emploie la majuscule dans tous les cas, pour l'adjectif et pour le nom.

1er groupe: le nom et l'adjectif ont la même forme.
Le nom pluriel prend un s.

un Allemand	=	a German *ou* (*s'il est nécessaire de distinguer*) a German man
une Allemande	=	a German *ou* a German woman
les Allemands (*en général*)	=	the Germans *ou* Germans *ou* German people
c'est un Allemand	=	he's German *ou* he's a German
il est allemand	=	he's German

Dans ce groupe: American, Angolan, Belgian, Brazilian, Chilean, Cypriot, Czech, Egyptian, Greek, Indian, Iranian, Italian, Jamaican, Mexican, Moroccan, Norwegian, Pakistani, Russian, Thai *etc.*

2e groupe: le nom s'obtient en ajoutant le mot man *ou* woman *à l'adjectif.*

un Japonais	=	a Japanese man
une Japonaise	=	a Japanese woman
les Japonais (*en général*)	=	the Japanese* *ou* Japanese people
c'est un Japonais	=	he's Japanese
il est japonais	=	he's Japanese

* Japanese *est un adjectif utilisé comme nom: il prend toujours l'article défini et ne prend jamais de* s.

Dans ce groupe: Burmese, Chinese, Congolese, Lebanese, Portuguese, Sudanese, Vietnamese *etc.*

3e groupe: le nom s'obtient en ajoutant le suffixe -man *ou* -woman *à l'adjectif.*

un Anglais	=	an Englishman
une Anglaise	=	an Englishwoman
les Anglais (*en général*)	=	the English† *ou* English people
c'est un Anglais	=	he's English *ou* he's an Englishman
il est anglais	=	he's English

† English *est un adjectif utilisé comme nom: il prend toujours l'article défini et ne prend jamais de* s.

Dans ce groupe: French, Dutch, Irish, Welsh *etc.*

4e groupe: le nom et l'adjectif sont des mots différents.
Le nom pluriel prend un s.

un Danois	=	a Dane *ou* a Danish man
une Danoise	=	a Dane *ou* a Danish woman
les Danois (*en général*)	=	Danes *ou* the Danes *ou* Danish people
c'est un Danois	=	he's Danish *ou* he's a Dane
il est danois	=	he's Danish

Dans ce groupe: Finn (*nom*): Finnish (*adjectif*); Icelander: Icelandic; Pole: Polish; Scot: Scottish; Spaniard: Spanish; Swede: Swedish; Turk: Turkish *etc.*

5e groupe: quelques cas particuliers, qui n'ont pas d'adjectif, par ex. la Nouvelle-Zélande:

un Néo-Zélandais	=	a New Zealander
une Néo-Zélandaise	=	a New Zealander
les Néo-Zélandais (*en général*)	=	New Zealanders
c'est un Néo-Zélandais	=	he's a New Zealander
il est néo-zélandais	=	he's a New Zealander

Quelques autres expressions permettant de parler de la nationalité de quelqu'un en anglais:

il est né en Angleterre	=	he was born in England
il vient d'Angleterre	=	he comes from England
il est d'origine anglaise	=	he's of English extraction
il est citoyen britannique	=	he's a British citizen
il est citoyen néo-zélandais	=	he's a New Zealand citizen
c'est un ressortissant britannique	=	he's a British national

bombardement au ~ napalm bomb/bombing.

naphtaline /naftalin/ *nf* Chimie naphthalene; Comm mothballs (*pl*); **boule de ~** mothball.

naphte /naft/ *nm* naphta.

napoléon /napɔleɔ̃/ *nm* (pièce) napoleon.

Napoléon /napɔleɔ̃/ *npr* Napoleon.

napoléonien, -ienne /napɔleɔnjɛ̃, ɛn/ *adj* Napoleonic.

napolitain, ~e /napɔlitɛ̃, ɛn/ **I** ▶ 857 *adj* Neapolitan.
II ▶ 462 *nm* Ling the Neapolitan dialect.

Napolitain, -e /napɔlitɛ̃, ɛn/ *nm,f* Neapolitan.

nappage /napaʒ/ *nm* **1** (en pâtisserie) fruit glaze; **2** (action) (avec de la confiture) glazing; (avec du chocolat, de la sauce) coating.

nappe /nap/ *nf* **1** (de table) tablecloth; **mets la ~** put the tablecloth on; **2** (couche) (de pétrole, gaz, d'huile) layer; (d'eau) sheet; Culin layer; **~ (d'eau) captive/libre** confined/unconfined ou free groundwater; **~ de mazout** oil slick; **~ de feu** sheet of flames; **~ de brouillard** (en mer) fog bank; (sur terre) layer of fog; **des ~s de brouillard** fog patches.
■ **~ d'autel** Relig altar cloth; **~ de charriage** Géol nappe.

napper /nape/ [1] *vtr* Culin (avec de la sauce, du chocolat) to coat (**de** with); (avec de la confiture) to glaze.

napperon /napʀɔ̃/ *nm* (pour couvert) place mat; (pour vase, lampe) mat.

narbonnais, ~e /naʀbɔnɛ, ɛz/ ▶ 857 *adj* of Narbonne.

Narbonnais, ~e /naʀbɔnɛ, ɛz/ ▶ 857 *nm,f* (natif) native of Narbonne; (inhabitant) inhabitant of Narbonne.

Narbonne /naʀbɔn/ ▶ 857 *npr* Narbonne.

narcisse /naʀsis/ *nm* **1** (fleur) narcissus; **2** pej (vaniteux) narcissist.

Narcisse /naʀsis/ *npr* Narcissus.

narcissique /naʀsisik/ *adj* narcissistic.

narcissisme /naʀsisism/ *nm* narcissism.

narco-dollars /naʀkodɔlaʀ/ *nmpl* drug money.

narcose /naʀkoz/ *nf* narcosis.

narco-terroriste, *pl* **~s** /naʀkoteʀɔʀist/ *nmf* terrorist (*involved in or financed by drug trafficking*).

narcotique /naʀkɔtik/ *adj, nm* narcotic.

narco(-)trafiquant, ~e, *mpl* **~s** /naʀko tʀafikɑ̃, ɑ̃t/ *nm,f* drug trafficker.

narghilé /naʀgile/ *nm* hookah.

narguer /naʀge/ [1] *vtr* to taunt [*personne*]; to flout [*autorité, tradition, danger*].

narguilé /naʀgile/ *nm* hookah.

narine /naʀin/ *nf* nostril.

narquois, ~e /naʀkwa, az/ *adj* mocking.

narquoisement /naʀkwazmɑ̃/ *adv* mockingly.

narrateur, -trice /naʀatœʀ, tʀis/ *nm,f* narrator.

narratif, -ive /naʀatif, iv/ *adj* narrative.

narration /naʀasjɔ̃/ *nf* **1** (action de raconter) narration; **2** (récit) narration, account; **interrompre sa ~** to break off one's account; **3** (en rhétorique) narration.

narrer /naʀe/ [1] *vtr* liter to relate; **~ qch par le menu** to relate sth in minute detail.

narthex /naʀtɛks/ *nm* narthex.

narval /naʀval/ *nm* narwhal.

nasal, ~e, *mpl* **-aux** /nazal, o/ **I** *adj* **1** Méd [*cloison, déformation, obstruction*] nasal; [*hémorragie, goutte*] nose; **2** Phon [*voyelle, son, voix*] nasal.
II nasale *nf* Phon nasal.

nasalisation /nazalizasjɔ̃/ *nf* Phon nasalization.

nasaliser /nazalize/ [1] *vtr* Phon to nasalize.

nasalité /nazalite/ *nf* Phon nasality.

nase° /nɑz/ **I** *adj* **1** (fatigué) [*personne*] shattered○; **2** (en mauvais état) [*personne, objet*] useless; **mon stylo est complètement ~** my pen has had it○.
II *nm* (nez) conk○, nose.

naseau, *pl* **~x** /nazo/ *nm* (de cheval, vache) nostril.

nasillard, ~e /nazijaʀ, aʀd/ *adj* [*voix*] nasal; [*instrument*] tinny.

nasillement /nazijmɑ̃/ *nm* **1** (manière de parler) nasal twang; **2** (de radio, d'instrument) tinny sound; **3** Méd (défaut phonatoire) nasal tone; **4** (de canard) quack.

nasiller /nazije/ [1] *vi* **1** [*personne*] to speak with a nasal voice; [*voix*] to have a nasal quality; [*appareil, instrument*] to make a tinny sound; **2** [*canard*] to quack.

nasse /nas/ *nf* **1** Pêche keepnet; **2** fig net.

natal, ~e, *mpl* **~s** /natal/ *adj* [*pays, village, terre, langue*] native.

Natal /natal/ ▶ 692 *nprm* Natal.

nataliste /natalist/ **I** *adj* [*politique, propagande*] pro-birth (*épith*), designed to increase the birthrate (*après n*).
II *nmf* advocate of a higher birthrate.

natalité /natalite/ *nf* birthrate; **taux de ~** birthrate.

natation /natasjɔ̃/ ▶ 449 *nf* swimming; **leçon de ~** swimming lesson; **concours de ~** swimming competition GB, swim meet US.

natatoire /natatwaʀ/ *adj* **vessie ~** Zool air bladder.

natif, -ive /natif, iv/ **I** *adj* (né) **~ de** native of.
II *nm,f* native (**de** of).

nation /nasjɔ̃/ *nf* nation.
■ **les Nations unies** the United Nations.

national, ~e, *mpl* **-aux** /nasjɔnal, o/ **I** *adj* (tous contextes) national.
II nationale *nf* trunk road GB, ≈ A road GB, highway US.
III nationaux *nmpl* nationals; **nationaux autrichiens/danois** Austrian/Danish nationals.

nationalement /nasjɔnalmɑ̃/ *adv* nationally.

nationalisable /nasjɔnalizabl/ *nf* Fin *company that could be nationalized in the near future.*

nationalisation /nasjɔnalizasjɔ̃/ *nf* nationalization.

nationaliser /nasjɔnalize/ [1] *vtr* to nationalize.

nationalisme /nasjɔnalism/ *nm* nationalism.

nationaliste /nasjɔnalist/ *adj, nmf* nationalist.

nationalité /nasjɔnalite/ *nf* nationality; **~ d'origine** original nationality; **acquérir la ~ canadienne** to acquire Canadian citizenship.

national-socialisme /nasjɔnalsɔsjalism/ *nm* National Socialism.

national-socialiste, *pl* **nationaux-socialistes** /nasjɔnalsɔsjalist, nasjɔnosɔsjalist/ *adj, nmf* National Socialist.

nativisme /nativism/ *nm* Philos nativism.

nativité /nativite/ *nf* **1** Relig nativity; **la Nativité** the Nativity; **2** Art Nativity scene.

natte /nat/ *nf* **1** (tresse) plait, braid US; **2** (sur le sol) mat; **3** (pain) plaited loaf.
■ **~ à billes de bois** bead cushion.

natter /nate/ [1] *vtr* to plait.

naturalisation /natyʀalizasjɔ̃/ *nf* **1** Jur naturalization; **faire une demande de ~** to apply for citizenship ou naturalization GB; **2** (acclimatation) introduction; **3** (taxidermie) stuffing.

naturalisé, **~e** /natyʀalize/ **I** *pp* ▶ **naturaliser**.
II *pp adj* Jur naturalized; **grec ~** naturalized Greek.
III *nm,f* naturalized citizen.

naturaliser /natyʀalize/ [1] *vtr* **1** Jur to naturalize [*étranger*]; **se faire ~ grec** to acquire Greek nationality; **elle est naturalisée française** she's acquired French nationality; **2** (adopter) to assimilate [*mot, usage, coutume*]; **3** (acclimater) to naturalize [*espèce, plante, animal*]; **4** (empailler) to stuff [*animal*].

naturalisme /natyʀalism/ *nm* (tous contextes) naturalism.

naturaliste /natyʀalist/ **I** *adj* Littérat, Art, Philos naturalist.
II ▶ **510** *nmf* **1** Littérat, Art, Philos naturalist; **2** (taxidermiste) taxidermist.

nature /natyʀ/ **I** *adj inv* **1** (sans additif) [*yaourt, fromage blanc*] natural; [*omelette*] plain; [*thé*] black; **à consommer avec du sucre ou ~** to be eaten with sugar or on its own; **2**○ (spontané) [*personne*] natural.
II *nf* **1** (forces nous gouvernant) nature; **laisser faire la ~** to let nature take its course; **les lois de la ~** the laws of nature; **la ~ fait bien les choses** the ways of nature are wonderful; **le pauvre n'a pas été aidé par la ~** nature didn't do the poor man any favours[GB]; **contre ~** against nature; **2** (environnement) nature; **une merveille de la ~** a wonder of nature; **les couleurs que l'on trouve dans la ~** the colours[GB] that are found in nature; **vivre au contact de la ~** to live close to nature; **protection** or **défense de la ~** protection of the environment ou the natural world; **une architecture bien intégrée à la ~** architecture that fits in well with the natural environment; **une ~ hostile/sauvage** a hostile/wild environment; **en pleine ~** in the heart of the countryside; **lâcher qn dans la ~** fig (en pleine campagne) to leave sb in the middle of nowhere, to let sb loose; **3** (caractère) nature; **une ~ généreuse** a generous nature; **une ~ impulsive/violente** an impulsive/a violent nature; **de ~ à faire** likely to do; **une découverte de ~ à révolutionner la technique** a discovery likely to revolutionize the world of technology; **des propositions de ~ à rassurer** proposals likely to reassure; **la vraie ~ de qn** sb's true ou real nature; **je n'y peux rien, c'est ma ~** I can't do anything about it, that's just the way I am; **il est anxieux de ~, il est d'une ~ anxieuse** he's nervous by nature, he's naturally nervous; **ce n'est pas dans ma ~ de m'énerver** it's not in my nature to get angry; **avoir une ~ fragile/robuste** to have a delicate/strong constitution; **cela tient à la ~ même du voyage** this is due to the very nature of the trip; **de même ~** of the same nature; **des offres de toute ~** offers of all kinds; **un déséquilibre de ~ économique et démographique** an imbalance of an economic and demographical nature; **4** (réalité) **peindre d'après ~** to paint from life; **plus grand/plus petit/plus vrai que ~** larger/smaller/more real than life; **5** (objets réels) **en ~** also hum [*payer, régler*] in kind; **avantages en ~** fringe benefits.
■ **~ humaine** human nature; **~ morte** Art still life.
IDIOMES **partir** or **disparaître dans la ~** to vanish into thin air.

naturel, **-elle** /natyʀɛl/ **I** *adj* (tous contextes) natural; **préserver l'équilibre ~** to preserve the natural balance; **constituer un frein ~ à qch** to be a natural brake to sth; **c'est ~ ta couleur de cheveux?** is your hair colour[GB] natural?; **ça ne fait pas très ~** it doesn't look very natural; **être dans son élément ~** to be in one's natural element; **son inquiétude est bien naturelle** her concern is quite natural; **essaie de rester naturelle** try to be natural; **il est ~ de faire/que qn fasse** it's natural to do/that sb should do; **trouver ~ que qn fasse** to find it natural that sb should do; **je t'en prie, c'est tout ~!** think nothing of it, it's perfectly natural ou normal!
II *nm* **1** (caractère) nature, disposition; **être d'un ~ craintif/gai** to be naturally timid/cheerful; **2** (spontanéité) **j'aime le ~ des enfants** I like the way children are so natural; **il manque de ~** he's not very natural; **annoncer qch à qn avec le plus grand ~** to tell sb sth in the most natural way; **le ~ de leurs réponses/manières** their unaffected answers/manners; **3** Culin **au ~** [*riz, pâtes*] plain; [*thon*] in brine; ▶ **galop**.

naturellement /natyʀɛlmɑ̃/ *adv* **1** (de nature) naturally; **un enfant ~ doué** a naturally gifted child; **2** (évidemment) of course; **~, il a plu** of course it rained.

naturisme /natyʀism/ *nm* **1** (nudisme) naturism GB, nudism; **faire du ~** to be a naturist GB ou nudist; **2** Philos, Relig naturism; **3** Méd naturopathy.

naturiste /natyʀist/ **I** *adj* **1** (nudiste) naturist GB, nudist; **2** Méd naturopathic.
II *nmf* **1** (nudiste) naturist GB, nudist; **2** (médecin) naturopath.

naufrage /nofʀaʒ/ *nm* shipwreck, sinking ¢; **le ~ du Titanic** the sinking of the Titanic; **faire ~** [*navire*] to be wrecked; [*marin*] to be shipwrecked; [*entreprise*] to collapse; **sauver qch du ~** to save sth from collapse [*entreprise, économie*]; **sauver qn du ~** fig to save sb from ruin; **le ~ de l'économie** the collapse of the economy.

naufragé, **~e** /nofʀaʒe/ **I** *adj* [*marin, équipage*] shipwrecked; **retrouver le navire ~** to find the wreck of the ship.
II *nm,f* (rescapé) survivor (of a shipwreck); (sur une île, une côte déserte) castaway.

Nauru /nauʀu/ ▶ **321**, **416** *nprf* Nauru.

nauséabond, **~e** /nozeabɔ̃, ɔ̃d/ *adj* **1** lit [*odeur*] sickening, nauseating; [*substance*] foul-smelling, stinking; **2** fig sickening, nauseating.

nausée /noze/ *nf* (dégoût) nausea ¢; (haut-le-cœur) bout of nausea; **donner la ~ à qn** to make sb feel sick; **avoir la ~** to feel sick or nauseous.

nauséeux, **-euse** /nozeø, øz/ *adj* nauseous.

nautile /notil/ *nm* nautilus.

nautique /notik/ *adj* [*art, science*] nautical; [*sports, fête*] water (*épith*).

nautisme /notism/ *nm* (sports) water sports (*pl*); (navigation) sailing, yachting.

naval, **~e**, *mpl* **~s** /naval/ *adj* **1** Ind [*industrie, secteur*] shipbuilding; **chantier ~** shipyard; **2** Mil naval; **école ~e** naval college GB, navy academy US.

navarin /navaʀɛ̃/ *nm* navarin.

Navarre /navaʀ/ ▶ **692** *nprf* **la ~** Navarre.

navet /navɛ/ *nm* **1** (légume) turnip; **2** pej (film) rubbishy film GB ou movie US.
IDIOMES **avoir du sang de ~ (dans les veines)**○ to be a weakling.

navette /navɛt/ *nf* **1** Transp (véhicule) shuttle; (liaison) shuttle (service); **faire la ~ entre Paris et Dijon** [*personne*] (pour le travail) to commute between Paris and Dijon; (pour raison personnelle) to travel back and forth between Paris and Dijon; [*bus*] to operate a shuttle service between Paris and Dijon; **il y a un car qui fait la ~** there is a shuttle service; **2** Tex shuttle; **3** Jur *movement of bill between two legislative assemblies*; **4** (plante) rape; (graine) rape seed.
■ **~ spatiale** space shuttle.

navetteur, **-euse** /navɛtœʀ, øz/ *nm,f* commuter.

navigabilité /navigabilite/ *nf* **1** (de rivière) navigability; **2** (de bateau) seaworthiness; (d'avion) airworthiness.

navigable /navigabl/ *adj* navigable.

navigant, **~e** /navigɑ̃, ɑ̃t/ **I** *adj* [*personnel*] Naut seagoing; Aviat flying; **mécanicien ~** flight engineer.
II *nm,f* **les ~s** Naut seagoing staff; Aviat air staff; **~s techniques** flight deck; **~s commerciaux** cabin crew.

navigateur, **-trice** /navigatœʀ, tʀis/ *nm,f* **1** (qui guide) navigator; **2** (marin) sailor; (au long cours) navigator.
■ **~ solitaire** solo yachtsman.

navigation /navigasjɔ̃/ *nf* **1** Aviat, Naut (techniques) navigation; **instrument de ~** navigational instrument; **2** (trafic sur l'eau) shipping, navigation; **ouvert à la ~** open to shipping ou navigation; **~ intérieure** or **fluviale** inland navigation; **salon de la ~** boat show; **3** (voyage) **plusieurs semaines de ~** several weeks on the water; **4** Ordinat browsing.
■ **~ aux instruments** Aviat instrument flying, IFR; **~ de plaisance** gén boating; (en voilier) sailing; **~ à vue** Aviat visual flying, VFR.

naviguer /navige/ [1] *vi* **1** [*bateau*] to sail; **être en état de ~** to be seaworthy; **2** [*personne*] (voyager sur l'eau) to sail; **avoir beaucoup navigué** to have spent a long time on the water; **3** (guider un bateau, un avion) to navigate; **~ au compas** or **à la boussole** to navigate by compass; **4** (voler) to fly; **5**○ (se déplacer) to travel; **elle a beaucoup navigué** she's been around a bit; **6** Ordinat to browse; **~ dans l'Internet** to surf the Internet.

navire /naviʀ/ *nm* ship, vessel spéc.
■ **~ amiral** Mil flagship; **~ de commerce** merchant ship; **~ de guerre** warship; **~ marchand** merchant ship.
IDIOMES **les rats quittent le ~** rats leave a sinking ship.

navire-citerne, *pl* **navires-citernes** /naviʀsitɛʀn/ *nm* tanker.

navire-école, *pl* **navires-écoles** /naviʀekɔl/ *nm* training ship.

navire-hôpital, *pl* **navires-hôpitaux** /naviʀɔpital, o/ *nm* hospital ship.

navire-usine, *pl* **navires-usines** /naviʀyzin/ *nm* factory ship.

navrant, **~e** /navʀɑ̃, ɑ̃t/ *adj* **1** (consternant) depressing; **2** (attristant) distressing, upsetting.

navré, **~e** /navʀe/ *adj* **1** (dans une formule de politesse) **je suis ~ de t'avoir fait attendre** I am sorry to have kept you waiting; **2** (triste, déçu) **avoir l'air ~** to look sad; **d'un ton ~** sadly; (en s'excusant) apologetically; **elle a pris un ton ~ pour me dire que...** she told me in apologetic tones that...

navrer /navʀe/ [1] *vtr* liter (contrarier) to upset.

nazaréen, **-éenne** /nazaʀeɛ̃, ɛn/ *adj* Nazarene.

naze◑ /naz/ = **nase**.

nazi, **~e** /nazi/ *adj, nm,f* Nazi.

nazisme /nazism/ *nm* Nazism.

NB (*written abbr* = **nota bene**) NB.

NdE *written abbr* ▶ **note**.

N'Djamena /dʒamena/ ▶ **857** *npr* Ndjamena.

NDLR *written abbr* ▶ **note**.

NdT *written abbr* ▶ **note**.

ne /nə/ (**n'** *before vowel or mute h*) *adv*

■ **Note** *ne*, adverbe de négation, n'a pas d'équivalent exact en anglais.
– Généralement, la forme négative se construit avec un auxiliaire ou un verbe modal accompagné d'une négation: *je ne sais pas* = I don't know; *je ne peux pas* = I can't, I cannot; *il n'a pas répondu* = he didn't answer.
– Pour *ne* utilisé avec *pas, jamais, guère, rien, plus, aucun, personne* etc, on se reportera à l'article correspondant.
– *ne + verbe + que* est traité dans l'article ci-dessous.

je n'ai que 100 francs I've only got 100 francs; **ce n'est qu'une égratignure** it's only a scratch, it's nothing but a scratch; **il n'y avait que lui dans la salle** there was nobody but him in the room, he was the only person in the room; **tu n'avais qu'à le dire!** you only had to say so!; **si tu veux que je t'aide tu n'as qu'à le dire** if you need help you only have to tell me; **il ne mange que des nouilles** he eats nothing but noodles, he only eats noodles; **il ne pense qu'à s'amuser** he only thinks of enjoying himself, he thinks of nothing but enjoying himself; **elle ne fait que (de) se plaindre** she does nothing but complain; **il n'y a qu'elle qui comprenne** only she understands; **il n'y a que lui pour être aussi désagréable** only he can be so unpleasant; **tu n'es qu'un raté** you're nothing but a loser○; **si l'avion est trop cher, il n'a qu'à prendre le train** if flying is too expensive he can take the train.

né, ~e /ne/ **I** *pp* ▶ **naître**.
II *pp adj* **bien/mal ~** highborn/lowborn (*épith*).
III (-)né (*in compounds*) **musicien(-)/écrivain(-)~** born musician/writer.

Néandertal /neɑ̃dɛʀtal/ *nprm* **l'homme de ~** Neanderthal man.

néandertalien, -ienne /neɑ̃dɛʀtaljɛ̃, ɛn/ *adj* [*homme, fossile*] Neanderthal.

néanmoins /neɑ̃mwɛ̃/ *conj, adv* nevertheless; **et ~** but nevertheless.

néant /neɑ̃/ *nm* **1** Philos **le ~** nothingness; **2** (absence de valeur) emptiness; **sombrer dans le ~** to sink into oblivion; **réduire à ~** to negate, to nullify [*effet, croissance, efforts, progrès*]; to destroy [*argument*]; to reduce [sth] to ashes [*espoir, rêve*]; to wipe out [*majorité*]; **'revenus: ~'** 'income: nil'.

Nebraska /nebʀaska/ ▶ 692 *nprm* Nebraska.

nébuleux, -euse /nebylø, øz/ **I** *adj* **1** (obscurci) [*ciel*] cloudy, overcast; [*masse*] nebulous; **2** (fumeux) [*idée, auteur, projet*] nebulous.
II nébuleuse *nf* **1** Astron nebula; **2** *fig* amorphous grouping.

nébuliseur /nebylizœʀ/ *nm* spray, atomizer.

nébulosité /nebylozite/ *nf* **1** (état du ciel) nebulosity; **2** (nuage) light cloud; **3** (de concept) nebulosity, haziness.

nécessaire /nesesɛʀ/ **I** *adj* **1** gén necessary (**à** for); **absolument/vraiment ~** absolutely/really necessary; **avoir les fonds ~s** to have the necessary funds (**pour qch** for sth; **pour faire** to do); **conditions ~s à la production/croissance/vie** conditions necessary for production/growth/life; **juger/croire ~ de faire** to deem sout/believe it necessary to do; **plus qu'il n'est ~** more than is necessary; **si ~** if necessary; **~ ou pas** whether necessary or not; **il est ~ de faire** is is necessary to do; **il n'est pas ~ de vérifier** there's no need to check, it isn't necessary to check; **est-ce bien ~?** is it really necessary?; **'faut-il réserver?'—'non, ce n'est pas ~'** 'is it necessary to book GB ou make a reservation?'—'no, there' s no need', 'no, it isn't necessary'; **il devient ~ de faire** it is becoming necessary to do; **il est ~ que tu y ailles** you have to go, you must go, it is necessary for you to go; **il n'est pas ~ que tu y ailles** you don't have to go, there is no need for you to go, it isn't necessary for you to go; **s'il était ~ que tu écrives** if you had ou needed to write, if it were necessary for you to write; **les voix ~s pour renverser le gouvernement** the votes needed in order to overthrow the government; **2** Philos necessary.
II *nm* **1** (ce qui s'impose) **faire le ~** to do what is necessary ou what needs to be done; **as-tu fait le ~ pour les billets/pour avoir des billets?** did you see about the tickets/about getting tickets?; **j'ai fait le ~** I've seen to it, I've dealt with it; **le ~ et le superflu** what is necessary and what is superfluous; **2** (biens et services) essentials (*pl*); **manquer du plus strict ~** to lack the bare essentials; **ne prendre que le ~** to take only the essentials; **3** Philos necessary; **le ~ et le contingent** the necessary and the contingent.
■ **~ de couture** sewing kit; **~ à ongles** manicure set; **~ de toilette** toiletries (*pl*).

nécessairement /nesesɛʀmɑ̃/ *adv* necessarily; **le progrès n'est pas ~ un bienfait** progress is not necessarily a blessing; **'y aura-t-il des licenciements?'—'pas ~/oui, ~'** 'will there be redundancies?'—'not necessarily/yes, it is unavoidable'; **cela finit ~ mal** it inevitably goes wrong; **passe-t-on ~ par Oslo?** do you have to go via Oslo?; **il s'ensuit ~ que** it necessarily follows that.

nécessité /nesesite/ **I** *nf* **1** (ce qui s'impose) necessity; **le téléphone est devenu une ~** the telephone has become a necessity; **~ absolue** or **impérative** absolute necessity; **~ urgente/impérieuse** urgent/pressing need; **~ de qch/de faire/d'être** need for sth/to do/to be; **d'où la ~ d'une coopération accrue/d'améliorer les transports publics** hence the need for closer cooperation/to improve public transport; **~ pour qn de qch/de faire** sb's need for sth/to do; **la ~ pour le parti d'une unanimité** the party's need for unanimity; **la ~ qu'il y a de lutter** the need to struggle; **je n'en vois pas la ~** I don't see that it is necessary, I don't see the need for it; **de première ~** vital; **produits/soins de première ~** vital commodities/care; **être de première ~** to be vital; **par ~** out of necessity; **par ~ de service** for internal reasons; **sans ~** unnecessarily; **être dans la ~ de faire** to have no choice but to do; ▶ **vertu**; **2** (pauvreté) need; **être dans la ~** to be in need; **3** (caractère inéluctable) necessity; **le hasard et la ~** chance and necessity.
II nécessités *nfpl* demands; **~s économiques/de gestion** economic/management demands; **les ~ de l'heure** the particular contingencies.
IDIOMES **~ fait loi** Prov necessity knows no law.

nécessiter /nesesite/ [1] *vtr* to require; **~ des pouvoirs accrus/une réforme** to require more powers/reform; **la situation nécessite qu'elle intervienne** the situation calls for her intervention.

nécessiteux, -euse /nesesitø, øz/ **I** *adj* needy; **les plus ~** the neediest.
II *nm,f* needy person; **les ~** the needy.

nec plus ultra /nɛkplyzyltʀa/ *nm inv* **le ~** the last word (**de** in).

nécrologie /nekʀɔlɔʒi/ *nf* **1** (liste) deaths column, obituary column; **2** (article) obituary.

nécrologique /nekʀɔlɔʒik/ *adj* obituary.

nécromancie /nekʀomɑ̃si/ *nf* necromancy.

nécromancien, -ienne /nekʀomɑ̃sjɛ̃, ɛn/ *nm,f* necromancer.

nécrophage /nekʀofaʒ/ *adj* necrophagous.

nécrophile /nekʀofil/ *adj, nmf* necrophiliac.

nécrophilie /nekʀofili/ *nf* necrophilia.

nécropole /nekʀɔpɔl/ *nf* necropolis.

nécrose /nekʀoz/ *nf* necrosis.

nécroser /nekʀoze/ [1] *vtr*, **se nécroser** *vpr* to necrose.

nectar /nɛktaʀ/ *nm* nectar.

nectarine /nɛktaʀin/ *nf* nectarine.

néerlandais, ~e /neɛʀlɑ̃dɛ, ɛz/ ▶ 462, 537 **I** *adj* Dutch.
II *nm* Ling Dutch.

Néerlandais, ~e /neɛʀlɑ̃dɛ, ɛz/ ▶ 537 *nm,f* Dutchman/Dutchwoman; **les ~** the Dutch (+ *v pl*).

nef /nɛf/ *nf* **1** Archit nave; **les ~s latérales** the side aisles; **2**‡ (embarcation) vessel, ship.

néfaste /nefast/ *adj* (nuisible) harmful (**à** to).

nèfle /nɛfl/ *nf* medlar.
IDIOMES **des ~s**○**!** no way○!, not on your life○!

néflier /neflije/ *nm* medlar (tree).

négateur, -trice /negatœʀ, tʀis/ *adj* [*esprit*] given to challenging everything (*après n*).

négatif, -ive /negatif, iv/ **I** *adj* **1** (non positif) negative; **2** (néfaste) negative, adverse.
II *adv* Aviat, Mil negative.
III *nm* gén, Ling, Phot negative; **au ~** in the negative.
IV négative *nf* **répondre par la négative** to reply in the negative; **dans la négative, nous aviserons** if not, we will think again.

négation /negasjɔ̃/ *nf* **1** (action de nier) negation; **2** Ling negative.

négationnisme /negasjɔnism/ *nm* revisionist ideas (*denying the Nazi Holocaust*).

négationniste /negasjɔnist/ *adj* revisionist (*denying the Nazi Holocaust*).

négativement /negativmɑ̃/ *adv* [*réagir*] negatively; [*répondre*] negatively, in the negative.

négativisme /negativism/ *nm* negativism.

négativité /negativite/ *nf* **1** (d'attitude) negativism, negativity; **2** (de particule) negativity.

négaton /negatɔ̃/ *nm* negatron.

négligé, ~e /negliʒe/ **I** *pp* ▶ **négliger**.
II *pp adj* [*personne, vêtement, apparence*] sloppy, scruffy○; [*cheveux, barbe*] unkempt; [*maison, intérieur*] neglected; [*travail*] careless, sloppy; [*blessure, infection*] untreated.
III *nm* **1** (vêtement) negligée; **2** (état) **le ~ de leur tenue** their sloppy way of dressing, their slovenly ou scruffy○ appearance.

négligeable /negliʒabl/ *adj* [*quantité, somme*] negligible, insignificant; [*personne*] insignificant, unimportant; [*opinion*] which does not count (*épith, après n*); **non ~** [*somme*] considerable; [*détail, rôle*] significant; [*atout, importance, perte*] significant, considerable.

négligemment /negliʒamɑ̃/ *adv* (avec nonchalance) nonchalantly; (avec indifférence) carelessly.

négligence /negliʒɑ̃s/ *nf* **1** (faute) negligence **¢**; **il y aurait eu des ~s** negligence is alleged; **~ professionnelle** professional negligence; **2** (laisser-aller) negligence, carelessness; **être d'une grande ~** to be very careless; **mettre** or **montrer de la ~ à faire** to be negligent in doing.

négligent, ~e /negliʒɑ̃, ɑ̃t/ *adj* [*personne, employé*] negligent, careless; [*élève, démarche*] careless; [*geste, coup d'œil*] casual.

négliger /negliʒe/ [13] **I** *vtr* **1** (ne pas s'occuper de) to neglect [*santé, corps, affaires, maison, travail, personne*]; to leave untreated [*affection, rhume*]; **une blessure négligée peut s'infecter** a wound which is not properly treated may become infected; **2** (ne pas tenir compte de) to ignore, to disregard [*résultat, fait, règle*]; **il n'a rien négligé pour réussir** he tried everything possible to succeed; **ne pas être à ~** [*chiffre*] to be worth taking into account; **une offre qui n'est pas à ~** an offer which is worth considering; **les avantages ne sont pas à ~** there are quite ou very substantial advantages; **3** (omettre) **~ de faire** to fail to do.
II se négliger *vpr* (dans sa tenue) to let

oneself go, not to take care of oneself; (pour sa santé) not to look after oneself.

négoce /negɔs/ *nm* trade (**avec** with); **faire du ~ avec** to trade with.

négociabilité /negɔsjabilite/ *nf* negotiability.

négociable /negɔsjabl/ *adj* negotiable.

négociant, **~e** /negɔsjɑ̃, ɑ̃t/ ▶510 *nm,f* gén merchant; (grossiste) wholesaler; **~ en textiles** textile merchant.

négociateur, **-trice** /negɔsjatœr, tris/ *nm,f* negotiator.

négociation /negɔsjasjɔ̃/ *nf* (principe) negotiation (**avec** with); (pourparlers) negotiations (*pl*) (**avec** with); **entamer des ~s**, **entrer en ~s** to enter into negotiations; **la table de ~** the negotiating table.

négocier /negɔsje/ [2] **I** *vtr* **1** Comm, Pol to negotiate (**avec** with); **2** Sport **~ un virage** to negotiate a bend.
II *vi* to negotiate (**avec** with).
III se négocier *vpr* to be negotiated.

nègre /nɛgr/ **I** *adj* [*art, musique*] Negro.
II *nm* **1** offensive Negro injur; **2** Édition ghostwriter.
■ **~ en chemise** *chocolate mousse with whipped cream piping.*

négresse /negrɛs/ *nf* offensive Negress injur.

négrier /negrije/ *nm* **1** Hist (personne) slave trader; (navire) slave ship; **2** pej slave driver.

négrillon /negrijɔ̃/ *nm* offensive piccaninny injur GB, little black Sambo injur US.

négrillonne /negrijɔn/ *nf* offensive piccaninny injur GB, little black Sambo injur US.

négritude /negrityd/ *nf* black identity, negritude.

négroïde /negrɔid/ *adj* Negroid.

negro(-)spiritual, *pl* **~s** /negrospiritɥɔl/ *nm* Negro spiritual.

Néguev /negɛv/ *nprm* **le ~** the Negev desert.

neige /nɛʒ/ *nf* **1** Météo snow; **~ fondue** (au sol) slush; (pluie) sleet; **aller à la ~** to go skiing; **paysage de ~** snow-covered landscape; **la ~ tombe depuis deux heures** it's been snowing for two hours; **battre les blancs en ~** beat the eggwhites until stiff; **blancs battus en ~** stiffly beaten eggwhites; **2**○ (drogue) snow○, cocaine.
■ **~ carbonique** carbon (dioxide) snow; **~s éternelles** eternal snows.
IDIOMES **être blanc comme ~** to be completely innocent; **fondre comme ~ au soleil** [*fortune, objections*] to melt away.

neiger /neʒe/ [13] *v impers* to snow; **il neige** it's snowing.

neigeux, **-euse** /nɛʒø, øz/ *adj* [*cime*] snow-covered; [*temps, hiver*] snowy.

nem /nɛm/ *nm* (Vietnamese) small spring roll.

Némésis /nemezis/ *npr* Nemesis.

néné● /nene/ *nm* boob●, breast.

nénette○ /nenɛt/ *nf* (jeune fille) bird● GB, chick○ US, girl.
IDIOMES **se casser la ~** to go to a lot of trouble.

nenni‡ /nɛnni, neni/ *adv* nay‡.

nénuphar /nenyfar/ *nm* waterlily.

néo /neo/ *préf* neo.

néo-calédonien, **-ienne**, *mpl* **~s** /neo kaledɔnjɛ̃, ɛn/ *adj* New Caledonian.

Néo-Calédonien, **-ienne**, *mpl* **~s** /neo kaledɔnjɛ̃, ɛn/ *nm,f* New Caledonian.

néoclassicisme /neoklasisism/ *nm* neoclassicism.

néoclassique /neoklasik/ *adj* neoclassical.

néocolonialisme /neokɔlɔnjalism/ *nm* neocolonialism.

néocolonialiste /neokɔlɔnjalist/ *adj, nmf* neocolonialist.

néodarwinisme /neodarwinism/ *nm* Neo-Darwinism.

néo-écossais, **~e** /neoekɔsɛ, ɛz/ *adj* Nova Scotian.

Néo-Écossais, **~e** /neoekɔsɛ, ɛz/ *nm,f* Nova Scotian.

néofascisme /neofaʃism/ *nm* neofascism.

néofasciste /neofaʃist/ *adj, nmf* neofascist.

néogothique /neogɔtik/ *adj, nm* neogothic.

néo-hellénique /neoelenik/ *adj* modern Greek.

néo-impressionnisme /neoɛ̃presjɔnism/ *nm* neoimpressionism.

néolibéral, **~e**, *mpl* **-aux** /neoliberal, o/ *adj* neoliberal.

néolibéralisme /neoliberalism/ *nm* neoliberalism.

néolithique /neɔlitik/ *adj, nm* Neolithic.

néologie /neɔlɔʒi/ *nf* neology.

néologique /neɔlɔʒik/ *adj* neological.

néologisme /neɔlɔʒism/ *nm* neologism.

néon /neɔ̃/ *nm* **1** (gaz) neon; **2** (appareil) neon light; (éclairage) neon lighting.

néonazi, **~e** /neonazi/ *adj, nm,f* neonazi.

néonazisme /neonazism/ *nm* neonazism.

néophyte /neɔfit/ *nmf* neophyte.

néoplasique /neɔplazik/ *adj* neoplastic.

néoplatonisme /neoplatɔnism/ *nm* Neo-Platonism.

néopositivisme /neopozitivism/ *nm* logical positivism.

néopositiviste /neopozitivist/ *adj, nmf* logical positivist.

néoprène® /neɔprɛn/ *nm* Neoprene®.

néoréalisme /neorealism/ *nm* neorealism.

néoréaliste /neorealist/ *adj, nmf* neorealist.

néo-zélandais, **~e** /neozelɑ̃dɛ, ɛz/ ▶537 *adj* New Zealand (*épith*).

Néo-Zélandais, **~e** /neozelɑ̃dɛ, ɛz/ ▶537 *nm,f* New Zealander.

Népal /nepal/ ▶321 *nprm* Nepal.

népalais, **~e** /nepalɛ, ɛz/ ▶462, 537 **I** *adj* Nepali.
II *nm* Ling Nepali.

Népalais, **~e** /nepalɛ, ɛz/ ▶537 *nm,f* Nepali, Nepalese.

néphrétique /nefretik/ *adj* nephritic; **coliques ~s** renal colic ¢.

néphrite /nefrit/ ▶271 *nf* **1** Méd nephritis; **2** Minér nephrite.

néphrologie /nefrɔlɔʒi/ *nf* nephrology.

néphrologue /nefrɔlɔg/ ▶510 *nmf* nephrologist.

népotisme /nepɔtism/ *nm* nepotism.

Neptune /nɛptyn/ **I** *npr* Mythol Neptune.
II *nprf* Astron Neptune.

neptunium /nɛptynjɔm/ *nm* neptunium.

néréide /nereid/ *nf* Zool nereis.

Néréide /nereid/ *npr* Mythol Nereid.

nerf /nɛr/ **I** *nm* **1** Anat nerve; **~ optique/sciatique/auditif** optic/sciatic/auditory nerve; **~ pneumogastrique** or **vague** vagus (nerve); **2** (vigueur) spirit, go○; **montrer que l'on a du ~** to show one has (a bit of) spirit ou go○; **redonner du ~ à qn** to put new heart into sb; **allez du ~! un peu de ~**○**!** come on, buck up○! GB, hang in there○!
II nerfs *nmpl* (système nerveux) nerves; **être malade des ~s** to suffer from nerves; **avoir les ~s solides** to have strong nerves.
■ **~ de bœuf** pizzle.
IDIOMES **jouer avec les ~s de qn** to be deliberately annoying; **ses ~s ont lâché** he went to pieces; **avoir les ~s à fleur de peau** to be very touchy, to have frayed nerves; **avoir les ~s en pelote**○ or **en boule**○ or **à vif** to be really wound up; **être sur les ~s**, **avoir ses ~s**○ to be on edge; **vivre sur les ~s** to live on one's nerves; **taper** or **porter sur les ~s de qn** to get on sb's nerves; **être à bout de ~s** to be at the end of one's tether ou rope US; **passer ses ~s sur qn/qch**○ to take it out on sb/sth; **avoir des ~s d'acier** to have nerves of steel; **l'argent est le ~ de la guerre** money is the sinews of war.

Néron /nerɔ̃/ *npr* Nero.

nerveusement /nɛrvøzmɑ̃/ *adv* **1** (avec impatience) nervously; **il conduit trop ~** he's too nervous when he drives; **2** (psychologiquement) **être épuisé ~** to be suffering from nervous exhaustion; **il n'est pas solide ~** he's rather highly strung GB ou high-strung US; **il faut qu'il récupère ~** he needs to have a good rest and calm down.

nerveux, **-euse** /nɛrvø, øz/ Méd **I** *adj* **1** (agité) [*personne, animal*] nervous, jumpy○; [*geste, rire*] nervous, tense; [*allure*] tense; [*toux*] nervous; **ne soyez pas si ~, tout se passera bien** don't be so nervous, it will all be fine; **2** (de nature émotive) [*personne, tempérament*] nervous, highly strung GB, high-strung US; **3** (vigoureux) [*corps, membre, main*] lean and muscular; [*moteur, voiture*] responsive; **4** (énergique) [*personne*] dynamic, full of go○; [*style, écriture, discours*] vigorous; **il n'est pas très ~** he hasn't got much go○, he isn't exactly dynamic; **5** Anat, Physiol [*cellule, centre, tissu*] nerve (*épith*); [*système, tension, excitabilité*] nervous; **lésion nerveuse** nerve damage; **être atteint de troubles ~** to be suffering from a nervous disorder; **fatigue nerveuse** nervous exhaustion; **6** Néol, Fin [*marché, Bourse*] nervous, jumpy○.
II *nm,f* Méd nervous person; **c'est un grand ~** he's a very nervous type.

nervi● /nɛrvi/ *nm* henchman, bully-boy.

nervosité /nɛrvozite/ *nf* **1** (appréhension) nervousness; **dans un état de grande ~** in a state of extreme nervous tension, in a very nervous state; **on sentait la ~ ambiante** (dans une réunion) you could feel the apprehension in the air; (dans la foule) you could feel the unrest in the air; **2** (surexcitation) excitability; **un cheval/enfant d'une grande ~** a very excitable horse/child; **3** Aut (de moteur) liveliness, bite○; **un moteur qui manque de ~** a sluggish engine.

nervure /nɛrvyr/ *nf* **1** Bot, Zool nervure; **2** Archit, Édition rib; **à fines ~s** finely ribbed; **3** Cout pin tuck.

nervuré, **~e** /nɛrvyre/ *adj* [*feuille, aile*] veined; [*voûte*] ribbed.

n'est-ce pas /nɛspa/ *adv* **1** (appelant l'acquiescement) **c'est joli, ~?** it's pretty, isn't it?; **tu es d'accord, ~?** you agree, don't you?; **vous-y penserez, ~?** you'll think about it, won't you?; **~ qu'il est gentil?** isn't he nice?; **2** (pour renforcer) of course; **la question, ~, reste ouverte** the question, of course, remains open.

net, **nette** /nɛt/ **I** *adj* **1** Compta, Écon, Fin (après déductions) net; **prix/salaire ~** net price/salary; **augmentation/perte nette** net increase/loss; **~ d'impôt** net of tax; **créations nettes d'emplois** net job creation; **immigration nette** net immigration; **2** (notable) [*changement, augmentation, recul*] marked; [*baisse*] sharp; [*tendance, odeur*] distinct; **ralentissement encore plus ~** even more marked slowdown; **3** (clair) [*personne, victoire, réponse, relation*] clear; [*situation*] clear-cut; **il a été très ~ à ce sujet** he was very clear on this subject; **il y a un ~ rapport entre les phénomènes** there's a clear relationship between the phenomena; **en avoir le cœur ~** to be clear in one's mind about it; **4** (distinct) [*souvenir, voix, forme*] clear; [*écriture*] neat; [*cassure, coupure*] clean; **avoir la nette impression que** to have the distinct impression that; **5** (impeccable) [*maison, vêtement*] neat; [*mains*] clean; **faire place nette** to clear everything out; **6** (irréprochable) [*personne*] clean; [*conscience*] clear; **personne pas nette** unsavoury person; **7**○ (lucide) **pas (très) ~** not quite with it○.
II *adv* [*s'arrêter*] dead; [*tuer*] outright; [*refuser*] flatly; [*dire*] straight out; **refuser tout ~** to refuse point blank; **la corde a cassé**

~ the rope snapped; **la clé s'est cassée ~** the key snapped in two.
III *nm* **1** Compta, Écon, Fin (revenu) net income; (bénéfices) net earnings (*pl*); **augmentation de 2% en ~** net 2% increase; **2** (propre) **copie au ~** clean copy; **mettre son texte au ~** to make a clean copy of one's text; **3** (clair) **mettre les choses au ~** to set matters straight.

nettement /nɛtmɑ̃/ *adv* **1** (indiscutablement) [*augmenter, se détériorer*] markedly; [*devancer*] clearly; [*préférer*] definitely; **~ meilleur/plus propre/moins froid** decidedly better/cleaner/warmer; **gagner ~** to be a clear winner; **2** (sans ambiguïté) [*soutenir, dire*] clearly; [*refuser*] flatly; **3** (distinctement) [*voir, sentir, séparer*] clearly; [*se souvenir*] distinctly.

netteté /nɛtte/ *nf* **1** (de voix, dessin, ciel) clarity; (de trait, d'image) sharpness; **s'exprimer avec ~/avec une grande ~** to express oneself clearly/very clearly; **2** (de résultat, corrélation, d'affirmation) definite nature; (de cassure) cleanness; **indiquer avec ~ un rapport** to show a relationship clearly; **3** (de lieu) cleanness; (de travail) neatness.

nettoiement /netwamɑ̃/ *nm* **1** (nettoyage) cleaning ¢; **~ des rues** street cleaning; **2** (enlèvement des ordures) refuse collection GB, garbage collection US; **service de ~** cleansing department GB, sanitation department US.

nettoyage /netwajaʒ/ *nm* **1** (opération) cleanup; **la maison a besoin d'un bon ~** the house needs a good cleanup; **campagne de ~** cleanup campaign; **~ de printemps** spring-cleaning ¢; **2** (action) cleaning ¢; **faire le ~** to do the cleaning; **~ à sec** dry-cleaning; **entreprise de ~** cleaning contractors (*pl*); **produit de ~** cleaner; **3** Cosmét (de la peau) cleansing ¢; **~ en profondeur** deep cleansing; **4** Mil mopping-up ¢; **opération de ~** mopping-up operation.
IDIOMES **faire le ~ par le vide**○ to have a good clearout○.

nettoyant, **~e** /nɛtwajɑ̃, ɑ̃t/ **I** *adj* cleaning.
II *nm* (produit) cleaning agent.

nettoyer /netwaje/ [23] **I** *vtr* **1** (rendre propre) to clean [*lieu, objet, légumes, mains, façade*]; to clean up [*jardin*]; to clean out [*rivière, conduit, oreilles*]; **donner une robe à ~** to take a dress to the cleaner's; **faire ~ qch à sec** to have sth dry-cleaned; **~ qch avec un chiffon/une éponge** to wipe/sponge sth; **2** (faire disparaître) to clean off [*tache*]; **3** (épurer) to clean up [*ville*]; **4**○ (dévaliser) to clean out○ [*appartement*]; **5**○ (ruiner) to clean out○ [*personne*].
II *vi* (faire du nettoyage) to clean; **passer sa journée à ~** to clean all day.
III se nettoyer *vpr* **1** (se laver soi-même) to get clean; **se ~ les mains** to clean one's hands; **se ~ les oreilles** to clean out one's ears; **2** (pouvoir être lavé) **le four/la tache se nettoie à l'eau chaude** the oven/the stain can be cleaned with hot water.

nettoyeur, **-euse** /netwajœʀ, øz/ **▶510** **I** *nm,f* (métier) cleaner; **~ de bureaux** office cleaner.
II *nm* (machine) cleaner.

Neuchâtel /nøʃatɛl/ *npr* **1** **▶857** Neuchâtel; **2** **▶692** (région) **le canton de ~** the canton of Neuchâtel.

neuf[1] /nœf/ **▶212**, **407**, **545** **I** *adj inv, pron* nine.
II *nm inv* nine; **faire la preuve par ~** Math to cast out the nines.

neuf[2], **neuve** /nœf, nœv/ **I** *adj* new; **comme ~** as new; **tout ~** brand new; **bonheur tout ~** new-found happiness; **voir qch d'un regard ~**, **porter un regard ~ sur qch** to look at sth in a new light; **'état ~'** 'as new'; **▶sang**.
II *nm inv* new; **quelque chose/rien de ~** something/nothing new; **il y a du ~** there's something new; **quoi de ~?** what's new?; **l'attrait du ~** the appeal of the new; **acheter du ~** to buy new; **être habillé de ~** to be dressed in new clothes; **refaire/remettre/repeindre qch à ~** to re-do/renovate/repaint sth completely; **donner un coup de ~ à qch** to spruce sth up; **redonner à qch le brillant** or **l'éclat du ~** to make sth look like new; **faire du ~ avec du vieux** to revamp things.
IDIOMES **faire peau neuve** [*bâtiment*] to undergo a transformation; [*personne*] to transform one's image; [*société*] to transform its image.

neurasthénie /nøʀasteni/ *nf* depression, neurasthenia†; **faire de la ~** to suffer from depression, to be depressed.

neurasthénique /nøʀastenik/ **I** *adj* depressed; (chroniquement) depressive.
II *nmf* depressive.

neurobiologie /nøʀobjɔlɔʒi/ *nf* neurobiology.

neurobiologique /nøʀobjɔlɔʒik/ *adj* neurobiological.

neurobiologiste /nøʀobjɔlɔʒist/ **▶510** *nmf* neurobiologist.

neurochirurgical, **~e**, *mpl* **-aux** /nøʀoʃiʀyʀʒikal, o/ *adj* neurosurgical.

neurochirurgie /nøʀoʃiʀyʀʒi/ *nf* neurosurgery.

neurochirurgien /nøʀoʃiʀyʀʒjɛ̃/ **▶510** *nm* neurosurgeon.

neuroleptique /nøʀolɛptik/ *adj, nm* neuroleptic.

neurologie /nøʀɔlɔʒi/ *nf* neurology.

neurologique /nøʀɔlɔʒik/ *adj* neurological.

neurologue /nøʀɔlɔg/ **▶510** *nmf* neurologist.

neuromusculaire /nøʀomyskylɛʀ/ *adj* neuromuscular.

neuronal, **~e**, *mpl* **-aux** /nøʀɔnal, o/ *adj* **1** Méd neuronal; **2** Ordinat neural.

neurone /nøʀɔn/ *nm* neurone.

neuropathie /nøʀopati/ *nf* neuropathy.

neuropathologie /nøʀopatɔlɔʒi/ *nf* neuropathology.

neurophysiologie /nøʀofizjɔlɔʒi/ *nf* neurophysiology.

neuropsychiatre /nøʀopsikjatʀ/ **▶510** *nmf* neuropsychiatrist.

neuropsychiatrie /nøʀopsikjatʀi/ *nf* neuropsychiatry.

neuropsychiatrique /nøʀopsikjatʀik/ *adj* neuropsychiatric.

neuropsychologie /nøʀopsikɔlɔʒi/ *nf* neuropsychology.

neurotoxine /nøʀotɔksin/ *nf* neurotoxin.

neurotransmetteur /nøʀotʀɑ̃smɛtœʀ/ *nm* neurotransmitter.

neurovégétatif, **-ive** /nøʀoveʒetatif, iv/ *adj* [*trouble*] vegetative; **système ~** autonomic nervous system.

neutralisation /nøtʀalizasjɔ̃/ *nf* (tous contextes) neutralization.

neutraliser /nøtʀalize/ [1] **I** *vtr* **1** Chimie to neutralize [*acide, solution*]; **2** (amoindrir) to neutralize [*concurrent, opposition, influence*]; to neutralize [*teinte, goût*]; **3** (empêcher d'agir) to overpower [*personne*]; **le forcené a été neutralisé** the maniac was overpowered; **4** Pol to neutralize [*territoire*].
II se neutraliser *vpr* [*effets*] to cancel each other out.

neutralisme /nøtʀalism/ *nm* neutralism.

neutraliste /nøtʀalist/ *adj, nmf* neutralist.

neutralité /nøtʀalite/ *nf* **1** Pol neutrality; **2** (d'individu, de texte) impartiality; **je préfère rester dans la ~** I prefer to remain neutral.

neutre /nøtʀ/ **I** *adj* **1** gén, Chimie, Phys, Pol neutral; **2** Ling, Zool neuter.
II *nm* Ling **le ~** the neuter.

neutron /nøtʀɔ̃/ *nm* neutron.

neuvaine /nœvɛn/ *nf* novena.

neuvième /nœvjɛm/ **I** **▶212**, **545** *adj* ninth.
II *nf* Scol *third year of primary school, age 8–9.*

Nevada /nevada/ **▶692** *nprm* Nevada.

névé /neve/ *nm* névé, firn.

Nevers /nəvɛʀ/ **▶857** *npr* Nevers.

neveu, *pl* **~x** /n(ə)vø/ *nm* nephew.
IDIOMES **un peu mon ~**○ hum not half!, and how!

névralgie /nevʀalʒi/ *nf* neuralgia ¢; **une ~ faciale** facial neuralgia; **des ~s** attacks of neuralgia.

névralgique /nevʀalʒik/ *adj* **1** Méd [*douleur*] neuralgic; **2** fig **point ~** key point.

névrite /nevʀit/ **▶271** *nf* neuritis ¢.

névritique /nevʀitik/ *adj* neuritic.

névropathe /nevʀɔpat/ *adj, nmf* neurotic.

névrose /nevʀoz/ **▶271** *nf* neurosis.

névrosé, **~e** /nevʀoze/ *adj, nm,f* neurotic.

névrotique /nevʀɔtik/ *adj* neurotic.

New Delhi /njudeli/ **▶857** *npr* New Delhi.

New Hampshire /njuɑ̃pʃiʀ/ **▶692** *nprm* New Hampshire.

New Jersey /njuʒɛʀzɛ/ **▶692** *nprm* New Jersey.

new-look /njuluk/ *adj inv, nm* New Look.

newton /njutɔn/ *nm* (unité) newton.

newtonien, **-ienne** /njutɔnjɛ̃, ɛn/ *adj* Newtonian.

New York /njujɔʀk/ *npr* **1** **▶857** (ville) New York City; **2** **▶692** **l'État de ~** New York (State).

new yorkais, **~e**, *mpl* **~**, *fpl* **~es** /njujɔʀkɛ, ɛz/ **▶857** *adj* of New York.

New Yorkais, **~e**, *mpl* **~**, *fpl* **~es** /njujɔʀkɛ, ɛz/ *nm,f* New Yorker.

nez /ne/ **▶188** *nm* **1** Anat nose; **~ droit/aquilin** or **en bec d'aigle** straight/aquiline nose; **~ en trompette** or **en pied de marmite** turned-up nose; **avoir le ~ bouché/qui coule** to have a blocked/runny nose; **respirer par le ~** to breathe through one's nose; **se boucher le ~** to hold one's nose; **tu saignes du ~** your nose is bleeding; **ça sent le parfum à plein ~**○ there's a strong smell of perfume; **regarder qn sous le ~** to stare rudely at sb; **mettre qch sous le ~ de qn**○ to put sth right under sb's nose; **mettre**○ or **fourrer**◑ **son ~ partout/dans qch** to poke one's nose into everything/into sth; **je n'ai pas mis le ~ dehors** I didn't set foot outside; **il fait un froid à ne pas mettre le ~ dehors** it's freezing cold; **mettre le ~ à la fenêtre** to show one's face at the window; **montrer** or **pointer le bout du ~** to show one's face; **lever à peine le ~** barely to look up; **ne pas lever le ~ de qch** never to lift one's head from sth; **elle travaille le ~ sur son ordinateur/sa feuille** she works hunched over her computer/her sheet of paper; **tu as le ~ dessus** it's staring you in the face; **se retrouver ~ à ~ avec qn** to find oneself face to face with sb; **avoir du ~**, **avoir le ~ fin** (odorat) to have a good sense of smell; (intuition) to be shrewd; **rire/fermer la porte au ~ de qn** to laugh/shut the door in sb's face; **▶lait**, **moutarde**, **ver**; **2** Aviat, Naut (partie avant) nose; **3** Géog (promontoire) headland; **4** Vin (arôme) nose.
IDIOMES **ça se voit** or **c'est gros comme le ~ au milieu du visage** or **de la figure**○ it's as plain as the nose on your face; **mener qn par le bout du ~**○ (dans un couple) to have sb under one's thumb; (plus général) to have sb wrapped round one's little finger○; **ton ~ bouge** or **remue** you're telling a lie; **avoir qn dans le ~**○ to have it in for sb; **avoir un coup** or **un verre dans le ~**○ to have had one too many○; **se manger**○ or **bouffer**◑ **le ~** to be at each other's throats; **ne pas voir plus loin que le bout de son ~** to see no further than the end of one's nose; **faire qch au ~ (et à la barbe) de qn** to do sth right under sb's nose; **filer** or **passer sous le ~ de qn** to slip through sb's fingers; **avoir le ~ creux**○ to be

canny; **se casser le ~**○ (trouver porte close) to find nobody at home; (échouer) to fail, to come a cropper○.

NF /ɛnɛf/ *adj, nf* (*abbr* = **norme française**) French manufacturing standard; **label ~** *label showing a product has been manufactured to standard.*

ni /ni/ *conj*

■ **Note** On observe que le français et l'anglais fonctionnent de la même façon: *il ne jure ni ne se met en colère* = he doesn't swear or lose his temper; *ni il jure ni il se met en colère* = he neither swears nor loses his temper; *elle ne veut pas le voir ni lui parler* = she doesn't wish to see him or to talk to him; *elle ne veut ni le voir ni lui parler* = she neither wishes to see him nor to talk to him.

il ne lui a pas offert de cadeau, ~ même envoyé de carte d'anniversaire he didn't give her a present or even send her a birthday card; **il ne pouvait pas venir chez moi ~ moi aller chez lui** he couldn't come to my house nor could I go to his house; **jamais il n'écrit ~ ne téléphone** he never writes or phones; **rien ~ personne ne le convaincra** nothing or nobody will convince him; **il est sorti sans parapluie ~ imperméable** he went out without an umbrella or a raincoat; **elle ne veut ~ ne peut changer** she doesn't want to change, nor can she; **il n'est ~ beau ~ laid** he's neither handsome nor ugly; **~ les menaces ~ les promesses ne le feront changer d'avis** neither threats nor promises will make him change his mind; **il ne parle ~ anglais, ~ allemand, ~ espagnol** he speaks neither English, nor German, nor Spanish; **il n'a ~ le temps ~ l'argent pour ce genre d'activité** he has neither the time nor the money for that sort of thing; **~ l'un ~ l'autre** neither one nor the other, neither of them; **~ elle ~ moi ne connaissons la réponse** neither she nor I know the answer; **il ne m'a dit ~ oui ~ non** he didn't say yes or no; **~ dans un sens ~ dans l'autre** in neither direction; **~ plus ~ moins** no more and no less; ▶ **foi, trompette**.

IDIOMES **faire qch ~ vu ~ connu**○ to do sth on the sly○; **c'est ~ fait ~ à faire**○ it's a botched○ job; **il n'a fait ~ une ~ deux**○ he didn't hesitate for a second.

niable /njabl/ *adj* deniable; **ce qui n'est pas ~** which can't be denied, which is undeniable.

Niagara /njagaʀa/ ▶**357** *nprm* Niagara; **chutes du ~** Niagara Falls.

niais, **~e** /njɛ, njɛz/ **I** *adj* [*personne*] stupid; [*air, visage*] stupid, inane.
II *nm,f* idiot, simpleton.

niaisement /njɛzmɑ̃/ *adv* stupidly, inanely.

niaiserie /njɛzʀi/ *nf* **1** (caractère) stupidity, silliness; **2** (propos) stupid ou inane remark; **débiter des ~s** to talk rubbish ou twaddle.

niaiseux, **-euse** /njɛzø, øz/ C **I** *adj* (stupide) moronic.
II *nm,f* (imbécile) moron.

Niamey /nijame/ ▶**857** *npr* Niamey.

Nicaragua /nikaʀagwa/ ▶**321** *nprm* Nicaragua.

nicaraguayen, **-enne** /nikaʀagwajɛ̃, ɛn/ ▶**537** *adj* Nicaraguan.

Nicaraguayen, **-enne** /nikaʀagwajɛ̃, ɛn/ ▶**537** *nm,f* Nicaraguan.

Nice /nis/ ▶**857** *npr* Nice.

niche /niʃ/ *nf* **1** (de chien) kennel, doghouse US; **à la ~**○**!** lit go to your kennel!; fig hum make yourself scarce○!; **2** Archit (de statue) niche; (alcôve) recess; **3**○ (farce) trick; **faire des ~s à qn** to play tricks on sb.
■ **~ écologique** ecological niche.

nichée /niʃe/ *nf* (d'oisillons, enfants) brood; (de souris) litter.

nicher /niʃe/ [1] **I** *vi* **1** Zool to nest; **2**○ (loger) to hang out○.
II se nicher *vpr* **1** Zool to nest; **2** (se blottir) [*personne, chaumière*] to nestle (**dans** in).

nichon● /niʃɔ̃/ *nm* boob●, breast.

nickel /nikɛl/ **I**○ *adj* [*objet*] spotless; [*logement*] spick and span (*jamais épith*), spick-and-span (*épith*).
II *nm* nickel.

nickelage /niklaʒ/ *nm* nickel-plating.

nickeler /nikle/ [19] *vtr* to nickel, to nickel-plate; **en acier nickelé** in nickel-plated steel.

niçois, **~e** /niswa, az/ ▶**857** *adj* of Nice.

Niçois, **~e** /niswa, az/ ▶**857** *nm,f* (natif) native of Nice; (habitant) inhabitant of Nice.

Nicosie /nikozi/ ▶**857** *npr* Nicosia.

nicotine /nikɔtin/ *nf* nicotine.

nid /ni/ *nm* (d'oiseaux, de fourmis, guêpes) nest; **faire son ~** to make its nest; **tomber du ~** to fall from the nest; **quitter le ~ familial** fig to leave the nest; **nous avons trouvé** or **surpris l'oiseau au ~** fig we caught him at home; **quand nous sommes arrivés, le ~ était vide** when we got there the bird(s) had flown.
■ **~ d'aigle** eyrie; **~ d'ange** snuggle suit; **~ de brigands** nest ou den of thieves; **~ d'espions** spy ring; **~ d'hirondelle** bird's nest; **potage aux ~s d'hirondelle** bird's-nest soup; **~ de mitrailleuses** machine gun nest; **~ de pie** Naut crow's nest; **~ à poussière** dust trap; **~ de résistance** pocket of resistance.

nid-d'abeilles, *pl* **nids-d'abeilles** /nidabɛj/ *nm* honeycomb weave; **des torchons en ~** tea towels in honeycomb weave.

nid-de-poule, *pl* **nids-de-poule** /nid pul/ *nm* pothole.

nidification /nidifikasjɔ̃/ *nf* nesting, nidification spéc.

nidifier /nidifje/ [2] *vi* to nest, to nidify spéc.

nièce /njɛs/ *nf* niece.

nielle /njɛl/ **I** *nm* Art niello.
II *nf* Agric (maladie) smut, bunt; (plante) **~ des blés** corncockle.

nieller /njelle/ [1] *vtr* Art to niello.

nième /ɛnjɛm/ *adj, nmf* = **énième**.

nier /nje/ [2] *vtr* to deny [*fait, existence, signature*]; to repudiate [*dette*]; **~ que** to deny that; **~ avoir fait qch** to deny doing sth; **~ à qn le droit de faire** to deny sb his/her right to do; **~ sa culpabilité** to deny one's guilt; **~ tout en bloc** to deny everything; **on ne peut ~ que** nobody can deny that; **~ un crime** to deny having committed a crime; **~ une faute** to deny having made a mistake; **~ l'évidence** to refuse to face up to the facts.

nietzschéen, **-éenne** /nitʃeɛ̃, ɛn/ *adj, nm,f* Nietzschean.

Nièvre /njɛvʀ/ ▶**357**, ▶**692** *nprf* (affluent, département) **la ~** the Nièvre.

nigaud, **~e** /nigo, od/ **I** *adj* silly.
II *nm,f* (silly) twit○ GB, goof○ US; **gros ~** silly billy○ GB, big goof○ US.

Niger /niʒɛʀ/ ▶**321**, **357** *nprm* (pays, fleuve) **le ~** the Niger.

Nigeria /niʒɛʀja/ ▶**321** *nprm* Nigeria.

nigérian, **~e** /niʒɛʀjɑ̃, an/ ▶**537** *adj* Nigerian.

Nigérian, **~e** /niʒɛʀjɑ̃, an/ ▶**537** *nm,f* Nigerian.

nigérien, **-ienne** /niʒɛʀjɛ̃, ɛn/ ▶**537** *adj* of Niger.

Nigérien, **-ienne** /niʒɛʀjɛ̃, ɛn/ ▶**537** *nm,f* (natif) native of Niger; (habitant) inhabitant of Niger.

nihilisme /ni'ilism/ *nm* Nihilism.

nihiliste /ni'ilist/ *adj, nmf* nihilist.

Nil /nil/ ▶**357** *nprm* **le ~** the Nile.

nilotique /nilɔtik/ *adj* Ling Nilotic.

nimbe /nɛ̃b/ *nm* nimbus, halo.

nimber /nɛ̃be/ [1] *vtr* [*soleil*] to halo (**de** with); [*brume*] to swathe.

nimbo-stratus /nɛ̃bostʀatys/ *nm inv* nimbostratus.

Nîmes /nim/ ▶**857** *npr* Nîmes.

nîmois, **~e** /nimwa, az/ ▶**857** *adj* of Nîmes.

Nîmois, **~e** /nimwa, az/ ▶**857** *nm,f* (natif) native of Nîmes; (habitant) inhabitant of Nîmes.

niobium /njɔbjɔm/ *nm* niobium.

nipper○: **se nipper** /nipe/ [1] *vpr* to get rigged out○ in one's Sunday best.

nippes○ /nip/ *nfpl* rags○, old clothes.

nippon, **-onne** /nipɔ̃, ɔn/ *adj* Japanese.

Nippon, **-onne** /nipɔ̃, ɔn/ *nm,f* Japanese.

nique○ /nik/ *nf* **faire la ~ à qn**○ to thumb one's nose at sb.

niquer● /nike/ [1] *vtr* **1** (posséder sexuellement) to lay●; **se faire ~** to get laid●; **2** (tromper) **se faire ~** to be had○.

nirvana /niʀvana/ *nm* nirvana.

nitouche○ /nituʃ/ *nf* **sainte ~** goody-goody○.

nitrate /nitʀat/ *nm* nitrate.

nitré, **~e** /nitʀe/ *adj* nitric.

nitreux, **-euse** /nitʀø, øz/ *adj* nitrous.

nitrifier /nitʀifje/ [2] *vtr* to nitrify.

nitrique /nitʀik/ *adj* nitric; **acide ~** nitric acid.

nitrite /nitʀit/ *nm* nitrite.

nitrobenzène /nitʀɔbɛ̃zɛn/ *nm* nitrobenzene.

nitroglycérine /nitʀɔglyseʀin/ *nf* nitroglycerine.

nival, **~e**, *mpl* **-aux** /nival, o/ *adj* **régime ~** snow melt dominated flow; **rétention ~e** snow storage.

niveau, *pl* **~x** /nivo/ *nm* **1** (hauteur) level; **~ de l'eau/d'huile** water/oil level; **au ~ du sol/de la chaussée** at ground/street level; **être de ~** to be level; **mettre de ~** to make [sth] level; **dix mètres au-dessus/au-dessous du ~ de la mer** ten metres[GB] above/below sea level; **être au même ~ que** to be level with; **arrivé au ~ du car** when he drew level with the coach GB ou bus; **l'eau nous arrivait au ~ des chevilles/genoux** the water came up to our ankles/knees; **au ~ du cou/de l'abdomen** [*blessures*] in the neck/abdominal region; **accroc au ~ du genou** tear at the knee; **2** (étage) storey GB, story US; **bâtiment sur deux ~x** two-storey GB ou two-story US building; **3** (degré) (d'intelligence) level; (de connaissances) standard; **~ culturel/intellectuel** cultural/intellectual level; **~ d'éducation/de formation** standard of education/of training; **~ bac**○ baccalaureate or equivalent; **'~ bac + 3'** baccalaureate or equivalent plus 3 years' higher education; **au-dessous du ~ exigé pour** below the required standard for; **~ de production/d'inflation** level of production/of inflation; **d'un bon ~** of a good standard; **mettre à ~** Ordinat to upgrade; **remise à ~** (d'élève) recap, refresher; **remettre qn à ~** to bring sb up to the required standard; **se mettre au ~ de qn** to put oneself on the same level as sb; **de haut ~** [*équipe, athlète*] top (*épith*); [*candidat*] high-calibre[GB] (*épith*); **~ des revenus/salaires** income/wage levels (*pl*); **4** (échelon) level; **à tous les ~x** at every level; **au ~ national/européen** at national/European level; **au plus haut ~** [*discussion, intervention*] top-level (*épith*); **les négociations se dérouleront au plus haut ~** there will be negotiations at the highest level; **au ~ de la commercialisation/des investissements** controv as regards marketing/investment; **5** Ling register; **~ familier/soutenu** informal/formal register; **6** Tech (instrument) level.
■ **~ (à bulle d'air)** spirit level; **~ de langue** Ling register; **~ à lunette** theodolite; **~ de maçon** mason's level; **~ de rémunération** wage level; **~ social** social status; **~ sonore** Audio sound level; **~ de vie** Écon standard of living, living standards.

nivelage /nivlaʒ/ *nm* **1** Gén Civ (de sol, route)

levelling[GB]; **2** (égalisation) (économique) standardization; (social) levelling[GB] out.

niveler /nivle/ [19] *vtr* **1** (aplatir) to level [*sol*]; to flatten [*relief*]; **2** (égaliser) to bring [sth] to the same level [*revenus*]; **~ par le bas/haut** to level down/up; **la souffrance nivelle les différences** suffering is a great leveller.

niveleuse /nivløz/ *nf* grading machine.

nivellement /nivɛlmɑ̃/ *nm* **1** Gén Civ (du sol) levelling[GB]; **2** Géog (mesure) land survey; **3** (égalisation) (économique) standardization; (social) levelling[GB]-out; **~ par le bas/haut** levelling[GB] down/up.

nivernais, **~e** /nivɛʀnɛ, ɛz/ **▶692**, **857** *adj* **1** (du Nivernais) of the Nevers region; **2** (de Nevers) of Nevers.

Nivernais, **~e** /nivɛʀnɛ, ɛz/ I **▶857** *nm,f* (natif) native of Nevers; (habitant) inhabitant of Nevers.

II **▶692** *nprm* **le ~** the Nevers region.

nivôse /nivoz/ *nm* Nivôse (*fourth month of the French revolutionary calendar*, ≈ *January*).

nobélisable /nɔbelizabl/ I *adj* worthy of a Nobel prize.

II *nmf* person who is worthy of a Nobel prize.

nobélium /nɔbeljɔm/ *nm* nobelium.

nobiliaire /nɔbiljɛʀ/ I *adj* [*titre, particule*] nobiliary; **prétention** or **revendication ~** claim to nobility.

II *nm* (registre) peerage list.

noble /nɔbl/ I *adj* **1** (aristocrate) [*personne*] of noble birth; [*famille*] aristocratic; **2** (qui a de la grandeur) [*sentiments, maintien*] noble; [*dessein, cause, tâche*] worthy, noble; **une mission ~** a worthy ou noble undertaking; **3** (supérieur) [*matériau*] (naturel) natural, non-synthetic; (raffiné) fine, delicate; [*filière, section*] prestige (*épith*), prestigious; [*activité, sport*] noble; **métaux ~s** precious metals; **morceaux ~s d'un animal** choice cuts of meat.

II *nmf* (personne) nobleman/noblewoman; **les ~s** the nobility (*sg*).

III *nm* Hist (monnaie) noble.

■ **~ art** Sport noble art.

noblement /nɔbləmɑ̃/ *adv* **1** (avec noblesse) nobly; **2** (avec générosité) handsomely.

noblesse /nɔblɛs/ *nf* **1** (qualité morale) nobility; **agir avec ~** to act nobly; **2** Hist (aristocratie) **la (haute) ~** the nobility; **la petite ~** the gentry; **prouver sa ~** to prove one's noble birth.

■ **~ de Cour** Hist Court nobility; **~ d'épée** Hist old nobility; **~ de robe** Hist noblesse de robe; **~ terrienne** Hist landed gentry.

IDIOMES **~ oblige** noblesse oblige.

nobliau, *pl* **~x** /nɔblijo/ *nm* minor nobleman.

noce /nɔs/ I *nf* **1**○ (fête) party; **faire la ~**○ fig to live it up○, to party○; **aujourd'hui je n'étais pas à la ~** fig today was no picnic; **2** (invités) wedding party.

II **noces** *nfpl* wedding (*sg*); **nuit/repas de ~s** wedding night/breakfast; **en premières ~s, il a épousé...** his first wife was...; **les Noces de Cana** the Wedding at Cana, the Marriage feast at Cana; **les Noces de Figaro** the Marriage of Figaro.

■ **~s d'argent** silver wedding (*sg*); **~s de diamant** diamond wedding (*sg*); **~s d'or** golden wedding (*sg*).

noceur○, **-euse** /nɔsœʀ, øz/ *nm,f* party animal○.

nocif, **-ive** /nɔsif, iv/ *adj* [*gaz, produit, effet*] noxious; [*théorie, thèse*] harmful.

nocivité /nɔsivite/ *nf* (de gaz, produit, d'effet, influence) noxiousness (**de** of); (de théorie, thèse) harmfulness (**de** of).

noctambule /nɔktɑ̃byl/ I *adj* [*promeneur*] late-night (*épith*); **ils sont ~s** they're night owls.

II *nmf* night-time reveller.

noctambulisme /nɔktɑ̃bylism/ *nm* night-time revelling[GB].

nocturne /nɔktyʀn/ I *adj* [*visite, spectacle, attaque*] night (*épith*); [*oiseau, animal*] nocturnal; [*sortie, promenade, équipée*] late-night (*épith*); **la vie ~ à Londres** nightlife in London.

II *nm* **1** Zool (oiseau) nocturnal bird; **2** Mus, Relig nocturne.

III *nf* **1** Sport (course, match) evening fixture; **jouer un match en ~** to play a match in the evening; **une réunion en ~** an evening fixture; **2** Comm (de magasin) late-night opening.

nodal, **~e**, *mpl* **-aux** /nɔdal, o/ *adj* nodal.

nodosité /nɔdɔzite/ *nf* **1** Méd nodule; **2** Bot nodosity.

nodule /nɔdyl/ *nm* nodule.

Noé /noe/ *npr* Noah.

noël /nɔɛl/ *nm* **1** (chant) Christmas carol; **2** (cadeau) **(petit) ~** Christmas present.

Noël /nɔɛl/ I *nm* Christmas; **'Joyeux ~'** 'Merry Christmas', 'Happy Christmas'; **à ~** at Christmas; **on y va pour ~** we are going there for Christmas; **de ~** [*arbre, cadeau, bûche*] Christmas (*épith*); **▶ tison**.

II *nf* **la (fête de) ~** Christmas.

■ **~ blanc** White Christmas.

nœud /nø/ I *nm* **1** (pour lier) knot; **faire un ~** to tie ou make a knot; **~ simple/double** single/double knot; **faire un ~ de cravate** to tie a tie; **2** (pour orner et lier) bow; **avoir des ~s rouges dans les cheveux** to have red bows ou ribbons in one's hair; **3** **▶860** Naut (unité de vitesse) knot; **4** (de branche, tige, planche) knot; **5** (point essentiel) crux; **6** Littérat (de pièce, de roman, d'intrigue) core; **7** Électrotech, Astron, Math node; **8●** (pénis) dick●, nob● GB.

II **nœuds** *nmpl* liter (d'amitié, affection) bonds, ties.

■ **~ coulant** slipknot; **~ ferroviaire** railway junction; **~ gordien** Gordian knot; **~ papillon** bow tie; **faire un/son ~ papillon** to do up a/one's bow tie; **~ routier** road junction; **~ de vipères** nest of vipers; **~ vital** Anat vital centre[GB]; **~s marins** Naut sailors' knots.

noir, **~e** /nwaʀ/ **▶193** I *adj* **1** (couleur) [*peinture, fumée, cheveux*] black; [*yeux*] dark; **être ~ de coups** to be black and blue; **être ~ de monde** [*rue, plage*] to be swarming ou teeming with people; **2** (sale) [*mains, col*] black, filthy; **être ~ de crasse/saleté** to be black with grime/dirt; **3** (obscur) [*ruelle, cachot*] dark; **les eaux ~es d'un lac** the dark waters of a lake; **il fait ~** it's dark; **4** (d'Afrique) [*personne, race, peau, quartier*] black; **avoir du sang ~ dans les veines** to have African ancestry; **5** (bronzé) **être ~, avoir la peau ~e** to have a dark tan; **6** (catastrophique) [*époque, année*] bad, bleak; [*misère*] dire, abject; [*désespoir*] deep; [*idée*] gloomy, dark; **dans le désespoir le plus ~** in deepest despair; **tout n'est pas ~ dans sa vie/ce livre** his life/this book is not all doom and gloom; **dresser** or **faire un tableau ~ de la situation** to paint a very black picture of the situation; **7** (méchant) [*regard*] black; [*âme, dessein*] dark; **regarder qn d'un œil ~** to give sb a black look; **entrer** or **se mettre dans une colère ~e** to fly into a towering rage; **8**○ (ivre) drunk.

II *nm* **1** (couleur) black; **le ~ te va bien** black suits you; **un ~ brillant/mat** a shiny/matt black; **il s'habille toujours en ~** he always wears black; **il était en ~** or **vêtu de ~** he was in black; **le ~ du velours sur le blanc du satin** black velvet against white satin; **2** (saleté) (tache noire) black mark; (crasse) dirt; **avoir du ~ sur le visage** to have a black mark on one's face; **avoir du ~ sous les ongles** to have dirt under one's nails; **3** (obscurité) dark; **dans le ~** in the dark; **avoir peur du ~** to be afraid of the dark; **4** Art (d'un tableau) the dark areas; **5** (clandestinement) **au ~** [*acheter, vendre*] on the black market; **travail au ~** gén work for which no earnings are declared; (deuxième emploi, non déclaré) moonlighting○; **travailler au ~** gén to work without declaring one's earnings; (deuxième emploi, non déclaré) to moonlight ○, to work on the side; **faire une réparation/des travaux au ~** to do repairs/work on the side; **6**○ (café) **un (petit) ~** an espresso.

III **noire** *nf* Mus crochet GB, quarter note US.

■ **~ d'aniline** aniline black; **~ animal** boneblack; **~ au blanc** reverse; **~ de carbone** carbon black; **~ et blanc** Phot black and white photography; **faire du ~ et blanc** to do black and white photography; **film/photographie en ~ et blanc** black and white film/photography; **le film est en ~ et blanc** the film is in black and white; **~ de fumée** lampblack.

IDIOMES **c'est écrit ~ sur blanc** it's there in black and white; **être ~ comme de l'ébène/du cirage** to be as black as ebony/boot polish; **voir tout en ~** to look on the black side (of things).

Noir, **~e** /nwaʀ/ *nm,f* black (man/woman); **les ~s** the blacks, black people; **~ Américain** black American, African American.

noirâtre /nwaʀɑtʀ/ **▶193** *adj* blackish.

noiraud, **~e** /nwaʀo, od/ I *adj* [*personne, teint, visage*] swarthy.

II *nm,f* swarthy person.

noirceur /nwaʀsœʀ/ *nf* **1** (d'encre) blackness; (de cheveux, nuit, d'yeux) darkness; **2** (de personne, regard, projets, d'intentions) blackness; **3** C (obscurité) dark; **à la ~** in the dark.

noircir /nwaʀsiʀ/ [3] I *vtr* **1** (salir) [*charbon*] to make [sth] dirty; [*fumée, feu, pollution*] to blacken; [*métal*] to turn [sth] black; [*encre*] to stain [sth] black; **la carcasse noircie d'un camion** the blackened shell of a truck; **il avait le visage noirci par la suie** his face was black with soot; **~ du papier** fig to scribble away; **2** (assombrir) **~ la situation** or **le tableau** to paint a black picture of the situation; **~ qn** or **la réputation de qn** to blacken sb's name ou character; **3** (teindre) to darken [*cuir*].

II *vi* (devenir noir) [*banane*] to go black; [*mur*] to get dirty ou black; [*métal*] to tarnish; (bronzer) [*personne*] to get brown.

III **se noircir** *vpr* [*ciel*] to darken; [*temps*] to become threatening; **se ~ le visage** to blacken one's face.

noircissure /nwaʀsisyʀ/ *nf* dark smudge.

noise /nwaz/ *nf* **chercher ~** or **des ~s à qn** to pick a quarrel with sb.

noisetier /nwaztje/ *nm* hazel (tree).

noisette /nwazɛt/ I **▶193** *adj inv* [*couleur, yeux*] hazel; [*tissu*] light brown.

II *nf* **1** Bot, Culin hazelnut; **glace à la ~** hazelnut ice cream; **chocolat aux ~s** hazelnut chocolate; **2** (morceau) small knob (**de** of).

noix /nwa/ *nf* **1** Bot walnut GB, English walnut US; **pain/fromage aux ~** walnut bread/cheese; **~ verte** green walnut; **2** (morceau) knob; **une ~ de beurre** a knob of butter; **3** Culin **rôti dans la ~** ≈ roast fillet of veal; **~ de coquille Saint-Jacques** white flesh of scallop; **4**○ (imbécile) nut○; **salut vieille ~!** hi there, old pal○!; **à la ~** [*histoire, artiste*] crummy○, crap●.

■ **~ du Brésil** Brazil nut; **~ de cajou** cashew nut; **~ de coco** coconut; **~ de cola** kola nut; **~ de galle** oak apple, oak gall; **~ (de) muscade** nutmeg; **~ pâtissière** *tender fillet cut of veal*; **~ de pécan** pecan nut; **~ de veau** *fillet end of a leg of veal*.

nolisé, **~e** /nɔlize/ *adj* C [*vol*] charter.

nom /nɔ̃/ I *nm* **1** (désignation) name; **quel est le ~ de ces plantes?** what's the name of these plants, what are these plants called?; **digne de ce ~** worthy of the name; **une dictature qui n'ose pas dire son ~** a dictatorship masquerading as something else; **la maladie doit** or **emprunte son ~**

à the disease owes its name to; **la lexicographie, comme son ~ l'indique, est**... as its name implies, lexicography is...; **n'avoir de république que le ~** to be a republic in name only; **connu sous le ~ de** known as; **donner un ~ à** to name; **sans ~** péj unspeakable; **cela porte un ~: la fainéantise** there's a word for that: laziness; **~ de ~**○, **~ d'un chien**○ or **d'une pipe**○ hell○; **qu'est-ce que tu fais ici, ~ de ~?** what the hell are you doing here?; **2** (nom propre) name; (opposé à prénom) surname, second name; **quel est ton ~?** what's your name?; **demander/connaître le ~ de qn** to ask/know sb's name; **connaître qn de ~** to know sb by name; **mettre un ~ sur un visage** to put a name to a face; **porter le ~ de son mari** to use one's husband's surname; **quelqu'un du ~ de Grunard** somebody by the name of Grunard; **réserver au ~ de Grunard** to book GB ou make a reservation in the name of Grunard; **sous mon/leur ~** under my/their own name; **George Sand, de son vrai ~ Aurore Dupin** George Sand, whose real name was Aurore Dupin; **~ et prénom** full name; **(c'est) à quel ~?** under what name?; **répondre au ~ de** to answer to the name of; **~ à coucher dehors**○ impossible name; **~ à rallonge**○ or **tiroirs** impossibly long name; **Louis le neuvième du ~** Louis IX; **petit ~** first name; **parler en son propre ~** to speak for oneself; **rassembler les électeurs sous** or **sur son ~** to rally the voters behind one; **en France, le produit se vend sous le ~ de 'Calex'** in France, the product is marketed under the 'Calex' tradename; ▸**faux**; **3** (réputation) name; **se faire un ~** to make a name for oneself (**comme, en tant que** as); **il s'est fait un ~ dans la publicité** he made his name in advertising; **vouloir laisser un ~** to want to become famous; **4** Ling (partie du discours) noun; **~ propre/commun** proper/common noun; **~ composé/féminin** compound/feminine noun.

II au nom de *loc prép* **1** (en vertu de) in the name of; **au ~ de la loi/notre amour** in the name of the law/our love; **au ~ du Père, du Fils et du Saint-Esprit** in the name of the Father, of the Son and of the Holy Ghost; **2** (de la part de) on behalf of; **au ~ de tous vos collègues** on behalf of all your colleagues.

■ **~ de baptême** Christian name; **~ de code** code name; **~ commercial** corporate name; **~ déposé** Comm, Jur registered trademark; **~ double** double-barrelled name GB, hyphenated name; **~ d'emprunt** pseudonym; **~ de famille** surname; **~ de guerre** nom de guerre; **~ de jeune fille** maiden name; **~ de lieu** place-name; **~ de plume** pen name, nom de plume; **~ de théâtre** stage name; ▸**petit**.

IDIOMES **traiter qn de tous les ~s (d'oiseaux)** to call sb all the names under the sun; **appeler les choses par leur ~** to call a spade a spade.

nomade /nɔmad/ **I** *adj* [*personne, vie, tribu*] nomadic.

II *nmf* (du désert) nomad; **mener une vie de ~** to lead a nomadic existence.

nomadisme /nɔmadism/ *nm* nomadism.

no man's land /nomanslɑ̃d/ *nm* no-man's land.

nombrable /nɔ̃bʀabl/ *adj* numerable, countable.

nombre /nɔ̃bʀ/ *nm* **1** Math, Ling, Sci number; **un ~ à deux chiffres** a two-digit number; **~ positif/négatif** positive/negative number; **la théorie des ~s** number theory; **la loi des grands ~s** the law of large numbers; **s'accorder en genre et en ~** to agree in gender and number; **2** (quantité) number; **le ~ des chômeurs** the number of unemployed; **le ~ croissant/décroissant** the increasing/decreasing ou falling number; **un certain ~ de** some; **être égal en ~** or **en ~ égal** to be equal in number; **être inférieur en ~** or **en ~ inférieur** [*troupes, joueurs*] to be fewer in number; [*groupe*] to be smaller; **être supérieur en ~** or **en ~ supérieur** [*troupes, joueurs*] to be larger in number; [*groupe*] to be bigger; **nous sommes en ~ suffisant pour** there are enough of us to; **dans le ~**○ **il y aura bien quelqu'un qui me prêtera de l'argent** surely one of them will lend me some money; **ils sont du ~ de ceux qui** they are among those who; **ils étaient au ~ de 30** there were 30 of them; **3** (grande quantité) numbers (*pl*); **être écrasé** or **succomber sous le ~** (de personnes) to be overcome by sheer weight of numbers; (de dossiers, lettres) to be defeated by the sheer volume; **subir la loi du ~** to be overcome by sheer weight of numbers; **sans ~** [*ennemis, personnes*] countless; [*ennuis*] endless; **bon ~ de** a good many; **~ de fois** many times; **4** Bible, Relig **le Livre de Nombres/les Nombres** the Book of Numbers/Numbers.

■ **~ aléatoire** Ordinat random number; **~ algébrique** algebraic number; **~ atomique** atomic number; **~ d'Avogadro** Avogadro's number ou constant; **~ cardinal** cardinal number; **~ complexe** complex (number); **~ décimal** decimal; **~ entier** whole number; **~ entier naturel** natural number; **~ entier relatif** integer; **~ fractionnaire** fraction; **~ au hasard** = **~ aléatoire**; **~ hétérogène** mixed number; **~ imaginaire** Ordinat imaginary number; **~ impair** odd number; **~ irrationnel** irrational number; **~ de Mach** Mach (number); **~ de masse** nucleon ou mass number; **~ d'or** Art golden section; **~ ordinal** ordinal number; **~ pair** even number; **~ parfait** perfect number; **~ premier** prime number; **~ rationnel** rational number; **~ réel** real number.

nombrer /nɔ̃bʀe/ [1] *vtr* liter to number, to count.

nombreux, **-euse** /nɔ̃bʀø, øz/ *adj* **1** (important) [*communauté, population, collection*] large; **la foule était nombreuse** there was a large ou vast crowd; **2** (en grand nombre) many (*épith*); **de ~ spectateurs/accidents** many ou numerous spectators/accidents; **de nombreuses personnalités étaient présentes** there were many ou numerous personalities present; **l'usine ne sera pas mise en service avant de nombreuses années** it will be many years before the factory is put into operation; **nous étions très ~** there were a great many of us; **ils étaient peu ~** there were only a few of them, there weren't many of them; **ils étaient ~ à ignorer la date de la réunion** many of them didn't know the date of the meeting; **ils ont répondu ~ à l'appel** numerous ou a great many people responded to the appeal; **les clients/candidats étaient ~** there were a lot of customers/candidates; **les clients étaient peu ~** there weren't many customers; **les touristes sont de plus en plus/de moins en moins ~** there are more and more/fewer and fewer tourists; **les admirateurs étaient venus ~** crowds of fans had come; **les clients étaient moins/plus ~ qu'hier** there were fewer/more customers than yesterday; **ils arrivent toujours plus ~** they are arriving in ever greater numbers; **les touristes deviennent trop ~** the number of tourists is becoming excessive; **dans de ~ cas** in many ou numerous cases.

nombril /nɔ̃bʀil/ *nm* navel; **se regarder le ~, contempler son ~** fig to contemplate one's navel; **elle se prend pour le ~ du monde** fig she thinks she's God's gift to mankind.

nombrilisme○ /nɔ̃bʀilism/ *nm* pej (de personne) self-absorption, navel-gazing○; **faire du ~** to be completely wrapped up in oneself.

nombriliste○ /nɔ̃bʀilist/ *adj* pej [*personne*] egocentric; [*politique, repli*] inward-looking.

nomenclature /nɔmɑ̃klatyʀ/ *nf* **1** (ensemble de termes) nomenclature; (de dictionnaire) word list; **2** Ordinat nomenclature.

nomenklatura /nɔmɛnklatuʀa/ *nf* nomenklatura.

nominal, **~e**, *mpl* **-aux** /nɔminal, o/ **I** *adj* **1** Écon, Fin [*hausse, taux*] nominal; **salaire ~** money, nominal wages; (avant déductions) gross salary, pay; **valeur ~e** (d'action) par value; (de monnaie) face value; **2** (par nom) **liste ~e** list of names; **appel ~** roll call; **3** Tech (indiqué) [*puissance, rendement*] rated; **4** Ling [*forme, emploi*] nominal.

II *nm* Fin (d'action) par value; **action au ~ de 100 francs** share with a par value of 100 francs.

nominalement /nɔminalmɑ̃/ *adv* **1** (par le nom) [*appeler*] by name; [*inviter*] personally; **2** Ling nominally.

nominalisation /nɔminalizasjɔ̃/ *nf* Ling nominalization.

nominaliser /nɔminalize/ [1] *vtr, vi* Ling to nominalize.

nominalisme /nɔminalism/ *nm* Philos nominalism.

nominatif, **-ive** /nɔminatif, iv/ **I** *adj* **1** (par noms) [*fichier, liste*] of names; **2** (individual) [*invitation*] personal; [*inculpation*] individual; **3** Fin [*titre, action*] registered.

II *nm* Ling nominative; **au ~** in the nominative.

nomination /nɔminasjɔ̃/ *nf* **1** (affectation) appointment; **~ à un poste/une commission** appointment to a post/a committee; **~ à la tête de** appointment as head of; **~ aux affaires étrangères** (comme ministre) appointment as Foreign Secretary; (comme fonctionnaire) appointment to the Foreign Affairs Office; **obtenir sa ~** to be appointed; **2** (lettre d'affectation) **attendre/recevoir sa ~** to expect/receive one's letter of appointment; **3** (sélection) controv nomination.

nominativement /nɔminativmɑ̃/ *adv* by name.

nominer /nɔmine/ [1] *vtr* controv to nominate.

nommément /nɔmemɑ̃/ *adv* specifically by name.

nommer /nɔme/ [1] **I** *vtr* **1** (désigner pour une fonction) to appoint; **~ qn (au poste de) directeur** to appoint sb director; **~ qn d'office/à un poste** to appoint sb automatically/to a position; **être nommé à Paris/Berlin** to be posted to Paris/Berlin; **2** (dénommer) to name [*personne*]; to call [*chose*]; **ce qu'on nomme tanka** what is called tanka; **être nommé d'après sa grand-mère** to be named after one's grandmother; **comment l'ont-ils nommé?** what did they call him?; **le nommé Durand** the man named Durand; **nommé communément** commonly known as; **3** (citer) to name [*complice, arbre, peintre*]; **pour ne ~ personne** to name ou mention no names.

II se nommer *vpr* **1** (s'appeler) to be called; **2** (donner son nom) to give one's name.

non /nɔ̃/

■ **Note** En anglais la réponse *no* est généralement renforcée en reprenant le verbe utilisé pour poser la question: *'tu es déçu?'—'non'* = 'are you disappointed?'—'no, I'm not'; *'est-ce que vous aimez les concombres?'—'non'* = 'do you like cucumber?'—'no, I don't'.

I *adv* **1** (marque le désaccord) no; **mais ~, je n'ai pas dit ça!** no, that's not what I said!; **'encore du café?'—'je ne dis pas ~'** 'more coffee?'—'I wouldn't say no'; **~, ~ et ~!** absolutely not!; **ah, ça ~!** definitely not!, no way○!; **alors, c'est ~?** so the answer is no?; **certes ~** not at all; **~, assurément** most certainly not; **'il était**

Les nombres (1)

Les nombres cardinaux

0	nought (*GB*) zero (*US*)*
1	one
2	two
3	three
4	four
5	five
6	six
7	seven
8	eight
9	nine
10	ten
11	eleven
12	twelve
13	thirteen
14	fourteen
15	fifteen
16	sixteen
17	seventeen
18	eighteen
19	nineteen
20	twenty
21	twenty-one
22	twenty-two
30	thirty
31	thirty-one
32	thirty-two
40	forty†
50	fifty
60	sixty
70	seventy
73	seventy-three
80	eighty
84	eighty-four
90	ninety
95	ninety-five
100	a hundred *ou* one hundred‡
101	a hundred and one (*GB*)§ a hundred one (*US*)
111	a hundred and eleven (*GB*) a hundred eleven (*US*)
123	a hundred and twenty-three (*GB*) a hundred twenty-three (*US*)
200	two hundred

Noter que l'anglais utilise une virgule là où le français a un espace.

1,000	a thousand
1,002	a thousand and two (*GB*) a thousand two (*US*)
1,020	a thousand and twenty (*GB*) a thousand twenty (*US*)
1,200	a thousand two hundred
10,000	ten thousand
10,200	ten thousand two hundred
100,000	a hundred thousand
102,000	a hundred and two thousand (*GB*) *ou* a hundred two thousand (*US*)
1,000,000	one million
1,200,000	one million two hundred thousand
1,264,932	one million two hundred and sixty-four thousand nine hundred and thirty-two (*GB*) *ou* one million two hundred sixty-four thousand nine hundred thirty-two (*US*)
2,000,000	two million¶
3,000,000,000	three thousand million (*GB*) *ou* three billion‖ (*US*)
4,000,000,000,000	four billion‖ (*GB*) four thousand billion (*US*)

les nombres jusqu'à dix = numbers up to ten
compter jusqu'à dix = to count up to ten

* *En anglais, lorsqu'on énonce les chiffres un à un, on prononce en général le zéro* oh: mon numéro de poste est le 403 = my extension number is 403 (*dire* four oh three).
Pour la température, on utilise zero: il fait zéro = it's zero.
Pour les scores dans les jeux et les sports, on utilise en général nil (*GB*) zero (*US*), *sauf au tennis, où zéro se dit* love.

† *Noter que* forty *s'écrit sans* u, *alors que* fourteen *et* fourth *s'écrivent comme* four.

‡ *Les formes avec* one *s'utilisent lorsqu'on veut insister sur la précision du chiffre. Dans les autres cas, on utilise plutôt* a.

§ *Noter que* and *s'utilise en anglais britannique entre* hundred*ou* thousand *et le chiffre des dizaines ou des unités (mais pas entre* thousand *et le chiffre des centaines). Il ne s'utilise pas en anglais américain.*

¶ *Noter que* million *est invariable en anglais dans ce cas.*

‖ *Attention: un* billion *américain vaut un milliard (1000 millions), alors qu'un* billion *britannique vaut 1000 milliards. Le billion américain est de plus en plus utilisé en Grande-Bretagne.*

Les adresses, les numéros de téléphone, les dates etc.

Les adresses

	dire
29 Park Road	twenty-nine Park Road
110 Park Road	a hundred and ten Park Road (*GB*) *ou* one ten Park Road (*US*)
1021 Park Road	one oh two one Park Road (*GB*) *ou* ten twenty-one Park Road (*US*)

Les numéros de téléphone

	dire
071 392 1011	oh seven one, three nine two; one oh one one *ou* ... one oh double one
1-415-243 7620	one, four one five, two four three, seven six two oh
78 02 75 27	seven eight, oh two, seven five, two seven

Les dates ▶ 350

Combien?

combien d'enfants y a-t-il? = how many children are there?
il y a vingt-trois enfants = there are twenty-three children

Noter que l'anglais n'a pas d'équivalent du pronom français en *dans:*

combien est-ce qu'il y en a? = how many are there?
il y en a vingt-trois = there are twenty-three
nous viendrons à 8 = there'll be 8 of us coming
ils sont 8 = there are 8 of them
ils étaient 10 au commencement = there were 10 of them at the beginning

L'anglais million *s'utilise ici comme adjectif. Noter l'absence d'équivalent anglais de la préposition* de *après* million.

1 000 000 d'habitants = 1,000,000 inhabitants (*dire* a million inhabitants *ou* one million inhabitants)
2 000 000 d'habitants = two million inhabitants

L'anglais utilise aussi les mots hundreds, thousands, millions *etc. au pluriel, comme en français:*

j'en ai des centaines = I've got hundreds
des milliers de livres = thousands of books
les milliers de livres que j'ai lus = the thousands of books I have read
des centaines et des centaines = hundreds and hundreds
des milliers et des milliers = thousands and thousands

Pour les numéraux français en -aine (dizaine, douzaine, quinzaine, vingtaine, trentaine, quarantaine, cinquantaine, soixantaine et centaine) lorsqu'ils désignent une somme approximative, l'anglais utilise le chiffre avec la préposition about *ou* around.

une dizaine de questions = about ten questions
une quinzaine de personnes = about fifteen people
une vingtaine = about twenty
une centaine = about a hundred
presque dix = almost ten *ou* nearly ten
environ dix = about ten
environ 400 pages = about four hundred pages
moins de dix = less than ten
plus de dix = more than ten
tous les dix = all ten of them *ou* all ten
ils s'y sont mis à cinq = it took five of them
ou (*s'ils n'étaient que cinq en tout*) it took all five of them

Noter l'ordre des mots dans:

les deux autres = the other two
les cinq prochaines semaines = the next five weeks
mes dix derniers dollars = my last ten dollars

☛ Voir page suivante

content?'—'que ~°**!'** 'was he pleased?'—'not at all!'; **elle n'est pas contente, ~** she isn't at all pleased; **dire** or **faire ~ de la tête** to shake one's head; **▶oui**; **2** (remplace une proposition) **je pense que ~** I don't think so, I think not; **je te dis que ~** no, I tell you; **il paraît que ~** apparently not; **cela marche? elle affirme que ~** does it work? she claims it doesn't; **tu trouves ça drôle? moi ~** do you think that's funny? I don't; **ils ont tous aidé, lui ~** everyone helped, but he didn't; **certains ont aimé, d'autres ~** some people liked it and some didn't; **3** (dans une double négation) **~ sans raison** not without reason; **~ sans mal** or **peine** not without difficulty; **~ sans hésiter** or **hésitation** not without hesitation; **~ loin de** not far from; **~ moins difficile** just as difficult; **une situation ~ moins triste** an equally sad situation; **4** (introduisant une rectification, nuance) **j'ai vu ~ seulement lui mais encore elle** I saw not only him but her too; **~ (pas) que je sois d'accord** not that I agree; **~ pas 200 mais 2000** 2000, not 200; **elle est assez jolie, et ~ très belle** she is quite pretty, rather than very beautiful; **devant le café, ou plutôt ~, dedans** outside the café, or rather inside; **5** (dans une alternative) **qu'il soit d'accord ou ~** whether he agrees or not; **malade ou ~, je viendrai** I'll come even if I'm ill; **tu viens, oui ou ~?** are you coming or not?; **va-t-il, oui ou ~, accepter?** will he accept or not?; **plaisanterie ou ~, cela ne m'a pas plu** even if it was supposed to be a joke, I didn't like it; **6** (interrogatif, exclamatif) **c'est difficile, ~?** (n'est-ce pas) it's difficult, isn't it?; **vous écrirez, ~?** you will write, won't you?; **~?** (de scepticisme) oh no?; **~!** (de surprise) no!; **sois un peu plus poli, ~ mais** °**!** be a bit more polite, for heaven's sake!; **7** (avec adjectif) non; **~ alcoolisé** nonalcoholic; **~ négligeable** [*atout, somme*] considerable; [*rôle*] important; **augmentation ~ prévue** unforeseen increase; **objet ~ identifié** unidentified object; **peur ~ feinte** genuine fear; **les choses ~ dites** things left unsaid; **être déclaré ~ coupable** to be found not guilty.

II *nm inv* **1** (désaccord) no; **ne dire ni oui ni ~** not to give a definite answer; **répondre ~** to say no; **dire ~ à la guerre** to say 'no' to war; **un ~ catégorique** an emphatic no; **2** (vote négatif) 'no' vote; **il y a eu 60 ~** (votes) there were 60 votes against ou 60 'no' votes; **répondez par oui ou par ~** answer yes or no; **mon ~ est définitif** no and that's final.

III non plus *loc adv* **je ne suis pas d'accord ~ plus** I don't agree either; **il n'a pas aimé le film, moi ~ plus** he didn't like the film and neither did I, he didn't like the film and I didn't either.

non-acceptation /nɔnaksɛptasjɔ̃/ *nf* non-acceptance.

Les nombres (2)

Quel numéro? Lequel?

le volume numéro 8 de la série	=	volume 8 of the series *ou* the 8th volume of the series
le cheval numéro 11	=	horse number 11
miser sur le 11	=	to bet on number 11
le nombre 7 porte bonheur	=	7 is a lucky number
la ligne 8 du métro	=	line number 8 of the underground (*GB*) *ou* subway (*US*)
la (chambre numéro) 8 est libre	=	room 8 is free
le 8 de pique	=	the 8 of spades
Louis XIV	=	Louis the Fourteenth

Les opérations

	dire
10 + 3 = 13	ten and three are thirteen *ou* ten plus three make thirteen
10 − 3 = 7	ten minus three is seven *ou* three from ten leaves seven
10 × 3 = 30	ten times three is thirty *ou* ten threes are thirty
30 ÷ 3 = 10*	thirty divided by three is ten *ou* three into thirty is ten
3^2	three squared
3^3	three cubed *ou* three to the power of three
3^4	three to the fourth *ou* three to the power of four
3^{100}	three to the hundredth *ou* three to the power of a hundred
3^n	three to the nth (dire [ɛnθ]) *ou* three to the power of n
√12	the square root of 12
√25 = 5	the square root of twenty-five is 5
B > A	B is greater than A
A < B	A is less than B

Les nombres décimaux

Noter que l'anglais utilise un point (the decimal point) *là où le français a une virgule. Noter également qu'en anglais britannique* zéro *se dit* nought, *et en américain* zero.

	dire
0.25	nought point two five *ou* point two five
0.05	nought point nought five *ou* point oh five
0.75	nought point seven five *ou* point seven five
3.33	three point three three
8.195	eight point one nine five
9.1567	nine point one five six seven

Les pourcentages

	dire
25%	twenty-five per cent
50%	fifty per cent
100%	a hundred per cent *ou* one hundred per cent
200%	two hundred per cent
365%	three hundred and sixty-five per cent (*GB*) *ou* three hundred sixty-five per cent (*US*)
4.25%	four point two five per cent
4.025%	four point oh two five per cent

Les fractions

	dire		dire
½	a half† *ou* one half	1/11	one eleventh
⅓	a third *ou* one third	1/12	one twelfth (*etc.*)
¼	a quarter *ou* one quarter etc.	⅔	two thirds
⅕	a fifth	⅖	two fifths
⅙	a sixth	2/10	two tenths (*etc.*)
1/7	a seventh	¾	three quarters
⅛	an eighth	⅝	five eighths
1/9	a ninth	3/10	three tenths (*etc.*)
1/10	a tenth		

* *Noter que le signe* divisé par *est différent dans les deux langues: au " : " français correspond le " ÷ " anglais.*

† *Pour les fractions jusqu'à 1/10, on utilise normalement* a (*a third*)*; on utilise* one (*one third*) *en mathématiques et pour les calculs précis.*

‡ *Noter que l'anglais utilise une virgule là où le français a un espace.*

Noter l'utilisation en anglais de l'article indéfini dans les expressions suivantes:

1½	one and a half
1⅓	one and a third
1¼	one and a quarter
1⅙	one and a sixth
1 1/7	one and a seventh (*etc.*)
5⅔	five and two thirds
5¾	five and three quarters
5⅘	five and four fifths (*etc.*)
45/100	forty-five hundredths

Noter que l'anglais n'utilise pas l'article défini dans:

les deux tiers d'entre eux = two thirds of them

Mais noter l'utilisation de l'article indéfini anglais dans:

quarante-cinq centièmes de seconde	=	forty-five hundredths of a second
dix sur cent	=	ten out of a hundred

Les nombres ordinaux

français	abréviation	en toutes lettres anglaises
1er	1st	first
2e	2nd	second
3e	3rd	third
4e	4th	fourth
5e	5th	fifth
6e	6th	sixth
7e	7th	seventh
8e	8th	eighth
9e	9th	ninth
10e	10th	tenth
11e	11th	eleventh
12e	12th	twelfth
13e	13th	thirteenth
20e	20th	twentieth
21e	21st	twenty-first
22e	22nd	twenty-second
23e	23rd	twenty-third
24e	24th	twenty-fourth
30e	30th	thirtieth
40e	40th	fortieth
50e	50th	fiftieth
60e	60th	sixtieth
70e	70th	seventieth
80e	80th	eightieth
90e	90th	ninetieth
99e	99th	ninety-ninth
100e	100th	hundredth
101e	101st	hundred and first
102e	102nd	hundred and second (*GB*) hundred second (*US*)
103e	103rd	hundred and third (*GB*) hundred third (*US*)
196e	196th	hundred and ninety-sixth (*GB*) hundred ninety-sixth (*US*)
1 000e	1,000th	thousandth
1 000 000e	1,000,000th	millionth

le premier	=	the first *ou* the first one
le quarante-deuxième	=	the forty-second *ou* the forty-second one
il y en a un deuxième	=	there is a second one
le second des deux	=	the second of the two

Noter l'ordre des mots dans:

les trois premiers	=	the first three
le troisième pays le plus riche du monde	=	the third richest nation in the world
les quatre derniers	=	the last four

non-accomplissement /nɔnakɔ̃plismɑ̃/ *nm* nonfulfilment[GB].

nonagénaire /nɔnaʒenɛʀ/ **I** *adj* **être ~** to be in one's nineties, to be a nonagenarian. **II** *nmf* nonagenarian.

non-agression /nɔnagʀesjɔ̃/ *nf* nonaggression; **pacte de ~** nonaggression pact.

non-aligné, **~e**, *mpl* **~s** /nɔnaliɲe/ *nm,f* nonaligned country.

non-alignement /nɔnaliɲmɑ̃/ *nm* nonalignment.

nonante /nɔnɑ̃t/ **▶ 545**, **212** *adj inv, pron* B, C, H ninety.

nonantième /nɔnɑ̃tjɛm/ *adj, nmf* B, C, H ninetieth.

non-assistance /nɔnasistɑ̃s/ *nf* **~ à personne en danger** failure to render assistance.

nonce /nɔ̃s/ *nm* nuncio; **~ apostolique** or **du Pape** papal nuncio.

nonchalamment /nɔ̃ʃalamɑ̃/ *adv* nonchalantly.

nonchalance /nɔ̃ʃalɑ̃s/ *nf* nonchalance; **avec ~** nonchalantly.

nonchalant, **~e** /nɔ̃ʃalɑ̃, ɑ̃t/ *adj* (personne) nonchalant; (enfant, élève) apathetic; **c'est un ~** he shows no enthusiasm for anything.

nonciature /nɔ̃sjatyʀ/ *nf* **1** (charge) nunciature; **2** (résidence) Apostolic Nunciature.

non-combattant, **~e** *mpl* **~s** /nɔ̃kɔ̃batɑ̃, ɑ̃t/ *nm,f* noncombatant.

non-comparution /nɔ̃kɔ̃paʀysjɔ̃/ *nf* nonappearance.

non-conciliation /nɔ̃kɔ̃siljasjɔ̃/ *nf* absence of agreement, failure to agree.

non-conformisme /nɔ̃kɔ̃fɔʀmism/ *nm* nonconformism.

non-conformiste, *pl* **~s** /nɔ̃kɔ̃fɔʀmist/ *nm,f* nonconformist.

non-conformité /nɔ̃kɔ̃fɔʀmite/ *nf* nonconformity (to standards ou regulations).

non-croyant, **~e**, *mpl* **~s** /nɔ̃kʀwajɑ̃, ɑ̃t/ *nm,f* nonbeliever, unbeliever.

non-discrimination /nɔ̃diskʀiminasjɔ̃/ *nf* nondiscrimination.

non-dissémination /nɔ̃diseminasjɔ̃/ *nf* nonproliferation.

non-dit /nɔ̃di/ *nm inv* **le ~** what is left unsaid.

non-être /nɔnɛtʀ/ *nm inv* nonbeing.

non-événement, *pl* **~s** /nɔnevɛnmɑ̃/ *nm* nonevent.

non-exécution /nɔnɛgzekysjɔ̃/ *nf* **~ des clauses d'un contrat** failure to comply with the clauses of a contract.

non-figuratif, **-ive**, *mpl* **~s** /nɔ̃figyʀatif, iv/ *nm,f* abstract artist.

non-fonctionnement /nɔ̃fɔ̃ksjɔnmɑ̃/ *nm* failure to operate.

non-fumeur, *pl* **~s** /nɔ̃fymœʀ/ *nm* nonsmoker; **parmi les ~s** among nonsmokers.

non-gage /nɔ̃gaʒ/ *nm* **certificat de ~** *certificate of freedom from lien.*

non-gréviste, *pl* **~s** /nɔ̃gʀevist/ *nmf* nonstriker.

non-imposition /nɔnɛ̃pozisjɔ̃/ *nf* nontaxation.

non-ingérence /nɔnɛ̃ʒeʀɑ̃s/ *nf* noninterference.

non-initié, **~e**, *mpl* **~s** /noninisje/ *nm,f* gén layman, lay person; (dans une secte) uninitiated person; **les ~s** the uninitiated.

non-inscrit, **~e**, *mpl* **~s** /nɔnɛ̃skʀi, it/ *nm,f* independent.

non-interférence /nɔnɛ̃tɛʀfeʀɑ̃s/ *nf* noninterference.

non-intervention /nɔnɛ̃tɛʀvɑ̃sjɔ̃/ *nf* nonintervention.

non-interventionniste, *pl* **~s** /nɔnɛ̃tɛʀvɑ̃sjɔnist/ *nmf* noninterventionist.

non-jouissance /nɔ̃ʒwisɑ̃s/ *nf* absence of rights of owner.

non-lieu, *pl* **~x** /nɔ̃ljø/ *nm* Jur dismissal (of a charge); **rendre un ~** to dismiss a case (because of a lack of evidence); **il y a eu ~** the judge dismissed the case.

non-moi /nɔ̃mwa/ *nm inv* nonego.

nonne† /nɔn/ *nf* nun.

nonnette /nɔnɛt/ *nf* Culin small iced gingerbread.

nonobstant† /nɔnɔpstɑ̃/ *adv, prép* notwithstanding.

non-paiement /nɔ̃pɛmɑ̃/ *nm* nonpayment.

nonpareilles /nɔ̃paʀɛj/ *nfpl* Culin hundreds and thousands.

non-participation /nɔ̃paʀtisipasjɔ̃/ *nf* nonparticipation.

non-présentation /nɔ̃pʀezɑ̃tasjɔ̃/ *nf* **~ d'enfant** denial of access to a child.

non-prolifération /nɔ̃pʀɔlifeʀasjɔ̃/ *nf* nonproliferation.

non-recevoir /nɔ̃ʀəsəvwaʀ/ *nm* **fin de ~** flat refusal.

non-reconduction, *pl* **~s** /nɔ̃ʀəkɔ̃dyksjɔ̃/ *nf* (de contrat, mesure) nonrenewal; (de personne) failure to reappoint.

non-représentation /nɔ̃ʀəpʀezɑ̃tasjɔ̃/ *nf* **~ d'enfant** denial of access to a child.

non-respect /nɔ̃ʀɛspɛ/ *nm* **~ de** failure to comply with, failure to observe [*clause, contrat, accord*]; failure to respect [*personne*].

non-responsabilité /nɔ̃ʀɛspɔ̃sabilite/ *nf* nonliability.

non-retour /nɔ̃ʀətuʀ/ *nm* **point de ~** point of no return.

non-rétroactivité /nɔ̃ʀetʀoaktivite/ *nf* (principle of) nonretrospectiveness.

non-salarié, **~e**, *mpl* **~s** /nɔ̃salaʀje/ *nm,f* non wage-earner.

non-sens /nɔ̃sɑ̃s/ *nm inv* **1** (absurdité) nonsense ₵; **ce que vous dites est un ~** what you are saying is nonsense; **cette politique est un ~** this policy is nonsensical; **2** (dans une traduction) meaningless phrase.

non-spécialiste, *pl* **~s** /nɔ̃spesjalist/ *nmf* layman; **pour les ~s** for the layman.

non-syndiqué, **~e**, *mpl* **~s** /nɔ̃sɛ̃dike/ *nm,f* non union member.

non-tissé, *pl* **~s** /nɔ̃tise/ *nm* Tex nonwoven cloth.

non-versement /nɔ̃vɛʀsəmɑ̃/ *nm* nonpayment.

non-violence /nɔ̃vjɔlɑ̃s/ *nf* nonviolence.

non-violent, **~e**, *mpl* **~s** /nɔ̃vjɔlɑ̃, ɑ̃t/ *nm,f* advocate of nonviolence.

non-votant, **~e**, *mpl* **~s** /nɔ̃vɔtɑ̃, ɑ̃t/ *nm,f* nonvoter.

non-voyant, **~e**, *mpl* **~s** /nɔ̃vwajɑ̃, ɑ̃t/ *nm,f* visually handicapped person; **les ~s** the visually handicapped.

nord /nɔʀ/ ▶ 621 **I** *adj inv* [*façade, versant, côté*] north; [*frontière, zone*] northern.
II *nm* **1** (point cardinal) north; **au ~ de Paris** [*être, habiter*] north of Paris; **vers le ~** [*aller, naviguer*] north, northward; **vent de ~** northerly wind; **le vent du ~** the north wind; **exposé au ~** north-facing (*épith*); **2** (région) north; **dans le ~ de la France** [*se situer, avoir lieu, habiter, voyager*] in the north of France; [*aller, se rendre*] to the north of France; **le ~ de l'Europe/du Japon** northern Europe/Japan; **3** Géog, Pol **le Nord** the North; **vivre dans le Nord** to live in the North; **venir du Nord** to come from the North; **du Nord** [*ville, accent*] northern.
III Nord *nprm* ▶ 692 (région, département) **le Nord** the Nord.
■ **~ géographique** geographic north; **~ magnétique** magnetic north; **~ vrai** true north; **le Nord Viêt Nam** Hist North Vietnam; ▶ **grand**.
IDIOMES **il ne perd pas le ~**○! he's got his head screwed on (the right way)○!

nord-africain, **~e**, *mpl* **~s** /nɔʀafʀikɛ̃, ɛn/ *adj* North African.

Nord-Africain, **~e**, *mpl* **~s** /nɔʀafʀikɛ̃, ɛn/ *nm,f* North African.

nord-américain, **~e**, *mpl* **~s** /nɔʀameʀikɛ̃, ɛn/ *adj* North American.

Nord-Américain, **~e**, *mpl* **~s** /nɔʀameʀikɛ̃, ɛn/ *nm,f* North American.

nord-coréen, **-éenne**, *mpl* **~s** /nɔʀkɔʀeɛ̃, ɛn/ ▶ 537 *adj* North Korean.

Nord-Coréen, **-éenne**, *mpl* **~s** /nɔʀkɔʀeɛ̃, ɛn/ ▶ 537 *nm,f* North Korean.

nord-est /nɔʀ(d)ɛst/ ▶ 621 **I** *adj inv* [*façade, versant*] northeast; [*frontière, zone*] northeastern.
II *nm* northeast; **vent de ~** northeasterly wind.

nordique /nɔʀdik/ *adj* Géog [*pays, population, économie*] Nordic; Ling Scandinavian, Nordic.

nordiste /nɔʀdist/ *adj, nmf* Hist US Unionist.

nord-ouest /nɔʀ(d)wɛst/ ▶ 621 **I** *adj inv* [*façade, versant*] northwest; [*frontière, zone*] northwestern.
II *nm* northwest; **vent de ~** northwesterly wind.

nord-sud /nɔʀsyd/ *adj inv* north-south; **les rapports Nord-Sud** North-South relations.

Nord-Sud /nɔʀsyd/ *adj inv* Pol [*dialogue, relations, affrontements*] North-South.

nord-vietnamien, **-ienne**, *mpl* **~s** /nɔʀvjɛtnamjɛ̃, ɛn/ *adj* North Vietnamese.

Nord-Vietnamien, **-ienne**, *mpl* **~s** /nɔʀvjɛtnamjɛ̃, ɛn/ *nm,f* Hist North Vietnamese.

Norfolk ▶ 692 *nprm* **le ~** Norfolk.

noria /nɔʀja/ *nf* Tech noria.

normal, **~e**, *mpl* **-aux** /nɔʀmal, o/ **I** *adj* **1** (sain) [*personne, comportement*] normal; **ne pas être dans son état ~** not to be oneself; **2** (non exceptionnel) [*situation, événement*] normal; (habituel) [*âge, tarif*] normal; **il est ~ que** it is natural that (+ *subj*); **il n'est pas ~ que** it is not right that (+ *subj*); **trouver ~ que** to find it natural that (+ *subj*); **c'est pas ~!** it's not right!; **quoi de plus ~?** what could be more natural?; **pas de quoi, c'est ~** not at all, it's natural; **3** Math (perpendiculaire) normal (**à** to).
II normale *nf* **1** (moyenne) average; **une intelligence au-dessous/au-dessus de la ~e** a below-average/an above-average intelligence; **la température est au-dessous/au-dessus de la ~e** the temperature is below/above average; **inférieur de 20% à la ~e** 20% below average; **les ~es saisonnières** Météo seasonal averages; **2** (norme) norm; **retour à la ~e** return to normal; **3** Math perpendicular.

Normale○ /nɔʀmal/ *nf*: *abbr* = **École normale supérieure**.

normalement /nɔʀmalmɑ̃/ *adv* [*fonctionner*] normally; **~ elle devrait être là** she should be here by now.

normalien, **-ienne** /nɔʀmaljɛ̃, ɛn/ *nm,f* student at an École normale supérieure.

normalisateur, **-trice** /nɔʀmalizatœʀ, tʀis/ **I** *adj* normalizing.
II *nm,f* leveller.

normalisation /nɔʀmalizasjɔ̃/ *nf* **1** Pol (régularisation) normalization; **~ des relations diplomatiques** normalization of diplomatic relations; **2** Tech (standardisation) standardization.

normaliser /nɔʀmalize/ [1] **I** *vtr* **1** Pol (régulariser) to normalize; **~ ses relations** to normalize relations; **2** Tech (standardiser) to standardize.
II se normaliser *vpr* **1** Pol (revenir à la normale) to get back to normal; (devenir normal) to normalize; **2** Tech (devenir standard) to be standardized.

normalité /nɔʀmalite/ *nf* normality.

normand, **~e** /nɔʀmɑ̃, ɑ̃d/ **I** ▶ 692 *adj* Hist Norman.
II *nm* Ling Norman (French).

Normand, **~e** /nɔʀmɑ̃, ɑ̃d/ *nm,f* **1** (de Normandie) Norman; **2** Hist (de Scandinavie) Norseman/Norsewoman.
IDIOMES **une réponse de ~** a noncommittal reply.

Normandie /nɔʀmɑ̃di/ ▶ 692 *nprf* **la ~** Normandy; **la basse/haute ~** Lower/Upper Normandy.

normatif, **-ive** /nɔʀmatif, iv/ *adj* normative, prescriptive.

normativisme /nɔʀmativism/ *nm* prescriptivism.

norme /nɔʀm/ *nf* **1** (règle) norm; **s'écarter de la ~** to deviate from the norm; **rester dans la ~** to remain within the norm; **revenir à la ~** to return to normal; **avoir valeur de ~** to be the norm; **2** Tech Ind Comm standard; **être conforme à la ~ européenne** to comply with European (Community) standard; **~s de sécurité** safety standards; **hors ~** lit nonstandard; **une œuvre/un réalisateur hors ~** fig an extraordinary work/film director; **3** Math norm.
■ **~ juridique** legal rule; **~ morale** moral standards (*pl*).

normographe /nɔʀmɔgʀaf/ *nm* stencil.

noroît /nɔʀwa/ *nm* northwester.

norrois /nɔʀwa/ ▶ 462 *nm* Norse; **le vieux ~** Old Norse.

Northamptonshire ▶ 692 *nprm* **le ~** Northamptonshire.

Northumberland ▶ 692 *nprm* **le ~** Northumberland.

Northumbrie ▶ 692 *nprf* **la ~** Northumbria.

Norvège /nɔʀvɛʒ/ ▶ 321 *nprf* Norway.

norvégien, **-ienne** /nɔʀveʒjɛ̃, ɛn/ ▶ 462, 537 **I** *adj* Norwegian.
II *nm* Ling Norwegian.

Norvégien, **-ienne** /nɔʀveʒjɛ̃, ɛn/ ▶ 537 *nm,f* Norwegian.

nos ▶ **notre**.

nosographie /nɔzɔgʀafi/ *nf* nosography.

nosologie /nɔzɔlɔʒi/ *nf* nosology.

nostalgie /nɔstalʒi/ *nf* nostalgia (**de** for); **avoir la ~ de son pays/de sa maison** to be homesick; **avoir** or **garder la ~ des années 30** to be nostalgic for the 1930's.

nostalgique /nɔstalʒik/ **I** *adj* (mélancolique) nostalgic (**de** for); (loin de son pays) homesick.
II *nm* **les ~s des années 20** those who are nostalgic for the 1920's.

nota bene /nɔtabene/ *nm inv* nota bene.

notabilité /nɔtabilite/ *nf* notability.

notable /nɔtabl/ **I** *adj* [*fait, différence*] notable; [*progrès*] significant.
II *nm* notable.

notablement /nɔtabləmɑ̃/ *adv* significantly.

notaire /nɔtɛʀ/ **▶510** *nm* ≈ lawyer, notary public.

notamment /nɔtamɑ̃/ *adv* **1** (entre autres) notably; **la Reine a visité la ville accompagnée ~ de**... the Queen visited the town accompanied, among others, by...; **2** (plus particulièrement) in particular, more particularly.

notarial, **~e**, *mpl* **-aux** /nɔtaʀjal, o/ *adj* notarial.

notariat /nɔtaʀja/ *nm* **1** (profession) profession of notary (public); **il se destine au ~** he intends to become a notary; **2** (corps) notaries public (*pl*).

notarié, **~e** /nɔtaʀje/ *adj* notarized.

notation /nɔtasjɔ̃/ *nf* **1** (système) notation; **~ algébrique/chimique** algebraic/chemical notation; **2** (appréciation) (d'élève, de devoir) marking GB, grading US; (de fonctionnaire, militaire) grading; **3** (observations) observation.

note /nɔt/ *nf* **1** (facture) bill, check US; **~ d'hôtel/de restaurant** hotel/restaurant bill ou check US; **~ d'électricité** electricity bill; **payer** or **régler une ~** to pay a bill GB ou check US; **mettez cela sur ma ~** put it on my bill; **faire la ~ de qn** to write out sb's bill; **2** Mus note; **je sais lire les ~s** I can read music; **▶faux**; **3** (évaluation) mark GB, grade US; **obtenir une bonne/mauvaise ~ en anglais** to get a good/bad mark GB ou grade US in English; **mettre** or **donner une bonne ~ à qn** to give sb a good mark GB ou grade US; **~ éliminatoire** fail mark GB; **c'est une bonne ~ pour lui** fig that's a point in his favour[GB]; **c'est une mauvaise ~ pour lui** fig that's a blot on his copybook; **4** (communication écrite) note; **~ manuscrite/officielle** handwritten/official note; **5** (transcription) **~s de cours** (lecture) notes; **prendre des ~s** to take notes; **prendre qch en ~** to make a note of sth; **lire ses ~s** to read (from) one's notes; **prendre (bonne) ~ de qch** fig to take due note of sth; **6** (détail) fig note; **une ~ triste/originale** a note of sadness/originality; **cette réflexion est bien dans la ~ du personnage** that comment is typical of him; **forcer la ~** fig to overdo it; **7** Imprim, Édition (commentaire) note; **~ en bas de page** footnote; **~ dans la marge** note in the margin; **faire une remarque en ~** (en marge) to put a note in the margin; (en bas de page) to put an observation in a footnote.
■ ~ diplomatique diplomatic note; **~ de l'éditeur**, **NdE** publisher's note; **~ de frais** expense account; **~ d'honoraires** (de médecin, traducteur etc) bill; **~ interne** memorandum, memo○; **~ de la rédaction**, **NDLR** editor's note; **~ de service** = **~ interne**; **~ du traducteur**, **NdT** translator's note.

noter /nɔte/ [1] *vtr* **1** (inscrire) to note down, to make a note of [*adresse, date, renseignement*]; to write down [*idée, citation, souvenir*]; **~ une commande** to write down an order; **c'est (bien) noté?** have you got that?; **2** (remarquer) to notice [*changement, différence, ressemblance*]; to notice, to note [*progrès, présence, erreur*]; **ceci est à ~** this should be noted; **il me déplaît, notez (bien) que je n'ai rien à lui reprocher** I don't like him, though mind you I haven't got anything particular against him; **il faut quand même ~** it has to be said; **3** (évaluer) to mark GB, to grade US [*devoir, exercice*]; to give a mark GB ou a grade US to [*élève, étudiant*]; to grade [*employé, fonctionnaire, militaire*]; **élève bien/mal noté** pupil who got good/bad marks GB ou grades US; **~ sur 20** to mark GB ou grade US out of 20; **fonctionnaire bien/mal noté** civil servant who obtains a high/low rating in progress reports; **4** (marquer) to mark [*texte, passage, citation*]; **~ qch d'une croix** to mark sth with a cross; **5** Mus to write down, to take down [*air, notes*].

notice /nɔtis/ *nf* **1** (exposé) note; **2** (instructions) instructions (*pl*); **~ de montage** assembly instructions; **~ explicative** instructions (*pl*) (for use).
■ ~ biographique biographical information ¢; **~ nécrologique** obituary.

notificatif, **-ive** /nɔtifikatif, iv/ *adj* notifying; **lettre notificative** letter of notification.

notification /nɔtifikasjɔ̃/ *nf* gén notification; Jur notice; **avoir** or **recevoir ~ de** to be notified of.

notifier /nɔtifje/ [2] *vtr* **~ qch à qn** gén to notify sb of sth; Jur to give sb notice of sth; **on m'a notifié mon licenciement** I was given my redundancy GB or dismissal US notice; **être notifié à qn** to be made known to sb.

notion /nosjɔ̃/ *nf* **1** (de danger, temps, réalité) notion; **perdre la ~ de qch** to lose all sense of sth; **2** (concept) notion; **3** (de langue, science) basic knowledge ¢; **avoir des ~s de** to have a basic knowledge of; **'Notions de botanique'** 'A Botany Primer'.

notionnel, **-elle** /nosjɔnɛl/ *adj* notional.

notoire /nɔtwaʀ/ *adj* [*fait, position*] well-known; [*escroc, bêtise*] notorious; [*inconduite*] Jur manifest; **il est ~ que** it's common knowledge that.

notoirement /nɔtwaʀmɑ̃/ *adv* manifestly; pej notoriously péj.

notoriété /nɔtɔʀjete/ *nf* **1** (de personne, lieu, d'œuvre) fame; (de produit) reputation; **il est de ~ (publique) que** it's common knowledge that; **2** (personne célèbre) celebrity.

notre, *pl* **nos** /nɔtʀ, no/ *adj poss*

■ Note En anglais, on ne répète pas le possessif coordonné: *notre adresse et notre numéro de téléphone* = our address and phone number.

---

our; **nos ancêtres** our ancestors; **nos enfants à nous**○ our children; **à nos âges** when you're our age; **nous sommes tous retournés dans ~ chambre** we all went back into our rooms; **un de nos amis** a friend of ours; **ils sont venus pendant ~ absence** they came while we were away; **~ retour s'est bien passé** we got back safely; **~ installation est provisoire** we're not permanently settled; **~ population vieillit** we have an ageing population; **c'était ~ avis à tous** we all felt the same; **c'est ~ maître à tous** he's the master of us all.

nôtre /notʀ/ **I** *adj poss* **nous avons fait ~s ces idées** we've adopted these ideas; **cette terre est ~** this land is our land.
II le nôtre, **la nôtre**, **les nôtres** *pron poss* ours; **un métier comme le ~** a job like ours; **leur alimentation est très différente de la ~** their diet is very different from our own; **quelle erreur était la ~** how wrong we were!; **à la ~** cheers!; **soyez des ~s!** won't you join us?; **les ~s** (notre peuple) our own people; (notre équipe) our side (*sg*); **es-tu des ~s?** are you on our side?

Nottinghamshire **▶692** *nprm* **le ~** Nottinghamshire.

nouba◑ /nuba/ *nf* party; **faire la ~** to live it up○.

nouer /nwe/ [1] **I** *vtr* **1** (faire un nœud à) to tie [*lacets, ceinture en tissu, cravate*]; to tie up, to tie [sth] up [*chaussure, colis*]; **~ deux ficelles (ensemble)** to tie ou knot two pieces of string (together); **2** (attacher) **~ qch autour de qch** to tie sth round GB ou around US sth; **~ ses cheveux** to tie one's hair back, to tie back one's hair; **3** (avec les bras) **~ ses bras autour du cou/de la taille de qn** to put one's arms around sb's neck/waist; **4** (contracter) **l'émotion me nouait la gorge** I felt choked with emotion; **avoir la gorge nouée** to have a lump in one's throat; **avoir l'estomac noué** to have a knot in one's stomach; **5** (établir) to establish [*relations*] (**avec** with); to engage in [*dialogue*] (**avec** with); **6** Cin, Littérat, Théât to weave [*action dramatique, intrigue, machination*].
II se nouer *vpr* **1** Cin, Littérat, Théât [*intrigue*] to take shape; **2** [*relations diplomatiques*] to be established; [*dialogue*] to begin; **3** (se contracter) **ma gorge se nouait** I had a lump in my throat; **mon estomac se nouait** my stomach knotted; **tous les muscles de mon corps se nouaient** all the muscles in my body were knotted.

noueux, **-euse** /nuø, øz/ *adj* **1** [*arbre, branche*] gnarled; **2** [*planche*] knotty; **3** [*doigts, mains*] gnarled.

nougat /nuga/ *nm* nougat.

nougatine /nugatin/ *nf* nougatine.

nouille /nuj/ **I**○ *adj* **ce qu'il est ~!** what a drip○!
II *nf* **1** (pâtes alimentaires) (tagliatelle) tagliatelle ¢; (génériquement) **des ~s** noodles, pasta ¢; **2**○ (niais) noodle○.
IDIOMES **avoir le cul bordé de ~s**◑ to be a lucky devil○ ou bastard◑.

noumène /numɛn/ *nm* noumenon.

nounou /nunu/ *nf* nanny GB, nurse.

nounours○ /nunuʀs/ *nm* teddy bear.

nourri, **~e** /nuʀi/ **I** *pp* **▶nourrir**.
II *pp adj* **1** [*tir*] heavy; [*applaudissements*] sustained; **2** [*conversation*] lively; [*style*] luxuriant.

nourrice /nuʀis/ *nf* **1** (gardienne) (chez elle) childminder GB, babysitter US; (chez l'enfant) nanny, babysitter US; (qui allaite) wet nurse; **être en ~** to be with a wet nurse; **2** (bidon) jerrycan.
■ ~ sèche dry nurse.

nourricier, **-ière** /nuʀisje, ɛʀ/ *adj* **1** liter [*terre, sève*] nourishing; **2**† [*père*] foster.

nourrir /nuʀiʀ/ [3] **I** *vtr* **1** (fournir des aliments à) to feed [*personne, plante*] (**de** on; **avec** with); to nourish [*cuir, épiderme*]; **bien nourri** well-fed, well-nourished; **mal nourri** undernourished; **~ au sein/au biberon** to breast-/bottle-feed; **poulet nourri au maïs** corn-fed chicken; **2** (subvenir aux besoins de) to keep [*famille, enfant*]; to provide a living for [*région*]; **avoir cinq bouches à ~** to have five mouths to feed; **mon travail ne me nourrit pas** I don't make enough to live on; **la poésie, ça ne nourrit pas son homme** you can't make a living out of poetry; **3** (entretenir) to harbour[GB] [*sombres desseins, espoir, crainte*]; to nurture [*projet*]; to feed [*incendie*]; to fuel [*passion, préjugés*]; to feed [*idéologie, stéréotypes*]; **4** (enrichir) to fuel [*discussion*]; to feed [*esprit*]; **elle fut nourrie d'histoire classique** she was brought up on classical history.
II se nourrir *vpr* **1** [*personne*] to eat; [*animal, plante*] to feed; **se ~ de** [*personne*] to live on; [*animal*] to live ou feed on; **2** fig **la spéculation/le racisme se nourrit de**... speculation/racism feeds on...; **il se nourrit de rêves** he lives on dreams.

nourrissant, **~e** /nuʀisɑ̃, ɑ̃t/ *adj* nourishing.

nourrisson /nuʀisɔ̃/ *nm* (nouveau-né) new-born baby; (enfant jusqu'à deux ans) infant.

nourriture /nuʀityʀ/ **I** *nf* **1** (aliments) food; **donner de la ~ à** to feed; **2** (régime) diet; **une ~ adaptée à nos besoins** a diet adapted to our needs.
II nourritures *nfpl* liter nourishment ¢; **des ~s intellectuelles** intellectual nourishment.

nous[1] /nu/ *pron pers* **1** (sujet) we; **~ sommes en avance** we're early; **~ n'avons pas terminé** we haven't finished; **~ qui n'étions pas prêts avons dû faire** we weren't ready and we still had to do; **il sait que ce n'est pas ~ qui avons cassé la vitre** he knows that it wasn't us that broke the window, he knows that we weren't the ones who broke the window; **c'est ~ les premiers**○ we're first; **2** (dans une comparaison) **il travaille plus que ~** he works more than us ou than we do; **elles sont plus âgées que ~** they are older than us ou than we are; **ils les voient plus souvent que ~** (que nous ne les voyons) they see them more often than we do; (qu'ils ne nous voient) they see them more often than us ou than they see us; **3** (objet) **des policiers ~ ont arrêtés à l'entrée** some police officers stopped us at the entrance; **elle ~ déteste** she hates us; **~ entendez-vous?** can you hear us?; **4** (nous = à nous) **il ne ~ a pas fait mal** he didn't hurt us; **elle ne ~ a pas tout dit** she didn't tell us everything; **tu ~ en veux?** do you bear a grudge against us?; **5** (après une préposition) us; **à cause de/autour de/après ~** because of/around/after us; **un cadeau pour ~** a present for us; **pour ~, c'est très important** it's very important to us; **entre ~, il n'est pas très intelligent** between ourselves ou you and me, he isn't very intelligent; **elle n'écrit à personne sauf à ~** she doesn't write to anyone but us; **sans ~, ils n'auraient pas pu s'en sortir** they couldn't have come through without us; **à ~** (en jouant) our turn; **ce sont des amis à ~** they're friends of ours; **nous n'avons pas encore de maison à ~** we haven't got a house of our own yet; **à ~, il a raconté une histoire très différente** he told us quite a different story; **la voiture bleue est à ~** the blue car is ours; **c'est à ~** (appartenance) it's ours, it belongs to us; (séquence) (it's) our turn; **(c'est) à ~ de choisir** (notre tour) it's our turn to choose; (notre responsabilité) it's up to us to choose; **6** (pronom réfléchi) ourselves; **reprenons-~ et recommençons** let's pull ourselves together and start again; **nous ne ~ soignons que par les plantes** we only use herbal medicines; **7** (nous = nous-mêmes) ourselves; **pensons à ~** let's think of ourselves; **8** (de majesté, modestie) we; **dans cet ouvrage ~ avons tenté de faire** in this work we have tried to do; **~ sommes arrivés à la conclusion suivante** (locuteur féminin) we arrived at the following conclusion.

nous[2] /nu/ *nm* **le ~ de majesté** the royal we.

nous-même, *pl* **nous-mêmes** /numɛm/ *pron pers* **1** (pluriel) ourselves; **nous avons décidé de les former ~s** we have decided to train them ourselves; **nous cherchons par ~s** we're looking ourselves; **c'est en ~s que nous devons chercher la solution** we must look within ourselves for the solution; **les animaux souffrent de la chaleur et ~s évitons de sortir au soleil** the animals are suffering from the heat and we ourselves are avoiding going out in the sun; **on s'en chargera ~s**○ we'll see to it ourselves; **2** (de majesté, modestie) **~ sommes convaincu de l'importance de la découverte** we are convinced of the importance of the discovery.

nouveau (**nouvel** *before vowel or mute h*), **nouvelle**, *mpl* **~x** /nuvo, nuvɛl/ **I** *adj* **1** (qui remplace, succède, s'ajoute) new; **le ~ modèle/système/locataire** the new model/system/tenant; **où se trouve la nouvelle entrée?** where's the new entrance?; **c'est le ~ Nijinsky** he's the new ou a second Nijinsky; **se faire faire un ~ costume** (pour remplacer) to have a new suit made; (supplémentaire) to have another ou a new suit made; **il a subi une nouvelle opération** he's had another ou a new operation; **il y a eu un nouvel incident** there's been another ou a new ou a fresh incident; **faire une nouvelle tentative** to make another ou a new ou a fresh attempt; **ces ~x attentats** these new ou fresh attacks; **procéder à de nouvelles arrestations** to make further arrests; **nous avons de nouvelles preuves de leur culpabilité** we have further evidence of their guilt; **une nouvelle fois** once again; **2** (d'apparition récente) [*mot, virus, science, ville*] new; (de la saison) [*pommes de terre, vin*] new; **tiens, tu fumes! c'est ~?** you're smoking! is this a new habit?; **c'est ~ ce manteau?** is this a new coat?; **ce genre de travail est ~ pour moi** this sort of work is new to me, I'm new to this sort of work; **tout ~** brand-new; **les ~x élus** the newly-elected members; **les ~x mariés** the newlyweds; **la nouvelle venue** the newcomer; **les ~x venus** the newcomers; ▶ **pauvre III**; **3** (original) [*ligne, conception, méthode*] new, original; **voir qch sous un jour ~** to see sth in a new light; **c'est une façon très nouvelle d'aborder le problème** it's a very novel approach to the problem; **ce n'est pas ~** this is nothing new; **il n'y a rien de ~** there's nothing new; **4** (novice) **être ~ dans le métier/en affaires** to be new to the job/in business.

II *nm,f* **1** (à l'école) new student; **tu as vu la nouvelle?** have you seen the new student?; **2** (dans une entreprise) new employee; **il y a trois ~x dans le bureau** there are three new people in the office; **je ne sais pas, je suis ~** I don't know, I'm new here; **3** (à l'armée) new recruit.

III *nm* **1** (rebondissement) **il y a du ~** (dans un processus) there's been a new development; (dans une situation) there' s been a change; **téléphone-moi s'il y a du ~** give me a ring GB ou call if there is anything new (to report); **j'ai du ~ pour toi** I've got some news for you; **2** (nouveauté) **il nous faut du ~** we want something new.

IV nouvelle *nf* **1** (annonce d'un événement) news ¢; **une nouvelle** gén a piece of news; Presse, TV, Radio a news item; **une bonne/mauvaise nouvelle** some good/bad news; **j'ai une grande nouvelle (à t'annoncer)** I've got some exciting news (for you); **j'ai appris deux bonnes nouvelles** I've heard two pieces of good news; **tu connais la nouvelle?** have you heard the news?; **première nouvelle**○! that's news to me!, that's the first I've heard of it!; **la nouvelle de qch** the news of [*décès, arrestation, mariage*]; **la nouvelle de sa mort nous a beaucoup peinés** we were very sad to hear about his/her death; ▶ **faux**; **2** Littérat short story; **un recueil de nouvelles** a collection of short stories.

V à nouveau, **de nouveau** *loc adv* (once) again.

VI nouvelles *nfpl* **1** (renseignements) news (*sg*); **recevoir des nouvelles de qn** (par la personne elle-même) to hear from sb; (par un intermédiaire) to hear news of sb; **il y a un mois que je suis sans nouvelles de lui** I haven't heard from him for a month; **on est sans nouvelles des prisonniers** we've had no news of the prisoners; **je prendrai de tes nouvelles** I'll hear how you're getting on; **donne-moi de tes nouvelles** let me know how you're getting on; **il m'a demandé de tes nouvelles** he asked after you; **faire prendre des nouvelles d'un malade** to send for news of a patient; **je viens aux nouvelles**○ (de ce qui s'est passé) I've come to see what's happened; (de ce qui se passe) I've come to see what's happening; **aux dernières nouvelles, il se porte bien**○ the last I heard he was doing fine; **il aura de mes nouvelles**○! he'll be hearing from me!; **goûte ce petit vin, tu m'en diras des nouvelles**○ have a taste of this wine, it's really good!; **2** Presse, Radio, TV **les nouvelles** the news (*sg*); **les nouvelles sont mauvaises** the news is bad; **les nouvelles du front** news from the front.

■ **~ franc** new franc; **~ philosophe** Philos *member of a French school of philosophy developed in the 70's*; **~ riche** nouveau riche; **~ roman** nouveau roman; **Nouveau Monde** New World; **Nouveau Réalisme** New Realism; **Nouveau Testament** New Testament; **Nouveaux pays industrialisés, NPI** Newly industrialized Countries, NIC; **Nouvel An** New Year; **le Nouvel An chinois/juif** the Chinese/Jewish New Year; **nouvelle année** = **Nouvel An**; **nouvelle cuisine** Culin nouvelle cuisine; **Nouvelle Vague** Cin New Wave.

IDIOMES **tout ~ tout beau** the novelty will soon wear off; **pas de nouvelles, bonnes nouvelles!** Prov no news is good news!

Nouveau-Brunswick /nuvobʀœswik/ ▶ 692 *nprm* New Brunswick.

Nouveau-Mexique /nuvomɛksik/ ▶ 692 *nprm* New Mexico.

nouveau-né, **~e**, *mpl* **~s** /nuvone/ **I** *adj* [*enfant, agneau*] newborn (*épith*).

II *nm,f* newborn baby.

nouveauté /nuvote/ *nf* **1** (caractère récent) newness, novelty; (originalité) novelty; **la ~ du produit/de la loi** the novelty of the product/of the law; **2** (chose nouvelle) novelty; **aimer/être à la recherche de la ~** to like/to look for novelty; **la (grande) ~, c'est que les femmes sont admises** the (great) novelty ou what's really new is that women are admitted; **ce n'est pas une ~!** that's nothing new!; **se défier des ~s** to be suspicious of anything new; **il s'est excusé? c'est une ~!** he apologized? that's new!; **3** (objet nouveau) gén new thing; (livre) new publication; (disque) new release; [*appareil, voiture*] new model; **~s d'automne** Mode new autumn fashions.

nouvel ▶ **nouveau I**.

Nouvelle-Angleterre /nuvɛlɑ̃glətɛʀ/ ▶ 692 *nprf* New England.

Nouvelle-Calédonie /nuvɛlkaledɔni/ ▶ 416 *nprf* New Caledonia.

Nouvelle-Écosse /nuvɛlekɔs/ ▶ 692 *nprf* Nova Scotia.

Nouvelle-Galles du Sud /nuvɛlgaldy syd/ ▶ 692 *nprf* **la ~** New South Wales.

Nouvelle-Guinée /nuvɛlgine/ ▶ 416 *nprf* New Guinea.

nouvellement /nuvɛlmɑ̃/ *adv* [*publié, révisé*] recently; [*bâti*] newly; **les personnes ~ domiciliées dans la ville** people who have recently taken up residence in the town.

Nouvelle-Orléans /nuvɛlɔʀleɑ̃/ ▶ 857 *nprf* **la ~** New Orleans.

Nouvelles-Hébrides /nuvɛlzebʀid/ *nprfpl* Hist **les ~** the New Hebrides.

Nouvelle-Zélande /nuvɛlzelɑ̃d/ ▶ 321, 416 *nprf* New Zealand.

nouvelliste /nuvelist/ ▶ 510 *nmf* short-story writer.

nova, *pl* **novae** /nɔva, nɔve/ *nf* nova.

novateur, **-trice** /nɔvatœʀ, tʀis/ **I** *adj* innovative.

II *nm,f* innovator, pioneer.

novation /nɔvasjɔ̃/ *nf* Jur novation.

novembre /nɔvɑ̃bʀ/ ▶ 521 *nm* November; **le 11 ~** Armistice Day.

novice /nɔvis/ **I** *adj* inexperienced, green.

II *nmf* **1** (débutant) novice, greenhorn○; **2** Relig novice.

noviciat /nɔvisja/ *nm* **1** Relig noviciate; **2** fig apprenticeship.

noyade /nwajad/ *nf* (meurtre, accident) drowning ¢; **il y a eu 20 ~s** there were 20 people drowned.

noyau, *pl* **~x** /nwajo/ *nm* **1** (de fruit) stone GB, pit US; **fruits à ~** stone fruit GB, fruit with pits US; **~ de prune/d'olive** plum/olive stone ou pit; **2** (groupe humain) core; **~ de fidèles/d'artistes** core of faithful supporters/of artists; **~x de résistance** pockets of resistance; **~x d'agitateurs** small groups of agitators; **3** (partie centrale) Astron, Biol, Nucl nucleus; Électrotech, Géol core; Constr newel; Ling (de phrase) kernel; (d'intonation) nucleus; Ordinat kernel.

■ **~ dur** hard core.

noyautage /nwajotaʒ/ *nm* infiltration.

noyauter /nwajote/ [1] *vtr* to infiltrate.

noyé, **~e** /nwaje/ **I** *pp* ▶ **noyer II, III**.

II *pp adj* **1**○ fig (perdu) **mes enfants sont (complètement) ~s en algèbre** my children are (completely) out of their depth with algebra; **2** liter (couvert) **vallée ~e dans la brume/l'obscurité** valley shrouded in mist/darkness; **visage ~ de larmes** face bathed in tears; **yeux ~s de larmes** eyes swimming with tears.

III *nm,f* drowned person; **il y a eu trois ~s** three people drowned; **retrouver des ~s** to find drowned people; **repêcher un ~** to recover a drowned body.

noyer /nwaje/ [23] **I** *nm* **1** (arbre) walnut (tree); **2** (bois) walnut; **~ noir** (**d'Amérique**) black walnut; **table en ~** walnut table.

II *vtr* **1** (tuer) to drown [*personne, animal*]; ▶**poisson**, **rage**; **2** (inonder) to flood [*village, champ, mine*]; **3** (mettre trop de liquide) to flood [*moteur*]; to drown [*pastis, whisky*]; to douse [*feu, incendie*]; **~ son chagrin** or **sa peine dans l'alcool** hum to drown one's sorrows; **4** (accabler, étourdir) **~ qn sous une multitude de renseignements** to swamp sb with a mass of information; **~ qn sous un flot de paroles** to talk sb' s head off; **5** (faire disparaître) **~ une idée dans qch** to lose ou bury an idea in sth; **~ une révolte dans le sang** to spill blood in quashing a revolt; **6** Tech (intégrer) to embed [*armature*]; (mettre à niveau) to countersink [*vis, clou*]; **~ une poutrelle dans du béton** to embed a girder in concrete; **7** Art to blend [*couleurs*]; to merge [*contours*].

III **se noyer** *vpr* **1** (accidentellement) to drown; (volontairement) to drown oneself; **noyé en mer** drowned at sea; **mourir noyé** to die by drowning; **2** (pour oublier) **se ~ dans les plaisirs** to throw oneself into a life of mindless enjoyment; **3** (disparaître) **se ~ dans la foule** to get swallowed up in the crowd; **mes cris se sont noyés dans le brouhaha général** my shouts were drowned in the general hubbub; **quelques acteurs connus noyés dans la foule** some well-known actors lost in the crowd; **4** (être dépassé) to get bogged down (**dans** in); **se ~ dans des détails** to get bogged down in details.

IDIOMES **se ~ dans un verre d'eau** to make a mountain out of a molehill.

NPI /ɛnpei/ *nmpl* ▶**nouveau**.

NTSC /ɛnteɛsse/ *nm* TV (*abbr* = **national television system committee**) NTSC; **système ~** NTSC standard.

nu, **~e** /ny/ **I** *adj* **1** (dévêtu) [*corps*] naked; [*partie du corps*] bare; **être ~** to be naked, to be in the nude; **être complètement** or **tout ~** to be completely naked, to be stark naked; **être à demi** or **à moitié ~** to be half-naked; **avoir la tête ~e** to be bareheaded; **avoir les jambes ~es** to have bare legs; **avoir les bras ~s** to have bare arms; **avoir les pieds ~s** to be barefoot; **être torse ~** to be stripped to the waist; **avoir les épaules ~es** to have bare shoulders; **2** (sans ornement) [*mur, pièce*] bare; (sans végétation) [*arbre, côte*] bare; (non enveloppé) [*fil électrique*] bare; (dépouillé) [*style*] unadorned; **l'épée ~e** with (a) drawn sword; **faire ~** to look ou seem bare; **voilà la vérité toute ~e** that is the plain truth.

II *nm inv* (lettre) nu.

III *nm* Art nude; **le ~** the nudes.

IV **à nu** *loc adv* **être à ~** [*fil électrique*] to be bare ou exposed; [*personne, vice, activité*] to be exposed; **mettre à ~** to strip [*fil électrique*]; to expose [*personne, vice, activité*]; **mettre son cœur à ~** to open one's heart.

V **nues** *nfpl* **les ~es** liter the heavens littér; (nuages) the clouds.

IDIOMES **tomber des ~es**○ to be flabbergasted○; **porter qn aux ~es** to praise sb to the skies.

nuage /nyaʒ/ *nm* **1** Météo lit, fig cloud (**sur** over); **~s de grêle** hail clouds; **un ciel sans ~s** a cloudless sky; **un bonheur sans ~s** unclouded happiness; **de lourds ~s s'amoncellent à l'horizon** lit, fig dark clouds are gathering on the horizon; **2** (de poussière, fumée, sauterelles) cloud (**de** of); **~ de lait** dash of milk.

IDIOMES **être dans les ~s** to have one's head in the clouds; **descendre de son ~** to come back to earth.

nuageux, **-euse** /nyaʒø, øz/ *adj* [*ciel, temps*] cloudy; [*système, masse*] cloud (*épith*).

nuance /nyɑ̃s/ *nf* **1** (de couleur) shade; **2** (de sens) nuance; **les ~s d'un texte/mot** the nuances of a text/word; **le roman est tout en ~s** the novel is full of subtle touches ou nuances; **sans ~** [*commentaire, prise de position, bilan*] clearcut; [*personnalité*] straightforward; pej unsubtle; [*affirmer, défendre*] unreservedly; **3** (différence) slight ou subtle difference; **apporter quelques ~s à un avis** to qualify an opinion slightly; **à quelques ~s près** apart from the odd slight difference; **à cette ~ près que** with the small reservation that; **4** Mus nuance.

nuancé, **~e** /nyɑ̃se/ **I** *pp* ▶**nuancer**.

II *pp adj* [*avis*] qualified; **peu ~** unsubtle, black-and-white (*épith*), black and white (*jamais épith*).

nuancer /nyɑ̃se/ [12] *vtr* **1** (avec un élément nouveau) to qualify [*avis*]; to modify [*vision des choses*]; **2** (modérer) to moderate [*propos*]; **~ son jugement** to moderate one's stance.

nuancier /nyɑ̃sje/ *nm* **1** (de peintures) colour[GB] chart; **2** Cosmét (de démonstration) make-up colour[GB] display chart.

Nubie /nybi/ *nprf* Nubia.

nubien, **-ienne** /nybjɛ̃, ɛn/ *adj* Nubian.

Nubien, **-ienne** /nybjɛ̃, ɛn/ *nm,f* Nubian.

nubile /nybil/ *adj* nubile.

nubilité /nybilite/ *nf* nubility.

nucléaire /nykleɛʀ/ **I** *adj* **1** Phys [*arme, centrale*] nuclear (*épith*); **2** Sociol [*famille*] nuclear.

II *nm* **le ~** (énergie) nuclear energy; (technologie) nuclear technology.

nucléé, **~e** /nyklee/ *adj* nucleate.

nucléique /nykleik/ *adj* nucleic.

nucléon /nykleɔ̃/ *nm* nucleon.

nudisme /nydism/ *nm* nudism.

nudiste /nydist/ *nmf* nudist.

nudité /nydite/ *nf* **1** (de personne) nakedness, nudity; **2** (de lieu, mur) bareness.

nuée /nye/ *nf* **1** (multitude) (de moucherons) swarm (**de** of); (de photographes, d'assaillants) horde (**de** of); **2** Météo dense cloud ₵.

■ **~ ardente** Météo nuée ardente.

nue-propriété, *pl* **nues-propriétés** /nypʀɔpʀijete/ *nf* ownership without usufruct.

nues ▶**nu** V.

nuire /nɥiʀ/ [69] **I** *vtr ind* **~ à** to harm [*voisin, famille*]; to be harmful ou prejudicial sout to [*santé, intérêts, réputation*]; to damage [*récoltes*]; to take away from [*plaisir, qualité, beauté*]; to be detrimental to [*déroulement*]; **son égoïsme lui a beaucoup nui** his selfishness has done him a lot of harm; **elle a fait cela dans l'intention de nuire** she did that maliciously.

II **se nuire** *vpr* (mutuellement) to do each other a lot of harm; (à soi-même) to do oneself a lot of harm.

IDIOMES **trop parler nuit** you should know when to keep your mouth shut.

nuisance /nɥizɑ̃s/ *nf* nuisance ₵; **~s sonores/chimiques** noise/chemical nuisance.

nuisette /nɥizɛt/ *nf* baby doll nightie.

nuisible /nɥizibl/ *adj* [*déchets*] dangerous; [*influence*] harmful; **rongeur ~** dangerous rodent; **insecte ~** insect pest; **~ à** detrimental to.

nuit /nɥi/ *nf* **1** (période) night; **en hiver, les ~s sont longues** in winter the nights are long; **cette ~** tonight; **en une ~** in one night; **toute la ~** all night (long); **en pleine ~** in the middle of the night; **au cœur de la ~** at dead of night; **travailler/étudier/conduire la ~** to work/study/drive at night; **après une ~ de voiture/train** after a night spent travelling[GB] in the car/train; **une ~ d'hôtel** a night in a hotel; **une chambre à 250 francs la ~** a room at 250 francs a night; **une ~ de débauche/travail** a night of debauchery/work; **il passe ses ~s à lire** he spends his nights reading; **ils ont voyagé de ~** they travelled by night; **vol/train/équipe de ~** night flight/train/shift; **ouvert toute la ~** open all night; **il n'a pas dormi de la ~** he didn't sleep a wink last night; **elle a passé une ~ d'angoisse** she spent an anxious night; **une ~ d'attente** a night of waiting; **faire une ~ complète**, **faire sa ~** to sleep right through the night; **ce malade ne passera pas la ~** this patient won't last (out) the night; **~ et jour** night and day; **souhaiter bonne ~ à qn** to wish sb goodnight; **2** (date) night; **la ~ dernière** last night; **dans la ~ de samedi à dimanche** during the night of Saturday to Sunday; **par une ~ d'orage/de pleine lune/d'été** on a stormy/moonlit/summer night; **3** (obscurité) **la ~ tombe** it's getting dark, night is falling; **la ~ tombe vite en décembre** night falls quickly in December; **la ~ est tombée sur la ville** night fell over the town; **avant la ~** before dark ou nightfall ; **à la ~ tombante** or **à la tombée de la ~** at nightfall; **à la ~** (**tombée**) after dark ou nightfall; **il fait ~** it's dark; **il faisait ~ noire, il faisait une ~ d'encre** it was pitch dark; ▶**gris**.

■ **~ américaine** Cin day for night; **~ blanche** sleepless night; **~ bleue** *night of terrorist bomb attacks*; **la ~ éternelle** eternal night; **~ de noces** wedding night; **la ~ des Rois** Théât Twelfth Night; **la ~ des temps** the dawn of time; **cette tradition se perd dans la ~ des temps** this tradition is lost in the mists of time.

IDIOMES **c'est le jour et la ~** they're as different as chalk and cheese; **attends demain pour donner ta réponse: la ~ porte conseil** wait till tomorrow to give your answer: sleep on it first.

nuitamment /nɥitamɑ̃/ *adv* liter by night.

nuitée /nɥite/ *nf* Tourisme night.

nul, **nulle** /nyl/ **I** *adj* **1** (dépourvu d'intelligence, de valeur) [*personne, élève*] hopeless, useless; [*travail, raisonnement, étude*] worthless; [*film, roman*] trashy○; **être ~ en français/sciences/sport/dans une matière/dans un domaine** to be hopeless at French/science/sports/at a subject/in a field; **elle est complètement nulle** she's completely hopeless ou useless; **il est trop ~ pour ce travail** he's too useless for the job; **2** Jur (sans effet légal) [*contrat, mariage*] void; [*testament*] invalid; [*élections*] null and void; [*vote, bulletin*] spoiled; **le contrat est ~ en cas de fausse déclaration** the contract is voidable in case of false declaration; **~ et non avenu** null and void; **3** Sport, Jeux **match/score ~** (équipes à égalité) tie, draw GB; (zéro partout) nil-all draw/score; **4** (qui n'existe pas) [*différence, danger, résultat, effet*] nil (*jamais épith*); [*récolte*] nonexistent; **vent ~** no wind.

II *adj indéf* (aucun) [*personne, idée, valeur, endroit*] no; **nulle autre ville** no other town; **je n'ai ~ besoin de tes conseils** I've no need of your advice, I don't need your advice; **je n'ai nulle envie de partir** I've no desire to leave, I don't want to leave; **~ autre que vous ne peut m'aider** no-one else but you can help me; **sans ~ doute** without any doubt; **~ doute que ces résultats auront de graves conséquences** these results will undoubtedly have serious consequences.

III○ *nm,f* idiot○; **c'est un ~** he's an idiot○ ou a dead loss○, he's completely useless.

IV *pron indéf* no one; **~ ne savait** no one knew; **les victimes, ~ n'en doute, sont des prisonniers politiques** no one is in any doubt that the victims are political prisoners; **~ n'est censé ignorer la loi** ignorance of the law is no excuse; **~ n'ignore que** everyone knows that.

V **nulle part** *loc adv* nowhere; **il n'a nulle**

part où aller he has nowhere to go; ▶ **impossible**, **prophète**.

nullard○, **~e** /nylaʀ, aʀd/ *nm,f* idiot○.

nullement /nylmɑ̃/ *adv* not at all; **je ne suis ~ impressionné** I'm not at all impressed; **~ effrayé, il pénétra dans la pièce** not at all frightened, he went into the room; **il n'est ~ question de faire** there's absolutely no question of doing; **n'avoir ~ l'intention de faire** to have absolutely no intention of doing; **il n'est ~ homme d'affaires** he is not a business man at all.

nullité /nylite/ *nf* **1** Jur nullity; **~ d'un mariage** nullity of a marriage; **~ de droit** nullity in law; **frapper de ~** to render void; **sous peine de ~** under pain of being declared null and void; **2** (d'argument, de théorie) invalidity; (d'œuvre, de personne) worthlessness; **c'est d'une totale ~** it's absolutely awful; **il est d'une ~ totale en français** he's absolutely useless at French; **3**○ (personne incapable) nonentity.

numéraire /nymeʀɛʀ/ **I** *adj* **espèces ~s** cash ¢.
II *nm* cash; **paiement en ~** payment in cash.

numéral, **~e**, *mpl* **-aux** /nymeʀal, o/ ▶ **545** *adj, nm* numeral.

numérateur /nymeʀatœʀ/ *nm* numerator.

numération /nymeʀasjɔ̃/ *nf* Math numeration.
■ **~ globulaire** Méd blood count.

numérique /nymeʀik/ *adj* **1** Tech [*enregistrement, affichage*] digital; **clavier ~** Télécom keypad; **commande ~** numerical control; **2** Math [*valeur*] numerical.

numériquement /nymeʀikmɑ̃/ *adv* numerically.

numériser /nymeʀize/ [1] *vtr* to digitize.

numériseur /nymeʀizœʀ/ *nm* digitizer.

numéro /nymeʀo/ *nm* **1** (nombre) number; **~ de téléphone/télécopie/compte** telephone/fax/account number; **le ~ 7** number 7; **2** (indiquant l'importance) **le ~ deux du parti** number two in the party; **objectif ~ un** primary objective; **le ~ un français de la chimie** the number one French chemical company; **le ~ un de l'opposition** the leader of the opposition; **3** Presse issue; **un vieux ~** a back number ou issue; **suite au prochain ~** lit to be continued; fig hum watch this space; **4** (dans un spectacle) act; (de chant) number; **faire son ~** lit to do one's act ou number; **5**○ (personne drôle) **quel ~**! what a character!
■ **~ d'abonné** customer's number; **~ d'appel** telephone number; **~ d'appel gratuit** freefone number GB, toll-free number US; **~ atomique** Chimie atomic number; **~ d'ordre** (queue GB ou line US) number; **~ de série** serial number; **~ vert** = **~ d'appel gratuit**; **~ zéro** Presse trial issue.
IDIOMES **tirer le bon ~** to be fortunate; **tirer le mauvais ~** to be unfortunate.

numérologie /nymeʀɔlɔʒi/ *nf* numerology.

numérotage /nymeʀɔtaʒ/ *nm* numbering.

numérotation /nymeʀɔtasjɔ̃/ *nf* numbering; **~ téléphonique** telephone numbering system; **~ abrégée** abbreviated dialling[GB].

numéroter /nymeʀɔte/ [1] *vtr* to number; **gravure numérotée** numbered print; **compte numéroté** secret bank account.

numerus clausus /nymeʀysklozys/ *nm inv* quota.

numide /nymid/ *adj* Numidian.

Numide /nymid/ *nm,f* Numidian.

Numidie /nymidi/ *nprf* Numidia.

numismate /nymismat/ *nm* numismatist.

numismatique /nymismatik/ **I** *adj* numismatic.
II *nf* numismatics (+ *v sg*), numismatology.

nunuche○ /nyny∫/ *adj* pej bird-brained○, silly.

nu-pied, *pl* **~s** /nypje/ *nm* (sandale) (open) sandal.

nu-propriétaire, **nue-propriétaire**, *mpl* **nus-propriétaires** /nypʀɔpʀijetɛʀ/ *nm,f* owner without usufruct.

nuptial, **~e**, *mpl* **-iaux** /nypsjal, o/ *adj* [*messe, bénédiction*] nuptial; [*chambre*] bridal; **cérémonie ~e** wedding.

nuptialité /nypsjalite/ *nf* **taux de ~** marriage rate.

nuque /nyk/ *nf* nape (of the neck).

nurse /nœʀs/ *nf* nanny GB, nurse.

nu-tête /nytɛt/ *adv* bareheaded.

nutritif, **-ive** /nytʀitif, iv/ *adj* [*aliment, repas*] nutritious; [*crème*] nourishing; [*valeur*] nutritive, nutritional.

nutrition /nytʀisjɔ̃/ *nf* nutrition.

nutritionnel, **-elle** /nytʀisjɔnɛl/ *adj* nutritional (*épith*).

nutritionniste /nytʀisjɔnist/ ▶ **510** *nmf* nutritionist.

Nyassaland /njasalɑ̃d/ *nprm* Hist Nyasaland.

nyctalope /niktalɔp/ *adj* [*animal*] having good night vision (*épith, après n*).

nyctalopie /niktalɔpi/ *nf* night vision.

nylon® /nilɔ̃/ *nm* nylon®; **en ~** [*chemise, sous-vêtement*] nylon (*épith*); **des bas en ~** nylons, nylon stockings.

nymphe /nɛ̃f/ *nf* **1** Mythol nymph; **2** Zool nymph; **3** Anat nympha; **les ~s** nymphae, labia minora.

nymphéa /nɛ̃fea/ *nm* waterlily.

nymphette /nɛ̃fɛt/ *nf* nymphet.

nymphomane /nɛ̃fɔman/ *adj, nf* nymphomaniac.

nymphomanie /nɛ̃fɔmani/ *nf* nymphomania.

Oo

o, O /o/ *nm inv* o, O.

ô /o/ *excl* liter o!

OAS /oaɛs/ *nf* (*abbr* = **Organisation armée secrète**) OAS (*terrorist organization opposed to Algerian independence*).

oasis /ɔazis/ *nf* oasis.

obédience /ɔbedjɑ̃s/ *nf* persuasion; **ils sont de même ~** they are of the same persuasion; **pays d'~ catholique** a Catholic country; **elle est d'~ marxiste** she is a Marxist.

obéir /ɔbeiʀ/ [3] *vtr ind* **1** (se soumettre) **~ à** to obey [*ordre, devoir, principe, règles*]; to follow [*norme, impulsion, émotion*]; to observe [*coutume*]; **~ à qn** [*soldat*] to obey sb; [*enfant, employé*] to do what one is told by sb; **ne discute pas, obéis!** don't argue, do as you're told!; **elle se fait ~ de ses enfants** her children always do as she says; **~ à une décision** to comply with a decision; **nous obéissons au moindre de ses caprices** we give in to his ou her slightest whim; **2** (être soumis) [*freins, véhicule*] to respond (**à** to).
IDIOMES **~ à qn au doigt et à l'œil** to obey sb slavishly.

obéissance /ɔbeisɑ̃s/ *nf* obedience (**à** to); **~ passive** blind obedience.

obéissant, ~e /ɔbeisɑ̃, ɑ̃t/ *adj* obedient.

obélisque /ɔbelisk/ *nm* obelisk.

obérer /ɔbeʀe/ [14] *vtr* to burden [sth/sb] with debt; **~ le budget de l'État** to be a heavy drain on the country's budget; **~ l'avenir du pays** to weigh heavily on the future of the country.

obèse /ɔbɛz/ *adj* obese.

obésité /ɔbezite/ *nf* obesity.

objecter /ɔbʒɛkte/ [1] *vtr* to object (**que** that); **~ à qn que** to object to sb that; **'c'est injuste,' objectera-t-on** some will object that it's not fair; **elle m'objecta que** she objected that; **tu as quelque chose à (m')~?** do you have any objections?; **~ un mal de tête pour refuser une invitation** to give a headache as an excuse for refusing an invitation.

objecteur /ɔbʒɛktœʀ/ *nm* objector.
■ **~ de conscience** conscientious objector.

objectif, -ive /ɔbʒɛktif, iv/ **I** *adj* objective; **tu n'es pas ~** you're not being objective.
II *nm* **1** (dessein) objective; **nous avons pour ~ de faire** our objective is to do; **se donner pour ~ de faire** to set oneself the objective of doing; **se donner qch pour ~** to set oneself sth as an objective; **l'~ est double** there are two objectives; **2** Phot lens; (de microscope, jumelles, télescope) objective; **~ à focale variable** zoom lens; **braquer son ~ sur qn** to point one's camera at sb; **3** (cible) target; (position à saisir) objective.

objection /ɔbʒɛksjɔ̃/ *nf* objection; **soulever des ~s** to raise objections.

objectivement /ɔbʒɛktivmɑ̃/ *adv* **1** (de façon objective) objectively; **2** (évidemment) clearly.

objectiver /ɔbʒɛktive/ [1] *vtr* to objectify.

objectivisme /ɔbʒɛktivism/ *nm* objectivism.

objectivité /ɔbʒɛktivite/ *nf* objectivity; **faire preuve d'~** to be objective; **en toute ~** objectively.

objet /ɔbʒɛ/ **I** *nm* **1** (chose) object; **~ en bois/métal** wooden/metal object; **~ fragile/décoratif** fragile/decorative item; **~ manufacturé** manufactured article; **~s personnels** gén personal possessions; Admin personal effects; **2** (sujet) (de pensée, débat, recherches, science) subject; (de désir, haine, d'amour) object; (de désaccord) source; (d'enquête) subject, focus; **faire l'~ de** to be the subject of [*enquête, recherche, critique*]; to be subjected to [*moquerie, surveillance*]; to be the object of [*convoitise, haine, lutte, poursuite*]; **être un ~ d'admiration/de respect pour qn** to be admired/respected by sb; **le débat de ce soir a pour ~** the subject of tonight's debate is; **3** (but) purpose, object; **cette lettre a pour ~ d'attirer votre attention sur qch** the purpose of this letter is to bring sth to your attention; **la linguistique a pour ~** the purpose of linguistics is; **'~: réponse à votre lettre du...'** (en haut d'une lettre) 're: your letter of...'; **être sans ~** [*plainte*] to be groundless ou unfounded; [*inquiétude, angoisse*] to be groundless; **4** Ling, Philos object; **5** Jur **~ d'un litige** matter at issue; **~ d'un procès** subject of an action.
II -objet (*in compounds*) as an object (*après n*); **la femme-~** woman as an object; **des livres-~s** books as objects.
■ **~ d'art** objet d'art; **~ du culte** liturgical object; **~ du délit** hum the offending object; **~ sexuel** sex object; **~s trouvés** lost property ₵; **aller aux ~s trouvés** to go to lost property GB ou to lost and found US; **~ volant non identifié, ovni** unidentified flying object, UFO.

objurgations /ɔbʒyʀgasjɔ̃/ *nfpl* **1** (reproches) objurgations; **2** (prières) entreaties.

oblat, ~e /ɔbla, at/ **I** *nm,f* oblate.
II oblats *nmpl* oblations.

oblation /ɔblasjɔ̃/ *nf* oblation.

obligataire /ɔbligatɛʀ/ Fin **I** *adj* [*marché, émission, rendement*] bond; **emprunt ~** bond issue.
II *nmf* bondholder.

obligation /ɔbligasjɔ̃/ *nf* **1** (devoir) (professionnel, moral, familial) obligation, responsibility; (légal) obligation; (militaire) obligation, duty; **vos ~s de citoyen** your obligations as a citizen; **faire honneur à ses ~s** to honour[GB] one's obligations; **satisfaire à ses ~s** to fulfil[GB] one's obligations ou duties; **faire face à ses ~s** to face up to one's responsibilities; **manquer à ses ~s** to fail in one's responsibilities; **sans ~ d'achat** with no obligation to buy; **avec ~ d'achat** with the obligation to buy; **sans ~ de votre part** with no obligation; **avec ~ de faire** with the obligation to do; **ce n'est pas une ~ de les inviter lundi** you don't have to invite them on Monday; **être dans l'~ de faire** to be under an obligation to do, to be obliged to do; **se faire une ~ de faire** to feel it one's duty to do; **avoir une ~** or **des ~s envers qn** to feel an obligation toward(s) sb; **2** (nécessité) necessity; **se voir** or **trouver dans l'~ de faire** to be forced into doing; **3** Fin bond; **~ convertible** convertible bond; **~ d'État** government bond; **~ de pacotille** junk bond; **~ à taux variable** floating rate note; **4** Jur obligation; **contracter une ~ envers qn** to contract an obligation toward(s) sb; **s'aquitter d'une ~** to carry out ou meet an obligation; **~ alimentaire** maintenance obligation; **5** liter (devoir de reconnaissance) obligation (**envers** toward, towards GB); **avoir d'immenses ~s envers qn** to be very grateful to sb; **6** Relig **fête d'~** (holy) day of obligation; **jeûne d'~** obligatory Fast Day.
■ **~ de réserve** duty of confidentiality; **~ scolaire** compulsory school attendance; **~s militaires, OM** military service ₵; **être dégagé** or **libéré des ~s militaires** to have done one's military service.

obligatoire /ɔbligatwaʀ/ *adj* **1** lit compulsory, obligatory; **service militaire ~** compulsory military service; **instruction ~ jusqu'à 16 ans** compulsory education up to the age of 16; **l'étude du latin n'est pas ~** Latin is not a compulsory subject; **tenue de soirée ~** evening dress is obligatory; **avoir un caractère ~** to be compulsory; **2**○ (inévitable) inevitable; **c'était ~** it was inevitable, it was bound to happen.

obligatoirement /ɔbligatwaʀmɑ̃/ *adv* **1** (par règlement) **une lettre doit ~ accompagner la demande** the application must be accompanied by a letter; **vous indiquerez ~ sur votre copie le nombre de mots de votre résumé** you must indicate the number of words in your summary on your paper; **sans des mesures ~ prises à l'échelle mondiale, l'humanité court à la catastrophe** it is imperative that measures be taken on a worldwide scale, otherwise humanity is heading for disaster; **2** (inévitablement) inevitably, necessarily; **cette route conduit ~ à la gare** this road leads you to the station; **il y a ~ une erreur** there must be a mistake.

obligé, ~e /ɔbliʒe/ **I** *pp* ▸ **obliger**.
II *pp adj* **1** (contraint) **~ de faire** forced to do; **être ~ de faire** to have to do; **je suis ~ de partir** I must go now, I have to go now; **se voir ~ de faire** to be forced to do; **je suis bien ~ de vous croire** I have no choice ou option but to believe you; **vous n'êtes pas ~ d'accepter** you don't have to accept; **ne te crois pas ~ d'être désagréable** iron you don't have to be unpleasant; **2** (reconnaissant) **être ~ à qn de qch/d'avoir fait** to be obliged ou grateful to sb for sth/for doing; **3**○ (fatal) inevitable; **c'était ~** it was inevitable, it was bound to happen; **4** (indispensable) essential; **un passage ~ (pour)** fig a prerequisite (for).
III *nm,f* **1** fml (personne) **être l'~ de qn** to be obliged ou indebted to sb; **2** Jur (débiteur) obligor; **principal ~** principal obligor.

obligeamment /ɔbliʒamɑ̃/ *adv* obligingly, very kindly.

obligeance /ɔbliʒɑ̃s/ *nf* **avec l'~ de qn**

through sb's good offices; **avoir l'~ de faire** to be kind enough to do; **ayez l'~ de m'écouter** be so kind as to listen to me, be kind enough to listen to me.

obligeant, ~e /ɔbliʒɑ̃, ɑ̃t/ *adj* [*personne*] obliging; [*manières*] pleasing; [*offre, mot*] kind.

obliger /ɔbliʒe/ [13] **I** *vtr* **1** (contraindre) **~ qn à faire** gén to make sb do; [*personne, police*] to force ou compel sb to do; [*autorité, règlement*] to make it compulsory for sb to do; [*devoir, prudence*] to compel sb to do; [*circonstance, événement*] to force sb to do; **comme la loi vous y oblige** as required by law; **rien ne t'oblige à accepter** you don't have to accept; **'tu vas l'aider?'—'bien obligé'** 'are you going to help him?'—'I've got no choice ou alternative'; **2** Jur [*bail, contrat, accord*] to bind [sb] legally [*personne*] (**à faire** to do); **un contrat oblige toutes les parties signataires** a contract is binding on all parties; **être obligé de faire** to be bound to do; **le bail m'oblige à réparer les dégâts** the lease makes me legally responsible for repairs; **3** (rendre service à) to oblige (**en faisant** by doing); **vous m'obligez beaucoup** I am much obliged to you; **je vous serais (très) obligé de bien vouloir faire** I should GB ou would be very much obliged if you would be so kind as to do.
II s'obliger *vpr* **1** (se contraindre) **s'~ à faire** to force oneself to do, to make oneself do; **2** (s'aider) to help one another; **c'est naturel de s'~ entre amis** it's only natural for friends to help one another.
IDIOMES **tradition oblige!** tradition demands it!

oblique /ɔblik/ **I** *adj* [*trait, rayon*] slanting; [*regard*] sidelong (*épith*); **en ~** [*avancer*] diagonally; [*poser*] crosswise; **cas ~** Ling oblique case; **muscle ~** Anat oblique muscle.
II *nf* Math oblique.

obliquement /ɔblikmɑ̃/ *adv* [*enfoncer, poser*] at an angle; [*déplacer*] diagonally; **regarder qn ~** to look sidelong at sb.

obliquer /ɔblike/ [1] *vi* **~ vers la droite/gauche** (légèrement) to bear right/left; (nettement) to veer right/left; **~ après l'école** to turn off past the school.

obliquité /ɔblikɥite/ *nf* **1** (de rayon, pluie, terrain) obliqueness; **2** Astron, Math obliquity.

oblitération /ɔbliteʀasjɔ̃/ *nf* **1** Postes (action) cancelling[GB] ₵; **avec ~ du 4 juin 1991** postmarked 4 June 1991; **(cachet d')~** postmark; **2** Méd occlusion; **3†** (effacement) obliteration.
■ **~ premier jour** Postes first day cover.

oblitérer /ɔbliteʀe/ [14] *vtr* **1** Postes to cancel, to obliterate [*timbre*]; **2** Méd to obstruct [*vaisseau*]; **3†** (effacer) to obliterate [*texte, souvenir*].

oblong, -ongue /ɔblɔ̃, ɔ̃g/ *adj* oblong.

obnubiler /ɔbnybile/ [1] *vtr* **1** (obséder) to obsess [*personne*]; **obnubilé par** obsessed by; **2** (obscurcir) to cloud [*jugement, émotion*].

obole /ɔbɔl/ *nf* small donation; **apporter son ~** to make one's modest contribution (**à** to).

obscène /ɔpsɛn/ *adj* obscene.

obscénité /ɔpsenite/ *nf* obscenity.

obscur, ~e /ɔpskyʀ/ *adj* **1** (sans lumière) [*pièce, rue, nuit*] dark; **2** (peu connu) [*personne, lieu*] obscure; **3** (incompréhensible) [*texte, comparaison, question*] obscure; **4** (mystérieux) [*rôle, affaire, raison, lutte*] obscure; **5** (humble) [*labeur, vie*] lowly; **6** (vague) vague; **un ~ désir/sentiment** a vague desire/feeling.

obscurantisme /ɔpskyʀɑ̃tism/ *nm* obscurantism.

obscurantiste /ɔpskyʀɑ̃tist/ *adj, nmf* obscurantist.

obscurcir /ɔpskyʀsiʀ/ [3] **I** *vtr* **1** (priver de lumière) to make [sth] dark [*lieu*]; **2** (ternir) to overshadow [*relations*]; **3** (rendre confus) to blur [*situation, dessein*]; **4** (rendre hermétique) to make [sth] obscure [*texte, œuvre*]; **5** (affaiblir) [*âge*] to dim [*vue*]; [*fumée*] to obscure [*vue*]; **6** (foncer) to deepen [*couleur*].
II s'obscurcir *vpr* **1** (devenir sombre) [*ciel, lieu*] to darken; **2** (devenir triste) [*regard*] to become sombre[GB]; **3** (devenir confus) [*situation*] to become confused.

obscurcissement /ɔpskyʀsismɑ̃/ *nm* fml **1** (de ciel) darkening; **2** (d'esprit) clouding; **3** (de vue) dimming.

obscurément /ɔpskyʀemɑ̃/ *adv* **1** [*sentir*] vaguely; **2** [*vivre*] in obscurity.

obscurité /ɔpskyʀite/ *nf* **1** (de lieu) darkness; **dans l'~** in the darkness; **2** (d'œuvre, de texte) obscurity; **3** (de personne, travail) obscurity; **4** (de situation) vagueness.

obsédant, ~e /ɔpsedɑ̃, ɑ̃t/ *adj* [*souvenir, rêve, musique*] haunting; [*rythme*] insistent; [*problème*] nagging (*épith*).

obsédé, ~e /ɔpsede/ *nm,f* **~ (sexuel)** sex maniac; **un ~ du vélo/du ski** a cycling/ski freak.

obséder /ɔpsede/ [14] *vtr* [*souvenir, rêve, peur, remords*] to haunt; [*idée, problème*] to obsess; **être obsédé par un souvenir** to be haunted by a memory; **être obsédé par un désir de vengeance** to be obsessed with a desire for revenge; **il est obsédé** he has sex on the brain○.

obsèques /ɔpsɛk/ *nfpl* funeral (*sg*); **~ civiles/nationales/religieuses** civil/state/religious funeral.

obséquieusement /ɔpsekjøzmɑ̃/ *adv* obsequiously.

obséquieux, -ieuse /ɔpsekjø, øz/ *adj* obsequious.

obséquiosité /ɔpsekjɔzite/ *nf* obsequiousness.

observable /ɔpsɛʀvabl/ *adj* observable, which can be observed (*épith, après n*).

observance /ɔpsɛʀvɑ̃s/ *nf* observance; **d'étroite** or **de stricte ~** of strict observance.

observateur, -trice /ɔpsɛʀvatœʀ, tʀis/ **I** *adj* observant; **avoir l'œil ~** to be very observant.
II *nm,f* observer.

observation /ɔpsɛʀvasjɔ̃/ *nf* **1** (fait de regarder) observation; **l'~ de la nature/des étoiles** the observation of nature/of the stars; **avion d'~** Mil reconnaissance plane; **satellite d'~** observation satellite; **satellite destiné à l'~ de la Terre** satellite for surveying the Earth; **mission d'~** Pol observer mission; **l'~ des oiseaux** birdwatching; **2** Méd (surveillance médicale) observation; **mettre qn en ~** to put sb under observation; **3** (résultat) observation; **noter ses ~s dans un carnet** to note (down) one's observations in a notebook; **4** (de règle, politique) observance; **5** (remarque) gén observation, remark; (sur un devoir) comment; **pas d'~s** no comment; **6** (reproche) reproach; **faire une ~ à qn** to reproach sb (**sur** for).

observatoire /ɔpsɛʀvatwaʀ/ *nm* **1** Astron observatory; **2** Mil observation post, look-out post; **3** (organisme) watchdog; **~ de la concurrence** competition watchdog.

observer /ɔpsɛʀve/ [1] **I** *vtr* **1** (regarder) to watch, to observe [*personne, mouvement, adversaire*]; to observe [*phénomène, situation*]; **se sentir observé** to feel one is being watched; **~ qch au microscope** lit to examine sth under a microscope; fig to scrutinize sth; **2** (remarquer) to notice, to observe [*chose, phénomène, réaction*]; **'la situation s'aggrave,' observa-t-il** 'the situation is worsening,' he observed; **faire ~ qch à qn** to point sth out to sb; **3** (suivre) to observe [*règle, usage, repos*]; to observe, to abide by [*trêve, traité*]; to keep, to observe [*jeûne, régime*]; to maintain [*stratégie, politique*]; to observe, to maintain [*grève*]; **~ le silence** to keep ou remain quiet; **~ une minute de silence** to observe a minute's silence; **4** (contrôler) to watch [*propos, manières, gestes*].
II s'observer *vpr* **1** (se regarder) [*personnes, armées, ennemis*] to watch each other, to observe each other; **2** (se surveiller) to keep a check on oneself; **s'~ beaucoup** to keep a close check on oneself.

obsession /ɔpsesjɔ̃/ *nf* obsession; **avoir l'~ de la maladie/mort** to be obsessed with sickness/death.

obsessionnel, -elle /ɔpsɛsjɔnɛl/ *adj* obsessional.

obsidienne /ɔpsidjɛn/ *nf* obsidian.

obsolescence /ɔpsɔlɛsɑ̃s/ *nf* obsolescence; **~ planifiée** built-in obsolescence.

obsolescent, ~e /ɔpsɔlɛsɑ̃, ɑ̃t/ *adj* obsolescent.

obsolète /ɔpsɔlɛt/ *adj* obsolete.

obstacle /ɔpstakl/ *nm* **1** (difficulté) obstacle (**à** to); **contourner l'~** to get around the obstacle; **se heurter à un ~** to come up against an obstacle; **faire ~ aux négociations/au développement** to obstruct the negotiations/the development; **elle a fait ~ à ma promotion** she stood in the way of my promotion; **2** Équit fence.

obstétrical, ~e, *mpl* **-aux** /ɔpstetʀikal, o/ *adj* obstetric.

obstétricien, -ienne /ɔpstetʀisjɛ̃, ɛn/ **▶510** *nm,f* obstetrician.

obstétrique /ɔpstetʀik/ *nf* obstetrics (+ *v sg*).

obstination /ɔpstinasjɔ̃/ *nf* obstinacy; **avec une incroyable ~** with amazing obstinacy; **~ à faire** stubborn insistence on doing, obstinacy in doing; **~ dans l'erreur** wrongheadedness; **avec ~** stubbornly.

obstiné, ~e /ɔpstine/ **I** *adj* **1** (entêté) [*personne, caractère, refus*] stubborn; **2** (acharné) [*efforts, chercheur*] dogged; **3** (durable) [*toux, pluie*] persistent.
II *nm,f* pigheaded person péj.

obstinément /ɔpstinemɑ̃/ *adv* obstinately.

obstiner: **s'obstiner** /ɔpstine/ [1] *vpr* to persist (**dans** in; **à faire** in doing); **il a tort, mais il s'obstine** he's wrong, but he persists; **s'~ à ne pas faire qch** to refuse obstinately to do sth; **s'~ dans le silence** to maintain a stubborn silence; **s'~ dans une opinion** to cling stubbornly to an opinion; **s'~ sur une question** to worry at a question.

obstruction /ɔpstʀyksjɔ̃/ *nf* gén, Méd, Pol, Sport obstruction; Tech (de conduit, canalisation) blockage; **~ intestinale** obstruction of the bowels, intestinal blockage; **faire ~ à qch** to obstruct sth; **faire de l'~ parlementaire** to filibuster.

obstructionnisme /ɔpstʀyksjɔnism/ *nm* obstructionism.

obstructionniste /ɔpstʀyksjɔnist/ *adj, nmf* obstructionist.

obstruer /ɔpstʀye/ [1] **I** *vtr* to obstruct, to block [*conduit, passage*]; **un tracteur accidenté obstrue la route** an accident involving a tractor is blocking the road; **les valises obstruent le passage** the suitcases are in the way.
II s'obstruer *vpr* to get ou become blocked.

obtempérer /ɔptɑ̃peʀe/ [14] *vtr ind* to comply (**à** with); **refus/refuser d'~** refusal/to refuse to comply.

obtenir /ɔptəniʀ/ [36] **I** *vtr* to get, to obtain [*informations, prix, permission, résultat, diplôme*]; to secure [*silence*]; to get, to arrive at [*total, somme*]; **~ qch de/pour qn** to get ou obtain sth from/for sb; **~ de faire** to gain permission to do; **~ de qn qu'il fasse** to get sb to do; **elle a obtenu qu'il reste** she got him to stay.
II s'obtenir *vpr* [*total, résultat*] to be arrived at, to be obtained.

obtention /ɔptɑ̃sjɔ̃/ *nf* **l'~ d'un diplôme/permis** getting a diploma/licence[GB]; **l'~ d'un visa/d'une nationalité** obtaining a visa/a citizenship.

obturateur, -trice /ɔptyʀatœʀ, tʀis/ **I** *adj*

1 Tech obturating (*épith*); **2** Anat [*membrane*] obturator (*épith*); **muscle ~ externe/interne** obturator externus/internus.
II *nm* **1** Phot shutter; **~ focal** or **à rideau** focal plane shutter; **~ central** between-the-lens shutter; **2** Dent obturator; **3** Tech (clapet) stopcock; **~ antiéruption** blowout preventer.

obturation /ɔptyʀasjɔ̃/ *nf* **1** (accidentelle) blocking (up); (volontaire) stopping up; **2** (résultat) blockage; **3** Phot **vitesse d'~** shutter speed; **4** Dent filling; **~ radiculaire** root filling GB, root canal; **faire une ~ dentaire** to fill a tooth.

obturer /ɔptyʀe/ [1] *vtr* **1** gén to block (up) [*trou, conduit*]; to stop [*fuite*]; to fill in [*fissure*]; **2** Dent to fill [*cavité*].

obtus, **~e** /ɔpty, yz/ *adj* (tous contextes) obtuse.

obus /oby/ *nm* Mil shell; **un éclat d'~** a piece of shrapnel; **des éclats d'~** shrapnel ¢; **tirs d'~** shellfire ¢.
■ **~ éclairant** star shell; **~ explosif** high explosive shell; **~ perforant** armour[GB]-piercing shell.

obusier /obyzje/ *nm* howitzer.

obvier /ɔbvje/ [2] *vtr ind* fml **~ à** to obviate sout, to guard against [*obstacle, mal, inconvénient*].

oc: **d'oc** /dɔk/ *loc adj* **langue d'~** langue d'oc (*group of southern French medieval dialects*).

OC (*written abbr* = **ondes courtes**) SW.

ocarina /ɔkaʀina/ **▶534** *nm* ocarina.

occase○ /ɔkaz/ = **occasion** 2, 3.

occasion /ɔkazjɔ̃/ *nf* **1** (circonstance) occasion; (moment favorable) opportunity, chance; **une ~ manquée/rêvée** a missed/undreamed-of opportunity; **à la moindre ~** at the first opportunity; **à la première ~** at the first ou earliest opportunity; **toute ~ leur est bonne pour faire** they'll find any excuse to do; **saisir l'~ pour faire** to seize the opportunity to do; **rater l'~** to miss one's opportunity ou chance; **laisser passer l'~ de faire** to miss the opportunity to do ou of doing; **à l'~** (si le cas se présente) some time; (parfois) occasionally; **à l'~ de** on the occasion of; **à** ou **en plusieurs ~s** on several occasions; **en certaines ~s** on certain occasions; **en toute ~** on all occasions; **par la même ~** at the same time; **pour l'~** for the occasion; **les grandes ~s** special occasions; **avoir/perdre** or **manquer l'~ de faire** to have/miss the opportunity to do ou the chance of doing; **être l'~ de qch** to give rise to sth, to occasion sth sout; **être l'~ de faire** to be a chance ou an opportunity to do; **profiter de l'~ pour faire** to take the opportunity to do; **d'~** [*héroïsme*] incidental; [*rencontre, aventure*] chance; **pour elle, toutes les ~s sont bonnes pour s'amuser** she won't miss an opportunity to have a good time; **j'ai encore raté une bonne ~ de me taire** I should have kept my mouth shut; **2** (marché) **(le marché de) l'~** the secondhand market; **une voiture/télévision d'~** a secondhand car/television; **je l'ai acheté d'~** I bought it secondhand; **3** (objet) secondhand buy; (bonne affaire) bargain; **ce n'est qu'une ~, mais elle marche bien** it's only secondhand, but it works well.

occasionnel, **-elle** /ɔkazjɔnɛl/ *adj* occasional; **utiliser qch de façon occasionnelle** to use sth occasionally.

occasionnellement /ɔkazjɔnɛlmɑ̃/ *adv* occasionally.

occasionner /ɔkazjɔne/ [1] *vtr* to cause, to occasion sout; **~ qch à qn** to cause sb sth.

occident /ɔksidɑ̃/ *nm* **1** (direction) west; **2** (pays) **l'Occident** the West.

occidental, **~e**, *mpl* **-aux** /ɔksidɑ̃tal, o/ *adj* **1** Géog western; **2** Pol Western; **le monde ~** the Western world.

Occidental, **~e**, *mpl* **-aux** /ɔksidɑ̃tal, o/ *nm,f* Westerner.

occidentaliser /ɔksidɑ̃talize/ [1] **I** *vtr* to westernize.
II s'occidentaliser *vpr* to become westernized.

occipital, **~e**, *mpl* **-aux** /ɔksipital, o/ **I** *adj* occipital.
II *nm* occipital bone.

occiput /ɔksipyt/ *nm* occiput.

occire† /ɔksiʀ/ *vtr* to slay sout, to kill.

occitan, **~e** /ɔksitɑ̃, an/ **I** *adj* of the langue d'oc.
II *nm* Ling langue d'oc.

occlure /ɔklyʀ/ [78] *vtr* to occlude.

occlusif, **-ive** /ɔklyzif, iv/ **I** *adj* stop (*épith*), occlusive.
II occlusive *nf* stop consonant, occlusive; **occlusive sourde/sonore** voiceless/voiced occlusive.

occlusion /ɔklyzjɔ̃/ *nf* **1** Méd occlusion; **2** Chimie, Dent, Météo occlusion; **3** Phon closure.
■ **~ intestinale** intestinal obstruction, obstruction of the bowels.

occultation /ɔkyltasjɔ̃/ *nf* **1** (dissimulation) (involontaire) eclipsing, overshadowing; (volontaire) (de question) obscuring; (de vérité) concealment; **2** Astron, Tech occultation; **3** Mil blackout.

occulte /ɔkylt/ *adj* **1** (relatif à l'occultisme) occult; **2** (secret) secret, clandestine.

occulter /ɔkylte/ [1] *vtr* **1** fml (involontairement) to eclipse, to overshadow; (volontairement) to obscure [*sujet, question, problème*]; to conceal [*vérité, fait*]; to conceal, to mask [*inquiétude, malaise*]; **2** Astron to occult; **3** Mil to blackout.

occultisme /ɔkyltism/ *nm* occultism.

occultiste /ɔkyltist/ *adj, nmf* occultist.

occupant, **~e** /ɔkypɑ̃, ɑ̃t/ **I** *adj* [*forces, troupes*] occupying.
II *nm,f* **1** gén (de maison) occupier, occupant; (de siège, véhicule) occupant; **premier ~** Jur first occupier.
III *nm* Mil **l'~**, **les ~s** the occupying forces (*pl*).
■ **~ de bonne foi** Jur occupier (*without a lease*).

occupation /ɔkypasjɔ̃/ *nf* **1** (passe-temps, tâche) occupation; (emploi) occupation, job; **trouve-toi une ~** find yourself an occupation; **avoir de multiples ~s** to have numerous occupations; **mes ~s professionnelles** my professional activities; **2** (fait d'habiter un lieu) occupancy, occupation; **le taux d'~ des lits d'hôpital** the occupancy rate of hospital beds; **3** (pour protester) occupation; **décider l'~ des locaux** to decide to stage a sit-in; **4** Mil occupation (**de** of; **par** by); **l'armée d'~** the army of occupation; **l'Occupation** Hist the Occupation; **pendant** or **sous l'Occupation** during ou under the Occupation.

occupé, **~e** /ɔkype/ **I** *pp* ▶ **occuper**.
II *pp adj* **1** [*personne, vie*] busy; **être très ~** to be very busy; **2** [*siège*] taken; [*ligne téléphonique*] engaged GB, busy; [*toilettes*] engaged; **ça sonne ~** Télécom it's engaged GB ou busy; **'toutes nos lignes sont ~es, veuillez patienter'** 'all our lines are busy, please hold'; **3** Mil [*pays*] occupied.

occuper /ɔkype/ [1] **I** *vtr* **1** (se trouver dans) [*personne*] to live in, to occupy [*appartement, maison*]; to be in, to occupy [*douche, cellule*]; to sit in, to occupy [*siège*]; **les locataires qui occupent actuellement la villa** the tenants who live in the villa at the moment; **ça fait deux heures qu'il occupe la salle de bains** he's been in the bathroom for two hours; **il occupe les lieux depuis six mois** he's been in the premises for six months; **~ la sixième place du classement/championnat** to be sixth in the ranking/championship; **2** (remplir) [*local, meuble*] to take up, to occupy [*espace*]; [*activité*] to take up, to fill [*temps*]; **le jardin potager occupe tout mon temps/trop de place** the vegetable garden takes up all my time/too much space; **aller au cinéma pour ~ la soirée** to go to the cinema to fill the evening; **Paul/le sport occupe une grande place dans sa vie** Paul/sport plays a great part in his/her life; **~ son temps/ses journées à faire** to spend one's time/one's days doing; **à quoi occupes-tu tes soirées?** how do you spend your evenings?; **3** (donner une activité à) to occupy [*personne, esprit*]; **ça l'occupe!** it keeps him/her occupied ou busy!; **mes études m'occupent beaucoup** my studies keep me very busy ou take up a lot of my time; **le sujet qui nous occupe aujourd'hui** the matter which we are dealing with today; **4** (exercer) to have [*emploi*]; to hold [*poste, fonctions*]; **ceux qui occupent des emplois précaires** those who have no job security; **~ le fauteuil présidentiel** to be President; **5** (employer) [*entreprise, secteur*] to employ [*personnes*]; **6** (se rendre maître de) [*grévistes, armée*] to occupy [*lieu*]; **~ les locaux** to stage a sit-in; **commencer à ~ le terrain** fig to have a foot in the door.
II s'occuper *vpr* **1** (ne pas être oisif) [*personne*] to keep oneself busy ou occupied; **savoir s'~** to know how to keep oneself busy; **j'ai de quoi m'~** I've got plenty to do; **chercher/trouver à s'~** to look for/find sth to do; **2** (prendre en charge) **s'~ de** to see to, to take care of [*dîner, billets*]; **je m'occupe de le leur faire savoir** I'll see that they are told; **3** (consacrer ses efforts à) **s'~ de** to be dealing with [*dossier, question*]; **l'avocat qui s'est occupé/s'occupe de l'affaire** the lawyer who dealt/is dealing with the case; **il s'occupe de leur faire obtenir un visa** he's trying to get them a visa; **4** (prodiguer des soins à) **s'~ de** to take care of [*enfant, animal, plante*]; to attend to [*client*]; **tu ne t'occupes pas assez de toi-même** you don't take enough care of yourself; **on s'occupe de vous?** are you being attended to?; Comm are you being served?; **je m'occupe de vous tout de suite** I'll be with you in a minute; **5** (avoir pour emploi) **s'~ de** to be in charge of [*financement, bibliothèque*]; to work with [*handicapés, enfants*]; **6** (se mêler) **s'~ des affaires des autres** to poke one's nose into other people's business○; **occupe-toi de tes affaires**○ or **de ce qui te regarde**○! mind your own business!; **de quoi je m'occupe**○! mind your own business!; **ne t'occupe pas de ça!**, **t'occupe**○! keep your nose out○! GB, keep your butt out○! US; **ne t'occupe pas d'elle/de ce qu'elle dit** don't take any notice of her/of what she says.

occurrence /ɔkyʀɑ̃s/ *nf* **1** (cas) case, instance; **en l'~** in this case ou instance; **2** Ling occurrence.

OCDE /osedeə/ *nf* (*abbr* = **Organisation de coopération et de développement économiques**) OECD.

océan /oseɑ̃/ **▶555** *nm* **1** lit ocean; **l'~ Antarctique** or **Austral** the Antarctic Ocean; **l'~ Arctique** the Arctic Ocean; **l'~ Atlantique** the Atlantic Ocean; **l'~ Indien** the Indian Ocean; **l'~ Pacifique** the Pacific Ocean; **2** (en France) **l'Océan** the Atlantic; **3** fig **un ~ de** a sea of.

Océanie /oseani/ **▶321** *nprf* **l'~** Oceania.

océanien, **-ienne** /oseanjɛ̃, ɛn/ *adj, nm,f* Oceanian.

océanique /oseanik/ *adj* oceanic.

océanographe /oseanɔgʀaf/ **▶510** *nmf* oceanographer.

océanographie /oseanɔgʀafi/ *nf* oceanography.

océanographique /oseanɔgʀafik/ *adj* oceanographic.

océanologie /oseanɔlɔʒi/ *nf* oceanology.

océanologue /oseanɔlɔg/ **▶510** *nmf* oceanologist.

ocelle /ɔsɛl/ *nm* ocellus.

ocelot /ɔslo/ *nm* **1** (animal) ocelot; **2** (fourrure) ocelot (fur).

ocre /ɔkʀ/ ▶193 *adj inv, nm* ou *f* ochre[GB].

ocré, ~e /ɔkʀe/ ▶193 *adj* ochred[GB].

ocreux, -euse /ɔkʀø, øz/ ▶193 *adj* ochreous[GB].

octaèdre /ɔktaɛdʀ/ **I** *adj* octahedral.
II *nm* octahedron.

octaédrique /ɔktaedʀik/ *adj* octahedral.

octal, ~e, *mpl* **-aux** /ɔktal, o/ *adj* octal.

octane /ɔktan/ *nm* octane; **indice d'~** octane number ou rating.

octante /ɔktɑ̃t/ ▶545 *adj inv, pron* dial eighty.

octave /ɔktav/ *nf* (tous contextes) octave.

octet /ɔktɛt/ *nm* **1** Ordinat byte; **2** Phys octet.

octobre /ɔktɔbʀ/ ▶521 *nm* October; **en ~** in October; **à la mi-~** in mid-October; **la révolution d'~** the October Revolution.

octogénaire /ɔktɔʒenɛʀ/ **I** *adj* **être ~** to be in one's eighties, to be an octogenarian.
II *nmf* octogenarian.

octogonal, ~e, *mpl* **-aux** /ɔktɔgɔnal, o/ *adj* octagonal.

octogone /ɔktɔgon/ *nm* octagon.

octopode /ɔktɔpɔd/ **I** *adj* octopod (*épith*).
II *nm* octopod; **les ~s** the Octopoda.

octosyllabe /ɔktɔsilab/ **I** *adj* octosyllabic.
II *nm* octosyllable.

octosyllabique /ɔktɔsilabik/ *adj* octosyllabic.

octroi /ɔktʀwa/ *nm* **1** (fait d'accorder) granting; **les procédures/conditions d'~ de qch** the procedures/conditions for granting sth; **2** Hist octroi.

octroyer /ɔktʀwaje/ [23] **I** *vtr* **~ qch à qn** to grant sb sth [*pardon, temps, faveur, bourse, augmentation*]; to allocate sb sth [*budget*].
II s'octroyer *vpr* to allow oneself [*répit, sursis*]; to win [*victoire*]; to achieve [*succès, place*].

octuor /ɔktɥɔʀ/ *nm* (œuvre, formation) octet.

oculaire /ɔkylɛʀ/ **I** *adj* **1** Méd **nerf moteur ~** oculomotor nerve; **avoir des troubles ~s** to have eye trouble; **2 témoin ~** eyewitness.
II *nm* ocular, eyepiece.

oculiste /ɔkylist/ ▶510 *nmf* oculist, ophthalmologist.

odalisque /ɔdalisk/ *nf* odalisque.

ode /ɔd/ *nf* ode (**à qn** to sb; **à qch** to sth, on sth).

odeur /ɔdœʀ/ *nf* smell (**de** of); (**bonne**) **~** nice smell; (**mauvaise**) **~** smell; **une ~ de gaz/de brûlé/de cigarette** a smell of gas/of burning/of cigarettes; **une ~ acide/âcre/sucrée** an acid/an acrid/a sweet smell; **l'~ d'une fleur** the scent of a flower; **dégager** or **avoir une bonne ~** to smell nice; **dégager** or **avoir une mauvaise ~** to smell; **chasser/combattre les mauvaises ~s** to get rid of/to combat unpleasant odours[GB]; **sans ~** [*crème, lotion, pommade*] fragrance-free; [*produit de nettoyage*] odourless[GB]; **les chiens retrouvent leur chemin à l'~** dogs find their way by scent; ▶**sainteté**.
IDIOMES **l'argent n'a pas d'~** money has no smell.

odieusement /ɔdjøzmɑ̃/ *adv* **1** (atrocement) horribly; **2** (de façon insupportable) obnoxiously.

odieux, -ieuse /ɔdjø, øz/ *adj* **1** (abject) [*personne, meurtre, action, mensonge*] horrible, odious; **2** (insupportable) obnoxious (**avec qn** to sb); **ta conduite a été odieuse** you were obnoxious.

odontologie /ɔdɔ̃tɔlɔʒi/ *nf* odontology.

odorant, ~e /ɔdɔʀɑ̃, ɑ̃t/ *adj* **1** (exhalant une odeur) odorous littér, which has a smell (*épith*); **2** (exhalant une bonne odeur) sweet-smelling.

odorat /ɔdɔʀa/ *nm* sense of smell; **l'organe de l'~** the olfactory organ.

odoriférant, ~e /ɔdɔʀifeʀɑ̃, ɑ̃t/ *adj* fragrant.

Les océans et les mers

Les noms d'océans et de mers

En anglais, les mots Ocean *et* Sea *prennent toujours une majuscule lorsqu'ils accompagnent un nom propre.*

l'océan Atlantique	=	the Atlantic Ocean
la mer Baltique	=	the Baltic Sea

Ocean *et* Sea *peuvent être omis en anglais dans la plupart des cas où* océan *et* mer *peuvent également être omis en français.*

l'Atlantique	=	the Atlantic
la Baltique	=	the Baltic

En cas de doute, consulter l'article dans le dictionnaire.

De avec les noms de mers et d'océans

Les expressions françaises avec de *se traduisent en général par l'emploi des noms de mers et d'océans en position d'adjectifs.*

le climat de l'Atlantique	=	the Atlantic climate
le climat de la mer du Nord	=	the North Sea climate
une traversée de l'Atlantique	=	an Atlantic crossing
une traversée de la mer du Nord	=	a North Sea crossing

Noter aussi:

une croisière sur l'Atlantique	=	an Atlantic cruise
une croisière en mer du Nord	=	a North Sea cruise

odyssée /ɔdise/ *nf* odyssey.

Odyssée /ɔdise/ *nf* **l'~** the Odyssey.

OEA /ɔəa/ *nf* (*abbr* = **Organisation des États américains**) OAS.

OECE /ɔəseə/ *nf* (*abbr* = **Organisation européenne de coopération économique**) OEEC.

œcuménique /ekymenik/ *adj* ecumenical.

œcuménisme /ekymenism/ *nm* ecumenism.

œdémateux, -euse /edematø, øz/ *adj* oedematous.

œdème /edɛm/ ▶271 *nm* Méd oedema; **souffrir d'un ~** to suffer from oedema.
■ **~ pulmonaire** pulmonary oedema; **~ de Quincke** angioneurotic oedema.

œdipe /edip/ *nm* Psych Oedipus complex.

Œdipe /edip/ *npr* Mythol Oedipus.

œil, *pl* **yeux** /œj, jø/ *nm* ▶188 **1** Anat eye; **avoir les yeux cernés** to have shadows ou rings under one's eyes; **enfant aux yeux verts** child with green eyes; **avoir de bons yeux** to have good eyesight ou eyes; **ouvrir un ~** lit to open one eye; **ouvrir l'~** fig to keep one's eyes open; **ouvrir les yeux à qn** fig to open sb's eyes; **ouvrez grand les yeux!** open your eyes wide!; **fermer les yeux** lit to shut one's eyes; **fermer les yeux sur qch** fig to turn a blind eye to sth; **fermer les yeux à qn** (à un mort) to close sb's eyes; **faire qch les yeux fermés** (très facilement) to be able to do sth with one's eyes closed; **acheter qch les yeux fermés** (avec confiance) to buy sth with complete confidence; **je n'ai pas fermé l'~ (de la nuit)** I haven't slept a wink; **il faut l'avoir à l'~** or **le tenir à l'~** you have to keep an eye on him; **avoir l'~ à tout** to keep an eye on everything; **cligner des yeux** to blink; **visible à l'~ nu** visible to the naked eye; **voir qch de ses propres yeux** to see sth with one's own eyes; **cela s'est passé sous mes yeux** it happened before my very eyes; **je n'en crois pas mes yeux** I can't believe my eyes; **chercher qch des yeux** to look around for sth; **il l'a suivie des yeux** his eyes followed her; **ne regarder qch que d'un ~** to be half-watching sth; **jeter un ~ à** or **sur qch** to have a quick look at sth; **elle avait l'~ rivé sur la pendule** her eyes were riveted on the clock; **n'avoir d'yeux que pour qn** to have eyes only for sb; **sans lever les yeux** [*parler, répondre*] without looking up; [*travailler*] without a break; **lever les yeux vers/sur qch** to look up toward(s)/at sth; **je l'ai sous les yeux** I have it in front of me; **mes yeux sont tombés sur qch** my eyes lit ou fell on sth; **faire qch aux yeux de tous** to do sth in public; **les yeux dans les yeux** gazing into each other's eyes; **être agréable à l'~** to be easy on the eye○ ou nice to look at; **coup d'~** (regard rapide) glance; (vue) view; **jeter un coup d'~ à qch** to glance at sth; **jette un coup d'~ pour voir s'il dort** have a quick look to see if he is asleep; **cela vaut le coup d'~** it's worth seeing; **avoir le coup d'~** to have a good eye; **yeux de biche** doe eyes; **yeux de braise** sparkling dark eyes; **yeux de chat** eyes like a cat; **yeux de cochon** piggy eyes; ▶**dent, doigt, loin, merlan, paille, taper**; **2** (exprimant des sentiments) eye; **des yeux rieurs/tristes** laughing/sad eyes; **avoir l'~ fourbe** to have a shifty look; **avoir l'~ vif** to have an intelligent look in one's eye; **elle le regardait d'un ~ amusé** she was looking at him with amusement in her eye; **d'un ~ compatissant** with a look of compassion; **d'un ~ méfiant** with a suspicious look, suspiciously; **d'un ~ inquiet** anxiously; **d'un ~ jaloux** jealously; **d'un ~ distrait** absent-mindedly; **d'un ~ attentif** attentively; **d'un ~ critique** critically; **d'un ~ froid** coldly; **regarder qch d'un ~ neuf** to see sth in a new light; **voir qch d'un ~ défavorable** or **d'un mauvais ~** to take a dim view of sth; **il ne voyait pas ça d'un bon ~** he took a dim view of it; **sous l'~ vigilant de** under the watchful eye of; **voir qn avec les yeux de l'amour** to look at sb with the eyes of love; **à mes yeux, il a tort** in my opinion he's wrong; **à leurs yeux, c'était un échec** in their eyes it was a failure; **voir qch d'un autre ~** to take a different view of sth; **3** (boucle, trou) gén eye; (dans une porte) peephole; **4** Imprim face; **5** Culin (de bouillon) bead of fat; (de pomme de terre) eye; **6** Météo eye; **7** Hort bud. ▶**paille, quatre.**
■ **~ composé** Zool compound eye; **~ électrique** electric eye; **~ à facettes** = **~ composé**; **~ magique** magic eye; **~ poché** black eye; **~ de verre** glass eye.
IDIOMES **mon ~**○**!** (marquant l'incrédulité) my eye○, my foot○; **à l'~**○ [*manger, être logé, voyager*] for nothing, for free○; **faire les gros yeux à qn** to glare at sb; **faire les yeux ronds** to look surprised; **manger** or **dévorer qch/qn des yeux** to gaze longingly at sth/sb; **faire de l'~ à qn** to make eyes at sb; **faire les yeux doux à qn** to make (sheep's) eyes at sb; **tourner de l'~**○ to faint, to keel over; **cela me sort par les yeux**○ I've had it up to here○; **elle avait les yeux qui lui sortaient de la tête** she was absolutely fuming; **il ne l'a pas fait pour tes beaux yeux**○ he didn't do it for your sake ou just to please you; **être tout yeux tout oreilles** to be very attentive; **avoir bon pied bon ~** to be as fit as a fiddle; **sauter aux yeux** to be obvious; **avoir l'~ américain** to have a keen eye; **avoir le mauvais ~** to be jinxed○.

œil-de-bœuf, *pl* **œils-de-bœuf** /œjdəbœf/ *nm* (lucarne) bull's eye.

œil-de-chat, *pl* **œils-de-chat** /œjdəʃa/ *nm* cat's eye.

œil-de-perdrix, *pl* **œils-de-perdrix** /œjdəpɛʀdʀi/ *nm* Méd corn.

œil-de-tigre, *pl* **œils-de-tigre** /œjdətigʀ/ *nm* tiger's-eye.

œillade /œjad/ *nf* (clin d'œil) wink; (regard furtif) glance; **lancer** or **décocher une ~ à qn** to wink at sb.

œillère /œjɛʀ/ *nf* **1** (du cheval) blinker, blinder US; **avoir** or **porter des ~s** fig to have a blinkered attitude, to wear blinders US; **2** (pour bain d'yeux) eyebath GB, eyecup US.

œillet /œjɛ/ *nm* **1** Bot carnation; **2** (de chaussure, bâche) eyelet; (de ceinture, bracelet) hole; (pour renforcer) reinforcement, reinforcing ring; (de métal) grommet.
■ **~ d'Inde** Bot French marigold; **~ mignardise** Bot wild pink; **~ de poète** Bot sweet william.

œilleton /œjtɔ̃/ *nm* **1** (de porte) peephole; **2** (d'instrument optique) eyepiece.

œnologie /enɔlɔʒi/ *nf* oenology.

œnologique /enɔlɔʒik/ *adj* oenological.

œnologue /enɔlɔg/ ▶ **510** *nmf* oenologist.

œsophage /ezɔfaʒ/ *nm* oesophagus.

œstral, **~e**, *mpl* **-aux** /ɛstʀal, o/ *adj* oestrous.

œstrogène /ɛstʀɔʒɛn/ **I** *adj* oestrogenic.
II *nm* oestrogen.

œstrus /ɛstʀys/ *nm* oestrus.

œuf /œf, *pl* ø/ *nm* **1** Zool, Culin egg; **~ de poule/de cane/de caille/d'autruche** hen's/duck's/quail's/ostrich egg; **un ~ entier** a whole egg; **un ~ de porcelaine/plâtre** a china/plaster egg; **en forme d'~** egg-shaped; **~s de cabillaud/d'esturgeon/de saumon** Culin cod's/sturgeon/salmon roe ¢; **des ~s de grenouille** frogspawn ¢; **2**○ (imbécile) idiot○; **faire l'~** to play the fool.
■ **~ au bacon** egg and bacon; **~ clair** Méd unfertilized egg; **~ en chocolat** chocolate egg; **~ (en) cocotte** baked egg (*cooked in ramekin*); **~ à la coque** boiled egg; **~ dur** hard-boiled egg; **~ frais** fresh egg; **~ en gelée** egg in aspic; **~ du jour** new-laid egg; **~ à la liqueur** liqueur-filled egg; **~ mayonnaise** egg mayonnaise; **~ mimosa** egg mimosa (*chopped egg garnish*); **~ mollet** soft-boiled egg; **~ de Pâques** Easter egg; **~ au plat** or **sur le plat** fried egg; **~ poché** poached egg; **~ à repriser** darning egg; **~ en sucre** sugar egg; **~s brouillés** scrambled eggs; **~s à la neige** Culin floating islands.
IDIOMES **plein comme un ~** full to bursting; **étouffer qch dans l'~** to nip sth in the bud; **marcher sur des ~s** to be walking on eggs; **va te faire cuire un ~**○**!** go and take a running jump○!

œuvre /œvʀ/ **I** *nm* (ensemble spécifié) **l'~ sculpté de Rodin** the sculptures (*pl*) of Rodin; **l'~ peint de Michel-Ange** the paintings (*pl*) of Michelangelo; ▶ **gros**.
II *nf* **1** Art, Littérat, Mus (production unique) work; (production générale) works (*pl*); **deux ~s antérieures à 1500** two works dating from before 1500; **~s complètes** complete works; **il a laissé une ~ imposante** he left an imposing body of work; **2** (besogne) work; **être à l'~** to be at work; **se mettre à l'~** to get down to work; **voir qn à l'~** to see sb in action; **mettre en ~** to implement [*programme, réforme*]; to display [*grande ingéniosité*]; **mise en ~** (de programme, stratégie) implementation; **tout mettre en ~ pour faire** to make every effort to do; **faire ~ de pacificateur** to act as a peacemaker; **faire ~ de paix** to work actively for peace; **le temps a fait son ~** time has wrought changes; **3** (résultat d'un travail) work; **être l'~ de** to be the work of; **faire ~ durable** fml to create a work of lasting significance.
■ **~ d'art** work of art; **~ de bienfaisance** or **de charité** charity; **~s mortes** Naut topsides; **~s vives** Naut quick-works, underwater parts; fig (d'entreprise) vitals; ▶ **bon**.
IDIOMES **être à pied d'~** to be ready to get down to work; **à l'~ on connaît l'ouvrier** or **l'artisan** Prov we judge the man by his work.

œuvrer /œvʀe/ [1] *vi* fml to work; **~ pour sa libération** or **pour qu'il soit libéré** to work for his release.

off○ /ɔf/ *adj inv* **1** Cin (hors écran) off-screen; **voix ~** voice-over; **2** (hors programme officiel) alternative; **le festival ~** the fringe festival.

offensant, **~e** /ɔfɑ̃sɑ̃, ɑ̃t/ *adj* offensive (**pour, à l'égard de** to).

offense /ɔfɑ̃s/ *nf* **1** (affront) insult; **pardonner/venger une ~** to forgive/to avenge an insult; **faire ~ à qn** to offend sb; **2** Relig trespass; **'pardonnez-nous nos ~s'** 'forgive us our trespasses'.
■ **~ envers un chef d'État** contempt of the head of state.

offensé, **~e** /ɔfɑ̃se/ *nm,f* **1 les ~s** the injured; **2** Jur injured party.

offenser /ɔfɑ̃se/ [1] **I** *vtr* **1** (blesser) to offend [*personne*]; **2** Relig to offend against [*Dieu, ciel*]; **'ceux qui nous ont offensés'** 'those who trespass against us'; **3** liter to offend against [*goût, principe, justice, raison*]; to be an offence[GB] to [*sens, yeux, oreille*]; to offend [*sensibilité, délicatesse*]; to tarnish [*souvenir, réputation*]; to injure [*sentiment, honneur, amour-propre*].
II s'offenser *vpr* to take offence[GB] (**de qch** at sth).

offenseur /ɔfɑ̃sœʀ/ *nm* offending party.

offensif, **-ive** /ɔfɑ̃sif, iv/ **I** *adj* Mil offensive.
II offensive *nf* Mil, fig offensive; **lancer une offensive** Mil, fig to launch an offensive (**contre** against); **offensive de charme** charm offensive; **l'offensive du froid/de l'hiver** the onslaught of the cold/of winter.

offertoire /ɔfɛʀtwaʀ/ *nm* offertory.

office /ɔfis/ **I** *nm* **1** (rôle) **remplir son ~** [*objet*] to fulfil[GB] its purpose, to do the job○; [*employé*] to carry out one's duty; **faire ~ de table** to serve as a table; **faire ~ d'interprète** to act as an interpreter; ▶ **bon**; **2** Admin, Jur (charge) office; **3** Relig (cérémonie) service; (prières) office; **l'~ divin** the divine office; **4** (salle) butlery.
II d'office *loc adv* (autorité) **d'~** without consultation; **mesure appliquée d'~** measure implemented without consultation; **on m'a muté d'~ aux archives** I was transferred to records without being consulted; **nos propositions ont été rejetées d'~** our proposals were dismissed out of hand; **commis** or **nommé d'~** [*avocat, expert*] appointed by the court (*après n*).
■ **~ culturel** *combined arts centre and tourist information office*; **~ ministériel** *office conferred for life by a public authority*; **~ du tourisme** tourist information office.

officialisation /ɔfisjalizasjɔ̃/ *nf* **~ de qch** making sth official.

officialiser /ɔfisjalize/ [1] *vtr* to make [sth] official.

officiant /ɔfisjɑ̃/ **I** *adj m* officiating; **prêtre ~** officiating priest, officiant.
II *nm* officiating priest, officiant.

officiel, **-ielle** /ɔfisjɛl/ **I** *adj* gén official; **c'est la version officielle** that's the official story; **être en visite officielle** [*envoyé*] to be on an official visit; [*chef d'État*] to be on a state visit.
II *nm* (fonctionnaire, organisateur) official.

officiellement /ɔfisjɛlmɑ̃/ *adv* officially.

officier /ɔfisje/ [2] **I** *nm* officer; **~ de réserve/d'active** reserve/serving officer; **~ général/supérieur** general/field officer; **~ subalterne** subaltern; **~ des pompiers/de police** fire/police officer; **~ de liaison** liaison officer; **~ de semaine** duty officer of the week; **~ de marine** naval officer; **~ de la marine marchande** officer in the merchant navy GB ou merchant marine US.
II *vi* Relig, hum to officiate.
■ **~ de l'état civil** registrar; **~ de la Légion d'honneur** officer of the Legion of Honour[GB]; **~ marinier** petty officer; **~ ministériel** *holder of an office conferred for life by a public authority*; **~ d'ordonnance** aide-de-camp; **~ de police judiciaire** law enforcement officer; **~ public** *office-holder whose statements are deemed authentic*; **~ de renseignement** intelligence officer; ▶ **grand**.

officieusement /ɔfisjøzmɑ̃/ *adv* unofficially.

officieux, **-ieuse** /ɔfisjø, øz/ *adj* unofficial; **à titre ~** unofficially.

officinal, **~e**, *mpl* **-aux** /ɔfisinal, o/ *adj* **1** (utilisé en pharmacie) [*herbe, plante*] officinal; **2** (inscrit dans une pharmacopée) [*remède*] official.

officine /ɔfisin/ *nf* **1** (laboratoire) dispensary; (magasin) pharmacy; **2** (organisation) organization.

offrande /ɔfʀɑ̃d/ *nf* offering; **en ~** as an offering; **faire l'~ de** to make an offering of.

offrant /ɔfʀɑ̃/ *nm* **vendre qch au plus ~** to sell sth to the highest bidder.

offre /ɔfʀ/ *nf* **1** (proposition) offer; **faire une ~** to make an offer; **~ d'achat/de vente** offer to buy/to sell; **leur ~ de dialogue/de compromis** their offer to talk/to compromise; **présenter ses ~s de service** fml to offer one's services; **'~ d'emploi'** 'situation vacant'; **répondre à une ~ d'emploi** to reply to a job advertisement; **faire paraître une ~ d'emploi** to advertise a job; **'cadres: ~s d'emploi'** 'managerial appointments'; **'locations: ~s'** 'accommodation to let' GB, 'rentals' US; **2** Écon supply; **l'équilibre entre l'~ et la demande** the balance between supply and demand; **l'excédent de l'~** surplus supply.
■ **~ d'achat** bid; **lancer une ~ d'achat** to launch a bid (**sur** for); **~ publique d'achat**, **OPA** takeover bid; **lancer une ~ publique d'achat** to make a takeover bid; **~ publique d'échange**, **OPE** share exchange offer; **~ publique de vente**, **OPV** public offer.

offrir /ɔfʀiʀ/ [4] **I** *vtr* **1** (en cadeau) **~ qch à qn** to give sth to sb, to give sb sth; **le plaisir d'~** the pleasure of giving; **c'est pour ~?** (cadeau) do you want it gift-wrapped?; (fleurs) would you like them specially wrapped?; **objets à ~** gifts; **2** (acheter) to buy (**à qn** for sb); **tu aimes ce chapeau? je te l'offre!** do you like this hat? I'll buy it for you!; **je t'offre un verre?** can I buy you a drink?; **il m'a offert le restaurant** he took me out for a meal; **c'est moi qui offre** I'm paying, it's my treat; **j'offre la tournée** it's my round; **3** (mettre à la disposition) to offer [*rôle, crédit*]; **~ qch à qn** to offer sb sth; **~ à manger/à boire à qn** to offer sb something to eat/a drink; **~ son bras/ses services à qn** to offer sb one's arm/one's services; **il a offert de nous aider** he offered to help us; **elle m'a offert de repeindre les volets** she offered to repaint the shutters for me; **'tu veux boire?'—'qu'est-ce que tu m'offres?'** 'would you like a drink?'—'what have you got?'; **4** (à titre d'échange) to offer [*récompense, somme d'argent*]; **tu m'en offres combien?** how much are you offering?; **je t'en offre 200 francs** I'll give you 200 francs for it; **5** (présenter) to offer, to give [*choix*]; to offer, to tender sout [*démission*]; to present [*difficultés*]; **n'avoir rien à ~** to have nothing to offer; **n'~ aucune résistance** to put up ou offer no resistance; **cela offre un avantage** there is one advantage; **ceci t'offrira l'occasion de faire** this will give you the opportunity to do; **~ le spectacle de la désolation** to be a sorry sight; **6** (exposer) **~ sa poitrine aux baïonnettes** to bare one's chest to the bayonets; **~ son visage au vent** to turn one's face up to feel the wind.

II **s'offrir** *vpr* **1** (se payer) **s'~** to buy oneself [*chapeau, fleurs*]; **ils ne peuvent pas s'~ une secrétaire/le théâtre** they can't afford a secretary/to go to the theatre[GB]; **je me suis offert le restaurant** I treated myself to a meal out; **2** (s'accorder) **s'~ un jour de vacances** to give oneself a day off; **3** (se proposer) **s'~ comme chauffeur** to offer ou volunteer to drive; **4** (se présenter) [*solution*] to present itself (**à** to); **c'est une grande chance qui s'offre à toi** it's a wonderful opportunity for you; **le paysage qui s'offrait à nous était féerique** the landscape before us was magical; **s'~ en spectacle** to make an exhibition of oneself.

offset /ɔfsɛt/ **I** *adj* offset.

II *nm* offset (printing); **livre imprimé en ~** book printed by offset.

offshore /ɔfʃɔʀ/ controv **I** *adj inv* **1** (en mer) offshore; **2** (hors lieu) [*banque*] offshore.

II *nm inv* **1** (exploitation pétrolière) **l'~** the offshore oil industry; **2** ▶449 Sport (activité) offshore racing; (bateau) offshore racer.

offusquer /ɔfyske/ [1] **I** *vtr* to offend (**en faisant** by doing).

II **s'offusquer** *vpr* to be offended (**de** by); to take offence[GB] (**de** at).

ogival, **~e**, *mpl* **-aux** /ɔʒival, o/ *adj* [*arc, voûte*] ribbed, ogival spéc; [*architecture, art*] Gothic.

ogive /ɔʒiv/ *nf* **1** Archit rib, ogive spéc; **croisée d'~s** intersecting ribs (*pl*); **arc d'~s** ogival arch; **voûte en ~** or **d'~s** diagonal rib vault, ogival vault; **2** Mil nose cone.

■ **~ nucléaire** nuclear warhead.

ogre /ɔgʀ/ *nm* **1** (géant) ogre; **2** (gros mangeur) big eater.

IDIOMES **manger comme un ~** to eat like a horse; **avoir un appétit d'~** to have a hearty appetite.

ogresse /ɔgʀɛs/ *nf* **1** (géante) ogress; **2** (grosse mangeuse) big eater.

oh /o/ **I** *nm inv* **pousser un ~ de surprise/d'indignation** to give a cry of surprise/of indignation; **pousser des ~** to cry out (**de** in).

II *excl* oh!; **~ hisse!** heave-ho!

ohé /ɔe/ *excl* hey (there)!; **~! du bateau!** ahoy there!

Ohio /ɔajo/ ▶692, 357 *nprm* Ohio.

ohm /om/ *nm* ohm.

ohmmètre /ommɛtʀ/ *nm* ohmmeter.

OHQ /oaʃky/ *nm*: *abbr* ▶ **ouvrier**.

oïdium /ɔidjɔm/ *nm* Bot oidium.

oie /wa/ *nf* **1** Zool goose; **2**○ (personne) goose.

■ **~ blanche** naïve young girl; **~ cendrée** Zool greylag (goose) GB, gray lag (goose) US; **~ sauvage** Zool wild goose.

oignon /ɔɲɔ̃/ *nm* **1** Bot, Culin onion; **soupe/tarte à l'~** onion soup/tart; **2** Bot (de fleur) bulb; **~ de tulipe** tulip bulb; **3** (montre) turnip watch, fob watch; **4** Méd bunion.

■ **~ grelot** pickling onion.

IDIOMES **faire qch aux petits ~s**○ to do sth with great attention to detail; **ce n'est pas tes ~s**○ it's none of your business; **occupe-toi de tes ~s**○ mind your own business.

oïl: **d'oïl** /dɔjl/ *loc adj* langue d'oïl (*group of northern French medieval dialects*).

oindre /wɛ̃dʀ/ [56] *vtr* **1** Relig to anoint; **2** to rub [sb] with ointment [*athlète*].

oint, **ointe** /wɛ̃, wɛ̃t/ **I** *pp* ▶ **oindre**.

II *pp adj* anointed.

III *nm* **l'~ du Seigneur** the Lord's anointed.

OIPC /oipese/ *nf* (*abbr* = **Organisation internationale de police criminelle**) ICPO.

Oise /waz/ ▶357, 692 *nprf* (rivière, département) **l'~** the Oise.

oiseau, *pl* **~x** /wazo/ *nm* **1** Zool bird; **2** fig (type)○ oddball○; **un drôle d'~** an oddball○; ▶ **nom**.

■ **~ chanteur** songbird; **~ exotique** or **des îles** exotic bird; **~ de malheur** or **de mauvais augure** bird of ill omen; **~ marin** or **de mer** seabird; **~ de nuit** night owl; **~ de paradis** bird of paradise; **~ de passage** lit, fig bird of passage; **~ de proie** bird of prey.

IDIOMES **attention le petit ~ va sortir!** watch the birdie!; **chercher/trouver l'~ rare** to look for/find the one (person) in a million; **être comme l'~ sur la branche** to be in a precarious situation; **manger comme un ~** to eat like a bird; **petit à petit l'~ fait son nid** Prov with time and effort you achieve your goals.

oiseau-lyre, *pl* **oiseaux-lyres** /wazoliʀ/ *nm* lyrebird.

oiseau-mouche, *pl* **oiseaux-mouches** /wazomuʃ/ *nm* hummingbird.

oiseleur /wazlœʀ/ *nm* bird-catcher.

oiselier, **-ière** /wazəlje, ɛʀ/ ▶510 *nm,f* bird-seller.

oisellerie /wazɛlʀi/ *nf* (boutique) birdshop; (profession) bird-selling.

oiseux, **-euse** /wazø, øz/ *adj* [*propos*] idle (*épith*); [*dispute, explication*] pointless, unnecessary.

oisif, **-ive** /wazif, iv/ **I** *adj* [*personne, capital*] idle; **vie oisive** life of idleness; **passer des journées oisives** to idle the days away.

II *nm,f* idler péj; **les ~s** the idle rich.

oisillon /wazijɔ̃/ *nm* fledgling.

oisiveté /wazivte/ *nf* idleness; **vivre dans l'~** to live in idleness; **perdre son temps dans l'~** to idle one's time away.

IDIOMES **l'~ est (la) mère de tous les vices** Prov the devil makes work for idle hands (to do) Prov.

oison /wazɔ̃/ *nm* Zool gosling.

OIT /oite/ *nf* (*abbr* = **Organisation internationale du travail**) ILO.

OK○ /oke/ *adj, adv* OK○, okay○.

okapi /ɔkapi/ *nm* okapi.

Oklahoma /ɔklaɔma/ ▶692 *nprm* Oklahoma.

okoumé /ɔkume/ *nm* (bois) gaboon (mahogany).

olé: **olé olé**○ /ɔleɔle/ *adj inv* [*plaisanterie*] naughty (*épith*); [*personne*] racy○.

oléacées /ɔlease/ *nfpl* Oleaceae.

oléagineux, **-euse** /ɔleaʒinø, øz/ **I** *adj* oleaginous.

II *nm* oleaginous plant.

oléfine /ɔlefin/ *nf* olefin(e).

oléiculture /ɔleikyltyʀ/ *nf* olive-growing.

oléine /ɔlein/ *nf* olein.

oléique /ɔleik/ *adj* oleic.

oléoduc /ɔleɔdyk/ *nm* (oil) pipeline.

oléum /ɔleɔm/ *nm* oleum.

olfactif, **-ive** /ɔlfaktif, iv/ *adj* olfactory.

olfaction /ɔlfaksjɔ̃/ *nf* olfaction.

olibrius○ /ɔlibʀijys/ *nm* oddball○, weirdo●.

olifant /ɔlifɑ̃/ *nm* oliphant.

oligarchie /ɔligaʀʃi/ *nf* oligarchy.

oligarchique /ɔligaʀʃik/ *adj* oligarchic(al).

oligarque /ɔligaʀk/ *nm* oligarch.

oligocène /ɔligɔsɛn/ *adj, nm* oligocene.

oligo-élément, *pl* **~s** /ɔligoelemɑ̃/ *nm* trace element.

oligopole /ɔligɔpɔl/ *nm* oligopoly.

olivaie /ɔlivɛ/ *nf* olive grove.

olivâtre /ɔlivɑtʀ/ ▶193 *adj* gén olive-greenish; [*teint*] sallow.

olive /ɔliv/ **I** ▶193 *adj inv* olive green; **vert ~** olive green.

II *nf* **1** (fruit) olive; **huile d'~** olive oil; **2** Électrotech (interrupteur) switch; **3** Archit bead moulding GB ou molding US.

oliveraie /ɔlivʀɛ/ *nf* olive grove.

olivette /ɔlivɛt/ *nf* **1** (tomate) plum tomato; **2** (raisin) olive-shaped grape.

olivier /ɔlivje/ *nm* **1** (arbre) olive tree; **jardin des Oliviers** Bible Garden of Gethsemane; **mont des Oliviers** Bible Mount of Olives; **2** (bois) olive wood.

olivine /ɔlivin/ *nf* olivine.

ollaire /ɔlɛʀ/ *adj* **pierre ~** serpentine.

olographe /ɔlɔgʀaf/ *adj* **testament ~** handwritten will, holograph will.

OLP /oɛlpe/ *nf* (*abbr* = **Organisation de libération de la Palestine**) PLO.

Olympe /ɔlɛ̃p/ *nprm* **1** Géog, Mythol **l'~** Mount Olympus; **2** Mythol (dieux) **les dieux de l'~** the gods of ou on Olympus, the Olympians.

olympiade /ɔlɛ̃pjad/ **I** *nf* Antiq Olympiad.

II **olympiades** *nfpl* Sport Olympics; **les ~ de Tokyo** the Tokyo Olympics.

olympien, **-ienne** /ɔlɛ̃pjɛ̃, ɛn/ *adj* lit, fig Olympian.

olympique /ɔlɛ̃pik/ *adj* Olympic.

olympisme /ɔlɛ̃pism/ *nm* Olympic spirit.

OM /oɛm/ **I** *nfpl* ▶ **obligation**.

II (*written abbr* = **ondes moyennes**) MW.

Oman /ɔmɑ̃/ ▶321 *nprm* (**le Sultanat d'**)**~** (the Sultanate of) Oman.

omanais, **~e** /ɔmanɛ, ɛz/ ▶537 *adj* Omani.

Omanais, **~e** /ɔmanɛ, ɛz/ ▶537 *nm,f* Omani.

ombelle /ɔ̃bɛl/ *nf* umbel.

ombellifère /ɔ̃bɛlifɛʀ/ **I** *adj* umbelliferous.

II *nf* umbellifer; **les ~s** Umbelliferae.

ombilic /ɔ̃bilik/ *nm* **1** Anat umbilicus, navel; **2** (de bouclier) boss.

ombilical, **~e**, *mpl* **-aux** /ɔ̃bilikal, o/ *adj* umbilical.

omble /ɔ̃bl/ *nm* Zool **~ chevalier** char.

ombrage /ɔ̃bʀaʒ/ *nm* shade ¢.

IDIOMES **faire** or **porter ~ à qn** to offend sb; **prendre ~ de qch** liter to take umbrage at sth.

ombrager /ɔ̃bʀaʒe/ [13] *vtr* [*feuillage*] to shade; liter [*cheveux, cils*] to fringe; **route ombragée** shady road.

ombrageux, **-euse** /ɔ̃bʀaʒø, øz/ *adj* [*personne*] tetchy; [*cheval*] skittish.

ombre /ɔ̃bʀ/ **I** *nm* (poisson) grayling.

II *nf* **1** (ombrage) shade; **30° à l'~** 30° in the shade; **rester à l'~** to stay in the shade; **à l'~ d'un figuier** in the shade of a fig tree; **l'arbre (nous) fait** or **donne de l'~** the tree provides shade; **tu leur fais de l'~** lit you're (standing) in their light; fig you're putting them in the shade; **à l'~ de qn/qch** fig (tout près) near sb/sth; (protégé par) under the protection of sb/sth; **rester dans l'~ de qn** to be in sb's shadow; **2** (forme portée) shadow; **faire/projeter des ~s sur le mur** to make/cast shadows on the wall; **avoir peur de son ~** to be scared of one's own shadow; **suivre qn comme une ~** to be sb's shadow; **n'être plus que** or **être l'~ de soi-même** to be the shadow of one's former self; ▶ **proie**; **3** liter (pénombre) darkness; **4** (anonymat, clandestinité) **peintres réputés ou dans l'~** renowned or obscure painters; **laisser certains détails dans l'~** to be deliberately vague about certain details; **agir dans l'~** to operate behind the scenes; **rester dans l'~** [*manipulateur*] to stay behind the scenes; [*poète*] to remain in obscurity; [*détail*] to be left vague; **combattants de l'~** underground fighters; **5** liter (trace) hint; **une ~ de moustache** a hint of a moustache; **l'~ d'un reproche/d'un accord** a hint of reproach/of an agreement; **une ~ de regret/tristesse passa dans son regard** a shadow of regret/a look of sadness crossed his/her face; **sans l'~ d'un doute** without a shadow of a doubt; **sans l'~ d'une preuve** without the slightest shred of evidence; **6** Art **l'~** (procédé) shading ¢; **faire des ~s** to shade; **7** (silhouette indécise) shadowy figure; **le royaume** or **séjour des ~s** the Kingdom of the Shades.

■ **~ chinoise** shadow puppet; **se découper en ~ chinoise sur le mur** to be silhouetted against the wall; **~ à paupières** eye shadow; **~ portée** shadow; **~ propre** dark side.

IDIOMES **mettre qn/être à l'~**○ euph to put sb/be behind bars○; **marcher à l'~**○ to keep out of the limelight; **l'homme qui tire plus vite que son ~** the fastest gun in the West; **passer comme une ~** to be ephemeral; **courir après une ~** to chase rainbows; **il y a une ~ au tableau** there is only one thing wrong; **jeter une ~ au tableau** to spoil the picture fig; **la seule ~ au tableau** the only snag.

ombrelle /ɔ̃bʀɛl/ *nf* **1** (objet) parasol, sunshade; **2** (de méduse) umbrella.

ombreux, **-euse** /ɔ̃bʀø, øz/ *adj* shady.

Ombrie /ɔ̃bʀi/ ▶ 692 *nprf* **l'~** Umbria.

ombrien, **-ienne** /ɔ̃bʀijɛ̃, ɛn/ **I** *adj* Umbrian.

II ▶ 462 *nm* Ling Umbrian.

Ombrien, **-ienne** /ɔ̃bʀijɛ̃, ɛn/ *nm,f* Umbrian.

OMC /oɛmse/ *nf* ▶ **organisation**.

oméga /ɔmega/ *nm inv* omega.

omelette /ɔmlɛt/ *nf* Culin omelette; **~ au jambon/aux fines herbes** ham/herb omelette.

■ **~ baveuse** runny omelette; **~ norvégienne** baked Alaska.

IDIOMES **on ne fait pas d'~ sans casser des œufs** Prov your can't make an omelette without breaking eggs Prov.

omettre /ɔmɛtʀ/ [60] *vtr* to leave out, to omit; **~ de faire** to fail ou omit to do; **à cause d'un mot omis** because of a word being left out; **n'omettez aucun détail** don't leave out any detail.

omicron /ɔmikʀɔn/ *nm* Ling omicron.

omission /ɔmisjɔ̃/ *nf* omission; **mentir par ~** to lie by omission.

omnibus /ɔmnibys/ **I** *adj inv* [*train*] slow, local.

II *nm* **1** Rail slow ou local train; **2** Hist Transp omnibus.

omnidirectionnel, **-elle** /ɔmnidiʀɛksjɔnɛl/ *adj* omnidirectional.

omnipotence /ɔmnipɔtɑ̃s/ *nf* omnipotence.

omnipotent, **~e** /ɔmnipɔtɑ̃, ɑ̃t/ *adj* omnipotent, all-powerful.

omnipraticien, **-ienne** /ɔmnipʀatisjɛ̃, ɛn/ ▶ 510 *nm,f* general practitioner, GP.

omniprésence /ɔmnipʀezɑ̃s/ *nf* omnipresence.

omniprésent, **~e** /ɔmnipʀezɑ̃, ɑ̃t/ *adj* omnipresent.

omniscience /ɔmnisjɑ̃s/ *nf* omniscience.

omniscient, **~e** /ɔmnisjɑ̃, ɑ̃t/ *adj* omniscient.

omnisports /ɔmnispɔʀ/ *adj inv* **salle ~** sports hall; **club ~** (multi-)sports club.

omnium /ɔmnjɔm/ *nm* **1** Sport (en cyclisme) omnium; Turf open handicap; **2** Fin holding company.

omnivore /ɔmnivɔʀ/ **I** *adj* omnivorous.

II *nmf* omnivore.

omoplate /ɔmɔplat/ *nf* shoulder blade, scapula spéc.

OMS /oɛmɛs/ *nf* (*abbr* = **Organisation mondiale de la santé**) WHO.

on /ɔ̃/ *pron pers* **1** (complètement indéfini) **~ a refait la route** the road was resurfaced; **~ a prétendu que** it was claimed that; **~ a affirmé des choses extraordinaires sur ce médicament** some extraordinary claims have been made for this drug; **~ a appris que**... it came out that...; **~ a beaucoup construit dans le centre de la ville** the centre[GB] of the town has become very built-up; **une démission dont ~ a beaucoup parlé** a much talked-about resignation; **~ a arrêté le voleur** the thief was arrested; **~ le dit très malade** he's said to be very ill; **~ dit qu'il a une maîtresse** it's said he has a mistress; **~ a refusé de me laisser entrer** I was refused admittance; **~ peut le dire** you can say that; **il pleut des cordes, comme ~ dit** it's raining cats and dogs, as they say; **2** (signifiant nous) **~ est à cinq minutes du centre-ville** we're only five minutes away from the town centre[GB]; **mon copain et moi, ~ va en Afrique** my boyfriend and I are going to Africa; **à quelle heure doit-~ y aller?** at what time do we have to go?; **où en est-~ avec l'Europe?** where do we stand on Europe?; **~ est peu de chose** death comes to us all; **au lycée ~ n'a pas le droit de fumer** smoking is not allowed at school; **toi et moi, ~ est faits pour s'entendre** we're two of a kind; **~ en parlait avec Janet hier** I was discussing it with Janet yesterday; **~ n'est pas des robots!** we're not robots!; **nous, ~ n'avait pas de bagages** we didn't have any luggage; **qu'est-ce qu'~ mange ce soir?** what's for tea tonight?; **~ a tout notre temps** there's plenty of time; **~ recherche une secr étaire de direction bilingue** bilingual personal assistant required; **~ se serait crus en plein hiver** it felt like the depths of winter; **il y a tellement de bruit qu'~ ne s'entend plus** there's so much noise that you can't hear yourself think; **3** (signifiant tu ou vous) **alors, ~ se promène?** so you're taking a stroll then?; **~ ne peut pas tout prévoir** you can't think of everything; **~ ne comprend rien à ce qu'il vous raconte** you can't understand a word of what he says to you; **~ se calme!** calm down!; **~ se dépêche!** hurry up!; **quand ~ veut, ~ peut** where there's a will, there's a way; **4** (signifiant je) **~ fait ce qu'~ peut!** one does what one can!; **toi, ~ ne t'a rien demandé** nobody asked you for your opinion; **~ dirait que c'est de l'or** it looks like gold; **5** (signifiant ils ou elles) **~ nous prend pour des imbéciles** they must think we're stupid; **~ ne m'a pas demandé mon avis** they didn't ask me for my opinion; **est-ce qu'~ nous a livré le piano?** has the piano been delivered?; **6** (signifiant quelqu'un) **~ t'appelle** someone's calling you, there's someone calling you; **~ m'a dit de m'adresser à vous** I was told to come and see you; **~ frappe** there's someone at the door; **~ a sonné à la porte** the doorbell rang; **si ~ me demande au téléphone, dites que je ne suis pas là** if anybody phones, tell them I'm out; **que dois-je dire si ~ vient pendant que vous êtes sorti?** what shall I say if somebody comes while you're out?; **7** (signifiant les gens) **~ ne peut pas vivre avec 2 000 francs par mois** you can't live on 2,000 francs a month; **~ a toujours int érêt à s'expliquer** it always pays to make oneself clear; **ce sont des choses que l'~ a du mal à comprendre quand elles vous arrivent** these things are hard to understand when they happen to you; **en Mongolie ~ boit du lait d'ânesse** in Mongolia they drink asses milk.

onagre /ɔnagʀ/ **I** *nm* Hist Mil, Zool onager.

II *nf* Bot evening primrose.

onanisme /ɔnanism/ *nm* onanism.

onc = **oncques**.

once /ɔ̃s/ *nf* **1** ▶ 620 Mes, fig ounce; **sans une ~ de méchanceté** without an ounce of malice; **2** Zool snow leopard, ounce‡.

oncial, **~e**, *mpl* **-iaux** /ɔ̃sjal, o/ **I** *adj* uncial.

II onciale *nf* uncial.

oncle /ɔ̃kl/ *nm* uncle; **oui, mon ~** yes uncle; **l'~ Robert** Uncle Robert; **~ d'Amérique** fig rich uncle (*often fictional*); **l'~ Sam** Uncle Sam.

oncogène /ɔ̃kɔʒɛn/ **I** *adj* oncogenic.

II *nm* oncogene.

oncologie /ɔ̃kɔlɔʒi/ *nf* oncology.

oncologiste /ɔ̃kɔlɔʒist/ *nmf*, **oncologue** /ɔ̃kɔlɔg/ ▶ 510 *nmf* oncologist.

oncques‡ /ɔ̃k/ *adv* never.

onction /ɔ̃ksjɔ̃/ *nf* **1** Relig unction, anointing; **l'~ des malades** the anointing of the sick; **2** (onctuosité) unction; **plein d'~** unctuous.

onctueusement /ɔ̃ktɥøzmɑ̃/ *adv* unctuously.

onctueux, **-euse** /ɔ̃ktɥø, øz/ *adj* **1** [*pâte, mélange*] smooth, creamy; [*couleur*] rich; **2** pej [*gestes, propos, personne*] unctuous.

onctuosité /ɔ̃ktɥozite/ *nf* **1** (de pâte, mélange) smoothness, creaminess; **2** péj (de gestes, propos, personne) unctuousness.

onde /ɔ̃d/ *nf* **1** (vibration) wave; **~ lumineuse/sonore** light/sound wave; **grandes ~s** long wave (*sg*); **sur les ~s** on the air; **sur les ~s de la BBC** on the BBC; **2** (vague marine) wave; **3** (eau) waters (*pl*) littér.

■ **~ de choc** Phys, fig shock wave; **~ entretenue** Phys continuous wave; **~s courtes** Radio short wave (*sg*); **~s moyennes** Radio medium wave (*sg*).

ondée /ɔ̃de/ *nf* shower; **~s orageuses/passagères** thundery/scattered showers.

ondine /ɔ̃din/ *nf* **1** Mythol undine; **2** (nageuse) female swimmer.

on-dit /ɔ̃di/ *nm inv* **les ~** hearsay ¢; **ne pas se préoccuper des ~** not to worry oneself about hearsay.

ondoiement /ɔ̃dwamɑ̃/ *nm* **1** (ondulation) (de collines) undulation; (de blé, d'herbes) swaying; **2** Relig baptism (*without the usual rites*).

ondoyant, **~e** /ɔ̃dwajɑ̃, ɑ̃t/ *adj* (ondulant) [*blé, chevelure*] rippling; [*corps, personne*] lithe; [*démarche*] swaying.

ondoyer /ɔ̃dwaje/ [23] **I** *vtr* Relig to baptize [*personne*] (*without the usual rites*).

II *vi* [*paysage, chevelure*] to undulate; [*démarche, blé*] to sway; [*flamme, rideau*] to flutter.

ondulant, **~e** /ɔ̃dylɑ̃, ɑ̃t/ *adj* [*démarche*] wave-like; [*paysage*] undulating.

ondulation /ɔ̃dylasjɔ̃/ *nf* **1** (mouvement) (de chevelure, musique) undulation; (de corps) swaying ¢; **~s du corps** swaying movements of the body; **2** (courbe) (de contour) curves (*pl*); (de chevelure) wave.

ondulatoire /ɔ̃dylatwaʀ/ *adj* [*mouvement*] undulatory.

ondulé, **~e** /ɔ̃dyle/ **I** *adj* [*cheveux, forme*] wavy; [*collines, terrain, chaussée*] undulating; [*carton, tôle*] corrugated.

II *nm* (carton) corrugated cardboard.

onduler /ɔ̃dyle/ [1] **I** *vtr* to curl [*cheveux*]; **se faire ~ les cheveux** to have one's hair curled.

II *vi* (ondoyer) [*colline, route*] to roll; [*herbe*] to ripple; [*chevelure*] to fall in waves; [*corps*] to sway.

onduleur /ɔ̃dylœʀ/ *nm* inverter.

onduleux, **-euse** /ɔ̃dylø, øz/ *adj* [*ligne, paysage*] undulating.

onéreux, **-euse** /ɔneʀø, øz/ *adj* **1** (coûteux) [*dépense, impôt*] onerous, heavy; [*achat*] expensive; [*entretien, rénovation*] costly; **2**† (lourd) [*devoir*] onerous.

ONG /oɛnʒe/ *nf* (*abbr* = **organisation non gouvernementale**) NGO.

ongle /ɔ̃gl/ *nm* (de personne) nail; (de quadrupède) claw; (de rapace) talon; **~s des mains** fingernails; **~s des pieds** toenails; **se faire les ~s** to do one's nails; **avoir les ~s en deuil** to have very dirty fingernails; ▶ **rubis**.

IDIOMES **défendre qch bec et ~s** to defend sth fiercely; **jusqu'au bout des ~s** through and through.

onglée /ɔ̃gle/ *nf* **avoir l'~** to have fingers numb with cold.

onglet /ɔ̃glɛ/ *nm* **1** (sur un livre) (échancré) thumb cut-out; (qui déborde) tab; **avec ~s** (échancrés) with thumb-index; (qui débordent) with step index; **2** (de moulure) mitre[GB]; **tailler en ~** to mitre[GB]; **boîte à ~s** mitre[GB] box; **3** Culin *prime cut of beef*; **4** (de lame, couvercle) groove; **5** Bot (de pétale) unguis; **6** Math ungula.

onguent /ɔ̃gɑ̃/ *nm* **1** Pharm ointment, salve; **2**† (parfum) unguent sout.

ongulé, **~e** /ɔ̃gyle/ Zool I *adj* ungulate.
II *nm* ungulate.

onirique /ɔniʀik/ *adj* (analogue au rêve) [*scène, atmosphère*] dream-like, oneiric sout; (relatif au rêve) [*symbole*] dream (*épith*).

onirisme /ɔniʀism/ *nm* **1** Art, Cin, Littérat dream-like nature; **2** Méd hallucinosis.

onomasiologie /ɔnɔmazjɔlɔʒi/ *nf* onomasiology.

onomastique /ɔnɔmastik/ I *adj* onomastic.
II *nf* onomastics (+ *v sg*).

onomatopée /ɔnɔmatɔpe/ *nf* onomatopoeia.

onomatopéique /ɔnɔmatɔpeik/ *adj* onomatopoeic.

onques = **oncques**.

Ontario /ɔ̃taʀjo/ ▶ **692**, **459** *nprm* Ontario; **le lac ~** Lake Ontario.

ontogenèse /ɔ̃tɔʒənɛz/ *nf* ontogeny.

ontologie /ɔ̃tɔlɔʒi/ *nf* ontology.

ontologique /ɔ̃tɔlɔʒik/ *adj* ontological.

ONU /ɔny, oɛny/ *nf* (*abbr* = **Organisation des Nations unies**) UN, UNO.

onusien, **-ienne** /ɔnyzjɛ̃, ɛn/ I *adj* [*troupes*] UN (*épith*).
II *nm,f* UN official.

onychophagie /ɔnikɔfaʒi/ *nf* nail-biting, onychophagia spéc.

onyx /ɔniks/ *nm* onyx; **en ~** onyx (*épith*).

onze /ɔ̃z/ ▶ **545**, **407**, **212** *adj inv, pron* eleven.
IDIOMES **faire prendre à qn le bouillon d'~ heures** to poison sb.

onzième /ɔ̃zjɛm/ ▶ **545**, **212** I *adj* eleventh; ▶ **ouvrier**.
II *nf* Scol *first year of primary school, age 6–7*.

oocyte /ɔɔsit/ *nm* = **ovocyte**.

oogénèse /ɔɔʒenɛz/ *nf* = **ovogénèse**.

oolithe /ɔɔlit/ *nf* oolite.

oolithique /ɔɔlitik/ *adj* oolitic.

OP /ope/ *nm*: *abbr* ▶ **ouvrier**.

OPA /opea/ *nf*: *abbr* ▶ **offre**.

opacification /ɔpasifikasjɔ̃/ *nf* opacification.

opacifier /ɔpasifje/ [2] I *vtr* to make [sth] opaque.
II **s'opacifier** *vpr* Méd to opacify.

opacité /ɔpasite/ *nf* **1** lit opacity; **2** fig (de texte) opacity, impenetrability; (de nuit) darkness; (de forêt, brouillard) impenetrability; (de montage financier) impenetrability.

opale /ɔpal/ *nf* opal.

opalescence /ɔpalɛsɑ̃s/ *nf* opalescence.

opalescent, **~e** /ɔpalɛsɑ̃, ɑ̃t/ *adj* opalescent.

opalin, **~e** /ɔpalɛ̃, in/ I *adj* opaline.
II **opaline** *nf* (substance) opaline; (objet) object made of opaline.

opaque /ɔpak/ *adj* **1** lit opaque; **2** fig [*texte*] opaque; [*nuit*] dark; [*forêt, brouillard*] impenetrable; [*combinaison financière, milieu*] impenetrable.

op'art /ɔpaʀ/ *nm* op art.

OPE /opeə/ *nf*: *abbr* ▶ **offre**.

opéable○ /opeabl/ *adj* [*compagnie*] ripe for a takeover bid○ (*après n*); **une société ~** a potential takeover target.

open /ɔpɛn/ I *adj inv* Sport open (*épith*); Transp [*billet*] open.
II *nm* Sport open.

OPEP /ɔpɛp/ *nf* (*abbr* = **Organisation des pays producteurs de pétrole**) OPEC; **un pays membre de l'~** an OPEC state.

opéra /ɔpeʀa/ *nm* **1** Mus opera; **j'aime l'~** I like opera; **grand ~** grand opera; **~ rock** rock opera; **2** (bâtiment) opera house.
■ **~ bouffe** opéra bouffe.

opérable /ɔpeʀabl/ *adj* [*malade, tumeur*] operable.

opéra-comique, *pl* **opéras-comiques** /ɔpeʀakɔmik/ *nm* opéra comique.

opérande /ɔpeʀɑ̃d/ *nm* operand.

opérant, **~e** /ɔpeʀɑ̃, ɑ̃t/ *adj* [*remède, mesure, pression*] effective.

opérateur, **-trice** /ɔpeʀatœʀ, tʀis/ I ▶ **510** *nm,f* (tous contextes) operator.
II *nm* **1** Ling, Math operator; **2** Télécom (exploitant) private telecommunications company.
■ **~ de prise de vue** cameraman; **~ radio** radio operator; **~ de saisie** keyboarder.

opération /ɔpeʀasjɔ̃/ *nf* **1** Méd **~ (chirurgicale)** operation, surgery ⊄; **c'était une petite/grosse ~** it was a minor/major operation; **elle a dû avoir une grosse ~** she had to undergo major surgery ou have a major operation; **2** Math (type de calcul) operation; (calcul) calculation; **les quatre ~s** the four basic operations; **le résultat d'une ~** the result of a calculation; **faire des ~s** (pour calculer) to do calculations; Scol to do sums; **3** (étape d'un processus) operation, process; **les diverses ~s dans la production de la soie** the various operations ou processes involved in silk manufacture; **4** (fonctionnement) process; **l'~ de l'esprit/de la digestion** the thought/digestive process; **5** Fin (transaction) transaction; **~ boursière/de banque** stock/banking transaction; **6** Fin (arrangement) **~ (financière)** deal; **~ immobilière** property deal; **7** (suite d'actions concrètes) gén, Mil operation; Pub campaign; **~ de police** police operation; **~ 'non à la misère'** anti-poverty campaign; **~ de prestige** prestige venture.
■ **~ à la baisse** bear transaction; **~ à cœur ouvert** open-heart surgery ⊄; **~ au comptant** gén cash transaction; (en bourse) spot transaction; **~ escargot** *strike strategy whereby truck drivers drive deliberately slowly to obstruct traffic*; **~ à la hausse** bull transaction; **~ à terme** (Bourse des valeurs) forward transaction; (Bourse des matières premières) futures transaction; **~s de couverture** hedging ⊄.

opérationnel, **-elle** /ɔpeʀasjɔnɛl/ *adj* operational.

opératoire /ɔpeʀatwaʀ/ *adj* **1** Méd [*technique*] surgical; [*risque*] in operating (*après n*); [*maladie*] post-operative; **les suites ~s** the aftermath ⊄ of surgery; **2** (qui fonctionne) operative.

opercule /ɔpɛʀkyl/ *nm* **1** Bot, Zool operculum; **2** (de hublot) deadlight; **3** (de pot) lid.

opéré, **~e** /ɔpeʀe/ *nm,f* person who has had an operation.

opérer /ɔpeʀe/ [14] I *vtr* **1** Méd to operate on [*malade, organe*]; **~ qn du genou/foie** to operate on sb's knee/liver; **~ qn d'un kyste/d'une tumeur** to operate on sb to remove a cyst/a tumour[GB]; **~ qn d'un cancer à la gorge** to operate on sb for cancer of the throat; **~ qn des amygdales/de l'appendicite** to remove sb's tonsils/appendix; **il faut l'~** he/she needs surgery ou an operation; **se faire ~** to have an operation, to have surgery; **on l'a opéré du cœur/foie** he's had a heart/liver operation; **il s'est fait ~ de l'appendicite** he's had his appendix out; **2** (effectuer) to make [*choix, changement, distinction*]; to carry out [*redistribution, restructuration*]; **3** (produire) to bring about [*changement*]; **~ des miracles** [*personne*] to work ou perform miracles; [*remède*] to work wonders.
II *vi* **1** Méd to operate; **il faut ~** an operation is necessary; **2** (avoir un effet) [*remède, charme*] to work (**sur** on); **3** (procéder) to proceed; **comment allons-nous ~?** how are we going to proceed?, how are we going to go about it?; **leur façon d'~** the way they go about things; **4** (mener des activités) [*voleur*] to operate.
III **s'opérer** *vpr* (se produire) to take place.

opérette /ɔpeʀɛt/ *nf* operetta, light opera ⊄; **j'aime l'~** I like light opera ou operettas.

ophidien, **-ienne** /ɔfidjɛ̃, ɛn/ *adj*, *nm* ophidian.

ophtalmie /ɔftalmi/ ▶ **271** *nf* ophthalmia.

ophtalmique /ɔftalmik/ *adj* ophthalmic.

ophtalmo○ /ɔftalmo/ I *nmf* (spécialiste) ophthalmologist.
II *nf* (spécialité) ophthalmology.

ophtalmologie /ɔftalmɔlɔʒi/ *nf* ophthalmology.

ophtalmologique /ɔftalmɔlɔʒik/ *adj* ophthalmological.

ophtalmologiste /ɔftalmɔlɔʒist/, **ophtalmologue** /ɔftalmɔlɔg/ ▶ **510** *nmf* ophthalmologist.

ophtalmoscope /ɔftalmɔskɔp/ *nm* ophthalmoscope.

ophtalmoscopie /ɔftalmɔskɔpi/ *nf* ophthalmoscopy.

opiacé, **~e** /ɔpjase/ I *adj* [*médicament*] opiate (*épith*); [*odeur*] of opium (*épith, après n*).
II *nm* opiate.

opinel® /ɔpinɛl/ *nm* pocket knife.

opiner /ɔpine/ [1] *vi* **~ du bonnet** or **de la tête** to nod in agreement.

opiniâtre /ɔpinjɑtʀ/ *adj* [*résistance*] dogged; [*travail*] relentless; [*personne*] tenacious; [*toux*] persistent.

opiniâtrement /ɔpinjɑtʀəmɑ̃/ *adv* doggedly.

opiniâtreté /ɔpinjɑtʀəte/ *nf* doggedness, tenacity.

opinion /ɔpinjɔ̃/ *nf* **1** (jugement, idée) opinion; **il se moque de l'~ des autres** he doesn't care what other people think; **je me fiche**○ **de votre ~** I don't give a damn○ about your opinion; **avoir bonne/mauvaise ~ de** to have a high/low opinion of; **je n'ai pas d'~ sur la question** I have no opinion on the matter; **être de l'~ que** to be of the opinion that; **mon ~ est faite** my mind is made up; **se faire une ~** to form an opinion (**de, sur** on); **'sans ~'** (dans un résultat de sondage) 'don't know'; **2** (sentiment général) **l'~ (publique)** public opinion; **braver l'~** to go against public opinion.

opiomane /ɔpjɔman/ *nmf* opium addict.

opiomanie /ɔpjɔmani/ *nf* opium addiction.

opium /ɔpjɔm/ *nm* opium.

opossum /ɔpɔsɔm/ *nm* opossum, possum○.

opportun, **~e** /ɔpɔʀtœ̃, yn/ *adj* [*moment*] opportune sout, appropriate; [*remarque, visite*] opportune sout; **il est ~ de faire** it's appropriate to do.

opportunément /ɔpɔʀtynemɑ̃/ *adv* opportunely.

opportunisme /ɔpɔʀtynism/ *nm* opportunism.

opportuniste /ɔpɔʀtynist/ I *adj* opportunistic.
II *nmf* opportunist.

opportunité /ɔpɔʀtynite/ *nf* **1** (bien-fondé) appropriateness (**de qch** of sth; **de faire** of doing); **2** (occasion) controv opportunity.

opposabilité /ɔpozabilite/ *nf* opposability.

opposable /ɔpozabl/ *adj* **1** Anat [*pouce*] opposable (**à** to); **2** Jur [*argument, contrat*] which can be used as evidence (*après n*).

opposant, **~e** /ɔpozɑ̃, ɑ̃t/ I *adj* Jur [*tiers, parties*] opposing.
II *nm,f* Pol opponent (**à** of); **les ~s au régime** the opponents of the regime.
III *nm* Anat opponent.

opposé, **~e** /ɔpoze/ I *pp* ▶ **opposer**.
II *pp adj* **1** (inverse) [*direction*] opposite; **nombres/angles ~s** opposite numbers/angles; **du côté ~ de la rue** on the opposite side of the street; **aller dans le sens ~** (volontairement) to go in the opposite direction; (par erreur) to go in the wrong direction; **2** (en contradiction) [*avis, opinion*] opposite; [*partis, forces, côtés, intérêts*] opposing; [*intérêts, buts, stratégies*] conflicting; **ils maintiennent des positions ~es sur la question** they maintain conflicting positions on the matter; **les deux partis restent ~s** the two parties remain opposed to each other; **des versions diamétralement ~es** diametrically opposed versions; **ils ont des opinions ~es aux nôtres** they are of the

opposite opinion to us; **3** (défavorable) opposed (**à** to); **êtes-vous ~e aux relations sexuelles avant le mariage?** are you opposed to sex before marriage?; **je ne suis pas ~ au principe** I'm not opposed to the idea.

III *nm* opposite; **elle est l'~ de sa sœur** she's the opposite of her sister; **il fait toujours l'~ de ce qu'on lui dit de faire** he always does the opposite of what he's told.

IV **à l'opposé** *loc* **1** (contrairement à) **à l'~ de mes frères** in contrast to my brothers; **à l'~ de ce qu'on pourrait croire** contrary to what one might think; **2** (à l'inverse) on the other hand; **à l'~, il peut subvenir à ses propres besoins** on the other hand he can support himself; **3** (dans l'autre sens) **il est parti exactement à l'~** (volontairement) he went off in exactly the opposite direction; (par erreur) he went off in completely the wrong direction; **vous vous trompez, la poste est à l'~** you're wrong, the post office is the other way.

opposer /ɔpoze/ [1] I *vtr* **1** (poser en obstacle) to put up [*résistance, argument*]; **~ un refus à qn** to refuse sb; **~ son veto à qch** to veto sth; **~ un démenti à qch** to deny sth, to issue a denial to sth sout; **~ que** fml to object that; **2** (mettre en compétition) to match ou pit [sb] against [*personne, équipe*]; **la finale opposait deux Américains** the final was between two Americans; **un match amical opposera les élèves aux** or **et les professeurs** students and teachers will meet in a friendly; **3** (séparer) [*litige, problème*] to divide [*personnes*]; **tout les oppose** they're divided on everything; **ce qui les oppose** what they're divided on ; **le conflit qui a opposé les deux pays** the conflict which set the two countries against each other; **4** (comparer) to compare (**à** to, with); **il serait ridicule d'~ Einstein à Newton** it would be ridiculous to set Einstein beside Newton ou to compare Einstein to Newton; **si l'on oppose la somme de travail fourni et le résultat** if one sets the amount of work done off against the result, if one compares the amount of work done to the result.

II **s'opposer** *vpr* **1** (ne pas accepter) **s'~ à qch** (montrer son désaccord) to be opposed to sth; (désapprouver activement) to oppose sth; **ils s'opposent fermement à ce que l'usine se construise** they are strongly opposing the building of the factory; **2** (empêcher) **s'~ à** to stand in the way of [*développement, changement*]; **plus rien ne s'oppose à notre réussite** nothing stands in the way of our success; **le temps s'opposait à la marche de l'expédition** the weather hindered the progress of the expedition; **3** (contraster) to contrast (**with** à); **leur optimisme béat s'oppose aux prévisions économiques** their smug optimism contrasts with the economic forecasts; **4** (diverger) [*idées, opinions*] to conflict; [*personnes*] to disagree; [*partisans, clans*] to be divided; **deux théories s'opposent à ce sujet** two theories conflict on this matter; **5** (s'affronter) [*équipes, concurrents*] to confront each other; **les deux joueurs s'opposeront en demi-finale** the two players will confront each other in the semifinals.

opposition /ɔpozisjɔ̃/ *nf* **1** (en politique) opposition; **les partis de l'~** the opposition parties; **être dans l'~** to be in the opposition; **d'~** [*député, parti*] opposition (*épith*); **journal d'~** newspaper of the opposition; **2** (désaccord) opposition; **être en ~ avec** to be in opposition to; **manifester son ~ à** to show one's opposition to; **rencontrer une faible/forte ~** to meet with little/strong opposition (**chez, de la part de** from); **faire de l'~ systématique** to put up systematic opposition; **3** (contraste) contrast (**entre** between); **~ de couleurs** contrast in colours[GB]; **par ~ à** in contrast with ou to; **4** Jur objection; **faire ~ à un mariage** to raise an objection to a marriage; **faire ~ à un chèque/paiement** to stop a cheque GB ou check US/payment; **5** Ling, Phon opposition; **unités en ~** units in opposition; **6** Phys opposition; **en ~ de phase** out of phase; **7** Astron opposition; **planète en ~** planet in opposition; **8** Psych opposition.

oppositionnel, **-elle** /ɔpozisjɔnɛl/ Pol I *adj* [*caractère, nature*] oppositional; [*groupe, membre*] opposition (*épith*).

II *nm,f* oppositionist.

oppressant, **~e** /ɔpʀɛsɑ̃, ɑ̃t/ *adj* oppressive.

oppressé, **~e** /ɔpʀese/ I *pp* ▶ **oppresser**.

II *pp adj* **être/se sentir ~** (physiquement) to be/feel breathless; (psychiquement) to be/feel oppressed.

oppresser /ɔpʀese/ [1] *vtr* to oppress; **la chaleur l'oppresse** he/she finds the heat oppressive.

oppresseur /ɔpʀesœʀ/ *nm* oppressor.

oppressif, **-ive** /ɔpʀesif, iv/ *adj* oppressive.

oppression /ɔpʀɛsjɔ̃/ *nf* **1** (contrainte) oppression; **2** (malaise) **avoir des ~s** to feel suffocated.

opprimé, **~e** /ɔpʀime/ I *pp* ▶ **opprimer**.

II *pp adj* [*peuple, classe*] oppressed.

III *nm,f* **les ~s** the oppressed (+ *v pl*).

opprimer /ɔpʀime/ [1] *vtr* **1** to oppress [*peuple*]; **2** to stifle [*conscience*].

opprobre /ɔpʀɔbʀ/ *nm* fml **1** (déshonneur) opprobrium sout; **couvrir qn d'~, jeter l'~ sur qn** to hold sb up to public opprobrium; **2** (déchéance) disgrace; **vivre dans l'~** to live in disgrace.

optatif, **-ive** /ɔptatif, iv/ I *adj* Ling optative.

II *nm* optative.

opter /ɔpte/ [1] *vi* to opt (**pour** for).

opticien, **-ienne** /ɔptisjɛ̃, ɛn/ ▶ **510** *nm,f* (dispensing) optician GB, optician US.

optimal, **~e**, *mpl* **-aux** /ɔptimal, o/ *adj* optimum.

optimalisation /ɔptimalizasjɔ̃/ *nf* controv optimization.

optimaliser /ɔptimalize/ [1] *vtr* controv to optimize.

optimisation /ɔptimizasjɔ̃/ *nf* optimization.

optimiser /ɔptimize/ [1] *vtr* to optimize.

optimisme /ɔptimism/ *nm* optimism; **démentir l'~ des commentaires** to give the lie to the optimistic views expressed; **faire preuve d'un ~ prudent** to be cautiously optimistic; **pécher par excès d'~** to be over-optimistic; **afficher un ~ raisonnable** to appear reasonably optimistic.

optimiste /ɔptimist/ I *adj* optimistic (**sur** about); **de façon ~** optimistically.

II *nmf* optimist.

optimum /ɔptimɔm/ I *adj* [*température*] optimum, optimal sout.

II *nm* optimum.

option /ɔpsjɔ̃/ *nf* **1** gén option (**sur** on); **abandonner une ~** to abandon an option; **le toit ouvrant est en ~** the sunroof is an optional extra ou an option US; **à ~** optional; **en ~** optional; **2** Fin option GB, stock option US.

■ **~ d'achat** Fin call (option); **~ de vente** Fin put (option).

optionnel, **-elle** /ɔpsjɔnɛl/ *adj* optional.

optique /ɔptik/ I *adj* **1** Anat optic; **2** Phys, Tech optical.

II *nf* **1** (étude, industrie) optics (+ *v sg*); **2** (point de vue) perspective; **dans cette ~** from this perspective; **changer d'~** to change one's perspective ou outlook; **3** (partie d'instrument) optical components (*pl*).

optométriste /ɔptɔmetʀist/ ▶ **510** *nmf* ophthalmic optician GB, optometrist.

opulence /ɔpylɑ̃s/ *nf* **1** (richesse) opulence, affluence; **2** (rondeur) ampleness.

opulent, **~e** /ɔpylɑ̃, ɑ̃t/ *adj* **1** [*pays*] opulent, affluent, wealthy; [*train de vie*] affluent; **2** [*poitrine, formes*] ample.

opus /ɔpys/ *nm* opus.

opuscule /ɔpyskyl/ *nm* opuscule.

OPV /opeve/ *nf*: *abbr* ▶ **offre**.

OQ /oky/ *nm*: *abbr* ▶ **ouvrier**.

or[1] /ɔʀ/ *conj* **1** (indiquant une opposition) and yet; **il dit avoir passé la soirée au cinéma, ~ personne ne peut le confirmer** he says he spent the evening at the cinema and yet nobody can confirm it; **tu m'as dit que tu serais à la bibliothèque, ~ tu n'y étais pas** you told me you'd be at the library and you weren't there; **~ ça, jeune homme, où vous croyez-vous?** hum now then, young man, where do you think you are?; **2** (introduisant un nouvel élément) **les musées sont fermés le mardi, ~ c'était justement un mardi** museums are closed on Tuesdays, and it just so happened that it was a Tuesday; **~, ce jour-là, il était sorti sans son parapluie** now, on that particular day, he went out without his umbrella; **il a commencé à me parler du livre, ~ je l'avais lu une semaine plus tôt** he started talking about the book and as it happened I'd read it a week before; **on lui avait offert une bouteille d'alcool, ~ Grovagnard était un ancien alcoolique**... he'd been given a bottle of spirits as a present; now Grovagnard was a former alcoholic...; **tous les hommes sont mortels, ~ je suis un homme, donc je suis mortel** all men are mortal, I am a man, therefore I am mortal; **3** (pour récapituler) **~ donc, c'était la nuit et nous étions perdus** now, it was night and we were lost.

or[2] /ɔʀ/ I ▶ **193** *adj inv* [*couleur, peinture*] gold; [*cheveux*] golden.

II *nm* **1** (métal) gold ¢; **~ pur/fin/massif** pure/fine/solid gold; **gravé à l'~ fin** engraved in fine gold; **~ (à) 18/24 carats** 18-/24-carat gold; **~ en feuille** sheet gold; **fil d'~** gold thread; **~ en barres** gold bullion; **~ en lingots** gold ingots (*pl*); **en ~** [*dent, bague*] gold (*épith*); [*patron, mari*] marvellous[GB]; [*occasion*] golden; **avoir un cœur d'~** or **en ~** fig to have a heart of gold; **avoir un caractère en ~** fig to be pure gold; **tout ce qui brille n'est pas d'~** all that glitters is not gold; ▶ **poule**; **2** Archit, Art (d'encadrement, église, de dôme) gilding ¢; **les ~s d'une icône** the gilding of an icon; **3** (couleur) **cheveux d'~** golden hair; **l'~ de tes cheveux** your golden hair; **les ~s de l'automne/des champs** the golden tints of autumn GB ou fall US/of the fields; **4** Hérald or.

■ **~ blanc** white gold; **~ dentaire** dental gold; **~ gris** = **~ blanc**; **~ jaune** yellow gold; **~ natif** native gold; **~ noir** black gold, oil; **~ rouge** red gold.

IDIOMES **la parole est d'argent, le silence est d'~** Prov speech is silver, silence is golden; **je ne le ferais pas pour tout l'~ du monde** I wouldn't do it for all the money in the world ou all the tea in China; **rouler sur l' ~, être cousu d'~** to be rolling in it○ ou in money; **elle parle d'~** what she says is so true!

oracle /ɔʀakl/ *nm* oracle.

orage /ɔʀaʒ/ *nm* storm; **le temps est à l'~, il va y avoir de l'~, il y a de l'~ dans l'air** lit, fig there's a storm brewing; **pluie d'~** thundery shower GB, thundershower US; **temps/ciel/vent d'~** stormy weather/sky/wind; **l'~ de la passion** fig the tumult of passion.

■ **~ de chaleur** summer storm; **~ de grêle** hailstorm; **~ magnétique** magnetic storm.

orageux, **-euse** /ɔʀaʒø, øz/ *adj* **1** Météo [*été*] stormy; [*temps*] thundery; **zone orageuse** storm belt; **2** (agité) [*discussion, réunion*] stormy; [*ambiance*] threatening; [*humeur*] angry.

oraison /ɔʀɛzɔ̃/ *nf* prayer, orison sout.

■ **~ funèbre** funeral oration.

oral, **~e**, *mpl* **-aux** /ɔʀal, o/ I *adj* **1** (non écrit) [*tradition, interrogation, compte-rendu*] oral; **transmettre un message ~** to transmit a message verbally; **2** Méd (par la bouche) **médicament administré par voie ~e** medicine to be taken orally; **3** Psych [*stade*] oral.

II *nm* Scol, Univ oral (examination).

■ **~ de rattrapage** resit oral (*taken by student who has failed a written exam*).

oralement /ɔʀalmɑ̃/ *adv* **1** Méd orally; **2** (pas par écrit) verbally; **communiquer des informations ~** to pass on information verbally.

orange /ɔʀɑ̃ʒ/ ▶ **193** I *adj inv* orange; Transp [*feu*] amber GB, yellow US.

II *nm* (couleur) orange; **passer à l'~** to go through when the light is amber GB ou yellow US.

III *nf* (fruit) orange.

■ **~ givrée** orange sorbet; **~ pressée** freshly squeezed orange juice; **~ sanguine** blood orange.

IDIOMES **apporter des oranges à qn** hum to visit sb in prison.

orangé, **~e** /ɔʀɑ̃ʒe/ ▶ **193** I *adj* orangy[GB].

II *nm* orangy[GB] colour[GB].

orangeade /ɔʀɑ̃ʒad/ *nf* orangeade.

oranger /ɔʀɑ̃ʒe/ *nm* orange tree; **fleur d'~** orange blossom; **eau de fleur d'~** orange-flower water.

orangeraie /ɔʀɑ̃ʒʀɛ/ *nf* orange grove.

orangerie /ɔʀɑ̃ʒʀi/ *nf* orangery.

orangiste /ɔʀɑ̃ʒist/ *nmf* (en Irlande) Orangeman/-woman.

orang-outan, *pl* **orangs-outans** /ɔʀɑ̃utɑ̃/ *nm* orang-utang GB, orangutan US.

orateur, **-trice** /ɔʀatœʀ, tʀis/ *nm,f* (intervenant) speaker; (tribun) orator.

oratoire /ɔʀatwaʀ/ I *adj* oratorical.

II *nm* Relig oratory.

oratorio /ɔʀatɔʀjo/ *nm* oratorio.

orbe /ɔʀb/ *nm* orb.

orbital, **~e**, *mpl* **-aux** /ɔʀbital, o/ I *adj* Astron [*vitesse, station*] orbital.

II **orbitale** *nf* Phys orbital.

orbite /ɔʀbit/ *nf* **1** Astron orbit; **en ~** in orbit; **mettre sur ~** to put [sth] into orbit [*satellite*]; fig to launch; **la mise en** or **sur ~** launching into orbit; **2** Anat eye-socket, orbit spéc; **il a les yeux qui sortent des orbites** lit he has bulging eyes; fig his eyes are popping out of his head; **avoir les yeux enfoncés dans les ~s** to have deep-set eyes; **3** (zone d'influence) **être dans/tomber dans l'~ de** to be in/to fall within the sphere of influence of; **4** Phys orbit.

orbiter /ɔʀbite/ [1] *vi* to orbit.

Orcades /ɔʀkad/ ▶ **416** *nprfpl* Géog **les ~** the Orkney islands.

orchestral, **~e**, *mpl* **-aux** /ɔʀkɛstʀal, o/ *adj* orchestral.

orchestrateur, **-trice** /ɔʀkɛstʀatœʀ, tʀis/ *nm,f* orchestrator.

orchestration /ɔʀkɛstʀasjɔ̃/ *nf* orchestration.

orchestre /ɔʀkɛstʀ/ *nm* **1** (classique) orchestra; (de bal, d'harmonie) band; **~ de jazz** jazz band; **~ symphonique** symphony orchestra; **~ de chambre/de cuivres** chamber/brass orchestra; **~ à cordes** string orchestra; **2** (fosse pour les musiciens) orchestra pit; **3** Cin, Théât (partie de la salle) orchestra stalls (*pl*) GB, orchestra US; **une place d'~** a seat in the stalls GB, an orchestra seat US.

orchestrer /ɔʀkɛstʀe/ [1] *vtr* to orchestrate.

orchidée /ɔʀkide/ *nf* orchid.

orchis /ɔʀkis/ *nm* orchid.

■ **~ mâle** male orchid; **~ pourpre** lady orchid.

ordalie /ɔʀdali/ *nf* Hist ordeal.

ordinaire /ɔʀdinɛʀ/ I *adj* **1** (ni spécial, ni anormal) gén ordinary; [*qualité, modèle*] standard; [*lecteur, touriste*] average, ordinary; [*vaisselle*] everyday; [*journée*] normal, ordinary; **séance ~** ordinary session; **procédure ~** ordinary court procedure; **en temps ~** in normal times; **ça n'a rien d'~** it's pretty unusual; **journée peu ~** unusual day; **d'une bêtise/audace peu ~** incredibly stupid/daring; **2** péj (médiocre) [*vie*] humdrum (*épith*); **très ~** [*repas, vin*] very average; [*personne*] very ordinary; **3** (coutumier) [*qualité, défaut*] usual; **avec sa politesse ~** with his usual politeness.

II *nm* **1** (menu habituel) **l'~** everyday fare; **2** (moyenne) **l'~** the commonplace; **sortir de l'~** [*livre, film*] to be out of the ordinary; **au-dessous/au-dessus de l'~** below/above average; **3** Relig **l'~ de la messe** the ordinary of the mass; **4** (essence) 2-star (petrol) GB, regular (gasoline) US.

III **à l'ordinaire**, **d'ordinaire** *loc adv* usually; **plus tard que d'~** or **qu'à l'~** later than usual; **comme à l'~** as usual.

ordinairement /ɔʀdinɛʀmɑ̃/ *adv* **1** (d'habitude) usually; **2** (normalement) normally.

ordinal, **~e**, *mpl* **-aux** /ɔʀdinal, o/ I *adj* ordinal.

II *nm* ordinal.

ordinateur /ɔʀdinatœʀ/ *nm* Ordinat computer; **travailler sur ~** to work with a computer; **~ individuel** or **personnel/de bureau** personal/desktop computer; **~ portatif** laptop computer; **~ central** mainframe; **~ frontal/dorsal** front-end/back-end computer; **conception/ingéniérie assistée par ~** computer-aided design/engineering; **transactions programmées par ~** computer-programmed[GB] transactions; **création d'images par ~** computer-generated graphics; **simulation par** or **sur ~** computer simulation.

ordination /ɔʀdinasjɔ̃/ *nf* ordination.

ordinogramme /ɔʀdinɔgʀam/ *nm* flowchart, flow diagram.

ordonnance /ɔʀdɔnɑ̃s/ I† *nm* ou *f* Mil batman; **d'~** [*revolver*] regulation (*épith*).

II *nf* **1** (document) prescription; **faire une ~ à qn** to give sb a prescription; **délivré uniquement sur ~** only available on prescription; **on peut l'acheter sans ~** you can buy it over the counter; **médicament vendu sans ~** over-the-counter medicine; **2** (agencement) (de salle, meubles) layout; (de cérémonie, banquet) order; **3** Jur ruling.

ordonnancement /ɔʀdɔnɑ̃smɑ̃/ *nm* **1** Compta order to pay; **2** (en gestion) scheduling; **3** fml (de cérémonie, phrases) order.

ordonnancer /ɔʀdɔnɑ̃se/ [12] *vtr* **1** (organiser) fml to organize [*fête, cérémonie*]; to plan [*discours*]; **2** (en gestion) to schedule; **3** Compta to authorize [*paiement, dépense*].

ordonnancier /ɔʀdɔnɑ̃sje/ *nm* **1** (de médecin) prescription pad; **2** (de pharmacien) prescription book.

ordonnateur, **-trice** /ɔʀdɔnatœʀ, tʀis/ *nm, f* **1** fml (organisateur) organizer; **~ des pompes funèbres** funeral director; **le grand ~ du monde** the great architect; **2** Compta *official with power to authorize payment*.

ordonné, **~e** /ɔʀdɔne/ I *pp* ▶ **ordonner**.

II *pp adj* **1** (rangé) [*chambre, armoire, personne*] tidy; **2** (méthodique) [*personne*] methodical; **3** (structuré) **bien ~** [*texte*] well-ordered; **4** (pas désorganisé) [*manifestation, grève*] orderly; **vie bien ~e** well-ordered life; ▶ **charité**; **5** Math ordered.

III **ordonnée** *nf* Math ordinate.

ordonner /ɔʀdɔne/ [1] I *vtr* **1** (commander) gén to order; [*médecin*] to prescribe [*repos*]; **~ à qn de faire qch** to order sb to do sth; **~ que qn soit libéré** to order sb to be set free; **~ le silence à qn** to order sb to be silent; **2** (mettre en ordre) to put [sth] in order [*objets*]; to order [*paragraphes*]; **~ qch par ordre alphabétique/chronologique** to put sth in alphabetical/chronological order; **~ sa réflexion autour d'un thème principal** to organize one's ideas around a central theme; **~ un polynôme** to arrange a polynomial; **3** Relig to ordain; **il a été ordonné** (**prêtre**) he has been ordained.

II **s'ordonner** *vpr* **s'~ facilement** [*paragraphes*] to fall into order easily; **ses idées s'ordonnent autour d'un thème principal** his/her ideas are organized around one main theme.

ordre /ɔʀdʀ/ *nm* **1** (commandement) order; **donner un ~ à qn** to give sb an order; **donner à qn l'~ de faire** to give sb the order to do, to order sb to do; **recevoir l'~ de faire qch** to be given the order to do sth, to be ordered to do sth; **je n'ai d'~ à recevoir de personne** I don't take orders from anybody; **j'ai des ~s** I'm acting under orders; **agir sur ~ de qn** to act on sb's orders; **travailler sous les ~s de qn** to work under sb; **elle a 30 personnes sous ses ~s** she has 30 people (working) under her; **être aux ~s de qn** Mil to serve under sb, to be under sb's command; (employé de maison) to be in sb's service; **prendre qn à ses ~s** to take sb on; **à vos ~s!** Mil yes, sir!; hum (à un ami, parent) at your service! hum; **jusqu' à nouvel ~** until further notice; **2** (disposition régulière) order; **par ~ alphabétique/chronologique** in alphabetical/chronological order; **en ~ croissant/décroissant** in ascending/descending order; **par ~ de préférence** in order of preference; **par ~ d'entrée en scène** in order of appearance; **l'~ des mots** word order; **l'~ des cérémonies** the order of ceremonies; **procédons par ~** let's do things in order; **tu dois, dans l'~, téléphoner à la gare, à l'aéroport, à l'hôtel** you've got to phone the station, the airport and the hotel, in that order; **selon un ~ strict** in strict order; **en bon ~** [*être aligné, avancer*] in an orderly fashion ; **avancer en ~ dispersé/serré** to advance in scattered/close formation; **~ de bataille** battle order; **3** Ordinat command; **4** (fait d'être rangé) tidiness, orderliness; (fait d'être bien organisé) order; **être en ~** [*maison, armoire*] to be tidy; [*comptes*] to be in order; **tenir une pièce en ~** to keep a room tidy; **mettre de l'~ dans** to tidy up [*pièce, placard*]; **mettre de l'~ dans ses comptes** to get one's accounts in order; **mettre de l'~ dans ses idées** to get one's ideas straight; **mettre de l'~ dans sa vie** to sort out one's life○; **mettre ses affaires en ~** (avant de mourir) to put one's affairs in order; **5** (qualité) tidiness; **elle n'a pas beaucoup d'~** (rangé) she' s not very tidy; (méthodique) she's not very methodical; **mettre bon ~ à qch** to sort out sth; **remettre une pièce en ~** to put everything back where it was in a room; **remise en ~** fig rationalization; **6** (comme valeur) order; **aimer l'~ et le travail sérieux** to like order and hard work; **7** (état stable et normal) order; **maintenir l'~ dans sa classe** to keep order in the classroom; **rappeler qn à l'~** to reprimand sb; **tout est rentré dans l'~** gén everything is back to normal; (après des émeutes) order has been restored; **l'~ public** public order; **maintenir/rétablir l'~ (public)** to maintain/restore law and order; **troubler l'~ public** [*individu*] to cause a breach of the peace; [*groupe d'insurgés*] to disturb the peace; **le respect de l'~ établi** respect for the established order; **c'est dans l'~ des choses** it's in the nature of things; **en ~ de marche** in working order; **8** (nature) nature; **un problème de cet ~** a problem of that nature; **un problème de cet ~ (de grandeur)** a problem on that scale; **c'est un problème d'~ économique** it's a problem of an economic nature; **d'~ officiel/personnel** of an official/a personal nature; **de l'~ de 30%** in ou of the order of 30% GB, on the order of 30% US; **~ de prix** price range; **de quel ~ de grandeur?** [*somme*] how much approximately?; **pour vous donner un ~ de grandeur** to give you a rough idea; **de premier ~** first-rate; **de**

second ~ second-rate; **dans le même ~ d'idées, je voudrais vous demander** talking of which, I would like to ask you; **c'est du même ~** it's the same kind of thing; **c'est d'un tout autre ~** it's a completely different kind of thing; **des préoccupations d'un tout autre ~** very different worries; **9** Archit, Biol, Zool order; **10** (confrérie) order; **~ de chevalerie** order of chivalry; **l'~ des médecins** the medical association; **l'~ des avocats** the lawyers' association; **être rayé de l'~** [*avocat*] to be disbarred; [*médecin*] to be struck off (the medical register) GB, to lose one's license US; **11** Relig order; **~ monastique** monastic order; **entrer dans les ~s** to take (holy) orders; **l'~ des cisterciens** the Cistercian order; **l'~ des Templiers** the Knights Templar; **les ~s majeurs/mineurs** major/minor orders; **12** (sous l'Ancien Régime) estate; **13** Fin order; **~ d'achat/de vente** order to buy/to sell; **libellez le chèque à l'ordre de X** make the cheque GB ou check US payable to X; **c'est à quel ~?** who do I make it payable to?; **14** Comm (commande) order; **carnet d'~s** order book.

■ ~ du jour (de réunion) agenda; **être à l'~ du jour** lit to be on the agenda; fig to be talked about; **inscrire qch à l'~ du jour** to put sth on the agenda; **~ de mobilisation** Mil marching orders (*pl*).

ordure /ɔʀdyʀ/ **I** *nf* **1** liter (abjection) filth; **se complaire dans l'~** to wallow in filth; **2**◑ (personne méprisable) **quelle ~ ce type!** that guy's a real bastard◑!

II ordures *nfpl* **1** (déchets) refuse ¢ GB, garbage ¢ US; **les ~s ménagères** household refuse GB, household garbage US; **ramassage des ~s ménagères** collection of household refuse GB ou garbage US; **mettre/jeter qch aux ~s** to put/throw sth in the bin GB ou in the garbage US; **défense de déposer des ~s** no dumping; **tas d'~s** rubbish heap GB, pile of garbage US; **2** (grossièretés) filth ¢; **cet article est un tissu d'~s** this article is sheer filth.

ordurier, **-ière** /ɔʀdyʀje, ɛʀ/ *adj* [*propos, langage*] filthy; **des lettres ordurières** hate mail.

orée /ɔʀe/ *nf* **1** lit edge; **2** fig start.

Oregon /ɔʀegɔ̃/ **▶692** *nprm* Oregon.

oreillard /ɔʀɛjaʀ/ *nm* long-eared bat.

oreille /ɔʀɛj/ **▶188** *nf* **1** Anat ear; **l'~ externe/moyenne/interne** the outer/middle/inner ear; **avoir les ~s décollées** to have sticking out ears; **elle a des perles aux ~s** she is wearing pearl earrings; **dire qch à l'~ de qn, dire qch à qn dans le creux de l'~** to whisper sth in sb's ear; **dresser l'~** lit, fig to prick up one's ears; **porter la casquette sur l'~** to wear one's cap over one eye; **emmitouflé jusqu'aux ~s** all wrapped up; **rougir jusqu'aux ~s** to blush to the roots of one's hair; **tendre l'~** to strain one's ears; **entrer par une ~ et sortir par l'autre** to go in one ear and out the other; **c'est arrivé** or **parvenu à leurs ~s** they got to hear of it, it came to their ears; **écouter de toutes ses ~s, être tout ~s** to be all ears, to listen intently; **n'écouter que d'une ~, écouter d'une ~ distraite** to half-listen, to listen with half an ear; **ouvre-bien les ~s!** listen carefully; **il m'en a glissé** or **soufflé un mot à l'~** he had a word with me about it; **en avoir plein les ~s de qch** to have had an earful of sth; **arrête de crier, tu me casses les ~s** stop yelling, you're bursting my eardrums; **ne prête pas l'~ à** don't listen to; **▶ affamé**, **dormir**, **fendre**, **puce**, **sourd**; **2** (ouïe) hearing; **avoir l' ~ fine** to have keen hearing ou sharp ears; **avoir de l'~** Mus to have a good ear (for music); **n'avoir pas d'~** Mus to be tone-deaf; **avoir l'~ juste** to have perfect pitch; **3** (personne) **les ~s sensibles** or **pudiques** people who are easily shocked; **à l'abri** or **loin des ~s indiscrètes** where no-one can hear; **4** (de marmite, plat) handle; (de vis, fauteuil) wing; **5** (de serviette, ballot) floppy end.

■ ~ d'ours Bot bear's ear, auricula; **~s en feuille de chou** cauliflower ears.

IDIOMES **avoir l'~ basse** to look sheepish; **avoir l'~ de qn** to have sb's ear; **s'il y a une ~ qui traîne** if anybody' s listening; **tirer** or **frotter les ~s à qn** to tell sb off, to give sb a ticking off○ GB; **se faire tirer l'~ pour faire** to drag one's feet about doing; **montrer le bout de l'~** (être vu) [*animal*] to peep out; (se trahir) to reveal a little bit of one's true self; **les ~s ont dû te siffler** or **tinter** your ears must have been burning.

oreiller /ɔʀeje/ *nm* pillow; **se réconcilier sur l'~** to make it up in bed.

oreillette /ɔʀɛjɛt/ *nf* **1** Anat auricle; **2** Mode (de casquette) earflap.

oreillons /ɔʀɛjɔ̃/ **▶271** *nmpl* mumps; **avoir les ~** to have mumps.

ores: **d'ores et déjà** /dɔʀzedeʒa/ *loc adv* already.

Oreste /ɔʀɛst/ *npr* Orestes.

orfèvre /ɔʀfɛvʀ/ **▶510** *nmf* goldsmith; **être ~ en la matière** fig to be an expert in the field.

orfèvrerie /ɔʀfɛvʀəʀi/ *nf* (métier) goldsmith's art; (commerce) goldsmith's and silversmith's; **article** or **pièce d'~** (en argent) piece of silverware; (en or) piece of gold work.

orfraie /ɔʀfʀɛ/ *nf* sea eagle.

IDIOMES **pousser des cris d'~** to scream blue murder.

organdi /ɔʀgɑ̃di/ *nm* organdie; **robe en ~** organdie dress.

organe /ɔʀgan/ *nm* **1** (de la vue, l'ouïe) organ; **2** (publication) organ; **~ officiel d'un parti** official organ of a party; **3** (institution) organ; **les ~s de l'État** the organs of the State; **~ consultatif/exécutif** consultative/executive body; **~ de presse** press organ; **4** Mécan system; **~s de freinage/direction** braking/steering system (*sg*); **5** (voix) voice; **6** (instrument) instrument; **les lois sont les ~s de la justice** laws are the instruments of justice.

organigramme /ɔʀganigʀam/ *nm* **1** Entr organization chart; **2** Ordinat flowchart.

organique /ɔʀganik/ *adj* organic.

organiquement /ɔʀganikmɑ̃/ *adv* organically.

organisateur, **-trice** /ɔʀganizatœʀ, tʀis/ **I** *adj* organizing (*épith*).

II *nm,f* organizer.

organisation /ɔʀganizasjɔ̃/ *nf* organization; **manquer d'~** to lack organization; **tu devrais faire un effort d'~** you should try to be more organized; **cette année ils ont fait un effort d'~** this year they made an effort at organizing things; **comité d'~** organizing committee.

■ Organisation mondiale du commerce, OMC World Trade Organization, WTO.

organisationnel, **-elle** /ɔʀganizasjɔnɛl/ *adj* organizational.

organisé, **~e** /ɔʀganize/ **I** *pp* **▶ organiser**.

II *pp adj* organized; **une réunion bien/mal ~e** a well-/badly-organized meeting.

organiser /ɔʀganize/ [1] **I** *vtr* to organize.

II s'organiser *vpr* **1** (se regrouper) [*dissidents, chômeurs, opposition*] to get organized; **s'~ en** to organize oneself into; **2** (être méthodique) to organize oneself; **3** (être mis sur pied) [*lutte, secours*] to get organized; **4** (être conçu) **le livre s'organise en 12 chapitres** the book is organized into 12 chapters; **l'histoire s'organise autour de deux thèmes principaux** the plot revolves ou is organized around two main themes.

organisme /ɔʀganism/ *nm* **1** (corps humain) body, organism spéc; **les défenses naturelles de l'~** the body's natural defences[GB]; **2** (être vivant) organism; **~ vivant** living organism; **3** (organisation) organization, body; **~ de surveillance** watchdog body.

organiste /ɔʀganist/ **▶510** *nmf* organist.

orgasme /ɔʀgasm/ *nm* orgasm; **~ clitoridien/vaginal** clitoral/vaginal orgasm; **avoir un ~** to have an orgasm.

orge /ɔʀʒ/ **I** *nm* Culin barley; **~ perlé** pearl barley.

II *nf* Agric, Bot barley.

orgeat /ɔʀʒa/ *nm* (**sirop d'**)**~** barley water.

orgelet /ɔʀʒəlɛ/ *nm* stye.

orgiaque /ɔʀʒjak/ *adj* orgiastic.

orgie /ɔʀʒi/ *nf* lit, fig orgy; **faire une ~ de fruits** to gorge oneself on fruit.

orgue /ɔʀg/ **▶534** **I** *nm* Mus organ; **tenir l'~** to be at the organ; **~ électronique** electronic organ.

II orgues *nfpl* Mus organ (*sg*); **les grandes ~s de Notre-Dame** the great organ in Notre Dame.

■ ~ de Barbarie barrel organ; **~s basaltiques** Géol basalt columns; **~s de Staline** Hist Mil Stalin organs.

orgueil /ɔʀgœj/ *nm* pride; **l'~ national** national pride; **être l'~ de qn** to be sb's pride and joy; **pécher par ~** to be too proud; **un sursaut d'~** a flash of pride.

orgueilleusement /ɔʀgœjøzmɑ̃/ *adv* proudly.

orgueilleux, **-euse** /ɔʀgœjø, øz/ **I** *adj* gén proud; (trop) overproud.

II *nm,f* overproud person; **c'est un ~** he's overproud.

oriel /ɔʀjɛl/ *nm* oriel window.

orient /ɔʀjɑ̃/ *nm* **1** (direction) east; **2** (pays) **l'Orient** the East; **▶ grand**.

orientable /ɔʀjɑ̃tabl/ *adj* [*miroir, bras de machine*] swivelling[GB], swivel (*épith*); [*antenne, projecteur*] adjustable.

oriental, **~e**, *mpl* **-aux** /ɔʀjɑ̃tal, o/ *adj* [*côte*] eastern; [*civilisation, langues, art, type*] oriental.

Oriental, **~e**, *mpl* **-aux** /ɔʀjɑ̃tal, o/ *nm,f* Asian; **les Orientaux** Asians.

orientaliser /ɔʀjɑ̃talize/ [1] **I** *vtr* to orientalize.

II s'orientaliser *vpr* to become orientalized.

orientalisme /ɔʀjɑ̃talism/ *nm* orientalism.

orientaliste /ɔʀjɑ̃talist/ *adj, nmf* Orientalist.

orientation /ɔʀjɑ̃tasjɔ̃/ *nf* **1** (position) (de maison) aspect; (d'antenne) angle; (de projecteur) direction; **la maison a une ~ plein sud** the house faces directly south; **2** (d'enquête, de recherche, politique) direction; **prendre une nouvelle ~** to change direction; **les ~s de l'art moderne** modern art trends; **3** Scol, Univ **l'~** (conseils) advice to students on which courses to follow; **changer d'~** to change courses; **faire une erreur d'~** to choose the wrong course; **l'~ des jeunes vers les carrières scientifiques** encouraging young people toward(s) careers in the sciences; **4** (tendance politique) leanings (*pl*); **5** (action de s'orienter) finding one's bearings; **l'~** Sport orienteering; **faire de l'~** to go orienteering; **6** Math orientation.

■ ~ professionnelle (pour un emploi) careers advice; (plus général) vocational counselling ou guidance; **~ scolaire** curriculum counselling GB, counselling US.

orienté, **~e** /ɔʀjɑ̃te/ **I** *pp* **▶ orienter**.

II *pp adj* **1** (disposé) **maison ~e d'est en ouest** house which has an east-west aspect; **bien/mal ~** [*maison*] in a good/bad position ou situation; [*phare*] shining in the right/wrong direction; **région ~e vers le tourisme et l'agriculture** region geared to tourism and farming; **2** (non objectif) [*reportage*] biased[GB], slanted; **3** Géog [*carte, plan*] showing grid north (*après n*); Math [*vecteur, axe*] directed.

orienter /ɔʀjɑ̃te/ [1] **I** *vtr* **1** (positionner) to decide on the aspect of [*maison*]; to adjust [*antenne, lampe, bras de machine*] (**vers** to); **~ la maison/terrasse vers le sud** or (**face**) **au sud** to make the house/terrace south-facing; **~ le spot vers le fond** to direct the spotlight toward(s) the back; **~ l'antenne vers l'ouest** to make the aerial face west; **2** (faire porter) to channel [*fonds publics*]; **~ qch sur qch** [*enquête, fonds publics*] to focus sth on sth; **~ la conversation sur** to bring the conversation around to; **3** (donner un sens idéologique à) to slant [*cours, conférence*]; **4** (guider) to direct [*personne*] (**vers** to); **5** Scol, Univ (conseiller) to give [sb] some career advice; **~ qn vers un spécialiste** to send sb to a specialist; **~ qn vers les sciences** to direct ou steer sb towards science subjects; **6** (flécher) to show grid north on [*carte, plan*]; Math to direct [*axe*]; **7** Naut to trim [*voile*].

II **s'orienter** *vpr* **1** (se repérer) to get ou to find one's bearings; **2** (se diriger) **s'~ vers** lit to turn toward(s); fig [*pays, mouvement*] to move toward(s); [*conversation*] to turn to; **s'~ vers les sciences/carrières scientifiques** to go in for science subjects/a career in science.

orienteur, **-euse** /ɔʀjɑ̃tœʀ, øz/ ▶510 *nm,f* careers adviser.

orifice /ɔʀifis/ *nm* **1** Anat orifice; **2** gén (de tuyau) mouth; (de puits) opening; (de tube) neck.

oriflamme /ɔʀiflam/ *nf* Hist oriflamme; (bannière d'apparat) banner.

origami /ɔʀigami/ *nm* origami.

origan /ɔʀigɑ̃/ *nm* oregano.

originaire /ɔʀiʒinɛʀ/ *adj* **1** (provenant) [*plante, animal*] native (**de** to); **produit ~ d'Afrique** product from ou originating from Africa; **famille ~ d'Asie** Asian family; **il est ~ d'Afrique** he is originally from Africa; **le pays dont il est ~** his native country; **2** (d'origine) [*tare, état*] original; [*déformation*] inherent.

originairement /ɔʀiʒinɛʀmɑ̃/ *adv* originally.

original, **~e**, *mpl* **-aux** /ɔʀiʒinal, o/ I *adj* **1** (authentique) [*document, tableau*] original; **2** (créatif) [*esprit, personnalité, œuvre, idée, décor*] original; **c'est ~ comme idée** that's an original idea; **3** (bizarre) [*personne, manières, vêtements*] eccentric.

II *nm,f* (personne excentrique) eccentric, oddball°.

III *nm* (œuvre primitive) original; **l'~ est au Prado** the original is in the Prado.

originalement /ɔʀiʒinalmɑ̃/ *adv* **1** (de façon créative) in an original way; **2** (à l'origine) originally.

originalité /ɔʀiʒinalite/ *nf* **1** (créativité) originality; **écrivain d'une grande ~** writer of great originality; **sans ~** unoriginal; **2** (aspect original) original aspect; **les ~s d'un livre** the original aspects of a book; **3** (excentricité) eccentricity.

origine /ɔʀiʒin/ *nf* **1** (provenance) origin; **toutes ~s confondues** of all origins; **tradition/mot/tissu d'~ italienne** tradition/word/fabric of Italian origin; **de toutes les ~s sociales** [*personnes*] from all walks of life; **être d'~ modeste/noble** to come from a modest/noble background; **famille d'~ modeste/noble** family of modest/noble origins; **être d'~ grecque** [*personne*] to be of Greek extraction; **être d'~ paysanne** [*personne*] to come from a farming family; **2** (commencement) origin; **l'~ de la vie/l'univers** the origin of life/the universe; **l'histoire de la Chine des ~s à nos jours** the history of China from its origins to the present day; **l'~ des temps** the beginning of time; **dès l'~** (de projet, technique) right from the start; (du monde) from the very beginning; **à l'~** originally; **d'~** [*pays*] of origin; [*moteur, objet, vitraux*] original; **3** (source) origin; **produit d'~ végétale/animale** product of vegetable/animal origin; **conflit d'~ raciale** conflict of racial origin; **à l'~ du conflit il y a un problème frontalier** the conflict has its origins in a border dispute; **trouver** or **avoir son ~ dans** to have its roots in; **maladie d'~ virale** viral disease; **pollution d'~ agricole/industrielle** agricultural/industrial pollution; **4** Math origin.

originel, **-elle** /ɔʀiʒinɛl/ *adj* original.

originellement /ɔʀiʒinɛlmɑ̃/ *adv* **1** (au début) originally; **2** (dès le début) from the start.

orignal, *pl* **-aux** /ɔʀiɲal, o/ *nm* moose (*inv*).

oripeaux /ɔʀipo/ *nmpl* faded finery ¢.

ORL /oɛʀɛl/ I *nmf* (*abbr* = **oto-rhino-laryngologiste**) ENT specialist.

II *nf* (*abbr* = **oto-rhino-laryngologie**) ENT.

orléanais, **~e** /ɔʀleanɛ, ɛz/ *adj* **1** ▶692 (de l'Orléanais) of the Orléans region; **2** ▶857 (d'Orléans) of Orléans.

Orléanais, **~e** /ɔʀleanɛ, ɛz/ ▶857 I *nm,f* (natif) native of Orléans; (habitant) inhabitant of Orléans.

II ▶692 *nm*: the Orléans region.

orléaniste /ɔʀleanist/ *adj, nmf* Orleanist.

Orléans /ɔʀleɑ̃/ ▶857 *npr* Orléans.

orlon® /ɔʀlɔ̃/ *nm* Orlon®.

orme /ɔʀm/ *nm* **1** (arbre) elm (tree); **2** (bois) elm (wood); **en ~** in elm.

ormeau, *pl* **~x** /ɔʀmo/ *nm* **1** Bot young elm tree; **2** Zool ormer GB, abalone US.

Orne /ɔʀn/ ▶357, 692 *nprf* (fleuve, département) **l'~** the Orne.

orné, **~e** /ɔʀne/ I *pp* ▶ **orner**.

II *pp adj* [*style*] ornate.

ornement /ɔʀnəmɑ̃/ *nm* **1** gén ornament; **jardin/arbres/plantes d'~** ornamental garden/trees/plants; **2** (de texte) embellishment; **3** Archit, Art decorative detail; **dessin d'~** decorative illustration; **4** Mus ornament, grace note.

■ **~s sacerdotaux** vestments.

ornemental, **~e**, *mpl* **-aux** /ɔʀnəmɑ̃tal, o/ *adj* ornamental.

ornementation /ɔʀnəmɑ̃tasjɔ̃/ *nf* ornamentation.

ornementer /ɔʀnəmɑ̃te/ [1] *vtr* to decorate (**de** with), to adorn (**de** with).

orner /ɔʀne/ [1] *vtr* **1** (décorer) [*personne*] to decorate [*maison, jardin*] (**de** with); to trim [*vêtement, chapeau*] (**de** with); **2** (embellir) [*ornement*] to adorn [*maison, jardin, vêtement, chapeau*]; [*personne*] to embellish [*style, texte*] (**de** with); **de belles gravures ornaient les murs** the walls were hung with beautiful prints.

ornière /ɔʀnjɛʀ/ *nf* rut; **le chemin est plein d'~s** lit the track is full of ruts; fig the way is full of pitfalls; **sortir de l'~** fig (de la routine) to get out of a rut; (d'une situation difficile) to get out of a difficult ou tricky° situation.

ornithologie /ɔʀnitɔlɔʒi/ *nf* ornithology.

ornithologique /ɔʀnitɔlɔʒik/ *adj* ornithological.

ornithologue /ɔʀnitɔlɔg/ ▶510 *nmf* ornithologist; **~ amateur** birdwatcher.

ornithorynque /ɔʀnitɔʀɛ̃k/ *nm* (duck-billed) platypus, duckbill US.

orogénèse /ɔʀɔʒenɛz/ *nf* orogeny.

orogénie /ɔʀɔʒeni/ *nf* Géol, Sci orogeny.

orogénique /ɔʀɔʒenik/ *adj* orogenic.

orographie /ɔʀɔgʀafi/ *nf* orography.

orographique /ɔʀɔgʀafik/ *adj* orographic.

oronge /ɔʀɔ̃ʒ/ *nf* agaric; **fausse ~** fly agaric.

orpaillage /ɔʀpajaʒ/ *nm* panning for gold.

orpailleur /ɔʀpajœʀ/ ▶510 *nm* gold panner.

Orphée /ɔʀfe/ *npr* Orpheus.

orphelin, **~e** /ɔʀfəlɛ̃, in/ I *adj* **1** lit (de père et mère) orphan; **être ~** to be an orphan; **être ~ de père/mère** to be fatherless/motherless; **2** fig **se sentir ~** to feel abandoned.

II *nm,f* orphan.

IDIOMES **défendre la veuve et l'~** to defend the weak.

orphelinat /ɔʀfəlina/ *nm* orphanage.

orphéon /ɔʀfeɔ̃/ *nm* town band.

orphie /ɔʀfi/ *nf* garfish.

orphisme /ɔʀfism/ *nm* Orphism.

orpin /ɔʀpɛ̃/ *nm* stonecrop.

orque /ɔʀk/ *nm* ou *f* killer whale.

ORSEC /ɔʀsɛk/ *adj* (*abbr* = **organisation des secours**) **plan ~** *official measures set up for major civil emergencies.*

orteil /ɔʀtɛj/ ▶188 *nm* toe; **gros ~** big toe.

ORTF /oɛʀteɛf/ *nf* (*abbr* = **Office de la radiodiffusion-télévision française**) *former name of French broadcasting service.*

orthocentre /ɔʀtɔsɑ̃tʀ/ *nm* orthocentre[GB].

orthodontie /ɔʀtɔdɔ̃ti/ *nf* orthodontics (+ *v sg*).

orthodontiste /ɔʀtɔdɔ̃tist/ ▶510 *nmf* orthodontist.

orthodoxe /ɔʀtɔdɔks/ I *adj* **1** (accepté) orthodox; **méthodes peu ~s** rather unorthodox methods; **2** Relig Orthodox.

II *nmf* Relig Orthodox.

orthodoxie /ɔʀtɔdɔksi/ *nf* **1** (conformisme) orthodoxy; **2** Relig **l'~** Orthodoxy.

orthogénèse /ɔʀtɔʒenɛz/ *nf* orthogenesis.

orthogénie /ɔʀtɔʒeni/ *nf* birth control; **centre d'~** family planning clinic.

orthogonal, **~e**, *mpl* **-aux** /ɔʀtɔgɔnal, o/ *adj* orthogonal.

orthographe /ɔʀtɔgʀaf/ ▶564 *nf* **1** (forme écrite) spelling; **quelle est l'~ de...?** how do you spell...?; **avoir une bonne/mauvaise ~** to be good/bad at spelling; **2** Scol (matière) spelling ¢; **être bon en ~** to be good at spelling; **avoir une bonne note en ~** to have a good mark GB ou grade US for spelling.

orthographier /ɔʀtɔgʀafje/ [2] I *vtr* to spell; **mot mal orthographié** misspelled word.

II **s'orthographier** *vpr* to be spelled.

orthographique /ɔʀtɔgʀafik/ *adj* [*règle*] spelling (*épith*), orthographic; **correcteur ~** Ordinat spellchecker.

orthonormé, **~e** /ɔʀtɔnɔʀme/ *adj* orthonormal.

orthopédie /ɔʀtɔpedi/ *nf* orthopedics (+ *v sg*); **~ néo-natale/dento-faciale** pediatric/dento-facial orthopedics; **service d'~** orthopedic department.

orthopédique /ɔʀtɔpedik/ *adj* orthopedic.

orthopédiste /ɔʀtɔpedist/ ▶510 *nmf* **1** Méd orthopedic specialist, orthopedist; **chirurgien ~** orthopedic surgeon; **2** (fabricant d'appareils) manufacturer of orthopedic appliances.

orthophonie /ɔʀtɔfɔni/ *nf* speech therapy.

orthophoniste /ɔʀtɔfɔnist/ ▶510 *nmf* speech therapist.

ortie /ɔʀti/ *nf* (stinging) nettle; **se piquer aux ~s** to get stung in the nettles; **soupe d'~** nettle soup; ▶ **froc**.

■ **~ blanche** white nettle.

IDIOMES **faut pas pousser pépé** or **mémé dans les ~s**° that's going a bit far.

ortolan /ɔʀtɔlɑ̃/ *nm* ortolan.

orvet /ɔʀvɛ/ *nm* slowworm, blindworm.

os /ɔs, *pl* o/ I *nm inv* **1** (élément) bone; **avoir de gros ~** to be big-boned; **en chair et en ~** in the flesh; **n'avoir que la peau sur les ~**° to be all skin and bone; **se rompre les ~**° to break one's neck°; **de la viande vendue avec/sans ~** meat sold on/off the bone; **2** (matière) bone; **un peigne/manche de couteau en ~** a bone comb/knife handle; **un couteau avec un manche en ~** a bone-handled knife; **3** Géol esker.

II *nmpl* (restes mortuaires) **les ~** the remains.

■ **~ à moelle** Culin marrowbone; **~ de seiche** Zool cuttlebone.

IDIOMES **l'avoir dans l'~**◑ to be screwed◑, to be unlucky; **il y a un ~**° there's a hitch;

L'orthographe et la ponctuation

L'alphabet anglais

La liste suivante indique la prononciation de chaque lettre, et donne pour chacun un moyen, parmi d'autres, d'épeler clairement en cas de difficultés. Certains utilisent pour cela l'alphabet des pilotes, d'autres celui des téléphonistes présenté ci-dessous.

A	[eɪ]	A for Alfred	O	[əʊ]	O for Oliver
B	[bi:]	B for beautiful	P	[pi:]	P for Peter
C	[si:]	C for cat	Q	[kju:]	Q for quite
D	[di:]	D for dog	R	[ɑ:(r)]	R for Robert
E	[i:]	E for elephant	S	[es]	S for sugar
F	[ef]	F for father	T	[(t)i:]	T for Tommy
G	[dʒi:]*	G for George	U	[ju:]	U for uncle
H	[eɪtʃ]	H for Harry	V	[vi:]	V for victory
I	[aɪ]	I for Ireland	W	['dʌblju:]	W for Walter
J	[dʒeɪ]*	J for John	X	[eks]	X for X-ray
K	[keɪ]	K for kangaroo	Y	[waɪ]	Y for yellow
L	[el]	L for London	Z	[zed] (*GB*)	Z for zoo
M	[em]	M for mother	*ou*	[zi:] (*US*)	
N	[en]	N for nothing			

Pour épeler

A majuscule	= capital A	
a minuscule	= small a	
ça s'écrit avec un A majuscule	= it has got a capital A	
en majuscules	= in capital letters *ou* in capitals	
en minuscules	= in small letters	
deux l	= double l	
deux n	= double n	
deux t	= double t	
à (a accent grave)	= a grave	[eɪ grɑ:v]
é (e accent aigu)	= e acute	[i: ə'kju:t]
è (e accent grave)	= e grave	[i: grɑ:v]
ê (e accent circonflexe)	= e circumflex	[i: 'sɜ:kəmfleks]
ë (e tréma)	= e diaeresis (*on dira parfois, plus simplement:* e with two dots)	[i: daɪ'erəsɪs]
ù (u accent grave)	= u grave	[ju: grɑ:v]
ç (c cédille)	= c cedilla	[si: sɪ'dɪlə]
l' (l apostrophe)	= l apostrophe	[el ə'pɒstrəfi]
d' (d apostrophe)	= d apostrophe	[di: ə'pɒstrəfi]
- (trait d'union)	= hyphen	['haɪfn]
"rase-mottes" s'écrit avec un trait d'union	= "rase-mottes" has a hyphen	

Pour dicter la ponctuation

un point	.	= full stop (*GB*) *ou* period (*US*)
à la ligne		= new paragraph
virgule	,	= comma
deux points	:	= colon†
point-virgule	;	= semi-colon†
point d'exclamation	!	= exclamation mark (*GB*) *ou* exclamation point (*US*)†
point d'interrogation	?	= question mark†
ouvrez la parenthèse	(	= open brackets
fermez la parenthèse	)	= close brackets
entre parenthèses	( )	= in brackets
entre crochets	[ ]	= in square brackets
tiret	-	= dash
points de suspension	...	= three dots (*GB*) *ou* suspension points (*US*)
ouvrez les guillemets	" *ou* ' ‡	= open inverted commas (*GB*) *ou* open quotation marks (*US*)
fermez les guillemets	" *ou* '	= close inverted commas (*GB*) close quotation marks (*US*)
entre guillemets	" " *ou* ' '	= in inverted commas (*GB*) in quotation marks (*US*) *ou* in quotes

La ponctuation des dialogues

La ponctuation des dialogues n'est pas la même dans les deux langues.

En français, le dialogue commence par le signe « *(maintenant souvent remplacé par un tiret, ou par* "*), chaque prise de parole est signalée par un tiret, le dialogue est clos par* » *(ou par* "*) et les interventions du narrateur (dit-il, remarqua-t-elle etc.) ne sont pas séparées du dialogue par un quelconque signe de ponctuation. En anglais, chaque prise de parole commence par* " *ou* ', *et se termine par* " *ou* '. *Ces mêmes signes sont utilisés avant et après chaque intervention du narrateur à l'intérieur d'une réplique. Exemple:*

"Well, I don't know," she said, "what to make of all this!"

* *Noter que les francophones confondent souvent les prononciations anglaises de G et de J.*

† *Noter qu'en anglais les deux points, le point-virgule, le point d'exclamation et le point d'interrogation ne sont pas précédés par un espace.*

Il a dit oui ; je ne sais pas pourquoi. = He said he would; I don't know why.
Voici pourquoi : je n'ai pas pu ! = This is why: I could not!

‡ *Noter que les guillemets anglais (*" *ou* '*) sont placés au dessus de la ligne.*

jusqu'à l'~○ completely; **donner un ~ à ronger à qn**○ to keep sb busy; **tomber sur un ~**○ to come across a snag; **être trempé jusqu'aux ~**○ to be soaked to the skin○; **s'il continue à boire ainsi, il ne va pas faire de vieux ~** (ne pas vivre longtemps) if he goes on drinking like this, he'll never make old bones; **je ne vais pas faire de vieux ~ ici** (ne pas s'éterniser) I'm not going to hang around here forever.

OS /ɔɛs/ *nm*: *abbr* ▶ **ouvrier**.

oscar /ɔskaʀ/ *nm* Cin Oscar; Mus, Pub award.

oscillateur /ɔsilatœʀ/ *nm* oscillator.

oscillation /ɔsilasjɔ̃/ *nf* **1** Phys, Télécom oscillation; **2** (balancement) (de pendule, métronome) swinging; (de navire) rocking; (du corps) swaying; **3** (variation) fluctuation; **les ~s de température** temperature fluctuations ou swings.

oscillatoire /ɔsilatwaʀ/ *adj* oscillatory.

osciller /ɔsile/ [1] *vi* **1** (se balancer) [*pendule*] to swing; [*navire*] to rock; [*foule*] to sway; [*tête*] to roll from side to side; **2** (fluctuer) [*monnaie*] to fluctuate; **3** (hésiter) to vacillate (**entre** between).

oscillogramme /ɔsilɔgʀam/ *nm* oscillogram.

oscillographe /ɔsilɔgʀaf/ *nm* oscillograph.

oscilloscope /ɔsilɔskɔp/ *nm* oscilloscope.

osé, **~e** /oze/ **I** *pp* ▶ **oser**.
II *pp adj* **1** (licencieux) [*livre, film*] risqué; **2** (audacieux) [*comportement*] daring; [*paroles*] outspoken.

oseille /ozɛj/ *nf* **1** Bot, Culin sorrel; **2**○ (argent) dough○, money; **avoir de l'~** to be rolling in it○, to be loaded○.

oser /oze/ [1] *vtr* to dare; **elle ose partir** she dares leave; **je n'ose pas demander** I daren't ask, I don't dare ask; **il a osé rester** he dared to stay; **ils n'ont pas osé répondre** they dared not answer, they didn't dare answer; **elle n'osait plus leur parler** she no longer dared speak to them; **comment oses-tu demander?** how dare you ask?; **comment as-tu osé partir?** how did you dare leave?; **répète si tu l'oses!** don't you dare repeat that!; **tu n'oserais pas!** you wouldn't dare!; **je n'ose croire/espérer que** I hardly dare believe/hope that; **j'ose croire que** I'd go so far as to believe that; **j'ose espérer que** I would hope that; **j'oserais dire que** I would venture to say that; **si j'ose dire** if I may say so.

oseraie /ozʀɛ/ *nf* willow bed.

osier /ozje/ *nm* **1** (arbre) osier; **2** (bois) osier, wicker; **une chaise en ~** a wicker chair.

Osiris /oziʀis/ *npr* Osiris.

Oslo /ɔslo/ ▶ **857** *npr* Oslo.

osmose /ɔsmoz/ *nf* lit, fig osmosis.

osmotique /ɔsmɔtik/ *adj* osmotic.

osque /ɔsk/ *adj, nm* Oscan.

ossature /ɔsatyʀ/ *nf* **1** Anat skeleton; **avoir une forte ~** to be big-boned; **~ du visage** bone structure; **2** Archit, Littérat, Mus, Tech framework; **3** Géol backbone.

osséine /ɔsein/ *nf* ossein.

osselet /ɔslɛ/ *nm* **1** Anat small bone; **~ de l'oreille** ossicle; **2** ▶ **449** Jeux (pièce) jack, knucklebone; (jeu) **les ~** jacks.

ossements /ɔsmɑ̃/ *nmpl* remains.

ossète /ɔsɛt/ **I** *adj* Osset.
II ▶ **462** *nm* Ling Ossetic.

Ossétie /ɔseti/ ▶ **692** *nprf* **l'~** Ossetia; **~ du Nord/Sud** North/South Ossetian region.

osseux, **-euse** /ɔsø, øz/ *adj* **1** [*personne, visage, charpente*] bony; **2** [*masse, croissance, système, maladie*] bone (*épith*).

ossification /ɔsifikasjɔ̃/ *nf* Biol, Méd ossification.

ossifier /ɔsifje/ [2] **I** *vtr* to ossify.
II s'ossifier *vpr* Biol, Méd to ossify.

osso buco /ɔsobuko/ *nm* osso bucco.

ossu, **~e** /ɔsy/ *adj* big-boned.

ossuaire /ɔsɥɛʀ/ *nm* ossuary.

ostéite /ɔsteit/ ▶ **271** *nf* osteitis.

ostensible /ɔstɑ̃sibl/ *adj* obvious.

ostensiblement /ɔstɑ̃sibləmɑ̃/ *adv* (manifestement) obviously; (sans se cacher) openly.

ostensoir /ɔstɑ̃swaʀ/ *nm* monstrance.

ostentation /ɔstɑ̃tasjɔ̃/ *nf* ostentation.

ostentatoire /ɔstɑ̃tatwaʀ/ *adj* ostentatious.

ostéoblaste /ɔsteoblast/ *nm* osteoblast.

ostéogenèse /ɔsteoʒənɛz/ *nf* osteogenesis.

ostéologie /ɔsteolɔʒi/ *nf* osteology.

ostéomyélite /ɔsteɔmjelit/ ▶ **271** *nf* osteomyelitis.

ostéopathe /ɔsteɔpat/ ▶ **510** *nmf* osteopath.

ostéopathie /ɔsteɔpati/ *nf* osteopathy.

ostéophyte /ɔsteɔfit/ *nm* osteophyte.

ostéoplastie /ɔsteɔplasti/ *nf* osteoplasty.

ostéoporose /ɔsteɔpɔʀoz/ ▶ **271** *nf* osteoporosis.

ostéotomie /ɔsteɔtɔmi/ *nf* osteotomy.

ostracisme /ɔstʀasism/ *nm* ostracism; Pol **être frappé d'~** to be ostracized.

ostréiculteur, **-trice** /ɔstʀeikyltœʀ, tʀis/ ▶ **510** *nm,f* oyster farmer.

ostréiculture /ɔstʀeikyltyʀ/ *nf* oyster farming, ostreiculture spéc.

ostrogoth, **~e** /ɔstʀɔgo, ɔt/ **I** *adj* Ostrogothic.
II *nm* fig barbarian.

Ostrogoths /ɔstʀɔgo/ *nprmpl* Ostrogoths.

otage /ɔtaʒ/ *nm* gén, Pol hostage; **être pris en ~** to be taken hostage; **prise d'~s** hostage-taking; **plusieurs prises d'~s** several instances of hostage-taking; **les grévistes tiennent les voyageurs en ~** fig the strikers are holding the passengers to ransom.

OTAN /ɔtɑ̃/ *nf* (*abbr* = **Organisation du traité de l'Atlantique Nord**) NATO.

otarie /ɔtaʀi/ *nf* eared seal, otary.

OTASE /ɔtaz/ *nf* (*abbr* = **Organisation du traité de l'Asie du Sud-Est**) SEATO.

ôter /ote/ [1] **I** *vtr* **1** (se débarrasser de) to take off [*vêtement, lunettes*]; to remove [*arête, étiquette, tache*] (**de** from); **~ le couvert** to clear the table; **ôte tes pieds du fauteuil** take your feet off the chair; **cela m'ôte un poids (de la poitrine)** that's a load off my mind; **ça ôte de son amertume au thé** it makes tea less bitter; ▶ **épine**, **pain**; **2** (retirer) fml **~ qch à qn** to take sth away from sb; **~ l'appétit à qn** to take away ou spoil sb's appetite; **~ tout espoir à qn** to dash sb's hopes; **~ la vie à qn** to take sb's life; **~ à qn l'envie de recommencer** to cure sb of any desire to try it again; **ôtez-leur cette idée de la tête** get that idea out of their heads; **on ne m'ôtera pas de l'idée qu'ils le savaient** I'm still convinced that they knew; **ce qui ne lui ôte rien de son charme/sa saveur** which doesn't in any way detract from its charm/flavour[GB]; **3** Math (retrancher) to take [sth] (**à** away from); **4 ôté de 9, il reste 5** 9 minus ou less ou take away 4 leaves 5.

II s'ôter *vpr* **1** (s'enlever) fml **s'~ qch de l'esprit** or **la tête** to get sth out of one's mind ou head; **2** (se déplacer) **ôte-toi de là!** move!

otite /ɔtit/ ▶ **271** *nf* inflammation of the ear, otitis spéc; **avoir une ~** to have earache, to have otitis spéc; **~ externe/interne** inflammation of the outer/inner ear.

oto-rhino○, *pl* **~s** /otoʀino/ *nmf* (*abbr* = **oto-rhino-laryngologiste**) ENT specialist.

oto-rhino-laryngologie /otoʀinolaʀɛ̃gɔlɔʒi/ *nf* ENT, otorhinolaringology.

oto-rhino-laryngologiste, *pl* **~s** /otoʀinolaʀɛ̃gɔlɔʒist/ ▶ **510** *nmf* ENT specialist.

otoscope /ɔtɔskɔp/ *nm* otoscope.

Ottawa /ɔtawa/ ▶ **857** *npr* Ottawa.

ottoman, **~e** /ɔtɔmɑ̃, an/ **I** *adj* Hist Ottoman.

II *nm* Tex ottoman.

III ottomane *nf* (fauteuil) ottoman.

Ottoman, **~e** /ɔtɔmɑ̃, an/ *nm,f* Ottoman.

ou /u/ *conj* **1** (choix) or; **désirez-vous boire de la bière ~ (bien) du vin?** would you like to drink beer or wine?; **tu pourrais lui offrir un collier, ~ (bien) une montre** you could give her a necklace, or (else) a watch; **tu entres ~ tu sors?** are you coming in or are you going out?; **est-ce que tu viens ~ pas?** are you coming or not?; **Istanbul ~ Constantinople** Istanbul or Constantinople; **tu te moques de moi ~ quoi?** are you making fun of me or what?; **donnons-nous rendez-vous à la Sorbonne, ~ plutôt non, au Panthéon** let's meet at the Sorbonne, or rather at the Pantheon; **je me contenterais d'un petit appartement ~ même d'une chambre** I would be happy with a small apartment, or even just a room; **tu peux venir me prendre chez moi, ~ alors on s'attend devant le cinéma** you can pick me up at home or else we'll meet outside the cinema; **fatigué ~ pas, il faut bien rentrer à la maison** tired or not, we have to go home; **que ça vous plaise ~ non** whether you like it or not; **je peux vous proposer du gin, du cognac ~ (encore) de la vodka** I can offer you gin, brandy or vodka; **2** (choix unique) or; **~ (bien)... ~ (bien)...** either... or...; **~ (bien) vous éteignez votre cigarette, ~ (bien) vous sortez** either you put out your cigarette or you leave the room; **~ bien il est très timide, ~ il est très impoli** he's either very shy or very rude; **de deux choses l'une, ~ il est étourdi ~ (bien) il est bête** it's one of two things, he's either absent-minded or he's stupid; **3** (évaluation) or; **il y avait trois ~ quatre cents personnes dans la salle** there were three or four hundred people in the room; **ils vont rester deux ~ trois jours** they'll stay two or three days.

où

où adverbe de lieu se traduit généralement par *where* dans les interrogations directes ou indirectes:

où es-tu? = where are you?
sais-tu où il est? = do you know where he is?

Lorsque la traduction du verbe de la proposition relative introduite par *où* pronom relatif est un verbe à particule, trois traductions sont possibles:

la ville où nous sommes passés = the town we passed through
ou the town that we passed through
ou the town which we passed through
ou the town through which we passed

Les trois premières traductions sont utilisées dans la langue courante, parlée ou écrite; la quatrième traduction sera préférée dans une langue plus soutenue, surtout écrite.

Pour simplifier la lecture des exemples, une seule traduction sera fournie mais il est toujours possible de générer les variantes sur les modèles donnés ci-dessus.

Lorsque *où* pronom relatif a une valeur temporelle, souvent il ne se traduit pas:

au moment où j'allais partir = at the moment I was about to leave

ou bien il se traduit par *when*:

c'était l'époque où j'habitais à Oxford = that was (the time) when I lived in Oxford

Attention, lorsque la proposition relative est au futur en français, elle est au présent en anglais:

le jour où elle arrivera = the day she arrives
un jour où tu auras le temps = one day when you have time

Pour les emplois abstraits et temporels de *où*, reportez-vous à l'article ci-dessous.

où /u/ **I** *adv inter* **1** lit where; **~ travailles-/vas-tu?** where do you work/are you going?; **je me demande/j'aimerais savoir ~...** I wonder/I'd like to know where...; **~ est-ce que tu vas?** where are you going?; **~ ça?** where's that?; **~ donc?** where on earth○?; **je l'ai perdu je ne sais ~** I've lost it somewhere or other; **elle l'a rencontré je ne sais ~** God knows where she met him; **par ~ êtes-vous passés pour venir?** which way did you come?; **pour ~ est-il parti?** where has he left for?; **vers ~ s'est-il dirigé?** which way did he go?; **je ne sais pas d'~ elle vient** I don't know where she comes from; **2** fig where; **~ en étais-je?** where was I?; **~ en êtes-vous?** (à quel stade) where have you got to?; (comment ça va) how is it going?; **tu vois ~ je veux en venir?** you see what I am getting at?; **~ allons-nous?** (quelle époque!) what are things coming to!; **d'~ vient cette habitude?** where does this habit come from?; **d'~ tenez-vous que?** where did you get the idea that?

II *pron rel* **1** (locatif) where; **le quartier ~ nous habitons** the area we live in, the area in which we live; **un lieu** or **endroit ~ faire** a place ou somewhere to do; **trouver un endroit ~ dormir** to find a place ou somewhere to sleep; **la région d'~ ils se sont enfuis** the area from which they escaped ou they escaped from; **nous sommes montés jusqu'au sommet, d'~ il y a une vue magnifique** we went all the way to the summit, from where there was a magnificent view; **d'~ s'élevait de la fumée** out of which smoke was rising; **les villes par ~ nous sommes passés** the towns we passed through; **~ tu iras, j'irai** where ou wherever you go, I'll go ; **ils sont allés ~ vous leur avez dit** they went where you told them to; **j'ai décidé de rester ~ je suis** I've decided to stay where I am; **~ qu'ils aillent/qu'elle soit** wherever they go/she is; **d'~ que vous veniez** wherever you come from; **2** (abstrait) **le monde ~ j'allais pénétrer** the world (which ou that) I was about to enter; **le chagrin ~ elle se trouvait** the grief (which ou that) she was experiencing; **la misère ~ elle se trouvait** the poverty in which she was living, the poverty she was living in; **elle entre dans une famille ~ tout est différent** she's joining a family where ou in which everything's different; **l'école d'~ elle sort est très réputée** the school she went to is very well-known; **au train** or **au rythme** or **à l'allure ~ vont les choses** (at) the rate things are going; **le travail s'est accumulé, d'~ ce retard** there is a backlog of work, hence the delay; **d'~ l'on peut conclure que** from which we can conclude that; **d'~ leur colère** hence their anger; **3** (temporel) when; **il fut un temps/je me souviens de la fois ~** there was a time/I remember the time when; **elle est à l'âge ~** she's at the age when ou where; **le matin ~ je l'ai rencontré** the morning I met him; **~ il se trompe, c'est lorsqu'il s'imagine que** where he goes wrong is in thinking that; **à l'instant ~ tu m'as appelé** just when you rang; **~ j'ai craqué, c'est quand on m'a refusé une augmentation** what made me flip was when they refused to give me a rise; **~ on voit le héros...** (en tête de chapitre) where we see the hero...

OUA /oya/ *nf* (*abbr* = **Organisation de l'unité africaine**) OAU.

Ouagadougou /uagadugu/ ▶ **857** *npr* Ouagadougou.

ouah○ /wa/ *excl* wow○!

ouailles /waj/ *nfpl* Relig flock (*sg*); **une de mes ~** one of my flock.

ouais○ /wɛ/ *adv* yes, yeah○; **ah ~?** oh yeah?; **~, ~, j'arrive!** OK, OK○, I'm coming!; **~, moi je n'y crois pas** well, I don't believe it myself.

ouananiche /wananiʃ/ *nf* C landlocked salmon.

ouaouaron /wawaʀɔ̃/ *nm* C bull frog.

ouate /wat/ *nf* **1** Pharm cotton wool GB, cotton US; **2** Tex wadding; **~ de cellulose** cellulose wadding; **doublé d'~** wadded.

■ **~ chirurgicale** Pharm surgical cotton wool GB, surgical cotton US; **~ hydrophile** Pharm cotton wool GB, absorbent cotton US.

ouaté, **~e** /wate/ **I** *pp* ▶ **ouater**.

II *pp adj* **1** Tex [*vêtement, tissu*] wadded; **2** fig [*ambiance*] cocoon-like; [*bruit, pas*] muffled.

ouater /wate/ [1] *vtr* Tex to wad.

ouatine /watin/ *nf* wadding, padding.

ouatiné, **~e** /watine/ *adj* Tex [*doublure, robe de chambre*] quilted.

oubli /ubli/ *nm* **1** (fait d'oublier) **l'~ de qch** gén forgetting sth; (de devoir) neglect of sth; **l'~ des autres** forgetting other people; **elle cherche l'~ dans la boisson** she drinks to forget; **le temps apporte l'~** time passes and men forget; **2** (omission) **c'est un simple ~** it's just an oversight;

cet ouvrage contient de regrettables ~s there are some regrettable omissions in this work; **3** (anonymat après la mort) oblivion littér; **tirer qch/qn de l'~** to rescue sth/sb from oblivion; **tomber dans l'~** to be completely forgotten, to sink into oblivion.
■ **~ de soi(-même)** selflessness.

oublié, **~e** /ublije/ *nm,f* **les ~s de la société** those who are overlooked by society ou left out in the cold.

oublier /ublije/ [2] **I** *vtr* **1** (ne pas se souvenir de) to forget [*nom, date, fait*]; (ne pas penser à) to forget about [*soucis, famille, incident*]; (ne pas prendre) to leave; **j'ai oublié mes clés/mon parapluie chez elle** I've left my keys/my umbrella at her house; **n'oublie pas ton parapluie** don't forget your umbrella; **quand je travaille, j'oublie l'heure** when I'm working, I forget about the time; **le plombier nous a oubliés** the plumber has forgotten us; **ah, j'oubliais, Isabelle a téléphoné** oh, I nearly forgot, Isabelle phoned; **elle a oublié ce qu'elle voulait dire** she's forgotten ou she can't remember what she wanted to say; **rien ne pourra me faire ~ ce moment** I shall never forget that moment, nothing can efface the memory of that moment litt ér; **son enthousiasme fait ~ son âge** she is so enthusiastic, you forget her age; **~ de faire/pourquoi/comment** to forget to do/why/how; **~ que** to forget that; **se faire ~** to keep a low profile, to lie low○; **2** (omettre) to leave [sth] out, to forget [*personne, détail, virgule*]; **tu oublies de dire que** you forget ou omit to mention that; **mon nom a été oublié de la liste** they've left my name off the list; **3** (négliger) to forget, to neglect [*devoir, ami*].
II s'oublier *vpr* **1** [*souvenir, fait*] to be forgotten; **ce sont des choses qui ne s'oublient pas** these things can't be forgotten, it's not the sort of thing you forget; **2** (négliger de se servir) to leave oneself out; **3** fml (perdre le sens des convenances) to forget oneself; **4** euph (faire ses besoins) [*enfant, chien*] to have an accident euph.

oubliettes /ublijɛt/ *nfpl* oubliette (*sg*).
IDIOMES **tomber dans les ~** to be forgotten; **tomber dans les ~ de l'histoire** to become a forgotten page in the history books; **mettre** or **jeter qch aux ~** to consign sth to oblivion.

oublieux, **-ieuse** /ublijø, øz/ *adj* forgetful (**de** of).

oued /wɛd/ *nm* Géog wadi.

ouest /wɛst/ **▶621** **I** *adj inv* [*façade, versant, côte*] west; [*frontière, zone*] western.
II *nm* **1** (point cardinal) west; **à l'~ de Paris** [*être, habiter*] west of Paris; **vers l'~** [*aller, naviguer*] west, westward; **un vent d'~** a westerly wind; **exposé à l'~** west-facing (*épith*); **2** (région) west; **dans l'~ de la France** [*se situer, avoir lieu, habiter, voyager*] in the west of France; [*aller, se rendre*] to the west of France; **l'~ du Japon** western Japan; **3** Géog, Pol **l'Ouest** the West; **vivre dans l'Ouest** to live in the West; **venir de l'Ouest** to come from the West; **de l'Ouest** [*ville, accent*] western.

ouest-allemand, **~e**, *mpl* **~s** /wɛstalmɑ̃, ɑ̃d/ *adj* West German.

ouf /uf/ **I** *nm* **faire ~, pousser un ~ (de soulagement)** to breathe a sigh of relief; **pousser un grand ~** to heave a great sigh of relief; **je n'ai pas eu le temps de dire ~ de toute la matinée** (souffler) I haven't had time to turn round all morning; **je n'ai pas eu le temps de dire ~, il était déjà parti** before I could say Jack Robinson, he'd gone.
II *excl* phew!

Ouganda /ugɑ̃da/ **▶321** *nprm* Uganda.

ougandais, **~e** /ugɑ̃dɛ, ɛz/ **▶537** *adj* Ugandan.

Ougandais, **~e** /ugɑ̃dɛ, ɛz/ **▶537** *nm,f* Ugandan.

ougrien, **-ienne** /ugʀijɛ̃, ɛn/ *adj* Ling Ugric.

oui /wi/

■ **Note** En anglais la réponse *yes* est généralement renforcée en reprenant le verbe utilisé pour poser la question: *are you happy? yes, I am; do you like Brahms? yes, I do.*

I *adv* **1** (marque l'accord) yes; (dans la marine) aye, aye; (à la cérémonie du mariage) I do; **mais ~!** yes!; **~ mais** yes, but; **bien sûr que ~!** yes, of course!; **alors c'est ~?** so the answer is yes?; **~ et non** yes and no; **acceptera-t-il ~ ou non de me rencontrer?** will he agree to meet me or not?; **découvrir si ~ ou non** to discover whether or not; **êtes-vous d'accord? si ~, dites pourquoi** do you agree? if so, say why; **dire ~ à qch** (par conviction) to welcome sth; (par nécessité) to agree to sth; **~ à l'Europe** 'yes' to Europe; **j'ai dit ~ tout de suite** I said yes ou I agreed at once; **j'ai attendu avant de dire ~ à leur proposition** I waited before agreeing to their proposal; **ne dire ni ~ ni non** to say neither yes nor no; **répondez par ~ ou par non** answer yes or no; **faire ~ de la tête** to nod; **2** (renforce une constatation) yes; **un changement, ~, mais surtout une amélioration** a change, yes, but above all an improvement; **lui, prudent? un lâche, ~!** him, cautious? a coward, more like○!; **elle est radin○, ~, radin!** she's stingy, she really is stingy!; **eh ~, c'est comme ça!** well, that's just the way it is!; **eh bien ~, j'ai triché, et alors?** OK, I cheated—so what?; **3** (marque l'insistance) yes; **~, nous voulons la guerre** yes, we do want war; **dans un livre que j'ai lu récemment, oui, je lis des livres** in a book I read recently, because I do read books you know; **tu viens, ~?** are you coming?; **tu viens, ~ ou non?** are you coming? yes or no?; **tu viens, ~ ou merde●?** are you coming or not, damn it●?; **c'est bientôt fini, ~?** are you going to stop that or not?; **4** (marque une transition) yes; **~, tu disais?** yes, you were saying?; **'je voudrais...'—'~, vas-y, dis-le!'** 'I'd like...'—'yes ou well, go on, say it!'; **~, ~, tu dis ça et puis tu ne le feras pas** yeah, yeah○, that's what you say, but you won't do it; **5** (remplace une proposition) **je crois que ~** or **qu'~**○ I think so; **'il a réussi?'—'je crois que ~'** 'has he succeeded?'—'I think so'; **'ils sont partis?'—'je crains que ~'** 'have they left?'—'I'm afraid so'; **tu ne le crois pas, moi ~** you don't believe it, but I do.
II *nm inv* **1** (accord) yes; **elle répondit d'un ~ timide** she answered with a timid yes; **le '~ mais' de M. Axel à notre proposition** Mr Axel's qualified 'yes' to our proposal; **2** (vote positif) 'yes' vote; **en votant ~, vous dites ~ à la démocratie** a 'yes' vote is a vote for democracy; **le '~' a recueilli 60% des suffrages** the 'yes' vote was 60%, 60% voted 'yes' ou in favour[GB]; **50 ~ sur 57 votants** 50 votes in favour[GB] out of 57 votes cast; **l'éclatante victoire des '~'** the sweeping victory of those in favour[GB]; **le ~ l'a emporté** the ayes have it.
IDIOMES **pour un ~ (ou) pour un non** [*s'absenter, s'énerver*] for the slightest thing; [*changer d'avis*] at the drop of a hat.

oui-da† /wida/ *adv* yes indeed.

ouï-dire /widiʀ/ *nm inv* hearsay; **par ~** by hearsay.

ouïe /wi/ *nf* **1** Physiol hearing ¢; **avoir l'~ fine** to have good hearing; **être tout ~** to be all ears; **2** Zool (de poisson) gill; **3** Mus (de violon) sound hole; **4** Mécan inlet; **5** Aviat (prise d'air) gill.

ouïgour /wiguʀ/ **▶462** *adj inv, nm* Uighur.

ouille /uj/ **I** *nm inv* ouch; **pousser un ~ de douleur** to cry out in pain.
II *excl* ouch!

ouïr† /wiʀ/ [38] *vtr* to hear; **oyez bonnes gens!** oyez! oyez! oyez!; **j'ai ouï dire que** word has reached me that.

ouistiti /wistiti/ *nm* **1** Zool marmoset; **2**○ (personne) **un (drôle de) ~** a funny character.

oukase /ukɑz/ *nm* **1** Hist ukase; **2** (ordre) decree.

Oulan-Bator /ulɑ̃batɔʀ/ **▶857** *npr* Ulan Bator.

Oulipo /ulipo/ *nm* (*abbr* = **Ouvroir de littérature potentielle**) Workshop of Potential Literature (*French literary circle created in 1960*).

ouragan /uʀagɑ̃/ *nm* **1** Météo hurricane; **2** (tumulte) storm; **déclencher un ~** to create a storm.
IDIOMES **arriver/passer comme un ~** to arrive/pass through like a hurricane.

Oural /uʀal/ *nprm* **1** **▶692** (région) **l'~** the Urals (*pl*); **les monts ~** the Ural mountains; **2** **▶357** (fleuve) **l'~** the Ural.

ouralo-altaïque /uʀaloaltaik/ *adj, nm* Ling Uralic-Altaic.

ourdir /uʀdiʀ/ [3] *vtr* **1** (tramer) to hatch [*complot, conspiration*]; to weave [*intrigue*]; **2** Tex to warp.

ourdou /uʀdu/ **▶462** *adj inv, nm* Ling Urdu.

ourler /uʀle/ [1] *vtr* to hem; **mouchoir/drap ourlé** hemmed handkerchief/sheet.

ourlet /uʀlɛ/ *nm* **1** Cout hem; **faire un ~ à** to put a hem on; **~ à festons/plat** scallop/plain hem; **▶faux**[1]; **2** Tech (de plaque, tôle) rim.
■ **~ de l'oreille** Anat helix.

ours /uʀs/ *nm* **1** Zool bear; **chasse à l'~** bear hunting ¢; **▶cage**; **2** (personne) **il est un peu ~** he's a bit surly; **3** Presse ≈ masthead.
■ **~ blanc** Zool polar bear; **~ brun** Zool brown bear; **~ mal léché** boor; **~ de mer** Zool Northern fur seal; **~ en peluche** Jeux teddy bear; **~ polaire** = **~ blanc**.
IDIOMES **vendre la peau de l'~ avant de l'avoir tué** Prov to count one's chickens before they're hatched.

ourse /uʀs/ *nf* Zool she-bear.

Ourse /uʀs/ *nprf* Astron **la Grande ~** the Plough GB, the Big Dipper US, Ursa Major spéc; **la Petite ~** the Little Bear GB, the Little Dipper US, Ursa Minor spéc.

oursin /uʀsɛ̃/ *nm* Zool (sea) urchin.

ourson /uʀsɔ̃/ *nm* Zool bear cub.

oust(e) /ust/ *excl* **(allez) ~!** out!

outarde /utaʀd/ *nf* Zool gén bustard; (oie sauvage) Canada goose.

outil /uti/ *nm* Tech tool; **~s de jardinage/de plombier** gardening/plumbing tools.
■ **~ logiciel** software tool; **~ pédagogique** teaching tool; **~ de production** production tool; **~ de travail** work tool.
IDIOMES **à méchant ouvrier point de bon ~** Prov a bad workman always blames his tools.

outillage /utijaʒ/ *nm* tools (*pl*); **~ agricole/industriel** farming/industrial tools.

outiller /utije/ [1] **I** *vtr* to equip [*personne, usine*]; **nous ne sommes pas outillés pour faire** we do not have the right tools to do.
II s'outiller *vpr* [*personne*] to equip oneself.

outilleur /utijœʀ/ **▶510** *nm* toolmaker.

outrage /utʀaʒ/ *nm* insult; **faire ~ à** to be an insult to [*personne, réputation, mémoire*]; to be an affront to [*raison, morale*].
■ **~ à agent** *verbal assault of a policeman*; **~ aux bonnes mœurs** affront to public decency; **~ à magistrat** contempt ¢ of court; **~ à la pudeur** indecency ¢.

outragé, **~e** /utʀaʒe/ **I** *pp* **▶outrager**.
II *pp adj* [*personne*] outraged; **prendre un air ~** to assume an air of outrage.

outrageant, **~e** /utʀaʒɑ̃, ɑ̃t/ *adj* [*parole, comportement*] offensive.

outrager /utʀaʒe/ [13] *vtr* **1** gén to offend [*personne*]; to be an affront to [*bonnes mœurs, morale*]; **se sentir outragé** to feel affronted; **2** (physiquement) to abuse [*personne*].

outrageusement /utʀaʒøzmɑ̃/ *adv* (de façon outrageuse) in an outrageous manner; (excessivement) outrageously.

outrageux, -euse /utʀaʒø, øz/ *adj* liter outrageous.

outrance /utʀɑ̃s/ *nf* **1** (excès) excess; **les ~s d'une comédie/d'un adolescent** the excesses of a comedy/of a teenager; **commettre une ~ de langage** to use extreme language ¢; **2** (caractère excessif) excessiveness; **l'~ de tes propos/ton langage** the extreme nature of your remarks/your language; **pousser la conscience professionnelle jusqu'à l'~** to take one's conscientiousness to extremes; **polémiquer/manger à ~** to argue/eat excessively; **le sport/la lecture à ~** excessive sport/reading; **investir/licencier à ~** to make too many investments/redundancies.

outrancier, -ière /utʀɑ̃sje, ɛʀ/ *adj* [*personne, propos, caractère*] extreme.

outre[1] /utʀ/ **I** *prép* (en plus de) in addition to; **~ les problèmes mentionnés/cette mesure** in addition to the problems mentioned/this measure; **~ (le fait) qu'il écrit, il illustre ses livres** as well as writing, he also illustrates his books; **~ (le fait) qu'elles sont illégales, ces activités ne sont pas rentables** as well as being illegal, the activities are not profitable.
II *adv* **passer ~** to pay no heed; **elle sait que c'est interdit mais elle passe ~** she knows it's forbidden but she pays no heed ou carries on regardless; **passer ~ à** to disregard ou override [*loi, décision, objection*].
III outre mesure *loc adv* unduly; **cela ne m'inquiète/m'étonne pas ~ mesure** it doesn't worry me/surprise me unduly.
IV en outre *loc adv* in addition; **cette machine nous permettra, en ~, de faire** in addition, this machine will allow us to do.

outre[2] /utʀ/ *nf* goatskin.
IDIOMES **être plein comme une ~**○ to be full to bursting.

outré, ~e /utʀe/ **I** *pp* ▶ **outrer**.
II *pp adj* **1** (indigné) [*personne, regards, protestations*] outraged; **être ~** to be outraged (**par, de** at); **prendre un air ~** to look deeply offended; **2** (exagéré) [*compliments, propos, description*] extravagant.

outre-Atlantique /utʀatlɑ̃tik/ *adv* across the Atlantic, in America; **d'~** [*presse, chanteur*] American.

outrecuidance /utʀəkɥidɑ̃s/ *nf* **1** (impertinence) impertinence; **avec ~** impertinently; **2** (présomption) presumptuousness; **avec ~** presumptuously.

outrecuidant, ~e /utʀəkɥidɑ̃, ɑ̃t/ *adj* **1** (impertinent) impertinent; **2** (présomptueux) presumptuous.

outre-Manche /utʀəmɑ̃ʃ/ *adv* across the Channel, in Britain; **d'~** [*presse, chanteur*] British.

outremer /utʀəmɛʀ/ ▶ **193** *adj inv, nm* ultramarine.

outre-mer /utʀəmɛʀ/ *adv* overseas.

outrepasser /utʀəpase/ [1] *vtr* to exceed [*droits, fonctions, prérogatives, devoir, pouvoir*]; to overstep [*limites, ordres*].

outrer /utʀe/ [1] *vtr* **1** (indigner) to outrage; **je suis outré par leur attitude, leur attitude m'a outré** I was outraged by their attitude; **2** (exagérer) [*personne*] to exaggerate [*comportement, vérité, description*].

outre-Rhin /utʀəʀɛ̃/ *adv* across the Rhine; **la presse d'~** the German press.

outre-tombe /utʀətɔ̃b/ *adv* **d'~** [*pâleur*] deathly; **une voix d'~** a voice from beyond the grave.

outsider /utsajdœʀ/ *nm* (tous contextes) outsider.

ouvert, ~e /uvɛʀ, ɛʀt/ **I** *pp* ▶ **ouvrir**.
II *pp adj* **1** (non fermé) [*porte, bouche, magasin, blessure, chemise*] open; **rester ~** to stay open; **c'est ~** it's open; **grand ~** wide open; **~ au public** open to the public; **~ à la circulation/à la navigation** open to traffic/for shipping; **chemise à col ~** open-necked shirt; **(la) bouche ~e** [*rester, écouter, regarder*] gén with one's mouth open; (d'étonnement) open-mouthed; **il avait la bouche ~e** gén his mouth was open; (d'étonnement) he was open-mouthed; **avoir/garder les yeux ~s** (ne pas s'endormir) to be/stay awake; (être attentif) to have/keep one's eyes open; ▶ **porte, tombeau**; **2** (en marche) [*lumière, gaz*] on (*jamais épith*); [*robinet*] running; **laisser la lumière ~e** to leave the light on; **laisser le robinet (d'eau) ~** to leave the tap GB ou faucet US running; **3** (inauguré) [*saison, séance, tunnel*] open; **4** (destiné) **~ à** [*centre, service*] open to; **~ aux jeunes de 13 à 19 ans** open to teenagers; **5** (déclaré) [*guerre, conflit, hostilité*] open; **être en conflit ~ avec qn** to be in open conflict with sb; **6** (franc) [*personne, caractère, jeu, dialogue*] open; **7** (réceptif) [*personne, esprit*] open (**à** to); **être ~ aux idées nouvelles/compromis** to be open to new ideas/compromise; **à l'esprit très ~** very open-minded; **8** (épanoui) [*fleur*] open; **9** (non résolu) [*question*] open; **la question reste ~e** the question remains open; **10** (non limitatif) [*série, question, programme*] open-ended; **11** Ling, Phon [*classe, voyelle, syllabe*] open.

ouvertement /uvɛʀtəmɑ̃/ *adv* gén openly; (de manière éhontée) blatantly.

ouverture /uvɛʀtyʀ/ *nf* **1** (action d'ouvrir) opening; **soyez prudent à l'~ du paquet** be careful when opening the parcel; **l'~ de la porte/de mon compte n'a pas été facile** opening the door/my account was not easy; **~ du testament** Jur reading of the will; **~ d'une information judiciaire** Jur opening of a judicial investigation; **~ d'un droit** Prot Soc granting of entitlement to benefits; **2** (fait de s'ouvrir) opening; **l'~ des vannes est automatique** the opening of the sluices is automatic, the sluices open automatically; **boîte/couvercle à ~ facile** ring-pull can/top; **3** (début) opening; **à l'~** at the opening; **~ de la campagne officielle** Pol opening of the election campaign; **~ de la chasse** Chasse opening of the shooting GB ou hunting US season; **~ de la pêche** Pêche opening of the fishing season; **4** (inauguration) opening; **~ d'un nouvel hôtel** opening of a new hotel; **cérémonie/jour/séance d'~** opening ceremony/day/session; **dès l'~** right from the opening; **5** Admin, Comm (fonctionnement) opening; **heures d'~** opening hours; **~ au public** opening to the public; **permettre l'~ des supermarchés le dimanche** to permit Sunday trading for supermarkets; **à l'~** at opening time; **6** (occasion) opportunity; **à la première ~** at the first opportunity; **7** (mise en œuvre) opening; **~ de négociations** opening of negotiations; **8** Constr opening; (accidentel) gap; **ménager une ~** to leave an opening; **calfeutrer les ~s** to fill in the gaps; **9** (tolérance) openness (**à** to); **atmosphère/esprit d'~** atmosphere/spirit of openness; **~ aux idées nouvelles/sur le monde** openness to new ideas/to the world; **(grande) ~ d'esprit** (great) open-mindedness; **10** Pol (transparence) openness; **politique d'~** policy of openness; **11** Pol (libéralisation) opening-up; (élargissement) opening-up (**à** to); (proposition) overture (**à, en direction de** to; **de, de la part de** from); **~ à l'Ouest/à gauche** opening-up to the West/to the left; **faire des ~s aux rebelles** to make overtures to the rebels; **politique d'~** policy of opening-up; **12** Écon opening (**à** to); **~ du marché national aux transporteurs étrangers** opening of the national market to foreign carriers; **13** Mus overture; **~ de Guillaume Tell** overture to William Tell; **14** Jeux (aux cartes) opening bid; (aux échecs) opening.

ouvrable /uvʀabl/ *adj* [*jour*] working; [*heure*] business; **aux heures ~s** during business hours.

ouvrage /uvʀaʒ/ **I** *nm* **1** (travail) work; **se mettre à l'~** to get down to work; **se tuer à l'~** to work oneself to death; **~ du temps** work of time; **2** (livre) book, work; (œuvre) work; **~ de référence** reference book, work of reference; **~ collectif** joint publication; **3** Cout (objet) piece of work; **un ~ de broderie** a piece of embroidery; **4** (produit par un artisan, un ouvrier) piece of work; **~ d'ébénisterie/de mosaïque** piece of cabinet work/of mosaic work; **~ de marqueterie** piece of marquetry.
II○ *nf* controv **c'est de la belle ouvrage** it's a very nice piece.
■ **~ d'art** Gén Civ civil engineering structure; **~ de maçonnerie** (en briques) brickwork; (en pierres) stonework, masonry; **~ militaire** fortification; **~ de soutènement** retaining work.
IDIOMES **mettre** or **avoir du cœur à l'~** to work with a will; **ne pas avoir le cœur à l'~** not to have one's heart in one's work.

ouvragé, ~e /uvʀaʒe/ *adj* [*bois, métal*] finely wrought; **meuble trop ~** over-elaborate piece of furniture.

ouvrant, ~e /uvʀɑ̃, ɑ̃t/ **I** *adj* **toit ~** Aut sunroof.
II *nm* Constr (de porte, fenêtre) (opening) leaf.

ouvré, ~e /uvʀe/ *adj* **1** (ouvragé) [*bois, bijou, linge*] finely worked; **2** Admin, Jur **jour ~** working day.

ouvre-boîtes /uvʀəbwat/ *nm inv* tin-opener GB, can-opener.

ouvre-bouteilles /uvʀəbutɛj/ *nm inv* bottle-opener.

ouvreur, -euse /uvʀœʀ, øz/ ▶ **510** *nm,f* **1** Cin, Théât usher/usherette; **2** Jeux (joueur qui commence) opener; **3** Sport (en rugby) stand-off half; (skieur) trailmaker.

ouvrier, -ière /uvʀije, ɛʀ/ **I** *adj* **1** Pol, Sociol [*contestation*] of the workers (*après n*); **classe ouvrière** working class; **pavillon ~** workman's cottage; **syndicat ~** trade union; **2** Zool [*abeille, fourmi*] worker (*épith*).
II ▶ **510** *nm,f* gén worker; (dans le bâtiment) workman; **~ maçon** building worker; **~ menuisier** carpenter (*employed by a builder*); **les ~s du bâtiment/des chantiers navals** the construction/shipyard workers; **avoir 50 ~s** to have a workforce of 50, to employ 50 workers; ▶ **œuvre, outil**.
III ouvrière *nf* Zool worker.
■ **~ agricole** agricultural labourer; **~ hautement qualifié, OHQ** highly skilled worker; **~ professionnel, OP** highly skilled worker (*specialized in a trade*); **~ qualifié, OQ** skilled worker; **~ spécialisé, OS** unskilled worker.
IDIOMES **les ~s de la onzième** or **dernière heure** people who arrive when the work is virtually done.

ouvrir /uvʀiʀ/ [32] **I** *vtr* **1** gén to open [*boîte, porte, bouteille, tiroir, huître, parachute, lettre*]; to draw back [*verrou*]; to undo [*col, chemise, fermeture à glissière*]; **~ la bouche** to open one's mouth; **ne pas ~ la bouche** (ne rien dire) not to say a word; **~ le bec**○ or **sa gueule**◑, **l'~**◑ to open one's trap○ ou gob◑ GB; **il faut toujours qu'il l'ouvre**◑ **au mauvais moment** he always opens his trap○ ou big mouth○ at the wrong time; **~ ses oreilles** to keep one's ears open; **~ les bras** to open one's arms; **~ les bras à qn** (accueillir) to welcome sb with open arms; **~ sa maison à qn** (accueillir) to throw one's house open to sb; **(se) faire ~ une porte** to get a door open; ▶ **grand III**; **2** (commencer) to open [*débat, négociation, spectacle, cérémonie, marque, chantier*]; to initiate [*période, dialogue, processus, campagne*]; **~ la marque à la cinquième minute** to open the scoring in the fifth minute; **3** (mettre en marche) to turn on [*radio, chauffage, gaz, lumière*]; **4** (créer) to open [*compte , magasin, école, souscription, poste*]; to open up [*possibilité, perspective, marché, passage*]; to initiate [*cours*] ; **~ une ligne de crédit** to open a line of credit; **~ un nouveau cours de gestion** to initiate a new management course; **~ la route** to open up the road; **~ une route** to build a road; **~ la route** or **voie à qch** to pave the way for sth; **5** (élargir) to open [*capital, actionnariat, jeu politique, rangs*] (**à** to); to open up [*compétition, marché*] (**à** to); **~ le ciel européen aux compagnies américaines** to open up the European skies to American carriers; **~ ses rangs aux femmes** to welcome women into one's ranks; **~ l'esprit à qn** to open sb's mind; **6** (entailler) to open [*abcès*]; to cut open [*joue*]; **~ le ventre à qn**○ (opérer) to cut sb open○.

II *vi* **1** (ouvrir la porte) to open the door (**à** to); **va ~** go and open the door; **n'ouvre à personne** don't open the door to anyone; **ouvrez!** (injonction) open up!; **ouvre-moi!** let me in!; **se faire ~** to be let in; **2** (fonctionner) [*magasin, service*] to open; **~ le dimanche** to open on Sundays; **3** (être créé) [*magasin, service*] to be opened; **une succursale ouvrira bientôt** a branch will soon be opened; **4** (déboucher) [*chambre, tunnel*] to open (**sur** onto); **~ sur le jardin** to open on to the garden GB ou yard US; **5** Fin **la Bourse a ouvert en baisse/hausse** the exchange opened down/up; **6** (aux cartes, échecs) to open.

III s'ouvrir *vpr* **1** gén [*boîte, porte, fenêtre, tiroir, huître, parachute*] to open; (sous un souffle) [*fenêtre*] to blow open; (sous un choc) [*porte, boîte, sac*] to fly open; (inopinément) [*vêtement*] to come undone; **2** (commencer) [*négociation, spectacle, chantier*] to open (**sur, avec** with); [*période, dialogue, processus*] to be initiated (**sur, avec** with); **le film s'ouvre sur un paysage** the film opens with a landscape; **le festival s'ouvrira sur un discours** the festival will open with a speech; **3** (s'élargir) [*pays, économie, capital, institution*] to open up (**à, vers** to); **s'~ à l'Est/aux nouvelles technologies** to open up to the East/to new technologies; **4** (se confier) to open one's heart (**à** to); **ouvrez-vous en à elle** open your heart to her about it; **5** (être ouvrant) [*fenêtre, toit*] to open; **ma valise/jupe s'ouvre sur le côté** my suitcase/skirt opens at the side; **6**○ (être mis en marche) **comment est- ce que le chauffage s'ouvre?** how do you turn on the heating?; **où est-ce que la lumière s'ouvre?** where do you turn on the light?; **7** (être créé) [*magasin, métro, possibilité*] to open; **un garage va s'~ ici** there's going to be a garage here; **8** (créer pour soi) [*personne*] to open up [*passage*]; **9** (se dérouler) [*chemin, voie, espace*] to open up; **une nouvelle voie s'ouvre devant nous** a new path is opening up before us; **10** (s'épanouir) [*fleur*] to open; **11** (se fendre) [*sol, cicatrice*] to open up; [*mer*] to part; **la mer s'ouvrit devant eux** the sea parted in front of them; **12** (se blesser) [*personne*] to cut open [*crâne, pied*]; **il a réussi à s'~ le crâne** he managed to cut his head open; **s'~ les veines** or **poignets** (pour se suicider) to slash one's wrists.

ouvroir /uvʀwaʀ/ *nm* **1** (cercle de dames) sewing circle; **2** (dans un couvent) workroom.

ouzbek /uzbɛk/ **▶ 537**, **462** *adj, nm* Uzbek.

Ouzbek /uzbɛk/ **▶ 537** *nmf* Uzbek.

Ouzbekistan /uzbekistɑ̃/ **▶ 321** *nprm* Uzbekistan.

ovaire /ɔvɛʀ/ *nm* ovary; **un kyste de** or **à l'~** an ovarian cyst.

ovale /ɔval/ **I** *adj* [*table, surface*] oval.

II *nm* oval; **en ~** oval, oval-shaped.

ovariectomie /ɔvaʀjɛktɔmi/ *nf* ovariectomy.

ovarien, -ienne /ɔvaʀjɛ̃, ɛn/ *adj* ovarian.

ovariotomie /ɔvaʀjɔtɔmi/ *nf* ovariotomy.

ovarite /ɔvaʀit/ **▶ 271** *nf* ovaritis.

ovation /ɔvasjɔ̃/ *nf* **1** (applaudissements) ovation; **faire une ~ à qn** to give sb an ovation; **il a fini son discours sous les ~s de la foule** he finished his speech to wild applause from the crowd; **2** (reconnaissance) accolade; **recevoir une ~** to receive an accolade.

ovationner /ɔvasjɔne/ [1] *vtr* (pour accueillir) to greet [sb/sth] with wild applause [*vedette, arrivée*]; **ils se levèrent pour ~ le candidat/spectacle** they gave the candidate/show a standing ovation.

ove /ɔv/ *nm* Archit, Art ovum.

overdose /ɔvəʀdoz/ *nf* lit, fig overdose; **mourir d'une** or **par ~** to die from an overdose; **avoir** or **faire une ~** to overdose; **regarder la télévision/manger du chocolat jusqu'à l'~** to overdose on television/on chocolate.

overdrive /ɔvəʀdʀajv/ *nm* overdrive.

Ovide /ɔvid/ *npr* Ovid.

ovin, ~e /ɔvɛ̃, in/ **I** *adj* ovine; **la viande ~e** mutton; **les producteurs ~s** sheep farmers.

II *nm* sheep; **les ~s** sheep; **les éleveurs d'~s** sheep farmers.

ovipare /ɔvipaʀ/ **I** *adj* egg-laying, oviparous spéc.

II *nm* egg-laying animal, oviparous animal spéc.

ovni /ɔvni/ *nm*: *abbr* **▶ objet**.

ovocyte /ɔvɔsit/ *nm* oocyte.

ovogenèse /ɔvɔʒənɛz/ *nf* oogenesis.

ovoïde /ɔvɔid/ *adj* egg-shaped, ovoid.

ovulaire /ɔvylɛʀ/ *adj* ovular.

ovulation /ɔvylasjɔ̃/ *nf* ovulation.

ovule /ɔvyl/ *nm* **1** Biol, Physiol ovum; **2** Bot ovule; **3** Pharm pessary.

ovuler /ɔvyle/ [1] *vi* to ovulate.

oxacide /ɔksasid/ *nm* oxyacid.

oxalique /ɔksalik/ *adj* **acide ~** oxalic acid.

oxalis /ɔksalis/ *nm inv* wood sorrel.

oxford /ɔksfɔʀd/ *nm* Tex Oxford (cloth).

Oxford /ɔksfɔʀd/ **▶ 857** *npr* Oxford.

oxfordien, -ienne /ɔksfɔʀdjɛ̃, ɛn/ **▶ 857** *adj* of Oxford.

Oxfordien, -ienne /ɔksfɔʀdjɛ̃, ɛn/ **▶ 857** *nm,f* (natif) native of Oxford; (habitant) inhabitant of Oxford.

Oxfordshire **▶ 692** *nprm* **l'~** Oxfordshire.

oxhydrique /ɔksidʀik/ *adj* oxyhydrogen (*épith*).

oxyacétylénique /ɔksiasetilenik/ *adj* oxyacetylene (*épith*).

oxydable /ɔksidabl/ *adj* [*métal*] liable to rust, oxidizable spéc.

oxydant, ~e /ɔksidɑ̃, ɑ̃t/ **I** *adj* oxidizing.

II *nm* oxidizer, oxidizing agent.

oxydase /ɔksidɑz/ *nf* oxidase.

oxydation /ɔksidasjɔ̃/ *nf* oxidation.

oxyde /ɔksid/ *nm* oxide.

■ **~ de carbone** carbon monoxide.

oxyder /ɔkside/ [1] *vtr*, **s'oxyder** *vpr* to oxidize.

oxydoréduction /ɔksidoʀedyksjɔ̃/ *nf* oxidation-reduction.

oxygénation /ɔksiʒenasjɔ̃/ *nf* Méd oxygenation.

oxygène /ɔksiʒɛn/ *nm* **1** Chimie oxygen; **~ liquide** liquid oxygen; **à ~** [*masque, tente*] oxygen (*épith*); **2** (air) air; **faire provision d'~** to get some fresh air; **je manque d'~ ici** I'm suffocating here.

oxygéné, ~e /ɔksiʒene/ **I** *pp* **▶ oxygéner**.

II *pp adj* **cheveux ~s** bleached-blond hair; **eau ~e** hydrogen peroxide.

oxygéner /ɔksiʒene/ [14] **I** *vtr* Chimie, Méd to oxygenate.

II s'oxygéner *vpr* to get some fresh air.

oxyhémoglobine /ɔksiemɔglɔbin/ *nf* oxyhaemoglobin.

oxymoron /ɔksimɔʀɔ̃/ *nm* oxymoron.

oyez /ɔje/ **▶ ouïr**.

ozone /ozon/ *nf* ozone; **la couche d'~** the ozone layer.

ozoniser /ɔzɔnize/ [1] *vtr* to ozonize.

Pp

p, **P** /pe/ *nm inv* p, P.

PACA /paka/ *nprf*: *abbr* = **Provence-Alpes-Côte d'Azur**.

pacage /pakaʒ/ *nm* **1** (lieu) pasture, grazing land; **2** (action) grazing.

pacager /pakaʒe/ [13] **I** *vtr* (faire paître) to pasture, to graze [*bétail*].
II *vi* [*bétail*] to graze.

pacha /paʃa/ *nm* Hist pasha.
IDIOMES **jouer les ~s**○ to expect to be waited on hand and foot; **mener une vie de ~** to live the life of Riley.

pachtou /paʃtu/ **▶ 462⌋** *nm* Afghan.

pachyderme /paʃidɛʀm/ *nm* **1** Zool pachyderm; **2** (personne massive) elephant; **de ~** [*physique, pas*] heavy.

pacificateur, **-trice** /pasifikatœʀ, tʀis/ **I** *adj* [*action, discours*] placatory; [*rôle*] peacemaking, pacificatory littér; **la mission pacificatrice de notre grand pays** the peacemaking mission of our great country.
II *nm,f* peacemaker.

pacification /pasifikasjɔ̃/ *nf* Mil, Pol pacification, peacemaking; **la ~ d'une région** the re-establishment of peace in a region.

pacifier /pasifje/ [1] *vtr* to establish peace in, to pacify [*pays, région*]; **il rêve d'un monde pacifié** he dreams of a world at peace.

pacifique /pasifik/ **I** *adj* **1** [*coexistence, solution, manifestation*] peaceful; [*peuple, personne*] peaceful, peace-loving; **2** Géog Pacific.
II *nmf* (personne) peace-loving person.

Pacifique /pasifik/ **▶ 555⌋** *nprm* **l'océan ~, le ~** the Pacific (Ocean); **le ~ Sud** the South Pacific.

pacifiquement /pasifikmɑ̃/ *adv* peacefully, pacifically littér.

pacifisme /pasifism/ *nm* pacifism.

pacifiste /pasifist/ *adj, nmf* pacifist.

pack /pak/ *nm* **1** (lot) pack (**de** of); **2** (au rugby) pack; **3** (glaces flottantes) pack ice.

pacotille /pakɔtij/ *nf* pej **de la ~** cheap rubbish, junk○; **bijou de ~** cheap piece of jewellery GB ou jewelry US; **montre de ~** cheap watch; **héroïsme de ~** bogus heroism.

pacson◐ /paksɔ̃/ *nm* **1** (grosse quantité) **un ~ de** a whole load○ of GB, a whole slew○ of; **2** (paquet) parcel; **3** (fortune) packet○ GB, bundle○.

pacte /pakt/ *nm* pact; **conclure un ~ avec qn/contre qch** to make a pact with sb/against sth; **~ de défense** ou **défensif** defence[GB] pact; **~ de non-agression** nonaggression pact; **le ~ de Varsovie** the Warsaw pact; **~ d'union sacrée** pact of sacred union.
■ **~ d'actionnaires** shareholders' alliance.

pactiser /paktize/ [1] *vi* to treat (**avec qn** with sb); **~ avec sa conscience** to stifle one's conscience.

pactole /paktɔl/ *nm* gold mine; **ramasser** or **toucher le ~**○ to make a fortune ou mint○.

paddock /padɔk/ *nm* **1** Turf paddock; **2**◐ (lit) bed; **aller au ~** to hit the sack○, to go to bed.

paddy /padi/ *nm* (**riz**) **~** paddy.

Padoue /padu/ **▶ 857⌋** *npr* Padua.

paf /paf/ **I**◐ *adj inv* plastered○, drunk.
II *excl* wham!

PAF /paf/ **I** *nm*: *abbr* **▶ paysage**.
II *nf*: *abbr* **▶ police**.

pagaie /pagɛ/ *nf* paddle.

pagaille○ /pagɑj/ **I** *nf* mess; **ils ont mis la ~ dans leur chambre** they have made a real mess in their room, they have messed up their room; **elle a mis la ~ dans mes papiers** she messed up my papers; **la grève a semé la ~ dans le pays** the strike has caused chaos throughout the country.
II en pagaille *loc adv* **1** (en désordre) in a mess; **2** (à profusion) **pêcher du poisson en ~** to catch loads○ of fish.

paganiser /paganize/ [1] *vtr* to paganize.

paganisme /paganism/ *nm* paganism.

pagaye○ = **pagaille**.

pagayer /pageje/ [21] *vi* to paddle.

page /paʒ/ **I** *nm* page (boy).
II *nf* page; **suite ~ 36** continued on page 36; **en première/dernière ~** on the front/back page; **marquer/perdre sa ~** to mark/lose one's page; **tournez la ~ SVP** please turn over; **tourner la ~** fig to turn over a new leaf; **faire la mise en ~, mettre en ~** Imprim, Presse to make up a page; **mise en ~** (résultat) layout; **les plus belles ~s de la poésie irlandaise** the finest passages of Irish poetry; **une ~ sombre de leur existence** a dark chapter in their lives; **▶ plein**.
■ **~ de garde** endpaper; **une ~ de publicité** Radio a commercial break; **Pages Jaunes**® Yellow Pages.
IDIOMES **éprouver l'angoisse de la ~ blanche** [*écrivain*] to have writer's block; **être à la ~** to be up to date; **se mettre à la ~** to bring oneself up to date.

page-écran, *pl* **pages-écrans** /paʒekʀɑ̃/ *nf* Ordinat page.

pageot○ /paʒo/ *nm* bed.

pagination /paʒinasjɔ̃/ *nf* **1** (numérotation) pagination; **2** Ordinat paging.

paginer /paʒine/ [1] *vtr* to paginate.

pagne /paɲ/ *nm* **1** (en tissu) loincloth; **2** (en paille) grass skirt.

pagode /pagɔd/ *nf* pagoda.

paie /pɛ/ *nf* pay; **ma ~ me suffit pour vivre** I can live on my pay ou wages; **toucher une bonne ~** to be well paid, to get a good wage; **bulletin** or **fiche** or **feuille de ~** payslip; **livre de ~** payroll; **faire la ~ des ouvriers** to do the workers' payroll.
IDIOMES **ça fait** or **il y a une ~**○**!** it was ages○ ago; **ça fait une ~**○ **que je ne l'ai pas vu** it's ages○ since I've seen him.

paiement /pɛmɑ̃/ *nm* payment; **faire** or **effectuer un ~** to make a payment; **~ comptant** or **en espèces** or **liquide** cash payment; **~ par chèque** payment by cheque GB ou check US; **en ~ de** in payment for [*article*]; in payment of [*facture*]; **après le ~ de leurs impôts** after they have paid their taxes; **le ~ de la dette extérieure** repayment ou paying off of the foreign debt.

païen, **-ïenne** /pajɛ̃, ɛn/ *adj, nm,f* pagan.

paierie /pɛʀi/ *nf* paymaster's office.

paillage /pajaʒ/ *nm* **1** (d'arbre, de sol) ≈ mulching; **2** (de chaise) seat.

paillard, **~e** /pajaʀ, aʀd/ *adj* bawdy.

paillardise /pajaʀdiz/ *nf* **1** (libertinage) bawdiness; **2** (propos) bawdy remark; (histoire) bawdy story.

paillasse /pajas/ **I** *nm* Théât clown.
II *nf* **1** (matelas) straw mattress; **2** (de laboratoire) lab bench; (d'évier) draining board.
IDIOMES **se crever la ~**○ to break one's back○ (**à faire** doing).

paillasson /pajasɔ̃/ *nm* **1** (tapis) doormat; **2** (personne servile) doormat; **3** Agric matting ¢; **4** Culin grated and sautéed potatoes (*pl*).

paille /pɑj/ **I ▶ 193⌋** *adj inv* (couleur) **cheveux (couleur) ~** straw-coloured[GB] hair; **jaune ~** straw yellow.
II *nf* **1** Agric straw; (de chaise) straw; **~ fraîche** fresh straw; **tapis de ~** straw mat; **un brin de ~** a wisp of straw; **~ de riz/seigle** rice/rye straw; **▶ bête**; **2** (pour boire) straw; **boire avec une ~** to drink through a straw; **3** Tech (défaut) flaw; **4**○ (presque rien) iron **trois ans, une ~!** three years, that's nothing at all! iron.
■ **~ de fer** steel wool.
IDIOMES **être sur la ~** to be penniless; **se retrouver sur la ~** to find oneself destitute; **mettre qn sur la ~** to ruin sb; **tirer à la courte ~** to draw lots; **voir la ~ qu'il y a dans l'œil de son voisin mais pas la poutre dans le sien** to see the mote in one's neighbour's[GB] eye but not the beam in one's own.

pailler /pɑje/ [1] *vtr* **1** Hort ≈ to mulch [*sol, arbuste*]; **2** (garnir) to put a straw seat in [*chaise*]; **chaise paillée** chair with a straw seat.

pailleté, **~e** /pajte/ *adj* **1** (avec des disques brillants) sequined, spangled US; **2** (avec de la poudre brillante) [*tissu*] glittery; **cheveux ~s d'or** hair sprayed with gold; **yeux ~s d'or** eyes flecked with gold.

paillette /pajɛt/ *nf* **1** (disque brillant) sequin, spangle US; **robe à ~s** a sequined ou spangled US dress; **2** (poudre brillante) glitter ¢; **3** (de roche) splinter; **savon en ~s** soap flakes.
■ **~ de sperme** sperm straw; **~s d'or** gold particles.

paillis /pɑji/ *nm* Hort ≈ mulch.

paillon /pɑjɔ̃/ *nm* (de bouteille) straw cover.

paillote /pajɔt/ *nf* grass hut.

pain /pɛ̃/ *nm* **1** (aliment) bread ¢; **le ~ frais/rassis** fresh/stale bread; **morceau/tranche de ~** piece/slice of bread; **des miettes de ~** breadcrumbs; **notre ~ quotidien** fig our daily bread; **le ~ et le vin** Relig the bread and wine; **être au ~ sec et à l'eau** to be on bread and water; **2** (miche) loaf; **un ~ rond** a round loaf; **acheter deux ~s** to buy two loaves; **un petit ~** a (bread) roll; **3** Culin **~ de légumes/viande/poisson** vegetable/meat/fish loaf;

4 (bloc) (de savon, cire) bar; (de glace) block; (de plastic, dynamite) stick; **5**◑ (coup) punch, sock○; **mettre un ~ à qn** to sock○ sb.
■ **~ bénit** Relig consecrated bread; **être ~ béni(t) pour qn** to be a godsend for sb; **~ bis** brown bread; **~ blanc** white bread; (miche) white loaf; **manger son ~ blanc le premier** to have it easy at the start; **~ brioché** brioche bread; (miche) brioche loaf; **~ à cacheter** bar of sealing wax; **~ de campagne** farmhouse bread; (miche) farmhouse loaf; **~ au chocolat** pastry with chocolate filling; **~ complet** wholemeal bread; (miche) wholemeal loaf; **~ d'épices** gingerbread; **~ de Gênes** Genoa cake; **~ grillé** toast; **~ au lait** milk roll; **~ au levain** sourdough bread; **~ de mie** sandwich loaf; **~ noir** rye bread; **~ perdu** French toast; **~ aux raisins** currant bun; **~ de seigle** rye bread; (miche) rye loaf; **~ sans sel** unsalted (white) bread; **~ de son** bran loaf; **~ de sucre** Culin, Géol sugar loaf; **en ~ de sucre** (crâne) egg-shaped; (montagne) sugar loaf (*épith*); **le Pain de Sucre** Géog Sugar Loaf Mountain; **~ viennois** Viennese bread; (miche) Viennese loaf.
IDIOMES **se vendre comme des petits ~s** to sell like hot cakes; **ça ne mange pas de ~**○ it doesn't cost anything; **je ne mange pas de ce ~-là** I won't have anything to do with it, I want no part of it; **enlever** or **ôter le ~ de la bouche à qn** to take the bread out of sb's mouth; **être bon comme du (bon) ~** to have a heart of gold; **long comme un jour sans ~** [*personne*] very tall; [*pantalon*] very long; **faire passer le goût du ~ à qn**○ to teach sb a lesson they won't forget.

pair, **~e** /pɛʀ/ **I** *adj* [*nombre, jours, fonction*] even; **le côté des numéros ~s d'une rue** the even-numbered side of a street.
II *nm* **1** (égal) peer; **être jugé/élu par ses ~s** to be judged/elected by one's peers; **c'est une cuisinière hors ~** she's an excellent cook; **elle a un mari hors ~!** she has a marvellous[GB] husband!; **aller** or **marcher de ~ avec qch** to go hand in hand with sth; **2** Hist, Pol peer; **3** Écon, Fin par, par value; **~ du change** par of exchange; **actions au ~** shares at par.
III au pair *loc* **travailler au ~** to work as an au pair; **jeune fille au ~** au pair (girl); **placer sa fille au ~ chez qn** to put one's daughter to work as an au pair with sb.
IV paire *nf* pair; **donner une ~e de gifles à qn** to box sb's ears.
IDIOMES **se faire la ~e**○ to hop it○ GB, to clear out○; **les deux font la ~e!** they're two of a kind!

pairesse /pɛʀɛs/ *nf* peeress.

pairie /pɛ(e)ʀi/ *nf* (dignité) peerage.

paisible /pezibl/ *adj* **1** (doux) [*animal, personne, caractère*] gentle; **d'une voix ~** in a gentle voice; **2** (tranquille) [*existence, vie, quartier*] peaceful, quiet; [*personne*] calm, easygoing; [*eau*] calm, untroubled; [*sommeil*] peaceful; **les eaux ~s d'une rivière** the calm waters of a river; **il dormait d'un sommeil ~** he was sleeping peacefully.

paisiblement /pezibləmɑ̃/ *adv* **1** (sans agressivité) [*manifester, défiler*] peacefully, peaceably; **2** (tranquillement) [*lire*] quietly, peacefully; [*dormir*] peacefully; **3** (sans s'inquiéter) quietly.

paître /pɛtʀ/ [74] *vi* to graze.
IDIOMES **envoyer ~ qn**○ hum to send sb packing○.

paix /pɛ/ *nf inv* **1** Pol, Mil peace; **en temps de ~** in peacetime, in times of peace; **œuvrer pour la ~ dans le monde** to work for world peace; **homme de ~** man of peace; **vivre en ~ avec son prochain** to live in peace with one's neighbour[GB]; **demander la ~** to sue for peace; **signer/négocier la ~** to sign/to negotiate a peace treaty; **conférence/traité/pourparlers de ~** peace conference/treaty/talks; **faire la ~ avec qn** to make peace with sb; **2** (calme intérieur) peace; **être en ~ avec soi-même** to be at peace with oneself; **la ~ de l'âme** peace of mind; **avoir la conscience** or **l'esprit en ~** to have peace of mind; **3** (tranquillité) peace; **avoir la ~** to have some peace; **il s'enferme dans son bureau pour avoir la ~** he shuts himself away in his office to get some peace; **laisser qn en ~** to leave sb alone, to leave sb in peace; **foutre**◑ **la ~ à qn** to leave sb alone; **fous-moi**◑ **la ~!** leave me alone!, get lost○!; **la ~!** be quiet!; **~ à ses cendres** or **à son âme** God rest his/her soul; **allez-en ~** go in peace; **qu'il repose en ~** may he rest in peace.
■ **~ armée** armed peace; **~ des braves** Mil honourable[GB] surrender; **~ éternelle** eternal rest; **~ sociale** social stability.
IDIOMES **si tu veux la ~, prépare la guerre** Prov if you want peace, prepare for war.

Pakistan /pakistɑ̃/ ▶321 *nprm* Pakistan.

pakistanais, **~e** /pakistanɛ, ɛz/ ▶537 *adj* Pakistani.

Pakistanais, **~e** /pakistanɛ, ɛz/ ▶537 *nm,f* Pakistani.

pal /pal/ *nm* **1** (pieu) aussi Hérald pale; **2** (supplice) impalement; **subir le supplice du ~** to undergo torture by impalement.

PAL /pal/ *nm* TV (*abbr* = **phase alternation line**) PAL; **système ~** PAL standard.

palabre /palabʀ/ *nm* ou *f* **1** (discussion) endless discussion; **perdre son temps en ~s** to waste one's time in endless discussions; **2** (assemblée) ≈ council.

palabrer /palabʀe/ [1] *vi* to discuss endlessly.

palace /palas/ *nm* luxury hotel.

paladin /paladɛ̃/ *nm* **1** Hist paladin; **2** fig (défenseur) champion.

palais /palɛ/ *nm inv* **1** Anat palate; **~ dur/mou/fendu** hard/soft/cleft palate; **2** (goût) palate; **avoir le ~ fin** to have a fine palate; **délicat au ~** delicate to the palate; **vin qui flatte le ~** wine that delights the palate; **3** Archit (de souverain, particulier) palace; **~ nationaux** *state-owned historic buildings in Paris*; **Grand Palais** *19th century exhibition centre in Paris*; **4** Jur law courts; **~ de justice** law courts; **dans le style du ~** in legal parlance.
■ **~ Bourbon** *seat of the French National Assembly*; **~ Brongniart** *home of the French Stock Exchange*; **~ du Luxembourg** *seat of the French Senate*; **~ des sports** sports centre[GB].

palan /palɑ̃/ *nm* hoist.

palanquin /palɑ̃kɛ̃/ *nm* palanquin.

palatal, **~e**, *mpl* **-aux** /palatal, o/ *adj* Phon palatal.

palatalisation /palatalizasjɔ̃/ *nf* palatalization.

palatalisé, **~e** /palatalize/ *adj* palatalized.

palatin, **~e** /palatɛ̃, in/ *adj* **1** Anat palatine; **2** Hist [*comte, Electeur*] Palatine; **le mont Palatin** Mount Palatine.

Palatinat /palatina/ *nprm* Palatinate.

pale /pal/ *nf* **1** (d'hélice, de rame, roue) blade; **2** Tech (vanne) paddle.

pâle /pɑl/ *adj* **1** lit [*couleur, teint, lueur*] pale; **vert/bleu ~** pale green/blue; **tu es toute ~, ça ne va pas?** you look really pale, is something wrong?; **~ de jalousie** green with envy; **être ~ comme un linge** to be as white as a sheet; **2** fig **une ~ imitation** a pale imitation; **faire ~ figure à côté de** to pale into insignificance beside.
IDIOMES **se faire porter ~**○ to go sick○.

palefrenier, **-ière** /palfʀənje, ɛʀ/ *nm,f* groom.

palefroi† /palfʀwa/ *nm* palfrey†.

paléochrétien, **-ienne** /paleokʀetjɛ̃, ɛn/ *adj* [*art*] early Christian.

paléographe /paleɔgʀaf/ ▶510 *nmf* paleographer.

paléographie /paleɔgʀafi/ *nf* paleography.

paléographique /paleɔgʀafik/ *adj* paleographic.

paléolithique /paleɔlitik/ *adj, nm* Paleolithic.

paléomagnétisme /paleomaɲetism/ *nm* paleomagnetism.

paléontologie /paleɔ̃tɔlɔʒi/ *nf* paleontology.

paléontologique /paleɔ̃tɔlɔʒik/ *adj* paleontological.

paléontologiste /paleɔ̃tɔlɔʒist/, **paléontologue** /paleɔ̃tɔlɔg/ ▶510 *nmf* paleontologist.

paléozoïque /paleozɔik/ *nm* Paleozoic.

Palerme /palɛʀm/ ▶857 *nprm* Palermo.

paleron /palʀɔ̃/ *nm* chuck (steak).

Palestine /palɛstin/ ▶692 *nprf* Palestine.

palestinien, **-ienne** /palɛstinjɛ̃, ɛn/ ▶692 *adj* Palestinian.

Palestinien, **-ienne** /palɛstinjɛ̃, ɛn/ *nm,f* Palestinian.

palet /palɛ/ *nm* **1** Sport (au hockey sur glace) puck; **2** Jeux (pierre) quoit; (jeu) quoits (+ *v sg*).

paletot /palto/ *nm* jacket.
IDIOMES **tomber sur le ~ de qn**○ to lay into sb○.

palette /palɛt/ *nf* **1** Art (objet, couleurs) palette; **2** fig range; **une ~ de services/d'activités** a range of services/activities; **la ~ d'un musicien/acteur** a musician's/an actor's range; **3** Culin (de porc, mouton) ≈ shoulder; **4** (plateau de chargement) pallet.
■ **~ de maquillage** make-up palette.

palétuvier /paletyvje/ *nm* (arbre) mangrove; (bois) mangrove (wood).

pâleur /pɑlœʀ/ *nf* **1** (de ciel) paleness; **2** (de malade) pallor; **il est d'une ~ maladive** his face has a sickly pallor.

pâlichon○, **-onne** /pɑliʃɔ̃, ɔn/ *adj* [*personne, teint*] peaky○ GB, peaked US; [*ciel, éclairage*] watery.

palier /palje/ *nm* **1** (d'escalier) landing; **mon voisin de ~** my neighbour[GB] on the same floor; **2** fig (stade) level; (phase stable) plateau; **l'inflation a atteint un ~** inflation has reached a plateau; **avancer par ~s** to proceed by stages; **3** Sport (en plongée) **~ (de décompression)** (decompression) stage; Aviat **vol en ~** horizontal flight; **4** Mécan bearing.

palière /paljɛʀ/ *adj f* **porte ~** entry door.

palimpseste /palɛ̃psɛst/ *nm* palimpsest.

palindrome /palɛ̃dʀom/ **I** *adj* palindromic.
II *nm* palindrome.

palinodie /palinɔdi/ *nf* **1** Antiq, Littérat palinode; **2** (rétractation) recantation.

pâlir /pɑliʀ/ [3] *vi* **1** [*coloris, photo, jour*] to fade; [*ciel, soleil*] to grow pale; [*personne*] to turn pale (**de** with); **il pâlit de jour en jour** he's growing paler every day; **faire ~ qn d'envie** or **de jalousie** to make sb green with envy; **un succès à faire ~ les concurrents** a success that would make the competition green with envy; **2** [*souvenirs*] to fade; [*gloire, prestige*] to fade (**à côté de** beside); **son étoile pâlit** his/her star is fading.

palissade /palisad/ *nf* (de jardin) fence; Mil palisade.

palissandre /palisɑ̃dʀ/ *nm* (arbre) rosewood; (bois) rosewood; (couleur) the colour[GB] of rosewood.

pâlissant, **~e** /pɑlisɑ̃, ɑ̃t/ *adj* [*jour, lueur*] fading.

palliatif, **-ive** /paljatif, iv/ **I** *adj* **1** gén [*mesure*] palliative; **2** Méd [*soin*] palliative; **unité de soins ~s** (établissement) hospice; (service hospitalier) unit for terminally ill patients.
II *nm* gén, Méd palliative.

pallier /palje/ [2] **I** *vtr* to compensate for [*problème, manque, inconvénient*].
II pallier à *vtr ind* controv = **pallier I**.
palmarès /palmaʀɛs/ *nm inv* **1** (classement) honours[GB] list; (d'acteurs, auteurs, etc) list of award winners; (de sportifs) list of winners; **premier au ~** first in the honours list; **2** (liste de succès) (tous contextes) record of achievements; **il a trois tournois à son ~** he has three tournament wins to his credit; **3** (meilleures ventes) hit parade.
palme /palm/ *nf* **1** Bot (feuille) palm leaf; (palmier) palm; **huile/sucre de ~** palm oil/sugar; **2** Sport (pour nager) flipper; **3** (décoration) Mil ≈ bar; **décoration avec ~** decoration and bar; **4** fig prize; **décerner la ~ de la politesse à qn** to award sb the prize for politeness; **remporter la ~** to take the prize.
■ **la ~ d'or** Cin the Palme d'or; **~s académiques** Univ *academic decoration for services to education.*
palmé, **~e** /palme/ *adj* **1** Zool [*pattes, doigts*] webbed, palmate spéc; **2** Bot [*feuille*] palmate.
palmer /palmɛʀ/ *nm* micrometer calliper.
palmeraie /palməʀɛ/ *nf* palm grove.
palmier /palmje/ *nm* **1** Bot palm (tree); **2** Culin (pâtisserie) large pastry biscuit.
■ **~ dattier** date palm; **~ à huile** oil palm.
palmipède /palmipɛd/ **I** *adj* web-footed.
II *nm* palmiped.
palmiste /palmist/ *nm* (arec) cabbage palm; (palmier à huile) oil palm.
palois, **~e** /palwa, az/ ▶857 *adj* of Pau.
Palois, **~e** /palwa, az/ *nm,f* (natif) native of Pau; (habitant) inhabitant of Pau.
palombe /palɔ̃b/ *nf* wood pigeon.
palonnier /palɔnje/ *nm* **1** Aviat rudder bar; Aut compensator; **2** Agric swingletree, singletree US.
palot◑ /palo/ *nm* French kiss; **rouler un ~ à qn**◑ to give sb a French kiss.
pâlot○, **-otte** /pɑlo, ɔt/ *adj* rather pale; **elle est un peu pâlotte ces jours-ci** she's been looking rather pale lately.
palourde /paluʀd/ *nf* clam.
palpable /palpabl/ *adj* [*objet, bonheur, brouillard*] palpable; [*vérité, preuve, avantage*] tangible.
palpation /palpasjɔ̃/ *nf* Méd palpation.
palpébral, **~e**, *mpl* **-aux** /palpebʀal, o/ *adj* Anat palpebral.
palper /palpe/ [1] *vtr* **1** [*médecin*] to palpate [*partie du corps*]; [*client, aveugle*] to feel [*objet, fruit*]; **2**○ (gagner de l'argent) **~ (de l'argent)** to rake it in○.
palpeur /palpœʀ/ *nm* **1** (de cuisinière électrique) heat sensor; **2** Tech sensor head.
palpitant, **~e** /palpitɑ̃, ɑ̃t/ **I** *adj* **1** (captivant) [*histoire, vie, ambiance, journée*] thrilling; **2** [*cœur*] fluttering; [*chair, corps*] twitching; **3** (qui respire par saccades) panting (**de** with).
II◑ *nm* (cœur) ticker○, heart.
palpitation /palpitasjɔ̃/ *nf* **1** Méd palpitation; **avoir des ~s** to have palpitations; **2** (de paupière, muscle) twitching; **3** liter (de lumière, de flamme, d'étoile) flickering; (de feuille, voile) fluttering; (d'eau) quivering; **4** liter (exaltation) thrill (**de** of); **~ de la vie/de l'aventure** thrill of life/adventure.
palpiter /palpite/ [1] *vi* **1** (battre) [*cœur*] to beat; [*chair, corps*] to twitch; [*veine*] to pulse; **2** (avoir des mouvements convulsifs) [*cœur*] to flutter; [*paupière, tempe*] to twitch; **3** liter (frémir) [*personne, eau*] to quiver (**de** with); [*lumière, flamme*] to flicker; [*feuille, voile*] to flutter.
palplanche /palplɑ̃ʃ/ *nf* Constr, Mines sheet pile, pile plank.
palsambleu‡ /palsɑ̃blø/ *excl* zounds‡!
paltoquet† /paltɔkɛ/ *nm* **1** (rustre) boor; **2** (prétentieux) wise guy○.
paluche◑ /palyʃ/ *nf* mitt◑, hand.
paludéen, **-éenne** /palydeɛ̃, ɛn/ *adj* Méd malarial; Géog paludal.
paludisme /palydism/ ▶271 *nm* malaria, paludism spéc.
palustre /palystʀ/ *adj* Géog paludal; Méd malarial.
pâmer: **se pâmer** /pɑme/ [1] *vpr* liter **se ~ de plaisir** to swoon with pleasure; **se ~ (d'admiration) devant qch** to swoon over sth; **il se pâmait d'aise** he was pleased as Punch.
pâmoison /pɑmwazɔ̃/ *nf* liter swoon; **tomber en ~ (devant qch)** to swoon (over sth).
pampa /pɑ̃pa/ *nf* pampas (+ *v sg*).
pamphlet /pɑ̃flɛ/ *nm* satirical tract.
pamphlétaire /pɑ̃fletɛʀ/ **I** *adj* pamphleteering.
II *nmf* pamphleteer.
pampille /pɑ̃pij/ *nf* **1** (de lustre) drop; **2** (en bijouterie) (forme de pierre taillée) pear-shape; (pendeloque) pendant stone.
pamplemousse /pɑ̃pləmus/ *nm* grapefruit.
pamplemoussier /pɑ̃pləmusje/ *nm* grapefruit tree.
pampre /pɑ̃pʀ/ *nm* **1** Bot vine branch (*with leaves and fruit*); **2** Archit pampre.
pan /pɑ̃/ *nm* (*also onomat*) **1** (partie) (de falaise, maison) section; (de vie, problème) part; (d'obscurité, de ciel) patch; **~ de mur** section of wall; **~ de vitre** glass panel; **2** (côté) (de tour, prisme) side; **relever les ~s d'un rideau** to tie back the curtains; **~s d'un manteau** coat-tails; **à ~s coupés** with cut-off corners; **3** (bruit) (de coup de feu) bang!; (de coup de poing) thump!; (de fessée) whack!; **je vais faire ~ ~** baby talk I'll give you a smack; **4** (marquant la soudaineté) pow!; **tout allait bien, et ~! on nous a dit que**... everything was fine, and pow! we were told that...
■ **~ de chemise** shirttail.
pan(-) /pɑ̃, pan/ *préf* Pol Pan; **pan-russe** Pan-Russian; **pan-européen** Pan-European.
Pan /pɑ̃/ *npr* Pan.
panacée /panase/ *nf* panacea.
panachage /panaʃaʒ/ *nm* Pol *voting for candidates from more than one party.*
panache /panaʃ/ *nm* **1** (élégance) panache; **avec ~** with panache; **2** (plumes) plume; **3** (de fumée, d'eau) plume (**de** of).
panaché, **~e** /panaʃe/ **I** *pp* ▶ **panacher**.
II *pp adj* [*bouquet, salade*] mixed; [*tulipe, lierre*] variegated.
III *nm* (bière et limonade) shandy.
panacher /panaʃe/ [1] *vtr* **1** to mix [*couleurs, fleurs, styles*]; **2** Pol **~ une liste électorale** to vote for a split ticket.
panade /panad/ *nf* bread soup.
IDIOMES **être dans la ~**○ to be in the soup○ ou in a tight corner.
panafricain, **~e** /panafʀikɛ̃, ɛn/ *adj* Pan-African.
panafricanisme /panafʀikanism/ *nm* Pan-Africanism.
panama /panama/ *nm* (chapeau) panama (hat).
Panama /panama/ ▶321, 857 *nprm* (pays) Panama; (ville) Panama City; **le canal de ~** the Panama Canal.
panaméen, **-éenne** /panameɛ̃, ɛn/ ▶537 *adj* Panamanian.
Panaméen, **-éenne** /panameɛ̃, ɛn/ ▶537 *nm,f* Panamanian.
panaméricain, **~e** /panameʀikɛ̃, ɛn/ *adj* Pan-American.
panaméricanisme /panameʀikanism/ *nm* Pan-Americanism.
panarabe /panaʀab/ *adj* Pan-Arab.
panarabisme /panaʀabism/ *nm* Pan-Arabism.
panard◑ /panaʀ/ *nm* foot.
panaris /panaʀi/ ▶271 *nm inv* whitlow.
pancarte /pɑ̃kaʀt/ *nf* **1** (sur un mur) notice GB, sign US; (sur un piquet) sign; **2** (dans une manifestation) placard GB, sign US.
pancréas /pɑ̃kʀeas/ *nm inv* pancreas.
pancréatique /pɑ̃kʀeatik/ *adj* pancreatic.
pancréatite /pɑ̃kʀeatit/ ▶271 *nf* pancreatitis.
panda /pɑ̃da/ *nm* panda.
Pandore /pɑ̃dɔʀ/ *npr* Pandora; **la boîte de ~** Pandora's box.
panégyrique /paneʒiʀik/ *nm* panegyric.
panel /panɛl/ *nm* **1** (de spécialistes) panel; **2** (échantillon) sample group.
paner /pane/ [1] *vtr* to coat with ou in breadcrumbs.
pangermanisme /pɑ̃ʒɛʀmanism/ *nm* Pan-Germanism.
pangermaniste /pɑ̃ʒɛʀmanist/ *adj* Pan-German.
panhellénique /panɛlenik/ *adj* Pan-hellenic.
panhellénisme /panɛlenism/ *nm* Pan-hellenism.
panicule /panikyl/ *nf* panicle.
panier /panje/ *nm* **1** (en osier, rotin, etc) basket; (corbeille à papier) wastepaper basket; (dans lave-vaisselle) rack; **mettre** or **jeter au ~** lit to throw [sth] out; fig to get rid of; **2** Sport (au basket-ball) basket; **marquer** or **réussir un ~** to score a basket; **3** Phot (de projecteur) magazine; **4** Mode pannier; **robe à ~s** dress with panniers.
■ **~ à bouteilles** bottle carrier; **~ à frites** chip basket GB, French-fry basket US; **~ garni** *small basket of fine food*; **~ à linge** linen basket; **le ~ de la ménagère** Écon the housewife's shopping basket; **~ de monnaies** Écon, Fin basket of currencies; **~ à salade** (ustensile) salad shaker; ○(fourgon de police) Black Maria GB, paddy wagon US.
IDIOMES **être un ~ percé**○ to spend money like water; **mettre tout le monde dans le même ~**○ to lump everybody together; **ils sont tous à mettre dans le même ~**○ they are all much of a muchness GB, they are all about the same; **mettre tous ses œufs dans le même ~**○ to put all one's eggs in one basket; **le haut** or **dessus du ~**○ the pick of the bunch, the cream of the crop; **mettre la main au ~ de qn**○ to feel sb's bottom; **ce bureau est un vrai ~ de crabes**○ the people in this office are always at each other's throats.
panière /panjɛʀ/ *nf* large basket.
panier-repas, *pl* **paniers-repas** /panjeʀəpa/ *nm* packed lunch GB, box lunch US.
panifiable /panifjabl/ *adj* suitable for making bread.
panification /panifikasjɔ̃/ *nf* bread-making.
panifier /panifje/ [2] *vtr* to make bread from [*céréale, farine*].
panique /panik/ **I** *adj* panic; **ventes ~s** panic selling; **trouble ~** panic attack; **sensibilité ~ au bruit** panic reaction to noise; **peur ~ (de qch)** terror (of sth).
II *nf* panic; **mouvement de ~** panic; **il y eut un mouvement de ~** there was panic; **début de ~** moment of panic; **semer** or **jeter la ~** to spread panic; **pas de ~!** don't panic!; **être pris de ~** to panic; **provoquer la ~ chez qn** to make sb panic.
paniquer○ /panike/ [1] **I** *vtr* to throw [sb] into a panic.
II *vi* to panic; **il a paniqué** he panicked.
III se paniquer *vpr* to panic.
panislamique /panislamik/ *adj* Pan-Islamic.
panislamisme /panislamism/ *nm* Pan-Islamism.
panjabi /pɑ̃ʒabi/ ▶462 *nm* Ling Punjabi, Panjabi.
panne /pan/ *nf* **1** (de véhicule, machine) breakdown; (de moteur, d'électricité) failure; **~ de courant** power failure; **avoir une ~** to

have a breakdown; **machine/voiture en ~** broken-down machine/car; **tomber en ~** [*voiture, appareil, instrument*] to break down; fig [*artiste, écrivain*] to run out of inspiration; **la machine/voiture est (tombée) en ~** the machine/car has broken down; **tomber en ~ sèche** or **d'essence** to run out of petrol GB ou gas US; **être à la merci d'une ~** to run the risk of breaking down; **lorsque la ~ survint...** (de voiture) when the car broke down...; (d'électricité) when the power failed...; **être en ~**○ fig [*recherche, projet*] to have come to a standstill; [*idéologie, pensée*] to be in a rut; **être en ~ de**○ to be out of [*objet, main-d'œuvre*]; to have run out of [*idées, imagination*]; **2** Constr (poutre) purlin; (tuile) pantile; **3** Tex panne; **4** Culin fat; **5** Naut **mettre en ~** to heave [sth] to [*voilier*]; **6** Tech (de marteau) peen.

IDIOMES **faire le coup de la ~** to pretend to break down (*so as to make advances to sb*).

panneau, *pl* **~x** /pano/ *nm* **1** (permanent) sign; (temporaire) board; (d'information) noticeboard; **il y a un ~ à l'entrée** there's a sign at the entrance; **mettre une annonce sur le ~** to put a notice on the board; **2** (élément) panel; **jupe à trois ~x** skirt made in three panels; **~ préfabriqué/en bois** prefabricated/wooden panel; **3** Art panel; **peint sur ~** painted on panel; **~ de Giotto** panel by Giotto.

■ **~ d'affichage** notice board GB, bulletin board; **~ électoral** Pol election signboard (*outside polling stations*); **~ indicateur** Aut signpost; **~ publicitaire** hoarding GB, billboard; **~ de signalisation routière** road sign; **~ solaire** solar panel.

IDIOMES **tomber** or **donner dans le ~**○ to fall for it○.

panonceau, *pl* **~x** /panɔ̃so/ *nm* (permanent) sign; (temporaire) board.

panoplie /panɔpli/ *nf* **1** Jeux (pour se déguiser) outfit; **une ~ de Zorro/docteur** a Zorro/doctor outfit; **2** (de professionnel) paraphernalia; **3** (ornementale) display; **4** (gamme) (d'objets usuels) array; (d'armements) arsenal; (de mesures, moyens) range; **le pays dispose d'une ~ d'armes nucléaires** the country has an arsenal of nuclear weapons; **il ont mis en œuvre toute une ~ de moyens** they have instigated a range of measures.

panorama /panɔrama/ *nm* **1** lit panorama; **2** fig (culturel) panorama; (politique, international, industriel) overview; **brosser un ~ de l'art contemporain** to paint a panorama of contemporary art.

panoramique /panɔramik/ **I** *adj* **1** gén [*vue, visite, route*] panoramic; **tour/restaurant ~** tower/restaurant with a panoramic view; **2** Aut [*vitre, pare-brise*] wrap-around; **toit ouvrant ~** sunroof; **3** Cin [*écran*] wide.

II *nm* Cin pan (shot); **~ horizontal/vertical** horizontal/vertical pan (shot).

panosse /panɔs/ *nf* H **1** (serpillière) floor cloth; **2** (chiffon) cloth.

pansage /pɑ̃saʒ/ *nm* (de cheval) grooming.

panse /pɑ̃s/ *nf* **1** Zool paunch; **2**○ hum (estomac) belly○; **s'en mettre plein la ~**○ to stuff one's face○; **3** (de cruche) belly.

pansement /pɑ̃smɑ̃/ *nm* **1** (avec compresse) dressing; **~ (adhésif)** plaster GB, Band-Aid®; **faire un ~ à qn** to put a dressing on sb's wound; **je vais te refaire ton ~** I'm going to change your dressing; **2** (action) dressing.

panser /pɑ̃se/ [1] *vtr* **1** Méd to dress [*blessure*]; to put a dressing on [*partie du corps*]; **2** fig [*temps*] to heal [*blessure morale*]; **~ ses blessures** to lick one's wounds; **3** Agric (étriller) to groom [*cheval*]; (prendre soin de) to muck out and feed [*vaches*]; to feed [*poules, lapins*].

panslavisme /pɑ̃slavism/ *nm* Pan-Slavism.

panslaviste /pɑ̃slavist/ **I** *adj* Pan-Slavic.

II *nm* Panslavist.

pansu, **~e** /pɑ̃sy/ *adj* [*personne, objet*] pot-bellied.

pantagruélique /pɑ̃tagʀyelik/ *adj* [*repas, appétit*] Pantagruelian.

pantalon /pɑ̃talɔ̃/ *nm* **1** (culotte longue) trousers GB (*pl*), pants US (*pl*); **acheter un ~** to buy a pair of trousers GB ou pants US; **mon ~ est sale** my trousers GB ou pants US are dirty; **~ à pinces** peg-top trousers GB ou pants US; **~ en toile** canvas trousers GB ou pants US; **~ à revers** trousers with turn-ups GB, cuffed pants US; **~ de** or **en flanelle/cuir** flannel/leather trousers GB ou pants US; **~ de pyjama** pyjama GB ou pajama US bottoms; **~ de** or **en velours** cords (*pl*); **2**† (sous-vêtement) bloomers (*pl*).

■ **~ corsaire** pedal pushers (*pl*); **~ de golf** plus-fours (*pl*).

Pantalon /pɑ̃talɔ̃/ *npr* Pantaloon.

pantalonnade /pɑ̃talɔnad/ *nf* **1** Théât slapstick comedy; **2** fig play-acting ¢.

pantelant, **~e** /pɑ̃tlɑ̃, ɑ̃t/ *adj* **1** (haletant) [*personne*] panting; (palpitant) [*chair*] quivering; **2** (ému) overcome (**de** with); **la nouvelle l'a laissé tout ~** he was overcome at the news.

panthéisme /pɑ̃teism/ *nm* pantheism.

panthéiste /pɑ̃teist/ **I** *adj* pantheistic.

II *nmf* pantheist.

panthéon /pɑ̃teɔ̃/ *nm* pantheon.

panthère /pɑ̃tɛʀ/ *nf* **1** (animal) panther; **2** (fourrure) panther skin.

■ **~ d'Afrique** African panther; **~ noire** black panther.

pantin /pɑ̃tɛ̃/ *nm* (jouet, fantoche) puppet.

IDIOMES **gesticuler comme un ~** to wave one's arms around.

pantographe /pɑ̃tɔgʀaf/ *nm* Tech, Rail pantograph.

pantois, **~e** /pɑ̃twa, az/ *adj* flabbergasted; **rester ~** to be flabbergasted; **ça m'a laissé ~** I was flabbergasted.

pantomime /pɑ̃tɔmim/ *nf* (art) mime; (spectacle) mime show; **faire la ~** fig to play it up.

pantouflard○, **~e** /pɑ̃tuflaʀ, aʀd/ **I** *adj* **personne ~e** stay-at-home○; **qu'est-ce que tu es ~!** what a stay-at-home you are!

II *nm,f* stay-at-home.

pantoufle /pɑ̃tufl/ *nf* slipper; **être en ~s** to be in one's slippers.

pantoufler○ /pɑ̃tufle/ [1] *vi* [*haut fonctionnaire*] to work in the private sector.

panure /panyʀ/ *nf* breadcrumbs (*pl*).

PAO /peao/ *nf* **1** *abbr* ▶ **production**; **2** *abbr* ▶ **publication**.

paon /pɑ̃/ *nm* **1** Zool peacock; **une plume de ~** a peacock feather; **2** (orgueilleux) peacock; **faire le ~** to play the peacock.

IDIOMES **être fier comme un ~** to be as proud as a peacock; **se parer des plumes du ~** to take all the credit for oneself.

paonne /pan/ *nf* peahen.

papa /papa/ *nm* dad○, daddy○, father; **placement à la ~**○ safe investment; **jouer au ~ et à la maman** to play mummies and daddies GB, to play house; **fils** or **fille à ~** spoiled little rich kid○.

■ **~ gâteau** doting father; **~ poule** overprotective father.

papal, **~e**, *mpl* **-aux** /papal, o/ *adj* papal.

papauté /papote/ *nf* papacy.

papaye /papaj/ *nf* papaya.

papayer /papaje/ *nm* papaya (tree).

pape /pap/ *nm* **1** ▶ **813** Relig pope; **le ~ Jean-Paul II** Pope John Paul II; **2** fig (personne influente) high priest (**de qch** of sth).

IDIOMES **être sérieux comme un ~** to be solemn-faced.

papelard, **~e** /paplaʀ, aʀd/ **I** *adj* liter (hypocrite) smooth.

II○ *nm* (papier) paper.

papelardise /paplaʀdiz/ *nf* liter smoothness.

paperasse○ /papʀas/ *nf* pej **1** (papiers) bumph○ ¢ GB, documents (*pl*); **2** (activité) paperwork ¢.

paperasserie○ /papʀasʀi/ *nf* paperwork.

paperassier○, **-ière** /papʀasje, ɛʀ/ *adj* [*employé*] fond of red tape (*jamais épith*); [*système, organisme*] full of red tape (*jamais épith*).

papeterie /papɛtʀi/ *nf* **1** ▶ **510** (commerce) stationer's (shop), stationery shop GB ou store US; **2** (articles) stationery; **3** (industrie) papermaking industry; **4** (usine) paper mill.

papetier, **-ière** /paptje, ɛʀ/ **I** *adj* papermaking.

II ▶ **510** *nm,f* **1** (fabricant) papermaker; **2** (commerçant) stationer.

papette /papɛt/ *nf* H **1** (neige fondue) slush; **2** (boue) mud.

papi /papi/ *nm* **1** (grand-père) granddad○, grandpa○; **2** (vieil homme) granddad○, old man.

papier /papje/ **I** *nm* **1** (matière) paper; **du ~ blanc/de couleur** white/coloured[GB] paper; **bout/feuille/morceau de ~** scrap/sheet/piece of paper; **jeter** or **coucher des idées sur le ~** to get ou put one's ideas down on paper; **sortie sur ~** Ordinat hardcopy output; **pâte à ~** pulp; **2** (document) paper; **jeter de vieux ~s à la poubelle** to throw out some old papers; **classer/ranger des ~s** to file/sort some papers; **~s personnels** personal ou private papers; **3**○ (article de journal) article, piece○.

II papiers *nmpl* Admin documents, papers; **~s d'identité** (identity) papers ou documents; **avoir des ~s en règle** to have one's papers in order.

■ **~ absorbant** kitchen towel, paper towel US; **~ (d')aluminium** (aluminium GB ou aluminum US) foil, kitchen foil; **~ alu**○ **~ d'argent** silver paper; **~ d'Arménie** incense paper; **~ par avion** airmail paper; **~ bible** India ou bible paper; **~ brouillon** rough paper GB, scrap paper; **~ bulle** unbleached paper; **~ buvard** blotting paper; **~ cadeau** gift wrap, wrapping paper; **~ canson**® drawing paper; **~ carbone** carbon paper; **~ chiffon** rag paper; **~ à cigarettes** cigarette paper; **fin comme du ~ à cigarettes** [*tarte, tranche*] wafer-thin; **~ collant** adhesive tape; **~ court** Fin short exchange; **~ crépon** crepe paper; **~ à dessin** drawing paper; **~ d'emballage** wrapping paper; **~ à en-tête** headed notepaper; **~ glacé** glossy ou shiny paper; **~ goudronné** tar paper; **~ hygiénique** toilet paper ou tissue; **~ Japon** Japanese paper; **~ journal** newsprint; **~ kraft** Manila paper; **~ à lettres** writing paper, notepaper; **~ libre** plain paper; **~ mâché** papier-mâché; **~ machine** typing paper; **~ millimétré** graph paper; **~ ministre** foolscap paper; **~ à musique** music paper; **être réglé comme du ~ à musique** [*vie*] to be highly regimented; **~ offset** offset paper; **~ paraffiné** wax paper; **~ peint** wallpaper; **~ pelure** onionskin (paper); **~ pH** litmus paper; **~ photographique** photographic paper; **~ de riz** rice paper; **~ de soie** tissue paper; **~ timbré** stamped paper; **~ toilette** = **~ hygiénique**; **~ sulfurisé** greaseproof paper; **~ tournesol** litmus paper; **~ tue-mouche** flypaper; **~ vélin** vellum paper; **~ vergé** laid paper; **~ de verre** sandpaper, glasspaper; **~s gras** litter ¢.

IDIOMES **être dans les petits ~s de qn** to be in sb's good books; **avoir une mine de ~ mâché** to be pasty faced, to have a pasty complexion.

papier-calque, *pl* **papiers-calque** /papjekalk/ *nm* tracing paper.

papier-émeri, *pl* **papiers-émeri** /papjeɛmʀi/ *nm* emery paper.

papier-filtre, *pl* **papiers-filtres** /papjefiltʀ/ *nm* filter paper.

papier-monnaie, *pl* **papiers-monnaies** /papjemɔnɛ/ *nm* paper money.

papille /papij/ *nf* papilla.

■ **~s gustatives** taste buds, lingual papillae spéc.
papillon /papijɔ̃/ *nm* **1** Zool butterfly; **2**○ (contravention) parking ticket; **3** Sport (**brasse**) **~** butterfly (stroke); **le 100 mètres ~** the 100 metres[GB] butterfly; **nager en ~** to swim the butterfly; **4** (personne) **ta sœur est un ~** your sister is flighty; **5** (écrou) wing nut, butterfly nut; **6** Aut (de carburation) butterfly valve.
■ **~ adhésif** (pour notes) self-stick note; (pour affichage) sticker; **~ de nuit** moth.
IDIOMES **minute ~**○ hang on a minute○.
papillonnant, ~e /papijɔnɑ̃, ɑ̃t/ *adj* flighty.
papillonner /papijɔne/ [1] *vi* **1** (voleter) to flit about (**de qch à qch** from sth to sth); **2** (être volage) to flirt incessantly.
papillote /papijɔt/ *nf* **1** Culin (papier aluminium) foil parcel; (confiserie) chocolate sweet GB ou candy US (*wrapped in silver paper*); (sur côtelette) frill; **faire du saumon en ~** to cook salmon in a foil parcel; **2** Cosmét curlpaper; **3** Relig (dans judaïsme) lock.
papillotement /papijɔtmɑ̃/ *nm* flickering **¢**.
papilloter /papijɔte/ [1] *vi* [*lumière*] to flicker; [*personne, yeux*] to blink; **~ des paupières** to blink.
papisme /papism/ *nm* popery.
papiste /papist/ *adj, nmf* papist.
papotage○ /papɔtaʒ/ *nm* **1** (activité) chattering; **2** (conversation) idle chatter **¢**.
papoter○ /papɔte/ [1] *vi* to chatter.
papou, ~e /papu/ **I** ▶**537** *adj* Papuan.
II ▶**462** *nm* Papuan.
Papou, ~e ▶**537** /papu/ *nm,f* Papuan.
Papouasie-Nouvelle-Guinée /papwazinuvɛlgine/ ▶**321** *nprf* Papua New Guinea.
papouille○ /papuj/ *nf* tickle **¢**; **faire des ~s à qn** to tickle sb.
paprika /papʀika/ *nm* paprika.
papule /papyl/ *nf* papule.
papy = **papi**.
papyrus /papiʀys/ *nm* Bot, Hist papyrus.
pâque /pɑk/ **I** *nf* **la ~ juive** Passover.
II pâques *nfpl* Easter; (**je vous souhaite de**) **joyeuses ~s** (I wish you a) happy Easter; **faire ses ~s** to do one's Easter duty.
Pâque /pɑk/ *nf* **la ~** (**juive**) Passover.
paquebot /pakbo/ *nm* liner; **~ transatlantique** transatlantic liner.
pâquerette /pɑkʀɛt/ *nf* daisy.
IDIOMES **être au ras des ~s**○ to be very basic.
Pâques /pɑk/ **I** *nm* Relig (fête) Easter; **les fêtes de ~** Easter; **le jour de ~** on Easter Sunday; **les vacances de ~** the Easter holidays GB ou vacation US; **à/pour ~** at/for Easter; **la semaine de ~** Easter week; **le lundi de ~** Easter Monday.
II ▶**416** *nprf* Géog **île de ~** Easter Island.
IDIOMES **faire ~ avant Carême** or **les Rameaux** to get pregnant before one is married.
paquet /pakɛ/ *nm* **1** Comm (de sucre, lessive, riz) packet GB, package US; (de cigarettes, café) packet GB, pack US; (d'enveloppes) pack; (de bonbons) bag; **mettre en ~** to package; **2** (colis) parcel; **faire/défaire/envoyer un ~** to wrap/undo/send a parcel; ▶**petit**; **3** (assemblage) (de vêtements, linge, billets) bundle; (de lettres) packet; **faire un ~ de journaux** to put together a bundle of newspapers; **4**○ (grande quantité) masses (*pl*); **il y avait des fraises par ~s** there were masses of strawberries; **5**○ (grosse somme) packet○ GB, bundle○ US; **gagner un ~** to make a packet○ ou bundle○; **6** Sport (au rugby) **~** (**d'avants**) pack (of forwards); **7** Ordinat, Télécom packet; **transmission par ~s** packet transmission; **8** Pol package.
■ **~ d'actions** Fin block of shares; **~ de données** Ordinat data packet; **~ d'erreurs** Ordinat error burst; **~ de mer** big wave; **~ de muscles** muscleman; **~ de nerfs**○ bundle of nerves○; **~ d'os**○ bag of bones○.
IDIOMES **faire ses ~s**○ to pack one's bags; **mettre le ~**○ to pull out all the stops; **risquer le ~**○ to go for the big one○.
paquetage /paktaʒ/ *nm* Mil pack.
paquet-cadeau, *pl* **paquets-cadeaux** /pakɛkado/ *nm* gift-wrapped present; **est-ce que vous pouvez faire un ~?** could you gift-wrap it?
par /paʀ/ **I** *prép* **1** (indiquant un trajet) **entre ~ le garage/~ la porte du garage** lit come in through the garage/by the garage door; **il a pris ~ les champs** he cut across the fields; **il est entré dans la compagnie ~ la petite porte** fig he got into the company through the back door; **il est passé ~ tous les échelons** fig he worked his way up through the ranks; **pour aller à Rome, je passe ~ Milan** to get to Rome, I go via ou by Milan; **prends** or **passe ~ le chemin au lieu de passer ~ la route** take the path instead of going by the road; **elle est arrivée ~ la droite** she came from the right; **errer ~ les rues** to wander through the streets; **voyager ~ le monde** to travel all over ou throughout the world; **le peintre a terminé** or **fini ~ la cuisine** the painter did the kitchen last; **2** (indiquant un lieu) **~ endroits** in places; **~ chez moi/nous**○ where I/we come from; **3** (indiquant une circonstance) **~ le passé** in the past; **~ une belle journée d'été** on a beautiful summer's day; **~ ce froid/cette chaleur** in this cold weather/this heat; **ils sortent même ~ moins 40°C** they go outdoors even when it's minus 40°C; **~ deux/trois fois** on two/three occasions; **4** (indiquant une répartition) **~ jour/semaine/an** a day/week/year; **les conférences auront lieu un lundi ~ mois** the lectures will take place once a month on a Monday; **~ personne** or **habitant** per person ou head; **~ tête** Écon per capita; **travailler ~ petits groupes** to work in small groups; **deux ~ deux** [*travailler*] in twos; [*marcher*] two by two; **les touristes sont arrivés ~ centaines/bus entiers** tourists arrived by the hundred/the coachload; **5** (introduit un complément d'agent) by; **baignée ~ une douce lumière** bathed in soft light; **être pris ~ son travail** to be taken up with one's work; **6** (indiquant le moyen) by; **régler/payer ~ carte de crédit** to pay by credit card; **7** (indiquant la manière) by; **le vent souffle ~ rafales** the wind blows in gusts; ▶**mont, saint**; **8** (indiquant la cause) **l'accident est arrivé ~ sa faute** it was his/her fault that the accident happened; **~ ennui/jalousie** out of boredom/jealousy; **9** (indiquant un intermédiaire) through; **tu peux me faire passer le livre ~ ta sœur** you can get the book to me via your sister.
II de par *loc prép* fml **1** (partout dans) throughout, all over; **avoir des amis de ~ le monde** to have friends throughout ou all over the world; **2** (à cause de) **de ~ sa fonction** by virtue of his/her/its office; **de ~ la loi** by law.
para○ /paʀa/ *nm* (*abbr* = **parachutiste**) para○.
parabole /paʀabɔl/ *nf* **1** Bible parable; **~ du Semeur** parable of the Sower; **2** Math parabola.
parabolique /paʀabɔlik/ *adj* parabolic.
parachèvement /paʀaʃɛvmɑ̃/ *nm* (bouclage) completion.
parachever /paʀaʃve/ [16] *vtr* (terminer) to complete; (fignoler) to put the finishing touches to.
parachutage /paʀaʃytaʒ/ *nm* **1** (de vivres, soldats) airdrop; **2**○ (nomination) **le ~ d'un enseignant** the appointment of a teacher from outside; **mon ~ en Normandie** my sudden transfer to Normandy.
parachute /paʀaʃyt/ *nm* **1** (voile) parachute; **~ ventral** lap-pack parachute; **~ dorsal** back(-pack) parachute; **~ de secours** safety parachute; **sauter en ~** to make a parachute jump; **saut en ~** parachute jump; **2** (sport) parachuting; **faire du ~** to go parachuting.
■ **~ ascensionnel** (sport) parascending.
parachuter /paʀaʃyte/ [1] *vtr* **1** Mil, Sport to parachute [*soldat, vivres*]; **2**○ (envoyer) to bring [sb] in from outside; **je n'ai pas envie d'être parachuté en Normandie** I don't want to be shunted off○ to Normandy.
parachutisme /paʀaʃytism/ ▶**449** *nm* parachuting; **faire du ~** to go parachuting.
■ **~ ascensionnel** parascending.
parachutiste /paʀaʃytist/ ▶**510** **I** *adj* [*troupes, escadron*] parachute.
II *nmf* **1** Sport parachutist; **2** Mil paratrooper.
parade /paʀad/ *nf* **1** (défilé) Mil, Théât parade; **de ~** [*costume, uniforme*] parade (*épith*); **faire une ~** to parade; **2** (défense) Sport, fig parry; **chercher/trouver une ~** to look for/find a parry (**à** to; **pour faire** to do); **3** (étalage) parade; **une indignation/un enthousiasme de ~** a show of indignation/enthusiasm; **faire ~ de** to flaunt [*richesse, connaissances*]; **4** (d'animal) display; **5** Équit pulling up.
■ **~ nuptiale** mating display.
parader /paʀade/ [1] *vi* pej to strut about.
paradigmatique /paʀadigmatik/ *adj* paradigmatic.
paradigme /paʀadigm/ *nm* paradigm.
paradis /paʀadi/ *nm inv* **1** Relig heaven; **l'enfer et le ~** heaven and hell; **être/aller au ~** to be in/go to heaven; **2** (lieu idéal) paradise; **le ~ de la voile/des sportifs** a paradise for sailors/sports enthusiasts; **un petit ~ antillais** a little bit of paradise in the West Indies; **c'est le ~ sur terre** it's heavenly; **c'est un ~ perdu** it's a garden of Eden; **3** Théât **le ~** the gods (*pl*).
■ **~ fiscal** Fisc tax haven; **~ terrestre** Bible Garden of Eden.
IDIOMES **tu ne l'emporteras pas au ~** you'll live to regret it.
paradisiaque /paʀadizjak/ *adj* heavenly.
paradisier /paʀadizje/ *nm* bird of paradise.
paradoxal, ~e, *mpl* **-aux** /paʀadɔksal, o/ *adj* paradoxical.
paradoxalement /paʀadɔksalmɑ̃/ *adv* paradoxically.
paradoxe /paʀadɔks/ *nm* paradox.
parafe = **paraphe**.
parafer = **parapher**.
paraffine /paʀafin/ *nf* (liquide) paraffin GB, kerosene US; (solide) paraffin wax; **huile de ~** paraffin oil GB, kerosene US.
paraffiner /paʀafine/ [1] *vtr* to paraffin.
parafiscal, ~e, *mpl* **-aux** /paʀafiskal, o/ *adj* [*taxe*] parafiscal.
parafiscalité /paʀafiskalite/ *nf* parafiscal funding.
parages /paʀaʒ/ *nmpl* neighbourhood[GB] (*sg*); **les ~ sont peu sûrs** the neighbourhood[GB] is not very safe; **dans les ~** around; **elle est dans les ~** she is around somewhere; **j'ai perdu mon chat quelque part dans les ~** I lost my cat somewhere around here; **j'étais dans les ~, alors je suis passé** I was in the neighbourhood[GB], so I stopped by○.
paragraphe /paʀagʀaf/ *nm* **1** (division) paragraph; **2** (signe typographique) section mark.
Paraguay /paʀagwɛ/ ▶**321** *nprm* Paraguay.
paraguayen, -enne /paʀagwejɛ̃, ɛn/ ▶**537** *adj* Paraguayan.
Paraguayen, -enne /paʀagwejɛ̃, ɛn/ ▶**537** *nm,f* Paraguayan.
paraître /paʀɛtʀ/ [73] **I** *nm* **le ~** appearance.
II *vi* **1** Édition, Presse [*publication*] to come out, to be published; **revue paraissant le jeudi/chaque semaine** magazine which

comes out on Thursdays/weekly; **mon livre a paru l'an dernier** my book came out ou was published last year; **mon livre paraîtra aux éditions Hachette** my book will be published by Hachette; **faire ~ un article** to publish an article; **un article paru dans une revue** an article which appeared in a magazine; **'à ~'** 'forthcoming titles'; **prochains ouvrages à ~ dans cette collection** coming out soon in this collection; **'vient de ~'** 'just out', 'just published'; **dans la rubrique 'vient de ~'** in the 'latest titles'; **2** (sembler) to appear, to seem; (avoir l'air) to look; **cela peut ~ ridicule** this may appear ou seem ridiculous; **il ne craint pas de ~ ridicule** he's not afraid of looking silly; **la situation paraît s'améliorer** the situation appears ou seems to be improving; **cette affaire me paraît louche** this business looks ou seems fishy to me; **aussi évident que cela puisse ~** however obvious this may appear ou seem (to be); **3** (devenir visible) [*personne, objet, véhicule, soleil*] to appear; **quand elle parut à la fenêtre** when she appeared at the window; **avec le temps, la cicatrice ne paraîtra plus** with time, the scar won't show any more; **avec un peu de maquillage, il n'en paraîtra rien** with a little make-up, it won't show at all; **elle ne laisse rien ~ de ses sentiments** she doesn' t let her feelings show at all; **sans qu'il n'y paraisse rien, elle a fini par gagner tout le monde à sa cause** without anyone realizing, she ended up winning everyone round GB ou over to her cause; **ce qu'ils font ~ à l'écran n'a rien à voir avec la réalité** what they show us on the screen has nothing to do with reality; **4** (se montrer) to appear; **~ en public** to appear in public; **il n'a pas paru à son bureau de la semaine** he hasn't shown up at his office all week; **~ à son avantage** to look one's best; **chercher à/aimer ~** to try/like to be seen in one's best light.

III *v impers* **il paraît que** apparently; **il paraîtrait que** it would seem that; **il me paraît inutile de faire** it seems useless to me to do; **ce n'est peut-être pas aussi grave qu'il (n'y) paraît** it may not be as serious as it seems; **paraît-il** it seems; **il paraît qu'elle a déménagé** (information) apparently she's moved; (question) I hear she's moved; **oui, il paraît** so I hear; **il paraît que les Français adorent la musique** the French are supposed to love music; **à ce qu'il paraît** apparently.

paralangage /paʀalɑ̃gaʒ/ *nm* paralanguage.

paralinguistique /paʀalɛ̃gɥistik/ **I** *adj* paralinguistic.

II *nf* paralinguistics (+ *v sg*).

paralittérature /paʀaliteʀatyʀ/ *nf* popular literature.

parallactique /paʀalaktik/ *adj* parallactic.

parallaxe /paʀalaks/ *nf* parallax.

parallèle /paʀalɛl/ **I** *adj* **1** [*lignes, plans*] parallel (**à** to); **la rue est ~ au fleuve** the street runs parallel to the river; **2** (distinct) parallel; (semblable) similar; **en ~ à** (distinctement) in parallel with; (semblablement) similarly to; **organiser un concours/une manifestation ~** to organize a parallel competition/demonstration; **nos concurrents ont suivi une démarche ~** our competitors took similar steps; **3** (en marge) [*marché, police*] unofficial; [*médecine, éducation*] alternative; [*monde, univers*] parallel; **mener une activité ~** (comme dérivatif) to have an activity as a sideline; (en fraude) to have a sideline; **4** Ordinat parallel; **traitement/imprimante ~** parallel processing/printer.

II *nm* **1** (comparaison) parallel; **établir** or **dresser un ~** to draw a parallel (**entre** between); **mettre deux événements en ~** to draw a parallel between two events; **2** Géog parallel; **3** Électrotech **en ~** in parallel.

III *nf* Math parallel line.

parallèlement /paʀalɛlmɑ̃/ *adv* **1** Math **~ à** parallel to; **2** (simultanément) at the same time (**à** as).

parallélépipède /paʀalelepipɛd/ *nm* parallelepiped.

parallélépipédique /paʀalelepipedik/ *adj* parallelepipedal.

parallélisme /paʀalelism/ *nm* **1** Math parallelism; **2** Aut (wheel) alignment; **vérifier le ~ (des roues)** to check the wheel alignment; **3** (correspondance) parallelism (**entre** between).

parallélogramme /paʀalelɔgʀam/ *nm* parallelogram.

paralysé, **~e** /paʀalize/ **I** *pp* ▶ **paralyser**.

II *pp adj* paralyzed; **rester ~** to be left paralyzed; **être ~ des jambes/du côté droit** to be paralyzed in the legs/on the right side; **~ par une grève** fig paralyzed by a strike.

III *nm,f* paralytic.

paralyser /paʀalize/ [1] *vtr* **1** Méd to paralyze; **2** (bloquer) to paralyze [*pays, entreprise, marché*]; to bring [sth] to a halt [*production, circulation*].

paralysie /paʀalizi/ *nf* paralysis; **être frappé de ~** to be paralyzed.

paralytique /paʀalitik/ *adj, nmf* paralytic.

paramécie /paʀamesi/ *nf* paramecium.

paramédical, **~e**, *mpl* **-aux** /paʀamedikal, o/ *adj* paramedical.

paramètre /paʀamɛtʀ/ *nm* parameter.

paramétrer /paʀametʀe/ [1] *vtr* to define.

paramilitaire /paʀamilitɛʀ/ *adj* paramilitary.

parangon /paʀɑ̃gɔ̃/ *nm* **un ~ de vertu** a paragon of virtue.

parano° /paʀano/ **I** *adj, nmf* paranoiac.

II *nf* paranoia.

paranoïa /paʀanɔja/ *nf* paranoia.

paranoïaque /paʀanɔjak/ *adj, nmf* paranoiac.

paranoïde /paʀanɔid/ *adj* paranoid.

paranormal, **~e**, *mpl* **-aux** /paʀanɔʀmal, o/ **I** *adj* paranormal.

II *nm* **le ~** the paranormal.

parapente /paʀapɑ̃t/ ▶ **449** *nm* Sport **1** (voile) paraglider; **2** (sport) paragliding.

parapet /paʀapɛ/ *nm* parapet.

paraphe /paʀaf/ *nm* (initiales) initials (*pl*); (trait de plume) flourish; (signature) signature; **veuillez apposer votre ~** (initiales) please initial; (signature) please sign.

parapher /paʀafe/ [1] *vtr* **1** (avec ses initiales) to initial; **2** (d'un trait de plume) to flourish; **3** fml (avec sa signature) to sign.

parapheur /paʀafœʀ/ *nm* signature book.

paraphrase /paʀafʀɑz/ *nf* paraphrase.

paraphraser /paʀafʀɑze/ [1] *vtr* to paraphrase.

paraphrastique /paʀafʀastik/ *adj* paraphrastic.

paraplégie /paʀapleʒi/ *nf* paraplegia.

paraplégique /paʀapleʒik/ *adj, nmf* paraplegic.

parapluie /paʀaplɥi/ *nm* lit, fig umbrella; **~ nucléaire** nuclear umbrella.

parapsychique /paʀapsiʃik/ *adj* parapsychological.

parapsychologie /paʀapsikɔlɔʒi/ *nf* parapsychology.

parapsychologue /paʀapsikɔlɔg/ *nmf* parapsychologist.

parascolaire /paʀaskɔlɛʀ/ *adj* extracurricular.

parasismique /paʀasismik/ *adj* **construction ~** earthquake-resistant construction.

parasitage /paʀazitaʒ/ *nm* **1** Radio, TV interference; **2** (exploitation) exploitation (**de** of).

parasitaire /paʀazitɛʀ/ *adj* parasitic(al).

parasite /paʀazit/ **I** *adj* [*plante, organisme*] parasitic(al); [*idée*] intrusive; **bruits ~s** Radio, TV interference ¢.

II *nm* **1** lit, fig parasite; **2** Radio, Télécom, TV **~s** (brouillage) interference ¢; (électricité statique) static ¢; **provoquer** or **faire des ~s dans la radio** to cause interference on the radio.

parasiter /paʀazite/ [1] *vtr* **1** Biol, Bot, Méd, Vét to live as a parasite on [*plante, animal*]; **2** (exploiter) to exploit; **3** Radio, TV to cause interference on [*radio, télévision*].

parasitique /paʀazitik/ *adj* parasitic(al).

parasitisme /paʀazitism/ *nm* parasitism.

parasitose /paʀazitoz/ ▶ **271** *nf* parasitosis.

parasol /paʀasɔl/ *nm* **1** (de plage) beach umbrella; (de café, jardin) sun umbrella; **2**† (ombrelle) parasol, sunshade.

parasympathique /paʀasɛ̃patik/ *adj* parasympathetic.

parataxe /paʀataks/ *nf* parataxis.

parathyroïde /paʀatiʀɔid/ *nf* parathyroid gland.

paratonnerre /paʀatɔnɛʀ/ *nm* lightning conductor GB, lightning rod.

paratyphique /paʀatifik/ *adj* paratyphoid.

paratyphoïde /paʀatifɔid/ ▶ **271** *nf* paratyphoid (fever).

paravent /paʀavɑ̃/ *nm* lit, fig screen.

parbleu† /paʀblø/ *excl* good Lord!

parc /paʀk/ *nm* **1** (jardin) park; **aller se promener au ~** to go for a walk in the park; **2** (enclos) (pour enfant) playpen; (pour bestiaux) pen; **~ à moutons** sheep pen; **3** (ensemble) (d'installations) (total) number (**de** of); (de biens d'équipement) stock (**de** of); **~ automobile** (d'une entreprise) fleet of cars; (d'un pays) number of cars (on the road); **~ ferroviaire** rolling stock; **~ immobilier** housing stock.

■ **~ d'attractions** amusement ou theme park; **~ à huîtres** oyster bed; **~ de loisirs** theme park; **~ marin (naturel)** *area of sea run as a national park*; **~ national** national park ; **~ naturel** nature park; **~ (naturel) régional** *national park run on a regional basis*; **~ relais** park and ride; **~ de stationnement** car park GB, parking lot US; **~ zoologique** zoological gardens (*pl*).

parcage /paʀkaʒ/ *nm* **1** (d'animaux) penning (**de** of); **2** (de voitures) parking (**de** of).

parce: **parce que** /paʀs(ə)k(ə)/ *loc conj* because; **'pourquoi est-ce que je ne peux pas aller à la plage avec eux?'—'~ que!'** 'why can't I go to the beach with them?'—'because I say so ou you can't!'; **'pourquoi ne lui as-tu pas téléphoné?'—'~ que!'** 'why haven't you phoned him?'—'because I haven't, that's why', 'just because!'; **il est déçu, d'abord ~ qu'il pleut, ensuite...** he's disappointed, one because it's raining and two...; **c'est ~ que j'aime le bois que je fais ce métier** I'm doing this job because I like wood; **s'il a réussi, c'est aussi ~ qu'on l'a aidé** if he succeeded, it's because he had help; **c'est bien ~ que c'est toi!** only because it's you!; **c'est justement ~ que** it's precisely because; **ne serait-ce que ~ que** if only because.

parcellaire /paʀsɛl(l)ɛʀ/ *adj* [*travail*] fragmented; [*connaissance*] patchy; **découpage ~** division into plots.

parcelle /paʀsɛl/ *nf* **1** (petit morceau) **~ de verre/plâtre** fragment of glass/plaster; **~ d'or** particle of gold; **2** (petite quantité) **une ~ de bonheur/d'autorité** a bit of happiness/of authority; **il n'y a pas une ~ de vérité là-dedans** there isn't a scrap of truth in it; **3** (portion de terrain) plot (of land).

parcellisation /paʀsɛl(l)izasjɔ̃/ *nf* (de terrain) parcelling[GB] out (**de** of); **~ du travail** division of labour[GB].

parcelliser /paʀsɛl(l)ize/ [1] *vtr* to parcel out [*terrain*]; to divide [*opinion publique*]; **~ le travail** to break down work into individual operations; **tâches/activités parcellisées** fragmented tasks/activities.

parchemin /paʀʃəmɛ̃/ *nm* **1** (peau, document) parchment; **2**○ (diplôme) bit of paper○ GB, sheepskin○ US, diploma.

parcheminé, **~e** /paʀʃəmine/ **I** *pp* ▶ **parcheminer**.
II *pp adj* **1** [*papier*] with a parchment finish (*épith*); **2** [*peau*] papery; **3** [*visage, main*] shrivelled[GB].

parcheminer /paʀʃəmine/ [1] **I** *vtr* to give a parchment finish to [*papier*].
II se parcheminer *vpr* [*visage*] to shrivel.

par-ci /paʀsi/ *adv* **~ par-là** here and there; **un gâteau ~ un bonbon par-là** a cake here, a sweet GB ou candy US there.

parcimonie /paʀsimɔni/ *nf* parsimony sout; **avec ~** sparingly, parsimoniously; **accorder des éloges avec ~** to be sparing with one's praise.

parcimonieusement /paʀsimɔnjøzmɑ̃/ *adv* parsimoniously, sparingly.

parcimonieux, **-ieuse** /paʀsimɔnjø, øz/ *adj* [*personne*] sparing (*jamais épith*), parsimonious sout; [*répartition*] stingy (*jamais épith*).

parcmètre /paʀkmɛtʀ/ *nm* parking meter.

parcourir /paʀkuʀiʀ/ [26] *vtr* **1** (sillonner) to travel all over [*pays, continent*]; **~ la ville** to go all over town; **~ un lieu à la recherche de** to scour a place in search of; **2** (franchir) to cover [*distance*]; **il a parcouru à pied la route jusqu'à Berlin** he walked all the way to Berlin; **il reste un long chemin à ~** there's still a long way to go; **3** (traverser) **la chemin de fer parcourt toute la région** the railway runs right across the region; **un frisson me parcourut le dos** a shiver ran down my spine; **4** (examiner rapidement) to glance through, to skim [*lettre, offres d'emploi*]; to scan [*horizon*]; **~ un endroit des yeux** or **du regard** to have a quick glance around a place.

parcours /paʀkuʀ/ *nm inv* **1** (trajet) (d'autobus, de personne) route; (de fleuve) course; **~ balisé** or **fléché** marked path; **2** Sport course; **reconnaître un ~** to go over ou walk a course (*before a race*); **~ de golf** round of golf; **elle a fait un excellent ~** (dans une course) she had an excellent race; **3** (cheminement) (professionnel) career; **son ~** (d'artiste) the development of his/her art; **incident de ~** hitch; **il expose le ~ personnel de l'auteur** he describes the author's personal development.
■ **~ du combattant** Mil assault course; fig obstacle course; **~ santé** fitness trail.

par-dedans /paʀdədɑ̃/ *adv* (par l'intérieur) **tu n'as pas besoin de faire la tour de la maison, tu peux passer ~ pour aller dans le jardin** you don't need to go round the outside, you can come through the house to get to the garden GB ou yard US.

par-dehors /paʀdəɔʀ/ *adv* (par l'extérieur) **je dois passer ~ pour aller dans ma chambre** I have to go around the outside to get to my room.

par-delà /paʀdəla/ *prép* liter **1** (de l'autre côté de) beyond; **~ les montagnes/mers** beyond the mountains/seas; **j'irais ~ l'océan pour te rejoindre** I would cross the widest ocean to be by your side; **2** fig (à travers) **~ les siècles** down the centuries; **cette statue est restée intacte ~ le temps** this statue has survived the passage of time.

par-derrière /paʀdɛʀjɛʀ/ *adv* **1** (par la partie postérieure) **passer ~** to go round GB ou to the back; **entrer ~** to come in round GB ou from the back; **ils m'ont attaqué ~** they attacked me from behind; **2** fig (sournoisement) behind sb's back; **critiquer/calomnier qn ~** to criticize/slander sb behind his/her back.

par-dessous /paʀdəsu/ **I** *adv* (par en dessous) underneath; **la barrière est trop haute, passe ~** the barrier is too high, go underneath; **tu auras froid avec ta veste, mets un pull ~** you'll be cold in just your jacket, put a sweater on underneath; **la porte est fermée à clé, glisse la lettre ~** the door is locked, slide the letter underneath; **le carton n'est pas solide, prends-le ~** the cardboard box isn't very strong, take hold of it underneath ou by the bottom.
II *prép* (sous quelque chose) underneath.

pardessus /paʀdəsy/ *nm* overcoat.

par-dessus /paʀdəsy/ **I** *adv* **1** (sur la chose en question) **tu vas avoir froid en chemise, mets un pull ~** you'll be cold in a shirt, put a sweater on; **pose ton sac dans un coin et mets ton manteau ~** put your bag in a corner and put your coat on top of it; **2** (par le dessus) **le mur n'est pas haut, passe/saute ~** the wall isn't high, climb/jump over it.
II *prép* **1** (par l'espace au-dessus de quelque chose) over; **il lisait ~ mon épaule** he was reading over my shoulder; **saute ~ le ruisseau** jump over the stream; **jeter qn/qch ~ bord** Naut to throw sb/sth overboard; ▶ **tête**; **2** fig (surtout) **ce que j'aime ~ tout, c'est le soleil/être dehors/voyager** what I like best of all is the sun/being outside/travelling[GB]; **je te recommande la prudence ~ tout** I advise you to be cautious above all else.

par-devant /paʀdəvɑ̃/ **I** *adv* **1** (par l'avant) **la porte de derrière est fermée, passe ~** the back door is locked, come round by the front; **2** fig (en face) **il te fait des sourires ~ mais dit du mal de toi dans ton dos** he's all smiles to your face but says nasty things about you behind your back.
II *prép* Jur (en présence de) **~ notaire** in the presence of a notary.

par-devers /paʀdəvɛʀ/ *prép* fml (en la possession de) **garder/conserver qch ~ soi** to keep sth in one's possession.

pardi○ /paʀdi/ *excl* of course!

pardieu† /paʀdjø/ *excl* good Lord!

pardon /paʀdɔ̃/ **I** *nm* **1** (fait de pardonner) forgiveness; Relig pardon; **demander ~ à qn** (pour une faute très grave) to ask sb for forgiveness; **je te demande ~** I'm sorry; **tu lui as demandé ~?** did you apologize ou say you were sorry?; **accorder son ~ à qn** fml to forgive sb; ▶ **grand**; **2** (dans une formule de politesse) **~!** sorry!; **~? qu'est-ce que tu as dit?** sorry ou I beg your pardon? GB what did you say?; **~ madame, je cherche...** excuse me please, I'm looking for...; **~ de vous avoir interrompu** I'm sorry for interrupting you.
II *excl* **ma mère est déjà grande mais alors ma sœur, ~!** if you think my mother is tall, you should see my sister !

pardonnable /paʀdɔnabl/ *adj* [*faute, délit*] forgivable; **ils ne sont pas ~s** it's unforgivable of them.

pardonner /paʀdɔne/ [1] **I** *vtr* **1** (accorder son pardon à) [*personne*] to forgive [*faute, erreur, écart*]; [*Dieu*] to pardon, to forgive [*péché*]; **~ à qn** to forgive sb; **~ qch à qn** to forgive sb sth; **~ à qn d'avoir fait** to forgive sb for doing; **je voudrais me faire ~** I'd like to be forgiven; **2** (dans une formule de politesse) **pardonnez-moi, mais je voudrais intervenir** excuse me, but I'd like to say something; **pardonne-moi ma curiosité** excuse my curiosity; **pardonne-moi de te déranger** I'm sorry if I'm disturbing you; **pardonnez-moi si je fais du bruit** excuse me if I'm being noisy.
II *vi* **ne pas ~** to be fatal; **une faute pareille ça ne pardonne pas** that kind of mistake can be fatal.
III se pardonner *vpr* [*personne*] to forgive oneself; **je ne me le pardonnerai jamais** I'll never forgive myself for that.
IDIOMES **faute avouée est à moitié pardonnée** Prov a fault confessed is half redressed Prov.

pare-balles /paʀbal/ *adj inv* bulletproof; **gilet ~** bulletproof vest.

pare-boue /paʀbu/ *nm inv* mud flap.

pare-brise /paʀbʀiz/ *nm inv* windscreen GB, windshield US.

pare-chocs /paʀʃɔk/ *nm inv* bumper; **rouler ~ contre ~** to drive along bumper to bumper.

pare-éclats /paʀekla/ *nm inv* Mil traverse.

pare-étincelles /paʀetɛ̃sɛl/ *nm inv* fireguard GB, fire screen US.

pare-feu /paʀfø/ *nm inv* (bande déboisée) firebreak.

parégorique /paʀegɔʀik/ *adj* **élixir ~** paregoric.

pareil, **-eille** /paʀɛj/ **I** *adj* **1** (semblable) similar (**à** to); **mon frère et ma sœur sont ~s** (l'un à l'autre) my brother and sister are alike; (que moi) my brother and sister are the same; **les deux chapeaux sont presque ~s** the two hats are almost identical; **ils sont tous ~s dans cette famille** they're all the same in that family; **je veux une robe pareille à la tienne** I want a dress the same as ou just like yours; **il est ~ à un avocat plaidant une cause perdue** he's just like a lawyer defending a lost cause; **elle est toujours pareille à elle-même** she's always the same; **c'est toujours ~ avec toi, tu compliques tout!** it's always the same with you, you just have to complicate everything!; **rien n'est plus ~** nothing is the same any more; **pour moi, c'est ~** it's all the same to me; **ce n'est pas ~ (du tout)!** it's not the same thing (at all)!; **à nul autre ~** liter without equal; **une beauté à nulle autre pareille** a beauty without equal; **'comment va-t-il aujourd'hui?'—'c'est toujours ~'** 'how is he today?'—'still the same', 'no change'; **il n'y en a pas deux ~s** [*objet, vêtement*] no two are alike; [*personne*] there's no-one quite like you/her/him; **2** (de telle nature) such; **je n'ai jamais dit une chose pareille** I never said any such thing; **je n'ai jamais rien vu de ~** I've never seen anything like it; **il n'avait jamais connu ~ bonheur** he had never known such happiness; **~ événement doit rester exceptionnel** there must be no repetition of this; **en ~ cas, dans un cas ~** in such cases; **en pareille circonstance** in similar circumstances; **tu travailles encore à une heure pareille!** you're still working at this hour!; **on ne peut rien faire par un temps ~** there's nothing we can do in weather like this.
II *nm,f* **1** (égal) equal; **on n'a jamais retrouvé son ~** we've never found his equal; **sa beauté est sans pareille** her beauty is without equal; **c'est un homme sans ~** he's a man without equal; **il est d'un dynamisme sans ~** he's incredibly dynamic; **il n'a pas son ~ pour semer le doute** he's second to none for spreading doubt; **on va où tu veux, pour moi c'est du ~ au même**○ we can go wherever you like, it makes no odds GB ou difference to me; **elle ou son mari, c'est du ~ au même**○ her or her husband, it's six of one and half-a-dozen of the other; **2** (personne semblable) **nos ~s** our fellows, our peers.
III○ *adv* **1** (identiquement) the same; **faire ~** to do the same; **les deux mots s'écrivent ~** both words are written ou spelled the same; **ils ont fait ~ avec nous** they acted the same (way) with us; **nous étions habillées ~** we were dressed the same (way); **2**○ C (néanmoins) all the same; **je l'ai fait ~** I did it all the same.

pareillement /paʀɛjmɑ̃/ *adv* **1** (de la même manière) (in) the same way; **la question a été traitée ~ chez les deux auteurs** the question has been treated in the same way ou similarly by the two authors; **partisans et adversaires se félicitent ~ de la décision prise** both partisans and opponents are happy about the decision that has been reached; **2** (également) too; **vous le pensez et moi ~** you think so and so do I ou and me too.

parement /paʀmɑ̃/ *nm* Constr, Mode facing.

■ ~ **d'autel** Relig frontal.

parenchyme /paʀɑ̃ʃim/ *nm* Anat, Bot parenchyma.

parent, **~e** /paʀɑ̃, ɑ̃t/ **I** *adj* [*conceptions, langues*] similar (**de** to); **~ à** or **avec** [*personne*] related to; **familles ~es** families which are related.
II *nm,f* **1** relative, relation; **~ proche/éloigné** close/distant relative ou relation; **~s et amis** friends and relations; **ils sont ~s par alliance** they're related by marriage; **plus proche ~(e)** next of kin; **2** Zool parent.
III *nm* **1** (le père ou la mère) parent; **il a un ~ étranger** he has one foreign parent; **un ~ d'élève** a (pupil's) parent; **mes ~s** my parents; **~s adoptifs** adoptive parents; **de ~s inconnus** of unknown parentage; **2** liter (ancêtres) forebears.
■ **~ pauvre** poor relation; **faire figure de ~ pauvre** to look like a poor relation; **~s d'élèves** (schoolchildren's) parents; **réunion de ~s d'élèves** parents' evening.

parental, **~e**, *mpl* **-aux** /paʀɑ̃tal, o/ parental.

parenté /paʀɑ̃te/ *nf* **1** (rapport) (entre personnes) blood relationship; (entre projets, histoires) connection; **l'importance des liens de ~** the importance of family ties; **il n'y a pas de lien de ~ entre eux** they are not related; **2** (parents et alliés) relations (*pl*).

parentèle /paʀɑ̃tɛl/ *nf* relations (*pl*).

parenthèse /paʀɑ̃tɛz/ *nf* **1** (digression) **je fais une ~ pour vous expliquer...** if I may just explain briefly...; **ouvrir une ~** to digress; **refermons la ~** but to come back to what we were talking about; (**soit dit**) **par ~** or **entre ~s** incidentally; **2** (signe typographique) bracket; **ouvrir/fermer la ~** to open/close brackets; **mettre qch entre ~s** lit to put sth in brackets; fig to put sth aside; **3** (épisode) interlude.

paréo /paʀeo/ *nm* ≈ sarong.

parer /paʀe/ [1] **I** *vtr* **1** (esquiver) to ward off, to parry [*coup*]; to ward off, to fend off [*attaque, danger*]; (en boxe, escrime) to parry; Naut to steer clear of [*grain, navire*]; **2** (protéger) to protect (**contre** against); **je suis paré, j'ai ma trousse à pharmacie** I'm well prepared, I've got my first-aid kit; **3** (orner) [*objet*] to adorn [*chose, personne*]; [*personne*] to adorn, to array [*chose, personne*] (**de** with); **4** (attribuer) **~ qn/qch de qch** to attribute sth to sb/sth; **5** Naut to get [sth] ready; **~ à virer** to prepare to go about; **6** (en boucherie, peausserie) to dress.
II parer à *vtr ind* (prévenir) to guard against; (remédier à) to deal with; **~ à toute éventualité** to be prepared for all contingencies; **~ au plus pressé** to deal with the most urgent matters first; **~ au grain** to prepare to meet a squall.
III se parer *vpr* **1** (se protéger) to take precautions (**contre** against); **2** (se vêtir) to array oneself; **elle s'est parée de fourrures/de bijoux** she arrayed herself in furs/with jewels; **3** (être recouvert) to be bedecked (**de** with); **4** (s'attribuer) **se ~ de** to invest oneself with; **il se pare de tous les talents** he claims to be ou makes himself out to be very clever. ▶ **paon**.

pare-soleil /paʀsɔlɛj/ *nm inv* Aut visor.

paresse /paʀɛs/ *nf* **1** (fainéantise) laziness; (dans la Bible) sloth; **par ~** out of laziness; **~ intellectuelle** ou **d'esprit** intellectual laziness; **être d'une ~ incorrigible** to be incorrigibly lazy; **2** (d'organe) sluggishness (**de** of); **~ intestinale** slow bowel.

paresser /paʀese/ [1] *vi* to laze; **arrête de ~!** stop lazing around!

paresseusement /paʀesøzmɑ̃/ *adv* lazily.

paresseux, **-euse** /paʀɛsø, øz/ **I** *adj* [*personne, geste, rivière*] lazy; [*organe*] sluggish; **ce qu'il est ~ pour faire le ménage!** he's so lazy about doing the housework!
II *nm,f* lazy person; **c'est une vraie paresseuse** she's really lazy.
III *nm* Zool sloth.

pare-vent /paʀvɑ̃/ *nm inv* windbreak.

parfaire /paʀfɛʀ/ [10] *vtr* **1** (achever) to complete, to round off [*éducation, œuvres*]; to perfect [*connaissance, technique*]; **~ sa forme** to reach a peak of ou top form; **2** (compléter) to make up [*somme d'argent*].

parfait, **~e** /paʀfɛ, ɛt/ **I** *adj* **1** (insurpassable) [*personne, beauté, travail, accord*] perfect; **elle est d'une beauté ~e** she is absolutely beautiful; **pendant ma maladie il a été ~** during my illness he was wonderful; **2** (total) [*ressemblance*] exact; [*imbécile*] complete; [*discrétion, égalité*] absolute; [*ignorance*] total; **3** (typique) [*estivant, touriste*] archetypal; [*exemple*] classic.
II *nm* **1** Culin parfait; **~ au chocolat** chocolate ice cream; **2** Ling (temps) perfect; **3** Relig (cathare) perfect.
IDIOMES **filer le ~ amour** to spin out love's sweet dream.

parfaitement /paʀfɛtmɑ̃/ *adv* **1** (à la perfection) perfectly; **elle parle ~ l'italien** she speaks Italian perfectly; **2** (absolument) [*savoir*] perfectly well; [*tolérer, admettre*] fully; [*bien, heureux, capable, simple*] perfectly; [*correct, égal*] absolutely; [*faux, incompréhensible*] totally; [*absurde, choquant*] utterly; **tout cela m'est ~ égal** it makes absolutely no difference to me; **j'ai ~ conscience de/que** I'm well aware of that; **3** (certainement) absolutely; **'tu y es allé tout seul?'—'~!'** 'you went by yourself?'—'absolutely!'

parfois /paʀfwa/ *adv* sometimes; **il est ~ difficile de se faire comprendre** it's sometimes hard to make oneself understood.

parfum /paʀfœ̃/ *nm* **1** (pour se parfumer) perfume, scent; **une bouteille de ~** a bottle of perfume; **2** (senteur) (de fleur, forêt) scent; (de sels de bain) fragrance; (de vin) bouquet; (de café) aroma; (de fruit) scent, (sweet) smell; **3** (goût) flavour[GB]; **des glaces à tous les ~s** icecreams in all flavours[GB]; **4** fig **un ~ du terroir** a rural flavour[GB]; **un ~ de scandale** a whiff of scandal; **un ~ de nostalgie** a touch of nostalgia.
IDIOMES **être au ~**○ to be in the know○ (**de** about), to be hip○ (**de** to) US; **mettre qn au ~**○ to put sb in the picture, to clue sb in○.

parfumé, **~e** /paʀfyme/ **I** *pp* ▶ **parfumer**.
II *pp adj* **1** [*fleur*] sweet-scented; [*thé*] flavoured[GB]; [*fruit*] fragrant; [*air, chambre*] fragrant; **2** [*mouchoir*] scented; **3** [*glace*] flavoured[GB]; **~ à la vanille** [*savon*] vanilla-scented; [*yaourt*] vanilla-flavoured[GB].

parfumer /paʀfyme/ [1] **I** *vtr* **1** (embaumer) **les fleurs parfument la pièce** the room is fragrant with flowers; **2** (imprégner de parfum) to put scent on [*mouchoir*]; to put scent in [*bain*]; **3** (aromatiser) to flavour[GB] (**à** with).
II se parfumer *vpr* (en général) to wear perfume; (pour l'occasion) to put perfume on; **à quoi te parfumes-tu?** what perfume do you wear?

parfumerie /paʀfymʀi/ ▶ **510** *nf* (boutique, industrie) perfumery; (usine) perfume factory; (secteur) perfume industry.

parfumeur, **-euse** /paʀfymœʀ, øz/ ▶ **510** *nm,f* **1** (vendeur) perfume salesman/saleswoman; **2** (fabricant) perfumer.

pari /paʀi/ *nm* **1** Sport bet; (gageure) bet, wager; **un ~ de 500 francs** a 500-franc bet; **faire/tenir un ~** to make/take up a bet; **prendre des ~s sur** to take bets on; **le ~ de Pascal** Philos Pascal's wager; **~ tenu!** you're on!; **les ~s sont ouverts** lit bets are now being taken; fig it's anyone's guess; **2** (activité) betting ¢; **les ~s sont interdits** betting is prohibited; **3** (défi) gamble; **un ~ commercial** a commercial gamble; **un ~ sur l'avenir** a gamble with the future.

paria /paʀja/ *nm* **1** Relig pariah; **2** (de société) outcast.

parier /paʀje/ [2] *vtr* **1** (faire un pari) to bet; **tu paries?** do you want to bet?; **~ qch avec qn** to bet sb sth; **~ avec qn que** to bet sb that; **je te parie 50 francs/tout ce que tu veux qu'il ne sera pas élu** I bet you 50 francs/anything that he won't be elected; **je (te) parie que tu ne le feras pas** I bet you won't do it; **2** Sport to bet [*argent*]; **~ sur** to bet on, to back [*cheval, boxeur*]; **~ qch sur** to bet sth on; **~ gros sur un cheval** to bet heavily on a horse, to place a large bet on a horse; **on parie sur lui à quatre contre un** they are backing him at four to one; **il y a fort** or **gros à ~ que** it's a safe bet that, the odds are that; **3** (compter) to bank (**sur** on) [*personne, méthode*]; **~ sur l'énergie solaire** to bank on solar energy; **4** (être sûr) to bet; **je parie qu'il a encore oublié** I bet he has forgotten again; **je l'aurais parié!** I knew it!; **j'aurais pourtant parié que c'était lui le coupable** I could have sworn he was the culprit.

pariétal, **~e**, *mpl* **-aux** /paʀjetal, o/ **I** *adj* **1** Anat parietal; **2** Archéol [*peinture*] (dans des grottes) cave (*épith*); (sur parois rocheuses) rock (*épith*).
II *nm* parietal bone.

parieur, **-ieuse** /paʀjœʀ, øz/ *nm,f* (joueur) gambler; (aux courses) better GB, bettor US, punter○ GB.

parigot○, **~e** /paʀigo, ɔt/ *adj, nm,f* Parisian.

Paris /paʀi/ ▶ **857** *npr* Paris.
IDIOMES **avec des si, on mettrait ~ en bouteille** Prov ≈ if wishes were horses, beggars would ride Prov.

paris-brest /paʀibʀɛst/ *nm inv*: *pastry with praline filling sprinkled with almonds.*

parisianisme /paʀizjanism/ *nm* **1** (attitude) pej Parisian conceit; **2** Ling Parisian expression.

parisien, **-ienne** /paʀizjɛ̃, ɛn/ ▶ **857** *adj* [*agglomération, accent, vie*] Parisian; [*bassin, banlieue, région*] Paris (*épith*).

Parisien, **-ienne** /paʀizjɛ̃, ɛn/ *nm,f* Parisian.

paritaire /paʀitɛʀ/ *adj* [*commission*] joint (*épith*).

parité /paʀite/ *nf* Fin, Math, Ordinat parity; **à ~** at parity.
■ **~ du change** parity of exchange.

parjure /paʀʒyʀ/ **I** *adj* [*témoignage*] perjured.
II *nmf* (personne) perjurer.
III *nm* (faux serment) perjury ¢; **commettre un ~** to commit perjury.

parjurer: **se parjurer** /paʀʒyʀe/ [1] *vpr* to perjure oneself.

parka /paʀka/ *nm* ou *f* parka.

parking /paʀkiŋ/ *nm* **1** (parc de stationnement) car park GB, parking lot US; (place de stationnement) parking space; **~ à étages** multistorey car park GB, multistory parking lot US; **2** (stationnement) controv parking; **~ interdit** no parking.

Parkinson /paʀkinsɔn/ ▶ **271** *npr* **maladie de ~** Parkinson's disease.

parkinsonien, **-ienne** /paʀkinsɔnjɛ̃, ɛn/ **I** *adj* [*symptômes*] of Parkinson's disease (*épith, après n*).
II *nm,f* man/woman suffering from Parkinson's disease.

par-là /paʀla/ *adv* ▶ **par-ci**.

parlant, **~e** /paʀlɑ̃, ɑ̃t/ **I** *adj* **1** (éloquent) [*attitude, geste*] eloquent, meaningful; [*comparaison*] vivid; [*preuve, chiffre, résultat, fait*] which speaks for itself; [*portrait*] lifelike; **les faits sont ~s** the facts speak for themselves; **ça me paraît suffisamment ~** it looks convincing enough to me; **2** (accompagné de paroles) **le cinéma ~** the talkies○ (*pl*); **un film ~** a talkie○; **horloge ~e** speaking clock; **3** (doué de parole) [*personne*] talkative; **être très/peu ~** to be very/not very talkative.
II *nm* Cin **le ~** the talkies○ (*pl*).

parlé, **~e** /paʀle/ **I** *pp* ▶ **parler**.

II *pp adj* [*langue, style, français*] spoken; (familier) colloquial.

Parlement /paʀləmɑ̃/ *nm* **le ~ européen/de Strasbourg/de Westminster** the European/Strasbourg/British Parliament; **au ~** [*majorité, siège, vote*] in Parliament; [*élu*] to Parliament; [*passer, présenter*] through Parliament; **voter qch au ~** to vote on sth in Parliament; **débattu/soumis au ~** discussed in/put before Parliament; **entrer au ~ européen** to go into the European Parliament.

parlementaire /paʀləmɑ̃tɛʀ/ **I** *adj* [*débat, groupe, majorité, immunité*] parliamentary.
II *nmf* **1** (membre du Parlement) member of Parliament; **les ~s français/européens** members of the French/European Parliament; **2** (médiateur) negotiator.

parlementariste /paʀləmɑ̃taʀist/ *adj, nmf* parliamentarian.

parlementer /paʀləmɑ̃te/ [1] *vi* to negotiate (**avec** with).

parler /paʀle/ [1] **I** *nm* **1** (manière de s'exprimer) way of talking; (langage) speech; **elle a un ~ vulgaire** she has a common way of talking; **~ négligé/soigné** sloppy/polished speech; **un ~ vrai qui ne plaît pas à tous** an outspokenness that some people don't like; **2** Ling dialect.
II *vtr* **1** (savoir manier) to speak [*langue*]; **~ (l')italien** to speak Italian; ▶**vache**; **2** (discuter) **~ affaires/politique** to talk (about) business/politics; **~ littérature/cinéma** to talk books/films; **~ boulot**○ or **boutique**○ to talk shop○.
III parler à *vtr ind* (s'adresser) **~ à qn** to talk ou speak to sb; (ne pas être brouillé avec) to be on speaking terms with sb; **j'ai à vous ~** I must talk ou speak to you; **il ne leur parle plus** he's no longer on speaking terms with them; **c'est ~ à un mur** it's like talking to a brick wall; **trouver à qui ~** fig to meet one's match; **moi qui vous parle, je n'aurais jamais cru ça**○! I'm telling you, I'd never have believed it!; **ça parle au cœur** it has a strong emotional appeal; **ça parle à l'imagination** it fires the imagination.
IV parler de *vtr ind* **1** (discuter) **~ de qch/qn** to talk about sth/sb; (mentionner) to mention sth/sb; **~ de tout et de rien, ~ de choses et d'autres** to talk about one thing and another; **ils parlent encore de politique** they're talking (about) politics again; **on ne parle que de ça** everybody is talking about it; **toute la ville en parle** it's the talk of the town; **faire ~ de soi** gén to get oneself talked about; (dans les médias) to make the news; **la France et l'Italie, pour ne ~ que des pays de la CEE** France and Italy, to mention only EC countries; **j'ai tous les soucis, sans ~ des frais** I have all the worry, not to mention the expense; **c'est d'épidémie qu'il faut ~** we're talking about an epidemic here; **le spécialiste parle d'une opération/d'opérer** the consultant is talking of an operation/of operating; **on parle d'un gymnase/de construire un gymnase** there's talk of a gymnasium/of building a gymnasium; **on en parle** there's talk of it; **on parle d'un écologiste pour ce poste** they're talking of giving the job to an ecologist ; **qui parle de vous expulser?** who said anything about throwing you out?; **~ mal de qn** to badmouth○, to speak ill of sb; **tu parles d'une aubaine**○! (admiratif, iron) talk about a bargain○!; **ta promesse/son travail, parlons-en!** iron some promise/work!; **n'en parlons plus!** (ça suffit) let's drop it; (c'est oublié, pardonné) that's the end of it; **finis-le, comme ça on n'en parle plus** finish it, then it's done; **'c'était dur?'—'n'en parlons pas**○**!'** 'was it hard?'—'unbelievable○!'; **2** (traiter) [*article, film, livre*] **~ de** to be about; **de quoi ça parle**○? what' s it about?; **les journaux en ont parlé** it was in the papers; **3** (s'entretenir) **~ de qch/qn avec qn** to talk to sb about sth/sb; **on peut ~ de tout avec eux** you can talk to them about anything; **il faut que j'en parle avec mes collègues** I must talk to my colleagues about it; **~ de qch/qn à qn** (l'entretenir de) to talk to sb about sth/sb, to tell sb about sth/sb; (lui souffler mot de) to mention sth/sb to sb; **il va ~ de toi à son chef** he'll put in a word for you with his boss; **de quoi va-t-il nous ~?** what is he going to talk to us about?; **il nous a parlé de vous** he's told us about you; **parle-moi de tes projets/amis** tell me about your plans/friends; **ne leur en parle pas** don't tell them about it, don't mention it to them; **il ne m'a jamais parlé de sa famille** he's never mentioned his family to me; **on m'a beaucoup parlé de vous** I've heard a lot about you; **ne m'en parlez pas!** don't talk to me about it!; **je ne veux pas qu'on m'en parle** I don't want to hear about it, I don't want to know; **avec le café, parlez-moi d'un bon cognac** with coffee, a good brandy is just the thing○; **la lecture? parle-lui plutôt de football!** books? he would rather hear about football GB ou soccer!
V *vi* **1** (articuler des mots) [*enfant, perroquet, poupée*] to talk; (d'une certaine façon) to speak, to talk; **elle a parlé à 14 mois** she started to talk at 14 months; **~ vite/fort/en russe** to speak ou talk fast/loudly/in Russian; **parle plus fort** speak up, speak louder; **~ du nez/avec un accent** to speak with a nasal twang/with an accent, to have a nasal twang/an accent; **~ entre ses dents** to mumble; **2** (s'exprimer) to speak; **~ en public** to speak in public; **laisse-le ~** let him speak, let him have his say; **~ pour qn** (en son nom) to speak for sb; (en sa faveur) to speak up on sb's behalf; **parle pour toi!** speak for yourself! ; **c'est à vous de ~** (dans débat) it's your turn to speak; (aux cartes) it's your bid; **parle, on t'écoute** come on ou speak up, we're listening; **écologiquement/économiquement parlant** ecologically/economically speaking; **~ sincèrement** to speak sincerely; **les faits parlent d'eux-mêmes** the facts speak for themselves; **laisser ~ son cœur** fig to speak from the heart; **~ avec les mains** hum to gesticulate a great deal, to talk with one's hands; **~ par gestes** to communicate by means of gestures; **les muets parlent par signes** the speech-impaired use sign language; **tu parles sérieusement?** are you serious?; **si l'on peut ~ ainsi** if one can put it like that; **~ en connaissance de cause** to know what one is talking about; **bien parlé!** well said!; **elle n'a qu'à ~, il obéit** he obeys her every word; **une prime? tu parles**○! a bonus? you must be joking○!; **tu parles si je viens**○! (bien sûr) you bet I'm coming○!; **faire ~ la poudre** (dans une bagarre) to start shooting; (entrer en guerre) to go to war; **3** (bavarder) to talk; **~ avec qn** to talk ou speak to sb (**de** about); **~ pour ne rien dire** to talk for the sake of talking, to talk drivel; **~ à tort et à travers** to talk through one's hat○; **il s'écoute ~** he loves the sound of his own voice; **parlons peu et parlons bien** let's get down to business; ▶**nuire**; **4** (faire des aveux) to talk, to blab○; (dénoncer) to grass○ GB, to squeal; **faire ~ qn** to make sb talk.
VI se parler *vpr* **1** (communiquer) to talk ou speak (to each other); **ils se sont parlé au téléphone** they spoke on the telephone; **on s'est parlé deux minutes** we spoke ou talked for a couple of minutes; **2** (ne pas être brouillés) to be on speaking terms; **ils ne se parlent pas** they're not on speaking terms; **3** (être utilisé) [*langue, dialecte*] to be spoken.

parleur /paʀlœʀ/ *nm* speaker, talker; ▶**beau**.

parloir /paʀlwaʀ/ *nm* (d'école, hôpital) visitors' room; (de prison) visiting room; (pour avocat) interview room; (de maison, couvent) parlour[GB]; (de théâtre) greenroom; **détenu privé de ~** prisoner who is not allowed visitors.

parlot(t)e○ /paʀlɔt/ *nf* chit-chat ₵.

parme /paʀm/ ▶**193** *adj inv, nm* mauve.

Parme /paʀm/ ▶**857** *npr* Parma; **jambon de ~** Parma ham.

Parmentier /paʀmɑ̃tje/ *npr* **hachis ~** cottage pie, shepherd's pie.

parmesan /paʀməzɑ̃/ *nm* Parmesan (cheese).

parmi /paʀmi/ *prép* among, amongst; **~ les invités/la population** among the guests/the population; **un exemple ~ tant d'autres** one example among many; **demain il sera ~ nous** he'll be with us tomorrow; **le plus important ~ les écrivains de ce siècle** the most important of this century's writers; **choisir ~ huit destinations** to choose from eight destinations.

Parnasse /paʀnas/ *nprm* **1** Géog **le (mont) ~** (Mount) Parnassus; **2** Littérat, Mythol **le ~** Parnassus.

parnassien, **-ienne** /paʀnasjɛ̃, ɛn/ *adj, nm,f* Parnassian.

parodie /paʀɔdi/ *nf* **1** Littérat (pastiche) parody; **2** (simulacre) mockery; **une ~ de procès** a travesty of justice.

parodier /paʀɔdje/ [2] *vtr* to parody.

parodique /paʀɔdik/ *adj* parodic.

paroi /paʀwa/ *nf* **1** (face interne) (de tunnel) side; (de grotte) wall; (de tube, tuyau) inner surface; **2** Constr (cloison) wall; **3** (de montagne) **~ rocheuse** rock face; **la ~ nord** the north face; **4** Anat, Bot wall; **~ utérine/abdominale** uterine/abdominal wall.

paroisse /paʀwas/ *nf* parish; **curé/réunion de la ~** parish priest/meeting.

paroissial, **~e**, *mpl* **-iaux** /paʀwasjal, o/ *adj* parish (*épith*).

paroissien, **-ienne** /paʀwasjɛ̃, ɛn/ *nm,f* parishioner; **un drôle de ~**○† a strange fellow, a queer fish○.

parole /paʀɔl/ *nf* **1** (faculté) speech; **les organes de la ~** the organs of speech; **être doué de ~** to have the power of speech, to be endowed with speech; **perdre/retrouver la ~** to lose/regain the power of speech, to lose/regain one's speech; **il ne lui manque que la ~** (animal) it can almost talk; **avoir la ~ facile** to have the gift of the gab○; **avoir le don de la ~** to be a good talker; ▶**or**[2]; **2** (possibilité de s'exprimer) **avoir droit à la ~** to have the right to speak; **prendre la ~** to speak; **laisser la ~ à qn** to let sb speak; **tu ne me laisses jamais la ~** you never let me speak; **lorsqu'il eut la ~** when his turn came to speak; (dans un débat) when he took the floor; **temps de ~** speaking time; **et maintenant, je donne** or **laisse la ~ à mon collègue** and now I hand over to my colleague; **3** (mot) word; **il n'a pas dit une ~** he didn't say a word; **~s en l'air** empty words; **belles ~s** fine words; **une ~ blessante** a hurtful remark; **joindre le geste à la ~** to suit the action to the word; **si tu crois que tu vas t'en tirer avec des ~s**○! you're not going to talk your way out of this one!; **sur ces bonnes ~s, je m'en vais** hum on that (philosophical) note, I'm off; **en ~s, ils sont tous tolérants** to hear them talk, they all hold the broadest ou most liberal views; **en ~s, tout est facile** it's easy to talk; ▶**payer**; **4** (assurance verbale) word; **reprendre/manquer à/donner sa ~** to go back on/break/give one's word; **tenir ~** to keep one's word; **il n'a qu'une ~, c'est un homme de ~** he's a man of his word; **il n'a aucune ~** you can't trust him; **je t'ai cru sur ~** I took you at your word; **~ d'honneur!** cross my heart!, I promise!; **je l'ai envoyé, ~ d'honneur!** I swear I sent it!; **je te donne ma ~ d'honneur que ce n'est pas vrai** I swear it's not true; **ma ~!** (upon) my word!; **5** (sentence, aphorisme) words (*pl*); **connaissez-vous cette ~ de Pascal?** do you know that saying of Pascal's?; **la ~ divine** the holy word of God; **prêcher la bonne ~** to spread the good word; **c'est ~ d'évangile** it's gospel truth, it's gospel○; **6** (texte) **~s** (de chanson) words, lyrics; (de dessin) words; **film sans**

~s silent film; **7** Ling speech, parole spéc; **8** Jeux **~!** pass!; **vous avez la ~** it's your bid.

IDIOMES **les ~s s'envolent, les écrits restent** (faites promettre par écrit) get it in writing; (ne vous engagez pas par écrit) never put anything in writing.

parolier, **-ière** /paʀɔlje, ɛʀ/ ▶ 510 *nm,f* (de chansons) lyric writer; (d'opéra) librettist.

paronyme /paʀɔnim/ *nm* paronym.

paronymie /paʀɔnimi/ *nf* paronymy.

paronymique /paʀɔnimik/ *adj* paronymous.

parotide /paʀɔtid/ *nf* parotid (gland).

paroxysme /paʀɔksism/ *nm* **1** (plus haut degré) (de plaisir) paroxysm; (de bataille) climax; (de ridicule) height; **atteindre/être à son ~** [*douleur*] to reach/to be at its height; [*conflit, combat*] to reach/to be at its climax; **au ~ de la fureur** in a frenzy of rage; **2** Méd crisis.

paroxystique /paʀɔksistik/ *adj* fml extreme, paroxysmal sout.

parpaillot†, **~e** /paʀpajo, ɔt/ *nm,f* Protestant.

parpaing /paʀpɛ̃/ *nm* **1** (en béton) breeze-block GB, cinder block US; **2** (en pierre) perpend.

Parque /paʀk/ *npr* **la ~** Fate; **les trois ~s** the three Fates.

parquer /paʀke/ [1] *vtr* **1** (mettre dans un parc) to pen [*bestiaux*]; **2** pej (entasser) to coop up [*personnes*]; **3** (garer) to park [*voiture*].

parquet /paʀkɛ/ *nm* **1** (plancher) parquet (floor); **~ de chêne** oak parquet; **poser du** or **un ~** to lay parquet; **2** Jur **le ~** ≈ the prosecution; **3** (à la Bourse) **le ~ de la Bourse** the floor of the Stock Exchange.

■ **~ à bâtons rompus** herringbone parquet floor; **~ de chauffe** Naut stokehold floor; **~ damier** chequered GB ou checkered US woodblock flooring; **~ mosaïque** = **~ damier**; **~ à points de Hongrie** mitred[GB] herringbone flooring.

parqueter /paʀkəte/ [20] *vtr* to lay parquet in, to parquet; **parqueté** [*pièce, salon*] with a parquet floor (*épith, après n*).

parrain /paʀɛ̃/ *nm* **1** Relig godfather; **être (le) ~ de qn** to be godfather to sb; **2** (de candidat, projet, d'enfant défavorisé, initiative) sponsor; (d'œuvre, de fondation) patron; **3** (de navire) *man who ceremonially launches a ship*; **4** (d'organisation criminelle) godfather.

■ Note En anglais *godfather* n'est jamais une forme d'adresse.

parrainage /paʀɛnaʒ/ *nm* **1** (caution morale) (de candidat, projet) sponsorship, backing ¢; (de fondation) patronage; **2** (soutien financier) sponsorship; **sous le ~ de...** sponsored by...

parrainer /paʀene/ [1] *vtr* **1** (moralement) to be patron of [*fondation*]; to back, to sponsor [*candidature, exposition*]; **2** (financièrement) to sponsor [*émission, championnat, enfant*].

parricide /paʀisid/ **I** *adj* parricidal.

II *nmf* (personne) parricide.

III *nm* (crime) parricide.

parsec /paʀsɛk/ *nm* parsec.

parsemer /paʀsəme/ [16] *vtr* **1** (éparpiller) **parsemez-la de persil haché** sprinkle some chopped parsley over it; **2** liter [*étoiles*] to stud [*ciel*]; **des feuilles parsèment la pelouse** the lawn is strewn with leaves; **une pelouse parsemée de fleurs** a lawn scattered ou dotted with flowers; **les obstacles ont parsemé sa vie** his/her life was strewn with obstacles; **les pièges qui parsèment la route vers la victoire** the obstacles on the path to victory.

parsi, **~e** /paʀsi/ **I** *adj* Parsee.

II ▶ 462 *nm* Ling Parsee.

part /paʀ/ **I** *nf* **1** (portion) (de tarte, gâteau) slice, portion; (de viande, riz) helping, portion; (d'héritage) share; **couper qch en six ~s égales** to cut sth into six equal portions; **vouloir/mériter une ~ du gâteau** fig to want/deserve a slice ou share of the cake; **avoir sa ~ de misères/souffrances/soucis** to have one's (fair) share of misfortunes/suffering/worries; **la ~ du pauvre** some food for the unexpected guest; **2** (élément d'un tout) proportion, part; **une ~ des bénéfices/du budget** a proportion of the profits/of the budget; **une ~ non négligeable de leur revenu** a significant proportion of their income; **une grande ~ de qch** a high proportion ou large part of sth; **une ~ de chance/jeu/sacrifice** an element of chance/risk/sacrifice; **il y a une grande ~ de fiction/de réel dans son récit** his account is highly fictional/very much based on reality; **le hasard n'a aucune ~ là-dedans** chance has nothing to do with it; **pour une ~** to some extent; **pour une bonne** or **grande ~** to a large ou great extent; **faire la ~ de qch** to take sth into account ou consideration; **faire la ~ des choses** to put things in perspective; **faire la ~ belle à qch** to place ou put great emphasis on sth; **faire la ~ belle à qn** to give sb the best deal; **à ~ entière** [*membre, citoyen*] full (*épith*); [*science, sujet*] in its own right; **ils sont français à ~ entière** they are full French nationals; **c'est un art à ~ entière** it's an art in its own right; **participer aux travaux/discussions à ~ entière** to participate fully in the work/discussions; **3** (contribution) share; **payer sa ~** to pay one's share; **chacun paie sa ~, c'est mieux** everyone pays their share, it's better that way; **faire sa ~ de travail/ménage** to do one's share of the work/housework; **prendre ~ à** to take part in [*activité, discussion, travail, conflit*]; **nous prenons ~ à votre douleur** or **peine** we share your grief; **il m'a fait ~ de ses projets/son inquiétude** he told me about his plans/concern; **je vous ferai ~ de mes intentions** I'll let you know my intentions; **Hélène et Roger Moulin sont heureux de vous faire ~ de la naissance de leur fille Zoé** Hélène and Roger Moulin are pleased to announce the birth of their daughter Zoé; **4** (partie d'un lieu) **de toute(s) ~(s)** [*surgir, arriver*] from all sides; **être attaqué de toutes ~s** to be attacked from all sides; **de ~ et d'autre** on both sides, on either side (**de qch** of sth); **il y a une volonté de dialogue de ~ et d'autre** there is a willingness to talk on both sides; **de ~ en ~** [*traverser, transpercer*] right ou straight through; ▶ **autre**[1] **III**, **nul V**, **quelque IV**; **5** (point de vue) **pour ma/ta/notre ~** for my/your/our part; **il a pour sa ~ déclaré que...** for his part he declared that...; **d'une ~..., d'autre ~...** (marquant une énumération) firstly..., secondly...; (marquant une opposition) on (the) one hand... on the other hand; **d'autre ~** (de plus) moreover; **prendre qch en bonne/mauvaise ~** to take sth in good part/take sth badly; **6** Fin, Écon **~ (sociale** or **d'intérêt)** share; **avoir des ~s dans une société** to have shares in a company; **une ~ de marché** a market share; **~ de fondateur** founder's share; **7** Fisc *unit on which the calculation of personal tax is based*; **8** Scol, Univ *unit on which the calculation of student grants is based*.

II à part *loc* **1** (à l'écart) [*ranger, classer*] separately; **mettre qch à ~** to put sth to one side; **si on met à ~ cette partie de la population** leaving aside this section of the population; **préparez une sauce/des légumes à ~** prepare a sauce/some vegetables separately; **prendre qn à ~** to take sb aside ou to one side; **2** (séparé) **une salle à ~** a separate room; **faire lit/chambre à ~** to sleep in separate beds/rooms; **3** (différent) **être un peu à ~** [*personne*] to be out of the ordinary; **un cas/lieu à ~** a special case/place; **un personnage à ~** a unique character; **4** (excepté) apart from; **(mis) à ~ ça il est charmant** apart from that he's charming; **à ~ ça, quoi de neuf**○**?** apart from that, what's new?; **la semaine s'est bien passée à ~ un jour de pluie** the week went well apart from one rainy day; **à ~ que** apart from the fact that; **blague à ~** joking aside.

III de la part de *loc prép* **1** (à la place de) [*agir, écrire, téléphoner*] **de la ~ de** on behalf of; **je vous souhaite bonne chance de la ~ de toute l'équipe** on behalf of the whole team I wish you good luck; **je vous appelle de la ~ de M. Pichon** I'm phoning on behalf of Mr Pichon; **2** (venant de) **de la ~ de qn** from sb; **il y a un message de la ~ de ton père** there's a message from your father; **j'ai un cadeau pour toi de la ~ de ma sœur** I've got a present for you from my sister; **donne-leur le bonjour de ma ~** say hello to them for me; **ce n'est pas très gentil de ta ~** that wasn't very nice of you; **sans engagement de votre ~** with no obligation on your part; **de leur ~, rien ne m'étonne** nothing they do surprises me; **c'est de la ~ de qui?** (au téléphone) who's calling ou speaking please?

IDIOMES **faire la ~ du feu** to cut one's losses.

partage /paʀtaʒ/ *nm* **1** (découpage) dividing, sharing; **le ~ des gains se fera entre 20 personnes** the profits will be split between ou shared out among 20 people; **ils ont eu des problèmes de ~ familial** they have had family problems in dividing up the inheritance; **ils ont toujours eu le souci du ~** they were always careful to share things out; **2** (distribution) distribution; **le ~ des terres n'était pas équitable** the lands had not been shared out fairly; **les enfants ont fait eux-mêmes le ~ des gâteaux** the children shared out the cakes between themselves; **le ~ du pain** the breaking of the bread; **3** (répartition) sharing (**avec** with), division (**avec** with); **régner/gouverner sans ~** to reign/to govern absolutely; **avec une joie sans ~** with unadulterated delight; **une victoire sans ~** a total victory; **le ~ des voix** Pol the division of votes; **comment se présente le ~ des voix entre les candidats?** how are the votes split between the candidates?; **4** (séparation) division (**en** into), partition (**en** into); **le ~ d'un territoire en deux** the division ou partition of a territory into two; **un plan de ~ d'un territoire en deux zones** a plan to divide or partition a territory into two zones; **5** (part) share; fig (sort) lot; **recevoir qch en ~** to be left sth (in a will); **il a reçu la malchance en ~** fig his lot is an unhappy one.

■ **~ de poste** job sharing; **~ proportionnel** Math proportional factorization.

partagé, **~e** /paʀtaʒe/ **I** *pp* ▶ **partager**.

II *pp adj* **1** (divisé) [*avis, opinions, presse, syndicats*] divided (**sur** on); **les médecins restent ~s** the doctors remain divided; **2** (ambivalent) [*réactions, sentiments*] mixed; **3** (indécis) **être ~** [*personne*] to be torn (**entre** between); **être ~ entre la colère et les larmes** to be torn between anger and tears; **4** (commun) [*chagrin*] shared; **leurs torts sont ~s** they are both to blame; **5** (réciproque) [*tendresse*] mutual; **amour ~** requited love.

partageable /paʀtaʒabl/ *adj* **1** [*domaine, terres, dépenses*] that can be divided (up) (**entre** between); **2** [*sentiment, optimisme, joie*] that can be shared (in); **ton optimisme n'est guère ~ dans les circonstances actuelles** I can hardly share your optimism in the present circumstances.

partager /paʀtaʒe/ [13] **I** *vtr* **1** (donner une partie de ce qui est à soi) to share [*jouets, nourriture*] (**entre** between; **avec** with); **il ne sait pas ~** he doesn't know how to share; **les enfants doivent apprendre à ~** children must learn to share; **2** (séparer) to divide [*pays, pièce*] (**en** into); **un rideau partage la chambre en deux** a curtain divides the bedroom into two; **3** (diviser) to divide [sth] (up), to split [*fortune, héritage, gâteau, terres, tâches*] (**entre** between, among; **en** into); **il a partagé ses biens entre ses trois enfants** he divided (up) ou split his belongings among his three children; **je partage mon temps entre la lecture et la musique** I divide my time between reading and music; **4** (avoir en commun) to share [*appartement, repas, goûts, avis, idées, responsabilités*]; (prendre part à) to share [*émotion, angoisse*]; **il a partagé ma vie pendant cinq ans** he shared my life for five years; **je partage ton inquiétude** I share your anxiety; **ils partagent le même goût de l'aventure** they share a love ou have a common love of adventure; **~ les mêmes valeurs** to have common values, to share values; **ton optimisme n'est pas partagé** no-one shares your optimism; **je partage votre avis** I agree with you, I'm of the same opinion; **5** (communiquer) to share [*chagrin, problème, joie*] (**avec** with); **faire ~ qch à qn** to let sb share in sth; **j'aimerais vous faire ~ ma joie** I'd like to let you share in my happiness; **il sait nous faire ~ ses émotions** he knows how to get his feelings across; **6** (opposer) [*problème, question*] to divide, to split [*population, politiciens, opinion publique*] (**en** into).

II se partager *vpr* **1** (se répartir) to share [*argent, travail, responsabilité*]; **les deux sociétés se partagent le marché** the two companies share the market; **les gagnants se sont partagé la somme de 10000 francs** the winners shared the sum of 10,000 francs; **deux sujets se partagent la 'une' des journaux** two topics share the front page; **2** (être divisé) to be divided (**en** into; **entre** between); to be split (**en** into); **le mouvement se partage en deux grandes tendances** the movement is divided ou split into two broad tendencies; **le groupe se partage entre adeptes du théâtre et fans de télévision** the group is divided between theatre[GB] enthusiasts and TV fans; **elle partage son temps entre son travail et ses enfants** she divides her time between her job and her children; **3** (se diviser) [*frais, responsabilités, nourriture*] to be shared; [*gâteau, tarte*] to be cut (up) (**en** into); **c'est le genre de travail qui ne se partage pas** it's the kind of work that cannot be shared; **4** (se communiquer) to be shared; **c'est un bonheur qui ne se partage pas** it's the sort of happiness one cannot share; **un tel chagrin ne peut se ~** such grief cannot be shared.

partageur, -euse /paʀtaʒœʀ, øz/ *adj* [*personne, enfant*] **être ~** to be good at sharing, to know how to share.

partance /paʀtɑ̃s/ *nf* **en ~** [*avion*] about to take off; [*navire*] about to sail; [*train, personne*] about to leave; **être en ~ pour** or **vers** [*avion, navire, train, voyageurs*] to be bound for; **sur un navire en ~ pour la Chine** on a ship bound for China.

partant¹ /paʀtɑ̃/ *conj* liter consequently.

partant², ~e /paʀtɑ̃, ɑ̃t/ **I**○ *adj* (enthousiaste) **être ~** to be game○ (**pour faire** to do); **quand il s'agit de faire la fête elle est toujours ~e** when it comes to living it up, she's always game.

II *nm,f* **1** gén person leaving ou departing; **les arrivants et les ~s** the arrivals and departures; **2** Sport, Turf starter.

partenaire /paʀtənɛʀ/ **I** *nmf* partner; **une bonne ~ au bridge** a good bridge partner; **qui était le ~ d'Arletty?** Cin who played opposite Arletty?

II *nm* Fin, Pol partner; **~ commercial/financier** trading/financial partner; **nos ~s de la CEE** our partners in the EC.

■ **~s sociaux** ≈ union and management.

partenariat /paʀtənaʀja/ *nm* partnership (**avec** with); **en quête de ~** seeking partnerships.

parterre /paʀtɛʀ/ *nm* **1** (de jardin) bed; **~ de fleurs** flower bed; **~ de bégonias** bed of begonias; **2** Théât (places) stalls (*pl*) GB, orchestra US; (spectateurs) people in the stalls GB ou orchestra US; **être au ~** to be in the stalls GB, to have orchestra seats US; **3** (assemblée) panel; **devant un ~ de journalistes** before a panel of journalists; **4**○ (sol) floor.

parthe /paʀt/ *adj, nm* Parthian.

Parthe /paʀt/ *nm* Parthian; **les ~s** the Parthians.

IDIOMES **décocher la flèche du ~** to fire a Parthian ou parting shot.

parthénogénèse /paʀtenɔʒenɛz/ *nf* parthenogenesis.

parthénogénétique /paʀtenɔʒenetik/ *adj* parthenogenetic.

Parthénon /paʀtenɔ̃/ *nprm* **le ~** the Parthenon.

parti, ~e /paʀti/ **I**○ *adj* (ivre) **être ~** to be tight○; **être un peu ~** to be tipsy○; **être complètement ~** to be plastered○.

II *nm* **1** (groupe de personnes) group; **le ~ des mécontents** the dissatisfied; **2** Pol party; **les ~s de l'opposition** the opposition parties; **avoir la carte d'un ~** to be a card-carrying member of a party; **le système du ~ unique** the one-party system; **3** (solution) option; **hésiter entre deux ~s** to hesitate between two options; **prendre ~** to commit oneself (**sur qch** on sth); **prendre ~ pour qn** to take sb's side; **prendre ~ contre qn** to be against sb; **prendre ~ pour/contre qch** to be for/against sth; **prendre le ~ de qn** to side with sb (**contre qn** against sb); **prendre le ~ de qch** to opt for sth; **prendre le ~ de faire** to decide to do; **il a pris le ~ de ne rien dire** he decided not to say anything; **ne pas savoir quel ~ prendre** not to know what to do for the best; **4**† (personne à marier) suitable match; **être un beau** or **bon ~** [*homme*] to be an eligible bachelor; [*homme, femme*] to be a catch○.

III partie *nf* **1** (élément d'un tout) gén part; (d'une somme, d'un salaire) proportion, part; **une ~e de la population/des électeurs** a proportion ou section of the population/of the voters; **une ~e des bénéfices/salaires** a proportion of the profits/wages; **les ~es du corps** the parts of the body; **la première/deuxième ~e de** the first/second part of [*livre, film, spectacle*]; **un feuilleton en six ~es** a television serial in six parts; **une bonne** or **grande ~e de** a good ou large number of [*personnes, objets, éléments*]; a high proportion of [*masse, ensemble, ressources*]; **la majeure ~e des gens** most people; **la majeure ~e de la population/des cas** the majority of the population/of cases; **en ~e** partly, in part; **en grande ~e** to a large ou great extent; **pour ~e** liter partly, in part; **tout ou ~e de** all or part of; **se faire rembourser tout ou ~e des frais** to have all or some of one's expenses paid; **faire ~e de** to be part of [*groupe, processus, idéologie, pays*]; **il fait ~e de la famille** he's one of the family; **faire ~e des premiers/derniers** to be among the first/last; **cela fait ~e de leurs avantages** that's one of their advantages; **faire ~e du passé** to belong to the past; **être** or **faire ~e intégrante de qch** to be an integral part of sth; **2** (division de l'espace) part; **dans cette ~e du monde/de l'Afrique** in this part of the world/of Africa; **la ~e est/ouest de Jérusalem** the eastern/western part of Jerusalem; **3** (division temporelle) part; **il a plu une ~e de la journée/nuit** it rained for part of the day/night; **ça m'a occupé une bonne ~e de la matinée** it took me a good part of the morning; **il leur consacre une ~e de son temps libre** he devotes some of his free time to them; **elle passe la majeure ~e de son temps au travail/à dormir** she spends most of her time at work/sleeping; **4** (profession) line (of work); **dans ma ~e** in my line (of work); **il est de la ~e** it's in his line (of work); **je ne suis pas du tout de la ~e** that's not at all in my line; **5** ▶ **449** Jeux, Sport game; **une ~e de poker/de billard/d'échecs** a game of poker/of billiards/of chess; **une ~e de tennis** a game of tennis; **une ~e de cache-cache** a game of hide-and-seek; **une ~e de golf** a round of golf; **faire** or **jouer une ~e** to have a game; **la ~e qui se joue entre les deux pays est difficile** fig the ongoing situation between the two countries is tense; **gagner/perdre une ~e** Jeux, Sport to win/lose a game; **gagner/perdre la ~e** fig to win/lose the day; **abandonner la ~e** Jeux, Sport to abandon the game; fig to give up (the fight); **avoir la ~e belle** or **facile** fig to have an easy time of it; **être de la ~e** fig to be in on it○; **je fête mes trente ans, j'espère que tu seras de la ~e** I'm having a thirtieth birthday party, I hope you can come; **nous ne pouvons pas venir à votre fête mais ce n'est que ~e remise** we can't make it to your party but maybe next time; **6** (dans une négociation, un contrat) party; **les ~es en présence/conflit** the parties (involved)/the opposing parties; **les ~es contractantes/concernées** the contracting/interested parties; **les deux ~es ont signé un accord** the two parties signed an agreement; **les ~es belligérantes** the warring parties ou factions; **être ~e prenante dans qch** to be actively involved in [*conflit, contrat, négociation*]; **7** Jur party; **la ~e adverse** the opposing party; **8** Mus part; **la ~e de soprano/basse** the soprano/bass part; **9** Math part.

IV parties○ *nfpl* privates○.

■ **~ pris** bias; **~ pris esthétique/politique** aesthetic/political bias; **~ pris de réalisme/modernité** bias toward(s) realism/modernity; **Parti conservateur** Conservative Party; **Parti communiste, PC** Communist Party; **Parti communiste français, PCF** French Communist Party; **Parti démocrate** Democrat Party; **Parti républicain** Republican Party; **Parti socialiste, PS** Socialist Party; **Parti travailliste** Labour Party; **~e carrée**○ wife-swapping party; **~e de chasse** Chasse hunting party; **~e civile** Jur plaintiff; **l'avocat de la ~e civile** the counsel for the plaintiff; **se constituer** or **porter ~e civile** to take civil action; **~e du discours** Ling part of speech; **~e fine** orgy; **~e de jambes en l'air**○ legover◑ GB, screw◑; **~e de pêche** fishing trip; **~e de plaisir** fun; **tu parles d'une ~e de plaisir!** iron that's not my idea of fun!; **~es génitales** or **honteuses**† private parts.

IDIOMES **prendre son ~ de qch** to come to terms with sth; **tirer ~ de qch** to take advantage of [*situation, événement*]; to turn [sth] to good account [*leçon, invention*]; **faire un mauvais ~ à qn** to ill-treat sb; **avoir affaire à forte ~e** to have a tough opponent; **prendre qn à ~e** to take sb to task; ▶ **lier**.

partial, ~e, *mpl* **-iaux** /paʀsjal, o/ *adj* [*personne, public, jugement*] biased[GB] (**envers** toward, towards GB, against).

partialement /paʀsjalmɑ̃/ *adv* in a biased[GB] way.

partialité /paʀsjalite/ *nf* (de personne, jugement) bias; **~ envers qn** (au profit de) bias toward(s) sb; (au détriment de) bias against sb; **avec ~** in a biased[GB] way; **accuser qn de ~** to accuse sb of being biased[GB].

participant, ~e /paʀtisipɑ̃, ɑ̃t/ *nm,f* (à un concours, une course) participant, entrant (**à** in); (à un débat, une conférence, une cérémonie) participant, person taking part (**à** in); (à un complot) person taking part, person involved (**à** in).

participatif, -ive /paʀtisipatif, iv/ *adj* **gestion participative** participative management; **titre ~** non-voting share (*in public sector companies*); **prêt ~** loan entitling the lender to an interest in the company.

participation /paʀtisipasjɔ̃/ *nf* **1** (à une réunion, un projet, festival, soulèvement) participation (**à** in); (à un complot, attentat) involvement (**à** in); **la ~ au gala de plusieurs vedettes a attiré les photographes** the appearance of several stars at the gala attracted the photographers; **la ~ au scrutin** or **aux élections a été très faible** there was a very low turnout at the polls; **2** (contribution) contribution; **acceptez ma modeste ~** accept my modest contribution; **~ aux frais** (financial) contribution; **entreprise en ~ mixte** joint partnership; **3** Fin (part financière) stake, holding; **~ de 17%** 17% stake; **prendre une ~ dans une société** to take a stake in a company; **entreprise en ~** joint venture.

■ **~ aux bénéfices** profit-sharing; **~ majoritaire/minoritaire** majority/minority stake; **~s croisées** reciprocal shareholding **₵**.

participe /paʀtisip/ *nm* Ling participle; **~ présent/passé** present/past participle.

participer /paʀtisipe/ [1] **I participer à** *vtr ind* **1** (prendre part) **~ à** to participate in, to take part in [*travail, réunion, soulèvement, manifestation*]; to be involved in [*crime, complot, attentat*]; **il ne participe pas assez en classe** he doesn't participate enough in class; **ce projet est immoral, je n'y participerai pas** this project is immoral, I will have no part in it; **~ à la destruction de l'environnement** to contribute to the destruction of the environment; **2** (contribuer financièrement à) **~ à** to contribute to; **~ à l'aide internationale** to contribute to international aid; **3** Écon, Entr **~ aux bénéfices** to share in the profits; **~ aux frais** to share in the cost, to contribute to the cost; **4** (partager) **~ à la joie/tristesse/douleur de qn** to share sb's joy/sadness/pain.

II participer de *vtr ind* fml **son comportement participe de la névrose** his/her behaviour is akin to ou has some of the characteristics of neurosis; **des idées qui participent de l'idéologie dominante** ideas which draw on the dominant ideology.

participial, **~e**, *mpl* **-iaux** /paʀtisipjal, o/ *adj* Ling participial.

particulariser: **se particulariser** /paʀtikylaʀize/ [1] *vpr* to be characterized (**par** by).

particularisme /paʀtikylaʀism/ *nm* distinctive identity; **~ national/régional/religieux** distinctive national/regional/religious identity.

particularité /paʀtikylaʀite/ *nf* **1** (caractéristique) special feature; **les ~s climatiques/géologiques d'une région** the special climatic/geological features of an area; **les ~s historiques d'un pays** a country's particular historical background; **un accord qui présente la ~ d'être** an agreement that has the special feature of being; **2** (de maladie, régime politique, situation) particular nature; (de coutume) uniqueness.

particule /paʀtikyl/ *nf* **1** gén, Phys particle; **2** Ling (mot) particle; (devant un patronyme) **~ (nobiliaire)** (nobiliary) particle, handle○; **nom à ~** aristocratic name (*preceded by a particle such as 'de'*).

■ **~ séparable** Ling separable prefix.

particulier, **-ière** /paʀtikylje, ɛʀ/ **I** *adj* **1** (propre) **l'entreprise a une façon particulière de procéder** the company has its own (particular) procedures; **il a ceci de ~ qu'il aime son indépendance** the thing is with him, he has to be independent; **il a une manière particulière de s'exprimer** he has a particular way of expressing himself; **2** (spécifique) [*droits, statut, privilèges, rôle*] special; [*exemple, thème, objectif*] specific; **les agriculteurs ont un régime d'imposition ~** the farmers have a special tax status; **3** (personnel) [*maison, voiture, professeur, secrétaire*] private; **je dois vous parler à titre ~** I must speak to you privately ou in private; **collection particulière** private collection; **4** (inhabituel) [*cas, situation, phénomène*] unusual; [*talent, jour, effort*] special; [*style, mœurs*] odd; [*accent*] distinctive, unusual; **il a examiné ce cas avec une attention particulière** he gave this case his particular attention; **un épisode très ~** a very unusual episode; **c'est quelqu'un de très ~** (admiratif) he's/she's somebody out of the ordinary; péj he's/she's weird; **'quoi de neuf?'—'rien de ~'** 'what's new?'—'nothing in particular, nothing special'; **il a des amis assez ~s** he has some friends who are definitely different; **elle a un genre ~** she's a bit weird; **cela a un goût assez ~** it tastes weird.

II en particulier *loc adv* **1** (en privé) in private; **puis-je vous voir en ~?** can I see you in private?; **2** (séparément) individually; **s'occuper de chaque cas en ~** to consider each case individually; **3** (surtout) particularly; (notamment) in particular ; **il a fait très froid, dans le nord en ~** it's been very cold, particularly in the north; **voir en ~ le chapitre 5** see chapter 5 in particular; **tous les pays sont concernés, la France en ~** all countries are concerned and France in particular.

III *nm* **1** (personne) (**simple**) **~** private individual; **loger chez des ~s** to stay with a family; **vente de ~ à ~** private sale; **vendre de ~ à ~** to sell privately; **2** (détail) **le ~** the particular; **du ~ au général** from the particular to the general.

particulièrement /paʀtikyljɛʀmɑ̃/ *adv* **1** (hautement) [*fatigué, honteux, important*] particularly; [*intelligent*] exceptionally; [*aimer, souffrir*] really; **il est ~ désagréable aujourd'hui** he's in a particularly nasty mood today; **pas ~** not particularly; **2** (spécialement) particularly, in particular; **campagne qui vise ~ les jeunes** campaign aimed at the young in particular, campaign particularly aimed at the young; **la crise économique frappe ~ cette région** the economic crisis is hitting this area particularly hard; **plus** or **tout ~** more particularly; **je ne la connais pas ~** I don't know her particularly well.

partiel, **-ielle** /paʀsjɛl/ **I** *adj* (non complet) [*paiement*] part (*épith*); [*montant, remboursement, destruction, accord, résultat*] partial; **une levée partielle des barrages routiers** a partial lifting of roadblocks; **des solutions très partielles** very incomplete solutions.

II *nm* Univ exam based on a module.

III partielle *nf* Pol ≈ by-election.

partiellement /paʀsjɛlmɑ̃/ *adv* partially.

partir /paʀtiʀ/ [30] **I** *vi* **1** (quitter un lieu) [*personne*] to leave, to go; **~ sans manger** to leave ou go without eating; **partez devant, je vous rejoins** go on ahead, I'll catch you up; **tu pars déjà?** are you leaving already?; **~ à pied/en voiture/en avion** to leave on foot/in a car/in a plane; **est-ce qu'ils sont partis en avion ou en train?** did they fly or did they take the train?; **il est parti en ville à bicyclette** he went to town on his bicycle; **il est parti il y a cinq minutes** he left five minutes ago; **ils sont partis en Écosse en stop** (ils sont encore en voyage) they're hitchhiking to Scotland; (dans le passé) they hitchhiked to Scotland; **~ de** to leave ou go from [*ville, gare, aéroport*]; **de quelle gare pars-tu?** which station are you leaving ou going from?; **je suis partie de chez moi à 20 heures** I left my house at 8 pm; **faire ~ qn** to make sb leave; **j'espère que je ne vous fais pas ~?** I hope I'm not driving you away?; **fais ~ ce chien!** get that dog out of here!; **~ en courant/boitant/hurlant** to run off/to limp off/to go off screaming; **~ fâché** to go off in a huff○; **~ content** to go away happy; **~ avec qn** to go off with sb; **elle est partie avec un autre** she went off with another man; **~ sans laisser d'adresse** lit to go away without leaving a forwarding address; (sans laisser de traces) to disappear without trace; **2** (pour une destination) to go, to leave; **~ loin/dans un pays lointain** to go far away/to a far-off country; **~ à Paris/à New York/au Mexique** to go to Paris/to New York/to Mexico; **je pars à Paris demain** I'm going to Paris tomorrow, I'm off to Paris tomorrow; **~ pour le Mexique/l'Australie** to leave for Mexico/Australia; **tu pars pour combien de temps?** how long are you going for?; **~ pour une semaine/six mois** to go for a week/six months; **est-ce que tu sais que je pars pour une semaine?** did you know I was going away for a week?; **~ en vacances** to go on holiday GB ou vacation US (**à** to); **nous partons en vacances dans les Vosges** we're going on holiday GB ou vacation to the Vosges; **~ en week-end** to go away for the weekend; **~ en week-end à Chamonix** to go to Chamonix for the weekend; **~ en voyage/expédition/croisière** to go on a trip/an expedition/a cruise; **~ à la guerre/au front** to go off to war/to the front; **~ au travail** to go to work; **~ à la pêche/chasse** to go fishing/hunting; **~ faire** to go to do; **elle est partie se reposer** she's gone for a rest; **~ en tournée** to set off on tour GB ou on a tour US; **~ en retraite** to retire; **3** (se mettre en mouvement) [*voiture, car, train*] to leave; [*avion*] to take off; [*moteur*] to start; [*personne*] to be off, to leave; **les coureurs sont partis** the runners are off; **le train à destination de Dijon va ~** the train to Dijon is about to depart ou leave; **à vos marques, prêts, partez!** on your marks, get set, go!; **4** (être projeté) [*flèche, balle*] to be fired; [*bouchon*] to shoot out; [*capsule*] to shoot off; [*réplique*] to slip out; **il jouait avec le fusil et le coup de feu est parti** he was playing with the gun and it went off; **la balle est partie, le blessant à l'épaule** the shot was fired, wounding him in the shoulder; **le bouchon est parti d'un seul coup** the cork suddenly shot out; **elle était tellement énervée que la gifle est partie toute seule** she was so angry that she slapped him/her before she realized what she was doing ou before she could stop herself; **5** (commencer) [*chemin, route*] to start; **le sentier part d'ici** the path starts here; **les branches qui partent du tronc** the branches growing out from the trunk; **les avenues qui partent de la Place de l'Étoile** the avenues which radiate outwards from the Place de l'Étoile; **~ favori** [*concurrent, candidat*] to start favourite[GB] (**à une course** for a race); **~ gagnant/battu d'avance** to be the winner/loser before one has even started; **~ dernier** (dans une course) to start last; **le troisième en partant de la gauche** the third (starting) from the left; **~ de rien** to start from nothing; **c'est parti!** (si l'on donne un ordre) go!; (si l'on constate) here we go!; **et voilà, c'est parti, il pleut!** here we go, it's raining!; **être bien parti**○ lit [*coureur, cheval*] to have got GB ou gotten US off to a good start; fig [*projet, travail, personne*] to have got GB ou gotten US off to a good start; **être bien parti pour gagner** lit, fig to seem all set to win; **l'entreprise a l'air bien partie** the firm seems to have got off to a good start; **être mal parti**○ lit [*coureur, cheval*] to have got off to a bad start; fig [*personne, pays, projet*] to be in a bad way; **avec la récession le pays est mal parti** what with the recession the country is in a bad way; **c'est mal parti**○ things don't look too good; **il faudrait qu'il fasse beau mais c'est mal parti** it would be nice if the weather was fine but it doesn't look too promising; **il a l'air parti pour réussir**○ he seems to be heading for success; **le mauvais temps est parti pour durer**○ it looks as if the bad weather is here to stay; **6** (se fonder) **~ de qch** to start from sth; **je suis parti d'une idée/observation très simple** I started from a very simple idea/observation; **l'auteur est parti d'un fait divers pour écrire son roman** the author used a news snippet as a starting point for his novel; **~ du principe que** to work on the assumption that; **~ d'une bonne intention** or **d'un**

bon sentiment [*idée, geste*] to be well-meant; **(en) partant de là**○... on that basis...; **7** (s'enlever) [*tache , saleté*] to come out; [*émail, peinture*] to come off; [*odeur*] to go; [*bouton , écusson, décoration*] to come off; **j'ai beau frotter, ça ne part pas** no matter how hard I rub, it won't come out; **la saleté part bien/mal** the dirt's coming off nicely/ won't come out; **l'étiquette est partie** the label has come off; **faire ~ une tache/un graffiti** to remove a stain/a piece of graffiti; **8** (être expédié) [*colis, lettre, rapport, candidature*] to be sent (off); **9** (se lancer) **quand il est parti on ne l'arrête plus** once he starts ou gets going there's no stopping him; **~ dans des explications/un monologue** to launch into explanations/a monologue; **~ dans des digressions** to start digressing; **10** (mourir) euph to go, to pass away euph.

II **à partir de** *loc prép* **1** (dans l'espace) from; **à ~ d'ici/du feu rouge/du carrefour** from here/the traffic lights/the crossroads; **2** (dans le temps) from; **à ~ de 16 heures/du 5 février** from 4 o'clock/5 February (onwards); **à ~ de maintenant** from now on; **à ~ du moment où** (sens temporel) as soon as; (sens conditionnel) as long as; **c'est possible à ~ du moment où tu résides dans le pays** it's possible as long as you are resident in the country; **à ~ de là, tout a basculé** from then on everything changed radically; **3** (supérieur ou égal) from; **à ~ de 2 000 francs** from 2,000 francs; **les enfants ne sont admis qu'à ~ de huit ans** children under eight are not admitted; **4** (en utilisant) from; **fabriqué à ~ de pétrole/d'un alliage** made from oil/an alloy; **5** (en se basant sur) from, on the basis of; **faire une étude à ~ de statistiques** to base a study on statistics; **à ~ de cet exemple il a démontré que** using ou from this example he proved that; **à ~ de ces chiffres/résultats il est possible de**... on the basis of these figures/results it is possible to...; **à ~ d'un échantillon représentatif** from ou on the basis of a representative sample; ▶ **courir**, **maille**, **mourir**.

partisan, **~e** /paʀtizɑ̃, an/ **I** *adj* **1** (de parti pris) pej [*esprit, discours, querelle*] partisan; **2** (en faveur de) **~ de qch/de faire** in favour[GB] of sth/of doing; **un homme ~ des réformes** a man who is in favour[GB] of the reforms; **être ~ du moindre effort** (être paresseux) to be lazy; (dans une décision) to go for the easy option.

II *nm,f* **1** gén supporter, partisan (**de** of); **un ~ acharné du libéralisme** a staunch supporter of liberalism; **2** Mil partisan.

partitif, **-ive** /paʀtitif, iv/ **I** *adj* partitive.

II *nm* partitive.

partition /paʀtisjɔ̃/ *nf* **1** Mus score; **la ~ chorale/d'orchestre** the choral/orchestral score; **jouer sans ~** to play without the music; **2** (partage) partition (**de** of); **3** Math partition.

partousard◑ = **partouzard**.

partouse◑ = **partouze**.

partouser◑ = **partouzer**.

partout /paʀtu/ *adv* **1** (en tous lieux) [*sévir, traîner, chercher*] everywhere; [*avoir mal, démanger, s'enduire*] all over; **comme ~ ailleurs** like everywhere else; **un peu ~ dans le monde** more or less all over the world; **il y avait de la boue ~** there was mud all over the place; **~ sur ton passage** wherever you go; **~ où je vais** wherever I go; **2** (dans tous les domaines) **il est le premier ~** he's the best at everything; **3** Sport **trois (points/buts) ~** three all.

IDIOMES **fourrer son nez ~**○ to stick one's nose into everything○.

partouzard◑, **~e** /paʀtuzaʀ, aʀd/ *nm,f* orgy-lover, swinger◑.

partouze◑ /paʀtuz/ *nf* (sexual) orgy; **faire une ~** to have an orgy, to swing◑.

partouzer◑ /paʀtuze/ [1] *vi* to take part in orgies.

parturiente /paʀtyʀjɑ̃t/ *nf* parturient.

parturition /paʀtyʀisjɔ̃/ *nf* parturition.

parure /paʀyʀ/ *nf* **1** (toilette) finery ¢; **~ de mariée** bridal finery; **les femmes avaient mis leurs plus belles ~s** the women had dressed up in all their finery; **la nature revêtue de la ~ du printemps** littér nature arrayed in her spring finery; **2** (bijoux) set of jewels; **~ de diamants** set of diamonds; **3** (ensemble assorti) set; **~ de lit/de table** set of bed linen/table linen; **4** Tech (en boucherie, peausserie) trimming.

parution /paʀysjɔ̃/ *nf* (de livre, journal, revue) publication; **à sa ~, le livre a fait scandale** when it came out ou was published, the book caused a scandal; **la ~ a été reportée en mars** the publication date has been put back till March; **vous en recevrez un exemplaire dès ~** you will receive an issue as soon as it is published.

parvenir /paʀvəniʀ/ [36] **I parvenir à** *vtr ind* **1** (atteindre) **~ à** to reach [*lieu, stade*]; [*lettre, nouvelle, rumeur, bruit*] to reach [*personne, groupe*]; **un fruit parvenu à maturité** a fruit which has reached maturity; **faire ~ qch à qn** (par voie postale) to send sth to sb; (par messager) to get sth to sb; **2** (au prix d'efforts) **~ à** to reach [*accord, solution, conclusion*]; to gain [*pouvoir*]; to get [*poste*]; to achieve [*équilibre*]; **~ à faire** to manage to do; **il veut ~ à ce qu'ils acceptent** he wants to get them to accept; **~ à ses fins** to achieve one's ends; **~ à son but** to achieve one's aim ou goal.

II *vi* (réussir socialement) to succeed.

parvenu, **~e** /paʀvəny/ **I** *adj* **un homme ~** an upstart.

II *nm,f* upstart.

parvis /paʀvi/ *nm inv* (d'église) square; **~ de cathédrale** cathedral square; (de bâtiment) forecourt.

pas¹ /pa/ *adv*

■ **Note** Dans la langue parlée ou familière, *not* utilisé avec un auxiliaire ou un modal prend parfois la forme *n't* qui est alors accolée à l'auxiliaire: *he hasn't finished, he couldn't come.* On notera que *will not* devient *won't*, que *shall not* devient *shan't* et *cannot* devient *can't*.

1 gén **sur les 15 employés, ~ un ne parle anglais** out of the 15 employees not one speaks English; **c'est un Autrichien, ~ un Allemand** he's an Austrian, not a German; **je ne prends ~ de sucre avec mon café** I don't take sugar in coffee; **ils n'ont ~ le téléphone** they haven't got a phone; **ils n'ont ~ d'enfants/de principes** they haven't got any children/principles, they have no children/principles; **il n'y a ~ de café dans le placard** there isn't any coffee in the cupboard, there's no coffee in the cupboard; **ce n'est ~ de l'amour, c'est de la possessivité** it isn't love, it's possessiveness; **ce n'est ~ du cuir, c'est du plastique** it isn't leather, it's plastic; **ce n'est ~ un lâche** gén he isn't a coward; (pour insister) he's no coward; **ce n'est ~ un ami à moi** gén he isn't a friend of mine; (pour insister) he's no friend of mine; **ce n'est ~ une raison pour crier comme ça!** that's no reason to shout like that!; **ce n'est ~ une vie pour un gamin de son âge** it's no life for a child of his age; **ce n'est ~ un endroit pour s'arrêter** it's no place to stop; **ce n'est ~ qu'il soit désagréable, mais il est tellement ennuyeux!** it's not that he's unpleasant, but he's so boring!; **elle n'est ~ très bavarde** she's not very talkative; **il n'est ~ plus intelligent qu'un autre** he's no brighter than anybody else; **je ne pense ~** I don't think so, I think not sout; **alors, tu viens ou ~**○**?** so, are you coming or not?; **elle a aimé le film, mais lui ~** or **mais ~ lui**○ she liked the film but he didn't; **ma voiture a un toit ouvrant, la leur ~** or **~ la leur**○ gén my car has a sunroof, theirs doesn't; (pour rectifier une erreur) my car has a sunroof, not theirs; **il m'a dit de ne ~ y aller** he told me not to go there; **du pain ~ cuit** unbaked bread; **des tomates ~ mûres** unripe tomatoes; **des chaussures ~ cirées** unpolished shoes; **une radio ~ chère**○ a cheap radio set; **je fouille dans ma poche... ~ de portefeuille!** I searched in my pocket... no wallet!; **~ d'augmentation pour vous, Pichon!** no raise for you, Pichon!; **non mais t'es ~ dingue**○**?** are you mad or what?; **2** (dans des expressions, exclamations) **~ du tout** not at all; **~ le moins du monde** not in the slightest ou in the least; **absolument ~** absolutely not; **~ vraiment** not really; **~ tellement** not much; **~ tant que ça** not all that much; **~ plus que ça** so-so○, not all that much; **~ d'histoires!** I don't want any arguments ou fuss about it!; **~ de chance!** hard luck!, tough luck!; **~ possible!** I can't believe it!; **~ croyable!** incredible!; **~ vrai**○**?** gén isn't that so?; **3** (n'est-ce pas) **elle est jolie la petite Pivachon, ~**○**?** the Pivachon girl is pretty, isn't she?; **on s'est bien amusé, ~**○**?** we had a good time, didn't we?; **on a bien travaillé, ~ vrai**○**?** we did good work, didn't we?

pas² /pa/ *nm inv* **1** (enjambée) step; **faire un grand/petit ~** to take a long/small step; **faire des petits ~** to take small steps; **faire des grands ~** to stride along; **marcher** or **avancer à grands ~** to stride along; **marcher** or **avancer à petits ~** to edge forward; **faire un ~ en avant/en arrière** to take a step forward/backward; **l'industrie a fait un grand ~ en avant** industry has taken a big step forward; **l'hiver arrive à grands ~** winter is fast approaching; **avancer à ~ de géant (dans qch)** to make giant strides (in sth); **avancer à ~ de fourmi (dans qch)** to progress at a snail's pace (in sth); **marcher à ~ de loup** or **de velours** to move stealthily; **marcher à ~ feutrés** to walk softly; **marcher à ~ comptés** to walk with measured steps; **faire ses premiers ~** [*enfant*] to take one's first steps; **faire ses premiers ~ dans la société mondaine** to make one's debut in society; **faire le premier ~** fig to make the first move; **suivre qn ~ à ~** to follow sb everywhere; **avancer ~ à ~ dans une enquête** to proceed step by step in an inquiry; **il n'y a qu'un ~** there's a fine line; **de là à dire qu'il s'en fiche**○**, il n'y a qu'un ~** there's only a fine line between that and saying he doesn't care; **j'habite à deux ~ (d'ici)** I live just a step away (from here); **le magasin est à deux ~ de chez elle** the shop is just a step away from her house; ▶ **cent¹**; **2** (allure) pace; **marcher d'un bon ~** to walk at a brisk pace; **allonger** or **hâter le ~** to quicken one's pace; **marcher d'un ~ lourd** to walk with a heavy tread; **marcher d'un ~ hésitant/gracieux** to walk hesitantly/gracefully; **se diriger vers sa voiture d'un ~ pressé** to walk hurriedly toward(s) one's car; **marcher du même ~** to walk in step; **ralentir le ~** to slow down; **marcher au ~** Mil to march; Équit to walk; **marquer le ~** Mil to mark time; **rouler** or **circuler au ~** to crawl (along); **'roulez au ~'** (sur panneau) 'dead slow' GB, '(very) slow' US; **mettre qn au ~** to bring sb to heel; **partir au ~ de course** to rush off, to race off; **faire qch au ~ de charge** to do sth in double-quick time; **j'y vais de ce ~** I'll do it straightaway; **3** (bruit) footstep; **j'ai entendu un bruit de ~** I heard footsteps; **reconnaître le ~ de qn** to recognize sb's (foot)step; **4** (trace de pied) footprint; **des ~ dans la neige/sur le sable** footprints in the snow/in the sand; **revenir** or **retourner sur ses ~** lit, fig to retrace one's steps, to backtrack; **marcher sur les ~ de qn** fig to follow in sb's footsteps; **5** Danse step; **un ~ de danse** a dance step; **le ~ de valse** the waltz step; **apprendre les ~ du tango** to learn how to tango; **6** Tech (d'une hélice) pitch; (d'un écrou, d'une vis) thread; **7** Aut, Aviat (distance entre les sièges) seat pitch.

■ **~ accéléré** quick march; **~ cadencé** slow time; **marcher au ~ cadencé** to march in slow time; **~ de deux** Danse pas de deux; **~ de l'oie** goosestep; **marcher au ~ de l'oie** to goosestep; **~ de patineur** (au ski) skating; **~ de porte** doorstep; **rester sur le ~ de la porte** to stay on the doorstep; **~ redoublé** double time, quick march; **marcher au ~ redoublé** to quick march; **~ de route** walking pace; **~ de tir** Mil Sport shooting range; Astronaut launch(ing) pad; **~ de vis** Tech thread.

IDIOMES **tirer qn/se tirer d'un mauvais ~** to get sb/to get out of a tight corner; **faire** or **sauter le ~** to take the plunge; **céder le ~ à qn** to make way for sb; **prendre le ~ sur qch/qn** to overtake sth/sb.

pascal[1], **~e**, *mpl* **~s** or **-aux** /paskal, o/ *adj* Relig [*week-end, fêtes*] Easter (*épith*); [*cierge, agneau*] paschal.

pascal[2] /paskal/ *nm* Mes pascal.

Pascal /paskal/ **I** *nm* Ordinat PASCAL, Pascal.
II *npr* Pascal.

pascalien, **-ienne** /paskaljɛ̃, ɛn/ *adj* [*pensée*] of Pascal (*après n*).

Pas-de-Calais /padkalɛ/ ▶ 692 *nprm* (département) **le ~** the Pas-de-Calais.

pas-de-porte /padpɔʀt/ *nm inv* (somme) key money.

passable /pasabl/ *adj* **1** [*exposé, film, soirée*] not bad (*jamais épith*), fairly good; [*production, résultats*] reasonable, acceptable; **2** Scol (notation) fair.

passablement /pasabləmɑ̃/ *adv* **1** (considérablement) [*ivre, énervé, flou*] rather, pretty○; [*boire, s'inquiéter*] quite a lot, quite a bit○; **2** (moyennement) [*jouer au tennis*] reasonably well.

passade /pasad/ *nf* **1** (engouement) fad; **une simple ~** just a passing fad; **2** (liaison amoureuse) brief affair.

passage /pasaʒ/ *nm* **1** (circulation) **interdire le ~ des camions dans la ville** to ban trucks from (driving through) the town; **une rue où il y a beaucoup de ~** (piétons) a street where there are a lot of passers-by; (véhicules) a street where there's a lot of traffic; **isoler les fenêtres pour empêcher le ~ de l'air** to seal the windows to prevent draughts GB ou drafts US; **2** (séjour) **ton bref ~ dans la ville a été très remarqué** your stay in the town was brief but did not go unnoticed; **lors de son ~ ici il a oublié son parapluie** when he was here he left his umbrella; **un petit ~ chez le teinturier ne lui ferait pas de mal** a visit to the dry-cleaners' wouldn't do it any harm; **après un bref ~ dans la fonction publique** after a short spell in the civil service; **3** (visite en chemin) **attendre le ~ du boulanger** to wait for the baker's van to come; **était-ce avant ou après le ~ du facteur?** was it before or after the postman had been?; **manquer le ~ des cigognes** to miss the storks going over; **le ~ du prochain bus est à 10 heures** the next bus is at 10 o'clock; **je peux te prendre au ~** I can pick you up on the way; **il est de ~ en France/dans notre ville** he is passing through France/our town; **des voyageurs de ~** travellers who are passing through; **des hôtes de ~** short-stay guests; **elle n'a que des amants de ~** she only has casual relationships; **4** (franchissement) **'~ interdit, voie privée'** 'no entry, private road'; **pour permettre le ~ de la lumière** in order to let the light in; **les voitures se sont garées pour laisser** or **céder le ~ à l'ambulance** the cars pulled over to let the ambulance go past; **on se retourne sur ton ~** you make people's heads turn as you go past; **notons au ~ que...** fig let's note in passing that...; **se servir au ~** lit (en passant) to help oneself; fig (légalement) to take a cut (of the profits); (illégalement) to pocket some of the profits; **~ en ferry/hovercraft** ferry/hovercraft crossing; **le ~ à gué du bras de mer est possible à marée basse** the sound can be forded at low tide; **la voiture a peiné lors du ~ du col** the car had a hard time crossing the pass; **5** (à la radio, télévision, au théâtre) **c'est leur troisième ~ à l'Olympia** it's the third time they've been to the Olympia; **ton ~ sur scène/à la télévision a été très remarqué** you made a great impact on stage/on the television; **chaque ~ de votre chanson à la radio vous rapportera des droits d'auteur** you'll get royalties every time your song is played on the radio; **6** (chemin emprunté) (par une personne) way; (par une chose) path; **prévoir le ~ du tout-à-l'égout/de câbles** to plan the route of the main sewer/of cables; **pour aller jusqu'au sommet il y a plusieurs ~s possibles** there are several possible ways of getting to the summit; **pousse-toi tu es dans mon ~** move! you're in my way!; **barrer le ~ à qn** to bar sb's way; **7** (à une situation nouvelle) **~ (de qch) à qch** transition (from sth) to sth; **~ à la deuxième étape/la phase suivante** progression to the second stage/the next phase; **son ~ dans la classe supérieure est compromis** he/she won't be allowed to move up into the next class GB ou grade US; **les rites initiatiques de ~ à l'âge adulte** the rites of passage into adulthood; **8** (petite rue) alley; (dans un bâtiment) passageway; **9** (de roman, symphonie) passage; (de film) sequence; **10** Équit passage.

■ **~ à l'acte** Psych acting out; **~ clouté**† = **~ pour piétons**; **~ à niveau** level crossing GB, grade crossing US; **~ obligé** prerequisite (**pour** for); **~ pour piétons** pedestrian crossing, crosswalk US; **~ protégé** right of way; **~ souterrain** underground passage; (sous une rue) subway; **~ à tabac** beating; **subir un ~ à tabac** to be beaten up; **~ à vide** gén bad patch; (pour un acteur, artiste) unproductive period.

passager, **-ère** /pasaʒe, ɛʀ/ **I** *adj* **1** (de courte durée) [*situation, crise*] temporary; [*sentiment, engouement*] passing; [*averse*] brief; [*fièvre, malaise*] slight, short-lived (*épith*); [*amours*] casual; **sa mauvaise humeur n'est que passagère** his/her bad mood won't last long; **2** (très fréquenté) [*avenue, endroit*] busy.
II *nm,f* Transp passenger (**à destination de** to; **en provenance de** from).
■ **~ clandestin** stowaway.

passagèrement /pasaʒɛʀmɑ̃/ *adv* temporarily.

passant, **~e** /pasɑ̃, ɑt/ **I** *adj* [*rue*] busy.
II *nm,f* passer-by; **quelques ~s** a few passers-by.
III *nm* (anneau de ceinture, bracelet-montre) loop.

passation /pasasjɔ̃/ *nf* Jur (conclusion d'acte) signing ₵; **~ d'écriture** Compta posting of an entry; **~ des pouvoirs** Jur, Pol transfer of power.

passavant /pasavɑ̃/ *nm* **1** Jur, Comm permit; **2** Naut catwalk.

passe /pɑs/ **I**○ *nm* **1** (passe-partout) master key; **2** (laissez-passer) pass.
II *nf* **1** Sport pass; **faire une ~** to pass the ball (**à** to); **2** (de prestidigitateur, torero) pass; **3** (de magnétiseur, d'hypnotiseur) pass; **il m'a fait des ~s** he made passes over me; **4**○ (de prostituée) trick○; **faire une ~** to turn a trick○; **le prix d'une ~** the cost of a trick; **5** (situation) **être dans une ~ difficile/une mauvaise ~** to be going through a difficult/bad patch; **être en ~ de faire** to be (well) on the way to doing; **c'est une méthode révolue ou en ~ de l'être** it's an outdated method or soon will be; **6** Naut (chenal) channel; **7** Géog (col) pass.
■ **~ d'armes** Mil passage of arms; fig heated exchange.

passé, **~e** /pɑse/ **I** *pp* ▶ **passer**.
II *pp adj* **1** (qui est révolu) [*années, siècles, expériences, amours*] past; **au cours des siècles ~s** in bygone centuries, in past centuries; **regretter le temps ~** to regret the past; **des vêtements ~s de mode** dated clothes; **2** (dernier en date) [*an, semaine*] last; **l'an/le mois ~** last year/month; **3** (plus de) **il était cinq heures ~es** it was past five o'clock; **il est 14 heures ~es de 3 minutes** it's 3 minutes past 2; **elle doit avoir trois ans ~s maintenant** she must be over three now; **j'ai 18 ans ~s, je fais ce que je veux!** I've turned 18 ou I'm over 18! I can do what I want!; **je me suis couchée à minuit ~** it was past ou turned midnight when I went to bed; **cela fait un mois ~ que je vous ai demandé de le faire** it was more than a month ago that I asked you to do it; **4** (usé par le temps) [*couleur, tissu*] faded.
III *nm* **1** (division du temps) past; **c'est du ~ maintenant** it's all in the past now; **dans** or **par le ~** in the past; **rompre avec le ~** to break with the past; **2** (de civilisation, d'individu) past; **les vestiges d'un ~ prestigieux** the vestiges of a prestigious past; **que sais-tu de son ~?** what do you know about her past?; **mon ~ de syndicaliste/comédien** my past as a trade unionist/an actor; **3** Ling past (tense); **mettre ce texte au ~** put this text into the past (tense); **il parle d'elle au ~** he talks about her in the past tense.
IV *prép* after; **~ 10 heures, ne faites plus de bruit** after 10 o'clock don't make any noise; **~ la poste c'est tout droit** after the post office you go straight on; **~ 8 heures il s'endort dans son fauteuil** come eight o'clock he goes to sleep in his armchair; **~ la rivière vous serez libre** once you've crossed the river, you'll be free.
■ **~ antérieur** past anterior; **~ composé** perfect; **~ empiétant** Cout embroidery stitch; **~ plat** Cout satin stitch; **~ simple** past historic.

passe-crassane /paskʀasan/ *nf inv* Passe Crassane (*variety of pear*).

passe-droit, *pl* **~s** /pasdʀwa/ *nm* preferential treatment ₵; **bénéficier d'un ~** to get preferential treatment.

passéisme /paseism/ *nm* pej attachment to the past; **une exposition qui sent le ~ à plein nez**○ an exhibition that smacks of nostalgia; **son discours électoral était d'un ~!** his election address really harked back to the past!

passéiste /paseist/ *adj* pej [*image, conservatisme, méthode*] old-fashioned; [*organisation, politicien, artiste, idée*] backward-looking péj.

passe-lacet, *pl* **~s** /paslasɛ/ *nm* bodkin.
IDIOMES **raide comme un ~** as straight ou stiff as a ramrod.

passement /pasmɑ̃/ *nm* braid ₵.

passementer /pasmɑ̃te/ [1] *vtr* to braid, to trim [sth] with braid.

passementerie /pasmɑ̃tʀi/ *nf* **1** (accessoires) passementerie, trimmings (*pl*); **2** (commerce) passementerie trade.

passe-montagne, *pl* **~s** /pasmɔ̃taɲ/ *nm* balaclava.

passe-partout /paspaʀtu/ **I** *adj inv* [*formule, réponse*] catch-all; [*vêtement*] for all occasions (*après n*); [*outil, instrument*] all-purpose.
II *nm inv* (clé) master key; (scie) two-man saw.

passe-passe /paspas/ *nm inv* **tour de ~** conjuring trick; fig wangling ₵; **faire qch par des tours de ~ juridiques/statistiques** to do sth by legal/statistical wangling; **il a usé d'un remarquable tour de ~ politique** he managed a remarkable bit of political wangling.

passe-plat, *pl* **~s** /paspla/ *nm* serving hatch.

passepoil /paspwal/ *nm* Cout piping ₵.

passepoilé, **~e** /paspwale/ *adj* [*boutonnière*] piped; [*poche*] bound.

passeport /paspɔʀ/ *nm* **1** Jur passport; **délivrer/renouveler un ~** to issue/to renew a passport; **être muni/détenteur d'un ~ diplomatique** to carry/to hold a diplomatic passport; **contrôle des ~s** passport control; **2** (ouverture) passport (**pour** to); **~ pour l'emploi** passport to employment; **cette compétence leur sert de ~ professionnel** these skills are a passport to the professional world.

passer /pɑse/ [1] **I** *vtr* **1** (franchir) to cross [*fleuve, pont, frontière, col*]; to go through [*porte, douane*]; to get over [*haie, obstacle*]; **ils ont fait ~ la rivière au troupeau** they took the herd across the river; **il m'a fait ~ la frontière** he got me across the border; **2** (faire franchir) **~ qch à la douane** to get sth through customs; **~ qch en fraude** or **contrebande** to smuggle sth; **~ qn en fraude** (vers l'intérieur) to smuggle sb in; (vers l'extérieur) to smuggle sb out; ▶**gauche**; **3** (dépasser) to go past, to pass; **quand vous aurez passé le feu, tournez à droite** turn right after the lights; **~ la barre des dix francs** to pass the ten franc mark; **on a passé l'heure** it's too late; **j'ai passé l'âge** I'm too old; **le malade ne passera pas la nuit** the patient won't last the night; **4** (mettre) **~ le doigt sur la table** to run one's finger over the table-top; **~ la tête à la fenêtre** to stick one's head out of the window; **elle m'a passé le bras autour des épaules** she put her arm around my shoulders; **elle m'a passé la main dans les cheveux** she ran her fingers through my hair; **5** (transmettre) to pass [*objet*] (**à** to); to pass [sth] on [*consigne, maladie*] (**à** to); (prêter)○ to lend (**à qn** to sb); (donner)○ to give (**à qn** to sb); **~ le ballon au gardien de but** to pass the ball to the goalkeeper; **passe-moi le sel** pass me the salt; **passe le vin à ton père** pass your father the wine; **faites ~ le plat entre vous** pass the dish around; **fais ~ la bonne nouvelle à tes amis** pass the good news on to your friends; **elle a attrapé la grippe et l'a passée à son mari** she caught flu and gave it to her husband; **il m'a passé son vélo**○ (prêté) he lent me his bike; (donné) he gave me his bike; **il m'a passé son rhume** he's given me his cold; **6** (au téléphone) **tu peux me ~ Chris?** can you put Chris on?; **attends, je te la passe** hold on, here she is, I'll put her on; **je vous le passe** (sur un autre poste) I'm putting you through; **pourriez-vous me ~ le poste 4834/le service de traduction?** could you put me through to extension 4834/the translation department, please?; **il est sorti, je vous passe sa secrétaire** he's out, I'll put you through to his secretary; **7** (se présenter à) to take, to sit [*examen scolaire, test*]; to have [*visite médicale, entretien*]; **~ son permis de conduire** to take one's driving test; **faire ~ un test à qn** to give sb a test; **c'est moi qui fais ~ l'oral de français aux nouveaux** I'm taking the new pupils for the French oral; **8** (réussir) to pass [*examen, test*]; **9** (dans le temps) to spend [*temps, jour, vie, vacances*] (**à faire** doing); **~ une nuit à l'hôtel** to spend a night at a hotel; **nous avons passé de bons moments ensemble** we've had some good times together; **dépêche-toi, on ne va pas y ~ la nuit**○! hurry up, or we'll be here all night!; **~ sa colère sur son chat/ses collègues** to take one's anger out on the cat/one's colleagues; **10** (pardonner) **~ qch à qn** to let sb get away with sth; **il ne me passe rien** he doesn't let me get away with anything; **elle leur passe tout** she lets them get away with murder; **passez-lui ses écarts de langage** excuse his/her strong language; **il passe tous ses caprices à sa fille** he indulges his daughter's every whim; **passez-moi l'expression/le terme** if you'll pardon the expression/the word; **11** (omettre) to skip [*mot, page, paragraphe*]; **je vous passe les détails** I'll spare you the details; **j'en passe et des meilleures** (après énumération) and so on and so forth, I could go on; **12** (utiliser) **~ un chiffon humide sur les meubles** to go over the furniture with a damp cloth; **~ un coup de fer sur une chemise** to give a shirt a quick press; **n'oublie pas de ~ l'aspirateur dans le salon** don't forget to hoover® GB ou vacuum the lounge; **13** (étendre) **en passant un peu de cire, les rayures disparaîtront** if you go over it with a bit of wax, the scratches will disappear; **~ un peu de baume sur une brûlure** to dab some ointment on a burn; **~ une couche de peinture sur qch** to give sth a coat of paint; **14** (soumettre) **passez le plat au four** put the dish in the oven; **~ la pointe d'une aiguille à la flamme** to hold the point of a needle over a flame; **~ le plancher à la cire** to put some wax on the floor; **~ qch à l'eau** (pour rincer) to give sth a rinse; (pour obtenir une réaction) to soak sth briefly in water; **qu'est-ce qu'elle nous a passé**○! she really went for us○!; ▶**peigne**; **15** (à travers une grille) to filter [*café*]; to strain [*jus de fruit, sauce*]; to purée [*légumes*]; **~ des légumes au moulin à légumes** to purée vegetables; **16** (enfiler) to slip [sth] on [*vêtement, anneau*]; to slip into [*robe*]; **ils ont essayé de me ~ la camisole** they tried to put me in a straitjacket; **17** (faire jouer) to play [*disque, cassette audio*]; (projeter) to show [*film, diapositives, cassette vidéo*]; (diffuser) to place [*annonce*]; **18** (signer) to sign [*contrat*]; to enter into [*accord*]; to place [*commande*]; to pass [*loi, décret*]; **~ un marché**○ to make a deal; **19** Compta (entrer) to enter, to post spéc [*somme, dépense*]; **20** Aut (enclencher) to go into [*vitesse*]; **~ la troisième/la marche arrière** to go into third gear/into reverse; **21** Jeux (renoncer à) **~ son tour** to pass.

II *vi* **1** (parcourir son chemin) [*personne, animal, véhicule, ballon*] to go past ou by, to pass; **~ entre** to pass between; **regarder ~ les trains** to watch the trains go past ou by; **nous sommes passés devant le palais/près du lac** we went past the palace/the lake; **~ sous/sur un pont** to go under/over a bridge; **l'autobus vient juste de ~** the bus has just gone; **le facteur n'est pas encore passé** the postman hasn't been yet; **quand passe le prochain car pour Caen?** when is the next coach GB ou bus for Caen?; **je suis passé à côté de lui/du monument** I passed him/the monument; **nous sommes passés près de chez toi ce matin** we were near your house this morning; **~ à pied/à cheval/en voiture/à bicyclette** to walk/ride/drive/cycle past; **un avion est passé** a plane flew past overhead; **il est passé en courant/boitant** he ran/limped past; **j'ai renversé le vase en passant** I knocked over the vase as I went by; **en passant, achète du lait** buy some milk while you're out; **le ballon est passé tout près des buts** the ball narrowly missed the goal; **2** (se trouver, s'étendre) **la route passe à côté du lac** the road runs alongside the lake; **le ruisseau passe derrière la maison** the stream runs behind the house; **ils ont fait ~ la route devant chez nous/près de l'église/derrière le village** they built the road in front of our house/near the church/behind the village; **ligne qui passe par les centres de deux cercles** line that connects the centres[GB] of two circles; **en faisant ~ une ligne par ces deux villes** drawing a line through these two towns; **3** (faire un saut) **je ne fais que ~** I've just popped in GB ou dropped by for a minute; **quand je suis passé au marché** when I went down to the market; **quand je suis passé à l'école** when I dropped by the school; **quand je suis passé chez lui** when I called in to see him GB, when I dropped by his place; **~ à la banque** to call in at the bank GB, to drop by the bank; **il est passé déposer un dossier** he came to drop off a file; **il est passé quelqu'un pour toi** someone was looking for you; **je passerai un de ces jours** I'll drop by one of these days; **~ dans la matinée** [*plombier, représentant*] to call in the morning GB, to come over in the morning; **passe nous voir plus souvent!** come and see us more often!; **~ prendre qn/qch** to pick sb/sth up; **je passerai te prendre à six heures** I'll pick you up at six; **je passerai prendre le gâteau dans une heure** I'll pick up the cake in an hour; **4** (se rendre) to go; **passez au guichet numéro 3** go to counter 3; **passons au salon** let's go into ou through to the lounge; **les contrebandiers sont passés en Espagne** the smugglers have crossed into Spain; **passez derrière moi, je vous montrerai le chemin** follow me, I'll show you the way; **il est passé devant moi, il m'est passé devant**○ (dans une queue) he pushed in front of me; **~ à la visite médicale** to go for a medical examination; **~ devant une commission** to come before a committee; **5** (aller au-delà) to get through; **tu ne passeras pas, c'est trop étroit** you'll never get through, it's too narrow; **on ne peut pas ~ à cause de la neige** we can't get through because of the snow; **impossible de ~ tant il y avait de monde** you couldn't get through, there were so many people; **il est passé au rouge** he went through the red lights; **il n'a pas attendu le feu vert pour ~** he didn't wait for the lights to turn green; **il m'a fait signe de ~** he waved me on; **il a fait ~ la vieille dame devant lui** he let the old lady go first; **vas-y, ça passe!** (à un automobiliste) go on, there's plenty of room!; **laisser ~ qn** to let sb through; **laisser ~ une ambulance** to let an ambulance through; **le volet laisse ~ un peu de lumière** the shutter lets in a chink of light; **la cloison laisse ~ le bruit** the partition doesn't keep the noise out; **~ par-dessus bord** to fall overboard; **il est passé par la fenêtre** (par accident) he fell out of the window; (pour entrer) he got in through the window; **il est passé sous un train** he was run over by a train; **nous n'avons pas pu faire ~ l'armoire par la porte** we couldn't get the wardrobe through the door; **à cause des travaux, on ne peut pas ~ derrière la maison** because of the road works, we can't get round GB ou around US the back of the house; ▶**caravane**, **casser**; **6** (transiter) **~ par** [*personne*] lit to pass ou go through; fig to go through; **nous sommes passés par Édimbourg** we went via Edinburgh; **ça ira plus vite en passant par la Belgique** it'll be quicker to go via Belgium; **la manifestation passera dans cette avenue** the demonstration will come along this avenue; **~ par qn pour faire qch** to do sth through sb; **~ par de rudes épreuves** to go through the mill, to have a rough time; **~ par l'opératrice** to go through the operator; **~ par une rue** to go along a street; **~ par l'escalier de service** to use the service stairs; **nous sommes passés par une agence matrimoniale** we met through a marriage bureau; **il est passé par tous les stades de la formation** he went through the various different stages of training; **~ au bord de la faillite** to come very close to bankruptcy; **il est passé par une très bonne école** he went to a very good school; **la formation par laquelle il est passé** the training (that) he had; **il dit tout ce qui lui passe par la tête** he always says the first thing that comes into his head; **je ne sais jamais ce qui te passe par la tête** I never know what's going on in your head; **une idée m'est passée par la tête** an idea occurred to me; **mais qu'est-ce qui lui est passé par la tête?** what on earth was he/she thinking of?; **ça fait du bien par où ça passe**○! [*aliment, boisson*] I needed that!; **un éclair de malice passa dans ses yeux** his/her eyes gleamed with mischief, he/she had a mischievous glint in his/her eyes; **un sourire passa sur ses lèvres** he/she smiled for a second; **en passant par** including; **des**

reptiles à l'homme, en passant par le singe from reptiles to man, including apes; ▸**maire**; **7**○ (avoir son tour) **il accuse le patron, ses collègues, le cuisinier, bref, tout le monde y passe** he's accusing the boss, his colleagues, the cook—in other words, everyone in sight; **le rock, le blues, la musique classique, tout y passe** rock, blues, classical music, you name it; **que ça te plaise ou non, il va falloir y ~** whether you like it or not, there's no alternative; **la nouvelle secrétaire va y ~ aussi** the new secretary will get it as well; **on ne peut pas faire autrement que d'en ~ par là** there is no other way around it; **je sais, j'en suis déjà passé par là** I know all about that, I've been there○; **8** (négliger) **~ sur** to pass over [*question, défaut, erreur*]; **je préfère ~ sur ce point pour l'instant** I'd rather not dwell on that point for the moment; **il est** or **a passé sur les détails** he didn't go into the details; **si l'on passe sur les frais de déplacement** if we ignore the travel expenses; **passons (là-dessus)!** (injonction) let's hear no more about it!; (pardon) let's say no more about it!; **~ à côté d'une question** (volontairement) to sidestep a question; (involontairement) to miss the point; **laisser ~ qch** (délibérément) to let sth pass, to overlook sth; (par inadvertance) to let sth slip through, to overlook sth; **laisser ~ une occasion, ~ à côté d'une occasion** to miss an opportunity, to let an opportunity slip ou go by; **laisser ~ quelques erreurs par gentillesse** to overlook a few errors out of soft-heartedness; **on ne peut pas laisser ~ une telle erreur** we cannot let a mistake like that through; **le réviseur a laissé ~ plusieurs fautes** the proofreader let several mistakes slip through; **il leur laisse ~ tous leurs caprices** he indulges their every whim; **9** (ne pas approfondir) **en passant** in passing; **notons en passant que** we should note in passing that; **en passant, il a ajouté que** in passing, he added that; **soit dit en ~** incidentally; **10** (être admis, supporté) [*aliment, repas*] to go down; [*commentaires, discours, critiques*] to go down well (**auprès de** with); [*loi, règlement, mesure*] to get through; [*attitude, pensée, doctrine*] to be accepted; [*candidat*] to get through; **je ne me sens pas bien, ce doit être le concombre qui passe mal** I don't feel well, it must be the cucumber; **prends un peu de cognac, ça fait ~!** have a drop of brandy, it's good for the digestion; **vos critiques sont mal passées/ne sont pas passées** your criticism went down badly/didn't go down well; **ils n'ont jamais pu faire ~ leur réforme/leurs idées** they never managed to get their reform through/their ideas accepted; **que je sois critiqué, passe encore, mais calomnié, non!** criticism is one thing, but I draw the line at slander; **avec lui, la flatterie, ça ne passe pas** flattery won't work with him; **~ au premier tour** Pol to be elected in the first round; **~ dans la classe supérieure** to move up to the next year ou grade US; **(ça) passe pour cette fois**○ this time, I'll let it go; **11** (se déplacer) **~ de France en Espagne** to leave France and enter Spain; **~ de la salle à manger au salon** to move from the dining room to the lounge; **~ à l'ennemi** to go over to the enemy; **~ dans le camp adverse** to go over to the other side; **~ sous contrôle de l'ONU/de l'État** to be taken over by the UN/the government; **~ sous contrôle ennemi** to fall into enemy hands; **~ de main en main** to be passed around; **~ constamment d'un sujet à l'autre** to flit from one subject to another; **~ d'un amant à un autre** to go from one lover to the next; **~ de l'opulence à la misère** to go from extreme wealth to extreme poverty; **~ de la théorie à la pratique** to put theory into practice; **leur nombre pourrait ~ à 700** their number could reach 700; **~ à un taux supérieur/inférieur** to go up to a higher rate/down to a lower rate; **faire ~ qch de 200 à 300** to increase sth from 200 to 300; **faire ~ qch de 300 à 200** to decrease sth from 300 to 200; **expression passée en proverbe** expression that has become a proverb; **12** (être pris) **~ pour un imbécile/pour être une belle ville** to be generally thought of as stupid/as a beautiful town (**auprès de** by); **~ pour un génie** to pass as a genius; **son excentricité passe pour de l'intelligence** his/her eccentricity passes for intelligence; **il passe pour l'inventeur de l'ordinateur** he's supposed to have invented computers; **~ pour quelqu'un d'autre** to be taken for someone else; **il pourrait ~ pour un Américain** he could be taken for an American; **il veut ~ pour un grand homme** he wants to be seen as a great man; **faire ~ qn/qch pour exceptionnel/exemplaire** to make sb/sth out to be exceptional/a model of perfection; **se faire ~ pour malade** to pretend to be ill; **se faire ~ pour mort** to fake one's own death; **il se fait ~ pour mon frère** he passes himself off as my brother; **se faisant ~ pour un agent d'assurance** by passing himself off as ou by impersonating an insurance salesman; **il m'a fait ~ pour un imbécile** he made me look like a fool; **13** (disparaître) [*douleur, événement*] to pass; **quand l'orage sera** or **aura passé** lit when the storm is over; fig when the storm dies down; **ça passera** (sa mauvaise humeur) it'll pass; (ton chagrin) you'll get over it; **la première réaction passée, il a été possible de faire** once we/they calmed down it was possible to do; **nous avons dû attendre que sa colère soit passée** we had to wait for his/her anger to subside; **~ de mode** [*vêtement, style, chanson, expression*] to go out of fashion; **cette mode est vite passée** or **a vite passé** that fashion was short-lived; **faire ~ à qn l'envie** or **le goût de faire** to cure sb of the desire to do; **les sales gosses, je vais leur faire ~ l'envie** or **l'habitude de tirer sur ma sonnette!** those damn kids, I'll teach them to ring my bell!; **ce médicament fait ~ les maux d'estomac** this medicine relieves stomach ache; **cette mauvaise habitude te passera** it's a bad habit you'll grow out of; **ça lui passera avant que ça me reprenne**○ it won't last; **14** (apparaître, être projeté, diffusé) [*artiste, groupe*] (sur une scène) to be appearing; (à la télévision, radio) to be on; [*spectacle, film*] to be on; [*cassette, musique*] to be playing; **mon ami passe à la télévision ce soir** my friend is on television tonight; **les films portugais qui passent à la télévision/au Rex/à Paris** the Portuguese films (that are) on television/on at the Rex/on in Paris; **15** (être placé) **~ avant/après** (en importance) to come before/after; **la santé passe avant tout** health comes first; **il fait ~ sa famille avant ses amis** he puts his family before his friends; **16**○ (disparaître) **où étais-tu (encore) passé?** where (on earth) did you get to?; **où est passé mon livre/le chat?** where has my book/the cat got to?; **17** (s'écouler) [*temps*] to pass, to go by; **deux ans ont passé depuis l'événement** two years have passed since it happened; **le temps a passé, et les gens ont oublié** time has passed and people have forgotten; **je ne vois pas le temps ~** I don't know where the time goes; **le week-end a** or **est passé trop vite** the weekend went too quickly; **18** (se mettre à) to turn to; **passons aux choses sérieuses** let's turn to serious matters; **nous pouvons ~ à l'étape suivante** we can move on to the next stage; **passons à autre chose** let's change the subject; **nous allons ~ au vote** let's vote now; **~ à l'offensive** to take the offensive; **19** (être transmis) **~ de père en fils/de génération en génération/à ses héritiers** to be handed down from father to son/from generation to generation/to one's heirs; **l'expression est passée dans la langue** the expression has become part of the language; **ça finira par ~ dans les mœurs** it'll eventually become common practice; **il a fait ~ son émotion dans la salle** he transmitted his emotion to the audience; **20** (être promu) to be promoted to ; **il est passé général** he's been promoted to general; **elle est passée maître dans l'art de mentir** she's an accomplished liar; **21** (être dépensé) [*argent, somme*] to go on ou in ou into; [*produit, matière*] to go into; **la moitié de mon salaire passe en remboursement de mes dettes** half my salary goes on paying off my debts; **toutes mes économies y sont passées**○ all my savings went into it; **22**○ (mourir) **y ~** to die; **si tu continues à conduire comme ça, tu vas finir par y ~** if you keep driving like that, you'll kill yourself; **on y passera tous, mais le plus tard sera le mieux** we've all got to go sometime, the later the better; **23** (se décolorer) [*teinte, tissu*] to fade; **~ au soleil** to fade in the sun; **24** (filtrer) [*café*] to brew; **faire ~ la soupe** to put the soup through the vegetable mill; **25** (changer de vitesse) **~ en troisième/marche arrière** to go into third/reverse; **la troisième passe mal** or **a du mal à ~** third gear is a bit stiff; **~ de seconde en troisième** to go from second into third; **26** Jeux (au bridge, poker) to pass.

III se passer *vpr* **1** (se produire) to happen; **ça s'est passé en Chine/à Pékin/le matin/au bon moment** it happened in China/in Beijing/in the morning/at the right time; **il ne se passe jamais rien dans ce village** nothing ever happens in this village; **que se passe-t-il?, qu'est-ce qui se passe?** what's happening, what's going on?; **tout se passe comme si le franc avait été dévalué** it's as if the franc was devalued; **2** (être situé) to take place; **la scène se passe au Viêt Nam/dans les années trente/de nos jours** the scene is set in Vietnam/in the thirties/in the present day; **3** (se dérouler) [*opération, examen, négociations*] to go; **comment s'est passée la réunion?** how did the meeting go?; **tout s'est bien passé** everything went well; **ça s'est mal passé** it didn't go well; **la réunion s'est très mal passée** the meeting went very badly; **tout s'est passé très vite** it all happened very fast; **ça va mal se ~ pour toi si tu continues!** you're going to be in trouble if you carry on GB ou continue doing that!; **ça ne se passera pas comme ça!** I won't leave it at that!; **4** (s'écouler) [*période*] to go by, to pass; **il s'est passé deux ans depuis, deux ans se sont passés depuis** that was two years ago; **il ne se passe guère de jour (sans) qu'elle ne trouve à se plaindre** hardly a day goes by without her finding something to complain about; **attendons que ça se passe** let's wait till it's over; **nos soirées se passaient à regarder la télévision** we spent the evenings watching television; ▸**jeunesse**; **5** (se dispenser) **se ~ de** [*personne*] to do without [*objet, activité, personne*]; to go without [*repas, nourriture, sommeil*]; **nous nous sommes passés de voiture** we did without a car; **nous nous passerons de lui** we'll do without him; **je me passerais bien de tes remarques** I can do without your comments; **se ~ de commentaires** to speak for itself; **ne pas pouvoir se ~ de faire** not to be able to help oneself from doing; **se ~ des services de qn** to do without sb's services; **6** (se mettre) **se ~ la langue sur les lèvres/la main dans les cheveux** to run one's tongue over one's lips/one's fingers through one's hair; **se ~ la main sur le front** to put a hand to one's forehead; **7** (l'un à l'autre) **ils se sont passé des documents** they exchanged some documents; **nous nous sommes passé le virus** we caught the virus from each other.

passereau, *pl* **~x** /pasʀo/ *nm* **1** gén passerine; **2**† (moineau) sparrow.

passerelle /pasʀɛl/ *nf* **1** (petit pont) footbridge; **2** fig (lien) link; **jeter une ~ entre qch et qch** to provide a link between sth and sth; **classe ~** conversion course;

3 (pour embarquer) Naut gangway; Aviat (escalier) steps; (tunnel) gangway; **jeter la ~** Naut to lower the gangway; **4** Naut (pour piloter) bridge; **~ de navigation** navigation bridge.

passe-temps /pastɑ̃/ *nm inv* pastime, hobby.

passe-thé /paste/ *nm inv* tea strainer.

passeur, **-euse** /pasœʀ, øz/ *nm,f* **1** ▶**510** Naut ferryman/ferrywoman; **2** (pour passer une frontière) smuggler; (de drogue) courier, mule○; **3** Sport passer.

passe-vue, *pl* **~s** /pasvy/ *nm* slide carrier ou changer.

passible /pasibl/ *adj* **1** Jur **~ de** [*délit*] punishable by; [*personne*] liable to; **2** Comm, Fisc **~ d'impôt** [*personne*] liable for tax; [*revenu*] taxable; **marchandises ~s de droits** dutiable goods, goods liable for duty.

passif, **-ive** /pasif, iv/ **I** *adj* **1** gén [*personne*] passive (**devant, face à** in the face of); **2 à la voix passive** Ling in the passive (voice); **3** Ordinat **mémoire passive** read-only memory, ROM.

II *nm* **1** Ling passive (voice); **2** Compta Fin liabilities (*pl*), debit; **au ~ du bilan** on the debit side.

■ **~ couru** accruals (*pl*); **~ éventuel** contingent liability; **~ exigible** current liabilities; **~ non exigible** non-current liabilities.

IDIOMES **mettre qch au ~ de qn** to count sth amongst sb's failures.

passiflore /pasiflɔʀ/ *nf* passiflora, passion-flower.

passing-shot, *pl* **~s** /pasiŋʃɔt/ *nm* controv passing shot.

passion /pasjɔ̃/ *nf* passion; **avoir une grande ~ pour** to have a great passion for; **avoir la ~ des voyages/du jeu/ d'écrire** to have a passion for travel/gambling/writing; **être esclave de ses ~s** to be a slave to one's passions; **les fleurs sont ma ~** flowers are my passion; **les élections ont déchaîné les ~s** the elections have made passions run high; **aimer à la** or **avec ~** to love passionately; **sans ~** (objectivement) dispassionately; (sans enthousiasme) without enthusiasm; **se prendre de ~ pour qn** to become infatuated with sb; **se prendre de ~ pour qch** to develop a passion for sth.

Passion /pasjɔ̃/ *nf* Passion; Relig **la ~ selon St Jean** the Passion according to St John; Mus the St John Passion.

passionnant, **~e** /pasjɔnɑ̃, ɑ̃t/ *adj* [*voyage, métier, découverte, match*] exciting; [*personne, dossier, information, musée*] fascinating; [*roman, film*] gripping, fascinating.

passionné, **~e** /pasjɔne/ **I** *pp* ▶**passionner**.

II *pp adj* [*amour*] passionate; [*débat, argument*] impassioned; **être ~ de** or **pour qch** to have a passion for sth; **un journaliste ~ d'opéra** a journalist with a passion for opera.

III *nm,f* enthusiast; **c'est un ~ de tennis/ calligraphie** he's a tennis/calligraphy enthusiast.

passionnel, **-elle** /pasjɔnɛl/ *adj* [*débat*] passionate; [*sujet, langage*] emotive; [*crime*] of passion.

passionnément /pasjɔnemɑ̃/ *adv* passionately.

passionner /pasjɔne/ [1] **I** *vtr* **1** (intéresser) to fascinate; **le débat m'a passionné** the debate fascinated me; **la botanique/littérature le passionne** he has a passion for botany/literature; **2** (rendre passionné) to inflame [*débat*].

II se passionner *vpr* (subitement) to develop a passionate interest (**pour** in); (habituellement) to have a passion (**pour** for).

passivation /pasivasjɔ̃/ *nf* passivation.

passivement /pasivmɑ̃/ *adv* passively.

passivité /pasivite/ *nf* passivity.

passoire /paswaʀ/ *nf* (pour légumes) colander; (pour infusion) strainer; (tamis) sieve; **troué comme une ~** riddled with holes; **être une vraie ~**○ [*frontière*] to be like an open door; [*gardien de buts*] to let anything through.

IDIOMES **avoir la tête comme une ~**○ to have a mind like a sieve○.

pastel /pastɛl/ **I** *adj inv* [*teinte*] pastel; **bleu ~** pastel blue.

II *nm* **1** (technique, crayon) pastel; **2** (œuvre) pastel; **3** (teinte) pastel tint ou tone.

pastelliste /pastelist/ *nmf* pastellist.

pastenague /pastənag/ *nf* stingray.

pastèque /pastɛk/ *nf* watermelon.

pasteur /pastœʀ/ ▶**510** *nm* **1** (protestant) minister; **2** (prêtre) priest; **3** (berger) shepherd; **le Bon Pasteur** Bible the Good Shepherd.

pasteurien, **-ienne** /pastœʀjɛ̃, ɛn/ **I** *adj* [*méthodes*] Pasteur (*épith*).

II *nm,f* researcher at the Pasteur Institute.

pasteurisation /pastœʀizasjɔ̃/ *nf* pasteurization.

pasteuriser /pastœʀize/ [1] *vtr* **1** (traiter à la chaleur) to pasteurize; **2** (expurger) to sanitize.

pastiche /pastiʃ/ *nm* pastiche.

pasticher /pastiʃe/ [1] *vtr* to imitate the style of [*auteur, œuvre*]; to imitate [*style*].

pasticheur, **-euse** /pastiʃœʀ, øz/ *nm,f* imitator.

pastille /pastij/ *nf* **1** Pharm pastille, lozenge; **des ~s pour la gorge** throat lozenges; **~ contre la toux** cough drop; **2** (petit bonbon) **~ de chocolat** chocolate drop; **~ de menthe** peppermint; **3** (motif) spot; **4** (rondelle) (de tissu, caoutchouc) patch; (de plastique) disc; (d'aquarelle) pastille.

■ **~ adhésive** (round) sticker; **~ de silicium** silicon chip.

pastis /pastis/ *nm inv* **1** (boisson) pastis; **2**○ (gâchis) mess.

pastoral, **~e**, *mpl* **-aux** /pastɔʀal, o/ **I** *adj* gén pastoral.

II pastorale *nf* **1** Littérat, Mus pastoral; **2** Relig pastoralia (*pl*).

pastorat /pastɔʀa/ *nm* pastorate.

pastoureau, *pl* **~x** /pastuʀo/ *nm* littér (berger) shepherd.

pastourelle /pastuʀɛl/ *nf* **1** littér (bergère) shepherdess; **2** Littérat pastoral song.

pat /pat/ **I** *adj inv* stalemate.

II *nm* stalemate; **faire (un) ~** to end in (a) stalemate.

patachon /pataʃɔ̃/ *nm* **mener une vie de ~**○ to live in the fast lane.

patafix® /patafiks/ *nm* blu-tak®.

patagon, **-onne** /patagɔ̃, ɔn/ *adj* Patagonian.

Patagon, **-onne** /patagɔ̃, ɔn/ *nm,f* Patagonian.

Patagonie /patagɔni/ ▶**692** *nprf* Patagonia.

pataphysique /patafizik/ Littérat **I** *adj* pataphysical (*épith*).

II *nf* pataphysics.

patapouf /patapuf/ **I**○ *nm* (**gros**) **~** fatso○.

II *excl* baby talk splat!

pataquès /patakɛs/ *nm inv* **1** Ling incorrect liaison; **2** (discours confus) **être un ~** to be unintelligible.

patata○ /patata/ *excl* ▶**patati**.

patate /patat/ *nf* **1**○ (pomme de terre) spud○; **2**○ (idiot) blockhead, idiot; **se débrouiller comme une ~** to make a complete hash of things; **3** (plante) sweet potato.

■ **~ douce** sweet potato.

IDIOMES **ça m'est resté sur la ~** it left me feeling bitter; **en avoir gros sur la ~**○ to be terribly upset○.

patati○ /patati/ *excl* **~, patata** and so on and so forth.

patatras○ /patatʀa/ *excl* crash○!; **et ~! le gosse**○ **tombe malade** and then, bang! the kid falls ill○.

pataud, **~e** /pato, od/ **I** *adj* lumbering [*allure, personne*]; clumsy [*geste, chien*].

II *nm* oaf.

pataugas® /patogas/ *nm inv* fell boots GB, canvas hiking boots.

pataugeoire /patoʒwaʀ/ *nf* paddling pool GB, baby pool US.

patauger /patoʒe/ [13] *vi* **1** (jouer) (dans une flaque) to splash about; (au bord de la mer) to paddle; (dans la boue) to squelch around; (piétiner) **~ dans la boue/neige** to flounder around in the mud/snow; **2** (s'embrouiller) to flounder.

patchouli /patʃuli/ *nm* patchouli; **essence de ~** patchouli oil.

patchwork /patʃwœʀk/ *nm* lit, fig patchwork; **coussin en ~** patchwork cushion.

pâte /pɑt/ **I** *nf* **1** Culin (à tarte) pastry; (levée) dough; (à friture, crêpes) batter; ▶**bon**; **tous les hommes sont faits de la même ~** fig all men are made the same; **2** (substance pâteuse) paste; **produit en ~** paste; **3** Tech (en céramique) paste.

II pâtes *nfpl* Culin **~s (alimentaires)** gén pasta **₵**.

■ **~ d'amandes** marzipan; **~ d'anchois** anchovy paste; **~ à beignets** batter; **~ briochée** brioche-style dough; **~ brisée** shortcrust pastry GB, pie crust US; **~ de coing** quince cheese; **~ à choux** choux pastry GB, cream puff pastry US; **~ dentifrice** toothpaste; **~ dure** (en céramique) hard paste; (fromage) hard cheese; **~ feuilletée** puff pastry; **~ à frire** = **~ à beignets**; **~ de fruit(s)** fruit paste; **~ à joints** gasket-seal compound; **~ à modeler** modelling[GB] clay, Plasticine®; **~ molle** (personne) pushover; (fromage) soft cheese; **~ à papier** Ind pulp; **~ sablée** riche shortcrust pastry GB, sugar crust US; **~ à tartiner** spread; **~ tendre** (en céramique) soft paste; **~ de verre** pâte-de-verre, decorative sintered glass.

IDIOMES **mettre la main à la ~** to pitch in.

pâté /pɑte/ *nm* **1** Culin pâté; **~ de foie** liver pâté; **~ en croûte** ≈ pie; **~ de gibier en croûte** game pie; **2** Constr (ensemble) block; **~ de maisons** block (of houses); **3** (tache d'encre) blot; **4** (à la plage) **~ de sable** sandpie; **faire des ~s** to make sandpies.

■ **~ de campagne** farmhouse pâté GB, *coarse pâté*.

pâtée /pɑte/ *nf* **1** (nourriture) (pour un chien) food; (pour les cochons) swill; (pour la volaille) mash; **2**○ (râclée, défaite) hiding; **prendre la ~** to get a hiding.

patelin, **~e** /patlɛ̃, in/ **I**† *adj* [*personne*] smooth-tongued; [*manières, voix*] oily.

II○ *nm* small village; **habiter dans un ~ perdu** to live at the back of beyond○ GB, to live in Podunk○ US.

patelle /patɛl/ *nf* Zool limpet.

patène /patɛn/ *nf* paten.

patenôtres† /patnotʀ/ *nfpl* prayers.

patent, **~e** /patɑ̃, ɑ̃t/ fml **I** *adj* manifest, obvious; **il est ~ que** it is patently obvious that.

II patente *nf* **1** (permis) *licence*[GB] *to exercise a trade or profession*; (taxe) business rates; **payer ~e** to be duly licensed; **2** Naut **~e de santé** bill of health.

patenté, **~e** /patɑ̃te/ *adj* **1** (agréé) [*fournisseur, transporteur*] licensed, authorized; **2**○ iron [*critique, défenseur*] established; **menteur ~** inveterate liar.

pater /pateʀ/ *nm inv* **1** Relig paternoster; **dire** or **réciter un ~** to say a paternoster; **2**○ (père) old man○, dad○.

■ **~ familias** paterfamilias.

patère /patɛʀ/ *nf* peg, hook.

paternalisme /patɛʀnalism/ *nm* paternalism.

paternaliste /patɛʀnalist/ *adj* paternalistic.

paterne† /patɛʀn/ *adj* paternal.

paternel, **-elle** /patɛʀnɛl/ I *adj* **1** (du père) paternal; **mon oncle ~** my paternal uncle; **2** (affectueux) fatherly.
II *nm*○ (père) old man○, dad○.

paternellement /patɛʀnɛlmɑ̃/ *adv* in a fatherly way.

paternité /patɛʀnite/ *nf* **1** (état de père) fatherhood; Jur paternity; **recherche de ~ naturelle** paternity suit; **2** (d'œuvre) authorship.

pâteux, **-euse** /pɑtø, øz/ *adj* **1** [*substance*] doughy; [*bouillie*] mushy; **2** [*voix*] thick; [*discours, style*] turgid; **j'ai la bouche pâteuse** my mouth feels all furry.

pathétique /patetik/ I *adj* **1** (émouvant) moving; **2** Anat pathetic.
II *nm* pathos.

pathétiquement /patetikmɑ̃/ *adv* touchingly.

pathétisme /patetism/ *nm* pathos.

pathogène /patɔʒɛn/ *adj* pathogenic.

pathologie /patɔlɔʒi/ *nf* pathology; **ça relève de la ~** it's pathological.

pathologique /patɔlɔʒik/ *adj* pathological.

pathologiquement /patɔlɔʒikmɑ̃/ *adv* pathologically.

pathologiste /patɔlɔʒist/ **▶ 510** *nmf* pathologist.

pathos /patos/ *nm* pathos; **faire du ~** to pile on the pathos○.

patibulaire /patibylɛʀ/ *adj* [*individu*] sinister-looking; **un homme à la mine ~** a sinister-looking fellow.

patiemment /pasjamɑ̃/ *adv* patiently.

patience /pasjɑ̃s/ *nf* **1** (qualité) patience; **manquer de/perdre ~** to lack/lose patience; **elle n'a aucune ~** she has no patience at all; **ma ~ a des limites** there are limits to my patience; **il faut vraiment de la ~ pour le supporter** you need a lot of patience to put up with him; **avec une grande/beaucoup de ~** with great/a lot of patience; **avoir de la ~ avec** to be patient with; **être d'une ~ infinie** or **sans bornes** to be endlessly patient; **s'armer de** or **prendre ~** to be patient; **avec ~** patiently; **~, c'est presque cuit** be patient, it's almost cooked; **2 ▶ 449** Jeux patience ¢ GB, solitaire ¢ US; **faire des ~s** to play patience GB ou solitaire US; **3** (plante) dock.
IDIOMES **prendre son mal en ~** to resign oneself to one's fate.

patient, **~e** /pasjɑ̃, ɑ̃t/ I *adj* patient.
II *nm,f* Méd patient.

patienter /pasjɑ̃te/ [1] *vi* to wait; **puis-je vous demander de ~?** would you mind waiting?; **faire ~ qn** to make sb wait; **patientez un instant/quelques minutes** wait a moment/a few minutes.

patin /patɛ̃/ *nm* **1 ▶ 449** (sport) skate; **2** (pour parquet) *felt pad used for walking on parquet floors*; **3** Tech (de meuble) furniture glide; (d'hélicoptère) skid; Rail **~ (de rail)** rail foot; (de luge) runner; **4**○ (baiser) French kiss; **rouler un ~ à qn** to give sb a French kiss.
■ **~ à glace** (chaussure) ice skate; (activité) ice-skating; **~ de frein** Aut brake block; **~ en ligne** (chaussure) rollerblade; (activité) rollerblading; **~ à roulettes** (chaussure) roller skate; (activité) roller-skating; **en ~s à roulettes** on roller skates.

patinage /patinaʒ/ *nm* **1 ▶ 449** (sport) skating; **~ sur glace** ice-skating; **2** Tech (de roue) spinning; (d'embrayage) slipping.
■ **~ artistique** figure skating; **~ de vitesse** speed skating.

patine /patin/ *nf* (naturelle) patina; (artificielle) finish, sheen; **la ~ du temps** or **de l'âge** the patina of age.

patiner /patine/ [1] I *vtr* (couvrir de patine) (artificiellement) to apply a finish to, to patinate spéc [*métal, meuble*]; (naturellement) to give a patina to [*bois, statue*]; **chêne/bronze patiné** oak/bronze shiny with age.
II *vi* **1** Sport to skate; **2** Aut [*roue*] to spin; [*embrayage*] to slip; **la voiture patinait dans la boue** the wheels of the car were spinning in the mud; **faire ~ l'embrayage** to slip the clutch; **3** (piétiner) [*discussion, projet*] to flounder; **4** C (tergiverser) to skirt the issue, to hedge.
III **se patiner** *vpr* [*bois, statue*] to acquire a patina.

patinette /patinɛt/ *nf* (child's) scooter.

patineur, **-euse** /patinœʀ, øz/ *nm,f* (sur glace, à roulettes) skater.

patinoire /patinwaʀ/ *nf* ice rink; **ton parquet est une vraie ~!** your floor is like an ice rink!

patio /patjo, pasjo/ *nm* patio.

pâtir /pɑtiʀ/ [3] *vi* **~ de** to suffer as a result of.

pâtisserie /pɑtisʀi/ *nf* **1 ▶ 510** (magasin) cake shop, pâtisserie; **2** (gâteau) pastry, cake; **3** (gâteaux) **la ~** pastries (*pl*), cakes (*pl*); **faire de la ~** to do some baking; **4** (confection de gâteaux) pastry-making, cake-making; **5** (secteur) confectionery; **6** Archit decorative moulding GB ou molding US.
■ **~ industrielle** mass-produced pastries (*pl*) ou cakes (*pl*); **~ maison** homemade pastries (*pl*) ou cakes (*pl*).

pâtissier, **-ière** /pɑtisje, ɛʀ/ **▶ 510** *nm,f* **1** (commerçant) confectioner; **elle a commandé un dessert chez le ~** she ordered a dessert from the confectioner's ou cake shop; **2** (fabricant) (dans une boutique, usine) confectioner; (dans un restaurant, hôtel) pastry cook.

pâtisson /pɑtisɔ̃/ *nm* custard marrow GB ou squash US.

patois, **~e** /patwa, az/ I *adj* [*mot*] dialect (*épith*).
II *nm inv* patois, dialect; **parler ~** to speak patois.

patoisant, **~e** /patwazɑ̃, ɑ̃t/ I *adj* [*région, habitant*] patois-speaking.
II *nm,f* patois speaker.

patraque○ /patʀak/ *adj* **être/se sentir ~** to be/to feel under the weather○.

pâtre /pɑtʀ/ *nm* shepherd.

patriarcal, **~e**, *mpl* **-aux** /patʀijaʀkal, o/ *adj* patriarchal.

patriarcat /patʀijaʀka/ *nm* **1** Relig patriarchate; **2** Sociol patriarchy.

patriarche /patʀijaʀʃ/ *nm* patriarch.

patricien, **-ienne** /patʀisjɛ̃, ɛn/ *adj, nm,f* patrician.

patrie /patʀi/ *nf* **1** (pays natal) homeland, native land; (nation) country; **mourir pour/défendre sa ~** to die/to fight for one's country; **2** fig (lieu d'origine) birthplace.

patrimoine /patʀimwan/ *nm* **1** Jur (de personne, famille) patrimony; (d'une entreprise) capital; **~ des ménages** household capital; **~ financier/immobilier** financial/property holdings; **2** (biens communs) heritage; **~ architectural** architectural heritage; **~ écrit** literary heritage.
■ **~ génétique** Biol gene pool; **~ héréditaire** Biol genetic inheritance.

patrimonial, **~e**, *mpl* **-iaux** /patʀimɔnjal, o/ *adj* patrimonial.

patriotard○ /patʀijɔtaʀ/ *adj* pej jingoistic○.

patriote /patʀijɔt/ I *adj* patriotic.
II *nmf* **1** gén patriot; **en ~** patriotically; **2** Hist (en France en 1789) Patriot.

patriotique /patʀijɔtik/ *adj* patriotic.

patriotiquement /patʀijɔtikmɑ̃/ *adv* patriotically.

patriotisme /patʀijɔtism/ *nm* patriotism.

patron, **-onne** /patʀɔ̃, ɔn/ I *nm,f* **1** Comm, Entr (directeur, gérant) manager, boss○; (propriétaire) owner, boss○; (artisan) **être son propre ~** to be one's own boss○; **les ~s et les salariés** management and workers; **2**○ (responsable) boss○; **chez lui, c'est lui le ~**○ at home, he's the boss○; **le ~**○ **du service** the boss○ of the department; **▶ grand**; **3**○ (conjoint) (époux) old man○; (épouse) old lady○; **4** Hist, Relig **(saint) ~** patron saint.
II *nm* **1** Cout pattern; **2** (taille) large; **grand ~** extra-large; **3** Art (pochoir) stencil.
■ **~ d'industrie** captain of industry; **~ de pêche** skipper, master; **~ de presse** newspaper proprietor; **~ de thèse**○ thesis supervisor.

patronage /patʀɔnaʒ/ *nm* **1** (soutien) patronage; **sous le ~ de** under the patronage of; **2**† (centre de loisirs) ≈ youth club; **humour/spectacle de ~** feeble humour[GB]/show.

patronal, **~e**, *mpl* **-aux** /patʀɔnal, o/ *adj* [*organisation, représentant*] employers'; [*cotisations*] employer.

patronat /patʀɔna/ *nm* employers (*pl*).

patronne ▶ patron.

patronner /patʀɔne/ [1] *vtr* to sponsor [*manifestation, soirée, spectacle*].

patronnesse /patʀɔnɛs/ *adj* **dame ~** Lady Bountiful.

patronyme /patʀɔnim/ *nm* patronymic.

patronymique /patʀɔnimik/ *adj* patronymic.

patrouille /patʀuj/ *nf* (tous contextes) patrol; **~ de reconnaissance/de chasse** reconnaissance/fighter patrol; **être en ~** to be on patrol; **être/partir/aller en ~** to be/to set off/to go on patrol.

patrouiller /patʀuje/ [1] *vi* to be on patrol; **~ dans la forêt** to patrol the forest.

patrouilleur /patʀujœʀ/ *nm* **1** (avion) patrol plane; **2** (navire) patrol boat; **3** (soldat) soldier on patrol.

patte /pat/ *nf* **1** Zool (jambe) leg; (pied) (de mammifère avec ongles ou griffes) paw; (d'oiseau) foot; **~ de devant** (jambe) foreleg; **~ de derrière** (jambe) hind leg; **donner la ~** to raise its paw; **▶ canard**, **chat**; **retomber sur ses ~s** [*chat*] to fall on its feet; fig [*personne*] to fall on one's feet; **2**○ (jambe) leg; (pied) foot; (main) hand; **tu es toujours dans mes ~s** you are always getting under my feet; **aller à ~s** to go on foot; **marcher à quatre ~s** [*enfant, adulte*] to walk on all fours; [*bébé*] to crawl; **se mettre à quatre ~s** to get down on all fours; **traîner** or **tirer la ~** to limp; **en avoir plein les ~s**○ to be dead on one's feet; **avoir 100 km dans les ~s**○ to have done 100 km; **avoir les ~s sales** to have dirty hands; **bas les ~s!** (ne me touchez pas) keep your hands to yourself!; (n'y touchez pas) hands off!; **3**○ (style) hand; **on reconnaît ta ~** one can recognize your hand; **4** Tech (languette) tab; (d'attache) lug; **5** Mode (de sac) tab; (de vêtement, bonnet) flap; (de col) tab; (de chaussure) tongue; (d'épaule) epaulette; **~ de boutonnage** button flap; **6** (favori) sideburn.
■ **~ d'araignée** Tech oil groove; **~s d'éléphant** Mode flares; **pantalon (à) ~s d'éléphant** flared trousers GB ou pants US; **~ de fixation** Tech (pour cadre) mounting bracket; (pour conduit) saddle; **~ folle**○ gammy leg GB, game leg US; **~ de lapin** (porte-bonheur) rabbit's foot; (favori) sideburn; **~ de mouche** (écriture) spidery scrawl ¢; **faire des ~s de mouche** to write in a spidery scrawl; **~ de scellement** Tech swallowtail.
IDIOMES **faire ~ de velours** [*chat*] to draw in its claws; [*personne*] to switch on the charm; **lever la ~** [*chien*] to lift its leg; **tomber dans les ~s de qn** to fall into sb's clutches; **se tirer des ~s de qn** to get out of sb's clutches; **montrer ~ blanche** to prove one is acceptable; **tomber sous la ~ de qn**○ to fall under sb's dominion; **avoir un fil à la ~** to be tied down; **se tirer dans les ~s** to pull dirty tricks on each other.

patte-d'oie, *pl* **pattes-d'oie** /patdwa/ *nf* **1** (ride) crow's-foot; **2** (carrefour) junction.

pattemouille /patmuj/ *nf* damp cloth (*for ironing*).

pâturage /pɑtyʀaʒ/ *nm* **1** (terrain) pasture; **2** (droit) pasturage.

pâture /pɑtyʀ/ *nf* (nourriture animale) feed; (terrain) pasture; **un scandale donné en ~ au public** fig a scandal used to satisfy the public's baser instincts; **être jeté en ~** fig to be thrown to the lions ou wolves.

pâturin /pɑtyʀɛ̃/ *nm* meadow grass, poa spéc.

pâturon /pɑtyʀɔ̃/ *nm* pastern.

Pau /po/ ▶ **857** *npr* Pau.

paulinien, -ienne /polinjɛ̃, ɛn/ *adj* Relig Pauline.

paulownia /polɔnja/ *nm* paulownia.

paume /pom/ *nf* **1** Anat palm (of the hand); **2** Sport real tennis, court tennis US.

paumé○, **~e** /pome/ **I** *adj* **1** [*personne*] (perdu) lost; (inadapté) mixed up GB, out of it○ US; **2** [*endroit*] pej godforsaken, jerkwater US.

II *nm,f* misfit.

paumelle /pomɛl/ *nf* lift-off hinge.

paumer○ /pome/ [1] **I** *vtr, vi* to lose.

II se paumer *vpr* to get lost.

paupérisation /popeʀizasjɔ̃/ *nf* pauperization.

paupériser /popeʀize/ [1] *vtr* to pauperize, to reduce to abject poverty.

paupérisme /popeʀism/ *nm* pauperism.

paupière /popjɛʀ/ *nf* eyelid; **~ inférieure/supérieure** lower/upper eyelid; **battre des ~s** to flutter one's eyelashes; **fermer les ~s** lit to close one's eyes; fig (mourir) to pass on ou away.

paupiette /popjɛt/ *nf* **~ de veau** stuffed escalope of veal.

pause /poz/ *nf* **1** (dans une activité) break; **faire une ~** to take a break; **~ thé/repas/pipi**○ tea/meal/toilet break; **~ de midi** lunch break; **~ publicitaire** commercial break; **2** (dans un discours) pause; **faire une ~** to pause; **3** (période calme) pause; **une ~ dans la course aux armements** a pause in the arms race; **4** Mus rest.

pause-repas, *pl* **pauses-repas** /pozʀəpɑ/ *nf* lunch break.

pauvre /povʀ/ **I** *adj* **1** (sans ressources) [*personne, quartier, pays*] poor; **les ~s gens** the poor; **2** (déficient) [*sol, alimentation, vocabulaire*] poor; [*végétation*] sparse; [*minerai*] poor quality; [*mélange*] Aut lean; [*langue, style*] impoverished; **~ en éléments nutritifs/oxygène** poor ou lacking in nutrients/oxygen; **régime ~ en sucre** (insuffisant) diet lacking in sugar; (conseillé) low-sugar diet; **minerai ~ en métal** ore with a low metal content; **~ en main-d'œuvre** with a shortage of labour[GB]; **3** (malheureux) [*personne*] poor; [*sourire*] weak, sad; **~ enfant!** poor child!; **un ~ type**○ (à plaindre) a poor chap○ GB ou guy○ US; (incapable) a dead loss○; **~ type** or **imbécile**○**!** (idiot) you jerk◑!; **~ de moi!** poor me!; **c'est comme ça, ma ~ dame**○ that's the way it goes, my dear; **4** (défunt) **mon ~ mari disait...** my poor husband used to say...; **son ~ mari** her late husband.

II○ *nmf* (à plaindre) **le/la ~!** poor man/woman!; (attendri) poor thing!; **ah, ma ~, si tu m'avais vu!** well, my dear, you should have seen me!

III *nm* **un ~** a poor man, a pauper†; **il y a beaucoup de ~s** there are a lot of poor people; **donner aux ~s** to give to the poor; **les nouveaux ~s** the new poor; **la technologie du ~** rudimentary technology; **plat de ~** humble dish; **~ d' esprit** half-wit.

pauvrement /povʀəmɑ̃/ *adv* poorly.

pauvresse† /povʀɛs/ *nf* poor wretch, pauper†.

pauvret, -ette /povʀɛ, ɛt/ **I** *adj* [*air*] pitiful.

II *nm,f* poor little thing.

pauvreté /povʀəte/ *nf* **1** (misère) (de personne, pays) poverty; **vivre dans la ~** to live in poverty; **2** (de mobilier, vêtements) shabbiness; **3** (médiocrité) (de sol, vocabulaire, d'imagination) poverty; (de débat, programme) poor quality; (de raisonnement) thinness; **~ intellectuelle** intellectual poverty; **~ de moyens** lack of means; **~ en idées** paucity of ideas; **la ~ de la récolte** the poor harvest.

IDIOMES **~ n'est pas vice** Prov poverty is no disgrace ou sin Prov.

pavage /pavaʒ/ *nm* **1** (travail) paving; **2** (revêtement) (de cour) paving; (de route) road surface.

pavane /pavan/ *nf* pavane.

pavaner: se pavaner /pavane/ [1] *vpr* [*personne*] to strut about; [*paon*] to strut.

pavé /pave/ *nm* **1** (de rue) cobblestone, sett spéc; **2** (rues) **se retrouver sur le ~** to find oneself out on the street; **battre le ~** to wear out one's shoe leather; **faire le ~** to walk the streets; **3** Presse display; **~ publicitaire** display advertisement; **4** Ordinat pad; **5** Culin (de viande, gâteau) slab; **~ au chocolat** chocolate slab cake; **6**○ (gros livre) huge tome.

■ **~ numérique** Ordinat numeric keypad.

IDIOMES **c'est le ~ de l'ours** ≈ it is more of a hindrance than a help; **jeter** or **lancer un ~ dans la mare** to set the cat among the pigeons; **sous les ~s, la plage** beneath the harsh reality lies a brighter tomorrow; **tenir le haut du ~** to head the field.

paver /pave/ [1] *vtr* to lay [sth] with cobblestones ou setts spéc [*chaussée, route*].

IDIOMES **l'enfer est pavé de bonnes intentions** the road to hell is paved with good intentions.

paveur /pavœʀ/ *nm* paver.

pavillon /pavijɔ̃/ *nm* **1** (bâtiment) (maison) (detached) house; (de parc, exposition) pavilion; (d'hôpital) pavilion, wing; (d'hôtel etc) chalet GB, bungalow US; **~ de banlieue** suburban house; **le ~ de la Suisse** the Swiss pavilion; **le ~ des sidéens** the Aids ward; **2** (d'oreille) auricle, pinna; (d'instrument) bell; (de haut-parleur, phonographe) horn; **3** Naut flag; **sous ~ français** under the French flag; **~ amiral/national** admiral's/national flag; **~ de complaisance** flag of convenience; **~ de quarantaine/signalisation** quarantine/signal flag; **baisser ~** lit to lower the flag; fig to admit defeat (**devant qn** to sb); **battre ~ russe/hollandais** Naut to fly the Russian/Dutch flag; **4** Aut roof; **5** Turf enclosure, stand; **6** Relig veil; **7** Hérald pavilion.

■ **~ de beaupré** Naut jack; **~ de chasse** hunting lodge; **~ noir** black flag, Jolly Roger; **~ de poupe** Naut ensign.

pavillonnaire /pavijɔnɛʀ/ *adj* **zone ~** residential area; **banlieue ~** suburb consisting of houses (*as opposed to high-rise buildings*).

pavlovien, -ienne /pavlɔvjɛ̃, ɛn/ *adj* Pavlovian.

pavois /pavwa/ *nm inv* **1** Naut **hisser le grand ~** to dress a ship overall; **navire en grand ~** ship dressed overall; **petit ~** identification signals (*pl*); **2** Hist (bouclier) shield; **élever** or **hisser qn sur le ~** fig to elevate sb to heroic status.

pavoiser /pavwaze/ [1] **I** *vtr* to decorate [sth] with flags [*édifice, rue*]; Naut to dress [*navire*]; **rue pavoisée** street decorated with flags; **~ pour une fête** to put out the flags for a festival.

II○ *vi* (exulter) to be jubilant; (chanter victoire) to crow péj; **il n'y a pas de quoi ~!** it's nothing to crow about!

pavot /pavo/ *nm* poppy; **fleur de ~** poppy flower; **graines de ~** poppy seeds.

■ **~ somnifère** opium poppy.

payable /pɛjabl/ *adj* [*somme, dû*] payable; [*marchandise, achat*] which must be paid for (*épith, après n*); **~ en six versements** [*somme, dû*] payable in six instalments[GB]; [*marchandise, achat*] that can be paid for in six instalments[GB]; **~ à la livraison** payable cash on delivery; **~ à la commande** payable cash with order; **le travail est ~ d'avance** the work must be paid for in advance.

payant, ~e /pɛjɑ̃, ɑ̃t/ *adj* **1** (qui paie) [*personne*] paying; **2** (qu'il faut payer) [*billet, spectacle*] for which you have to pay (*après n*), not free (*jamais épith*); **l'entrée est-elle ~e?** do you have to pay to get in?, is there a charge for admission?; **chaîne ~e** TV subscription channel; **le stationnement est ~** there is a charge for parking; **parking ~** ≈ pay and display car park; **3** (avantageux) [*affaire*] lucrative, profitable; [*mesures*] worthwhile; [*efforts, stratégie*] which pays off (*épith, après n*); **sa tactique a été ~e** his strategy paid off; **notre attente a été ~e** it was worth the wait.

paye /pɛj/ = **paie**.

payement /pɛjmɑ̃/ = **paiement**.

payer /peje/ [21] **I** *vtr* **1** (régler) to pay for [*article, billet, achat, travail, service*]; to pay, to settle [*facture, note, dette*]; to pay [*somme, impôt, intérêt, salaire*]; **combien as-tu payé le livre?** how much did you pay for the book?; **~ le gaz/téléphone** to pay the gas/phone○ bill; **elle m'a payé le loyer/une matinée de travail** she paid me the rent/for a morning's work; **~ 500 francs de loyer** to pay 500 francs in rent; **~ 200 francs de fournitures** to pay 200 francs for the materials; **il m'a payé le terrain 10 000 francs** he paid me 10,000 francs for the land; **j'ai payé le vendeur** I paid the shop assistant GB ou salesclerk US; **il m'a fait ~ 10 francs/la ficelle** he charged me 10 francs/for the string; **travail bien/mal payé** well-/poorly-paid job; **~ par chèque/carte de crédit** to pay by cheque GB ou check US/credit card; **être payé à coups de pied dans les fesses**○ or **avec un lance-pierres** to be paid peanuts○; **2** (s'acquitter envers) to pay, to settle up with [*fournisseur, artisan*]; to pay [*employé*]; **~ l'entrepreneur** to settle up with ou pay the builder; **~ qn pour faire** or **pour qu'il fasse** to pay sb to do; **je ne suis pas payé pour ça!** that's not what I'm paid to do!; **être payé à ne rien faire** to be paid for doing nothing; **~ qn de ses services** to pay sb for their services; **avoir du mal à se faire ~** to have trouble getting paid; **être payé à l'heure/à l'année** to be paid on an hourly/annual basis; **être trop/trop peu payé** to be overpaid/underpaid; **ça ne paie pas son homme!** it's a poorly-paid job; **il est payé pour le savoir!** fig he knows that to his cost!; **3**○ (offrir) **~ qch à qn** to buy sb sth; **~ un verre** or **à boire à qn** to buy sb a drink; **~ l'avion à qn** to pay for sb's plane ticket; **viens, je te paie le restaurant** come on, I'll treat you to a meal; **4** (subir des conséquences) to pay for [*faute, imprudence*]; **~ cher sa réussite/d'avoir hésité** to pay dearly for one's success/for dithering; **tu me le paieras (cher)!** you'll pay for this!, I'll make you pay for this!; **~ de sa vie** to pay with one's life; **il a payé sa témérité de sa vie** his rashness cost him his life; **~ pour les autres** to take the rap○, to carry the can○ for the others; **5** (compenser) to cover; **ça me paie mon loyer** it covers the ou my rent; **leur réussite la paie de tous ses sacrifices** their success makes all her sacrifices worthwhile.

II *vi* **1** (récompenser) [*efforts, peine, sacrifice*] to pay off; **2** (rapporter) [*profession, activité*] to pay; **c'est un métier qui paie bien** it's a job that pays well; **c'est un métier qui paie mal** it's not a job that pays well; **3**○ (prêter à rire) to look funny ou comical; **il payait dans son imitation du patron** he did a funny imitation of the boss.

III se payer *vpr* **1** (être payable) [*service, marchandise*] to have to be paid for; [*personne, salaire*] to have to be paid; **2**○ (à soi-même) to treat oneself to [*voyage, dîner etc*]; iron to get [*rhume, mauvaise note*]; to get landed with [*travail, importun*]; **se ~ une cuite**○ to get plastered○; **se ~ qn**◑ (lui régler son compte) to give sb what for○; (coucher avec) to bed sb○, to have it off with sb◑; **se ~ un mur/arbre**○ to crash into a wall/tree; **se ~ un piéton**○ to knock down ou to slam○ a pedestrian; **3** (prendre son dû) **payez-vous sur ce billet** take what I owe you out of this note GB ou bill US.

IDIOMES **~ qn de promesses/belles paroles** to fob sb off with promises/fine words; **se ~ de mots** to talk a lot of hot air○; **se ~ d'illusions** to delude oneself; **se ~ du bon temps**○ to have a good time; **se ~ la tête**○ or **la gueule**◑ or **la tronche**◑ **de qn** (se moquer) to take the piss◑ out of sb, to take the mickey○ out of sb GB, to razz sb US; (duper) to take sb for a ride; **il aime sa femme et il est bien payé de retour** he loves his wife and she returns his love; **il me déteste et il est payé de retour** he hates me and the feeling's mutual; **il a payé de sa personne** it cost him dear.

payeur, **-euse** /pɛjœʀ, øz/ **I** *adj* **organisme** or **service ~** paying authority; **officier ~** paymaster.

II *nm,f* **1** (trésorier) Admin, Mil paymaster; **2** (client) payer; **mauvais ~** gén bad payer; Comm bad debtor.

pays, **~e** /pei, iz/ **I** *nm,f* (compatriote) someone from back home; **c'est ma ~e** she's from back home.

II *nm* **1** (État) country; **~ industriel/riche** industrial/rich country; **les ~ lointains** distant countries; **l'Italie est le ~ du soleil** Italy is the land of sun; **dans mon ~** where I come from, in my country; ▶ **conquérir**; **2** (région) **la Bourgogne est le ~ du bon vin** Burgundy is the home of good wine; **fromage du ~** locally-produced cheese; **gens/produit du ~** local people/product; **il n'est pas du ~** he is not local; **rentrer au ~** (vu du point de départ) to go back home; (vu du point d'arrivée) to come back home; **3** (village) village; **un petit ~ des Landes** a small village in the Landes.

■ **~ d'accueil** host country; **~ de cocagne** Cockaigne; **~ hôte** host country; **~ d'origine** country of origin; **~ des rêves** dreamland; **Pays du Soleil levant** Land of the Rising Sun; **~ en (voie de) développement** developing country.

IDIOMES **voir du ~** to do some travelling[GB]; **être en ~ connu** or **de connaissance** (dans un lieu) to be in familiar surroundings; (parmi des gens) to be among familiar faces; (sur un sujet) to be on one's home ground.

paysage /peizaʒ/ *nm* **1** (site) landscape; (vue) scenery ¢, landscape; **~ morne/industriel** bleak/industrial landscape; **~ accidenté** uneven landscape; **~s méditerranéens/de montagne** mediterranean/mountain landscapes; **~ urbain** lit, fig urban landscape GB, cityscape; **nous avons vu de magnifiques ~s** we saw some beautiful scenery; **les cheminées gâchent le ~** the chimneys spoil the view; **2** fig (milieu) scene; **le ~ politique/économique/culturel** the political/economic/cultural scene ou landscape; **~ universitaire/scolaire** university/educational world; **ça fait bien dans le ~ de dire qu'on est sportif** it looks good if you say that you're into sports; **3** Art (genre, tableau) landscape (painting).

■ **~ audiovisuel français**, **PAF** French radio and TV scene.

paysagé, **~e** /peizaʒe/ = **paysager**.

paysager, **-ère** /peizaʒe, ɛʀ/ *adj* **1** (relatif à l'environnement) environmental; **projet ~** environmental project; **2** (aménagé) [*jardin, parc*] landscaped; [*bureau*] open-plan.

paysagiste /peizaʒist/ *nmf* **1** (peintre) landscape artist, landscapist; **2** ▶ **510** (concepteur) **(jardinier) ~** landscape gardener; **(architecte) ~** landscape architect.

paysan, **-anne** /peizɑ̃, an/ **I** *adj* **1** (agricole) [*classe, milieu*] farming; [*syndicat, revendications*] farmers'; **2** (de la campagne) [*monde, vie*] rural; [*allure, façons*] peasant; Hist [*vie, misère*] peasant; **3** (naturel) aussi Culin [*soupe, pain*] country.

II *nm,f* ▶ **510** **1** (cultivateur) ≈ small farmer; Géog peasant farmer; Hist peasant/peasant woman; **2** (campagnard) pej peasant péj.

paysannat /peizana/ *nm* rural population.

paysannerie /peizanʀi/ *nf* gén ≈ small farmers (*pl*); **la ~** Géog, Hist the peasantry (+ *v sg* ou *pl*).

Pays-Bas /peibɑ/ ▶ **321** *nprmpl* **les ~** The Netherlands.

PC /pese/ *nm* **1** Pol (*abbr* = **parti communiste**) CP, Communist Party; **2** Ordinat (*abbr* = **personal computer**) PC; **3** (*abbr* = **poste de commandement**) (dans la police) division; Mil CP.

PCC (*written abbr* = **pour copie conforme**) Admin *certified true and accurate*.

PCF /peseɛf/ *nm* (*abbr* = **parti communiste français**) French Communist Party.

PCV /peseve/ *nm* (*abbr* = **paiement contre vérification**) reverse charge call GB, collect call US; **appelle-moi en ~** phone me and reverse the charges, call me collect US.

PDG /pedeʒe/ *nm* (*abbr* = **président-directeur général**) chairman and managing director GB, chief executive officer, CEO US.

péage /peaʒ/ *nm* **1** (taxe) toll; **autoroute à ~** toll motorway GB, toll road US; **2** (lieu) tollbooth.

péagiste /peaʒist/ *nmf* toll collector.

peau, **~x** /po/ *nf* **1** Anat skin; **avoir la ~ grasse/sèche/ridée** to have greasy/dry/wrinkled skin; **avoir la ~ douce** to have soft skin; **avoir une belle ~** to have lovely skin; **avoir une ~ de pêche** to have lovely soft skin; **~ morte** dead skin; **avoir la ~ dure** fig to be thick-skinned; **n'avoir que la ~ sur les os** to be all skin and bone; **prendre une/deux balles dans la ~** to be shot once/twice; ▶ **neuf**[2] **ours**; **2** (d'animal) gén skin; (pour faire du cuir) hide; (fourrure) pelt; **la ~ du porc est couverte de soies** the skin of the pig ou pig's skin is all covered in bristles; **veste en ~ de mouton** sheepskin jacket; **sac en ~ de porc/~ de serpent** pigskin/snakeskin bag; **ils étaient vêtus de ~x de bêtes** they were dressed in animal skins ou hides; **gants/veste en** or **de ~** leather gloves/jacket; **3** (de fruit, légume) skin, peel; (d'orange, de citron, pamplemousse) peel ¢; **les oranges ont une ~ épaisse** oranges have thick peel ou have a thick rind; **enlever la ~ d'un légume/fruit** to peel a vegetable/fruit; **4** (pellicule) (de lait, peinture) skin; **5**○ (vie) **jouer** or **risquer sa ~** to risk one's life; **faire la ~ à qn** to kill sb, to bump sb off○; **sauver sa ~** to save one's skin; **tenir à sa ~** to value one's life; **vouloir la ~ de qn** to want sb dead; **changer de ~** to turn over a new leaf; **craindre pour sa ~** to fear for one's life; **tu y laisseras ta ~** it'll kill you.

■ **~ d'âne** hum diploma; **~ de banane** lit banana skin; fig trap; **~ de chagrin** Mode shagreen; **rétrécir comme une ~ de chagrin** to shrink away to nothing; **~ de chamois** chamois leather, shammy (leather); **~ d'orange** orange peel skin, cellulite; **~ de tambour** Mus drumhead; **tendu comme une ~ de tambour** as taut as a drumskin; **~ de vache** lit cowhide; fig○ nasty piece of work GB, shit◑.

IDIOMES **~ de balle** or **de zébi**○! no way!, nothing doing○!; **je n'aimerais pas être dans sa ~** I wouldn't like to be in his/her shoes; **être** or **se sentir bien dans sa ~**○ (dans sa tête) to feel good about oneself; (dans son corps) to feel good; **être** or **se sentir mal dans sa ~**○ (physiquement) to feel lousy○; (psychologiquement) not to feel good about oneself; (gêné) to feel ill-at-ease; **avoir qn dans la ~**○ to be crazy about sb; **prendre** or **recevoir douze balles dans la ~**○ to be shot by a firing squad.

peaucier /posje/ **I** *adj m* **muscle ~** orofacial muscle.

II *nm* platysma.

peaufinage /pofinaʒ/ *nm* fine tuning fig.

peaufiner /pofine/ [1] *vtr* to refine [*politique, système*]; to put the finishing touches to [*contrat, travail, texte*].

peau-rouge, *pl* **peaux-rouges** /poʀuʒ/ *adj* Red Indian.

Peau-Rouge, *pl* **Peaux-Rouges** /poʀuʒ/ *nmf* Red Indian.

peausserie /posʀi/ *nf* leatherwork; **les ~s** leather goods.

peaussier, **-ière** ▶ **510** /posje, ɛʀ/ *nm,f* leather-worker.

pébroc◑, **pébroque**◑ /pebʀɔk/ *nm* brolly○ GB, umbrella.

pécari /pekaʀi/ *nm* **1** (animal) peccary; **2** (cuir) peccary skin; **en ~** peccary-skin (*épith*).

peccadille /pekadij/ *nf* peccadillo.

pechblende /pɛʃblɛ̃d/ *nf* pitchblende.

pêche /pɛʃ/ **I** ▶ **193** *adj inv* (couleur) peach; **murs ~** peach walls.

II *nf* **1** Bot peach; **~ blanche** white peach; **~ jaune** or **abricot** yellow peach; **~ de vigne** vineyard peach; **2** (activité) fishing; **~ en mer/en rivière/côtière** sea/freshwater/inshore fishing; **grande ~ (au large)** deep-sea fishing; **~ au thon/à la truite/au saumon** tuna/trout/salmon fishing; **'~ gardée'** 'private fishing'; **aller à la ~** lit to go fishing (**à** for); **aller à la ~ à la truite** to go fishing for trout; **aller à la ~ aux voix/informations** fig to angle for votes/information; **la ~ est ouverte** the fishing season is open; **3** (poissons capturés) catch; **une belle ~** a good ou fine catch; **la ~ a été bonne?** lit caught anything?; fig did you find anything interesting?; **4**○ (coup) clout○; **recevoir une ~** to get a clout; **5**○ (forme) **avoir la ~**○ to be feeling great; **ne pas avoir la ~**○ to be feeling low.

■ **~ à la baleine** whaling; **~ au chalut** trawling; **~ à la crevette** shrimping; **~ à la cuillère** spinning; **~ au harpon** harpoon fishing; **~ au lancer** casting; **~ à la ligne** angling; **~ miraculeuse** Relig miraculous draught of fishes; **~ à la mouche** fly-fishing; **~ aux moules** mussel gathering ou picking; **~ à la traîne** trolling; **~ au vif** live-bait fishing.

péché /peʃe/ *nm* **1** (faute) sin; **commettre un ~** to commit a sin; **~ mortel/véniel** mortal/venial sin; **le ~ originel** original sin; **les septs ~s capitaux** the seven deadly sins; **le ~ de gourmandise** the sin of gluttony; **vivre dans le ~** gén to live a sinful life; hum (vivre maritalement) to live in sin; **mourir en état de ~** to die in a state of sin; **~ de jeunesse** youthful indiscretion; **à tout ~ miséricorde** all sins will be forgiven; **2** (aberration) crime; **ce serait un ~ de rater ça** it would be a crime to miss that.

■ **~ mignon** (little) weakness; **le chocolat, c'est mon ~ mignon** I've got a little weakness for chocolate.

pécher /peʃe/ [14] *vi* **1** Relig to sin; **~ par gourmandise/colère** to be guilty of the sin of gluttony/anger; **2** (ne pas respecter) to offend (**contre** against); **~ contre la bienséance/le bon goût** to offend against propriety/good taste; **3** (ne pas être parfait) **~ par ignorance/négligence** to err through ignorance/carelessness; **~ par excès de confiance/de prudence** to be overconfident/overcareful; **le film pèche par manque de réalisme** the film falls down through a lack of realism; **le roman pèche sur un point** the novel has one major failing.

pêcher /pɛʃe/ [1] **I** *nm* Bot peach tree.

II *vtr* **1** Pêche to go fishing for [*poissons*]; to catch [*crustacés*]; **j'ai pêché une truite dans la Tamise** I caught a trout in the Thames; **~ la baleine/la crevette** to go whaling/shrimping; **2**○ (chercher) to get; **où est il allé ~ cet accoutrement/cette idée?** where did he get that outfit/idea from?

III *vi* to fish; **~ à la mouche** to fly-fish; **~ au vif** to fish with live bait; **~ en haute mer** to go deep-sea fishing; **~ à la ligne** to angle.

IDIOMES **~ en eau trouble** to stir up the mud.

pécheresse /peʃʀɛs/ *nf* sinner.

pêcherie /pɛʃʀi/ *nf* **1** Tech (usine) fish factory; **2** (zone de pêche) fishing ground.

pécheur /peʃœʀ/ *nm* sinner.

pêcheur /pɛʃœʀ/ ▶ 510 *nm* fisherman.

■ **~ de baleines** whaler; **~ de crevettes** shrimper; **~ d'hommes** Relig fisher of men; **~ à la ligne** angler; **~ de perles** pearl diver.

pécore /pekɔʀ/ *nf* pej silly goose○ péj.

pecten /pɛktɛn/ *nm* pecten.

pectine /pɛktin/ *nf* pectin.

pectique /pɛktik/ *adj* pectic.

pectoral, **~e**, *mpl* **-aux** /pɛktɔʀal, o/ **I** *adj* **1** Anat, Zool pectoral; **2** [*sirop*] cough (*épith*).

II *nm* **1** Anat pectoral muscle; **gonfler les pectoraux** to stick out one's chest; **2** Antiq (pendentif) pectoral; (d'armure) breastplate.

pécule /pekyl/ *nm* **1** (économies) savings (+ *v pl*), nest egg○; **amasser un petit ~** to put a little money by; **2** (de militaire) gratuity; (de détenu) **~ de libération** Jur allowance paid on release (*to prisoner*).

pécuniaire /pekynjɛʀ/ *adj* financial.

pécuniairement /pekynjɛʀmɑ̃/ *adv* financially.

pédagogie /pedagɔʒi/ *nf* **1** (science) education, pedagogy; **2** (qualité de pédagogue) teaching skills (*pl*); **il a le sens de la ~** he's a born teacher; **la ~ n'est pas son fort** he's not a very good teacher; **3** (méthode) teaching method.

pédagogique /pedagɔʒik/ *adj* [*activité, recherche, but, valeur*] educational, pedagogic; [*système, projet*] education (*épith*); [*personnel, matériel, méthode*] teaching (*épith*), pedagogic; [*dossier, frais*] teaching (*épith*); **formation ~** teacher training; **responsable ~** teacher in charge; **réunion ~** teachers' meeting.

pédagogiquement /pedagɔʒikmɑ̃/ *adv* pedagogically.

pédagogue /pedagɔg/ **I** *adj* good at explaining (*jamais épith*).

II *nmf* **1** (enseignant) teacher; **2** (spécialiste) educationalist.

pédale /pedal/ *nf* **1** (de bicyclette, piano, frein) pedal; (de machine à coudre, tour) treadle; **poubelle à ~** pedal bin; **auto à ~s** pedal car; **2**◑ (homosexuel) offensive queer◑ injur.

IDIOMES **perdre les ~s**○ (s'affoler) to lose one's grip; (s'embrouiller) to get muddled up; **se mélanger** or **s'emmêler les ~s**○ to get mixed up.

■ **~ douce** Mus soft pedal; **mettre la ~ douce** fig to soft pedal; **~ forte** loud ou sustaining pedal.

pédaler /pedale/ [1] *vi* **1** lit to pedal; **2** fig (se dépêcher)○ to get a move on○.

IDIOMES **~ dans la choucroute**○ or **la semoule**○ or **le yaourt**○ to flounder around.

pédaleur○, **-euse** /pedalœʀ, øz/ *nm,f* cyclist.

pédalier /pedalje/ *nm* (de bicyclette) chain transmission; (de piano) pedals (*pl*).

pédalo® /pedalo/ *nm* pedalo GB, pedal boat; **faire du ~** to go out on a pedalo.

pédant, **~e** /pedɑ̃, ɑ̃t/ **I** *adj* pedantic.

II *nm,f* pedant.

pédanterie /pedɑ̃tʀi/ *nf* pedantry.

pédantisme /pedɑ̃tism/ *nm* pedantry.

pédé◑ /pede/ *nm* offensive queer◑ injur, homosexual, gay.

IDIOMES **il est ~ comme un phoque** he's queer as a coot○ GB ou a three-dollar bill US.

pédéraste /pedeʀast/ *nm* **1** (pédophile) pederast; **2** (homosexuel) homosexual.

pédérastie /pedeʀasti/ *nf* **1** (pédophilie) pederasty; **2** (homosexualité masculine) homosexuality.

pédérastique /pedeʀastik/ *adj* pederastic.

pédestre /pedɛstʀ/ *adj* **randonnée ~** ramble; **association/itinéraire ~** ramblers' association/route; **circuit ~** (signed) walk.

pédiatre /pedjatʀ/ ▶ 510 *nmf* paediatrician.

pédiatrie /pedjatʀi/ *nf* paediatrics (+ *v sg*).

pedibus: **pedibus cum jambis**○ /pedibyskɔmʒɑ̃bis/ *adv* hum on foot, on ou by shank's pony hum.

pédicule /pedikyl/ *nm* peduncle.

pédicure /pedikyʀ/ ▶ 510 *nmf* chiropodist GB, podiatrist US.

pedigree /pedigʀe/ *nm* pedigree; **chien à ~** pedigree dog.

pédiluve /pedilyv/ *nm* footbath.

pédologie /pedɔlɔʒi/ *nf* pedology.

pédologique /pedɔlɔʒik/ *adj* pedological.

pédologue /pedɔlɔg/ ▶ 510 *nmf* pedologist.

pédoncule /pedɔ̃kyl/ *nm* peduncle.

pédonculé, **~e** /pedɔ̃kyle/ *adj* pedunculate.

pédophile /pedɔfil/ *adj, nmf* paedophile.

pédophilie /pedɔfili/ *nf* paedophilia.

pedzouille◑ /pɛdzuj/ *nm* pej country bumpkin○ péj GB, hick○ péj US.

peeling /piliŋ/ *nm* exfoliation.

Pégase /pegaz/ *npr* Pegasus.

PEGC /peəʒese/ *nmf* (*abbr* = **professeur d'enseignement général des collèges**) secondary school teacher GB, junior high school teacher US (*up to age 15*).

pègre /pɛgʀ/ *nf* **la ~** the underworld.

peignage /pɛɲaʒ/ *nm* Tex combing.

peigne /pɛɲ/ *nm* **1** (à cheveux) comb; **se donner un coup de ~** to run a comb through one's hair; **se faire donner un coup de ~** to have one's hair-do tidied up; **2** Tex (sur un métier) reed; (pour carder) carder; **3** Zool pecten; **4** (pour peindre) graining comb.

■ **~ africain** Afro comb GB, pick US; **~ à poux** fine-tooth comb (for headlice).

IDIOMES **passer qch au ~ fin** to go over ou through sth with a fine-tooth comb.

peigné, **~e** /peɲe/ **I** *pp* ▶ **peigner**.

II *pp adj* **1** Tex [*tissu*] brushed; [*fil*] combed; **2** [*cheveux*] **bien ~s** neatly combed; **mal ~s** tousled.

III *nm* (tissu) brushed fabric; (ruban) **le ~** combed slivers (*pl*).

IV peignée○ *nf* hiding○.

peigne-cul◑, *pl* **~s** /pɛɲky/ *nm* pej lout péj.

peigner /peɲe/ [1] **I** *vtr* **1** to comb [*cheveux*]; **2** Tex to card.

II se peigner *vpr* to comb one's hair.

IDIOMES **~ la girafe** hum to fiddle about doing nothing GB, to do busy work US.

peigneur, **-euse** /pɛɲœʀ, øz/ **I** ▶ 510 *nm,f* (ouvrier) carder.

II peigneuse *nf* (machine) carding machine.

peignoir /pɛɲwaʀ/ *nm* **1** (déshabillé) dressing gown GB, robe US; (de boxeur) dressing gown; **~ de bain** bathrobe; **2** (chez coiffeur) cape GB, robe US.

peinard○, **~e** /penaʀ, aʀd/ *adj* [*travail*] cushy○; [*endroit*] snug; **j'ai trouvé un boulot/coin ~** I've found a cushy○ job/a snug little spot; **être ~** to take things easy; **se tenir ~** [*personne*] to stay out of trouble; **en père ~** indolently.

peinardement○ /penaʀdəmɑ̃/ *adv* casually.

peindre /pɛ̃dʀ/ [55] **I** *vtr* **1** (avec de la peinture) to paint [*mur, motif, paysage*]; **~ qch en blanc** to paint sth white; **~ qch de motifs/personnages** to paint motifs/figures on sth; **une cravate en soie peinte** a tie made of painted silk; **l'œuvre peinte de Picasso** Picasso's paintings; **2** (avec des mots) to depict [*personnage, situation, époque*] (**comme** as).

II *vi* to paint; **~ au pinceau/couteau** to paint with a brush/palette knife; **~ sur bois/soie** to paint on wood/silk.

III se peindre *vpr* **1** [*peintre*] to paint a self-portrait; **2** [*auteur*] to depict oneself (**comme** as); **3** (apparaître) **se ~ sur qch** [*gêne, joie*] to be written on.

peine /pɛn/ **I** *nf* **1** (chagrin) sorrow, grief; **avoir de la ~** to feel sad ou upset; **faire de la ~ à qn** to hurt sb; **ça me fait de la ~ de le voir si triste** it hurts me to see him so sad; **tu leur as fait de la ~ en leur disant ça** you hurt their feelings when you said that; **il faisait ~ à voir** he looked a sorry sight; **cela faisait ~ à voir** it was sad to see; **2** (effort) effort, trouble; **c'est ~ perdue** it's a waste of effort; **en être pour sa ~** to waste one's time and effort; **se donner de la ~ pour faire** to go to a lot of trouble to do; **se donner** or **prendre la ~ de faire** to take the trouble to do; **tu pourrais réussir si seulement tu te donnais la ~ d'essayer** you could succeed if only you tried ou if only you made the effort; **il ne s'est même pas donné la ~ de nous prévenir** he didn't even bother to tell us; **il a quand même pris la ~ de te remercier/de venir** he still took the trouble to thank you/to come; **donnez-vous** or **prenez la ~ d'entrer** fml please do come in; **il n'est pas au bout de ses ~s** (dans une situation pénible) his troubles are far from over; (pour accomplir une tâche) he's still got a long way to go; **me voilà au bout de mes ~s!** (dans une situation difficile) my troubles are over now; (en finissant un travail) there, I've finished!; **se mettre en ~ pour qn** to go out of one's way for sb('s sake); **ce n'est pas la ~ de crier, je ne suis pas sourd** there's no need to shout, I'm not deaf; **ce n'est pas la ~ de te fâcher comme ça!** there's no need to get so angry!; **est-ce vraiment la ~ que je vienne?** do I really need to come?; **ce n'est pas la ~ d'aller voir ce film, il est nul** there's no point in going to see that film, it's awful; **ce n'est pas la ~ qu'il se déplace, le bureau est fermé** there's no point in him going, the office is closed; **c'était bien la ~ que je me donne tant de mal!** I went to all that trouble for nothing!; **c'est/c'était bien la ~!** what's/what was the point!; **c'était bien la ~ de venir de si loin pour trouver porte close!** what was the point of coming all this way to find nobody home!; **ça en valait vraiment la ~** it was really worth it; **ce n'est pas la ~ de faire un si long voyage pour un jour** it's not worth travelling[GB] so far just for one day; **la pièce vaut la ~ d'être vue** the play is worth seeing; **concentrez vos efforts sur ce qui en vaut la ~** concentrate on worthwhile activities; **cette idée vaut la ~ d'être soumise à qn** it's worth ou worthwhile submitting the idea to sb; **pour la ~** or **ta/votre ~** (en récompense) for your trouble; **tu m'as bien aidé, pour la ~ je t'offre à boire** you've been a great help to me, I'll buy you a drink for your trouble; ▶ **suffire**; **3** (difficulté) difficulty; **sans ~** easily; **avec ~** with difficulty; **avoir** or **éprouver de la ~ à faire** to have difficulty doing, to find it hard to do; **j'ai eu toutes les ~s du monde à le persuader/à trouver la maison** I had the greatest difficulty (in) persuading him/(in) finding the house; **j'ai ~ à le croire** I find it hard to believe; **l'allemand/le jardinage sans ~** German/gardening without tears; **il n'est pas en ~ pour trouver du travail** he has no difficulty finding work; **être bien en ~ de faire** to be hard put to do; **il serait bien en ~ de te prêter de l'argent, il n'a pas un sou** he would be hard put to lend you any money, he doesn't have a penny; **4** (punition) gén punishment; Jur penalty, sentence; **~ de prison** prison sentence; **une ~ de cinq ans de prison** a five-year prison sentence; **'défense de fumer sous ~ d'amende'** 'no smoking, offenders will be fined'; **'défense d'entrer sous ~ de poursuites'** 'trespassers will be prosecuted'; **sous ~ de mort** on pain of death; **sous ~ de décevoir** because of the risk of causing disappointment; **sous ~ de perdre de l'argent** at the risk of losing money; **pour la** or **ta ~** (comme punition) as punishment; **pour la ~, tu feras la vaisselle** as punishment, you'll do the dishes.

II **à peine** *loc adv* hardly, barely; **tu pars déjà, il est à ~ cinq heures!** you're not leaving already? it's barely five o'clock; **il est resté à ~ une heure** he stayed (for) barely an hour; **on a à ~ de quoi finir le mois** we've barely ou hardly enough to get by on until the end of the month; **une allusion à ~ voilée** a thinly veiled allusion; **il gagne à ~ 20 francs de l'heure** he barely earns 20 francs an hour; **c'est à ~ si je l'ai reconnu** I hardly recognized him; **il a à ~ touché à son assiette** he hardly touched his food; **il sait à ~ lire** he can hardly read; **il tenait à ~ debout** he could hardly stand; **c'est à ~ si elle dit bonjour/répond quand on lui parle** she barely says hello/replies if you speak to her; **il exagère à ~!** he's not really exaggerating! ; **à ~ était-il arrivé** or **il était à ~ arrivé qu'il pensait déjà à repartir** no sooner had he arrived than he was thinking of leaving again; **'je t'assure que je n'étais pas au courant'—'à ~○!'** (exprimant l'incrédulité) 'I tell you I didn't know about it'—'I don't believe it!', 'I don't buy that○!'

■ **~ capitale** Jur capital punishment; **condamné à la ~ capitale** sentenced to death; **~ de cœur** heartache ₵; **il a des ~s de cœur** his heart is aching; **~ correctionnelle** Jur penalty of two months to five years imprisonment; **~ criminelle** sentence for serious crime; **~ incompressible** Jur *prison term with no provision for remission*; **~ de mort** Jur death penalty; **~ de police** Jur penalty of one day to two months imprisonment; **~ de substitution** Jur alternative sentence.

peiner /pene/ [1] I *vtr* to sadden, to upset [*personne*]; **la nouvelle m'a beaucoup peiné** the news upset me greatly; **être/avoir l'air peiné** to be/to look sad ou upset; **je l'ai peiné en refusant** I hurt his feelings by refusing.

II *vi* [*personne*] to struggle; [*machine, voiture*] to labour[GB]; **elle peinait sur sa dissertation** she was struggling with her essay; **le cycliste peine dans les montées** the cyclist struggles on the uphills.

peintre /pɛ̃tʀ/ **▶510** *nm* **1** (artiste, artisan) painter; **~ abstrait/figuratif/paysagiste** abstract/representational/landscape painter; **2** (auteur) portrayer; **un ~ de la vie parisienne** a portrayer of Parisian life.

■ **~ en bâtiment** house painter, painter and decorator GB.

peintre-décorateur, *pl* **peintres-décorateurs** /pɛ̃tʀdekɔʀatœʀ/ **▶510** *nm* interior decorator.

peinture /pɛ̃tyʀ/ *nf* **1** (matériau) paint; **'~ fraîche'** 'wet paint'; **~ brillante/mate** gloss/matt paint; **~ satinée** satin paint; **2** (revêtement) paintwork; **la ~ de la voiture** the car's paintwork; **les rideaux ne vont pas avec la ~** the curtains don't match the paintwork; **refaire les ~s d'une pièce** to repaint a room; **3** (art, technique) painting; **~ abstraite/figurative/murale** abstract/representational/wall painting; **~ sur toile/soie** painting on canvas/silk; **~ au couteau** painting with a palette knife; **~ au pistolet** spray painting; **la ~ flamande** Flemish painting; **investir dans la ~** to invest in paintings; **faire de la ~** to paint; **je ne peux pas le voir en ~○** fig I can't stand the sight of him; **4** (tableau) painting; **une ~ de Van Gogh** a painting by Van Gogh; **5** (description) portrayal; **il a laissé une ~ vivante de son époque** he left a vivid portrayal of his times.

■ **~ acrylique** acrylic paint, emulsion (paint); **~ à l'eau** water-based paint; **~ de genre** genre painting; **~ gestuelle** action painting; **~ à l'huile** (revêtement) oil paint; (technique) painting in oils; (tableau) oil painting; **~ murale** mural.

peinturlurer /pɛ̃tyʀlyʀe/ [1] I *vtr* to daub; **~ qch de** or **en blanc** to daub sth with white paint; **un mur peinturluré** a wall that has been daubed with paint; **des clowns peinturlurés** clowns with their faces daubed in paint.

II **se peinturlurer** *vpr* **se ~ le visage** [*acteur, clown*] to cake one's face in greasepaint; pej [*femme*] to cake one's face in makeup.

péjoratif, -ive /peʒɔʀatif, iv/ I *adj* pejorative.

II *nm* pejorative.

péjoration /peʒɔʀasjɔ̃/ *nf* pejoration.

péjorativement /peʒɔʀativmɑ̃/ *adv* pejoratively.

pékin○ = **péquin**.

Pékin /pekɛ̃/ **▶857** *npr* Beijing, Peking.

pékiné /pekine/ *nm* pekin.

pékinois, ~e /pekinwa, az/ I **▶857** *adj* of Beijing, Pekinese.

II **▶462** *nm* **1** Ling Pekinese; **2** Zool Pekinese.

Pékinois, ~e /pekinwa, az/ *nm,f* (natif) native of Beijing; (habitant) inhabitant of Beijing.

PEL /peəɛl/ *nm*: *abbr* **▶plan**.

pelade /pəlad/ **▶271** *nf* alopecia.

pelage /pəlaʒ/ *nm* coat.

pélagique /pelaʒik/ *adj* pelagic.

pélargonium /pelaʀgɔnjɔm/ *nm* pelargonium.

pelé, ~e /pəle/ *adj* [*animal*] mangy; [*vêtement*] threadbare; [*colline*] bare.

IDIOMES **il y avait quatre** or **trois ~s et un tondu** there was hardly anybody ou a soul.

pêle-mêle /pɛlmɛl/ I *adv* [*entasser*] higgledy-piggledy.

II *nm inv* **1** (désordre) jumble; **2** (cadre) photo frame (for several photos).

peler /pəle/ [17] I *vtr* to peel.

II *vi* **1** [*peau, nez*] to peel; **2○** (avoir froid) to freeze; **on pèle ici!** it's freezing here!; **~ de froid** to freeze.

pèlerin, ~e /pɛlʀɛ̃, in/ I *nm* **1** Relig pilgrim; **2** Zool **faucon ~** peregrine falcon; **requin ~** basking shark; **3○** (individu) bloke○ GB, guy○ US.

II **pèlerine** *nf* cape.

pèlerinage /pɛlʀinaʒ/ *nm* **1** (voyage) pilgrimage; **aller en/faire un ~ à Lourdes** to go on/to make a pilgrimage to Lourdes; **2** (lieu) place of pilgrimage.

pélican /pelikɑ̃/ *nm* Zool pelican.

pelisse /pəlis/ *nf* fur-trimmed coat, pelisse.

pellagre /pelagʀ/ **▶271** *nf* pellagra.

pelle /pɛl/ *nf* **1** gén shovel; (jouet) spade; (de boulanger) peel; **à la ~○** fig by the dozen; **2◑** (baiser) French kiss; **rouler une ~ à qn◑** to give sb a French kiss.

■ **~ à charbon** coal shovel; **~ à gâteau** cake slice; **~ mécanique** mechanical digger; **~ à poussière** dustpan; **~ à tarte** pie server.

IDIOMES **ramasser une ~○** to come a cropper○.

pellet /pɔlɛ, pelɛ/ *nm* pellet.

pelletage /pɛltaʒ/ *nm* **le ~ du sable/de la terre** shovelling[GB] sand/earth.

pelletée /pɛlte/ *nf* **1** (de sable, charbon) shovelful; **2** (grande quantité) heap (**de** of).

pelleter /pɛlte/ [20] *vtr* to shovel.

pelleterie /pɛltʀi/ *nf* (préparation) fur preparation; (commerce) fur trade; (fourrures) furs (*pl*).

pelleteuse /pɛltøz/ *nf* mechanical digger.

pelletier, -ière /pɛltje, ɛʀ/ *nm,f* furrier.

pellicule /pelikyl/ I *nf* **1** Phot, Cin film; **~ couleur/noir et blanc** colour[GB]/black-and-white film; **~ vierge** unexposed film; **2** (de poussière, d'huile) film (**de** of); (de givre, glace, peinture) thin layer (**de** of).

II **pellicules** *nfpl* Physiol, Pharm dandruff ₵.

pelliculé, ~e /pelikyle/ *adj* [*support, reliure*] plastic-coated (*épith*).

Péloponnèse /pelopɔnɛz/ *nprm* Peloponnese GB, Peloponnesus.

pelotage○ /p(ə)lɔtaʒ/ *nm* groping○.

pelotari /p(ə)lɔtaʀi/ *nm* pelota player.

pelote /p(ə)lɔt/ **▶449** *nf* **1** Tex, Cout ball; **vendu en ~s de 50 g** sold in balls of 50 g; **2** Sport (balle) pelota ball; (jeu) pelota.

■ **~ basque** pelota; **~ à épingles** pin cushion.

peloter /p(ə)lɔte/ [1] I *vtr* **1○** (caresser) to grope○ [*personne*]; **se faire ~** to be groped○; **2** Tex to wind [sth] into a ball.

II **se peloter○** *vpr* to grope each other○.

peloteur○, -euse /p(ə)lɔtœʀ, øz/ *nm,f* pej groper○ péj.

peloton /p(ə)lɔtɔ̃/ *nm* **1** Tex ball; **un ~ de laine/ficelle** a ball of string/wool; **2** Mil platoon; **3** (en cyclisme) pack; **se détacher du ~** to get clear of the pack; **dans le ~ de tête** Sport in the leading pack; fig [*entreprise*] up among the leaders; **être en tête de ~** to be leading the pack, to be at the front of the pack; **en queue de ~** Sport at the back of the pack; fig lagging behind.

■ **~ d'exécution** firing squad; **~ d'instruction** ≈ NCO training; **faire** or **suivre le ~** ≈ to undergo NCO training.

pelotonner /p(ə)lɔtɔne/ [1] I *vtr* Tex to wind [sth] into a ball.

II **se pelotonner** *vpr* [*personne, chat*] (de bien-être) to snuggle up (**contre** against; **dans** in); (de peur) to huddle up (**contre** against; **dans** in).

pelouse /p(ə)luz/ *nf* **1** (gazon) lawn; **'~ interdite'** 'keep off the grass'; **2** Sport (terrain) pitch GB, field US; **3** Turf public enclosure.

peluche /p(ə)lyʃ/ *nf* **1** (matière) plush; **jouet en ~** cuddly toy GB, stuffed animal US; **couverture en ~** soft blanket; **2** (jouet) cuddly toy GB, stuffed animal US; **3** (sur un lainage) fluff.

pelucher /p(ə)lyʃe/ [1] *vi* [*lainage*] to become fluffy.

pelucheux, -euse /p(ə)lyʃø, øz/ *adj* [*vêtement, tissu*] fluffy.

pelure /p(ə)lyʀ/ *nf* **1** (de légume, fruit) peel ₵, piece of peel; (d'oignon) skin; **2○** (manteau) coat.

■ **~ d'oignon** Vin *adj inv* (couleur) pale rosé; *nm* (vin) rosé (wine).

pelvien, -ienne /pɛlvjɛ̃, ɛn/ *adj* pelvic.

pelvis /pɛlvis/ *nm inv* pelvis.

pénal, ~e, *mpl* **-aux** /penal, o/ I *adj* [*justice, enquête, poursuites*] criminal; **▶sanction**.

II *nm* (voie pénale) criminal justice system; (juridiction pénale) criminal courts (*pl*); **passer au ~** to appear before a criminal court.

pénalisant, ~e /penalizɑ̃, ɑ̃t/ *adj* **des mesures ~es pour les pays les plus pauvres** measures which penalize the poorest countries.

pénalisation /penalizasjɔ̃/ *nf* **1** Sport (pénalité) penalty; (action) penalizing ₵; **2** (sanction) **~ (fiscale)** taxation; **les experts prévoient une ~ des entreprises par...** observers expect companies will be penalized by...

pénaliser /penalize/ [1] *vtr* (tous contextes) to penalize.

pénalité /penalite/ *nf* **1** Jur, Fin (sanction) penalty; **2** Sport penalty; **réussir une ~** (en rugby) to score a penalty goal.

■ **~ de retard** Comm, Fisc penalty.

penalty /penalti/ *nm* penalty; **siffler un ~** to award a penalty; **point de ~** penalty spot.

pénard, ~e = **peinard**.

pénardement = **peinardement**.

pénates /penat/ *nmpl* **1○** hum (domicile)

home; **regagner ses ~** to go back home; **2** Mythol (dieux) Penates; (statuettes) penates.

penaud, **~e** /pəno, od/ *adj* [*personne, air*] sheepish.

pence ▶ **penny**.

penchant /pɑ̃ʃɑ̃/ *nm* **1** (inclination) fondness (**pour** for), penchant sout (**pour** for); (faible) weakness (**pour** for); **éprouver un doux ~ pour qn** to be fond of sb; **2** (disposition) tendency, inclination; **des ~s suicidaires/sadiques** suicidal/sadistic tendencies; **donner libre cours à ses mauvais ~s** to give way to one's baser instincts.

penché, **~e** /pɑ̃ʃe/ **I** *pp* ▶ **pencher**.
II *pp adj* (incliné) [*mur*] sloping; [*arbre, tour, colonne*] leaning; [*écriture*] slanting; **le pylône est de plus en plus ~** the pylon is leaning more and more; **être ~** [*personne*] to be bent over; [*colonne, mur, arbre*] to be leaning over; **~ à la fenêtre** leaning out of the window; **~ sur mon ouvrage** bent over my work.

pencher /pɑ̃ʃe/ [1] **I** *vtr* to tilt [*meuble, objet*]; to tip [sth] up [*bouteille, verre*]; **~ la tête** [*personne*] (en avant) to bend one's head forward(s); (en arrière) to lean ou tilt one's head back; **~ la tête sur le côté** to tilt one's head to one side; **~ le corps en avant/en arrière** to lean forward(s)/backward(s); **~ la tête** [*fleur*] to wilt.
II *vi* **1** (être incliné) [*objet, tour, arbre, mur*] to lean; [*bateau*] to list; [*tableau*] to slant, to tilt; **le tableau penche un peu du côté gauche** the painting is slanting ou tilting a little to the left; **2** (préférer) **~ pour** to incline toward(s) [*opinion, théorie*]; to be in favour[GB] of [*solution, fermeté*].
III se pencher *vpr* **1** (s'incliner) [*personne*] to lean; (se baisser) to bend down; **se ~ en avant/en arrière/vers** to lean forward(s)/backward(s)/(over) toward(s); **se ~ à la fenêtre** to lean out of the window; **'défense de se ~ au-dehors'** 'do not lean out of GB ou out US the window'; **se ~ sur qn/qch** to bend over sb/sth; **2** (analyser) **se ~ sur** to look into [*problème, passé*]; **se ~ avec indulgence sur le cas de qn** to take a lenient view of sb's case.

pendable /pɑ̃dabl/ *adj* **cas ~**† Jur hanging case ou offence[GB]; fig **c'est un cas ~** it's deplorable.
IDIOMES **jouer un tour ~ à qn** to play a rotten trick on sb.

pendaison /pɑ̃dɛzɔ̃/ *nf* Jur hanging.
■ **~ de crémaillère** house-warming (party).

pendant[1] /pɑ̃dɑ̃/ **I** *prép* **1** (pour exprimer une durée) for; **je t'ai attendu ~ des heures** I waited for you for hours; **~ les trois premières années** for the first three years; **~ un instant** for a moment; **~ longtemps** for a long time; **~ toute la durée des vacances** for the entire ou throughout the vacation; **~ tout le trajet** for the whole journey, throughout the journey; **il a été malade ~ tout le trajet** he was sick throughout the journey; **l'hôtel est seulement ouvert ~ l'été** the hotel is only open in summer ou during the summer; **~ combien de temps avez-vous vécu à Versailles?** how long did you live in Versailles?; **2** (au cours de) during; **ils viendront nous voir ~ l'été** they are coming to see us during ou in the summer; **le temps s'est refroidi ~ la nuit** it got colder during the night ou overnight; **avant la guerre et ~** before and during the war; **~ tout le temps où mon père était malade j'allais le voir tous les jours** all the time my father was ill I visited him every day, I visited my father every day during his illness; **~ ce temps(-là)** meanwhile; **~ ce temps, à quelques kilomètres de là** meanwhile, a few kilometres[GB] away; **prendre le médicament ~ toute la durée du séjour** take the medicine throughout the whole stay.
II pendant que *loc conj* while; **~ qu'il dort je peux travailler** while he's asleep I can work; **voyage ~ qu'il est temps** travel while you have the chance; **~ que j'y pense, ton père a téléphoné il y a une heure** while I think of it, your father called an hour ago; **~ que tu y es/nous y sommes** while you're at it/we're at it.

pendant[2], **~e** /pɑ̃dɑ̃, ɑ̃t/ **I** *adj* **1** (qui pend) **être assis les jambes ~es** to be sitting with one's legs dangling; **assis sur une chaise les jambes ~es** sitting on a chair with one's legs dangling down; **l'oreille ~e** with one ear drooping; **le chien avait la langue ~e** the dog's tongue lolled ou was hanging out; **2** Jur, Admin (en instance) [*cas, procès*] pending (*épith*); [*question*] outstanding.
II *nm* **1** (objet) **~ (d'oreille)** drop earring; **2** (équivalent) **le ~ de** the counterpart of [*personne, institution*]; **le ~ d'un vase** the matching vase; **être le ~ de, faire ~ à** to match [*objet*]; to be the counterpart of [*personne, institution*]; **se faire ~** [*objets*] to match; [*personnes, institutions*] to be counterparts; **son discours fait ~ à la déclaration de Paul** his/her speech parallels Paul's declaration.

pendard†, **~e** /pɑ̃daʀ, aʀd/ *nm,f* hum rogue, scoundrel†.

pendeloque /pɑ̃dlɔk/ *nf* (de bijou) pendant, drop (*on earring*); (de lustre) lustre[GB], (glass) pendant.

pendentif /pɑ̃dɑ̃tif/ *nm* (bijou) pendant; Archit pendentive.

penderie /pɑ̃dʀi/ *nf* (meuble) wardrobe; (local) walk-in cupboard GB ou closet US.

pendiller /pɑ̃dije/ [1] *vi* to flap about.

Pendjab /pɛndʒab/ ▶ 692 *nprm* Punjab.

pendouiller○ /pɑ̃duje/ [1] *vi* to dangle down.

pendre /pɑ̃dʀ/ [6] **I** *vtr* **1** (exécuter) to hang [*condamné*]; **~ qn haut et court** to hang sb; **va te faire ~!** go to hell○!; **qu'il aille se faire ~ ailleurs**○**!** he can go to hell○!; **je veux bien être pendu s'il rembourse ses dettes** if he pays off his debts I'll eat my hat; **2** (accrocher) to hang [*tableau, rideau*]; to hang up [*vêtement, clé, jambon*]; **~ qch à** to hang sth from [*plafond*]; to hang sth (up) on [*clou, mur*]; **~ un rideau à la fenêtre** to put up a curtain at the window.
II *vi* **1** (être suspendu) [*objet, vêtement*] to hang (**à** from); [*jambe, bras*] to dangle; **des corps pendaient encore aux arbres** bodies were still hanging from the trees; **du linge pendait aux fenêtres** washing was hanging from the windows; **~ jusqu'au sol** to be hanging down to the ground; **laisser ~ ses jambes** to dangle one's legs; **2** (pendiller) [*lambeaux, mèche*] to hang down; [*joue, sein*] to sag; [*pan de jupe*] to droop; **ta jupe pend devant** your skirt is drooping at the front.
III se pendre *vpr* **1** (se tuer) to hang oneself; **2** (s'accrocher) **se ~ à** to hang from [*branche*]; **se ~ au cou de qn** to throw one's arms around sb's neck.
IDIOMES **ça te pend au (bout du) nez** you've got it coming to you.

pendu, **~e** /pɑ̃dy/ **I** *pp* ▶ **pendre**.
II *pp adj* **1** (mort) [*personne*] hanged; **2** (accroché) [*objet*] hung (**à** on), hanging (**à** from); **~ à son micro** fig clutching the microphone; **~ au bras de sa femme** clinging to his wife's arm; **être ~ aux lèvres de qn** to hang on sb's every word; **être toujours ~ au téléphone** to spend all one's time on the telephone.
III *nm,f* hanged man/woman; **une haie de ~s** a line of hanging bodies.
IV *nm* Jeux **jouer au ~** to play hangman.
IDIOMES **parler de corde dans la maison d'un ~** to make a tactless remark.

pendulaire /pɑ̃dylɛʀ/ *adj* [*mouvement*] pendular.

pendule /pɑ̃dyl/ **I** *nm* **1** Phys pendulum; **2** (de radiesthésie) pendulum.
II *nf* (horloge) clock.
IDIOMES **remettre les ~s à l'heure** to set the record straight.

pendulette /pɑ̃dylɛt/ *nf* small clock; **~ de voyage** travelling[GB] clock.

pêne /pɛn/ *nm* bolt; **~ demi-tour** sash.

Pénélope /penelɔp/ *npr* Mythol, fig Penelope.

pénéplaine /peneplɛn/ *nf* peneplain.

pénétrabilité /penetʀabilite/ *nf* penetrability.

pénétrable /penetʀabl/ *adj* **1** (qui peut être pénétré) penetrable; **2** (intelligible) understandable.

pénétrant, ~e /penetʀɑ̃, ɑ̃t/ **I** *adj* **1** lit [*vent, air, son, voix, bruit*] penetrating; [*pluie*] drenching; [*froid*] piercing; [*humidité*] pervasive; **2** fig (perspicace) [*personne, remarque, étude*] shrewd; [*esprit, regard*] penetrating.
II pénétrante *nf* urban motorway GB ou freeway US.

pénétration /penetʀasjɔ̃/ *nf* lit, fig penetration; **~ d'un marché** market penetration; **taux de ~** level of market penetration; **la ~ des eaux dans le sol** the seepage of water into the soil.

pénétré, **~e** /penetʀe/ **I** *pp* ▶ **pénétrer**.
II *pp adj* [*air, ton*] earnest, intense; **être ~ de** to be imbued with [*idée, sentiment*]; **être ~ de reconnaissance** to be full of gratitude; **être ~ de son importance** to be full of one's own importance.

pénétrer /penetʀe/ [14] **I** *vtr* **1** (s'infiltrer dans) [*pluie, liquide*] to soak into, to seep into [*terre, tissu*]; [*soleil, lumière*] to penetrate [*feuillage*]; **la pluie a pénétré nos vêtements** the rain soaked through our clothes; **le froid m'a pénétré jusqu'aux os** the cold went right through me; **2** (percer à jour) to fathom [*mystère, secret, intentions, pensée*]; **3** (sexuellement) to penetrate; **4** (atteindre) [*idée, mode*] to reach [*milieu, groupe*]; **5** (remplir) to fill; **son courage me pénétrait d'admiration** his/her courage filled me with admiration; **il était pénétré d'un sentiment de reconnaissance** he was filled with gratitude.
II *vi* **1** (entrer) **~ dans** or **à l'intérieur de** [*personne, animal*] to enter, to get into [*lieu*]; [*balle, éclat d'obus*] to penetrate [*organe*]; [*armée, soldats*] to penetrate [*lignes ennemies, pays*]; [*personne*] to penetrate [*cercle, groupe, organisation*]; **~ en territoire ennemi** to enter ou penetrate enemy territory; **ils ont pénétré dans le bâtiment sans se faire repérer** they got into the building without anyone noticing them; **il est interdit de ~ sur le chantier** it is forbidden to enter the building site; **~ dans une maison par effraction** to break into a house; **l'auteur nous fait ~ dans l'univers des sociétés secrètes** the author takes us into the world of secret societies; **2** (s'infiltrer) **~ dans** [*lumière, froid, odeur*] to get into, to penetrate [*lieu*]; [*eau, vent, fumée*] to get into [*lieu*]; **c'est par là que le froid/l'eau pénètre** that's where the cold/the water gets in; **pour empêcher le froid de ~** to keep the cold air out; **3** (s'imprégner) **~ dans** [*crème, lotion*] to penetrate [*peau, cuir chevelu*]; [*cire, vernis*] to penetrate [*meuble, bois*]; **faire ~ la pommade en massant doucement** to rub the ointment in by massaging gently.
III se pénétrer *vpr* **se ~ d'une idée** to get an idea firmly rooted in one's mind.

pénibilité /penibilite/ *nf* strenuousness.

pénible /penibl/ *adj* **1** (difficile) [*effort, impression*] painful; [*travail*] hard; [*voyage, ascension*] difficult; **c'est une situation ~ à supporter** the situation is difficult to bear; **2** (agaçant) [*personne*] tiresome; **être ~** to be tiresome ou a pain○; **c'est un enfant ~** he's a difficult child; **c'est ~, ces retards constants!** these constant delays are so tiresome!; **c'est ~!** it's such a pain○!

péniblement /peniblәmɑ̃/ *adv* **1** (tout juste) [*atteindre, se vendre*] barely; **2** (avec peine) [*marcher, élaborer, préserver*] with difficulty.

péniche /peniʃ/ **I** *nf* Naut barge.
II○ **péniches** *nfpl* (chaussures) clodhoppers○, shoes.
■ **~ de débarquement** landing craft.

pénicilline /penisilin/ *nf* penicillin.

pénil /penil/ *nm* mons veneris.

péninsulaire /penɛ̃sylɛʀ/ *adj* peninsular.

péninsule /penɛ̃syl/ *nf* peninsula; **la ~ ibérique** the Iberian Peninsula.

pénis /penis/ *nm inv* penis.

pénitence /penitɑ̃s/ *nf* **1** Relig (peine) penance; **faire ~** to do penance; **2** (punition) punishment; **mettre qn en ~** to punish sb; **pour ta ~...** as a punishment...; **3** (gage) forfeit.

pénitencier /penitɑ̃sje/ *nm* prison, penitentiary US.

pénitent, **~e** /penitɑ̃, ɑ̃t/ *adj, nm,f* penitent.

pénitentiaire /penitɑ̃sjɛʀ/ *adj* [*établissement, institution*] penal; [*personnel, régime, médecine*] prison (*épith*).

penne /pɛn/ *nf* **1** (d'oiseau) quill, penna spéc; **2** (de flèche) feather.

Pennines /pɛnin/ *nprfpl* **les ~** the Pennines.

Pennsylvanie /pɛnsilvani/ ▶ **692** *nprf* Pennsylvania.

penny, *pl* **pence** /peni, pɛns/ *nm* penny.

pénologue /penɔlɔg/ ▶ **510** *nmf* Jur penologist.

pénombre /penɔ̃bʀ/ *nf* **1** (obscurité) half-light; **dans la ~** in the half-light; **2** Astron penumbra.

pensable /pɑ̃sabl/ *adj* thinkable; **ce n'est pas ~** it's unthinkable.

pensant, **~e** /pɑ̃sɑ̃, ɑ̃t/ *adj* thinking.

pense-bête, *pl* **pense-bêtes** /pɑ̃sbɛt/ *nm* reminder, aide-mémoire.

pensée /pɑ̃se/ *nf* **1** (faculté) thought; **le cerveau, siège de la ~** the brain, seat of thought; **la ~ distingue l'homme de l'animal** thought distinguishes man from animals; **2** (ce que l'on pense) thought; **être perdu dans ses ~s** to be lost in thought; **faites-nous part de vos ~s sur** or **à ce sujet** let us know your thoughts on this matter; **voilà une ~ très profonde!** iron how profound!; **à la ~ de** at the thought of; **j'enrage à la ~ qu'elle puisse être avec lui** I'm furious at the thought that she might be with him; **je frémis rien qu'à la ~ de devoir y aller** I shudder at the very thought of having to go there; **j'aimerais connaître le fond de ta ~** I'd like to know what you really think deep down; **il l'a fait dans la ~ de vous être agréable** he did it thinking that it would please you; **dire sa ~** to speak one's mind, to say what one thinks; **lire dans les ~s de qn** to read sb's mind ou thoughts; **il a eu une ~ pour les victimes de l'accident** he remembered the victims of the accident; **j'ai eu une ~ émue pour mes grands-parents** I thought fondly of my grandparents; **3** (esprit) mind; **venir à la ~ de qn** to come to sb's mind; **elle essayait de chasser l'image de sa ~** she was trying to get the image out of her mind; **en ~**, **par la ~** [*se représenter, voir*] in one's mind; **nous serons avec vous par la ~** we'll be with you in spirit; **4** (manière de penser) thinking; **~ claire/confuse** clear/muddled thinking; **5** (philosophie) thought; **la ~ moderne/grecque/marxiste** modern/Greek/Marxist thought; **la ~ de Hegel/Machiavel** the thought of Hegel/Machiavelli; **une ~ politique très pauvre** impoverished political ideas (*pl*); **6** (fleur) pansy.

penser /pɑ̃se/ [1] **I** *vtr* **1** (avoir une opinion) to think (**de** of, about); **~ du bien/du mal de qn/qch** to think well/badly ou ill of sb/sth; **qu'est-ce que tu en penses?** what do you think of it?; **il m'a dit ce qu'il pensait du professeur/film** he told me what he thought of the teacher/film; **je ne sais pas quoi ~ de ce livre/de lui/de la situation** I don't know what to make ou think of this book/of him/of the situation; **je n'en pense rien** I have no opinion about it; **dire ce que l'on pense** to say what one thinks, to speak one's mind; **qu'est-ce que tu penserais d'un week-end en Normandie?** what would you say to a weekend in Normandy?; **il ne disait rien mais n'en pensait pas moins** he said nothing but it didn't mean that he agreed; **2** (croire) to think; **~ que** to think that; **je pense qu'il a raison** I think (that) he's right; **c'est bien ce que je pensais!** I thought as much!; **je (le) pense, je pense que oui** I think so; **je ne (le) pense pas, je pense que non** I don't think so; **je le pensais plus intelligent** I thought he was more intelligent than that; **je pense avoir fait du bon travail** I think I did a good job; **je n'aurais jamais pensé ça de lui** I would never have thought that of him; **il n'est pas aussi bête qu'on le pense** he's not as stupid as people think (he is); **je te le dis comme je le pense** I'm telling you (just) what I think; **quand on dit 'culture' il pense 'ennui'** to him culture spells boredom; **elle ne pense pas un mot de ce qu'elle dit** she doesn't believe a word of what she's saying; **tu penses vraiment ce que tu dis?** do you really mean what you're saying?; **tout laisse** or **porte à ~ que** there's every indication that; **je pense bien!** you bet○!, for sure; **vous pensez (bien) que si j'avais su ça...** you can well imagine that if I'd known that...; **vous pensez si j'étais content/furieux!** you can imagine how pleased/angry I was!; **'il s'est excusé?'—'penses-tu!'** 'did he apologize?'—'you must be joking!', 'some hope!'; **pensez donc!** just imagine!; **3** (se rappeler) **pense que ça ne sera pas facile** remember that it won't be easy; **ça me fait ~ qu'il faut que je lui écrive** that reminds me that I must write to him/her; **4** (avoir l'intention de) **~ faire** to be thinking of doing, to intend to do; **il pense venir demain** he's thinking of coming tomorrow, he intends to come tomorrow; **elle pense déménager bientôt** she intends to move soon; **qu'est-ce que tu penses faire maintenant?** what do you think you'll do now?, what do you intend to do now?; **5** (concevoir) to think [sth] up [*appareil, dispositif, projet*]; **c'est bien pensé!** it's well thought out!; **il faut ~ l'avenir, non l'improviser** we've got to plan for the future, not improvise[GB] it.
II penser à *vtr ind* **1** (songer) **~ à** to think of ou about [*personne, endroit*]; (réfléchir à) to think about [*problème, proposition, offre*]; **à quoi penses-tu?** what are you thinking about?; **je pense à elle** I'm thinking of ou about her; **on ne peut pas ~ à tout** you can't think of everything; **faire/dire qch sans y ~** to do/say sth without thinking; **il ne pense qu'à lui/à l'argent/à s'amuser** he only thinks of himself/about money/about enjoying himself; **il faudrait ~ à rentrer, il se fait tard** we'd better think about going back, it's getting late; **pense à ce que tu dis!** think about what you're saying!; **pensez aux conséquences/à votre carrière!** think of the consequences/of your career!; **maintenant que j'y pense** now that I (come to) think of it; **ça me rend malade rien que d'y ~** it makes me ill just thinking about it; **c'est simple, il fallait y ~** or **il suffisait d'y ~** it's simple, it just required some thinking; **regardez le pendule et ne pensez plus à rien** look at the pendulum and empty your mind; **sans ~ à mal** without meaning any harm; **tu n'y penses pas! c'est trop dangereux!** you can't be serious! it's too dangerous!; **n'y pensons plus!** let's forget about it!; **votre argent vous pouvez vous le mettre où je pense**◐! you can stuff your money you know where○!; **il a reçu le ballon où je pense**○ the ball hit him you know where○; **il ne pense qu'à ça**○! he's got a one-track mind!; **2** (se souvenir) **~ à** to remember; **pense à écrire à ton grand-père/changer l'ampoule** remember to write to your grandfather/change the lightbulb; **est-ce que tu as pensé à arroser les plantes?** did you remember to water the plants?; **pense à ton rendez-vous** remember your appointment; **pense à ce que t'a dit le docteur!** remember what the doctor told you!; **mais j'y pense, c'est ton anniversaire aujourd'hui!** now I come to think of it it's your birthday today!; **tant que j'y pense** while I think of it; **il me fait ~ à mon père** he reminds me of my father; **fais-moi ~ à acheter du beurre** remind me to buy some butter; **3** (envisager) **~ à faire** to be thinking of doing; **elle pense à s'installer en France** she's thinking of moving to France.
III *vi* to think; **je pense donc je suis** I think therefore I am; **avec mes films, j'essaie de faire ~ le public** in my films, I try to make people think; **façon de ~** way of thinking; **je lui ai dit ma façon de ~!** I gave him a piece of my mind!; **~ tout haut** to think out loud; **je pense comme vous** I agree with you.

penseur /pɑ̃sœʀ/ *nm* thinker.

pensif, **-ive** /pɑ̃sif, iv/ *adj* pensive, thoughtful.

pension /pɑ̃sjɔ̃/ *nf* **1** (rente) pension; **2** (hôtel) boarding house; (séjour) board; **frais de ~** accommodation charges; **prendre qn en ~** to take sb as a lodger; **j'ai pris ~ chez eux pendant trois mois** I boarded with them for three months; **3** Scol (école) boarding school; (frais d'école) boarding fees (*pl*); **mettre qn en ~** to send sb to boarding school.
■ **~ alimentaire** Jur alimony; **~ complète** Tourisme full board; **~ de famille** Tourisme family hotel; **~ d'invalidité** Assur disability pension; Jur disablement benefit; **~ de retraite** = **~ de vieillesse**; **~ de réversion** Prot Soc reversion benefit; **~ viagère** Fin life annuity; **~ de vieillesse** Prot Soc old-age pension.

pensionnaire /pɑ̃sjɔnɛʀ/ *nmf* **1** (résident) (d'hôtel) resident; (de prison) inmate; **2** Scol boarder; **3** Théât resident member.

pensionnat /pɑ̃sjɔna/ *nm* boarding school.

pensionné, **~e** /pɑ̃sjɔne/ **I** *pp* ▶ **pensionner**.
II *pp adj* pensioned-off.
III *nm,f* pensioner.

pensionner /pɑ̃sjɔne/ [1] *vtr* to grant a pension to.

pensivement /pɑ̃sivmɑ̃/ *adv* pensively.

pensum† /pɛ̃sɔm/ *nm* (punition) imposition GB, punishment; (tâche pénible) chore; (ouvrage ennuyeux) laborious book.

pentaèdre /pɛ̃taɛdʀ/ **I** *adj* pentahedral.
II *nm* pentahedron.

pentagonal, **~e**, *mpl* **-aux** /pɛ̃tagɔnal, o/ *adj* pentagonal.

pentagone /pɛ̃tagɔn/ *nm* pentagon.

Pentagone /pɛ̃tagɔn/ *nprm* **le ~** the Pentagon.

pentamètre /pɛ̃tamɛtʀ/ *nm* pentameter.

pentane /pɛ̃tan/ *nm* pentane.

Pentateuque /pɛ̃tatøk/ *nm* **le ~** the Pentateuch.

pentathlon /pɛ̃tatlɔ̃/ *nm* pentathlon.

pentatonique /pɛ̃tatɔnik/ *adj* [*gamme*] pentatonic.

pente /pɑ̃t/ *nf* **1** (déclivité) slope; **~ douce/raide** gentle/steep slope; **une ~ de 10%** a gradient of 1 in 10 GB, 10% gradient US; **toit/rue en ~** sloping roof/street; **terrain en ~** sloping plot; **jardin en ~** garden on a slope; **descendre** or **aller en ~ douce** to slope gently down; **2** Math gradient; **3** (direction) direction; **être sur la bonne ~** to be going in the right direction; **l'économie est sur la ~ ascendante** the economy is showing an upward trend.
IDIOMES **avoir la dalle** or **le gosier en ~**○ to drink like a fish○; **être sur la mauvaise**

~, être sur une ~ savonneuse [*délinquant*] to be on the slippery slope GB, to be going astray; [*entreprise, économie*] to be going downhill; **remonter la ~** to get back on one's feet.

Pentecôte /pɑ̃tkot/ *nf* **1** (chrétienne) (événement) Pentecost; (période) Whitsun; **à la ~** at Whitsun; **week-end/lundi de ~** Whit weekend/Monday; **2** (juive) Pentecost.

penthotal® /pɛ̃tɔtal/ *nm* Pentothal®.

pentu, **~e** /pɑ̃ty/ *adj* [*toit*] pitched (*épith*), sloping; [*chemin*] steep.

penture /pɑ̃tyʀ/ *nf* strap hinge.

pénultième /penyltjɛm/ **I** *adj* penultimate.
II *nf* penultimate (syllable).

pénurie /penyʀi/ *nf* **1** (manque) shortage (**de** of); **~ pétrolière/alimentaire** oil/food shortage; **~ de main-d'œuvre/de talents** shortage of labour[GB]/talent; **~ de logements** housing shortage; **2** (disette) scarcity, shortage.

PEP /pɛp/ *nm* (*abbr* = **plan d'épargne populaire**) *long-term savings plan*.

pépé○ /pepe/ *nm* **1** (grand-père) granddad, grandpa○; **2** (vieil homme) granddad○, old man; ▶ **ortie**.

pépée○ /pepe/ *nf* chick○, pretty girl.

pépère○ /pepɛʀ/ **I** *adj* [*vie, travail*] cushy○; [*endroit*] nice.
II *nm* **1** (grand-père) granddad○, grandpa○; **2** (vieillard) granddad○, old man; **3** (homme) pej fatty○ péj; (bébé) chubby little chap.

pépettes○† /pepɛt/ *nfpl* dough○ ₵, money ₵.

pépie /pepi/ *nf* Vét the pip.
IDIOMES **avoir la ~** [*personne*] to be parched.

pépiement /pepimɑ̃/ *nm* chirping.

pépier /pepje/ [2] *vi* to chirp.

pépin /pepɛ̃/ *nm* **1** Bot pip; **sans ~s** seedless; **2**○ (ennui) slight problem; **avoir des ~s** to have problems; **3**○ (parapluie) brolly○ GB, umbrella.

pépinière /pepinjɛʀ/ *nf* **1** Hort nursery; **2** fig breeding-ground (**de** for).

pépiniériste /pepinjeʀist/ ▶ **510** *nmf* nurseryman/nurserywoman.

pépite /pepit/ *nf* (d'or) nugget.
■ **~s de chocolat** Culin chocolate chips.

péplum /peplɔm/ *nm* **1** Antiq peplos; **2** Cin historical epic.

pepsine /pɛpsin/ *nf* pepsin.

peptide /pɛptid/ *nm* peptide.

peptique /pɛptik/ *adj* peptic.

péquenaud○, **~e** /pɛkno, od/ *nm,f* pej country bumpkin○, hick○ US.

péquenot○ = **péquenaud**.

péquin○ /pekɛ̃/ *nm* **1** Mil soldier's slang civvy○; **s'habiller en ~** to wear civvies○; **2** (individu) fellow○.

perborate /pɛʀbɔʀat/ *nm* perborate.

perçage /pɛʀsaʒ/ *nm* (de trou) drilling, boring; (de paroi) boring through.

percale /pɛʀkal/ *nf* percale.
■ **~ glacée** chintz.

percaline /pɛʀkalin/ *nf* percaline.

perçant, **~e** /pɛʀsɑ̃, ɑ̃t/ *adj* **1** [*cri, voix*] shrill; [*regard*] piercing; **2** [*vue*] sharp.

perce /pɛʀs/ *nf* **mettre en ~** to broach, to tap [*tonneau*].

percée /pɛʀse/ *nf* **1** (dans une forêt, un mur, un quartier) opening; **2** (progrès rapide) breakthrough; **3** Mil breakthrough; **4** Sport (au rugby) break.

percement /pɛʀsəmɑ̃/ *nm* (de tunnel) boring; (de route) (ouverture) clearing; (construction) building; **le ~ de trois fenêtres** making three window openings.

perce-neige /pɛʀsənɛʒ/ *nm* or *f inv* snowdrop.

perce-oreille, *pl* **~s** /pɛʀsɔʀɛj/ *nm* earwig.

percepteur, **-trice** /pɛʀsɛptœʀ, tʀis/ **I** *adj* [*organe*] sensory.
II *nm* tax inspector.

perceptibilité /pɛʀsɛptibilite/ *nf* perceptibility.

perceptible /pɛʀsɛptibl/ *adj* **1** [*son, nuance*] perceptible (**à** to); **2** Fisc [*somme, montant, impôt*] payable.

perceptif, **-ive** /pɛʀsɛptif, iv/ *adj* **1** [*interprétation*] perceptual; **2** [*personne*] perceptive.

perception /pɛʀsɛpsjɔ̃/ *nf* **1** Fisc (bureau) tax office; **2** (d'impôt) collection; **3** Psych perception.

percer /pɛʀse/ [12] **I** *vtr* **1** (transpercer) to pierce [*corps, surface, armure*]; (crever) to burst [*abcès, tympan*]; **se faire ~ les oreilles** to have one's ears pierced; **avoir les oreilles percées** to have pierced ears; **un cœur percé d'une flèche** a heart pierced by an arrow; **cela me perce le cœur** it breaks my heart; **~ qn de coups de couteau** to stab sb repeatedly with a knife; **il avait la poitrine percée de coups de couteau** he had knife-wounds in the chest; **2** (faire un trou dans) **~ qch, ~ un trou dans qch** gén to make a hole in [*seau, poche*]; (avec une perceuse) to drill ou bore a hole through [*mur, bois*]; (avec une pointe fine) to pierce a hole in [*coquille, couvercle*] ; **~ un coffre-fort** to break open a safe; **ma poche est percée** there's a hole in my pocket; **avoir des souliers percés** to have holes in one's shoes; **3** (créer une ouverture, une voie) to make [*fenêtre, porte*] (**dans** in); to build [*route, canal, tunnel*] (**dans, à travers** through); **percer le front ennemi** to break through the enemy front lines; **un mur percé de meurtrières** a wall with loopholes in it; **4** (traverser) to pierce [*silence, air*]; to break through [*nuages*]; **une lumière perça l'obscurité** a ray of light pierced the darkness; **mes yeux avaient du mal à ~ l'obscurité** I had difficulty in making anything out in the darkness; **5** (découvrir) to penetrate [*secret, mystère*]; to uncover [*complot*]; **~ qn à jour** to see through sb; **6** Physiol **~ ses** or **des dents** to be teething; **il a percé une dent** he's cut a tooth.
II *vi* **1** (apparaître) [*soleil, rayon*] to break through; [*plante*] to come up; [*dent*] to come through; **elle a une dent qui perce** she is cutting a tooth; **2** Mil, Sport to break through; **3** (se révéler) [*agacement, inquiétude*] to show; **laisser ~** to show [*dépit, émotion*]; **rien n'a percé de leur rencontre** nothing has emerged about their meeting; **4** (réussir) [*acteur, écrivain*] to become known, to make it○.

perceuse /pɛʀsøz/ *nf* drill.
■ **~ à percussion** hammer drill.

percevable /pɛʀsəvabl/ *adj* [*taxe*] payable.

percevoir /pɛʀsəvwaʀ/ [5] *vtr* **1** (recouvrer) to collect [*impôt*]; (recevoir) to receive [*pension, droits d'auteur, salaire, loyer*]; **2** Physiol (par les sens) to perceive [*couleur, odeur, bruit*]; to experience [*sensation, douleur*]; to feel [*vibration*]; **3** (par l'esprit) to appreciate [*signification, gravité*]; to become aware of, to perceive [*changement*]; **être perçu comme** to be seen as; **4** (accepter) **être bien/mal perçu** to be well/badly received.

perche /pɛʀʃ/ *nf* **1** (bâton) gén pole; (de téléski) T-bar; (pour micro) (microphone) boom; **2**○ (personne) (**grande**) **~** beanpole○; **3** Sport (activité) pole-vaulting; **4** (poisson) perch; **5** (de trolley bus) current collector; **6** (mesure de longueur) rod, perch.
IDIOMES **tendre la ~ à qn** to throw sb a line.

perché, **~e** /pɛʀʃe/ **I** *pp* ▶ **percher**.
II *pp adj* **1** [*maison, village, antenne, girouette*] perched (**sur** on); **village haut ~ dans les montagnes** village high up in the mountains; **voix haut ~e** high-pitched voice; **2** [*personne*] perched (**sur** on); **~ sur des échasses** standing on stilts; **~e sur de hauts talons** teetering on high heels; **ma valise est ~e en haut de l'armoire** my suitcase is on top of the wardrobe.

percher /pɛʀʃe/ [1] **I** *vtr* **~ qch sur une étagère** to stick sth up on a shelf; **~ un enfant sur un mur** (asseoir) to perch a child on a wall; (mettre debout) to stand a child on a wall.
II *vi* **1** [*oiseau*] (se poser) to perch (**sur** on); (pour la nuit) to roost (**dans** in; **sur** on); **les oiseaux qui perchent** perching birds; **2**○ [*personne*] (loger) to live; (passer la nuit) to kip○ GB, to crash○; **3**○ [*maison, lieu*] to be; **où elle perche, ta maison**○**?** where exactly is your house?
III se percher *vpr* [*oiseau*] to perch (**sur** on); [*personne*] (sur un mur, une échelle) to perch (**sur** on); (sur des échasses) to stand (**sur** on).

percheron, **-onne** /pɛʀʃəʀɔ̃, ɔn/ **I** *adj* **1** ▶ **692** [*population*] of the Perche; **2** [*cheval, jument, race*] Percheron.
II *nm* (cheval) Percheron.

Percheron, **-onne** /pɛʀʃəʀɔ̃, ɔn/ *nm,f* (natif) native of the Perche; (habitant) inhabitant of the Perche.

percheur, **-euse** /pɛʀʃœʀ, øz/ *adj* **oiseau ~** perching bird.

perchiste /pɛʀʃist/ ▶ **510** *nmf* **1** (sauteur) pole-vaulter; **2** Cin, Radio, TV boom operator; **3** (de télésiège) ski-lift attendant; **4** (de cirque) perch artist.

perchlorate /pɛʀklɔʀat/ *nm* perchlorate.

perchman, *pl* **perchmen** /pɛʀʃman, mɛn/ ▶ **510** *nm* controv **1** TV, Cin, Radio boom operator; **2** (de télésiège) ski-lift attendant.

perchoir /pɛʀʃwaʀ/ *nm* **1** (pour se poser) lit, fig perch; (pour la nuit) lit roost; **2**○ Pol Speaker's Chair; **au ~** in the Speaker's chair.

perclus, **~e** /pɛʀkly, yz/ *adj* crippled (**de** with); fig paralyzed (**de** with).

percolateur /pɛʀkɔlatœʀ/ *nm* (espresso) coffee machine.

percussion /pɛʀkysjɔ̃/ *nf* **1** Mus **les ~s** (instruments) the percussion instruments; (dans un orchestre) percussion section; (tambours) drums; **2** Méd, Mil percussion; **3** Phys impact.

percussionniste /pɛʀkysjɔnist/ *nmf* ▶ **510** percussionist.

percutant, **~e** /pɛʀkytɑ̃, ɑ̃t/ *adj* **1** fig [*critique, attaque*] hard-hitting; [*logique, style*] trenchant; [*portrait, démonstration*] striking; [*personne*] forceful; [*slogan*] punchy○; **2** Mus [*son*] percussive; **3** Mil percussion (*épith*).

percuter /pɛʀkyte/ [1] **I** *vtr* **1** Aut [*voiture, chauffeur*] to hit; **2** Tech to strike; **3** Méd to percuss [*organe, articulation*].
II *vi* **~ contre** [*véhicule*] to crash into; [*obus*] to explode against.
III se percuter *vpr* [*véhicules*] to collide.

percuteur /pɛʀkytœʀ/ *nm* (de fusil, mitrailleuse) firing pin; (de fusil de chasse) hammer.

perdant, **~e** /pɛʀdɑ̃, ɑ̃t/ **I** *adj* [*numéro*] losing (*épith*); **être ~** (désavantagé) to have lost out; (ne pas gagner) to have lost; **partir ~** (désavantagé) to be at a disadvantage from the word go; (défaitiste) to have a defeatist attitude from the word go.
II *nm,f* loser.

perdition /pɛʀdisjɔ̃/ *nf* **lieu de ~** den of iniquity; **en ~** [*pays, entreprise*] in trouble (*après n*); [*navire*] in distress (*après n*); **âme en ~** damned soul.

perdre /pɛʀdʀ/ [6] **I** *vtr* **1** (égarer) to lose; **~ un bouton à sa chemise** to lose a button from one's shirt; **~ qch/qn de vue** lit, fig to lose sight of sth/sb; **2** (ne pas conserver) to lose [*argent, ami, emploi, droit, place, tour, vue, voix*]; **~ 10 000 francs sur une vente** to lose 10,000 francs on a sale; **~ la vie/la mémoire** to lose one's life/one's memory; **~ du poids/du sang** to lose weight/blood; **je perds mes cheveux** I'm losing my hair; **j'ai quelques kilos à ~** I need to lose a few kilos; **tu n'as rien/tu as tout à ~** you've got nothing/you've got everything to lose; **~ le soutien/l'estime de qn** to lose sb's support/respect; **j'en ai perdu le sommeil/l'appétit** I've lost sleep/my appetite over it; **~ patience/courage** to lose patience/heart; **~ son calme** to lose one's temper; **il a perdu de son arrogance** he's become more humble; **~ le contrôle de son véhicule** to lose control of one's vehicle; **~ de l'importance** to become less important; **~ toute son importance** to lose all importance; **leurs actions ont perdu 9%** their shares have dropped 9%; **sans ~ le sourire, elle a continué** still smiling, she went on; ▶ **dix**; **3** (se débarrasser de) to shed [*feuilles, fleurs, emplois*]; **ton chien perd ses poils** your dog is moulting GB ou molting US; **ton manteau perd ses poils** your coat is shedding (its) hairs; **4** (voir mourir) to lose [*parents, ami*]; **5** (ne pas remporter) to lose [*élections, bataille, procès*]; **6** (manquer) to miss [*chance*]; **tu n'as rien perdu (en ne venant pas)** you didn't miss anything (by not coming); **tu ne les connais pas? tu n'y perds rien** don't you know them? you're not missing much; **ne pas (vouloir) ~ un mot de ce que qn dit** to hang on sb's every word; **7** (gaspiller) to waste [*journée, mois, années*]; **perdre son temps** to waste one's time; **il n'y a pas de temps à ~** there's no time to lose; **tu as de l'argent à ~!** you've got money to burn!; **elle a du temps à ~** she's got nothing better to do; **sans ~ un instant** immediately; **il est venu sans ~ une minute** he didn't waste any time in coming; **venez sans ~ une minute** ou **un instant** come straight away; **8** (ne plus suivre) to lose; **~ son chemin** or **sa route** to lose one's way, to get lost; **~ la trace d'une bête** to lose the trail of an animal; **9** (mal retenir) **je perds mon bracelet** my bracelet is coming off; **je perds mes chaussures** my shoes are too big; **je perds mon pantalon** my trousers are coming down ou falling down; **10** (ruiner) to bring [sb] down; **cet homme te perdra** that man will be your undoing.

II *vi* **1** (être perdant) to lose; **~ aux élections** to lose the election; **j'y perds** I lose out; **2** (diminuer) **~ en gentillesse/crédibilité** to be less kind/credible; **~ en anglais** to lose ou forget (some of) one's English.

III **se perdre** *vpr* **1** (s'égarer) to get lost; **2** (s'embrouiller) to get mixed up; **toutes ces dates, je m'y perds** all these dates, I'm all mixed up ou confused; **ne vous perdez pas dans des détails** don't get bogged down in details; **je me perdais dans mes explications** I was getting bogged down in my explanation; **3** (être absorbé) **se ~ dans ses pensées** to be lost in thought; **se ~ dans la contemplation de qch** to gaze contemplatively at sth; **4** (disparaître) (cesser d'être vu) to disappear; (cesser d'être entendu) [*cri, appel*] to be lost; **une tradition dont les origines se perdent dans la nuit des temps** a tradition whose origins are lost in the mists of time; **5** (ne pas être utilisé) [*aliment, récolte*] to go to waste; **il y a des claques qui se perdent**○! somebody's looking for a good smack!; **6** (tomber en désuétude) [*coutume, tradition*] to die out; **le sens littéral s'est perdu** the literal meaning has been lost.

IDIOMES **~ la tête** or **la raison** or **l'esprit** (devenir fou) to go out of one's mind; (paniquer) to lose one's head.

perdreau, *pl* **~x** /pɛʀdʀo/ *nm* **1** Zool young partridge; **2** Culin partridge.

perdrix /pɛʀdʀi/ *nf inv* partridge.

perdu, **~e** /pɛʀdy/ **I** *pp* ▶ **perdre**.

II *pp adj* **1** [*bracelet, enfant, liberté, illusion*] lost; **chien ~** stray dog; **balle ~e** stray bullet; **2** [*match, élection*] lost; **tout n'est pas ~** all is not lost; **tout est ~** it's all over; **c'est ~ d'avance** it's hopeless; **3** [*journée, occasion*] wasted; **c'est un samedi de ~** that was a wasted Saturday; **c'est du temps ~** it's a waste of time; **à tes moments ~s** in your spare ou free time; **4** (condamné) **il est ~** (face au danger, en cas de maladie) there's no hope for him; (ruiné) he's ruined, he's had it○; **les fraisiers sont ~s** the strawberry plants have died ou have had it○; **5** (embrouillé) [*personne*] lost; **6** (endommagé) [*récolte, vêtement*] ruined; [*aliment*] spoiled; **7** (vague) **le regard ~ dans le vide** staring into space.

III *adj* **1** (isolé) [*endroit, village*] remote, isolated; **vivre dans un coin ~** to live in a godforsaken spot; **~ au milieu de l'océan/des bois** lost in the middle of the ocean/of the woods; **maison ~e dans l'obscurité/la brume** house shrouded in darkness/mist; **salle ~e au bout d'un couloir** room tucked away at the end of a corridor; **2** (non réutilisable) disposable; (non consigné) non returnable.

IDIOMES **se lancer à corps ~ dans** to throw oneself headlong into; **ce n'est pas ~ pour tout le monde** somebody will do all right out of it; **crier/courir comme un ~** to shout/run like a madman.

perdurer /pɛʀdyʀe/ [1] *vi* liter [*situation, conflit*] to continue; [*sentiment, phénomène*] to endure.

père /pɛʀ/ **I** *nm* **1** (géniteur) father; **devenir ~** to become a father; **il est marié et ~ de deux enfants** he is married with two children; **de ~ en fils** [*transmis, passer*] from father to son; **ils sont banquiers de ~ en fils** they have been bankers for generations; **Dupont ~** Dupont senior; ▶ **avare**; **2** Zool, Biol (d'animal) gén male parent; (de cheval, d'animal domestique) sire; **3** Relig (titre) Father; **le ~ Joseph** Father Joseph; **mon ~** Father; **un ~ dominicain** a dominican friar; **un ~ jésuite** a Jesuit priest; **4** fig (inventeur) father; **le ~ fondateur** the founding father; **5**○ (monsieur) **le ~ Dupont** old○ Dupont.

II **pères** *nmpl* (ancêtres) forefathers.

■ **~ abbé** abbot; **~ adoptif** adoptive father; **~ biologique** biological father; **~ blanc** White Father; **~ de famille** father; **être ~ de famille** to have a family to look after; **placement/valeur de ~ de famille** safe ou low-risk investment; **en bon ~ de famille** as a responsible tenant; **le ~ Noël** Father Christmas GB, Santa Claus; **~ peinard**○ easy-going bloke○ GB ou guy; **~ spirituel** spiritual father; **~ tranquille** mild-mannered fellow; **Père de l'Église** Church Father, Father of the Church.

pérégrinations /peʀegʀinasjɔ̃/ *nfpl* peregrinations, travels.

péremption /peʀɑ̃psjɔ̃/ *nf* **1** Comm **date de ~** use-by date; **2** Jur extinction.

péremptoire /peʀɑ̃ptwaʀ/ *adj* **1** [*ton*] peremptory; **sur un ton ~** peremptorily; **2** [*preuve, argument*] conclusive.

pérenniser /peʀenize/ [1] *vtr* **1** gén to perpetuate; **2** Admin to confirm [sb] in an appointment.

pérennité /peʀenite/ *nf* liter permanence; **croire à la ~ de la paix** to believe that the peace is permanent.

péréquation /peʀekwasjɔ̃/ *nf* **1** Admin (des pensions, salaires) adjustment; Fisc cross-subsidization; **2** Écon adjustment.

perestroïka /peʀɛstʀɔika/ *nf* perestroika.

perfectibilité /pɛʀfɛktibilite/ *nf* perfectibility.

perfectible /pɛʀfɛktibl/ *adj* perfectible.

perfectif, **-ive** /pɛʀfɛktif, iv/ Ling **I** *adj* perfective.

II *nm* perfective.

perfection /pɛʀfɛksjɔ̃/ *nf* perfection; **à la ~** to perfection; **être une ~** [*personne, chose*] to be a gem.

perfectionné, **~e** /pɛʀfɛksjɔne/ **I** *pp* ▶ **perfectionner**.

II *pp adj* [*machine, système*] advanced.

perfectionnement /pɛʀfɛksjɔnmɑ̃/ *nm* improvement (**de** of); **un rapide ~ des moyens de production** a rapid improvement in the means of production.

perfectionner /pɛʀfɛksjɔne/ [1] **I** *vtr* to perfect [*technique, machine*]; to refine [*art*].

II **se perfectionner** *vpr* [*technique, outils*] to improve; **se ~ en allemand** to improve one's German.

perfectionnisme /pɛʀfɛksjɔnism/ *nm* perfectionism.

perfectionniste /pɛʀfɛksjɔnist/ *adj, nmf* perfectionist.

perfecto® /pɛʀfɛkto/ *nm* black biker's jacket.

perfide /pɛʀfid/ **I** *adj* liter [*personne, conseil, propos*] perfidious, treacherous; [*eaux*] treacherous; **et il ajoute, ~...** he adds, treacherously...

II *nmf* liter gén traitor; (amant) faithless lover.

■ **la ~ Albion** perfidious Albion.

perfidement /pɛʀfidmɑ̃/ *adv* liter treacherously.

perfidie /pɛʀfidi/ *nf* liter **1** (caractère) perfidy, treachery; **2** (action) treachery.

perforant, **~e** /pɛʀfɔʀɑ̃, ɑ̃t/ *adj* [*instrument*] perforating; [*ulcère, lésion*] perforated; [*projectile*] armour^GB^-piercing; [*insecte, mollusque*] boring.

perforateur, **-trice** /pɛʀfɔʀatœʀ, tʀis/ **I** *nm,f* Ordinat (employé) punch card operator.

II *nm* Méd perforator.

III **perforatrice** *nf* **1** (pour papier, carton) punch; Ordinat card punch; **2** Tech (outil) drill; (machine) drilling machine.

■ **~ à air comprimé** pneumatic drill.

perforation /pɛʀfɔʀasjɔ̃/ *nf* **1** gén, Méd perforation; **2** Ordinat (opération) punching; (trou) punched hole.

perforer /pɛʀfɔʀe/ [1] *vtr* **1** (percer) gén to pierce; (de trous réguliers) to perforate; Méd to perforate; **ulcère perforé** perforated ulcer; **2** (poinçonner) to punch; **bande perforée** Ordinat punched tape; **carte perforée** Ordinat punch card.

perforeuse /pɛʀfɔʀøz/ *nf* Ordinat **1** (machine) card punch; **2** ▶ **510** (employée) card punch operator.

performance /pɛʀfɔʀmɑ̃s/ *nf* **1** (résultat) result, performance; (record, exploit) achievement; **réaliser une belle ~** to achieve a good result; **améliorer sa ~** to improve one's performance; **c'est une véritable ~** it's a real achievement; **~ d'acteur** acting performance; **2** Écon, Fin (résultats, rendement) **~s** performance ₵; **les ~s des actions sont bonnes** the shares have performed well; **3** Tech (d'avion, de machine) performance; **voiture de haute ~** high-performance car; **4** Psych performance; **test de ~** performance test; **5** Ling performance.

performant, **~e** /pɛʀfɔʀmɑ̃, ɑ̃t/ *adj* **1** Tech [*voiture*] performance (*épith*); [*personne, techniques*] efficient; [*matériel*] high-performance (*épith*); **2** Fin [*action*] performing; [*investissement*] high-return (*épith*); **3** Écon [*entreprise, société*] competitive.

performatif /pɛʀfɔʀmatif/ *nm* performative.

perfusion /pɛʀfyzjɔ̃/ *nm* Méd drip GB, IV US; **sous ~** on a drip GB ou an IV US.

pergola /pɛʀgɔla/ *nf* (tonnelle) pergola.

périanthe /peʀjɑ̃t/ *nm* Bot perianth.

péricarde /peʀikaʀd/ *nm* pericardium.

péricardite /peʀikaʀdit/ ▶ **271** *nf* pericarditis.

péricarpe /peʀikaʀp/ *nm* pericarp.

péricliter /peʀiklite/ [1] *vi* [*affaire, économie*] to be on the decline; **son affaire a périclité** his business collapsed.

péridot /peʀido/ *nm* Minér peridot.

péridural, **~e**, *mpl* **-aux** /peʀidyʀal, o/ **I** *adj* epidural.

II **péridurale** *nf* epidural.

périf○ /peʀif/ *nm* ring road GB, beltway US.

périgée /peʀiʒe/ *nm* perigee.

périglaciaire /peʀiglasjɛʀ/ *adj* periglacial.

Périgord /peʀigɔʀ/ ▶ 692 *nprm* **le ~** Périgord.

périgourdin, **~e** /peʀiguʀdɛ̃, in/ ▶ 692 I *adj* from Périgord.
II *nm* Ling **le ~** the Périgord dialect.

Périgourdin, **~e** /peʀiguʀdɛ̃, in/ ▶ 692 *nprm,f* (natif) native of Périgord; (habitant) inhabitant of Périgord.

Périgueux /peʀigø/ ▶ 857 *npr* Périgueux.

péril /peʀil/ *nm* liter peril littér, danger; **affronter des ~s** to confront danger; **les ~s de la mer** the perils of the sea; **il y a ~ à faire** it is dangerous to do; **au ~ de sa vie** at the risk of one's life; **à ses risques et ~s** at one's own risk; **il n'y a pas ~ en la demeure** what's the hurry?; **mettre en ~** to imperil littér [*démocratie, liberté, indépendance*]; to jeopardize [*avenir, chances*]; to threaten [*survie, patrimoine*]; to endanger [*santé, qualité*].
■ **le ~ jaune** Pol the yellow peril.

périlleusement /peʀijøzmɑ̃/ *adv* liter perilously littér, dangerously.

périlleux, **-euse** /peʀijø, øz/ *adj* liter perilous littér, dangerous.

périmé, **~e** /peʀime/ I *pp* ▶ **périmer**.
II *pp adj* **1** [*passeport, billet*] out-of-date (*épith*); **son passeport est ~** his passport has expired; **2** Comm **ce produit est ~** this product has passed its use-by date; **3** (désuet) [*idée, coutume, institution*] outdated.

périmer /peʀime/ [1] I *vtr* to make [sth] obsolete [*idéal, théorie*].
II **se périmer** *vpr* **1** (expirer) [*billet, passeport*] to expire; **laisser ~ qch** to let sth expire; **2** (se démoder) [*idée, style, meuble*] to become dated; [*institution*] to become old-fashioned; **3** Jur [*instance*] to lapse; **laisser ~ une instance** to allow proceedings to lapse.

périmètre /peʀimɛtʀ/ *nm* **1** Math (contour) perimeter; **2** (espace enclos) area; **à l'intérieur de ce ~** within this area ou zone; **dans le ~ de l'usine/l'école** on the factory/school premises; **dans un ~ de 30 km autour de la centrale nucléaire** within a 30 km radius of the nuclear power station.
■ **~ de sécurité** safety zone.

périnatal, **~e**, *mpl* **~s** /peʀinatal/ *adj* perinatal.

périnatalité /peʀinatalite/ *nf* perinatal period; **programme de ~** perinatal programme[GB].

périnéal, **~e**, *mpl* **-aux** /peʀineal, o/ *adj* perineal.

périnée /peʀine/ *nm* perineum.

période /peʀjɔd/ *nf* **1** gén period; **pendant la ~ d'essai/de Pâques** during the trial/Easter period; **la ~ Brejnev** the Brezhnev era; **elle traverse une ~ Elvis** hum she's going through an Elvis phase; **en ~ de crise** at a time of crisis; **en ~ électorale** at election time; **on est en (pleine) ~ électorale/de crise** we are (right) in the middle of an election/a crisis; **par ~s** periodically; **2** Météo period; (plus court) spell; **3** Mil **~ (d'instruction)** training; **4** Math (de fonction) period; (de fraction) repetend; **5** Sport (de match) half.

périodicité /peʀjɔdisite/ *nf* periodicity.

périodique /peʀjɔdik/ I *adj* **1** Chimie, Phys periodic; **2** Presse periodical; **3** Méd [*fièvre, maladie*] recurring; **4** (hygiénique) [*protection, garniture*] sanitary; **5** Math [*fonction*] periodic; **fraction ~** recurring decimal.
II *nm* periodical.

périodiquement /peʀjɔdikmɑ̃/ *adv* periodically.

périoste /peʀjɔst/ *nm* periosteum.

péripatéticien, **-ienne** /peʀipatetisjɛ̃, ɛn/ I *adj, nm,f* Philos Peripatetic.
II **péripatéticienne** *nf* hum streetwalker.

péripétie /peʀipesi/ *nf* **1** (incident) incident; (événement) event; (aventure) adventure; **après maintes ~s** (incidents) after many ups and downs; (aventures) after many adventures; **les ~s de** (procès, voyage, etc) the eventful moments of; **séjour plein de** or **riche en ~s** eventful stay; **2** Littérat, Théât **la ~** the peripeteia; **les ~s de l'intrigue** the twists and turns of the plot.

périphérie /peʀifeʀi/ *nf* periphery; **à la ~ de la capitale** on the periphery of the capital.

périphérique /peʀifeʀik/ I *adj* **1** gén peripheral; (quartier) outlying (*épith*); **2** Radio **radio ~** *broadcasting station situated outside the territory to which it transmits*.
II *nm* **1** Transp ring road GB, beltway US; **2** Ordinat peripheral; **~ d'entrée/de sortie** input/output device.

périphrase /peʀifʀɑz/ *nf* circumlocution, periphrasis spéc.

périphrastique /peʀifʀastik/ *adj* circumlocutory, periphrastic spéc.

périple /peʀipl/ *nm* gén journey; (en bateau) voyage.

périr /peʀiʀ/ [3] *vi* **1** (mourir) liter to die (**de** of); **faire ~ qn/qch** to kill sb/sth; **il a péri noyé** he was drowned, he drowned; **2** Naut [*navire*] to go down; **3** (disparaître) liter [*œuvre*] to be destroyed; [*culture, liberté, espoir, souvenir*] to perish littér; [*empire, régime*] to fall; **4** (se détériorer) [*denrées*] to perish.

périscolaire /peʀiskɔlɛʀ/ *adj* extracurricular.

périscope /peʀiskɔp/ *nm* periscope.

périscopique /peʀiskɔpik/ *adj* periscopic.

périssable /peʀisabl/ *adj* **1** Comm perishable; **denrées ~s** perishable goods; **2** fig [*œuvre*] ephemeral; [*sentiment, être*] transient.

périssoire /peʀiswaʀ/ *nf* canoe.

péristaltique /peʀistaltik/ *adj* peristaltic.

péristaltisme /peʀistaltism/ *nm* peristalsis.

péristyle /peʀistil/ *nm* peristyle.

Péritel® /peʀitɛl/ *nf* **prise ~** (femelle) scart socket; (mâle) scart plug.

péritoine /peʀitwan/ *nm* peritoneum.

péritonite /peʀitɔnit/ ▶ 271 *nf* peritonitis.

perle /pɛʀl/ I ▶ 193 *adj inv* **(gris) ~** pearl grey GB ou gray US.
II *nf* **1** (d'huître) pearl; (de verre, bois, plastique) bead; **collier de ~s** string of pearls; ▶ **faux**[1]; **2** (être ou chose d'exception) gem; **c'est la ~ des maris/cuisiniers** he's a gem of a husband/cook; **~ de bon sens/d'économie** paragon of common sense/of thrift; **épouser une ~** to marry a wonderful man/woman; **ma femme de ménage est une vraie ~** my cleaning lady is a real treasure; **3**○ (erreur grossière) howler○ (**de** in); **4** liter (goutte) **~ de rosée** dewdrop; **~ de sang** drop(let) of blood; **~ de sueur** bead of sweat.
■ **~ de culture** cultured pearl; **~ fine** real pearl; **~ naturelle** = **~ fine**; **~ rare** fig real treasure; **chercher/trouver la ~ rare** to look for/to find someone special; **~s de bain** Cosmét bath pearls.
IDIOMES **il n'est pas ici pour enfiler des ~s** he's not here to amuse himself; **jeter des ~s aux cochons** or **pourceaux** to cast one's pearls before swine.

perlé, **~e** /pɛʀle/ *adj* **1** [*orge*] pearl (*épith*); [*riz*] polished; **2** Tex **coton ~** pearl cotton; [*laine*] pearlized; **3** Cout [*broderie, vêtement*] beaded; **4** fig **rire ~** rippling laugh.

perler /pɛʀle/ [1] *vi* [*goutte, larme*] to appear; **la sueur perlait sur son front** beads of sweat stood out on his/her brow.

perliculture /pɛʀlikyltyʀ/ *nf* pearl farming.

perlier, **-ière** /pɛʀlje, ɛʀ/ *adj* pearl (*épith*).

perlimpinpin /pɛʀlɛ̃pɛ̃pɛ̃/ *nm* **poudre de ~** hum magical cure.

perlouze◑ /pɛʀluz/ *nf* (perle) pearl.

perm○ /pɛʀm/ *nf* **1** soldiers' slang = **permission 2**; **2** schoolchildren's slang = **permanence I 4**.

permafrost /pɛʀmafʀɔst/ *nm* permafrost.

permanence /pɛʀmanɑ̃s/ I *nf* **1** (absence d'interruption) permanence; (répétition) persistence; **2** (service) **'~ de 8 à 9 heures'** open from 8 am till 9 am; **~ téléphonique** manned line; **être de ~** to be on duty; **assurer** or **tenir une ~** [*personne*] to be on duty; [*député, avocat*] to hold a surgery GB, to have office hours US; **3** (local) permanently manned office; **~ du parti** party offices (*pl*); **4** Scol (salle) (private) study room GB, study hall US; (période) (private) study period.
II **en permanence** *loc adv* **1** (sans interruption) permanently; **siéger en ~** to be in permanent session; **ouvert en ~** open around the clock; **2** (très fréquemment) constantly; **donner des informations en ~** [*chaine, radio*] to give continuous ou round-the-clock news coverage.

permanent, **~e** /pɛʀmanɑ̃, ɑ̃t/ I *adj* **1** (qui reste en fonction) [*bureau, personnel, exposition, assemblée*] permanent; [*comité, armée*] standing (*épith*); **2** (qui se maintient) [*tension, contact, effort, danger*] constant; [*spectacle, formation*] continuous; [*invalidité, incapacité*] permanent; **cinéma ~ de 13 à 23 heures** continuous performances from 1 pm to 11 pm; **de façon ~e** [*séjourner*] permanently; [*augmenter, se succéder*] constantly; **3** Phys [*aimant, gaz*] permanent; **4** Cout [*pli, plissé*] permanent.
II *nm,f* (employé) permanent employee; (membre) permanent member.
III **permanente** *nf* perm; **~e à chaud/à froid** hot/cold perm; **faire une ~e à qn** to give sb a perm; **se faire faire une ~e** to have one's hair permed.

permanenté, **~e** /pɛʀmanɑ̃te/ *adj* permed.

permanenter /pɛʀmanɑ̃te/ [1] *vtr* to perm [*cheveux*]; **se faire ~** to have a perm; **cheveux permanentés** permed hair.

permanganate /pɛʀmɑ̃ganat/ *nm* permanganate.

perméabilité /pɛʀmeabilite/ *nf* **1** (de matière) permeability (**à** to); **2** fig (de personne) susceptibility (**à** to); (de frontière, marché) openness; **à cause de la ~ des frontières** because the frontiers are easily crossed.

perméable /pɛʀmeabl/ *adj* **1** (à l'air, l'eau) permeable (**à** to); **2** fig [*frontière*] easily crossed; [*marché*] easily penetrated; **être ~ à une influence** to be susceptible to an influence.

permettre /pɛʀmɛtʀ/ [60] I *vtr* **1** (donner l'autorisation) to allow; **je ne le permettrai pas** I won't allow it; **je ne permets pas qu'on dise du mal d'elle** I won't hear a word against her; **~ à qn de faire qch** to allow sb to do sth, to give sb permission to do sth; **il nous a permis de sortir ce soir** he allowed us ou gave us permission to go out tonight; **est-ce que vous savez s'il est permis de fumer/prendre des photos ici?** do you know if smoking is allowed here?/if you're allowed to take photos here?; **permettez-moi de vous accompagner** allow me to accompany you; **permets-moi de te dire que** let me tell you that; **permettez-moi d'ajouter que** I would like to add that; **vous permettez que j'ouvre la fenêtre /que je fume?** do you mind if I open the window/if I smoke?; **(vous) permettez! j'étais là avant!/je n'ai pas dit cela!** excuse me! I was here first!/I didn't say that!; **ça, permettez-moi d'en douter** I'm sorry, I have my doubts about that; **c'est pas permis**○ **d'être aussi pingre/hypocrite!** how can anyone be so stingy/such a hypocrite?; **il est pingre/menteur comme c'est pas permis**○ he's incredibly stingy/an incredible liar; **il est permis de se poser des questions** one is entitled to wonder; **tous les espoirs sont permis** there is every hope of success; **2** (donner les moyens) **des mesures pour ~ une reprise rapide de l'économie/la création de nouveaux emplois** measures to ensure rapid economic recovery/the creation of new jobs; **ça permet une meilleure tenue de route** it ensures ou makes for better road-holding; **si le temps le permet** weather permitting; **dès que les circonstances le permettront** as soon as circumstances allow ou permit; **je viendrai si mon emploi du temps (me) le permet** I'll come if my schedule allows ou permits; **ce procédé permet de consommer moins d'énergie** this system makes it possible to use less energy; **~ à qn de faire** to allow ou enable sb to do, to give sb the opportunity to do; **ça m'a permis de travailler plus longtemps/d'économiser** it allowed ou enabled me ou gave me the opportunity to work longer/to save money; **un accord qui devrait ~ à la France d'exporter davantage** an agreement that should enable ou allow France to export more; **leurs moyens ne le leur permettent pas** they can't afford it; **ma santé ne me permet pas de faire du sport** my health prevents me from doing any sport; **autant qu'il est permis d'en juger** as far as one can tell.

II **se permettre** *vpr* **je peux me ~ ce genre de plaisanterie avec lui** I can get away with telling him that kind of joke; **il se permet bien des choses** or **bien des familiarités avec elle** he takes a lot of liberties with her; **puis-je me ~ une remarque?** might I say something?; **se ~ de faire** to take the liberty of doing; **il s'est permis d'entrer sans frapper/d'utiliser mon ordinateur** he took the liberty of coming in without knocking/of using my computer; **je me suis permis de lui faire la remarque/de lui dire ce que je pensais** I ventured to point it out to him/to tell him what I thought, I took the liberty of pointing it out to him/of telling him what I thought; **tu ne peux pas te ~ d'être en retard à ton rendez-vous** you can't afford to be late for your appointment; **je ne peux pas me ~ d'acheter une nouvelle voiture** I can't afford to buy a new car; **puis-je me ~ de vous offrir un verre?** would you care for a drink?; **puis-je me ~ de vous raccompagner?** fml might I be allowed to escort you home?; **'je me permets de vous écrire au sujet de...'** 'I'm writing to you about...'

permien, **-ienne** /pɛʀmjɛ̃, ɛn/ I *adj* Permian.
II *nm* Permian.

permis, **~e** /pɛʀmi, iz/ I *pp* ▶ **permettre**.
II *pp adj* [*limites*] permitted.
III *nm inv* permit, licence GB, license US.
■ **~ de chasse** hunting permit; **~ de conduire** (document) driver's licence[GB]; (examen) driving test; **~ de construire** planning permission GB, building permit US; **~ de démolition** demolition consent; **~ d'inhumer** burial certificate; **~ moto** motorcycle licence[GB]; **~ de navigation** certificate of seaworthiness; **~ de pêche** fishing permit; **~ poids lourd** heavy goods vehicle licence GB, HGV licence GB, articulated-vehicle license US; **~ de port d'armes** gun licence[GB]; **~ de séjour** Jur residence permit; **~ de travail** Jur work permit.

permissif, **-ive** /pɛʀmisif, iv/ *adj* permissive.

permission /pɛʀmisjɔ̃/ *nf* **1** gén permission; **demander la ~** to ask permission; **demander à qn la ~ de faire** to ask sb's permission to do; **accorder à qn la ~ de faire** to grant sb permission to do; **je leur ai donné la ~ de le faire** I gave them permission to do it; **avec votre ~** with your permission; **avoir la ~ de faire** to have permission to do; **avoir la ~ de qn pour faire** to have sb's permission to do; **il a ma ~** he has my permission; **2** Mil leave ₵; **partir en ~** to go on leave; **avoir quelques jours de ~** to have a few days' leave; **j'ai pris une ~ de dix jours** I took ten days' leave; **les ~s sont supprimées** all leave has been cancelled[GB].
■ **la ~ de minuit** permission to stay out late.

permissionnaire /pɛʀmisjɔnɛʀ/ *nm* soldier on leave.

permissivité /pɛʀmisivite/ *nf* permissiveness.

permutabilité /pɛʀmytabilite/ *nf* Math permutability; gén interchangeability.

permutable /pɛʀmytabl/ *adj* **1** gén [*élément, fonction*] interchangeable (**avec** with); [*emploi*] which can be switched (*épith, après n*) (**avec** with); [*employé*] who can be switched (*épith, après n*) (**avec** with); **2** Math permutable.

permutation /pɛʀmytasjɔ̃/ *nf* **1** Jeux, Math permutation; **2** Admin, Mil (échange de poste) exchange of posts.

permuter /pɛʀmyte/ [1] I *vtr* **1** gén to switch [sth] around [*lettres, étiquettes*]; **2** Sci, Math to permute.
II *vi* [*personnes*] to exchange posts (**avec** with).

pernicieusement /pɛʀnisjøzmɑ̃/ *adv* perniciously; **conseiller ~** to give pernicious advice.

pernicieux, **-ieuse** /pɛʀnisjø, øz/ *adj* pernicious.

péroné /peʀɔne/ *nm* fibula.

péroniste /peʀɔnist/ *adj, nmf* Peronist.

péronnelle† /peʀɔnɛl/ *nf* pej flibbertigibbet○ péj.

péroraison /peʀɔʀɛzɔ̃/ *nf* **1** (conclusion) (de discours) peroration; (de cantate) finale; **2** (discours ennuyeux) pej long-winded speech.

pérorer /peʀɔʀe/ [1] *vi* pej to hold forth péj.

Pérou /peʀu/ ▶ **321** *nprm* Peru.
IDIOMES **ce n'est pas le ~** it's not a fortune.

Pérouse /peʀuz/ ▶ **857** *npr* Perugia.

peroxyde /peʀɔksid/ *nm* peroxide; **~ d'hydrogène** hydrogen peroxide.

perpendiculaire /pɛʀpɑ̃dikylɛʀ/ *adj, nf* perpendicular (**à** to).

perpendiculairement /pɛʀpɑ̃dikylɛʀmɑ̃/ *adv* **1** (à angle droit) at right angles (**à** to); **2** (verticalement) vertically.

perpète○ /pɛʀpɛt/ *nf* **être condamné à ~**, **avoir la ~** prisoners' slang to get life○; **habiter à ~** to live miles away; **jusqu'à ~** forever and a day○.

perpétration /pɛʀpetʀasjɔ̃/ *nf* perpetration.

perpétrer /pɛʀpetʀe/ [14] *vtr* to perpetrate.

perpette = **perpète**.

perpétuation /pɛʀpetɥasjɔ̃/ *nf* perpetuation.

perpétuel, **-elle** /pɛʀpetɥɛl/ *adj* **1** gén perpetual; **2** (à vie) [*poste, secrétaire*] permanent; **réclusion perpétuelle** life imprisonment.

perpétuellement /pɛʀpetɥɛlmɑ̃/ *adv* constantly, perpetually.

perpétuer /pɛʀpetɥe/ [1] I *vtr* to perpetuate [*espèce, souvenir*].
II **se perpétuer** *vpr* **1** [*espèce*] to perpetuate itself; **2** [*usages, culture*] to be perpetuated.

perpétuité /pɛʀpetɥite/ *nf* (durée) perpetuity; (perpétuation) perpetuation; **à ~** Jur [*réclusion*] life; Admin [*concession*] in perpetuity (*après n*).

Perpignan /pɛʀpiɲɑ̃/ ▶ **857** *npr* Perpignan.

perpignanais, **~e** /pɛʀpiɲanɛ, ɛz/ ▶ **857** *adj* of Perpignan.

Perpignanais, **~e** /pɛʀpiɲanɛ, ɛz/ *nm,f* (natif) native of Perpignan; (habitant) inhabitant of Perpignan.

perplexe /pɛʀplɛks/ *adj* perplexed, baffled; **rendre ~** to perplex.

perplexité /pɛʀplɛksite/ *nf* perplexity, confusion; **jeter qn dans la ~** to throw sb into confusion; **je suis dans une grande ~** I'm totally perplexed.

perquisition /pɛʀkizisjɔ̃/ *nf* search; **effectuer une ~ au domicile de qn** to carry out a search of ou at sb's house.

perquisitionner /pɛʀkizisjɔne/ [1] I *vtr* to search [*maison*].
II *vi* to (carry out a) search; **la police perquisitionne à leur domicile** the police are searching their home.

perron /pɛʀɔ̃/ *nm* flight of steps.

perroquet /pɛʀɔkɛ/ *nm* **1** Zool parrot; **tout répéter comme un ~** to repeat everything parrot-fashion; **2** Naut topgallant sail; **petit/grand ~** fore/main topgallant sail; **3** (apéritif) *pastis with crème de menthe*; **4** (portemanteau) hat and coat stand.
■ **~ de mer** (oiseau) puffin; (poisson) parrotfish.

perruche /peʀyʃ/ *nf* **1** Zool budgerigar GB, budgie○ GB, parakeet US; **2** Naut mizzen topgallant sail.
■ **~ à collier** ring-necked parakeet; **~ ondulée** budgerigar GB, parakeet US.

perruque /peʀyk/ *nf* **1** (postiche) wig; **2** Pêche tangle (*of fishing line*); **3**○ (travail) **faire de la ~** to do one's own work on company time.

perruquier /peʀykje/ ▶ **510** *nm* wigmaker.

pers /pɛʀ/ liter *adj m* blue-green.

persan, **~e** /pɛʀsɑ̃, an/ I *adj* [*chat, tapis*] Persian.
II *nm* **1** ▶ **462** Ling Persian; **2** Zool Persian (cat).

Persan, **~e** /pɛʀsɑ̃, an/ *nm,f* Persian.

perse /pɛʀs/ *adj* Persian.

Perse /pɛʀs/ I *nmf* Persian.
II *nprf* Hist Persia.

persécuté, **~e** /pɛʀsekyte/ *nm,f* **1** lit victim of persecution; **2** Psych person with a persecution complex.

persécuter /pɛʀsekyte/ [1] *vtr* to persecute [*peuple, chrétiens*]; **se sentir persécuté** to feel persecuted.

persécuteur, **-trice** /pɛʀsekytœʀ, tʀis/ *nm,f* persecutor.

persécution /pɛʀsekysjɔ̃/ *nf* persecution; **manie/complexe de ~** persecution mania/complex.

Persée /pɛʀse/ *npr* Perseus.

persévérance /pɛʀseveʀɑ̃s/ *nf* perseverance (**à faire** in doing; **dans qch** in sth); **avec ~** with determination.

persévérant, **~e** /pɛʀseveʀɑ̃, ɑ̃t/ *adj* [*personne*] persevering (*épith*); **de façon ~e** with determination; **être ~ dans l'effort** to be determined in one's efforts; **tu n'es pas très ~!** you give up too easily!

persévérer /pɛʀseveʀe/ [14] *vi* **1** [*personne, équipe*] to persevere (**dans qch** in sth); **2** liter (persister) [*fièvre*] to persist.

persienne /pɛʀsjɛn/ *nf* (louvred[GB]) shutter.

persiflage /pɛʀsiflaʒ/ *nm* mockery, persiflage.

persifler /pɛʀsifle/ [1] *vtr, vi* to mock.

persifleur, **-euse** /pɛʀsiflœʀ, øz/ liter I *adj* [*ton, propos*] mocking.
II *nm,f* disparager.

persil /pɛʀsi(l)/ *nm* parsley; **~ frisé/commun** curly-leaved/common parsley; **~ haché** chopped parsley; **un brin de ~** a sprig of parsley.

persillade /pɛʀsijad/ *nf* parsley and garlic garnish.

persillé, **~e** /pɛʀsije/ *adj* [*carottes, pommes de terre*] garnished with chopped parsley (*après n*); **fromage ~** blue cheese; **viande ~e** marbled meat.

persique /pɛʀsik/ *adj* Persian; **le golfe Persique** the Persian Gulf.

persistance /pɛʀsistɑ̃s/ *nf* persistence; **ta ~ à vouloir faire** your persistent attempts to do; **avec ~** persistently; **ta ~ à nier l'évidence** or **les faits** your persistent denial of the facts.
■ **~ optique** Physiol persistence of vision.

persistant, **~e** /pɛʀsistɑ̃, ɑ̃t/ *adj* **1** gén [*chaleur, problème, désaccord*] continuing; [*odeur, neige*] lingering; [*toux, symptôme*] persistent; **2** Bot [*calice*] persistent; **arbre à feuilles ~es** evergreen.

persister /pɛʀsiste/ [1] *vi* **1** (durer) [*symptôme, douleur*] to persist; [*mauvais temps, inflation, pénurie*] to continue; [*doute, problème*] to remain; [*odeur*] to linger; **le mauvais temps persistera sur la Bretagne** the bad weather will continue in Brittany; **2** (s'obstiner) **~ dans son erreur/sa tentative** to persist in one's error/attempt; **~ dans son refus** or **à refuser** to continue to refuse; **je persiste à croire que...** I still believe that...; **~ dans le mensonge** to lie persistently; **~ dans son opinion** to stick to one's opinion; **ils persistent dans leur intention de sortir par ce mauvais temps** they still insist on going out in this bad weather; **je persiste à vouloir les embaucher** I still insist on employing them.
IDIOMES **il persiste et signe**○ he's sticking to his guns○.

persona /pɛʀsɔna/ *nf* **~ grata/non grata** persona grata/non grata.

personnage /pɛʀsɔnaʒ/ *nm* **1** (personne fictive) also Cin, Théât character; **les ~s d'un roman/d'une pièce** the characters in a novel/in a play; **les ~s de Zola** Zola's characters; **un rôle de ~ secondaire** the role of a secondary character; **la liste des ~s** the cast list, the dramatis personae (*pl*) Théât; **se mettre dans la peau de son ~** to get inside one's part ou character; **2** (personne représentée) figure; **les ~s d'une crèche de Noël** the figures in a Christmas crib GB ou manger; **un ~ allégorique qui représente le temps** an allegorical figure representing time; **3** (personne importante) figure; **un ~ influent** an influential figure; **un ~ important des sciences/du XXe siècle** a prominent figure in science/in the 20th century; **un ~ haut placé** a high-placed person; **les ~s importants de la ville** the local dignitaries; **un ~ célèbre** a celebrity; **4** (personne curieuse) character; **c'est un drôle de ~** he's an odd character; **c'est un ~ extraordinaire/singulier** he's an amazing/a strange character; **5** (personne affectée) image; **cet air distant fait partie de son ~** this air of aloofness is part of his image; **se composer un ~** to adopt a persona.

personnalisation /pɛʀsɔnalizasjɔ̃/ *nf* personalization.

personnaliser /pɛʀsɔnalize/ [1] *vtr* **1** (donner une note personnelle) to add a personal touch to [*maison, uniforme*]; to customize [*voiture*]; **2** (adapter) **~ un contrat** to tailor a contract to the individual; **offre/lettre personnalisée** personal offer/letter.

personnalité /pɛʀsɔnalite/ *nf* **1** Psych personality; **~ effacée** retiring personality; **forte ~** strong personality; **2** (personne influente) important person.

personne[1] /pɛʀsɔn/ *pron indéf* **1** (nul) **~ n'est parfait** nobody's ou no-one's perfect; **~ ne te dérangera** nobody ou no-one will disturb you; **je n'accuse ~** I'm not accusing anybody ou anyone; **~ n'a vu mon stylo?** has anybody seen my pen?; **il n'y avait presque/jamais ~** there was hardly/never anybody there; **tu n'as oublié ~?** you haven't forgotten anybody, have you?; **plus ~ ne les a vus** nobody else saw them; **ni lui ni ~ n'est satisfait** neither he nor anyone else is satisfied; **je n'ai parlé à ~** I didn't talk to anybody ou anyone; **je n'en ai parlé à ~ d'autre que toi** I told nobody ou no-one but you; **~ d'autre que lui ne pourrait le faire** nobody but him could do it; **tu ne connais ~ d'autre?** don't you know anybody else?; **n 'y a-t-il ~ ici qui parle l'anglais?** is there no-one here who speaks English?; **il n'y a ~?** (dans le lieu) is anybody there?; (depuis la porte) is anybody in?; **'qui a sonné/parlé?'—'~'** 'who rang/spoke?'—'no-one'; **que ~ ne sorte!** nobody leave!; **que ~ n'aille croire que** don't let anybody think that; **~ de sensé/sérieux ne ferait** no sensible/serious person would do; **ce n'est un mystère pour ~** it's no mystery; **je n'y suis pour ~** if anybody asks for me, I'm not here; **il n'y est pour ~** he's not in for anyone; **quand il s'agit de faire le ménage, il n'y a plus ~**○ when it comes to doing the housework, there's nobody around; **dès qu'on parle de travail, il n'y a plus ~**○ as soon as you mention work, everybody disappears; **2** (quiconque) anyone, anybody; **faire qch comme** or **mieux que ~** to do sth better than anyone ou anybody (else); **sans ~ pour m'aider** without anyone ou anybody to help me; **avant que ~ (ne) réagisse** before anyone had time to react; **~ de blessé?** anyone ou anybody hurt?

personne[2] /pɛʀsɔn/ *nf* **1** (individu) person; **la ~ de votre choix** the person of your choice; **la ~ de la réception** the person at reception; **cinquante francs par ~** fifty francs per person; **un groupe de dix ~s** a group of ten people; **les ~s concernées** those concerned; **50% des ~s interrogées** 50% of those interviewed; **un voyage pour deux ~s** a trip for two; **logement pour ~ seule** accommodation for a single person; **lit/chambre d'une ~** single bed/room; **la ~ aimée** the loved one; **une ~ âgée** an elderly person; **les ~s âgées** the elderly; **il était accompagné d'une charmante jeune ~** he was accompanied by a charming young lady; **en cas d'empoisonnement, si la ~ ne respire plus** in case of poisoning, if the person has stopped breathing; **si une ~ tombe à l'eau** if someone falls into the water; **si une ~ te demande son chemin** if anybody asks you the way; **une ~ de confiance** someone trustworthy; **toute ~ désirant des informations supplémentaires** anyone wishing further information; **il doit y avoir erreur sur la ~** it must be the wrong person ou a case of mistaken identity; **il y avait erreur sur la ~ de leur client** their client was a victim of mistaken identity; ▶ **grand**; **2** (individu en lui-même) **satisfait/content de sa (petite) ~** satisfied/pleased with oneself; **bien fait de sa ~** good-looking; **trouver un allié en la ~ de mon frère/du ministre** to find an ally in the person of my brother/of the minister; **c'est bien suffisant pour mon humble** ou **ma modeste ~** it's quite enough for my humble self; **le respect de/les droits de la ~ (humaine)** respect for/the rights of the individual; **la ~ et la pensée de Confucius** Confucius, the man and his thought; **j'apprécie en lui le poète, pas la ~** I like him as a poet, not as a person; **toute sa ~ inspirait le respect** his/her whole being inspired respect; **le Christ en tant que ~** Christ as a person; **le ministre en ~** the minister in person; **il s'en occupe en ~** he's dealing with it personally; **c'est la cupidité en ~** he/she is greed personified; **3** Ling person; **troisième ~ du pluriel** third person plural; **écrit à la première ~** written in the first person.
■ **~ à charge** Jur dependant; **~ civile** Jur artificial person; **~ déplacée** Pol displaced person; **~ morale** Jur = **~ civile**; **~ physique** Jur natural person.

personnel, **-elle** /pɛʀsɔnɛl/ **I** *adj* **1** (individuel) [*ami, effets, ordinateur*] personal; [*engagement, papiers*] private; **fortune personnelle** private ou personal fortune; **pour son usage ~** for one's personal ou private use; **adresse personnelle** home ou private address; **c'est urgent et ~** it's urgent and confidential; **'personnelle'** (sur une lettre) 'private'; **'strictement personnelle'** (sur une lettre) 'private and confidential'; **sur le plan ~** on a personal level; **2** (original) [*style, langage*] individual; **il écrit de façon personnelle** he writes in an individual way; **3** (égoïste) [*enfant, joueur*] selfish; **avoir un jeu ~** to play a selfish game; **4** Ling [*forme, pronom, verbe*] personal; [*mode*] finite.
II *nm* (d'industrie, usine) workforce; (de compagnie, d'administration) employees (*pl*), personnel; (d'hôpital, hôtel, ambassade, école) staff; **l'usine a un ~ de 40 personnes** the factory has a payroll ou workforce of 40; **nous manquons de ~** we are understaffed; **le ~ militaire/civil** the military/civilian personnel; **le ~ en civil/en tenue** plain-clothes/uniformed staff; **service/directeur du ~** personnel department/manager; **~ navigant/au sol** Aviat flight/ground personnel; **~ de santé des armées** army medical personnel; **~ enseignant** teaching staff; **le ~ féminin** female staff ou employees.

personnellement /pɛʀsɔnɛlmɑ̃/ *adv* personally; **il nous a reçus ~** he received us in person.

personnification /pɛʀsɔnifikasjɔ̃/ *nf* personification (**de** of).

personnifier /pɛʀsɔnifje/ [2] *vtr* to personify.

perspective /pɛʀspɛktiv/ *nf* **1** Archit, Art perspective; **en ~** [*dessin*] perspective (*épith*); [*dessiner*] in perspective; **2** (vue) view; **3** (optique) perspective, angle; **dans une ~ historique/sociologique** from a historical/sociological angle; **4** (probabilité) prospect (**de** of; **de faire** of doing); **~s d'avenir/de carrière** future/career prospects (*pl*); **dans cette ~** at this prospect; **dans une ~ européenne** in terms of European prospects; **en ~** [*réjouissances, problèmes*] in prospect.
■ **~ aérienne** aerial perspective; **~ cavalière** isometric projection; **~ démographique** demographic projection.

perspicace /pɛʀspikas/ *adj* perceptive, perspicacious.

perspicacité /pɛʀspikasite/ *nf* insight, perspicacity; **manquer de ~** to lack insight.

persuader /pɛʀsɥade/ [1] **I** *vtr* to persuade (**de** of; **de faire** to do; **que** that); **se laisser ~** to let oneself be persuaded.
II se persuader *vpr* to persuade oneself (**de** of; **que** that).

persuasif, **-ive** /pɛʀsɥazif, iv/ *adj* persuasive.

persuasion /pɛʀsɥazjɔ̃/ *nf* persuasion.

perte /pɛʀt/ **I** *nf* **1** (fait d'égarer) loss, losing; **la ~ d'une bague** losing a ring, the loss of a ring; **2** (fait de ne pouvoir garder) loss; **~ de contrôle** loss of control; **~s d'emploi** job losses; **~ de vitesse** Aviat loss of speed; **être en ~ de vitesse** lit to be losing speed; fig to be slowing down, to be running out of steam; **la ~** or **les ~s de poids/de mémoire** weight/memory loss; **avoir des ~s de sang** Méd to bleed; **la plaine s'étend à ~ de vue** the plain stretches as far as the eye can see; **3** Fin (somme perdue, fait de perdre) loss; **~ d'argent** financial loss; **vendre à ~** to sell at a loss; **profits et ~s** profits and losses; **subir des ~s importantes** to lose large sums of money, to sustain heavy losses; **4** (fait d'être perdant) (de match, bataille, d'élection) loss; **5** (disparition) loss; (mort) loss; **la ~ de trois avions** the loss of three aircraft; **la ~ d'un être cher** the loss of a loved one; **ce n'est pas une (grande** or **grosse) ~** that's not much of a loss; **6** (gaspillage) waste; **c'est une ~ de temps** it's a waste of time; **réduire les ~s de temps** to cut down on time-wasting; **~ d'énergie** (de personne) waste of energy; (de machine, d'installation) energy loss; **~ de chaleur** heat loss; **ce serait en pure ~** (inutile) it would be futile; **agir en pure ~** to do something that is a complete waste of time; **le crabe c'est bon, mais il y a de la ~** crab is nice, but there's a lot of waste; **7** (ruine) ruin; **cela causera sa ~** it will be his/her ruin; **courir** or **aller à sa (propre) ~** to be on the road to ruin, to be heading ou riding for a fall; **vouloir la ~ de qn** to try to bring about sb's downfall; **jurer la**

~ de qn to vow to bring about sb's downfall.

II **pertes** *nfpl* losses; **de lourdes ~s** heavy losses; **causer des ~s en vies humaines** to take a heavy toll in human life.

■ **~ de connaissance** loss of consciousness, blackout; **~ sèche** Fin dead loss; **~s blanches** vaginal discharge ¢, leucorrhea ¢ spéc; **~s séminales** involuntary emission ¢ of semen, spermatorrhea ¢ spéc.

pertinemment /pɛʀtinamɑ̃/ *adv* **1** (avec justesse) pertinently; **2** (parfaitement) [*savoir*] perfectly well.

pertinence /pɛʀtinɑ̃s/ *nf* pertinence; **avec ~** pertinently.

pertinent, **~e** /pɛʀtinɑ̃, ɑ̃t/ *adj* **1** (à-propos) [*question, remarque*] pertinent; **2** Ling **un trait ~** a relevant feature.

perturbant, **~e** /pɛʀtyʀbɑ̃, ɑ̃t/ *adj* [*nouvelle, phénomène*] disturbing.

perturbateur, **-trice** /pɛʀtyʀbatœʀ, tʀis/ I *adj* [*élément, rôle*] disruptive.

II *nm,f* troublemaker.

perturbation /pɛʀtyʀbasjɔ̃/ *nf* **1** (d'un service, du marché) disruption; **légères ~s sur les vols intérieurs** slight disruption to domestic flights; **2** Météo disturbance; **3** (agitation) (politique) upheaval; (sociale) disturbance.

perturber /pɛʀtyʀbe/ [1] *vtr* **1** (dérégler) to disrupt [*trafic, marché, études*]; to interfere with [*sommeil, développement*]; **cela m'a un peu perturbé** it has unsettled me a bit; **2** (inquiéter) to perturb sout; **cela ne m'a pas perturbé** it didn't bother me; **être perturbé**○ to be very disturbed; **3** (semer le trouble) to disrupt [*réunion, ordre, cérémonie*].

péruvien, **-ienne** /peʀyvjɛ̃, ɛn/ ▶537 *adj* Peruvian.

Péruvien, **-ienne** /peʀyvjɛ̃, ɛn/ ▶537 *nm,f* Peruvian.

pervenche /pɛʀvɑ̃ʃ/ I ▶193 *adj inv* (**bleu**) ~ periwinkle blue.

II *nf* **1** (fleur) periwinkle; **2**○ (contractuelle) (female) traffic warden GB, meter maid○ US.

pervers, **~e** /pɛʀvɛʀ, ɛʀs/ I *adj* **1** (méchant) wicked; **2** (dépravé) perverted; **3** (négatif) [*effet, conséquence*] pernicious.

II *nm,f* pervert.

perversion /pɛʀvɛʀsjɔ̃/ *nf* perversion (**de** of).

perversité /pɛʀvɛʀsite/ *nf* perversity.

pervertir /pɛʀvɛʀtiʀ/ [3] *vtr* to corrupt.

pesage /pəzaʒ/ *nm* **1** (d'objet) weighing; **2** Sport (de sportif) weigh-in; (salle) weighing room; **3** Turf (de jockey) weigh-in; (enceinte) enclosure.

pesamment /pəzamɑ̃/ *adv* [*chargé, tomber*] heavily; [*marcher, se déplacer*] with a heavy step; **monter ~ un escalier** to go upstairs with a heavy tread.

pesant, **~e** /pəzɑ̃, ɑ̃t/ *adj* **1** (lourd) [*objet*] heavy; [*pas, allure, démarche*] heavy; **d'un pas ~** with a heavy step; **2** (pénible) [*hiérarchie, réglementation*] cumbersome, unwieldy; [*contrainte, obligation*] burdensome; [*atmosphère, silence*] oppressive; [*joug, mainmise, incertitude*] heavy; **3** (massif) [*architecture, monument, personne*] ungainly; **4** (ennuyeux) [*personne, écrivain*] dull, ponderous; [*style*] heavy.

IDIOMES **valoir son ~ d'or** to be worth its weight in gold.

pesanteur /pəzɑ̃tœʀ/ *nf* **1** (lourdeur) (de style) heaviness; (d'esprit) dullness; (de bureaucratie, d'administration, de régime) inertia ¢; **les ~s administratives** administrative inertia; **2** Phys gravity; **l'action de la ~** the pull of gravity; **défier les lois de la ~** [*acrobate*] to defy the laws of gravity.

pèse-acide, *pl* **~s** /pɛzasid/ *nm* acidimeter.

pèse-alcool /pɛzalkɔl/ *nm inv* alcoholometer.

pèse-bébé, *pl* **~s** /pɛzbebe/ *nm* baby scales (*pl*); **trois ~s** three pairs of baby scales.

pesée /pəze/ ▶620 *nf* **1** (opération) weighing; **~ de précision** precision weighing; **de quand date votre dernière ~?** when were you last weighed?; **2** (poussée) shove; **3** (quantité) weight; **une ~ de 50 kg** a weight of 50 kg, a 50 kg weight.

pèse-lettre, *pl* **~s** /pɛzlɛtʀ/ *nm* letter scales (*pl*).

pèse-personne, *pl* **~s** /pɛzpɛʀsɔn/ *nm* bathroom scales (*pl*); **j'ai acheté un deuxième ~ pour les enfants** I bought a second pair of bathroom scales for the children.

peser /pəze/ [16] ▶620 I *vtr* **1** (mesurer le poids de) to weigh [*personne, objet*]; **2** (apprécier) to weigh up; **~ le pour et le contre** to weigh up the pros and cons; **~ ses mots** or **paroles** to choose one's words carefully; **tout bien pesé** all things considered.

II *vi* **1** (avoir un poids) to weigh; (être lourd) to be heavy; **combien pèses-tu?** how much do you weigh?; **je pèse 70 kg** I weigh 70 kg; **~ lourd** to weigh a lot; **cette valise pèse trop** this suitcase is too heavy; **elle ne pèse rien!** she doesn't weigh a thing!; **ça pèse des tonnes!** fig it weighs a ton!; **2** (avoir de l'importance) to carry weight; **ceux qui pèsent dans la vie publique** those who carry weight in public life; **leurs voix ne pèseront pas lourd dans la balance** their votes won't carry much weight; **~ dans/sur une décision** to have a decisive influence in/on a decision; **3** (faire sentir son poids) **~ sur** [*menaces, soupçons, risques, incertitudes*] to hang over [*personne, projet*]; [*impôts, charges, contraintes*] to weigh [sb/sth] down [*personne, pays*]; [*personne, décision*] to influence (greatly) [*politique, stratégie, situation*]; **~ lourd sur** to weigh heavily on; **faire ~ un danger sur qn/un pays** to be a danger to sb/a country; **faire ~ un risque sur** to threaten; **4** (être pénible) **la solitude me/leur pèse** loneliness weighs heavily on me/them; **5** (exercer une poussée) **~ contre/sur** to push against/ down on.

III **se peser** *vpr* to weigh oneself.

IDIOMES **envoyez, c'est pesé**○! off it goes.

pèse-sirop, *pl* **~s** /pɛzsiʀo/ *nm* saccharometer GB, saccharimeter US.

peseta /pezeta/ ▶46 *nf* peseta.

peson /pəzɔ̃/ *nm* spring balance.

pessaire /pesɛʀ/ *nm* pessary.

pessimisme /pesimism/ *nm* pessimism.

pessimiste /pesimist/ I *adj* pessimistic.

II *nmf* pessimist.

peste /pɛst/ I *nf* **1** ▶271 Méd plague; **2**○ (personne insupportable) pest○; **espèce de petite ~!** you little pest!

II† *excl* Heavens†!; **~ soit de**... a plague on†...

■ **~ bubonique** or **noire** bubonic ou black plague.

IDIOMES **fuir qn/qch comme la ~** to avoid sb/sth like the plague; **je me méfie de lui comme de la ~** I don't trust him an inch.

pester /pɛste/ [1] *vi* to curse (**contre qch/qn** sth/sb).

pesticide /pɛstisid/ I *adj* [*produit*] pesticidal.

II *nm* pesticide.

pestiféré, **~e** /pɛstifeʀe/ I *adj* Méd [*personne*] plague-stricken; [*lieu*] plague-infested.

II *nm,f* Méd plague-stricken person; **les ~s** the plague-stricken; **il me traite comme un ~** fig he avoids me like the plague.

pestilence /pɛstilɑ̃s/ *nf* stench.

pestilentiel, **-ielle** /pɛstilɑ̃sjɛl/ *adj* pestilential.

pet○ /pɛ/ *nm* fart○; **lâcher un ~** to fart○.

IDIOMES **ça ne vaut pas un ~ (de lapin)**○ it's not worth a damn○; **il a toujours un ~ de travers**○ he's always got something wrong with him.

pétainiste /petenist/ I *adj* [*régime*] Pétain (*épith*); [*discours*] pro-Pétain (*épith*).

II *nmf* supporter of Maréchal Pétain.

pétale /petal/ *nm* petal.

pétanque /petɑ̃k/ ▶449 *nf* petanque, boules.

pétant○, **~e** /petɑ̃, ɑ̃t/ *adj* on the dot (*après n*); **il est arrivé à midi ~/à six heures ~es** he arrived at twelve on the dot/at six on the dot.

pétaradant, **~e** /petaʀadɑ̃, ɑ̃t/ *adj* [*moto, moteur, machine*] sputtering, backfiring.

pétarade /petaʀad/ *nf* (de moteur, véhicule) backfiring ¢.

pétarader /petaʀade/ [1] *vi* [*moteur, véhicule*] (avec un bruit irrégulier) to backfire; (avec un bruit régulier) to sputter; **les karts pétaradent sur le circuit** the karts are sputtering around the circuit.

pétard /petaʀ/ *nm* **1** (explosif) banger GB, firecracker US; **tirer un ~** to let off a banger; **un ~ mouillé** fig a damp squib; **2**○ (tapage) racket○; **faire du ~** (faire scandale) to make a hell of a row○; (protester) to kick up a fuss○; **être en ~** (en colère) to be hopping mad○ GB, to be real mad○ US; **3**◑ (pistolet) shooter◑; **4**◑ (derrière) bum◑ GB, ass◑ US; **5**○ (cigarette de marijuana) joint○.

pétasse● /petas/ *nf* offensive tart◑ GB, slut◑ injur.

pétaudière /petodjɛʀ/ *nf* bedlam; **une ~** bedlam.

pet-de-nonne, *pl* **pets-de-nonne** /pɛdnɔn/ *nm* Culin fritter (*made from choux pastry*).

péter /pete/ [14] I○ *vtr* (casser) to break, to bust○ [*appareil, circuit*]; to snap [*cordon, fil*]; **~ la gueule à qn**◑ to beat the hell out of sb◑.

II *vi* **1**◑ (lâcher un pet) to fart○; **2**○ (éclater) [*ballon, tuyau*] to burst; [*explosif*] to go off; **l'arme lui a pété à la figure** the weapon went off in his face; **faire ~ une grenade/un pétard** to let off a grenade/a banger GB ou firecracker US; **la situation est grave, ça va ~ d'un jour à l'autre** fig the situation is serious, it could blow up any day now; **3** (casser) [*appareil, circuit, crayon, lampe*] to break, to bust○; [*cordon, fil*] to snap; [*bouton, couture*] to burst.

III **se péter**◑ *vpr* (se casser) [*appareil, circuit, crayon, lampe*] to break, to bust○; [*cordon, fil*] to snap; **se ~ la gueule** (avoir un accident) to get smashed up; (se soûler) to get pissed◑ GB ou stoned◑ US; (se droguer) to get high○; **être pété** (soûl) to be pissed GB ou stoned US; (drogué) to be high○.

IDIOMES **envoyer qn ~**○ to send sb packing○; **~ le feu**○ [*personne*] to be full of beans; **ça va ~ le feu**○ there's going to be all hell let loose○; **~ la santé**○ to be bursting with health; **vouloir ~ plus haut que son cul**◑ to be too big for one's boots; **~ dans la soie**◑ to live in the lap of luxury.

pète-sec○ /pɛtsɛk/ I *adj inv* [*ton, manières*] abrupt.

II *nmf inv* pej abrupt person.

péteux○, **-euse** /petø, øz/ I *adj* **1** (poltron) cowardly; **2** (prétentieux) stuck-up○.

II *nm,f* **1** (poltron) coward; **2** (prétentieux) cocky (little) upstart○.

pétillant, **~e** /petijɑ̃, ɑ̃t/ *adj* [*vin*] sparkling; [*eau*] sparkling; [*regard, yeux*] sparkling (**de** with); [*personne*] bubbly.

pétillement /petijmɑ̃/ *nm* (de champagne) fizziness; (de feu) crackling; **un ~ de malice se lisait dans ses yeux** you could see a mischievous twinkle in his/her eyes.

pétiller /petije/ [1] *vi* [*champagne*] to fizz; [*bois*] to crackle; [*yeux, regard*] to sparkle (**de** with).

pétiole /petjɔl/ *nm* petiole.

petiot○, **~e** /pətjo, ɔt/ I *adj* [*enfant*] tiny.

II *nm,f* (enfant) little boy/little girl.

petit, **~e** /p(ə)ti, it/ I *adj* **1** (en taille) [*personne, pied, objet, arbre, entreprise*] (objectivement) small; (subjectivement) little; **il est ~ pour son âge** he's small for his age; **les mêmes, mais en plus ~** the same ones, but smaller; **le 36, c'est trop ~** 36 is too small; **le monde est ~!** it's a small world!; **un homme de ~e taille**, **un homme ~** a short ou small man; **~ et trapu** short and stocky; **un ~ homme timide** a shy little man; **la ~e blonde, là-bas** the little blonde, over there; **une toute ~e pièce/femme** a tiny room/woman; **se faire tout ~** fig to try to make oneself inconspicuous; **c'est Versailles en plus ~** it's a miniature Versailles; ▶**bête**, **doigt**, **lorgnette**, **plat**, **ruisseau**; **2** (en longueur, durée) [*foulée, promenade, distance, paragraphe*] short; **par ~es étapes** in easy stages; ▶**semaine**; **3** (en âge) (objectivement) young; (subjectivement) little; **il est trop ~ pour comprendre** he's too young to understand; **c'est la plus ~e** she's the youngest; **je t'ai connu ~** I knew you when you were little; **mon ~ frère** my little brother; (bébé) my baby brother; **le ~ Jésus** baby Jesus; **~ garçon** little boy; **petite fille** little girl; **une ~e Française** a French girl; **le ~ nouveau** the new boy; **les ~s enfants** small ou young children; **c'est notre ~ dernier** he's our youngest; **~ chat** kitten; **~ chien** puppy; **~ ours/renard/lion** bear/fox/lion cub; **4** (en quantité, prix, force) [*somme, appétit, majorité, volume, quantité, groupe*] small; [*mangeur, buveur*] light; [*salaire, loyer*] low; [*tape, vent, averse*] light; [*cri, rire, sourire*] little; [*goût, espoir, chance*] slight; **d'une ~e voix timide** in a timid little voice; **une ~e pluie fine** a fine drizzle; **ça a un ~ goût de cerise** it tastes slightly of cherries; **avoir une ~e santé** to have poor health; **fais un ~ effort** make an effort; **un (tout) ~ peu de sel** (just) a little salt; **un ~ sourire coquin/supérieur** a mischievous/superior little smile; ▶**feu**[2]; **5** (en gravité) [*inconvénient, détail, défaut, opération*] minor; [*rhume*] slight; [*égratignure, souci*] little; **6** (dans une hiérarchie) [*marque, cru*] lesser known; [*situation, emploi*] modest; [*fonctionnaire, dignitaire*] low-ranking; [*poète*] minor; **les ~es routes** minor roads; **le ~ personnel** low-grade staff; **les ~es gens** ordinary people; **un ~ escroc** a small-time crook; ▶**soldat**; **7** (pour minimiser) little; **chante-nous une ~e chanson** give us a little song; **un ~ coup de rouge** a little glass of red wine; **un ~ visage triste** a sad little face; **un bon ~ vin/restaurant** a nice little wine/restaurant; **un ~ cadeau/secret** a little gift/secret; **une ~e faveur** a little favour[GB]; **de bons ~s plats** tasty dishes; **un ~ coin tranquille** a quiet spot; **envoie-moi un ~ mot** drop me a line; **passe-moi un ~ coup de fil**○ give me a ring GB ou call; **avoir de ~es attentions pour qn** to make a fuss of sb GB, to fuss over sb; **il faut une ~e signature ici** could I ask you to sign here, please?; **je n'ai eu que deux ~es semaines de congé!** I only had two short weeks off!; **j'en ai pour une ~e minute/heure** it won't take me a minute/more than an hour; **une ~e trentaine de personnes** under thirty people; **8** (en sentiment) **mon ~ Pierre** my dear Pierre; **mon ~ papa** darling daddy; **mon ~ chéri/ange** my darling/angel; **mon ~ chou**○ or **poulet**○ sweetie○, honey○; **une ~e garce**◑ a bitch◑; **un ~ imbécile** an idiot; **très préoccupée de sa ~e personne** very taken up with herself; **il tient à sa ~e tranquillité** he likes a nice quiet life; **9** (mesquin) [*personne, procédé*] petty, mean; (étroit) [*conception*] narrow; **les ~s esprits** small-minded people.

II *nm,f* **1** (enfant) little boy/girl, child; (benjamin) **le ~** (de deux) the younger one; (de plus de deux) the youngest one; **les ~s** the children, the kids○; **pauvre ~!** poor thing!; **la ~e Martin** the Martin girl; **les ~s Martin** the Martin children; **ils ont deux ~s** they have two children; **elle a eu un ~** she's had a baby; **n'aie pas peur, mon ~** don't be afraid; **2** (adulte de petite taille) small man/woman; **les ~s** small people.

III *adv* **voir ~** (sous-estimer) to underestimate; (être sans ambition) to have no ambition; **chausser/tailler ~** [*chaussures, vêtements*] to be small-fitting; **~ à ~** little by little, gradually; ▶**oiseau**.

IV *nm* **1** (jeune animal) **~s** young; (chats) kittens; (chiens) puppies; (loups, lions, ours) cubs, young; **le mammifère allaite ses ~s** mammals suckle their young; **la lionne et ses ~s** the lioness and her cubs ou young; **comment s'appelle le ~ de la chèvre?** what do you call a baby ou young goat?; **faire des ~s** [*chienne*] to have puppies; fig (se multiplier) [*argent*] to grow; (se briser) [*vase*] to end up in bits; **2** (personne modeste) **les ~s** ordinary people; **un ~ de la finance** a minor figure in the world of finance.

■ **~ aigle** Zool scops owl; **~ ami** boyfriend; **~ bassin** Anat lower pelvis; (de piscine) small pool; **~ blanc** (vin) small glass of white wine; **~ bleu**† Postes telegram; **~ bois** (d'allumage) kindling; **~ cacatois** fore royal sail; **~ chef** petty tyrant; **jouer au ~ chef** to throw one's weight around○; **~ coin**○ euph (toilettes) loo○ GB, bathroom US; **aller au ~ coin** to go to the loo○ GB ou bathroom US; **~ commerçant** small trader; **~ commerce** small traders (*pl*); **~ crème** small espresso with milk; **~ déjeuner** breakfast; **~ endroit** = **~ coin**; **~ four** petit four; **~ hunier** Naut fore topsail; **~ juif**○ funny bone; **~ linge** underwear; **laver son ~ linge** to wash one's smalls○; **~ maître** minor master; **~ noir** coffee; **~ nom**○ (prénom) first name; **~ paquet** small packet; **~ perroquet** Naut fore topgallant sail; **~ peuple** lower classes (*pl*); **~ point** petit point; **~ pois** (garden) pea, petit pois; **~ porteur** small shareholder; **~ pot** (pour bébés) jar of baby food; **~ quart** Naut dogwatch; **~ rat (de l'Opéra)** *pupil at Paris Opéra's ballet school*; **~ roque** (aux échecs) castling short; **~ salé** streaky salted pork; **~ trot** jog trot; **~e amie** girlfriend; **~e annonce** Presse classified advertisement ou ad○; **~e caisse** petty cash; **~e école**○ ≈ nursery school; **~e main** seamstress (*at a top fashion house*); **~e mort** orgasm; **~e nature** weakling; **~e phrase** (memorable) saying; **~e reine** Sport cycling; **~e souris** tooth fairy; **~e vérole** smallpox; **~e voiture** toy car; **~es annonces matrimoniales** personal ads; **~es classes**○ Scol younger children; **~es et moyennes entreprises**, **PME** small and medium enterprises, SMEs; **~es sœurs des pauvres** Little Sisters of the Poor; **~s chevaux** Jeux ≈ ludo (*sg*); **~s métiers du passé** traditional crafts.

petit-beurre, *pl* **petits-beurre** /p(ə)tibœʀ/ *nm* crisp all-butter biscuit GB ou cookie US.

petit-bourgeois, **petite-bourgeoise**, *pl* **petits-bourgeois**, **petites-bourgeoises** /p(ə)tibuʀʒwa, p(ə)titbuʀʒwaz/ pej **I** *adj* petit bourgeois péj, lower middle class.
II *nm,f* lower middle class person.

petit-cousin, **petite-cousine**, *pl* **petits-cousins**, **petites-cousines** /p(ə)tikuzɛ̃, p(ə)titkuzin/ *nm,f* (issu de cousin germain) first cousin once removed, second cousin; (cousin éloigné) distant relation.

petite-fille, *pl* **petites-filles** /p(ə)titfij/ *nf* granddaughter.

petitement /p(ə)titmɑ̃/ *adv* **1** (à l'étroit) **être logé ~** to live in cramped accommodation; **2** (chichement) [*vivre, recevoir*] in a penny-pinching way; (maigrement) **être ~ bénéficiaire** [*entreprise*] to show only a small profit; **3** (avec mesquinerie) [*penser, agir*] pettily.

petite-nièce, *pl* **petites-nièces** /p(ə)titnjɛs/ *nf* great-niece.

petitesse /p(ə)titɛs/ *nf* **1** (mesquinerie) pettiness; **~ d'esprit** small-mindedness; **~ de cœur** mean-spiritedness; **2** (petite taille) small size; **la ~ de notre savoir** our limited knowledge.

petit-fils, *pl* **petits-fils** /p(ə)tifis/ *nm* grandson.

pétition /petisjɔ̃/ *nf* petition (**contre** against; **en faveur de** in favour[GB] of); **signer/faire circuler une ~** to sign/to circulate a petition.

pétitionnaire /petisjɔnɛʀ/ *nm,f* petitioner.

pétitionner /petisjɔne/ [1] *vi* to petition.

petit-lait /p(ə)tilɛ/ *nm* whey.
IDIOMES **ça se boit comme du ~!** it slips down nicely!

petit-nègre○ /p(ə)tinɛgʀ/ *nm inv* offensive pidgin French.

petit-neveu, *pl* **petits-neveux** /p(ə)tin(ə)vø/ *nm* great-nephew.

petits-enfants /p(ə)tizɑ̃fɑ̃/ *nmpl* grandchildren.

petit-suisse, *pl* **petits-suisses** /p(ə)tisɥis/ *nm* petit-suisse, individual fromage frais.

pétochard◑, **~e** /petɔʃaʀ, aʀd/ pej *nm,f* coward, yellowbelly○.

pétoche◑ /petɔʃ/ *nf* **avoir la ~** to be scared stiff○; **flanquer la ~ à qn** to scare sb stiff○.

pétoire○ /petwaʀ/ *nf* (fusil) rusty old gun.

peton /pətɔ̃/ *nm* baby talk tootsie lang enfantin, foot.

pétoncle /petɔ̃kl/ *nm* small scallop.

pétouiller○ /petuje/ [1] *vi* H (avoir des problèmes) [*personne*] to be struggling; [*voiture*] to run rough.

Pétrarque /petʀaʀk/ *npr* Petrarch.

pétrel /petʀɛl/ *nm* petrel.

pétri, **~e** /petʀi/ **I** *pp* ▶**pétrir**.
II *pp adj* **~ de** péj steeped in [*ignorance*]; puffed up with [*orgueil*]; full of [*contradictions, défauts*].

pétrifiant, **~e** /petʀifjɑ̃, ɑ̃t/ *adj* petrifying.

pétrification /petʀifikasjɔ̃/ *nf* lit petrification; fig fossilization[GB].

pétrifier /petʀifje/ [2] **I** *vtr* **1** lit to petrify; **forêt pétrifiée** petrified forest; **2** fig to transfix; **cette nouvelle nous a pétrifiés** we were transfixed by the news.
II se pétrifier *vpr* **1** lit to become petrified; **2** fig [*personne*] to be transfixed; [*cœur*] to harden; [*sourire*] to freeze.

pétrin /petʀɛ̃/ *nm* **1** (récipient) dough trough; **~ mécanique** kneading machine; **2**○ (ennuis) fix○; **je suis dans un beau ~!** I'm in a real fix○!; **se mettre** or **se fourrer**○ **dans le ~** to get into a fix○; **mettre** or **fourrer**○**/laisser qn dans le ~** to put/leave sb in a fix○; **tirer qn du ~** to get sb out of a fix○.

pétrir /petʀiʀ/ [3] *vtr* **1** Culin to knead [*pâte*]; **2** [*masseur*] to knead [*épaules, mollets*]; **3** fig to mould GB ou mold US [*personnalité*].

pétrochimie /petʀɔʃimi/ *nf* petrochemistry.

pétrochimique /petʀɔʃimik/ *adj* petrochemical.

pétrochimiste /petʀɔʃimist/ ▶**510** *nmf* petrochemist.

pétrodollar /petʀɔdɔlaʀ/ *nm* petrodollar.

pétrographie /petʀɔgʀafi/ *nf* petrography.

pétrole /petʀɔl/ *nm* oil, petroleum spéc; **du ~** [*industrie, prix*] oil (*épith*); [*dérivés*] petroleum (*épith*); **~ brut** crude oil.

pétrolette○ /petʀɔlɛt/ *nf* (vélomoteur) moped.

pétroleuse /petʀɔløz/ *nf* **1** Hist (female) fire-raiser (*during the Commune*); **2** (militante) (female) activist.

pétrolier, **-ière** /petʀɔlje, ɛʀ/ **I** *adj* [*producteur, prospection, embargo, compagnie*] oil; [*produits*] petroleum; [*pays*] oil-producing; [*port*] oil-exporting.
II *nm* **1** (navire) oil tanker; **2** (industriel)

▶ 510 | oil man; (ingénieur) petroleum engineer.

pétrolifère /petʀɔlifɛʀ/ *adj* [*roche*] oil-bearing; [*région*] oil-producing; [*gisement*] oil.

pétulance /petylɑ̃s/ *nf* exuberance.

pétulant, ~e /petylɑ̃, ɑ̃t/ *adj* exuberant.

pétunia /petynja/ *nm* petunia.

peu /pø/

■ **Note** Les emplois de *peu* avec *avant, d'ici, depuis, sous* sont traités respectivement sous chacun de ces mots.
– Il sera également utile de se reporter à la note d'usage sur les quantités ▶ 662 |.

I *adv* **1** (modifiant un verbe) not much; **il travaille/dort/parle ~** he doesn't work/sleep/talk much; **elle gagne assez ~** she doesn't earn very much; **elle gagne très/trop ~** she earns very/too little; **le radiateur chauffe ~** the radiator doesn't give out much heat; **je sors assez/très ~** I don't go out very much/very much at all; **je sais me contenter de ~** I'm satisfied with very little; **40 francs/un demi-litre/1,50 m, c'est (bien) ~** 40 francs/half a litre[GB]/1,50 m, that's not (very) much; **20 personnes, c'est ~** 20 people, that's not many; **dix minutes/deux mois ça fait ~** ten minutes/two months, that's not long; **deux semaines c'est trop ~** two weeks isn't long enough; **si ~ que ce soit** however little, no matter how little; **tu ne vas pas t'en faire pour si**○ **~** you're not going to worry about such a little thing; **je ne vais pas me casser la tête pour si ~** I'm not going to rack my brains over such a little thing; **il leur en faut ~ pour pleurer/paniquer** it doesn't take much to make them cry/panic; **la catastrophe a été évitée de ~** disaster was only just avoided; **tu les as ratés de ~** you've just missed them; **il est mon aîné de ~** he's slightly older than me; **j'aime ~ sa façon de dévisager les gens** I don't much care for the way he stares at people; **ça compte** or **importe ~** it doesn't really matter; **la cuisine n'est pas très bonne , et c'est ~ dire** the food isn't very good to say the least; **il est aussi borné que son père et ce n'est pas ~ dire**○! he's as narrow-minded as his father and that's saying a lot!; **un homme comme on en voit** or **fait**○ **~** the kind of man you don't often come across; **très ~ pour moi**○! fig no thanks○!; **2** (modifiant un adjectif) not very; **~ soigneux/ambitieux/fier** not very tidy/ambitious/proud; **il est très ~ jaloux** he's not at all jealous; **c'est un endroit assez ~ connu** it's a relatively little-known spot; **cet endroit trop ~ connu des touristes** this spot which is sadly little known to tourists; **pour les personnes trop ~ qualifiées** for people who haven't got enough qualifications; **ils se sentent très** ou **fort ~ concernés par**... they feel quite unconcerned about...; **nous étions ~ nombreux** there weren't many of us; **nous étions très/trop ~ nombreux** there were very/too few of us; **un individu ~ recommandable** a disreputable character; **elle n'est pas ~ fière** she's more than a little proud.

II *pron indéf* **~ lui font confiance** few ou not many people trust him/her; **il a écrit beaucoup de livres, ~ lui survivront** he has written many books, few will outlive him.

III **peu de** *dét indéf* **1** (avec un nom dénombrable) **~ de mots/d'occasions** few words/opportunities; **2** (avec un nom non dénombrable) **~ de temps/d'espoir** little time/hope; **en ~ de temps** in next to no time; **j'ai ~ de temps pour le faire** I haven't got much time to do it; **il y a ~ de changement** there's little change; **il y a ~ de bruit** there's not much noise; **il est tombé ~ de neige/pluie cet hiver** there hasn't been much snow/rain this winter; **il a ~ de patience** he's not very patient; **c'est ~ de chose** it's not much; **cela représente ~ de chose** it stands for little; **avec ~ de chose elle a fait un repas délicieux** with very little she made a delicious meal; **on est bien ~ de chose!** we're so insignificant!; **il y a ~ de visiteurs/divergences** there are few ou not many visitors/differences; **très ~ de personnes sont atteintes** very few people are affected; **en ~ de mots/jours** in a few words/days; **je sais ~ de choses sur lui** I don't know much about him; **il y a ~ de chances qu'il accepte** he's unlikely to accept; **la proposition a ~ de chances d'aboutir** the proposal has little chance of getting through.

IV *nm* **1** (petite quantité) **le ~ de** the little [*importance, confiance, pluie, liberté*]; the few [*livres, souvenirs, amis*]; **il a oublié le ~ d'anglais qu'il savait** he's forgotten the ou what little English he knew; **elle s'est fait voler le ~ d'objets qu'il lui restait** she was robbed of the few things she had left; **je vais dépenser le ~ d'argent qu'il me reste** I'm going to spend the ou what little money I've got left; **il a voulu montrer le ~ d'importance qu'il attachait à l'affaire** he wanted to show how unimportant the matter was to him; **je leur ai dit le ~ que je savais** I told them the ou what little I knew; **il a dépensé le ~ qu'il lui restait** he spent what little he had left; **2** (manque) **le ~ de** the lack of; **malgré le ~ d'intérêt manifesté** despite the lack of interest; **j'ai remarqué ton ~ d'enthousiasme** I've noticed your lack of enthusiasm; **ton ~ d'appétit m'inquiète** your lack of appetite is worrying me.

V **un peu** *loc adv* **1** (dans une mesure faible) a little, a bit; **mange un ~** eat a little; **cela m'inquiète/m'énerve/m'ennuie un ~** it worries me/annoys me/bothers me a little ou a bit; **ça m'agace plus qu'un ~**○ it annoys me to say the least; **le rôti est un ~ brûlé** the roast is a bit ou slightly burned; **elle est un ~ médium/poète**○ she's a bit of a ou something of a medium/poet; **tu ne serais pas un ~ casse-cou?** you're a bit of a daredevil, aren't you?; **dors/attends/reste encore un ~** sleep/wait/stay a little longer; **'il a plu?'—'pas qu'un ~**○**!'** 'did it rain?'—'did it ever○!'; **'elle aime le fromage?'—'oui, pas qu'un ~!'** 'does she like cheese?'—'does she ever○!'; **2** (modifiant un adverbe) a little, a bit; **mange un ~ plus/moins** eat a bit more/less; **parle un ~ plus fort** speak a little ou a bit louder; **parle un ~ moins fort** keep your voice down; **va un ~ moins/plus vite** go a bit slower/faster; **il fait un ~ moins froid qu'hier** it's a little less cold than yesterday; **il fait un ~ plus froid qu'hier** it's slightly ou a little colder than yesterday; **un ~ au-dessous/au-dessus de la moyenne** slightly below/above average; **elle se maquille un ~ trop** she wears a bit too much make-up; **un ~ plus de bruit/vent** a bit more noise/wind; **un ~ plus de gens/problèmes** a few more people/problems; **un ~ moins de** slightly less [*pluie, humour*]; slightly fewer [*gens, tableaux*] ; **peux-tu me donner un tout petit ~ plus de carottes** can you give me just a few more carrots; **amène tes amis, un ~ plus un ~ moins tu sais**... bring your friends, another two or three people won't make much difference; **donne-moi ton linge à laver, un ~ plus un ~ moins**... give me your laundry, a bit more won't make any difference; **'il avait l'air un ~ contrarié'—'un ~ beaucoup même**○**'** 'he looked a bit annoyed'—'more than a bit'; **3** (emploi stylistique) just; **arrête un ~ de faire l'idiot!** just stop behaving like an idiot!; **répète un ~ pour voir**○**!** you just try saying that again!; **vise un ~ la perruque**○**!** just look at the wig!; **réfléchis un ~** just think; **je vous demande un ~**○**!** I ask you!; **il sait un ~ de quoi il parle**○ he does know what he' s talking about; **4** (emploi par antiphrase) a little; **tu ne serais pas un ~ jaloux toi?** aren't you just a little jealous?; **ton histoire est un ~ tirée par les cheveux** your story is a little far-fetched to say the least; **c'est un ~ tard!** it's a bit late!; **tu exagères** ou **pousses**○ **un ~!** you're pushing it a bit○!; **5**○ (pour renforcer une affirmation) **il est un ~ bien ton copain!** your boyfriend is a bit of all right○!; **'tu le ferais toi?'—'un ~ (que je le ferais)!'** 'would you do it?'—'I sure would○!'; **comme organisateur il se pose un ~ là!** as an organizer he's great!

VI **peu à peu** *loc adv* gradually, little by little; **les nuages se dissiperont ~ à ~** the clouds will gradually clear.

VII **pour un peu** *loc adv* very nearly; **pour un ~ ils se seraient battus** they very nearly had a fight; **pour un ~ il m'aurait insulté!** he very nearly insulted me!

VIII **pour peu que** *loc conj* if; **pour ~ qu'il ait bu, il va nous raconter sa vie** if he's had anything at all to drink, he'll tell us his life story.

peuchère /pøʃɛʀ/ *excl* dial poor thing!

peuh /pø/ *excl* huh!

peul, ~e /pøl/ I *adj* Fulani.
II ▶ 462 | *nm* Ling Fulani.

Peul, ~e /pøl/ *nm,f* Fula.

peuplade /pœplad/ *nf* small tribe.

peuple /pœpl/ I *adj inv* pej [*personne*] common; [*expression, mot*] vulgar; **ça fait ~** (accent) it sounds common; (style, allure) it looks common.

II *nm* **1** Pol people (+ *v sg* ou *pl*); **le ~ français** the French people; **les ~s opprimés** oppressed peoples; **être un élu du ~** to be elected by the people; **le ~ de droite/gauche** the right-wing/left-wing element of the population; **2** Sociol **le ~** the people (+ *v pl*); **un homme du ~** a man of the people; **le ~ des campagnes** country people (+ *v pl*); **le ~ des villes** townspeople (+ *v pl*); ▶ **petit**; **3** (foule) lots of people (*pl*); **il y a du ~ dans les rues** there are lots of people in the streets; **tu te fous**● **du ~** what do you think you're doing?; **que demande le ~?** what more could anyone want?

■ **~ élu** Chosen People.

peuplé, ~e /pœple/ I *pp* ▶ **peupler**.
II *pp adj* **1** (habité) [*pays, région*] populated; **un pays très/peu ~** a densely/sparsely populated country; **2** (rempli) **~ de** peopled with [*personnes, monstres*]; filled with [*rêves, souvenirs, dangers*].

peuplement /pœpləmɑ̃/ *nm* population.

peupler /pœple/ [1] I *vtr* **1** (faire occuper) to populate [*pays, région, île*] (**de** with); to stock [*bois, étang, région*] (**de** with); **2** (occuper) [*personnes, population*] to populate [*pays, région, île*]; [*animaux, plantes*] to colonize [*pays, région, île*]; [*spectateurs, délinquants, étudiants*] to fill [*salle, rue*]; **3** (remplir) [*souvenirs, rêves, visions*] to fill; **fantasmes qui peuplent l'esprit** fantasies which fill the mind.

II **se peupler** *vpr* [*ville, région*] to fill up (**de** with).

peupleraie /pøpləʀɛ/ *nf* poplar grove.

peuplier /pøplije/ *nm* poplar.

■ **~ blanc** white poplar; **~ d'Italie** Lombardy poplar.

peur /pœʀ/ *nf* gén fear; (soudaine) fright, scare; **la ~ de l'inconnu/de la mort/du ridicule** fear of the unknown/of death/of ridicule; **être mort** or **vert de ~** to be scared to death; **être pris de** or **prendre ~** to take fright; **une ~ panique s'empara de lui** he was panic-stricken; **vivre dans la ~ de** to live in fear ou dread of; **avoir ~** to be afraid ou scared ou frightened (**de** of); **avoir ~ que** to be afraid that; **il a ~ des chiens/de son père/de sa femme/du chômage** he's afraid ou frightened of dogs/of his father/of his wife/of unemployment; **j'ai eu une de ces ~s!** I got such a scare!, I got ou had a terrible fright; **elle a ~ de prendre l'avion/mourir** she's afraid of flying/dying; **je n'ai qu'une ~, c'est qu'il pleuve** I 'm only afraid of one thing, that it will rain; **j'ai (bien) ~ qu'il ne soit trop tard!** I'm afraid it may be too late!; **j'en ai bien ~** I'm afraid so; **j'ai toujours ~ qu'il ait un accident** I'm always afraid that he'll have an accident; **il n'a ~ de rien** lit he's not afraid of anything, he's fearless; iron he knows no shame; **il veut courir le marathon sans s'être préparé? il n'a pas ~!** he wants to run the marathon without having trained? he's being very optimistic!; **il n'a pas ~ de se contredire/se ridiculiser** it doesn't seem to worry him if he contradicts himself/makes a fool of himself; **n'ayez pas ~** (ne soyez pas effrayé) don't be afraid; (ne vous inquiétez pas) don't worry; **avoir ~ pour qn** to be afraid for sb; **avoir plus de ~ que de mal** to be more frightened than hurt; **faire ~ à qn** to frighten ou scare sb; **il s'amuse à faire ~ aux petits enfants** he enjoys frightening ou scaring small children; **tu ne me fais pas ~!** I'm not afraid ou frightened of you!; **je ne t'ai pas entendu entrer, tu m'as fait ~** I didn't hear you coming in, you gave me a fright ou a scare; **le bruit a fait ~ aux biches qui se sont enfuies** the noise frightened the deer away; **être laid à faire ~** to be hideously ugly; **maigre** or **d'une maigreur à faire ~** terribly thin; **le travail ne nous fait pas ~** we're not afraid of hard work; **trois heures de marche ça ne me fait pas ~!** I'm not afraid of a three-hour walk!; **il est poli/généreux ça fait ~**○**!** iron he's not exactly the most polite/generous man in the world; **de** or **par ~ de** for fear of; **il n'a rien dit de ~ de le contrarier** he said nothing for fear of annoying him ou lest he annoy him sout; **il l'a tuée de ~ qu'elle ne parle** he killed her for fear that she might talk ou lest she talk; ▶ **bleu**.

peureusement /pœʀøzmɑ̃/ *adv* fearfully.

peureux, **-euse** /pœʀø, øz/ **I** *adj* fearful.
II *nm,f* fearful person.

peut-être /pøtɛtʀ/ *adv* perhaps, maybe; **il a ~ oublié, ~ a-t-il oublié** fml perhaps ou maybe he's forgotten; **il y avait ~ 200 personnes** there were maybe 200 people; **on finira dans deux ans, ~ trois** we'll finish in two, maybe ou possibly three years' time; **je me suis ~ mal fait comprendre** perhaps I haven't made myself clear; **tu crois ~ que je vais laisser tomber!** perhaps you think that I'm going to give (it) up!; **il faudrait ~ te dépêcher!** iron perhaps you ought to get a move on○!; **je ne sais pas lire, ~?** iron I do know how to read, you know!; **tu veux m'apprendre à conduire, ~?** iron I do know how to drive, you know!; **si tout va bien, on arrivera ~ demain** if all goes well, we may arrive tomorrow; **elle travaille ~ lentement mais avec soin** she might work slowly, but she's careful; **il est ~ bourru, mais il est serviable** he may be a bit surly, but he is helpful; **c'est ~ bien lui qui a appelé** perhaps ou maybe it was he who rang GB ou called; **~ bien que la cérémonie se fera le matin** the ceremony may well take place in the morning; **'tu viendras?'—'~ bien'** 'will you come?'—'I may well do' GB, 'I just might'; **~ bien que oui, ~ bien que non**○ maybe yes, maybe no.

peyotl /pɛjɔtl/ *nm* Bot peyote.

pèze○ /pɛz/ *nm* dough○, money; **il a du ~** he's loaded○.

pfennig /pfɛnig/ *nm* ▶**46** pfennig.

PGCD /peʒesede/ *nm* (*abbr* = **plus grand commun diviseur**) HCF, hcf.

pH /peaʃ/ *nm* pH.

phacochère /fakɔʃɛʀ/ *nm* warthog.

phaéton /faetɔ̃/ *nm* **1** (calèche) phaeton; **2**† (cocher) coachman.

phagocyte /fagɔsit/ *nm* phagocyte.

phagocyter /fagɔsite/ [1] *vtr* **1** Biol to ingest by phagocytosis; **2** fig to swallow up.

phagocytose /fagɔsitoz/ *nf* phagocytosis.

phalange /falɑ̃ʒ/ *nf* **1** Anat phalanx; **2** liter (groupe) phalanx littér; **3** (en Espagne) Falange; (au Liban) **les ~s** the (Christian) Phalangists; **4** Antiq phalanx.

phalangien, **-ienne** /falɑ̃ʒjɛ̃, ɛn/ *adj* phalangeal.

phalangiste /falɑ̃ʒist/ *adj, nmf* (au Liban) Phalangist; (en Espagne) Falangist.

phalanstère /falɑ̃stɛʀ/ *nm* phalanstery.

phalarope /falaʀɔp/ *nm* phalarope.

phalène /falɛn/ *nf* or *m* geometer moth.

phallique /falik/ *adj* phallic.

phallocentrisme /falɔsɑ̃tʀism/ *nm* phallicism.

phallocrate /falɔkʀat/ **I** *adj* male chauvinist (*épith*), phallocratic.
II *nm* male chauvinist, phallocrat.

phallocratie /falɔkʀasi/ *nf* male chauvinism, phallocracy.

phallocratique /falɔkʀatik/ *adj* male chauvinist (*épith*), phallocratic.

phalloïde /falɔid/ *adj* **amanite ~** death cap.

phallus /falys/ *nm* phallus.

phanérogame /faneʀɔgam/ **I** *adj* phanerogamic.
II *nm* phanerogam.

phantasme = **fantasme**.

pharamineux, **-euse** = **faramineux**.

pharaon /faʀaɔ̃/ *nm* pharaoh.

pharaonien, **-ienne** /faʀaɔnjɛ̃, ɛn/ *adj* Pharaonic.

phare /faʀ/ **I** *nm* **1** Aut headlight, headlamp; **allumer** or **mettre ses ~s** to switch on one's headlights; **se mettre en pleins ~s** to switch the headlights on full beam GB, to put the high beams on US; **2** Naut lighthouse; **gardien de ~** lighthouse keeper; **3** fig (guide) beacon.
II (-)phare (*in compounds*) **film/œuvre(-)~** seminal film/work; **pays(-)~** influential country; **action/année/site(-)~** key share/year/site.
■ **~ antibrouillard** fog-light; **~ à iode** quartz halogen light; **~ à longue portée** high-intensity light.

pharisaïsme /faʀizaism/ *nm* pharisaism.

pharisien, **-ienne** /faʀizjɛ̃, ɛn/ *nm,f* **1** fig pharisee; **2** Antiq, Relig Pharisee.

pharmaceutique /faʀmasøtik/ *adj* pharmaceutical.

pharmacie /faʀmasi/ *nf* **1** ▶**510** Comm chemist's (shop) GB, drugstore US, pharmacy; **vendu exclusivement en ~** available only at the chemist's GB ou pharmacy US; **~ de nuit** duty chemist's GB, night pharmacy US; **~ de garde** duty chemist's GB, *pharmacy open on a Sunday or a holiday according to a rotating schedule*; **~ allopathique/homéopathique** allopathic/homeopathic pharmacy; **2** (dans un hôpital) dispensary, pharmacy; **3** (meuble) medicine cabinet; **4** (discipline) pharmacy; (science des médicaments) pharmacy; **elle est en troisième année de ~** she's in her third year studying pharmacy; **5** (produits) **la ~** medicines (*pl*); (dans un supermarché) health-care products (*pl*); Ind pharmaceuticals (*pl*); **le numéro un de la ~ en France** France's top pharmaceuticals company; **~ allopathique/homéopathique** allopathic/homeopathic remedies (*pl*).
■ **~ portative** or **de voyage** first-aid kit.

pharmacien, **-ienne** /faʀmasjɛ̃, ɛn/ ▶**510** *nm,f* (dans un magasin) (dispensing) chemist GB, pharmacist; (ailleurs) pharmacist.

pharmacodépendance /faʀmakodepɑ̃dɑ̃s/ *nf* drug-dependence.

pharmacologie /faʀmakɔlɔʒi/ *nf* pharmacology.

pharmacologique /faʀmakɔlɔʒik/ *adj* pharmacological.

pharmacopée /faʀmakɔpe/ *nf* pharmacopeia.

pharyngal, **~e**, *mpl* **-aux** /faʀɛ̃gal, o/ **I** *adj* Phon pharyngeal.
II pharyngale *nf* pharyngeal.

pharyngé, **~e** /faʀɛ̃ʒe/ *adj* pharyngeal.

pharyngien, **-ienne** /faʀɛ̃ʒjɛ̃, ɛn/ *adj* Anat pharyngeal.

pharyngite /faʀɛ̃ʒit/ ▶**271** *nf* pharyngitis.

pharynx /faʀɛ̃ks/ *nm inv* pharynx.

phase /fɑz/ *nf* **1** (d'évolution) stage; **2** Astron, Chimie, Phys phase; **3** Électrotech (**conducteur de**) **~** live wire; **en ~** in phase; **être en ~ avec qn** fig to be on sb's wavelength.

phasme /fasm/ *nm* stick insect, walking stick US.

Phébus /febys/ *npr* Phoebus.

Phèdre /fɛdʀ/ *npr* Phaedra.

Phénicie /fenisi/ *nprf* Phoenicia.

phénicien, **-ienne** /fenisjɛ̃, ɛn/ **I** *adj* Phoenician.
II *nm* Ling Phoenician.

Phénicien, **-ienne** /fenisjɛ̃, ɛn/ *nm,f* Phoenician.

phéniqué, **~e** /fenike/ *adj* **eau ~e** phenol solution.

phénix /feniks/ *nm inv* **1** Mythol phoenix; **2**† (personne) liter phoenix; **3** Bot = **phœnix**.

phénobarbital /fenobaʀbital/ *nm* phenobarbitone.

phénol /fenɔl/ *nm* phenol.

phénoménal, **~e**, *mpl* **-aux** /fenɔmenal, o/ *adj* phenomenal.

phénoménalement /fenɔmenalmɑ̃/ *adv* phenomenally.

phénomène /fenɔmɛn/ *nm* **1** (fait) phenomenon; **des ~s inexpliqués** unexplained phenomena; **des ~s de racisme** manifestations of racism; **le ~ Gorbatchev** the Gorbatchev phenomenon; **2**○ (original) **c'est un ~!** he/she's quite a character!; **3** (de cirque) freak; **4** Philos phenomenon.

phénoménologie /fenɔmenɔlɔʒi/ *nf* phenomenology.

phénoménologique /fenɔmenɔlɔʒik/ *adj* phenomenological.

phénoménologue /fenɔmenɔlɔg/ *nmf* phenomenologist.

phénotype /fenɔtip/ *nm* phenotype.

phényle /fenil/ *nm* phenyl.

phéromone /feʀɔmɔn/, **phérormone** /feʀɔʀmɔn/ *nf* pheromone.

Philadelphie /filadɛlfi/ ▶**857** *npr* Philadelphia.

philanthrope /filɑ̃tʀɔp/ *nmf* philanthropist.

philanthropie /filɑ̃tʀɔpi/ *nf* philanthropy.

philanthropique /filɑ̃tʀɔpik/ *adj* philanthropic.

philatélie /filateli/ *nf* stamp collecting, philately.

philatélique /filatelik/ *adj* philatelic.

philatéliste /filatelist/ *nmf* stamp collector, philatelist.

philharmonie /filaʀmɔni/ *nf* philharmonic society.

philharmonique /filaʀmɔnik/ *adj* [*orchestre, société*] philharmonic.

philhellène /filelɛn/ **I** *adj* philhellenic.
II *nmf* philhellene.

philhellénisme /filelenism/ *nm* philhellenism.

Philippe /filip/ *npr* Philippe.
■ **~ Auguste** Philip Augustus; **~ le Bel** Philip the Fair; **~ le Bon** Philip the Good.

philippin, **~e** /filipɛ̃, in/ ▶**537** *adj* Philippine (*épith*).

Philippin, **~e** /filipɛ̃, in/ **I** ▶**537** *nm,f* Filipino.
II Philippines ▶**555**, **321** *nprfpl* **les**

~es the Philippines; **mer des ~es** Philippine Sea.

philippique /filipik/ *nf* liter philippic littér.

philistin, ~e /filistɛ̃, in/ **I** *adj* liter philistine.
II *nm* philistine.

Philistins /filistɛ̃/ *nprmpl* **les ~** the Philistines.

philo○ /filo/ *nf* students' slang *abbr* = **philosophie**.

philodendron /filodɛ̃dʀɔ̃/ *nm* philodendron.

philologie /filɔlɔʒi/ *nf* philology.

philologique /filɔlɔʒik/ *adj* philological.

philologue /filɔlɔg/ ▶510 *nmf* philologist.

philosophale /filɔzɔfal/ *adj f* **la pierre ~** the philosopher's stone.

philosophe /filɔzɔf/ **I** *adj* philosophical.
II *nmf* philosopher; **prendre les choses en ~** to take things philosophically.

philosopher /filɔzɔfe/ [1] *vi* to philosophize (**sur** about).

philosophie /filɔzɔfi/ *nf* **1** (doctrine) philosophy; **la ~ grecque/de Platon** Greek/Plato's philosophy; **la ~ du renoncement** the philosophy of renunciation; **prendre/supporter qch avec ~** to take/bear sth philosophically; **2** (conception) philosophy; **une nouvelle ~ des transports** a new philosophy of transport; **3** Scol, Univ (matière) philosophy; (classe)† *humanities stream in final year of secondary school*; **faire une licence de ~** to do a philosophy degree GB, to major in philosophy US; **avoir une licence de ~** to have a degree in philosophy.

philosophique /filɔzɔfik/ *adj* philosophical.

philosophiquement /filɔzɔfikmɑ̃/ *adv* philosophically.

philtre /filtʀ/ *nm* philtre; **~ d'amour** love potion.

phimosis /fimozis/ *nm inv* phimosis.

phlébite /flebit/ ▶271 *nf* phlebitis.

phlébologie /flebɔlɔʒi/ *nf* vascular medicine.

phlébologue /flebɔlɔg/ ▶510 *nmf* vascular specialist.

phlébotomie /flebɔtɔmi/ *nf* venesection, phlebotomy spéc.

phlegmon /flɛgmɔ̃/ ▶271 *nm* acute inflammation, phlegmon spéc (**à** of).

phlox /flɔks/ *nm inv* phlox.

phlyctène /fliktɛn/ *nf* blister.

Phnom Penh /pnɔmpɛn/ ▶857 *npr* Phnom Penh.

phobie /fɔbi/ *nf* gén, Psych phobia (**de** about); **avoir la ~ de qch** to have a phobia about sth.

phobique /fɔbik/ *adj* phobic.

phocéen, -éenne /fɔseɛ̃, ɛn/ **I** *adj* Antiq Phocean.
II *nm,f* Antiq Phocean; **les ~s** journ the people of Marseilles.
■ **la cité phocéenne** journ Marseilles.

phœnix /feniks/ *nm inv* Phœnix.

phonateur, -trice /fɔnatœʀ, tʀis/ *adj* phonatory.

phonation /fɔnasjɔ̃/ *nf* phonation.

phonatoire /fɔnatwaʀ/ *adj* phonatory.

phonématique /fɔnematik/ **I** *adj* phonemic.
II *nf* phonemics (+ *v sg*).

phonème /fɔnɛm/ *nm* phoneme.

phonémique /fɔnemik/ **I** *adj* phonemic.
II *nf* phonemics (+ *v sg*).

phonéticien, -ienne /fɔnetisjɛ̃, ɛn/ ▶510 *nm,f* phonetician.

phonétique /fɔnetik/ **I** *adj* [*transcription, alphabet*] phonetic; **loi ~** sound law; **altération ~** sound change.
II *nf* phonetics (+ *v sg*); **~ acoustique/articulatoire** acoustic/articulatory phonetics.

phonétiquement /fɔnetikmɑ̃/ *adv* phonetically.

phoniatre /fɔnjatʀ/ ▶510 *nmf* phoniatrician.

phoniatrie /fɔnjatʀi/ *nf* phoniatrics (+ *v sg*).

phonie /fɔni/ *nf* radiotelegraphy.

phonique /fɔnik/ *adj* phonic.

phono○ /fɔno/ *nm* gramophone GB, phonograph US.

phonogramme /fɔnɔgʀam/ *nm* phonogram.

phonographe /fɔnɔgʀaf/ *nm* gramophone GB, phonograph US.

phonographique /fɔnɔgʀafik/ *adj* [*industrie*] record (*épith*); **œuvre ~** recorded works (*pl*).

phonologie /fɔnɔlɔʒi/ *nf* phonology.

phonologique /fɔnɔlɔʒik/ *adj* phonological.

phonologue /fɔnɔlɔg/ *nmf* phonologist.

phonothèque /fɔnɔtɛk/ *nf* sound archive.

phoque /fɔk/ *nm* Zool **1** (animal) seal; **2** (peau) sealskin; **un manteau en ~** a sealskin coat.
IDIOMES **souffler comme un ~** to puff and pant.

phosphatage /fɔsfataʒ/ *nm* treatment with phosphates.

phosphate /fɔsfat/ *nm* phosphate; **lessive sans ~s** phosphate-free detergent.

phosphaté, ~e /fɔsfate/ *adj* **1** [*engrais*] phosphate (*épith*); **2** Culin [*bouillie, aliment*] containing calcium phosphate (*après n*).

phosphater /fɔsfate/ [1] *vtr* to apply phosphates to [*terre*].

phosphène /fɔsfɛn/ *nm* phosphene.

phosphore /fɔsfɔʀ/ *nm* phosphorus.

phosphoré, ~e /fɔsfɔʀe/ *adj* phosphorous.

phosphorer○ /fɔsfɔʀe/ [1] *vi* to beaver away.

phosphorescence /fɔsfɔʀesɑ̃s/ *nf* phosphorescence.

phosphorescent, ~e /fɔsfɔʀesɑ̃, ɑ̃t/ *adj* phosphorescent.

phosphoreux, -euse /fɔsfɔʀø, øz/ *adj* [*acide*] phosphorous; [*alliage*] phosphor (*épith*).

phosphorique /fɔsfɔʀik/ *adj* phosphoric.

phosphure /fɔsfyʀ/ *nm* phosphide.

photo /fɔto/ *nf* (*abbr* = **photographie**) **1** (technique) photo; **faire de la ~** (en amateur) to take photos; (en professionnel) to be a photographer; **2** (image) photo, photograph, picture; **faire une ~** to take a photograph ou picture; **~s de vacances** holiday GB ou vacation US photographs; **prendre qn/qch en ~** to take a photo ou picture of sb/sth; **être pris en ~** to be photographed; **se faire prendre en ~** to have one's photo taken.
■ **~ d'identité** passport photo; **~ de mode** fashion photo, fashion shot; **~ satellite** satellite picture; **~ souvenir** souvenir photograph.

photo(-) /fɔto/ *préf* Sci photo(-); **photocathode** photocathode; **phototaxie** phototaxis.

photobiologie /fɔtobjɔlɔʒi/ *nf* photobiology.

photochimie /fɔtoʃimi/ *nf* photochemistry.

photochimique /fɔtoʃimik/ *adj* photochemical.

photochromique /fɔtokʀɔmik/ *adj* photochromic, photosensitive.

photocomposer /fɔtokɔ̃poze/ [1] *vtr* to filmset GB, to photocompose US.

photocomposeuse /fɔtokɔ̃pozøz/ *nf* filmsetter GB, photocomposer US.

photocomposition /fɔtokɔ̃pozisjɔ̃/ *nf* film setting GB, photocomposition US.

photoconducteur, -trice /fɔtokɔ̃dyktœʀ, tʀis/ **I** *adj* photoconductive.
II *nm* photoconductor.

photoconduction /fɔtokɔ̃dyksjɔ̃/ *nf* photoconductivity.

photocopie /fɔtokɔpi/ *nf* **1** (copie) photocopy, photostat, xerox® US; **2** (procédé) photocopying; **3** (service) (dans magasin, université) photocopying service; (dans administration) **envoyer qch à la ~** to send sth to be photocopied.

photocopier /fɔtokɔpje/ [2] *vtr* to photocopy, to xerox® US.

photocopieur /fɔtokɔpjœʀ/ *nm* photocopier.

photocopieuse /fɔtokɔpjøz/ *nf* photocopier.

photocopillage /fɔtokɔpijaʒ/ *nm* illegal photocopying.

photodégradable /fɔtodegʀadabl/ *adj* photodegradable.

photodissociation /fɔtodisɔsjasjɔ̃/ *nf* photodisintegration.

photoélectricité /fɔtoelɛktʀisite/ *nf* photoelectricity.

photoélectrique /fɔtoelɛktʀik/ *adj* [*cellule, effet*] photoelectric.

photo-finish, *pl* **photos-finish** /fɔtofiniʃ/ *nf* **c'est la ~ qui a désigné le vrai vainqueur de la course** the winner was decided on a photofinish; **contrôler l'arrivée d'une course à la ~** to verify the result of a race by examining the photofinish.

photogénique /fɔtoʒenik/ *adj* [*personne, couleur, matière*] photogenic.

photographe /fɔtogʀaf/ ▶510 *nmf* **1** (qui prend des photos) photographer; **~ de presse/de mode** press/fashion photographer; **2** (commerçant) **aller chez le ~** to go to the camera shop GB ou store US.
■ **~ de plateau** Cin stills man.

photographie /fɔtogʀafi/ *nf* **1** (technique) photography; **la ~ en noir et blanc** black and white photography; **2** (image) photograph, picture; **prendre une ~** to take a photograph; **3** (aperçu représentatif) picture; **une ~ de la société contemporaine** a picture of contemporary society.
■ **~ aérienne** (technique) aerial photography; (cliché) aerial photograph; **~ d'art** art photography; **~ de plateau** Cin still; **~ de reportage** photojournalism.

photographier /fɔtogʀafje/ [2] *vtr* **1** (prendre en photo) to photograph, to take photos ou a photo of [*personne, lieu, objet*]; **se faire ~** to have one's photo or picture taken; **se laisser ~** to let oneself be photographed; **2** (mémoriser) to fix [sth/sb] in one's mind, to make a mental picture of [*endroit, personne*].

photographique /fɔtogʀafik/ *adj* [*art, papier, image, documents*] photographic.

photographiquement /fɔtogʀafikmɑ̃/ *adv* photographically.

photograveur /fɔtogʀavœʀ/ ▶510 *nm* photoengraver, process engraver.

photogravure /fɔtogʀavyʀ/ *nf* photoengraving.

photo-interprétation /fɔtoɛ̃tɛʀpʀetasjɔ̃/ *nf* photo interpretation.

photojournalisme /fɔtoʒuʀnalism/ ▶510 *nm* photojournalism.

photojournaliste /fɔtoʒuʀnalist/ ▶510 *nmf* photojournalist.

photolithographie /fɔtolitɔgʀafi/ *nf* photolithography.

photoluminescence /fɔtolyminesɑ̃s/ *nf* photoluminescence.

photolyse /fɔtoliz/ *nf* photolysis.

photomaton® /fɔtomatɔ̃/ *nm* (appareil) photo booth.

photomètre /fɔtomɛtʀ/ *nm* photometer.

photométrie /fɔtometʀi/ *nf* photometry.

photométrique /fɔtometʀik/ *adj* photometric.

photomontage /fɔtomɔ̃taʒ/ *nm* photomontage.

photomultiplicateur /fɔtomyltiplikatœʀ/ *nm* photomultiplier.

photon /fɔtɔ̃/ *nm* photon.

photonique /fɔtɔnik/ *adj* photonic.

photopériodique /fɔtopeʀjɔdik/ *adj* photoperiodic.

photopériodisme /fɔtopeʀjɔdism/ *nm* photoperiodism.

photophobie /fɔtofɔbi/ *nf* photophobia.

photophore /fɔtofɔʀ/ *nm* (de mineur, spéléologue) miner's lamp; (décoratif) (decorative) candle holder.

photopile /fɔtopil/ *nf* solar cell.

photorésistance /fɔtoʀezistɑ̃s/ *nf* photoresistance.

photosensibilisation /fɔtosɑ̃sibilizasjɔ̃/ *nf* photosensitization.

photosensible /fɔtosɑ̃sibl/ *adj* photosensitive.

photostat® /fɔtosta/ *nm* Photostat®.

photostoppeur, **-euse** /fɔtostɔpœʀ, øz/ ▶ 510 *nm,f* street photographer.

photostyle /fɔtostil/ *nm* light pen.

photosynthèse /fɔtosɛ̃tɛz/ *nf* photosynthesis.

photothèque /fɔtotɛk/ *nf* **1** (lieu) picture library; **2** (collection) photographic collection.

photothérapie /fɔtoteʀapi/ *nf* phototherapy.

phototropisme /fɔtotʀɔpism/ *nm* phototropism.

phototype /fɔtotip/ *nm* phototype.

photovoltaïque /fɔtovɔltaik/ *adj* photovoltaic.

phrase /fʀɑz/ *nf* **1** Ling (assemblage de mots) sentence; **2** (propos) phrase; **une ~ célèbre/ampoulée** a well-known/highflown phrase; **une ~ qui veut tout dire** a revealing phrase; **il eut cette ~ admirable** he came out with this wonderful phrase; **avoir une ~ malheureuse** to say the wrong thing; **faire des ~s** or **de grandes ~s** to use flowery words; **sans ~s** without mincing one's words; **pas de ~s** no fine phrases; **tour de ~** turn of phrase; ▶ **petit**; **3** Mus phrase.
■ **~ toute faite** stock phrase, set expression.

phrasé /fʀɑze/ *nm* Mus phrasing.

phraséologie /fʀazeɔlɔʒi/ *nf* **1** (ensemble de termes) phraseology; **2** (verbiage) verbosity.

phraséologique /fʀazeɔlɔʒik/ *adj* **1** Ling phraseological; **dictionnaire ~** dictionary of idioms; **2** pej [*style*] pretentious.

phraser /fʀɑze/ [1] **I** *vtr* Mus [*musicien*] to phrase [*air, mouvement*].
II *vi* (faire des phrases) to be wordy.

phraseur, **-euse** /fʀɑzœʀ, øz/ *nm,f* phrasemonger, phrasemaker.

phrastique /fʀastik/ *adj* phrasal.

phréatique /fʀeatik/ *adj* **nappe ~** ground water ¢.

phrénique /fʀenik/ *adj* phrenic.

phrénologie /fʀenɔlɔʒi/ *nf* phrenology.

Phrygie /fʀiʒi/ *nprf* Phrygia.

phrygien, **-ienne** /fʀiʒjɛ̃, ɛn/ *adj* Phrygian; **bonnet ~** Phrygian cap.

phtaléine /ftalein/ *nf* phthalein.

phtisie† /ftizi/ *nf* consumption, phthisis spéc.
■ **~ galopante** galloping consumption.

phtisiologie /ftizjɔlɔʒi/ *nf* phthisiology.

phtisiologue /ftizjɔlɔg/ ▶ 510 *nmf* tuberculosis specialist, phthisiologist spéc.

phtisique† /ftizik/ *adj, nmf* consumptive.

phycologie /fikɔlɔʒi/ *nf* phycology.

phylactère /filaktɛʀ/ *nm* **1** (de bande dessinée) speech ou thought bubble; **2** (de vitrail) phylactery, scroll; **3** (étui) phylactery.

phylloxéra /filɔksera/ *nm* (insecte, maladie) phylloxera.

phylogenèse /filɔʒənɛz/ *nf* **1** (formation des espèces) phylogenesis; **2** (science) phylogeny.

phylogénétique /filɔʒenetik/ **I** *adj* phylogenetic, phyletic.
II *nf* phylogenetics (+ *v sg*).

phylum /filɔm/ *nm* phylum.

physalis /fizalis/ *nm inv* Chinese lantern, physalis spéc.

physicien, **-ienne** /fizisjɛ̃, ɛn/ ▶ 510 *nm,f* physicist; **un ~ nucléaire** a nuclear physicist.

physico-chimique, *pl* **~s** /fizikoʃimik/ *adj* physicochemical.

physico-mathématique, *pl* **~s** /fizikomatematik/ *adj* physicomathematical.

physiocrate /fizjɔkʀat/ *nmf* physiocrat.

physiocratie /fizjɔkʀasi/ *nf* physiocracy.

physiologie /fizjɔlɔʒi/ *nf* **1** Physiol physiology (**de** of); **2** littér (structure) anatomy (**de** of).

physiologique /fizjɔlɔʒik/ *adj* physiological.

physiologiquement /fizjɔlɔʒikmɑ̃/ *adv* physiologically.

physiologiste /fizjɔlɔʒist/ ▶ 510 *nmf* physiologist.

physionomie /fizjɔnɔmi/ *nf* (traits du visage) facial appearance, physiognomy sout; (visage) face; fig (de pays) face; (de quartier) appearance, look; **la ~ de l'Europe/de la France a beaucoup changé** the face of Europe/France has greatly changed; **~ politique d'un pays** political complexion of a country; **~ du marché** Fin state of the market.

physionomiste /fizjɔnɔmist/ *nmf* **1** (amateur) **c'est un bon ~** (personne douée de mémoire) he has a good memory for faces; (personne qui sait juger) he's a good judge of faces; **2** ▶ 510 (profession) *casino employee responsible for recognizing people who are banned from gaming halls.*

physiopathologie /fizjɔpatɔlɔʒi/ *nf* physiopathology.

physiothérapie /fizjɔteʀapi/ *nf* physiotherapy GB, physical therapy US.

physique /fizik/ **I** *adj* physical; **pour les cyclistes, c'est une étape très ~** for cyclists, this is a stage which requires a lot of physical effort; **un acteur qui a un jeu très ~** an actor with a very physical way of acting; **le squash provoque une énorme dépense ~** squash involves an enormous expenditure of energy.
II *nm* (apparence) physical appearance; (corps) physique; **avoir un ~ séduisant/banal** to look attractive/ordinary; **jouer de son ~** to play on one's good looks; **au ~** physically.
III *nf* (discipline) physics (+ *v sg*); **de ~** [*livre, professeur, examen, laboratoire*] physics; **la ~ nucléaire/des particules** nuclear/particle physics.
IDIOMES **avoir le ~ de l'emploi** to look the part.

physiquement /fizikmɑ̃/ *adv* physically.

phytobiologie /fitobjɔlɔʒi/ *nf* phytobiology.

phytogéographie /fitoʒeɔgʀafi/ *nf* phytogeography.

phytopathologie /fitopatɔlɔʒi/ *nf* phytopathology.

phytophage /fitofaʒ/ *adj* phytophagous.

phytoplancton /fitoplɑ̃ktɔ̃/ *nm* phytoplankton.

phytosanitaire /fitosanitɛʀ/ *adj* phytosanitary; **produit ~** pesticide.

phytothérapeute /fitoteʀapøt/ ▶ 510 *nmf* herbalist.

phytothérapie /fitoteʀapi/ *nf* herbal medicine.

pi /pi/ *nm inv* pi.

piaf○ /pjaf/ *nm* **1** (petit oiseau) little bird; **2** (moineau) sparrow.

piaffement /pjafmɑ̃/ *nm* **on entendait les ~s d'un cheval** we could hear a horse pawing the ground.

piaffer /pjafe/ [1] *vi* **1** [*cheval*] to paw the ground; **2** [*personne*] to be impatient (**de faire** to do); **~ d'impatience** to be champing at the bit.

piaillement /pjajmɑ̃/ *nm* **1** (d'oiseau) chirping ¢; **2**○ (d'enfant) squealing ¢.

piailler /pjaje/ [1] *vi* **1** [*oiseau*] to chirp; **2**○ [*personne*] to squeal.

piaillerie○ /pjajʀi/ *nf* = **piaillement**.

piailleur, **-euse** /pjajœʀ, øz/ *adj* [*oiseau*] chirping; [*enfant*] squealing (*épith*).

pianissimo /pjanisimo/ **I** *adv* **1** Mus [*jouer, chanter*] pianissimo; **2**○ very gently; **allez-y ~** easy does it!
II *nm* Mus pianissimo passage.

pianiste /pjanist/ *nmf* **1** ▶ 510 (professionnel) pianist; **un ~ de talent** a talented pianist; **2** (amateur) piano player.
■ **~ de jazz** jazz pianist.

pianistique /pjanistik/ *adj* **1** (de pianiste) [*technique, qualité*] pianistic; **2** (de piano) [*musique, études*] piano.

piano /pjano/ **I** *nm* **1** ▶ 534 (instrument) piano; **jouer qch au ~** to play sth on the piano; **se mettre au ~** (s'asseoir) to sit down at the piano; (apprendre) to take up the piano; **2** (passage joué doucement) piano passage; **3**○ (fourneau de restaurant) cooker GB, stove.
II *adv* **1** Mus piano; **2**○ fig (doucement) softly-softly○ GB, gently; **vas-y ~** take it easy.
■ **~ acoustique** acoustic piano; **~ bastringue** honky-tonk piano; **~ de concert** concert grand (piano); **~ crapaud** small baby grand; **~ demi-queue** boudoir grand GB, parlor grand US; **~ droit** upright piano; **~ électrique** electric piano; **~ mécanique** Pianola®, player piano; **~ numérique** player piano; **~ quart de queue** baby grand; **~ à queue** grand piano.

pianoforte /pjanofɔʀte/ ▶ 534 *nm* pianoforte.

pianotage /pjanɔtaʒ/ *nm* (sur un piano) tinkling; (sur une machine à écrire, un téléphone, ordinateur) tapping; (sur une table) drumming.

pianoter /pjanɔte/ [1] **I** *vtr* **1** (sur un piano) to tinkle [*air, mélodie*]; **2**○ (taper) to tap in; **pianotez**○ **3615 sur votre Minitel®** tap in 3615 on your Minitel®.
II *vi* **1** (sur un piano) to tinkle; **2** (sur un ordinateur, une machine à écrire) to tap (**sur** at); **je pianote sur mon clavier toute la journée** I tap away at the keyboard all day long; **3** (sur une table) to drum.

piastre /pjastʀ/ ▶ 46 *nf* **1** gén piastre[GB]; **2** C (dollar) dollar.

piaule◑ /pjol/ *nf* pad○, room.

piaulement /pjolmɑ̃/ *nm* **1** (d'oiseau) cheeping ¢; **2**○ (d'enfant) bawling○ ¢.

piauler /pjole/ [1] *vi* **1** (oiseau) to cheep; **2**○ (enfant) to bawl○.

PIB /peibe/ *nm*: *abbr* ▶ **produit**.

pic /pik/ **I** *nm* **1** (montagne, sommet) peak; **2** (outil) pick; (de mineur) pickaxe[GB]; **3** fig (de courbe) peak; **~ de natalité** peak in the birthrate; **4** (oiseau) woodpecker.
II à pic *loc adj* [*paroi, falaise*] sheer; [*montagne, gorge, ravin*] very steep.
III à pic *loc adv* **1** (en pente raide) **s'élever à ~** [*paroi, falaise*] to rise sheer; **tomber à ~** [*falaise*] to fall in a sheer drop; **couler à ~** [*personne, objet*] to go straight down ou straight to the bottom; **2**○ [*arriver, se trouver*] (juste à temps) in the nick of time; (au bon moment) just at the right moment.
■ **~ à glace** ice pick; **~ noir** Zool black woodpecker.

pica /pika/ *nm* (tous contextes) pica.

picador /pikadɔʀ/ *nm* picador.

picaillons◑ /pikajɔ̃/ *nmpl* **des ~** dough○ ¢, money ¢.

picard, **~e** /pikaʀ, aʀd/ ▶ 692 **I** *adj* of Picardy.
II *nm* Ling Picardy dialect.

Picard, **~e** /pikaʀ, aʀd/ ▶ 692 *nm,f* (natif) native of Picardy; (habitant) inhabitant of Picardy.

Picardie /pikaʀdi/ ▶692 *nprf* **la ~** Picardy.

picaresque /pikaʀɛsk/ Littérat **I** *adj* [*roman, genre, héros*] picaresque.

II *nm* (genre) **le ~** the picaresque.

piccolo /pikɔlo/ ▶534 *nm* piccolo.

Pic de la Mirandole /pikdəlamiʀɑ̃dɔl/ *npr* Pico della Mirandola.

pichenette /piʃnɛt/ *nf* flick; **donner une ~ à qn** to give sb a flick; **enlever une poussière d'une ~** to flick off a speck of dust.

pichet /piʃɛ/ *nm* **1** (cruche) jug GB, pitcher; **2** (contenu) jugful GB, pitcherful.

pickpocket /pikpɔkɛt/ *nm* pickpocket.

pick-up○ /pikœp/ *nm inv* record player.

picoler◑ /pikɔle/ [1] *vi* to booze○, to drink; **~ sec** or **dur** to be a real boozer○ ou pisshead◑ GB; **qu'est-ce qu'il picole**◑! what a boozer○ ou pisshead◑ GB!

picoleur○, **-euse** /pikɔlœʀ, øz/ *nm,f* boozer○, drunkard.

picorer /pikɔʀe/ [1] **I** *vtr* [*volaille, oiseau*] to peck at [*graines, miettes*].

II *vi* [*oiseau, poule*] to peck about, to forage; [*personne, enfant*] to nibble.

picot /piko/ *nm* **1** Tech (dent) tooth; **entraînement à ~s** sprocket drive, tractor feed; **2** (pointe restant sur du bois) splinter; **3** (dentelle) picot; **une dentelle à ~** picot(-edged) lace.

picotement /pikɔtmɑ̃/ *nm* (de peau, membres) tingling ¢; (de gorge) tickling ¢; (d'yeux) smarting ¢; **ressentir des ~s dans les bras/la gorge** to feel one's arms tingling/one's throat tickling.

picoter /pikɔte/ [1] **I** *vtr* **1** (irriter) [*fumée, gaz, vent*] to sting, to make [sth] sting [*yeux, nez*]; to tickle [*gorge*]; [*herbe*] to sting [*peau, membres*]; **le froid me picote les joues/la peau** the cold makes my cheeks/skin tingle; **le gaz me picote les yeux** the gas is stinging my eyes ou makes my eyes sting; **j'ai la gorge qui me picote** my throat is tickling; **2** (piquer) [*oiseau*] to peck [*fruit, pain*]; [*personne*] to prick [*feuille, carton*].

II *vi* [*gorge*] to tickle; [*yeux*] to sting; **j'ai la peau qui picote** my skin is prickling.

picotin /pikɔtɛ̃/ *nm* **1** (ration) **~ d'avoine** ration of oats; **2** (mesure) peck.

picouse◑ /pikuz/ *nf* (piqûre) jab○ GB, shot○, injection.

picrate /pikʀat/ *nm* **1**◑ (vin) plonk○ GB, cheap wine; **un petit coup de ~** a drop of plonk; **2** Chimie picrate.

picrique /pikʀik/ *adj* picric.

pictogramme /piktɔgʀam/ *nm* pictograph, pictogram.

pictographie /piktɔgʀafi/ *nf* pictography, picture writing.

pictographique /piktɔgʀafik/ *adj* pictographic.

pictural, **-e**, *mpl* **-aux** /piktyʀal, o/ *adj* pictorial.

pidgin /pidʒin/ *nm* pidgin.

pie /pi/ **I** ▶193 *adj inv* [*cheval*] **~ noir** piebald; **~ alezan** skewbald; [*vache*] black and white.

II *adj f* liter **œuvre ~** charitable act; **faire œuvre ~** to be charitable.

III *nf* **1** (oiseau) magpie; **2** (bovin) **la race ~ rouge** (bovins) the breed of red and white cattle; **3**○ (bavard) chatterbox○.

IDIOMES **être bavard comme une ~**○ to be a chatterbox○; **être voleur comme une ~**○ to be a thieving magpie○.

Pie /pi/ *npr* Pius.

pièce /pjɛs/ **I** *nf* **1** (d'habitation) room; **maison de quatre ~s** four-room(ed) house (*excluding kitchen and bathroom*); **2** ▶46 (monnaie) **~ (de monnaie)** coin; **~ d'or/d'argent** gold/silver coin; **~ d'un franc** one franc coin ou piece; **donner** or **glisser la ~ à qn**○ to tip sb, to give sb a tip; ▶**monnaie**; **3** Théât play; Littérat, Mus piece; **4** (morceau) bit, piece; **en ~s** in bits; **mettre en ~s** (briser) to smash [sth] to pieces; (déchirer) to pull [sth] to pieces; fig to pull [sth/sb] to pieces; **fait d'une seule ~** made in one piece; **~ à ~** bit by bit; **5** (élément d' un assemblage) part; **~ de rechange** spare part; **~s de charpente** roofing timbers; **créé de toutes ~s** fig created from nothing; **c'est forgé** or **inventé de toutes ~s** fig it's a complete fabrication; **6** (pour réparer) patch; **poser une ~ sur un vêtement** to put a patch on a garment; **7** (document) document; **juger avec ~s à l'appui** to judge on the basis of supporting documents; **~s jointes** enclosures; **juger sur ~s** to judge on the actual evidence; **8** (unité, objet) piece, item; (de jeu d'échecs, puzzle) piece; **service de table de 18 ~s** 18-piece dinner service; **vendu à la ~** sold separately ou individually; **20 francs (la) ~** 20 francs each ou apiece ; **travailler à la ~** or **aux ~s** to do piecework; **être à la ~** or **aux ~s** to be on piecework; **9** (quantité) (d'étoffe) length; **~ de bois** piece of timber; **~ de viande** (large) piece of meat; **10** (parcelle) **~ de luzerne/d'avoine** field of lucerne/of oats; **~ de terre** field, piece of land; **11** (animal) **~ de bétail** head of cattle; Chasse, Culin, Pêche **une belle ~ (de poisson)** a handsome fish; **plusieurs ~s de poisson et de gibier** a variety of fish and game.

II -pièces (*in compounds*) **1** (habitation) **un deux/trois-~s cuisine** a two-/three-roomed flat GB ou apartment US with kitchen; **2** (vêtement) **un (maillot/costume) deux-~s** a two-piece swimsuit/suit; **trois-~s** three-piece suit.

■ **~ d'artifice** firework; **~ d'artillerie** cannon; **~ de collection** collector's item; **~ à conviction** Jur exhibit; **~ d'eau** ornamental lake; (plus petit) ornamental pond; **~ détachée** spare part; **en ~s détachées** (en kit) in kit form; (démonté) dismantled; **~ d'identité** identity papers (*pl*); **vous avez une ~ d'identité?** do you have some identification ¢?; **~ maîtresse** (de collection) showpiece; (de plaidoyer) key element; (de politique) cornerstone; **~ montée** (gâteau) layer cake; (choux) *pyramid-shaped arrangement of cream puffs*; **~ de musée** museum piece; **~ rapportée** lit patch; **la famille et les ~s rapportées**○ hum the family and all the in-laws; **~ de résistance** pièce de résistance; **~ de théâtre** play; **~ de vers** short poem; **~ de vin** cask of wine.

IDIOMES **il est tout d'une ~** he's a very straightforward man; **on n'est pas aux ~s**○ we're not in a sweat-shop; **faire ~ à qn** to thwart sb.

piécette /pjesɛt/ *nf* small coin.

pied /pje/ *nm* **1** ▶188 Anat foot; **avoir les ~s plats** to have flat feet; **avoir les ~s cambrés** to have high-arched feet ou high arches; **marcher avec les ~s tournés en dedans/en dehors** to be pigeon-toed/splay-footed; **être ~s nus** to have bare feet, to be barefoot(ed); **il était ~s nus dans ses chaussures** his feet were bare inside his shoes; **aimer rester (les) ~s nus** to like to go barefoot(ed); **marcher/courir (les) ~s nus** to walk about/to run around barefoot(ed); **sauter à ~s joints** lit to jump with one's feet together; fig to jump in with both feet; **il a sauté à ~s joints dans le piège** he jumped into the trap with both feet; **coup de ~** kick; **donner un coup de ~ à qn** to kick sb; **donner un coup de ~ dans qch** to kick sth; **tuer qn à coups de ~** to kick sb to death; **casser qch à coups de ~** to kick sth to pieces; **écarter qch d'un coup de ~** to kick sth aside; **je lui ai mis mon ~ aux fesses**◑**/au cul**● I kicked him up the backside○/arse● GB ou ass◑ US; **à ~** gén on foot; **être à ~** to be on foot; **aller quelque part à ~** to go somewhere on foot; **promenade à ~** walk; **randonnée à ~** ramble; **être aux ~s de qn** lit, fig to be at sb's feet; **se jeter aux ~s de qn** to throw oneself at sb's feet; **son chien au ~** with his dog at his heels; **au ~!** (ordre à un chien) heel!; **bottes aux ~s** wearing boots; **ne plus pouvoir mettre un ~ devant l'autre** to be unable to go another step ou to put one foot in front of the other; **traîner les ~s** lit, fig to drag one's feet; **ne plus tenir sur ses ~s** to be about to keel over; **taper du ~** (de colère) to stamp one's foot; (d'impatience) to tap one's foot; **repousser qch du ~** to push sth away with one's foot; **mettre ~ à terre** (de cheval) to dismount; (de camion) to get out; (de moto, bicyclette) to dismount, to get off; **avoir le ~ alerte** to have a spring in one's step; **de la tête aux ~s, des ~s à la tête, de ~ en cap** from head to foot, from top to toe; **portrait en ~** full-length portrait; **statue en ~** standing figure; **je n'ai jamais mis les ~s chez elle** I've never set foot in her house; **avoir un ~ dans l'édition** to have a foothold in publishing; **avoir conscience de là où on met les ~s**○ fig to be aware of what one is letting oneself in for; **2** (d'animal) Zool gén foot; (de cheval) hoof; Culin trotter; **~s de porc/de mouton** pig's/sheep's trotters; **animaux sur ~** livestock on the hoof; **3** (de collant, chaussette) foot; **4** (base) (de colline, falaise, d'escalier) foot, bottom; (de mât, colonne) foot, base; **habiter au ~ des montagnes** to live at the foot of the mountains; **au ~ de l'arbre** at the foot of the tree; **5** (de meuble) (pris dans sa totalité) leg; (extrémité) foot; (de verre) stem; (de lampe) base; (d'appareil photo) gén stand; (trépied) tripod; **table à trois ~s** three-legged table; **~ de table** table-leg; **~ de lampe** lampstand; **au ~ du lit** (opposé à la tête) at the foot of the bed; **6** (de champignon) stalk; **7** (plant) (de céleri, salade) head; **~ de vigne** vine; **récolte sur ~** standing crop; **8** ▶477 Mes (anglais) foot (*0,3048 metres*[GB]); (autrefois) foot (*0,3248 metres*[GB]); ▶**six**; **9** Littérat (en métrique) foot; **10** (niveau) **sur un ~ d'égalité** on an equal footing; **sur le même ~** on the same level.

■ **~ de col** collarstand; **~ à coulisse** calliper rule; **~ de lit** footboard; **~ tendre** tenderfoot.

IDIOMES **~ à ~** [*céder, se défendre*] inch by inch; **être sur ~** [*personne*] to be up and about; [*affaires*] to be up and running; **mettre qch sur ~** to set sth up; **mise sur ~** setting up; **remettre qch sur ~** [*pays, affaire*] to get sth back on its feet again; **j'ai ~** I can touch the bottom; **je n'ai plus ~** I'm out of my depth; **perdre ~** lit to go out of one's depth; fig to lose ground; **lâcher ~** to give up; **prendre ~ quelque part** to get a foothold somewhere; **ne pas mettre les ~s dehors** not to set foot outside; **avoir toujours un ~ en l'air** to be always on the go; **être à ~ d'œuvre** to be ready to get down to work; **je me suis débrouillé comme un ~**○ I've made a mess of it; **elle joue au tennis comme un ~**○ she's hopeless at tennis; **faire un ~ de nez à qn** to thumb one's nose at sb; **faire un ~ de nez à la tradition/aux conventions** to cock a snook at tradition/at conventions; **faire du ~ à qn** to play footsy with sb○; **faire des ~s et des mains pour obtenir qch** to work really hard at getting sth; **ça lui fera les ~s**○ that will teach him a lesson; **c'est le ~**○ (très bien) that's terrific○; **c'est pas le ~ aujourd'hui**○ things aren't so hot today○; **prendre son ~**○ gén to have a good time; (au lit) to have it away◑; **sortir les ~s devant** to leave feet first; **partir du bon/mauvais ~** to get off on the right/wrong foot; **mettre à ~** (mesure disciplinaire) to suspend; (mesure économique) to lay [sb] off; **lever le ~**○ (aller moins vite) to slow down; (s'arrêter) to stop.

pied-à-terre /pjetatɛʀ/ *nm inv* pied-à-terre.

pied-bot, *pl* **pieds-bots** /pjebo/ *nm* club-footed person.

pied-d'alouette, *pl* **pieds-d'alouette** /pjedalwɛt/ *nm* larkspur.

pied-de-biche, *pl* **pieds-de-biche** /pjedbiʃ/ *nm* **1** (de machine à coudre) presser foot; **2** (levier) crowbar; **3** (arrache-clous) claw head.

pied-de-coq, *pl* **pieds-de-coq** /pjedkɔk/ **I** *adj inv* [*tissu*] large houndstooth.

II *nm* large houndstooth check.

pied-de-poule, *pl* **pieds-de-poule** /pjedpul/ **I** *adj inv* houndstooth.

II *nm* houndstooth check.

piédestal, *pl* **-aux** /pjedɛstal, o/ *nm* (socle) pedestal; **placer/mettre qn sur un ~** fig to put sb on a pedestal; **descendre/tomber de son ~** fig to come down from/to fall off one's pedestal.

pied-noir○, *pl* **pieds-noirs** /pjenwaʀ/ **I** *adj* [*accent*] pied-noir, of a French colonial born in Algeria.

II *nmf* pied-noir (*French colonial born in Algeria*).

pied-plat, *pl* **pieds-plats** /pjepla/ *nm* flat-footed individual.

piège /pjɛʒ/ *nm* **1** (dispositif) (engin) trap; (collet) snare; (fosse) pit; **poser/tendre un ~** to set/to lay a trap; **prendre un animal au ~** to catch an animal in a trap; **être pris au ~** to be caught in a trap; **relever un ~** to check a trap; **le ~ tendu n'a pas fonctionné** the trap that had been set didn't work; **l'animal pris au ~** the trapped animal; **2** (stratagème) trap; **tendre un ~ à qn** to set a trap for sb; **il s'est laissé prendre au ~** he walked into the trap; **tomber dans un ~** to fall into a trap; **être pris au ~** to get caught in a trap, to be trapped; **être pris à son propre ~** to fall into one's own trap; **le ~ s'est refermé sur lui** he was caught in the trap; **3** (difficulté) pitfall; **les ~s de la traduction** gén the pitfalls of translation; (d'un texte spécifique) the pitfalls in the translation; **c'est un texte sans ~** it's a straightforward text; **la dictée comporte quelques ~s orthographiques** the dictation has some tricky spellings; **il y a un ~ dans la formulation du sujet de dissertation** there's a trap in the way the subject of the essay is formulated.

■ **~ à cons**◑ con○; **~ à ions** Électron ion trap GB, beam bender US; **~ à lapins** rabbit snare; **~ à loups** mantrap; **~ à oiseaux** gin trap; **~ à poux**◑ beard; **~ à rats** lit rattrap; **~ à renards** gin trap.

piégé, **~e** /pjeʒe/ **I** *pp* ▶ **piéger**.

II *pp adj* (muni d'un dispositif) [*objet, valise, sac*] booby-trapped; **une lettre ~e** a letter bomb; **un colis ~** a parcel GB ou package US bomb; **une voiture ~e** a car bomb; **le colis était-il ~?** was the parcel GB ou package US booby-trapped?

piégeage /pjeʒaʒ/ *nm* **1** (d'animaux) trapping; **2** (de valise, voiture, colis) booby-trapping (**de** of).

piéger /pjeʒe/ [15] *vtr* **1** lit (capturer) gén to trap [*animal, criminel*]; (avec un collet) to snare [*animal*]; **se faire** or **se laisser ~** to get trapped; **2** (tromper) to trick, to trap [*personne*]; **je me suis fait ~ par une question à double sens** I let myself be tricked by a double-edged question; **3** (munir d'un dispositif) to booby-trap [*lettre, colis, voiture*].

pie-grièche, *pl* **pies-grièches** /pigʀijɛʃ/ *nf* shrike.

pie-mère, *pl* **pies-mères** /pimɛʀ/ *nf* pia mater.

piémont /pjemɔ̃/ *nm* Géog piedmont plain.

Piémont /pjemɔ̃/ ▶ **692** *nprm* Piedmont.

piémontais, **~e** /pjemɔ̃tɛ, ɛz/ ▶ **692** *adj* Piedmontese.

Piémontais, **~e** /pjemɔ̃tɛ, ɛz/ *nm,f* Piedmontese.

piéride /pjeʀid/ *nf* pierid (butterfly).

■ **~ du chou** cabbage white.

pierraille /pjɛʀɑj/ *nf* loose stones (*pl*).

pierre /pjɛʀ/ *nf* **1** (matière) stone; **un pont/mur de** or **en ~** a stone bridge/wall; **une maison en ~ de la région** a house in local stone; **2** (morceau) stone, rock; **un mur en ~s sèches** a drystone wall; **un désert de ~s** a rocky ou stony wilderness; **'attention, chute de ~s'** 'beware of falling rocks'; **poser la première ~** to lay the foundation stone; fig to lay the foundations (**de** of); **être amateur de vieilles ~s** fig to be fascinated by old buildings; **3** (immobilier) property GB, real-estate US; **investir dans la ~** to invest in bricks and mortar; ▶ **blanc, faux**[1], **jardin, mousse**.

■ **~ à aiguiser** whetstone; **~ angulaire** lit, fig cornerstone; **~ à bâtir** building stone; **~ à briquet** flint; **~ à chaux** limestone; **~ dure** semiprecious stone; **~ à feu** = **~ à briquet**; **~ fine** gemstone; **~ à fusil** gun flint; **~ gravée** engraved stone, intaglio spéc; **~ levée** standing stone; **~ de lune** moonstone; **~ à plâtre** gypsum; **~ ponce** pumice stone; **~ précieuse** precious stone; **~ de Rosette** Archéol Rosetta Stone; **~ de taille** dressed stone; **~ tombale** tombstone, gravestone; **~ de touche** touchstone.

IDIOMES **jeter la ~ à qn** to accuse sb; **jeter la première ~** Bible to cast the first stone (**à** at); **apporter sa ~ à qch** to make one's contribution to sth; **faire d'une ~ deux coups** to kill two birds with one stone.

Pierre /pjɛʀ/ *npr* Pierre.

■ **~ le Grand** Peter the Great.

pierreries /pjɛʀʀi/ *nfpl* gems.

pierreux, **-euse** /pjɛʀø, øz/ *adj* **1** [*chemin, champ*] stony (*épith*); **2** [*poire*] gritty; **3** Méd [*concrétion*] stony.

pietà /pjeta/ *nf inv* pietà.

piétaille /pjetɑj/ *nf* **1** (subalternes) **la ~** (de fonction subalterne) the underlings (*pl*) péj; (de petite condition) the riff-raff péj; **2** hum (piétons) footsloggers péj; **3** (infanterie) **la ~** the infantry.

piété /pjete/ *nf* piety; **~ filiale** filial piety; **de ~** [*articles, livres*] devotional.

piétinement /pjetinmɑ̃/ *nm* **1** (mouvement) **le ~ de la foule dans les rues en fête** the crowd shuffling through the festive streets; **2** (bruit) **les ~s dans le couloir** the sound of feet in the corridor; **3** (de négociations, d'enquête) lack of progress.

piétiner /pjetine/ [1] **I** *vtr* **1** lit to trample [sth] underfoot [*bouquet, fraisiers, drapeau*]; **~ le sol** (d'impatience, de rage) to stamp one's feet; **périr piétiné** to be trampled to death; **2** fig to trample on [*droits, croyances*].

II *vi* **1** (sur place) **~ d'impatience/de rage** to hop up and down with impatience/with fury; **2** (marcher lentement) (à cause de la foule) to shuffle along; (à cause de la boue, la neige) to trudge along; **~ dans la boue** to trudge through the mud; **3** (ne pas avancer) [*négociations, enquête*] to make no headway; **je piétine** I'm not getting anywhere.

piétisme /pjetism/ *nm* pietism.

piétiste /pjetist/ Relig **I** *adj* pietistic.

II *nmf* pietist.

piéton, **-onne** /pjetɔ̃, ɔn/ **I** *adj* [*rue, zone, voie*] pedestrianized.

II *nm,f* pedestrian; **passage pour ~s** pedestrian crossing.

piétonnier, **-ière** /pjetɔnje, ɛʀ/ *adj* **1** [*rue, zone, voie*] pedestrianized; **2** [*circulation*] pedestrian (*épith*).

piètre /pjɛtʀ/ *adj* [*médecin, acteur, écrivain*] very mediocre; [*santé, résultats*] very poor; [*avantage*] negligible; [*début, performance*] sorry; **c'est une ~ consolation** it's not much comfort; **avoir ~ allure** to cut a sorry figure.

piètrement /pjɛtʀəmɑ̃/ *adv* badly.

pieu, *pl* **~x**[1] /pjø/ *nm* **1** (poteau pointu) stake; **une clôture de ~x** a picket fence; **2** Archit, Constr pile; **3**◑ (lit) bed; **se mettre** or **aller au ~** to hit the hay◑ ou the sack◑.

pieusement /pjøzmɑ̃/ *adv* **1** Relig piously; **2** (avec respect) devotedly; **des documents ~ conservés** documents religiously kept.

pieuter◑ /pjøte/ [1] **I** *vi* (dormir, être hébergé) to kip○ GB, to sleep.

II se pieuter *vpr* to hit the hay○, to hit the sack○.

pieuvre /pjœvʀ/ *nf* **1** Zool octopus; **2** (entreprise tentaculaire) octopus; **3** (personne) **quelle ~!** he's so clingy○!

pieux[2], **pieuse** /pjø, øz/ *adj* **1** Relig [*personne*] pious, religious; [*acte, pensée, livre, lecture*] pious; [*peinture*] religious; **croyance pieuse** religious belief; **avoir une pensée pieuse pour qn** to remember sb in one's prayers; **2** liter [*devoirs*] loving; [*affection, silence*] reverent.

■ **~ mensonge** white lie.

piézoélectricité /pjezoelɛktʀisite/ *nf* piezoelectricity.

piézoélectrique /pjezoelɛktʀik/ *adj* piezoelectric.

piézomètre /pjezomɛtʀ/ *nm* piezometer.

pif /pif/ **I** *nm* **1**◑ (nez) nose, conk○ GB, schnozzle○ US; **2**◑ (flair) intuition; **j'ai eu du ~** I had a hunch○; **au ~** [*mesurer*] roughly; [*trouver*] by chance; [*décider*] just like that.

II *excl* **1** (détonation) bang!; **2** (gifle) whack!

IDIOMES **avoir qn dans le ~**○ to have it in for sb○.

pifer◑ /pife/ [1] *vtr* **elle ne peut pas le ~** she can't stand○ him.

pifomètre◑ /pifɔmɛtʀ/ *nm* intuition; **au ~** [*mesurer*] roughly; [*décider*] just like that.

pige /piʒ/ *nf* **1** Édition, Presse **travailler à la ~, faire des ~s** to do freelance work; **2**◑ (année) **avoir 40 ~s** to be 40; **3** (tige) measuring rod; **4** (longueur) length.

IDIOMES **faire la ~ à qn**○ to leave sb standing, to beat sb.

pigeon /piʒɔ̃/ *nm* **1** (oiseau) pigeon; **2**◑ (naïf) sucker○.

■ **~ d'argile** clay pigeon; **~ biset** pigeon, rock dove; **~ colombin** stock dove; **~ ramier** wood pigeon, ring dove; **~ vole** Simon says; **jouer à ~ vole** to play Simon says; **~ voyageur** carrier pigeon; **envoyer un message par ~ voyageur** to send a message by carrier pigeon ou pigeon post GB.

pigeonnant, **~e** /piʒɔnɑ̃, ɑ̃t/ *adj* [*soutien-gorge*] uplift (*épith*); [*poitrine*] with a lot of cleavage (*épith, après n*).

pigeonne /piʒɔn/ *nf* Zool hen pigeon.

pigeonneau, *pl* **~x** /piʒɔno/ *nm* young pigeon.

pigeonner◑ /piʒɔne/ [1] *vtr* to take [sb] for a ride○; **se faire ~** to be taken for a ride○.

pigeonnier /piʒɔnje/ *nm* **1** (pour pigeons) gén pigeon house; (en haut d'un bâtiment) pigeon loft; (bâtiment circulaire) dovecote; **2** hum (appartement) garret.

piger /piʒe/ [13] *vtr* **1**○ (comprendre) to understand; **tu as pigé?** did you get it?; **je ne pige rien à l'informatique** I haven't got a clue○ ou I'm completely clueless○ about computing; **2** (mesurer) to measure [sth] with a measuring rod [*distance*].

pigiste /piʒist/ *nmf* freelance.

pigment /pigmɑ̃/ *nm* pigment.

pigmentaire /pigmɑ̃tɛʀ/ *adj* pigmentary.

pigmentation /pigmɑ̃tasjɔ̃/ *nf* pigmentation (**de** of).

pigmenter /pigmɑ̃te/ [1] *vtr* [*soleil, maladie*] to alter the pigmentation of [*peau*].

pigne /piɲ/ *nf* pine cone.

pignon /piɲɔ̃/ *nm* **1** (de maison) gable; **une maison à ~** a gabled house; **2** (roue dentée) gearwheel, cogwheel; (petite roue) pinion; **~ de renvoi** transmission gearwheel; **3** (de pin) pine kernel.

IDIOMES **avoir ~ sur rue** [*entreprise, notaire, architecte*] to be well-established.

pignouf◑ /piɲuf/ *nm* pej oaf, lout.

pilaf /pilaf/ *nm* pilau; **riz ~** pilau rice.

pilage /pilaʒ/ *nm* (de noix, céréales) grinding; (de glace, verre) crushing; (avec un pilon) pounding.

pilaire /pilɛʀ/ *adj* [*atrophie*] of the hair (*après n*); [*acné*] of the follicles.

pilastre /pilastʀ/ *nm* pilaster.

Pilate /pilat/ *npr* **Ponce ~** Pontius Pilate.

pilchard /pilʃaʀ/ *nm* pilchard.

pile /pil/ **I**○ *adv* **1** (brusquement) **s'arrêter ~** [*voiture, conducteur, appareil, machine*] to stop dead; **elle s'est arrêtée ~ de faire** she suddenly stopped doing; **2** (exactement) exactly; **à 10 heures et demie ~** at ten-thirty sharp ou on the dot○; **être ~ à l'heure** to be bang○ GB ou right on time; **tu tombes ~**○ (au bon moment) you've come just at the right time; (la personne qu'il faut) you're just the person I wanted to see ou we need; **tu es tombé ~** (en devinant) you hit the nail on the head○; **ça tombe ~** (au bon moment) that's lucky; **elle est arrivée ~ au moment où je devais partir** she turned up precisely as I was about to leave; **c'est tombé ~ dans mon assiette** it fell straight ou right into my plate.

II *nf* **1** (tas) (désordonné) pile; (régulier) stack; **2** Électrotech **~ (électrique)** battery; **~ rechargeable** rechargeable battery; **~ longue durée/plate** long-life/flat battery; **~ alcaline** alkaline battery; **~ au cadmium** cadmium cell; **à ~s** [*jouet, réveil, perceuse*] battery-operated (*épith*); **fonctionner sur ~s et sur secteur** to work on batteries and off the mains; **3** Archit (de pont) pier; **4** (de monnaie) **le côté ~ est abîmé** the reverse side is damaged; **~ je gagne, face tu perds** tails I win, heads you lose; **jouer à ~ ou face** Jeux to play heads or tails; **ils ont joué** or **décidé** or **tiré à ~ ou face** (choix de personne) they tossed for it; (choix d'option) they decided it on the flip ou toss of the coin; **'comment choisir?'—'à ~ ou face'** 'how can I/we etc choose?'—'toss a coin'; **ça s'est joué à ~ ou face** it was a toss-up○; **5** Ordinat stack; **6**○ (défaite) **prendre une ~** to take a hammering○.

■ **~ atomique** atomic pile; **~ bouton** button battery; **~ Leclanché** Leclanché cell; **~ sèche** dry cell; **~ solaire** solar cell; **~ Volta** voltaic pile.

piler /pile/ [1] **I** *vtr* to grind [*noix, céréales*]; to crush [*gousse d'ail, glace*]; **verre pilé** crushed glass.

II○ *vi* (s'arrêter net) [*voiture*] to pull up short, to stop suddenly; [*conducteur*] to slam on the brakes.

pileux, **-euse** /pilø, øz/ *adj* **système ~** hair (*épith*).

pilier /pilje/ *nm* **1** Constr pillar; **2** fig (de doctrine, d'économie, institution) mainstay; (personne) (de communauté, d'église) pillar; (de parti) stalwart; (habitué)○ **~ de bar** or **bistrot** bar fly○; **c'est un ~ de bistrot** he's always propping up the bar; **3** (au rugby) prop forward; **jouer ~** to play prop forward; **quel ~!** what an excellent prop forward!; **4** Anat pillar.

pillage /pijaʒ/ *nm* **1** (de ville, région) pillage, plundering; (de magasins) looting; **2** (des caisses de l'État) pillaging; **3** (plagiat) plagiarism.

pillard, **~e** /pijaʀ, aʀd/ **I** *adj* [*hordes, bandes*] pillaging, plundering; [*oiseaux*] thieving.

II *nm,f* (de magasin) looter; (pendant une guerre) pillager, looter.

piller /pije/ [1] *vtr* **1** Mil [*soldats, bandes*] to pillage [*ville, région*]; to loot [*maison, magasin*]; **~ et violer** to rape and plunder; **2** gén [*personne*] to pillage [*objets d'art*]; to plunder [*temple*]; to ransack [*maison, réfrigérateur, placard*]; [*oiseau*] to plunder [*arbre, verger*]; **~ les caisses de l'État** to plunder the treasury coffers; **3** (plagier) to plagiarize [*œuvre, auteur*].

pilleur, **-euse** /pijœʀ, øz/ *nm,f* (de magasin) looter; (d'église) plunderer.

pilon /pilɔ̃/ *nm* **1** (outil) pestle; **2** (jambe de bois) wooden leg; **3** (de volaille) drumstick; **4** Édition pulping; **mettre qch au ~** to pulp sth.

pilonnage /pilɔnaʒ/ *nm* Mil bombardment; **le ~ d'artillerie** shelling.

pilonner /pilɔne/ [1] *vtr* **1** Mil to bombard; **2** (écraser) to grind, to pound [*graines, céréales*]; **3**○ Sport to give [sb] a pounding○ [*adversaire, équipe*]; to pound away at [*buts*]; **4** Édition to pulp.

pilori /pilɔʀi/ *nm* Hist stocks (*pl*); **être condamné au ~** to be sentenced to the stocks; **mettre** or **clouer qn au ~** fig to pillory sb.

pilosité /pilozite/ *nf* hairiness ¢; hum growth.

pilotage /pilɔtaʒ/ *nm* **1** Aviat, Naut piloting ¢; Aut driving ¢; **un accident dû à une erreur de ~** an accident caused by pilot error; **le ~ à trois** flying with two co-pilots; **2** (gestion) (d'entreprise) running ¢; (de négociation) leading ¢; **le ~ d'une entreprise** running a company.

■ **~ automatique** Aviat automatic piloting system.

pilote /pilɔt/ **I** *nm* **1** ▶ 510 (conducteur) Aviat, Naut pilot; Aut driver; **2** (guide) guide; **servir de ~ à qn** to show sb around; **3** (dirigeant) Pol leader; Entr manager.

II **(-)pilote** (*in compounds*) **étude/projet(-)~** pilot study/project; **ferme/hôpital/école(-)~** experimental farm/hospital/school.

■ **~ automatique** automatic pilot; **~ automobile** racing driver; **~ de chasse** fighter pilot; **~ de course** = **~ automobile**; **~ d'essai** test pilot; **~ de ligne** airline pilot.

piloter /pilɔte/ [1] **I** *vtr* **1** (conduire) to pilot [*avion, navire*]; to drive [*voiture*]; **2** (guider) to show [sb] around [*personne*]; **3** (diriger) to run [*entreprise*]; to lead [*négociation*].

II *vi* **1** Aviat to fly; **~ à deux** to fly with dual controls; **2** Aut to drive.

pilotis /pilɔti/ *nm inv* stilts (*pl*), pilotis (*pl*); **bâti sur ~** built on stilts.

pilou /pilu/ *nm* cotton flannel, flannelette.

pilule /pilyl/ *nf* **1** (médicament) pill; **2** (contraceptif) **~ (contraceptive)** (contraceptive) pill; **~ abortive** abortion pill; **je prends la ~** I'm on the pill.

IDIOMES **avaler la ~**○ to grin and bear it; **la ~ est dure à avaler**○ it's a bitter pill to swallow; **faire passer la ~**○ to sweeten the pill; **trouver la ~ amère**○ to find it a bitter pill to swallow; **dorer la ~ à qn** to butter sb up; **se dorer la ~**○ to sunbathe.

pimbêche /pɛ̃bɛʃ/ *nf* stuck-up madam○.

piment /pimɑ̃/ *nm* **1** (plante) capsicum; **2** (condiment) hot pepper; **3** (stimulation) **du ~** a bit of spice; **le risque met du ~ dans la vie** danger adds a bit of spice to life.

■ **~ doux** sweet pepper; **~ rouge** red hot pepper, chilli; **~ vert** hot pepper.

pimenter /pimɑ̃te/ [1] *vtr* **1** Culin to put chillies[GB] in, to put chilli[GB] powder in [*plat*]; **un plat très pimenté** a very hot dish; **2** (animer) to give a bit of spice to [*situation, réunion, spectacle*].

pimpant, **~e** /pɛ̃pɑ̃, ɑ̃t/ *adj* [*femme, robe, village*] spruce, smart; [*voiture, bicyclette*] smart.

pimprenelle /pɛ̃pʀənɛl/ *nf* burnet.

pin /pɛ̃/ *nm* pine (tree); **du bois de ~** pine; **chaise/cuisine en ~** pine chair/kitchen; **pomme de ~** pine cone.

■ **~ laricio** Corsican pine; **~ maritime** maritime pine; **~ d'Oregon** Oregon pine, Douglas fir; **~ parasol** or **pignon** stone pine; **~ sylvestre** Scots pine.

pinacle /pinakl/ *nm* Archit pinnacle.

IDIOMES **porter** or **mettre qn au ~** to praise sb to the skies; **être/monter au ~** to be at/to reach the top.

pinacothèque /pinakɔtɛk/ *nf* art gallery.

pinaillage○ /pinɑjaʒ/ *nm* hairsplitting, quibbling.

pinailler○ /pinɑje/ [1] *vi* to split hairs, to quibble (**sur** about).

pinailleur○, **-euse** /pinɑjœʀ, øz/ **I** *adj* [*personne*] pernickety○ GB, persnickety US.

II *nm,f* hairsplitter, quibbler.

pinard● /pinaʀ/ *nm* plonk○ GB, wine.

pinardier○ /pinaʀdje/ *nm* **1** (bateau) wine tanker; **2** (marchand) wine merchant.

pinasse /pinas/ *nf* Naut (flat-bottomed) fishing smack.

pince /pɛ̃s/ **I** *nf* **1** (outil) (de plombier, d'électricien) pliers (*pl*), pair of pliers; (de forgeron) tongs (*pl*), pair of tongs; ▶ **serrer**; **2** Cout dart; **faire des ~s à la taille** (par style) to put darts in at the waist; (pour ajuster) to take [sth] in at the waist [*robe, pantalon*]; **faire des ~s à une veste** to put darts in a jacket; **un pantalon à ~** trousers (*pl*) GB ou pants (*pl*) US with a pleated waist; **3** Zool (de homard, crabe, d'écrevisse) pincer, claw; (dent de cheval) incisor; **4** (levier) crowbar.

II pinces○ *nfpl* **aller/être à ~s**○ to be on foot; **faire 5 km à ~s** to do 5 km on foot, to walk for 5 km; **je ne peux pas te ramener, je suis à ~s** I can't give you a lift GB ou ride US, I'm on foot.

■ **~ à charbon** coal tongs (*pl*); **~ à cheveux** hair grip; **~ coupante** wire cutters (*pl*); **~ crocodile** crocodile clip; **~ à dessin** bulldog clip; **~ à épiler** tweezers; **~ à escargot** snail tongs (*pl*); **~ à glaçons** ice tongs (*pl*); **~ hémostatique** haemostatic forceps; **~ à linge** clothes peg; **~ multiprise** adjustable pliers (*pl*); **~ à ongles** nail clippers (*pl*); **~ à sucre** sugar tongs (*pl*); **~ universelle** universal pliers (*pl*); **~ à vélo** bicycle clip.

pincé, **~e** /pɛ̃se/ **I** *pp* ▶ **pincer**.

II *pp adj* **1** (contraint) [*sourire*] tight-lipped; **prendre un air ~** to become stiff ou starchy; **2** (serré) [*lèvres*] thin; [*narines*] pinched.

III pincée *nf* (de poivre, sel) pinch (**de** of).

pinceau, *pl* **~x** /pɛ̃so/ *nm* **1** (instrument) brush; (à peinture) (paint) brush; **se maquiller au ~** to apply make-up with a brush; **passer un coup de ~ sur qch**, **donner un coup de ~ à qch** to give sth a lick of paint; **2** (manière de peindre) brushwork; **3**○ (pied) foot; **4** (faisceau) **~ de lumière** thin beam of light; **~ lumineux** Phys pencil beam.

pince-fesses○ /pɛ̃sfɛs/ *nm inv* (fête) do○, bash○, cocktail party.

pincement /pɛ̃smɑ̃/ *nm* **1** (de peau, personne) pinch; **2** (serrement) pang; **avoir un ~ de cœur** to feel a pang ou a twinge of sadness; **3** Mus (de corde) plucking.

pince-monseigneur, *pl* **pinces-monseigneur** /pɛ̃smɔ̃sɛɲœʀ/ *nf* (levier) jemmy GB, slim jim US.

pince-nez /pɛ̃sne/ *nm inv* pince-nez.

pince-oreilles /pɛ̃sɔʀɛj/ *nm inv* earwig.

pincer /pɛ̃se/ [12] **I** *vtr* **1** (pour faire mal) [*personne*] to pinch; [*crabe*] to nip; **se faire ~ par un crabe** to get nipped by a crab; **2**○ (attraper) to nab○, to catch [*voleur, criminel*]; **sa mère l'a pincé**○ **en train de voler des chocolats dans le placard** his mother caught him stealing chocolates from the cupboard; **il s'est fait ~**○ **à** or **en train de tricher à l'examen** he got caught cheating in the exam; **se faire ~** to get nabbed○ ou caught; **3** (serrer) **~ les lèvres** or **la bouche** to purse (up) one's lips; **une veste qui pince la taille** a jacket which hugs the waist; **4** Mus to pluck [*corde, guitare*]; **5** Hort to pinch out, to pinch off [*bourgeon*].

II○ *vi* [*vent, froid*] to be nippy○; **ça pince, aujourd'hui!** it's (pretty) nippy○ today!

III se pincer *vpr* **1** (accidentellement) to catch oneself; **elle s'est pincée en refermant le tiroir** she caught her fingers closing the drawer; **je me suis pincé les doigts dans la porte** I caught ou trapped my fingers in the door; **2** (volontairement) to pinch oneself; **j'ai dû me ~ pour y croire** I

had to pinch myself to make sure I wasn't dreaming; **se ~ le nez** to hold one's nose.
IDIOMES **en ~ pour qn**○ to be stuck○ on sb, to be in love with sb.

pince-sans-rire /pɛ̃ssɑ̃ʀiʀ/ I *adj inv* [*personne, ton*] deadpan; **être ~** to be deadpan, to have a deadpan sense of humour^GB.
II *nmf inv* **c'est un ~** he has a deadpan sense of humour^GB.

pincette /pɛ̃sɛt/ *nf* **1** (petite pince) tweezers (*pl*), pair of tweezers; **2** (de cheminée) fire tongs (*pl*), pair of fire tongs.
IDIOMES **il n'est pas à prendre avec des ~s** he's like a bear with a sore head.

pinçon /pɛ̃sɔ̃/ *nm* pinch-mark.

Pindare /pɛ̃daʀ/ *npr* Pindar.

pindarique /pɛ̃daʀik/ *adj* Pindaric.

pine● /pin/ *nf* prick●, cock●, penis.

pinède /pinɛd/ *nf* pine forest.

pingouin /pɛ̃gwɛ̃/ *nm* auk; (manchot) controv penguin; **grand ~** great auk; **petit ~** razorbill.

ping-pong®, *pl* **~s** /piŋpɔ̃ŋ/ ▶ **449** *nm* **1** (jeu) table tennis, ping-pong; **jouer au ~** to play table tennis; **raquette de ~** table tennis bat; **2** (table) table tennis table.

pingre /pɛ̃gʀ/ I *adj* stingy, niggardly (**à l'égard de, envers** towards, with).
II *nmf* skinflint.

pingrerie /pɛ̃gʀəʀi/ *nf* stinginess.

pinotte /pinɔt/ *nf* C **beurre de ~** peanut butter.

pin-pon /pɛ̃pɔ̃/ *nm* (*also onomat*) *sound of a two-tone siren.*

pin's /pins/ *nm inv* lapel badge.

pinson /pɛ̃sɔ̃/ *nm* chaffinch.
■ **~ des Ardennes** brambling; **~ des neiges** snow finch; **~ du Nord** = **~ des Ardennes**.
IDIOMES **être gai comme un ~** to be as happy as a lark.

pintade /pɛ̃tad/ *nf* guinea fowl.

pintadeau, *pl* **~x** /pɛ̃tado/ *nm* young guinea fowl, guinea poult spéc.

pinte /pɛ̃t/ *nf* **1** ▶ **117** (mesure anglo-saxonne) pint; (ancienne mesure) ≈ US quart (= 0,94 litre); **2** (récipient) pot, tankard; **3** H (bar) bar.
IDIOMES **se payer une ~ de bon sang** (s'amuser) to have a good time; (rire) to have a good laugh.

pinté, **~e** /pɛ̃te/ I *pp* ▶ **pinter**.
II *pp adj* plastered○, sloshed○, drunk.

pinter○ /pɛ̃te/ [1] I *vtr* to get [sb] plastered○ ou drunk.
II **se pinter** *vpr* **1** (s'enivrer) to get plastered○ ou drunk; **2** H (boire un verre) to have a drink.

pin-up○ /pinœp/ *nf inv* **1** (personne) glamour girl, sexy girl; **2** (photo) pin-up.

pioche /pjɔʃ/ *nf* **1** (de cultivateur) mattock; (de terrassier) pickaxe; **2** Jeux stock.

piocher /pjɔʃe/ [1] I *vtr* **1** (creuser) to dig [sth] over [*sol*]; **2**○ (potasser) to swat at○ GB, to slave away at [*matière*]; to cram for○ [*examen*]; **3** Jeux to take [sth] from the stock [*carte, domino*].
II *vi* **1** (creuser) to dig; **2**○ (potasser) to swot○ GB, to slave away○; **3** (prendre) Jeux to take [sth] from the stock [*carte, domino*]; **~ dans** to dip into [*économies, fonds*]; to dig into [*tas, porte-monnaie*]; **pioche!** (aux cartes) take a card!; (à table) help yourself, dive in○!; **~ dans la caisse** to have one's hand in the till.

piolet /pjɔlɛ/ *nm* ice axe GB ou ax US.

pion, **pionne** /pjɔ̃, pjɔn/ I○ *nm,f* Scol *student paid to supervise pupils.*
II *nm* Jeux (aux échecs) pawn; (aux dames) draught GB, checker US; **n'être qu'un ~ sur l'échiquier** fig to be a mere pawn.

pioncer◑ /pjɔ̃se/ [12] *vi* to sleep.

pionnier, **-ière** /pjɔnje, ɛʀ/ *adj, nm,f* pioneer.

pioupiou○† /pjupju/ *nm* tommy○† GB, grunt◑ US, common soldier.

pipe /pip/ *nf* **1** (à fumer) pipe; **fumer la ~** to smoke a pipe; **~ de bruyère/en terre** briar/clay pipe; **2**◑ (cigarette) fag○ GB, cig○; **3**● (fellation) blow job●; **tailler** or **faire une ~ à qn** to give sb a blow job.
IDIOMES **casser sa ~**○ to die, to kick the bucket○; **se fendre la ~** to laugh one's head off○.

pipeau, *pl* **~x** /pipo/ *nm* **1** ▶ **534** (petite flûte) (reed-)pipe; **2** (appeau) birdcall.
IDIOMES **c'est du ~**○ it's no great shakes○; **c'est pas du ~**○ it's for real○.

pipelette○ /piplɛt/ *nf* **1** (bavard) gossip(-monger); **2** (concierge) **la ~** the concierge.

pipeline /piplin, pajplajn/ *nm* pipeline.

piper /pipe/ [1] *vtr* **1**○ (dire) **ne pas ~ (mot)** not to say a word (**de** about); **2** Jeux to load [*dés*]; to mark [*cartes*]; **les dés sont pipés** lit, fig the dice are loaded.

piperade /pipeʀad/ *nf* piperade, Spanish omelette.

pipette /pipɛt/ *nf* pipette.

pipi○ /pipi/ *nm* wee○ GB, pee○; (langage enfantin) wee-wee○; **faire ~** to have a pee; (langage enfantin) to have a wee-wee; **faire ~ dans sa culotte** to wet oneself; **j'en ai fait ~ dans ma culotte** I wet myself laughing; **c'est à faire ~ dans sa culotte** it's hilarious; **faire ~ au lit** to wet the bed; **le chat a fait ~ dans mes pantoufles** the cat has weed in my slippers.
IDIOMES **c'est du ~ de chat**○ (boisson) it's gnat's piss○; (spectacle, livre) it's as dull as dishwater.

pipi-room○, *pl* **~s** /pipiʀum/ *nm* loo○ GB, bathroom US.

pipistrelle /pipistʀɛl/ *nf* pipistrelle.

pipit /pipit/ *nm* pipit.
■ **~ des prés** meadow pipit.

piquage /pikaʒ/ *nm* Cout stitching; **le ~ d'une veste à la machine** the machine-stitching of a jacket.

piquant, **~e** /pikɑ̃, ɑ̃t/ I *adj* **1** (acéré) [*feuilles, tige, chardon*] prickly; [*aiguille, clou*] sharp; [*barbe*] bristly; **2** (fort) [*moutarde, plat, sauce*] hot; [*odeur*] pungent; [*vin, fromage*] sharp; **3** (vif, mordant) [*froid*] biting; [*air*] sharp; **4** fig (acerbe) [*remarque, ton*] cutting, biting; **5** fig, liter (émoustillant) [*histoire, aventure*] spicy, piquant; [*charme, femme*] heady.
II *nm* **1** (épine, pointe) (de feuille, tige, chardon) prickle; (d'oursin, de hérisson, cactus) spine; (de barbelés) spike, barb; **2** fig (d'histoire, aventure, de conversation) spiciness; (de situation) piquancy; **mettre** or **donner du ~ à la situation/conversation** to add spice to the situation/conversation; **le ~ de cette histoire** what was so piquant ou spicy about the story.

pique /pik/ I *nf* **1** (allusion blessante) cutting remark; **envoyer des ~s à qn** to level cutting remarks at sb; **2** (arme) pike; **3** (lance de picador) lance; **recevoir des coups de ~** [*taureau*] to be stuck with a lance; **4** (à cocktail) swizzle stick.
II *nm* Jeux (carte) spade; (couleur) spades (*pl*); **avoir du ~** to be holding spades; **avoir des ~s dans son jeu** to be holding spades; **jouer ~** to play spades; **neuf/roi de ~** nine/king of spades.

piqué, **~e** /pike/ I *pp* ▶ **piquer**.
II *pp adj* **1** Cout [*couvre-lit, couverture*] quilted; **2** (marqué) [*meuble, bois*] worm-eaten; [*linge, miroir, fruit*] spotted; [*papier, livre*] foxed; **un livre ~ de moisissures** a foxed book; **du linge tout ~ de taches de rouille** linen spotted with rust marks; **un visage ~ de taches de rousseur** a face dotted with freckles; **3** (aigre) [*vin, bière*] sour; **4**○ (fou) [*personne*] dotty○, eccentric; **5** Mus [*note, phrase*] staccato; **les trois dernières mesures sont ~es** the last three bars are to be played staccato.
III○ *nm,f* (extravagant) nutcase○; **c'est une vieille ~e**○ she's an old nutcase○.
IV *nm* **1** (tissu) piqué; **en ~ de coton** in cotton piqué; **2** Aviat (nose)dive; **faire un ~** to do a (nose)dive, to (nose)dive; **descendre en ~** to come down in a nosedive; **(faire) une descente en ~** (to do) a nosedive; **3** Danse piqué; **exécuter un ~** to execute a piqué; **4** (de photographie) sharpness.

pique-assiette○ /pikasjɛt/ *nmf inv* sponger○, freeloader○.

pique-feu /pikfø/ *nm inv* poker.

pique-fleurs /pikflœʀ/ *nm inv* flower holder.

pique-nique, *pl* **~s** /piknik/ *nm* picnic; **aller faire un ~ à la campagne** to go for GB ou on a picnic in the country.

pique-niquer /piknike/ [1] *vi* to have a picnic; **aller ~ à la campagne** to go for GB ou on a picnic in the country.

pique-niqueur, **-euse**, *mpl* **~s** /piknikœʀ, øz/ *nm,f* picnicker.

piquer /pike/ [1] I *vtr* **1** (blesser) [*guêpe, scorpion, méduse, ortie*] to sting; [*moustique, puce, araignée, serpent*] to bite; [*chardon, rosier*] to prick; **le scorpion l'a piqué au bras** the scorpion stung his arm; **il s'est fait ~ par une méduse** he was ou got stung by a jellyfish; **2** (enfoncer une pointe) [*personne, bec, aiguille*] to prick [*animal, fruit*]; **~ qn avec une aiguille** to prick sb with a needle; **~ son cheval** to spur one's horse; **~ un rôti avec une fourchette** to prick a roast with a fork; **~ un couteau dans le gâteau** to prick the cake with a knife; **~ des petits pois avec sa fourchette** to stab peas with one's fork; **~ (son cheval) des éperons** to urge one's horse on with one's spurs; **3** Méd to give [sb] an injection; **~ qn à l'épaule/au bras** to give sb an injection in the shoulder/in the arm; **je me suis fait ~ contre la grippe** I've had a flu injection; **faire ~ un animal** to have an animal put down; **on a dû faire ~ le chat** we had to have the cat put down; **4** Culin **~ un gigot d'ail** to stud a leg of lamb with garlic; **~ un oignon de clous de girofle** to stick an onion with cloves; **un gigot d'agneau piqué d'ail** a leg of lamb studded with garlic; **5** (fixer) to stick [*épingle, peigne*] (**dans** into); (épingler) to pin [*carte, badge*] (**à** to; **sur** on); **~ des fleurs dans ses cheveux** to stick flowers in one's hair; **~ une photo au mur/une médaille sur une veste** to pin a photo to the wall/a medal on a jacket; **6** (parsemer) (de trous) [*insecte, ver*] to make holes in [*bois, meuble*]; (de taches) [*moisissure, rouille*] to spot [*linge, miroir*]; to fox [*papier, livre*]; **7** (irriter) [*vent, froid*] to be biting; **mon pull me pique la peau** my sweater feels scratchy; **le froid me pique le visage** the cold is making my face tingle; **la fumée me pique la gorge/les yeux** the smoke is stinging my throat/eyes; **sa gorge le pique** his throat is prickling ou stinging; **ses yeux la piquaient** her eyes were stinging; **ça me pique partout** I'm itchy all over; **8**○ (voler) to pinch○ GB, to steal [*livre, idée*] (**à** from); (emprunter) to pinch○ GB, to borrow [*crayon, pull*]; (choisir) to pick [*nombre, personne*]; **il a piqué cette invention à son professeur** he pinched the invention from his professor; **il pique (dans les magasins)** he's always pinching things (from shops GB ou stores US); **il n'arrête pas de me ~ mes fringues**○ he's always pinching my clothes; **je me suis fait ~ mon sac à main** I had my handbag pinched; **~ un numéro au hasard** to pick a number at random; **9**○ (arrêter) [*police*] to nab○, to nick○ GB [*bandit, voleur*]; (surprendre) to get [*personne*]; **il s'est fait ~ à la sortie du magasin** he was nabbed ou nicked GB as he left the store; **ils se sont fait ~ à tricher pendant l'examen** they got caught cheating during the exam; **10**○ (attraper) to catch [*maladie, virus*]; **11** Cout to stitch [*tissu, vêtement*]; **~ une robe à la machine** to machine(-stitch) a dress; **est- ce que tu sais ~?** do you know how to use a sewing-machine?; **12** (toucher, affecter) [*propos, attitude, personne*] to needle [*personne*]; to sting [*orgueil, fierté*]; **cette remarque m'a piquée** this remark wounded me; **~ qn au vif** to cut sb to the quick; **13** (éveiller) to arouse [*curiosité, intérêt*]; **14**○ (commencer) **~ un fou rire** to have a fit of the giggles; **~ une crise de nerfs** to throw a fit○; **~ un cent mètres** to break into a run; **~ un galop** to break into a gallop; **15** (plonger) **~ une tête (dans l'eau)** to dive (into the water); **16** Mus **~ une note** to play a note staccato.

II *vi* **1** (irriter) [*barbe*] to be bristly; [*vêtement, laine*] to be scratchy; [*gorge, yeux, nez*] to sting; **ça pique!** [*ortie, seringue*] it stings!; [*plante épineuse*] it pricks!; [*fumée*] it stings!; [*barbe*] it's bristly!; **j'ai la gorge qui pique** my throat is stinging; **tu piques ce matin** you are all bristly this morning; **2** (exciter les sens) [*moutarde, sauce*] to be hot; [*vin, fromage*] to be sharp; [*boisson, soda*]○ to be fizzy○ GB ou sparkling; **c'est de l'eau qui pique** this is fizzy GB ou sparkling water; **3** (descendre) [*oiseau*] to swoop down; [*avion*] to dive; **l'aigle piqua droit sur sa proie** the eagle swooped on its prey; **~ du nez** (s 'endormir) to nod off, to doze off; (baisser la tête) to look down; (chuter) [*avion*] to go into a nosedive; [*marché, Bourse, actions*] to take a nosedive; [*fleur*] to droop; **4** (prendre) **arrête de ~ dans le plat** stop picking (things out of the serving dish); **il y a plein de livres/vêtements dans le grenier, pique dans le tas si tu veux** there are lots of books/clothes in the attic, help yourself from the pile; **5**○ (s'élancer) **le taureau piqua droit sur nous** the bull came straight for us; **il piqua à travers bois pour échapper à la police** he cut across the woods to escape (from) the police.

III se piquer *vpr* **1** (se blesser) to prick oneself; **se ~ avec** to prick oneself with [*aiguille*]; to prick oneself on [*clou*]; **se ~ aux ronces** to scratch oneself on the brambles; **se ~ aux orties** to get stung by nettles; ▶**frotter**; **2** (se faire une piqûre) to inject oneself; (se droguer)○ to shoot up○, to inject oneself; **il se pique** he shoots up○; **je n'ai pas besoin d'infirmière, je me pique moi-même** I don't need a nurse, I do my own injections; **il se pique à l'héroïne** he injects himself ou shoots up○ with heroin; **3** (se couvrir de taches) [*miroir*] to go spotty GB, to become spotted; [*papier, livre*] to become foxed; [*confiture*] to go GB ou become mouldy GB ou moldy US; [*linge*] to become spotted; [*métal*] to become spotted (with rust); **le papier mural de la salle de bains est en train de se ~** the bathroom wallpaper is becoming mildewed; **4** fml (par prétention) **se ~ de philosophie** to like to make out GB ou pretend one is a philosopher; **se ~ de peindre/d'écrire** to like to make out GB ou pretend that one is a painter/writer; **se ~ de réussir seul** to claim that one can manage on one's own; **5** (se vexer) to take offence[GB] **(de** at); **elle s'est piquée de ta plaisanterie** she took offence[GB] at your joke; **il se pique facilement** he takes offence[GB] easily.

IDIOMES **quelle mouche t'a piqué**○? what's eating○ you?; **~ des deux** Équit to spur on one's horse; (s'enfuir)○ to beat it○; **son article n'était pas piqué des vers**○ or **hannetons**○ his/her article didn't pull any punches; **c'est une petite maison pas piquée des vers**○ ou **hannetons**○ it's a really lovely little house; **se ~ le nez**○ or **la truffe**◑ to booze○, to knock it back○.

piquet /pikɛ/ *nm* **1** (pieu) stake; (très court) peg; (pour slalom) gate pole; (de parasol) pole; **2** (groupe de gens) picket; **3** (punition) **mettre un élève au ~** to make a pupil stand in the corner; **4** ▶**449** (jeu de cartes) piquet.
■ **~ de grève** Entr (strike) picket, picket line; **~ d'incendie** Mil fire picket; **~ de tente** tent peg.
IDIOMES **rester planté comme un ~**○ to stand like a dummy; **raide comme un ~** stiff as a post.

piquetage /piktaʒ/ *nm* **1** (de terrain) staking out; **2** (de roche) pecking.

piqueter /pikte/ [20] *vtr* **1** (pour délimiter) to stake out, to stake [sth] out [*chemin*]; **2** (parsemer) to dot **(de** with); **piqueté de (taches de) rouille** spotted with rust; **ciel piqueté d'étoiles** sky spangled with stars.

piquette /pikɛt/ *nf* **1** (vin) pej plonk○ GB, cheap wine; **2**○ (défaite) hammering○; **prendre une ~** to take a hammering○.

piqueur, -euse /pikœʀ, øz/ **I** *adj* Zool [*insectes*] stinging.
II ▶**510** *nm,f* **1** Cout (ouvrier) (sewing) machinist; **2** Équit head stableman/stable girl.
III *nm* Tech (agent) foreman.

piquier /pikje/ *nm* Hist pikeman.

piqûre /pikyʀ/ *nf* **1** (injection) injection, shot; **une ~ de pénicilline** an injection ou a shot of penicillin; **faire une ~ à qn** to give sb an injection; **se faire faire des ~s** to have ou get (a course of) injections; **2** (blessure) (d'épine, épingle) prick; (d'ortie, abeille, de scorpion) sting; (de moustique) bite; **ce sont des ~s de puces** those are flea-bites; **3** (petit trou) (dans le bois) hole; (dans le cuir) tooling; **des ~s de vers** worm holes; **des chaussures à ~s** tooled leather shoes; **4** (petite tache) (sur un miroir, du papier) spot; (sur du métal) spot, speck; (sur un livre) spot, stain; **des ~s de rouille** specks ou spots of rust; **des ~s de moisissure sur les pages d'un livre** mould GB ou mold US spots ou stains on the pages of a book; **5** Cout (point) stitch; (couture) stitching ¢; **découdre les ~s d'un vêtement** to unpick (the stitching of) a garment; **faire des ~s à la main/à la machine** to do hand stitching/machine stitching.
■ **~ de rappel** Méd booster (injection).
IDIOMES **une ~ d'amour-propre** a wound to one's pride.

piranha /piʀana/ *nm* piranha.

piratage /piʀataʒ/ *nm* piracy, pirating; **~ de cartes bancaires** credit card fraud; **~ de cassettes vidéo** video piracy; **~ informatique** computer hacking.

pirate /piʀat/ **I** *adj* [*émetteur, édition, radio*] pirate (*épith*).
II *nm* Naut pirate; fig (à un enfant) **quel ~!** what a little rascal!
■ **~ de l'air** hijacker, skyjacker; **~ informatique** computer hacker.

pirater /piʀate/ [1] *vtr* to pirate.

piraterie /piʀatʀi/ *nf* **1** (activité) piracy ¢; (acte) act of piracy; **2** (escroquerie) (activité) swindling ¢; (acte) swindle; **c'est de la ~** it's a swindle.
■ **~ aérienne** hijacking, skyjacking; **~ informatique** computer hacking.

pire /piʀ/ **I** *adj* **1** (comparatif) worse **(que** than); **c'est bien ~** it's much worse; **c'est encore ~** it's even worse; **c'est dix fois ~** it's ten times as bad; **il y a bien ~ encore** there's much worse; **2** (superlatif) worst; **un escroc de la ~ espèce** a swindler of the worst kind; **il a raconté les ~s mensonges** he told the most wicked lies.
II *nm,f* worst; **les ~s** the worst; **le ~ des imbéciles** the biggest fool; **le ~ des deux** the worse of the two.
III *nm* **le ~** the worst; **s'attendre au ~** to expect the worst; **craindre le ~** to fear the worst; **le ~ c'est que** the worst of it all is that; **au ~** at the very worst; **le ~ est à venir** there's worse in store.
IDIOMES **il n'y a ~ eau que l'eau qui dort** Prov still waters run deep Prov.

Pirée /piʀe/ ▶**857** *npr* **le ~** Piraeus.

piriforme /piʀifɔʀm/ *adj* pear-shaped.

pirogue /piʀɔg/ *nf* dugout canoe, pirogue spéc.

piroguier /piʀɔgje/ *nm* canoeist.

pirouette /piʀwɛt/ *nf* **1** Danse, Équit pirouette; **faire des ~s** (danseur) to pirouette; **les ~s d'un clown** the cavortings of a clown; **2** (réponse évasive) skilful evasion; (revirement) U-turn, flip-flop○ US; **s'en tirer par une ~** to dodge the question skilfully[GB].

pirouetter /piʀwete/ [1] *vi* **1** [*danseur*] to pirouette; **~ sur ses talons** to spin on one's heels; **faire ~ qch** to spin sth around; **2** (faire volte-face) to do a U-turn, to flip-flop○ US.

pis /pi/ **I** *adj inv* liter worse; **ce qui est ~ (encore)** what is (even) worse; **elle est laide, et, qui ~ est, méchante** she is ugly and, what is worse, she is nasty; **c'est ~ que jamais** it's worse than ever.
II *adv* liter worse; **il y a ~** there's worse; **aller de mal en ~** or **de ~ en ~** to go from bad to worse.
III *nm inv* **1** (de vache) udder; **2** liter **le ~** the worst; **le ~ est que** the worst thing is that; **en mettant** or **prenant les choses au ~** if the worst comes to the worst; **au ~ (aller)** at the worst.
IDIOMES **dire ~ que pendre de qn** to vilify sb.

pis-aller /pizale/ *nm inv* lesser evil; **considérer qn/qch comme un ~** to consider sb/sth as the lesser evil; **ces matériaux sont des ~** we'll have to make do with these materials.

piscicole /pisikɔl/ *adj* fish-farming, piscicultural spéc; **l'élevage ~** fish farming.
■ **ferme ~** fish farm.

pisciculteur, -trice /pisikyltœʀ, tʀis/ ▶**510** *nm,f* fish farmer, pisciculturist spéc.

pisciculture /pisikyltyʀ/ *nf* fish farming, pisciculture spéc.

pisciforme /pisifɔʀm/ *adj* fish-shaped.

piscine /pisin/ *nf* swimming pool; **~ couverte** indoor swimming pool.
■ **~ de désactivation** deactivation pool.

piscivore /pisivɔʀ/ **I** *adj* fish-eating (*épith*), piscivorous spéc.
II *nm* fish eater.

Pise /piz/ ▶**857** *npr* Pisa.

pisé /pize/ *nm* ≈ adobe.

pisse◑ /pis/ *nf* piss◑.
IDIOMES **c'est de la ~ de chat** or **d'âne** (boisson) it's gnat's piss.

pisse-copie○ /piskɔpi/ *nmf inv* pej (journaliste) hack journalist péj; (écrivain) hack writer péj.

pisse-froid○ /pisfʀwa/ *nm inv* cold fish.

pissenlit /pisɑ̃li/ *nm* dandelion.
IDIOMES **manger** or **sucer les ~s par la racine**○ to be pushing up the daisies○.

pisser /pise/ [1] **I**◑ *vtr* **~ du sang** to pass blood; **~ le sang** [*personne, nez, blessure*] to pour with blood; **mon moteur pissait l'huile** my engine was leaking oil all over the place.
II *vi* **1**◑ (uriner) [*personne, animal*] to pee◑; (plus vulgaire) to piss◑; **j'ai envie de ~** I want to pee◑; **~ de rire** to piss◑ oneself laughing; **~ dans sa culotte** to wet one's pants; **rire à en ~ dans sa culotte** to wet ou piss◑ one's pants laughing; **~ au lit** to wet the bed; ▶**mérinos, violon**; **2**○ (fuir) [*récipient*] to leak; **un tonneau qui pisse de partout** a cask that leaks like a sieve; **l'eau pisse de partout** water is pouring out from everywhere.
IDIOMES **il pleut comme vache qui pisse**◑ it's pissing down◑, it's pouring down○; **se regarder** or **s'écouter ~**◑, **ne plus se sentir ~**◑ to be full of oneself; **ça lui a pris comme une envie de ~**◑ he had a sudden urge to do it; **laisse ~**◑**!** forget it!

pissette /pisɛt/ *nf* Chimie wash bottle.

pisseur○, **-euse**[1] /pisœʀ, øz/ **I** *nm,f* lit (enfant) bedwetter.
II pisseuse *nf* **1** (fillette) minx; **2** (prétentieuse) fig little madam○ GB, pretentious little twit○.

pisseux○, **-euse**[2] /pisø, øz/ *adj* pej (sale, terne) [*mur, papier peint, couleur*] dingy; **jaune ~** dingy yellow.

pisse-vinaigre○ /pisvinɛgʀ/ *nm inv* grouser○, grouch.

pissoir◑ /piswaʀ/ *nm* urinal.

pissotière○ /pisɔtjɛʀ/ *nf* street urinal, pissoir US.

pistache /pistaʃ/ **I** ▶193 *adj inv* **(vert) ~** pistachio (green).
II *nf* pistachio; **une ~** a pistachio nut; **glace à la ~** pistachio ice cream.

pistachier /pistaʃje/ *nm* pistachio tree.

pistage /pistaʒ/ *nm* tracking, trailing.

pistard, **~e** /pistaʀ, aʀd/ *nm,f* track racer, track cyclist.

piste /pist/ *nf* **1** (trace) lit, fig (d'animal, de personne, d'objet) trail; **suivre/perdre la ~ de** to follow/to lose the trail of; **être sur la ~ de** to be on the trail of; **être sur une bonne/mauvaise ~** to be on the right/wrong track; **être sur une fausse ~** to be on the wrong track; **2** (ensemble d'indices) lead; **avoir plusieurs ~s** to have several leads; **3** Sport (de stade, d'autodrome) track; (d'hippodrome) racecourse GB, racetrack US; (de danse) floor; (de patinage) rink; (de cirque) ring; (de ski) piste; (de ski de fond) trail; (pour course automobile) racetrack; **~ d'élan** (au ski) takeoff track; **~ (de ski) pour débutants** nursery slope; **skier hors ~** to go off-piste skiing; **épreuve sur ~** track event; **faire un tour de ~** to do a lap; **entrer en ~** (au cirque) to come into the ring; fig to enter the fray; **en ~!** fig get cracking○!; **être en ~** fig to be in the running; **4** (chemin) (de brousse) track; (de désert) trail; **5** Aviat runway; **~ d'envol/d'atterrissage** takeoff/landing strip ou runway; **6** (de disque, cassette) track; **~ sonore** sound track.
■ **~ artificielle** (avec neige artificielle) artificial slope; (en matière plastique) dry ski slope; **~ cavalière** bridle path, bridleway; **~ cyclable** (sur route) cycle lane; (à côté d'une route) cycle way, cycle path; (à la campagne) cycle track.

pister /piste/ [1] *vtr* to trail, to track [*animal*]; **~ qn** (suivre) to trail sb; (être sur la trace de) to be on the trail of sb.

pisteur, **-euse** /pistœʀ, øz/ ▶510 *nm,f* member of the ski patrol.

pistil /pistil/ *nm* pistil.

pistole /pistɔl/ *nf* pistole.

pistolet /pistɔlɛ/ *nm* **1** (arme) pistol, gun; **tirer au ~** to fire a pistol; **c'est un excellent tireur au ~** he's an excellent shot with a pistol; **2** Tech (outil) gun; **3**○ (urinal) bed-bottle; **4**† fig **un drôle de ~** an odd customer; **5** B (petit pain) roll.
■ **~ à air comprimé** air gun; **~ d'alarme** alarm gun; **~ automatique** automatic gun; **~ à peinture** spray gun.

pistolet-mitrailleur, *pl* **pistolets-mitrailleurs** /pistɔlɛmitʀajœʀ/ *nm* submachine gun.

piston /pistɔ̃/ *nm* **1** Tech piston; **moteur à ~s** piston engine; **2**○ (relations) contacts (*pl*); **avoir du ~** to have connections ou contacts in the right places; **il a un ~ au ministère** he knows somebody ou he has connections in the Ministry; **il a obtenu son poste par ~** he got his job because he has connections in the right places, someone got him the job by pulling strings; **3** Mus (d'instrument) valve; **cornet à ~s** cornet.

pistonner○ /pistɔne/ [1] *vtr* pej to pull strings for [*candidat*]; **elle l'a pistonné auprès du directeur/au ministère** she pulled strings for him with the director/at the Ministry; **se faire ~** to get someone to pull a few strings; **il a été pistonné** someone pulled strings for him.

pistou /pistu/ *nm* (condiment) pesto.

pitance† /pitɑ̃s/ *nf* fare ₵; **se contenter d'une maigre ~** to make do with meagre[GB] fare.

pitchpin /pitʃpɛ̃/ *nm* pitch pine.

piteusement /pitøzmɑ̃/ *adv* [*se comporter*] pathetically; [*se plaindre, gémir*] pitifully, pathetically; [*échouer*] miserably.

piteux, **-euse** /pitø, øz/ *adj* **1** (piètre) [*résultats*] poor, pitiful; [*aspect*] sorry (*épith*); **dans un ~ état**, **en ~ état** in a sorry state; **avoir piteuse allure** to be a sorry sight; **2** (penaud) [*personne, air*] crestfallen; **la mine piteuse** looking crestfallen.

pithécanthrope /pitekɑ̃tʀɔp/ *nm* pithecanthropus.

pithiviers /pitivje/ *nm inv* (gâteau) *puff pastry with almond paste filling.*

pitié /pitje/ *nf* **1** (compassion) pity; (indulgence) pity, mercy; **éprouver** or **avoir de la ~ pour qn** to feel pity for sb, to pity sb; **avoir ~ de qn** (plaindre) to feel sorry for sb; (se montrer charitable) to take pity on sb; **ayez ~ de nous!** (soyez bon) take ou have pity on us!; (épargnez-nous) have mercy on us!; **prendre qn en ~** to take pity on sb; **faire ~ à qn**, **inspirer de la ~ à qn** to fill sb with pity; **il me fait ~** I feel sorry for him; **il fait ~ (à voir)** he's a pitiful sight; **maigre à faire ~** pitifully thin; **ça fait ~ de voir ça** it's pitiful to see that; **ça me fait ~ de la voir dans cet état** it makes me sad to see her in that state; **c'est (grand) ~ qu'il ait abandonné** it's a (great) pity that he gave up; **sans ~** [*vainqueur*] merciless, pitiless; [*huer, critiquer*] mercilessly; [*concurrence*] ruthless; **un monde sans ~** a cruel world; **par ~, tais-toi!** for pity's sake, be quiet!; **~!** (grâce) (have) mercy!; (ça suffit)○ for pity's sake!; **~ pour nos forêts/la nature!** save our forests/the environment!; **~ pour mes pauvres oreilles!** think of my poor ears!; **2** (avec mépris) pity; **sourire de ~** pitying smile; **regarder qn avec ~** to look pityingly at sb.
IDIOMES **il vaut mieux faire envie que ~** Prov it's better to be envied than pitied.

piton /pitɔ̃/ *nm* **1** (à crochet) hook; (à anneau) eye; **2** (d'alpinisme) piton; **3** Géog peak; **4**○ C (touche d'ordinateur) key; (touche de téléphone) button; (interrupteur) switch; (bouton) knob; (jeton) counter.

pitonner○ /pitɔne/ [1] C **I** *vtr* **~ un numéro de téléphone** to dial a number.
II *vi* (sur un ordinateur) to use the keyboard; (sur une télécommande) to use the remote control; **~ sur une sonnette** to ring a bell.

pitoyable /pitwajabl/ *adv* **1** (digne de pitié) pitiful; **2** (lamentable) pathetic.

pitoyablement /pitwajabləmɑ̃/ *adv* **1** (de façon pitoyable) pitifully; **2** (lamentablement) [*échouer*] miserably; [*se comporter, chanter*] pathetically.

pitre /pitʀ/ *nm* (tous contextes) clown, buffoon; **c'est le ~ de la classe** he's the class clown; **faire le ~** to clown around.

pitrerie /pitʀəʀi/ *nf* clowning ₵.

pittoresque /pitɔʀɛsk/ **I** *adj* [*lieu*] picturesque; [*personnage*] colourful[GB]; [*histoire, anecdote, scène*] colourful[GB]; [*expression, style, œuvre*] vivid, picturesque.
II *nm* **le ~** the picturesque; **le ~ de qch** the picturesque quality of sth, the vividness of sth; **le ~ dans tout cela** the amusing thing about all that.

pive /piv/ *nf* H (pomme de pin) pine cone.

pivert /pivɛʀ/ *nm* green woodpecker.

pivoine /pivwan/ *nf* peony.
IDIOMES **être rouge comme une ~** to be as red as a beetroot GB ou a beet US.

pivot /pivo/ *nm* **1** Tech pivot; **2** fig (d'économie, de gouvernement) linchpin; (de complot, d'affaire) kingpin; **société ~** key firm; **3** Sport (joueur) pivot, post; **4** Dent post and core.

pivotant, **~e** /pivɔtɑ̃, ɑ̃t/ *adj* [*fauteuil*] swivel; [*panneau*] pivoting; [*porte*] revolving.

pivoter /pivɔte/ [1] *vi* [*personne, animal*] to pivot, turn; [*panneau, mur*] to pivot; [*porte, table*] to revolve; [*fauteuil, chaise*] to swivel; **~ sur ses talons** to turn on one's heel; **faire ~ qch** to swivel sth round[GB] [*fauteuil*]; to swing sth round GB ou around US [*avion*]; to set sth revolving [*porte*].

pixel /piksɛl/ *nm* pixel.

pizza /pidza/ *nf* pizza; **~ au fromage et à la tomate** cheese and tomato pizza.

pizzeria /pidzeʀia/ ▶510 *nf* pizzeria.

pizzicato, *pl* **~s** or **pizzicati** /pidzikato, ti/ *nm* pizzicato.

PJ /peʒi/ *nf* **1** *abbr* ▶ **police**; **2** (*written abbr* = **pièce jointe**) enc(l).

PL (*written abbr* = **poids lourd**) HGV GB, heavy truck US.

placage /plakaʒ/ *nm* **1** (feuille de bois) veneer; **2** (revêtement) (en bois) veneer; (en métal) plating; (en marbre, pierre) facing; **~ en acajou** mahogany veneer; **3** Sport (technique) tackling ₵; **un ~** a tackle.

placard /plakaʀ/ *nm* **1** (meuble) cupboard; **~ à balais/de cuisine** broom/kitchen cupboard; **ranger** or **mettre au ~** fig (de côté) to put [sth] on ice [*projet*]; to shunt [sb] aside [*personne*]; (au rebut) to ditch [*projet*]; to pension [sb] off [*personne*]; **sortir du ~** fig to come in from the cold; **2** Pub (affiche) poster, bill; (dans un journal) **~ publicitaire** advertisement; **3** Imprim (épreuve) galley (proof); **4**○ (prison) clink○; **faire un an de ~** to do a year inside ou in clink○.

placarder /plakaʀde/ [1] *vtr* **1** (afficher) to post, to stick [*avis, affiche, photo*]; **2** (décorer) to cover [sth] with posters [*mur*]; **placardé de** covered with.

place /plas/ *nf* **1** (espace) room, space; **avoir de la ~** to have room ou space **(pour faire** to do); **il y a encore assez de ~ pour deux personnes/valises** there's enough room ou space left for two people/suitcases; **avoir la ~ de faire** to have enough room ou space to do; **prendre de la ~** to take up room ou space; **(faire) perdre/gagner de la ~** to waste/to save space; **faire de la ~** to make room ou space **(à qn/qch** for sb/sth; **pour faire** to do); **se faire de la ~** to make room ou space for oneself; **laisser de la ~** (pour une personne, un meuble) to leave room ou space; (pour un écrit) to leave enough space; **laisse-moi un peu de ~ pour leur écrire un mot** leave me a bit of space to write them a few lines; **2** (emplacement, espace défini) gén place; (pour s'asseoir) seat; **chaque chose à sa ~** everything in its place; **il est resté une heure à la même ~** he stayed in the same place for an hour; **remettre qch à sa ~** to put sth back in its place; **les dictionnaires ne sont pas à la bonne/à leur ~** the dictionaries aren't in the right place/where they should be; **j'ai deux ~s pour 'Le Lac des Cygnes'** I've got two tickets for 'Swan Lake'; **il reste une ~ en première** there's one seat left in first class; **laisse ta ~ à la dame!** give the lady your seat!; **est-ce que cette ~ est libre?** is this seat free?; **une salle de 200 ~s** a 200 seat auditorium; **j'ai eu une ~ gratuite** I got a free seat; **garde-moi ma ~** (dans une file) keep my place; (dans un train, au cinéma) keep my seat ; **garde-moi une ~** (dans le train, au cinéma) keep me a seat; **payer sa ~** (au cinéma, théâtre) to pay for one's ticket; Transp to pay one's fare; **payer ~ entière** (au cinéma, théâtre) to pay full price; Transp to pay full fare; **les ~s sont chères** fig (parking difficile) parking spaces are hard to find; (âpre concurrence dans l'emploi) jobs are hard to come by; **prenez ~** (sur un siège) take a seat; (chacun à son siège) take your seats; (chacun à son poste) take your places; **prendre ~** (s'asseoir) to take a seat; (s'installer) [*exposant, stand*] to set up; [*tireur, policier*] to position oneself; (s'intégrer) to take one's place; **roman qui a pris ~ parmi les plus grands** novel that has taken its place among the greatest; **sur ~** [*aller, envoyer, se rendre*] to the scene; [*arriver*] on the scene; [*être, trouver, sautiller, étudier*] on the spot; [*enquête, recherche, tournage*] on-the-spot (*épith*); **de ~ en ~** here and there; **voiture de quatre ~s** four-seater car; **divan à trois ~s** three-seater sofa; ▶ **chasse**; **3** (emplacement pour se garer) parking place; **appartement avec ~ de parking** apartment with parking space; **je n'ai pas trouvé de ~ pour** or **où me garer** I couldn't find a parking space ou a place to park; **un parking de 500 ~s** a car park for 500 cars; **4** (rang dans un classement, la société) place; (position dans un ordre) position; **prendre la ~ de qn** to take sb's place; **prendre** or **obtenir la deuxième ~** to take second place (**à** in); **il est dans les premières/dernières ~s** he's up toward(s) the top/down toward(s) the bottom; **la ~ d'un mot dans une phrase** the position of a word in a sentence; **se faire une ~ dans le monde de la finance** to carve out a place for oneself in the world of finance; **être en bonne ~ pour gagner/réussir** to be well-placed ou in a good position to win/succeed; **il occupe une ~ éminente** he holds a very high position (**à, dans** in); **chacun (à) sa ~** everyone should know his place; **il faut savoir rester à sa ~** you must know your place; **il n'est pas à sa ~ dans cette réception** he looks out of place at this reception; **je ne me sens pas à ma ~ dans ce milieu** I feel out of place in this environment; **remettre qn à sa ~** to put sb in his/her place; **quelle ~ faire à l'art?** what place can be afforded to art?; **avoir sa ~ dans** to deserve a place in; **il n'y a pas de ~ pour eux dans notre système** there is no place for them in our system; **avoir une ~ à part** or **de choix dans** to have a special place in; **tenir une grande ~/une ~ très importante dans la vie de qn** to play a large part/a very important part in sb's life; **donner** or **consacrer** or **faire une large ~ à qch** to put a lot of emphasis on sth; **la ~ croissante de l'environnement en politique** the growing emphasis on the environment in politics; **notre travail laisse peu de ~ à l'imagination** our work leaves little room for the imagination; **faire ~ à** to give way to; **~ aux jeunes** or **à la jeunesse!** lit, fig make way for the young!; **5** (substitution) **à la ~ de** instead of, in place of; **il a mis de la vodka à la ~ du cognac** he's used vodka instead of brandy; **il y a maintenant un comité à la ~ de l'ancien directeur** there's now a committee in place of the former manager; **ils sont partis/ont été récompensés à notre ~** they went/were rewarded instead of us; **qu'aurais-tu fait à ma ~?** what would you have done in my place?; (**si j'étais**) **à ta ~** if I were in your position ou shoes; **mets-toi à leur ~** put yourself in their position ou shoes; **téléphone-lui toi-même, je ne peux pas le faire à ta ~!** phone him yourself, I can't do it for you!; **j'ai mis le vase à la ~ du cendrier** I put the vase where the ashtray was; **construire une école à la ~ de la gare** (où était la gare) to build a school where the station used to be; (où était prévue la gare) to build a school where the station should have been; (au lieu de) to build a school instead of a station; **6** (situation définie) **en ~** [*système, structures*] in place (*après n*); [*troupes*] in position (*après n*); [*dirigeant, pouvoir, régime, partie*] ruling (*épith*); **les gens en ~** the powers that be; **nos hommes sont en ~** our men are in position; **ne plus tenir en ~** to be restless ou fidgety; **les enfants ne tiennent plus en ~** the children keep fidgeting; **mettre en ~** to put [sth] in place [*grillage, programme, règlement, stratégie*]; to put [sth] in ou into position [*satellite, troupes, équipe*]; to establish, to set up [*réseau , marché, régime, institution*]; to install [*ligne téléphonique, canalisations*]; **se mettre en ~** [*plan, politique, système, structure*] to be put in place; [*forces, troupes, police*] (être mis en position) to be put in ou into position; (soi-même) to position oneself; [*réseau, marché, régime*] to be established, to be set up; **mise en ~** (de grillage, système, normes, services) putting in place; (de satellite, forces, d'équipe) positioning; (de réseau, marché, régime, d'institution) establishment, setting up; (de ligne téléphonique, canalisation) installation[GB]; **remettre en ~** to put [sth] back in place; **on se retrouve sur ~** we'll meet up there; **je suis sur ~, je peux le faire** I'm on the spot, I can do it; **dépannage/inscriptions sur ~** on-the-spot repairs/registration; **ouvrage à consulter sur ~** reference book; **laisser qn sur ~** to leave sb standing; **7** (dans une agglomération) square; **la ~ du village** the village square; **sur la ~ Tiananmen/Rouge** in Tiananmen/Red Square; **la ~ de la Concorde** the Place de la Concorde; **la ~ du marché** the market-place; **8** Fin market; **~ financière** financial market; **sur la ~ parisienne** or **de Paris** on the Paris market; **9** (emploi) job; **avoir une bonne ~ chez** to have a good job with; **perdre sa ~** to lose one's job; **c'est une ~ très recherchée** or **demandée** it's a highly sought-after job ou position; **il y a des ~s à prendre** there are good job opportunities; **10** (forteresse) **entrer dans la ~** to get in on the inside; **être dans la ~** to be on the inside; **être maître de la ~** lit to be in control; fig to rule the roost; **se rendre maître de la ~** to take control; **avoir un pied dans la ~** fig to have a foot in the door.

■ **~ d'armes** Mil parade ground; **~ assise** seat; **~ forte** Mil fortified town; **~ d'honneur** (à table) place ou seat of honour[GB]; **la ~ publique** the public; **intéresser la ~ publique** to interest the public; **sur la ~ publique** [*célébrer, apprendre, entendre*] in public; **mettre** or **porter** or **étaler qch sur la ~ publique** to bring sth out in the open [*information, projet*].

IDIOMES **je ne lâcherais** or **donnerais pas ma ~ pour un empire** I wouldn't change places for the world ou for all the tea in China; **une ~ pour chaque chose et chaque chose à sa ~** Prov a place for everything and everything in its place.

placé, ~e /plase/ **I** *pp* ▶ **placer**.

II *pp adj* **1** (situé géographiquement) **être ~** [*objet, robinet, fenêtre*] to be; [*chaise, table, statue*] to be placed; [*bâtiment, boutique*] to be situated ou placed; [*personne*] gén to be; (au théâtre, cinéma) to be sitting; **le magasin est ~ près de l'église** the shop GB ou store US is situated ou located near the church; **être bien/mal ~** [*objet*] to be in a good/bad position; [*bâtiment, boutique*] to be well ou conveniently/badly ou inconveniently situated; [*personne*] (à table, à une cérémonie) to have a good/bad place; (au théâtre, cinéma) to have a good/bad seat; **être mieux ~** [*objet, robinet, fenêtre*] to be in a better position; [*chaise, table, statue*] to be in a better place, to be better placed; [*bâtiment, boutique*] to be better situated; [*personne*] (à table, à une cérémonie) to have a better place; (assis) (au théâtre, cinéma) to have a better seat; **la couche de cellules ~e juste sous la peau** the layer of cells (which is) right under the skin; **être ~ face à** [*personne, siège, objet*] to be facing; **2** (situé dans une hiérarchie) **être bien/mal ~** to be well/badly placed; **être bien/mal ~ sur une liste** to have a good/bad position on the list; **les étudiants les mieux ~s** the students with the best results; **3** (dans la société, une hiérarchie) **bien/haut ~** in a good/high position (*après n*); **un ami bien ~/haut ~ dans la hiérarchie** a friend who is well placed/high up in the hierarchy; **avoir des amis haut ~s** to have friends in high places; **4** (être dans une position) **être bien/mal ~ pour faire** (pour obtenir, bénéficier, réussir) to be well/badly placed to do; (pour savoir, revendiquer, juger) to be in a (good)/in no position to do; **être mal ~ pour critiquer** to be in no position to criticize; **être particulièrement mal** ou **bien mal ~ pour juger** to be in absolutely no position to judge; **il est bien ~ pour le poste** he's a likely candidate for the job; **être mieux ~ pour bénéficier de** to be better placed to benefit from; **5** (fondé) **mal ~** [*orgueil, fierté*] misplaced; [*remarque, plaisanterie*] misplaced; **6** (mis) **être ~ à la tête** or **direction de** to be placed at the head of [*groupe, entreprise*]; **être ~ sous les ordres** or **le commandement de** to be placed under the orders of; **être ~ sous la direction de** [*orchestre*] to be conducted by; [*troupe de théâtre*] to be directed by; **7** Prot Soc [*enfant*] in care; **8** Turf [*cheval*] placed; **jouer un cheval ~ et gagnant** to back a horse each way GB, to back a horse across the board US; **non ~** unplaced.

placebo /plasebo/ *nm* placebo; **administrer un ~ à qn** to give a placebo to sb; **l'effet ~** the placebo effect.

placement /plasmɑ̃/ *nm* **1** Fin investment; **2** (emploi) **assurer le ~ des diplômés** to ensure that the graduates find employment; **le ~ de nos étudiants est de plus en plus difficile** finding employment for our students is getting more and more difficult; **3** Prot Soc (d'enfant) fostering; **prendre en ~** to foster.

placenta /plasɛ̃ta/ *nm* placenta.

placentaire /plasɛ̃tɛʀ/ *adj* placental.

placer /plase/ [12] **I** *vtr* **1** (mettre à un endroit) to put, to place [*objet*]; to seat [*personne*] (**à côté de** beside); **~ ses doigts sur le clavier** to place one's fingers on the keyboard; **le metteur en scène a placé cette scène au début du film** the director put this scene at the beginning of the film; **~ des gardes** to post guards; **~ des hommes autour d'une maison** to position men around a house; **place l'antenne dans cette direction** position the aerial in this direction; **~ sa balle** (au tennis) to place one's ball; **2** (mettre dans une situation) to put, to place; **le directeur m'a placé à la tête du service informatique** the manager put me in charge of the data-processing department; **~ qn dans l'obligation de faire** to place sb under an obligation to do; **~ qn sous la protection de** to place sb under the protection of; **~ un service sous la responsabilité de qn** to make a department responsible for sb; **~ qn/être placé devant un choix difficile** to present sb/to be faced with a difficult choice; **3** (procurer un emploi) to place, to find a job for; **l'école place ses élèves** the school places ou finds employment for its students; **~ qn comme domestique chez qn** to place sb as a servant in sb's household; **~ qn auprès de qn comme garde du corps** to place sb with sb as a bodyguard; **4** Fin (investir) to invest; (mettre en dépôt) to deposit, to put; **~ une partie de ses revenus à la caisse d'épargne** to deposit ou put part of one's income in a savings bank; **5** (attribuer) to place ou to put [*confiance*] (**en** in); to pin [*espoirs*] (**dans, en** on); **6** (introduire) to slip in [*remarque, anecdote*]; **je n'arrive pas à en ~ une avec elle!** I can't get a word in edgeways GB ou edgewise US with her!; **elle ne me laisse pas en ~ une!** she won't let me get a word in edgeways GB ou edgewise US!; **il s'arrange toujours pour ~ cette plaisanterie dans la conversation** he always manages to get ou work that joke into the conversation; **7** Prot Soc to place [sb] in care [*enfant*]; **8** (vendre) to place, to sell [*produit, marchandise*].

II se placer *vpr* **1** (à un endroit) **se ~ près de** (debout) to stand next to; (assis) to sit next to; **placez-vous au milieu** gén get in the middle; (debout) stand in the middle; (assis) sit in the middle; **se ~ autour d'une maison** [*policiers*] to position oneself around a house; **où se placent les verres?** where do the glasses go?; **sais-tu comment se placent les piles?** do you know which way round GB ou around US the batteries go?; **2** (dans une situation) **se ~ sous la protection de qn** to place oneself under sb's protection; **se ~ sous une perspective**

nouvelle to look at things from a new perspective; **ça dépend de quel point de vue on se place** it depends on your point of view; **il s'est placé comme apprenti** he found ou got himself an apprenticeship[GB]; **notre démarche/intervention se place dans le cadre de l'aide au tiers-monde** our action/intervention comes within the context of Third World aid; **3** (dans une hiérarchie) **se ~ premier** [*coureur, cheval*] to come first; **il s'est placé dans les premiers** (en classe) he got one of the top places; (dans une course) he finished among the first.

placet /plasɛ/ *nm* **1** Jur (plaintiff's) writ and statement of claim; **2**† petition.

placeur, **-euse** /plasœʀ, øz/ ▶**510** *nm,f* usher/usherette.

placide /plasid/ *adj* placid, calm.

placidement /plasidmɑ̃/ *adv* placidly, calmly.

placidité /plasidite/ *nf* placidity, calmness.

placier, **-ière** /plasje, ɛʀ/ ▶**510** *nm,f* **1** (représentant) sales representative; **2** (sur un marché) market superintendent, market toby○.

placoter○ /plakɔte/ [1] *vi* C (bavarder) to chat.

plafond /plafɔ̃/ **I** *nm* **1** (de pièce) ceiling; (de tente, véhicule, souterrain) roof; **~ à caissons** coffered ceiling; **salle haute/basse de ~** high-/low-ceilinged room; **~ nuageux** cloud ceiling, cloud cover; ▶**faux**[1]; **2** (limite) ceiling, limit; **~ des prix/d'importation** price/import ceiling; **~ de crédit/ressources** lending/funding limit; **fixer un nouveau ~ de production** to set a new maximum production level; **crever le ~** (dépasser la limite) to go through the ceiling; (battre les records) to break all previous records.

II **(-)plafond** (*in compounds*) **niveau/vitesse(-)~** maximum level/speed.

plafonnement /plafɔnmɑ̃/ *nm* **1** (action de limiter) setting a ceiling on [*salaires, forces armées*]; setting a limit on [*dépenses*]; **2** (atteinte de la limite) (de prix, salaires) ceiling (**de** on); (de dépenses) limitation (**de** of).

plafonner /plafɔne/ [1] **I** *vtr* **1** Constr [*ouvrier*] to put a ceiling in [*pièce*]; [*matériau*] to form a ceiling over [*pièce*]; **la grange est plafonnée** the barn has had a ceiling put in; **2** (limiter) to put a ceiling on [*prix, salaire, production*]; **l'augmentation des salaires est plafonnée à 3%** wage increases are limited to a maximum of 3%; **loyer plafonné** protected rent; **salaire plafonné** *upper limit of salary on which contributions are payable.*

II *vi* **1** (atteindre une limite) [*production, dépenses, chômage*] to reach a ceiling, to peak out (**à** at; **autour de** at about); [*élève, employé*] to reach a maximum level of attainment; (se stabiliser) [*prix, chômage*] to level off (**à** at; **autour de** at about); **la production plafonne autour de 15 tonnes par an** production remains constant at about 15 tons a year; **~ très bas** to remain at a low level; **2** Aviat **l'avion plafonne à 15000 m** (est limité à) the plane has an absolute ceiling of 15,000 m; (culmine à) the plane has reached its ceiling of 15,000 m.

plafonnier /plafɔnje/ *nm* (au plafond) flush-fitting ceiling lamp; (dans une voiture) interior light.

plagal, **~e**, *mpl* **-aux** /plagal, o/ *adj* plagal.

plage /plaʒ/ *nf* **1** Géog (de mer, rivière, lac) beach; **~ de galets/de sable** pebble/sandy beach; **aller à la ~** to go to the beach; **sac/chaussures de ~** beach bag/shoes; **2** (zone) range; **~ de choix** range of choice; **~ de prix** price range; **3** (tranche horaire) slot; **4** (de disque) track.

■ **~ arrière** Aut rear window shelf; Naut quarterdeck; **~ avant** Naut forecastle, fo'c'sle; **~ horaire** Radio, TV time slot; **~ image** Vidéo video track; **~ musicale** Radio, TV musical interval; **~ sous-marine** bank.

plagiaire /plaʒjɛʀ/ *nmf* plagiarist.

plagiat /plaʒja/ *nm* plagiarism.

plagier /plaʒje/ [2] *vtr* to plagiarize [*œuvre, auteur*].

plagiste /plaʒist/ ▶**510** *nmf* (employé) beach attendant; (exploitant) beach manager.

plaid /plɛd/ *nm* (couverture) tartan rug GB, plaid blanket US.

plaidant, **~e** /plɛdɑ̃, ɑ̃t/ *adj* Jur [*parties*] litigant.

plaider /plede/ [1] **I** *vtr* **1** (défendre) to plead [*cause, affaire*]; **~ la cause de qn** to plead sb's case; **~ la cause de qch** to put the case for sth, to plead the cause of sth; **2** (faire valoir) **~ la légitime défense** to plead self-defence[GB]; **~ l'irresponsabilité** to plead diminished responsibility; **~ coupable/non coupable** to plead guilty/not guilty.

II *vi* to plead (**contre** against; **pour qn** on sb's behalf); **~ pour** or **en faveur de qn/qch** fig to plead for ou in favour[GB] of sb/sth.

plaideur, **-euse** /plɛdœʀ, øz/ *nm,f* Jur litigant.

plaidoirie /plɛdwaʀi/ *nf* Jur plea.

plaidoyer /plɛdwaje/ *nm* **1** Jur (d'avocat, de défense) speech for the defence[GB]; **2** fig (défense passionnée) plea (**en faveur de** in favour[GB] of; **contre** against).

plaie /plɛ/ *nf* **1** (blessure physique) wound; (ulcération) sore; (coupure) cut; **~ vive** open sore; **2** (blessure morale) wound; (calamité) scourge; **la ~ du chômage** the scourge of unemployment; **les sept ~s d'Égypte** Bible the seven plagues of Egypt; **3**○ (chose ou personne pénible) pain○; **cette circulation/cet enfant, quelle ~!** this traffic/that child is such a pain!

IDIOMES **ne rêver que ~s et bosses** to be very aggressive; **~ d'argent n'est pas mortelle** Prov money isn't everything; **remuer** or **retourner le couteau dans la ~** to twist the knife in the wound; **mettre le doigt sur la ~** to put one's finger on the problem.

plaignant, **~e** /plɛɲɑ̃, ɑ̃t/ **I** *adj* Jur litigant.

II *nm,f* Jur plaintiff, complainant.

plain† /plɛ̃/ *nm* Naut high tide.

plain-chant, *pl* **plains-chants** /plɛ̃ʃɑ̃/ *nm* plainchant ¢, plainsong ¢.

plaindre /plɛ̃dʀ/ [54] **I** *vtr* to pity, to feel sorry for [*personne, animal*]; **je te plains d'avoir à supporter cela** I feel sorry for you, having to put up with that; **elle aime se faire ~** she likes to be pitied; **il est (bien) à ~** he is (very much) to be pitied; **il n'est vraiment pas à ~** (il mérite son sort) he got what he deserved; (il a de la chance) he's got nothing to complain about.

II **se plaindre** *vpr* **1** (protester) to complain; (pleurnicher) to whinge péj, to complain; **arrête donc un peu de te ~** stop complaining ou whingeing○; **se ~ de** to complain of [*douleurs, maux de tête*]; to complain about [*personne, temps, situation, bruit*]; **se ~ à qn** to complain to sb; **se ~ que** to complain that; **je n'ai pas à me ~ de lui, il a toujours bien fait son travail** I've no complaints about him, he's always worked well; **allez vous ~ à la direction** go and complain to the management; **celui-là, il faut toujours qu'il se plaigne!** that guy○ is forever complaining!; **je t'ai prévenu, maintenant ne viens pas te ~ s'il t'arrive quelque chose** I warned you, so don't come complaining to me if something happens to you; **c'est bien ce que tu voulais, de quoi te plains-tu?** it's what you wanted, so what are you complaining about?; **les affaires vont bien, il n'y a pas à se ~** business is going well, I can't complain ou I've no complaints; **il n'y a pas lieu de se ~** there's no reason to complain, there are no grounds for complaint; **2** (geindre) [*blessé, malade*] to moan.

plaine /plɛn/ *nf* plain; ▶**grand**.

plain-pied: **de plain-pied** /dəplɛ̃pje/ **I** *loc adj* **1** (à un étage) **un bâtiment de ~** a single-storey GB ou single-story US building; **une maison de ~** a single-storey GB ou single-story US house, a bungalow GB; **l'école est de ~** the school only has one storey GB ou story US; **la cuisine est de ~ avec le jardin** the kitchen is at the same level as the garden GB ou yard US ou is on a level with the garden GB ou yard US; **2** (à égalité) **être de ~ avec qn** to be on an equal footing with sb.

II *loc adv* **entrer de ~ dans le monde politique** to have an easy passage into the world of politics; **passer de ~ de la philosophie à la finance** to be equally at home discussing philosophy or finance.

plainte /plɛ̃t/ *nf* **1** (réclamation) complaint; **2** (de malade, blessé) moan, groan; **la ~ de l'oiseau au soir tombé** the plaintive cry of the bird at nightfall; **la ~ du vent dans les arbres** the moaning of the wind in the trees; **la ~ des violons** the wail of the violins; **3** Jur complaint; **déposer une ~** or **porter ~ contre qn** to lodge a complaint against sb (**auprès de** with); **retirer une ~** to withdraw a complaint; **~ contre X** Jur complaint against person or persons unknown.

plaintif, **-ive** /plɛ̃tif, iv/ *adj* [*cri, voix, ton, parole*] plaintive, doleful; [*note, musique, son*] plaintive, mournful.

plaintivement /plɛ̃tivmɑ̃/ *adv* plaintively, dolefully.

plaire /plɛʀ/ [59] **I plaire à** *vtr ind* **1** (être séduisant) **elle plaît aux hommes** men find her attractive; **elle m'a plu tout de suite** I liked her straight ou right away; **il cherche trop à ~** he tries too hard to be liked; **à son âge elle plaît encore** she's still attractive even at her age; **il a tout pour ~** lit he is attractive in every way; iron he is not exactly God's gift; **2** (être apprécié) **mon nouveau travail me plaît** I like my new job; **la veste/maison me plaît** I like the jacket/house; **le film leur a beaucoup plu** they liked the film a lot; **il ne m'a jamais plu ce type**○ I have never liked that guy○; **si ça ne te plaît pas, c'est pareil** or **c'est le même prix**○ if you don't like it, that's tough○ ou that's too bad; **offre-leur des fleurs, ça plaît toujours** give them flowers, they're always welcome; **c'est un modèle/produit qui plaît beaucoup** it's a very popular model/product; **le spectacle a beaucoup plu** the show was very popular; **ça te plairait de partir en week-end?** would you like to go away for the week-end?; **ça ne me plaît guère de la voir sortir avec ce voyou** I don't really like her going out with that lout GB ou hoodlum US.

II se plaire *vpr* **1** (à soi-même) to like oneself; **je me plais bien avec ce chapeau** I like myself in this hat; **2** (l'un l'autre) [*personnes, couple*] to like each other; **ils se sont plu tout de suite** or **immédiatement** they hit it off○ straight GB ou right away; **3** (être bien) **ils se plaisent ici/dans leur nouvelle maison** they like it here/in their new house; **cette plante/cet animal se plaît dans un environnement marécageux** this plant/this animal thrives in a marshy environment; **4** (aimer) **se ~ à faire** to enjoy doing; **il se plaît à contredire tout le monde** he enjoys contradicting everyone; **il se plaît à dire qu'il est issu du peuple** he likes to say that he's a son of the people.

III *v impers* **il me plaît de penser que** I like to think that; **vous plairait-il de vous joindre à nous?** fml would you like to join us?; **comme il vous plaira** just as you like ou please; **s'il te plaît, s'il vous plaît** please; **il s'est acheté une montre en or, s'il vous plaît!** he bought himself a gold watch, if you please!; **plaît-il?** I beg your pardon?; **plût**

au ciel or à Dieu qu'il soit sain et sauf! fml God grant he's safe and sound!; ▶ avril.

plaisamment /plɛzamɑ̃/ *adv* **1** (de manière agréable) agreeably; **2** (d'une manière comique) amusingly.

plaisance /plɛzɑ̃s/ *nf* **la (navigation de) ~** gén boating; (sur voilier) sailing; **bateau de ~** pleasure boat.

plaisancier, **-ière** /plɛzɑ̃sje, ɛʀ/ *nm,f* amateur sailor.

plaisant, **~e** /plɛzɑ̃, ɑ̃t/ *adj* **1** (agréable) pleasant; **2** (amusant) amusing, funny; ▶ **mauvais**.

plaisanter /plɛzɑ̃te/ [1] **I** *vtr* (railler) to tease [*personne*] (**sur** about).
II *vi* to joke; **elle aime ~** she likes joking; **tu plaisantes!** you're joking ou kidding○!; **~ sur qch/qn** to joke ou make jokes about sth/sb; **~ de qch** to joke ou make jokes about sth; **il plaisante volontiers de ses soucis** he's quite ready to make a joke of his troubles; **être d'humeur à ~** to be in the mood for jokes ou joking; **ce matin, je ne suis pas d'humeur à ~** I'm in no mood for joking this morning; **faire/dire qch en plaisantant** or **pour ~** to do/to say sth as a joke; **on ne plaisante pas avec ces choses-là** these things are no laughing matter; **il ne faut pas ~ avec sa santé** one shouldn't take chances with one's health.

plaisanterie /plɛzɑ̃tʀi/ *nf* **1** (fait de plaisanter) **il ne comprend pas la ~** he can't take a joke; **aimer la ~** to be fond of a joke; **pousser trop loin la ~** to take ou carry the joke too far; **~ (mise) à part** joking aside; **2** (blague) joke; **une ~ de bon/mauvais goût** a joke in good/bad taste; **faire/lancer des ~s** to make/to crack jokes; **être l'objet des ~s de qn** to be a figure of fun to sb; **être en butte aux ~s de qn** to be the butt of sb's jokes; **les ~s les plus courtes sont les meilleures** the shortest jokes are the best; **la ~ a assez duré!** this has gone on long enough!; **3** (chose facile à faire) **c'est une ~** it's a piece of cake○.
■ **~ de corps de garde** barrack room joke.

plaisantin /plɛzɑ̃tɛ̃/ *nm* **1** (blagueur) practical joker; **petit ~!** wise guy○!; **2** (fumiste) skiver○.

plaisir /plɛziʀ/ *nm* **1** (sensation agréable) pleasure; **le ~ des sens/des yeux** sensual/aesthetic pleasure; **le ~ d'offrir/de lire/de jouer** the pleasure of giving/of reading/of playing; **prendre** or **avoir (du) ~ à faire** to enjoy doing; **prendre un malin ~ à faire** to take a wicked delight in doing; **chacun prend son ~ où il le trouve** one must take one's pleasure where one finds it; **j'ai eu le ~ de faire leur connaissance/de dîner avec eux** I had the pleasure of meeting them/of dining with them; **M. et Mme Grovagnard ont le ~ de vous faire part du mariage/de la naissance de leur fille Nicole** Mr. and Mrs. Grovagnard are pleased to announce the marriage/birth of their daughter Nicole; **de ~** [*rougir, frémir, défaillir*] with pleasure; [*cris, gémissements, frémissements*] of pleasure; **avec (grand) ~** with (great) pleasure; **j'ai appris avec ~ que** I was delighted to hear that; **gâcher le ~ de qn** to spoil sb's pleasure; **pour le ~** for pleasure; **je ne te punis pas pour le ~ mais parce que tu le mérites** I'm not punishing you for the sake of it, but because you deserve it; **à ~** [*se tourmenter, exagérer, mentir*] a lot; **tout le ~ est pour moi** the pleasure's all mine; **pour le plus grand ~ des auditeurs/du public** for the enjoyment of the listeners/of the audience; **faire ~ à qn** to please sb; **elle aime faire ~** she likes to please; **ça me ferait (très) ~ de la revoir** I would be very pleased ou I would be delighted to see her again; **qu'est-ce qui te/leur ferait ~?** what would you/they like?; **si ça peut te faire ~** if it'll make you happy; **je viendrai, mais c'est bien pour te faire ~** I'll come, but only because you want me to; **ça fait toujours ~!** iron isn't that nice!; **me ferez-vous le ~ d'accepter mon invitation?** fml would you do me the pleasure of accepting my invitation?; **tu vas me faire le ~ de ranger ta chambre/de me parler sur un autre ton!** you'll tidy up your room/speak to me more politely if you know what's good for you!; **faites-moi le ~ de vous taire!** would you please shut up○!; **il se fera un ~ de vous faire visiter la ville/de vous aider** he will be delighted to show you around town/to help you; **faire durer le ~** lit to make the pleasure last; iron to prolong the agony; **ce sera selon mon bon ~** that will be according to my pleasure; **car tel est notre bon ~** for such is my pleasure; **je vous/lui/leur souhaite bien du ~** iron I wish you/him/them joy of it!; **2** (source d'agrément) pleasure; **des ~ raffinés** refined pleasures; **les menus ~s de l'existence** the simple pleasures of life; **à mon âge les ~s sont rares** at my age there are few pleasures left to enjoy; **une vie de ~s** a life devoted to pleasure; **c'est un ~ que je ne me refuse jamais** it's a pleasure that I never deny myself; **les ~s charnels** the pleasures of the flesh, carnal pleasures; **les ~s défendus** forbidden pleasures; **aimer les ~s de la table** to enjoy good food; **3** (sexuel) pleasure; **donner/éprouver du ~** to give/to experience pleasure; **le ~ solitaire** masturbation.

plan, **~e** /plɑ̃, plan/ **I** *adj* **1** gén [*surface*] flat, even; **2** Math, Phys plane.
II *nm* **1** (carte) (de région, ville, métro) map; (dans bâtiment, domaine, paquebot) plan, map; **je te fais un ~ pour que tu ne te perdes pas** I'll draw you a map so you won't get lost; **2** Archit, Constr plan; **tirer des ~s** to draw up plans; **c'est lui qui a fait les ~s de sa maison** he drew up the plans for his house himself; **acheter/vendre une maison sur ~** to buy/sell a house on architect's plans; **3** Ind, Tech (de machine, d'appareil) (schéma directeur) blueprint; (après construction) plan; **les ~s du nouvel avion de chasse** the blueprint for the new fighter plane; **4** Math, Phys plane; **5** (canevas) outline, framework, plan; **fais un ~ au lieu de rédiger directement** draw up a plan before you start writing; **~ détaillé** detailed plan; **6** Cin, Phot (image) shot; **montage ~ par ~** shot-to-shot editing; **premier ~** foreground; **second ~** middle-distance; **au premier ~** in the foreground; **au second ~** in the middle distance; ▶ **gros**; **7** (niveau) level; **mettre deux personnes sur le même ~** fig to put two people at the same level; **cette question vient au premier ~ de sa campagne électorale** this issue is at the forefront of his electoral campaign; **ce dossier est au premier ~ de l'actualité** this issue is front-page news ou is at the forefront of the news; **être relégué au second ~** [*personne, problème*] to be relegated to the background, to take a back seat; **de (tout) premier ~** [*personnalité*] leading (*épith*); [*œuvre*] key, major; **de second ~** second-rate; **sur le ~ politique/économique/personnel** from a political/an economic/a personal point of view, in political/economic/personal terms; **sur le ~ de l'efficacité** from the point of view of efficiency, in terms of efficiency; **au ~ régional/national** at regional/national level; **8** (projet) plan, programme[GB]; **un ~ pour l'emploi** a plan for employment, an employment programme[GB]; **un ~ anti-inflation** an anti-inflation plan ou programme[GB]; **le gouvernement a présenté son ~ de relance économique** the government has presented its plan to boost the economy; **j'ai un ~, voilà ce qu'on va faire** I have a plan, here's what we'll do; **j'ai un bon ~○ pour voyager pas cher/entrer gratuitement** I know a good way of travelling[GB] cheaply/getting in free; **on se fait un ~ restaurant○?** shall we go out for a meal?; ▶ **comète**.
■ **~ d'action** plan of action; **~ américain** Cin thigh shot; **~ d'amortissement** repayment schedule ou plan; **~ de campagne** plan of campaign; **~ de carrière** career plan; **~ comptable** code of legal requirements in accounting practice; **~ directeur** Mil battle map; Écon master plan; **~ d'eau** man-made lake; **~ d'ensemble** Cin long shot; **~ d'épargne** savings plan; **~ d'épargne logement**, **PEL** *savings scheme entitling depositor to cheap mortgage*; **~ d'épargne retraite** top-up pensions scheme; **~ de faille** fault plane; **~ fixe** Cin static shot; **~ incliné** inclined plane; **en ~ incliné** sloping; **~ de masse** overall building plan; **~ de métro** map of the underground GB ou subway US; **~ moyen** Cin medium close-up; **~ d'occupation des sols**, **POS** land use plan; **~ quinquennal** five-year plan; **~ rapproché** Cin waist shot; **~ social** Écon, Entr planned redundancy scheme GB, scheduled lay-off program US; **~ de travail** (pour projet) working schedule; (surface) worktop; **~ d'urbanisme** urban planning policy; **~ de vol** flight plan.
IDIOMES **laisser qn en ~○** to leave sb in the lurch, to leave sb high and dry; **laisser qch en ~○** to leave sth unfinished; **il a tout laissé en ~ pour la rejoindre à Rome** he dropped everything to go and join her in Rome; **rester en ~○** [*personne*] to be left stranded ou high and dry; [*projets*] to be left unfinished.

planant○, **~e** /planɑ̃, ɑ̃t/ *adj* [*drogue, musique*] mind-blowing○.

planche /plɑ̃ʃ/ **I** *nf* **1** (pièce de bois) plank; (pour pétrir, laver etc) board; **un sol en ~s** a wooden floor; **2** (en gravure) (plaque) plate; **3** Édition, Imprim (illustration) plate; **4** (en natation) floating on one's back; **faire la ~** to float on one's back; **5** Agric, Hortic bed.
II planches *nfpl* **les ~s** (de bord de mer) the boardwalk (*sg*).
■ **~ à billets** minting plate; **faire marcher la ~ à billets○** to print money; **~ à découper** chopping-board; (plus épaisse) butcher's block; **~ à dessin** drawing board; **~ à laver** washboard; **~ à pain** breadboard; **~ à pâtisserie** pastry board; **~ à repasser** ironing-board; **~ à roulettes** Sport skateboard; **faire de la ~ à roulettes** to skateboard; **~ de salut** fig lifeline; **~ de surf** surfboard; **~ à voile** (engin) windsurfing board; (activité) windsurfing; **faire de la ~ à voile** to windsurf.
IDIOMES **monter sur les ~s** Théât to go on the stage, to tread the boards; **brûler les ~s** Théât to bring the house down; **avoir du pain sur la ~○** to have one's work cut out.

planche-contact, *pl* **planches-contact** /plɑ̃ʃkɔ̃takt/ *nf* Phot contact print.

plancher /plɑ̃ʃe/ [1] **I** *nm* **1** (sol) floor; **2** Écon, Fin (seuil inférieur) floor, minimum; **atteindre un ~** [*prix, cours*] to bottom out; **3** Anat (paroi) floor; **~ buccal** floor of the mouth.
II (-)plancher (*in compounds*) **prix(-)~** bottom price; **cours(-)~** Fin (de monnaie) floor ou bottom rate; (de valeur) floor ou bottom price.
III○ *vi* students' slang to work (**sur** on).
■ **le ~ des vaches○** land, terra firma.
IDIOMES **mettre le pied au ~○** Aut to put one's foot down on the accelerator.

planchette /plɑ̃ʃɛt/ *nf* **1** (petite planche) small board; **2** (rayon) (small) shelf.

planchiste /plɑ̃ʃist/ *nmf* windsurfer.

plan-concave, *pl* **~s** /plɑ̃kɔ̃kav/ *adj* plano-concave.

plan-convexe, *pl* **~s** /plɑ̃kɔ̃vɛks/ *adj* plano-convex.

plancton /plɑ̃ktɔ̃/ *nm* plankton.

plané, **~e** /plane/ **I** *adj* **vol ~** lit glide; **faire un vol ~** fig to go flying, to fall.
II *nm* glide.

planéité /planeite/ *nf* gén levelness, flatness; (en optique) planeness.

planer /plane/ [1] *vi* **1** [*avion, oiseau*] to glide (**sur** over); [*oiseau de proie*] to hover (**sur** over); [*vapeur*] to float (**sur** over), to waft (**sur** over); **2** [*tristesse, menace*] to hang (**sur** over); **laisser ~ le doute** to allow uncertainty to persist; **3**○ [*rêveur*] to have one's head in the clouds; **~ au-dessus de** [*esprit*] to soar above; **il plane au-dessus des détails** he is above petty details; **4**○ [*drogué*] to be spaced out○, to be high○.

planétaire /planetɛʀ/ *adj* Astron, Mécan, Phys planetary; fig global.

planétarium /planetaʀjɔm/ *nm* planetarium.

planète /planɛt/ *nf* planet.
■ **~ inférieure** inferior planet; **~ supérieure** superior planet.

planétologie /planetɔlɔʒi/ *nf* planetology.

planeur /planœʀ/ *nm* **1** (engin) glider; **2** ▶ **449** (sport) gliding.

planifiable /planifjabl/ *adj* **évolution économique ~** economic development that can be planned.

planificateur, **-trice** /planifikatœʀ, tʀis/ **I** *adj* planning.
II *nm,f* planner.

planification /planifikasjɔ̃/ *nf* planning.
■ **~ familiale** or **des naissances** family planning.

planifier /planifje/ [2] *vtr* to plan [*production, vacances, semaine, attaque*]; to schedule, to programme[GB] [*traitement*]; **~ à court/long terme** to draw up a short-/long-term plan; **~ l'économie à moyen terme** to draw up a medium-term economic plan.

planimétrie /planimetʀi/ *nf* planimetry.

planimétrique /planimetʀik/ *adj* planimetric.

planisphère /planisfɛʀ/ *nm* planisphere.

planning○ /planiŋ/ *nm* controv schedule; **respecter le ~** to keep to schedule.
■ **~ familial** family planning service.

plan-plan○ /plɑ̃plɑ̃/ *adj inv* [*vie, existence*] dull, humdrum.

planque○ /plɑ̃k/ *nf* **1** (cachette) (de personne) hideout; (de chose) hidey-hole○ GB, stash○ US; **2** (emploi confortable) cushy number○; **il a trouvé la ~** he's got GB ou gotten US himself a cushy number.

planqué○ /plɑ̃ke/ *nm* soldiers' slang skiver.

planquer○ /plɑ̃ke/ [1] **I** *vtr* to hide [*personne*]; to hide [sth] away [*objet*]; **~ de l'argent** to stash money away.
II se planquer *vpr* (pour ne pas être vu) to hide; (plus longtemps) to go into hiding; (pour se protéger) to hide; (par lâcheté) to skive.

plan-relief, *pl* **plans-reliefs** /plɑ̃ʀəljɛf/ *nm* scale model.

plan-séquence, *pl* **plans-séquences** /plɑ̃sekɑ̃s/ *nm* sequence shot.

plant /plɑ̃/ *nm* **1** (plante) young plant; (plus jeune) seedling; **~ de tomate** young tomato plant; (plus jeune) tomato seedling; **un ~ de vigne** a young vine; **des ~s de fleurs** bedding plants; **2** (plantation) (d'arbres) plantation; **~ de légumes** vegetable patch; **~ de fleurs** flower bed.

Plantagenêt /plɑ̃taʒnɛ/ *npr* Plantagenet.

plantain /plɑ̃tɛ̃/ *nm* plantain.

plantaire /plɑ̃tɛʀ/ *adj* Anat plantar.

plantation /plɑ̃tasjɔ̃/ *nf* **1** (propriété agricole) plantation; **2** (terrain planté) (d'arbres, de café) plantation; (de fleurs) bed; (de légumes) patch; **3** (végétaux) **mes ~s de tomates** the tomatoes I've planted; **tu as fait des ~s?** have you planted anything?; **4** (activité) planting.

plante /plɑ̃t/ *nf* **1** Bot plant; **~ carnivore/médicinale** carnivorous/medicinal plant; **~ grimpante** climber, climbing plant; **~ d'appartement** or **verte** houseplant; **~ grasse** succulent; **~ textile** fibre[GB] plant; **~ de serre** lit, fig hothouse plant; **~ annuelle** annual; **~ vivace** perennial; **soigner par les ~s** to use herbal medicine; **2** Anat **~ (des pieds)** sole (of the foot).

planté, **~e** /plɑ̃te/ **I** *pp* ▶ **planter**.
II *pp adj* **1** (enraciné) **dents bien/mal ~es** regular/uneven teeth; **avoir les cheveux ~s bas sur le front** to have a low forehead; **2**○ (debout) standing; **il était ~ devant le magasin** he was standing outside the shop; **rester ~ devant un tableau** to stand gazing at a painting; **ne reste pas ~ là, rentre!** don't just stand there, come in!; **ne reste pas ~ comme un piquet!** don't just stand there like a lemon ou dummy!

planter /plɑ̃te/ [1] **I** *vtr* **1** Agric, Hort to plant [*rosier, pommes de terre, tomates, jardin*]; **route plantée d'arbres** tree-lined road, road lined with trees; **2** (ficher) to drive in [*pieu*]; to knock in [*clou*]; **~ un pieu dans qch** to drive a stake into sth; **~ un couteau/une fourchette dans** to stick a knife/a fork into; **~ ses dents/ses griffes dans le bras de qn** to sink one's teeth/to dig one's claws into sb's arm; **~ une flèche dans une cible** to shoot an arrow into a target; **clou mal planté** nail which has not gone in straight; **~ un drapeau au pôle Sud** to put up a flag at the South Pole; **3** (dresser) to pitch [*tente*]; **~ un décor** lit to put up a set; fig to set the scene; **~ une échelle contre un mur** to stand a ladder against a wall; **bâtiment planté en rase campagne** building stuck in the middle of nowhere; **4** (mettre) to put, to stick○; **~ la bouteille sur la table** to stick the bottle on the table; **~ un baiser sur la joue de qn** to plant a kiss on sb's cheek; **5**○ (abandonner) **~ là** to drop [*outil*]; to dump○, to abandon [*voiture*]; to pack in○, to chuck in○ GB [*travail*]; to walk out on, to ditch○ [*époux*]; **il m'a planté là et a sauté dans un taxi** he left me standing there and jumped into a taxi; **il a tout planté là et est parti en Inde** he dropped everything ou he chucked○ it all in and went off to India.
II se planter *vpr* **1** Hort [*fleur, parterre*] to be planted; **se ~ au printemps** to be planted in the spring; **2** (se ficher) [*clou, pieu*] to go in; **3** [*personne*] **se ~ une épine/un clou dans le pied** to get a thorn/a nail in one's foot; **avoir une épine plantée dans le pied** to have a thorn in one's foot; **4**○ (se tenir) **aller se ~ devant qch/qn** to go and stand in front of sth/sb; **5**○ (avoir un accident) to crash; **se ~ en planeur** to crash in a glider; **se ~ en vélo** to have a bicycle accident; **6**○ (se tromper) to get it wrong; (se perdre) to get lost; **se ~ dans une addition** to get a sum all wrong; **il s'est planté en histoire** he made a mess of the history paper ou exam.

planteur /plɑ̃tœʀ/ ▶ **510** *nm* (exploitant) planter; **~ de thé** tea planter.

planteuse /plɑ̃tøz/ *nf* (machine) potato planter.

plantigrade /plɑ̃tigʀad/ *adj, nm* plantigrade.

plantoir /plɑ̃twaʀ/ *nm* dibble.

planton /plɑ̃tɔ̃/ *nm* (sentinelle) sentry; (ordonnance) orderly; **être de ~** to be on sentry ou orderly duty; **faire le ~** fig to wait around.

plantureusement /plɑ̃tyʀøzmɑ̃/ *adv* [*manger*] abundantly.

plantureux, **-euse** /plɑ̃tyʀø, øz/ *adj* **1** [*déjeuner*] lavish; [*poitrine*] generous; [*femme*] buxom, well-endowed hum; **2** [*pays, terre*] fertile; [*année, récolte*] bumper (*épith*).

plaquage /plakaʒ/ *nm* **1** Tech (de bois) veneering; (de métal) plating; (de pierre) facing; **2** Sport (technique) tackling ¢; **un ~** a tackle.

plaque /plak/ *nf* **1** (de moisissure, d'humidité) patch; **~ de verglas** patch of ice; **2** (sur la peau) blotch; (plus grand) patch; ▶ **sclérose**; **3** (de verre, de métal) plate; (plus grand) sheet; (de marbre) slab; (plus petit) plaque; (de chocolat) slab; (au jeu) chip; (de cabinet médical, d'étude de notaire) brass plate; (de policier) badge; **4** Électron anode; **5** Géol (tectonic) plate.
■ **~ d'accumulateur** accumulator plate; **~ chauffante** hotplate; **~ de cheminée** fireback; **~ commémorative** (commemorative) plaque; **~ dentaire** plaque; **~ d'égout** manhole cover; **~ de four** drip tray; **~ de garde** guard plate; **~ d'identité** (de soldat) ID tag; (de chien) name tag, dog tag; **~ d'immatriculation** or **minéralogique** number plate GB, license plate US; **~ à pâtisserie** baking tray; **~ de propreté** finger plate; **~ sensible** plate; **~ tournante** lit turntable; fig crossroads (*sg*).
IDIOMES **être à côté de la ~**○ (se tromper) to be completely mistaken; (être distrait) to be not with it○; **elle répond toujours à côté de la ~**○ her answers are always slightly off beam○.

plaqué, **~e** /plake/ **I** *pp* ▶ **plaquer**.
II *pp adj* **1** (recouvert) [*bijou*] plated; **~ or** gold-plated; **~ argent** silver-plated; **~ acajou/noyer** with a mahogany/walnut veneer; **2** (appliqué) **poche ~e** patch pocket.
III *nm* **le ~** (bijoux) plated jewellery GB ou jewelry US; (couverts) plated cutlery; (revêtement) plating; **en ~** plated.

plaqueminier /plakminje/ *nm* persimmon.

plaquer /plake/ [1] **I** *vtr* **1** (appuyer, aplatir) **~ qn contre qch/au sol** to pin sb against sth/to the ground; **~ sa main sur** to put one's hand on; **le vent plaquait sa jupe contre ses cuisses** the wind made her skirt stick to her legs; **~ une mèche sur son front** to plaster a lock of hair onto one's forehead; **2**○ (rompre avec) to ditch○, to get rid of [*amant*]; (quitter) to walk out on○, leave; **~ un emploi** to chuck in a job○ GB, to chuck a job○ US; **tout ~** to chuck it all in○ GB, to chuck everything○ US; **3** (en rugby) to tackle; **4** (rajouter) péj to tack [*citation, commentaire*] (**sur** onto); **5** Tech to veneer [*meuble, bois ordinaire*]; to plate [*bijou, métal ordinaire*]; **6** Mus to strike [*accord*].
II se plaquer *vpr* **se ~ contre un mur** to flatten oneself against a wall; **se ~ au sol** to lie flat on the ground; **se ~ contre qn** to press oneself up against sb.

plaquette /plakɛt/ *nf* **1** Comm (de chocolat) bar; (de beurre) packet; (de pilules) ≈ blister strip; **2** Tech (de métal) small plate; **3** Physiol platelet; **4** Édition (publicitaire) brochure; (en prose) pamphlet; **une ~ de vers** a slim volume of poetry.
■ **~ de frein** brake shoe.

plasma /plasma/ *nm* Phys, Physiol plasma.

plastic /plastik/ *nm* plastic explosive; **attentat au ~** bomb attack.

plasticage /plastikaʒ/ *nm* bomb attack (**de** on).

plasticien, **-ienne** /plastisjɛ̃, ɛn/ ▶ **510** *nm,f* **1** Méd plastic surgeon; **2** Art visual artist.

plasticité /plastisite/ *nf* **1** (de matériau) plasticity; **2** (d'esprit) plasticity; (de caractère) malleability.

plastifiant, **~e** /plastifjɑ̃, ɑ̃t/ **I** *adj* plasticizing (*épith*).
II *nm* plasticizer.

plastification /plastifikasjɔ̃/ *nf* **1** (de carte, document) plastic coating; **2** Chimie, Tech plasticizing.

plastifier /plastifje/ [2] *vtr* to coat [sth] with plastic; **carte plastifiée** plastic-coated card.

plastiquage = **plasticage**.

plastique /plastik/ **I** *adj* **1** [*beauté*] formal, plastic; **2** [*chirurgie, chirurgien*] plastic; **3** (malléable) plastic.
II *nm* (matière) plastic; **c'est du ~** it's plastic; **sac en ~** plastic bag.
III *nf* **1** (arts) **la ~** the plastic arts (*pl*); (sculpture) the art of sculpture; **2** (esthétique)

(d'objet, de statue) formal beauty; (de personne) physique.

plastiquement /plastikmɑ̃/ *adv* in terms of form, visually.

plastiquer /plastike/ [1] *vtr* to carry out a bomb attack on; **il s'est fait ~ trois fois** there have been three bomb attacks on his place.

plastiqueur, **-euse** /plastikœʀ, øz/ *nm,f* terrorist, bomber.

plastron /plastʀɔ̃/ *nm* **1** (de chemise) shirt front; (faux) dicky○, false shirt front; (de corsage) ornamental front; **2** (d'escrimeur) plastron; (d'armure) breast-plate; **3** (d'oiseau) breast-shield.

plastronner /plastʀɔne/ [1] **I** *vtr* to cover (**de** with).
II *vi* to be full of oneself.

plasturgie /plastyʀʒi/ *nf* plastics processing.

plat, **~e** /pla, plat/ **I** *adj* **1** (sans relief) [*fond, surface, pays, terrain*] flat; [*mer*] smooth; **un terrain parfaitement ~** a perfectly flat plot of land; **être ~e, avoir la poitrine ~e** to be flat-chested; **électroencéphalogramme ~** electroencephalograph showing a flat trace; **2** (peu profond) [*chapeau*] flat; [*bateau, embarcation*] flat-bottomed; (sans épaisseur) [*caillou, paquet*] flat; [*montre, calculatrice, briquet*] slimline; [*cheveux*] limp; **3** (sans talon) [*chaussure, soulier*] flat; ▶**couture**; **4** (fade) [*saveur, goût*] bland; [*vin*] insipid; (sans caractère) [*style, description*] lifeless; [*traduction*] flat; [*texte, discours*] dull; **5** (humble) **faire de ~es excuses à qn** to apologize abjectly to sb.
II *nm* **1** (pour cuire, servir) dish; **~ de porcelaine/d'argent** china/silver dish; **2** (aliments servis) dish; **~ froid/chaud** cold/hot dish; **un ~ de spaghetti/viande** a dish of spaghetti/meat; **un bon petit ~** a tasty dish; ▶**vengeance**; **3** (partie d'un repas) course; **plusieurs ~s au choix** a choice of several courses; **4** (partie plate) **le ~ de la main** the flat of one's hand; **le ~ d'un couteau** the flat of a knife; **5** (terrain plat) flat ground; **courir sur du ~** to run on the flat.
III plate *nf* **1** Naut flat-bottomed boat; **2** Hist piece of plate armour[GB].
IV à plat *loc adv* **1** (horizontalement) [*mains, pieds*] flat; **poser** or **mettre qch à ~** to lay sth down flat; **pose les livres à ~ sur mon bureau** lay the books down flat on my desk; **dormir à ~** to sleep without a pillow; **à ~ ventre** lit flat on one's stomach; **dormir à ~ ventre** to sleep flat on one's stomach; **se mettre à ~ ventre devant qn** fig to grovel in front of sb; **tomber à ~** [*plaisanterie, remarque*] to fall flat; **2** (hors d'usage) [*pneu*] flat; [*batterie*] flat GB, dead; **3**○ (sans énergie) **être à ~** [*personne*] to be run down; **sa maladie l'a mis à ~** his illness really took it out of him○; **4** (en ordre) **mettre/remettre qch à ~** [*comptes, activité, dossier*] to review sth from scratch; **une mise à ~ du système fiscal est envisagée** a complete review of the tax system is planned.
■ **~ de côtes** top rib of beef; **~ cuisiné** Comm ready-cooked meal; (chez soi) dish that takes time and trouble; **~ du jour** today's special, dish of the day; **~ à légumes** vegetable dish; **~ de nouilles**○ pej drip○ pej; **~ à poisson** serving dish for fish; **~ de résistance** Culin main course; fig main item; **~ à tarte** pie dish; **~es côtes** Culin top rib ₵ of beef.
IDIOMES **faire un ~**○ (en natation) to do a belly flop○; **faire du ~ à qn**○ to chat sb up○ GB, to come on to sb○; **mettre les petits ~s dans les grands**○ to go to town on a meal○; **mettre les pieds dans le ~**○ to put one's foot in it; **faire tout un ~ de qch**○ to make a song and dance about sth○ GB, to make a big deal about sth.

platane /platan/ *nm* plane tree; **rentrer dans** or **se payer**○ **un ~** to crash into a tree.

plat-bord, *pl* **plats-bords** /plabɔʀ/ *nm* gunwale.

plateau, *pl* **~x** /plato/ **I** *nm* **1** (pour servir, porter) tray (**de** of); **2** Théât stage; Cin, TV set; **et sur le ~ ici ce soir...** and in our panel tonight...; **3** (niveau constant) plateau; **arriver à un ~** [*fièvre, inflation*] to level off; [*talent, capacités*] to reach a plateau; **4** Géog plateau; **5** (de balance) pan; (de table) top; (de tourne-disques) turntable.
II plateau(-) (*in compounds*) **~(-)télé**○ TV dinner; **~(-)repas** meal on tray.
■ **~ de chargement** loading platform; **~ continental** continental shelf; **~ d'embrayage** clutch disc; **~ de frein** backplate; **~ à fromage** (objet) cheeseboard; **~ de fromages** (assortiment) cheeseboard; **~ de fruits de mer** seafood platter; **~ de pédalier** chainwheel; **~ de tournage** film set.
IDIOMES **il faut qu'on t'apporte tout sur un ~?** do you expect everything to be handed to you on a plate?; **servir qch sur un ~ d'argent** to serve sth on a silver platter.

plateau-repas, *pl* **plateaux-repas** /platoʀ(ə)pɑ/ *nm* meal tray.

plate-bande, *pl* **plates-bandes** /platbɑ̃d/ *nf* (dans un jardin) border, flower bed; **marcher sur** or **piétiner les plates-bandes de qn**○ fig to encroach on sb's territory.

platée○ /plate/ *nf* plateful (**de** of).

plate-forme, *pl* **plates-formes** /platfɔʀm/ *nf* **1** Constr platform; **~ d'hélicoptère** helicopter platform; **toit en ~** flat roof; **2** Transp (de bus, tramway) platform; **3** Comm (pour marchandises) skid; **4** Pol platform; **la ~ électorale** the party platform; **5** Géog platform.
■ **~ continentale** continental shelf; **~ de forage** drilling rig; **~ littorale** coastal shelf; **~ pétrolière** oil rig.

platement /platmɑ̃/ *adv* **s'excuser ~** to apologize abjectly; **s'exprimer ~** to express oneself unimaginatively ou in bland terms.

platine /platin/ ▶**193** **I** *adj inv* platinum; **blond ~** platinum blond.
II *nm* platinum.
III *nf* **1** (d'horloge, de serrure) plate; (de microscope) stage; (de presse) platen; **2** (tourne-disques) turntable.
■ **~ iridié** platiniridium.

platiné, **~e** /platine/ *adj* **1** (plaqué) platinum-plated; **2** (blond) [*cheveux*] platinum blond.

platitude /platityd/ *nf* **1** (caractère banal) (de remarque, texte) banality; (de personne) dreariness; (de style) triteness; **des remarques d'une ~ désolante** unbearably trite remarks; **2** (propos banal) platitude; **débiter**○ **des ~s** to spout platitudes.

Platon /platɔ̃/ *npr* Plato.

platonicien, **-ienne** /platɔnisjɛ̃, ɛn/ **I** *adj* Platonic.
II *nm,f* Platonist.

platonique /platɔnik/ *adj* **1** [*amour*] platonic; **2** [*revendication*] token (*épith*).

platoniquement /platɔnikmɑ̃/ *adv* platonically.

platonisme /platɔnism/ *nm* Platonism.

plâtrage /plɑtʀaʒ/ *nm* **1** Constr (action) plastering; (résultat) plasterwork, plaster; **2** Agric liming.

plâtras /plɑtʀɑ/ *nm inv* Constr rubble ₵.

plâtre /plɑtʀ/ *nm* **1** Constr (matériau) plaster; **les ~s** plasterwork ₵; **ton Brie, c'est du ~** your Brie is like chalk; **2** Méd, Art (objet) plaster cast; **on lui a mis la jambe dans le ~** they've put his leg in plaster ou in a cast; **~ de marche** walking cast.
IDIOMES **battre qn comme ~**○ to beat the living daylights out of sb○; **essuyer les ~s** to put up with the initial problems.

plâtrer /plɑtʀe/ [1] *vtr* **1** Constr to plaster [*mur*]; **2** Méd **~ le bras de qn** to put sb's arm in plaster ou in a cast; **il a la jambe plâtrée** his leg is in plaster; **se faire ~ le bras** to have one's arm put in plaster.

plâtrerie /plɑtʀəʀi/ *nf* (usine) plasterworks (+ *v sg* ou *pl*); (travail) plastering.

plâtreux, **-euse** /plɑtʀø, øz/ *adj* **1** [*mur*] plastered; fig [*teinte*] chalky; **2** Culin [*fromage*] chalky.

plâtrier, **-ière** /plɑtʀije, ɛʀ/ **I** ▶**510** *nm,f* plasterer.
II plâtrière *nf* (carrière) gypsum quarry; (four) gypsum kiln; (usine) plasterworks (+ *v sg* ou *pl*).

plausibilité /plozibilite/ *nf* plausibility.

plausible /plozibl/ *adj* plausible.

plausiblement /plozibləmɑ̃/ *adv* plausibly.

Plaute /plot/ *npr* Plautus.

playback /plɛbak/ *nm inv* miming, lip syncing; **chanter en ~** to mime to a tape, to lip-sync (a song).

play-boy, *pl* **~s** /plɛbɔj/ *nm* playboy.

plèbe /plɛb/ *nf* **1** péj plebs (+ *v pl*), hoi polloi (+ *v pl*); **2** Hist plebeians (*pl*).

plébéien, **-ienne** /plebejɛ̃, ɛn/ *adj, nm,f* plebeian.

plébiscitaire /plebisitɛʀ/ *adj* [*régime*] plebiscitary; **vote ~** plebiscite.

plébiscite /plebisit/ *nm* plebiscite.

plébisciter /plebisite/ [1] *vtr* **1** (élire) to elect [sb] with a huge majority; **se faire ~** to be elected by an overwhelming majority; **2** (approuver) to vote overwhelmingly in favour[GB] of [*personne, mesure*]; to acclaim [*mode, programme*]; **les auditeurs ont plébiscité l'émission** the programme[GB] has proved popular with the vast majority of listeners.

plectre /plɛktʀ/ *nm* plectrum.

pléiade /plejad/ *nf* liter (groupe) group; (de personnes remarquables) galaxy, pleiad.

Pléiade /plejad/ *nprf* **1** Littérat **la ~** the Pleiad; **2** Astron Pleiad; **les ~s** the Pleiades.

plein, **~e** /plɛ̃, plɛn/ **I** *adj* **1** (rempli) full (**de** of); **être ~ à craquer** to be full to bursting; **j'ai les mains ~es** my hands are full; **il avait les yeux ~s de larmes** his eyes were full of tears; **être ~ de vie/d'idées/de fraîcheur** to be full of life/of ideas/of freshness; **être ~ d'humour** [*personne, film, livre*] to be amusing; **des huîtres bien ~es** nice fat oysters; **une jupe ~e de taches** a skirt covered with stains; **avoir le nez ~**○ to need to blow one's nose; **2** (indiquant une quantité maximale) **un ~ verre/panier/pot** a glassful/basketful/potful (**de** of); **une ~e assiette/valise/salle** a plateful/suitcaseful/roomful (**de** of); **il a une ~e cave de vin/chambre de jouets** he has a cellar full of wine/bedroom full of toys; **un ~ carton de vieux journaux** a boxful of old newspapers; **prendre** or **saisir qch à ~es mains** to take hold of sth with both hands [*objet massif*]; to pick up a handful of sth [*terre, sable, pièces de monnaie*]; **3** (non creux) [*brique, mur, cloison*] solid; [*joues, visage*] plump; [*forme*] rounded; **4** (total) [*pouvoir, accord, effet, adhésion*] full; [*succès, satisfaction, confiance*] complete; **confier** or **voter les ~s pouvoirs à qn** to grant sb full power; **avec le ~ accord de qn** with sb's full agreement; **avoir la ~e maîtrise/utilisation de qch** to have full control/use of sth; **~ et entier** [*accord, adhésion, responsabilité*] full; **avoir la responsabilité ~e et entière de qch** to have full responsibility for sth; **5** (entier) [*jour, mois, année*] whole, full; [*lune*] full; **il faut compter un mois ~** you should allow a full month; **c'est la ~e mer** it is high tide; **6** (milieu) **en ~e poitrine/tête** (right) in the middle of the chest/head; **en ~e réunion/nuit/crise** (right) in the middle of the meeting/night/crisis; **en ~e ville/forêt/campagne** (right) in the middle of the town/forest/countryside; **en ~ cœur** right in

the heart; **en ~ centre-ville** right in the centre[GB] of town; **en ~ mois d'août** right in the middle of August; **en ~ jour** in broad daylight; **en ~ été** at the height of summer; **en ~ hiver** in the depths of winter; **en ~e mer** on the open sea; **être en ~e mutation** or **évolution** to be experiencing radical change; **être en ~e récession** to be in a deep recession; **7** Zool **~e** [*femelle*] pregnant; [*vache*] in calf; [*jument*] in foal; [*truie*] in pig; **8**○ (ivre) sloshed○, drunk; **9** (en parlant de cuir) **reliure ~e peau** full leather binding; **un livre avec une reliure ~e peau** a fully leather-bound book; **manteau/veste ~e peau** coat/jacket made out of full skins.
II *adv* **1** (exprimant une grande quantité) **avoir des billes ~ les poches** to have one's pockets full of marbles; **il a des idées ~ la tête** he's full of ideas; **2** (directement) **être orienté ~ sud/nord** to face due south/north.
III *nm* **1** (de réservoir) **faire le ~ de** lit to fill up with [*eau, carburant*]; fig to get a lot of [*idées, voix, visiteurs*]; **s'arrêter pour faire le ~** to stop to fill up; **j'ai fait deux ~s** or **deux fois le ~ pour venir ici** I took two tankfuls to get here; **le ~ s'il vous plaît** fill it up please; **2** Phys **les ~s et les vides** plenums and vacuums; **3** (en calligraphie) downstroke; **les ~s et les déliés** the downstrokes and upstrokes.
IV○ **plein de** *dét indéf* **~ de** lots of, loads○ of [*choses, argent, bises, amis*]; **tu veux des timbres? j'en ai (tout) ~** do you want any stamps? I've got loads.
V à plein *loc adv* [*bénéficier, utiliser*] fully; **tourner** or **marcher à ~** [*machine , entreprise*] to work flat out, to work to capacity.
VI en plein *loc adv* **en ~ devant** right in front of; **atterrir en ~ dans le jardin/sur le toit** to land right in the middle of the garden GB ou yard US/on top of the roof; **l'avion s'est écrasé en ~ sur l'immeuble** the plane crashed straight into the building; **il m'est rentré en ~ dedans**○ he crashed right into me.
VII○ **tout plein** *loc adv* really; **gentil/mignon tout ~** really nice/sweet.
■ **~e page** Imprim full page; **~e propriété** Jur freehold.
IDIOMES **en avoir ~ les jambes** or **pattes**○ to be worn out, to be fit to drop○; **en avoir ~ le dos**○ or **les bottes**○ or **le cul**● to be fed up (to the back teeth) (**de** with); **(s')en prendre ~ les gencives**○ or **la gueule**● to get it in the neck○.

plein-air /plɛnɛʀ/ *nm inv* Scol (outdoor) games (*pl*).

pleinement /plɛnmɑ̃/ *adv* fully; **avoir ~ conscience de qch** to be fully aware of sth.

plein-emploi /plɛnɑ̃plwɑ/ *nm inv* full employment.

plein-temps, *pl* **pleins-temps** /plɛ̃tɑ̃/ *nm* gén full-time job; Méd full-time consultancy.

pléistocène /pleistɔsɛn/ *adj, nm* Pleistocene.

plénier, -ière /plenje, ɛʀ/ *adj* plenary.

plénipotentiaire /plenipɔtɑ̃sjɛʀ/ *adj, nm* plenipotentiary.

plénitude /plenityd/ *nf* **1** (intégrité) **exercer la ~ de ses fonctions/pouvoirs** to exercise one's functions/powers to the full; **garder la ~ de ses droits** to retain all one's rights; **donner à qn la ~ de sa responsabilité** to give sb full responsibility; **2** (sensation de bien-être) bliss; **un sentiment de ~** a blissful feeling; **3** (ampleur) liter fullness, ampleness.

plénum /plenɔm/ *nm* plenary meeting.

pléonasme /pleɔnasm/ *nm* pleonasm.

pléonastique /pleɔnastik/ *adj* pleonastic.

plésiosaure /plezjɔzɔʀ/ *nm* plesiosaurus.

pléthore /pletɔʀ/ *nf* (de marchandises, d'exemples) superabundance, plethora; **il y a ~ d'offres** there is a deluge ou plethora of offers.

pléthorique /pletɔʀik/ *adj* [*quantité, trafic*] excessive; [*classe*] overcrowded; [*personnel*] surplus to requirement (*jamais épith*); **aux effectifs ~s** [*société, service*] overstaffed.

pleurage /plœʀaʒ/ *nm* Tech wow.

pleural, ~e, *mpl* **-aux** /plœʀal, o/ *adj* pleural.

pleurant /plœʀɑ̃/ *nm* Art mourner.

pleurer /plœʀe/ [1] **I** *vtr* **1** (regretter) to mourn [*mort, ami*]; to lament [*absence*]; **~ ses parents** to mourn one's parents; **~ sa jeunesse perdue** to lament one's lost youth; **~ la mort de qn** to lament the death of sb; **2**○ (économiser) **ne pas ~ sa peine/son argent** to spare no effort/expense; **elle n'a pas pleuré le beurre dans sa tarte!** she hasn't skimped on the butter in the tart!
II *vi* **1** (après une émotion) [*enfant, adulte*] to cry, to weep; **il pleure pour un rien** he cries at the slightest thing; **faire ~ qn** [*personne, histoire, film*] to make sb cry; **~ en silence/en public** to cry silently/in public; **j'en aurais pleuré!** I could have wept!; **~ de joie/rage** to cry ou weep with joy/rage; **~ de rire, rire à en ~** to laugh until one cries; **c'est une histoire triste/bête à ~** this story is too sad/stupid for words; **2** (involontairement) [*yeux*] to water; **la fumée/le maquillage me fait ~ (les yeux)** smoke/make-up makes my eyes water; **j'ai les yeux qui pleurent** my eyes are watering; **3** (s'affliger) **~ sur qch/qn** to shed tears over sth/sb; **arrête de ~ sur ton sort!** stop feeling sorry for yourself!; **je ne risque pas de ~ sur ton sort!** I won't shed any tears over you!; **4**○ (se plaindre) [*personne*] to whine; **aller ~ auprès de qn** to go whining to sb; **~ après qch**○ to beg for sth [*augmentation, faveur*]; **5** liter [*violon*] to sob; [*vent*] to sigh; **6** Agric [*arbre, vigne*] to exude sap.
IDIOMES **~ comme un bébé** to cry like a baby; **elle n'a que ses yeux pour ~** all she can do is cry ou weep.

pleurésie /plœʀezi/ ▶**271** *nf* pleurisy.

pleurétique /plœʀetik/ *adj, nmf* pleuritic.

pleureur /plœʀœʀ/ *adj m* **saule ~** weeping willow.

pleureuse /plœʀøz/ *nf* (hired) mourner.

pleurnichard○, **~e** /plœʀniʃaʀ, aʀd/ **I** *adj* [*ton, personne*] whining.
II *nm,f* cry-baby○.

pleurnichement○ /plœʀniʃmɑ̃/ *nm* = **pleurnicherie**.

pleurnicher○ /plœʀniʃe/ [1] *vi* to snivel○.

pleurnicherie /plœʀniʃʀi/ *nf* snivelling[GB]○ ¢.

pleurnicheur, -euse /plœʀniʃœʀ, øz/ *nm,f* pej sniveller[GB]○ péj.

pleuropneumonie /plœʀɔpnømɔni/ ▶**271** *nf* pleuropneumonia.

pleurote /plœʀɔt/ *nm* pleurotus.

pleurs /plœʀ/ *nmpl* **1** (larmes) tears; **en ~** in tears; **2** (récriminations) outcry; **il va y avoir des ~ chez les enseignants** there will be an outcry from schoolteachers; **il y aura des ~ et des grincements de dents** there will be wailing and gnashing of teeth.

pleutre /pløtʀ/ liter **I** *adj* cowardly.
II *nm* coward.

pleutrerie /pløtʀəʀi/ *nf* liter **1** (caractère) cowardice; **2** (acte) act of cowardice.

pleuvasser○ /pløvase/ [1] *v impers* to drizzle.

pleuvoir /pløvwaʀ/ [39] **I** *v impers* to rain; **il pleut** it's raining; **il pleut à grosses gouttes** the rain is falling in big drops; **il pleut à torrents** or **à seaux** it's pouring with rain; **il pleut des cordes**○ or **des hallebardes** it's coming down in buckets; **il pleut à ne pas mettre un chat dehors** it's coming down in buckets; **des gâteaux comme s'il en pleuvait**○ loads of cakes○.
II *vi* [*obus, coups*] to rain down; [*demandes d'emploi*] to pour in; **les compliments pleuvaient** compliments were being handed out left, right and centre[GB]; **les mauvaises nouvelles pleuvent** bad news is coming in thick and fast.

pleuvoter○ /pløvɔte/ [1] *v impers* to drizzle.

plèvre /plɛvʀ/ *nf* pleura.

plexiglas® /plɛksiglas/ *nm* plexiglass®.

plexus /plɛksys/ *nm* plexus; **~ solaire** solar plexus.

pli /pli/ *nm* **1** (ondulation) (de feuille de papier, carte routière, rideau, drap, d'éventail) fold; **2** (de jupe) pleat; (de pantalon) (trouser) crease; (de chemise, veste) crease; (involontaire) crease; **jupe à ~s** pleated skirt; **ta veste/ton pantalon fait un ~** there is a crease in your jacket/your trousers; **ta chemise/veste fait des ~s** your shirt/jacket is all creased; **3** (ligne sur la peau) (de bouche, d'yeux) line; (bourrelet) (de ventre, double-menton) fold; **le ~ de l'aine** (the fold of) the groin; **4** Géol fold; **5** Jeux (levée) trick; **faire un ~** to take a trick; **6** (lettre) letter; **un ~ urgent** an urgent letter; **sous ~ cacheté** in a sealed envelope; **sous ~ séparé** under separate cover; **7** Constr (couche de contreplaqué) veneer sheet; **panneau à trois ~s** three-ply board.
■ **~ d'aisance** kick pleat; **~ couché** flat pleat; **~ creux** Cout box pleat.
IDIOMES **ça ne fait pas un ~**○ there's no doubt about it; **c'est un ~ à prendre** it's something you've got to get used to; **il a pris un mauvais ~** he's got into a bad habit.

pliable /plijabl/ *adj* pliable, flexible.

pliage /plijaʒ/ *nm* folding.

pliant, ~e /plijɑ̃, ɑ̃t/ **I** *adj* folding.
II *nm* folding stool, campstool.

plie /pli/ *nf* plaice.

plié /plije/ *nm* Danse plié.

plier /plije/ [2] **I** *vtr* **1** (rabattre) to fold [*papier, vêtement, parapluie*]; to fold up [*chaise, table, lit, tente*]; **~ qch en deux/trois** to fold sth in two/three; **2** (courber) to bend [*tige, roseau, objet*]; **il a plié la fourchette en deux** he bent the fork in half; **je n'arrive pas à ~ le bras/les genoux** I can't bend my arm/my knees; **3** (ranger) to pack [*affaires*]; **~ bagages**○ to pack one's things and go; **4** (soumettre) to submit; **~ qn à la discipline** to subject ou submit sb to discipline; **~ qn à sa volonté** to bend ou submit sb to one's will.
II *vi* **1** (ployer) [*arbre, branche, articulation*] to bend; [*paroi, planche, plancher*] to sag; **la branche plie sous le poids des fruits** the branch bends ou sags under the weight of fruit; **~ sous le poids des ans** to be bowed with age; **2** (céder) to give in; **faire ~ qn** to make sb give in; **~ devant la détermination de l'ennemi** to yield to the determination of the enemy; **~ sous les menaces/coups de qn** to yield to sb's threats/blows.
III se plier *vpr* **1** (être pliant) [*chaise, mètre, parapluie*] to fold; **la table se plie facilement** the table folds (down) easily ou is easy to fold; **2** (se soumettre) **se ~ à** to submit to; **se ~ à la discipline** to yield ou submit to discipline; **se ~ au règlement** to submit to the rules; **se ~ à la volonté du plus grand nombre** to yield ou submit to the wishes of the majority ; **se ~ à des exigences** to bow to necessity.
IDIOMES **être plié (en deux** or **quatre)** (de rire) to be doubled up with laughter; (de douleur) to be doubled up with pain.

plieuse /plijøz/ *nf* (machine) folder.

Pline /plin/ *npr* **~ l'Ancien** Pliny the Elder; **~ le Jeune** Pliny the Younger.

plinthe /plɛ̃t/ *nf* **1** (de mur) skirting board GB, baseboard US; **2** (de statue) plinth.

pliocène /plijɔsɛn/ *adj, nm* Pliocene.

plissage /plisaʒ/ *nm* pleating.

plissé /plise/ *nm* pleats (*pl*); **~ soleil** sunray pleats (*pl*).

plissement /plismɑ̃/ *nm* **1** Géol **~ de terrain** fold; **~ alpin/hercynien** Géol

Alpine/Hercynian orogeny; **2** (action de plisser) (des yeux) screwing up; (de peau, cou) wrinkling, puckering.

plisser /plise/ [1] **I** *vtr* **1** (volontairement) to fold [*papier*]; to pleat [*tissu, étoffe*]; **2** (involontairement) to crease [*vêtement*]; **ta robe est toute plissée** your dress is all creased; **3** (froncer) **~ le front** to knit one's brows; **~ le nez** to wrinkle one's nose; **~ les yeux** or **paupières** to screw up one's eyes; **~ la bouche** or **les lèvres** to purse one's lips; **une douce brise plissait la surface de l'étang** a gentle breeze ruffled the surface of the pond; **4** Géol to fold.

II *vi* (faire des plis) [*bas*] to wrinkle; [*jupe, veste*] to be creased ou puckered.

III se plisser *vpr* **1** (se froisser) [*vêtement, tissu*] to crease ou get creased; **ce tissu se plisse très facilement** this fabric creases very easily ou is very easily creased; **2** [*nez*] to wrinkle; [*bouche, lèvres*] to pucker up.

pliure /plijyʀ/ *nf* (de feuille, tissu) fold; **la ~ du genou** the back of the knee; **la ~ du coude** the crook of the elbow.

ploc /plɔk/, **plof** /plɔf/ *excl* plop!; **~ ~!** plip plop!; **ça a fait ~!** it went plop!

ploiement /plwamɑ̃/ *nm* (de jambe) bending; Géol folding.

plomb /plɔ̃/ *nm* **1** (métal) lead; **de** or **en ~** lead (*épith*); **sans ~** [*essence*] unleaded; **chaleur/soleil de ~** fig burning heat/sun; **ciel de ~** liter leaden sky; **mer de ~** liter grey GB ou gray US sea; **j'ai des jambes de ~** my legs feel like lead; **2** (de chasse) **un ~** a lead pellet; **du ~** lead shot ¢; **du gros ~** buckshot ¢; **3** (fusible) fuse; **les ~s ont sauté** the fuses have blown; **faire sauter les ~s** to blow the fuses; **4** Cout piece of lead; Pêche sinker; **5** (sceau) customs seal; (sur un compteur) seal; **6** (de vitrail) lead; **7** Imprim type.

■ **~ de sonde** Naut lead line.

IDIOMES **avoir du ~ dans l'aile**○ to be in a bad way○; **cela va leur mettre du ~ dans la tête** or **cervelle**○ that will knock some sense into them.

plombage /plɔ̃baʒ/ *nm* Dent filling.

plombe◐ /plɔ̃b/ *nf* hour; **à trois ~s** at three o'clock.

plombé, **~e** /plɔ̃be/ **I** *pp* ▶ **plomber**.

II *pp adj* [*dent*] with a filling.

III *adj* [*teint, visage*] ashen; [*couleur, ciel*] leaden.

plomber /plɔ̃be/ [1] **I** *vtr* **1** Dent to fill [*dent*]; **2** (sceller) to seal; **3** (pour alourdir) to weight [sth] [*filet de pêche, rideaux*]; **4** Constr to plumb.

II se plomber *vpr* liter [*ciel*] to become leaden; [*visage*] to grow ashen.

plomberie /plɔ̃bʀi/ *nf* (tuyaux, métier) plumbing.

plombier /plɔ̃bje/ ▶ **510** *nm* plumber.

plombières /plɔ̃bjɛʀ/ *nf inv* tutti-frutti ice cream.

plombier-zingueur, *pl* **plombiers-zingueurs** /plɔ̃bjezɛ̃gœʀ/ ▶ **510** *nm* zinc-roofer.

plombifère /plɔ̃bifɛʀ/ *adj* plumbiferous.

plonge○ /plɔ̃ʒ/ *nf* washing up, dishwashing US; **faire la ~** to wash the dishes, to wash up GB; **il fait la ~ dans un restaurant** he works as a dishwasher in a restaurant.

plongeant, **~e** /plɔ̃ʒɑ̃, ɑ̃t/ *adj* [*tir, décolleté*] plunging; **une vue ~e** a bird's eye view (**sur** of).

plongée /plɔ̃ʒe/ *nf* **1** ▶ **449** Sport (discipline) gén (skin) diving; (avec scaphandre autonome) scuba diving; (avec tube respiratoire) snorkelling[GB]; **~ sous-marine** deep-sea diving; **faire de la ~** to go diving; **~ en apnée** diving without an aqualung; **2** Pêche, Sport, Tech (séjour sous l'eau) dive; **3** Naut (de sous-marin) dive; **effectuer une ~** to do a dive; **un sous-marin en ~** a submerged submarine; **4** Cin high-angle shot; **prendre qch en ~** to take a high-angle shot of sth.

plongeoir /plɔ̃ʒwaʀ/ *nm* gén diving-board; (planche) springboard.

plongeon /plɔ̃ʒɔ̃/ *nm* **1** Sport (discipline) diving; **2** Sport (de nageur, gardien de but) dive; **il a fait un magnifique ~** he did a magnificent dive; **3** (chute) fall; **la voiture a fait un ~ de 200 mètres** the car plunged ou plummeted 200 metres; **le dollar a fait un ~ hier à la Bourse** the dollar took a dive yesterday on the stock exchange; **4** (oiseau) diver.

■ **~ de haut** Sport high diving; **~ du tremplin** Sport springboard diving.

plonger /plɔ̃ʒe/ [13] **I** *vtr* to plunge (**dans** into); **~ des crustacés dans l'eau bouillante** to plunge shellfish into boiling water; **~ un couteau dans la poitrine de qn** to plunge a knife into sb's breast; **~ la ville dans l'obscurité** to plunge the city into darkness; **elle plongea son regard dans le mien** she stared deep into my eyes; **il a plongé la tête dans le moteur** he stuck his head into the engine; **~ qn dans le désarroi/désespoir** to throw sb into great confusion/despair; **~ le pays dans la crise/pagaille**○ to throw the country into crisis/chaos; **l'arbre plonge ses racines très profond dans le sol** the tree thrusts its roots deep into the ground.

II *vi* **1** gén [*nageur, sous-marin, scaphandrier, animal, avion*] to dive (**dans** into); [*oiseau*] to swoop down (**sur** on); [*gardien de but, rugbyman*] to dive; **~ sous la table** to dive under the table; **~ dans la rivière** [*voiture*] to plunge into the river; **de ce sommet, le regard plonge vers la vallée** from this mountain top, you can get a bird's eye view of the valley; **2** (péricliter) [*affaire, commerce*] to flounder; [*action, monnaie*] to take a dive; [*élève*] to go downhill; **3**○ (se faire incarcérer) to be sent down○.

III se plonger *vpr* **1** (s'immerger) to plunge (**dans** into); **se ~ dans l'eau** to plunge into the water; **2** (s'absorber) to bury oneself (**dans** in); **se ~ dans un roman/son travail** to bury oneself in a novel/one's work; **plongés dans leur lecture** buried in their books; **être plongé dans ses pensées** or **réflexions** to be deep in thought; **être plongé dans un sommeil profond** to be in a deep sleep.

plongeur, **-euse** /plɔ̃ʒœʀ, øz/ ▶ **510** **I** *nm,f* **1** Pêche, Sport, Tech diver; **2** (laveur de vaisselle) dishwasher.

II *nm* **1** Tech plunger piston; **2** (oiseau) diver.

plosive /ploziv/ *nf* plosive.

plot /plo/ *nm* **1** Électrotech contact; **2** (de bois) block.

■ **~ de départ** Sport starting block.

Plotin /plɔtɛ̃/ *npr* Plotinus.

plouc○ /pluk/ pej **I** *adj inv* [*manières, personne*] uncouth, hick (*épith*) US; **ça fait ~ de dire ça** that's a red neck○ thing to say.

II *nm* country bumpkin○.

plouf /pluf/ **I** *nm inv* splash; **faire un ~** to go splash.

II *excl* splash!

ploutocrate /plutɔkʀat/ *nm* plutocrat.

ploutocratie /plutɔkʀasi/ *nf* plutocracy.

ploutocratique /plutɔkʀatik/ *adj* plutocratic.

ployer /plwaje/ [23] liter **I** *vtr* to bow, to bend [*genou, branche*]; to bow [*tête*]; **il ploya les épaules** his shoulders sagged.

II *vi* [*planche, toit*] to sag; [*branche, personne*] to bend; [*jambes, genoux*] to buckle, give way; **~ sous un fardeau** to be weighed down by a burden; **~ sous le joug** to bend under the yoke; **faire ~ qch** lit to make sth bend; **faire ~ l'ennemi** to force the enemy to yield.

plucher [1] = **pelucher**.

pluches /plyʃ/ *nfpl* **être de corvée de ~** to be on spud-bashing○ duty GB, to be doing KP○ US.

plucheux, **-euse** = **pelucheux**.

pluie /plɥi/ *nf* **1** (eau, phénomène) **la ~** rain; **sous la ~** in the rain; **sous une ~ battante/torrentielle** in driving/torrential rain; **il tombait une ~ fine** it was drizzling; **jour de ~** rainy day; **par temps de ~** when it rains, in rainy weather; **2** (averse) **après la ~** after the rain; **des ~s intermittentes/violentes/d'été** periodic/heavy/summer showers; **la saison des ~s** the rainy season, the rains; **3** (de missiles, d'injures) hail (**de** of); (d'étincelles, de cadeaux, compliments) shower (**de** of); (de lettres, d'offres) lots (**de** of); **tomber en ~** [*projectiles, étincelles*] to rain down; **jeter le riz en ~ dans le lait bouillant** sprinkle the rice into the boiling milk.

■ **~s acides** acid rain ¢.

IDIOMES **il n'est pas né** or **tombé de la dernière ~**○ he wasn't born yesterday○; **parler de la ~ et du beau temps** to make small talk; **elle fait la ~ et le beau temps dans le parti** she calls the shots○ in the party; **après la ~ le beau temps** Prov every cloud has a silver lining Prov.

plumage /plymaʒ/ *nm* plumage.

plumard◐ /plymaʀ/ *nm* bed; **aller au ~** to turn in○, to hit the hay○.

plume /plym/ **I** *nf* **1** (d'oiseau) feather; **léger comme une ~** light as a feather; **soulever qch comme une ~** to pick sth up as though it were as light as a feather; **chapeau à ~s** feathered hat; **oreiller de ~s** feather pillow; **2** (pour écrire) (d'oiseau) quill (pen); (en métal) (pen) nib; **~ d'oie** goose quill; **prendre la ~ pour...** to put pen to paper to..., to take up one's pen to...; **d'un coup de ~** with a single stroke of the pen; **je lui passe la ~** I'm handing over to him/her; **écrire au fil de la ~** to write as the thoughts come into one's head; **elle a la ~ facile** words flow easily from her pen; **vivre de sa ~** to earn a living by one's pen; **prendre sa plus belle ~** to get out one's smartest notepaper; **dessin à la ~** pen-and-ink drawing.

II◐ *nm* = **plumard**.

IDIOMES **perdre ses ~s**○ to lose one's hair, to go bald; **elle y a laissé** or **perdu des ~s**○ she did not come off unscathed; **voler dans les ~s de qn**○ to fly at sb.

plumeau, *pl* **~x** /plymo/ *nm* **1** (ustensile) feather duster; **2** (touffe) tuft.

plumer /plyme/ [1] *vtr* **1** to pluck [*oiseau*]; **2**○ to fleece○ [*personne*]; **se faire ~** to be ripped off○ ou fleeced○.

plumet /plymɛ/ *nm* plume.

plumetis /plymti/ *nm inv* (broderie) satin stitch; (tissu) Swiss cotton.

plumette /plymɛt/ *nf* feather.

plumier /plymje/ *nm* pencil box.

plumitif /plymitif/ *nm* péj (employé) penpusher; (auteur) hack, scribbler.

plupart: **la plupart** /laplypaʀ/ *nf inv* (le plus grand nombre) **la ~ des gens/maisons/oiseaux** most people/houses/birds; **dans la ~ des cas** in most cases; **pour la ~** for the most part; **la ~ des hommes présents** most of the men present; **la ~ s'en allèrent tôt** most people left early; **la ~ d'entre eux** most of them; **il a écrit des quantités d'articles mais la ~ sont sans intérêt** he wrote numerous articles, most of them devoid of interest; **la ~ du temps** most of the time, mostly.

plural, **~e**, *mpl* **-aux** /plyʀal, o/ *adj* [*vote*] plural.

pluralisme /plyʀalism/ *nm* pluralism.

pluraliste /plyʀalist/ *adj* **1** Pol pluralist; **2** Philos pluralistic.

pluralité /plyʀalite/ *nf* multiplicity, plurality.

pluriannuel, **-elle** /plyʀianɥɛl/ *adj* **1** [*plante*] perennial; **2** [*plan, contrat*] long-term.

pluricellulaire /plyʀiselylɛʀ/ *adj* multicellular.

pluriculturel, **-elle** /plyʀikyltyʀɛl/ *adj* multicultural.

pluridisciplinaire /plyʀidisiplinɛʀ/ *adj* multidisciplinary.

pluridisciplinarité /plyʀidisiplinaʀite/ *nf* multidisciplinary approach.

pluriel, **-ielle** /plyʀjɛl/ **I** *adj* plural.
II *nm* plural; **au ~** in the plural; **à la troisième personne du ~** in the third person plural; **le ~ de majesté** the royal 'we'.

pluriethnique /plyʀiɛtnik/ *adj* multiethnic.

plurifonctionnalité /plyʀifɔ̃ksjɔnalite/ *nf* (de matériau) versatility; (de service) flexibility.

plurifonctionnel, **-elle** /plyʀifɔ̃ksjɔnɛl/ *adj* [*salle, matériau*] multipurpose; [*service*] flexible.

plurilatéral, **~e**, *mpl* **-aux** /plyʀilateʀal, o/ *adj* multilateral.

plurilingue /plyʀilɛ̃g/ **I** *adj* multilingual.
II *nmf* polyglot.

plurilinguisme /plyʀilɛ̃gɥism/ *nm* multilingualism.

plurinominal, *pl* **-aux** /plyʀinɔminal, o/ *adj m* **scrutin ~** plurinominal system.

pluripartisme /plyʀipaʀtism/ *nm* multiparty system.

plurivalent, **~e** /plyʀivalɑ̃, ɑ̃t/ *adj* polyvalent.

plus[1] /ply, plys, plyz/ **I** *pr ép* **1** (dans une addition) **8 ~ 3 égale 11** 8 and 3 equals 11, 8 plus 3 equals 11; **on nous a servi du fromage, un dessert ~ du café** we were served cheese, a dessert and coffee (as well); **2** (pour exprimer une valeur) **un jour il faisait moins 5°, le lendemain ~ 10°** one day it was minus 5°, the next plus 10°.
II *adv de comparaison* **1** (modifiant un verbe) (comparatif) more; (superlatif) **le ~** the most; **il mange/travaille ~ (que moi)** he eats/works more (than I do ou than me); **tu devrais demander ~** you should ask for more; **je ne peux pas faire ~** I can do no more, I can't do any more, I can't do more than that; **elle en sait ~ que lui sur le sujet** she knows more about the subject than he does; **c'est ~ que je ne peux supporter** it's more than I can bear; **elle l'aime ~ que tout** she loves him/her more than anything; **il est ~ à plaindre qu'autre chose** he's more to be pitied than anything else; **c'est ~ que bien** it's more than just good; **elle est ~ que jolie** she's more than just pretty; **il a fait ~ que l'embaucher, il l'a aussi formé** he did more than just hire him, he also trained him; **j'en ai ~ qu'assez** I've had more than enough; **elle mange deux fois/trois fois ~ que lui** she eats twice/three times as much as he does; **~ je gagne, ~ je dépense** the more I earn, the more I spend; **~ j'y pense, moins je comprends** the more I think about it, the less I understand; **~ ça va** as time goes on; **qui ~ est** furthermore, what's more; **c'est lui qui m'a le ~ appris** he's the one who taught me the most; **quel pays aimes-tu le ~?** which country do you like best?; **de ~ en ~** more and more; **il fume de ~ en ~** he smokes more and more; **2** (modifiant un adjectif) (comparatif) more; (superlatif) most; **deux fois ~ vieux/cher** twice as old/expensive (**que** as); **trois/quatre fois ~ cher** three/four times as expensive (**que** as); **il n'est pas ~ riche que moi** he's no richer than I am ou than me, he isn't any richer than I am ou than me; **c'est le même modèle en ~ petit** it's the same model, only smaller; **il est on ne peut ~ gentil/désagréable** he's as nice/unpleasant as can be; **il est ~ ou moins fou** he's more or less insane; **il est ~ ou moins artiste** he's an artist of sorts; **la cuisine était ~ ou moins propre** the kitchen wasn't particularly clean, the kitchen was clean after a fashion; **il a été ~ ou moins poli** he wasn't particularly polite; **ils étaient ~ ou moins ivres** they were a bit drunk; **le ~ heureux des hommes** the happiest of men; **la ~ belle de toutes** the most beautiful of all; **mon vœu le ~ cher** my dearest wish; **l'arbre le ~ gros que j'aie jamais vu** the biggest tree I've ever seen; **son livre le ~ court** his shortest book; **c'est ce qu'il y a de ~ beau/important au monde** it's the most beautiful/important thing in the world; **un livre des ~ intéressants** a most interesting book; **un individu des ~ méprisables** a most despicable individual; **de ~ en ~ difficile** more and more difficult; **de ~ en ~ chaud** hotter and hotter; **3** (modifiant un adverbe) (comparatif) more; (superlatif) most; **trois heures ~ tôt/tard** three hours earlier/later; **deux fois ~ longtemps** twice as long (**que** as); **trois/quatre fois ~ longtemps** three/four times as long (**que** as); **ils ne sont pas restés ~ longtemps que nous** they didn't stay any longer than we did ou than us; **il l'a fait ~ ou moins bien** he didn't do it very well; **de ~ en ~ loin** further and further; **~ tu te coucheras tard, ~ tu auras de mal à te lever** the later you go to bed, the harder it'll be for you to get up; **~ tu te coucheras tôt, moins tu seras fatigué** the earlier you go to bed, the less tired you'll be; **c'est moi qui y vais le ~ souvent** I go there the most often; **ça s'est passé le ~ simplement/naturellement du monde** it happened quite simply/naturally.
III *adv de négation* **elle ne fume ~** she doesn't smoke any more ou any longer, she no longer smokes, she's given up smoking; **il n'habite ~ ici** he no longer lives here, he doesn't live here any more ou any longer; **le grand homme n'est ~** the great man is no more; **elle ne veut ~ le voir** she doesn't want to see him any more ou any longer, she no longer wants to see him; **il a décidé de ne ~ y aller** he decided to stop going there; **je ne veux ~ en entendre parler** I don't want to hear any more about it; **il n'y est ~ (jamais) retourné** he never went back there (again); **~ jamais ça!** never again!; **nous ne faisons ~ ce modèle** we no longer do this model, we don't do this model any more ou any longer; **il n'a ~ vingt ans** (il n'est plus très jeune) he's not twenty any more, he's no longer twenty; **nous n'avons ~ d'espoir** we've no more hope, we no longer have any hope,

---

plus[1]

Formation du comparatif des adjectifs et des adverbes en anglais

Deux cas peuvent se présenter:

1 ***Adjectifs et adverbes courts***

En règle générale on ajoute *'-er'* à la fin de l'adjectif/adverbe:

plus grand	=	taller
plus petit	=	smaller
plus simple	=	simpler
plus longtemps	=	longer
plus vite	=	faster

Remarques:

Pour certains mots dont l'unique voyelle est une voyelle brève, on double la consonne finale:

big → *bigger*
sad → *sadder*
dim → *dimmer*
wet → *wetter* etc.

Attention aux adjectifs en *'y'*:

sunny → *sunnier*
pretty → *prettier*
happy → *happier* etc.

2 ***Adjectifs et adverbes longs***

On ajoute *more* devant le mot:

plus beau	=	more beautiful
plus compétent	=	more competent
plus intéressant	=	more interesting
plus facilement	=	more easily
plus sérieusement	=	more seriously

Remarques:

Certains mots de deux syllabes admettent les deux formes: *simple* peut produire *simpler* ou *more simple*

handsome → *handsomer*
ou more handsome etc.

Certains mots de deux syllabes n'admettent que la forme avec *more*:

callous → *more callous*
cunning → *more cunning*

Les adverbes se terminant par *'-ly'* n'admettent que la forme avec *more*:

quickly → *more quickly*
slowly → *more slowly* etc.

Formation du superlatif des adjectifs et des adverbes en anglais

Deux cas peuvent se présenter:

1 ***Adjectifs et adverbes courts***

En règle générale on ajoute *'(e)st'* à la fin du mot:

le plus grand	=	the tallest
le plus petit	=	the smallest
le plus simple	=	the simplest
le plus longtemps	=	the longest
le plus vite	=	the fastest

Remarques:

Pour certains mots dont l'unique voyelle est une voyelle brève, on double la consonne finale:

big → *the biggest*
sad → *the saddest*
dim → *the dimmest* etc.

Attention aux adjectifs en *'y'*:

sunny → *the sunniest*
pretty → *the prettiest*
happy → *the happiest* etc.

2 ***Adjectifs et adverbes longs***

On ajoute *the most* devant le mot:

le plus beau	=	the most beautiful
le plus compétent	=	the most competent
le plus intéressant	=	the most interesting
le plus facilement	=	the most easily
le plus sérieusement	=	the most seriously

Remarques:

Certains mots de deux syllabes admettent les deux formes:

simple → *the simplest*
ou the most simple
clever → *the cleverest*
ou the most clever etc.

Certains mots de deux syllabes n'admettent que la forme avec *the most*:

callous → *the most callous*
cunning → *the most cunning* etc.

Les adverbes en *'-ly'* n'admettent que la forme avec *the most*:

quickly → *the most quickly*
slowly → *the most slowly* etc.

Attention: lorsque la comparaison ne porte que sur deux éléments on utilise la forme du comparatif:

le plus doué des deux = the more gifted of the two
la voiture la plus rapide des deux = the faster car

L'expression *le plus possible* est traitée avec *possible*.

On trouvera ci-dessous exemples et exceptions illustrant les différentes fonctions de *plus*. On trouvera également des exemples de *plus* dans les notes d'usage répertoires ▶ **1920**.

we've given up hoping; **~ besoin de se presser**○ there's no longer any need to hurry, there's no more need to hurry, there's no need to hurry any more; **il n'y a ~ de pain/d'œufs** there is no more bread/ there are no more eggs, there isn't any bread left/there aren't any eggs left; **je ne veux ~ de vin** I don't want any more wine; **il n'y a ~ rien** there's nothing left; **~ rien ne m'intéresse** nothing interests me any more; **je ne voyais ~ rien** I could no longer see anything, I couldn't see a thing any more; **il n'y a ~ personne dans la pièce** there's nobody left in the room, there's no longer anybody in the room; **il n'y a ~ aucun crayon** there aren't any pencils left, there are no more pencils; **il n'y a ~ aucun problème** there's no longer any problem; **ce n'est ~ du courage, c'est de la folie** it's no longer bravery, it's foolhardiness; **j'entre dans le garage, ~ de voiture**○! I went into the garage, the car was gone○!; **ce n'est ~ qu'une question de jours** it's only a matter of days now; **il n'y a ~ qu'une solution** there's only one solution left; **il ne restait ~ que quelques bouteilles** there were only a few bottles left, there was nothing left but a few bottles; **il n'y a ~ que lui qui puisse nous aider** only he can help us now; **~ que trois jours avant les vacances!** only three days left ou to go until the vacation!; **nous n'avons ~ qu'à rentrer à la maison** all we can do now is go home; **il ne me reste ~ qu'à vous remercier** it only remains for me to thank you.

IV plus de *dét indéf* **1** (avec un nom dénombrable) **trois/deux fois ~ de livres/verres que** three times/twice as many books/ glasses as; **c'est là que j'ai vu le ~ de serpents** that's where I saw the most snakes; **c'est lui qui a le ~ de livres** he's got the most books; **le joueur qui a le ~ de chances de gagner** the player who is most likely to win; **les jeunes qui posent le ~ de problèmes** the young people who pose the most problems; **c'est le candidat qui a remporté le ~ de voix** he's the candidate who won the most votes; **~ tu mangeras de bonbons, ~ tu auras de caries** the more sweets GB ou candy US you eat, the more cavities you'll have; **il y en a ~ d'un qui voudrait être à sa place** quite a few people would like to be in his/her position; **2** (avec un nom non dénombrable) **je n'ai pas pris ~ de crème que toi** I didn't take any more cream than you did, I took no more cream than you did; **il n'a pas ~ d'imagination que sa sœur** he has no more imagination than his sister, he hasn't got any more imagination than his sister; **trois/ deux fois ~ de vin/talent** three times/ twice as much wine/talent (**que** as); **le joueur qui a gagné le ~ d'argent** the player who won the most money; **3** (avec un numéral) **elle ne possède pas ~ de 50 disques** she has no more than 50 records; **une foule de ~ de 10000 personnes** a crowd of more than ou over 10,000 people; **il a ~ de 40 ans** he's over 40, he's more than 40 years old; **les gens de ~ de 60 ans** people over 60; **les ~ de 60 ans** the over-sixties; **il était déjà bien ~ de onze heures/midi** it was already well past ou after eleven o'clock/midday.

V au plus *loc adv* at the most; **tout au ~** at the very most, at the outside.

VI de plus *loc adv* **1** (en outre) furthermore, moreover, what's more; **2** (en supplément) **j'ai mangé deux pommes de ~ qu'elle** I ate two apples more than she did; **donnez-moi deux pommes de ~** give me two more apples; **ça nous a pris deux heures de ~ que la dernière fois** it took us two hours longer than last time; **j'ai besoin de deux heures de ~** I need two more hours; **il a trois ans de ~ que sa sœur** he's three years older than his sister; **une fois de ~** once more, once again; **l'augmentation représente 9% de ~ que l'année précédente** the rise is 9% more than last year.

VII en plus *loc* **en ~ (de cela)** on top of that; **il est arrivé en retard et en ~ (de cela) il a commencé à se plaindre** he arrived late and what' s more ou on top of that he started complaining; **c 'est le même modèle avec le toit ouvrant en ~** it's the same model, only with a sunroof; **c'est tout le portrait de son père, la moustache en ~** he's the image of his father, only with a moustache GB ou mustache US; **il a reçu 2000 francs en ~ de son salaire habituel** he got 2,000 francs on top of his usual salary; **en ~ de son métier d'ingénieur il élève des tatous** besides his job as an engineer, he breeds armadillos; **les taxes en ~** plus tax, tax not included; **il s'est passé quelque chose en ~** something else happened as well.

■ Note *A note on pronunciation*:
plus/*le plus* used in comparison (meaning more/the most) is pronounced [ply] before a consonant and [plyz] before a vowel. It is pronounced [plys] when at the end of a clause. In the *plus de* and *plus que* structures both [ply] and [plys] are generally used.
plus used in *ne plus* (meaning no longer/not any more) is always pronounced [ply] except before a vowel, in which case it is pronounced [plyz]: *il n'habite plus ici* [plyzisi].

---

plus² /plys/ *nm* **1** Math plus; **le signe ~** the plus sign; **2**○ (avantage) plus○; **son expérience d'enseignant constitue un ~ pour lui** his teaching experience is a point in his favour[GB] ou is a plus○.

plusieurs /plyzjœʀ/ **I** *adj* several; **~ fois/ autres** several times/others; **~ centaines de personnes** several hundred people; **il y en avait ~ centaines** there were several hundred of them; **en ~ endroits** in several places; **une ou ~ personnes** one or more people; **à ~ reprises** several times.
II *pron indéf* **~ ont déjà signé** several people have already signed; **vous êtes ~ à vouloir faire** there are several of you who want to do; **ils avaient invité de nombreuses personnes, mais ~ ont refusé de venir** they had invited a lot of people but several refused to come.

plus-que-parfait /plyskəpaʀfɛ/ *nm inv* pluperfect.

plus-value, *pl* **~s** /plyvaly/ *nf* **1** Écon, Fin (de biens mobiliers) increase in value; (d'actif, de monnaie) appreciation; (profit à la vente) capital gain; **réaliser** or **dégager une ~** to make a capital gain; **être en ~** [*action*] to be up; **2** Fin (excédent) surplus; **3** (majoration) surcharge; **4** (dans le marxisme) surplus value.
■ **~ financière** capital gain.

Plutarque /plytaʀk/ *npr* Plutarch.

Pluton /plytɔ̃/ **I** *npr* Mythol Pluto.
II *nprf* Astron Pluto.

plutonium /plytɔnjɔm/ *nm* plutonium.

plutôt /plyto/ *adv* **1** (de préférence) rather; **je préfère t'appeler ~ que (de) t'écrire** I'd rather phone you than write to you; **pourquoi lui ~ qu'un autre?** why him rather than anybody else?; **mangez des produits frais ~ que surgelés** eat fresh products rather than frozen ones; **prenez les cachets ~ avant les repas** take the tablets preferably before eating; **passe ~ le matin** call round GB ou come by US in the morning preferably; **2** (au lieu de) instead; **~ mourir (que d'accepter)!** I'd rather ou sooner die (than accept)!; **demande ~ à Corinne** ask Corinne instead; **prends ~ celui-là** take that one instead; **ne viens pas demain, viens ~ après-demain** don't come tomorrow, make it the day after; **j'ai ~ tendance à ne pas m'en faire/grossir** I'm more the kind not to worry/to put on weight; **il aurait ~ tendance à croire le contraire** he'd tend to think the opposite; **tout ~ que de vivre ici** anything but live here; **~ que de rêvasser, aide-moi** instead of daydreaming why don't you help me?; **3** (plus précisément) rather; **elle est blonde ou ~ châtain clair** she's got blond, or rather light brown hair; **dis ~ que tu n'as pas envie de le faire** why don't you just say that you don't want to do it?; **c'est ~ une corvée qu'un plaisir** it's a chore rather than a pleasure; **il n'est pas timide mais ~ réservé, il est ~ réservé que timide** he's more reserved than shy, he's reserved rather than shy; **4** (ayant une valeur intensive) rather; **~ agréable/décevant/ gêné** rather nice/disappointing/embarrassed; **la nouvelle a été ~ bien/mal accueillie** the news went down rather well/ badly; **'tu prends des vacances cet été?' —'~ oui**○**!'** 'are you taking a vacation this summer?'—'too right○!', 'you bet○!'

pluvial, **~e**, *mpl* **-iaux** /plyvjal, o/ *adj* [*régime, érosion*] pluvial.

pluvier /plyvje/ *nm* plover.

pluvieux, **-ieuse** /plyvjø, øz/ *adj* [*année, semaine, jour*] wet, rainy; **par temps ~** in rainy weather.

pluviner○ /plyvine/ [1] *v impers* to drizzle.

pluviomètre /plyvjɔmɛtʀ/ *nm* rain gauge, pluviometer.

pluviométrie /plyvjɔmetʀi/ *nf* pluviometry.

pluviométrique /plyvjometʀik/ *adj* [*carte, courbe*] rainfall.

pluviôse /plyvjoz/ *nm* Pluviôse (*fifth month of the French revolutionary calendar*, ≈ *February*).

pluviosité /plyvjozite/ *nf* rainfall level.

PLV /peɛlve/ *nf*: *abbr* ▶ **publicité**.

PM /peɛm/ **I** *nm* (*abbr* = **pistolet-mitrailleur**) submachine gun.
II *nf*: *abbr* ▶ **préparation**.

PMA /peɛma/ *nf*: *abbr* ▶ **procréation**.

PME /peɛmə/ *nfpl*: *abbr* ▶ **petit**.

PMI /peɛmi/ *nfpl* **1** (*abbr* = **petites et moyennes industries**) small and medium-sized industries; **2** *abbr* ▶ **protection**.

PMU /peɛmy/ *nm* (*abbr* = **Pari mutuel urbain**) *French state-controlled betting system*; **un ~** a betting office.

PNB /peɛnbe/ *nm*: *abbr* ▶ **produit**.

pneu /pnø/ *nm* **1** Aut tyre GB, tire US; **~ clouté** or **à clous** studded tyre GB ou tire US; **~ neige** snow tyre GB ou tire US; **~ tendre** slick tyre GB ou tire US; **2**○ *abbr* = **pneumatique II**.

pneumatique /pnømatik/ **I** *adj* **1** Tech pneumatic; **2** (gonflable) inflatable.
II *nm* **1** (message) *letter sent by pneumatic tube*; **2**† = **pneu 1**.

pneumectomie /pnømɛktɔmi/ *nf* pneumonectomy.

pneumoconiose /pnømokɔnjoz/ ▶ **271** *nf* pneumoconiosis.

pneumocoque /pnømɔkɔk/ *nm* pneumococcus.

pneumogastrique /pnømɔgastʀik/ **I** *adj* pneumogastric.
II *nm* vagus nerve.

pneumologie /pnømɔlɔʒi/ *nf* chest medicine.

pneumologue /pnømɔlɔg/ ▶ **510** *nmf* lung specialist, chest physician.

pneumonie /pnømɔni/ ▶ **271** *nf* pneumonia.

pneumonique /pnømɔnik/ **I** *adj* pneumonic.
II *nmf* pneumonia patient.

pneumothorax /pnømotɔʀaks/ *nm inv* pneumothorax.

Pô /po/ ▶ **357** *nprm* Po.

pochade /pɔʃad/ *nf* **1** Art quick (colour[GB]) sketch; **2** Littérat humorous sketch.

pochard○, **~e** /pɔʃaʀ, aʀd/ *nm,f* soak○, drunk.

poche /pɔʃ/ **I** *nf* **1** (de vêtement) pocket; **une ~ de veste** a jacket pocket; **en ~** lit in one's pocket; **il est revenu le contrat en ~** fig he came back with the contract in the bag○ ou all sewn up○; **son diplôme en ~, il est parti aux États-Unis** armed with his diploma, he set off for the States; **il avait 1000 francs en ~** lit he had 1,000 francs on him; fig (à sa disposition) he had 1,000 francs available; **je n'ai pas un sou en ~** lit I haven't got a penny on me; fig (à ma disposition) I haven't got a penny to my name; **avoir de l'argent plein les ~s**○ to be loaded○, to have plenty of money; **se remplir** or **s'en mettre plein les ~s**○ to line one's pockets; **faire les ~s de qn** (vider) to empty out sb's pockets; (voler) to pick sb's pocket; **une ~ pleine de pièces de monnaie** a pocket full of coins; **un couteau de ~** a pocket knife; **édition/guide de ~** pocket edition/guide; **format de ~** pocket-size (*épith*); **2** (de sac, portefeuille) pocket; **3** (sac) bag; **4** (accumulation) **~ de gaz/d'air** gas/air pocket; **~ de pus** accumulation of pus; **5** (déformation) **avoir des ~s sous les yeux** to have bags under one's eyes; **mon pantalon fait des ~s aux genoux** my trousers GB ou pants US are baggy at the knees; **6** Zool (de kangourou, pélican) pouch; **7** (secteur) fig Mil pocket; **~ de résistance** pocket of resistance; **~ de pauvreté** pocket of poverty; **8** Méd (appareillage) colostomy bag.
II *nm* Édition, Imprim **1** (livre)○ paperback; **2** (format) pocket size; **paraître/être édité en ~** to come out/to be published in paperback.
■ **~ à douille** piping bag; **~ des eaux** amniotic sac; **~ de glace** ice pack; **~ passepoilée** bound pocket; **~ plaquée** patch pocket; **~ revolver** hip pocket.
IDIOMES **avoir qn dans sa ~**○ to have sb in one's pocket; **mettre qn dans sa ~**○ to get sb on one's side; **c'est dans la ~**○ it's in the bag○, it's all sewn up○; **en être de sa ~**○ to be out of pocket; **payer (qch) de sa ~**○ to pay (for sth) out of one's own pocket; **mettre la main à la ~** to put one's hand in one's pocket, to fork out○; **ne pas avoir les yeux dans sa ~**○ not to miss a thing○; **ne pas avoir sa langue dans sa ~**○ never to be at a loss for words; **mettre sa fierté** or **son orgueil dans sa ~**○ to swallow one's pride; **connaître un endroit comme sa ~**○ to know a place like the back of one's hand.

pocher /pɔʃe/ [1] **I** *vtr* **1** Culin to poach; **2** (meurtrir) **~ un œil à qn** to give sb a black eye; **se faire ~ un œil** to get a black eye.
II *vi* (se déformer) [*vêtement*] (à l'arrière) to seat at the back; (aux genoux) to go baggy at the knees.

pochette /pɔʃɛt/ *nf* **1** (enveloppe) (de crayons, feutres, ciseaux, compas) case; (de document) folder; **une ~ de stylos** a pen case; **une ~ de disque** a record sleeve; **une ~ d'allumettes** a book of matches; **une ~ de diapositives** a slide pack; **une ~ de serviette de table** a napkin case; **article présenté sous ~ plastique** item sold in a plastic cover; **2** Mode (mouchoir décoratif) pocket handkerchief; **3** (petit sac à main) clutch bag; (pour papiers d'identité, argent) pouch.

pochette-surprise, *pl* **pochettes-surprises** /pɔʃɛtsyʀpʀiz/ *nf: child's novelty consisting of several small surprise items in a cone.*

pocheuse /pɔʃøz/ *nf* egg poacher.

pochoir /pɔʃwaʀ/ *nm* (plaque, dessin) stencil; **travailler au ~** to work with a stencil; **marquer son nom au ~** to stencil one's name; **exécuté au ~** stencilled[GB].

podagre‡ /pɔdagʀ/ **I** *adj* gouty, suffering from gout (*après n*).
II *nmf* gout sufferer.
III *nf* gout.

podium /pɔdjɔm/ *nm* gén podium; (de défilé de mannequins) catwalk GB, runway US; **monter sur le ~** to mount the podium.

podologie /pɔdɔlɔʒi/ *nf* chiropody.

podologue /pɔdɔlɔg/ ▶**510** *nmf* chiropodist.

podomètre /pɔdɔmɛtʀ/ *nm* pedometer.

podzol /pɔdzɔl/ *nm* podzol.

poêle /pwal/ **I** *nm* **1** (pour chauffer) stove; **~ à bois/mazout** wood-burning/oil stove; **2** (de cercueil) pall; **tenir les cordons du ~** to be a pall-bearer.
II *nf* frying pan; **passer qch à la ~** to fry sth; **œuf à la ~** fried egg.
■ **~ à frire** frying pan.

poêlée /pwale/ *nf* **une ~ de** a whole pan of.

poêler /pwale/ [1] *vtr* (dans une poêle) to fry; (dans un poêlon) to braise.

poêlon /pwalɔ̃/ *nm* heavy saucepan (*earthenware or cast iron*).

poème /pɔɛm/ *nm* poem; **~ en prose** prose poem; **c'est tout un ~**○ it's quite something.
■ **~ symphonique** symphonic poem.

poésie /pɔezi/ *nf* **1** (art) poetry; **2** (poème) poem; **3** (qualité) **la ~ de son œuvre** the poetic quality of his work.

poète /pɔɛt/ *nm* **1** (auteur) poet; **2** (rêveur) poet, dreamer.

poétesse† /pɔetɛs/ *nf* poetess†.

poétique /pɔetik/ **I** *adj* [*œuvre, lieu*] poetic; [*personne*] romantic.
II *nf* poetics (+ *v sg*).

poétiquement /pɔetikmɑ̃/ *adv* poetically.

poétiser /pɔetize/ [1] *vtr* to poeticize.

pogne◑ /pɔɲ/ *nf* mitt○, hand.

pogner○ /pɔɲe/ [1] *vtr* C to take, to get, to catch.

pognon◑ /pɔɲɔ̃/ *nm* dough○, money; **être plein de ~** to be loaded○.

pogrom(e) /pɔgʀɔm/ *nm* pogrom.

poids /pwa/ ▶**620** *nm inv* **1** Phys weight; **vaciller sous le ~ de qch** to stagger under the weight of sth; **peser de tout son ~ contre/sur qch** to put all one's weight against/on sth; **vendre au ~** to sell by the weight; **surveiller son ~** to watch one's weight; **prendre/perdre du ~** to put on/lose weight; **elle a pris un peu de ~** she's put on a bit of weight; **peser son ~** to be very heavy; **et voici deux kilos d'orange, bon ~!** here's two good kilos of oranges for you!; **2** (importance) (de personne) influence, stature; (de pays, parti, d'électorat) influence; (de paroles, mots, d'arguments) weight; **le ~ de l'État dans l'économie** the influence of the state in the economy; **argument de ~** weighty argument; **donner du ~ à ses arguments** to give ou lend weight to one's arguments; **personne de ~** person who carries a lot of weight; **adversaire de ~** opponent to be reckoned with; **il n'y a aucune personnalité de ~ pour la remplacer** there's nobody of sufficient stature to replace her; **il n'a aucun ~ politique** he hasn't got any political stature; **peser de tout son ~ dans la balance politique** to carry great weight in the political balance; **il ne fait pas le ~ devant un adversaire aussi redoutable** he's no match for ou he's out of his league against such a formidable opponent; **je ne crois pas qu'il fera le ~ à ce poste** I don't think he's up to this job, I think this job is out of his league; **3** (fardeau) lit weight; fig burden; **un ~ de 200 kg** a 200 kg weight; **il est capable de soulever des ~ énormes** he can lift a terrific weight; **le ~ des ans/du passé/des habitudes** the burden of the years/of the past/of habit; **le ~ des impôts** the tax burden; **être un ~ pour qn** to be a burden on sb; **4** (gêne) weight; **vous m'ôtez un ~ de la conscience** you've taken a weight off my mind; **avoir un ~ sur la conscience** to have a guilty conscience; **avoir un ~ sur la poitrine** to feel as though there's a weight (pressing down) on one's chest; **5** (masse métallique) (pour peser) weight; **des ~ en laiton** brass weights; **6** (en athlétisme) shot; **lancer le ~** to put the shot; **le lancer du ~** the shot put; **lanceur de ~** shot-putter; **7** (pièce de mécanisme) weight; **remonter les ~ d'une horloge** to wind up the weights in a clock; **équilibrer les ~ d'une bascule** to balance the weights of a set of scales.
■ **~ atomique** atomic weight; **~ brut** gross weight; **~ coq** Sport bantamweight; **~ et haltères** Sport weightlifting ¢; **faire des ~ et haltères** to do weightlifting; **un champion de ~ et haltères** a champion weightlifter; **~ léger** Sport lightweight; **~ lourd** Sport heavyweight; Transp heavy goods vehicle GB, heavy truck; **~ mi-lourd** Sport light heavyweight; **~ mi-moyen** Sport welterweight; **~ moléculaire** molecular weight; **~ mort** Tech dead weight, dead load; fig dead weight, drag○; **~ mouche** Sport flyweight; **~ moyen** Sport middleweight; **~ net** Ind net weight; **~ net égoutté é** Ind net weight drained; **~ plume** Sport featherweight; **~ spécifique** specific gravity; **~ superléger** Sport light middleweight; **~ total en charge, PTC** Transp gross weight; **~ total à vide, PTAV** Transp tare; **~ volumique** = **~ spécifique**; **~ welter** Sport welterweight.
IDIOMES **faire bon ~ bonne mesure** to be evenhanded; **avoir** or **faire deux ~ deux mesures** [*personne, institution, gouvernement*] to have double standards; **cette réglementation fait deux ~ deux mesures** these regulations show evidence of double standards.

poignant, **~e** /pwaɲɑ̃, ɑ̃t/ *adj* (émouvant) poignant; (déchirant) heart-rending, harrowing.

poignard /pwaɲaʀ/ *nm* dagger; **coup de ~** stab; **tué à coups de ~** stabbed to death; **coup de ~ dans le dos** lit, fig stab in the back.

poignarder /pwaɲaʀde/ [1] *vtr* (blesser) to stab, to knife; (tuer) to stab [sb] to death; **~ qn dans le dos** lit, fig to stab sb in the back.

poigne /pwaɲ/ *nf* (direction) firm hand; **avoir de la ~** lit to have a strong grip; fig to be firm-handed; **avoir une ~ de fer** to have an iron grip; **homme à ~** fig strong man.

poignée /pwaɲe/ *nf* **1** lit (quantité) gén handful; (de billets) fistful; **à** or **par ~s** in handfuls; **une ~ de gens** a handful of people; **2** (de porte, tiroir, sac) handle; (de sabre) hilt.
■ **~ de main** handshake; **échanger une ~ de main** to shake hands.

poignet /pwaɲɛ/ *nm* **1** ▶**188** Anat wrist; **au ~** on the wrist; **à la force des ~s** [*se hisser*] using the strength of one's arms; **à la force du ~** [*réussir*] by sheer hard work; **2** Cout cuff.
■ **~ mousquetaire** French cuff.

poil /pwal/ *nm* **1** (chez l'être humain) hair; **~s superflus** unwanted hair; **arracher les ~s (blancs) de sa barbe** to pull the (white) hairs out of one's beard; **avoir le ~ blond**○ to have blond hair; **avoir du ~ aux jambes** to have hairy legs; **avoir du ~ au menton** lit to have a hairy chin; (être adulte) to be a grown man; **à ~**◑ (nu) stark naked, starkers○; **se mettre à ~**○ to strip, to strip off GB; **'à ~!'** 'get your clothes off!'; **de tout ~**○ of all kinds; **'au (petit) ~**○**!'** 'fine!'; **être au ~**○ [*objet*] to be just the ticket○; [*personne*] to be fantastic; **ça marche au ~**○ it works like a dream; **arriver** or **tomber au (quart de) ~**○ to arrive at just the right moment; **travailler au ~**○ to be a great worker; **démarrer au quart de ~**○ to start straight away; **ne plus avoir un ~ de sec**○ to be soaked to the skin; **2**○ (cheveux) **avoir le ~ long/ras/rare** to have long/short/thin hair; **homme au ~ ras** short-haired man; **homme au ~ rare** bald-

Le poids

dire				dire
one gram	1 g*	=	0.35† oz	*ounces*
one hundred grams	100 g	=	0.22 lbs	*pounds‡*
		=	3.52 oz	*ounces*
one kilogram	1 kg	=	2.20 lbs	
		=	35.26 oz	
one hundred kilograms	100 kg	=	220 lbs	
		=	15.76 st§	*stones*
		=	1.96 cwt	*hundredweight*
One ton ou *one metric ton*		=	0.98 ton¶	*tons (GB)*
		=	1.10 tons‖	*tons (US)*

* *Pour les mesures du système métrique, les abréviations sont les mêmes en anglais qu'en français. Mais attention à* ton: *voir ci-dessous.*

† *Noter que l'anglais a un point là où le français a une virgule. Pour la prononciation des nombres, voir* **les nombres ▶ 066**.

‡ *Noter que la* pound *anglaise, que nous appelons couramment* livre, *vaut en fait 454 grammes.*

§ *Les* stones *ne sont pas utilisées aux États-Unis.*

¶ *Il n'y a pas d'abréviation pour* ton.

‖ *La tonne anglaise et la tonne américaine ne correspondent pas au même poids. Attention, car les anglophones peuvent en outre utiliser le mot* ton *pour la tonne de 1 000 kilos; pour éviter cette ambiguïté, on peut dire* metric ton.

Les équivalences suivantes peuvent être utiles:

1 oz	=	28,35 g				
1 lb	=	16 ozs	=	453,60 g		
1 st	=	14 lbs	=	6,35 kg		
1 cwt	=	8 st (*GB*)	=	112 lbs (*GB*)	=	50,73 kg
			=	100 lbs (*US*)	=	45,36 kg
1 ton	=	20 cwt (*GB*)	=	1014,6 kg		
	=	20 cwt (*US*)	=	907,2 kg		

Le poids des choses

combien pèse le colis?	=	what does the parcel weigh? *ou* how much does the parcel weigh?
quel est son poids?	=	how much does it weigh? *ou* how heavy is it? *or* what is its weight?
il pèse 5 kg	=	it weighs 5 kilos *ou* it is 5 kilos in weight
le colis fait 5 kg	=	the parcel weighs 5 kilos
il fait à peu près 5 kg	=	it is about 5 kilos
presque 6 kg	=	almost 6 kilos
plus de 5 kg	=	more than 5 kilos
moins de 6 kg	=	less than 6 kilos
A est plus lourd que B	=	A is heavier than B
A pèse plus lourd que B	=	A weighs more than B
B est plus léger que A	=	B is lighter than A
B est moins lourd que A	=	B is lighter than A
A est aussi lourd que B	=	A is as heavy as B
A fait le même poids que B	=	A is the same weight as B
A pèse autant que B	=	A is the same weight as B
A et B font le même poids	=	A and B are the same weight
A et B pèsent le même poids	=	A and B are the same weight

Noter:

il pèse deux kilos de trop	=	it is 2 kilos overweight
six kilos de sucre	=	six kilos of sugar
vendu au kilo	=	sold by the kilo

Noter l'ordre des mots dans l'adjectif composé anglais, et l'utilisation du trait d'union. Noter aussi que pound *et* kilo, *employés comme adjectifs, ne prennent pas la marque du pluriel.*

une pomme de terre de 3 livres	=	a 3-lb potato (*dire* a three-pound potato)
un colis de 5 kg	=	a 5-kilo parcel (*dire* a five-kilo parcel)

On peut aussi dire a parcel 5 kilos in weight.

Le poids des personnes

En anglais britannique, le poids des personnes est donné en stones, *chaque* stone *valant 6,35 kilos; en anglais américain, on le donne en* pounds (*livres*), *chaque* livre *valant 454 grammes.*

combien pèses-tu?	=	how much do you weigh? *ou* what is your weight?
je pèse 63 kg 500	=	I weigh 10 st (*ten stone*) (*GB*) *ou* I weigh 140 lbs (a hundred forty pounds) (*US*) I weigh 63 kg 500
il pèse 71 kg	=	he weighs 10 st 3 (ten stone three) (*GB*) *ou* he weighs 160 lbs (a hundred sixty pounds) (*US*) *ou* he weighs 71 kg
il pèse 82 kg	=	he weighs 13 st (thirteen stone) (*GB*) *ou* he weighs 180 lbs (a hundred eighty pounds) (*US*) he weighs 82 kg
il fait trois kilos de trop	=	he is three kilos overweight

Noter l'ordre des mots dans l'adjectif composé anglais, et l'utilisation du trait d'union. Noter aussi que stone, *employé comme adjectif, ne prend pas la marque du pluriel.*

un athlète de 125 kg	=	a 20-stone athlete *ou* a 125-kg athlete

ing man; **3** (d'animal) hair; **il y a des ~s de chien sur le fauteuil** there are dog hairs on the armchair; **perdre ses ~s** to moult GB ou molt US, to shed (its) hairs; **manteau en ~ de chameau** camel hair coat; **animal à ~s** furry animal; **avoir le ~ long/court** to have long/short hair; **animal à ~ ras/long** short-/long-haired animal; **animal au ~ soyeux/gris** animal with a silky/grey coat; **caresser dans le sens du ~** lit to stroke [sb/sth] the way the fur lies; fig to butter [sb] up○; **4** Bot hair, down ¢; **5**○ (petite quantité) (d'humour, ironie) touch; (de bon sens, d'intelligence, de courage) shred; **un ~ plus grand/trop petit** a shade larger/too small; **à un ~ près** by a whisker; **il s'en est fallu d'un ~ que je fasse** I was within a whisker of doing; **il s'en est fallu d'un ~ que la balle me touche** the bullet missed me by a whisker; **6** Tex (de tapis) pile ¢; (de tissu) nap ¢; (de brosse, balai) bristle.

■ **~ à gratter** itching powder; **~s tactiles** vibrissae.

IDIOMES **être de bon/mauvais ~**○ to be in a good/bad mood; **j'ai le ~ qui se hérisse**○ my hackles rise; **hérisser le ~**○ **de qn** to put sb's back up○; **avoir un ~ dans la main**○ to be bone idle; **ne plus avoir un ~ sur le caillou**○ to be as bald as a coot○; **tomber sur le ~ de qn**○ (se fâcher contre) to have a real go at sb○; (frapper) to give sb what's coming to him/her.

poilant◐, **~e** /pwalɑ̃, ɑ̃t/ *adj* killingly funny○, hilarious.

poil-de-carotte /pwaldəkaʀɔt/ **▶ 193** *adj inv* (couleur) [*cheveux*] ginger.

poiler: **se poiler**◐ /pwale/ [1] *vpr* to laugh one's head off○.

poilu, **~e** /pwaly/ **I** *adj* hairy.

II○ *nm*: *French soldier in World War I.*

poinçon /pwɛ̃sɔ̃/ *nm* **1** (pour creuser) (de brodeuse) stiletto; (de cordonnier) awl; (de menuisier) bradawl; (de graveur) burin; (d'orfèvre, de sculpteur) punch; (de scribe) stylus; **2** (pour marquer) die, stamp; (marque) hallmark; **3** (matrice) die.

poinçonnage /pwɛ̃sɔnaʒ/, **poinçonnement** /pwɛ̃sɔnmɑ̃/ *nm* **1** (de billet) punching, clipping; **2** (de l'or, argent) hallmarking; (de marchandise) stamping; **3** Tech (de tôle) punching out.

poinçonner /pwɛ̃sɔne/ [1] *vtr* **1** (perforer) to punch, clip [*billet*]; **2** (marquer) to hallmark [*or, argent*]; to stamp [*marchandise*].

poinçonneur, **-euse** /pwɛ̃sɔnœʀ, øz/ **I ▶ 510** *nm,f* (employé des transports) ticket-puncher; (ouvrier) punching-machine operator.

II poinçonneuse *nf* (à billets) ticket-punch; (machine-outil) punching machine.

poindre /pwɛ̃dʀ/ [56] *vi* [*jour*] to dawn, to break; [*aube*] to break; [*soleil*] to peep through; [*plante*] to peep through, to come up; [*idée, sentiment*] to dawn.

poing /pwɛ̃/ *nm* fist; **coup de ~** punch; **asséner** or **flanquer**○ **un coup de ~ à qn** to punch sb; **opération** or **action coup de ~** fig (police) raid; **des images coup de ~** fig shocking images; **il a pris mon ~ dans la figure**○ I punched him in the face; **taper du ~ sur la table** lit, fig to bang one's fist on the table; **les ~s sur les hanches** with (one's) arms akimbo, with one's hands on one's hips; **montrer le ~** to shake one's fist; **lever le ~** to give the clenched-fist salute; **pieds et ~s liés** lit, fig bound hand and foot; **l'épée au ~** sword in hand.

IDIOMES **dormir à ~s fermés** to sleep like a log.

point /pwɛ̃/ **I** *nm* **1** (endroit) point; **un ~ précis du globe/sur une carte** a particular point on the earth/on a map; **un ~ de ravitaillement/ralliement** a staging/rallying point; **un ~ de rencontre** a meeting point; **~ de vente** (sales) outlet; **serrure 3 ~s** 3 point lock; **2** (situation) point; Naut position; **être sur le ~ de faire** to be just about to do, to be on the point of doing; **j'étais sur le ~ de leur dire/d'abandonner/de partir** I was just about to tell them/to give up/to leave, I was on the point of telling them/giving up/leaving; **j'en suis toujours au même ~ (qu'hier/qu'il y a un an)** I'm still exactly where I was (yesterday/last year); **au ~ où j'en suis, ça n'a pas d'importance!** I've reached the point where it doesn't matter any more!; **il en est au ~ où il allume une cigarette en se levant** he's got GB ou gotten US to the stage ou point where he lights a cigarette as soon as he gets up; **faire le ~** Naut to take bearings; fig to take stock of the situation; **faire le ~ sur la situation économique/sur la recherche scientifique** fig to take stock of the economic situation/of scientific research; **faire le ~ sur la circulation (routière)/l'actualité** to give an up-to-the-minute report on the traffic news/current situation; **3** (degré) **il m'agace/m'inquiète au plus haut ~** he annoys me/worries me intensely; **la circulation était à ce ~ bloquée que j'ai dû laisser ma voiture au bord de la route** the traffic was so bad that I had to leave my car on the side of the road; **je ne le pensais pas bête/coléreux à ce ~** I didn't think he was that stupid/quick-tempered; **'j'en aurais pleuré'—'ah bon, à ce ~?'** 'I could have cried'—'really? it was that bad?'; **je sais à quel ~ elle est triste/sensible** I know how sad/sensitive

Les points cardinaux

nord	north	N
sud	south	S
est	east	E
ouest	west	W

Noter que la liste des quatre points cardinaux est traditionnellement donnée dans cet ordre dans les deux langues.

nord-est	northeast	NE
nord-ouest	northwest	NW
nord-nord-est	north northeast	NNE
est-nord-est	east northeast	ENE

etc.

Dans les expressions suivantes, nord *est pris comme exemple; les autres noms de points cardinaux s'utilisent de la même façon.*

Où?

vivre dans le Nord	=	to live in the North
dans le nord de l'Écosse	=	in the north of Scotland
au nord du village	=	north of the village *ou* to the north of the village
à 7 km au nord	=	7 kilometres north *ou* 7 kilometres to the north
droit au nord	=	due north
la côte nord	=	the north coast
la face nord (d'une montagne)	=	the north face
le mur nord	=	the north wall
la porte nord	=	the north door
passer au nord d'Oxford	=	to go north of Oxford

Les mots en -ern et -erner

Les mots anglais en -ern *et* -erner *sont plus courants que les adjectifs français* septentrional, occidental, oriental *et* méridional.

une ville du Nord	=	a northern town
l'accent du Nord	=	a northern accent
le dialecte du Nord	=	the northern dialect
l'avant poste le plus au nord	=	the most northerly outpost *ou* the northernmost outpost
quelqu'un qui habite dans le Nord	=	a northerner
un homme du Nord	=	a northerner
les gens du Nord	=	northerners

Les adjectifs en -ern *sont normalement utilisés pour désigner des régions à l'intérieur d'un pays ou d'un continent* (▶ 692).

le nord de l'Europe	=	northern Europe
l'est de la France	=	eastern France
le sud de la Roumanie	=	southern Romania
le nord d'Israël	=	northern Israel

Mais noter:

l'Asie du Sud-Est	=	South-East Asia

Pour les noms de pays qui utilisent les points cardinaux (*Corée du Nord, Yemen du Sud*) *se reporter au dictionnaire.*

Dans quelle direction?

Noter les adverbes en -ward *ou* -wards (*GB*) *et les adjectifs en* -ward, *utilisés pour indiquer une direction vague.*

aller vers le nord	=	to go north *ou* to go northward *ou* to go in a northerly direction
naviguer vers le nord	=	to sail north *ou* to sail northward
venir du nord	=	to come from the north
un mouvement vers le nord	=	a northward mouvement

Pour décrire le déplacement d'un object, on peut utiliser un composé avec -bound.

un bateau qui se dirige vers le nord	=	a northbound ship
les véhicules qui se dirigent vers le nord	=	northbound traffic

Noter aussi:

les véhicules qui viennent du nord	=	traffic coming from the north
des fenêtres qui donnent au nord	=	north-facing windows *ou* windows facing north
une pente orientée au nord	=	a north-facing slope
nord quart nord-est	=	north by northeast

Noter ces expressions servant à donner la direction des vents:

le vent du nord	=	the north wind
un vent de nord	=	a northerly wind *ou* a northerly
des vents dominants de nord	=	prevailing north winds
le vent est au nord	=	the wind is northerly *ou* the wind is in the north
le vent vient du nord	=	the wind is blowing from the north

she is; **si tu savais à quel ~ il m'agace!** if you only knew how much he annoys me!; **au ~ que** to the extent that; **à tel ~ que** to such an extent that...; **douloureux/endommagé à (un) tel** or **au ~ que** so painful/badly damaged that; **la situation s'est aggravée au ~ qu'ils ont dû appeler la police** the situation became so bad that the police had to be called in; **le temps s'est rafraîchi au ~ qu'il a fallu remettre le chauffage** the weather got so cold that the heating had to be put back on; **il est têtu à un ~!** he's so incredibly stubborn!; **jusqu'à un certain ~** up to a (certain) point, to a certain extent; **4** (question particulière) point; (dans un ordre du jour) item, point; **un programme en trois ~s** a three-point plan; **un ~ fondamental/de détail (d'un texte)** a basic/minor point (in a text); **sur ce ~** on this point; **j'aimerais revenir sur ce dernier ~** I would like to come back to that last point; **un ~ de désaccord/litige** a point of disagreement/contention; **reprendre un texte ~ par ~** to go over a text point by point; **en tout ~, en tous ~s** in every respect ou way; **une politique en tous ~s désastreuse** a policy that is disastrous in every respect; **les deux modèles sont semblables en tous ~s** the two models are alike in every respect; **5** (marque visible) gén dot; **les villes sont marquées par un ~** towns are marked by a dot; **il y a un ~ sur le i et le j** there's a dot on the i and the j; **un ~ lumineux/rouge dans le lointain** a light/a red dot in the distance; **bientôt, le navire ne fut qu'un ~ à l'horizon** soon, the ship was a mere dot ou speck on the horizon; **un ~ de colle** a spot of glue; **un ~ de rouille** a speck of rust; **~s de graissage** lubricating points; ▶ **i**; **6** Jeux, Sport point; **marquer/perdre des ~s** lit, fig to score/lose points; **compter les ~s** to keep (the) score; **un ~ partout!** one all!; **battre son adversaire aux ~s** to beat one's opponent on points; **remporter une victoire aux ~s** to win on points; **7** (pour évaluer) mark GB, point US; **avoir sept ~s d'avance** to be seven marks ahead; **avoir dix ~s de retard** to be ten marks behind; **il m'a manqué trois ~s pour réussir** I failed by three marks; **enlever un ~ par faute** to take a mark off for each mistake; **obtenir** or **avoir 27 ~s sur 40** to get 27 out of 40; **être un bon ~ pour** to be a plus point for; **être un mauvais ~ pour qn/qch** to be a black mark against sb/sth; **8** (dans un système de calcul) point; **la livre a perdu trois ~s** the pound lost three points; **le taux de chômage a augmenté de 0,8 ~s** the unemployment rate rose by 0.8 points; **le permis à ~s** *system whereby driving offender gets penalty points*; **il a perdu sept ~s dans les sondages** he's gone down seven points in the polls; **9** Math point; **~ d'intersection/d'inflexion** point of intersection/of inflection; **10** Ling (en ponctuation) full stop GB, period US; **mettre un ~** to put a full stop; **~ à la ligne** (dans une dictée) full stop, new paragraph; **~ final** (dans une dictée) full stop; **mettre un ~ final à qch** fig to put a stop ou an end to sth; **je n'irai pas, ~ final**○! I'm not going, full stop GB ou period US!; **tu vas te coucher un ~ c'est tout**○! you're going to bed and that's final!; **11** Mus dot; **12** Imprim point; **13** Méd (douleur) pain; **avoir un ~ à la poitrine/à l'aine** to have a pain in the chest/in the groin; **14** (en couture, tricot) stitch; **faire un ~ à qch** to put a few stitches in sth; **dentelle au ~ de Venise** Venetian lace.

II† *adv* not; **tu ne tueras ~** Bible thou shalt not kill; **je n'en ai ~** I don't have any; **'tu es fâché?'—'non ~!'** 'are you angry?'—'not at all'.

III à point *loc adv* **venir/arriver à ~** to come/arrive just in time; **venir/arriver** or **tomber à ~ nommé** to come/arrive just at the right moment; **faire cuire à ~** to cook [sth] medium rare [*viande*]; **bifteck (cuit) à ~** medium rare steak; **le camembert est à ~** the camembert is ready to eat.

IV au point *loc adv, loc adj* **être au ~** [*système, méthode, machine*] to be well designed; [*spectacle, émission*] to be well put together; **leur système/machine/spectacle n'est pas encore très au ~** their system/machine/show still needs some working on; **le nouveau modèle est très au ~** the new model is very well designed; **le spectacle n'était pas du tout au ~** the show wasn't up to scratch; **le prototype n'est pas encore au ~** the prototype isn't quite ready yet; **ça fait des semaines qu'ils répètent mais leur numéro n'est pas encore au ~** they've been rehearsing for weeks but they still haven't got GB ou gotten US it quite right; **je ne suis pas au ~ pour les examens** I'm not ready for the exams; **mettre [qch] au ~** (inventer) to perfect [*théorie, système, méthode, technique*]; to work out, to devise [*accord, plan de paix, stratégie*]; to develop [*vaccin, médicament, appareil*]; (régler) to adjust [*machine, mécanisme*]; **il leur reste deux semaines pour finir de mettre leur spectacle au ~** they've got two more weeks to put the finishing touches to their show; **mettre au ~ sur qch** Phot to focus on sth; **mise au ~** Phot focus; fig (déclaration) clarifying statement; **la mise au ~ est automatique sur mon appareil** my camera has automatic focus; **faire la mise au ~** Phot to focus (**sur** on); **faire une mise au ~** fig to set the record straight (**sur** about); **mise au ~** (invention) (de théorie, système, méthode, technique) perfecting; (de médicament, vaccin) development; (réglage) (de machine, mécanisme) adjusting; Phot focus.

■ **~ d'acupuncture** Méd acupuncture point; **~ d'ancrage** Aut anchor; fig base; **~ d'appui** Mil base of operations; Phys fulcrum; gén support; **les piliers servent de ~ d'appui à la charpente** the roof structure is supported by the pillars; **trouver un ~ d'appui à une échelle** to find a support for a ladder; **~ arrière** Cout back stitch; **~ d'attache** base; **~ de bâti** Cout tacking stitch; **~ blanc** whitehead; **~ de blé** (en tricot) double moss stitch; **~ de boutonnière** Cout buttonhole stitch; **~ cardinal** Phys, Géog compass ou cardinal point; **~ de chaînette** (en broderie) chain stitch; **~ de chausson** (en broderie)

herringbone stitch; ~ **chaud** trouble ou hot spot; **les ~s chauds du globe** the world's trouble spots; ~ **de chute** fig port of call; ~ **commun** mutual interest; **nous avons beaucoup de ~s communs** we have a lot in common; **ils n'ont aucun ~ commun** they have nothing in common; ~ **de congestion**† Méd *slight congestion of the lung*; ~ **de côtes** (en tricot) rib; ~ **de côté** (douleur) stitch; (en couture) slip stitch; **avoir un ~ de côté** to have a stitch in one's side; ~ **de croix** (en broderie) cross stitch; ~ **de départ** lit, fig starting point; **nous revoilà à notre ~ de départ** fig we're back to square one; ~ **de devant** Cout running stitch; ~ **d'eau** (naturel) watering place; (robinet) water tap GB ou faucet US; ~ **d'ébullition** boiling point; ~ **d'épine** (en broderie) featherstitch; ~ **d'exclamation** Ling exclamation mark; ~ **faible** weak point; ~ **de feston** (en broderie) blanket stitch; ~ **fort** strong point; ~ **de fuite** Art, Archit vanishing point; ~ **de fusion** melting point; ~ **G** G-spot; ~ **d'interrogation** Ling question mark; ~ **de jersey** (en tricot) stocking stitch; ~ **du jour** daybreak; **au ~ du jour** at daybreak; ~ **de liquéfaction** liquefaction point; ~ **de mire** Mil target; fig focal point; ~ **mousse** (en tricot) garter stitch; ~ **mort** Aut neutral; **se mettre** or **passer/être au ~ mort** Aut to put the car into/to be in neutral; **être au ~ mort** fig [*affaires, consommation*] to be at a standstill; [*négociations*] to be in a state of deadlock; ~ **noir** (comédon) blackhead; (problème) problem; (sur la route) blackspot; **l'inflation reste le seul ~ noir** inflation is the only problem; ~ **de non-retour** point of no return; ~ **d'orgue** Mus pause sign; ~ **d'ourlet** Cout hemstitch; ~ **de penalty** penalty spot; ~ **de piqûre** Cout back stitch; ~ **de presse** Journ press briefing; ~ **de repère** (spatial) landmark; (temporel, personnel) point of reference; ~ **de reprise** Cout darning stitch; ~ **de retraite** Prot Soc *point which counts towards a retirement pension scheme*; ~ **de riz** (en tricot) moss stitch; ~ **de surfil** Cout whipstitch; ~ **de suture** Méd stitch; ~ **de tige** (en broderie) stem stitch; ~ **de torsade** (en tricot) cable stitch; ~ **de vue** (paysage) viewpoint; (opinion) point of view; **du ~ de vue de la direction** from the management's point of view; **du ~ de vue de l'efficacité/du sens** as far as efficiency/meaning is concerned; **d'un ~ de vue économique c'est rentable/intéressant** from a financial point of view it's profitable/attractive; **~s de suspension** suspension points.
IDIOMES **être mal en ~** to be in a bad way.

pointage /pwɛ̃taʒ/ *nm* **1** (vérification) gén checking; (en cochant) ticking off GB, checking off US; **faire un ~ des personnes présentes** to tick off GB ou check off US the names of those present; **le ~ des voix** (dans un vote) the tally of the votes; **2** Entr (en entrant) clocking on, clocking in; (en sortant) clocking off; **une feuille de ~** a time sheet; **3** (avec une arme à feu) aiming, pointing.

pointe /pwɛ̃t/ **I** *nf* **1** (bout piquant) point; **se piquer le doigt sur la ~ d'un couteau** to cut one's finger on the point of a knife; **2** (extrémité qui s'amenuise) (de col, clocher, crayon, sein) point; (de chaussure) toe; (des cheveux) end; **en ~** pointed; **une barbe en ~** a pointed beard; **tailler un buisson en ~** to shape a bush into a point; **3** (objet pointu) (de grille) spike; (de lance, flèche) tip, point; **un casque à ~** a helmet with a spike; **4** (niveau très avancé) **de ~** [*technologie, technique*] advanced, state-of-the-art; [*domaine, secteur, industrie*] high-tech; [*formation, idées*] advanced; [*entreprise, spécialiste*] leading; **un système électronique à la ~ du progrès** a state-of-the-art electronic system; **être à la ~ de la mode** [*personne*] to be up with the latest fashion; **une entreprise à la ~ de la modernité** an extremely modern company; **5** (niveau supérieur à la moyenne) high; **une ~ de 20% sur la courbe du chômage** a 20% high on the unemployment curve; **une activité qui connaît de fortes ~s saisonnières** an activity with seasonal highs; **un enfant qui a des ~s de température de 40°** a child whose temperature shoots up to 40°C; **une vitesse de ~ de 200 km/h** a maximum or top speed of 200 km/h; **il a poussé une ~ de 180 km/h** he touched a top speed of 180 km/h; **aux heures de ~** at peak time; **le métro est bondé parce que c'est l'heure de ~** the metro is packed because it's the rush hour; **évitez les heures de ~** avoid peak times; **6** (petite quantité) touch; **ajoutez une ~ d'ail/de cannelle** add a touch of garlic/of cinnamon; **une ~ d'ironie** a hint of irony; **une ~ d'accent italien** a hint of an ou a slight Italian accent; **7** (clou) nail; **8** (allusion désagréable) pointed ou barbed remark; **lancer des ~s à qn** to level cutting remarks at sb; **9** Géog (cap) **~ (de terre)** headland; **10** (foulard) (triangular) scarf; **11** (couche) (triangular) nappy; **12** Naut (de compas) pointer; **13** (outil) (pour tailler) cutter; (pour graver) metal point; **14** Danse (extrémité du chausson) point; (chausson) blocked shoe; **15** Hérald base.
II pointes *nfpl* **1** Sport (**chaussures à**) **~s** spikes; **courir avec des ~s** to run in spikes; **2** Danse **faire des ~s** to dance on points.
■ ~ **d'asperge** asparagus tip; ~ **de diamant** diamond cutter; ~ **de feu** Méd ignipuncture; ~ **du jour** daybreak; ~ **du pied** toes (*pl*), tiptoe; **tendre la ~ du pied** to point one's toes; **marcher sur la ~ des pieds** to walk on tiptoe; **elle est entrée sur la ~ des pieds** she tiptoed in; **aborder une question sur la ~ des pieds** fig to broach a matter carefully; ~ **sèche** Art metal point.
IDIOMES **tailler** or **couper les oreilles en ~ à qn** to give sb a thick ear.

pointé, **~e** /pwɛ̃te/ **I** *pp* ▶ **pointer**[1].
II *pp adj* Mus [*note*] dotted; **une blanche ~e** a dotted minim GB ou half-note US.

pointeau /pwɛ̃to/ *nm* **1** Tech awl; **2** Aut needle; **3** (contrôleur) timekeeper.

pointer[1] /pwɛ̃te/ [1] **I** *vtr* **1** (en cochant) to tick off GB, to check off US [*noms, mots, chiffres*]; to check [*liste*]; to time [*sportif*]; **2** (diriger) to point [*arme*] (**sur qch/qn** at sth/sb); ~ **un** or **son doigt vers qch/qn** to point at sth/sb; ~ **un doigt accusateur sur qch/qn** to point an accusing finger at sth/sb; ~ **sa tête par la porte/par la fenêtre** to stick one's head round the door GB ou in US/out of the window; ~ **son museau** [*animal*] to peep out; ~ **son nez**○ to show one's face; **3** (dresser en pointe) ~ **ses oreilles** [*chien*] to prick up its ears.
II *vi* **1** Entr [*employé*] (en arrivant) to clock in; (en sortant) to clock out; **nous ne sommes pas obligés de ~** we don't have to clock in and out; ~ **à l'usine**○ to work in a factory; **2** Prot Soc ~ **à l'agence pour l'emploi** to sign on at the unemployment office; **3** Sport (aux boules) *to aim at positioning a boule as close to the jack as possible*; **4** (se dresser) [*clocher, tour, arbre, antenne*] to rise up; [*seins*] to stick out; **le clocher pointait au-dessus des toits** the steeple was visible above the roofs; ~ **à l'horizon** to rise up on the horizon; **5** (apparaître) [*soleil*] to come up, to rise; [*aube, jour*] to break; [*fleur, plante*] to come up; [*bourgeons*] to open; **les crocus commencent à ~** the crocuses are starting to come up.
III○ **se pointer** *vpr* [*personne*] to turn up; **il s'est pointé en jean à la cérémonie** he turned up at the ceremony in jeans.

pointer[2] /pwɛ̃tɛʀ/ *nm* (chien) pointer.

pointeur, **-euse** /pwɛ̃tœʀ, øz/ **I** *nm,f* gén checker; Entr, Sport timekeeper; (aux boules) *player whose role is to position his own boule.*
II *nm* Mil gun-layer.
III pointeuse *nf* Entr time clock.

pointillage /pwɛ̃tijaʒ/ *nm* stipple, stippling.

pointillé, **~e** /pwɛ̃tije/ **I** *pp* ▶ **pointiller**.
II *pp adj* dotted (**de** with).
III *nm* **1** (ligne) dotted line; (perforation) perforation(s); **plier suivant le ~** fold along the dotted line; **en ~** lit dotted; **message en ~** fig underlying message; **2** Art stippling; **dessin au ~** stippled drawing.

pointiller /pwɛ̃tije/ [1] *vtr, vi* Art to stipple.

pointilleux, **-euse** /pwɛ̃tijø, øz/ *adj* pej [*personne*] fussy (**sur** about), pernickety.

pointillisme /pwɛ̃tijism/ *nm* pointillism.

pointilliste /pwɛ̃tijist/ *adj, nmf* pointillist.

pointu, **~e** /pwɛ̃ty/ **I** *adj* **1** (qui se termine en pointe) [*bout*] pointed; [*couteau, ciseaux*] with a sharp point (*épith*); [*clocher, toit, chapeau*] pointed; [*nez, menton*] pointed, sharp péj; **mes ciseaux sont ~s** my scissors have a sharp point; **des objets ~s** sharp objects; **2** (pointilleux) [*détail*] precise; [*contrôle*] close, thorough; **3** (de spécialiste) [*secteur, travail, activité*] highly specialized; [*approche, question*] precise; **4** (aigu) [*voix*] piercing; [*ton*] shrill.
II *adv* **parler ~** *to sound like a Parisian to a native of the south of France.*

pointure /pwɛ̃tyʀ/ ▶ **793** *nf* (de gant, chaussure) size; **quelle est sa ~?**, **quelle ~ fait-il?** what size does he take?; **des chaussures de quelle ~?** what size shoes?

point-virgule, *pl* **points-virgules** /pwɛ̃viʀgyl/ *nm* semicolon.

poire /pwaʀ/ *nf* **1** (fruit) pear; **tarte aux ~s** pear tart GB ou pie US; **2** (en boucherie) *cut of topside of beef used for steaks*; **3** (objet) (interrupteur) (pear-shaped) light switch; (en bijouterie) pear-shaped stone; **visage/seins en forme de ~** pear-shaped face/breasts; **4**○ (visage) face; **prendre un coup en pleine ~** to be hit right in the middle of the face; **se ficher de la ~ de qn** to take the mickey out of sb○ GB, to make fun of sb; **5**○ (personne naïve) mug○ GB, sucker○; **il a trouvé la bonne ~** he's found a real sucker○.
■ ~ **Belle-Hélène** *stewed pear with ice cream and chocolate sauce*; ~ **à injections** or **à lavement** bulb syringe.
IDIOMES **couper la ~ en deux** to split the difference; **parler de qch entre la ~ et le fromage** to discuss sth very casually; **garder une ~ pour la soif** to save something for a rainy day.

poiré /pwaʀe/ *nm* perry.

poireau, *pl* **~x** /pwaʀo/ *nm* leek; **~x (en) vinaigrette** leeks in a vinaigrette dressing; **tarte aux ~x** leek quiche.
IDIOMES **faire le ~**○ to hang about○.

poireauter○ /pwaʀɔte/ [1] *vi* to hang about○; **faire ~ qn** to keep sb hanging about○.

poirée /pwaʀe/ *nf* Swiss chard.

poirier /pwaʀje/ *nm* **1** (arbre) pear (tree); **2** (bois) pear.
IDIOMES **faire le ~** to do a headstand.

pois /pwa/ *nm inv* **1** Bot, Culin pea; **petit ~** (garden) pea, petit pois; **petit ~ à écosser** shelling pea; **une boîte de petits ~** a can of peas; **2** Mode (motif) dot; **à ~** polka dot (*épith*), spotted.
■ ~ **cassé** split pea; ~ **chiche** chickpea; ~ **gourmand** or **mange-tout** mangetout pea GB, snow pea US; ~ **sauteur** jumping bean; ~ **de senteur** sweet pea; ~ **de sept ans** butterbean.

poiscaille○ /pwaskɑj/ *nf* fish.

poison /pwazɔ̃/ **I**○ *nmf* (personne agaçante) pest.
II *nm* lit, fig poison.

poissard, **~e** /pwasaʀ, aʀd/ **I** *adj* (grossier) coarse.
II poissarde‡ *nf* fishwife.

poisse○ /pwas/ *nf* (malchance) rotten luck○; (chose contrariante) drag○; **quelle ~, ce**

temps! this weather is a real drag!; **porter la ~ à qn** to bring sb bad luck.

poisser /pwase/ [1] **I** *vtr* to make [sth] sticky.
II *vi* to be sticky.
IDIOMES **se faire ~**○ to get caught.

poisseux, **-euse** /pwasø, øz/ *adj* [*mains, table*] sticky; [*atmosphère*] muggy; [*restaurant*] greasy.

poisson /pwasɔ̃/ *nm* **1** Zool, Culin fish; **des ~s** fish ou fishes; **les ~s d'eau douce/de mer** freshwater/saltwater fish; **du ~ cru/surgelé** raw/frozen fish; **manger du ~** to eat fish; **2** Astrol (natif des Poissons) Pisces; **il est ~s** he is a Pisces.
■ **(petit) ~ d'argent** (insecte) silverfish; **~ d'avril** (exclamation) April fool; (blague) April fool's joke; **faire un ~ d'avril à qn** to make an April fool of sb; **~ cartilagineux** cartilaginous fish; **~ électrique** electric eel; **~ osseux** bony fish; **~ pané** breaded fish; (en bâtonnets) fish fingers; **~ perroquet** parrot-fish; **~ rouge** goldfish; **~ volant** flying fish.
IDIOMES **être comme un ~ dans l'eau** to be in one's element; **essayer de noyer le ~** to fudge the issue; **petit ~ deviendra grand** mighty oaks from little acorns grow; **les gros ~s mangent les petits** it is the survival of the fittest; ▶ **engueuler**.

poisson-chat, *pl* **poissons-chats** /pwasɔ̃ʃa/ *nm* catfish.

poisson-lune, *pl* **poissons-lunes** /pwasɔ̃lyn/ *nm* sunfish.

poissonnerie /pwasɔnʀi/ ▶510 *nf* **1** (magasin) fishmonger's (shop) GB, fish shop US; (dans supermarché) fish counter, fish market US; **2** (industrie) fish trade.

poissonneux, **-euse** /pwasɔnø, øz/ *adj* [*eaux, rivière*] well stocked with fish (*après n*).

poissonnier, **-ière** /pwasɔnje, ɛʀ/ ▶510
I *nm,f* fishmonger GB, fish vendor US, **aller chez le ~** to go to the fishmonger's.
II poissonnière *nf* Culin fish kettle.

Poissons /pwasɔ̃/ ▶874 *nprmpl* Pisces.

poisson-scie, *pl* **poissons-scies** /pwasɔ̃si/ *nm* sawfish.

poitevin, **~e** /pwatvɛ̃, in/ ▶692 *adj* **la région ~e** the Poitou region; **le marais ~** the Poitou marshes (*pl*).

Poitevin, **~e** /pwatvɛ̃, in/ *nm,f* (natif) native of the Poitou region; (habitant) inhabitant of the Poitou region.

Poitiers /pwatje/ ▶857 *npr* Poitiers.

Poitou /pwatu/ ▶692 *nprm* **le ~** the Poitou region.

Poitou-Charentes /pwatuʃaʀɑ̃t/ ▶692 *nprm* **le ~** the Poitou-Charentes.

poitrail /pwatʀaj/ *nm* chest.

poitrinaire† /pwatʀinɛʀ/ *adj, nm,f* consumptive†.

poitrine /pwatʀin/ ▶188, 793 *nf* **1** (thorax) chest; (seins) breasts (*pl*); **sa ~ se soulevait** his/her chest was rising up; **tour de ~** (pour un homme) chest size; (pour une femme) bust size; **une belle ~** a nice bust, nice breasts; **un cri jaillit de sa ~** she uttered a cry; **se frapper la ~** fig to beat one's breast; **elle n'a pas beaucoup de ~** she is rather flat-chested; **2** Culin, Zool breast; **~ d'agneau** breast of lamb; **~ de bœuf** brisket; **~ de porc** ≈ belly of pork.
■ **~ fumée/salée** ≈ smoked/unsmoked streaky bacon.

poivrade /pwavʀad/ *nf*: *dressing with crushed peppercorns*.

poivre /pwavʀ/ *nm* pepper; **~ moulu** ground pepper; **~ en grains** whole peppercorns; **~ blanc/noir/vert** white/black/green pepper; **un steak au ~ vert** a steak with green peppercorns; **~ de Cayenne** cayenne pepper; **~ et sel** salt-and-pepper (*épith*); **il est ~ et sel** he has salt-and-pepper hair; **~ rose** pink pepper berries.

poivré, **~e** /pwavʀe/ **I** *pp* ▶ **poivrer**.
II *pp adj* [*sauce, odeur*] peppery; [*plaisanterie*] racy.

poivrer /pwavʀe/ [1] *vtr* to add pepper to [*plat, sauce*].

poivrier /pwavʀije/ *nm* **1** Culin (récipient) pepper pot GB, pepper shaker US; (moulin) pepper mill; **2** Bot (arbuste) pepper tree.

poivrière /pwavʀijɛʀ/ *nf* **1** Culin (récipient) pepper pot GB, pepper shaker US; **2** (plantation) pepper plantation.

poivron /pwavʀɔ̃/ *nm* sweet pepper, capsicum; **~ vert/rouge** green/red pepper; **~s farcis** stuffed peppers; **mettre du ~ dans** to put peppers in.

poivrot○, **~e** /pwavʀo, ɔt/ *nm,f* drunk, drunkard.

poix /pwa/ *nf inv* pitch; **~ bitumineuse** coal-tar pitch.

poker /pɔkɛʀ/ ▶449 *nm* poker; **~ de dames/valets/rois** four queens/jacks/kings; **une partie de ~** fig a game of bluff; **coup de ~** fig gamble; **tenter un coup de ~** to gamble.
■ **~ d'as** (jeu de dés) poker dice; **~ menteur** liar poker (*similar to liar dice*).

polaire /pɔlɛʀ/ **I** *adj* **1** gén (du pôle) [*faune, flore, région*] polar; (digne du pôle) [*froid, paysage*] arctic; **2** Chimie, Math polar; **3** Tex **laine** or **fibre ~** fleece.
II *nf* Math polar.

polar○ /pɔlaʀ/ *nm* detective novel.

polarisant, **~e** /pɔlaʀizɑ̃, ɑ̃t/ *adj* polarizing.

polarisation /pɔlaʀizasjɔ̃/ *nf* **1** Électrotech, Phys polarization; **2** (d'attention, de sentiment) focusing, polarization.

polariser /pɔlaʀize/ [1] **I** *vtr* **1** Électrotech, Phys to polarize; **2** (concentrer) to focus [*attention, sentiment, débat, opinion*] (**sur** on); **toute l'attention est polarisée sur les mineurs** all attention is focused on the miners; **3** (attirer à soi) to attract [*intérêt, regards*]; to be a focus for [*soupçon*]; **pourra-t-il ~ les électeurs de gauche?** will he be able to attract left-wing voters?; **le projet polarise tous leurs efforts** all their efforts are going into the project.
II se polariser *vpr* **1** Phys, Électrotech to polarize; **2** (se concentrer) [*attention, débat*] to focus, to concentrate (**sur, autour de** on, around); [*personne*] to focus one' s attention (**sur** on); **le débat politique se polarise sur cette question** the political debate centres[GB] ou focuses[GB] on ou around this question.

polarité /pɔlaʀite/ *nf* polarity.

polaroid® /pɔlaʀɔid/ *nm* Polaroid®; **une photo prise au ~** a polaroid (photo).

polder /pɔldɛʀ/ *nm* polder.

pole /pol/ *adj* controv **~ position** pole position.

pôle /pol/ *nm* **1** Astron, Géog, Math, Phys pole; **le ~ Nord/Sud** the North/South Pole; **~ magnétique** magnetic pole; **2** fig (centre) centre[GB] (**de qch** of sth); (tendance) pole; **un ~ d'attraction** a centre[GB] of attraction.

polémique /pɔlemik/ **I** *adj* [*œuvre, déclaration*] polemical.
II *nf* debate; **l'affaire suscite de violentes ~s** the affair has sparked off fierce debate.

polémiquer /pɔlemike/ [1] *vi* to enter into a debate (**avec** with).

polémiste /pɔlemist/ *nmf* polemicist.

polémologie /pɔlemɔlɔʒi/ *nf* war studies (*pl*).

polenta /pɔlɛnta/ *nf* polenta.

poli, **~e** /pɔli/ **I** *pp* ▶ **polir**.
II *pp adj* **1** (lisse) [*bois, métal, pierre*] polished; **2** (travaillé) [*style*] polished.
III *adj* (courtois) [*personne*] polite (**avec qn** to sb); [*demande, refus*] polite; **trop ~ pour être honnête** too polite to be genuine.
IV *nm* shine; **donner du ~ à qch** to polish sth up.

police /pɔlis/ *nf* **1** (force) police (+ *v pl*); **il est dans la ~** he is in the police; **voiture de ~** police car; **coopération des ~s** cooperation between police forces; **toutes les ~s du pays** every police force in the country; **2** (organisme privé) security service; **3** (maintien de l'ordre) policing; **pouvoirs de ~** powers to enforce law and order; **faire la ~** to keep order; **faire la ~ dans un quartier/une zone** to police a district/an area; **faire sa propre ~** to do one's own policing; **4** Assur **~ (d'assurance)** (contrat) (insurance) policy; (document) policy (document); **contracter une ~ d'assurance-vie** to take out life insurance ou a life insurance policy; **5** Imprim, Ordinat **~ (de caractères)** fonts (*pl*); **6** (tribunal) **passer en simple ~** to be tried in a police court.
■ **~ de l'air et des frontières**, **PAF** border police; **~ judiciaire**, **PJ** *detective division of the French police force*; **~ militaire** military police; **~ des mœurs** or **mondaine** vice squad; **~ montée** mounted police; **~ municipale** city police; **~ nationale** national police force; **~ parallèle** *unofficial government police*; **~ des polices** *police internal investigative body*; **~ politique** political police; **~ privée** private police force; **~ de la route** traffic police; **~ secours** ≈ emergency services (*pl*); **appeler ~ secours** to call the emergency services; **~ secrète** secret police.

policer /pɔlise/ [12] *vtr* liter to civilize.

polichinelle /pɔliʃinɛl/ *nm* (jouet) Punch.
IDIOMES **avoir un ~ dans le tiroir**◑ to have a bun in the oven◑.

Polichinelle /pɔliʃinɛl/ *npr* Punchinello.

policier, **-ière** /pɔlisje, ɛʀ/ **I** *adj* [*surveillance, chien, régime, mesure, enquête*] police; [*film, roman*] detective.
II *nm* **1** ▶510 (personne) policeman; **femme ~** policewoman; **2** (film) detective film; (roman) detective novel.

policlinique /pɔliklinik/ *nf* ≈ outpatients' clinic.

poliment /pɔlimɑ̃/ *adv* politely.

polio /pɔljo/ **I** *nmf* (*abbr* = **poliomyélitique**) person handicapped by polio.
II ▶271 *nf* (*abbr* = **poliomyélite**) polio; **vaccin contre la ~** polio vaccine.

poliomyélite /pɔljomjelit/ ▶271 *nf* poliomyelitis.

poliomyélitique /pɔljomjelitik/ **I** *adj* handicapped by polio (*jamais épith*); [*virus*] polio (*épith*); **il est ~** he has polio.
II *nmf* polio sufferer.

polir /pɔliʀ/ [3] *vtr* to polish [*bois, pierre, métal*]; to polish (up) [*style*]; **se ~ les ongles** to buff one's nails.

polissage /pɔlisaʒ/ *nm* polishing.

polisseur, **-euse** /pɔlisœʀ, øz/ **I** ▶510 *nm,f* (personne) polisher.
II polisseuse *nf* (machine) electric polisher.

polissoir /pɔliswaʀ/ *nm* **1** gén electric polisher; **2** Archéol polishing stone.
■ **~ à ongles** nail buffer.

polisson, **-onne** /pɔlisɔ̃, ɔn/ **I** *adj* **1** [*enfant*] naughty; **2** (licencieux) naughty, saucy.
II *nm,f* (enfant) naughty child.

polissonnerie /pɔlisɔnʀi/ *nf* **1** (d'enfant) naughty trick; **des ~s** mischief ¢, naughty tricks; **2** (propos licencieux) naughty remark.

politesse /pɔlitɛs/ *nf* politeness; **par ~** out of politeness; **le 'vous' de ~** the polite 'vous' form; **tu pourrais avoir la ~ de t'excuser** you might have the decency to apologize; **rendre la ~ à qn** to return the compliment; **échanger** or **se faire des ~s** to exchange pleasantries; **échanger des ~s** iron to exchange insults.
IDIOMES **l'exactitude est la ~ des rois** Prov punctuality is the hallmark of a gentleman; **brûler** or **griller la ~ à qn** to push in ahead of sb.

politicard○ /pɔlitikaʀ/ *nm* pej political wheeler-dealer.

politicien, **-ienne** /pɔlitisjɛ̃, ɛn/ **I** *adj*

(purely) political; **politique politicienne** pej politicking.

II *nm,f* politician.

politico(-) /pɔlitiko/ *préf* politico; **politico-culturel** politico-cultural; **politico-économique** politico-economic; **politico-militaire** politico-military; **affaire politico-financière** financial scandal.

politique /pɔlitik/ I *adj* **1** (relatif aux affaires publiques) political; **la semaine ~** the week's political developments; **2** (habile) [*concession*] tactical; [*comportement, acte*] calculating.

II *nm* **1** (aspect) political aspect; **2** (personne qui s'intéresse aux affaires de l'État) politician; **3** (personne habile) **un (fin) ~** a shrewd operator.

III *nf* Pol **1** (science, art) politics (+ *v sg*); **faire de la ~** (en faire son métier) to go into politics, to be in politics; (en tant que militant) to be involved in politics; (dans une discussion) to talk politics; **2** (manière de gouverner) policy; **la ~ du gouvernement en matière d'éducation** the government's education policy; **~ étrangère/intérieure/agricole/sociale** foreign/domestic/agricultural/social policy; **déclaration de ~ générale** statement of general policy; **3** (stratégie) policy; **nouvelle ~ de recrutement** new recruiting ou recruitment policy; **notre ~ des prix** our pricing policy.

■ **~ contractuelle** *contractual undertaking between the state and a private body*; **~ de la terre brûlée** scorched earth policy.

IDIOMES **pratiquer la ~ de l'autruche** to stick ou hide one's head in the sand; **pratiquer la ~ du pire** to envisage the worst-case scenario.

politique-fiction, *pl* **politiques-fictions** /pɔlitikfiksjɔ̃/ *nf* Cin, Littérat *literary or film genre describing an imaginary political future.*

politiquement /pɔlitikmɑ̃/ *adv* **1** lit politically; **2** (habilement) shrewdly.

politisation /pɔlitizasjɔ̃/ *nf* politicization.

politiser /pɔlitize/ [1] I *vtr* to politicize.

II **se politiser** *vpr* [*personne, mouvement, association, conflit*] to become politicized.

politologie /pɔlitɔlɔʒi/ *nf* political science.

politologue /pɔlitɔlɔg/ ▶ **510** *nmf* political scientist.

polka /pɔlka/ *nf* polka; **danser une ~** to do a polka.

pollen /pɔl(l)ɛn/ *nm* pollen.

pollinique /pɔl(l)inik/ *adj* pollen (*épith*).

pollinisateur, -trice /pɔl(l)inizatœʀ, tʀis/ I *adj* pollinating (*épith*).

II *nm* pollinator.

pollinisation /pɔl(l)inizasjɔ̃/ *nf* pollination.

polluant, ~e /pɔl(l)ɥɑ̃, ɑ̃t/ I *adj* polluting.

II *nm* pollutant.

polluer /pɔl(l)ɥe/ [1] *vtr* to pollute.

pollueur, -euse /pɔl(l)ɥœʀ, øz/ I *adj* polluting.

II *nm,f* (usine) polluter, factory responsible for pollution.

pollution /pɔl(l)ysjɔ̃/ *nf* lit, fig pollution ¢ (**par** caused by); **~ de l'air/l'eau** air/water pollution; **taux de ~** pollution level; **~s d'origine agricole** pollution from agricultural sources.

■ **~ nocturne** wet dream, nocturnal emission spéc.

polo /pɔlo/ *nm* **1** (vêtement) polo shirt; **2** ▶ **449** (sport) polo.

polochon○ /pɔlɔʃɔ̃/ *nm* bolster; **bataille (à coups) de ~s** pillow fight.

Pologne /pɔlɔɲ/ ▶ **321** *nprf* Poland.

polonais, ~e /pɔlɔnɛ, ɛz/ I ▶ **537** *adj* Polish.

II ▶ **462** *nm* Ling Polish.

III **polonaise** *nf* **1** Danse, Mus polonaise; **2** Culin *pastry with meringue topping, flavoured*GB *with Kirsch.*

Polonais, ~e /pɔlɔnɛ, ɛz/ ▶ **537** *nm,f* Pole.

poltron, -onne /pɔltʀɔ̃, ɔn/ I *adj* cowardly.

II *nm,f* coward.

poltronnerie /pɔltʀɔnʀi/ *nf* cowardice.

polyacide /pɔliasid/ *adj, nm* polyacid.

polyacrylique /pɔliakʀilik/ *adj* polyacrylic.

polyalcool /pɔlialkɔl/ *nm* polyalcohol.

polyamide /pɔliamid/ *nm* polyamide; **en ~** polyamide (*épith*).

polyandre /pɔliɑ̃dʀ/ *adj* polyandrous.

polyandrie /pɔliɑ̃dʀi/ *nf* polyandry.

polyarthrite /pɔliaʀtʀit/ ▶ **271** *nf* polyarthritis.

Polybe /pɔlib/ *npr* Polybius.

polycarbonate /pɔlikaʀbɔnat/ *nm* polycarbonate.

polychlorure /pɔliklɔʀyʀ/ *nm* **~ de vinyle** polyvinyl chloride, PVC.

polychrome /pɔlikʀom/ *adj* polychrome.

polychromie /pɔlikʀomi/ *nf* polychromy.

polyclinique /pɔliklinik/ *nf* private hospital.

polycop○ /pɔlikɔp/ *nm* students' slang duplicated notes (*pl*).

polycopie /pɔlikɔpi/ *nf* **1** (procédé) duplicating; **2** (feuille) duplicate copy.

polycopié, ~e /pɔlikɔpje/ I *adj* duplicated.

II *nm* duplicated notes (*pl*).

polycopier /pɔlikɔpje/ [2] *vtr* to duplicate.

polyculture /pɔlikyltyʀ/ *nf* mixed farming.

polyèdre /pɔliɛdʀ/ I *adj* polyhedral.

II *nm* polyhedron.

polyédrique /pɔliedʀik/ *adj* polyhedral.

polyester /pɔliɛstɛʀ/ *nm* polyester; **en ~** polyester (*épith*).

polyéthylène /pɔlietilɛn/ *nm* polythene GB, polyethylene US; **~ basse/haute densité** low-/high-density polythene ou polyethylene.

polygame /pɔligam/ I *adj* polygamous.

II *nmf* polygamist.

polygamie /pɔligami/ *nf* polygamy.

polyglobulie /pɔliglɔbyli/ ▶ **271** *nf* polycythemia.

polyglotte /pɔliglɔt/ *adj, nmf* polyglot.

polygonal, ~e, *mpl* **-aux** /pɔligɔnal, o/ *adj* polygonal.

polygone /pɔligon/ *nm* **1** Math polygon; **2** Mil firing range.

polygraphe /pɔligʀaf/ *nm* (appareil) polygraph.

polyhandicapé, ~e /pɔliɑ̃dikape/ I *adj* multiply handicapped.

II *nm,f* multiply handicapped person; **les ~s** the multiply handicapped.

polyinsaturé, ~e /pɔliɛ̃satyʀe/ *adj* polyunsaturated.

polymère /pɔlimɛʀ/ I *adj* polymeric.

II *nm* polymer.

polymérisation /pɔlimeʀizasjɔ̃/ *nf* polymerization.

polymériser /pɔlimeʀize/ [1] *vtr, vi* to polymerize.

polymétallique /pɔlimetalik/ *adj* polymetallic.

Polymnie /pɔlimni/ *npr* Polyhymnia.

polymorphe /pɔlimɔʀf/ *adj* polymorphous.

polymorphisme /pɔlimɔʀfism/ *nm* polymorphism.

Polynésie /pɔlinezi/ ▶ **692** *nprf* Polynesia.

polynésien, -ienne /pɔlinezjɛ̃, ɛn/ I *adj* Polynesian.

II *nm* Ling Polynesian.

Polynésien, -ienne /pɔlinezjɛ̃, ɛn/ *nm,f* Polynesian.

polynévrite /pɔlinevʀit/ ▶ **271** *nf* polyneuritis.

polynôme /pɔlinom/ *nm* polynomial.

polynucléaire /pɔlinykleɛʀ/ I *adj* polynuclear.

II *nm* polymorphonuclear leucocyte GB ou leukocyte US.

polype /pɔlip/ *nm* Méd, Zool polyp.

polypeptide /pɔlipɛptid/ *nm* polypeptide.

polyphasé, ~e /pɔlifaze/ *adj* polyphase (*épith*).

polyphonie /pɔlifɔni/ *nf* Mus polyphony.

polyphonique /pɔlifɔnik/ *adj* Mus polyphonic.

polypier /pɔlipje/ *nm* polypary.

polypode /pɔlipɔd/ *nm* polypody.

polypore /pɔlipɔʀ/ *nm* polypore, pore fungus.

■ **~ du bouleau** birch polypore; **~ écailleux** scaly polypore; **~ luisant** lucid bracket.

polypropylène /pɔlipʀɔpilɛn/ *nm* polypropylene.

polyptyque /pɔliptik/ *nm* polyptych.

polysémie /pɔlisemi/ *nf* polysemy.

polysémique /pɔlisemik/ *adj* polysemous.

polystyrène /pɔlistiʀɛn/ *nm* polystyrene; **~ expansé** expanded polystyrene GB, cellular polystyrene US, Styrofoam® US.

polysyllabe /pɔlisil(l)ab/ *nm* polysyllable.

polysyllabique /pɔlisil(l)abik/ *adj* polysyllabic.

polytechnicien, -ienne /pɔlitɛknisjɛ̃, ɛn/ *nm,f*: *graduate of the École Polytechnique.*

polytechnique /pɔlitɛknik/ *adj* polytechnic.

Polytechnique /pɔlitɛknik/ *nf*: *Grande École of Science and Technology.*

polythéisme /pɔliteism/ *nm* polytheism.

polythéiste /pɔliteist/ I *adj* polytheistic.

II *nmf* polytheist.

polytransfusé, ~e /pɔlitʀɑ̃sfyse/ *nm,f*: *person who has undergone repeated blood transfusions.*

polyuréthane /pɔliyʀetan/ *nm* polyurethane.

polyvalence /pɔlivalɑ̃s/ *nf* **1** (d'appareil, de matériel) versatility; **2** (d'employé, de professeur) flexibility; **3** Chimie, Méd polyvalence.

polyvalent, ~e /pɔlivalɑ̃, ɑ̃t/ I *adj* Chimie, Méd polyvalent; [*matériel, appareil*] multipurpose (*épith*), multifunctional; [*employé, secrétaire*] who does several jobs (*après n*); [*professeur*] teaching several subjects (*après n*); **inspecteur ~** Fisc tax inspector (*checking company tax returns*).

II *nm* tax inspector (*checking company tax returns*).

III **polyvalente** *nf* C comprehensive school.

polyvinyle /pɔlivinil/ *nm* polyvinyl.

polyvinylique /pɔlivinilik/ *adj* polyvinyl (*épith*).

polyvision /pɔlivizjɔ̃/ *nf* multiple screen projection.

Poméranie /pɔmeʀani/ ▶ **692** *nprf* Pomerania.

pommade /pɔmad/ *nf* Méd ointment.

IDIOMES **passer de la ~**○ **à qn** to butter sb up○.

pomme /pɔm/ *nf* **1** (fruit) apple ▶ **trois**; **2** (d'arrosoir) rose; (de douche) shower-head; (de canne) pommel, knob; (de mât) truck; (d'escalier) knob; **3**○ (benêt) mug○ GB, sucker○; **ça va encore être pour ma ~** (ennui) I'm in for it again○; (tour de payer) it looks like it's my turn to pay again.

■ **~ d'Adam** Anat Adam's apple; **~ d'amour** tomato; (confiserie) toffee apple GB, candy apple US; **~ d'api** ≈ small apple; **~ de cajou** cashew apple; **~ cannelle** sweetsop; **~ à cidre** cider apple; **~ à couteau** eating apple; **~ à cuire** cooking apple; **~ de discorde** fig bone of contention; **~ épineuse** thorn apple; **la ~ de Newton** fig Newton's apple; **~ de pin** pine cone; **~ rose** rose apple; **~ de terre** potato; **~ de terre en robe des champs** potato boiled in its skin; **~s allumettes** potato straws GB, shoestring potatoes US; **~s chips** crisps GB, potato chips US; **~s dauphine** dauphine potatoes;

~s frites chips GB, (French) fries; **~s à l'huile** ≈ potato salad; **~s mousseline** creamed potatoes (*with egg yolk and cream*); **~s vapeur** steamed potatoes.

IDIOMES **tomber dans les ~s**○ to faint, to pass out○; **être dans les ~s**○ to be out cold○, to have fainted.

pommé, **~e** /pɔme/ *adj* [*chou, laitue*] with a firm heart (*épith, après n*).

pommeau, *pl* **~x** /pɔmo/ *nm* (de canne, rampe) knob; (d'épée, de selle) pommel.

pommelé, **~e** /pɔmle/ *adj* **cheval ~** dappled horse; **cheval gris ~** dapple-grey GB ou dapple-gray US horse; **un ciel ~** a mackerel sky.

pommelle /pɔmɛl/ *nf* filter (*over a pipe*).

pommer /pɔme/ [1] *vi* [*chou, salade*] to form a heart.

pommeraie /pɔmʀɛ/ *nf* apple orchard.

pommette /pɔmɛt/ ▶ **188** *nf* cheekbone; **~s saillantes** high cheekbones.

pommier /pɔmje/ *nm* (arbre) apple tree; (bois) apple, apple-wood.

■ **~ du Japon** Japanese crab apple (tree); **~ sauvage** crab apple tree.

Pomone /pɔmɔn/ *npr* Pomona.

pompage /pɔ̃paʒ/ *nm* pumping.

■ **~ optique** Phys optical pumping.

pompe /pɔ̃p/ **I** *nf* **1** (appareil) pump; **~ à bicyclette** bicycle pump; **2**○ (chaussure) shoe; **3** (apparat) pomp; **en grande ~** with great pomp; **4**○ Sport (exercice) press-up GB, push-up; **faire des ~s** to do push-ups; **5**● soldiers' slang (classe) **soldat de première ~** ≈ lance corporal; **soldat de seconde ~** private.

II pompes *nfpl* Relig vanities; **les ~s de Satan** Satan's pomps.

■ **~ à air** air pump; **~ auxiliaire** backing pump; **~ à eau** water pump; **~ à chaleur** heat pump; **~ à essence** petrol pump GB, gas pump US; **~ à fric**○ fig *drain on one's funds* ou *resources*; **~ à incendie** fire engine; **~ à vide** vacuum pump; **~s funèbres** (lieu) undertaker's (*sg*) GB, funeral home (*sg*) US; (entreprise) undertaker's GB, funeral director's.

IDIOMES **avoir un coup de ~** to be knackered○ GB ou pooped○; **à toute ~**○ at top speed, as quickly as possible; **marcher** or **être à côté de ses ~s**○ not to be with it, to be away with the fairies○.

Pompée /pɔ̃pe/ *npr* Pompey.

Pompéi /pɔ̃pei/ ▶ **857** *npr* Pompeii.

pompéien, **-ienne** /pɔ̃pejɛ̃, ɛn/ ▶ **857** *adj* Pompeian.

Pompéien, **-ienne** /pɔ̃pejɛ̃, ɛn/ *nm,f* Pompeian.

pomper /pɔ̃pe/ [1] *vtr* **1** (aspirer) to pump [*liquide, air*]; (pour vider) to pump out; (pour faire monter) to pump up; **~ de l'eau** to pump water; **2**○ students' slang (copier) to copy (**sur** from), to crib (**sur** from); **il leur a pompé toutes ses idées** he cribbed all their ideas; **3**○ (fatiguer) to knacker○ GB, to poop○; **je suis pompé aujourd'hui** I'm knackered○ GB ou pooped○ today.

IDIOMES **~ l'air de qn**○ to get on sb's nerves.

pompette○ /pɔ̃pɛt/ *adj* tipsy○, drunk.

pompeusement /pɔ̃pøzmɑ̃/ *adv* pompously.

pompeux, **-euse** /pɔ̃pø, øz/ *adj* pompous.

pompier, **-ière** /pɔ̃pje, ɛʀ/ **I** *adj* [*style, artiste, écrivain*] pompous.

II ▶ **510** *nm* fireman, firefighter; **appeler les ~s** to call the fire brigade GB or fire department US; **femme ~** female firefighter.

pompiste /pɔ̃pist/ ▶ **510** *nmf* petrol GB ou gas US pump attendant.

pompon /pɔ̃pɔ̃/ *nm* (de bonnet, frange) bobble; (de pantoufle) pompom; **bonnet à ~** bobble hat.

IDIOMES **à toi le ~**○**!** iron you beat the lot!; **c'est le ~**○**!** iron that's the limit!; **remporter** or **décrocher le ~** to come top, to win first prize.

pomponner /pɔ̃pɔne/ [1] **I** *vtr* **~ un bébé** to get a baby dressed up.

II se pomponner *vpr* to get dolled up; **toujours bien pomponné** always nicely turned out.

ponant /pɔnɑ̃/ *nm* **1** (vent) west wind; **2**† (ouest) liter west.

ponçage /pɔ̃saʒ/ *nm* **1** Tech (de bois, mur) sanding; (de cuir) smoothing; **2** (à la pierre ponce) pumicing.

ponce /pɔ̃s/ *nf* Art (sachet) pounce bag; (morceau de feutre) pounce pad; **pierre ~** pumice stone.

Ponce /pɔ̃s/ *npr* **~ Pilate** Pontius Pilate.

poncer /pɔ̃se/ [12] *vtr* **1** Tech (pour décaper) to sand; **2** Art (pour reproduire) to pounce; **3** (à la pierre ponce) to pumice.

ponceuse /pɔ̃søz/ *nf* sander; **~ à bande/vibrante** belt/orbital sander.

poncho /pɔ̃ʃo/ *nm* poncho.

poncif /pɔ̃sif/ *nm* **1** (banalité) cliché, commonplace; **2** Art stencil (*for pouncing*).

ponction /pɔ̃ksjɔ̃/ *nf* **1** Méd puncture; **~ lombaire** lumbar puncture; **2** (en argent) levy; **les ~s fiscales** tax levies.

ponctionner /pɔ̃ksjɔne/ [1] *vtr* **1** Méd (perforer) to puncture; (extraire) to tap [*liquide*]; **2** (de l'argent) to levy [*somme*]; **~ 5 millions** to levy 5 million; **~ le budget de la Défense** to tap the Defence[GB] budget.

ponctualité /pɔ̃ktɥalite/ *nf* **1** (exactitude) punctuality; **avec ~** punctually; **2** (minutie) liter meticulousness; **avec ~** meticulously.

ponctuation /pɔ̃ktɥasjɔ̃/ *nf* Ling punctuation; **signes de ~** punctuation marks.

ponctuel, **-elle** /pɔ̃ktɥɛl/ *adj* **1** (à l'heure) [*personne*] punctual; [*paiement*] prompt; **2** (méticuleux) meticulous; **3** (ne portant pas sur l'ensemble) [*action, opération*] (limitée) limited; (localisée) localized; (ciblée) selective; [*problème*] isolated; **débrayages ~s dans une usine** selective stoppages in a factory; **4** Ling punctual.

ponctuellement /pɔ̃ktɥɛlmɑ̃/ *adj* **1** (à l'heure) [*arriver, répondre*] punctually; [*payer*] promptly; **2** (avec assiduité) meticulously; **3** (en ciblant) selectively.

ponctuer /pɔ̃ktɥe/ [1] *vtr* lit, fig to punctuate (**de** with).

pondéral, **~e**, *mpl* **-aux** /pɔ̃deʀal, o/ *adj* weight (*épith*).

pondérateur, **-trice** /pɔ̃deʀatœʀ, tʀis/ *adj* [*élément*] stabilizing.

pondération /pɔ̃deʀasjɔ̃/ *nf* **1** (de personne) levelheadedness; **elle fait preuve de beaucoup de ~** she is very levelheaded; **2** (équilibrage) balancing; (équilibre) balance (**entre** between); **3** Stat (d'indice) weighting.

pondéré, **~e** /pɔ̃deʀe/ *adj* **1** [*personne, attitude*] levelheaded; **2** Stat [*indice*] weighted.

pondérer /pɔ̃deʀe/ [14] *vtr* **1** (équilibrer) to balance; **2** Stat to weight [*indice*].

pondéreux, **-euse** /pɔ̃deʀø, øz/ **I** *adj* [*matière*] heavy.

II *nmpl* **les ~** heavy goods.

pondeur○ /pɔ̃dœʀ/ *nm* péj prolific writer; **c'est un ~ d'articles** he churns out○ articles.

pondeuse /pɔ̃døz/ **I** *adj f* **poule ~** layer, laying hen.

II *nf* **1** (poule) **bonne ~** good layer; **2**○ (mère) pej prolific breeder.

pondre /pɔ̃dʀ/ [6] *vtr* **1** Zool to lay [*œuf*]; **la poule ne pond pas en ce moment** the hen is not laying at the moment; **où les oiseaux/poissons pondent-ils?** where do birds/fish lay their eggs?; **2**○ (produire) to produce [*poème, article*]; to churn out○ péj [*poèmes, articles*]; to produce [*enfant*]; **j'ai pondu mon rapport en deux heures** I produced my report in two hours.

poney /pɔnɛ/ *nm* pony; **faire du ~** to go pony-riding.

pongé /pɔ̃ʒe/ *nm* pongee.

pongiste /pɔ̃ʒist/ ▶ **449** *nmf* table-tennis player.

pont /pɔ̃/ **I** *nm* **1** Archit, Constr bridge; **franchir un ~** to cross a bridge; **2** (liens) fig link (**avec** with), tie (**avec** with); **couper les ~s** to break off all contact; **il a coupé les ~s avec sa famille** he has broken with his family; **3** (vacances) extended weekend (*including day(s) between a public holiday and a weekend*); **faire le ~** to make a long weekend of it; **lundi je fais le ~** I'm taking Monday off; **4** Naut deck; **tout le monde sur le ~!** all hands on deck!; **~ principal/supérieur** main/upper deck; **~ avant/~ arrière** foredeck/reardeck; **bâtiment à deux ~s** two-decker; **5** Aut axle; **~ avant/arrière** front/rear axle; **6** Sport crab; **faire le ~** to do the crab; **7** Électrotech bridge (circuit).

II ponts *nmpl* **~s (et chaussées)** highways department; ▶ **école**.

■ **~ aérien** airlift; **~ aux ânes** lit pons asinorum; fig truism; **~ basculant** bascule bridge; **~ de bateaux** pontoon bridge; **~ à béquilles** portal bridge; **~ élévateur** hydraulic ramp; **~ d'envol** flight deck; **~ flottant** pontoon bridge; **~ de graissage** hydraulic ramp; **~ levant** vertical-lift bridge; **~ mobile** movable bridge; **~ à péage** toll bridge; **~ roulant** (overhead) travelling[GB] crane; **~ suspendu** suspension bridge; **~ thermique** thermal bridge; **~ tournant** swing bridge; **~ transbordeur** transporter bridge; **Pont des Soupirs** Bridge of Sighs.

IDIOMES **coucher sous les ~s** to sleep rough, to be a tramp; **il coulera beaucoup d'eau sous les ~s avant que...** it will be a long time before...; **brûler les ~s derrière soi** to burn one's boats ou bridges; **faire un ~ d'or à qn** to offer sb a large sum to accept a job.

Pont /pɔ̃/ *nprm* Antiq **le (royaume du) ~** Pontus.

pontage /pɔ̃taʒ/ *nm* Méd bypass (operation); **faire un ~ à qn** to carry out ou to do a bypass operation on sb; **il a eu un ~** he had a bypass operation.

Pont-à-Mousson /pɔ̃tamusɔ̃/ ▶ **857** *npr* Pont-à-Mousson.

ponte /pɔ̃t/ **I** *nm*○ **1** (personnage) big shot○; **2** (au jeu) punter.

II *nf* (action) laying (*of eggs*); (œufs) clutch; **~ ovulaire** ovulation.

ponter /pɔ̃te/ [1] **I** *vtr* **1** Naut to deck; **2** Jeux (miser) to bet.

II *vi* Jeux to punt, to play against the bank.

Pont-Euxin /pɔ̃tøksɛ̃/ *nprm* Antiq **le ~** the Euxine Sea, Pontus Euxinus.

pontife /pɔ̃tif/ *nm* **1** Relig pontiff; **le souverain ~** the pope; **2**○ (personnage important) pundit○.

pontifical, **~e**, *mpl* **-aux** /pɔ̃tifikal, o/ **I** *adj* [*trône, autorité, garde*] papal; [*messe, célébration*] pontifical; **la visite ~e** the pope's visit.

II *nm* (livre) pontifical.

pontificat /pɔ̃tifika/ *nm* pontificate.

pontifier /pɔ̃tifje/ [2] *vi* to pontificate.

pont-levis, *pl* **ponts-levis** /pɔ̃ləvi/ *nm* drawbridge.

ponton /pɔ̃tɔ̃/ *nm* Naut (débarcadère) (floating) landing stage; (plate-forme) pontoon; (vieux navire) hulk.

pontonnier /pɔ̃tɔnje/ *nm* Mil pontonier.

pool /pul/ *nm* Écon pool.

■ **~ de dactylos** Admin typing pool.

pop /pɔp/ *adj inv*, *nm* ou *nf* pop.

■ **~ music** pop music.

pop'art /pɔpaʀ(t)/ *nm* pop art.

pop-corn, *pl* **~s** /pɔpkɔʀn/ *nm* popcorn ₵.

pope /pɔp/ *nm* pope, orthodox priest.

popeline /pɔplin/ *nf* poplin; **une chemise en ~** a poplin shirt.

popote○ /pɔpɔt/ **I** *adj inv* péj **c'est un type du genre ~** he's the stay-at-home type.

II *nf* **1** (cuisine) cooking; **faire la ~** to do the cooking; **2** Mil† mess; **faire la tournée des ~s** fig to go on a tour of inspection.

popotin○ /pɔpɔtɛ̃/ *nm* bum○ GB, rear○, bottom.

populace /pɔpylas/ *nf* **la ~** the masses (*pl*); **une ~** a rabble.

populaire /pɔpylɛʀ/ *adj* **1** (ouvrier) [*quartier, banlieue*] working-class; [*littérature, art, roman*] popular; [*édition*] cheap; [*restaurant*] basic; **être d'origine ~** to be from a working-class background; **il écrit pour un public ~** he writes for ordinary people; **classe ~** working class; **2** (entériné par la tradition) [*tradition*] folk; **culture ~** folklore; **le bon sens ~** popular wisdom; **3** (estimé) popular (**chez, parmi** with); **4** (venant du peuple) [*révolte, mouvement*] popular; [*volonté, colère, pouvoir, souveraineté*] of the people; **5** Ling (utilisé par le peuple) popular; (grossier)vulgar; **6** Géog, Pol [*république, démocratie*] people's.

populairement /pɔpylɛʀmɑ̃/ *adv* popularly; **~ appelé** popularly known as; **parler ~** to speak commonly.

popularisation /pɔpylaʀizasjɔ̃/ *nf* **1** (propagation) popularization; **2** (popularité) increasing popularity.

populariser /pɔpylaʀize/ [1] **I** *vtr* to popularize.

II se populariser *vpr* to become very popular.

popularité /pɔpylaʀite/ *nf* popularity (**auprès de** with, among); **avoir une grande ~ auprès des élèves** to be very popular with ou among the pupils.

population /pɔpylasjɔ̃/ *nf* population; **la ~ du globe** the population of the world; **la ~ étudiante/carcérale/agricole** the student/prison/farming population; **la ~ locale** the local community; **l'hôpital peut recevoir une ~ de mille malades** the hospital can take one thousand patients; **la prison a été construite pour une ~ de mille prisonniers** the prison was built for one thousand inmates.

■ **~ active** Sociol working population.

populeux, **-euse** /pɔpylø, øz/ *adj* densely populated, populous.

populisme /pɔpylism/ *nm* **1** Pol populism; **2** Littérat Populism (*French literary movement founded in 1929*).

populiste /pɔpylist/ **I** *adj* **1** Pol populist; **2** Littérat *relating to the Populism movement in French literature.*

II *nmf* **1** Pol populist; **2** Littérat *adherent of Populism in French literature.*

populo○ /pɔpylo/ *nm* masses (*pl*); **attirer du ~** to pull in the crowds; **il y a du ~** there are crowds of people.

porc /pɔʀ/ *nm* **1** (animal) pig, hog US; (viande) pork; (peau) pigskin; **2**○ péj (personne) pig○.

porcelaine /pɔʀsəlɛn/ *nf* **1** (matière) porcelain, china; **en ~** porcelain ou china (*épith*); **~ de Chine** china; **~ de Sèvres/Limoges** Sèvres/Limoges china ou porcelain; **~ vitreuse** vitreous china; ▸**éléphant**; **2** (objet) piece of porcelain; **3** Zool cowrie.

porcelainier, **-ière** /pɔʀsəlɛnje, ɛʀ/ **I** *adj* porcelain.

II ▸**510** *nm,f* porcelain manufacturer.

porcelet /pɔʀsəlɛ/ *nm* piglet.

porc-épic, *pl* **~s** /pɔʀkepik/ *nm* porcupine.

porche /pɔʀʃ/ *nm* porch; **sous le ~** in the porch.

porcher /pɔʀʃe/ ▸**510** *nm* pig keeper.

porcherie /pɔʀʃəʀi/ *nf* lit, fig pigsty.

porcin, **~e** /pɔʀsɛ̃, in/ **I** *adj* **1** Agric [*race*] porcine; **élevage ~** pig breeding; **viande ~e** pork; **2** fig [*visage, yeux*] piggy, porcine; [*manières*] swinish.

II *nm* pig; **les ~s** pigs.

pore /pɔʀ/ *nm* pore; **suant la peur par tous les ~s** fig exuding fear.

poreux, **-euse** /pɔʀø, øz/ *adj* porous.

porion /pɔʀjɔ̃/ ▸**510** *nm* Mines foreman.

porno○ /pɔʀno/ **I** *adj* porno○, porn○.

II *nm* Cin (genre) porn○; (film) blue movie○.

pornographe /pɔʀnɔgʀaf/ **I** *adj* pornographic.

II *nmf* pornographer.

pornographie /pɔʀnɔgʀafi/ *nf* pornography.

pornographique /pɔʀnɔgʀafik/ *adj* pornographic.

porosité /pɔʀozite/ *nf* porosity.

porphyre /pɔʀfiʀ/ *nm* porphyry.

porphyrique /pɔʀfiʀik/ *adj* porphyritic.

port /pɔʀ/ *nm* **1** (pour accoster) harbour[GB]; (avec installations portuaires) port; **~ naturel/artificiel** natural/artificial harbour[GB]; **~ maritime** or **de mer** maritime port, seaport; **~ fluvial** river port; **~ de commerce** commercial ou trading port; **~ industriel** industrial port; **les restaurants du ~** the restaurants along the harbour[GB]; **flâner sur le ~** to stroll around the harbour[GB]; **travailler au ~** to work in ou at the port; **ouvriers du ~** port workers; **entrer au ~** to come into port; **sortir du ~** to leave port; **entrée au ~** entering port; **2** (ville portuaire) port; **3** (refuge) haven; **4** (fait de porter) **le ~ de l'uniforme** wearing uniform; **~ illégal de décorations** wearing medals fraudulently; **le ~ du casque est obligatoire** helmets must be worn at all times; **le ~ de la barbe est interdit** beards may not be worn; **~ d'armes** carrying arms; **5** (maintien) carriage; (démarche) bearing; **un joli ~ de tête** a graceful carriage of the head; **6** Transp carriage; Postes postage; **~ dû/payé** or **gratuit** Transp carriage forward/paid; Postes postage due/paid; **7** Ordinat port.

■ **~ d'aéroglisseurs** hoverport; **~ artificiel** Mil artificial harbour[GB]; **~ d'attache** Naut port of registry; fig home base; **~ autonome** autonomous port; **~ de bras** Danse port de bras; **~ d'entrée** port of entry; **~ d'escale** port of call; **~ franc** free port; **~ militaire** naval base; **~ de pêche** (installations) fishing harbour[GB]; (ville) fishing port; **~ pétrolier** tanker terminal; **~ de plaisance** marina; **~ de salut** haven.

IDIOMES **arriver à bon ~** to arrive safe and sound.

portable /pɔʀtabl/ *adj* **1** (portatif) portable; **2** (pas trop lourd) **c'est ~** it can be carried; **3** (mettable) [*robe, pull*] wearable; **ce n'est pas ~** it's unwearable.

portage /pɔʀtaʒ/ *nm* **1** (transport à dos d'homme) porterage; **2** Naut (halage à sec) portage.

portail /pɔʀtaj/ *nm* (de parc, jardin) gate; (d'église, de temple) great door.

portance /pɔʀtɑ̃s/ *nf* Aviat lift.

portant, **~e** /pɔʀtɑ̃, ɑ̃t/ **I** *adj* **1** [*mur*] load-bearing; [*roue*] carrying; **2** [*personne*] **bien ~** in good health; **mal ~** in poor health; **être mieux ~** to be in better health.

II *nm* **1** Théât side strut; **2** Naut (d'aviron) rigger.

IDIOMES **à bout ~** at point-blank range.

portatif, **-ive** /pɔʀtatif, iv/ *adj* portable; **ordinateur ~** laptop computer.

porte /pɔʀt/ **I** *adj* [*veine*] portal.

II *nf* **1** (entrée) (de bâtiment) door; (de parc, stade, jardin) gate; **la ~ de derrière/devant** the back/front door; **la ~ du jardin** the garden gate; **devant la ~ de l'hôpital** outside the hospital; **je me suis garée devant la ~** I've parked right outside; **avoir une gare à sa ~** to have a station on one's doorstep; **Grenoble est aux ~s des Alpes** Grenoble is the gateway to the Alps; **aux ~s du désert** at the edge of the desert; **passer la ~** to enter the house; **ouverture/fermeture des ~s à 18 heures** doors open/close at 6 o'clock; **ouvrir sa ~ à qn** to let sb in; **ouvrir la ~ à la critique** to invite criticism; **c'est la ~ ouverte à la criminalité** it's an open invitation to crime; **ouvrir/fermer ses ~s (au public)** [*salon, exposition, magasin*] to open/close (to the public); **l'entreprise a fermé ses ~s** the company has gone out of business; **la Communauté a ouvert ses ~s au Portugal** the Community has admitted Portugal; **mettre à la ~** (exclure d'un cours) to throw [sb] out; (renvoyer) to expel [*élève*]; to fire, to sack○ GB [*employé*]; **ce n'est pas la ~ à côté**○ it's quite far; **voir qn entre deux ~s** to see sb very briefly; **trouver ~ close** or **de bois** to find nobody in; **j'ai mis deux heures, de ~ à ~** it took me two hours (from) door to door; **2** (panneau mobile) (de maison, meuble, d'avion) door; (de jardin, parc, stade) gate; **une ~ en bois/fer** a wooden/an iron door; **se tromper de ~** lit to get the wrong door; fig to come to the wrong place; **frapper à la ~ de qn** lit, fig to knock at sb's door; **frapper à la bonne/mauvaise ~** to come to the right/wrong place; **3** (de ville fortifiée) gate; **aux ~s de la ville** at the city gates; **4** (moyen d'accès) gateway; **la ~ des honneurs** the gateway to honours[GB]; **la victoire leur ouvre la ~ de la finale** the victory clears the way to the final for them; **5** (possibilité) door; **cela ouvre/ferme bien des ~s** it opens/closes many doors; **6** (dans un aéroport) gate; **~ numéro 10** gate number 10; **7** Sport (en ski) gate; **8** (portière) door; **une voiture à deux/cinq ~s** a two-/five-door car; **9** Électron gate.

■ **~ basculante** up-and-over door; **~ bâtarde** medium-sized door; **~ battante** swing door; **~ coulissante** sliding door; **~ d'écluse** lock gate; **~ d'entrée** (de maison) front door; (d'église, hôpital, immeuble) main entrance; **~ pliante** folding door; **~ de service** tradesmen's entrance GB, service entrance; **~ de sortie** lit exit; fig escape route; **~ à tambour** revolving door; **~ tournante** = **~ à tambour**; **~ vitrée** glass door; **les ~s de l'Enfer** Relig the gates of Hell; **~s ouvertes** open day GB, open house US; **journée** or **opération ~s ouvertes à l'école** the school is organizing an open day GB ou open house US; **les ~s du Paradis** Relig the gates of Heaven.

IDIOMES **prendre la ~** to leave; **entrer par la petite/grande ~** to start at the bottom/top; **enfoncer une ~ ouverte** to state the obvious; **il faut qu'une ~ soit ouverte ou fermée** Prov you've got to decide one way or the other; ▸**balayer**.

porté, **~e** /pɔʀte/ **I** *pp* ▸**porter**.

II *pp adj* **être ~ à se plaindre** to be inclined to complain; **être ~ au pessimisme** to be inclined to be pessimistic; **je suis ~ à croire que** I'm inclined to think that; **être ~ sur qch** to be keen on sth; **être ~ sur la chose** or **la bagatelle**† euph to like it○, to be keen on sex.

III *nm* Danse porté.

IV portée *nf* **1** (distance) range; **arme de longue/courte/moyenne ~e** long-/short-/medium-range weapon; **être à ~e de canon** to be within firing range; **missile d'une ~e de 900 kilomètres** missile with a range of 900 kilometres[GB]; **être hors de ~e** to be out of reach; **être à la ~e de qn** to be within sb's reach; **'tenir hors de ~e des enfants'**, **'ne pas laisser à la ~e des enfants'** 'keep out of reach of children'; **être à ~e de main** or **à la ~e de la main** (accessible) to be within reach; (dans endroit commode) to be to hand; **je le garde à ~e de main** (accessible) I keep it where I can reach it; (dans endroit commode) I keep it to hand; **être à ~e de voix** to be within earshot; **ne pas être à ~e de voix** to be out of earshot; **2** (niveau) **c'est à ta ~e** (faisable) you can do it; (compréhensible) you're capable of understanding it; (en prix) it's within your means; **c'est à la ~e de**

n'importe qui (faisable) anybody can do it; (compréhensible) anybody can understand it; (en prix) anybody can afford it; **ce n'est pas à la ~e de toutes les bourses** not everybody can afford it; **se mettre à la ~e de qn** to come down to sb's level; **3** (effet) impact; **la ~e d'une décision/des paroles de qn** the impact of a decision/of sb's words; **4** (d'animaux) litter; **une ~e de six chatons** a litter of six kittens; **5** Mus staff, stave GB; **6** (de pont, d'arc) span; **7** Mécan (surface d'appui) seat.
■ **~e de noyau** (en métallurgie) core print.

porte-aéronefs /pɔʀtaeʀɔnɛf/ *nm inv* aircraft carrier.

porte-à-faux /pɔʀtafo/ *nm inv* **être en porte à faux** lit [*mur*] to be out of plumb; [*rocher*] to be precariously balanced; Archit [*construction*] to be cantilevered; fig [*personne*] to be in an awkward position.

porte-aiguilles /pɔʀteguij/ *nm inv* needle-case.

porte-à-porte /pɔʀtapɔʀt/ *nm inv* Comm door-to-door selling; Pol door-to-door canvassing; **faire du ~** Comm to be a door-to-door salesperson; Pol to canvas from door to door.

porte-autos /pɔʀtɔto/ *nm inv* (wagon) car-carrier; (camion) car-transporter.

porte-avions /pɔʀtavjɔ̃/ *nm inv* aircraft carrier.

porte-bagages /pɔʀt(ə)bagaʒ/ *nm inv* (sur un vélo) carrier; (dans un train) luggage rack; (dans un avion) overhead locker; (sur un toit de voiture) roof rack.

porte-bébé /pɔʀt(ə)bebe/ *nm inv* (panier) carrycot GB, carrier US; (kangourou®) (baby) sling, baby carrier; (sac à dos) baby carrier.

porte-billets /pɔʀt(ə)bijɛ/ *nm inv* wallet.

porte-bonheur /pɔʀt(ə)bɔnœʀ/ *nm inv* lucky charm, good-luck charm; **offrir du muguet ~** to give lily-of-the-valley for good luck.

porte-bouteilles /pɔʀt(ə)butɛj/ *nm inv* (panier) bottle-carrier, bottleholder; (égouttoir) bottle-drainer.

porte-cartes /pɔʀt(ə)kaʀt/ *nm inv* (pour carte de crédit etc) card wallet; (pour carte routière ou d'état-major) map holder.

porte-char, *pl* **~s** /pɔʀt(ə)ʃaʀ/ *nm* Mil tank transporter.

porte-chéquier /pɔʀt(ə)ʃekje/ *nm inv* cheque book GB ou checkbook US holder.

porte-cigares /pɔʀt(ə)sigaʀ/ *nm inv* cigar case.

porte-cigarettes /pɔʀt(ə)sigaʀɛt/ *nm inv* cigarette case.

porte-clés, porte-clefs /pɔʀt(ə)kle/ *nm inv* key ring.

porte-conteneurs /pɔʀt(ə)kɔ̃tənœʀ/ *nm inv* container ship.

porte-couteau, *pl* **~x** /pɔʀt(ə)kuto/ *nm* knife rest.

porte-crayons /pɔʀt(ə)kʀɛjɔ̃/ *nm inv* pencil holder.

porte-documents /pɔʀt(ə)dɔkymɑ̃/ *nm inv* briefcase, attaché case.

porte-drapeau /pɔʀt(ə)dʀapo/ *nm inv* lit, fig standard-bearer.

porte-étendard /pɔʀtetɑ̃daʀ/ *nm inv* standard-bearer.

portefaix† /pɔʀt(ə)fɛ/ **▶ 510 |** *nm inv* porter.

porte-fenêtre, *pl* **portes-fenêtres** /pɔʀt(ə)fənɛtʀ/ *nf* French window.

portefeuille /pɔʀtəfœj/ **I** *adj* **jupe/robe ~** wrap-over skirt/dress.
II *nm* **1** (à billets) wallet, billfold US; **2** Pol portfolio; **avoir le ~ de la Défense** to hold the defence[GB] portfolio; **3** Fin portfolio; **un ~ d'actions** a portfolio of shares.
IDIOMES **faire un lit en ~** to make an apple pie bed; **avoir le ~ bien garni** to be well-off; **avoir toujours la main au ~** to be very generous.

porte-fusible /pɔʀt(ə)fyzibl/ *nm inv* fuse holder.

porte-greffes /pɔʀt(ə)gʀɛf/ *nm inv* stock (for graft).

porte-hélicoptères /pɔʀtelikɔptɛʀ/ *nm inv* helicopter carrier.

porte-jarretelles /pɔʀt(ə)ʒaʀtɛl/ *nm inv* suspender belt GB, garter belt US.

portemanteau, *pl* **~x** /pɔʀt(ə)mɑ̃to/ *nm* **1** (au mur) (patère) (coat) peg ou hook; (collectif) coat rack; (sur pied) coat stand, clothes tree US; **donne-moi ta veste, je vais la mettre au ~** give me your jacket, I'll hang it up for you; **2** (cintre) coat hanger.

porte-menu, *pl* **~s** /pɔʀt(ə)məny/ *nm* menu holder.

portemine /pɔʀt(ə)min/ *nm* propelling GB ou mechanical US pencil.

porte-monnaie /pɔʀt(ə)mɔnɛ/ *nm inv* purse GB, coin purse US; **faire appel au ~ de qn** fig to ask sb to dip into his/her pocket.

porte-musique /pɔʀt(ə)myzik/ *nm inv* music case.

porte-outil /pɔʀtuti/ *nm inv* Tech chuck.

porte-parapluies /pɔʀt(ə)paʀaplɥi/ *nm inv* umbrella stand.

porte-parole /pɔʀt(ə)paʀɔl/ *nm inv* (personne) spokesperson, spokesman/spokeswoman; (journal) mouthpiece; **se faire le ~ de** [*personne*] to act as a spokesperson for; [*journal*] to be the mouthpiece of.

porte-pipes /pɔʀt(ə)pip/ *nm inv* pipe rack.

porte-plume /pɔʀt(ə)plym/ *nm inv* penholder.

porter /pɔʀte/ [1] **I** *vtr* **1** (transporter) to carry [*chose, personne*]; **~ qn sur son lit** to get sb into bed; **~ qn sur son dos** to carry sb on one's back, to give sb a piggyback○; **tu ne dois rien ~** you mustn't carry anything heavy; **2** (apporter) **~ qch quelque part** to take sth somewhere [*lettre, paquet*]; **~ qch à qn** to take sb sth, to bring sb sth US; **~ des messages** to run messages; **~ la bonne nouvelle** to spread the word; **~ une affaire devant les tribunaux** to bring a case to court; **3** (soutenir) [*mur, chaise*] to carry, to bear [*poids*]; **mes jambes ne me portent plus** my legs are giving out; **l'eau te portera** the water will hold you up; **être porté par le vent** [*sable , papier*] to be blown along by the wind; **~ qn à bout de bras** fig to take on sb's problems; **mes parents sont lourds à ~** my parents are emotionally demanding; **~ l'espoir de millions d'hommes** to be the focus for the hopes of millions; **être porté par un mouvement d'espoir** to be carried along by a surge of optimism; **4** (avoir sur soi) to wear [*robe, bijou, verres de contact*]; to have [*cheveux longs, balafre*]; to have, to wear [*barbe, moustache*]; **~ les armes** to bear arms; **~ une arme** to be armed; **5** (avoir) to have [*initiales, date, titre*]; to bear [*sceau*]; **ne pas ~ de date** not to have a date, to be undated; **ne pas ~ de titre** not to have a title, to be untitled; **portant le numéro 300** with the number 300; **le document porte la mention 'secret '** the document is marked 'secret'; **ils ne portent pas le même nom** they have different names; **quel prénom porte-t-elle?** what's her first name?; **elle porte le nom de son mari** she has taken her husband's name; **le nom que je porte est celui de ma grand-mère** I'm named after my grandmother; **il porte bien son nom** the name suits him; **bien ~ son âge** to look good for one's age; **~ des traces de sang** to be blood-stained; **l'arbre ne portait plus de feuilles** the tree was bare of leaves; **portant une expression de découragement sur son visage** looking discouraged; **~ en soi une grande volonté de réussir** to be full of ambition; **cela ~ en soi quelques risques** it's inherently risky; **6** (produire) to bear [*fleurs*]; **~ des fruits** lit, fig to bear fruit; **l'enfant qu'elle porte** the child she is carrying; **le roman qu'il porte en lui** his great unwritten novel; **7** (amener) **~ qch à** [*situation, événement*] to bring sth to; [*personne, entreprise, administration*] to put sth up to; **cela porte la cotisation/le prix du billet d'avion/le nombre des victimes à...** this brings the subscription/the price of the plane ticket/the death toll to...; **~ un taux/une cotisation à** to put a rate/a subscription up to; **~ la température de l'eau à 80°C** to heat the water to 80°C; **~ qn au pouvoir** to bring sb to power; **~ qn à la tête d'une entreprise** to take sb to the top of a company; **8** (diriger) **~ son regard vers** to look at; **~ qch à sa bouche** to raise sth to one's lips; **~ qch à son oreille** to hold sth to one's ear; **~ la main à son chapeau** to lift one's hat; **si tu portes la main sur elle** if you lay a finger on her; **~ de l'intérêt à qch** to be interested in sth; **l'estime/l'amour qu'elle te porte** her respect/love for you; **~ ses efforts sur qch** to devote one's energies to sth; **~ un jugement sur qch** to pass judgment on sth; **faire ~ ses accusations sur** to direct one's accusations at; **9** (inscrire) **~ qch sur un registre** to enter sth on a register; **~ une somme au crédit de qn** to credit a sum to sb's account; **être porté disparu** to be reported missing; **se faire ~ malade** or **pâle**○ to go○ ou report sick; **~ témoignage** to bear witness; **~ plainte** to lodge a complaint; **10** (inciter) **~ qn à être méfiant** or **à se méfier** to make sb cautious; **tout le porte à la méfiance** everything inclines him to caution; **tout nous porte à croire que** everything leads us to believe that; **11** (donner, causer) **~ partout la mort et la destruction** to spread death and destruction; **~ bonheur** or **chance** to be lucky; **~ malheur** to be unlucky; **ça m'a porté bonheur** it brought me luck; **ça m'a porté malheur** it was unlucky; ▶ **nuit**.
II porter sur *vtr ind* **1** (concerner) **~ sur** [*débat, article*] to be about; [*mesure, accord*] to concern, to apply to; [*interdiction*] to apply to; **l'impôt porte sur les objets de luxe** the tax applies to luxury goods; **l'accent porte sur la deuxième syllabe** the accent is on the second syllable; **2** (reposer sur) **~ sur** [*structure*] to be resting on; **3** (heurter) **~ sur** to hit.
III *vi* **une voix qui porte** a voice that carries; **des arguments qui portent** convincing arguments; **ta critique a porté** your criticism hit home; **le coup a porté** the blow hit home; **~ contre un mur** to hit a wall; **un canon qui porte à 500 mètres** a cannon with a range of 500 metres[GB]; **les mortiers ne portent pas jusqu'ici** we are out of mortar range.
IV se porter *vpr* **1** (se sentir) **elle se porte bien/mal/mieux** [*personne*] she is well/ill/better; [*affaire*] it's going well/badly/better; **comment se porte votre femme?** how is your wife?; **je ne m'en porte pas plus mal** I'm none the worse for it; **je me porte à merveille** I'm absolutely fine; **2** (être mis) [*vêtement, bijou, chapeau*] **cela se porte avec des chaussures plates** you wear it with flat shoes; **les jupes se portent juste au-dessus du genou cet hiver** skirts are being worn just above the knee this year; **cela ne se porte plus** it has gone out of fashion; **3** (aller, se diriger) **se ~ à la rencontre de qn** (aller) to go to meet sb; (venir) to come to meet sb; **se ~ sur** [*soupçon*] to fall on; **le choix se porta sur le vase bleu** they/she etc chose the blue vase; **tous les regards se sont portés vers le ciel/vers lui** everyone looked toward(s) the sky/in his direction; **se ~ à des excès** to overindulge; **4** (se propager) **se ~ sur** to spread to; **ça s'est porté sur les poumons** it spread to the lungs.

porte-revues /pɔʀt(ə)ʀəvy/ *nm inv* magazine rack.

porte-rouleau, *pl* **~x** /pɔʀtʀulo/ *nm* (de papier hygiénique) toilet roll holder; (de papier absorbant) kitchen roll holder.

porte-savon /pɔʀt(ə)savɔ̃/ *nm inv* soapdish.

porte-serviettes /pɔʀt(ə)sɛʀvjɛt/ *nm inv* towel rail.

porte-skis /pɔʀt(ə)ski/ *nm inv* ski rack.

porteur, **-euse** /pɔʀtœʀ, øz/ **I** *adj* **1** gén **être ~ d'espoir** to bring hope; **être ~ d'un passeport grec** to hold a Greek passport; **être ~ d'un virus** to carry a virus; **2** Tech **mur/essieu ~** load-bearing wall/axle; **roue porteuse** Rail carrying wheel; **3** Écon (en expansion) [*marché*] buoyant; [*métier*] booming; **4** Radio, Télécom [*courant, fréquence, onde*] carrier (*épith*); **5** Astronaut, Aviat, Mil **missile ~ d'une charge nucléaire** missile carrying a nuclear payload; **appareil gros ~** jumbo aircraft; **6** Fin **être ~ d'intérêts** [*compte*] to bear interest; **7** Ling **être ~ de sens** to have a meaning; **unité porteuse de sens** meaningful unit.

II *nm,f* **1** (possesseur) holder, bearer; **~ d'une carte de crédit** credit-card holder; **les ~s de diplômes étrangers** people who hold foreign qualifications; **2** Méd carrier.

III *nm* **1** ▶510 (de bagages) porter; (coursier) messenger; **2** Fin (de chèque) bearer; **~ d'actions** shareholder; **~ d'obligations** bondholder; **titre/chèque au ~** bearer security/cheque GB ou check US; ▶**petit**; **3** Télécom carrier current.

IV porteuse *nf* Télécom carrier wave.

■ **~ d'eau** water carrier; **~ sain** Méd symptom-free carrier.

porte-vélo /pɔʀt(ə)velo/ *nm inv* bicycle rack.

porte-verre /pɔʀt(ə)vɛʀ/ *nm inv* (wall) glass holder.

porte-voix /pɔʀt(ə)vwa/ *nm inv* megaphone; **les mains en ~** his/her hands cupped around his/her mouth.

portier /pɔʀtje/ *nm* **1** ▶510 (concierge) porter; **~ de nuit** night porter; **2**○ (gardien de but) goalkeeper.

■ **~ électronique** numeric keypad.

portière /pɔʀtjɛʀ/ *nf* **1** Aut door; **jeter qch par la ~** to throw sth out of the car window; **2** (tenture) portiere; **3** Mil raft.

portillon /pɔʀtijɔ̃/ *nm* gate.

IDIOMES **se bousculer au ~**○ [*personnes*] to fall over each other; [*idées, événements*] to crowd in; **ça ne se bouscule pas au ~**○ people are not exactly queueing GB ou lining US up.

portion /pɔʀsjɔ̃/ *nf* **1** Culin (part) portion; (quantité servie) helping; **10 francs la ~** 10 francs per portion; **double ~ pour tout le monde!** double helpings for everyone!; **2** (dans un partage) share; **3** (partie) gén portion; (de route) stretch; (de territoire) part.

■ **~ congrue** (nourriture) minute portion of food; (revenu) minimal income; **réduire qn à la ~ congrue** to give sb the strict minimum.

portique /pɔʀtik/ *nm* **1** Archit portico; **2** Sport frame (in gym); **3** (pour enfants) climbing frame.

■ **~ électronique de sécurité** Aviat antimetal detector frame; Aut **~ de lavage** (automatic) car-wash.

porto /pɔʀto/ *nm* port.

■ **~ flip** egg flip (*with port*).

Porto-Novo /pɔʀtonovo/ ▶857 *npr* Porto Novo.

portoricain, **~e** /pɔʀtoʀikɛ̃, ɛn/ ▶537 *adj* Puerto Rican.

Portoricain, **~e** /pɔʀtoʀikɛ̃, ɛn/ ▶537 *nm,f* Puerto Rican.

Porto Rico /pɔʀtoʀiko/ ▶321, 416 *nprf* Puerto Rico.

portrait /pɔʀtʀɛ/ *nm* **1** Art, Phot portrait; **c'est un ~ fidèle** it's a good likeness; **un ~ peu flatteur** an unflattering portrait; **~ de famille** family portrait; **2** gén, Littérat (description) description, picture; **faire le ~ de qn/qch** to paint a picture of sb/sth; **3** (réplique) spitting image; **tu es tout le ~ de ton père** you're the spitting image of your father; **4**○ (visage) face; **s'abîmer le ~** to smash one's face up; **se faire abîmer** or **rectifier le ~** to have one's face bashed○ in ou smashed○ in; **se faire tirer le ~** to have one's photo taken.

portraitiste /pɔʀtʀɛtist/ ▶510 *nmf* **1** Art portrait painter; **2** Phot portrait photographer.

portrait-robot, *pl* **portraits-robots** /pɔʀtʀɛʀɔbo/ *nm* photofit® (picture), identikit; **le ~ du criminel** a photofit (picture) of the murderer; **faire le ~ de qn** lit to make up a photofit (picture) of sb; fig to give a profile of sb.

portuaire /pɔʀtɥɛʀ/ *adj* port (*épith*).

portugais, **~e** /pɔʀtygɛ, ɛz/ **I** ▶537 *adj* Portuguese.

II ▶462 *nm* Ling Portuguese.

III portugaise *nf* (huître) common Portuguese oyster.

IDIOMES **tu as les ~es ensablées**○**?** are you deaf or what○?

Portugais, **~e** /pɔʀtygɛ, ɛz/ ▶537 *nm,f* Portuguese.

Portugal /pɔʀtygal/ ▶321 *nprm* Portugal.

POS *written abbr* ▶**plan**.

pose /poz/ *nf* **1** (mise en place) (de compteur, vitre) putting in, installation (**de** of); (de placard, serrure, dentier) fitting (**de** of); (de parquet, carrelage, moquette) laying (**de** of); (de signalisation routière) installation (**de** of); (de rideau) hanging, putting up (**de** of); Mil (de mine) laying (**de** of); **après la ~ du parquet nous pourrons nous installer** when the floor has been laid we can move in; **la ~ d'un amalgame** Dent the filling of a tooth; **2** (manière de se tenir) pose; **prendre une ~ provocante/solennelle** to strike a provocative/solemn pose; **3** Art pose; **garder** or **tenir la ~** to keep ou hold the pose; **une séance de ~** a sitting; **4** (affectation) pretention, affectation; **s'exprimer avec ~** to speak in an affected manner; **5** Phot exposure; **temps de ~** exposure time; **une pellicule de 24 ~s** a 24 exposure film.

posé, **~e** /poze/ **I** *pp* ▶**poser**.

II *pp adj* [*air, personne, manière*] composed; [*geste*] controlled; [*voix*] controlled, calm; **d'une voix ~e** in a calm voice, calmly.

Poséidon /pozeidɔ̃/ *npr* Poseidon.

posément /pozemɑ̃/ *adv* carefully, thoughtfully; **il parlait très ~** he weighed his words (carefully); **il a toujours agi ~** he has always trodden carefully.

posemètre /pozmɛtʀ/ *nm* Phot exposure meter, light meter.

■ **~ à cellule** photocell light ou exposure meter.

poser /poze/ [1] **I** *vtr* **1** (mettre) to put down, to lay down [*livre, journal*]; to put down, to set down [*verre, tasse*]; **il a posé son verre** he put ou set down his glass; **pose ton manteau et assieds-toi** put your coat somewhere and sit down; **ils ont posé un échafaudage contre le mur** they've put some scaffolding up against the wall; **~ la main sur le bras de qn** to lay ou place one's hand on sb's arm; **dès qu'il a posé le pied en Italie il a su qu'il y serait bien** as soon as he set foot in Italy he knew he would be happy there; **j'ai posé une lettre sur votre bureau** I've put a letter on your desk; **s'endormir dès qu'on pose la tête sur l'oreiller** to fall asleep as soon as one's head hits ou touches the pillow; **~ les yeux sur qn/qch** to look at sb/sth; **~ son regard sur qn** to look at sb; **~ un baiser sur la joue de qn** to plant a kiss on sb's cheek; **une grande bâtisse posée au mileu d'un parc** a large mansion set in the middle of a park; **2** (mettre en place) to put in, to install [*compteur, vitre*]; to install [*signalisation, radiateur*]; to fit [*serrure, dentier, prothèse*]; to lay [*carrelage, mine, pierre, câble*]; to plant [*bombe*]; to fit, to lay [*moquette*]; to put up [*papier peint, tableau, rideau, cloison*]; to put up, to post [*affiches*]; to fit, to insert [*stérilet*]; to apply [*garrot*]; **3** (établir) to assert, to postulate sout [*théorie, hypothèse*]; to lay down [*principes, règles, limites*]; **~ la supériorité de l'homme sur l'animal** to assert the superiority of human beings over animals; **le syndicat a posé un préavis de grève** the trade union has given notice of a strike; **je vais accepter leur proposition mais je vais ~ mes conditions** I'll accept their proposal but I'm going to lay down my conditions; **~ sa candidature à un poste** to apply for a job; **~ sa candidature à une élection** to stand GB ou run for election; **~ une addition** to write a sum down, to write down a sum; **je pose 3 et je retiens 2** I put ou write down (the) 3 and carry (the) 2; **~ que** to suppose that; **~ comme hypothèse que** to put forward the theory that; **4** (soulever) to ask [*question*] (**sur, au sujet de** about); to set [*devinette*]; **la question reste posée** the question (still) remains; **~ (un) problème à qn** to pose a problem for sb; **ça ne pose aucun problème** that's no problem at all ; **ça leur pose des problèmes** that poses problems for them; **5** Mus to place [*voix*]; **j'ai appris à ~ ma voix** I've learned to place my voice.

II *vi* **1** Art, Phot to pose; **~ nu** to pose (in the) nude; **2** (être affecté) to put on airs; **il fallait la voir ~ devant le ministre!** you should have seen how she put on airs in front of the minister!; **~ pour la galerie** to play to the gallery; **~ au génie méconnu** to act ou play the misunderstood genius.

III se poser *vpr* **1** [*oiseau, insecte*] to settle, to alight (**sur** on); **2** [*avion*] to land, to touch down; **se ~ en catastrophe** to make an emergency landing; **3**○ (s'asseoir) to plant oneself (**sur** on); **pose-toi quelque part et attends-moi** park○ yourself somewhere and wait for me; **4** (s'arrêter) [*yeux, regard*] to fall (**sur** on); **5** (être installé) **une fenêtre se pose plus facilement à deux** it' s easier to fit ou install a window if there are two of you; **6** (s'affirmer) **se ~ en qch** to claim to be sth; **se ~ en victime/exemple** to present oneself as a victim/an example; **se ~ comme le successeur** to present oneself as the successor; **7** (se demander) **se ~ des questions** to ask oneself questions; **se ~ des questions au sujet de qn/qch** (s'interroger) to wonder about sb/sth; (douter) to have doubts about sb/sth; **se ~ la question de l'efficacité de qn/l'efficacité de qch** to wonder ou have doubts about sb's efficiency/ the efficiency of sth; **il faut se ~ la question de savoir si le projet a des chances d'aboutir** we must ask ourselves whether this project has any chance of success; **ils vivent sans se ~ de questions** they accept things as they are; **8** (exister) [*problème, cas, question*] to arise; **le problème se pose régulièrement** the problem arises regularly; **la question ne se pose pas** (c'est impossible) there's no question of it; (c'est évident) it goes without saying; **la question se pose aussi en termes d'argent** there is also a financial side to the question.

IDIOMES **comme imbécile/hypocrite il se pose là**○! he's a prime example of an idiot/a hypocrite!

poseur, **-euse** /pozœʀ, øz/ ▶510 **I**○ *adj* **elle est (trop) poseuse** she's (too much of) a poser○.

II *nm,f* (snob) poser○.

■ **~ d'affiches** billsticker, billpost; **~ de bombes** bomber, bomb planter; **~ de carrelage** tiler; **~ de moquette** carpet fitter.

positif, **-ive** /pozitif, iv/ **I** *adj* **1** (affirmatif) [*réponse*] affirmative; **2** (constructif) [*entretien, climat*] constructive; [*évolution, effet, conséquence*] positive; **3** (favorable) [*critique, réaction, bilan*] favourable[GB]; [*point, image*] positive; **il a parlé de lui en termes très ~s** he spoke of him in highly favourable[GB] terms ou very positively; **4** (réaliste) [*personne, esprit, attitude*] positive; **5** Méd, Math, Électrotech, Phot positive.

II *nm* **1** (résultat concret) **je veux du ~** I need something positive; **2** (points favorables) positive points (*pl*); **3** Phot positive; **4** Ling positive (degree).

position /pozisjɔ̃/ *nf* **1** (dans l'espace) position (**de** of); **la ~ géographique d'une ville** the geographical position of a town; **veuillez indiquer votre ~** Naut, Aviat please state your position; **il faut revoir la ~ des joueurs** Sport the positioning of the players has to be rethought; **en ~ horizontale/verticale** horizontally/vertically; **attention, l'échelle est en ~ instable** be careful, the ladder isn't steady; **2** Mil position; **bombarder les ~s ennemies** to bomb the enemy's positions; **la troupe a pris ~ sur la crête** the troop has taken up its position on the ridge; **3** (posture) position (**de** of); **faire l'amour dans toutes les ~s** to make love ou have sex in every (possible) position; **la ~ des doigts sur une guitare** the positioning of the fingers on a guitar; **rien de pire que de rester en ~ assise toute la journée** there's nothing worse than sitting down all day; **4** (situation) position; **placer qn dans une ~ difficile** to put sb in a difficult ou an awkward position; **être/se sentir en ~ de force** to be/feel oneself to be in a position of strength; **nous ne sommes pas en ~ de vous aider/d'agir** we are in no position to help you/to act; **être en ~ minoritaire/majoritaire** to be in the minority/majority; **se trouver dans une ~ délicate** to be in a tricky situation; **être en ~ dominante sur le marché** to be a market leader; **5** (professionnelle, sociale) position; **il occupe une ~ très en vue** he's in a very public position; **sa ~ est très enviée** his/her position is widely envied; **6** (au classement) place, position; **être en deuxième/troisième ~** to be in second/third place ou position; **7** (point de vue) position, stance; **maintenir/durcir sa ~** to maintain/harden one's position ou stance; **définir une ~ commune** to reach a common position; **~ de principe** position ou stance taken on principle; **adopter une ~ de principe** to make a stand on principle; **revenir sur/réviser ses ~s** to reconsider/review one's position; **prendre ~ sur un problème** to take a stand on an issue; **prise de ~** stance, stand (**sur qch** on sth); **camper** or **rester sur ses ~s** to stand one's ground; **8** Fin (bank) balance; **demander sa ~** to ask for the balance of one's account; **être en ~ créditrice/débitrice** [*compte*] to be in credit/debit; **9** Danse position; **première/cinquième ~** first/fifth position.

■ **~ acheteur** Fin bull position; **~ du missionnaire** missionary position; **~ de repli** fallback; **~ vendeur** Fin bear position.

positionnement /pozisjɔnmɑ̃/ *nm* **1** Mécan (de pièce) positioning (**de** of); **2** Aviat, Mil, Naut positioning (**de** of); **3** Comm, Pub **le ~ d'un produit sur le marché** the positioning of a product.

positionner /pozisjɔne/ [1] *vtr* **1** Tech, Mécan to position; **2** Mil, Naut, Aviat **~ qn** to establish sb's position; **3** Comm, Pub **~ un produit** to position a product; **4** Fin **~ un compte bancaire** to draw up a statement of account.

positivement /pozitivmɑ̃/ *adv* [*répondre*] positively; [*réagir, juger*] favourably[GB].

positiver /pozitive/ [1] *vi* to think positive.

positivisme /pozitivism/ *nm* positivism.

positiviste /pozitivist/ *adj, nmf* positivist.

positivité /pozitivite/ *nf* positivity.

positon /pɔzitɔ̃/, **positron** /pɔzitʀɔ̃/ *nm* positron.

posologie /pɔzɔlɔʒi/ *nf* dosage.

possédant, **~e** /pɔsedɑ̃, ɑ̃t/ **I** *adj* wealthy; **les classes ~es** the rich, the wealthy.

II *nm,f* **les ~s** the rich, the wealthy.

possédé, **~e** /pɔsede/ *nm,f* **les ~s** the possessed; **crier/hurler/se débattre comme un ~** to shout/scream/struggle like one possessed.

posséder /pɔsede/ [14] **I** *vtr* **1** (détenir) to own, to possess sout [*propriété, œuvre d'art, voiture, fortune, armée, arme, matériel*]; to hold [*charge*]; **il possède 10% du capital** he owns 10% of the capital; **sa famille ne possède plus rien** his/her family has nothing left; **2** (être équipé de) to have; **cette voiture possède des sièges en cuir** this car has leather seats; **un jardin qui possède un bassin** a garden with a fish pond; **3** (jouir de) to have [*habileté, diplôme, connaissance, qualité, talents*]; **plante qui possède des vertus curatives** plant with healing properties; **~ un grand savoir** to be extremely knowledgeable; **4** (maîtriser) to speak [sth] fluently [*langue*]; to have a thorough knowledge of [*sujet, matière, technique*]; **elle possède parfaitement son métier** she is extremely skilled at her job; **il possède parfaitement son art** he is a perfect master of his art; **5** (sexuellement) to have, to possess sout [*femme*]; **6** (dominer) [*sentiment, colère, douleur*] to overwhelm; **la haine le possédait** he was overwhelmed with hatred; **un démon le possède** he is possessed by a demon; **7**○ (duper) to have○; **il nous a bien possédés** he really had○ us there; **se faire ~ par qn** to be had○ by sb.

II se posséder *vpr* liter (se dominer) to control oneself; **il ne se possédait plus** he was beside himself.

possesseur /pɔsesœʀ/ *nm* (de biens, d'objets) owner, possessor sout; (de véhicule) owner; (de diplôme, carte d'identité, d'actions) holder; (de secret) keeper; (de passeport) bearer.

■ **~ de bonne foi** Jur person in bona fide possession.

possessif, **-ive** /pɔsesif, iv/ **I** *adj* Ling, Psych possessive.

II *nm* Ling possessive.

possession /pɔsesjɔ̃/ *nf* **1** (de maison, terres, fortune) possession, ownership; (de diplôme, drogue, d'arme) possession; **la ~ d'un passeport est obligatoire** you must have a passport; **avoir qch en sa ~** to have sth in one's possession; **tomber en la ~ de qn** [*objet*] to come into sb's possession; **entrer en** or **prendre ~ de qch** to take possession of sth; **prendre ~ d'un héritage** to come into one's inheritance; **être en ~ de toutes ses facultés** to be in possession of all one's faculties; **être en pleine ~ de ses moyens** to be on top form; **2** (maîtrise) (de langue) fluency (**de** in); (de métier, technique) mastery (**de** of); **3** (chose possédée) (bien) possession; (territoire) possession; **4** (ensorcellement) possession.

possessivité /pɔsesivite/ *nf* possessiveness.

possibilité /pɔsibilite/ **I** *nf* **1** (éventualité) possibility; **c'est une ~** it's a possibility; **~ de faire** possibility of doing; **~ que** possibility that; **il y a la ~ qu'il vienne** there's a possibility that he might come; **2** (occasion) opportunity; (solution) option; **~ d'embauche** job opportunity; **cette ~ pourrait ne pas se reproduire** the chance may never come again; **les ~s de trouver un emploi** the chances of finding a job; **évaluer toutes les ~s** to weigh up all the options; **je n'ai pas d'autre ~ que d'accepter** I have no choice ou option but to accept; **offrir** or **donner à qn la ~ de faire** to give sb the chance ou option of doing; **offrir à qn une grande ~ de choix** to give sb a wide range of options; **cela te laisse la ~ de rester à Oxford quelques jours supplémentaires** it gives you the chance of staying in Oxford a few more days; **se réserver la ~ de faire** to reserve the right to do.

II possibilités *nfpl* **1** (potentiel) (de personne) abilities; (d'appareil) potential ou possible uses; **avoir de nombreuses ~s** [*personne, appareil*] to be versatile; **2** (moyens) resources; **dans la mesure de ses ~s** according to one's means.

possible /pɔsibl/ **I** *adj* **1** (réalisable) possible; **si (c'est) ~** if possible; **dès que ~** as soon as possible; **un accord devrait être ~** it should be possible to come to an agreement; **la construction d'un tel bâtiment dans notre ville n'est pas ~** it is not possible to build such a building in our town; **nous avons fait tout ce qui était ~ pour les aider** we did everything possible to help them; **techniquement c'est ~** it's technically possible; **je viendrai chaque fois que cela sera ~** I'll come whenever I can; **il est toujours ~ de renoncer** it's always possible to give up; **ce n'est pas ~ autrement** there's no other way of doing it; **il ne me sera pas ~ de me déplacer aujourd'hui** I won't be able to get out today; **il ne lui sera pas ~ d'être chez vous avant midi** he won't be able to get to you before noon; **cela ne me sera pas ~ si on ne m'accorde pas plus de moyens financiers** I won't be able to do it unless I'm given more funds; **rendre qch ~** to make sth possible; **désolé, ce n'est pas ~** (refus) I'm sorry, it's just not possible; **toutes les précautions ~s** every possible precaution; **tout le courage ~** the utmost courage; **toute la volonté ~** every determination; **tous les cas ~s et imaginables** every conceivable case; **faire preuve de toute l'énergie ~ et imaginable** to be extremely energetic; **le plus cher ~** [*vendre*] at the highest possible price; **se lever le plus tôt ~** to get up as early as possible; **le plus ~ près de la gare** as close to the station as possible; **recule le plus ~** go back as far as you can; **en faire le plus/moins ~** to do as much/little as possible; **je vous souhaite un séjour le plus agréable ~** I wish you a most pleasant stay; **le plus de renseignements ~** as much information as possible; **diffuser une revue le plus largement ~** to distribute a magazine as widely as possible; **hachez le plus finement ~** chop as finely as possible; **aller le plus loin ~** to go as far away as possible ou as one can; **je vais retarder le plus ~ mon départ** I'm going to delay my departure as much as I can; **le plus rapidement/tôt ~** as quickly/soon as possible; **payer le moins ~** to pay as little as possible; **faire le moins de fautes ~ dans une dictée** to make as few mistakes as possible in a dictation; **essayer de faire le moins de mal ~** to try to do the least possible harm; **autant que ~** as much as possible; **limiter les déplacements autant que ~** to keep travelling down to a minimum; **2** (potentiel) possible; **il n'y a pas d'erreur ~, c'est lui** it's him, without a shadow of a doubt; **il n'y a aucune erreur ~ sur l'identité du meurtrier** there can be no doubt as to the identity of the murderer; **on annonce de ~s perturbations sur les lignes aériennes** there is a possibility of disruptions to airlines; **nous avons sélectionné de ~s candidats** we have selected some potential candidates; **tout est ~** anything is possible; **(ce n'est) pas ~**○ (surprise) I don't believe it; (ironie) you're joking; **est-ce ~!** iron can this be possible?, did I hear you correctly?; **il m'attend? (c'est) ~, mais il...** he's waiting for me? maybe he is, but he...; **que vous ayez des ennuis cela est fort ~, mais...** I'm sure you do have problems, but...; **ce n'est pas ~ d'être aussi bête** how can anyone be so stupid?; **ce n'est pas ~, il pleut encore** I don't believe it, it's raining again!; **'tu vas acheter une voiture?'—'~'** 'are you going to buy a car?'—'maybe'; **3**○ (acceptable) **pas ~** impossible, awful; (croyable) **pas ~** unbelievable; **il a une femme pas ~** his wife is impossible ou awful; **il a un accent pas ~** he has an atrocious accent; **être d'une lenteur pas ~** to be awfully ou unbelievably slow; **être d'une bêtise pas ~** to be incredibly stupid; **il a une chance pas ~** he's incredibly ou unbelievably lucky.

II *nm* **le ~** that which is possible; **rester dans le domaine du ~** to be within the realms of possibility; **faire (tout) son ~** to do one's best; **faire (tout) son ~ pour faire** to do everything in one's power to do; **je ferai mon ~ pour venir** I'll do my best to come; **elle est bête au ~**○ she's as stupid as they come.

post(-) /pɔst/ *préf* post(-); **postdoctoral** post-doctoral; **postféodal** postfeudal; **postfreudien** post-Freudian; **postromantique** post-Romantic.

postal, **~e**, *mpl* **-aux** /pɔstal, o/ *adj* [*train, bateau, avion*] mail; [*fourgonnette, fourgon*] post office GB, mail US; [*services*] postal.

postcure /pɔstkyʀ/ *nf* aftercare.

postdater /pɔstdate/ [1] *vtr* to postdate.

poste /pɔst/ **I** *nm* **1** (fonction) (dans une entreprise) position, job; (dans la fonction publique) post; **~ d'enseignement** Scol teaching post; Univ university teaching post; **un ~ de secrétaire/comptable** a position as a secretary/an accountant; **un ~ à** or **de responsabilité** a position of responsibility; **supprimer dix ~s** to cut ten jobs; **suppression de ~** job cut; **trois ~s vacants** or **à pourvoir** three vacancies; **être en ~ à Moscou/en Russie** [*diplomate*] to be posted to Moscow/to Russia; **2** Sport position; **3** (lieu) post; **~ (de travail)** work station; **être à son ~** to be at one's post; **4** (commissariat) **~ de police** police station; **5** Radio, TV (appareil) **~ de radio** radio (set); **~ de télévision** television (set); (station de radio) (radio) station; **~ émetteur** transmitter; **6** Télécom (appareil) (tele)phone; (ligne) extension; **numéro de ~** extension number; **pourrais-je avoir le ~ 426?** could I have extension 426?; **7** Entr, Ind (période de travail) shift; **les ouvriers se relaient par ~s de huit heures** the workers do eight-hour shifts; **8** Fin, Compta item; **9** Mil post; **l'abandon de ~** abandoning one's post; **~ d'écoute/d'observation/de commandement** listening/observation/command post; **~ de garde** or **police** guard-house; **il est toujours fidèle au ~** you can always rely on him, you can count on him through thick and thin.

II *nf* **1** Admin (bureau) post office; **la Poste** the Post Office; **la ~** (service) the post GB, the mail US; **envoyer par la ~** to send [sth] by post GB, to mail US; **mettre qch à la ~** to post sth GB, to put sth in the post GB, to mail sth US; **la ~ marche très bien** the postal service is very good; **la Poste recrute** there are vacancies for postal workers; **privatiser la ~** to privatize postal services; **fourgonnette de la ~** post office van GB, mail truck US; ▶ **lettre**; **2** Hist, Transp mail; **cheval de ~** post horse.

■ **~ aérienne** airmail; **~ d'aiguillage** Rail signal box; **~ budgétaire** budget item; **~ cellulaire** cellphone; **~ de contrôle** control centre[GB]; **~ de douane** customs post; **~ d'équipage** Naut crew's quarters (*pl*); **~ à essence** filling station, gas station US; **~ à galène** Radio crystal set; **~ d'incendie** fire hydrant; **~ de lavage** carwash; **~ de péage** toll booth; **~ de pilotage** Aviat flight deck; **~ restante** poste restante GB, general delivery US; **~ de secours** first-aid post GB ou station; **~ de soudure** or **à souder** welding equipment.

posté, **~e** /pɔste/ **I** *pp* ▶ **poster**[1].

II *pp adj* [*emploi, ouvrier*] shift (*épith*); **travail ~** shift work.

poste-frontière, *pl* **postes-frontières** /pɔstfʀɔ̃tjɛʀ/ *nm* frontier post, customs post.

poster[1] /pɔste/ [1] **I** *vtr* **1** (expédier) to post GB, to mail US [*lettre, colis*]; **2** (placer) to post, to station [*soldat, garde, policier*]; to station [*complice*]; to put [sb] in place [*espion*].

II se poster *vpr* **se ~ devant** (debout) to station oneself in front of; (assis) to sit in front of.

poster[2] /pɔstɛʀ/ *nm* (affiche) poster.

postérieur, **~e** /pɔsteʀjœʀ/ **I** *adj* **1** (dans le temps) [*date*] later (*épith*); [*événement, œuvre*] subsequent; **un écrivain ~ à Flaubert** a writer who came after Flaubert; **cette invention est ~e à 1960** this invention dates from after 1960; **un événement ~ à la guerre** an event which took place after the war; **2** (dans l'espace) [*partie, section*] posterior; [*pattes*] hind (*épith*); **3** Phon back.

II○ *nm* behind○, posterior hum; **un coup de pied au ~** lit, fig a kick up the behind○.

postérieurement /pɔsteʀjœʀmɑ̃/ *adv* subsequently; **~ à** after, subsequent to sout.

postériorité /pɔsteʀjɔʀite/ *nf* posteriority.

postérité /pɔsteʀite/ *nf* **1** (immortalité) posterity; **passer à** or **entrer dans la ~** [*nom, personne*] to go down in history; [*œuvre*] to become part of the cultural heritage; **2** (lignée) descendants (*pl*); **mourir sans ~** to die without issue; **il se situe dans la ~ de Balzac** he's part of the Balzac tradition.

postface /pɔstfas/ *nf* postface.

post-formation /pɔstfɔʀmasjɔ̃/ *nf* continuing training.

postglaciaire /pɔstglasjɛʀ/ *adj, nm* postglacial.

posthume /pɔstym/ *adj* posthumous.

postiche /pɔstiʃ/ **I** *adj* **1** (faux) [*barbe*] false; [*sentiment*] fake; **2** Art (ajouté) [*ornement, vêtement*] postiche.

II *nm* (de cheveux) hairpiece; (pour un chauve) toupee; (perruque) wig; (fausse moustache) false moustache GB ou mustache US; (fausse barbe) false beard.

postier, **-ière** /pɔstje, ɛʀ/ ▶ **510** *nm,f* postal worker.

postillon /pɔstijɔ̃/ *nm* **1** (de salive) drop of saliva; **lancer des ~s** to spit (saliva); **2** ▶ **510** (cocher) postillion.

postillonner /pɔstijɔne/ [1] *vi* to spit (saliva).

postimpressionnisme /pɔstɛ̃pʀesjɔnism/ *nm* postimpressionism.

postimpressionniste /pɔstɛ̃pʀesjɔnist/ *adj, nmf* postimpressionist.

postindustriel, **-ielle** /pɔstɛ̃dystʀiɛl/ *adj* postindustrial.

postmodernisme /pɔstmɔdɛʀnism/ *nm* postmodernism.

postmoderniste /pɔstmɔdɛʀnist/ *adj, nmf* postmodernist.

postnatal, **~e**, *mpl* **~s** ou **-aux** /pɔstnatal, o/ *adj* postnatal; **soins postnataux** postnatal care ₵; **allocation ~e** maternity allowance.

postopératoire /pɔstɔpeʀatwaʀ/ *adj* post-operative.

post-partum /pɔstpaʀtɔm/ *nm inv* post-partum period.

postposer /pɔstpoze/ [1] *vtr* to place [sth] after the verb [*sujet*]; to place [sth] after the noun [*adjectif*]; **sujet/adjectif postposé** postpositive subject/adjective.

postposition /pɔstpozisjɔ̃/ *nf* postposition.

postprandial, **~e**, *mpl* **-iaux** /pɔstpʀɑ̃djal, o/ *adj* postprandial.

postscolaire /pɔstskɔlɛʀ/ *adj* **enseignement ~** continuing education.

post-scriptum /pɔstskʀiptɔm/ *nm inv* post-script; **en ~ à** as a postscript to.

postsynchronisation /pɔstsɛ̃kʀɔnizasjɔ̃/ *nf* dubbing.

postsynchroniser /pɔstsɛ̃kʀɔnize/ [1] *vtr* to dub, to add the soundtrack to.

postulant, **~e** /pɔstylɑ̃, ɑ̃t/ *nm,f* **1** gén candidate (**à** for); **~ au titre mondial** contestant for the world title; **2** Relig postulant.

postulat /pɔstyla/ *nm* gén premise; Math, Philos postulate; **~ de départ** gén basic premise; Philos postulate.

postuler /pɔstyle/ [1] **I** *vtr* **1** (solliciter) to apply for [*emploi*] (**auprès de** to); **2** (affirmer) to postulate; **~ que** to postulate that.

II *vi* to apply (**à, pour** for).

posture /pɔstyʀ/ *nf* (pose) posture; (situation) position; **être en mauvaise ~** to be in a difficult position.

pot /po/ *nm* **1** Art, Ind (récipient, contenu) gén container; (en verre) jar; (en plastique) carton, tub; (en faïence, terre) pot; (pichet) jug; **~ de verre** glass jar; **mettre qch en ~** to put [sth] into jars [*confiture, fruits*]; to pot [*plante*]; **plante en ~** potted plant; **~ de marmelade** jar of marmalade; **~ de yaourt** (en verre) jar of yoghurt; (en plastique) carton of yoghurt; **acheter un ~ de peinture** to buy a tin of paint; **garder les ~s de confiture** to save jam jars; **réutiliser les ~s de peinture** to re-use the paint tins; **il a fallu trois ~s de peinture** it took three tins of paint; ▶ **cuiller**; **2** (de chambre) pot; (de bébé) potty; **aller sur le ~** (ponctuellement) to go on the potty; **depuis un mois il va sur le ~** he's been potty-trained for a month now; **3**○ (boisson) drink; **prendre un ~** to have a drink; **4**○ (réunion) do○ GB, drinks party; **~ d'accueil/d'adieu** welcoming/farewell party; **5**○ (chance) luck; **elle n'a pas eu de ~** she hasn't had much luck; **avoir du ~** to be lucky; **avoir un coup de ~** to have a stroke of luck; **(par un) coup de ~, la porte était ouverte** as luck would have it, the door was open; **6** (argent commun) kitty; **ramasser le ~** Jeux to win the kitty.

■ **~ catalytique** Aut catalytic converter; **~ de chambre** chamber pot; **~ de colle** lit pot of glue; fig○ leech; **~ à eau** water jug GB, pitcher US; **~ d'échappement** (silencieux) silencer GB, muffler US; (système) exhaust; **~ de fleurs** flowerpot, plantpot; **~ à lait** (de table) milk jug GB, creamer; (de transport) milk can; **~ au noir** Naut dead calm zone; fig deathtrap; **~ à tabac** lit tobacco jar; fig○ potbellied person.

IDIOMES **payer les ~s cassés** to pick up the pieces; **c'est le ~ de terre contre le ~ de fer** it's an unequal contest; **ce sera à la fortune du ~** you'll have to take pot luck; **découvrir le ~ aux roses** to stumble on what's been going on; **être sourd comme un ~**○ to be as deaf as a post; **tourner autour du ~** to beat about the bush; **payer plein ~**○ to pay full price; **partir** or **démarrer plein ~**○ to be off ou go off like a shot○.

potable /pɔtabl/ *adj* **1** (buvable) **eau ~** drinking water; **eau non ~** not drinking water; **2**○ (passable) decent; **il n'y a pas un seul film ~** there isn't a single decent film; **à peine ~** [*hôtel, film*] tolerable.

potache○ /pɔtaʃ/ *nm* schoolboy.

potage /pɔtaʒ/ *nm* soup.

potager, **-ère** /pɔtaʒe, ɛʀ/ **I** *adj* [*plante, herbe, racine*] edible; **jardin ~** kitchen garden; **culture potagère** vegetable growing ₵.

II *nm* kitchen garden.

potasse /pɔtas/ *nf* potash.

■ **~ d'Alsace** Agric muriate of potash; **~ caustique** caustic potash.

potasser○ /pɔtase/ [1] **I** *vtr* to mug up○ GB, to bone up on○ US [*dossier, manuel*]; to swot up○ GB, to bone up on○ US [*matière, histoire*].

II *vi* to swot○ GB, to bone up○ US.

potassique /pɔtasik/ *adj* potassium (*épith*).

potassium /pɔtasjɔm/ *nm* potassium.

pot-au-feu /pɔtofø/ *nm inv* **1** (plat) pot-au-feu, boiled beef (*with vegetables*); **2** (viande) boiling beef.

pot-de-vin, *pl* **pots-de-vin** /podvɛ̃/ *nm* bribe, backhander○ GB; **toucher des pots-de-vin** to take bribes.

pote○ /pɔt/ *nm* mate○ GB, pal○ US.

poteau, *pl* **~x** /pɔto/ *nm* **1** (grand piquet) post; (au football, rugby) goalpost; **~ de départ/d'arrivée** starting/finishing post; **coiffer qn au ~** lit, fig to overtake GB ou pass US sb at the finishing line; **les traîtres au ~!** death to the traitors!; **avoir des**

jambes comme des ~x○ to have legs like tree trunks; **2**◑ (ami) mate○ GB, pal○ US.
■ **~ électrique** electricity pole (*supplying domestic power lines*); **~ d'exécution** execution post; **~ indicateur** signpost; **~ télégraphique** telegraph pole.

potée /pɔte/ *nf*: *boiled meat with cabbage.*

potelé, **~e** /pɔtle/ *adj* chubby.

potence /pɔtɑ̃s/ *nf* **1** (gibet) gallows; (pendaison) gallows (*sg*); **il mérite la ~** he deserves to hang; **2** (équerre) bracket; **3** (bras de levage) jib; **~ pivotante** swing jib.

potencé, **~e** /pɔtɑ̃se/ *adj* Hérald potent; **croix ~e** cross potent.

potentat /pɔtɑ̃ta/ *nm* potentate.

potentialité /pɔtɑ̃sjalite/ *nf* **1** (virtualité) potential; **2** (possibilité) potentiality.

potentiel, **-ielle** /pɔtɑ̃sjɛl/ **I** *adj* potential.
II *nm* **1** (possibilité) potential (**de** for); **~ de production** production capacity ou potential; **2** Ling (mode) potential mood; **3** Phys potential.

potentiellement /pɔtɑ̃sjɛlmɑ̃/ *adv* potentially.

potentille /pɔtɑ̃tij/ *nf* potentilla.

potentiomètre /pɔtɑ̃sjɔmɛtʀ/ *nm* potentiometer.

poterie /pɔtʀi/ *nf* **1** (production) pottery; **cours de ~** pottery class; **2** (produit) piece of pottery; **des ~s** pottery ¢; **une ~ de Picasso** a piece of pottery by Picasso; **les ~s de Picasso** Picasso's pottery; **3** (atelier) pottery.

poterne /pɔtɛʀn/ *nf* postern.

potiche /pɔtiʃ/ *nf* **1** (vase) vase; **2** (en politique) pej **n'être qu'une** or **faire figure de ~** to be a mere puppet; **être réduit au rôle de ~** to be reduced to nothing more than a puppet; **3** (en société) pej **être une ~** to look merely decorative.

potier, **-ière** /pɔtje, ɛʀ/ ▶ 510 *nm,f* potter.

potin○ /pɔtɛ̃/ *nm* **1** (commérage) gossip ¢; **les derniers ~s** the latest gossip; **2** (tapage) din○ ¢; **faire du ~** to make a din○.

potiner○ /pɔtine/ [1] *vi* to gossip.

potion /posjɔ̃/ *nf* potion; **la ~ était amère** fig it was a bitter pill to swallow.
■ **~ magique** lit magic potion; fig magic formula.

potiron /pɔtiʀɔ̃/ *nm* pumpkin GB, winter squash US.

potlatch /pɔtlatʃ/ *nm* potlatch.

pot-pourri, *pl* **pots-pourris** /popuʀi/ *nm* **1** Mus medley; **2** (pour parfumer) potpourri.

potron-minet /pɔtʀɔ̃minɛ/ *nm inv* **dès ~** at the crack of dawn.

Pott /pɔt/ *npr* **mal de ~** Pott's disease.

pou, *pl* **~x** /pu/ *nm* louse; **avoir des ~x** to have lice.
■ **~ de corps** body louse; **~ du pubis** crab louse; **~ de tête** headlouse.
IDIOMES **chercher des ~x**○ to nitpick○; **chercher des ~x dans la tête de qn**○ to find fault with sb; **être laid** or **moche**○ **comme un ~** to be as ugly as sin; **être vexé comme un ~**○ to be extremely offended.

pouah○ /pwa/ *excl* ugh!, yuck!

poubelle /pubɛl/ *nf* **1** (de cuisine, salle de bains) bin GB, trash can US; (d'extérieur) dustbin GB, garbage can US; **~ à pédale/à couvercle basculant** pedal/swing-top bin GB ou garbage can US; **mettre** or **jeter qch à la ~** to throw sth away; **sortir la ~** to take the rubbish out; **faire les ~s** to go through dustbins GB ou trash cans US; **2** (à grande échelle) dumping ground; **~ nucléaire** nuclear dumping ground; **la ville refuse d'être une ~** the town isn't prepared to become a mere dumping ground; **aller dans les ~s de l'histoire** to be consigned to the scrap heap of history.

pouce /pus/ **I** *nm* **1** ▶ 188 (de la main) thumb; (du pied) big toe; **se faire mal au ~** to hurt one's thumb; **2** ▶ 477 (unité de mesure) inch; **ne pas progresser/céder d'un ~** not to move forward/give an inch; **ne pas bouger d'un ~** not to budge an inch.
II *excl* schoolchildren's slang pax! GB, truce!
IDIOMES **se tourner** or **rouler les ~s** to twiddle one's thumbs; **manger/déjeuner sur le ~** to have a quick bite to eat/to have a quick bite to eat at lunchtime; **manger une soupe sur le ~** to have a quick bowl of soup; **mettre les ~s**○, **dire ~** to give up; **donner un coup de ~ à qn/à qch** (au départ) to help sb/sth get started; (pour relancer) to give sb/sth a boost.

Poucet /pusɛ/ *npr* **le petit ~** Hop o'my Thumb.

Pouchkine /puʃkin/ *npr* Pushkin.

poudingue /pudɛ̃g/ *nm* pudding stone.

poudre /pudʀ/ *nf* **1** gén powder; **réduire qch en ~** to grind sth to a powder; **2** Cosmét powder; **se mettre de la ~** to put on powder; **~ libre/compacte** loose/pressed powder; **3** (explosif) **~ (à canon)** gunpowder; **un baril de ~** a barrel of gunpowder.
■ **~ à éternuer** sneezing powder; **~ à laver** washing powder; **~ à lever** raising agent; **~ de perlimpinpin** hum magical cure; **~ à récurer** scouring powder; **~ de riz** Cosmét rice powder.
IDIOMES **mettre le feu aux ~s** to bring things to a head; **jeter de la ~ aux yeux** to try to impress; **c'est de la ~ aux yeux** it's all a front; **se répandre comme une traînée de ~** to spread like wildfire.

poudrer /pudʀe/ [1] **I** *vtr* to powder; **cheveux poudrés** powdered hair.
II *vi* C [*neige*] to drift.
III se poudrer *vpr* to powder oneself; **se ~ le visage/le nez** to powder one's face/one's nose.

poudrerie /pudʀəʀi/ *nf* **1** (d'explosifs) explosives factory; **2** C (de neige) driven snow.

poudreux, **-euse** /pudʀø, øz/ **I** *adj* [*neige*] powdery.
II poudreuse *nf* (neige) powdery snow; **skier dans la poudreuse** to ski in the powdery snow.

poudrier /pudʀije/ *nm* powder compact.

poudrière /pudʀijɛʀ/ *nf* **1** (entrepôt) powder magazine; **2** fig time bomb.

poudroiement /pudʀwamɑ̃/ *nm* liter shimmer.

poudroyer /pudʀwaje/ [23] *vi* liter [*neige, route*] to shimmer.

pouêt-pouêt /pwɛtpwɛt/ *nm inv* (*also onomat*) honk-honk.

pouf /puf/ **I** *nm* **1** (siège) pouffe; **2**◑ (maison de prostitution) brothel; **3** (bruit) **faire ~** to fall with a soft thud.
II *excl* oopsadaisy!

pouffer /pufe/ [1] *vi* **~ (de rire)** (une fois) to burst out laughing; (continuellement) to be in stitches○.

pouf(f)iasse◑ /pufjas/ *nf* slut◑.

Pouilles /puj/ ▶ 692 *nprfpl* Apulia (*sg*).

pouilleux, **-euse** /pujø, øz/ **I** *adj* **1**○ (sale) seedy; **2** (couvert de poux) flea-ridden.
II *nm,f* seedy character; **bande de ~** scruffy lot.

pouillot /pujo/ *nm* warbler.
■ **~ siffleur** wood warbler; **~ véloce** chiffchaff.

poujadisme /puʒadism/ *nm* Poujadism (*right-wing movement of the 1950s*).

poulaga◑ /pulaga/ *nm* cop○; **la maison Poulaga** the cop shop○.

poulailler /pulaje/ *nm* **1** Agric (abri) henhouse; (enclos) hen run; (oiseaux) hens (*pl*); **2**○ Théât (lieu) **le ~** the Gods (*pl*) GB, the gallery; (spectateurs) the audience in the Gods (*pl*) GB, the gallery.

poulain /pulɛ̃/ *nm* **1** Zool colt; (très jeune) foal; **2** (débutant) protégé.

poulaine /pulɛn/ *nf* **1** (chaussure) piked shoe; **2** Naut (ship's) head.

poularde /pulaʀd/ *nf* fattened chicken.

poulbot /pulbo/ *nm* (street) urchin.

poule /pul/ *nf* **1** Zool hen; ▶ **poussin**; **2** Culin boiling fowl; **3**◑ (compagne) **sa ~** his woman○; **4**○ (terme d'affection) **ma ~** my pet○, honey US; **5**◑ (prostituée) hooker◑, whore; **une ~ de luxe** a high-class hooker◑; **6** Sport (groupe d'adversaires) group; (tournoi) tournament; **7** Jeux pool, kitty.
■ **~ de bruyère** greyhen GB, grayhen US; **~ d'eau** moorhen; **~ d'essai** Turf race for three-year olds; **~ faisane** hen pheasant; **~ mouillée**○ pej wimp○ péj; **~ naine** bantam; **~ pondeuse** laying hen; **~ au pot** Culin chicken casserole.
IDIOMES **quand les ~s auront des dents** when pigs fly; **se coucher avec les ~s** to go to bed early; **se lever avec les ~s** to get up with the lark; **être comme une ~ qui a trouvé un couteau** to be completely nonplussed; **tuer la ~ pour avoir l'œuf, tuer la ~ aux œufs d'or** to kill the goose that lays the golden egg.

poulet /pulɛ/ *nm* **1** Zool, Culin chicken; **2**◑ (policier) cop○; **3**○ (terme d'affection) **mon ~** my pet○, honey US; **4**† (lettre) billet-doux†.
■ **~ d'élevage** ≈ battery chicken; **~ fermier** ≈ free-range chicken; **~ de grain** corn-fed chicken.
IDIOMES **et mon cul, c'est du ~**◑**?** you're pulling my leg○!

poulette /pulɛt/ *nf* **1** Zool young hen; Culin pullet; **sauce ~** white sauce (*containing egg and lemon juice*); **2**○ (fille) bird○ GB, chick○ US; **ma ~** (terme d'affection) my pet○, honey US.

pouliche /puliʃ/ *nf* filly.

poulie /puli/ *nf* pulley; **~ étagée** stepped pulley; **~ de tension** idler.

pouliner /puline/ [1] *vi* to foal.

poulinière /pulinjɛʀ/ *adj f* **jument ~** brood mare.

pouliot /puljo/ *nm* **(menthe) ~** pennyroyal.

poulpe /pulp/ *nm* octopus.

pouls /pu/ *nm inv* Méd, Physiol pulse; **prendre/tâter le ~ de qn** lit to take/to feel sb's pulse; fig to sound sb out.

poumon /pumɔ̃/ *nm* ▶ 188 Anat lung; **à pleins ~s** [*crier*] at the top of one's voice; [*aspirer*] deeply; **avoir du ~** to have a good pair of lungs; **les forêts sont le ~ de la terre** forests are the lungs of the earth.
■ **~ d'acier** or **artificiel** iron lung.
IDIOMES **cracher ses ~s**◑ to cough one's lungs up.

poupard† /pupaʀ/ *nm* chubby baby.

poupe /pup/ *nf* stern; **avoir le vent en ~** lit, fig to have the wind in one's sails.

poupée /pupe/ ▶ 449 *nf* **1** (jouet) doll; **jouer à la ~** to play dolls; **avoir un visage de ~** to have a doll-like face; **~ de chiffon/de cire** rag/wax doll; **2**○ (forme d'adresse) poppet GB, toots○ US; **3**○ (pansement) finger bandage.
■ **~ de cabestan** capstan drum; **~ fixe** (de tour) headstock; **~ gonflable** inflatable doll; **~ du loess** loess doll; **~ mannequin** Barbie® doll; **~ mobile** (de tour) tailstock; **~ régionale** doll in traditional dress; **~ de son** rag doll; **~s gigognes** or **russes** set (*sg*) of Russian dolls.
IDIOMES **être une vraie ~** to be really cute.

poupin, **~e** /pupɛ̃, in/ *adj* chubby.

poupon /pupɔ̃/ *nm* (bébé) tiny baby; (jouet) baby doll.

pouponner○ /pupɔne/ [1] *vi* **1** (s'occuper d'un bébé) [*homme*] to play the doting father; [*femme*] to play the doting mother; [*couple*] to play the doting parents; **2** (être enceinte) to be pregnant.

pouponnière /pupɔnjɛʀ/ *nf* children's home (*for under-threes*).

pour[1] /puʀ/ *prép* **1** (indiquant le but) to; **~ cela, il faudra faire** to do that, you'll have to do; **~ bien faire il faudrait partir tôt** to be really sure we should leave early; **c'était ~ rire** or **plaisanter** it was a joke; **il est**

pour[1]

pour + verbe

Lorsque *pour* sert à indiquer un but il se traduit généralement par *to* devant un verbe à l'infinitif:

sortir pour acheter un journal = to go out to buy a newspaper
pour faire des meringues, il faut des œufs = to make meringues, you need eggs

Il peut également se traduire par *in order to*, qui est plus soutenu:

pour mettre fin aux hostilités = in order to put an end to hostilities

Quand *pour* est suivi d'une forme négative, il se traduira par *so as not to* ou *in order not to*:

pour ne pas oublier = so as not to forget
pour ne pas rater le train = so as not to miss the train *ou* in order not to miss the train

Lorsque *pour* relie deux actions distinctes sans relation de cause à effet, il sera traduit par *and* et le verbe conjugué normalement:

elle s'endormit pour se réveiller deux heures plus tard = she fell asleep and woke up two hours later

Quand la deuxième action n'est pas souhaitable ou qu'une notion de hasard malheureux est sous-entendue, on traduira par *only to*:

elle s'endormit pour se réveiller deux heures plus tard = she fell asleep only to wake up two hours later
il partit à la guerre pour se faire tuer trois jours plus tard = he went off to war only to be killed three days later

pour + nom ou pronom

Lorsque *pour* sert à indiquer la destination au sens large il se traduit généralement par *for*:

le train pour Pau = the train for Pau
pour vendredi = for Friday
il travaille pour elle = he works for her

Lorsque *pour* signifie *en ce qui concerne*, il se traduira le plus souvent par *about*:

tu te renseignes pour une assurance voiture? = will you find out about car insurance?
tu te renseignes pour samedi? = will you find out about Saturday?

Attention:
pour placé en début de phrase se traduira par *as regards*:

pour l'argent, rien n'est décidé = as regards the money, nothing has been decided *ou* nothing has been decided about the money

Lorsque *pour* signifie *comme* il se traduit souvent par *as*:

je l'ai eu pour professeur = I had him as a teacher

Attention à la présence de l'article en anglais.

Lorsque *pour* relie un terme redoublé il se traduit parfois par *for*:

mot pour mot = word for word

Mais ce n'est pas toujours le cas:

jour pour jour = to the day

On se reportera au nom dans le dictionnaire.

On trouvera ci-dessous exemples supplémentaires et exceptions.

seul mais il a tout fait ~○ he's on his own, but it's entirely his own doing; **~ que** so that; **que faire ~ qu'elle comprenne?** how can we get her to understand?; **~ ainsi dire** so to speak; **2** (indiquant une destination) for; **le train ~ Paris** (prêt à partir) the train for Paris; (plus général) the train to Paris; **l'avion ~ Paris** the Paris plane, the plane to Paris; **c'est le train ~ où?** where does this train go?; **il faut une heure pour Oloron** it's an hour to Oloron; **quelque chose ~ le mal de tête/le rhume** something for headaches/colds; **c'est fait** or **étudié ~**○! (c'est sa fonction) that's what it's for; **bien sûr tu peux en manger, c'est fait ~!** of course you can eat some, that's what it's there for!; **3** (en ce qui concerne) **j'ai choisi le sujet d'étude mais ~ l'université je ne sais pas encore** I've decided on my subject but as regards the university I'm not sure yet ou but I'm not sure about the university yet; **c'est bien payé mais ~ la sécurité de l'emploi...** the pay is good but as regards job security ou as far as job security goes...; **oui, c'est ~ quoi?** yes, what is it?; (plus poli) yes, what can I do for you?; **~ moi, il a tort** as far as I am concerned, he's wrong; **qu'est-il ~ toi, un ami?** how do you see him? as a friend?; **4** (en faveur de) for; **voter ~ un candidat** to vote for a candidate; **120 voix ~ et 95 contre** 120 votes for and 95 against; **c'est ~ la recherche contre le cancer** it's for ou in aid of cancer research; **je suis ~**○ I'm in favour[GB]; **être ~ qch/faire qch** gén to be in favour[GB] of sth/doing sth; **je suis ~ que Catherine reste** I'm in favour[GB] of Catherine staying; **je suis ~ les Verts** I'm for the ecologists; **je suis ~ Paris** Sport I support Paris; **5** (avec une indication de temps) for; **ce sera prêt ~ vendredi?** will it be ready for ou by Friday?; **~ plus tard/aujourd'hui** for later/today; **~ toujours** forever; **~ le moment** or **l'instant** for the moment, for the time being; **le bébé/le baptême c'est ~ quand?** when is the baby due/the christening?; **6** (comme) **elle a ~ ambition d'être pilote** her ambition is to be a pilot; **elle a ~ principe de ne jamais emprunter de l'argent** it's a rule with her ou it's one of her principles never to borrow money; **ils ont ~ habitude de déjeuner tard** they usually have a late lunch; **n'avoir ~ toute arme qu'un bâton** to be armed only with a stick; **il n'avait qu'un pantalon ~ tout vêtement** he was wearing nothing but a pair of trousers GB ou pants US; **7** (à la place de) for; **écrire qch ~ qch** to write sth instead of sth; **je l'ai pris ~ plus bête qu'il n'est** I thought he was more stupid than he really is; **je suis ici ~ ma collègue** I'm here in place of my colleague; **8** (à son avantage) **elle avait ~ elle de savoir écouter/la patience** she had the merit of being a good listener/being patient; **9** (introduisant une concession) **~ intelligent qu'il soit** intelligent though he may be; **'il te parlera du Japon'—'~ ce que ça m'intéresse!'** 'he'll talk to you about Japan'—'I can't say I'm very interested'; **~ peu qu' il y ait du monde sur la route nous serons en retard** there only has to be a bit of traffic and we'll be late; **~ autant que je sache** as far as I know; **10** (marquant l'emphase) **~ être intelligente, ça elle l'est!** she really is intelligent!, intelligent she certainly is!; **11** (indiquant une quantité) **j'ai mis ~ 200 francs d'essence** I've put in 200 francs' worth of petrol GB ou gas US; **merci ~ tout** thank you for everything; **pleurer ~ un rien** to cry over nothing; **s'inquiéter ~ un rien** to fret about nothing; **je n'y suis ~ rien** I had nothing to do with it; **ne t'inquiète pas ~ si peu** don't worry about a little thing like that; **tu y es bien ~ quelque chose si elle est malheureuse** if she's miserable, it has certainly got something to do with you; **il y est ~ beaucoup si elle est malheureuse** if she's miserable, he's largely to blame; **elle y est ~ beaucoup s'il a réussi** if he has succeeded a lot of the credit should go to her; **je n'en ai pas ~ longtemps** it won't take long; **il n'en a plus ~ longtemps** (mourant) he doesn't have long to live; **j'en ai encore ~ deux heures** it'll take another two hours; **j'en ai ~ une minute** it'll only take a minute; **12** (indiquant une cause) for; **se battre ~ une femme** to fight over a woman; **être battu ~ avoir menti** to be beaten for lying; ▶**oui**; **13** (introduisant une proportion) **dix ~ cent** ten per cent; **~ 250 employés, seulement 28 sont des femmes** out of 250 employees only 28 are female; **une cuillère de vinaigre ~ quatre d'huile** one spoonful of vinegar to four of oil; **~ une large part** to a large extent.

pour[2] /puʀ/ *nm* **le ~ et le contre** pros and cons (*pl*).

pourboire /puʀbwaʀ/ *nm* tip; **donner un ~ à qn** to tip sb; **être payé au ~** to be on tips only.

pourceau, *pl* **~x** /puʀso/ *nm* **1** (cochon) swine; ▶**confiture, perle**; **2** (homme) pej swine péj.

pourcentage /puʀsɑ̃taʒ/ *nm* **1** Math, Stat percentage; **2** (rémunération) commission; **payer qn au ~** to pay sb by commission; **être au ~** to be on commission; **3** (profit illicite) pej cut○; **prendre un ~** to take one's cut (**sur** of); **la pratique des ~s** the practice of taking cuts.

pourchasser /puʀʃase/ [1] *vtr* **1** (traquer) to hunt [*animal, criminel*]; **2** (harceler, faire des avances) to pursue.

pourfendeur, -euse /puʀfɑ̃dœʀ, øz/ *nm,f* (de fraudes, d'injustices) scourge.

pourfendre /puʀfɑ̃dʀ/ [6] *vtr* **1** (dénoncer) to lambast, to castigate sout; **2** (tuer) liter to cleave [sb] in two littér.

pourlécher: **se pourlécher** *vpr* /puʀleʃe/ [14] **se ~ (les babines**○**)** to lick ou smack one's lips.

pourparlers /puʀpaʀle/ *nmpl* talks (**entre** between); **entrer en ~ avec qn** to start talks with sb; **ouvrir des ~** to start talks; **dès l'ouverture des ~** (right) from the start of the talks; **~ de paix** peace talks; **être en ~** [*personnes*] to be engaged in talks; [*affaire*] to be under discussion.

pourpier /puʀpje/ *nm* purslane.

pourpoint /puʀpwɛ̃/ *nm* Hist doublet; (matelassé) pourpoint.

pourpre /puʀpʀ/ ▶**193**| **I** *adj* crimson.
II *nm* **1** (couleur) crimson; **2** Zool murex; **3** Hérald purpure.
III *nf* (colorant) Tyrian purple; (étoffe, dignité) purple.
■ **~ impériale** Hist imperial purple; **~ rétinien** Anat visual purple.

pourpré, ~e /puʀpʀe/ ▶**193**| *adj* crimson; **ciel ~** sky tinged with crimson.

pourquoi[1] /puʀkwa/ **I** *adv, conj* **1** (dans une interrogation directe) why?; **~ est-ce qu'il répète toujours la même chose?** why does he keep repeating the same thing?; **~ ce livre?** why this book?; **dis ~ tu t'en vas sans moi?** why are you going without me?; **~ ça?** why?; **~ donc?** but why?; **~ pas** or **non?** why not?; **~ pas un week-end à Paris?** what ou how about a weekend in Paris?; **~ moi?** why me?; **~ des cris?** why all the shouting?; **~ je ris?** why am I laughing?; **~ cette prudence/tant de mystère?** why so cautious/so mysterious?; **~ est-ce que je ne t'ai pas vu?** why didn't I see you?; **~ ne pas imaginer un**

système différent? why not imagine a different system?; **~ ne pas l'avoir fait plus tôt?** why didn't you/we etc do it before?; **~ as-tu décidé de partir?** why have you decided to leave?; **~ s'en priver?** why deny yourself?; **2** (dans une interrogation indirecte) why; **dis-moi ~ tu pleures** tell me why you are crying; **sans savoir ~** without knowing why; **sans savoir (ni) ~ ni comment** without knowing how or why; **va donc savoir ~!** God knows why!

II c'est pourquoi *loc adv* that's why; **il semble que vous n'avez pas reçu ma première lettre, c'est ~ je vous adresse ci-joint une photocopie** it appears that you didn't receive my first letter, so I enclose a photocopy.

pourquoi[2] /puʀkwa/ *nm inv* **le ~ et le comment** the why and the wherefore; **quel est le ~ de toute cette agitation?** what is the reason for all this disturbance?; **nous ne pouvons répondre à tous les ~** we cannot go into all the whys and wherefores.

pourri, ~e /puʀi/ **I** *pp* ▶ **pourrir**.

II *pp adj* **1** (avarié) [*aliment*] rotten; [*végétal*] decayed, rotting; ▶ **engueuler**; **2** (décomposé) [*bois*] rotten; [*mur, roche*] rotten, crumbling; **3**○ (mauvais) [*temps, climat, été*] rotten○, dismal; **4**○ (de mauvaise qualité) [*appareil, objet, véhicule, système*] rotten○, lousy○; **5** (déplaisant) [*lieu, quartier, coin*] awful; **6**○ (corrompu) [*personne, mentalité*] crooked○, corrupt; [*société*] corrupt, rotten○; [*magistrat, policier*] crooked○, bent○; **7**○ (gâté) [*enfant*] spoiled rotten○ (*jamais épith*), spoiled; **être ~ de fric**○ to be filthy○ rich.

III *nm* (pourriture) rotten part; **ça sent le ~** it smells rotten.

IV◑ *nm,f* swine◑.

IDIOMES **être ~ jusqu'à l'os** to be rotten to the core.

pourrir /puʀiʀ/ [3] **I** *vtr* **1** (faire se décomposer) [*eau, humidité*] to rot [*bois*]; **2** (corrompre) [*luxe, succès*] to spoil [*personne*]; **3**○ (gâter excessivement) to spoil [sb] rotten○ [*enfant*].

II *vi* **1** (s'abîmer) [*œuf, viande*] to go bad ou off GB; [*fruit*] to go bad, to rot; **2** (se décomposer) to rot; **3** fig (végéter) to rot; **~ en prison** to rot in prison; **4** fig (se dégrader) [*situation, grève*] to deteriorate; **laisser ~ la situation** to let the situation deteriorate.

pourrissement /puʀismɑ̃/ *nm* (de situation, conflit) deterioration.

pourriture /puʀityʀ/ *nf* **1** (décomposition) rot, decay; **2** (corruption) corruption, rottenness; **3**◑ (personne) pej swine◑; **4** Agric, Bot rot.

■ **~ grise** Agric grey mould GB, gray mold US; **~ noble** Vin noble rot.

poursuite /puʀsɥit/ *nf* **1** (action de poursuivre) pursuit (**de** of); **se lancer à la ~ de qn** to set off in pursuit of sb; **être à la ~ de** to be in pursuit of [*bonheur, idéal, passé*]; **2** (chasse) chase; **une ~ en hélicoptère** a helicopter chase; **une folle ~** a wild chase; **3** (continuation) continuation; **la ~ d'un dialogue/d'une politique/des conflits** the continuation of a dialogue[GB]/of a policy/of fighting; **4** Sport (en cyclisme) pursuit; **5** Jur **~ (judiciaire)** (judicial) proceedings (*pl*); **engager** or **intenter des ~s contre qn** to take proceedings against sb; **abandonner les ~s** to drop the charges; **6** Astronaut tracking; **dispositif de ~** tracking device.

■ **~ disciplinaire** disciplinary action.

poursuiteur, -euse /puʀsɥitœʀ, øz/ *nm,f* Sport pursuit cyclist.

poursuivant, ~e /puʀsɥivɑ̃, ɑ̃t/ *nm,f* **1** (personne qui poursuit) pursuer; **échapper à ses ~s** to escape one's pursuers; **2** Jur (personne qui exerce des poursuites) plaintiff.

poursuivre /puʀsɥivʀ/ [62] **I** *vtr* **1** (traquer) to chase [*animal, personne, voiture*]; **~ qn en voiture** to chase sb in a car; **qu'est-ce que tu fais là? mais tu me poursuis!** what are you doing here? are you following me?; **2** (harceler) [*personne*] to hound [*personne*]; [*cauchemar, rêve*] to haunt [*personne*]; **~ qn de sa haine/rancune** to be consumed by hatred/resentment toward(s) sb; **~ qn de ses assiduités** liter to force one's attentions on sb; **la malchance le poursuit, il est poursuivi par la malchance** he's dogged by misfortune; **cette histoire de vol m'a longtemps poursuivie** that stealing business dogged me for a long time; **le remords le poursuit** he's haunted by feelings of remorse; **3** (rechercher) to seek (after) [*honneurs, vérité*]; to pursue [*but*]; **4** (continuer) to continue [*marche, voyage, chemin*]; to pursue [*négociations, travaux, réflexion, objectif, tâche*]; to continue [*efforts, activité, tentative, conflit*]; **~ une enquête policière** to proceed with a police enquiry; **~ la modernisation de qch** to continue modernizing sth; **~ des** or **ses études** to continue studying ou one's studies; **~ une carrière politique/scientifique** to pursue a political career/a career in science; **5** Jur **~ qn (en justice** or **devant les tribunaux)** (en droit civil) to sue sb; (en droit pénal) to take sb to court.

II *vi* **1** (continuer) [*personne*] to continue; **poursuivez, nous vous écoutons** please continue, we're listening; **~ sur un sujet** to continue talking on a subject; **2** (persévérer) **'en progrès, poursuivez'** (sur un bulletin scolaire) 'good progress, keep it up'.

III se poursuivre *vpr* **1** (continuer) [*négociations, tendance, conflit, voyage, réformes*] to continue; **les combats se sont poursuivis dans la nuit** fighting continued into the night; **2** (l'un l'autre) [*enfants, adultes*] to chase (after) each other.

pourtant /puʀtɑ̃/ *adv* though; **et ~** and yet; **c'était ~ une bonne idée** and yet it was a good idea, it was a good idea though; **c'est ~ vrai** it's true though, it's true all the same; **inimaginable et ~ vrai** inconceivable yet true, inconceivable but true nevertheless; **il faudra ~ le leur dire** they'll have to be told though; **il n'est ~ pas bête** and yet he's not stupid; **ce n'est ~ pas difficile!** (and yet) it's not so difficult!; **~ il avait tout pour réussir** and yet he had everything going for him; **il avait travaillé dur et ~ il a échoué** he worked hard and yet ou even so he failed; **tout avait ~ bien commencé** and yet everything had got off to a good start; **des prévisions optimistes et ~ réalistes** optimistic yet realistic forecasts, forecasts which are optimistic but nevertheless realistic; **techniquement ~, le film est parfait** technically, however, the film is perfect; **techniquement, le film est ~ parfait** the film is nevertheless technically perfect; **il a été critiqué par Paul, ~ un ami de longue date** he was criticized by Paul, though ou and yet he was an old friend.

pourtour /puʀtuʀ/ *nm* **1** (bords extérieurs) perimeter; (de cercle) circumference; **2** (région avoisinante) surrounding area; **plantes cultivées sur le ~ de la Méditerranée** plants cultivated in the areas surrounding the Mediterranean.

pourvoi /puʀvwa/ *nm* appeal; **~ en cassation** appeal to the court of cassation; **~ en révision** appeal on new evidence; **~ pour vice de forme** appeal on grounds of procedural error; **~ en grâce** petition for mercy.

pourvoir /puʀvwaʀ/ [40] **I** *vtr* **1** (attribuer) to fill [*poste, emploi, place, siège*]; **siège/poste à ~** available seat/position; **être à ~** [*poste, bourse, siège*] to be available; **2** (doter) **~ qn de** to endow sb with [*qualité, trait, ressources*]; **~ une région en ressources** to provide a region with resources; **~ une maison en équipement** to fit out a house; **bien pourvu** (financièrement) well-off; (physiquement) well-endowed; **être pourvu de diplômes** to hold qualifications.

II pourvoir à *vtr ind* (assurer) to provide for [*besoin, dépense, sécurité, remplacement*]; **j'y pourvoirai** I'll see to it; **Dieu y pourvoira** God will provide.

III se pourvoir *vpr* **1** (se munir) **se ~ de** to provide oneself with [*monnaie*]; to equip oneself with [*véhicule, bottes*]; **je m'étais pourvu de mon passeport et de mon billet d'avion** I had armed myself with my passport and my plane ticket; **2** Jur (faire appel) **se ~ en** or **devant** to appeal to; **se ~ en cassation** or **devant la Cour de cassation** to appeal to the Court of cassation.

pourvoyeur, -euse /puʀvwajœʀ, øz/ *nm,f* **1** (source) **~ de** source of [*emplois, matière première, fonds*]; **grand ~** major source; **2** (fournisseur) **~ de** purveyor of [*capital, spectacle*]; **~ de drogue** drug dealer; **~ de ragots** gossipmonger.

pourvu: **pourvu que** /puʀvyk(ə)/ *loc conj* **1** (à condition que) provided (that), as long as; **2** (dans une phrase exclamative) let's hope; **~ qu'il fasse beau dimanche!** let's hope it'll be fine on Sunday!; **~ qu'il ne neige pas!** let's hope it doesn't snow!; **~ que ça dure!** let's hope it lasts!

poussah /pusa/ *nm* **1** (jouet) tumbler; **2** (homme) pej fatty pej.

pousse /pus/ *nf* **1** (rejet) Bot shoot; fig offshoot; **2** (croissance) growth; **la ~ des ongles/cheveux** nail/hair growth; **3** Bot (apparition) **la ~ des bourgeons/feuilles** the sprouting of buds/leaves; **4** Vét heaves (+ *v sg*).

■ **~s de bambou** Culin bamboo shoots.

poussé, ~e /puse/ **I** *pp* ▶ **pousser**.

II *pp adj* **1** (de haut niveau) [*étude, enquête*] thorough, exhaustive; [*formation, études, technologie*] advanced; **interrogatoire ~** grilling; **2** (exagéré) **être un peu ~** [*plaisanterie*] to go a bit too far; [*comparaison, conclusion*] to be a bit forced; **3** Aut [*moteur*] modified, souped up○.

III poussée *nf* **1** (pression, poids) (d'eau, de foule) pressure; (de vent) force; Constr, Géol, Mécan (force) thrust; **~e latérale** Mécan lateral thrust; **~e verticale de l'eau** Phys buoyancy in water; **sous la ~e de** lit beneath the pressure of; fig under the pressure of, under pressure from; **2** (bourrade) push, shove; Mil (avancée) thrust; **d'une ~e** with a push ou shove; **renverser/écarter qch d'une ~e** to push sth over/aside; **résister aux ~es de l'ennemi** to withstand enemy pressure; **3** Méd (accès) attack (**de** of); **~e de fièvre** sudden high temperature; **~e d'urticaire** rash; **4** (augmentation) (de prix) (sharp) rise ou increase (**de** in); (de racisme, violence, nationalisme) upsurge (**de** of); **~e démographique** rise in population; **la ~e du vote vert** the greens' increased share of the vote; **~e inflationniste** inflationary trend.

■ **~e radiculaire** Bot root pressure; **~e des terres** Constr earth pressure.

pousse-café /puskafe/ *nm inv* (after-dinner) liqueur.

pousse-pousse /puspus/ *nm inv* **1** (taxi) rickshaw; **2** (manège) swing boat.

pousser /puse/ [1] **I** *vtr* **1** (déplacer) to push [*brouette, vélo, meuble, personne*]; (écarter ce qui gêne) to move, to shift, to push [sth] aside [*objet*]; **tu m'as poussé!** you pushed me!; **~ une voiture en panne** to push a broken-down car; **~ le lit contre le mur/vers la gauche** to push the bed (up) against the wall/over to the left; **~ une porte** (pour la fermer) to push a door to; (pour l'ouvrir) to push a door open; **~ un verrou** to push ou slide a bolt home; **peux-tu ~ ta voiture? elle gêne** can you move your car? it's in the way; **pousse tes fesses◑!** shove over○!; **le vent pousse les nuages vers l'est** the wind is blowing ou pushing the clouds in an easterly direction; **le vent poussait le bateau vers la côte** the wind was driving the boat toward(s) the shore; **~ les enfants vers la sortie** to hustle the children toward(s) the exit; **~ un ballon du pied** (l'écarter) to kick a ball out of the way; (le faire avancer) to kick a ball along; **~ qn du coude** to give sb a dig ou to nudge sb with one's elbow; ▶ **bouchon**, **ortie**; **2** (entraîner) **c'est la jalousie/l'ambition qui le pousse** he's driven by jealousy/ambition; **poussé par la pitié** stirred by pity; **poussé par le désir de les aider** prompted by a desire to help them; **c'est sa femme qui le pousse à boire** it's his wife who drives him to drink; **~ qn à faire qch** (encourager) to encourage sb to do sth; (vivement) to urge sb to do sth; (contraindre) [*faim, désespoir, haine*] to drive sb to do sth; **~ qn à la dépense** to encourage sb to spend more money; **~ à la consommation** to encourage people to buy more; (au bar) to encourage people to drink more; **son professeur le pousse (à s'orienter) vers la biologie** his teacher is encouraging him to do biology; **mes amis me poussent à accepter** my friends are urging me to accept; **~ qn au désespoir/suicide** to drive sb to despair/suicide; **c'est ce qui m'a poussé vers l'enseignement/à écrire cette lettre** that's what made me take up teaching/write this letter; **elle ne voulait pas vendre, on l'y a poussée** she didn't want to sell, she was pushed into it; **tout me pousse à croire que** everything leads me to believe that; **il n'a pas fallu le ~ beaucoup pour qu'il parle** he didn't need much prompting to talk; **3** (faire travailler plus) to push [*élève*]; to keep [sb] at it [*employé*]; to ride [sth] hard [*monture*]; to drive [sth] hard [*voiture*]; to flog○ [*moteur*]; **on ne pousse pas assez les élèves** pupils are not pushed hard enough; **~ les feux** to stoke up; **4** (promouvoir) to push [*produit, protégé*]; **5** (porter plus avant) to pursue [*recherches, études, raisonnement*]; **si l'on pousse plus loin cette logique** if we pursue this line of reasoning (further); **c'est ~ un peu loin la modestie/la plaisanterie** that's carrying ou taking modesty/the joke a bit far; **~ le perfectionnisme à l'extrême** to be too much of a perfectionist; **~ le courage jusqu'à la folie** to be insanely brave; **~ la bêtise/l'abnégation/la prudence jusqu'à faire** to be stupid/self-denying/cautious enough to do; **~ son effort jusqu'aux limites de l'endurance** to push oneself to the limit; **6** (émettre) to let out [*cri*]; to heave [*soupir*]; **~ un hurlement/miaulement/rugissement** to howl/miaow/roar; **~ une gueulante**○ to yell and scream○; **~ la chansonnette** or **romance**, **en ~ une**○ to sing a song.

II *vi* **1** (croître) [*enfant, plante, barbe, ongle*] to grow; (apparaître) [*plante*] to sprout; [*dent*] to come through; fig [*immeuble, ville*] to spring up; **l'arbre a poussé de 50 cm** the tree has grown 50 cm; **les radis commencent à ~** the radishes are coming up ou sprouting; **sa première dent pousse** his/her first tooth is coming through, he's/she's cutting his/her first tooth; **les villes nouvelles ont poussé comme des champignons** new towns have sprung up like mushrooms; **je fais ~ des légumes** I grow vegetables; **ça fait ~ le gazon/les cheveux** it makes the grass/your hair grow; **se laisser** or **se faire ~ les cheveux** to grow one's hair; **se laisser** or **se faire ~ la barbe/moustache** to grow a beard/moustache GB ou mustache US; **et le bébé, ça pousse**○**?** how's your baby doing?; ▶ **aile**; **2** (aller) **~ plus loin/jusqu'à la ville** to go on further/as far as the town; **on a poussé jusqu'au village suivant** we carried on as far as the next village; **3** (pour accoucher, aller à la selle) to push; **4** (faire pression) **le juge a poussé pour qu'on les acquitte** the judge pressed the jury for an acquittal; **5**○ (exagérer) to overdo it, to go too far; **tu ne crois pas que tu pousses un peu?** don't you think you're overdoing it?; **cinq francs pièce, faut pas ~**○**!** five francs each, that's a bit steep○!

III se pousser *vpr* **1** (pour faire de la place) to move over; **2**○ (pour réussir) to try to get on in life.

IDIOMES **à la va comme je te pousse** any old how; **se ~ du col**○ to push oneself forward, to be pushy; **~ qn au cul●** or **aux fesses**○ to give sb a kick up the backside○.

poussette /pusɛt/ *nf* **1** (de bébé) pushchair GB, stroller US; **2** (à provisions) shopping trolley GB, cart US; **3**○ Sport little push (*when cheating in a cycle race*).

poussette-canne, *pl* **poussettes-cannes** /pusɛtkan/ *nf* buggy (*with umbrella fold action*).

pousseur /pusœʀ/ *nm* **1** Aviat booster; **2** Naut pusher tug.

poussier /pusje/ *nm* coal dust.

poussière /pusjɛʀ/ *nf* **1** (poudre) dust; **nuage/grain de ~** cloud/speck of dust; **~ d'or/d'amiante** gold/asbestos dust; **~ interstellaire/radioactive** cosmic/radioactive dust; **réduire en ~** to reduce to dust; **tomber en ~** lit to crumble away; fig to fall to bits; **~ d'étoiles** stardust; **2** (grain) speck of dust.

IDIOMES **10 francs/20 ans et des ~s** just over 10 francs/20 years; **mordre la ~** to bite the dust.

poussiéreux, **-euse** /pusjeʀø, øz/ *adj* **1** lit [*local, chaussures, route*] dusty; **2** fig pej [*idée, bureaucratie*] outdated, fossilized.

poussif, **-ive** /pusif, iv/ *adj* **1** [*personne, véhicule*] wheezy; [*cheval*] broken-winded; **2** [*allure*] labouring[GB]; **une vieille voiture à l'allure poussive** an old car that wheezes along; **3** [*récit*] laboured[GB].

poussin /pusɛ̃/ *nm* **1** Zool chick; **2** Culin poussin GB, spring chicken; **3**○ (terme d'affection) **mon ~** my poppet○ GB, honey(-bunch)○ US; **4** Sport player under the age of 11; **les ~s** the under-elevens.

IDIOMES **une poule n'y retrouverait pas ses ~s** it's a real mess.

poussine /pusin/ *nf* Sport girl under the age of 11; **les ~s** the under-elevens.

poussivement /pusivmɑ̃/ *adv* wheezily.

poussoir /puswaʀ/ *nm* **1** (bouton) (push) button; **2** Mécan pushrod, tappet.

poutre /putʀ/ *nf* **1** Constr (en bois, béton) beam; (en métal) girder; **~s apparentes** exposed beams; **plafond à ~s apparentes** timbered ceiling with exposed beams; ▶ **paille**; **2** Sport beam; **exercices à la ~** exercises on the beam.

■ **~ maîtresse** (en bois) main beam; (en métal) main girder.

poutrelle /putʀɛl/ *nf* girder.

poutzer /putse/ [1] *vtr* H (astiquer) to shine up.

pouvoir[1] /puvwaʀ/ [49]

■ **Note** *can* et *may* qui peuvent traduire le verbe *pouvoir* ne s'emploient ni à l'infinitif, ni au futur.

I *v aux* **1** (être capable de) to be able to; **peux-tu soulever cette boîte?** can you lift this box?; **nous espérons ~ partir cette année** we hope to be able to go away this year; **dès que je pourrai** as soon as I can; **il ne pourra pas venir** he won't be able to come; **je suis content que vous ayez pu venir** I'm glad you could come; **il ne pouvait pas cacher son irritation** he couldn't conceal his annoyance; **il pourrait mieux faire** he could do better; **elle aurait pu le faire** she could have done it; **tu peux/pourrais bien me rendre ce service** you can/could at least do this for me; **tu ne pouvais pas me le dire tout de suite!** why couldn't you have told me ou didn't you tell me that right away?; **on ne pourrait mieux dire** that's very well put; **je n'en peux plus** (épuisement , exaspération) I've had it○; (satiété) I'm full○; ▶ **vieillesse**; **2** (être autorisé à) to be allowed to; **les élèves ne peuvent pas quitter l'établissement sans autorisation** pupils can't ou may not ou are not allowed to leave the school without permission; **est-ce que je peux me servir de ta voiture?** can I use your car?; **puis-je m'asseoir?** may I sit down?; **est-ce qu'on peut fumer ici?** is smoking allowed here?; **nous ne pouvons tout de même pas les laisser faire** we can't just stand by and do nothing; **tu peux toujours essayer** you can ou could always try; **on peut dire que** it can be said that; **après ce qui est arrivé on peut se poser des questions** after what happened questions are bound to be asked; **3** (avoir le choix de) **on peut écrire clef ou clé** the word can be written clef or clé; **on peut ne pas faire l'accord** the agreement is optional; **il ne peut pas ne pas accepter** he has no option but to accept; **il peut être malade après tout ce qu'il a mangé** after the amount he ate it's no wonder that he is ill; **4** (avoir l'obligeance de) **pourriez-vous me tenir la porte s'il vous plaît?** can ou could you hold the door (open) for me please?; **si tu pouvais garder la petite, je sortirais un peu** if you could keep an eye on the baby, I could go out for a while; **peux-tu me dire quelle heure il est s'il te plaît?** could you tell me the time please?; **5** (être susceptible de) **tout peut arriver** anything could happen; **cela pourrait arriver à n'importe qui** it could happen to anybody; **il ne peut pas ne pas gagner** he's bound to win; **où peut-il bien être?** where can he be?; **où pouvait-il bien être?** where could he be?; **que peut-il bien faire?** what can he be doing?; **tout le monde peut se tromper** anyone can make a mistake; **puisse cette nouvelle année exaucer vos vœux les plus chers** wishing you everything you could want for the new year; **puisse-t-il revenir sur sa décision** we can only hope that he goes back on his decision; **puissiez-vous dire vrai** let us hope you are right; **rien ne pourra l'arrêter** nothing can stop him/her; **qu'est-ce que cela peut (bien) te faire?** what business is it of yours?; **il peut toujours espérer** there's no harm in wishing ou hoping; **s'il croit que je vais payer ses dettes il peut toujours attendre** if he thinks I'm going to pay his debts he's got another think coming; **elle pouvait mentir, il l'aimait toujours** no matter how much she lied, he still loved her; **qu'est-ce qu'il peut y avoir comme monde!** what a crowd there is!; **qu'est-ce qu'il peut faire froid ici!** it's so cold here!; **ce qu'il peut être grand!** how tall he is!; **peux-tu être bête!** how silly you can be!

II *vtr* **que puis-je pour vous?** what can I do for you?; **je ne peux rien pour vous/contre eux** there's nothing I can do for you/about them; **je n'y peux rien** I can't do anything about it, there's nothing I can do about it; **je fais ce que je peux** I'm doing my best; **'je sais que c'est difficile mais qu'y puis-je?'—'vous pouvez beaucoup'** 'I know it's hard, but what can I do?'—'plenty'.

III *v impers* **il peut faire très froid en janvier** it can get very cold in January; **il pourrait arriver que je parte** I could ou might leave; **il pouvait être 10 heures** it was probably about 10 o'clock; **il peut neiger comme il peut faire beau** it might snow or it might be fine; **c'est inimaginable ce qu'il a pu pleuvoir!** you can't imagine ou wouldn't believe how much it rained!; **ce qu'il peut pleuvoir en ce moment!** it's raining really hard at the moment.

IV il se peut *vpr impers* **il se peut que les prix augmentent en juin** prices may ou might rise in June; **il se peut** or **pourrait que j'accepte leur offre** I may ou might accept their offer; **se peut-il qu'il m'ait oublié?** can he really have forgotten me?; **se peut-il que vous ayez fait cela?** how could you do such a thing?; **'est-ce que tu viendras ce soir?'—'cela se peut'** 'are you coming this evening?'—'I may do'; **cela se pourrait bien** very possibly so; **il** or **cela se pourrait (bien) qu'il soit fâché** he might (well) be angry; **ça ne se peut pas**○ it's impossible.

V on ne peut plus *loc adv* **il est on ne peut plus timide** he is as shy as can be; **c'est on ne peut mieux** it couldn't be better; **il travaille on ne peut plus sérieusement** you couldn't ask for a more conscientious worker; **il est on ne peut plus désagréable** he's thoroughly unpleasant.

IDIOMES **qui peut le plus peut le moins** if you can do something complicated, you can do something simple; **autant que faire se peut** as far as possible.

pouvoir[2] /puvwaʀ/ *nm* **1** (puissance) power; **~s surnaturels** supernatural powers; **~ blanchissant d'un détergent** whitening power of a detergent; **~ d'évocation d'un mot** evocative power of a word; **2** (faculté) ability; **avoir un remarquable ~ d'adaptation** to be remarkably adaptable; **avoir le ~ de faire** to be able to do; **3** (ascendant) power (**sur** over); **le ~ de qn sur qn** sb's power over sb; **il la tient en son ~** he's got her in his power; **4** (autorité) power, authority; **n'avoir aucun ~ sur qn** to have no power over sb; **je n'ai pas le ~ de décider** it's not up to me to decide; **il n'est pas en mon ~ de prendre une telle décision** I'm not the one who decides; **5** Pol power; **~ absolu/royal** absolute/royal power; **après 15 ans de ~** after 15 years in power; **avoir le ~** to be in power; **exercer le ~** to exercise power; **prendre le ~** to take power; **arriver au ~** to come to power; **se maintenir au ~** to stay in power; **séparation des ~s** separation of powers; **en vertu des ~s qui nous sont conférés** by reason of ou in exercise of the powers invested in us; **avoir tous ~s** to have ou exercise all powers; **donner tous ~ à qn** to give sb full powers, to confer full powers on sb; **les pleins ~s** full powers; **le ~ en place** the government in power; **6** Admin, Jur power; **déléguer ses ~s à qn** to delegate powers to sb; **~ par-devant notaire** power of attorney; **donner ~ à qn** to give sb a proxy.

■ **~ d'achat** purchasing power; **~ calorifique** calorific value; **~ exécutif** executive power; **le ~ judiciaire** (corps) the judiciary; **~ législatif** legislative power; **~ séparateur** Phys resolving power; **~ spirituel** spiritual power; **~ temporel** temporal power; **les ~s constitués** the powers that be; **~s exceptionnels** emergency powers; **~s publics** authorities.

pouzzolane /puzɔlan/ *nf* pozzuolana.

Powys ▶ 692 *nprm* **le ~** Powys.

PPCM /pepeseɛm/ *nm* (*abbr* = **plus petit commun multiple**) LCM, lcm.

PQ° /peky/ *nm* toilet paper; **rouleau de ~** loo roll GB, roll of toilet paper.

PR /peɛʀ/ *nm* (*abbr* = **parti républicain**) *French Republican Party.*

practice /pʀaktis/ *nm* (au golf) driving range.

præsidium /pʀezidjɔm/ *nm* presidium.

■ **~ du Soviet suprême** Presidium of the Supreme Soviet.

pragmatique /pʀagmatik/ **I** *adj* pragmatic. **II** *nf* pragmatics (+ *v sg*).

pragmatisme /pʀagmatism/ *nm* pragmatism.

pragmatiste /pʀagmatist/ *adj, nmf* pragmatist.

Prague /pʀag/ ▶ 857 *npr* Prague.

praire /pʀɛʀ/ *nf* clam.

prairial /pʀɛʀjal/ *nm* Prairial (*ninth month in the French Revolutionary calendar,* ≈ *June*).

prairie /pʀɛʀi/ *nf* gén meadow; (aux États-Unis) **la ~** the prairie(s).

pralin /pʀalɛ̃/ *nm* Culin praline.

praline /pʀalin/ *nf* **1** (amande) sugared GB ou sugar-coated US almond; **2**° (balle) slug°, bullet; **3** B (chocolat) chocolate.

praliné, **~e** /pʀaline/ **I** *adj* **1** (enrobé de sucre) sugared GB, sugar-coated US; **2** [*dessert, crème*] praline (*épith*).

II *nm* (mélange, arôme, bonbon) praline.

praliner /pʀaline/ [1] *vtr* Culin to flavour[GB] [sth] with praline.

praséodyme /pʀazeɔdim/ *nm* praseodymium.

praticable /pʀatikabl/ **I** *adj* **1** (où l'on peut passer) [*chemin, route, sentier*] passable, practicable, negotiable; **avec la neige les routes ne sont pas ~s** the roads are not passable due to snow; **à peine** or **difficilement ~** [*chemin*] scarcely passable; **2** (réalisable) [*sport*] that can be played (*après n*); [*analyse*] practicable sout.

II *nm* **1** Cin platform; **2** Théât working scenery, practicable scenery spéc; **3** Sport (en gymnastique) *space used for floor exercises.*

praticien, **-ienne** /pʀatisjɛ̃, ɛn/ *nm,f* **1** Méd general practitioner, GP; **demandez à votre ~** ask your GP; **les ~s hospitaliers** hospital doctors; **2** (personne de métier) practitioner.

pratiquant, **~e** /pʀatikɑ̃, ɑ̃t/ **I** *adj* Relig [*personne, catholique*] practising[GB]; **il n'est pas ~** he doesn't practise[GB] (his religion); **être très ~** to be very devout; **musulman non ~** non-practising[GB] Muslim.

II *nm,f* Relig (catholique) practising[GB] Catholic; (musulman) practising[GB] Muslim; (juif) practising[GB] Jew.

pratique /pʀatik/ **I** *adj* **1** (commode) [*appareil, objet*] handy, practical; [*endroit, itinéraire*] convenient; [*technique, vêtement, meuble*] practical; **c'est ~ ce tissu, ça ne se repasse pas** this material is practical, you don't have to iron it; **voir le côté ~ des choses** to see the practical side of things; **2** (utile) [*manuel, renseignement, conseil, moyen*] practical; **3** (non théorique) [*application, exercice, mesure*] practical; **quelles sont vos connaissances ~s dans ce domaine?** how much practical experience do you have in the field?; **4** (concret) [*problème, détail, raison*] practical; **en termes ~s** in practical terms; **5** (pragmatique) [*personne*] practical; **avoir le sens** or **l'esprit ~** to be practical; **n'avoir aucun sens** or **esprit ~** to be totally impractical.

II *nf* **1** (exercice d'une activité) **inciter les jeunes à la ~ d'un sport** to encourage young people to play a sport; **la ~ des arts martiaux est très répandue** many people practise[GB] martial arts; **la ~ des langues vivantes** speaking foreign languages; **cela nécessite de longues heures de ~** it takes hours of practice; **avoir une bonne ~ de l'anglais** to have a good working knowledge of English; **la ~ religieuse** religious observance; **2** (expérience) practical experience; **manquer de ~** to lack practical experience; **avoir une longue ~ de la médecine** to have many years of experience in medicine; **avoir la ~ des affaires** to have practical business experience; **3** (application de principes) practice; **la théorie et la ~** theory and practice; **mettre qch en ~** to put sth into practice; **dans la ~, en ~** in practice; **4** (habitude) practice; **une ~ courante/frauduleuse/déloyale** a common/fraudulent/disloyal practice; **certaines ~s culturelles/funéraires** certain cultural/funerary practices; **les ~s religieuses** religious practices.

pratiquement /pʀatikmɑ̃/ *adv* **1** (en pratique) in practice; **2** (quasiment) practically, virtually; **elle a ~ tout essayé** she's tried practically ou virtually everything; **~ jamais** hardly ever; **elles n'ont ~ pas évolué** they have hardly evolved at all.

pratiquer /pʀatike/ [1] **I** *vtr* **1** (exercer régulièrement) to play [*tennis, squash, basket*]; to do [*athlétisme, canoë, tir à l'arc, yoga*]; **~ l'équitation/l'aviron/le ski/l'escalade** to ride/row/ski/climb; to take part in [*activité, discipline*]; to practise[GB] [*langue*]; **~ la médecine** to practise[GB] medicine; **il ne pratique plus** he doesn't practise[GB] any more; **il est croyant mais ne pratique pas** he believes in God but doesn't practise[GB] his faith; **2** (mettre à exécution) to use [*méthode, chantage*]; to pursue [*politique*]; to charge [*taux d'intérêt*]; **toutes les entreprises pratiquent cette stratégie** all companies use ou follow this strategy; **~ la concertation/l'ouverture** to pursue a policy of consultation/openness ; **ils pratiquent des tarifs très compétitifs** they offer very competitive rates; **3** (effectuer) to carry out [*examen, greffe, transfusion*]; to administer [*soins*]; to make [*passage, trou*]; to clear [*chemin*]; to carry out [*expulsion*]; **~ un sentier dans un taillis** to clear a path through a thicket; **4** fml (lire régulièrement) **~ Queneau/Sartre** to read a lot of Queneau/Sartre.

II se pratiquer *vpr* (être en usage) [*tennis, football, billard*] to be played; [*technique, politique, stratégie*] to be used; [*prix, tarif*] to be charged; **c'est un sport qui se pratique beaucoup** it's a very popular sport; **le volley-ball se pratique essentiellement en salle** volley-ball is mainly played indoors; **ici le ski/l'équitation/l'aviron se pratique toute l'année** here people can go skiing/riding/rowing throughout the year.

praxis /pʀaksis/ *nf inv* praxis.

Praxitèle /pʀaksitɛl/ *npr* Praxiteles.

pré /pʀe/ *nm* **1** Agric meadow; **2** (terrain de duel) duelling[GB] ground; **aller sur le ~** lit to fight a duel; fig to do battle.

■ **~ carré** preserve, reserved area.

pré(-) /pʀe/ *préf* pre(-); **préclassique** preclassical; **préindustriel** preindustrial; **prévictorien** pre-Victorian; **précommande** advance order; **précontrat** advance contract; **pré-accord** preliminary agreement.

préadolescent, **~e** /pʀeadɔlesɑ̃, ɑ̃t/ **I** *adj* preteenage.

II *nm,f* preteenager.

préalable /pʀealabl/ **I** *adj* (qui précède) [*permission, avis*] prior; (qui prépare) [*entretien, étude*] preliminary; **sans avis ~** without prior notice; **~ à** preceding; **les entretiens ~s aux négociations** the talks preceding the negotiations; **poser des conditions ~s à une nomination** to lay down certain preconditions for an appointment.

II *nm* (condition) precondition (**à** for, of); (préliminaire) preliminary; **en ~ à** (avant) prior to; (en préliminaire) as a preliminary to; **poser qch en** or **comme ~** to lay sth down as a precondition ou prior condition.

III au préalable *loc adv* first, beforehand.

préalablement /pʀealabləmɑ̃/ *adv* beforehand; **~ à toute décision** prior to ou before any decision; **coupez en petits dés les légumes ~ épluchés** dice the previously peeled vegetables.

Préalpes /pʀealp/ *nprfpl* Pre-Alps.

préalpin, **~e** /pʀealpɛ̃, in/ *adj* of the Pre-Alps.

préambule /pʀeɑ̃byl/ *nm* **1** (introduction) preamble; **2** (avertissement) forewarning; **sans ~** with no forewarning.

préamplificateur /pʀeɑ̃plifikatœʀ/ *nm* preamplifier, preamp°.

préapprentissage /pʀeapʀɑ̃tisaʒ/ *nm* Scol work experience; **je suis en ~** I'm on a work experience programme[GB].

préau, *pl* **~x** /pʀeo/ *nm* (d'école) covered playground; (de prison) exercise yard; (d'hôpital, de cloître) inner courtyard.

préavis /pʀeavi/ *nm inv* notice; **sans ~** without notice; **un ~ d'un mois, un mois de ~** a month's notice; **~ de licenciement** dismissal notice; **déposer un ~ de grève** to give notice of strike action.

prébende /pʀebɑ̃d/ *nf* **1** (revenu) liter income derived from a sinecure; **2** Relig prebend.

prébendé, **~e** /pʀebɑ̃de/ *adj* prebendal.

prébendier /pʀebɑ̃dje/ *nm* prebendary.

précaire /pʀekɛʀ/ *adj* **1** [*existence, position, bonheur*] precarious; [*emploi*] insecure; [*construction, structure*] flimsy; **le travail ~** casual work; **2** Jur [*possession*] precarious; **détention (d'un bien à titre) ~** precarious holding (of a property); **location/occupant à titre ~** precarious tenancy/occupier.

précairement /pʀekɛʀmɑ̃/ *adv* liter, Jur precariously.

précambrien, **-ienne** /pʀekɑ̃bʀijɛ̃, ɛn/ I *adj* Precambrian.

II *nm* **le ~** the Precambrian (era).

précarisation /pʀekaʀizasjɔ̃/ *nf* **~ de l'emploi** casualization of labour^GB; **la ~ des salariés gagne du terrain** the habit of using casual labour^GB is increasing.

précariser /pʀekaʀize/ [1] I *vtr* **~ l'emploi** to casualize labour^GB; **~ la situation de qn** to make sb's position insecure.

II **se précariser** *vpr* [*emploi*] to become insecure.

précarité /pʀekaʀite/ *nf* gén, Jur precariousness; **la ~ de l'emploi** job insecurity; **prime de ~** *bonus given to temporary staff as compensation for lack of job security.*

précaution /pʀekosjɔ̃/ *nf* **1** (mesure) precaution; **~s d'hygiène** hygiene precautions; **prendre la ~ de faire** to take the precaution of doing; **les ~s d'emploi d'un médicament** the precautions to be taken in using a medicine; **prendre ses ~s** gén to take precautions; euph (en allant aux toilettes) to go to the toilet just in case; euph (avec un contraceptif) to take precautions euph; **prendre toutes ses ~s** (pour garder un secret, mener une enquête) to take every precaution; **sans aucune/la moindre ~** without any/the slightest precaution; **manipuler un objet avec mille** or **d'infinies ~s** to handle an object extremely carefully; **s'entourer de ~s** to take a great number of precautions; **2** (prévoyance) caution; **sans ~** without caution; **avec ~** (attention) with caution; (méfiance) cautiously; **par ~** as a precaution; **par mesure de ~** as a precautionary measure; **pour plus de ~** as an added precaution; **faire des achats de ~** to stockpile; **un stock de ~** a stockpile.

■ **~s oratoires** carefully chosen words.

IDIOMES **deux ~s valent mieux qu'une** Prov better safe than sorry Prov.

précautionneusement /pʀekosjɔnøzmɑ̃/ *adv* [*poser, manipuler*] very carefully; [*avancer, marcher*] (avec attention) with caution; (avec méfiance) cautiously.

précautionneux, **-euse** /pʀekosjɔnø, øz/ *adj* fml careful.

précédemment /pʀesedamɑ̃/ *adv* previously, before.

précédent, **~e** /pʀesedɑ̃, ɑ̃t/ I *adj* previous; **la fois ~e** the time before, on the previous occasion.

II *nm,f* **le ~** the previous one.

III *nm* (fait antérieur) precedent; **créer un ~** to create a precedent; **sans ~** without precedent, unprecedented.

précéder /pʀesede/ [14] *vtr* **1** (dans un groupe en mouvement) [*personne, groupe*] to go in front of, to precede; [*véhicule*] to be in front of, to precede; **la voiture/l'homme qui me précédait** the car/the man in front of me; **il était dans la voiture qui précédait** he was in the car in front; **2** (dans un lieu) **il m'avait précédé de cinq minutes** he'd got there five minutes ahead of me; **il est arrivé vite mais on l'avait précédé** he arrived quickly but someone had got there first; **3** (être placé avant) [*paragraphe, mot, chapitre*] to precede; **dans le paragraphe qui précède** in the above ou preceding paragraph; **ne tenez pas compte de ce qui précède** ignore the above; **4** (se produire avant) [*événement, période, mois, crise*] to lead up to, to precede; [*film*] to precede; **les six mois qui précèdèrent la guerre/leur mort** the six months leading up to the war/their death; **le mois précédant Noël** the month before Christmas; **la semaine qui a précédé votre départ** the week before you left; **les générations qui nous ont précédés** the generations that came before us; **faire ~ une opération d'un traitement** to administer a course of treatment before an operation; **5** (dans un classement, une hiérarchie) to be higher than, to come higher than; **Pierre précède Paul au classement** Pierre comes before Paul in the ranking; **Tours précède Grenoble de trois points** Tours is three points ahead of Grenoble.

précepte /pʀesɛpt/ *nm* precept.

précepteur, **-trice** /pʀesɛptœʀ, tʀis/ ▶ 510 *nm,f* (private) tutor.

préceptorat /pʀesɛptɔʀa/ *nm* **1** (état, titre) tutorship; **2** (méthode d'enseignement) (private) tutoring.

préchauffage /pʀeʃofaʒ/ *nm* (d'aliments, de feu) preheating; (de moteur) warming up; (de goudron, pièce à souder) heating up.

préchauffer /pʀeʃofe/ [1] *vtr* to preheat [*aliment*]; to warm up [*moteur*]; to heat [*goudron, pièce à souder*].

prêche /pʀɛʃ/ *nm* sermon.

prêcher /pʀeʃe/ [1] I *vtr* **1** Relig to preach [*Évangile*]; **~ la bonne parole** to spread the Word; **2** (recommander) to advocate [*patience, modération*]; **elle prêche l'impossible** she is advocating the impossible; **~ la patience à qn** to urge sb to be patient.

II *vi* to preach.

IDIOMES **~ le faux pour savoir le vrai** to tell a lie in order to get at the truth; **~ pour son saint** or **sa paroisse** to promote one's own cause.

prêcheur, **-euse** /pʀɛʃœʀ, øz/ I *adj* pej preachy° péj.

II *nm,f* preacher.

prêchi-prêcha /pʀɛʃipʀɛʃa/ *nm inv* pej sermonizing.

précieusement /pʀesjøzmɑ̃/ *adv* **1** [*garder, conserver*] carefully; [*graver*] minutely; **2** [*parler*] in an affected manner.

précieux, **-ieuse** /pʀesjø, øz/ I *adj* **1** (coûteux) [*pierre, métal, livre*] precious; [*meuble*] valuable; **chaque minute est précieuse** every moment is precious; **2** (utile) [*information*] very useful; [*collaborateur*] valued; **vous m'avez été d'un ~ secours** you've helped me immeasurably; **votre aide m'a été précieuse** your help was most valuable; **3** (chéri) [*amitié, droit, qualité*] precious; [*ami*] very dear; **4** (affecté) [*style, langage, geste*] precious; **5** Littérat [*littérature, salon*] précieuse.

II **précieuse** *nf* (femme) précieuse.

préciosité /pʀesjozite/ *nf* preciosity.

précipice /pʀesipis/ *nm* precipice; **être au bord du ~** fig [*pays, compagnie*] to be on the brink of collapse.

précipitamment /pʀesipitamɑ̃/ *adv* [*partir, s'enfuir*] hurriedly; **il nous a quittés ~** he left us in a hurry; **rentrer** or **revenir ~** to rush back; **se lever ~** to leap to one's feet.

précipitation /pʀesipitasjɔ̃/ I *nf* **1** (hâte) haste; **la ~ de leur départ nous a surpris** their hasty departure surprised us; **dans ma ~** in my haste; **il faut se garder de toute ~** we mustn't rush things; **avec ~** hurriedly; **sans ~** unhurriedly; **sans grande ~** with no great haste; **2** Chimie precipitation.

II **précipitations** *nfpl* Météo rainfall ¢, precipitation ¢ spéc.

précipité, **~e** /pʀesipite/ I *pp* ▶ **précipiter**.

II *pp adj* **1** (rapide) [*course, pas, respiration, rythme*] rapid, fast; [*battement du cœur, mouvement*] rapid; **des coups ~s à la porte** an impatient knocking at the door; **2** (hâtif) [*décision, départ, retour, diagnostic*] hasty, precipitate; **un jugement ~** a snap judgment.

III *nm* Chimie precipitate.

précipiter /pʀesipite/ [1] I *vtr* **1** (jeter) **~ qn d'un balcon** to push sb off a balcony; **~ qn par la fenêtre** to push sb out of the window; **~ qn dans le vide** (du haut d'un bâtiment, palier) to push sb off; (du haut d'une falaise) to push sb over; (par la fenêtre) to push sb out; **~ qn dans l'escalier** to push sb down the stairs; **~ qn contre** to throw sb against; **le vent l'a précipité contre l'arbre** the wind blew him against the tree; **2** fig (plonger) **~ qn dans le désarroi** to throw sb into confusion; **~ qn/un pays dans le chaos** to throw sb's life/a country into chaos; **~ qn dans le malheur** or **la misère** to plunge sb into hardship; **3** (hâter) to hasten [*départ, décision, réforme*]; to precipitate [*révolte, événement*]; **~ le vote d'une loi** to speed up the passage of a bill; **mieux vaut ne pas ~ les choses** it is better not to rush things; **4** Chimie to precipitate [*solution*].

II *vi* Chimie to precipitate.

III **se précipiter** *vpr* **1** (se jeter) **il s'est précipité dans le vide** he jumped off; **se ~ du haut d'un immeuble** to jump off ou throw oneself off the top of a building; **se ~ du haut d'une falaise** to jump off ou throw oneself over the edge of a cliff; **2** (se ruer) to rush; **se ~ à la porte/fenêtre** to rush to the door/window; **en le voyant tomber, je me suis précipité** when I saw him fall, I rushed over; **se ~ au secours de qn** to rush to sb's aid, to rush to help sb; **se ~ dans les bras de qn** to throw oneself into sb's arms; **se ~ sur** [*personne*] to rush at, to throw oneself on [*personne*]; [*animal*] to rush at [*personne*]; to rush for [*objet*]; fig to pounce on [*idée, théorie*]; **se ~ sur les soldes/sur les bonnes affaires** to rush to the sales/for bargains; **se ~ vers qn** to rush toward(s) sb; **se ~ pour faire** to rush to do; **3** (se dépêcher) to rush, to hurry; **pas la peine de se ~**° no point in rushing ou hurrying; **4** (affluer) [*spectateurs, clients, candidats*] to pour in; [*investisseurs*] to come running; **les clients ne se précipitent pas** customers are not exactly pouring in; **5** (s'accélérer) [*action, événement*] to move faster; **les choses se précipitent à l'Est** things are moving faster in the East.

précis, **~e** /pʀesi, iz/ I *adj* **1** (bien défini) [*programme, critère, motif, réglementation*] specific; [*idée, engagement, date*] definite; [*moment*] particular; **dans le cas ~ de** in the specific case of; **à ce moment ~ de l'année** at this particular time of year; **aucune date ~e n'a été fixée** no definite date has been fixed ou set; **2** (exact) [*personne, geste, langue, travail, horaire, réponse*] precise; [*chiffre, donnée, calcul*] accurate; [*souvenir*] clear; [*endroit, moment*] exact; **à douze centimètres, pour être ~** twelve centimetres^GB away, to be precise; **adresse ~e** exact address; **à l'endroit ~ où** at the exact place where; **au moment ~ où** at the exact time when; **à deux heures ~es** at exactly two o'clock; **3** (de précision) [*instrument de mesure*] accurate; **une montre très ~e** a very accurate watch.

II *nm inv* Édition handbook.

précisément /pʀesizemɑ̃/ *adv* **1** (justement) precisely; **c'est ~ ce que je pense** that's precisely what I think; **2** (avec précision) precisely; **impossible de le dater plus ~** impossible to date it more precisely; **3** (pour être précis) **à la page 6 plus ~** on page 6 to be more precise; **l'Europe et plus ~ la France** Europe and more precisely France.

préciser /pʀesize/ [1] I *vtr* **1** (ajouter) [*personne, rapport*] to add (**que** that); **il a précisé que son pays était déçu** he added that his country was disappointed; **a-t-il précisé** he added; **faut-il le** or **est-il besoin de ~** needless to say; **2** (faire état de) [*personne, communiqué*] to state (**que** that); **~ ses intentions** to state one's intentions; **précise le gouvernement** the government states; **3** (indiquer avec précision) to specify [*lieu, date, nombre*]; **~ si/pourquoi/comment** to specify whether/why/how; **pouvez-vous ~?** could you be more specific?; **lieu/moment/nombre non précisé** unspecified place/time/number; **4** (rendre plus précis) to clarify [*idées, programme*].

II **se préciser** *vpr* **1** (se concrétiser) [*danger, avenir, menace*] to become clearer; [*projet, mariage, voyage*] to take shape; **mon départ se précise** all the arrangements have been made for my departure; **2** (devenir apparent) [*forme, réalité*] to become clear.

précision /pʀesizjɔ̃/ *nf* **1** (minutie) precision; **doser/ciseler avec ~** to measure out/ chisel with precision; **~ du détail** detailed precision; **2** Mes, Sci (justesse) accuracy; **avec une ~ d'un millimètre** with an accuracy to within one millimetre[GB]; **se révéler d'une grande ~** to prove to be very accurate; **avec ~** accurately; **localiser avec ~** to pinpoint; **mesurer avec ~** to measure accurately; **instrument de ~** precision instrument; **3** (détail) detail; **apporter quelques ~s** to give a few details (**sur** about); **sans autres ~s** without further details; **ils n'ont pas donné de ~s sur la réunion** they didn't provide any details about the meeting; **pour plus de ~ contacter** for further details please contact.

précité, **~e** /pʀesite/ *adj* aforementioned (*épith*), mentioned previously (*après n*).

précoce /pʀekɔs/ *adj* **1** (mûr avant l'âge) [*enfant, intelligence, sexualité*] precocious; **2** (en avance) [*légume, saison, diagnostic, vision, dépistage*] early (*épith*); **3** (prématuré) [*rides, sénilité, démence*] premature.

précocement /pʀekɔsmɑ̃/ *adv* **1** (très tôt) early; **2** (trop tôt) prematurely.

précocité /pʀekɔsite/ *nf* **1** (d'enfant, intelligence) precociousness, precocity sout; **2** (d'action) **la ~ du dépistage** early detection; **3** (de fruit, saison) earliness.

précolombien, **-ienne** /pʀekɔlɔ̃bjɛ̃, ɛn/ *adj* pre-Columbian.

précombustion /pʀekɔ̃bystjɔ̃/ *nf* precombustion.

précompte /pʀekɔ̃t/ *nm* deduction; **~ de l'impôt** deduction of tax at source.

précompter /pʀekɔ̃te/ [1] *vtr* to deduct [*cotisation*] (**sur** from).

préconception /pʀekɔ̃sɛpsjɔ̃/ *nf* preconception.

préconçu, **~e** /pʀekɔ̃sy/ *adj* preconceived; **avoir des idées ~es** to have preconceived ideas.

préconisation /pʀekɔnizasjɔ̃/ *nf* **1** (de traitement) recommendation; **2** Relig preconization.

préconiser /pʀekɔnize/ [1] *vtr* **1** (conseiller) to recommend [*méthode, solution*]; (prôner) to advocate [*doctrine, jeûne*]; **~ que nous fassions** to recommend that we should do; **il préconise d'intervenir militairement** he recommends military intervention; **2** Relig to preconize [*évêque*].

préconscient, **~e** /pʀekɔ̃sjɑ̃, ɑ̃t/ **I** *adj* preconscious.

II *nm* preconscious.

précontraint, **~e** /pʀekɔ̃tʀɛ̃, ɛ̃t/ **I** *adj* [*béton, poutre*] prestressed.

II *nm* prestressed concrete.

précuit, **~e** /pʀekɥi, it/ *adj* precooked.

précurseur /pʀekyʀsœʀ/ **I** *adj m* precursory fml; **signes ~s de l'orage** signs that herald a storm.

II *nm* (dans un domaine) pioneer; **~ de** [*discipline*] forerunner of; [*personne*] precursor of.

prédateur, **-trice** /pʀedatœʀ, tʀis/ **I** *adj* predatory.

II *nm* **1** (animal) predator; **2** (homme préhistorique) hunter-gatherer.

prédation /pʀedasjɔ̃/ *nf* **1** (par les animaux) predation; **2** (de l'homme préhistorique) hunting and gathering.

prédécesseur /pʀedesesœʀ/ *nm* predecessor.

prédélinquant, **~e** /pʀedelɛ̃kɑ̃, ɑ̃t/ *nm,f*: *young person likely to become an offender*.

prédestination /pʀedɛstinasjɔ̃/ *nf* littér, Relig predestination.

prédestiné, **~e** /pʀedɛstine/ **I** *pp* ▶ **prédestiner**.

II *pp adj* [*nom, prénom*] appropriate; **être ~ à qch** to be predestined for sth.

prédestiner /pʀedɛstine/ [1] *vtr* to predestine; **~ qn à qch/à faire** to predestine sb for sth/to do.

prédétermination /pʀedetɛʀminasjɔ̃/ *nf* predetermination.

prédéterminer /pʀedetɛʀmine/ [1] *vtr* to predetermine.

prédicant† /pʀedikɑ̃/ *nm* preacher.

prédicat /pʀedika/ *nm* predicate.

prédicateur, **-trice** /pʀedikatœʀ, tʀis/ *nm,f* preacher.

prédicatif, **-ive** /pʀedikatif, iv/ *adj* predicative.

prédication /pʀedikasjɔ̃/ *nf* **1** Ling, Philos predication; **2** Relig (fait de prêcher) preaching; (sermon) sermon.

prédictif, **-ive** /pʀediktif, iv/ *adj* predictive.

prédiction /pʀediksjɔ̃/ *nf* prediction.

prédigéré, **~e** /pʀediʒeʀe/ *adj* predigested.

prédilection /pʀedilɛksjɔ̃/ *nf* predilection (**pour** for), liking (**pour** for); **de ~** favourite[GB] (*épith*).

prédire /pʀediʀ/ [65] *vtr* **1** (par divination) to predict [*avenir*]; **~ qch à qn** to predict sth for sb; **il m'a prédit que je ferais** he predicted that I would do; **2** (par réflexion) to predict.

prédisposer /pʀedispoze/ [1] *vtr* to predispose (**à** to).

prédisposition /pʀedispozisjɔ̃/ *nf* predisposition (**à faire** to do); **~ au diabète** predisposition to diabetes; **montrer des ~s pour la musique** to show a talent for music.

prédominance /pʀedɔminɑ̃s/ *nf* predominance (**sur** over).

prédominant, **~e** /pʀedɔminɑ̃, ɑ̃t/ *adj* predominant.

prédominer /pʀedɔmine/ [1] *vi* to predominate (**sur** over); **ce qui prédomine à mes yeux, c'est...** what strikes me most is...

préélectoral, **~e**, *mpl* **-aux** /pʀeelɛktɔʀal, o/ *adj* pre-election (*épith*).

préemballé, **~e** /pʀeɑ̃bale/ *adj* prepacked.

prééminence /pʀeeminɑ̃s/ *nf* preeminence (**sur** over).

prééminent, **~e** /pʀeeminɑ̃, ɑ̃t/ *adj* preeminent.

préemption /pʀeɑ̃psjɔ̃/ *nf* preemption; **droit de ~** pre-emptive right.

préencollé, **~e** /pʀeɑ̃kɔle/ *adj* [*enveloppe*] gummed; [*papier peint*] prepasted; [*carreau, affiche*] self-adhesive.

préenregistrer /pʀeɑ̃ʀəʒistʀe/ [1] *vtr* to prerecord; **cassette préenregistrée** prerecorded tape ou cassette.

préétablir /pʀeetabliʀ/ [3] *vtr* to pre-establish.

préexistant, **~e** /pʀeɛgzistɑ̃, ɑ̃t/ *adj* preexisting.

préexistence /pʀeɛgzistɑ̃s/ *nf* pre-existence.

préexister /pʀeɛgziste/ [1] *vi* to pre-exist; **~ à qch** to predate sth.

préfabrication /pʀefabʀikasjɔ̃/ *nf* prefabrication.

préfabriqué, **~e** /pʀefabʀike/ **I** *adj* prefabricated; **baraquement ~** prefabricated building, terrapin.

II *nm* **1** (matériau) prefabricated material; **2** (maison) prefabricated house, prefab○; (bâtiment) prefabricated building, prefab○.

préface /pʀefas/ *nf* preface; **~ d'un livre** preface to a book; **~ de Paul George** preface by Paul George.

préfacer /pʀefase/ [12] *vtr* to write a ou the preface to; **ouvrage préfacé par** book with a preface by.

préfacier, **-ière** /pʀefasje, ɛʀ/ *nm,f* preface writer.

préfectoral, **~e**, *mpl* **-aux** /pʀefɛktɔʀal, o/ *adj* [*niveau, autorisation*] prefectorial; [*administration, locaux*] prefectural; **mouvement ~** prefectural reshuffle.

préfecture /pʀefɛktyʀ/ *nf* **1** Admin prefecture; **2** (chef-lieu) *main city of a department*; **3** Mil Naut **~ maritime** naval prefecture.

■ **~ de police** *police headquarters in some large French cities*.

préférable /pʀefeʀabl/ *adj* preferable; **il est ~ que** it is preferable ou better that; **il est ~ que tu n'y ailles pas** it is preferable ou better that you don't go; **il est/serait ~ de faire** it is/would be preferable ou better to do; **~ à** preferable to; **la déception est ~ à l'incertitude** disappointment is preferable to uncertainty.

préféré, **~e** /pʀefeʀe/ **I** *pp* ▶ **préférer**.

II *pp adj, nm,f* favourite[GB].

préférence /pʀefeʀɑ̃s/ *nf* preference; **avoir une ~ (marquée) pour qn/qch** to have a (clear) preference for sb/sth; **ne pas avoir de ~** to have no preference; **donner la ~ à qn/qch** to give preference to sb/sth; **de ~** preferably; **achète cette marque de ~** if you can, buy this brand; **par ordre de ~** in order of preference.

préférentiel, **-ielle** /pʀefeʀɑ̃sjɛl/ *adj* preferential; **bénéficier d'un tarif ~** to obtain a preferential rate.

préférer /pʀefeʀe/ [14] *vtr* to prefer; **~ Pierre à Paul** to prefer Pierre to Paul; **~ le jazz à la musique classique** to prefer jazz to classical music; **~ faire** to prefer to do ou doing; **je préfère téléphoner plutôt qu'écrire** I prefer phoning to writing; **je préfère que tu viennes plus tard** I would rather you came later, I would prefer it if you came later; **(c'est) comme tu préfères** (it's) as you prefer ou wish; **j'aurais préféré ne jamais l'apprendre** I wish I'd never heard it.

préfet /pʀefɛ/ *nm* **1** Admin prefect; **~ de police** prefect of police, police chief; **~ maritime** post admiral; **~ apostolique** prefect apostolic; **~ de région** regional prefect; **2** Scol (dans un établissement privé) prefect; **~ des études** prefect of studies; **3** ▶ **510** B Scol headmaster.

préfète /pʀefɛt/ *nf* **1** (femme du préfet) prefect's wife; **2** B Scol headmistress.

préfiguration /pʀefigyʀasjɔ̃/ *nf* prefiguration (**de** of).

préfigurer /pʀefigyʀe/ [1] *vtr* to prefigure.

préfixal, **~e**, *mpl* **-aux** /pʀefiksal, o/ *adj* prefixal.

préfixation /pʀefiksasjɔ̃/ *nf* prefixation.

préfixe /pʀefiks/ *nm* prefix.

préfixer /pʀefikse/ [1] *vtr* **1** Ling to prefix; **2** Jur to prearrange.

préglaciaire /pʀeglasjɛʀ/ *adj* preglacial.

préhenseur /pʀeɑ̃sœʀ/ *adj m* prehensile.

préhensile /pʀeɑ̃sil/ *adj* prehensile.

préhension /pʀeɑ̃sjɔ̃/ *nf* prehension, grasping.

préhistoire /pʀeistwaʀ/ *nf* prehistory.

préhistorique /pʀeistɔʀik/ *adj* lit, fig prehistoric.

préindustriel, **-ielle** /pʀeɛ̃dystʀijɛl/ *adj* [*société*] pre-industrial.

préinscription /pʀeɛ̃skʀipsjɔ̃/ *nf* preregistration.

préjudice /pʀeʒydis/ *nm* harm ¢, damage ¢; **un grave ~** serious harm ou damage; **~ financier** financial loss; **~ matériel** material loss; **~ moral** moral wrong; **causer un ~ à qn** to harm sb, to cause harm to sb; **porter ~ à qn** to harm sb, to cause harm to sb; **porter ~ à qch** gén to damage sth, to be detrimental to sth; Jur to be prejudicial to sth; **subir un ~** to suffer harm; **au ~ de qn** to the detriment of sb; **il a vendu l'affaire au ~ de ses frères** he sold the business to the detriment of his brothers; **sans ~ de** Jur without prejudice to; **il a été condamné à 10 000 francs d'amende, sans ~ des dommages et intérêts** he was ordered to pay 10,000 francs without prejudice to damages.

préjudiciable /pʀeʒydisjabl/ *adj* prejudicial, detrimental (**à** to).

préjugé /pʀeʒyʒe/ *nm* prejudice; **~ de classe/race** class/racial prejudice; **il est plein de ~s** he's very prejudiced; **~(s) en faveur de qn** bias (*sg*) in favour[GB] of sb; **avoir un ~ en défaveur de** or **contre qn/qch** to have a prejudice against sb/sth; **bénéficier d'un ~ favorable auprès de** or **de la part de qn** to be looked on favourably[GB] by sb.

préjuger /pʀeʒyʒe/ [13] **I** *vtr* to prejudge.
II préjuger de *vtr ind* to prejudge; **nous ne pouvons ~ de l'avenir** we can't tell what the future holds.

prélasser: **se prélasser** /pʀelase/ [1] *vpr* to lounge; **elle se prélassait dans son lit** she was lounging in her bed; **se ~ au soleil** to laze in the sun.

prélat /pʀela/ *nm* prelate.

prélature /pʀelatyʀ/ *nf* prelacy.

prélavage /pʀelavaʒ/ *nm* prewash; **~ inutile** do not prewash.

prélaver /pʀelave/ [1] *vtr* to prewash.

prêle /pʀɛl/ *nf* Bot horsetail, equisetum.

prélèvement /pʀelɛvmɑ̃/ *nm* **1** Géol, Méd, Sci (action) sampling; **faire** or **effectuer un ~ de sang** to take a blood sample; **le ~ doit se faire le matin** the sample should be taken in the morning; **2** (échantillon) sample; **3** Fin (opération) debiting; **faire** or **effectuer un ~ bancaire de 100 francs** to make a debit of 100 francs; **faire faire un ~ sur son compte** to have money debited from one's account; **4** Fin (somme) debit; **5** Fin, Fisc deduction.
■ **~ automatique** direct debit; **~ exceptionnel** exceptional levy; **~ fiscal** deduction of tax; **~ forfaitaire** deduction of tax at the basic rate; **~ libératoire** tax withholding with full discharge; **~ social** social security contributions (*pl*); **~ à la source** deduction at source; **~s obligatoires** tax and social security deductions.

prélever /pʀelve/ [16] *vtr* **1** Méd, Sci, Géol (pour une analyse) to take a sample of [*sang, moelle, eau*] (**de** from); (pour une greffe) to remove [*organe*]; **~ un échantillon de** to take a sample of; **2** Fin (sur un compte bancaire) to debit (**sur** from); **3** Fisc to deduct [*cotisation, impôt*] (**sur** from); **4** (prendre) to take [*argent, pourcentage*] (**sur** from); to remove [*pièce, matériel*] (**sur** from).

préliminaire /pʀelimineʀ/ **I** *adj* preliminary (**à** to).
II préliminaires *nmpl* preliminaries.

prélude /pʀelyd/ *nm* **1** Mus prelude; **2** fig prelude; **en ~ à** as a prelude to.

préluder /pʀelyde/ [1] **I préluder à** *vtr ind* to be a prelude to.
II *vi* Mus to warm up.

prématuré, **~e** /pʀematyʀe/ **I** *adj* premature; **il serait ~ de faire** it would be premature to do.
II *nm,f* premature baby.

prématurément /pʀematyʀemɑ̃/ *adv* [*naître, vieillir*] prematurely.

prémédication /pʀemedikasjɔ̃/ *nf* premedication.

préméditation /pʀemeditasjɔ̃/ *nf* premeditation; **avec/sans ~** [*agir*] with/without premeditation; [*crime*] premeditated/unpremeditated.

préméditer /pʀemedite/ [1] *vtr* to premeditate [*coup, meurtre*]; **~ de faire** to plan to do.

prémenstruel, **-elle** /pʀemɑ̃stʀɥɛl/ *adj* premenstrual.

prémices /pʀemis/ *nfpl* liter beginnings.

premier, **-ière** /pʀəmje, ɛʀ/ ▶212, 545
I *adj* **1** (qui commence une série) [*habitant, emploi, automobile, symptôme*] first; **Adam fut le ~ homme** Adam was the first man; **c'est la première fois que je viens ici** this is the first time I've been here; **la première et la dernière fois** the first and last time; **les ~s temps de** the initial period of; (**dans**) **les ~s temps tout allait bien** at first things went well; **2** (qui précède dans l'espace) [*porte, rue, visage, carrefour*] first; **les trois premières rues** the first three streets; **les premières marches (de l'escalier)** the first few steps; **3** (dans une série) [*numéro, chapitre, mot, candidat*] first; **première personne du singulier/du pluriel** first person singular/plural; **le ~ janvier/juin** the first of January/of June; **article ~ du code pénal** first article of the penal code; **'livre ~'** 'book one'; **Napoléon Ier** Napoleon I ou the First; **Elisabeth Ire** Elizabeth I ou the First; **4** (par sa supériorité) [*artiste, écrivain, producteur, puissance*] leading; [*élève, étudiant*] top; **le ~ producteur mondial de vin** the world's leading wine producer; **être ~** [*élève, étudiant*] to be top; [*coureur*] to be first; **il est ~ en physique** he's top in physics; **terminer** or **arriver ~** [*coureur*] to come first; **une affaire de première importance/urgence** a matter of the utmost importance/urgency; **article de première nécessité** an absolutely essential item; **5** (par son infériorité) [*billet, ticket, place*] cheapest; **nos ~s prix** or **tarifs** (pour voyages) our cheapest holidays GB ou package tours US; (pour billets) our cheapest tickets; **6** (originel) [*impression*] first, initial; [*vivacité, éclat*] initial; [*aspect*] original; **recouvrer sa santé première** to recover one's health; **7** (essentiel) [*qualité*] prime; [*objectif*] primary, basic; [*conséquence*] primary, main; **8** Philos [*terme, notion, proposition, donnée*] basic, fundamental; [*vérité, principe*] first.
II *nm,f* **1** (qui se présente d'abord) first; **vous êtes le ~ à me le dire** you are the first to tell me; **il est toujours le ~ à se plaindre** he's always the first to complain; **sortir le ~** to go out first; **arriver le ~**, **arriver les ~s** to arrive first; **les ~s arrivés seront les ~s servis** first come, first served; **2** (dans une énumération) first; **je préfère le ~** I prefer the first one; **le ~ de mes fils** (sur deux fils) my elder son; (sur plus de deux fils) my eldest son; **3** (dans un classement) **arriver le ~** [*coureur*] to come first; **être le ~ de la classe** [*élève*] to be top of the class; **il est le ~ en latin** he's top in Latin.
III *nm* **1** (dans un bâtiment) first floor GB, second floor US; **monter/descendre au ~** to go up/to go down to the first GB ou second US floor; **habiter au ~** to live on the first GB ou second US floor; **2** (jour du mois) first; **être payé tous les ~s du mois** to be paid on the first of every month; **le ~ de l'an** New Year's Day; **3** (arrondissement) first arrondissement; **habiter dans le ~** to live in the first arrondissement; **4** (dans une charade) first; **mon ~ est** my first is.
IV en premier *loc adv* **faire qch en ~** to do sth first; **faire passer son travail en ~** to put one's work first; **recourir à l'arme nucléaire en ~** to resort to nuclear weapons in the first instance; **citons en ~ le livre de notre collègue** first of all there's our colleague's book; **il faut en ~ baisser l'impôt sur les bénéfices** first of all it is necessary to reduce taxes on profits.
V première *nf* **1** (événement important, exploit) first; **première mondiale** world first; **2** Théât, Cin première; **3** Scol Univ *sixth year of secondary school, age 16–17*; **4** Aut first (gear); **être en première** to be in first (gear); **passer la première** to go into first (gear); **rouler en première** to drive in first (gear); **5**○ Rail, Aviat first class; **voyager en première** to travel first class; **un billet de première** a first-class ticket; **6** (couturière dirigeant un atelier) head seamstress; **7** (en alpinisme) first ascent; **~ solitaire** first solo-ascent; **8** (dans une chaussure) insole.
VI de première○ *loc adj* first-rate; **c'est de première** it's first-class ou first-rate.
■ **~ âge** [*produits, vêtements*] for babies up to six months (*après n*); **~ clerc** chief clerk; **~ communiant** boy making his first communion; **~ de cordée** leader; **~ danseur** leading dancer; **~ jet** first ou rough draft; **~ maître** *intermediate rank between chief petty officer and fleet chief petty officer* GB, ≈ master chief petty officer US; **~ ministre** prime minister; **~ secrétaire** (d'un parti, organisme) first secretary; **~ venu** just anybody; **elle s'est jetée dans les bras du ~ venu** she threw herself into the arms of the first man to come along; **~ violon** Mus first violin, leader; **première classe** Mil ≈ private; **première communiante** Relig girl making her first communion; **première communion** Relig first communion; **première épreuve** Imprim first proof; **première nouvelle!** that's the first I've heard about it; **~s secours** first aid ₵.

premièrement /pʀəmjɛʀmɑ̃/ *adv* **1** (dans une énumération) firstly, first; **2** (introduisant une objection) for a start, for one thing, to begin with; **~ je n'étais pas à Paris à cette époque** for a start I was not in Paris at that time.

premier-né, **première-née**, *mpl* **premiers-nés**, *fpl* **premières-nées** /pʀəmjene, pʀəmjɛʀne/ *nm,f* **1** (premier enfant) first born; **le ~ de leurs enfants était un garçon** their first born was a son; **2** (première production) first.

prémisse /pʀemis/ *nf* premise, premiss GB.

prémolaire /pʀemɔlɛʀ/ *nf* premolar.

prémonition /pʀemɔnisjɔ̃/ *nf* premonition; **avoir la ~ d'un drame** to have a premonition of tragedy.

prémonitoire /pʀemɔnitwaʀ/ *adj* premonitory.

prémunir /pʀemyniʀ/ [3] **I** *vtr* (protéger) to protect (**contre** against).
II se prémunir *vpr* to protect oneself (**contre** against, from).

prenant, **~e** /pʀənɑ̃, ɑ̃t/ *adj* **1** (captivant) [*intrigue, spectacle*] fascinating; [*voix*] captivating; (absorbant) [*travail, métier*] absorbing; **2** Zool [*queue*] prehensile.

prénatal, **~e**, *mpl* **~s** ou **-aux** /pʀenatal, o/ *adj* [*chirurgie*] prenatal; [*surveillance*] antenatal; **un examen ~** an antenatal○.

prendre /pʀɑ̃dʀ/ [52] **I** *vtr* **1** (saisir) to take; **~ un vase sur l'étagère/dans le placard** to take a vase off the shelf/out of the cupboard; **~ le bras de son mari** to take one's husband's arm; **~ qn par la taille** (des deux mains) to take sb by the waist; (d'un bras) to put one's arm around sb's waist; **puis-je ~ votre manteau?** may I take your coat?; **prenez donc une chaise** do have ou take a seat; ▶ **clique**, **courage**, **jambe**; **2** (se donner, acquérir) **~ un air/une expression** to put on an air/an expression; **~ le nom de son mari** to take one's husband's name; **~ une identité** to assume an identity; **~ un accent** (involontairement) to pick up an accent; (volontairement) to put on an accent; **~ une habitude** to develop ou pick up a habit; **~ une voix grave** to adopt a solemn tone; **~ un rôle** to assume a role; **ta remarque prend tout son sens** you comment begins to make sense; **~ une nuance** to take on a particular nuance; **3** (dérober) to take; **~ de l'argent dans la caisse/à ses parents** to take money from the till GB ou cash register/from one's parents; **on m'a pris tous mes bijoux** I had all my jewellery GB ou jewelry US stolen; **il m'a pris ma petite amie** he stole my girlfriend; **la guerre leur a pris deux fils** they lost two sons in the war; **la guerre leur a pris tout ce qui leur était cher** the war robbed them of all they held most dear; **4** (apporter) to bring; **n'oublie pas de ~ des bottes** don't forget to bring boots; **je n'ai pas pris assez d'argent** I haven't brought enough money; **5** (emporter) to take; **j'ai pris ton parapluie** I took your umbrella; **ne prends rien sans demander** don't take anything without asking; **prends ton écharpe, il fait froid** take your scarf, it's cold; **6** (retirer) **~ de l'argent au distributeur** to get some money out of the cash dispenser; **~ de l'eau au puits** to get water from the well; **~ quelques livres à la bibliothèque** to get a few books out of the library; **7** (consommer) to have [*boisson, aliment, repas*]; to take [*médicament, drogue*]; **vous prendrez bien quelque chose/un peu de gâteau?** won't you have something to eat or drink/some cake?; **je vais ~ du poisson** I'll have fish; **mais tu n'as rien pris!** you've hardly taken any!; **aller ~ un café/une bière** to go for a coffee/a beer; **je prends des calmants depuis la guerre** I've been on tranquillizers[GB] since the war; **le médecin me fait ~ des antibiotiques** the doctor has put me on antibiotics; **je ne prends jamais d'alcool/de drogue** I never touch alcohol/take drugs; **8** (s'accorder) to take; **~ un congé** to take a vacation; **je vais ~ mon mercredi**○ I'm going to take Wednesday off; ▶**temps**; **9** (choisir) to take [*objet*]; to choose [*sujet, question*]; **~ la rouge/le moins cher des deux/la chambre double** to take the red one/the cheaper one/the double room; **j'ai pris la question sur Zola** I chose the question on Zola; **la romancière a pris comme sujet une histoire vraie** the writer based her novel on a true story; **~ qn pour époux/épouse** to take sb to be one's husband/wife; **10** (faire payer) to charge; **elle prend combien de l'heure/pour une coupe?** how much does she charge an hour/for a cut?; **on m'a pris très cher** I was charged a lot; **il prend 15% au passage** he takes a cut of 15%; **11** (nécessiter) to take [*temps*]; (user) to take up [*espace, temps*]; **le voyage m'a pris moins de deux heures** the trip took me less than two hours; **tes livres prennent trop de place** your books take up too much room; **mes enfants me prennent tout mon temps/toute mon énergie** my children take up all my time/all my energy; **12** (acheter, réserver, louer) to get [*aliments, essence, place*]; **prends aussi du jambon** get some ham too; **j'ai pris deux places pour ce soir** I've got two tickets for tonight; **~ une chambre en ville** to get a room in town; **j'en prendrai un kilo** I'll have a kilo; **13** (embaucher) (durablement) to take [sb] on [*employé, assistant, apprenti*]; (pour une mission) to engage [*personne*]; **ils ne m'ont pas pris** they didn't take me on; **~ qn comme nourrice** to take sb on as a nanny; **~ un avocat/guide** to engage a lawyer/guide; **être pris chez** or **par Hachette** to get a job with Hachette; **~ une maîtresse** to take a mistress; **14** (accueillir) to take; **ils ont pris la petite chez eux** they took the little girl in; **l'école n'a pas voulu la ~** the school wouldn't take her; **ce train ne prend pas de voyageurs** this train doesn't take passengers; **~ un client** [*taxi*] to pick up a customer; [*prostituée*] to pick up a client; [*coiffeur*] to take a customer; **~ un patient** [*médecin*] to see a patient; **~ un nouveau patient** [*médecin, dentiste*] to take on a new patient; **~ un élève** [*professeur*] to take on a student; **15** (ramasser au passage) to pick up [*personne, pain, clé, journal, ticket*]; **je passe te ~ à midi** I'll come and pick you up at 12; **~ un auto-stoppeur** to pick up a hitchhiker; **~ les enfants à l'école** to collect the children from school; **16** (emmener) to take [*personne*]; **je prends les enfants cet après-midi** I'll take the children this afternoon; **je peux te ~** (en voiture) I can give you a lift; **17** (attraper) to catch [*personne, animal*]; **elle s'est fait ~ en train de voler** she got caught stealing; **~ un papillon avec ses doigts** to pick up a butterfly; **~ un papillon entre ses mains** to cup a butterfly in one's hands; **je vous y prends**○**!** caught you!; **on ne m'y prendra plus**○**!** I won't be taken in○ again!; **se laisser ~ par un attrape-nigauds/une histoire** to fall for a trick/a story; **je ne me suis pas laissé ~** (tromper) I wasn't going to be taken in○; **se laisser ~ dans une bagarre** to get drawn into a fight; **se faire ~ par l'ennemi** to be captured by the enemy; **~ un poisson** to catch a fish; ▶**flagrant**, **sac**, **taureau**, **vinaigre**; **18** (assaillir) **une douleur le prit** he felt a sudden pain; **qu'est-ce qui te prend**○**?** what's the matter with you?; **ça te/leur prend souvent**○**?** are you/they often like this? **ça te prend souvent de gueuler**○ **comme ça?** do you often yell○ like that?; **19** (captiver) to involve [*spectateur, lecteur*]; **être pris par un livre/film** to be involved in a book/film; **20** (subir) to get [*gifle, coup de soleil, décharge, contravention*]; to catch [*rhume*]; **j'ai pris le marteau sur le pied** the hammer hit me on the foot; **qu'est-ce qu'ils ont pris**○**!** (coups, défaite) what a beating○ they got!; (reproches) what a telling-off○ they got!; **~ une quinte de toux** to have a coughing fit; **21** Transp (utiliser) to take [*autobus, métro, train, ferry, autoroute*]; **~ le train/la voiture/l'avion** to take the train/the car/the plane; **~ le** or **un taxi** to take a taxi; **il a pris l'avion pour aller à Bruxelles** he went to Brussels by air; **je ne prends plus la voiture pour aller à Paris** I've given up driving to Paris; **s'il fait beau, je prendrai la bicyclette** if the weather's nice, I'll cycle; **en général je prends mon vélo pour aller travailler** I usually cycle to work; **22** (envisager) to take; **prenons par exemple Nina** take Nina, for example; **si je prends une langue comme le chinois/un pays comme la Chine** if we take a language like Chinese/a country like China; **à tout ~** all in all; **23** (considérer) to take; **ne le prends pas mal** don't take it the wrong way; **il a plutôt bien pris ta remarque** he took your comment rather well; **il me prend pour un imbécile** he takes me for a fool; **pour qui me prends-tu?** (grossière erreur) what do you take me for?; (manque de respect) who do you think you're talking to?; **tu me prends pour ton esclave?** I'm not your slave, you know!; **excusez-moi, je vous ai pris pour quelqu'un d'autre** I'm sorry, I thought you were someone else; ▶**argent**, **canard**, **vessie**; **24** (traiter) to handle; **il est très gentil quand on sait le ~** he's very nice when you know how to handle him; **savoir ~ son enfant** to know how to handle one's child; **on ne sait jamais par où la ~**○ you never know how to handle her; **25** (mesurer) to take [*mensurations, température, tension, pouls*]; **je vais ~ votre pointure** let me measure your foot; **26** (noter) to take down; **je vais ~ votre adresse** let me just take down your address; **il s'est enfui mais j'ai pris le numéro de sa voiture** he drove off but I took down his registration GB ou license US number; **27** (apprendre) **~ que** to get the idea (that); **où a-t-il pris qu'ils allaient divorcer?** where did he get the idea they were going to get divorced ?; **28** (accepter) to take; **~ les cartes de crédit** to take credit cards; **il a refusé de ~ l'argent** he refused to take the money; **il faut ~ les gens comme ils sont** you must take people as you find them; **~ les choses comme elles sont** to take things as they come; **à 1 500, je prends, mais pas plus** at 1,500, I'll take it, but that's my best offer; **29** (endosser) to take over [*direction, pouvoir*]; to assume [*contrôle, poste*]; **je prends ça sur moi** I'll see to it; **~ sur soi de faire** to take it upon oneself to do, to undertake to do; **elle a pris sur elle de leur parler/de leur cacher la vérité** she took it upon herself to talk to them/to hide the truth from them; **je prends sur moi tes dépenses** I'll cover your expenses; **30** (accumuler) to put on [*poids*]; to gain [*avance*]; **~ trois minutes (d'avance)** to gain three minutes; **~ des forces** to build up one's strength; **31** (contracter) to take on [*bail*]; to take [*emploi*]; **32** (défier) to take [sb] on [*concurrent*]; **je prends le gagnant/le perdant** I'll take on the winner/the loser; **33** (conquérir) Mil to take, to seize [*ville, forteresse*]; to capture [*navire, tank*]; Jeux to take [*pièce, carte*]; **34** (posséder sexuellement) to take [*femme*].

II *vi* **1** (aller) **~ à gauche/vers le nord** to go left/north; **prenez tout droit** keep straight on; **~ à travers champs** to strike out GB ou head off across the fields; **~ au plus court** to take the shortest route; **~ par le littoral** to follow the coast; **2** (s'enflammer) [*feu, bois, mèche*] to catch; [*incendie*] to break out; **3** (se solidifier) [*gelée, flan, glace, ciment, plâtre, colle*] to set; [*blancs d'œufs*] to stiffen; [*mayonnaise*] to thicken; **4** (réussir) [*grève, innovation*] to be a success; [*idée, mode*] to catch on; [*teinture, bouture, vaccination, greffe*] to take; [*leçon*] to sink in; **5** (prélever) **~ sur ses économies pour entretenir un neveu** to draw on one's savings to support a nephew; **~ sur son temps libre pour traduire un roman** to translate a novel in one's spare time; **6** (se contraindre) **~ sur soi** to take a hold on oneself; **~ sur soi pour faire** to make oneself do; **~ sur soi pour ne pas faire** to keep oneself from doing; **j'ai pris sur moi pour les écouter** I made myself listen to them; **j'ai pris sur moi pour ne pas les insulter** I kept myself from insulting them; **7**○ (être cru) **ça ne prend pas!** it won't wash○ ou work!; **ton explication ne prendra pas avec moi** that explanation won't wash with me○; **8**○ (subir) **~ pour qn** to take the rap○ for sb; **c'est toujours moi qui prends!** I'm always the one who gets it in the neck○!; **tu vas ~!** you'll catch it○!; **il en a pris pour 20 ans** he got 20 years.

III se prendre *vpr* **1** (devoir être saisi, consommé, mesuré) **un marteau se prend par le manche** you hold a hammer by the handle; **les pâtes ne se prennent pas avec les doigts** you don't eat pasta with your fingers; **en Chine le thé se prend sans sucre** in China they don't put sugar in their tea; **la vitamine C se prend de préférence le matin** vitamin C is best taken in the morning; **la température se prend le matin** your temperature should be taken in the morning; **2** (pouvoir être acquis, conquis, utilisé, attrapé) **les mauvaises habitudes se prennent vite** bad habits are easily picked up; **le roi ne se prend jamais** (aux échecs) the king can't be taken; **un avion ne se prend pas sans réservation** you can't take a plane without making reservation; **3** (s'attraper) **se ~ le pied gauche avec la main droite** to take one's left foot in one's right hand; **certains singes se prennent aux arbres avec leur queue** some monkeys can swing from trees by their tails; **4** (se tenir l'un l'autre) **se ~ par la taille** to hold each other around the waist; **5** (se coincer) **se ~ les doigts dans la porte** to catch one's fingers in the door; **mon écharpe s'est prise dans les rayons** my scarf got caught in the spokes; **6**○ (recevoir) **il s'est pris quinze jours de prison/une gifle** he got two weeks in prison/a smack in the face; **tu vas te ~ l'étagère sur la tête** the shelf is going to come down on your head; **je me suis pris une averse** I got caught in a shower; **7** (commencer) **se ~ à faire** to find oneself doing; **elle s'est prise à aimer** she found herself falling in love; **se ~ de sympathie pour qn** to take to sb; **8** (se considérer) **elle se prend pour un génie** she thinks she's a genius; **il se prend pour James Dean** he fancies himself as James Dean; **pour qui est-ce que tu te prends?** who do you think you are?; ▶**Dieu**; **9** (agresser) **s'en ~ à qn** (par des reproches ou des coups) to set about sb; (pour passer sa colère) to take it out on sb; **s'en ~ à qch** (habituellement) to carry on about sth; (à l'occasion) to lay into sth; **10** (se comporter) **savoir s'y ~ avec** to have a way with [*enfants, femmes, vieux*]; to know how to handle [*employés, élèves*]; **11** (agir) **il faut s'y ~ à l'avance pour avoir des places** you have to book ahead to get seats; **tu t'y es pris trop tard** you left it too late (**pour faire** to do); **il**

s'y est pris à plusieurs fois he tried several times; **ils s'y sont pris à trois contre lui** it was three against one; **on s'y est pris à trois pour faire** it took the three of us to do; **regarde comment elle s'y prend** look how she's doing it; **elle s'y prend bien/mal** she sets ou goes about it the right/wrong way; **j'aime bien ta façon de t'y ~** I like the way you go about it; **comment vas-tu t'y ~?** how will you go about it?; **comment vas-tu t'y ~ pour les convaincre?** how will you go about convincing them?

IDIOMES **c'est toujours ça de pris**○ that's something at least; **il y a à ~ et à laisser** it's like the curate's egg; **c'est à ~ ou à laisser** take it or leave it; **tel est pris qui croyait ~** the tables are turned; **bien m'en a pris**○ it was a good job○; **mal m'en a pris**○ it was a mistake.

preneur, -euse /pʀənœʀ, øz/ *nm,f* Comm (acheteur) taker; **les ~s étaient nombreux** there were plenty of takers; **il n'y a pas ~** there are no takers (**pour** for); **trouver ~** [*article*] to attract a buyer; [*personne*] to find a buyer (**pour** for); **ne pas trouver ~** [*article*] to remain unsold; **je suis ~** (acheteur) I'll take it; (intéressé par la proposition) count me in; (intéressé par un plat) I'd love some.

■ **~ à bail** lessee; **~ d'otages** hostage taker; **~ de son** sound recordist.

prénom /pʀenɔ̃/ *nm* gén first name, christian name GB; Admin forename, given name; **deuxième ~** middle name; **~ usuel** name by which one is known.

IDIOMES **se faire un ~** hum to become the famous child of a famous parent.

prénommé, ~e /pʀenɔme/ **I** *pp* ▶**prénommer**.

II *pp adj* **un ~ Jules** somebody called Jules; **la ~e Isabelle** the girl known as Isabelle.

III *nm,f* Jur **le ~** the aforementioned.

prénommer /pʀenɔme/ [1] **I** *vtr* to name, to call; **un garçon prénommé Olivier** a boy named Olivier; **M. Martin, prénommé Henri** Mr Martin, first name Henri; **comment l'ont-ils prénommé?** what did they call him?

II se prénommer *vpr* to be called.

prénotion /pʀenosjɔ̃/ *nf* foreknowledge ₵.

prénuptial, ~e, *pl* **-iaux** /pʀenypsjal, o/ *adj* [*examen*] pre-marriage.

préoccupant, ~e /pʀeɔkypɑ̃, ɑ̃t/ *adj* [*situation, événement, pensées*] worrying; **son état de santé est ~** his/her condition is giving cause for concern.

préoccupation /pʀeɔkypasjɔ̃/ *nf* (souci) worry, concern; (pensée dominante) concern; **de graves ~s** serious problems ou concerns; **c'est l'une de nos ~s majeures** or **essentielles** this is one of our major ou main concerns.

préoccupé, ~e /pʀeɔkype/ **I** *pp* ▶**préoccuper**.

II *pp adj* (soucieux) preoccupied; **il a l'air très ~ en ce moment** he seems very preoccupied ou he's got a lot on his mind at the moment; **être ~ par qch** to be concerned about sth; **il semble peu ~ par les problèmes de l'entreprise** he seems to have little concern for the company's problems.

préoccuper /pʀeɔkype/ [1] **I** *vtr* **1** (inquiéter) to worry; **qu'est-ce qui te préoccupe?** what's worrying you?; **ma santé le préoccupe** he's been worried about my health; **2** (occuper) to concern; **la question qui nous préoccupe** the question which concerns us.

II se préoccuper *vpr* **se ~ de** to be concerned about [*problème, situation*]; to think about [*avenir, opinion*]; **agir sans se ~ des autres** to act without thinking about other people; **il ne s'est pas préoccupé de savoir si cela m'arrangeait** he didn't think to ask if it would suit me; **la ville se préoccupe surtout de tourisme** the town's main concern is tourism; **se ~ de sa petite personne** to think only of oneself, to be self-centred[GB].

préopératoire /pʀeɔpeʀatwaʀ/ *adj* preoperative.

prépa○ /pʀepa/ *nf* student's slang *class preparing students for entrance exams to the Grandes Écoles*.

préparateur, -trice /pʀepaʀatœʀ, tʀis/ ▶**510** *nm,f* (dans un laboratoire) laboratory assistant; (dans une pharmacie) **~ en pharmacie** pharmacist's assistant.

préparatifs /pʀepaʀatif/ *nmpl* preparations (**de** for).

préparation /pʀepaʀasjɔ̃/ *nf* **1** (mise au point) preparation; **en ~** [*livre, film, spectacle, loi*] in preparation; **ceci exige un long travail de ~** this requires lengthy preparation; **2** (résultat) preparation; **~ pharmaceutique/chimique** pharmaceutical/chemical preparation; **3** Scol homework, prep○ GB; **faire une ~ de français/latin** to prepare one's French/Latin homework; **4** Tech (de peaux, laines) dressing.

■ **~ militaire, PM** *training course prior to military service*.

préparatoire /pʀepaʀatwaʀ/ *adj* [*réunion, entretien, phase*] preliminary; [*travail*] preparatory, preliminary.

préparer /pʀepaʀe/ [1] **I** *vtr* **1** (apprêter) to prepare [*affaires, chambre, cours, loi, discours, plat, surprise*] (**pour** for); to get [sth] ready [*vêtements, outils, dossier, documents*] (**pour** for); to prepare, to plan [*réunion, campagne électorale, spectacle*]; to plan [*vacances, avenir*]; to prepare for [*rentrée, transition*]; to draw up [*projet*]; to hatch [*complot*]; to prepare, to lay [*piège*]; **il est en train de ~ le dîner** he's getting dinner ready, he's fixing dinner US; **~ le terrain** fig to prepare the ground; **il est en train de ~ un mauvais coup** he's cooking something up○; **il prépare un livre/un disque pour l'année prochaine** he's working on a book to be published/a record to be released next year; **tu me prépareras mon costume pour demain?** would you get my suit ready for tomorrow?; **des plats préparés** ready-to-eat meals; **je me demande ce que l'avenir nous prépare** I wonder what the future has in store for us; **il a l'air bizarre en ce moment, je me demande ce qu'il nous prépare** he's been acting oddly recently, I wonder what he's up to; **toutes ces grèves, ça nous prépare une belle pagaille**○**!** with all these strikes we're in for complete chaos!; **il nous prépare une bonne grippe**○ he's coming down with the flu; **~ ses effets** [*comédien, orateur*] to time one's effects; **2** (mettre en condition) to prepare [*personne, pays, économie*] (**à** for); **~ qn à un examen** to prepare sb for an exam; **~ qn à une épreuve sportive** to coach sb for a (sports) competition; **être bien/mal préparé à qch** to be well-/ill-prepared for sth; **l'éducation devrait ~ à la vie** education should be a preparation for life; **essaie de la ~ avant de lui annoncer la nouvelle** try and break the news to her gently; **~ qn à faire** to prepare sb to do; **ses parents ne l'ont pas préparé à affronter le monde extérieur** his parents did not prepare him for the world; **3** Scol, Univ to prepare for, to study for [*examen, concours*]; **il prépare une école d'ingénieurs** he's studying for the engineering school entrance examinations; **4** Tech to dress [*laine, cuir*]; **5** Culin to dress [*poisson, volaille*].

II se préparer *vpr* **1** (s'apprêter) [*personne*] to get ready (**pour qch** for sth; **à faire** to do); **je me préparais à sortir quand le téléphone a sonné** I was just getting ready to go out when the phone rang; **l'armée se prépare à envahir le pays voisin** the army is getting ready ou gearing up○ to invade the neighbouring[GB] country; **2** (se mettre en condition) to prepare (**à** for); **l'athlète s'est préparé pour la course** the athlete prepared for ou trained for the race; **se ~ pour un examen** to prepare for ou study for an exam; **se ~ à qch/à faire qch** to prepare for sth/to do sth; **se ~ au pire** to prepare for the worst; **je ne m'étais pas préparé à cette éventualité** I was not prepared for this to happen; **prépare-toi à recevoir une mauvaise nouvelle** prepare yourself for some bad news; **la population se prépare à passer un rude hiver** the people are preparing for a harsh winter; **3** (être imminent) [*orage, malheurs, troubles*] to be brewing; [*changements*] to be in the offing; **un remaniement ministériel se prépare** a cabinet reshuffle is in the offing; **un coup d'État se prépare dans le pays** a coup d'état is imminent in the country; **il se prépare quelque chose de louche** something fishy○ is going on; **4** (faire pour soi) **se ~ une tasse de thé/de la soupe** to make ou fix US oneself a cup of tea/some soup.

prépayé, ~e /pʀepeje/ *adj* prepaid.

prépondérance /pʀepɔ̃deʀɑ̃s/ *nf* predominance (**sur** over); **acquérir/avoir la ~** to gain/to have predominance; **à ~ étrangère** predominantly foreign.

prépondérant, ~e /pʀepɔ̃deʀɑ̃, ɑ̃t/ *adj* predominant; **jouer un rôle ~** to play a predominant role; **la voix du président est ~e** the chairman has the casting vote.

préposé, ~e /pʀepoze/ *nm,f* **1** gén official; **~ à qch** official responsible for sth; **~ aux écritures** clerk; **~ des douanes** customs official; **~ au vestiaire** cloakroom attendant; **~ aux toilettes** lavatory attendant; **2** (facteur) postman/postwoman.

préposer /pʀepoze/ [1] *vtr* **~ qn à qch/faire qch** to assign sb to sth/to do sth.

prépositif, -ive /pʀepozitif, iv/ *adj* prepositional.

préposition /pʀepozisjɔ̃/ *nf* preposition.

prépositionnel, -elle /pʀepozisjɔnɛl/ *adj* prepositional.

prépositivement /pʀepozitivmɑ̃/ *adv* prepositionally.

préprofessionnel, -elle /pʀepʀɔfesjɔnɛl/ *adj* vocational; **enseignement ~** vocational training; **classes préprofessionnelles** vocational classes.

préprogrammé, ~e /pʀepʀɔgʀame/ *adj* Ordinat **ordinateur ~** stored memory computer.

prépuce /pʀepys/ *nm* foreskin, prepuce spéc.

préraphaélisme /pʀeʀafaelism/ *nm* Pre-Raphaelitism.

préraphaélite /pʀeʀafaelit/ *adj, nmf* Pre-Raphaelite.

prérentrée /pʀeʀɑ̃tʀe/ *nf* Scol *preparatory day for teachers before school year begins*.

préretraite /pʀeʀətʀɛt/ *nf* **1** (situation) early retirement; **être en ~** to have taken early retirement; **être mis en ~** to be asked to take early retirement; **2** (allocation) early retirement pension.

préretraité, ~e /pʀeʀətʀɛte/ *nm,f*: *person who has taken early retirement*; **ce sont des ~s** they've taken early retirement.

prérévolutionnaire /pʀeʀevɔlysjɔnɛʀ/ *adj* prerevolutionary.

prérogative /pʀeʀɔgativ/ *nf* **1** (avantage) prerogative (**de faire** to do); **~ de qn/qch sur** primacy of sb/sth over; **s'arroger des ~s** to claim prerogatives; **2** (don) liter gift.

préromantique /pʀeʀɔmɑ̃tik/ *adj, nmf* pre-Romantic.

préromantisme /pʀeʀɔmɑ̃tism/ *nm* pre-Romanticism.

près /pʀɛ/ **I** *adv* **1** (non loin dans l'espace) close; **la ville est tout ~** it's no distance to the town, the town is close by; **ce n'est pas tout ~** it's quite a way; **c'est plus ~ qu'on ne pense** it's closer than you'd think; **se raser de ~** to have a close shave; **2** (non loin dans le temps) **les vacances sont tout ~ maintenant** the vacation is nearly here ou upon us; **3** fig **cela pèse 10 kg, à**

quelques grammes ~ it weighs 10 kg, give or take a few grams; **ce roman est plutôt bon, à quelques détails ~** this novel is quite good, apart from the odd detail; **à ceci** or **cela ~ que** except that; **il m'a remboursé au centime ~** he paid me back to the very last penny; **à une minute ~, j'avais mon train/je battais mon record** I was within a minute of catching my train/breaking my record; **à une voix ~, le projet aurait été adopté** the project would have been adopted but for one vote; **gagner/perdre à deux voix ~** to win/lose by two votes; **elles sont semblables, à la couleur ~** they're the same but for the colour[GB]; **prends ton temps, on n'est pas à cinq minutes ~** take your time, five minutes won't make any difference; **ils ne sont plus à un vol ~** one more theft won't make any difference to them; **je ne suis pas à un paquet de cigarettes ~** what does the odd packet of cigarettes matter?; **précis au millimètre ~** accurate to within a millimetre[GB]; **à une exception ~** with only one exception; **à quelques exceptions ~** with a few rare exceptions.

II près de *loc prép* **1** (dans l'espace) near; **j'aimerais être ~ de toi** I'd like to be with you; **elle habite ~ d'ici** she lives nearby ou near here; **être ~ du but** fig to be close to achieving one's goal; **la balle est passée très ~ du cœur** the bullet just missed the heart; **~ d'elle, un enfant jouait** a child was playing near her ou beside her; **elle est ~ de lui** (à ses côtés) she's with him; **2** (dans le temps) near, nearly; **il est ~ de l'âge de la retraite** he's near retirement age; **il est ~ de minuit** it's nearly midnight; **elle est ~ de la cinquantaine** she's nearly fifty; **on est ~ des vacances maintenant** the holidays are nearly here ou upon us; **être ~ de faire** to be about to do; **je ne suis pas ~ de recommencer/d'y retourner** I'm not about to do that again/to go back there again ; **être ~ de partir/sombrer** to be about to leave/sink; **le jour est ~ de se lever** dawn is about to break; **je suis ~ de penser/croire que** I almost think/believe that; **être ~ de réussir/de refuser/d'accepter** to be about to succeed/to refuse/to accept, to be on the point of succeeding/of refusing/of accepting; **ils étaient ~ de la victoire** they were close to victory; **le problème n'est pas ~ d'être résolu** the problem is nowhere near solved; **3** (par les idées, les sentiments) close; **elle a toujours été très ~ de sa mère** she has always been very close to her mother; **ils sont très ~ l'un de l'autre** they are very close; **vivre ~ de la nature** to live close to nature; **4** (presque) nearly, almost; **cela coûte ~ de 1 000 francs** it costs nearly ou almost 1,000 francs; **il a cessé de fumer pendant ~ de 20 ans** he didn't smoke for nearly 20 years; **cela a nécessité ~ d'un an de travail** it involved nearly a year's work; **le chômage touche ~ de 3 millions de personnes** unemployment affects nearly ou almost 3 million people; **une toile de ~ de 2 m sur 3** a canvas measuring almost 2 m by 3; **cela fait ~ d'un mois que j'attends** I've been waiting close to ou for nearly a month.

III de près *loc adv* closely; **regarder de plus ~** to take a closer look; **regarder/examiner qch de ~** to look at/to examine sth closely; **observer/suivre qn de ~** to observe/to follow sb closely; **surveiller qn/qch de ~** to keep a close eye on sb/sth; **le coup de fusil a été tiré de très ~** the shot was fired at close range; **voir de ~** to see clearly close up; **vu de ~, cela rassemble à**… seen from close quarters, it looks like…; **les examens/concurrents se suivent de ~** the exams/competitors are close together; **les explosions se succédèrent de ~** the explosions came in close succession; **être lié de ~ à qch** to be closely linked with sth; **s'intéresser de ~ à qch** to take a close interest in sth; **frôler de ~ la catastrophe** to come close to disaster; **ne pas y regarder de trop ~** not to look too closely; **voir la mort de ~** to look death in the face, to come close to death; **à y regarder de plus ~** on closer examination.

IV à peu près *loc adv* (presque) **la rue est à peu ~ vide** the street is practically ou virtually empty; **cela coûte à peu ~ 200 francs** it costs about ou around 200 francs; **il y a à peu ~ une heure qu'il est parti** he left about an hour ago, it's about an hour since he left; **un groupe d'à peu ~ 50 personnes** a group of about ou some 50 people; **je pense à peu ~ comme toi** I think more or less the same as you; **à peu ~ de la même façon** in much the same way; **à peu ~ semblables** pretty much the same; **cela désigne à peu ~ n'importe quoi** it refers to just about anything; **c'est à peu ~ tout** that's about the size of it; **c'est à peu ~ tout ce qu'on sait sur cette affaire** that's just about all we know about this matter.

présage /prezaʒ/ *nm* **1** (signe) omen; **~ de malheur** omen of doom; **oiseau de mauvais ~** bird of ill omen; **~ de mort** omen of death; **heureux ~** happy omen; **bon/mauvais ~** good/bad omen; **2** (signe avant-coureur) harbinger; **~ de** harbinger of; **c'est le ~ d'une brillante carrière** it's the harbinger of a brilliant career; **ce coup de téléphone est le ~ d'une catastrophe** this phone call is the harbinger of a disaster; **3** (prédiction) prediction.

présager /prezaʒe/ [13] *vtr* (annoncer) [*événement, nouvelle*] to presage; (prévoir) [*personne*] to predict; **laisser ~** to suggest (**à** to); **cela ne présage rien de bon** this does not bode well.

pré-salé, *pl* **prés-salés** /presale/ *nm* **1** (animal) salt-meadow sheep; **2** (viande) salt-meadow lamb.

presbyte /prɛsbit/ **I** *adj* longsighted GB, farsighted US, presbyopic spéc.
II *nmf* longsighted person GB, farsighted person US, presbyopic spéc; **c'est un ~** he's longsighted GB ou farsighted US.

presbytère /prɛsbitɛr/ *nm* presbytery.

presbytérianisme /prɛsbiterjanism/ *nm* Presbyterianism.

presbytérien, -ienne /prɛsbiterjɛ̃, ɛn/ **I** *adj* Presbyterian; **il est ~** he's a Presbyterian.
II *nm,f* Presbyterian.

presbytie /prɛsbisi/ *nf* longsightedness GB, farsightedness US, presbyopia spéc.

prescience /presjɑ̃s/ *nf* liter **1** (connaissance de l'avenir) foresight, prescience; **2** (intuition) premonition; **3** Relig prescience.

prescient, ~e /presjɑ̃, ɑ̃t/ *adj* prescient.

préscientifique /presjɑ̃tifik/ *adj* prescientific.

préscolaire /preskɔlɛr/ *adj* preschool.

préscolarisation /preskɔlarizasjɔ̃/ *nf* preschool education.

préscolariser /preskɔlarize/ [1] *vtr* to send [sb] to nursery school [*enfant*].

prescripteur, -trice /prɛskriptœr, tris/ *nm,f* prescriber.

prescriptible /prɛskriptibl/ *adj* [*dette, droit*] subject to limitation of action by lapse of time; [*peine, crime*] time-barred.

prescription /prɛskripsjɔ̃/ *nf* **1** Méd prescription; (sur un emballage) **'se conformer aux ~s du médecin'** 'to be taken in accordance with doctor's instructions'; **2** (ordre) prescript; **3** Jur (de droit) prescription; (de peine, crime) limitation of action by lapse of time; (de dette) barring by lapse of time; **délai de ~** period of limitation.

prescrire /prɛskrir/ [67] **I** *vtr* **1** Méd to prescribe [*médicament, repos*] (**à qn** for sb); **'ne pas dépasser la dose prescrite'** (sur un emballage) 'do not exceed stated dose'; **2** (imposer) to stipulate; **au jour prescrit** on the day stipulated; **à la date prescrite** on the date stipulated; **ce que l'honneur prescrit** what honour[GB] dictates; **3** (requérir) [*circonstance, événement*] to call for; **4** Jur to subject [sth] to limitation by lapse of time [*peine, crime, dette, droit*].
II se prescrire *vpr* **1** Jur [*crime, peine, dette*] to be subject to limitation by lapse of time; **2** Méd to be prescribed.

préséance /preseɑ̃s/ *nf* precedence; **avoir la ~ sur qn** to take precedence over sb.

présélecteur /preselɛktœr/ *nm* **1** Aut preselector; **2** Tech preset device.

présélection /preselɛksjɔ̃/ *nf* **1** (de personnes, livres) shortlisting; **être admis** or **retenu en ~** to be shortlisted; **2** Tech presetting; **bouton de ~** preset button; **boîte de vitesses à ~** Aut preselector gearbox.

présélectionner /preselɛksjɔne/ [1] *vtr* **1** to shortlist [*personnes, livres*]; **2** Tech to preselect [*vitesse*]; TV, Radio to preset.

présence /prezɑ̃s/ **I** *nf* **1** (de personne) presence; (au bureau, à l'usine) attendance; **elle nous a honorés de sa ~** she honoured[GB] us with her presence; **il ignore ta ~** he doesn't know you are here; **il fait de la ~, c'est tout** he's present and not much else; **il me suffit de faire de la ~** I just need to turn up; **fuir/éviter la ~ de qn** to shun/to avoid sb; **trois mois de ~ dans l'entreprise sont nécessaires** it is necessary to have been with the company for three months; **en ~ du maire/d'un avocat** in the presence of the mayor/of a lawyer; **il l'a fait en ma ~/hors de ma ~** he did it in my presence/while I wasn't there; **en ~ d'un acide il se produit une réaction** a reaction occurs when an acid is present; **en ~ d'une foule énorme** in front of a huge crowd; **en ~ de la reine** in the presence of the Queen; **les forces en ~ dans le conflit** the forces involved in the conflict; **en ~ d'un tel désastre** faced with such a disaster; **les parties en ~** Jur the litigants, the opposing parties; **mettre deux personnes en ~** to bring two people together ou face to face; **2** (de pays) presence; **la ~ française en Afrique** the French presence in Africa; **3** (de substance, phénomène, d'industrie) presence (**dans** in); **4** Relig **la ~ réelle** real presence; **5** (être animé) **sentir une ~** to feel a presence; **il a besoin d'une ~** he needs company; **6** (personnalité) presence; **avoir beaucoup de ~ (sur scène)** to have great stage presence; **7** (influence d'auteur) liter influence.
■ **~ d'esprit** presence of mind.

présent, ~e /prezɑ̃, ɑ̃t/ **I** *adj* **1** (sur les lieux) [*personne*] present; **j'étais ~ quand cela est arrivé** I was present ou there when it happened; **les personnes ~es** those present; **les personnes ici ~es** the persons here present sout; **M. Glénat, ici ~** Mr Glénat, who is here with us; **être ~ à une cérémonie** to be present at ou to attend a ceremony; **il était ~ aux obsèques** he was present at ou he attended the funeral; **il ne sera pas ~ à l'audience** Jur he will not appear in court; **'~!'** (à l'école) 'here'!, 'present'!; **j'étais ~ en pensée** or **par le cœur** I was there in spirit; **aux prochaines élections le nouveau parti sera ~** fig at the next elections the new party will be represented; **pour aller au cinéma il est toujours ~!** fig he's always ready to go to the cinema GB ou movies US!; **2** (existant) present; **la violence est ~e à toutes les pages** violence is present on every page; **la faim est toujours ~e dans cette partie du monde** there's still hunger in that part of the world; **la société, ~e depuis peu dans ce secteur** the company, which has recently moved into this sector; **avoir ~ à l'esprit** to have [sth] in mind [*conseil*]; to have [sth] fresh in one's mind [*souvenir*]; **le souvenir toujours ~ de** the ever present memory of; **gardez** or **ayez bien ~ à l'esprit que** bear in mind that; **3** (actif) actively involved; **être très ~ dans une organisation** to be actively involved in an organization; **la société reste très ~e sur le marché** the company is still very active on the market; **ma mère a toujours été très ~e** (dans ma vie) my mother has always been there for me; **un acteur/un chanteur très ~ sur scène** an actor/a singer with a strong stage presence; **4** (actuel) [*moment, situation, état*] present; **ne penser qu'au moment ~** not to look beyond the present; **le 5 du mois ~** on the 5th instant GB ou of this month; **faire qch dans la minute ~e** to do sth instantly; **5** (en cause) present; **la ~e déclaration** the present statement; **par la ~e lettre** by the present (letter), hereby Jur; **6** Ling [*temps, participe*] present.

II *nm,f* (personne) **il n'y avait que 10 ~s** there were only 10 people present; **la liste des ~s** the list of those present.

III *nm* **1** (période) **le ~** the present; **pour le ~** for the moment ou present; **2** Ling (temps) present (tense); **le verbe est au ~ du subjonctif** the verb is in the present subjunctive; **3** (cadeau) gift, present; **faire ~ de qch à qn** to present sb with sth.

IV présente *nf* (lettre) **par la ~e** hereby; **joint à la ~e** herewith.

V à présent *loc adv* (en ce moment) at present; (maintenant) now; **d'à ~** of today; **à ~ que** now that.

présentable /pʀezɑ̃tabl/ *adj* [*personne, tenue*] presentable; **ce devoir n'est pas ~** this is a very untidy piece of work.

présentateur, -trice /pʀezɑ̃tatœʀ, tʀis/ **▶510** *nm,f* Radio, TV (de spectacle, d'émission) presenter, anchor; **le ~ (du journal)** the newsreader GB, the newscaster US.

présentation /pʀezɑ̃tasjɔ̃/ *nf* **1** (d'ami, de conférencier) gén introduction; (à un souverain, la cour) presentation; **faire les ~s** to make the introductions; **2** (apparence) appearance; **'excellente ~ exigée'** 'smart appearance required'; **3** (arrangement) (de plat, devoir, d'idées) presentation; (de magazine, lettre) presentation, layout; (de produits) display, presentation; **4** (manifestation, spectacle) show, showing; **~ des collections d'hiver** Mode showing of the winter collections; **~ de mode** fashion show; **5** (d'émission, de journal, jeu) presentation; **il est chargé de la ~ d'une nouvelle émission à la télévision** he's to be the presenter of a new television programme; **6** (de carte, ticket, bagage) production, showing; (de pièces justificatives) production, presentation; Fin (de chèque) presentation; **sur ~ de** on production of; **7** (exposé) presentation; **lundi aura lieu la ~ du budget à l'Assemblée nationale** on Monday the budget will be presented to the National Assembly; **8** Relig **la Présentation de la Vierge/l'Enfant Jésus** Presentation of the Virgin/the Child; **fête de la Présentation de Jésus** Candlemas; **9** Méd (de bébé) presentation; **~ par le siège** breech presentation.

présentement /pʀezɑ̃tmɑ̃/ *adv* at present GB, at the moment GB, presently US.

présenter /pʀezɑ̃te/ [1] **I** *vtr* **1** (faire connaître) to introduce (**à** to); (de manière officielle) to present (**à qn** to sb); **~ un conférencier à l'auditoire** to introduce a speaker to the audience; **permettez-moi de vous ~ mon collègue** fml may I introduce my colleague?; **je vous présente mon fils** this is my son, may I introduce my son?; **on vous a présentés?** have you been introduced?; **il l'a présentée comme sa secrétaire** he introduced her as his secretary; **il n'est pas nécessaire de vous ~ Pierre** Pierre needs no introduction from me; **être présenté au roi/à la cour** to be presented to the king/at court; **2** (montrer) to show [*ticket, carte, menu*]; **~ une troupe à** to parade troops before; **'présentez armes!'** 'present arms!'; **3** (proposer au public) to present [*spectacle, vedette, rétrospective, collection*]; Radio, TV to present [*journal, émission*]; Comm to display [*marchandises*]; **4** (soumettre) to present [*chèque, facture, addition*]; to submit [*devis, rapport, thèse*]; to table [*motion*]; to introduce [*proposition, projet de loi*]; **~ qn à** to put sb forward for [*poste, élection*]; to enter sb for [*examen, concours*]; **~ une liste pour les élections** to put forward a list (of candidates) for the elections; **~ une proposition à un comité** to put a proposal to a committee; **~ sa candidature à un poste** to apply ou put in an application for a job; **~ un enfant au baptême** to have a child christened; **5** (exposer) to present [*situation, faits, budget, conclusions*]; to expound, to present [*théorie*]; to present, to set out [*idée*]; to set out [*objections, point de vue*]; **rapport mal/bien présenté** badly-/well-presented report; **~ qn comme (étant) un monstre** to portray sb as a monster; **être présenté comme miraculeux** to be described as miraculous; **être présenté comme un modèle** to be held up as a model; **être présenté comme une simple mesure provisoire** to be described as just a temporary measure; **~ la victoire comme acquise** to speak of victory as already won; **comment allez-vous leur ~ l'affaire?** how are you going to put the matter to them?; **~ une affaire devant les tribunaux** to take a case to court; **~ la note** or **l'addition** to present the bill GB ou check US; **6** (exprimer) to offer [*condoléances*] (**à** to); **~ des excuses** to apologize (**à** to); **7** (comporter) to involve, to present [*risque, difficulté*]; to show [*différences, signe, trace*]; to show, to present [*symptôme*]; to offer [*avantage*]; to have [*aspect, particularité, défaut*]; **un coffret qui présente des incrustations de nacre** a box set with mother of pearl; **~ un grand intérêt/peu d'intérêt** to be of great interest/of little interest; **8** (orienter) **~ son visage au soleil** to turn one's face to the sun; **~ le flanc à l'ennemi** to turn the flank to the enemy; **~ les voiles au vent** to set the sails into the wind.

II *vi* **~ bien** to have a smart appearance; **~ mal** to be badly turned out.

III se présenter *vpr* **1** (paraître) to appear; (aller) to go; (venir) to come; **tu ne peux pas te ~ dans cette tenue** you can't appear dressed like that; **se ~ à l'audience** Jur to appear in court; **en arrivant, il faut se ~ à la réception** when you arrive you must go ou report to reception; **personne ne s'est présenté** nobody came ou appeared ou turned up○; **présentez-vous à 10 heures** come at 10; **quand il s'est présenté chez le directeur** when he presented himself sout at the manager's office; **on ne se présente pas chez les gens à minuit** you don't call on people at midnight; **comment oses-tu te ~ chez moi?** how dare you show your face at my house?; **'ne pas écrire, se ~'** 'please apply in person'; **2** (se faire connaître) to introduce oneself (**à** to); **je me présente, Jacques Roux** may I introduce myself? Jacques Roux; **il s'est présenté (à moi) comme (un) employé de la banque** he introduced himself (to me) as a bank employee; **se ~ comme le** or **en libérateur du pays** to make oneself out to be the country's saviour; **3** (se porter candidat) **se ~ à** to take [*examen, concours*]; to stand for [*élections*]; **se ~ aux élections présidentielles** to stand in the presidential elections, to run for president US; **en 1988 il ne s'est pas présenté** in 1988 he didn't stand; **se ~ sur la même liste que** to stand GB ou run US alongside sb; **se ~ pour un emploi** to put in ou apply for a post; **4** (survenir) [*occasion, difficulté, problème*] to arise, to present itself; [*solution*] to emerge; **peu d'occasions se sont présentées** there were few opportunities; **lire/manger tout ce qui se présente** to read/eat anything that comes along; **les difficultés qui se présentent à nous** the difficulties with which we are faced ou confronted; **les possibilités qui se présentent à nous** the possibilities available to us; **cette idée s'était présentée à mon esprit** the idea had crossed my mind; **un spectacle étonnant se présenta à mes yeux** an amazing sight met my eyes; **5** (exister) [*médicament, produit*] **se ~ en, se ~ sous forme de** to come in the form of; **se ~ sous forme de cachets/en sirop/en granulés** to come ou be available in tablet form/as a syrup GB ou sirup US/in the form of granules; **6** (s'annoncer) **l'affaire se présente bien/mal** things are looking good/bad; **comment se présente la situation sur le front?** what is the situation at the front?; **7** Méd **comment se présente l'enfant?** how is the baby presenting?; **le bébé se présente par le siège** the baby is in the breech position.

présentoir /pʀezɑ̃twaʀ/ *nm* (meuble) display stand ou unit; (rayon) display shelf; **~ à tourniquet** rotating display rack; **~ de caisse** check-out display.

présérie /pʀeseʀi/ *nf* test batch.

préservateur, -trice /pʀezɛʀvatœʀ, tʀis/ *nm* Chimie, Ind preservative; **sans ~** preservative-free.

préservatif /pʀezɛʀvatif/ *nm* condom; **~ féminin** female condom.

préservation /pʀezɛʀvasjɔ̃/ *nf* (de personne, d'environnement) protection; (de bâtiment, site) preservation, conservation; (de pouvoir, d'État) preservation; **la ~ de la nature** nature conservation.

préserver /pʀezɛʀve/ [1] **I** *vtr* to preserve [*tradition, unité, patrimoine, jeunesse, paix*] (**de** from, against); to protect [*intérêt, droit, emploi, environnement, corps*] (**de** from, against).

II se préserver *vpr* **se ~ de** to protect oneself against [*intempéries*].

IDIOMES **jamais je ne l'épouserai, Dieu** or **le ciel m'en préserve!** God forbid I should ever marry him/her!

présidence /pʀezidɑ̃s/ *nf* **1** (fonction) (d'État, association, de club, syndicat) presidency; (d'entreprise, de parti, commission, jury, tribunal, cour) chairmanship; (d'université) vice-chancellorship GB, presidency US; **exercer la ~** Pol to hold the presidency; Entr to hold the chairmanship; **votre candidature à la ~ de la République** your candidacy for the presidency of the Republic; **candidat à la ~** Pol presidential candidate; **être candidat à la ~** Pol to stand GB ou run US for presidency; **2** (résidence) presidential palace; (bureaux) presidential offices (*pl*).

■ **~ du Parlement Européen** presidency of the European Parliament.

président /pʀezidɑ̃/ **▶813** *nm* (d'État, association, de club, syndicat) president; (d'entreprise, de conseil d'administration) chairman; (de parti, commission) chairperson; (de jury d'examen ou de prix) chairman; (d'université) vice-chancellor GB, president US; **'Ducostar, ~!'** Pol 'Ducostar for president!'; **Monsieur le Président** Pol Mr President; Entr Mr Chairman; Jur Your Honour[GB]; **Madame le Président** fml Pol Madam President; Entr Madam Chairman; Jur Your Honour[GB].

■ **~ de l'Assemblée nationale** Pol President of the National Assembly; **~ du Conseil** Hist head of government (*during the third and fourth Republics in France*) ; **~ du Parlement européen** President of the European Parliament; **~ de la République** gén President of the Republic; **~ de séance** (à une réunion) chair, chairperson; **~ du Sénat** Pol President of the Senate.

président-directeur, *pl* **présidents-directeurs** /pʀezidɑ̃diʀɛktœʀ/ *nm* **~ général** chairman and managing director GB, chief executive officer US.

présidente /pʀezidɑ̃t/ **▶813** *nf* **1** (d'État, de club, syndicat) president; (de parti, commission) chair, chairwoman; (d'entreprise, de conseil d'administration) chairman; **2** (épouse du chef d'État) First Lady.

présidentiable /pʀezidɑ̃sjabl/ **I** *adj* [*minis-*

tre, chef de parti] who is a potential presidential candidate (*épith, après n*).

II *nmf* potential presidential candidate.

présidentialisme /pʀezidɑ̃sjalism/ *nm* presidentialism.

présidentiel, **-ielle** /pʀezidɑ̃sjɛl/ I *adj* presidential; **l'entourage ~** the president's entourage.

II **présidentielles** *nfpl* presidential election (*sg*).

présider /pʀezide/ [1] I *vtr* **1** (diriger) to chair [*commission, débat, jury d'examen*]; **2** (être président de) to be the president of [*club, association*]; to be the chairman/chairwoman of [*entreprise, parti, conseil d'administration*]; Jur to preside over [*cour*]; to be the vice-chancellor GB ou president US of [*université*]; **3** (être à l'honneur) **~ un dîner** to be the guest of honour[GB] at a dinner.

II **présider à** *vtr ind* **1** (régir) fml **~ à** [*astre, divinité, règle*] to govern [*destinées, naissances, guerre*]; to oversee [*évolution*]; **2†** (superviser) **~ à** [*personne*] to preside over [*réunion, cérémonie, préparatifs*].

présidium = **præsidium**.

présocratique /pʀesɔkʀatik/ I *adj* pre-Socratic.

II *nm* pre-Socratic (philosopher).

présomptif, **-ive** /pʀezɔ̃ptif, iv/ *adj* **héritier ~** heir apparent.

présomption /pʀezɔ̃psjɔ̃/ *nf* **1** Jur presumption (**de** of); **condamner qn sur de simples ~s** to condemn sb on presumptive grounds alone; **~ d'innocence/de paternité** presumption of innocence/of paternity; **2** (supposition) assumption; **3** (prétention) presumption; **être plein de ~** to be full of presumption, to be presumptuous.

présomptueusement /pʀezɔ̃ptɥøzmɑ̃/ *adv* presumptuously.

présomptueux, **-euse** /pʀezɔ̃ptɥø, øz/ I *adj* [*personne, air*] arrogant; [*action, propos*] presumptuous; **il serait ~ de dire** it would be presumptuous to say.

II *nm,f* presumptuous person.

présonorisation /pʀesɔnɔʀizasjɔ̃/ *nf* Cin, TV playback.

presque /pʀɛsk/ *adv* **nous sommes ~ arrivés** we're almost ou nearly there; **~ tout le monde/chaque semaine** almost everybody/every week; **~ la moitié** almost half; **~ toujours** almost always; **la ~ totalité des étudiants** almost all the students; **il y a trois ans ~ jour pour jour** it's nearly three years to the day; **la même histoire ou ~** the same story or almost the same; **tout le monde ou ~** everybody or almost everybody; **il n'y avait personne ou ~, il n'y avait ~ personne** there was hardly anyone there; **c'était le bonheur ou ~** it was as close to happiness as one can get; **il ne reste ~ rien** there's hardly anything left; **cela n'arrive ~ jamais** it hardly ever happens; **il n'a ~ pas plu** it hardly rained at all; **il ne neige ~ plus** it has almost stopped snowing; **elle n'a rien mangé ou ~** she ate hardly anything; **il ne se passe ~ pas de jour sans que quelque chose arrive** hardly a day goes by without something happening.

presqu'île /pʀɛskil/ *nf* peninsula.

pressage /pʀɛsaʒ/ *nm* pressing.

pressant, **~e** /pʀɛsɑ̃, ɑ̃t/ *adj* [*besoin, demande, invitation, danger, problème*] pressing; [*appel*] urgent; [*créancier, vendeur*] insistent; **demander qch de manière ~e** to press for sth.

presse /pʀɛs/ I *nf* **1** (journaux) press; (journalistes) press; (magazines) magazines (*pl*); **~ écrite/économique** written/economic press; **article de ~** press article; **présenter à** or **devant la ~** to present to the press; **convoquer la ~** to summon the press; **~ automobile/féminine/du cœur** motoring GB ou car US/women's/romantic magazines; **avoir bonne/mauvaise ~** to be well/not well thought of (**auprès** among); **que dit la ~?** what do the papers say?; ▶ **grand**; **2** (machine à presser) press; **~ hydraulique/de 100 tonnes** hydraulic/100-ton press; **~ à la main/à vis/mécanique** hand/screw/power press; **~ à relier/à emboutir** holding/stamping press; **3** (machine à imprimer) press; **~ à cylindres** or **rotative** cylinder press; **~ à bras** hand press; **~ à platine** platen press; **mettre sous ~** to send [sth] off to press; **être mis sous ~** to go to press; **'sous ~'** 'in preparation'; **4** (hâte) **dans les moments de ~** when things get busy.

II **presses** *nfpl* (maison d'édition) press (*sg*).

pressé, **~e** /pʀese/ I *pp* ▶ **presser**.

II *pp adj* **1** (qui n'a pas le temps) [*personne, client, visiteur, automobiliste*] impatient; [*pas, air*] hurried; **être/avoir l'air ~** to be/look in a hurry; **avoir l'air bien ~** to seem to be in a great hurry; **les gens ~s dans la rue** people rushing about in the street; **2** (désireux) **~ de faire** keen to do; **peu ~ de prendre des risques** in no great hurry to take (any) risks; **3** (urgent) [*affaire*] urgent; **elle n'a rien eu de plus ~ que de faire** she couldn't wait to do; **aller** or **parer au plus ~** to do the most urgent thing(s) first.

presse-agrumes /pʀɛsagʀym/ *nm inv* (électrique) juice extractor GB, juicer US; (manuel) fruit squeezer GB, juicer US.

presse-ail /pʀɛsaj/ *nm inv* garlic press.

presse-bouton /pʀɛsbutɔ̃/ *adj inv* **guerre ~** push-button warfare; **usine ~** fully automated factory.

presse-citron /pʀɛssitʀɔ̃/ *nm inv* lemon squeezer.

presse-étoupe /pʀɛsetup/ *nm inv* Tech gland.

pressentiment /pʀɛsɑ̃timɑ̃/ *nm* premonition; **avoir le ~ de/que** to have a premonition about/that; **mes ~s se confirment** it's all turning out as I expected; **j'ai été pris d'un ~** I had a premonition.

pressentir /pʀɛsɑ̃tiʀ/ [30] *vtr* **1** (deviner) to have a premonition about [*malheur, changement*]; **~ que** to have a premonition that; **2** fml (sonder) **~ qn pour un emploi** to approach sb about a job; **la seule personne pressentie** the only person who was approached.

presse-papiers /pʀɛspapje/ *nm inv* paperweight.

presse-purée /pʀɛspyʀe/ *nm inv* potato masher.

presser /pʀese/ [1] I *vtr* **1** (inciter) **~ qn de faire** to urge sb to do; **2** (harceler) [*personne*] to press [*personne, débiteur*]; [*armée*] to harry [*ennemi*]; **cessez de me ~** stop pestering me; **~ qn de questions** to ply sb with questions; **3** (tourmenter) [*faim, nécessité*] to drive [sb] on [*personne*]; **4** (hâter) to increase [*cadence, rythme*]; **~ le pas** or **mouvement** to hurry; **~ son départ** to hurry one's departure; **qu'est-ce qui vous presse tant?** what's the hurry?; **5** (appuyer sur) to press [*bouton*]; **~ qch contre** or **sur** to press sth against; **6** (serrer) to squeeze [*main, bras, objet*]; **~ qn dans ses bras/contre sa poitrine** to clasp sb in one's arms/to one's chest; **7** (comprimer) to squeeze [*orange, éponge, peau*]; to press [*raisin*]; **8** Tech to press [*disque*].

II *vi* (être urgent) [*affaire, temps*] to be pressing; [*travail, tâche*] to be urgent; **le temps presse** time is running out; **rien ne presse** there's no hurry ou rush.

III **se presser** *vpr* **1** (se serrer) **se ~ sur** or **contre** to press oneself against; **se ~ autour de qn/qch** to press around sb/sth; **2** (se hâter) to hurry up; **se ~ de faire** to hurry up and do; **presse-toi de terminer** hurry up and finish; **pressons, pressons**○**!** get a move on○!; **presse-toi un peu** get a move on; **3** (être en nombre) [*foule*] to throng; (aller en nombre) [*foule*] to flock (**à, dans, sur, vers** to); **on ne se presse pas cette année dans les cinémas** people aren't flocking to the cinemas GB ou movies US this year.

presse-raquette /pʀɛsʀakɛt/ *nm inv* racket press.

pressing /pʀɛsiŋ/ ▶ **510** *nm* (teinturerie) dry-cleaner's; **porter sa veste au ~** to take one's jacket to the dry-cleaner's.

pression /pʀɛsjɔ̃/ *nf* **1** (force physique) pressure; **régler la ~** to adjust the pressure; **~ atmosphérique** atmospheric pressure; **hautes/basses ~s** high/low pressure ₵; **~ d'huile/des pneus** oil/tyre GB ou tire US pressure; **~ artérielle** blood pressure; **sous ~** (sans compression) under pressure; (avec compression) pressurized; **eau sous haute ~** water under high pressure; **2** (contrainte) pressure ₵; **travailler sous ~** to work under pressure; **être sous ~** to be under pressure; **céder aux ~s** to give in to (the) pressure; **être soumis à des ~s** to come under pressure; **faire l'objet de ~s** to be put under pressure; **faire ~** or **exercer des ~s sur qn/qch** to put pressure on sb/sth; **ils ont fait ~ sur lui pour qu'il signe** they pressurized him into signing; **~ sur le patronat/les prix** pressure on (the) employers/prices; **multiplier les ~s sur** to increase (the) pressure on; **~ à la hausse/baisse** upward/downward pressure; **forte ~** intense pressure; **~ démographique/inflationniste** population/inflationary pressure; **~ des partis/étudiants** pressure from the parties/students; **sous la ~ populaire** under pressure from the public; **~ fiscale** tax burden; **3** (action d'appuyer) pressure; **~ de la main** manual pressure; **exercer une (légère) ~ avec la main** to press (gently) with one's hand; **à la moindre ~** under the slightest pressure; **faire ~ sur** [*objet, os*] to be pushing ou pressing against; **4** Cout (bouton) press stud GB, popper GB, snap (fastener); **5**○ (bière) **une ~, un demi** ≈ a half (of draught GB ou draft US beer).

pressoir /pʀɛswaʀ/ *nm* **1** (bâtiment) pressing shed; **2** (machine) press; **~ à vin/olives** wine/olive press.

pressurer /pʀɛsyʀe/ [1] *vtr* **1** Agric (presser) to press; **2**○ (exploiter) to milk○.

IDIOMES **se ~ le cerveau**○ to rack one's brain(s)○; **~ qn comme un citron**○ to squeeze sb dry○.

pressurisation /pʀɛsyʀizasjɔ̃/ *nf* pressurization.

pressuriser /pʀɛsyʀize/ [1] *vtr* to pressurize.

prestance /pʀɛstɑ̃s/ *nf* presence, bearing; **avoir une belle ~, avoir beaucoup de ~** to have a confident bearing ou manner.

prestataire /pʀɛstatɛʀ/ *nm* **1** Comm **~ de service** (service) contractor, service provider; **2** (bénéficiaire de prestations) recipient (*of a state benefit*).

prestation /pʀɛstasjɔ̃/ *nf* **1** Admin (aide) benefit; **avoir droit à des ~s** to be entitled to benefits; **~ financière** financial benefit; **2** Mil allowance (*paid to servicemen*); **3** (prêt, fourniture) provision; **~ de capitaux** provision of capital; **~ de service** (provision of a) service; **société de ~s de services** contractor; **4** (service) service; **hôtel qui offre de bonnes ~s** hotel providing various services; **5** (de personne) controv performance; **il a fait une bonne ~** he gave a good performance; **~ télévisée** televised appearance.

■ **~ de serment** swearing-in; **la ~ de serment du président aura lieu lundi** the President will be sworn in on Monday; **~s familiales** *benefits available to families with children*; **~s en nature** benefits in kind; **~s de sécurité sociale** welfare payments.

preste /pʀɛst/ *adj* liter [*mouvement*] nimble; [*réplique*] prompt.

prestement /pʀɛstəmɑ̃/ *adv* liter [*agir, répliquer*] promptly; [*se mouvoir*] nimbly.

prestidigitateur, **-trice** /pʀɛstidiʒitatœʀ, tʀis/ ▶ **510** *nm,f* conjurer.

prestidigitation /pʀɛstidiʒitasjɔ̃/ *nf* conjuring; **c'est de la ~** fig it's (like) magic.

prestige /pʀɛstiʒ/ *nm* gén prestige; **être sensible au ~ de l'uniforme** to be susceptible to the glamour of a uniform; **de ~** [*réalisation*] prestige; [*voiture*] luxury.

prestigieux, **-ieuse** /pʀɛstiʒjø, øz/ *adj* prestigious.

prestissimo /pʀɛstisimo/ *adv, nm* prestissimo.

presto /pʀɛsto/ **I** *adv* **1** Mus presto; **2**○ quickly; ▶ **illico**.
II *nm* Mus presto.

présumer /pʀezyme/ [1] **I** *vtr* to presume, to assume (**que** that); **présumé innocent** presumed innocent; **auteur présumé** presumed author; **le père présumé** the putative father; **le présumé coupable/terroriste** the alleged culprit/terrorist.
II présumer de *vtr ind* (**trop**) **~ de ses forces/possibilités** to overestimate one's strength/capabilities.

présupposé /pʀesypoze/ *nm* presupposition.

présupposer /pʀesypoze/ [1] *vtr* to presuppose.

présupposition /pʀesypozisjɔ̃/ *nf* presupposition.

présure /pʀezyʀ/ *nf* rennet.

prêt, **~e** /pʀɛ, pʀɛt/ **I** *adj* **1** (préparé) ready (**à, pour** for; **à faire, pour faire** to do); **~ à l'emploi** ready for use; **le pays n'est pas ~ pour l'indépendance** the country isn't ready for independence; **être fin ~** [*personne*] to be all set; **tout est fin ~ pour la réception/l'arrivée des invités** everything is ready for the reception/the guests' arrival; **se tenir ~** to be ready (**à faire** to do); **2** (disposé) **être ~ à faire** to be ready ou prepared to do; **ils sont ~s à faire grève** they are ready ou prepared to go on strike; **il est toujours ~ à rendre service** he's always ready ou willing to oblige; **il est ~ à tout pour atteindre son but** he will stop at nothing ou he will do anything to get what he wants; **il est ~ à toutes les bassesses pour de l'argent** he will do anything ou he will stoop to anything for money.
II *nm* **1** (action) lending; **le service de ~ de la bibliothèque** the library loans service; **2** (somme) loan; Mil soldier's pay; **demander un ~** to apply for a loan; **obtenir un ~** to secure a loan; **un ~ de 20000 francs** a 20,000 franc loan; **un ~ à 10%** a loan at 10%, a 10% loan.
■ **~ bancaire** bank loan; **~ à la consommation** consumer loan; **~ sur gage** (activité) pawnbroking; (somme) collateral loan; **~ d'honneur** loan on trust; **~ personnel** personal loan; **~ relais** bridging loan.

prêt-à-monter, *pl* **prêts-à-monter** /pʀɛtamɔ̃te/ *nm* kit, flat-pack; **bureau en ~** flat-packed desk.

prêt-à-porter, *pl* **prêts-à-porter** /pʀɛtapɔʀte/ *nm* **1** (vêtements) ready-to-wear, ready-to-wear clothes (*pl*); **acheter du ~** to buy clothes off the peg GB ou rack US; **2** (secteur) ready-to-wear.

prêté /pʀete/ *nm* **c'est un ~ pour un rendu** it's tit for tat.

prétendant, **~e** /pʀetɑ̃dɑ̃, ɑ̃t/ **I** *nm,f* **1** (à un titre, poste) candidate (**à** for); **2** (royal) pretender; **~ au trône** pretender to the throne.
II *nm* (soupirant) suitor.

prétendre /pʀetɑ̃dʀ/ [6] **I** *vtr* **1** (affirmer) to claim (**que** that); **il prétend tout ignorer de cette affaire** he claims to know nothing about the matter; **à ce qu'il prétend** according to him; **aussi belle qu'on le prétend** as beautiful as they say; **on le prétend très spirituel** he is said to be very witty; **2** (s'attendre à) to expect; **~ être obéi** to expect to be obeyed.
II prétendre à *vtr ind* **~ à des indemnités** to claim damages; **~ aux honneurs** to aspire to honours[GB]; **~ à un poste/salaire** to seek a job/salary.
III se prétendre *vpr* **elle se prétend indisposée/offensée** she claims she is indisposed/offended; **il se prétend artiste/médecin** he makes out he is an artist/a doctor.

prétendu, **~e** /pʀetɑ̃dy/ **I** *adj* [*coupable, terroriste, voleur*] alleged; [*démocratie, égalité, crise*] alleged, so-called; [*médecin, policier, expert, artiste*] would-be; **la ~e reprise de l'économie** the alleged ou so-called economic upturn.
II† *nm,f* intended†.

prétendument /pʀetɑ̃dymɑ̃/ *adv* supposedly, allegedly.

prête-nom, *pl* **~s** /pʀɛtnɔ̃/ *nm* frontman, man of straw.

prétentaine† /pʀetɑ̃tɛn/ *nf* **courir la ~** to go gallivanting.

prétentieusement /pʀetɑ̃sjøzmɑ̃/ *adv* pretentiously.

prétentieux, **-ieuse** /pʀetɑ̃sjø, øz/ **I** *adj* [*personne, ton, style*] pretentious.
II *nm,f* pretentious person; **petit ~** pretentious little idiot.

prétention /pʀetɑ̃sjɔ̃/ **I** *nf* **1** (vanité) pretentiousness, conceit; **être plein de ~** to be very pretentious ou conceited; **être sans ~** to be unpretentious ou unassuming; **2** (revendication) claim; **avoir des ~s sur** or **à qch** to have a claim to sth; **renoncer à ses ~s** to renounce one's claims; **3** (présomption) **avoir une ~ à l'intelligence/à l'élégance** to have pretentions to intelligence/elegance; **avoir la ~ de faire** to claim to do; **il a la ~ de pouvoir faire** he claims he can do.
II prétentions *nfpl* (salaire demandé) **quel les sont vos ~s?** what salary are you asking for?; **avoir des ~s acceptables/excessives** to ask for a reasonable/an excessive salary; **indiquez vos ~s** state salary required.

prêter /pʀete/ [1] **I** *vtr* **1** (fournir un bien matériel) to lend [*argent, objet*] (**à qn** to sb); **~ à 10%** Fin to lend (money) at 10%; **peux-tu me rendre le livre que je t'ai prêté?** can you give me back the book I lent you?; **~ sur gages** to loan against security; **des toiles prêtées par le Louvre à un musée américain** paintings on loan from the Louvre to an American museum; **des toiles prêtées au Louvre par un musée américain** paintings on loan to the Louvre from an American museum; **2** (accorder) **~ son aide à qn** to give sb some help; **~ son appui/assistance à qn** to give ou lend sb one's support/assistance; **~ attention à** to pay attention to; **ils ont prêté leur concours à cette entreprise** they lent their support to this venture; **~ la main à qn** to lend sb a hand; **~ l'oreille** to listen, to lend an ear hum; **~ serment** to take an oath; **~ son nom à** to lend one's name to, to allow one's name to be used by; **si Dieu me prête vie** if God spares me; ▶ **flanc**; **3** (attribuer) **~ qch à qn** to attribute ou ascribe sth to sb [*intention, desseins, propos, vertus*]; **les intentions que l'on prête au président** the president's supposed intentions; **on lui prête des qualités qu'il n'a pas** qualities are attributed ou ascribed to him which he does not have; **on me prête des propos que je n'ai jamais tenus** I'm credited with remarks I never made; **on prête à l'entreprise l'intention de se réimplanter à l'étranger** it is said that the company intends to relocate abroad.
II prêter à *vtr ind* **~ à** to give rise to, to cause; **déclaration qui prête à confusion** statement that gives rise to ou causes confusion; **sujet qui prête à l'inquiétude** issue which is cause for concern; **conduite qui prête à la critique** behaviour[GB] that is open to ou invites criticism; **son attitude prête à rire** his/her attitude is laughable ou ridiculous; **tout prête à croire** or **penser que la crise est finie** all the indications would suggest that the recession is over.
III *vi* Tech [*cuir, tissu*] to stretch.
IV se prêter *vpr* **1** (consentir) **se ~ à** to take part in [*machination, manœuvre, arrangement, jeu*]; **jamais je ne me prêterai à ce genre de manigances!** I would never have anything to do with that kind of skulduggery○!; **2** (convenir) **se ~ à** to lend itself to; **le roman se prête à une interprétation psychanalytique/une adaptation cinématographique** the novel lends itself to a psychoanalytic interpretation/a film adaptation; **le lieu ne se prêtait pas à une déclaration d'amour** the surroundings were ill-suited to ou did not lend themselves to a declaration of love; **3** (donner) **se ~ assistance** [*personnes*] to assist one another; **se ~ une assistance mutuelle** [*pays*] to provide mutual assistance to one another.

prétérit /pʀeteʀit/ *nm* preterite; **au ~** in the preterite.

prétérition /pʀeteʀisjɔ̃/ *nf* paralipsis.

préteur /pʀetœʀ/ *nm* Antiq praetor.

prêteur, **-euse** /pʀɛtœʀ, øz/ **I** *adj* **il n'est pas ~** he doesn't like lending his things, he's very possessive about his belongings.
II ▶ **510** *nm,f* lender.
■ **~ sur gages** pawnbroker.

prétexte /pʀetɛkst/ *nm* excuse, pretext; **un bon/mauvais ~** a good/poor excuse (**pour faire** for doing); **c'est un ~ pour s'esquiver** it's just an excuse for getting away; **il a saisi le premier ~ venu pour refuser** he gave the first excuse that came into his head to refuse; **être le ~ de qch** to be used as an excuse for sth; **tout est ~ à sortir** any excuse will do to go out; **sous ~ de faire** on the pretext of doing; **sous (le) ~ que** on the pretext that; **donner qch comme ~, prendre ~ de qch** to use sth as a pretext ou an excuse (**pour faire** to do, for doing); **donner à qn un ~, servir de ~ à qn** to give sb an excuse (**pour faire** to do, for doing); **servir de ~ à qch** to be an excuse for sth; **sous aucun ~** on no account; **n'y allez sous aucun ~** on no account are you to go; **n'ouvrez la porte sous aucun ~** don't open the door on any account.

prétexter /pʀetɛkste/ [1] **I** *vtr* to use [sth] as an excuse, to plead; **il a prétexté un rendez-vous urgent pour s'éclipser** he pleaded an urgent engagement in order to get away; **prétextant qu'il était trop vieux/qu'il faisait froid** using his age/the cold as an excuse.
II prétexter de *vtr ind* **~ de qch pour faire** to use sth as an excuse for doing.

prétoire /pʀetwaʀ/ *nm* **1** Jur courtroom; **2** Antiq (tribunal) praetorium.

Pretoria /pʀetɔʀja/ ▶ **857** *npr* Pretoria.

prétorien, **-ienne** /pʀetɔʀjɛ̃, ɛn/ **I** *adj* praetorian.
II *nm* Antiq praetorian.

prétraiter /pʀetʀete/ [1] *vtr* to pretreat; **bois prétraité** pretreated wood.

prêtre /pʀɛtʀ/ *nm* priest; ▶ **grand**.

prêtre-ouvrier, *pl* **prêtres-ouvriers** /pʀɛtʀuvʀije, pʀɛtʀəzuvʀije/ *nm* worker priest.

prêtresse /pʀɛtʀɛs/ *nf* priestess.

prêtrise /pʀɛtʀiz/ *nf* priesthood.

preuve /pʀœv/ *nf* **1** (argument) proof ¢; **une ~** a piece of evidence; **~ légale/mathématique/incontournable** legal/mathematical/incontrovertible proof; **~ probante** conclusive proof; **apporter la ~ de/que** to offer proof of/that; **ne pas avoir de ~(s)** to have no proof; **demander/fournir des ~s** to ask for/to provide proof; **fournir une autre ~** to provide further proof; **être la ~ supplémentaire de** to be further proof of; **~ d'achat/de propriété** proof of purchase/of ownership; **sur ~ d'identité** upon proof of identity; **par manque de ~** for lack of proof; **la meilleure ~ c'est que** the most compelling proof is that; **la ~ est**

faite de/que now there is proof of/that; **pour ~ de** as proof of; **~ en main** with concrete proof; **renverser la charge de la ~** to reverse the onus of proof; **faire la ~ de** to show proof of; **donner la ~ que** to prove that; **faire ses ~s** [*personne*] to prove oneself; [*chose*] to prove itself; **jusqu'à ~ du contraire** until proved otherwise; **il a rougi, ~ qu'il t'aime** he blushed which proves that he loves you; **il t'aime, la ~ en est qu'il a rougi** he loves you, otherwise he would not have blushed; **il doit être malade, la ~, c'est qu'il n'a pas mangé** he must be ill, the fact that he has not eaten proves it; **2** (expression) demonstration; **~ d'amour** demonstration of love; **être la ~ vivante de** to be living proof of; **faire ~ de** to show; **faire ~ que** to show that; **~ de bonne volonté (de la part de)** goodwill gesture (from).

■ ~ par l'absurde Sci reductio ad absurdum.

preux‡ /pʀø/ **I** *adj m inv* valiant.

II *nm inv* valiant knight.

prévaloir /pʀevalwaʀ/ [45] **I** *vi* to prevail (**sur** over; **contre** against); **faire ~ la vérité** to make truth prevail; **faire ~ son point de vue** to gain acceptance for one's point of view.

II se prévaloir *vpr* **1** (se fonder) **se ~ d'un règlement/précédent** to cite a rule/precedent (**auprès de qn** to sb; **pour faire** as grounds for doing); **se ~ de son ancienneté** to claim seniority (**pour faire** to do); **2** (tirer vanité) **se ~ de** to boast [*succès, expérience, diplômes*].

prévaricateur, -trice /pʀevaʀikatœʀ, tʀis/ fml or Jur **I** *adj* corrupt.

II *nm,f* corrupt official.

prévarication /pʀevaʀikasjɔ̃/ *nf* Jur breach of trust.

prévariquer /pʀevaʀike/ [1] *vi* Jur to fail in one's duty.

prévenance /pʀevnɑ̃s/ *nf* consideration (**envers, à l'égard de** toward, towards GB); **manquer de ~** to show a lack of consideration; **être plein de ~** to be extremely considerate.

prévenant, ~e /pʀevnɑ̃, ɑ̃t/ *adj* considerate (**envers, à l'égard de** toward, towards GB).

prévenir /pʀevniʀ/ [36] *vtr* **1** (informer) to tell (**de** about; **que** that); **prévenez-nous de votre visite** tell us when you're coming; **partir sans ~** to leave without telling anybody; **arriver sans ~** to arrive without warning; **2** (téléphoner à) to call [*médecin, police*]; **prévenez la police** call the police; **3** (donner un avertissement) to warn (**de** about; **que** that); **je te préviens, si tu fais ça je m'en vais!** I warn you, if you do that I'm off!; **~ la population des risques d'explosion** to warn the population about the risk of explosion; **je vous aurai prévenu!** I have warned you!; **4** (éviter) to prevent [*catastrophe, maladie*]; **5** (aller au devant de) to anticipate [*désir*]; **elle prévient leurs moindres désirs** she anticipates their every wish.

IDIOMES **mieux vaut ~ que guérir** prevention is better than cure.

préventif, -ive /pʀevɑ̃tif, iv/ **I** *adj* [*action, pouvoir, traitement*] preventive; **à titre ~** as a preventive measure.

II○ **préventive** *nf* Jur custody.

prévention /pʀevɑ̃sjɔ̃/ *nf* **1** (action préventive) prevention; **~ de la délinquance/des incendies/du sida** crime/fire/Aids prevention; **~ de la carie dentaire/des accidents du travail** prevention of tooth decay/of accidents at work; **méthodes/campagne/opération de ~** prevention methods/campaign/plan; **faire de la ~** to take preventive action; **2** fml (préjugé) prejudice (**contre** against); **3** Jur (détention préventive) detention on suspicion; (temps de détention préventive) remand in custody.

■ Prévention routière Admin *French national road safety organization.*

préventivement /pʀevɑ̃tivmɑ̃/ *adv* as a precautionary measure; **agir ~** to take preventive action.

prévenu, ~e /pʀevny/ **I** *adj* Jur **être ~ de** to be accused of.

II *nm,f* Jur defendant.

préverbe /pʀevɛʀb/ *nm* (verb) prefix.

prévisibilité /pʀevizibilite/ *nf* predictability.

prévisible /pʀevizibl/ *adj* [*développement, événement*] foreseeable, predictable; [*chiffre, réaction, personne*] predictable; **leur échec était ~** their failure was predictable; **un accident difficilement ~** an accident which could hardly have been foreseen.

prévision /pʀevizjɔ̃/ *nf* **1** (action de prévoir) forecasting; **la ~ du temps** weather forecasting; **~ économique** economic forecasting; **la ~ de la demande** the forecasting of demand; **faire des ~s** to make forecasts; **en ~ de** in anticipation of; **2** (ce qu'on prévoit) gén prediction; Compta, Écon, Fin, Entr forecast; **les chiffres confirment les ~s** the figures confirm the forecasts; **les ~s de croissance pour 1995** (economic) growth forecasts for 1995; **les résultats vont au-delà de toutes nos ~s** the results go beyond all our expectations; **~s météorologiques** weather forecast (*sg*).

prévisionnel, -elle /pʀevizjɔnɛl/ *adj* projected; **comptes ~s** projected accounts.

prévisionniste /pʀevizjɔnist/ **▶510** *nmf* (economic) forecaster

prévoir /pʀevwaʀ/ [42] *vtr* **1** (annoncer comme probable) to predict [*changement, amélioration, augmentation, arrivée, inflation*]; to foresee [*événement, échec, victoire*]; to anticipate [*conséquence, réaction*]; to forecast [*résultat, temps*]; **qui pouvait ~ ce qui se passerait?** who could have foreseen what would happen?; **nous ne pouvions pas ~ qu'il démissionnerait** we couldn't anticipate that he would resign; **la participation au vote a été moins forte que prévue** the turn-out has been lower than anticipated; **rien ne laissait ~ un tel résultat** there was no prior indication of such a result; **c'était à ~!** that was predictable!; **2** Jur (envisager) [*loi, texte, règlement*] to make provision for, to provide for [*cas, infraction, possibilité*]; [*personne, législateur*] to make provision for, to allow for [*cas, infraction, possibilité*]; **le texte ne prévoit rien en cas de litige** the text makes no provision in case of litigation; **les cas prévus par la loi** cases provided for by the law; **3** (fixer dans le temps) to plan [*réunion, rendez-vous, assemblée*] (**pour** for); to set the date for [*rentrée, déménagement*] (**pour** for); **la réunion prévue (pour) le 17 avril** the meeting planned for 17 April; **rendez-vous comme prévu le 17** meeting on the 17th as planned or arranged; **le début des travaux est prévu pour le 20 mai** the work is scheduled to start on 20 May; **4** (planifier) [*architecte, organisateur, concepteur, éditeur*] to plan [*pièce, construction, édition*]; [*propriétaire, client*] to plan to have [*pièce*]; **l'architecte prévoit deux escaliers de secours** the architect is planning two emergency staircases; **nous prévoyons deux chambres d'amis** we plan to have two spare rooms; **il n'a pas prévu de sortie de secours** he didn't make provision for an emergency exit; **être prévu** to be planned; **ce n'était pas prévu!** that wasn't meant to happen!; **le (petit) dernier n'était pas prévu** the youngest wasn't planned; **rien n'est prévu pour l'année prochaine** there's no plan for next year; **une salle a été prévue pour les fumeurs** provision has been made for a smoking room; **rien n'a été prévu pour les enfants** no provision has been made for the children; **nous prévoyons la construction d'une usine** we're planning to build a factory; **nous prévoyons la visite de Venise** we're planning to visit Venice; **~ de faire** to plan to do; **il prévoit de rentrer le 17 avril** he plans to come back on 17 April; **ils ont prévu de privatiser** they have made plans to privatize; **je dois ~ un repas pour 30 personnes** I have to organize a meal for 30 people; **l'accord prévu entre les deux compagnies** the projected agreement between the two companies; **un plan de réorganisation prévoyant 500 suppressions d'emploi** a reorganization plan which entails the projected loss of 500 jobs; **remplissez le formulaire prévu à cet effet** fill in the appropriate form; **tout a été prévu pour qch/pour faire** all the arrangements have been made for sth/to do; **la salle a été prévue pour 100 personnes** the room has been designed for 100 people; **'~ deux jours pour le trajet'** 'allow two days to get there'; **les travaux n'ont pas été terminés dans les délais prévus** the work was not completed within the allotted time or the deadline; **5** (se munir de) **~ qch** to make sure one takes sth [*vêtement, parapluie*] ; **~ le repas de midi** to bring a packed lunch; **6** (s'attendre à) [*organisateur, hôte, gouvernement*] to expect [*personne*]; to expect, to anticipate [*postes d'emploi, pénurie, grève*]; **7** (allouer) to allow [*somme d'argent*]; [*touriste, client*] to allow [*temps, durée*]; [*réparateur, déménageur, organisateur*] (fixer) to assign [*durée*].

prévôt /pʀevo/ *nm* **1** **▶813** Hist, Relig provost; **2** Mil ≈ provost marshal.

prévôté /pʀevote/ *nf* **1** Hist (juridiction) provosty; (fonction) provostship; **2** Mil military police; **3** Relig provostship.

prévoyance /pʀevwajɑ̃s/ *nf* foresight; **manque de ~** lack of foresight.

prévoyant, ~e /pʀevwajɑ̃, ɑ̃t/ *adj* far-sighted; **être ~** to be far-sighted, to think ahead.

Priam /pʀijam/ *npr* Priam.

priapisme /pʀijapism/ *nm* priapism.

prie-Dieu /pʀidjø/ *nm inv* prie-dieu.

prier /pʀije/ [2] **I** *vtr* **1** (demander à) **~ qn de faire** to ask sb to do; **je l'ai prié de sortir** I asked him to leave; **je vous prie d'excuser mon retard** I'm so sorry I'm late; **je vous prie de vous taire** will you kindly be quiet; **il a vite accepté, je vous prie de le croire**○! he accepted quick enough, believe me!; **être prié de faire** (ordre) to be requested to do; (requête) to be kindly requested to do; (invitation) to be invited to do; **vous êtes priés de vous abstenir de fumer** you are kindly requested to refrain from smoking; **vous êtes prié d'assister à l'inauguration** you are invited to attend the opening; **pouvez-vous me passer le sel, je vous prie** would you mind passing the salt, please?; **pas d'histoires, je vous prie!** no nonsense, please!; **je vous en prie, laissez-nous** please, leave us alone; **'puis-je entrer?'—'je vous en prie'** 'may I come in?'—'please do!'; **je vous en prie, ce n'est rien** don't mention it, it's nothing; **je vous en prie, (après vous)** after you; **elle ne s'est pas fait ~** she didn't have to be asked twice; **il aime se faire ~** he likes to be coaxed; **il a accepté sans se faire ~** he accepted without hesitation; **2** Relig to pray to [*Dieu, saint*]; **~ que** to pray that; **prions que tout aille bien** let's keep our fingers crossed○.

II *vi* Relig to pray; **~ pour qn/qch** to pray for sb/sth; **~ pour la paix** to pray for peace; **~ pour que la paix revienne** to pray for peace to be restored; **~ sur la tombe de qn** to pray at sb's grave.

prière /pʀijɛʀ/ **I** *nm* Édition **~ d'insérer** review slip.

II *nf* **1** Relig prayer; **lieu de ~** place of prayer; **appeler les fidèles à la ~** to call the faithful to prayer; **une journée placée sous le signe de la ~** a day of prayer; **être absorbé dans sa ~** to be absorbed in prayer ou one's prayers; **faire sa ~** or **ses ~s** to say one's prayers; **conduire la ~** to lead the prayers; **la ~ du soir** evening prayers (*pl*); **2** (demande) request; (plus insistant) plea, entreaty; **céder à la ~ de qn** to give in to sb's request, to yield to sb's plea ou entreaty; **~ de fermer la porte** please close the door; **~ de ne pas fumer** no smoking please; **~ de ne pas se pencher à la portière** do not lean out of the window.

prieur /pRijœR/ *nm* (père) ~ prior.

prieuré /pRijœRe/ *nm* (couvent) priory; (église) priory church; (maison du prieur) prior's house, priory.

prima donna /pRimadɔna/ *nf inv* prima donna.

primaire /pRimɛR/ **I** *adj* **1** (par opposition à secondaire) primary; **2** (simpliste) [*personne*] limited, of limited outlook (*après n*); [*réaction*] kneejerk° (*épith*), simplistic; [*raisonnement, anticommunisme, opinion*] simplistic; **3** Jur **délinquant ~** first offender.

II *nm* **1** Scol **le ~** primary education; **2** Écon **le ~** the primary sector; **3** Géol **le ~** the palaeozoic era.

III *nf* Pol (élection) primary.

primal, **~e**, *pl* **-aux** /pRimal, o/ *adj* primal; **cri ~** primal scream.

primat /pRima/ *nm* **1** (archevêque) primate; **2** (primauté) primacy.

primate /pRimat/ *nm* **1** Zool primate; **les ~s** the primates; **2** (homme grossier) pej ape° péj.

primauté /pRimote/ *nf* **1** (supériorité de fait) primacy, supremacy (**sur** over); **2** (autorité) primacy.

prime /pRim/ **I** *adj* **1** (premier) **de ~ abord** at first, initially; **de ~ abord, je l'ai trouvé antipathique** at first, I disliked him; **dans sa ~ jeunesse** in the first flush of youth, in the early days of his/her youth; **la ~ enfance** early childhood; **2** Math prime; **A ~** A prime.

II *nf* **1** (récompense) bonus; **en ~ avec votre abonnement, recevez ce magnifique réveil** as a free gift to new subscribers, we're offering this fabulous alarm clock; **financer de telles émissions, c'est donner une ~ à la bêtise** giving financial backing to programmes[GB] like that amounts to actively encouraging idiocy; **et en ~ il a reçu un coup de pied aux fesses** and, for good measure, he got a kick in the backside; **2** (indemnité) allowance; **3** (subvention) subsidy; **4** Assur, Fin premium; **faire ~** to rise; **5** (en escrime) prime.

■ **~ d'ancienneté** seniority bonus; **~ à la construction** building subsidy; **~ de déménagement** removal allowance GB, relocation allowance; **~ à l'embauche** recruitment premium; **~ d'encouragement** incentive bonus; **~ d'équipement** development subsidy; **~ à l'exportation** export subsidy; **~ de fin d'année** Christmas bonus; **~ de licenciement** redundancy payment GB, severance pay; **~ de précarité** *allowance to compensate for insecurity of employment*; **~ de rendement** productivity bonus; **~ de risque** danger money; **~ de transport** transport allowance GB, transportation allowance US; **~ de vie chère** cost-of-living allowance.

primer /pRime/ [1] **I** *vtr* **1** (l'emporter sur) to take precedence over, to prevail over; **chez cet auteur, l'émotion prime la réflexion** in this author's work emotion prevails over thought; **2** (récompenser) to award a prize to [*œuvre, animal*]; **ce chien a été primé** this dog won a prize; **bête primée** prize-winning animal; **film primé** award-winning film; **ce film a été primé** this film won an award.

II primer sur *vtr ind* controv = **primer I 1**.

III *vi* (dominer) **dans ce sorbet, c'est le cassis qui prime** blackcurrant is the dominant flavour[GB] in this sorbet; **chez lui, c'est l'imagination qui prime** with him, imagination is all-important ou is of prime importance; **pour eux, c'est la quantité qui prime** for them, it's quantity that matters most ou that takes priority.

primesautier, **-ière** /pRimsotje, ɛR/ *adj* impulsive.

primeur /pRimœR/ **I** *nf* **1** (nouveauté) **avoir la ~ de qch** (apprendre) to be the first to hear sth; (bénéficier de) to be the first to benefit from sth; **c'est une grande nouvelle dont je te réserve la ~** it's a great piece of news and you are the first to hear it; **2** Comm **fruits/légumes de ~** new season's fruit/vegetables; **vin (de) ~** new season's wine.

II primeurs *nfpl* early fruit and vegetables, early produce ¢; **marchand de ~s** greengrocer (*specializing in early produce*).

primevère /pRimvɛR/ *nf* primrose.

primipare /pRimipaR/ **I** *adj* primiparous.

II *nf* primipara.

primitif, **-ive** /pRimitif, iv/ **I** *adj* **1** (d'origine) [*budget, différence*] initial; [*projet, état*] original; **2** Anthrop [*société, art*] primitive; **tout ce qui est ~ et sauvage** all that is primitive and savage; **3** (peu évolué) [*plante, animal, langue*] primitive; **4** (rudimentaire) [*outil, moyen, méthode*] primitive; **5** (simpliste) [*personne*] primitive; [*raisonnement*] crude; **6** Math [*fonction*] primitive; **7** Phys [*couleur*] primary; **8** Ling [*temps*] basic.

II *nm,f* **1**† Anthrop [*personne*] primitive; **2** (personne fruste) uncouth person.

III *nm* Art **les ~s italiens/flamands** Italian/Flemish Primitives.

IV primitive *nf* Math primitive.

primitivement /pRimitivmɑ̃/ *adv* originally, initially.

primo /pRimo/ *adv* firstly.

primogéniture /pRimoʒenityR/ *nf* primogeniture.

primo-infection, *pl* **~s** /pRimoɛ̃fɛksjɔ̃/ *nf* primary infection.

primordial, **~e**, *mpl* **-iaux** /pRimɔRdjal, o/ *adj* **1** (essentiel) essential, vital; **2**† (origine) primordial, primitive.

prince /pRɛ̃s/ *nm* **1** ▶ **813** (membre d'une famille souveraine) prince; **le ~ de Monaco/Galles** the Prince of Monaco/Wales; **le ~ Charles** Prince Charles; **2** (numéro un) king; **le ~ de la mode** the king of fashion.

■ **le ~ charmant** Prince Charming; **~ consort** prince consort; **~ de l'Église** prince of the Church; **~ héritier** crown prince; **~ du sang** royal prince; **le ~ des Ténèbres** the Prince of Darkness.

IDIOMES **vivre comme un ~** or **en ~** to live like a king; **vêtu comme un ~** dressed like a prince; **être** or **se montrer bon ~** to be magnanimous.

prince-de-galles /pRɛ̃sdəgal/ **I** *adj inv* prince-of-wales check; **tissu ~** cloth with a prince-of-wales check.

II *nm inv* prince-of-wales check.

princeps /pRɛ̃sɛps/ *adj inv* **édition ~** first printed edition, editio princeps.

princesse /pRɛ̃sɛs/ *nf* **1** ▶ **813** (titre) princess; **la ~ de Monaco** the Princess of Monaco; **la ~ Anne** Princess Anne; **2** (en couture) **ligne ~** princess line; **une robe ~** a princess-line dress.

IDIOMES **aux frais de la ~** (de l'État) at the taxpayer's expense; (d'une société) at the company's expense; (d'une personne) at sb's expense; **faire sa ~**° to give oneself airs.

princier, **-ière** /pRɛ̃sje, ɛR/ *adj* [*titre, goûts, somme*] princely; [*luxe*] dazzling.

princièrement /pRɛ̃sjɛRmɑ̃/ *adv* [*recevoir, être logé*] in grand style.

principal, **~e**, *mpl* **-aux** /pRɛ̃sipal, o/ **I** *adj* **1** (le plus important) [*facteur, danger, souci*] main; [*tâche, objection, autorité*] principal; **c'est l'œuvre ~e de l'auteur** it's the author's major work; **2** (de tête) [*pays, rôle, personnage*] leading; **les principaux pays industrialisés** the leading industrial countries; **3** Admin [*commissaire, inspecteur, clerc*] chief; **4** Ling [*proposition*] main.

II *nm* **1** (l'essentiel) **le ~** the main thing; **c'est le ~** that's the main thing; **le ~ c'est qu'il soit sain et sauf** the main thing is that he is safe and sound; **2** Scol principal; **3** Fin principal.

III principale *nf* **1** Ling main clause; **2** Scol principal.

principalement /pRɛ̃sipalmɑ̃/ *adv* mainly.

principat /pRɛ̃sipa/ *nm* reign.

principauté /pRɛ̃sipote/ *nf* principality.

principe /pRɛ̃sip/ **I** *nm* **1** (règle) principle; **avoir des ~s** to have principles; **par ~** on principle; **pour le ~** as a matter of principle; **c'est une question de ~** it's a matter of principle; **objection de ~** objection on the grounds of principle; **~ de non-ingérence** principle of noninterference; **il a pour ~ de ne jamais emprunter d'argent** he never borrows money as a matter of principle; **accord de ~** provisional agreement; **2** (hypothèse) assumption; **partir du ~ que**, **poser comme ~ que** to work on the assumption that; **3** (concept) principle; **ils ont accepté le ~ d'une conférence de paix** they have accepted the principle of a peace conference; **quel est le ~ de la machine à vapeur** how does a steam engine work?, what's the principle behind the steam engine?; **selon quel ~ cette machine fonctionne-t-elle?** on what principle does this machine work?; **les ~s d'une science/d'un art** (rudiments) the rudiments of a science/an art; **4** Chimie, Pharm principle; **les ~s actifs contenus dans un médicament** the active principles of a medicine; **5** (origine) principle; **Dieu comme ~ de toute chose** God as the principle behind all things; **remonter au ~ des choses** to go back to first principles.

II en principe *loc adv* **1** (habituellement) as a rule; **en ~ je rentre chez moi vers 18 heures** as a rule I get home at around six o'clock; **2** (en théorie) in theory; **en ~ on part vendredi** in theory we're leaving on Friday.

■ **~ d'Archimède** Phys Archimedes' principle; **~ de causalité** Philos causality; **~ d'exclusion de Pauli** Nucl, Phys Pauli exclusion principle; **~ de plaisir** Psych pleasure principle; **~ de réalité** Psych reality principle.

printanier, **-ière** /pRɛ̃tanje, ɛR/ *adj* [*fleur, soleil*] spring (*épith*); [*journée, temps, tenue, couleur*] springlike.

printemps /pRɛ̃tɑ̃/ ▶ **738** *nm inv* **1** (saison) spring; **au ~ de la vie** fig in the springtime of life; **le ~ de Prague** the Prague spring; **2**° hum (an) **mes 60 ~** my 60 summers.

priori ▶ **a priori**.

prioritaire /pRijɔRitɛR/ *adj* **1** [*dossier, projet*] priority (*épith*); **être ~** to have priority; **2** [*voiture, chauffeur*] with right GB ou the right US of way (*épith, après n*); **être ~, être sur une route ~** to have right GB ou the right US of way.

priorité /pRijɔRite/ *nf* **1** (importance) priority; **donner la ~ à qch** to give priority to sth; **en ~** (avant le reste) first; (par-dessus tout) first and foremost; **venir en ~** to come first; **penser en ~ à soi** to put oneself first; **en ~, ils ont besoin de médicaments** first and foremost they need medicines; **nous nous en occuperons en ~** we'll make it a priority; **le projet a ~/prend la ~ sur tout le reste** the project has/takes precedence over everything else; **2** (fait plus important) priority; **être une ~ absolue, être la ~ numéro un** to be the top priority; **3** (en voiture) priority, right of way; **avoir ~** to have right GB ou the right US of way (**sur** over); **laisser/refuser la ~ à un véhicule** to give way/to refuse to give way to a vehicle; **~ à droite** priority to the right.

pris, **~e** /pRi, pRiz/ **I** *pp* ▶ **prendre**.

II *pp adj* **1** (occupé) busy; **nous sommes**

très ~ cette semaine we're very busy this week; **si vous n'êtes pas ~** if you're not doing anything; **je suis ~** (pour l'instant) I'm busy; (pour la période qui vient) I've got something on; **ma journée est ~e** I'm busy all day; **j'ai les mains ~es** I've got my hands full; **les places sont toutes ~es** all the seats are taken; **2** (vendu) sold; **tout a été ~ en une heure** everything was sold in one hour; **toutes les places sont ~es** it's sold out; **3** (gelé) frozen; **les eaux du lac sont ~es** the lake is frozen; **4** (encombré) [*nez*] stuffed up; [*bronches*] congested; **j'ai la gorge ~e** I'm hoarse; **5** (affecté) **~ de** overcome with [*inquiétude, remords, envie*]; **~ de panique** panic-stricken; **être ~ de fièvre** to have a temperature; **être ~ de regrets/terreur/désespoir** to be full of ou overcome with regret/terror/despair; **être ~ de nausées** to feel sick GB ou nauseous US; **~ de boisson** under the influence.

III prise *nf* **1** Mil (capture) capture; (assaut) storming; **la ~e de Monastir** the capture of Monastir; **la ~e de la Bastille** the storming of the Bastille; **2** Jeux (aux échecs) **être en ~e** [*pièce*] to be threatened; **3** Chasse, Pêche (au filet, piège) catching ¢; **~e d'une panthère au filet** catching a panther in a net; **une belle ~e** (pêche sportive) a fine catch; (pêche commerciale) a fine haul; **4** Sport (au judo, catch) hold; **se dégager d'une ~e** to break a hold; **5** (point permettant de saisir) hold; **avoir du mal à trouver une ~e** to have trouble finding a hold; **n'offrir aucune ~e** lit (pour la main) to have no handholds; (pour le pied) to have no footholds; fig [*personne*] to be impossible to pin down; **avoir ~e sur qn** to have a hold over sb; **avoir ~e sur qch** to have leverage on sth; **donner** or **laisser ~e à** [*personne*] to lay oneself open to; **être en ~e** Aut [*moteur, conducteur*] to be in gear; **être en ~e (directe) avec qch** [*personne*] to be in (close) touch with sth; **être en ~e avec l'actualité** [*journal*] to have its finger on the pulse of events; **6** (absorption) **la ~e d'alcool est déconseillée pendant le traitement** do not take alcohol during the course of treatment; **à ingérer en trois ~es quotidiennes** to be taken three times daily; **7** (solidification) setting ¢; **8** Électrotech (femelle) socket GB, outlet US; (mâle) plug; **~e à deux fiches** two-pin plug; **~e multiple** (domino) (multiplug) adaptor; (sur une rallonge) trailing socket; **~e triple** (domino) three-way adaptor; (sur une rallonge) three-way trailing socket; **9** Électron (femelle) jack; (mâle) plug.

■ **~e d'air** gén air inlet; Aviat air intake; **~e d'antenne** Radio, TV (femelle) aerial socket; (mâle) aerial plug; **~e d'armes** Mil military parade; **~e d'assaut** Mil storming ¢; **~e de bec**○ row○, argument; **~e en charge** Prot Soc granting¢ of benefits; Transp (dans un taxi) minimum fare; **~e en compte** consideration (**de** of); **~e de conscience** realization; **~e de contact** initial contact; **~e de contrôle** Fin takeover; **~e de corps** Jur arrest; **~e de courant** Électrotech (femelle) socket GB, outlet US; **~e de décision** decision-making ¢; **~e d'eau** Constr water supply point; **~e de guerre** Mil spoils (*pl*) of war; **~e de fonctions** (de président, dirigeant) inauguration; (d'employé) first day at work; **~e d'otages** Mil hostage-taking ¢; **~e de participation** Fin acquisition of a stake (**dans** in); **~e de pouvoir** Pol takeover; **~e de position** Pol stand; **~e de sang** Méd blood test; **faire une ~e de sang à qn** to take a blood sample from sb; **~e de son** Cin, Radio, TV sound recording ¢; **~e de terre** Électrotech earth GB, ground US; **~e de vue** Cin, Vidéo shooting ¢; Phot shot.

IDIOMES **être aux ~es avec des difficultés** to be grappling with difficulties; **être aux ~es avec ses concurrents** to be doing battle with one's competitors.

priser /pʀize/ [1] *vtr* **1** liter (apprécier) to hold [sth] in esteem [*œuvre, qualité*]; **il prise fort/peu ce genre de divertissement** this kind of entertainment is very much/is not to his taste; **chanteur très prisé du public** singer very popular with the public; **animal prisé pour sa fourrure** animal prized for its fur; **2** (aspirer par le nez) to snort [*drogue*]; **~ (du tabac)** to take snuff.

prismatique /pʀismatik/ *adj* prismatic.

prisme /pʀism/ *nm* prism; **voir (les choses) à travers un ~** fig to see through a distorting lens.

prison /pʀizɔ̃/ *nf* lit, fig prison; **punissable d'une peine de ~** punishable by a prison sentence; **envoyer qn/aller en ~** to send sb/to go to prison; **elle a fait de la ~** she has been in prison; **elle a fait trois ans de ~** she spent three years in prison; **depuis leur entrée en ~** since they went into prison; **sortir de ~** to get out of prison; **à leur sortie de ~** (demain) when they get out of prison; **tirer** or **sortir qn de ~** to get sb out of prison; **mettre/jeter qn en ~** to put/to throw sb in prison; **mise en ~** imprisonment; **condamné à trois ans de ~** sentenced to three years' imprisonment; ▶ **aimable**.

prisonnier, **-ière** /pʀizɔnje, ɛʀ/ **I** *adj* **il est ~** he is a prisoner; **les soldats ~s** soldiers taken prisoner; **être ~ de** to be held prisoner by [*personne, groupe*]; to be a prisoner of [*éducation, croyance*]; **je me sentais prisonnière** I felt like a prisoner; **ma main était prisonnière** my hand was trapped.

II *nm,f* lit, fig prisoner; **faire un ~** to take a prisoner; **ils ne font pas de ~s** they don't take prisoners; **faire qn ~** to take sb prisoner; **on l'a** or **il a été fait ~** he was taken prisoner; **retenir qn ~** to hold sb prisoner.

■ **~ de guerre** Mil prisoner of war, POW; **~ d'opinion** Pol prisoner of conscience; **~ politique** Pol political prisoner.

privatif, **-ive** /pʀivatif, iv/ *adj* **1** (privé) [*jardin, terrasse*] private; **2** Jur (qui prive) privatory sout; **peine privative de liberté** custodial sentence; **3** Ling [*particule, préfixe, suffixe*] privative.

privation /pʀivasjɔ̃/ *nf* **1** (suppression) (de droit, liberté) deprivation, forfeiture; (de salaire) suspension; **2** (manque) want, privation sout; **souffrir de ~s** to suffer want; **mener une vie** or **vivre de ~s** to live a life of privation; **s'imposer des ~s** to make sacrifices; **économiser à force** or **au prix de dures ~s** to scrimp and save.

■ **~ des droits civiques** Jur forfeiture of civil rights.

privatisation /pʀivatizasjɔ̃/ *nf* privatization; **~ partielle** partial privatization.

privatiser /pʀivatize/ [1] *vtr* to privatize.

privautés /pʀivote/ *nfpl* fml liberties; **se permettre des ~ avec qn** to take liberties with sb.

privé, **~e** /pʀive/ **I** *pp* ▶ **priver**.

II *pp adj* **~ de** deprived of; **une région peu à peu ~e d'arbres/d'eau** an area gradually deprived of trees/of water; **~ de tout** deprived of everything; **un style ~ d'humour/d'imagination** a humourless[GB]/an unimaginative style; **je suis resté ~ de téléphone pendant deux jours** I had to do without a phone for two days; **tu seras ~ de dessert/télévision!** you'll go without dessert/television!

III *adj* **1** (non étatique) [*secteur, investisseur, compagnie, intérêt*] private; **2** (non destiné au public) [*lieu, projection, collection*] private; **3** (non officiel) [*visite, entretien, consultation, source*] unofficial; [*accord, déclaration*] unofficial; [*clientèle, détective, diner*] private; **à titre ~** unofficially; **en visite à Londres à titre ~** on an unofficial visit to London; **chez lui, l'homme ~ est tout différent du personnage officiel** his private face is very different from his public one; **4** (personnel) [*vie, correspondance, affaire*] private; **se mêler de la vie ~e des autres** to meddle in other people's private lives.

IV *nm* **1** (secteur) Écon, Pol private sector; **dans le ~** [*travailler, exercer*] in the private sector; **2** Scol **le ~** private schools (*pl*); **aller dans le ~** [*élève*] to go to a private school; **3** (activité) **dans le ~, le maire est directeur d'une société** apart from his official position, the mayor is a company director; **dans le ~ il est très sympathique** as a person he's really nice; **en ~** (seul à seul) in private; (non officiellement) off the record; **puis-je vous parler en ~?** may I speak to you in private?; **le porte-parole a déclaré en ~ que** off the record, the spokesman announced that; **4**○ (détective) private eye○, private detective.

priver /pʀive/ [1] **I** *vtr* **1** (déposséder) **~ qn de** to deprive sb of; **sa mort nous prive d'un grand homme** his death deprives us of a great man; **son attaque l'a privée de la parole/de l'usage d'un bras** she lost the power of speech/the use of an arm after her stroke; **2** (interdire à) **~ qn de** to deprive sb of; **~ qn de nourriture** to deprive sb of food; **~ qn de télévision/de sorties** to forbid sb to watch TV/to go out; **3** (faire manquer) **la seule chose qui me prive** the only thing I miss; **cela me prive de ne pas (pouvoir) faire** I miss being able to do; **cela me priverait beaucoup de ne plus aller au théâtre** I would really miss going to the theatre[GB]; **elle a arrêté de fumer, mais ça ne la prive pas** she has given up GB ou quit US smoking, but she doesn't miss it; **~ qn/qch de** to deprive sb/sth of; **~ qn du plaisir de faire** to deprive sb of the pleasure of doing; **~ une région d'eau** to deprive an area of water; **l'orage nous a privés d'électricité** we had no electricity because of the thunderstorm; **ça ne te prive pas beaucoup de ne pas pouvoir te laver!** hum it's no hardship for you, not being able to wash!; **si ça ne vous prive pas, pourriez-vous me prêter votre voiture?** could you lend me your car if you don't need it?; **tu peux prendre ces revues, cela ne me privera pas** you can take these magazines, I don't need them.

II se priver *vpr* **1** (s'abstenir) **se ~ pour ses enfants** to go without for the sake of one's children; **pourquoi se ~?** why stint ourselves?; **se ~ de qch/de faire** to go ou do without sth/doing; **se ~ de cinéma** to do without visits to the cinema GB ou movies US; **c'est gratuit, j'aurais tort de m'en ~!** it's free, I'd be a fool not to take it!; **elle ne se privera pas du plaisir de le raconter à tout le monde** she won't be able to resist telling everyone about it; **eh bien, tu ne te prives de rien!** hum you certainly don't believe in stinting yourself!; **2** (se refuser, perdre) **se ~ de** to lose, to give up; **en faisant cela, ils se privent d'un moyen de contrôle** by doing this, they're losing ou they are giving up one means of control; **3** (se défaire) **se ~ de** to do without [*personne*]; to dispense with [*services*]; **4** (se retenir) **se ~ de faire** to hesitate to do; **elle ne s'est pas privée de leur dire les choses en face** she didn't hesitate to tell them a few home truths; **il y avait beaucoup à critiquer dans ce projet, et il ne s'en est pas privé** there was a lot to criticize in that project, and criticize it he did.

privilège /pʀivilɛʒ/ *nm* privilege; **le ~ de l'âge** the privilege of age; **l'abolition des ~s** the abolition of privileges; **avoir le ~ de faire** to have the privilege of doing; **c'est un ~ de faire** it's a privilege to do; **c'est un ~ de le connaître** I am honoured[GB] to know him; **j'ai le triste ~ de devoir annoncer que** it is my sad duty to announce that; **avoir le triste ~ d'être toujours dernier** hum to have the misfortune of always being last.

privilégié, **~e** /pʀivileʒje/ **I** *pp* ▶ **privilégier**.

II *pp adj* **1** (avantagé) [*personne, quartiers*] privileged; **2** (chanceux) fortunate; **être ~ par le sort** to be blessed by fortune; **3** (exceptionnel) [*moment, liens*] special; [*traitement*] preferential; [*position, conditions de travail*] privileged; **4** (préféré) [*mode d'expression, cible*] preferred.

III *nm,f* **1** Hist **un ~** a privileged member of society; **les ~s** the privileged classes; **2** (favorisé) **un ~** a privileged person; **les ~s** the privileged; **les quelques ~s qui ont pu assister au concert** the privileged few who were able to go to the concert.

privilégier /pʀivileʒje/ [2] *vtr* **1** (favoriser) to favour[GB] [*personne, organisme*]; **~ qn sur qn d'autre** to give sb an advantage over sb else; **2** (donner priorité) to give priority to [*question sociale, objectif*]; **~ qch sur qch d'autre** to give more importance to sth than to sth else; **3** Hist to privilege, to bestow privileges on [*groupe social*].

prix /pʀi/ *nm inv* **1** (coût) price; **~ d'achat/de vente** purchase/selling price; **~ de détail/de gros** retail/wholesale price; **~ fixe** set price; **~ affiché/conseillé/demandé** posted/recommended/asking price; **~ de revient** cost price; **vendre à** or **au ~ coûtant** to sell at cost price; **au prix où sont les appartements nous ne pourrons jamais acheter** at the price apartments are we'll never be able to buy anything; **~ à la production/à la consommation** producer/consumer price; **~ de sortie d'usine** factory(-gate) price; **c'est à quel ~?** how much is it?; **ton ~ sera le mien** name your price; **c'est mon dernier ~** that's my final offer; **tu me fais un ~ (d'ami)?** can you do GB ou make US me a special price○? ; **qu'il soit d'accord ou pas, c'est le même ~○!** fig it doesn't matter whether he agrees or not!; **trouver qch dans mes ~** (fourchette de prix) to find sth within my price-range; (dans mes moyens) to find sth I can afford; **meubles anciens vendus au ~ fort** antiques sold at a premium (price); **acheter une maison au ~ fort** to buy a house when prices are at their highest; **à bon ~** [*vendre*] at a good price; **de ~** expensive; **hors de ~** extremely expensive; **cela n'a pas de ~** it's priceless; **acheter qch à ~ d'or** to pay a small fortune for sth; **c'est joli, mais j'y ai mis le ~** it's pretty, but I paid a lot for it; **si tu veux de la soie, il faut être prêt à y mettre le ~** if you want silk, you have to be prepared to pay for it; **mettre qch à ~ à 50 francs** [*commissaire- priseur*] to start the bidding at 50 francs; **mettre à ~ la tête de qn** to put a price on sb's head; **2** (coût en efforts, sacrifices) price; **le ~ de la réussite** the price of success; **à tout ~** at all costs; **je ne le ferai à aucun ~** I will not do it at any price; **au ~ de nombreux sacrifices** by dint of much sacrifice; **3** (valeur affective, morale) price; **son amitié n'a pas de ~ pour moi** his/her friendship is very precious to me; **j'attache beaucoup de ~ à son amitié** I value his/her friendship greatly; **cela donne du ~ à ta visite** it makes your visit all the more precious; **apprécier l'amabilité de qn à son juste ~** to appreciate sb's kindness fully; **4** (honneur, récompense) prize; **obtenir le premier/deuxième ~** to win first/second prize; **il n'a pas eu de ~** he didn't get a prize; **~ de consolation** consolation prize; **~ d'encouragement** special ou consolation prize; **obtenir le premier ~ d'interprétation** to get the award for best actor; **le ~ Nobel** (récompense) the Nobel prize; (personne) the Nobel prize-winner; **c'est le premier ~ du concours Chopin** (personne) he/she won first prize in the Chopin competition; **lire le ~ Goncourt** to read the book which won the Prix Goncourt; **5** Turf race; ▶ **grand**.

■ **~ d'appel** loss leader; **~ d'excellence** *prize for top academic achievement*; **~ de retrait** reserve price.

IDIOMES **au ~ où sont les choses** or **où est le beurre○!** prices being what they are!

pro /pʀo/ *nmf* (*abbr* = **professionnel**) pro○.

pro(-) /pʀo/ *préf* Pol pro(-); **~-européen** pro-European.

probabilisme /pʀɔbabilism/ *nm* probabilism.

probabiliste /pʀɔbabilist/ I *adj* probabilistic.

II *nmf* probabilist.

probabilité /pʀɔbabilite/ *nf* **1** (d'événement, accident) probability, likelihood; **selon toute ~** in all probability; **2** Math probability ₵; **les ~s** probability theory; **calcul des ~s** calculation of probability.

probable /pʀɔbabl/ *adj* **1** (vraisemblable) [*événement, cause, hypothèse*] probable, likely; **c'est peu/fort ~** it's not very probable ou likely/highly probable ou likely; **il est ~ qu'il viendra** it is probable that he will come; **il est peu/fort peu ~ qu'il vienne** it's rather/highly unlikely that he will come; **2** (prévisible) likely; **Berg est le vainqueur ~** Berg is likely to win.

probablement /pʀɔbabləmɑ̃/ *adv* probably.

probant, **~e** /pʀɔbɑ̃, ɑ̃t/ *adj* [*argument, démonstration*] convincing; [*force, preuve*] conclusive; **une pièce ~e** a piece of conclusive evidence; **en forme ~e** Jur duly certified.

probation /pʀɔbasjɔ̃/ *nf* **1** Jur probation; **pendant sa ~** while on probation; **2** Relig probation; **année de ~** probationary year.

probatoire /pʀɔbatwaʀ/ *adj* **examen ~** assessment test; **épreuve ~** aptitude test; **stage ~** probation period; **délai ~** Jur probation.

probe /pʀɔb/ *adj* liter upright, honest.

probité /pʀɔbite/ *nf* integrity, probity.

problématique /pʀɔblematik/ I *adj* [*situation*] problematic; [*chances*] doubtful; [*issue, dénouement*] in doubt (*jamais épith*); [*succès*] unlikely (*jamais épith*); **sa libération apparaît comme ~** his/her release seems to be in doubt.

II *nf* problems (*pl*), issues (*pl*); **la ~ contemporaine** contemporary issues; **la ~ de l'identité** the problems of identity.

problème /pʀɔblɛm/ *nm* (difficulté) problem; (sujet) issue; **~ d'algèbre** algebra problem; **le ~ du chômage** the problem of unemployment; **c'est tout un ~** it's a big problem; **ça pose un ~** it is a problem; **sans ~!, pas de ~!** no problem!; **~ moral** moral issue; **peau à ~s** problem skin.

procédé /pʀɔsede/ *nm* **1** (méthode) technique; **mettre au point/améliorer un ~** to develop/refine a technique; **~ de lyophilisation/fabrication** freeze-drying/manufacturing technique; **~ révolutionnaire/chirurgical** revolutionary/surgical technique; **~ destiné à faire** technique for doing; **2** (manière d'agir) practice[GB]; **~ scandaleux** appalling practice; **je suis choqué par le ~** I am shocked by such a practice; **se livrer à des ~s odieux** to engage in despicable practices; **échange de bons ~s** exchange of courtesies; **3** Littérat device; **~ littéraire/rhétorique** literary/rhetorical device.

procéder /pʀɔsede/ [14] **I procéder à** *vtr ind* (se livrer) **~ à** to carry out [*analyse, vérification, sondage*]; to undertake [*réforme, création d'emplois*]; **~ à des opérations financières** to carry out financial transactions; **~ à un tirage au sort/un vote** to hold a draw/a vote; **~ à l'arrestation de qn** to arrest sb; **~ à des arrestations** to make arrests.

II procéder de *vtr ind* (relever) **~ de** to be a product of; **imagination qui procède d'un esprit pervers** imagination which is the product of a perverted mind; **évaluation qui procède de l'intuition** assessment which is a product of intuition.

III *vi* (agir) to go about things; **~ par ordre** to go about things methodically; **comment allez-vous ~?** how are you going to go about it?; **~ par élimination** to use a process of elimination.

procédure /pʀɔsedyʀ/ *nf* **1** (action judiciaire) proceedings (*pl*); **engager une ~ contre** to take ou institute proceedings against; **entamer une ~** to start proceedings; **~ judiciaire/disciplinaire** legal/disciplinary proceedings; **~ d'extradition/en diffamation/de divorce** extradition/defamation/divorce proceedings; **2** (méthode) procedure; **~ d'obtention du permis de conduire** procedure for obtaining a driving licence; **quelle est la ~ à suivre?** what's the procedure?; **réformer la ~** Jur to reform the procedure; **~ prescrite** Jur prescribed procedure; **~ judiciaire/disciplinaire** judicial/disciplinary procedure.

■ **~ d'atterrissage** Aviat approach procedure.

procédurier, **-ière** /pʀɔsedyʀje, ɛʀ/ I *adj* [*personne*] litigious.

II *nm,f* litigious person.

procès /pʀɔsɛ/ *nm inv* **1** Jur (pénal) trial (**contre** against); **~ d'un criminel de guerre** trial of a war criminal; **~ pour corruption/meurtre** trial for corruption/murder; **~ pour incitation à la violence** trial for incitement to violence; **2** Jur (civil) lawsuit, case; **gagner/perdre son ~** to win/lose one's lawsuit ou case; **être en ~ avec qn** to be involved in a lawsuit with sb; **intenter un ~ à qn** to take sb to court, to sue sb; **menacer qn de ~** to threaten to take sb to court; **3** (critique) indictment; **mauvais ~** unjustified indictment; **~ d'une institution/d'une personne** indictment of an institution/of a person; **faire le ~ de qch/qn** to put sth/sb in the dock; **faire un mauvais ~ à qn** to accuse sb unjustly; **faire un ~ d'intention à qn** to judge sb on mere intent; **4** Ling process.

■ **~ de sorcière** witch trial.

IDIOMES **sans autre forme de ~** without further ado.

processeur /pʀɔsesœʀ/ *nm* Ordinat processor.

procession /pʀɔsesjɔ̃/ *nf* **1** (file) procession; **~ de chameaux/prisonniers** procession of camels/prisoners; **2** (défilé) stream; **~ de créanciers/clients** stream of creditors/customers; **3** Relig procession.

processionnaire /pʀɔsesjɔnɛʀ/ *adj* **chenille ~** processionary caterpillar.

processus /pʀɔsesys/ *nm* **1** gén process; **~ de fabrication** manufacturing process; **2** Anat process; **3** Méd (évolution) evolution.

procès-verbal, *pl* **-aux** /pʀɔsɛvɛʀbal, o/ *nm* **1** (compte-rendu) (de réunion) minutes (*pl*); (d'interrogatoire) transcript; **2** Jur statement of offence[GB]; **dresser un ~ à qn** to give sb a ticket, to book sb GB; **3** (amende) controv fine; **avoir un ~** to get a ticket.

prochain, **~e** /pʀɔʃɛ̃, ɛn/ I *adj* **1** (suivant) next; **l'an/le mois ~** next year/month; **en juin ~** next June; **le 15 juin ~** next June 15th; **au printemps ~** next spring; **dans les ~es heures** in the next few hours; **au cours des jours ~s, dans les jours ~s** in the next few days; **la ~e fois** next time; **la ~e fois que tu fais cela** (the) next time you do that; **ce sera pour une ~e fois** some other time, then!; **il n'y aura pas de ~e fois** there won't be a next time; **à la ~e○!** see you!; **je descends à la ~e** (dans le train, métro) I'm getting off at the next station; **j'ai acheté une voiture noire, la ~e sera rouge** I've bought a black car, my next one will be red; **vous êtes le ~ sur la liste** you're next on the list; **2** (imminent) [*publication, promulgation*] forthcoming; [*réunion, sommet*] coming, forthcoming; [*mort, retour, départ, guerre, crise*] imminent, impending (*épith*); **un jour ~** one day soon; **3** Philos [*cause*] immediate.

II *nm* gén fellow man; Relig neighbour[GB]; **tu aimeras ton ~ comme toi-même** thou shalt love thy neighbour[GB] as thyself.

prochainement /pʀɔʃɛnmɑ̃/ *adv* soon, shortly; **'~ sur vos écrans'** 'coming soon to a cinema GB ou theater US near you'.

proche /pʀɔʃ/ **I** *adj* **1** (dans l'espace) [*bâtiment, maison, rue*] nearby (*épith*); **~ de** close to, near; **c'est tout ~** it's very close; **dans une maison toute ~** in a nearby house; **le plus ~** the nearest; **c'est notre plus ~ voisin** he's our nearest neighbour[GB]; **ce n'est pas très ~** it's quite a way (off); **assez ~** not far away; **un village assez ~** a village not far away; **les bureaux sont très ~s les uns des autres** the desks are very close together; **2** (dans le futur) [*moment, départ, événement*] imminent; [*souvenir*] real, vivid; **la nuit est ~** it'll soon be dark; **le temps est ~ où** the time will soon come when; **la victoire est ~** victory is at hand; **la mort est ~** death is imminent; **être ~ de la mort** to be near ou close to death; **la fin est ~** the end is (drawing) near; **3** (récent) [*événement*] recent; **c'est encore trop ~** it's still too recent; **4** (voisin) [*chiffres, valeurs, taux*] similar; [*langues*] closely related; [*sens, idées, théories, résultats, partis*] similar; **ces deux mots sont de sens très ~s** these two words mean much the same; **~ de** [*chiffre, valeur, taux, inflation, langue*] close to; [*idée, théorie*] close ou similar to; [*résultat, conclusion, parti, mouvement*] similar to; [*attitude, comportement*] verging on; **une ignorance ~ de la bêtise** ignorance bordering ou verging on stupidity; **5** (sur le plan affectif) [*personnes*] close (**de** to); Admin (sur un formulaire) (**plus**) **~ parent** next of kin.

II de proche en proche *loc adv* little by little, gradually.

III *nm* (parent) close relative; (ami) close friend; (collègue, associé) close associate; **un ~ du président** a close aide to the president; **mes ~s** my nearest and dearest.

Proche-Orient /pʀɔʃɔʀjɑ̃/ *nprm* **le ~** the Near East.

proclamation /pʀɔklamasjɔ̃/ *nf* (action, texte) proclamation, declaration; **la ~ de l'état d'urgence/des résultats** the proclamation of the state of emergency/the results.

proclamer /pʀɔklame/ [1] **I** *vtr* **1** (reconnaître officiellement) to proclaim [*souveraineté, état d'urgence*]; **il a été proclamé roi** he was proclaimed king; **2** (annoncer) [*personne*] to declare [*confiance, intention, conviction*]; to proclaim [*innocence*]; [*affiche, document*] to proclaim [*liberté, souveraineté*].

II se proclamer *vpr* [*personne*] to proclaim oneself [*roi, chef*].

proconsul /pʀɔkɔ̃syl/ *nm* proconsul.

procrastination /pʀɔkʀastinasjɔ̃/ *nf* fml procrastination.

procréateur, **-trice** /pʀɔkʀeatœʀ, tʀis/ **I** *adj* liter procreative.

II *nm,f* procreator.

procréation /pʀɔkʀeasjɔ̃/ *nf* procreation.

■ **~ artificielle** artificial reproduction; **~ médicalement assistée**, **PMA** assisted reproduction.

procréer /pʀɔkʀee/ [11] *vi* to procreate; **être en âge de ~** to be of childbearing age.

procuration /pʀɔkyʀasjɔ̃/ *nf* **1** (pouvoir) power of attorney; (pour une élection) proxy; **par ~** [*voter*] by proxy; [*vivre*] vicariously; **2** (formulaire) power of attorney; (pour une élection) proxy form; **donner une ~ à qn** gén to give sb power of attorney; (pour une élection) to appoint sb proxy.

procurer /pʀɔkyʀe/ [1] **I** *vtr* **1** (être la cause de) to bring [*plaisir, sensation*]; to give [*argent, avantages*]; **~ qch à qn** to give sb sth; **2** (fournir) [*personne*] **~ qch à qn** to get sb sth.

II se procurer *vpr* (obtenir) to obtain; (acheter) to buy.

procureur /pʀɔkyʀœʀ/ *nm* prosecutor.

■ **~ général** public prosecutor; **~ de la République** state prosecutor.

prodigalité /pʀɔdigalite/ *nf* **1** (propension) extravagance; **2** (abondance) liter abundance (**de** of); **3** (dépenses) extravagance.

prodige /pʀɔdiʒ/ *nm* **1** (génie) prodigy; **guitariste ~** guitar prodigy; **enfant ~** child prodigy; **2** (exploit) feat; **réussir le ~ de faire** to achieve the remarkable feat of doing; **faire des ~s** to work wonders; **tenir du ~** to be a miracle; **~ technique** technical miracle.

prodigieusement /pʀɔdiʒjøzmɑ̃/ *adv* prodigiously.

prodigieux, **-ieuse** /pʀɔdiʒjø, øz/ *adj* [*intelligence, mémoire, quantité*] prodigious; [*personne*] wonderful; **d'une bêtise prodigieuse** prodigiously stupid.

prodigue /pʀɔdig/ **I** *adj* **1** (gaspilleur) extravagant; **2** (libéral) **être ~ de conseils** to be free with advice; **être ~ de promesses** to be good at making promises; **être ~ de compliments/de son argent** to be lavish with one's praise/one's money; **être ~ de son temps/ses efforts** to be generous with one's time/one's efforts; **il est peu ~ de compliments** he's not one to give praise; **3** Relig **l'enfant** or **le fils ~** the prodigal son.

II *nmf* spendthrift.

prodiguer /pʀɔdige/ [1] *vtr* **1** (distribuer sans compter) to lavish [*attentions, affection, soins, compliments*] (**à** on); to make lots of [*promesses*] (**à** to); to give lots of [*conseils, encouragements*] (**à** to); **~ des excuses à qn** to apologize profusely to sb; **~ ses efforts** to spare no effort; **malgré les efforts prodigués par l'équipe** despite the team's heroic effort; **2** (donner) to give [*soins*] (**à** to); **pendant qu'il prodiguait ses soins aux blessés** while he was attending to the wounded; **~ des soins adéquats aux malades** to care adequately for the patients.

producteur, **-trice** /pʀɔdyktœʀ, tʀis/ **I** *adj* **une région productrice de thé/café** tea-/coffee-growing area; **un pays ~ de viande** a meat-producing country; **pays ~ de pétrole/charbon** oil-/coal-producing country.

II *nm,f* **1** Écon (de matériel, pétrole, d'objet, énergie) producer; (de plante, céréale, café, coton) grower, producer; **ce pays est un ~ agricole** this country is an agricultural producer; **du ~ au consommateur** from the producer to the consumer; **2** ▶510 Cin, TV (personne) producer; (société) production company; **un ~ de radio/télévision** a radio/television producer; **un ~ réalisateur** a producer and director.

productible /pʀɔdyktibl/ *adj* that can be produced (*épith, après n*).

productif, **-ive** /pʀɔdyktif, iv/ **I** *adj* [*travail, réunion, journée*] productive; [*investissement, capital*] profitable; **capital ~ d'intérêts** interest-bearing capital; **placement ~** high-yield ou profitable investment; **actions productives d'un dividende de...** shares yielding a dividend of...

II *nm* Ind **les ~s** people working in production.

production /pʀɔdyksjɔ̃/ *nf* **1** (fait de produire) (de marchandise, produit agricole, d'objet) production; (d'électricité) production, generation; (d'énergie) generation; **mise en ~** putting into production; **la ~ du nouveau modèle débutera le mois prochain** the new model will go into production next month; **arrêter la ~ d'un modèle** to stop producing a model; **la ~ d'anticorps/d'enzymes par l'organisme** the production of antibodies/of enzymes by the body; **2** (produits) gén products (*pl*), goods (*pl*); (produits agricoles) produce; **3** (quantités produites) (de produits agricoles, matières premières) production; (de produits manufacturés, d'énergie) output, production; **la ~ de café a chuté** coffee production has fallen; **augmenter la ~ de pétrole** to increase oil production; **la ~ de notre entreprise s'élève à 5 millions de machines par an** our firm's output is 5 million machines per year; **le pays exporte 30% de sa ~ agricole** the country exports 30% of its agricultural production; **chiffres de la ~** production figures; **4** (dans une entreprise) (**service de**) **la ~** production; **directeur de la ~** production manager; **il est à la ~ maintenant** he is in production now; **5** Cin, TV (processus, film) production; **directeur de ~** production manager; **~ à grand spectacle** spectacular; **6** (d'écrivain, auteur) (ouvrage) work; (ensemble de l'œuvre) works (*pl*), output; **~ littéraire** literary output; **toute la ~ d'un auteur** an author's complete works; **la ~ dramatique du XIXe siècle** 19th-century drama; **7** (présentation) Jur, Admin presentation; **sur ~ de votre carte** on presentation of your card.

■ **~ assistée par ordinateur**, **PAO** computer-aided manufacturing, CAM.

productique /pʀɔdyktik/ *nf* industrial automation.

productivité /pʀɔdyktivite/ *nf* Ind, Fin productivity; **avoir une faible ~** to show low productivity.

produire /pʀɔdɥiʀ/ [69] **I** *vtr* **1** (fabriquer) to produce [*marchandise, objet, pétrole*]; to produce, to generate [*électricité, énergie, chaleur, fumée, gaz*]; **cette usine produit peu** this factory has a low output; **2** Agric (cultiver) to produce, to grow [*céréales, café, coton*]; (donner) [*arbre, terre*] to yield; [*région, pays*] to produce [*vin, blé, maïs*]; **cet arbre ne produit plus** this tree no longer bears fruit; **3** (causer, provoquer) to produce, to have [*effet, résultat*]; to produce, to bring about [*changement*]; to create, to make [*impression*]; to cause, to create [*sensation, émotion*]; **ces mesures mettront du temps à ~ leurs effets** it will be some time before the effects of these measures are felt; **~ une bonne/mauvaise impression** to create a good/bad impression; **4** Cin, Radio, Théât, TV to produce [*film, pièce, disque, émission*]; **5** (créer) to produce [*œuvre, tableau*]; to produce, to make [*logiciel*]; **un artiste/écrivain qui produit beaucoup** a prolific artist/writer; **6** (donner naissance à) [*pays, système, époque*] to produce [*génie, scientifique*]; **un club qui produit d'excellents athlètes** a club that turns out ou produces great athletes; **7** Fin (rapporter) to bring in [*argent, richesse*]; to yield [*intérêt*]; **faire ~ qch** to make sth yield a return; **8** Admin, Jur (montrer) to produce [*papier d'identité, certificat*]; to produce, to bring [sb] forward [*témoin*].

II se produire *vpr* **1** (survenir) [*catastrophe, changement*] to occur, to happen; **cela se produit souvent** that happens a lot; **2** (donner un spectacle) [*groupe, chanteur*] to perform.

produit /pʀɔdɥi/ *nm* **1** (article) product; **des ~s** gén goods, products; Agric produce ⊄; **~ végétal/alimentaire/surgelé/pharmaceutique** vegetable/food/frozen/pharmaceutical product; **~s alimentaires** foodstuffs; **~s agricoles** agricultural ou farm produce; **~s laitiers/pétroliers** dairy/petroleum products; **2** Fin (revenu) income; (bénéfice) profit; **vivre du ~ de son travail** to live on the income from one's work; **vivre du ~ de sa terre** to live off the land; **vivre du ~ de ses investissements** to live on the income from one's investments; **vivre du ~ de ses biens** to live on the income from one's property; **le ~ de la vente** the proceeds (*pl*) of the sale; **3** (résultat) (de recherche) result; (d 'activité, état, de hasard) product; **c'est le ~ de ton imagination** it's a figment of your imagination; **c'est un pur ~ des médias** he's/she's a media creation; **c'est un pur ~ des années 90** he's/she's very much a product of the 90s; **4** Biol, Chimie, Phys product; **un ~ chimique** a chemical; **~ de combustion** product of combustion; **~ de décomposition** product of decomposition; **~ de substitution** product of substitution; **~ de fission/fissile** fission/fissile product; **5** Math product; **le ~ de deux nombres** the product of two numbers.

■ ~ d'assurance insurance product; **~ de base** (aliment) staple food; **~ de beauté** beauty product; **~ chimique** chemical; **~ de consommation courante** consumer product; **~ dérivé** by-product; **~ d'entretien** cleaning product, household product; **~ d'épargne** savings product; **~ financier** financial product; **~ fini** finished product; **~ intérieur brut**, **PIB** gross domestic product, GDP; **~ de luxe** luxury product; **~ manufacturé** manufactured product; **~ de marque** Comm branded article; **~ national brut**, **PNB** gross national product, GNP; **~ de substitution** substitute.

proéminence /pʀɔeminɑ̃s/ *nf* **1** (saillie) protuberance; **2** (aspect saillant) prominence.

proéminent, **~e** /pʀɔeminɑ̃, ɑ̃t/ *adj* prominent.

prof○ /pʀɔf/ *nmf*: *abbr* = **professeur** 1.

profanateur, **-trice** /pʀɔfanatœʀ, tʀis/ I *adj* [*acte*] sacrilegious.
II *nm,f* profaner.

profanation /pʀɔfanasjɔ̃/ *nf* (de temple, tombe) desecration; (de sentiment, mémoire, beauté) defilement; (de famille, d'institution) debasement.

profane /pʀɔfan/ I *adj* **1** (non religieux) [*fête, art, littérature*] secular; **amour ~** profane love; **2** (non initié) **être ~ en la matière** to know nothing about the subject, to be a layman.
II *nmf* **1** (non-initié) layman/laywoman; **2** Relig nonbeliever.
III *nm* **le ~ et le sacré** the sacred and the profane.

profaner /pʀɔfane/ [1] *vtr* to desecrate [*temple, tombe*]; to defile [*sentiment, mémoire, nom, beauté*]; to debase [*famille, institution*]; to violate [*innocence*].

proférer /pʀɔfeʀe/ [14] *vtr* to hurl [*insultes, obscénités*]; to make [*menaces*] (**contre** against).

professer /pʀɔfese/ [1] *vtr* **1** (déclarer) to declare [*admiration, amour*]; to state, to profess [*opinion*]; to profess [*théorie, idée*]; **il dit le contraire de ce qu'il professait hier** he is saying the opposite of what he professed yesterday; **~ que** to declare ou profess that; **2**† (enseigner) to teach [*matière*].

professeur /pʀɔfesœʀ/ **▶510** *nm* **1** (enseignant) (de collège, lycée) teacher; (dans l'enseignement supérieur) teacher, lecturer GB, professor US; (titulaire) professor; **elle est ~ d'histoire** (dans un collège, un lycée) she's a history teacher; (dans une université) she teaches history; **le ~ remplaçant** the supply GB ou substitute US teacher; **2 ▶813** (titre) Méd, Univ professor; **le ~ Nimbus** Professor Nimbus.

■ ~ des écoles primary school teacher; **~ émérite** or **honoraire** Univ emeritus professor; **~ principal** Scol form GB ou homeroom US teacher.

profession /pʀɔfesjɔ̃/ *nf* **1** (métier) occupation; **quelle est votre ~?** what's your occupation?; **embrasser la ~ médicale** to join ou enter the medical profession; **ceux qui décident d'embrasser la ~ d'enseignant** those who decide to join the teaching profession; **exercer la ~ d'infirmière** to be a nurse by profession; **sans ~** gén unemployed; (femme au foyer) housewife; **il est bibliothécaire de ~** he's a librarian by profession; **2** (corporation) profession; **appeler la ~ à cesser le travail** to call on those who work in the profession to stop work; **3** (déclaration publique) declaration, profession; **faire ~ de libéralisme/d'anarchisme** to profess one's liberalism/anarchism; **il a fait ~ de défendre cette cause** he professed to defend this cause.

■ ~ de foi gén declaration of faith; Relig *solemn declaration of faith made at the age of 11*; **~ libérale** profession.

professionnalisation /pʀɔfesjɔnalizasjɔ̃/ *nf* professionalization.

professionnalisé, **~e** /pʀɔfesjɔnalize/ I *pp* ▶ **professionnaliser**.
II *pp adj* **1** Mil [*régiment, unité*] professional; **2** Scol, Univ [*formation, institut*] vocational.

professionnaliser /pʀɔfesjɔnalize/ [1] I *vtr* to professionalize.
II **se professionnaliser** *vpr* to become professionalized.

professionnalisme /pʀɔfesjɔnalism/ *nm* **1** (qualité) professionalism; **2** (statut) **après dix ans de ~** after ten years as a professional.

professionnel, **-elle** /pʀɔfesjɔnɛl/ I *adj* **1** (relatif au métier) [*qualification, catégorie, objectif, prétention, réussite*] professional; [*vie, milieu*] working (*épith*), professional; [*maladie*] occupational; [*enseignement, baccalauréat, formation*] vocational; [*exposition, salon*] trade; **j'ai eu de la chance dans le domaine** or **sur le plan ~** I've been lucky in my professional life; **pour raisons professionnelles** for work ou professional reasons; **revendications professionnelles** workers' demands; **jargon ~** specialist jargon; **l'avenir ~** career prospects (*pl*); **avoir une activité professionnelle** to have an occupation, to be in work; **en dehors de mes activités professionnelles** outside my work; **il s'occupe de leur réinsertion professionnelle** he's responsible for finding them jobs; **local à usage ~** business premises (*pl*); **2** (non amateur) [*joueur, club, statut, danseur*] professional; **tricheur ~** hum professional cheat; **acteur/sportif non ~** amateur ou nonprofessional actor/sportsman.
II *nm,f* **1** (spécialiste d'un métier) professional; **le salon est réservé aux ~s** the show is restricted to people in the trade; **un ~ du cinéma** a professional film-maker; **un ~ du bâtiment** a person working in the building trade; **les ~s de la santé** health professionals; **c'est du travail de ~** lit, fig it's a professional job; **2** (non-amateur) professional; **passer ~** to turn professional.
III **professionnelle**○ *nf* (prostituée) prostitute, pro○.

professionnellement /pʀɔfesjɔnɛlmɑ̃/ *adv* professionally.

professoral, **~e**, *mpl* **-aux** /pʀɔfesɔʀal, o/ *adj* **1** (dogmatique) [*ton, orateur*] professorial; **2** (relatif aux professeurs) **le corps ~** (la profession) the teaching profession; (d'un établissement) the teaching staff.

professorat /pʀɔfesɔʀa/ *nm* teaching; **choisir le ~** to opt for teaching.

profil /pʀɔfil/ *nm* **1** (contour physique) profile; (coupe verticale) profile, cross profile; **être de ~** to be in profile; **se mettre de ~** to position oneself in profile; **garder/adopter un ~ bas** to keep/adopt a low profile; **2** (qualifications) **vous avez le ~ requis pour ce poste** you have the right qualifications for the job; **'~ exigé'** 'qualifications required'; **3** Psych profile; **avoir un ~ de gagnant/patron/ministre** to have the profile of a winner/boss/minister.

■ ~ grec Greek profile.

profilage /pʀɔfilaʒ/ *nm* profiling.

profilé, **~e** /pʀɔfile/ I *pp* ▶ **profiler**.
II *pp adj* [*pièce*] profiled; [*aile, voile*] streamlined.
III *nm* profile; **~ aluminium/plastique** aluminium GB ou aluminum US/plastic profile.

profiler /pʀɔfile/ [1] I *vtr* **1** Tech to profile [*pièce, aile*]; **2** (représenter en profil) to draw a section of [*édifice*]; **3** (présenter) **la tour profile sa silhouette dans le ciel** the tower is silhouetted ou outlined against the sky.
II **se profiler** *vpr* [*forme, relief*] to stand out (**contre, sur** against); [*danger, candidat, problème, changements*] to emerge; [*événements*] to approach.

profit /pʀɔfi/ *nm* **1** (avantage) benefit, advantage; **faire qch avec ~** to benefit from doing sth; **vous consulterez ce guide avec ~** you'll find this guide very useful; **il a appliqué avec ~ les nouvelles méthodes** he's made good use of the new methods; **tirer ~ de** to make the most of, to take advantage of; **il a tiré ~ de mes conseils** he put my advice to good use; **il n'a pas su tirer ~ de ce qui lui est arrivé il y a deux ans** he didn't learn from what happened to him two years ago; **faire son ~ de qch** to use sth to one's advantage, to make use of sth; **faire du ~**○ [*nourriture*] to go a long way; [*objet, appareil*] to be good value; **ce manteau m'a fait du ~**○ I've had a lot of wear out of this coat; **être d'un grand ~ à qn** to be of great benefit ou value to sb, to benefit sb greatly; **ce stage linguistique leur a été d'un grand ~** that language course has been of great benefit ou value to them, they got a lot out of that language course; **pour le plus grand ~ de** to the great benefit of; **trouver (son) ~ à faire** to find it to one's advantage to do; **s'il le fait c'est qu'il y trouve son ~** he's doing it because he gets something out of it; **organiser un concert au ~ des handicapés/de la recherche sur le cancer** to organize a concert in aid of the handicapped/of cancer research; **accusé d'espionnage au ~ d'un pays étranger** accused of spying for a foreign country; **la réforme s'est faite au ~ des grands propriétaires** the reform benefited land owners; **abandonner le charbon au ~ du nucléaire** to drop coal in favour[GB] of nuclear energy; **le candidat de la majorité a perdu des voix au ~ des écologistes** the ruling party's candidate lost votes to the ecologists; **tourner au ~ de qn** to work in sb's favour[GB]; **mettre à ~** to make the most of, to take advantage of [*temps libre, stage*]; to turn [sth] to good account ou to one's advantage [*situation*]; to make good use of [*idée, découverte, résultat*]; **2** Écon (gains) profit; **dégager des ~s**, **faire des ~s** to make a profit; **réaliser 10 millions de ~** to make a profit of 10 million; **~s illicites/illimités** illicit/unlimited profits; **~s pétroliers** oil revenues; **être une source de ~ pour** to be a source of wealth for.

IDIOMES **il n'y a pas de petits ~s** Prov look after the pennies and the pounds will look after themselves Prov GB, a penny saved is a penny earned Prov GB, a dollar is a dollar US.

profitable /pʀɔfitabl/ *adj* **1** (utile) beneficial, profitable (**à** to); **son départ n'est ~ à personne** his/her leaving doesn't make things better for anybody; **2** (rentable) profitable.

profiter /pʀɔfite/ [1] I **profiter à** *vtr ind* **1** (être utile) **~ à qn** [*leçon, expérience, conseil, affaire, circonstances*] to benefit sb, to be of benefit to sb; **ça profite toujours aux mêmes** it's always the same people who reap the benefit; **à qui profite le crime?** who benefits by ou from the crime?; **2** (faire grossir) **~ à qn** [*aliment*] to make sb put on weight; **la nourriture ne lui profite pas** he doesn't get the benefit of his food.
II **profiter de** *vtr ind* **1** (tirer avantage) **~ de** to use, to make the most of [*avantage*]; to make the most of, to take advantage of [*privilège, occasion, situation*]; to take advantage of [*visite, faiblesse, vente*]; **~ de qn** to take advantage of sb; **profite bien de tes vacances!** have a good holiday!; **j'ai profité de mon passage à Paris pour visiter le Louvre** I took the opportunity of visiting the Louvre when I was in Paris; **j'ai profité de ce qu'il était là pour lui demander de m'aider** since he was there I took the opportunity of asking him to help me; **il a profité de ce que je ne regardais pas pour voler**

les documents he took advantage of the fact that I was not looking to steal the documents; **~ de l'obscurité pour s'enfuir** to flee under cover of darkness; **2** (tirer agrément) **~ de qch** to make the most of sth, to enjoy sth; **la vie est courte, profitez-en** life is short, make the most of it ou live it to the full; **les enfants ont profité de leurs vacances** the children got a lot out of their holidays GB ou vacation US; **~ de qn**○ to make the most of being with sb; **j'étais tellement occupé que je n'ai pas pu ~ de mes petits-enfants** I was so busy that I didn't have time to enjoy (being with) my grandchildren.

III○ *vi* (se fortifier) [*personne, enfant, animal*] to grow; [*plante, arbre*] to thrive, to grow.

profiterole /pʀɔfitʀɔl/ *nf* profiterole; **~s au chocolat** chocolate profiteroles.

profiteur, **-euse** /pʀɔfitœʀ, øz/ *nm,f* profiteer.

profond, **~e** /pʀɔfɔ̃, ɔ̃d/ **I** *adj* **1** ▶ 477 lit deep; **~ de 10 mètres** 10 metres[GB] deep; **au plus ~ de** lit, fig in the depths of; **au plus ~ de la nuit** in the dead of night; **peu ~** shallow; **2** (intense) [*joie, désespoir*] overwhelming; [*ennui*] acute; [*soupir*] heavy; [*sentiment, tristesse, chagrin, amour*] deep, profound; [*bleu*] deep; [*sommeil*] deep; **3** (très grand) [*signification, cause, changement, désaccord*] profound; [*intérêt*] keen; [*foi*] deep; [*mépris, ignorance*] profound; [*silence*] deep; **4** (pénétrant) [*esprit, réflexion, remarque*] profound; [*regard*] penetrating; **c'est ~ ce que tu dis** what you say is profound; **5** (réfléchi) [*personne*] deep; **6** (provincial) **la France ~e** provincial France; **l'Amérique ~e** small-town America.

II *adv* deeply, deep down; **creuser ~** to dig deeply.

profondément /pʀɔfɔ̃demɑ̃/ *adv* **1** (loin) [*creuser, pénétrer, s'enfoncer*] deeply; **2** (intensément) [*dormir, respirer, éprouver, aimer*] deeply; [*souffrir*] greatly; [*détester, haïr*] utterly, completely; [*convaincu*] utterly; [*marqué, affecté*] profoundly; [*choqué, ému, vexé*] deeply; **s'ennuyer ~** to be profoundly bored.

profondeur /pʀɔfɔ̃dœʀ/ **I** *nf* **1** ▶ 477 lit (de mer, trou) depth; **avoir une ~ de 3 mètres** to be 3 metres deep ou in depth; **creuser à 2 mètres de ~** to dig 2 metres down; **en ~** [*analyse, réforme, réflexion*] in-depth (*épith*); **étudier/analyser qch en ~** to study/analyse[GB] sth in depth; **travail en ~** thorough work; **2** (d'armoire, étagères) depth; **3** (de sentiment, d'amour) depth.

II profondeurs *nfpl* liter **~s de la mer/d'une forêt** the depths of the sea/of a forest; **les ~s de l'âme** the (innermost) depths of the soul.

■ **~ de champ** Phot depth of field.

pro forma /pʀofɔʀma/ *loc adj inv* **facture ~** pro forma invoice.

profus, **~e** /pʀɔfy, yz/ *adj* liter abundant.

profusément /pʀɔfyzemɑ̃/ *adv* profusely.

profusion /pʀɔfyzjɔ̃/ *nf* (de détails, chiffres, couleurs) profusion; (de nourriture, boisson) abundance; **avoir tout à ~** to have everything in abundance.

progéniture /pʀɔʒenityʀ/ *nf* progeny.

progestatif /pʀɔʒɛstatif/ *nm* progestin, progestogen.

progestérone /pʀɔʒɛsteʀɔn/ *nf* progesterone.

progiciel /pʀɔʒisjɛl/ *nm* software package.

programmable /pʀɔgʀamabl/ *adj* programmable.

programmateur, **-trice** /pʀɔgʀamatœʀ, tʀis/ **I** ▶ 510 *nm,f* Radio, TV programme[GB] planner.

II *nm* gén timer; (de machine à laver) programme[GB] selector.

programmation /pʀɔgʀamasjɔ̃/ *nf* **1** Ordinat programming; **2** Radio, TV (diffusion) programming; **3** Radio, TV (planification) programme[GB] planning.

programme /pʀɔgʀam/ *nm* **1** Radio, Théât, TV, Cin programme[GB]; **ce n'est pas au ~** lit it's not on the programme[GB]; fig that wasn't planned; **changement de ~** lit change in the ou of programme[GB]; fig change of plan; **2** (emploi du temps) programme[GB]; **le ~ de la journée** the programme[GB] for the day; **avoir un ~ très chargé** to have a very busy schedule; **quel est le ~ des réjouissances aujourd'hui?** hum what delights are in store (for us) today?; **3** (projet) (d'action) plan; (de travail) programme[GB]; **~ électoral** electoral programme[GB] ou platform; **~ de gouvernement** government programme[GB] ou platform; **c'est tout un ~!** hum that'll take some doing!; **4** Scol, Univ syllabus; **le ~ d'histoire** the History syllabus; **le ~ de première année** the first-year syllabus; **au ~** on the syllabus; **5** Ordinat program; **~ d'exploitation/de compilation** operating/compiling program; **~ machine/d'assemblage** computer/assembly program.

programmer /pʀɔgʀame/ [1] *vtr* **1** (prévoir) to schedule, to bill [*émission*]; to plan [*travail, vacances, visite*]; **il a bien programmé son coup!** that was well planned!; **2** Ordinat to program [*ordinateur, données*].

programmeur, **-euse** /pʀɔgʀamœʀ, øz/ ▶ 510 *nm,f* (computer) programmer.

progrès /pʀɔgʀɛ/ *nm inv* **1** (pas en avant) (de personne) progress ¢; (de recherche, technique, science) progress ¢, advance; (d'enquête, affaire, de négociation) progress ¢; **marquer un ~ dans le domaine technique** to mark an advance in the field of technology; **les ~ de la médecine/de l'informatique** advances in medicine/in computer technology; **faire des ~** to make progress; **être en ~** [*personne*] to be making progress; [*résultats*] to be improving; **être en net/en léger ~** to be making clear/slight progress; **il y a du ~**○! things are improving!; **2** (résultat chiffré) increase; **afficher un ~ de 2%** to show an increase of 2%; **être en ~ de 10%** to be up by 10%; **3** (concept) **le ~** progress; **on n'arrête pas le ~!** iron that's progress for you!; **4** (progression) (de maladie) progression; (d'homme politique) progress; (d'armée) advance.

progresser /pʀɔgʀese/ [1] *vi* **1** (atteindre un niveau supérieur) [*taux, indice, bénéfice, résultat, inflation, salaires*] to rise, to go up; [*emploi, chômage*] to rise; [*pouvoir d'achat, budget*] to increase; [*économie, marché, Bourse*] to improve; [*entreprise*] to make progress; [*homme politique*] to make gains; **nos ventes ont bien progressé ce mois-ci** there has been a marked increase in our sales this month; **la mortalité infantile ne progresse plus** infant mortality is no longer rising; **~ de 3%/3 points** [*exportations, production, nombre, taux*] to rise by 3%/3 points; [*candidat, parti*] to gain 3%/3 points; **le franc a progressé de 3% par rapport à la lire** the franc has risen by 3% against the lira; **2** (dans son développement) [*enquête, affaire, négociations*] to make progress ou headway; [*relations*] to improve; [*réformes, analyse, pays, ville*] to make progress, to develop; [*science, technologie*] to progress; [*connaissances*] to increase; **le dossier des otages progresse** progress is being made in the hostage issue; **l'enquête ne progresse plus** the inquiry is no longer making progress; **3** (gagner du terrain) [*marcheur, alpiniste, anticyclone, dépression*] to make progress; [*ennemi, adversaire, armée*] to move forward; **~ de 200 m/3 km** [*personne, véhicule*] to advance by 200 m/3 km; **son livre continue de ~ dans les ventes** his/her book continues to move up the best seller list; **~ dans sa carrière** [*personne*] to progress in one's career; **4** (se propager) [*maladie, épidémie*] to spread; [*idéologie*] to gain ground; [*criminalité, délinquance, toxicomanie*] to be on the increase; **5** (s'améliorer) [*élève, sportif, équipe*] to make progress, to improve; **l'équipe a beaucoup progressé** the team has made a lot of progress; **~ dans un domaine** to make progress in a field.

progressif, **-ive** /pʀɔgʀesif, iv/ *adj* **1** gén progressive; **2** Fin, Fisc [*impôt, taux*] progressive; **3** Ling continuous, progressive.

progression /pʀɔgʀɛsjɔ̃/ *nf* **1** (avancée) (de marcheur, d'alpiniste) progress (**dans** in; **vers** toward, towards GB); (d'ennemi, orage, de cyclone) advance; **2** (propagation) (d'épidémie, idéologie) spread; (de criminalité, délinquance) increase; **3** (obtention de résultats supérieurs) (de taux, résultats, dépenses) increase; (de pouvoir d'achat, salaires) increase; (de chômage, d'inflation) increase; (de candidat, parti) progress, progression; **on enregistre une ~ annuelle de 5%** an annual increase of 5% is recorded; **rien ne peut arrêter la ~ du parti** nothing can stop the party's progress; **être en ~** [*résultat*] to be up; [*tendance*] to be increasing; **les ventes sont en ~ constante** sales are increasing steadily; **leur chiffre d'affaires est en ~ de 10%** their turnover is up by 10%; **en termes de ~** in terms of growth; **4** Math progression; **~ arithmétique/géométrique** arithmetic/geometric progression; **5** Mus progression.

progressiste /pʀɔgʀesist/ *adj, nmf* progressive.

progressivement /pʀɔgʀesivmɑ̃/ *adv* progressively.

progressivité /pʀɔgʀesivite/ *nf* progressiveness.

prohibé, **~e** /pʀɔibe/ **I** *pp* ▶ **prohiber**.

II *pp adj* [*marchandise, substance, arme*] prohibited; [*commerce, action*] illegal; **port d'arme ~** illegal possession of a firearm.

prohiber /pʀɔibe/ [1] *vtr* to prohibit.

prohibitif, **-ive** /pʀɔibitif, iv/ *adj* **1** (excessif) [*prix, taxe*] prohibitive; **2** (qui interdit) [*loi, système*] prohibition (*épith*).

prohibition /pʀɔibisjɔ̃/ *nf* prohibition (**de** of); **loi de ~** prohibition law.

prohibitionnisme /pʀɔibisjɔnism/ *nm* prohibitionism.

prohibitionniste /pʀɔibisjɔnist/ *adj, nmf* prohibitionist.

proie /pʀwɑ/ *nf* lit, fig prey; **l'aigle s'est abattu sur sa ~** the eagle swooped down on its prey; **sa générosité en fait une ~ facile pour les parasites** his/her generosity makes him/her an easy prey for scroungers; **il a été la ~ des journaux à scandale quand il a divorcé** he fell prey to ou was hounded by the gutter press when he got divorced; **toute la région est la ~ des promoteurs immobiliers** the whole area has fallen prey to property salesmen GB ou real estate developers US; **le bâtiment était la ~ des flammes** the building was in flames; **être en ~ au doute** to be prey to doubt, to be beset by doubts; **être en ~ à l'angoisse/aux remords/au désespoir** to be racked by anguish/remorse/despair; **être en ~ à la maladie** to be stricken by illness; **pays en ~ à une grave crise économique/la guerre civile** country in the grip of a serious economic crisis/civil war; **entreprise en ~ à des difficultés insurmontables** company beset ou plagued by overwhelming difficulties.

IDIOMES **lâcher la ~ pour l'ombre** to give up what one has already got to go chasing after shadows.

projecteur /pʀɔʒɛktœʀ/ *nm* **1** (pour éclairer) (de DCA, mirador) searchlight; (spot) spotlight; (de véhicule) headlight; (de stade) floodlight; **être sous les ~s** fig to be in the spotlight; **2** (pour projeter) Cin, Tech projector; **~ de cinéma/de diapositives** film/slide projector; **~ réflecteur** overhead projector.

projectif, **-ive** /pʀɔʒɛktif, iv/ *adj* projective.

projectile /pʀɔʒɛktil/ *nm* **1** gén missile, projectile; **2** (balle, obus) projectile.

projection /pʀɔʒɛksjɔ̃/ *nf* **1** (processus) **l'éruption commença par une ~ de cendres** the eruption began with a discharge ou emission of ashes; **nettoyer qch par ~ de sable** to sandblast sth; **2** (éclaboussures) **le cuisinier a reçu des ~s d'huile bouillante** the cook got spattered with scalding oil; **il y avait des ~s de boue sur toute la voiture** there was mud spattered all over the car; **3** Cin (fait de projeter) projection; (séance) showing; **salle de ~** screening room; **cabine de ~** projection room; **appareil de ~** projector; **4** Math, Psych projection (**sur** onto); **5** (prévision) forecast.

■ **~s volcaniques** volcanic emissions.

projectionniste /pʀɔʒɛksjɔnist/ ▶510 *nmf* projectionist.

projet /pʀɔʒɛ/ *nm* **1** (plan) plan; **faire** or **former/concevoir un ~** to form/to conceive a plan; **faire des ~s d'avenir** to make plans for the future; **réaliser un ~** to carry out a plan; **vous avez des ~s pour l'été?** do you have any plans for the summer?; **en ~, à l'état de ~** at the planning stage, on the drawing board; **espérons que ces réformes/améliorations ne resteront pas à l'état de ~** let us hope that these reforms/improvements get past the planning stage ou drawing board; **j'ai un film et un roman en ~** I'm planning a film and a novel; **2** (entreprise en cours) project; **le ~ prend du retard** the project is falling behind schedule; **~ de dictionnaire/chaîne de télévision/navette spatiale** dictionary/TV channel/space shuttle project; **~ d'investissement** investment project ou scheme; **3** (esquisse) (de roman, contrat) (rough) draft; **4** Archit (plan d'exécution) execution plan ou drawing.

■ **~ de budget** budget proposal; **~ de contrat** draft contract; **~ de loi** (government) bill; **~ de réforme** Pol reform bill.

projeter /pʀɔʒte/ [20] *vtr* **1** (lancer) **en nous doublant, le camion a projeté des gravillons sur notre voiture** when it passed us the truck threw some gravel up against the car; **~ du sable sur des bâtiments pour les nettoyer** to sandblast buildings; **le geyser projetait des gerbes d'eau** the geyser was spouting jets of water; **le volcan projetait de la fumée** the volcano was belching smoke; **~ du vitriol au visage de qn** to throw acid in sb's face; **le choc l'a projeté par terre/par-dessus bord/hors de son véhicule** the shock sent him hurtling to the ground/overboard/out of his vehicle; **le feu/chalumeau projette des étincelles** the fire/blowtorch throws out sparks; **2** (jeter) to cast [*ombre, reflet*] (**sur** on); **3** Cin, Phot to show, to project [*film, diapositives*] (**sur** onto); **un documentaire sera projeté** a documentary will be shown; **4** (prévoir) to plan [*voyage, vacances, mariage*]; **je projette de faire le tour du monde** I'm planning to go round the world; **5** Math, Psych to project (**sur** onto).

projeteur /pʀɔʒtœʀ/ ▶510 *nm* design technician.

prolapsus /pʀɔlapsys/ *nm* prolapse.

prolégomènes /pʀɔlegɔmɛn/ *nmpl* prolegomena.

prolepse /pʀɔlɛps/ *nf* prolepsis.

prolétaire /pʀɔletɛʀ/ **I** *adj* proletarian.

II *nmf* proletarian; **'~s de tous les pays, unissez-vous!'** 'workers of the world, unite!'

prolétariat /pʀɔletaʀja/ *nm* proletariat.

prolétarien, **-ienne** /pʀɔletaʀjɛ̃, ɛn/ *adj* proletarian.

prolétarisation /pʀɔletaʀizasjɔ̃/ *nf* proletarianization.

prolétariser /pʀɔletaʀize/ [1] *vtr* proletarianize.

prolifération /pʀɔlifeʀasjɔ̃/ *nf* proliferation; **~ cellulaire** cell proliferation.

proliférer /pʀɔlifeʀe/ [14] *vi* to proliferate.

prolifique /pʀɔlifik/ *adj* prolific.

prolixe /pʀɔliks/ *adj* verbose, prolix.

prolixité /pʀɔliksite/ *nf* prolixity.

prolo° /pʀɔlo/ **I** *adj* [*vêtement, style*] modest; péj cheap and nasty; **ça fait ~** that's a bit common.

II *nmf* pleb°, prole.

prologue /pʀɔlɔg/ *nm* prologue.

prolongateur /pʀɔlɔ̃gatœʀ/ *nm* extension cable GB, extension cord US.

prolongation /pʀɔlɔ̃gasjɔ̃/ *nf* **1** (de trêve, bataille) continuation; (de congé, spectacle) extension; **2** Sport extra time; **jouer les ~s** to play ou go into extra time GB, to play overtime US.

prolonge /pʀɔlɔ̃ʒ/ *nf* **1** (véhicule) **~ (d'artillerie)** gun carriage; **2** (corde) rope (*for a gun carriage*).

prolongé, **~e** /pʀɔlɔ̃ʒe/ **I** *pp* ▶**prolonger**.

II *pp adj* [*effort*] sustained; [*arrêt*] lengthy; [*séjour*] extended; [*week-end*] long; [*exposition*] prolonged, extended; **c'est un adolescent ~** he's an overgrown teenager, he's still a teenager at heart; **'pas d'utilisation ~e sans avis médical'** (sur des médicaments) 'if symptoms persist, consult your doctor'.

prolongement /pʀɔlɔ̃ʒmɑ̃/ *nm* **1** (agrandissement) extension; **le ~ d'une voie ferrée** the extension of a railway; **2** (direction) **la rue Berthollet se trouve dans le ~ de la rue de la Glacière** Rue de la Glacière becomes Rue Berthollet; **3** (suite) outcome, consequence; **la guerre a été le ~ logique de la crise** war was the inevitable outcome ou consequence of the crisis; **une affaire aux ~s multiples** a case with wide-ranging repercussions.

prolonger /pʀɔlɔ̃ʒe/ [13] **I** *vtr* **1** (faire durer) to extend, to prolong [*vacances, séjour, voyage, promenade*] (**de** by); to prolong [*débat, séance, vie*] (**de** by); to continue [*traitement*] (**de** for); **2** (agrandir) to extend [*route, voie ferrée, ligne électrique, clôture*] (**de** by; **jusqu'à** as far as); **3** (être le prolongement de) to be an extension of; **le nouveau bâtiment prolonge l'ancien** the new building is an extension of the old one; **la nouvelle bretelle prolonge l'autoroute jusqu'à Clermont-Ferrand** the new motorway GB ou freeway US link brings the motorway GB ou freeway US right up to Clermont-Ferrand.

II se prolonger *vpr* **1** (dans le temps) (durer) [*maladie, symptôme, effet*] to persist, to last; [*situation*] to go on, to last; [*spectacle, réunion, discussion*] to go on, to continue (**jusqu'à** until); (déborder) to overrun (**de** by); **2** (dans l'espace) **se ~ jusqu'à** [*chemin, route, voie ferrée, mur, clôture*] to go as far as, to extend as far as; **l'artiste se prolonge dans ses œuvres** fig the artist lives on in his/her works.

promenade /pʀɔmnad/ *nf* **1** (sortie) (à pied) walk; (à cheval, moto) ride; (à bicyclette) (bike-ride; (voiture) drive, ride; (en bateau) gén ride (in a boat); **partir en/faire une/être en ~** to go for a/to go out for a/to be out for a walk ou ride ou drive; **2** (lieu aménagé) gén walkway; (en bord de mer) promenade; **la Promenade des Anglais à Nice** the Promenade des Anglais in Nice.

promener /pʀɔmne/ [16] **I** *vtr* **1** (faire sortir) to take [sb] out [*enfant, personne*]; to take [sth] out for a walk, to walk [*chien, animal*]; (faire visiter) to show [sb] around [*personne, visiteur*]; **il est sorti ~ le chien** he's taken the dog out for a walk; **nous l'avons promené partout** we took him all over the place; **va chez le boulanger, ça te promènera** go to the baker's, it'll get you out; **il m'a promené dans toute l'usine avant de trouver le bon service** he dragged me around the whole factory before finding the right department; **le pianiste promenait ses mains sur le clavier** the pianist's fingers flowed over the keyboard; **2** (transporter) to lug° [*valise, sac, pancarte, objet encombrant*]; to carry [*objet, parapluie, sac à main, carnet*]; **à 13 ans il promène encore son ours en peluche** he's 13, but he still carries his teddy bear around with him; **il promène sa tristesse/son ennui partout** he carries his misery/his boredom around with him wherever he goes; **~ son regard** or **œil sur qn/qch** to cast an eye over sb/sth; **~ une loupe sur qch** to look over sth with a magnifying glass.

II se promener *vpr* **1** (pour se distraire) (à pied) to go for a walk; (en voiture) to go for a drive; (en bateau) to go out in a boat; (à bicyclette, à cheval) to go for a ride; **nous sommes allés nous ~ dans la vieille ville** we went for a walk around the old town; **ils sont partis se ~ dans les bois** they've gone (off) for a walk in the woods; **le dossier s'est promené dans toute l'usine** the file did the rounds of the factory.

promeneur, **-euse** /pʀɔmnœʀ, øz/ *nm,f* (randonneur) walker; **quelques ~s attardés se trouvaient encore dans le parc** a few people were still out taking a stroll ou walk in the park, there were still a few people in the park taking a stroll ou walk.

promenoir /pʀɔm(ə)nwaʀ/ *nm* (de couvent, prison, collège) covered walk(way); (de théâtre) gallery.

promesse /pʀɔmɛs/ *nf* **1** (engagement) promise; **faire une ~ à qn** to make sb a promise, to give sb one's word; **faire de grandes ~s** to make grand promises; **avoir la ~ de qn** to have sb's word; **tenir ses ~s** to keep one's promises; **ne pas tenir ses ~s** to break one's promises; **manquer à sa ~** to break one's promise ou word; **fausses ~s** empty promises; **~ de mariage** promise of marriage; **faire la ~ à qn que** to promise sb that, to give sb one's word that; **2** Jur, Comm **honorer ses ~s** to honour[GB] one's commitments; **~ de vente/d'achat** agreement to sell/to buy; **3** (espérance) promise; **être plein de ~s** [*personne, auteur, athlète*] to be full of promise, to have great promise; **un magnifique coucher de soleil qui est la ~ de beau temps** a beautiful sunset which promises fine weather to come.

■ **~ en l'air** or **de Gascon** or **d'ivrogne** empty ou idle promise.

Prométhée /pʀɔmete/ *npr* Prometheus.

prométhium /pʀɔmetjɔm/ *nm* promethium.

prometteur, **-euse** /pʀɔmɛtœʀ, øz/ *adj* promising.

promettre /pʀɔmɛtʀ/ [60] **I** *vtr* **1** (s'engager à donner) **~ qch à qn** to promise sb sth; **ils ont promis beaucoup pour être réélus** they promised great things in order to get re-elected; **'pourrais-tu le faire pour demain?'—'je ne (te) promets rien'** 'could you do it by tomorrow?'—'I can't promise anything'; **~ son cœur/son amour/sa main à qn** to pledge one's heart/one's love/one's hand to sb; **~ fidélité (à qn)** to pledge fidelity (to sb); **~ le secret** to promise to keep a secret; **promets-moi d'être prudent sur la route** promise you'll drive carefully; **'promets-moi de n'en parler à personne'—'je te le promets'** 'promise me (that) you won't tell anybody about it'—'I promise!'; **je te promets que tu le paieras cher** you'll pay for that, I promise you ; **je te promets qu'il le regrettera** he'll regret it, I guarantee you; **2** (annoncer) **une soirée qui promet bien des surprises** an evening that holds a few surprises in store; **voilà qui nous promet de nombreux débats télévisés** it looks as though we'll be getting a lot of televised debates; **cette grève nous promet une belle pagaille** this strike is guaranteed to cause chaos; **ses diplômes lui promettent un bel avenir** his/her diplomas guarantee him/her a fine future; **la journée promet d'être chaude** it promises to be a hot day; **un débat/match qui promet d'être intéressant** a debate/match that promises to be interesting; **3** (destiner) **ce jeune cadre est promis à un bel**

avenir this young executive has a fine future ahead of him.
II *vi* **1** (avoir de l'avenir) to show promise; **un jeune musicien qui promet** a promising young musician; **un film qui promet** a film which sounds (as though it should be) interesting; **2**○ iron (présager des ennuis) **cet enfant promet** that child is going to be a handful; **ça promet!** that's going to be fun!; **ça promet pour l'hiver** winter's got GB ou gotten US off to a good start.
III **se promettre** *vpr* **1** (à soi-même) to promise oneself [*plaisir, voyage*]; **se ~ du bon temps** to decide to have a bit of fun; **2** (être résolu) **se ~ de faire** to resolve to do; **il s'est promis de ne plus la revoir** he has resolved ou made up his mind not to see her again; **3** (l'un l'autre) [*personnes, couple*] **se ~ de faire** to promise each other to do; **ils se sont promis fidélité** they have promised to be faithful to each other; **ils se sont promis de ne plus se quitter** they (have) vowed never to be parted.
IDIOMES **~ monts et merveilles** or **la lune (à qn)** to promise (sb) the moon ou the earth.

promis†, **~e** /pʀɔmi, iz/ *nm,f* betrothed†.

promiscuité /pʀɔmiskɥite/ *nf* (dans un dortoir, une cellule) lack of privacy; (dans le métro, un bidonville) overcrowding.

promo○ /pʀɔmo/ *nf*: *abbr* = **promotion** 2, 4.

promontoire /pʀɔmɔ̃twaʀ/ *nm* promontory.

promoteur, **-trice** /pʀɔmɔtœʀ, tʀis/ *nm,f* **1** ▶ **510** Constr property developer; **2** (de théorie, d'idée) instigator; (de mouvement, d'exposition) promoter; **3** Chimie promoter.

promotion /pʀɔmɔsjɔ̃/ *nf* **1** (avancement) promotion (**à** to); (personnes promues) promotion list; **2** Comm (special) offer; **en ~** on (special) offer; **faire des ~s** to have (special) offers; **3** (développement) promotion; **assurer la ~ de** to promote; **4** Univ *year group of students admitted to higher education institutes* GB, class US; **il est sorti major de sa ~** he graduated first in his year.
■ **~ sociale** further (vocational) education.

promotionnel, **-elle** /pʀɔmɔsjɔnɛl/ *adj* promotional; **grande vente promotionnelle** big promotion GB, big sale US; **prix ~** special offer.

promouvoir /pʀɔmuvwaʀ/ [43] *vtr* **1** (faire la promotion de) to promote [*produit, idée, action, paix, investissement*]; **2** (dans la hiérarchie) to promote; **~ qn (au rang de) sergent** to promote sb (to the rank of) sergeant; **3** (honorifiquement) to elevate; **~ qn héros national** to elevate sb to the status of national hero.

prompt, **~e** /pʀɔ̃, pʀɔ̃t/ *adj* [*action, réaction, intervention*] prompt; [*geste, coup d'œil*] swift; [*repartie, esprit*] ready; [*retournement, départ*] sudden; **avoir l'esprit ~** to have a ready ou quick wit; **meilleurs vœux de ~ rétablissement** best wishes for a speedy recovery; **être ~ à agir/réagir** to act/react swiftly; **être ~ à la riposte** or **à riposter** to be always ready with a reply; **avoir la répartie ~e** to be quick at repartee; **avoir le geste ~/la main ~e** to be quick to act/to strike.

promptement /pʀɔ̃tmɑ̃/ *adv* (sans délai) [*expédier, répondre, remplacer, licencier*] promptly; [*réagir, intervenir*] swiftly; (vite) [*juger, comprendre, décider*] quickly.

prompteur /pʀɔ̃ptœʀ/ *nm* autocue GB, Teleprompter® US.

promptitude /pʀɔ̃tityd/ *nf* (de réponse, réaction) promptness; (de décision) rapidity; (de guérison) speed; (de geste) swiftness; (de départ, changement) suddenness; **leur ~ à réagir/accepter** their prompt reaction/acceptance; **leur ~ à croire/pardonner** their readiness to believe/to forgive.

promulgation /pʀɔmylgasjɔ̃/ *nf* promulgation.

promulguer /pʀɔmylge/ [1] *vtr* to promulgate.

prône /pʀon/ *nm* prone.

prôner /pʀone/ [1] *vtr* to advocate, to extol the virtues of.

pronom /pʀɔnɔ̃/ *nm* pronoun; **~ réfléchi/complément** reflexive/object pronoun.

pronominal, **~e**, *mpl* **-aux** /pʀɔnɔminal, o/ *adj* pronominal; **verbe ~** reflexive ou pronominal verb.

pronominalement /pʀɔnɔminalmɑ̃/ *adv* pronominally; **verbe employé ~** verb used reflexively ou pronominally.

prononçable /pʀɔnɔ̃sabl/ *adj* pronounceable; **c'est difficilement ~** it's difficult to pronounce.

prononcé, **~e** /pʀɔnɔ̃se/ I *pp* ▶ **prononcer**.
II *pp adj* [*accent*] strong, pronounced; [*saveur, odeur*] strong; [*rides*] marked; **avoir un goût ~ pour** to be particularly fond of.
III *nm* pronouncement.

prononcer /pʀɔnɔ̃se/ [12] I *vtr* **1** Phon to pronounce [*son, mot*]; **un mot souvent mal prononcé** a word which is often mispronounced ou pronounced wrongly; **2** (proférer) to mention [*name*]; to say [*mot, phrase*]; **sans ~ une parole** without saying ou uttering a word; **3** (dire publiquement) to deliver [*discours, allocution*]; **~ ses vœux** Relig to take one's vows; **4** (déclarer) to pronounce [*peine de mort*]; to pass [*mesure d'expulsion*]; **~ la dissolution du parlement** to dissolve parliament; **~ le divorce** to grant a divorce; **~ un non-lieu en faveur de qn** to nonsuit sb.
II *vi* Jur to make known a decision.
III **se prononcer** *vpr* **1** Phon to be pronounced; **la lettre ne se prononce pas** you don't pronounce the letter, the letter isn't pronounced; **2** (faire connaître un avis, une décision) **se ~ contre qch** to declare oneself against sth, to come down against sth; **se ~ en faveur de** or **pour qch** to declare oneself in favour[GB] of sth, to come down in favour[GB] of sth; **se ~ sur qch** to give one's opinion on sth, to pronounce on sth sout; **il ne s'est pas encore prononcé** he hasn't yet given his opinion, he has yet to pronounce sout.

prononciation /pʀɔnɔ̃sjasjɔ̃/ *nf* **1** Phon pronunciation; **faire des fautes** or **des erreurs de ~** to make pronunciation errors ou mistakes; **il a une bonne/mauvaise ~** his pronunciation is good/bad; **la mauvaise ~ du mot 'province'** the mispronunciation of the word 'province'; ▶ **défaut**; **2** Jur pronouncement.

pronostic /pʀɔnɔstik/ *nm* **1** (sportif, financier) forecast; **faire des ~s** to make forecasts; **2** (dans un conflit) prediction; **3** (médical) prognosis.

pronostiquer /pʀɔnɔstike/ [1] *vtr* **1** Sport, Turf to forecast [*résultat*]; **2** (prévoir) to herald [*défaite, victoire, taux de chômage*].

pronostiqueur, **-euse** /pʀɔnɔstikœʀ, øz/ *nm,f* tipster.

pronunciamiento /pʀɔnunsjamjɛnto/ *nm* army coup.

propagande /pʀɔpagɑ̃d/ *nf* propaganda; **~ électorale** election propaganda; **film/affiche de ~** propaganda film/poster; **faire de la ~ pour** to campaign for [*cause*]; to plug, to push [*produit*]

propagandiste /pʀɔpagɑ̃dist/ *nmf* propagandist.

propagateur, **-trice** /pʀɔpagatœʀ, tʀis/ *nm,f* proponent; **~ de mauvaises nouvelles** spreader of bad news.

propagation /pʀɔpagasjɔ̃/ *nf* **1** (d'incendie, de nouvelle, maladie) spread (**de** of); **2** Phys (de son, d'onde) propagation (**de** of); **3** (d'espèce) propagation (**de** of).

propager /pʀɔpaʒe/ [13] I *vtr* **1** to spread [*rumeur, haine, idée, maladie*]; **2** to propagate [*espèce*]; **3** Phys to propagate [*onde, son*].
II **se propager** *vpr* **1** gén to spread; **2** Phys to propagate.

propane /pʀɔpan/ *nm* propane.

propanier /pʀɔpanje/ *nm* propane tanker.

propédeutique /pʀɔpedøtik/ *nf*: *formerly, first year at university in arts and science faculties*.

propène /pʀɔpɛn/ *nm* propene.

propension /pʀɔpɑ̃sjɔ̃/ *nf* propensity (**à qch** for sth; **à faire** to do).

propergol® /pʀɔpɛʀgɔl/ *nm* (rocket) propellant.

prophète, **prophétesse** /pʀɔfɛt, pʀɔfetɛs/ *nm,f* prophet/prophetess; **~ de malheur** prophet of doom GB, doomsayer US; ▶ **faux**[1].
IDIOMES **nul n'est ~ en son pays** Prov no-one is a prophet in his own land Prov.

prophétie /pʀɔfesi/ *nf* prophecy.

prophétique /pʀɔfetik/ *adj* prophetic.

prophétiquement /pʀɔfetikmɑ̃/ *adv* prophetically.

prophétiser /pʀɔfetize/ [1] *vtr* to prophesy.

prophylactique /pʀɔfilaktik/ *adj* prophylactic.

prophylaxie /pʀɔfilaksi/ *nf* prophylaxis.

propice /pʀɔpis/ *adj* favourable (**à** for), propitious (**à** for); **peu ~** scarcely propitious; **trouver le moment ~** to find the right moment (**à qch** for sth; **pour faire qch** to do sth).

propitiation /pʀɔpisjasjɔ̃/ *nf* propitiation.

propitiatoire /pʀɔpisjatwaʀ/ *adj* propitiatory.

proportion /pʀɔpɔʀsjɔ̃/ *nf* **1** (quantité relative) proportion; **une ~ croissante/relative de femmes** a growing/relative proportion of women; **une ~ de 10 chômeurs pour 35 salariés** 10 unemployed workers for every 35 in work; **dans une ~ de cinq contre un** in a ratio of five to one; **en ~ de** in proportion to; **dépenses en ~ du revenu** spending in proportion to income; **en ~, ils sont mieux payés** they are proportionately better paid; **c'est calculé en ~** it is calculated proportionately; **2** (équilibre) proportion; **être sans ~ avec** to be out of (all) proportion to; **être hors de ~ avec** to be out of proportion to; **il n'y a aucune ~ entre l'incident et sa mauvaise humeur** the bad temper he showed was out of all proportion to the incident; **ramener le débat à de plus justes ~s** to put things back in perspective; **cela a pris de telles ~s que** it has become so serious that; **la criminalité a augmenté dans des ~s considérables/inquiétantes** crime has increased considerably/alarmingly; **toutes ~s gardées** relatively speaking; **3** Art, Archit proportion; **armoire de belles ~s** well-proportioned wardrobe.

proportionnalité /pʀɔpɔʀsjɔnalite/ *nf* proportionality; **~ de l'impôt** proportional taxation.

proportionné, **~e** /pʀɔpɔʀsjɔne/ I *pp* ▶ **proportionner**.
II *pp adj* **bien/mal ~** [*personne, bâtiment*] well-/badly-proportioned.

proportionnel, **-elle** /pʀɔpɔʀsjɔnɛl/ I *adj* (tous contextes) proportional (**à** to); **être directement/inversement ~ à qch** to be directly/inversely proportional to sth; **prime proportionnelle au rendement** productivity bonus.
II **proportionnelle** *nf* Pol proportional representation.

proportionnellement /pʀɔpɔʀsjɔnɛlmɑ̃/ *adv* proportionately; **augmenter les salaires ~ au rendement** to raise salaries in proportion to output.

proportionner /pʀɔpɔʀsjɔne/ [1] *vtr* **~ qch à qch** to make sth proportional to sth; **être proportionné à qch** [*impôt, récompense*] to be proportional ou proportionate to sth.

propos /pʀɔpo/ **I** *nm inv* **1** (sujet) **à ~, je**... by the way, I...; **à ~ de votre travail** about ou regarding your work; **'je voudrais te parler'—'à quel ~?'** or **'à ~ de quoi?'** 'I would like to speak to you'—'what about?'; **à ~ de qui?** about who?; **à ~ de tout** about everything; **à ~ de rien** about nothing in particular; **il dit ça à ~ de tout et de rien** he says that about everything; **à ce ~, je voudrais**... in this connection, I would like...; **à ~** [*arriver, parler*] at the right moment ou time; **mal à ~** [*arriver, parler*] at (just) the wrong moment ou time; **être hors de ~** [*commentaire*] to be inopportune; **à tout ~** constantly; **juger à ~ de faire qch** to see fit to do sth; ▶ **à-propos**; **2** (projet) fml intention; **avoir le ferme ~ de** to have the firm intention of; **faire qch de ~ délibéré** to do sth deliberately ou on purpose.

II *nmpl* comments; **tenir des ~ grossiers** to make vulgar comments; **'~ recueillis par J. Brun'** 'interview by J. Brun'.

proposer /pʀɔpoze/ [1] **I** *vtr* **1** (suggérer) to suggest [*réunion, débat, solution, promenade*]; **je propose qu'on aille se promener** I suggest we take a walk; ▶ **Dieu**; **2** (offrir) to offer [*aide, argent*] (**à qn** to sb); Tourisme, Pub to offer [*stage, excursion*]; **on m'a proposé un poste intéressant** I've been offered an interesting job; **'que veux-tu manger?'—'qu'est-ce que tu me proposes?'** 'what would you like to eat?'—'what is there?'; **'nous vous proposons de dîner aux chandelles'** 'enjoy a candlelight supper'; **je te propose de travailler avec nous** why don't you come and work with us?; **~ un bébé à l'adoption** to put a child up for adoption; **3** (soumettre) to put forward [*solution, mesure*]; to propose [*stratégie, projet*]; **~ la candidature de qn** to put sb's name forward as a candidate; **4** (à un examen) to set [*sujet, question*]; **5** to present [*loi*].

II se proposer *vpr* **1** (être volontaire) **se ~ pour faire** to offer to do; **se ~ pour peindre la cuisine** to offer to paint the kitchen; **je me suis proposé comme cuisinier** I offered to do the cooking; **2** (avoir l'intention) **se ~ de** to intend to [*étudier, voyager*].

proposition /pʀɔpozisjɔ̃/ **I** *nf* **1** (suggestion) suggestion; **2** (offre) offer, proposal; **faire des ~s concrètes** to make concrete proposals; **~ technique/commerciale** technical/business proposal; **3** (soumis à l'approbation) proposal; **sur (la) ~ du maire** at the mayor's instigation; **~ de loi** ≈ bill; **4** Philos proposition; **5** Ling clause; **~ principale/subordonnée/relative** main/subordinate/relative clause.

II *nfpl* **faire des ~s à qn** to proposition sb.

propositionnel, -elle /pʀɔpozisjɔnɛl/ *adj* propositional.

propre /pʀɔpʀ/ **I** *adj* **1** (hygiénique, sans souillure, nettoyé) [*personne, objet*] clean; (qui ne salit pas) [*travail, manipulation*] clean; (qui ne pollue pas) clean; **tu n'as pas les mains ~s!** your hands aren't clean!; **je n'ai plus rien de ~ à me mettre** I haven't got anything clean to wear; **la menuiserie est plus ~ que la plomberie** carpentry is not such a dirty job as plumbing; **une voiture ~** lit a clean car; fig a car which runs on unleaded petrol GB ou gas US; **nous voilà ~s!** fig, iron we're in a fine mess now!; ▶ **sou**; **2** (soigné, soigneux) tidy, neat; **3** (moral) [*personne, vie*] decent; [*affaire*] honest; **des affaires pas très ~s** unsavoury[GB] business (+ *v sg*); **4** (personnel) **ma ~ voiture** my own car; **il n'y a que ses ~s recherches qui l'intéressent** he's/she's only interested in his/her own research; **ce sont tes ~s paroles** (rapport) you said so yourself; (insistance) those were your very words; **de mes ~s yeux** with my own eyes; **5** (spécifique) of one's own; **avoir son style ~** to have a style of one's own; **il manque de personnalité ~** he doesn't have a personality of his own; **chaque pays a des lois qui lui sont ~s** each country has its own particular laws ou has laws of its own; **pour des raisons qui leur sont ~s** for reasons of their own; **6** (approprié) [*terme, expression*] right, proper; **7** (continent) [*bébé*] toilet-trained; [*animal*] housetrained GB, housebroken US.

II propre à *loc adj* **1** (spécifique) **~ à qch/qn** peculiar to sth/sb; **faculté/maladie ~ aux êtres humains** faculty/illness peculiar to human beings; **terme/style ~ au jargon administratif** terms/style peculiar to bureaucracy; **2** (capable de) **~ à faire** (résultat attendu) likely to do; (résultat étonnant) liable to do; **trouver les arguments ~s à convaincre/~s à convaincre les plus sceptiques** to find arguments which are likely to convince/liable to convince even the most sceptical GB ou skeptical US; **les mesures ~s à limiter le chômage** measures to curb unemployment; **il n'est ~ à rien** he's a good-for-nothing; **3** (adapté) **~ à qch** appropriate for; **prendre les dispositions ~s à la sécurité des passagers** to take appropriate measures to ensure passengers' safety; **produit déclaré ~ à la consommation** product fit for consumption.

III *nm* **1** (ce qui est nettoyé) **ça sent le ~** it smells nice and clean; **2** (copie, texte) fair copy; **mettre qch au ~** to make a fair copy of sth; **relire un rapport avant sa mise au ~** to reread a report before making a fair copy of it; **3** (ce qui est moral) **c'est du ~!** iron that's very nice!; **4** (ce qui est spécifique) **être le ~ de** to be peculiar to; **le rire est le ~ de l'homme** laughter is peculiar to humans; **le ~ de cette nouvelle technologie est de faire** what is peculiar to this new technology is that it does; **c'est le ~ de la jeunesse que d'être insouciante** lightheartedness is a peculiarly youthful quality; **la maison leur appartient en ~** they are the sole owners of the house; **disposer en ~ d'un ordinateur** to have one's own individual computer; **les titres détenus en ~ par la banque** the securities held solely by the bank.

IDIOMES **bon à tout, ~ à rien** Prov Jack of all trades (and master of none) Prov.

proprement /pʀɔpʀəmɑ̃/ *adv* **1** (au sens strict) purely; **les institutions ~ financières** purely financial institutions; **à ~ parler** strictly speaking; **~ dit** (sans considérations annexes) as such (*après n*); (au sens restreint) in the strict sense of the word (*après n*); **quant au procès/au village ~ dit** as for the trial/the village itself ou proper; **la psychiatrie/physique ~ dite** psychiatry/physics proper; **2** (absolument) [*honteux, insupportable, scandaleux*] absolutely; **3** (véritablement) really; **c'est ~ de la bassesse** that's really low; **il s'est ~ moqué de toi** he made a proper fool of you; **4** (littéralement) literally; **l'air est devenu ~ irrespirable** the air has become literally unbreathable; **5** (spécifiquement) specifically; **une question ~ européenne** a specifically European issue; **une maladie ~ infantile** a disease of childhood; **6** (comme il faut) well and truly; **le professeur l'a ~ remis à sa place** he was well and truly put in his place by the teacher; **7** (avec soin) [*écrire, s'habiller, vêtu*] neatly; **faire son travail** or **travailler ~** to do a neat job; **il tient son cahier très ~** he keeps his exercise book very neat; **mange ~!** eat cleanly!; **8** (honnêtement) [*gagner sa vie*] honestly; [*vivre, se comporter, agir*] decently.

propret, -ette /pʀɔpʀɛ, ɛt/ *adj* neat and tidy.

propreté /pʀɔpʀəte/ *nf* **1** (absence de souillure) cleanliness; **il n'est pas très regardant sur la ~** he isn't very fussy about cleanliness; **d'une ~ douteuse** not very clean; **d'une ~ éblouissante** sparkling clean; **veiller à la ~ d'un bâtiment** to make sure ou see to it that a building is kept clean; **en parfait état de ~** perfectly clean; **habituer un chat à la ~** to house-train GB ou housebreak US a cat; **avec ~** [*manger*] cleanly; [*repeindre*] neatly; **2** (honnêteté) honesty; **on l'estime pour sa ~ morale** he's/she's respected for his/her scrupulousness.

propriétaire /pʀɔpʀijetɛʀ/ *nmf* **1** (de terres, bien, d'immeubles, objet) owner; (d'hôtel, de restaurant, journal, commerce) proprietor, owner; **un petit ~** a small-scale property owner; **dans ce pays, il y a plus de ~s que de locataires** in this country there are more homeowners than tenants; **ils sont ~s de leur maison** they own their own house; **faire le tour du ~** to look round GB ou around US the house; **faire faire le tour du ~ à qn** to show sb round GB ou around US the house; **2** (de propriété louée) landlord/landlady, owner; **mon ~ a encore augmenté mon loyer** my landlord has put up the rent again.

■ **~ foncier** landowner; **~ indivis** joint owner; **~ terrien** = **~ foncier**.

propriété /pʀɔpʀijete/ *nf* **1** (droit) ownership, property; **l'abolition de la ~ privée** the abolition of private ownership; **certificat de ~** certificate of ownership; **posséder qch en toute ~** to be the sole ou exclusive owner of sth, to have sole ownership of sth; **2** (biens possédés) property; **être la ~ de qn** to be the property of sb; **toutes ces richesses sont la ~ d'un seul individu** all this wealth is the property of one person; **ces véhicules sont la ~ de la compagnie** these vehicles are company property; **3** (bien immobilier) gén property; (domaine) estate, property; (maison) house, property; **4** (caractéristique) property; **une plante aux ~s anti-inflammatoires** a plant with anti-inflammatory properties; **5** (exactitude) aptness.

■ **~ artistique et littéraire** intellectual property right, copyright; **~ bâtie** developed property; **~ commune** joint ownership; **~ foncière** landed estate; **~ immobilière** real estate, realty; **~ industrielle** patent rights (*pl*); **~ mobilière** movable property; **~ non bâtie** undeveloped property; **~ privée** private property; **~ publique** public property.

proprio◐ /pʀɔpʀio/ *nmf* landlord/landlady.

propulser /pʀɔpylse/ [1] **I** *vtr* **1** (faire mouvoir) [*moteur*] to propel [*véhicule, projectile*]; **2** (promouvoir) to propel [*personne*]; **3**○ (déplacer violemment) to hurl [*personne, objet*].

II se propulser○ *vpr* to propel oneself○.

propulseur /pʀɔpylsœʀ/ **I** *adj m* [*mécanisme, engin*] propellent, propelling (*épith*).

II *nm* **1** Tech propelling device; (moteur) engine; **~ (de fusée)** (rocket) engine; **2** (produit chimique) propellant.

■ **~ à hélice** propeller; **~ à réaction** jet engine.

propulsif, -ive /pʀɔpylsif, iv/ *adj* propulsive.

propulsion /pʀɔpylsjɔ̃/ *nf* propulsion; **~ par réaction** jet propulsion; **à ~ nucléaire** nuclear-powered.

propylène /pʀɔpilɛn/ *nm* propylene.

prorata /pʀɔʀata/ *nm inv* proportion; **au ~ de** in proportion to, proportionally to; **distribuer les dividendes au ~** to distribute the dividends pro rata.

prorogatif, -ive /pʀɔʀɔgatif, iv/ *adj* [*décret, mesure*] of prolongation (*après n*).

prorogation /pʀɔʀɔgasjɔ̃/ *nf* **1** (de délai, durée) extension; (d'échéance) deferment; (de bail, passeport) renewal; **2** (de session, d'assemblée) adjournment.

proroger /pʀɔʀɔʒe/ [13] *vtr* **1** (reculer) to defer [*date, échéance*]; (prolonger) to renew [*contrat, passeport*]; (rallonger) to extend [*validité, délai*]; **2** (suspendre) to adjourn [*assemblée*].

prosaïque /pʀɔzaik/ *adj* [*existence, personnage*] prosaic.

prosaïquement /pʀɔzaikmɑ̃/ *adv* prosaically.

prosaïsme /pʀɔzaism/ *nm* mundaneness; **le ~ du quotidien** the mundaneness of the everyday.

prosateur /pʀɔzatœʀ/ *nm* prose writer.

proscription /pʀɔskʀipsjɔ̃/ *nf* **1** (interdiction) proscription; **2** Pol (exil) banishment; **frapper qn de ~** to impose banishment on sb.

proscrire /pʀɔskʀiʀ/ [67] *vtr* **1** (interdire) to ban [*œuvres, alcool, féculents*]; **2** Pol (bannir) to banish [*personne*].

proscrit, **~e** /pʀɔskʀi, it/ **I** *pp* ▸ **proscrire**.
II *pp adj* banned.
III *nm,f* outlaw; **une vie de ~** the life of an outlaw.

prose /pʀoz/ *nf* **1** (forme littéraire) prose; **poème en ~** prose poem; **2** hum (style personnel) prose style; (texte) masterpiece.

prosélyte /pʀozelit/ *nmf* proselyte.

prosélytisme /pʀozelitism/ *nm* proselytizing; **faire du ~ politique/féministe** to try to convert people to one's politics/to feminism.

prosodie /pʀɔzɔdi/ *nf* prosody.

prosodique /pʀɔzɔdik/ *adj* prosodic.

prosopopée /pʀɔzɔpɔpe/ *nf* prosopopeia.

prospect /pʀɔspɛ(kt)/ *nm* **1** (en urbanisme) *minimum legal distance between two buildings*; **2** Comm prospective buyer.

prospecter /pʀɔspɛkte/ [1] *vtr* **1** Comm (pour vendre) to canvass [*région, clientèle*]; **2** (pour trouver) to prospect; **~ un sol pour y trouver du pétrole** to prospect for oil in an area of ground; **3** (examiner) to scrutinize [*fichier*]; **~ les petites annonces** to search through ou trawl the small ads.

prospecteur, **-trice** /pʀɔspɛktœʀ, tʀis/ *nm,f* **1** Comm canvasser; **2** (de terrain) prospector; **3** (d'idées) explorer.

prospecteur-placier, *pl* **prospecteurs-placiers** /pʀɔspɛktœʀplasje/ ▸ **510** *nm* ≈ employment officer.

prospectif, **-ive** /pʀɔspɛktif, iv/ **I** *adj* long-term.
II prospective *nf* futurology.

prospection /pʀɔspɛksjɔ̃/ *nf* **1** Comm (de clientèle, région) canvassing; **2** Géol prospecting.

prospective ▸ **prospectif**.

prospectus /pʀɔspɛktys/ *nm inv* leaflet.

prospère /pʀɔspɛʀ/ *adj* [*société, personne*] thriving; [*année, saison*] prosperous.

prospérer /pʀɔspeʀe/ [14] *vi* [*entreprise, plante, personne*] to thrive.

prospérité /pʀɔspeʀite/ *nf* prosperity; **en pleine ~** (fortune) prosperous; (santé) in flourishing health.

prostaglandine /pʀɔstaglɑ̃din/ *nf* prostaglandin.

prostate /pʀɔstat/ *nf* prostate (gland).

prostatectomie /pʀɔstatɛktɔmi/ *nf* prostatectomy.

prostatique /pʀɔstatik/ **I** *adj* (de la prostate) prostatic; (concernant la prostate) prostate (*épith*).
II *nm* prostate patient.

prostatite /pʀɔstatit/ ▸ **271** *nf* prostatitis.

prosternation /pʀɔstɛʀnasjɔ̃/ *nf* **1** lit prostration (**devant** before); **2** fig self-abasement (**devant** in front of).

prosternement /pʀɔstɛʀnəmɑ̃/ *nm* **1** (attitude) prostrate position; **2** (action) prostration (**devant** before).

prosterner: **se prosterner** /pʀɔstɛʀne/ [1] *vpr* **1** lit to prostrate oneself (**devant** before); **être prosterné devant l'autel** to be prostrate before the altar; **2** fig to grovel (**devant** to).

prostitué /pʀɔstitɥe/ ▸ **510** *nm* male prostitute GB, prostitute US.

prostituée /pʀɔstitɥe/ ▸ **510** *nf* prostitute.

prostituer /pʀɔstitɥe/ [1] **I** *vtr* **1** lit to send [sb] out to work as a prostitute; **2** fig to prostitute [*talent*].
II se prostituer *vpr* lit, fig to prostitute oneself.

prostitution /pʀɔstitysjɔ̃/ *nf* lit, fig prostitution.

prostration /pʀɔstʀasjɔ̃/ *nf* Méd, Relig prostration; **un état de ~** a state of shock.

prostré, **~e** /pʀɔstʀe/ *adj* gén prostrate; Méd prostrated.

protagoniste /pʀɔtagɔnist/ *nmf* protagonist.

protecteur, **-trice** /pʀɔtɛktœʀ, tʀis/ **I** *adj* **1** (qui protège) protective; **crème protectrice** protective cream; **sous l'œil ~ de leur père** under the protective gaze of their father; **une mère trop protectrice** an overprotective mother; **2** (supérieur) [*ton, air*] patronizing.
II *nm,f* protector; **~ de la nature** protector of nature; **~ des arts** patron of the arts.
III *nm* Hist protector.

protection /pʀɔtɛksjɔ̃/ *nf* **1** (action de protéger) protection (**contre** against); **~ de l'environnement** protection of the environment; **~ électrique/thermique** electric/thermal protection; **assurer la ~ de qn** to ensure sb's protection; **être sous la ~ de qn** to be under sb's protection; **être sous la ~ de la police** to be under police protection; **être sous la ~ de la loi** to be protected by the law; **être sous haute ~** to be under tight security; **de ~** [*écran, lunettes, grille, mesures*] protective; [*zone, système, indice*] protection; **l'indice de ~ d'une crème solaire** the protection factor of a sun cream; **2** (dispositif qui protège) protective device; **3** (appui) **bénéficier de ~s** to have friends in high places.
■ **~ civile** civil defence[GB]; **~ féminine** sanitary protection; **~ maternelle et infantile**, **PMI** ≈ mother and infant welfare; **~ rapprochée** bodyguard; **~ sociale** social welfare system; **~ solaire** Cosmét sun cream.

protectionnisme /pʀɔtɛksjɔnism/ *nm* protectionism; **~ d'État** state protectionism.

protectionniste /pʀɔtɛksjɔnist/ *adj, nmf* protectionist.

protectorat /pʀɔtɛktɔʀa/ *nm* protectorate.

protégé, **~e** /pʀɔteʒe/ *nm,f* protégé.

protège-cahier, *pl* **~s** /pʀɔtɛʒkaje/ *nm* exercise-book cover.

protège-dents /pʀɔtɛʒdɑ̃/ *nm inv* Sport gumshield.

protège-matelas /pʀɔtɛʒmatla/ *nm inv* mattress cover.

protéger /pʀɔteʒe/ [15] **I** *vtr* **1** (préserver) to protect [*espèce, frontière, droit*] (**contre** against; **de** from); **se sentir protégé** to feel protected; **le vaccin protège pour dix ans** the vaccine provides protection for ten years; **2** (favoriser) to encourage, to promote [*art, sport, artisanat*].
II se protéger *vpr* to protect oneself (**de** from; **contre** against).

protège-slip, *pl* **~s** /pʀɔtɛʒslip/ *nm* pantyliner.

protège-tibia, *pl* **~s** /pʀɔtɛʒtibja/ *nm* shinpad, shinguard.

protéide /pʀɔteid/ *nm* protein.

protéiforme /pʀɔteifɔʀm/ *adj* protean.

protéine /pʀɔtein/ *nf* protein.

protéique /pʀɔteik/ *adj* protein (*épith*), proteinic spéc.

protestable /pʀɔtɛstabl/ *adj* Jur liable to protest (*après n*).

protestant, **~e** /pʀɔtɛstɑ̃, ɑ̃t/ *adj, nm,f* Protestant.

protestantisme /pʀɔtɛstɑ̃tism/ *nm* Protestantism.

protestataire /pʀɔtɛstatɛʀ/ **I** *adj* [*personne*] protesting (*épith*); [*défilé, mouvement, parti, vote*] protest (*épith*).
II *nmf* protester.

protestation /pʀɔtɛstasjɔ̃/ *nf* **1** (réclamation) protest (**contre** against); **en signe de ~** as a (mark of) protest; **paroles/gestes de ~** words/gestures of protest; **2** liter (assurance) protestation; **~s d'amitié** protestations of friendship; **3** Jur protesting.

protester /pʀɔtɛste/ [1] **I** *vtr* Jur to protest [*effet, billet*].
II protester de *vtr ind* **~ de son innocence** to protest one's innocence.
III *vi* to protest (**contre** against; **auprès de** to).

protêt /pʀɔtɛ/ *nm* protest; **~ faute de paiement** protest on nonpayment; **~ faute d'acceptation** protest on nonacceptance.

prothèse /pʀɔtɛz/ *nf* **1** Méd (appareil) gén prosthesis spéc; (membre artificiel) artificial limb; (dentier) dentures (*pl*), false teeth (*pl*); **~ auditive** hearing aid; **~ de la hanche** hip replacement; **2** (technique, spécialisation) prosthetics (+ *v sg*); Dent prosthodontics (+ *v sg*).

prothésiste /pʀɔtezist/ ▸ **510** *nmf* gén prosthetist; **~ dentaire** prosthodontist.

prothrombine /pʀɔtʀɔ̃bin/ *nf* prothrombin.

protide /pʀɔtid/ *nm* protein.

protocolaire /pʀɔtɔkɔlɛʀ/ *adj* (cérémonieux) formal; (officiel) official; **question ~** question of protocol; **de façon peu ~** unceremoniously.

protocole /pʀɔtɔkɔl/ *nm* **1** (cérémonial) formalities (*pl*); (d'État) protocol; **sans ~** gén informally; hum unceremoniously; **2** Pol (accord) protocol; **~ d'accord** draft agreement; **3** (méthode) gén procedure; Ordinat protocol; (liste de conventions) style guide.

proton /pʀɔtɔ̃/ *nm* proton.

protoplasme /pʀɔtɔplasm/ *nm* protoplasm.

protoplasmique /pʀɔtɔplasmik/ *adj* protoplasmic.

prototype /pʀɔtɔtip/ *nm* prototype.

protoxyde /pʀɔtɔksid/ *nm* protoxide; **~ d'azote** nitrous oxide.

protozoaire /pʀɔtɔzɔɛʀ/ *nm* protozoan.

protubérance /pʀɔtybeʀɑ̃s/ *nf* gén bump, protuberance sout; Anat protuberance spéc; **~s solaires** solar prominences.

protubérant, **~e** /pʀɔtybeʀɑ̃, ɑ̃t/ *adj* gén protruding, protuberant sout; [*estomac*] bulging; [*yeux*] protruding, bulging.

prou /pʀu/ *adv* **peu ou ~** more or less.

proue /pʀu/ *nf* prow, bow(s).

prouesse /pʀuɛs/ *nf* lit feat; iron exploit; **faire** or **réaliser une ~** to perform a feat.

prout○ /pʀut/ *nm* fart○; **faire un ~** to fart○, to break wind.

prouvable /pʀuvabl/ *adj* provable.

prouver /pʀuve/ [1] **I** *vtr* **1** (établir la réalité de) to prove; **ton hypothèse reste à ~** your hypothesis is yet to be proved; **il faudrait qu'il accepte, et ça n'est pas prouvé**○ he has to accept and there's no guarantee that he will; **~ par l'absurde** to prove by reductio ad absurdum; **~ à qn que** to prove to sb that; **~ qch à qn** to prove sth to sb; **2** (indiquer) to show; **tout prouve qu'il est sincère** everything shows that he's sincere; **3** (exprimer) to demonstrate [*sentiment*].
II se prouver *vpr* **1** (à soi-même) **elle cherche à se ~ qu'elle a raison** she's trying to prove to herself that she's right; **2** (être démontré) **un axiome ne se prouve pas** an axiom cannot be proved; **3** (l'un l'autre) **ils se sont prouvé qu'ils s'aimaient** they demonstrated their love for one another.
IDIOMES **n'avoir plus rien à ~** to have proved oneself.

provenance /pʀɔvnɑ̃s/ *nf* origin; **indiquer la ~ des marchandises** to indicate the country of origin of the goods; **un bateau de ~ inconnue** a boat whose country of origin is unknown; **en ~ de** [*marchandise, personne, menace*] from; **le train 217 en ~**

de Roanne à destination de Grenoble train number 217 from Roanne to Grenoble.

provençal, **~e**, *mpl* **-aux** /pʀɔvɑ̃sal, o/ I ▶692 *adj* Provençal; **à la ~e** Culin (à la) Provençale.
II ▶462 *nm* Ling Provençal.

Provençal, **~e**, *mpl* **-aux** /pʀɔvɑ̃sal, o/ *nm,f* Provençal.

Provence /pʀɔvɑ̃s/ ▶692 *nprf* **la ~** Provence.

Provence-Alpes-Côte d'Azur /pʀɔvɑ̃salpkotdazyʀ/ ▶692 *nprf* **la région ~** Provence-Alpes-Côte d'Azur.

provende /pʀɔvɑ̃d/ *nf* feed.

provenir /pʀɔvniʀ/ [36] *vi* **1** [*marchandise, importation, capitaux, profit*] to come (**de** from); **les tableaux proviennent de collections privées** the paintings come from private collections; **la viande provenant de France** meat from France; **2** [*situation, déséquilibre*] to stem (**de** from).

proverbe /pʀɔvɛʀb/ *nm* proverb; **le livre des Proverbes** Bible the Book of Proverbs; **comme dit le ~** as the saying goes; **passer en ~** to become proverbial.

proverbial, **~e**, *mpl* **-iaux** /pʀɔvɛʀbjal, o/ *adj* proverbial.

proverbialement /pʀɔvɛʀbjalmɑ̃/ *adv* proverbially.

providence /pʀɔvidɑ̃s/ I *nf* **1** salvation; **être la ~ de qn** to be sb's salvation; **2** Relig providence.
II **(-)providence** (*in compounds*) **État-~** welfare state; **remède-~** heaven-sent remedy.

Providence /pʀɔvidɑ̃s/ *nf* Providence.

providentiel, **-ielle** /pʀɔvidɑ̃sjɛl/ *adj* providential.

providentiellement /pʀɔvidɑ̃sjɛlmɑ̃/ *adv* providentially.

province /pʀɔvɛ̃s/ *nf* **1** (région) province; **2** (pays hormis la capitale) **la ~** the provinces (*pl*); **vivre/s'installer en ~** to live/settle in the provinces; **ville de ~** provincial town; **elle sort de sa ~, elle arrive du fond de sa ~** pej she's up from the country.
■ **Provinces Maritimes** Maritime Provinces; **Provinces des Prairies** Prairie Provinces.

provincial, **~e**, *mpl* **-iaux** /pʀɔvɛ̃sjal, o/ I *adj* provincial.
II *nm,f* provincial; **les provinciaux** people from the provinces.
III *nm* Relig provincial.

provincialisme /pʀɔvɛ̃sjalism/ *nm* provincialism.

proviseur /pʀɔvizœʀ/ *nm* headteacher GB ou principal US (*of a lycée*).

provision /pʀɔvizjɔ̃/ I *nf* **1** (de nourriture, conserves, bois, papier) stock, supply; (d'eau) supply; **faire ~ de qch** to stock up with sth, to lay in a stock ou supplies of sth; **faire ~ d'énergie** [*personne*] to build up a reserve of energy; **2** Comm, Fin (acompte) deposit; (sur un compte en banque) credit (balance); **3** Jur (arrhes) retainer, retaining fee.
II **provisions** *nfpl* shopping ₵; **faire ses ~s, aller aux ~s**○ to go shopping; **sac à ~s** shopping bag; **placard à ~s** food cupboard.

provisionnel, **-elle** /pʀɔvizjɔnɛl/ *adj* provisional.

provisoire /pʀɔvizwaʀ/ I *adj* [*accord, bilan, gouvernement, jugement*] provisional; [*solution, mesure*] provisional, temporary; [*construction, installation, situation*] temporary; **à titre ~** on a temporary basis.
II *nm* **s'installer dans le ~** to become settled in a temporary situation; **c'est du ~ qui dure** it's a case of the temporary become permanent.

provisoirement /pʀɔvizwaʀmɑ̃/ *adv* provisionally.

provitamine /pʀɔvitamin/ *nf* provitamin.

provocant, **~e** /pʀɔvɔkɑ̃, ɑ̃t/ *adj* provocative.

provocateur, **-trice** /pʀɔvɔkatœʀ, tʀis/ I *adj* provocative.
II *nm,f* agitator, agent provocateur sout.

provocation /pʀɔvɔkasjɔ̃/ *nf* provocation (**à l'égard de** to); **c'est de la ~!** he's/she's etc just being provocative!; **faire de la ~** to be provocative.

provoquer /pʀɔvɔke/ [1] *vtr* **1** (causer) to cause [*accident, explosion, dégâts, mort*]; to arouse [*intérêt, curiosité*]; to provoke [*réaction, gaieté, colère*]; to trigger off [*discussion*]; to prompt [*explications, aveux*]; **~ une rencontre entre** to set up a meeting between; **2** (défier) to provoke; **~ qn en duel** to challenge sb to a duel; **3** (déclencher) **~ l'accouchement** to induce labour; **4** (exciter sexuellement) to arouse.

proxénète /pʀɔksenɛt/ *nm* procurer.

proxénétisme /pʀɔksenetism/ *nm* procuring sout; **inculpé de ~** Jur charged with living off immoral earnings.

proximité /pʀɔksimite/ *nf* **1** (voisinage) nearness, proximity; **à ~** nearby, close by; **un commerce** or **magasin de ~** a corner shop GB, a convenience store US; **le commerce de ~** corner shops (*pl*) GB, convenience stores (*pl*) US; **à ~ de** near, close to; **2** (imminence) imminence; **à cause de la ~ de Noël** because it is so close to Christmas.

prude /pʀyd/ I *adj* prudish.
II *nf* prude.

prudemment /pʀydamɑ̃/ *adv* [*conduire, observer*] carefully; [*réagir, admettre, progresser, avancer, attendre*] cautiously.

prudence /pʀydɑ̃s/ *nf* caution, prudence fml; **donner des conseils de ~** to advise caution; **faire preuve de ~** to show caution; **inciter à la ~** to call for caution; **~ verbale** verbal caution; **avec ~** [*avancer, parler, réagir*] cautiously; [*manier, utiliser*] with caution; **avec la plus grande ~** with the greatest caution; **par ~** as a precaution; **redoubler de ~** to be doubly careful; **manquer de ~** to be imprudent; **automobilistes, ~!** drivers, beware!
IDIOMES **~ est mère de sûreté** Prov better safe than sorry Prov.

prudent, **~e** /pʀydɑ̃, ɑ̃t/ *adj* **1** (soucieux de sa sécurité) careful; **on n'est jamais trop ~** you can't be too careful; **ce n'est pas ~ de faire** it isn't safe to do; **2** (réservé) [*candidat, attitude, déclaration*] cautious (**dans** in; **sur** on, about); **se montrer ~ dans son analyse/ses prévisions** to appear cautious in one's analysis/one's forecasts; **il faut être ~** one must be cautious; **3** (sage) wise; **il est ~ de réserver/d'arriver tôt** it would be wise to book/to arrive early; **juger ~ de ne pas accepter/de ne rien dire** to think it wise not to accept/not to say anything; **tu as raison, c'est plus ~** you're right, it's wiser.

pruderie /pʀydʀi/ *nf* prudishness, prudery.

prud'homal, **~e**, *mpl* **-aux** /pʀydɔmal, o/ *adj* of an industrial tribunal (*après n*) GB, of a labor relations board (*après n*) US.

prud'homme /pʀydɔm/ *nm* ≈ member of an industrial tribunal GB ou of a labor relations board US; **Conseil des ~s** ≈ industrial tribunal GB, labor relations board US.

prudhommesque /pʀydɔmɛsk/ *adj* pompous.

prune /pʀyn/ I ▶193 *adj inv* plum-coloured[GB].
II *nf* (fruit) plum; (eau-de-vie) plum brandy.
IDIOMES **des ~s**●! no way○!; **pour des ~s**○ for nothing.

pruneau, *pl* **~x** /pʀyno/ *nm* **1** (fruit) prune; **2**● (balle) slug○, bullet.

prunelle /pʀynɛl/ *nf* **1** (fruit) sloe; **2** (liqueur) ≈ sloe gin; **3** Anat pupil; **4** (œil) eye.
IDIOMES **jouer de la ~** to give come-hither looks; **j'y tiens comme à la ~ de mes yeux** it's the apple of my eye.

prunellier /pʀynelje/ *nm* blackthorn.

prunier /pʀynje/ *nm* plum (tree).
IDIOMES **secouer qn comme un ~** to shake sb until their teeth rattle.

prunus /pʀynys/ *nm* prunus.

prurigineux, **-euse** /pʀyʀiʒinø, øz/ *adj* pruriginous.

prurigo /pʀyʀigo/ ▶271 *nm* prurigo.

prurit /pʀyʀit/ *nm* pruritus.

Prusse /pʀys/ Hist *nprf* Prussia.
IDIOMES **travailler pour le roi de ~** to work for nothing.

prussien, **-ienne** /pʀysjɛ̃, ɛn/ I *adj* Prussian; **à la prussienne** in the Prussian manner.
II *nm* (soldat) Prussian.

prussique† /pʀysik/ *adj* [*acide*] prussic.

prytanée /pʀitane/ *nm* Mil *school reserved for children of the military.*

PS /peɛs/ *nm* **1** Pol *abbr* ▶ **parti**; **2** (*written abbr* = **post-scriptum**) PS.

psalmiste /psalmist/ *nm* psalmist.

psalmodie /psalmɔdi/ *nf* **1** Relig psalmody; **2** fig, littér chanting.

psalmodier /psalmɔdje/ [2] I *vtr* to chant [*texte*].
II *vi* **1** Relig (réciter) to say psalms; (chanter) to chant psalms; **2** gén to chant.

psaume /psom/ *nm* psalm; **le livre des Psaumes** Bible the Book of Psalms.

psautier /psotje/ *nm* Psalter.

pseudo- /psødo/ *préf* pseudo; **~-scientifique** pseudo-scientific; **~-philosophique** pseudo-philosophical; **~-équilibre** so-called balance; **~-savant** self-styled scientist.

pseudonyme /psødɔnim/ *nm* pseudonym; **sous un ~** under a pseudonym; **sous le ~ d'Ajar** under the pseudonym Ajar.

psi /psi/ *nm inv* psi.

psitt /psit/ *excl* psst!

psittacisme /psitasism/ *nm* parrotry.

psittacose /psitakoz/ ▶271 *nf* psittacosis.

psoriasis /psɔʀjazis/ ▶271 *nm inv* psoriasis.

psy○ /psi/ *nmf* (*abbr* = **psychanalyste**) shrink○, psychoanalyst.

psychanalyse /psikanaliz/ *nf* psychoanalysis; **faire une ~** to have psychoanalysis, to be in (psycho)analysis; (d'une œuvre) psychoanalytical criticism.

psychanalyser /psikanalize/ [1] *vtr* to psychoanalyse[GB] [*personne*]; to make a psychoanalytical study of [*texte*]; **se faire ~** to get oneself psychoanalysed[GB].

psychanalyste /psikanalist/ ▶510 *nmf* psychoanalyst.

psychanalytique /psikanalitik/ *adj* psychoanalytic(al).

psyché /psiʃe/ *nf* **1** (miroir) cheval glass; **2** Psych psyche.

Psyché /psiʃe/ *npr* Psyche.

psychédélique /psikedelik/ *adj* psychedelic.

psychédélisme /psikedelism/ *nm* **1** Méd psychedelic state; **2** (phénomène) psychedelia.

psychiatre /psikjatʀ/ ▶510 *nmf* psychiatrist.

psychiatrie /psikjatʀi/ *nf* psychiatry; **le service de ~** the psychiatric department.

psychiatrique /psikjatʀik/ *adj* psychiatric.

psychique /psiʃik/ *adj* [*activité, troubles*] mental.

psychisme /psiʃism/ *nm* psyche.

psycho○ /psiko/ *nf* psychology; **il a fait ~** he studied psychology.

psychodrame /psikodʀam/ *nm* **1** Psych psychodrama; **2** (drame) drama.

psycholinguistique /psikolɛ̃gɥistik/ *nf* psycholinguistics (+ *v sg*).

psychologie /psikɔlɔʒi/ *nf* **1** (discipline) psychology; **~ du développement/sociale** developmental/social psychology;

licence de ~ degree in psychology; **2** (intuition) (psychological) insight; **3** (mentalité) psychology.
psychologique /psikɔlɔʒik/ *adj* psychological; **c'est ~!** it's all in the mind!, it's psychological!
psychologiquement /psikɔlɔʒikmɑ̃/ *adv* psychologically.
psychologue /psikɔlɔg/ **I** *adj* **il n'est pas très ~** he's not much of a psychologist.
II ▶510 *nmf* psychologist.
psychométrie /psikometʀi/ *nf* psychometrics (+ *v sg*).
psychométrique /psikometʀik/ *adj* psychometric.
psychomoteur, -trice /psikɔmɔtœʀ, tʀis/ *adj* psychomotor.
psychopathe /psikɔpat/ *nmf* **1** (atteint de psychopathie) psychopath; **2**† (malade mental) mentally ill person.
psychopathie /psikɔpati/ *nf* psychopathy.
psychopathologie /psikopatɔlɔʒi/ *nf* psychopathology.
psychopédagogie /psikopedagɔʒi/ *nf* educational psychology.
psychophysiologie /psikofizjɔlɔʒi/ *nf* psychophysiology.
psychoprophylactique /psikopʀɔfilaktik/ *adj* **accouchement ~** natural childbirth.
psychose /psikoz/ *nf* **1** Méd, Psych psychosis; **2** gén (obsession) **~ du cambriolage/de la guerre** obsessive fear of robbery/of war; **~ collective** mass panic.
psychosensoriel, -ielle /psikosɑ̃sɔʀjɛl/ *adj* psychosensory.
psychosocial, ~e, *mpl* **-iaux** /psikosɔsjal, o/ *adj* psychosocial.
psychosociologie /psikosɔsjɔlɔʒi/ *nf* psychosociology.
psychosociologue /psikosɔsjɔlɔg/ ▶510 *nmf* social psychologist.
psychosomatique /psikosɔmatik/ **I** *adj* psychosomatic.
II *nf* psychosomatic medicine.
psychotechnicien, -ienne /psikotɛknisjɛ̃, ɛn/ ▶510 *nm,f* psychotechnician.
psychotechnique /psikotɛknik/ **I** *adj* [*tests*] psychotechnic(al).
II *nf* psychotechnics (+ *v sg*).
psychothérapeute /psikoteʀapøt/ ▶510 *nmf* psychotherapist.
psychothérapie /psikoteʀapi/ *nf* psychotherapy; **faire une ~** to be in ou have (psycho)therapy.
psychothérapique /psikoteʀapik/ *adj* psychotherapeutic.
psychotique /psikɔtik/ *adj, nmf* psychotic.
psychotrope /psikɔtʀɔp/ **I** *adj* [*médicament*] psychotropic, psychoactive.
II *nm* psychotropic drug.
PTAV *written abbr* ▶ **poids.**
PTC *written abbr* ▶ **poids.**
ptérodactyle /pteʀɔdaktil/ *nm* pterodactyl.
Ptolémée /ptɔleme/ *npr* Ptolemy.
ptôse /ptoz/ *nf* ptosis; **des ~s** ptoses.
ptôsis /ptozis/ *nm inv* ptosis.
PTT /petete/ *nfpl* (*abbr* = **Administration des postes et télécommunications et de la télédiffusion**) *former French postal and telecommunication service.*
ptyaline /ptialin/ *nf* ptyalin.
ptyalisme /ptialism/ *nm* Méd ptyalism.
puant, ~e /pɥɑ̃, ɑ̃t/ *adj* **1** lit [*bêtes*] stinking; [*fromage*] smelly; **2**○ fig, péj (déplaisant) **un type ~** an incredibly arrogant guy○; **~ de fierté** disgustingly proud.
puanteur /pɥɑ̃tœʀ/ *nf* stench.
pub[1] /pœb/ *nm* pub.
pub[2]○ /pyb/ *nf*: *abbr* ▶ **publicité.**
pubère /pybɛʀ/ *adj* pubescent.
puberté /pybɛʀte/ *nf* puberty; **à la ~** at puberty.
pubien, -ienne /pybjɛ̃, ɛn/ *adj* pubic.
pubis /pybis/ *nm inv* (région) pubes; (os) pubis.
public, -ique /pyblik/ **I** *adj* [*lieu, vente, argent*] public; [*école, enseignement*] state (*épith*) GB, public US; [*entreprise, chaîne*] state-owned (*épith*); **rendre qch ~** to make sth public; **la dette publique** the national debt; **hôpital ~** state-run hospital; **les cours sont ~s** the lectures are open to the public; **en audience publique** in open court; **homme** or **personnage ~** public figure; **femme** or **fille publique** prostitute.
II *nm* **1** (tout le monde) public; **en ~** in public; **ouvert au ~** open to the public; **'interdit au ~'** 'no admittance'; **'avis au ~'** 'public notice'; **porter qch à la connaissance du ~** to make sth public; ▶ **grand**; **2** (de spectacle, conférence, d'émission) audience; (de manifestation sportive) spectator; **s'adresser à un ~ jeune/un large ~** to be directed at a young audience/a wide audience; **il lui faut un ~** he/she has to have an audience; **être bon ~** to be easily pleased; **être mauvais ~** to be hard to please; **tous ~s** for all ages; **on entendait des rires dans le ~** there was laughter in the audience; **3** (lecteurs) readership; **4** (adeptes) **avoir un ~** to have a following; **elle ne veut pas décevoir son ~** she doesn't want to disappoint her fans ou public; **5** Écon **le ~** the public sector.
publicain /pyblikɛ̃/ *nm* Antiq publican.
publication /pyblikasjɔ̃/ *nf* **1** (parution) publication; **date de ~** date of publication, publication date; **suspendre sa ~** [*périodique*] to suspend publication; **la ~ du livre est prévue pour mai** the book is due to be published ou to come out in May; **2** (ouvrage) publication; **~s universitaires/obscènes** academic/obscene publications.
■ **~ assistée par ordinateur, PAO** desktop publishing, DTP; **~ des bans (de mariage)** publishing the banns.
publiciste /pyblisist/ **I** ▶510 *nmf* (personne) advertising executive, adman○; **elle est ~** she's in advertising.
II *nm* (entreprise) advertising agency.
publicitaire /pyblisitɛʀ/ **I** *adj* [*campagne, budget*] advertising; [*objet, vente, voiture, jeu*] promotional; **cadeau ~** free gift.
II ▶510 *nmf* (personne) advertising executive; **il est ~** he's in advertising.
III *nm* (société) advertising agency.
publicité /pyblisite/ *nf* **1** (activité, profession) advertising; **il travaille dans la ~** he's in advertising; **faire de la ~ pour un produit** to advertise a product; **service (de) ~** advertising department; **coup de ~** publicity stunt; **c'était un beau coup de ~** it was good publicity; **2** (annonce) Presse advertisement, advert GB, ad; Cin, Radio, TV commercial, advertisement, advert GB, ad; **passer une ~ à la télévision/radio** to run an advert GB ou ad on television/the radio; **3** (diffusion) publicity; **donner** or **faire de la ~ à qn/qch** to give sb/sth publicity; **faire une mauvaise ~ à qn/qch** to give sb/sth a bad press.
■ **~ comparative** comparative advertising; **~ des débats** open debate; **~ directe** direct mail advertising; **~ institutionnelle** corporate advertising; **~ sur les lieux de vente, PLV** point-of-sale advertising; **~ mensongère** misleading advertising; **~ des prix** publishing of prices; **~ rédactionnelle** advertising feature GB, reading notice US.
publier /pyblije/ [2] *vtr* to publish [*livre, revue, auteur*]; to issue ou release [*communiqué*]; **~ les bans** Admin to publish the banns; **se faire ~** to get published.
publiphone® /pyblifɔn/ *nm* public telephone, payphone; **~ à pièces/carte** coin-/card-operated phone.
publipostage /pyblipɔstaʒ/ *nm* **1** (principe) direct mail advertising; **2** (opération) mail shot; **3** (documents) mailing pack.
publiquement /pyblikmɑ̃/ *adv* publicly.
puce /pys/ **I** ▶193 *adj inv* puce.
II *nf* **1** Zool flea; **2** (terme d'affection) **ma ~**○ my pet○, honey○ US; **3** ▶449 Jeux **jeu de ~** tiddlywinks (+ *v sg*); **4** Ordinat (silicon) chip.
■ **~ d'eau** water flea; **~ de sable** sand flea.
IDIOMES **ça m'a mis la ~ à l'oreille** that set me thinking; **se secouer les ~s**○ to stir one's stumps○ GB, to get the lead out○ US; **secoue-toi les ~s!** get a move on○!; **secouer les ~s à qn**○ (gronder) to give sb a good ticking off○ GB, to bawl sb out○.
puceau○, *pl* **~x** /pyso/ **I** *adj* **il est encore ~** he's still a virgin.
II *nm* virgin.
pucelage○ /pyslaʒ/ *nm* virginity.
pucelle /pysɛl/ **I**○ *adj* **être ~** to be a virgin.
II‡ *nf* virgin, maid†; **la Pucelle (d'Orléans)** the Maid of Orleans.
puceron /pysʀɔ̃/ *nm* aphid.
pucier● /pysje/ *nm* bed.
pudding /pudiŋ/ *nm* heavy fruit sponge.
pudeur /pydœʀ/ *nf* **1** (relative au corps) sense of modesty; **n'avoir aucune ~** to have no sense of modesty ou no shame; **blesser/offenser la ~ de qn** to offend sb's sense of decency; **outrage public à la ~** indecent exposure; **sans ~** shamelessly; **2** (relative aux sentiments) (considération) decency; (retenue) sense of propriety; **ayez la ~ de vous taire** have the decency to keep quiet; **par ~ elle ne pleura pas** her sense of propriety stopped her from crying.
pudibond, ~e /pydibɔ̃, ɔ̃d/ *adj* prudish.
pudibonderie /pydibɔ̃dʀi/ *nf* prudishness.
pudicité /pydisite/ *nf* liter modesty.
pudique /pydik/ *adj* modest, self-conscious; (discret) discreet.
pudiquement /pydikmɑ̃/ *adv* **1** (chastement) modestly; **2** (par timidité ou discrétion) discreetly; **3** (en termes pudiques) discreetly.
puer /pɥe/ [1] **I** *vtr* to stink of [*essence, gaz*]; **il pue le parvenu** he has upstart written all over him; **ça pue l'hypocrisie** it reeks of hypocrisy.
II *vi* to stink; **il puait des pieds** his feet stank.
puéricultrice /pɥeʀikyltʀis/ ▶510 *nf* pediatric nurse.
puériculture /pɥeʀikyltyʀ/ *nf* childcare.
puéril, ~e /pɥeʀil/ *adj* [*conduite, réaction*] childish; [*attitude, activité*] puerile.
puérilement /pɥeʀilmɑ̃/ *adv* [*réagir*] childishly; [*juger*] in a puerile manner.
puérilité /pɥeʀilite/ *nf* (de conduite) childishness; (d'attitude) puerility.
puerpéral, ~e, *mpl* **-aux** /pɥɛʀpeʀal, o/ *adj* puerperal; **fièvre ~e** puerperal fever.
pugilat /pyʒila/ *nm* lit fist fight; fig open combat.
pugiliste /pyʒilist/ *nm* pugilist.
pugnace /pygnas/ *adj* fml pugnacious.
pugnacité /pygnasite/ *nf* fml pugnacity.
puîné, ~e‡ /pɥine/ **I** *adj* younger.
II *nm,f* younger brother/sister.
puis /pɥi/ *adv* **1** (ensuite) then; **aller à Paris ~ à Milan** to go to Paris then to Milan; **et ~ il est parti** and then he left; **et ~?** then what?; **des pommes, des poires et ~ des pêches** apples, pears and peaches; **et ~ quoi encore**○**!** what(ever) next?; **2** (d'ailleurs) **et ~ je m'en fiche**○**!** anyway, I don't care!; **et ~ c'est facile de critiquer** anyway, it's easy to criticize; **il va être en colère? et ~ (après)?** he's going to be angry? so what?; **tu vas ranger ta chambre et ~ c'est tout!** you'll go and tidy your room and that's the end of the matter.
puisard /pɥizaʀ/ *nm* (égout) soakaway GB, sink hole US.
puisatier /pɥizatje/ ▶510 *nm* well-digger.
puiser /pɥize/ [1] *vtr* lit, fig **puiser qch dans qch** to draw sth from sth; **~ à pleines**

mains dans qch to draw heavily on sth; **~ dans ses économies/réserves** to draw on one's savings/reserves; **~ dans son porte-monnaie** to put one's hand in one's purse; **~ ses informations aux meilleures sources** to get one's information from the best sources.

puisque (**puisqu'** *before vowel or mute h*) /pɥisk(ə)/ *conj* **1** (attendu que) since; **~ c'est comme ça, je m'en vais** since it's like that I'm going; **puisqu'il pleut je reste ici** since ou as it's raining, I'm staying here; **2** (dans une phrase exclamative) **mais ~ je te dis que c'est impossible** but I'm telling you it's impossible; **mais puisqu'il te dit qu'il a peur** but he did tell you he's frightened.

puissance /pɥisɑ̃s/ **I** *nf* **1** Phys, Électrotech power; **la ~ d'un moteur** the power of an engine; **un amplificateur d'une ~ de 60 watts** a 60-watt amplifier; **une bombe d'une forte ~** a very powerful bomb; **mon aspirateur n'a pas assez de ~** my vacuum cleaner isn't powerful enough; **2** (intensité) (de lumière) intensity; (de son) volume; **régler la ~ d'une radio/lampe halogène** to adjust the volume on a radio/the intensity of a halogen lamp; **3** Math power; **dix ~ trois** ten to the power (of) three; **élever un nombre à la ~ neuf** to raise a number to the power (of) nine; **4** (pouvoir) power; **fonder** or **asseoir sa ~ sur qch** to build one's power on sth; **volonté de ~** will to power; **assassin/héros en ~** potential killer/hero; **5** (capacité) power; **la ~ militaire/nucléaire d'un pays** the military/nuclear power of a country; **leur ~ industrielle est supérieure à la nôtre** their industrial power is superior to ours; **ta ~ de concentration/d'imagination** your powers (*pl*) of concentration/imagination; **il a une ~ de travail remarquable** his capacity for work is remarkable; **6** (vigueur) power, strength; **7** (pays) power; **la première ~ nucléaire/commerciale du monde** the foremost nuclear/commercial power in the world; **une ~ étrangère** a foreign power; **une ancienne ~ coloniale** a former colonial power; **une grande ~** a superpower; **le sommet des grandes ~s** the great powers summit.

II puissances *nfpl* Relig **les ~s** the powers; **les ~s occultes** the occult powers; **les ~s infernales** or **des ténèbres** the powers of darkness; **les ~s célestes** the heavenly powers.

■ **~ administrative** Aut engine rating; **~ effective** effective power; **~ de feu** firepower; **~ fiscale** = **~ administrative**; **~ au frein** Aut brake horsepower; **~ nominale** Aut nominal horsepower; **~s d'argent** financial powers.

puissant, **~e** /pɥisɑ̃, ɑ̃t/ **I** *adj* **1** Tech [*moteur, véhicule, ordinateur, bombe, freins*] powerful; **2** (intense) [*voix*] powerful; [*sentiment, émotion*] strong; [*parfum, arôme*] hum powerful; **3** (fort) [*personne, animal, épaules, mâchoires, mouvement*] powerful; **un ~ athlète** a powerful athlete; **4** (influent) [*personne, pays, syndicat, secteur*] powerful; **un organisme très ~** a very powerful organization; **5** (efficace) [*antidote, détergent*] powerful.

II puissants *nmpl* **les ~s** the powerful, the mighty.

puits /pɥi/ *nm* **1** (d'eau) well; **~ de pétrole** oil well; **2** (conduit) shaft.

■ **~ d'aération** Mines ventilation shaft; **~ d'ascenseur** Constr lift GB ou elevator US shaft; **~ d'érudition** fount of knowledge; **~ de mine** mine shaft; **~ perdu** soakaway GB, sink hole US; **~ de science** = **~ d'érudition**.

pull○ /pyl/ *nm* (*abbr* = **pull-over**) jumper GB, sweater, pullover.

pullman /pylman/ *nm* Pullman.

pull-over, *pl* **~s** /pylɔvɛʀ/ *nm* jumper GB, sweater, pullover.

pullulement /pylylmɑ̃/ *nm* **1** (multiplication) proliferation; **2** (grand nombre) (d'insectes, de gens) swarm; (de fautes, problèmes) multitude.

pulluler /pylyle/ [1] *vi* **1** (se multiplier) to proliferate; **depuis dix ans les romans de mauvaise qualité pullulent** for the last ten years there has been an abundance of poor quality novels; **2** (grouiller) **les touristes/insectes pullulent dans la région** the area is swarming with tourists/insects; **les poissons pullulent dans la rivière** the river is teeming with fish; **les erreurs pullulent dans le texte** the text abounds with mistakes.

pulmonaire /pylmɔnɛʀ/ **I** *adj* [*maladie, infection*] lung (*épith*), pulmonary spéc; [*artère, veine*] pulmonary.

II *nf* Bot lungwort.

pulpe /pylp/ *nf* **1** (de fruit) pulp; (de pomme de terre) flesh; **2** Anat (de doigt) fleshy part; (de dent) pulp; **3** (pâte à papier) pulp; **réduire en ~** to pulp.

pulpeux, **-euse** /pylpø, øz/ *adj* [*corps, lèvres*] luscious; [*fruit*] pulpy.

pulsar /pylsaʀ/ *nm* pulsar.

pulsation /pylsasjɔ̃/ *nf* **1** Méd, Physiol (fait de battre) beating ₵, pulsation spéc; (battement) beat; **~s cardiaques** (rythme) heartbeat (*sg*); (battement) heartbeats; **2** Électrotech, Phys pulse.

pulser /pylse/ [1] *vtr* to blow [*air*]; **chauffage à air pulsé** hot air heating.

pulsion /pylsjɔ̃/ *nf* impulse, urge; **des ~s violentes** violent impulses ou urges; **~ de mort** death wish, death instinct spéc; **acheter par ~** to be an impulse buyer.

pulvérisable /pylveʀizabl/ *adj* [*liquide*] sprayable; [*matériau*] pulverable.

pulvérisateur /pylveʀizatœʀ/ *nm* gén spray; Agric sprayer.

pulvérisation /pylveʀizasjɔ̃/ *nf* **1** (de liquide) spraying; **'utiliser en ~s nasales'** 'for use as nasal spray'; **2** (de matériau) pulverization[GB]; **3** (d'investissements, de responsabilités) breaking up.

pulvériser /pylveʀize/ [1] **I** *vtr* **1** (projeter) to spray [*liquide*]; **2** (broyer) to pulverize [*solide*]; **3** (anéantir) to pulverize [*bâtiment, ennemi*]; to demolish○ [*argument*]; **4** (battre) Sport to shatter○ [*record*].

II se pulvériser *vpr* [*matériau*] to crumble (into powder).

pulvériseur /pylveʀizœʀ/ *nm* disc harrow.

pulvérulent, **~e** /pylveʀylɑ̃, ɑ̃t/ *adj* pulverulent.

puma /pyma/ *nm* puma.

punaise /pynɛz/ **I** *nf* **1** (pointe) drawing pin GB, thumbtack US; **2** Zool bug; **3**○ (femme méchante) pej bitchy woman; **c'est une vraie ~** she's really bitchy.

II○ *excl* (de surprise) blimey○! GB, gee○! US; (de dépit) heck○!

■ **~ des bois** stink bug; **~ des lits** bedbug; **~ de sacristie** pej churchy woman.

punaiser○ /pyneze/ [1] *vtr* to pin ou tack US [sth] up.

punch[1] /pɔ̃ʃ/ *nm* (boisson) punch; **boire du ~** to drink punch.

punch[2] /pœnʃ/ *nm* **1** (de boxeur) punch; **avoir du ~** to pack quite a punch; **2** (énergie) energy; (dynamisme) drive; **manquer de ~** [*slogan, film*] to lack punch; [*personne*] to lack drive; **avoir du ~** [*slogan, discours*] to be punchy○; [*personne*] to have drive.

puncheur /pœnʃœʀ/ *nm* **c'est un ~** lit he has a powerful punch; fig○ he's a (real) go-getter○.

punching-ball, *pl* **~s** /pœnʃiŋbol/ *nm* punchball GB, punching bag US.

punique /pynik/ *adj* Punic.

punir /pyniʀ/ [3] *vtr* gén, Jur, Scol to punish [*criminel, crime*]; **tu ne sors pas, tu es puni** you're not going out, you're being punished; **toute la classe est punie** the whole class is being punished; **être puni pour vol** to be punished for stealing; **il a été puni de sa paresse** he has been punished for his laziness; **je voulais qu'il ait des regrets mais c'est moi qui suis puni** I wanted him to feel sorry but it is me who is being punished.

punissable /pynisabl/ *adj* punishable (**de** by).

punitif, **-ive** /pynitif, iv/ *adj* punitive; **expédition punitive** punitive strike.

punition /pynisjɔ̃/ *nf* **1** (châtiment) punishment; **~ collective** collective punishment; **comme ~** or **pour ta ~ tu feras** as a punishment you will do; **donner** or **infliger une ~ à qn** to punish sb; **avoir une ~** to be punished; **2** (tâche) **il n'a pas fait sa ~** he hasn't done the task he was given as punishment.

punk /pœ̃k/ *adj, nmf* punk.

pupille /pypij/ **I** *nmf* (mineur sous tutelle) ward.

II *nf* Anat pupil.

■ **~ de l'État** child in care; **~ de la Nation** war orphan.

pupitre /pypitʀ/ *nm* **1** (tableau de commande) control panel; Ordinat console; **2** (de musicien) music stand; (de piano) music rest; **qui est au ~?** who's conducting?; **l'orchestre de la Scala de Milan avec, au ~, Arturo Toscanini** the orchestra of La Scala in Milan conducted by Arturo Toscanini; **3** (bureau) desk; **4** (d'orateur) lectern.

pupitreur, **-euse** /pypitʀœʀ, øz/ ▶510 *nm,f* Ordinat system operator.

pur, **~e** /pyʀ/ **I** *adj* **1** (sans mélange) [*substance, laine, héroïne, race*] pure; (non dilué) [*whisky, pastis*] straight; **c'est de l'or ~** it's pure gold; **un métal à l'état ~** metal in its pure state; **boire son vin ~** to drink one's wine undiluted; **une confiture ~ sucre** a jam with no artificial sweetening; **une confiture ~ fruit** a real fruit jam; **fromages ~ chèvre/vache** pure goat's/cow's milk cheese; **~ porc** [*saucisson*] pure pork (*épith*); **2** (non altéré) [*eau, air*] pure; [*diamant*] flawless; [*ciel*] clear; [*son, voix*] pure, clear; **respirer l'air ~** to breathe the pure air; **3** (sans fioritures) [*ligne, style*] pure; [*beauté*] unsullied; **4** (total) [*méchanceté, fantasme, vérité*] pure; [*coïncidence, plaisir, ignorance, folie, inconscience*] sheer; **c'est du ~ masochisme** it's sheer ou pure masochism; **en ~e perte** to no avail; **de ~e forme** token (*épith*); **question/propos de ~e forme** token question/words; **~ et simple** [*mensonge, refus, ignorance, élimination*] outright; **on envisage le retrait ~ et simple des troupes** they simply envisage the withdrawal of the troops; **c'est de la paresse/fiction ~e et simple** it's laziness/fiction, pure and simple; **~ et dur** hardline; **le militarisme ~ et dur** hardline militarism; **un militant ~ et dur** a hardline militant; **5** (théorique) [*sciences, recherche, mathématiques*] pure; **6** (d'origine) [*tradition*] true; **dans la ~e tradition populaire** in the true popular tradition; **un ~ produit de qch** lit, fig a typical product of sth; **un Parisien de ~e souche** a Parisian born and bred; **à l'état ~** [*génie, bêtise*] sheer; **c'est de la bêtise à l'état ~** it's sheer stupidity; **7** (sans défaut moral) [*personne, cœur*] pure.

II *nm,f* **1** (personne irréprochable) virtuous person; **2** (fidèle à un parti) hardliner; **les ~s et durs** the hardliners.

purée /pyʀe/ **I** *nf* Culin (de fruits, légumes) purée; (aliment trop cuit) pej mush; **~ (de pommes de terre)** mashed potatoes (*pl*); **~ de marrons/tomates** chestnut/tomato purée; **~ de carottes et de pommes de terre** purée of carrots and potatoes.

II○ *excl* heck○!

■ **~ en flocons** instant mash GB, instant mashed potatoes (*pl*); **~ de pois** (brouillard) pea souper GB, fog.

IDIOMES **être dans la ~**○ to be in a mess.

purement /pyʀmɑ̃/ *adv* purely; **~ et simplement** purely and simply.

pureté /pyʀte/ *nf* (de diamant, son, d'eau) purity; (de sentiment, personne) purity; (de forme, style) purity; **la ~ du style roman** the purity of the Roman style; **la ~ de l'air** the purity of the air.

purgatif, **-ive** /pyʀgatif, iv/ **I** *adj* purgative.
II *nm* purgative.

purgatoire /pyʀgatwaʀ/ *nm* Relig **le ~** purgatory; **faire son ~** fig to do one's penance; **cet enfant, c'est mon ~** fig this child was sent to try me.

purge /pyʀʒ/ *nf* **1** Méd purgative; **2** Pol purge; **3** Tech (de radiateur, freins) bleeding; (de tuyau) draining; **4** Jur redemption.

purger /pyʀʒe/ [13] **I** *vtr* **1** Méd to purge; **2** Tech to bleed [*radiateur, freins*]; to drain [*tuyau*]; to purify [*métal*]; **3** liter (débarrasser) to purge (**de** of); **4** Jur to serve [*peine*]; to redeem [*hypothèque*].
II se purger *vpr* [*personne*] to take a purgative.

purgeur /pyʀʒœʀ/ *nm* (de radiateur, tuyauterie) bleed valve; (de locomotive à vapeur) purge ou drain valve.

purifiant, **~e** /pyʀifjɑ̃, ɑ̃t/ *adj* [*air*] purifying; [*crème, lotion*] cleansing.

purificateur, **-trice** /pyʀifikatœʀ, tʀis/ **I** *adj* [*rite, cérémonie*] purificatory.
II *nm* **~ d'atmosphère** or **d'air** air purifier.

purification /pyʀifikasjɔ̃/ *nf* purification; **La Purification** the Purification.
■ **~ ethnique** ethnic cleansing.

purifier /pyʀifje/ [2] **I** *vtr* **1** gén to purify [*eau, air, sang*]; to cleanse [*peau*]; to purify [*langage*]; **2** (moralement) liter to purify [*personne, esprit*].
II se purifier *vpr* [*organisme, métal*] to purify itself; [*personne*] to cleanse oneself.

purin /pyʀɛ̃/ *nm* slurry.

purisme /pyʀism/ *nm* purism.

puriste /pyʀist/ *nmf* purist.

puritain, **~e** /pyʀitɛ̃, ɛn/ **I** *adj* (austère) puritanical; Relig Puritan.
II *nm,f* (rigoriste) puritan; Hist Relig Puritan.

puritanisme /pyʀitanism/ *nm* puritanism.

purpura /pyʀpyʀa/ *nm* purpura.

purpurin, **~e** /pyʀpyʀɛ̃, in/ ▶193 *adj* crimson.

pur-sang /pyʀsɑ̃/ *nm inv* thoroughbred, purebred.

purulence /pyʀylɑ̃s/ *nf* purulence.

purulent, **~e** /pyʀylɑ̃, ɑ̃t/ *adj* purulent.

pus /py/ *nm* pus.

pusillanime /pyzilanim/ *adj* pusillanimous.

pusillanimité /pyzilanimite/ *nf* pusillanimity.

pustule /pystyl/ *nf* pustule.

pustuleux, **-euse** /pystylø, øz/ *adj* pustular.

putain● /pytɛ̃/ **I** *nf* **1** (prostituée) offensive whore, hooker◑ injur; (femme facile) slag● injur GB, slut◑; **2** (juron) **~ de voiture/stylo** fucking● car/pen.
II *excl* fuck●!, fucking hell●!

putatif, **-ive** /pytatif, iv/ *adj* Jur [*enfant, père*] putative.

pute● /pyt/ *nf* **1** (prostituée) whore, hooker◑; (femme facile) slag● GB, slut◑; **faire la ~** lit to be a prostitute; fig to prostitute oneself; **2** fig (personne méchante) shit◑.

putois /pytwa/ *nm inv* **1** (animal) polecat; **2** (fourrure) skunk (fur).
IDIOMES **crier comme un ~** to scream one's head off.

putréfaction /pytʀefaksjɔ̃/ *nf* putrefaction; **odeur de ~** smell of rotting; **cadavre en état de ~** putrefying corpse.

putréfier: **se putréfier** /pytʀefje/ [2] *vpr* [*cadavre*] to putrefy; [*viande*] to rot.

putrescence /pytʀesɑ̃s/ *nf* putrescence sout.

putrescent, **~e** /pytʀesɑ̃, ɑ̃t/ *adj* [*chair*] putrescent sout; [*matière*] rotting.

putrescible /pytʀesibl/ *adj* putrescible sout.

putride /pytʀid/ *adj* lit, fig putrid.

putridité /pytʀidite/ *nf* (de matière) putridity; (d'écrit) foulness.

putsch /putʃ/ *nm inv* putsch.

putschiste /putʃist/ **I** *adj* [*officier*] involved in the putsch (*après n*).
II *nmf* **les ~s** those involved in the putsch.

Puy-de-Dôme /pɥiddom/ ▶692 *nprm* (département) **le ~** the Puy-de-Dôme.

puzzle /pœzl, pyzl/ *nm* Jeux jigsaw puzzle; fig jigsaw; **un ~ de 2000 pièces** a 2,000-piece jigsaw puzzle; **reconstituer un ~** to piece a jigsaw together.

PV○ /peve/ *nm inv* (*abbr* = **procès-verbal**) gén fine; (pour stationnement illégal) parking ticket; (pour excès de vitesse) speeding ticket; **payer ses ~** to pay one's fines; **attraper un ~** to get a ticket; **avoir un ~ pour stationnement illégal/excès de vitesse** to get a parking/speeding ticket.

PVC /pevese/ *nm* (*abbr* = **chlorure de polyvinyle**) PVC; **tuyaux en ~** PVC pipes.

pygargue /pigaʀg/ *nm* sea eagle.

Pygmalion /pigmaljɔ̃/ *npr* Pygmalion; **il a été leur ~** he made them.

pygmée /pigme/ *nmf* pygmy.

pyjama /piʒama/ *nm* pyjamas (*pl*) GB, pajamas (*pl*) US, pair of pyjamas GB ou pajamas US; **se mettre en ~** to put on one's pyjamas GB ou pajamas US; **sortir en ~** to go out in one's pyjamas GB ou pajamas US.

pylône /pilon/ *nm* Électrotech pylon; Radio, TV mast; Archit (de temple) pylon; (de pont) tower.

pylore /pilɔʀ/ *nm* pylorus.

pylorique /pilɔʀik/ *adj* pyloric.

pyorrhée /pjɔʀe/ *nf* pyorrhea.

pyramidal, **~e**, *mpl* **-aux** /piʀamidal, o/ *adj* **1** lit [*construction*] pyramid-shaped, pyramidal; fig [*hiérarchie*] pyramid (*épith*); **2** Anat pyramidal.

pyramide /piʀamid/ *nf* lit, fig pyramid; **~ des âges** age pyramid.

pyrénéen, **-éenne** /piʀeneɛ̃, ɛn/ ▶692 *adj* Pyrenean.

Pyrénéen, **-éenne** /piʀeneɛ̃, ɛn/ *nm,f* Pyrenean.

Pyrénées /piʀene/ ▶692 *nprfpl* **les ~** the Pyrenees.

Pyrénées-Atlantiques /piʀeneatlɑ̃tik/ ▶692 *nprfpl* (département) **les ~** the Pyrénées-Atlantiques.

Pyrénées-Orientales /piʀeneɔʀjɑ̃tal/ ▶692 *nprfpl* (département) **les ~** the Pyrénées-Orientales.

pyrex® /piʀɛks/ *nm inv* Pyrex®; **en ~** Pyrex (*épith*).

pyrite /piʀit/ *nf* (iron) pyrites, fool's gold.

pyrographe /piʀogʀaf/ *nm* heated point (*for pokerwork*).

pyrograver /piʀogʀave/ [1] *vtr* **~ un dessin** to make a design in pokerwork.

pyrograveur, **-euse** /piʀogʀavœʀ, øz/ ▶510 *nm,f* pokerwork artist.

pyrogravure /piʀogʀavyʀ/ *nf* pokerwork.

pyrolyse /piʀɔliz/ *nf* pyrolysis; **four à ~** self-cleaning oven.

pyromane /piʀɔman/ *nmf* **1** Jur arsonist; **2** Psych pyromaniac.

pyromanie /piʀɔmani/ *nf* pyromania.

pyromètre /piʀomɛtʀ/ *nm* pyrometer; **~ optique** optical pyrometer.

pyrométrie /piʀometʀi/ *nf* pyrometry.

pyrométrique /piʀometʀik/ *adj* [*cône*] pyrometric; **canne/sonde ~** pyrometer rod/probe.

pyrotechnicien, **-ienne** /piʀotɛknisjɛ̃, ɛn/ ▶510 *nm,f* pyrotechnist.

pyrotechnie /piʀotɛkni/ *nf* pyrotechnics (+ *v sg*).

pyrotechnique /piʀotɛknik/ *adj* pyrotechnic.

Pyrrhon /piʀɔ̃/ *npr* Pyrrho.

pyrrhonien, **-ienne** /piʀɔnjɛ̃, ɛn/ **I** *adj* Pyrrhonian.
II *nm,f* Pyrrhonist.

Pyrrhus /piʀys/ *npr* Pyrrhus; **victoire à la ~** Pyrrhic victory.

Pythagore /pitagɔʀ/ *npr* Pythagoras; **théorème de ~** Pythagoras' theorem, Pythagorean theorem US; **table de ~** multiplication table.

pythagoricien, **-ienne** /pitagɔʀisjɛ̃, ɛn/ *adj, nm,f* Pythagorean.

pythagorisme /pitagɔʀism/ *nm* Pythagoreanism.

pythie /piti/ *nf* **la ~** Pythia.

python /pitɔ̃/ *nm* python.
■ **~ réticulé** reticulated python; **~ royal** royal python; **~ vert** green python.

pythonisse /pitɔnis/ *nf* pythoness.

pyxide /piksid/ *nf* Archéol, Bot pyxis.

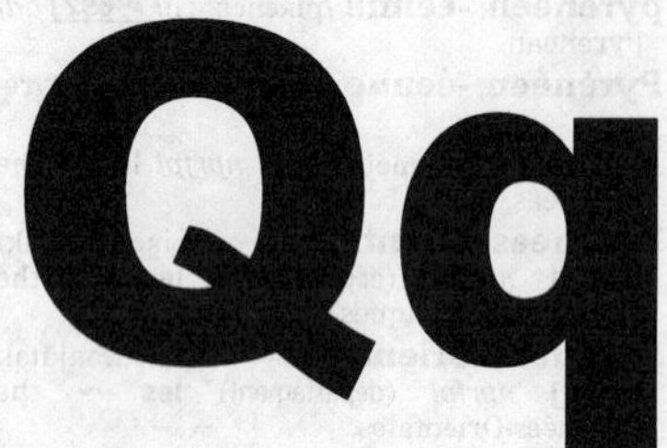

q, **Q** /ky/ *nm inv* q, Q.

Qatar /kataʀ/ ▶ **321** *nprm* Qatar.

qatari, **~e** /kataʀi/ ▶ **537** *adj* Qatari.

Qatari, **~e** /kataʀi/ ▶ **537** *nm,f* Qatari.

qcm /kyseɛm/ *nm* (*abbr* = **questionnaire à choix multiple**) multiple-choice questionnaire, mcq.

QG /kyʒe/ *nm*: *abbr* ▶ **quartier**.

QHS /kyaʃɛs/ *nm*: *abbr* ▶ **quartier**.

QI /kyi/ *nm* (*abbr* = **quotient intellectuel**) IQ.

qsp (*written abbr* = **quantité suffisante pour**) qs.

qu' ▶ **que**.

quadragénaire /kwadʀaʒenɛʀ/ **I** *adj* **être ~** to be in one's forties.

II *nmf* person in his/her forties.

quadragésime /kwadʀaʒezim/ *nf* Quadragesima.

quadrangle /kwadʀɑ̃gl/ *nm* quadrangle.

quadrangulaire /kwadʀɑ̃gylɛʀ/ *adj* quadrangular.

quadrant /kadʀɑ̃/ *nm* quadrant.

quadrature /kadʀatyʀ/ *nf* quadrature.

IDIOMES **c'est la ~ du cercle** it's like squaring the circle.

quadrette /kadʀɛt/ *nf* team of four boules players.

quadriceps /kwadʀisɛps/ *nm* quadriceps.

quadrichromie /kwadʀikʀɔmi/ *nf* four-colour[GB] printing process; **imprimer en ~** to print in four colours[GB].

quadriennal, **~e**, *mpl* **-aux** /kwadʀijɛnal, o/ *adj* **1** (de quatre ans) [*plan*] four-year (*épith*); **2** (tous les quatre ans) quadrennial.

quadrijumeaux /kwadʀiʒymo/ *adj mpl* quadrigeminal.

quadrilatère /kwadʀilatɛʀ/ *nm* quadrilateral.

quadrillage /kadʀijaʒ/ *nm* **1** (de papier) cross-ruling; **2** (occupation) **le ~ de la ville par l'armée** the taking of control of the town by the army; **le ~ du terrain** Mil the chequering of the terrain.

quadrille /kadʀij/ *nm* quadrille.

quadrillé, **~e** /kadʀije/ **I** *pp* ▶ **quadriller**.

II *pp adj* [*papier*] squared; **une feuille ~e** a sheet of squared paper.

quadriller /kadʀije/ [1] *vtr* **1** (occuper) [*armée*] to take control of [*ville, secteur*]; [*police*] to spread one's net over [*ville, région*]; **2** (faire des carrés sur) to cross-rule [*papier*].

quadrimoteur /k(w)adʀimɔtœʀ/ **I** *adj* four-engined.

II *nm* four-engined plane.

quadriparti, **~e** /k(w)adʀipaʀti/ *adj* = **quadripartite**.

quadripartite /k(w)adʀipaʀtit/ *adj* quadripartite.

quadriphonie /kwadʀifɔni/ *nf* quadraphony; **en ~** in quadraphonic sound.

quadriphonique /kwadʀifɔnik/ *adj* quadraphonic.

quadriréacteur /k(w)adʀiʀeaktœʀ/ *nm* four-engined jet plane.

quadrisyllabe /k(w)adʀisillab/ *nm* (vers) four-syllable line; (mot) four-syllable word.

quadrisyllabique /k(w)adʀisillabik/ *adj* [*vers*] four-syllable (*épith*).

quadrumane /k(w)adʀyman/ **I** *adj* [*animal*] quadrumanous.

II *nm* quadrumane; **les ~s** Quadrumana.

quadrupède /k(w)adʀypɛd/ *adj, nm* quadruped.

quadruple /kwadʀypl/ **I** *adj* [*nombre, rangée, somme*] quadruple; **~ champion de France** four times champion of France, quadruple champion of France; **il a un salaire ~ du mien** his salary is four times mine, he earns four times as much as I do; **l'objectif est ~** the aims are fourfold; **en ~ exemplaire** in four copies.

II *nm* **le ~ de cette quantité** four times this amount, quadruple this amount; **le nombre des sans-abri est le ~ d'il y a 20 ans** the number of homeless people is four times what it was twenty years ago.

quadruplé, **~e** /kwadʀyple/ *nm,f* quadruplet, quad.

quadruplement /kwadʀypləmɑ̃/ *nm* quadrupling (**de** of).

quadrupler /kwadʀyple/ [1] **I** *vtr* to quadruple.

II *vi* to quadruple, to increase fourfold.

quadruplex /kwadʀyplɛks/ *nm* quadruplex.

quai /kɛ/ *nm* **1** Naut quay; **le navire est à ~** the ship has docked; **2** (berge aménagée) bank; **se promener sur les ~s de la Seine** to walk along the banks of the Seine; **3** (de gare, métro) platform; **attends-moi sur le ~** wait for me on the platform.

■ **~ de débarquement** Naut unloading dock; **~ d'embarquement** Naut loading dock; **Quai des Orfèvres** Paris police HQ; **Quai d'Orsay** French Foreign Office.

quaker, **quakeresse** /kwɛkœʀ, kwɛkʀɛs/ *nm,f* Quaker/Quakeress.

quakerisme /kwɛkəʀism/ *nm* Quakerism.

qualifiable /kalifjabl/ *adj* Sport [*équipe, joueur*] able to qualify (*jamais épith*).

qualificatif, **-ive** /kalifikatif, iv/ **I** *adj* **1** Ling [*adjectif*] qualifying; **2** Sport [*épreuve*] qualifying.

II *nm* **1** Ling qualifier; **2** gén term; **il a employé des ~s peu flatteurs à mon égard** he described me in rather unflattering terms.

qualification /kalifikasjɔ̃/ *nf* **1** Sport qualification (**pour** for); **un match de ~** a qualifying match ou game; **2** gén (compétence pratique) skills (*pl*); (diplôme) qualification; **la ~ des ouvriers s'est élevée** the level of skills among workers has risen; **on demande de hautes ~s pour cet emploi** you need good qualifications for this job; **être sans ~** to be unskilled; **3** Jur determination of the proper law.

qualifié, **~e** /kalifje/ **I** *pp* ▶ **qualifier**.

II *pp adj* **1** (compétent) [*personnel, main-d'œuvre, salarié*] skilled; (diplômé) qualified; **les jeunes non ~s** (sans diplôme) young people without qualifications; (sans compétences) young people without skills; **2** (demandant des compétences) [*emploi, poste*] skilled; **3** Jur [*vol*] aggravated.

qualifier /kalifje/ [2] **I** *vtr* **1** (caractériser) to describe [*personne, situation, méthode*]; **~ qn/qch de qch** to describe sb/sth as sth; **elle qualifie son œuvre de moderne** she describes her work as modern; **je ne peux ~ votre conduite!** your conduct defies description!; **comment ~ sa conduite?** how can we describe his/her behaviour[GB]?; **2** (donner la compétence à) [*travail*] to qualify [*personne*] (**pour** for); **je ne suis pas qualifiée pour vous répondre** I'm not qualified to give you an answer; **3** Sport [*victoire, but*] to qualify [*équipe, sportif*] (**pour** for); **l'équipe/la joueuse est qualifiée pour la finale** the team/player has qualified for the final; **4** Ling [*adjectif*] to qualify [*nom*].

II se qualifier *vpr* [*joueur, pays*] to qualify (**pour** for); **ils se sont facilement qualifiés** they qualified easily.

qualitatif, **-ive** /kalitatif, iv/ *adj* [*étude, enquête*] qualitative; **contrôle ~** quality control; **sur le plan ~**, **en termes ~s** in terms of quality.

qualitativement /kalitativmɑ̃/ *adv* qualitatively.

qualité /kalite/ *nf* **1** (valeur) quality; **du cuir de bonne/mauvaise/meilleure ~** good/poor/better quality leather; **de ~** [*produit, spectacle, médecine, matériel*] quality (*épith*); **être de ~** to be of good quality; **de première ~** of the highest quality; **~ de la vie** quality of life; **2** (aptitude) quality; **avoir beaucoup de ~s** to have many qualities; **la franchise n'est pas sa ~ première** frankness isn't his greatest quality; **avoir les ~s requises** to have the necessary qualities; **avoir des ~s de dirigeant** to have leadership qualities; **ses ~s de gestionnaire** his skills as an administrator; **3** Entr, Ind quality; **système/audit de ~** quality system/audit; **gestion/assurance/maîtrise de la ~** quality management/assurance/control; **certificat de ~** certificate of quality; **service ~** quality department; **4** (statut) status; (fonction) position; **la ~ de citoyen/réfugié** the status of citizen/refugee; **sa ~ de directeur l'autorise à faire** his position as manager allows him to do; **avoir ~ pour faire** to be entitled to do; **en (sa) ~ de représentant** in his capacity as representative; **nom, prénom et ~** surname, first name and occupation; **ès ~s** ex officio; **5** (sorte) quality; **nous avons plusieurs ~s de champagne/papier** we have several qualities of champagne/paper.

qualiticien, **-ienne** /kalitisjɛ̃, ɛn/ ▶ **510** *nm,f* quality controller.

quand /kɑ̃, kɑ̃t/

■ **Note** *when* traduisant *quand* conjonction ne peut pas être suivi du futur: *quand il aura terminé* = when he has finished; *quand je serai guérie, j'irai te voir* = when I'm better, I'll come and see you.

I *conj* **1** (lorsque) when; **~ il arrivera, vous lui annoncerez la nouvelle** when he gets here, you can tell him the news; **appelez-moi ~ la voiture sera prête** call me when the car is ready; **~ il arriva sur place, il comprit** when he got there, he understood; **~ il prend son poste en 1980, la situation est déjà catastrophique** when he took up his post in 1980, the situation was already catastrophic; **~ il termine son repas, nous partons** when he has finished his meal, we're going; **tu auras ton dessert ~ tu auras fini ta viande** you'll have your dessert when you have finished your meat; **~ il est fatigué et qu'il boit** when he is tired and he drinks; **cela date de ~ j'étais étudiante** it goes back to when I was a student, it goes back to my student days; **emporte une pomme pour ~ tu auras faim**○ take an apple with you in case you get hungry; **2** (valeur exclamative) **~ je pense que ma fille va avoir dix ans!** to think that my daughter's almost ten (years old)!; **~ je vous le disais!** I told you so!; **3** (toutes les fois que) whenever; **~ elle doit prendre l'avion elle est toujours très nerveuse** whenever she has to fly she gets nervous; **~ il pleut plus de trois jours la cave est inondée** whenever it rains for more than three days, the cellar floods; **~ il se mettait en colère, tout le monde tremblait** everybody shook with fear whenever he got angry; **~ il s'agit de boire un verre, il ne dit jamais non** when he's offered a drink, he never refuses it; **son attitude change ~ il s'agit de son fils** his attitude changes when it comes to his son; **savoir sévir ~ il faut** to be strict when necessary; **4** (alors que) fml when; **pourquoi partir ~ tout nous incite à rester?** why leave when there's every reason to stay?; **tu oses te plaindre ~ des gens meurent de faim!** you dare to complain when there are people starving!; **elle l'a laissé tomber ~ elle aurait dû l'aider** she let him down when she should have helped him; **5** (même si) fml even if; **~ (bien même) la terre s'écroulerait, il continuerait à dormir** even if the earth opened up, he'd carry on sleeping; **'tu ne vas pas faire ça?'—'et ~ bien même?'** 'you're not going to do that?'—'what if I do?'

II *adv* when; **~ arrive-t-il/viendras-tu?** when does he arrive/will you come?; **~ est-ce que tu reviens?, tu reviens ~○?** when are you coming back?; **je ne sais pas ~ elle arrivera** I don't know when she'll get here; **depuis ~ habitez-vous ici?** how long have you been living here?; **ça date de ~ cette histoire?** when did all this happen?; **de ~ date votre dernière réunion?** when was your last meeting?; **de ~ est la lettre?** what is the date on the letter?; **je me demande pour ~ est prévue la publication du dictionnaire** I wonder when the dictionary is due to be published; **c'est prévu pour ~?** when is it scheduled for?; **c'est pour ~ le bébé?** when is the baby due?; **à ~ la semaine de 30 heures?** when will we have the 30-hour week?

III quand même *loc adv* **ils étaient occupés mais ils nous ont ~ même rendu visite** they were busy but even so they came to visit us; **ils ne veulent pas de moi, mais j'irai ~ même!** they don't want me, but I'll go all the same; **elle est ~ même bête d'avoir fait ça!** it's really stupid of her to have done that!; **~ même, tu as vu ça?** really, did you see that?; **~ même, tu exagères!** (tu n'es pas objectif) come on, you're exaggerating!; (tu vas trop loin) come on, that's going too far!; **tu ne vas pas faire ça ~ même?** you're not going to do that, are you?

quant: **quant à** /kɑ̃ta/ *loc prép* **1** (pour ce qui est de) as for; **~ à vous/lui/Paul** as for you/him/Paul; **la France, ~ à elle, n'a pas pris position** as for France, it did not take a stand; **~ au dîner/aux enfants, rien ne presse** as for dinner/the children, there's no hurry; **~ à partir/me marier, jamais!** as for leaving/getting married, never!; **~ à dire que** as for saying that; **~ à moi, j'en suis sûr** personally ou as for me, I'm sure of it; **2** (au sujet de) about, concerning; **elle ne m'a rien dit ~ à l'heure de la réunion** she didn't say anything to me about what time the meeting would be ou concerning the time of the meeting; **il est très discret ~ à sa vie sentimentale** he is very discreet about ou when it comes to his love life.

quanta *nmpl* ▶ **quantum**.

quant-à-soi /kɑ̃taswa/ *nm inv* dignity; **rester sur son ~** to remain aloof.

quantième /kɑ̃tjɛm/ *nm* Admin **préciser le ~ du mois** to specify which day of the month.

quantifiable /kɑ̃tifjabl/ *adj* quantifiable.

quantificateur /kɑ̃tifikatœʀ/ *nm* quantifier.

quantification /kɑ̃tifikasjɔ̃/ *nf* quantification.

quantifier /kɑ̃tifje/ [2] *vtr* **1** Écon, Math to quantify; **2** Phys to quantize.

quantifieur /kɑ̃tifjœʀ/ *nm* quantifier.

quantique /kɑ̃tik/ *adj* Phys quantum.

quantitatif, -ive /kɑ̃titatif, iv/ *adj* quantitative.

quantitativement /kɑ̃titativmɑ̃/ *adv* quantitatively.

quantité /kɑ̃tite/ ▶ 662 *nf* **1** (mesure) quantity (**de** of), amount (**de** of); **de grosses ~s** huge quantities; **en grande/petite ~** in large/small quantities; **faire qch en ~s industrielles** Ind to mass-produce sth; hum to make vast quantities of sth; **~ négligeable** lit, fig negligible quantity; **2** (grand nombre) **des ~s de** hosts ou scores of [*personnes*]; masses○ ou a lot of [*choses*]; **(une) ~ de** masses○ ou a lot of [*choses*]; **il y avait une ~ de gens incroyable** there was an incredible number of people; **en ~** [*du pain, du vin*] in large amounts; [*des livres*] in large numbers; **il y a des fruits en ~ au marché** there is plenty ou an abundance of fruit at the market; **3** Sci, Ling, Mus quantity.

quantum, *pl* **quanta** /k(w)ɑ̃tɔm, k(w)ɑ̃ta/ *nm* quantum.

quarantaine /kaʀɑ̃tɛn/ *nf* **1** (environ quarante) about forty; **une ~ de lits** about forty beds; **2** (âge) **il a la ~** he's in his forties; **elle approche la ~** she's getting on for forty; ▶ **cinquantaine**; **3** Méd (isolement) quarantine; **être en ~** lit to be in quarantine; fig to be ostracized, to have been sent to Coventry GB; **mettre qn en ~** lit to quarantine sb; fig to ostracize sb, to send sb to Coventry GB.

quarante /kaʀɑ̃t/ ▶ 545, 212 *adj inv, pron* forty; ▶ **moquer**.

quarante-cinq /kaʀɑ̃tsɛ̃k/ ▶ 545, 212 *adj inv, pron* forty-five.

■ **~ tours** Mus single.

quarantenaire /kaʀɑ̃tnɛʀ/ *adj* **1** (de quarante ans) forty-year (*épith*); **2** Méd quarantine (*épith*).

quarantième /kaʀɑ̃tjɛm/ ▶ 545 *adj* fortieth.

quark /kwaʀk/ *nm* quark.

quart /kaʀ/ ▶ 407 *nm* **1** (quatrième partie) quarter (**de** of); **un ~ d'heure** lit a quarter of an hour; **faire passer un mauvais ~ d'heure à qn** to give sb a hard time; **un kilo un ~** a kilo and a quarter; **un ~ de siècle** a quarter century; **un ~ de poulet/fromage** a quarter chicken/cheese; **il possède les trois ~s du capital** he owns three quarters of the capital; **les trois ~s du temps** most of the time; **les trois ~s des gens** most people; **un portrait de trois ~s** Art a portrait in three-quarter profile; **se tenir de trois ~s** to stand three quarters on; **2** (bouteille) a quarter-litre[GB] bottle (**de** of); (pichet) a quarter-litre[GB] pitcher (**de** of); **3** (gobelet) beaker (of a quarter-litre[GB] capacity); **4** Naut watch; **être de ~** to be on watch; **rendre/prendre le ~** to hand over the/go on watch.

■ **~ de cercle** quadrant; **~ de queue** baby grand (piano); **~ de soupir** semiquaver; **~ de ton** quarter tone; **~ de tour** lit a 90° ou ninety-degree turn; **faites un ~ de tour (sur vous-même)** turn 90° ou ninety degrees; **faire qch au ~ de tour** fig to do sth immediately; ▶ **petit**, **grand**.

quart-de-rond, *pl* **quarts-de-rond** /kaʀdəʀɔ̃/ *nm* ovolo, quarter round.

quarte /kaʀt/ *nf* **1** Mus fourth; **2** Sport (en escrime) quarte; **3** Jeux (aux cartes) quart.

quarté /kaʀte/ *nm*: *betting based on forecasting the first four horses in a race*.

quarteron /kaʀtəʀɔ̃/ *nm* (petit nombre) pej handful (**de** of).

quartette /kwaʀtɛt/ *nm* jazz quartet.

quartier /kaʀtje/ *nm* **1** (partie d'une ville) area, district; (zone administrative) district; (zone ethnique) quarter; **un ~ populaire/commerçant/résidentiel** a working-class/shopping/residential area ou district; **le ~ des affaires** the business area ou district; **dans mon ~** in my area; **le plan du ~** a map of the area; **le ~ arabe/indien** the Arab/Indian quarter; **les beaux ~s** fashionable districts; **de ~** [*commerçant, médecin, cinéma*] local; **la vie de ~** local community life; **les gens du ~** the locals; **êtes-vous du ~?** are you from around here?; **2** (portion) quarter; **un ~ de pommes** an apple quarter; **un ~ de bœuf** a quarter of beef; **un ~ d'orange** an orange segment; **3** Astron quarter; **premier/dernier ~ de la lune** the moon's first/last quarter; **4** (de noblesse) quarter; **huit ~s de noblesse** eight quarters of nobility; **avoir ses ~s de noblesse** to be of noble lineage; **5** Mil **~s** quarters; **être consigné dans ses ~s** to be confined to quarters; **prendre ses ~s d'hiver/d'été** Mil to go into winter/summer quarters; fig to go to one's winter/summer residence; **avoir ~ libre** Mil to be off duty; fig to have time off ou free time.

■ **~ général**, **QG** Mil, fig headquarters, HQ; **~ de haute sécurité**, **QHS** Admin maximum security wing; **~ de selle** Équit saddle flap.

IDIOMES **ne pas faire de ~** to show no mercy, to give no quarter†.

quartier-maître, *pl* **quartiers-maîtres** /kaʀtjemɛtʀ/ *nm* leading seaman GB, petty officer third class US.

quart-monde /kaʀmɔ̃d/ *nm inv* underclass.

quarto /kwaʀto/ *adv* fourthly.

quartz /kwaʀts/ *nm* quartz; **à ~** quartz (*épith*); **montre/pendule à ~** quartz watch/clock.

quartzite /kwaʀtsit/ *nm* quartzite.

quasar /kazaʀ/ *nm* quasar.

quasi /kazi/ **I** *adv* almost; **~ immédiat/parfait** almost immediate/perfect; **le projet a été accueilli avec un enthousiasme ~ général** the project met with almost universal enthusiasm.

II *nm* Culin **~ (de veau)** fillet of veal.

III quasi- (*in compounds*) **~-monopole/indifférence** virtual monopoly/indifference; **~-certitude** near certainty; **la ~-totalité de** almost all of; **à la ~-unanimité** almost unanimously.

quasiment○ /kazimɑ̃/ *adv* practically.

Quasimodo /kazimodo/ **I** *npr* Littérat Quasimodo.

II *nf* Relig Low Sunday.

quaternaire /kwatɛʀnɛʀ/ **I** *adj* **1** Géol Quaternary; **2** Chimie quaternary.

II *nm* Géol Quaternary.

quatorze /katɔʀz/ ▶ 545, 407, 212 *adj inv, pron* fourteen.

IDIOMES **chercher midi à ~ heures** to complicate matters; **c'est reparti comme en 14!** here we go again!

quatorzième /katɔʀzjɛm/ ▶ 545, 212 *adj* fourteenth.

quatrain /katʀɛ̃/ *nm* quatrain.

quatre /katʀ/ ▶ 545, 407, 212 *adj inv, pron, nm inv* four; ▶ **saigner**, **jeudi**.

Les quantités

Dénombrables ou non-dénombrables?

L'anglais, comme le français, distingue deux catégories de noms: ceux qui désignent des éléments pouvant se compter par unités, se dénombrer (les dénombrables), comme les pommes, les chaises etc., et ceux qui désignent des éléments toujours à l'état de masse, non dénombrable en éléments séparés (les non-dénombrables), comme le lait ou le sable.

Comment distinguer un dénombrable d'un non-dénombrable? Précédés de «assez de», un dénombrable se met au pluriel (assez de pommes) et un non-dénombrable se met au singulier (assez de lait) (**recette pour francophones uniquement**). *«beaucoup», «peu» et «moins» exigent, en anglais, des traductions différentes, selon qu'ils spécifient un nom dénombrable, ou un nom non dénombrable.*

		pour les dénombrables	**pour les non-dénombrables**
beaucoup de	=	a lot of *ou* lots of *ou* many*	a lot of *ou* lots of *ou* much*
peu	=	few *ou* not many	little *ou* not much
plus	=	more	more
moins	=	fewer *ou* (*familier*) less	less
assez	=	enough	enough

* *Attention:* not many *et* not much *s'emploient couramment, mais* many *et* much *sont peu utilisés à la forme affirmative.*

Les noms dénombrables

combien y a-t-il de pommes?	=	how many apples are there?
il y a beaucoup de pommes	=	there are lots of apples

Noter l'absence d'équivalent anglais du français en *dans les expressions suivantes:*

combien y en a-t-il ?	=	how many are there?
il y en a beaucoup	=	there are a lot
il n'y en a pas beaucoup	=	there aren't many
il y en a deux kilos	=	there are two kilos (*on peut aussi dire, dans la conversation,* there's two kilos)
il y en a vingt	=	there are twenty
j'en ai vingt	=	I've got twenty
A a plus de pommes que B	=	A has got more apples than B

Noter l'ordre des mots dans:

quelques pommes de plus	=	a few more apples
quelques personnes de plus	=	a few more people
A a moins de pommes que B	=	A doesn't have as many apples as B
beaucoup moins de pommes	=	far fewer apples *ou* not nearly as many apples

Les noms non-dénombrables

combien y a-t-il de lait?	=	how much milk is there?
il y a beaucoup de lait	=	there is a lot of milk

Noter l'absence d'équivalent anglais du français en *dans les expressions suivantes.*

combien y en a-t-il?	=	how much is there?
il y en a beaucoup	=	there is a lot
il n'y en a pas beaucoup	=	there isn't much *ou* there's only a little
j'en ai deux kilos	=	I've got two kilos
A a plus de lait que B	=	A has got more milk than B
beaucoup plus de lait	=	much more milk
un peu plus de lait	=	a little more milk
A a moins de lait que B	=	A has got less milk than B
beaucoup moins de lait	=	much less milk *ou* far less milk
un peu moins de lait	=	a little less milk

Quantités relatives

combien y en a-t-il par kilo?	=	how many are there to the kilo?
il y en a dix par kilo	=	there are ten to the kilo
il y en a cinq pour dix francs	=	you get five for ten francs

Pour toutes les expressions utilisées pour donner un prix par unité de mesure (longueur, poids etc.), l'anglais utilise l'article indéfini là où le français utilise l'article défini.

combien coûte le litre?	=	how much does it cost a litre? *ou* how much does a litre cost?
vingt francs le litre	=	twenty francs a litre
combien coûte un kilo de pommes?	=	how much do apples cost a kilo? *ou* how much does a kilo of apples cost?
dix francs le kilo	=	ten francs a kilo
elles sont à dix francs le kilo	=	they are ten francs a kilo
combien coûte le mètre?	=	how much does it cost a metre?
dix livres le mètre	=	£10 a metre

Mais noter:

la voiture fait huit litres aux cent	=	the car does 35 miles to the gallon†
combien y a-t-il de verres par bouteille?	=	how many glasses are there to the bottle?
il y a six verres par bouteille	=	there are six glasses to the bottle

† *En anglais, on compte la consommation d'une voiture en mesurant non pas le nombre de litres nécessaires pour parcourir 100 kilomètres, mais la distance parcourue (en miles) avec 4,54 litres (un gallon) de carburant (mpg).*
Pour convertir la consommation exprimée en litres aux 100 km en mpg (miles per gallon) et vice versa il suffit de diviser 280 par le chiffre connu.

IDIOMES **dire à qn ses ~ vérités** to tell sb a few home truths; **faire les ~ volontés de qn** to give in to sb's every whim; **être tiré à ~ épingles** to be dressed up to the nines○; **manger comme ~** to eat like a horse; **ne pas y aller par ~ chemins** not to beat about the bush; **ils se sont dispersés aux ~ vents** they scattered to the four winds; **je vais leur parler entre ~ yeux** or **quat'zyeux**○ I'm going to talk to them face to face; **monter/descendre (un escalier) ~ à ~** to go up/down the stairs four at a time; **être entre ~ planches** to be six feet under.

quatre-cent-vingt-et-un /katsɑ̃vɛ̃teœ̃/ *nm inv*: *game of dice.*

quatre-épices /katʀepis/ *nm inv* allspice.

quatre-heures /katʀœʀ/ *nm inv* afternoon snack (*for children*).

quatre-mâts /katʀəmɑ/ *nm inv* four-master.

quatre-quarts /kat(ʀə)kaʀ/ *nm inv* pound cake.

quatre-vingt(s) /katʀəvɛ̃/ ▶545, 212 *adj, pron* eighty.

quatre-vingt-dix /katʀəvɛ̃dis/ ▶545, 212 *adj inv, pron* ninety.

quatre-vingt-dixième /katʀəvɛ̃dizjɛm/ ▶545 *adj* ninetieth.

quatre-vingtième /katʀəvɛ̃tjɛm/ ▶545 *adj* eightieth.

quatrième /katʀijɛm/ ▶545, 212 **I** *adj* fourth; **voulez-vous faire le ~?** (aux cartes) will you make a fourth?
II *nf* **1** Scol *third year of secondary school, age 13–14*; **2** Aut fourth gear; **passer en ~** to change ou go into fourth gear.
■ **le ~ âge** very old people.

IDIOMES **faire qch en ~ vitesse**○ to do sth in double quick time○.

quatrillion /katʀiljɔ̃/ ▶545 *nm* quadrillion GB, septillion US.

quatuor /kwatɥɔʀ/ *nm* (œuvre, formation) quartet; **un ~ à cordes** a string quartet.

que (**qu'** *before vowel or mute h*) /kə/ **I** *conj* **1** (reprenant une autre conjonction) **comme tu ne veux pas venir et ~ tu ne veux pas dire pourquoi** since you refuse to come and (since you) refuse to say why; **si vous venez et ~ vous avez le temps** if you come and (if you) have the time; **2 je crains ~ tu (ne) fasses une bêtise** I'm worried (that) you might do something silly; **le fait qu'il se soit enfui prouve sa culpabilité** the fact that he has run away is proof of his guilt; **qu'il soit le meilleur, nous nous en sommes déjà rendu compte** we were already well aware that he's the best; **taisez-vous ~ j'entende ce qu'il dit** stop talking so (that) I can hear what he's saying; **approche, ~ je te regarde** come closer so I can look at you; **qu'il pleuve et toute la récolte est détruite** if it rains the harvest will be ruined; **~ vous le vouliez ou non, ~ cela vous plaise ou non** whether you like it or not; **il voudrait faire échouer le projet qu'il ne s'y prendrait pas autrement** if he wanted to ruin the project he couldn't have chosen a better way to do it; **il l'aurait fait qu'il ne voudrait pas l'admettre** even if he did do it he wouldn't admit it; **il n'était pas sitôt parti qu'elle appela la police** no sooner had he left than she called the police; **vous dormiez encore ~ j'avais déjà fait une longue promenade** you were still asleep, while I had already been for a long walk; **j'avais déjà lu 10 pages qu'il n'avait toujours pas commencé** I had already read 10 pages while he hadn't even started; **il ne se passe pas de jour qu'il ne pleuve** not a day goes by without rain ou when it doesn't rain; **~ tout le monde sorte!** everyone must leave!; **qu'on veuille bien m'excuser mais...** you must excuse me but...; **qu'il se taise!** I wish he would be quiet!; **que n'êtes vous-arrivés hier soir!** fml if only you'd arrived last night!; **~ ceux qui n'ont pas compris le disent** let anyone who hasn't understood say so; **qu'on le pende!** hang him!; **qu'il crève**○**!** let him rot○!, he can rot○!; **~ j'aille le voir!** you expect me to go and see him!; **~ je leur prête ma voiture!** you expect me to lend them my car!; **~ je sache** as far as I know; **3**○ (à la place de l'inversion du sujet) **et alors? ~ je lui ai dit** so? I said to him; **approche! qu'il m'a dit** come closer! he says to me○.

II *pron inter* what; **~ fais-tu ?** what are you doing?; **~ dire?** what can you ou one say?; **~ faire?** (maintenant) what shall I do?, what am I to do?; (au passé) what could I do?, what was I to do?; **~ veux-tu pour ton anniversaire?** what do you want for your birthday?; **qu'est-ce que tu en penses?** what do you think?; **je ne sais ~ dire** I don't know what to say; **je ne sais pas ce qu'il a dit** I don't know what he said; **~ sont ces traces?** what are those tracks?; **qu'est-ce que c'est que ça?** what's that?; **qu'importe?** what does it matter?

III *pron rel* **1** (ayant un nom de personne pour antécédent) **Pierre, ~ je n'avais pas vu depuis 20 ans, est venu me voir hier** Pierre, whom I had not seen for 20 years, came to see me yesterday; **c'est la plus belle femme ~ j'aie jamais vue** she's the most beautiful woman (that) I've ever seen; **2** (ayant un nom de chose ou d'animal pour antécédent) **je n'aime pas la voiture ~ tu as achetée** I don't like the car (that) you've bought; **le livre qu'il a écrit juste après la guerre** the book that he wrote just after the war; **les photos ~ vous regardez ont été prises à Rome** the photographs that ou which you are looking at were taken in Rome; **c'est la plus belle fleur ~ j'aie jamais vue** it's the most beautiful flower (that) I've ever seen; **3** (employé comme attribut) that; **la vieille dame qu'elle est devenue** the old lady that she has become; **énervé qu'il était il n'a pu terminer son discours** he was so worked up that he couldn't finish his speech; **de petite fille sage qu'elle était elle est devenue une petite peste** she's changed from the good little girl that she was into a real pest; **bête ~ je suis** fool that I am; **stupide ~ tu es!** you silly thing!

IV *adv* **~ vous êtes jolie!** how pretty you are!; **~ c'est difficile/ennuyeux** how difficult/boring it is; **~ c'est joli** it's so pretty; **ce ~ vous êtes jolie!** you're so pretty!; **~ de monde/d'eau** what a lot of people/water; **qu'avait-il besoin de faire?** why did he have to do?; **~ ne le disais-tu plus tôt?** fml why didn't you say so earlier?; **'vous ne leur en avez pas parlé?'—'oh ~ si!'** 'haven't you spoken to them about it?'—'oh yes I have!'; **~ non!** definitely not!; **'tu en as besoin?'—'~ oui!'** 'do you need it'—'indeed I do!'; **c'était une époque turbulente ~ le XVIe siècle** what a turbulent period the 16th century was.

Québec /kebɛk/ **I** ▶ **692** *nprm* **le ~** Quebec.

II ▶ **857** *npr* Quebec.

québécois, **~e** /kebekwa, az/ *adj* of Quebec.

Québécois, **~e** /kebekwa, az/ *nm,f* Quebecois, Quebecker.

quechua /ketʃwa/ ▶ **462** **I** *adj* Quechuan (*épith*).

II *nm* Ling Quechua.

quel, **quelle** /kɛl/ **I** *dét inter* **~s sont les pays membres de la CEE?** what are the member countries of the EEC?; **je me demande quelle est la meilleure solution** I wonder what the best solution is; **de ces deux médicaments, ~ est le plus efficace?** which of these two medicines is more effective?; **de tous les employés, ~ est le plus compétent?** of all the employees, who is the most competent?

II *adj inter* **dans ~s pays as-tu vécu?** what countries have you lived in?; **~s peintres appartenaient à cette école?** what ou which painters belonged to this school?; **de ~ étage a-t-il sauté?** which floor did he jump from?; **de quelle couleur est ta voiture?** what colour[GB] is your car?; **quelle heure est-il?** what time is it?; **à quelle heure le film commence-t-il?** (at) what time does the film start?; **mais ~ monstre êtes-vous donc?** what kind of monster are you?; **~ âge as-tu?** how old are you?; **si tu savais à ~ point il m'agace!** if you only knew how much he irritates me!; **tu as remarqué avec quelle méchanceté elle lui a répondu?** did you notice how snappily she answered him?; **tout le monde sait avec ~ courage vous avez accompli votre mission** everybody knows how bravely you carried out your mission.

III *adj excl* what; **~ imbécile!** what an idiot!; **~ homme!** what a man!; **quelle idée bizarre!** what a weird idea!; **quelle coïncidence!** what a coincidence!; **~ bonheur (que) de les voir enfin réunis!** how delightful it is to see them together again at last!; **quelle horreur!** how dreadful!

IV *adj rel* **j'accepte votre proposition, ~s qu'en soient les risques** I accept your offer whatever the risks may be; **quelles qu'aient pu être tes raisons, tu n'aurais jamais dû faire cela** whatever your reasons may have been you should never have done that; **quelle que soit la route que l'on prenne** whatever ou whichever road we take; **~ que soit l'hôtel où ils sont descendus** whatever ou whichever hotel they are staying at; **~ que soit le vainqueur** whoever the winner may be; **~ que soit l'endroit où il se sont arrêtés** wherever they stopped; **quelle que soit mon admiration pour lui** however much I admire him, much as I admire him.

que

que conjonction de subordination se traduit généralement par *that*:

elle a dit qu'elle le ferait	= she said that she would do it
il est important qu'ils se rendent compte que ce n'est pas simple	= it's important that they should realize that it's not simple

On notera que *that* est souvent omis:

je pense qu'il devrait changer de métier	= I think he should change jobs

Quand *que* suit un verbe exprimant un souhait, une volonté l'anglais utilise un infinitif:

je voudrais que tu ranges ta chambre	= I'd like you to tidy your room
elle veut qu'il fasse un stage de formation	= she wants him to do a training course

On trouvera ci-dessous quelques exemples supplémentaires mais on pourra toujours se reporter aux verbes, adjectifs et substantifs qui peuvent être suivis de *que*, comme ***montrer***, ***comprendre***, ***apparaître***, ***certain***, ***évident***, ***idée*** etc. De même les locutions *ainsi que*, *alors que*, *bien que* sont traitées respectivement à ***ainsi***, ***alors***, ***bien***. Pour les emplois de *que* avec *ne*, *plus*, *moins* etc. on se reportera à ***ne***, ***plus***, ***moins*** etc. Voir **I** ci-dessous.

que pronom relatif se traduit différemment selon qu'il a pour antécédent un nom de personne:

l'homme que je vois	= the man that I can see *ou* the man I can see *ou* the man who I can see *ou* the man whom I can see
les amis que j'ai invités	= the friends that I've invited *ou* the friends I've invited *ou* the friends who I have invited *ou* the friends whom I have invited

(dans les deux cas ci-dessus la traduction avec *whom* appartient au registre de la langue écrite); ou un nom de chose, concept, animal:

le chien que je vois	= the dog that I can see *ou* the dog I can see *ou* the dog which I can see
l'invitation que j'ai reçue	= the invitation that I received *ou* the invitation I received *ou* the invitation which I received

Voir **III** ci-dessous.

quel

quel déterminant interrogatif se traduit généralement par *who* lorsque la question porte sur des personnes:

quel est ce jeune homme?	= who is that young man?

et par *what* dans les autres cas:

quelle est la capitale du Togo?	= what is the capital of Togo?

Toutefois lorsque la question porte sur un nombre de possibilités que l'on sait restreint, on utilisera *which*:

quel est le musicien français qui a composé 'le Boléro'?	= what French musician composed the 'Bolero'?

mais:

quel est le musicien français qui a composé 'le Boléro'? Debussy, Ravel ou Poulenc?	= which French musician composed 'the Bolero'? Debussy, Ravel or Poulenc?

On remarquera par ailleurs que l'inversion du sujet dans les propositions interrogatives indirectes en français n'est pas reproduite en anglais:

je me demande quel est son avis sur la question	= I wonder what his opinion on the matter is

quel adjectif interrogatif se traduit soit par *what* lorsque le contexte est vague et les possibilités infinies:

quel musicien vas-tu écouter?	= what musician are you going to listen to?

soit par *which* lorsque le contexte est spécifique et le nombre de possibilités limité:

dans quel tiroir as-tu mis la lettre?	= which drawer did you put the letter in?

On remarquera qu'en anglais lorsque la question comporte une préposition plusieurs cas sont possibles:

dans quel pays habite-t-elle?	= what country does she live in? *ou* in what country does she live?

La première traduction est utilisée dans la langue courante, parlée ou écrite. La deuxième sera préférée dans une langue plus soutenue, surtout écrite. Voir **II** ci-dessous.

Les autres fonctions de *quel* sont traitées ci-dessous en **III** et **IV**.

Par ailleurs certains emplois de *quel* sont traités dans les notes d'usage, notamment celles concernant ***l'âge***, ***l'heure*** etc. ▶ **1920**

quelconque /kɛlkɔ̃k/ **I** *adj* (ordinaire) [*personne*] ordinary, nondescript; [*livre, acteur*] poor, second-rate; [*restaurant, hôtel, produit, vin*] second-rate; [*endroit, intérieur, décor*] characterless, dull; (qui manque de charme) [*personne*] ordinary-looking, plain-looking; **j'ai trouvé le film très ~** I thought the film was very poor.

II *adj indéf* (n'importe lequel) any; **je doute qu'il y ait un ~ rapport entre les deux événements** I doubt that there's any link between the two events; **si tu as un problème ~, n'hésite pas à me prévenir** if you have any problem whatsoever, don't hesitate to tell me; **si pour une raison ~ il ne pouvait pas venir** if for some reason or other he couldn't come, if for any reason he couldn't come; **sous un prétexte ~** on some pretext or other; **si le livre avait un intérêt ~, je te le prêterais** if the book was in any way interesting, I would lend it to you; **est-ce que vous avez une ~ idée de combien ça peut coûter?** have you got any idea how much it costs?

quelle ▶ **quel**.

quelque

Remarques à propos de *quelque chose*

Dans les phrases affirmatives *quelque chose* se traduit par *something*:

quelque chose m'a frappé	= something struck me
j'ai vu quelque chose qui va te plaire	= I saw something that you will like

Dans les phrases interrogatives et conditionnelles, l'anglais fait une distinction entre une vraie question dont la réponse peut être *oui* ou *non* ou une vraie supposition:

avez-vous quelque chose à ajouter?	= have you got anything to add?
si tu vois quelque chose de louche	= if you see anything suspicious
si quelque chose leur arrivait	= if anything happened to them

et une supposition formulée sous forme de question:

tu fais une drôle de tête, tu as quelque chose à dire?	= you don't look too pleased, have you got something to say?

ou de suggestion:

si tu as vu quelque chose que tu aimerais pour ton anniversaire	= if you have seen something that you'd like for your birthday
si quelque chose te déplaît, dis-le	= if there's something you don't like, say so.

Voir exemples supplémentaires et exceptions ci-dessous ▶ 1920

quelqu'un

Dans les phrases affirmatives *quelqu'un* se traduit par *someone* ou *somebody*:

quelqu'un m'a dit qu'elle était malade	= someone told me she was ill
j'ai rencontré quelqu'un qui te connaissait	= I met someone who knew you

Dans les phrases interrogatives et conditionnelles l'anglais fait une distinction entre une vraie question dont la réponse peut être oui ou non ou une vraie supposition:

est-ce que quelqu'un parle grec?	= does anybody speak Greek?
est-ce que quelqu'un a vu mes clés?	= has anybody seen my keys?
est-ce que quelqu'un connaît la réponse?	= does anyone know the answer?
si quelqu'un téléphone, dites que je serai absent jusqu'à demain	= if anyone calls, say that I'll be away until tomorrow
si quelqu'un touche à mon ordinateur, il sera puni	= if anyone touches my computer, they'll be punished

et une supposition, un soupçon formulé sous forme de question:

est-ce que quelqu'un a touché à mon ordinateur?	= has somebody been playing with my computer?
est-ce que quelqu'un t'a donné la réponse?	= did someone give you the answer?

ou bien une requête ou une offre polie:

est-ce que quelqu'un pourrait fermer la fenêtre?	= could somebody close the window?
est-ce que quelqu'un veut encore du gâteau?	= would somebody like another piece of cake?
si quelqu'un voulait bien ouvrir la porte au chien	= if someone would please let the dog in

Dans les deux derniers cas, la réponse attendue est *oui*.

Voir exemples supplémentaires et exceptions ci-dessous.

quelque /kɛlk/ **I** *adj indéf* **1** (au singulier) (dans les phrases affirmatives) some; (dans les phrases interrogatives) any; **nous avons eu ~ difficulté à nous comprendre** we had some difficulty in understanding each other; **j'ai eu ~ peine à le convaincre** I had some trouble persuading him; **il sera probablement allé voir ~ ami** he's probably gone to see some friend of his; **il trouvera bien ~ autre moyen d'y parvenir** he's sure to find some other way of managing it; **il y a ~ temps** some time ago; **depuis ~ temps il est déprimé** for some time he has been depressed; **il y aurait ~ contradiction à dire que** it would be somewhat contradictory to say that; **si pour ~ raison que ce soit tu ne pouvais pas venir** if for whatever reason you were unable to come; **~ décision que tu prennes** whatever decision you come to; **de ~ côté que nous allions** whichever way we go; **2** (au pluriel) (dans les phrases affirmatives) some, a few; (dans les phrases interrogatives) any; **~s jours/chaises/étudiants** some ou a few days/chairs/students; **je voudrais ajouter ~s mots** I'd like to add a few words; **~s instants** a few moments; **la police a dispersé les ~s manifestants qui restaient** the police dispersed the few remaining demonstrators; **est-ce qu'il vous reste ~s cartons?** do you have any boxes left?; **ça dure trois heures et ~s** it lasts over three hours.

II *adv* **1** (environ) **les ~ deux mille spectateurs** the two thousand odd spectators, the two thousand or so spectators; **il y a ~ 20 ans de cela** it was about 20 years ago; **ça lui a coûté ~ 300 francs** it cost him about 300 francs; **ils étaient ~ deux cents hommes** they numbered some two hundred men; **2** (si) however; **~ compétents qu'ils soient** however competent they may be; **~ admirable que soit son attitude** however admirable his attitude may be.

III quelque chose *pron indéf inv* (affirmatives) something; **vous mangerez/boirez bien ~ chose?** you'll eat/drink something won't you?; **vous avez fait tomber ~ chose** you've knocked something over; **elle lui a offert un petit ~ chose** she gave him a little something; **il faut faire ~ chose!** we've got to do something!; **il y a ~ chose qui ne va pas** something's wrong; **~ chose me dit que** something tells me that; **ils y sont pour ~ chose** they've got something to do with it; **il se passe ~ chose** there's something going on; **il leur est peut-être arrivé ~ chose** maybe something's happened to them; **elle est restée ~ chose comme trois heures** she stayed for something like ou for about three hours; **il me reste ~ chose comme 200 francs** I've got about 200 francs left; **~ chose d'autre** something else; **~ chose de mieux/de moins cher** something better/cheaper; **il m'a dit ~ chose d'incroyable** he told me something amazing; **il y a ~ chose d'inquiétant chez elle, elle a ~ chose d'inquiétant** there's something strange about her; **il y aurait ~ chose d'absurde à refuser sa proposition** it would be ridiculous to turn down his offer; **il boit, c'est ~ chose d'inimaginable!** he drinks such a lot, it's unbelievable!; **il a ~ chose de son grand-père** he's got a look of his grandfather about him; **faire ~ chose à qn** [*événement, substance*] to have an effect on sb; **il y a ~ chose comme vent aujourd'hui**○! there's quite a wind blowing today!; **il y avait ~ chose comme monde en ville**○ there was quite a crowd in town; **c'est ~ chose! tu es toujours en retard!** for crying out loud! you're always late; **en ce temps-là, être instituteur, c'était ~ chose** in those days it was quite something to be a primary school teacher; **leur faire ranger leur chambre, c'est ~ chose!** getting them to tidy their room is quite an operation!; **c'est déjà ~ chose!** that's something at least!; **ça me dit ~ chose** it reminds me of something, it rings a bell.

IV quelque part *loc adv* somewhere; **ils sont ~ part en Autriche** they're somewhere in Austria; **il lui a mis son pied ~ part**○ euph he gave him a kick in the behind; **tu n'aurais pas vu mes clés ~ part?** you haven't seen my keys anywhere, have you?

V quelque peu *loc adv* somewhat; **ma remarque l'a ~ peu décontenancé** he was somewhat taken aback by my remark; **il était ~ peu surpris/gêné** he was somewhat surprised/embarrassed; **il a accepté après avoir ~ peu hésité** he accepted after some hesitation.

quelquefois /kɛlkəfwa/ *adv* sometimes.

quelques-uns, **-unes** /kɛlkəzœ̃, yn/ *pron indéf pl* some, a few; **la plupart des tableaux ont brûlé mais ils ont réussi à en sauver ~** most of the paintings were burned but they managed to save some ou a few; **parmi tous les soldats, seuls ~ ont survécu** of all the soldiers, only a few survived; **l'artiste présentera quelques-unes de ses œuvres** the artist will present some ou a few of his/her works.

quelqu'un /kɛlkœ̃/ *pron indéf* **1** (dans les phrases affirmatives) someone, somebody; **~ d'autre** somebody else, someone else; **c'est ~ de très doué/de compétent** he/she is very gifted/competent; **un jour, il deviendra ~** one day, he'll be somebody; **cette fille-là, c'est ~!** that girl isn't just anybody; **2** (dans les phrases interrogatives et conditionnelles) **il y a ~?** is there anybody here?; **le téléphone sonne, est-ce que ~ pourrait répondre?** the telephone is ringing, could somebody answer?; **si ~ téléphone pendant mon absence** if anybody phones while I'm out.

quémander /kemɑ̃de/ [1] *vtr* to beg; **~ qch auprès de qn** to beg sth from sb, to beg sb for sth.

quémandeur, **-euse** /kemɑ̃dœʀ, øz/ *nm,f* pej scrounger○ péj.

qu'en-dira-t-on /kɑ̃diʀatɔ̃/ *nm inv* gossip; **je me moque du ~** I don't care what people say; **sans souci du ~** heedless of what people might say.

quenelle /kənɛl/ *nf*: *dumpling made of flour and egg, flavoured*[GB] *with meat or fish.*

quenotte○ /kənɔt/ *nf* baby talk toothy-peg○ GB lang enfantin, tooth.

quenouille /kənuj/ *nf* distaff.

IDIOMES **tomber en ~** to die out.

quéquette○ /kekɛt/ *nf* baby talk willy○ GB, weenie○ US.

querelle /kəʀɛl/ *nf* **1** (dispute) quarrel (**entre** between); (chamaillerie) squabble; **~ de famille** family quarrel; **chercher ~ à qn** to pick a quarrel with sb; **~s intestines** internal squabbling; **2** (débat) dispute; **la ~ sur les nationalisations** the dispute over nationalization.

■ **~ d'Allemand** quarrel about nothing; **~ d'amoureux** lovers' tiff; **~ de clocher** parish-pump quarrel.

quereller /kəʀele/ [1] **I**† *vtr* (gronder) to tell [sb] off.

II se quereller *vpr* to quarrel (**à propos de, au sujet de** about, over).

querelleur, **-euse** /kəʀɛlœʀ, øz/ *adj* quarrelsome.

quérir† /keʀiʀ/ [35] *vtr* liter **aller ~ qn/qch** to fetch sb/sth; **envoyer ~ qn/qch** to send for sb/sth.

questeur /kɛstœʀ/ *nm* **1** Antiq quaestor; **2** Admin *member of a parliamentary assembly responsible for internal finances and administration.*

question /kɛstjɔ̃/ *nf* **1** (interrogation) question (**sur** about); **répondre à/poser une ~** to answer/ask a question; **répondre à la ~ de qn** to answer sb's question; **poser une ~ à qn** to ask sb a question; **les ~s posées à l'examen** the questions asked in the exam; **cette** or **quelle ~!** what a question!; **je ne me suis jamais posé la ~** I've never really thought about it; **je me posais justement la ~** I was just wondering about that; **je ne sais pas, pose-leur la ~** I don't know, ask them; **je me pose des ~s sur** I'm wondering about; **sans se poser de ~s** unthinkingly; **2** (sujet) matter, question; (ensemble de problèmes) issue, question; **c'est une ~ de temps/goût/bon sens** it's a matter ou question of time/taste /common sense; **~ d'habitude!** it's a matter of habit; **c'est une ~ de vie ou de mort** it's a matter of life and death; **il en fait une ~ de principe** he's making an issue of it; **la ~ (du) nucléaire/de la drogue** the nuclear/drug issue ou question; **la ~ n'est pas de savoir qui/comment/si** the question is not who/how/whether; **en ~** (dont il s'agit) in question; (qui pose problème) at issue; **(re)mettre en ~** (réexaminer) to reappraise; (repenser) to reassess; **remise en ~** (réexamen) reappraisal; (critique) reassessment; **se remettre en ~** to take a new look at oneself; **là n'est pas la ~, la ~ n'est pas là** that's not the point; **les ~s à l'ordre du jour** the items on the agenda; **il est bien ~ de ça!** iron of course! iron; **il est ~ d'elle dans l'article** she's mentioned in the article; **il est ~ qu'il prenne sa retraite** there's some talk of him retiring; **un film où il est ~ de l'environnement** a film about the environment; **ce dont il est ~ dans mon article** what my article is about; **de quoi sera-t-il ~ dans votre livre?** what will your book be about?; **il n'est pas ~ que tu partes** (à un invité) you can't possibly leave; **il est hors de ~ d'accepter/que vous acceptiez** to accept/for you to accept is out of the question; **c'est tout à fait hors de ~!** that's absolutely out of the question!; **pas ~!** no way○!; **3**○ (pour ce qui est de) **~ argent/santé, ça va** where money/health is concerned, things are OK; **la maison est jolie, mais ~ quartier...** the house is pretty, but as for the area...; **4** Hist (torture) question; **soumettre qn à la ~** to put sb to the question.

■ **~ de confiance** Pol vote of confidence; **poser la ~ de confiance** to call for a vote of confidence; **~ écrite** Pol written question (*by French deputy to minister*); **~ fermée** yes/no question; **~ orale** Pol oral question (*written by French deputy to minister, who answers orally*); **~ orale avec/sans débat** oral question with/without subsequent debate (*with other deputies*); **~ orientée** leading question; **~ ouverte** open-ended question; **~ piège** trick question; **~ préalable** Pol preliminary question; **~ subsidiaire** tiebreaker; **~s d'actualité**† Pol = **~s au gouvernement**; **~s au gouvernement** Pol questions to ministers in parliament.

IDIOMES **faire les ~s et les réponses** to do all the talking.

questionnaire /kɛstjɔnɛʀ/ *nm* questionnaire.

questionnement /kɛstjɔnmɑ̃/ *nm* questioning ₵.

questionner /kɛstjɔne/ [1] *vtr* to question.

questure /kɛstyʀ/ *nf* **1** Antiq quaestorship; **2** Admin *financial and administrative duties in a parliamentary assembly.*

quête /kɛt/ *nf* **1** (d'aumônes) collection; **faire**

---

qui

qui pronom interrogatif sujet se traduit par *who*:

qui est-ce?	=	who is it?
qui a cassé la vitre?	=	who broke the window?
qui vous a reçu?	=	who met you?

qui pronom interrogatif dans des fonctions autres que sujet se traduit par *who* ou *whom*:

qui avez-vous rencontré?	=	who did you meet? *ou* whom did you meet?
qui vas-tu inviter?	=	who are you going to invite? *ou* whom are you going to invite?

La traduction avec *whom* appartient au registre de la langue écrite.

Lorsque le pronom interrogatif est utilisé avec une préposition, deux cas sont possibles:

avec qui voulez-vous un rendez-vous?	=	who do you want an appointment with? *ou* with whom do you want an appointment?
pour qui as-tu acheté cette montre?	=	who did you buy that watch for? *ou* for whom did you buy that watch?

Voir la remarque ci-dessus concernant *whom*. Voir exemples supplémentaires et exceptions en **I** ci-dessous.

qui pronom relatif sujet se traduit par *who* lorsqu'il remplace un nom de personne:

je remercie ceux qui m'ont aidé	=	my thanks to those who helped me
j'ai rencontré Pierre qui m'a parlé de toi	=	I met Pierre who talked to me about you

et par *that* ou *which* (ce dernier étant plus spécifique à l'anglais britannique) dans la plupart des autres cas:

le vase qui était sur la table	=	the vase that (*ou* which) was on the table
une idée qui n'était pas mauvaise	=	an idea that (*ou* which) wasn't bad
un chien qui avait l'air affamé	=	a dog that (*ou* which) looked hungry

Voir exemples supplémentaires et exceptions en **II 1** ci-dessous.

qui pronom relatif ayant une fonction autre que sujet et remplaçant un nom de personne se traduit par *that, who* ou *whom*, cette dernière traduction étant du domaine de la langue écrite:

un ami en qui je peux avoir confiance	=	a friend that I can trust *ou* a friend who I can trust *ou* a friend whom I can trust *ou* (le pronom relatif peut parfois s'omettre en anglais) a friend I can trust

---

la ~ (à l'église) to take the collection; [*saltimbanque*] to pass the hat round; (pour une œuvre) to collect for charity; **2** (recherche) search (**de** for); **sa ~ de justice** his search for justice; **en ~ de nouvelles** in search of news; **être/se mettre en ~ de qch** to be/go looking for sth; **la ~ du Graal** liter the quest for the Holy Grail.

quêter /kete/ [1] **I** *vtr* to look for, to seek [*approbation, pitié, soutien*]; to try to get [*sourire*]; to fish for [*compliment*]; to canvass for [*suffrages*].

II *vi* (à l'église) to take the collection; (pour une cause) **~ pour une œuvre/pour les réfugiés** to collect for a charity/for the refugees.

quêteur, -euse /kɛtœʀ, øz/ *nm,f* collector.

quetsche /kwɛtʃ/ *nf* (sweet purple) plum.

queue /kø/ *nf* **1** Zool tail; **2** Bot (de feuille, fleur) stem; (de cerise, pomme) stalk GB, stem US; (de fraise) hull; **3** (manche) (de casserole, poêle) handle; **4** (de billard) cue; **5** (partie terminale) (d'animal, avion, de cerf-volant) tail; (de cortège, procession) tail(-end); (de train) rear, back; **les wagons de ~** the rear carriages GB ou cars US; **monter en ~ de train** to get on at the rear ou back of the train; **6** (dans un classement) **~ de classe** bottom of the class; **ce pays est en ~ des pays industrialisés** this country is lagging behind other industrialized nations, this country is at the bottom of the league of industrialized nations ; **ils arrivent en ~ de peloton des grandes entreprises européennes** they come at the bottom of the league table of European companies; **7** (file d'attente) queue GB, line US; **faire la ~** to stand in a queue GB, to stand in line US; **se mettre à la ~** to join the queue GB, to get in line US; **à la ~!** go to the back of the queue GB ou line US; **il y avait 200 mètres de ~** there was a 200-metre[GB] queue GB ou line US; **j'ai fait deux heures de ~** I queued GB or stood in line US for two hours; **8** Mode (traîne) train; **9●** (pénis) cock●, prick●.

IDIOMES **une histoire sans ~ ni tête** a cock and bull story; **ce film n'a ni ~ ni tête** you can't make head or tail of this film; **la ~ basse** or **entre les jambes**○ with one's tail between one's legs; **il n'y en avait pas la ~ d'un(e)**○ there were none to be seen, there wasn't a trace of one; **faire une ~ de poisson à qn** Aut to cut in front of sb; **finir** or **se terminer en ~ de poisson** to fizzle out, to peter out.

queue-d'aronde, *pl* **queues-d'aronde** /kødaʀɔ̃d/ *nf* dovetail; **assemblage à ~** dovetailing.

queue-de-cheval, *pl* **queues-de-cheval** /kødʃəval/ *nf* ponytail; **elle se fait une ~** she puts her hair in a ponytail.

queue-de-morue, *pl* **queues-de-morue** /kødmɔʀy/ *nf* paintbrush.

queue-de-pie○, *pl* **queues-de-pie** /kødpi/ *nf* tails (*pl*), tailcoat.

queue-de-rat, *pl* **queues-de-rat** /kødʀa/ *nf* rat-tail file.

queuter○ /køte/ [1] *vi* (échouer) to fail.

queux† /kø/ *nm* **maître ~** chef.

qui /ki/ **I** *pron inter* (fonction sujet) who; (fonction complément) whom; **~ a fait ça?** who did that?; **~ ça?** who's that?; **~ va là?** who goes there?; **~ veut-elle voir?** who does she want to speak to?; **à ~ sont ces chaussures?** whose shoes are these?; **de ~ est ce roman?** who is this novel by?; **faites-moi savoir ~ vous désirez rencontrer** let me know who you wish to meet; **dis-moi à ~ tu penses** tell me who you are thinking about; **dites-moi avec ~ vous voulez un rendez-vous** tell me who you want an appointment with; **sais-tu à ~ sont ces lunettes?** do you know whose glasses these are?

II *pron rel* **1** (fonction sujet) (l'antécédent est un nom de personne) who; (autres cas) that, which; **le gouvernement qui a été formé par** the government (which was) formed by; **le chien, qui m'avait reconnu, s'approcha de moi** the dog, which recognized me, came up to me; **lui ~ s'intéresse aux armes à feu devrait aimer cette exposition** since he is so interested in firearms he should enjoy this exhibition; **toi qui pensais faire des économies!** you were the one who thought you were going to save money!; **celui ~ a pris le livre aurait pu le dire** whoever took the book could have said so; **ceux ~ n'ont pas fini pourront revenir demain** those who haven't finished can come back tomorrow; **que ceux ~ ne sont pas d'accord lèvent le doigt** let anyone who doesn't agree raise their hand; **il y a quelqu'un ~ veut vous parler** there's someone here who wants to speak to you; **est-ce vous ~ venez d'appeler?** was it you who called just now?; **un homme apparut ~ portait un chapeau** a man appeared, wearing a hat; **2** (fonction autre que sujet) **invitez ~ vous voulez** invite whoever ou anyone you like; **viens avec ~ tu veux** come with whoever you want; **j'ai vu ~ tu sais** I saw you know who; **c'est à ~ des deux criera le plus fort** each (one) is trying to shout louder than the other; **quelqu'un en ~ j'ai confiance** someone I trust; **quelqu'un sans ~ on ne peut rien (faire)** someone without whom one can do nothing; **ce ~ me plaît chez lui c'est son sens de l'humour** what I like about him is his sense of humour[GB]; **je suis allé à la poste ce ~ m'a pris un quart d'heure** I went to the post office which took me a quarter of an hour; **3 ~ que vous soyez** whoever you are; **~ que ce soit** whoever it is, anybody; **je n'ai jamais frappé ~ que ce soit** I've never hit anybody; **~ que ce soit ~ a fait cela** whoever (it was who) did that; **~ que ce soit, je ne suis pas là** I'm not here for anybody; **4** fml **les enfants étaient déguisés ~ en indien, ~ en pirate, ~ en prince** the children were dressed up, one as an Indian, one as a pirate, one as a prince.

quia: **à quia** /akɥija/ *loc adv* liter **être (réduit) à ~** to be left speechless.

quiche /kiʃ/ *nf* quiche, flan.
■ **~ lorraine** egg and bacon quiche.

quick /kwick/ *nm* tennis quick®, macadam.

quiconque /kikɔ̃k/ **I** *pron rel* whoever, anyone who; **une brochure sera envoyée à ~ en fera la demande** a brochure will be sent to whoever requests one ou anyone who requests one; **le règlement interdit à ~ de fumer dans le bâtiment** the regulations forbid smoking in the building; **~ refusera d'obéir sera sanctionné** whoever refuses ou anyone who refuses to obey will be punished.
II *pron indéf* anyone, anybody; **il le fait mieux que ~** he does it better than anybody (else).

quidam○ /kidam/ *nm* hum individual.

quiet†, **quiète** /kjɛ, ɛt/ *adj* calm.

quiétisme /kjetism/ *nm* Quietism.

quiétiste /kjetist/ *adj, nmf* Quietist.

quiétude /kjetyd/ *nf* tranquillity (**de** of); **travailler en toute ~** to work undisturbed; **partez en toute ~, je m'occupe des chats** don't worry about a thing, I'll look after the cats while you're away.

quignon /kiɲɔ̃/ *nm* crusty end (of a loaf).

quille /kij/ *nf* **1** ▶449 (objet) skittle; **jouer aux ~s** to play skittles; **2** Naut keel; **3**○ soldiers' slang end of military service; **4**○ (jambe) leg.
IDIOMES **être reçu comme un chien dans un jeu de ~s** to be given a very unfriendly welcome.

quincaillerie /kɛ̃kajʀi/ *nf* **1** (magasin) hardware shop GB ou store US, ironmonger's GB; **2** (articles) hardware; (industrie) hardware business; **3**○ (bijoux) junk jewellery GB ou jewelry US.

quincaillier, **-ère** /kɛ̃kaje, ɛʀ/ ▶510 *nm,f* owner of a hardware shop GB ou store US, ironmonger GB.

quinconce /kɛ̃kɔ̃s/ *nm* **en ~** [*arbres, boutons*] in staggered rows.

quinine /kinin/ *nf* quinine.

quinquagénaire /kɛ̃kaʒenɛʀ/ **I** *adj* **être ~** to be in one's fifties.
II *nmf* person in his/her fifties.

quinquagésime /kɛ̃kaʒezim/ *nf* Quinquagesima.

quinquennal, **~e**, *mpl* **-aux** /kɛ̃kenal, o/ *adj* **1** (de cinq ans) [*plan*] five-year (*épith*); **2** (tous les cinq ans) five-yearly (*épith*).

quinquennat /kɛ̃kena/ *nm* **1** (plan) five-year plan; **2** (mandat) five-year mandate, five-year term.

quinquet /kɛ̃kɛ/ *nm* **1** (lampe) oil lamp; **2**† (œil) eye; **ouvre tes ~s** open your peepers○ ou eyes.

quinquina /kɛ̃kina/ *nm* Bot **1** (arbre) cinchona; **2** (écorce) cinchona-bark; **3** (vin) *wine flavoured*[GB] *with cinchona bark*.

quintal, *pl* **-aux** /kɛ̃tal, o/ ▶620 *nm* quintal, one hundred kilos.

quinte /kɛ̃t/ *nf* **1** Mus fifth; **2** Jeux (aux cartes) quint; **~ royale** royal flush; **3** Sport (en escrime) quinte; **4** Méd **une ~ (de toux)** a coughing fit.

Quinte-Curce /kɥɛ̃tkyʀs/ *npr* Curtius.

quintessence /kɛ̃tesɑ̃s/ *nf* also Philos quintessence (**de** of).

quintette /kɛ̃tɛt/ *nm* (œuvre, formation) quintet; **~ à cordes** string quintet.

quintillion /k(ɥ)ɛ̃tiljɔ̃/ ▶545 *nm* quintillion GB, nonillion US.

quintuple /kɛ̃typl/ **I** *adj* [*nombre, rangée*] quintuple; **une somme ~ d'une autre** an amount five times more than another; **en ~ exemplaire** in five copies.
II *nm* **le ~ de cette quantité** five times the amount; **leur mise leur a rapporté le ~** they got five times their bet back.

quintuplé, **~e** /kɛ̃typle/ *nm,f* quintuplet, quin GB, quint US.

quintupler /kɛ̃typle/ [1] **I** *vtr* to quintuple.
II *vi* to quintuple, to increase fivefold.

quinzaine /kɛ̃zɛn/ *nf* **1** (environ quinze) about fifteen; ▶ **cinquantaine 1**; **2** (deux semaines) fortnight GB, two weeks; **la première/deuxième ~ de mars** the first/second half of March; **~ commerciale** two-week sale; **~ littéraire** two-week book promotion; **~ tchèque/anglaise** two-week promotion of Czech/English goods.

quinze /kɛ̃z/ ▶545, 407, 212 **I** *adj inv* fifteen; **~ jours** two weeks, a fortnight GB; **téléphone-moi dans ~ jours** call me in two weeks ou a fortnight GB; **je pars mardi en ~** I'm leaving two weeks on GB ou from US Tuesday; **tous les ~ jours** every fortnight GB ou two weeks.
II *pron* fifteen.

quinzième /kɛ̃zjɛm/ ▶545, 212 *adj* fifteenth.

quiproquo /kipʀɔko/ *nm* (sur des personnes) case of mistaken identity; (sur choses) misunderstanding.

Quito /kito/ ▶857 *npr* Quito.

quittance /kitɑ̃s/ *nf* (reçu) receipt; (facture) bill; **~ de loyer/d'électricité** rent/electricity receipt.

quitte /kit/ **I** *adj* **1** (sans dette) **nous sommes ~s, je suis ~ avec lui** lit, fig we're quits; **tenir qn ~ d'une dette/promesse** to release sb from a debt/promise; **2 en être ~ pour la peur/un rhume** to get off with a fright/a cold; **il en est ~ à bon compte** he has got off lightly.
II quitte à *loc prép* **1** (au risque de) **nous voulons un barrage, ~ à inonder quelques fermes** we want a dam even if it means flooding a few farms; **j'ai décidé de vendre ma voiture, ~ à en racheter une plus tard** I've decided to sell my car, I can always buy another one later; **2** (tant qu'à) **~ à aller à Londres, autant** or **il vaut mieux** or **au moins que ce soit pour quelques jours** if you're going to London anyway, you might as well go for a few days; **~ à se mettre en grève, au moins que ce soit pour de bon** if you're going to go on strike, you might as well do it properly.
■ **~ ou double** it's double or quits; **jouer à ~ ou double** to play double or quits.

quitter /kite/ [1] **I** *vtr* **1** (sortir de) [*personne*] to leave [*endroit, pays, ville, bureau, chaussée*]; **il a quitté son domicile à 8 h** he left his house at 8; **elle ne quitte plus sa chambre/son lit** she doesn't leave her bedroom/bed any more; **~ l'école à 16 ans** to leave school at 16; **il faut ~ la nationale 7 à Valence** you have to come off the nationale 7 at Valence; **2** (se séparer de) [*personne*] to leave [*personne, famille*]; **il nous a quittés vers 22 h** he left us at about 10 pm; **sa femme l'a quitté il y a un an** his wife left him a year ago; **il faut que je vous quitte, j'ai une réunion** I must go now, I have a meeting; **3** (abandonner) [*personne*] to leave [*travail, poste*] ; to leave [*service, parti, organisation , entreprise*] ; **j'ai quitté mon emploi de serveur** I left my job as a waiter; **~ le confort de qch** to leave the comforts of sth; **~ le monde des affaires** to leave the world of business; **~ l'enseignement** to give up teaching; **~ la politique** to retire from ou to give up politics; **~ la scène** fig [*acteur*] to give up acting; **tout en cuisinant, elle ne quittait pas ses enfants des yeux** while cooking, she didn't let the children out of her sight; **il ne l'a pas quittée des yeux de tout le repas** he didn't take his eyes off her throughout the meal; **ne quittez pas** (au téléphone) hold the line, please; **4** (déménager) [*personne*] to leave [*lieu*]; [*entreprise*] to move from [*rue*]; to move out of [*bâtiment*]; **l'ambassade quitte la place Vendôme** the embassy is moving from the place Vendôme; **5** (laisser en mourant) euph **un grand homme nous a quittés** a great man has passed away euph; **quand je vous aurai quittés**... when I've gone...; **6** (enlever) [*personne*] to take off [*vêtement, chapeau*]; **~ le deuil** to come out of mourning.
II se quitter *vpr* (se séparer) [*personnes*] to part; **nous nous sommes quittés bons amis/très fâchés** we parted the best of friends/on angry terms; **ils ne se quittent plus** they're inseparable now. ▶ **navire**.

quitus /kitys/ *nm* auditor's certificate of correct record.
■ **~ fiscal** ≈ tax certificate.

qui-vive /kiviv/ **I** *nm inv* **être sur le ~** to be on the alert.
II *excl* Mil **~?** who goes there?

quoi /kwa/ **I** *pron inter* **1** (dans une interrogation directe) what; **~? je n'ai pas entendu** what? I didn't hear; **à ~ penses-tu?** what are you thinking about?; **avec ~ peut-on abattre ce mur?** what can we knock this wall down with?; **à ~ bon?** what's the point?; **à ~ bon recommencer?** what's the point of starting again?; **en ~ suis-je responsable?** in what way ou how am I responsible?; **par ~ voulez-vous commencer?** (à table) what would you like to start with?; (tâche, travail) where would you like to start?; **pour ~ faire?** what for?; **je veux bien le rencontrer mais pour lui dire ~?** I don't mind meeting him but what shall I say to him?; **~ de neuf?** what's new?; **~ encore?** what now?; **~ de plus beau/difficile (que...)?** what could be more beautiful/difficult (than...)?; **de ~ (de ~)**○**?** what?; **~ d'étonnant si leurs enfants sont comme ça** it's hardly surprising that their children are like that; **c'est ~ ça là-bas**○**?** what's that over there?; **~ d'autre?** what else?
II *pron rel* **1 il n'y a rien sur ~ vous puissiez fonder vos accusations** there's nothing on which you can base your accusations; **voilà sur ~ je fonde mes accusations** that's what I base my accusations on; **il prétend tout savoir, ce en ~ il se trompe** he claims he knows everything, which is where he's wrong; **il se moque de tout ce en ~ elle croit** he laughs at everything she believes in; **ce en ~ il avait raison** and he was quite right; **ce à ~ vous pensez** what you are thinking about; **à ~ il a répondu** to which he replied; **après ~ ils sont partis** after which they left; **ce contre ~ ils se battent** what they are fighting against; **de ~ nous pouvons conclure que** from this we can conclude that; **(il n'y a) pas de ~!** (formule de politesse) think nothing of it, my pleasure, don't

mention it; **il n'y a pas de ~ se fâcher/crier** there's no reason to get angry/to shout; **il n'a (même) pas de ~ s'acheter un livre** he hasn't (even) got enough money to buy a book; **emporte de ~ lire** take something to read with you; **il a de ~**° (de l'argent) he's got plenty of money; **il a de ~ être satisfait** he's got good reason to be satisfied; **'tu ne devrais pas t'inquiéter'—'il y a de ~'** 'you shouldn't worry'—'I've got good reason'; **dis-moi à ~ tu penses** tell me what you are thinking about; **dis-nous avec ~ tu as payé cette voiture** tell us how you paid for this car; **2 ~ qu'elle puisse en dire** whatever she may say; **~ qu'il ait pu faire dans sa jeunesse** whatever he may have done in his youth; **~ qu'il arrive** whatever happens; **si je peux faire ~ que ce soit pour vous aider** if I can do anything to help you; **je ne m'étonne plus de ~ que ce soit** nothing surprises me any more; **~ que ce soit, dis-le-moi** whatever it is, tell me; **~ que ce soit qu'il ait dit** whatever he said; **~ qu'il en soit** be that as it may; **~ qu'il en ait** fml in spite of his wishes to the contrary.

III *excl* what; **alors, ~!** what then!; **ou ~!** or what!; **tu rentres ou ~!** so, are you coming in, or what?; **il est prétentieux, stupide, agaçant, pas du tout intéressant ~!** he's pretentious, stupid, irritating, in short he's pretty uninteresting.

quoique (**quoiqu'** *before vowel or mute h*) /kwak(ə)/ *conj* although, though; **nous sommes mieux ici qu'à Paris, ~** we're better off here than in Paris, but then (again); **quoiqu'il soit malade, il travaille beaucoup** although he's ill GB ou sick US, he's doing a lot of work; **~ pauvre, elle est généreuse** although she's poor she is generous, she's generous although ou though poor; **il joue un rôle important, ~ discret** he plays an important, though discreet, role; **j'irai avec toi..., ~, c'est assez loin** I'll come with you...it's quite a long way though.

quolibet /kɔlibɛ/ *nm* gibe GB, jibe US.

quorum /kɔʀɔm/ *nm* quorum.

quota /kɔta/ *nm* quota (**sur** on); **~ d'exportation/de production** export/production quota; **les ~s laitiers** milk quotas.

quote-part, *pl* **quotes-parts** /kɔtpaʀ/ *nf* share; **payer sa ~** to pay one's share.

quotidien, -ienne /kɔtidjɛ̃, ɛn/ **I** *adj* (de chaque jour) daily; (ordinaire) everyday (*épith*); **les dépenses/tâches quotidiennes** daily expenses/tasks; **un problème de la vie quotidienne** an everyday problem; **le temps de travail ~** the working day.

II *nm* **1** Presse daily (paper); **un grand ~ national** a big national daily; **2** (vie quotidienne) everyday life; **'L'Inde au ~'** 'everyday life in India'; **vivre le racisme/la pauvreté au ~** to experience racism/poverty everyday.

quotidiennement /kɔtidjɛnmɑ̃/ *adv* every day, daily; **les transactions sont effectuées ~** transactions are carried out every day.

quotidienneté /kɔtidjɛnte/ *nf* everyday nature (**de** of).

quotient /kɔsjɑ̃/ *nm* Math quotient.

■ **~ électoral** Pol electoral quota; **~ familial** Fisc dependents' allowance (*in assessing tax liability*); **~ intellectuel** intelligence quotient; **~ respiratoire** respiratory quotient.

quotité /kɔtite/ *nf* share; **~ disponible** disposable share of estate.

QWERTY /kwɛʀti/ *adj inv* **clavier ~** QWERTY keyboard.

r, **R** /ɛʀ/ *nm inv* r, R; **rouler les ~** Phon to roll one's r's; **les mois en ~** the months with an 'r' in them.

rab○ /ʀab/ *nm* **1** (ce qui est en trop) extra; **en ~** extra (*épith*); **il y a du ~** there's some extra; **il y a du ~ de viande**, **il y a de la viande en ~** there's some extra meat; **qui veut du ~?** who wants a bit extra?; **j'ai eu 10 minutes de ~ pour le faire** I got an extra 10 minutes to do it; **faire du ~** (au travail) to do extra hours; (à l'armée) to serve extra time; **2** (portion supplémentaire) seconds; **demander/prendre du ~** to ask for/to have seconds.

rabâchage /ʀabɑʃaʒ/ *nm* (d'orateur) harping (on) péj; (d'élève) repetition; **il fait du ~** [*orateur*] he goes over and over the same old thing; [*élève*] he learns by repetition.

rabâcher /ʀabɑʃe/ [1] **I** *vtr* to keep repeating [*histoires, faits*].
II *vi* to keep harping (on); **il passe son temps à ~** he's always harping on.

rabâcheur, **-euse** /ʀabɑʃœʀ, øz/ pej **I** *adj* **il est un peu ~** he tends to repeat himself.
II *nm,f* repetitive bore péj.

rabais /ʀabɛ/ *nm inv* (réduction) discount; **obtenir un ~ de 20%/100 francs sur qch** to get a 20%/100 francs discount on sth; **accorder un ~ à qn sur l'achat de qch** to give sb a discount on sth; **au ~** [*achat, vente*] at a discount; [*matériel, vêtements*] cheap; [*travail*] badly paid; [*formation, culture*] on the cheap (*après n*) GB, bargain-basement (*épith*) US; [*chef, acteur*] third-rate; **vendre qch au ~** to sell sth at a discount; **acheter qch au ~** to buy sth cheap; **travailler au ~** to work for low wages.

rabaisser /ʀabese/ [1] **I** *vtr* **1** to lower [*prétentions*]; to belittle [*mérite, valeur*]; to belittle [*personne*]; **~ l'orgueil de qn** to humble sb's pride; **2** to reduce [*taux*].
II se rabaisser *vpr* (en paroles) to belittle oneself; (par son comportement) to demean oneself (**devant qn** before sb).

rabane /ʀaban/ *nf* raffia matting.

rabat /ʀaba/ *nm* **1** (de sac, meuble, poche) flap; **2** (de magistrat, religieux) bands (*pl*); **3** = **rabattage**.

Rabat /ʀaba/ **▶857** *npr* Rabat.

rabat-joie /ʀabajwa/ **I** *adj inv* **être ~** to be a killjoy.
II *nmf inv* killjoy.

rabattable /ʀabatabl/ *adj* [*siège, banquette*] folding (*épith*).

rabattage /ʀabataʒ/ *nm* beating.

rabatteur, **-euse** /ʀabatœʀ, øz/ *nm,f* **1** Chasse beater; **2** (de clients) pej tout○.

rabattre /ʀabatʀ/ [61] **I** *vtr* **1** (refermer) [*personne*] to shut [*capot, couvercle*]; to fold [*tablette*]; to put up [*strapontin*]; [*vent*] to blow [sth] back [*volet*]; **2** (plier) to turn [sth] down [*col*]; to take in [*coutures*]; to take up [*ourlet*]; to turn [sth] back [*couverture*]; to turn [sth] down [*drap*] (**sur** over); **3** (faire descendre) [*personne*] to pull [sth] down [*chapeau, visière, jupe*] (**sur** over); [*vent*] to beat [sth] down [*fumée*] (**sur** over); [*joueur*] to smash [*balle*]; **le chapeau rabattu jusqu'aux yeux** his/her hat pulled down over his/her eyes; **d'un geste elle a rabattu sa jupe sur ses genoux** she quickly pulled her skirt down over her knees; **~ l'orgueil de qn** to wound sb's pride; **~ les prétentions de qn** to thwart sb's ambitions; **~ la prétention de qn** to cut sb down to size; **4** (retrancher) to knock [sth] off [*pourcentage, somme*]; **~ 10%/20 francs sur qch** to knock 10%/20 francs off sth; **il n'a rien voulu ~** he wouldn't knock anything off; **5** Chasse [*personne, chien*] to beat [*gibier*]; **6** (racoler) to tout for○ [*clientèle*]; **~ des clients/électeurs** to tout for custom/votes; **7** (en tricot) to cast off [*maille*]; **8** Hort to cut back [*plante*].
II se rabattre *vpr* **1** (se refermer) [*capot, couvercle*] to shut; [*tablette*] to fold up; [*volet*] to bang to; **le siège se rabat automatiquement** the seat goes back automatically; **se ~ brutalement** [*couvercle, capot*] to come down suddenly; **2** (se plier) [*couverture, drap*] to fold down; **le col peut se ~** the collar can be turned down; **3** (s'incliner) [*chapeau, visière*] to be pulled down; **4** (rentrer dans sa file) [*automobiliste, véhicule*] to pull back in; **5** (s'accommoder) **se ~ sur** (faute de mieux) to make do with; (après réflexion) to settle for; **j'ai dû me ~ sur le modèle le moins cher** I had to make do with the cheapest model; **n'étant pas assez bon en mathématiques, ils s'est rabattu sur l'archéologie** not being good enough at mathematics, he settled for archeology.

rabbin /ʀabɛ̃/ **▶813** *nm* rabbi; **grand ~** chief rabbi.

rabbinat /ʀabina/ *nm* rabbinate.

rabbinique /ʀabinik/ *adj* rabbinical.

rabelaisien, **-ienne** /ʀablezjɛ̃, ɛn/ *adj* Rabelaisian.

rabibocher○ /ʀabibɔʃe/ [1] **I** *vtr* **~ Pierre avec Paul** to bring Pierre and Paul together.
II se rabibocher *vpr* to make up.

rabiot○ /ʀabjo/ *nm* extra; **faire du ~** [*soldat*] to serve extra time; [*employé*] to do extra hours.

rabioter○ /ʀabjɔte/ [1] **I** *vtr* (obtenir) to wangle○ [*temps*]; **~ une portion** to get an extra portion.
II *vi* to skimp○; **restaurateur qui rabiote sur la quantité** restaurateur who skimps on portions.

rabique /ʀabik/ *adj* rabies (*épith*).

râble /ʀɑbl/ *nm* (de lapin, lièvre) saddle.
IDIOMES **ils nous sont tombés sur le ~**○ they laid into us○.

râblé, **~e** /ʀɑble/ *adj* **1** [*animal*] sturdy; **2** [*personne*] stocky.

rabot /ʀabo/ *nm* plane.

rabotage /ʀabɔtaʒ/ *nm* planing (down).

raboter /ʀabɔte/ [1] *vtr* **1** Tech to plane; **2** (érafler) to scrape.

raboteur /ʀabɔtœʀ/ *nm* planer.

raboteux, **-euse** /ʀabɔtø, øz/ **I** *adj* **1** [*planche, terrain*] rough; **2** [*style*] unpolished.
II raboteuse *nf* (machine) planing machine, planer.

rabougri, **~e** /ʀabugʀi/ *adj* [*arbre, tronc*] stunted; [*fruit*] shrunken; [*enfant, adulte*] shrivelled[GB] up; [*vieillard*] wizened.

rabougrir /ʀabugʀiʀ/ [3] **I** *vtr* [*froid, sécheresse*] to stunt [*plantes*].
II se rabougrir *vpr* [*plante*] to become stunted; [*vieillard*] to become wizened.

rabougrissement /ʀabugʀismɑ̃/ *nm* **1** (de plante) stunting; **2** (de personne) wizening.

rabouter /ʀabute/ [1] *vtr* to join [sth] (end to end) [*planches*]; to splice [*cordages, bandes*].

rabrouer /ʀabʀue/ [1] *vtr* to snub; **se faire ~ par qn** to be snubbed by sb.

racaille /ʀakɑj/ *nf* scum.

raccommodage /ʀakɔmɔdaʒ/ *nm* **1** (réparation) (de vêtements, filets) mending; (de chaussettes, bas) darning; (résultat) repair; **2**○ (réconciliation) reconciliation.

raccommoder /ʀakɔmɔde/ [1] **I** *vtr* **1** (réparer) to mend [*chaussettes, filet*]; to darn [*chaussettes, bas*]; **2**○ (réconcilier) to reconcile [*personnes*]; **~ X avec Y** to patch things up between X and Y○.
II○ **se raccommoder** *vpr* (se réconcilier) to make it up○ (**avec** with); **ils se sont finalement raccommodés** they made it up in the end.

raccommodeur, **-euse** /ʀakɔmɔdœʀ, øz/ **▶510** *nm,f* repairer of linen; **~ de faïences et de porcelaines** repairer of pottery.

raccompagner /ʀakɔ̃paɲe/ [1] *vtr* (à pied) to walk [sb] (back) home; (en voiture) to drive [sb] (back) home.

raccord /ʀakɔʀ/ *nm* **1** (de planche, papier peint) join; **faire un ~** (en posant du papier peint) to line up the pattern; **2** (retouche) (en peinture) touch-up; **3** (transition) (de texte) connecting passage; (dans un film) link shot; **4** Tech joint.

raccordement /ʀakɔʀdəmɑ̃/ *nm* **1** (activité) (de route, voie ferrée) linking; Télécom connecting, hookup US; (de tubes) joining; **demander le ~ au réseau** Télécom to apply to have the phone connected ou hooked up US; **2** (jonction) (de route) link road; (de voie ferrée) loop line; Télécom connection, hookup US; (de tubes) joint.

raccorder /ʀakɔʀde/ [1] **I** *vtr* **1** gén to connect (**à** to); to link together [*chapitres, parties*]; to join up [*motifs de papier peint*]; **2** Télécom (par câble) to connect, to hook up US; (par satellite) to link up; **3** Cin to link [sth] together [*scènes, plans*].
II se raccorder *vpr* gén to be connected (**à** to); (par satellite) to be linked up; [*chapitres, scènes*] to be linked (together).

raccourci /ʀakuʀsi/ *nm* **1** (chemin) shortcut; **prendre un ~** to take a shortcut; **2** (version abrégée) summary; (image réductrice) **c'est un peu un ~** it's a bit simplistic; **en ~** in short; **3** (en peinture) foreshortening; **Christ en ~** foreshortened figure of Christ.
IDIOMES **taper sur qn à bras ~s**○ lit to hit sb very hard; **tomber sur qn à bras ~s**○ fig to lay into sb○.

raccourcir /ʀakuʀsiʀ/ [3] **I** *vtr* to shorten, to reduce [*trajet, temps imparti*]; to shorten, to take up [*pantalon, jupe*] (**de** by); to cut [*texte, discours*]; **~ un texte de dix lignes** to cut ten lines out of a text; **ça raccourcit**

le trajet de dix kilomètres it shortens the journey by ten kilometres[GB], it knocks ten kilometres[GB] off the journey; **~ sa visite d'une semaine** to cut one's visit short by one week; **prenons cette route, ça va nous ~**○ let's take that road, it'll get us there quicker.

II *vi* [*vêtement*] (au lavage) to shrink (**de** by); (avec la mode) to get shorter; [*jours*] to get shorter (**de** by), to draw in.

raccourcissement /ʀakuʀsismɑ̃/ *nm* **1** (de vêtement) (au lavage) shrinking; (par un couturier) shortening; **2** (de distance, délai) shortening.

raccrocher /ʀakʀɔʃe/ [1] **I** *vtr* **1** (remettre) to hang [sth] back up [*rideaux, manteau, tableau etc*] (**à, sur** on); **2** Télécom **~ le combiné** or **le téléphone** to put the telephone down; **elle avait mal raccroché (le téléphone)** she hadn't replaced the receiver properly; **3**○ Sport (en boxe) **~ les gants** lit, fig to hang up one's gloves; **4** (rattacher) to reattach (**à** to); **~ un collier** to do up ou fasten a necklace again; **5** (solliciter) to pull in [*passants*]; **~ le client** [*vendeur*] to tout for custom, to drum up business○; [*prostituée*] to solicit; **6**○ (reprendre) to rescue [*affaire*].

II *vi* **1** Télécom to hang up; **~ au nez de qn**○ to hang up on sb; **2**○ Sport to give up competition.

III se raccrocher *vpr* **se ~ à** lit to grab hold of [*bras, rebord*]; fig to cling on to [*personne, prétexte*]; **il se raccroche à n'importe quoi** he's clutching at straws.

race /ʀas/ *nf* **1** (d'êtres humains) race; **2** Zool breed; **cheval de ~** thoroughbred (horse); **chien de ~** pedigree (dog); **les ~s bovines/canines** (the) breeds of cattle/dog; **3** (espèce) controv species; **la ~ bovine** the bovine species; **la ~ humaine** the human race; **4**○ (catégorie de personnes) race; **une ~ guerrière** a race of warriors; **sale ~!** offensive rotten○ lot! injur; **5** littér (lignée) line; **la ~ de David** the line of David; **être le dernier de sa ~** to be the last of one's line.
IDIOMES **avoir de la ~** to have breeding; **bon chien chasse de ~** Prov like father like son Prov.

racé, ~e /ʀase/ *adj* **1** [*personne*] distinguished; **2** [*cheval*] thoroughbred; [*chien*] pedigree (*épith*); **3** [*objet*] of classically elegant lines.

rachat /ʀaʃa/ *nm* **1** (d'objet vendu) buying back, buyback; Jur **vente avec faculté de ~** sale with option of repurchase; **2** (de société) buyout; **3** (d'actions) repurchase; **4** (de dette, rente) redemption; **5** (de prisonnier) ransoming; **6** (pardon) fml redemption.
■ **~ d'entreprise par l'encadrement** management buyout, MBO; **~ d'entreprise par les salariés**, **RES** employee buyout.

rachetable /ʀaʃtabl/ *adj* [*objet*] repurchasable; [*dette, erreur, péché*] redeemable.

racheter /ʀaʃte/ [18] **I** *vtr* **1** (récupérer un objet vendu) to buy [sth] back; **2** (acheter encore) **je vais ~ du vin/une bouteille/deux bouteilles** I'll buy some more wine/another bottle/two more bottles; **3** (pour renouveler) **mes draps sont usés, il faut que j'en rachète** my sheets are worn out, I'll have to buy new ones; **4** (acheter) **je rachète votre voiture 5 000 francs** I'll buy your car off you for 5,000 francs; **5** (effectuer une opération commerciale) to buy out [*société, usine*]; to buy up [*ensemble d'actions*]; **6** (pour se dégager) to redeem [*dette, rente*]; **7** (contre rançon) to redeem [*esclave*]; to ransom [*otage*]; **8** Relig [*pécheur*] to atone for [*faute, péché*] (**par** by); [*Dieu*] to redeem [*humanité*] (**par** through); **9** (compenser) [*personne*] to make amends for [*impolitesse*]; [*qualité*] to make up for, to compensate for [*défaut*]; **il n'y en a pas un pour ~ l'autre** they're as bad as each other; **10** Scol [*examinateur*] to mark up [*candidat, copie*].

II se racheter *vpr* to redeem oneself (**par** through); **se ~ aux yeux de qn** to redeem oneself in sb's eyes.

rachidien, -ienne /ʀaʃidjɛ̃, ɛn/ *adj* spinal, rachidian spéc.

rachis /ʀaʃi/ *nm inv* Anat rachis; Bot (d'épi) rachis; Zool (de plume) shaft.

rachitique /ʀaʃitik/ *adj* **1** Méd [*personne*] rachitic spéc; **il est ~** he suffers from rickets; **2** fig [*animal, plante*] scrawny.

rachitisme /ʀaʃitism/ *nm* rickets (+ *v sg*), rachitis spéc.

racial, ~e, *mpl* **-iaux** /ʀasjal, o/ *adj* racial; **émeutes ~es** race riots; **relations ~es** race relations.

racine /ʀasin/ **I** *nf* **1** Bot root; **prendre ~** lit, fig to take root; **2** (source) root; **être à la ~ de** to be at the root of; **prendre** or **attaquer le mal à la ~** to strike at the root of the problem; **3** Anat root; **rougir jusqu'à la ~ des cheveux** to blush to the roots of one's hair; **4** Math root; **~ carrée/cubique** square/cube root; **5** Ling root.

II racines *nfpl* (de personne) roots; **il n'a de ~s nulle part** he hasn't got any roots; **une croyance qui a de profondes ~s** a deep-rooted belief.
■ **~ comestible** root vegetable.

racinette /ʀasinɛt/ *nf* C root beer.

racinien, -ienne /ʀasinjɛ̃, ɛn/ *adj* Racinian.

racisme /ʀasism/ *nm* **1** (doctrine) racism; **2** (discrimination) prejudice; **~ anti-étudiants** prejudice against students.

raciste /ʀasist/ *adj, nmf* racist.

rack /ʀak/ *nm* (de chaîne hi-fi) system stand.

racket /ʀakɛt/ *nm* (organisation) extortion racket; (activité) racketeering; **c'est du ~!** it's extortion!; **le ~ des commerçants** the extortion of money from shopkeepers.

racketter /ʀakɛte/ [1] *vtr* to extort money from, to shake [sb] down◑ US; **se faire ~** to be the victim of extortion.

racketteur /ʀakɛtœʀ/ *nm* racketeer.

raclage /ʀɑklaʒ/ *nm* scraping.

raclée○ /ʀɑkle/ *nf* (tous contextes) hiding○; **recevoir une ~** to get a hiding; **flanquer une ~ à qn** to give sb a hiding.

raclement /ʀɑkləmɑ̃/ *nm* (action, bruit) scraping; **elle entendit un ~ de gorge** she heard somebody clearing their throat.

racler /ʀɑkle/ [1] **I** *vtr* **1** (nettoyer) to scrape [sth] clean [*plat, assiette*]; ▶ **tiroir**; **2** (enlever) to scrape off [*vernis, rouille*]; **~ la boue de ses semelles** to scrape the mud off the soles of one's shoes; **3** (frotter) [*pneu*] to scrape against [*trottoir*]; **~ le gosier** [*vin*] to be rough on the throat; **4** pej (jouer) to scrape away at péj.

II se racler *vpr* **se ~ la gorge** to clear one's throat.

raclette /ʀɑklɛt/ *nf* **1** Culin raclette (*Swiss cheese dish*); **(fromage à) ~** raclette cheese; **2** (petit racloir) scraper.

racloir /ʀɑklwaʀ/ *nm* scraper.

raclure /ʀɑklyʀ/ **I**◑ *nf* (racaille) louse○, despicable person.

II raclures *nfpl* (de bois) shavings.

racolage /ʀakɔlaʒ/ *nm* **1** (d'électeurs, de partisans) touting (**de** for); **le ~ publicitaire** canvassing; **2** (par prostituée) soliciting (**de** for); **se livrer au ~ sur la voie publique** to solicit in a street.

racoler /ʀakɔle/ [1] *vtr* **1** [*politicien*] to tout for [*électeurs*]; (pour un spectacle) to tout for, to bark for○ [*passants*]; **2** [*prostituée*] to solicit for [*clients*]; **elle racole en voiture** she solicits in a car.

racoleur, -euse /ʀakɔlœʀ, øz/ **I** *adj* [*affiche*] eye-catching; [*slogan à la radio*] catchy; [*regard, sourire*] enticing.

II *nm* (pour des élections, un parti) canvasser; (pour un spectacle, un commerce) tout, barker.

III racoleuse *nf* streetwalker.

racontable /ʀakɔ̃tabl/ *adj* **histoire pas/à peine ~** a story which is not/hardly repeatable.

racontar○ /ʀakɔ̃taʀ/ *nm* piece of idle gossip; **des ~s** idle gossip.

raconter /ʀakɔ̃te/ [1] **I** *vtr* **1** (relater) [*personne*] to tell [*histoire*]; [*film, livre*] to tell [*histoire*]; to describe [*fait, épisode*]; to recount [*bataille*]; to describe [*rencontre, amitié, vie*]; **~ en détail** to describe in detail; **alors! raconte!** tell me all about it then!; **après l'accident les témoins racontent** after the accident, witnesses describe how it happened; **la pièce raconte l'histoire d'une femme** the play tells the story of a woman; **ne nous raconte pas ta vie** don't tell us your life-story; **racontenous ce qui s'est passé** tell us what happened; **~ à qn comment/pourquoi/où** to tell sb how/why/where; **il leur a raconté comment il s'était échappé** he told them how he had escaped; **il raconte bien/mal** he's a good/bad storyteller; **je suis tombée en panne, je te raconte pas**○! my car broke down, I'll spare you the details!; **tu racontes n'importe quoi!** you're talking nonsense!; **2** (prétendre) to say; **~ que** to say that; **on raconte que** it is said that; **il nous a raconté qu'il s'était perdu** he told us that he had got GB ou gotten US lost; **tu sais ce qu'on raconte sur toi?** do you know what people are saying about you?; **qu'est-ce que tu racontes?** what are you talking about?; **on raconte beaucoup de sottises à son sujet** a lot of silly things are said about him/her; **3** (dépeindre) liter [*personne*] to describe [*époque, mœurs, pays*].

II se raconter *vpr* (parler de soi) to talk about oneself.

raconteur, -euse /ʀakɔ̃tœʀ, øz/ *nm,f* storyteller.

racornir /ʀakɔʀniʀ/ [3] **I** *vtr* **1** (durcir) to harden [*peau*]; to stiffen [*cuir*]; fig to harden [*personne, cœur*]; **mains que le travail manuel a racornies** hands horny with manual work; **2** (rabougrir) [*âge*] to wizen [*personne*]; [*sécheresse*] to shrivel [*plante*].

II se racornir *vpr* **1** (devenir dur) [*peau*] to harden; fig [*personne, cœur*] to harden; [*cuir*] to stiffen; **2** (se rabougrir) [*plante*] to shrivel; [*personne*] to grow wizened.

racornissement /ʀakɔʀnismɑ̃/ *nm* **1** (du cuir) stiffening; **2** (de plante) shrivelling[GB].

rad /ʀad/ *nm* **1** Math (*written abbr* = **radian**) rad; **2**† Phys rad.

radar /ʀadaʀ/ *nm* radar; **au ~** by radar; **effectuer des contrôles ~** to carry out radar speed checks; **marcher au ~**○ fig to be on autopilot.

radariste /ʀadaʀist/ ▶ **510** *nmf* radar operator.

rade /ʀad/ *nf* roads (*pl*); **en ~ de Toulon** in Toulon roads; **mouiller en ~** to lie at anchor (*in a roadstead*).
IDIOMES **laisser qn en ~**○ to leave sb stranded; **rester en ~**○ [*personne*] to be left stranded; [*projet*] to be shelved.

radeau, *pl* **~x** /ʀado/ *nm* **1** (embarcation) raft; **2** (train de bois) (timber) raft.
■ **~ pneumatique** rubber dinghy.

radial, ~e, *mpl* **-iaux** /ʀadjal, o/ **I** *adj* **1** [*pneu, carcasse*] radial(-ply); **2** [*vitesse*] radial, line-of-sight (*épith*); **3** [*nerf, artère*] radial.

II *nm* (nerf) radial nerve; (muscle) radial muscle.

III radiale *nf* **1** Aut (route) radial road; **2** Anat (artère) radial artery; (veine) radial vein.

radian /ʀadjɑ̃/ *nm* radian.

radiant, ~e /ʀadjɑ̃, ɑ̃t/ **I** *adj* (tous contextes) radiant.

II *nm* radiant.

radiateur /ʀadjatœʀ/ *nm* (de chauffage central, voiture) radiator.
■ **~ à convection** convector heater; **~ électrique** electric heater; **~ soufflant** fan heater.

radiation /ʀadjasjɔ̃/ *nf* **1** Phys radiation; **2** (de personne) gén expulsion; (de médecin) striking off from the register GB, loss of the license to practice medicine US; (d'avocat) disbarring; **après leur ~ du comité** after their expulsion from the committee; **après leur ~ du club** after the withdrawal of their club membership; **la faute de Me Nadaud a entraîné sa ~ (du barreau)** Mr Nadaud was disbarred for malpractice.

radical, **~e**, *mpl* **-aux** /ʀadikal, o/ **I** *adj* **1** [*méthode, solution, changement*] radical; [*mesure, remède*] drastic; **2** Pol [*parti, député*] radical; **3** Bot, Math radical.
II *nm,f* **1** Pol (personne) radical; **2** Ling, Chimie radical; **3** Math root sign.

radicalement /ʀadikalmɑ̃/ *adv* [*opposé, différent*] radically; [*nouveau*] completely; [*efficace*] extremely; [*changer*] radically; [*détruire*] completely.

radicalisation /ʀadikalizasjɔ̃/ *nf* **1** (de parti, régime, d'attitude) toughening; **2** (de réformes, changements) stepping up.

radicaliser /ʀadikalize/ [1] **I** *vtr* **1** [*syndicat, parti*] to toughen [*attitude*]; to harden [*politique*]; to step up [*revendications*]; **2** [*répression*] to cause [sb] to become more radical.
II se radicaliser *vpr* **1** [*personne, groupe*] to become more radical; **2** [*attitude, exigences*] to toughen; [*politique*] to harden.

radicalisme /ʀadikalism/ *nm* radicalism.

radical-socialisme /ʀadikalsɔsjalism/ *nm* radical socialism.

radicelle /ʀadisɛl/ *nf* rootlet.

radiculaire /ʀadikylɛʀ/ *adj* radicular.

radicule /ʀadikyl/ *nf* radicle.

radié, **~e** /ʀadje/ **I** *pp* ▶ **radier**.
II *pp adj* Bot rayed.

radier /ʀadje/ [2] *vtr* **~ qn d'une liste** to remove sb from a list; **~ un nom d'une liste** to cross a name off a list; **~ un médecin** to strike off a doctor GB, to take away a doctor's license US; **~ un avocat** to disbar a lawyer.

radiesthésie /ʀadjɛstezi/ *nf* dowsing.

radiesthésiste /ʀadjɛstezist/ ▶ **510** *nmf* dowser.

radieux, **-ieuse** /ʀadjø, øz/ *adj* **1** (éclatant) [*soleil*] dazzling; **2** (ensoleillé) [*temps, matinée*] glorious; **3** (heureux) [*visage, air, sourire*] radiant; [*personne*] radiant with joy; [*souvenir*] glorious; **4** (prometteur) [*avenir*] glorious.

radin○, **~e** /ʀadɛ̃, in/ **I** *adj* stingy○; **elle est très ~(e)** she's very stingy.
II *nm,f* skinflint○, cheapskate◑.

radiner◑ /ʀadine/ [1] *vtr*, **se radiner**◑ *vpr* to turn up○.

radinerie○ /ʀadinʀi/ *nf* stinginess○.

radio /ʀadjo/ **I** *adj inv* [*équipement, contact, signal*] radio.
II ▶ **510** *nm* (opérateur) radio operator.
III *nf* **1** (appareil) radio; **2** (radiodiffusion) radio; **un poste de ~** a radio; **écouter qn/qch à la ~** to listen to sb/sth on the radio; **il travaille à la ~** he works in the radio; **3** (station) radio (station); **4** (radiotéléphonie) (d'un avion, d'un bateau) radio; **5** Méd (radiographie) X-ray; **passer une ~ des poumons** to have a chest X-ray; **à la ~ on peut voir**... on the X-ray you can see...
■ **~ libre** independent local radio station; **~ locale** local radio (station); **~ pirate** pirate radio (station).

radioactif, **-ive** /ʀadjoaktif, iv/ *adj* radioactive; **déchets ~s** radioactive waste ¢.

radioactivité /ʀadjoaktivite/ *nf* radioactivity.

radioalignement /ʀadjoaliɲmɑ̃/ *nm* radio navigation system.

radioamateur /ʀadjoamatœʀ/ *nm* radio ham.

radioastronome /ʀadjoastʀɔnɔm/ *nm* radio astronomer.

radioastronomie /ʀadjoastʀɔnɔmi/ *nf* radio astronomy.

radiobalisage /ʀadjobalizaʒ/ *nm* radio beacon signalling[GB].

radiobalise /ʀadjobaliz/ *nf* radio beacon.

radiobiologie /ʀadjobjɔlɔʒi/ *nf* radiobiology.

radiocarbone /ʀadjokaʀbɔn/ *nm* radiocarbon.

radiocassette /ʀadjokasɛt/ *nm* ou *f* (lecteur) radio cassette player; (enregistreur) radio cassette recorder.

radiocobalt /ʀadjokɔbalt/ *nm* radiocobalt.

radiocommande /ʀadjokɔmɑ̃d/ *nf* radio control.

radiocommunication /ʀadjokɔmynikasjɔ̃/ *nf* radiocommunication.

radiocompas /ʀadjokɔ̃pa/ *nm inv* radio compass.

radioconducteur /ʀadjokɔ̃dyktœʀ/ *nm* radioconductor.

radiodiagnostic /ʀadjodjagnɔstik/ *nm* Méd X-ray diagnosis.

radiodiffuser /ʀadjodifyze/ [1] *vtr* to broadcast; **journal radiodiffusé** news broadcast; **publicité radiodiffusée** radio commercial.

radiodiffusion /ʀadjodifyzjɔ̃/ *nf* broadcasting; **de ~** radio (*épith*).

radioélectricien, **-ienne** /ʀadjoelɛktʀisjɛ̃, ɛn/ ▶ **510** *nm,f* radio engineer.

radioélectricité /ʀadjoelɛktʀisite/ *nf* radio engineering.

radioélectrique /ʀadjoelɛktʀik/ *adj* radio.

radioélément /ʀadjoelemɑ̃/ *nm* radioelement.

radiofréquence /ʀadjofʀekɑ̃s/ *nf* radio frequency.

radiogalaxie /ʀadjogalaksi/ *nf* radio galaxy.

radiogoniomètre /ʀadjogɔnjɔmɛtʀ/ *nm* Télécom radiogoniometer; Aviat, Naut radio direction finder.

radiogoniométrie /ʀadjogɔnjɔmetʀi/ *nf* Télécom radiogoniometry; Aviat, Naut radio direction finding.

radiogramme /ʀadjɔgʀam/ *nm* radio-telegram.

radiographie /ʀadjɔgʀafi/ *nf* **1** (procédé) radiography, X-ray photography; **2** (cliché) X-ray (photograph).

radiographier /ʀadjɔgʀafje/ [2] *vtr* to X-ray.

radiographique /ʀadjɔgʀafik/ *adj* X-ray.

radioguidage /ʀadjogidaʒ/ *nm* Aviat, Naut radio control; **~ des automobilistes** traffic information service.

radioguider /ʀadjogide/ [1] *vtr* to control by radio; **fusée radioguidée** radio-controlled rocket.

radio-isotope, *pl* **~s** /ʀadjoizotɔp/ *nm* radioisotope.

radiologie /ʀadjɔlɔʒi/ *nf* radiology.

radiologique /ʀadiɔlɔʒik/ *adj* radiological.

radiologiste /ʀadjɔlɔʒist/, **radiologue** /ʀadjɔlɔg/ ▶ **510** *nmf* radiologist.

radiomessageur /ʀadjomesaʒœʀ/ *nm* pager.

radiomètre /ʀadjomɛtʀ/ *nm* radiometer.

radionavigateur /ʀadjonavigatœʀ/ *nm* radio officer.

radionavigation /ʀadjonavigasjɔ̃/ *nf* radio navigation.

radiophare /ʀadjofaʀ/ *nm* radio beacon.

radiophonie /ʀadjofɔni/ *nf* radiotelephony.

radiophonique /ʀadjofɔnik/ *adj* [*programme, production*] radio (*épith*); **techniques ~s** (radio) broadcasting techniques.

radioprotection /ʀadjopʀɔtɛksjɔ̃/ *nf* Nucl radiation hygiene.

radioreportage /ʀadjoʀəpɔʀtaʒ/ *nm* radio report.

radioreporter /ʀadjoʀəpɔʀtɛʀ/ ▶ **510** *nm* radio reporter.

radio-réveil, *pl* **radios-réveils** /ʀadjoʀevɛj/ *nm* clock radio.

radioscopie /ʀadjɔskɔpi/ *nf* fluoroscopy.

radioscopique /ʀadjɔskɔpik/ *adj* fluoroscopic.

radiosondage /ʀadjosɔ̃daʒ/ *nm* Météo radiosonde investigation.

radiosonde /ʀadjosɔ̃d/ *nf* Météo radiosonde.

radiosource /ʀadjosuʀs/ *nf* radio source.

radio-taxi, *pl* **~s** /ʀadjotaksi/ *nm* radio taxi.

radiotechnique /ʀadjotɛknik/ **I** *adj* radiotechnological.
II *nf* radio technology.

radiotélégraphie /ʀadjotelegʀafi/ *nf* radiotelegraphy.

radiotélégraphiste /ʀadjotelegʀafist/ ▶ **510** *nmf* radiotelegraphist.

radiotéléphone /ʀadjotelefɔn/ *nm* radiotelephone.

radiotéléphonie /ʀadjotelefɔni/ *nf* radiotelephony.

radiotélescope /ʀadjoteleskɔp/ *nm* radio telescope.

radiotélévisé, **~e** /ʀadjotelevize/ *adj* broadcast (simultaneously) on radio and television.

radiothérapeute /ʀadjoteʀapøt/ ▶ **510** *nmf* radiotherapist.

radiothérapie /ʀadjoteʀapi/ *nf* radiotherapy.

radis /ʀadi/ *nm inv* radish.
■ **~ noir** black radish.
IDIOMES **je n'ai plus un ~**○ I haven't got a penny.

radium /ʀadjɔm/ *nm* radium.

radiumthérapie /ʀadjɔmteʀapi/ *nf* radium therapy.

radius /ʀadjys/ *nm inv* radius.

radjah /ʀadʒa/ *nm* rajah.

radôme /ʀadom/ *nm* radome.

radon /ʀadɔ̃/ *nm* radon.

radotage /ʀadɔtaʒ/ *nm* drivel ¢.

radoter /ʀadɔte/ [1] **I** *vtr* to tell [sth] again and again.
II *vi* (parler beaucoup) to ramble (on); (se répéter) to repeat oneself; (dire des bêtises) to talk drivel○.

radoteur, **-euse** /ʀadɔtœʀ, øz/ *nm,f* driveller[GB].

radoub /ʀadu/ *nm* graving; **navire au ~** ship in dry dock.
■ **bassin de ~** dry dock, graving dock.

radouber /ʀadube/ [1] *vtr* to grave [*navire*]; to mend [*filet*].

radoucir /ʀadusiʀ/ [3] **I** *vtr* to soften [*voix*]; to soften up [*personne*]; to improve [*humeur*]; to make milder [*temps*].
II se radoucir *vpr* [*voix*] to become softer; [*personne*] to soften up; [*humeur*] to improve; [*temps*] to turn milder.

radoucissement /ʀadusismɑ̃/ *nm* (de la voix) softening; (d'humeur) improvement (**de** in); **le ~ de son caractère est dû à l'influence de sa femme** he has mellowed under his wife's influence; **la météo annonce un ~** the weather forecast says the weather's turning milder.

rafale /ʀafal/ *nf* **1** (de vent, pluie) gust; (de neige) flurry; **vent qui souffle en ~s** gusty wind; **2** (de mitraillette) burst; **tir en ~s** firing in bursts.

raffermir /ʀafɛʀmiʀ/ [3] **I** *vtr* **1** lit [*lotion, crème*] to tone [*épiderme*]; [*sport*] to tone up, to firm up [*musculature*]; [*eau froide*] to firm (up) [*tissus*]; **2** fig [*personne*] to strengthen [*autorité, position*]; [*mesure*] to steady [*marché, cours boursier*].
II se raffermir *vpr* [*tissus, chairs, peau*] to become firmer; [*voix*] to steady; [*cours boursier*] to become steady; [*sol*] to harden.

raffermissement /ʀafɛʀmismɑ̃/ *nm* **1** lit (de peau) (naturel) firming up; (avec crème, lotion) toning; **2** fig (de monnaie, taux) steadying; (d'autorité) strengthening; **le ~ du franc vis-à-vis du mark** the steadying of the franc against the deutschmark.

raffinage /ʀafinaʒ/ *nm* refining; **~ du pétrole** oil refining.

raffiné, **~e** /ʀafine/ **I** *pp* ▶ **raffiner**.

II *pp adj* [*personne, civilisation*] refined; [*cuisine*] sophisticated; **personne ~e dans ses goûts** person of refined tastes; **un type**○ **pas très ~** a rather uncouth character; **un mets ~** a delicacy.

raffinement /ʀafinmɑ̃/ *nm* **1** (de personne, civilisation) refinement; **faire preuve de ~ dans ses manières** to have refined manners; **2** (de décor, d'habillement) sophistication (**de** of); **3** (détail) refinement; **~s de style** stylistic refinements.

raffiner /ʀafine/ [1] **I** *vtr* to refine; **sucre raffiné/non raffiné** refined/unrefined sugar.
II *vi* to be fastidious (**sur** about); **~ sur la toilette** to be fastidious about one's appearance.

raffinerie /ʀafinʀi/ *nf* refinery; **~ de pétrole** oil refinery.

raffineur, -euse /ʀafinœʀ, øz/ **▶ 510** *nm,f* refiner.

raffoler○ /ʀafɔle/ [1] *vtr ind* **~ de** to be crazy○ about.

raffut○ /ʀafy/ *nm* **1** (bruit) racket○; **faire un ~ de tous les diables** to make one hell○ of a racket; **2** (scandale) stink○; **faire du ~** to raise a stink.

rafiot○ /ʀafjo/ *nm* boat, (old) tub○.

rafistolage○ /ʀafistɔlaʒ/ *nm* **1** (action) patching up; **2** (réparation) makeshift repair; fig stop-gap solution.

rafistoler○ /ʀafistɔle/ [1] *vtr* to patch up.

rafle /ʀɑfl/ *nf* **1** (opération policière) raid; (arrestation massive) roundup; **effectuer** or **faire une ~** to carry out a raid (**dans, chez** on); **2** (d'objets) clean sweep; **faire une ~** to make a clean sweep (**sur** of).

rafler○ /ʀɑfle/ [1] *vtr* **1** (emporter) to make off with, to swipe○ [*bijoux, gâteaux, provisions*]; **2** (obtenir) to walk off with [*médaille, récompense*]; to snap up [*contrat, marché*].

rafraîchir /ʀafʀɛʃiʀ/ [3] **I** *vtr* **1** (refroidir) [*pluie*] to cool [*atmosphère*]; [*glaçons*] to chill [*eau*]; **bois un verre d'eau, ça te rafraîchira** have a glass of water, it'll refresh you ou it'll cool you down; **le thé glacé/l'air frais te rafraîchira** the iced tea/the fresh air will cool you down; **2** (rénover) [*personne*] to restore [*tableau*]; to give a fresh coat of paint to [*mur, maison*]; **~ la mémoire de qn** to refresh sb's memory; **je me suis fait ~ la frange** I had my fringe GB ou bangs US trimmed.
II *vi* **mettez la salade de fruits à ~** put the fruit salad to chill.
III se rafraîchir *vpr* [*temps, atmosphère*] to become ou get cooler; [*personne*] to refresh oneself.

rafraîchissant, ~e /ʀafʀɛʃisɑ̃, ɑ̃t/ *adj* refreshing.

rafraîchissement /ʀafʀɛʃismɑ̃/ *nm* **1** Météo drop in temperature; **2** (boisson) refreshment.

ragaillardir /ʀagajaʀdiʀ/ [3] *vtr* to cheer [sb] up [*personne*]; **je me sens (tout) ragaillardi** I feel much brighter.

rage /ʀaʒ/ *nf* **1** Méd, Vét rabies ¢; **être atteint de la ~** to have rabies; **vaccin contre la ~** rabies vaccine; **2** (fureur) rage; **être en ~ contre qn/qch** to be furious with sb/about sth; **être pris d'une ~ aveugle/meurtrière/impuissante** to go into a blind/murderous/helpless rage; **être fou de ~** to be in a mad rage; **être ivre de ~** to be beside oneself with rage; **étouffer/écumer de ~** to choke/foam with rage; **se mettre** or **entrer dans une ~ folle** to fly into a rage; **serrer les poings de ~** to clench one's fists with rage; **avoir la ~ au cœur** ou **au ventre** to (inwardly) seethe with rage; **accepter qch la ~ au cœur** to accept sth while inwardly seething (with rage); **mettre qn en ~** to make sb's blood boil; **faire ~** [*maladie, concurrence, spéculation*] to be rife; [*épidémie, incendie, tempête, bataille*] to rage; **3** (passion) passion; **la ~ du jeu** a passion for gambling; **la ~ de réussir/de gagner** a passion for success/for winning; **il s'entraîne/travaille avec ~** he trains/works with passionate dedication.
■ **~ de dents** raging toothache; **~ furieuse** furious rabies; **~ paralytique** dumb rabies.
IDIOMES **qui veut noyer son chien l'accuse de la ~** give a dog a bad name and hang him.

rageant, ~e /ʀaʒɑ̃, ɑ̃t/ *adj* infuriating; **c'est ~** it's infuriating (**de faire** to do).

rager /ʀaʒe/ [13] *vi* (enrager) to rage; (être en rage) to be in a rage; **faire ~ qn** to make sb's blood boil.

rageur, -euse /ʀaʒœʀ, øz/ *adj* furious.

rageusement /ʀaʒøzmɑ̃/ *adv* **1** [*s'écrier*] furiously; [*écrire*] (avec colère) angrily; **2**○ (sans relâche) furiously.

raglan /ʀaglɑ̃/ *adj inv, nm* raglan.

ragondin /ʀagɔ̃dɛ̃/ *nm* **1** (animal) coypu; **2** (fourrure) coypu, nutria.

ragot○ /ʀago/ *nm* malicious gossip ¢; **faire circuler des ~s** to spread malicious gossip.

ragoût /ʀagu/ *nm* stew, ragout; **~ de poisson** fish; **viande en ~** meat stew.

ragoûtant, ~e /ʀagutɑ̃, ɑ̃t/ *adj* **peu** or **pas très ~** [*cuisine, mets*] rather unappetizing; [*affaire*] rather unsavoury[GB]; [*tâche, travail*] rather unappealing.

ragtime /ʀagtajm/ *nm* ragtime.

rahat-loukoum, *pl* **~s** /ʀaatlukum/ *nm* piece of Turkish delight; **des ~s** Turkish delight.

rai /ʀɛ/ *nm* **~ de lumière** ray of light.

raï /ʀaj/ *nm*: *music from the Maghreb with Western influences.*

raid /ʀɛd/ *nm* **1** Mil raid; **~ aérien** air raid; **2** Sport (à pied, ski, VTT) trek; **faire un ~ en traîneau à chien** to go dog-sleigh trekking, to go mushing US; **3** Fin raid (**sur** on); **~ boursier** raid on the stock exchange; **lancer un ~ sur** to mount a raid on.

raide /ʀɛd/ **I** *adj* **1** (sans souplesse) [*personne*] stiff; [*dos, jambe, col*] stiff; [*allure, attitude*] stiff; [*cheveux*] straight; [*fil, corde*] taut; **marcher d'un pas ~** to walk stiffly; **2** (à pic) [*pente, escalier*] steep; **3**○ (exagéré) **elle est ~ celle-là!** that's completely out of order; **je trouve ça un peu ~** that's a bit out of order; **4**○ (fauché) broke○; **5**○ (âpre) [*boisson*] rough; **6**○ (scabreux) [*plaisanterie, scène*] racy; **7**○ (soûl) plastered○, blind drunk○; **8**† (inflexible) liter inflexible.
II *adv* **1** (abruptement) [*monter, descendre*] steeply; **côte/escalier qui monte ~** steep slope/staircase; **2**○ (brutalement) **tomber ~ mort** to drop dead.
IDIOMES **être/se tenir ~ comme un piquet** to be/stand stiff as a ramrod; **tomber ~** to be flabbergasted.

raider /ʀɛdɛʀ/ *nm* controv (personne) raider; (compagnie) corporate raider.

raideur /ʀɛdœʀ/ *nf* **1** (de jambe, dos) stiffness; **avec ~** [*marcher, saluer*] stiffly; [*répondre, acquiescer*] stiffly; **2** (de caractère, principes) inflexibility; **3** (de pente, d'escalier) steepness.

raidillon /ʀɛdijɔ̃/ *nm* steep path.

raidir /ʀɛdiʀ/ [3] **I** *vtr* **1** lit to tighten [*cordage*]; to stiffen [*tissu*]; to tense [*bras, corps*]; **2** fig to harden [*attitude*].
II se raidir *vpr* **1** lit [*cordage*] to get tighter; [*bras, corps*] to tense up; [*tissu*] to stiffen; **les membres raidis par le froid** limbs stiffened by the cold; **2** fig [*attitude, mouvement*] to harden; **se ~ contre la douleur** to brace oneself against pain.

raidissement /ʀɛdismɑ̃/ *nm* (de muscle, corps) stiffening; (d'attitude) hardening.

raidisseur /ʀɛdisœʀ/ *nm* **1** Tech (pour tendre) stretcher; **2** Constr, Naut stiffener.

raie /ʀɛ/ *nf* **1** (dans coiffure) parting GB, part US; **se faire la ~ au milieu/sur le côté** to part one's hair in the middle/on the side; **2** (ligne) line; (griffure) scratch; **la ~ des fesses**○ hum the cleavage of the buttocks; **3** (rayure) stripe; **tissu à ~s** striped material; **4** (poisson) skate.
■ **~ d'absorption** Phys absorption line; **~ blanche** Zool white skate; **~ bouclée** thornback ray; **~ électrique** Zool electric ray; **~ d'émission** Phys emission line; **~ miroir** Zool brown ray.

raifort /ʀɛfɔʀ/ *nm* horseradish; **sauce au ~** horseradish sauce.

rail /ʀɑj/ *nm* **1** Rail (barre) rail, track; **sortir des ~s** lit to leave the track GB, to jump the track US; **être sur les ~s** fig [*projet*] to be on course; **remettre qch sur les ~s** fig to put sth back on the rails GB ou on (the) track [*projet*]; **2** (moyen de transport) rail; **transport par ~** rail transport; **3** (de tringle, porte) rail.
■ **~ de sécurité** crash barrier.

railler /ʀɑje/ [1] **I** *vtr* to make fun of; **ils ont raillé leur camarade sur son accent** they made fun of their friend's accent.
II se railler *vpr* **se ~ de** to make fun of.

raillerie /ʀɑjʀi/ *nf* **1** (attitude) mockery ¢; **dire qch sur le ton de la ~** to say sth in a mocking tone; **2** (propos) mocking remark; **être l'objet de ~s** to be a laughing stock; **être l'objet des ~s de qn** to be the butt of sb's jokes; **être l'objet de cruelles ~s** to be the butt of cruel jokes.

railleur, -euse /ʀɑjœʀ, øz/ **I** *adj* mocking.
II *nm,f* mocker.

rail-route /ʀɑjʀut/ *adj inv* road-rail.

rainer /ʀene/ [1] *vtr* to groove.

rainette /ʀɛnɛt/ *nf* tree frog.

rainurage /ʀenyʀaʒ/ *nm* **1** (action) grooving; **2** (surface) grooved surface.

rainure /ʀenyʀ/ *nf* groove.

rainurer /ʀenyʀe/ [1] *vtr* to groove.

rais = **rai**.

raisin /ʀɛzɛ̃/ *nm* **1** (fruit) grapes (*pl*); **~ blanc/noir** white/black grapes; **manger du ~** to eat grapes; **une grappe de ~** a bunch of grapes; **un grain de ~** a grape; **2** (variété) grape; **cette région produit un ~ sucré** this region produces a sweet grape; **3** (format) ≈ royal (*format 50 x 65 cm*).
■ **~ de table** dessert grapes (*pl*); **~s de Corinthe** currants; **~s de Malaga** Malaga raisins; **~s secs** raisins; **~s de Smyrne** sultanas.

raisiné /ʀɛzine/ *nm* preserve made from grape juice and various fruits.

raison /ʀɛzɔ̃/ *nf* **1** (motif) reason; **n'avoir aucune ~ de** to have no reason to; **non sans quelque ~** not without reason; **pour la bonne/la simple ~ que** for the very good/the simple reason that; **pour ~(s) de santé** for health reasons; **pour des ~s économiques/humanitaires/politiques** for economic/humanitarian/political reasons; **pour des ~s d'économie/d'hygiène** for reasons of economy/of hygiene; **on ne sait pour quelle ~** for unknown reasons; **il y a une ~ à cela** there's a reason for that; **avoir toutes les ~s de penser/d'être inquiet** to have every reason to believe/be worried; **avoir de bonnes ~s de penser/soupçonner que** to have good reasons for believing/suspecting that; **~ d'agir** reason for action; **~ d'accepter/d'acheter/d'emprunter/d'interdire** reason for accepting/buying/borrowing /prohibiting; **~ de plus pour faire/ne pas faire** all the more reason to do/not to do; **en ~ d'une panne/d'un désaccord/de la situation** owing to a breakdown/a disagreement/the situation; **à plus forte ~** even more so, especially; **à juste ~** quite rightly; **avec ~** justifiably; **comme de ~** as one might expect; **~ d'inquiétude/d'optimisme** cause for alarm/for optimism; **~ d'espoir** grounds (*pl*) for hope; **se rendre aux ~s de qn** to yield to sb's arguments; **2** (opposé à tort) **avoir ~** to be right; **ne pas avoir entièrement ~** not to be completely right; **avoir un peu/mille fois ~** to be partly/absolutely right; **à** or **avec ~** rightly; **donner (entière-**

ment) **~ à qn** to agree with sb (completely); **obtenir ~** to obtain satisfaction; **3** (rationalité) reason **¢**; **contraire à la ~** contrary to reason; **la folie l'a emporté sur la ~** madness got the better of reason; **se rendre à la ~** to see reason; **faire entendre ~ à qn** to make sb see reason; **il ne veut pas entendre ~** he won't see reason; **ramener qn à la ~** to bring sb to his/her senses; **perdre la ~** to lose one's mind; **en appeler à la ~** to appeal to people's common sense; **ne plus avoir toute sa ~** to be no longer in full possession of one's faculties; **il faut se faire une ~** you just have to resign yourself to it; **elle s'est fait une ~** she resigned herself to it; **se faire une ~ de qch** to resign oneself to sth; **conforme à la ~** rational; **plus que de ~** more than is sensible; **avoir ~ de qn/qch** to get the better of sb/sth; ▶ **rime**; **4** Math (rapport) ratio; **~ d'une progression** ratio of a progression; **à ~ de** at the rate of; **trente films à ~ de trois films par jour** thirty films at the rate of three films a day; **en ~ directe/inverse de** in direct/inverse proportion to.

■ **~ d'État** Pol reasons (*pl*) of State; **~ d'être** Philos raison d'être; (de vivre) reason for living; **n'avoir plus de ~ d'être** to be no longer justified; **n'avoir aucune ~ d'être** to have no justification; **avoir sa ~ d'être** to have its justification; **~ sociale** Jur company ou corporate name.

IDIOMES **la ~ du plus fort est toujours la meilleure** Prov might is right Prov; **il nous faut ~ garder** we must keep a cool head.

raisonnable /ʀɛzɔnabl/ *adj* **1** (pas trop élevé) [*prix, distance*] reasonable; [*consommation, natalité*] moderate; **ils vendent des voitures à des prix ~s** the cars they sell are reasonably priced, they sell cars at reasonable prices; **2** (mesuré) [*personne, objectif*] reasonable; [*politique, enthousiasme*] moderate; **3** (sensé) [*personne, idée, solution*] sensible; **sortir avec de la fièvre, est-ce bien ~?** is it really sensible to go out when you're running a temperature?; **à ce prix, est-ce bien ~?** is it sensible at that price?; **il est/n'est pas ~ de faire** it is/isn't sensible to do; **les délais paraissent ~s** the deadlines seem reasonable; **4** Philos (doué de raison) rational; **un être ~** a rational being.

raisonnablement /ʀɛzɔnabləmɑ̃/ *adv* **1** (légitimement) [*supposer, exiger*] reasonably; **être ~ inquiet** to be justifiably anxious; **2** (rationnellement) [*consentir, expliquer*] reasonably; **on peut ~ penser que** it is reasonable to think that; **3** (assez) [*précis, propre, confiant*] reasonably; **4** (modérément) [*boire, fumer*] in moderation; [*travailler*] at a reasonable pace; **5** (avec sagacité) [*gérer, parler*] sensibly.

raisonné, **~e** /ʀɛzɔne/ **I** *pp* ▶ **raisonner**.

II *pp adj* **1** (prudent) [*optimisme, attitude, déclaration*] cautious; [*décision*] carefully thought out; [*expansion, politique*] moderate; **2** (contrôlé) [*passion*] controlled[GB]; [*enthousiasme*] measured; **3** (sensé) [*gestion, stratégie*] sensible; **4** (rationnel) **grammaire ~e** analytical grammar; **histoire/biographie ~e** critical history/biography.

raisonnement /ʀɛzɔnmɑ̃/ *nm* **1** (suite d'arguments) reasoning **¢** (**sur** about); **un ~ confus/solide** confused/sound reasoning; **les lacunes de ton ~** the gaps in your reasoning; **suivre le ~ de qn** to follow sb's reasoning; **tous les ~s sous-jacents** all the underlying reasoning; **faire le même ~ pour** to apply the same reasoning to; **selon le même ~** by the same argument; **faire le ~ que** to argue that; **il tient le ~ suivant** his argument is as follows; **je ne tiens pas le même ~** I have a different way of reasoning; **tu ne feras jamais rien avec ce genre de ~** you won't get anywhere with that sort of thinking; **2** (opération de la pensée) reasoning; **~ logique/analogique/pratique** logical/analogical/practical reasoning; **mode/forme /méthode de ~** way/form/method of reasoning; **fondé sur le ~** based on reason; **3** (type de pensée) thinking; **~ économique/politique** economic/political thinking.

■ **~ par l'absurde** reductio ad absurdum.

raisonner /ʀɛzɔne/ [1] **I** *vtr* to reason with [*personne*]; to rationalize [*sentiment*]; **essayer de ~ ses enfants** to try to reason with one's children; **~ sa peur** to rationalize one's fear; **se laisser ~** to let oneself be talked round GB ou persuaded.

II *vi* **1** (penser) to think; **~ juste/faux** to think correctly/incorrectly; **~ à court terme** to think in the short term; **~ en termes économiques** to think in economic terms; **~ sur** to consider; **~ sur l'histoire/un problème** to consider history/ a problem; **2** (réfléchir soigneusement) to think carefully; **~ avant d'agir** to think carefully before acting.

III se raisonner *vpr* **1** (être raisonnable) [*personne*] to reason with oneself; **2** (être contrôlé) [*sentiment*] to be subject to reason.

raisonneur, **-euse** /ʀɛzɔnœʀ, øz/ **I** *adj* [*personne, air, esprit*] argumentative.

II *nm,f* **1** (par habitude) quibbler; **2** (rigoureux) reasoner.

rajeunir /ʀaʒœniʀ/ [3] **I** *vtr* **1** (physiquement) to make [sb] look younger; (moralement) to make [sb] feel younger; **cette cure en montagne m'a rajeuni de dix ans** my health cure in the mountains has made me feel ten years younger; **sa nouvelle coiffure la rajeunit d'au moins cinq ans** her new hairstyle makes her look at least five years younger ou takes at least five years off her; **2** (attribuer un âge moindre à) **~ qn** to make sb out to be younger; **les journaux l'ont rajeuni de cinq ans** the papers have made him out to be five years younger (than he is); **40 ans! vous me rajeunissez, c'est gentil!** 40! you're giving me the benefit of a few years, that's nice of you!; **déjà grand-père! cela ne me rajeunit pas!** a grandfather already! it doesn't make me feel any younger; **votre fils a déjà 25 ans! cela ne nous rajeunit pas** your son is 25! we're not getting any younger; **3** (rendre plus moderne) to give a new look to, to brighten up [*bâtiment, fauteuil*]; to modernize [*secteur économique, organisation*]; to update, to modernize [*installation, équipement*]; to update, to bring [sth] up to date [*livre, guide, règlement*]; **4** (abaisser la moyenne d'âge) to bring ou inject new blood into [*parti, corps de métier*]; to bring down the average age of [*population*].

II *vi* **1** (moralement) [*personne*] to feel younger; **2** (physiquement) [*personne*] to look younger; **3** (redevenir plus gai) [*quartier*] to become a lot livelier; **4** (retrouver l'éclat du neuf) [*meuble, matière*] to look as good as new.

III se rajeunir *vpr* **1** (essayer de paraître plus jeune) to make oneself look younger; **2** (se dire plus jeune) to make oneself out to be younger (than one is).

rajeunissant, **~e** /ʀaʒœnisɑ̃, ɑ̃t/ *adj* rejuvenating.

rajeunissement /ʀaʒœnismɑ̃/ *nm* **1** (de groupe, population) **on assiste à un ~ du corps enseignant** these days teachers are getting younger; **nous avons enregistré un ~ de la population** we see that the population is getting younger; **2** (d'entreprise) modernization; (de bâtiment) modernization, renovation; (d'équipement) modernization, updating; (de livre, manuel, règlements) updating; **3** (de personnes) rejuvenation; **cure de ~** rejuvenating treatment.

rajout /ʀaʒu/ *nm* addition.

rajouter /ʀaʒute/ [1] *vtr* to add (**à** to); **~ du beurre/des légumes** to add some more butter/vegetables; **~ un paragraphe** to add a paragraph; **en ~** (mentir) to exaggerate; (en faire trop) to overdo it.

rajustement /ʀaʒystəmɑ̃/ *nm* = **réajustement**.

rajuster /ʀaʒyste/ [1] **I** *vtr* to straighten [*chapeau, vêtement*]; to push [sth] back up [*lunettes*]; **~ sa coiffure** to tidy one's hair.

II se rajuster *vpr* to straighten one's clothes.

râlant○, **~e** /ʀɑlɑ̃, ɑ̃t/ *adj* infuriating; **c'est ~ qu'il pleuve** it's infuriating that it's raining.

râle /ʀɑl/ *nm* **1** (bruit pulmonaire) rale; **2** (de mourant, blessé) groan; **3** Zool rail.

■ **~ d'eau** Zool water rail; **~ des genêts** Zool corncrake; **~ de la mort** death rattle.

ralenti, **~e** /ʀalɑ̃ti/ **I** *pp* ▶ **ralentir**.

II *pp adj* [*geste, rythme, croissance*] slower.

III *nm* **1** Cin slow motion; **scène/chute (filmée) au ~** scene/fall (filmed) in slow motion; **tourner au ~** to shoot [sth] in slow motion; **2** (pas à pleine capacité) **fonctionner au ~** [*machine, entreprise*] to be just ticking over; [*personne*] to be running at half-speed; **avancer au ~** [*automobiliste, circulation*] to crawl along; **vivre au ~** to live at a slow pace; **3** Aut idle; **tourner au ~** [*moteur*] to be ticking over GB, to idle; **moteur qui tient bien le ~** engine that ticks over GB ou idles well.

ralentir /ʀalɑ̃tiʀ/ [3] *vtr, vi*, **se ralentir** *vpr* to slow down.

ralentissement /ʀalɑ̃tismɑ̃/ *nm* **1** (processus) slowing down; **~ de l'activité économique** slowdown in ou slowing down of the economy; **on assiste à un ~ de la croissance du travail temporaire** there is a slowdown in the growth of temporary work; **2** (sur les routes) tailback.

ralentisseur /ʀalɑ̃tisœʀ/ *nm* **1** (système de freins) engine brake; **2** (sur la chaussée) sleeping policeman GB, speed ramp.

râler /ʀɑle/ [1] *vi* **1**○ (protester) to moan○ (**contre** about); **qu'est-ce que tu as encore à ~?** what are you moaning about now?; **ça me fait ~** it annoys ou bugs○ me; **2** (gémir) [*mourant, blessé*] to groan.

râleur○, **-euse** /ʀɑlœʀ, øz/ **I** *adj* **qu'est-ce que tu peux être ~!** what a moaner○ you are!; **c'est un type assez ~** he's a bit of a moaner.

II *nm,f* moaner○.

ralingue /ʀalɛ̃g/ *nf* boltrope.

ralliement /ʀalimɑ̃/ *nm* rallying (**de qn à qch** of sb to sth); **de ~** [*cri, point, signe*] rallying.

rallier /ʀalje/ [2] **I** *vtr* **1** (rassembler) to rally [*troupes, navires*]; **2** (convaincre) to rally [*partisans*]; to win over [*opposants*] (**à** to); **solution qui rallie tous les suffrages** solution that has unanimous support; **~ qn à qch** to win sb over to sth; **~ qn à sa cause** to win sb over; **3** (adhérer) to rejoin [*groupe, parti*]; **4** (rejoindre) [*militaire*] to rejoin [*poste*]; [*diplomate, fonctionnaire*] to take up [*poste*]; **~ le bord** [*marin*] to rejoin (one's) ship; **~ la terre** [*navire*] to make landfall.

II se rallier *vpr* **1** (faire cause commune) **se ~ à** to rally to [*républicains*]; to join [*parti*]; **2** (être favorable) **se ~ à** to come round to [*avis, opinion*]; **elle s'est ralliée à notre cause** she was won over; **3** [*troupes, navires*] to rally.

rallonge /ʀalɔ̃ʒ/ *nf* **1** (de fil électrique) extension cord, extension lead GB; (de table) leaf; **table à ~s** extending table; **discours à ~**○ interminable speech; **nom à ~(s)**○ double-barrelled name GB, hyphenated name; **2**○ (d'argent) additional sum; (à une subvention) additional grant; (de temps) extension; **obtenir une ~ de 50 000 francs/d'une semaine de congé** to get an extra 50,000 francs/week off.

rallonger /ʀalɔ̃ʒe/ [13] **I** *vtr* **1** (en longueur, durée) to extend [*fil, table, période*]; to make [sth] longer [*paragraphe*]; **~ une jupe** (par l'ourlet) to let a skirt down; **~ qch de 2**

mètres to make sth 2 metres[GB] longer; **~ son séjour d'une semaine** to extend one's stay by a week; **2**○ (en argent) **~ la paie de 500 francs** to increase wages by 500 francs.
II *vi* **les jours rallongent** the days are getting longer ou drawing out.
III se rallonger *vpr* to lie down again.

rallumer /ʀalyme/ [1] **I** *vtr* **1** to relight [*feu, pipe*]; **~ la lumière** to put the light on again; **2** (raviver) to rekindle [*querelles, passions*]; **3** (faire reprendre) to trigger off again [*lutte, guerre*].
II se rallumer *vpr* **1** [*incendie*] to flare up again; **les lumières se sont rallumées** the lights went on again; **2** fig [*querelles, passions*] to be rekindled; [*lutte, guerre*] to flare up again.

rallye /ʀali/ *nm* **1** Sport (car) rally; **2** (réunion mondaine) party.

RAM /ʀam/ *nf* (*abbr* = **random access memory**) RAM.

ramadan /ʀamadɑ̃/ *nm* Ramadan; **faire le ~** to keep Ramadan.

ramage /ʀamaʒ/ **I** *nm* liter (d'oiseau) song.
II ramages *nmpl* (motif) foliage pattern; **à ~s** with a foliage pattern.

ramassage /ʀamasaʒ/ *nm* **1** (action de prendre par terre) (de coquillages, cailloux, d'œufs) collecting; (de champignons) picking; (de fruits, feuilles mortes, débris) picking up; **2** (fait de collecter) (de cahiers, copies) taking in, collection; (d'ordures ménagères, de vieux journaux) collection; (d'enfants) collection GB, picking up; **le ~ des ordures ménagères s'effectue deux fois par semaine** household rubbish GB ou garbage US is collected twice a week; **car de ~** (pour employés) work bus; (scolaire) school bus.

ramassé, **~e** /ʀamase/ **I** *pp* ▸ **ramasser**.
II *pp adj* **1** (trapu) stocky, squat; **2** (recroquevillé) (pour se protéger) huddled up; (accroupi) crouched, crouching; **être ~ sur soi-même** to be hunched up; **être ~ en chien de fusil** to be curled up; **3** (concis) [*style, formule, expression*] concise, condensed.

ramasse-miettes /ʀamasmjɛt/ *nm inv* crumb collector, silent butler US.

ramasse-monnaie /ʀamasmɔnɛ/ *nm inv* change tray.

ramasse-poussière /ʀamaspusjɛʀ/ *nm inv* dust trap.

ramasser /ʀamase/ [1] **I** *vtr* **1** (prendre par terre) to collect [*bois, coquillages, œufs*]; to pick up [*cailloux, crayon, prunes*]; to dig up [*pommes de terre*]; to pick up [*paille, foin*]; **~ à la pelle** lit to shovel [sth] up [*sable, terre*]; fig (en grande quantité) to get bucketfuls of [*argent*]; **2** (collecter) Scol to take [sth] in, to collect [*cahiers, devoirs, livres*]; to collect [*ordures ménagères, vieux journaux*]; to collect GB, to pick up [*enfants, écoliers*]; **3** (rassembler) to pick up, to collect up [*objets, jouets*]; to pick up [*feuilles mortes, débris*]; **4**○ (relever) to pick up [*enfant, vieillard, ivrogne*]; **~ qn dans le ruisseau** fig péj to pick sb up out of the gutter; **5** (recueillir) to collect GB, to take in [*personne, animal, chien perdu*]; **6**○ (arrêter) [*police*] to nick○ sb; **se faire ~ dans une rafle** to get picked up in a (police) raid; **7**○ (attraper) to get [*réprimande, gifle, mois de prison*]; to catch [*rhume*]; **~ un coup** to get hit; **se faire ~** to get a telling-off; **8** (réunir en une masse) to gather up [*jupe*]; **~ ses cheveux en un chignon** to put up one's hair in a chignon; **9** (gagner) to scoop up [*prix*]; **10** (condenser) to condense [*récit*] (**en** into).
II se ramasser *vpr* **1** (se replier) to huddle up, to shrink into oneself; (se pelotonner) to curl up; **2**○ (tomber) [*personne*] to fall over ou down; **3**○ (échouer) to come a cropper○.
IDIOMES **~ une bûche**○ or **un gadin**○ to come a cropper○; **se faire ~ à un examen**○ to fail ou flunk○ US an exam; **~ ses forces** to muster one's strength.

ramasseur, **-euse** /ʀamasœʀ, øz/ *nm,f* **~ de champignons** mushroom picker; (au tennis) **~ de balles** ball boy.

ramasseuse-presse, *pl* **ramasseuses-presses** /ʀamasøzpʀɛs/ *nf* baler.

ramassis /ʀamasi/ *nm inv* péj (de vauriens) bunch; (d'idées, objets) jumble.

ramassoire /ʀamaswaʀ/ *nf* H (pelle à poussière) dustpan.

rambarde /ʀɑ̃baʀd/ *nf* guardrail.

ramdam○ /ʀamdam/ *nm* **1** lit racket○, noise; **2** fig fuss; **faire du ~** [*personne*] to kick up ou make a fuss; [*affaire*] to cause an uproar.

rame /ʀam/ *nf* **1** Naut oar; **la traversée de l'Atlantique à la ~** the crossing of the Atlantic in a rowing boat; **2** (de papier) ream; **3** (métro, train) train; **une ~ de métro** a metro train; **4** Agric stake; **5** Tex tenter.
IDIOMES **il n'en fiche pas une ~**○ he doesn't do a stroke○.

rameau, *pl* **~x** /ʀamo/ *nm* gén branch; Bot branch, bough littér; **~ d'olivier** olive branch.

Rameaux /ʀamo/ *nmpl* **les ~, le dimanche des ~** Palm Sunday.

ramée /ʀame/ *nf* liter leafy branches.

ramenard○, **~e** /ʀamnaʀ, aʀd/ *adj* boastful (*épith*).

ramener /ʀamne/ [16] **I** *vtr* **1** (réduire) **~ l'inflation à 5%** to reduce inflation to 5 per cent; **~ les impôts au-dessous de 30%** to reduce taxation to below 30 per cent; **~ qch de 10%/20 personnes/30 francs à** to reduce sth from 10%/20 people/30 francs to; **~ la semaine de travail de 39 à 32 heures** to reduce the working week from 39 to 32 hours; **~ qch à de justes proportions** or **à sa juste mesure** to get sth into proportion; **2** (faire revenir) **~ qn/qch à** to bring sb/sth back to; **~ qn à la réalité** to bring sb back to reality; **~ qn à l'obéissance** to bring sb back into line; **~ les prix à leur niveau antérieur** to restore prices to their previous levels; **~ l'ordre/la paix/le calme** to restore order/peace/calm; **~ qn à de bons** or **meilleurs sentiments** to put sb into a better frame of mind; **~ qn sur terre** to bring sb down to earth; **~ qn à la vie** or **à soi** to bring sb round; **~ qn à la raison** to bring sb to his/her senses; **~ toujours tout à soi** always to relate everything to oneself; **3** (reconduire) to take [sb/sth] back; **~ qn à la maison** to take sb home; **l'avion qui les ramenait s'est écrasé** the plane which was taking them back crashed; **~ un malade à l'hôpital** to take a patient back to hospital; **~ qn en voiture** to give sb a lift GB ou ride US home; **~ un fugitif en prison** to take an escapee back to prison; **4** (faire rentrer) to bring [sb/sth] back; **j'attends qu'on ramène ma sœur/voiture** I'm waiting for my sister/car to be brought back; **~ qn sur la Terre** to bring sb back to Earth; **5** (rapporter) to bring back [*pain, souvenir, photos, maladie*] (**de** from); to return [*objet prêté*]; to win [*médaille, titre*]; **~ un cadeau de Paris** to bring back a gift from Paris; **~ des livres à la bibliothèque** to return books to the library; **~ qch dans ses bagages** fig to bring back sth from one's trip [*accord, expérience*]; **6** (déplacer) **~ les genoux vers le menton** draw your knees up to your chin; **~ la farine des bords vers le centre** draw the flour into the centre[GB] from around the edge; **~ ses cheveux en arrière/sur le côté** (avec un peigne) to comb one's hair back/to the side; (avec la main) to sweep one's hair back/to the side; **~ son manteau sur ses genoux** to pull one's coat over one's knees; **~ sa couverture sur son menton** to pull one's blanket up to one's chin.
II se ramener *vpr* **1** (être réductible) **se ~ à** to come down to, to boil down to; **se ~ à une question d'argent** to come ou boil down to a question of money; **2**○ (venir) to come over; (revenir) to come back; **ramène-toi!** come over here!
IDIOMES **la ~**○ (intervenir intempestivement) to stick one's oar in○; (se vanter avec ostentation) to show off○.

ramequin /ʀamkɛ̃/ *nm* ramekin.

ramer /ʀame/ [1] **I** *vtr* Agric to stake.
II *vi* **1** Naut to row; **2**○ (travailler dur) to work like a dog○.

ramette /ʀamɛt/ *nf* ream.

rameur, **-euse** /ʀamœʀ, øz/ *nm,f* gén rower; Sport oarsman/oarswoman.

rameuter /ʀamøte/ [1] **I** *vtr* to round up.
II se rameuter *vpr* to regroup.

rami /ʀami/ ▸ **449** *nm* Jeux rummy.

ramie /ʀami/ *nf* Bot, Tex ramie.

ramier /ʀamje/ **I** *adj* **pigeon ~** woodpigeon.
II *nm* woodpigeon.

ramification /ʀamifikasjɔ̃/ *nf* **1** (d'organisation) **les ~s d'une société secrète** the network of a secret society; **une société ayant de nombreuses ~s en Europe** a company with several offshoots in Europe; **2** (d'histoire, de complot) ramification; **3** (subdivision) subdivision; **4** Bot ramification.

ramifier: **se ramifier** /ʀamifje/ [2] *vpr* **1** lit [*tronc, tige, nerf, veine*] to branch (**en** into); [*branche*] to divide (**en** into); **2** fig [*secte, société*] to be divided into branches; **famille très ramifiée** family with many branches; **problème très ramifié** problem with many ramifications.

ramille /ʀamij/ *nf* small branches (*pl*).

ramolli, **~e** /ʀamɔli/ *adj* **1** [*substance*] (devenu mou) soft; (rendu mou) softened; **2**○ [*personne*] (avachi) limp; (apathique) spineless; (gâteux) soft in the head; **il est complètement ~** (gâteux) he's completely gaga○; **avoir le cerveau ~**○ péj to be soft in the head.

ramollir /ʀamɔliʀ/ [3] **I** *vtr* **1** (rendre mou) to soften [*matière*]; **2** (affaiblir) to make [sb] soft [*personne*]; to weaken [*volonté*].
II se ramollir *vpr* **1** [*matière*] to become soft, soften; **2**○ [*personne*] (s'avachir) to grow soft; (devenir gâteux) to go soft in the head○.

ramollissement /ʀamɔlismɑ̃/ *nm* lit, fig softening; **~ cérébral** or **du cerveau** softening of the brain.

ramollo○ /ʀamɔlo/ **I** *adj* (gâteux) doddery; (mou) spineless○.
II *nmf* (vieillard) dodderer; (mou) wet rag○.

ramonage /ʀamɔnaʒ/ *nm* **1** (de cheminées) chimney-sweeping; **entreprise de ~** chimney sweeps (*pl*); **les frais de ~** the cost of having the chimneys swept; **2** (en alpinisme) (action) chimney-climbing; (technique) laybacking.

ramoner /ʀamɔne/ [1] *vtr* **1** to sweep [*cheminée*]; **2** (en alpinisme) to back up.

ramoneur /ʀamɔnœʀ/ ▸ **510** *nm* chimney sweep.

rampant, **~e** /ʀɑ̃pɑ̃, ɑ̃t/ **I** *adj* **1** [*animal, insecte*] crawling; [*tige*] prostrate; [*plante*] creeping; **2** (servile) [*manières, personne*] grovelling[GB]; **3** (insidieux) [*idéologie, mal, inflation*] creeping; **4**○ Aviat **personnel ~** ground staff; **5** Archit [*arc, voûte*] rampant; **6** Hérald rampant (*après n*).
II *nm* **1**○ Aviat member of the ground staff; **les ~s** the ground staff; **2** (de pignon, fronton) sloping end; **toit à deux ~s** saddleback roof GB, saddle roof US.

rampe /ʀɑ̃p/ *nf* **1** (d'escalier) (sur balustres) banister; (fixée au mur) hand-rail; **2** (plan incliné) ramp; (côte) Rail incline; **3** Théât **la ~** the footlights.
■ **~ d'accès** (d'autoroute) sliproad GB, entrance ramp US; (de bâtiment) ramp; **~ d'arrosage** irrigation line; **~ de balisage** runway lights (*pl*), ramp; **~ de chargement** loading ramp; **~ d'embarquement** embarcation ramp; **~ de lancement** launchpad.
IDIOMES **passer la ~** Théât (dialogue) to

work; (plaisanterie) to come off; **tenir bon la ~**○ to hold out; **lâcher la ~**○ to kick the bucket○.

ramper /ʀɑ̃pe/ [1] *vi* **1** [*reptile, personne*] to crawl; [*chat, fauve*] to creep; **s'approcher/s'éloigner en rampant** to crawl near/away; **2** [*plante*] to creep; **3** fig (s'humilier) to grovel (**devant** to).

ramure /ʀamyʀ/ *nf* **1** (d'arbre) branches (*pl*); **2** ₵ (de cerf) antlers (*pl*).

rancard◐ /ʀɑ̃kaʀ/ *nm* **1** (rendez-vous) appointment; (amoureux) date; **avoir un ~ avec qn** to have an appointment ou a date with sb; **2** (renseignement) tip.

rancarder○ /ʀɑ̃kaʀde/ [1] *vtr* to arrange to meet.

rancart /ʀɑ̃kaʀ/ *nm* **1**○ **mettre au ~** to scrap [*objet, projet*]; to ditch [*personne*]; **bon à mettre au ~** ready for the scrap heap; **2**◐ = **rancard**.

rance /ʀɑ̃s/ **I** *adj* [*odeur, graisse*] rancid.

II *nm* **odeur/goût de ~** rancid smell/taste; **sentir le ~** to smell rancid.

ranch /ʀɑ̃tʃ/ *nm* ranch.

ranci, ~e /ʀɑ̃si/ **I** *pp* ▸ **rancir**.

II *pp adj* [*graisse*] rancid.

rancir /ʀɑ̃siʀ/ [3] *vi* [*huile, graisse*] to go rancid.

rancœur /ʀɑ̃kœʀ/ *nf* **1** (grief) resentment ₵ (**envers qn, contre qn** against sb); **éprouver de la ~ contre qn** to be full of resentment against sb; **accumuler des ~s** to store up resentment; **2** (amertume) rancour[GB].

rançon /ʀɑ̃sɔ̃/ *nf* **1** (somme d'argent) ransom; **moyennant ~** for a ransom; **mettre qn à ~** to hold sb to ransom GB ou for ransom US; **2** (contrepartie) **la ~ de qch** the price you have to pay for sth; **la ~ de la gloire/du succès** the price of fame/of success; **la ~ du péché** the wages of sin.

rançonner /ʀɑ̃sɔne/ [1] *vtr* **1** (exiger de l'argent de) [*brigand*] to rob [*voyageurs*]; [*racketteur*] to extort money from [*commerçants*]; **2**○ (exploiter) to fleece○ [*client, contribuable*]; **3**† (demander une rançon à) **~ un otage/navire** to hold a hostage/ship to ransom.

rançonneur, -euse /ʀɑ̃sɔnœʀ, øz/ *nm,f* (brigand) robber; (exploiteur) extortionist.

rancune /ʀɑ̃kyn/ *nf* **1** (sentiment) resentment ₵; **avoir de la ~ contre qn** to bear a grudge against sb; **sans ~!** no hard feelings; **2** (grief) grudge; **entretenir des ~s** to bear grudges; **garder ~ à qn d'avoir fait qch** to bear a grudge against sb for having done sth.

rancunier, -ière /ʀɑ̃kynje, ɛʀ/ *adj* **être ~** to be a person who holds grudges.

rand /ʀɑ̃d/ ▸ **46** *nm* rand.

randonnée /ʀɑ̃dɔne/ *nf* **1** (activité) (à pied) walking; (plus pénible) hiking; (de plusieurs jours) backpacking; **la ~ à cheval** pony-trekking; **~ à ski** off-piste skiing; **2** (promenade) (à pied) walk; (plus pénible) hike; **~ équestre** pony trek; **faire une ~** (à pied) to go walking; (à cheval) to go pony-trekking; (à skis) to go off-piste skiing; **ils sont en ~ en Espagne** (en voiture) they are touring Spain by car; **3** (trajet) (pour marcheurs) walk; (pour cavaliers) trail; (pour automobilistes) scenic route for motorists; **une ~ classique** (à pied) a well-known walk.

randonneur, -euse /ʀɑ̃dɔnœʀ, øz/ **I** *nm,f* (personne) (à pied) hiker, rambler GB; (à bicyclette) (touring) cyclist.

II randonneuse *nf* (bicyclette) mountain bike.

rang /ʀɑ̃/ *nm* **1** (rangée) (de personnes, chaises, légumes) row; (de collier) strand; **les enfants étaient en ~s** the children were in rows; **mettre les enfants en ~s** to make the children line up; **se mettre en ~s** [*enfants*] to get into (a) line; **(mettez-vous) en ~s deux par deux/trois par trois** line up in twos/threes; **Paul est au premier/dernier ~** Paul is in the first/last row; **2** Mil rank; **placer des soldats sur deux ~s** to draw up soldiers in two ranks; **silence dans les ~s!** silence in the ranks!; **les ~s d'une armée** the rank and file, the ranks; **rompre les ~s** (sur ordre) to fall out; (sans ordre) to break ranks; **servir dans le ~** to serve in the ranks; **sortir du ~** Mil, fig to rise ou come up through the ranks; **serrer les ~s** Mil to close ranks; Scol [*élèves*] to crowd together; fig (être solidaires) to close ranks; **ramener qn dans le ~** fig to bring sb into line, to make sb toe the line; **rentrer dans le ~** lit to fall into line; fig to toe the line; **rejoindre les ~s de l'opposition** fig to join the ranks of the opposition; **venir grossir les ~s des mécontents** fig to swell the ranks of the discontented; **3** (place) **arriver au 20e ~ mondial des exportations de café** to rank 20th in the world for coffee exports; **être au 5e ~ mondial des exportateurs de coton** to be the 5th largest exporter of cotton in the world; **ce problème vient au premier/dernier ~ des préoccupations du gouvernement** the problem is at the top/bottom of the government's list of priorities ; **reléguer qn/qch au ~ de** to relegate sb/sth to the rank of; **être sur les ~s pour un poste** to be in the running for a job; **acteur/auteur de second ~** second-rate actor/author; **4** (ordre) order; **par ~ d'ancienneté/de taille** in order of seniority/of height; **5** (dans une hiérarchie) rank; **~ inférieur, ~ subalterne** lower rank; **avoir ~ de** to have the rank of; **accéder au ~ de** to rise to ou to attain the rank of; **élevé au ~ de** promoted to the rank of; **fonction de très haut ~** high-ranking post; **ne fréquenter que des personnes de son ~** to mix only with people of one's own station; **garder** or **tenir son ~** to behave in a way appropriate to one's position; **mettre sur le même ~ que** to put in the same class as; **6** (au tricot) row; **un ~ à l'endroit/l'envers** one row knit/purl.

rangé, ~e /ʀɑ̃ʒe/ **I** *pp* ▸ **ranger**[1].

II *pp adj* (de bonne conduite) [*vie*] orderly; [*personne*] well-behaved.

III rangée *nf* (de maisons, d'arbres) row, line; (de sièges, spectateurs, soldats, d'élèves) row; **la première ~e vous pouvez sortir** Scol the first row can leave.

rangement /ʀɑ̃ʒmɑ̃/ *nm* **1** (action) (de dossier, pièce) tidying up; (dans un meuble) putting away; **le ~ du garage m'a pris toute la journée** it took me the whole day to tidy up the garage; **c'est un maniaque du ~** he's obsessively tidy; **2** (meuble, espace) storage space ₵; **meuble/espace de ~** storage unit/space; **boîte de ~** storage box.

ranger[1] /ʀɑ̃ʒe/ [13] **I** *vtr* **1** (remettre à sa place) to put away; **range les ciseaux!** put the scissors away!; **avant de partir range tes jouets** before leaving put away your toys; **~ un livre sur une étagère** to put a book back on a shelf; **le dossier était mal rangé** the file had been put in the wrong place; **où as-tu rangé ma veste?** where did you put my jacket?; **où ranges-tu tes verres?** where do you keep the glasses?; **~ les produits dangereux hors de la portée des enfants** keep (all) dangerous products out of the reach of children; **~ sa voiture au garage** to put one's car in the garage; **2** (ordonner) (par classement) to arrange; (en ligne) to line up; **~ qch dans l'ordre alphabétique/chronologique** to put ou arrange sth in alphabetical/chronological order; **~ des élèves deux par deux/trois par trois** to line pupils up in pairs/threes; **3** (situer) **~ un poète parmi les romantiques** to consider a poet as one of the Romantics; **on le range dans le camp des marxistes** he is regarded as a marxist; **~ qn dans la catégorie des imbéciles** to consider sb an idiot; **~ un animal dans la catégorie des mammifères** to class an animal as a mammal; **~ qn de son côté** to win sb over to one's side; **4** (mettre en ordre) to tidy [*maison, pièce, meuble*]; **il passe son temps à ~** he spends his time tidying up; **tout est bien rangé ici** everything is nice and tidy here; **ton bureau est toujours parfaitement rangé** your desk is always perfectly tidy.

II se ranger *vpr* **1** (se mettre en rang) [*soldats, prisonniers*] to line up, to get in line; [*élèves, enfants*] to line up, to form a line; **se ~ derrière qn** lit, fig to line up behind sb; **2** (se mettre sur le côté) [*véhicule, conducteur*] to pull over; [*cycliste*] to pull in; [*piéton*] to step aside, to make way; **3** (se garer) [*véhicule, conducteur*] to park; **se ~ à quai** [*navire*] to dock; **4** (se placer) **se ~ parmi** or **au côté de** to side with; **se ~ sous l'autorité de qn** to abide by sb's authority; **se ~ à l'avis** or **l'opinion de qn** to go along with sb; **5** (être mis à sa place) [*vaisselle, livres*] to be kept; **où se rangent les assiettes?** where are the plates kept?; **un couteau ça se range!** there's a place for knives!; **6** (s 'assagir) to settle down; **avec l'âge il a fini par se ~** he has settled down with age.

ranger[2] /ʀɑ̃dʒɛʀ/ *nm* **1** (soldat américain) ranger; **2** (chaussure) heavy-duty boot, Doc Marten® boot GB, stogie US.

Rangoun /ʀɑ̃gun/ ▸ **857** *npr* Rangoon.

ranimation /ʀanimasjɔ̃/ *nf* = **réanimation**.

ranimer /ʀanime/ [1] **I** *vtr* **1** (faire reprendre conscience à) to resuscitate [*personne*]; **2** (revigorer) [*air, promenade*] to revive [*personne*]; **3** (raviver) to rekindle [*feu, ardeur, espoir, débat*]; to stir up [*querelle, inquiétude*]; to restore [*confiance*]; to revive [*marché financier, région*]; to liven up [*conversation*].

II se ranimer *vpr* **1** (reprendre conscience) to come round, to regain consciousness; **2** (se raviver) [*feu*] to flare up; [*ardeur, flamme, débat*] to be rekindled; [*conversation*] to liven up.

RAO /ɛʀao/ *nf*: *abbr* ▸ **recherche**.

raout† /ʀaut/ *nm* rout‡, reception.

rap /ʀap/ *nm* Mus rap.

rapace /ʀapas/ **I** *adj* [*personne*] rapacious.

II *nm* Zool bird of prey.

rapacité /ʀapasite/ *nf* **1** (d'animal) ferocity; **2** (de marchand) rapacity, greed; **marchander avec ~** to haggle ferociously.

râpage /ʀɑpaʒ/ *nm* (de carotte, fromage) grating; (de bois, métal) rasping; (de pierre) grinding.

rapatrié, ~e /ʀapatʀije/ *nm,f* repatriate (**de** from); **les ~s d'Afrique du Nord** *people who returned to France after the Algerian war*.

rapatriement /ʀapatʀimɑ̃/ *nm* repatriation.

rapatrier /ʀapatʀije/ [2] *vtr* to repatriate [*exilés, fonds*].

râpe /ʀɑp/ *nf* **1** Culin grater; **2** Tech rasp.
■ **~ à fromage** cheese grater.

râpé, ~e /ʀɑpe/ **I** *pp* ▸ **râper**.

II *pp adj* [*carotte, fromage*] grated; [*vêtement*] worn.

III◐ *adj* (loupé) **c'est ~** it's off○.

IV *nm* Culin grated cheese.

râper /ʀɑpe/ [1] *vtr* to grate [*fromage, carotte*]; to rasp [*bois*]; to grind [*pierre, tabac*]; **~ le gosier**○ fig to be rough on the throat.

rapetassage○ /ʀap(ə)tasaʒ/ *nm* patching up.

rapetasser○ /ʀap(ə)tase/ [1] *vtr* to patch up [*vêtement, soulier*].

rapetissement /ʀap(ə)tismɑ̃/ *nm* diminishing size.

rapetisser /ʀap(ə)tise/ [1] **I** *vtr* lit **la distance/ce miroir rapetisse les objets** distance/this mirror makes things look smaller.

II *vi* [*jours*] to get shorter, to draw in; [*vêtement*] to shrink; [*personne*] to shrink, to get shorter.

III se rapetisser *vpr* [*vieillard*] to shrink, to get shorter.

râpeux, -euse /ʀɑpø, øz/ *adj* [*langue, vin*] rough; [*voix*] rasping.

Raphaël /ʀafaɛl/ *npr* Raphael.

raphia /ʀafja/ *nm* **1** (fibre) raffia; **une natte en ~** a raffia mat; **un brin de ~** a piece of raffia; **2** (arbre) raffia palm.

rapiat○ /ʀapja/ **I** *adj* (avare) stingy○, mean, cheap○ US.

II *nmf* skinflint○, cheapskate○.

rapide /ʀapid/ **I** *adj* **1** (qui se déplace très vite) fast; **le plus ~** the fastest; **le moins ~** the slowest; **être ~ à la course** to be a fast runner; **2** (qui coule vite) [*rivière, eau*] fast-flowing; [*courant*] strong; **3** (fortement incliné) [*pente, descente*] steep; **4** (fait en peu de temps) [*progrès, développement, disparition, transformation, vieillissement*] rapid; [*moyen, victoire*] quick; [*livraison, succès, amélioration, aggravation*] quick, rapid; [*réaction, intervention*] quick, swift; [*réponse, décision*] prompt; [*service*] quick, speedy; **jeter un coup d'œil ~ à sa montre** to take a quick look at ou to glance at one's watch; **une ~ montée du chômage** a rapid rise in unemployment; **avec une machine c'est ~** with a machine it's quick; **je vais y aller en avion, c'est plus ~** I'm going by plane ou I'm flying, it's quicker; **5** (au rythme soutenu) [*mouvement, geste*] quick; [*allure*] quick, rapid; [*course*] fast; [*rythme, respiration, pouls*] fast, rapid; [*musique, danse*] fast; **sa respiration était ~, il avait une respiration ~** he was breathing rapidly; **il a un pouls trop ~** his pulse is too fast; **6** (qui agit vite) [*personne, esprit*] quick; **à effet ~** [*médicament, substance*] quick-acting, fast-acting.

II *nmf* **être un ~** (pour penser, comprendre) to be a quick thinker; (pour agir) to have quick reactions.

III *nm* **1** (cours d'eau) rapids (*pl*); **descendre un ~** to shoot the rapids; **2** Rail express; **le ~ Paris-Maubeuge** the Paris-Maubeuge express.

IDIOMES **être ~ comme l'éclair** to be as quick as lightning.

rapidement /ʀapidmɑ̃/ *adv* rapidly, quickly; [*livrer*] quickly; [*intervenir, réagir*] quickly, swiftly; [*jouer*] Mus fast.

rapidité /ʀapidite/ *nf* **1** (promptitude) speed; **la ~ avec laquelle il a réagi m'a surpris** his quick reaction surprised me; **la ~ de son coup d'œil/geste** his quick glance/movement; **2** (concision) littér (de style, narration) briskness.

IDIOMES **réagir avec la ~ de l'éclair** to react with lightning speed.

rapiéçage /ʀapjesaʒ/, **rapiècement** /ʀapjɛsmɑ̃/ *nm* **1** (action) patching; **2** (pièce) patch.

rapiécer /ʀapjese/ [14] *vtr* to patch.

rapière /ʀapjɛʀ/ *nf* rapier.

rapine /ʀapin/ *nf* littér **1** (action) plundering; **2** (butin) plunder; **vivre de ~s** to live by plundering.

rapiner /ʀapine/ [1] *vi* littér to plunder; Mil to pillage.

raplapla○ /ʀaplapla/ *adj inv* (fatigué) worn out, wiped out○ (*jamais épith*).

rappel /ʀapɛl/ *nm* **1** (remise en mémoire) reminder (**de** of; **à** to); **~ utile/douloureux du passé** useful/grim reminder of the past; **~ historique** historical reminder; **2** (avis de facturation) reminder; **lettre de ~** reminder; **recevoir/envoyer un ~** to receive/to send a reminder; **'dernier ~'** 'final reminder'; **~ d'impôts** tax reminder; **3** (salaire différé) back pay; (impôt restitué) **~ (d'impôt)** tax refund; **recevoir deux mois de ~** to get two months' back pay; **4** (appel à revenir) (d'ambassadeur) recall; (de réservistes) call-up; (d'acteurs) Théât curtain call; **recevoir son ~** or **sa feuille de ~** [*soldat*] to get one's call-up papers; **avoir trois ~s** [*acteur*] to take three curtain calls; **~ à l'ordre/à la décence/au devoir** call to order/to decency/to duty; **battre** or **sonner le ~** lit, fig to call to arms; **5** Méd (de vaccination) booster; **6** Art (répétition de couleur, motif) repeat; **7** Sport (en alpinisme) abseiling ₵, rappel spéc; **descendre en ~** to abseil, to rappel spéc; **8** Naut righting ₵; **se mettre au ~, faire du ~** to sit out.

rappelé, ~e /ʀaple/ *nm,f* Mil recalled reservist.

rappeler /ʀaple/ [19] **I** *vtr* **1** (remettre en mémoire) to remind [sb] of; **~ l'importance de** to remind people of the importance of; **~ qch à qn** to remind sb of sth; **~ leurs devoirs aux enseignants** to remind teachers of their duties; **~ à qn que** to remind sb that; **~ que** to remind (sb) that; **nous rappelons qu'il est interdit de fumer** may we remind you that smoking is prohibited; **~ le souvenir de qn** to evoke the memory of sb; **~ le souvenir d'un événement** to recall an event; **livre/exposition rappelant la vie de Proust** book/exhibition recalling Proust's life; **rappelez-moi au bon souvenir de** remember me to; **il en a profité pour ~ au bon souvenir des sénateurs la crise précédente/que** he took the opportunity to remind the senators of the preceding crisis/that; **2** (dire) to say; **comme le rappelait hier le premier ministre** as the Prime Minister said yesterday; **a-t-il rappelé** he said; **rappelons-le** let's not forget; **3** (évoquer par ressemblance) to remind [sb] of; **vous me rappelez votre sœur** you remind me of your sister; **4** (par téléphone) to call back; **Pierre demande que tu le rappelles à son bureau** Pierre would like you to call him back at the office; **veuillez ~ plus tard** please call back later; **5** (appeler à revenir) to call [sb] back [*personne*]; Mil, Pol to recall [*ambassadeur, réserviste*]; Théât to call back [*acteur*]; **être rappelé à Dieu** to pass away; **~ qn à l'ordre** to call sb to order; **~ qn au devoir** to remind sb of his/her duty; **~ qn à l'obéissance** to bring sb to heel.

II se rappeler *vpr* **1** (se souvenir de) to remember [*fait, mot, visage*]; **se ~ avoir vu/lu** to remember seeing/reading; **se ~ comment/pourquoi** to remember how/why; **se ~ que** to remember that; **2** (se manifester) **se ~ au bon souvenir de qn** or **à l'attention de qn** [*personne*] to send one's regards to sb; **se ~ au bon souvenir de** iron [*réalité*] to come vividly back to sb's mind.

rappliquer○ /ʀaplike/ [1] *vi* (arriver) to turn up○; (revenir) to come back.

rapport /ʀapɔʀ/ **I** *nm* **1** (lien) connection, link; **faire/établir le ~ entre** to make/to establish the connection ou link between; **avoir ~ à qch** to have something to do with sth; **être sans ~ avec** to bear no relation to; **n'avoir aucun ~ avec** to have nothing to do with, to have no connection with; **les deux événements sont sans ~ (entre eux)** the two events are unrelated ou unconnected; **il y a un ~ étroit entre ces deux phénomènes** there is a close connection between the two phenomena; **je ne vois pas le ~!** I don't see the connection!; **il n'y a aucun ~ de parenté entre eux** they're not related; **un emploi/salaire en ~ avec mes qualifications** a job/salary appropriate to ou that matches my qualifications; **un emploi en ~ avec tes goûts** a job suited to ou that matches your interests; **il faut que la peine soit en ~ avec le délit** the punishment must fit the crime; **~ de cause à effet** relation of cause and effect; **~ à**○ about, concerning; **je viens vous voir ~ à mon augmentation** I'm coming to see you about my rise GB ou raise US; **2** (relations) **~s** relations; **~ amicaux** or **d'amitié** friendly relations; **avoir** or **entretenir de bons/mauvais ~s avec qn** to be on good/bad terms with sb; **les ~s entre les deux pays sont tendus/amicaux** relations between the two countries are strained/friendly; **il a des ~s difficiles avec sa mère** he has a difficult relationship with his mother; **avoir des ~s**○ euph to have intercourse ou sex; **3** (contact) **être en ~ avec qn** to be in touch with sb; **nous sommes en ~ avec d'autres entreprises** we have dealings with other companies; **se mettre en ~ avec qn** to get in touch with sb; **mettre des gens en ~** to put people in touch with each other; **4** (point de vue) **sous le ~ de** from the point of view of; **sous ce ~** in this respect; **sous tous les ~s** in every respect; **il est bien sous tous (les) ~s** he's a decent person in every way ou respect; **5** (compte-rendu) report; **~ officiel** official report; **~ de police/commission d'enquête** police/select committee report; **~ confidentiel** confidential report; **rédiger un ~** to draw up a report; **6** Mil daily briefing (*with roll-call*); **7** (rendement) return, yield; (de pari) **les ~s** the winnings (**de** on); **investissement d' un bon ~** investment that offers a good return or yield; **produire un ~ de 4%** to produce a return ou yield of 4%; **immeuble de ~** block of flats GB ou apartment block US that is rented out; **être en plein ~** [*arbres, terres*] to be in full yield; **8** Math, Tech ratio; **dans un ~ de 1 à 10** in a ratio of 1 to 10; **le ~ hommes/femmes est de trois contre un** the ratio of men to women is three to one; **bon/mauvais ~ qualité prix** good/poor value for money; **changer de ~** Aut, Mécan to change gear.

II par rapport à *loc prép* **1** (comparé à) compared with, in comparison with; **le chômage a augmenté par ~ à l'an dernier** unemployment increased compared with last year; **il est généreux/petit par ~ à son frère** he' s generous/small compared with his brother; **par ~ au dollar/mark** against the dollar/German mark; **2** (en fonction de) **le nombre de voitures par ~ au nombre d'habitants** the number of cars in relation to the number of inhabitants; **un angle de 40° par ~ à la verticale** an angle of 40° to the vertical; **un changement par ~ à la position habituelle du parti** a change from the usual party line; **3** (vis-à-vis de) with regard to, toward(s); **notre position par ~ à ce problème** our position with regard to this problem; **l'attitude de la population par ~ à l'immigration** people's attitude toward(s) immigration.

■ **~ d'engrenage** Aut, Mécan gear ratio; **~ de force** (équilibre) balance of power; (lutte) power struggle; **ils veulent créer un ~ de force en leur faveur** they want to tilt the balance of power in their favour[GB]; **je rêve d'une relation sans ~ de force** I dream of a relationship free of any power struggle; **~s sexuels** sexual relations.

rapportage○ /ʀapɔʀtaʒ/ *nm* tale-telling.

rapporter /ʀapɔʀte/ [1] **I** *vtr* **1** (remettre en place) (ici) to bring back; (là-bas) to take back; (rendre) (ici) to bring back (**à** to), to return (**à** to); (là-bas) to take back (**à** to), to return (**à** to); **as-tu rapporté le livre à la bibliothèque?** did you take back ou return the book to the library?; **rapporte-moi mes disques dès que possible** bring back my records as soon as possible; **je vous rapporte votre sac à main** I've brought back your handbag; **chien dressé à ~ le gibier** dog trained to retrieve game; **2** (prendre avec soi) to bring back [*objet, cadeau, nouvelle*] (**à** to, **de** from); **il nous a rapporté des cadeaux de son voyage** he brought us back presents from his trip; **est-ce que vous rapportez de bonnes nouvelles?** have you brought back good news?; **3** (procurer un bénéfice) to bring in [*somme, revenu*] (**à** to); **la vente de la maison leur a rapporté beaucoup d'argent** they made a lot of money on the sale of the house, the sale of the house brought them a lot of money; **les actions rapportent 10%** the shares yield ou return 10%; **mes vignobles/terres me rapportent beaucoup d'argent** my vineyards/lands bring me in a good income ou a lot of money; **leurs investissements leur rapportent beaucoup d'argent** their investments give them a high return on their money; **ça ne rapporte rien** it doesn't pay; **qu'est-ce que ça va te ~ sinon des ennuis?** what can you gain from it except trouble?; **4** (ajouter) to add; Cout to sew [sth] on [*poche, pièce*]; **5** (relater) to report (**à** to); (citer) to quote [*bon mot*]; **je ne fais que ~ ses propos** I'm only reporting what he said; **on m'a rapporté que** I was told that; **la légende rapporte que** legend has it that; **6** (rattacher) to relate to; **si on rapporte les événements au contexte de l'époque** if you put the events in the context of the period; **~ qch à sa cause** to relate sth to its cause; **il rapporte tout à sa petite personne** he brings everything back to himself; **7** (convertir) **~ les mesures à l'échelle qui convient** to bring the measurements into scale; **8**○ (moucharder) Scol **ce n'est pas beau de ~ ce qu'ont fait tes petits camarades** it's not nice to tell on your friends; **9** Math **~ un angle** to plot an angle; **10** Jur to rescind, to revoke [*décret, mesure, acte*]; to cancel [*nomination*]; to reverse [*décision*].

II *vi* **1** (procurer un bénéfice) to bring in money, to be lucrative; **un métier/investissement qui rapporte** a lucrative job/investment; **ça rapporte beaucoup** it's lucrative; **ça rapporte peu** it's not very lucrative; **2**○ (moucharder) to tell tales.

III se rapporter *vpr* **1** (être en relation avec) **se ~ à** to relate to, to bear a relation to; **votre réponse ne se rapporte pas à la question posée** your answer does not relate to ou is not relevant to the question asked; **tout ce qui se rapporte à ce chanteur la passionne** she's mad about everything that's got to do with this singer; **le pronom se rapporte au nom** Ling the pronoun is related to the noun; **2** (faire confiance à) **s'en ~ à** to rely on; **je m'en rapporte à vous/à votre jugement** I rely on you/on your judgment.

rapporteur, **-euse** /ʀapɔʀtœʀ, øz/ **I**○ *adj* **ce qu'il peut être ~ ce gamin!** that kid is a regular little telltale GB ou tattletale US!

II *nm,f* **1** Pol reporter; **2**○ (mouchard) telltale GB ou tattletale US.

III *nm* Math protractor.

rapprendre /ʀapʀɑ̃dʀ/ [52] *vtr* = **réapprendre**.

rapproché, **~e** /ʀapʀɔʃe/ **I** *pp* ▸ **rapprocher**.

II *pp adj* **1** (dans l'espace) close together; **il a les yeux ~s** his eyes are set close together, his eyes are close-set; **elle a les sourcils ~s** her eyebrows are close together; **2** (dans le temps) close together; **les jours de livraison sont plus ~s** delivery days are closer together; **il a eu deux crises d'asthme ~es** he had two asthma attacks close together; **à intervalles ~s** in quick succession; **deux coups de fusil ~s** two gunshots in quick succession.

rapprochement /ʀapʀɔʃmɑ̃/ *nm* **1** (entente) rapprochement Pol; **il n'y a pas eu de ~ entre leurs positions** they have failed to narrow the gap between their positions; **le groupe né du ~ entre la firme Dubois et la société Laforêt** the group formed from the links established between the Dubois firm and the Laforêt company; **2** (comparaison) connection; **ton ~ est inattendu** the connection you make is surprising; **faire** or **établir un ~** to make ou establish a connection (**entre** between; **avec** with); **je n'avais pas fait le ~** I hadn't seen ou made the connection.

rapprocher /ʀapʀɔʃe/ [1] **I** *vtr* **1** (rendre plus proche) to move [sth] closer [*objet*] (**de** to); **peux-tu ~ la lampe, je n'y vois rien** can you move the lamp a bit closer, I can't see a thing; **si tu n'y vois rien, rapproche la lampe** if you can't see, move the lamp closer; **rapproche la chaise du mur** move the chair closer to the wall; **le courant nous rapproche de la côte** the current is taking us toward(s) the coast; **le prolongement de la ligne va me ~ de mon travail** the extension of the line will take me closer to my work; **il faut ~ les électrodes pour que l'étincelle se produise** the electrodes must be moved closer together in order to produce a spark; **j'ai dû ~ mon fauteuil de la fenêtre** I had to move my armchair closer to the window; **rapproche les deux vases** move the two vases closer together; **les jumelles rapprochent les objets** fig binoculars make objects seem closer ou nearer; **2** (dans le temps) to bring [sth] forward(s) [*date, rendez-vous*] (**de** to); **ils veulent ~ la date des négociations** they want to bring the date of the negotiations forward; **cette date nous rapproche trop des élections** this date brings us too close to the elections; **3** (disposer à l'entente) to bring [sb] (closer) together [*personnes*]; **leur passion pour la musique les rapproche** they are drawn together by their passion for music; **ses épreuves l'ont rapprochée des pauvres** her hardships have brought her closer to the poor; **ils ont réussi à ~ les deux pays** they managed to improve relations between the two countries; **4** (réunir) to bring together [*personnes*]; **activité/club rapprochant des gens d'horizons très différents** activity/club which brings together people from very different walks of life; **5** (pour comparer) to compare; **la situation est à ~ de ce qui s'est passé en 1951** the situation can be compared to what happened in 1951; **6** (apparenter) **ses caractéristiques le rapprochent plus des mammifères** its characteristics make it closer to the mammals.

II se rapprocher *vpr* **1** (devenir plus proche) to get closer, to get nearer (**de** to); **l'avion/l'orage/l'ennemi se rapproche** the plane/the storm/the enemy is getting closer; **j'ai choisi ce travail pour me ~ d'elle** I chose this job so that I could be nearer to her; **2** (améliorer des relations) to get closer (**de** to); **ils n'ont rien fait pour se ~ de nous** they did nothing to get closer to us; **il semble que les deux pays se rapprochent** relations between the two countries seem to be improving; **3** (s'apparenter) **se ~ de** (processus) to get close to; (état) to be close to; **leurs peintures se rapprochent des fresques antiques** their paintings are similar to ancient frescoes; **le chimpanzé se rapproche plus de l'homme que du babouin** the chimpanzee is more closely related to man than to the baboon.

rapprovisionnement /ʀapʀɔvizjɔnmɑ̃/ *nm* = **réapprovisionnement**.

rapprovisionner /ʀapʀɔvizjɔne/ [1] *vtr* = **réapprovisionner**.

rapsode = **rhapsode**.

rapsodie = **rhapsodie**.

rapt /ʀapt/ *nm* **1** (enlèvement) kidnapping[GB], abduction; **2** Phys, Nucl pick-up.

raquer○ /ʀake/ [1] *vi* (payer) to cough up○, pay up.

raquette /ʀakɛt/ *nf* **1** (de tennis, badminton) racket; (de tennis de table) bat GB, paddle US; **2** (joueur) player; **c'est une fine ~** he's a good player; **3** (pour marcher dans la neige) snowshoe; **4** Bot prickly pear.

rare /ʀɑʀ/ *adj* **1** (peu commun) [*personne, objet, animal, plante*] rare; [*matière première, denrée, main-d'œuvre, produit*] scarce; [*minerai*] rare, scarce; **être l'un des ~s qui** to be one of the few (people) who; **2** (peu fréquent) [*cas, mot, maladie*] rare; [*moment*] rare; [*visites*] infrequent; [*occasion*] rare, unusual; [*emploi, utilisation*] unusual, uncommon; [*voyages, trains*] infrequent; [*voitures, passants, clients, amis*] few; **les clients sont ~s à cette époque-ci de l'année** we have very few customers at this time of year; **devenir** or **se faire ~** [*argent, produit, denrée*] to be ou become scarce; **vous vous faites ~ ces temps-ci** you are not around much these days; **il se fait de plus en plus ~ dans le village** he comes to the village less and less (frequently); **quelques ~s visiteurs** a few occasional visitors; **~s étaient ceux qui faisaient** there were few who did; **il est ~ de faire** it is unusual to do; **il n'est pas ~ de faire** it isn't uncommon ou unusual to do; **il est ~ qu'il vienne en train** it's unusual for him to come by train; **il n'est pas ~ qu'il reste pour dîner** it's not unusual for him to stay for dinner; **cela n'a rien de ~** there's nothing unusual about it; **à de ~s exceptions près** with few exceptions; **3** (exceptionnel) [*qualité, beauté, talent*] rare; [*maîtrise, intelligence, énergie, courage*] exceptional; [*bêtise, impudence, inconséquence*] singular; **combat d'une ~ violence** exceptionally violent fight ou fighting; **être d'une bêtise ~** or **d'une ~ bêtise** to be singularly ou exceptionally stupid; **être d'une intelligence ~** to be exceptionally intelligent; **il est l'exemple ~ de** he is a rare example of; **4** (clairsemé) [*cheveux, barbe, végétation*] sparse; [*air*] thin.

raréfaction /ʀɑʀefaksjɔ̃/ *nf* (de gaz, d'air) rarefaction; (pénurie) growing shortage.

raréfiable /ʀɑʀefjabl/ *adj* rarefiable.

raréfier /ʀɑʀefje/ [2] **I** *vtr* **1** (rendre moins dense) to rarefy [*air, gaz*]; **2** (rendre rare) to make [sth] rare.

II se raréfier *vpr* [*air*] to become thinner; [*gaz, atmosphère*] to rarefy; [*nourriture, denrée, argent*] to become scarce; [*espèce animale, végétale*] to become rare.

rarement /ʀɑʀmɑ̃/ *adv* rarely, seldom.

rareté /ʀɑʀte/ *nf* **1** (d'argent, de crédit, denrées) shortage, scarcity; (d'édition, de médaille, mot) rarity; (d'offre, de demande) shortage; **édition d'une grande ~** very rare edition; **la ~ des visiteurs** the small number of visitors; **2** (de phénomène, d'événement) rarity; (de lettres, d'appels) infrequency; **être d'une grande ~** [*objet*] to be very rare; [*action*] to be very infrequent.

rarissime /ʀɑʀisim/ *adj* extremely rare; **les occasions sont ~s** opportunities are few and far between.

ras, **~e** /ʀɑ, ʀɑz/ **I** *adj* **1** (naturellement court) [*poils, pelage*] short; [*végétation*] low-growing; **à poil ~** [*animal, fourrure*] short-haired; **2** (coupé court) [*barbe*] short; [*gazon*] cut short (*après n*); [*étoffe, tapis*] short-piled; **en ~e campagne** in (the) open country; **3** [*mesure*] level; **une cuillère à café ~e de levure** a level teaspoonful of baking powder; **plein/remplir à ~ bord** filled/to fill to the brim (**de** with).

II *adv* short; **coupé ~** [*cheveux, barbe, gazon*] cut short (*après n*); **couper qch (à) ~** to cut sth very short [*cheveux, gazon*].

III au ras de *loc prép* **au ~ de l'eau/des arbres** at water/tree level; **au ~ de la terre** or **du sol** lit at ground level; **couper une plante au ~ du sol** to cut a plant down to ground level.

IDIOMES **être à ~ de terre** or **du sol** or **des pâquerettes**○ [*propos, idées, débat*] to be rather basic; **faire table ~e de** to make a clean sweep of; **en avoir ~ le bol**○ or **cul**● to be fed up○ (**de qn/qch** with sb/sth).

RAS /ɛʀaɛs/ (*abbr* = **rien à signaler**) nothing to report.

rasade /ʀɑzad/ *nf* (dans un verre) glassful; (au goulot) swig○.

rasage /ʀɑzaʒ/ *nm* **1** (action) shaving; **2** (résultat) shave; **~ de près** close shave.

rasant, **~e** /ʀɑzɑ̃, ɑ̃t/ *adj* **1** (frôlant) [*lumière, rayon*] oblique; [*tir, balle*] grazing; [*vol*] low; **2**○ (ennuyeux) boring.

rascasse /ʀaskas/ *nf* scorpion fish.

ras-de-cou /ʀɑdku/, **ras-du-cou** /ʀɑdyku/ *nm inv* **1** (pull) crew-neck sweater; **2** (collier) choker.

rasé, **~e** /ʀɑze/ **I** *pp* ▸ **raser**.

II *pp adj* **1** [*poil, cheveux, tête*] shaven; [*menton*] clean-shaven; [*jambe*] shaved; **il a les cheveux ~s** he's had his hair shaved off; **être bien/mal ~** to be well/badly shaven; **être ~ de près/de frais** to be close/freshly shaven; **2** (détruit) Mil razed to the ground; Constr [*bâtiment, quartier*] demolished.

rase-mottes /ʀɑzmɔt/ *nm inv* **le (vol en) ~** hedgehopping, low flying; **faire du ~, voler en ~** to fly low.

raser /ʀɑze/ [1] **I** *vtr* **1** to shave [*personne, tête, joue, jambe*] (**à** with); to shave off [*barbe, cheveux, moustache*]; **ce rasoir rase bien/mal** this razor shaves well/badly; **~ de près** to give [sb] a close shave; **se faire ~** to get shaved; **crème/mousse à ~** shaving cream/foam; **2** (abattre) Constr to demolish [*bâtiment, quartier*]; Mil to raze [sth] to the ground [*fortification, ville, quartier*]; **3** (effleurer) [*projectile*] to graze; [*avion, oiseau*] to skim; **4**○ (ennuyer) to bore [sb] stiff○.

II se raser *vpr* **1** to shave (**à** with); **se ~ les jambes** to shave one's legs; **se ~ de près** to give oneself a close shave; **se ~ la barbe/moustache** to shave off one's beard/moustache GB ou mustache US; **2**○ (s'ennuyer) to be bored stiff○.

IDIOMES **demain on rase gratis!** and pigs will fly!; **~ les murs** to hug the walls.

raseur○, **-euse** /ʀɑzœʀ, øz/ **I** *adj* [*personne*] boring.

II *nm,f* bore; **quel ~!** what a bore he is!

rasibus○ /ʀɑzibys/ *adv* short.

ras-le-bol○ /ʀɑlbɔl/ *nm inv* discontent; **le ~ étudiant** student discontent.

rasoir /ʀɑzwaʀ/ **I**○ *adj* [*personne, situation, film*] boring.

II *nm* (objet) **~ mécanique** razor; **~ électrique** electric shaver; **~ à main** cut-throat GB ou straight US razor; **~ mécanique** or **de sûreté** safety razor; **~ jetable** disposable razor; **~ à pile(s)** battery shaver; **~ rechargeable** (mécanique) razor with replacement blades; (électrique) rechargeable shaver; **lame de ~** razor blade; **une coupure de ~** a nick with a razor; **~ à deux lames** twin-blade razor; **coupe au ~** razor cut; **il lui a tranché la gorge d'un coup de ~** he cut his/her throat with a razor; **il l'a tuée d'un coup de ~** he killed her with a razor; ▶**lame**.

Raspoutine /ʀasputin/ *npr* Rasputin.

rassasier /ʀasazje/ [2] **I** *vtr* [*nourriture*] to fill [sb] up; [*personne*] to stuff (**de** with); **ce repas m'a vraiment rassasié** the meal has really filled me up; **être rassasié** (de nourriture) to have eaten one's fill (**de** of), to be replete (**de** with); **être rassasié de** to have had one's fill of [*spectacle, activité*].

II se rassasier *vpr* to eat one's fill (**de** of).

rassemblement /ʀasɑ̃bləmɑ̃/ *nm* **1** (manifestation) rally; (attroupement) gathering; (plus organisé) meeting; **2** (fait de se rassembler) gathering; **~ devant l'hôtel à cinq heures** meet in front of the hotel at five; **~!** Mil fall in!; **sonner le ~** Mil, hum to sound the rallying call; **3** (fait de rassembler) gathering together; **4** (union) uniting; **travailler au ~ des électeurs** to work on uniting voters.

rassembler /ʀasɑ̃ble/ [1] **I** *vtr* **1** (pour former un groupe) to gather [sb] together [*personnes*]; (pour mettre en contact) to bring [sb] together [*personnes*]; Mil to muster, assemble [*troupes*]; to round up [*moutons, troupeau*]; **~ des personnes dans une pièce/autour d'une estrade** to gather people in a room/around a platform; **2** (autour d'une cause commune) to unite [*citoyens, nation*]; **3** (réunir) to gather [sth] together [*effets personnels, documents*]; to gather, collect [*informations, preuves*]; **~ des poèmes en un seul volume** to collect poems together in one volume; **~ ses forces/son courage** to summon up one's strength/one's courage (**pour faire** to do); **~ ses idées** to collect one's thoughts.

II se rassembler *vpr* gén [*personnes*] to gather; (dans un but précis) to assemble; **se ~ autour de qn** to gather around sb; **tous les villageois rassemblés** all the assembled villagers.

rassembleur /ʀasɑ̃blœʀ/ *nm* rallying point.

rasseoir /ʀaswaʀ/ [41] **I** *vtr* to sit [sb] down again [*personne debout*]; to sit [sb] up again [*personne couchée*].

II se rasseoir *vpr* to sit down (again); **faire ~ qn** to make sb sit down (again).

rasséréné /ʀaseʀene/ **I** *pp* ▶**rasséréner**.

II *pp adj* reassured.

rasséréner /ʀaseʀene/ [14] **I** *vtr* to reassure, to calm [sb] down [*personne*].

II se rasséréner *vpr* [*personne*] to calm down; [*visage*] to clear.

rassir /ʀasiʀ/ [3] *vi*, **se rassir** *vpr* [*pain, gâteau*] to go stale.

rassis, **~e** /ʀasi, iz/ **I** *pp* **1** ▶**rassir**; **2** ▶**rasseoir**.

II *pp adj* [*pain, gâteau*] stale.

rassortiment /ʀasɔʀtimɑ̃/ *nm* = **réassortiment**.

rassortir /ʀasɔʀtiʀ/ [30] *vtr* = **réassortir**.

rassurant, **~e** /ʀasyʀɑ̃, ɑ̃t/ *adj* reassuring; **en compagnie d'un individu peu ~** with a dubious individual.

rassurer /ʀasyʀe/ [1] **I** *vtr* to reassure; **~ qn** to reassure sb, to put sb's mind at rest; **~ qn sur qch** to put sb's mind at rest about sth.

II se rassurer *vpr* to reassure oneself; **rassure-toi, tout va bien maintenant** don't worry, everything's all right now; **que l'on se rassure** set your mind at rest; **'ce n'est pas grave,' rassure Jean** 'it's no real problem,' John said reassuringly; **je suis rassuré de te savoir guéri** I'm relieved to hear you're better; **je n'étais pas très rassuré** (à un examen) I wasn't exactly confident; (devant un danger) it was quite frightening.

rasta○ /ʀasta/ *adj, nm* Rasta○.

rastafari /ʀastafaʀi/ *adj inv, nm* Rastafarian.

rastaquouère◐ /ʀastakwɛʀ/ *nm* pej flashy foreigner péj.

rat /ʀa/ *nm* **1** Zool rat; ▶**navire**; **2** (terme d'affection) **mon petit ~**○ my little darling; ▶**petit**; **3** péj skinflint, cheapskate; **quel ~**○**!** (avare) he is so tight-fisted.

■ **~ d'Amérique** Zool muskrat; **~ de bibliothèque** bookworm; **~ des bois** Zool wood rat; **~ des champs** Zool field mouse; **~ d'eau** Zool water rat; **~ d'égout** Zool brown rat, sewer rat; **~ d'hôtel** sneak thief; **~ musqué** = **~ d'Amérique**; **~ palmiste** Zool African ground squirrel.

IDIOMES **on est fait comme des ~s**○ we're caught like rats in a trap; **s'ennuyer comme un ~ mort**○ to be bored stiff○; **à bon chat bon ~** Prov you/they etc have met your/their etc match.

rata†○ /ʀata/ *nm* soldiers' slang grub○.

ratafia /ʀatafja/ *nm* (liqueur) ratafia (*liqueur*).

ratage○ /ʀataʒ/ *nm* failure, disaster○; **après ces ~s en série** after this series of failures ou disasters.

ratatiné, **~e** /ʀatatine/ **I** *pp* ▶**ratatiner**.

II *pp adj* [*carotte, poire*] shrivelled[GB]; [*visage, personne*] wizened.

ratatiner /ʀatatine/ [1] **I**◐ *vtr* to kill, to bump [sb] off; **se faire ~** to get bumped off.

II se ratatiner *vpr* **1** [*carotte, poire*] to shrivel; **2** [*visage, personne*] to become wizened.

ratatouille /ʀatatuj/ *nf* **1** Culin ratatouille; **2**○ (en sport, au jeu) thrashing○; **prendre une ~** to be thrashed○.

rate /ʀat/ *nf* **1** Zool female rat; **2** Anat spleen.

IDIOMES **se dilater la ~**○ to kill oneself laughing○; **ne pas se fouler la ~**○ not to strain oneself○.

raté, **~e** /ʀate/ **I** *pp* ▶**rater**.

II *pp adj* **1** (pas réussi) [*acteur, politicien, peintre*] failed; **une vie ~e** a wasted life; **mon dîner était ~** my dinner party was a disaster; **des photos ~es** photos that didn't come out; **la dernière photo est ~e** the last photo didn't come out; **2** [*occasion*] missed.

III *nm,f* (personne) failure.

IV *nm* Mil **avoir un ~** [*arme*] to fail to fire.

V ratés *nmpl* **1** fig (de négociations, système) hiccups; **2** Aut **avoir des ~s** [*voiture, moteur*] to backfire, to misfire GB.

râteau, *pl* **~x** /ʀɑto/ *nm* rake.

râtelier /ʀɑtəlje/ *nm* **1** Agric hayrack; **2**○ (dentier) false teeth (*pl*).

■ **~ d'armes** gun rack; **~ à pipes** pipe rack.

IDIOMES **manger à tous les ~s** to run with the hare and hunt with the hounds.

rater /ʀate/ [1] **I** *vtr* **1** (ne pas réussir) to fail, to flunk○ US [*examen*]; **j'ai raté ma vie/ma carrière** my life/my career is a failure; **j'ai raté mon gâteau/ma photo** my cake/my photo is a failure; **je rate toujours les gâteaux** my cakes are never a success; **~ un saut en hauteur** to fail a high-jump; **elle a raté son coup**○ she has failed; **2** (ne pas être présent pour) to miss [*train, début de film, rendez-vous*]; **~ son train de cinq minutes** to miss the train by five minutes; **3** (ne pas atteindre, ne pas voir) to miss [*cible, objectif, marche, personne*]; **il n'en rate pas une**○ he can be relied upon to put his foot in it○; **4**○ (ne pas sanctionner) **la prochaine fois je ne le raterai pas** next time I won't let him get away with it; **elle ne l'a pas raté**○ fig she put him in his place○.

II *vi* **1** [*plan, opération*] to fail, flop○; **il dit toujours des bêtises, ça ne rate jamais**○ he can be relied upon to say something stupid; **ça va tout faire ~**○ it'll spoil everything; **2** [*arme*] to misfire.

III se rater *vpr* **1** (soi-même) to bungle one's suicide attempt; **2** (ne pas se voir) **nous nous sommes ratés** we missed each other.

ratiboiser◐ /ʀatibwaze/ [1] *vtr* (voler) to clean [sb] out; **~ qch à qn** to pinch sth from sb○; **être complètement ratiboisé** to be cleaned out○.

raticide /ʀatisid/ *nm* rat poison.

ratier /ʀatje/ *nm* Zool ratter.

ratière /ʀatjɛʀ/ *nf* rat trap.

ratification /ʀatifikasjɔ̃/ *nf* (action) ratification (**de** of; **par** by); (document) instrument of ratification.

ratifier /ʀatifje/ [2] *vtr* **1** Jur, Admin to ratify [*traité, contrat*]; **2** (confirmer) liter to confirm [*projet, propos*].

ratine /ʀatin/ *nf* ratine.

ratio /ʀasjo/ *nm* ratio.

ratiocination /ʀasjɔsinasjɔ̃/ *nf* liter endless cogitation.

ratiociner /ʀasjɔsine/ [1] *vi* liter to cogitate endlessly (**sur** about).

ration /ʀasjɔ̃/ *nf* **1** (portion) ration; **une ~ alimentaire** a daily food ration; **une ~ de pain/riz par personne** a ration of bread/rice to each person; **une ~ de foin** a hay ration; **2** Physiol diet; **une ~ de croissance** a healthy diet for a growing child; **3** fig share (**de** of).

rationalisation /ʀasjɔnalizasjɔ̃/ *nf* rationalization.

rationaliser /ʀasjɔnalize/ [1] *vtr* to rationalize.

rationalisme /ʀasjɔnalism/ *nm* rationalism.

rationaliste /ʀasjɔnalist/ *adj, nmf* rationalist.

rationalité /ʀasjɔnalite/ *nf* rationality.

rationnel, **-elle** /ʀasjɔnɛl/ **I** *adj* rational.

II *nm* **1** Math rational number; **2** Philos **le ~** the rational.

rationnellement /ʀasjɔnɛlmɑ̃/ *adv* rationally.

rationnement /ʀasjɔnmɑ̃/ *nm* rationing ¢; **~ d'eau** water rationing; **malgré les ~s** despite rationing; **ticket/carte de ~** ration coupon/card.

rationner /ʀasjɔne/ [1] **I** *vtr* Écon to ration [*essence*]; to impose rationing on [*population*]; **~ la population en eau** to impose water rationing on the population; **je te rationne le chocolat** I'm rationing your chocolate supply.

II se rationner *vpr* to cut down (**en** on).

ratissage /ʀatisaʒ/ *nm* **1** (de jardin) raking; **2** (fouille) search; **procéder au ~ d'une région** to carry out a search of an area, to comb an area.

ratisser /ʀatise/ [1] *vtr* **1** (égaliser) to rake over [*jardin, allée*]; (enlever) to rake up [*feuilles mortes*]; **2** (fouiller) to comb [*quartier, région*]; **~ large** to cast one's net wide.

raton /ʀatɔ̃/ *nm* **1** Zool young rat; **2**◑ (Maghrébin) *offensive term applied to North Africans living in France*.

■ **~ laveur** racoon.

raton(n)ade /ʀatɔnad/ *nf* racial attack (*on Arabs or other minorities*).

RATP /ɛʀatepe/ *nf* (*abbr* = **Régie autonome des transports parisiens**) *Paris public transport system*.

rattachement /ʀataʃmɑ̃/ *nm* **1** (de territoire) unification (**à** with); **2** Admin (de personne) **demander son ~ à** Admin to ask to be posted to.

rattacher /ʀataʃe/ [1] **I** *vtr* **1** (faire dépendre) to attach [*service, région*] (**à** to); to link [*devise*] (**à** to); to post [*employé*] (**à** to); **il est rattaché au directeur des ventes** he reports to the sales director; **2** (associer) to associate [*œuvre, artiste*] (**à** with); **3** (attacher de nouveau) to retie [*lacets, poignets*]; to fasten [sth] again [*ceinture de sécurité, collier*]; to re-attach [*wagon, remorque*]; **~ un chien** to tie a dog up again; (avec une chaîne) to chain a dog up again; **4** (affectivement) **plus rien ne la rattache à Lyon/à ses parents** she no longer has any ties with Lyons/her parents; **c'est ce qui me rattache à la vie** it's what keeps me alive.

II se rattacher *vpr* **1** [*œuvre, artiste*] to be linked (**à** to); [*thème, problème*] to relate (**à** to); **2** [*passager*] to fasten one's seat belt again.

rattrapable /ʀatʀapabl/ *adj* **1** (réparable) [*dommage, perte*] recoverable; [*erreur, gaffe*] redeemable; [*tache*] removable; [*sauce*] which can be rescued (*épith*); [*maille*] which can be picked up (*épith*); **2** Admin, Entr (pouvant être travaillé ultérieurement) [*heure, journée*] which can be made up (*épith, après n*); (pouvant être conservé pour plus tard) [*congé*] which can be held over (*épith, après n*).

rattrapage /ʀatʀapaʒ/ *nm* **1** Comm, Écon (remise à jour) adjustment; (avec effet rétroactif) retroactive adjustment; **~ des salaires/prix** adjustment of wage rates/prices; **~ du déséquilibre** adjustment of the imbalance; **~ des salaires pour l'année en cours** retroactive adjustment of wage rates for the current year; **2** Fin (remontée) recovery; (hausse technique) **~ de cours** overdue increase in prices; **3** (de retard) catching up ¢ (**de** with); **~ des pays développés** catching up with developed countries; **opération/processus de ~** catching-up exercise/process; **4** Scol **cours/classe de ~** remedial lesson/class.

rattraper /ʀatʀape/ [1] **I** *vtr* **1** (rejoindre) to catch up with [*concurrent, passant, niveau*]; **~ son adversaire/le reste de la classe** to catch up with one's opponent/the rest of the class; **il a été rattrapé par la gloire/son passé/son âge** fame/his past/his age has caught up with him; **2** (capturer) to catch [*fugitif, animal*]; **3** (compenser) to make up for [*absence, temps perdu, déficit, différence*]; to make up [*points, arriérés, temps de retard, distance*] (**on** sur); **~ son retard** to catch up; **~ son retard sur qn** to catch up with sb; **~ du sommeil/du courrier en retard** to catch up on one's sleep/one's correspondence; **4** (réparer) to make good [*dommage, omission*]; to put right [*problème, tort, erreur*]; to smooth over [*paroles, gaffe verbale*]; to get over [*inconvénient*]; to save [*situation*]; to rescue [*sauce*]; to pick up [*maille*]; **~ le coup**○ to put things right; **5** (saisir) to catch [*objet*]; **~ le vase in extremis** to catch the vase at the last second; **6**○ Scol, Univ (permettre de passer) to let [sb] through, to let [sb] pass [*élève, étudiant*].

II se rattraper *vpr* **1** (se faire pardonner) to redeem oneself (**auprès de qn** with sb); **se ~ de ses erreurs** to make up for one's mistakes; **2** (compenser son désavantage) to make up for it; **elle se rattrape en travaillant deux fois plus** she makes up for it by working twice as hard; **3** Scol (atteindre le niveau requis) to catch up; **il faudra te ~ avant la fin de l'année** you'll have to catch up before the end of the year; **4** (compenser une perte) to make up one's losses (**avec** on); (compenser le temps perdu) to make up for lost time; (compenser ce qu'on n'a pas mangé) to make up for it; **se ~ sur le dessert** to make up for it by eating a big dessert; **5** (éviter une catastrophe) **se ~ de justesse** to stop oneself just in time; **se ~ à une branche** to save oneself by catching hold of a branch.

rature /ʀatyʀ/ *nf* crossing-out; **sans ~s ni surcharges** Admin without deletions or alterations.

raturer /ʀatyʀe/ [1] *vtr* **1** (barrer) to cross out [*mot, phrase*]; **deux mots raturés** two words crossed out; **2** (corriger) to correct [*page, texte*].

rauque /ʀok/ *adj* [*voix*] (naturellement) husky; (momentanément) hoarse; [*cri*] harsh.

ravage /ʀavaʒ/ *nm* **les ~s de la guerre/du temps** the ravages of war/time; **faire des ~s** [*troupes, incendie, pollution*] to wreak havoc; [*épidémie*] to take a terrible toll; **l'ampleur des ~s** the extent of the damage; **tu vas faire des ~s avec ta mini-jupe** hum you'll knock them dead in that mini-skirt.

ravagé○, **~e** /ʀavaʒe/ *adj* (fou) crazy.

ravager /ʀavaʒe/ [13] *vtr* **1** [*incendie, guerre, insectes*] to devastate, to ravage; **2** [*maladie, alcool*] to ravage [*personne, visage*]; [*chagrin*] to tear [sb] apart; [*passions*] to consume.

ravageur, **-euse** /ʀavaʒœʀ, øz/ *adj* **1** [*désir, passion*] all-consuming; [*humour*] destructive; [*mèche, sourire*] stunning; **2** [*insecte, animal*] destructive; [*incendie*] devastating.

ravalement /ʀavalmɑ̃/ *nm* **1** (de façades en pierre, brique) cleaning; (de façades crépies) refacing; **entreprise de ~** firm specializing in renovating façades; **faire le ~ d'un bâtiment** to renovate the façade of a building; **2** fig (amélioration) facelift; **faire un ~ de façade**◑ hum to do a repair job○ on one's face○.

ravaler /ʀavale/ [1] **I** *vtr* **1** Constr to clean [*façade en pierre, brique*]; to reface [*façade crépie*]; to renovate [*bâtiment*]; **2** fig to give [sth] a facelift [*image*]; **3** to swallow [*colère, indignation*]; **~ ses larmes** to hold back one's tears; **~ ses reproches** to keep one's criticisms to oneself; **faire ~ ses paroles à qn** to make sb eat his/her words; **4** (déprécier) **~ qch au rang de** to reduce sth to the level of.

II se ravaler *vpr* **1** (s'avilir) **se ~ au rang de**... to reduce oneself to the level of...; **2 se ~ la façade**◑ hum to do a repair job○ on one's face○.

ravaudage /ʀavodaʒ/ *nm* (d'habits) mending; (de chaussettes) darning.

ravauder /ʀavode/ [1] *vtr* to mend [*chemise*]; to darn [*chaussette, pull*].

rave /ʀav/ *nf* turnip.

ravenelle /ʀavnɛl/ *nf* wallflower.

Ravenne /ʀavɛn/ ▶ **857** *npr* Ravenna.

ravi, **~e** /ʀavi/ **I** *pp* ▶ **ravir**.

II *pp adj* delighted (**de** with); (plus fort) thrilled (**de** with); **je suis ~ de mon séjour/mon cadeau/ma nouvelle voiture** I'm delighted with my stay/my present/my new car; **~ de faire** delighted to do; **~ de vous avoir rencontré** delighted to have met you; **avoir un air ~** to look delighted ou thrilled.

ravier /ʀavje/ *nm* small dish (*for hors d'oeuvres*).

ravigotant, **~e** /ʀavigɔtɑ̃, ɑ̃t/ *adj* invigorating.

ravigote /ʀavigɔt/ *nf*: *highly-seasoned sauce with herbs and shallots*.

ravigoter○ /ʀavigɔte/ [1] *vtr* [*air frais*] to invigorate; [*alcool, boisson*] to perk [sb/sth] up; **la pluie a ravigoté mes plantes** the rain made my flowers perk up.

ravin /ʀavɛ̃/ *nm* ravine.

ravine /ʀavin/ *nf* gully.

ravinement /ʀavinmɑ̃/ *nm* **1** (érosion) gully erosion; **2** (sillons) gullies (*pl*).

raviner /ʀavine/ [1] *vtr* **1** (creuser) to furrow [*sol, terrain*]; **collines ravinées** hillsides full of ravines; **2** (marquer) to line [*visage*].

ravioli /ʀavjɔli/ *nm* ravioli ¢; **un ~** a piece of ravioli.

ravir /ʀaviʀ/ [3] *vtr* **1** (plaire beaucoup) to delight; **elle est belle à ~** she's ravishing; **le bleu lui va à ~** blue really suits him/her; **2** fml (dérober) to abduct [*personne*]; to steal [*bien*]; **~ qch à qn** to rob sb of sth; **~ la première place à qn** to rob sb of first place.

raviser: **se raviser** /ʀavize/ [1] *vpr* to change one's mind.

ravissant, **~e** /ʀavisɑ̃, ɑ̃t/ *adj* beautiful, delightful.

ravissement /ʀavismɑ̃/ *nm* **1** (enchantement) rapture; **écouter avec ~** to listen with rapture; **manger qch avec ~** to eat sth with great delight; **2** (rapt) abduction.

ravisseur, **-euse** /ʀavisœʀ, øz/ *nm,f* kidnapper[GB], abductor.

ravitaillement /ʀavitajmɑ̃/ *nm* **1** (activité) (en vivres) provision of fresh supplies (**de qn** to sb; **en qch** of sth); **le ~ en eau/en essence** the provision of supplies of water/of fuel; **aller au ~** to go and stock up; **~ en vol** Aviat in-flight refuelling[GB]; **2** (vivres) supplies (*pl*).

ravitailler /ʀavitaje/ [1] **I** *vtr* (en vivres) to provide [sb] with fresh supplies [*armée, ville*] (**en qch** of sth); (en carburant) to refuel [*avion, navire*]; **~ une troupe en eau/carburant** to provide a unit with supplies of water/fuel; **~ en vol** to refuel in flight.

II se ravitailler *vpr* (en vivres) to obtain fresh supplies (**en qch** of sth).

ravitailleur /ʀavitajœʀ/ *nm* **1** (en carburant) (avion) tanker aircraft; (camion) bowser; **2** (navire) submarine mother-ship.

raviver /ʀavive/ [1] *vtr* [*personne*] to rekindle [*feu*]; [*produit*] to revive [*couleur*]; [*événement*] to rekindle [*colère, chagrin, passion, désir*]; to bring back [*mémoire, souvenir*]; to revive [*querelle, hostilité, malentendu*]; **~ une douleur** (physique) to bring the pain back; (mentale) to re-open an old wound.

ravoir /ʀavwaʀ/ *vtr* **1** (avoir à nouveau) **~ qn/qch** to get sb/sth back; **elle va ~ ses enfants** (après un divorce) she's going to get her children back; **2**○ (remettre à neuf) **je n'arrive pas à ~ cette chemise** I can't get this shirt clean; **~ une casserole** to get a saucepan clean again.

rayé, **~e** /ʀeje/ **I** *pp* ▶ **rayer**.

II *pp adj* [*tissu, pull*] striped; **canapé ~ blanc et jaune** sofa with white and yellow stripes.

rayer /ʀeje/ [21] *vtr* **1** (barrer) to cross [sth] out [*mot, phrase*]; **'~ la mention inutile'** 'delete whichever does not apply'; **~ qch/qn d'une liste** to cross sth/sb's name off a list; **2** (supprimer) **~ qch de sa conscience** to blot sth out from one's mind; **la ville a été rayée de la carte** the town was wiped off the map; **3** (abîmer) to scratch [*meuble, disque*]; **4** Mil **~ le canon d'une arme** to rifle a gun barrel.

rayon /ʀɛjɔ̃/ *nm* **1** Math radius; **un ~ de 10 cm** a radius of 10 cm; **tracer un cercle de ~ r** draw a circle with radius r; **2** (limite) radius; **dans un ~ de 10 km** within a 10 km radius; **~ d'action** lit range; fig sphere of activity ou activities; **~ d'action d'une arme** range of action of a weapon; **avion à grand ~ d'action** long-range aircraft; **3** (de lumière, lune) ray; **les ~s du soleil, les ~s solaires** the sun's rays; **un ~ de soleil** lit a ray of sunlight; fig (personne) a ray of sunshine; **ma fille c'est mon ~ de soleil** my daughter is the light of my life; **j'ai profité qu'il y avait un ~ de soleil pour sortir** I took advantage of a moment's sunshine to go out; **4** Méd, Phys (radiation) radiation ₵, ray; **les ~s X** X-rays; **les ~s alpha/bêta/gamma/ ultraviolets/infrarouges** alpha/beta/gamma/ultraviolet/infrared rays; **~ laser** laser beam; **être traité** or **soigné aux ~s** to undergo radiation treatment; **avoir une série de ~s**○ to undergo a course of radiation treatment; **passer un objet aux ~s** (**X**) to X-ray an object; **5** (de roue) spoke; **6** (étagère) shelf; **~ de bibliothèque** (book)shelf; **7** Comm (dans un grand magasin) department; (dans un petit magasin) section; **aller voir au ~ alimentation** to try the food section ou department; **au ~** (**des**) **jouets** in the toy department; **avoir des chemises en ~** to have shirts out on the shelves; **tous nos modèles sont en ~s** all our styles are on display; **la littérature de second ~** top-shelf magazines; **8** (domaine) **c'est mon ~** (responsabilité) that's my department○; **ce n'est pas mon ~** (affaire) that's not my concern; (compétence) it's ou that's not (really) my line; **il en connaît un ~ à ce sujet** he knows a lot about it; **9** Zool **un ~** (**de ruche**) a honeycomb.

■ **~ de braquage** Aut turning circle; **~ cathodique** cathode ray; **~s cosmiques** Astron cosmic rays; **~ lumineux** light ray, ray of light; **~ de la mort** death ray; **~ terrestre** radius of the Earth; **~ vert** green flash; **~ visuel** visual ray.

rayonnage /ʀɛjɔnaʒ/ *nm* shelves (*pl*).

rayonnant, **~e** /ʀɛjɔnɑ̃, ɑ̃t/ *adj* **1** (radieux) [*air, personne, beauté, joie*] radiant; [*sourire*] beaming; [*visage*] shining; **~ de** [*personne*] glowing ou radiant with; [*visage*] shining ou radiant with; **2** Phys (qui produit des radiations) [*chaleur, lumière, énergie*] radiant; **3** (disposé en rayons) [*décor*] that radiates outwards; **chapelles ~es** radiating chapels; **gothique ~** High Gothic.

rayonne /ʀɛjɔn/ *nf* rayon.

rayonnement /ʀɛjɔnmɑ̃/ *nm* **1** Phys (radiation) radiation; **~ solaire** solar radiation; **~ radio-actif** radiation, radioactivity; **le ~ de la Terre** the Earth's radiation; **2** (éclat) radiance; **un ~ de joie/bonheur illuminait son visage** his/her face was shining with joy/happiness; **3** (prestige) fig (de pays, civilisation, personne, pensée) influence; **le ~ mondial/européen d'un pays** a country's influence in the world/in Europe.

■ **~ thermique** thermal radiation.

rayonner /ʀɛjɔne/ [1] *vi* **1** (se propager) [*lumière, chaleur*] to radiate (**de** from); **une chaleur qui rayonne** (a) radiant heat; **2** (émettre de la lumière) liter [*astre, étoile*] to shine (forth); [*mer*] to glisten, sparkle; **~ de mille feux** fig [*mer, paillettes*] to shimmer; [*diamants*] to flash; **3** (resplendir) [*personne*] to glow (**de** with); **4** (manifester son influence) [*personne, penseur, œuvre*] to be an influence (**sur** on; **dans** throughout); [*ville, pays, cité*] to exert its influence, to hold sway (**sur** over; **dans** throughout); [*circulation*] to extend (**sur** over; **dans** throughout); [*grâce*] to shine forth (**sur** over); **5** (se déplacer) [*militaires, véhicule militaire*] to patrol; [*personnes, touristes*] to tour around; [*véhicule*] to tour; **nous avons rayonné dans toute la région** from our base we toured around the region; **6** (être disposé en rayons) [*avenues, allées, lignes*] to radiate out (**de** from); **7** (se manifester dans toutes les directions) [*douleurs*] to spread; **j'ai une douleur ici et elle rayonne dans tout le côté** I've got a pain here, and it spreads all down my side.

rayure /ʀɛjyʀ/ *nf* **1** (motif) stripe; **à ~s** striped; **à ~s blanches et jaunes** with white and yellow stripes; **2** (éraflure) scratch; **3** (d'arme) groove.

raz-de-marée /ʀɑdmaʀe/ *nm inv* lit, fig tidal wave; **~ électoral** electoral landslide.

razzia /ʀazja/ *nf* raid; **faire une ~ dans le réfrigérateur** to raid the fridge.

RDA /ɛʀdea/ *nprf* (*abbr* = **République démocratique allemande**) Hist German Democratic Republic, GDR.

rdc *written abbr* = **rez-de-chaussée**.

re: **et re**○ /əʀə/ *loc excl* here we go again!

ré /ʀe/ *nm inv* (note) D; (en solfiant) re.

réabonnement /ʀeabɔnmɑ̃/ *nm* Presse subscription renewal; Transp, Théât season ticket renewal.

réabonner /ʀeabɔne/ [1] **I** *vtr* Presse **~ qn à une revue** to renew sb's subscription to a magazine.

II se réabonner *vpr* Presse to renew one's subscription; Théât to renew one's season ticket.

réac○ /ʀeak/ *adj, nmf* reactionary.

réaccoutumer /ʀeakutyme/ [1] *vtr* **~ qn à qch** to get sb used to sth again.

II se réaccoutumer *vpr* **se ~ à qch** to get used to sth again.

réactance /ʀeaktɑ̃s/ *nf* **bobine de ~** reactor.

réacteur /ʀeaktœʀ/ *nm* **1** Nucl **~** (**nucléaire**) (nuclear) reactor; **2** Aviat jet engine; **3** Chimie reactor.

réactif, **-ive** /ʀeaktif, iv/ **I** *adj* reactive; **papier ~** reagent paper, test paper.

II *nm* reagent.

réaction /ʀeaksjɔ̃/ *nf* **1** (en paroles, actions) reaction (**à** to; **contre** against); (plus posé, réfléchi) response; **en ~ à** in reaction to; **accepter sans ~** to accept with no reaction; **il est demeuré sans ~** he didn't react; **sans ~** [*moteur, instrument*] unresponsive; **la ~ naturelle est de...** the natural reaction is to...; **sa ~ à la question fut de...** he responded to the question by...; **cela va provoquer des ~s** people are bound to react; **cela va susciter de vives ~s auprès du public** it will provoke a strong public reaction; **il a eu une ~ inattendue** his reaction was surprising; **2** Chimie, Méd, Phys reaction; Mécan (de machine) response; **~ en chaîne** lit, fig chain reaction; **moteur à ~** jet engine; **avion à ~** jet aircraft; **3** (mouvement d'idées) reaction; **4** Psych response; **~ de défense** defence[GB] response.

■ **~ officielle** Pol official response; **~ de rejet** Psych rejection response; fig negative response.

réactionnaire /ʀeaksjɔnɛʀ/ *adj, nmf* reactionary.

réactivation /ʀeaktivasjɔ̃/ *nf* (d'appareil) reactivation; (de négociations) relaunching.

réactiver /ʀeaktive/ [1] *vtr* to rekindle [*feu*]; to reactivate [*appareil*]; to relaunch [*négociations*]; to increase [*emploi*]; to revive [*contacts, économie*].

réactualisation /ʀeaktɥalizasjɔ̃/ *nf* gén updating; (de débat) relaunch.

réactualiser /ʀeaktɥalize/ [1] *vtr* gén to update; to relaunch [*débat*].

réadaptation /ʀeadaptasjɔ̃/ *nf* readjustment.

réadapter /ʀeadapte/ [1] **I** *vtr* **~ qn à qch** to help sb to readjust to sth.

II se réadapter *vpr* to readjust (**à qch** to sth).

réadmettre /ʀeadmɛtʀ/ [60] *vtr* to readmit [*élève, étudiant*].

réadmission /ʀeadmisjɔ̃/ *nf* readmission.

réaffectation /ʀeafɛktasjɔ̃/ *nf* **1** (de personnes) redeployment; **2** (de fonds) transfer.

réaffecter /ʀeafɛkte/ [1] *vtr* to redeploy [*personne*] (**à** to); to transfer [*subvention*].

réaffirmer /ʀeafiʀme/ [1] *vtr* to reaffirm (**que** that), to reassert (**que** that).

réagir /ʀeaʒiʀ/ [3] *vi* **1** [*personne, groupe*] to react (**à** to; **contre** against); (de façon plus posée, réfléchie) to respond (**à** to); **~ de façon exagérée** to overreact; **2** (avoir des répercussions) **~ sur** to have an effect on; **3** Chimie to react (**à** to).

réajustement /ʀeaʒystəmɑ̃/ *nm* readjustment (**de** of).

réajuster /ʀeaʒyste/ [1] *vtr* to readjust [*salaire, prévision*].

réalignement /ʀealiɲəmɑ̃/ *nm* Fin, Pol realignment.

réaligner /ʀealiɲe/ [1] *vtr* Fin, Pol to realign.

réalisable /ʀealizabl/ *adj* **1** [*projet*] feasible; [*innovation*] workable; **ce n'est pas ~** [*étude*] it can't be carried out; **2** Fin realizable.

réalisateur, **-trice** /ʀealizatœʀ, tʀis/ **▶ 510** *nm,f* Radio, TV, Cin director.

réalisation /ʀealizasjɔ̃/ *nf* **1** (de rêve, d'ambition) (action, résultat) fulfilment[GB]; **2** (d'étude, de sondage) carrying out; **conception et ~** [*de meuble, satellite, hôtel*] design and construction; **se lancer dans la ~ d'un projet** to become involved in a project; **projet en cours de ~** project in progress; **amener un projet jusqu'à sa ~** (après sa conception) to get a project underway; (terminer) to bring a project to completion; **3** (ce qui est réalisé) achievement; **les ~s d'entreprises régionales** achievements of local firms; **des ~s mieux adaptées à notre région** constructions more suited to our region; **4** TV, Radio, Cin production; (film) film.

réaliser /ʀealize/ [1] **I** *vtr* **1** (rendre réel) to fulfil[GB] [*rêve, ambition, promesses*]; to achieve [*équilibre, idéal, exploit*]; **~ des économies** to save money; **~ une vente/des bénéfices** to make a sale/a profit; **pour ~ un bon score** to achieve a good score; **elle a réalisé un exploit en faisant** it was no mean feat to do; **pour que chacun puisse ~ son potentiel** so that everyone can realize his/her potential; **2** (exécuter, fabriquer) to make [*maquette, meuble*]; to carry out [*sondage, projet, tâche*]; **3** Radio, TV, Cin to direct; **4** (se rendre compte de) controv to realize (**que** that); **5** Fin to realize [*bien*].

II se réaliser *vpr* **1** (devenir réel) [*rêve*] to come true; [*promesses, prédictions*] to be fulfilled[GB]; **2** (s'épanouir) **se ~** (**dans qch**) to find fulfilment[GB] (in sth).

réalisme /ʀealism/ *nm* realism.

réaliste /ʀealist/ **I** *adj* **1** [*personne, approche*] realistic; **2** Art realist.

II *nmf* realist.

réalité /ʀealite/ *nf* **1** (réel) **la ~** reality; **en ~** in reality; **dans la ~, c'est impossible** in practice, it's impossible; **cela fait partie de notre ~ quotidienne** it's part of our everyday life; **2** (caractère réel) **la ~ du problème/du marché** the real nature of the problem/of the market; **la ~ américaine** the realities of American life; **3** (fait réel) reality; **devenir** (**une**) **~** [*rêve, projet*] to become (a) reality; **c'est déjà une ~** [*nouvelle autoroute, chômage*] it is already a reality; **les ~s économiques** economic realities; **tenir compte des ~s** to take the facts into consideration; **être confronté aux ~s** to come face to face with reality.

réaménagement /ʀeamenaʒmɑ̃/ *nm* **1** (de site, ville) redevelopment; **coûts/plans de ~**

redevelopment costs/plans; **2** (de pièce, maison) rearrangement.

réaménager /ʀeamenaʒe/ [13] *vtr* to redevelop [*site, ville*]; to rearrange [*pièce, maison*].

réanimateur, **-trice** /ʀeanimatœʀ, tʀis/ *nm,f* member of an intensive care team.

réanimation /ʀeanimasjɔ̃/ *nf* **1** (service) intensive care; **service de ~** intensive care unit; **être en ~** to be in intensive care; **2** (technique) resuscitation.

réanimer /ʀeanime/ [1] *vtr* = **ranimer**.

réapparaître /ʀeapaʀɛtʀ/ [73] *vi* [*soleil, mot*] to reappear; [*phénomène, maladie*] to recur; **~ en public** to reappear in public; **~ après une longue absence** to return ou reappear after a long absence.

réapparition /ʀeapaʀisjɔ̃/ *nf* (de maladie, symptôme) recurrence; (de personne) reappearance; **la ~ des criquets** the return of locusts; **faire une ~** to reappear; **après plusieurs mois de pénurie le beurre a fait sa ~ dans les magasins** after several months of shortages butter is back on sale in the shops.

réapprendre /ʀeapʀɑ̃dʀ/ [52] *vtr* to learn [sth] again; **~ à faire** to learn (how) to do again.

réapprentissage /ʀeapʀɑ̃tisaʒ/ *nm* **le ~ de qch** relearning sth; **cela demande un long ~** it takes a long time to relearn.

réapprovisionnement /ʀeapʀɔvizjɔnmɑ̃/ *nm* **1** (en vivres, munitions) renewal of supplies; (en carburant) refuelling[GB]; **2** (de magasin) restocking.

réapprovisionner /ʀeapʀɔvizjɔne/ [1] **I** *vtr* to restock [*magasin*]; **~ qn en qch** to provide sb with fresh supplies of sth.

II se réapprovisionner *vpr* to stock up (**en** on).

réargenter /ʀeaʀʒɑ̃te/ [1] *vtr* to replate [*couverts*].

réarmement /ʀeaʀməmɑ̃/ *nm* **1** (de pays) rearmament; **une politique de ~** a policy of rearmament; **~ moral** moral rearmament; **2** (de navire) refit.

réarmer /ʀeaʀme/ [1] **I** *vtr* **1** (munir d'armes) to rearm; **2** (mettre en ordre de marche) to reload [*fusil, appareil photo*]; **3** Naut (équiper) to refit [*navire*].

II *vi* to rearm [*pays, groupe*].

réarrangement /ʀeaʀɑ̃ʒmɑ̃/ *nm* rearrangement; **réaction de ~** rearrangement reaction.

réarranger /ʀeaʀɑ̃ʒe/ [13] *vtr* to rearrange.

réassignation /ʀeasiɲasjɔ̃/ *nf* resummons (*sg*).

réassigner /ʀeasiɲe/ [1] *vtr* gén to reassign [*mission*]; Jur to resummon.

réassort /ʀeasɔʀ/ *nm* **1** (activité) restocking; **2** (marchandise) new ou fresh stock.

réassortiment /ʀeasɔʀtimɑ̃/ *nm* (de stock) replacement; (de marchandises) restocking.

réassortir /ʀeasɔʀtiʀ/ [3] **I** *vtr* **1** to match up [*tissu*] (**avec** with); **2** Comm to replace [*stock*].

II se réassortir *vpr* to stock up (**en** on).

réassurance /ʀeasyʀɑ̃s/ *nf* reinsurance.

réassurer /ʀeasyʀe/ [1] **I** *vtr* to reinsure.

II se réassurer *vpr* to reinsure oneself (**à** with).

rebaisser /ʀ(ə)bese/ [1] **I** *vtr* **1** (une fois) to lower [*rideau*]; **2** (à nouveau) to turn [sth] down again [*chauffage*]; to reduce [sth] a second time [*prix*].

II *vi* [*prix, température*] to go down again, to drop again.

rebaptiser /ʀ(ə)batize/ [1] *vtr* to rechristen [*personne*]; to rename, to rechristen [*rue, parti, ville*].

rébarbatif, **-ive** /ʀebaʀbatif, iv/ *adj* [*travail, activité*] offputting; [*visage, apparence*] forbidding, rebarbative sout.

rebâtir /ʀ(ə)bɑtiʀ/ [3] *vtr* to rebuild.

rebattre /ʀ(ə)batʀ/ [61] *vtr* to reshuffle [*cartes de jeu*].

IDIOMES **~ les oreilles de qn avec une histoire** to go on (and on) about something.

rebattu, **~e** /ʀ(ə)baty/ **I** *pp* ▶ **rebattre**.

II *pp adj* [*sujet, thème*] hackneyed.

IDIOMES **avoir les oreilles ~es de qch** to be tired of hearing about sth.

rebec /ʀəbɛk/ ▶ **534** *nm* rebec.

Rébecca /ʀebɛka/ *npr* Rebecca.

rebelle /ʀəbɛl/ **I** *adj* **1** Mil, Pol [*forces, chef, soldat*] rebel (*épith*); **2** (refusant l'autorité) [*fils, artiste*] rebellious; **être ~ à** to be resistant to [*compromis*]; to have a mental block about [*musique, langues étrangères*]; **être ~ à la discipline** to be intractable; **3** [*mèche*] unruly; [*tache*] stubborn; **4** Méd resistant.

II *nmf* rebel.

rebeller: **se rebeller** /ʀəbɛle/ [1] *vpr* to rebel (**contre** against).

rébellion /ʀebɛljɔ̃/ *nf* **1** (action) rebellion; **entrer en ~** to rebel (**contre** against); **2** (personnes) **la ~** the rebels (*pl*).

rebelote○ /ʀəbəlɔt/ *excl* here we go again!

rebiffer○: **se rebiffer** /ʀ(ə)bife/ [1] *vpr* to rebel; **se ~ contre un règlement idiot** to rebel against a stupid rule; **se ~ contre qn** to refuse to take any more from sb.

rebiquer○ /ʀ(ə)bike/ [1] *vi* [*mèche de cheveux, col*] to stick up.

reblanchir /ʀ(ə)blɑ̃ʃiʀ/ [3] *vtr* **~ un mur/une façade** to whitewash a wall/a façade again.

reblochon /ʀəblɔʃɔ̃/ *nm* Culin *soft cheese made with cow's milk*.

reboisement /ʀ(ə)bwazmɑ̃/ *nm* reafforestation, reforestation.

reboiser /ʀ(ə)bwaze/ [1] *vtr* to reafforest, to reforest.

rebond /ʀ(ə)bɔ̃/ *nm* **1** (de balle) bounce; **frapper la balle au ~** to hit the ball on the rebound; **2** (ressaisissement) recovery (**de** of); (augmentation) increase (**de** in); **un ~ des cours** a sudden recovery of share ou stock prices.

rebondi, **~e** /ʀ(ə)bɔ̃di/ *adj* **1** [*vase, cruche, forme*] round, rounded; [*joue*] chubby; [*visage*] plump; [*ventre*] fat; [*poitrine*] ample; [*fesses, hanches*] generously proportioned; [*cuisse, muscle*] bulging; **enfant aux joues ~es** chubby-cheeked child; **femme aux formes ~es** generously proportioned woman; **homme au ventre ~** portly man; **2** fig [*portefeuille*] bulging.

rebondir /ʀ(ə)bɔ̃diʀ/ [3] *vi* **1** [*balle*] to bounce, to rebound; [*rayon, son, onde*] to bounce (**contre, sur** off); **fais ~ la balle par terre/contre le mur** bounce the ball on the ground/against the wall; **2** (repartir) [*conversation, polémique*] to start up again; [*économie, pays*] to pick up; [*procès, intrigue*] to take a new turn; **débat qui n'en finit pas de ~** debate which won't die down; **faire ~** to start [sth] up again [*conversation, débat*]; to give a new twist to [*procès*].

rebondissement /ʀ(ə)bɔ̃dismɑ̃/ *nm* (de polémique) sudden revival (**de** of); (de procès, d'affaire) new development (**de** in); **les ~s de l'intrigue** the twists and turns of the plot; **feuilleton à ~s** action-packed soap opera.

rebord /ʀ(ə)bɔʀ/ *nm* **1** (partie en saillie) ledge; **2** (bord surélevé) gén raised edge; (d'objet rond) rim; **3** (bord arrondi) lip; **4** (bord) edge.

■ **~ de cheminée** mantelpiece; **~ de fenêtre** windowsill; (plus large) (window) ledge.

reborder /ʀ(ə)bɔʀde/ [1] *vtr* (au lit) to tuck [sb] in ou up again.

reboucher /ʀ(ə)buʃe/ [1] **I** *vtr* (avec un bouchon de liège) to recork [*bouteille*]; (avec un bouchon en verre) to replace the stopper of [*flacon*]; (avec un capuchon) to put the cap back on [*stylo*]; to put the top back on [*tube de dentifrice*]; **~ un trou** to fill (up) a hole again.

II se reboucher *vpr* [*lavabo, tuyauterie*] to clog up again; [*artère, canal*] to block up again.

rebours: **à rebours** /aʀ(ə)buʀ/ **I** *loc adv* **1** (à l'envers) [*compter, marcher*] backward(s); **prendre l'ennemi à ~** to attack the enemy from the rear; **caresser un chat à ~** to stroke a cat the wrong way; **brosser une étoffe à ~** to brush a cloth against the nap; **prendre qn à ~** to rub sb up the wrong way; **2** (de travers) **comprendre à ~** to misunderstand, to get the wrong end of the stick○ GB.

II à rebours de *loc prép* **à ~ de la tendance actuelle, cette entreprise se porte très bien** contrary to the current trend, this business is doing very well; **aller à ~ de** to go against [*mode, tendance*]; ▶ **compte**.

rebouteux○, **-euse** /ʀ(ə)butø, øz/ ▶ **510** *nm,f* bonesetter.

reboutonner /ʀ(ə)butɔne/ [1] **I** *vtr* to button [sth] up again.

II se reboutonner *vpr* to do up one's buttons back up again.

rebroussement /ʀəbʀusmɑ̃/ *nm* **gare de ~** dead-end GB ou stub-end US station.

rebrousse-poil: **à rebrousse-poil** /aʀ(ə)bʀuspwal/ *loc adv* the wrong way; **caresser un chat à ~** to stroke a cat's fur the wrong way; **brosser à ~** to brush [sth] the wrong way [*manteau*]; to brush [sth] against the pile [*tapis*]; to brush [sth] against the nap [*velours*]; **prendre qn à ~** fig to rub sb up the wrong way.

rebrousser /ʀ(ə)bʀuse/ [1] *vtr* [*personne*] to brush [sth] the wrong way [*poil*]; **le vent rebroussait sa crinière** the wind swept back its mane; **~ chemin** to turn back.

rebuffade /ʀ(ə)byfad/ *nf* fml rebuff.

rébus /ʀebys/ *nm inv* Jeux rebus; **déchiffrer un ~** to solve a rebus.

rebut /ʀ(ə)by/ *nm* **1** lit (déchet) rubbish ¢; **il ne reste que le ~** there is nothing left but rubbish; **essayer de réduire les ~s d'une production** to try to cut down waste in production; **bon pour le ~** fit ou ready for the scrapheap; **des matériaux** or **objets de ~** junk ¢; **mettre qch/qn au ~** to throw sth/sb on the scrapheap; **le ~ de la société** fig the dregs of society; **2** Postes dead mail.

rebutant, **~e** /ʀ(ə)bytɑ̃, ɑ̃t/ *adj* [*travail, exercice, démarche*] unpleasant.

rebuter /ʀ(ə)byte/ [1] *vtr* **1** (dégoûter) [*travail, activité*] to disgust; [*personne*] to repel; **son apparence/il me rebute** his appearance/he repels me; **2** (décourager) [*obstacle, difficulté*] to put off; **rien ne la rebute** nothing puts her off.

recacheter /ʀ(ə)kaʃte/ [20] *vtr* to reseal.

recalcification /ʀ(ə)kalsifikasjɔ̃/ *nf* increased calcification.

récalcitrant, **~e** /ʀekalsitʀɑ̃, ɑ̃t/ *adj* recalcitrant.

recaler /ʀ(ə)kale/ [1] **I** *vtr* **1**○ Scol, Univ to fail [*candidat*]; **être recalé à une épreuve** to fail a test; **2** Aut **~ (le moteur)** to stall (the engine) again.

II *vi* to stall again.

récapitulatif, **-ive** /ʀekapitylatif, iv/ **I** *adj* **tableau ~** summary table.

II *nm* (texte) summary of the main points.

récapitulation /ʀekapitylasjɔ̃/ *nf* summing up, recap○; **faire une ~ de qch** to sum up sth.

récapituler /ʀekapityle/ [1] *vtr* to sum up, to recapitulate.

recarreler /ʀ(ə)kaʀle/ [19] *vtr* to retile.

recaser○ /ʀ(ə)kaze/ [1] **I** *vtr* **1** (dans un emploi) to find another job for [*personne*]; **2** (remarier) **~ un ami** to find a friend a new wife.

II se recaser○ *vpr* **1** (dans un emploi) to find another job; **2** (se remarier) [*femme*] to find a new husband; [*homme*] to find a new wife.

recauser /ʀ(ə)koze/ [1] *vtr ind* **~ de qch avec** or **à**○ **qn** to talk to sb about sth again.

recéder /ʀ(ə)sede/ [14] *vtr* **1** (rétrocéder) to give sth back again; **2** (revendre) **~ qch à qn** to let sb have sth back.

recel /ʀəsɛl/ *nm* (d'objets volés) (fait d'accepter) receiving stolen goods; (fait de garder) being in possession of stolen goods; **~ de malfaiteur** concealment of a criminal.

receler /ʀəsle, ʀsəle/ [17] *vtr* **1** Jur to conceal [*criminel*]; (accepter) to receive [*marchandise*]; (garder) to possess [*marchandise*]; **2** (contenir) to contain; **~ un trésor** to contain hidden treasure.

receleur, -euse /ʀəsløʀ, ʀsəlœʀ, øz/ *nm,f* (qui accepte) receiver of stolen goods, fence○; (qui garde) possessor of stolen goods.

récemment /ʀesamɑ̃/ *adv* recently; **tout ~** very recently.

recensement /ʀ(ə)sɑ̃smɑ̃/ *nm* **1** Sociol census; **faire un ~** to take a census; **2** (inventaire) inventory; **le ~ des ressources pétrolières** an inventory of oil resources.

recenser /ʀ(ə)sɑ̃se/ [1] *vtr* **1** Sociol to take a census of [*population*]; **2** (inventorier) to list [*objets, problèmes*]; to draw up an inventory of [*armes, arsenaux*].

récent, ~e /ʀesɑ̃, ɑ̃t/ *adj* [*incident, nouvelle, découverte*] recent; [*maison*] new, newly built; **son livre le plus ~** his/her latest book.

recentrage /ʀəsɑ̃tʀaʒ/ *nm* refocusing.

recentrer /ʀəsɑ̃tʀe/ [1] **I** *vtr* to refocus.

II se recentrer *vpr* to refocus.

récépissé /ʀesepise/ *nm* receipt; **~ de demande de carte de séjour** receipt acknowledging an application for a resident's permit.

réceptacle /ʀesɛptakl/ *nm* **1** (récepteur) **c'est le ~ des eaux fluviales** it receives the fluvial waters; **le ~ des immondices de la ville** the town tip; **2** Géog catchment basin; **3** Bot receptacle; **4** (récipient) container.

■ **~ à verre** bottle bank.

récepteur, -trice /ʀesɛptœʀ, tʀis/ **I** *adj* receiving; **poste ~** receiver.

II *nm* **1** Biol receptor; **2** Radio, TV (appareil) receiver.

réceptif, -ive /ʀesɛptif, iv/ *adj* receptive (**à** to).

réception /ʀesɛpsjɔ̃/ *nf* **1** (réunion) reception; **donner une ~** to hold a reception; **donner une petite ~** to give a party; **salle de ~** reception room, function room; **2** (manière d'accueillir) reception, welcome; **une ~ glaciale/courtoise** an icy/a polite reception; **une ~ chaleureuse** a warm welcome; **3** (fait d'être admis) **la ~ d'un écrivain à l'Académie française** the induction of a writer into the Académie française; **discours de ~** welcoming speech; **4** (bureau d'accueil) reception; **demander à la ~** ask at reception ou at the reception desk; **5** (de courrier, marchandises) receipt; **~ d'une lettre/d'un colis** receipt of a letter/of a parcel; **il faut payer dès ~ de la facture** payment is due on receipt of the bill; **s'occuper de la ~ des marchandises** to take delivery of the goods; **6** Radio, TV (de signaux, d'ondes) reception; **7** Sport (après un saut) landing; (de ballon) catching.

■ **~ des travaux** Constr official acceptance of work (*upon completion and after checking*).

réceptionnaire /ʀesɛpsjɔnɛʀ/ **▶510** *nmf* **1** Comm receiving clerk; **2** (dans un hôtel) chief receptionist GB, head receptionist US.

réceptionner /ʀesɛpsjɔne/ [1] **I** *vtr* **1** Comm **~ des marchandises** to take delivery of goods; **2** (accueillir) to welcome [*personne, voyageur*]; **3** Sport to catch, to field [*ballon*].

II se réceptionner *vpr* to land; **il s'est mal réceptionné et s'est cassé la cheville** he landed badly and broke his ankle.

réceptionniste /ʀesɛpsjɔnist/ **▶510** *nmf* receptionist.

réceptivité /ʀesɛptivite/ *nf* **1** gén receptivity; **2** Méd sensitivity (**à** to).

récessif, -ive /ʀesesif, iv/ *adj* recessive.

récession /ʀesesjɔ̃/ *nf* Écon, Astron recession; **une phase de ~** a recessionary period.

récessivité /ʀesesivite/ *nf* recessiveness.

recette /ʀ(ə)sɛt/ *nf* **1** Culin **~ (de cuisine)** recipe; **tu me donneras la ~ du gâteau?** will you give me the recipe for the cake?; **livre de ~s** recipe book; **2** (méthode) formula, recipe; **il n'y a pas de ~ pour faire fortune/pour être heureux** there's no (magic) formula for making a fortune/for happiness; **3** Pharm formula; **4** Comm (argent encaissé) takings (*pl*); **aujourd'hui la ~ a été bonne** the takings have been good today; **faire ~** lit to bring in money; fig to be a success; **5** Compta (rentrée d'argent) **les ~s** receipts; **les ~s et (les) dépenses** receipts and expenses; **6** Fisc (bureau) tax collector's office, revenue office; (recouvrement) collection; **7** Tech (de matériel, d'équipement) acceptance; **8** Mines landing; **~ du jour/du fond** top/bottom landing.

■ **~s publicitaires** Pub advertising revenue ¢; **~s publiques** Fisc tax revenue ¢.

recevabilité /ʀəsvabilite, ʀ(ə)səvabilite/ *nf* admissibility.

recevable /ʀəsvabl, ʀ(ə)səvabl/ *adj* **1** gén [*excuse, offre*] acceptable; **2** Jur [*demande, appel, pourvoi*] admissible.

receveur, -euse /ʀəs(ə)vœʀ, øz/ *nm,f* **1** **▶510** (d'autobus, de tramway) conductor; **2** Méd recipient; **~ universel** universal recipient.

■ **~ des contributions** tax collector, tax officer; **~ municipal** rate collector; **~ des postes** postmaster.

recevoir /ʀəsvwaʀ, ʀ(ə)səvwaʀ/ [5] **I** *vtr* **1** (être le destinataire de) to receive, to get [*lettre, argent, appel téléphonique, compliment, récompense, conseil, ordre, autorisation, formation, blessure*] (**de** from); **nous avons bien reçu votre lettre** we acknowledge receipt of your letter; **~ une gifle** to get a slap; **~ un coup de pied/coup de poing dans le ventre** to get kicked/punched in the stomach; **~ une fessée** to get a spanking; **il a reçu le ballon dans le visage** he was hit in the face by the ball; **il a reçu une tuile/un caillou sur la tête** he got hit ou struck on the head by a tile/a stone; **j'ai reçu le marteau sur le pied** the hammer landed on my foot; **je n'ai pas de leçons à ~ de cet imbécile** I'm not going to be lectured by that idiot; **je n'ai d'ordre à ~ de personne** I don't take orders from anyone; **la mesure a reçu un accueil favorable de la part des enseignants** the measure met with approval from teachers; **je n'ai reçu aucun encouragement de sa part** he/she gave me no encouragement at all; **~ les ordres** Relig to take holy orders; **2** (accueillir) to welcome, to receive [*amis, invités*]; (de façon officielle) (brièvement) to receive [*ministre, ambassadeur, délégation*]; (plus longuement) to play host to [*ministre, ambassadeur, délégation*]; **être bien/mal reçu** [*proposition*] to be well/badly received; [*invités*] to get a good/bad reception; **il nous a très gentiment reçus dans sa villa** he very kindly welcomed us into his villa; **~ qn froidement** to give sb a cold reception; **je vous remercie de nous avoir si bien reçus** thank you for giving us such a warm welcome ou for being so welcoming; **demain nous les recevons à dîner** tomorrow we're having them to dinner; **on a reçu mon frère pour les vacances** we had my brother staying with us for the holidays GB ou vacation US; **ils reçoivent beaucoup** they do a lot of entertaining, they entertain a lot; **ils reçoivent très peu** they don't do a lot of entertaining; **ces gens-là ne savent pas ~!** those people don't know how to entertain!; **le délégué syndical a été reçu par le ministre** the union representative was received by the minister; **Laval reçoit Caen** Sport Laval is playing host to Caen; **il va se faire ~**○ he's going to get it○; **3** (pour consultation) to see [*patients, clients*]; **il reçoit uniquement sur rendez-vous** he only sees people by appointment; **elle reçoit entre 14 et 17 heures** she's available for consultation between 2 and 5 pm; **le directeur va vous ~ dans son bureau** the manager will see you in his office; **4** Radio, TV (capter) to receive [*signal, ondes*]; **on reçoit mal cette chaîne** we get bad reception on that channel; **je vous reçois cinq sur cinq** Radio I'm receiving you loud and clear; **reçu!** Roger!; **5** (contenir) [*hôtel, refuge*] to accommodate [*personne*]; [*salle de spectacle, stade*] to hold [*spectateurs*]; **6** (recueillir) to get [*soleil, pluie*]; **cette région reçoit 500 millimètres de pluie par an** this region gets 500 millimetres[GB] of rain a year; **la pièce ne reçoit jamais le soleil** the room never gets the sun; **le fleuve reçoit plusieurs affluents** several tributaries flow into the river; **des bassins reçoivent l'eau de pluie** pools collect the rainwater; **7** Scol, Univ (admettre) to pass [*élève, candidat*]; **être reçu à un examen** to pass an exam; **il a été reçu premier/second au concours** he came first/second in the examination; **il a été reçu à l'Académie française** he was admitted to the Académie française.

II se recevoir *vpr* (après un saut, une chute) to land; **il s'est reçu sur les mains** he landed on his hands; **il s'est mal reçu et s'est cassé le poignet** he landed badly and broke his wrist.

rechange: **de rechange** /dəʀ(ə)ʃɑ̃ʒ/ *loc adj* [*pièce*] spare; [*solution*] alternative; **c'est ma chemise de ~** it's my spare shirt; **j'ai pris une chemise de ~** I have a change of shirt.

rechanger /ʀ(ə)ʃɑ̃ʒe/ [13] **I** *vtr* to change [sth] again; **~ qch de place** to move sth again.

II rechanger de *vtr ind* **~ d'avis/de coiffure** to change one's mind/one's hairstyle again; **~ de place** to change places again.

III se rechanger *vpr* to change one's clothes again.

rechapage /ʀ(ə)ʃapaʒ/ *nm* remoulding GB, retreading.

rechaper /ʀ(ə)ʃape/ [1] *vtr* to remould GB, retread; **pneu rechapé** remould GB, retread.

réchapper /ʀeʃape/ [1] **I réchapper de** *vtr ind* to come through [*maladie, accident*]; **personne n'en a** or **est réchappé** nobody came through it alive.

II se réchapper *vpr* to escape again.

recharge /ʀ(ə)ʃaʀʒ/ *nf* **1** (de briquet, stylo) refill; (d'arme) reload; **2** (processus) recharging; **mettre une batterie en ~** to recharge a battery.

rechargeable /ʀ(ə)ʃaʀʒabl/ *adj* [*briquet, stylo*] refillable; [*pile, appareil ménager*] rechargeable.

rechargement /ʀ(ə)ʃaʀʒəmɑ̃/ *nm* **1** (de camion) reloading; **2** (de batterie) recharging; **3** (de route) remetalling[GB]; (de voie ferrée) reballasting.

recharger /ʀ(ə)ʃaʀʒe/ [13] **I** *vtr* **1** (avec cargaison) to reload [*véhicule*]; **2** (regarnir) to reload [*arme, appareil photo*]; to refill [*stylo, briquet*]; **3** Électrotech to recharge [*batterie, pile*]; **4** Constr to remetal [*route*]; to reballast [*voie ferrée*].

II se recharger *vpr* **1** (qualité) [*batterie, pile*] to be rechargeable; [*stylo, briquet*] to be refillable; **2** (processus) [*batterie, pile*] to recharge.

réchaud /ʀeʃo/ *nm* stove.

■ **~ à alcool** spirit stove; **~ électrique** electric ring GB, hotplate; **~ à gaz** (d'appartement) gas ring; (de camping) camping stove.

réchauffage /ʀeʃofaʒ/ *nm* reheating.

réchauffé, ~e /ʀeʃofe/ **I** *pp* ▶ **réchauffer**.

II *pp adj* **1** (rebattu) [*histoire, plaisanterie*] hackneyed; **2**○ (pas frileux) **il est drôlement**

~ pour être en chemise par ce froid he can't feel the cold if he's only wearing a shirt in this chilly weather.

III *nm* **ça sent le ~, c'est du ~** there's nothing new about it, it's old hat.

réchauffement /ʀeʃofmɑ̃/ *nm* warming (up); **le ~ de la planète** global warming; **la météo annonce un prochain ~** according to the weather forecast it's going to warm up ou get warmer soon; **le ~ des relations entre les deux pays** fig the improvement in relations between the two countries.

réchauffer /ʀeʃofe/ [1] I *vtr* **1** Culin to reheat, to heat [sth] up [*plat, nourriture*]; **2** (rendre chaud) to warm up [*personne, pieds*]; to heat up, to warm up [*pièce*]; **une bonne promenade, ça réchauffe!** a good walk warms you up!; **le soleil a réchauffé l'eau de la piscine** the sun warmed up ou heated up the water in the swimming pool; **les effluents ont réchauffé les eaux du fleuve** the effluent raised the temperature of the water in the river; ▸**serpent**; **3** (détendre) **ses plaisanteries ont réchauffé l'atmosphère** his/her jokes livened up the atmosphere.

II *vi* Culin **le plat réchauffe** the dish is being heated up; **faire ~ qch** to heat sth up, reheat sth; **elle a mis le ragoût à ~** she's heating up the stew.

III **se réchauffer** *vpr* **1** (soi-même) [*personne*] to warm oneself up; **se ~ les mains/pieds** to warm one's hands/feet; **2** (pour soi) **il s'est réchauffé un reste de soupe** he heated up some left-over soup for himself; **3** (devenir chaud) [*temps*] to warm up; **ça se réchauffe depuis deux jours** the weather's started to warm up in the last couple of days; **les eaux du lac se sont réchauffées à cause de la pollution** the temperature of the water in the lake has risen because of pollution.

IDIOMES **ça m'a réchauffé le cœur** it warmed my heart

réchauffeur /ʀeʃofœʀ/ *nm* heater.

rechausser /ʀ(ə)ʃose/ [1] I *vtr* **1** (chausser de nouveau) **~ un enfant** to put a child's shoes back on; **~ ses skis** to put one's skis on again; **2** Agric to earth [sth] up again; Constr to line the foot of.

II **se rechausser** *vpr* to put one's shoes back on.

rêche /ʀɛʃ/ *adj* [*mains, tissu*] rough.

recherche /ʀ(ə)ʃɛʀʃ/ *nf* **1** (étude) research ¢; **la ~ et le développement** research and development; **~ fondamentale/appliquée** basic/applied research; **~ scientifique/militaire/spatiale** scientific/military/space research; **fonds pour la ~** research funds; **être/travailler dans la ~** to be/to work in research; **faire des ~s en biologie/sur le cancer/pour améliorer un produit** to do research in biology/into cancer/into improving a product; **2** (fouille) search; **après deux heures de ~** after a two-hour search; **tout le monde a participé aux ~s** everyone took part in the search; **les ~s pour retrouver l'enfant n'ont rien donné** the search for the child drew a blank; **la ~ d'un livre/d'un criminel** the search for a book/for a criminal; **la ~ de vos renseignements lui a pris deux heures** he spent two hours searching for the information you wanted; **à la ~ de qn/qch** in search of sb/sth; **être à la ~ de** to be looking for, to be in search of; **aller** or **partir** or **se mettre à la ~ de** to go looking for, to go in search of; **ils sont à la ~ d'un logement** they're looking for somewhere to live; **être à la ~ d'un emploi** to be looking for a job, to be job-hunting; **se mettre à la ~ d'un emploi** to go job-hunting; **travailler à la ~ d'une solution** to work on finding a solution; **3** (volonté d'atteindre) **~ de** pursuit of; **être à la ~ d'un bonheur idéal** to be in pursuit of ideal happiness; **4** (soin) (raffinement) meticulousness; (affectation) pej affectation; **avec ~** [*habillé, décoré, écrit*] with meticulous care; **sans ~** (non affecté) without affectation; (négligé) carelessly; **il y a trop de ~ dans votre style/votre tenue** you are too fastidious about your style/your dress.

■ **~ assistée par ordinateur**, **RAO** computer-aided retrieval, CAR; **~ dichotomique** Ordinat binary ou dichotomizing search; **~ d'emploi** job-hunting; **c'est sa première ~ d'emploi** he's looking for his first job; **~ opérationnelle** operations ou operational research; **~ de paternité** Jur establishment of paternity; **action en ~ de paternité** paternity suit.

recherché, **~e** /ʀ(ə)ʃɛʀʃe/ I *pp* ▸**rechercher**.

II *pp adj* **1** (rare) sought-after (**pour** for); **un livre/fruit très ~** a highly ou much sought-after book/fruit; **2** (demandé) in demand (*après n*); **un mannequin très ~** a model very much in demand; **3** (soigné) [*toilette*] meticulous; péj affected; [*style, écrit, expression*] original, inventive; péj recherché; [*décor*] meticulously arranged (*épith*); **4** (visé) [*but, objectif, effet*] intended; **ce n'était pas le but ~** that wasn't the object of the exercise.

rechercher /ʀ(ə)ʃɛʀʃe/ [1] *vtr* **1** (tâcher de trouver) to search out [*objet convoité*]; to look for [*objet égaré*]; to look for [*logement, emploi, explication*]; Ordinat to search for [*donnée*]; **collectionneur qui recherche un livre rare** collector searching out ou trying to track down a rare book; **~ un terme dans une banque de données** to search a data bank for a term; **~ les causes d'un accident/d'un phénomène** to look into the causes of an accident/of a phenomenon; **il est recherché pour meurtre/par la police/dans le monde entier** he's wanted for murder/by the police/the world over; **'recherchons vendeuse qualifiée'** 'qualified sales assistant GB ou clerk US required'; **2** (tâcher d'obtenir) to seek [*sécurité, bonheur, paix*] (**auprès de qn** with sb); to seek, to look for [*alliances, alliés, soutien*]; to fish for [*compliments*].

rechigner /ʀ(ə)ʃiɲe/ [1] I **rechigner à** *vtr ind* **~ à qch/à faire** to balk at sth/at doing; **elle ne rechigne pas à la tâche** she's not afraid of hard work.

II *vi* to grumble; **sans ~** without grumbling ou a murmur; **en rechignant** grudgingly, with a bad grace.

rechristianiser /ʀ(ə)kʀistjanize/ [1] *vtr* to rechristianize.

rechute /ʀ(ə)ʃyt/ *nf* **1** Méd, fig relapse; **faire une ~** to have a relapse; **2** Écon (de monnaie, ventes) new fall (**de** in).

rechuter /ʀ(ə)ʃyte/ [1] *vi* **1** Méd to have a relapse; fig to relapse (**dans** into); **2** Écon [*prix, monnaie*] to fall again, drop again; [*ventes*] to fall off again.

récidivant, **~e** /ʀesidivɑ̃, ɑ̃t/ *adj* Méd recurring.

récidive /ʀesidiv/ *nf* **1** Jur second offence[GB]; **en cas de ~** in the event of a second offence[GB]; **la ~ entraîne une aggravation des peines** sentences are stiffer for a second offence[GB]; **il est accusé de vol avec ~** he has been charged with a second offence[GB] of theft; **2** fig repetition; **3** Méd recurrence.

récidiver /ʀesidive/ [1] *vi* **1** Jur (la première fois) to commit a second offence[GB]; (plusieurs fois) to commit subsequent offences; **2** (recommencer) fml to do it again; **il récidive dans ses accusations** he's gone back to making his accusations; **il avait arrêté de boire mais maintenant il a récidivé** he had given up drinking but now he has slipped back into his old ways; **3** Méd to recur.

récidiviste /ʀesidivist/ *nmf* **1** Jur (au second délit) second offender, recidivist; (après plusieurs délits) habitual offender, repeater US, recidivist; **2** fig backslider.

récidivité /ʀesidivite/ *nf* Méd tendency to recur, recurring nature.

récif /ʀesif/ *nm* reef; **~ corallien** coral reef; **~ frangeant** fringing reef.

récif-barrière, *pl* **récifs-barrières** /ʀesifbaʀjɛʀ/ *nm* barrier reef.

récipiendaire /ʀesipjɑ̃dɛʀ/ *nmf* recipient (*of a diploma or medal*); (dans académie) member elect.

récipient /ʀesipjɑ̃/ *nm* container (**à** for).

réciprocité /ʀesipʀɔsite/ *nf* reciprocity; **à titre de ~** in return.

réciproque /ʀesipʀɔk/ I *adj* **1** gén [*aide, accord*] reciprocal, mutual; [*sentiment, confiance*] mutual; **je ne peux pas le supporter et c'est ~** I can't stand him and the feeling's mutual; **2** Ling, Math reciprocal; **3** Philos (en logique) converse.

II *nf* **1** gén reverse; **la ~ est vraie** the reverse is true; **ne vous attendez pas à la ~ de sa part** don't expect anything from him in return; **il fallait t'attendre à la ~** you should have known he'd pay you back for it; **2** Math reciprocal; **3** Philos (en logique) converse.

réciproquement /ʀesipʀɔkmɑ̃/ *adv* **se respecter ~** to respect one another; **et ~** and vice versa; **j'ai mis l'armoire à la place du lit et ~** I put the wardrobe where the bed was and vice versa.

récit /ʀesi/ *nm* **1** (narration) story; (genre) narrative; **un ~ d'aventures** an adventure story; **le ~ de mes aventures** the account of my adventures; **faire le ~ de** to give an account of; **2** Théât narrative monologue; **3** (d'orgue) récit.

récital /ʀesital/ *nm* recital; **~ de piano/chansons** piano/song recital; **donner des ~s** to give recitals.

récitant, **~e** /ʀesitɑ̃, ɑ̃t/ I *adj* solo.

II *nm,f* narrator.

récitatif /ʀesitatif/ *nm* recitative.

récitation /ʀesitasjɔ̃/ *nf* **1** (texte littéraire) **apprendre une ~** to learn a text (off) by heart; **2** (matière) **être fort en ~** to be good at reciting (texts off by heart); **3** (action de réciter) reciting.

réciter /ʀesite/ [1] *vtr* **1** lit to recite [*leçon, poème, prière*]; **faire ~ qch à qn** to make sb recite sth; **2** fig, pej to trot out○ [*raisons, faits*] péj.

réclamation /ʀeklamasjɔ̃/ *nf* **1** (plainte) complaint; **~ injustifiée** unjustified complaint; **lettre de ~** letter of complaint; **faire/déposer/recevoir une ~** to make/lodge/receive a complaint; **service des ~s** customer complaints department; **2** (demande) claim (**de** for); **sur ~** on request.

■ **~ d'état** Jur claim to ownership.

réclame /ʀeklam/ *nf* **1** (réputation) publicity; **faire une bonne/mauvaise ~ à qn/qch** to be good/bad publicity for sb/sth; **2**† Pub (annonce) advertisement; (activité) advertising; **faire de la ~** to advertise (**pour** for); **'en ~'** 'on offer' GB, 'on sale' US.

réclamer /ʀeklame/ [1] I *vtr* **1** (demander) to ask for [*personne, chose, argent*]; to call for [*réforme, aide, silence, enquête*]; to beg [*indulgence*]; to claim [*dû, indemnité*]; to demand [*justice, augmentation*]; **~ de l'argent à qn** to ask sb for money; **~ des indemnités à qn** to claim damages from sb; **~ que** to demand that (+ *subj*); **~ qu'elle s'en aille** to demand that she go; **~ la parole** gén to ask to speak; (dans un débat) to ask to take the floor; **se voir ~ qch** to be asked for sth; **~ à cor et à cri** to clamour[GB] for; **2** (en pleurant) [*bébé*] to cry for [*biberon, mère*]; **3** (nécessiter) to require [*qualité*]; **travail qui réclame de l'attention** work that requires attention.

II *vi* **1** (se plaindre) to complain; **il n'arrête pas de ~** he keeps complaining.

III **se réclamer** *vpr* **1** (s'affirmer) **se ~ de** [*parti*] to be an expression of [*démocratie*]; [*organisation, personne*] to claim to be representative of [*parti, organisme, religion*]; **2** (se fonder sur) [*personne*] to claim to follow [*principe, idéologie, personne*]; **se ~ de ses**

ancêtres to involve the memory of one's ancestors; **3** (se prévaloir) **se ~ de qn** to use sb's name; **il s'est réclamé de mon père pour se faire inviter** he used my father's name to get himself invited.

reclassement /ʀəklasmɑ̃/ *nm* **1** (de dossiers) reclassifying; **2** (d'employé) redeployment (**dans** to); **3** (de salaires) regrading.

reclasser /ʀəklase/ [1] **I** *vtr* **1** (classer de nouveau) to reclassify [*dossiers*]; **2** (affecter à un nouveau poste) to redeploy (**dans** to); **3** (réajuster le salaire de) to regrade.

II se reclasser *vpr* to find new employment (**dans** in).

reclus, **~e** /ʀəkly, yz/ **I** *adj* [*personne, existence*] reclusive; **vivre ~** to live as a recluse; **elle passe ses journées, ~e dans sa maison** she spends her days shut up in her house.

II *nm,f* recluse.

réclusion /ʀeklyzjɔ̃/ *nf* **1** Jur imprisonment; **~ à perpétuité** or **à vie** life sentence; **condamné à dix ans de ~ (criminelle)** sentenced to ten years' imprisonment; **2** Relig reclusion.

réclusionnaire /ʀeklyzjɔnɛʀ/ *nmf* convict.

recoiffer /ʀ(ə)kwafe/ [1] **I** *vtr* **~ qn** to tidy sb's hair.

II se recoiffer *vpr* to tidy one's hair.

recoin /ʀəkwɛ̃/ *nm* lit corner; fig recess; **tous les coins et les ~s** every nook and cranny, every corner.

recoller /ʀ(ə)kɔle/ [1] **I** *vtr* **1** (coller de nouveau) **~ les morceaux d'un vase** to stick the pieces of a vase together again; **~ une enveloppe** to reseal an envelope; **2○** (remettre) **ils l'ont rattrapé et recollé en prison** they caught him and put him back in jail; **il lui a recollé un coup de poing** he punched him/her again.

II recoller à○ *vtr ind* **~ à** to catch up with; **le cycliste a réussi à ~ au groupe de tête** the cyclist managed to catch up with the leaders.

récoltant, **~e** /ʀekɔltɑ̃, ɑ̃t/ *adj* **propriétaire ~** (wine) producer.

récolte /ʀekɔlt/ *nf* **1** Agric (activité) harvest; (produits récoltés) crop, harvest; **la date de la ~ varie** the date of the harvest varies; **nous avons fait trois ~s cette année** we've had three crops this year; **400 tonnes de ~ ont été perdues** 400 tonnes of the crop was lost; **la ~ de maïs/raisins est excellente** the corn/grape crop is excellent; **2** fig (collecte) collection; (fruits de la collecte) (argent) takings (*pl*); (documents) crop.

récolter /ʀekɔlte/ [1] *vtr* **1** Agric to harvest [*maïs, raisin*]; to dig up [*pommes de terre*]; **2** (ramasser) [*abeille*] to collect [*pollen*]; [*personne*] to win [*voix, points*]; to collect [*somme d'argent, informations*]; to reap [*avantage*]; **~○ des mauvaises notes** to get bad marks; **à l'aider, je n'ai récolté que des ennuis** I got nothing but trouble in return for helping him; **~ les fruits de son travail** ou **ses efforts** to reap the fruits of one's labour[GB]; ▶ **semer**.

recommandable /ʀəkɔmɑ̃dabl/ *adj* commendable; **un individu peu ~** a disreputable individual; **il est peu ~** he's a disreputable character.

recommandation /ʀəkɔmɑ̃dasjɔ̃/ *nf* **1** (conseil) also Jur Pol recommendation; **faire des ~s à qn** to make recommendations to sb; **voir un film sur les ~s de qn** to see a film on sb's recommendation; **2** (parrainage) recommendation; **lettre de ~** letter of recommendation, reference; **sur la ~ de qn** on the recommendation of sb; **avoir une ~ de qn** to be recommended by sb; **3** Postes registration.

recommandé, **~e** /ʀəkɔmɑ̃de/ **I** *pp* ▶ **recommander**.

II *pp adj* **1** Postes [*colis, lettre*] registered; **sous pli ~** by registered post GB ou mail; **2 il est ~ de faire** it is advisable to do, you are advised to do; **il est ~ de boire un litre et demi par jour** you are advised to drink one and a half litres a day; **il est ~ à la population d'être vigilante** the public is advised to be vigilant.

III *nm* (lettre) registered letter; (colis) registered parcel; **envoyer qch en ~** to send sth by registered post GB ou mail.

recommander /ʀəkɔmɑ̃de/ [1] **I** *vtr* **1** (conseiller fortement) to advise; **~ la prudence à qn**, **~ à qn d'être prudent** to advise sb to be cautious; **~ à qn la plus grande discrétion** to advise sb to be extremely discreet; **je recommande la prudence** I would advise caution; **~ à qn de ne rien dire** to advise sb not to say anything; **les précautions recommandées par**... precautions recommended by...; **la vaccination est recommandée pour les séjours en Afrique** vaccination is recommended for visits to Africa; **ce n'est pas très recommandé** it is not really advisable; **2** (formuler un avis) [*président, organisme international*] to recommend (**qch à qn** sth to sb); **3** (signaler pour sa qualité) to recommend [*film, médecin, méthode*] (**à qn** to sb); **les restaurants recommandés par ce guide** the restaurants recommended by ou in this guide; **le chef vous recommande de boire un vin de Cahors avec ce plat** the chef recommends a Cahors wine with this dish; **4** (parrainer) to recommend (**à, auprès de** to); **on l'a recommandé?** was he recommended?; **5** Postes to send [sth] by registered post GB ou mail; **6** Relig **~ son âme à Dieu** to commend one's soul to God.

II se recommander *vpr* **1** (invoquer l'appui de) **se ~ de qn** to use sb's name; **2** (demander l'aide de) **se ~ à Dieu** to commend oneself to God; **3** fml (se faire estimer) **se ~ par** [*personne, lieu*] to be well known for.

recommencement /ʀəkɔmɑ̃smɑ̃/ *nm* **le ~ d'un exercice** starting an exercise again; **le ~ d'un traitement** the resumption of treatment; **la vie n'est qu'une suite de ~s** life is just a series of new beginnings; **l'histoire est un éternel ~** history is constantly repeating itself.

recommencer /ʀəkɔmɑ̃se/ [12] **I** *vtr* **1** (complètement) to start [sth] again [*rapport, tâche*]; **il faut tout ~, tout est à ~** the whole thing will have to be done again; **~ qch à zéro** to start sth again from scratch; **~ depuis le début** to start [sth] again from the beginning; **2** (après une pause) to start [sth] again [*traitement, travail*]; **~ à travailler/à vivre** to start working/living again; **on recommence les cours en octobre** classes start again ou resume in October; **3** (faire à nouveau) to do [sth] again [*rapport, action*]; to rewrite [*letter*]; **recommence!** do it again!; **promettre de ne jamais ~** to promise never to do it again; **je ne recommencerai plus** I'll never do it again; **et ne recommence plus!** don't you ever do that again!

II *vi* to start again, to begin again; **le bruit recommence** the noise is starting again; **mon mal de tête recommence** my headache's coming back; **il recommence à neiger** it is starting to snow again; **l'année universitaire recommence en octobre** the academic year starts again in October.

récompense /ʀekɔ̃pɑ̃s/ *nf* (matérielle ou morale) reward; (honorifique) award; **en ~** as a reward (**de** for).

récompenser /ʀekɔ̃pɑ̃se/ [1] *vtr* to reward (**de** for; **par** with); **elle a été récompensée d'avoir persévéré** her perseverance was rewarded.

recomposer /ʀ(ə)kɔ̃poze/ [1] **I** *vtr* gén to reconstruct [*scène*]; Imprim to reset [*page*]; TV to reconstitute [*image*]; Télécom **~ un numéro** to dial a number again.

II se recomposer *vpr* to re-form.

recomposition /ʀ(ə)kɔ̃pozisjɔ̃/ *nf* gén reconstruction; Imprim resetting; TV reconstitution.

recompter /ʀ(ə)kɔ̃te/ [1] *vtr* **~ son argent** to count one's money again; **~ une addition** to add up a bill GB ou check US again.

réconciliateur, **-trice** /ʀekɔ̃siljatœʀ, tʀis/ **I** *adj* reconciliatory.

II *nm,f* peacemaker.

réconciliation /ʀekɔ̃siljasjɔ̃/ *nf* aussi Jur reconciliation (**de X et de Y** of X with Y); **la ~ des deux familles** the reconciliation between the two families.

réconcilier /ʀekɔ̃silje/ [2] **I** *vtr* lit **~ Pierre et Paul**, **~ Pierre avec Paul** to bring Pierre and Paul back together; **~ la morale et la politique** to reconcile morality with politics.

II se réconcilier *vpr* [*couple, amis*] to make up; [*nations*] to be reconciled; **se ~ avec** to make up with [*ennemi*]; to be reconciled with [*nation, doctrine*]; **se ~ avec soi-même** to learn to live with oneself.

reconductible /ʀ(ə)kɔ̃dyktibl/ *adj* renewable.

reconduction /ʀ(ə)kɔ̃dyksjɔ̃/ *nf* renewal; **renouvelable par tacite ~** renewable by tacit agreement.

reconduire /ʀ(ə)kɔ̃dɥiʀ/ [69] *vtr* **1** (accompagner) (à la porte) to see [sb] out; **~ qn chez lui/à la gare** gén to take sb home/to the station; (à pied) to walk sb home/to the station; (en voiture) to drive sb home/to the station; **la police l'a reconduit à la frontière** the police escorted him back to the border; **2** (prolonger) to extend [*grève, cessez-le-feu*]; (renouveler) to renew [*mandat, accord*]; **~ qn dans ses fonctions** to re-elect sb; **être reconduit dans ses fonctions** to be re-elected, to remain in office; **3** (piloter) to drive [sth] again.

réconfort /ʀekɔ̃fɔʀ/ *nm* comfort; **il m'a été d'un grand ~** he was a great comfort to me; **avoir besoin de ~** to need comforting.

réconfortant, **~e** /ʀekɔ̃fɔʀtɑ̃, ɑ̃t/ *adj* **1** (consolant) comforting; (rassérénant) cheering; **2** (revigorant) fortifying.

réconforter /ʀekɔ̃fɔʀte/ [1] **I** *vtr* **1** (consoler) to comfort; (rasséréner) **~ qn** to cheer sb up; **2** (revigorer) to fortify.

II se réconforter *vpr* to restore one's strength.

reconnaissable /ʀ(ə)kɔnɛsabl/ *adj* recognizable; **être ~ à qch** to be recognizable by sth.

reconnaissance /ʀ(ə)kɔnɛsɑ̃s/ *nf* **1** (gratitude) gratitude; **être plein de ~** to be full of gratitude, to be very grateful; **exprimer/témoigner sa ~ à qn** to express/to show one's gratitude to sb; **ma ~ envers lui n'a pas de bornes** I'm infinitely grateful to him; **geste de ~** mark of gratitude; **en ~ de** in appreciation of [*aide, services*]; **avoir** or **éprouver de la ~ pour qn** to be ou feel grateful to sb; **2** (action d'identifier) recognition; **~ des formes/de la parole** Ordinat pattern/speech recognition; **faire un signe de ~** to give a sign of recognition; **3** (fait d'admettre) (de torts, d'erreurs) admission, admitting; (de qualités, mérite) recognition, recognizing; **la ~ de sa propre faiblesse** admitting one's own weakness; **4** (de droit, d'indépendance, d'un État) recognition; **~ de l'autorité de qn** acknowledgement of sb's authority; **~ d'un enfant** legal recognition of a child; **5** (fait d'explorer) Mil reconnaissance; **mission/patrouille/avion de ~** reconnaissance mission/patrol/plane; **après une ~ des lieux** Mil after reconnoitring the area; fig after having a look around; **aller** or **partir en ~** Mil to go on reconnaissance; fig to go and have a look around, to go and have a recce○; **envoyer qn en ~** Mil to send sb on reconnaissance; fig to send sb to have a look around; **faire la ~ du parcours** Équit to walk the course.

■ **~ de dette** acknowledgement of debt, IOU○; **~ optique de caractères**, **ROC** optical character recognition, OCR.

IDIOMES **avoir la ~ du ventre** hum to love the person who feeds one.

reconnaissant, **~e** /R(ə)kɔnɛsɑ̃, ɑ̃t/ *adj* grateful; **être ~ à qn de qch/d'avoir fait** to be grateful to sb for sth/for doing; **je vous serais ~ de bien vouloir faire** fml I should ou would be grateful if you would do.

reconnaître /R(ə)kɔnɛtR/ [73] **I** *vtr* **1** (retrouver) to recognize; (identifier) to identify; **je t'ai reconnu à ta voix/ton pas/ta cicatrice** I recognized you by your voice/your walk/your scar; **~ une odeur** to recognize a smell; **je ne sais pas ~ les champignons** I can't identify different kinds of mushrooms; **excuse-moi, je ne t'avais pas reconnu** sorry, I didn't recognize you; **~ le mâle de la femelle** to tell the male from the female; **je reconnais bien là leur grande générosité/leur manque de courage** it's just like them to be so generous/to be such cowards; **je te reconnaîtrais entre mille** I'd recognize ou know you anywhere; **2** (admettre) to admit [*faits, torts, erreurs*]; **il reconnaît avoir menti** or **qu'il a menti** he admits he lied; **il faut ~ que ce n'est pas un travail passionnant** you have to admit that it's not exciting work; **~ qch comme une évidence** to accept sth as a fact; **être reconnu comme douteux** to be far from certain; **~ qn comme son chef** to acknowledge ou recognize sb as one's leader; **~ qn comme le meilleur économiste du pays** to acknowledge sb to be the best economist in the country; **~ qn coupable** to find sb guilty; **~ des qualités à qn** to recognize that sb has their good points; **il faut leur ~ une certaine franchise** you have to admit that they are quite open; **3** (considérer comme légitime) to recognize [*syndicat, régime, droit de grève*]; (comme valable) to recognize [*diplôme étranger*]; **~ le droit de qn à qch/de faire** to recognize sb's right to sth/to do; **~ un enfant** to recognize a child legally; **l'enfant a-t-il été reconnu?** has the child been legally recognized?; **~ une dette** to acknowledge a debt; **4** (explorer) **~ les lieux** Mil to reconnoitre[GB] the area; fig to have a look round[GB], to go on a recce○.

II se reconnaître *vpr* **1** (soi-même) to recognize oneself; **se ~ dans qn** to see oneself in sb; **je me reconnais en elle** I see myself in her; **2** (l'un l'autre) to recognize each other; **3** (être identifiable) **se ~ à qch** to be recognizable by sth; **4** (s'orienter) to know where one is; **je ne me reconnais plus** I don't recognize a thing; **5** (s'avouer) to admit; **se ~ coupable** to admit one is guilty; **6** (considérer comme légitime) **nous nous reconnaissons le droit de** we feel we have the right to.

reconnu, **~e** /R(ə)kɔny/ **I** *pp* ▶ **reconnaître**.

II *pp adj* [*fait, diplôme, médecin*] recognized; **pays ~ depuis 1990** country that was recognized in 1990; **~ par la loi** recognized by law; **il est ~ que** it is recognized that; **~ citoyen français** recognized as a French citizen; **être ~ fiable** [*méthode, modèle, machine*] to be known to be reliable.

reconquérir /R(ə)kɔ̃keRiR/ [35] *vtr* **1** Mil to reconquer, recover [*territoire*]; **2** fig to regain [*dignité, estime, liberté*]; to win back [*personne, droit*].

reconquête /R(ə)kɔ̃kɛt/ *nf* **1** (de territoire) reconquest; **2** (de personne, droit) winning back; (de liberté) regaining.

reconsidérer /R(ə)kɔ̃sideRe/ [14] *vtr* to reconsider.

reconstituant, **~e** /R(ə)kɔ̃stitɥɑ̃, ɑ̃t/ **I** *adj* fortifying.

II *nm* tonic.

reconstituer /R(ə)kɔ̃stitɥe/ [1] **I** *vtr* to re-form, to reconstitute [*armée, association*]; to reconstruct [*crime, événement*]; to recreate [*époque, décor*]; to piece [sth] together again [*objet en morceaux*]; to build up again [*réserves, forces*].

II se reconstituer *vpr* to re-form.

reconstitution /R(ə)kɔ̃stitysjɔ̃/ *nf* (d'armée, association) re-forming, reconstitution; (de crime, d'événement) reconstruction; (d'époque, de décor) re-creation; **~ des faits** reconstruction; **~ de carrière** career record.

reconstruction /R(ə)kɔ̃stRyksjɔ̃/ *nf* (d'édifice, de ville) reconstruction; (de pays, société) rebuilding.

reconstruire /R(ə)kɔ̃stRɥiR/ [69] *vtr* to reconstruct [*édifice, ville*]; to rebuild [*pays, économie, société*].

reconventionnelle /R(ə)kɔ̃vɑ̃sjɔnɛl/ *adj f* **demande ~** Jur counter-claim.

reconversion /R(ə)kɔ̃vɛRsjɔ̃/ *nf* (de travailleur) redeployment; (de région) redevelopment; (d'économie) restructuring; (d'usine) conversion.

reconvertir /R(ə)kɔ̃vɛRtiR/ [3] **I** *vtr* to redeploy [*personnel*]; to redevelop [*région*]; to restructure [*économie, industrie*]; to convert [*usine, bâtiment*]; to adapt [*équipement*]; **taxi reconverti en ambulance** taxi converted into an ambulance.

II se reconvertir *vpr* [*personnel*] to switch to a new type of employment; [*entreprise*] to switch to a new type of production; [*bâtiment, installations*] to be converted; **se ~ dans l'enseignement** to switch to teaching; **l'usine s'est reconvertie dans le textile** the factory has switched to textiles.

recopier /R(ə)kɔpje/ [2] *vtr* **1** (retranscrire) to copy out [*texte, citations*]; (noter) to copy down [*adresse*]; **2** (mettre au propre) to write up [*brouillon, devoir*].

record /R(ə)kɔR/ **I** *adj* [*niveau, vitesse, prix, année, croissance*] record.

II *nm* **1** Sport record; **battre/établir le ~ du monde** to break/to set the world record; **détenir le ~ masculin de natation/le ~ de France** to hold the men's swimming record/the French record; **2** fig record (**de** for); **en un temps ~** in record time; **on a battu tous les ~s d'affluence** (pour film, exposition) attendance figures have reached record levels.

recorder /R(ə)kɔRde/ [1] *vtr* to restring [*guitare, raquette*].

recordman, *pl* **-men** /Rəkɔrdman, mɛn/ *nm* (men's) record-holder (**de** for).

recordwoman, *pl* **-men** /Rəkɔrdwuman, mɛn/ *nf* (women's) record-holder (**de** for).

recoucher /R(ə)kuʃe/ [1] **I** *vtr* to put [sb] back to bed.

II se recoucher *vpr* to go back to bed.

recoudre /R(ə)kudR/ [76] *vtr* **1** Cout to sew up [*ourlet, doublure*]; to sew [sth] back on [*bouton*]; **2** Méd to stitch up [*plaie, blessé*]; **il est recousu de partout** he's covered in stitches.

recoupement /R(ə)kupmɑ̃/ *nm* **1** (vérification) cross-check, cross-checking ¢; **après plusieurs ~s** after cross-checking several times; **faire des ~s** to cross-check; **par ~s** by cross-checking; **selon un ~ des informations de sources serbe et croate** according to both Serbian and Croatian sources; **2** (intersection) intersection.

recouper /R(ə)kupe/ [1] **I** *vtr* **1** (de nouveau) to cut [sth] again [*cheveux, haie*]; (davantage) to cut some more [*viande*]; to recut [*vêtement*]; **2** (comparer) to tie in ou tally with [*version, témoignage*]; **3** Jeux to cut [sth] again [*cartes*].

II se recouper *vpr* (s'accorder) [*versions, témoignages*] to tally; [*résultats*] to add up; (se couper) [*lignes, cercles*] to intersect.

recourbé, **~e** /R(ə)kuRbe/ **I** *pp* ▶ **recourber**.

II *pp adj* [*bec, nez*] hooked; [*cils, ongles*] curved; [*tige de métal*] curved.

recourber /R(ə)kuRbe/ [1] **I** *vtr* to bend [sth] back.

II se recourber *vpr* **1** (état) [*cils, ongles*] to be curved; **2** (processus) [*tige de métal*] to curve.

recourir /R(ə)kuRiR/ [26] **I recourir à** *vtr ind* **~ à** to use, to have recourse to [*remède, technique*]; to resort to [*expédient, stratagème, violence*]; to turn to [*parent, ami*]; to go to [*agence, expert*]; **~ à la justice** to go to court.

II *vi* **1** Sport to run again; **2** Jur to lodge an appeal (**contre** against).

recours /R(ə)kuR/ *nm inv* **1** (moyen quelconque) recourse; (moyen extrême) resort; **le ~ à qch** resorting to sth, recourse to sth; **sans autre ~ que** with no other way out but; **avoir ~ à** to have recourse to [*remède, technique*]; to resort to [*expédient, stratagème*]; to turn to [*parent, ami*]; to go to [*agence, expert*]; **en dernier ~** as a last resort; **c'est sans ~** there's no way out; **2** Jur appeal; **déposer un ~ auprès d'un** or **devant un tribunal** to lodge an appeal (**contre** against); **~ en annulation** application ou motion for annulment; **~ en révision** application to reopen proceedings; **~ en grâce** petition for reprieve.

recouvrable /R(ə)kuvRabl/ *adj* [*somme, créance*] recoverable, retrievable; [*impôt*] collectable.

recouvrement /R(ə)kuvRəmɑ̃/ *nm* **1** Fin, Fisc (d'impôt, de cotisation) collection; (de somme, dette) recovery; **2** Constr (d'une ardoise) lap; **3** (de toit) (processus) covering; (résultat) cover; **4** (de santé, faculté, vue) recovery.

recouvrer /R(ə)kuvRe/ [1] *vtr* **1** Fin, Fisc to recover [*somme, créance*]; to collect [*impôt, cotisation*]; **2** (retrouver) to recover [*santé, forces*]; to regain [*liberté*]; **~ la raison** to regain one's sanity.

recouvrir /R(ə)kuvRiR/ [32] **I** *vtr* **1** (couvrir complètement) to cover (**de** with); **la campagne était recouverte d'une épaisse couche de neige** the countryside was covered with ou in a thick blanket of snow; **~ des meubles avec des housses** to cover furniture with dust sheets; **une table recouverte d'une nappe** a table with a cloth, a table covered with a cloth; **le sol était recouvert de débris** the ground was covered ou strewn with debris; **leurs affiches ont été recouvertes par celles de leurs adversaires** their posters were covered up ou papered over by those of their opponents; **2** (couvrir de nouveau) to cover [sb] up again [*malade, enfant*]; to re-cover [*chaise, fauteuil*]; **3** (masquer) to hide, to conceal; **son attitude nonchalante recouvre une volonté inflexible** his/her easygoing manner conceals an iron will; **4** (inclure) **cela recouvre en partie ce que j'allais dire** this partly covers what I was about to say; **une réalité qui recouvre deux problèmes fondamentaux** a situation that encompasses two fundamental problems.

II se recouvrir *vpr* **1** (devenir couvert) to become covered (**de** with); **2** (se chevaucher) [*tuiles*] to overlap; **3** (correspondre) [*concepts*] to overlap; **4** (remettre son chapeau) to put one's hat back on.

recracher /R(ə)kRaʃe/ [1] *vtr* to spit out.

récré○ /RekRe/ *nf* schoolchildren's slang (*abbr* = **récréation**) break, recess US.

récréatif, **-ive** /RekReatif, iv/ *adj* [*jeu, activité, film, soirée*] entertaining; [*zone, parc*] recreation (*épith*).

récréation /RekReasjɔ̃/ *nf* **1** (à l'école primaire) playtime GB, recess US; (dans le secondaire) break GB, recess US; **ils sont en ~** they are having their break; **à la ~** at break, during playtime; **2** (loisir) recreation.

recréer /R(ə)kRee/ [11] *vtr* to recreate.

recrépir /R(ə)kRepiR/ [3] *vtr* to roughcast.

recreuser /RəkRøze/ [1] *vtr* to dig [sth] deeper.

récrier: **se récrier** /RekRije/ [2] *vpr* to exclaim; **se ~ d'admiration** to exclaim in admiration; **se ~ contre qch** to protest volubly against sth.

récriminateur, **-trice** /RekRiminatœR, tRis/ **I** *adj* remonstrative.

II *nm,f* remonstrator.

récrimination /RekRiminasjɔ̃/ *nf* bitter remonstration, recrimination.

récriminatoire /ʀekʀiminatwaʀ/ *adj* remonstrative.

récriminer /ʀekʀimine/ [1] *vi* to rail sout (**contre qn/qch** against sb/sth).

récrire /ʀekʀiʀ/ [67] *vtr* = **réécrire**.

recroqueviller: **se recroqueviller** /ʀ(ə)kʀɔkvije/ [1] *vpr* **1** [*personne*] to huddle up; **elle était toute recroquevillée** she was all huddled up; **2** [*objet, feuille*] to shrivel up.

recru, **~e** /ʀ(ə)kʀy/ **I** *adj* liter **~ (de fatigue)** exhausted.
II recrue *nf* lit, fig recruit; **faire une nouvelle ~e** to get a new recruit.

recrudescence /ʀ(ə)kʀydesɑ̃s/ *nf* (de violence, d'intérêt) fresh upsurge (**de** of); (de bombardements, peur, pessimisme, demandes, grèves) new wave (**de** of); (d'incendie, de combats) renewed outbreak (**de** of); **la ~ du froid** the return of even colder weather; **la ~ de la tempête** the storm's sudden increase in violence; **on craint une ~ de la fièvre** it is feared that the fever may recur with renewed intensity.

recrudescent, **~e** /ʀ(ə)kʀydesɑ̃, ɑ̃t/ *adj* **être ~** to be on the increase.

recrue ▶ **recru**.

recrutement /ʀ(ə)kʀytmɑ̃/ *nm* recruitment.

recruter /ʀ(ə)kʀyte/ [1] **I** *vtr* (engager) to recruit; **~ qn comme enseignant** to take sb on as a teacher; **~ qn par concours/sur titres** (pour un travail) to appoint sb on the basis of competitive examination/of sb's qualifications; (pour une école) to accept sb on the basis of competitive examination/of sb's qualifications.
II se recruter *vpr* **1** (s'embaucher) to be recruited (**dans, parmi** from); **2** (provenir de) **se ~ dans** or **parmi** to come from.

recruteur, **-euse** /ʀ(ə)kʀytœʀ, øz/ **I** *adj* [*officier, agent*] recruiting; [*bureau, agence*] recruitment (*épith*).
II *nm,f* **1** gén recruitment specialist, recruiter US; **2** Mil recruiting officer.

recta○ /ʀɛkta/ *adv* **c'est ~** you can bet on it; **chaque fois que je lave mes vitres, c'est ~, il pleut** every time I clean the windows it rains, you can bet on it; **payer ~** to pay there and then; **partir ~** to leave on the dot.

rectal, **~e**, *mpl* **-aux** /ʀɛktal, o/ *adj* rectal.

rectangle /ʀɛktɑ̃gl/ **I** *adj* Math [*trapèze, triangle*] right-angled, right US.
II *nm* gén, Math rectangle.
■ **~ blanc** *'suitable for adults only' sign on French TV*.

rectangulaire /ʀɛktɑ̃gylɛʀ/ *adj* rectangular, oblong.

recteur /ʀɛktœʀ/ *nm* **1** Scol, Univ (d'académie) ≈ chief education officer GB, ≈ superintendent (of schools) US; **2** (d'institution catholique) rector.

rectifiable /ʀɛktifjabl/ *adj* [*erreur*] rectifiable, that can be corrected (*jamais épith*).

rectificateur /ʀɛktifikatœʀ/ *nm* Chimie rectifier.

rectificatif, **-ive** /ʀɛktifikatif, iv/ **I** *adj* (corrigé) corrected, amended, revised; (qui corrige) of correction; **article ~** Comm correcting entry.
II *nm* **1** Presse correction; **2** (à une loi) amendment (**à** to).

rectification /ʀɛktifikasjɔ̃/ *nf* **1** (correction) (d'erreur) correction; (de contrat) rectification; (modification) (de liste, décret) amendment; (de chiffres) adjustment; (de limites) rectification; **2** (de tracé, route) straightening; (de virage) straightening out; **3** (rectificatif) correction; **4** Chimie, Math rectification; **5** Tech (de pièce) making true; (à la meule) grinding.

rectifier /ʀɛktifje/ [2] *vtr* **1** (corriger) to correct, rectify [*erreur*]; **'un seul,' rectifia-t-il** 'only one,' he corrected; **2** (rendre conforme) to adjust [*assaisonnement, dimension, position, chiffres*]; to rectify [*limites, contrat, ouvrage défectueux*]; to amend [*facture, document*]; **~ sa cravate** to adjust one's tie; **~ la position** Mil to straighten up; **~ sa conduite** fig to mend one's ways; **~ le tir** lit to adjust one's aim; fig to change one's approach; **il a rectifié le tir** fig he adopted a new approach; **3** (redresser) to straighten [*tracé, route*]; to straighten out [*virage*]; **4** Chimie, Math to rectify; **5** Tech to true, straighten [*pièce*] ; (à la meule) to grind; **6**◑ (tuer) **être rectifié, se faire ~** to get bumped off○.

rectifieur, **-ieuse** /ʀɛktifjœʀ, øz/ **I** ▶ **510** *nm,f* (ouvrier) grinding machine operator.
II rectifieuse *nf* (machine) grinding machine.

rectiligne /ʀɛktiliɲ/ **I** *adj* **1** gén straight; [*propagation*] rectilinear; **2** Math rectilinear.
II *nm* dihedral (angle).

rectilinéaire /ʀɛktilineɛʀ/ *adj* Phot rectilinear.

rection /ʀɛksjɔ̃/ *nf* Ling government.

rectitude /ʀɛktityd/ *nf* **1** (de caractère, jugement) rectitude; **2** (de ligne) straightness.

recto /ʀɛkto/ *nm* front, recto spéc; **au ~** on the front; **~ verso** on both sides, recto verso spéc.

rectoral, **~e**, *mpl* **-aux** /ʀɛktɔʀal, o/ *adj* [*décision*] of the local education authority (*après n*) GB, of the board of education (*après n*) US; **services rectoraux** local education services GB, services of the board of education US.

rectorat /ʀɛktɔʀa/ *nm* **1** (administration) ≈ local education authority GB, ≈ board of education US; **2** (bureaux) local education offices.

rectoscope /ʀɛktɔskɔp/ *nm* proctoscope.

rectrice /ʀɛktʀis/ *nf* Zool rectrix.

rectum /ʀɛktɔm/ *nm* rectum.

reçu, **~e** /ʀ(ə)sy/ **I** *pp* ▶ **recevoir**.
II *pp adj* **1** [*candidat*] successful; **~ à un examen** successful in GB ou on US an exam; **2** [*usage*] accepted; **3** Radio **message ~** message received and understood.
III *nm,f* Scol, Univ successful candidate.
IV *nm* **1** (quittance) receipt; **2** (réception) **au ~ de ta lettre** upon receipt of your letter, on receiving your letter.
■ **~ pour solde de tout compte** received in full and final payment.

recueil /ʀ(ə)kœj/ *nm* (d'un auteur) collection; (de divers auteurs) anthology; (de documents, lois) compendium.
■ **~ de jurisprudence** Jur casebook.

recueillement /ʀəkœjmɑ̃/ *nm* **1** (méditation) contemplation; **2** (attitude respectueuse) reverence; **dans un profond ~** in reverential silence.

recueilli, **~e** /ʀəkœji/ **I** *pp* ▶ **recueillir**.
II *pp adj* [*air, visage*] rapt; [*fidèle*] rapt in prayer; [*foule, silence*] reverential; **une vie solitaire et ~e** a life of solitary contemplation.

recueillir /ʀəkœjiʀ/ [27] **I** *vtr* **1** (rassembler) to collect [*dons, signatures, anecdotes*]; to gather, to collect [*témoignages, renseignements*]; **2** (obtenir) to obtain, to get [*voix, nouvelles*]; to gain [*consensus*]; to achieve [*unanimité*]; to win [*louanges*]; **~ des applaudissements** [*personne, proposition*] to be greeted with applause; **3** (récupérer) to collect [*eau, résine*]; to gather [*miel*]; **cuvette pour ~ l'eau** bowl to catch the water; **~ le fruit de son travail** to reap the fruit of one's labour[GB]; **4** (prendre avec soi) to take in [*orphelin*]; to pick up [*naufragé*]; **5** (enregistrer) to record [*impression, opinions*]; (par écrit) to take down [*déposition*]; **6** (hériter) to inherit [*fortune*]; to receive [*héritage*].
II se recueillir *vpr* **1** (méditer) to commune with oneself; (se concentrer) **se ~ avant d'entrer en scène** to collect oneself before going on stage; **se ~ sur la tombe de qn** to stay some time in silent contemplation at sb's grave [*parent*]; to pay homage to sb's memory [*héros*]; **se ~ au monument aux morts** to stand in silent remembrance before the war memorial; **2** (prier) to engage in private prayer.

recuire /ʀ(ə)kɥiʀ/ [69] **I** *vtr* **1** Culin to reboil [*confiture*]; **~ un steak/gâteau** to cook a steak/cake a bit more; **2** Tech to anneal [*métal*]; to refire [*poterie*].
II *vi* **il faut que je fasse ~ le ragoût** I must finish off cooking the stew.

recuit, **~e** /ʀ(ə)kɥi, it/ **I** *pp* ▶ **recuire**.
II *pp adj* Culin **cuit et ~**○ hum done to a frazzle○.
III *nm* Tech annealing.

recul /ʀ(ə)kyl/ *nm* **1** (détachement) detachment; **avec le ~** with hindsight ou in retrospect; **manquer de ~** to be incapable of being objective; **prendre du ~** to stand back; **prendre du ~ par rapport à une situation** to look at a situation objectively; **prendre un peu de ~** to distance oneself slightly; **il faut du ~ pour juger son propre travail** you need to stand back to judge your own work; **2** (baisse) (d'investissements, de production, nombre) drop (**de** in), fall (**de** in); (de doctrine) decline (**de** in); **~ du dollar** fall in the dollar; **~ de la maladie** decline in the disease; **le ~ d'un homme politique** a politician's decline in popularity; **être en ~** [*investissements, exportations, ventes*] to be dropping ou falling; [*racisme, tendance*] to be on the decline; [*parti*] to be in decline; **être en léger/net ~** [*investissements, exportations, ventes*] to show a slight/definite drop; [*racisme, tendance*] to be declining slightly/to be definitely on the decline; **un ~ de 3 points/5%** a 3 point/5% drop; **3** (dans l'espace) (de voiture, wagon) reversing GB, backing up; (d'armée) pulling ou drawing back; (des eaux, de la mer) recession; **avoir un mouvement de ~** to recoil; **feu de ~** Aut reversing light; **manquer de ~** to be too close; **prendre du ~** to step back; **le ~ de la forêt amazonienne** the gradual disappearance of the Amazonian forest; **4** (de date, réunion) postponement; (d'âge de la retraite) raising; **5** (dérobade) backing down; **6** (d'une arme) recoil.

reculade /ʀ(ə)kylad/ *nf* climb-down.

reculé, **~e** /ʀ(ə)kyle/ *adj* **1** [*quartier, zone, village*] remote; **2** [*temps, époque*] distant, remote.

reculer /ʀ(ə)kyle/ [1] **I** *vtr* **1** (pousser) to move back [*vase, lampe*]; to move ou push back [*meuble*]; **pour ~ les frontières du possible** fig to push back the frontiers of what we thought was possible; **~ les pendules d'une heure** to put the clocks back an hour; **2** (faisant marche arrière) to reverse GB, to back up; **3** (dans le temps) to put off [*moment du départ*]; to put off, to postpone [*événement, décision*]; to put back [*date*]; to raise [*âge*].
II *vi* **1** [*personne, groupe, joueur*] (aller en arrière) to move back; (pour mieux voir quelque chose, pour être vu) to stand back; [*chauffeur*] to reverse; **~ d'un pas** to step back; **~ de trois pas** to take three steps back(wards); **~ de quelques pas** to take a few steps back(wards); **~ de quelques mètres** to move back a few yards; **~ lentement vers qch** to retreat slowly toward(s) sth; **faire ~ un groupe de personnes** to move a group of people back; **j'ai l'impression de ~** lit, fig I feel as if I'm going backward(s); **~ d'une case** Jeux to go back a square; **~ à la vue du sang** to recoil at the sight of blood; **~ pour mieux sauter** (prendre son élan) to move back to get a better run-up; **c'est ~ pour mieux sauter** fig it's just putting off the inevitable; **2** [*voiture, chariot*] to move backward(s); (dans une pente) to roll backward(s); (délibérément) to reverse GB, to back up; **3** [*armée*] to pull ou draw back; **4** [*falaise*] to be eroded; [*forêt*] to be gradually disappearing; [*eaux*] to go down; [*mer*] to recede; **5** (régresser) [*franc, valeurs boursières*] to fall; [*production, exportation*] to fall,

to drop; [*doctrine, mouvement*] to decline; [*parti, politicien*] to suffer a drop in popularity; **faire ~** to cause a fall in [*franc, exportation*]; **faire ~ le chômage** to reduce unemployment; **faire ~ le racisme** to curb racism; **faire ~ la maladie** to reduce the incidence of the disease; **~ de cinq places** [*élèves, sportif*] to fall back ou to drop five places; **6** (céder, se dérober) to back down; (hésiter) to shrink back; **cela m'a fait ~** it put me off; **~ devant une difficulté** to shrink from a difficulty; **ne ~ devant rien** to stop at nothing; **il ne reculera devant rien pour réussir** he'll stop at nothing to succeed; **ne pas ~ devant les manœuvres frauduleuses** to be quite prepared to use fraudulent measures; **7** [*arme*] to recoil; **8** Équit to rein back.

III se reculer *vpr* gén to move back; (d'un pas) to step back; (pour mieux voir) to stand back; **se ~ de quelques pas** to take a few steps back.

reculons: **à reculons** /aʀ(ə)kylɔ̃/ *loc adv* **avançer** or **aller à ~** lit to go backward(s); fig to go reluctantly; **monter un escalier à ~** to go upstairs backward(s).

récupérable /ʀekypeʀabl/ *adj* **1** (réutilisable) [*matériau*] reusable; **2** (réparable) [*objet, vêtement*] which can be made good again (*épith, après n*); **la voiture n'est pas ~** the car is beyond repair; (après accident) the car is a write-off; **3** (réformable) [*délinquant*] who can be rehabilitated (*épith, après n*); **non ~** beyond redemption; **4** (argent) recoverable; **5** Entr (heures de travail) which can be made up.

récupérateur, **-trice** /ʀekypeʀatœʀ, tʀis/ **I** *adj* **1** (réparateur) **le pouvoir ~ du sommeil** the healing powers of sleep; **2** Pol péj [*discours, tactique*] designed to absorb dissenting opinion.

II *nm* **1** Tech (de chaleur, aussi en armurerie) recuperator; **2** **▶510|** (personne) salvage dealer; **~ de métaux** scrap metal dealer, scrap merchant.

récupération /ʀekypeʀasjɔ̃/ *nf* **1** (de ferraille) salvage; (de chiffons) reclamation; **une cabane construite à partir de matériaux de ~** a shack built of salvaged materials; **2** (de l'organisme) recovery; **capacité de ~** recuperative power; **3** (recouvrement) (d'argent, de prêt) recovery; **4** (d'heures de travail) making up; **la ~ des heures travaillées le dimanche** time off in lieu of hours worked on Sunday; **5** Pol (de mouvement) taking over, hijacking; (d'idées) appropriation.

récupérer /ʀekypeʀe/ [14] **I** *vtr* **1** (rentrer en possession de) to get back, to recover [*argent, objet, force*]; **j'aimerais bien ~ les disques que je t'ai prêtés** I'd like to get back those records I lent you; **2** (aller chercher) to fetch; **elle doit ~ son fils chez la nourrice** she must go and pick up ou fetch her son from the childminder GB ou babysitter US; **je suis allé ~ le ballon chez les voisins** I went to get ou fetch the ball back from the neighbours'[GB]; **il a récupéré le ticket de caisse au fond de la poubelle** he retrieved the receipt from the bottom of the bin GB ou garbage can US; **3** (ramasser pour réutiliser) to salvage [*ferraille*]; to reclaim [*chiffons, vieux journaux*]; **j'ai pu ~ quelques pommes pas trop abîmées** I managed to salvage a few apples that weren't too bruised; **j'ai récupéré quelques planches sur le chantier** I picked up a few planks from the building site; **4** (garder) to save [*timbres, boites*]; **5** Entr to make up [*journées, heures de travail*]; **il faudra que je récupère les heures perdues** I'll have to make up the hours; **6** Pol to take over, to hijack [*mouvement, personne*]; to appropriate [*idées*]; **7** (réinsérer) to rehabilitate [*délinquant*]; **8**○ (recouvrer) [*personne*] to recover [*santé, mobilité, forces*].

II *vi* (après un effort physique) to recover (**de** from); (après une maladie) to recover, to recuperate (**de** from); **il n'a jamais vraiment récupéré après son accident** he never really recovered after his accident.

récurage /ʀekyʀaʒ/ *nm* (de casserole) scouring; (de lavabo) scrubbing.

récurer /ʀekyʀe/ [1] *vtr* to scour [*casserole*]; to scrub [*lavabo*]; **poudre à ~** scouring powder.

récurrence /ʀekyʀɑ̃s/ *nf* **1** (répétition) recurrence; **2** Math recursion.

récurrent, **~e** /ʀekyʀɑ̃, ɑ̃t/ *adj* **1** gén, Anat, Méd recurrent; **2** Phys **image ~e** afterimage; **3** Math **série ~e** recursion formula ou clause.

récursif, **-ive** /ʀekyʀsif, iv/ *adj* recursive.

récursivité /ʀekyʀsivite/ *nf* recursion.

récusable /ʀekyzabl/ *adj* open to challenge.

récusation /ʀekyzasjɔ̃/ *nf* challenging, challenge; **~ de juré** Jur challenging a juror, objection to a juror; **droit de ~** right of challenge.

récuser /ʀekyze/ [1] **I** *vtr* to challenge, to object to [*juré, témoin, arbitre*].

II se récuser *vpr* gén to declare oneself incompetent; Jur [*juge*] to decline to act in a case.

recyclable /ʀ(ə)siklabl/ *adj* [*matériau*] recyclable; [*personne*] retrainable.

recyclage /ʀ(ə)siklaʒ/ *nm* **1** (de matériau) recycling; **~ du verre** recycling of glass; **2** (de personnel) retraining; **stage de ~** retraining course; **3** Fin (de capitaux) recycling; (de profits) reinvestment; (d'argent sale) laundering; **4** Tech (de gaz, liquide) recirculation.

recycler /ʀ(ə)sikle/ [1] **I** *vtr* **1** (pour réutiliser) to recycle [*matériau*]; **2** **~ le personnel** (former de nouveau) to retrain the staff; (perfectionner) to provide refresher courses for the staff; **3** (réinvestir) to recycle [*capitaux*]; to reinvest [*profits*]; (blanchir) pej to launder [*argent*]; **4** Tech to recirculate [*gaz, liquide*].

II se recycler *vpr* **1** (se perfectionner) to update one's skills; (faire un stage) to attend a refresher course; **2** (se reconvertir) to retrain; (changer d'emploi) to change jobs; **se ~ dans l'enseignement** (se reconvertir) to retrain as a teacher; (changer d'emploi) to go into teaching.

rédacteur, **-trice** /ʀedaktœʀ, tʀis/ **▶510|** *nm,f* **1** (de texte) gén author, writer; (dans un ministère) parliamentary draftsman/draftswoman; **2** Presse, Édition editor; **~ sportif/politique** sports/political editor; **3** Ordinat programmer[GB].

■ **~ en chef** editor in chief; **~ publicitaire** copywriter.

rédaction /ʀedaksjɔ̃/ *nf* **1** (activité) (d'article, ouvrage) (écriture) writing; (correction) editing; (de liste, bilan) compilation; (de document, décret) drafting; (manière de rédiger) wording; **2** Presse (bureaux) editorial offices; (personnel) editorial staff; **3** Scol essay GB, theme US.

■ **~ publicitaire** copywriting.

rédactionnel, **-elle** /ʀedaksjɔnɛl/ **I** *adj* editorial.

II *nm* text (*of advertisement*).

reddition /ʀɛdisjɔ̃/ *nf* **1** (capitulation) surrender; **2** Jur **~ de comptes** rendering of accounts.

redécoupage /ʀ(ə)dekupaʒ/ *nm* Admin, Pol **~ électoral** constituency boundary changes GB, redistricting US.

redécouverte /ʀ(ə)dekuvɛʀt/ *nf* rediscovery.

redécouvrir /ʀ(ə)dekuvʀiʀ/ [32] *vtr* to rediscover.

redéfaire /ʀ(ə)defɛʀ/ [10] **I** *vtr* to undo [sth] again.

II se redéfaire *vpr* to come undone again.

redéfinir /ʀ(ə)definiʀ/ [3] *vtr* to redefine.

redéfinition /ʀədefinisjɔ̃/ *nf* (d'objectif, de concept) redefining (**de** of); (d'institution, de pays) reshaping (**de** of).

redemander /ʀədmɑ̃de, ʀ(ə)dəmɑ̃de/ [1] *vtr* **1** (demander de nouveau) **~ qch à qn** to ask sb for sth again; **2** (se faire rendre) **~ qch à qn** to ask sb for sth back; **3** (demander davantage) **~ des fruits à qn** to ask sb for more fruit.

redémarrage /ʀ(ə)demaʀaʒ/ *nm* **1** Aut (de moteur) restarting; **2** (reprise) upturn (**de** in); **3** (réouverture) **le ~ de l'usine a été lent** it took a long time for the factory to get going again.

redémarrer /ʀ(ə)demaʀe/ [1] *vi* **1** Aut [*voiture*] to move off again; [*moteur*] to start again; [*chauffeur*] to drive off again; **2** Écon [*marché, économie*] to take off again; [*entreprise*] to relaunch itself; **le gouvernement a réussi à faire ~ l'économie** the government managed to restart the economy.

rédempteur, **-trice** /ʀedɑ̃ptœʀ, tʀis/ *adj* Relig redemptive; fig liter redeeming.

Rédempteur /ʀedɑ̃ptœʀ/ *nm* **le ~** the Redeemer.

rédemption /ʀedɑ̃psjɔ̃/ *nf* redemption.

Rédemption /ʀedɑ̃psjɔ̃/ *nf* **la ~** the Redemption.

redéploiement /ʀ(ə)deplwamɑ̃/ *nm* **1** (de forces, personnel, ressources) redeployment; **2** (d'industrie) restructuring; **~ industriel/politique** industrial/political restructuring.

redéployer /ʀ(ə)deplwaje/ [23] **I** *vtr* **1** to redeploy [*forces, personnel, ressources*]; **2** to restructure [*budget, économie*].

II se redéployer *vpr* [*entreprise*] to expand (abroad); [*capitaux*] to be redirected.

redescendre /ʀədesɑ̃dʀ/ [6] **I** *vtr* **1** (transporter de nouveau) (en bas) gén to take [sb/sth] back down [*personne, objet*] (**à** to); (à l'étage) to take [sb/sth] back downstairs [*personne, objet*]; (d'en haut) gén to bring [sb/sth] back down [*personne, objet*] (**de** from); (de l'étage) to bring [sb/sth] back downstairs [*personne, objet*]; **~ les bouteilles à la cave** to take the bottles back down to the cellar; **~ les valises du grenier** to bring the suitcases back down from the attic; **je peux vous ~ au village** I can take you back down to the village; **redescends-moi mes pantoufles** bring my slippers back down (to me); **je leur ai fait ~ les bouteilles à la cave** I made them take the bottles back down to the cellar; **j'ai fait ~ le piano dans le salon** I had the piano taken ou brought back down to the living room; **faites-moi ~ les dossiers secrets** get the secret files brought back down to me; **2** (remettre en bas) to get [sth] back down [*valise, boîte*]; **redescends-moi cette boîte** get me that box back down; **~ un seau dans un puits** to lower a bucket back into a well; **3** (rabaisser) to lower [*étagère, tableau, store*] (**de** by); to wind [sth] back down [*vitre de véhicule*]; to roll [sth] back down [*manches, jambes de pantalon*]; to pull [sth] back down [*jupe, robe*]; to turn down [*col*]; **~ une étagère de 20 centimètres/d'un cran** to lower a shelf another 20 centimetres[GB]/by another notch; **4** (parcourir de nouveau) [*personne*] (en allant) to go back down [*pente, rue, étage*]; to go ou climb back down [*escalier, marches, échelle*]; (en venant) to come back down [*pente, rue, marches, échelle*]; [*voiture, automobiliste*] to drive back down [*pente, route*]; [*bateau*] to sail back down [*fleuve*]; **nous avons redescendu la colline à pied** (en marchant) we walked back down the hill; (et non à bicyclette) we went back down the hill on foot; **~ la colline en rampant/à bicyclette** to crawl/cycle back down the hill; **il m'a fait ~ l'escalier en courant** he made me run back down the stairs.

II *vi* (descendre de nouveau) [*personne*] (en allant) gén to go back down, to go down again (**à** to); (de l'étage) to go back downstairs, to go downstairs again; (en venant) gén to come back down, to come down again (**de** from) ; (de l'étage) to come back downstairs, to come downstairs again; (après être remonté) (en allant) to go back down again; (en venant) to come back down again; [*train, ascenseur, téléphérique, avion, hélicoptère*] (en allant) to go back down; (en venant) to come back down; [*oiseau*] to fly down again; [*prix, taux,* *monnaie*] to go down again; [*mer*] to go back out; [*température, baromètre*] to fall again, to go down again; **reste ici, je redescends à la cave** stay here, I'm going back down to the cellar; **peux-tu ~ chercher mon sac?** can you go back downstairs and get my bag?; **tu es redescendu à pied?** gén did you walk back down?; (plutôt que par l'ascenseur) did you come back down on foot?; **je préfère ~ par l'escalier** I prefer to go back down by the stairs; **nous sommes redescendus par le sentier/la route** (à pied) we walked back down by the path/the road; (à cheval) we rode back down by the path/road; **il est redescendu vers moi en rampant** he crawled back down to me; **il est redescendu du col à bicyclette/en voiture** he cycled/drove back down from the pass; **où est l'écureuil? il a dû ~ de l'arbre** where's the squirrel? it must have climbed back down from the tree; **je suis redescendu au fond du puits/au bas de la falaise** I went back down to the bottom of the well/to the foot of the cliff; **~ de** [*personne*] to step back off [*trottoir, marche*]; [*personne, animal*] to climb back down from [*mur, tabouret*]; **~ de l'échelle/la corde** to climb back down from the ladder/the rope; **il est redescendu du toit** [*enfant, chat*] he's come back down off the roof; **~ de son lit** to get out of bed again; **~ de cheval/bicyclette** to get off one's horse/bicycle again; **~ de voiture** to get out of the car again; **~ du train** to get off the train again; **on nous a fait ~ de l'avion** we were made to get out of the plane again; **~ à Marseille** (retourner) to go back down to Marseilles; **~ dans les sondages** [*politicien, parti*] to drop ou to move down in the opinion polls; **l'opposition redescend dans la rue** the opposition is taking to the streets again; **~ en deuxième position** [*équipe*] to go back down to second place; **les cours sont redescendus de 20%** prices have gone down another 20%; **faire ~ les cours** to bring the prices down again; **faire ~ le dollar** to send ou put the dollar down again; **le franc est redescendu par rapport à la livre** the franc has gone down ou dropped against the pound again; **faire ~ la température** gén to lower the temperature; Méd to lower one's temperature.

IDIOMES **~ sur terre** to come (back) down to earth.

redevable /ʀədvabl, ʀ(ə)dəvabl/ *adj* **1 être ~ de qch à qn** (d'une faveur, d'un succès) to owe sth to sb, to be indebted to sb for sth; (d'une somme) to owe sth to sb; **2** Fisc **être ~ de l'impôt** to be liable for tax.

redevance /ʀədvɑ̃s, ʀ(ə)dəvɑ̃s/ *nf* **1** (taxe) gén charge; (de télévision) licence GB ou license US fee; (de téléphone) rental charge; **2** (droit d'exploitation) royalty.

■ **~s fermières** rent (*on a farm, often paid in kind*).

redevenir /ʀ(ə)dəvniʀ, ʀədvəniʀ/ [36] *vi* **~ normal** to become normal again.

rédhibitoire /ʀedibitwaʀ/ *adj* **1** [*coût*] prohibitive; [*obstacle*] insurmountable; [*condition*] unacceptable; [*timidité*] crippling; **être d'une bêtise ~** to be stupid beyond redemption; **2** Jur **vice ~** latent ou redhibitory defect.

rediffuser /ʀ(ə)difyze/ [1] *vtr* to repeat GB, to rerun [*émission*]; **émission rediffusée** repeat GB, rerun.

rediffusion /ʀ(ə)difyzjɔ̃/ *nf* repeat GB, rerun.

rédiger /ʀediʒe/ [13] *vtr* (écrire) to write [*article, texte*]; (en développant ses notes) to write up [*notes, thèse*]; to draft [*décret, contrat*]; **ainsi rédigé** expressed in such terms.

redingote /ʀ(ə)dɛ̃gɔt/ *nf* (d'homme) frock coat; (de femme) fitted coat.

redire /ʀ(ə)diʀ/ [65] *vtr* to repeat; **il a redit sa désapprobation** he reiterated ou repeated his disapproval; **~ qch à qn** (répéter) to tell sth to sb again; **je ne te le redirai pas une autre fois!** I won't tell you again!; **je le lui ai dit et redit** I've told him over and over again; **~ à qn de faire** to remind sb to do; **~ à qn que** to remind sb that; **avoir** or **trouver quelque chose à ~ à qch** to find fault with sth; **avez-vous quelque chose à ~ à leur travail?** have you got any complaints about their work?; **qu'avez-vous à ~ à notre décision?** what have you got against our decision?; **je ne vois rien à y ~** I've got nothing against it; **côté qualité, (il n'y a) rien à ~** from the point of view of quality, it can't be faulted.

rediscuter /ʀ(ə)diskyte/ [1] *vtr* **~ qch** (discuter de nouveau) to discuss sth again; (approfondir) to discuss sth further.

redistribuer /ʀ(ə)distʀibɥe/ [1] *vtr* **1** to redistribute [*richesses*]; to reallocate [*tâches, terres*]; **2** Jeux **~ les cartes** to deal the cards again.

redistribution /ʀ(ə)distʀibysjɔ̃/ *nf* (de richesses) redistribution; (de tâches) reallocation.

redite /ʀ(ə)dit/ *nf* (needless) repetition.

redondance /ʀ(ə)dɔ̃dɑ̃s/ *nf* **1** (dans un style) verbosity; **2** (terme superflu) superfluous term; **3** Ling redundancy; **4** Ordinat, Télécom redundancy.

redondant, ~e /ʀ(ə)dɔ̃dɑ̃, ɑ̃t/ *adj* **1** [*style*] verbose; [*terme*] superfluous, redundant; **2** Ling redundant; **3** Ordinat [*code*] redundant; **système ~** back-up system.

redonner /ʀ(ə)dɔne/ [1] *vtr* **1** (donner de nouveau) **~ qch à qn** to give sb sth again, to give sth to sb again; **redonne-moi ton numéro de téléphone** give me your phone number again; **ça m'a redonné faim** it made me hungry again; **ça lui a redonné envie de peindre/voyager** it made him/her feel like painting/travelling[GB] again; **redonne-lui un verre d'eau** give him/her another glass of water; **il m'a redonné de la soupe** he gave me some more soup, he gave me another helping of soup; **~ un coup de balai dans la cuisine** to give the kitchen another sweep; **~ une couche de vernis à une porte** to give a door another coat of varnish; **2** (rétablir) **~ courage/confiance à qn** to restore sb's courage/confidence; **~ espoir à qn** to give sb renewed hope, to restore sb's hopes; **~ des forces/de l'énergie à qn** to restore sb's strength/energy; **produit qui redonne de l'éclat aux cheveux** product which puts the shine back in one's hair; **~ vigueur à l'économie d'un pays** to revive a country's economy; **~ vie à une ville/un quartier** to breathe new life into a town/an area; **3** (rendre) to give [sth] back, to return [*objet, argent*] (**à** to); **4** (rediffuser) to show [sth] again [*film, émission*].

redorer /ʀ(ə)dɔʀe/ [1] *vtr* to regild.

IDIOMES **~ son blason** [*personne*] to restore one's image; [*ville, groupe*] to restore its image.

redormir /ʀ(ə)dɔʀmiʀ/ [30] *vi* **1** (se rendormir) to go back to sleep; **2** (après une période d'insomnies) to sleep again.

redoublant, ~e /ʀ(ə)dublɑ̃, ɑ̃t/ *nm,f* student repeating a year.

redoublé, ~e /ʀ(ə)duble/ **I** *pp* ▶**redoubler**.

II *pp adj* **des attaques ~es** increasingly violent attacks; **il s'est mis à l'ouvrage avec un zèle ~** he threw himself into the work with redoubled vigour[GB]; **frapper qch/qn à coups ~s** to hit sth/sb very hard.

redoublement /ʀ(ə)dubləmɑ̃/ *nm* **1** Scol **il va falloir envisager le ~ pour cet élève** we'll have to think about this student repeating a year; **après deux ~s il n'était toujours pas au niveau** after repeating a year twice he was still not up to standard; **2** Ling reduplication; **3** (intensification) intensification.

redoubler /ʀ(ə)duble/ [1] **I** *vtr* **1** Scol **~ une classe** to repeat a year; **2** Ling to reduplicate [*consonne, syllabe*]; **3** (intensifier) **les événements récents ont redoublé sa méfiance** recent events have made him/her twice as wary ou have made her even more wary.

II redoubler de *vtr ind* **~ de prudence/d'égards** to be twice as ou much more careful/attentive; **~ d'efforts** to redouble one's efforts, to work twice as hard; **il te faut ~ de vigilance** you need to be twice as vigilant ou extra vigilant; **la bataille/tempête a redoublé de violence** the fighting/storm has got GB ou gotten US even fiercer.

III *vi* **1** Scol to repeat a year; **2** (s'intensifier) to intensify; **la pluie a redoublé** it's raining even harder; **sa rage a redoublé** he became even more enraged.

redoutable /ʀ(ə)dutabl/ *adj* [*arme, examen, concurrent*] formidable; [*mal*] dreadful; **il est d'une lucidité ~** he is frighteningly clear-sighted.

redouter /ʀ(ə)dute/ [1] *vtr* (craindre) to fear [*ennemi, mort*]; (appréhender) to dread [*événement, conséquence, avenir*]; **je redoute d'y aller** I dread going there.

redoux /ʀ(ə)du/ *nm inv* mild spell.

redressement /ʀədʀɛsmɑ̃/ *nm* **1** (reprise) recovery; **un net ~ des exportations/de l'économie** a clear upturn ou recovery in exports/in the economy; **2** (remise sur pied) re-establishment; **plan de ~** recovery plan; **3** (remise en forme) straightening out; **4** (manœuvre) straightening up; **5** Électrotech rectification; **6†** (rééducation) **maison de ~** reformatory.

■ **~ fiscal** tax adjustment; **~ judiciaire** receivership; **être mis en ~ judiciaire** to go into receivership.

redresser /ʀ(ə)dʀese/ [1] **I** *vtr* **1** (remettre d'aplomb) to straighten up [*barrière, piquet*]; (remettre debout) to put [sth] up again [*barrière, piquet*]; (détordre) to straighten [sth] out [*barre de métal, pare-chocs*]; to straighten [*dent*]; **~ des fleurs dans un vase** to put flowers straight in a vase; **~ un malade** to sit a sick person up; **~ les épaules** to straighten one's shoulders; **~ la tête** lit to lift one's head up; fig (tenir tête) to stand up for oneself; **2** (après une crise) to put [sth] back on its feet [*économie*]; to turn [sth] round GB ou around US [*entreprise*]; to improve [*performance*]; **~ la situation** to put the situation right; **3** (après une baisse) to aid the recovery of [*monnaie*] ; to improve [*marge de bénéfices*]; **~ le score** to even up the score; **4** (après une manœuvre) to straighten up [*voilier, planeur, volant*]; **~ la barre** lit to right the helm; fig to put things back on an even keel; **redresse!** straighten up!; **5** (après une erreur) to rectify [*erreur*]; **~ un compte** to adjust an account; **~ les torts** fml to right (all) wrongs sout; **~ les injustices sociales** fml to redress social injustice; **6** Électrotech to rectify.

II se redresser *vpr* **1** [*personne*] (se mettre debout) to stand up; (s'asseoir) to sit up; (se mettre droit) (en position debout) to stand up straight; (en position assise) to sit up straight; **2** (reprendre de la vigueur) [*industrie, économie, plante*] to pick up again, to recover; [*pays, compagnie*] to get back on its feet; **3** (après une manœuvre) [*voilier, planeur*] to straighten up; **4** (être fier) to give oneself airs.

redresseur /ʀədʀɛsœʀ/ *nm* **1** (justicier) **~ de torts** redresser of wrongs; **2** Électrotech rectifier.

réducteur, -trice /ʀedyktœʀ, tʀis/ **I** *adj* **1** (simplificateur) [*analyse, slogan*] reductionist, simplistic; **2** Chimie reducing; **3** Mécan **engrenage ~** reduction gear.

II *nm* **1** Chimie reducing agent; **2** Mécan **~ de vitesse** speed reducer.

■ **~ de têtes** Anthrop head shrinker.

réductibilité /ʀedyktibilite/ *nf* reducibility.

réductible /ʀedyktibl/ *adj* **1** (en diminuant) [*frais, dépenses*] which can be reduced ou cut (*après n*); [*délai*] which can be shortened or reduced (*après n*); **2** (qui peut être réduit) **ce**

n'est pas ~ à it cannot simply be seen as; **3** Chimie, Math, Méd reducible.

réduction /ʀedyksjɔ̃/ *nf* **1** (remise) discount, reduction; (consentie à un groupe particulier) concession (**sur** on); **~ de 5%** 5% reduction; **faire une ~ à qn** to give sb a discount; **je vous fais une ~ de 50 francs/5%** I'll give you a 50 franc/5% discount; **~ de fractions au même dénominateur** reduction of fractions to a common denominator; **~ étudiants/familles nombreuses** concession for students/large families; **avoir droit à une ~** to have a concession; **2** (action de diminuer) (de dépenses, coût, subventions, production) cutting, reducing; (de délais) shortening, reducing; (d'armements, inégalités) reducing; **~ d'impôts** cutting taxes; **~ de l'écart entre** narrowing the gap between; **3** (diminution) (de dépenses, coût, d'armements) reduction, cut (**de** in); **~ d'impôts** tax cut; **~s d'effectifs** staff cuts; **4** (simplification) **la ~ d'une théorie à quelques principes de base** reducing a theory to a few basic principles; **5** Art (reproduction réduite) small replica; **6** Chimie, Culin, Math, Méd reduction.

■ **~ chromatique** Biol reduction division; **~ de peine** Jur remission.

réduire /ʀedɥiʀ/ [68] **I** *vtr* **1** (diminuer) to reduce [*impôt, coût, vitesse, distance, stocks, inégalités*]; to reduce, to cut [*dépenses*]; to reduce, to shorten [*délai, durée*]; to reduce, to lessen [*chances, risques*]; to reduce, to limit [*choix*]; to reduce, to bring down [*chômage*]; to limit [*influence*]; **~ le personnel** to cut (down on) staff; **~ un article de 3%** to reduce ou cut the price of an article by 3%; **~ d'un quart** to reduce by a quarter; **~ qch de peu/de beaucoup** to reduce sth slightly/greatly; **~ qch au minimum** to reduce sth to a minimum; **~ les subventions de moitié** to cut subsidies by half; **~ qch en taille/en longueur** to make sth smaller/shorter, to reduce the size/length of sth; **les jeans sont réduits de 20%** jeans are reduced by 20%; **~ le nombre de succursales** to cut down the number of branches; **je dois ~ mes dépenses** I must cut down on my spending; **~ l'écart entre** to narrow the gap between; **2** (en reproduisant) to reduce [*photographie, document*]; to scale down [*dessin*]; (en faisant des coupures) to cut [*texte*]; **3** (transformer) **~ qch en poudre** to crush sth to powder; **~ qch en bouillie** to reduce sth to a pulp; **~ le blé en farine** to grind wheat into flour; **être réduit en cendres** lit [*bâtiment, ville*] to be reduced to ashes; fig [*espoirs, rêves*] to turn to ashes; **être réduit à rien** ou **à néant** [*efforts, travail, fortune*] to be wiped out; **4** (en simplifiant) **~ qch à** to reduce sth to; **~ un problème à l'essentiel** to reduce a problem to its bare essentials; **vous avez tort de ~ ce conflit à...** it is wrong to consider this conflict as no more than...; **5** (obliger) **~ qn à qch** to reduce sb to sth; **~ qn au silence** to reduce sb to silence; **~ qn à la mendicité** to reduce sb to begging; **en être réduit à se taire/mendier** to be reduced to silence/begging; **voilà à quoi j'en suis réduit!** this is what I've been reduced to!; **~ un peuple en esclavage** to reduce a nation to slavery; **6** (vaincre) to subdue [*ennemi, tribu*]; to silence [*opposition*]; to crush [*émeute, mouvement de résistance*]; **7** Culin, Chimie to reduce [*composé*]; **8** Méd to set, to reduce spéc [*os fracturé*]; **9** Math to reduce [*fraction*]; **~ des fractions au même dénominateur** to reduce fractions to a common denominator.

II *vi* Culin [*sauce, sirop*] to reduce; [*champignons, épinards*] to shrink; **faites ~ le mélange** allow the mixture to reduce; **les champignons réduisent à la cuisson** mushrooms shrink when cooked.

III se réduire *vpr* **1** (diminuer) [*coûts*] to be reduced ou cut; [*délais*] to be reduced ou shortened; [*importations*] to be cut; **l'écart se réduit** the gap is narrowing; **2** (consister seulement en) **se ~ à** to consist merely of; **leur contribution se réduit à quelques sacs de blé** their contribution consists merely of a few sacks of wheat; **cela se réduit à bien peu de chose** it doesn't amount to very much; **3** (se restreindre) **se ~ dans ses dépenses** to cut down on one's spending.

réduit, **~e** /ʀedɥi, it/ **I** *pp* ▶ **réduire**.

II *pp adj* **1** (diminué) [*taux, cotisation, vitesse*] reduced, lower; [*délai*] shorter; [*activité*] reduced; [*main-d'œuvre*] smaller, reduced; [*groupe*] smaller; **à vitesse ~e** at a lower speed; **billets à prix ~** tickets at a reduced price; **vendre des objets à prix ~** to sell things at cut-price; **l'essor des magasins à prix ~s** the boom in discount stores; **avec un personnel ~** with fewer staff; **à mobilité ~e** with restricted ou reduced mobility; **visibilité ~e** restricted visibility; **2** (peu important) [*moyens, choix*] limited; [*groupe*] small; **3** (petit) [*taille*] small; **de taille ~e** small; **ses dimensions ~es** its small size; **occuper une place ~e** not to take up much room; **en format ~** [*objet*] in a scaled down ou reduced format; **4** Math [*équation*] reduced.

III *nm* **1** (placard) cubbyhole; **2** pej (petite pièce) cubbyhole péj.

rééchelonnement /ʀeeʃlɔnmɑ̃/ *nm* (de dette) rescheduling.

rééchelonner /ʀeeʃlɔne/ [1] *vtr* to reschedule [*dette*].

réécrire /ʀeekʀiʀ/ [67] *vtr* to rewrite.

réécriture /ʀeekʀityʀ/ *nf* rewriting, rewrite; **règle de ~** Ling rewrite rule.

réédification /ʀeedifikasjɔ̃/ *nf* lit, fig rebuilding.

réédifier /ʀeedifje/ [2] *vtr* lit, fig to rebuild.

rééditer /ʀeedite/ [1] *vtr* **1** Édition to reissue, to reprint [*livre*]; **2**○ (refaire) to repeat [*action, exploit*].

réédition /ʀeedisjɔ̃/ *nf* **1** Édition reissue; **2**○ (de situation, d'œuvre) carbon copy.

rééducation /ʀeedykasjɔ̃/ *nf* **1** Méd (des mouvements) physiotherapy, physical therapy; (de handicapé) rehabilitation; **~ de la parole** speech therapy; **faire de la ~** to have physiotherapy ou physical therapy; **2** (de délinquant) rehabilitation; **centre de ~** rehabilitation centre[GB]; **3** (nouvelle éducation) re-education.

■ **~ motrice analytique** Méd restoration of motor reflexes; **~ motrice fonctionnelle** Méd restoration of motor function.

rééduquer /ʀeedyke/ [1] *vtr* **1** Méd to restore normal functioning to [*membre*]; to rehabilitate [*handicapé*]; **~ la parole** to treat speech disorder; **2** Jur to rehabilitate [*délinquant*]; **3** (éduquer différemment) to re-educate [*personne*]; to retrain [*animal*].

réel, **réelle** /ʀeɛl/ **I** *adj* **1** (non imaginaire) [*besoin, risque, événement, être*] real; (véritable) [*cause, motif, coût*] true, actual; [*fait*] true; **2** (grand) [*émotion, difficultés, effort*] real; **3** Fin [*revenu*] real; [*taux d'intérêt*] effective; **4** Astron, Math, Ordinat, Philos, Phys real; **5** Jur real; **garantie réelle** pledge of real property.

II *nm* liter, Philos **le ~** the real.

réélection /ʀeelɛksjɔ̃/ *nf* re-election.

rééligibilité /ʀeeleʒibilite/ *nf* reeligibility.

rééligible /ʀeeliʒibl/ *adj* reeligible.

réélire /ʀeeliʀ/ [66] *vtr* to reelect.

réellement /ʀeɛlmɑ̃/ *adv* really.

réembarquer /ʀeɑ̃baʀke/ [1] **I** *vtr* to re-embark [*passagers*]; to reload [*marchandises*].

II *vi* [*passagers*] to re-embark, to go back on board (ship); **faire ~ les troupes** to re-embark the troops.

III se réembarquer *vpr* to re-embark, to go back on board (ship).

réembaucher /ʀeɑ̃boʃe/ [1] *vtr* to take [sb] on again; **on réembauche à l'usine** the factory is taking on labour[GB] again.

réémetteur /ʀeemɛtœʀ/ *nm* relay station.

réemploi /ʀeɑ̃plwa/ *nm* (de matériaux) reuse; (de fonds) Fin reinvestment; (de personnel) re-employment.

réemployer /ʀeɑ̃plwaje/ [23] *vtr* to reuse [*matériaux*]; to reinvest [*fonds*]; to re-employ [*personnel*].

réendosser /ʀeɑ̃dose/ [1] *vtr* to take [sth] on again [*responsabilité*].

réenfiler /ʀeɑ̃file/ [1] *vtr* to rethread [*aiguille, perles*].

réengagement /ʀeɑ̃gaʒmɑ̃/ *nm* = **rengagement**.

réengager /ʀeɑ̃gaʒe/ [13] *vtr* = **rengager**.

réenregistrer /ʀeɑ̃ʀʒistʀe/ [1] *vtr* to rerecord [*disque, film*].

réentendre /ʀeɑ̃tɑ̃dʀ/ [6] *vtr* **1** gén to listen to [sth] again; **2** Jur to re-examine [*témoin*].

rééquilibrage /ʀeekilibʀaʒ/ *nm* Tech readjustment; **~ des roues** Aut wheel-balancing.

rééquilibrer /ʀeekilibʀe/ [1] *vtr* **1** Tech to readjust [*chargement*]; **2** Aut to balance [*wheels*]; **3** Écon to balance [*budget*]; **~ la balance des paiements** to restore the balance of payments; **~ les pouvoirs** Pol to restore the balance of power.

réescompte /ʀeɛskɔ̃t/ *nm* rediscount.

réescompter /ʀeɛskɔ̃te/ [1] *vtr* to rediscount.

réessayer /ʀeɛseje/ [21] *vtr* **1** Cout **~ un vêtement** to try a garment on again; **2** (tenter) **~ de faire qch** to try doing sth again.

réétudier /ʀeetydje/ [2] *vtr* to reconsider [*situation, proposition*].

réévaluation /ʀeevalɥasjɔ̃/ *nf* **1** Fin (de monnaie, taux) revaluation; **2** (de forces, recettes, patrimoine) reappraisal, re-evaluation.

réévaluer /ʀeevalɥe/ [1] *vtr* **1** Fin to revalue [*monnaie*]; to revise [*salaire, impôt, taux (de crédit)*]; **2** (estimer à nouveau) to reappraise, reevaluate [*patrimoine, dépenses, forces, emploi*].

réexamen /ʀeegzamɛ̃/ *nm* (de projet, situation, dossier, budget) re-examination; (de décision, candidature) reconsideration.

réexaminer /ʀeegzamine/ [1] *vtr* to re-examine [*projet, situation, dossier, budget*]; to reconsider [*décision, candidature*].

réexpédier /ʀeɛkspedje/ [2] *vtr* **1** (faire suivre) to forward, to redirect; **2** (retourner) to send [sth] back.

réexpédition /ʀeɛkspedisjɔ̃/ *nf* **1** (fait de faire suivre) forwarding, redirection; **enveloppe de ~** *envelope provided by the Post Office for forwarding mail*; **2** (retour à l'envoyeur) returning to sender; **frais de ~** return postage.

réexportation /ʀeɛkspɔʀtasjɔ̃/ *nf* re-exportation; **le volume des ~s** the volume of re-exports.

réexporter /ʀeɛkspɔʀte/ [1] *vtr* to re-export.

réf (*written abbr* = **référence**) ref.

refaire /ʀəfɛʀ/ [10] **I** *vtr* **1** (faire de nouveau) to do [sth] again, to redo [*exercice, calcul, travail, vêtement*]; to repack [*bagage*]; to redo [*maquillage*]; **~ les mêmes erreurs** to make the same mistakes again; **~ le même voyage** to make the same journey again; **~ le même chemin** (en sens inverse) to go back the same way; **~ du cinéma** [*ancien acteur*] to get back into films GB ou movies US; **tout est à ~** it will have to be done all over again; **'à ~'** (sur une copie d'élève) 'do it again'; **~ un numéro de téléphone** to redial a number, to dial a number again; **si c'était à ~** if I had to do it all over again; **je vais ~ les rideaux de ta chambre** I'll make some new curtains for your bedroom; **~ des mathématiques/de l'espagnol** to do maths/Spanish again; **2** (faire en plus) **je vais ~ un gâteau** I'll make another cake; **je vais ~ de la soupe** I'll make some more soup; **~ trois exercices** to do three more exercises; **~ trois gâteaux** to make three more cakes; **3** (changer complètement) **vouloir ~ le monde/la société** to want to change the world/society; **on ne peut pas ~ l'histoire** you can't rewrite history; **se faire ~ le nez** to have one's nose re-modelled[GB]; **se faire ~ les seins/le visage** to have plastic surgery on one's breasts/one's face; **on ne le refera pas** there's no changing him; **~ sa vie (avec quelqu'un d'autre)** to start all over again (with somebody else); **4** (rénover) to redo [*toit, gouttière, sol*]; to redecorate [*pièce*]; to resurface [*route*] ; **~ la peinture dans le couloir** to repaint the corridor; **~ les peintures** to repaint; **la pièce est à ~** the room will have to be redone; **appartement refait à neuf** completely refurbished apartment; **5**○ (voler, tromper) **se faire ~ de dix francs** to be done out○ of ou diddled out○ of ten francs; **il est refait, il s'est fait ~** he's been had○.

II **se refaire** *vpr* **1** (fabriquer pour soi) **se ~ une robe** to make oneself another dress; **se ~ une tasse de thé** to make (oneself) another cup of tea; **2** (retrouver) **se ~ des amis** to make new friends; **se ~ une santé** to recuperate; **se ~ une beauté** to redo one's make-up; **3** (se réhabituer) **se ~ à** to get used to [sth] again [*pays , activité*]; **4** (changer) **on ne se refait pas** a person can't change; **5**○ (financièrement) to recoup one's losses.

III *v impers* **il refait froid/beau** it's cold/fine again.

réfection /ʀefɛksjɔ̃/ *nf* (de toiture, façade, bâtiment) repairing; (de route) mending; (de pièce, maison) redoing; **'en ~'** [*église, clocher*] 'restoration work in progress'.

réfectoire /ʀefɛktwaʀ/ *nm* (d'institution) refectory; Mil mess.

référé /ʀefeʀe/ *nm* Jur summary judgment; **jugement/ordonnance de** or **en ~** summary judgment[GB]/order; **intenter une action en ~ contre qn, assigner qn en ~** to apply for a summary judgment to be heard against sb; **plainte en ~** summary action; **juge des ~s** judge in chambers.

référence /ʀefeʀɑ̃s/ I *nf* **1** (renvoi) reference (à to); **en** or **par ~ à** in reference to; **faire ~ à** to refer to, to make reference to; **les ouvrages cités en ~** the works referred to; **2** (modèle) (prime) example; **être cité comme la ~** to be cited as prime example; **lui? ce n'est pas une ~!** who, him? well, he's not much of an example!; **date/année de ~** date/year of reference; **point de ~** point of reference, reference point; **prix/livre de ~** reference price/book; **brut de ~** base crude; **produit de ~** leading product; **3** (identification) reference; (numéro) reference number; **notre/votre ~** our/your reference; **notre catalogue compte 5000 ~s bibliographiques** there are 5,000 entries in our catalogue[GB]; **4** Ling reference.

II **références** *nfpl* (pour emploi, location) references; **~s exigées** references required.

référencé, **~e** /ʀefeʀɑ̃se/ I *pp* ▶ **référencer**.

II *pp adj* **la commande ~e ci-dessous** the order quoted below.

référencer /ʀefeʀɑ̃se/ [12] *vtr* to classify [*document*].

référendaire /ʀefeʀɑ̃dɛʀ/ *adj* [*campagne, projet*] referendum (*épith*); **consultation ~** referendum.

référendum /ʀefeʀɛ̃dɔm/ *nm* referendum (**sur** on).

référent /ʀefeʀɑ̃/ *nm* referent.

référentiel, **-ielle** /ʀefeʀɑ̃sjɛl/ I *adj* Ling, gén referential.

II *nm* fml frame of reference.

référer /ʀefeʀe/ [14] I **référer à** *vtr ind* **1 en ~ à** to consult; **il doit en ~ au ministre** he must refer the matter to ou consult the minister; **2** Ling **~ à** to refer to.

II **se référer** *vpr* **1** (faire référence à) **se ~ à** to refer to [*date, personne, article, loi*]; **si on se réfère à cette période/loi** if one refers to this period/law; **2** (consulter) **se ~ à** to consult [*livre, publication, chapitre*]; **référez-vous au texte original** consult the original text.

refermer /ʀ(ə)fɛʀme/ [1] I *vtr* **1** (fermer) to close [*boîte, porte, tiroir, porte-monnaie, main*]; to put the lid back on [*pot*]; to put the top back on [*bouteille, bidon*]; to close [*livre, dossier*]; **~ une porte derrière qn** to close the door behind sb; **~ qch sur qch/qn** to close sth on sth/sb; **~ une porte sur qn** to close the door on sb; **2** (fermer de nouveau) to close [sth] again [*boîte, porte, tiroir, coffre*]; to put the lid back on [sth] again [*pot*]; to put the top back on [sth] again [*bouteille, bidon*]; **~ à clé** to lock (again).

II **se refermer** *vpr* [*piège, porte, fenêtre, tombe, fleur*] to close (**sur** on); [*coquille*] to close (**sur** on); [*eau*] to close (**sur** over); [*blessure*] to close up.

refiler○ /ʀ(ə)file/ [1] *vtr* to pass [*vêtement, livre, notes, renseignement, maladie*] (**à qn** onto sb); to palm [sth] off [*fausse monnaie*] (**à qn** on sb); **on m'a refilé un faux billet** someone palmed a forged note off on me; **il m'a refilé son rhume** he gave me his cold.

réfléchi, **~e** /ʀefleʃi/ I *adj* **1** (posé) [*personne*] reflective, thoughtful; [*regard*] thoughtful; [*ton*] deliberate; **2** (mûri) [*décision*] considered; [*action*] well-considered; **tout bien ~** all things considered; **c'est tout ~** my mind is made up; **3** Phys [*image, onde*] reflected; **4** Ling reflexive.

II *nm* Ling reflexive.

réfléchir /ʀefleʃiʀ/ [3] I *vtr* to reflect [*onde, chaleur*].

II **réfléchir à** *vtr ind* **~ à** to think about; **plus j'y réfléchis** the more I think about it; **j'y ai mûrement réfléchi** I have thought it through ou over very carefully; **sans ~ au fait qu'il n'y avait pas d'eau** quite forgetting that there was no water; **puis j'ai réfléchi au fait que ce serait fermé** then it occurred to me that it would be shut.

III *vi* to think (**sur qch** about sth); **parler sans ~** to speak without thinking; **ça fait ~** it makes you think; **si on réfléchit** or **en réfléchissant, on voit bien** if you (stop and) think about it, you realize; **et puis, en réfléchissant, j'ai décidé de rester** but then, on reflection, I decided to stay; **réfléchis et donne-moi ta réponse demain** think about it ou think it over and give me your answer tomorrow; **ça leur donnera à ~** it'll give them something to think about; **mais réfléchis donc un peu, ça va fondre au soleil!** use your brain, it will melt in the sun!

IV **se réfléchir** *vpr* [*onde, image*] to be reflected (**dans** in; **sur** on).

réfléchissant, **~e** /ʀefleʃisɑ̃, ɑ̃t/ *adj*, reflective.

réflecteur, **-trice** /ʀeflɛktœʀ, tʀis/ I *adj* reflecting.

II *nm* reflector.

réflectorisé, **~e** /ʀeflɛktɔʀize/ *adj* [*peinture, revêtement, casque*] reflective; [*route*] with cat's eyes (*épith, après n*).

reflet /ʀ(ə)flɛ/ *nm* **1** (image) lit, fig reflection; **voir son ~ dans l'eau** to see one's reflection in the water; **le ~ d'un rayon de soleil sur l'étang** the reflections of sunlight on the pond; **être le ~ d'une époque** to reflect a period, to be a reflection of a period; **être le pâle ~ de qn/qch** fig to be a mere shadow of sb/sth; **2** (lueur) glint; (plus délicat) shimmer ¢; **~s dorés** golden glints; **feuillage à ~s argentés** foliage with a silvery shimmer; **3** (nuance de couleur) sheen ¢; **les ~s du satin** the sheen of satin; **fourrure noire à ~s bleus** black fur with a bluish sheen; **cheveux châtains aux ~s roux** brown hair with red highlights; **pierre grise à ~s bleus** grey stone with a bluish sparkle.

refléter /ʀ(ə)flete/ [14] I *vtr* **1** (renvoyer) to reflect, to mirror; **2** (traduire) to reflect; **son visage reflétait son émotion** his/her emotion showed in his/her face.

II **se refléter** *vpr* lit, fig to be reflected (**dans** in).

refleurir /ʀ(ə)flœʀiʀ/ [3] *vi* **1** (fleurir à nouveau) [*fleur*] to flower again; [*arbre*] to blossom again; **2** (réapparaître) [*vêtement, slogan, affiche*] to reappear.

reflex /ʀeflɛks/ I *adj* Phot reflex; **appareil ~** reflex camera.

II *nm inv* reflex camera.

réflexe /ʀeflɛks/ I *adj* reflex.

II *nm* **1** Physiol reflex; **avoir de bons ~s** to have quick ou good reflexes; **2** (réaction, habitude) reaction; **manquer de ~** to be slow to react, to react slowly; **elle a eu le ~ de freiner** her instinctive reaction was to brake; **un ~ de bureaucrate** a typically bureaucratic reaction; **c'est un ~ normal** it's a normal reaction; **faire qch par ~** to do sth automatically ou without thinking.

■ **~ conditionné** conditioned reflex; **~ professionnel** professional conditioning ¢; **~ de succion** sucking reflex.

réflexibilité /ʀeflɛksibilite/ *nf* reflexibility.

réflexible /ʀeflɛksibl/ *adj* reflexible.

réflexif, **-ive** /ʀeflɛksif, iv/ *adj* reflexive.

réflexion /ʀeflɛksjɔ̃/ *nf* **1** (pensée) thought (**sur** on), reflection (**sur** on); **faire part de ses ~s à qn** to share one's thoughts with sb; **inspirer des ~s amères** to give rise to bitter feelings; **2** (méditation) thinking (**sur** on), reflection (**sur** on); **faire naître une ~ nouvelle sur l'histoire** to give rise to some fresh thinking on history; **leur offre mérite ~** their offer is worth thinking about; **cela demande ~** it needs ou requires thinking about; **prendre le temps de la ~** to take time to think; **sans ~** without thinking; **~ faite** or **à la ~, je n'irai pas** on reflection ou on second thoughts, I won't go; **à la ~, on s'aperçoit que c'est absurde** when you really think about it, you realize that it is absurd; **après mûre ~** after careful consideration, after much thought; **donner matière à ~** to be food for thought; **3** (remarque) remark (**sur** about), comment (**sur** on); **faire des ~s** gén to make remarks; **fais-nous grâce de tes ~s** spare us your comments; **elle t'a fait une ~?** did she say anything to you?; **on m'a fait des ~s sur votre attitude** I've had complaints about your attitude; **s'attirer des ~s** to attract criticism ou adverse comment; **il a eu une ~ bizarre/étonnante** he said something odd/surprising; **elle a des ~s parfois!** she says some funny things sometimes!; **4** (étude) study (**sur** of); **document de ~** discussion paper; **5** Phys reflection.

réflexivité /ʀeflɛksivite/ *nf* reflexiveness, reflexivity.

refluer /ʀ(ə)flye/ [1] *vi* **1** (couler en sens inverse) [*liquide*] to flow back; **2** (reculer) [*foule, groupe*] to surge back(wards); [*inflation, chômage*] to go down; **faire ~** to push back [*foule*]; to push down [*chômage*].

reflux /ʀ(ə)fly/ *nm inv* **1** (marée) ebb tide; **2** (de foule, manifestants) surging away; (de chômage, devise) decline.

refondre /ʀ(ə)fɔ̃dʀ/ [6] *vtr* **1** lit to melt down again [*métal*]; to recast [*objet*]; to remint [*monnaie*]; to remix [*papier*]; **2** fig to rework [*structure, règles*]; to recast [*édition*]; to reorganize [*organisme*].

refonte /ʀ(ə)fɔ̃t/ *nf* gén overhaul; (de contrat) rewriting.

reforestation /ʀ(ə)fɔʀɛstasjɔ̃/ *nf* reafforestation.

reformage /ʀ(ə)fɔʀmaʒ/ *nm* Ind reforming.

réformateur, **-trice** /ʀefɔʀmatœʀ, tʀis/ I *adj* [*dirigeant, parti, idéologie*] reforming; [*milieu, courant, force*] of reform.

II *nm,f* reformer.

réforme /ʀefɔʀm/ *nf* **1** (modification) reform; **~ de l'enseignement/de l'orthographe**

teaching/spelling reform; **2** Mil discharge; **3** Relig **la Réforme** the Reformation; **4** Agric **bête de ~** cull; **vache/truie de ~** cull cow/sow.

réformé, **~e** /ʀefɔʀme/ **I** *adj* **1** Mil (inapte) unfit for service; (invalide) invalided out; **2** Relig Reformed.

II *nm* Mil [*appelé*] person who has been declared unfit for service; [*soldat*] discharged soldier.

III *nm,f* Relig Protestant.

reformer /ʀ(ə)fɔʀme/ [1] **I** *vtr* to re-form; **~ les rangs** [*soldats*] to fall in again; [*élèves*] to fall into line again.

II se reformer *vpr* [*glace, végétation*] to re-form; [*équipe*] to re-form; [*soldats*] to form up again; [*peau, foie*] to renew itself.

réformer /ʀefɔʀme/ [1] **I** *vtr* **1** (changer) to reform; **~ les abus** to weed out abuses; **2** Mil to declare [sb] unfit for service [*appelé*]; to discharge [*soldat*]; **se faire ~** to get oneself discharged; **3** Jur to overturn [*décision*].

II se réformer *vpr* **1** (changer) to reform; **2** (s'amender) liter to reform one's behaviour[GB].

réformette○ /ʀefɔʀmɛt/ *nf* pej nominal reform.

réformisme /ʀefɔʀmism/ *nm* reformism.

réformiste /ʀefɔʀmist/ *adj, nmf* reformist.

reformuler /ʀ(ə)fɔʀmyle/ [1] *vtr* to reformulate.

refoulé, **~e** /ʀ(ə)fule/ Psych **I** *pp* ▶ **refouler**.

II *pp adj* [*personne*] repressed, inhibited.

III *nm,f* **1** (psychologiquement) repressed person; **2** (sexuellement) sexually repressed person.

IV *nm* Psych **retour du ~** return of the repressed.

refoulement /ʀ(ə)fulmɑ̃/ *nm* **1** Psych repression; (refus des pulsions sexuelles) sexual repression; **2** (expulsion) (d'ennemi) pushing back; (d'immigrant) turning back; (de la foule) driving back; **3** Rail backing, reversing; **4** Tech (de liquide) forcing back.

refouler /ʀ(ə)fule/ [1] *vtr* **1** (contenir) to suppress [*émotion, souvenir*]; to repress [*tendance*]; to hold back [*larmes*]; to stifle [*sanglots*]; **colère refoulée** suppressed anger; **2** (repousser) to force [sth] back [*liquide*]; to push back [*ennemi*]; to turn back [*immigrant*]; to drive back [*foule*]; **3** (refuser) to reject [*candidat*]; to turn away [*spectateur*]; **4** Rail to back, to reverse; **5** Naut to stem.

réfractaire /ʀefʀaktɛʀ/ **I** *adj* **1** (opposé) recalcitrant (**à** to); (insensible) impervious (**à** to); Méd resistant (**à** to); **2** (résistant à la chaleur) [*matériau*] refractory; **brique ~** firebrick, refractory brick; **argile ~** fireclay; **3** Hist [*prêtre*] nonjuring; [*conscrit*] draft-dodging.

II *nmf* **1** (opposant) recalcitrant; **les ~s à l'aventure/au progrès** those resistant to adventure/to progress; **2** Hist (prêtre) nonjuring priest; (conscrit) draft dodger; (travailleur) *French civilian who refused to be drafted to work in Germany in 1942–44.*

réfracter /ʀefʀakte/ [1] **I** *vtr* to refract.

II se réfracter *vpr* to be refracted.

réfracteur, **-trice** /ʀefʀaktœʀ, tʀis/ **I** *adj* refractive.

II *nm* Astron refracting telescope.

réfraction /ʀefʀaksjɔ̃/ *nf* refraction.

refrain /ʀ(ə)fʀɛ̃/ *nm* **1** (de chanson) chorus; **2** (rengaine) pej (old) refrain; **ils nous resservent toujours le même ~** they're always giving us the same old refrain.

■ **~ publicitaire** advertising jingle.

refréner /ʀ(ə)fʀene/, **réfréner** /ʀefʀene/ [14] **I** *vtr* to curb.

II se réfréner *vpr* to restrict oneself.

réfrigérant, **~e** /ʀefʀiʒeʀɑ̃, ɑ̃t/ **I** *adj* **1** [*appareil, système*] cooling; **2** [*accueil, attitude*] frosty.

II *nm* (appareil) cooler.

réfrigérateur /ʀefʀiʒeʀatœʀ/ *nm* refrigerator; **mettre un projet au ~** fig to put a project on ice.

réfrigérateur-congélateur, *pl* **réfrigérateurs-congélateurs** /ʀefʀiʒeʀatœʀkɔ̃ʒelatœʀ/ *nm* fridge-freezer.

réfrigération /ʀefʀiʒeʀasjɔ̃/ *nf* refrigeration.

réfrigérer /ʀefʀiʒeʀe/ [14] *vtr* **1** lit to refrigerate [*aliment*]; to cool [*local*]; **entrepôt réfrigéré** cold store; **2** fig to have a dampening effect on [sb].

réfringence /ʀefʀɛ̃ʒɑ̃s/ *nf* refractiveness.

réfringent, **~e** /ʀefʀɛ̃ʒɑ̃, ɑ̃t/ *adj* refractive.

refroidir /ʀəfʀwadiʀ/ [3] **I** *vtr* **1** (faire baisser la température de) [*personne, mécanisme*] to cool down [*mélange, moteur*]; [*brouillard*] to cool [*atmosphère*]; **2** (calmer) [*personne, nouvelle*] to dampen [*ardeur, enthousiasme*]; **3** (décourager) **~ qn** [*nouvelle, échec, accueil*] to dampen sb's spirits; **4**● (tuer) to bump [sb] off○; **se faire ~** to be bumped off; **5** Jeux (à cache-tampon) **'tu refroidis!'** 'you're getting colder!'

II *vi* **1** (devenir moins chaud) [*bain, soupe*] to cool down; **attendez que le mélange refroidisse** wait until the mixture has cooled (down); **faire** or **laisser ~ qch** to leave sth to cool; **2** (devenir trop froid) [*bain, soupe, café*] to get cold; **commencez de manger sinon ça va ~** start eating or it will get cold; **va te laver, ton bain va ~** go and wash, your bath will be getting cold.

III se refroidir *vpr* [*temps*] to get colder; [*muscle, articulation*] to stiffen up; [*personne*] to get cold; **je me suis refroidi en t'attendant dehors** I got cold waiting for you outside.

refroidissement /ʀəfʀwadismɑ̃/ *nm* **1** Météo drop in temperature; **~ du temps** cooler weather; **on prévoit un ~ du temps pour lundi** on Monday the weather will be cooler ou colder; **2** gén, Tech, Nucl cooling; **circuit/tuyau/appareil/cuve de ~** cooling circuit/pipe/system/tower; **liquide de ~** coolant; **3** Méd chill; **avoir un ~** to have a chill; **4** (de relations, sentiment) cooling.

refroidisseur /ʀəfʀwadisœʀ/ *nm* coolant, cooling agent.

refuge /ʀ(ə)fyʒ/ **I** *nm* **1** (abri, réconfort) refuge; **chercher/trouver ~** to seek/find refuge (**auprès de qn** with sb; **contre qch** from sth); **trouver (un) ~ dans la solitude/la religion** to find (a) refuge in solitude/religion; **un bon livre est un ~ contre l'ennui** a good book guards against boredom; **2** (en montagne) (mountain) refuge; **nous allons coucher en ~** we'll spend the night in a (mountain) refuge; **3** (pour animaux) sanctuary; **4** Gén Civ (de chaussée) traffic island; (de pont) refuge.

II (-)refuge (*in compounds*) **investissement/monnaie ~** safe investment/currency; **pays ~** country of refuge.

réfugié, **~e** /ʀefyʒje/ *nm,f* refugee.

réfugier: **se réfugier** /ʀefyʒje/ [2] *vpr* lit, fig to take refuge (**dans** in; **chez qn** with sb).

refus /ʀ(ə)fy/ *nm* refusal (**de qch** of sth; **de faire** to do); Équit refusal; **c'est un motif valable de ~** it's a valid reason for refusing; **en cas de ~ de ta part** if you refuse; **opposer un ~ à qn** to refuse sb's request; **~ de la mort/maladie** refusal to accept the idea of death/being ill; **ce n'est pas de ~**○ I wouldn't say no.

■ **~ d'obéissance** Mil insubordination; Jur contempt of court; **~ d'obtempérer** refusal to comply; **~ de priorité** failure to give way.

refuser /ʀ(ə)fyze/ [1] **I** *vtr* **1** (ne pas accepter) to refuse [*offre, don, invitation*]; to turn down [*poste, emploi*]; **~ l'obstacle** Équit to refuse a fence; **~ le combat** to refuse to fight; **~ la facilité** to refuse to take the easy way out; **~ de faire qch** [*personne*] to refuse to do sth; **ce rosier refuse de fleurir** this rose bush refuses to flower; **2** (ne pas accorder) to refuse [*permission, aide, crédit, entrée*]; **~ qch à qn** to refuse sb sth; **se voir ~ qch** to be refused sth; **il a refusé qu'on vende la maison** he wouldn't allow the house to be sold; **~ sa porte à qn** to bar one's door to sb; **je lui refuse le droit de me juger** he has no right to judge me; **~ l'accès d'un bâtiment à qn** to deny sb admittance to a building; **3** (rejeter) to reject [*budget, injustice, racisme*]; to refuse to accept [*fait, réalité, évidence*]; to turn away [*spectateur, client*]; to reject, to turn down [*manuscrit*]; **~ un candidat** (à un poste) to turn down ou reject a candidate; (à un examen) to fail a candidate; **~ du monde** to turn people away; **être refusé à un concours** to fail an examination.

II *vi* [*vent*] to veer forward, to haul.

III se refuser *vpr* **1** (être décliné) **ça ne se refuse pas** (occasion, avantage) it's too good to pass up○ ou miss; (verre, bonbon) I wouldn't say no○; **2** (se priver de) to deny oneself [*plaisir*]; **on ne se refuse rien!** you're certainly not stinting yourself!; **3** (dire non) **se ~ à** to refuse to accept [*évidence*] ; to refuse to adopt [*solution, procédé*]; **se ~ à faire** to refuse to do; **4** (ne pas se livrer) [*femme*] **se ~ à un homme** to refuse to give oneself to a man.

réfutable /ʀefytabl/ *adj* refutable.

réfutation /ʀefytasjɔ̃/ *nf* refutation.

réfuter /ʀefyte/ [1] *vtr* to refute; **~ avoir fait** to deny having done.

refuznik /ʀəfyznik/ *nm* refuznik.

regagner /ʀ(ə)gaɲe/ [1] *vtr* **1** (rejoindre) to get back to [*lieu, poste*]; **~ son domicile** to return home; **~ sa place** to return to one's seat; **2** (recouvrer) to regain, to win back [*estime, confiance*]; to pick up [*point*]; **pour ~ l'électorat** to win back the electorate; **~ du terrain** [*armée, équipe, idéologie*] to regain ground; [*chômage, inflation*] to creep ou go up again.

regain /ʀ(ə)gɛ̃/ *nm* **1** Écon (reprise) (de marché) recovery (**de** of); (d'inflation, de chômage) rise (**de** in); **~ de la consommation** upturn in consumer spending; **craindre un ~ de l'inflation** to fear a rise in inflation; **2** (recrudescence) (d'intérêt) revival; (de violence, tension) resurgence, renewal; **possibilité d'un ~ de violence** possibility of renewed violence; **susciter un ~ d'intérêt pour la région** to create renewed interest in the region; **connaître un ~ de popularité/prestige** to enjoy renewed popularity/prestige; **3** Agric second crop.

régal /ʀegal/ *nm* **1** (mets savoureux) culinary delight; **c'est un (vrai) ~!** it's (absolutely) delicious!; **sa soupe, quel ~!** her soup is delicious!; **le dessert a fait le ~ des convives** the guests thought that the dessert was delicious; **2** fig delight; **un ~ pour les oreilles** a delight to listen to; **un ~ pour les yeux** a feast for the eyes; **le spectacle est un vrai ~** the show is an absolute delight.

régalade /ʀegalad/ *nf* **boire à la ~** *to drink without letting one's lips touch the bottle.*

régaler /ʀegale/ [1] **I** *vtr* [*personne*] to treat [sb] to a delicious meal; **~ qn de** lit to treat sb to [*vin, mets*]; fig to regale sb with [*anecdotes*].

II○ *vi* (payer l'addition) to pay the bill GB ou check US; **laisse, c'est moi qui régale** leave it, it's my treat.

III se régaler *vpr* **1** (de nourriture) **je me régale** it's delicious; **les enfants se sont régalés avec ton dessert** the children really enjoyed your dessert; **Jean fait un gâteau, je me régale à l'avance** Jean is making a cake, I can taste it already; **2** fig **le spectacle était grandiose, ils se sont régalés** the show was stunning, they thoroughly enjoyed it; **se ~ avec** to enjoy [sth] thoroughly [*film, spectacle, personnage*]; **se ~ de** to love [*anecdote, histoire, personnage*];

se ~ à l'avance de qch to look forward to sth.

régalien, -ienne /ʀegaljɛ̃, ɛn/ *adj* (inhérent à la royauté) regalian; (digne d'un roi) kingly.

regard /ʀ(ə)gaʀ/ **I** *nm* **1** (action de regarder) look; **porter son ~ sur qch** to look at sth; **diriger son ~ vers qch** to look toward(s) sth; **détourner le ~** to look away; **chercher qch/qn du ~** to look around for sth/sb; **interroger qn du ~** to look enquiringly GB ou inquiringly US at sb; **suivre qch/qn du ~** to follow sth/sb with one's eyes; **'suivez mon ~'** 'follow my eyes'; **avertir qn du ~** to give sb a warning look; **elle attire tous les ~s** everyone looks at her; **jeter un ~ rapide à** or **sur qch** to have a quick look at sth, to glance at sth; (en feuilletant) to glance through sth; **~ en coin** sidelong glance; **~ fixe** stare; **avoir le ~ fixe** to have a fixed stare; **avoir le ~ perdu** to have a blank ou vacant look; **j'ai croisé son ~** our eyes met; **échanger des ~s** to exchange looks; **soutenir le ~ de qn** to look sb straight in the eyes without flinching; **loin** or **à l'abri des ~s indiscrets** far from prying eyes; **soustraire qch aux ~s** to conceal sth from view; **elle ne m'a pas accordé un seul ~** she didn't even look at me; **2** (yeux) eyes; **un ~ clair** light-coloured[GB] eyes; **3** (expression) expression; **son ~ triste** her sad expression; **un ~ timide** a shy expression; **un ~ de colère** an angry expression; **elle a un ~ intelligent** she looks intelligent; **d'un ~ admiratif/inquiet** admiringly/anxiously; **sous le ~ amusé/anxieux/envieux de qn** under the amused/anxious/jealous eye of sb; **jeter un ~ noir à qn** to give sb a black look; **~ méchant** glare; **lancer** or **jeter un ~ méchant à qn** to glare at sb; **son ~ se durcissait** his/her eyes hardened; **on lisait la tristesse/joie dans son ~** you could tell by his/her expression that he/she was sad/happy; **4** (manière de juger) eye; **le ~ de l'anthropologue** the anthropologist's eye; **le ~ des autres** other people's opinion; **c'est un autre ~ sur la situation** it's another way of looking at the situation; **porter un ~ critique sur qch** to look critically at sth; **porter un ~ nouveau sur qch** to take a fresh look at sth; **5** (fait de fixer son attention sur) look; **un bref ~ sur l'actualité** a quick look at the news; **6** Tech (ouverture) spyhole; (trappe) manhole.

II au regard de fml *loc prép* with regard to; **au ~ du chômage/du règlement** with regard to unemployment/to the rules; **au ~ de la loi/du parti** in the eyes of the law/of the party.

III en regard de fml *loc prép* (en comparaison) compared with.

IV en regard *loc adv* **avec une carte en ~** with a map on the opposite page; **texte original avec la traduction en ~** parallel text.

regardant, ~e /ʀ(ə)gaʀdɑ̃, ɑ̃t/ *adj* **ne pas être très ~** (exigeant) not to be very particular ou fussy (**sur** about); (économe) not to care about what things cost; **être ~ avec son argent** to be careful with one's money.

regarder /ʀ(ə)gaʀde/ [1] **I** *vtr* **1** (diriger son regard vers) to look at; **~ qch par la fenêtre** to look out of the window at sth; **~ qch avec inquiétude/admiration** to look at sth anxiously/admiringly; **regarde qui vient!** look who's coming!; **~ qch méchamment** to glare at sth; **~ rapidement** to have a quick look ou to glance at [*bâtiment, paysage*]; (en feuilletant) to glance through [*document, livre*]; **~ qn en face** lit, fig to look sb in the face; **~ la réalité** or **les choses en face** to face facts, to face up to things; **~ qn de haut** fig to look down one's nose at sb; **~ qn de travers** fig to look askance at sb; ▶**lorgnette, vache**; **2** (fixer avec attention) to watch, to look at [*personne, scène*]; to look at [*tableau, diapositives, paysage*]; to watch [*film, télévision, émission*]; **~ qn faire** to watch sb doing; **~ les enfants jouer** or **qui jouent** to watch the children playing; **regarde bien comment je fais** watch what I do carefully; **~ une pièce à la télévision** to watch a play on television; **~ qch fixement** to stare at sth; **~ qn/qch longuement** to gaze at sb/sth; **~ qn dans les yeux** to look sb in the eye(s); **3** (pour vérifier, savoir) to look at [*montre, carte*]; to have a look at, to check [*pneus, niveau d'huile*]; **~ dans** to look up, to consult [*dictionnaire, annuaire, livre de cuisine*]; **~ si** to have a look to see if; **regarde si elle arrive** have a look to see if she is coming, see if you can see her coming; **regarde voir s'il reste du pain**○ look and see if there's any bread left; **4** (examiner, considérer) to look at [*statistiques, pays, situation*]; **~ qch de plus près** to look more closely at sth; **si on regarde les choses calmement** if we look at things calmly; **~ pourquoi/si/qui** to see why/if/who; **~ qch comme douteux** to regard sth as doubtful; **5** (constater) to look; **regarde-moi ça!** just look at that!; **regarde-moi ce désordre!** look at this mess!; **regarde comme c'est beau!** look! isn't that lovely!; **6** (concerner) to concern [*personne*]; **ça ne vous regarde pas** that doesn't concern you; (moins poli) it's none of your business; **mêle-toi de ce qui te regarde!** mind your own business○!; **ça ne regarde que moi** that's nobody's business but mine; **7** (prendre en compte, envisager) **elle ne regarde que ses intérêts** she thinks only of her own interests; **~ l'avenir avec confiance** to view the future with confidence; **8** (faire face à) [*maison*] to overlook [*baie, mer*].

II regarder à *vtr ind* to think about; **~ à la dépense** to watch what one spends; **ne pas ~ à la dépense** to spare no expense; **sans ~ à la dépense/à la qualité** without worrying about the cost/about quality; **quand on y regarde de trop/très près** when you look at it too/very closely; **à y ~ de plus près** on closer examination; **tu devrais y ~ à deux fois avant de l'acheter** you should think twice before buying it.

III *vi* **1** (diriger son regard) to look; **~ en l'air** to look up; **~ par terre** to look down; **~ dehors/dedans** to look outside/inside; **~ par la fenêtre** (de l'intérieur) to look out of the window; (de l'extérieur) to look in through the window; **regarde derrière toi** look behind you; **regarde droit devant toi** look straight ahead; **regarde autour de toi** lit, fig look around; **regarde ailleurs** (détourne le regard) look away; **~ du côté de qn** to look toward(s) sb; **regarde bien** have a good look; **2** (en cherchant) to look; **~ partout/ailleurs** to look everywhere/somewhere else; **3** (faire attention) to look; **regarde où tu vas** look ou watch where you're going; **regarde où tu mets les pieds** look ou watch where you put your feet.

IV se regarder *vpr* **1** (soi-même) to look at oneself; **se ~ dans la glace** to look at oneself in the mirror; **se ~ les ongles** to look at one's nails; **2** (l'un l'autre) to look at one another; ▶**blanc, faïence**; **3** (être vis-à-vis) [*bâtiments*] to face one another.

IDIOMES **il ne s'est pas regardé**○! he ought to take a look at himself!; **tu ne m'as pas bien regardé**○! you must be joking!

regarnir /ʀ(ə)gaʀniʀ/ [3] *vtr* to restock [*étalage, réfrigérateur*]; to refill [*trousse de secours*]; **~ un stock** to restock.

régate /ʀegat/ *nf* regatta.

régence /ʀeʒɑ̃s/ **I** *adj inv* [*style, mobilier*] French Regency; **~ anglais** Regency.

II *nf* **1** Pol regency; **exercer la ~** to act as regent; **2** Hist **la Régence** the Regency.

régénérateur, -trice /ʀeʒeneʀatœʀ, tʀis/ **I** *adj* gén regenerative; Cosmét rejuvenating.

II *nm* Tech, Télécom regenerator.

régénération /ʀeʒeneʀasjɔ̃/ *nf* lit, fig regeneration.

régénérer /ʀeʒeneʀe/ [14] **I** *vtr* **1** Biol, aussi fig to regenerate; **2** Chimie to reactivate.

II se régénérer *vpr* **1** Biol [*cellules*] to regenerate; **2** fig [*corps, personne*] to regain one's forces.

régent, ~e /ʀeʒɑ̃, ɑ̃t/ *nm,f* **1** Pol regent; **2** Hist (de la Banque de France) director.

régenter /ʀeʒɑ̃te/ [1] *vtr* (diriger) to regiment; (contrôler) to regulate.

reggae /ʀege/ *adj inv, nm* reggae.

régicide /ʀeʒisid/ **I**† *adj* liter regicidal.

II *nmf* (personne) regicide.

III *nm* (crime) regicide.

régie /ʀeʒi/ *nf* **1** (gestion) (par l'État) state control (**de** over); (par la commune) local authority control GB, local government control US (**de** over); **en** or **à ~ directe** (de l'État) under state control; (de la commune) under local authority GB ou government US control; **2** (entreprise) **~ d'État** public corporation, state-owned company; (de spectacle) Théât stage management; Cin, TV production department; **3** local central control room.

■ **~ d'abonné** Télécom switchboard; **~ directe** Admin (mode de gestion) direct management of a public service; (service) directly managed public service; **~ intéressée** Admin (mode de gestion) management of a public service on a concessionary basis; (service) public service managed on a concessionary basis; **~ de presse** advertising agency (*handling press advertising only*); **~ publicitaire** advertising agency (*selling advertising space*); **Régie française des tabacs** *French State tobacco industry*.

regimber /ʀ(ə)ʒɛ̃be/ [1] *vi* **1** [*personne*] to balk (**contre** at); **2** [*cheval, âne*] to jib.

régime /ʀeʒim/ *nm* **1** (alimentation) diet; **~ sans sel/sucre/graisse** salt-/sugar-/fat-free diet; **~ lacté/hautes calories** milk/high-calorie diet; **être/se mettre au ~** to be/to go on a diet; **suivre un ~** to be on a diet; **être au ~ jockey**○ hum to be on a starvation diet; **être au ~ sec** hum to be on the wagon○; **produit de ~** dietary product; **2** Pol (mode de gouvernement) system (of government); (gouvernement) government; (totalitaire) regime; **~ parlementaire** parliamentary system; **3** (conditions) system, regime; **~ pénitentiaire/scolaire** prison/school system; **~ de faveur** preferential treatment; **4** Admin (organisation) scheme; (règlement) regulations; **~ d'assurances/de retraite** insurance/pension scheme; **~ des changes/d'échanges** exchange/trade regulations; **~ complémentaire** *private pension scheme that supplements the state scheme*; **5** Jur **~ matrimonial** marriage settlement; **~ de la communauté des biens** *agreement whereby a married couple's property is jointly owned*; **~ de la séparation des biens** *agreement whereby each spouse retains ownership of his/her property*; **6** Mécan (rythme) (running) speed; **bas/haut ~** low/high revs; **tourner à plein ~** [*moteur*] to run at top speed; [*usine*] to work at full capacity; **à ce ~** fig at this rate; **7** Phys (débit) rate of flow; **8** Géog, Météo regime; **9** (de bananes) bunch; (de dattes) cluster, bunch; **10** Ling object; **~ direct/indirect** direct/indirect object; **cas de ~** objective case.

régiment /ʀeʒimɑ̃/ *nm* **1** Mil (unité) regiment; **2**○ (service militaire) military service; **3**○ (multitude) army; **elle avait (tout) un ~ de domestiques** she had a whole army of servants; **il y en a pour un ~!** there's enough to feed an army!

régimentaire /ʀeʒimɑ̃tɛʀ/ *adj* regimental.

région /ʀeʒjɔ̃/ ▶ 692 *nf* **1** Admin region; **la ~ parisienne** the Paris region; **2** Géog (territoire) region; (autour d'un lieu) area; **les ~s tropicales/froides** tropical/cold regions; **le Vésuve et sa ~** Vesuvius and the surrounding area; **le vin de la ~** the local wine; **en ~** journ in the regions; **3** Anat region; **la ~ lombaire** the lumbar region; **4** Mil district; **~ militaire** military district ou command; **5** fig region; **les ~s supérieures**

Les régions

Les indications ci-dessous valent pour les noms des états américains, des provinces canadiennes, des comtés anglais, des départements français, des provinces françaises, des régions administratives d'autres pays comme les cantons suisses ou les provinces belges, et même pour les noms de régions géographiques qui ne sont pas des entités politiques.

Les noms de régions

En général, l'anglais n'utilise pas l'article défini devant les noms de régions.

aimer l'Alabama = to like Alabama
aimer la Californie = to like California
visiter le Nouveau-Mexique = to visit New Mexico
visiter le Texas = to visit Texas
le Lancashire = Lancashire
la Bourgogne = Burgundy
la Provence = Provence
la Savoie = Savoy

Mais l'article est utilisé pour les noms de certaines provinces ou régions françaises, certains cantons suisses et beaucoup de départements français. En cas de doute, consulter le dictionnaire.

le Berry = the Berry
le Limousin = the Limousin
le Valais = the Valais
les Alpes-Maritimes = the Alpes-Maritimes
l'Ardèche = the Ardèche
les Landes = the Landes
le Loir-et-Cher = the Loir-et-Cher
le Loiret = the Loiret
le Rhône = the Rhône
le Var = the Var

À, au, aux, dans, en

À, au, aux, dans *et* en *se traduisent par* to *avec les verbes de mouvement* (*par ex.* aller, se rendre *etc*) *et par* in *avec les autres verbes* (*par ex.* être, habiter *etc.*).

vivre au Texas = to live in Texas
aller au Texas = to go to Texas
vivre en Californie = to live in California
aller en Californie = to go to California
vivre dans les Rocheuses = to live in the Rockies
aller dans les Rocheuses = to go to the Rockies

De avec les noms de régions

Quelques noms de régions ont donné naissance à des adjectifs, mais il y en a beaucoup moins qu'en français. En cas de doute, consulter le dictionnaire.

les habitants de la Californie = Californian people
les vins de Californie = Californian wines

Ces adjectifs sont tous utilisables comme des noms.

les habitants de la Californie = Californians *ou* Californian people

Lorsqu'il n'y a pas d'adjectif, on peut, la plupart du temps, utiliser le nom de la région en position d'adjectif.

l'accent du Texas = a Texas accent
le beurre de Normandie = Normandy butter
les églises du Yorkshire = Yorkshire churches
les paysages de la Californie = the California countryside

Mais en cas de doute, il est plus sûr d'utiliser la tournure avec of*, toujours possible.*

la frontière du Texas = the border of Texas
les habitants de l'Auvergne = the inhabitants of the Auvergne
les rivières du Dorset = the rivers of Dorset
les villes du Languedoc = the towns of Languedoc

Les adjectifs dérivés

Les adjectifs dérivés des régions n'ont pas toujours d'équivalent en anglais. Plusieurs cas sont possibles mais on pourra presque toujours utiliser le nom de la région placé avant le nom qualifié:

la région dauphinoise = the Dauphiné region

Pour souligner la provenance on choisira from + *le nom de la région:*

l'équipe dauphinoise = the team from the Dauphiné region

Pour parler de l'environnement on optera pour of + *le nom de la région:*

l'économie vendéenne = the economy of the Vendée

Pour situer on utilisera in + *le nom de la région:*

mon séjour vendéen = my stay in the Vendée

---

du savoir the loftier realms of knowledge.

régional, **~e**, *mpl* **-aux** /ʀeʒjɔnal, o/ *adj* Admin, Géog regional; **directeur ~** Comm area manager.

régionalisation /ʀeʒjɔnalizasjɔ̃/ *nf* regionalization.

régionaliser /ʀeʒjɔnalize/ [1] *vtr* to regionalize.

régionalisme /ʀeʒjɔnalism/ *nm* **1** Pol regionalism; **2** Ling regional expression, regionalism.

régionaliste /ʀeʒjɔnalist/ *adj*, *nmf* regionalist.

régir /ʀeʒiʀ/ [3] *vtr* gén, aussi Jur, Ling to govern.

régisseur /ʀeʒisœʀ/ ▶510 *nm* **1** (de domaine) steward, manager; **2** Théât stage manager; **3** Admin Jur *person holding a concession to manage a public service.*

■ **~ de plateau** Cin studio manager; TV floor manager; **~ de presse** Pub advertising director (*of an agency selling press advertising*); **~ publicitaire** Pub advertising director (*of an agency selling multi-media advertising*).

registre /ʀ(ə)ʒistʀ/ *nm* **1** (cahier) register; **~ électoral/des actionnaires** electoral/shareholders' register; **~ des absences** Scol attendance register; **~ d'état civil** register of births, marriages and deaths; **tenir un ~** to keep a register; **les ~s de la police** police records; **être inscrit au ~ du commerce** to be a registered company; **2** (de roman, film, discours) style; **dans le même ~, le candidat propose** fig along the same lines, the candidate proposes; **3** (étendue) register; **cet acteur a un ~ limité** this actor has a limited range; **4** Ordinat, Tech register; **5** Ling register.

réglable /ʀeglabl/ *adj* **1** [*hauteur, pression*] adjustable; **siège à dossier ~** reclining seat; **2** Fin (payable) payable; **~ en 6 mensualités** payable in 6 monthly instalments[GB].

réglage /ʀeglaʒ/ *nm* **1** (mise au point) (de vitesse) regulating; (de compteur, thermostat) setting; (de moteur) tuning; **avec ~ automatique** (chauffage, four) with a timing device; **2** (de pression, tir, volume, siège) adjustment; **3** (de papier) ruling.

règle /ʀɛgl/ **I** *nf* **1** (instrument) ruler, rule; **à la ~** with a ruler; **2** (consigne) rule; **~ de grammaire** grammatical rule; **~ de conduite** rule of conduct; **les ~s de la bienséance** the rules of propriety; **la ~ du jeu** lit, fig the rules of the game; **respecter les ~s du jeu** lit, fig to play the game according to the rules; **dans** or **selon les ~s** according to the rules; **dans** or **selon les ~s de l'art** by the rule book; **il se fait une ~** or **il a pour ~ de payer comptant** he makes it a rule to pay cash; **3** (usage établi) rule; **c'est la ~** that's the rule; **en ~ générale** as a (general) rule; **il est de ~ de répondre** or **qu'on réponde** it is customary to reply.

II règles *nfpl* Physiol period; **est-ce qu'elle a ses ~s?** (en ce moment) is she having her period?; (en général) is she having periods?, is she menstruating?

III en règle *loc adj* [*demande*] formal; [*avertissement*] official; [*papiers, comptes*] in order; **subir un interrogatoire en ~** to be given a thorough interrogation.

IV en règle *loc adv* **pour passer la frontière, il faut être en ~** to cross the frontier, your papers must be in order; **se mettre en ~ avec le fisc** to get one's tax affairs properly sorted out.

■ **~ à calcul** slide rule; **~ graduée** graduated ruler; **~ d'or** golden rule; **~ de trois** rule of three; **~s de sécurité** safety regulations.

réglé, **~e** /ʀegle/ **I** *pp* ▶ **régler**.

II *pp adj* **1** (à lignes) [*papier*] ruled, lined; **2** (organisé) [*vie, maison*] well-ordered; [*défilé*] well-organized; **3** (décidé) **c'est une affaire ~e, l'affaire est ~e** the matter is settled; **c'est ~** it's settled; **4** Physiol [*adolescente*] who has started having periods (*épith, après n*); **elle est bien ~e** her periods are regular.

IDIOMES être ~ comme du papier à musique or **comme une horloge** to be as regular as clockwork.

règlement /ʀɛgləmɑ̃/ *nm* **1** (règles) regulations (*pl*), rules (*pl*); **~ administratif/militaire** administrative/military regulations; **c'est contraire au ~** it's against the regulations ou rules; **le ~ c'est le ~** rules are rules; **2** (paiement) payment; **mode de ~** method of payment; **effectuer un ~** to make a payment; **~ en liquide** cash settlement ou payment; **faire un ~ par chèque** to pay ou settle by cheque GB ou check US; **en ~ de** in settlement ou payment of; **veuillez joindre votre ~** please enclose your remittance; **3** (résolution) settlement; **l'affaire est en voie de ~** the matter is being settled; **~ à l'amiable** amicable settlement; Jur out-of-court settlement.

■ **~ de comptes** settling of scores (**entre** between); **~ direct** direct debit; **~ interne** rules and regulations; **~ judiciaire** compulsory liquidation; **être en ~ judiciaire** to be in the hands of the receiver; **~ de police** by(e)-law, police regulation; **~ de procédure** rules (*pl*) of procedure; **~ de sécurité** safety regulations (*pl*).

réglementaire /ʀɛgləmɑ̃tɛʀ/ *adj* **1** (requis) [*tenue, taille*] regulation (*épith*); [*format*] prescribed; [*procédure*] statutory; **2** (légiférant) [*pouvoir*] regulatory; **dispositions ~s du territoire** law of the territory; **les textes ~s** rules and regulations.

réglementation /ʀɛgləmɑ̃tasjɔ̃/ *nf* **1** (règles) rules (*pl*), regulations (*pl*); **la ~ en vigueur** the rules ou regulations in force; **2** (contrôle) regulation, control.

réglementer /ʀɛgləmɑ̃te/ [1] *vtr* to regulate, to control [*prix*]; to regulate [*commerce, industrie*]; to control [*publicité*]; **prix réglementé** government-controlled[GB] price.

régler /ʀegle/ [14] **I** *vtr* **1** (payer) to settle [*compte, dette*]; to pay [*facture, montant*]; to settle, to pay [*dette*]; to pay [*créancier, fournisseur, notaire*]; to pay for [*achat, travaux, fournitures*]; **~ en espèces/par chèque** to pay cash/by cheque GB ou check

US; **réglons nos comptes** lit let's settle up; **on va ~ nos comptes**○ fig we're going to have it out○; **avoir des comptes à ~ avec qn** fig to have a score ou account to settle with sb; **~ son compte à qn**○ (frapper) to sort sb out; (tuer) to bump sb off○, to kill sb; **2** (résoudre) to settle [*question*]; to settle, to sort out [*litige, problème*]; **~ ses affaires** to sort out one's affairs; **réglez ça entre vous** sort it out between you; **3** (mettre au point) to settle [*détails, modalités, ordre*]; to fix, to decide on [*programme, calendrier*]; to arrange [*mise en scène, chorégraphie*]; to organize [*défilé*]; **~ le sort de qn** to decide sb's fate; **4** (ajuster) to adjust [*hauteur, dossier, micro, chauffage*]; to regulate, to adjust [*vitesse, mécanisme*]; to tune [*moteur*]; (fixer d'avance) to set [*allumage*]; **~ la pression sur 3** to set the pressure at 3; **5** (adapter) **~ sa conduite sur celle de qn** to model one's behaviour[GB] on sb's; **~ sa montre sur celle de qn** to set one's watch by sb's; **~ sa vitesse sur celle de qn** to adjust one's speed to sb's; **6** (tracer des lignes) to rule (lines on) paper.

II se régler *vpr* **1** (être ajusté) [*hauteur, température*] to be adjusted; **2** (se modeler) **se ~ sur qn/qch** to model oneself on sb/sth.

réglette /ʀeglɛt/ *nf* (de règle à calcul) slide; (de balance) graduated beam.

■ **~ (jauge)** Aut dipstick.

réglisse /ʀeglis/ **I** *nm* ou *f* (racine, saveur) liquorice GB ou licorice US; **de** or **à la ~** liquorice GB ou licorice (*épith*) US.

II *nf* (plante) liquorice GB ou licorice US.

réglo○ /ʀeglo/ *adj inv* [*personne*] on the level○ (*jamais épith*), straight○; **c'est ~** it's OK○; **ce n'est pas très ~** it's not legit○.

réglure /ʀeglyʀ/ *nf* **papier à ~ fine** narrow-ruled paper.

régnant, ~e /ʀeɲɑ̃, ɑ̃t/ *adj* [*dynastie, famille*] reigning; [*idéologie*] prevailing.

règne /ʀɛɲ/ *nm* **1** Pol (de monarque, pape) reign; (de général, président) rule; **sous le ~ d'Henri IV** under the reign of Henri IV; **à la fin du ~ des généraux** at the end of the generals' rule; **une atmosphère de fin de ~** lit, fig a sense of the end of an era; **2** fig (de peur, d'hypocrisie) reign; **3** Biol kingdom; **le ~ animal/végétal** the animal/vegetable kingdom.

régner /ʀeɲe/ [14] *vi* **1** Pol [*souverain*] to reign, to rule; **~ sur** to reign over, to rule; **2** (imposer sa domination) [*chef, personnalité*] to be in control; **diviser pour ~** divide and rule; **~ en maître sur** to reign supreme over; **3** (prédominer) [*confusion, optimisme, crainte, harmonie*] to reign; [*atmosphère, odeur, ambiance*] to prevail; **il régnait une odeur fétide** a foul smell pervaded the place; **la confiance règne!** iron there's trust for you!; **faire ~** to give rise to [*insécurité, injustice*]; to impose [*ordre*]; **les rebelles font ~ la terreur/violence dans le pays** the rebels have brought terror/violence to the country; **il faisait ~ la terreur dans l'entreprise** he imposed a reign of terror on the company; **l'inquiétude règne chez les jeunes** there is anxiety among the youth.

regonflage /ʀ(ə)gɔ̃flaʒ/, **regonflement** /ʀ(ə)gɔ̃fləmɑ̃/ *nm* (de pneu, ballon) reinflation.

regonfler /ʀ(ə)gɔ̃fle/ [1] **I** *vtr* **1** (gonfler de nouveau) to reinflate [*pneu*]; to blow [sth] up again [*ballon, bouée*]; (avec une pompe à main) to pump [sth] up again; **2** (gonfler davantage) to put more air into; **3**○ fig (remonter) to increase [*effectifs*]; to boost [*ventes, profits*]; **~ qn** to boost sb's morale; **être regonflé à bloc**○ to be back in top form○.

II *vi* **1** [*rivière*] to rise again; **2** [*jambe, doigt*] to swell up again.

regorger /ʀ(ə)gɔʀʒe/ [13] *vi* [*magasin, maison, entrepôt*] to be packed (**de** with); [*ville, pays, région*] to have an abundance (**de** of); [*discours, film*] to be crammed (**de** with); **ses livres regorgent d'anecdotes/de clichés** his books are crammed with anecdotes/with clichés; **le lac regorge de poissons** the lake is brimming with fish.

régresser /ʀegʀese/ [1] *vi* **1** (diminuer) [*eaux, inondation*] to recede; [*production, chômage*] to go down (**de** by); **faire ~ le chômage** to push down unemployment; **2** (décliner) [*culture, enseignement, industrie*] to be in decline; [*programme, spectacle*] to deteriorate; [*vedette, personnalité*] to lose ground; **il a régressé en maths** his work in maths GB ou math US has deteriorated; **3** (disparaître) [*épidémie, fléau*] to die out.

régressif, -ive /ʀegʀesif, iv/ *adj* [*évolution*] regressive.

régression /ʀegʀesjɔ̃/ *nf* **1** gén (diminution) decline; **être en ~** to be in decline; **2** Biol, Géog, Psych, Stat regression; **~ linéaire** linear regression; **~ marine** marine regression; **de ~** [*courbe, coefficient*] regression (*épith*).

regret /ʀəgʀɛ/ *nm* **1** (remords) regret; **sans ~s** with no regrets; **je n'ai qu'un ~, c'est de ne pas l'avoir écouté** my only regret is that I didn't listen to him; **je n'ai aucun ~ à ne pas les avoir rencontrés** I don't regret at all not having met them; **tu n'as pas à avoir de ~s** you have no cause for regret; **2** (insatisfaction) regret; **il a remarqué avec ~ que** he observed with regret that; **j'apprends avec ~ que** I'm sorry to hear that; **c'est avec ~ que j'apprends la démission de notre collègue** I was sorry to hear of our colleague's resignation; **à ~** [*consentir, abandonner, avouer, vendre*] with regret; **comme à ~** as if with regret; **à mon/notre grand ~** to my/our great regret; **j'ai le** or **je suis au ~ de vous annoncer que/qch** I regret to inform you that/of sth; **j'ai le** or **je suis au ~ de ne pouvoir vous aider** I regret that I cannot help you; **mille ~s** I'm terribly sorry; **'~s éternels'** 'greatly missed'.

regrettable /ʀəgʀɛtabl/ *adj* [*incident, erreur, pratique*] regrettable; **il est tout à fait ~ qu'il soit absent** it is extremely regrettable that he is not present.

regrettablement /ʀəgʀɛtabləmɑ̃/ *adv* regrettably; **il semble, fort ~, que ce ne soit pas le cas** it seems, most regrettably, that this is not the case.

regretté, ~e /ʀəgʀete/ **I** *pp* ▶ **regretter.**

II *pp adj* fml late lamented; **notre ~ collègue** our late lamented colleague.

regretter /ʀəgʀete/ [1] *vtr* **1** (déplorer) to regret [*situation, agissement*]; **~ l'absence de débat** to regret the absence of debate; **~ que qn fasse** to regret ou to be sorry that sb does; **il a regretté qu'on n'ait pas parlé de l'avenir** he regretted that nobody spoke about the future; **nous regrettons que tu ne sois pas parmi nous** we are sorry that you're not among us; **je regrette de ne pas pouvoir t'aider** I'm sorry I can't help you; **nous regrettons de ne pouvoir donner suite à votre demande** we regret to inform you that your application has been unsuccessful; **je regrette de partir, mais il le faut** I'm sorry to be leaving, but I have to; **j'ai beaucoup regretté leur départ** I was very sorry that they left; **'il n'y a pas de dialogue,' regrette un employé** 'there's no dialogue[GB],' complains one employee; **2** (se repentir de) to regret [*colère, erreur, impatience*]; **~ sa décision** to regret one's decision; **~ son argent/sa peine** to regret having spent one's money/having gone to some trouble; **tu n'as rien à ~** you have nothing to regret; **~ d'avoir fait** to regret doing, to be sorry for doing; **ils regrettent d'avoir abandonné/d'abandonner leurs études** they regret giving up/that they'll have to give up their studies; **elle regrette ce qu'elle a fait/ce qui s'est passé** she regrets what she did/what happened; **viens avec nous, tu ne le regretteras pas!** come with us, you won't regret it!; **elle m'a menti mais elle va le ~!** she lied to me but she'll regret it!; **je ne regrette rien** I have no regrets; **3** (ressentir l'absence de) to miss [*passé, personne, lieu*]; **je regrette cette époque** I miss that time; **il a été beaucoup regretté** he was sorely ou greatly missed; **4** (pour s'excuser) to be sorry; **je regrette, il est absent** I'm sorry but he's not here; **je regrette, j'étais là avant vous!** excuse me ou I'm sorry but I was here before you!

regrossir /ʀ(ə)gʀosiʀ/ [3] *vi* [*personne*] to put on weight again.

regroupement /ʀ(ə)gʀupmɑ̃/ *nm* **1** (rassemblement) (de mots, services, d'usines) grouping; (d'intérêts) pooling; (de personnes) bringing together; (de provinces, terrains) grouping together, regrouping; (de sociétés) grouping, consolidation; **lieu de ~** meeting point; **2** (fusion) merger; **favoriser les ~s** to encourage mergers; **3** (fait de remettre ensemble) (de personnes, pièces de collection) getting [sth] back together; (de troupes) rallying; (de troupeau) rounding up.

■ **~ familial** Admin family entry and settlement; **~ pédagogique** Admin school merger, school consolidation US.

regrouper /ʀ(ə)gʀupe/ [1] **I** *vtr* **1** (mettre ensemble) to group [sth] together [*objets, mots, services, terrains*]; to bring [sth] together [*personnes*]; to group [sth] together, to consolidate [*provinces, territoires*]; to pool [*intérêts*]; (amalgamer) to merge; **l'exposition regroupe vingt tableaux de Monet** the exhibition brings together twenty Monets; **~ deux chapitres en un seul** to merge two chapters into one; **les trois écoles regroupent 3 000 élèves** the three schools have a combined roll of 3,000 pupils; **questions regroupées autour d'un thème** questions based on a theme; **2** (remettre ensemble) to reassemble [*élèves*]; to rally [*partisans, armée*]; to regroup [*parti*]; to round up [*animaux*].

II se regrouper *vpr* **1** (se mettre ensemble) [*groupes, entreprises*] to group together; [*mécontents*] to gather (together) (**autour de** around; **derrière** behind); **se ~ en association** to form an association; **2** (se remettre ensemble) [*personnes*] to regroup; [*coureurs*] to bunch together again.

régularisation /ʀegylaʀizasjɔ̃/ *nf* **1** (de situation) sorting out, regularization; **2** Fin equalization; **fonds de ~** equalization fund; **~ des cours** price stabilization; **mesure de ~ des marchés** measure designed to stabilize the market; **3** Compta adjustment; **4** (de cours d'eau) regulation.

régulariser /ʀegylaʀize/ [1] **I** *vtr* **1** (rendre légal) to sort out, to regularize [*position*]; to put [sth] in order [*papiers*]; **~ sa situation auprès des autorités** to get oneself sorted out with the authorities, to regularize one's position with the authorities; **~ sa situation**○ hum (se marier) to make it legal○, to tie the knot○; **2** (ajuster) to regulate [*flux, fonctionnement*]; to even out [*pente*]; **3** Compta to adjust; **4** Fin to equalize [*dividende*]; to stabilize [*cours, marché*].

II se régulariser *vpr* [*pouls, circulation*] to return to normal.

régularité /ʀegylaʀite/ *nf* **1** (caractère répétitif) regularity; **se produire avec une certaine ~** to occur fairly regularly ou with some regularity; **2** (caractère constant) (de rythme, production, progrès) steadiness; (de traits du visage) regularity; (d'écriture, de surface) evenness; (de qualité) consistency; **avec ~** [*progresser*] steadily; [*tracer*] evenly; **3** (légalité) legality, correctness.

régulateur, -trice /ʀegylatœʀ, tʀis/ **I** *adj* regulating; **jouer un rôle ~** to act as a regulator; **avoir une influence régulatrice sur les prix** to have a steadying influence on prices.

II *nm* (mécanisme) regulator (**de** of); **~ de croissance/débit** growth/flow regulator.

régulation /ʀegylasjɔ̃/ *nf* regulation, control; **mécanisme de ~ des changes** exchange control mechanism; **avoir une**

fonction de ~ to have a regulatory function; **système sans ~** unregulated system.
■ **~ des naissances** birth control.

réguler /ʀegyle/ [1] *vtr* to regulate.

régulier, -ière /ʀegylje, ɛʀ/ I *adj* **1** (en fréquence) [*versements, arrivages, choc, battement*] regular; **à intervalle(s) ~(s)** at regular intervals; **être en contact ~ avec qn** to be regularly in touch with sb; **2** (habituel) [*lecteur, client*] regular; Transp [*train, ligne, service*] regular, scheduled; **vol ~** scheduled flight; **3** (de qualité constante) [*flux, rythme, demande, hausse, effort, production*] steady; [*pouls, respiration*] steady; [*qualité, progrès*] consistent; [*épaisseur, surface, ligne*] even; [*écriture*] regular; [*vie*] (well-)ordered; **être ~ dans ses habitudes** to be regular in one's habits; **être ~ dans son travail** to be a consistent worker; **4** (symétrique) [*traits*] regular; [*façade*] symmetrical; **5** (honnête) [*affaire*] above board (*jamais épith*), legit○; [*personne*] honest, on the level○ (*jamais épith*); **être ~ en affaires** to be a straight○ person to deal with; **ce n'est pas très ~** it's rather irregular; **6** (conforme) [*papiers, scrutin*] in order (*jamais épith*); [*gouvernement*] legitimate; **il est en situation régulière** his official documents ou papers are in order; **7** Ling [*pluriel, verbe*] regular; **8** Mil [*armée, troupes*] regular; **9** Relig [*clergé*] regular.

II **régulière**○ *nf* **ma régulière** (épouse) my missus○; (petite amie) my steady○.

régulièrement /ʀegyljɛʀmɑ̃/ *adv* **1** (périodiquement, habituellement) [*expédier, rencontrer, se produire*] regularly; **2** (sans à-coups) [*progresser, couler*] steadily; **3** (en formant un motif répété) [*disposer, espacer*] evenly; **4** (selon les règles) [*inscrit, élu*] properly, duly; [*effectué*] in the proper manner; **5** (en principe, d'habitude) normally.

régurgitation /ʀegyʀʒitasjɔ̃/ *nf* regurgitation.

régurgiter /ʀegyʀʒite/ [1] *vtr* lit, fig to regurgitate.

réhabilitation /ʀeabilitasjɔ̃/ *nf* **1** (réinsertion) rehabilitation; **2** Jur rehabilitation; **3** (d'immeuble, de quartier) renovation.

réhabiliter /ʀeabilite/ [1] I *vtr* **1** (réinsérer) to rehabilitate [*personne*]; (revaloriser) to redeem [*passé, institution*]; **2** Jur to rehabilitate [*accusé*]; **3** (en urbanisme) to renovate [*immeuble, quartier*].

II **se réhabiliter** *vpr* [*personne*] to recover one's reputation.

réhabituer /ʀeabitɥe/ [1] I *vtr* to reaccustom (**qn à qch** sb to sth; **qn à faire** sb to doing).

II **se réhabituer** *vpr* to become reaccustomed (**à** to).

rehausse /ʀəos/ *nf* **1** (de chariot, remorque) side extension; **2** (de vêtement) yoke; **~ dos** back yoke.

rehaussement /ʀəosmɑ̃/ *nm* Constr, Fisc raising.

rehausser /ʀəose/ [1] *vtr* **1** (surélever) to raise; **2** (accentuer) to enhance [*prestige, beauté*] (**de** by); **3** (souligner) to set off [*contour, motif*] (**de** by).

réhausseur /ʀeosœʀ/ *nm* booster cushion.

rehaut /ʀəo/ *nm* Art light.

réhydratant, ~e /ʀeidʀatɑ̃, ɑ̃t/ *adj* Cosmét moisturizing.

réhydratation /ʀeidʀatasjɔ̃/ *nf* rehydration.

réhydrater /ʀeidʀate/ [1] *vtr* to rehydrate [*plante, sol*]; to moisturize [*peau*].

réification /ʀeifikasjɔ̃/ *nf* reification.

réifier /ʀeifje/ [2] *vtr* to reify.

réimperméabiliser /ʀeɛ̃pɛʀmeabilize/ [1] *vtr* to reproof.

réimplantation /ʀeɛ̃plɑ̃tasjɔ̃/ *nf* **1** (d'usine, industrie) re-establishment; **2** (de dent, cellules) reimplantation.

réimplanter /ʀeɛ̃plɑ̃te/ [1] I *vtr* **1** to re-establish [*usine, industrie*]; **2** to reimplant [*dent, cellule*].

II **se réimplanter** *vpr* [*usine, industrie*] to re-establish itself.

réimportation /ʀeɛ̃pɔʀtasjɔ̃/ *nf* reimportation.

réimporter /ʀeɛ̃pɔʀte/ [1] *vtr* to reimport.

réimposer /ʀeɛ̃poze/ [1] *vtr* **1** Fisc reimpose; **2** Imprim to reimpose.

réimpression /ʀeɛ̃pʀesjɔ̃/ *nf* **1** (activité) reprinting; **l'ouvrage est en ~** the book is being reprinted; **2** (ouvrage) reprint.

réimprimer /ʀeɛ̃pʀime/ [1] *vtr* to reprint.

Reims /ʀɛ̃s/ **▶ 857** *npr* Reims.

rein /ʀɛ̃/ Anat I *nm* (organe) kidney.

II **reins** *nmpl* **les ~s** (bas du dos) the small of the back; liter (bas ventre) the loins (*pl*) littér; **avoir mal aux ~s** to have backache GB ou a backache US; **une serviette autour des ~s** a towel around the waist; **se redresser d'un coup de ~s** to heave oneself up; **c'est un travail qui vous casse les ~s** fig it's backbreaking work; **avoir les ~s solides** fig to be strong; **casser les ~s à qn** fig to break sb; **il risque de se casser les ~s dans cette affaire** he may come a cropper○ GB ou he may fall flat on his face○ in this business.
■ **~ artificiel** kidney machine.

réincarcération /ʀeɛ̃kaʀseʀasjɔ̃/ *nf* reimprisonment.

réincarcérer /ʀeɛ̃kaʀseʀe/ [14] *vtr* to reimprison.

réincarnation /ʀeɛ̃kaʀnasjɔ̃/ *nf* reincarnation.

réincarner: **se réincarner** /ʀeɛ̃kaʀne/ [1] *vpr* to be reincarnated; **c'est Cicéron réincarné** he is the reincarnation of Cicero.

réincorporer /ʀeɛ̃kɔʀpɔʀe/ [1] *vtr* Mil to re-enlist.

reine /ʀɛn/ *nf* **1 ▶ 813** (souveraine) queen; **la ~ Anne** Queen Anne; **la ~ d'Espagne** the Queen of Spain; **2** (première) **la ~ du bal** fig the belle of the ball; **être la ~ des imbéciles/des pommes**○ to be a complete idiot/a prize mug○; **3** Zool queen; **4** Jeux (aux échecs) queen.
■ **~ de beauté** beauty queen; **~ mère** queen mother; **~ des reinettes** Hort (eating) apple.

reine-claude, *pl* **reines-claudes** /ʀɛnklod/ *nf* greengage.

reine-des-prés /ʀɛndepʀe/ *nf inv* Bot meadowsweet.

reine-marguerite, *pl* **reines-marguerites** /ʀɛnmaʀgəʀit/ *nf* China aster.

reinette /ʀɛnɛt/ *nf* rennet apple.

réinfecter /ʀeɛ̃fɛkte/ [1] I *vtr* to reinfect.

II **se réinfecter** *vpr* to become reinfected.

réinfection /ʀeɛ̃fɛksjɔ̃/ *nf* reinfection.

réinjecter /ʀeɛ̃ʒɛkte/ [2] *vtr* to reinject [*liquide, capitaux*].

réinscription /ʀeɛ̃skʀipsjɔ̃/ *nf* re-enrolment[GB].

réinscrire /ʀeɛ̃skʀiʀ/ [67] I *vtr* to re-enrol[GB].

II **se réinscrire** *vpr* to re-enrol.

réinsérer /ʀeɛ̃seʀe/ [14] I *vtr* **1** to reintegrate [*personne*]; **2** to reinsert [*annonce, objet*].

II **se réinsérer** *vpr* [*personne*] to become reintegrated.

réinsertion /ʀeɛ̃sɛʀsjɔ̃/ *nf* **1** (de personne) reintegration; **2** (d'annonce, objet) reinsertion.

réinstallation /ʀeɛ̃stalasjɔ̃/ *nf* **1** (dans un lieu) move, relocation; **indemnité de ~** resettlement allowance; **2** (dans une fonction) reinstatement (**dans** in); (après une élection) **depuis sa ~ à la présidence** since being re-elected as president.

réinstaller /ʀeɛ̃stale/ [1] I *vtr* **1** (réaménager) to refit [*pièce*]; (changer de lieu) **~ les bureaux au premier étage** to move the offices back to the first GB ou second US floor; **2** (rétablir) (dans une ville, une région) to resettle [*personne*] (**dans** to); (dans une maison) to move [sb] back [*personne*] (**dans** to); (à un poste) **~ qn dans ses fonctions** to reinstate someone in his/her old job; (à un mandat) **~ qn à la présidence** to re-elect sb as president.

II **se réinstaller** *vpr* **1** (dans un lieu) **se ~ dans un fauteuil** to settle (oneself) back into an armchair; **se ~ en banlieue** [*habitant*] to move back to the suburbs; [*compagnie, commerçant*] to set up business again in the suburbs; **2** (dans une situation) **se ~ à la présidence** to become president again; **se ~ en tête** to get back into the lead.

réintégration /ʀeɛ̃tegʀasjɔ̃/ *nf* **1** (réadmission) (au travail) reinstatement (**de** of); (dans un système, un service) reintegration (**dans** into); (à une nationalité) Jur reestablishment of nationality; **demander sa ~ dans la nationalité française** to apply for reestablishment of French nationality; **2** (retour) **~ à la vie civile** return to civilian life; **~ du domicile conjugal** Jur return to the marital home.

réintégrer /ʀeɛ̃tegʀe/ [14] *vtr* **1** (rejoindre) to return to [*lieu, groupe, système*]; **~ le domicile conjugal** to return to the marital home; **2** (rétablir) **~ qn (dans ses fonctions)** to reinstate sb (in his/her job); **~ qn dans le tissu social** or **la société** to reintegrate sb into society; **~ qn dans ses droits** to restore sb's rights; **~ qn dans la nationalité française** to reestablish sb's French nationality; **~ les chômeurs de longue durée** to reintegrate the long-term unemployed.

réintroduction /ʀeɛ̃tʀɔdyksjɔ̃/ *nf* reintroduction.

réintroduire /ʀeɛ̃tʀɔdɥiʀ/ [69] I *vtr* to reintroduce [*sujet, contrôle, erreurs*] (**dans** in); to reinsert [*clé, tube*] (**dans** in).

II **se réintroduire** *vpr* (dans un lieu) to get back (**dans** into); (dans un milieu) to reestablish oneself (**dans** in).

réinventer /ʀeɛ̃vɑ̃te/ [1] *vtr* **1** (renouveler) to reinvent [*genre, art*]; **~ le monde** to dream of changing the world iron; **il a réinventé la roue!** iron he thinks he invented the wheel!; **en matière de pédagogie, tout est à ~** where teaching is concerned, everything needs to be thought through again from scratch; **2** (recréer) to recreate [*personnage, enfance*].

réinvestir /ʀeɛ̃vɛstiʀ/ [3] *vtr* to reinvest, to plough GB ou plow US back [*profits, argent*].

réinviter /ʀeɛ̃vite/ [1] *vtr* to invite back, to reinvite.

réitératif, -ive /ʀeiteʀatif, iv/ *adj* reiterative.

réitération /ʀeiteʀasjɔ̃/ *nf* reiteration, repetition.

réitérer /ʀeiteʀe/ [14] *vtr* to reiterate [*demande, appel, ordre, erreur*]; to repeat [*attaque, exploit, opération*]; **s'il réitère, ce sera la prison** if he re-offends, he will go to jail.

reître /ʀɛtʀ/ *nm* liter thuggish soldier.

rejaillir /ʀ(ə)ʒajiʀ/ [3] *vi* **1** [*liquide*] to splash back (**sur** onto); (sous pression) to spurt back (**sur** onto); [*lumière*] to be reflected (**sur** on); **l'eau m'a rejailli au visage** the water splashed back in my face; **2** fig **~ sur qn** [*succès, gloire*] to reflect on sb; [*scandale, discrédit*] to affect sb adversely; **les bienfaits de la science rejaillissent sur tous** the benefits of science are felt by all.

rejaillissement /ʀ(ə)ʒajismɑ̃/ *nm* liter (de liquide) splashing; fig (de scandale) adverse effect; (de gloire, succès) reflection.

rejet /ʀ(ə)ʒɛ/ *nm* **1** (refus) gén rejection; Admin, Jur (de recours, résolution, plainte, charges) dismissal; (de motion, proposition, projet de loi) defeat; (de requête) denial; (de demande) rejection; **exprimer son ~ du régime** to voice one's rejection of the regime; **ce fut un vote de ~** it was a protest vote; **après le ~ de la réforme** after the reform had been defeated; **en cas**

de ~ de la demande d'asile if the request for asylum should be denied ou rejected; **2** (exclusion de personne, race, religion) rejection; **le ~ d'un enfant/étranger** the rejection of a child/foreigner; **réaction de ~** gén hostile reaction (**à l'égard de** to) ; Psych rejection response; **3** École, Ind (production) discharge ¢; (évacuation) disposal; (déchets) **~s** waste ¢; **région polluée par les ~s d'une usine** area polluted by the discharge from a factory; **traiter les ~s d'une usine** to process the waste from a factory; **les ~s toxiques/radioactifs** toxic/radioactive waste; **le ~ des déchets/des eaux usées** waste/wastewater disposal; **les ~s en mer** (**de déchets**) dumping (of waste) at sea; **les ~s polluants** pollutants; **4** Ling (en fin de phrase) end positioning; (en poésie) enjambement; **5** Méd (de greffon) rejection; **faire un ~** to reject a transplanted organ; **6** Agric, Hort **~ de souche** stump, shoot; **7** Géol (de faille) downthrow; (de couche) leap.

rejeter /ʀəʒte, ʀʒəte/ [20] **I** *vtr* **1** (refuser) gén to reject [*théorie, initiative, alliance, conseil, pièce défectueuse, candidature*]; to turn down [*offre*]; Admin, Jur to dismiss [*recours, plainte, charges, résolution*]; to defeat [*motion, proposition, projet de loi*]; to deny [*requête*]; to reject [*demande*]; to set aside [*décision, verdict*]; **~ une proposition de paix** to reject a peace proposal; **~ des accusations** to dismiss accusations; **sa candidature a été rejetée** his application was rejected; **2** (exclure) to reject [*enfant, étranger, marginal*]; **se sentir rejeté** to feel rejected; **3** (renvoyer) **~ qch** to shift sth [*tort, faute, responsabilité*] (**sur** onto); **elle rejette tous les torts sur son mari** she shifts all the blame onto her husband; **~ la responsabilité de qch sur qn** to shift the blame for sth onto sb; **4** (restituer) [*malade*] to bring up [*nourriture, bile, sang*]; [*organisme*] to reject [*greffon*]; [*machine*] to reject [*jetons, pièces*]; **5** (produire) [*usine, zone industrielle*] to discharge [*déchets, eaux usées*]; to eject [*fumée, gaz*]; [*volcan*] to spew out [*lave*]; **~ des déchets dans une rivière/à la mer** to discharge waste into a river/into the sea; **~ du chlore/soufre dans l'atmosphère** to eject chlorine/sulphur[GB] into the atmosphere; **6** (se débarrasser de) [*personne, compagnie*] to dispose of [*déchets*]; [*pêcheur*] to throw [sth] back [*poisson*]; [*mer, marée*] to wash up [*corps, débris*]; **~ un poisson à l'eau/dans une rivière** to throw a fish back into the water/into a river; **épave rejetée sur le rivage** flotsam washed ashore; **~ des déchets en mer** to dump waste at sea; **7** (déplacer) **~ un mot en fin de phrase/au début d'un vers** to put a word at the end of the sentence/at the beginning of a line of verse; **8** (chasser) [*armée, troupes*] to push ou drive back [*ennemi, assaillants*] (**hors de** out of); **9** (bouger brutalement) [*personne*] to throw [*tête, cheveux, épaules*] (**en arrière** back); **il rejeta le buste en arrière pour éviter le coup** he threw his body back to avoid being hit.

II se rejeter *vpr* **1** (se reculer) **se ~ en arrière** to throw ou fling oneself back; **2** (se renvoyer) **se ~ les torts** or **la faute** to blame each other; **se ~ la responsabilité de qch** to blame each other for sth.

rejeton /ʀəʒtɔ̃, ʀʒətɔ̃/ *nm* **1**○ hum (enfant) offspring (*inv*); **2** Bot offshoot; **3** fig offshoot.

rejoindre /ʀ(ə)ʒwɛ̃dʀ/ [56] **I** *vtr* **1** (à un rendez-vous) to meet up with; **2** (rattraper) to catch up with; **3** (se joindre à) to join [*personne, groupe, mouvement*]; (de nouveau) to rejoin; **le sentier rejoint la route** the path joins the road; **4** (aller à) [*personne*] to get to [*endroit*]; (de nouveau) to get back to [*endroit*]; to return to [*domicile, caserne*]; **~ son poste** to take up one's appointment; (de nouveau) to return to one's duties; **5** (s'accorder avec) [*personnes*] **~ qn sur qch** to concur sout with sb on sth; **vos idées/conclusions rejoignent les miennes** your ideas/conclusions are akin to mine; **ça rejoint ce qu'il a dit** it ties up with what he said.

II se rejoindre *vpr* **1** (se rencontrer) [*personnes*] to meet up; [*routes*] to meet; **2** (s'accorder) [*personnes*] to be in agreement (**sur** on); [*opinions, goûts*] to be similar; **3** (se fondre) **la musique et la poésie se rejoignent** music and poetry merge.

rejointoyer /ʀ(ə)ʒwɛ̃twaje/ [23] *vtr* to repoint.

rejouer /ʀ(ə)ʒwe/ [1] **I** *vtr* **1** gén, Mus to play [sth] again; **2** Sport to replay [*match, point*]; **le match sera rejoué** there will be a replay; **3** Cin, Théât to play [sth] again, act [sth] again [*rôle*]; to do [sth] again, to run [sth] again [*scène*]; **~ une pièce** [*compagnie*] to perform a play again; [*théâtre*] to put on a play again; **4** Jeux (aux cartes) **~ (du) pique** to lead spades again; (au casino) **~ le 9** to bet on the 9 again.

II *vi* [*enfant, sportif, musicien*] to play again; [*acteur*] to act again; [*compagnie*] to perform again.

réjoui, **~e** /ʀejwi/ **I** *pp* ▸ **réjouir**.

II *pp adj* [*personne, air, mine*] cheerful; **tout ~ de son succès** delighted with his success; **tout ~ à l'idée de** delighted at the thought of.

réjouir /ʀeʒwiʀ/ [3] **I** *vtr* **1** (faire plaisir à) to delight [*personne, regard*]; **ça me réjouit le cœur** it gladdens my heart; **l'idée du départ me réjouit/ne me réjouit pas** I am delighted/less than delighted at the thought of leaving; **2** (divertir) to amuse.

II se réjouir *vpr* to rejoice; **il n'y a pas de quoi se ~** there is no cause for rejoicing; **se ~ de qch** to be delighted at [*nouvelle*]; to be delighted with [*succès, projet*]; to delight in [*bonheur, malheur*]; **se ~ de faire** to be delighted to do; **se ~ que** to be delighted that; **se ~ à l'idée** or **à la pensée que** to be delighted at the thought that; **se ~ à l'avance de** to look forward to [*événement*] ; **je me réjouis à l'avance du dépit qu'il va éprouver** I can't wait to see how disappointed he'll be.

réjouissance /ʀeʒwisɑ̃s/ **I** *nf* rejoicing.

II réjouissances *nfpl* celebrations; **quel est le programme des ~s**○**?** iron what delights are in store for us?; **au programme des ~s** iron on the fun-packed agenda.

réjouissant, **~e** /ʀeʒwisɑ̃, ɑ̃t/ *adj* **1** (qui fait plaisir) heartening, delightful; **la nouvelle n'a rien de bien ~** it's not exactly cheerful news; **eh bien, c'est ~!** iron well, that's just wonderful!; **2** (divertissant) amusing.

relâche /ʀ(ə)lɑʃ/ *nf* **1** Théât, Cin closure; (sur un panneau) 'no performance'; **le jeudi est jour de ~** it's closed on Thursdays; **demain c'est jour de ~** Cin it's closed tomorrow; Théât there's no performance tomorrow; **faire ~** to be closed; **2** (pause) break, rest; **sans ~** relentlessly; **3** Naut port of call; **faire ~** (dans un port) to put in; (au large) to drop anchor.

relâché, **~e** /ʀ(ə)lɑʃe/ **I** *pp* ▸ **relâcher**.

II *pp adj* [*surveillance, discipline, morale, mœurs*] lax, slack; [*style*] slipshod.

relâchement /ʀ(ə)lɑʃmɑ̃/ *nm* **1** (de discipline, surveillance) slackening, relaxation; (d'attention, effort, de zèle) slackening; (de morale, mœurs) loosening, relaxation; **il y a du ~ dans la discipline/surveillance** discipline/supervision is getting lax ou slack; **il y a du ~ dans le travail** the work is slacking off; **2** (de muscle) slackening.

relâcher /ʀ(ə)lɑʃe/ [1] **I** *vtr* **1** (desserrer) to loosen, to relax [*étreinte, lien, muscle*]; to loosen [*ressort, entrave, intestins*]; **2** (libérer) to release, to set [sb/sth] free [*personne, otage, animal*]; to let [sth] go [*poisson*]; **3** (diminuer) to relax, to let up on [*discipline, surveillance*]; **~ son attention** to let one's attention wander; **il a relâché son zèle** his zeal has flagged; **~ ses efforts** to let up.

II *vi* Naut (dans un port) to put in; (au large) to drop anchor.

III se relâcher *vpr* **1** (se détendre) [*étreinte, lien, ressort*] to loosen; [*muscle*] to relax, to loosen up; **2** (faiblir) [*surveillance, effort, discipline*] to slacken; [*zèle*] to flag; [*élève*] to grow slack; **se ~ dans son travail** to grow slack in one's work; **se ~ dans son effort** to let up.

relais /ʀ(ə)lɛ/ **I** *nm inv* **1** (intermédiaire) intermediary; **c'est lui le ~ du ministère** he's the ministry's intermediary; **prendre le ~ (de qn/qch)** to take over (from sb/sth); **passer le ~ à qn** to hand over to sb; **2** Sport relay; **course de ~** relay race; **le ~ 4 fois 100 mètres** the 4 by 100 metres[GB] relay; **3** (restaurant) restaurant; (hôtel) hotel; **4** Tech, Télécom relay; **~ radioélectrique** radio electric relay; **~ de temporisation** time delay relay; **~ de télévision** television relay station; **~ hertzien** radio relay station.

II (-)relais (*in compounds*) **usine-/atelier-~** intermediary factory/workshop.

relance /ʀ(ə)lɑ̃s/ *nf* **1** (reprise) (d'industrie, idée) revival; (d'économie) reflation; (impulsion donnée) boost (**de** to); (de débat, négociations) reopening; (recrudescence) (de terrorisme) upsurge; (d'inflation) rise; **mesures de ~** reflationary measures; **entraîner la ~ de** to give a boost to [*construction, commerce*]; to lead to an upsurge of [*terrorisme*]; to lead to a rise in [*inflation*]; **2** (par créancier) (action) chasing up ¢; (lettre) reminder; (par importun) pestering ¢; **~ du client** Comm follow-up; **3** (au poker) (action) raising the stakes; (mise) raise; **faire une ~** to raise the stakes.

relancer /ʀ(ə)lɑ̃se/ [12] **I** *vtr* **1** (lancer de nouveau) to throw [sth] again [*balle*]; (renvoyer) to throw [sth] back (again) [*balle*]; **2** (faire repartir) to restart [*moteur*]; to relaunch [*compagnie, campagne, offensive, projet*]; to revive [*idée, tradition*]; to reopen [*débat, négociations*]; to boost [*investissement, production*]; to reflate [*économie*]; **~ le gibier** to start the game (again); **c'est lui qui a relancé la mode de...** he was the one who brought back the fashion for...; **3** (poursuivre) [*créancier*] to chase [sb] up; [*importun*] to pester.

II *vi* (au poker) to raise the stakes (**de** by).

relaps, **~e** /ʀ(ə)laps/ **I** *adj* relapsed (*épith*).

II *nm,f* (hérétique) relapsed heretic; (criminel) relapsed criminal.

relater /ʀ(ə)late/ [1] *vtr* fml to recount [*événements, histoire, aventure*].

relatif, **-ive** /ʀ(ə)latif, iv/ **I** *adj* **1** (non absolu) [*vérité, majorité, importance, succès, silence*] relative; **tout est ~** it's all relative; **une amélioration toute relative** a purely relative improvement; **le risque est très ~** the risk is relatively slight; **jouir d'une estime relative** to enjoy a limited amount of respect; **un confort très ~** limited comfort; **2** (qui se rapporte) relating (**à** to); **dans un article ~ aux droits des employés** in an article relating to employees' rights; **les lois relatives au divorce** the laws relating to divorce, divorce laws; **3** Ling [*pronom, proposition*] relative; **4** (respectif) [*position, poids*] relative.

II *nm* Ling relative (pronoun).

III relative *nf* Ling relative (clause).

relation /ʀ(ə)lasjɔ̃/ **I** *nf* **1** (rapport) connection (**avec** with); **il n'y a aucune ~ entre les deux affaires** there is no connection between the two cases; **faire la ~ entre deux événements** to make the connection between two events; **je n'avais pas fait la ~ entre les deux** I hadn't made the connection between the two; **faire la ~ avec qch/qn** to make the connection with sth/sb; **un projet établi en ~ avec l'industrie** a project set up in partnership with industry; **2** (personne) acquaintance; **c'est une de mes ~s** he/she is an acquaintance of mine; **une vague ~** a vague acquaintance; **des ~s d'affaires** business acquaintances; **renouer avec d'anciennes ~s** to catch up with some old acquaintances; **3** (personne puissante) connection; **avoir des ~s** to have connections;

obtenir qch grâce à ses or **par ~s** to obtain sth through one's connections; **4** (lien) relationship (**avec** with; **entre** between); **une ~ amicale/sentimentale** a friendly/romantic relationship; **entretenir/avoir de bonnes ~s avec qn** to keep up/to have a good relationship with sb; **avoir une ~ très conflictuelle/tendre avec qn** to have a very stormy/tender relationship with sb; **la ~ parent-enfant/médecin-patient** the parent-child/doctor-patient relationship; **être/entrer en ~ avec qn** to be/get in touch with sb; **être en ~ d'affaires avec qn** to have business dealings with sb; **mettre deux personnes en ~** to put two people in contact ou touch (with each other); **5** Math relation; **~ d'équivalence** equivalence relation.

II **relations** *nfpl* (échanges) relations (**avec** with); **les ~s culturelles/diplomatiques/commerciales** cultural/diplomatic/trade relations; **ministre chargé des ~s avec le Parlement** *minister responsible for organizing parliamentary agenda.*

■ **~s extérieures** Pol foreign affairs; **~s publiques** public relations; **~s sexuelles** sexual relations.

relationnel, **-elle** /ʀ(ə)lasjɔnɛl/ *adj* **1** Psych [*aptitudes, qualités*] relational; **avoir des problèmes ~s** to have relational problems or difficulties; **2** Ling, Ordinat relational.

relativement /ʀ(ə)lativmɑ̃/ I *adv* relatively.

II **relativement à** *loc prép* in relation to, relative to.

relativiser /ʀ(ə)lativize/ [1] *vtr* to put [sth] into perspective.

relativisme /ʀəlativism/ *nm* relativism.

relativiste /ʀ(ə)lativist/ I *adj* Philos relativist; Phys relativistic.

II *nmf* relativist.

relativité /ʀ(ə)lativite/ *nf* relativity.

relaver /ʀ(ə)lave/ [1] *vtr* to wash [sth] again.

relax○ /ʀəlaks/ I *adj inv* [*personne*] (détendu) relaxed; (insouciant) laid-back○; [*tenue*] casual; **petite soirée ~** informal little gathering.

II *excl* take it easy○!, calm down!

relaxant, **~e** /ʀ(ə)laksɑ̃, ɑ̃t/ I *adj* [*bain, vacances*] relaxing; [*médicament*] relaxant.

II *nm* relaxant.

relaxation /ʀ(ə)laksasjɔ̃/ *nf* relaxation.

relaxe /ʀəlaks/ *nf* Jur discharge.

relaxer /ʀ(ə)lakse/ [1] I *vtr* **1** (relâcher) to discharge [*prévenu*]; **2** (détendre) to relax [*muscle, personne*].

II **se relaxer** *vpr* to relax.

relayer /ʀ(ə)leje/ [21] I *vtr* **1** (remplacer) to take over from, relieve; **se faire ~ par qn** to get [sb] to take over from one GB ou for one US; **2** TV, Télécom to relay [*signal, émission*].

II **se relayer** *vpr* **1** gén to take turns (**pour faire** doing); **ils se relaient toutes les heures** they change over every hour; **2** Sport gén to take over from each other.

relayeur, **-euse** /ʀ(ə)lejœʀ, øz/ *nm,f* relay runner.

relecteur, **-trice** /ʀ(ə)lɛktœʀ, tʀis/ *nm,f* proofreader.

relecture /ʀ(ə)lɛktyʀ/ *nf* (de livre) rereading; (d'épreuves) proofreading; (de cassette) replaying.

relégation /ʀ(ə)legasjɔ̃/ *nf* **1** Sport relegation GB; **2** Hist Jur (travaux forcés) transportation; (prison) imprisonment.

reléguer /ʀ(ə)lege/ [14] *vtr* **1** fig (mettre à l'écart) to relegate [*personne, question*] (**à, dans** to); to banish, consign [*objet*] (**à, dans** to); **~ qn/qch au second plan** to push sb/sth into the background; **2** Sport to relegate (**en** to) GB; **3** Hist Jur (emprisonner) to jail (*for a minimum of one year*); (transporter) ≈ to sentence [sb] to transportation.

relent /ʀ(ə)lɑ̃/ *nm* **1** (puanteur) lingering odour[GB]; **2** fig (trace) whiff; **il s'en dégage un ~ de racisme** there's a whiff of racism about it.

relevable /ʀələvabl/ *adj* [*dossier*] adjustable.

relève /ʀ(ə)lɛv/ *nf* **1** (action) **la ~ de qn** relieving sb; **la ~ s'effectue à 20 heures** the changeover takes place at 8 pm, the relief occurs at 8 pm; **la ~ de la garde** the changing of the guard; **prendre** or **assurer la ~** lit, fig to take over; **2** (personne) relief; (équipe) relief team.

relevé, **~e** /ʀəlve, ʀlәve/ I *pp* ▶ **relever**.

II *pp adj* **1** Culin spicy; **2** (raffiné) [*propos*] refined; **peu ~** [*jeu de mot, style*] rather coarse.

III *nm* **1** (action de noter) taking down, noting down; **faire le ~ de** to take down [*noms*]; to pick out [*verbes, passages intéressants*]; to list [*erreurs*]; **faire le ~ des dépenses** to make a note of expenses; **faire le ~ du compteur** to read the meter; **le ~ du compteur s'effectue tous les six mois** the meter is read every six months; **2** (compte-rendu) statement; **~ de gaz/d'électricité/de téléphone** gas/electricity/telephone bill; **3** Archit plan.

■ **~ bancaire** or **de compte** bank statement; **~ d'identité bancaire**, **RIB** *slip giving official details of a bank account*; **~ d'identité postal**, **RIP** *slip giving official details of a post office account*; **~ de notes** Scol report GB, grades (*pl*) US.

relèvement /ʀ(ə)lɛvmɑ̃/ *nm* **1** (hausse) (action) increasing; (résultat) increase; **~ de l'impôt** (action) increasing taxes; (résultat) tax increase; **un ~ de 13%** a 13% increase; **2** (de statue, clôture, mât) putting up; **3** Naut bearing; **4** Math projecting.

relever /ʀəlve, ʀ(ə)ləve/ [16] I *vtr* **1** (remettre debout) to pick up [*personne tombée, tabouret*]; to put [sth] back up (again) [*statue, clôture*]; **2** (mettre à la verticale) to raise [*dossier de siège, manette*]; **3** (bouger à nouveau) **~ la main** (pour parler) to put up one's hand again; **~ les yeux** or **le nez** or **le front** to look up; **~ la tête** (redresser) to raise one's head; (pour voir) to look up; (ne pas être vaincu) to refuse to accept defeat; **4** (mettre plus haut) to turn up [*col*]; to lift [*jupe*]; to wind up [*vitre de voiture*]; to raise [*voile, store*]; (à nouveau) to raise [sth] again [*store, rideau de théâtre*]; **~ un coin du rideau** to lift up a corner of the curtain; **~ ses cheveux** to put one's hair up; **elle a toujours les cheveux relevés** she always wears her hair up; **5** (constater) to note, to notice [*erreur, contradiction, signe*]; to notice [*fait, absence*]; (faire remarquer) to point out [*erreur, contradiction*]; **~ que** to note that; **'il t'a encore critiqué'—'je n'ai pas relevé'** 'he criticized you again'—'I didn't notice'; **~ la moindre inexactitude** to seize on the slightest inaccuracy; **6** (prendre note de) to take down, to note down [*date, nom, dimensions, numéro d'immatriculation*]; to take [*empreinte*]; to note down [*citation, passage*]; **~ le compteur** to read the meter; **7** (collecter) to take in [*copies d'examen*]; **8** (réagir à) to react to [*remarque*]; **~ la gageure** or **le défi** to take up the challenge; **~ un pari** to take on a bet; **9** (reconstruire) to rebuild [*mur*]; to put sth back on its feet [*pays, institution, industrie, économie*]; **10** (augmenter) to raise [*niveau de vie, niveau d'études*]; to raise, to increase [*taux d'intérêt, prix, productivité*]; **~ les salaires de 3%** to put up ou increase salaries by 3%; **~ toutes les notes de trois points** to put all the grades up by three marks; **11** (remplacer) to relieve [*équipe*]; **~ la garde** to change the guard, to relieve the guard; **12** (donner plus d'attrait à) to spice up [*plat*]; **~ une sauce avec de la moutarde** to spice a sauce up with mustard; **~ un récit de détails amusants** to enliven a tale with amusing details; **13** fml (libérer) **~ qn de** to release sb from [*vœux, obligation*]; **~ qn de ses fonctions** to relieve sb of their duties; **14** (en tricot) **~ une maille** to pick up a stitch.

II **relever de** *vtr ind* **1** (dépendre de) **notre service relève du ministère de la Défense** our department comes under the Ministry of Defence; **2** (être de la compétence de) **l'affaire relève de la Cour européenne de justice** the case comes within the competence of the European Court of Justice; **cela ne relève pas de ma compétence/mes fonctions** this doesn't come within my competence/my duties; **3** (s'apparenter à) **cela relève de la gageure/du mythe** this comes close to being impossible/to being a myth; **4** (se rétablir) **~ de** to be recovering from [*maladie*].

III **se relever** *vpr* **1** (après une chute) to pick oneself up; (après avoir été assis) to get up again; **2** (sortir du lit) to get up again, to get out of bed again; **3** (être mis à la verticale) **se ~ facilement** [*dossier*] to be easy to raise; **se ~ automatiquement** to be raised automatically; **4** (être remonté) [*store*] to be raised; **la vitre ne se relève plus** the window won't wind GB ou roll US up; **5** (se remettre) **se ~ de** to recover from [*maladie, chagrin, crise, scandale*]; **il ne s'en relèvera pas** he'll never recover from it; **se ~ de ses ruines** to rise from the ruins.

releveur /ʀəlvœʀ, ʀləvœʀ/ I *adj m* **muscle ~** elevator muscle.

II *nm* Anat elevator.

relief /ʀəljɛf/ I *nm* **1** Géog relief ¢; **étude des ~s montagneux** study of mountain relief; **le ~ sous-marin** the relief of the sea bed; **un ~ accidenté/monotone** a hilly/an unrelieved landscape; **région au ~ accidenté** mountainous region; **2** (de surface, paroi) relief ¢; (de médaille, monnaie) raised pattern; **globe terrestre en ~** globe of the world in relief; **carte en ~** relief map; **lettres/motifs en ~** embossed letters/patterns; **le braille est une écriture en ~** Braille is a type of raised ou relief script; **mettre qch en ~** to accentuate sth, to throw sth into relief; **3** Archit, Art (en sculpture) relief; **4** (profondeur) depth; **l'effet de ~ est bien rendu dans ce tableau** the effect of depth is well done in this painting; **5** (caractère) **personnage qui manque de ~** one-dimensional ou flat character; **donner du ~ à un discours/texte** to enliven a speech/text; **6** Cin, Phot **cinéma/photographie en ~** three-dimensional cinema/photography.

II **reliefs**† *nmpl* (de repas) leftovers.

relier /ʀəlje/ [2] *vtr* **1** (réunir) to link up, to link [sb/sth] together [*personnes, objets, piquets*] (**à** to); to join up [*points*] (**à** to); to connect [*appareils électriques*] (**à** to; **par** with); **2** (faire communiquer) to link [*ville, personne, organisme*] (**à** to); to link (up ou together) [*lieux, berges*]; **3** (rassembler) to link [*idées, faits*] (**à** to, with); to link together [*mots, propositions*] (**par** with); **~ les faits entre eux** to find a link between the facts; **4** Imprim to bind; **livre relié** hardback (book); **un livre relié cuir** a leather-bound book; **5** Tech to hoop [*tonneau*].

relieur, **-ieuse** /ʀəljœʀ, øz/ ▶**510** *nm,f* (book)binder; **~ d'art** fine bookbinder.

religieusement /ʀ(ə)liʒjøzmɑ̃/ *adv* **1** (consciencieusement) [*obéir*] religiously; **2** (avec recueillement) [*écouter*] with rapt attention; **3** (pieusement) [*se marier*] in church; **élever ~ ses enfants** to bring up one's children in the faith.

religieux, **-ieuse** /ʀ(ə)liʒjø, øz/ I *adj* **1** Relig [*culte, édifice, cérémonie, fête*] religious; [*école, mariage*] (chrétien) church (*épith*); [*ordre, vie, personne, pays, éducation, art*] religious; [*musique*] sacred; **l'habit ~** the monk's/nun's habit; **2** fig [*silence*] reverent; [*vénération*] religious; [*soin*] conscientious; **avec un soin ~** most conscientiously.

II *nm,f* monk/nun.

III **religieuse** *nf* Culin round éclair.

religion /ʀ(ə)liʒjɔ̃/ *nf* **1** (sens du sacré) religion; (culte organisé) religion; **Guerres de Religion** Hist Wars of Religion; **2** (piété) religion, (religious) faith; **avoir de la ~** to be religious; **sa ~ est sincère** he is a sincere believer; **3** fig (culte d'une valeur) **avoir la ~ du progrès/de l'art** to be a great believer in progress/in art; **se faire une ~ de la ponctualité** iron to make a fetish of punctuality; **ma ~ est faite là-dessus** I'm absolutely convinced of that; **4** (vie monastique) monastic life; **entrer en ~** to enter the Church.

religiosité /ʀ(ə)liʒjozite/ *nf* religious inclination; péj piousness, religiosity.

reliquaire /ʀ(ə)likɛʀ/ *nm* reliquary.

reliquat /ʀ(ə)lika/ *nm* **1** Compta (de somme) remainder, rest; (de compte) balance; (de dette) outstanding amount ou balance; **s'il y a un ~** (de somme) if there is anything left over; **2** Méd (de maladie) after-effects (*pl*).

relique /ʀ(ə)lik/ *nf* Relig, fig relic; **garder qch comme une ~** to treasure sth.

relire /ʀ(ə)liʀ/ [66] **I** *vtr* (de nouveau) to reread; (pour corriger) to read [sth] over [*texte*]; to proofread [*épreuves*].

II se relire *vpr* (de nouveau) to reread what one has written; (pour corriger) to read over what one has written.

reliure /ʀəljyʀ/ *nf* **1** (couverture) binding; **une ~ en cuir/carton** a leather/board binding; **2** (métier, action) bookbinding; **la ~ d'art** (fine) bookbinding.

relogement /ʀ(ə)lɔʒmɑ̃/ *nm* rehousing.

reloger /ʀ(ə)lɔʒe/ [13] *vtr* to rehouse.

relouer /ʀəlwe/ [1] *vtr* **1** [*locataire*] to rent [sth] (**à qn** from sb) again; **2** [*propriétaire*] to relet (**à qn** to sb).

réluctance /ʀelyktɑ̃s/ *nf* Électrotech reluctance.

reluire /ʀ(ə)lɥiʀ/ [69] *vi* [*bois, cuir*] to shine; [*surface mouillée*] to glisten; [*métal*] to shine; (au soleil) to glitter; **~ de propreté** to be sparkling clean.

IDIOMES **il sait passer la brosse à ~** he's a real flatterer.

reluisant, ~e /ʀ(ə)lɥizɑ̃, ɑ̃t/ *adj* lit [*meuble*] shining, shiny; [*surface mouillée*] glistening; [*métal*] shiny; fig **peu ~** [*situation*] far from brilliant.

reluquer◐ /ʀ(ə)lyke/ [1] *vtr* (regarder) to stare at [*personne*]; (avec convoitise) to eye [*objet*]; to eye up○ GB, check out○ US [*personne*]; **~ l'héritage** fig to have one's eye on the inheritance.

rem /ʀɛm/ *nm* rem.

remâcher /ʀ(ə)mɑʃe/ [1] *vtr* **1** (mâcher de nouveau) [*ruminant*] to chew [sth] again; [*personne*] to chew on [*bétel, chique*]; **2**○ (ressasser) to ruminate over, to brood over [*problème, passé*]; to nurse [*rancœur, dépit*].

remaillage /ʀəmajaʒ/ *nm* (de filet) mending the mesh (**de** of); (de bas) mending a ladder GB ou run US (**de** in).

remailler /ʀəmaje/ [1] *vtr* to mend the mesh of [*filet*]; to mend a ladder GB ou run US in [*bas*].

remake /ʀimɛk/ *nm* Cin remake.

rémanence /ʀemanɑ̃s/ *nf* gén persistence; (en magnétisme) remanence; **~ des images visuelles** persistence of vision; **effets de ~ des images visuelles** after-imagery.

rémanent, ~e /ʀemanɑ̃, ɑ̃t/ *adj* [*magnétisme*] residual; [*odeur*] persistent; **image ~e** after-image.

remanger /ʀ(ə)mɑ̃ʒe/ [13] **I** *vtr* to have [sth] again.

II *vi* to eat again.

remaniement /ʀ(ə)manimɑ̃/ *nm* **1** (de plan, projet) modification; **2** (de manuscrit) revision; (radical) redrafting; **3** (d'équipe) reorganization.

■ **~ ministériel** Pol cabinet reshuffle.

remanier /ʀ(ə)manje/ [2] *vtr* **1** to modify, to revise [*plan, projet*]; **2** to alter [*manuscrit*]; (radicalement) to redraft [*manuscrit*]; **3** to reorganize [*équipe*]; Pol to reshuffle [*cabinet, ministère*].

remaquiller /ʀ(ə)makije/ [1] **I** *vtr* to make [sb] up again.

II se remaquiller *vpr* to redo one's make-up; (faire des retouches) to touch up one's make-up.

remarcher /ʀ(ə)maʀʃe/ [1] *vi* **1** [*personne, animal*] to walk again; **2** [*appareil, machine*] to work again.

remariage /ʀ(ə)maʀjaʒ/ *nm* second marriage, remarriage.

remarier /ʀ(ə)maʀje/ [2] **I** *vtr* **elle voudrait ~ son fils** she would like to see her son married again; **elle est remariée à** or **avec un dentiste** her second husband is a dentist.

II se remarier *vpr* to remarry; **se ~ avec** to remarry.

remarquable /ʀ(ə)maʀkabl/ *adj* **1** (exceptionnel) [*qualité, personne, œuvre, produit*] remarkable (**par** for); **d'une intelligence/beauté ~** remarkably intelligent/beautiful; **2** (frappant) [*caractère, trait*] striking; **il est ~ que** it is amazing that; **3** (méritant mention) [*événement, parole, produit*] noteworthy; **je n'ai rien vu ni entendu de ~** I haven't seen or heard anything of note.

remarquablement /ʀ(ə)maʀkabləmɑ̃/ *adv* remarkably.

remarque /ʀ(ə)maʀk/ *nf* **1** (propos) remark; **~s judicieuses/désobligeantes** pertinent/unkind remarks; **faire des ~s** to comment; **elle m'en a fait la ~** she commented on it to me; **je m'en suis fait la ~** I thought the same thing; **2** (note) **mettre des ~s dans la marge** to put a few comments in the margin; **3** Art (en gravure) remarque.

remarqué, ~e /ʀ(ə)maʀke/ **I** *pp* ▶ **remarquer**.

II *pp adj* [*initiative*] noteworthy; [*hausse*] noticeable; **leur entrée/Éva a été très ~e** their entrance/Eva attracted a lot of attention; **ta présence sera sans doute assez ~e** your presence will probably attract quite a lot of attention; **elle a fait un discours particulièrement ~** she gave a speech which attracted particular attention.

remarquer /ʀ(ə)maʀke/ [1] **I** *vtr* **1** (signaler) to point out; **faire ~** to point out; **comme le remarquait** or **faisait ~ Hegel** as Hegel pointed out; **remarque-t-il** he points out; **(faire) ~ que** to point out that; **faire ~ à qn que** to point out to sb that; **elle lui a fait ~ qu'il était en retard** she pointed out to him that he was late; (reproche) **je te ferai ~ que c'était ton idée** may I remind you that it was your idea; **2** (dire) liter to observe (**que** that); **les jours raccourcissent, remarqua-t-il tristement** the days are growing shorter, he observed sadly; **on remarquera que** you will observe that; **3** (voir) to notice [*personne, événement, situation, objet*]; **~ que/comment** to notice that/how; **remarque, ce n'est pas très important** mind you, it's not very important; **remarquons que ce n'est pas la première fois** let us note that it is not the first time; **se faire ~** to draw attention to oneself; **ne te fais pas ~** don't draw attention to yourself; **entrer/sortir sans se faire ~** to come in/to leave unnoticed; **le roman/film mérite d'être remarqué** the novel/film is worthy of attention ou notice; **4** (distinguer) **~ un visage dans la foule** to spot a face in the crowd.

II se remarquer *vpr* **1** (attirer l'attention) [*personne, vêtement, caractéristique*] to attract attention; **2** (se voir) [*qualité, défaut, sentiment*] to show; **mon émotion se remarquait à ma pâleur** one could tell from my pallor that I was deeply affected.

remballer /ʀɑ̃bale/ [1] *vtr* **1** (emballer de nouveau) to pack [sth] up again; (dans du papier) to rewrap; **il peut ~ sa marchandise**○ he can pack up and clear off○ GB ou clear out US; **remballe tes compliments**○ you can stuff◐ your compliments; **2**○ (rabrouer) to send [sb] packing○.

rembarquer /ʀɑ̃baʀke/ [1] *vtr, vi* = **réembarquer**.

rembarrer○ /ʀɑ̃baʀe/ [1] *vtr* to send [sb] packing○; **se faire ~** to be sent packing○.

remblai /ʀɑ̃blɛ/ *nm* **1** (talus) embankment; **route en ~** raised road; (dans marais) causeway; **2** (action) (de fossé) filling in; (de talus) banking up; **travaux de ~** (pour surélever) embankment work; **3** (matériau) **(terre de) ~** (pour rail, route) ballast; (pour fossé) fill; (pour excavation) backfill.

remblaver /ʀɑ̃blave/ [1] *vtr* Agric to resow.

remblayage /ʀɑ̃blɛjaʒ/ *nm* = **remblai 1**, **3**.

remblayer /ʀɑ̃bleje/ [21] *vtr* to fill in [*fossé*]; to bank up [*route, voie ferrée*].

rembobinage /ʀɑ̃bɔbinaʒ/ *nm* rewinding.

rembobiner /ʀɑ̃bɔbine/ [1] *vtr* to rewind.

remboîter /ʀɑ̃bwate/ [1] *vtr* **1** gén **~ qch dans qch** to fit sth back into sth; **~ le pied dans la table** to fit the leg back into the table; **~ des tubes** to fit tubes back together; **2** Méd to relocate [*os*].

rembourrage /ʀɑ̃buʀaʒ/ *nm* (de siège, coussin) stuffing; (d'épaules) Cout padding.

rembourrer /ʀɑ̃buʀe/ [1] *vtr* to stuff [*siège, coussin*]; Cout to pad [*épaules*]; **bien rembourré** hum [*personne*] well-padded.

remboursable /ʀɑ̃buʀsabl/ *adj* [*emprunt, dette, avance*] repayable; [*billet, médicament, soins*] refundable; **~ à 75%** [*médicament, soin*] refundable at 75%; **~ en 10 ans** [*emprunt*] repayable over 10 years.

remboursement /ʀɑ̃buʀsəmɑ̃/ *nm* **1** (de dette, d'emprunt) repayment; **2** (par un commerçant) refund; **votre ticket de caisse sera nécessaire en cas d'échange ou de ~** keep your till receipt in case of exchange or refund; **'le spectacle est annulé, ~ des billets à la caisse'** 'the performance is cancelled, tickets will be refunded at the box office'; **3** (d'argent déboursé) reimbursement, refund; **~ des frais sur justificatif** expenses will be reimbursed ou refunded on production of receipts; **~ des frais médicaux** reimbursement ou refunding of medical expenses; **faire une demande de ~ à la sécurité sociale** to claim for reimbursement ou a refund by the social security services; **je te prête 5 000 francs, pour le ~ on peut s'arranger** I'll lend you 5,000 francs and we can come to an agreement on how you'll pay me back.

rembourser /ʀɑ̃buʀse/ [1] **I** *vtr* **1** (rendre de l'argent prêté par un organisme) to pay off, to repay [*emprunt, dette*]; **~ une dette sur 10 ans** to pay off a debt over 10 years; **2** (en reprenant des marchandises) to give a refund to [*client*]; to refund the price of [*vêtement, article, appareil*]; **~ qch à qn** to give sb a refund on sth; **se faire ~ qch** to get a refund on sth; **votre garantie 'satisfait ou remboursé'** your guarantee 'your money refunded if not completely satisfied'; **nous vous rembourserons tous vos achats sans discuter** the price of all returned goods will be refunded on demand; **le magasin ne rembourse pas mais il donne des avoirs** we do not give refunds on returned goods but we will issue a credit note; **ils m'ont remboursé mon billet d'avion** they gave me a refund for my plane ticket; **les spectateurs ont été remboursés** the spectators have been given a refund; **remboursez! remboursez!** we want our money back!; **3** (rendre de l'argent déboursé) to reimburse [*frais professionnels, employé*]; **~ qn de qch** to pay sb back for sth, to reimburse sb for sth; **~ les frais de qn** to reimburse sb; **la sécurité sociale ne rembourse pas certains médicaments** certain medicines are non-refundable ou are not reimbursed by the social security; **~ une opération** to reimburse the cost of an operation; **médicament remboursé à 40%** medicine refundable ou reimbursed at 40%; **~ un ami** to pay a friend back; **je ne peux te ~ que la moitié de ce que tu m'as prêté hier** I can only pay you back half of what you lent me yesterday; **achète-moi des cigarettes et je te rembourserai** buy me some cigarettes and I'll pay you back; **se faire ~ par sa société** to be reimbursed by one's company; **4** (payer la différence) to refund; **si vous trouvez le même article moins cher ailleurs, nous vous remboursons la différence** if you find the same article cheaper elsewhere, we will refund the difference.

II se rembourser *vpr* to get one's money back; **je me suis remboursé en gardant sa montre** I kept his/her watch by way of payment.

rembrunir: **se rembrunir** /Rɑ̃bRyniR/ [3] *vpr* [*visage*] to darken, cloud over; **elle s'est rembrunie** her face clouded over.

rembrunissement /Rɑ̃bRynismɑ̃/ *nm* littér (de visage) darkening.

remède /R(ə)mɛd/ *nm* **1** (médicament) medicine; **as-tu pris tes ~s?** have you taken your medicines?; **un ~ universel** a universal panacea; **2** (solution) cure (**à, contre** for), remedy (**à, contre** for); **porter ~ à qch** to find a cure ou remedy for sth; **le ~ est pire que le mal** the cure is worse than the disease.

■ **~ de bonne femme** old wives' remedy; **~ de cheval** strong medicine; **~ miracle** miracle cure.

IDIOMES **aux grands maux les grands ~s** desperate times call for desperate measures.

remédier /R(ə)medje/ [2] *vtr ind* **~ à** to remedy [*défaillance, déficit, situation*].

remembrement /R(ə)mɑ̃bRəmɑ̃/ *nm* regrouping of lands.

remembrer /R(ə)mɑ̃bRe/ [1] *vtr* to regroup [*terres*]; to reconstitute [*domaine*].

remémoration /R(ə)memɔRasjɔ̃/ *nf* recall, recollection.

remémorer: **se remémorer** /R(ə)me mɔRe/ [1] *vpr* to recall, to recollect.

remerciement /R(ə)mɛRsimɑ̃/ *nm* thanks (*pl*); **je n'ai pas eu un seul ~** I didn't get a word of thanks; **tous mes ~s** many thanks; **cadeau/lettre de ~** thank you present/letter; **adresser ses ~s à qn** to thank sb; **en ~ de leur aide, elle leur a fait un cadeau** she gave them a present by way of thanks for the help they'd given her; **se confondre en ~s** to thank profusely.

remercier /R(ə)mɛRsje/ [2] *vtr* **1** (dire merci à) to thank (**de, pour** for; **d'avoir fait** for doing); **est-ce que tu as remercié tout le monde?** did you thank everybody?; **je voudrais ~ mes amis/toute l'équipe** I would like to thank my friends/all the team; **nous remercions tout particulièrement M. X** we would particularly like to thank Mr X; **je vous remercie** thank you; **elle l'a remercié chaleureusement/de tout cœur** she thanked him warmly/wholeheartedly; **tu peux me ~!** you have me to thank for that!; **il nous a remerciés de l'avoir accueilli/conseillé** he thanked us for having welcomed/advised him; **remercions le ciel d'être encore en vie** thank God we are still alive; **nous vous remercions d'adresser votre courrier à...** please address your letters to...; **2** (congédier) iron to dismiss, to let [sb] go.

réméré /RemeRe/ *nm* Jur right of reemption; **vendre à ~** to sell with a right of reemption.

remettant /Rəmɛtɑ̃/ *nm* Fin remitter; **signature du ~** remitter's signature.

remettre /R(ə)mɛtR/ [60] **I** *vtr* **1** (replacer) **~ qch dans/sur** to put sth back in/on; **remettez la bouteille au frais** put the bottle back to cool; **remets ce livre là où tu l'as pris!** put that book back where you found it!; **~ qch à cuire** (sur la cuisinière) to put sth back on the ring; (dans le four) to put sth back in the oven; **~ qch à sécher** (dehors) to hang the washing ou wash US out again; **~ la main sur qch** to put one's hands on sth again; **~ qch en mémoire à qn** to remind sb of sth; **~ qn en prison/en pension** to send sb back to prison/to boarding school; **~ qn dans un service** to put sb back in a department; **2** (donner) **~ qch à qn** to hand sth over to sb [*clés, rançon*]; to hand sth in to sb [*lettre, colis, rapport, devoir*]; to present sth to sb [*récompense, trophée, médaille*]; **~ sa démission** to hand in one's resignation (**à qn** to sb); **~ sa vie entre les mains de qn** to put one's life in sb's hands; **~ qn entre les mains de la justice** to hand sb over to the law; **3** (rétablir) **~ qch droit** or **d'aplomb** to put sth straight again; **~ qch à plat** to lay sth down again; **~ qch sur le côté** to put sth back on its side; **~ qch debout** to stand sth back up; **4** (différer) to postpone, to put off [*visite, voyage, rendez-vous, réunion*]; to defer [*jugement*]; **~ une visite à une date ultérieure** to postpone a visit until a later date; **nous avons remis la réunion à jeudi** we've put the meeting off until Thursday; **~ qch au lendemain/à plus tard** to put sth off until tomorrow/until later; **5** (faire fonctionner de nouveau) to put [sth] on again, to put [sth] back on [*gaz, électricité, chauffage, ventilateur*]; to play [sth] again [*disque, cassette, chanson*]; to turn [sth] on again [*contact*]; **tu peux ~ le courant, j'ai terminé** you can put the electricity back on, I've finished; **~ les essuie-glaces/phares** to switch the windscreen GB ou windshield US wipers/headlights on again; **6** (remplacer) **~ un bouton à qch** to put a new button on sth; **~ une poignée** to put a new handle on; **~ une vis/vitre** to put a new screw/windowpane in; **7** (ajouter) to add some more [*sel, poivre, bois, plâtre, papier*]; to add another [*bouton, vis, clou*]; to put in another [*suppositoire*]; **remets un peu d'eau/d'huile** add a bit more water/oil; **~ de l'argent dans qch** to put some more money in sth; **j'ai remis 15 francs** I've put in another 15 francs; **remettez-moi quelques tomates**○ give me a few more tomatoes; **8** (porter de nouveau) (ce que l'on vient d'enlever) to put [sth] back on [*chaussures, manteau, bijou*]; (ce que l'on portait dans le passé) to wear [sth] again [*chaussures, manteau, bijou*]; **tu peux ~ tes chaussures, on s'en va** you can put your shoes back on, we're going; **ne remets pas ces chaussettes, elles sont sales** don't wear these socks again, they're dirty; **il va falloir ~ les bottes, c'est l'hiver** we'll have to start wearing our boots again, it's winter; **9** Méd to put [sth] back [*épaule, cheville*]; **10** (réconforter) [*remontant, médicament*] to make [sb] feel better; **buvez, cela vous remettra** drink up, it'll make you feel better; **11** (se souvenir de) **~ qn/le visage de qn** to remember sb/sb's face; **12** (faire grâce de) **~ une dette à qn** to let sb off a debt; **~ une peine à qn** to give sb remission; **~ ses péchés à qn** to forgive sb's sins; **13**○ (recommencer) **~ ça** to start again; **tu ne vas pas ~ ça!** you're not going to start again, are you?; **on s'est bien amusé, quand est-ce qu'on remet ça?** that was fun, when are we going to do it again?

II se remettre *vpr* **1** (retourner) **se ~ à un endroit** to go ou get back to a place; **remets-toi là/devant lui** get back there/in front of him; **se ~ au lit/à sa place/à table** to go back to bed/to one's seat/to the table; **se ~ en rang** to get back in line; **se ~ debout** to get up and stand up again; **se ~ en selle** to get back in the saddle; **2** (s'appliquer à nouveau) **se ~ du mascara/rouge à lèvres** to put on some more mascara/lipstick; **se ~ un suppositoire** to put in another suppository; **3** (recommencer) **se ~ au travail** to go back to work; **se ~ au dessin/tennis/piano** to start drawing/playing tennis/playing the piano again; **se ~ à faire** to start doing again; **se ~ à boire/espérer/pleurer** to start drinking/hoping/crying again; **il s'est remis à neiger/faire du vent** it's started to snow/to get windy again; **4** (porter sur soi à nouveau) **se ~ en jean/jupe** to wear jeans/a skirt again; **5** (se rétablir) **se ~ de** to recover from [*maladie, accouchement, accident*]; to get over [*déception, émotion, échec, décès*]; **il ne s'est jamais vraiment remis de sa chute** he never really recovered from his fall; **remets-toi vite!** get well soon!; **t'es-tu remis de tes émotions?** have you got over the shock?; **il ne se remet pas de son divorce** he can't get over his divorce; **6** (faire confiance) **s'en ~ à qn** to leave it to sb; **s'en ~ à la décision/aux conclusions de qn** to accept sb's decision/conclusions; **7** (reprendre une vie de couple) **se ~ avec qn** to get back together with sb; **ils se sont remis ensemble après un an de séparation** they got back together after splitting up for a year; **8** (se rappeler) **se ~ qn/le visage de qn** to remember sb/sb's face.

remeubler /R(ə)mœble/ [1] **I** *vtr* to refurnish [*logement*]; to supply [sb] with new furniture [*personne*].

II se remeubler *vpr* to replace one's furniture.

rémige /Remiʒ/ *nf* remex.

remilitarisation /Rəmilitarizasjɔ̃/ *nf* remilitarization.

remilitariser /Rəmilitarize/ [1] *vtr* to remilitarize.

reminéraliser /RəmineRalize/ [1] *vtr* **~ son organisme** to replenish the minerals in one's body.

réminiscence /Reminisɑ̃s/ *nf* **1** Philos, Psych (faculté de rappel) reminiscence; **2** (souvenir) recollection; **sauf quelques vagues ~s** apart from a vague recollection; **3** (rappel) **il y a dans cette œuvre des ~s de Bach** this work is reminiscent of Bach.

remise /R(ə)miz/ *nf* **1** (transmission) **la ~ de la rançon est prévue à 20 heures** the ransom is due to be handed over at 8 pm; **attendre la ~ des clés/du matériel** to wait for the keys/material to be handed over; **~ des clés au locataire à 14 heures** keys will be handed over to the tenant at 2 pm; **la date limite de ~ des mémoires/rapports est fixée au 15 juin** the deadline for handing in the dissertations/reports is 15 June; **~ des prix** prizegiving; **~ des médailles/récompenses** medals/awards ceremony; **être invité à la ~ des coupes** to be invited to the presentation of the trophies; **2** Comm (rabais) discount; **faire** or **accorder une ~ de 50 francs/20%** to give a 50 franc/20% discount (**sur qch** on sth); **3** (de dette, péchés) remission; **une ~ de peine** a remission; **bénéficier d'une ~ de peine** to get remission; **4** Fin remittance; **~ de fonds** remittance of funds; **~ d'un effet à l'encaissement** remittance of a bill for collection; **5** (bâtiment) shed; **6** Chasse cover.

■ **~ de cause** Jur adjournment (of hearing).

remiser /R(ə)mize/ [1] *vtr* to put [sth] away [*skis, vieux vêtements, livres*] (**dans** in); **~ des jouets au grenier** to put toys away in the attic.

remisier /R(ə)mizje/ ▶ 510 *nm* (intermediate) broker.

rémissible /Remisibl/ *adj* remissible.

rémission /Remisjɔ̃/ *nf* **1** (de faute, péchés) remission, forgiveness; **sans ~** (sans indulgence) [*punir, condamner*] mercilessly; (sans interruption) [*pleuvoir, travailler*] without stopping; **2** Méd remission; **être en (phase de) ~** [*patient, maladie, douleur*] to be in remission; **3** fig (amélioration) recovery.

rémittence /Remitɑ̃s/ *nf* remission.

rémittent, ~e /Remitɑ̃, ɑ̃t/ *adj* [*fièvre*] remittent.

remmaillage /Rɑ̃mɑjaʒ/ *nm* = **remaillage**.

remmailler /Rɑ̃mɑje/ [1] *vtr* = **remailler**.

remmancher /Rɑ̃mɑ̃ʃe/ [1] *vtr* to put the handle back on.

remmener /Rɑ̃mne/ [16] *vtr* to take [sb] back.

remobiliser /ʀəmɔbilize/ [1] *vtr* lit, fig to remobilize.

remodelage /ʀəmɔdlaʒ/ *nm* (de nez, d'ébauche) reshaping; (d'administration) restructuring; (de quartier) replanning.

remodeler /ʀəmɔdle/ [17] *vtr* to restructure [*administration*]; to reshape [*nez, ébauche*]; to replan [*quartier*].

rémois, **~e** /ʀemwa, az/ ▶857 *adj* of Reims.

Rémois, **~e** /ʀemwa, az/ ▶857 *nm,f* (natif) native of Reims; (habitant) inhabitant of Reims.

remontage /ʀ(ə)mɔ̃taʒ/ *nm* (de moteur, pièces) reassembly; (d'un tuyau) reconnection; **le ~ du mécanisme/de la montre** winding up the mechanism/the watch.

remontant, **~e** /ʀ(ə)mɔ̃tɑ̃, ɑ̃t/ **I** *adj* Hort [*rosier, fraisier*] remontant.
II *nm* pick-me-up○, tonic; **j'ai besoin d'un petit ~** I need a pick-me-up○.

remonte /ʀ(ə)mɔ̃t/ *nf* **1** Naut **la ~ d'un fleuve/du Nil** travelling[GB] upstream/up the Nile; **2** Zool (des saumons) run; **3** Équit, Mil remount.

remontée /ʀ(ə)mɔ̃te/ *nf* **1** (action de remonter) climb up; **la ~ des spéléologues de la grotte** the potholers' GB ou spelunkers' US climb up from the cave; **la ~ au village fut difficile** the climb back up to the village was difficult; **la ~ de la Saône en péniche** going up the Saône by barge; **2** (après une baisse) (de prix, taux, bénéfices) rise (**de** of); (de sportif, d'homme politique) recovery (**de** of); (d'influence, de parti) rise (**de** of); (de violence, d'incidents) increase (**de** in); **la ~ des eaux** the rise in the water levels; **faire une belle ~** [*coureur, candidat*] to make a good recovery; **les cours du pétrole poursuivent leur ~** oil prices continue to rise; **la ~ du candidat de la majorité dans les sondages est spectaculaire** the rise of the ruling party's candidate in the opinion polls is spectacular.
■ **~ mécanique** Sport, Tech ski lift.

remonte-pente, *pl* **~s** /ʀ(ə)mɔ̃tpɑ̃t/ *nm* ski-tow.

remonter /ʀ(ə)mɔ̃te/ [1] **I** *vtr* **1** (transporter de nouveau) (en haut) gén to take [sb/sth] back up [*personne, objet*] (**à** to); (à l'étage) to take [sb/sth] back upstairs [*personne, objet*]; (d'en bas) gén to bring [sb/sth] back up [*personne, objet*] (**de** from); (de l'étage) to bring [sb/sth] back upstairs [*personne, objet*]; **~ les valises au grenier** to take the suitcases back up to the attic; **~ les bouteilles de la cave** to bring the bottles back up from the cellar; **je peux vous ~ au village** I can take you back up to the village; **remonte-moi mes pantoufles** bring my slippers back up (to me); **je leur ai fait ~ les valises au grenier** I made them take the suitcases back up to the attic; **j'ai fait ~ le piano dans la chambre** I had the piano taken back up to the bedroom; **faites-moi ~ les dossiers secrets** get the secret files brought back up to me; **2** (remettre en haut) to put [sth] back up [*valise, boîte*]; **~ la valise sur l'armoire** to put the suitcase back up on the wardrobe; **~ un seau d'un puits** to pull a bucket up from a well; **3** (relever) to raise [*étagère, store, tableau*] (**de** by); to wind [sth] back up [*vitre de véhicule*]; to roll up [*manches, jambes de pantalon*]; to hitch up [*jupe, pantalon*]; to turn up [*col*]; to pull up [*chaussettes*]; **~ une étagère de 20 centimètres/d'un cran** to raise a shelf another 20 centimetres[GB]/by another notch; **~ une note de deux points** to raise a mark GB ou grade US by two points; **4** (parcourir de nouveau) [*personne*] (en allant) to go back up [*pente, rue, étage*]; to go ou climb back up [*escalier, marches, échelle*]; (en venant) to come back up [*pente, rue, marches, échelle*]; [*voiture, automobiliste*] to drive back up [*pente, route*]; **nous avons remonté la colline à pied** (en marchant) we walked back up the hill; (et non à bicyclette) we went back up the hill on foot; **~ la colline en rampant/à bicyclette** to crawl/cycle back up the hill; **il m'a fait ~ l'escalier en courant** he made me run back up the stairs; **5** (parcourir en sens inverse) [*bateau*] to sail up [*fleuve, canal*]; [*poisson*] to swim up [*rivière*]; [*personne, voiture*] to go up [*rue, boulevard*]; **tu remontes l'avenue jusqu'à la banque** you go up the avenue until you get to the bank; **~ un canal en péniche** to go up a canal in a barge; **~ une rivière en canoë/en yacht/à la nage** to canoe/sail/swim up a river; **~ un boulevard à bicyclette/en voiture** to cycle/drive up a boulevard; **~ le flot de voyageurs** to walk against the flow of passengers; **~ une filière** or **piste** fig to follow a trail (**jusqu'à qn** to sb); **~ le temps par la pensée** or **l'imagination** to go back in time in one's imagination; **6** (rattraper dans un classement) [*cycliste*] to catch up with [*peloton, concurrent*]; **7** (réconforter) **~ qn** or **le moral de qn** to cheer sb up, to raise sb's spirits; **la nouvelle/il m'a remonté le moral** the news/he cheered me up; **8** (assembler de nouveau) to put [sth] back together again [*armoire, table, jouet*]; to re-erect [*échafaudage*]; to reassemble [*moteur, machine*]; to put [sth] back [*roue*]; **il s'amuse à démonter et ~ ses jouets** he's having fun taking his toys apart and putting them back together again; **9** (retendre le ressort de) to wind [sth] up [*mécanisme, montre, réveil*]; to wind [sth] up [*boîte à musique*] (**avec** with); **être remonté à bloc**○ fig [*personne*] to be full of energy; **10** (remettre en scène) to revive [*pièce, spectacle*].
II *vi* **1** (monter de nouveau) [*personne*] (en allant) gén to go back up, to go up again (**à** to); (à l'étage) to go back upstairs, to go upstairs again; (en venant) gén to come back up, to come up again (**de** from); (à l'étage) to come back upstairs, to come upstairs again; (après être redescendu) (en allant) to go back up again; (en venant) to come back up again; [*train, ascenseur, téléphérique*] (en allant) to go back up; (en venant) to come back up; [*avion, hélicoptère*] to climb again; [*oiseau*] to fly up again; [*prix, taux, monnaie*] to go up again; [*chemin, route*] to rise again; [*mer*] to come in again; [*température, baromètre*] to rise again, to go up again; **reste ici, je remonte au grenier** stay here, I'm going back up to the attic; **peux-tu ~ chercher mon sac?** can you go back upstairs and get my bag?; **tu es remonté à pied?** gén did you walk back up?; (plutôt que par l'ascenseur) did you come back up on foot?; **je préfère ~ par l'escalier** I prefer to go back up by the stairs; **nous sommes remontés par le sentier/la route** (à pied) we walked back up by the path/the road; (à cheval) we rode back up by the path/the road; **il est remonté vers moi en rampant** he crawled back up to me; **il est remonté au col à bicyclette/en voiture** he cycled/drove back up to the pass; **où est l'écureuil? il a dû ~ à l'arbre** where's the squirrel? it must have gone back up the tree; **je suis remonté en haut de la tour/au sommet de la falaise** I went back up to the top of the tower/to the top of the cliff; **elle est remontée dans sa chambre** she went back up to her bedroom; **~ à l'échelle/la corde** to climb back up the ladder/the rope; **~ sur** [*personne*] to step back onto [*trottoir, marche*]; [*personne, animal*] to climb back onto [*mur, tabouret*]; **il est remonté sur le toit** [*enfant, chat*] he's gone back up onto the roof; **~ dans son lit** to get back into bed; **~ à la surface** lit [*plongeur*] to surface; [*huile, objet*] to rise to the surface; fig [*scandale*] to resurface; [*souvenirs*] to surface again; **~ à cheval** to get back on a horse; **~ en voiture/dans le train** to get back in the car/on the train; **~ à bord d'un avion** to board a plane again; **~ dans les sondages** [*politicien, parti*] to move up in the opinion polls; **~ de la quinzième à la troisième place** [*sportif, équipe*] to move up from fifteenth to third position; **~ à Paris** (retourner) to go back up to Paris; **la criminalité remonte** crime is rising again; **les cours sont remontés de 20%** prices have gone up another 20%; **faire ~ le dollar** to send ou put the dollar up again; **faire ~ les cours** to put prices up again; **le franc est remonté par rapport à la livre** the franc has gone up ou risen against the pound again; **faire ~ la température** gén to raise the temperature; Méd to raise one's temperature; **2** (pour retrouver l'origine) **~ dans le temps** to go back in time; **~ à** [*historien*] to go back to [*époque, date*]; [*événement, œuvre, tradition*] to date back to [*époque, date, personnage historique*]; [*habitude*] to be carried over from [*enfance, période*]; [*enquêteur, police*] to follow the trail back to [*personne, chef de gang*]; **~ 20 ans en arrière** [*historien*] to go back 20 years; **l'histoire remonte à quelques jours** the story goes back a few days; **il nous a fallu ~ jusqu'en 1770** we had to go back to 1770; **les manuscrits remontent au XIe siècle** the manuscripts date back to the 11th century; **~ à l'époque où** to date back to the days when; **~ aux causes de qch** to identify the causes of sth; **faire ~** to trace (back) [*origines, ancêtres*] (**à** to); **3** (se retrousser) [*pull, jupe*] to ride up; **4** (se faire sentir) **les odeurs d'égout remontent dans la maison** the smell from the drains reaches our house; **j'ai mon petit déjeuner qui remonte**○ my breakfast is repeating on me○; **5** Naut **~ au** or **dans le vent** to sail into the wind.
III se remonter *vpr* **1** (se réconforter) **se ~ le moral** (seul) to cheer oneself up; (à plusieurs) to cheer each other up; **2** (s'équiper de nouveau) **se ~ en meubles/draps** to get some new furniture/sheets; **se ~ en vin** to replenish one's stock ou supply of wine.

remontoir /ʀ(ə)mɔ̃twaʀ/ *nm* (de jouet, d'horloge) winder, key; (de montre, réveil) winder.

remontrance /ʀ(ə)mɔ̃tʀɑ̃s/ *nf* **1** (reproche) reprimand, remonstrance ¢ sout; **faire des ~s à qn à propos de qch** to reprimand sb for sth; **2** Hist remonstrance.

remontrer /ʀ(ə)mɔ̃tʀe/ [1] **I** *vtr* to show [sth] again (**à qn** to sb).
II *vi* **en ~ à qn** (lui donner une leçon) to teach sb a thing or two; (montrer sa supériorité) to prove one's superiority to sb.
III se remontrer *vpr* to show one's face again.

remords /ʀ(ə)mɔʀ/ *nm inv* remorse ¢; **rongé par le ~** eaten up with remorse; **manifester du** or **des ~** to show remorse; **sans le moindre ~** without the slightest remorse; **plein de ~** filled with remorse, remorseful; **avoir** or **éprouver quelque ~ à avoir fait** to feel some remorse for doing; **~ de conscience** twinge of conscience.

remorquage /ʀ(ə)mɔʀkaʒ/ *nm* towing; **'dépannage, ~'** Aut 'breakdown and recovery service' GB, 'towing service' US.

remorque /ʀ(ə)mɔʀk/ *nf* **1** (câble) towrope; (action) tow; **'véhicule en ~'** 'on tow' GB, 'in tow' US; **prendre une voiture en ~** to tow a car; **être à la ~** fig to trail behind; **être à la ~ de qn** fig to tag along behind sb; **2** (vehicule) trailer; **~ de secours routier** breakdown truck GB, tow truck US.

remorquer /ʀ(ə)mɔʀke/ [1] *vtr* **1** lit to tow [*véhicule*] (**jusqu'à** to); **~ un navire au port/jusqu'à la sortie du port** to tow a ship into harbour[GB]/out of the harbour[GB]; **se faire ~** to be towed; **2** fig to drag [sb] along.

remorqueur /ʀ(ə)mɔʀkœʀ/ *nm* tug.

rémoulade /ʀemulad/ *nf* rémoulade, mayonnaise-type dressing; **céleri ~** celeriac in rémoulade.

remoulage /ʀ(ə)mulaʒ/ *nm* **1** Art (action) recasting; (résultat) recast; **2** (de grain) regrinding; (de farine) remilling.

remouler /ʀ(ə)mule/ [1] *vtr* Art to recast.

rémouleur /ʀemulœʀ/ ▶510 *nm* grinder.

remous /ʀ(ə)mu/ *nm inv* **1** (dans l'eau, l'air) eddy; **2** (sillage) backwash (*tjrs sg*); (contre la rive) wash (*tjrs sg*); **3** Aviat (sillage) slipstream (*tjrs sg*); **4** (agitation) (de sentiments, d'idées) turmoil **¢**; (dans foule) movement; (dans opinion, auditoire) stir **¢**; **les grands ~ de l'histoire** the great upheavals of history; **le parti est agité par des ~** the party is troubled by unrest.

rempaillage /ʀɑ̃pɑjaʒ/ *nm* reseating.

rempailler /ʀɑ̃pɑje/ [1] *vtr* to reseat [*chaise*].

rempailleur, -euse /ʀɑ̃pɑjœʀ, øz/ **▶510** *nm,f* repairer of rush seats.

rempaqueter /ʀɑ̃pakte/ [20] *vtr* to pack [sth] up again.

rempart /ʀɑ̃paʀ/ *nm* **1** (mur) rampart; (de château-fort) battlements (*pl*); **les ~s de la ville** the city walls, the ramparts; **2** (défense) defence[GB] (**contre** against); **faire un ~ de son corps à qn** to shield sb with one's body.

rempiler /ʀɑ̃pile/ [1] **I** *vtr* to restack [*boîtes*].
II *vi*○ soldiers' slang to re-enlist.

remplaçable /ʀɑ̃plasabl/ *adj* replaceable.

remplaçant, ~e /ʀɑ̃plasɑ̃, ɑ̃t/ **I** *adj* [*professeur, instituteur*] supply GB, substitute US; [*joueur, footballeur*] substitute, reserve.
II *nm,f* **1** (provisoire) gén substitute, replacement; (professeur, instituteur) supply GB, substitute US; (acteur) stand-in; Sport substitute, reserve; **2** (définitif) successor.

remplacement /ʀɑ̃plasmɑ̃/ *nm* **1** (de personne) replacement; **le ~ de Pierre par Paul à la direction** the replacement of Pierre by Paul as director; **il a été nommé en ~ de M. Robin** he was appointed as a replacement for Mr Robin ou to replace Mr Robin; **assurer le ~ d'un collègue pendant ses vacances/son congé de maladie** to stand in for ou cover for a colleague during his vacation/his sick leave; **faire des ~s** [*enseignant*] to do supply teaching GB, to do substitute teaching US; [*intérimaire*] to do temporary work, to do temping jobs○; **il a fait trois ~s ce mois-ci** [*enseignant*] he had three supply GB ou substitute US teaching assignments this month; [*intérimaire*] he had three temporary ou temping jobs this month; **2** (de chose) replacement; **le ~ d'une pièce usée/de carreaux cassés** the replacement of a worn part/of broken windowpanes; **ils m'ont donné une télévision neuve en ~ de la vieille** they gave me a new television to replace the old one; **émission diffusée en ~ d'une autre** programme[GB] broadcast in place of another; **produit de ~** substitute.

remplacer /ʀɑ̃plase/ [12] **I** *vtr* **1** (prendre momentanément la place de) to stand in for, to cover for [*collègue, docteur, professeur, employé, acteur*]; **~ qn à une réunion** to stand in for sb at a meeting; **c'est lui qui remplace le docteur Dubois** he's standing in for ou covering for Doctor Dubois; **elle s'est fait ~ par un collègue ce jour-là** she got a colleague to stand in for her that day; **elle a été remplacée par M. Pichon pendant son absence** Mr Pichon stood in for her while she was away; **est-ce que tu peux me ~ au standard cinq minutes?** can you take over from me at the switchboard for five minutes?; **2** (succéder à) to replace, to succeed [*personne*]; to replace, to take over from [*méthode, technologie, tradition*]; **M. Bon remplace Mme Roux à la direction** Mr Bon is replacing ou succeeds Mrs Roux as director; **~ qn comme patron** to take over from sb as the boss; **l'ancien moteur a été remplacé par un nouveau** the old engine has been replaced by a new one; **le disque laser remplace peu à peu le disque vinyle** the compact disc is gradually taking over from ou replacing the record; **3** (changer) to replace [*pièce, matériel, personne*] (**par** with); **~ un carreau** to replace ou change a windowpane; **tous les téléphones à pièces ont été remplacés par des téléphones à cartes** all the coinbox telephones have been replaced with cardphones; **~ qn comme ministre** to remove sb from the post of minister; **remplacez le nom par le pronom qui convient** replace the noun with the appropriate pronoun; **ils m'ont remplacé ma télévision** they gave me a replacement for my TV set; **4** (tenir lieu de) to replace; **le pronom remplace le nom** the pronoun takes the place of ou replaces the noun; **on peut ~ le vinaigre par du jus de citron** you can use lemon juice as a substitute for vinegar; **ce produit n'est pas mal mais ne remplace pas le vrai sel** this product isn't bad but it's no substitute for real salt.

rempli, ~e /ʀɑ̃pli/ **I** *pp* **▶ remplir**.
II *pp adj* **récit ~ de détails amusants** story full of ou filled with amusing details; **texte ~ d'erreurs/de fautes/de clichés** text full of ou riddled with errors/with mistakes/with clichés; **une vie bien ~e** a full life; **une journée bien ~e** a busy day; **un emploi du temps ~** a busy schedule; **avoir le portefeuille bien ~**○ to be well-heeled○, to be rich.
III *nm* Cout tuck.

remplir /ʀɑ̃pliʀ/ [3] **I** *vtr* **1** (dans l'espace) to fill (up) [*récipient, verre, assiette, sac, tiroir*] (**de** with); to fill in ou out [*formulaire, questionnaire*]; **un verre rempli à ras bord** a glass filled to the brim; **il vida son verre d'un trait et le remplit à nouveau** he drained his glass and refilled it ou filled it up again; **~ qch à moitié** to half fill sth; **un verre à moitié rempli** a half-filled glass; **~ qch aux deux tiers** to fill sth two thirds full; **les manifestants ont rempli les rues de la ville** the demonstrators filled the streets; **sa vie est remplie de petites contrariétés** fig his life is full of small vexations; **~ qn de joie/d'espoir/d'amertume** fig to fill sb with joy/with hope/with bitterness; **~ qn d'aise** fig to delight sb; **il a rempli des centaines de pages sur un sujet qui n'intéresse personne** he wrote hundreds of pages on a subject nobody's interested in; **une barque remplie d'eau** a waterlogged boat; **le chanteur remplit des salles de 10 000 places** the singer draws in ou pulls in crowds of 10,000; **il n'a pas réussi à ~ l'Olympia lors de son unique concert** he didn't manage to fill the Olympia when he gave his only concert; **2** (s'acquitter de) [*personne*] to carry out, to perform [*rôle, mission, fonction*]; to fulfil[GB], to carry out [*devoir, obligations, objectifs*]; to fulfil[GB] [*engagements*]; [*objet, dispositif*] to fulfil[GB] [*rôle, fonction*]; **~ les conditions** to fulfil[GB] ou meet the conditions.
II se remplir *vpr* [*récipient, salle, rues, ciel*] to fill (up) (**de** with).

remplissage /ʀɑ̃plisaʒ/ *nm* **1** (de récipient) filling; **coefficient** or **taux de ~** Transp occupancy rate; **2** pej (par manque d'inspiration) padding; **il y a beaucoup de ~ dans ce film/livre** there's a lot of padding in this film/book; **faire du ~** to pad out one's work.

remplumer: **se remplumer** /ʀɑ̃plyme/ [1] *vpr* **1**○ [*personne*] (en argent) to get back on one's feet; (en poids) to put some weight back on; **2** [*oiseau*] to grow new feathers.

rempocher /ʀɑ̃pɔʃe/ [1] *vtr* to put [sth] back in one's pocket [*argent*]; **rempoche tes compliments**○ you can keep your compliments○.

remporter /ʀɑ̃pɔʀte/ [1] *vtr* **1** (gagner) to win [*épreuve, siège, titre, victoire*]; **la pièce a remporté un vif succès** the play was a great success; **2** (reprendre) to take [sth] away again.

rempotage /ʀɑ̃pɔtaʒ/ *nm* repotting.

rempoter /ʀɑ̃pɔte/ [1] *vtr* to repot.

remuant, ~e /ʀ(ə)mɥɑ̃, ɑ̃t/ *adj* **1** (agité) [*spectateur, adolescent, partisan*] rowdy; **2** (actif) [*enfant*] boisterous; [*adulte*] energetic.

remue-ménage /ʀ(ə)mymenaʒ/ *nm inv* **1** (désordre et confusion) chaos **¢**; **faire du ~** to cause chaos; **2** (mouvements en tous sens) bustle **¢**; **3** (changements) upheaval; **~ au gouvernement** upheaval in the government.

remue-méninges /ʀəmymenɛ̃ʒ/ *nm inv* brainstorming.

remuer /ʀ(ə)mɥe/ [1] **I** *vtr* **1** (mouvoir) to move; **~ les doigts/la main/le bras** to move one's fingers/one's hand/one's arm; **je ne peux plus ~ les orteils** I can't wiggle ou move my toes; **il remuait les lèvres en silence** his lips moved silently; **elle marche en remuant les hanches** she wiggles her hips when she walks; **peux-tu ~ les oreilles?** can you wiggle your ears?; **le chien remuait la queue** the dog was wagging its tail; **2** (secouer) [*personne*] to shake [*objet*]; [*vent*] to shake [*branche, feuilles, arbres*]; [*vagues, vent*] to toss [*bateau*]; **arrête de ~ la table** stop shaking the table; **3** (déplacer) [*personne*] to move [*personne, objet lourd*]; **il a tout remué dans le tiroir pour retrouver la clé** he turned the whole drawer upside down to find the key; **▶ ciel**; **4** Culin to stir [*soupe, sauce, café, pâtes*]; to toss [*salade*]; **remuez sans arrêt** stir constantly; **5** (brasser) lit to turn over [*terre*]; to poke [*cendres*]; fig to mull over [*pensées, chimères, idées*]; to handle [*argent*]; **6** (évoquer) to rake up [*passé, vieille histoire*]; to stir up [*souvenirs*]; **7** (bouleverser) to upset [*personne*]; (émouvoir) to move; **j'en suis encore toute remuée** I still feel very upset by it.
II *vi* (bouger) [*personne*] to move; [*enfant*] to fidget; [*feuilles*] to flutter; [*bateau*] to bob up and down; **entendre ~** to hear movement; **le vent fait ~ les feuilles** the leaves flutter in the wind; **le vent fait ~ les arbres** the trees sway in the wind.
III se remuer○ *vpr* **1** (sortir de son apathie) to get a move on○; **allez, remue-toi!** come on, get a move on○!; **2** (faire des efforts) **se ~ pour faire** to make an effort to do; **il s'est beaucoup remué pour avoir ce travail** he made a big effort to get this job.

remugle /ʀ(ə)mygl/ *nm* stale smell; **sentir le ~** to smell stale.

rémunérateur, -trice /ʀemyneʀatœʀ, tʀis/ *adj* lucrative.

rémunération /ʀemyneʀasjɔ̃/ *nf* (de travail) pay (**de** for); (de service) payment (**de** for); (d'investissement) return (**de** on); (de compte) interest (**de** on); **toucher une forte ~** (pour un travail, service) to be very well paid; (sur un compte) to receive high interest.
■ **~ du capital** Fin return on capital.

rémunérer /ʀemyneʀe/ [14] *vtr* to pay [*personne*]; to pay for [*service, travail*]; **bien/mal rémunéré** well/poorly paid.

renâcler /ʀ(ə)nɑkle/ [1] *vi* **1** [*personne*] to show reluctance; **~ à qch/à faire** to balk at sth/at doing; **~ devant un plat** to turn up one's nose at a dish; **sans ~** without complaining; **en renâclant** grudgingly; **~ à la besogne** to be workshy; **elle ne renâcle pas à la besogne** she's not afraid of hard work; **2** [*animal*] to snort.

renaissance /ʀ(ə)nɛsɑ̃s/ *nf* Relig rebirth; fig revival.

Renaissance /ʀ(ə)nɛsɑ̃s/ *nf* Hist Renaissance; **meubles ~** Renaissance furniture.

renaissant, ~e /ʀ(ə)nɛsɑ̃, ɑ̃t/ *adj* [*idéologie, violence, démocratie*] re-emergent.

renaître /ʀ(ə)nɛtʀ/ [74] *vi* **1** [*personne, région, théâtre, nature*] to come back to life; **il se sent ~** he feels he's coming back to life; **faire ~ une région/une activité** to revive a region/an activity; **~ à la vie/à l'amour** to rediscover life/love; **~ de ses cendres** to rise from the ashes; **2** (réapparaître) [*désir, peur, espoir, forces*] to return; [*violence, idéologie*] to re-emerge; **faire ~ l'espoir/l'amour** to bring new hope/love; **faire ~ la peur/les passions** to renew fear/passions.

rénal, **~e**, *mpl* **-aux** /ʀenal, o/ *adj* [*artère, veine*] renal; [*infection*] kidney (*épith*).

renard /ʀ(ə)naʀ/ *nm* **1** (animal, fourrure) fox; **2** (personne) cunning devil.

■ **~ argenté** silver fox; **~ bleu** blue fox; **~ de mer** thresher shark.

IDIOMES **être rusé comme un ~** to be as cunning as a fox.

renarde /ʀ(ə)naʀd/ *nf* vixen.

renardeau, *pl* **~x** /ʀ(ə)naʀdo/ *nm* fox cub.

renardière /ʀ(ə)naʀdjɛʀ/ *nf* fox's earth.

renauder†○ /ʀ(ə)node/ [1] *vi* to grouse○.

rencaisser /ʀɑ̃kese/ [1] *vtr* **1** Hort to rebox; **2**○ **rencaisse ton argent/tes compliments** you can keep your money/your compliments; **rencaisse tes affaires** pack your things; **rencaisse ta guitare** put that guitar away.

rencard○ = **rancard**.

rencarder○ /ʀɑ̃kaʀde/ [1] *vtr* = **rancarder**.

renchérir /ʀɑ̃ʃeʀiʀ/ [3] **I** *vtr* (rendre plus cher) [*dépréciation, réévaluation, hausse*] to increase, to put [sth] up [*prix, coût*]; to make [sth] more expensive, to put [sth] up [*exportations, biens, produits*].

II *vi* **1** (ajouter) to add; **'nous sommes très satisfaits,' renchérit-il** 'we are very satisfied,' he added; **peu après Pierre renchérissait en disant...** soon after Pierre went further, saying...; **~ sur ce que dit qn** to add something to what sb says; **il renchérit sur tout ce que je dis** he takes everything I say (one step) further; **et son ami de ~: 'tu as absolument raison'** 'you're absolutely right,' his friend added; **2** (aller plus loin) to go one step further; **il a renchéri en cassant une assiette/en envoyant l'armée** he went one step further and broke a plate/and sent in the army; **3** (dans une vente) to raise the bidding; **~ sur le prix de qch** to make a higher bid for sth; **il a renchéri sur la dernière offre** he raised the bidding.

renchérissement /ʀɑ̃ʃeʀismɑ̃/ *nm* increase, rise; **le ~ des loyers/du pétrole** the increase in rents/in the price of oil; **un ~ de 16%** an increase of 16%.

rencontre /ʀɑ̃kɔ̃tʀ/ *nf* **1** (réunion) meeting (**avec** with; **entre** between); **~ de Londres** London meeting; **~ des deux présidents** meeting between the two presidents; **aller/venir à la rencontre de qn** to go/to come to meet sb; **aller à la ~ de problèmes** to be heading for trouble; **2** (contact) meeting; (non prévu) encounter; **première ~** first meeting; **~ étrange/inattendue** strange/unexpected encounter; **~ de hasard** chance meeting ou encounter; **~ mémorable/exceptionnelle** memorable/exceptional encounter; **aimer les ~s** to like meeting people; **rechercher les ~s** to try to meet people; **faire la ~ de qn** to meet sb; **au hasard des ~s** through chance meetings ou encounters; ▶**mauvais**; **3** Sport (match) match GB, game US; (réunion) meeting GB, meet US; **~ de football** football ou soccer match GB, soccer game US; **~ d'athlétisme** athletics meeting GB, track meet US; **4** Mil encounter (**de, entre** between); **~ des deux armées** encounter between the two armies.

■ **~ plénière** Pol plenary meeting; **~ au sommet** Pol summit meeting.

rencontrer /ʀɑ̃kɔ̃tʀe/ [1] **I** *vtr* **1** (voir) to meet [*personne*]; **le président a rencontré son homologue américain hier** the president met his American counterpart yesterday; **~ sur son chemin** to come across; **2** (faire connaissance avec) to meet [*personne*]; **je l'ai rencontrée en 1965** I met her in 1965; **3** (être en présence de) to meet with [*réaction, opposition*]; [*personne*] to find [*amour, sympathie*]; to encounter [*obstacle, problème*]; [*objet mobile*] to hit [*personne, mur, objet*]; **ma main a rencontré la sienne** my hand met his/hers; **4** (trouver) [*personne*] to come across [*qualité, objet, personne*]; **on ne rencontre pas souvent des gens aussi généreux** you don't often come across ou meet such generous people; **5** Sport to meet, to play [*joueur, équipe*]; to meet GB, to fight [*boxeur*].

II se rencontrer *vpr* **1** (se voir) to meet; **je propose que nous nous rencontrions demain** I suggest that we meet tomorrow; **2** (faire connaissance) to meet; **nous nous sommes rencontrés au Caire** we met in Cairo; **3** (être en présence) [*yeux, mains*] to meet; **leurs yeux se rencontrèrent** their eyes met; **4** (se trouver) [*qualité, objet, personne*] to be found; **genre de générosité/vase qui se rencontre rarement** kind of generosity/vase which is seldom found; **ça se rencontre rarement, des gens aussi doués** you don't often come across such gifted people; **5** Sport [*joueurs, équipes*] to meet, to play each other.

IDIOMES **les grands esprits se rencontrent** Prov great minds think alike Prov.

rendement /ʀɑ̃dmɑ̃/ *nm* **1** (production) (de terre, d'élevage, investissement) yield; (de machine, travailleur) output **¢**; **~ laitier/agricole** milk/farm yield; **~ à l'hectare** yield per hectare; **~ de 8%** yield of 8%; **~ des obligations** yield of bonds; **tourner à plein ~** to run at full capacity; **2** (productivité) (d'usine, entreprise) productivity **¢**; (de machine, travailleur, source d'énergie) efficiency **¢**; **~ énergétique** energy efficiency; **3** (résultat) (de sportif, publicité, d'élève) performance; **~ scolaire** performance at school; **~ musculaire** muscular performance.

rendez-vous /ʀɑ̃devu/ *nm inv* **1** (chez un médecin, coiffeur, avocat etc) appointment (**avec** with; **chez** at); **prendre/avoir ~ avec un spécialiste** to make/have an appointment with a specialist; **j'ai ~ chez le médecin/coiffeur** I've got an appointment at the doctor's/hairdresser's; **recevoir les malades sur ~** to see patients by appointment; **'consultations sur ~ seulement'** 'consultations by appointment only'; **2** (avec des amis) **j'ai ~ avec un ami** I'm meeting a friend; **on peut se fixer un ~?** shall we meet?; **je leur ai donné ~ à minuit** I've arranged to meet them at midnight; **~ demain!** see you tomorrow!; **'~ à 10 heures à la gare'** 'meet at the station at 10 am'; **le soleil n'était pas au ~** the sun didn't shine; **la croissance est au ~** growth is the order of the day; **3** (réunion professionnelle) meeting; **vous avez deux ~ cet après-midi avec nos représentants d'Asie et de Scandinavie** you have two meetings this afternoon, with our Asian and Scandinavian representatives; **4** (rassemblement) gathering; (lieu) meeting place; **ce café est le ~ des joueurs d'échecs** that café is a meeting place for chess players; **5** (émission) programme[GB], slot; **notre prochain ~ sur les ondes** our next programme[GB].

rendormir /ʀɑ̃dɔʀmiʀ/ [30] **I** *vtr* to put [sb] back to sleep.

II se rendormir *vpr* to go back to sleep.

rendosser /ʀɑ̃dose/ [1] *vtr* **~ son manteau** to put one's coat on again.

rendre /ʀɑ̃dʀ/ [6] **I** *vtr* **1** (retourner) (pour restituer) to give back, to return [*objet emprunté*] (**à** to); to take back [*objet consigné*] (**à** to); to return [*otage, territoire annexé*] (**à** to); (pour refuser) to return, to give back [*cadeau*] (**à** to); to return [*article défectueux*] (**à** to); (pour s'acquitter) to repay, to pay back [*emprunt, somme, dette*] (**à** to); to return [*salut, invitation*] (**à** to); **elle m'a rendu mon livre** she gave me back my book; **je dois ~ la voiture à mon père/à l'agence de location** I have to give the car back to my father/take the car back to the car hire GB ou rental US agency; **ils ont rendu les tableaux volés au musée** they returned the stolen paintings to the museum; **l'enfant sera rendu contre rançon** the child will be returned for a ransom; **prête-moi 500 francs, je te les rendrai demain** lend me 500 francs, I'll pay you back tomorrow; **elle m'a rendu mon baiser** she kissed me back; **elle ne m'a pas rendu la monnaie** she didn't give me my change; **~ la pareille à qn** to pay sb back; **il la déteste mais elle le lui rend bien** he hates her and she feels the same about him; ▶**César**, **monnaie**; **2** (redonner) **~ la santé/vue à qn** to restore sb's health/sight; **~ l'espoir à qn** to give sb hope again; **~ le sourire à qn** to put the smile back on sb's face; **~ son indépendance à un pays** to restore a country's independence; **~ des locaux à leur utilisation première** to return premises to their original use; **une nouvelle méthode de relaxation qui vous rendra le sommeil** a new relaxation method that will help you sleep; **3** (faire devenir) to make; **~ qn heureux/célèbre** to make sb happy/famous; **~ qch possible/difficile/obligatoire** to make sth possible/difficult/compulsory; **l'éclairage rend la chambre lugubre** the lighting makes the room look gloomy; **~ qn fou** to drive sb mad; **ce bruit rend fou** that noise is enough to drive you mad ou crazy○; **4** (remettre) [*élève, étudiant*] to hand in, to give in [*copie, devoir*] (**à** to); **ne rends pas tes devoirs en retard** don't hand ou give your homework in late; **il a rendu (une) copie blanche à son examen** he handed ou gave in a blank paper at the end of his exam; **5** (produire) [*terre, champ*] to yield [*récolte, quantité*]; **ferme qui rend 100 000 francs par an** farm which brings in 100,000 francs a year; **~ peu** not to produce much; **6** (exprimer, traduire) [*auteur, mots*] to convey [*pensée, sentiment, atmosphère*]; [*traducteur*] to translate, to render [*texte, terme*]; to convey, to render [*nuance*]; [*peintre*] to depict [*lumière, relief, scène*]; [*traduction, tableau*] to convey [*atmosphère, style*]; **résumé/traduction qui ne rend pas la subtilité/le rythme de l'original** summary/translation that fails to catch the subtlety/the rhythm of the original; **savoir ~ une émotion/un personnage** [*acteur*] to be good at putting across ou over an emotion/a character; **~ l'expression d'un visage** [*peintre, photographe*] to capture the expression on a face; **un poème chinois merveilleusement rendu en anglais** a Chinese poem beautifully translated into English, a marvellous[GB] translation into English of a Chinese poem; **~ un mot par une périphrase** to paraphrase a word; **ça rend mieux/ne rendra rien en couleurs** it comes out better/won't come out in colour[GB]; **7** (vomir) to bring up [*aliment, déjeuner, bile*]; **8** (prononcer) to pronounce [*jugement, sentence, arrêt, décision, décret*]; to return [*verdict*]; to pronounce [*oracle*]; **9** (émettre) [*instrument, objet creux*] to give off [*son*]; **10** (exsuder) **les tomates rendent de l'eau (à la cuisson)** tomatoes give out water when cooked; **~ du jus** to be juicy; **saler les concombres pour leur faire ~ l'eau** salt the cucumbers to draw out the water; **11** Sport [*concurrent*] **~ du poids** to have a weight handicap (**à** compared with); **~ de la distance à qn** to give sb a (distance) handicap; **~ 3 kilos** to carry 3 kilos ou a 3 kilo-handicap; **~ 10 mètres à qn** to give sb a 10-metre[GB] handicap; **il vous rendrait des points** he's more than a match for you.

II *vi* **1** (produire) **~ (bien)** [*terre*] to be productive; [*plante*] to produce a good crop, to be productive; [*culture, céréale*] to do well; [*activité, commerce*] to be profitable; **2** (vomir) to be sick, to throw up○; **le médicament m'a fait ~** the medicine made me sick; **avoir envie de ~** to feel sick GB ou nauseous.

III se rendre *vpr* **1** (aller) to go; **se ~ à Rome/en Chine/en ville** to go to Rome/to China/to town; **se ~ à Vienne en voiture/avion** to go to Vienna by car/plane, to drive/fly to Vienna; **se ~ chez des amis** to go to see friends; **en me rendant à Lima** on my way to Lima; ▶**bagage**; **2** (devenir) to make oneself; **se ~ indispensable/malade** to make oneself indispensable/ill; **se ~ ridicule** to make a fool of oneself; **3** (capituler) [*criminel*] to give oneself up (**à** to); [*troupe, armée, ville*] to surrender (**à** to); **rendez-vous, vous êtes cernés!** give yourselves up, you're surrounded!; **4** (se soumettre) **se ~ à qch** to bow to [*argument, avis*]; to yield to [*prières, supplique*]; to answer [*appel*]; **il ne se rend jamais** (dans une discussion) he never gives in.

IDIOMES **~ l'âme** or **l'esprit** to pass away; **~ le dernier soupir** or **souffle** to breathe one's last; **le bon Dieu te le rendra au centuple** your reward will be great in Heaven.

rendu, **~e** /ʀɑ̃dy/ **I** *pp* ▶ **rendre**.

II *pp adj* **1** (arrivé) [*marchandise*] to be delivered (**à** to); **nous étions déjà ~s quand il a téléphoné** we had already arrived when he phoned; **nous serons plus vite ~s en taxi** we'll get there more quickly by taxi; **le prix des articles ~s à domicile** the price of home-delivered items; **2**† (fatigué) **être ~** to be exhausted.

III *nm* **1** Art depiction; **le ~ des chairs/de la lumière** the depiction of flesh/of light; **2** Comm (objet rapporté) return, returned article.

rêne /ʀɛn/ *nf* rein; **tenir les ~s** lit, fig to hold the reins; **rendre les ~s à un cheval** Équit to give a horse its head; **lâcher les ~s** lit to slacken the reins; fig to let go; **prendre les ~s du gouvernement** to take over the reins of government; **prendre les ~s d'une affaire** to assume control of a business.

renégat, **~e** /ʀənega, at/ *nm,f* Relig, fig renegade.

renégociation /ʀənegɔsjasjɔ̃/ *nf* renegotiation.

renégocier /ʀ(ə)negɔsje/ [2] *vtr* to renegotiate.

renfermé, **~e** /ʀɑ̃fɛʀme/ **I** *pp* ▶ **renfermer**.

II *pp adj* [*personne*] withdrawn; [*sentiment*] hidden.

III *nm* **odeur de ~** musty smell; **ça sent le ~** it smells musty.

renfermer /ʀɑ̃fɛʀme/ [1] **I** *vtr* **1** (receler) to contain; **2**† (ranger sous clé) to lock [sth] away.

II se renfermer *vpr* [*personne*] to become withdrawn; **se ~ dans le mutisme/sa coquille** to retreat into silence/one's shell.

renfiler /ʀɑ̃file/ [1] *vtr* to put [sth] on again [*vêtement*]; to re-string [*collier, perles*]; to re-thread [*aiguille*].

renflé, **~e** /ʀɑ̃fle/ **I** *pp* ▶ **renfler**.

II *pp adj* [*vase*] rounded; [*dome*] bulbous; [*estomac*] bulging.

renflement /ʀɑ̃fləmɑ̃/ *nm* bulge.

renfler /ʀɑ̃fle/ [1] **I** *vtr* to puff out [*joues*].

II se renfler *vpr* to bulge.

renflouage /ʀɑ̃fluaʒ/, **renflouement** /ʀɑ̃flumɑ̃/ *nm* **1** (de navire) raising; **2** (de personne, d'entreprise) bailing out.

renflouer /ʀɑ̃flue/ [1] *vtr* **1** to raise [*navire*]; **2** to bail out [*personne, entreprise*].

renfoncement /ʀɑ̃fɔ̃smɑ̃/ *nm* **1** (de mur) recess; **~ de porte** doorway; **2** Imprim indentation.

renfoncer /ʀɑ̃fɔ̃se/ [12] *vtr* **1** (enfoncer plus) to drive [sth] further in [*clou*]; to push [sth] further in [*bouchon*]; **~ son chapeau** to pull down one's hat; **il aurait voulu leur ~ leurs paroles dans la gorge** he would have liked to ram their words back down their throats; **2** Imprim to indent.

renforcement /ʀɑ̃fɔʀs(ə)mɑ̃/ *nm* **1** (de construction) reinforcement, strengthening (**de** of); (d'équipe, effectifs) strengthening (**de** of); **des matériaux de ~** materials for reinforcement; **2** (intensification) (de rôle) strengthening; (d'activité) increase; (de sécurité) tightening (**de** of).

renforcer /ʀɑ̃fɔʀse/ [12] **I** *vtr* **1** (rendre plus solide) to reinforce [*construction, vêtement*]; to strengthen [*muscles, tissus*]; **~ un vêtement aux coudes/genoux** to reinforce the elbows/knees of a garment; **2** (accroître le nombre de) to strengthen [*équipe, effectifs, troupe*]; **nos équipes techniques sont renforcées par des ingénieurs** our technical crews are backed up by engineers; **3** (intensifier) to strengthen, reinforce [*pouvoir, loi, sanctions, amitié, défense*]; to reinforce [*contrôle, dépendance, image, doute, déséquilibre*]; to step up [*surveillance*]; **4** (donner plus de pouvoir à) to strengthen [*groupe, ville, monnaie*]; **ce qui s'est passé me renforce dans mes positions/certitudes** what has happened strengthens my position/convictions.

II se renforcer *vpr* [*pouvoir*] to increase; [*contrôle*] to become tighter; [*équipe, effectifs, groupe*] to grow; [*amitié, haine*] to grow stronger; [*pays, influence, secteur*] to grow stronger; **la tendance à la baisse s'est renforcée en 1993** the downward trend increased in 1993; **notre groupe industriel continue de se ~** our industrial group continues to grow stronger.

renfort /ʀɑ̃fɔʀ/ *nm* **1** Mil reinforcement; **envoyer/attendre des ~s** to send/wait for reinforcements; **en ~** as reinforcements; **2** gén support ¢; **avoir besoin de ~** to need support; **aller chercher/attendre des ~s** to go and get/to wait for support; **en ~** in support; **à grand ~ de qch** with a lot of sth; **la campagne a débuté à grand ~ de publicité** the campaign started with a lot of publicity; **annoncé à grand ~ de publicité** much heralded; **3** Sport substitute; **4** Tech support; **une pièce de ~** a support piece; **5** Cout (de coude) elbow patch; (de genou) knee patch; (d'ourlet) hemming tape; (de poche) reinforcement.

renfrogné, **~e** /ʀɑ̃fʀɔɲe/ *adj* [*visage, air, personne*] sullen.

renfrogner: **se renfrogner** /ʀɑ̃fʀɔɲe/ [1] *vpr* to become sullen.

rengagé, **~e** /ʀɑ̃gaʒe/ Mil **I** *adj* re-enlisted.

II *nm,f* re-enlisted man/woman.

rengagement /ʀɑ̃gaʒmɑ̃/ *nm* (d'un soldat) re-enlistment; (d'un employé) re-engagement.

rengager /ʀɑ̃gaʒe/ [13] **I** *vtr* **1** (embaucher de nouveau) to take [sb] on again [*employé*]; Mil to re-enlist [*soldat*]; **2** (reprendre) to renew [*hostilités*]; to reopen [*discussion*]; Sport to resume [*partie*].

II *vi* Mil to re-enlist, to sign up again.

III se rengager *vpr* Mil to re-enlist, to sign up again.

rengaine /ʀɑ̃gɛn/ *nf* (chanson) corny old song○; (air) corny old tune○; fig **c'est toujours la même ~** fig it's always the same old song.

rengainer /ʀɑ̃gɛne/ [1] *vtr* **1** lit to sheathe [*épée, poignard*]; to put [sth] back in its holster [*pistolet*]; **2**○ fig **j'ai rengainé mes excuses**○ I kept my apologies to myself.

rengorgement /ʀɑ̃gɔʀʒəmɑ̃/ *nm* liter overweening conceit.

rengorger: **se rengorger** /ʀɑ̃gɔʀʒe/ [13] *vpr* [*oiseau*] to puff out its breast; [*personne*] to swell with conceit (**de qch** at sth; **d'avoir fait** at having done).

reniement /ʀənimɑ̃/ *nm* disavowal.

■ **~ de saint Pierre** Bible Denial of Saint Peter.

renier /ʀənje/ [2] **I** *vtr* to renounce [*religion, opinion, cause*]; to disown [*ami, enfant, signature, œuvre*]; to disclaim [*obligation*].

II se renier *vpr* (désavouer ses opinions) to go back on one's opinions; (désavouer le passé) to go back on everything one has stood for.

reniflard /ʀ(ə)niflaʀ/ *nm* (crankcase) breather.

reniflement /ʀ(ə)nifləmɑ̃/ *nm* **1** (action) sniffing; **2** (bruit) sniff.

renifler /ʀ(ə)nifle/ [1] **I** *vtr* **1** (sentir) [*personne, animal*] to sniff [*odeur, piste*]; [*cochon*] to sniff for [*truffes*]; **2** (absorber par le nez) to snort○ [*cocaïne*]; to sniff [*vapeur, colle*]; **~ du tabac** to take snuff; **3**○ (pressentir) to sniff out [*bonne affaire*]; **~ un mauvais coup** to smell trouble.

II *vi* to sniff.

rennais, **~e** /ʀɛnɛ, ɛz/ ▶ **857** *adj* of Rennes.

Rennais, **~e** /ʀɛnɛ, ɛz/ ▶ **857** *nm,f* (natif) native of Rennes; (habitant) inhabitant of Rennes.

renne /ʀɛn/ *nm* reindeer.

Rennes /ʀɛn/ ▶ **857** *npr* Rennes.

renom /ʀənɔ̃/ *nm* **1** (bonne reputation) fame, renown; **avoir du ~** to be famous ou renowned; **de** or **en ~** [*marque, styliste*] famous (*épith*); **2** (réputation) reputation; **~ d'honnêteté/de qualité** reputation for honesty/for quality.

renommé, **~e** /ʀənɔme/ **I** *pp* ▶ **renommer**.

II *pp adj* famous, renowned (**pour qch** for sth; **pour faire** for doing).

III renommée *nf* **1** (réputation) reputation; **gagner/engager/défendre sa ~e** to earn/to stake/to defend one's reputation; **2** (célébrité) fame; **faire la ~e de qch/qn** to make sth/sb famous; **peintre/musée de ~e mondiale** world-famous painter/museum, painter/museum of world renown; **3** (opinion publique) liter reports (*pl*); **à en croire la ~e** judging by the reports.

IDIOMES **bonne ~e vaut mieux que ceinture dorée** Prov a good name is worth more than great wealth.

renommer /ʀ(ə)nɔme/ [1] *vtr* to reappoint [*personne*] (**à qch** to sth).

renonce /ʀ(ə)nɔ̃s/ *nf* Jeux **faire une ~** to revoke.

renoncement /ʀ(ə)nɔ̃smɑ̃/ *nm* renunciation (**à qch** of sth; **de** or **par qn** by sb).

renoncer /ʀ(ə)nɔ̃se/ [12] *vtr ind* **1** (après expérience) **~ à** to give up; **c'est trop difficile, je renonce!** it's too difficult, I give up!; **~ à** to give up [*poste, activité, plaisir, lutte, action*]; **~ à faire** to give up doing; **je renonce à chercher une maison** I'm giving up looking for a house; **elle a renoncé à lui** she finished with him; **2** (avant de commencer) **~ à** to abandon [*projet, objectif, principes*]; **~ à faire** to abandon the idea of doing; **l'athlète a renoncé à participer aux épreuves** the athlete has abandoned the idea of taking part in the trials; **3** (abandonner la possession de) **~ à** to relinquish [*mandat, pouvoir*]; to waive [*privilèges*]; to give up [*liberté*]; to end [*amitié*]; relinquish [*capital*]; **4** (abandonner un droit sur) **~ à** to renounce [*honneurs, couronne*]; **5** Jeux (aux cartes) to revoke; **6** littér **~ à** to renounce [*monde*].

renonciation /ʀ(ə)nɔ̃sjasjɔ̃/ *nf* **1** Jur, gén (à une fonction) giving up (**à** of; **de** by); (au trône) relinquishment (**à** of; **de** by); (à une succession) renunciation (**à** of; **de** by); **2** liter renunciation (**à** of; **de** by).

renoncule /ʀənɔ̃kyl/ *nf* (bouton d'or) (meadow) buttercup.

■ **~ des champs** corn buttercup; **~ des fleuristes** ranunculus; **~ des marais** marsh marigold.

renouée /ʀənwe/ *nf* bistort.

■ **~ des oiseaux** knotgrass.

renouer /ʀənwe/ [1] **I** *vtr* **1** lit to retie [*lacets, ficelle*]; **2** fig to renew [*amitié*]; to pick up the thread of [*conversation*].

II renouer avec *vtr ind* **~ avec** (après dispute) to make up with [*personne*]; (après perte de contact) to get back in touch with [*personne*]; to revive [*tradition*]; to re-establish [*pratique*]; to go back to [*passé*]; **j'ai renoué avec d'anciennes connaissances** I've got GB ou gotten US back in touch with old acquaintances of mine.

III se renouer *vpr* **des liens se sont renoués entre eux** they have re-established close ties.

renouveau, *pl* **~x** /ʀənuvo/ *nm* **1** (renaissance) (de nationalisme, genre, mode) revival; (de communauté) rebirth; (de politique) regeneration; **2** (regain) **un ~ d'intérêt pour** a renewal of interest in; **3** liter (printemps) springtime.

renouvelable /ʀənuvlabl/ *adj* **1** [*permis, contrat*] renewable; **mandat non ~** nonrenewable mandate; **élu pour cinq ans non ~s** elected for a nonrenewable five-year mandate; **2** École [*source d'énergie*] renewable; **3** [*exploit, expérience*] which can be repeated (*after n*).

renouvelé, **~e** /ʀənuvle/ **I** *pp* ▶ **renouveler**.

II *pp adj* **1** (neuf) [*joie, vitalité, ardeur, énergie*] renewed; **2** (changé) [*équipe, édition*] remodelled[GB]; **3** (répété) **controverse maintes fois ~e** recurring controversy.

renouveler /ʀənuvle/ [19] **I** *vtr* **1** (proroger) to renew [*passeport, abonnement, bail, pacte*]; **elle a renouvelé son mandat** Pol she has been re-elected; **2** (refaire) to renew, to repeat [*suggestion, expérience, promesse, commande*]; to renew [*forces, efforts*]; **3** (remplacer) to replace [*matériel, garde-robe, équipe*]; to change [*eau*]; to renew [*stocks*]; **~ l'air dans une chambre** to air a room; **4** (redonner) to renew [*soutien, prêt*]; **~ sa confiance en qn** gén to reaffirm one's faith in sb; (élire à nouveau) to re-elect sb; **5** (rendre nouveau) to revitalize [*genre, style*]; to revive [*sentiment*].

II se renouveler *vpr* **1** (être remplacé) [*générations, techniques*] to be replaced; **une pièce où l'air ne se renouvelle pas** a room which isn't aired; **2** (varier) [*auteur, artiste*] to try something new, to try out new ideas; **3** (se reproduire) [*exploit, expérience*] to happen again; **que cela ne se renouvelle pas!** don't let it happen again!

renouvellement /ʀənuvɛlmɑ̃/ *nm* **1** (de passeport, pacte, d'abonnement) renewal; **2** (de matériel, mobilier, garde-robe, d'équipe) replacement; **être responsable du ~ des stocks** to be responsible for replacing the stock; **opérer un ~ au sein d'une équipe** to make changes in a team; **3** (de cellules, générations) renewal; **4** (de style, doctrine) revitalization; (de langue) renewal; **5** (de demande, suggestion, promesse) reiteration; **le ~ d'un exploit** the repetition of a feat.

rénovateur, **-trice** /ʀenɔvatœʀ, tʀis/ **I** *adj* [*théorie, attitude*] reforming.

II *nm,f* gén (de coutume) modernizer; (de science, religion) reformer.

III *nm* **~ du bois** furniture restorer.

rénovation /ʀenɔvasjɔ̃/ *nf* **1** Constr (de quartier) renovation; (de maison, immeuble) (pour gros travaux) renovation; (pour simples travaux) refurbishment; (de route) repairs (*pl*); **2** fig [*politique*] reform; (de secteur économique/industriel) revitalization.

rénover /ʀenɔve/ [1] *vtr* **1** Constr (avec de gros travaux) to renovate [*quartier, maison, immeuble*]; (avec des travaux simples) to refurbish [*maison, immeuble*]; to restore [*meuble*]; **appartement entièrement rénové** fully renovated flat GB ou apartment US; **2** (remettre à jour) to reform [*institution, politique, loi*]; to revamp [*projet, procédure*]; to overhaul [*système technique*].

renseignement /ʀɑ̃sɛɲmɑ̃/ **I** *nm* **1** (information) information ¢, piece of information; **des ~s** information; **des ~s utiles** useful information; **nous n'avons aucun ~ là-dessus** we have no information on the matter; **les ~s fournis sont inexacts** the information given is incorrect; **prendre des ~s sur qch/qn** to find out about sth/sb; **merci pour le ~** thank you for the information; **demander des ~s à qn** to ask sb for information; **est-ce que je peux vous demander un ~?** can I ask you something?; **les ~s demandés par qn** the information requested by sb; **il est allé aux ~s** he went to find out (about it); **~s pris, il semblerait que** upon investigation, it would appear that; **'pour tous ~s, s'adresser à…'** 'all inquiries to…'; **2** Mil intelligence; **service/officier de ~** intelligence service/officer; **il travaille dans le ~** he works in intelligence.

II renseignements *nmpl* (service, bureaux) information ¢; Télécom directory enquiries GB, information US, directory assistance US; **adressez-vous aux ~s** ask at information ou at the information desk; **demande le numéro aux ~s** ask directory enquiries GB ou directory assistance US for the number.

■ **~s généraux**, **RG** *branch of the French police force dealing with political security*.

renseigner /ʀɑ̃seɲe/ [1] **I** *vtr* [*réceptionniste, personne*] to give information to [*client, touriste, passant*] (**sur** about); [*agent, informateur*] to give ou supply information to [*police, gouvernement*] (**sur** about); **la brochure/le documentaire nous renseigne sur…** the brochure/the documentary gives us information about ou tells us about…; **il vous renseignera sur les différentes formules proposées** he'll give you information about ou he'll tell you about the different schemes available; **être bien renseigné** to be well-informed; **être mal renseigné** to be ill-informed, to have the wrong information; **on l'a mal renseigné** he was given the wrong information, he was misinformed; **demandez au rayon accessoires, ils vous renseigneront** ask at the accessories department, they' ll be able to help you.

II se renseigner *vpr* (demander des informations) to find out, to enquire (**sur** about; **auprès de** from); (faire des recherches) to make enquiries (**sur** about; **auprès de** from); **renseigne-toi auprès d'un employé sur les horaires des trains** ask somebody who works here about the train times; **se ~ sur les activités de qn** to make enquiries about ou to look into sb's activities; **renseigne-toi avant de prendre une décision** find out about it before you decide; **je vais me ~ auprès d'elle** I'll ask her about it.

rentabilisation /ʀɑ̃tabilizasjɔ̃/ *nf* **la ~ de l'entreprise est notre premier objectif** our primary aim is to make the company profitable.

rentabiliser /ʀɑ̃tabilize/ [1] *vtr* to secure a return on [*investissement*]; to make a profit on [*produit*]; to make [sth] profitable [*affaire*]; **~ la recherche** to make research pay; **les gros investissements sont parfois longs à ~** large-scale investment is sometimes slow to yield a profit; **l'isolation de ma maison sera vite rentabilisée** my home insulation will soon pay for itself.

rentabilité /ʀɑ̃tabilite/ *nf* **1** (caractère rentable) profitability; **2** (profit) return; **~ de 4%** return of 4%; **avoir une forte ~** to yield a high return.

■ **~ économique** Fin return on capital employed; **~ financière** Fin ratio of sales to fixed assets.

rentable /ʀɑ̃tabl/ *adj* [*affaire, activité, produit, créneau*] profitable; [*placement, investissement*] profitable; [*découverte*] fruitful; **il n'est pas ~ de faire** it does not pay to do.

rente /ʀɑ̃t/ *nf* **1** (revenu personnel) private income; **vivre de ses ~s** to have a private income ou private means; **~ de situation** (financièrement) guaranteed income; (privilège) privileged position, advantages; **2** (contrat financier) annuity; **~ viagère** life annuity; **~ temporaire** terminable annuity; **~ mensuelle** monthly allowance; **faire une ~ à qn** to give sb an allowance; **3** Fin (emprunt d'État) government stock; **~ à 5%** 5% stock; **~ perpétuelle/amortissable** non-redeemable/redeemable stock.

rentier, **-ière** /ʀɑ̃tje, ɛʀ/ *nm,f* person of independent means; **mener une vie de ~** to lead a life of leisure.

rentrant, **~e** /ʀɑ̃tʀɑ̃, ɑ̃t/ *adj* **1** Aviat [*train d'atterrissage*] retractable; **2** Math [*angle, polygone, secteur*] re-entrant.

rentré, **~e** /ʀɑ̃tʀe/ **I** *pp* ▶ **rentrer**.

II *pp adj* **1** (retenu) [*colère, envie, rire*] suppressed; **2** (en retrait) [*joues, yeux*] sunken; [*ventre, fesses*] held in (*après n*).

III *nm* Cout **faire un ~** to turn in ou fold under the raw edge (*of a hem*).

IV rentrée *nf* **1** (reprise d'activité) (general) return to work (*after the slack period of the summer break, in France*); (début d'année scolaire) start of the (new) school year; (début de trimestre) beginning of term; (pour une institution) reopening; **la ~e de septembre a été agitée** the return to work after the Summer holidays was turbulent; **des grèves sont prévues pour la ~e** strikes are expected after the summer break; **la mode/les livres de la ~e** the autumn ou new season's fashion/books; **mon livre sera publié à la ~e** my book will be published in the autumn GB ou fall US; **il s'est cassé la jambe le jour de la ~e** he broke his leg on the first day of term; **2** (retour) (de vacancier, voitures) return; (d'employés, élèves) return (to work); **la ~e à Paris un dimanche soir** going back to Paris on a Sunday evening; **la ~e du personnel après le déjeuner** the staff coming in at the end of lunch hour; **surveiller la ~e des enfants à la fin de la récréation** to supervise the children at the end of break GB ou recess US; **3** (réapparition publique) comeback; **~e politique** political comeback; **faire sa ~e** [*homme politique, artiste, sportif*] to make one's comeback; **4** (d'argent) (recette) receipts (*pl*); (revenu) income ¢; (dans une caisse) takings (*pl*); **les ~es** Compta receipts; **leur seule ~e d'argent étant le loyer de leurs ateliers** their only income being the rent from the workshops; **il n'y a pas eu de ~e importante depuis deux mois** there hasn't been any significant amount of money coming in for two months; **~e de fonds** cash inflow; **~es fiscales** (annuelles) tax revenue ¢; (ponctuelles) tax revenues; **5** Astronaut, Mil (de vaisseau, capsule, missile) re-entry; **à sa** or **lors de sa ~e dans l'atmosphère** on re-entry into the atmosphere; **point de ~e d'un missile** re-entry point of a missile; **6** Agric (mise à l'abri) **la ~e des foins/de la récolte se fera la semaine prochaine** the hay/the harvest will be brought in next week.

■ **~e des classes** start of the school year; **~e littéraire** the beginning of the literary year; **~e parlementaire** reassembly of Parliament; **~e scolaire** = **~e des classes**; **~e sociale** *opening of a new season of trade union activity and negotiation*; **~e universitaire** start of the academic year.

rentre-dedans° /ʀɑ̃tdədɑ̃/ *nm inv* **faire du ~ à qn** to try to get off with sb° GB, to come on to sb°.

rentrer /ʀɑ̃tʀe/ [1] **I** *vtr* **1** (mettre à l'abri) gén to put [sth] in [*objet, animal*]; (en venant) to bring [sth] in [*objet, animal*]; (en allant) to take [sth] in [*objet, animal*]; **rentre la bicyclette/voiture au garage** put the bike/car in the garage; **rentre le linge, il va pleuvoir** bring the washing in, it's going to rain; **2** (rétracter) [*pilote*] to raise [*train d'atterrissage*]; [*félin*] to draw in [*griffes*]; **rentrez le ventre!** hold your stomach in!; **3** (faire pénétrer) to put [*clé*] (**dans** in, into); to tuck [*pan de chemise*] (**dans** into); **4** (refouler) to suppress [*colère*]; to hold back [*larmes*]; **5** Imprim to indent [*ligne*].

II *vi* (+ *v être*) **1** (pénétrer) (dans une pièce, une cabine téléphonique) to go in; (dans une voiture, un ascenseur) to get in; (tenir, s'adapter) to fit; (percuter)° **~ dans** to hit; **~ dans le salon** to go into the living room; **~ dans un arbre**° to hit a tree; **2** (entrer de nouveau) (en allant) to go back in; (en venant) to come back in; **~ dans** to go/to come back into; **ils sont sortis puis rentrés cinq minutes plus tard** they went out only to come back in (again) five minutes later; **le satellite va ~ dans l'atmosphère** the satellite is about to re-enter the atmosphere; **3** (revenir) gén to get back, to come back, to return (**de** from) ; (chez soi) to come home (**de** from); **il est rentré tard dans la nuit** he got back late at night; **il ne va pas tarder à ~ du travail** he'll be back from work soon; **ne rentre pas trop tard!** don't stay out too late!; **quand es-tu rentré en France/à Paris?** when did you get back to France/to Paris?; **mon mari rentrera le 17** my husband will be home on the 17th; **rentre à la maison tout de suite!** come home immediately!; **4** (repartir) gén to get back, to go back, to return; (chez soi) to go home (**de** from); **nous rentrons en France/à Paris le 17** we're going back to France/to Paris on the 17th; **il est tard, je dois ~ (chez moi)** it's late, I must get back; **il fait trop froid, je rentre** (à l'intérieur) it's too cold, I'm going (back) inside; (de plus loin) it's too cold , I'm going (back) home; **se dépêcher de ~** (chez soi) to hurry home; **~ en classe** [*élèves*] to go back to school; **5** (récupérer) **~ dans qch** to recover ou recoup sth [*dépense*]; **6** (être encaissé) [*argent, loyer, créance*] to come in; **faire ~ l'argent** to get the money in; **des fonds vont me ~ bientôt** I'll be getting some money in soon; **7** (pouvoir trouver place) to fit; **mes chaussures ne rentrent pas dans ma valise** my shoes won't fit into my case, I can't get my shoes into my case; **faire ~ qch dans la tête de qn** to get sth into sb's head; **il n'y a rien à faire pour leur faire ~ ça dans la tête** there's no way of getting it into their heads; **~ dans la serrure** to fit the lock; (être compris) **l'algèbre/l'économie, ça ne rentre pas!** algebra/economics just won't go in!; **'ça marche l'anglais?'—'ça commence à ~'** 'how's the English going?'—'I'm beginning to get the hang of it○'.

IDIOMES **~ en soi-même** to withdraw; **je vais leur ~ dedans◑** or **dans le lard◑** or **dans le chou◑** (physiquement, verbalement) I'm going to lay into them○; **il s'est fait ~ dans le lard par la critique◑** the critics laid into him○; **il m'est rentré dedans◑** (en voiture) (légèrement) he bumped ou ran into me; (violemment) he crashed into me; **il s'est fait ~ dedans** another car crashed into him; **se ~ dedans◑** [*adversaires*] to lay into each other○; [*automobilistes, voitures*] (légèrement) to bump ou run into each other; (violemment) to crash into each other.

renversant, **~e** /Rɑ̃vɛRsɑ̃, ɑ̃t/ *adj* astounding, astonishing.

renverse /Rɑ̃vɛRs/ *nf* (de vent, marée) turning; (de courant) change of direction.

IDIOMES **tomber à la ~** to fall flat on one's back; **il y a de quoi tomber à la ~!** it's absolutely astounding!

renversé, **~e** /Rɑ̃vɛRse/ **I** *pp* ▶ **renverser**.

II *pp adj* **1** (image, pyramide, cône) inverted; **2** (stupéfait) staggered, astounded.

renversement /Rɑ̃vɛRsəmɑ̃/ *nm* **1** (inversion) (de tendance, situation, termes, d'ordre, alliance) reversal; (d'image) inversion, reversal; (de marée, vent) turning; (de courant) change of direction; Math (de fraction) inversion; Mus (d'intervalle, accord) inversion; **2** (de gouvernement, dirigeant) (par la force) overthrow; (par un vote) removal from office.

renverser /Rɑ̃vɛRse/ [1] **I** *vtr* **1** (faire tomber) to knock over [*meuble, bouteille, vase, seau*]; [*automobiliste, véhicule*] to knock down, to run over [*piéton, cycliste*]; [*manifestants*] to topple [*statue*]; [*manifestants, vandales*] to overturn [*voiture*]; [*vague*] to overturn [*bateau*]; **il courait sans regarder devant lui et a renversé une vieille dame** he was running without looking where he was going and knocked over an old lady; **2** (répandre) to spill [*liquide, contenu*]; **~ du vin sur la moquette** to spill wine on the carpet; **il m'a renversé du jus sur la manche** he spilled some juice on my sleeve; **3** (mettre à l'envers) to turn [sth] upside down [*sablier, flacon*]; **4** (pencher) **~ la tête en arrière** to tip ou tilt one's head back; **~ le buste en arrière** to lean back; **5** (inverser) to reverse [*termes, ordre, situation, rôles, tendance*]; Phys to invert, to reverse [*image*]; Math to invert [*fraction*]; Électrotech to reverse [*courant*]; **6** Pol (mettre fin à) (par la force) to overthrow, to topple [*régime, gouvernement, dirigeant*]; (par un vote) to vote [sth] out of office [*gouvernement, dirigeant, ministère*]; **7**○ (stupéfier) [*événement, nouvelle*] to stagger, to astound [*personne*]; **il avait l'air renversé par la nouvelle** he seemed staggered by the news.

II se renverser *vpr* [*véhicule*] to overturn; [*bateau*] to capsize; [*objet, bouteille*] to fall over; [*liquide, contenu*] to spill.

renvoi /Rɑ̃vwa/ *nm* **1** (d'élève, étudiant, immigré, de joueur) expulsion (**de** from); (d'employé, ambassadeur) dismissal (**de** from); **~ de l'université/l'équipe** expulsion from the university/the team; **~ de l'usine/du gouvernement** dismissal from the factory/from the government; **~ pour indiscipline** Mil dismissal for insubordination; **~ d'un élève pour trois jours** suspension of a pupil from school for three days; **~ des immigrés dans leur pays** repatriation of immigrants to their own country; **2** (retour à l'expéditeur) return; **~ d'un colis/de marchandises** return of a parcel/of goods; **3** Sport (au tennis, ping-pong, volley-ball) return; (au football, rugby) clearance; **~ en touche** clearance into touch; **mauvais ~ d'un défenseur** poor clearance by a defender; **4** (report) gén postponement; Jur, Pol (envoi) referral (**devant** to); (ajournement) adjournment (**à** until); **~ de l'affaire devant la Cour d'appel** referral of the case to the court of appeal; **~ en commission d'un projet de loi** referral of a bill GB ou committal of a bill US to the competent committee; **demander le ~ de son procès** to ask for one's trial to be adjourned; **~ à huitaine** adjournment for a week; **~ d'une discussion à la prochaine session** postponement of a discussion until the next session; **5** (référence) (dans un dictionnaire, livre, fichier) cross-reference (**à** to); (dans un discours, une discussion) reference (**à** to); **6** Mus repeat sign; **7** (éructation) belch, burp○; **avoir un ~** gén to burp○; [*bébé*] to posset; **avoir des ~s** to belch, to burp○; **donner des ~s** [*nourriture, plat*] to repeat (**à** on).

■ **~ temporaire de ligne** Télécom call diversion.

renvoyer /Rɑ̃vwaje/ [24] *vtr* **1** (relancer) to throw [sth] back [*projectile, ballon*]; (répercuter) to reflect [*lumière, chaleur*]; to echo [*son*]; **~ une image déformée** to reflect a distorted image; **2** (réexpédier) to return [*courrier, marchandises*]; **3** (faire retourner) to send [sb] back [*personne*]; **~ qn à l'école/à l'hôpital** to send sb back to school/to hospital GB ou to the hospital US; **~ qn dans son pays** to send sb back to his/her own country; **~ qn chez lui** or **dans ses foyers** to send sb home; **~ qn de bureau en bureau** to send sb from one office to another; **~ un projet de loi en commission** to send a bill to committee, to commit a bill US; **~ un patient à un spécialiste** to refer a patient to a specialist; **4** (expulser) to expel [*élève, étudiant, immigré, joueur*] (**de** from); to dismiss [*employé, ambassadeur*] (**de** from); **se faire ~ de son travail** to get oneself dismissed from one's job; **~ un élève pour trois jours** to suspend a pupil (from school) for three days; **5** (faire partir) to send [sb] away [*personne, hôtes*]; **6** Jur **~ un accusé** to discharge a defendant; **~ un accusé devant les assises** to send a defendant before the criminal court; **7** (ajourner) to postpone [*débat, décision*] (**à** until); to adjourn [*affaire*] (**à** until); **~ un projet sine die** to postpone a project indefinitely; ▶ **calendes**; **8** (faire se reporter) **~ à** to refer to; **l'astérisque renvoie aux notes** the asterisk refers to the notes; **~ le lecteur à un article/un livre** to refer the reader to an article/a book; **9** (faire référence) **~ à** to relate back to; **la notion de justice renvoie à la morale** the notion of justice relates back to ethics.

réoccupation /Reɔkypasjɔ̃/ *nf* reoccupation.

réoccuper /Reɔkype/ [1] *vtr* to reoccupy [*pays, local*]; to take up [sth] again [*poste*].

réorchestration /ReɔRkɛstRasjɔ̃/ *nf* reorchestration.

réorchestrer /ReɔRkɛstRe/ [1] *vtr* to reorchestrate.

réorganisation /ReɔRganizasjɔ̃/ *nf* reorganization.

réorganiser /ReɔRganize/ [1] **I** *vtr* to reorganize.

II se réorganiser *vpr* [*personne*] to reorganize oneself; [*industrie*] to reorganize itself.

réorientation /ReɔRjɑ̃tasjɔ̃/ *nf* reorientation (**vers** toward, towards GB).

réorienter /ReɔRjɑ̃te/ [1] **I** *vtr* to reorientate [*élève, étudiant*] (**vers** toward, towards GB); to reshape [*politique*]; to reorientate [*fusée*].

II se réorienter *vpr* [*élève*] to transfer (**vers** to); [*étudiant*] to transfer (**vers** to) GB, to change majors US.

réouverture /ReuvɛRtyR/ *nf* reopening.

repaire /R(ə)pɛR/ *nm* (d'animal) den; (de brigands) den; (de trafiquants, terroristes) hideout.

repaître: **se repaître** /RəpɛtR/ [74] *vpr* **se ~ de qch** [*animal*] to feed on sth [*personne*] to revel in sth.

répandre /Repɑ̃dR/ [6] **I** *vtr* **1** (mettre) to spread [*substance, matériau*] (**sur** on; **dans** in); to pour [*liquide*] (**sur** on; **dans** in); (accidentellement) to spill [*liquide*]; **~ du gravier dans une allée** to spread gravel on a path; **~ son contenu/un chargement** to empty its contents/a load; **2** (disperser) [*personne, vent*] to scatter [*graines, farine, déchets*]; **3** (propager) to spread [*nouvelle, sentiment, enseignement, religion*] (**dans, à travers** throughout); to give off [*chaleur, fumée, odeur*] (**dans** into); to distribute [*bienfait, richesse*]; **~ la bonne parole** to spread the good word; **~ la terreur** to spread terror.

II se répandre *vpr* **1** (se propager) [*nouvelle, maladie, usage, enseignement, religion, substance, odeur*] to spread (**dans, à travers** throughout); **2** (déverser) **se ~ en invectives** to let out a stream of abuse (**contre** at); **se ~ en compliments/louanges** to be lavish with one's compliments/praise.

répandu, **~e** /Repɑ̃dy/ *adj* (commun) widespread; **très** or **largement ~** very widespread; **peu ~** not very widespread.

réparable /RepaRabl/ *adj* **1** [*objet, appareil, montre, sac, dégâts*] repairable; **cette montre est-elle ~?** can this watch be repaired?; **c'est facilement/difficilement ~** it's easy/hard to repair; **ce n'est pas ~** it can't be repaired; **2** [*perte, faute*] which can be made up for (*épith, après n*); [*dommage, sottise, erreur*] which can be put right (*épith, après n*).

reparaître /R(ə)paRɛtR/ [73] *vi* **1** (apparaître de nouveau) = **réapparaître**; **2** (être publié à nouveau) [*journal, hebdomadaire*] to be back in print; [*œuvre, texte*] to be republished.

réparateur, **-trice** /RepaRatœR, tRis/ **I** *adj* [*repos, sommeil*] refreshing; [*crème, lotion, produit*] soothing; **crème réparatrice de nuit** night treatment cream.

II ▶ **510** *nm,f* (d'appareil, de machine) engineer; **un ~ de télévision/machine à laver** a TV/washing machine engineer.

réparation /RepaRasjɔ̃/ **I** *nf* **1** (de montre, d'appareil, de machine) repairing, mending; (de véhicule, mur, bâtiment, route, d'avarie) repairing; (de vêtement, chaussure) mending; **la ~ de la télévision m'a coûté 500 francs** it cost me 500 francs to get the television repaired; **en dix ans une seule ~ a été effectuée sur cette machine** in ten years this machine has only been repaired once; **cela ne vaut pas la ~** it's not worth getting it repaired; **travaux de ~** repair work; **~ automobile/navale** car/naval repairs; **être en ~** [*bâtiment, maison, route*] to be under repair; **ma voiture/ chaîne stéréo est en ~** my car/stereo is being repaired; **'en ~'** 'out of order'; **2** Jur (de tort, préjudice, dommage) compensation (**de** for); **demander/obtenir ~ de** to seek/to obtain compensation for; **en ~ de** to compensate for; **en ~ de la perte de** to compensate for the loss of; **en ~ de tout le mal que tu as commis** to make up for all the harm you've done; **3** (d'injustice) redress (**de** for).

II réparations *nfpl* **1** (travaux) repairs, repair work **¢**; **~s de qch** (de toiture, mur, charpente) repairs to sth; **~s de menuiserie/plomberie** carpentry/plumbing repairs; **grosses ~s** major repairs; **2** (dommages et intérêts) compensation; **10 000 francs de ~s** 10,000 francs compensation; **3** Hist Mil reparations.

■ ~ par les armes duel; **demander ~ par les armes** to challenge sb to a duel.

réparer /Repare/ [1] **I** *vtr* **1** (remettre en état) to repair [*bâtiment, véhicule, route, maison*]; to repair, to mend [*appareil, accroc, vêtement, chaussure*]; **donner ses chaussures à ~** to take one's shoes to be mended ou repaired; **~ sommairement qch** to patch sth up; **2** (compenser les effets) to put [sth] right [*erreur, injustice*] (**en faisant** by doing); to make up for [*oubli, maladresse*]; **tu n'arriveras jamais à ~ le mal que tu as fait** you'll never (be able to) make up for what you've done; **3** Jur (dédommager) to compensate for [*faute, préjudice, dommage, perte*] (**en faisant** by doing; **par** through); **4** (restaurer) **~ ses forces** to get one's strength (back).

II se réparer *vpr* **se ~ facilement** [*montre, machine, appareil*] to be easy to repair ou mend; **ça ne se répare pas** it can't be repaired ou mended.

reparler /R(ə)parle/ [1] **I** *vtr ind* **1** (après interruption) **~ de** to discuss [sth] again (**à qn, avec qn** with sb); **on reparle de l'affaire de l'hôpital** the hospital scandal is in the news again; **nous reparlerons de ce problème demain** we'll come back to this problem again tomorrow; **on reparlera certainement de lui** he's definitely a name to look out for; **on en reparlera**○! you haven't heard the last of this○; **2** (après dispute) **~ à** to be back on speaking terms with.

II se reparler *vpr* (après dispute) to speak to each other again.

repartie /Reparti/ *nf* rejoinder fml; **une vigoureuse ~** a spirited rejoinder; **elle a de la ~** she always has a ready reply; **avoir la ~ facile** or **l'esprit de ~** to have a quick wit.

repartir /R(ə)partir/ [30] **I** *vtr* to retort (**que** that).

II *vi* **1** (quitter un endroit) to leave again; (regagner un lieu) to go back; **tu repars déjà?** you're leaving already?; **il est reparti chez lui** he's gone back home; **2** (après un arrêt) [*personne*] to set off again; [*machine*] to start again; [*bus*] to leave; [*emploi, secteur économique*] to pick up again; [*végétation*] to start to grow again; **3** (recommencer) **~ sur de nouvelles bases** to start all over again; **~ à zéro** to start again from scratch; **~ à la charge** to launch another offensive; **~ en campagne** to start campaigning again; **c'est reparti pour un tour** here we go again○!; **c'est reparti comme en 14**○ it' s taken off again.

répartir /Repartir/ [3] **I** *vtr* **1** (distribuer) to share [sth] out [*somme, biens, travail, financement, objets*] (**entre** among, between); to split [*bénéfices, frais*] (**entre** among, between); to distribute [*poids, masse, bagages*]; **~ des gens dans des salles** to dispatch up into several rooms; **~ des pays/peuples en plusieurs catégories** to divide countries/peoples into several categories; **~ les rôles** to distribute the roles; **être bien réparti** [*argent, tâches*] to be shared out evenly; [*poids, bagages*] to be evenly distributed; **les capitaux ont été mal répartis** the capital hasn't been shared out evenly; **~ un plan sur deux ans** to spread a plan over two years; **huit séances réparties sur toute l'année** eight sessions spread out over the year ; **~ l'impôt** to spread taxes; **2** (étaler) to spread [*produit, crème*].

II se répartir *vpr* **1** (partager) [*personnes*] to share out, to split [*travail, avantages, tâche, objets*]; **2** (être distribué) [*personnes*] to divide up; [*dépenses, rôles, travaux, tâches*] to be split ou shared; [*voix, votes*] to be split; **se ~ en** [*personnes, objets, tâches, exemples*] to divide (up) into, to split up into; **se ~ autour/dans** [*personnes*] to spread out around/in.

répartiteur /Repartitœr/ *nm* distributor.

répartition /Repartisjɔ̃/ *nf* **1** (d'argent, de biens, travail, rôles) sharing out (**entre** among, between; **en** into); (de personnes, terres, d'emplois) dividing up (**entre** among; **en** into); (de l'impôt) distribution (**de** of); **la ~ des terres/personnes se fera** the land/people will be divided up; **la ~ des tâches doit se faire selon**... tasks should be distributed according to...; **2** (résultat) distribution; **la ~ des richesses** the distribution of wealth; **3** Math distribution.

repas /R(ə)pɑ/ *nm inv* meal; **faire un bon ~** to have a good meal; **~ de famille** family meal; **manger/boire en dehors des ~** or **entre les ~** to eat/drink between meals; **médicament à prendre pendant les ~** medicine to be taken with meals; **~ à la carte** à la carte meal; **~ de midi/du soir** midday/evening meal; **~ de noces** wedding breakfast; **~ de Noël** Christmas dinner; **~ d'affaires** (à midi) business lunch; (le soir) business dinner; **le ~ des anciens** *meal in honour*[GB] *of local senior citizens*; **il m'a téléphoné à l'heure du ~** he phoned me while I was eating; **téléphoner aux heures des ~** please call at mealtimes.

repassage /R(ə)pasaʒ/ *nm* **1** (tâche ménagère) ironing; **faire du ~** to do some ironing; **2** Tech (aiguisage) sharpening.

repasser /R(ə)pase/ [1] **I** *vtr* **1** (avec un fer) to iron, to press [*vêtement, tissu*]; **~ à la vapeur** to iron with a steam iron; **~ les coutures à fer chaud** press the seams with a hot iron; **'~ à fer doux'** 'cool iron'; **2** (franchir de nouveau) to cross [sth] again [*pont, fleuve, frontière*]; **3** (se soumettre de nouveau à) to take [sth] again [*permis de conduire, oral*]; to retake, to resit GB [*examen écrit*]; **4** (donner, passer de nouveau) to pass [sth] again [*outil, sel*] (**à qn** to sb); **~ l'aspirateur** to vacuum again; **repasse la salade** (à toute la table) pass the salad round GB ou around US again; **~ un disque à qn** to play a record for sb again; **ils repassent 'les Liaisons dangereuses'** (au cinéma) 'Dangerous Liaisons' is on again, they're showing 'Dangerous Liaisons' again; **je te repasse Jean** (au téléphone) I'll pass you back to Jean; **je vous repasse le standard** I'm putting you back to the switchboard; **~ qch dans son esprit** to think back over sth; **5**○ (transmettre) to pass on [*virus*] (**à qn** to sb); to give [*rhume*] (**à qn** to sb); **~ un client à qn** to pass on a customer to sb; **6** (aiguiser) to sharpen [*ciseaux*].

II *vi* **1** (dans un même lieu) [*cyclistes, procession*] to go past again; **~ en voiture/en vélo** to drive/to cycle past again; **~ devant qch** (à pied) to go past sth again; (en voiture) to drive past sth again; **~ en courant** to run past again; **il passait et repassait devant ma maison** he was going up and down in front of my house; **~ par le même chemin** to go back the same way; **tu n'as pas besoin de ~ par Lyon** you don't have to go back through Lyons; **si tu repasses à Lyon, viens me voir** if you're ever back in Lyons, come and see me; **je repasserai demain** I'll call in again GB ou stop by tomorrow; **je dois ~ au bureau** I have to call in at the office again ou pop○ back into the office ou stop by at the office; **s'il croit que je vais accepter, il repassera**○ or **il peut toujours ~**○! if he thinks I'm going to agree, he's got another think coming○!; **~ en commission** to be re-examined by the commission; **2** (être montré, diffusé) **~ au cinéma/à Paris** [*film*] to be showing again at the cinema GB ou movies US/in Paris; **3** (pour terminer un travail) **quand elle fait la vaisselle, je dois ~ derrière elle** I always have to do the dishes again after she's done them; **4** (pour accentuer) **~ sur un trait** to go over a line; **5** Aut **~ en seconde/troisième** to go back into second/ third gear; **~ au point mort** to go back into neutral.

III se repasser *vpr* **cela se repasse?** can it be ironed?; **une chemise qui se repasse facilement** a minimum-iron shirt.

repasseuse /R(ə)pasøz/ **▶510** *nf* **1** (ouvrière) presser; **2** (machine) ironing machine.

repaver /R(ə)pave/ [1] *vtr* to repave.

repayer /R(ə)peje/ [21] *vtr* to pay [sth] again; **tu me repayes un coup à boire?** will you stand me another drink?

repêchage /R(ə)pɛʃaʒ/ *nm* **1** (dans l'eau) recovery (*from water*); **2** Scol, Univ (de candidat) awarding of a pass by discretion GB, raising to a passing grade US; **examen** or **épreuve de ~** resit GB, retest US; **question (de) ~** supplementary question (*giving another chance to pass*).

repêcher /R(ə)peʃe/ [1] *vtr* **1** (dans l'eau) to recover [*corps, véhicule*] (*from water*); to fish out [*objet*]; **2** Scol, Univ to award a discretionary pass to GB, to raise [sb] to a passing grade US [*candidat*]; Sport to allow to qualify.

repeindre /R(ə)pɛ̃dR/ [55] *vtr* to repaint.

repenser /R(ə)pɑ̃se/ [1] **I** *vtr* to rethink [*travail, théorie, organisation*]; to take a fresh look at [*pratiques, système*]; **il faut ~ le lycée** we must take a fresh look at secondary schools.

II repenser à *vtr ind* **~ à** to think back to [*enfance, vacances*]; to think again about [*discussion, anecdote*]; **maintenant que j'y repense, il était au courant** now I think about it again, he did know.

repentant, **~e** /R(ə)pɑ̃tɑ̃, ɑ̃t/ *adj* repentant.

repenti, **~e** /R(ə)pɑ̃ti/ **I** *adj* repentant.

II *nm,f* penitent.

repentir /R(ə)pɑ̃tiR/ **I** *nm* **1** gén, Relig repentance; **2** Art pentimento.

II se repentir [30] *vpr* **1** gén to regret (**de qch** sth; **d'avoir fait** having done); **2** Relig to repent (**de qch** of sth; **d'avoir fait** having done).

repérable /R(ə)peRabl/ *adj* gén that can be spotted (*après n*); Aviat, Mil that can be located (*après n*); **facilement ~** easy to spot ou to pick out; **difficilement ~** difficult to spot; Aviat, Mil difficult to locate.

repérage /R(ə)peRaʒ/ *nm* Aviat, Mil location (**de** of); Cin finding a location (**de** for); **le ~ d'un lieu sur une carte** locating a place on a map.

répercussion /RepɛRkysjɔ̃/ *nf* **1** fig repercussion (**de** of; **sur** on), knock-on effect (**de** of; **sur** on); **la baisse du dollar a eu des ~s sur la Bourse** the fall in the dollar had a knock-on effect on the Stock Exchange; **2** (de choc) repercussion; (de son) reverberation.

répercuter /RepɛRkyte/ [1] **I** *vtr* **1** (transmettre) to pass [sth] on [*information, mauvaise humeur, hausse, baisse*]; **la baisse de la TVA sera répercutée sur les tarifs des transports** the drop in VAT will be reflected in transport charges; **la hausse sera répercutée sur le client** the increase will be passed on to the customer; **2** Phys to send back [*son, onde*].

II se répercuter *vpr* **1** [*son*] to echo; [*augmentation, baisse, transformation*] to be reflected (**sur** in); **2** [*sentiment*] to have repercussions (**sur** on), to have a knock-on effect (**sur** on); **ses problèmes se répercutent sur son équilibre nerveux** his/her problems are affecting his/her nerves.

reperdre /ʀ(ə)pɛʀdʀ/ [6] *vtr* to lose [sth] again.

repère /ʀ(ə)pɛʀ/ *nm* **1** (balise, jalon) marker; (arbre, bâtiment) landmark; (encoche, trait) (reference) mark; (en arpentage) **~ de niveau** benchmark; **la statue sert de ~** the statue is a useful landmark; **2** (événement) landmark; (date) reference point; (référence) reference point, criterion; **la société a perdu ses ~s traditionnels** society has lost its traditional points of reference; **société sans ~s** society which has lost its bearings.

repérer /ʀ(ə)peʀe/ [14] **I** *vtr* **1**○ (discerner) to spot [*personne, erreur, endroit*]; **~ les lieux** to check out a place; **si tu ne veux pas te faire ~** if you don't want to get noticed ou to attract attention; **se faire ~ par la police** to be spotted by the police; **2** (situer) to locate [*avion, cible, ennemi*]; to pinpoint [*endroit précis*]; **3** (marquer) to mark [*niveau, alignement*].

II se repérer○ *vpr* **1** (s'orienter) lit, fig (dans un lieu, un livre) to get one's bearings; **je n'arrive pas à me ~ dans cette théorie** I can't make head or tail of this theory; **je n'arrive pas à me ~ dans tous ces documents/mensonges** I don't know where I am with all these documents/lies; **2** (se remarquer) [*erreur, qualité*] to stand out; **ça se repère facilement** it stands out clearly, it's easy to pick out ou to spot.

répertoire /ʀepɛʀtwaʀ/ *nm* **1** (carnet) notebook with thumb index; **2** (liste) **~ téléphonique** (imprimé) telephone directory; (personnel) telephone book; **~ d'adresses** (imprimé) directory; (personnel) address book; **~ des métiers/fournisseurs** trade/suppliers directory; **~ alphabétique des métiers** trade directory in alphabetical order; **3** Mus, Théât repertoire; **inscrire un morceau/rôle à son ~** to add a piece/role to one's repertoire; **avoir tout un ~ d'anecdotes/d'insultes** fig to have an extensive repertoire of anecdotes/of insults; **une pièce du ~** Théât a stock play; **le ~ classique** Mus, Théât, Danse the classics; **4** Ordinat directory.

répertorier /ʀepɛʀtɔʀje/ [2] *vtr* **1** (faire la liste de) to list [*titres, entreprises, informations*]; to index [*ouvrages*]; **non répertorié** unlisted; **2** (recenser) to identify [*espèces, cas, risques*]; **on a répertorié trois cas de rage** three cases of rabies have been identified; **un genre musical non répertorié** a musical genre that isn't in the standard repertoire.

repeser /ʀ(ə)pəze/ [16] *vtr* to weigh [sth] again.

répéter /ʀepete/ [14] **I** *vtr* **1** (redire) to repeat; **voulez-vous ~, s'il vous plaît?** would you please repeat that?; **on ne saurait assez ~ que** it cannot be repeated often enough that; **répétez après moi** repeat after me; **faire ~ des élèves** to make pupils repeat aloud; **il se fait toujours ~ une question avant de répondre** he always asks for a question to be repeated before replying; **j'ai dû me faire ~ la question trois fois avant de comprendre** I had to have the question repeated three times before I understood; **~ qch à qn** to say sth to sb again, to tell sb sth again; **je ne me le suis pas fait ~ deux fois!** I didn't need to be told twice!; **répète (un peu pour voir)!** say that again!; **je l'ai dit et je le répète encore** I've said it once and I'll say it again; **tu répètes toujours la même chose** you keep saying the same thing over and over again; **je te répète que tu as tort** I keep telling you that you're wrong; **2** (rapporter) to tell; **ne le répète à personne** don't tell anyone; **elle répète tout à sa mère** she tells her mother everything she hears; **promets-moi de ne rien ~** promise me you won't say anything ou repeat this to anyone; **elle répète tout ce qu'on lui dit** she repeats everything you tell her; **3** (refaire) to repeat [*essai, expérience, geste*]; **attaques/menaces/tentatives répétées** repeated attacks/threats/attempts; **4** (rejouer) (pour harmoniser) to rehearse [*pièce*]; to rehearse for [*concert*]; (pour apprendre) to practise[GB] [*passage, morceau*]; **~ son rôle** to go over ou through one's lines; **5** (reproduire) to repeat [*forme, son, image*]; **thème/motif répété indéfiniment** theme/pattern repeated indefinitely.

II se répéter *vpr* **1** (redire) (en rabâchant) to repeat oneself; (pour se rappeler) to repeat [sth] to oneself [*phrase, conseil*]; **tu l'as déjà dit, tu te répètes!** you've already said that, you're repeating yourself!; **je me répète tous les jours tes conseils** I repeat your advice to myself every day; **j'ai beau me ~ que** however often I tell myself that; **2** (se reproduire) [*phénomène, événement*] to be repeated; **le sinistre scénario s'est répété hier** the dreadful scenario was repeated yesterday; **cycle qui se répète tous les 60 ans** cycle which is repeated every 60 years; **l'histoire ne se répète pas** history doesn't repeat itself; **si ce genre d'accident se répète...** if this kind of accident happens again...; **que cela ne se répète pas!** don't let it happen again!

répétiteur, -trice /ʀepetitœʀ, tʀis/ *nm,f* coach; (d'opéra) répétiteur.

répétitif, -ive /ʀepetitif, iv/ *adj* [*tâche, geste*] repetitive; [*phénomène*] recurrent.

répétition /ʀepetisjɔ̃/ *nf* **1** (dans un texte) repetition; **2** (de geste, d'erreur) repetition; **3** Mus, Théât (mise au point) rehearsal; **4**† (leçon particulière) (private) coaching; **donner des ~s à qn** to give private coaching to sb.

■ **~ des couturières** Théât dress rehearsal; **~ générale** Théât dress rehearsal; Mus final rehearsal; **~ technique** Théât technical rehearsal.

répétitivité /ʀepetitivite/ *nf* repetitiveness.

repeuplement /ʀ(ə)pœpləmɑ̃/ *nm* **1** Géog repopulation; **2** (de forêt) reforestation (**en** with); **3** (de rivière) restocking (**en** with).

repeupler /ʀ(ə)pœple/ [1] **I** *vtr* **1** Géog to repopulate [*pays, ville, région*]; **2** Pêche, Chasse to restock [*étang, parc*] (**de** with); **3** Agric to reforest [*lieu*] (**en** with); **~ une forêt** to replant a forest.

II se repeupler *vpr* Géog to become repopulated.

repiquage /ʀ(ə)pikaʒ/ *nm* **1** (de riz) transplanting; (de salade, géranium) pricking out; **2** (de bande, disque) rerecording; **3** (de photo) retouching ¢; **4** (de rue, cour) repaving; **5** Biol subculturing; **effectuer un ~** to subculture (**de qch** sth); **6** Imprim overprinting.

repiquer /ʀ(ə)pike/ [1] **I** *vtr* **1** to transplant [*riz*]; to prick out [*salade, géranium*]; **2** (piquer encore) [*insecte*] to bite again; **3** to retouch [*photo*]; **4** to rerecord [*bande, disque*]; **5** to repave [*rue, cour*]; **6** Imprim to overprint; **7** Constr to key [*mur, paroi*]; **8**◑ (reprendre) [*voleur*] to pinch○ again [*objet*]; [*policier*] to nab○ again [*malfaiteur*]; **se faire ~** to get nabbed○ again.

II◑ **repiquer à** *vtr ind* **1** (reprendre) **~ au plat** to have another helping; **2** (recommencer) **~ au truc** to be at it again○.

répit /ʀepi/ *nm* respite; **travailler sans ~** to work ceaselessly ou without respite; **il pleut sans ~ depuis deux jours** it has been raining continuously for two days; **j'ai eu un (moment de) ~ à l'heure du déjeuner** I had a break at lunch time; **leur travail ne leur laisse aucun ~** they never get a break from work; **accorder/s'accorder un instant de ~** to give/take a moment off (**pour faire** to do); **laisser un ~ de cinq jours à qn** to give sb five days' grace.

replacer /ʀ(ə)plase/ [12] **I** *vtr* **1** (placer à nouveau) to put [sth] back, to replace [*objet*] (**dans** in; **sur** on); **on l'a replacé dans sa position initiale** it was put back in its original position; **2** fig (situer) **~ qch dans son contexte** to set sth back in context; **~ un débat dans un contexte international** to set a debate back in an international context; **3** (redonner un emploi) to find [sb] another job; **4**○ (citer à nouveau) to repeat, to trot out [sth] again [*blague, expression*].

II se replacer *vpr* **1** (retrouver un emploi) to find another job (**dans** in); **2** fig (s'imaginer) **se ~ dans une période/un contexte** to imagine oneself back in a period/context.

replanter /ʀ(ə)plɑ̃te/ [1] *vtr* **1** (changer de terre) to transplant [*rosier, arbre*]; **2** (après destruction) to replant [*arbre*]; **3** (reboiser) to replant [*parc, forêt*] (**en** with); **il faudra ~ pour éviter l'érosion** we must replant trees to avoid erosion.

replat /ʀəpla/ *nm* shelf.

replâtrage○ /ʀ(ə)plɑtʀaʒ/ *nm* fig pej **leur réconciliation, c'est du ~**○ their reconciliation is just papering over the cracks.

replâtrer /ʀ(ə)plɑtʀe/ [1] *vtr* **1** Constr to replaster [*mur*]; **2** fig to patch up [*groupe, union*]; **~ la situation financière** to paper over the cracks in the financial situation.

replet, -ète /ʀəplɛ, ɛt/ *adj* [*personne*] plump; [*visage, joues*] plump, chubby.

réplétion /ʀeplesjɔ̃/ *nf* (d'estomac) repletion; (de vessie) fullness.

repleuvoir /ʀ(ə)plœvwaʀ/ [39] *v impers* to rain again; **il repleut** it's raining again.

repli /ʀ(ə)pli/ *nm* **1** (double pli) double fold; **faire un ~ à qch** (sur un poignet) to fold sth back; (sur un rideau) to fold sth up; **2** (pli profond) fold; **les ~s du terrain/vêtement** the folds of the land/garment; **les ~s de sa conscience** fig the recesses of his/her conscience littér; **3** (recul) Mil (**mouvement de**) **~** withdrawal (**sur** to); **effectuer un ~ stratégique/tactique** to effect a strategic/tactical withdrawal; **une position de ~** fig a fallback position; **on note un ~ des actionnaires sur les valeurs sûres** it has become apparent that shareholders are falling back on blue chip securities; **4** (mouvement de retrait) retreat; **après le ~ des manifestants devant la police** after the demonstrators retreated from the police; **~ sur soi(-même)** Psych withdrawal; **5** (régression) fall; **être en ~ de 10%** to be down 10%; **accuser un ~ de 10%** to show a fall of 10%; **le ~ du dollar/des valeurs/des exportations** the fall in the dollar/in share prices/in exports.

repliable /ʀ(ə)plijabl/ *adj* folding (*épith*).

réplication /ʀeplikasjɔ̃/ *nf* Biol replication.

repliement /ʀ(ə)plimɑ̃/ *nm* **~ (sur soi-même)** withdrawal.

replier /ʀ(ə)plije/ [2] **I** *vtr* **1** (plier à nouveau) to fold up [*dépliant, plan*]; **2** (rabattre) to turn down [*page*]; to fold [sth] back [*drap*] (**sur** over); **3** (refermer) to fold up [*chaise-longue, éventail*]; to close [*parapluie, canif*]; **4** (remettre en place) [*personne*] to fold [*bras*]; **~ ses jambes** to tuck one's legs under; **~ ses ailes** [*oiseau*] to fold its wings; **5** Mil to pull back [*armée*]; to evacuate [*civils*].

II se replier *vpr* **1** [*lame, canapé-lit*] to fold up; **2** [*troupe, armée*] to withdraw (**sur** to; **dans** into); **3 se ~ sur soi-même** [*personne*] to become withdrawn; [*institution, pays*] to shut itself off from the rest of the world.

réplique /ʀeplik/ *nf* **1** (riposte verbale) retort, rejoinder; **faire qch en ~ à un discours/une action** to do sth in response to a speech/an action; **il a la ~ facile** he's never stuck for an answer, he's always ready with an answer; **2** (objection) **faire qch sans ~** to do sth without arguing; **pas de ~!** don't answer back!, no arguments!; **argument**

sans ~ irrefutable argument; **3** Théât line; **oublier une ~** to forget a line; **supprimer quelques ~s** to cut some lines; **donner la ~ à qn** (pour faire apprendre un rôle) to go through sb's lines with them; (dans une représentation) to play opposite sb; **manquer sa ~** to miss one's cue; **les deux politiciens se sont donné la ~ pendant une heure** there was an hour-long sparring session between the two politicians; **4** (copie) Art replica; (personne) **elle est la ~ de sa mère** she is the image of her mother.

répliquer /ʀeplike/ [1] **I** *vtr* **1** (répondre) to retort; **'jamais,' répliqua-t-elle** 'never,' she retorted; **elle répliqua que ce n'était pas possible** she retorted that it wasn't possible; **elle m'a répliqué que je mentais** she retorted that I was lying; **2** Biol to replicate.

II répliquer à *vtr ind* **~ à qn** (en objectant) to argue with sb; **il n'aime pas qu'on lui réplique** he doesn't like to be argued with; **~ à** to respond to [*objections, critique, attaques*].

III *vi* **1** (verbalement) to answer back; **ne réplique pas!** don't answer back!, don't argue!; **2** (par une action) to retaliate, to respond; **~ en lançant une bombe** to respond by dropping a bomb.

replonger /ʀ(ə)plɔ̃ʒe/ [13] **I** *vtr* **~ qch dans l'eau** to plunge sth back into the water; **~ le pays dans le désordre/la misère** fig to plunge the country back into chaos/poverty.

II *vi* **1** [*nageur*] to dive again (**dans** into); **2** fig **~ dans la dépression/le désespoir** to plunge ou sink back into depression/despair; **il a replongé**○ **après la mort de son père** after his father's death he sank back into depression.

III se replonger *vpr* **se ~ dans son travail/sa lecture** to immerse oneself in one's work/one's book again.

répondant, ~e /ʀepɔ̃dɑ̃, ɑ̃t/ *nm,f* **1** (d'une personne) referee; Fin, Jur (caution) surety, guarantor; **être le ~ de qn** Fin, Jur to stand surety ou guarantor for sb; (pour références) to be sb's referee; fig to vouch for sb; **2** Relig server.

IDIOMES **avoir du ~**○ (de l'argent) to have money; (de la repartie) to be good at repartee.

répondeur /ʀepɔ̃dœʀ/ *nm* Télécom **~ (téléphonique)** (telephone) answering machine, answerphone.

répondre /ʀepɔ̃dʀ/ [6] **I** *vtr* **1** (dire, écrire) to answer, to reply; **~ une injure** to answer ou reply with an insult; **~ une bêtise** to give a silly answer ou reply; **je n'ai rien répondu** I didn't reply, I didn't say anything in reply; **tu réponds n'importe quoi** you just give any answer that comes into your head; **mais enfin, réponds quelque chose!** well, for heaven's sake, say something!; **réponds-leur que je m'en occupe** tell them I'm dealing with it; **je me suis vu ~ que, il m'a été répondu que** I was told that; **tu me demandes si c'est possible et je te réponds que oui/non** you're asking me if it is possible, and I'm telling you it is/isn't; **que peut-elle ~ à cette accusation?** how can she answer the accusation?; **qu'as-tu à ~ (à cela)?** what' s your answer (to that)?, what do you have to say to that?; **il m'a répondu que** he answered that, he replied (to me) that; **qu'est-ce qu'il t'a répondu?** what was his answer?; **bien répondu!** well said!; **2** Relig to respond [*messe*].

II répondre à *vtr ind* **1** (être conforme à) **~ à** to answer, to meet [*besoin, exigences*]; to fulfil [*souhait, désir*]; to answer, to fit [*signalement*]; to come up to, to meet [*attente, espérances*]; **pour ~ aux nouvelles règles** in order to conform to the new ruling; **la maison ne répond pas à leurs exigences** the house falls short of ou does not meet their requirements; **ça ne répond pas à mon attente** it falls short of ou does not come up to my expectations; **le château répond à l'idée que je m'en faisais** the castle is just as I imagined it; **2** (agir en retour) **~ à** to respond to [*avances, appel, critique, attaque*]; to return [*affection, salut, politesse*]; to deal with [*situation, frustrations*]; **~ aux critiques de qn par le mépris** to treat sb's criticism with contempt; **~ à un sourire** to smile back; **~ à la violence par la violence** to meet violence with violence.

III répondre de *vtr ind* (servir de caution) **~ de qn** to vouch for sb; Fin, Jur to stand surety for sb; **~ d'une action** to answer for an action; **je réponds de lui/son honnêteté** I can vouch for him/his honesty; **~ de ses actes devant la justice** to answer for one's actions in court; **il doit ~ des dettes de sa femme** he is liable for his wife's debts; **je ne réponds plus de rien** it's out of my hands from now on; **ça sera fini, j'en** or **je vous en réponds**○ it will be finished, take my word for it ou you can be sure of that.

IV *vi* **1** (donner une réponse) **~ à** to reply to, to answer [*personne, question, lettre*]; to reply to [*ultimatum*]; **~ à un questionnaire** to fill in a questionnaire; **~ à un chef d'accusation** Jur to answer a charge; **~ par oui ou par non** to answer yes or no; **si le téléphone sonne, réponds** if the telephone rings, answer it; **~ par écrit/par lettre/par téléphone** to reply in writing/by letter/by phone; **il m'a répondu par une longue lettre** he sent me a long letter back ou in reply; **je n'ai pas encore répondu à ta lettre** I've not written back to you yet; **~ par un sourire/clin d'œil** to answer with a smile/wink; **~ en levant les bras au ciel** to throw up one's hands by way of reply ou of an answer; **j'attends qu'il réponde** I'm waiting for his reply; **seul l'écho me répondit** there was no answer but an echo; **la flûte répond au piano** the flute answers the piano; **2** (se manifester) **~ au téléphone/à la porte** to answer the phone/the door; **ça ne répond pas** there's no answer ou reply; **3** (être insolent) **~ à qn** to answer sb back GB, to talk back to sb; **ose ~!** just you say a word!; **4** liter (se nommer) **elle répond au (doux) nom de Flore** she answers to the (charming) name of Flore; **5** (réagir) Physiol, Tech [*mécanisme, organe, muscle*] to respond (**à** to); **la direction n'a pas répondu** Aut the steering failed; **les freins ne répondent plus** the brakes have failed ou aren' t working any more.

V se répondre *vpr* **1** (se faire pendant) [*parterres, fontaines*] to match; **2** (se faire entendre) [*oiseaux*] to call to each other; [*instruments de musique*] to answer each other.

répons /ʀepɔ̃/ *nm inv* Relig response.

réponse /ʀepɔ̃s/ *nf* **1** (à une question, lettre, objection) answer (**à** to), reply (**à** to); (à un questionnaire) reply; **~ à une accusation** answer to an accusation; Jur answer to a charge; **la ~ est oui** the answer is yes; **pour toute ~ il haussa les épaules** his only reply ou response was to shrug his shoulders; **en ~ à votre question** in answer ou reply to your question; **en ~ à votre lettre** in reply to your letter; **ma lettre est restée sans ~** my letter remained unanswered; **télégramme avec ~ payée** reply paid telegram; ▶**berger**; **2** (solution) answer (**à** to); **3** (réaction) response (**à** to); **en ~ à notre appel télévisé** in response to our televised appeal; **temps de ~** response time; **la ~ du public/marché a été favorable** the public/market has responded favourably[GB]; **4** Mus answer.

■ **~ manuelle** manual answering; **~ de Normand** noncommittal reply; **~ des primes** Fin declaration of options.

IDIOMES **avoir ~ à tout** to have all the answers, to have an answer for everything.

repopulation /ʀ(ə)pɔpylasjɔ̃/ *nf* repopulation.

report /ʀ(ə)pɔʀ/ *nm* **1** (de procès) adjournment (**à** until); (de rendez-vous, départ, mariage, réunion, d'inscription, élection) postponement (**à** to, until); (de jugement) deferment (**à** to, until); **le ~ de la date d'examen a contrarié beaucoup de gens** the fact that the date of the exam was put back upset a lot of people; **2** (de dessin, d'image) transfer (**sur** onto); **3** (aux élections) transfer; **le ~ des voix au bénéfice de** or **en faveur de** the transfer of votes to; **4** (de somme) carrying forward; (somme reportée) amount carried forward; **faire le ~ d'une somme** to carry a sum forward.

■ **~ d'incorporation** Mil deferment of military service.

reportage /ʀ(ə)pɔʀtaʒ/ *nm* **1** Presse, TV, Radio report (**sur** on); **lire notre ~ page 18** read our report on page 18; **~ télévisé/radio** television/radio report; **partir en ~** to go to cover a story; **rentrer de ~** to come back from covering a story; **2** (technique) reporting; **les techniques du ~** the techniques of reporting; **un spécialiste du ~** an expert reporter.

■ **~ photo(graphique)** photo-reportage.

reporter[1] /ʀ(ə)pɔʀte/ [1] **I** *vtr* **1** (différer) to put back [*date*] (**à** to); to postpone, to put back [*rendez-vous, événement*] (**à** until); to extend [*délai*] (**à** to); to postpone [*départ, match*] (**à** until); to defer [*jugement*] (**à** until); **~ une décision** to postpone making a decision; **~ son départ d'une semaine** to postpone one's departure by a week; **~ la réunion de lundi à vendredi** to postpone Monday's meeting until Friday; **2** (copier sur un autre support) to carry forward [*calcul, résultat*]; to copy out [*texte, nom*]; to transfer [*dessin, photo*]; **~ des noms sur une liste** to copy out names on a list; **3** (déplacer) **~ un paragraphe/chapitre en début d'un texte** to move a paragraph/chapter to the beginning of a text; **4** (aller remettre) to take [sth] back [*marchandise, objet*]; **~ un livre à la bibliothèque** to take a book back to the library; **5** (dans le passé) **cela nous reporte longtemps en arrière** that's going back a long time; **~ qn plusieurs années en arrière** to take sb back several years; **6** (transférer) to transfer [*affection*] (**sur** to); **~ des voix sur un autre candidat** to transfer votes to another candidate; **~ son agressivité sur qn** to take one's aggression out on sb; **7** (porter à nouveau) to wear [sth] again [*vêtement, chapeau*].

II se reporter *vpr* **1** (consulter) to refer to, to see; **reportez-vous à la page 3** refer to page 3; **reportez-vous au règlement** refer to the rules; **2** (revenir en pensée) **se ~ à** to think back to, to cast one's mind back to; **reportez-vous aux jours précédant le meurtre** cast your mind back to the days leading up to the murder; **3** (être transféré) [*affection*] to be transferred (**sur** to); [*voix*] to be transferred (**sur** to).

reporter[2] /ʀ(ə)pɔʀtɛʀ/ ▶**510** *nm* Presse, TV reporter; **une femme ~** a woman reporter; **un grand ~** a special correspondent.

reporter-cameraman, *pl* **reporters-cameramen** /ʀ(ə)pɔʀtɛʀkameʀaman, mɛn/ ▶**510** *nm* reporter and cameraman.

reporter-photographe, *pl* **reporters-photographes** /ʀ(ə)pɔʀtɛʀfɔtɔgʀaf/ ▶**510** *nm* press photographer.

reporteur /ʀ(ə)pɔʀtœʀ/ ▶**510** *nm* TV, Presse reporter.

repos /ʀ(ə)po/ *nm inv* **1** (inactivité, délassement) rest; **s'accorder du ~** to have a rest; **s'accorder un instant de ~** to have a little rest; **observez un ~ complet pendant six semaines** you must have six weeks of complete rest; **après un jour/une heure de ~** after a day's/an hour's rest; **mon jour de ~** (sans travail) my day off; **ce n'est pas de tout ~** it's no easy task, it's no picnic○; **sans ~** [*travailler*] without respite; [*voyager*] constantly; [*marcher*] without stopping; **muscle au ~** relaxed muscle; **machines au ~** machines which are not working; **terres au ~** fallow land;

~! Mil at ease!; **soldats au ~** soldiers standing at ease; **2** (absence de soucis) peace littér; **chercher/trouver le ~** to search for/ to find peace; **troubler le ~ des morts** to disturb the slumbers of the dead.

■ **~ compensateur** *extra time off for extra hours worked*; **le ~ éternel** euph eternal rest.

reposant, **~e** /ʀ(ə)pozɑ̃, ɑ̃t/ *adj* [*occupation*] peaceful, restful; [*lumière*] soothing; [*position, lecture*] relaxing.

repose /ʀ(ə)poz/ *nf* (de moquette) relaying; **la ~ d'une vitre** putting in a new windowpane.

reposé, **~e** /ʀ(ə)poze/ **I** *pp* ▶ **reposer**.
II *pp adj* **avoir les traits ~s** or **le visage ~** to look rested; **lire qch à tête ~e** to read sth at one's leisure.

repose-pied, *pl* **~s** /ʀ(ə)pozpje/ *nm* footrest.

reposer /ʀ(ə)poze/ [1] **I** *vtr* **1** (d'une fatigue) to rest [*jambes, esprit*]; **cela me repose de mon travail habituel** it's a rest from my usual work; **cela repose de ne pas parler** saying nothing can be restful; **lumière qui repose** soothing light; **2** (appuyer) **~ sa tête sur qch** to rest one's head on sth; **~ sa tête sur l'épaule de qn** to rest ou lean one's head on sb's shoulder; **3** (placer) to put [sth] down [*téléphone, verre*]; (à nouveau) to put [sth] down again [*bibelot*]; **~ qch à sa place** to put sth back in its place ou where it belongs; **4** (soulever à nouveau) to ask [sth] again [*question*]; **cela repose le problème du chômage** this raises the problem of unemployment again; **~ sa candidature** (pour un emploi) to reapply; **5** (fixer de nouveau) to re-lay [*moquette*]; **~ une vitre** to put in a new pane of glass.
II *vi* **1** (être enterré) **qu'elle repose en paix** may she rest in peace; **où reposent de nombreux soldats** where many soldiers are buried; **le corps/le défunt repose dans la chambre funéraire** the body/the deceased man is lying in the funeral parlour[GB]; **'ici repose Victor Hugo'** (sur tombe) 'here lies Victor Hugo'; **2** (être inactif) **laisser ~ la terre** to rest the land; **la nature repose** liter nature is at rest littér; **3** [*navire, épave*] to lie; **4** Culin **puis laisser ~** [*pâte*] then let it rest; **5 ~ sur** [*idée, expérience*] to be based on; **le bâtiment repose sur...** the building is built on...; **la poutre repose sur...** the beam is supported by...; **tout repose sur elle** (être sa responsabilité) it all rests with her.
III se reposer *vpr* **1** (d'une fatigue) to have a rest, to rest; **repose-toi bien** have a good rest; **laisser ~ son cheval** to let one's horse rest; **2** (faire confiance, avoir besoin de) **se ~ sur qn** to rely on sb; **3** (à nouveau) [*montgolfière, avion*] to touch down again; **le problème va se ~** the problem will recur.

repose-tête /ʀ(ə)poztɛt/ *nm inv* **1** gén head rest; **2** Aut head restraint.

reposoir /ʀ(ə)pozwaʀ/ *nm* Relig altar of repose.

repoussage /ʀ(ə)pusaʒ/ *nm* Tech repoussé work.

repoussant, **~e** /ʀ(ə)pusɑ̃, ɑ̃t/ *adj* [*laideur*] hideous; [*saleté, odeur*] revolting; **être ~ de laideur** to be hideously ugly.

repousse /ʀ(ə)pus/ *nf* **1** (de cheveux, d'herbe) regrowth; **2** Agric (jeune pousse) new growth.

repousser /ʀ(ə)puse/ [1] **I** *vtr* **1** (remettre en place) to push [sth] back into [*tiroir*]; to push [sth] to [*verrou, porte, fenêtre*]; to push back [*meuble, objet*]; **~ la porte d'un coup de pied** to kick the door to ou shut; **2** (déplacer, éloigner) to push away [*papiers, livres, objets*]; to push back [*mèche de cheveux*]; **3** (obliger à reculer) to push ou drive back [*individu, attaquant, foule, manifestants, animal*]; Mil to repel [*attaquant*]; **il faut ~ l'ennemi hors de nos frontières** we must push the enemy back beyond our borders; **4** (s'opposer avec succès à) to repel [*attaque, charge, offensive*] (**de** with); to fight off, to resist [*tentation, tentative*]; **5** (rejeter) to dismiss [*objection, argument, conseil, offre*]; to decline [*aide*]; to turn down [*demande, requête, candidature*]; to reject [*candidat*]; **~ les avances de qn** to spurn sb's advances; **6** (dégoûter) [*physique, manière, saleté, odeur*] to revolt; **7** (différer) to postpone, to put [sth] back [*départ, rendez-vous*] (**jusqu'à** until); to put GB ou move [sth] back, to defer sout [*date*] (**jusqu'à** until); to postpone [*événement*] (**jusqu'à** until); **~ une réunion du lundi au vendredi** to postpone a Monday meeting until Friday; **~ son départ d'un mois** to put one's departure back by a month; **8** Tech to decorate [sth] with repoussé design [*cuir, métal*]; **en cuir/métal repoussé** in ou made of repoussé leather/metal.
II *vi* [*cheveux, barbe, herbe*] (après une coupe) to grow again; (après disparition) to grow back; [*feuille*] to grow again; [*dent*] to come up; **se laisser ~ la barbe/les cheveux** to let one's beard/hair grow (back) again.
III se repousser *vpr* [*électrons, aimants*] to repel each other.

repoussoir /ʀ(ə)puswaʀ/ *nm* **1** Tech (pour la pierre) burin; (pour le cuir) embossing tool; **2** Art (en peinture) repoussoir; **3**○ (mettant en valeur) foil; **servir de ~ à** to act as a foil to; **4**○ (personne très laide) ugly person.

répréhensible /ʀepʀeɑ̃sibl/ *adj* [*geste, acte*] reprehensible; **moralement ~** morally reprehensible; **il n'y a rien de ~ à dire ce que tu penses** there's nothing wrong with speaking your mind; **dans l'accident le conducteur était ~** the driver was to blame for the accident.

reprendre /ʀ(ə)pʀɑ̃dʀ/ [52] **I** *vtr* **1** (se resservir) **~ du pain/vin** to have some more bread/wine; **je reprendrais bien de ce ragoût** I would love some more (of that) stew; **reprenez un peu de poulet** have some more chicken; **j'en ai repris deux fois** I had three helpings; **2** (prendre de nouveau) to pick up again [*objet, outil*]; to take [sth] back [*cadeau, objet prêté*]; to retake, to recapture [*ville*]; to recapture [*fugitif*]; to go back on [*parole, promesse*]; (aller chercher) to pick [sb/ sth] up, to collect [*personne, voiture*]; **il reprit son balai et continua son travail** he picked up his broom again and carried on GB ou continued with his work; **tu passes me ~ à quelle heure?** what time will you come back for me?; **~ sa place** (son siège) to go back to one's seat; **~ sa place de numéro un/deux** to regain one's position as number one/two; **j'ai repris les kilos que j'avais perdus** I've put back on the weight I'd lost; **~ son nom de jeune fille** to revert to one's maiden name; **3** (accepter de nouveau) to take [sb] on again [*employé*]; to take [sb] back [*mari, élève*]; Comm to take [sth] back [*article*]; (contre un nouvel achat) to take [sth] in part GB ou partial US exchange; **si on me reprend ma vieille voiture** if I can trade in my old car, if they take my old car in part exchange; **les marchandises ne sont ni reprises ni échangées** goods cannot be returned or exchanged; **4** (recommencer) to resume, to continue [*promenade, récit, conversation*]; to pick up [sth] again, to go back to [*journal, tricot*]; to take up [sth] again, to resume [*fonctions, études*]; to take up [sth] again [*lutte*]; to reopen [*hostilités*]; to revive [*pièce, opéra, tradition*]; **~ le travail** or **son service** (après un congé, une grève) to go back to work; **on quitte à midi et on reprend à 14 heures** we stop at 12 and start again at 2; **ils ont repris les travaux de rénovation** the renovation work has started again ou has resumed; **~ sa lecture** to go back to one's book, to resume one's reading; **~ (le chemin de) l'école** to go back to school; **on reprend le bateau ce soir** (après une escale) we're sailing again tonight; (pour le retour) we're sailing back tonight; **tu reprends le train à quelle heure?** (de retour) what time is your train back?; **~ la parole** to start speaking again; **~ le fil de son discours/ses pensées** to carry on with one's speech/one's original train of thought; **~ le fil de la conversation** to pick up the thread of conversation; **~ une histoire au début** to go back to the beginning of a story; **~ les arguments un à un** to go over the arguments one by one; **5** (acquérir) to take over [*cabinet, commerce, entreprise*]; **~ une affaire à son compte** to take over a firm, to take a firm over; **6** (surprendre de nouveau) **~ qn à faire qch** to catch sb doing sth again; **que je ne t'y reprenne plus!** don't let me catch you doing that again!; **on ne m'y reprendra plus** you won't catch me doing that again; **on ne me reprendra plus à lui rendre service!** you won't catch me doing him/her any favours[GB] again!; **7** (recouvrer) **~ confiance** to regain one's confidence; **~ ses vieilles habitudes** to get back into one's old ways; **la nature reprend ses droits** nature reasserts itself; **elle a repris sa liberté** she's a free woman again; ▶ **bête**; **8** (retoucher) to alter [*vêtement, couture*]; Constr to repair [*mur*]; **~ le travail de qn** to correct sb's work; **~ cinq centimètres en longueur/largeur** Cout to take sth up/in 5 cm; **il y a tout à ~ dans ce chapitre** the whole chapter needs re-writing; **9** (utiliser de nouveau) to take up [*idée, thèse, politique*]; Littérat to re-work [*intrigue, thème*]; **~ une thèse à son compte** to adopt a theory as one's own; **10** (répéter) to repeat [*argument*]; to take up [*slogan, chant*]; **reprenons à la vingtième mesure** Mus let's take it again from bar 20; **~ la leçon précédente** Scol to go over the previous lesson again; **tous les médias ont repris la nouvelle** all the media took up the report; **pour ~ le vieil adage** as the saying goes; **11** (corriger) to correct [*élève*]; (pour langage grossier) to pull [sb] up; **permettez-moi de vous ~** excuse me, but that is not correct; **12** (resurgir) **mon mal de dents m'a repris** my toothache has come back; **la jalousie le reprend** he's feeling jealous again; **les soupçons le reprirent** he began to feel suspicious again; **voilà que ça le reprend**○**!** iron there he goes again!
II *vi* **1** (retrouver sa vigueur) [*commerce, affaires*] to pick up again; [*plante*] to recover, to pick up; **les affaires ont du mal à ~** business is only picking up slowly; **mon camélia reprend bien** (après une maladie) my camellia is recovering nicely; (après transplantation) my camellia has taken nicely; **la vie reprend peu à peu** life is gradually getting back to normal; **2** (recommencer) [*école, cours, bombardement, bruit, pluie*] to start again; [*négociations*] to resume; **le froid a repris** it's turned cold again; **la pluie a repris** it's started raining again; **nos émissions reprendront à 7 heures** Radio, TV we shall be back at 7 o'clock; **3** (continuer) **'c'est bien étrange,' reprit-il** 'it's very strange,' he continued.
III se reprendre *vpr* **1** (se corriger) to correct oneself; **se ~ à temps** to stop oneself in time; **2** (se ressaisir) [*personne*] to pull oneself together; Fin [*action, titre*] to rally, to pick up; **3** (recommencer) **s'y ~ à trois fois pour faire qch** to make three attempts to do ou at doing sth; **j'ai dû m'y ~ à plusieurs fois pour allumer le feu** it took me several attempts to get the fire going; **il se reprend à penser/espérer que c'est possible** he's gone back to thinking/ hoping it might be possible; **se ~ à craindre le pire** to begin to fear the worst again.

repreneur /ʀ(ə)pʀənœʀ/ *nm* Écon buyer; péj raider; (qui sauve l'entreprise) rescuer.

représailles /ʀ(ə)pʀezaj/ *nfpl* gén, Mil, Pol reprisals (*pl*), (moins violentes) retaliation ¢ (**contre, à l'égard de** against; **de la part de** on the part of); **user de** or **exercer des ~ contre l'ennemi** to take reprisals against the enemy; **par** or **en ~** in retaliation; **par peur de ~** for fear of reprisals; **nous nous attendons à des ~ de leur part** we expect them to retaliate.

représentable /ʀ(ə)pʀezɑ̃tabl/ *adj* **les résultats sont ~s par un graphique** the results can be shown in the form of a graph.

représentant, ~e /ʀ(ə)pʀezɑ̃tɑ̃, ɑ̃t/ *nm,f* **1** (délégué) (tous contextes) representative (**de** of); **~ syndical/des professeurs/du parti** trade union/teachers'/party representative; **~ des forces de l'ordre** police officer; **2** ▶ **510** Comm sales representative, sales rep; **le ~ de la maison** or **marque Hachette** the Hachette representative; **~ en vins/produits de beauté** representative for a wine merchant/a cosmetics firm; **3** (type, modèle) representative; **~ d'une espèce** representative example of a species.
■ **~ de commerce** sales representative, sales rep; **~ exclusif** sole agent; **~ en justice** Jur legal representative; **~ multicarte** (sales) representative for several firms.

représentatif, -ive /ʀ(ə)pʀezɑ̃tatif, iv/ *adj* **1** Pol [*assemblée, système*] representative; **2** (qui représente) representative (**de** of); **échantillon ~ de la population** representative cross-section ou sample of the population; **très/peu ~** very/not very typical (**de** of); **courbe représentative d'une fonction** curve representing ou which represents a function; **emblème/symbole ~ de la monarchie** emblem/symbol of the monarchy.

représentation /ʀ(ə)pʀezɑ̃tasjɔ̃/ *nf* **1** (action de représenter) representation (**de** of); **~ d'un son par un symbole** representation of a sound by a symbol; **~ graphique** graphic representation; **~ en arbre** tree diagram; **~ spatiale d'un objet** three-dimensional representation of an object; **2** Théât (séance) performance; **3** Psych (perception, image mentale) perception; **~ auditive/intellectuelle** auditory/mental perception; **4** (rôle de mandataire, délégué) representation; (mandataires, délégation) representatives (*pl*); **~ proportionnelle/diplomatique/en justice** proportional/diplomatic/legal representation; **la ~ nationale** Pol the representatives of a country; **mandataire qui assure la ~ de son mandant** Jur proxy who represents his/her principal; **5** Comm (activité) (de distributeur) representation; (de voyageur de commerce) commercial travelling[GB]; **~ exclusive** sole agency; **faire de la ~** to be a sales representative ou rep.

représentativité /ʀ(ə)pʀezɑ̃tativite/ *nf* representativeness; **la faible ~ d'un syndicat** the weak representation of a union; **reconnaître la ~ d'un syndicat/parti** to acknowledge that a union/party is representative; **partis ayant fait la preuve de leur ~** parties having proved their status as representatives.

représenter /ʀ(ə)pʀezɑ̃te/ [1] **I** *vtr* **1** (figurer) [*tableau, dessin*] to depict, to show; [*peintre*] to depict [*paysage, scène, milieu, situation*]; to portray [*personne*]; **le décor représente un jardin** Théât the scene shows a garden; **le peintre l'a représenté en empereur romain** the painter has portrayed him as a Roman emperor; **on l'a représenté comme un héros** he has been portrayed as a hero; **2** (exprimer) to represent; **~ les sons par des symboles** to represent sounds by symbols; **que représente ce signe?** what does this sign represent?; **face au reste, il représente la modération** compared to the rest, he represents the moderate position; **elle représente bien l'esprit de son époque** she typifies the spirit of her age; **3** (équivaloir à) to represent; (signifier) to mean; **le prix d'une voiture représente deux ans de salaire** a car represents two years' salary; **cela représente trop de sacrifices/frais** it means too many sacrifices/too much expense; **il représente, à leurs yeux, le parfait employé** in their eyes he is the perfect employee; **les enfants représentent les deux tiers de la population** children make up two thirds of the population; **le vin représente 60% de la consommation d'alcool** wine accounts for 60% of alcohol consumption; **ce qui, à mes yeux, représente un exploit** which, to my mind, is a considerable achievement; **4** (être mandataire de) to represent [*personne, communauté, organisation*]; **se faire ~ par** to be represented by; **~ la France à l'ONU/un congrès** to represent France at the UN/a conference; **~ qn auprès d'un tribunal** to represent sb in court; **5** Comm to represent [*entreprise*]; **6** Théât (jouer) to perform [*pièce*]; to put on [*spectacle*]; **7** (faire percevoir) fml **~ qch à qn** to point sth out to sb; **représentez-lui les avantages de ce contrat** point out the advantages of the contract to him/her.
II se représenter *vpr* **1** (s'imaginer) to imagine [*conséquences, scène, personne*]; **je me représente comment ça s'est produit** I can imagine how it happened; **on se la représente très bien en premier ministre** one can just see her as Prime Minister; **on a du mal à se le ~ en vaincu** it's hard to see him as a beaten man; **représentez-vous cette pauvre femme** just picture that poor woman; **2** (survenir à nouveau) [*occasion*] to arise again; [*problème*] to crop up again; **se ~ à qn** or **à l'esprit de qn** [*idée*] to occur to sb again, to cross sb's mind again; **lorsque l'occasion se représentera** next time the opportunity arises; **l'occasion ne se représentera pas** there won't be another opportunity; **3** (être à nouveau candidat) **se ~ à un examen** to resit GB or retake an examination; **se ~ aux élections** to stand GB ou run US for election again.

répressif, -ive /ʀepʀesif, iv/ *adj* [*action, régime, loi*] repressive; [*personne, éducation*] strict; **la psychiatrie répressive** psychiatric treatment involving restraint.

répression /ʀepʀesjɔ̃/ *nf* **1** Pol, Jur suppression (**de, contre** of); **la ~ sanglante contre les opposants** the bloody suppression of opponents; **la ~ des substances dopantes/du banditisme** the suppression of drugs/of crime; **mesures de ~** repressive measures; **l'Office de la ~ des fraudes** the Fraud Squad; **2** Psych (d'élan, de pulsion) repression; (en psychanalyse freudienne) suppression.

réprimande /ʀepʀimɑ̃d/ *nf* gén, Mil reprimand; **faire de sévères ~s à qn** to reprimand sb severely (**pour** for).

réprimander /ʀepʀimɑ̃de/ [1] *vtr* to reprimand (**qn d'avoir fait** sb for doing).

réprimer /ʀepʀime/ [1] *vtr* to repress [*envie, nervosité, penchant*]; to suppress [*bâillement, sourire*]; to suppress [*révolte*]; to crack down on [*fraude, trafic*].

repris /ʀ(ə)pʀi/ *nm inv* **~ de justice** ex-convict; **un dangereux ~ de justice** a hardened criminal.

reprisage /ʀ(ə)pʀizaʒ/ *nm* (de tissu) mending; (de chaussettes) darning.

reprise /ʀ(ə)pʀiz/ *nf* **1** (récupération) (de ville, place forte) recapture; Jur (de concession, bien) repossession; **procédure de ~** Jur repossession proceedings; **2** (recommencement) (de travaux, cours, vols, dialogue, négociations, d'hostilités) resumption (**de** of); (de froid, mauvais temps) return (**de** of); (de pièce, film) rerun; (d'émission) Radio, TV repeat; (d'œuvre rarement jouée) revival; **~ du travail** resumption of work; (après une grève) return to work; **~ des cours le 10 mars** school starts again on 10 March; **à deux ~s** on two occasions, twice; **à plusieurs** or **maintes ~s** on several occasions, repeatedly, again and again; **3** Écon, Fin (nouvel essor) (de demande, production) increase (**de** in); (de commerce) revival (**de** of); **~ de la Bourse** stock market rally ou recovery; **la ~ économique/des affaires/des cours** economic/business/stock market recovery; **on assiste à une ~ de l'économie/du marché** we're seeing an upturn in the economy/in the market; **la ~ de l'emploi** the fall in unemployment; **les actions sont en ~ à 20 francs** shares are up at 20 francs; **4** Comm (de marchandise) return, taking back; (contre un nouvel achat) trade-in, part exchange GB; Comm, Écon (d'entreprise, de commerce) takeover, acquisition; **marchandise en dépôt avec ~ des invendus** goods on sale or return; **la maison ne fait pas de ~** goods cannot be returned; **donner une voiture en ~** to trade in a car; **accepter une voiture en ~** to take a car in part GB ou partial US exchange; **250 francs de ~ sur votre vieille machine à laver contre achat d'une neuve** 250 francs for your old washing machine when you buy a new one; **valeur de ~** part exchange GB ou trade-in value; **5** (dans l'immobilier) key money; **payer 10 000 francs de ~ au locataire partant** to pay the outgoing tenant 10,000 francs key money; **6** Aut acceleration ¢; **avoir de bonnes ~s** to have good acceleration; **7** Cout (de tissu) mend; (de chaussette, lainage) darn; **faire une ~ à qch** to mend [*tissu, robe*]; to darn [*chaussette, lainage*]; **8** Sport (en boxe) round; (au football) start of second half; (en escrime) bout; Équit riding lesson; **combat en 10 ~s** fight over 10 rounds; **9** (réutilisation) taking up; **10** Mus (phrase, signe, exécution) repeat; **11** Constr **faire la ~ d'un mur** to repair a wall.
■ **~ d'une entreprise par l'encadrement** management buyout; **~ d'une entreprise par les salariés**, **RES** employee buyout.

repriser /ʀ(ə)pʀize/ [1] *vtr* to mend [*vêtement, rideau, accroc*]; to darn [*chaussette*].

réprobateur, -trice /ʀepʀɔbatœʀ, tʀis/ *adj* reproachful, disapproving.

réprobation /ʀepʀɔbasjɔ̃/ *nf* **1** gén disapproval, reprobation sout; **devant la ~ de qn** faced with sb's disapproval; **2** Relig reprobation.

reproche /ʀ(ə)pʀɔʃ/ *nm* **1** (remontrance) reproach, reprimand; **faire** or **adresser des ~s à qn** to reproach ou reprimand sb (**sur, au sujet de** for); **j'ai un ou deux ~s à vous faire** I've one or two criticisms to make; **essuyer des ~s** to come under attack (**de la part de** from), to be criticized (**de la part de** by); **attitude qui mérite des ~s** reprehensible attitude; **un ton/regard de ~** a reproachful tone/look; **sans ~** beyond reproach; **sans peur et sans ~** liter dauntless; **sans vouloir vous faire de ~, soit dit sans ~** fml without wishing to criticize ou reproach you; **2** (critique) (à l'égard de qch) **faire des ~s à qch** to find fault with sth; **il n'y a aucun ~ à faire à cette maison** there's nothing wrong with this house; **3** liter **être un ~ permanent pour qn** to be a living reproach to sb.

reprocher /ʀ(ə)pʀɔʃe/ [1] **I** *vtr* **1** (parlant de personnes) **~ qch à qn** to criticize ou reproach sb for sth; **~ à qn sa malhonnêteté/son ingratitude/son égoïsme** to criticize ou to reproach sb for his/her dishonesty/ingratitude/selfishness; **qu'est-ce que tu lui reproches?** what have you got against him/her?; **je ne vous reproche rien, mais...** I'm not criticizing ou reproaching you but...; **on ne peut rien lui ~** he's/she's beyond reproach; **sur le plan personnel je n'ai rien à te ~** I've got nothing against you on a personal level; **pour ce qui est de votre travail il n'y a rien à vous ~** as far as your work goes, you are beyond reproach; **~ à qn de faire** (ponctuellement) to criticize ou to reproach sb for doing; **je lui reproche de ne jamais tenir compte des autres** I hate the way he/she never considers other people; **elle me reproche de ne jamais lui écrire** she complains that I never write to her; **2** (parlant de choses) **ce que je reproche à cette voiture c'est sa consommation d'essence** what I don't like about this car is its fuel consumption; **je n'ai rien à ~ à cette maison si ce n'est que...** the only thing I don't like about this house is that...; **est-ce que tu me reproches le pain que je mange?** so you even begrudge me a bit of bread!; **tu ne peux pas**

me ~ les erreurs des autres you can't blame me for other people's mistakes; **qu'est-ce que tu reproches à ma cravate orange?** what's wrong with my orange tie?; **ce que je reproche à votre devoir c'est...** what's wrong with your paper is...; **il n'y a** or **je n'ai rien à ~ à votre devoir** there's nothing wrong with your paper; **les faits qui lui sont reprochés** the charges against him/her.

II **se reprocher** *vpr* **se ~ qch** to blame ou reproach oneself for sth; **je n'ai rien à me ~** I've done nothing wrong; **se ~ de faire** to blame ou reproach oneself for doing.

reproducteur, **-trice** /ʀ(ə)pʀɔdyktœʀ, tʀis/ I *adj* **1** Biol [*organe, appareil, fonction*] reproductive; **2** Agric [*animal, vache, porc*] breeding (*épith*); **taureau ~** bull for service.

II *nm* Agric breeding animal.

reproductible /ʀ(ə)pʀɔdyktibl/ *adj* reproducible.

reproductif, **-ive** /ʀ(ə)pʀɔdyktif, iv/ *adj* reproductive.

reproduction /ʀ(ə)pʀɔdyksjɔ̃/ *nf* **1** Biol (d'animaux, de plantes) reproduction; (de bactéries) multiplication; **la ~ artificielle** assisted reproduction; **2** (action de copier) (d'objet, œuvre) reproduction; (de clé) duplication; **droit de ~** copyright; **droits de ~ réservés** all rights reserved; **toute ~ intégrale** or **partielle de ce livre est illicite** no part of this book may be reproduced; **~ interdite** no unauthorized reproduction ou copying; **3** (copie) reproduction, copy; **4** Tech (restitution) reproduction; **~ des sons** sound reproduction.

reproduire /ʀ(ə)pʀɔdɥiʀ/ [69] I *vtr* **1** (répéter) to repeat [*erreur, expérience*]; to imitate, to copy [*habitude, comportement*]; to recreate [*condition, milieu*]; to copy, to imitate [*geste*]; to reproduce [*son, voix*]; **2** (copier) to reproduce, to copy [*tableau, motif, meuble, photo*] (**sur** on); to duplicate [*clé*]; to reproduce [*texte, déclaration*] (**sur** on; **dans** in); to recreate [*style, condition, atmosphère*]; **sa déclaration sera reproduite dans les journaux** his/her declaration will be printed (in full) in the papers; **ils reproduisent à la craie/à l'encre des tableaux célèbres** they reproduce famous paintings in chalk/in ink; **3** Biol to breed [*animal, plante, espèce*]; **4** Tech (restituer) to reproduce [*son*].

II **se reproduire** *vpr* **1** Biol [*homme*] to reproduce; [*animal, plante*] to reproduce, to breed; **2** (se répéter) [*processus, changement, situation, phénomène*] to recur; [*faute, scandale, faits*] to happen again, to recur; **pour éviter que ces faits ne se reproduisent** to make sure that this doesn't happen again; **si cela devait se ~...** if it were to happen again...; **et que cela ne se reproduise plus!** and don't let it happen again!

reprographie /ʀəpʀɔgʀafi/ *nf* (reproduction) reprography; (département) reprographics (+ *v sg*).

reprographier /ʀəpʀɔgʀafje/ [2] *vtr* to reproduce.

réprouvé, **~e** /ʀepʀuve/ *nm,f* outcast.

réprouver /ʀepʀuve/ [1] *vtr* to condemn.

reps /ʀɛps/ *nm* Tex rep.

reptation /ʀɛptasjɔ̃/ *nf* crawling ¢.

reptile /ʀɛptil/ *nm* Zool reptile.

reptilien, **-ienne** /ʀɛptiljɛ̃, ɛn/ *adj* reptilian.

repu, **~e** /ʀəpy/ I *pp* ▶ **repaître**.

II *pp adj* **1** (qui a bien mangé) replete (*jamais épith*); **~, il s'endormit** replete, he fell asleep; **je suis ~** I'm full; **les convives ~s** the well-fed guests; **l'animal ~ n'était plus à craindre** the animal had eaten its fill and was no longer dangerous; **2** fig **~ de** replete with; **~ d'honneurs/de plaisirs** replete with honours[GB]/pleasures; **elle est ~e d'art classique** she has had her fill of classical art.

républicain, **~e** /ʀepyblikɛ̃, ɛn/ I *adj, nm,f* republican.

II *nm* Zool social weaver.

republier /ʀ(ə)pyblije/ [2] *vtr* to republish.

république /ʀepyblik/ *nf* Pol republic; **après tout, on vit en ~** after all, it's a free country; **~ des lettres** republic of letters.

République /ʀepyblik/ *nf* Géog, Hist Republic; **la Cinquième ~** Hist the Fifth Republic; **la ~ d'Irlande/du Bénin** the Republic of Ireland/of Benin; **la ~ française** the French Republic.

répudiation /ʀepydjasjɔ̃/ *nf* **1** (d'épouse) repudiation; **2** (de droit, nationalité) renunciation (**de** of); **3** littér (d'engagement) reneging; (d'opinion, idée) repudiation; (de foi) renunciation.

répudier /ʀepydje/ [2] *vtr* **1** to repudiate [*épouse*]; **2** to renounce [*droit, nationalité*]; **3** littér (rejeter) to renege on [*engagement*]; to repudiate [*idée, opinion*]; to renounce [*foi, croyance*].

répugnance /ʀepyɲɑ̃s/ *nf* **1** (aversion) repugnance; **~ pour** loathing of [*aliment, odeur, saleté, crasse, personne*]; disgust for [*comportement*]; loathing of, disgust for [*mensonge, violence*]; **avoir** or **éprouver de la ~ pour** to loathe ou detest [*aliment, odeur, idée, théorie*]; to find [sth] repugnant ou disgusting [*comportement, mensonge, violence*]; to find [sth] disgusting [*saleté*]; to find [sb] repugnant, to loathe [*personne*]; **je n'ai que de la ~ pour ce genre de personne** I feel nothing but disgust ou loathing for that sort of person; **inspirer de la ~ à qn** to fill sb with loathing ou disgust; **2** (hésitation) reluctance (**à faire** to do); **avec ~** reluctantly, with reluctance.

répugnant, **~e** /ʀepyɲɑ̃, ɑ̃t/ *adj* [*personne*] repugnant; [*laideur, saleté, travail*] disgusting, revolting; [*lieu, milieu*] repugnant, disgusting; [*comportement*] disgusting, loathsome; [*œuvre, article, idée*] repugnant, loathsome; **être d'une laideur/saleté ~e** to be disgustingly ugly/dirty.

répugner /ʀepyɲe/ [1] I *vtr* [*nourriture, personne*] to be repugnant to, to disgust [*personne*]; **vivre ici me répugne** I loathe ou detest living here; **il me répugne profondément** I find him deeply repugnant.

II **répugner à** *vtr ind* to be averse to [*tâche, effort, violence*]; **il ne répugne pas à la tâche** he is not averse to work; **~ à faire** to be reluctant to do, to be loath to do; **il ne répugne pas à faire** it doesn't bother him to do; **il ne répugne pas à mentir** he has no qualms about lying.

III *v impers* **il me répugne de vous le dire, mais...** I hate to have to tell you, but...; **il me répugne de devoir faire** I am loath to do.

répulsif, **-ive** /ʀepylsif, iv/ I *adj* gén, Phys repulsive.

II Agric, Hort *nm* repellent; **~ à insectes** insect repellent.

répulsion /ʀepylsjɔ̃/ *nf* **1** (répugnance) feeling of repulsion; **éprouver de la/un sentiment de ~ pour qn** to be repelled by sb; **il m'inspire de la ~** I find him repulsive; **2** Phys repulsion.

réputation /ʀepytasjɔ̃/ *nf* **1** (honorabilité) reputation; **nuire à** or **ternir la ~ de qn** to damage sb's reputation; **2** (renom) reputation; **avoir bonne/mauvaise ~** to have a good/bad reputation; **se faire une ~** to make a name for oneself; **leur ~ n'est plus à faire** their reputation is well-established; **connaître qn/qch de ~** to know sb/sth by reputation; **sa ~ d'efficacité/de chanteur** his reputation for efficiency/as a singer; **avoir la ~ d'être** to have a reputation for being; **œuvre de grande ~** highly regarded work.

réputé, **~e** /ʀepyte/ *adj* **1** (renommé) [*compagnie, école, club*] reputable; [*écrivain, peintre*] of repute; [*produit*] well-known; **~ pour qch** renowned for sth; **c'est l'avocat le plus ~ de Paris** he's regarded as the best lawyer in Paris; **elle n'est pas ~e pour sa bonté** she's not renowned for her kindness; **2** (tenu pour) **~ cher/honnête** reputed ou reckoned to be expensive/honest; **il est ~ avoir une excellente cave** he is reputed ou reckoned to have an excellent cellar.

requérable /ʀəkeʀabl/ *adj* [*créance, rente*] which must be collected in person (*épith, après n*).

requérant, **~e** /ʀəkeʀɑ̃, ɑ̃t/ I *adj* **partie ~e** claimant.

II *nm,f* (qui sollicite) applicant; (qui réclame) claimant.

requérir /ʀəkeʀiʀ/ [35] *vtr* **1** (solliciter) to request [*secours, protection*]; **2** (nécessiter) (au besoin) to call for [*qualité*]; (impérativement) to require [*soin, compétences, unanimité, preuve*]; **3** (réquisitionner) Admin to requisition [*voitures, chevaux*]; to conscript [*civils, travailleurs*]; **le maire peut ~ la force publique** the mayor can summon the police; **4** Jur to call for [*peine, inculpation*]; **pendant que le procureur requérait** while the prosecutor was making his closing speech ou summation US.

requête /ʀəkɛt/ *nf* **1** (sollicitation) request; **à** or **sur la ~ de qn** at sb's request; **2** Jur petition; **déposer une ~** to file a petition; **adresser une ~ au juge** to petition the judge; **~ en faillite** petition in bankruptcy; **~ civile** *appeal to a Court against a judgment.*

requiem /ʀekwijɛm/ *nm inv* requiem.

requin /ʀ(ə)kɛ̃/ *nm* **1** (poisson) shark; **2** (personne cupide) shark.

■ **~ baleine** whale shark; **~ blanc** great white shark; **~ marteau** hammerhead (shark); **~ pèlerin** basking shark.

requinquer○ /ʀ(ə)kɛ̃ke/ [1] I *vtr* to buck [sb] up○; **ça (vous) requinque** [*boisson*] it peps you up○; [*repos, air frais*] it does you good.

II **se requinquer** *vpr* to perk up○.

requis, **~e** /ʀəki, iz/ I *pp* ▶ **requérir**.

II *pp adj* **1** (nécessaire) [*patience, tact, conditions*] necessary; (exigé) [*diplôme, âge, conditions*] required; **satisfaire aux conditions ~es** to meet the requirements; **2** [*personne*] conscripted for forced labour[GB]

III *nm inv* Hist **les ~** *civilians conscripted for forced labour[GB] during German Occupation 1939–45.*

réquisition /ʀekizisjɔ̃/ *nf* Admin, Mil (de biens, locaux) (officiellement) requisitioning; (officieusement) commandeering; (de personnes) conscription (*for forced labour[GB]*).

réquisitionner /ʀekizisjɔne/ [1] *vtr* Admin, Mil (officiellement) to requisition; (officieusement) to commandeer [*biens, locaux*]; to conscript [*ouvriers, civils*]; hum **elle m'a réquisitionné pour le ménage** she conscripted me to do the housework.

réquisitoire /ʀekizitwaʀ/ *nm* **1** Jur (discours) closing speech for the prosecution (*requesting a specific sentence*); (acte écrit) information laid by public prosecutor (*to start criminal proceedings*); **2** (dénonciation) indictment (**contre** of).

RER /ɛʀəɛʀ/ *nm*: *abbr* ▶ **réseau**.

RES /ɛʀəɛs/ *nm* ▶ **rachat**.

rescapé, **~e** /ʀɛskape/ I *adj* [*personne*] surviving.

II *nm,f* survivor (**de** from).

rescousse: **à la rescousse** /alaʀɛskus/ *loc adv* **venir/aller à la ~ de qn** to come/go to sb's rescue; **appeler qn à la ~** to call to sb for help.

réseau, *pl* **~x** /ʀezo/ *nm* **1** Tech (de fils, conduits, routes) network; **~ câblé/routier/de communications/de vente/électrique** cable/road/communications/sales/electricity network; **~ de transport** transport system; **~ hydrographique** river system; **sur l'ensemble du ~** throughout the network; **les abonnés du ~** Télécom telephone customers; **2** (de personnes) network; **~ d'espions/de trafiquants de drogue** spy/drugs ring; **3** Ordinat network; **~ local**

local area network; **4** Phys **~ cristallin** crystal lattice; **~ de diffraction** diffraction grating; **5** Zool reticulum.

■ **~ express régional**, **RER** *rapid-transit rail system in the Paris region*; **~ numérique à intégration de services**, **RNIS** Integrated Services Digital Network, ISDN.

résection /ʀesɛksjɔ̃/ *nf* resection.

réséda /ʀezeda/ *nm* mignonette, reseda spéc.

réservataire /ʀezɛʀvatɛʀ/ *nmf* Jur *heir who cannot be completely dishinherited.*

réservation /ʀezɛʀvasjɔ̃/ *nf* (d'hôtel, de restaurant, spectacle, transport) reservation, booking GB; **j'ai fait trois ~s pour demain** (pour le théâtre) I've reserved ou booked GB three seats for tomorrow; (pour l'avion) I've reserved ou booked GB three seats on tomorrow's flight; (pour le restaurant) I've reserved ou booked GB for three for tomorrow; (pour le train) I've reserved ou booked GB three seats on the train tomorrow; (pour l'hôtel) I've reserved ou booked GB for three people for tomorrow night.

réserve /ʀezɛʀv/ *nf* **1** (restriction) reservation (**au sujet de, à l'égard de** about); **le projet de loi suscite les plus grandes ~s dans l'opposition** the opposition have very strong reservations about the bill; **adhésion sans ~** unreserved support; **je me range sans ~ de votre côté** you have my unreserved support; **se confier à qn sans ~** to confide in sb totally; **avec une ~ importante** with one important condition; **sous ~ d'approbation du budget/de disponibilité/de changement** subject to budget approval/availability/alteration; **sous ~ que tout aille bien** provided everything goes well; **'sous (toute) ~'** (dans un programme) 'to be confirmed'; **je vous le dis sous toutes ~s** I'm telling you for what it's worth; **nouvelle donnée sous toutes ~s** unconfirmed news (report); **2** (provision) stock; **des ~s de sucre/d'eau** a stock of sugar/water; **faire des ~s de farine/sucre** to lay in a stock of flour/sugar; **~(s) d'argent** money in reserve; **j'ai toujours une bonne bouteille en ~** I always have a good bottle put by; **il a toujours une ou deux histoires drôles en ~** he's always got some funny story up his sleeve; **il peut sauter un repas, il a des ~s** he can afford to miss a meal; **3** École, Écon **~s de charbon/pétrole** coal/oil reserves; **~s d'eau** water supply (*sg*); **~s prouvées/probables/possibles** proved/indicated/inferred reserve; **4** (discrétion) reserve; **sortir de sa ~** to drop one's reserve; **manquer de ~** to be too outspoken; **garder une certaine ~ avec qn** to keep a certain distance with sb; **devoir** or **obligation de ~** Admin, Mil duty of confidentiality; **manquement à l'obligation de ~** breach of confidentiality; **5** (local de stockage) stockroom; **6** (section de bibliothèque) stacks (*pl*); (section de musée) storerooms (*pl*); **7** (territoire protégé) reserve; **~ naturelle/de chasse/de pêche** nature/game/fishing reserve; **~ ornithologique** bird sanctuary; **8** (territoire alloué) reservation; **~ indienne** Indian reservation; **9** Mil (réservistes) **la ~** the reserves (*pl*); **armée/officier de ~** reserve army/officer; **10** Art, Imprim blank; **laisser/garder en ~** to leave/to keep blank.

■ **~ alcaline** alkali reserve; **~ légale** Compta legal reserve; Jur *portion of inheritance that cannot be witheld from legal heir*; **~ de puissance** power reserve; **~ statutaire** statutory reserve; **~s en devises** currency reserves; **~s métalliques** bullion reserves; **~s monétaires** monetary reserves; **~s nutritives** nutritional reserves; **~s récupérables** exploitable reserves.

réservé, **~e** /ʀezɛʀve/ **I** *pp* ▶ **réserver**.

II *pp adj* **1** (privé) [*chasse, pêche*] private; **2** (attribué) **~ à la clientèle** (reserved) for patrons only; **~ aux invalides** (reserved) for the disabled; **voie ~e aux taxis/autobus** taxi/bus lane; **'tous droits de traduction et de reproduction ~s'** Jur 'all rights reserved'; **'~'** 'reserved'; **3** (réticent) [*personne, caractère*] reserved; (réticent) [*attitude, propos*] reticent; [*accueil*] restrained; **se montrer ~ sur les résultats/le succès de qch** to be guarded about the results/success of sth.

réserver /ʀezɛʀve/ [1] **I** *vtr* **1** (retenir à l'avance) to reserve [*chambre, table*]; to reserve, to book GB [*place, billet*]; **'pour ~ s'adresser à l'accueil'** 'reservations can be made at reception'; **2** (mettre de côté) to keep [*place*]; to put aside [*journal, pain, marchandise*]; (faire mettre de côté) to reserve, to have [sth] put aside [*journal, pain, marchandise*]; **~ qch pour les grandes occasions** to keep sth for special occasions; **3** (garder pour plus tard) to set aside [*argent*]; to save [*énergie, explications*]; **est-ce que tu peux me ~ une heure cet après-midi?** can you set aside an hour for me this afternoon?; **4** (destiner) **~ un mauvais accueil à qn** to give sb a chilly reception; **~ un bon accueil à qn** to give sb a warm welcome; **sans savoir ce que l'avenir nous réserve** without knowing what the future has in store ou holds for us; **je leur réserve une (mauvaise) surprise** I've got a (nasty) surprise in store for them; **il ignorait le (triste) sort qui lui était réservé** he knew nothing of the sad fate that awaited him; **l'année passée m'a réservé bien des déceptions/surprises** last year was full of disappointments/surprises for me; **on lui a réservé la place d'honneur** he's the guest of honour[GB]; **l'honneur de présider la séance t'est réservé** you are to have the honour[GB] of chairing the meeting; **5** (remettre à plus tard) **~ son jugement** to reserve judgement[GB]; **~ son diagnostic** to defer diagnosis; **le patron réserve sa décision jusqu'à lundi** the boss is postponing his decision until Monday.

II se réserver *vpr* **elle se réserve quelques instants de repos après le déjeuner** she sets aside a few minutes after lunch to relax; **se ~ la meilleure chambre/les meilleurs morceaux** to save the best room/the best bits for oneself; **se ~ le droit de faire** to reserve the right to do; **se ~ la faculté de faire** to keep the option open to do; **se ~ pour une meilleure occasion** to wait for a better opportunity; **se ~ pour le dessert** to save some room for dessert; **il se réserve pour la candidature à la présidence** he's saving himself for the presidential race.

réserviste /ʀezɛʀvist/ *nmf* reservist.

réservoir /ʀezɛʀvwaʀ/ *nm* **1** (cuve) gén tank; **~ à eau** water tank; **~ à essence** petrol tank GB, gas tank US; **~ de secours** reserve tank; **~ de stockage** storage tank; **2** (lac artificiel) reservoir; **3** fig (source) **~ de main-d'œuvre/compétences** reservoir of labour[GB]/ability.

résidant, **~e** /ʀezidɑ̃, ɑ̃t/ *adj* resident.

résidence /ʀezidɑ̃s/ *nf* **1** (maison) residence; **2** (domicile) place of residence; **changer de ~** to change one's place of residence; **établir sa ~ en France** to take up residence in France; **il faut 5 ans de ~ dans le pays** you must have been resident in the country for 5 years; **en ~ surveillée**, **assigné à ~** under house arrest; ▶ **certificat**; **3** (immeuble) (luxury) apartment building; **4** (groupe d'immeubles) residential development, apartment complex US.

■ **~ principale/secondaire** main/second home; **~ universitaire** (university) hall of residence GB, residence hall US.

résidence-hôtel, *pl* **résidences-hôtels** /ʀezidɑ̃sotɛl/ *nm* residential hotel.

résident, **~e** /ʀezidɑ̃, ɑ̃t/ *nm,f* **1** (étranger) foreign resident, resident alien US; **les ~s français en Italie** French nationals resident in Italy; **statut de ~ permanent** permanent resident status; **2** (habitant d'une résidence) resident; **3** (diplomate) resident.

résidentiel, **-ielle** /ʀezidɑ̃sjɛl/ *adj* residential.

résider /ʀezide/ [1] *vi* **1** (vivre) to reside sout, to live; **il réside à Paris/à cette adresse** he resides in Paris/at this address; **2** (se trouver) **~ dans qch** to lie in sth; **la difficulté réside en ce que** the difficulty lies in the fact that; **c'est là** or **en cela que réside la difficulté** that's where the difficulty lies.

résidu /ʀezidy/ *nm* **1** (dépôt) Chimie, fig residue **¢**; **~s de combustion** residue from combustion; **2** (reste) remnant; (détritus) waste **¢**; **~s industriels** industrial waste.

résiduel, **-elle** /ʀezidɥɛl/ *adj* residual; **valeur résiduelle** residual value.

résignation /ʀeziɲasjɔ̃/ *nf* **1** (acceptation) resignation (**à** to); **sa ~ n'est qu'apparente** he only seems to be giving in; **2** (abandon) Jur relinquishment (**de** of).

résigné, **~e** /ʀeziɲe/ *adj* [*ton, air, remarques*] resigned; **être ~ à qch/à son sort** to be resigned to sth/to one's fate; **il est ~** he's resigned to it; **des gens ~s** people resigned to their fate.

résigner /ʀeziɲe/ [1] **I** *vtr* liter to relinquish [*fonction*].

II se résigner *vpr* to resign oneself (**à qch** to sth; **à faire** to doing); **je ne peux m'y ~** I can't resign myself to it; **dans la vie, il faut se ~** in life you have to learn to accept things.

résiliable /ʀeziljabl/ *adj* [*contrat, bail*] which can be terminated (*épith, après n*).

résiliation /ʀeziljasjɔ̃/ *nf* (de contrat, bail) termination.

résilience /ʀeziljɑ̃s/ *nf* (en métallurgie) impact strength.

résilient, **~e** /ʀeziljɑ̃, ɑ̃t/ *adj* [*métal*] resilient.

résilier /ʀezilje/ [2] *vtr* to terminate [*contrat, bail*].

résille /ʀezij/ *nf* **1** gén net; (pour cheveux) hairnet; **bas ~** fishnet stockings; **2** Tech (de vitrail) leads (*pl*).

résine /ʀezin/ *nf* resin.

résiné /ʀezine/ *nm* resinated wine.

résineux, **-euse** /ʀezinø, øz/ **I** *adj* resinous.

II *nm inv* conifer.

résistance /ʀezistɑ̃s/ *nf* **1** (opposition) resistance (**à** to); **se rendre sans ~ aux policiers** to give oneself up to the police without a fight ou without putting up any resistance; **~ passive/non-violente** passive/nonviolent resistance; **faire de la ~** to resist; **la ~ au changement** resistance to change; **opposer** or **offrir une ~ à** to put up resistance to; **2** (groupe de personnes) resistance; **la Résistance** Hist the Resistance; **3** (fait de supporter physiquement) (de personne, soldat, sportif) resistance; (à la fatigue, douleur) resistance (**à** to); (de plante) hardiness; (de germe, cellule) resistance (**à** to); **athlète qui fait preuve d'une grande ~** athlete who has a lot of stamina; **manquer de ~** to lack stamina; **4** (fait de supporter moralement) resistance (**à** to); **5** Psych resistance (**à** to); **6** Phys (de matériau, métal) strength; (de tissu, d'appareil) strength; **~ à la corrosion** resistance to corrosion; **~ au choc** shock-resistance; **étudier la ~ des matériaux** to study the strength of materials; **~ de l'air** air ou wind resistance; **7** Électrotech (propriété) resistance; (conducteur) resistance, resistor; (d'appareil ménager) element; **une ~ de 75 ohms** a resistance ou resistor of 75 ohms; **une des ~s a grillé**○ one of the elements has gone.

résistant, **~e** /ʀezistɑ̃, ɑ̃t/ **I** *adj* **1** [*personne, sportif, animal*] tough, resilient; [*plante*] hardy; **être ~ à** [*personne, animal*] to be able to stand [*effort, froid, chaleur, fatigue*]; to be resistant to [*maladie*]; [*plante, maladie, cellule*] to be resistant to;

2 (solide) [*matériau, métal*] resistant; [*tissu, vêtement, cuir, plastique*] hard-wearing; **~ à** resistant to [*haute température, usure*]; **~ à l'eau/la chaleur/la rouille** waterproof/ heatproof/rustproof; **3** Hist Mil [*organisation, mouvement*] resistance (*épith*).

II *nm,f* Hist Mil resistance fighter; **il a été ~** he was in the Resistance.

résister /ʀeziste/ [1] *vtr ind* **1** (s'opposer par la force) **~ à** to resist [*agresseur, assaut, attaque, occupation, régime*]; **le voleur a tenté de ~** the thief tried to resist arrest; **~ par la violence** to put up armed resistance; **~ par la non-violence** to resist by nonviolent means; **~ passivement** to use passive resistance; **2** (supporter physiquement) **~ à** [*personne, cœur, organe, animal*] to stand [*effort physique*]; to be able to stand [*soif, climat*]; [*matériau*] to withstand [*force, poussée, vent*]; [*mur, bâtiment, bateau*] to stand up to, to withstand [*force, poussée, corrosion, explosion*]; [*tissu, vêtement*] to stand [*lavage*]; [*bâtiment, mur, bois, objet*] to stand up to, to resist [*intempéries, chaleur, traitement*] ; **l'appareil ne résistera pas longtemps à un tel traitement** the machine won't last long if you treat it like that; **tissu qui résiste à des lavages fréquents** material that will stand frequent washing; **couleur qui résiste au soleil** colour[GB] that won't fade in the sun; **le bâtiment/mur n'a pas résisté** the building/wall collapsed ou gave; **crème qui résiste à l'eau** waterproof cream; **matériau qui résiste à la chaleur/rouille** heatproof/rustproof material; **le coffre-fort a bien résisté** the safe remained intact; **rien ne lui résiste, il casse tout** he breaks everything in sight, and I mean everything!; **3** (supporter moralement) **~ à** [*personne*] to get through, to endure [*épreuve, chagrin, tragédie*]; to bear [*angoisse*]; **4** (être plus fort que) **~ à** [*amour, entente, amitié*] to withstand [*séparation, différences*]; to overcome [*conventions, opposition*]; [*économie, pays, régime, industrie*] to withstand [*crise, invasion, changement, grève, scandale*]; **~ à la concurrence de** to stand the competition from; **le gouvernement n'a pas résisté à la pression de l'opinion** the government had to give in to public opinion; **~ au temps** or **à l'épreuve du temps** to stand the test of time; **théorie qui ne résiste pas à l'analyse** theory that doesn't bear ou stand up to analysis; **leur amour a résisté à l'opposition de leurs parents** their love was stronger than their parents' opposition; **5** (tenir tête) **~ à** to resist [*personne, influence, pression, charme*]; **il ne supporte pas qu'on lui résiste** he can't bear resistance; **personne ne peut lui ~** nobody dares stand up to him/her; **6** (repousser) **~ à la tentation** to resist temptation; **je n'ai pas pu ~, j'ai acheté un nouveau chapeau** I couldn't resist (it), I bought a new hat.

résistivité /ʀezistivite/ *nf* resistivity.

résistor /ʀezistɔʀ/ *nm* resistor.

résolu, ~e /ʀezɔly/ I *pp* ▸ **résoudre**.

II *pp adj* resolute, determined.

résoluble /ʀezɔlybl/ *adj* [*contrat*] voidable.

résolument /ʀezɔlymɑ̃/ *adv* [*opposé, favorable*] resolutely; [*confiant*] totally; [*croire*] firmly.

résolutif, -ive /ʀezɔlytif, iv/ *adj* resolvent.

résolution /ʀezɔlysjɔ̃/ *nf* **1** (décision) resolution; **prendre une ~** to make a resolution; **prendre de bonnes ~s** to make (good) resolutions; **mes bonnes ~s pour la nouvelle année** my New Year's resolutions; **c'est une bonne ~** it's a good resolution; **prendre la ~ de faire** to make a resolution to do, to resolve to do; **2** Pol (proposition retenue) resolution; **voter une ~** to pass a resolution; **la ~ 687 de l'ONU** UN resolution 687; **3** (solution) resolution; **pour une ~ pacifique du conflit** for a peaceful resolution of the conflict; **4** (fermeté) resolve, resolution; **manquer de ~** to lack resolve; **agir avec ~** to act with resolve; **5** Math, Mus, Méd, Ordinat resolution.

résolutoire /ʀezɔlytwaʀ/ *adj* resolutive.

résonance /ʀezɔnɑ̃s/ *nf* **1** gén, Électrotech, Phys, Télécom resonance; **être/entrer en ~** to be/start resonating; **2** littér (de poème, musique) echo; **ça éveille une ~ en moi** it strikes a chord.

résonant, ~e = **résonnant**.

résonateur /ʀezɔnatœʀ/ *nm* Phys resonator.

résonnance = **résonance**.

résonnant, ~e /ʀezɔnɑ̃, ɑ̃t/ *adj* **1** Électrotech, Phys, Télécom resonant; **2** littér echoing (**de** with).

résonner /ʀezɔne/ [1] *vi* **1** (faire du bruit) [*pas, rire, cloche*] to ring out; [*sonnerie*] to resound; [*cymbales*] to clash; **2** (renvoyer un bruit) [*salle*] to echo; **~ de** to resound with.

résorber /ʀezɔʀbe/ [1] I *vtr* **1** fig to absorb [*excédent, déficit*]; to reduce, to bring [sth] down [*inflation, chômage*]; to use up [*stocks*]; to bring down [*sureffectif*]; to reduce [*misère, inégalités*]; **2** Méd to resorb [*épanchement, tumeur*].

II **se résorber** *vpr* **1** fig [*excédent, déficit*] to be reduced; [*inflation, chômage*] to be coming down; [*colère*] to fade; **2** Méd [*hématome*] to be resorbed.

résorption /ʀezɔʀpsjɔ̃/ *nf* **1** Méd resorption (**de** of); **2** fig (de chômage, d'inflation) reduction (**de** of); **le chômage est en ~** unemployment is coming down.

résoudre /ʀezudʀ/ [75] I *vtr* **1** (trouver la solution à) to solve [*équation, mystère*]; to resolve [*crise, conflits, désaccord*]; to solve, to resolve [*problème*]; **cela ne résoudra rien** that won't solve anything; **ce n'est pas résolu** it's unresolved; **2** fml (décider) to resolve ou decide to do; **il résolut d'attendre** he resolved to wait; **~ la destruction de qch** to decide to destroy sth; **~ qn à faire** [*personne*] to prevail on sb to do; **3** (décomposer) to resolve (**en** into); **4** Jur to rescind; **5** Méd to resolve.

II **se résoudre** *vpr* **1** (se décider) **se ~ à faire** to resolve ou make up one's mind to do; **il ne s'est toujours pas résolu à l'appeler** he still hasn't made up his mind to call him/her; **être résolu à faire** to be determined to do; **se montrer résolu à faire qch** to show one's determination to do sth; **2** (se résigner) **je ne peux pas me ~ à la renvoyer** I can't bring myself to dismiss her; **être résolu à attendre** to be resigned to waiting; **se ~ à l'attente/à l'idée que** to resign oneself to waiting/to the idea that.

respect /ʀɛspɛ/ I *nm* gén respect (**de, pour** for); **avoir du ~ pour** to respect, to have respect for [*personne, mémoire, opinion, croyance*]; **avoir peu/beaucoup de ~ pour** to have little/a lot of respect for; **devoir le ~ à qn** to owe sb (some) respect; **avec tout le ~ qui leur est dû** with all the respect due to them; **malgré tout le ~ qu'on lui doit** with all due respect to him/ her; **témoigner du ~ à qn** to show respect to ou toward(s) sb; **manquer de ~ à qn** to be disrespectful to ou toward(s) sb; **le ~ de soi** self-respect; **le ~ mutuel** mutual respect.

II **respects** *nmpl* respects; **présenter ses ~s à qn** to pay one's respects to sb; **je suis allé présenter mes ~s à** I went to pay my respects to; **transmettez** or **présentez mes ~s à votre épouse** give my regards to your wife.

IDIOMES **sauf votre ~** with all due respect; **tenir qn en ~** to keep sb at bay.

respectabilité /ʀɛspɛktabilite/ *nf* respectability.

respectable /ʀɛspɛktabl/ *adj* **1** (estimable) respectable; **2** (important) [*taille, somme d'argent*] respectable; [*embonpoint*] generous.

respecter /ʀɛspɛkte/ [1] I *vtr* **1** (considérer avec respect) to respect [*personne, mémoire*]; **se faire ~** to command respect; **il s'est toujours fait ~ par ses élèves** he has always commanded the respect of his pupils; **savoir se faire ~** to know how to command respect; **2** (ne pas porter atteinte à) to respect, to have respect for [*opinion, croyance, action, lieu, nature*]; to treat [sth] with respect [*objet, matériel*]; to respect [*promesse, ordre, style, loi, contrat*]; to honour[GB] [*engagement*]; to respect, to have respect for [*vie privée, coutumes, règle*]; **classer qch en respectant l'ordre alphabétique/chronologique** to classify sth in alphabetical/chronological order; **quand vous rangerez les livres, respectez l'ordre alphabétique** when you put the books away, place them in alphabetical order; **faire ~ l'ordre/la loi** to enforce order/the law; **respectez le sommeil des gens, ne courez pas dans les escaliers** remember people are sleeping, do not run down the stairs.

II **se respecter** *vpr* to respect oneself; **tout homme/médecin qui se respecte** any self-respecting man/doctor.

respectif, -ive /ʀɛspɛktif, iv/ *adj* respective.

respectivement /ʀɛspɛktivmɑ̃/ *adv* respectively.

respectueusement /ʀɛspɛktɥøzmɑ̃/ *adv* respectfully; **~ vôtre** yours respectfully.

respectueux, -euse /ʀɛspɛktɥø, øz/ *adj* **1** (plein de révérence) respectful (**envers** to, toward, towards GB); **être ~ de qch** to be respectful of sth, to respect sth; **se montrer ~ de qch** to show respect for sth, to respect sth; **être/se montrer peu ~ de qch** to have/to show little respect for sth; **des propos peu ~** some rather disrespectful remarks; **citoyen ~ de la loi** law-abiding citizen; **2** (dans une lettre) **veuillez agréer, Monsieur, mes salutations respectueuses** (à une personne non nommée) yours faithfully; (à une personne nommée) yours sincerely.

■ **~ de l'environnement** environment-friendly.

respirable /ʀɛspiʀabl/ *adj* **1** lit [*air*] breathable; **l'air n'est pas ~** the air is unbreathable; **2** fig [*ambiance*] bearable; **pendant tout le repas l'atmosphère n'était pas ~** throughout the meal the atmosphere was unbearable.

respirateur /ʀɛspiʀatœʀ/ *nm* **1** Méd (masque, appareil) respirator; **un ~ artificiel** artificial breathing apparatus ¢; **2** Tech respirator.

respiration /ʀɛspiʀasjɔ̃/ *nf* **1** (fonction) breathing, respiration spéc; (souffle) breath; **~ externe/pulmonaire** external/ pulmonary respiration; **avoir une ~ haletante** to be panting; **avoir une ~ courte** to be short of breath; **avoir une ~ oppressée** to have difficulty breathing; **avoir une ~ difficile** to have breathing difficulties; **une ~ bruyante** heavy breathing; **avoir une ~ bruyante** to breathe heavily; **retenir sa ~** to hold one's breath; **reprendre sa ~** to get one's breath back; **faire trois ~s** to breathe in and out three times; **2** (inhalation) **la ~ de qch** breathing in sth; **la ~ d'un gaz nocif** breathing in a noxious gas.

■ **~ artificielle** artificial respiration; **~ assistée** assisted ventilation.

respiratoire /ʀɛspiʀatwaʀ/ *adj* [*voie, système, appareil*] respiratory; [*troubles, difficulté*] breathing, respiratory spéc.

respirer /ʀɛspiʀe/ [1] I *vtr* **1** (inhaler) to breathe in [*air, gaz, fumée, poussière*]; **2** (sentir) to smell [*parfum, odeur*]; **3** (exprimer) [*personne, visage, sourire*] to exude, to radiate [*honnêteté, bonheur, gentillesse*]; to exude [*méchanceté*]; [*maison, lieu*] to exude [*richesse, bonheur, honnêteté*]; **il respire la santé** he's a picture of health.

II *vi* **1** lit to breathe; **~ par le nez/la bouche** to breathe through one's nose/one's mouth; **'respirez!'** 'breathe in!'; **'respirez bien fort'** 'take a deep breath'; **~ avec**

difficulté to have difficulty breathing; **2** fig (se reposer) to catch one's breath; **nous n'avons pas une minute pour ~** fig we don't have a moment to catch our breath; **laisse-moi ~** fig let me get my breath back; **3** (être soulagé) to breathe; **enfin je respire!** at last I can breathe again!.

resplendir /ʀɛsplɑ̃diʀ/ [3] *vi* **1** (briller) [*astre, lumière*] to shine brightly; [*surface neigeuse, surface mouillée*] to sparkle; [*surface métallique*] to gleam; **2** (rayonner) **la joie resplendit sur son visage** his/her face is beaming with joy; **~ de bonheur/santé** to be glowing with happiness/health.

resplendissant, **~e** /ʀɛsplɑ̃disɑ̃, ɑ̃t/ *adj* **1** (brillant) [*soleil, lumière*] brilliant; [*surface neigeuse, surface mouillée*] sparkling; [*surface métallique*] gleaming; **fleur d'un rouge ~** brilliant red flower; **~ de lumière** ablaze with lights; **2** (rayonnant) [*santé, beauté, mine*] radiant; **~ de santé/bonheur** glowing with health/happiness.

resplendissement /ʀɛsplɑ̃dismɑ̃/ *nm* (d'astre) brilliance; (de surface neigeuse, mouillée) sparkle; (de surface métallique) gleam; (de personne, visage) glow; (de gloire) splendour[GB].

responsabilisation /ʀɛspɔ̃sabilizasjɔ̃/ *nf* **le principe est basé sur la ~ des salariés** the principle is based on staff being given a sense of responsibility.

responsabiliser /ʀɛspɔ̃sabilize/ [1] *vtr* to give [sb] a sense of responsibility.

responsabilité /ʀɛspɔ̃sabilite/ *nf* **1** (participation) gén responsibility; **avoir sa part de ~ dans qch** to share some of the responsibility for sth; **rejeter** or **nier toute ~ dans qch** to deny all responsibility for sth; **avoir/partager la ~ de qch** to have/to share the responsibility for sth; **porter seul toutes les ~s** to have all the responsibilities; **il en porte l'entière ~** he bears full responsibility for it; **se renvoyer la ~** to blame each other; **2** (charge) responsibility; **c'est une lourde ~** it's a great responsibility; **avoir beaucoup de ~s** to have many responsibilities; **avoir la ~ de qch** to be responsible for sth; **confier la ~ de qch à qn** to give sb responsibility for sth; **un poste de** or **à ~** a position of responsibility; **sous la ~ de qn** under the supervision of sb; **fuir les ~s** to shun responsibility; **donner des ~s à qn** to give sb responsibilities; **prendre ses ~s** to face up to one's responsibilities; **3** (fait de devoir répondre de ses actions) responsibility; (légalement) liability; **~ civile/collective/contractuelle/pénale** civil/collective/contractual/criminal liability; **la ~ d'un employeur** an employer's liability; **'la direction décline toute ~ en cas de vol'** 'the management disclaims all responsibility for loss due to theft'; **votre ~ est engagée** you're responsible; **faute grave engageant la ~ de la société** serious mistake for which the company is liable to be held responsible; **engager la ~ du gouvernement sur un projet de loi** *to bring a bill before parliament which will involve a motion of confidence in the government*; **4** Assur liability; **~ civile** personal liability.

responsable /ʀɛspɔ̃sabl/ **I** *adj* **1** (coupable) [*personne, défaillance, erreur*] responsible (*après n*) (**de qch** for sth); **il est ~ de l'incendie** he's responsible for the fire; **l'alcool est ~ de nombreux accidents** alcohol is responsible ou is to blame for many accidents; **2** (devant répondre de ses actes) responsible, accountable (**de qch** for sth); (légalement) responsible, liable (**de qch** for sth); **être ~ de ses actes** to be responsible for one's actions; **on est ~ de ce que l'on dit/écrit** you are responsible for what you say/write; **3** (ayant la charge) **être ~ de qch/qn** to be responsible for sth/sb, to be in charge of sth/sb; **je suis ~ du magasin** I am responsible for the shop GB ou store US; **qui est la personne ~ ici?** who is in charge here?; **4** (raisonnable) [*personne, attitude, acte*] responsible; **être très ~** to be very responsible; **un vote/rapport ~** a sensible vote/report.

II *nmf* **1** (personne en charge) gén person in charge; (gérant, directeur) manager; (chef de parti) leader; (chef de service) head; (administrateur) official; **je voudrais parler au ~** I'd like to talk to the person in charge; **selon un ~ politique** according to a political leader; **M. Doucet, ~ d'une petite entreprise** Mr Doucet, the manager of a small company; **plusieurs ~s communistes/catholiques** several communist/catholic leaders; **un haut ~ de la Banque Mondiale** a high-ranking official at the World Bank; **des ~s de la police** senior police officers; **2** (personne coupable) **les ~s de la catastrophe** the people responsible ou to blame for the catastrophe; **les ~s seront punis** those responsible ou those who are to blame will be punished; **c'est lui le ~** he is responsible ou to blame; **3** (cause) **le grand ~ c'est le tabac/le manque d'amour** smoking/lack of love is the main cause.

■ **le ~ de classe** form representative (*elected by the pupils to represent them*).

resquillage○ /ʀɛskijaʒ/ *nm*, **resquille**○ /ʀɛskij/ *nf* (en train, car, métro) fare dodging○ GB, free loading◑ US; (au spectacle) sneaking in○; (dans queue) queue-jumping GB; **c'est le roi de la resquille** he's an expert at getting things for free○, he's a freeloader◑.

resquiller○ /ʀɛskije/ [1] **I** *vtr* (obtenir frauduleusement) **~ une place** to get in for free○.

II *vi* (en train, métro) to dodge paying the fare○; (au spectacle) to sneak in○, to get in for free; (dans queue) to queue-jump○ GB, to cut in line US.

resquilleur○, **-euse** /ʀɛskijœʀ, øz/ *nm,f* **1** Transp fare dodger○ GB, freeloader◑ US; **2** (au spectacle) person who gets in for free○; **3** (dans queue) queue-jumper○ GB.

ressac /ʀəsak/ *nm* backwash.

ressaisir /ʀ(ə)seziʀ/ [3] **I** *vtr* [*peur, rire, envie, passion*] to take hold of [sb] again [*personne*].

II se ressaisir *vpr* [*personne, candidat, sportif*] to pull oneself together; [*équipe sportive*] to recover; [*marché, valeurs boursières*] to recover, to make a recovery; **allons, ressaisis-toi!** come on, pull yourself together!; **l'équipe s'est ressaisie en fin de match** the team recovered toward(s) the end of the match ou game; **appeler la foule à se ~** to call on the people in the crowd to come to their senses.

ressaisissement /ʀ(ə)sezismɑ̃/ *nm* **on espère un ~ de l'électorat/l'opinion** it is hoped that the electorate/the public will come to its senses.

ressasser /ʀ(ə)sase/ [1] *vtr* (ruminer) to brood over [*échec, pensées*]; to dwell on [*regrets, malheurs*]; (rabâcher) to keep trotting out○ [*griefs, conseils*] (**à qn** to sb); **phrase mille fois ressassée** phrase that has been trotted out a thousand times○; **théorie ressassée** hackneyed theory.

ressaut /ʀ(ə)so/ *nm* **1** Géog (palier) ledge; **2** Archit projection; **faire ~** to form a projection.

ressayer /ʀeseje/ [21] *vtr* = **réessayer**.

ressemblance /ʀ(ə)sɑ̃blɑ̃s/ *nf* **1** (entre personnes) resemblance, likeness (**avec qn** to sb); **une grande/vague ~ entre les deux sœurs** a strong/faint resemblance ou likeness between the two sisters; **la ~ avec ton père est frappante** your resemblance to your father is striking; **tu leur trouves des ~s?** can you see any resemblance ou likeness between them?; **'toute ~ avec des personnes existant ou ayant existé...'** 'any similarity to persons living or dead...'; **2** (entre choses) similarity; **les différences et ~s entre les civilisations** the differences and similarities between civilizations; **3** Art (de tableau, sculpture) likeness (**avec l'original** to the original); **un portrait d'une grande ~** a portrait that is a very good likeness.

ressemblant, **~e** /ʀ(ə)sɑ̃blɑ̃, ɑ̃t/ *adj* **c'est très ~** it's a good likeness; **un portrait ~/peu ~** a portrait which is a good likeness/isn't a very good likeness.

ressembler /ʀ(ə)sɑ̃ble/ [1] **I ressembler à** *vtr ind* **1** (en parlant de personnes) (physiquement) **~ à** to look like, to resemble [*personne, animal*]; (psychiquement) to be like [*personne*]; **à quoi ressemble-t-il?** (physiquement) what does he look like?; (de caractère) what is he like?; **tu as vu à quoi tu ressembles?** have you any idea what you look like?; **il ne ressemble pas à l'image que j'en avais** he's not how I imagined him; **cela ne te ressemble pas de perdre patience** it's not like you to get impatient; **2** (en parlant de choses) (d'apparence visuelle) to look like; (par le contenu) to be like, to resemble; **ça ressemble à de la lavande mais ça n'en est pas** it looks like lavender but it isn't; **~ fort à qch** to be very like sth; **~ un peu à qch** to be a bit like sth; **cela ressemblait à un coup monté** it all looked like a put-up job; **cela ne ressemble à rien** [*spectacle, robe*] it's like nothing on earth; (n'avoir aucun sens) it makes no sense; **à quoi ça ressemble de dire cela?** what a thing to say!

II se ressembler *vpr* **1** (parlant de personnes) (physiquement) to look alike, to look like each other; (psychiquement) to be alike; **vous ne vous ressemblez pas beaucoup** (physiquement) you don't really look alike; **ils se ressemblent trop pour s'entendre** they are too (much) alike to get on; **2** (parlant de choses) [*lieux, soirées, méthodes, techniques*] to be alike; **toutes les villes se ressemblent** all towns are alike ou the same; ▸ **assembler**, **goutte**.

IDIOMES **les jours se suivent et ne se ressemblent pas** no two days are the same.

ressemelage /ʀ(ə)səmlaʒ/ *nm* resoling.

ressemeler /ʀ(ə)səmle/ [19] *vtr* to resole; **faire ~ une paire de chaussures** to have a pair of shoes resoled.

ressemer /ʀəs(ə)me, ʀsəme/ [16] **I** *vtr* to sow [sth] again [*grain, champ*].

II se ressemer *vpr* [*plante*] to seed itself.

ressentiment /ʀ(ə)sɑ̃timɑ̃/ *nm* resentment (**contre** against; **à l'égard de** toward, towards GB); **éprouver du ~ de qch** to feel resentful about sth; **il en a gardé un ~ féroce** he feels deeply resentful about it.

ressentir /ʀ(ə)sɑ̃tiʀ/ [30] **I** *vtr* to feel [*amour, inquiétude, chagrin*]; **ressenti comme une urgence/insulte** felt to be an emergency/insult; **les mesures sont bien/mal ressenties** the measures have been well/badly received.

II se ressentir *vpr* **se ~ de** [*personne, pays*] to feel the effects of, to suffer from; [*travail, performances, qualité*] to show the effects of, to suffer from; **la qualité s'en ressent** the quality is suffering.

resserre /ʀ(ə)sɛʀ/ *nf* (pièce) storeroom; (remise, cabane) shed.

resserrement /ʀ(ə)sɛʀmɑ̃/ *nm* **1** (action) (de nœud, boulon, tissus humains) tightening; (de vaisseau sanguin) constricting; (de crédit) tightening up; (d'amitié, de relation) strengthening; **2** (de chemin, vallée, rivière) narrowing.

resserrer /ʀ(ə)seʀe/ [1] **I** *vtr* **1** (serrer de nouveau) to tighten [*nœud, vis, étreinte*]; **2** (réduire le développement de) to compress [*texte, narration*] (**en qch** into sth); **~ un chapitre en deux pages** to compress a chapter into two pages; **3** (rendre plus étroit) lit to narrow [*passage, route*]; to take [sth] in [*vêtement*]; to tighten [*pores*]; **4** (renforcer) to strengthen [*amitié, relation*]; **5** (faire regrouper) to make [sb/sth] draw closer; **resserrez les rangs!** close up a bit!; **6** (rendre plus sévère) to tighten up (on) [*discipline, surveillance*].

II se resserrer *vpr* **1** (devenir plus étroit) [*chemin, vallée, rivière*] to narrow; **2** (devenir plus fort) [*amitié, relation*] to become stronger; **3** (devenir plus serré) [*lien, nœud*] to tighten; **4** (se refermer) [*troupes, personnes*] to close in; [*étreinte, piège*] to tighten; [*écart*] to close; **5** (se regrouper) [*personnes, cercle*] to draw closer together; **6** (devenir plus sévère) [*discipline, surveillance*] to become stricter.

resservir /ʀ(ə)sɛʀviʀ/ [30] **I** *vtr* **1** (servir de nouveau) to serve [sth] (up) again; **~ qch à qn** to serve sb with sth again; **2** (à table) to give [sb] another helping (**de** of); **~ de la soupe à qn** to give sb another helping of soup; **3**○ (utiliser à nouveau) to trot○ [sth] out again [*explication, thème, argument*].

II *vi* **1** (être réutilisé) [*objet, outil, vêtement*] to be used again; **cela peut toujours ~** it may come in handy○ again; **ne jette pas ce sac, il pourra me ~** don't throw away that bag, I could get some more use out of it; **ne le jette pas, il pourra me ~ l'an prochain** don't throw it away, I could use it again next year; **2** Mil to serve again.

III se resservir *vpr* **1** (d'un plat) to help oneself again, to take another helping; **resservez-vous!** help yourself to some more!, have another helping!; **'puis-je me ~?'** 'can I help myself to some more?'; **se ~ du poulet** to help oneself to some more chicken; **2** (réutiliser) **se ~ de qn/qch** to use sb/sth again.

ressort /ʀ(ə)sɔʀ/ *nm* **1** Tech spring; **un mécanisme à ~** a spring mechanism; **un matelas à ~** a sprung mattress; **~ de compression/flexion/traction** compression/flexion/tension spring; **2** (énergie) resilience; **avoir du/manquer de ~** to have/lack resilience; **3** (force agissante) **les ~s du pouvoir/de la haine** the impulse behind power/hatred; **~s dramatiques/du comique** dramatic/comic impulse; **les ~s psychologiques du personnage** the character's psychological motivation; **4** (compétence) **être du ~ de qn** to be within sb's province; **ce n'est pas de mon ~** (en mon pouvoir) it's outside my province; (ma responsabilité) it's not my responsibility; **l'affaire est du ~ de la Cour européenne** the case falls within the jurisdiction of the European court; **en premier/dernier ~** in the first/last resort; **des sanctions économiques et, en dernier ~, militaires** economic and, in the last resort, military sanctions.

■ **~ à boudin** coil spring; **~ hélicoïdal** helical spring; **~ à lames** leaf spring; **~ spiral** spiral spring.

ressortir /ʀ(ə)sɔʀtiʀ/ [30] **I** *vtr* **1** (sortir à nouveau) to take [sth] out again; (plus d'effort) to get [sth] out again; **on ressort les manteaux pour l'hiver** we're getting our coats out for the winter; **2** (ce qu'on ne sortait plus) to bring [sth] out again [*vieux vêtement*] (**de** from); to dig out○ [*affaire de corruption*] (**de** from); **3** (redire) to come out with [*plaisanterie, phrase, idée*]; **il nous ressort toujours les mêmes histoires** he's always coming out with the same stories; **4** (remettre sur le marché) to re-release [*disque, film*].

II ressortir à, **ressortir de** *vtr ind* **1 ~ à** Jur to be ou fall within the jurisdiction of [*tribunal*]; **2 ~ à** or **de** fml (concerner) to pertain to sout.

III *vi* **1** (sortir à nouveau) [*personne*] to go out again; **il est ressorti vers 20 heures** he went out again at around 8 pm; **2** (après être entré) [*balle, tige*] to come out again (**par** through); [*personne*] to come back out (**de** of); **la balle est ressortie par la nuque** the bullet came out through the back of his/her neck; **je ne t'avais pas vu ~ (du magasin)** I hadn't seen you come back out (of the shop GB ou store US); **3** (se distinguer nettement) [*ornement, couleur, dessin*] to stand out; **cela ressort bien/mal sur ce fond** it shows up very well/doesn't show up very well against that background; **voici ce qui ressort de l'étude: premièrement...** the results of the study are as follows, firstly...; **faire ~** to revive [*souvenirs*]; to bring out [*rivalités*]; to bring to light [*contradiction*]; [*maquillage*] to bring out [*couleur des yeux*]; [*cadre, couleur*] to set [sth] off well [*photo, tableau, couleur*]; **faire ~ que** [*étude, rapport*] to bring out the fact that; **4** (être remis sur le marché) [*film, disque*] to be re-released; [*journal, revue*] to be back in circulation.

IV *v impers* **il ressort que** it emerges that; **il ressort de l'enquête que 70% des usagers...** it emerges from the survey that 70% of users...

ressortissant, **~e** /ʀ(ə)sɔʀtisɑ̃, ɑ̃t/ *nm,f* national; **~ français/étranger** French/foreign national.

ressouder /ʀ(ə)sude/ [1] **I** *vtr* Tech (par soudure autogène) to reweld; (par brasure) to solder [sth] again [*joint*]; to solder [sth] together again [*pièces*].

II se ressouder *vpr* [*os*] to knit (together); [*fracture*] to mend.

ressource /ʀ(ə)suʀs/ *nf* **1** (richesse) resource; **la principale ~ du Brésil** Brazil's main resource; **les ~s naturelles** or **de la nature** natural resources; **les ~s énergétiques/forestières/minérales** energy/forest/mineral resources; **2** (option) option; **elle n'a pas d'autre ~ que de fuir** she has no option but to flee; **en dernière ~** as a last resort; **être à bout de ~** to be at one's wits' end; **3** fig (réserves) **avoir de la ~**○ to be resourceful; **puiser dans ses propres ~s** to fall back on one's inner resources; **une personne de ~s** a resourceful person; **4** (revenus) **~s** resources; **35% de ses ~s** 35% of his/her resources; **vous avez des ~s?** do you have any means of support?; **être sans ~s**, **n'avoir aucune ~** to have no means of support; **quelles sont vos ~s?** what is your financial position?; **mes maigres ~s** my slender means; **5** (possibilités) (de lieu, technique) possibilities; **toutes les ~s de l'imaginaire** all the powers of the imagination.

■ **~s humaines** human resources.

ressourcer: **se ressourcer** /ʀ(ə)suʀse/ [12] *vpr* to recharge one's batteries.

ressurgir /ʀ(ə)syʀʒiʀ/ [3] *vi* = **resurgir**.

ressusciter /ʀesysite/ [1] **I** *vtr* **1** (exhumer du passé) to revive [*style, tradition, passé, auteur*]; to rekindle [*haine, amour*]; **2** Relig to raise [sb] from the dead; fig to bring [sb] back to life; **ton alcool de poire ressusciterait un mort**○ your pear brandy would bring the dead back to life; **le traitement m'a ressuscité** the treatment gave me a new lease of GB ou on US life.

II *vi* **1** Relig [*mort*] to rise from the dead; **ressuscité d'entre les morts** risen from the dead; **2** (revenir à la vie) fig [*nature, ville*] to come back to life; [*pass é, souvenir*] to come alive again; [*haine, amour*] to be rekindled.

restant, **~e** /ʀɛstɑ̃, ɑ̃t/ **I** *adj* remaining; **l'argent ~** the remaining money, the money that's left; **avec les 100 francs ~s** with the 100 francs that's left.

II *nm* **1** (ce qui est encore à venir) **le ~** the rest, the remainder; (solde) the balance, the remainder; **mets-en trois ici et le ~ dans le jardin** put three here and the rest in the garden GB ou yard US; **payer le ~ en six mensualités** to pay the balance ou remainder in six monthly instalments[GB]; **pour le ~ de mes jours** for the rest of my life ou days; **passer le ~ de la journée à lire** to spend the rest of the day reading; **2** (ce qui subsiste) **un ~ de tissu** a bit of material left over; **un ~ de poulet/jambon** some left-over chicken/ham; **un ~ de clarté** a last glimmer of light.

restau○ /ʀɛsto/ *nm*: *abbr* = **restaurant**.

restaurant /ʀɛstɔʀɑ̃/ *nm* restaurant; **on mange** or **va souvent au ~** we often eat out.

■ **~ d'entreprise** staff canteen; **~ gastronomique** gourmet restaurant; **~ rapide** fast-food restaurant; **~ self-service** self-service restaurant; **~ universitaire**, **RU** university canteen GB, cafeteria.

restaurateur, **-trice** /ʀɛstɔʀatœʀ, tʀis/ *nm,f* **1** (hôtelier) restaurant owner; (de restaurant gastronomique) restaurateur; **2** Art, Hist restorer.

restauration /ʀɛstɔʀasjɔ̃/ *nf* **1** (hôtellerie) catering; **être dans la ~** to be in the catering business; **2** Art, Hist restoration.

■ **~ rapide** fast-food industry.

Restauration /ʀɛstɔʀasjɔ̃/ *nf* Hist **la ~** the Restoration.

restaurer /ʀɛstɔʀe/ [1] **I** *vtr* **1** (nourrir) to feed; **2** Art, Hist to restore [*tableau, monarchie, paix*].

II se restaurer *vpr* to have something to eat.

restau-U○ /ʀɛstoy/ *nm* university canteen GB, cafeteria.

reste /ʀɛst/ **I** *nm* **1** (ce qui subsiste) **le ~** the rest (**de** of); (argent) the balance; Math the remainder; **le ~ du monde/du temps/des livres** the rest of the world/of the time/of the books; **payer un tiers d'avance, le ~ (de la somme) à la fin des travaux** to pay a third in advance and the balance on completion of the work; **s'il y a un ~ de lait/quiche** if there is a bit of milk/quiche left; **il m'a proposé un ~ de poulet** he offered me some left-over chicken; **avec le ~, je ferai une salade** I'll make a salad out of what's left; **faire une ceinture avec un ~ de tissu** to make a belt out of some left-over material; **il a un ~ d'affection pour elle** he still feels a bit of affection for her; **conserver un ~ de dignité/lucidité** to preserve a vestige of dignity/lucidity; **2** (ce qui est encore à dire, faire etc) **le ~** the rest; **tu imagines le ~** you can imagine the rest; **prépare le repas, je me charge du ~** you get the meal ready, leave the rest to me; **avec le loyer, les assurances et (tout) le ~**○, **je ne m'en sors pas** with the rent, the insurance and everything else, I just can't manage; **je te souhaite santé, bonheur et tout le ~**○ I wish you health, happiness and all the rest; **pour le ~**, **quant au ~** (as) for the rest; **au ~** liter, **du ~** besides; **du ~, c'est trop cher** besides, it's too expensive; **avoir du temps/de l'argent de ~** to have time/money to spare.

II restes *nmpl* **1** (de fortune, bâtiment, d'armée) remains (**de** of); **2** Culin **les ~s** the leftovers; **l'art d'accommoder les ~s** how to use leftovers; **les ~s d'un gigot** the remains of a joint; **je ne veux pas de tes ~s** lit, fig I don't want your leftovers; **3** (cadavre) **les ~s de qn** the remains of sb.

IDIOMES **elle a encore de beaux ~s**○ hum she's still well preserved; **partir sans demander** or **attendre son ~** to leave without further ado; **être** or **demeurer en ~ avec qn** to feel indebted to sb; **pour ne pas être en ~** so as not to be outdone; **je ne voulais pas être en ~, alors j'ai acheté le gâteau** not wanting to be outdone, I bought the cake.

rester /ʀɛste/ [1] (+ *v être*) **I** *vi* **1** (dans un lieu) to stay, to remain; **~ chez soi/à l'intérieur/en ville** to stay at home/indoors/in town; **il est resté un an à Rome** he stayed a year in Rome, he stayed in Rome for a year; **ne reste pas au soleil/sous la pluie** don't stay in the sun/out in the rain; **reste où tu es/tant que tu veux** stay where you are/for as long as you like; **les autres sont partis, mais elle est restée pour m'aider** the others left but she stayed behind to help me; **je ne peux pas ~ longtemps** I can't stay long; **~ un moment à bavarder** to stay chatting for a while; **~ (à) dîner** to stay for dinner; **la clé est restée coincée dans la serrure** the key got stuck in the lock; **la bière est restée au soleil** the beer was left in the sun; **le linge est resté dehors toute la nuit** the washing was left out all night; **c'est resté dans ma mémoire** I still remember it; **cet enfant ne peut pas ~ en place!** the child can't keep still!; **que ça reste entre nous!** this is strictly between you and me!; **j'y suis, j'y reste** here I am and here I stay; **2** (dans une position, un état) to remain; **~ assis/debout** to remain seated/standing; **restez assis!** (par mesure de sécurité) remain seated!; (ne vous dérangez pas) don't get up!; **je suis resté debout pendant tout le voyage** I had to stand for the whole journey; **~ indécis/impassible/attentif/fidèle** to remain undecided/impassive/alert/faithful; **un auteur resté méconnu** an author who went unrecognized; **~ au chômage/au pouvoir** to remain unemployed/in power; **~ silencieux** to remain ou keep silent; **~ sans bouger** (debout) to stand still; (assis) to sit still; (couché) to lie still; **reste tranquille!** keep still!; **~ sans manger** to go without food; **elle est restée très naturelle** she's stayed very natural; **~ paralysé après un accident** to be left paralysed after an accident; **~ veuve** to be left a widow, to be widowed; **~ orphelin** to be orphaned; **~ les bras croisés** lit to keep one's arms folded; fig to stand idly by; **ne reste pas là les bras croisés** don't just stand there, do something!; ▶**flan**; **3** (subsister) to be left, to remain; **le peu de temps qui reste** the little time that's left; **c'est le seul ami qui me reste** he's the only friend I have left; **ce qui reste de la ville** what remains ou is left of the town; **ce qui reste du repas** the leftovers; **dis-moi ce qui reste à faire** tell me what there is left to do; **il reste 50 km à parcourir/100 francs à payer** there's still another 50 km to go/100 francs to pay; **4** (survivre) [*œuvre, souvenir*] to live on; **sa musique restera** his/her music will live on; **~ comme l'un des grands de ce siècle** to live on as one of the great men of our age; **les années passent, le souvenir reste** the years go by, but the memories don't fade; **l'habitude lui en est restée** the habit stuck, he/she never lost the habit; **5** (s'arrêter) **~ sur une bonne/mauvaise impression** to be left with a good/bad impression; **leur refus m'est resté sur le cœur** their refusal still rankles; **6** (ne pas aller au-delà de) **en ~ à** to go no further than; **nous en sommes restés aux préliminaires** we didn't get beyond the preliminaries; **il en est resté au XIXe siècle** pej he's stuck in the 19th century; **nous en étions restés à la page 12** we had got GB ou gotten US as far as page 12; **restons-en là pour le moment** let's leave it at that for now; **l'affaire aurait pu en ~ là** the matter needn't have gone any further; **je compte bien ne pas en ~ là** I won't let the matter rest there.

II *v impers* **il reste encore quelques minutes/pommes** there are still a few minutes/apples left; **il m'en reste un** I've got one left; **il ne me reste que 100 francs** I've only got 100 francs left; **il ne me reste plus que lui** he's all I've got left; **il me reste juste de quoi payer le loyer** I've just got enough left to pay the rent; **il me reste à peine le temps/la force de m'habiller** I've barely got time/the strength to get dressed; **que reste-t-il de la ville?** what remains ou is left of the town?; **il reste beaucoup à faire** there's still a lot to do ou to be done; **il ne te reste plus qu'à t'excuser** it only remains for you to apologize; **il reste entendu que** it goes without saying that; **(il) reste à savoir/décider si** it remains to be seen/it still has to be decided whether; **reste à résoudre le problème du logement** the housing problem remains to be solved; **il reste que, il n'en reste pas moins que** the fact remains that.

IDIOMES **y ~**○ to meet one's end ou Maker.

restituer /ʀɛstitɥe/ [1] *vtr* **1** (rendre) to restore [*bien*] **(à qn** to sb); to restore [*souvenir, qualité, différences*]; **~ au peuple sa souveraineté** to restore sovereignty to the people; **2** (rétablir) to reconstruct [*texte*]; to restore [*fresque*]; **3** (recréer) to reproduce [*son, image*]; to recreate [*ambiance*]; **une traduction qui restitue toutes les nuances de l'original** a translation which catches all the nuances of the original; **4** (libérer) Phys to release [*énergie*].

restitution /ʀɛstitysjɔ̃/ *nf* **1** (action de rendre) (de bien, terre) return, restitution sout; (de droit, qualité) restoration; **2** (de texte) reconstruction; (de fresque) restoration; **3** (de son, d'image) reproduction; **4** (libération) Phys release.

resto○ /ʀɛsto/ *nm* restaurant; **~ du cœur** ≈ soup kitchen.

restreindre /ʀɛstʀɛ̃dʀ/ [55] **I** *vtr* to cut back [*dépenses, nombre*]; to curb [*dépenses*]; to limit [*possibilités, choix*]; to restrict [*champ d'action, importations, subventions, liberté, droit*]; **~ ses recherches à** to restrict ou limit one's research to; **~ sa vie/ses activités à** to limit one's existence/one's activities to.

II se restreindre *vpr* **1** (devenir plus petit) [*champ d'action, possibilités*] to become restricted; [*production, revenus, territoire*] to shrink; [*influence*] to wane; **2** (se limiter) **se ~ (dans ses dépenses)** to cut back (on one's expenses).

restreint, **~e** /ʀɛstʀɛ̃, ɛ̃t/ **I** *pp* ▶**restreindre**.

II *pp adj* [*public, vocabulaire*] limited; [*équipe*] small; **être en nombre ~** to be few in number; **nous étions en comité ~** there were just a few of us; **cela a été décidé en comité ~** it was decided by just a few people.

restrictif, **-ive** /ʀɛstʀiktif, iv/ *adj* restrictive.

restriction /ʀɛstʀiksjɔ̃/ *nf* **1** (limitation) restriction; **~s commerciales/de crédit/budgétaires** trade/credit/budget restrictions; **~s salariales** wage restraints; **pendant les ~s** (de guerre) when there was rationing; **sans ~** [*voyager*] freely; [*commercialiser*] without restriction; **ils sont, et sans ~, des citoyens comme les autres** they are, with absolutely no exception, citizens like everybody else; **2** (réserve) qualification; **apporter une ~ à ce qui est dit** to qualify a statement; **sans ~** [*accepter, approuver*] without reservations; [*soutenir*] unreservedly.

restructuration /ʀ(ə)stʀyktyʀasjɔ̃/ *nf* **1** Admin, Écon restructuring; **plan de ~** restructuring plan; **2** (en urbanisme) redevelopment.

restructurer /ʀ(ə)stʀyktyʀe/ [1] **I** *vtr* Admin, Écon to restructure [*service, organisation*]; to redevelop [*ville, quartier*].

II se restructurer *vpr* [*service, organisation*] to restructure itself; [*quartier*] to be redeveloped.

resucée○ /ʀ(ə)syse/ *nf* pej **1** (de boisson) **une ~ (de gin)** a drop more (gin); **2** (de spectacle, livre) rehash○.

résultante /ʀezyltɑ̃t/ *nf* **1** Math, Sci resultant; **2** (conséquence) (end) result.

résultat /ʀezylta/ **I** *nm* **1** Math, Phys (d'opération, de problème) result; **2** (bilan) (d'élection, de compétition) result; (de recherches) results (*pl*), findings (*pl*); (de négociations, d'enquête) result, outcome; (de travail, sondage, d'analyse) result(s); **obtenir un ~** to get a result; **le ~ de deux ans de travail** the result of two years' work; **beau ~!** great work, well done!; **sans ~** without success; **le mauvais ~ de l'équipe de France** the poor showing of the French team; **3** (réalisation positive) result; **nous voulons des ~s** we want results; **4** (conséquence) result(s), outcome; **être le ~ de** to be the result of; **avoir pour ~ de faire** to have the effect of doing; **tu n'as pas voulu m'écouter: ~, tu as fait des bêtises** you wouldn't listen to me, and now you've done something stupid.

II résultats *nmpl* **1** (chiffres) (d'examen, élection, de compétition) results (*pl*); Scol, Univ (d'élève, de mois) marks GB, grades US; **les ~s partiels de l'élection** the election results so far; **~s en baisse ce trimestre** Scol lower marks GB ou grades US this term; **2** Méd (d'analyse, examen) results; **3** Fin, Compta (d'entreprise) results; **les ~s de l'année 1990** the results for 1990.

résulter /ʀezylte/ [1] **I** *vi* **~ de** to be the result of, to result from; **votre échec résulte d'un manque de travail** the reason for your failure is that you didn't do enough work; **la colère qui résulte de cette décision** the anger resulting from this decision; **la colère qui en résulte** the resulting anger; **ce qui résulte de cette politique fiscale** the result of this fiscal policy.

II *v impers* **il résulte de tout ceci que** the result of all this is that, as a result of all this; **il résulte de ce que vous venez de dire que** it follows from what you have just said that; **il en résulte que nous pouvons compter sur leur appui** as a result we can count on their support; **qu'en résultera-t-il?** what will be the result of this?

résumé /ʀezyme/ *nm* **1** (version courte) summary, résumé; **faire le ~ de qch** to summarize sth; **pour faire un ~ de la situation** to summarize ou to sum up the situation; **en ~** (pour finir) to sum up; (en bref) in brief; **2** (exposé succint) rundown; **faire un ~ de qch (à qn)** to give (sb) a rundown of ou on sth; **'~ des épisodes précédents'** 'the story so far'; **3** (ouvrage) gén brief guide; (pour examen) study notes (*pl*).

■ **~ de texte** précis, summary; **faire un ~ de texte** to write a précis ou summary.

résumer /ʀezyme/ [1] **I** *vtr* **1** (raccourcir) to summarize [*texte, pensée, délibération*]; **2** (récapituler) to sum up [*nouvelle, match, état d'esprit*]; **il l'a résumé en deux mots** he summed it up in two words; **3** (refléter) to sum up; **cette anecdote résume le personnage** this anecdote sums up the character.

II se résumer *vpr* **1** (être bref) [*personne*] to sum up; **pour me ~ je dirai que** to sum up I'll say that; **2** (se limiter) **se ~ à** [*vie, action, événement, opinion*] to come down to; **le match de hockey s'est résumé à un long pugilat** what the match came down to was one long fight; **3** (se raccourcir) [*texte, pensée, discours*] to be summarized, to be summed up.

résurgence /ʀezyʀʒɑ̃s/ *nf* **1** Géol re-emergence (*of river*); **2** fig (d'idéologie) resurgence; (de mode) revival.

résurgent, **~e** /ʀezyʀʒɑ̃, ɑ̃t/ *adj* [*eaux*] re-emergent.

resurgir /ʀ(ə)syʀʒiʀ/ [3] *vi* [*rivière*] to re-emerge; [*idéologie, problème, personne*] to reappear; [*souvenir*] to come back.

résurrection /ʀezyʀɛksjɔ̃/ *nf* **1** (de mort) resurrection; **la Résurrection** Relig the Resurrection; **la ~ de Lazare** Relig the raising of Lazarus; **2** (renaissance) (de cinéma, tradition) revival; (de personne) rebirth.

retable /ʀətabl/ *nm* altarpiece.

rétablir /ʀetabliʀ/ [3] **I** *vtr* **1** (ramener) to restore [*électricité, ordre, confiance, régime, impôt*]; to restore [*forces, santé*]; **~ la situation** to restore normality; **~ la circulation** to get the traffic moving again; **2** (restituer) to re-establish [*vérité, faits*]; to restore [*texte*]; **3** (guérir) to restore [sb] to health [*malade*]; **4** (réintégrer) **~ qn dans ses fonctions** to reinstate sb in his/her job; **~ qn dans ses droits/son titre** to restore sb's rights/title; **~ qn sur le trône** to restore sb to the throne.

II se rétablir *vpr* **1** lit, fig (s'améliorer) [*malade, monnaie, devise*] to recover; **2** (être restauré) [*ordre, silence*] to be restored; [*calme*] to return; [*situation*] to return to normal; **3** Sport [*gymnaste*] to pull oneself up.

rétablissement /ʀetablismɑ̃/ *nm* **1** (d'électricité, de paix, relations, loi) restoration; **~ de qn dans son emploi** reinstatement of sb in his/her post; **2** (de faits, vérité) re-establishment; **3** (de malade, monnaie) recovery; **4** Sport pull-up; **faire un ~** to pull oneself up.

retailler /R(ə)taje/ [1] *vtr* Cout to recut; **faire ~ qch** to have sth recut.

rétamé○, **~e** /Retame/ *adj* (épuisé) knackered◑ GB, beat○; (battu) hammered○; (ivre) plastered○.

rétamer /Retame/ [1] **I** *vtr* **1** (réparer) to retin [*casseroles*]; **2**○ (épuiser) to wear [sb] out○; (battre) to hammer○.

II se rétamer○ *vpr* **1** (tomber) to come a cropper○; **2** (se blesser en voiture) to crash (**contre** into).

rétameur /RetamœR/ *nm* tinker, mender of pots and pans.

retape◑ /R(ə)tap/ *nf* **1** (de prostituée) soliciting; **elle fait de la ~** she's a streetwalker; **2** (recrutement) **faire de la ~ pour qch** to beat the drum for sth; **il fait de la ~ pour sa fête de charité** he's drumming up support for his charity fete.

retaper /R(ə)tape/ [1] **I** *vtr* **1**○ (réparer) to do up [*maison, auto*]; **une vieille ferme retapée** an old farmhouse which has been done up; **2**○ (rétablir) [*séjour, traitement*] **~ qn** to put sb on his/her feet again; **3** (dactylographier) to retype [*lettre*]; **4** (arranger) to straighten [*lit*].

II se retaper○ *vpr* [*convalescent*] to recover, to get better.

retapisser /R(ə)tapise/ [1] *vtr* (de papier peint) to repaper (**de** with); (de tissu, toile) to redecorate [*pièce*] (**de** with); to recover, to redecorate [*mur*]; to reupholster [*fauteuil, canapé*] (**de** with).

retard /R(ə)taR/ **I** *adj* Méd delayed; **insuline ~** delayed insulin; **faire une injection ~** to give a delayed injection.

II *nm* **1** (absence de ponctualité) lateness; (temps écoulé) delay; **le ~ du train/courrier/facteur** the fact that the train/post/postman was late; **vos ~s répétés sont inacceptables** your continual lateness is unacceptable; **trois ~s en une semaine c'est trop!** being late three times in a week is too much!; **votre ~ de ce matin est inexcusable** you've no excuse for being late this morning; **un ~ de 10 minutes sur le vol en provenance de Nice** a ten-minute delay in the flight from Nice; **des ~s sont à prévoir sur les trains de banlieue** delays are likely on commuter trains; **léger/important ~** slight/major delay; **avoir du ~** to be late; **avoir un ~ d'une heure, avoir une heure de ~** (avant échéance) to be one hour behind schedule; (après échéance) to be one hour late; **en ~** late; **être/arriver en ~** to be/to arrive late; **être en ~ dans son travail** to be behind with one's work; **je me suis mis en ~ dans mon travail** I've fallen behind with my work; **tu vas nous mettre en ~ si tu ne te dépêches pas!** you're going to make us late if you don't hurry up!; **nous sommes en ~ sur l'emploi du temps** we're behind schedule; **elle rend toujours son travail en ~** she's always handing her work in late; **il a rendu sa dissertation avec une semaine de ~** he handed his essay in one week late; **prendre du ~** to fall ou get behind (**dans** with); **il a pris du ~ dans son travail** he has fallen behind with his work; **le cycliste a pris du ~ sur le groupe de tête** the cyclist has fallen behind the leaders; **rattraper** or **combler son ~** to catch up; **nous avons beaucoup de ~ à rattraper** we've got a lot to catch up; **être en ~ pour faire qch** to be late doing sth; **elle est toujours en ~ pour payer ses factures** she's always late paying her bills; **il lui a souhaité son anniversaire en ~** he wished her a belated happy birthday; **avoir du courrier/travail en ~** to have a backlog of mail/work; **après bien des ~s** after a lot of delay; **sans ~** without delay, straight away; ▶ **métro**; **2** (développement moins avancé) backwardness ¢; **~ industriel/technologique** industrial/technological backwardness; **il est en ~ en mathématiques** he's behind in maths GB ou math US; **il a deux ans de ~** Scol he's two years behind at school; **ils ont vingt ans de ~ sur le reste de l'Europe** they're twenty years behind the rest of Europe; **être en ~ sur son temps** to be behind the times; **3** Mus retardation.

■ **~ à l'allumage** Aut, Tech delayed ignition; **~ intellectuel** backwardness.

retardataire /R(ə)taRdatɛR/ **I** *adj* **1** (non ponctuel) **les élèves ~s** students who are late; **les spectateurs ~s** latecomers; **2** (qui date) [*méthode, pédagogie, théorie*] outdated.

II *nmf* latecomer.

retardateur, **-trice** /R(ə)taRdatœR, tRis/ **I** *adj* Tech retarding.

II *nm* Chimie retarder.

retardé, **~e** /R(ə)taRde/ **I** *pp* ▶ **retarder**.

II *pp adj* [*personne*] backward.

retardement /R(ə)taRdəmɑ̃/ **I** *nm* delaying.

II à retardement *loc adj* [*appareil photo, dispositif*] delayed-action (*épith*); **bombe à ~** time-bomb; **des compliments/applaudissements à ~** belated compliments/applause.

III à retardement *loc adv* [*se fâcher, agir*] after the event; **il comprend toujours à ~** he's slow on the uptake○.

retarder /R(ə)taRde/ [1] **I** *vtr* **1** (par rapport à une heure convenue) to make [sb] late; **tu vas au théâtre, je ne veux pas te ~** I don't want to make you late for the theatre[GB]; **dépêche-toi, tu vas nous ~!** hurry up, you're going to make us late!; **être retardé** [*train, avion*] to be delayed; **le brouillard a retardé le décollage** fog delayed take-off; **2** (par rapport à un emploi du temps) to hold [sb] up; **je ne veux pas vous ~** I don't want to hold you up ou delay you; **il a été retardé par un client/les embouteillages** he was held up by a customer/the traffic; **ça l'a retardé dans son travail/ses recherches** this held up his work/his research; **le mauvais temps a retardé les opérations de sauvetage** the bad weather held up the rescue operation; **3** (reporter) to put off, to postpone [*départ, opération*]; **il a retardé son départ de deux jours** he put his departure off ou he postponed his departure for two days; **elle retarde toujours le moment de prendre une décision** she always puts off making decisions; **4** (reculer) to put back [*réveil, horloge*]; **cette nuit n'oubliez pas de ~ vos montres d'une heure** don't forget to put your watches back one hour tonight.

II *vi* **1** [*pendule, réveil, montre*] (être en retard) to be slow; (prendre de plus en plus de retard) to lose time; **ma montre retarde de cinq minutes par jour** my watch loses five minutes a day; **ce réveil retarde de 20 minutes** this alarm clock is 20 minutes slow; **je retarde de cinq minutes** my watch is five minutes slow; **2** (être rétrograde) **~ sur son temps** or **son époque** to be behind the times; **ils retardent de 50 ans!** they're 50 years behind the times!; **3** (ne pas être au courant) to be out of touch; **Léningrad? tu retardes, c'est Saint-Pétersbourg maintenant!** Leningrad? you're out of touch, it's Saint Petersburg now!

reteindre /R(ə)tɛ̃dR/ [55] *vtr* to redye [*cheveux, vêtement*]; to restain [*meuble, bois*]; **faire ~ qch** to have sth redyed [*cheveux, vêtement*]; to have sth restained [*meuble, bois*].

retéléphoner /R(ə)telefɔne/ [1] **I** *vtr* to phone [sb] again; (retourner un appel) to call ou phone [sb] back.

II *vi* **1** (de nouveau) to call ou phone again; **2** (retourner un appel) **~ à qn** to call ou phone sb back.

III se retéléphoner *vpr* to phone each other again.

retendre /R(ə)tɑ̃dR/ [6] **I** *vtr* **1** (de nouveau) to tighten up (again) [*corde, fil, toile*]; **2** (davantage) to tighten up [*corde, ressort*]; **faire ~ les cordes** to have the strings tightened; **3** (présenter de nouveau) **~ un plat** to offer a dish again; **~ la main** to hold out one's hand again.

II se retendre *vpr* [*corde*] to tighten up.

retenir /Rətniʀ, Rtəniʀ/ [36] **I** *vtr* **1** (empêcher de partir) to keep [*personne*]; (retarder) to hold [sb] up, to detain [*personne*]; **il m'a retenu plus d'une heure avec ses bavardages** he kept me chatting for over an hour; **son travail l'a retenu à Paris** his job kept him in Paris; **je ne vous retiendrai pas longtemps** I won't keep you long; **je ne vous retiens pas!** iron don't let me keep you!; **j'ai été retenu** I was held up; **~ qn prisonnier** to hold sb captive ou prisoner; **~ qn à dîner** to ask sb to stay for dinner; **2** (maintenir fixe) lit, fig to hold [*objet, attention*]; (en arrière) to hold back [*cheveux, volet, chien, personne, foule*]; to retain [*sol*]; (empêcher une chute) to stop [*personne*]; to rein in [*cheval*]; **un crochet retient le volet contre le mur** a hook holds the shutter back against the wall; **~ sa langue** fig to hold one's tongue; **la prudence/ma timidité m'a retenu** fig caution/my shyness held me back; **si tu ne l'avais pas retenu, il serait tombé** if you hadn't stopped him, he would have fallen; **si je ne l'avais pas retenu, il aurait tout avoué** if I hadn't helded on to him, he would have confessed everything; **retenez-moi ou je fais un malheur**○! hold me down or I'll go berserk○!; **~ qn par la manche** to catch hold of sb's sleeve; **votre réclamation a retenu toute notre attention** fml your complaint is receiving our full attention; **3** (réprimer) to hold back [*larmes*]; to hold [*souffle*]; to stifle [*cri, rire, soupir, bâillement*]; to bite back [*exclamation*] ; to suppress [*sourire*]; to contain, to suppress [*colère*]; to check [*geste*]; **elle ne put ~ un bâillement** she tried in vain to stifle a yawn; **colère retenue** suppressed anger; **4** (capturer) to retain [*chaleur, humidité, eau, odeur*]; to absorb [*lumière*]; **5** (réserver) to reserve, to book GB [*table, chambre, place*]; to set [*date*]; **la date retenue est jeudi prochain** the date set is next Thursday; **6** (confisquer) to withhold, to retain [*caution, bagages*]; to stop [*salaire*]; (prélever) to deduct [*somme, cotisation, impôt*] (**sur** from); **~ l'impôt à la source** Fisc to deduct tax at source; **7** (mémoriser) to remember [*numéro, nom, date, formule*]; to be left with, to get [*impression*]; (absorber) to take in [*enseignement*]; **retiens-bien ceci** remember this; **cet enfant ne retient rien** that child doesn't take anything in; **je retiens de cet échec que** the lesson I learned from that failure is that; **je retiens qu'on peut leur faire confiance** I've learned that they can be trusted; **toi, je te retiens**○! I won't forget this!, you'll live to regret this!; **8** (agréer) to accept [*argument, plan, proposition*]; Jur to uphold [*chef d'accusation*]; (considérer favorablement) **votre candidature a été retenue** you're being considered for the post; **être retenu comme critère/un indice valable** to be used as a criterion/a reliable indication; **c'est la solution retenue par le gouvernement** that's the solution the government has decided on; **être retenu comme solution** to be the solution adopted; **9** Math to carry (over); **je pose 5 et je retiens 1** I put down 5 and carry 1.

II se retenir *vpr* **1** (se rattraper) to stop oneself; **se ~ à qch** to hang on to sth; **j'ai essayé de me ~ dans ma chute** I tried to stop myself from falling; **2** (réprimer une envie psychique) to stop oneself; **se ~ de faire** to stop oneself from doing; **se ~ de pleurer/rire** to try not to cry/laugh; **je n'ai pas pu me ~ de pleurer** I couldn't hold back the tears; **il ne put se ~ de rire** he couldn't help laughing; **je me suis retenu de leur dire ce que je pensais** I refrained from telling them what I thought; **j'ai dû me ~ pour ne pas la gifler** it was all I could do not to slap her; **3**○ (réprimer un besoin physiologique) to control oneself; **retiens-toi, nous sommes presque arrivés** hold on, we're nearly there; **ne le gronde pas, il n'a pas pu se ~** don't scold him, he couldn't help it.

retenter /ʀ(ə)tɑ̃te/ [1] *vtr* to reattempt [*exploit, ascension*]; **~ de faire** to make another attempt at doing; **~ sa chance** to try one's luck again; **~ le coup**○ (pour réussir) to have another go○; (pour tromper) to try it on again○.

rétenteur /ʀetɑ̃tœʀ/ **I** *adj m* **muscle ~** retentor muscle.
II *nm* Jur lienor.

rétention /ʀetɑ̃sjɔ̃/ *nf* **1** Méd retention; **faire de la ~ d'eau/d'urine** to suffer from water/urine retention; **2** (refus de communiquer) withholding (**de** of); **~ d'information** Jur withholding of information; **pratiquer une politique de ~** Écon to impose limits on exports (*in order to raise prices*); **3** Géog retention (**de** of).

retentir /ʀ(ə)tɑ̃tiʀ/ [3] *vi* **1** (résonner) to ring out; (plus fort) to resound; **~ aux oreilles de qn** to ring in sb's ears; **~ en qn** liter to strike a chord in sb; **2** (affecter) **~ sur** [*fatigue, drogue, état*] to have an impact on; [*événement, situation*] to have repercussions on.

retentissant, **~e** /ʀ(ə)tɑ̃tisɑ̃, ɑ̃t/ *adj* **1** (éclatant) [*déclaration, échec, succès*] resounding; [*procès, film, découverte, discours*] sensational; **2** (sonore) [*cri, voix, bruit*] ringing; (plus fort) resounding.

retentissement /ʀ(ə)tɑ̃tismɑ̃/ *nm* **1** (bruit) (de pas, voix, d'instrument) ringing; (de tonnerre, canon) boom; **2** (répercussions) effect (**sur** on); (d'artiste, d'œuvre) impact (**sur** on); **3** (succès) sensation; **avoir un (grand) ~** to cause a (great) sensation.

retenu, **~e** /ʀətny, ʀtəny/ **I** *adj* liter [*élégance, charme*] discreet.
II retenue *nf* **1** (modération) restraint; **faire preuve/manquer de ~e** to show/to lack restraint; **critiquer avec ~e** to be restrained in one's criticism(s); **perdre toute ~e** to lose one's inhibitions; **n'avoir aucune ~e dans son langage** to use very immoderate language; **n'avoir aucune ~e dans sa conduite** to behave wildly; **boire/manger sans ~e** to drink/to eat to excess; **rire sans ~e** to laugh uproariously; **2** (prélèvement) deduction (**sur** from); **opérer** or **faire une ~e de 10% sur le salaire de qn** to make a deduction of 10% ou to deduct 10% from sb's salary; **la ~e pour la retraite/au titre des cotisations sociales** ≈ pension/national insurance contributions; **3** Scol detention; **être en ~e** to be in detention; **j'ai eu deux heures de ~e** I got two hours' detention; **4** Math **tu as oublié la ~e des dizaines** you forgot to carry over from the tens column; **5** Transp (ralentissement) tailback; **6** Tech (masse d'eau) reservoir; **ouvrage de ~e** dam; **barrage à faible ~e** low-capacity dam.
■ **~e de garantie** Comm retention money; **~e à la source** Fisc deduction of tax at source GB, withholding tax US; **système de ~e à la source** pay as you earn system, PAYE system GB, withholding system US.

rétiaire /ʀetjɛʀ/ *nm* Antiq retiarius.

réticence /ʀetisɑ̃s/ *nf* **1** (répugnance) reluctance; **avec ~** reluctantly; **sans ~** (parler) openly; (accepter) unreservedly; **2** liter (réserve) reticence ¢; **ses ~s en ce qui concerne le passé** his/her reticence about the past; **3** (chose omise) non-disclosure, omission; **relever des ~s dans les témoignages** to point out omissions in the evidence; **'toute ~ de la part de l'assuré'** 'failure on the part of the insured to declare all relevant facts'.

réticent, **~e** /ʀetisɑ̃, ɑ̃t/ *adj* **1** (qui hésite) hesitant (**à faire** about doing); (qui rechigne) reluctant (**à faire** to do); **se montrer/être ~ à une idée** to seem/to be hostile to an idea; **2** (peu communicatif) [*personne*] reticent; (de nature) reserved.

réticulaire /ʀetikylɛʀ/ *adj* reticular.

réticule /ʀetikyl/ *nm* **1** (en optique) reticle; **2** (petit sac) reticule; **3** Mode (filet) hairnet.

réticulé, **~e** /ʀetikyle/ *adj* **1** Anat, Bot, Géol reticulate; **2** Archit reticulated.

rétif, **-ive** /ʀetif, iv/ *adj* [*âne, cheval*] restive; [*personne, humeur*] rebellious.

rétine /ʀetin/ *nf* retina.

rétinien, **-ienne** /ʀetinjɛ̃, ɛn/ *adj* retinal.

rétinite /ʀetinit/ ▶ **271** *nf* retinitis.

rétinographie /ʀetinoɡʀafi/ *nf* retinography.

retirage /ʀ(ə)tiʀaʒ/ *nm* **1** (action) reprinting; **2** (résultat) reprint.

retiré, **~e** /ʀ(ə)tiʀe/ *adj* (solitaire) [*endroit, vie*] secluded; (éloigné) [*endroit*] remote; **vivre ~e dans un couvent** to live the secluded life of a nun; **mener une vie ~e** to live a life of seclusion, to lead a secluded life; **vivre ~ de la société** to live the life of a recluse.

retirer /ʀ(ə)tiʀe/ [1] **I** *vtr* **1** (se débarrasser de) to take off [*vêtement, bijou*]; **retire-lui ses gants** take his/her gloves off; **2** (faire sortir) to take out, to remove (**de** from); **~ les arêtes** to take out ou remove the bones; **~ une balle d'une blessure** to remove ou extract a bullet from a wound; **~ les mains de ses poches/le poulet du four** to take one's hands out of one's pockets/the chicken out of the oven; **~ un enfant d'une école** to take a child away from a school, to remove a child from a school; **~ un filet de l'eau** to pull a net out of the water; **~ un corps des décombres** to pull a body from ou out of the rubble; **~ un mouchoir de sa poche** to pull a handkerchief out of one's pocket; **~ un gâteau d'un moule** to turn a cake out of a tin GB ou pan US; **~ ses troupes d'un pays** to withdraw one's troops from a country; **je n'arrive pas à ~ la cuillère du bocal** I can't get the spoon out of the jar; ▶ **épine**; **3** (écarter) to withdraw [*pied, main, tête*]; **retire ta main, tu vas te brûler** move your hand away, you'll burn yourself; **4** (supprimer, enlever) to withdraw [*permission, privilège*] (**à** from); to take away, to remove [*droit, bien, objet*] (**à** from); **~ un produit de la vente** Comm to recall a product; **~ la garde d'un enfant à qn** to withdraw custody of a child from sb; **on m'a retiré la garde de mon fils** I've lost custody of my son; **il s'est fait ~ son permis de conduire** he had his driver's licence[GB] taken away from him; **~ [qch] de la circulation** to withdraw [sth] from circulation [*monnaie*]; **retire-lui ce livre des mains** take that book away from him/her; **~ un livre du programme** to take a book off the syllabus; **~ ses affaires de la table** to take one's things off the table; **~ sa confiance à qn** not to trust sb any more; **je lui ai retiré mon estime** I no longer have any respect for him/her; **~ une pièce de l'affiche** to close a play; **5** (ne pas maintenir) to withdraw [*plainte, accusation, offre, soutien*]; **~ sa candidature** (à un poste) to withdraw one's application; (à une élection) to stand down (**en faveur de** in favour[GB] of); **je retire ce que j'ai dit** I take back what I said; **6** (rentrer en possession de) to collect, to pick up [*billet, bagages, dossier, inscription*] ; to withdraw [*argent*] (**d'un compte** from an account); **~ les billets au guichet/à l'agence de voyages** to collect one's tickets at the counter/from the travel agent's; **7** (recueillir) to get, to derive [*bénéfice*] (**de** from); **il en retire 10 000 francs par an** he gets 10,000 francs a year out of it; **espérant en ~ un profit/avantage** hoping to get some benefit/advantage out of it; **je n'en ai retiré que des ennuis** it brought me nothing but trouble, I got nothing but trouble out of it; **tout ce qu'il a retiré de sa baignade/de son refus de payer, c'est...** all he got out of his swim/of refusing to pay was...; **8** (extraire) to extract [*minerai, huile*] (**de** from); **graine dont on retire de l'huile** seed from which oil is extracted.
II se retirer *vpr* **1** (partir) to withdraw, to leave; (aller se coucher)† to retire to bed; **se ~ dans son bureau/un coin** to withdraw to one's study/a corner; **se ~ en province/sur ses terres** to retire to the country/to one's estate; **se ~ de** to withdraw from [*groupement, parti, territoire, compétition*]; to retire from [*affaires, politique*]; **se ~ du monde** to withdraw from society; **se ~ du barreau** to retire from the bar; **un homme retiré de la politique** a man retired from political life; **depuis qu'il est retiré des affaires** since he retired, since his retirement; **se ~ du combat/de la partie** to pull out; **se ~ sur la pointe des pieds** to tiptoe out ou away; **se ~ sans bruit** to slip away quietly; **2** (après accouplement) to withdraw; **3** (reculer) [*eaux de crue*] to subside, to recede; [*glacier*] to retreat; [*personne*] to step back; (pour laisser passer) to step aside; **se ~ sur ses arrières** or **positions** Mil to retreat; **la foule se retira vers la mairie** the crowd retreated to the town hall; **la mer se retire** the tide is going out.

retombée /ʀ(ə)tɔ̃be/ **I** *nf* Archit springing.
II retombées *nfpl* **1** (pluie) **~s radioactives** radioactive fallout ¢; **2** (conséquences) effects (*pl*) (**sur** on), consequences (*pl*) (**sur** for); **~s catastrophiques** disastrous consequences; **~s positives/bénéfiques** positive/beneficial effects; **les mesures auront des ~s favorables sur l'emploi** the measures will have a favourable[GB] effect on employment; **~s médiatiques** consequences of media coverage; **3** (d'une invention) spin-offs (*pl*).

retomber /ʀ(ə)tɔ̃be/ [1] *vi* **1** (faire une nouvelle chute) [*personne, objet*] to fall again; **~ malade/amoureux** fig to fall ill/in love again; **~ dans la misère/l'anarchie/la facilité** fig to sink back into poverty/anarchy/a state of complacency; **~ dans le péché** fig to fall back into evil ways; **~ en enfance** fig to regress to childhood; **la conversation retombe toujours sur le même sujet** fig the conversation always comes back to the same subject; **2** (retourner au sol après s'être élevé) [*personne, chat, projectile*] to land; [*ballon, capot, rideau métallique*] to come down; [*brouillard*] to set in again; **elle sauta et retomba sur le ventre** she jumped and landed on her stomach; **~ sur ses pattes** [*chat*] to land on its feet; **~ sur ses pieds** or **pattes**○ fig to land on one's feet; **les fumées toxiques retombent en pluie acide** toxic fumes come down as acid rain; **laisser ~ le capot/ses bras** to let the bonnet GB ou hood US/one's arms drop; **ça va te ~ sur le nez**○ fig it'll come down on your head; **3** (s'affaisser) [*personne*] to fall back; [*soufflé*] to collapse; fig [*colère, exaltation*] to subside; [*enthousiasme, intérêt*] to wane; **elle tenta de se redresser et retomba** she tried to get up and fell back; **sa colère retomba d'elle-même** his/her anger subsided; **se laisser ~ sur le sable/dans son fauteuil** to fall ou flop back onto the sand/into one's chair; **4** (diminuer) [*valeur, monnaie*] to fall; [*température*] to go down, to fall; **le dollar est retombé à 4 francs** the dollar has fallen to 4 francs; **5** (pendre) **sa chevelure retombait sur ses épaules** his/her hair fell ou flowed over his/her shoulders; **elle écarta la mèche qui lui retombait sur le front** she pushed back the hair which was hanging in her eyes; **les rideaux retombent en plis gracieux** the curtains hang gracefully; **6** (incomber à) **~ sur qn** [*responsabilité, ennui*] to fall on sb; **toutes les responsabilités retombent sur moi** all the responsibility falls on me; **la faute du père retombera sur le fils** Bible the sins of the fathers will be visited on the sons; **tu fais des bêtises et c'est sur moi que ça retombe** you behave stupidly, and I'm the one who has to pay for it; **faire ~ la responsabilité sur qn** to pass the buck○ to sb; **7** (rencontrer de nouveau) **~ sur** to run into [sb] again [*personne*]; to come across [sth] again [*occasion*].

retordre /R(ə)tɔRdR/ [6] *vtr* Tex to twist [*fil*].
IDIOMES **donner du fil à ~ à qn** to give sb a hard time.

rétorquer /RetɔRke/ [1] *vtr* (répliquer) to retort (**que** that).

retors, ~e /Rətɔʀ, ɔRs/ *adj* **1** pej [*personne*] crafty; [*argument*] devious; **2** Tex [*fil*] twisted.

rétorsion /RetɔRsjɔ̃/ *nf* Jur, Pol retaliation; **user de ~** to retaliate; **mesure de ~** retaliatory measure.

retouche /R(ə)tuʃ/ *nf* (de vêtement, texte) alteration; (de photo, tableau) retouch; **faire des ~s** Cout to do alterations; Phot to retouch photographs.

retoucher /R(ə)tuʃe/ [1] **I** *vtr* **1** (modifier) to make alterations to [*vêtement*]; to alter [*col, manches*]; to retouch, to touch up [*photographie, tableau*]; **~ un texte** to make alterations to a text; **ces photographies ont été retouchées** these photographs have been touched up ou retouched; **faire ~** to have [sth] altered [*vêtement*]; **2** (de nouveau) (pour sentir) to touch again; (obtenir) **~ 100 francs** to get another 100 francs.
II retoucher à *vtr ind* **1** (pour sentir) **~ à qch** to touch sth again; **2** (reprendre) **~ à l'alcool/la drogue** to start drinking again/taking drugs again; **il a juré qu'il ne retoucherait jamais à l'alcool** he vowed that he would never touch alcohol again.

retoucheur, -euse /R(ə)tuʃœR, øz/ ▶ **510** *nm,f* Phot, Cin retoucher.

retour /R(ə)tuR/ *nm* **1** (trajet) return; (**billet de**) **~** return ticket GB, round trip (ticket) US; **ils me payent l'aller, non le ~** they're paying for my outward journey but not for the return; **au ~ nous nous sommes arrêtés pour déjeuner** we stopped for lunch on the way back; **la pluie s'est mise à tomber pendant notre ~** it started raining as we were on our way back; **être sur le chemin du ~** to be on one's way back; **notre ~ s'est bien passé** we got back safely; **il faut penser au ~** (à rentrer) we must think about getting back; (au voyage pour rentrer) we must think about the return journey; **il vient juste d'arriver mais il pense déjà à son ~** he's only just arrived but he's already thinking about going back; **il prépare son ~ dans son pays** he's getting ready to return ou to go back to his own country; **il y a des embouteillages à cause des ~s de vacances** there are traffic jams because of people coming back from their holidays GB ou vacations US; **2** (au point de départ) return; **~ sur terre** return to earth; **à mon ~ à Paris/dans la région** on ou upon my return to Paris/to the area; **à son ~ du front/de l'étranger** on his return from the front/from abroad; **être de ~** to be back; **je serai de ~ avant minuit** I'll be back by midnight; **de ~ à Paris, elle a ouvert un magasin** back in Paris, she opened a shop GB ou store US; **de ~ à la maison** back home; **à son ~, elle m'a téléphoné** when she got back, she phoned me; **il attend le ~ de sa femme pour prendre une décision** he's waiting for his wife to return ou to come back before making a decision; **un ~ triomphal** a triumphant return; **fêter le ~ de qn** to celebrate sb's return; **partir sans espoir de ~** to leave for good; **3** (à un stade antérieur) return; **~ à la normale** return to normal; **on attend le ~ au calme** people are waiting for things to calm down; **~ à la vie civile** return to civilian life; **~ à la terre** going back to the land; **~ à la nature** return to nature; **'~ à la case départ'** 'back to square one'; **~ aux sources** (aux principes) return to basics; (à la nature) return to the simple life; (vers ses racines) return to one's roots; **il connaît maintenant le succès et c'est un juste ~ des choses** he's successful now, and deservedly so; **donner qch en ~** to give sth in return; **4** (réapparition) return; **le ~ du beau temps/de l'hiver** the return of the fine weather/of winter; **le ~ des hirondelles** the swallows' return; **le ~ de la mode des années 60** the return of 60s fashions; **le ~ d'un chanteur après 15 ans de silence** a singer's comeback after 15 years of silence; **faire un ~ en force** [*chanteur, artiste*] to make a big comeback; [*idéologie*] to be back with a vengeance; [*cycliste, coureur*] to make a strong comeback; **5** (échange) **elle s'engage, en ~, à payer la facture** she undertakes for her part to pay the bill; **aimer sans ~** liter to suffer from unrequited love littér; **6** Comm (objets invendus) return; (de récipient, bouteille) return; (**clause de**) **~ sans frais** no protest clause; **'sans ~ ni consigne'** 'no deposit or return'; **7** (renvoi) **~ à l'expéditeur** or **à l'envoyeur** return to sender; **par ~ du courrier** by return of post GB, by the next mail US; **8** (au tennis) return; **~ de service** return of service; **9** Tech return; **~ automatique du chariot** automatic carriage return.
■ **~ d'âge** change of life; **~ en arrière** Cin, Littérat flashback; **ce serait un ~ en arrière** (pas souhaitable) it would be a step backward(s); **un ~ en arrière s'impose** (souhaitable) we must go back to the previous state of affairs; **~ de balancier** or **de bâton**○ backlash; **en ~ d'équerre** at a right angle; **~ de flamme** Tech flashback; Aut, fig backfiring; **~ de manivelle**○ = **~ de balancier**; **~ de marée** undertow; **~ à la masse** or **à la terre** earth GB ou ground US return; **~ offensif** renewed attack; **'~ rapide'** fast rewind; **~ sur soi-même** soul-searching; **faire un ~ sur soi-même** to do some soul-searching.
IDIOMES **être sur le ~**○ to be over the hill○.

retournement /R(ə)tuRnəmɑ̃/ *nm* (de situation) reversal (**de** of); **il y a eu un ~ de l'opinion publique** there was a turn around ou swing in public opinion.

retourner /R(ə)tuRne/ [1] **I** *vtr* (+ *v avoir*) **1** (changer de côté) to turn [sth] over [*seau, caisse, steak, poisson*]; to turn [*matelas*]; **~ une carte à jouer** (figure visible) to turn up a playing card; (figure pas visible) to put a playing card face down; **~ un tableau contre le mur** to turn a painting to the wall; **2** (mettre à l'envers) to turn [sth] inside out [*vêtement, sac*]; Cout to turn [*vêtement, coussin, col*]; **un coup de vent a retourné son parapluie** a gust of wind turned his umbrella inside out; **il a retourné ses poches à la recherche de quelques sous** he turned his pockets inside out looking for some change; **3** (tourner à plusieurs reprises) to turn over [*terre*]; to toss [*salade, foin*]; **~ une idée** or **pensée dans sa tête** to turn an idea ou a thought over in one's mind; **4** (changer d'orientation) to return [*compliment, critique*]; **~ la situation** to reverse the situation; **elle a retourné le pistolet contre elle-même** she then turned the gun on herself; **si tu retournes l'argument contre lui** if you turn his own argument against him; **5** (bouleverser) [*personne*] to turn [sth] upside down [*maison, pièce*]; [*nouvelle, spectacle*] to shake [*personne*]; **elle a retourné toute la maison pour retrouver la facture** she turned the house upside down trying to find the bill; **je suis encore tout retourné**○ I'm still quite shaken; **6** (renvoyer) to send [sth] back, to return [*colis, lettre, marchandise*].
II *vi* (+ *v être*) **1** (aller à nouveau) to go back, to return (**à** to); **~ dans son village natal** to return to the village where one was born; **~ chez le dentiste/médecin pour une nouvelle visite** to go back to the dentist's/doctor's for another visit; **~ à l'école/au bureau** to go back to school/to the office; **je n'y suis jamais retourné depuis** I've never been back ou never returned since; **2** (à un état antérieur) to go back (**à** to), to return (**à** to); **animal qui est retourné à l'état sauvage** animal that has gone back ou returned to its wild state; **~ à ses premières amours** liter to return to one's first love; **il est retourné à son laboratoire et à ses expériences** he went back to his laboratory and to his experiments; **les biens retournent à leur légitime possesseur** the property reverts to its rightful owner.
III se retourner *vpr* **1** (tourner la tête) to turn around, to turn round GB; **je l'ai appelée et elle s'est retournée** I called her and she turned around; **partir sans se ~** lit, fig to leave without once looking back; **elle est tellement grande que tout le monde se retourne sur son passage** she's so tall that everybody turns to look as she goes past; **2** (changer de position) [*personne couchée*] to turn over; [*véhicule, automobiliste*] to turn over, to overturn; **se ~ sur le dos/ventre** to turn over onto one's back/stomach; **il n'a pas arrêté de se ~ (dans son lit) pendant toute la nuit** he kept tossing and turning all night long; **la voiture s'est retournée dans un fossé** the car overturned into a ditch; **3** (s'organiser) to get organized; **ça lui laissera le temps de se ~** it'll give her time to sort things out ou to get organized; **4** (prendre un tour inverse) **se ~ contre qn** [*personne, animal*] to turn against sb; [*situation, agissements*] to backfire on sb; **se ~ contre ses alliés** to turn on one's allies; **ses arguments se sont retournés contre lui** his arguments backfired on him; **5** (se tordre) **elle s'est retourné le doigt/un ongle** she bent back her finger/a nail; **6** (repartir) **s'en ~** to go back; **s'en ~ chez soi** to go back home; ▶ **plaie.**
IV *v impers* **j'aimerais savoir de quoi il retourne** I'd like to know what's going on.
IDIOMES **~ qn comme une crêpe**○ or **un gant**○ to make sb change their mind completely.

retracer /RətRase/ [12] *vtr* **1** (marquer) to redraw [*ligne, dessin*]; **2** (narrer) to recount [*événement, vie*].

rétractable /RetRaktabl/ *adj* [*pointe, embout*] retractable; [*offre*] revocable.

rétractation /RetRaktasjɔ̃/ *nf* (de pointe, d'embout) retraction; (d'offre) revocation.

rétracter /RetRakte/ [1] **I** *vtr* (tous contextes) to retract; **il a rétracté ses injures** he retracted his insults; **le chat a rétracté ses griffes** the cat retracted its claws.
II se rétracter *vpr* (tous contextes) to retract.

rétractile /RetRaktil/ *adj* retractile.

retraduction /RətRadyksjɔ̃/ *nf* (nouvelle) new translation; (à partir d'une traduction) translation of a translation; (vers la langue de départ) translation back into the original language.

retraduire /RətRadɥiR/ [69] *vtr* (de nouveau) to retranslate; (vers la langue de départ) to translate [sth] back into the original language; **~ du grec** to translate back from the Greek.

retrait /R(ə)tRɛ/ **I** *nm* **1** (de valise, paquet, commande, dossier) collection; (d'argent) withdrawal; **s'adresser au guichet nº 2 pour le ~ des colis** parcels can be collected for counter nº. 2; **présentez un reçu pour le ~ de toute commande** a receipt must be produced when collecting orders; **2** (annulation, suppression) (d'autorisation, de soutien, monnaie) withdrawal (**de** of); Comm (d'article défectueux) recall (**de** of); **réclamer le ~ d'une mesure** to call for a measure to be lifted; **après le ~ de la candidature du maire sortant** after the outgoing mayor stood down; **~ du permis (de conduire)** disqualification from driving; **3** (départ) withdrawal; **le ~ des troupes de la zone occupée** the withdrawal of the troops from the occupied zone; **le ~ du pilote du championnat** the driver's withdrawal from the championships; **faire un ~ de fonds** to withdraw funds; **le ~ des eaux a révélé l'ampleur du désastre** when the water went down ou subsided, the scale of the disaster became apparent; **4** (après accouplement) withdrawal.

II en retrait *loc adv* **1** (à l'écart) **maison (située) en ~ de** house set back from [*route*]; house a little way out of [*village*]; **se tenir en ~** lit to stand back; **se mettre/tenir en ~** fig to take/to occupy a back seat; **rester en ~** fig to stay in the background; **la police reste en ~** the police are keeping a low profile; **ce secteur reste en ~ de l'automobile** this sector is somewhat behind the automotive sector; **le texte est en ~ par rapport aux déclarations du ministre** fig the bill is less drastic than the minister had led us to expect; **2** (en baisse) **les recettes sont en ~ de 10% par rapport à** or **sur l'année dernière** takings are 10% down on last year; **3** Tech (contraction) (de béton, tissu) shrinkage; (de métal) contraction.

■ **~ à vue** withdrawal on demand.

retraite /ʀ(ə)tʀɛt/ *nf* **1** (cessation d'activité) retirement; **la ~ à 60 ans** retirement at 60; **l'âge de la ~** retirement age; **~ anticipée** early retirement; **prendre sa ~** to retire; **prendre sa ~ de commandant de l'armée de terre** to retire from the army with the rank of major; **il est resté à Paris jusqu'à sa ~** he stayed in Paris until he retired; **mettre qn à la ~** to make sb take retirement, to retire sb; **il a été mis à la ~ anticipée** he was made to take early retirement; **mise à la ~ d'office** compulsory retirement; **il y aura des mises à la ~** a number of people will be asked to retire; **à la ~** retired; **sa mise à la ~ l'a beaucoup déprimé** he was very depressed at being retired; **il est en ~ depuis deux ans** he has been retired for two years; **partir en ~** to retire; **départ à la ~** retirement; **2** (pension) pension; **une ~ d'ouvrier** a worker's pension; **toucher sa ~** to draw one's pension; **régime de ~ par capitalisation** funded pension plan, pension plan by capitalization; **régime de ~ par répartition** contributory pension scheme ou plan; **~ complémentaire** supplementary pension; **3** Mil retreat; **~ en bon ordre** orderly retreat; **sonner la ~** to sound the retreat; **~ de Russie** retreat from Russia; **battre en ~** Mil to beat a retreat, to retreat; fig to beat a hasty retreat; **4** Relig retreat; **une ~ d'une semaine** a week's retreat; **être en ~** to be in retreat; **faire ~** to go into retreat; **5** (lieu retiré) littér (d'écrivain) retreat; (de brigands) refuge; **sortir de sa ~** to come out of one's retreat.

retraité, ~e /ʀ(ə)tʀete/ I *pp* ▶ **retraiter**.
II *pp adj* [*personne*] retired.
III *nm,f* retired person; **les ~s** retired people.

retraitement /ʀ(ə)tʀɛtmɑ̃/ *nm* reprocessing.

retraiter /ʀ(ə)tʀete/ [1] *vtr* Phys Nucl to reprocess.

retranché, ~e /ʀ(ə)tʀɑ̃ʃe/ *adj* [*village, cap, position*] entrenched.

retranchement /ʀ(ə)tʀɑ̃ʃmɑ̃/ *nm* entrenched position, entrenchment; **pousser qn (jusque) dans ses derniers ~s** fig to drive sb into a corner.

retrancher /ʀ(ə)tʀɑ̃ʃe/ [1] **I** *vtr* **1** (enlever) to cut out [*mot, phrase, passage*] (**de** from); **2** (soustraire) to subtract, to take away [*somme, montant*] (**de** from); to deduct [*cotisations, frais*] (**de** from); **il faut ~ 10% du total** you must subtract 10% from the total; **tu ajoutes dix et tu retranches trois** you add ten and take away three.

II se retrancher *vpr* **1** Mil (s'installer) to take up position; (pour être à l'abri) to entrench oneself; **être retranché dans un village/bâtiment** [*soldats*] to have taken up position in a village/building; **2** (se cacher) **se ~ derrière** to hide behind [*idéologie, décision, loi*]; **il se retranche derrière l'article 14/les décisions patronales** he hides behind article 14/management decisions; **il se retranche derrière le directeur** he says it's a matter for the manager; **se ~ dans** to take refuge in [*silence, rêve, attitude*]; **elle se retranche dans une attitude soumise** she retreats into a submissive attitude.

retranscription /ʀ(ə)tʀɑ̃skʀipsjɔ̃/ *nf* retranscription.

retranscrire /ʀ(ə)tʀɑ̃skʀiʀ/ [67] *vtr* to retranscribe.

retransmetteur /ʀ(ə)tʀɑ̃smɛtœʀ/ *nm* relay.

retransmettre /ʀ(ə)tʀɑ̃smɛtʀ/ [60] *vtr* **1** (transmettre) Radio, TV to broadcast [*nouvelles, émission*]; **~ (qch) en direct** to broadcast sth live; **~ qch en différé** to broadcast a recording of sth; **2** (par relais) to relay; **retransmis par satellite** relayed by satellite; **3** Télécom, Radio to retransmit [*message, appel*].

retransmission /ʀ(ə)tʀɑ̃smisjɔ̃/ *nf* **1** (d'émission) broadcast; **~ en direct/différé** live/recorded broadcast; **la ~ de la cérémonie se fera à 15 heures** the ceremony will be broadcast at 3 pm; **2** (relais) relay; **assurer la ~ d'un signal** to relay a signal; **3** Télécom, Radio (de message, d'appel) retransmission.

retravailler /ʀ(ə)tʀavaje/ [1] **I** *vtr* to revise [*œuvre*].
II *vi* (après chômage, démission) to start working again; (après vacances, maladie) to go back to work.

retraverser /ʀ(ə)tʀavɛʀse/ [1] *vtr* **1** (de nouveau) to cross [sth] again; **2** (en sens inverse) to cross back over.

rétréci, ~e /ʀetʀesi/ I *pp* ▶ **rétrécir**.
II *pp adj* [*vêtement*] shrunken; [*champ d'investigation*] narrowed down; **'attention! chaussée ~e'** 'warning! road narrows'.

rétrécir /ʀetʀesiʀ/ [3] **I** *vtr* **1** Tex [*lavage*] to shrink; **le lavage l'a rétréci en longueur/largeur** it has got GB ou gotten US shorter/narrower in the wash; ▶ **peau**; **2** Cout [*couturier*] **~ en largeur** to take in (**de** by); **~ en longueur** to take up (**de** by); **3** Bot to shrivel [*plante*]; **4** Anat, Méd to contract [*pupille*]; **5** Constr (en largeur) to make [sth] narrower [*route*]; (de tous côtés) to make [sth] smaller [*terrain, parc*]; **6** (minimiser) to narrow down [*sujet, champ d'investigation*]; to narrow [*question, idée, domaine*].
II *vi* to shrink (**de** by) ; **ne rétrécit pas au lavage** does not shrink in the wash.
III se rétrécir *vpr* **1** [*route, berge, champ d'investigation*] to narrow (**en** into); [*cercle de fidèles*] to shrink; **2** Anat [*pupille*] to contract; **3** [*pensée*] to become more restricted.

rétrécissement /ʀetʀesismɑ̃/ *nm* **1** Tex, Cout (au lavage) (action) shrinking (**de** of); (résultat) shrinkage; (par couturier) **~ en largeur** taking in; **~ en longueur** taking up; **2** Constr (de route, embouchure, vallée) narrowing; **3** Anat, Méd (de pupille) contraction; (d'œsophage, urètre, intestin) stricture.

retrempe /ʀətʀɑ̃p/ *nf* requenching.

retremper: **se retremper** /ʀətʀɑ̃pe/ [1] *vpr* **1** (baigneur) to have ou take another dip; **2** (dans un milieu, une ambiance) **se ~ dans l'ambiance familiale** to reimmerse oneself in the family atmosphere.

rétribuer /ʀetʀibɥe/ [1] *vtr* to remunerate [*personne, travail*].

rétribution /ʀetʀibysjɔ̃/ *nf* **1** (paiement) remuneration; **2** (récompense) reward (**de** for).

rétro /ʀetʀo/ **I** *adj inv* imitating the styles of an earlier period.
II *nm* **1** (style) Archit Art nostalgic style; **2** Mode retro fashions (*pl*); **3**○ Aut (*abbr* = **rétroviseur**) rear-view mirror.

rétroactif, -ive /ʀetʀoaktif, iv/ *adj* Admin, Jur [*effet, mesure*] retrospective, retroactive; [*loi*] retrospective, ex post facto; [*augmentation*] backdated; **augmentation rétroactive à compter du** increase backdated to; **la loi n'a pas d'effet ~** the law cannot be applied retrospectively; **avec effet ~** [*mesure*] retrospective; [*augmentation*] backdated.

rétroaction /ʀetʀoaksjɔ̃/ *nf* **1** Admin, Jur retrospective effect; **2** Biol, Écon, Phys feedback; **effet de ~** feedback effect.

rétroactivement /ʀetʀoaktivmɑ̃/ *adv* Admin, Jur retrospectively, retroactively.

rétroactivité /ʀetʀoaktivite/ *nf* Admin, Jur retroactivity; (de jugement) ex post facto effect.

rétrocéder /ʀetʀɔsede/ [14] *vtr* **1** Jur to retrocede [*territoire*] (**to** à); to restore [*bien*] (**to** à); to reassign [*droit*] (**to** à); **2** (revendre) **~ ses parts à qn** to sell one's shares back to sb.

rétrocession /ʀetʀɔsɛsjɔ̃/ *nf* (de territoire) retrocession.

rétroflexe /ʀetʀoflɛks/ *adj* Ling retroflex.

rétrofusée /ʀetʀofyze/ *nf* retro-rocket.

rétrogradation /ʀetʀogʀadasjɔ̃/ *nf* **1** (de militaire, fonctionnaire) demotion; **la ~ de qn à l'échelon inférieur** the demotion of sb by one grade; **2** Sport (de sportif, cheval) relegation; **3** Astron retrogradation.

rétrograde /ʀetʀogʀad/ *adj* **1** (réactionnaire) [*personne, gouvernement*] reactionary; [*politique, loi, pensée*] retrograde; **2** (qui va en sens inverse) [*mouvement, marche*] retrograde.

rétrograder /ʀetʀogʀade/ [1] **I** *vtr* **1** Mil, Admin to demote [*militaire, fonctionnaire*] (**à** to); **~ qn à l'échelon inférieur** to demote sb by one grade; **2** Sport to relegate [*sportif, cheval*].
II *vi* **1** Aut to change down GB, to downshift US; **2** Sport [*équipe, club*] to be relegated GB ou demoted US (**à, en** to); **3** Astron to retrograde.

rétropédalage /ʀetʀopedalaʒ/ *nm* lit backpedalling[GB]; **frein à ~** backpedal brake.

rétropédaler /ʀetʀopedale/ [1] *vi* lit to backpedal.

rétroprojecteur /ʀetʀopʀɔʒɛktœʀ/ *nm* overhead projector.

rétropropulsion /ʀetʀopʀɔpylsjɔ̃/ *nf* reverse thrust.

rétrospectif, -ive /ʀetʀɔspɛktif, iv/ **I** *adj* [*analyse, exposition*] retrospective; **avoir une peur ~** to be frightened after the event.
II rétrospective *nf* Art retrospective; Cin festival; **rétrospective Bergman/Tati** Bergman/Tati season GB ou festival; **rétrospective des événements de l'année** review of the year's events.

rétrospectivement /ʀetʀɔspɛktivmɑ̃/ *adv* **1** (après coup) [*avoir peur*] after the event; **2** (après réflexion) in retrospect.

retroussé, ~e /ʀ(ə)tʀuse/ I *pp* ▶ **retrousser**.
II *pp adj* **1** [*robe*] hitched up GB, hiked up US (**jusqu'à** to); [*manche*] rolled up; **2** [*nez*] turned up; [*lèvre*] curling (*épith*); **il a le nez ~** he's got a turned up nose.

retrousser /ʀ(ə)tʀuse/ [1] *vtr* to hitch up GB, to hike up US [*robe*] (**jusqu'à** to); to roll up [*pantalon*]; **~ ses manches** lit, fig to roll up one's sleeves; **le chien retroussa ses babines** the dog bared its teeth.

retroussis /ʀ(ə)tʀusi/ *nm inv* **1** (de chapeau) turned-up brim; **2** (de lèvre, moustache) liter curl; (de nez) tilt.

retrouvailles /ʀ(ə)tʀuvaj/ *nfpl* (après une séparation) reunion (**avec** with); (après une brouille) reconciliation (**avec** with).

retrouver /ʀ(ə)tʀuve/ [1] **I** *vtr* **1** (ce qui était perdu) to find [*sac, chien, cadavre, fugitif*]; **~ son chemin** to find one's way; **~ qn vivant** to find sb alive; **2** (trouver à nouveau) to find [sth] again [*travail, conditions, objet*]; to come across [sth] again [*idée, thème*]; **je voudrais ~ le même tissu** I would like to find the same fabric again; **on retrouve ce thème dans votre dernier roman** we come across this theme again in your last novel; **3** (redécouvrir) to rediscover [*formule, technique, recette*]; **4** (recouvrer) to get [sth] back [*assurance*]; to regain, to recover [*force, santé*]; **~ son sang-froid** to regain one's composure; **il a retrouvé le sourire** he's smiling again; **ton teint a retrouvé son éclat** your skin has got GB ou gotten US its natural radiance back; **~ le sommeil** (après s'être réveillé) to get back to sleep; (après période d'insomnie) to be able to sleep again; **5** (se rappeler) to remember [*nom, air, code secret*]; **6** (revoir) to meet [sb] again [*connaissance*]; to see [sth] again, to be back in [*lieu*]; (regagner) to be back in [*lieu*]; **un ami que j'ai retrouvé 20 ans après** a friend I met again after 20 years; **j'ai hâte de ~ Paris/ma maison** I can't wait to be back in Paris/to be back home; **il avait laissé un enfant, il retrouva un homme** he had left a child and returned to find a man; **~ les choses telles qu'elles étaient** to find things as they were; **7** (reconnaître) to recognize [*personne, trait, style*]; **je retrouve sa mère en elle** I can see her mother in her; **on le retrouve dans cette œuvre** you can see his hand in this work; **quand tu souris, je te retrouve** that's more like you to be smiling; **8** (rejoindre) to join, to meet [*personne*]; **viens nous ~ à la plage** come and join us on the beach; **je vous retrouverai plus tard** I'll join ou meet you later; **je te retrouve pour déjeuner?** shall I meet you for lunch?; **je te retrouverai!** (menace) I'll get my own back on you!

II se retrouver *vpr* **1** (se réunir) to meet; (se voir de nouveau) to meet again; **on se retrouvera devant le cinéma** let's meet (up) outside the cinema; **on se retrouvera l'an prochain** we'll meet again next year; **de temps en temps on se retrouve entre amis** we get together with a few friends once in a while; **on s'est retrouvé en famille** the family got together; **comme on se retrouve!** fancy seeing you here!; **on se retrouvera!, nous nous retrouverons!** (menace) I'll get my own back on you!; **2** (être) to find oneself; **se ~ couché par terre/coincé** to find oneself lying on the floor/trapped; **se ~ enceinte** to find oneself pregnant; **se ~ à la tête d'une entreprise** to find oneself at the head of a company; **se ~ nez à nez avec qch/qn** to find oneself face to face with sth/sb; **se ~ orphelin/veuf/sans argent** to be left an orphan/a widower/penniless; **se ~ confronté à** to be faced with; **se ~ seul** to be left on one's own; **se ~ à l'hôpital/au chômage/en prison** to end up in hospital/unemployed/in prison; **je me retrouve toujours en bout de table/dernier** I always end up at the far end of the table/last; **se ~ au même point** to be back to square one; **3** (s'orienter) **se** or **s'y ~ dans** lit to find one's way around in [*lieu , fouillis*]; fig to follow, to understand [*explication*]; **tu t'y retrouves entre tous ces emplois/amants?** can you cope with all these jobs/lovers?; **il y a trop de changements, on ne s'y retrouve plus** there are too many changes, we don't know if we're coming or going; **4**○ (rentrer dans ses frais) **s'y ~** to break even; (faire un bénéfice) to do well; **je m'y retrouve très bien en étant indépendante** I'm doing very well as a freelance; **5** (être présent) [*personne, qualité*] to be found; [*problème*] to occur; **cet instinct se retrouve chez tous les animaux** it's an instinct found in all animals; **ce type de construction syntaxique se retrouve en français** the same syntactic construction exists ou is found in French; **le même amour de la musique se retrouve chez les deux enfants** both children have the same love of music; **6** (se reconnaître) **se ~ dans qn/qch** to see ou recognize oneself in sb/sth; **se ~ dans ses enfants** to see oneself in one's children.

IDIOMES **un de perdu, dix de retrouvés** there are plenty more fish in the sea.

rétrovirus /ʀetʀoviʀys/ *nm inv* retrovirus.

rétroviseur /ʀetʀovizœʀ/ *nm* **1** (intérieur) rear-view mirror; **2** (extérieur) wing mirror GB, outside rear-view mirror US.

rets† /ʀɛ/ *nmpl* littér toils†.

IDIOMES **prendre qn dans ses ~** fig to catch sb in one's toils.

réuni, **~e** /ʀeyni/ **I** *pp* ▶ **réunir**.

II *pp adj* **1** (mis ensemble) [*forces, qualités, salaires*] combined; **pouvoirs ~s en une seule main** concentration of power in a single hand; **2** (assemblé) [*conseil, personnes*] assembled; **le comité central, ~ depuis la semaine dernière** the central committee, which has been in session since last week; **3** (remis ensemble) reunited; **les deux Berlin ~s** (a) reunited Berlin; **4** Comm (associés) **les Exportateurs Réunis** Associated Exporters.

réunificateur, **-trice** /ʀeynifikatœʀ, tʀis/ *adj* [*politique*] of reunification (*épith, après n*).

réunification /ʀeynifikasjɔ̃/ *nf* reunification.

réunifier /ʀeynifje/ [2] **I** *vtr* to reunify; **pays réunifié** reunified country.

II se réunifier *vpr* to be reunified, to reunite.

réunion /ʀeynjɔ̃/ *nf* **1** Admin, Pol (séance) meeting (**entre** between); **~ publique** public meeting; **~ du conseil d'administration** board meeting; **être en ~** [*personne*] to be at ou in a meeting; [*comité*] to be meeting; **tenir une ~** to hold a meeting; **2** Sport meeting; **~ sportive/hippique** sports/race meeting; **3** (rencontre) gathering, get-together; **~ amicale/mondaine** friendly/social gathering; **~ familiale** or **de famille** family gathering ou reunion; **4** (retrouvailles) (après une séparation) reunion; (après une brouille) reconciliation; **5** (groupement) (de talents, volontés) combination; (de poèmes, d'œuvres) collection; (d'objets) assembly; **par la ~ d'indices multiples** by getting ou putting together various pieces of evidence; **6** (fusion) Hist, Pol (rattachement) union (**à** with); (après séparation) reunification; Écon, Entr (de sociétés) merger; **la ~ des deux Allemagnes** the reunification of Germany; **7** (intersection) (de routes) junction; (de fleuves) confluence; **8** Math (d'ensembles) union.

Réunion /ʀeynjɔ̃/ ▶ **416** *nprf* **la ~** Reunion.

réunionite○ /ʀeynjɔnit/ *nf* pej obsession with holding meetings.

réunion-téléphone, *pl* **réunions-téléphone** /ʀeynjɔ̃telefɔn/ *nf* telephone link-up.

réunir /ʀeyniʀ/ [3] **I** *vtr* **1** (assembler) [*congrès, manifestation*] to bring together [*participants*]; [*organisateur*] to get [sb] together [*participants*]; **2** (convoquer) to call [sb] together [*délégués, collaborateurs*]; to convene [*conseil, assemblée*]; **3** (inviter) to have [sb] round GB ou over [*amis, parents*]; **~ ses amis pour son anniversaire** to have friends round[GB] to celebrate one's birthday; **4** (rapprocher) to join [*bords*]; (en tirant) to draw [sth] together; to bring [sb] together [*personnes*]; (après une brouille) to bring [sb] together again, to reunite; (après une séparation) to reunite; **la passion pour les livres les a réunis** a love of books brought them together; **5** (fusionner) Entr to merge [*sociétés*]; Pol to unite [*États, province*] (**à** with); **~ un territoire à un État** to join a territory to a state; **~ deux provinces en une seule** to unite ou merge two provinces; **6** (cumuler) liter **~ les qualités nécessaires** to have all the necessary qualifications; **~ les conditions nécessaires** to fulfil[GB] all the necessary conditions; **7** (recueillir) to raise [*fonds*]; to collect [*œuvres, preuves, lettres, articles*]; **8** (regrouper) to assemble [*éléments, preuves*]; to gather [sth] together [*documents, papiers*]; **~ des tickets avec un trombone/avec une épingle** to clip/to pin tickets together; **9** (relier) [*galerie, route, canal*] to connect [*lieux*]; **~ les deux extrémités par un nœud** to knot the two ends together.

II se réunir *vpr* **1** (s'assembler) [*délégués, comité*] to meet; [*amis, parents*] to get together; **se ~ entre amis** to get together with friends, to have a get-together with friends; **2** (se joindre) [*routes, fleuves*] to meet; **3** (s'associer) Écon [*sociétés*] to merge; Pol [*nations*] to unite.

réussi, **~e** /ʀeysi/ **I** *pp* ▶ **réussir**.

II *pp adj* **1** (mené à bien) [*expérience, opération, révolution*] successful; **2** (apprécié) [*soirée, exposition*] successful; **3** (bien fait) [*spectacle, œuvre*] accomplished; [*photo*] good; [*phrase*] well-constructed; **le soufflé est bien ~** the soufflé has come out beautifully; **comme mari, il est ~**○**!** iron he's a fine husband all right! iron, he's a dead loss○ as a husband!

réussir /ʀeysiʀ/ [3] **I** *vtr* to achieve [*unification, modernisation*]; to carry off [sth] successfully [*coup politique, OPA*]; to carry out [sth] successfully [*fabrication, opération*]; to make a success of [*vie, éducation*]; to win [*pari*]; to pass [*examen*]; **~ une mayonnaise** to make a successful mayonnaise; **~ un film** to make a good film; **~ la prouesse de faire** to achieve the feat of doing; **elle a réussi la performance de gagner** she managed to win; **~ l'impossible** to manage the impossible; **~ son coup**○ to pull it off○; **~ un gros coup**○ to pull off a major deal.

II réussir à *vtr ind* **1** (parvenir à) **~ à faire** to succeed in doing, to manage to do; **~ à atteindre ses objectifs** to manage to achieve one's goals; **~ à garder son équilibre** to manage to keep one's balance; **~ à ne pas tomber** to manage not to fall; **~ à un examen** to pass an exam; **ne ~ à rien** not to succeed in anything; **2** (être favorable à) **~ à qn** [*vie, politique, méthode*] to turn out well for sb; [*aliment, mode de vie, repos*] to do sb good; **tout leur réussit** everything turns out well for them; **la mer me réussit** the sea does me good; **le vin blanc/le climat ne me réussit pas** white wine/the climate doesn't agree with me.

III *vi* **1** (atteindre le but recherché) [*personne, action, projet*] to succeed; **la patience peut ~** patience can succeed; **ça n'a pas réussi** it didn't work, it didn't come off; **2** (être couronné de succès) [*opération chirurgicale, tentative, commerce*] to be successful; **3** (obtenir un bon résultat) [*personne*] to do well (**en, dans** in); **~ en latin/dans la vie/en affaires** to do well in Latin/in life/in business.

réussite /ʀeysit/ *nf* **1** gén success (**dans** in); **~ sociale** social success; **~ scolaire** success at school; **~ à un examen** success in an examination; **~ dans sa carrière** success in one's career; **nous leur devons nos ~s** we owe our successes to them; **2** Jeux patience ¢ GB, solitaire ¢ US; **faire des ~s** to play patience GB ou solitaire US.

réutiliser /ʀeytilize/ [1] *vtr* to reuse.

revacciner /ʀ(ə)vaksine/ [1] *vtr* to revaccinate.

revaloir /ʀ(ə)valwaʀ/ [45] *vtr* **je te/leur revaudrai ça** (hostile) I'll get even with you/them for that; (reconnaissant) I'll return the favour[GB].

revalorisation /ʀ(ə)valɔʀizasjɔ̃/ *nf* **1** (augmentation) **un accord prévoyant une ~ des salaires de 3%** an agreement which allows for a 3% wage increase; **la ~ des honoraires médicaux aura pour effet...** the increase in doctors' fees will result in...; **crédits consacrés à la ~ des bas salaires/des retraites** funds allocated to increase ou to raise low salaries/pensions; **2** (retour de l'estime) **la ~ de la fonction enseignante/des études littéraires/des enseignants** the enhanced prestige of the teaching profession/literary studies/teachers; **3** (amélioration) **ils réclament une ~ de leur statut** they are demanding an improvement in ou an enhancement of their status; **les retraités attendent une ~ de leur niveau de vie** pensioners are waiting for an improvement in their standard of living; **4** (remise en état) **crédits pour la ~ des quartiers défavorisés** funds to renovate run-down areas.

revaloriser /R(ə)valɔRize/ [1] *vtr* **1** (augmenter) to increase, to raise [*salaire, pension*]; to revalue, to revalorize [*monnaie*]; to increase the value of [*titre*]; **en revalorisant le titre de 15%** by increasing the bond by 15%; **2** (rendre l'estime envers) **~ le travail manuel/les filières techniques** to enhance the prestige of ou to reassert the value of manual work/technical studies; **~ les traditions locales** to reassert the value of ou to promote local traditions; **3** (améliorer) **~ les conditions de travail** to improve working conditions; **4** (remettre en état) **~ un quartier/un bâtiment** to renovate an area/a building.

revanchard, ~e /R(ə)vɑ̃ʃaR, aRd/ pej *adj, nm,f* revanchist.

revanche /R(ə)vɑ̃ʃ/ **I** *nf* **1** revenge; **désir de/esprit de ~** desire for/spirit of revenge; **avoir sa ~** to get one's revenge; **prendre sa ~** to take one's revenge, to get even; **2** Sport return match GB ou game US; Jeux return game.

II en revanche *loc adv* on the other hand.

IDIOMES **à charge de ~** provided you'll let me return the favour[GB].

revanchisme /R(ə)vɑ̃ʃism/ *nm* revanchism.

rêvasser /Rɛvase/ [1] *vi* to (day)dream.

rêvasserie /RɛvasRi/ *nf* (day)dreaming ₵.

rêve /Rɛv/ *nm* **1** (de dormeur) (activité) dreaming; (résultat) dream; **faire un ~** to have a dream; **j'ai fait un ~ affreux** I had a horrible dream; **fais de beaux ~s!** sweet dreams!; **j'ai l'impression de vivre un ~** I feel as if I'm dreaming; **s'évanouir comme un ~** to fade away like a dream; **en ~** in a dream; **2** (fantasme) dream; **~ de jeunesse** youthful dream; **~ de grandeur** dream of greatness; **avoir des ~s de grandeur/vengeance** to dream of greatness/vengeance; **la femme de mes ~s** the woman of my dreams; **la maison de mes ~s** my dream house; **une maison/voiture de ~** a dream house/car; **un temps de ~** unbelievably good weather, wonderful weather; **une créature de ~** a dream-like creature; **3** (idéal) **cet endroit, c'est le ~** this place is just perfect; **ce n'est pas le ~** it's not ideal.

■ **~ éveillé** daydream.

rêvé, ~e /Reve/ **I** *pp* ▶ **rêver**.

II *pp adj* ideal, perfect.

revêche /Rəvɛʃ/ *adj* [*air, ton*] sour; [*personne*] crabby.

réveil /Revɛj/ *nm* **1** (après un somme) waking (up); **à mon ~, il neigeait** when I woke up, it was snowing; **au ~/dès son ~, il allume la radio** on waking up/as soon as he wakes up, he turns on the radio; **les cauchemars provoquent des ~s en sursaut** nightmares wake you up with a start; **2** (après malaise, anesthésie) **j'ai eu des nausées au ~** I felt nauseous when I came to ou when I regained consciousness; **salle de ~** recovery room; **3** (de la nature, la passion, d'un sentiment) reawakening; (de nation, mouvement) resurgence; (de la foi) revival; (de douleurs) return, recurrence; (de la conscience) awakening; (de volcan) return to activity; **le ~ des minorités** the new activism of minorities; **le ~ du nationalisme** the revival ou resurgence of nationalism; **4** (retour à la réalité) awakening; **le ~ a été brutal après le boom des années 80** it was a rude awakening after the boom of the eighties; **5** Mil reveille; **sonner le ~** to sound the reveille; **~ en fanfare** fig rousing start to the day; **6** (pendule) alarm clock; **remonter un ~** to wind up an alarm (clock); **mettre le ~ pour 7 h** to set the alarm for 7 (o'clock).

■ **~ automatique** reminder call; **~ par téléphone** alarm call (through the operator); **~ de voyage** travel alarm (clock).

réveille-matin /Revɛjmatɛ̃/ *nm inv* alarm clock.

réveiller /Reveje/ [1] **I** *vtr* **1** (tirer du sommeil, de rêverie, d'hypnose) to wake [sb] up, to wake; **être réveillé en sursaut** to wake up with a start ou jump; **être réveillé par l'orage** to be woken by the storm; **se faire ~ à 6 heures** to arrange to be woken at 6; **faire un bruit à ~ les morts** to make enough noise to wake the dead; **2** (ranimer) to revive, to bring [sb] round GB [*malade*]; to bring some sensation back into [*membre ankylosé*]; to whet [*appétit*]; to awaken [*sentiment, passion*]; to arouse [*crainte, curiosité*]; to bring out [*instinct*]; to awaken, to stir up [*souvenir*]; to arouse [*crainte, polémique*]; **~ la douleur** to bring back the pain; **exercises pour ~ vos muscles** exercises to tone up your muscles; **~ les consciences** to stir people's consciences.

II se réveiller *vpr* **1** (après un somme) to wake up; (après une rêverie, une hypnose) to awaken (**de** from); **se ~ en sursaut/en sueur** to wake up with a start ou jump/in a sweat; **2** (après anesthésie, malaise) [*personne*] to come round GB ou to, to regain consciousness; **ma jambe se réveille** the feeling is coming back into my leg; **3** (après période d'inertie) [*personne, peuple*] to wake up; [*nature*] to reawaken; [*volcan*] to become active again; **4** (se raviver) [*douleur, appétit*] to come back; [*jalousie, passion, souvenir*] to be reawakened; ▶ **chat**.

réveillon /Revɛjɔ̃/ *nm* **~ de Noël/du Nouvel An** (dîner) Christmas Eve/New Year's Eve dinner; (fête) Christmas Eve/New Year's Eve party; (date) Christmas Eve/New Year's Eve.

réveillonner /Revɛjɔne/ [1] *vi* (pour Noël) to celebrate Christmas (*with a midnight meal and a party on Christmas Eve*); (pour Nouvel An) to see the New Year in.

réveillonneur, -euse /Revɛjɔnœr, øz/ *nm,f* (Christmas/New Year's Eve) reveller[GB].

révélateur, -trice /RevelatœR, tRis/ **I** *adj* [*détail, fait*] revealing, telling; **être ~ de qch** to reveal sth; **un incident ~ du climat actuel** an incident which says a lot about the current social climate.

II *nm* **1** Phot developer; **2** (fait, détail) pointer (**de** to); **être le ~ du malaise économique** to be a pointer to the current economic malaise; **ce film a été le ~ de son talent** this film revealed his/her talent.

révélation /Revelasjɔ̃/ *nf* **1** (de scandale, secret) revelation; **ce voyage fut pour moi une véritable ~** fig this trip was a real revelation to me; **2** (aveu) revelation, disclosure; **faire des ~s** to make revelations ou disclosures; **il nous a fait des ~s** he made certain disclosures to us; **3** (œuvre, auteur) discovery, find; **être la ~ de l'année** to be the discovery of the year; **4** Phot development.

révélé, ~e /Revele/ **I** *pp* ▶ **révéler**.

II *pp adj* [*religion, vérité*] revealed.

révéler /Revele/ [14] **I** *vtr* **1** (dévoiler) [*presse, personne*] to reveal, to disclose [*fait, chiffres, nom*] (**à** to); to give away [*secret*] (**à** to); **~ le contenu d'un dossier** to disclose the contents of a file; **~ que** to reveal that; **2** (indiquer) to reveal, to show [*nature, personnalité*]; to show [*talent, sentiment*]; **les sondages révèlent un changement d'attitude** the polls show a shift in attitude; **ce livre révèle un grand écrivain** this book shows the author to be a major writer; **sa robe révèle la finesse de sa taille** her dress shows off her slender waist; **3** (faire connaître) [*œuvre*] to make [sb] known [*éditeur, acteur*] (**à** to); [*éditeur, impresario*] to discover, to launch [*auteur, artiste*]; **cela l'a révélée à elle-même** it gave her a great deal of personal insight; **4** Phot to develop.

II se révéler *vpr* **1** (devenir célèbre) to make one's name ou mark; **2** (être finalement) **se ~ faux/important** to turn out to be wrong/important; **se ~ être** to turn out ou prove to be; **3** Relig **Dieu s'est révélé à** God revealed Himself to; **se ~ comme un grand pianiste** to emerge as a great pianist; **4** (se manifester) [*goût, sensation*] to be revealed (**à** to).

revenant, ~e /Rəvnɑ̃, ɑ̃t/ *nm,f* ghost; **tiens, une ~e**○! hum long time no see○!

revendeur, -euse /R(ə)vɑ̃dœR, øz/ ▶ **510** *nm,f* **1** (détaillant) stockist; **en vente chez votre ~ habituel** available at your usual stockist; **un ~ de drogue** a drug dealer; **2** (d'objets d'occasion) secondhand dealer; **3** (d'objets volés) seller (of stolen goods).

revendicateur, -trice /R(ə)vɑ̃dikatœR, tRis/ **I** *adj* [*lettre, discours*] full of demands (*jamais épith*).

II *nm,f* protester.

revendicatif, -ive /R(ə)vɑ̃dikatif, iv/ *adj* [*action, mouvement, campagne*] protest (*épith*); [*dossier, programme*] of demands; **journée revendicative** day of protest.

revendication /R(ə)vɑ̃dikasjɔ̃/ *nf* **1** (réclamation) (d'ouvrier, de catégorie sociale) demand; (de pays, d'héritier, de population) claim (**sur, de** to); **~s sociales** social demands; **~s salariales** wage demands ou claims; **~s territoriales** territorial claims; **la ~ d'un territoire par un État** the claim of a state to a territory; **la ~ d'un droit** the demanding of a right; **2** (reconnaissance) claiming of responsibility (**de** for).

revendiquer /R(ə)vɑ̃dike/ [1] **I** *vtr* **1** (réclamer) to demand [*droit, augmentation, égalité*]; to claim [*héritage, trône, territoire*]; **2** (s'affirmer l'auteur de) to claim responsibility for [*attentat, action*]; to claim authorship of [*livre*]; **~ un tableau** to claim to be the painter of a painting; **~ la paternité** to claim paternity; **l'attentat n'a pas été revendiqué** no-one has claimed responsibility for the attack; **~ la responsabilité de** to take (full) responsibility for; **3** (affirmer avoir) to claim; **un syndicat qui revendique 30 000 membres** a union which claims a membership of 30,000; **4** (être fier de) to proclaim [*origines, condition*].

II se revendiquer *vpr* **se ~ comme catholique** to declare one's catholic loyalties.

revendre /R(ə)vɑ̃dR/ [6] **I** *vtr* **1** (vendre au détail) to sell [sth] retail, to retail (**à** to); **2** (vendre ce qui est à soi) to sell [*objet, voiture, maison*] (**à** to); to sell (off) [*actions, parts, or*]; (vendre des objets volés) to sell on [*bijoux, tableaux*]; **il a dû ~ sa voiture neuve** he had to sell his new car; **il m'a revendu la voiture qu'il m'avait achetée l'année dernière** he sold me back the car he bought from me last year; **avoir des crayons/pommes à ~** to have pencils/apples galore; **avoir de l'énergie/du courage à ~** to have energy/courage to spare.

II se revendre *vpr* (se vendre d'occasion) to resell; **c'est un modèle qui se revend facilement** it's a model which is easy to resell.

revenez-y /Rəvnezi, Rvənezi/ *nm inv* **le gâteau a un petit goût de ~** the cake is rather moreish○ GB, the cake is so good I'd like seconds.

revenir /RəvniR, RvəniR/ [36] **I** *vi* (+ *v être*) **1** (fréquenter de nouveau) to come back; (venir une fois encore) to come again; **un client mal servi ne revient pas** a dissatisfied customer won't come back; **elle revient chaque année en France** she comes back to France every year; **elle revient en France cette année** she's coming to France again this year; **nous fermons, revenez demain** we're closing, come back tomorrow; **tu reviendras nous voir?** will you come and see us again?; **~ (pour) faire** to come back to do; **2** (rentrer) [*personne, animal, véhicule*] to come back, to return; **~ à/de** to come back ou return to/from; **~ de Tokyo** to come back from Tokyo; **~ chez soi** to come back ou return home; **~ sur terre** fig to come back to earth; **~ à sa place** to return to one's seat; **partir pour ne jamais**

~ to leave never to return; **~ de loin** lit to come back from far away; fig to have a close shave; **son mari lui est revenu** her husband came back to her; **en revenant du bureau** (en route) coming home from the office, on the way home from the office; (à l'arrivée) on getting home from the office; **je reviens tout de suite** I'll be back in a minute, I'll be right back○; **il en est revenu vivant** he got back in one piece; **elle est revenue en vitesse à la maison** she rushed back home; **mon chèque m'est revenu parce qu'il n'était pas signé** my cheque GB ou check US was returned because I forgot to sign it; ▶ **galop**; **3** (reprendre, retourner à) **~ à** to return to, to come back to [*méthode, conception, histoire*]; **revenons à notre héros** let's return to our hero; **~ à la normale** to return to normal; **~ au pouvoir** to return to power; **ça revient à la mode** it's coming back into fashion; **le dollar est revenu à 5 francs** the dollar has gone back to 5 francs; **~ à la politique** to come back into politics; **~ à ses habitudes** to return ou revert to one's old habits; **~ aux frontières d'avant la guerre** to revert to pre-war borders; **pour (en) ~ à mon histoire/ce que je disais** to get back to my story/what I was saying; **~ à de meilleurs sentiments** to return to a better frame of mind; **n'y reviens pas!** (ne recommence pas) don't let it happen again!; (n'en parle plus) don't start that again!; **4** (réapparaître) [*tache, rhume, douleur*] to come back; [*soleil*] to come out again; [*saison*] to return; [*date, fête*] to come round again GB, to come again US; [*idée, thème*] to recur; [*mode*] to come back; **cette idée me revenait souvent** the idea kept occurring to me; **le mot revient souvent sous sa plume** the word keeps cropping up in his/her writing; **le calme est revenu** calm has been restored, things have calmed down; **5** (être recouvré) [*appétit, mémoire*] to come back; **l'appétit me revient** I'm getting my appetite back; **sa mémoire ne lui reviendra jamais comme avant** his/her memory will never be the same again; **6** (être remémoré) **~ à qn**, **~ à la mémoire** or **l'esprit de qn** to come back to sb; **ça me revient!** now I remember!, now it's coming back!; **cette journée me revient en mémoire** I remember that day; **si le nom me/te revient** if I/you remember the name, if the name comes to mind; **7** (coûter) **~ à 100 francs** to come to 100 francs, to cost 100 francs; **ça m'est revenu à 100 francs** it cost me 100 francs; **ça revient cher** it works out expensive; **8** (équivaloir à) **ça revient au même** it amounts ou comes to the same thing; **ce qui revient à dire que** which amounts to saying that; **9** (reconsidérer) **~ sur** to go back over [*question, différend, passé*]; (changer d'avis) to go back on [*décision, parole, promesse*]; to retract [*aveu*]; **ne revenons pas là-dessus** don't let's go over all that again; **10** (sortir d'un état) **~ de** to get over [*maladie, frayeur, surprise*]; to lose [*illusion*]; to abandon [*théorie*] ; **~ de ses illusions** to lose one's illusions; **~ de son erreur** to realize one's mistake; **la vie à la campagne, j'en suis revenu** as for life in the country, I've seen it for what it is; **je le croyais honnête mais j'en suis revenu** I thought he was honest but I've seen him for what he is; **être revenu de tout** to be blasé; **je n'en reviens pas**○! I can't get over it!, I'm amazed!; **je n'en reviens pas qu'il ait dit oui**○ I can't get over the fact that he said yes, I am amazed that he said yes; **je n'en reviens pas des progrès que tu as faits**○ I'm amazed at the progress you've made; **11** (être rapporté) [*propos, remarque*] **~ à qn**, **~ aux oreilles de qn** to get back to sb, to reach sb's ears; **12** (être attribué) **~ à qn** [*bien, titre*] to go to sb, to pass to sb; [*honneur*] to fall to sb; (de droit) to be due to sb; **le titre leur revient à la mort de leur père** the title goes ou passes to them on their father's death; **ce poste pourrait revenir à un écologiste** this post could go to an ecologist; **ça leur revient de droit** it's theirs by right; **les 10% qui me reviennent** the 10% that's coming to me; **la décision revient au rédacteur** it is the editor's decision, the decision lies with the editor; **13** Culin **faire ~** to brown [*ail, oignons, viande*].

II s'en revenir *vpr* liter to return (**de** from).

III *v impers* **1** (incomber) **c'est à vous qu'il revient de trancher** it is for you to decide; **2** (parvenir à la connaissance de) **il m'est revenu certains propos** certain remarks have reached my ears; **s'il leur en revenait quelque chose** if it reached their ears, if it got back to them; **il me revient de tous côtés qu'on me critique** I keep hearing that people are criticizing me; **3** (être remémoré) liter **il me revient que** I recall ou remember that.

IDIOMES **~ à soi** to come round, to come to; **~ à la vie** to come back to life; **il a une tête** or **un air qui ne me revient pas** I don't like the look of him.

revente /R(ə)vɑ̃t/ *nf* **1** (d'objet, de voiture, maison) resale; **cette voiture ne vaut rien à la ~** this car has no resale value; **2** (d'action, de parts, d'or) sale; **à la ~** on the sale.

revenu, **~e** /Rəvny, Rvəny/ *nm* **1** Fisc (de personne) income; (de l'État) revenue ₵; **~ brut/disponible/imposable/annuel** gross/disposable/taxable/annual income; **avoir de gros ~s** to have a large income; **être sans ~s** to have no income; **tirer un ~ de** to get an income from; **politique des ~s** incomes policy; **~s publics** or **de l'État** public ou state revenue; **2** Fin (rendement) income, yield; **à ~ fixe** fixed-income.

■ **~ minimum d'insertion, RMI** Prot Soc *minimum benefit paid to those with no other source of income*; **~ non salarial** unearned income; **~ salarial** earned income.

rêver /Reve/ [1] **I** *vtr* **1** (en dormant) to dream (**que** that); **2** (imaginer) to dream of [*succès, vengeance*]; **tu as dû le ~!** you must have dreamed it!

II *vi* **1** [*dormeur*] to dream (**de** about); **j'en rêve la nuit** I dream about it at night; **dis-moi que je ne rêve pas** tell me I'm not imagining things ou dreaming; **j'ai rêvé de cela il y a longtemps** I dreamed it ou had that dream a long time ago; **~ tout éveillé** to be lost in a daydream; **on croirait ~!** you'd think you were dreaming!; **2** (se faire des illusions) to dream; **tu rêves si tu penses qu'ils vont te garder** you're fooling yourself ou dreaming if you think (that) they will keep you; **3** (rêvasser) to dream (**à** of); **~ à l'été** to dream of summer; **4** (aspirer à) to dream (**de** of); **je rêve de rentrer dans mon pays** I dream of returning home ou to my own country.

III se rêver *vpr* **se ~ patron** to dream of being the boss.

réverbération /ReveRbeRasjɔ̃/ *nf* (de lumière) glare; (de chaleur) reflection; (de son) reverberation.

réverbère /ReveRbɛR/ *nm* **1** (lampadaire) street lamp ou light; **2** Tech reflector.

réverbérer /ReveRbeRe/ [14] **I** *vtr* [*surface*] to reflect [*lumière, chaleur*]; to make [sth] reverberate [*son*].

II se réverbérer *vpr* [*lumière, chaleur*] to be reflected; [*son*] to reverberate.

reverchon /RəvɛRʃɔ̃/ *nf* reverchon (*dark-red variety of sweet cherry*).

reverdir /R(ə)vɛRdiR/ [3] **I** *vtr* Tech to soak.

II *vi* to grow green again.

révérence /ReveRɑ̃s/ *nf* **1** (salut) (de femme) curtsey; (d'homme) bow; **faire la ~** [*femme*] to curtsey (**à** to); [*homme*] to bow (**à** to); **2** (respect) liter reverence; **traiter qn avec ~** to treat sb respectfully; **considérer qn/qch avec une ~ craintive** to regard sb/sth with awe.

IDIOMES **tirer sa ~**○ to take one's leave (**à qn** of sb).

révérencieux, **-ieuse** /ReveRɑ̃sjø, øz/ *adj* liter deferential (**envers** to); **attitude peu révérencieuse** irreverent attitude; **une crainte révérencieuse** reverential awe (**à l'égard de, envers** for).

révérend, **~e** /ReveRɑ̃, ɑ̃d/ **I** *adj* reverend; **le ~ Père Duval** the Reverend Duval; **ma ~e Mère** Reverend Mother.

II *nm,f* **1** (dans un couvent) Father/Mother Superior; **2** (pasteur) reverend.

révérer /ReveRe/ [14] *vtr* to revere.

rêverie /RɛvRi/ *nf* **1** (activité) daydreaming, reverie littér; **se laisser aller à la ~** to drift off into a dream; **2** (rêve éveillé) daydream.

revérifier /R(ə)veRifje/ [2] *vtr* to double-check.

revernir /R(ə)vɛRniR/ [3] **I** *vtr* Tech to revarnish [*meuble*].

II se revernir *vpr* **se ~ les ongles** to apply nail varnish GB ou polish.

revers /R(ə)vɛR/ *nm inv* **1** (dos) (de feuille) back, reverse; (de tissu) wrong side; (de main) back; (de médaille, pièce) reverse; **d'un ~ de la main** with the back of one's hand; **le ~ de la médaille** fig the downside○, the disagreeable aspect; **prendre une armée à ~** Mil to attack an army from the rear; **2** (repli) (de veste) lapel; (de pantalon) turn-up GB, cuff US; (de manche) cuff; **3** (au tennis) backhand (stroke); **faire un ~** to play a backhand (stroke); **4** fig (échec) setback, reversal.

■ **~ de fortune** reversal of fortune.

IDIOMES **toute médaille a son ~** Prov there is no rose without a thorn.

reverser /R(ə)vɛRse/ [1] *vtr* **1** Fin to transfer [*indemnité, somme*] (**à** to); **2** (retourner) **~ qch dans un récipient** to pour sth back into a container; **3** (une autre fois) **~ à boire à qn** to pour sb another drink.

réversibilité /ReveRsibilite/ *nf* **1** gén, Chimie, Phys reversibility; **2** Jur reversion.

réversible /ReveRsibl/ *adj* **1** gén, Mode reversible; **2** Chimie, Phys reversible; **3** Jur reversionary.

réversion /ReveRsjɔ̃/ *nf* **1** Jur (**droit de**) **~** reversion; **pension de ~** reversion benefit; **2** Biol reversion.

revêtement /R(ə)vɛtmɑ̃/ *nm* **1** Gén Civ, Tech (de route, terrain de sport, piste cyclable) surface; **~ routier** road surface; **2** Constr (peinture, crépi, ciment) coating; (en vinyl, plastique) covering; **~s muraux/de sol** wall/floor coverings; **3** Aviat, Naut (surface protectrice) skin; **4** Art (de fresque) coating.

revêtir /R(ə)vɛtiR/ [33] **I** *vtr* **1** (avoir) to have [*caractère, intérêt*]; to assume [*gravité, solennité*]; to take on [*aspect, allure, signification*]; to hold [*importance*]; to entail [*inconvénient*]; **~ la forme de** to take the form of; **2** (mettre) to put on [*vêtement, tunique, soutane, habit*]; **3** (vêtir) **~ qn de** to dress sb in; **~ un enfant d'habits neufs** to dress a child in new clothes; **revêtu de** wearing [*uniforme, médaille*]; **4** (compléter) **~ un document/contrat d'une signature** to affix a signature to a document/contract; **~ un document/contrat d'un tampon** to stamp a document/contract; **~ un passeport d'un visa** to stamp a passport with a visa; **document revêtu d'une signature** signed document; **document revêtu d'un tampon** document bearing a stamp; **5** (recouvrir) **~ qch de** to cover sth with [*moquette, parquet*]; **~ un mur de papier peint** to paper a wall; **~ un mur de tissu** to put a material covering on a wall; **~ un mur de boiseries** to face a wall with panelling^GB; **~ une route de bitume** to asphalt a road, to cover a road with asphalt.

II se revêtir *vpr* **1** (se vêtir) **se ~ de** to put on; **se ~ d'un châle** to put on a shawl; **2** lit (se recouvrir) to become covered with; **se ~ de neige** to become covered with snow.

rêveur, **-euse** /RɛvœR, øz/ **I** *adj* [*air,*

personne] dreamy; **cela laisse ~** it makes you wonder.
II *nm,f* dreamer.

rêveusement /ʀɛvøzmɑ̃/ *adv* (distraitement) absently; (pensivement) dreamily.

revient /ʀ(ə)vjɛ̃/ *nm* **prix de ~** cost price; **calculer** or **établir le prix de ~ de qch** to do the costing for sth.

revigorer /ʀ(ə)vigɔʀe/ [1] *vtr* **1** (physiquement) [*boisson*] to perk [sb] up, to revive; [*douche, air*] to revive; **2** (moralement) to hearten; **3** to revitalize [*entreprise*].

revirement /ʀ(ə)viʀmɑ̃/ *nm* (de situation, politique, d'opinion) turnaround (**de** in); **~ total** U-turn GB, flip-flop US.

réviser /ʀevize/ [1] *vtr* **1** (réexaminer) to revise [*position, code, contrat, tarifs*]; to review [*procès, Constitution*]; to redraw [*frontières*]; **~ qch à la hausse/à la baisse** to revise sth upward(s)/downward(s); **~ son jugement** to revise one's opinion; **2** (vérifier) to service, to overhaul [*machine, auto, chaudière*]; to overhaul [*montre*]; to revise [*manuscrit*]; to audit [*comptes*]; **faire ~** to have [sth] serviced [*voiture*]; to have [sth] overhauled [*montre*]; to have [sth] revised [*manuscrit*]; **donner sa voiture à ~** to take one's car in for servicing ou for a service; **3** Scol, Univ to revise GB, to review US; **il est en train de ~ pour son examen** he's busy revising GB ou reviewing US for his exam.

réviseur /ʀevizœʀ/ *nm* **1** Imprim proofreader; **2** Compta auditor.

révision /ʀevizjɔ̃/ *nm* **1** (réexamen) (de position, code, contrat, tarifs) revision; (de procès) review; (de frontière) redrawing; **la ~ d'un procès** the review of a case; **~ à la hausse/à la baisse** upward/downward revision; **2** (vérification du bon état) (de machine, voiture, chaudière) service; (de manuscrit) revision; (de comptes) audit; (de montre) overhauling; **la ~ d'une auto nous prend environ cinq heures** it takes us about five hours to service a car; **la ~ des 10000 km** the 10,000 km service; **à la ~ tout semblait normal** when it was serviced everything seemed all right; **3** Scol, Univ revision ¢ GB, review ¢ US; **commencer les** or **ses ~s** to start revising GB ou reviewing US; **faire des ~s** to revise GB ou review US; **faire ses ~s** to do one's revision GB ou reviewing US.

révisionnisme /ʀevizjɔnism/ *nm* revisionism.

révisionniste /ʀevizjɔnist/ *adj, nmf* revisionist.

revisser /ʀ(ə)vise/ [1] *vtr* to screw [sth] back on.

revitalisant, ~e /ʀ(ə)vitalizɑ̃, ɑ̃t/ *adj* revitalizing (*épith*).

revitalisation /ʀ(ə)vitalizasjɔ̃/ *nf* revitalization.

revitaliser /ʀ(ə)vitalize/ [1] *vtr* to revitalize.

revivifier /ʀ(ə)vivifje/ [2] *vtr* liter to revive [*sentiment*]; to revivify [*personne*].

revivre /ʀ(ə)vivʀ/ [63] **I** *vtr* **1** (se remémorer) to go over, relive [*événement, passé*]; **faire ~ qch à qn** to bring back memories of sth to sb; **2** (connaître à nouveau) to live through [sth] again [*époque*].
II *vi* **1** (être ragaillardi) to come alive again; **je me sens ~** I have come alive again; **l'air frais m'a fait ~** the fresh air (has) revived me; **2** (être soulagé) to be able to breathe again; **après l'examen de ce matin, je revis!** I can breathe again after this morning's exam!; **3** (renaître) [*idée, tradition, mode, institution*] to be reborn ou revived; **faire ~** to revive [*tradition, mode*]; **4** (être ressuscité) to live again (**dans , à travers** in); **elle voit son père ~ dans ses enfants** she sees her father again in her children; fig **faire ~** to bring [sth] back to life [*époque, événement*].

révocabilité /ʀevɔkabilite/ *nf* (de testament) revocability; (de personne) dismissibility.

révocable /ʀevɔkabl/ *adj* [*testament*] revocable; [*personne*] dismissible (*from office*).

révocation /ʀevɔkasjɔ̃/ *nf* (de testament, d'édit) revocation; (de personne) dismissal.

revoici○ /ʀ(ə)vwasi/ *présentatif* **~ Marianne!** Marianne's back, here's Marianne again!; **te ~!** so you're back!; **le ~ dans ses bouquins** he's back to his books again; **nous ~ au point de départ** we are ou it's back to square one.

revoilà /ʀ(ə)vwala/ = **revoici**.

revoir /ʀ(ə)vwaʀ/ [46] **I au revoir** *loc nom* goodbye, bye○; **au ~ Monsieur/Madame** goodbye; **dis au ~ à la dame** say goodbye ou bye-bye○ to the lady; **ce n'est qu'un au ~** it's just a temporary goodbye ou farewell; **faire au ~ de la main** to wave goodbye.
II *vtr* **1** (voir de nouveau) to see [sb/sth] again [*personne, lieu, film*]; **j'espère les ~ l'an prochain** I hope to see them again next year; **il ne l'avait pas revu depuis 10 ans** he hadn't seen him for 10 years; **~ la mer/qn une dernière fois** to see the sea/sb one last time; **je suis allé ~ la maison où je suis né** I went back to see the house where I was born; **je ne voudrais pas ~ ce genre de scène** I hope I never see anything like that again; **2** (en pensée) to see; **je la revois encore dans sa petite robe bleue** I can still see her in her little blue dress; **je revois bien la petite maison où nous vivions** I can just see the little house we lived in; **3** (réexaminer) to go over [*texte, devoir, épreuve*]; to review [*méthode, politique, action*]; to check through [*compte, comptabilité*]; **'à ~'** 'go over again'; **4** (corriger) to correct; **son devoir était à ~ entièrement** his/her paper had to be completely rewritten; **5** (réviser) Scol [*étudiant, élève*] to revise GB, to review [*matière*]; to go over [*leçon*].
III **se revoir** *vpr* **1** (se rencontrer de nouveau) [*personnes*] to see each other again; **ils ne se sont jamais revus** they never saw each other again; **nous ne nous sommes revus qu'une seule fois** we only saw each other again once; **2** (en pensée) to see oneself; **je me revois toujours entrant chez lui** I can still see myself going into his house.

revoler /ʀ(ə)vɔle/ [1] **I** *vtr* to steal [sth] again.
II *vi* to fly again.

révoltant, ~e /ʀevɔltɑ̃, ɑ̃t/ *adj* appalling.

révolte /ʀevɔlt/ *nf* **1** (soulèvement) revolt; **~ armée** armed revolt; **la ~ gronde** there are murmurings of revolt; **réprimer/écraser une ~ dans le sang** to put down/crush a revolt ou rebellion with bloodshed; **être en ~ contre** to be in revolt against; **2** (indignation, désobéissance) rebellion.

révolté, ~e /ʀevɔlte/ **I** *pp* ▶ **révolter**.
II *pp adj* **1** (qui s'est soulevé) rebel (*épith*); **2** (qui refuse d'obéir) rebellious; **3** (indigné) appalled.
III *nm,f* rebel.

révolter /ʀevɔlte/ [1] **I** *vtr* to appal[GB]; **~ qn en faisant qch** to appal[GB] sb by doing sth.
II **se révolter** *vpr* **1** (se soulever) to rebel; **le pays s'est révolté** the country rebelled; **les ouvriers/paysans se révoltent** the workers/peasants are in revolt; **2** (refuser d'obéir) [*personne, enfant*] to rebel (**contre** against); **3** (s'indigner) to be appalled (**contre, devant** by).

révolu, ~e /ʀevɔly/ *adj* **1** (passé) **ce temps est ~** those days are over ou past; **2** (achevé) **avoir 12 ans révolus** to be over 12 years of age; **après une année ~e** after a year has gone by; **pensant à l'année ~e** thinking of the year gone by.

révolution /ʀevɔlysjɔ̃/ *nf* **1** Pol revolution; **provoquer une ~** to bring about a revolution; **~ scientifique/industrielle** scientific/industrial revolution; **ce livre est une ~** this is a revolutionary book; **faire ~ dans** to revolutionize; **la Révolution (française** or **de 1789)** the French Revolution; **2** (effervescence) turmoil; **être en ~** to be in turmoil; **3** Astron, Math rotation; **4** (forces) **la ~** the revolutionary forces.
■ **~ culturelle** Cultural Revolution; **~ de juillet** French revolution of July 1830; **~ nationale** *France's social revolution directed by Maréchal Pétain beginning in 1940*; **la ~ d'octobre** the Russian Revolution ou the October Revolution; **~ de palais** palace revolution.

révolutionnaire /ʀevɔlysjɔnɛʀ/ *adj, nmf* Hist, Pol revolutionary.

révolutionner /ʀevɔlysjɔne/ [1] *vtr* **1** (transformer) to revolutionize [*sciences, pensée*] (**par** with); **2**○ (mettre en émoi) to upset; **3** (soulever) to revolutionize [*pays*].

revolver /ʀevɔlvɛʀ/ *nm* **1** (à barillet) revolver; (arme de poing) controv handgun; **coup de ~** gunshot; **abattre qn à coups de ~** to shoot sb, to gun sb down; **~ à six coups** six-shooter○; **2** (de microscope) revolving nosepiece.

revolving /ʀevɔlviŋ/ *adj inv* controv **crédit ~** revolving credit.

révoquer /ʀevɔke/ [1] *vtr* **1** to revoke [*testament*]; **2** to dismiss [*personne*].

revoter /ʀ(ə)vɔte/ [1] **I** *vtr* **~ un budget** to vote on a budget again.
II *vi* to vote again.

revoyure● /ʀ(ə)vwajyʀ/ *nf* **à la ~** be seeing you○.

revue /ʀ(ə)vy/ *nf* **1** (magazine) gén magazine; (spécialisé) journal; **~ d'art** art magazine; **~ scientifique** scientific journal; **2** Mil (parade) parade; (inspection) review; **la ~ du 14 juillet** the Bastille Day parade; **~ de détail** kit inspection; **~ d'armement** weapons inspection; **passer [qch] en ~** to review [*troupes, armées*]; to inspect [*matériel, équipement*]; **3** Mus (spectacle) revue; **4** (examen) examination; **faire la ~ de qch** to examine sth; **se livrer à une ~ minutieuse de ses papiers** to go through one's papers in minute detail; **passer qch en ~** to go over sth, to have a look at sth; **nous avons passé en ~ tous les grands restaurants de Paris** we went through a list of the best restaurants in Paris.
■ **~ de presse** TV, Radio, Presse review of the papers.
IDIOMES **être de la ~**○ to have to miss out○.

révulsé, ~e /ʀevylse/ **I** *pp* ▶ **révulser**.
II *pp adj* **1** (contracté) [*visage, membre*] contorted; **il gisait, les yeux ~s** there he lay, his eyes rolled upward(s); **2** (indigné) [*air*] appalled.

révulser /ʀevylse/ [1] **I** *vtr* (indigner) to appal[GB].
II **se révulser** *vpr* [*yeux*] to roll (upward(s)); [*visage, membre*] to contort.

révulsif, -ive /ʀevylsif, iv/ Méd **I** *adj* revulsive.
II *nm* revulsive.

révulsion /ʀevylsjɔ̃/ *nf* **1** Méd revulsion; **2** (indignation) revulsion.

Reykjavik /ʀɛkjavik/ **▶ 857** *npr* Reykjavik.

rez-de-chaussée /ʀɛdʃose/ *nm inv* **1** (niveau) ground floor GB, first floor US (**de** of); **du/au ~** on the ground GB ou first US floor; **2** (appartement) ground-floor flat GB, first-floor apartment US.

rez-de-jardin /ʀɛdʒaʀdɛ̃/ *nm inv* garden level; **chambre en ~** bedroom at garden level; **appartement en ~** garden flat GB, garden apartment US.

RF *nf*: *written abbr* = **République française**.

RFA /ɛʀɛfa/ *nprf*: *abbr* = **République fédérale d'Allemagne** Federal Republic of Germany, FRG.

RG /ɛʀʒe/ *nmpl*: *abbr* ▶ **renseignement**.

Rh /ɛʀaʃ/ *nm* (*written abbr* = **rhésus**) Rh.

rhabillage /ʀabijaʒ/ *nm* **1** (de personne) dressing again; **pendant leur ~** while they

were getting dressed again; **2** (de montre) repairing (**de** of).
rhabiller /ʀabije/ [1] **I** *vtr* **1** (habiller de nouveau) **~ qn** to dress sb again, to put sb's clothes back on; **2** (réparer) to repair [*bijou*].
II se rhabiller *vpr* to get dressed again, to put one's clothes back on.
IDIOMES **il peut aller se ~**○! he can go back where he came from!
rhapsode /ʀapsɔd/ *nm* (chanteur) rhapsodist, rhapsode.
rhapsodie /ʀapsɔdi/ *nf* rhapsody.
rhème /ʀɛm/ *nm* rheme.
rhénan, **~e** /ʀenɑ̃, an/ ▶692 *adj* of the Rhineland.
Rhénanie /ʀenani/ ▶692 *nprf* Rhineland.
Rhénanie-du-Nord-Westphalie /ʀenanidynɔʀvɛstfali/ ▶692 *nprf* North Rhine-Westphalia.
Rhénanie-Palatinat /ʀenanipalatina/ ▶692 *nprf* Rhineland-Palatinate.
rhéostat /ʀeɔsta/ *nm* rheostat.
rhésus /ʀezys/ *nm inv* **1** Biol rhesus; **facteur ~** rhesus (factor); **la mère est ~ positif** the mother is rhesus positive; **un sujet ~ négatif** a rhesus negative subject; **2** Zool (**macaque**) **~** rhesus monkey.
rhéteur /ʀetœʀ/ *nm* **1** Antiq rhetor; **2** liter, pej rhetorician.
rhétoricien, **-ienne** /ʀetɔʀisjɛ̃, ɛn/ *nm,f* rhetorician.
rhétorique /ʀetɔʀik/ **I** *adj* [*procédé, effet*] rhetorical.
II *nf* rhetoric (**de** of).
Rhin /ʀɛ̃/ ▶357 *nprm* **le ~** the Rhine.
rhinite /ʀinit/ ▶271 *nf* common cold, rhinitis spéc.
rhinocéros /ʀinɔseʀɔs/ *nm inv* rhinoceros.
■ **~ blanc** white rhinoceros.
rhino-laryngite, *pl* **~s** /ʀinolaʀɛ̃ʒit/ ▶271 *nf* rhinolaryngitis.
rhinologie /ʀinɔlɔʒi/ *nf* rhinology.
rhino-pharyngé, **~e**, *mpl* **~s** /ʀinofaʀɛ̃ʒe/ *adj* nasopharyngeal; **affection ~e** nasopharyngitis.
rhino-pharyngite, *pl* **~s** /ʀinofaʀɛ̃ʒit/ ▶271 *nf* nasopharyngitis.
rhino-pharynx /ʀinofaʀɛ̃ks/ *nm inv* nasopharynx.
rhizome /ʀizom/ *nm* rhizome.
rhô /ʀo/ *nm inv* rho.
rhodanien, **-ienne** /ʀɔdanjɛ̃, ɛn/ *adj* [*vallée, couloir*] Rhône (*épith*); [*capitale, club*] of the Rhône.
Rhode Island /ʀodajlɑ̃d/ ▶692 *nprm* Rhode Island.
Rhodes /ʀɔd/ ▶416 *nprf* (**l'île de**) **~** (the island of) Rhodes.
Rhodésie /ʀɔdezi/ *nprf* Hist Rhodesia.
rhodium /ʀɔdjɔm/ *nm* rhodium.
rhododendron /ʀɔdɔdɛ̃dʀɔ̃/ *nm* rhododendron.
rhombe /ʀɔ̃b/ *nm* **1** ▶534 (instrument de musique) rhombus; **2**† liter (losange) rhombus.
rhombique /ʀɔ̃bik/ *adj* rhombic.
rhomboïdal, **~e**, *mpl* **-aux** /ʀɔ̃bɔidal, o/ *adj* rhomboid.
rhomboïde /ʀɔ̃bɔid/ **I** *adj* **muscle ~** rhomboideus.
II *nm* **1** Math rhomboid; **2** Anat rhomboideus.
Rhône /ʀon/ ▶357, 692 *nprm* (fleuve, département) **le ~** the Rhône.
Rhône-Alpes /ʀonalp/ ▶692 *nprm* **la région ~** the Rhône-Alpes.
rhovyl® /ʀɔvil/ *nm* Rhovyl®; **une chemise en ~** a Rhovyl vest.
rhubarbe /ʀybaʀb/ *nf* rhubarb; **confiture de ~** rhubarb jam.
rhum /ʀɔm/ *nm* rum; **~ blanc/brun** white/dark rum; **au ~** with rum.
rhumatisant, **~e** /ʀymatizɑ̃, ɑ̃t/ *adj, nm,f* rheumatic.
rhumatismal, **~e**, *mpl* **-aux** /ʀymatismal, o/ *adj* rheumatic.
rhumatisme /ʀymatism/ ▶271 *nm* rheumatism ¢; **avoir des ~s dans les doigts** to have rheumatism in one's fingers.
■ **~ articulaire (aigu)** (acute) rheumatoid arthritis; **~ déformant** rheumatoid arthritis; **~ inflammatoire** inflammatory arthritis; **~ musculaire** fibrositis.
rhumatologie /ʀymatɔlɔʒi/ *nf* rheumatology.
rhumatologue /ʀymatɔlɔg/ ▶510 *nmf* rheumatologist.
rhume /ʀym/ ▶271 *nm* cold; **avoir un (gros) ~** to have a (bad) cold.
■ **~ de cerveau** head cold; **~ des foins** hay fever.
rhumerie /ʀɔmʀi/ *nf* **1** (distillerie) rum distillery; **2** (débit de boissons) rum cocktail bar.
rhyolit(h)e /ʀijɔlit/ *nf* rhyolite.
ria /ʀia/ *nf* ria.
riant, **~e** /ʀijɑ̃, ɑ̃t/ *adj* [*visage*] happy; [*paysage*] liter pleasant.
RIB /ʀib/ *nm*: *abbr* ▶ **relevé**.
ribambelle /ʀibɑ̃bɛl/ *nf* (d'enfants) flock (**de** of); (d'amis) host (**de** of); (de noms) whole string (**de** of); (de procès) series (**de** of).
ribaude‡ /ʀibod/ *nf* strumpet‡.
riboflavine /ʀiboflavin/ *nf* riboflavin.
ribonucléase /ʀibonykleaz/ *nf* ribonuclease.
ribonucléique /ʀibonykleik/ *adj* **acide ~** ribonucleic acid.
ribose /ʀiboz/ *nm* ribose.
ribosome /ʀibozom/ *nm* ribosome.
ribouldingue○† /ʀibuldɛ̃g/ *nf* binge○, spree; **faire la ~** to go on a binge ou spree.
ricain○, **~e** /ʀikɛ̃, ɛn/ offensive or hum **I** *adj* Yankee○.
II *nm,f* Yank○.
ricanement /ʀikanmɑ̃/ *nm* (rire moqueur) snigger; (rire sot) giggle; **des ~s** (de moquerie) sniggering ¢; (de sottise) giggling ¢.
ricaner /ʀikane/ [1] *vi* (méchamment) to snigger; (bêtement) to giggle.
ricaneur, **-euse** /ʀikanœʀ, øz/ **I** *adj* sniggering.
II *nm,f* sniggerer.
richard○, **~e** /ʀiʃaʀ, aʀd/ *nm,f* pej well-heeled○ person; **c'est un (gros) ~** he's loaded○, he's rolling in money○.
Richard /ʀiʃaʀ/ *npr* Richard; **~ Cœur de Lion** Richard the Lionheart GB, Richard the Lion-hearted US.
riche /ʀiʃ/ **I** *adj* **1** (fortuné) [*personne*] rich, wealthy, well-off; (prospère) [*pays, région, ville*] rich; **je ne suis pas bien ~** I'm not very well-off; **être ~ à millions** to be extremely rich; **2** (considérable) [*végétation, faune, palette, collection, vocabulaire, style*] rich; [*bibliothèque*] well-stocked; **disposer d'une documentation très ~** to have a wealth of information at one's disposal; **3** (par son contenu) [*terre, sujet, minerai, pensée, langue, aliment*] rich (**en** in); [*architecture, décoration*] elaborate, rich; [*roman*] richly textured; **4** (luxueuse) [*bijoux, habit*] fine; [*étoffe*] rich; [*demeure*] sumptuous; [*cadeau*] magnificent; **une ~ idée** an excellent idea; **être trop ~ en oxygène/fer** to contain too much oxygen/iron; **aliment ~ en fibres/protéines** food that is high ou rich in fibre[GB]/protein; **un pays ~ en pétrole/uranium** an oil-/uranium-rich country; **c'est une expérience ~ d'enseignements** it's an educational experience; **~ de promesses** full of promise; **~ de tout un passé médiéval, la petite ville** with its medieval past, the small town; **~ de son diplôme** armed with his diploma.
II *nmf* rich man/woman; **les ~s** the rich, the wealthy; **un gosse**○ **de ~s** a rich kid; **club/loisir de ~s** a club/hobby for the rich; **quartier de ~s** wealthy part of town; **nouveau ~** nouveau riche; **la parabole du mauvais ~** Relig, Bible the parable of Lazarus and the rich man.
IDIOMES **on ne prête qu'aux ~s** Prov unto those that have shall more be given.
richelieu /ʀiʃəljø/ *nm* brogue; **~ à bout fleuri** brogue with decorative stitching.
richement /ʀiʃmɑ̃/ *adv* **1** (luxueusement) [*meublé*] richly; [*vêtu, décoré*] lavishly, elaborately; [*illustré*] richly, lavishly; **~ dotée** [*fille*] provided with a large dowry; [*tombola*] with big prizes; **2** (pour pourvoir de biens) **marier ~ sa fille** to make a wealthy match for one's daughter.
richesse /ʀiʃɛs/ **I** *nf* **1** (de personne, pays) wealth; **être une source de ~ pour** to be a source of wealth for; **notre principale ~** our main source of wealth; **faire la ~ d'un pays/d'une ville** [*activité, pétrole*] to bring wealth to a country/a town; **étaler sa ~** to flaunt one's wealth; **vivre dans la ~** to live in (the lap of) luxury; **~ nationale** national wealth; **ce lopin de terre c'est toute notre ~** this plot of land is all we have; **2** (luxe, somptuosité) (de bijoux) magnificence; (d'étoffe, de vêtement) richness; (de mobilier, demeure) sumptuousness; **décoration d'une trop grande ~** over-elaborate decoration; **3** (teneur) richness (**en** in); **la ~ d'un aliment en sucre** the sugar content of a food ; **la trop grande ~ d'un aliment en sel** a food's excessive salt content; **4** (abondance) (de végétation, faune, vocabulaire, collection) richness; (de documentation) wealth.
II richesses *nfpl* **1** (biens matériels) wealth ¢; **accumuler des ~s** to accumulate wealth ou riches; **2** (objets de grande valeur) treasures; **les ~s d'un musée** the treasures of a museum; **3** (ressources) resources; **~s naturelles** natural resources.
richissime○ /ʀiʃisim/ *adj* fabulously rich ou wealthy.
ricin /ʀisɛ̃/ *nf* castor-oil plant; **huile de ~** castor oil.
ricocher /ʀikɔʃe/ [1] *vi* [*balle*] to ricochet (**sur** off); [*pierre*] (sur l'eau) to skim (**sur** on ou across); (sur un obstacle) to rebound (**sur** off); **faire ~ des cailloux sur le lac** to skim stones on ou across the lake.
ricochet /ʀikɔʃɛ/ *nm* (de balle) ricochet; (de pierre) (sur l'eau) bounce; (sur un obstacle) rebound; **faire ~** lit [*balle*] to ricochet (**sur** off); [*pierre*] to rebound (**sur** off); fig [*décision*] to have repercussions (**sur** on); **faire des ~s** to skim stones (**sur** on ou across); **elle a fait trois ~s** she made the stone bounce three times; **cela l'a touché par ~** (projectile) he was hit on the rebound; (chômage) he was indirectly affected.
ric-rac○ /ʀikʀak/ *loc adv* **1** (de justesse) [*réussir, s'échapper*] by the skin of one's teeth; **ça va être ~ pour prendre le train** it's going to be touch and go for the train; **2** (rigoureusement) [*payer*] on the dot.
rictus /ʀiktys/ *nm inv* (fixed) grin, rictus.
ride /ʀid/ *nf* **1** (sur un visage, fruit) wrinkle; **ne pas avoir pris une ~** [*visage*] not to have aged; [*œuvre*] not to have dated; **2** (sur l'eau) ripple.
ridé, **~e** /ʀide/ **I** *pp* ▶ **rider**.
II *pp adj* [*personne, fruit*] wrinkled; [*lac*] rippled.
rideau, *pl* **~x** /ʀido/ *nm* **1** (dans une maison) curtain; (voilage) net curtain; **ouvrir/fermer les ~x** to open/close the curtains; **tirer les ~x** to draw the curtains; **doubles ~x** curtains; **2** Théât curtain; **3** (de magasin, bâtiment) (plein) roller shutter; (grille) security grille; **4** (ensemble) (d'arbres, de brouillard) curtain; (de soldats, flammes) wall; **5** (de cheminée) register; **6** Phot (d'obturateur) shutter; **7** (de classeur) roll top.
■ **~ de bain** bath curtain; **~ bonne femme** net curtain with tiebacks; **~ de douche** shower curtain; **~ de fer** Hist Iron Curtain; **~ de fumée** lit blanket of smoke; fig smokescreen.
IDIOMES **tirer le ~ sur qch** to draw a veil

over sth; **~!** Théât curtain!; fig (let's) drop it!; **grimper aux ~x**○ to go up the wall○.

ridelle /ʀidɛl/ *nf* side rail.

rider /ʀide/ [1] **I** *vtr* **1** to wrinkle [*visage, peau*]; **2** to ripple [*surface, lac*].

II se rider *vpr* **1** [*visage, peau*] to wrinkle; **2** [*lac, surface*] to ripple.

ridicule /ʀidikyl/ **I** *adj* **1** (digne de moquerie) ridiculous; **il ne craint pas d'être ~** he's not afraid of looking silly ou appearing foolish; **c'est ~** it's ridiculous ou absurd; **2** (insensé) **il est ~ de faire** it's ridiculous ou madness to do; **vous seriez ~ de refuser** you would be mad to refuse; **3** (insignifiant) [*somme, salaire*] ridiculously low, pathetic.

II *nm* **1** (ce qui est grotesque) ridicule; **il n'a pas peur du ~** he isn't afraid of ridicule; **se couvrir de ~** to make oneself an object of ridicule; **couvrir qn de ~** to heap ridicule on sb, to ridicule sb; **tourner qch/qn en ~** to make sth/sb look ridiculous; **2** (de situation) ridiculousness, absurdity; **il est d'un ~!** he looks so ridiculous!; **la situation est d'un ~!** the situation is ridiculous!

III ridicules *nmpl* (travers) liter foibles.

IDIOMES **le ~ ne tue pas** Prov looking a fool never killed anyone.

ridiculement /ʀidikylmɑ̃/ *adv* **1** (de façon grotesque) in a ridiculous way, ridiculously; **~ vêtu** dressed ridiculously; **2** (de façon dérisoire) ridiculously; **un salaire ~ bas** a ridiculously low salary.

ridiculiser /ʀidikylize/ [1] **I** *vtr* [*personne*] to ridicule [*personne, théorie, propos*]; to annihilate [*équipe, adversaire, concurrent*]; [*comportement, situation*] to make [sb] look ridiculous [*personne*]; **il l'a ridiculisé auprès des invités** he ridiculed him in front of the guests; **il l'a ridiculisé auprès des téléspectateurs/électeurs** he made him look foolish ou ridiculous in the eyes of the viewers/electorate.

II se ridiculiser *vpr* [*personne*] to make a fool of oneself, to make oneself look ridiculous.

ridule /ʀidyl/ *nf* fine wrinkle.

rien[1] /ʀjɛ̃/ **I** *pron indéf* **1** (nulle chose) **~ n'est impossible** nothing is impossible; **un mois à ne ~ faire** a month doing nothing; **j'ai décidé de ne ~ dire** I decided to say nothing ou not to say anything; **il n'y a ~ qui puisse la consoler** nothing can console her; **il n'y a plus ~** there's nothing left; **il n'y a plus ~ à faire** (comme travail) there's nothing left ou else to do; (pour le sauver) there's nothing more ou else that can be done; **ce n'est ~** it's nothing; **elle n'est ~** she's a nobody; **il n'est ~ pour moi** he means ou is nothing to me; **ils ne nous sont ~** they're nothing to do with us; **il n'en est ~** it's nothing of the sort; **elle ne t'a ~ fait** she hasn't done anything to you; **n'avoir ~ à faire avec qn** to have nothing to do with sb; **~ n'y fait!** nothing's any good!; **il n'a ~ d'un intrigant** there's nothing of the schemer about him; **elle n'a ~ de sa sœur** she's nothing like her sister; **~ de bon** nothing good; **~ d'autre** nothing else; **~ de moins/de plus** nothing less/more (**que** than); **~ de meilleur/de pire/de mieux** nothing better/worse/better (**que** than); **il n'y a ~ de tel/de tel que la marche pour garder la forme** there's nothing like it/like walking to keep you fit; **il n'y a ~ eu de cassé** nothing was broken; **ça n'a ~ de luxueux** there's nothing luxurious about it; **je n'ai jamais ~ vu de pire** I've never seen anything worse; **~ à déclarer/signaler** nothing to declare/report; **partir de ~** to start from nothing; **faire un drame d'un ~** to make a drama out of nothing; **pour ~** (en vain) for nothing; (à bas prix) for next to nothing; **'pourquoi?'—'pour ~'** 'why?'—'no reason'; **ce n'est pas pour ~ que** it's not without reason ou not for nothing that; **parler pour ~** to waste one's breath; **'merci'—'de ~'** 'thank you'—'you're welcome', 'not at all'; **en moins de ~** in no time at all; **'que prends-tu?'—'~ du tout'** 'what are you having?'—'nothing at all'; **c'est ça ou ~** it's that or nothing, take it or leave it; **'mais vous avez un contrat'—'ça ou ~(, c'est pareil)'** 'but you have a contract'—'I might as well not have one', 'it makes no odds'; **c'est mieux que ~** it's better than nothing; **c'est moins que ~** it's nothing at all; **c'est trois fois ~** it's next to nothing; **~ à ~, ~ de ~**○ absolutely nothing; **faire qch comme ~** to do sth very easily; **2** (seulement) **~ que la bouteille pèse deux kilos** the bottle alone weighs two kilos; **j'en ai eu pour 220 francs ~ qu'avec les fleurs** the flowers alone cost me 220 francs; **c'est à lui et ~ qu'à lui** it's his and his alone; **elle voudrait un bureau ~ qu'à elle**○ she would like an office all to herself; **il n'est ~ qu'un scribouillard** he's nothing but ou he's just a penpusher; **'qu'y a-t-il à boire?'—'~ que de l'eau'** 'what is there to drink?'—'just water'; **la vérité, ~ que la vérité** the truth and nothing but the truth; **~ que pour te plaire** just to please you; **j'en ai la nausée ~ que d'y penser** I feel sick just thinking about it; **~ qu'à voir comment il s'habille** just by looking at the way he dresses; **~ que ça**○**?** (en réponse) is that all?; **ils habitent un château, ~ que ça!** iron they live in a castle, no less! ou if you please! iron; **3** (quoi que ce soit) anything; **avant de ~ signer** before signing anything; **sans que j'en sache ~** without my knowing anything about it; **il m'a demandé si je n'avais ~ vu** he asked me if I had seen anything; **as-tu jamais ~ fait pour eux?** have you ever done anything for them?; **4** Sport gén nil; (au tennis) love; **~ partout, ~ à ~** nil nil; **~ à 15** (au tennis) love 15.

II de rien (du tout) *loc adj* **fille de ~** worthless girl; **un petit bleu de ~ (du tout)** a tiny bruise; **une affaire de ~ du tout** a trivial matter.

III○ *adv* **c'est ~ moche!** it isn't half ugly○! GB, it's really ugly.

IV○ **un rien** *loc adv* a (tiny) bit; **un ~ pédant/trop cuit** a bit pedantic/overcooked.

V en rien *loc adv* at all, in any way; **cela ne me concerne en ~** that doesn't concern me at all ou in any way; **ce n'est en ~ nécessaire** it's not at all necessary, it's in no way necessary; **il ne te ressemble en ~** he's not at all like you, he's nothing like you.

IDIOMES **~ à faire!** (c'est impossible) it's no good ou use!; (refus) no way○!; **on n'a ~ pour ~** you get nothing for nothing; **ce n'est pas ~!** (exploit) it's quite something!; (tâche) it's no joke, it's not exactly a picnic○!; (somme) it's not exactly peanuts○!

rien[2] /ʀjɛ̃/ *nm* **1** (vétille) **être puni pour un ~** to be punished for the slightest thing; **un ~ le fâche** the slightest thing annoys him; **un ~ l'habille, elle s'habille d'un ~** she looks good in the simplest thing; **se disputer pour un ~** to quarrel over nothing; **perdre son temps à des ~s** to waste one's time on trivial things; **les petits ~s qui rendent la vie agréable** the little things which make life pleasant; **faire qch comme un ~** to do sth very easily; **2** (petite quantité) **un ~ de** a touch of; **un ~ d'humour** a touch of humour[GB]; **un ~ de sel** a tiny pinch of salt; **un ~ de cognac** a dash of brandy; **en un ~ de temps** in next to no time; **3** (personne) **un/une ~ du tout** (insignifiant) a nobody; (sans moralité) a nogood○, a worthless person.

rieur, **rieuse** /ʀijœʀ, øz/ **I** *adj* [*personne*] cheerful; [*visage, yeux*] laughing; [*ton*] cheerful.

II *nm,f* cheerful person.

IDIOMES **mettre les ~s de son côté** to win the audience over.

rififi○ /ʀififi/ *nm* fisticuffs (*pl*); **il va y avoir du ~** there's going to be some fisticuffs.

riflard○ /ʀiflaʀ/ *nm* umbrella, bumbershoot○ US.

rifle /ʀifl/ *nm* **un 22 long ~** a 22 calibre[GB] rifle.

rift /ʀift/ *nm* rift valley.

Riga /ʀiga/ ▶ 857 *npr* Riga.

rigaudon /ʀigodɔ̃/ *nm* Danse rigaudon; **danser le ~** to do ou dance the rigaudon.

rigide /ʀiʒid/ *adj* **1** [*personne, règlement*] rigid; **2** [*matériau, support*] rigid; [*carton*] stiff.

rigidement /ʀiʒidmɑ̃/ *adv* rigidly.

rigidifier /ʀiʒidifje/ [2] *vtr* to rigidify.

rigidité /ʀiʒidite/ *nf* rigidity.

rigodon = **rigaudon**.

rigolade○ /ʀigɔlad/ *nf* **1** (amusement) **aimer la ~** to like a laugh○; **quelle ~!** what a laugh○!; **ça a été une partie de (franche) ~** it was a really good laugh○; **prendre qch à la ~** to make a joke of sth; **ne pas être d'humeur à la ~** to be in no mood for laughter ou joking; **le moment n'est pas à la ~** this is no time for laughter ou for fun and games; **il prend tout à la ~** he makes a joke of everything; **2** (plaisanterie) joke; **cette histoire est une vaste ~** this story is one big joke; **prendre qch à la ~** to take ou treat sth as a joke; **3** (chose facile) **réparer ça, c'est de la ~!** repairing this is a piece of cake○ ou is dead easy○.

rigolard○, **~e** /ʀigɔlaʀ, aʀd/ **I** *adj* [*visage, air*] grinning; **c'est un type ~** he's a (good) laugh○.

II *nm,f* joker.

rigole /ʀigɔl/ *nf* (conduit) channel; (écoulement) rivulet.

■ **~ d'écoulement** drain.

rigoler○ /ʀigɔle/ [1] *vi* **1** (rire) to laugh; **on a bien rigolé** we had a good laugh○; **faire ~ qn** to make sb laugh, to give sb a good laugh; **ne me fais pas ~** iron don't make me laugh; **il n'y a pas de quoi ~** there is nothing to laugh about, this is no laughing matter; **2** (s'amuser) to have fun; **il aime bien ~** he likes a laugh; **ça ne rigole pas tous les jours ici** it's not much fun here; **3** (plaisanter) to joke, to kid○; **il ne faut pas ~ avec la sécurité** you mustn't mess about ou fool around with security; **il a dit ça pour ~** he said it as a joke.

rigolo○, **-ote** /ʀigɔlo, ɔt/ **I** *adj* **1** (amusant) funny; **2** (curieux) odd, funny.

II *nm,f* **1** (fumiste) joker; **2** (personne amusante) **c'est un petit ~** he's quite a little comedian.

rigorisme /ʀigɔʀism/ *nm* rigorism.

rigoriste /ʀigɔʀist/ **I** *adj* [*attitude*] unbending, rigoristic; [*morale*] rigorist, hardline.

II *nmf* rigorist.

rigoureusement /ʀiguʀøzmɑ̃/ *adv* **1** (incontestablement) absolutely; **c'est ~ faux/vrai** that's completely untrue/true; **c'est ~ défendu** or **interdit** it's strictly ou absolutely forbidden; **2** (durement) [*punir, traiter*] rigorously, harshly; **3** (scrupuleusement) [*obéir*] scrupulously; [*sélectionner, mesurer*] carefully; [*conforme*] strictly.

rigoureux, **-euse** /ʀiguʀø, øz/ *adj* **1** (sévère) [*morale, discipline*] strict, rigorous; [*règlement, personne*] strict; **2** (rude) [*climat, saison*] harsh, severe; [*froid*] severe; [*température*] harsh; [*conditions de travail*] difficult, hard; **3** (conduit avec précision) [*observations, recherches, démonstration, description*] meticulous; [*travail*] meticulous, scrupulous; [*logique, analyse, méthode, sélection, gestion, pensée*] rigorous; [*argumentation*] meticulous, rigorous; [*application*] strict; **de façon rigoureuse** rigorously; **la construction rigoureuse d'un roman** the tight structure of a novel; **un raisonnement ~** a closely reasoned argument; **4** (strict) [*obéissance, sens*] strict; [*personne*] rigorous; **être ~ dans ses observations/analyses** to be rigorous ou meticulous in one's observations/analysis.

rigueur /ʀigœʀ/ **I** *nf* **1** (sévérité) (de sanction,

règlement, loi, personne) strictness; (de discipline) strictness, harshness; (de répression) harshness; **se conformer à une morale d'une grande ~** to adhere to an extremely strict moral code; **être d'une extrême/grande ~ avec qn** to be extremely/very strict with sb; **traiter ses enfants avec trop de ~** to treat one's children too harshly ou strictly; **2** (dureté) (de climat, saison) harshness; (de condition) harshness; **3** (précision) (d'observation, de recherche, travail, style) meticulousness, rigour[GB]; (de logique, démonstration, d'analyse, argumentation) rigour[GB]; **une analyse d'une grande ~** a very rigorous analysis; **faire preuve de ~** to be rigorous; **étude faite avec ~** study meticulously carried out; **leur travail manque de ~** their work is not rigorous enough; **4** Pol, Écon austerity; **~ monétaire** monetary austerity; **plan de ~** austerity measures.
II rigueurs *nfpl* littér (de saison, climat) rigours[GB]; **affronter les ~s de l'hiver** to withstand the rigours[GB] of winter.
III de rigueur *loc adj* obligatory, essential; **précautions de ~** necessary precautions; **les gants blancs sont de ~** white gloves are to be worn ou must be worn; **la prudence reste de ~ au ministère** caution is the order of the day at the ministry; **visite de ~** obligatory social call; **les banalités de ~** the usual platitudes.
IV à la rigueur *loc adv* **nous pouvons à la ~ emprunter à mes parents** if we absolutely must we can borrow from my parents; **à la ~ je peux te prêter 100 francs** at a pinch GB ou in a pinch US I can lend you 100 francs; **je peux venir trois jours ou cinq à la ~** I can come for three days or five at the very outside; **qu'il ait gagné la médaille de bronze à la ~, mais pas la médaille d'or** he may well have deserved to win the bronze medal, but not the gold; **il est un peu excentrique à la ~, mais fou certainement pas** he may be a bit eccentric, but he's certainly not mad.
IDIOMES **tenir ~ à qn de qch** to bear sb a grudge for sth; **il lui tient ~ d'avoir dilapidé toute la fortune de leur père** he bears him/her a grudge for having frittered away their father's fortune; **il ne t'en tiendra pas ~** he won't hold it against you.

rikiki○ = **riquiqui**.

rillettes /rijɛt/ *nfpl* ≈ potted meat; **~ de porc/d'oie** potted pork/goose.

rillons /rijɔ̃/ *nmpl* sautéed pork morsels.

rilsan® /rilsɑ̃/ *nm* Rilsan®.

rimailler† /rimɑje/ [1] *vi* to write bad verse.

rimailleur†, **-euse** /rimɑjœr, øz/ *nm,f* pej poetaster†, rhymester†.

rimaye /rimɑj/ *nf* bergschrund.

rime /rim/ *nf* rhyme; **~ masculine/féminine** masculine/feminine rhyme; **~s embrassées** or **enlacées** enclosing rhyme; **des ~s en 'our'** rhymes in 'our'; **~ pour l'œil** eye rhyme; **'tu fais des ~s'** 'that rhymes'; **~s suivies** or **accouplées** or **plates** rhyming couplets.
IDIOMES **sans ~ ni raison** without rhyme or reason; **cela n'a ni ~ ni raison** it has neither rhyme nor reason.

rimer /rime/ [1] *vi* **1** (former une rime) to rhyme; **~ pour les yeux** or **pour l'œil** to form an eye rhyme; **2** (signifier) **cela ne rime à rien** it makes no sense; **ça ne rime à rien de faire** there's no sense in doing.

rimeur, **-euse** /rimœr, øz/ *nm,f* péj mediocre poet.

rimmel® /rimɛl/ *nm* mascara; **ton ~ coule** your mascara is running.

rinçage /rɛ̃saʒ/ *nm* (processus) rinsing; (de lave-linge, lave-vaisselle) rinse; **(ajouter à) l'eau de ~** (add to) rinsing water.

rince-bouteilles /rɛ̃sbutɛj/ *nm inv* bottle-washing machine.

rince-doigts /rɛ̃sdwa/ *nm inv* **1** (récipient) finger-bowl; **2** (en papier) finger wipe.

rincée○ /rɛ̃se/ *nf* **prendre une ~** (pluie) to get drenched; (coups) to get a thrashing○.

rincer /rɛ̃se/ [12] **I** *vtr* **1** (ôter le savon) to rinse; (laver) to rinse [sth] out; **2**○ [*pluie*] to drown; **3**◑ (offrir à boire à) to stand○ [sb] a drink; **il se fait toujours ~** he always gets drinks bought for him; **4**◑ (au jeu) to clean [sb] out.
II se rincer *vpr* **se ~ les mains/les cheveux** to rinse one's hands/hair; **se ~ la bouche** to rinse one's mouth out.
IDIOMES **se ~ l'œil**◑ to get an eyeful; **se ~ la dalle**◑ or **le gosier**◑ to have a drink.

rincette○ /rɛ̃sɛt/ *nf* drop of liqueur (*mixed with the dregs in one's coffee cup*).

ring /riŋ/ *nm* (boxing) ring.

ringard, **~e** /rɛ̃gar, ard/ **I** *adj* [*vêtement*] dated; [*idée, méthode, politique*] out of date; [*personne*] behind the times (*jamais épith*).
II *nm* (tisonnier) poker.

Rio de Janeiro /rjodəʒanero/ ▶857 *npr* Rio de Janeiro.

RIP /rip/ *nm*: *abbr* ▶ **relevé**.

ripaille○ /ripɑj/ *nf* blow-out○, feast; **faire ~** to have a blow-out○ ou feast.

ripailler○ /ripaje/ [1] *vi* to have a blow-out○, to feast.

ripaton◑ /ripatɔ̃/ *nm* foot.

riper◑ /ripe/ [1] *vi* **1** (déraper) [*pied*] to slip; [*bicyclette*] to skid; **2** (partir) to leave, to head off○.

ripoliner /ripɔline/ [1] *vtr* **1** (avec de la peinture) to paint; **2** (embellir) to give [sth] a face-lift.

riposte /ripɔst/ *nf* **1** (verbale) reply, riposte; **prompt à la ~** always ready with a reply; **2** (physique) response (**à** to); **~ graduée** flexible response; **3** Sport (en escrime) riposte; (en lutte, boxe) counter.

riposter /ripɔste/ [1] **I** *vtr* to retort (**que** that).
II *vi* **1** (verbalement) to retort; **~ à qn/qch par** to counter sb/sth with; **~ à qn/qch en faisant** to counter sb/sth by doing; **2** (par des coups) to respond (**à** to; **par** with; **en faisant** by doing); **3** Mil to return fire, to shoot back; **~ à qch par qch** to counter sth with sth; **~ à une attaque (en faisant)** to counter-attack (by doing); **4** (en sport) to ripost.

ripou○, *pl* **~x** /ripu/ *adj* [*personne, policier*] crooked○, bent○.

riquiqui○ /rikiki/ *adj inv* [*vêtement*] ridiculously small; [*logement, voiture*] poky○; [*portion, banquet*] measly○.

rire /rir/ [68] **I** *nm* **1** (éclat) laughter; **un ~** a laugh; **un ~ communicatif/énorme/gras/bête** an infectious/a loud/a vulgar/a stupid laugh; **avoir un ~ forcé** to give a forced laugh; **avoir le ~ facile** to laugh at the slightest thing; **il y eut des ~s et des applaudissements dans le public** there was laughter and applause in the audience; **il a eu un petit ~** he chuckled; **elle a eu un petit ~ nerveux** she laughed nervously; **il éclata d'un gros ~** (bref) he let out a guffaw; (qui dure) he gave a loud hearty laugh; **entendre des ~s** to hear laughter or laughing; **2** (hilarité) laughter.
II *vi* **1** (s'esclaffer) to laugh; **se mettre à ~** to burst out laughing; **faire ~ qn** to make sb laugh; **tu nous feras toujours ~!** you're a real scream○!; **il n'y a pas de quoi ~!** that's not funny!, that's no laughing matter!; **il vaut mieux en ~ (qu'en pleurer)** you might as well laugh as cry; **dit-il en riant** he laughed, he said, laughing; **j'ai bien** or **beaucoup ri** I laughed a lot; **on a ri un bon coup**○ we had a good laugh; **~ des plaisanteries de qn** to laugh at sb's jokes; **il me disputait, et moi de ~** he was telling me off and all I could do was laugh; ▶ **vendredi**; **2** (s'amuser) to have fun; **ils ne pensent qu'à ~** all they care about is having fun; **on va bien ~** we're going to have a lot of fun; **il faut bien ~ un peu** you need a bit of fun now and again; **~ de peu** or **de rien** to laugh at anything; **fini de ~, je ne ris plus** the fun's over; **tu veux ~!** you must be joking ou kidding○!; **j'ai fait ça pour ~** I was joking; **c'était pour ~** it was a joke; **sans ~**○ seriously, honestly; **sans ~, quand est-ce que tu pars?** seriously, when are you leaving?; **non! sans ~ elle t'a dit ça?** no! she really told you that?; **tu me fais ~ avec tes idées**○**!** you make me laugh with your ideas!; **elle me fait ~, partir en vacances... avec quel argent**○**!** go on vacation? she must be joking! how can I afford it?; **laisse-moi ~, ne me fais pas ~**○ don't make me laugh; **3** (se moquer) **~ de qch/qn** to laugh at sth/sb; **ne ris pas de mon chapeau** don't laugh at my hat; **on rit de lui** everybody's laughing at him; **~ aux dépens de qn** to laugh at sb's expense; **tu peux ~ mais c'est la vérité** laugh if you like, but it's true; **4** (avoir une expression gaie) liter **elle a les yeux qui rient, ses yeux rient** she has laughing eyes.
III se rire *vpr* **1** (se moquer) **se ~ de qn** fml to laugh at sb; **2** (surmonter aisément) **se ~ des obstacles/difficultés/dangers** fml to make light of obstacles/difficulties/dangers.
■ **~s préenregistrés** Radio, TV canned laughter.
IDIOMES **rira bien qui rira le dernier** Prov he who laughs last laughs longest Prov; **être mort** or **écroulé de ~**○ to be doubled up (with laughter).

ris /ri/ *nm inv* **1** Culin **~ (de veau)** calf's sweetbread; **des ~ de veau grillés** grilled calves' sweetbreads; **2** Naut reef; **prendre un ~** to take in a reef, to reef in; **3**‡ (rire) laugh.

risée /rize/ *nf* **1** (sujet de moquerie) **être la ~ de** to be the laughing stock of; **il est devenu la ~ des électeurs** he's become the laughing stock of the voters; **2** (vent) gust (of wind).

risette○ /rizɛt/ *nf* smile; **fais ~!** give me a smile!; **le bébé fait ~** the baby is smiling.

risible /rizibl/ *adj* ridiculous, laughable.

risque /risk/ *nm* **1** (danger) risk (**de** of); **comporter** or **présenter un ~** [*processus*] to carry a risk; [*décision, action*] to involve some risk; **il n'y a pas grand ~ à accepter leur proposition** there's not much risk involved in accepting their offer; **~ accru** increased risk; **gros ~s** major risks; **~ d'échec/d'infection/d'inflation** risk of failure/of infection/of inflation; **~ d'incendie** fire risk; **le grand ~, c'est le chômage** the major risk is unemployment; **le ~ que le conflit s'étende** the risk that the conflict might spread; **malgré le ~** in spite of the risk; **courir un ~** to run a risk; **prendre des ~s/un ~** to take risks/a risk; **il n'y a pas de ~s**○ **que ça leur arrive/de s'ennuyer!** there's no risk of that happening to them/of getting bored!; **c'est sans ~** it's safe; **agir sans ~** to act safely; **sans ~ de qch/de faire** with no risk of sth/of doing; **au ~ de faire** at the risk of doing; **au ~ d'être mal compris** at the risk of being misunderstood; **à (haut) ~, à ~s** [*personne, groupe, investissement, prêt*] high-risk (*épith*); **partenaire/obligation à ~** high-risk partner/bond; **2** Assur risk; **~ naturel/nucléaire** natural/nuclear risk; **~ maritime** risk at sea.
■ **~ de change** Fin foreign exchange risk; **les ~s du métier** occupational hazards; **les ~s professionnels** occupational hazards.

risqué, **~e** /riske/ *adj* **1** (aléatoire) [*entreprise, carrière, comportement*] risky; [*investissement*] high-risk; **2** (osé) [*plaisanterie, remarque*] risqué; [*hypothèse*] daring.

risquer /riske/ [1] **I** *vtr* **1** (être passible de) to face [*accusation, condamnation*]; **~ une amende/vingt ans de prison/la peine de mort** to face a fine/twenty years in prison/the death penalty; **~ des poursuites** to face criminal charges; **~ gros** to face a heavy sentence; **2** (s'exposer à) to risk [*mort, critique*]; **~ des ennuis** to risk trouble; **vas-y, tu ne risques rien** go ahead, you're safe; fig go ahead, you've got nothing to lose; **qu'est-ce qu'on risque?** lit what are the risks?; fig what have we got to lose?; **~ gros** to take a major risk; **tu risques qu'on t'abîme ta voiture** you run the risk of having your car damaged; **3** (mettre en danger) to risk [*vie, réputation, fortune, emploi*]; **~ sa peau**○ to risk one's neck○; **4** (oser) to venture [*regard, allusion, question*]; to risk [*geste*]; to attempt [*démarche, opération*]; **~ un œil** to venture a glance; **~ un pied dans l'obscurité** to take a tentative step into the dark; **~ le coup**○ to risk it, to chance it.

II **risquer de** *vtr ind* **1** (pouvoir) **tu risques de te brûler** you might burn yourself; **je/elle ne risque pas de faire** there's no danger of my/her doing; **elle risque fort d'être déçue** she may well be disappointed; **les taux d'intérêt ne risquent pas de baisser** there's no chance of interest rates falling; **ça ne risque pas de m'arriver!** there's no chance of that happening to me!; **ça ne risque pas**○! not a chance○!; **2** (prendre le risque) **~ de faire** to risk doing; **il ne veut pas ~ de perdre son travail** he doesn't want to risk losing his job.

III **se risquer** *vpr* **1** (s'aventurer) to venture; **se ~ sur le marché français/sur le balcon** to venture into the French market/on to the balcony; **se ~ à faire** to venture to do; **se ~ à sortir** to venture out; **se ~ à faire du ski** to have a go at skiing; **je ne m'y risquerais pas!** I wouldn't risk it; **2** (oser) **se ~ à dire** to dare to say; **je ne me risquerais pas à le contredire** I wouldn't dare to contradict him.

IV *v impers* **il risque de neiger/pleuvoir** it might snow/rain; **il risque d'y avoir du monde** there may well be a lot of people there.

IDIOMES **qui ne risque rien n'a rien** nothing ventured, nothing gained; **~ le tout pour le tout** to stake ou risk one's all.

risque-tout /ʀiskətu/ I *adj inv* daredevil; **être ~** to be a daredevil; **conducteur ~** daredevil driver.

II *nmf inv* daredevil.

rissole /ʀisɔl/ *nf* Culin rissole.

rissoler /ʀisɔle/ Culin [1] I *vtr* to brown.

II *vi* to brown; **faire ~** to brown.

ristourne /ʀistuʀn/ *nf* **1** Comm discount, rebate; **faire une ~ à qn** to give sb a discount ou rebate; **une ~ de 50 francs sur un produit** a 50-franc discount on a product; **2** (à un adhérent, associé) rebate; **bénéficier d'une ~** to benefit from a rebate.

ristourner /ʀistuʀne/ [1] *vtr* **~ qch à qn** to give sb a discount ou rebate of sth; **le commerçant m'a ristourné 100 francs** the shopkeeper gave me a discount of 100 francs.

rital◑, **~e** /ʀital/ *nm,f* offensive (Italien) wop◑ injur.

rite /ʀit/ *nm* lit, fig rite; **les ~s du baptême** the rites of baptism; **~ d'initiation** Anthrop initiation rite; fig (habitude) ritual.

ritournelle /ʀituʀnɛl/ *nf* **1** Mus ritornello; **2** fig (rabâchage) **j'en ai assez de sa sempiternelle ~!** I'm fed up with his constant harping on!

ritualiser /ʀitɥalize/ [1] *vtr* to ritualize.

rituel, **-elle** /ʀitɥɛl/ I *adj* ritual.

II *nm* ritual.

rituellement /ʀitɥɛlmɑ̃/ *adv* **1** (de manière rituelle) ritually; **2** (invariablement) invariably, ritually.

rivage /ʀivaʒ/ *nm* shore.

rival, **~e**, *mpl* **-aux** /ʀival, o/ I *adj* [*nations, équipes, personnes*] rival.

II *nm,f* rival; **être sans ~** to be without rival ou unrivalled[GB]; **être rivaux en** to be rivals in.

rivaliser /ʀivalize/ [1] *vi* to compete with; **~ avec qch** to rival sth; **~ d'adresse/d'esprit avec qn** to try to outdo sb in skill/wit, to vie with sb in skill/wit.

rivalité /ʀivalite/ *nf* rivalry (**entre** between; **avec** with).

rive /ʀiv/ *nf* **1** (de rivière, fleuve, détroit) bank; **la Rive gauche/droite** (à Paris) the Left/Right Bank; **2** (de mer, lac) shore; **la ~ sud de la Méditerranée** the southern shore of the Mediterranean.

river /ʀive/ [1] *vtr* to clinch [*clou, rivet*]; to rivet [*plaques de tôle*]; to fasten [*forçat, prisonnier*] (**à** to); **être rivé à qch** fig to be tied to [*travail, famille*]; to be glued to [*télévision*]; **je suis restée rivée sur place par la surprise** I stood riveted ou rooted to the spot with surprise; **avoir les yeux rivés sur** to have one's eyes riveted on.

IDIOMES **~ son clou à qn** to leave sb speechless.

riverain, **~e** /ʀivʀɛ̃, ɛn/ I *adj* **1** (de voie) [*maison, propriété*] bordering the street ou road; **2** (de cours d'eau) riverside (*épith*); riparian spéc; **3** (de lac) lakeside (*épith*).

II *nm,f* **1** (habitant) (de rue) resident; (de cours d'eau) riverside resident; (de bord de lac) lakeside resident; **'interdit sauf aux ~s'** 'residents only'; **2** (propriétaire) riparian.

riveraineté /ʀivʀɛnte/ *nf* Jur riparian rights (*pl*).

rivet /ʀivɛ/ *nm* rivet.

rivetage /ʀivtaʒ/ *nm* riveting.

riveter /ʀivte/ [20] *vtr* to rivet.

riveteuse /ʀivtøz/ *nf* (machine) riveting machine.

rivière /ʀivjɛʀ/ *nf* **1** (cours d'eau) river; **2** Sport, Turf (fossé) water jump.

■ **~ de diamants** diamond necklace, diamond rivière.

IDIOMES **les petits ruisseaux font les grandes ~s** Prov great oaks from little acorns grow Prov.

rixe /ʀiks/ *nf* brawl (**entre** between).

Riyad /ʀijad/ **▶ 857** *npr* Riyadh.

riz /ʀi/ *nm* rice; **un bol de ~** a bowl of rice.

■ **~ blanc** white rice; **~ cantonais** egg fried rice; **un grain de ~** a grain of rice; **~ Caroline** long grain rice; **~ complet** whole rice; **~ créole** creole rice; **~ au curry** curried rice; **~ long grain** long grain rice; **~ pilaf** pilau rice; **~ sauvage** wild rice, Indian rice.

rizerie /ʀizʀi/ *nf* (usine) rice-processing factory.

riziculture /ʀizikyltyʀ/ *nf* rice growing.

rizière /ʀizjɛʀ/ *nf* paddy field.

RMI /ɛʀɛmi/ *nm*: *abbr* ▶ **revenu**.

RMIste /ɛʀɛmist/ *nmf* person receiving minimum benefit payment.

RMN /ɛʀɛmɛn/ *nf* (*abbr* = **résonance magnétique nucléaire**) NMR.

RN /ɛʀɛn/ *nf* (*abbr* = **route nationale**) ≈ A road GB, highway US.

RNIS /ɛʀɛniɛs/ *nm*: *abbr* ▶ **réseau**.

roannais, **~e** /ʀɔanɛ, ɛz/ **▶ 857** *adj* of Roanne.

Roannais, **~e** /ʀɔanɛ, ɛz/ **▶ 857** *nm,f* (natif) native of Roanne; (habitant) inhabitant of Roanne.

Roanne /ʀɔan/ **▶ 857** *npr* Roanne.

robe /ʀɔb/ *nf* **1** (vêtement féminin) dress; **~ courte/longue** short/long dress; **2** (vêtement distinctif) (d'avocat) gown; (de prêtre) robe; (de moine) frock; **la ~** the Robe; **3** Hist, Anthrop (vêtement masculin) robes (*pl*); **4** Zool (pelage) coat; **5** Vin (couleur) colour[GB].

■ **~ de bal** ball gown; **~ de bure** habit; **~ bustier** (boned) strapless dress; **~ de chambre** dressing gown, robe US; **~ chasuble** pinafore dress, jumper US; **~ d'été** summer dress; **~ fourreau** sheath dress; **~ de grossesse** maternity dress ou smock; **~ d'intérieur** housecoat; **~ isabelle** dun coat; **~ longue** full-length dress; **~ de mariée** wedding dress ou gown; **~ du soir** evening dress GB, evening gown.

roberts◑ /ʀɔbɛʀ/ *nmpl* (seins) knockers◑, boobs○.

robe-sac, *pl* **robes-sacs** /ʀɔbsak/ *nf* sack dress.

robe-tablier, *pl* **robes-tabliers** /ʀɔbtablije/ *nf* overall.

Robin /ʀɔbɛ̃/ *npr* (prénom) Robin.

■ **~ des bois** Littérat Robin Hood.

robinet /ʀɔbinɛ/ *nm* tap GB, faucet US; **ouvrir/fermer un ~** to turn a tap GB ou faucet US on/off; **le ~ du lavabo** the basin tap GB ou faucet US; **le ~ de gaz** the gas tap GB ou valve US; **~ d'arrêt** stopcock; **~ d'eau chaude/froide** hot/cold (water) tap GB ou faucet US.

robinetterie /ʀɔbinɛtʀi/ *nf* **1** (dispositif) plumbing fixtures; **2** (usine) tap ou faucet US factory.

robineux○ /ʀɔbinø/ *nm inv* C (clochard) down-and-out GB, hobo US.

robinier /ʀɔbinje/ *nm* locust tree, false acacia.

roboratif, **-ive** /ʀɔbɔʀatif, iv/ *adj* (revigorant) [*climat, activité*] invigorating; [*vin, alcool*] fortifying; [*remède, nourriture*] restorative.

robot /ʀɔbo/ *nm* robot.

■ **~ ménager** Culin food processor.

robotique /ʀɔbɔtik/ *nf* robotics (+ *v sg*); **~ industrielle** industrial robotics.

robotisation /ʀɔbɔtizasjɔ̃/ *nf* automation, robotization US.

robotiser /ʀɔbɔtize/ [1] *vtr* to automate, to robotize US [*usine, atelier, production*]; **travailleurs robotisés** fig robotized workers.

robre /ʀɔbʀ/ *nm* (au bridge) rubber.

robusta /ʀɔbysta/ *nm* robusta.

robuste /ʀɔbyst/ *adj* [*personne, animal, machine, constitution*] robust, sturdy; [*plante, arbres*] sturdy; [*constitution, santé*] robust, sound; [*appétit*] healthy; [*foi, conviction*] strong, firm.

robustesse /ʀɔbystɛs/ *nf* (de personne, d'animal, de machine) robustness, sturdiness; (de constitution, santé) robustness, soundness; (d'arbre, de plante) sturdiness; (de foi, convictions) strength, firmness.

roc /ʀɔk/ *nm* **1** (rocher) rock; **il est solide comme un ~** he's solid as a rock; **2** (roche) rock; **un cœur dur comme le ~** a heart as hard as stone; **3** Mythol **oiseau ~** roc.

ROC /ʀɔk/ *nf*: *abbr* ▶ **reconnaissance**.

rocade /ʀɔkad/ *nf* **1** (de dérivation) bypass; (circulaire) ring road, beltway US; **2** Mil transversal route.

rocaille /ʀɔkaj/ I *nm* (style ornemental) rocaille; **un meuble ~** a rocaille piece of furniture.

II *nf* **1** (pierres) loose stones (*pl*) ou rocks (*pl*); **2** (terrain pierreux) rocky ou stony ground; **plantes de ~** rock plants; **3** (décor de jardin) rockery, rock garden; **4** (pierre d'ornement) rocaille; **grotte en ~s** rockwork grotto.

rocailleux, **-euse** /ʀɔkajø, øz/ *adj* **1** (pierreux) [*terrain*] rocky, stony; **2** (rauque) [*voix, sonorités*] harsh, grating.

rocambolesque /ʀɔkɑ̃bɔlɛsk/ *adj* [*aventure, affaire*] fantastic, incredible.

roche /ʀɔʃ/ *nf* rock; **~s éboulées/côtières** fallen/coastal rocks; ▶ **clair**, **Tarpéienne**.

■ **~ feuilletée** foliated rock; **~ mère** Géol, Mines parent rock; **~s calcaires** calcareous rocks; **~ sédimentaire** sedimentary rock; **~ volcanique** volcanic rocks.

rocher /ʀɔʃe/ *nm* **1** (bloc de roche) rock; **~ à fleur d'eau** rock just above the surface (of the water); **~ de Sisyphe** Mythol rock of Sisyphus; **2** (éminence rocheuse) rock; **le ~ de Gibraltar** the Rock of Gibraltar; **le Rocher** Monaco; **3** Anat (os) petrosal bone; **4** Culin praline chocolate.

rochet /ʀɔʃɛ/ *nm* **1** Tex (bobine) bobbin;

2 Mécan (roue dentée) ratchet; **roue à ~** ratchet wheel; **3** Relig (aube courte) rochet.

Rocheuses /Rɔʃøz/ *nprfpl* **les ~** the Rocky mountains, the Rockies.

rocheux, -euse /Rɔʃø, øz/ *adj* [*côte, récif, terrain*] rocky; **fond ~** rocky bottom; **paroi rocheuse** rock face.

rock /Rɔk/ **I** *adj inv* [*musique, concert, festival*] rock (*épith*).
II *nm* **1** (style musical) rock (music); **2** (danse) jive; **danser le ~** to jive, to dance the jive; **3** = **roc 3**.
■ **~ and roll**, **~'n'roll** rock and roll, rock 'n' roll.

rocker = **rockeur**.

rockeur, -euse /Rɔkœr, øz/ *nm,f* (chanteur) rock singer; (musicien) rock musician; (amateur) rock fan.

rocking-chair, *pl* **~s** /Rɔkiŋ(t)ʃɛR/ *nm* rocking chair.

rococo /Rɔkoko/ **I** *adj inv* **1** Art [*art, style, objets*] rococo; **2** pej (démodé) old-fashioned.
II *nm* rococo; **en ~** rococo.

rodage /Rɔdaʒ/ *nm* **1** (de véhicule, moteur) running in GB, breaking in US; **j'étais derrière une voiture en ~** I was following a car which was being run in GB ou broken in US; **2** (de pièce, soupapes) grinding; **le spectacle/l'équipe est encore en ~** fig the show/the team is still getting into its stride.

rodéo /Rɔdeo/ *nm* rodeo; **~ à la voiture volée** joyriding○; **faire du ~ à la voiture volée** to joyride○.

roder /Rɔde/ [1] *vtr* **1** Aut (user) to run in GB, to break in US [*véhicule, moteur*]; **2** Tech to grind [*pièce, soupapes*]; **3** (mettre au point) to bring [sth] up to scratch, to polish up [*spectacle, méthode, technique*]; **~ qn à** or **pour** Sport to train sb for [*épreuve*]; **être (bien) rodé** [*personne*] to have the hang of things; [*service*] to be running smoothly.

rôder /Rode/ [1] *vi* **1** (avec intention malfaisante) to prowl; **~ autour d'une maison** to prowl around a house; **~ autour de qn** to hang around sb; **un individu suspect rôdait autour de la maison** a suspicious individual was prowling around the house ou hanging around outside the house; **la mort rôde** death is on the prowl; **2** (au hasard) to roam around, to wander about.

rôdeur, -euse /RodœR, øz/ *nm,f* pej prowler.

rodomontade /Rɔdɔmɔ̃tad/ *nf* fml (action, propos) bragging ¢, boasting ¢.

rogatoire /Rɔgatwar/ *adj* **commission ~** Jur letters (*pl*) rogatory.

rogaton /Rɔgatɔ̃/ *nm* **1** (reste de repas) **~s** leftovers; **2** (objet de rebut) rubbish ¢, piece of junk; **il faut jeter ces vieux ~s** we must throw this old rubbish ou junk away.

rogne○ /Rɔɲ/ *nf* (colère) anger; **être en ~** to be (hopping) mad ou in a temper; **mettre qn en ~** to get sb mad○, to get sb's back up○; **se mettre en ~** to get mad, to lose one's temper ou rag○ GB.

rogner /Rɔɲe/ [1] *vtr* **1** (couper les bords de) to trim [*bâton, angle*]; to clip [*griffes*]; to clip, to trim [*ongles*]; **~ les ailes à qn** fig to clip sb's wings; **2** (prélever) **~ sur** to cut down ou back on sth [*budget*]; to whittle away [*économies*]; **3** Imprim (découper) to trim [*feuillet, feuille*].

rognon /Rɔɲɔ̃/ *nm* **1** Culin kidney; **~s de veau/d'agneau/de porc** veal/lamb/pork kidneys; **~s sauce madère** kidneys in Madeira sauce; **2** Géol (masse minérale) nodule.

rognure /RɔɲyR/ *nf* (de papier, carton) trimming; (d'ongles) clipping; (d'or, de peau) clipping.

rogomme◑ /Rɔgɔm/ *nm* brandy; **voix de ~** husky ou rasping voice.

rogue /Rɔg/ *adj* haughty, contemptuous.

roi /Rwa/ *nm* **1** ▶ **813** (souverain) king; **le ~ Louis** King Louis; **le ~ de France** the King of France; **le livre des Rois** Bible the Book of Kings; **mets/festin de ~** dish/feast fit for a king; **2** (sans rival en son genre) **le ~ des animaux/de la forêt** the king of beasts/of the forest; **le ~ du rock/de la mode** the king of rock/fashion; **le ~ de l'arnaque**○ a master swindler; **le ~ des imbéciles/salauds**○ a complete idiot/bastard◑; **le ~ des cons**◑ a prize bloody idiot◑ GB, a complete asshole◑ US; **3** (magnat) tycoon; **le ~ du béton/de l'épicerie** the concrete/supermarket tycoon; **4** Jeux (aux cartes, échecs) king.
■ **~ constitutionnel** Pol constitutional monarch; **les ~s fainéants** Hist *the last Merovingian kings*; **les ~s mages** Bible the (three) wise men, the three kings, the Magi; **le ~ Soleil** Hist the Sun King; **le Roi des Rois** Hist the King of Kings.
IDIOMES **tirer les Rois** to eat Twelfth Night cake; ▶ **royaume**.

roide /Rwad/ *adj* liter [*allure*] stiff; [*attitude*] rigid, inflexible.

roideur /RwadœR/ *nf* liter (d'allure) stiffness; (d'attitude) rigidity, inflexibility.

roitelet /Rwatlɛ/ *nm* **1** (oiseau) goldcrest, firecrest; **2** (petit roi) kinglet.

rôle /Rol/ *nm* **1** Théât, Cin, TV, Radio, Danse part, role; **un ~ de figurant** a walk-on part; **un ~ de servante** a servant's part; **apprendre/savoir son ~** to learn/to know one's part; **le ~ d'Hamlet** the role of Hamlet; **premier ~** lead, leading role; **second ~** supporting part ou role; **avoir le premier ~** to have the leading role, to play the lead; **avec Grovagnard dans le ~ de Zorro** with Grovagnard as Zorro ou in the role of Zorro; **~ de composition** character part; **distribuer les ~s** to do the casting; **tu n'es pas très crédible dans le ~ du père autoritaire** you are not very convincing when you try to come the heavy-handed father; **2** (fonction) gén role; (d'organe, de cœur, rein) function, role; **réduire le ~ de l'État** to reduce the role of the state; **renverser les ~s** to reverse roles; **le ~ de l'adverbe/de la ponctuation dans la phrase** the role of the adverb/of punctuation marks in the sentence; **le ~ de qn dans une affaire** sb's role ou part in an affair; **le comité/l'organisme a pour ~ de faire** the role of the committee/the organization is to do; **jouer un grand ~** or **un ~ important dans** to play a large ou major part ou role in; **les membres de l'organisation auront un ~ d'observateurs** the members of the organization will act as observers; **faire qch à tour de ~** to take it in turns to do sth, to do sth in turn; **faire la vaisselle à tour de ~** to take it in turns to do the washing up GB ou the dishes; **3** Jur (feuillet) roll; (registre) register.
■ **~ d'équipage** Naut muster roll.
IDIOMES **avoir** or **tenir le beau ~**○ to have the easy job.

rôle-titre, *pl* **rôles-titres** /RoltitR/ *nm* title role.

rollmops /Rɔlmɔps/ *nm inv* rollmop.

ROM /Rɔm/ *nf* (*abbr* = **read only memory**) ROM.

romain, ~e /Rɔmɛ̃, ɛn/ **I** *adj* **1** ▶ **857** (de la Rome moderne ou ancienne) Roman; **2** Relig **l'Église ~e** the Roman Catholic Church, the Church of Rome; **3** Imprim **caractères ~s** roman typeface.
II romaine *nf* **1** (salade) cos lettuce, romaine lettuce US; **2** (balance) steelyard.
IDIOMES **être bon comme la ~e** to be soft○ ou gullible.

Romain, ~e /Rɔmɛ̃, ɛn/ ▶ **857** *nm,f* Roman; ▶ **travail**[1].

romaïque /Rɔmaik/ ▶ **462** *adj, nm* Ling Romaic, Demotic.

roman, ~e /Rɔmɑ̃, an/ **I** *adj* **1** Archit Romanesque; (en Angleterre) Norman; **2** Ling [*langue*] Romance (*épith*).
II *nm* **1** (œuvre en prose) novel; **un ~ de Zola** a novel by Zola; **je ne lis jamais de ~s** I never read novels ou fiction; **on se croirait en plein ~** it's like something out of a novel; **sa vie est un vrai ~** his life is like something out of a novel; **ça n'existe que dans les ~s** that only happens in books; **c'est tout un ~** (c'est long, compliqué) it's a real saga; ▶ **nouveau**; **2** (genre) **le ~** the novel; **3** (œuvre du Moyen Âge) romance; **~ courtois** courtly romance; **4** Archit **le ~** the Romanesque; **5** ▶ **462** Ling **le ~ (commun)** late vulgar Latin.
■ **~ d'amour** love story, romance; **~ d'analyse** psychological novel; **~ d'anticipation** (œuvre) science fiction novel; (genre) science fiction; **~ d'aventures** adventure story; **~ de cape et d'épée** swashbuckling historical romance; **~ à clé** roman à clef; **~ épistolaire** epistolary novel; **~ d'épouvante** horror story; **~ d'espionnage** spy novel; **le ~ d'évasion** escapist fiction; **~ de gare** airport novel; **~ historique** historical novel; **~ par lettres** = **~ épistolaire**; **~ de mœurs** novel of manners; **~ noir** roman noir, crime novel; **~ policier** whodunnit, detective story; **~ de science-fiction** science fiction novel; **~ de série noire** thriller; **~ social** sociological novel; **~ à thèse** philosophical novel; **~ à tiroirs** episodic novel.

romance /Rɔmɑ̃s/ *nf* **1** (chanson) love song; **2** Littérat romance.

romancer /Rɔmɑ̃se/ [12] *vtr* **1** (déformer) to romanticize; **2** (présenter sous forme de roman) to fictionalize; **vie romancée de Mandrin** fictionalized account of the life of Mandrin.

romanche /Rɔmɑ̃ʃ/ ▶ **462** *nm, adj* Ling Romans(c)h.

romancier, -ière /Rɔmɑ̃sje, ɛR/ ▶ **510** *nm,f* novelist.

romand, ~e /Rɔmɑ̃, ɑ̃d/ ▶ **462** *adj* French-speaking.

Romand, ~e /Rɔmɑ̃, ɑ̃d/ *nm,f* French-speaking Swiss.

romanesque /Rɔmanɛsk/ **I** *adj* **1** (pas terre à terre) [*personne*] romantic; [*situation, histoire*] like something out of a novel; **2** Littérat [*récit, texte*] fictional; **la technique ~** the technique of the novel; **c'est une œuvre ~** it's a work of fiction, it's a novel; **l'œuvre ~ de Balzac** Balzac's novels.
II *nm* **1** (genre) **le ~** fiction; **2** (caractère) **le ~ d'une situation** the fantastical aspect of a situation.

roman-feuilleton, *pl* **romans-feuilletons** /Rɔmɑ̃fœjtɔ̃/ *nm* serial.

roman-fleuve, *pl* **romans-fleuves** /Rɔmɑ̃flœv/ *nm* roman-fleuve, saga.

romanichel, -elle /Rɔmaniʃɛl/ *nm,f* **1** (tzigane) offensive Romany, gypsy; **2** (vagabond) pej tramp.

romanisant, ~e /Rɔmanizɑ̃, ɑ̃t/ **I** *adj* **1** [*église*] Romanistic; **2** Ling [*étudiant*] specializing in Romance languages (*épith, après n*).
II *nm,f* (expert) specialist in Romance languages; (étudiant) student of Romance languages.

romaniser /Rɔmanize/ [1] *vtr* to Romanize.

romaniste /Rɔmanist/ *nmf* **1** Relig Romanist; **2** Ling specialist in Romance languages; **3** Art Romanist.

romano○ /Rɔmano/ *nmf* offensive gypsy.

roman-photo, *pl* **romans-photos** /Rɔmɑ̃foto/ *nm* photo-story.

romantique /Rɔmɑ̃tik/ *adj, nmf* romantic.

romantisme /Rɔmɑ̃tism/ *nm* **1** Art, Littérat, Mus (genre) Romanticism; **2** (sentimentalisme) romanticism.

romarin /RɔmaRɛ̃/ *nm* rosemary.

rombière◑ /Rɔ̃bjɛR/ *nf* pej **une vieille ~** an old bag○.

Rome /Rɔm/ ▶ **857** *npr* Rome.
IDIOMES **tous les chemins mènent à ~** Prov all roads lead to Rome Prov; **~ ne s'est pas faite en un jour** Prov Rome wasn't built in a day Prov.

roméique /ʀɔmeik/ *adj, nm* = **romaïque**.

rompre /ʀɔ̃pʀ/ [53] **I** *vtr* **1** (faire cesser) to break [*monotonie, charme, liens*]; to break off [*négociation, fiançailles, relation, conversation*]; to upset [*équilibre*]; to disrupt [*harmonie*]; to end [*isolement, logique infernale*]; to break up [*unité, complicité*]; to interrupt [*uniformité*]; **2** (cesser de respecter) to break [*contrat, accord, jeûne, silence, trêve*]; **3** (casser) to break [*branche, pain, digue*]; to break through [*ligne ennemie, barrage, cordon policier*]; **~ les rangs** to fall out; **rompez (les rangs)!** fall out!; **4** liter (habituer) **~ qn à/à faire** to train sb to/to do; **~ un soldat au maniement des armes** to accustom a soldier to handling arms.
II *vi* **1** (en finir) **~ avec** to break with [*habitude, tradition, doctrine*]; to make a break from [*passé*]; to break away from [*parti, milieu*]; to break up with [*fiancé*]; **2** Pol (interrompre les relations) **~ avec** to break away from; **~ avec Damas/un parti** to break away from Damascus/a party; **3** (se séparer) to break up; **ils ont rompu** they've broken up; **~ avec qn** to break up with sb; **elle a rompu avec lui** she's broken up with him; **ils ont rompu trois jours avant le mariage** they broke up three days before the wedding; **4†** (casser) to break; **la corde a rompu** the rope broke; **5** Sport (en escrime) to break.
III se rompre *vpr* **1** (se casser) [*corde, branche, axe*] to break; [*harmonie*] to be disrupted; **2†** (se fracturer) [*jambe, tibia*] to break.

rompu, **~e** /ʀɔ̃py/ **I** *pp* ▶ **rompre**.
II *pp adj* liter (habitué) **~ à** well accustomed to; **diplomate ~ aux négociations** diplomat well accustomed to negotiations; **~ aux techniques modernes** well-versed in modern techniques.
III *adj* (fatigué) **~ (de fatigue)** worn-out.

romsteck /ʀɔmstɛk/ *nm* rump steak.

ronce /ʀɔ̃s/ *nf* **1** (plante, tige) bramble; **2** (nœud du bois) burr; **~ de noyer** burr walnut.

ronceraie /ʀɔ̃sʀɛ/ *nf* bramble patch.

ronchon○, **-onne** /ʀɔ̃ʃɔ̃, ɔn/ **I** *adj* grouchy○, grumpy○.
II *nm,f* grouch○, grump○.

ronchonnement○ /ʀɔ̃ʃɔnmɑ̃/ *nm* grumbling ¢, grousing○ ¢.

ronchonner○ /ʀɔ̃ʃɔne/ [1] *vi* to grumble (**après** about), to grouse○ (**après** about).

ronchonneur○, **-euse** /ʀɔ̃ʃɔnœʀ, øz/ **I** *adj* grouchy○, grumpy○.
II *nm,f* grouch○, grump○.

rond, **~e** /ʀɔ̃, ʀɔ̃d/ **I** *adj* **1** gén [*objet, table, trou, chapeau, tête, œil*] round; [*tube, bâtiment*] circular; [*plat*] round, circular; [*écriture, lettres*] rounded; [*bras, mollet, ventre, cuisse, menton*] rounded; [*seins*] full; [*visage*] round; [*personne*] tubby; **un petit nez ~** a button nose; **un bébé tout ~** a chubby baby; **elle se trouve trop ~e** euph she thinks she's too fat; **2** (net) [*nombre, chiffre*] round; **un compte ~** a round sum; **ça fait trois cents francs tout ~** that's three hundred francs exactly; **elle a sept ans tout ~** she's seven years old exactly; **3**○ (ivre) drunk; **4** Vin [*vin*] round.
II *nm* **1** (cercle) circle; **tracer un ~** to draw a circle; **danser en ~** to dance (round) in a circle; **s'asseoir en ~** to sit in a circle ou ring; **faire des ~s de fumée** to blow smoke rings; **faire des ~s dans l'eau** lit to make ripples in the water; **un ~ de lumière** a patch of light; ▶ **baver**; **2**○ (argent) **ils ont des ~s** they're rich, they're loaded○; **n'avoir plus un ~** to be broke○; **tu as assez de ~s?** have you got enough dough○?; **coûter des ~s** to cost a bundle○!; **3** Culin (morceau de bœuf) round steak; **4** (tranche) slice.
III ronde *nf* **1** Danse, Mus round dance; **faire une ~e** to make ou form a circle; **entrer dans la ~e** lit, fig to join the dance; **2** (va-et-vient) **la ~e des voitures sur la place de la Concorde/le circuit** the cars whirling round Place de la Concorde/the circuit; **la ~e des notes de service dans un bureau** memos going the rounds in an office; **la ~e des saisons** the passing of the seasons; **3** (inspection) (de policiers) patrol; (de soldats, gardiens) watch; **faire sa ~e** to be on patrol ou watch; **4** Mus (note) semibreve GB, whole note US; **5** (écriture arrondie) roundhand.
IV à la ronde *loc adv* **1** (autour) around; **toutes les cloches à la ~e sonnaient** all the bells were ringing for miles around; **on entendait le bruit à trois kilomètres à la ~e** you could hear the noise three kilometres[GB] away; **2** (ici et là) around; **offrir des gâteaux à la ~e** to pass some cakes around.
■ **~ à béton** Constr reinforcing bar; **~ de jambe** Danse rond de jambe; **faire des ~s de jambe à qn** fig to be overly polite to sb; **~ de serviette** napkin ring; **~ de sorcière** fairy ring.
IDIOMES **être ~ en affaires**○ to be honest, to be on the level○; **ouvrir des yeux ~s** to be wide-eyed with astonishment; **être ~ comme une barrique** or **queue de pelle** or **un petit pois** to be blind drunk○.

rond-de-cuir, *pl* **ronds-de-cuir** /ʀɔ̃dkɥiʀ/ *nm* penpusher GB, pencil pusher US.

rondeau, *pl* **~x** /ʀɔ̃do/ *nm* Littérat, Mus rondeau.

ronde-bosse, *pl* **rondes-bosses** /ʀɔ̃d bɔs/ *nf* sculpture in the round.

rondel /ʀɔ̃dɛl/ *nm* Littérat rondel.

rondelet○, **-ette** /ʀɔ̃dlɛ, ɛt/ *adj* [*personne*] plump, tubby○; [*visage*] chubby; **une somme rondelette** quite a tidy○ sum.

rondelle /ʀɔ̃dɛl/ *nf* **1** (tranche ronde) slice; **un Perrier® ~**○ a Perrier® with a slice of lemon; **couper en ~s** to slice up; **je vais te couper en ~s**○ fig I'm going to wring your neck; **2** Tech washer; **~ d'étanchéité/de serrage/à ressort** seal/clamping/spring washer.

rondement /ʀɔ̃dmɑ̃/ *adv* **1** (avec efficacité) promptly; **mener ~ une affaire** to get something done fast; **elle mène ses affaires ~** she gets things done; **2**○ (généreusement) **être payé ~** to be well paid.

rondeur /ʀɔ̃dœʀ/ *nf* **1** (de corps) (de mollet, genou) roundness; (de bras, sein) curve; **~s féminines** womanly curves; **~s enfantines** puppy fat ¢; **2** (de caractère) openness; **avec ~** (franchement) frankly; **3** Vin roundness.

rondin /ʀɔ̃dɛ̃/ *nm* log; **cabane en ~s** log cabin.

rondo /ʀɔ̃do/ *nm* Mus rondo.

rondouillard○, **~e** /ʀɔ̃dujaʀ, aʀd/ **I** *adj* tubby○, podgy○ GB, pudgy○ US.
II *nm,f* tubby man/woman.

rond-point, *pl* **ronds-points** /ʀɔ̃pwɛ̃/ *nm* roundabout GB, traffic circle US.

ronéo® /ʀɔneo/ *nf* Roneo®.

ronéoter○ /ʀɔneɔte/, **ronéotyper** /ʀɔneɔtipe/ [1] *vtr* to duplicate, to Roneo®.

ronflant, **~e** /ʀɔ̃flɑ̃, ɑ̃t/ *adj* **1** [*poêle*] roaring; **2** [*style*] high-flown; [*discours*] grandiloquent; [*promesse*] fine-sounding.

ronflement /ʀɔ̃fləmɑ̃/ *nm* **1** (de dormeur) snore; **2** (de chaudière, poêle) roar ¢; (moins fort) purr ¢; (de moteur) purr ¢; (de petit avion) drone.

ronfler /ʀɔ̃fle/ [1] *vi* **1** (faire un bruit) [*dormeur*] to snore; [*chaudière, poêle*] to roar; (moins fort) to purr; [*moteur*] to purr; **2**○ (dormir) to be fast asleep, to be out for the count○.
IDIOMES **~ comme une toupie** or **un orgue** or **un sonneur** to snore like a pig.

ronflette○ /ʀɔ̃flɛt/ *nf* snooze○; **faire** or **piquer**○ **une ~** to have a snooze○.

ronfleur, **-euse** /ʀɔ̃flœʀ, øz/ *nm,f* **1** (personne) (qui ronfle) snorer; **2**○ (qui aime dormir) great sleeper; **3** (de téléphone) electric buzzer.

ronger /ʀɔ̃ʒe/ [13] **I** *vtr* **1** (grignoter) [*souris, chien*] to gnaw [*fromage, os*]; [*vers*] to eat into [*bois*]; [*chenille*] to eat away, to nibble [*feuilles*]; **table rongée par les vers** worm-eaten table; **2** (attaquer) [*eau, acide, rouille*] to erode, to eat away at; **3** fig [*maladie, querelles*] to wear down [*personne*]; **il est rongé par la maladie** he's wasted by illness, his illness is wearing him down; **4** (mordiller) to chew, to nibble; [*personne*] to pick [*os*].
II se ronger *vpr* **se ~ les ongles** to bite one's nails.
IDIOMES **se ~ les sangs** to worry oneself sick.

rongeur /ʀɔ̃ʒœʀ/ *nm* rodent.

ronron○ /ʀɔ̃ʀɔ̃/ *nm* (*also onomat*) **1** (de chat) purr, purring ¢; **faire ~** to purr; **2** (de moteur) purring ¢; **3** (routine) **le ~ de la vie quotidienne** the humdrum routine of daily life.

ronronnement /ʀɔ̃ʀɔnmɑ̃/ *nm* (de chat, moteur) purring ¢.

ronronner /ʀɔ̃ʀɔne/ [1] *vi* [*chat, moteur*] to purr; **~ de plaisir** [*chat*] to purr with pleasure; fig [*auditeurs*] to purr positively.

roque /ʀɔk/ *nm* (aux échecs) **1** (tour) rook, castle; **2** (action) castling; **grand/petit ~** castling long/short.

roquer /ʀɔke/ [1] *vi* Jeux **1** (aux échecs) to castle; **2** (au croquet) to roquet.

roquet /ʀɔkɛ/ *nm* **1** (chien) yappy little dog; **2** (personne) bad-tempered little runt.

roquette /ʀɔkɛt/ *nf* Mil rocket.

rosace /ʀozas/ *nf* (figure géométrique) rosette; (vitrail) rose window; (au plafond) rose.

rosacé, **~e** /ʀozase/ **I** *adj* Bot rosaceous.
II rosacée *nf* **1** Méd (couperose) rosacea; **2** Bot rosaceous plant; **les ~s** Rosaceae.

rosaire /ʀozɛʀ/ *nm* (chapelet, prières) rosary; **réciter son ~** to say one's rosary.

rosat /ʀoza/ *adj inv* Pharm rose (*épith*); **pommade ~** lip salve.

rosâtre /ʀozɑtʀ/ ▶ **193** *adj* pinkish.

rosbif /ʀɔsbif/ *nm* **1** (viande) (crue) joint of beef GB, roast of beef US; (cuite) roast beef; **2**○ †injur (Anglais) Englishman.

rose /ʀoz/ ▶ **193** **I** *adj* **1** (couleur) [*tissu, peinture*] pink; **~ pâle/vif/clair/foncé** pale/bright/light/dark pink; **vieux ~** dusty pink, old rose; **des tons ~ pâle** pale pink tones ou shades; **marbre/granit/pierre ~** pink marble/granite/stone; **2** (indiquant une bonne santé) rosy; **il a les joues toutes ~s** his cheeks are pink ou rosy.
II *nm* (couleur) pink; **le ~ te va si bien** pink really suits you; **les rideaux étaient d'un joli ~** the curtains were a lovely pink.
III *nf* **1** Bot rose; **~ artificielle/en soie/en papier** artificial/silk/paper rose; **confiture de ~** rose jam; **essence de ~** attar of roses; **2** (vitrail) rose window; **3** (en bijouterie) **diamant en ~** rose diamond.
■ **~ bonbon** candy pink; **~ d'Inde** African marigold; **~ indien** Indian rose; **~ de Jéricho** rose of Jericho, resurrection plant; **~ musquée** musk rose; **~ de Noël** Christmas rose; **~ pompon** button rose; **~ des sables** Minér gypsum flower; **~ trémière** hollyhock; **~ des vents** compass rose.
IDIOMES **ce n'est pas (tout) ~** it's not all roses, it's not roses all the way; **la vie n'est pas ~** life isn't a bed of roses; **voir la vie en ~** to see life through rose-coloured[GB] spectacles; **il n'y a pas de ~ sans épines** Prov there is no rose without a thorn; **envoyer qn sur les ~s**○ to send sb packing○; **découvrir le pot aux ~s** to find out what is going on.

rosé, **~e** /ʀoze/ **I** ▶ **193** *adj* pinkish.
II *nm* Vin rosé; **boire du ~** to drink rosé.
III rosée *nf* dew; **humide de ~e** [*herbe, fleur, nature*] covered with dew; [*objet, vêtement*] wet with dew.

roseau, *pl* **~x** /ʀozo/ *nm* Bot reed.

rose-croix /ROZKRWA/ *nm inv* Rosicrucian.
Rose-Croix /ROZKRWA/ *nf* (confrérie) **la ~** the Rosicrucians (*pl*).
roséole /ROZEOl/ ▶271 *nf* roseola.
roseraie /ROZRE/ *nf* rose garden.
rose-thé, *pl* **roses-thé** /ROzte/ *nf* Bot tea rose.
rosette /ROZEt/ *nf* **1** (ornement) rosette; **2** (nœud) bow; **3** (décoration) rosette; **avoir la ~** to have been awarded the order of the Legion of Honour[GB]; **4** Culin **~ (de Lyon)** rosette, slicing sausage.
rosicrucien, **-ienne** /ROZIKRYSJẼ, En/ Relig *adj, nm,f* Rosicrucian.
rosier /ROZje/ *nm* Bot rosebush, rose; **~ grimpant/nain** climbing/dwarf rose.
rosière /ROZJER/ *nf: young girl recognized for her virtue.*
rosiériste /ROZIeRist/ ▶510 *nmf* rose grower.
rosir /ROZIR/ [3] **I** *vtr* to turn [sth] pink.
II *vi* [*ciel, neige, paysage*] to turn pink; [*visage, personne*] to go pink.
rosse○ /ROS/ **I** *adj* [*professeur, critique, action*] mean; [*imitateur, chansonnier, humour*] nasty; **c'est ~ ce que tu m'as fait** that was a mean thing to do to me.
II *nf* **1** (cheval) nag○; **2** (personne) heel○, meanie○.
rossée○ /ROSE/ *nf* thrashing○.
rosser○ /ROSe/ [1] *vtr* **1** (battre) to beat [sb/ sth] up○ [*personne, animal*]; **se faire ~** to get beaten up○; **2** (vaincre) to thrash○ [*équipe, armée*].
rosserie /ROSRI/ *nf* **1** (parole) nasty remark; (action) mean trick; **2** (caractère) (de professeur, d'entraîneur) meanness; (d'imitateur, de chansonnier) nastiness; **il est d'une ~ incroyable** he's incredibly mean ou nasty.
rossignol /ROSiɲOl/ *nm* **1** (oiseau) nightingale; **avoir une voix de ~** to have the voice of a nightingale; **2**○ (de cambrioleur) picklock; **3**○ (marchandise invendable) bit of junk.
rostre /ROStR/ **I** *nm* **1** Naut ram, rostrum; **2** Zool rostrum.
II rostres *nmpl* Antiq (tribune) **les ~s** the rostrum (*sg*).
rot○ /RO/ *nm* burp○; **faire un ~** to burp○; **faire faire son ~ à un bébé** to wind ou burp a baby.
rôt† /RO/ *nm* Culin roast.
rotarien, **-ienne** /ROtARJẼ, En/ *adj, nm,f* Rotarian.
rotatif, **-ive** /ROtatif, iv/ **I** *adj* rotary.
II rotative *nf* Imprim rotary press.
rotation /ROtasjɔ̃/ *nf* **1** (mouvement sur soi) rotation; **~ autour d'un axe** rotation on an axis; **~ de la Terre autour de l'axe des pôles** rotation of the Earth on the Polar axis; **mouvement de ~** rotational movement; **effectuer une ~ complète** to rotate fully; **2** (voyage) round trip; (fréquence des voyages) round trip service; Mil, Aviat, Naut turnaround; **cet avion effectue 3 ~s par semaines** this plane does 3 round trips a week; **la ~ des avions sur une base aérienne** the turnaround of planes on an air base; **3** (de locataire, clients) turnover; (d'équipe, de pharmacien, médecin, tâche) rotation; (de stock) turnover; **système de ~** rota system; **4** Agric rotation; **~ des cultures** crop rotation.
rotatoire /ROtatwAR/ *adj* rotary.
roter○ /ROte/ [1] *vtr* to burp○, to belch.
rôti, **~e** /ROti/ **I** *pp* ▶ **rôtir**.
II *pp adj* Culin [*poulet, oie, lapin*] roast (*épith*).
III *nm* **1** (avant la cuisson) joint; **acheter un ~ de porc** to buy a joint of pork; **un ~ de veau de 2 kg** a 2 kg joint of veal; **2** (après la cuisson) roast; **du ~ de bœuf** roast beef; **un ~ de bœuf** a joint of roast beef.
IV rôtie *nf* dial, C piece of toast.
rotin /ROtẼ/ *nm* (matériau) rattan; **fauteuil de** or **en ~** rattan chair.
rôtir /ROtIR/ [3] **I** *vtr* Culin to roast [*viande*]; to toast, to grill [*pain, tartine*]; **faire ~** to roast [*viande*]; to toast, to grill [*pain, tartine*].
II *vi* **1** Culin to roast; **mettre un poulet à ~ au four** to put a chicken in the oven to roast; **2**○ (être exposé au soleil) to roast; **se faire ~ les pieds au soleil** to roast one's feet in the sun; **3**○ (subir une forte chaleur) [*personne*] to roast, to be roasting.
III se rôtir *vpr* **1** Culin to be roasted; **2**○ (s'exposer à la chaleur) to roast (oneself), to toast (oneself); **se ~ les pieds** to roast ou toast one's feet.
IDIOMES **il attend que ça lui tombe tout rôti dans le bec** he expects things to fall into his lap.
rôtisserie /ROtisRI/ *nf* rotisserie.
rôtisseur, **-euse** /ROtisœR, øz/ ▶510 *nm,f* (boutique, restaurant) seller of roast meat.
rôtissoire /ROtiswAR/ *nf* rotisserie, roasting spit.
rotonde /ROtɔ̃d/ *nf* **1** Archit (édifice) rotunda; **2** (dans un bus) back seat; **3** Rail roundhouse.
rotondité /ROtɔ̃dite/ *nf* (caractère) roundness.
rotor /ROtOR/ *nm* Électrotech, Aviat rotor.
rotule /ROtyl/ *nf* **1** Anat kneecap, patella spéc; **2** Tech ball-and-socket joint.
IDIOMES **être sur les ~s**○ to be on one's last legs; **mettre qn sur les ~s**○ to wear sb out○.
rotulien, **-ienne** /ROtyljẼ, En/ *adj* patellar; **réflexe ~** knee jerk, patellar reflex spéc.
roture /ROtyR/ *nf* **1** Hist (classe) common people, commoners; **2** (condition) common birth.
roturier, **-ière** /ROtyRje, ER/ **I** *adj* fig [*manières, langage*] common péj; Hist **la classe roturière** the common people.
II *nm,f* Hist commoner.
rouage /RWaʒ/ *nm* **1** (de machine, d'horlogerie) wheel; **les ~s** the parts ou works; **2** (d'État, d'administration) machinery ¢; **les ~s bureaucratiques** the wheels of bureaucracy; **être un ~ parmi d'autres** to be a cog in a machine; **n'être qu'un des ~s** to be a tiny cog in the machine.
Rouanda /RWɑ̃da/ ▶321 *nprm* Rwanda.
roubignoles● /Rubiɲɔl/ *nfpl* balls●, testicles.
roublard○, **~e** /RublaR, aRd/ **I** *adj* crafty, cunning.
II *nm,f* crafty devil○; **ce ~ de Paul** that crafty devil Paul.
roublardise○ /RublaRdiz/ *nf* **1** (caractère) craftiness, cunning; **avec** or **par ~** by cunning; **2** (action) cunning trick.
rouble /Rubl/ ▶46 *nm* rouble.
roucoulades /Rukulad/ *nfpl* (d'oiseau) cooing¢; (de chanteur) crooning¢; (d'amoureux) billing and cooing ¢; (d'homme politique) soothing words.
roucoulement /Rukulmɑ̃/ *nm* **1** (d'oiseau) cooing ¢; **2**○ (d'amoureux) billing and cooing ¢; (mots tendres) murmuring ¢.
roucouler /Rukule/ [1] **I** *vtr* to croon [*chanson*]; to coo [*mots d'amour*].
II *vi* **1** [*oiseau*] to coo; **2** [*amoureux*] to bill and coo.
roudoudou /Rududu/ *nm: hard sweet* GB ou *candy* US *set in a small container*.
roue /Ru/ *nf* **1** (de véhicule, loterie, jeu) wheel; **changer la ~ d'une voiture** to change the wheel on a car; **un véhicule à quatre/deux ~s** a four-/two-wheel vehicle; **~ avant/arrière** front/back ou rear wheel; **~ de gouvernail** helm; **être ~(s) à ~(s)** or **~ dans ~** to be neck and neck; **sur** or **dans la ~ de qn** hot on sb's tail; **avoir une ~ à plat** to have a flat tyre GB ou tire US; ▶ **grand**; **2** (en gymnastique) cartwheel; **faire une ~** to do a cartwheel; **3** (dans un mécanisme) wheel; **~ dentée** cog ou toothed wheel; **~ de transmission** toothed gear ou wheel; **~ de friction** frictional wheel; **~ hydraulique** water wheel; **4** (supplice) **(le supplice de) la ~** the wheel.
■ **~ à aube** paddle wheel; **~ directrice** leading ou guiding wheel; **~ de la fortune** wheel of fortune; **~ de l'histoire** wheel of history; **~ d'impression** print wheel; **~ libre** freewheel; **être** or **pédaler en ~ libre** to freewheel; **descendre une côte en ~ libre** to freewheel down a hill; **~ motrice** driving wheel; **véhicule à 4 ~s motrices** four-wheel-drive vehicle; **~ de secours** spare wheel ou tyre GB ou tire US.
IDIOMES **être la cinquième** or **dernière ~ du carrosse** or **de la charrette** (inutile) to be superfluous; (de trop) to feel unwanted; **pousser qn à la ~** to be behind sb; **faire la ~** [*paon*] to spread its tail, to display; [*personne*] pej to strut ou parade around; (en gymnastique) to do a cartwheel.
roué, **~e** /Rwe/ **I** *adj* cunning.
II *nm,f* (personne rusée) pej cunning devil.
rouelle /RwEl/ *nf* round; **~ de veau/porc** round of veal/pork (*cut across the leg*).
Rouen /Rwɑ̃/ ▶857 *npr* Rouen.
rouennais, **~e** /RwanE, Ez/ ▶857 *adj* of Rouen.
Rouennais, **~e** /RwanE, Ez/ ▶857 *nm,f* (natif) native of Rouen; (habitant) inhabitant of Rouen.
rouer /Rwe/ [1] *vtr* **~ qn de coups** to beat sb up.
rouerie /RuRI/ *nf* **1** (caractère) cunning; **2** (action) cunning trick, trickery ¢; **être victime des ~s de qn** to be the victim of sb's trickery.
rouet /RwE/ *nm* (machine à filer) spinning wheel; **filer au ~** to spin.
rouflaquettes○ /RuflakEt/ *nfpl* sideburns, sideboards GB.
rouge /Ruʒ/ ▶193 **I** *adj* **1** [*objet, peinture, couleur*] red; **une robe ~** a red dress; **2** [*personne, visage, joue*] (congestionné) red, flushed; (à cause du soleil, du froid) red; **elle était toute ~ d'avoir couru** she was flushed ou red in the face from having run; **avoir le teint ~** to have a high colour[GB]; **il avait les yeux ~** his eyes were red; **~ de honte/colère** red with shame/fury; **3** (roux) [*cheveux, barbe*] red, ginger; [*pelage*] ginger; **4** (porté à incandescence) [*charbon, braise, tison, fer*] red-hot; **les braises sont encore ~s** the embers are still glowing; **5** Pol (communiste) Red; **banlieue ~** Red suburb (*area of a city with a communist-controlled administration*).
II *nmf* Pol (communiste) Red.
III *adv* **voter ~**○ to vote communist.
IV *nm* **1** (couleur) red; **peindre qch en ~** to paint sth red; **le ~ ne lui va pas** red doesn't suit him/her; **~ clair/vif/foncé** light/bright/dark red; **sa robe était d'un ~ magnifique** her dress was a wonderful red colour[GB]; **toute la gamme des ~s** the whole range of reds; **s'habiller en ~** to dress in red; **porter du ~** to wear red; **2** (matière colorante) red; **les ~s organiques** natural red dyes; **les ~s d'origine végétale** reds of plant origin; **3** Cosmét (fard) **~ à joues** blusher, rouge†; (pour lèvres) **~ à lèvres** lipstick ; **un tube de ~ à lèvres** a lipstick; **4** Aut, Transp red; **le feu est au ~** the lights are red, the (traffic) light is red; **passer au ~** to jump the lights GB ou a red light; **5** (dû à l'incandescence) **chauffer** or **porter un fer au ~** to heat a piece of iron until it is red hot; **un fer porté au ~** a red-hot iron; **6** (coloration) **le ~ lui monta au visage** he/she went red in the face; **le ~ de la honte/colère** flush of shame/anger; **7**○ Vin red (wine); **préférer le blanc au ~** to prefer white (wine) to red; **gros ~ (qui tache)**○ cheap red wine, red plonk○ GB; **un coup de ~**○ a glass of red wine; **8** Compta, Fin, Ind red; **être dans le ~** to be in the red; **sortir du ~** to get out of the red.
■ **~ brique** brick red; **~ cardinal**

cardinal red; **~ cerise** cherry red; **~ sang** blood red.

IDIOMES **être ~ comme une tomate** or **un coq** or **une écrevisse** or **un coquelicot** (de timidité, honte) to be as red as a beetroot GB ou a beet US; (après avoir couru) to be red in the face; **voir ~** to see red.

rougeâtre /ʀuʒɑtʀ/ ▶ **193** *adj* reddish.

rougeaud, ~e /ʀuʒo, od/ **I** *adj* [*personne*] ruddy-faced, ruddy-cheeked; [*visage, teint*] ruddy.

II *nm,f* ruddy-faced ou ruddy-cheeked person.

rouge-gorge, *pl* **rouges-gorges** /ʀuʒgɔʀʒ/ *nm* robin (redbreast).

rougeoiement /ʀuʒwamɑ̃/ *nm* (de soleil, ciel, d'incendie) red ou reddish glow.

rougeole /ʀuʒɔl/ ▶ **271** *nf* measles (+ *v sg*).

rougeoyant, ~e /ʀuʒwajɑ̃, ɑ̃t/ *adj* [*reflet*] reddish; [*ciel*] reddening (*épith*), glowing red (*jamais épith*).

rougeoyer /ʀuʒwaje/ [23] *vi* [*ciel*] to take on a red glow; [*soleil couchant*] to glow fiery red; [*feu*] to glow red.

rouge-queue, *pl* **rouges-queues** /ʀuʒkø/ *nm* Zool redstart.

rouget /ʀuʒɛ/ *nm* red mullet, goatfish US.

■ **~ barbet** striped mullet; **~ grondin** gurnard; **~ de roche** red mullet.

rougeur /ʀuʒœʀ/ *nf* **1** (couleur, teinte) redness; **2** (congestion) (due à la chaleur) redness, flushing; (due à l'émotion) flushing; (due au froid) redness; **3** (sur la peau) C red blotch.

rougir /ʀuʒiʀ/ [3] **I** *vtr* **1** (donner une teinte rouge) [*personne*] (avec du fard) to redden [*joues*]; to turn [sth] red, to redden [*arbres, feuilles*]; **le froid rougissait leur visage** the cold turned their faces red; **~ son eau** to put a little red wine in one's water; **~ la terre du sang de ses ennemis/de son sang** to make the earth run red with one's enemies'blood/with one's blood; **2** (porter à incandescence) to heat [sth] until it is red hot, to make [sth] red hot [*métal*]; **il a rougi une barre de fer** he heated an iron bar until it was red hot.

II *vi* **1** [*personne, visage*] (d'émotion) to blush, to go red (in the face) (**de** with); (de colère) to flush, to go red (in the face) (**de** with) ; [*personne, peau, visage, main*] (à cause du froid, de la chaleur) to go red, to turn red; **~de honte** to go red with shame, to blush with shame; **~ jusqu'aux yeux** or **jusqu'aux oreilles** to turn ou go as red as a beetroot GB ou a beet US, to turn ou go bright red; **~ jusqu'à la racine des cheveux** to blush to the roots of one's hair; **faire ~ qn** to make sb blush ou go red; **tu devrais ~ de tes mensonges** you ought to be ashamed of your lies; **il n'a pas à en ~** that's nothing for him to be ashamed of; **sans ~** without shame, without feeling ashamed; **ne ~ de rien** to be utterly shameless, to have no shame; **2** (mûrir) [*fruit, légume*] to go ou turn red, to redden; [*feuille, arbre, forêt*] to turn red, to redden; (à la cuisson) [*crustacé, homard, carapace*] to turn red; **3** (devenir incandescent) [*métal, tison*] to glow (red ou red hot); [*ciel*] to turn ou glow red.

rougissant, ~e /ʀuʒisɑ̃, ɑ̃t/ *adj* [*personne*] blushing; [*feuille, forêt, arbre, ciel*] reddening.

rougissement /ʀuʒismɑ̃/ *nm* (de personne) blushing ₵; **le ~ des feuilles** the reddening ou turning of the leaves.

rouille /ʀuj/ **I** ▶ **193** *adj inv* [*couleur, peinture*] red-brown, russet; [*vêtement, tissu*] red-brown, rust(-coloured[GB]).

II *nf* **1** Chimie, Bot rust; **2** Culin rouille (*garlic mayonnaise made with red chillies*).

rouillé, ~e /ʀuje/ **I** *pp* ▶ **rouiller**.

II *pp adj* **1** lit [*objet, fer*] rusty, rusted; Bot rusty; **2** (pas en forme) [*athlète*] out of practice; [*corps, muscle, membre*] stiff; [*esprit, mémoire*] rusty○, shaky; [*cerveau, personne*] rusty○; [*technique, pratique*] rusty; **je suis un peu ~** I'm a bit out of practice; **je suis un peu ~ en russe** my Russian's a bit rusty.

rouiller /ʀuje/ [1] **I** *vtr* **1** lit to rust, to make [sth] go rusty [*objet, fer*]; **2** fig to slow [sb] down [*personne*]; to make [sth] soft [*corps, muscle*]; to make [sth] shaky ou rusty [*mémoire*]; to dull, to blunt [*esprit*].

II *vi* [*fer*] to rust, to go rusty; **laisser qch ~** to let sth rust ou go rusty.

III se rouiller *vpr* [*personne*] to slow down; [*sportif*] to get out of shape; [*muscle, corps*] to lose tone; [*mémoire, esprit*] to get shaky ou rusty; [*pratique, connaissance*] to become ou get rusty.

rouir /ʀwiʀ/ [3] *vtr* to ret; **faire ~** to ret.

rouissage /ʀwisaʒ/ *nm* retting.

roulade /ʀulad/ *nf* **1** Culin (de viande) stuffed rolled meat; **~ de veau/porc** stuffed rolled veal/pork, veal/pork roulade; **2** Sport roll; **~ avant/arrière** forward/backward roll; **faire des ~s** to do rolls; **3** (de chanteur) roulade; (d'oiseau) trill, trilling ₵.

roulage /ʀulaʒ/ *nm* **1** Agric rolling; **2** Transp (road) haulage GB, trucking US.

roulant, ~e /ʀulɑ̃, ɑ̃t/ **I** *adj* **1** (monté sur roues) **table ~e** trolley GB, serving cart US; **matériel ~** Rail rolling stock; **2** Transp **personnel ~** (dans le train) train crew; (dans le bus) bus crew.

II○ *nm* Transp (dans le train) member of a train crew; (dans le bus) member of a bus crew.

III roulante *nf* Mil field kitchen.

roulé, ~e /ʀule/ **I** *pp* ▶ **rouler**.

II *pp adj* **1** Culin **épaule ~e** rolled shoulder; **2** Phon **r ~** rolled r; **3**◑ (parlant d'une femme) **être bien ~e** to be a nice bit of stuff◑ GB, to be a nice piece◑ US.

III *nm* Culin roll; **~ au chocolat/à la confiture** chocolate/jam roll; **~ au fromage/jambon** *puff pastry filled with cheese/ham.*

rouleau, *pl* **~x** /ʀulo/ *nm* **1** (cylindre) roll; **~ de papier hygiénique/d'essuie-tout/de papier peint** roll of toilet paper/of paper towels/of wallpaper; **ce papier peint fait 150 francs le ~** this wallpaper is 150 francs a roll; **j'ai besoin de trois ~x pour refaire la cuisine** I need three rolls to do ou paper the kitchen; **un ~ de parchemin/fil électrique/papier aluminium** a roll of parchment/electrical cable/tin foil; **un ~ de pièces de monnaie** a roll of coins; **se vendre au ~** to be sold by the roll; **acheter de la moquette en ~** to buy a roll of carpet; **le revêtement existe en dalles ou en ~** you can get this covering in tiles or in a roll; **2** (grosse vague) breaker, roller; **3** Imprim, Tech, Agric roller; **4** (bigoudi) roller, curler; **5** Sport **~ ventral** straddle (roll); **~ dorsal** flop; **sauter en ~** (en ventral) to straddle; (en dorsal) to flop; **6** (pour peindre) roller.

■ **~ compresseur** Tech roadroller, steamroller; fig steamroller; **~ à pâtisserie** Culin rolling pin; **étendre la pâte au ~** roll out the pastry with a rolling pin; **~ de peintre** Tech paintroller; **peindre le plafond au ~** to paint the ceiling with a roller; **~ de printemps** Culin spring roll.

IDIOMES **être au bout du ~**○ (nerveusement) to be at the end of one's tether; (être mourant) to be at death's door.

roulé-boulé, *pl* **roulés-boulés** /ʀulebule/ *nm* roll; **faire un ~** to do a roll.

roulement /ʀulmɑ̃/ *nm* **1** (bruit sourd) (du train, des voitures) rumble; **un ~ de tambour** or **batterie** a drum roll; **on entendait le ~ lointain des tambours** you could hear the distant roll of drums; **un ~ de tonnerre** a rumble of thunder; **entendre les ~s du tonnerre** to hear the rumble of thunder; **il y eut plusieurs ~s de tonnerre** there were several rumbles of thunder; **2** (mouvement circulaire) **avoir un ~ d'épaules/d'yeux** to roll one's shoulders/eyes; **3** Fin turnover; **4** (alternance) rotation; **travailler par ~** to work (in) shifts; **faire** or **établir un ~** to draw up a rota GB ou schedule; **5** Tech bearing; **les ~s sont usés** the bearings are worn (out); **~ à billes** Tech ball bearing.

rouler /ʀule/ [1] **I** *vtr* **1** (faire tourner) [*personne*] to roll [*tonneau, pneu, tronc d'arbre*]; **~ des troncs d'arbre dans une pente** to roll tree trunks down a slope; **~ des truffes dans du cacao/des boulettes dans la farine** to roll truffles in cocoa powder/meatballs in flour; **le fleuve roule ses eaux boueuses** the muddy waters of the river swirl along; **les vagues roulent les galets** the waves shift the pebbles around; **2** (pousser) to wheel [*charrette, brouette, chariot*]; **3** (mettre en rouleau) to roll up [*tapis, papier, sac de couchage, tente, pâte*]; to roll [*cigarette*]; to roll up [*manche, col, pantalon*]; **~ qch en boule** to roll [sth] up into a ball [*pull, écharpe, chemise*]; to roll [sth] into a ball [*pâte à modeler, glaise*]; **~ son pull en boule pour faire un oreiller** to roll one's sweater (up) into a ball to make a pillow; **~ qn dans** to roll sb up in [*couverture, drap, tapis*]; **tabac à ~** rolling tobacco; **machine à ~ (les cigarettes)** cigarette roller; **s'en ~ une**○ to roll oneself a fag○; **4** (mouvoir circulairement) **~ les** or **des épaules** to roll one's shoulders; **~ les** or **des hanches** to wiggle one's hips; **~ les** or **des yeux** to roll one's eyes; **~ des yeux furieux à qn** to give sb a furious look; **il m'a roulé de ces yeux**○**!** (de colère) he gave me a filthy look!; (de surprise) his eyes were popping out of his head!; **5** (aplanir) to roll [*champ, gazon, terrain de tennis*]; to roll out [*pâte à tarte*]; **6** Phon **~ les 'r'** to roll one's 'r's; **7**○ (berner) **~ qn**○ to diddle○ GB ou cheat sb; **elle m'a roulé en me rendant la monnaie** she diddled ou cheated me when she gave me the change; **se faire ~ de 3 francs** to be diddled ou cheated out of 3 francs.

II ▶ **860** *vi* **1** (se déplacer en tournant sur soi-même) [*boule, pièce, pierre, tronc, personne*] to roll; **le stylo a roulé par terre/sous le bureau** the pen rolled across the floor/under the desk; **~ dans le ravin** [*personne, véhicule*] to roll down into the ravine; **~ dans la boue/l'herbe** to roll in the mud/the grass; **faire ~ qn par terre/dans la poussière** to make sb roll on the ground/in the dust; **les cailloux roulent sous nos pieds** our feet slip on the loose stones; **faire ~ les dés** to roll the dice; ▶ **mousse**; **2** (avancer sur des roues) [*train, bus, voiture, bicyclette*] to go; **la voiture est accidentée mais elle roule encore** the car is damaged but still goes; **les bus ne roulent pas le dimanche** buses don't run on Sundays, there aren't any buses on Sundays; **ma voiture ne roule plus** my car won't go; **mon vélo roule mal** there's something wrong with my bike; **ma voiture n'a pas roulé depuis deux ans** my car hasn't been driven for two years; **~ à grande vitesse** [*voiture, train*] to travel at high speed; **~ au super/à l'ordinaire** [*voiture*] to run on 4-star GB ou premium US/2-star GB ou regular US; **ça roule bien/mal sur l'autoroute**○ the traffic is light/bad on the motorway GB ou freeway US; **ça roule** ○**!** fig (c'est entendu) it's a deal!; **3** (conduire) [*conducteur*] to drive (**en direction de, vers** toward, towards GB); **les Anglais roulent à gauche** the English drive on the left; **~ toute la nuit** to drive all night; **~ doucement/vite** to drive slowly/fast; **~ au pas/à toute vitesse** to drive very slowly/at top speed; **~ en voiture** to drive a car; **~ en moto/à bicyclette** to ride a motorbike/bicycle; **~ en Cadillac®** to drive a Cadillac®; **~ à 20 km/h** to drive at 20 kilometres[GB] per hour; **roulez jeunesse**○**!** let's go○!; **tout le monde est prêt? allez, roulez jeunesse!** is everyone ready? then let's hit the road!; **~ pour qn**○ (soutenir politiquement) to be in sb's camp, to support sb; ▶ **tombeau**; **4** (bouger) [*muscles*] to ripple; **faire ~ ses épaules** to roll one's shoulders; **faire ~ ses biceps/pecto-**

raux to flex one's biceps/pectorals; **5** Naut [*bateau*] to roll; **6** (se relayer) [*personnes, équipes*] to work in rotation ou shifts; **7** (faire un bruit sourd) [*tonnerre, détonation*] to rumble.

III se rouler *vpr* **1** (en étant allongé) **se ~ dans** [*personne, animal*] to roll in [*herbe, boue, foin*]; **se ~ par terre** lit [*enfant*] to roll (about) on the floor; fig (rire beaucoup) to fall about laughing; **une blague à se ~ par terre** a hilarious joke; **c'était à se ~ par terre** it was hilarious; **se ~ en boule** [*animal, personne*] to curl up in a ball (**sur** on; **dans** in); **2** (s'envelopper dans) **se ~ dans** to wrap oneself in [*couverture, drap, manteau*]; **il dormait roulé dans une vieille couverture** he was sleeping wrapped in an old blanket.

IDIOMES **~ une pelle** or **un patin à qn●** to give sb a French kiss; **~ sous la table○** to be under the table; **~ la caisse** or **les** or **des mécaniques○** to swagger along.

roulette /ʀulɛt/ *nf* **1** (petite roue) caster; **table/lit à ~s** table/bed on casters; **2** ▶ 449 Jeux roulette; **à la ~** at roulette; **jouer à la roulette** to play roulette; **3** Dent (dentist's) drill; **4** Culin pastry wheel; Cout tracing wheel; **5** (en reliure) fillet.

■ **~ russe** Russian roulette.

IDIOMES **aller** or **marcher comme sur des ~s** to go smoothly ou like a dream.

rouleur, **-euse** /ʀulœʀ, øz/ *nm,f* cyclist; **c'est un bon ~** he's strong on the flat.

roulier /ʀulje/ *nm* **1** (navire) roll-on roll-off ship; **2** (voiturier) carter.

roulis /ʀuli/ *nm* (de bateau) rolling; (de voiture, train) swaying; **il y avait du ~** the ship was rolling.

roulotte /ʀulɔt/ *nf* (horse-drawn) caravan GB, trailer US.

roulotter /ʀulɔte/ [1] *vtr* Cout to roll a hem on [*tissu*]; to roll [*ourlet*].

roulure◑ /ʀulyʀ/ *nf* offensive slut◑ injur.

roumain, **~e** /ʀumɛ̃, ɛn/ **I** ▶ 537 *adj* Romanian.

II ▶ 462 *nm* Ling Romanian.

Roumain, **~e** /ʀumɛ̃, ɛn/ ▶ 537 *nm,f* Romanian.

Roumanie /ʀumani/ ▶ 321 *nprf* Romania.

round /ʀund, ʀawnd/ *nm* (tous contextes) round.

roupettes◑ /ʀupɛt/ *nfpl* balls◑, testicles.

roupie /ʀupi/ ▶ 46 *nf* rupee.

IDIOMES **c'est de la ~ de sansonnet** it's a load of rubbish○; **ce n'est pas de la ~ de sansonnet○** it's not just any old rubbish○.

roupiller○ /ʀupije/ [1] *vtr* to sleep.

roupillon○ /ʀupijɔ̃/ *nm* snooze○, nap; **piquer** or **faire un ~** to have a snooze○, to take a nap.

rouquin○, **~e** /ʀukɛ̃, in/ **I** *adj* [*personne*] red-haired; [*cheveux*] red.

II *nm,f* redhead.

III *nm* (vin) plonk○ GB, cheap red wine.

rouscailler○ /ʀuskɑje/ [1] *vi* to gripe○.

rouspétance○ /ʀuspetɑ̃s/ *nf* griping○.

rouspéter○ /ʀuspete/ [14] *vi* to grumble (**contre** about; **après** at).

rouspéteur○, **-euse** /ʀuspetœʀ, øz/ **I** *adj* **il est un peu ~** he's a bit of a grumbler.

II *nm,f* grumbler.

roussâtre /ʀusɑtʀ/ ▶ 193 *adj* [*pelage, terre, feuillage*] reddish.

rousse /ʀus/ *adj* ▶ **roux** I, II.

rousseauiste /ʀusoist/ *adj, nmf* Rousseauist.

rousserolle /ʀusʀɔl/ *nf* **~ effarvatte** reed warbler.

roussette /ʀusɛt/ *nf* **1** (poisson) spotted dogfish; **2** (chauve-souris) flying fox.

rousseur /ʀusœʀ/ *nf* (de cheveux, barbe) redness; (de feuille, d'arbre) brownness, redness; (de teinte, ton) russet colour[GB].

roussi /ʀusi/ *nm* **une odeur de ~** a slight smell of burning; **ça sent le ~** lit it smells of burning; fig○ there's trouble brewing.

roussir /ʀusiʀ/ [3] **I** *vtr* **1** (colorer) littér [*automne*] to turn [sth] brown ou red [*feuille*]; [*tabac*] to turn [sth] brown [*papier, moustache*]; [*soleil*] to turn [sth] yellow [*papier*]; **2** (brûler) [*fer à repasser, chaleur, soleil*] to scorch; [*flamme*] to singe.

II *vi* **1** [*forêt, feuille, arbre*] to go brown ou red; [*cheveux, barbe, moustache*] to go brown; [*papier, tissu*] to go yellow; **2** Culin **faire ~** to brown [*oignon, viande, beurre*].

roustons◑ /ʀustɔ̃/ *nmpl* balls◑, testicles.

routage /ʀutaʒ/ *nm* **1** (de journaux, colis) sorting and mailing; **société de ~** mailing house; **2** Ordinat routing.

routard○, **~e** /ʀutaʀ, aʀd/ *nm,f* backpacker.

route /ʀut/ *nf* **1** Gén Civ (voie terrestre) road, highway US; **construction/entretien des ~s** road construction/maintenance; **~ prioritaire** road with right of way; **~ à deux/trois voies** two-/three-lane road; **~ de Douai** (vers Douai) Douai road, road to Douai; (qui vient de Douai) road from Douai; **~ de l'aéroport** road to the airport; **demain je prends la ~** tomorrow I take to the road; **tenir la ~** lit [*voiture*] to hold the road; fig [*argument, raisonnement*] to hold water; [*équipement*] to be well-made; **2** Transp (moyen de transport) road; **le rail et la ~** road and rail; **par la ~** by road; **il y a six heures de ~** it's a six-hour drive; **je préfère prendre la ~** I prefer to go by road; **faire la ~○** (partir à l'aventure) to go on the road; **le rail est aussi rapide que la ~** it's just as quick to travel by rail as by road; **la ~ est meurtrière** the roads can kill; **faire de la ~○** to do a lot of mileage; **3** (itinéraire) route; **~ du pétrole/fer** oil/iron route; **~s aériennes/maritimes** air/sea routes; **changer de ~** to change route; **s'éloigner** or **dévier de sa ~** lit [*avion, bateau*] to go off course; [*voiture, piéton*] to go the wrong way; fig [*personne*] to stray from one's chosen path; **la ~ est toute tracée désormais** fig from now on, it's all plain sailing; **nos ~s se sont croisées** fig our paths crossed; **4** (parcours) lit, fig way; **la ~ est longue!** it's a long way!; **la ~ sera longue** it will be a long journey; **être/se mettre sur la ~ de qn** to be/to get in sb's way; **trouver un obstacle sur sa ~** to find an obstacle in one's way; **rencontrer qch en ~** lit to meet sth on the way; fig to meet sth along the way; **couper la ~ à qn** to bar sb's way; **j'ai changé d'avis en cours de ~** I changed my mind along the way; **je me suis arrêté en cours de ~** I stopped on the way; **j'ai perdu mon parapluie en ~** I lost my umbrella on the way; **finis ta phrase, ne t'arrête pas en (cours de) ~** finish your sentence, don't stop halfway through; **être en ~** [*personne*] to be on one's way; [*projet*] to be underway; [*plat*] to be cooking; **avoir qch en ~** to have [sth] underway [*projet*]; **avoir un enfant en ~** to have a baby on the way; **détruire tout sur sa ~** to destroy everything in one's path; **être sur la bonne ~** lit to be heading in the right direction; fig to be on the right track; **remettre qn sur la bonne ~** to put sb right; **~ du succès/de la démocratie** road to success/towards democracy; **faire ~ avec qn** to travel with sb; **faire ~ vers, être en ~ pour** [*avion, passager*] to be en route for; [*bateau*] to be sailing to; [*voiture, train, piéton*] to be heading for; **faire fausse ~** lit to go off course; fig to be mistaken; **se mettre en ~** to set off; **en ~!** let's go!; **bonne ~!** have a good journey GB ou a nice trip!; **mettre en ~** to start [*machine, voiture*]; to get [sth] going [*projet, fabrication*] ; **la mise en ~ des négociations a été difficile** it was difficult to get the negotiations going; **déclencher la mise en ~ du moteur** to start the engine; **5** Sport (cyclisme) **géants** or **rois de la ~** road-cycling champions; **épreuve** or **course sur ~** road race.

■ **~ pour automobiles** dual carriageway GB, divided highway US; **~ communale** public highway; **~ départementale** secondary road (*maintained by Local Authority*); **~ des épices** Hist spice route; **~ forestière** forest road; **~ à grande circulation** trunk road GB, highway US; **~ nationale** trunk road GB, ≈ A road GB, national highway US; **~ de navigation** shipping lane; **~ du rhum** Sport Rum route race; **~ rurale** country road; **~ secondaire** minor road; **~ de la soie** Hist Silk Route ou Road; **~ du vin** wine trail.

router /ʀute/ [1] *vtr* to sort [sth] for mailing [*magazines, journaux*].

routier, **-ière** /ʀutje, ɛʀ/ **I** *adj* **1** (de la route) road; **transport/trafic/tunnel ~** road transport/traffic/tunnel; **réseau ~** road network.

II *nm* **1** ▶ 510 Transp (chauffeur) lorry driver GB, truck driver; ▶ **vieux**; **2** Comm (restaurant) transport café GB, truck stop US; **3** Sport (en cyclisme) road racer; **4** Naut (carte nautique) navigation chart; **5** Hist, Mil (soldat irrégulier) campaigner; **6** (scout de plus de seize ans) venture scout GB, explorer US.

III routière *nf* **ma voiture n'est pas une très bonne routière** my car is not very good for long-distance driving.

routine /ʀutin/ *nf* **1** (habitude) routine; **s'installer dans une ~** to get into a routine; **tomber dans la ~** to get into a rut; **sortir de la ~** to get out of a rut; **travail/enquête/contrôle de ~** routine work/enquiry/check; **2** Ordinat routine.

routinier, **-ière** /ʀutinje, ɛʀ/ **I** *adj* [*personne*] set in one's ways (*jamais épith*), stuck in a rut (*jamais épith*); [*esprit, méthode, travail, vie*] routine (*épith*); **il est trop ~** he is too set in his ways.

II *nm,f* creature of habit.

rouvre /ʀuvʀ/ *nm* durmast (oak), sessile oak.

rouvrir /ʀuvʀiʀ/ [32] **I** *vtr* **1** [*personne*] to open [sth] again [*porte, rideau, coffre, yeux*]; to reopen [*blessure*]; to turn [sth] back on [*gaz, électricité*]; **2** (remettre en service) [*personne*] to reopen [*magasin, théâtre, route*]; **le théâtre rouvre ses portes en septembre** the theatre[GB] will reopen in September; **3** (après arrêt) [*personne*] to resume [*négociations, hostilités*]; [*personne, affaire, scandale*] to reopen [*débat, affaire*].

II *vi* [*magasin, école, musée, théâtre, route*] to reopen.

III se rouvrir *vpr* [*porte, fenêtre*] to open (again); [*blessure, parapluie*] to open up (again).

roux, **rousse** /ʀu, ʀus/ ▶ 193 **I** *adj* [*couleur*] russet; [*cheveux, barbe*] red; (plus clair) ginger; [*feuilles*] orange; [*personne*] red-haired (*épith*); [*animal, pelage*] ginger; **il est ~** he's a redhead.

II *nm,f* red-haired person, redhead; **les ~** redheads.

III *nminv* **1** (couleur) red; **ses cheveux étaient d'un ~ magnifique** she had beautiful red hair; **2** Culin roux.

IV rousse◑ *nf* (police) **la rousse** the law ou fuzz○.

royal, **~e**, *mpl* **-aux** /ʀwajal, o/ **I** *adj* **1** (de souverain) [*famille, pouvoir, décret*] royal [*dignité, autorité*] royal, regal; **2** (magnifique) [*accueil*] royal; [*cadeau*] fit for a king (*après n*); [*pourboire, salaire*] princely; **3** (suprême) [*indifférence*] supreme, lofty; [*mépris*] majestic, utter; [*paix*] blissful.

II royale *nf* **1** Culin royale (*savoury egg custard*); **~e de carotte/gibier/volaille** carrot/game/chicken royale; **à la ~e** à la royale; **2** Mil **la Royale** *the French Navy*; **3** (barbe) imperial.

royalement /ʀwajalmɑ̃/ *adv* **1** (avec magnificence) [*recevoir, traiter*] royally, like royalty; [*vivre*] royally, like a king ou queen;

j'espère être payé ~ pour ce travail I hope I will be paid handsomely for this work; **2** (complètement) **il se moque ~ de son travail** he really couldn't care less○ about his work; **il se fiche ~ de l'opinion des autres** he couldn't give a damn○ about what other people think.

royalisme /ʀwajalism/ *nm* royalism.

royaliste /ʀwajalist/ *adj, nmf* royalist.
IDIOMES **être plus ~ que le roi** to be more catholic than the pope.

royalties /ʀwajalti/ *nfpl* royalties.

royaume /ʀwajom/ *nm* lit, fig kingdom.
IDIOMES **au ~ des aveugles, les borgnes sont rois** Prov in the country of the blind, the one-eyed man is king Prov.

Royaume-Uni /ʀwajomyni/ ▶ 321 *nprm* **~ de Grande-Bretagne et d'Irlande du Nord** United Kingdom of Great Britain and Northern Ireland; **le ~** the United Kingdom.

royauté /ʀwajote/ *nf* **1** (dignité) kingship; **2** (régime) monarchy.

RPR /ɛʀpeɛʀ/ *nm* (*abbr* = **Rassemblement pour la République**) *main political party of the Gaullist Right.*

RSVP /ɛʀɛsvepe/ (*abbr* = **répondez s'il vous plaît**) RSVP.

ru /ʀy/ *nm* liter brook.

RU /ʀy/ *nm*: *abbr* ▶ **restaurant**.

ruade /ʀyad/ *nf* **1** (de cheval) buck; **décocher une ~** to buck; **2** fig (de parti, de personne) attack; **les ~s de l'opposition contre le gouvernement** the opposition's attacks on the government.

ruban /ʀybɑ̃/ *nm* gén (de cheveux, paquet, décoration, d'ornementation) ribbon; Cout binding tape; (de cérémonie) ribbon; (de fleuve, route) fig ribbon; (de machine à écrire) **~ (encreur)** typewriter ribbon; Ordinat **~ encreur** printer ribbon; **~ tricolore** tricolour[GB] ribbon; **couper le ~** to cut the ribbon.
■ **~ d'acier** steel band ou strip; **~ adhésif** adhesive tape, sticky tape GB; **~ bleu** blue ribbon; **détenir le ~ bleu de qch** to be the world champion at sth; **~ de chapeau** hat band; **~ correcteur** cover-up tape; **~ effaceur** lift-off tape; **~ isolant** insulating tape; **~ magnétique** magnetic tape; **~ de Möbius** Möbius strip; **~ perforé** Ordinat (punched) paper tape.

rubato /ʀubato/ *adv, nm* rubato.

rubéole /ʀybeɔl/ ▶ 271 *nf* German measles (+ *v sg*), rubella spéc.

Rubicon /ʀybikɔ̃/ *nprm* Rubicon.
IDIOMES **franchir le ~** to cross the Rubicon.

rubicond, **~e** /ʀybikɔ̃, ɔ̃d/ *adj* [*personne, visage, joues*] ruddy, rubicund.

rubidium /ʀybidjɔm/ *nm* rubidium.

rubis /ʀybi/ *nm inv* **1** (pierre, bijou) ruby; **2** ▶ 193 (couleur) ruby; **3** (de montre) jewel, ruby; **une montre montée sur ~** watch with a jewelled[GB] bearing.
IDIOMES **payer ~ sur l'ongle** to pay cash on the nail.

rubrique /ʀybʀik/ *nf* **1** Presse section; **~ littéraire/cinéma/sportive/financière/des spectacles** book(s)/film/sports/finance/entertainment(s) section; **tenir une ~ dans un journal** to have a column in a newspaper; **2** (catégorie) category; **sous la même ~** in the same category; **classer des papiers sous la ~ 'à suivre'** to file papers under 'further action'; **3** Relig rubric.
■ **~ mondaine** social column; **~ nécrologique** obituary column.

ruche /ʀyʃ/ *nf* **1** (habitation) beehive, hive; **2** fig hive of activity; **3** Cout ruche.

ruché /ʀyʃe/ *nm* ruche.

rucher /ʀyʃe/ *nm* apiary.

rude /ʀyd/ *adj* **1** (pénible) [*métier, travail, vie, journée, combat*] hard, tough; [*climat, hiver*] severe, harsh; [*épreuve*] severe; **mettre qn/qch à ~ épreuve** to put sb/sth to a severe test; **être mis à ~ épreuve** to be put to a severe test; **c'est un ~ coup pour lui** it's a harsh ou severe blow for him; **2** (au toucher) [*étoffe, barbe, peau*] rough; **3** (grossier) [*voix, manières*] harsh; [*traits, personne*] coarse; **4** (sévère) [*ton, personne, caractère*] harsh, severe; **5** (solide) [*appétit*] healthy; [*montagnard, marin*] rugged; **c'est un ~ gaillard** he's a strapping fellow; **6** (redoutable) [*adversaire, concurrent*] tough, formidable.
IDIOMES **en voir de ~s** to have a hard ou tough time of it; **en faire voir de ~s à qn** to put sb through it.

rudement /ʀydmɑ̃/ *adv* **1** (brutalement) [*frapper, pousser, secouer*] roughly; **2** (sans ménagements) [*parler, traiter*] roughly, harshly; **3**○ (très) [*cher, gentil, fatigant, bon, bien*] really, damn◐; [*content, mauvais*] really; **c'est ~ mieux!** it's a hell of a lot○ better!

rudesse /ʀydɛs/ *nf* **1** (de climat, vie, d'hiver, éducation) harshness, severity; **2** (de personne, ton) harshness, severity; **avec ~** harshly, severely; **3** (manque de raffinement) coarseness.

rudiment /ʀydimɑ̃/ **I** *nm* Anat rudiment; **un ~ de queue** a rudimentary tail.
II rudiments *nmpl* (de langue, matière, discipline) rudiments; **s'initier aux ~s de** to learn the rudiments of; **nous n'en sommes qu'au stade des ~s** we are still at the rudimentary stage; **avoir quelques ~s de** to have a rudimentary knowledge of.

rudimentaire /ʀydimɑ̃tɛʀ/ *adj* **1** (de base) basic; (limite) rudimentary; **au confort très ~** with basic comfort; **2** Anat rudimentary.

rudoyer /ʀydwaje/ [23] *vtr* to bully.

rue /ʀy/ *nf* **1** (voie, population) street; **~ à sens unique** one-way street; **scènes de la ~** street scenes; **2** (peuple) pej **la ~** the mob péj; **3** Bot rue.
■ **~ piétonne** or **piétonnière** pedestrianized ou pedestrian street.
IDIOMES **ça ne court pas les ~s**○ it's pretty thin on the ground○; **être à la ~** to be on the street, to be down-and-out; **jeter/mettre qn à la ~** to throw/put sb out on the street; **descendre dans la ~** to take to the street.

ruée /ʀɥe/ *nf* rush; **dans la ~, il a perdu son chapeau** he lost his hat in the rush; **à la fin des cours, c'est la ~ dans les couloirs** when the bell goes (off), everyone rushes down the corridors; **quand on leur demande un service, ce n'est pas la ~** iron if you ask them a favour[GB], they don't exactly rush to oblige.
■ **~ vers l'or** gold rush.

ruelle /ʀɥɛl/ *nf* alleyway, back street.

ruer /ʀɥe/ [1] **I** *vi* [*cheval*] to kick.
II se ruer *vpr* to rush; **se ~ vers** to rush for ou toward(s); **se ~ hors de/dans** to rush out of/into, to dash out of/into; **se ~ dans l'escalier** (pour monter) to rush ou tear up the stairs; (pour descendre) to rush ou tear down the stairs; **se ~ sur qn/qch** to pounce on sb/sth; **se ~ à l'assaut de qch** to launch an attack on sth; **les gens se ruent à l'assaut des magasins** fig there is a rush on the shops GB ou stores US.
IDIOMES **~ dans les brancards** to kick over the traces, to rebel.

rufian○ /ʀyfjɑ̃/ *nm* **1**† (souteneur) procurer; **2** (aventurier) adventurer.

rugby /ʀygbi/ *nm* Sport rugby; **jouer au ~** to play rugby; **un joueur de ~** a rugby player; **~ à treize** rugby league; **~ à quinze** rugby union.

rugbyman, *pl* **rugbymen** /ʀygbiman, mɛn/ *nm* Sport rugby player.

rugir /ʀyʒiʀ/ [3] **I** *vtr* to bellow (out) [*ordre, insulte*]; to growl [*menace*]; **'tuez-les tous!' rugit-il** 'kill them all!' he bellowed.
II *vi* **1** Zool to roar; **2** [*personne*] to howl; **~ de colère/fureur/douleur** to roar ou howl with anger/fury/pain; **~ de rage** to howl with rage; **3** fig [*vent*] to howl; [*moteur, mer, vague*] to roar; [*klaxon*] to blare; **faire ~** to rev up [*moteur*].

rugissant /ʀyʒisɑ̃/ *adj m* **les quarantièmes ~s** Géog, Naut the roaring forties.

rugissement /ʀyʒismɑ̃/ *nm* **1** (d'animal) roar; **pousser un ~** or **des ~s** to roar; **2** (de personne) roar, howl; **pousser un ~** to roar, to howl; **pousser un ~ de** to let out a roar ou howl of; **3** fig (de vague) roar(ing); (de vent) howling.

rugosité /ʀygozite/ *nf* **1** (état) roughness; **2** (aspérité) rough patch.

rugueux, **-euse** /ʀygø, øz/ *adj* [*écorce, peau, cuir, main, table, toile, drap*] rough; [*surface, bois*] rough, rugged; [*mur, vin*] rough; [*sol*] rough, bumpy.

Ruhr /ʀuʀ/ ▶ 692 *nprf* **la ~** the Ruhr.

ruine /ʀɥin/ **I** *nf* **1** (de bâtiment) ruin; **en ~(s)** ruined (*épith*); **être/tomber en ~(s)** to be in ruins/to fall into ruin; **menacer ~** to be threatening to collapse; **2** (bâtiment) ruin; **ils ont acheté une ~ en France** they bought a ruin in France; **leur maison n'était plus qu'une ~** their house was nothing more than a ruin; **3** (de personne, d'entreprise, de pays) ruin; **causer la ~ de qn/qch** to ruin sb/sth, to lead to sb's ruin/to the ruin of sth; **être au bord de la ~** to be on the brink of financial ruin; **aller** or **courir à la ~** to be heading for financial ruin; **c'est la ~** fig it's exorbitant; **ce n'est pas la ~** fig it's not that expensive; **les femmes seront sa ~** women will be the ruin of him; **4** (de civilisation) collapse; (de réputation, d'avenir) ruin; (d'espoir) death; **être la ~ de** (de civilisation, réputation, santé) to ruin; (de crédit) to destroy; (d'avenir, espoir) to ruin, to wreck; **courir** or **aller à la ~** [*civilisation*] to be heading for collapse; **5** (personne) péj wreck.
II ruines *nfpl* ruins; **les ~s de Carthage** the ruins of Carthage; **les ~s d'un empire** the ruins of an empire.

ruiner /ʀɥine/ [1] **I** *vtr* **1** (provoquer la banqueroute de) to ruin [*pays, personne, entreprise, économie*]; **2** (coûter cher à) **~ qn** to be a drain on sb's resources; **ça ne va pas le ~** iron that's not going to break the bank; **3** (détruire) to destroy, to wreck [*santé, forces*]; **l'alcool a ruiné ses forces** alcohol has turned him/her into a wreck; **4** (dévaster) [*bombardement*] to reduce [sth] to rubble [*ville, bâtiment*]; [*pluie, incendie, inondation, cyclone*] to ruin [*culture*]; **5** (causer la perte de) to ruin [*vie, réputation*]; to destroy [*argument, théorie, bonheur*]; to shatter [*espérances, rêve*].
II se ruiner *vpr* (perdre ses biens) to be ruined, to lose everything; (dépenser excessivement) to ruin oneself (**en faisant** doing); **se ~ à la Bourse** to lose everything on the stock exchange; **se ~ pour une femme** to spend everything one has on a woman; **se ~ au jeu/en livres** to spend all one's money gambling/on books; **se ~ la santé** to ruin one's health.

ruineux, **-euse** /ʀɥinø, øz/ *adj* [*entretien, dépense*] exorbitant; [*goût, plaisir, sortie, fête*] very expensive, extravagant; [*achat, guerre, affaire, objet*] ruinously expensive; **être ~** to be very expensive; **ce n'est pas ~** it's quite reasonable.

ruisseau, *pl* **~x** /ʀɥiso/ *nm* **1** (cours d'eau) stream, brook; **2** (flot) **~ de larmes/lave** stream of tears/lava; **~ de sang** trickle of blood; **un ~ de larmes coulait le long de ses joues** tears streamed down her cheeks; **3** (caniveau) gutter; **tomber dans le ~** to go to the dogs; **rouler dans le ~** to wallow in the gutter; **tirer** or **sortir qn du ~** to pull sb out of the gutter; **être élevé dans le ~** to be brought up in the gutter.
IDIOMES **les petits ~x font les grandes rivières** Prov great oaks from little acorns grow Prov.

ruisselant, **~e** /ʀɥislɑ̃, ɑ̃t/ *adj* [*eau, pluie*] streaming; [*mur, paroi, personne, visage,* *animal, habit, parapluie*] dripping wet; **~ de sueur** dripping with sweat.

ruisseler /ʀɥisle/ [19] *vi* **1** (écouler) [*eau, pluie, sueur, larme, sang*] to stream; [*graisse*] to drip; **2** littér [*chevelure*] to tumble down; **la lumière ruisselait sur** the light glistened on; **3** (être recouvert d'un liquide) [*personne, surface, habit, parapluie*] to stream, to be streaming (**de** with); **~ de sueur** to be dripping with sweat; **~ de graisse** to be dripping with fat; **les vitres ruisselaient de pluie** the rain was streaming down the windows; **ses joues ruisselaient de larmes** tears were streaming down his/her cheeks; **~ de lumière** to be flooded with light.

ruisselet /ʀɥislɛ/ *nm* littér rivulet, brooklet.

ruissellement /ʀɥisɛlmɑ̃/ *nm* **1** lit (de pluie, d'humidité) streaming (**sur** down); (de graisse) dripping (**sur** down); (de produits toxiques) seepage; **le ~ de l'eau sur les vitres** water streaming down the windows; **2** littér **~ de pierres précieuses** cascade of precious stones; **~ de chevelure sur des épaules** hair tumbling about sb's shoulders.

■ **~ pluvial** run-off.

rumba /ʀumba/ *nf* rumba.

rumeur /ʀymœʀ/ *nf* **1** (ouï-dire) rumour[GB] (**sur** about); **rien ne permet de confirmer cette ~** there is nothing to confirm this rumour[GB]; **selon certaines ~s, il aurait quitté le pays** rumour[GB] has it that he may have left the country; **les journaux font courir la ~ de leur séparation prochaine** the newspapers are spreading rumours[GB] ou the rumour[GB] that they're about to separate; **faire taire une ~** to put a stop to a rumour[GB]; **apprendre qch par la ~ publique** to learn sth through a rumour[GB] that is going around; **2** (de voix, mer, vent) murmur; **il y eut une ~ dans l'assistance** there was a murmur in the audience.

ruminant /ʀyminɑ̃/ *nm* ruminant.

rumination /ʀyminasjɔ̃/ *nf* **1** Zool chewing the cud, rumination spéc; **2** (méditation) brooding, rumination.

ruminer /ʀymine/ [1] **I** *vtr* **1** Zool to ruminate; **2** (penser constamment à) to brood on [*malheur*]; to chew over○ [*idée, projet*].

II *vi* **1** Zool to chew the cud, to ruminate spéc; **2** [*personne*] to brood.

rumsteck /ʀɔmstɛk/ *nm* rump steak.

rune /ʀyn/ *nf* rune.

runique /ʀynik/ *adj* runic.

rupestre /ʀypɛstʀ/ *adj* **1** [*plante, flore*] rock (*épith*); **2** [*peinture, art, dessin*] cave (*épith*), rock (*épith*).

rupin◐, **~e** /ʀypɛ̃, in/ **I** *adj* pej [*personne, quartier*] wealthy, posh○ GB.

II *nm,f* pej **les ~s** the rich; **épouser un ~** to marry somebody who is loaded○; **un restaurant de ~s** a posh○ GB ou fancy restaurant.

rupteur /ʀyptœʀ/ *nm* contact breaker; **~ d'allumage** contact breaker.

rupture /ʀyptyʀ/ *nf* **1** (de relations) breaking-off; **ils souhaitent la ~ des relations commerciales/négociations** they want to break off trade relations/the negotiations; **la ~ d'un accord** the breaking-off of an agreement; **2** (résultat) breakdown (**avec** in); **la ~ du dialogue avec l'OLP a entraîné...** the breakdown in the talks with the PLO led to...; **3** (de couple, coalition, d'amis) break-up; **si tu fais ça c'est la ~!** if you do that we're through○ ou splitting up!; **lettre de ~** letter ending a relationship; **4** (opposition) **être en ~ avec** to be at odds with [*hiérarchie, groupe*]; **il est en ~ avec cette idéologie/tradition** he's broken away from this ideology/tradition; **5** (cassure) gén break; (de barrage, digue) breaking; (de conduite) fracture; (de muscle, d'artère) rupture; (d'organe mécanique ou électrique) failure; **point de ~** breaking point; **accident dû à la ~ d'un essieu** accident caused by a broken axle ou by an axle breaking; **amener une situation au point de ~** to bring a situation to breaking point; **il y a ~ entre le passé et le présent** fig there's a break between the past and the present.

■ **~ d'anévrisme** Méd ruptured aneurysm; **~ de charge** Transp transshipment; **~ de contrat** Jur breach of contract; **~ de pente** Géol shelf break; **~ de stock** Comm stock shortage; **être en ~ de stock** [*produit, magasin*] to be out of stock.

rural, **~e**, *mpl* **-aux** /ʀyʀal, o/ **I** *adj* [*développement, exode, milieu*] rural; [*hôpital, chemin, vie, origine*] country; **l'espace ~** the countryside.

II *nm,f* **les ruraux** people who live in the country.

ruse /ʀyz/ *nf* **1** (procédé) trick, ruse; **imaginer une ~ pour faire qch** to think of a cunning way of doing sth; **connaître les ~s du métier** to know the tricks of the trade; **c'est une ~ de guerre** hum it's a cunning stratagem; **c'est une ~ de Sioux** hum it's a crafty trick; **2** (habileté) cunning, craftiness; **avec ~** cunningly; **faire preuve de** or **agir avec ~** to be cunning.

rusé, **~e** /ʀyze/ **I** *adj* cunning, crafty; **jouer au plus ~ avec qn** to try to outsmart sb; **ils jouent au plus ~** they try to outsmart each other.

II *nm,f* **c'est une ~e** she's a crafty one.

ruser /ʀyze/ [1] *vi* **1** (être rusé) to be crafty; **2** (être plus fin que) **~ avec** to trick [*ennemi, police*]; **3** (vaincre) **~ avec** to find a way around [*difficulté, obstacle*].

rush, *pl* **rushes** /ʀœʃ/ **I** *nm* **1** Sport (à la course) final burst; (en sport collectif) attack; **2**○ (ruée) rush; **le ~ sur l'immobilier a fait grimper les prix** the rush to buy property has pushed prices up.

II rushes *nmpl* Cin rushes.

russe /ʀys/ ▶ 462, 537 **I** *adj* Russian; **œufs à la ~** Russian eggs.

II *nm* Ling Russian.

Russe /ʀys/ ▶ 537 *nmf* Russian; **un ~ blanc** a White Russian.

Russie /ʀysi/ ▶ 321 *nprf* Russia.

russification /ʀysifikasjɔ̃/ *nf* Russification.

russifier /ʀysifje/ [2] **I** *vtr* to Russify.

II se russifier *vpr* Géog [*quartier, région*] to be settled by Russians.

russisant, **~e** /ʀysizɑ̃, ɑ̃t/ *nm,f* Russianist.

russisme /ʀysism/ *nm* Russianism.

rustaud, **~e** /ʀysto, od/ **I** *adj* rustic, coarse péj.

II *nm,f* pej (country) bumpkin péj, hick péj.

rusticité /ʀystisite/ *nf* **1** (d'un matériau, d'un lieu) rustic character (**de** of); **la ~ de leurs manières** their rustic manners (*pl*); **2** Agric hardiness (**de** of).

rustine® /ʀystin/ *nf* (puncture-repair) patch; **coller une ~** to stick on a patch; **boîte de ~s** puncture repair kit.

rustique /ʀystik/ **I** *adj* **1** (campagnard) [*meuble, crépi*] rustic; [*plat*] country (*épith*); [*maison, mode de vie, personne, manières*] rustic, country (*épith*); **2** Agric [*plante*] hardy (*épith*).

II *nm* **le ~** rustic style.

rustre /ʀystʀ/ **I** *adj* pej [*manières, personne*] uncouth péj.

II *nm* **1** (homme grossier) lout; **2**† (paysan) peasant.

rut /ʀyt/ *nm* Zool rutting season; **être en ~** to be in rut; **un cerf en ~** a rutting deer, a deer in rut.

rutabaga /ʀytabaga/ *nm* swede GB, rutabaga US; **manger des ~s** to eat swede.

ruthénium /ʀytenjɔm/ *nm* ruthenium.

rutilant, **~e** /ʀytilɑ̃, ɑ̃t/ *adj* [*diamant*] sparkling; [*carrosserie, chrome*] gleaming.

rutiler /ʀytile/ [1] *vi* [*chrome*] to gleam; [*diamant*] to sparkle.

RV *written abbr* = **rendez-vous**.

Rwanda = **Rouanda**.

rwandais, **~e** /ʀwɑ̃dɛ, ɛz/ ▶ 537 *adj* Rwandan.

Rwandais, **~e** /ʀwɑ̃dɛ, ɛz/ ▶ 537 *nm,f* Rwandan.

rythme /ʀitm/ *nm* **1** Littérat, Mus rhythm; **~ lent/rapide** slow/rapid rhythm; **avoir le sens du ~** to have a good sense of rhythm; **au ~ d'une rumba** to the rhythm of a rumba; **chanter/danser en ~** to sing/dance in time; **marquer le ~** to beat time; **~ binaire/ternaire** duple/triple time; **avoir le ~ dans la peau**○ to have a natural sense of rhythm; **2** (allure) (d'accroissement, de production) rate; (de vie, film) pace; **le ~ infernal de la vie citadine** the hectic pace of city life; **aller à son ~** to go at one's pace; **tenir le ~** to keep up with the pace; **vivre au ~ des saisons** to live according to the rhythm of the seasons; **changer au ~ des saisons** to change with the seasons; **la situation se dégrade à un ~ accéléré** the situation is deteriorating rapidly; **au ~ de** at a rate of; **au ~ de 300000 par an** at a rate of 300,000 per year; **3** (mouvement régulier) rate; **~ cardiaque/respiratoire** heart/respiratory rate; **la revue sort au ~ de quatre numéros par an** the magazine is published four times a year.

■ **~ biologique** biorhythm; **~ de croissance** growth rate; **~s scolaires** school timetables.

rythmé, **~e** /ʀitme/ **I** *pp* ▶ **rythmer**.

II *pp adj* rhythmic; **la musique est très ~e** the music has a very good rhythm.

rythmer /ʀitme/ [1] *vtr* **1** (scander) to put rhythm into [*phrase, poème*]; to give rhythm to [*tâche, marche*]; **2** (ponctuer) [*actions, événements*] to regulate [*vie, journée, travail*]; **les pauses-café rythment la vie du routier** a truck driver's life is punctuated by coffee breaks; **une vie rythmée par les saisons** a life regulated ou governed by the seasons.

rythmique /ʀitmik/ **I** *adj* [*battement, mouvement*] rhythmic, rhythmical; [*accent, schéma*] rhythmic.

II *nf* **1** Ling rhythmics (+ *v sg*); **2** Mus rhythm section.

Ss

s, S /ɛs/ *nm inv* s, S.
s' **1** ▶ **se**; **2** ▶ **si**[1].
sa ▶ **son**[1].
SA /ɛsa/ *nf*: *abbr* ▶ **société**.
Saba /saba/ *npr* Sheba; **la reine de ~** the Queen of Sheba.
sabayon /sabajɔ̃/ *nm* zabaglione.
sabbat /saba/ *nm* **1** Relig Sabbath; **2** (des sorcières) witching hour.
sabbatique /sabatik/ *adj* **1** Relig Sabbatical; **2** Univ, Entr, Admin [*année*] sabbatical; **être en congé ~** to be on sabbatical (leave).
Sabin, **~e** /sabɛ̃, in/ *nm,f* Sabine; **l'enlèvement des ~es** the rape of the Sabine women.
sabir /sabiʀ/ *nm* **1** (charabia) mumbo-jumbo; **2** (mélange) pidgin; **3** Hist sabir.
sablage /sablaʒ/ *nm* **1** (de chaussée) gritting; **2** (pour nettoyer) sandblasting.
sable /sɑbl/ **I** ▶ **193** *adj inv* sand-coloured[GB].
II *nm* **1** Minér sand; **bâtir sur le ~** fig to build on sand; **2** Hérald sable.
III sables *nmpl* sands.
■ **~s bitumineux** tar sands; **~s mouvants** quicksands.
IDIOMES **être sur le ~**○ to be on one's beam ends.
sablé, **~e** /sable/ **I** *pp* ▶ **sabler**.
II *pp adj* **1** [*route, allée*] covered with sand; **2** Culin **pâte ~e** rich (sweetened) shortcrust pastry.
III *nm* (biscuit) ≈ shortbread biscuit GB, cookie US.
sabler /sable/ [1] *vtr* **1** to grit [*chaussée*]; **2** Tech (pour nettoyer) to sandblast; (pour mouler) to sand-cast.
IDIOMES **~ le champagne** to crack open some champagne.
sableux, **-euse** /sablø, øz/ **I** *adj* sandy.
II sableuse *nf* **1** (pour la chaussée) gritter; **2** (pour décaper) sandblaster.
sablier /sablije/ *nm* hourglass; (pour cuire des œufs) egg timer.
sablière /sablijɛʀ/ *nf* **1** (carrière) sand quarry; **2** (poutre) stringpiece; **3** (de locomotive) sandbox.
sablonneux, **-euse** /sablɔnø, øz/ *adj* sandy.
sabord /sabɔʀ/ *nm* scuttle.
■ **~ de charge** cargo hatchway; **~ de coupée** gang port; **~ de pavois** bulwark port.
sabordage /sabɔʀdaʒ/ *nm* Naut scuttling.
saborder /sabɔʀde/ [1] **I** *vtr* Naut to scuttle; fig to scuttle, to scupper.
II se saborder *vpr* Naut [*équipage*] to scuttle ou scupper one's own ship; [*flotte*] to scuttle ou scupper its own ship; fig to sink oneself/itself.
sabot /sabo/ *nm* **1** (chaussure) clog; **2** Zool hoof; **coup de ~ de cheval/de vache** kick from a horse/from a cow; **recevoir un coup de ~ de cheval** to get kicked by a horse; **donner un coup de ~ à qn** to kick sb, to give sb a kick; **3** Aut shoe; **4** Tech (de pieu, poteau) shoe; (de pied de meuble) (metal) foot; **5**○ (objet sans valeur) old contraption.
■ **~ d'enrayage** Rail slipper brake; **~ de Denver®** wheel clamp; **mettre un ~ de Denver® à une voiture** to clamp a car; **~ de frein** brake shoe.
IDIOMES **jouer/travailler comme un ~**○ to play/to work very badly; **je te vois** or **t'entends venir avec tes gros ~s**○ I can see it coming a mile off○; **ne pas se trouver sous le ~ d'un cheval** to be hard to come by; **ne pas avoir les deux pieds dans le même ~** to be on one's toes.
sabotage /sabɔtaʒ/ *nm* **1** (méthode) sabotage; **faire du ~** to do acts of sabotage; **2** (acte) act of sabotage; **explosion due à un ~** explosion caused by sabotage.
saboter /sabɔte/ [1] *vtr* **1** (détériorer) to sabotage [*matériel, véhicule*]; **2** (faire échouer) to sabotage [*négociation, plan*]; **~**○ **un travail** to botch a job.
saboterie /sabɔtʀi/ *nf* clog factory.
saboteur, **-euse** /sabɔtœʀ, øz/ *nm,f* **1** (de matériel) saboteur; **2** (de travail) botcher.
sabotier, **-ière** /sabɔtje, ɛʀ/ ▶ **510** *nm,f* (fabricant) clog maker; (commerçant) clog seller.
sabre /sɑbʀ/ *nm* **1** (à lame droite) sword; (à lame courbée) sabre[GB]; **se battre au ~** to fight with swords; **~ au clair** Mil with sword(s) drawn; **mettre ~ au clair** to draw one's sword; **bruits de ~** fig sabre[GB]-rattling; **recevoir un coup de ~** to be struck by a sword ou a sabre[GB]; **le ~ et le goupillon** fig the Army and the Church; **2**○ fig (rasoir) cut-throat razor.
■ **~ d'abattage** or **d'abattis** machete; **~ d'abordage** cutlass; **~ de cavalerie** riding sabre[GB].
sabrer /sɑbʀe/ [1] *vtr* **1** Mil to sabre[GB], to cut down; **2** (écourter) to cut chunks out of [*article, manuscrit*]; (supprimer) to cut out [*phrase, paragraphe*]; to axe[GB] [*projet*]; **3** (critiquer) to tear [sb] to pieces [*auteur*]; to pan○ [*livre, film*]; **4**○ (recaler) to flunk○ [*étudiant*]; (licencier) to fire, to sack○ GB; **5** (rayer) liter to score [*page, dessin*] (**de** with); **la cicatrice qui sabre sa joue** the scar which is scored across his cheek; **6**○ (bâcler) to rush through [*travail*].
sabretache /sabʀətaʃ/ *nf* sabretache.
sabreur /sɑbʀœʀ/ *nm* **1** Mil, Sport swordsman; **2** péj (soldat) real fighter.
sac /sak/ *nm* **1** (contenant) gén bag; (grossier, à usage commercial) sack; **~ de sport** sports bag GB, gym bag US; **~ à charbon/à patates** coal/potato sack; **~ de farine** (petit) flour bag; (grand) flour sack; **2** (contenu) bag(ful), sack(ful); **j'ai consommé trois ~s de charbon cet hiver** I used three sacks of coal this winter; **3** Anat, Bot sac; **4** (pillage) sack; **mettre à ~** to sack [*ville, région*]; to ransack [*boutique, maison*]; **5**◐ (10 francs) *ten French francs*.
■ **~ d'aspirateur** dust bag, vacuum-cleaner bag; **~ à bandoulière** shoulder bag; **~ de congélation** freezer bag; **~ de couchage** sleeping bag; **~ à dos** rucksack GB, backpack; **~ à dos à claie** stretcher-frame rucksack GB ou backpack; **~ à dos promenade** daysack GB, knapsack US; **~ d'embrouilles** can of worms; **~ herniaire** Anat hernial sac; **~ isotherme** cool bag; **~ lacrymal** Anat lacrymal sac; **~ à main** handbag, purse US; **~ à malices** bag of tricks; **~ (de) marin** Naut kitbag GB, duffel bag US; **~ de montagne** rucksack GB, knapsack; **~ de nœuds** fig = **~ d'embrouilles**; **~ d'os**○ fig bag of bones; **~ à papier**○! nitwit○!; **~ penderie** suiter, suit bag; **~ de plage** beachbag; **~ en plastique** (sans poignées) polythene bag; (avec poignées) carrier bag; **~ pollinique** Bot pollen sac; **~ polochon** holdall; **~ postal** mail sack; **~ poubelle** bin liner GB, trash bag US, trash-can liner US; **~ à provisions** shopping bag, carry-all US; **~ à puces**○ fleabag○ GB, flea-infested animal; **~ reporter** bucket bag; **~ de sable** Constr, Mil sandbag; (pour la boxe) punchbag GB, punching bag US; **~ à viande**○ (sleeping bag) liner; **~ à vin**○ (old) soak○; **~ de voyage** travel bag.
IDIOMES **l'affaire est dans le ~**○ it's in the bag○; **avoir plus d'un tour dans son ~** to have more than one trick up one's sleeve; **être habillé comme un ~ (à patates)** to look like a sack of potatoes; **vider son ~**○ to get it off one's chest; **se faire prendre la main dans le ~** to be caught red-handed; **mettre dans le même ~** to lump [sth] together, to tar [sth] with the same brush pej.
saccade /sakad/ *nf* jerk; **avancer par ~s** to jerk along.
saccadé, **~e** /sakade/ *adj* [*mouvement, marche*] jerky; [*musique, rythme*] staccato; [*voix*] clipped.
saccage /sakaʒ/ *nm* (de région) devastation; (de bâtiment) vandalizing.
saccager /sakaʒe/ [13] *vtr* **1** (abîmer) to wreck, to devastate [*région, site, arbres*]; to vandalize [*bâtiment, tombe*]; **2** (mettre à sac) to sack.
saccharine /sakaʀin/ *nf* saccharin.
saccharose /sakaʀoz/ *nm* saccharose.
SACEM /sasɛm/ *nf* (*abbr* = **Société des auteurs, compositeurs et éditeurs de musique**) *association of composers and music publishers to protect copyright and royalties.*
sacerdoce /sasɛʀdɔs/ *nm* **1** Relig priesthood; **30 ans de ~** 30 years in the priesthood; **2** fig vocation.
sacerdotal, **~e**, *mpl* **-aux** /sasɛʀdɔtal, o/ *adj* priestly, sacerdotal sout.
sachem /saʃɛm/ *nm* sachem; **le (grand) ~** fig the boss.
sachet /saʃɛ/ *nm* (de poudre) packet, package; (d'aromates) sachet; (de confiseries) bag; **~ de pastilles/chocolats** bag of lozenges/chocolates; **~ de lavande** lavender-bag; **~ de thé** teabag; **elle achète son thé en ~s plutôt qu'en vrac** she buys teabags and not loose tea; **un ~ d'infusion** herbal teabag.
sacoche /sakɔʃ/ *nf* **1** (gros sac) bag; (banane) bumbag; **2** (de deux-roues) (contre la roue arrière) pannier GB, saddlebag US; (sous la selle) saddlebag; **3** (d'écolier) (school)bag; (avec bretelles) satchel.
■ **~ à outils** toolbag; **~ de plombier**

plumber's toolbag; **~ de postier** postbag GB, mailbag.

sacquer○ /sake/ [1] *vtr* **1** [*employeur*] to sack○, to fire○ [*employé*]; **2** [*enseignant*] to mark [sb] strictly; **se faire ~ en anglais** to get a really low mark in English; **se faire ~ à un examen** to be failed at an exam.
IDIOMES **je ne peux pas le ~** I can't stand the sight of him.

sacral, **~e**, *mpl* **-aux** /sakʀal, o/ *adj* sacral.

sacralisation /sakʀalizasjɔ̃/ *nf* **la ~ de la science** regarding science as sacred.

sacraliser /sakʀalize/ [1] *vtr* **1** (rendre sacré) to make [sth] sacred; **2** (considérer comme sacré) to regard [sth] as sacred.

sacramentel, **-elle** /sakʀamɑ̃tɛl/ *adj* **1** Relig [*onction, rite*] sacramental; **2** fig (rituel) ritual, sacred.

sacre /sakʀ/ *nm* (de roi) coronation; (d'évêque) consecration; **il a reçu le ~ du prix Nobel** fig he has been honoured[GB] with the Nobel prize; **le Sacre du Printemps** Mus The Rite of Spring.

sacré, **~e** /sakʀe/ **I** *pp* ▶ **sacrer**.
II *pp adj* **1** Relig [*art, objet, lieu, flamme*] sacred; [*cause, fureur*] holy; **2** (à respecter) [*règle, lien, droit*] sacred; **mes soirées, c'est ~** my evenings are sacred; **3**○ (remarquable) **être un ~ menteur/travailleur** to be a hell of a○ liar/worker; **avoir un ~ culot/une ~e patience** to have a hell of a nerve○/a hell of a lot○ of patience; **il a un ~ courage** he's really courageous; **en prendre un ~ coup**○ to get a hell of a knock○; **il a eu une ~e veine** or **chance** he's been damn○ lucky; **4**○ (maudit) blasted○, confounded○; **la ~e manie de faire qch** the infuriating habit of doing sth; **5**○ (d'admiration, de surprise) **~ Paul, va!** Paul, you old devil!; **ce ~ Pierre s'en est encore tiré** that old devil Pierre has got GB ou gotten US away with it again; **~ veinard** lucky devil○; **~ nom d'une pipe**○ ou **~ nom de nom**○**!** (de surprise) good grief!; (de colère) hell and damnation!
III *nm* **le ~** the sacred.
■ **le Sacré Collège** Relig the Sacred College.
IDIOMES **avoir le feu ~** to be full of zeal ou enthusiasm.

sacrebleu /sakʀəblø/ *excl* good grief○!

Sacré-Cœur /sakʀekœʀ/ *nm* Relig Sacred Heart.

sacrement /sakʀəmɑ̃/ *nm* sacrament; **mourir muni des derniers ~s de l'Église** to die having received the last rites of the Church; **le saint ~** the Blessed Sacrament.

sacrément○ /sakʀemɑ̃/ *adv* incredibly○.

sacrer /sakʀe/ [1] *vtr* **1** Relig to crown [*roi*]; to consecrate [*évêque*]; **2** fig **être sacré champion de ski** to be crowned ski champion; **elle fut sacrée meilleure actrice de sa génération** she was hailed as the best actress of her generation.

sacrificateur, **-trice** /sakʀifikatœʀ, tʀis/ *nm,f* sacrificer.

sacrifice /sakʀifis/ *nm* sacrifice; **faire de grands ~s** to make great sacrifices; **faire le ~ de qch** to sacrifice sth.

sacrificiel, **-ielle** /sakʀifisjɛl/ *adj* sacrificial.

sacrifier /sakʀifje/ [1] **I** *vtr* **1** (immoler) lit to sacrifice (**à** to); **2** (négliger) **~ ses loisirs pour étudier** to sacrifice ou to give up one's free time in order to study; **il a fallu ~ les deux derniers chapitres** we had to sacrifice the last two chapters; **~ sa famille à son travail** to put one's work before one's family; **3**○ Comm to give away, to sell [sth] off cheap [*marchandise*]; to slash [*prix*]; **'prix sacrifiés'** rock-bottom prices.
II sacrifier à *vtr ind* to conform to [*rite, coutume*].
III se sacrifier *vpr* **1** lit to sacrifice oneself (**pour qn** for sb); **2**○ fig (financièrement) to make sacrifices (**pour qn** for sb).

sacrilège /sakʀilɛʒ/ **I** *adj* sacrilegious.
II *nm* Relig sacrilege ₵; **un ~** an act of sacrilege.

sacripant○ /sakʀipɑ̃/ *nm* tearaway○.

sacristain /sakʀistɛ̃/ ▶ **510** *nm* sexton.

sacristie /sakʀisti/ *nf* (d'église) sacristy; (de temple protestant) vestry.

sacro-iliaque, *pl* **~s** /sakʀoiljak/ *adj* sacro-iliac.

sacro-lombaire, *pl* **~s** /sakʀolɔ̃bɛʀ/ *adj* sacrolumbar.

sacro-saint, **~e**, *mpl* **~s** /sakʀosɛ̃, ɛt/ *adj* sacrosanct.

sacro-sciatique, *pl* **~s** /sakʀosjatik/ *adj* sacrosciatic.

sacrum /sakʀɔm/ *nm* sacrum.

sadique /sadik/ **I** *adj* sadistic.
II *nmf* sadist.

sadiquement /sadikmɑ̃/ *adv* sadistically.

sadisme /sadism/ *nm* sadism.

sado-maso○ /sadomazo/ *adj inv* sadomasochistic.

sadomasochisme /sadomazɔʃism/ *nm* sadomasochism.

sadomasochiste /sadomazɔʃist/ **I** *adj* sadomasochistic.
II *nmf* sadomasochist.

safari /safaʀi/ *nm* safari.

safari-photo, *pl* **safaris-photos** /safaʀifɔto/ *nm* photographic safari.

safran /safʀɑ̃/ ▶ **193** **I** *adj inv* saffron (yellow).
II *nm* **1** (épice) saffron; **riz au ~** saffron rice; **2** (couleur) saffron; **3** Naut rudder blade.

safrané, **~e** /safʀane/ *adj* (pour le goût) saffron (*épith*); (pour la couleur) coloured[GB] with saffron.

saga /saga/ *nf* saga.

sagace /sagas/ *adj* sagacious, shrewd.

sagacité /sagasite/ *nf* sagacity, shrewdness.

sagaie /sagɛ/ *nf* assegai.

sage /saʒ/ **I** *adj* **1** (sensé) [*personne*] wise; [*paroles, décision, précaution, action*] wise, sensible; [*compromis*] sensible; **il serait ~ de faire** it would be wise ou sensible to do; **il serait ~ que vous le fassiez** you would be wise to do it; **2** (docile) [*enfant, chien*] good, well-behaved; [*public*] restrained; [*ville*] sedate; **sois ~!** be good!, behave yourself!; **3** (modéré) [*goût, mode*] sober; [*spectacle, esthétique*] tame; [*prix*] moderate, reasonable; [*idées*] sensible; **conduite ~** Aut sensible driving; **4** (pudique) [*vêtement*] sober.
II *nm* **1** (homme avisé) wise man; Antiq sage; **2** (conseiller) expert.
IDIOMES **être ~ comme une image** to be as good as gold.

sage-femme, *pl* **sages-femmes** /saʒfam/ ▶ **510** *nf* midwife; **un homme ~** a male midwife.

sagement /saʒmɑ̃/ *adv* **1** (avec bon sens) [*choisir, agir, conseiller*] wisely; **2** (avec docilité) [*attendre, écouter*] quietly; **aller ~ s'asseoir** to go and sit down quietly; **livres ~ rangés sur les rayons** books neatly arranged on the shelves; **3** (sans excès) **user ~ de qch** to use sth wisely; **le marché a réagi ~** Fin the market reacted quietly; **4** (avec décence) gén properly; [*s'habiller*] soberly; [*vivre*] quietly; **se conduire ~** to behave oneself.

sagesse /saʒɛs/ *nf* **1** (de sage) wisdom; **la ~ des nations** popular wisdom; ▶ **crainte**; **2** (bon sens) (de personne) wisdom, common sense; (de parole, décision, d'action) wisdom; (de conseil) soundness; **faire preuve de ~** to show common sense; **avoir la ~ de faire** to have the good sense to do; **la voix de la ~** the voice of reason; **avec ~** wisely ou sensibly; **3** (docilité) good behaviour[GB]; **être d'une ~ exemplaire** to be a model of good behaviour[GB]; **4** (modération) moderation; (manque d'audace) staidness; **user de qch avec ~** to use sth wisely; **la ~ de la façade** the unadventurousness of the façade; **la ~ de nos prix** our sensible ou moderate prices; **5** (réserve) sensible behaviour[GB]; (de vêtement) sobriety; **6** Relig **le Livre de la Sagesse** the Wisdom of Solomon.

Sagittaire /saʒitɛʀ/ ▶ **874** *nprm* Sagittarius.

sagittal, **~e**, *mpl* **-aux** /saʒital, o/ *adj* Anat, Math sagittal.

sagouin○, **~e** /sagwɛ̃, in/ *nm,f* (dirty) slob○; **travail de ~** sloppy ou slovenly work.

Sahara /saaʀa/ ▶ **692** *nprm* Sahara.
■ **~ occidental** Western Sahara.

saharien, **-ienne** /saaʀjɛ̃, ɛn/ **I** *adj* Saharan.
II saharienne *nf* (veste) safari jacket.

Sahel /saɛl/ ▶ **692** *nprm* Sahel.

sahélien, **-ienne** /saeljɛ̃, ɛn/ *adj* Sahelian.

saignant, **~e** /sɛɲɑ̃, ɑ̃t/ **I** *adj* **1** [*viande*] rare; **2** [*blessure*] lit bleeding; fig raw; **3**○ fig [*critique*] savage; Sport [*rencontre*] bloody; Presse [*manchette*] sensationalist.
II○ *nm* **le ~** Culin rare meat; Presse sensationalism.

saignée /sɛɲe/ *nf* **1** Méd bloodletting, bleeding; **faire une ~ à qn** to bleed sb; **2** (dans un budget) hole (**dans** in); **pratiquer une ~ dans son budget** to make a hole in one's budget; **3** (entaille) cut; (pour câble) groove; **4** Agric (rigole) drainage channel.
■ **la ~ du coude** the inside of the elbow.

saignement /sɛɲ(ə)mɑ̃/ *nm* bleeding ₵.
■ **~ de nez** nosebleed.

saigner /sɛɲe/ [1] **I** *vtr* **1** Méd to bleed; **2** (tuer) to kill [sth] (*by slitting its throat*) [*animal*]; **~ un cochon** to stick a pig.
II *vi* to bleed; **~ du nez** to have a nosebleed; **il saignait du nez** his nose was bleeding; **ça va ~**○ there'll be trouble○.
IDIOMES **~ comme un bœuf**○ to bleed heavily; **~ qn à blanc** to bleed sb dry; **se ~ (aux quatre veines) pour qn** to make big sacrifices for sb.

saillant, **~e** /sajɑ̃, ɑ̃t/ **I** *adj* **1** [*os, mâchoire*] prominent; [*muscle*] bulging; [*angle*] salient; **2** [*fait, épisode*] salient.
II *nm* Archit, Mil salient.

saillie /saji/ *nf* **1** (avancée) projection; **en ~** projecting (*épith*); **le balcon est en ~** the balcony juts out; **faire ~** to project; **2** Zool covering, serving; **3** (pointe d'esprit) sally.

saillir /sajiʀ/ [28] **I** *vtr* (couvrir) to cover, to serve.
II *vi* (avancer) to jut out; (ressortir) [*côtes, muscles*] to bulge.

sain, **~e** /sɛ̃, sɛn/ *adj* **1** (en bonne santé) lit, fig [*personne, corps, esprit, plante, économie*] healthy; [*dent*] sound, healthy; **~ d'esprit** sane; **~ de corps et d'esprit** sound in body and mind; **~ et sauf** [*revenir*] safe and sound; [*s'en tirer, s'en sortir*] unscathed; **2** (bénéfique) [*climat, alimentation, activité, vie*] healthy; [*affaire, entreprise*] sound; [*lecture*] wholesome, suitable; **c'est un divertissement ~** it's good clean fun; **3** (en bon état) [*plante*] healthy; [*fruit, maison, charpente*] sound; [*plaie*] clean; **4** (solide, fiable) [*jugement, bases, gestion*] sound; **5** (normal) [*curiosité, scepticisme, colère*] healthy; **6** Naut [*côte*] safe.

saindoux /sɛ̃du/ *nm inv* lard.

sainement /sɛnmɑ̃/ *adv* **1** [*vivre, s'alimenter*] healthily; **2** [*juger*] sensibly; [*raisonner*] soundly.

sainfoin /sɛ̃fwɛ̃/ *nm* sainfoin.
■ **~ des Alpes** French honeysuckle; **~ d'Espagne** or **d'Italie** sulla; **~ oscillant** telegraph plant.

saint, **~e** /sɛ̃, sɛ̃t/ **I** *adj* **1** (sacré) holy; **image ~e** holy image; **les ~s Apôtres** the holy apostles; **~es huiles** holy oils; **la ~e Bible** the Holy Bible; **semaine ~e** Holy Week; **vendredi ~** Good Friday;

jeudi ~ Maundy Thursday; **2** (canonisé) ~ **Paul/Ignace de Loyola/Thomas d'Aquin** Saint Paul/Ignatius Loyola/Thomas Aquinas; **3** (vertueux) good, godly; **4**○ (pour insister) **toute la ~e journée** the whole blessed○ day; **j'ai une ~e horreur de qch** I can't stand sth.

II *nm,f* saint; **ce n'est pas une ~e, il lui arrive de se mettre en colère!** she's no saint, she sometimes gets cross; **se prendre pour un ~/une ~e** to think one is perfect; **elle croit que son fils est un (petit) ~** she thinks her son is perfect, in her eyes her son can do no wrong; ▶ **prêcher, vouer.**

■ **le ~ des ~s** lit, fig the Holy of Holies; **les ~s de glace** the 11th, 12th and 13th May; **les ~s Innocents** the Holy Innocents; **le ~ suaire** the Holy Shroud; **la ~e Église catholique** the Holy Catholic Church; **la sainte famille** the Holy family; **~e nitouche** pej goody-goody○ péj; **ne fais pas ta ~e nitouche** don't be such a goody-goody○; **je ne supporte pas ses airs de ~e nitouche!** I can't stand it when she's doing her goody-goody○ act!; **~e table** communion rail ; **la Sainte Vierge** the Virgin Mary; **les ~es Écritures** the Holy Scriptures.

IDIOMES **jurer par tous les ~s (du Paradis)** to swear by all the saints.

Saint-André /sɛ̃tɑ̃dʀe/ *npr* **croix de ~** Saint Andrew's cross.

Saint-Antoine /sɛ̃tɑ̃twan/ *npr* **croix de ~** Saint Anthony's cross, tau cross.

Saint-Barthélémy /sɛ̃baʀtelemi/ *nf* **la ~** the St Bartholomew's Day massacre.

Saint-Benoît /sɛ̃bənwa/ *npr* **herbe de ~** avens.

saint-bernard /sɛ̃bɛʀnaʀ/ *nm inv* St Bernard; **c'est un vrai ~** fig he's/she's a real Good Samaritan.

Saint-Christophe et Nièves /sɛ̃kʀistɔfenjɛv/ ▶ **321**, **416** *nprm* Saint Christopher-Nevis.

Saint-Cyr /sɛ̃siʀ/ *npr*: *French military academy.*

saint-cyrien, *pl* **~s** /sɛ̃siʀjɛ̃/ *nm* (ancien élève) graduate of St Cyr; (élève) student at St Cyr.

Saint-Domingue /sɛ̃dɔmɛ̃g/ ▶ **857** *npr* Santo Domingo.

Sainte-Alliance /sɛ̃taljɑ̃s/ *nprf* **la ~** the Holy Alliance.

Sainte-Barbe /sɛ̃tbaʀb/ *npr* **herbe de ~** wintercress.

Sainte-Hélène /sɛ̃telɛn/ ▶ **416** *nprf* Saint Helena.

Saint-Elme /sɛ̃tɛlm/ *npr* **feu ~** Saint Elmo's fire.

Sainte-Lucie /sɛ̃tlysi/ ▶ **321**, **416** *nprf* St Lucia.

saintement /sɛ̃tmɑ̃/ *adv* **mourir ~** to die like a saint; **vivre ~** to live a saintly life.

Saint-Esprit /sɛ̃tɛspʀi/ *nprm* Holy Spirit; (en formule) Holy Ghost; **par l'opération du ~**○ by magic.

sainteté /sɛ̃tte/ *nf* **1** (de personne) saintliness, sanctity; (de lieu) holiness; **2** (titre) **Sa Sainteté** His Holiness.

IDIOMES **ne pas être en odeur de ~ (auprès de qn)** to be in sb's bad books.

Saint-Étienne /sɛ̃tetjɛn/ ▶ **857** *npr* Saint-Étienne.

Sainte-Trinité /sɛ̃ttʀinite/ *nf* the Holy Trinity.

Saint-Fiacre /sɛ̃fjakʀ/ *npr* **herbe de ~** heliotrope.

saint-frusquin○ /sɛ̃fʀyskɛ̃/ *nm inv* **tout le ~** the whole caboodle○.

Saint-Gall /sɛ̃gal/ *npr* **1** ▶ **857** (ville) Saint Gall; **2** ▶ **692** (région) **canton de ~** canton of Saint Gall.

Saint-Georges /sɛ̃ʒɔʀʒ/ *npr* **canal ~** Saint George's channel.

saint-glinglin○: **à la saint-glinglin** /asɛ̃glɛ̃glɛ̃/ *loc adv* probably never; **rester/attendre jusqu'à la ~** to stay/wait till the cows come home○.

Saint-Guy /sɛ̃gi/ ▶ **271** *npr* **la danse de ~** Méd Saint Vitus's dance; fig the fidgets (*pl*).

Saint-Hélier /sɛ̃telje/ ▶ **857** *npr* St Helier.

saint-honoré /sɛ̃tɔnɔʀe/ *nm inv* Culin Saint-Honoré (*cream-filled tart topped with choux and caramel*).

Saint-Jacques /sɛ̃ʒak/ *npr* **coquille ~** scallop.

Saint-Jacques-de-Compostelle /sɛ̃ʒakdəkɔ̃pɔstɛl/ ▶ **857** *npr* Santiago de Compostela.

Saint-Jean /sɛ̃ʒɑ̃/ *nf inv* **la ~** Midsummer Day; **feux de la ~** *bonfires lit on Midsummer Night.*

Saint-Laurent /sɛ̃lɔʀɑ̃/ ▶ **357** *nprm* **le ~** the Saint Lawrence; **le golfe du ~** the Gulf of Saint Lawrence.

Saint-Malo /sɛ̃malo/ ▶ **857** *npr* Saint-Malo.

Saint-Marin /sɛ̃maʀɛ̃/ ▶ **321** *nprm* San Marino.

Saint-Martin /sɛ̃maʀtɛ̃/ ▶ **212** *nf inv* **été de la ~** Indian summer.

Saint-Michel /sɛ̃miʃɛl/ *npr* **le mont ~** the Mont-Saint-Michel.

Saint-Nicolas /sɛ̃nikɔla/ *nf* **la ~** Saint Nicholas' Day, 6 December.

Saint-Office /sɛ̃tɔfis/ *nm* Holy Office.

Saint-Père /sɛ̃pɛʀ/ *nm* Holy Father.

Saint-Pétersbourg /sɛ̃petɛʀsbuʀ/ ▶ **857** *npr* St Petersburg.

Saint-Philippe /sɛ̃filip/ *npr* **herbe de ~** Bot woad.

saint-pierre /sɛ̃pjɛʀ/ *nm inv* Culin, Zool John Dory.

Saint-Pierre-et-Miquelon /sɛ̃pjɛʀemiklɔ̃/ ▶ **416** *nprf* Saint Pierre and Miquelon.

Saint-Roch /sɛ̃ʀɔk/ *npr* **herbe ~** fleabane.

Saint-Sépulcre /sɛ̃sepylkʀ/ *nm* Holy Sepulchre[GB].

Saint-Siège /sɛ̃sjɛʒ/ *nm* Holy See.

saint-simonisme /sɛ̃simɔnism/ *nm* Saint-Simonianism.

Saint-Sylvestre /sɛ̃silvɛstʀ/ *nf inv* **la ~** New Year's Eve.

saint-synode, *pl* **saints-synodes** /sɛ̃sinɔd/ *nm* holy synod.

Saint-Thomas et Prince /sɛ̃tɔmaepʀɛ̃s/ ▶ **321**, **416** *nprm* Sao Tomé e Principe.

Saint-Tropez /sɛ̃tʀope/ ▶ **857** *npr* Saint-Tropez.

Saint-Valentin /sɛ̃valɑ̃tɛ̃/ ▶ **212** *nf inv* **la ~** St Valentine's Day, Valentine's Day.

Saint-Vincent et les Grenadines /sɛ̃vɛ̃sɑ̃delegʀənadin/ ▶ **321**, **416** *nprm* St Vincent and the Grenadines.

saisie /sezi/ *nf* **1** (confiscation) seizure; **~ de drogue** seizure of drugs; **2** Jur seizure; **opérer une ~** to make a seizure; **3** Ordinat **~ (sur clavier)** keyboarding; **~ de données** data capture.

■ **~ conservatoire** sequester of property.

saisie-arrêt, *pl* **saisies-arrêts** /seziaʀɛ/ *nf* attachment.

saisine /sezin/ *nf* Jur *submission of a case before the court.*

saisir /seziʀ/ [3] **I** *vtr* **1** (prendre fermement) to seize, to grab [*objet*]; to grab [*personne, bras*]; **~ qn par le bras/la main/la manche/les cheveux** to grab ou seize sb by the arm/the hand/the sleeve/the hair; **2** (attraper) [*animal*] to seize [*proie*]; **~ au vol** lit to catch [*balle*]; fig to jump at [*affaire*]; (prendre) to snatch [sth] up; ▶ **bond**; **3** (profiter de) to seize [*occasion*]; **elle saisira le moindre prétexte pour le renvoyer**○ she'll use the slightest excuse to sack○ him; **'affaire à ~'** 'amazing bargain'; **4** (comprendre) to understand; **il n'a pas l'air de ~ la gravité de la situation** I don't think he understands how serious the situation is; **tu saisis?** do you understand?, do you get it○?; **5** (entendre) to catch [*bribes de conversation*]; **6** (s'emparer de) [*émotion, froid, envie, terreur*] to grip [*personne*]; **elle a été saisie par le froid en entrant dans l'eau** she was gripped by the cold as she went into the water; **elle a été saisie d'une envie de rire** she was seized with a desire to laugh; **7** (impressionner) to strike [*personne*]; **j'ai été saisi par leur maigreur** I was struck by how thin they were; **il a été saisi par la beauté du paysage** he was struck by the beauty of the landscape; **8** (confisquer) [*police, douane*] to seize [*drogue*]; **9** Jur to seize, to distrain [*biens*]; **~ la justice** to go to law; **~ la justice d'une affaire** to refer ou submit a matter to a court; **la Cour Suprême a été saisie de l'affaire** the matter was referred to the Supreme Court; **10** Ordinat to capture [*données*]; to keyboard [*texte*]; **11** Culin to sear [*viande*].

II se saisir *vpr* **se ~ de** to catch ou grab hold of [*objet*]; to annex [*territoire*].

saisissable /sezisabl/ *adj* **1** (perceptible) [*détail, nuance*] perceptible; **2** Jur [*biens*] distrainable; [*revenus*] attachable.

saisissant, **~e** /sezisɑ̃, ɑ̃t/ *adj* **1** [*froid*] piercing; **2** (frappant) [*effet, ressemblance, coïncidence*] striking; **un portrait ~ de ressemblance** a portrait which is a striking likeness.

saisissement /sezismɑ̃/ *nm* **1** (sensation de froid) sudden chill; **2** (émotion) sudden emotion, shock.

saison /sɛzɔ̃/ ▶ **738** *nf* **1** (division de l'année) season; **en cette ~** at this time of year; **en toute ~** all (the) year round; **il fait** or **c'est un temps de ~** it's typical weather for the time of year, it's seasonal weather; **porter des vêtements de ~** to wear the right clothes for the time of year; **fruits de ~** seasonal fruits; **la ~ nouvelle** springtime; **à la belle/mauvaise ~** in the summer/winter months; **remarque de ~** fig fitting remark; **il n'y a plus de ~s!** there are no real seasons any more; **2** (période) season; **~ des asperges/huîtres** asparagus/oyster season; **~ des pluies** rainy season; **~ froide** cold season; **~ des amours/de la pêche** mating/fishing season; **~ des foins/semailles** haymaking/sowing time; **3** Tourisme season; **~ touristique** tourist season; **~ des vacances** holiday GB ou vacation US season; **aller faire la ~ à Nice** to go and work in Nice during the holiday season; **en pleine ~** at the height of the season; **la haute/morte ~** the high/slack season; **en basse ~** in the off season; **prix hors ~** off-season prices; **4** Sport, Théât season; **~ hippique/théâtrale** horseracing/theatre season; **5** Méd **faire une ~ à Vichy** to take a cure at Vichy.

saisonnier, **-ière** /sɛzɔnje, ɛʀ/ **I** *adj* seasonal.

II *nm,f* (ouvrier) seasonal worker; (hôtelier) *hotelier who only opens during the season.*

saké /sake/ *nm* sake.

Sakhaline /sakalin/ ▶ **416** *npr* **île ~** Sakhalin.

salace /salas/ *adj* salacious.

salacité /salasite/ *nf* salaciousness.

salade /salad/ *nf* **1** (plante) lettuce; **planter des ~s** to plant lettuces; **2** (plat) salad; **~ verte** green salad; **~ de tomates/riz** tomato/rice salad; **~ composée** mixed salad; **haricots verts en ~** French bean salad; **3**○ (embrouillamini) muddle; (mensonge) yarn; (boniment de vendeur) sales patter ou pitch○; **raconter des ~s** to spin yarns○; **il a essayé de me vendre sa ~** he gave me his sales patter ou pitch○.

■ **~ de fruits** fruit salad; **~ niçoise** salade niçoise; **~ russe** Russian salad; **~ tiède** *green salad with warm garnish.*

saladier /saladje/ *nm* (récipient) salad bowl; (contenu) bowl.

Les saisons

En anglais, on trouve quelquefois les noms des saisons avec des majuscules, mais les minuscules sont préférables.

printemps = spring
été = summer
automne = autumn (*GB*) *ou* fall (*US*)
hiver = winter

Dans les expressions suivantes, summer *est pris comme exemple; les autres noms de saisons s'utilisent de la même façon.*

j'aime l'été = I like the summer *ou* I like summer
l'été a été pluvieux = the summer was wet *ou* summer was wet
un été pluvieux = a rainy summer
l'été le plus chaud = the warmest summer

Quand?

L'anglais emploie souvent in *devant les noms de saisons.*

en été = in the summer *ou* in summer
au début de l'été = in the early summer *ou* in early summer
à la fin de l'été = in the late summer *ou* in late summer
à la mi-été = in mid-summer

Mais in *peut être remplacé par une autre préposition, ou par* this, that, next, last *etc.*

pendant l'été = during the summer
pendant tout l'été = throughout the summer
tout au long de l'été = all through the summer
avant l'été = before the summer
jusqu'à l'été = until the summer
cet été = this summer
cet été-là = that summer
l'été prochain = next summer
l'été dernier = last summer
l'année prochaine en été = the summer after next
l'année dernière en été = the summer before last
tous les ans en été = every summer
un été sur deux = every other summer *ou* every second summer
presque tous les étés = most summers

De avec les noms de saisons

Les expressions françaises avec de se traduisent en anglais par l'emploi des noms de saisons en position d'adjectifs.

la collection d'été = the summer collection
une journée d'été = a summer day
une pluie d'été = a summer shower
un soir d'été = a summer evening
le soleil d'été = summer sunshine
les soldes d'été = the summer sales
des vêtements d'été = summer clothes
un temps d'été = summer weather

Enfin, comparer:

un matin d'été = one summer morning
par un matin d'été = on a summer morning
un matin en été = one morning in summer

salage /salaʒ/ *nm* **1** (de nourriture) salting; **2** (de route) gritting GB, salting US.

salaire /salɛʀ/ *nm* **1** (paie) salary; (à la journée, à l'heure, à la semaine) (taux) wage; (somme) wages (*pl*); **~ annuel/mensuel** annual/monthly salary; **~ horaire/journalier/hebdomadaire** hourly/daily/weekly wage ou salary; **~ brut/net** gross/take-home pay; **~ au rendement** incentive wages, efficiency wages US; **~ de misère** or **famine** starvation wage; **2** fig (récompense) reward (**de** for); (châtiment) punishment (**de** for).
■ **~ de base** basic salary GB, base pay US; **~ d'embauche** starting salary; **~ minimum interprofessionnel de croissance, SMIC** guaranteed minimum wage; **~ unique** single income.
IDIOMES **toute peine mérite ~** Prov hard work deserves a reward.

salaison /salɛzɔ̃/ *nf* **1** (viande) salt meat ¢; (poisson) salt fish ¢; **2** (action de saler) salting.

salamalecs /salamalɛk/ *nmpl* unctuousness ¢; **faire des ~** to be unctuous.

salamandre /salamɑ̃dʀ/ *nf* **1** Zool salamander; **2** ®(poêle) (slow-burning) stove.

Salamanque /salamɑ̃k/ ▶ **857** *npr* Salamanca.

salami /salami/ *nm* salami GB, boloney US.

salant /salɑ̃/ *adj m* **marais ~** saltern.

salarial, **~e**, *mpl* **-iaux** /salaʀjal, o/ *adj* **1** (des salaires) [*politique, législation, négociations, revendications, augmentation*] wage (*épith*); **allocations ~es** tax allowances; **revenu ~/non ~** earned/unearned income; **2** (des salariés) **cotisation ~e** employee's contribution; **charges ~es** payroll charges; **coût ~ unitaire** unit wage cost.

salariat /salaʀja/ *nm* **1** (ensemble des salariés) wage-earners (*pl*); **progression du ~ féminin** increase in the female workforce ou in the number of women at work; **2** (condition) **le ~ à temps partiel** part-time wage earning; **le ~ et le bénévolat** salaried and voluntary status; **3** (mode de rémunération) (au mois) payment by salary; (à l'heure, la semaine) payment by wages.

salarié, **~e** /salaʀje/ **I** *adj* [*ouvrier, employé*] wage-earning; [*emploi, travail*] salaried; **travailleur non ~** non-wage-earning worker; **travail non ~** unwaged work.
II *nm,f* (ouvrier) wage earner; (employé) salaried employee; **les ~s** wage earners; **les ~s d'une entreprise** the employees on a company's payroll.

salaud◑ /salo/ **I** *adj m* rotten○; **c'est ~ ce que tu as fait là** that was a rotten○ thing to do.
II *nm* offensive bastard◑; **t'en as d'la chance mon ~!** you lucky bastard◑!; **faire un coup de ~ à qn** to play sb a rotten trick.

sale /sal/ **I** *adj* **1** (*after n*) (pas propre) dirty; (obscène) dirty; ▶ **linge**; **2** (*before n*) (désagréable) [*individu*] horrible; [*bête, maladie, affaire, habitude*] nasty; [*temps*] filthy; [*métier, travail, endroit*] rotten; offensive dirty; **quel ~ gosse**○**!** what a horrible brat○!; **~ menteur!** you dirty liar!; **quel ~ bled**○**!** what a dump○!; **il a une ~ tête** or **gueule**◑ (antipathique) he's got a nasty face; (maladif) he looks dreadful; (mécontent) he's pulling GB ou making US an awful face; **faire une ~ tête** to pull GB ou make US an awful face; **l'événement fut un ~ coup pour lui** the event dealt him a very nasty blow; **jouer un ~ tour à qn** to play a dirty trick on sb; **elle a vraiment un ~ caractère** she's got a foul temper; **j'ai passé un ~ quart d'heure** or **de ~s moments** I had a pretty grim time (of it).
II *nm* **mettre qch au ~** to put sth in the wash; **aller au ~** to go in the wash.
IDIOMES **être ~ comme un peigne** or **un cochon** to be filthy dirty.

salé, **~e** /sale/ **I** *pp* ▶ **saler**.
II *pp adj* **1** (contenant du sel) salt (*épith*); salty (*jamais épith*); **eau ~e** salt water; **lac ~** salt lake; **la mer est ~e** the sea is salty; **2** (additionné de sel) [*alimentation, beurre, cacahuète, eau, plat*] salted; [*mets, amuse-gueule*] savoury[GB]; (conservé avec du sel) [*poisson, viande*] salt (*épith*); **manger ~** to eat savoury[GB] things; **non ~** unsalted; **trop ~** too salty; **3** (de sel) salty; **goût ~** salty taste.
III *adj* **1** (grivois) spicy; **propos ~s** spicy talk ¢; **2**○ (très élevé) [*prix*] steep; [*jugement*] stiff.
IV *nm* **le ~** savoury[GB] food; ▶ **petit**.

salement /salmɑ̃/ *adv* **1** (en salissant) **manger ~** to be a messy eater; **un ouvrier/peintre qui travaille ~** a worker/painter who does a messy job; **2**○ (gravement) badly, seriously; **il s'est fait ~ amocher**○ he's been badly ou seriously injured.

saler /sale/ [1] *vtr* **1** (mettre du sel sur) to salt [*mets*]; **~ et poivrer (qch)** to add salt and pepper (to sth); **2**○ (augmenter) to bump up○ [*facture, note, prix*]; **3** (en hiver) to grit GB, to salt US [*route*].

saleté /salte/ *nf* **1** (état) dirtiness; (crasse) dirt; **être d'une ~ repoussante** to be filthy, to be disgustingly dirty; **tu n'imagines pas la ~ de sa maison/ses vêtements** you can't imagine how dirty ou filthy his house is/his clothes are; **vivre dans la ~** to live in filth; **être couvert de ~** to be covered with dirt; **2** (impureté) dirt ¢; **il y a une ~ sur l'objectif** there's dirt on the lens; **3** (ordure) **ramasser les ~s qui traînent dans le jardin** to pick up the rubbish GB ou trash US in the garden GB ou yard US; **faire des ~s** to make a mess; **le chat a fait des ~s sur le tapis** euph the cat made a mess on the carpet; **raconter des ~s** fig to tell dirty stories; **4**○ (chose de mauvaise qualité) (objet) piece of junk; (aliment) junk food; **quelle ~ cette bagnole**○**!** this car is a real piece of junk!; **~ d'ordinateur!** damn computer!; **c'est une vraie ~ ce virus!** it's a rotten bug!; **~ de temps!** what lousy weather○!; **~, va! dégage!** fig scum◑, get lost○!; **5**○ (méchanceté) **faire une ~ à qn** to play a dirty trick on sb.

salicaire /salikɛʀ/ *nf* purple loosestrife.

salicylate /salisilat/ *nm* salicylate.

salicylique /salisilik/ *adj* salicylic.

salière /saljɛʀ/ *nf* **1** Culin (récipient ouvert) saltcellar; (avec couvercle percé) saltcellar GB, saltshaker US; **2**○ (creux des clavicules) saltcellar○ GB.

salifère /salifɛʀ/ *adj* saliferous.

salification /salifikasjɔ̃/ *nf* salification.

salifier /salifje/ [2] *vtr* to salify.

saligaud◑ /saligo/ *nm* **1** (salaud) offensive dirty bastard◑ injur; **2**† (personne sale) dirty pig○.

salin, **~e** /salɛ̃, in/ **I** *adj* saline.
II *nm* Géog salt marsh.
III saline *nf* Ind saltworks (+ *v sg*); Géog salt marsh.

salinité /salinite/ *nf* salinity.

salique /salik/ *adj* **loi ~** Salic law.

salir /saliʀ/ [3] **I** *vtr* **1** (rendre sale) to dirty [*sol, assiette*]; to soil [*draps, lit*]; **2** (flétrir) to sully [*mémoire, amour*]; to corrupt [*artiste, imagination*]; **toutes ces insinuations risquent de ~ cet homme** all these insinuations could sully the man's reputation.
II *vi* [*industrie, charbon*] to pollute.
III se salir *vpr* **1** (se couvrir de taches, de saleté) to get dirty, to dirty oneself; **se ~ les mains** lit, fig to get one's hands dirty; **2** (se compromettre) to sully ou tarnish one's reputation.

salissant, **~e** /salisɑ̃, ɑ̃t/ *adj* **1** (qui devient sale) [*couleur, tissu*] which shows the dirt (*épith, après n*); **le blanc est ~** white shows the dirt; **2** (qui rend sale) [*travail*] dirty.

salissure /salisyʀ/ *nf* (dirty) mark.

salivaire /salivɛʀ/ *adj* salivary.

salivation /salivasjɔ̃/ *nf* salivation.

salive /saliv/ *nf* saliva.
IDIOMES **perdre** or **dépenser inutilement sa ~** to waste one's breath.

saliver /salive/ [1] *vi* to salivate; **~ devant qch** to drool over sth.

salle /sal/ *nf* **1** (pièce) (de château, palais) hall; (de musée, bibliothèque, café) room; (de restaurant) (dining) room; (de cinéma, théâtre) auditorium; (de grotte) chamber; (d'hôpital) ward; **cinéma à cinq ~s** cinema with five screens; **le film passe en ~ 2** the film is on screen 2; **prochainement dans vos ~s** Cin coming soon to a cinema near you; **la ~ était comble** the place was packed; **faire ~ comble** [*spectacle*] to be packed; [*acteur*] to fill the house; **y a-t-il un médecin dans la ~?** is there a doctor in the house?; **'~ au sous-sol'** (dans restaurant) 'more seats downstairs'; **en ~** [*sport*] indoor; **'prix en ~'** (dans café) *tariff for drinks served at the tables in a café*; **2** (spectateurs) audience.
■ **~ d'armes** (pour exercice) drill hall GB, armory US; (pour entrepôt) armory; **~ d'arrêt(s)** Mil guardroom; **~ d'attente** waiting room; **~ d'audience** Jur courtroom; **~ audiovisuelle** audiovisual room; **~ de bains** bathroom; **~ de bal** ballroom; **~ de billard** billiard room; **~ blanche** Ind clean room; **~ capitulaire** chapter room; **~ de casino** gaming room; **~ de cinéma** cinema GB, movie theater US; **~ de classe** classroom; **~ de commandes** control room; **~ communale** village hall; **~ commune** (à l'hôpital) ward; **~ de concert** concert hall; **~ de conférences** (petite pièce) lecture room; (avec gradins) lecture theatre[GB], auditorium; **~ de congrès** conference hall; **~ de contrôle** control room; **~ des délibérations** committee room; **~ d'eau** shower room; **~ d'embarquement** Aviat departure lounge; **~ d'études** Scol private study room GB, study hall US; **~ d'exposition** (petite pièce) exhibition room; (grande pièce) exhibition hall; Comm showroom; **~ des fêtes** (de village) village hall; (en ville) community centre[GB]; **~ de garde** (d'hôpital) staff room; **~ des gardes** (de château) guardroom; **~ de gymnastique** gymnasium; **~ d'honneur** Mil trophy room; **~ informatique** computer room; **~ de jeu(x)** (de casino) gaming room; (pour enfants) playroom; **~ de lecture** reading room; **~ de loisirs** recreation room; **~ des machines** Naut engine room; **~ à manger** (pièce) dining room; (mobilier) dining-room suite; **~ des marchés** Fin (de banque) dealing room; (de Bourse) floor; **~ modulable** multi-purpose room; **~ de montage** Cin cutting room; **~ municipale** town hall; **~ omnisports** sports hall; **~ d'opération** Méd operating theatre GB, operating room US; **~ d'opérations** Mil operations room; **~ des pas perdus** waiting hall; **~ de police** Mil guardroom; **~ polyvalente** multi-purpose hall; **~ de presse** press room; **~ des professeurs** staff room; **~ de projection** projection room; **~ de quartier** local cinema GB, local movie theater US; **~ de réanimation** intensive care ward; **~ de rédaction** Presse (newspaper) office; **~ de régie** Cin, Théât control room; **~ de réunion** meeting room; **~ de réveil** Méd recovery room; **~ de séjour** living room; **~ de soins** Méd treatment room; **~ de spectacle** Cin cinema GB, movie theater US; Théât theatre[GB]; **~ de théâtre** theatre[GB]; **~ du trône** throne room; **~ des ventes** auction room; **~s obscures** cinemas GB, movie theaters US.

Salluste /salyst/ *npr* Sallust.

salmigondis○ /salmigɔ̃di/ *nm inv* (ramassis) hotchpotch GB, hodgepodge US.

salmis /salmi/ *nm* salmi.

salmonelle /salmɔnɛl/ *nf* salmonella.

salmonellose /salmɔnɛloz/ ▶271 *nf* salmonella poisoning, salmonellosis spéc.

salmoniculture /salmɔnikyltyʀ/ *nf* salmon farming.

salmonidé /salmɔnide/ *nm* salmonid; **les Salmonidés** Salmonidae.

saloir /salwaʀ/ *nm* salting tub.

Salomé /salome/ *npr* Salome.

Salomon /salomɔ̃/ *npr* **1** Hist Solomon; **2** ▶321, 416 Géog **îles ~s** Solomon Islands.

salon /salɔ̃/ *nm* **1** (pièce) gén lounge; (dans un château, palais) drawing room; **la pièce fait ~-salle à manger** the room is a combined living dining room; **2** (mobilier) living-room suite, sitting-room suite; **~ de jardin** garden furniture; **3** (exposition) (pour professionnels) (trade) show; (pour grand public) fair; (artistique) exhibition; **les organisateurs du ~** the trade show organizers; **le ~ de l'auto/de la gastronomie/de l'informatique** the car/food/computer show; **~ des collectionneurs/du livre/de l'emploi** collectors'/book/careers fair; **~ de l'habitat** home furnishings exhibition; **4** (réunion mondaine) salon; **faire** or **tenir ~** to hold a salon; **~ littéraire/politique** literary/political salon; **conversation de ~** polite conversation.
■ **~ de beauté** beauty salon; **~ de coiffure** hairdressing salon; **~ d'essayage** fitting room; **~ funéraire** C funeral parlour GB, funeral home US; **~ de thé** tearoom.

salonnard○, **~e** /salɔnaʀ, aʀd/ *nm,f* pej lounge lizard.

salopard◑ /salɔpaʀ/ *nm* offensive bastard◑ injur.

salope◑ /salɔp/ *nf* offensive **1** (garce) bitch◑ injur; (femme facile) tart○ injur, whore; **2** (salaud) bastard◑ injur.

saloper○ /salɔpe/ [1] *vtr* **1** (gâcher) to botch○ [*travail*]; **2** (salir) to muck up○.

saloperie◑ /salɔpʀi/ *nf* **1** (saleté) muck○ ¢; (matière visqueuse) gunge○ GB, goop◑ ¢ US; fig (produit nocif, drogue) muck○ ¢; **les peintres ont fait des ~s partout** the painters left muck all over the place; **2** (microbe, maladie) bug○; **elle a encore attrapé une ~ à l'école** she's caught a bug at school again; **3** (nourriture) (infecte) muck○ ¢ GB, slop○; (malsaine) junk (food)○ ¢; **ton régime ne vaut rien si tu continues à manger des ~s** it's useless dieting if you keep eating junk food; **c'est pas mauvais ces petites ~s!** iron this muck's not bad! iron; **4** (objet de rebut) junk○ ¢; **enlève-moi toutes les ~s qui traînent à la cave** clear up all that junk in the cellar; **cette ~ d'ordinateur est encore en panne** this bloody◑ GB ou damn○ computer's not working again; **5** (procédé) dirty trick; **il m'a fait une belle ~** he played me a really dirty trick; **6** (propos) filthy remarks; **cesse de dire des ~s** (grossièretés) stop that filthy language; (calomnies) stop those filthy comments.

salopette /salɔpɛt/ *nf* (pour protéger) overalls (*pl*); (pour s'habiller) dungarees (*pl*) GB, overalls (*pl*) US; (pour skier) salopettes (*pl*) GB, ski overalls (*pl*) US.

salpêtre /salpɛtʀ/ *nm* saltpetre[GB].
■ **~ du Chili** Chile saltpetre[GB].

salpingite /salpɛ̃ʒit/ ▶271 *nf* salpingitis.

salsa /salsa/ *nf* salsa; **danser la ~** to dance the salsa.

salsepareille /salsəpaʀɛj/ *nf* greenbrier.

salsifis /salsifi/ *nm inv* salsify.
■ **~ d'Espagne** or **noir** black salsify.

saltimbanque /saltɛ̃bɑ̃k/ *nmf* **1** (bateleur) street acrobat; **2** pej (comédien) entertainer; **il appartient au monde des ~s** he belongs to the world of entertainment.

salubre /salybʀ/ *adj* [*air, climat*] healthy; [*logement*] salubrious sout.

salubrité /salybʀite/ *nf* (d'air, de climat) healthiness; (de logement) salubrity sout.
■ **~ publique** public health.

saluer /salɥe/ [1] *vtr* **1** (dire bonjour) to greet [*personne*]; **~ qn de la main** to wave to ou at sb; **~ qn de la tête** to nod to sb; **~ qn de loin/en passant** to acknowledge sb from a distance/in passing; **saluez-la de ma part** say hello to her from me; **~ le public** to take a bow; **2** (dire au revoir) to say goodbye to [*personne*]; **je vous salue** I'll say goodbye; **je vous salue bien bas**† I take my humble leave of you; **3** (accueillir) to greet [*personne*]; **~ qn aux cris de** to greet sb with cries of; **~ qn par des applaudissements** to greet sb with applause; **4** Mil to salute [*soldat, officier, drapeau, navire*]; **5** (accueillir avec satisfaction) to welcome [*décision, nomination, nouvelle, résultat*]; **~ qch avec** or **par** to greet sth with; **~ l'annonce par des applaudissements** to greet the announcement with applause; **6** (rendre hommage) to salute [*personne en vie*]; to pay tribute to [*défunt, mémoire*]; to praise [*qualité, travail, rapport, attitude*]; **je vous salue Marie** hail Mary; **~ qn/qch comme** to hail sb/sth as; **salué comme un génie/une étape décisive** hailed as a genius/a breakthrough.

salure /salyʀ/ *nf* **1** Culin saltiness; **2** Chimie saltness.

salut /saly/ *nm* **1** (salutation) greeting; **~!** (bonjour) hello!, hi!; (au revoir) bye!; **~ à ta sœur!** say hello to your sister!; **~ les filles/les copains/beauté!** hi girls/pals/beautiful!; **~ amical** friendly greeting; **~ de la main** wave (of the hand); **~ de la tête** nod; **~ des acteurs** bow; **2** (geste) salute; **~ fasciste/militaire** fascist/military salute; **~ au drapeau** salute to the colours[GB] ou flag; **faire le ~ militaire** to salute; **3** (secours) salvation (**dans** in); **être le ~ de qn** to be sb's salvation; **apporter le ~** to offer salvation; **trouver son ~ dans qch** to find one's salvation in sth; **le ~ se trouve dans** salvation lies in; **devoir son ~ à** to owe one's salvation to; **~ national** or **public** national salvation; **4** Relig (rédemption) salvation; **obtenir son ~** to find salvation; **hors de l'Église point de ~** no salvation outside the Church; **5** (hommage) homage; **~ à** homage to.

salutaire /salytɛʀ/ *adj* **1** (bénéfique) [*choc, changement, expérience, leçon, rappel*] salutary; [*effet, environnement, effort*] beneficial; [*air, habitude*] healthy; **cela leur a été ~** it did them good; **2** (rédempteur) salutary.

salutation /salytasjɔ̃/ **I** *nf* **1** gén greeting; **2** Relig salutation.
II salutations *nfpl* **sincères ~s** (à une personne nommée) yours sincerely; (à une personne non nommée) yours faithfully.

salutiste /salytist/ *nmf* Salvationist.

Salvador /salvadɔʀ/ ▶321 *nprm* El Salvador.

salvadorien, **-ienne** /salvadɔʀjɛ̃, ɛn/ ▶537 *adj* Salvadorian.

Salvadorien, **-ienne** /salvadɔʀjɛ̃, ɛn/ ▶537 *nm,f* Salvadorian.

salvateur, **-trice** /salvatœʀ, tʀis/ *adj* saving (*épith*).

salve /salv/ *nf* **1** (d'armes à feu) salvo; **tirer une ~ d'honneur** to fire a salute; **2** (série) **~ d'applaudissements** burst of applause; **~ d'injures** volley of insults; **3** (attaque verbale) broadside; **lancer une ~ contre qn** to launch a broadside against sb.

Samaritain, **~e** /samaʀitɛ̃, ɛn/ *nm,f* Samaritan; **faire le bon ~**, **jouer les ~s** to act the good Samaritan.

samba /sɑ̃mba/ *nf* samba.

samedi /samdi/ ▶750 *nm* Saturday.
■ **~ saint** Holy Saturday.
IDIOMES **être né un ~** to be born lazy.

samizdat /samizdat/ *nm* samizdat.

Samoa /samɔa/ ▶321, 416 *nprm* Samoa.
■ **~ occidental** Western Samoa.

samoan, **~e** /samɔɑ̃, an/ ▶462, 537 **I** *adj* Samoan.
II *nm* Ling Samoan.

Samoan, **~e** /samɔɑ̃, an/ ▶537 *nm,f* Ling Samoan.

samouraï /samuʀaj/ *nm* samurai.

samovar /samɔvaʀ/ *nm* samovar.

samoyède /samɔjɛd/ *adj, nm* Samoyed.

Samson /sɑ̃sɔ̃/ *npr* Samson.

SAMU /samy/ *nm* (*abbr* = **Service d'assistance médicale d'urgence**) ≈ mobile accident unit GB, emergency medical service, EMS US.

sana○ /sana/ *nm* sanatorium GB, sanitarium US.

sanatorium /sanatɔʀjɔm/ *nm* sanatorium GB, sanitarium US.

Sancerre /sɑ̃sɛʀ/ ▶857 *npr* Sancerre.

sancerrois, **~e** /sɑ̃sɛʀwa, az/ ▶857 *adj* of Sancerre.

Sancerrois, **~e** /sɑ̃sɛʀwa, az/ **I** ▶857 *nm,f* (natif) native of Sancerre; (habitant) inhabitant of Sancerre.
II ▶692 *nm* **le ~** the Sancerre region.

Sancho Pança /sɑ̃ʃopɑ̃sa/ *npr* Sancho Panza.

sanctificateur, **-trice** /sɑ̃ktifikatœʀ, tʀis/ **I** *adj* sanctifying.
II *nm,f* sanctifier.

sanctification /sɑ̃ktifikasjɔ̃/ *nf* sanctification.

sanctifier /sɑ̃ktifje/ [1] *vtr* to sanctify; **que Ton nom soit sanctifié** hallowed be Thy name.

sanction /sɑ̃ksjɔ̃/ *nf* **1** (peine) Jur penalty, sanction; Admin disciplinary measure; Scol punishment; **la ~ de l'échec** the penalty for failure; **prendre des ~s contre qn** gén to discipline sb; Admin to take disciplinary action against sb; **prendre des ~s économiques contre** to impose economic sanctions on; **maintenir/lever les ~s** to maintain/lift sanctions; **prononcer une ~ contre un joueur** Sport to penalize a player; **2** (ratification, approbation) sanction; (jugement) verdict; **recevoir une ~ officielle** to be given official sanction; **la ~ des électeurs va tomber le 2 mars** voters will give their verdict on 2 March.
■ **~ disciplinaire** Admin disciplinary measure; **~ pénale** Jur penalty.

sanctionner /sɑ̃ksjɔne/ [1] *vtr* **1** (punir) to punish [*faute, coupable*]; **2** (ratifier) to sanction [*loi, usage, conduite*]; **3** (consacrer) to give official recognition to [*études, formation*]; **compétences sanctionnées par un diplôme** skills recognized by a diploma; **une année d'études sanctionnées par un diplôme** a one-year course leading to a diploma.

sanctuaire /sɑ̃ktɥɛʀ/ *nm* **1** (lieu saint) shrine; **2** (asile) sanctuary.

sanctus /sɑ̃ktus/ *nm* Sanctus.

sandale /sɑ̃dal/ *nf* sandal.

sandalette /sɑ̃dalɛt/ *nf* light sandal.

sandow® /sɑ̃do/ *nm* **1** (sangle) luggage elastic; **2** Aviat bungee.

sandre /sɑ̃dʀ/ *nm* pikeperch.

sandwich, *pl* **~s** or **~es** /sɑ̃dwitʃ/ *nm* **1** Culin sandwich; **~ au pâté** pâté sandwich; **prendre en ~** to sandwich [*personne, voiture*]; **(pris) en ~** sandwiched (**entre** between); **2** Tech (matériau) sandwich panel.

sang /sɑ̃/ *nm* **1** Physiol blood; **donner son ~** to give blood; **avoir de l'alcool dans le ~** to have alcohol in one's blood; **~ contaminé** contaminated blood; **perte de ~** loss of blood; **être en ~** to be covered with blood; **couleur de ~** blood-red; **taché de ~** bloodstained; **mordre jusqu'au ~** to bite through the skin; **animal à ~ chaud/froid** warm-/cold-blooded animal; **le ~ m'est monté à la tête** I had a rush of blood to the head; **au premier ~** (dans un duel) at the first cut; **coup de ~** apoplexy; **avoir le ~ qui monte au visage** to blush; **verser son ~ pour son pays** to shed blood for one's country; **faire couler le ~** fig to shed blood; **le ~ a coulé** fig blood flowed; **avoir du ~ sur les mains** fig to have blood on one's hands; ▶**navet**; **2** (vie) **~ des martyrs** martyrs' blood; **au prix du ~** with loss of life; **payer de son ~** to pay with one's blood; **3** (violence) bloodshed; **vouloir la guerre et le ~** to want war and bloodshed; **se terminer dans le ~** to end in bloodshed; **odeur de ~** smell of blood; **ivre de ~** lusting for blood; **4** (hérédité) blood; **un ~ royal** royal blood; **~ riche et généreux** blood of a rich and generous line; **de ~** [*frère, liens*] blood (*épith*); **être du même ~** to be kin; **vous êtes de mon ~** you and I are kin.
■ **~ bleu** blue blood; **~ du Christ** Relig blood of Christ; **~ rouge** arterial blood.
IDIOMES **avoir le ~ chaud** (être sensuel) to be hot-blooded; (être coléreux) to be hotheaded; **avoir un coup de ~** to have apoplexy; **avoir qch dans le ~**○ to have sth in one's blood; **il a ça dans le ~** it's in his blood; **mettre qch à feu et à ~** to put sth to fire and the sword; **mon ~ n'a fait qu'un tour** (d'émotion) my heart missed a beat; (de colère) I saw red; **se faire du mauvais ~**○ to worry; **apporter du ~ neuf** to bring new blood; **tourner les ~s à qn**○ to give sb a fright; **bon ~**○, **bon ~ de bon ~**○, **bon ~ de bonsoir**○! for God's sake○!

sang-froid /sɑ̃fʀwa/ *nm inv* composure; **garder/perdre son ~** to keep/lose one's composure; **garde ton ~!** keep calm!; **faire qch de ~** to do sth in cold blood.

sanglant, **~e** /sɑ̃glɑ̃, ɑ̃t/ *adj* **1** (violent) [*affrontement, incident, répression, putsch, époque*] bloody; **2** (outrageant) [*affront, défaite*] cruel; **3** (couvert de sang) [*plaie, main*] bloody; [*couteau, vêtement*] bloodstained.

sangle /sɑ̃gl/ *nf* **1** (pour attacher) strap; **2** Équit girth; **3** (de siège, lit) webbing ¢.
■ **~ abdominale** Anat abdominal muscles (*pl*).

sanglé, **~e** /sɑ̃gle/ **I** *pp* ▶**sangler**.
II *pp adj* **~ dans** squeezed into.

sangler /sɑ̃gle/ [1] *vtr* Équit to girth.

sanglier /sɑ̃glije/ *nm* wild boar.

sanglot /sɑ̃glo/ *nm* sob; **dire qch dans un ~** to say sth with a sob; **éclater en ~s** to burst out sobbing; **avec des ~s dans la voix** with a sob in one's voice.

sangloter /sɑ̃glɔte/ [1] *vi* to sob.

sangria /sɑ̃gʀija/ *nf* sangria.

sangsue /sɑ̃sy/ *nf* (tous contextes) leech.

sanguin, **~e** /sɑ̃gɛ̃, in/ **I** *adj* **1** Méd, Physiol blood; **examen/flux/prélèvement ~** blood test/flow/sample; **2** (rouge) [*visage*] ruddy; **3** (impétueux) impulsive; **tempérament ~** (en médecine ancienne) sanguine humour[GB]; gén impulsive character.
II *nm,f* (personne impétueuse) impulsive person; **c'est un ~** he's hotheaded.
III sanguine *nf* **1** (orange à pulpe rouge) blood orange; **2** Art (dessin) red chalk drawing; (crayon) red chalk; **3** Minér red chalk.

sanguinaire /sɑ̃ginɛʀ/ *adj* [*régime, dictature*] bloody, sanguinary sout; [*attaque, bataille, crime*] bloody; [*personne, goût*] bloodthirsty.

sanguinolent, **~e** /sɑ̃ginɔlɑ̃, ɑ̃t/ *adj* [*couteau, vêtement, pansements*] blood-stained; [*plaie*] from which blood is oozing (*après n*); [*pus*] blood-streaked.

sanisette® /sanizɛt/ *nf* automatic public toilet.

sanitaire /sanitɛʀ/ **I** *adj* **1** Méd [*règlement, service, personnel*] health (*épith*); [*conditions*] sanitary; **2** (en plomberie) [*système, ingénieur*] plumbing (*épith*); **installations ~s** sanitation (*sg*).
II *nm* (secteur d'activité) **le ~** bathroom equipment and installation.
III sanitaires *nmpl* **les ~s** (lieu) (dans un bâtiment) the bathroom; (dans un camping) the toilet block; (plomberie) the plumbing.

sans /sɑ̃/

■ **Note** Lorsque *sans* marque l'absence, le manque ou la privation, il se traduit généralement par *without*. Lorsqu'il fait partie d'une expression figée comme *sans concession, sans équivoque, sans emploi, sans intérêt* la traduction est donnée respectivement sous ***concession***, ***équivoque***, ***emploi***, ***intérêt*** etc.
– De même quand il est associé à un verbe, *compter sans, cela va sans dire etc* la traduction est donnée respectivement sous les verbes ***compter***, ***dire*** etc.
– La double négation *non sans* est traitée sous ***non***.
– On trouvera ci-dessous d'autres exemples et les usages particuliers de *sans*.

I *adv* (exprime l'absence, l'exclusion) without; **faire/se débrouiller ~** to do/manage without.
II *prép* **1** (absence, manque) without [*personne, accord, permission*]; **un jour ~ pluie** a day without rain, a dry day; **une maison ~ téléphone** a house without a telephone; **je suis ~ voiture aujourd'hui** I don't have a car today; **je bois mon thé ~ sucre** I don't take sugar in my tea; **du chocolat noir ~ sucre** sugar-free dark chocolate; **un visage ~ charme** an unattractive face; **un couple ~ enfant** a childless couple; **c'est un couple ~ enfant** they have no children; **une personne ~ fierté/scrupules** a person who has no pride/scruples; **~ cela** or **ça**○ otherwise; **il nous a dit ça ~ plus de précisions** he told us about it without going into details; **un jus d'orange ~ glaçons** an orange juice without ice ou with no ice; **2** (pour écarter une circonstance) **il est resté trois mois ~ téléphoner** he didn't call for three months; **~ être très perspicace, on pouvait s'en douter** you wouldn't have to be very astute to suspect it; **il est poli, ~ plus** he's polite, but that's as far as it goes; **~ plus de cérémonies** without further ado; **~ plus tarder** without further delay; **~ plus attendre** without waiting a moment longer; **~ plus de commentaires** without any further comment; **3** (à l'exclusion de) **on sera douze ~ les enfants** there'll be twelve of us not counting the children; **le total s'entend ~ la TVA** the price doesn't include VAT; **3500 francs ~ le voyage** 3,500 francs not including transport GB ou transportation US.
III sans que *loc conj* (+ *subj*) without; **~ que je m'en aperçoive** without my noticing; **pars ~ qu'on te voie** leave without anyone seeing you.
■ **~ domicile fixe**, **SDF** of no fixed abode, NFA; **les ~ domicile fixe** people of no fixed abode; **être ~ domicile fixe** to be of no fixed abode.

sans-abri /sɑ̃zabʀi/ *nmf inv* **un ~** a homeless person; **les ~** the homeless; **c'est un ~** he's homeless.

San Salvador /sɑ̃salvadɔʀ/ ▶857 *npr* San Salvador.

sans-cœur /sɑ̃kœʀ/ **I** *adj inv* [*personne*] heartless.
II *nmf inv* heartless person; **tu es un ~** you're heartless.

sans-culotte, *pl* **~s** /sɑ̃kylɔt/ *nm* Hist sans culotte.

sans-emploi /sɑ̃zɑ̃plwa/ *nmf inv* unemployed person; **les ~** the unemployed, the jobless; **trois millions de ~** three million unemployed ou jobless.

sans-faute /sɑ̃fot/ *nm inv* **1** Équit clear round; **faire un ~** to have a clear round; **2** fig faultless performance; **mon parcours politique/universitaire est un ~** my political/university career went off without a hitch.

sans-gêne /sɑ̃ʒɛn/ **I** *adj inv* [*personne*] cheeky, bad-mannered (*épith*).

II *nmf inv* cheeky person, bad-mannered person.
III *nm* cheekiness; **faire preuve de ~** to be cheeky ou bad-mannered.

sans-grade /sɑ̃gʀad/ *nm inv* nobody; **les ~** the nobodies.

sanskrit, ~e /sɑ̃skʀi, it/ I *adj* Sanskrit.
II *nm* Ling Sanskrit.

sans-le-sou○ /sɑ̃lsu/ *nmf inv* penniless person; **c'est un ~** he's penniless.

sansonnet /sɑ̃sɔnɛ/ *nm* starling.

sans-papiers /sɑ̃papje/ *nm inv* illegal immigrant.

santal /sɑ̃tal/ *nm* **1** (essence) sandalwood; **2** (arbre) sandalwood; **bois de ~** sandalwood.

santé /sɑ̃te/ *nf* **1** (de personne, pays, d'organisation) health; **~ mentale** mental health; **être en bonne/mauvaise ~** to be in good/bad health; **avoir la ~** lit to enjoy good health; fig to be full of bounce; **se refaire une ~** to build up one's strength; **il respire la ~** he's glowing with health; **avoir une petite ~** to be frail ou delicate; **avoir une ~ de fer** to have an iron constitution; **comment va la ~?** how are you?; **2** (en buvant) **à votre ~!** cheers!; **à la ~ de Janet!** here's to Janet!; **buvons à votre ~** let's drink to your (good) health; **3** Admin health; **la ~ publique** public health; **services de ~** health services; **les professionnels de la ~** health workers.

santiag○ /sɑ̃tjag/ *nf* cowboy boot.

Santiago /sɑ̃tjago/ **▶857** *npr* Santiago.

santon /sɑ̃tɔ̃/ *nm* Christmas crib figure.

Saône-et-Loire /sonelwaʀ/ **▶692** *nprf* (département) **la ~** the Saône-et-Loire.

saoudien, -ienne /saudjɛ̃, ɛn/ **▶537** *adj* Saudi (Arabian).

Saoudien, -ienne /saudjɛ̃, ɛn/ **▶537** *nm,f* Saudi (Arabian).

saoul, ~e = **soûl**.

saoulard○**, ~e** = **soûlard**.

sapajou /sapaʒu/ *nm* capuchin monkey.

sape /sap/ I *nf* **1** Mil (tranchée) sap; **2** (action de saper) lit, fig sapping; **travail de ~** Tech sap digging; fig sabotage.
II○ **sapes** *nfpl* (vêtements) clothes.

saper /sape/ [1] I *vtr* **1** (détruire) to undermine [*mur, falaise, moral*]; **2**○ (vêtir) to dress.
II○ **se saper** *vpr* **1** (s'habiller) to dress; **être bien/mal sapé** to be well/badly dressed; **2** (s'habiller bien) to dress up to the nines○.

saperlipopette○† /sapɛʀlipɔpɛt/ *excl* goodness me!

sapeur /sapœʀ/ *nm* sapper.
IDIOMES **fumer comme un ~** to smoke like a chimney.

sapeur-pompier, *pl* **sapeurs-pompiers** /sapœʀpɔ̃pje/ *nm* fireman; **les sapeurs-pompiers de Paris** the Paris Fire Brigade.

saphène /safɛn/ I *adj* [*veine, nerf*] saphenous.
II *nf* saphena.

saphique /safik/ *adj* Sapphic.

saphir /safiʀ/ *nm* **1** Minér sapphire; **2** (pointe de lecture) stylus.

saphisme† /safism/ *nm* sapphism†.

sapide /sapid/ *adj* sapid.

sapidité /sapidite/ *nf* sapidity; **agent de ~** flavouring[GB] agent.

sapin /sapɛ̃/ *nm* **1** fir tree; **2** (bois) deal; **des étagères en ~** deal shelves.
■ **~ de Noël** (arbre) Christmas tree; (fête) Christmas party (*for staff and their children*).
IDIOMES **ça sent le ~** hum you sound as though you're not long for this world.

sapinière /sapinjɛʀ/ *nf* fir plantation.

saponacé, ~e /sapɔnase/ *adj* saponaceous.

saponaire /sapɔnɛʀ/ *nf* saponin.

saponification /sapɔnifikasjɔ̃/ *nf* saponification.

saponifier /sapɔnifje/ [1] *vtr* to saponify.

sapristi○† /sapʀisti/ *excl* heavens!

saquer○ /sake/ [1] *vtr* **1** (noter sévèrement) students' slang to mark [sb] down GB, to grade [sb] hard US [*élève*]; **se faire ~** to be marked down (**à** in; **par** by); **2** (supporter) **je ne peux pas le ~** I can't stand him.

sarabande /saʀabɑ̃d/ *nf* **1** Danse, Mus saraband; **2** (ribambelle) (de chiffres) jumble; (d'images) flock; **~ de souvenirs** swirling memories; **~ de gens** swirling crowd of people; **3** (vacarme) racket; **faire la ~** to make a racket; **~ des sorcières** witches' rout.

Saragosse /saʀagɔs/ **▶857** *npr* Saragossa.

sarbacane /saʀbakan/ *nf* blowpipe.

sarcasme /saʀkasm/ *nm* **1** (dérision) sarcasm; **2** (remarque) sarcastic remark.

sarcastique /saʀkastik/ *adj* sarcastic.

sarcastiquement /saʀkastikmɑ̃/ *adv* sarcastically.

sarcelle /saʀsɛl/ *nf* teal.

sarclage /saʀklaʒ/ *nm* hoeing.

sarcler /saʀkle/ [1] *vtr* to hoe.

sarclette /saʀklɛt/ *nf* small hoe.

sarcloir /saʀklwaʀ/ *nm* hoe.

sarcomatose /saʀkomatoz/ **▶271** *nf* sarcomatosis.

sarcome /saʀkom/ **▶271** *nm* sarcoma.

sarcophage /saʀkɔfaʒ/ I *nm* Archéol sarcophagus.
II *nf* Zool flesh-fly.

Sardaigne /saʀdɛɲ/ **▶416** *nprf* Sardinia.

sardane /saʀdan/ *nf* Sardana.

sarde /saʀd/ **▶462** *adj, nm* Sardinian.

Sarde /saʀd/ *nm,f* Sardinian.

sardine /saʀdin/ *nf* **1** Zool sardine; **~ à l'huile** sardine in oil; **~s en boîte** tinned GB ou canned US sardines; **2**○ (piquet de tente) tent peg; **3**○ (galon) stripe.
IDIOMES **c'est la ~ qui a bouché le port de Marseille** that's a tall story; **être serrés comme des ~s** to be crammed together like sardines.

sardinerie /saʀdinʀi/ *nf* sardine cannery.

sardinier, -ière /saʀdinje, ɛʀ/ I *adj* sardine (*épith*); **industrie sardinière** sardine industry.
II *nm* **1** (pêcheur) sardine fisherman; **2** (bateau) sardine boat; **3** (ouvrier) sardine canner.

sardonique /saʀdɔnik/ *adj* sardonic.

sardoniquement /saʀdɔnikmɑ̃/ *adv* sardonically.

sargasse /saʀgas/ *nf* gulfweed.

Sargasses /saʀgas/ **▶555** *nprfpl* **mer des ~** Sargasso Sea.

sari /saʀi/ *nm* sari.

sarigue /saʀig/ *nf* opossum.

SARL /ɛsaɛʀɛl/ *nf: abbr* ▶ **société**.

sarment /saʀmɑ̃/ *nm* **1** (de vigne) **~ (de vigne)** vine shoot; **2** (tige grimpante) bine.

sarmenteux, -euse /saʀmɑ̃tø, øz/ *adj* [*vigne*] climbing; [*tige*] sarmentose.

saroual /saʀwal/ *nm* baggy (African) trousers (*pl*) GB ou pants (*pl*) US.

sarrasin, ~e /saʀazɛ̃, in/ I *adj* Hist Saracen.
II *nm* Bot, Culin buckwheat; **miel de ~** buckwheat honey.

Sarrasin, ~e /saʀazɛ̃, in/ *nm,f* Saracen.

sarrau /saʀo/ *nm* smock.

Sarre /saʀ/ **▶357**, **692** *nprf* (rivière, région) Saar.

sarriette /saʀjɛt/ *nf* savory.

Sarthe /saʀt/ **▶357**, **692** *nprf* (rivière, département) **la ~** the Sarthe.

sas /sɑs/ *nm inv* **1** (pièce étanche) airlock; **2** (d'écluse) lock; **3** (tamis) sieve.

Saskatchewan /saskatʃewan/ **▶692** *nprm* Saskatchewan.

sassafras /sasafʀa/ *nm inv* sassafras.

sasser /sase/ [1] *vtr* **1** (tamiser) to sift, to screen [*farine*]; **2** (passer par une écluse) to let [sth] through a lock [*péniche*].

Satan /satɑ̃/ *npr* Satan.

satané○**, ~e** /satane/ *adj* damned○.

satanique /satanik/ *adj* **1** (démoniaque) [*sourire, ruse*] fiendish; **2** (de Satan) [*culte*] Satanic.

satanisme /satanism/ *nm* Satanism.

satellisation /satɛlizasjɔ̃/ *nf* **1** Astronaut putting ¢ [sth] into orbit [*engin*]; **programme de ~** satellite launching programme[GB]; **2** fig **le pays a subi une ~ culturelle** the country has become a mere satellite in terms of culture.

satelliser /satɛlize/ [1] I *vtr* **1** Astronaut to put [sth] into orbit [*engin*]; **2** Entr, Pol (assujettir) to turn [sth] into a satellite [*pays, entreprise, parti*]; **être satellisé par** to become the satellite of; **se faire ~ par** to be turned into a satellite by.
II **se satelliser** *vpr* **1** Astronaut [*engin*] to go into orbit; **2** Entr, Pol [*ville, parti*] to become a satellite.

satellitaire /satɛlitɛʀ/ *adj* satellite (*épith*); **téléphone ~** satellite telephone.

satellite /satɛlit/ I *nm* **1** (astre, engin) satellite; **~ de transmission/télécommunications** broadcasting/telecommunications satellite; **~ météorologique** weather satellite; **~ d'observation** observation satellite; **2** Pol (pays) satellite; **3** Mécan (pignon) bevel pinion.
II **(-)satellite** (*in compounds*) **nation-~** satellite nation.

satellite-espion, *pl* **satellites-espions** /satɛlitɛspjɔ̃/ *nm* spy satellite.

satellite-relais, *pl* **satellites-relais** /satɛlitʀəlɛ/ *nm* communications satellite.

satiété /sasjete/ I *nf* satiation sout, satiety sout.
II **à satiété** *loc adv* **1** (jusqu'à satisfaction) **boire/manger à ~** to drink/to eat one's fill; **il avait mangé à ~** he was replete sout; **2** (jusqu'à saturation) [*dire, répéter*] ad nauseam.

satin /satɛ̃/ *nm* satin; **une peau de ~** a satin-smooth ou silky skin.
■ **~ de coton** satinized cotton; **~ de polyester** polyester satin.

satiné, ~e /satine/ I *adj* [*étoffe*] satiny (*épith*); [*doublure*] satin (*épith*); [*peinture*] satin-finish (*épith*); [*peau*] silky, satin-smooth (*épith*).
II *nm* (de tissu) sheen; (de peau) silkiness.

satinette /satinɛt/ *nf* satinette, sateen.

satire /satiʀ/ *nf* satire; **faire la ~ de qch/qn** to satirize sth/sb.

satirique /satiʀik/ *adj* satirical.

satiriste /satiʀist/ **▶510** *nmf* satirist.

satisfaction /satisfaksjɔ̃/ *nf* **1** (plaisir) satisfaction ¢; **mon travail m'apporte de réelles ~s** I get real satisfaction from my work; **constater/apprendre avec ~ que** to note/hear with satisfaction that; **à notre grande ~** to our great satisfaction; **à la ~ générale** to everyone's satisfaction; **pour ma ~ personnelle** for my own (personal) satisfaction; **motif de ~** reason to feel satisfied; **2** (contentement) satisfaction; **exprimer son entière ~** to express one's complete satisfaction; **la ~ de nos besoins** the fulfilment[GB] of our needs; **notre nouvelle secrétaire donne entière ~** we're very pleased with the new secretary; **si le lave-vaisselle ne vous donne pas ~** if you are not entirely satisfied with the dishwasher; **3** (réparation) satisfaction; **obtenir ~** to obtain satisfaction; **obtenir ~ sur tout** to obtain complete satisfaction; **4** Écon satisfaction.

satisfaire /satisfɛʀ/ [10] I *vtr* (contenter) to satisfy [*personne*]; to please [*électorat, client*]; to satisfy [*demande, curiosité*]; to meet [*besoin*]; to fulfil[GB] [*ambition, aspiration, exigence*]; **ton explication ne me satisfait pas** I'm not satisfied with your explanation; **cet employé vous satisfait-il?**

are you satisfied with this employee?; **~ les besoins d'un enfant** to meet the needs of a child; **~ l'attente d'un client** to come up to a customer's expectations; **~ les revendications des grévistes** to meet strikers' demands; **~ un besoin naturel** euph to answer a call of nature.

II satisfaire à *vtr ind* to fulfil[GB] [*obligation, ambition*]; to meet [*norme, condition*].

III se satisfaire *vpr* (se contenter) **se ~ de** [*personne*] to be satisfied with [*explication, excuse*]; to be content with [*bas salaire*]; **se ~ de peu** to be easily satisfied.

satisfaisant, **~e** /satisfəzɑ̃, ɑ̃t/ *adj* **1** (adéquat) satisfactory; **réponse peu ~e** unsatisfactory answer; **répondre de façon ~e** to give a satisfactory answer; **il travaille de façon ~e** his work is satisfactory; **2** (gratifiant) [*métier*] satisfying.

satisfait, **~e** /satisfɛ, ɛt/ **I** *pp* ▶ **satisfaire**.

II *pp adj* (contenté) [*client, curiosité, besoin*] satisfied; [*désir, envie*] gratified; **être ~ de** to be satisfied with [*réponse, employé*].

III *adj* (content) [*personne*] happy; [*sourire*] satisfied; **avoir un air ~** to look pleased with oneself; **être ~ de soi-même** to be pleased with oneself.

satisfecit /satisfesit/ *nm inv* **1** (approbation) **décerner un ~ à qn** to give sb a glowing report; **2** Scol† good mark GB, good grade US.

satrape /satʀap/ *nm* **1** fig despot, satrap; **2** Antiq satrap.

saturante /satyʀɑ̃t/ *adj f* **vapeur ~** Phys saturated vapour[GB].

saturateur /satyʀatœʀ/ *nm* **1** Chimie saturator; **2** (humidificateur) humidifier.

saturation /satyʀasjɔ̃/ *nf* Chimie saturation (**de** of); (de marché) saturation (**de** of); (de trains, d'hôtels) overcrowding; (de réseau téléphonique, routier) overloading; **arriver à ~** [*solution, marché, réseau*] to reach saturation point; [*public, personne*] to have had as much as one can take.

saturé, **~e** /satyʀe/ **I** *pp* ▶ **saturer**.

II *pp adj* **1** (imprégné) gén, Chimie saturated (**de** with); **terre ~e d'eau** waterlogged land; **atmosphère ~e d'humidité** saturated air; **2** (rassasié) **le public est ~ de publicité/discours** the public has had its fill of advertising/speeches; **la télé, j'en suis ~**○ I'm sick of television○; **j'ai trop travaillé, je suis ~**○ I've worked too hard, I can't do any more; **3** (surchargé) [*marché*] saturated; [*profession*] overcrowded; [*système, équipement*] overloaded; [*région, transports*] crowded out (**de** with); **entre 7 heures et 8 heures, le réseau est ~** Télécom between 7 and 8, all lines are busy.

saturer /satyʀe/ [1] **I** *vtr* **1** (imprégner) to saturate (**de** with); **2** (gorger) **~ les gens de publicité/discours** to overload people with advertising/speeches; **on nous sature de feuilletons** we're being inundated with soap operas; **traiter la demande et ~ le besoin** to cater to demand and meet people's needs.

II○ *vi* **je sature** I've had it up to here○.

saturnales /satyʀnal/ *nfpl* Antiq Saturnalia.

Saturne /satyʀn/ **I** *npr* Mythol Saturn.

II *nprf* Astron Saturn.

saturnien, **-ienne** /satyʀnjɛ̃, ɛn/ *adj* liter (mélancolique) saturnine littér.

saturnisme /satyʀnism/ ▶ 271 *nm* lead poisoning.

satyre /satiʀ/ *nm* **1** Mythol satyr; **2** (individu lubrique) lecher; **3** Zool satyr.

sauce /sos/ *nf* Culin sauce; **viande/plat en ~** meat/dish with sauce; **allonger une ~** to thin a sauce; **(r)allonger la ~** fig to spin things out.

■ **~ aigre-douce** sweet and sour sauce; **~ béarnaise** bearnaise sauce; **~ béchamel** béchamel sauce; **~ blanche** white sauce; **~ aux câpres** caper sauce; **~ chasseur** mushroom and wine sauce; **~ hollandaise** hollandaise sauce; **~ madère** madeira sauce; **rognons ~ madère** kidneys in madeira sauce; **~ marchand de vin** wine sauce; **~ piquante** piquant ou spicy sauce; **~ suprême** supreme sauce; **poulet ~ suprême** chicken supreme; **~ tomate** tomato sauce; **~ au vin** wine sauce.

IDIOMES **mettre qch à toutes les ~s** to adapt sth to any purpose; **je me demande à quelle ~ on va me manger** I wonder what's in store for me; **prendre la ~**○ to get soaked ou drenched.

saucée○ /sose/ *nf* downpour; **prendre une ~** to get soaked ou drenched.

saucer /sose/ [1] *vtr* **1** (éponger) to wipe [sth] with a piece of bread [*assiette, plat*]; **2**○ (tremper) **se faire ~** to get soaked ou drenched.

saucier /sosje/ ▶ 510 *nm* sauce chef, cook specializing in sauces.

saucière /sosjɛʀ/ *nf* sauceboat.

saucisse /sosis/ *nf* sausage; **chair à ~** sausage meat; **chapelet de ~s** string of sausages.

■ **~ de Francfort** frankfurter; **~ sèche** dried sausage; **~ de Strasbourg** knackwurst ¢; **~ de Toulouse** *coarse pork sausage*.

IDIOMES **ne pas attacher son chien avec des ~s** to be tight-fisted○.

saucisson /sosisɔ̃/ *nm* (slicing) sausage; **~ à l'ail** garlic sausage; **~ sec** ≈ salami, summer sausage US.

saucissonné, **~e** /sosisɔne/ **I** *pp* ▶ **saucissonner**.

II○ *pp adj* **se sentir ~** to feel trussed up like a chicken (**dans** in).

saucissonner○ /sosisɔne/ [1] *vi* ≈ to have a snack.

sauf[1] /sof/ **I** *prép* **1** (excepté, hormis) except, but; **ils avaient toutes les tailles ~ la mienne** they had every size but ou except mine; **je suis libre tous les jours ~ demain** I'm free every day except ou but tomorrow; **le film était bien ~ la fin** the film was good apart from the ending; **j'ai bien aimé ta famille ~ ton frère** I really liked your family apart from your brother; **2** (sous réserve de) **~ contrordre** failing an order to the contrary; **~ avis contraire** unless otherwise stated; **~ imprévu** all things being equal, unless anything unforeseen happens; **~ dispositions contraires** Jur except as otherwise provided; **~ erreur de ma part** if I'm not mistaken.

II sauf si *loc conj* (excepté si) unless; **nous mangerons dehors, ~ s'il pleut** we'll eat outside unless it rains; **je partirai en septembre, ~ si je rate mes examens** I'll leave in September unless I fail my exams.

III sauf que *loc conj* except that; **tout sera comme autrefois ~ que nous sommes plus vieux** everything will be the same as before except that we're older.

sauf[2], **sauve** /sof, sov/ *adj* **1** (sauvé) safe; **être ~** to be safe; **j'ai eu la vie sauve** my life was spared; **laisser la vie sauve à qn** to spare sb's life; **2** fig [*honneur, réputation*] intact.

sauf-conduit, *pl* **~s** /sofkɔ̃dɥi/ *nm* safe-conduct; **accorder un ~ à qn** to issue sb with a safe-conduct.

sauge /soʒ/ *nf* sage.

saugrenu, **~e** /sogʀəny/ *adj* crazy, potty○ GB.

Saül /sayl/ *npr* Saul.

saule /sol/ *nm* willow.

■ **~ pleureur** weeping willow.

saumâtre /somɑtʀ/ *adj* [*eau, dépôt*] brackish; [*goût*] bitter and salty; **je l'ai trouvée ~**○ fig it was hard to take.

saumon /somɔ̃/ **I** ▶ 193 *adj inv* salmon (pink).

II *nm* **1** Zool salmon; **~ fumé** smoked salmon; **2** (métal) nonferrous ingot.

saumonée /somɔne/ *adj f* **truite ~** salmon trout.

saumonette /somɔnɛt/ *nf* catshark.

saumure /somyʀ/ *nf* **1** Culin brine; **conserver dans la ~** to pickle in brine; **thon en ~** tuna in brine; **2** (dans un marais salant) bittern.

saumuré, **~e** /somyʀe/ *adj* Culin pickled in brine (*après n*).

sauna /sona/ *nm* sauna.

saupoudrer /sopudʀe/ [1] *vtr* **1** lit to sprinkle (**de** with); **2** fig to give [sth] sparingly.

saupoudreuse /sopudʀøz/ *nf* (à sucre) sugar sprinkler; (à farine) flour sprinkler.

saur /sɔʀ/ *adj m* **hareng ~** kipper, kippered herring.

saurien /sɔʀjɛ̃/ *nm* lacertilian; **les ~s** Lacertilia.

saut /so/ *nm* **1** (mouvement) jump; **~ en parachute** parachute jump; **faire un ~ en parachute** to make a parachute jump; **~ à pieds joints** jump with the feet together; **faire un petit ~** to skip; **faire un ~ de deux mètres** to jump two metres[GB]; **faire un ~ sur place** to leap in the air; **faire des ~s de puce** [*avion*] to do short-haul hops; **faire un ~ de 10 ans** to skip 10 years; **faire un ~ dix ans en arrière** to jump back ten years; **faire un ~ de 2%** to shoot up by 2%; **faire un ~ dans l'inconnu** to take a leap into the unknown; **au ~ du lit** first thing in the morning; **2** ▶ 449 Sport (activité) **le ~** jumping; **être bon en ~** to be a good jumper; **3**○ (visite) **faire un ~ à Paris** to make a flying visit to Paris; **faire un ~ chez qn** to pop in and see sb; **je ne fais qu'un ~** it'll only be a flying visit; **faire un ~ à la boulangerie** (de chez soi) to pop round to the baker's GB, to duck out to the bakery US; (en chemin) to pop in to the baker's; **4** Ordinat jump; **~ de page** page break.

■ **~ de l'ange** swallow dive GB, swan dive US; **~ carpé** pike, jackknife dive; **~ de chat** saut de chat; **~ de cheval** vaulting; **~ en chute libre** free-fall jump; **~ en ciseaux** scissors jump GB, scissor jump US; **~ à la corde** skipping; **~ à l'élastique** bungee jumping; **~ en hauteur** high jump; **être bon en ~ en hauteur** to be good at the high jump; **~ en longueur** long jump; **~ de la mort** salto mortale; **~ d'obstacles** Équit show jumping; **~ à la perche** pole vault; **faire du ~ à la perche** to pole vault; **~ périlleux** mid-air somersault; **~ en rouleau** straddle roll; (bond) ski jump; **~ à skis** (sport) ski jumping.

IDIOMES **faire le ~** to take the plunge; **faire le grand ~** (se suicider) to kill oneself.

saut-de-loup, *pl* **sauts-de-loup** /sodlu/ *nm* Archit ha-ha.

saut-de-mouton, *pl* **sauts-de-mouton** /sodmutɔ̃/ *nm* **1** Gén Civ flyover GB, overpass US; **2** Équit curvet.

saute /sot/ *nf* **~ de température** sudden change in temperature; **~ de vent** shifting ¢ of the wind; **~ d'humeur** mood swing; **avoir des ~s d'humeur** to have moods; **j'en ai assez de tes ~s d'humeur** I've had enough of your moods.

sauté, **~e** /sote/ **I** *pp* ▶ **sauter**.

II *pp adj* Culin sautéed.

III *nm* Culin **~ d'agneau/de veau** sautéed lamb/veal.

saute-mouton /sotmutɔ̃/ *nm inv* leapfrog; **jouer à ~** to play leapfrog.

sauter /sote/ [1] **I** *vtr* **1** (franchir) to jump [*distance, hauteur*]; to jump over [*ruisseau, barrière*]; **~ les trois dernières marches** to jump down the bottom three steps; **~ deux mètres en hauteur** Sport to clear two metres[GB] in the high jump; **~ quatre mètres en longueur** to do four metres[GB] in the long jump; **2** (omettre volontairement) to skip [*étape, repas, période*]; to leave out [*dé-

tails]; **~ un paragraphe** (en lisant) to skip a paragraph; (en recopiant) to leave out a paragraph; **3** (omettre involontairement) to miss out GB, to miss [*mot, ligne*]; **~ son tour** Jeux to miss one's turn; **4** Scol **~ une année** or **classe** to skip a year; **5●** (sexuellement) to screw●; **se faire ~** to get laid●.
II *vi* **1** (faire un saut) gén to jump; (vers le bas) to jump (down); (vers le haut) to jump (up); (vers l'extérieur) to jump (out); (vers l'intérieur) to jump (in); **~ dans qch** to jump into sth; **~ par-dessus qch** to jump over sth; **~ sur le banc** to jump onto the bench; **~ du banc** to jump off the bench; **~ d'une fenêtre** to jump out of a window; **~ d'un avion** to jump out of a plane; **saute!** (de haut) jump (down)!; (dans une piscine) jump (in)!; **~ à terre** to jump (down) to the ground; **~ d'une branche à l'autre** to leap from branch to branch; **~ d'un pied sur l'autre** to hop from one foot to the other; **~ à pieds joints** lit to jump with one's feet together; **~ à pieds joints dans un piège** fig to fall straight into a trap; **~ dans le vide** to jump; **~ en hauteur/en longueur** to do the high/long jump; **~ à la perche** to pole vault; **~ en parachute** (une fois) to make a parachute jump; (régulièrement) to go parachute jumping; **~ à la corde** to skip; **~ en ciseaux** to do a scissors jump GB ou scissor jump US; **faire ~ un enfant sur ses genoux** to dandle a child on one's knee; **~ dans l'inconnu** to take a leap ou to leap into the unknown; **~ sur qn** to pounce on sb; **~ sur son téléphone/pistolet** to grab one's telephone/gun; **~ sur l'occasion/une offre** to jump at the chance/an offer; **~ à la gorge de qn** to go for sb's throat; **le chien m'a sauté à la figure** the dog went for my face; **~ au cou de qn** to greet sb with a kiss; ▶**reculer**; **2** (aller vivement) to jump; **~ du lit** to jump out of bed; **~ dans un taxi/dans un train** to jump ou hop into a taxi/onto a train; **~ d'un avion à l'autre** to hop off one plane and onto the next; **3** (passer) **nos frais ont sauté de 20% à 32%** our costs have jumped from 20% to 32%; **~ d'un sujet à l'autre** to skip from one subject to another; **4○** (être supprimé) **faire ~ un paragraphe** (délibérément) to take out a paragraph; (par erreur) to miss out GB ou miss a paragraph; **faire ~ une réunion** to cancel a meeting; **l'émission/la réunion a sauté** the programme[GB]/the meeting was cancelled[GB]; **le poste va ~** the job is being axed; **faire ~ une contravention** to get out of paying a parking ticket; **5** (être délogé, instable) [*courroie, chaine de vélo*] to come off; [*images de télévision*] to jump; **la troisième vitesse saute** the third gear keeps slipping; **6** (céder) **faire ~ une serrure** to force a lock; **faire ~ une maille** to drop a stitch; **faire ~ les boutons** to burst one's buttons; **faire ~ une dent à qn** to knock one of sb's teeth out; **faire ~ les barrières** fig to break down the barriers; **7** (exploser) [*bombe, mine*] to blow up, to go off; [*pont, bâtiment*] to be blown up, to go up; **il a sauté sur une mine** he was blown up by a mine; **faire ~ qch** to blow sth up; **faire ~ les plombs** Électrotech to blow the fuses; **8** Culin **faire ~ des oignons** to sauté onions; **faire ~ une crêpe** to toss a pancake; **faire ~ les bouchons de champagne** to make the champagne corks pop; **9○** (être licencié) to be fired, to get the sack○ GB; **faire ~ qn** to fire sb; **10** (faire faillite) to go bust○.
IDIOMES **~ aux yeux** to be blindingly obvious; **et que ça saute○!** make it snappy○!; **~ en l'air○** or **au plafond○** (de joie) to jump for joy; (de colère) to hit the roof○; (de surprise) to be staggered; **la sauter◑** (avoir faim) to be starving○.

sauterelle /sotʀɛl/ *nf* **1** Zool grasshopper; (criquet) controv locust; **2○** (femme grande) **une grande ~○!** a beanpole○!

sauterie† /sotʀi/ *nf* party, hop†.

saute-ruisseau† /sotʀɥiso/ *nm inv* errand boy†.

sauteur, -euse /sotœʀ, øz/ **I** *adj* Zool [*oiseau*] hopping; [*insecte*] leaping.
II *nm* **1** Sport jumper; **~ en hauteur** high jumper; **~ en longueur** long jumper; **~ à la perche** pole vaulter; **2** Équit (cheval) show jumper.
III sauteuse *nf* **1** Culin (deep) frying pan; **2** (scie) jigsaw.

sautillant, ~e /sotijɑ̃, ɑ̃t/ *adj* [*démarche, rythme*] bouncy; [*oiseau*] hopping.

sautillement /sotijmɑ̃/ *nm* (d'enfant) skipping ¢ about; (d'oiseau) hopping ¢ about; **les ~s des enfants me faisaient rire** the way the children skipped about made me laugh.

sautiller /sotije/ [1] *vi* **1** [*oiseau*] to hop; (en avançant) to hop along; (d'un lieu à l'autre) to hop around; **2** [*enfant*] (en avançant) to skip along; (d'un lieu à l'autre) to skip around; (d'un pied sur l'autre) to hop from one foot to the other; (sur place) to jump up and down.

sautoir /sotwaʀ/ *nm* **1** (collier) long necklace; **porter une montre en ~** to wear a watch on a chain around one's neck; **2** Hérald saltire.

sauvage /sovaʒ/ **I** *adj* **1** (non apprivoisé) [*animal, plante, région*] wild; [*enfant, passion*] wild; [*peuplade, tribu*] primitive, savage; **2** (cruel, barbare) [*mœurs, cruauté*] savage; [*lutte*] fierce; [*rire, cri*] wild; **OPA ~** hostile takeover bid; **3** (timide) [*personne*] unsociable; **4** (illégal) [*immigration, affichage, vente*] illegal; **urbanisation ~** uncontrolled[GB] growth.
II *nmf* **1** (être primitif ou brutal) savage; **on n'est pas des ~s** we're not savages; **2** (être non sociable) unsociable person, loner.

sauvagement /sovaʒmɑ̃/ *adv* savagely.

sauvageon, -onne /sovaʒɔ̃, ɔn/ **I** *nm,f* (enfant) wild child.
II *nm* Bot wild stock.

sauvagerie /sovaʒʀi/ *nf* **1** (brutalité) savagery; **2** (insociabilité) unsociability.

sauvagin, ~e /sovaʒɛ̃, in/ **I** *adj* [*odeur, goût*] of wildfowl (*épith, après n*).
II sauvagine *nf* **1** Chasse (oiseaux) waterfowl; **2** Tech (peaux) pelts (of small animals); (animaux) small animals used in the fur trade.

sauve ▶**sauf²**.

sauvegarde /sovgaʀd/ *nf* **1** (de patrimoine, paix, valeurs) maintenance; (de droits, libertés) protection; **assurer la ~ de** to safeguard; **se placer sous la ~ de** to put oneself under the protection of; **2** Ordinat (action) saving; (copie de sécurité) back-up; **3** Naut (cordage) (pour personne) manrope; (pour gouvernail, écope) safety-rope.

sauvegarder /sovgaʀde/ [1] *vtr* **1** gén to safeguard; **2** Ordinat (provisoirement) to save; (recopier) to back [sth] up.

sauve-qui-peut /sovkipø/ *nm inv* stampede.

sauver /sove/ [1] **I** *vtr* **1** (garder en vie) to save; (porter secours à) to rescue; **~ la vie à qn** to save sb's life; **~ des vies** to save lives; **~ qn de la noyade** to save sb from drowning; **savoir faire le geste qui sauve** to know how to save somebody's life; **on est sauvés, j'ai une idée!** we're saved, I've just had an idea!; **~ sa peau○** to save one's skin○; **elle est sauvée** [*malade*] she has pulled through○; **2** (sauvegarder) to save [*personne, organe, honneur, ville, entreprise*] (**de** from); to salvage [*marchandises*] (**de** from); **3** Relig to save [*croyant, âme*]; **4** (rendre acceptable) to redeem; **ce qui le sauve à mes yeux, c'est sa générosité** his redeeming feature for me is his generosity.
II se sauver *vpr* **1** (s'enfuir) (de prison, d'une cage) to escape (**de** from); (de chez ses parents, de l'école) to run away (**de** from); (face à une situation difficile) to run away (**de** from); (face à un danger) to run; **je me suis sauvé à la nage** I escaped by swimming off; **se ~ en bateau/avion** to escape by boat/plane; **sauvez-vous!** run (for it)!; **2** (s'éloigner) [*enfant, mouton*] to run away; [*oiseau*] to fly away; **3○** (s'en aller) **il faut que je me sauve** I've got to rush off now; **sauve-toi, tu vas être en retard** you'd better run or you'll be late.
IDIOMES **~ la situation** to save the day; **sauve qui peut!** (à terre) run for your life; (en mer) it's every man for himself.

sauvetage /sovtaʒ/ *nm* **1** (de personnes) rescue; **~ en mer** sea rescue; **~ en montagne** mountain rescue; **équipe de ~** rescue team; **cours de ~** life-saving training; **2** (d'entreprise) rescue; **plan/tentatives de ~** rescue plan/attempts; **3** (de satellite) rescue; (de marchandises) salvage ¢.

sauveteur /sovtœʀ/ ▶**510** *nm* rescuer.

sauvette: **à la sauvette** /alasovɛt/ *loc adv* **1** (en hâte) [*préparer, signer*] in a rush, hastily; **2** (à la dérobée) [*filmer, enregistrer*] on the sly; **3** (illégalement) **vendre qch à la ~** to sell sth illegally on the street; **un vendeur à la ~** gén an illicit street vendor; (de billets de spectacle) ticket tout GB, scalper○ US.

sauveur /sovœʀ/ *nm* Relig saviour[GB].

SAV /ɛsave/ *nm*: *abbr* ▶**service**.

savamment /savamɑ̃/ *adv* **1** (avec érudition) learnedly, eruditely; **2** (avec habileté) [*mené*] adroitly; [*construit, choisi*] skilfully[GB].

savane /savan/ *nf* **1** (hautes herbes) savannah; **2** C (marécage) swamp.

savant, ~e /savɑ̃, ɑ̃t/ **I** *adj* **1** [*personne*] learned (**en** in), erudite; [*assemblée, groupement*] learned, scholarly; **2** [*édition, étude, émission*] scholarly; [*calcul*] complicated, involved; ▶**mot**; **3** (habile) [*manœuvre*] clever, skilful[GB]; [*action*] clever; [*mise en scène*] skilful[GB]; **4** [*animal*] performing.
II *nm,f* (personne cultivée) scholar.
III *nm* (scientifique) scientist.

savarin /savaʀɛ̃/ *nm* rum baba.

savate /savat/ *nf* **1○** (vieille pantoufle) old slipper; (vieille chaussure) old shoe; **2** (sport) ≈ kickboxing; **3** (personne maladroite) clumsy idiot○.

savetier‡ /savtje/ *nm* cobbler.

saveur /savœʀ/ *nf* (d'aliment, de boisson) flavour[GB]; **sans ~** flavourless[GB]; (plus critique) tasteless; **plein de ~** [*fruit*] full of flavour[GB]; [*plat cuisiné*] flavoursome[GB], tasty; [*remarque*] pungent.

Savoie /savwa/ ▶**692** *nprf* **1** (région) **la ~** Savoy; **2** (département) **la ~** Savoie.

savoir /savwaʀ/ [47] **I** *nm* **1** (érudition) learning ¢; **le ~ désintéressé** learning for its own sake; **un grand ~** great learning; **2** (science) knowledge ¢; **le ~ médical** medical knowledge; **le ~ et l'expérience** knowledge and experience; **les ~s et les savoir-faire** knowledge and know-how; **3** (culture) body ¢ of knowledge; **transmettre un ~** to pass on a body of knowledge.
II *vtr* **1** (connaître) to know [*vérité, réponse*]; **~ son texte** to know one's lines; **~ qch par cœur** to know sth by heart; **~ que** to know (that); **je sais qu'elle est pauvre** I know she's poor; **vous n'êtes pas sans ~ que** you are no doubt aware that; **elle sait bien que** she knows very well (that); **je la savais triste** I knew she was miserable; **~ quand/pourquoi** to know when/why; **~ qui/ce que** to know who/what; **~ combien il est difficile de faire** to know how difficult it is to do; **on ne sait où elle est** nobody knows where she is; **tu sais ce que tu veux, ou non?** do you know what you want or don't you?; **ne l'écoute pas, elle ne sait plus ce qu'elle dit** take no notice, she doesn't know what she's saying; **~ qch sur qn** to know sth about sb; **ne rien ~ de qch** to know nothing about sth; **il ne sait rien de** or **sur moi** he doesn't know anything about me, he knows nothing about me; **elle en sait plus/moins que moi** she knows more/less about it than I do; **il n'en saura rien** he'll never know (about it); **je n'en sais rien** I don't know; **la douleur, elle en sait quelque chose** she knows what

pain is; **c'est vrai, tu sais** that's true, you know; **va** or **allez ~!**, **qui sait!** who knows!; **on ne sait jamais** you never know; **si seulement j'avais su** if only I'd known; **je (le) sais bien** I know; **est-ce que je sais, moi!** how should I know!; **il est parti pour la raison que tu sais** you know very well why he left; **elle n'a rien voulu ~** she just didn't want to know; **fais-moi ~ si** let me know if; **parler sans ~** to talk about things one knows nothing about; **sans le ~** without knowing (it); **c'est faux, (pour autant) que je sache** as far as I know, it's not true; **pas que je sache** not as far as I know; **elle a fait ~ que** she let it be known that; **elle nous a fait ~ que** she informed us that; **je ne veux pas le ~** I don't want to know; **comment l'as-tu su?** how did you find out?; **je l'ai su par elle** she told me about it; **~ le chinois** to know Chinese; **bien ~ le japonais** to have a good knowledge of Japanese; **quelque chose qu'il sait être douloureux** something he knows is painful ou to be painful; **on la savait riche** she was known to be rich; **reste à ~ si** it remains to be seen if ou whether; **ne ~ que faire pour...** to be at a loss as to how to...; **on croit ~ qu'elle est à Paris** she is understood ou thought to be in Paris; **on ne leur savait pas d'ennemis** they had no known enemies; **sachant que** given that; **sache qu'il t'a menti/que j'avais raison** I'm telling you, he was lying/I was right; **sachez que fumer est interdit dans le bureau** you should know that smoking is forbidden in the office; **il a menti, et que sais-je encore!** he told lies, and goodness knows GB ou who knows what else!; **la personne que vous savez, qui vous savez** you-know-who; **je ne sais quel journaliste** some journalist or other; **je ne sais qui** somebody or other; **tu viens ou pas, il faudrait ~!** are you coming or not? make your mind up!; **on va avoir une augmentation ou pas, il faudrait ~!** are we getting more money or not? let's get it straight!; **elle a je ne sais combien de tableaux** she's got who knows how many pictures; **si tu savais** or **tu ne peux pas ~ comme je suis content!** you can't imagine how happy I am!; **tu en sais des choses!** you really know a thing or two!; ▶ **savoir, vieillesse**; **2** (être capable de) **~ faire** to be able to do, to know how to do; **~ comment faire** to know how to do; **je sais conduire/nager/taper à la machine** I can drive/swim/type; **je sais parler espagnol** I can speak Spanish; **il ne sait pas dire non** he can't say no; **~ pardonner** to be able to forgive; **~ écouter** to be a good listener; **elle sait bien/mal expliquer** she's good/bad at explaining things; **il a su nous parler** he was able to talk to us; **il a su la comprendre** he understood her; **on ne saurait tout prévoir** one cannot foresee everything; **je ne saurais vous dire pourquoi** I really can't say why; **on ne saurait mieux dire** I couldn't have put it better myself; **elle sait y faire avec les enfants** she's good with children; **elle sait y faire avec les hommes** she knows how to handle men; **il pleurait tout ce qu'il savait** he cried and cried; **3** B (pouvoir) **je ne sais pas soulever la valise** I can't lift the suitcase; **on ne sait pas ~ ce qui va se passer** it's impossible to know what will happen.

III se savoir *vpr* **1** (être connu) **ça se saurait** people would know about that; **à la campagne, tout se sait** in the country, people get to know all that goes on; **tout se sait ici** people get to know everything in this place; **cela a fini par se ~** word got around, it got out in the end; **ça s'est su tout de suite** word immediately got around; **2** (être conscient d'être) **se savoir aimé** to know one is loved; **se ~ perdu** to know one is done for.

IV *v impers* (pouvoir) **il ne saurait en être question** it's completely out of the question; **il ne saurait y avoir de démocratie sans égalité** there can be no democracy without equality.

V à savoir *loc adv* that is to say; **dans deux jours, à ~ lundi** in two days, that is to say on Monday.

IDIOMES **ne pas ~ où donner de la tête** not to know whether one is coming or going; **et Dieu** or **Diable sait quoi!** and God knows what else!

savoir-faire /savwarfɛr/ *nm inv* know-how.

savoir-vivre /savwarvivr/ *nm inv* manners (*pl*), mastery of the social graces, savoir faire; **~ téléphonique** telephone manners (*pl*); **manquer de ~** to be lacking in the social graces.

savon /savɔ̃/ *nm* **1** (produit) soap; **~ en paillettes** soap flakes; **2** (morceau) (bar of) soap; **où est le ~?** where is the soap?; **un ~ dermatologique** a (cake of) dermatological soap.

■ **~ à barbe** shaving soap; **~ liquide** liquid soap; **~ de Marseille** household soap; **~ noir** soft soap.

IDIOMES **passer un ~ à qn**○ to give sb a telling-off; **se faire passer un ~**○ to get a telling-off.

savonnage /savɔnaʒ/ *nm* soaping; **procédez à un ~ méticuleux** soap down carefully.

savonner /savɔne/ [1] **I** *vtr* to rub soap on [*linge*]; to soap [sb] all over [*enfant*]; **elle m'a savonné le dos** she soaped my back.

II se savonner *vpr* (pour se laver) to soap oneself all over; (pour se raser) to lather oneself; **se ~ les mains** to put soap on one's hands; **se ~ le visage** (pour se raser) to lather one's face.

savonnerie /savɔnri/ *nf* soap factory.

savonnette /savɔnɛt/ *nf* small cake of soap.

savonneux, -euse /savɔnø, øz/ *adj* soapy; **être sur une pente savonneuse** fig to be on the slippery slope.

savourer /savure/ [1] *vtr* to savour[GB] [*succès, moment, instant*]; to revel in ou delight in [*honneurs*]; to appreciate [*expression*]; **profitez de votre séjour pour ~ les produits régionaux** take advantage of your stay to enjoy local produce.

savoureux, -euse /savurø, øz/ *adj* [*plat*] tasty; [*anecdote*] juicy.

savoyard, ~e /savwajar, ard/ ▶**692** *adj* Savoyard.

Savoyard, ~e /savwajar, ard/ *nm,f* Savoyard.

saxe /saks/ *nm* Dresden china ¢; **un ~** a piece of Dresden china.

Saxe /saks/ ▶**692** *nprf* Saxony.

saxhorn /saksɔrn/ ▶**534** *nm* saxhorn.

saxifrage /saksifraʒ/ *nf* saxifrage.

saxo○ /sakso/ *nm* **1** (instrument) sax○; **2** (instrumentiste) sax○ player.

saxon, -onne /saksɔ̃, ɔn/ **I** *adj* Saxon.

II ▶**462** *nm* Ling Saxon.

Saxon, -onne /saksɔ̃, ɔn/ *nm,f* Saxon.

saxophone /saksɔfɔn/ ▶**534** *nm* **1** (instrument) saxophone; **2** (instrumentiste) saxophone player.

saxophoniste /saksɔfɔnist/ ▶**510** *nmf* saxophonist.

saynète /sɛnɛt/ *nf* playlet.

sbire /sbir/ *nm* pej henchman péj.

scabieux, -ieuse /skabjø, øz/ **I** *adj* [*éruption*] scabious.

II scabieuse *nf* Bot scabious.

scabreux, -euse /skabrø, øz/ *adj* risqué.

scalaire /skalɛr/ **I** *adj* [*grandeur*] scalar.

II *nm* Zool angelfish.

scalène /skalɛn/ *adj* Math scalene.

scalp /skalp/ *nm* **1** (cuir chevelu) scalp; **2** (pratique) scalping.

scalpel /skalpɛl/ *nm* scalpel; **donner un coup de ~ dans** to make a cut with a scalpel in.

scalper /skalpe/ [1] *vtr* to scalp.

scampi /skɑ̃pi/ *nmpl* scampi ¢.

scandale /skɑ̃dal/ *nm* scandal; **~ boursier** scandal on the Stock Exchange; **~ des pots-de-vin** bribery scandal; **le ~ de la faim dans le monde** the scandal of hunger in the world; **faire éclater un ~** to cause a scandal to break; **étouffer un ~** to hush up a scandal; **faire ~** to cause a scandal; **faire un** or **du ~** (réprobation générale) to cause a scandal; (scène individuelle) to cause a fuss; **faire du ~ sur la voie publique** to create a public disturbance; **celui par qui le ~ arrive** he who causes scandal; **l'opposition a crié au ~** there was a general outcry from the opposition; **au grand ~ de** to the great disgust of; **un journal à ~** a scandal sheet; **la presse à ~** the gutter press; **c'est un ~!** it's scandalous, it's outrageous!

scandaleusement /skɑ̃daløzmɑ̃/ *adv* outrageously.

scandaleux, -euse /skɑ̃dalø, øz/ *adj* (tous contextes) scandalous (**de faire** to do), outrageous (**de faire** to do); **c'est proprement ~!** it's absolutely scandalous!

scandaliser /skɑ̃dalize/ [1] **I** *vtr* to outrage, to scandalize [*personne*]; **être scandalisé par** to be outraged by.

II se scandaliser *vpr* to be shocked (**de qch** by sth); **personne ne s'en est scandalisé** nobody raised any objections.

scander /skɑ̃de/ [1] *vtr* **1** Littérat (faire l'analyse métrique) to scan; (déclamer) to declaim; **2** (rythmer) to accentuate, to give emphasis to [*phrase, mots*]; **3** to chant [*slogan, nom*].

scandinave /skɑ̃dinav/ *adj* Scandinavian; **il est d'origine ~** he is from Scandinavia.

Scandinave /skɑ̃dinav/ *nmf* Scandinavian.

Scandinavie /skɑ̃dinavi/ ▶**692** *nprf* **la ~** Scandinavia.

scandium /skɑ̃djɔm/ *nm* scandium.

scanner /skanɛr/ *nm* = **scanneur**.

scanneur /skanœr/ *nm* **1** (appareil) scanner; **2** Méd (scanographie) scan; **passer un ~** to have a scan.

scanographie /skanɔgrafi/ *nf* Méd **1** (technique) scanning; **2** (image) scan; **passer une ~** to have a scan.

scansion /skɑ̃sjɔ̃/ *nf* scansion.

scaphandre /skafɑ̃dr/ *nm* **1** Naut deep-sea diving suit; **2** Astronaut spacesuit.

■ **~ autonome** aqualung.

scaphandrier /skafɑ̃drije/ ▶**510** *nm* deep-sea diver.

scapulaire /skapylɛr/ **I** *adj* Anat scapular.

II *nm* **1** Anat scapula; **2** Relig scapular.

scarabée /skarabe/ *nm* **1** Zool beetle; **2** (bijou en archéologie) scarab.

■ **~ sacré** scarab.

scarificateur /skarifikatœr/ *nm* **1** Méd scarificator; **2** Agric scarifier.

scarification /skarifikasjɔ̃/ *nf* **1** Méd, Hort scarification; **2** Sociol (rite) scarification.

scarifier /skarifje/ [1] *vtr* to scarify.

scarlatine /skarlatin/ ▶**271** *nf* scarlet fever, scarlatina spéc.

scarole /skarɔl/ *nf* escarole.

scatologie /skatɔlɔʒi/ *nf* scatology.

scatologique /skatɔlɔʒik/ *adj* scatological.

sceau, *pl* **~x** /so/ *nm* **1** (objet, empreinte) seal; **apposer son ~** to affix one's seal; **sous le ~ du secret** [*dire, confier*] in confidence; **2** (marque distinctive) stamp, hallmark; **porter le ~ de** to bear the stamp ou hallmark of.

sceau-de-Salomon, *pl* **sceaux-de-Salomon** /sod(ə)salomɔ̃/ *nm* Solomon's seal.

scélérat, ~e /selera, at/ liter **I** *adj* villainous.

II *nm,f* villain.

scélératesse /selerates/ *nf* liter **1** (caractère) villainy; **2** (acte) act of villainy.

scellé /sele/ *nm* seal; **apposer les ~s** to

affix seals (*to doors, drawers, premises etc pending an enquiry*).

sceller /sele/ [1] *vtr* **1** (apposer un sceau) to seal [*document, acte*]; **2** (fixer solidement) to fix [sth] securely [*étagère, barreau*]; **~ un anneau dans le béton** to set a ring securely in concrete; **3** (consacrer) to seal [*amitié, alliance, réconciliation*].

scellofrais® /selɔfʀɛ/ *nm inv* clingfilm, Saran Wrap® US.

scénario /senaʀjo/ *nm* **1** Cin screenplay, script; **2** Théât scenario; **3** (déroulement) scenario; **~ catastrophe** nightmare ou doomsday scenario.

scénariste /senaʀist/ **▶510** *nmf* scriptwriter.

scène /sɛn/ *nf* **1** Théât (plateau) stage; **~ tournante** revolving stage; **être en** or **sur ~** to be on stage; **'en ~!'** 'on stage!'; **entrer en ~** to come on; **entrée en ~** entrance; **sortir de ~** to go off; **le rideau de ~** the curtain; **2** (subdivision, action) scene; **acte I ~ 3** act I scene 3; **la ~ se passe à Paris** the scene is set in Paris; **les ~s d'amour** the love scenes; **3** (activité théâtrale) stage; **quitter la ~** (métier) to give up the stage; **la ~ parisienne** Parisian theatre[GB]; **musique de ~** music for the theatre[GB]; **maquillage/costume de ~** theatrical make-up/costume; **mettre 'Phèdre' en ~** [*troupe*] to stage 'Phèdre'; [*personne*] to direct 'Phèdre'; **mettre en ~ un film** to direct a film; **mettre en ~ l'avarice** to portray greed; **une excellente mise en ~** an excellent production; **mise en ~ d'Ariane Mnouchkine** directed by Ariane Mnouchkine; **roman porté à la ~** novel adapted for the stage; **à la ~ comme à la ville** on stage and off; **4** (actualité) scene; **sur la ~ internationale/politique** on the international/political scene; **occuper le devant de la ~** fig to be in the news; **5** (esclandre) **faire (toute) une ~ (à qn)** to throw a fit○; **faire une ~ de jalousie** to throw a jealous fit○; **6** (épisode, spectacle) scene; **~s bibliques/de chasse** Biblical/hunting scenes; **~s de panique/torture** scenes of panic/torture; **un accident, c'est toujours une ~ pénible** an accident is always a terrible sight; **il a assisté à toute la ~** he saw the whole thing.

■ **~ d'intérieur** Art interior; **~ de ménage** domestic dispute; **~ originaire** or **primitive** primal scene.

IDIOMES **jouer la grande ~ du deux○ à qn** to make a grand drama of it.

scénique /senik/ *adj* [*répertoire*] stage (*épith*); [*musique*] for the stage; **le lieu ~** the stage; **jeu ~** stagecraft; **du point de vue ~** theatrically speaking.

scepticisme /sɛptisism/ *nm* **1** (incrédulité) scepticism GB, skepticism US (**sur, envers** about; **à l'égard de** toward, towards GB); **ils envisagent la réforme avec ~** they take a sceptical GB ou skeptical US view of the reform; **2** Philos (doctrine) scepticism GB, skepticism US.

sceptique /sɛptik/ **I** *adj* sceptical GB, skeptical US (**sur, à l'égard de** about); **laisser qn ~** to leave sb unconvinced.

II *nmf* **1** (personne incrédule) sceptic GB, skeptic US; **2** Philos sceptic GB, skeptic US.

sceptre /sɛptʀ/ *nm* sceptre[GB].

Schaffhouse /ʃafuz/ **▶692** *npr* **le canton de ~** the canton of Schaffhausen.

schapska /ʃapska/ *nm* (s)chapska.

schelem = **chelem**.

schéma /ʃema/ *nm* **1** (dessin) diagram; **2** (points principaux) outline; **3** (processus) pattern.

■ **~ corporel** body image; **~ directeur d'aménagement et d'urbanisme, SDAU** *regional planning and development programme*[GB].

schématique /ʃematik/ *adj* **1** (simplifié) [*vision, raisonnement*] simplistic; **2** (de schéma) schematic.

schématiquement /ʃematikmɑ̃/ *adv* **1** (avec un schéma) [*représenter, reproduire*] in a diagram; **2** (en simplifiant) [*exposer, expliquer*] in broad outline.

schématisation /ʃematizasjɔ̃/ *nf* simplification; (excessive) oversimplification.

schématiser /ʃematize/ [1] *vtr* **1** (simplifier) to simplify; (à l'excès) to oversimplify; **2** (faire un schéma) to make ou draw a diagram.

schématisme /ʃematism/ *nm* simplification; (excessif) oversimplification.

schème /ʃɛm/ *nm* Philos, Psych schema.

scherzando /skɛʀtzando/ *adv* scherzando.

scherzo /skɛʀtzo/ *nm* scherzo.

schilling /ʃiliŋ/ **▶46** *nm* schilling.

schismatique /ʃismatik/ *adj* schismatic.

schisme /ʃism/ *nm* schism.

schiste /ʃist/ *nm* schist.

■ **~ bitumineux** oil shale.

schisteux, -euse /ʃistø, øz/ *adj* schistose.

schizoïde /skizɔid/ *adj, nmf* schizoid.

schizoïdie /skizɔidi/ *nf* schizoid disorder.

schizophrène /skizɔfʀɛn/ *adj, nmf* schizophrenic.

schizophrénie /skizɔfʀeni/ **▶271** *nf* schizophrenia.

schlinguer◐ /ʃlɛ̃ge/ [1] *vi* to stink.

schnaps /ʃnaps/ *nm* schnap(p)s.

schnock◐ /ʃnɔk/ *nm* **un vieux ~** a fuddy-duddy; **du ~** what's-his-name.

schuss /ʃus/ *adv, nm* schuss; **descendre (en) ~** or **tout ~** to schuss down.

schwa /ʃva/ *nm* schwa.

Schwyz /ʃviz/ **▶692** *npr* **le canton de ~** the canton of Schwyz.

SCI /ɛssei/ *nf*: *abbr* ▶ **société**.

sciage /sjaʒ/ *nm* sawing; **~ mécanique** power sawing.

sciatique /sjatik/ **I** *adj* **nerf ~** sciatic nerve.

II **▶271** *nf* (douleur) sciatica; **avoir une ~** to have sciatica.

scie /si/ *nf* **1** (outil) saw; **2**○ (personne ou chose ennuyeuse) **quelle ~!** what a bore ou pain in the neck!; **3** (refrain) catch-tune.

■ **~ à chantourner** fretsaw; **~ circulaire** circular saw; **~ à dos** back saw; **~ égoïne** handsaw; **~ électrique** electric ou power saw; **~ à guichet** keyhole saw; **~ à métaux** hacksaw; **~ musicale** musical saw; **~ à refendre** ripsaw; **~ à ruban** band saw; **~ sauteuse** jigsaw; **~ de tailleur de pierre** stone saw.

sciemment /sjamɑ̃/ *adv* knowingly.

science /sjɑ̃s/ *nf* **1** (savoir) science; **dans l'état actuel de la ~** in the present state of science; **2** (domaine du savoir) science; **les ~s et les lettres** science and the arts; **la pêche, c'est toute une ~** fishing is a science all of its own; **3** (érudition) knowledge, erudition; **un homme de votre ~ devrait savoir cela** a man of your erudition should know that; **épater qn avec sa ~** to blind sb with science, to impress sb with one's knowledge.

■ **~s appliquées** applied sciences; **~s économiques** economics (+ *v sg*); **~s exactes** exact sciences; **~s de l'homme** human sciences; **~s humaines** = **~s de l'homme**; **~s mathématiques** mathematical sciences; **~s naturelles** ≈ biology (*sg*); **~s occultes** black arts; **~s physiques** physical sciences; **~s politiques** political science (*sg*); **~s sociales** social sciences; **~s de la Terre** Earth sciences; **~s de la vie** life sciences; **Sciences Po**○ Univ *Institute of Political Science*.

IDIOMES **être un puits de ~** to be a fount of knowledge.

science-fiction /sjɑ̃sfiksjɔ̃/ *nf* science fiction; **un roman de ~** a science-fiction ou sci-fi○ novel.

scientifique /sjɑ̃tifik/ **I** *adj* scientific.

II *nmf* scientist; **c'est plus un ~ qu'un littéraire** he's better at science subjects than at arts subjects.

scientifiquement /sjɑ̃tifikmɑ̃/ *adv* scientifically.

scientisme /sjɑ̃tism/ *nm* scientism.

scientiste /sjɑ̃tist/ **I** *adj* scientistic.

II *nmf* follower of scientism.

scientologie /sjɑ̃tɔlɔʒi/ *nf* Scientology; **l'Église de ~** the Church of Scientology.

scier /sje/ [2] *vtr* **1** to saw; **2**○ (abasourdir) [*nouvelle, personne*] to stun.

IDIOMES **~ la branche sur laquelle on est assis** to shoot oneself in the foot.

scierie /siʀi/ *nf* sawmill.

scieur /sjœʀ/ *nm* sawyer.

scille /sil/ *nf* spring squill.

scinder /sɛ̃de/ [1] **I** *vtr* to split [*organisation, groupe*]; to break down [*problème, question*]; **~ en deux/plusieurs parties** to split into two/several parts.

II se scinder *vpr* [*organisation, parti*] to split up; **se ~ en deux/plusieurs parties** to split into two/several parts.

scintillant, ~e /sɛ̃tijɑ̃, ɑ̃t/ *adj* [*étoile*] twinkling; [*langage, style*] scintillating.

scintillation /sɛ̃tijasjɔ̃, sɛ̃tillasjɔ̃/ *nf* scintillation.

scintillement /sɛ̃tijmɑ̃/ *nm* (d'un diamant) (fait de scintiller) sparkling; (des étoiles) twinkling; **le ~ de son regard** the way her eyes sparkle.

scintiller /sɛ̃tije/ [1] *vi* [*diamant*] to sparkle; [*regard, œil*] (de santé) to sparkle; (de malice) twinkle; [*étoile*] to twinkle; [*eau*] to glisten.

Scipion /sipjɔ̃/ *npr* **~ l'Africain** Scipio Africanus.

scission /sisjɔ̃/ *nf* **1** (sécession) split, schism (**au sein de** within); **faire ~** to break away ou to secede sout; **2** Biol, Phys fission.

scissionniste /sisjɔnist/ *adj, nmf* secessionist.

scissipare /sisipaʀ/ *adj* fissiparous.

scissiparité /sisipaʀite/ *nf* fissiparity, fission.

scissure /sisyʀ/ *nf* Anat fissure.

sciure /sjyʀ/ *nf* **~ (de bois)** sawdust.

scléreux, -euse /skleʀø, øz/ *adj* sclerotic.

sclérosant, ~e /skleʀozɑ̃, ɑ̃t/ *adj* **1** Méd [*traitement, substance*] sclerosant; **2** fig [*mode de vie, travail*] mind-numbing.

sclérose /skleʀoz/ *nf* **1** **▶271** Méd sclerosis; **2** (immobilisme) fossilization, ossification.

■ **~ en plaques, SEP** multiple sclerosis, MS.

scléroser /skleʀoze/ [1] **I** *vtr* Méd to sclerose [*varices*].

II se scléroser *vpr* **1** fig (se figer) [*institution, personne*] to become fossilized; **2** Méd [*tissu, organe, veine*] to become hardened ou sclerosed spéc.

sclérotique /skleʀotik/ *nf* sclera, sclerotic.

scolaire /skɔlɛʀ/ **I** *adj* **1** Scol [*vacances, programme, livre*] school (*épith*); [*réforme, publication*] educational; [*échec, réussite*] academic; **établissement ~** school; **2** pej (sans originalité) unimaginative.

II *nmf* schoolchild; **les ~s** schoolchildren.

scolarisable /skɔlaʀizabl/ *adj* **1** (par l'âge) [*enfant*] ready to start school; **2** (ayant les capacités nécessaires) **être ~** not to need special schooling; **il n'est pas ~** he needs special schooling.

scolarisation /skɔlaʀizasjɔ̃/ *nf* schooling, education; **~ des adultes** adult education; **le taux de ~** the percentage of children in full-time education; **la ~ plus poussée d'un grand nombre de jeunes** the increased numbers of young people staying on at school.

scolariser /skɔlaʀize/ [1] *vtr* **1** (envoyer à l'école) to send [sb] to school; **est-il scolarisé?** does he go to school?; **2** (pourvoir d'éco-

se

La traduction du pronom personnel *se* varie en fonction du verbe auquel il est associé et de son rôle; il sera traité automatiquement avec le verbe pronominal auquel on aura tout intérêt à se reporter.

se complément d'objet direct ou indirect d'un verbe pronominal réfléchi

se blesser	= to hurt oneself	*ils se sont brûlés*	= they burnt themselves
il se regarde	= he's looking at himself	*elles se sont brûlées*	= they burnt themselves
elle se regarde	= she's looking at herself	*le chien s'est brûlé*	= the dog burnt itself

Mais attention, très souvent en anglais le pronom ne sera pas exprimé:

se laver	= to wash *ou* to have a wash
elle s'habille	= she's getting dressed
il se rase	= he's shaving

Avec les parties du corps

il se lave les pieds	= he's washing his feet
elles se coupent les ongles	= they're cutting their nails
se ronger les ongles	= to bite one's nails
le chat se lèche les moustaches	= the cat is cleaning its whiskers
ils se bouchent les oreilles	= they put their fingers in their ears

se pronom réciproque

ils se détestent = they hate each other

On trouvera des exemples supplémentaires et des cas non envisagés ici dans l'article ci-dessous. En cas de doute, se reporter à l'article du verbe.

les) to provide [sth] with schools [*pays, région*].

scolarité /skɔlaʀite/ *nf* **1** (études) schooling; **durant ma ~** when I was at school; **après une ~ à** having been educated at; **arrêter sa ~ à 13 ans** to leave school at 13; **avoir une ~ difficile** not to do well at school; **la ~ obligatoire** compulsory education; **allonger la ~** to raise the school-leaving age; **l'allongement de la ~** (fait) staying on at school; **2** Univ (service administratif) university administration.

scolastique /skɔlastik/ **I** *adj* scholastic.
II *nf* scholasticism.

scoliose /skɔljoz/ *nf* scoliosis; **avoir une ~** to have scoliosis.

scolopendre /skɔlɔpɑ̃dʀ/ *nf* **1** Bot scolopendrium; **2** Zool scolopendrid.

sconse /skɔ̃s/ *nm* (fourrure) skunk (fur); **manteau de** or **en ~** skunk coat.

scoop○ /skup/ *nm* Presse scoop; **obtenir un ~** to score a scoop.

scooter /skutœʀ/ *nm* (motor) scooter.
■ **~ des mers** or **nautique** jetski; **~ des neiges** snowmobile.

scorbut /skɔʀbyt/ **▶ 271** *nm* scurvy.

score /skɔʀ/ *nm* **1** Scol, Sport score; **réaliser un bon/mauvais ~** to get a good/bad score; **~ nul** draw GB, tie US; **2** Pol result; **réaliser un bon ~ électoral** to get good results in the election; **réaliser un ~ de 38%** to get 38% of the vote.

scorie /skɔʀi/ *nf* **1** Géol scoria **¢**; **2** Mines slag **¢**, scoria **¢**; **3** (déchet) dross **¢**.

scorpion /skɔʀpjɔ̃/ *nm* Zool scorpion.
■ **~ aquatique** or **d'eau** water scorpion; **~ de mer** sea scorpion.

Scorpion /skɔʀpjɔ̃/ **▶ 874** *nprm* Scorpio.

scorsonère /skɔʀsɔnɛʀ/ *nf* scorzonera.

scotch, *pl* **~es** /skɔtʃ/ *nm* **1** (boisson) Scotch (whisky); **2** ®(ruban adhésif) Sellotape® GB, Scotch® tape US; **un rouleau** or **ruban de ~** a roll of Sellotape GB ou Scotch tape US.

scotcher /skɔtʃe/ [1] *vtr* to Sellotape® GB, to Scotch-tape® US.

scout, **~e** /skut/ **I** *adj* scout (*épith*).
II *nm,f* (Catholic) boy scout/(Catholic) girl scout; **matériel de ~** scouting gear.

scoutisme /skutism/ *nm* scouting; **faire du ~** to be a scout.

scrabble® /skʀabl/ **▶ 449** *nm* Scrabble®; **jouer au ~** to play Scrabble®.

scriban /skʀibɑ̃/ *nm* bureau cabinet.

scribe /skʀib/ *nm* **1** Antiq scribe; **2** (employé) pen pusher○ GB, pencil pusher US.

scribouillard○, **~e** /skʀibujaʀ, aʀd/ *nm,f* pen pusher○ GB, pencil pusher US.

script /skʀipt/ *nm* **1** (écriture) **écrire en ~** to print; **2** Cin, Radio, TV script.

scripte /skʀipt/ *nmf* Cin, Radio, TV continuity man/girl.

script-girl, *pl* **~s** /skʀiptgœʀl/ *nf* Cin, Radio, TV continuity girl.

scripturale /skʀiptyʀal/ *adj f* **monnaie ~** bank money.

scrofulaire /skʀɔfylɛʀ/ *nf* Bot figwort.
■ **~ aquatique** water figwort; **~ noueuse** common figwort.

scrofule /skʀɔfyl/ *nf* scrofula, king's evil.

scrofuleux, **-euse** /skʀɔfylø, øz/ *adj* scrofulous.

scrogneugneu /skʀɔɲøɲø/ *excl* humph!

scrotal, **~e**, *mpl* **-aux** /skʀɔtal, o/ *adj* scrotal.

scrotum /skʀɔtɔm/ *nm* Anat scrotum.

scrupule /skʀypyl/ *nm* scruple; **avoir ~ à faire** fml, **avoir des ~s à faire** to have scruples about doing; **n'avoir aucun ~** to have no scruples (**à faire** about doing); **être dénué de ~s** to be completely unscrupulous; **une personne sans ~s** an unscrupulous person; **faire taire ses ~s** to forget one's scruples; **être exact jusqu'au ~** to be scrupulously precise; **un ~ d'objectivité caractérise son exposé** his account is characterized by scrupulous objectivity.

scrupuleusement /skʀypyløzmɑ̃/ *adv* gén [*respecter, appliquer*] scrupulously; **se comporter ~ en affaires** to be scrupulous in one's business dealings.

scrupuleux, **-euse** /skʀypylø, øz/ *adj* scrupulous; **peu ~** unscrupulous; **veiller au respect ~ de qch** to ensure that sth is scrupulously respected.

scrutateur, **-trice** /skʀytatœʀ, tʀis/ **I** *adj* [*regard, air*] searching; [*nature*] inquiring; **d'un œil ~** with a searching look.
II *nm,f* (de vote) scrutineer.

scruter /skʀyte/ [1] *vtr* to scan [*mer, horizon, paysage*]; to scrutinize [*objet*]; to examine [*sol, personne, motif*]; to search [*mémoire*]; **~ la mer pour apercevoir qch** to scan the sea for sth.

scrutin /skʀytɛ̃/ *nm* **1** (vote) ballot; **par voie de ~** by ballot; **dépouiller le ~** to count the votes; **2** (élections) polls (*pl*); **ouverture/fermeture du ~** opening/closing of the polls; **date/jour du ~** polling date/day; **premier/deuxième tour de ~** first/second ballot; **mode de ~** electoral system.
■ **~ de liste** list system; **~ majoritaire** election by majority vote; **~ proportionnel** proportional representation, PR.

SCT /ɛssete/ *nm*: *abbr* ▶ **syndrome**.

sculpter /skylte/ [1] *vtr* **1** (réaliser) to sculpt, to carve [*statue, buste*] (**dans** in); to carve [*ornements, meuble*] (**dans** out of); **~ une statue dans du marbre** to sculpt ou carve a statue in marble; **~ une tête dans un rocher** to carve a head in the rock; **2** (travailler) to sculpt, to carve [*pierre, marbre*]; to carve [*bois*]; **~ au ciseau** to carve with a chisel; **cheminée en marbre sculpté** sculpted marble mantelpiece; **3** (éroder) [*mer, érosion*] to sculpt, to carve out [*roche, falaise*].

sculpteur /skyltœʀ/ **▶ 510** *nm* sculptor; **elle est ~** she's a sculptor; **~ sur bois** woodcarver.

sculptural, **~e**, *mpl* **-aux** /skyltyʀal, o/ *adj* [*art*] sculptural; [*forme, beauté, corps*] statuesque.

sculpture /skyltyʀ/ *nf* **1** (art) sculpture; **faire de la ~** (comme passe-temps) to do sculpture; (comme travail) to be a sculptor; **la ~ du bois** woodcarving; **2** (ouvrage) gén sculpture; (sur bois) woodcarving; **~ en marbre/bronze** marble/bronze sculpture; **~ sur bois** woodcarving; **une ~ de Rodin** a Rodin sculpture; **3** Aut (de pneu) tread **¢**.

Scylla /sila/ *npr* Scylla; ▶ **Charybde**.

scythe /sit/ *adj* Scythian.

Scythe /sit/ *nmf* Scythian.

SDAU /ɛsdeay/ *nm*: *abbr* ▶ **schéma**.

SDF /ɛsdeɛf/ *nmf*: *abbr* ▶ **sans**.

SDN /ɛsdeɛn/ *nf*: *abbr* ▶ **société**.

se (**s'** *before vowel or mute h*) /sə, s/ *pron pers* **1** (verbe réfléchi) **s'habiller** to get dressed, to dress; **~ cacher** to hide; **il ne faut pas ~ bloquer sur un mot** you shouldn't get stuck on one word; **2** (réciprocité) **ils ~ bousculent** they're jostling each other; **ils ~ sont injuriés** they insulted each other; **3** (verbe à valeur intransitive) **elle ~ comporte honorablement** she behaves honourably; **la voiture s'est bien comportée** the car performed well; **l'écart ~ creuse** the gap is widening; **l'épreuve ~ déroule en deux temps** the event takes place in two stages; **4** (verbe à valeur passive) **les exemples ~ comptent sur les doigts** the examples can be counted on the fingers of your hand; **le médicament ~ vend sans ordonnance** the medicine is sold without a prescription; **5** (avec un verbe impersonnel) **comment ~ fait-il que...?** how come...?, how is it that...?; **il ~ prépare actuellement une nouvelle édition** a new edition is being prepared at the moment; **il ~ produit une réaction chimique** there is a chemical reaction; **il ~ vend chaque jour plusieurs centaines d'appareils** several hundred appliances are sold every day.

séance /seɑ̃s/ *nf* **1** (réunion) (de tribunal, parlement, Bourse) session; (de comité, conseil municipal) meeting; **~ d'ouverture/de clôture** opening/closing session; **~ ordinaire/plénière** ordinary/plenary session; **être en ~** gén to be in session; [*parlementaires*] to sit; **tenir ~** to meet; **~ publique** public meeting; **~ des questions au gouvernement** session of questions to ministers in parliament; **~ tenante** immediately; **2** (période d'activité) session; **dix ~s de kinésithérapie** ten physiotherapy sessions; **organiser une ~ de travail** to organize a workshop; **3** Cin show; **~ supplémentaire à minuit** extra show at midnight; **une ~ privée** a private screening; **le film commence vingt minutes après le début de la ~** the film commences twenty minutes after the start of the programme[GB].
■ **~ de spiritisme** séance.

séant /seɑ̃/ **I** *adj m* **il est ~ de faire** it is fitting to do.
II *nm* **se mettre sur son ~** to sit up.

seau, *pl* **~x** /so/ *nm* (récipient) gén bucket, pail; (pour enfant) bucket; (contenu) bucket(-ful).
■ **~ à champagne** champagne bucket; **~ à charbon** coal scuttle; **~ à glace** ice bucket; **~ hygiénique** slop pail.
IDIOMES **pleuvoir à ~x**○ to pour; **la pluie tombe à ~x**○ it's pouring.

sébacé, **~e** /sebase/ *adj* sebaceous.

sébile /sebil/ *nf* begging bowl; **tendre la ~** to beg.

séborrhée /sebɔʀe/ *nf* seborrhoea.

sébum /sebɔm/ *nm* sebum; **excès de ~** excessive sebum.

sec, **sèche** /sɛk, sɛʃ/ **I** *adj* **1** (sans humidité) [*temps, matière, peau, cheveux*] dry; [*abricot, fruit*] dried; **bois ~** dry wood; **vapeur/chaleur sèche** dry steam/heat; **avoir la gorge sèche** to feel parched°; **à pied ~** without getting one's feet wet; **ne plus avoir un fil de ~**° to be soaked through ou drenched; **garder l'œil ~** not to shed a tear; **2** (pas doux) [*vin, cidre*] dry; (sans eau) **boire son gin ~** to like one's gin straight ou neat GB; **3** (austère) [*personne, communiqué*] terse; [*lettre, ton*] curt; [*style*] dry; [*élégance*] stark; [*traits*] sharp; **avoir un cœur ~** to be cold-hearted; ▶**trique**; **4** (net) [*bruit*] sharp; **se briser d'un coup ~** to snap; **donner un coup ~ à qch** to give sth a sharp tap.
II *nm* **être à ~** [*rivière, réservoir*] to have dried up; [*compte en banque*] to be empty; [*personne*] to have no money; **tenir qch au ~** to keep sth in a dry place; **mettre une mare à ~** to drain a pond; **avoir les pieds bien au ~** to have nice dry feet; **cacahuètes grillées à ~** dry roasted peanuts.
III *adv* **1** (avec netteté) **se briser ~** to snap; **2**° (beaucoup) [*cogner, pleuvoir, boire*] a lot.
IV sèche° *nf* (cigarette) fag GB, cig°.
IDIOMES **aussi ~**° immediately; **rester ~**° to be unable to reply; **je l'ai eu ~**° I was pretty choked°.

sécable /sekabl/ *adj* [*comprimé*] divisible.

SECAM /sekam/ *nm* (*abbr* = **séquentiel couleur à mémoire**) SECAM; **système ~** SECAM standard.

sécant, **~e** /sekɑ̃, ɑ̃t/ **I** *adj* secant (**de** to).
II sécante *nf* Math secant.

sécateur /sekatœʀ/ *nm* clippers (*pl*).
■ **~ à haie** shears (*pl*).

sécession /sesesjɔ̃/ *nf* secession ȼ; **le droit de ~** the right to secede; **faire ~** to secede.

sécessionniste /sesesjɔnist/ *adj, nmf* secessionist.

séchage /seʃaʒ/ *nm* gén drying ȼ; (du bois) seasoning ȼ.

sèche ▶**sec I, IV.**

sèche-cheveux /sɛʃʃəvø/ *nm inv* hairdrier GB, blow-dryer US.

sèche-linge /sɛʃlɛ̃ʒ/ *nm inv* (machine) tumble-drier GB, tumble-dryer US; (armoire) drying cupboard.

sèche-mains /sɛʃmɛ̃/ *nm inv* hand-drier GB, blower US.

sèchement /sɛʃmɑ̃/ *adv* drily, coldly; **très ~** curtly.

sécher /seʃe/ [1] **I** *vtr* **1** gén to dry [*cheveux, enfant, poisson, fruit, larme, linge*]; **2**° (manquer) to skip [*cours*]; **~ l'école** to skip school, to bunk off° GB.
II *vi* **1** (devenir sec) [*linge, cheveux*] to dry; [*plaie, herbe, boue*] to dry up; [*encre, peinture*] (normalement) to dry; (par négligence) to dry up; [*fleur*] to wither; [*jambon*] to get dried up; **fleur/viande/boue séchée** dried flower/meat/mud; **faire ~ des champignons/des fleurs/ses chaussures** to dry mushrooms/flowers/one's shoes; **mettre le linge à ~** (dehors) to hang out the washing; **mettre des vêtements à ~** (après un lavage) to hang clothes up to dry; (après la pluie) to dry out clothes; **'faire ~ à plat'** 'dry flat'; **mettre du bois à ~** to leave wood to season; **~ sur pied** [*plante*] to wilt; **2**° (ne pas savoir répondre) to dry up.
III se sécher *vpr* (avec une serviette) to dry oneself; **se ~ devant le poêle** to dry off in front of the stove; **se ~ les cheveux** to dry one's hair.

sécheresse /seʃʀɛs/ *nf* **1** (manque de pluie) drought; **une grave ~** a severe drought; **2** (de climat) dryness ȼ; **3** (austérité) (de personne) curt manner; (d'auteur, ouvrage) dryness; **la ~ de son ton** his/her curt tone; **avec ~** [*dire, répondre*] curtly.

séchoir /seʃwaʀ/ *nm* **1** (sèche-cheveux) hairdrier GB, blow-dryer US; **2** (pour le linge) (étendage) clothes airer, clothes horse; (armoire) drying cupboard; (machine) tumble-drier GB, tumble-dryer US; **3** Agric drier GB, dryer US.

second, **~e** /səgɔ̃, ɔ̃d/ **I** *adj* **1** (dans une séquence) second; **~e partie/fois** second part/time; **chapitre ~** chapter two; **en ~e lecture** at a second reading; **en ~ lieu** secondly; **dans un ~ temps, nous étudierons**... subsequently, we will study...; **c'est à prendre au ~ degré** it is not to be taken literally; **le second Empire** the Second Empire; **2** (dans une hiérarchie) second; **~ violon** second violin; **officier en ~** second officer; **être commandant en ~** to be second in command; **voyager en ~e classe** to travel second class; **billet de ~e classe** second-class ticket; **elle est arrivée en ~e position** she came second; **de ~ ordre** second-rate; **politicien de ~ plan** minor politician; **faire passer qch au ~ plan** to make sth take second place; **de ~ choix** of inferior quality; **jouer un ~ rôle** Théât to play a supporting role; **jouer les ~ rôles** fig to play second fiddle; **les causes ~es** the secondary causes; **3** (autre) second; **ma ~e patrie** my second home; **c'est une ~e Marie Curie** she is a second Marie Curie; **avoir le don de ~e vue** to have second sight.
II *nm,f* **le ~, la ~e** gén the second one; (enfant) the second child; **le ~ de la liste** the second one on the list; **mon ~ est**... (dans une charade) my second is...
III *nm* **1** (adjoint) second-in-command; **2** (étage) second floor GB, third floor US; **au ~** on the second floor GB, on the third floor US; **les gens du ~** the people on the second floor; **3** (dans un duel) second.
IV en second *loc adv* [*arriver, partir*] second; **passer en ~** [*travail, amis*] to come second.
V seconde *nf* **1** ▶**860** (unité de temps) second; **11 mètres par ~e** 11 metres[GB] per ou a second; **à la ~e près** to the nearest second; **2** (court laps de temps) second; **je reviens dans une ~e** I'll be back in a second ou sec°; **en une fraction de ~e** in a split second; **3** Scol (classe) *fifth year of secondary school, age 15–16*; **4** Transp **billet de ~e** standard ticket GB, second-class ticket; **voyager en ~e** to travel standard ou second class; **5** Aut second gear; **passer en** or **la ~e** to change into second; **6** Mus second.
■ **~ avènement** Bible Second Coming; **~ de cordée** second man (in a climbing party); **~ couteau** Cin, Théât cameo role; **~ maître** Mil Naut ≈ petty officer GB, ≈ petty officer first class US; **~ marché** secondary market.

secondaire /səgɔ̃dɛʀ/ **I** *adj* **1** (en deuxième position) secondary; **2** (de moindre importance) [*personnage, route*] minor; **3** Scol **école ~** secondary school GB, high school US; **enseignement ~** secondary school GB ou high school US education; **j'ai fait mes études ~s à**... I was in secondary school GB ou high school US at...; **4** Méd **lésions ~s** secondary lesions; **syphilis ~** the second stage of syphilis; **effets ~s** side effects; **5** Géol **ère ~** Mesozoic era; **6** Tech secondary.
II *nm* **1** Scol secondary school GB ou high school US education; **les enseignants du ~** secondary GB ou high US school teachers; **2** Géol **le ~** the Mesozoic.

secondairement /səgɔ̃dɛʀmɑ̃/ *adv* secondarily.

seconde ▶**second I, II, IV.**

secondement /səgɔ̃dmɑ̃/ *adv* secondly.

seconder /səgɔ̃de/ [1] *vtr* [*personne*] to assist; [*circonstance*] to aid.

secouer /səkwe/ [1] **I** *vtr* **1** (agiter) to shake [*bouteille, branche, personne*]; to shake out [*nappe, tapis, parapluie*]; **~ la tête** to shake one's head; **rire en secouant les épaules** to shake with laughter; **être un peu secoué** (dans une voiture, un avion) to have rather a bumpy ride; (sur un bateau) to have rather a rough trip; **secoué par un séisme** [*ville, région*] hit by an earthquake; **2** (se débarrasser de) to shake off [*poussière, neige, joug*]; **3** (ébranler) [*crise*] to shake [*personne, pays*]; **être un peu secoué** (par une nouvelle) to be rather shaken up; **la guerre/polémique qui secoue le pays** the war/controversy raging in the country; **4**° (activer) to give [sb] a shaking-up° [*personne*].
II se secouer *vpr* **1** (pour se dégager) [*personne*] to give oneself a shake; [*animal*] to give itself a shake; **2** (nerveusement) to jump about all over the place; **3**° (contre le découragement) to pull oneself together; (contre l'inertie) to wake up, to get moving°.

secourable /səkuʀabl/ *adj* **être ~** to be a good samaritan; **tendre une main ~ à qn** to give sb a helping hand.

secourir /səkuʀiʀ/ [26] *vtr* (aider) to help [*personne*]; (sauver) to rescue [*alpiniste, marin*]; (soigner) to give first aid to [*accidenté*]; (assister) to provide aid for [*réfugié*].

secourisme /səkuʀism/ *nm* first aid; **brevet/cours de ~** first aid certificate/class.

secouriste /səkuʀist/ ▶**510** *nmf* first-aid worker.

secours /səkuʀ/ **I** *nm inv* (aide) help; **au ~!** help!; **appeler** or **crier au ~** to shout for help; **appel au ~** cry for help; **avec/sans le ~ de** with/without the help of; **être d'un grand ~** to be a great help; **porter ~ à** to help; **il l'a appelée à son ~** he got her to help him; **porter ~ à, se porter au ~ de** to help [*blessé, réfugié*]; to come to the aid of [*personne critiquée, entreprise*]; to rescue [*animal*]; **aller/voler au ~ de qn** to go/to rush to sb's aid; **venir au ~ de qn** to come to sb's aid; **le ~ en mer/en montagne** sea/mountain rescue operations (*pl*); **~ financier** financial aid ȼ; **de ~** (de rechange) [*roue*] spare; (d'urgence) [*sortie*] emergency; (de soins) [*matériel*] first aid; (de sauvetage) [*équipe, opération*] rescue; (de sécurité) [*matériel*] back up.
II *nmpl* **1** (personnes) (secouristes) rescuers, rescue team (*sg*); (renforts) reinforcements; **2** (vivres, médicaments) relief supplies; **~ médicaux** medical supplies; **~ humanitaires** humanitarian aid ȼ; **premiers ~, ~ d'urgence** first aid ȼ; **3** Relig **les ~ de la religion** the consolation of religion.

secousse /səkus/ *nf* **1** (mouvement brusque) jolt; **une légère ~** a slight jolt; **éviter les ~s** (en voiture, avion) to avoid the bumps; **avancer par ~s** [*voiture, train*] to jerk forward; **avancer sans une ~** to move forward smoothly; **donner une ~ à qch** (en tirant) to give sth a tug; (en poussant) to give sth a push; **2** (émotion) (personnelle) shock; (dans un groupe) upheaval; **3** Géol **~ (sismique)** (earth) tremor; **4** Électrotech **~ (électrique)** (electric) shock.

secret, **-ète** /səkʀɛ, ɛt/ **I** *adj* **1** (non divulgué) [*dossier, code, rite, société*] secret; **tenir qch ~** to keep sth secret ou a secret; **2** (dissimulé) [*passage, mécanisme*] secret; **3** (intime, mystérieux) [*vie, sentiment, raisons*] secret; **avoir le ~ espoir de réussir** secretly to hope to succeed; **4** (réservé) [*personne*] secretive.
II *nm* **1** (ce qu'on cache) secret; **c'est un/mon ~** it's a/my secret; **garder un ~** to keep a secret; **c'est un ~ entre nous** it's our secret; **ne pas avoir de ~s pour qn** to have no secrets from sb; **confier un ~ à qn** to let sb into GB ou in on US a secret; **ce n'est un ~ pour personne** it's no secret (que that); **faire un ~ de qch** to make a secret of sth; **il n'en fait pas un ~** he makes no secret of it; ▶**tombe**; **2** (ce qui est caché) secret; **livrer ses ~s** [*nature, substance, tombe*] to yield up (its) secrets (**à**

to); **la mécanique n'a plus de ~s pour elle** mechanics holds no secrets for her; **3** (discrétion) secrecy; **dans le ~ de leur atelier** in the secrecy of their studio; **faire qch dans le plus grand ~** to do sth in the utmost ou greatest secrecy; **être tenu au ~** to be sworn to secrecy; **dans le ~ de ton cœur** in your heart of hearts; **être dans le ~ (des dieux)** to be in on the secret; **mettre qn dans le ~/le ~ de qch** to let sb into GB ou in on US the secret/a secret about sth; **garder le ~ sur qch** to keep sth a secret; **promettre le ~ absolu sur qch** to promise to keep sth strictly secret; **en ~** in secret; **4** (recette) secret; **le ~ du bonheur** the secret of happiness; **quel est ton ~ pour rester jeune?** what's your secret for staying young?; **avoir le ~ de qch** to know the secret of sth; **encore une de ces gaffes dont il a le ~** another of those blunders that only he knows how to make; **il a le ~ des solutions compliquées pour les problèmes simples** he has a knack of finding complicated answers to simple problems; **5** (prison) **mettre qn/être au ~** to put sb/to be in solitary confinement; **6** (réserve) secrecy; **leur goût du ~** their taste for secrecy; **7** (mécanisme) secret mechanism; **une serrure à ~** a secret lock.

■ **~ bancaire** Fin, Jur bank confidentiality; **~ d'État** Pol State secret; **~ de fabrication** industrial secret; **~ de Polichinelle** open secret; **~ professionnel** Jur professional confidentiality; **être tenu au ~ professionnel** to be sworn to professional confidentiality.

secrétaire /s(ə)kʀetɛʀ/ **I** *nmf* (employé administratif) secretary; **~ à mi-temps** part-time secretary.

II *nm* **1** (cadre politique) secretary; **2** (cadre diplomatique) secretary; **premier/deuxième ~** first/second secretary; **3** (meuble) secretaire GB, secretary US; **4** Zool secretary bird.

■ **~ adjoint** assistant secretary; **~ bilingue** bilingual secretary; **~ de direction** personal assistant; **~ d'État** (en France) minister; (en Grande-Bretagne, aux États-Unis) Secretary of State; **~ général** general secretary; **~ général de l'ONU** UN secretary-general; **~ médicale** medical secretary; **~ particulier** private secretary; **~ de production** Cin producer's assistant; **~ de rédaction** Presse subeditor GB, copy-editor; **~ de séance** committee secretary.

secrétariat /s(ə)kʀetaʀja/ *nm* (travail) secretarial work; **école de ~** secretarial college; (fonction) secretaryship; (mandat) term of office as secretary; (lieu) secretariat.

■ **~ d'État** ministry; **~ d'État à l'emploi** ministry for employment; **~ de mairie** city hall secretariat; **~ de rédaction** (activité) subediting GB, copy-editing; (bureau) subeditors' room GB, copy-editors' room.

secrète /səkʀɛt/ ▶ **secret I.**

secrètement /səkʀɛtmɑ̃/ *adv* secretly.

sécréter /sekʀete/ [1] *vtr* **1** Bot, Physiol to secrete; **2** (exuder) to exude [*goutte, liquide*]; **3** (produire) to foster [*inégalités, idéologie*]; to hatch [*réforme*]; **~ l'ennui** to exude boredom.

sécréteur, **-trice** /sekʀetœʀ, tʀis/ *adj* secretory.

sécrétion /sekʀesjɔ̃/ *nf* secretion.

sectaire /sɛktɛʀ/ *adj, nmf* sectarian.

sectarisme /sɛktaʀism/ *nm* sectarianism.

secte /sɛkt/ *nf* Relig sect; (clan) faction.

secteur /sɛktœʀ/ *nm* **1** Écon (d'activités générales) sector; **~ primaire/privé/public** primary/private/public sector; **~ secondaire** or **manufacturier** manufacturing (sector); **~ tertiaire** or **des services** service sector; **~ de l'industrie** industrial sector; **~ d'activité** sector; **~ agricole/bancaire/hospitalier** farming/banking/hospital sector; **les différents ~s économiques** the various sectors of the economy; **2** Admin (subdivision) area; **~ de recrutement scolaire** school's catchment area; **les représentants commerciaux ont chacun leur ~** each sales representative has his own territory; **3**° (parages) neighbourhood[GB]; **on a intérêt à changer de ~** we'd be better off somewhere else; **4** Électrotech **le ~** (réseau) the mains (*pl*); **appareil fonctionnant sur ~** mains-operated appliance; **panne de ~** power failure; **5** Math sector; **~ sphérique** sector of a sphere; **6** Mil sector; **~ d'opérations** operational sector; **~ de tir** field of fire.

■ **~ postal**, **SP** Mil *army postal area*; **~ sauvegardé** conservation area.

section /sɛksjɔ̃/ *nf* **1** (division) Admin, Mil section; (de parti, syndicat) branch; **~ locale** local branch; (de route, chemin de fer) section; (de livre) part; **2** Scol (selon les niveaux) stream GB, track US; **choisir une ~ littéraire/scientifique/technique** to choose a literary/scientific/technical option; **3** Univ department; **~ d'anglais/de biochimie** English/Biochemistry department; **4** Math, Tech (coupe) section; **~ conique/longitudinale/oblique/transversale** conical/longitudinal/oblique/transverse section; **un tube de 12 mm de ~** a 12 mm gauge tube; **5** (coupure) section.

■ **~ d'autobus** Transp fare stage; **~ d'or** Math golden section; **~ rythmique** Mus rhythm section.

sectionnement /sɛksjɔnmɑ̃/ *nm* (de tendon, membre) severing; (de territoire, service) division (**en** into).

sectionner /sɛksjɔne/ [1] *vtr* to sever [*membre, artère*]; to divide up [*service, administration*] (**en** into); to cut [*tuyau, câble, fil*].

sectoriel, **-ielle** /sɛktɔʀjɛl/ *adj* sectoral.

sectorisation /sɛktɔʀizasjɔ̃/ *nf* division.

sectoriser /sɛktɔʀize/ [1] *vtr* to divide [sth] into sectors.

séculaire /sekylɛʀ/ *adj* **1** (vieux) [*tradition, arbre*] ancient; **2** (vieux de cent ans) [*arbre, maison*] hundred-year-old; [*personne*] centenarian; **plusieurs fois ~** several hundred years old; **3** (tous les cent ans) [*cérémonie*] centennial; **4** Astron secular.

sécularisation /sekylaʀizasjɔ̃/ *nf* **1** (de religieux) (rendu séculier) secularization; (rendu laïque) laicization; **2** (de biens, fonctions) secularization.

séculariser /sekylaʀize/ [1] *vtr* **1** (rendre séculier) to secularize [*personne, monastère*]; **2** (rendre laïque) to laicize [*personne*]; to secularize [*biens, fonctions*].

séculier, **-ière** /sekylje, ɛʀ/ **I** *adj* [*clergé, prêtre*] secular.

II *nm* (prêtre) secular.

secundo /səgɔ̃do/ *adv* secondly.

sécurisant, **~e** /sekyʀizɑ̃, ɑ̃t/ *adj* **1** [*milieu, situation, équipement*] reassuring; **2** Psych [*père, mère*] who makes one feel secure (*épith, après n*).

sécuriser /sekyʀize/ [1] *vtr* **1** gén (rassurer) to reassure; **2** Psych to make [sb] feel secure [*personne*]; **un enfant/malade sécurisé** a secure child/patient; **se sentir sécurisé** to feel secure.

securit® /sekyʀit/ *nm* **(verre) ~** Triplex® (glass) GB, safety glass.

sécuritaire /sekyʀitɛʀ/ *adj* [*idéologie, discours*] security (*épith*).

sécurité /sekyʀite/ *nf* (absence de risques d'agression) security; (absence de danger fortuit) safety; **pour votre ~** for your own safety; **assurer la ~ de** (contre des agresseurs) to ensure the security of; (contre un accident, un sinistre) to ensure the safety of; **~ civile/publique** civil/public security; **en toute ~** [*travailler, voyager, se baigner*] in complete safety; **la ~ matérielle/financière** material/financial security; **~ de l'emploi** job security; **de ~** [*système, forces, services*] security; [*dispositif, garantie, zone*] safety; [*raisons, question, problème*] of security (*après n*); **règles** or **consignes de ~** safety regulations; **avoir une impression de ~** to feel secure; **être/se sentir en ~** to be/to feel secure ou safe (**auprès de** with).

■ **~ routière** road safety; **~ sociale**, **SS** *French national health and pensions organization.*

sédatif, **-ive** /sedatif, iv/ **I** *adj* [*propriété*] sedative; [*potion, effet*] soothing.

II *nm* sedative.

sédation /sedasjɔ̃/ *nf* sedation; **être sous ~** to be under sedation.

sédentaire /sedɑ̃tɛʀ/ **I** *adj* **1** gén [*vie, travail, personne*] sedentary; **emploi ~** sedentary ou desk job; **2** Anthrop [*population*] geographically stable; **3** Mil [*troupes*] garrison(ed) (*épith*).

II *nmf* **1** Entr person with a sedentary ou desk job; **2** (casanier) stay-at-home GB, homebody US; **3** Anthrop **les ~s** the indigenous population.

sédentarisation /sedɑ̃taʀizasjɔ̃/ *nf* settlement.

sédentariser /sedɑ̃taʀize/ [1] **I** *vtr* to settle; **nomades sédentarisés** settled nomads.

II se sédentariser *vpr* Anthrop to settle.

sédentarité /sedɑ̃taʀite/ *nf* (de population) settled way of life; (d'emploi, de condition) sedentary nature.

sédiment /sedimɑ̃/ *nm* sediment.

sédimentaire /sedimɑ̃tɛʀ/ *adj* sedimentary.

sédimentation /sedimɑ̃tasjɔ̃/ *nf* sedimentation.

séditieux, **-ieuse** /sedisjø, øz/ *adj* **1** [*personne*] rebellious; **2** [*écrit, esprit, propos*] seditious.

sédition /sedisjɔ̃/ *nf* insurrection.

séducteur, **-trice** /sedyktœʀ, tʀis/ **I** *adj* seductive.

II *nm,f* (trompeur) seducer/seductress; (charmeur) charmer; **c'est un grand ~** he's a real charmer.

séduction /sedyksjɔ̃/ *nf* (manœuvre) seduction; (charme naturel) charm; **manœuvres de ~** stratagems of seduction; **une femme pleine de ~** a woman of great charm; **pouvoir de ~** (de personne, d'acteur) power of seduction (**sur** over); (de la jeunesse, des mots) seductiveness; (de l'argent) lure; (du luxe) enticement; (du cinéma, de la télévision) seductive power (**sur** over).

séduire /sedɥiʀ/ [1] *vtr* **1** (attirer) [*personne*] gén to captivate; **il aime ~** he likes to charm people; **avec son physique, il séduira les filles** with his physique, he'll attract the girls; **2** (plaire à) to appeal to [*personne*]; (être plaisant) to be appealing; **cette solution séduit par sa simplicité** this solution is appealing in its simplicity; **ton projet me séduit plus que le leur** I find your plan more appealing than theirs; **les qualités qui séduisent le plus chez un homme** the most attractive qualities in a man; **3** (convaincre) [*personne*] to win over; **il a séduit l'électorat de gauche par...** he won over the left-wing electorate with...; **je me suis laissé ~ par leurs propositions** I let myself be won over by their offers; **4**† (pour des relations sexuelles) to seduce.

séduisant, **~e** /sedɥizɑ̃, ɑ̃t/ *adj* [*personne, produit, site, perspective*] attractive; [*projet, idée, mode de vie*] appealing.

séfarade /sefaʀad/ **I** *adj* Sephardic.

II *nmf* Sephardi (Jew).

segment /sɛgmɑ̃/ *nm* **1** Ling, Math, Ordinat, Zool segment; **~ de droite** line segment; **~ sphérique** segment of a sphere; **2** Sociol (groupe) group; **~ de la population/clientèle** population/client group; **3** Aut **~ (de piston)** piston ring; **~ de frein** brake shoe.

segmental, **~e**, *mpl* **-aux** /sɛgmɑ̃tal, o/ *adj* Ling segmental.

segmentation /sɛgmɑ̃tasjɔ̃/ *nf* **1** Ling, Math, Ordinat, Sociol segmentation; **2** Biol cleavage.

segmenter /sɛgmɑ̃te/ [1] **I** *vtr* to segment [*programme, énoncé, marché*] (**en** into).

II se segmenter *vpr* gén to split up, to segment (**en** into); Biol [*œuf*] to undergo cleavage.

ségrégatif, -ive /segʀegatif, iv/ *adj* (pour raison raciale) segregationist; (pour raison sociale, sexuelle, de santé) segregative.

ségrégation /segʀegasjɔ̃/ *nf* segregation.

ségrégationnisme /segʀegasjɔnism/ *nm* segregationism.

ségrégationniste /segʀegasjɔnist/ *adj, nmf* segregationist.

seiche /sɛʃ/ *nf* cuttlefish.

séide /seid/ *nm* (fanatical) henchman.

seigle /sɛgl/ *nm* rye; **pain/farine de ~** rye bread/flour.

seigneur /sɛɲœʀ/ *nm* **1** Hist (propriétaire, noble) lord; **vivre en grand** or **comme un ~** to live like a lord; **se conduire en grand ~** to behave in noble fashion; **jouer au grand ~** to flash one's money around; **être grand ~** to be generous; **2** fig (de la finance, l'industrie) heavyweight; (du sport) star; **le ~ des lieux** hum the boss; **mon ~ et maître** my lord and master.
■ ~ de la guerre warlord.
IDIOMES **à tout ~ tout honneur** Prov honour[GB] where honour[GB] is due.

Seigneur /sɛɲœʀ/ **I** *nm* Lord; **Notre ~ Jésus-Christ** Our Lord Jesus Christ; **le ~ l'a rappelé à lui** euph he has gone to meet his Maker; **il repose dans la paix du ~** euph he is at peace with the Lord; ▶ **impénétrable**.
II *excl* Good Lord!
IDIOMES **être dans les vignes du ~** hum to have been sampling the fruit of the vine.

seigneurial, ~e, *mpl* **-iaux** /sɛɲœʀjal, o/ *adj* **1** [*château, terres*] (en France) seigneurial; (en Angleterre) manorial; **2** fig [*demeure*] stately; [*manières*] lordly.

seigneurie /sɛɲœʀi/ *nf* **1** (terre) seigneury; **2** (autorité, droits) seigniory; **3** (titre) **votre ~** your Lordship.

sein /sɛ̃/ *nm* **1** Anat breast; **donner le ~ à un enfant** to give a child the breast; **~s tombants** sagging breasts; **avoir les ~s nus** to be topless; **se faire refaire les ~s** to have plastic surgery on one's breasts; **nourrir (son enfant) au ~** to breast-feed (one's baby); **serrer qn/qch contre** or **sur son ~** to clasp sb/sth to one's bosom; **2** (utérus) womb; **porter un enfant dans son ~** to carry a child in one's womb; **retour au** or **dans le ~ maternel** return to the womb; **3** (partie intérieure) bosom; **au ~ de** within.
IDIOMES **ça me ferait mal aux ~s○ (de faire)** it would make me feel sick (to do). ▶ **faux**[1], **serpent**.

seine /sɛn/ *nf* Pêche seine.

Seine /sɛn/ ▶ 357 *nprf* **la ~** the Seine.

Seine-et-Marne /sɛnemaʀn/ ▶ 692 *nprf* (département) **la ~** Seine-et-Marne.

Seine-Maritime /sɛnmaʀitim/ ▶ 692 *nprf* (département) **la ~** Seine-Maritime.

Seine-Saint-Denis /sɛnsɛ̃dni/ ▶ 692 *nprf* (département) **la ~** Seine-Saint-Denis.

seing /sɛ̃/ *nm* Jur signature; **acte sous ~ privé** private agreement.

séisme /seism/ *nm* **1** Géol earthquake, seism; **2** (bouleversement) upheaval.

seize /sɛz/ ▶ 545, 407, 212 *adj inv, pron* sixteen.

seizième /sɛzjɛm/ ▶ 545, 212 *adj* sixteenth.
■ ~s de finale Sport *round in competition with thirty-two competitors.*

séjour /seʒuʀ/ *nm* **1** (période) stay; **~ de trois semaines** three-week stay; **~ à l'étranger/à Paris/à l'hôtel** stay abroad/in Paris/in a hotel; **j'ai fait un ~ à l'hôpital** I had a stay in hospital GB ou in the hospital US; **il a fait plusieurs ~s/un ~ en prison** he has been in prison several times/ for a time; **faire un ~ à l'étranger/en France** to spend some time abroad/in France; **~s à l'étranger** (dans CV) time spent abroad; **faire un ~ touristique en Italie** to go touring in Italy; **2** (pièce) (dans une annonce) reception; (chez soi) living room; **3** fml (lieu) abode sout; **un ~ champêtre** a rural retreat; **le ~ des morts** the abode of the dead.
■ ~ culturel cultural holiday GB ou vacation; **~ linguistique** language study holiday GB ou vacation.

séjourner /seʒuʀne/ [1] *vi* **1** [*personne*] to stay; **nous avons séjourné à l'hôtel/chez des amis** we stayed in a hotel/with friends; **2** [*liquide, brouillard*] to lie; **l'eau a séjourné des mois après l'inondation** the water lay for months after the flood.

sel /sɛl/ **I** *nm* **1** Culin salt; **ajouter du ~** to add salt; **gros ~** coarse salt; **régime sans ~** salt-free diet; **pain sans ~** unsalted bread; **2** Chimie salt; **~ de sodium** sodium salt; **3** fig (esprit) savour[GB]; (piquant) piquancy; **les jeux de mots perdent de leur ~ à la traduction** puns lose some of their savour[GB] in translation; **la situation** or **ça ne manque pas de ~** the situation has a certain piquancy.
II sels *nmpl* Pharm smelling salts (*pl*); **respirer des ~s** to sniff smelling salts.
■ ~ de céleri celery salt; **~ de cuisine** cooking salt; **~ fin** fine ou table salt; **~ gemme** rock salt; **~ marin** sea salt; **le ~ de la terre** the salt of the earth; **~s de bain** Cosmét bath salts.

sélacien /selasjɛ̃/ *nm* Zool selachian.

sélect○, ~e /selɛkt/ *adj* [*club, bar*] exclusive; [*clientèle*] select.

sélecteur, -trice /selɛktœʀ, tʀis/ **I** *adj* selective.
II *nm* **1** Ordinat, Télécom, TV selector; **2** Mécan (de bicyclette, d'embrayage standard) gear lever, gearshift US; (de moto) gear change, gearshift US; (d'embrayage automatique) gearstick, gearshift US.
■ ~ de gammes band selector.

sélectif, -ive /selɛktif, iv/ *adj* (tous contextes) selective.

sélection /selɛksjɔ̃/ *nf* **1** (de candidats) gén selection; (pour un emploi) selection process; **opérer une ~ parmi** to make a selection from; **~ par** or **sur examen** selection by exam; **~ à l'entrée** selective entry; **2** (de titres, livres, films) selection, choice; **~ hebdomadaire** (de journal, revue) weekly choice; **3** Sport (choix) selection; (équipe) team; **comité de ~** selection committee; **~ nationale/française** national/French team; **match de ~** trial match; **épreuve de ~** trial (**pour** for); **avoir 20 ~s en équipe nationale** [*joueur*] to have been capped ou tapped 20 times for the national team; **4** Agric, Biol selection; **~ génétique/naturelle** genetic/natural selection.

sélectionné, ~e /selɛksjɔne/ *nm,f* Sport selected player.

sélectionner /selɛksjɔne/ [1] *vtr* **1** (choisir) to select (**pour qch** for sth; **pour faire** to do; **parmi** from); **~ des élèves pour un concours** to enter pupils for a competitive examination; **être sélectionné sur dossier** Univ Scol to be selected on the basis of one's academic record; **2** Ordinat to highlight [*texte, mot*].

sélectionneur, -euse /selɛksjɔnœʀ, øz/ *nm,f* Sport selector.
■ ~ entraîneur Sport team manager.

sélectivement /selɛktivmɑ̃/ *adv* selectively.

sélectivité /selɛktivite/ *nf* selectivity.

sélénite /selenit/ **I** *adj* lunar.
II *nmf* moondweller.

sélénium /selenjɔm/ *nm* selenium.

self○ /sɛlf/ *nm* (restaurant) self-service restaurant.

self-service, *pl* **~s** /sɛlfsɛʀvis/ *nm* (restaurant) self-service restaurant.

selle /sɛl/ **I** *nf* **1** (siège) Équit saddle; (de vélo, moto) saddle; **monter sans ~** to ride bareback; **(re)mettre en ~** fig firmly to (re)establish; **être bien en ~** fig to be firmly in the saddle; **2** (de sculpteur) turntable; **3†** (chaise percée) commode; **aller à la ~** euph to have a bowel movement.
II selles *nfpl* Méd stools (*pl*).
■ ~ d'agneau Culin saddle of lamb.

seller /sele/ [1] *vtr* to saddle.

sellerie /sɛlʀi/ *nf* **1** Comm (bourrellerie) saddlery; (articles) tack; (garnissage) upholstery; (maroquinerie) leatherwork; (articles de maroquinerie) hand-stitched leather goods (*pl*); **2** Équit (selles et harnais) tack; (local) tack room.

sellette /selɛt/ *nf* **1** (pour plante, statue) stand; (de sculpteur) small turntable; **2** (d'ouvrier) cradle.
IDIOMES **être sur la ~** to be in the hot seat; **mettre qn sur la ~** to put sb in the hot seat.

sellier /selje/ *nm* (bourrelier) saddler; (garnisseur) upholsterer; (maroquinier) maker of fancy leather goods.

selon /səlɔ̃/ **I** *prép* **1** (du point de vue de) according to [*personne, étude, sondage, gouvernement*]; **~ moi, il va pleuvoir** in my opinion, it's going to rain; ▶ **apparence, vraisemblance**; **2** (comme le dit) **~ les termes du président** in the President's words; **~ la formule** as people ou they say; **3** (conformément à) according to [*principe, règle, souhait*]; **~ la loi** under the law; **l'idée/la théorie ~ laquelle** the idea/ the theory that; **~ une pratique courante** in accordance with ou following a current practice; **4** (en proportion de) according to [*travail, taille*]; **contribuer ~ ses moyens** to contribute according to one's means; **dépenser ~ ses moyens** to spend within one's means; **5** (en fonction de) depending on [*heure, température, circonstance*]; **il décidera ~ son humeur** his decision will depend on his mood; **la situation varie ~ les régions** the situation varies from region to region; **c'est ~○** it all depends.
II selon que *loc conj* depending on whether; **le prix des fraises n'est pas le même ~ qu'on les achète en juin ou en décembre** the price of strawberries varies depending on whether you buy them in June or December.

Seltz /sɛlts/ *npr* **eau de ~** seltzer water.

semailles /səmaj/ *nfpl* (travail) sowing ¢; (époque) sowing season (*sg*); (graines semées) seeds; **faire les ~** to sow.

semaine /s(ə)mɛn/ ▶ 750, 801 *nf* **1** (de calendrier) week; **cette ~** this week; **la ~ prochaine** next week; **dans une ~** in a week's time; la **~ dernière** last week; **dans deux ~s** in two weeks' time, the week after next; **toutes les ~s** every week; **toutes les deux ~s** every two weeks, every fortnight GB; **toutes les quatre ~s** every four weeks; **un séjour de 6 ~s** a six-week stay; **louer/payer à la ~** to rent/pay by the week; **prendre trois ~s de vacances** to take three weeks' vacation; **2** (salaire hebdomadaire) week's wages; (argent de poche) (weekly) pocket money.
■ ~ anglaise† Entr five-day week; **~ commerciale** Comm trade week; **~ de travail** working week; **~ sainte** Relig Holy Week.
IDIOMES **vivre à la petite ~** to live from day to day.

semainier /səmɛnje/ *nm* **1** (agenda) week-to-a-page diary; **2** (meuble) chest of (seven) drawers; **3** (bracelet) seven-band bracelet.

sémanticien, -ienne /semɑ̃tisjɛ̃, ɛn/ ▶ 510 *nm,f* semanticist.

sémantique /semɑ̃tik/ **I** *adj* semantic.
II *nf* semantics (+ *v sg*).

sémaphore /semafɔʀ/ *nm* Naut, Télécom semaphore; Rail semaphore signal.

semblable /sɑ̃blabl/ **I** *adj* **1** (comparable) similar (**à** to); **des résultats à peu près/ tout à fait ~s** roughly/quite similar results; **ils sont ~s en tout** they are alike

Les jours de la semaine

Les noms des jours

L'anglais emploie la majuscule pour les noms de jours. Les abréviations sont courantes en anglais familier écrit, par ex. dans une lettre à un ami: I'll see you on Mon 17 Sept.

		abréviation anglaise
dimanche	Sunday	Sun
lundi	Monday	Mon
mardi	Tuesday	Tue *ou* Tues
mercredi	Wednesday	Wed
jeudi	Thursday	Thur *ou* Thurs
vendredi	Friday	Fri
samedi	Saturday	Sat

Noter que dans les pays anglophones on considère en général que la semaine commence le dimanche.

Dans les expressions suivantes, Monday *est pris comme exemple; les autres noms de jours s'utilisent de la même façon.*

quel jour sommes-nous? = what day is it?
nous sommes lundi = it's Monday
c'est aujourd'hui lundi = today is Monday

Pour l'expression de la date, **▶ 212**.

L'anglais emploie normalement on *devant les noms de jours, sauf lorsqu'il y a une autre préposition, ou un mot comme* this, that, next, last *etc.*

Lundi ou le lundi: un jour précis, passé ou futur

c'est arrivé lundi = it happened on Monday
lundi matin = on Monday morning
lundi après-midi = on Monday afternoon
lundi matin de bonne heure = early on Monday morning
lundi soir en fin de soirée = late on Monday evening
lundi, on va au zoo = on Monday, we're going to the zoo
lundi dernier = last Monday
lundi dernier dans la soirée = last Monday evening
lundi prochain = next Monday
lundi en huit = the Monday after next *ou* on Monday week
dans un mois lundi = a month from Monday
dans un mois à dater de lundi dernier = in a month from last Monday
à partir de lundi = from Monday onwards
c'est arrivé le lundi = it happened on the Monday
le lundi matin = on the Monday morning
le lundi après-midi = on the Monday afternoon
tard le lundi soir = late on the Monday evening
tôt le lundi matin = early on the Monday morning
elle est partie le lundi après-midi = she left on the Monday afternoon
ce lundi = this Monday
ce lundi-là = that Monday
précisément ce lundi-là = that very Monday

Le lundi: un même jour chaque semaine

quand est-ce que cela a lieu? = when does it happen?
cela a lieu le lundi = it happens on Mondays
le lundi, on va au zoo = on Mondays, we go to the zoo
elle ne travaille jamais le lundi = she never works on Mondays
le lundi après-midi, elle va à la piscine = she goes swimming on Monday afternoons
tous les lundis = every Monday
chaque lundi = each Monday
un lundi sur deux = every other Monday *ou* every second Monday
un lundi sur trois = every third Monday
presque tous les lundis = most Mondays
certains lundis = some Mondays
un lundi de temps en temps = on the occasional Monday
le deuxième lundi de chaque mois = on the second Monday in the month

Un lundi: un jour quelconque

c'est arrivé un lundi = it happened on a Monday *ou* it happened one Monday
un lundi matin = on a Monday morning *ou* one Monday morning
un lundi après-midi = on a Monday afternoon *ou* one Monday afternoon

Du avec les noms des jours de la semaine

Les expressions françaises avec du *se traduisent normalement par l'emploi du nom de jour en position d'adjectif.*

les cours du lundi = Monday classes
la fermeture du lundi = Monday closing
les programmes de télévision du lundi = Monday TV programmes
les trains du lundi = Monday trains
le vol du lundi = the Monday flight

Et comparer:

le journal du lundi = the Monday paper
le journal de lundi = Monday's paper

et de même the Monday classes *et* Monday's classes *etc.*

---

in all respects; **une réunion ~ à d'autres/à celles qu'on a connues** a meeting similar to others/to those we knew; **une journée ~ à tant d'autres** a day like any other; **elle est toujours ~ à elle-même** she's always the same; **je n'ai jamais rencontré quelqu'un de ~** I've never met anyone like him/her; **je n'ai jamais rien entendu/écrit de ~** I've never heard/written anything like it; **j'en ai vu de ~s** I've seen similar ones; **2** (identique) identical; **des maisons toutes ~s** identical looking houses; **3** (tel) (*before n*) such; **~ proposition** such a proposal; **~s propositions** such proposals; **une ~ théorie ne pouvait pas trouver de défenseurs** such a theory could not find anyone to defend it.

II *nmf* fellow creature; **il n'a pas son ~ pour faire rire les autres** there's nobody like him for making people laugh; **il n'a d'audience qu'auprès de ses ~s** he has no audience other than his own kind; **eux et leurs ~s** they and their kind.

semblant /sɑ̃blɑ̃/ *nm* **un ~ de légalité/d'honnêteté** a semblance of legality/of honesty; **faire ~ de croire à qch/d'être triste** to pretend to believe sth/to be sad; **faire ~ que** to pretend that; **il n'est pas triste, il fait ~** he isn't really sad, he's only pretending; **elle ne fait ~ de rien, mais elle t'a vu** she's seen you but she's not letting on○; **jouer à faire ~** to play 'let's pretend'.

sembler /sɑ̃ble/ [1] **I** *vi* to seem; **~ heureux/être heureux** to seem happy/to be happy; **elle semble croire que** she seems to believe that; **le voyage m'a semblé long** the journey seemed long to me; **le temps m'a semblé long** the time seemed to me to pass slowly; **la maison semble vide** the house seems empty; **tout semble possible** it seems anything is possible.

II *v impers* **il semble que** it seems that; **il semble bon de faire** it seems appropriate to do; **faites comme bon vous semble** do whatever you think best; **il semble que le problème soit réglé** it seems (that) the problem has been solved; **il semblerait que le problème soit réglé** it would seem that the problem has been solved; **le problème est réglé à ce qu'il me semble** the problem has been solved, or so it seems to me; **il me semble que c'est trop grand** it seems too big to me; **il me semble surprenant que** it strikes me as strange that; **il me semble important de faire** I think it is important to do; **elle a raison, me semble-t-il** or **il me semble** or **ce me semble** I think she's right; **il me semble l'avoir déjà rencontrée** I think I've met her before; **elle a, semble-t-il, refusé** apparently, she has refused; **si bon me semble** if I feel like it; **elle ne travaille que quand bon lui semble** she only works when she feels like it.

sème /sɛm/ *nm* seme.

semelle /s(ə)mɛl/ *nf* **1** Mode sole; **~ antidérapante** non-slip sole; **~ de crêpe** crepe sole; **2** Tech (de fer à repasser) soleplate; (de machine) bedplate; (de rail) flange; (de ski) midsection.

■ **~ compensée** wedge heel; **chaussures à ~s compensées** wedge shoes; **~ intérieure** insole.

IDIOMES **battre la ~** to stamp one's feet; **être (dur comme) de la ~** to be as tough as old boots○ GB ou leather US; **ne pas quitter** or **lâcher qn d'une ~** to stick to sb like a leech; **ne pas reculer d'une ~** not to budge an inch.

semence /s(ə)mɑ̃s/ *nf* **1** Agric, Hort seed; **de ~** seed (*épith*); **2** (ferment) seed; **3** (clou) tack; **4** (sperme)† semen, seed†.

■ **~ de perles** seed pearls.

semencier, **-ière** /səmɑ̃sje, ɛʀ/ **I** *adj* [*recherche, production*] seed.

II *nm* seed company.

semer /s(ə)me/ [1] *vtr* **1** Agric to sow [*graines*]; **~ à la volée** to sow, to broadcast; **champ semé de colza** field sown with rape; **2** (apporter) to sow [*discorde, trouble*]; to spread [*confusion, panique, désordre*]; [*arme, ouragan*] to bring [*mort*]; **~ le doute** to sow doubts; **3** (parsemer) **~ des clous sur la route** to strew the road with nails; **semé de** strewn with; **elle a semé ses jouets dans toute la maison** she has scattered her toys all over the house; **~ son argent** fig to throw one's money about; **mission semée de difficultés** mission bristling with difficulties; **copie semée de fautes** copy riddled with errors; **ciel semé d'étoiles** star-spangled sky; **on récolte ce qu'on a semé** as you sow so shall you reap; **4**○ (perdre) to drop; **j'ai dû ~ mes clés** I must have dropped my keys; **5** (distancer) to shake off [*poursuivant, gêneur*]; to leave [sb] behind [*concurrent*].

IDIOMES **qui sème le vent récolte la tempête** Prov he who sows the wind reaps the whirlwind.

semestre /s(ə)mɛstʀ/ **▶ 801** *nm* **1** (d'année civile) half-year; **au premier/second ~** in the first/second half of the year; **le premier ~ (de) 1993 a été difficile** the first half of 1993 was difficult; **tous les ~s, une fois par ~** twice a year; **2** (d'année universitaire) semester; **j'ai dû repasser les examens du premier/second ~** I had to re-take the first-/second-semester exams GB ou finals US; **3** (rente, pension) half-yearly payment.

semestriel, **-ielle** /səmɛstʀijɛl/ *adj* **1** [*revue, bulletin*] biannual; [*réunion, prévisions, perspectives*] twice-yearly (*épith*); [*résultats*] half-yearly (*épith*); **la présidence semestrielle de la CEE** the six-month presidency of the EC; **2** Univ [*examen*] end-of-semester (*épith*) GB, final US; [*cours*] one-semester (*épith*).

semeur, **-euse** /səmœʀ, øz/ **I** *nm,f* **1** Agric sower; **2** fig **~ de discorde** sower of discord; **~ de troubles** troublemaker.
II semeuse (also **Semeuse**) *nf*: *figure of a female sower on French stamps and coins.*

semi-annuel, **-elle**, *mpl* **~s** /səmianɥɛl/ *adj* semiannual.

semi-aride, *pl* **~s** /səmiaʀid/ *adj* semi-arid.

semi-automatique, *pl* **~s** /səmiɔtɔmatik/ *adj* semiautomatic.

semi-autonome, *pl* **~s** /səmiotɔnɔm/ *adj* semiautonomous.

semi-auxiliaire, *pl* **~s** /səmioksiljɛʀ/ *nm* Ling semiauxiliary.

semi-boycott, *pl* **~s** /səmibɔjkɔt/ *nm* partial boycott.

semi-circulaire, *pl* **~s** /səmisiʀkylɛʀ/ *adj* semicircular.

semi-clochard, **~e**, *mpl* **~s** /səmiklɔʃaʀ, aʀd/ *nm,f* virtual beggar.

semi-conducteur, **-trice**, *mpl* **~s** /səmikɔ̃dyktœʀ, tʀis/ **I** *adj* semiconducting.
II *nm* semiconductor.

semi-conserve, *pl* **~s** /səmikɔ̃sɛʀv/ *nf* Culin, Ind partially preserved product.

semi-consonne, *pl* **~s** /səmikɔ̃sɔn/ *nf* semiconsonant.

semi-démocratique, *pl* **~s** /səmidemɔkʀatik/ *adj* relatively democratic.

semi-désertique, *pl* **~s** /səmidezɛʀtik/ *adj* semidesert.

semi-échec, *pl* **~s** /səmieʃɛk/ *nm* partial failure.

semi-enterré, **~e**, *mpl* **~s** /səmiɑ̃teʀe/ *adj* half-buried.

semi-fini, **~e**, *mpl* **~s** /səmifini/ *adj* semifinished.

semi-industriel, **-elle**, *mpl* **~s** /səmiɛ̃dystʀijɛl/ *adj* partly industrialized.

semi-liberté, *pl* **~s** /səmilibɛʀte/ *nf* relative freedom.

semi-libre, *pl* **~s** /səmilibʀ/ *adj* relatively free.

sémillant, **~e** /semijɑ̃, ɑ̃t/ *adj* spirited; [*esprit*] sparkling.

semi-marathon, *pl* **~s** /səmimaʀatɔ̃/ *nm* half marathon.

semi-mort, **~e**, *mpl* **~s** /səmimɔʀ, ɔʀt/ *adj* half-dead.

séminaire /seminɛʀ/ *nm* **1** (réunion) seminar (**sur** on); **2** (institution) seminary; **il est entré au ~** he entered the seminary; **grand ~** seminary; **petit ~** junior seminary.

séminal, **~e**, *mpl* **-aux** /seminal, o/ *adj* seminal.

séminariste /seminaʀist/ *nm* seminarist, seminarian.

semi-officiel, **-ielle**, *mpl* **~s** /səmiɔfisjɛl/ *adj* semiofficial.

sémiologie /semjɔlɔʒi/ *nf* semiology.

sémiologique /semjɔlɔʒik/ *adj* semiological.

sémiologue /semjɔlɔg/ *nm* semiologist.

sémioticien, **-ienne** /semjɔtisjɛ̃, ɛn/ **▶510** *nm,f* semiotician.

sémiotique /semjɔtik/ **I** *adj* semiotic.
II *nf* semiotics (+ *v sg*).

semi-perméable, *pl* **~s** /səmipɛʀmeabl/ *adj* semipermeable.

semi-précieux, **-ieuse** /səmipʀesjø, øz/ *adj* [*pierre*] semiprecious.

semi-professionnel, **-elle**, *mpl* **~s** /səmipʀɔfɛsjɔnɛl/ *adj, nm,f* semiprofessional.

semi-public, **-ique**, *mpl* **~s** /səmipyblik/ *adj* Jur [*organisme, secteur*] semipublic.

semi-remorque, *pl* **~s** /səmiʀəmɔʀk/ **I** *nm* (camion) articulated lorry GB, tractor-trailer US.
II *nf* (remorque) semitrailer.

semi-retraité, **~e**, *mpl* **~s** /səmiʀətʀɛte/ *nm,f* person in part retirement; **les ~s** people in part retirement.

semi-rural, **~e**, *mpl* **-aux** /səmiʀyʀal, o/ *adj* largely rural.

semis /s(ə)mi/ *nm inv* **1** Agric (ensemencement) sowing; (jeune plant) seedling; (terrain) seedbed; **les ~ de printemps** spring sowings; **2** (ornement) small repeating pattern.

sémite /semit/ *adj* Semitic.

sémitique /semitik/ *adj* Ling Semitic.

semi-voyelle, *pl* **~s** /səmivwajɛl/ *nf* semivowel.

semoir /səmwaʀ/ *nm* **1** (machine) seed drill; **2†** (sac) seedbag.

semonce /səmɔ̃s/ *nf* reprimand; **coup de ~** lit, fig warning shot, shot across the bows.

semoule /səmul/ *nf* semolina; **sucre ~** caster sugar.

sempiternel, **-elle** /sɑ̃pitɛʀnɛl/ *adj* perpetual, endless.

sempiternellement /sɑ̃pitɛʀnɛlmɑ̃/ *adv* perpetually, endlessly.

sénat /sena/ *nm* senate.

sénateur /senatœʀ/ **▶813** *nm* senator; **train de ~** hum stately pace.

sénatorial, **~e**, *mpl* **-iaux** /senatɔʀjal, o/ **I** *adj* senatorial.
II sénatoriales *nfpl* **les ~es** the senatorial elections.

séné /sene/ *nm* senna.

sénéchal, *pl* **-aux** /seneʃal, o/ *nm* Hist, Jur seneschal.

séneçon /sɛnsɔ̃/ *nm* groundsel.

Sénégal /senegal/ **▶321** *nprm* Senegal.

sénégalais, **~e** /senegalɛ, ɛz/ **▶537** *adj* Senegalese.

Sénégalais, **~e** /senegalɛ, ɛz/ **▶537** *nm,f* Senegalese.

Sénèque /senɛk/ *npr* Seneca.

sénescence /senesɑ̃s/ *nf* senescence.

senestre /sənɛstʀ/ *adj* **1†** (gauche) left-hand; **2** Hérald sinister.

sénevé /senve/ *nm* wild mustard.

sénile /senil/ *adj* senile.

sénilité /senilite/ *nf* senility; **~ précoce** premature senility.

senior /senjɔʀ/ *adj, nmf* senior.

senne /sɛn/ *nf* Pêche seine.

sens /sɑ̃s/ **I** *nm inv* **1** (direction) lit, fig direction, way; **dans les deux ~** in both directions; **aller dans le bon/mauvais ~** to go the right/wrong way, to go in the right/wrong direction; **elle venait en ~ inverse** she was coming from the opposite direction; **mouvement en ~ contraire** backward movement; **en tous ~** in all directions; **dans le ~ Paris-Lyon** in the Paris to Lyons direction; **dans le ~ de la largeur** widthways, across; **dans le ~ de la longueur** lengthways, longways US; **être dans le bon/mauvais ~** to be the right/wrong way up; **des flèches dans tous les ~** arrows pointing in all directions; **retourner un problème dans tous les ~** to consider a problem from every angle; **courir dans tous les ~** to run all over the place; **dans le ~ de la marche** facing the engine; **dans le ~ des fils** Tex with the grain; **~ dessus dessous** /sɑ̃d(ə)sydəsu/ (à l'envers) upside down; (en désordre) upside down; (très troublé) very upset; **~ devant derrière** /sɑ̃dəvɑ̃dɛʀjɛʀ/ back to front; **aller dans le bon ~** [*réformes, mesures*] to be a step in the right direction; **des mesures qui vont dans le ~ de notre rapport** measures which are in line with our report; **le pays va dans le ~ d'une plus grande indépendance** the country is moving toward(s) greater independence; **le ~ de l'histoire** the tide of history; **nous travaillons dans ce ~** that's what we are working toward(s); **ces facteurs ont œuvré dans le ~ d'une baisse** these factors have contributed to a fall; **2** (d'une action) meaning; (de mythe, symbole) meaning; (de mot, d'expression) meaning; **le ~ figuré/littéral/péjoratif d'un mot** the figurative/literal/pejorative sense of a word; **employer un mot au ~ propre/figuré** to use a word literally/figuratively; **avoir un ~ péjoratif** to be pejorative, to have a pejorative sense; **le ~ premier de qch** the original meaning of sth; **au ~ large/strict du terme** in the broad/strict sense of the word; **au ~ propre du terme** literally; **au ~ fort du terme** in the fullest sense of the word; **c'est correct, dans tous les ~ du terme** it's correct, in every sense of the word; **prendre tout son ~** [*remarque, titre*] to take on its full meaning; **en un ~** in a sense; **en ce ~ que** in the sense that; **cela n'a pas de ~** gén it doesn't make sense; (idiot, ridicule) it's absurd; **cela n'a de ~ que si tu restes** it makes no sense unless you stay; **3** Physiol sense; **avoir un ~ de l'odorat très développé** to have a very keen sense of smell; **recouvrer** fml or **retrouver l'usage de ses ~** to regain consciousness; **avoir un sixième ~** fig to have a sixth sense; **4** (intuition) sense; **~ du rythme/devoir** sense of rhythm/duty; **avoir le ~ des responsabilités** to have a sense of responsibility; **avoir le ~ de l'orientation** to have a good sense of direction; **avoir le ~ pratique** to be practical; **ne pas avoir de ~ pratique** to be impractical; **avoir peu de ~ critique** to be uncritical; **avoir le ~ de l'organisation** to be a good organizer; **ne pas avoir le ~ du ridicule** not to realize when one looks silly; **avoir le ~ des affaires** to have a flair ou head for business; **ton ~ des affaires** your business sense; **ne pas avoir le ~ de la langue** to have no feeling for language; **n'avoir aucun ~ des réalités** to live in a dream world.
II *nmpl* senses; **plaisirs des ~** sensual pleasures.
■ **~ commun** common sense; **~ giratoire** roundabout GB, traffic circle US; **suivez le ~ giratoire** go round the roundabout GB, follow the traffic circle around US; **~ de l'humour** sense of humour[GB]; **avoir le ~ de l'humour** to have a sense of humour[GB]; **~ interdit** (panneau) no-entry sign; (rue) one-way street; **~ obligatoire** (panneau) one-way sign; **~ unique** (panneau) one-way sign; (rue) one-way street; **c'est à ~ unique** lit it's one-way; fig it's one-sided.
IDIOMES **tomber sous le ~** to be patently obvious.

sensation /sɑ̃sasjɔ̃/ *nf* **1** (impression physique) feeling, sensation; **~ de brûlure** burning feeling ou sensation; **~ de chaleur** hot feeling; **~ de détente** feeling of relaxation; **~ de bien-être** sense of well-being; **~ désagréable** unpleasant sensation; **cela ne procure pas les mêmes ~s** it doesn't have the same effect; **on a la ~ de flotter** you feel as if you're floating; **aimer/rechercher les ~s fortes** to like one's/to look for thrills; **2** (sentiment) feeling, sensation; **~ étrange** strange sensation, funny feeling; **~ de liberté/puissance** feeling ou sense of freedom/power; **~ d'euphorie** sense of euphoria; **3** (réaction) sensation; **la décision a fait ~** (a étonné) the decision caused a sensation; **le film a fait ~** (a plu) the film was a sensation; **tu vas faire ~ avec cette robe** you'll be a sensation in that dress; **un journal à ~** a tabloid; **la presse à ~** the tabloid press; **reportages à ~** keyhole journalism ¢.

sensationnel, **-elle** /sɑ̃sasjɔnɛl/ *adj* **1**○ (formidable) [*personne, vacances, succès*] fantastic○; **2** (créant surprise, intérêt) [*déclaration, nouvelle*] sensational, astonishing; **3** (à sensation) [*reportage*] sensational.

sensé, **~e** /sɑ̃se/ *adj* sensible.

sensément /sɑ̃semɑ̃/ *adv* sensibly.

sensibilisateur, **-trice** /sɑ̃sibilizatœʀ, tʀis/ *adj* sensitizing.

sensibilisation /sɑ̃sibilizasjɔ̃/ *nf* **1** (fait de rendre conscient) consciousness raising; **campagne de ~** awareness campaign;

une ~ des médecins au problème making doctors aware of the problem; **2** Méd, Phot sensitizing, sensitization.

sensibiliser /sɑ̃sibilize/ [1] *vtr* **1** (rendre conscient) **~ le public à un problème** to increase public awareness of an issue; **~ les jeunes/les entreprises à** to make young people/companies more aware of; **2** Chimie, Méd, Phot to sensitize.

sensibilité /sɑ̃sibilite/ **I** *nf* **1** (qualité) sensibility; **elle est d'une grande ~** she is very sensitive; **leur ~ artistique** their artistic sensibility; **2** Méd, Physiol, Phot sensitivity.
II sensibilités *nfpl* sensibilities; **les ~s politiques** political sensibilities.

sensible /sɑ̃sibl/ **I** *adj* **1** (non indifférent) [*personne, nature*] sensitive; **être ~ aux compliments** to like compliments; **être ~ aux charmes de qn** to be susceptible to sb's charms; **j'ai été très ~ à votre gentille attention** I was most touched by your kindness; **je suis ~ au fait que** I am aware that; **avoir le cœur ~** to be sensitive; **ce film est déconseillé aux personnes ~s** this film is not for the squeamish; **être ~ à un argument** to be swayed by an argument; **les natures ~s** pej the fainthearted; **2** (qui perçoit) [*organe, membrane, appareil, instrument*] sensitive; **avoir l'oreille ~** to have keen hearing; **un être ~** a sentient being; **être ~ au froid/à la lumière** [*membrane, appareil*] to be sensitive to cold/to light; **je suis très ~ au froid** I really feel the cold; **balance ~ au milligramme** scale which is accurate to a milligram; **marché ~ aux fluctuations économiques** (délicat) market sensitive to fluctuations in the economy; **3** (fragile) [*peau*] sensitive; (un peu douloureux) [*peau cicatrisée*] tender; [*membre blessé*] sore; **je suis ~ de la gorge**, **j'ai la gorge ~** I often get a sore throat; **j'ai les pieds ~s** I have tender feet; **4** (notable) [*recul, hausse, différence*] appreciable; [*effort*] real; **de manière ~** appreciably; **la différence est à peine ~** the difference is hardly noticeable; **5** Phot sensitive; **~ à la lumière** photosensitive; **6** (délicat) [*dossier, question, thème*] sensitive; **7** (perceptible) **le monde ~** the physical ou tangible world.
II *nmf* sensitive person; **c'est un grand ~** he's very sensitive.
III *nf* Mus leading note.

sensiblement /sɑ̃sibləmɑ̃/ *adv* **1** (considérablement) [*réduire, différer, modifier, augmenter*] appreciably, noticeably; [*différent*] perceptibly; **~ plus rapide** considerably faster; **2** (plus ou moins) [*pareil*] roughly; **~ le même nombre d'élèves** roughly the same number of pupils.

sensiblerie /sɑ̃sibləʀi/ *nf* pej sentimentality péj.

sensitif, **-ive** /sɑ̃sitif, iv/ **I** *adj* sensory.
II sensitive *nf* (mimosa) sensitive plant.

sensoriel, **-ielle** /sɑ̃sɔʀjɛl/ *adj* sensory; **organe ~** sense organ.

sensori-moteur, **-trice**, *mpl* **~s** /sɑ̃sɔʀimɔtœʀ, tʀis/ *adj* sensorimotor.

sensualisme /sɑ̃sɥalism/ *nm* sensualism.

sensualité /sɑ̃sɥalite/ *nf* sensuality.

sensuel, **-elle** /sɑ̃sɥɛl/ *adj* sensual.

sensuellement /sɑ̃sɥɛlmɑ̃/ *adv* sensually.

sente /sɑ̃t/ *nf* liter footpath.

sentence /sɑ̃tɑ̃s/ *nf* **1** (décision) sentence; **2** (propos) maxim.

sentencieusement /sɑ̃tɑ̃sjøzmɑ̃/ *adv* sententiously.

sentencieux, **-ieuse** /sɑ̃tɑ̃sjø, øz/ *adj* [*personne, discours*] sententious.

senteur /sɑ̃tœʀ/ *nf* liter scent.

senti, **~e** /sɑ̃ti/ *adj* **bien ~** [*paroles, remarques*] well-chosen; [*réplique, réponse*] blunt; [*discours, tirade*] forthright.

sentier /sɑ̃tje/ *nm* lit, fig path, track; **être sur le ~ de la guerre** fig to be on the warpath; **hors des ~s battus** off the beaten track.
■ ~ de grande randonnée long-distance footpath; **~ de petite randonnée** footpath.

sentiment /sɑ̃timɑ̃/ *nm* **1** (sensation) feeling; **éprouver un ~ d'injustice/de lassitude** to have a feeling of injustice/of tiredness; **2** (sensibilité) feeling; **il est incapable de ~** he's incapable of feeling ou emotion; **avec beaucoup de ~** [*chanter, jouer*] with great feeling; **agir par ~ plus que par raison** to be guided by one's feelings rather than by reason; **faire du ~** to sentimentalize; **tu ne m'auras pas au ~**○**!** you won't get round GB ou around US me like that!; **n'essaie pas de me le faire au ~**○ don't try to get round GB ou around US me; **il ne fait pas de ~ en affaires** he doesn't let sentiment get in the way of business; **pas de ~, soyons réalistes!** let's put feelings aside and be realistic!; **3** (connaissance intuitive) **le ~ de la nature/beauté** a feeling for nature/beauty; **le ~ religieux** religious feeling; **avoir le ~ de sa force/faiblesse** to have a sense of one's own strength/weakness; **j'ai le ~ de comprendre** I feel that I understand; **j'ai le ~ d'être suivi/qu'on m'observe** I've got the feeling (that) I'm being followed/that I'm being watched; **j'ai le ~ qu'il va pleuvoir** I've got a feeling it's going to rain; **donner le ~ de faire/qu'on fait** to give the impression of doing/that one does; **4** (inclination) feeling, sentiment sout; **cacher ses ~s** to hide one's feelings; **~s généreux** generous feelings; **~s nobles** noble sentiments; **les beaux** or **bons ~s** fine sentiments; **être animé de bons/mauvais ~s** to have good/bad intentions; **prendre qn par les ~s** to appeal to sb's better nature; **5** (opinion) feeling; **le ~ général est que** the general feeling is that; **~ sur** feeling about ou on; **donner son ~ sur qch** to state one's feelings about sth; **6** (dans les formules épistolaires) **~s affectueux** or **amicaux** best wishes; **veuillez croire à mes ~s dévoués** or **les meilleurs** (à une personne non nommée) yours faithfully; (à une personne nommée) yours sincerely.

sentimental, **~e**, *mpl* **-aux** /sɑ̃timɑ̃tal, o/ **I** *adj* **1** (relatif à l'amour) [*vie, intrigue*] love (*épith*); [*relations*] romantic; **dans le domaine ~, sur le plan ~** (dans un horoscope) on the romance front; **2** (affectif) [*attachement, raisons*] sentimental; **'pourquoi les gardes-tu?'—'c'est ~'** 'why do you keep them?'—'for sentimental reasons'; **3** (sensible) [*personne, public*] sentimental, romantic; **4** (d'une sensiblerie mièvre) [*attitude, chanson*] sentimental; **faire un portrait ~ de qn** to draw a sentimental picture of sb.
II *nm,f* sentimental person; **c'est un ~** he's very sentimental.

sentimentalement /sɑ̃timɑ̃talmɑ̃/ *adv* sentimentally.

sentimentalisme /sɑ̃timɑ̃talism/ *nm* sentimentalism.

sentimentalité /sɑ̃timɑ̃talite/ *nf* sentimentality.

sentinelle /sɑ̃tinɛl/ *nf* sentry; **être en ~** to be on sentry duty; **faire la ~** to stand guard, to keep watch.

sentir /sɑ̃tiʀ/ [30] **I** *vtr* **1** (percevoir par l'odorat) to smell [*parfum, fleur*]; **on sentait les foins** or **l'odeur des foins** we could smell the hay; **tu ne sens pas une odeur?** can't you smell something?; **je ne sens rien** I can't smell anything; **fais-moi ~ ce fromage** let me smell that cheese; **on sent que tu fumes le cigare** one can tell that you smoke cigars by the smell; **2** (percevoir par le toucher, le corps, le goût) to feel; **~ le froid/un caillou** to feel the cold/a stone; **je ne sens rien** I can't feel anything; **je ne sens plus mes orteils tellement j'ai froid** I'm so cold I can't feel my toes any more; **j'ai marché trop longtemps, je ne sens plus mes pieds** I've been walking for too long, my feet are numb; **elle m'a fait ~ sa bosse** she made me feel her lump; **on sent qu'il y a du vin dans la sauce** one can smell ou taste the wine in the sauce; **~ d'où vient le vent** lit, Naut to see how the wind blows ou lies; fig to see which way the wind is blowing; **le froid commence à se faire ~** the cold weather is setting in; **les effets du médicament se feront bientôt ~** the effects of the medicine will soon be felt; **3** (avoir conscience de) to be conscious of [*importance*]; (percevoir) to feel [*beauté, force*]; (apprécier) to appreciate [*difficulté*]; (percevoir intuitivement) to sense [*danger, désapprobation*]; **~ les beautés d'un texte/la force d'une expression** to feel the beauty of a text/the force of an expression; **as-tu bien senti le message de ce film?** did you fully appreciate the message of the film?; **~ que** (percevoir) to feel that; (avoir l'idée) to have a feeling that; **je sens qu'il est sincère** I feel that he's sincere; **je sens que ce livre te plaira** I have a feeling that you'll like this book; **on sent que l'hiver approche** it feels wintry; **il ne sent pas sa force** he doesn't know his own strength; **il ne sent pas (les subtilités de) l'art moderne** he has no feeling for (the subtleties of) modern art; **je te sens inquiet**, **je sens que tu es inquiet** I can tell you're worried; **faire ~ son autorité** to make one's authority felt; **les mesures commencent à faire ~ leurs effets** the effects of the measures are beginning to make themselves felt ou to be felt; **je leur ai fait ~ mon désaccord** I made it clear to them that I didn't agree; **faire ~ le rythme d'un poème** to bring out the rhythm of a poem; **se faire ~** [*besoin, présence, absence*] to be felt.
II *vi* **1** (avoir une odeur) to smell; **~ bon/mauvais/fort** to smell nice/bad/strong; **tu sens le vin!** you smell of wine!; **ça sent le chou/la charogne/la cigarette** it smells of cabbage/carrion/cigarettes; **herbes qui sentent bon la Provence** herbs smelling ou redolent sout of Provence; **ça sent bon le café** there's a nice smell of coffee; **ça sent drôle ici** there's a funny smell in here; **fleurs qui ne sentent pas** flowers which don't have a scent; **2** (puer) to smell; **le poisson commence à ~** the fish is beginning to smell; **qu'est-ce qui sent (comme ça)?** what's that smell?; **~ des pieds/aisselles** to have smelly feet/armpits; **~ de la bouche** to have bad breath; **3** (révéler) to smack of; **ta douleur/ton attitude sent la comédie** or **le théâtre** your grief/your attitude smacks of insincerity; **une fille qui sent la** or **sa province** a girl with a touch of the provinces about her; **ciel nuageux qui sent l'orage** cloudy sky that heralds a storm.
III se sentir *vpr* **1** (avoir la sensation de) to feel; **se ~ mieux/las/chez soi** to feel better/tired/at home; **se ~ surveillé** to feel that one is being watched; **elle ne s'est pas sentie visée par ma remarque** she didn't feel that my remark was aimed at her; **elle s'est sentie rougir** she felt herself blushing; **elle s'est senti piquer par un moustique** she felt a mosquito bite; **non mais tu te sens bien (dans ta tête)**○**?** are you feeling all right (in the head)○?; **ne plus se ~**○ (de joie) to be overjoyed; (de vanité) to get above oneself; **ne plus se ~ de joie**○ to be beside oneself with joy; **2** (se reconnaître) to feel; **se ~ assez fort pour faire, se ~ la force de faire** to feel strong enough to do; **se ~ libre de faire** to feel free to do; **se ~ victime d'une machination** to feel that one is the victim of a scheme; **se ~ une obligation envers qn** to feel an obligation towards sb; **3** (être perceptible) [*phénomène, amélioration, effet*] to be felt; **les sanctions commencent à se ~** the sanctions are beginning to bite, the effects of the sanctions are beginning to be felt.
IDIOMES **je ne peux pas le ~** I can't stand him; **je l'ai senti passer!** (piqûre, addition) it really hurt!; (réprimande) I really got it in the neck!; **elle va la ~ passer!** (piqûre, addition)

it's going to hurt!; (réprimande) she's going to get it in the neck!

seoir† /swaʀ/ [41] **I seoir à** *vtr ind* [*vêtement, coiffure*] to suit; **cette robe vous sied à ravir** that dress suits you beautifully.

II *v impers* **il sied** it is appropriate (**de faire** to do); **comme il sied** as is right and proper; **il vous sied bien de critiquer** iron it ill becomes you to criticize.

Séoul /seul/ ▶857 *npr* Seoul.

sep /sɛp/ *nm* (de charrue) frog.

SEP /sɛp/ *nf*: *abbr* ▶ **sclérose**.

sépale /sepal/ *nm* sepal.

séparable /sepaʀabl/ *adj* separable (**de** from); **être difficilement ~ de** to be difficult to separate from.

séparateur, -trice /sepaʀatœʀ, tʀis/ **I** *adj* [*mur*] dividing.

II *nm* Tech, Ordinat separator.

séparation /sepaʀasjɔ̃/ *nf* **1** (de groupes, genres, secteurs, d'objets) (fait d'être séparés) separation (**entre** between); (action de séparer) separating, separation; **la ~ des pouvoirs** Pol the separation of powers; **la ~ de l'Église et de l'État** the separation of Church and State; **ils envisagent la ~ de leurs activités commerciales et de recherche** they are thinking of separating their commercial and research activities; **après la ~ des composants du mélange** after separating out the constituents of the mixture; **la ~ du pays en deux États** the division ou splitting of the country into two states; **2** (de personnes) (fait d'être séparés) separation; (action de se quitter) parting; (rupture) aussi Jur separating, separation; **après deux ans de ~** after two years' separation; **depuis sa ~ d'avec sa femme** since he separated from his wife, since his separation from his wife; **3** (limite) (entre jardins) boundary; (entre pièces) partition; fig boundary, dividing line; **mur de ~** (extérieur) boundary wall; (intérieur) dividing wall; **établir une ~ (nette) entre sa vie privée et professionnelle** to keep one's private life (completely) separate from one's work.

■ **~ de biens** Jur matrimonial division of property; **~ de corps** Jur judicial separation; **~ de fait** Jur de facto separation.

séparatisme /sepaʀatism/ *nm* separatism.

séparatiste /sepaʀatist/ *adj, nmf* separatist.

séparé, ~e /sepaʀe/ **I** *pp* ▶ **séparer**.

II *pp adj* **1** (sans contact) [*personne*] **être ~** to be separated (**de** from); **vivre ~** to live apart (**de** from); **2** (de part et d'autre d'une limite) **~ (de qch) par** separated (from sth) by; **jardins séparés par une haie** gardens GB ou yards US separated by a hedge; **3** (éloigné) **nous ne sommes ~s du village que de quelques kilomètres** we're only a few kilometres[GB] away from the village; **les deux villages sont ~s de quelques kilomètres** the two villages are a few kilometres[GB] apart; **des événements ~s par plusieurs années** events (which are) several years apart.

III *adj* (distinct) [*affaires, mondes, accords, groupes*] separate; **pièce ~e qui sert de débarras** separate room which is used as a junk room; **faire l'objet d'une étude ~e** to form the object of a separate study.

séparément /sepaʀemɑ̃/ *adv* separately.

séparer /sepaʀe/ [1] **I** *vtr* **1** (ne pas laisser ensemble) to separate [*objets, concepts, rôles, amis, adversaires*]; to separate out [*composants*]; **~ les passagers et les bagages** to separate passengers and luggage; **~ qch/qn de** to separate sth/sb from; **~ le minerai de la gangue** to separate the ore from the valueless material; **~ les blancs des jaunes** Culin separate the whites from the yolks; **nous sommes obligés de les ~, sinon ils se battent** we have to separate them ou keep them apart, otherwise they fight; **on ne peut ~ le fond de la forme** form and content cannot be separated, you can't separate form and content; **~ l'aspect politique d'un problème de son aspect économique** to keep the political aspect of a problem separate from its economic aspect; **la mort les a séparés** they were parted by death; **la vie nous a séparés** we have gone our separate ways in life; **c'est un malentendu qui les a séparés** a misunderstanding came between them, a misunderstanding drove them apart; ▶ **ivraie**; **2** (distinguer) [*personne*] to distinguish between [*concepts, domaines, problèmes*]; **~ un problème d'un autre** to distinguish between one problem and another; **les deux affaires sont à ~** we must distinguish between the two matters ou cases; **on ne peut ~ ces deux problèmes** one cannot dissociate these two problems; **3** (former une limite entre) [*obstacle, cloison, espace*] to separate; **une haie sépare les deux jardins/mon jardin du leur** a hedge separates the two properties/my garden GB ou yard US from theirs; **une barrière séparait les spectateurs des** or **et les animaux** a fence separated the spectators from ou and the animals; **cinq secondes seulement séparaient les deux athlètes** only five seconds separated the two athletes; **quelques kilomètres nous séparent de la mer** we are a few kilometres[GB] away from the sea; **deux ans séparent les deux événements** there is a gap of two years between the two events; **encore deux mois nous séparent du départ** we still have two months to go before we leave; **le temps qui sépare le passage de deux véhicules** the time lapse between the passage of two vehicles; **c'est tout ce qui nous sépare de la victoire** it's the only thing standing between us and victory; **4** (constituer une inégalité entre) [*opinions, caractères*] to divide [*personnes*]; **la différence de milieu social qui les sépare** the difference in social background that divides them; **l'âge les séparait** age was a barrier between them; **les qualités qui séparent un bon musicien d'un virtuose** the qualities that make the difference between a good musician and a virtuoso; **tout les sépare** they are worlds apart; **5** (diviser) to divide [*surface*]; **~ une pièce en deux** to divide a room in two; **~ ses cheveux par une raie au milieu** to part one's hair in the middle.

II se séparer *vpr* **1** (se quitter) [*promeneurs, invités*] to part, to leave each other; [*conjoints, amants*] to split up, to separate aussi Jur; **nous nous sommes séparés au carrefour** we left each other ou parted at the crossroads; **les membres du groupe ont dû se ~** the members of the group had to split up; **2** (quitter) **se ~ de** to leave [*camarade, groupe, famille*]; to split up with, to separate from aussi Jur [*mari, femme*]; **ne te sépare pas de moi, on ne se retrouverait pas** don't leave my side, we would never find each other again; **3** (se disperser) [*manifestants, cortège, groupe*] to disperse, to split (up) (**en** into); [*assemblée*] to break up; **se ~ en petits groupes** to split (up) into small groups; **mes amis, il est temps de nous ~** my friends, it's time we broke up; **4** (se passer de) **se ~ de** to let [sb] go [*employé, collaborateur*]; to part with [*objet personnel*]; **il ne se sépare jamais de son parapluie** he takes his umbrella everywhere with him; **ne vous séparez pas de vos bagages** keep your luggage with you at all times; **5** (se diviser) [*chemin, rivière, branche, tige*] to divide (**en** into); **le fleuve se sépare en trois bras** the river divides into three; **la route se sépare (en deux)** the road forks.

sépia /sepja/ **I** ▶193 *adj inv* (couleur) sepia.

II *nf* **1** Art (pigment) sepia; (dessin) sepia drawing; **2** Zool (seiche) sepia; (sécrétion) (cuttlefish) ink.

sept /sɛt/ ▶545, 407, 212 *adj inv, pron, nm inv* seven.

■ **les ~ Familles** Jeux Happy Families.

IDIOMES **tourne ~ fois ta langue dans ta bouche avant de parler** think long and hard before you speak.

septain /sɛptɛ̃/ *nm* heptastich.

septante /sɛptɑ̃t/ ▶545, 212 *adj inv, pron* B, H seventy.

septantième /sɛptɑ̃tjɛm/ ▶545 *adj* B, H seventieth.

septembre /sɛptɑ̃bʀ/ ▶521 *nm* September.

septennal, ~e, *mpl* **-aux** /sɛptenal, o/ *adj* seven-year (*épith*).

septennat /sɛptena/ *nm* seven-year term (of office).

septentrion† /sɛptɑ̃tʀijɔ̃/ *nm* North.

septentrional, ~e, *mpl* **-aux** /sɛptɑ̃tʀijɔnal, o/ *adj* northern.

septicémie /sɛptisemi/ ▶271 *nf* blood-poisoning, septicemia spéc.

septicémique /sɛptisemik/ *adj* septicemic.

septicité /sɛptisite/ *nf* septicity.

septième /sɛtjɛm/ ▶545, 212 **I** *adj* seventh.

II *nf* Scol *fifth year of primary school, age 10–11.*

■ **le ~ art** the cinematographic art.

IDIOMES **être au ~ ciel** to be on cloud nine.

septique /sɛptik/ *adj* septic.

septuagénaire /sɛptɥaʒenɛʀ/ **I** *adj* **être ~** to be in one's seventies.

II *nmf* person in his/her seventies, septuagenarian.

septuagésime /sɛptɥaʒezim/ *nf* Septuagesima.

septum /sɛptɔm/ *nm* septum.

septuor /sɛptɥɔʀ/ *nm* (œuvre, formation) septet.

septuple /sɛptypl/ **I** *adj* **une somme ~ d'une autre** an amount seven times more than another.

II *nm* **leur mise leur a rapporté le ~** they got back seven times more than they had bet.

septuplé, ~e /sɛptyple/ *nm,f* septuplet.

septupler /sɛptyple/ [1] **I** *vtr* to increase [sth] sevenfold.

II *vi* to increase sevenfold.

sépulcral, ~e, *mpl* **-aux** /sepylkʀal, o/ *adj* **1** (funèbre) sepulchral; **clarté ~e** subterranean gloom; **silence ~** deathly silence; **visage ~** deathly pale face; **2**† (funéraire) [*pierre, caveau*] funerary.

sépulcre /sepylkʀ/ *nm* sepulchre[GB].

sépulture /sepyltyʀ/ *nf* **1** (tombe) grave; **2** (enterrement) burial.

séquelle /sekɛl/ *nf* **1** Méd (d'accident, opération) aftereffect; **2** (retombées) repercussion; (conséquence) consequence.

séquence /sekɑ̃s/ *nf* **1** gén sequence; **2** Chimie (de polymère) block.

séquenceur /sekɑ̃sœʀ/ *nm* sequencer.

■ **~ de vol** Aviat flight sequencer.

séquentiel, -ielle /sekɑ̃sjɛl/ *adj* sequential.

séquestration /sekɛstʀasjɔ̃/ *nf* **1** (détention) gén confinement; Jur **~ (arbitraire)** illegal detention; **2** Jur (saisie) sequestration; **~ de biens** sequestration of goods; **3** Chimie sequestration.

■ **~ pulmonaire** Méd pulmonary sequestration.

séquestre /sekɛstʀ/ *nm* **1** Jur sequestration; **mettre sous ~** to sequestrate [*biens*]; **biens (mis) sous ~** sequestrated property; **lever le ~** to lift the sequestration order; **2** Méd sequestrum.

séquestrer /sekɛstʀe/ [1] *vtr* **1** (détenir) gén to hold [*otage*]; Jur to confine [sb] illegally [*personne*]; **un mari qui séquestre sa femme** a husband who keeps his wife locked away; **~ son patron dans son bureau** to lock the boss in his office (*in industrial dispute*); **2** Jur (saisir) to sequestrate [*biens*].

sequin /səkɛ̃/ *nm* **1** (paillette) sequin; **à ~s** sequined; **2** (monnaie) sequin.

séquoia /sekɔja/ *nm* sequoia.

■ **~ géant** giant sequoia, big tree.

sérac /seʀak/ *nm* serac.

sérail /seʀaj/ *nm* **1** Hist seraglio; **2** (entourage) innermost circle.

IDIOMES **être nourri** or **élevé dans le ~** to be born to it.

séraphin /seʀafɛ̃/ *nm* **1** (ange) seraph; **les ~s** the seraphim; **2**○ C (avare) miser.

séraphique /seʀafik/ *adj* seraphic.

serbe /sɛʀb/ I ▶**692** *adj* Serbian.

II ▶**462** *nm* Ling Serbian.

Serbe /sɛʀb/ *nmf* Serb.

Serbie /sɛʀbi/ ▶**692** *nprf* Serbia.

serbo-croate /sɛʀbokʀɔat/ ▶**462** *nm* Serbo-Croatian.

Sercq /sɛʀk/ ▶**416** *nprf* Sark.

serein, ~e /səʀɛ̃, ɛn/ I *adj* [*ciel, temps*] clear; [*personne, visage*] serene; [*jugement*] dispassionate; [*critique*] objective.

II *nm* (pluie fine) serein.

sereinement /səʀɛnmɑ̃/ *adv* [*regarder*] serenely; [*réfléchir, parler*] calmly; [*voir l'avenir*] with equanimity; [*juger*] dispassionately.

sérénade /seʀenad/ *nf* **1** (concert) serenade; **donner une ~ à qn** to serenade sb; **2**○ (tapage) racket○.

sérénissime /seʀenisim/ I *adj* **son Altesse ~** His/Her Serene Highness; **la ~ République** Hist La Serenissima, the Venetian Republic.

II *nf* **la Sérénissime** Venice.

sérénité /seʀenite/ *nf* **1** (de visage, esprit) serenity; (de personne) equanimity; **envisager qch avec ~** to view sth with equanimity; **afficher une totale/grande ~** to display perfect/great composure; **2** (de juge, jugement) impartiality; **3** (de ciel, temps) calmness.

séreux, -euse /seʀø, øz/ I *adj* serous.

II **séreuse** *nf* serous membrane, serosa spéc.

serf, serve /sɛʀ, sɛʀv/ I *adj* **1** lit [*condition*] of serfdom; **2** fig [*âme, esprit*] slavish.

II *nm,f* serf.

serfouette /sɛʀfwɛt/ *nf* combined hoe and fork.

serge /sɛʀʒ/ *nf* Tex serge.

sergé /sɛʀʒe/ *nm* Tex twill.

sergent /sɛʀʒɑ̃/ *nm* **1** ▶**390** Mil (de terre) ≈ sergeant; (de l'air) ≈ sergeant GB, ≈ staff sergeant US; **~ instructeur** drill sergeant; **2** Tech (serre-joint) cramp.

■ **~ de ville**† policeman, town constable† GB.

sergent-chef, *pl* **sergents-chefs** /sɛʀʒɑ̃ʃɛf/ ▶**390** *nm* Mil (de terre) ≈ staff sergeant; (de l'air) ≈ flight sergeant GB, ≈ chief master sergeant US.

séricicole /seʀisikɔl/ *adj* silk (*épith*), sericultural spéc.

sériciculture /seʀisikyltyʀ/ *nf* silkworm rearing, sericulture spéc.

série /seʀi/ *nf* **1** (suite) series (*sg*) (**de qch** of sth); **une ~ de mesures/réactions** a series of measures/reactions; **catastrophes/meurtres en ~** a series of catastrophes/murders; **avoir des problèmes en ~, avoir toute une ~ de problèmes** to have one problem after another; **~ d'attentats** wave of attacks; **2** (de production) **numéro de ~** serial number; **~ limitée** limited edition; **modèle de ~** gén mass-produced model; (voiture) production model; **fabriqués** or **faits en ~** mass-produced; **production en ~** mass production; **voiture hors ~** custom-built car; **numéro hors ~** special issue; ▶**grand**; **3** (collection) set; **une ~ de casseroles/bandes dessinées** a set of saucepans/comics; **4** (programme télévisé) series (*sg*); **une ~ américaine** an American series; **une ~ sur la Chine** a series on China; **un film de ~ B** a B movie; **5** Sport (catégorie) division; (épreuve) heat; **tête de ~ numéro un** (au tennis) number one seed; **6** Chimie, Math, Mus series (*sg*); **7** Électrotech **montage en ~** series connection; **batteries montées en ~** batteries connected in series; **8** Scol (au baccalauréat) option; **~ A/C** literature/maths GB ou math US option; **9** Ordinat **en ~** serial.

■ **~ noire** Cin, Littérat thriller; fig (catastrophes) series of disasters (*pl*); (malchance) run of bad luck.

sériel, -ielle /seʀjɛl/ *adj* serial.

sérier /seʀje/ [2] *vtr* to classify.

sérieusement /seʀjøzmɑ̃/ *adv* **1** (avec application) [*apprendre, travailler*] seriously; **2** (sans plaisanter) [*parler, envisager*] seriously; **il pense ~ à déménager/démissionner** he's seriously thinking of moving/resigning; **3**○ (considérablement) [*affaiblir, compliquer*] seriously, considerably; **la conférence m'a ~ ennuyé** the lecture really ou utterly bored me.

sérieux, -ieuse /seʀjø, øz/ I *adj* **1** (réfléchi) [*élève, employé*] serious, serious-minded; [*activité, travail*] serious; [*politique, réforme*] serious; **Michel est un élève ~ et appliqué** Michel is serious and conscientious; **être ~ dans son travail** [*personne*] to be serious about one's work; **2** (qui ne rit pas) [*personne, air, visage*] serious; **dire qch d'un air très ~** to say sth in a very serious way; **c'est bien vrai, tu es ~?** is it really true, are you serious?; **soyons ~, cette idée est totalement idiote** let's be serious, this idea is totally stupid; **3** (qui mérite considération) [*affaire, raison, menace*] serious; [*piste, indice*] important; **passer aux choses sérieuses** to move on to serious matters, to get down to the nitty-gritty○; **4** (non fait pour l'amusement) [*étude, sujet, livre, conversation, débat, film*] serious; [*annonce, proposition*] genuine; **une enquête très sérieuse révèle** a very serious survey reveals; **avoir des lectures très sérieuses** to read very serious books; **5** (digne de confiance) [*personne, maison, établissement*] reliable; **tu peux lui faire confiance, c'est quelqu'un de ~** you can trust him, he's reliable; **'pas ~ s'abstenir'** (dans petite annonce) 'genuine inquiries only', 'no time-wasters'; **6** (grave) [*conséquences, blessure, problème, incident, crise*] serious; **être confronté à de ~ ennuis** to be faced with serious difficulties; **il souffre de ~ troubles de la vue** he has serious problems with his eyesight; **la situation est jugée très sérieuse par le gouvernement** the government is treating the situation as very serious; **7** (considérable) [*effort, besoin*] real, concerted; [*progrès*] considerable; [*handicap*] serious; **conserver une sérieuse avance** to retain a considerable lead; **opérer une sérieuse restructuration des services** to carry out a complete restructuring of services; **prendre un ~ retard dans son travail** to fall seriously behind with one's work; **avoir un ~ besoin de vacances** really to need a vacation, to be seriously in need of a vacation; **8** (responsable) [*personne*] responsible; **il n'est pas très ~ ce garçon** this boy is a bit irresponsible; **cela ne fait pas très ~** that doesn't make a very good impression.

II *nm* **1** (expression grave) seriousness; **dire qch avec beaucoup de ~** to say sth very seriously; **garder son ~** to keep a straight face; **perdre son ~** to start to laugh; **2** (caractère réfléchi) seriousness; **faire qch avec ~** to do sth carefully; **elle travaille avec ~ et application** she is serious and conscientious in her work; **il a fait preuve de beaucoup de ~ dans ses études** he's shown himself to be very serious about his studies; **3** (de situation) seriousness, gravity sout; (de projet, démarche) seriousness; **je mets en doute le ~ de leur proposition** I have my doubts about the seriousness of their proposal; **prendre qch/qn au ~** to take sth/sb seriously; **se prendre au ~** to take oneself seriously; **4** (chope de bière) beer mug (*1 litre*).

sérigraphie /seʀigʀafi/ *nf* **1** (procédé) silkscreen printing; **2** (œuvre) silkscreen print.

serin /səʀɛ̃/ *nm* **1** Zool canary; **2**† (benêt) (**grand**) **~** silly billy○.

seriner○ /səʀine/ [1] *vtr* **~ qch à qn** to drum sth into sb; **~ que** to harp on about the fact that.

seringa /səʀɛ̃ga/ *nm* syringa, mock orange.

seringue /səʀɛ̃g/ *nf* Culin, Hort, Méd syringe.

■ **~ à huile** Mécan oil squirt; **~ hypodermique** hypodermic syringe.

sérique /seʀik/ *adj* Méd serumal; **maladie ~** serum sickness.

serment /sɛʀmɑ̃/ *nm* **1** (devant une autorité) oath; **déclarer sous ~** to declare on GB ou under oath; **prêter ~** to take the oath; **un ~ professionnel** a professional oath; **2** (promesse) liter vow; **faire (le) ~ de faire** to make a solemn vow to do; **échanger des ~s** to exchange vows; ▶**faux**[1].

■ **le ~ d'Hippocrate** Méd the Hippocratic oath; **un ~ d'ivrogne** an empty promise; **le ~ du Jeu de Paume** Hist *vow taken in 1789 by the French Assembly to create a constitution.*

sermon /sɛʀmɔ̃/ *nm* **1** Littérat, Relig sermon; **le Sermon sur la montagne** Relig the Sermon on the Mount; **2** péj (discours) lecture; (remontrance) talking-to.

sermonner /sɛʀmɔne/ [1] *vtr* (conseiller) to lecture; (morigéner) to give [sb] a talking-to; **se faire ~** to get a talking-to.

sermonneur, -euse /sɛʀmɔnœʀ, øz/ I *adj* preachy.

II *nm,f* preachy individual.

sérodiagnostic /seʀodjagnɔstik/ *nm* serodiagnosis.

sérologie /seʀɔlɔʒi/ *nf* serology.

sérologique /seʀɔlɔʒik/ *adj* serological.

séronégatif, -ive /seʀonegatif, iv/ I *adj* HIV-negative; **être déclaré ~** to be found to be HIV-negative.

II *nm,f* HIV-negative person.

séropositif, -ive /seʀopozitif, iv/ I *adj* gén seropositive (**à** for); (dans le cas du sida) HIV positive.

II *nm,f* HIV positive person.

séropositivité /seʀopozitivite/ *nf* (dans le cas du sida) (HIV antibody) seropositivity.

sérosité /seʀozite/ *nf* serous fluid.

sérothérapie /seʀoteʀapi/ *nf* serotherapy.

sérotine /seʀɔtin/ *nf* **1** Zool serotin; **2** Méd (membrane) basal decidua.

sérotonine /seʀotɔnin/ *nf* serotonin.

serpe /sɛʀp/ *nf* billhook; **visage taillé à la ~** or **à coups de ~** craggy face.

serpent /sɛʀpɑ̃/ *nm* **1** Zool snake; **2** Bible serpent; **3** ▶**534** Mus serpent.

■ **~ d'airain** Bible brazen serpent; **~ d'eau** water snake; **~ à lunettes** cobra; **~ marin** Zool sea snake; **~ de mer** Mythol sea serpent; (histoire) hackneyed subject; **~ monétaire** Fin currency snake; **~ à plumes** Mythol plumed serpent; **~ à sonnette** rattlesnake.

IDIOMES **réchauffer** or **nourrir un ~ dans son sein** to take a viper to one's bosom; **c'est le ~ qui se mord la queue** things go round and round GB ou around and around US in circles.

Serpent /sɛʀpɑ̃/ *nprm* Astron Serpens.

serpentaire /sɛʀpɑ̃tɛʀ/ I *nm* Zool secretary bird.

II *nf* Bot stink dragon.

serpenteau, *pl* **~x** /sɛʀpɑ̃to/ *nm* **1** Zool baby snake; **2** (feu d'artifice) serpent.

serpenter /sɛʀpɑ̃te/ [1] *vi* [*route, fleuve*] to wind (**à travers, dans** through).

serpentin /sɛʀpɑ̃tɛ̃/ *nm* **1** (de fête) streamer; **2** Tech (de chauffage, refroidissement) coil.

serpentine /sɛʀpɑ̃tin/ *nf* Minér serpentine.

serpette /sɛʀpɛt/ *nf* pruning knife.

serpillière /sɛʀpijɛʀ/ *nf* floorcloth; **passer la ~** to wash the floor.

serpolet /sɛʀpɔlɛ/ *nm* wild thyme.

serrage /seʀaʒ/ *nm* (de vis, d'écrou) tightening.

serre /sɛʀ/ *nf* **1** (maison de verre) greenhouse; **mettre qch en** or **sous ~** to put sth in a greenhouse; **culture en ~** greenhouse cultivation; **effet de ~** greenhouse effect; **2** (de rapace) talon, claw.

serré, **~e** /seʀe/ **I** *pp* ▶ **serrer**.
II *pp adj* **1** (ajusté) [*vis, écrou*] tight; [*jupe, pantalon*] tight; **je suis ~e dans ma veste/jupe** my jacket/skirt is too tight; **robe ~e à la taille** dress fitted at the waist; **chemise ~e à la taille avec une ceinture** shirt pulled in at the waist by a belt; **2** (dense) (herbe) thick; (écriture) cramped; **en rangs ~s** in serried rows; **il tombait une pluie fine et ~e** it was drizzling; **3** (sans grande latitude) [*délais, emploi du temps, budget*] tight; [*virage*] sharp; **4** (rigoureux) [*analyse, étude, vérification*] close; [*contrôle, gestion*] strict; **5** (acharné) [*lutte*] hard; [*discussion, débat, négociation*] heated; [*partie, match*] close; **le score est ~** the scores are close; **le premier tour des élections va être ~** the first round of the elections is going to be a close contest; **6** (fort) [*café*] very strong.
III *adv* [*écrire*] in a cramped hand; [*tricoter*] tightly; **il va falloir jouer ~ si...** we can't take any chances if...

serre-file, *pl* **~s** /sɛʀfil/ *nm* Mil (personne) file-closer; (navire) tail-end Charlie○.

serre-joint, *pl* **~s** /sɛʀʒwɛ̃/ *nm* Tech clamp.

serre-livres /sɛʀlivʀ/ *nm inv* book end.

serrement /sɛʀmɑ̃/ *nm* **1** lit **~ de main** handshake; **2** fig **avoir** or **ressentir un ~ de cœur** to feel a pang; **3** Mines dam.

serrer /seʀe/ [1] **I** *vtr* **1** (maintenir vigoureusement) [*personne*] to grip [*volant, rame*]; **ne serrez pas le volant, détendez-vous** don't grip the steering wheel, relax; **si tu serres bien la corde tu ne risqueras rien** if you grip the rope tightly you'll be OK; **~ qch dans sa main** to grip [sth] in one's hand [*pièce, bonbon, crayon, clé*]; **~ qn/qch dans ses bras** to hug sb/sth; **~ qn/qch contre sa poitrine** to hug sb/sth to one's chest; **~ qch entre ses cuisses/genoux** to grip sth between one's thighs/knees; **~ qch entre ses dents** to clench sth between one's teeth; **~ le poignet/cou de qn** to squeeze sb's wrist/neck; **~ la main de** or **la pince**○ **à qn** to shake hands with sb; **elle a serré la main du ministre** she shook hands with the minister; **~ les poings** to clench one's fists; **la peur me serrait la gorge** my throat was constricted with fear; **ça me serre le cœur de voir ça** it wrings my heart to see that; **2** (ajuster) [*personne*] to tighten [*corset, ceinture, nœud*]; to tighten [*ficelle*]; **serre bien tes lacets** do your shoelaces up tight; **tu as trop serré ton nœud de cravate** your tie is too tight; **~ son peignoir autour de sa taille** to pull one's dressing-gown around oneself; **mon chignon n'est pas assez serré** my bun is (too) loose; **3** (tenir à l'étroit) [*chaussures, vêtement*] to be too tight; **mon pantalon me serre** my trousers GB ou pants US are too tight; **ça me serre à la taille/aux épaules/aux mollets** it's too tight around my waist/across my shoulders/around my calves; **4** (bloquer) to tighten [*écrou, vis, boulon*]; to turn [sth] off tightly [*robinet*]; **~ une pièce dans un étau** to grip a part in a vice GB ou vise US; **ne serrez pas trop** don't overtighten; **sans ~** [*fixer, visser*] loosely; **5** (être près de) **~ le trottoir** [*automobiliste*] to hug the kerb GB ou curb US; **~ l'accotement** to drive very close to the edge of the road; **~ à droite/gauche** [*véhicule*] to move close to the right/left of the road; **~ un cycliste contre le trottoir** [*voiture*] to force a cyclist up against the pavement GB ou sidewalk US; **~ qn de près** [*concurrent*] to be hot on sb's tail; **6** (rapprocher) to push [sth] closer together [*livres, tables, objets*] (**contre** against); to squeeze [*personne*] (**dans** in; **contre** against); **être serré** [*livres, personnes*] to be packed together; **nous sommes trop serrés dans la cuisine** there are too many of us in the kitchen; **~ les rangs** lit, fig to close ranks; **7** (étudier en profondeur) **~ un sujet/problème de près** to study a subject/problem closely; **8** (réduire) to cut [*budget, dépenses, prix*]; **essayer de ~ les coûts** to try to cut costs; **9** Naut to furl [*voile*]; **~ le vent** to sail close to the wind; **10** liter, dial (ranger) to stow [sth] away [*objet précieux, économies*].
II se serrer *vpr* **1** (se rapprocher de) [*personnes*] to squeeze up (**autour de** around; **dans** in); **serrez-vous pour faire de la place** squeeze up to make room; **ma voiture est petite, il va falloir se ~** my car is small, we'll have to squeeze up; **se ~ contre qch/qn** to squeeze up against sth/sb; **ils se sont serrés les uns contre les autres** they huddled together; **2** (se comprimer) **se ~ dans une jupe/un pantalon** to squeeze oneself into a skirt/a pair of trousers GB ou pants US; **nous nous sommes serré la main** we shook hands; **3** (se contracter) **avoir le cœur qui se serre** to feel deeply upset; **avoir la gorge qui se serre** (d'émotion) to have a lump in one's throat; (de peur, trac) to have one's heart in one's mouth.
IDIOMES **~ la pince**○ or **louche**○ or **cuiller**○ **à qn** to shake sb's hand.

serre-tête, *pl* **~s** /sɛʀtɛt/ *nm* hairband.

serrure /seʀyʀ/ *nf* (de porte, coffre, tiroir) lock; **~ en applique/à encastrer** rim/mortice lock; **~ de sécurité/à combinaison** safety/combination lock; **trou de ~** keyhole; **regarder par le trou de la ~** to look through the keyhole.
■ **~ à barillet** cylinder sashlock; **~ avec bouton de verrouillage** latchlock; **~ à pêne demi-tour** sashlock; **~ 3 points** multilock.

serrurerie /seʀyʀʀi/ *nf* **1** ▶ **510** (boutique) locksmith's; **2** (corps de métier) locksmith's trade; **3** (serrures) locks (*pl*).

serrurier /seʀyʀje/ ▶ **510** *nm* locksmith.

sertir /sɛʀtiʀ/ [3] *vtr* **1** (en joaillerie) to set [*pierre*]; **2** Tech to crimp [*tôles*].

sertissage /sɛʀtisaʒ/ *nm* **1** (en joaillerie) setting; **2** Tech crimping.

sertisseur, **-euse** /sɛʀtisœʀ, øz/ ▶ **510** *nm,f* **1** (en joaillerie) jewel setter; **2** Tech crimper.

sertissure /sɛʀtisyʀ/ *nf* (manière de sertir) setting; (partie du chaton) bezel.

sérum /seʀɔm/ *nm* Physiol, Pharm, Chimie serum; **~ antirabique** anti-rabies serum; **un ~ antivenimeux** an antivenin; **~ physiologique** physiological solution; **~ sanguin** blood serum; **~ de vérité** truth drug.

servage /sɛʀvaʒ/ *nm* Hist serfdom.

serval /sɛʀval/ *nm* serval.

servant /sɛʀvɑ̃/ **I** *adj m* **chevalier ~** devoted admirer.
II *nm* **1** Relig server; **2** Mil (au canon) member of a gun crew.

servante /sɛʀvɑ̃t/ ▶ **510** *nf* (domestique) maidservant.

serve ▶ **serf**.

serveur, **-euse** /sɛʀvœʀ, øz/ ▶ **510** **I** *nm,f* (dans café, restaurant) waiter/waitress.
II *nm* **1** Sport server; **2** (aux cartes) dealer; **3** Ordinat server.

servi, **~e** /sɛʀvi/ **I** *pp* ▶ **servir**.
II *pp adj* **1** (à table) **'prends de la viande'—'merci je suis déjà ~'** 'have some meat'—'I already have some, thank you'; **2**○ fig iron **nous voulions du soleil, nous sommes ~s** we wanted some sunshine and we've certainly got it.

serviabilité /sɛʀvjabilite/ *nf* helpfulness; **être d'une grande ~** to be very obliging ou helpful.

serviable /sɛʀvjabl/ *adj* obliging, helpful.

service /sɛʀvis/ **I** *nm* **1** (action serviable, faveur) **je peux te demander un ~?** (action serviable) can I ask you to do something for me?; (faveur) can I ask you a favour[GB]?; **pourrais-tu me rendre un petit ~?** could you do something for me?; **tu m'as rendu ~** (**en faisant cela**) that was a great help; **elle m'a rendu de nombreux ~s** she's been very helpful; **il est toujours prêt à rendre ~** he is always ready to help; **rendre un mauvais ~ à qn** to do sb a disservice; **ce n'est pas un ~ à leur rendre** or **ce n'est pas leur rendre ~ que de faire leurs devoirs** you are not helping them by doing their homework for them; **2** (liaison) service; **~ de bus** bus service; **le ~ d'été/d'hiver/de nuit** the summer/winter/night service; **le ~ n'est pas assuré le dimanche** there's no service on Sundays; **~ réduit** or **partiel** reduced service; **3** (fonctionnement) **être en ~** [*ascenseur*] (en train de fonctionner) to be working; (en état de fonctionner) to be in working order; **être en ~** [*autoroute*] to be open; [*ligne de métro, de bus*] to be running; [*aérogare*] to be open, to be in operation; **ne pas être en ~** [*ligne de métro*] to be closed; **être hors ~** [*ascenseur*] to be out of order; **entrer en ~** [*ligne de métro, aérogare, autoroute*] to be opened, to come into service; **mettre en ~** to bring [sth] into service [*appareil, véhicule*]; to open [*gare, aérogare, autoroute, ligne de bus*]; **remettre en ~** to bring [sth] back into service [*appareil*]; to reopen [*gare, autoroute*] ; **la mise** or **l'entrée en ~ de la ligne de bus** the start of the new bus service; **depuis la mise** or **l'entrée en ~ de cette route** since the opening of this road; **4** (aide) **rendre ~ à qn** [*machine, appareil*] to be a help to sb; [*route, passage, magasin*] to be convenient (for sb); **ça peut toujours rendre ~** it might come in handy; **5** (action de servir) gén service; **être au ~ de son pays** to serve one's country; **'décoré pour ~ rendu'** 'decorated for service to his/her country'; **je suis à leur ~** (employé) I work for them; (dévoué) I'm at their disposal; **travailler au ~ de la paix** to work for peace; **mettre son énergie/argent au ~ d'une cause** to devote all one's energy/money to a cause; **'à votre ~!'** (je vous en prie) 'don't mention it!', 'not at all!'; **'que puis- je faire** or **qu'y a-t-il pour votre ~?'** 'may I help you?'; **'(nous sommes) à votre ~ madame'** 'always pleased to be of assistance'; **6** (à table) service; **le ~ est rapide ici** the service here is quick; **130 francs ~ compris/non compris** 130 francs service included/not included; **le ~ n'est pas compris** service is not included; **12% pour le ~** 12% service charge; **faire le ~** (servir les plats) to serve; (desservir) to act as waiter; **manger au premier ~** to go to the first sitting; **7** (des gens de maison) (domestic) service; **être en ~ chez qn, être au ~ de qn** to be in sb's service; **entrer au ~ de qn** to go to work for sb; **prendre qn à son ~** to take sb on, to engage sb; **avoir plusieurs personnes à son ~** to have several people working for one; **escalier de ~** back stairs (*pl*), service stairs (*pl*); **entrée de ~** tradesmen's entrance GB, service entrance; **8** (obligations professionnelles) service; **avoir 20 ans de ~ dans une entreprise** to have been with a firm 20 years; **être de** or **en ~** to be on duty; **l'infirmière de ~** the duty nurse, the nurse on duty; **prendre son ~ à** to come on duty at; **elle n'avait pas assuré son ~ ce jour-là** she hadn't come on duty that day; **assurer le ~ de qn** to cover for sb; **il ne fume pas pendant les heures de ~** he doesn't smoke on duty; **son ~ se termine à** he comes off duty at; **être en ~ commandé** [*policier*] to be on an official assignment, to be acting under orders; **état de ~(s)** record of service, service record; **le ~ de nuit** night duty; **pharmacie de ~** duty chemist; **être de ~ de garde** (dans un hôpital) to be on duty; (médecin généraliste) to be on call; **~ en temps de paix** Mil peace time service; **être** or **jouer l'idiot de ~** to be the house clown; **9** (section administrative) department; **~ administratif/culturel/du personnel** administrative/cultural/personnel department; **le ~ de psychiatrie/de cardiologie** the psychiatric/cardiology department; **le ~ des urgences** the casualty department GB ou emergency room US; **les blessés furent conduits au ~ des urgences** the injured were taken to casualty GB ou to ER US; **~ de réanimation** intensive care unit; **les ~s de sécurité** the security services; **les ~s secrets** the secret service; **les ~s d'espionnage** or **de renseignements** the intelligence services; **~ de dépannage** breakdown service; **~ d'entretien** (département de l'entreprise) maintenance department; (personnel) maintenance staff; **les ~s du Premier Ministre se refusent à tout commentaire** the Prime Minister's office has refused to comment; **chef de ~** (dans une administration) section head; (dans un hôpital) senior consultant; **10** Mil (obligations militaires) **~ (militaire)** military ou national service; **~ national** national service; **faire son ~ (militaire)** to do one's military service; **~ actif** active service; **~ civil** non-military national service; **partir au ~**° to go off to do one's military service; **être bon pour le ~** lit to be passed fit for military service; fig hum to be passed fit; **reprendre du ~** to re-enlist ou sign up again; **quitter le ~** to be discharged, to leave the forces; **11** (vaisselle) set; **un ~ à thé** a tea set; **un ~ à café** a coffee set; **~ à dessert** or **gâteau** dessert set; **~ de table** dinner service; **12** Relig service; **~ religieux** church service; **13** Sport service, serve; **être au ~** to serve ou be serving; **Valérie au ~** Valérie to serve; **changement de ~** change of service; **faute de ~** fault.

II services *nmpl* services; **les biens et les ~s** goods and services; **avoir recours aux ~s de qn** to call on sb's services; **se passer** or **priver des ~s de qn** to dispense with sb's services.

■ **~ après-vente, SAV** (département) after-sales service department; (activité) after-sales service; **~ minimum** reduced service; **~ d'ordre** stewards (*pl*); **~ de presse** (de ministère, parti, d'entreprise) press office; (de maison d'édition) press and publicity department; (livre) review copy; **~ public** public service; **Service du travail obligatoire, STO** *compulsory labour*[GB] *organization set up in 1943 during the German occupation of France*; **~s sociaux** Prot Soc social services.

serviette /sɛʀvjɛt/ *nf* **1** (pour la toilette) towel; **2** (pour la table) **~ (de table)** (table) napkin, serviette GB; **mets ta ~!** put your napkin on; **3** (cartable) briefcase.

■ **~ de bain** bath towel; **~ hygiénique** sanitary towel; **~ d'invités** hand towel; **~ de plage** beach towel; **~ de toilette** towel.

IDIOMES **il ne faut pas mélanger les torchons et les ~s**° you've got to know what's what.

serviette-éponge, *pl* **serviettes-éponges** /sɛʀvjɛtepɔ̃ʒ/ *nf* terry towel.

servile /sɛʀvil/ *adj* **1** (soumis) [*personne, attitude*] servile; [*fidélité, obéissance*] slavish; **2** (peu original) [*adaptation*] slavish; [*traduction*] over-literal; **3** Hist (de serf) servile; (de domestique) menial.

servilement /sɛʀvilmɑ̃/ *adv* [*obéir*] slavishly; [*flatter*] obsequiously; (sans originalité) [*imiter, copier*] slavishly.

servilité /sɛʀvilite/ *nf* (soumission) servility.

servir /sɛʀviʀ/ [30] **I** *vtr* **1** (être au service de) to serve [*État, maître, société*]; **2** (fournir) [*commerçant, serveur*] to serve; **il n'y a personne pour ~** there's nobody to serve; **le boucher m'a mal servi aujourd'hui** the butcher didn't give me very good meat today; **je suis toujours très bien servi dans leur magasin** I'm always very happy with what I buy in their shop GB ou store US; **moi qui voulais du changement, je suis servie!** iron well I wanted a change and I certainly got it!; **3** (donner à boire, à manger) to serve [*invité, plat, boisson*]; **~ qch à qn** to serve sb (with) sth; **~ qn à table** to serve sb at table; **~ à manger/à dîner à qn** to serve food/dinner to sb; **qu'est-ce que je vous sers (à boire)?** what would you like to drink?; **~ qn en qch** (en légumes, viande) to serve sb sth; **il m'a servi une grosse part de gâteau** he served me a large slice of cake; **tu es mal servi** you haven't got much; **tu es bien servi?** have you got enough?; **tu as été bien servi en gâteau** you've been given a generous helping of cake; **'Madame est servie'** 'dinner is served Madam'; **au moment de ~** before serving; **'~ frais'** 'serve chilled'; **4** (être utile à) [*situation*] to help [*personne, projet, cause*]; to serve [*intérêt*]; [*personne*] to further [*cause, ambition, intérêt*]; **~ un but** or **une fin** to serve an end; **5**° (donner) **~ qch comme argument/excuse** to use sth as an argument/excuse; **6** Relig **~ la messe** to serve mass; **7** Écon (payer) to pay [*rente, pension, intérêt*]; **8** Jeux to deal [*cartes*]; **9** Mil to serve [*arme*].

II servir à *vtr ind* **1** (être utilisé) **~ à qn** [*pièce, maison, salle*] to be used by sb; **cela sert à mon père** my father uses it; **cette casserole me sert pour faire des confitures** I use this pan for making jam; **~ à qch** to be used for sth; **~ à la fabrication de qch** to be used for making sth; **cela ne sert à rien** it's not used for anything; **ces matériaux nous servent à fabriquer**... we use these materials for manufacturing...; **les exercices m'ont servi à comprendre la règle** the exercises helped me to understand the rule; **2** (être utile) [*connaissances, objet*] to come in useful; **cela te servira** it will come in useful (for you); **cela ne m'a servi à rien** this was of no use to me; **cela ne sert à rien** [*objet*] it's useless; [*action*] it's no good; **je les ai menacés mais cela n'a servi à rien** I threatened them but it didn't do any good; **cela ne sert à rien de faire** there's no point in doing; **~ à quelque chose** to serve a useful purpose; **~ à faire** to be used for doing.

III servir de *vtr ind* (avoir la fonction) **~ de** [*personne*] to act as; **~ d'intermédiaire/d'interprète à qn** to act as an intermediary/an interpreter for sb; **~ d'arme** to be used as a weapon; **la table nous sert de bureau** we use the table as a desk; ▶ **courir**.

IV *vi* **1** Mil (dans une armée) **~ dans** to serve in; **2** Sport to serve; **à toi de ~** it's your serve ou service; **3** (être employé comme domestique) **il a servi dix ans chez madame de la Poya** he was in Mrs de la Poya's service for ten years; **il a servi sous Turenne** he served under Turenne; **4** (être utilisé) to be used; **ne jette pas la boîte, elle peut encore ~** don't throw the box away, it might come in useful ou handy for something; **5** (travailler comme serveur) **~ dans un café** gén to work as a waiter in a café; (au bar) to work as a barman.

V se servir *vpr* **1** (à boire, à manger) to help oneself; **servez-vous** help yourself ou yourselves; **se ~ un verre de vin/une part de gâteau** to help oneself to a glass of wine/a slice of cake; **sers-toi bien** take plenty; **2** (faire ses courses) **se ~ chez le boucher du coin** to shop at the local butcher's; **pour le fromage nous nous servons chez Pauchon** we buy cheese at ou from Pauchon's; **3** (faire usage de) **se ~ de qch/qn** to use sth/sb (**comme** as); **se ~ d'un stratagème** to employ a stratagem; **se ~ d'une situation** to make use of a situation; **4** Culin, Vin to be served; **le vin se sert frais** wine should be served chilled; **5** (dans magasin) to help oneself (**de qch** to sth).

VI *v impers* **à quoi sert-il de faire?** what's the point ou use of doing?; **il ne sert à rien de crier** there's no point in shouting.

IDIOMES **on n'est jamais si bien servi que par soi même** Prov if you want something done it's better to do it yourself.

serviteur /sɛʀvitœʀ/ *nm* servant; **'votre ~!'** (à votre service) 'at your service, sir ou madam!'; **votre très humble ~** your most humble and obedient servant; **votre ~** (moi-même) yours truly.

IDIOMES **l'argent est un bon ~ et un mauvais maître** Prov money is a good servant but a bad master.

servitude /sɛʀvityd/ *nf* **1** (esclavage) servitude; **2** (obligation) constraint; **les ~s d'un métier** the constraints of a job; **3** Jur (en immobilier) **immeuble sans ~** building free from encumbrance.

servocommande /sɛʀvokɔmɑ̃d/ *nf* servomechanism.

servodirection /sɛʀvodiʀɛksjɔ̃/ *nf* power(-assisted) steering.

servofrein /sɛʀvofʀɛ̃/ *nm* power(-assisted) brakes (*pl*).

servomécanisme /sɛʀvomekanism/ *nm* servomechanism.

servomoteur /sɛʀvomɔtœʀ/ *nm* servomotor.

ses ▶ **son**[1].

sésame /sezam/ *nm* sesame; **un pain au ~** a sesame seed loaf.

IDIOMES **Sésame ouvre-toi!** open sesame!

session /sɛsjɔ̃/ *nf* **1** (réunion) session; **~ de printemps** spring session; **2** Scol, Univ examination session; **la première/deuxième ~** June/September examinations; **~ de rattrapage** retakes (*pl*); **3** (stage) course; **~ de formation** training course.

sesterce /sɛstɛʀs/ *nm* sestertium.

set /sɛt/ *nm* Sport set.

■ **~ de table** place mat.

Sète /sɛt/ ▶ **857** *npr* Sète.

sétois, ~e /setwa, az/ ▶ **857** *adj* of Sète.

Sétois, ~e /setwa, az/ ▶ **857** *nm,f* (natif) native of Sète; (habitant) inhabitant of Sète.

setter /setɛʀ/ *nm* setter.

■ **~ anglais** English setter; **~ irlandais** Irish setter, red setter.

seuil /sœj/ *nm* **1** (dalle) **~ (de la porte)** doorstep; (entrée) doorway (**de** of); **se tenir sur le ~** (de porte) to stand on the doorstep; (de maison) to stand in the doorway; **franchir le ~** to cross the threshold (**de** of); **moi vivant, il ne franchira pas le ~ de ma maison** he will come into my house over my dead body; **2** (limite) threshold (**de** of); **atteindre un ~** to reach a threshold; **3** liter (début) threshold littér (**de** of); **au ~ de** (saison, carrière) at the beginning of; (mort, adolescence) on the threshold of; **4** Psych threshold; **5** Géog bank.

■ **~ absolu** Physiol, Psych absolute threshold; **~ d'audibilité** Physiol, Psych difference threshold; **~ d'audition** Physiol threshold of hearing; **~ différentiel** = **~ d'audibilité**; **~ de la douleur** Physiol threshold of pain; **~ d'excitation** Physiol, Psych absolute threshold; **~ d'imposition** Fisc tax threshold; **~ de pauvreté** poverty line; **~ de rentabilité** break-even point; **~ de tolérance** Sociol immigration limit.

seul, ~e /sœl/ *adj* **1** (sans compagnie) alone, on one's own; **toute ~e** all alone, all on her own; **~ au monde** alone in the world; **vivre ~** to live alone ou on one's own; **elle n'aime pas rester ~e** she doesn't like being alone; **elle est venue toute ~e** she came alone; **elle m'a laissé ~** she left me on my own; **je les ai laissés tout ~s** I left them all alone ou all on their own; **une femme ~e dans la rue** a woman alone ou on her own in the street; **c'est dangereux pour les femmes ~es** it's dangerous for women on their own; **les femmes ~es étaient regardées de travers** single women used to be frowned upon; **vous êtes ~ dans la vie?** are you single?; **j'étais ~ avec elle/contre tous/face à eux** I was alone with her/against everyone else/in front of them; **j'étais ~ pour faire tout le travail** I did all the work alone ou on my own; **je préfère la rencontrer ~e** I'd rather meet her alone ou in private; **elle veut vous parler ~ à ~** or **~e à ~(e)** she wants to speak to you alone ou in private; **nous nous sommes retrouvés ~ à ~** we found ourselves alone together; **parler/rire/chanter tout ~** to talk/laugh/sing to oneself; **2** (sans aide) gén by oneself, on one's own; (avec idée de victoire) single-handedly; **je peux le faire/y aller ~** I can do it/go there by myself ou on my own; **elle l'a fait toute ~e** she did it all by herself ou all on her own; **elle a remporté tous les prix/conclu le marché/mené la révolution à elle ~e** she single-handedly carried off all the prizes/pulled off the deal/led the revolution; **le travail ne va pas se faire tout ~!** the work won't get done all by itself!; **(tout) ~s, les chiffres ne veulent pas dire grand-chose** on their own, the figures don't mean very much; **~, je n'aurais jamais pu le faire** I could never have done it alone ou by myself ou on my own; **il a mangé un poulet à lui tout ~** he ate a whole chicken all to himself; **le papier se détache tout ~** the paper comes off easily; **ça va tout ~** (c'est facile) it's really easy, it's a piece of cake○; (c'est moins pénible) it's much easier; (c'est sans problèmes) things are running smoothly; **3** (unique) only; **le ~ homme/avantage/problème** the only man/advantage/problem; **une ~e femme/façon/chaise** only one woman/way/chair; **un ~ d'entre eux/de tous les participants** only one of them/out of all the participants; **la ~e et unique personne/raison/chaise** the one and only person/reason/chair; **ils étaient les ~s Français du groupe** they were the only French people in the group; **les ~s élèves à avoir compris** the only pupils who understood; **à la ~e différence/condition que** the only difference/condition being that; **pas un ~ client/arbre/magasin** not a single customer/tree/shop GB ou store US; **l'espion et l'ambassadeur sont une ~e et même personne** the spy and the ambassador are one and the same person; **d'une ~e pièce** in one piece; **pour cette ~e raison** for this reason alone; **dans cette ~e ville** in this town alone; **au cours de cette ~e rencontre** during this meeting alone; **dans le ~ but de faire** with the sole aim of doing; **à la ~e idée/pensée de faire** at the very idea/thought of doing; **~ de son espèce** unique; **~ de sa catégorie** the only one in his/her category; **ils ont parlé d'une ~e voix** they were unanimous; **4** (solitaire) lonely; **c'est un homme ~** he's a lonely man; **elle est très ~e** she's very lonely; **se sentir ~** to feel lonely; **5** (avec valeur adverbiale) only; **~es les femmes peuvent comprendre ça** only women can understand that; **elle ~e pourrait vous le dire** only she could tell you; **~ un miracle pourrait la sauver** only a miracle could save her; **l'offre est réservée à nos ~s employés** the offer is open only to our employees; **6** (avec valeur nominale) **le ~, la ~e** the only one; **les ~s, les ~es** the only ones; **j'étais (le) ~ à manger** I was the only one eating; **j'étais (le) ~ à en manger** I was the only one who ate any; **j'étais le ~ à aimer le spectacle** I was the only one enjoying the show; **j'ai été le ~ à avoir aimé le spectacle** I was the only one who enjoyed the show; **nous étions les ~s à critiquer/rire** we were the only ones to criticize/laugh; **les ~s à comprendre** the only ones who understood; **la ~e qui n'a** or **n'ait pas compris** the only one who didn't understand; **les ~s que je connaisse/en qui je peux avoir confiance** the only ones I know/I can trust; **c'est le ~ qui nous reste** it's the only one (that) we've got left; **c'est la ~e qui puisse t'aider** she's the only one who can help you; **tu n'es pas la ~e!** you're not the only one!; **tu n'es pas la ~e à penser** or **croire que** you're not alone in thinking that; **ils sont les ~s à croire que** they're alone in thinking that; **j'étais le ~ en cravate** I was the only one wearing a tie; **c'est l'œuvre d'un ~** it's the work of one man; **il n'y en a pas un ~ qui se soit levé** not a single person stood up; ▶ **malheur**.

seulement /sœlmɑ̃/ *adv* **1** (pas davantage) only; **~ 13%** only 13%; **nous étions ~ deux** or **deux ~** there were only the two of us; **'nous étions dix'—'~?'** 'there were ten of us'—'is that all?'; **2** (pas avant) only; **il rentre ~ dans quelques jours** he won't be back for a few days; **j'ai compris ~ plus tard que** I only realized later that; **elle revient ~ demain/lundi** she's not coming back until tomorrow/Monday; **'vous le recevrez lundi'—'~ lundi?'** 'you'll get it on Monday'—'not before Monday?'; **3** (uniquement) only; **faire qch ~ pour aider qn** to do sth only to help sb; **ce n'est pas ~ une question de principe** it's not only a question of principle; **c'est non ~ idiot, mais (aussi) vulgaire** not only is it stupid, but it's also vulgar; **non ~ tu rentres tard mais en plus tu réveilles tout le monde!** not only do you come home late but you wake everybody up as well!; **4** (toutefois) only, but; **c'est possible, ~ je veux y réfléchir** it's possible, only ou but I'd like to think about it; **5** (au moins) **si ~** if only; **si ~ je pouvais leur parler** if only I could talk to them; **6** (même) **pas ~** not even; **il ne nous a pas ~ remerciés** he didn't even thank us; **elle est partie il n'y a pas ~ deux minutes** she left not two minutes ago.

seulet○, **-ette** /sœlɛ, ɛt/ *adj* lonely; **se sentir (un peu) ~** to feel (a bit) lonely.

sève /sɛv/ *nf* **1** Bot sap; **2** fig vigour[GB].

sévère /sevɛʀ/ *adj* **1** (dur) [*personne, éducation*] strict; [*sélection*] rigorous; [*jugement, décision, leçon*] harsh; [*punition*] severe; **la presse est de plus en plus ~** the press is becoming increasingly critical **(à l'égard de** of); **2** (austère) [*regard, ton*] stern, severe; [*architecture, beauté*] severe; **3** (important) [*défaite, pertes*] heavy; [*chute*] severe.

sévèrement /sevɛʀmɑ̃/ *adv* **1** (durement) [*punir*] harshly; [*frapper*] severely; [*critiquer, juger*] harshly, severely; [*réglementer*] strictly; [*regarder*] sternly; **2** (gravement) [*éprouver, endommager*] severely.

sévérité /seveʀite/ *nf* **1** (dureté) (de personne, d'éducation) strictness; (de verdict, décision) harshness; **manquer de ~ avec** to be not strict enough with; **2** (de visage, personne) sternness; (d'architecture, de vêtements) severity.

sévices /sevis/ *nmpl* physical abuse ¢; **être victime de ~ sexuels** to be a victim of sexual abuse.

Séville /sevil/ ▶ **857** *npr* Seville; **le Barbier de ~** the Barber of Seville.

sévir /seviʀ/ [3] *vi* **1** (punir) to clamp down **(contre** on); **2** (causer des ravages) [*tempête, guerre*] to rage; [*épidémie, pauvreté*] to be rife; [*voyous*] to be running wild; **la sécheresse sévit dans le pays** drought is ravaging the country; **3** fig [*doctrine*] to hold sway; [*délation*] to be rife; **mon ancien professeur sévit toujours au lycée** hum my former teacher is still pegging away at the school.

sevrage /səvʀaʒ/ *nm* weaning.

sevrer /səvʀe/ [16] *vtr* **1** lit to wean [*enfant, animal*]; **~ un toxicomane** to wean a drug addict off a drug; **2** hum (priver) **~ qn de qch** to deprive sb of sth.

sèvres /sɛvʀ/ *nm inv* Sèvres porcelain.

Sèvres /sɛvʀ/ ▶ **857** *npr* Sèvres; **la manufacture de ~** the Sèvres porcelain factory.

sexagénaire /segzaʒenɛʀ/ **I** *adj* **être ~** to be in one's sixties.

II *nmf* person in his/her sixties.

sexagésimal, **~e**, *mpl* **-aux** /segzaʒezimal, o/ *adj* sexagesimal.

sexagésime /segzaʒezim/ *nf* Sexagesima.

sex-appeal /sɛksapil/ *nm inv* sex appeal.

sexe /sɛks/ *nm* **1** (distinction mâle femelle) sex; **indépendamment du sexe, de l'ethnie, de l'âge** irrespective of gender, race, age; **des représentants des deux ~s** representatives of both sexes; **changer de ~** to have a sex change (operation); **un bébé de ~ féminin** a female baby; **les individus de ~ masculin** males; **2** (organes génitaux) genitals (*pl*); **3** (sexualité) sex.

■ **~ faible** weaker sex; **~ fort** stronger sex.

sexisme /sɛksism/ *nm* sexism; **c'est du ~!** it's sexist!

sexiste /sɛksist/ *adj, nmf* sexist.

sexologie /sɛksɔlɔʒi/ *nf* sexology.

sexologue /sɛksɔlɔg/ ▶ **510** *nmf* sex therapist.

sex-shop, *pl* **~s** /sɛksʃɔp/ *nm* sex shop.

sextant /sɛkstɑ̃/ *nm* Astron, Naut, Math sextant.

sextillion /sɛkstiljɔ̃/ *nm* sextillion GB, undecillion US.

sextuor /sɛkstɥɔʀ/ *nm* (œuvre, formation) sextet.

sextuple /sɛkstypl/ **I** *adj* **une somme ~ d'une autre** an amount six times more than another.

II *nm* **leur mise leur a rapporté le ~** they got back six times more than they had bet.

sextuplé, **~e** /sɛkstyple/ *nm,f* sextuplet.

sextupler /sɛkstyple/ [1] **I** *vtr* to multiply [sth] by six, to sextuplicate.

II *vi* [*bénéfices*] to increase sixfold.

sexualité /sɛksɥalite/ *nf* gén, Biol sexuality; **avoir une ~ épanouie/refoulée** to be sexually uninhibited/inhibited.

sexué, **~e** /sɛksɥe/ *adj* [*plante*] sexed; [*reproduction*] sexual.

sexuel, **-elle** /sɛksɥɛl/ *adj* [*comportement, plaisir, rapport, différenciation*] sexual; [*vie, éducation, hormone, glande*] sex.

sexuellement /sɛksɥɛlmɑ̃/ *adv* sexually.

sexy○ /sɛksi/ *adj inv* [*personne, vêtement*] sexy○.

seyant, **~e** /sɛjɑ̃, ɑ̃t/ *adj* becoming; **elle a une robe/coiffure ~e** her dress/hairstyle suits her.

Seychelles /seʃɛl/ ▶ **321**, **416** *nprfpl* **les ~** the Seychelles.

sézigue◐ /sezig/ *pron pers* him/her.

SF /ɛsɛf/ *nf* (*abbr* = **science-fiction**) sci-fi.

SFP /ɛsɛfpe/ *nf* (*abbr* = **société française de production et de création audiovisuelles**) *television and video production company*.

SGBD /ɛsʒebede/ *nm*: *abbr* ▶ **système**.

SGDG /ɛsʒedeʒe/ *loc adv* (*abbr* = **sans garantie du gouvernement**) *without the guarantee of the government*.

shah /ʃa/ *nm* shah; **le ~ d'Iran** the Shah of Iran.

shaker /ʃekœʀ/ *nm* cocktail shaker.

shakespearien, **-ienne** /ʃɛkspiʀjɛ̃, ɛn/ *adj* Shakespearean.

shako /ʃako/ *nm* shako.

shampooing /ʃɑ̃pwɛ̃/ *nm* (lavage, produit) shampoo; **faire un ~ à qn** to give sb a shampoo; **~ pour cheveux gras** shampoo for greasy ou oily US hair; **~ sec** dry shampoo; **~ à la camomille** camomile shampoo.

■ **~ colorant** shampoo-in hair colouring[GB].

shampouiner /ʃɑ̃pwine/ [1] *vtr* to shampoo [*personne, cheveux, animal, moquette*].

shampouineur, **-euse** /ʃɑ̃pwinœʀ, øz/ ▶ **510** **I** *nm,f*: *trainee hairdresser* (*who washes hair*).

II shampouineuse *nf* carpet cleaner.

shantung /ʃɑ̃tuŋ/ *nm* shantung.

shérif /ʃeʀif/ *nm* sheriff.

sherpa /ʃɛʀpa/ *nm* sherpa.

shetland /ʃɛtlɑ̃d/ *nm* **1** (laine) Shetland wool; **un pull en ~** a Shetland wool sweater; **2** (poney) Shetland pony.

Shetland /ʃɛtlɑ̃d/ **▶416** *nprfpl* **les ~** the Shetlands; **les îles ~** the Shetland Islands.

shintoïsme /ʃintɔism/ *nm* Shintoism.

shit○ /ʃit/ *nm* dope○, pot○.

shoot /ʃut/ *nm* **1** Sport shot; **2**○ (de drogue) fix○.

shooter /ʃute/ [1] **I** *vi* to shoot.
II○ **se shooter** *vpr* to shoot up○; **elle est complètement shootée** she's completely stoned.

shopping /ʃɔpiŋ/ *nm* controv shopping; **faire du ~** to go shopping.

short /ʃɔʀt/ *nm* shorts (*pl*).

show-biz○ /ʃobiz/ *nm inv* showbiz○.

shrapnel /ʃʀapnɛl/ *nm* shrapnel.

Shropshire **▶692** *nprm* **le ~** Shropshire.

shunt /ʃœt/ *nm* shunt.

shunter /ʃœte/ [1] *vtr* **1** Électrotech to shunt; **2**○ (éviter) to bypass.

si[1] /si/

■ **Note** *si* adverbe de degré modifiant un adjectif a deux traductions en anglais selon que l'adjectif modifié est attribut: *la maison est si jolie* = the house is so pretty, ou épithète: *une si jolie maison* = such a pretty house.
– Dans le cas de l'épithète il existe une deuxième possibilité, assez rare et littéraire, citée pour information: = so pretty a house.

I *nm inv* if; **des ~ et des mais** ifs and buts.
II *adv* **1** (marquant l'affirmation) yes; **'tu ne le veux pas?'—'~!'** 'don't you want it?'—'yes I do!'; **'ils n'ont pas encore vendu leur maison?'—'il me semble que ~'** 'haven't they sold their house yet?'—'yes, I think they have'; **il n'ira pas, moi ~** he won't go, but I will; **mais ~** yes, of course; **'tu ne le veux pas?'—'mais ~'** 'don't you want it?'—'yes, of course I do'; **~ fort** littér yes indeed; **2** (marquant l'intensité) so; **ce n'est pas ~ simple** it's not so simple; **de ~ bon matin** so early in the morning; **de ~ bonne heure** so early; **c'est un homme ~ agréable** he's such a pleasant man; **vous habitez un ~ joli pays** you live in such a lovely country; **je suis heureux de visiter votre ~ jolie ville** I'm glad to visit your town, it's so pretty; **j'ai eu ~ peur que** I was so afraid that; **~ bien que** (par conséquent) so; (à tel point que) so much so that; **elle n'a pas écrit, ~ bien que je ne sais pas à quelle heure elle arrive** she hasn't written, so I don't know what time she's arriving; **elle s'agitait en tous sens ~ bien qu'elle a fini par tomber** she was flapping about all over the place, so much so that she fell over; **tant et ~ bien que** so much so that; **3** (pour marquer la comparaison) **rien n'est ~ beau qu'un coucher de soleil** there's nothing so beautiful as a sunset; **est-elle ~ bête qu'on le dit?** is she as stupid as people say (she is)?; **4** (pour marquer la concession) **~ loin que vous alliez nous saurons bien vous retrouver** however far away you go ou no matter how far away you go, we will be able to find you; **~ intelligent qu'il soit** or **soit-il, il ne peut pas tout savoir** as intelligent as he is ou however intelligent he is, he can't know everything; **~ pénible que soit la situation** however hard the situation may be; **~ peu que ce soit** however little it may be.
III *conj* (**s'** *before* il *or* ils) **1** (marquant l'éventualité) if; **~ ce n'est (pas) toi, qui est-ce?** if it wasn't you, who was it?; **il n'a rien pris avec lui ~ ce n'est un livre et son parapluie** he didn't take anything with him apart from ou other than a book and his umbrella; **l'une des villes les plus belles, ~ ce n'est la plus belle** one of the most beautiful cities, if not the most beautiful; **personne n'a compris ~ ce n'est le meilleur de la classe** nobody understood except the best pupil in the class; **~ ce n'était la peur d'être malade j'irais avec vous** if it weren't for fear of getting ill I'd go with you; **à quoi servent ces réunions ~ ce n'est à nous faire perdre notre temps?** what purpose do these meetings serve other than to waste our time?; **~ c'est (comme) ça, je pars** if that's how it is, I'm leaving; **s'il vient demain et qu'il fait beau** if he comes tomorrow and the weather's fine; **lui seul peut trouver une solution, ~ solution il y a** only he can find a solution, if there is one ou a solution; **~ oui** if so; **était-il à Paris? ~ oui avec qui? ~ non pourquoi?** was he in Paris? if he was, who was he with? if he wasn't, why?; **explique-moi tout ~ tant est que tu puisses le faire** tell me everything, if you can do it that is; **je ne sais pas s'il pourra nous prêter la somme avant dimanche, ~ tant est qu'il veuille bien nous la prêter** I don't know if he will be able to lend us the money before Sunday, if he's willing to lend it to us at all (that is); **~ tant est qu'une telle distinction ait un sens** if such a distinction makes any sense; **c'est un brave homme s'il en est** he's a brave man if ever there was one; **c'était un homme cultivé s'il en fut** he was an educated man if ever there was one; **2** (marquant l'hypothèse dans l'avenir ou le présent) if; **~ j'étais riche** if I were rich; **~ j'étais toi**, **~ j'étais à ta place** if I were you; **s'il pleuvait je serais content** I would be glad if it rained; **3** (exprimant l'hypothèse dans le passé) if; **~ j'avais su qu'il était à Paris je l'aurais invité** if I had known that he was in Paris I would have invited him; **~ j'avais eu l'argent** if I had had the money; **4** (quand) if; **s'il pleurait elle le prenait tout de suite dans ses bras** if he cried she would pick him up straightaway; **enfant, ~ je lisais, je n'aimais pas être dérangé** when I was a child I used to hate being disturbed if ou when I was reading; **5** (dans une phrase exclamative) if only; **~ vous pouviez venir!** if only you could come!, I wish you would come!; **~ au moins vous m'aviez téléphoné!** if only you had phoned me!; **~ encore** or **enfin** or **seulement** or **même** if only; **~ j'avais su!** if only I'd known!, had I known!; **vous pensez ~ j'étais content!** you can imagine how happy I was!; **~ j'ai envie de partir? ah ça oui!** do I want to leave? but of course I do!; **et ~ je le rencontrais dans la rue!** just imagine if ou just suppose I meet him in the street!; **6** (introduit la suggestion) **~ tu venais avec moi?** how ou what about coming with me?, why don't you come with me?; **~ nous allions dîner au restaurant?** how ou what about going out for dinner?; **~ tu venais passer le week-end avec nous?** why don't you come and spend the weekend with us?; **et s'il décidait de ne pas venir?** and what if he decided not to come?; **et ~ tu lui écrivais?** why don't you write to him/her?; **7** (pour marquer l'opposition) whereas; **~ la France est favorable au projet, les autres pays y sont violemment opposés** whereas France is in favour[GB] of the project, the other countries are violently opposed to it; **8** (introduit une interrogation indirecte) if, whether; **je me demande s'il viendra** I wonder if ou whether he'll come.

si[2] /si/ *nm inv* (note) B; (en solfiant) ti.

Siam /sjam/ *nprm* Hist Siam.

siamois, **~e** /sjamwa, az/ **I** *adj* **1** Zool [*chat*] Siamese; **2** Méd **des frères ~** Siamese twin boys; **des sœurs ~es** Siamese twin girls.
II *nm* **1** **▶462** Ling Siamese; **2** Zool Siamese cat.

Siamois, **~e** /sjamwa, az/ *nm,f* Siamese.

Sibérie /sibeʀi/ **▶692** *nprf* Siberia.

sibérien, **-ienne** /sibeʀjɛ̃, ɛn/ **▶692** *adj* Siberian.

sibilant, **~e** /sibilɑ̃, ɑ̃t/ *adj* sibilant.

sibylle /sibil/ *nf* sibyl.

sibyllin, **~e** /sibilɛ̃, in/ *adj* lit, fig sibylline.

sic /sik/ *adv* sic.

sicaire /sikɛʀ/ *nm* sicarian.

SICAV /sikav/ *nf* (*abbr* = **société d'investissement à capital variable**) unit trust GB, mutual fund US.

siccatif, **-ive** /sikatif, iv/ **I** *adj* siccative.
II *nm* siccative.

Sicile /sisil/ **▶692**, **416** *nprf* **la ~** Sicily; **en ~** in Sicily.

sicilien, **-ienne** /sisiljɛ̃, ɛn/ **▶692** **I** *adj* Sicilian.
II **▶462** *nm* Ling Sicilian.

Sicilien, **-ienne** /sisiljɛ̃, ɛn/ *nm,f* Sicilian.

sida /sida/ **▶271** *nm* (*abbr* = **syndrome immunodéficitaire acquis**) Aids (+ *v sg*).

side-car, *pl* **~s** /sidkaʀ/ *nm* **1** (caisse) sidecar; **2** (moto et caisse) motorcycle combination.

sidéen, **-éenne** /sideɛ̃, ɛn/ *nm,f* Aids sufferer.

sidéral, **~e**, *mpl* **-aux** /sideʀal, o/ *adj* sidereal.

sidérant○, **~e** /sideʀɑ̃, ɑ̃t/ *adj* staggering○, astonishing.

sidérer○ /sideʀe/ [14] *vtr* to stagger○, to astonish.

sidérurgie /sideʀyʀʒi/ *nf* steel industry.

sidérurgique /sideʀyʀʒik/ *adj* steel (*épith*).

sidérurgiste /sideʀyʀʒist/ **▶510** *nm* **1** (ouvrier) steel worker; **2** (producteur) steel producer.

siècle /sjɛkl/ **▶801** *nm* **1** (cent ans) century; **leur dynastie a régné plus de trois ~s** their dynasty ruled for more than three centuries; **au Ve ~ avant/après J.-C.** in the 5th century BC/AD; **les dramaturges/l'art du XVIIe ~** 17th-century dramatists/art; **au ~ dernier** in the last century; **d'ici la fin du ~** by the turn of the century; **être né avec le ~** to be born at the turn of the century; **du ~**○ [*affaire, idée, projet*] of the century; **un ~ de photographie/danse moderne** one hundred years of photography/modern dance; **il y a des ~s que je ne suis venu ici**○ I haven't been here for ages; **depuis des ~s** for centuries; **2** (époque) age; **le ~ de Louis XIV** the age of Louis XIV; **les ~s futurs** future ages; **il est d'un autre ~** he belongs to another age; **il faut vivre avec** or **être de son ~** one must move with the times; **▶grand**; **3** Relig world; **vivre dans le ~** to be of the world; **renoncer au ~** to renounce the world; **s'abandonner aux tentations du ~** to give oneself over to worldly temptations; **dans** or **pour les ~s des ~s** for ever and ever.

sied **▶seoir**.

siège /sjɛʒ/ *nm* **1** (pour s'asseoir) seat; **prenez un ~** take ou have a seat; **~ avant/arrière** front/back seat; **~ d'une chaise/balançoire** seat of a chair/swing; **~ des w-c** toilet seat; **2** (d'entreprise) head office; (d'organisation) headquarters (*pl*); (d'évêché) see; (de tribunal) seat; **3** Pol (d'élu, de député) seat; **perdre son ~** to lose one's seat; **4** Mil (de ville, forteresse) siege; **mettre le ~ devant une ville** to lay siege to a town; **lever le ~** lit to raise the siege; fig ○(partir) to take off○; **faire le ~ d'une ville/d'une ambassade** to besiege a town/an embassy; **5** Anat seat; **le bébé se présente par le ~** the baby is in the breech position.
■ **~ d'appoint** extra seat; **~ baquet** bucket seat; **~ canné** cane chair; **~ de repos** recliner, reclining chair; **~ social** head office; **~ de soupape** valve seat.

siéger /sjeʒe/ [15] *vi* **1** (être membre) [*député, magistrat*] to sit; **~ au sénat/au conseil d'administration** to sit in the senate/on the board of directors; **2** (tenir séance) [*assemblée, commission*] to be in session; **3** (résider) [*assemblée, organisation*] to have its headquarters.

sien, **sienne** /sjɛ̃, sjɛn/

■ **Note** En anglais, le choix du possessif de la troisième personne du singulier est déterminé par le genre du 'possesseur'. Sont du masculin: les personnes de sexe masculin et les animaux domestiques mâles; sont du féminin: les personnes de sexe féminin, les animaux domestiques femelles et souvent les navires; sont du neutre les animaux non domestiques et les non-animés. La forme masculine est *his*: *il m'a donné le sien/la sienne/les siens/les siennes* = he gave me his. La forme féminine est *hers*: *elle m'a donné le sien/la sienne/les siens/les siennes* = she gave me hers. Pour le neutre on répète le nom avec l'adjectif possessif *its*.

I *adj poss* **cette maison est sienne à présent** the house is now his/hers.
II **le sien, la sienne, les siens, les siennes** *pron poss* his/hers; **celui-là, c'est le ~** that's his/hers; **l'enfant n'était pas le ~** the child was not his/hers; **alors que les taux baissent en Europe, le Canada augmente les ~s** while rates are coming down in Europe, Canada is putting its rates up; **être de retour parmi les ~s** (sa famille) to be back with one's family; (ses amis) to be back among one's own friends; **elle a encore fait des siennes!** she's been up to mischief again!; **mon ordinateur refait des siennes** the computer's started playing up GB ou acting up again; ▶ y[2].

Sienne /sjɛn/ ▶ 857 *npr* Siena.

sierra /sjɛʀa/ *nf* sierra.

sierra-léonais, **~e**, *mpl* **~** /sjɛʀaleɔnɛ, ɛz/ ▶ 537 *adj* Sierra Leonean.

Sierra-Léonais, **~e**, *mpl* **~** /sjɛʀaleɔnɛ, ɛz/ ▶ 537 *nm,f* Sierra Leonean.

Sierra Leone /sjɛʀaleɔn/ ▶ 321 *nprf* Sierra Leone.

sieste /sjɛst/ *nf* nap, siesta; **faire la ~** to have ou take a nap, to have a siesta; **une courte ~** a short nap ou siesta.

sieur† /sjœʀ/ *nm* **le ~ Alexandre** Jur Mr Alexandre; hum my honourable[GB] friend Alexandre.

sifflant, **~e** /siflɑ̃, ɑ̃t/ I *adj* **1** gén [*voix, son*] hissing; [*respiration, toux*] wheezing; **2** Phon sibilant.
II **sifflante** *nf* Phon sibilant.

sifflement /sifləmɑ̃/ *nm* (de personne, train, projectile) whistle; (de bouilloire, vent) whistling ¢; (d'oiseau, insecte) chirping ¢; (de serpent) hissing ¢; **émettre un ~ admiratif** to give a whistle of admiration; **les ~s et les huées du public** the hisses and boos of the audience.
■ **~ d'oreilles** Méd ringing in the ears ¢, tinnitus ¢.

siffler /sifle/ [1] I *vtr* **1** (avec la bouche) to whistle [*air, chanson*]; (appeler) to whistle for [*personne*]; to whistle GB ou whistle for [*chien*]; (interpeller) to whistle at [*personne*]; **se faire ~** [*femme*] to get wolf-whistles; **2** (dire) to hiss; **je te hais, siffla-t-il entre ses dents** I hate you, he hissed between clenched teeth; **3** Sport [*arbitre*] to blow one's whistle for [*faute, fin*]; **4** (huer) to hiss, to boo [*vedette, politicien*]; **elle s'est fait ~** she was hissed ou booed; **5**◑ (boire) to knock back○ [*verre, bouteille*]; **6**◑ (dérober) to steal, to pinch.
II *vi* **1** (produire un son) [*personne, vent, train, bouilloire*] to whistle; [*projectile*] to whistle through the air; [*oiseau, insecte*] to chirp; [*serpent*] to hiss; **2** (donner un coup de sifflet) to blow one's whistle.

sifflet /siflɛ/ *nm* **1** (instrument) whistle; **coup de ~** whistle; **coup de ~ final** Sport final whistle; **au (coup de) ~ vous vous arrêtez!** when the whistle blows, stop!; **2** (sifflement) (de locomotive) whistle; (de désapprobation) hiss, boo, catcalls (*pl*); (de bouilloire) whistling ¢; **s'en aller sous les ~s** [*joueur*] to be booed off the field; [*chanteur, acteur*] to be hissed off the stage.
IDIOMES **couper le ~ à qn**○ (faire taire) to shut sb up○; (interloquer) to take the wind out of sb's sails.

siffleur, **-euse** /siflœʀ, øz/ I *adj* [*oiseau*] chirping; [*serpent*] hissing.
II *nm,f* (personne qui siffle) whistler; (personne qui hue) booer.

siffleux /siflø/ *nm* C (marmotte) groundhog, woodchuck.

sifflotement /siflɔtmɑ̃/ *nm* whistling ¢.

siffloter /siflɔte/ [1] I *vtr* to whistle [sth] to oneself [*air, chanson*].
II *vi* to whistle away to oneself; **~ entre ses dents** to whistle a tune under one's breath.

sigillaire /siʒilɛʀ/ I *adj* [*anneau, histoire*] signet, sigillary spéc.
II *nm* sigillaria.

sigillographie /siʒilɔɡʀafi/ *nf* sigillography.

sigle /siɡl/ *nm* acronym.

sigma /siɡma/ *nm inv* sigma.

signal, *pl* **-aux** /siɲal, o/ *nm* signal; **~ convenu** agreed signal; **~ audio/radio/vidéo** audio/radio/video signal; **au ~ de qn** at sb's signal; **donner le ~ de qch** to give the signal for sth; **donner le ~ du départ** gén, Mil to give the signal to leave; Sport to give the starting signal; **donner le ~ d'entrée à qn** to cue sb in.
■ **~ d'alarme** alarm signal; **tirer le ~ d'alarme** lit to pull the alarm; fig to raise the alarm; **~ d'appel** Télécom call waiting service; **~ de danger** danger signal; **~ de détresse** Aviat, Naut distress signal; Aut emergency signal; **~ lumineux** traffic light; **~ de ralentissement** speed limit sign; **~ sonore** (de répondeur) tone.

signalement /siɲalmɑ̃/ *nm* (d'individu, objet) description.

signaler /siɲale/ [1] I *vtr* **1** (faire remarquer) **~ qch à qn**, **~ qch à l'attention de qn** to bring sth to sb's attention, to point sth out to sb; **~ à qn que** to point out to sb that; **je leur ai signalé qu'on était pressé** I pointed out to them that time was getting short; **2** (faire savoir) **~ qch à qn** to inform sb of sth; **on m'a signalé votre absence** I was informed of your absence; **~ à qn que** to inform sb that; **je leur ai signalé que je viendrais** I informed them that I would be coming; **3** (rappeler) **~ à qn que** to remind sb that; **je te signale que tu parles à ton père** may I remind you that you're speaking to your father; **4** (indiquer) to indicate [*travaux, danger, présence*]; **un virage mal/bien signalé** a badly/well signposted bend; **5** (rapporter) to report [*fait, événement*]; **rien à ~** nothing to report; **des vols sont parfois signalés** thefts are sometimes reported; **6** (dénoncer) to report [*personne*]; **~ qn à la police** to report sb to the police.
II **se signaler** *vpr* **se ~ par qch** to distinguish oneself by sth; **il s'est toujours signalé par son courage/intelligence** he's always been known for his bravery/intelligence; **se ~ à l'attention de qn** to get oneself noticed by sb.

signalétique /siɲaletik/ *adj* descriptive; **photo ~** identity photograph; **renseignement ~** detail of identity; **fiche ~** specification sheet; **plaque ~** rating plate.

signalisation /siɲalizasjɔ̃/ *nf* **1** (système) signalling[GB]; **2** (réseau) signals (*pl*).
■ **~ horizontale** road markings (*pl*); **~ de piste** Aviat runway lights and markings (*pl*); **~ routière** roadsigns and markings (*pl*); **~ verticale** roadsigns (*pl*).

signaliser /siɲalize/ [1] *vtr* to signpost [*route, itinéraire*]; to put up signals along [*chenal, voie ferrée*]; to mark out and light [*piste d'atterrissage*]; **la route est mal signalisée** the road is badly signposted.

signataire /siɲatɛʀ/ *nmf* (personne) signatory; **les pays ~s de l'accord** the countries who are signatories to the agreement.

signature /siɲatyʀ/ *nf* **1** (inscription) signature; **apposer sa ~** to append one's signature; **article publié sous la ~ de X** article published under the name of X; **2** (droit de signer) **avoir la ~ de qn** to have the right to sign for sb; **avoir la ~ sur un compte** to be authorized to sign on an account; **3** (fait de signer) signing (**de** of); **4** (engagement) **il a donné sa ~** he signed, he put his signature to it; **5** (caractéristique) hallmarks (*pl*); **cet acte porte la ~ de Zorro** this act bears all the hallmarks of Zorro.

signe /siɲ/ *nm* **1** (indice) sign; **~ précurseur** omen; **c'est bon/mauvais ~** it's a good/bad sign; **c'est ~ de pluie** it's a sign of rain; **c'est ~ que** it's a sign that; **donner des ~s de faiblesse** to show signs of weakness; **un ~ des temps** a sign of the times; **~ distinctif** or **particulier** distinguishing feature; **c'était un ~ du destin** it was fate; **2** (symbole) gén, Astrol sign; (d'écriture) mark; **le ~ égale/plus** the equals/plus sign; **~s de ponctuation** punctuation marks; **~ diacritique** diacritic mark; **~ typographique** typographic mark; **marquer qch d'un ~** to put a mark against sth; **~ cabalistique** cabalistic sign; **~ astral** star sign; **~ du zodiaque** sign of the zodiac; **~ de terre/d'eau/de feu/d'air** earth/water/fire/air sign; **être né sous le ~ du Cancer** to be born under (the sign of) Cancer; **placé sous le ~ de** fig, journ marked by [*violence, espoir*]; **3** (geste) sign; **faire ~ à qn** lit to wave to sb; (contacter) to get in touch with sb; **faire ~ à qn de faire** to motion sb to do [*parler, commencer, avancer, partir*]; to beckon sb to do [*avancer, reculer, tourner, s'arrêter*]; **faire (un) ~ de la main à qn** to gesture to sb; **il m'a fait ~ de la tête** (pour que je vienne) he beckoned to me; (pour approuver, me saluer) he nodded to me; (pour désapprouver) he shook his head; **d'un ~ de la main/tête, elle m'a montré la cuisine** she pointed to/nodded her head in the direction of the kitchen; **faire ~ que oui/que non** to indicate agreement/disagreement; **faire un ~ de refus** to indicate one's refusal; **faire comprendre par un ~ que** to indicate that; **on se faisait des ~s pendant que** we were making signs to each other while; **faire de grands ~s à qn** to gesticulate to sb; **faire un ~ amical** to give a friendly wave (**à** to); **échanger des ~s d'intelligence** or **de connivence avec qn** (regards) to exchange knowing looks with sb; (gestes) to gesture knowingly to sb; **en ~ de respect/protestation** as a sign of respect/protest; **4** Ling, Méd sign.
■ **~ de la croix** sign of the cross; **faire le ~ de la croix, faire un ~ de croix** to make the sign of the cross; **~ extérieur de richesse** outward sign of wealth.
IDIOMES **il n'a pas donné ~ de vie depuis six mois** there's been no sign of him for six months.

signer /siɲe/ [1] I *vtr* **1** (apposer sa signature sur) to sign [*contrat, traité, lettre, chèque, tableau*]; **~ de son nom de jeune fille/d'un pseudonyme** to sign with one's maiden name/with a pseudonym; **'signé Dupont'** 'signed Dupont'; **un tract non signé** an unsigned pamphlet; **il signe son troisième roman** he's written his third novel; **un parfum signé X** a perfume by X; **ça, c'est signé ta sœur**○! that's your sister all over○!; **~ son arrêt de mort** fig to sign one's own death warrant; **le disque compact a signé la fin du 33 tours** fig the compact disc signalled[GB] the end of the LP; **2** Tech to hallmark [*pièce d'orfèvrerie*].
II **se signer** *vpr* to cross oneself.

signet /siɲɛ/ *nm* bookmark.

signifiant, **~e** /siɲifjɑ̃, ɑ̃t/ I *adj* Ling significant, meaningful.
II *nm* Ling signifier.

significatif, **-ive** /siɲifikatif, iv/ *adj* **1** (porteur de sens) [*détail, exemple, titre, geste*] significant; **il est ~ que** it is significant that; **2** (important) [*recul, rôle, changement, consé-*

quences] significant; **de manière significative** [*changer, augmenter*] significantly.

signification /siɲifikasjɔ̃/ *nf* **1** (sens) gén meaning; Ling signification; **2** (portée) importance; **avoir une ~ politique** to be politically significant; **3** Jur notification.

significativement /siɲifikativmɑ̃/ *adv* significantly.

signifié /siɲifje/ *nm* Ling signified.

signifier /siɲifje/ [1] *vtr* **1** (avoir pour sens) to mean; **qu'est-ce que ça signifie?** (question normale) what does it mean?; (ton mécontent) what is the meaning of this?; **2** (impliquer) to mean; **cela signifie que** it means that; **3** fml (notifier) **~ qch à qn** to inform sb of sth [*décision, refus*]; **~ à qn que** to inform sb that; **~ son congé à qn** to give sb notice; **~ à un employé qu'il est congédié** to inform an employee of his/her dismissal; **~ à un ami de se tenir prêt à partir** to tell a friend to be ready to leave; **4** Jur **~ qch à qn** to notify sb of sth.

sikh /sik/ *adj, nm* Sikh.

silence /silɑ̃s/ *nm* **1** (absence de bruit) silence; **dans le ~ de la nuit** in the silence of the night; **la manifestation s'est déroulée dans le ~** the demonstration took place in silence; **un ~ de mort** a deathly silence ou hush; **le ~ absolu** absolute ou dead silence; ▶ **or²**; **2** (fait de se taire) silence; **~!** silence!; **'un peu de ~ s'il vous plaît'** 'quiet please'; **un ~ poli/gêné/pesant** a polite/an embarrassed/a heavy silence; **ses longs ~s** his/her long silences; **après six mois de ~** after six months' silence; **en ~** [*travailler, marcher, souffrir*] in silence; **garder le ~** to keep silent; **réduire qn au ~** (empêcher de s'exprimer) to reduce sb to silence; (tuer) to silence sb; **réduire un mouvement/l'opposition au ~** to silence a movement/the opposition; **passer qch sous ~** to pass over sth in silence; **ta nomination a été passée sous ~** your nomination was passed over in silence; **3** (pause dans propos) silence; **la conversation fut entrecoupée de ~s** the conversation was interspersed with silences; **4** Mus rest.

silencieusement /silɑ̃sjøzmɑ̃/ *adv* silently.

silencieux, **-ieuse** /silɑ̃sjø, øz/ **I** *adj* **1** (sans bruit) [*maison, ville, dîner, manifestation*] silent; **2** (qui ne parle pas) [*personne, public, classe*] silent; **rester ~** to remain silent (**sur** about); **la presse reste étonnamment silencieuse sur sa démission** the press remains surprisingly silent about his/her resignation; **3** (peu bruyant) [*aspirateur, moteur*] quiet.

II *nm* **1** (sur une arme) silencer; **2** Aut (de pot d'échappement) silencer GB, muffler US.

Silésie /silezi/ ▶ **692** *nprf* Silesia.

silex /silɛks/ *nm inv* (roche, objet) flint; **en/de ~** flint (*épith*).

silhouette /silwɛt/ *nf* (en contre-jour) silhouette; (dans l'obscurité) (de personne) figure; (d'objet) shape; (dans le lointain) outline.

silhouetter /silwete/ [1] **I** *vtr* to draw an outline of.

II se silhouetter *vpr* to be silhouetted (**sur** against).

silicate /silikat/ *nm* silicate.

silice /silis/ *nf* silica.

siliceux, **-euse** /silisø, øz/ *adj* siliceous.

silicium /silisjɔm/ *nm* silicon; **en/au ~** silicon (*épith*).

silicone /silikon/ *nf, nm* silicone.

■ **~ élastomère** silicone rubber.

silicose /silikoz/ ▶ **271** *nf* silicosis.

sillage /sijaʒ/ *nm* **1** (de navire) wake; (d'avion) (visible) vapour[GB] trail; (invisible) slipstream; **2** (de personne) wake; (de parfum) trail; **dans le ~ de qn/qch** in the wake of sb/sth; **3** Phys wake.

sillement /sijmɑ̃/ *nm* C (sifflement) buzzing.

siller○ /sije/ [1] *vi* C to buzz; **les oreilles me sillent** my ears are buzzing.

sillon /sijɔ̃/ *nm* **1** Agric furrow; **2** (rainure) line; **3** (ride profonde) furrow; **4** Anat, Zool fissure; **5** Audio (de disque) groove; **6** Géog line; Géol fissure.

sillonner /sijɔne/ [1] *vtr* **1** (parcourir) [*personne, bicyclette, automobile*] to go up and down; [*aéronef*] to fly to and fro across; [*navire*] to sail to and fro across; [*réseau*] to criss-cross; **2** (creuser) to furrow; **sillonné de rides** furrowed with wrinkles.

silo /silo/ *nm* silo; **~ à céréales** or **grains** grain silo; **mettre qch en ~** to load sth into a silo.

silure /silyʀ/ *nm* silurid.

simagrée /simagʀe/ *nf* play-acting ¢; **arrête tes ~s!** stop all that play-acting!; **se laisser prendre aux ~s de qn** to get taken in by sb's play-acting.

simien, **-ienne** /simjɛ̃, ɛn/ **I** *adj* simian.

II *nm* simian.

simiesque /simjɛsk/ *adj* ape-like.

similaire /similɛʀ/ *adj* similar (**à** to).

similarité /similaʀite/ *nf* similarity (**avec** with; **entre** between).

similicuir /similikɥiʀ/ *nm* imitation leather, Leatherette®.

similigravure /similigʀavyʀ/ *nf* halftone.

similitude /similityd/ *nf* gén, Math similarity (**entre** between).

simonie /simɔni/ *nf* simony.

simoun /simun/ *nm* simoon.

simple /sɛ̃pl/ **I** *adj* **1** (facile) [*problème, question, situation, idée*] simple, straightforward; [*choix, moyen, façon, explication, calcul*] simple; **son raisonnement est très ~** his/her reasoning is very simple; **je veux des phrases ~s mais correctes** I want simple but correct sentences; **la situation est loin d'être ~** the situation is far from (being) simple ou straightforward; **c'est (bien) ~, il ne fait plus rien** he simply doesn't do anything any more; **pourquoi faire ~ quand on peut faire compliqué?** iron why not make life even more difficult for yourself?; **2** (sans prétention) [*repas, cérémonie, mariage, vie, goûts*] simple; [*décoration, intérieur*] plain; [*vêtement*] simple, plain; [*personne, air*] unaffected, unpretentious; **elle portait une jupe toute ~** she was wearing a very simple ou plain skirt; **elle est ~ et naturelle** she's unaffected and natural; **il est resté très ~ malgré son succès** he's remained very unpretentious in spite of his success; **3** (modeste) [*origines*] modest; **venir d'un milieu ~** to come from a modest background; **4** (ordinaire) [*avertissement, remarque*] mere; [*fonctionnaire, travailleur*] ordinary; **c'est une ~ question d'honneur/de bon sens** it's simply ou purely a question of honour[GB]/of common sense; **un ~ tour de clé suffit** just one turn of the key does it; **il est ~ garçon de café/employé du bureau** he's just a waiter in a café/a clerk; **il l'a mis KO d'un ~ coup de poing** he knocked him out with a single blow; **même en hiver, il n'est vêtu que d'une ~ chemise** even in winter he only ou just wears a shirt; **pour la ~ raison que** for the simple reason that; **le ~ fait de poser la question** the mere fact of asking the question; **par ~ curiosité** out of pure curiosity; **sur ~ présentation du passeport** simply on presentation of one's passport; **ce ne sera qu'une ~ formalité/vérification** it will be a mere formality/a simple check; **réduire qch à sa plus ~ expression** to reduce sth to a minimum; **5** (peu intelligent) [*personne*] simple; **il est gentil mais un peu ~** he's nice but a bit simple; **6** Chimie, Nucl, Bot simple; **7** Ling [*passé, futur*] simple; **8** (non multiple) [*cornet de glace, nœud*] single.

II *nm* **1** (dans un calcul) **le prix varie du ~ au double** the price can turn out to be twice as high; **2** Sport **~ dames/messieurs** ladies'/men's singles (*pl*).

III simples *nmpl* Bot, Pharm medicinal herbs.

■ **~ d'esprit** simple-minded; **c'est un** or **il est ~ d'esprit** he's simple-minded; **~ soldat** private.

simplement /sɛ̃pləmɑ̃/ *adv* **1** (seulement) [*approuver, déclarer, rappeler*] simply; **vas-y, ~ fais attention** you can go, only be careful; **il faut ~ remplir cette page** you simply have to fill in GB ou out US this page; **2** (sans sophistication) [*se vêtir, vivre*] simply; (absolument) [*charmant, remarquable, inadmissible*] simply; **tout ~** quite simply; **3** (sans difficulté) easily.

simplet, **-ette** /sɛ̃plɛ, ɛt/ *adj* [*personne*] simple, simple-minded; [*raisonnement*] simplistic.

simplicité /sɛ̃plisite/ *nf* **1** (facilité) simplicity; **grâce à sa ~ d'utilisation** thanks to its ease of use; **c'est d'une ~ enfantine** it's so easy a child could do it; **2** (caractère) (de personne) unpretentiousness, lack of pretention; (de choses) simplicity; **recevoir qn en toute ~** to receive sb very simply; **la ~ du style/de la présentation** the simplicity of the style/of the presentation; **avec une grande ~ de moyens** with very limited resources ou means; **avec ~** simply.

■ **~ d'esprit** simpleness.

simplifiable /sɛ̃plifjabl/ *adj* **1** gén that can be simplified (*après n*); **2** Math reducible.

simplificateur, **-trice** /sɛ̃plifikatœʀ, tʀis/ *adj* [*méthode*] simplifying; pej [*propos, schéma*] simplistic.

simplification /sɛ̃plifikasjɔ̃/ *nf* **1** gén simplification; **2** Math reduction.

simplifier /sɛ̃plifje/ [2] **I** *vtr* **1** gén to simplify [*exercice, transaction, texte*]; **pour ~, on peut dire que** to simplify matters, one can say that; **~ la vie** or **l'existence de qn** to make life easier for sb; **ça te simplifiera la vie** it will make life easier for you; **2** Math to reduce [*fraction*].

II se simplifier *vpr* **se ~ la vie** or **l'existence** to make life easier for oneself.

simplisme /sɛ̃plism/ *nm* simplism; **un raisonnement d'un ~ désarmant** a disarmingly simplistic piece of reasoning.

simpliste /sɛ̃plist/ **I** *adj* simplistic.

II *nmf* **c'est un ~** he thinks in simplistic terms.

simulacre /simylakʀ/ *nm* liter **1** (action simulée) pretence[GB]; **~ de combat/d'exécution/de procès** mock fight/execution/trial; **2** (travesti) péj sham; **le référendum tient du ~** the referendum is a sham; **~ de justice** travesty of justice; **~ de bonheur/réussite** illusion of happiness/success.

simulateur, **-trice** /simylatœʀ, tʀis/ **I** *nm,f* (personne qui feint) shammer, faker; (faux malade) malingerer.

II *nm* Tech simulator; **~ de vol** flight simulator; **~ de conduite** driving simulator.

simulation /simylasjɔ̃/ *nf* **1** gén, Méd simulation; (pour éviter une corvée) malingering ¢; **c'est de la ~!** he/she's putting it on○ ou faking○!; **2** Sci (méthode) simulation; Ordinat (computer) modelling[GB]; (représentation) model; **étudier qch en ~** Ordinat to work sth out using a computer model; **3** Jur **~ de vente** fictitious sale.

simuler /simyle/ [1] *vtr* **1** (feindre) to feign, to simulate [*attaque, émotion, sentiment*]; **~ la folie** to feign madness; **~ la douleur** to pretend to be in pain; **2** (reproduire) Ordinat, Tech to simulate [*effets, conditions, situation*]; **3** Jur **~ une vente** to effect a fictitious sale; **~ des opérations** Compta to effect fictitious operations.

simultané, **~e** /simyltane/ *adj* [*traduction, transmission*] simultaneous; **en ~** simultaneously.

simultanéité /simyltaneite/ *nf* simultaneity.

simultanément /simyltanemɑ̃/ *adv* simultaneously, at the same time; **~, les**

demandes se font plus nombreuses at the same time, applications are getting more numerous; **le président a paru ~ hésitant et inquiet** the president appeared both hesitant and worried.

Sinaï /sinai/ *nprm* **le ~** Sinai; **le mont ~** Mount Sinai.

sinanthrope /sinɑ̃tʀɔp/ *nm* Sinanthropus.

sinapisme /sinapism/ *nm* mustard plaster.

sincère /sɛ̃sɛʀ/ *adj* **1** (dont on ne peut douter) [*personne, confession, regret, affection*] sincere; [*ami*] true (*épith*); (non feint) [*intérêt, émotion, offre, soutien, combat*] genuine; (franc) [*opinion, portrait*] honest; **sois ~ pour une fois!** be honest for once!; **2** (en correspondance) **~s condoléances** sincere ou heartfelt sympathy; **veuillez agréer mes ~s salutations** yours sincerely.

sincèrement /sɛ̃sɛʀmɑ̃/ *adv* **1** (sans feindre) [*regretter, croire*] sincerely; [*penser*] genuinely; [*remercier, parler, s'exprimer*] sincerely; **dis-moi ~ ce que tu en penses** tell me honestly what you think of it, give me your honest opinion of it; **je suis ~ désolé** I'm truly sorry; **2** (franchement) frankly; **~, j'aimerais mieux rester** frankly ou to be honest, I would rather stay; **~, tu n'en ferais pas autant?** be honest, wouldn't you do the same?

sincérité /sɛ̃seʀite/ *nf* (de personne, paroles, d'affection) sincerity; (de réponse, d'opinion) honesty; (d'offre, de soutien) genuineness.

sinécure /sinekyʀ/ *nf* sinecure; **ce n'est pas une ~** it's no sinecure.

sine die /sinedje/ *loc adv* sine die.

sine qua non /sinekwanɔn/ *loc adj* **condition ~** sine qua non (**pour** for).

Singapour /sɛ̃gapuʀ/ **▶ 321**, **416** *nprm* Singapore.

singapourien, **-ienne** /sɛ̃gapuʀjɛ̃, ɛn/ **▶ 537** *adj* Singaporean.

Singapourien, **-ienne** /sɛ̃gapuʀjɛ̃, ɛn/ **▶ 537** *nm,f* Singaporean.

singe /sɛ̃ʒ/ *nm* **1** Zool monkey; (sans queue) ape; **les grands ~s** the apes, the large primates; **2** fig (imitateur) mimic; (personne agile) **c'est un vrai ~** he's very agile; **faire le ~** to clown about GB ou around; **3**○ (bœuf de conserve) corned beef; **4**◐ (patron) boss.

IDIOMES **malin comme un ~** as cunning ou sly as a fox; **laid comme un ~** as ugly as sin; **payer en monnaie de ~** to let sb whistle for his/her money; **ce n'est pas à un vieux ~ qu'on apprend à faire la grimace** Prov don't teach your grandmother to suck eggs.

singer /sɛ̃ʒe/ [13] *vtr* to ape [*personne, manière*]; to feign, to fake [*attitude, sentiment*].

singerie /sɛ̃ʒʀi/ **I** *nf* (ménagerie) monkey house.

II singeries *nfpl* (grimaces) faces; (pitreries) antics; **faire des ~s** to monkey about GB ou around.

singleton /sɛ̃glətɔ̃/ *nm* Jeux, Math singleton.

singulariser /sɛ̃gylaʀize/ [1] **I** *vtr* (faire remarquer) to make [sb] conspicuous; (traiter différemment) to single [sb] out.

II se singulariser *vpr* to call attention to oneself; **se ~ par qch/en faisant qch** to distinguish oneself by sth/by doing sth.

singularité /sɛ̃gylaʀite/ *nf* **1** (chose anormale) peculiarity, singularity; **2** (caractère unique) uniqueness; **3** Phys singularity.

singulier, **-ière** /sɛ̃gylje, ɛʀ/ **I** *adj* **1** (insolite) peculiar; **un personnage ~** an unusual character; **2** (individuel) **combat ~** single combat.

II *nm* **1** Ling singular; **mettre au ~** to put into the singular; **à la deuxième personne du ~** in the second person singular; **2** (caractère étonnant) singularity.

singulièrement /sɛ̃gyljɛʀmɑ̃/ *adv* **1** (curieusement) [*vêtu, différent*] oddly; [*agir, penser, se comporter*] oddly; **2** (beaucoup) [*augmenter, accroître, contraster*] radically; **manquer ~ de** to be singularly lacking in.

sinistre /sinistʀ/ **I** *adj* **1** [*personnage, projet*] sinister; [*bruit, lueur*] sinister, ominous; [*lieu, paysage, avenir*] bleak; [*soirée, invité*] dreary; **2** (*before n*) **de ~s crétins**○**/crapules** absolute idiots/crooks.

II *nm* (désastre) disaster; (accident) accident; (incendie) blaze; **déterminer l'étendue du ~** to assess the extent of the damage.

sinistré, **~e** /sinistʀe/ **I** *adj* [*personne, famille, pays*] stricken (*épith*); **région ~e** disaster area.

II *nm,f* disaster victim.

sinistrose○ /sinistʀoz/ *nf* doom and gloom.

sinologie /sinɔlɔʒi/ *nf* sinology.

sinologue /sinɔlɔg/ *nmf* sinologist.

sinon /sinɔ̃/ **I** *conj* **1** (autrement) otherwise, or else; **j'y vais ~ je vais être en retard** I must go otherwise I'm going to be late; **arrête ~ je crie/je me fâche!** stop or (else) I'll scream/I'll get cross!; **2** (à part) except, apart from; **il ne s'intéresse à rien ~ à la musique** he has no interests except music; **personne n'est venu ~ quelques amis** nobody came apart from a few friends; **ça ne sert à rien, ~ à perdre du temps** not only is it pointless but it wastes time; **3** (pour ne pas dire) not to say; **c'est une réussite ~ un chef d'œuvre** it's a success, not to say a masterpiece; **c'est devenu difficile ~ impossible** it has become difficult if not impossible.

II sinon que *loc conj* except that, other than that; **je ne sais rien ~ qu'il est parti** I don't know anything except that he's gone.

sinople /sinɔpl/ *nm* Hérald vert.

sinoque○ /sinɔk/ **I** *adj* crazy○.

II *nmf* crazy person, headcase○.

sinueux, **-euse** /sinɥø, øz/ *adj* [*ligne*] sinuous; [*cours d'eau*] winding, meandering; [*sentier*] winding; [*approche*] tortuous.

sinuosité /sinɥozite/ *nf* **les ~s d'un cours d'eau/d'un sentier** the twists and turns of a river/of a path; **les ~s d'une ligne** the curves of a line.

sinus /sinys/ *nm inv* **1** Anat sinus; **2** Math sine (**de** of).

sinusite /sinyzit/ **▶ 271** *nf* sinusitis ¢.

sinusoïdal, **~e** /sinyzɔidal/ *adj* Math, Phys sinusoidal.

sinusoïde /sinyzɔid/ *nf* sine curve, sinusoid.

Sion /sjɔ̃/ *npr* Zion.

sionisme /sjɔnism/ *nm* Zionism.

sioniste /sjɔnist/ *adj, nmf* Zionist.

sioux /sju/ **I** *adj inv* Sioux.

II ▶ 462 *nm* Ling Sioux.

Sioux /sju/ *nmf inv* Sioux.

siphoïde /sifɔid/ *adj* siphon-like.

siphon /sifɔ̃/ *nm* **1** (tuyau) gén siphon; (d'évier, de lavabo) U-bend; **déboucher le ~** to unblock the U-bend; **2** (bouteille) siphon (bottle); **un ~ d'eau de Seltz** a soda-siphon; **3** Bot, Zool siphon.

siphonné○, **~e** /sifɔne/ *adj* nuts○, crazy○.

siphonner /sifɔne/ [1] *vtr* Tech to siphon (off).

sire /siʀ/ *nm* Hist Sire; **un triste ~** a disreputable character.

sirène /siʀɛn/ *nf* **1** gén, Mil siren; (de bateau) foghorn; (d'usine) hooter GB, siren; **~ des pompiers** (dans la ville) fire siren; (sur un camion) siren on a fire engine; **2** Mythol gén mermaid; (au chant fatal) siren; **être séduit par les ~s de l'argent/du pouvoir/d'Hollywood** to be seduced by the allure of money/of power/of Hollywood.

■ **~ d'alarme** fire alarm.

IDIOMES **écouter le chant des ~s** to listen to the sirens' song.

sirocco /siʀoko/ *nm* sirocco; **un vent de ~** a sirocco.

sirop /siʀo/ *nm* **1** Culin (pour dessert) syrup GB ou sirup US; (boisson) cordial; **~ d'érable** maple syrup GB ou sirup US; **~ de fraise/menthe/cassis** strawberry/mint/blackcurrant cordial; **~ de citron/d'orange** ≈ lemon/orange squash; **~ d'orgeat** barley water; **2** Pharm syrup GB ou sirup US, mixture; **~ pectoral** or **contre la toux** cough mixture.

siroter○ /siʀɔte/ [1] *vtr* to sip.

sirupeux, **-euse** /siʀypø, øz/ *adj* lit, fig syrupy GB, sirupy US.

sis, **~e** /si, siz/ *adj* located.

sisal /sizal/ *nm* sisal; **corde en ~** sisal rope; **tapis de ~** sisal matting.

sismicité /sismisite/ *nf* seismicity (**de** of).

sismique /sismik/ *adj* seismic.

sismogramme /sismɔgʀam/ *nm* seismogram.

sismographe /sismɔgʀaf/ *nm* seismograph.

sismographie /sismɔgʀafi/ *nf* seismography.

sismologie /sismɔlɔʒi/ *nf* seismology.

sismologique /sismɔlɔʒik/ *adj* **centre ~** seismological centre[GB]

sismologue /sismɔlɔg/ **▶ 510** *nmf* seismologist.

sistre /sistʀ/ **▶ 534** *nm* sistrum.

Sisyphe /sizif/ *npr* Sisyphus; **le mythe de ~** the myth of Sisyphus.

sitar /sitaʀ/ **▶ 534** *nm* sitar.

site /sit/ *nm* **1** (lieu pittoresque) gén area; **~ touristique** or **pittoresque** place of interest; **visitez les ~s d'Égypte** visit Egypt's places of interest; **les merveilleux ~s du Colorado/de la Côte d'Azur** the splendours[GB] of Colorado/of the Côte d'Azur; **~ archéologique** archeological site; **~ classé** conservation area; **2** Ind, Comm (lieu d'une implantation particulière) site; **aménager un ~ de barrage** to develop the site for a dam; **rechercher un ~ d'implantation pour une entreprise** to search for a site to start up a business; **hors ~** off-site; **3** Mil (**angle de**) **~** angle of sight.

■ **~ d'enfouissement** nuclear dump; **~ propre** (voie réservée) bus lane.

sit-in /sitin/ *nm inv* sit-in.

sitôt /sito/

■ **Note** *sitôt* conjonction et préposition se traduit le plus souvent par *as soon as*. Mais attention au choix du temps: *sitôt rentré de voyage* (qu'il rentrera) = as soon as he gets back from his trip; (qu'il est rentré) = as soon as he got back from his trip; *sitôt la fin du mauvais temps* (dans le passé) = as soon as the bad weather had passed; (dans l'avenir) = as soon as the bad weather has passed.

I *adv* **~ après** (tout de suite) immediately after; (peu de temps) soon after; **elle est arrivée ~ après** she arrived soon afterwards; **nous partirons ~ après** we'll leave immediately afterwards; **je n'y retournerai pas de ~** I won't go back there in a hurry○.

II *conj, prép* **~ que** as soon as; **~ qu'ils arriveront**, **~ leur arrivée** as soon as they come.

IDIOMES **~ dit, ~ fait**† no sooner said than done.

sittelle /sitɛl/ *nf* nuthatch.

situ: **in situ** /insity/ *loc adv* **étudier un animal/une plante in ~** to study an animal/a plant in its natural habitat; **faire un contrôle in ~** to do an on-the-spot check.

situation /sitɥasjɔ̃/ *nf* **1** (ensemble de conditions) situation; **analyser une ~ sous toutes ses faces** to analyse[GB] a situation from all sides; **renverser la ~** to reverse the situation; **être dans une ~ délicate/désespérée** to be in a delicate/hopeless situation; **200 personnes sont dans la même ~** 200 people are in the same situation ou position; **une population en ~ d'extrême pauvreté** a population suffering extreme poverty; **~ financière** financial standing ou status; **~ d'esclavage** slavery; **se retrouver en ~ de mendicité** to find oneself reduced to begging; **faire un stage en ~** to go on ou do work experience; ▶**intéressant**; **2** (emploi) job, position; **elle a une très bonne ~** she has a very good job; **se faire une ~** to get a good job; **il a perdu sa ~** he's lost his post ou job; **avoir une ~ stable** to have a steady job; **3** (emplacement) location (**de** of); **la ~ du magasin est idéale** the shop GB ou store US is ideally located ou has an ideal location.

■ **~ de compte** Fin bank statement; **~ de famille** Admin marital status, family status; **~ militaire** *status as regards military service*; **~ de trésorerie** Fin cash flow statement.

situer /sitɥe/ [1] **I** *vtr* **1** (déterminer la position de) (dans l'espace) to locate [*ville, pays*]; (dans le temps) to place; **notre maison est située dans le nord d'Oxford** our house is on the north side of Oxford; **l'hôtel est bien situé** the hotel is in a good location; **~ un événement dans le temps** to situate an event historically; **2** (définir) to situate [*écrivain, œuvre*]; **un homme qu'on a du mal à ~ politiquement** a man whose politics are difficult to define; **3** (placer) **~ une histoire en 2001/à Palerme** to set a story in 2001/in Palermo.

II se situer *vpr* **1** (se dérouler) **se ~ à Paris/à l'époque de la Révolution** to be set in Paris/at the time of the Revolution; **2** (être) **politiquement, je me situe plutôt à gauche/droite** politically I'm more to the left/right; **ses résultats se situent plutôt dans la moyenne** his/her results are more or less average.

SIVP /ɛsivepe/ *nm* (*abbr* = **stage d'initiation à la vie professionnelle**) *paid work experience for the young unemployed*.

six /sis, *but before consonant* si, *and before vowel* siz/ ▶545, 407, 212 *adj inv, pron, nm inv* six.

IDIOMES **faire une tête de ~ pieds de long** to pull a long face.

sixain = **sizain**.

six-huit /sisɥit/ *nm inv* Mus six-eight; **mesure à ~** six-eight time.

sixième /sizjɛm/ ▶545, 212 **I** *adj* sixth.

II *nf* Scol *first year of secondary school, age 11–12*.

six-quatre-deux○: **à la six-quatre-deux** /alasiskatdø/ *loc adv* sloppily; **faire un travail à la ~** to do a sloppy job.

sixte /sikst/ *nf* **1** Mus sixth; **2** Sport (en escrime) sixte.

sizain /sizɛ̃/ *nm* **1** Littérat hexastich; **2** Jeux *packet of six packs of cards*.

skaï® /skaj/ *nm* imitation leather, Leatherette®; **en ~** in imitation leather.

skate-board, *pl* **~s** /skɛtbɔʀd/ ▶449 *nm* (objet) skateboard; (activité) skateboarding; **faire du ~** to skateboard.

sketch, *pl* **~es** /skɛtʃ/ *nm* sketch (**sur** on, about).

ski /ski/ ▶449 *nm* **1** (matériel) ski; **des ~s courts** short skis; **une paire de ~s** a pair of skis; **on y va à ~s?** shall we go there on skis?; **chausser des ~s** to put on skis; **2** (activité) **le ~** skiing; **faire du ~** to ski, to go skiing; **station/chaussures/école de ~** ski resort/boots/school.

■ **~ acrobatique** aerial (in freestyle skiing); **~ alpin** Alpine skiing; **~ artistique** ballet (in freestyle skiing); **~ de descente** = **~ de piste**; **~ évolutif** short ski method (of skiing); **~ extrême** extreme skiing; **~ de fond** (activité) cross-country skiing; (matériel) cross-country ski; **~ sur gazon** turf skiing; **~ de haute montagne** high altitude skiing; **~ hors piste** off-piste skiing; **~ nautique** water skiing; **~ nordique** Nordic skiing; **~ de piste** (activité) downhill skiing; (matériel) downhill ski; **~ de randonnée** (activité) ski touring; (matériel) touring ski.

skiable /skjabl/ *adj* [*neige, domaine*] skiable.

ski-bob, *pl* **~s** /skibɔb/ ▶449 *nm* **1** (véhicule) skibob; **2** Sport skibobbing; **faire du ~** to skibob, to go skibobbing.

skier /skje/ [2] *vi* to ski; **~ hors piste** to go off-piste skiing, to ski off piste.

skieur, **-ieuse** /skjœʀ, øz/ *nm,f* skier.

skiff /skif/ ▶449 *nm* skiff; **course de ~** skiff race.

skipper /skipœʀ/ *nm* skipper.

slalom /slalɔm/ *nm* slalom; **~ géant/spécial** giant/special slalom; **faire du ~** lit to slalom; **faire du ~ entre les voitures** fig to zigzag between the cars.

slalomer /slalɔme/ [1] *vi* **1** Sport to slalom (**entre** between); **2** fig to zigzag (**entre** between).

slalomeur, **-euse** /slalɔmœʀ, øz/ *nm,f* slalom skier ou racer.

slave /slav/ *adj* Slavonic.

Slave /slav/ *nmf* Slav.

slavon /slavɔ̃/ ▶462 *nm* Ling Slavonic.

slavophile /slavɔfil/ *adj, nmf* Slavophile.

sleeping† /slipiŋ/ *nm* sleeping car.

slip /slip/ *nm* **1** (d'homme) underpants (*pl*), briefs (*pl*); (de femme) knickers (*pl*), pants (*pl*) GB, panties (*pl*) US; **2** Naut slipway.

■ **~ de bain** (d'homme) bathing trunks (*pl*); (de femme) bikini bottom; **~ brésilien** high-cut briefs (*pl*).

slogan /slɔgɑ̃/ *nm* slogan.

slovaque /slɔvak/ ▶462, 537 *adj, nm* Slovak.

Slovaque /slɔvak/ ▶537 *nmf* Slovak.

Slovaquie /slɔvaki/ ▶321 *nprf* Slovakia.

slovène /slɔvɛn/ ▶462, 537 **I** *adj* Slovene, Slovenian.

II *nm* Ling Slovene, Slovenian.

Slovène /slɔvɛn/ ▶537 *nmf* Slovene.

Slovénie /slɔveni/ ▶321 *nprf* Slovenia.

slow /slo/ *nm* slow dance; **danser un ~ avec qn** to have a slow dance with sb.

smala○ /smala/ *nf* (famille) tribe○; **ils ont débarqué avec toute la ~** they arrived with the whole tribe.

smalt /smalt/ *nm* smalt.

smaltine /smaltin/ *nf* smaltite.

smash, *pl* **~es** /smaʃ/ *nm* smash.

smasher /smaʃe/ [1] **I** *vtr* to smash [*balle*].

II *vi* to play a smash.

SME /ɛsəmə/ *nm*: *abbr* ▶**système**.

SMIC /smik/ *nm*: *abbr* ▶**salaire**.

smicard○, **~e** /smikaʀ, aʀd/ *nm,f* person on a minimum wage.

smocks /smɔk/ *nmpl* smocking ¢; **une robe à ~** a smocked dress.

smoking /smɔkiŋ/ *nm* dinner jacket GB, tuxedo.

snack○ /snak/, **snack-bar**, *pl* **~s** /snakbaʀ/ *nm* snack bar.

SNC /ɛsɛnse/ *nf*: *abbr* ▶**société**.

SNCF /ɛsɛnseɛf/ *nf* (*abbr* = **Société nationale des chemins de fer français**) *French national railway company*.

SNI /sni/ *nm* (*abbr* = **Syndicat national des instituteurs**) *French national union of primary-school teachers*.

sniff /snif/ *excl* boo-hoo!

sniffer◐ /snife/ [1] *vtr* drug users' slang to snort○ [*poudre*]; to sniff [*vapeurs*]; **~ de la cocaïne** to snort○ cocaine; **~ de la colle** to sniff glue.

snob /snɔb/ **I** *adj* [*personne*] stuck-up○; [*endroit, restaurant, soirée*] posh; **elle est très ~** she's very stuck-up○, she's a real snob.

II *nmf* snob; **c'est un ~** he's a snob.

snober /snɔbe/ [1] *vtr* to snub [*personne*].

snobinard○, **~e** /snɔbinaʀ, aʀd/ **I** *adj* [*personne*] snobby○, stuck-up○.

II *nm,f* snob.

snobisme /snɔbism/ *nm* snobbery.

sobre /sɔbʀ/ *adj* **1** (qui mange et boit peu) abstemious; (qui ne boit jamais d'alcool) teetotal; (qui n'a pas trop bu) sober; **il est très ~ ce soir** he's being very abstemious tonight; **je dois rester ~, c'est moi qui conduis** I can't drink much, I'm driving; **je suis ~, je peux conduire** I'm sober, so I can drive; **2** (mesuré) [*personne*] temperate, sober, moderate; [*discours, récit, langage*] sober, low-key; [*vie*] simple; **3** (simple) [*style*] plain, sober; [*architecture, décoration, vêtement, mise en scène*] sober.

IDIOMES **être ~ comme un chameau** to be abstemious.

sobrement /sɔbʀəmɑ̃/ *adv* **1** (avec modération) [*manger, boire*] in moderation; **2** (simplement) [*s'habiller*] plainly, soberly; [*dire*] soberly.

sobriété /sɔbʀijete/ *nf* **1** (fait de ne pas boire) temperance, sobriety sout; **2** (réserve) (de personne) restraint, sobriety sout; (de discours, critique) moderation; **3** (de style, ligne, mise en scène, d'art) sobriety sout.

sobriquet /sɔbʀikɛ/ *nm* nickname; **donner un ~ à qn** to give sb a nickname, to nickname sb.

soc /sɔk/ *nm* ploughshare GB, plowshare US.

sochalien, **-ienne** /sɔʃaljɛ̃, ɛn/ ▶857 *adj* of Sochaux.

Sochalien, **-ienne** /sɔʃaljɛ̃, ɛn/ *nm,f* (natif) native of Sochaux; (habitant) inhabitant of Sochaux.

Sochaux /sɔʃo/ ▶857 *npr* Sochaux.

sociabilité /sɔsjabilite/ *nf* **1** (aptitude) sociability; **2** (caractère) sociability, outgoing nature.

sociable /sɔsjabl/ *adj* **1** gén [*personne, tempérament*] sociable; **c'est quelqu'un de très ~** he/she's a very sociable person; **2** Sociol social.

social, **~e**, *mpl* **-iaux** /sɔsjal, o/ **I** *adj* **1** (relatif à la vie en société) [*rapports, phénomène, conventions, climat, politique*] social; **sur le plan ~** in social terms; **mesures ~es** social policy measures; **2** (propre à la société) [*catégorie, classe, inégalités, justice, cohésion*] social; **les origines ~es de qn, le milieu ~ de qn** sb's social background; **3** (relatif au travail) **conflit ~** industrial ou trade dispute; **revendications ~es** workers' demands.

II *nm* **le ~** social issues (*pl*); **faire du ~** [*gouvernement*] to take a keen interest in social issues.

social-démocrate, **sociale-démocrate**, *mpl* **sociaux-démocrates** /sɔsjaldemɔkʀat, sɔsjodemɔkʀat/ *adj, nm,f* social democrat.

social-démocratie /sɔsjaldemɔkʀasi/ *nf* social democracy.

socialement /sɔsjalmɑ̃/ *adv* socially; **être ~ pris en charge** to be under care of the social services.

socialisant, **~e** /sɔsjalizɑ̃, ɑ̃t/ *adj* with socialist leanings.

socialisation /sɔsjalizasjɔ̃/ *nf* **1** Sociol socialization; **2** Écon, Pol collectivization.

socialiser /sɔsjalize/ [1] *vtr* **1** Sociol to socialize [*individus*]; **2** Écon, Pol to collectivize.

socialisme /sɔsjalism/ *nm* socialism; **le ~ démocratique/scientifique/ révolutionnaire** democratic/scientific/revolutionary socialism; **le ~ utopique/d'État** utopian/State socialism.

socialiste /sɔsjalist/ *adj, nmf* socialist.

sociétaire /sɔsjetɛʀ/ *nmf* member.

société /sɔsjete/ *nf* **1** Sociol society; **vivre en ~** to live in society; **la vie en ~** life in society; **2** (communauté humaine) society; **la place de l'enfant dans la ~** the place of children in society; **3** (groupe humain) society; **les ~s primitives/modernes** primitive/modern societies; **dans notre ~** in our society; **4** (groupe spécifique) society; **~ savante/secrète** learned/secret society; **~ d'écrivains/d'artistes** writers'/artists' society; **~ de chasse/pêche/tir** hunting/angling/shooting club; **5** Ind, Jur, Fin company; **constituer une ~** to set up a

company; **~ d'emballage/de nettoyage** packaging/cleaning company; **6** (vie mondaine) society; **en ~** in society; **faire ses débuts dans la ~** to make one's debut in society; **la bonne/haute ~** polite/high society; **7** (compagnie) company, society sout; **rechercher la ~ de qn** to seek sb's company; **dans la ~ de qn** in sb's company.
■ **~ d'abondance** affluent society; **~ par actions** Jur, Fin joint stock company; **~ anonyme**, **SA** public company; **~ d'assistance** Assur motoring organization GB, automobile club; **~ de Bourse** Fin broking firm; **~ civile** Sociol society; Jur, Fin non-trading company; **~ civile immobilière**, **SCI** *investment company that rents out property*; **~ commerciale** Jur, Fin business firm; **~ de consommation** consumer society; **~ d'économie mixte** semipublic company; **~ écran** dummy company; **~ d'exploitation** development company; **~ fiduciaire** trust company; **~ d'investissement** investment company; **~ en nom collectif**, **SNC** general partnership; **~ à responsabilité limitée**, **SARL** private company; **~ de services** service company; **~ à succursales multiples** chain store; **Société de Jésus** Relig Society of Jesus; **Société des Nations**, **SDN** Hist League of Nations.

Société /sɔsjete/ ▶416 *nprf* **îles de la ~** Society Islands.

socioculturel, **-elle** /sɔsjokyltyʀɛl/ *adj* [*rapports*] sociocultural; **centre/animateur ~** recreation centre[GB]/officer.

socio-démocrate, *pl* **~s** /sɔsjodemɔkʀat/ **I** *adj* social democratic.
II *nmf* social democrat.

socio-économique, *pl* **~s** /sɔsjoekɔnɔmik/ *adj* socioeconomic.

socio-éducatif, **-ive**, *mpl* **~s** /sɔsjo edykatif, iv/ *adj* [*programme, système*] socio-educational.

sociogramme /sɔsjɔgʀam/ *nm* sociogram.

sociolinguistique /sɔsjolɛ̃gɥistik/ **I** *adj* sociolinguistic.
II *nf* sociolinguistics (+ *v sg*).

sociologie /sɔsjɔlɔʒi/ *nf* sociology.

sociologique /sɔsjɔlɔʒik/ *adj* sociological.

sociologiquement /sɔsjɔlɔʒikmɑ̃/ *adv* sociologically.

sociologue /sɔsjɔlɔg/ ▶510 *nmf* sociologist.

sociométrie /sɔsjometʀi/ *nf* sociometry.

socioprofessionnel, **-elle** /sɔsjopʀɔfɛsjɔnɛl/ *adj* social and occupational.

socle /sɔkl/ *nm* **1** (base) (de statue, pilier) pedestal, plinth; (de lampe, construction) base; (d'appareil) stand; **2** fig (base) basis; **3** Géol platform.
■ **~ continental** Géol continental platform.

socque /sɔk/ *nm* (chaussure) clog.

socquette /sɔkɛt/ *nf* ankle sock, anklet US.

Socrate /sɔkʀat/ *npr* Socrates.

socratique /sɔkʀatik/ *adj* Socratic.

soda /sɔda/ *nm* (eau gazeuse) soda water; (boisson gazeuse sucrée) fizzy drink GB, soda US.

sodé, **~e** /sɔde/ *adj* with soda (*épith, après n*).

sodique /sɔdik/ *adj* with sodium (*épith, après n*).

sodium /sɔdjɔm/ *nm* sodium.

Sodome /sɔdɔm/ ▶857 *npr* Sodom.

sodomie /sɔdɔmi/ *nf* sodomy, buggery.

sodomiser /sɔdɔmize/ [1] *vtr* to sodomize, to bugger.

sodomite /sɔdɔmit/ *nm* sodomite.

sœur /sœʀ/ *nf* **1** (dans la famille) sister; **c'est ma grande/petite ~**○ she's my big/little sister; **l'ignorance est souvent ~ de la misère** fig ignorance often goes hand in hand with poverty; **2** Relig sister; **une ~** a nun; **~ Anne** Sister Anne; **bonjour, ma ~** good morning, Sister; **elle est allée à l'école chez les ~s** she went to a convent school; **une ~ infirmière** a nursing sister.
■ **~ jumelle** twin sister; **~ de lait** foster sister.
IDIOMES **ils sont comme frère et ~** they are like brother and sister; **et ta ~**◐**!** piss off◐, go to hell◐!

sœurette○ /sœʀɛt/ *nf* sis○, sister.

sofa /sɔfa/ *nm* sofa.

Sofia /sɔfja/ ▶857 *npr* Sofia.

SOFRES /sɔfʀɛs/ *nf* (*abbr* = **Société française d'enquêtes par sondage**) *French national institute for market research and opinion polls.*

software /sɔftwɛʀ/ *nm* controv software package.

soi¹ /swa/ *pron pers* **1** (personne) **il faut avoir des amis autour de ~** one should have friends around one; **pour une meilleure connaissance de ~** for better self-knowledge; **apprendre la maîtrise de ~** to learn self-control; **rester maître de ~** to keep in control of oneself; **laisser la porte se refermer derrière ~** to let the door shut behind one; **développer sa confiance en ~** to build up one's self-confidence; **la haine de ~** self-hatred; **trouver en ~ les ressources nécessaires** to find the necessary resources within oneself; **garder qch pour ~** to keep sth to oneself; **malgré ~ on est ému** one is moved in spite of oneself; **choisir de rester entre ~**† to choose to keep to themselves; **2** (objet, concept, idée) **un épisode banal en ~** an episode that is in itself commonplace; **une activité considérée non comme un moyen mais comme une fin en ~** an activity that is considered not as a means but as an end in itself; **la logique n'est pas un objectif en ~** logic is not an aim in itself; **en ~, le sujet est intéressant** the subject is interesting in itself; **aller de ~** to go without saying; **cela va de ~** it goes without saying; **il va de ~ que je paie ma part** it goes without saying that I'll pay my share; **il va de ~ que sans votre soutien rien n'est possible** it goes without saying that nothing would be possible without your support; **ça devrait aller de ~** it should be obvious; **le parallèle allait de ~ entre...** the parallel was obvious between...; **publier une œuvre de cette nature ne va pas de ~** publishing a work of this kind is not so straightforward.

soi² /swa/ *nm* **1** Philos self; **2** Psych (ça) id.

soi-disant /swadizɑ̃/ **I** *adj inv* (*before n*) **1** (qui prétend être) self-styled; **2** (prétendu) controv [*démocratie, liberté, miracle*] so-called (*épith*).
II *loc adv* **1** (prétendument) supposedly; **il n'est pas allé à l'école ~ parce qu'il est malade** he hasn't gone to school, supposedly because he's ill; **elle a ~ la migraine** she has a migraine, or so she says; **~ que** it would appear that.

soie /swa/ *nf* **1** Tex silk; **~ grège/sauvage/artificielle** raw/wild/artificial silk; **2** (poil) bristle; **une brosse à cheveux en ~s naturelles** a bristle hairbrush; **3** Bot awn; **4** Tech (de couteau) tang.

soierie /swaʀi/ *nf* **1** (étoffe) silk; **une ~ légère** a light silk; **2** Ind silk industry; **3** Comm silk trade.

soif /swaf/ *nf* **1** (besoin de boire) thirst; **avoir ~** to be thirsty; **avoir une ~ terrible**○ to be terribly thirsty; **mourir de ~** lit to die of thirst; fig to be dying of thirst; **étancher sa ~** to quench one's thirst; **boire jusqu'à plus ~** to drink one's fill; **donner ~** to make one thirsty; **la terre a ~** the soil is thirsty; **il fait ~**○**!** hum it's thirsty work! hum; **2** (désir) **~ de** thirst for [*justice, liberté, revanche, amour*]; hunger or lust for [*pouvoir, richesses*]; **la ~ d'apprendre** the thirst for knowledge; **avoir ~ d'affection/de bonheur** to crave affection/happiness; **la ~ de sang** bloodthirstiness; **faire qch jusqu'à plus ~**○ to do sth until one has had enough.
IDIOMES **conserver une poire pour la ~** to save something for a rainy day.

soiffard○, **~e** /swafaʀ, aʀd/ *nm,f* boozer○; **quel ~ ce Zorec!** what a boozer that Zorec is!

soignant, **~e** /swaɲɑ̃, ɑ̃t/ *adj* [*personnel, équipe*] medical (*épith*); **médecin ~** doctor, GP GB.

soigné, **~e** /swaɲe/ **I** *pp* ▶ **soigner**.
II *pp adj* **1** (bien entretenu) [*mains, ongles*] well-manicured; [*coiffure, vêtements, tenue*] immaculate; **il est très ~ de sa personne** he's very well-groomed; **individu peu ~** unkempt person; **2** (bien fait) [*catalogue, revue, édition*] carefully produced; [*emballage, maquette*] carefully done; [*conception, organisation, tactique*] carefully thought out; [*réglage, alignement*] careful, meticulous; [*travail*] meticulous; **peu ~** [*emballage*] carelessly done; [*travail*] careless.
III○ *adj* (d'importance) **avoir une grippe ~e** to have terrible flu; **faire des reproches ~s à qn** to give sb a thorough dressing-down; **l'addition était ~e!** the bill GB ou check US was astronomical○!

soigner /swaɲe/ [1] **I** *vtr* **1** (chercher à guérir) to treat [*personne, animal, maladie*]; **~ un rhume avec de l'aspirine**® to treat a cold with aspirin; **sa patte n'est pas cassée, on pourra la ~** its paw isn't broken, we can treat it; **faire ~ qn** to get sb treatment; **se faire ~** to get treatment; **il n'y a pas moyen de se faire ~ correctement ici** you just can't get the proper treatment here; **il faut te faire ~**○**!** hum you should have your head examined!; **2** (s'occuper de) to look after [*personne, animal, client*]; **3** (faire attention à) to take care over [*tenue, présentation*]; to look after [*mains*]; **soignez votre écriture/orthographe** take care over your writing/spelling.
II se soigner *vpr* **1** (chercher à guérir) to treat oneself; **je me soigne aux antibiotiques** I'm treating myself with antibiotics; **elle n'aime pas se ~** she doesn't like to take anything when she's ill; **soigne-toi bien!** look after yourself!; **je ne suis pas très intelligent mais je me soigne** hum I'm not very clever but I'm working on it!; **2** (pouvoir être guéri) [*maladie*] to be treatable; **infection qui se soigne facilement aux antibiotiques** infection that can easily be treated with antibiotics; **ça se soigne, tu sais!** hum (time to) get the men in white coats! hum; **3** (veiller à sa tenue) to take care over one's appearance; (veiller à son bien-être) to take care of oneself.

soigneur /swaɲœʀ/ ▶510 *nm* Sport gén trainer; (de boxeur) second.

soigneusement /swaɲøzmɑ̃/ *adv* [*ranger, laver, examiner, décrire, choisir, préparer, éviter*] carefully; [*travailler*] meticulously; [*écrire, colorier*] neatly.

soigneux, **-euse** /swaɲø, øz/ *adj* **1** (consciencieux) conscientious; (précautionneux) careful; **être ~ dans ses choix** to choose carefully; **un utilisateur ~ de la langue** someone who is careful in his/her use of language; **2** (propre et ordonné) [*personne*] neat, tidy; **il est ~ de sa personne** he takes a lot of care with his appearance; **3** (bien fait) [*examen, recherche, ajustement*] careful.

soi-même /swamɛm/ *pron pers* **être ~** to be oneself; **rester fidèle à ~** to be true to oneself; **la connaissance de ~** knowing oneself, self-knowledge; **apprendre à se connaître ~** to learn to know oneself; **donner le meilleur de ~** to give the best of oneself, to give of one's best; **le plaisir de faire ~ des confitures** the pleasure of making one's own jam; **faire des pizzas ~, c'est facile** it's easy to make your own pizza; **le directeur ~ était là**○ the manager himself was there.

soin /swɛ̃/ I *nm* **1** (application) care; **avec ~** [*choisir, préparer, travailler*] carefully; **sans ~** carelessly; **avec beaucoup de** or **un grand ~** very carefully; **le ~ apporté (par qn) à qch** the care taken (by sb) over sth; **mettre un ~ infini à faire** to take infinite care in doing; **prendre ~ de qch** to take care of sth; **prendre ~ de qn/sa santé** to look after sb/one's health; **avoir** or **prendre ~ de faire** (s'appliquer) to be careful to do; (s'assurer) to make sure to do; **prends ~ de ne pas réveiller les enfants** be careful not to wake the children; **nous avons pris ~ d'éviter toute confrontation** we were careful to avoid any confrontation; **prendre ~ de sa petite personne** to coddle oneself; **son premier ~ a été d'appeler sa femme** the first thing he did was to call his wife; **laisser à qn/à d'autres le ~ de faire** to leave it to sb/to others to do; **je laisse au lecteur le ~ d'imaginer la suite** I leave it to the reader to imagine the rest; ▶ **apporter**, **confier**; **2** Cosmét (produit) product; **~ aux extraits cellulaires** product with cellular extracts; **~ de bronzage** suncare product; **~ antipelliculaire** dandruff treatment.

II **soins** *nmpl* **1** Méd (traitement) treatment ¢; (ensemble d'activités, service) care ¢; **recevoir/donner des ~s** to receive/give treatment; **~s intensifs/d'urgence/médicaux/dentaires** intensive/emergency/medical/dental care; **les premiers ~s à donner aux brûlés** first-aid treatment for burns; **~s à domicile** homecare ¢; **laisser qn sans ~s** to neglect sb; **laisser qn mourir sans ~s** to let sb die of neglect; **2** Cosmét care ¢; **~s corporels** or **du corps** body care ¢; **~s esthétiques** or **de beauté** beauty care ¢; **~s du cheveu** haircare ¢; **~s du visage** skincare ¢; **~s de la peau** body care ¢; **3** (attention) care ¢; **confier** or **laisser qch/qn aux bons ~s de qn** to leave sth/sb in sb's care; **'aux bons ~s de'** (sur une enveloppe) 'care of', 'c/o'; **publié par leurs/mes ~s** published by their/my good offices; **organisé par les ~s de l'association** organized through the good offices of the association; **les ~s domestiques/du ménage** domestic/household tasks.

IDIOMES **être aux petits ~s pour qn** to attend to sb's every need.

soir /swaʀ/ *nm* **1** (fin du jour) evening; (partie de la nuit) night; **la réunion est le ~** the meeting is in the evening; **travailler le ~** to work in the evening, to work evenings; **le ~ du 3, le 3 au ~** on the evening of the 3rd; **par un beau ~ d'été** on a fine summer evening; **le ~ venu** when evening fell; **le ~ des événements** on the evening of the events; **nous partirons samedi ~** we'll leave on Saturday evening; **il sort tous les samedis ~** he goes out every Saturday night; **6 heures du ~** 6 (o'clock) in the evening; (pour un horaire) 6 pm; **passe me voir un de ces ~s** come round[GB] and see me some evening; **à ce ~!** see you tonight!; **2** (soirée) evening; **3** (déclin) liter twilight; **au ~ de l'Empire** in the twilight ou last days of the Empire; **le ~ de la vie** the evening of one's life.

IDIOMES **être du ~** to be a night person.

soirée /swaʀe/ *nf* **1** (période) evening; **la ~ a été calme** it was a quiet evening; **dans** or **pendant la ~, en ~** in the evening; **les chaudes ~s d'été** hot summer evenings; **en début/fin de ~** at the beginning/end of the evening; **en ~** in the evening; **la pièce sera jouée en ~** the play will have an evening performance; **2** (réception) party; **aller dans une** or **en ~** to go to a party; **donner une ~** to give a party; **charmante ~!** iron great party! iron; **3** (spectacle) evening performance ou show; **~ littéraire** literary evening; **~ chant et poésie** evening of music and poetry; **dernière ~** last show ou performance.

soit I /swa/ ▶ **être**[1].

II /swa/ *conj* **1** (marque une alternative) **~, ~** either, or; **~ du fromage, ~ un gâteau, ~ des fruits** either cheese, or a cake, or fruit; **~ que, ~ que** (pour proposer) either, or; (pour supposer) either because, or because; **elle suggère ~ que vous veniez chez nous, ~ qu'on aille au restaurant** she suggests that either you come to our place, or (else) we go to a restaurant; **il le savait, ~ qu'il l'avait lu dans les journaux, ~ qu'on le lui avait dit** he knew it, either because he had read it in the newspapers, or because someone had told him; **c'est ~ l'un ~ l'autre, pas les deux** it's got to be one thing or the other, not both; **2** (à savoir) that is, ie; **toutes mes économies, ~ 200 francs** all my savings, ie ou that is, 200 francs; **il y a dix gâteaux, ~ deux chacun** there are ten cakes, ie ou that is, two each; **3** Math **~ un triangle ABC** let ABC be a triangle.

III /swat/ *adv* very well; **je me suis trompé, ~, mais là n'est pas la question** very well, I was wrong, but that's not the point; **eh bien ~, puisque tu y tiens** very well then, since you insist.

■ Note L'usage hésite, en mathématiques, entre la forme invariable de la conjonction et la forme verbale qui se met facultativement au pluriel (*soit* ou *soient* deux vecteurs), mais la traduction reste la même.

soixantaine /swasɑ̃tɛn/ *nf* about sixty; ▶ **cinquantaine**.

soixante /swasɑ̃t/ ▶ **545**, **212** *adj inv, pron* sixty.

soixante-dix /swasɑ̃tdis/ ▶ **545**, **212** *adj inv, pron* seventy.

soixante-dix-huit /swasɑ̃tdizɥit/ ▶ **545**, **212** *adj inv, pron* seventy-eight.

■ **~ tours** 78; **collectionner les ~ tours** to collect 78s.

soixante-dixième /swasɑ̃tdizjɛm/ ▶ **545** *adj* seventieth.

soixante-huitard, **~e**, *mpl* **~s** /swasɑ̃twitaʀ, aʀd/ *nm,f*: *participant in the student and workers' protest movement of May 1968*.

soixantième /swasɑ̃tjɛm/ ▶ **545** *adj* sixtieth.

soja /sɔʒa/ *nm* soya bean GB, soybean US; **planter du ~** to plant soya beans GB ou soybeans; **saucisse/pâté de** or **au ~** soya GB ou soybean sausage/pâté; **sauce de ~** soy sauce; **salade de (germes** or **pousses de) ~** bean sprout salad.

sol /sɔl/ *nm* **1** (à l'extérieur) ground; (dans une maison) floor; **la télévision est posée à même le ~** the television is on the floor; **l'avion a tué 5 personnes au ~** the aeroplane GB ou airplane US killed 5 people on the ground; **une maison au ~ en terre battue** a house with a trodden earth floor; **son adversaire l'a plaqué au ~** his opponent knocked him to the floor ou ground; **sentir le ~ se dérober sous ses pieds** lit to feel the ground giving way; fig to feel the ground giving way beneath one; **vitesse au ~ d'un avion** ground speed of an aeroplane; **la surface au ~ d'un bâtiment** the floor surface of a building; **exercices au ~** Sport floor exercises; **2** (territoire) soil; **le ~ africain/américain** African/American soil; **revenir sur son ~ natal** to come back to one's native soil; **3** (terrain) soil; **~ fertile/argileux** fertile/clay soil; **~ lunaire** lunar soil; **4** Mus (note) G; (en solfiant) soh; **5** (monnaie) sol.

sol-air /sɔlɛʀ/ *adj inv* [*engin, missile*] surface-to-air.

solaire /sɔlɛʀ/ I *adj* [*jour, calendrier, énergie*] solar; [*moteur, radio*] solar-powered; [*lumière, produit*] sun (*épith*).

II *nm* (énergie) solar energy.

solarium /sɔlaʀjɔm/ *nm* solarium.

soldanelle /sɔldanɛl/ *nf* **~ des Alpes** alpine snowbell.

soldat /sɔlda/ ▶ **390**, **510** *nm* soldier, serviceman; **~ de réserve** reserve soldier; **~ de métier** regular soldier; **~ d'infanterie** ≈ infantryman; **un simple ~** a private; **~ de 2e classe** ≈ private; **~ de 1e classe** ≈ private.

■ **Soldat inconnu** Unknown Soldier; **~ de plomb** tin ou toy soldier; **~s du feu** firemen.

IDIOMES **jouer au petit ~** to act brave.

soldatesque /sɔldatɛsk/ *nf* pej soldiery.

solde /sɔld/ I *nm* Fin balance; **~ créditeur/débiteur** credit/debit balance; **il y a un ~ de 100 francs en votre faveur** there is a balance of 100 francs in your favour[GB]; **~ positif** or **excédentaire/négatif** or **déficitaire** credit/debit balance; **faire le ~ d'un compte** to settle an account; **'pour ~ de tout compte'** 'in settlement'; **reçu pour ~ de tout compte** received in full and final payment.

II *nf* Mil pay; **toucher/dépenser sa ~** to get/to spend one's pay; **~ à l'air** *danger money for aviators and parachutists*; **avoir qn à sa ~** fig to have sb in one's pay; **être à la ~ de l'ennemi** fig to be in the pay of the enemy ou the enemy's pay.

III **en solde** *loc adv* **acheter une veste en ~** to buy a jacket in a sale ou at sale price GB ou on sale US; **mettre des marchandises en ~** to sell goods at sale price GB, to put goods on sale US.

IV **soldes** *nmpl* sales; (écrit en vitrine) sale (*sg*); **~s d'été/d'hiver** summer/winter sales; **faire les ~s**○ to go to the sales; **faire/annoncer des ~s sur qch** to have/to announce a sale on sth.

solder /sɔlde/ [1] I *vtr* **1** Comm to sell off, to clear [*marchandises*]; **~ des articles à prix coûtant** to sell items off at cost price; **2** Compta to settle the balance of [*compte*].

II **se solder** *vpr* **1** (finir) **se ~ par qch** to end in sth; **le procès s'est soldé par un non-lieu** the trial ended in the dismissal of the charge; **se ~ par un échec** [*efforts, démarche*] to end in failure; **2** Écon **se ~ par qch** to show sth; **le bilan se solde par un déficit de 10 000 francs** the statement shows a deficit of 10,000 francs.

solderie /sɔldəʀi/ *nf* discount shop.

soldeur, **-euse** /sɔldœʀ, øz/ ▶ **510** *nm,f* discount trader.

sole /sɔl/ *nf* **1** Zool sole; **2** (de four) hearth; **3** (de sabot) sole; **4** Naut sole, (flat) bottom.

solécisme /sɔlesism/ *nm* Ling solecism.

soleil /sɔlɛj/ *nm* **1** gén, Astron, Astrol sun; **~ de minuit** midnight sun; **au ~** in the sun; **se mettre au ~** [*personne, animal*] (s'exposer) to go into the sun; (rester) to sit in the sun; **prendre le ~** to get some sun; **un radieux ~ de printemps** a brilliant spring sun; **le ~ se lève à l'est** the sun rises in the east; **un week-end sans ~** a weekend without any sun; **sous un ~ de plomb** under a blazing sun; **en plein ~** [*travailler, marcher, être assis*] in hot sun; [*laisser un produit, exposer*] in direct sunlight; **la pièce était pleine de ~** the room was filled with sunlight; **nous avons eu deux jours de ~** we've had two sunny days; **quand il y a du ~** when it's sunny; **il fait ~** it's sunny; **soigner ses coups de ~** to treat one's sunburn; **ses coups de ~ la font souffrir** her sunburn is really painful; **attraper un coup** or **des coups de ~** to get sunburned; ▶ **neige**; **2** (à la barre fixe) grand circle; **3** (tournesol) sunflower; **4** (pièce d'artifice) Catherine wheel GB, pinwheel US.

IDIOMES **avoir du bien au ~** to own property; **avoir/se faire une place au ~** to have done/to do well for oneself; **(il n'y a) rien de nouveau sous le ~** there is nothing new under the sun; **le ~ brille** or **luit pour tout le monde** Prov the sun shines upon all alike.

solennel, **-elle** /sɔlanɛl/ *adj* **1** (empreint de gravité) solemn; **prendre des airs ~s** to put on solemn airs; **dire qch d'un ton ~** to say sth solemnly; **2** (officiel) [*cérémonie*] solemn; [*appel, déclaration, cadre*] formal; **des funérailles solennelles** funeral service; (nationales) state funeral.

solennellement /sɔlanɛlmɑ̃/ *adv* [*promettre, s'engager*] solemnly; [*célébrer, inaugurer, défiler, déclarer, démentir*] formally.

solennité /sɔlanite/ *nf* solemnity; **chef d'État reçu avec ~** head of state received with solemn ceremonies; **donner à une cérémonie une ~ particulière** to make a ceremony particularly solemn.

solénoïde /sɔlenɔid/ *nm* solenoid.

Soleure /sɔlœʀ/ *npr* **1** ▶ 857 (ville) Solothurn; **2** ▶ 692 (région) **le canton de ~** the canton of Solothurn.

Solex® /sɔlɛks/ *nm inv* (vélomoteur) (Solex®) moped.

solfège /sɔlfɛʒ/ *nm* **1** (exercice) music theory; **apprendre le ~** to learn music theory; **~ chanté** sol-fa; **2** (manuel) music theory book.

solfier /sɔlfje/ [2] *vtr* to sing using the tonic sol-fa system.

soli ▶ **solo**.

solidaire /sɔlidɛʀ/ *adj* **1** (lié par des intérêts communs) [*équipe, groupe*] united; **ils forment un groupe très ~** they really stand together; **être ~ de qn** to be behind sb, to support sb; **se sentir/montrer ~ de qn** to feel/to show solidarity with sb; **2** Mécan [*pièces*] interdependent; **3** Jur **un contrat ~** a contract binding on all parties; **débiteurs ~s** jointly liable debtors.

solidairement /sɔlidɛʀmɑ̃/ *adv* **employés qui agissent ~** employees acting in common; **travailler ~** to work together; **associés ~ responsables** Jur jointly liable partners.

solidariser /sɔlidaʀize/ [1] **I** *vtr* Jur to make [sb] jointly liable.
II se solidariser *vpr* **se ~ avec qch/qn** to stand by sth/sb, to make common cause with sth/sb.

solidarité /sɔlidaʀite/ *nf* solidarity (**entre** between); **~ professionnelle/de classe** professional/class solidarity; **liens/sentiment de ~** ties/feeling of solidarity; **faire qch par ~ avec qn** to do sth out of solidarity with sb.

solide /sɔlid/ **I** *adj* **1** (consistant) [*état, corps, aliment, carburant*] solid; **2** (résistant) [*maison, échafaudage, amitié, lien, union*] solid; [*chaussures, sac*] sturdy; [*lien, fixation, lame, mécanisme*] strong; [*position, base*] firm; **la chaise/l'étagère n'est pas très ~** the chair/the shelf is a bit rickety; **être ~ au poste** to be dependable at work; **3** (vigoureux) [*personne, constitution*] strong; [*poignée de main*] firm; [*cœur, poumons*] strong, sound; **être ~ sur ses jambes** lit, fig to be steady on one's legs; **elle a les nerfs ~s** she's got nerves of steel; **avoir la tête ~** fig to have one's head screwed on; **ma tête n'est plus très ~** my mind is going a bit; **un ~ appétit** hum a hearty appetite; **il a un ~ coup de fourchette** hum he likes his food; **4** (sérieux) [*affaire, connaissances, expérience, raisons*] sound; [*garanties*] firm; [*qualités*] solid; [*partenaire*] dependable; **elle a une ~ formation en informatique** she's had a sound training in computer science; **ton rapport n'est pas assez ~** your report isn't very convincing; **il a une ~ réputation d'agressivité/de raseur**° he has a reputation for being aggressive/for being a bore; **5** (substantiel) hearty; **un ~ petit déjeuner** a hearty breakfast.
II *nm* **1** Math, Phys solid; **2** (fiable) **ce qu'il te dit, c'est du ~** what he says is sound, you can believe what he says; **ce secteur, c'est du ~** that industry is solid; **3** (consistant) **manger du ~** to eat solids; **marcher sur du ~** to walk on firm ground; **4** (durable) **les meubles anciens, c'est du ~** antique furniture is solidly built.

solidement /sɔlidmɑ̃/ *adv* **1** (fermement) [*lier, accrocher, soutenu*] firmly; **des maisons ~ construites** solidly-built houses; **2** (fortement) [*s'établir, implanter, ancré*] firmly; [*barricadé*] securely; [*armé*] heavily; **un rapport/témoignage ~ documenté** a soundly-documented report/testimony; **elle a ~ établi sa réputation** she has established quite a reputation (**de, en tant que** as).

solidification /sɔlidifikasjɔ̃/ *nf* solidification.

solidifier /sɔlidifje/ [2] **I** *vtr* to solidify; **laves solidifiées** solidified lava ¢.
II se solidifier *vpr* to solidify.

solidité /sɔlidite/ *nf* **1** (de construction) solidity; (de machine) strength; (de lien) firmness; (de vêtement) hard-wearing quality; **d'une grande ~** [*construction*] well-built; [*machine*] sturdy; [*lien*] strong; [*vêtement*] hard-wearing; **2** (de raisonnement, démonstration, thèse) soundness; **3** (d'institution, économie) stability.

soliloque /sɔlilɔk/ *nm* soliloquy (**sur** on ou about).

soliloquer /sɔlilɔke/ [1] *vi* to soliloquize (**sur** on ou about).

solipède /sɔlipɛd/ *adj* solipedal.

solipsisme /sɔlipsism/ *nm* solipsism.

soliste /sɔlist/ *nmf* soloist.

solitaire /sɔlitɛʀ/ **I** *adj* **1** (sans compagnie) [*personne, vie, promenade*] solitary (*épith*); [*vieillesse, enfance*] lonely; **navigateur ~** Sport single-handed ou solo yachtsman; **2** (non fréquenté) [*sentier, lieu*] lonely (*épith*); **3** (isolé) [*maison, hameau*] isolated; [*arbre*] lone (*épith*).
II *nmf* (personne) solitary person, loner; (ermite) hermit; **vivre en ~** to live alone; **voler/naviguer en ~** to fly/sail solo; **traversée/course en ~** solo crossing/race.
III *nm* **1** (diamant) solitaire; **2** (sanglier) rogue boar; **3** ▶ 449 Jeux solitaire; **jouer au ~** to play solitaire.

solitude /sɔlityd/ *nf* **1** (fait d'être seul) solitude; **aimer la ~** to enjoy solitude, to enjoy being on one's own; **2** (sentiment) loneliness.

solive /sɔliv/ *nf* joist.

sollicitation /sɔlisitasjɔ̃/ *nf* **1** (requête) appeal, request; **répondre** or **céder aux ~s de qn** to give in to sb's appeals ou requests; **2** (impulsion donnée) (à un cheval) prompting; (à une machine) touch; **répondre à la moindre ~ du cavalier** to respond to the slightest prompting from the rider; **la voiture répond à la moindre ~ de l'accélérateur/du chauffeur** the car responds to the slightest touch on the accelerator/from the driver.

solliciter /sɔlisite/ [1] *vtr* **1** (demander) fml to seek [*entretien, poste, avis*]; to seek, to solicit sout [*contributions*]; to canvass, to solicit sout [*voix*]; **~ du Parlement des pouvoirs spéciaux** to seek special powers from Parliament; **j'ai l'honneur de ~ de votre bienveillance l'autorisation de faire** I would respectfully request your permission to do; **son avis est très sollicité** his/her advice is much ou highly sought-after; **2** (démarcher) to approach, to call on ou upon [*personne, organisation*]; to canvass [*client, électeur*]; **être sollicité par des collecteurs de fonds** to be approached ou asked for contributions by fund raisers; **~ les clients à domicile** to sell to people in their own homes; **être très sollicité** [*député, bienfaiteur*] to be assailed by requests; [*chanteur, orateur*] to be very much in demand; **3** (faire appel à) to attract [*attention, intérêt, regard*]; to call upon [*mémoire, logique*]; **4** (agir sur) to prompt [*cheval*]; to try [*mécanisme*]; to stimulate [*muscle, organe*].

solliciteur, -euse /sɔlisitœʀ, øz/ *nm,f* supplicant sout.

sollicitude /sɔlisityd/ *nf* concern, solicitude (**envers** for); **avec une ~ toute maternelle** with (truly) maternal concern; **entourer qn de ~** to cosset sb.

sol-mer /sɔlmɛʀ/ *adj inv* [*engin, missile*] surface-to-sea.

solo, *pl* **~s** or **soli** /sɔlo, *pl* sɔli/ **I** *adj inv* solo; **piano/album ~** solo piano/album; **spectacle ~** one-man/-woman show.
II *nm* solo; **~ de trompette** trumpet solo; **jouer/chanter en ~** to play/sing solo.

sol-sol /sɔlsɔl/ *adj inv* [*engin, missile*] surface-to-surface.

solstice /sɔlstis/ *nm* solstice; **~ d'hiver/d'été** winter/summer solstice.

solubiliser /sɔlybilize/ [1] *vtr* to make [sth] soluble.

solubilité /sɔlybilite/ *nf* solubility.

soluble /sɔlybl/ *adj* **1** [*comprimé*] soluble; **2** [*problème*] solvable, soluble.

soluté /sɔlyte/ *nm* Chimie, Pharm solution.

solution /sɔlysjɔ̃/ *nf* **1** (action de résoudre) (de difficulté, mots croisés, d'énigme) solution (**de** of), solving (**de** of); (de crise, conflit) resolution (**de** of); **pour faciliter la ~ du problème** in order to solve the problem ou to get the problem solved more easily; **2** (réponse) solution (**de, à** to); **tenir la ~ de qch** to have the solution to sth; **une ~ de facilité** an easy way out; **~ de compromis** compromise; **la ~ n'est pas la force** force is not the solution ou the answer; **la situation est sans ~** there's no way out of the situation, the situation can't be resolved; **trouver une ~ pour assurer la sécurité dans la région** to find a way of making the area safe; **3** Chimie, Pharm solution; **sel en ~** salt in solution; **vendu en comprimé ou ~** sold in tablet or liquid form.
■ **~ finale** Hist Final Solution.

solutionner /sɔlysjɔne/ [1] *vtr* controv to solve.

solvabilité /sɔlvabilite/ *nf* (de débiteur) solvency; (de client, d'emprunteur) creditworthiness.

solvable /sɔlvabl/ *adj* [*débiteur*] solvent; [*emprunteur, client*] creditworthy.

solvant /sɔlvɑ̃/ *nm* solvent.

soma /sɔma/ *nm* soma.

somali /sɔmali/ ▶ 462 *nm* Ling Somali.

Somali, ~e /sɔmali/ ▶ 537 *nm,f* Somali.

Somalie /sɔmali/ ▶ 321 *nprf* Somalia.

somalien, -ienne /sɔmaljɛ̃, ɛn/ ▶ 537 *adj* Somalian.

Somalien, -ienne /sɔmaljɛ̃, ɛn/ ▶ 537 *nm,f* Somalian.

somatique /sɔmatik/ *adj* Biol, Méd somatic.

somatisation /sɔmatizasjɔ̃/ *nf* somatization.

somatiser /sɔmatize/ [1] **I** *vtr* to have a psychosomatic reaction to [*problème*].
II° *vi* **tu somatises!** it's psychosomatic!

sombre /sɔ̃bʀ/ *adj* **1** (obscur) dark; **vert/rouge ~** dark green/red; **il fait ~** it's dark; **2** (triste) [*pensée, avenir, période*] dark, black; [*tableau, conclusion*] depressing, grim; [*air, personne, visage*] solemn, sombre^GB; **une ~ vision du monde** a gloomy ou depressing view of the world; **une période ~ s'annonce pour eux** things are looking gloomy for them; **d'un air ~** sombrely^GB, gloomily; **3**° (déplorable) (*before n*) [*crétin, brute*] absolute; [*affaire*] murky; **c'est une ~ histoire d'inceste** it's a grim story of incest; **4** Ling [*voyelle*] dark.

sombrement /sɔ̃bʀəmɑ̃/ *adv* liter (avec pessimisme) sombrely^GB, gloomily; (de façon inquiétante) darkly; **envisager ~ l'avenir** to see a dark future ahead.

sombrer /sɔ̃bʀe/ [1] *vi* **1** (couler) [*navire*] to sink; **2** (s'engloutir) **~ dans** [*personne*] to sink into [*désespoir, folie, oubli, débauche, alcoolisme*]; **~ dans le ridicule** to lapse into the ridiculous; **le pays/leur industrie est en train de ~** the country/their industry is going under.

sombrero /sɔ̃bʀeʀo/ *nm* sombrero.

Somerset ▶ 692 *nprm* **le ~** Somerset.

sommaire /sɔmmɛʀ/ **I** *adj* [*enquête*] perfunctory; [*examen, analyse, explication*] cursory;

[*description*] rough; [*installation, éducation, repas*] rough and ready (*épith*); [*vision, conception*] shallow; [*toilette*] token; [*compte-rendu, jugement, procès, exécution*] summary.

II *nm* **1** (table des matières) contents (*pl*); **au ~ de notre numéro de juillet** featured in our July issue; **2**○ (programme) **au ~: un débat sur le chômage** in the programme[GB]: a debate on unemployment.

sommairement /sɔmmɛʀmɑ̃/ *adv* [*exposer, juger, exécuter*] summarily; **répondre/expliquer ~** to give a cursory answer/explanation; **évaluer ~** to make a brief assessment; **parcourir ~ un livre/rapport** to skim through a book/report.

sommation /sɔmmasjɔ̃/ *nf* **1** Jur (acte d'huissier) notice; **~ de quitter les lieux/de payer** notice to quit/to pay; **~ de comparaître en justice** summons to appear in court; **2** (avertissement) (de policier) warning; (de sentinelle) challenge; **faire les ~s d'usage** (tous contextes) to issue the customary warnings; **tirer sans ~s** (tous contextes) to shoot without warning.

■ **~ sans frais** Fisc second demand for payment, second notice to pay.

somme /sɔm/ **I** *nm* nap, snooze○; **faire un (petit) ~** to have ou take a nap, to have a snooze○.

II *nf* **1** (argent) sum; **une ~ de 1000 francs** a sum of 1,000 francs; **ça fait○ une ~!** it's quite a sum!; **une grosse/petite ~ (d'argent)** a large/small sum; **dépenser de grosses ~s d'argent** to spend vast amounts ou huge sums of money; **2** (quantité) sum total; **la ~ de nos connaissances** the sum total of our knowledge; **ce n'est pas avec une ~ de vérités qu'on fait une philosophie** you can't make a philosophy out of a collection of truths; **il a fourni une grosse ~ de travail** he did a great quantity of work; **en ~, ~ toute** all in all; **3** Math sum; **faire la ~ de deux nombres/vecteurs** to add two numbers/vectors together; **4** (œuvre) summa.

Somme /sɔm/ **▶357**, **692** *nprf* (fleuve, département) **la ~** the Somme.

sommeil /sɔmɛj/ *nm* **1** Physiol sleep **¢**; **~ profond/léger/réparateur** deep ou sound/light/refreshing sleep; **trouver/perdre le ~** to get to/to lose sleep; **j'ai du ~ à rattraper** I've got to catch up on lost sleep; **avoir ~** to be ou feel sleepy; **nuit sans ~** sleepless night; **avoir le ~ agité** to sleep fitfully; **avoir le ~ léger/lourd** to be a light/heavy sleeper; **tirer qn de son ~** to wake [sb] up, to rouse sb sout; **2** (attente) **être en ~** [*projet, activité, affaire*] to have been put on ice; **laisser** or **mettre un projet en ~** to put a project on ice.

■ **~ crépusculaire** twilight sleep, seminarcosis spéc; **~ éternel** eternal rest; **~ à ondes lentes** slow-wave sleep; **~ paradoxal** REM sleep; **~ profond** = **~ à ondes lentes**; **~ rapide** = **~ paradoxal**.

IDIOMES **dormir d'un ~ de plomb** to sleep like a log○; **dormir du ~ des justes** to sleep the sleep of the just; **dormir de son dernier ~** to sleep one's last ou final sleep.

sommeiller /sɔmeje/ [1] *vi* (somnoler) [*personne, animal*] to doze; [*nature, campagne, passion, désir*] to lie dormant.

sommelier, **-ière** /sɔməlje, ɛʀ/ **▶510** **I** *nm,f* wine steward, sommelier.

II sommelière *nf* H (serveuse) waitress.

sommer /sɔmme/ [1] *vtr* **~ qn de faire** to command sb to do; **~ qn de comparaître** Jur to summons sb to appear.

sommet /sɔmmɛ/ *nm* **1** Géog (de montagne indéfinie) peak; (de montagne définie) summit; (montagne pointue) peak; **les ~s sont enneigés toute l'année** the peaks are covered with snow all year; **le plus haut ~ de France/des Alpes** the highest peak in France/in the Alps; **atteindre le ~ (du mont Blanc)** to reach the summit (of Mont Blanc); **2** (d'arbre, de bâtiment, tour, mur, crâne, colline) top; (de vague) crest; (de courbe) peak; (de hiérarchie, organisation) top; (de carrière) summit; **3** (summum) (de gloire, réussite, bêtise) height; **c'est un ~ de mauvais goût** it's the height of bad taste; **atteindre les ~s de la perfection** to attain the heights of perfection; **atteindre un ~** or **des ~s** [*prix, ventes*] to peak; **un des ~s de la littérature suédoise** (écrivain, texte) one of the greats of Swedish literature; **4** (rencontre) summit; **~ franco-allemand** Franco-German summit; **conférence au ~** summit meeting; **se réunir au ~** to meet at the summit; **le ~ européen de Bruxelles** the European summit in Brussels; **5** Math (de triangle, d'angle) apex; (de cône, volume) vertex.

sommier /sɔmje/ *nm* **1** (de lit) (bed) base; **~ tapissier** or **à ressorts** bed base GB, box spring US; **~ métallique** wire bed frame; **~ à lattes de bois** slatted bed base; **2** Mus (d'orgue) wind chest; (de piano, clavecin) pin block; **3** Constr (d'arc, de voûte) springer; (de porte, fenêtre) lintel; (de grille) crossbar; **4** Jur (fichier) criminal records (*pl*).

sommité /sɔmmite/ *nf* (expert) leading expert (**en** in); **~ de la médecine** leading medical expert; **~ des sciences sociales** leading expert in social science.

somnambule /sɔmnɑ̃byl/ **I** *adj* **être ~** to sleepwalk; **elle a un enfant ~** one of her children sleepwalks.

II *nmf* sleepwalker, somnambulist spéc; **agir en** or **comme un ~** to act as if in a trance.

somnambulisme /sɔmnɑ̃bylism/ *nm* sleepwalking, somnambulism spéc.

somnifère /sɔmnifɛʀ/ **I** *adj* [*produit, propriété*] soporific.

II *nm* (médicament) sleeping drug; (comprimé) sleeping pill; **ce livre est un ~** fig this book is soporific.

somnolence /sɔmnɔlɑ̃s/ *nf* **1** lit drowsiness; **en état de ~** in a drowsy state; **2** fig lethargy; **un pays en état de ~** a country in a state of lethargy.

somnolent, **~e** /sɔmnɔlɑ̃, ɑ̃t/ *adj* **1** lit [*personne*] drowsy; **2** fig [*attention*] flagging; [*ville*] sleepy; [*industrie, pays, marché*] lethargic.

somnoler /sɔmnɔle/ [1] *vi* **1** lit [*personne*] to drowse; **2** fig [*ville*] to be sleepy; [*marché, industrie, pays*] to be lethargic.

somptuaire /sɔ̃ptɥɛʀ/ *adj* **1** Antiq, Hist [*loi, édit*] sumptuary; **2** (excessif) controv [*dépense*] lavish.

somptueusement /sɔ̃ptɥøzmɑ̃/ *adv* sumptuously.

somptueux, **-euse** /sɔ̃ptɥø, øz/ *adj* sumptuous.

somptuosité /sɔ̃ptɥozite/ *nf* liter sumptuousness.

son[1], **sa**, *pl* **ses** /sɔ̃, sa, se/ *adj poss*

■ **Note** En anglais, le choix du possessif de la troisième personne du singulier est déterminé par le genre du 'possesseur'. Sont du masculin: les personnes de sexe masculin et les animaux domestiques mâles; sont du féminin: les personnes de sexe féminin, les animaux domestiques femelles et souvent les navires; sont du neutre: les animaux non domestiques et les non-animés. La forme masculine est *his*: *sa femme/moustache* = his wife/moustache; *son ordinateur* = his computer; *sa niche* = his kennel. La forme féminine est *her*: *son mari/ordinateur* = her husband/computer; *sa robe* = her dress; *sa niche* = her kennel. La forme neutre est *its*. Quand le 'possesseur' est indéterminé on peut dire *one's*: *faire ses devoirs* = to do one's homework. On ne répète pas le possessif coordonné: *sa robe et son manteau* = her dress and coat.

---

ses enfants à elle○ her children; **~ étourdie de sœur**○ his/her absent-minded sister; **Sa Majesté** His/Her Majesty; **il nous a fait sa crise** he threw one of his fits; **un de ses amis** a friend of his/hers; **elle a ~ lundi** (cette semaine) she's off on Monday; (toutes les semaines) she gets Mondays off; **elle doit gagner ses 30000 francs** she must make 30,000 francs; **il en est à sa troisième grippe** it's the third time he's had flu GB ou the flu; **elle sait parfaitement sa géographie** she's awfully good at geography; **je ne sais pas ce qu'elle lui trouve, à ~ Georges**○ I don't know what she sees in Georges; **il n'arrête pas de parler de ~ Zola**○ he keeps talking about his beloved Zola; **à sa vue, j'ai compris** when I saw him/her/it, I understood.

son[2] /sɔ̃/ *nm* **1** (bruit) sound; **un ~ caverneux/plein/étouffé** a hollow/full/muffled sound; **émettre/percevoir un ~** to emit/to detect a sound; **le timbre et la hauteur d'un ~** the tone and pitch of a sound; **être réveillé au ~ du clairon** to be woken up by the sound of the bugle; **défiler au ~ d'une fanfare** to march to the beat of a band; **danser au ~ d'un orchestre** to dance to the music of a band; **2** (volume) volume; **baisser le ~** to turn the volume down; **3** Radio, Mus, TV, Cin sound; **équipe/ingénieur du ~** sound team/engineer; **4** (enveloppe du blé) bran; **des céréales au ~** cereals with bran; **pain au ~** bran loaf.

IDIOMES **faire l'âne pour avoir du ~** to play stupid to get at the truth; **entendre plusieurs ~s de cloche** to hear several different versions (of the same thing).

■ **~ et lumière** son et lumière.

sonal /sonal/ *nm* jingle.

sonante /sonɑ̃t/ *nf* resonant vowel.

sonar /sɔnaʀ/ *nm* Naut sonar; **détection au ~** detection by sonar.

sonate /sɔnat/ *nf* sonata; **~ en sol mineur** sonata in G minor; **~ pour piano** piano sonata; **~ pour clarinette et piano** sonata for clarinet and piano.

sonatine /sɔnatin/ *nf* sonatina.

sondage /sɔ̃daʒ/ *nm* **1** (enquête) (pour opinion) poll Pol; (pour étude) survey; **~ d'opinion** Pol opinion poll; **faire un ~ auprès d'un groupe sur les habitudes alimentaires des Français** to carry out a survey among a group on the eating habits of the French; **je vais faire un ~ parmi mes collègues** I'm going to sound out my colleagues (**pour faire** to do); **2** Méd (pour évacuer, introduire) catheterization; (pour examiner) probing; **~ vésical** urinary ou bladder catheterization; **3** Météo, Naut, Pêche sounding; **~ par ballon** balloon sounding; **4** Géol, Mines (creusement) drilling; (trou de sonde) borehole; **~ destructif/diamant/rotatif** destructive/diamond core/rotary drilling.

■ **~ d'écoute** Radio, TV audience ratings poll.

sonde /sɔ̃d/ *nf* **1** Méd (pour évacuer, introduire) catheter; (pour examiner) probe; **2** Naut, Pêche (plomb) sounding lead; (ligne) sounding line; **jeter la ~** to heave the lead; **naviguer à la ~** to navigate by sounding; **3** Météo sonde; **4** Géol, Mines drill; **5** Ind (pour produits alimentaires) taster; **~ à vin/fromage** wine/cheese taster.

■ **~ gastrique** Méd stomach tube; **~ pyrométrique** Tech pyrometer probe; **~ spatiale** Astronaut space probe; **~ thermométrique** Tech thermometer probe; **~ urétérale** Méd ureteric catheter; **~ urétrale** Méd urethral catheter.

sondé, **~e** /sɔ̃de/ *nm,f* Sociol **les ~s** those polled; **20% des ~s** 20% of those polled.

sonder /sɔ̃de/ [1] *vtr* **1** (enquêter) (pour opinion) to poll [*personne, groupe*]; (pour étude) to survey [*personne, groupe*]; (pour dévoiler) to sound [sb] out [*personne*]; to sound out [*intentions*]; **8% des personnes sondées avant les élections** 8% of those polled before the elections; **2** (fouiller) to probe [*ballot, couche de neige, mare*]; **3** Méd (pour évacuer, introduire dans) to catheterize [*organe*]; (pour examiner) to probe [*organe*]; **4** Météo to take soundings in [*atmosphère*]; **5** Naut to sound [*fond*]; **6** Géol, Mines to make test drills in [*sol, couche*].

sondeur, **-euse** /sɔ̃dœʀ, øz/ **I** *nm,f* **1** ▶ 510 (enquêteur) pollster; **2** Naut (personne) sounder; **3** Géol, Mines (personne) driller.
II *nm* (appareil) Météo, Naut sounder; Géol, Mines driller.
III sondeuse *nf* Géol, Mines (machine) drilling machine.
■ **~ acoustique** Mil, Naut echo sounder; **~ à ultrasons** Naut, Sci ultrasonic depth finder.

songe /sɔ̃ʒ/ *nm* liter dream; **faire un ~** to have a dream; **en ~** [*voir, apparaître*] in a dream.

songe-creux /sɔ̃kʀø/ *nm inv* dreamer.

songer /sɔ̃ʒe/ [13] **I songer à** *vtr ind* **~ à qch/qn** to think of sth/sb; **~ à faire** to think of doing; **~ que** to think that; **si l'on songe que** if one thinks that; **quand on** or **si l'on y songe** when you come to think of it; **tant que j'y songe** while I'm thinking of it; **quand j'y songe** when I think of it; **il songe à changer de métier** he's thinking of changing jobs, he's contemplating a change of job; **songe qu'il ne te reste qu'un mois pour finir** remember that you've only got a month left to finish; **tu n'y songes pas!** you can't be serious!; **songez-y** (n'oubliez pas) bear it in mind; (réfléchissez) think about it; **je n'y avais même pas songé** it hadn't even occurred to me; **songe à ta réputation/ton avenir** think of ou consider your reputation/your future; **songe aux conséquences /à ce que tu leur dois** think of ou consider the consequences/how much you owe them; **songe à ta famille avant d'accepter cette offre** think of ou consider your family before you accept this offer; **je songeais à lui pour ce poste** I was thinking of ou considering him for the post.
II† *vi* liter to daydream.

songerie /sɔ̃ʒʀi/ *nf* daydreaming.

songeur, **-euse** /sɔ̃ʒœʀ, øz/ **I** *adj* pensive; **avoir l'air ~** to look pensive; **dit-il, l'air ~** he said pensively; **ça me laisse ~** it has set me thinking.
II *nm,f* liter dreamer.

sonique /sɔnik/ *adj* [*barrière*] sound (*épith*).

sonnant, **~e** /sɔnɑ̃, ɑ̃t/ *adj* **à trois heures ~es** on the stroke of three.
IDIOMES **payer/être payé en espèces ~es et trébuchantes** to pay/to be paid in cash.

sonné, **~e** /sɔne/ **I** *pp* ▶ **sonner**.
II *pp adj* **1** (étourdi) (physiquement) groggy; (moralement) shattered; **au deuxième round, il était déjà ~** he was already groggy in the second round; **il avait l'air ~ par son échec** he looked shattered at having failed; **2** (révolu) **il est six heures ~es** it has just struck six o'clock; **elle a quarante ans bien ~s**○ she's well into her forties; **3**○ (fou) nuts○.

sonner /sɔne/ [1] **I** *vtr* **1** (faire tinter) to ring [*cloche*]; **2** (annoncer) [*horloge*] to strike [*heure*]; [*personne*] to sound [*charge, retraite, alarme*]; to ring out [*vêpres, angélus*]; **l'horloge sonne les heures et les demies** the clock strikes on the hour and on the half-hour; **3** (faire venir) to ring for [*domestique, gardien, infirmière*]; **on ne t'a pas sonné**○! did anyone ask you?; **4**○ (faire vaciller) [*coup, boxeur*] to make [sb] dizzy [*personne*]; [*nouvelle, événement*] to stagger [*personne*]; [*vin, alcool*] to knock [sb] out [*personne*].
II sonner de *vtr ind* to sound [*cor, trompette*]; to play [*cornemuse*].
III *vi* **1** (se faire entendre) [*cloches, téléphone*] to ring; [*heure*] to strike; [*réveil*] to go off; [*alerte, alarme, trompette*] to sound; **minuit vient de ~** midnight has just struck; **l'heure n'a pas encore sonné** it hasn't struck the hour yet; **leur dernière heure a sonné** their last hour has come; **ta dernière heure a sonné**○! (menace) your time's run out!; **le temps de la retraite a sonné** the time has come to retire; **la fin des cours va ~ dans cinq minutes** the bell for the end of lessons will ring in five minutes; **il fait ~ son réveil à 5 heures** he sets his alarm for 5 o'clock; **les bottes faisaient ~ les dalles du palais** the floor of the palace rang with the sound of boots; **2** (rendre un son) [*mot, expression*] to sound; **ça sonne bien/mal** that sounds good/bad; **ta remarque sonnerait mal aux oreilles d'un peintre** your comment isn't the sort of thing a painter likes to hear; **mots qui sonnent mal dans la bouche d'un prêtre** words that are most unsuitable coming from a priest; **3** (actionner une sonnerie) to ring; **pour appeler l'infirmière, sonnez deux fois** to call the nurse, ring twice; **on a sonné à la porte** the doorbell has just rung; **va voir qui sonne** go and see who's at the door; **ça sonne chez le voisin** (à la porte) the neighbour[GB]'s bell's ringing; (au téléphone) the neighbour[GB]'s phone's ringing.

sonnerie /sɔnʀi/ *nf* **1** (son) ringing; (de carillon) chimes (*pl*); **une ~ stridente** a clamorous ringing; **le réveil n'a pas marché ou je n'ai pas entendu la ~** the alarm-clock didn't go off or I didn't hear it; **je n'ai pas entendu la ~ du téléphone** I didn't hear the telephone ring; **système qui déclenche une ~ dès qu'on approche** system that sets off an alarm as soon as you go near it; **2** (air) sounding.
■ **~ électrique** electric bell; **~ militaire** (bugle) call.

sonnet /sɔnɛ/ *nm* sonnet.

sonnette /sɔnɛt/ *nf* **1** (de bicyclette, d'intérieur) bell; (de porte) doorbell; **actionner la ~** to ring the bell; **~ d'alarme/de nuit** alarm/night bell; **j'ai entendu un coup de ~** I heard the bell ring; **il y a eu un coup de ~** the bell rang; **tirer la ~ d'alarme** lit to pull the emergency cord; fig to sound the alarm; **2** Gén Civ pile-driver.

sonneur /sɔnœʀ/ *nm* (de cloches) bell-ringer; (d'autres instruments) player.
IDIOMES **dormir** or **ronfler comme un ~**○ to sleep like a log.

sono○ /sono/ *nf*: *abbr* = **sonorisation 1, 2**.

sonore /sɔnɔʀ/ *adj* **1** (éclatant) [*rire, baiser, gifle*] resounding; [*formules, paroles*] high-sounding; **2** (qui résonne) [*paroi*] resonant; [*pièce, couloir, voûte*] echoing; [*plancher*] hollow-sounding (*épith*); **3** (relatif au son) [*vibrations, source*] sound (*épith*); **le volume ~ est tel qu'il faut crier pour s'entendre** the noise level is so high that you have to shout to hear each other; **4** Cin, Radio **effets ~s** sound effects; **un document ~** a recording; **5** Phon [*consonne, phonème*] voiced.

sonorisation /sɔnɔʀizasjɔ̃/ *nf* **1** Tech (matériel) public address system, PA system; **installer la ~ dans une salle de conférence/une aérogare/une rue** to install a public address system in a conference room/an air terminal/a street; **installer la ~ dans un cinéma/une salle de bal** to install the sound system in a cinema/a ballroom; **2** Cin **la ~ d'un film** adding the soundtrack to a film; **3** Phon voicing (**de** of).

sonoriser /sɔnɔʀize/ [1] *vtr* **1** (équiper d'une sonorisation) to install a public address system ou PA system in [*salle de conférences, rue*]; to install a sound system in [*salle de concert, cinéma*]; **2** Cin **~ un film** to add the soundtrack to a film; **3** Phon to voice [*consonne, phonème*].

sonorité /sɔnɔʀite/ *nf* **1** Mus (d'un instrument, d'une voix) tone (**de** of); **la ~ grave d'un saxophone** the deep tone of a saxophone; **les ~s de l'italien** the sound of Italian; **2** Audio (d'une chaîne hi-fi) sound quality (**de** of); **3** (d'un plancher, mur) resonance (**de** of); **la ~ d'une maison vide** the hollow sound of an empty house; **4** Phon voicing (**de** of).

sonothèque /sɔnɔtɛk/ *nf* sound (effects) library.

Sonotone® /sɔnɔtɔn/ *nm* hearing aid.

sophisme /sɔfism/ *nm* sophism.

sophiste /sɔfist/ *nm* sophist.

sophistication /sɔfistikasjɔ̃/ *nf* sophistication.

sophistique /sɔfistik/ **I** *adj* sophistic.
II *nf* sophistry.

sophistiqué, **~e** /sɔfistike/ *adj* (complexe) sophisticated; (artificiel) artificial, mannered.

Sophocle /sɔfɔkl/ *npr* Sophocles.

sophrologie /sɔfʀɔlɔʒi/ *nf* relaxation therapy.

soporifique /sɔpɔʀifik/ **I** *adj* **1** Pharm soporific; **2** fig [*livre, cours*] soporific.
II *nm* (médicament) sleeping drug.

soprane /sɔpʀan/ = **soprano**.

soprano /sɔpʀano/ ▶ 134 **I** *nm* (voix) soprano.
II *nmf* (chanteur) (femme) soprano; (enfant) treble, soprano; **un(e) ~ lyrique/dramatique** a lyric/dramatic soprano.

sorbet /sɔʀbɛ/ *nm* sorbet; **~ (au) citron** lemon sorbet.

sorbetière /sɔʀbətjɛʀ/ *nf* ice-cream maker.

sorbier /sɔʀbje/ *nm* service tree; **~ des oiseleurs** rowan, mountain ash.

sorbonnard○, **~e** /sɔʀbɔnaʀ, aʀd/ *nm,f* students' slang *student or teacher at the Sorbonne.*

sorcellerie /sɔʀsɛlʀi/ *nf* witchcraft; (maléfique) sorcery; **c'est de la ~!** fig it must be magic!

sorcier /sɔʀsje/ **I**○ *adj m* **ce n'est (pourtant) pas ~!** (but) it's dead○ easy!
II *nm* **1** (magicien) wizard; (maléfique) sorcerer; **2** (guérisseur) witch doctor.

sorcière /sɔʀsjɛʀ/ *nf* witch; **c'est une vraie ~** she's a real old witch.

sordide /sɔʀdid/ *adj* [*habitation, rue, quartier*] squalid, sordid; [*conditions de vie, crime, détails*] sordid; [*avarice, égoïsme*] base.

sordidement /sɔʀdidmɑ̃/ *adv* [*vivre*] squalidly, sordidly; [*agir, se comporter*] basely.

sorgho /sɔʀgo/ *nm* sorghum.

Sorlingues /sɔʀlɛ̃g/ ▶ 416 *nprfpl* **les (îles) ~** the Scilly Isles, the Scillies.

sornettes /sɔʀnɛt/ *nfpl* tall stories.

sort /sɔʀ/ *nm* **1** (condition) lot; **se plaindre de son ~** to complain of one's lot; **être satisfait de son ~** to be satisfied with one's lot; **améliorer son ~** to improve one's lot; **2** (destin) fate ₵; **remettre son ~ entre les mains de qn** to put one's fate in sb's hands; **le ~ en a décidé autrement** fate decided otherwise; **c'est un coup du ~** it's just one of those things; **il sera bientôt fixé sur son ~** he'll soon know his fate; **le ~ est contre moi** I'm ill-fated; **il a eu un ~ tragique** he came to a tragic end; **tirer au ~** to draw lots; **tirer qch au ~** to draw lots for sth; **le ~ des armes** the fortunes (*pl*) of war; **faire un ~ à**○ **un plat/une bouteille** fig to polish off○ a dish/a bottle.
IDIOMES **jeter un ~ à qn** to put a curse ou jinx on sb; **le ~ en est jeté** the die is cast.

sortable /sɔʀtabl/ *adj* **1** (supportable) **mon mari n'est pas ~** I can't take my husband anywhere; **2** (présentable) **tu n'es pas ~ dans cet état!** you're not fit to be seen!

sortant, **~e** /sɔʀtɑ̃, ɑ̃t/ *adj* (susceptible d'être reconduit) [*député, président*] sitting; (non reconduit) [*député, président, équipe, champion*] outgoing.

sorte /sɔʀt/ **I** *nf* sort (**de** of), kind (**de** of); **des gens/problèmes de toutes ~s, toutes ~s de gens/problèmes** all sorts ou kinds of people/problems; **d'aucune ~** of any sort ou kind ou type; **une ~ de fenêtre/clé** a sort ou kind of window/key.
II de la sorte *loc adv* [*agir, se comporter, mentir*] in this way; **je n'ai rien fait de la ~** I haven't done anything of the kind ou sort; **il ne l'entendent pas de la ~** they don't see it that way.
III de sorte à *loc prép* (de manière à) so as to, in order to; **de ~ à ne pas faire** so as not to do.

IV de sorte que *loc conj* **1** (de but) so that; **de ~ que je puisse venir** so that I might come; **2** (de manière) in such a way that; **la toile est peinte de ~ que** the canvas is painted in such a way that; **3** (de conséquence) with the result that; **de ~ que je n'ai pas pu venir** with the result that I couldn't come.

V en quelque sorte *loc adv* (pour ainsi dire) in a way.

VI en sorte de *loc prép* **fais en ~ d'être à l'heure** try to be on time.

VII en sorte que *loc conj* **1** (de but) **fais en ~ que tout soit en ordre** make sure everything is tidy; **faire en ~ qu'il comprenne** to make sure that he understands; **2** (de conséquence) so; **en ~ qu'il n'a rien compris** so he understood nothing.

sortie /sɔʀti/ *nf* **1** (lieu) exit; **la ~ est à gauche** the exit is to the left; **je t'attendrai à la ~** I'll wait for you outside (the building); **prenez la première ~** (sur une route) take the first exit; **'~'** (sur un panneau) 'exit', 'way out' GB; **trouver la ~** (de l'intérieur) to find one's way out; **la ~ est indiquée par une flèche** the exit ou way out GB is shown by an arrow; **raccompagner qn jusqu'à la ~** to see sb out; **à la ~ de la ville** (extra-muros) on the outskirts of the town; (intra-muros) on the edge of the town; **à la ~ ouest de la ville** on the western edge of the town; **les ~s de Paris sont encombrées** the roads out of Paris are busy; **surveiller la ~ des écoles** to patrol the school gates; **à la ~ du canal de Suez** at the mouth of the Suez canal; **2** (moment) **à ma ~ du tribunal/de l'armée/de la réunion** when I left the court/the army/the meeting; **sa femme l'attendait à sa ~ de prison** his wife was waiting for him when he came out of prison; **depuis ma ~ de prison** since I came out of prison; **à leur ~ d'hôpital** when they came out of hospital; **prendre ses enfants à la ~ de l'école** to pick the children up after school; **se retrouver à la ~ de l'école/du théâtre** to meet after school/the play; **mendier à la ~ des cinémas/églises** to beg outside cinemas/churches; **être arrêté à sa ~ du territoire** to be arrested as one is leaving the country; **six mois après leur ~ de l'université** six months after they left college; **à la ~ de l'hiver** at the end of winter; **~ des usines/bureaux/magasins** knocking-off○ time; **à la ~ des usines/bureaux/magasins** when the factories/offices/shops GB ou stores US turn out GB ou lock up US; **l'heure de la ~** Scol home time; Entr knocking-off○ time; **3** (départ) **faire une ~ fracassante/remarquée** [*personne*] to make a sensational/conspicuous exit; **je suis las de tes entrées et ~s continuelles** I'm tired of your constant comings and goings; **~ d'un navire** departure of a boat; **la ~ de la récession/crise** the end of the recession/crisis; **la ~ de la livre hors du SME** the withdrawal of the pound from the ERM; **la ~ des Républiques hors de l'union** the republics' withdrawal from the union; **le droit à la libre ~ du territoire** the right to travel freely abroad; **être interdit de ~ (du territoire)** to be forbidden to leave the country; **jusqu'à la ~ du ventre maternel** until the moment of birth; **4** (activité) gén outing; **économiser sur les ~s** to cut down on outings; **faire une ~** to go on an outing; **être de ~**○ [*élèves*] to be on an outing; **faire une ~ avec l'école** to go on a school outing; **~ à la campagne** outing to the country; **ce soir, c'est mon soir de ~** tonight is my evening out; **le samedi est mon jour de ~** Saturday is my day out; **c'est la ~ du samedi soir** it's Saturday night out; **priver qn de ~** to forbid sb to go out; **première ~ d'un convalescent** a convalescent's first time out; **le patron est de ~**○ the boss is out; **première ~ en coupe du monde** Sport first game in the world cup; **5** (commercialisation) (de nouveau modèle) launching ₵; (de film, disque) release; (de livre) publication; (de collection) presentation; (de nouveau journal) publication; **le film/livre a été interdit dès sa ~** the film/book was banned as soon as it came out; **lors de la ~ parisienne du film** when the film was released in Paris; **la ~ du journal est à six heures** the newspaper comes out at six o'clock; **le numéro a été entièrement vendu dès sa ~** the issue sold out as soon as it went on sale; **6**○ (déclaration) remark; **faire une ~ désagréable** to make a nasty remark; **7** Électron, Électrotech, Ordinat output; **données de ~** output data; **puissance de ~** output power; **signal de ~** output signal; **~ sur imprimante** (processus) printing; **faire une ~ sur imprimante** to print; **~ laser** (processus) hardcopy laser output; (feuille imprimée) laser hardcopy; **8** Pol (retraite) retirement; **~ de la vie politique** retirement from political life; **9** Théât (d'acteur) **~ (de scène)** exit; **il a été applaudi à sa ~ (de scène)** he was applauded as he left the stage; **rater**○ **sa ~** to fluff○ one's exit; ▶**faux**[1]; **10** Mil sortie; **~ de nuit** night sortie; **faire/tenter une ~** to make/to attempt a sortie; **11** Compta (dépense) expenditure; **12** Fin (de capitaux) outflow; **~ de fonds** cash outflow; **13** Écon (de marchandises) export; **14** Tech (orifice) outlet; **~ des gaz d'échappement** (processus) discharge of exhaust gases; **~ des eaux usées** (emplacement) sewage outfall; (processus) discharge of sewage.

■ **~ des artistes** Théât stage-door; **~ d'autoroute** exit; **~ de bain** Mode bathrobe; **être en ~ de bain** to be wearing a bathrobe; **~ de but** (au football) goal-kick; **~ en corner** corner; **'~ d'école'** (sur un panneau) 'school'; **~ éducative** field trip; **~ dans l'espace** spacewalk; **faire une ~ dans l'espace** to walk in space; **~ de mêlée** (au rugby) heel-out; **~ scolaire** (d'un jour) school outing; (de plus d'un jour) school trip; **~ en touche** (au football) throw-in; **~ (en touche) pour Pau** Pau throw-in; **'~ de véhicules'** (sur un panneau) 'vehicle exit'.

IDIOMES **je t'attends** or **tu vas voir à la ~**○! I'll get you outside!

sortilège /sɔʀtilɛʒ/ *nm* spell; **jeter un ~** to cast a spell; **les ~s de l'Orient** the magic of the East.

sortir /sɔʀtiʀ/ [30] **I** *nm* **au ~ de** at the end of; **au ~ de l'adolescence/mes études** at the end of adolescence/my studies.

II *vtr* **1** (promener) to take [sb/sth] out [*personne, chien, cheval*]; **~ un malade/son caniche** to take a patient/one's poodle out; **j'y vais moi-même, ça me sortira** I'll go myself, it'll give me a chance to get outside; **2**○ (inviter) to take [sb] out [*personne*]; **~ sa petite amie** to take one's girlfriend out; **3**○ (expulser) to throw [sb] out, to chuck○ [sb] out [*personne*] (**de** of); to send [sb] out [*élève*]; **se faire ~ en quart de finale** to be knocked out in the quarterfinal; **4** (mettre à l'extérieur) to get [sb/sth] out [*personne, papiers, parapluie, meubles de jardin, voiture, vêtements*] (**de** of); **~ l'argenterie** to get out the silverware; **~ qn du lit** to get sb out of bed; **~ une bille de sa poche** to take a marble out of one's pocket; **~ sa voiture en marche arrière** to reverse one's car out; **~ les mains de ses poches** to take one's hands out of one's pockets; **~ un couteau/revolver** to pull out a knife/revolver; **~ le drapeau** to hang out the flag; **~ les draps pour les aérer** to put out the sheets to air; **~ du pus** to squeeze out pus; **~ un point noir** to squeeze a blackhead; **~ la poubelle/les ordures** to put the bin/the rubbish GB ou garbage US out; **~ sa tête/langue** to poke one's head/tongue out; **~ une carte** to bring out a card; **5** (délivrer) **~ qn de** to get sb out of; **~ un ami de prison** to get a friend out of jail; **~ un ami de sa dépression** to pull a friend out of his depression; **~ une entreprise de ses difficultés** to get a company out of difficulties; **~ qn de sa léthargie** to shake sb out of his/her lethargy; **6** (commercialiser) to bring out [*livre, disque, modèle, nouveau produit, nouveau journal*]; to release [*film*]; to present [*collection*]; **7** (produire) to turn out [*livre, disque, film, produit*]; **~ mille téléviseurs par jour** to turn out one thousand televisions a day; **8** Imprim to bring [sth] out [*exemplaire, numéro, journal*]; **9** Ordinat [*ordinateur*] to output [*données, résultats*]; **10** (exporter) (légalement) to export [*marchandises*] (**de** from); (illégalement) to smuggle [sth] out [*marchandises*] (**de** of); **11**○ (dire) to come out with○ [*paroles*]; **~ des énormités/insultes/âneries** to come out with rubbish/insults/nonsense; **il (nous) sort toujours des excuses** he's always coming out ou up with excuses; **~ une blague** to crack a joke.

III *vi* (+ *v être*) **1** (aller dehors) [*personne, animal*] to go out; (venir dehors) [*personne, animal*] to come out (**de** of); **~ par la fenêtre/la porte de derrière** to go out through the window/the back door; **~ dans la rue/sur le balcon** to go out in the streets/on the balcony; **~ faire un tour** (à pied) to go out for a walk; (à vélo, cheval) to go out for a ride; (en voiture) to go out for a drive; **~ faire des courses** to go out shopping; **~ déjeuner** to go out for lunch; **être sorti** to be out; **sortez les mains en l'air!** come out with your hands up!; **sortez et ne revenez pas!** get out and don't come back!; **~ discrètement** to slip out (**de** of); **~ en vitesse** to rush out; **~ en courant** to run out; **~ en trombe de sa chambre** to burst out of one's room; **faire ~ qn** to get sb outside; **faire ~ son chien** to take one's dog out; **laisser ~ qn** to allow sb out; **laisser ~ les élèves** (à la fin de la classe) to dismiss the class; **empêcher de ~** to keep [sb/sth] in [*personne, animal*]; **~ dans l'espace** to space walk; **~ de scène** to leave the stage; **Figaro sort** exit Figaro; **Figaro et Almaviva sortent** exeunt Figaro and Almaviva; ▶**devant**[1], **œil**; **2** (passer du temps dehors) to go out; **~ tous les soirs/avec des amis** to go out every night/with friends; **~ au restaurant** to go out to a restaurant; **~ avec qn** to go out with sb; **inviter qn à sortir** to ask sb out; **~ en ville** to go out on the town; **3** (quitter un lieu) **~ de** to leave; **~ de chez qn** to leave sb's house; **~ d'une réunion** to leave a meeting; **~ du port** [*navire*] to leave port; **~ du pays** [*personne, marchandise*] to leave the country; **~ de chez soi** to go out; **~ de la pièce** to walk out of the room; **sortez d'ici/de là!** get out of here/of there!; **~ de son lit/son bain** [*personne*] to get out of bed/the bath; **~ de la route** [*véhicule*] to leave the road; **~ de la famille** [*bijou, tableau*] to go out of the family; **~ tout chaud du four** to be hot from the oven; ▶**loup**; **4** (venir d'un lieu) **~ de** to come out of; **~ de chez le médecin** to come out of the doctor's; **~ de sa chambre en chemise de nuit** to come out of one's room in one's nightgown; **5** (quitter un état, une situation) **~ d'un profond sommeil/d'un rêve** to wake up from a deep sleep/from a dream; **~ de son mutisme** or **silence** to break one's silence; **~ de l'adolescence** to come out of adolescence ; **~ de la récession** to pull out of the recession; **~ d'un cercle vicieux** to break out of a vicious circle; **~ de soi** to lose control of oneself; **~ de l'hiver** to reach the end of winter; **on n'en sort jamais**○ there's no end to it; **on n'en sortira jamais!** (problème) we'll never see the end of it!; (embouteillage) we'll never get out of it!; **il refuse d'en ~**○ (changer d'avis) he won't budge an inch○; **il n'y a pas à ~ de là**○ there's no two ways about it○; **6** (venir de quitter un état) **~ à peine de l'enfance** to be just emerging from childhood; **~ de maladie/d'une dépression** to be recovering from an illness/from a bout of depression; **~ d'une**

crise/guerre to emerge from a crisis/war; **7** (émerger) to come out; **~ différent/désenchanté/déçu** to come out different/disenchanted/disappointed; **elle est sortie de sa dépression très affaiblie** after her depression she was a mere shadow of her former self; **8** (s'échapper) [*eau, air, étincelle, fumée*] to come out (**de** of; **par** through); **le bouchon ne sort pas** the cork won't come out; **l'eau sort du robinet** the water comes out of the tap GB ou faucet US; **une odeur sort de la pièce** there's a smell coming from the room; **faire ~** to squeeze [sth] out [*pâte, colle, eau, jus*] (**de** of); to eject [*cassette*] (**de** from); **~ en masse** [*personnes*] to pour out; ▶ **vérité**; **9** (pousser) [*plante, insecte*] to come out; [*dent*] to come through; **les bourgeons sortent** the buds are coming out; **~ de terre** [*plante*] to spring up; [*bâtiment*] to rise from the ground; **il lui est sorti une dent** he/she's cut a tooth; **10** (dépasser) to stick out; **il y a un clou qui sort** there's a nail sticking out; **~ de l'eau à marée basse** [*roche*] to stick out of the water at low tide; **11** (être commercialisé) [*film, disque, livre, nouveau modèle, nouveau produit, collection*] to come out; **Le Monde sort l'après-midi** Le Monde goes on sale in the afternoon; **~ tous les jours/toutes les semaines/tous les mois** [*journal, périodique*] to be published daily/weekly/monthly; **~ de la chaîne** [*produit industriel*] to come off the production line; **~ des presses** [*journal, livre*] to come off the press; **ça sort tout juste des presses** it's hot off the press; **12** (provenir) [*personne, produit*] to come from; **~ d'un milieu intellectuel/d'une famille de banquiers** to come from an intellectual background/from a family of bankers; **~ de Berkeley** Univ to have graduated from Berkeley; **~ de chez Hachette** to have been with Hachette previously; **d'où sors-tu à cette heure**○? where have you been?; **d'où sors-tu comme ça**○? what have you been doing to look like that?; **d'où sort-il celui-là**○? what planet's he from○?; **13** (être en dehors) **~ du sujet** [*personne*] to wander off the subject; [*remarque*] to be beside the point; **cela sort de ma compétence/de mes fonctions** that's not in my brief/within my authority; **14** (être tiré) [*numéro, sujet*] to come up; **c'est le 17 qui est sorti** it was (number) 17 that came up; **15** Ordinat to exit.

IV se sortir *vpr* **1** (échapper) **se ~ d'une situation difficile** to get out of a predicament; **se ~ de la pauvreté** to escape from poverty; **se ~ d'une dépression** to come out of a bout of depression; **se ~ d'une épreuve** to come through an ordeal; **s'en ~** (situation difficile) to get out of it; (maladie) to get over it; **s'en ~ vivant** to escape with one's life; **2** (se débrouiller) **s'en ~** gén to pull through; (financièrement) to cope; (intellectuellement, manuellement, physiquement) to manage; **tu t'en sors?** can you manage?; **s'en ~ tant bien que mal** to struggle through; **s'en ~ à peine** (financièrement) to scrape a living.

IDIOMES **~ par les trous de nez**○ to get up one's nose○.

SOS /ɛsoɛs/ *nm* **1** (signal) SOS; **lancer un ~** to send out an SOS; **2** (service) emergency service; **~ médecins/poisons** doctors'/poison emergency service; **~ dépannage** emergency breakdown service; **3** (ligne téléphonique) helpline; **~ enfants battus/tabac** child abuse/smokers' helpline.

■ **~ racisme** *anti-racist organization in France.*

sosie /sɔzi/ *nm* double; **Paul est le ~ de son père** Paul is the spitting image of his father; **c'est ton ~!** he/she's the spitting image of you!

sot, sotte /so, sɔt/ **I** *adj* [*personne, idée, projet*] silly.

II *nm,f* silly thing; **tu es un ~** you're a silly thing; **petit ~!** you silly thing!

IDIOMES **il n'y a pas de ~s métiers** Prov no profession is without merit.

sotie = **sottie**.

sot-l'y-laisse /solilɛs/ *nm inv* oyster (*of fowl*).

sottement /sɔtmɑ̃/ *adv* foolishly, stupidly.

sottie /sɔti/ *nf*: *satirical farce of 15th and 16th centuries.*

sottise /sɔtiz/ *nf* **1** (manque de jugement) silliness, foolishness; **d'une ~ impensable** incredibly silly; **avoir la ~ de faire/dire** to be silly enough to do/say; **2** (parole) silly ou foolish remark; **dire des ~s** to talk rubbish; **il a encore dit une ~** he made another silly remark; **3** (acte) **c'est une ~ de faire** it's silly to do; **faire une ~** to do something silly; **commettre la ~ de faire** to be silly enough to do; **faire des ~s** [*enfants*] to be naughty.

sottisier /sɔtizje/ *nm* collection of howlers○.

sou /su/ *nm* **1** fig (petite monnaie) penny GB, cent US; **ça ne m'a pas coûté un ~** it didn't cost me a penny; **je ne veux pas payer un ~ de plus** I don't want to pay a penny more; **cette affaire ne rapporte pas un ~** this business doesn't make a penny; **il est arrivé/reparti sans le** or **un ~** he arrived/left without a penny; **je n'ai pas le premier ~** I haven't got a single penny GB ou a red cent US; **je n'ai pas un ~** I haven't got two pennies to rub together GB, I'm broke○; **être sans le ~** to be penniless; **un touriste sans le ~** a penniless tourist; **économiser ~ par** or **à ~** to scrimp and save; **il est près de ses ~s** he's a penny-pincher; **c'est une affaire de gros ~s** there's big money involved; **un manteau de quatre ~s** a cheap coat; ▶ **vaillant**; **2** fig (petite quantité) **il n'a pas un ~** or **deux ~s de bon sens/talent** he hasn't got a scrap of common sense/talent; **il n'a pas un ~ de méchanceté** he hasn't got a hint of malice in him; **3** Hist (pièce) sou; ▶ **appareil, machine**; **4** C (centième de dollar) cent; **5** H (cinq centimes suisses) five Swiss centimes.

IDIOMES **un ~ est un ~** every penny counts; **être propre comme un ~ neuf** to be clean as a new pin○; **s'embêter**○ or **s'ennuyer à cent ~s de l'heure** to be bored to death.

soubassement /subasmɑ̃/ *nm* **1** Constr (de bâtiment) base, base course; (de colonne) base; **2** Géol bedrock; **3** (d'affaire, de montage financier) bedrock.

soubresaut /subʀəso/ *nm* (de personne, animal) start; (de véhicule) jolt; **avoir un ~** [*personne, animal*] to give a start; [*véhicule*] to give a jolt; **les derniers ~s** (de personne, d'animal, empire) the death throes.

soubrette /subʀɛt/ *nf* maid.

souche /suʃ/ *nf* **1** (d'arbre) (tree) stump; (de vigne) stock; **2** (origine) stock; **de ~ paysanne** of peasant stock; **de vieille/bonne ~** of old/good stock; **être français de ~** to be French born and bred; **faire ~** to establish a line; **3** Biol strain; **~ virale/bactérienne** virus/bacterial strain; **4** (de carnet, livret) stub.

IDIOMES **dormir comme une ~** to sleep like a log; **rester (planté) comme une ~** to be rooted to the spot.

souci /susi/ *nm* **1** (inquiétude) **se faire du ~** to worry (**pour, à propos de** about); **se faire beaucoup de ~** to worry a lot; **ne te fais pas de ~** don't worry; **je ne me fais pas de ~ pour lui** I'm not worried about him; **tu te fais du ~ pour rien** there's nothing to worry about; **oh, lui il ne se fait pas de ~** oh, he doesn't worry too much about things; **donner (bien) du ~ à qn** to be a (great) worry to sb; **2** (problème) problem; **avoir des ~s** to have problems; **avoir de gros ~s d'argent/de santé/financiers** to have serious money/health/financial problems; **cela t'évitera bien des ~s** you'll save yourself a lot of problems ou trouble; **j'ai d'autres ~s (en tête)** I've got other things to worry about; **être sans ~s** to have no worries; **c'est le cadet** or **le moindre de mes ~s** that's the least of my worries; **leur unique ~ est de faire** all they care about is doing; **3** fml (soin) **avoir le ~ de qch** to care about sth; **avoir le ~ de faire** to be anxious to do; **leur ~ de la qualité/du réalisme** their concern for quality/realism; **avoir le ~ de la qualité/du réalisme** to care about quality/realism; **dans le ~ de qch/de faire** with a view to sth/to doing; **dans un ~ de diversification** with a view to diversification; **dans le seul ~ de plaire/de nous être agréable** with the sole desire of pleasing/of being nice to us; **répondre à un ~ de justice** to satisfy a desire for justice; **il a agi dans l'unique ~ de vos intérêts** he acted solely out of concern for your interests; **sans ~ de qch/de faire** with no thought for sth/of doing; **4** Bot marigold; **~ d'eau** marsh marigold; **~ des jardins** pot marigold.

soucier: **se soucier** /susje/ [2] *vpr* to care (**de qch** about sth; **de faire** about doing); **il ne se soucie guère de sa santé/son avenir** he cares little about his health/his future; **il ne se soucie pas de réussir/paraître** he doesn't care about success/his appearance; **sans se ~ de qch/faire** without concerning oneself with sth/doing.

soucieux, -ieuse /susjø, øz/ *adj* [*personne, air, visage, ton*] worried; **il avait l'air ~** he looked worried; **rendre qn ~** to worry sb; **ça me rend ~ de voir** it worries me to see; **être ~ de** to be concerned about [*réputation, santé*]; to care about [*indépendance, qualité, avenir*]; **être peu ~ de** to care little about [*convenances, apparences*]; **être ~ de faire** to be anxious to do; **être peu ~ de faire** to care little about doing.

soucoupe /sukup/ *nf* saucer.

■ **~ volante** flying saucer.

IDIOMES **ouvrir des yeux (grands) comme des ~s** to open one's eyes wide (in amazement).

soudage /sudaʒ/ *nm* gén welding; (brasage) soldering; **~ autogène** autogenous welding; **~ à l'arc** arc welding; **~ par points** spot welding.

soudain, ~e /sudɛ̃, ɛn/ **I** *adj* sudden, unexpected.

II *adv* suddenly, all of a sudden.

soudainement /sudɛnmɑ̃/ *adv* suddenly.

soudaineté /sudɛnte/ *nf* suddenness.

Soudan /sudɑ̃/ ▶ **321** *nprm* Sudan.

soudanais, ~e /sudanɛ, ɛz/ ▶ **462**, **537**

I *adj* Sudanese.

II *nm* Ling Sudanic.

Soudanais, ~e /sudanɛ, ɛz/ ▶ **537** *nm,f* Sudanese man/woman; **les ~** the Sudanese.

soudard /sudaʀ/ *nm* **1** (individu grossier) liter boor; **2** Hist soldier.

soude /sud/ *nf* **1** Chimie soda; **~ caustique** caustic soda; **~ du commerce** or **ménagère** washing soda; **2** Bot saltwort.

souder /sude/ [1] **I** *vtr* **1** Tech (travail du métal) gén to weld; (braser) to solder; (travail des plastiques) to seal; **2** (réunir) to join [*bords, extrémités*] (**à** to); fig to bind [sb] together [*personnes*]; **comité bien soudé autour de son président** committee united behind its chairman; **3** Culin to seal [*bords, pâte, couvercle*].

II se souder *vpr* **1** lit [*vertèbres*] to fuse; [*os*] to knit together; **2** fig [*équipe*] to become united; [*personnes*] to be brought closer together.

soudeur /sudœʀ/ ▶ **510** *nm* welder.

soudoyer /sudwaje/ [23] *vtr* to bribe; **se faire ~** to be bribed.

soudure /sudyʀ/ *nf* **1** Tech (joint) weld, join; (fil à souder) solder; (opération) gén welding; (brasage) soldering; **~ autogène** welding; **~ à l'arc** arc welding; **2** Méd (de vertèbres) fusing; Bot (de pétales) fusing; **3** (transition) **faire la ~** (entre deux systèmes, récoltes) to bridge the gap (**entre** between); (entre deux rentrées d'argent) to make ends meet.

soufflage /suflaʒ/ *nm* **~ du verre** glass-blowing; **~ à la bouche** hand-blowing; **~ de la fonte** iron-blowing.

soufflant, **~e** /suflɑ̃, ɑ̃t/ **I** *adj* **1** (essoufflé) breathless; **2** Tech **machine ~e** blowing apparatus; **3**○ (étonnant) stunning.

II◑ *nm* (arme) gun-shooter○.

III soufflante *nf* **1** Ind (en verrerie) blowing machine; (en métallurgie) blower; **2** Mécan blowing-down engine.

souffle /sufl/ *nm* **1** Physiol (respiration) breath; **retenir/reprendre son ~** to hold/ to catch one's breath; **avoir le ~ court** to be short of breath; **retrouver son ~** lit, fig to get one's breath back; **couper le ~ à qn** lit to wind sb; fig to take sb's breath away; **à couper le ~** [*beauté, vitesse*] breathtaking; [*beau*] breathtakingly; **(en) avoir le ~ coupé** lit to be winded; fig to be speechless; **être à bout de ~** [*personne*] to be out of breath; [*pays, économie*] to be running out of steam; **travailler jusqu'à en perdre le ~** to work till one drops; **jusqu'au dernier ~** till one's dying breath; **dire qch dans un ~** to say sth in a whisper; **parler dans un même ~ de ceci et de cela** to speak in the same breath of this and that; **retrouver un deuxième** or **second** or **nouveau ~** (après un effort) [*personne*] to get one's second wind; (après un marasme, vieillissement) [*pays, entreprise, activité, personne, machine*] to get a new lease of GB ou on US life; **donner un deuxième** or **second** or **nouveau ~ à qn/ qch** [*personne, décision, changement*] to put new life into sb/sth; **avoir du ~** lit [*trompettiste*] to have good lungs; [*acteur, chanteur*] to have a powerful voice; [*sportif*] to be fit; fig (avoir de l'endurance) [*personne*] to have staying power; [*moteur*] to be powerful; (avoir de l'esprit) [*auteur, œuvre*] to be inspired; (avoir de l'audace)○ to have nerve; **avoir un ~ de marathonien** to have the stamina of a marathon runner; **manquer de ~** lit [*personne*] to be short of breath; fig (manquer d'endurance) [*personne*] to lack staying power; (manquer d'esprit) [*œuvre*] to lack that vital spark; ▶**rendre**; **2** (bruit de respiration) breathing; **~ léger/précipité** light/ rapid breathing; **3** (brise) breeze; **~ parfumé** scented breeze; **pas un ~ (de vent/d'air)** not a breath of wind/of air; **au moindre ~** at the slightest breeze; **4** (esprit) spirit; **~ révolutionnaire/ olympique** revolutionary/Olympic spirit; **~ de la liberté/révolte** spirit of freedom/ rebellion; **5** (force) inspiration; **~ d'un film/roman/discours** inspiration of a film/ novel/speech; **~ créateur** creative inspiration; **~ vital** breath of life; **6** (élément) touch; **~ de génie** touch of genius; **7** Phys (d'explosion, de réacteur, ventilateur) blast; **8** Méd (en cardiologie) murmur; **~ au cœur** heart murmur; **~ diastolique/systolique** diastolic/systolic murmur.

IDIOMES **être battu/échouer d'un ~** to be beaten/to fail by a whisker GB ou hair US; **sentir le ~ de la mort** to feel the cold hand of death.

soufflé, **~e** /sufle/ **I** *pp* ▶**souffler**.

II *pp adj* **1**○ (stupéfait) flabbergasted; **en rester ~** to be flabbergasted; **2** Ind [*bitume, huile, pâte*] blown; **3** Culin [*omelette, pommes de terre*] souffléed.

III *nm* Culin soufflé; **~ au fromage/chocolat** cheese/chocolate soufflé.

IDIOMES **retomber comme un ~** to come to nothing, to fall flat○.

souffler /sufle/ [1] **I** *vtr* **1** (éteindre) to blow out [*bougie, lampe*]; **2** (envoyer) to blow [*air, odeur, poussière*]; **le ventilateur souffle de l'air froid** the fan is blowing cold air; **~ de la fumée au visage/dans les yeux de qn** to blow smoke in sb's face/eyes; **ne me souffle pas ton haleine au visage** don't breathe all over me; **3** (chuchoter) to whisper [*mots, texte*] (**à qn** to sb; **que** that); **~ qch à l'oreille de qn** to whisper sth into sb's ear; **je t'aime, souffla-t-il** I love you, he whispered; **~ la réplique à un acteur** Théât to prompt an actor, to give an actor a prompt; **4** (suggérer) to suggest [*idée, nom*] (**à** to); **elle m'a soufflé l'idée** she suggested the idea to me; **on lui a soufflé la réponse** sb told him/her the answer; **5** Ind to blow [*verre, bouteille*]; to blast [*métal*]; **6** (détruire) [*explosion, bombe*] to blow out [*vitre*]; to blast [*construction*]; **7** Jeux (aux dames) to huff [*pièce*]; **8**○ (prendre) to pinch○ [*travail, propriété*] (**à** from); to whip away○ [*contrat*] (**à** from); **mon meilleur ami m'a soufflé mon poste et ma femme** my best friend pinched my job and my wife; **9**○ (stupéfier) to flabbergast; **j'ai été soufflé d'apprendre la nouvelle** I was flabbergasted to hear the news.

II *vi* **1** Météo [*vent*] to blow; **~ en** or **par rafales** to blow in gusts; **le vent souffle fort** there's a strong wind; **ça souffle** it's windy; **le vent souffle en tempête** there's a gale-force wind; **2** (se propager) [*vent de révolte, liberté*] to blow; **le vent de la liberté souffle dans le pays/sur tout le continent** the wind of freedom is sweeping through the country/through the continent; **un vent de folie souffle sur le stade** frenzy is sweeping through the stadium; **3** (reprendre sa respiration) to get one's breath back; [*cheval*] to get its wind back; fig [*personne, économie*] to take a breather○; **laisse-moi ~!** let me get my breath back!; (pour rembourser) give me a breather!; **le pays peut enfin ~** the country can relax at last; **4** (respirer difficilement) to puff; **suant et soufflant** huffing and puffing; **5** (produire un souffle) [*personne, animal*] to blow; **~ doucement** to blow gently; **~ dans une trompette** to blow a trumpet; **~ sur son thé** to blow on one's tea; **~ sur une bougie** to blow out a candle; **souffle fort!** (pour te moucher) have a good blow!; **~ sur le feu** lit to blow on the fire; fig to inflame the situation; **il suffirait de lui ~ dessus pour qu'elle tombe** one puff of wind would blow her over; **6** (donner la réponse) to tell sb the answer; **on ne souffle pas!** no prompting!

IDIOMES **~ le chaud et le froid** to blow hot and cold; **~ comme un bœuf** or **un phoque** or **une locomotive** to puff and pant.

soufflerie /sufləʀi/ *nf* **1** Tech (d'expérimentation) wind tunnel; **essais en ~** wind tunnel testing; **2** (d'orgue, de forge, four) bellows (*pl*); **3** (machine) blower; (lieu) blower house; **4** (de verre) (machine) glassblower; (entreprise) glass-blowing company.

soufflet /suflɛ/ *nm* **1** Tech (de cheminée, forge, d'orgue, appareil photo) bellows (*pl*); **2** Rail (de wagon) concertina vestibule; **3** (de chaussure, poche) gusset; **4**† (gifle) slap; **donner/recevoir un ~** to give/to get a slap.

■ **~ de vitesses** Aut gear-lever GB ou gear-shift US grommet.

souffleter† /suflәte/ [20] *vtr* **~ qn** to slap sb's face.

souffleur, **-euse** /suflœʀ, øz/ **I** *nm,f* **1** ▶**510** Théât prompter; **2** Ind **~ (de verre)** glassblower.

II *nm* Zool (dauphin) bottle-nosed dolphin.

III souffleuse *nf* Agric (à grains) seed blower.

souffrance /sufʀɑ̃s/ *nf* suffering ¢; **la ~ physique/morale** physical/moral suffering; **abréger les ~s d'un animal** to put an animal out of its misery; **en ~** [*projet, dossier*] pending; **laisser une affaire en ~** to leave a matter pending; **colis en ~** (non livré) parcel awaiting delivery; (non réclamé) unclaimed parcel.

souffrant, **~e** /sufʀɑ̃, ɑ̃t/ *adj* unwell; **être ~** to be unwell; **le patron, ~, a dû annuler la réunion** the boss was unwell and had to cancel the meeting.

souffre-douleur /sufʀәdulœʀ/ *nm inv* punch-bag GB, punching-bag US.

souffreteux, **-euse** /sufʀәtø, øz/ *adj* [*enfant, vieillard*] sickly.

souffrir /sufʀiʀ/ [4] **I** *vtr* **1** (supporter) **~ tout de qn** to put up with anything from sb; **il ne souffre pas la critique** he can't take criticism; **il ne souffre pas d'être interrompu/contredit** he can't stand being interrupted/contradicted; **elle ne peut plus le ~** she can't stand him any more; **2** (permettre) fml **souffrez que je vous dise** allow me to tell you; **cette affaire ne peut ~ aucun retard** this matter brooks no delay sout; **la règle souffre quelques exceptions** this rule does admit of a few exceptions sout.

II *vi* **1** (physiquement) [*personne, animal*] to suffer; **il a beaucoup souffert** he has suffered a great deal ou a lot; **~ en silence** to suffer in silence; **faire ~ qn/un animal** to cause sb/an animal suffering; **~ de qch** to suffer from [*cancer, rhumatismes, diabète, malformation*]; **~ du dos/de l'estomac/ du genou** to suffer from back/stomach/knee problems; **les enfants qui souffrent de malnutrition** children suffering from malnutrition; **~ du froid/de la chaleur/du manque d'eau** to suffer from the cold/from the heat/from lack of water; **ma blessure/ cheville me fait ~** my wound/ankle hurts; **mes chaussures me font ~** my shoes are hurting me; **j'ai souffert chez le dentiste** I suffered at the dentist's; **est-ce qu'il souffre?** is he in pain?; **2** (moralement) [*personne*] to suffer; **faire ~** [*personne*] to make [sb] suffer; [*problème, situation*] to upset; **~ de** to suffer from [*trac*]; **~ de la discrimination/du racisme** to be a victim of discrimination/of racism; **ils souffrent de l'éloignement d'avec leurs enfants** they are finding it painful to be separated from their children; **~ d'être rejeté/d'être incompris** to suffer the pain of rejection/of being misunderstood; **ils souffrent de ne pas se voir/de ne rien pouvoir faire** they find it painful to be separated/to be unable to do anything; **elle souffre de voir que** it upsets her to see that; **3** (être endommagé) [*cultures, vigne, secteur, économie*] to be badly affected (**de** by); [*pays, région, ville*] to suffer (**de** from); **4**○ (peiner) [*personne, équipe*] to have a hard time (**pour faire** doing); **j'ai fini la course mais j'ai souffert!** I finished the race but it was tough!

III se souffrir *vpr* **ils ne peuvent pas se ~** they can't stand each other.

soufisme /sufism/ *nm* Sufism.

soufrage /sufʀaʒ/ *nm* sulphurization[GB].

soufre /sufʀ/ *nm* sulphur[GB]; **odeur de ~** lit, fig smell of sulphur[GB]; **jaune ~** sulphur[GB]-yellow.

IDIOMES **sentir le ~** to smack of heresy.

soufrer /sufʀe/ [1] *vtr* to sulphurate[GB] [*étoffe, laine*]; to sulphur[GB] [*allumette*]; to treat [sth] with sulphur[GB] [*vigne*].

soufrière /sufʀijɛʀ/ *nf* sulphur[GB] mine.

souhait /swɛ/ *nm* wish; **c'est mon ~ le plus cher** it's my dearest wish; **émettre/ formuler un ~** to express/to make a wish; **exaucer un ~** to grant a wish; **répondre aux ~s de qn** [*proposition, situation*] to suit sb; **à ~** [*stupide, beau*] incredibly; **fruit doré à ~** perfectly ripe fruit.

IDIOMES **à vos ~s!** bless you!

souhaitable /swɛtabl/ *adj* desirable; **il est/ serait ~ de faire** it is/would be desirable to do.

souhaiter /swete/ [1] *vtr* **1** (espérer) to hope for; **~ la fin de la crise** to hope for an end to the crisis; **~ que** to hope that; **il est à ~ que tout se passe bien** it is to be hoped that everything will go well; **c'est une expérience que je ne souhaite à personne** it's an experience I wouldn't wish on anyone; **2** (exprimer) **~ qch à qn** to wish sb sth; **je souhaite un avenir prospère à cette entreprise** I wish the company a prosperous future; **~ bonne chance/(la) bonne année à qn** to wish sb luck/a happy New Year; **je vous souhaite une bonne et heureuse année** I wish you a happy New Year; **~ la bienvenue à qn** to welcome sb, to bid sb welcome; **~ beaucoup de bonheur à qn** to wish sb every happiness; **je vous souhaite d'obtenir très bientôt votre diplôme** I hope you get your degree very soon; **3** (désirer) **il souhaite** or **souhaiterait se rendre là-bas en voiture** he would like to go by car; **nous souhaiterions que vous veniez dès que possible** we would like you to come as soon as possible.

souillé, ~e /suje/ **I** *pp* ▶ **souiller**.
II *pp adj* dirty, soiled; **être ~ de** to be stained with.

souiller /suje/ [1] *vtr* **1** (salir, polluer) to soil, to make [sth] dirty; **~ son lit** to soil one's bed; **~ qch de qch** to soil sth with sth; **2** (rendre impur) liter to defile [*lieu, personne*]; to sully [*mémoire, réputation*].

souillon /sujɔ̃/ *nf* sloven, slob○, slattern†.

souillure /sujyʀ/ *nf* **1** (flétrissure morale) stain, taint; **2** (saleté) stain.

souk /suk/ *nm* **1** (marché arabe) souk; **2**○ (désordre) mess; (bruit) racket○; **mettre le ~ dans qch** to make a mess of [*placard, papiers*]; to make a mess in [*pièce*]; **faire le ~** to make a racket○.

soul /sul/ Mus **I** *adj inv* soul.
II *nf* soul (music).

soûl, ~e /su, sul/ **I** *adj* **1** (ivre) drunk; **un peu/complètement ~** a bit/completely drunk; **être fin ~**○ to be blind drunk; **2** fig (grisé) drunk (**de** with); **être ~ de grand air** to be drunk with fresh air; **j'étais ~ de leurs paroles** I was drunk with their words.
II tout son soûl *loc adv* [*boire, manger*] one's fill; [*pleurer, rire*] as much as one wants; **dormir tout son ~** to sleep as much as one wants.
IDIOMES **être ~ comme une bourrique** or **un cochon**○ to be drunk as a lord GB ou skunk○.

soulagement /sulaʒmɑ̃/ *nm* relief; **ce fut un immense ~** it was an enormous relief; **au ~ de qn** to sb's relief; **à mon grand ~** to my great relief; **au ~ général** to everyone's relief.

soulager /sulaʒe/ [13] **I** *vtr* **1** (décharger) to relieve [*personne, entreprise, étagère*] (**de** of); **passe-moi une valise, ça te soulagera** let me relieve you of one of your suitcases; **il faut le ~ des tâches administratives** we'll have to relieve him of administrative duties; **suppression d'une taxe pour ~ les entreprises exportatrices** tax relief for exporters; **2** (apaiser) to relieve [*personne*]; to relieve, to ease [*peine, conscience*]; **~ qn d'un mal de tête** to relieve sb's headache; **pleure un bon coup, ça soulage** have a good cry, you'll feel better; **la mort de l'assassin ne soulagera pas ma peine** the death of the murderer will not assuage my grief; **tu m'as soulagé d'un grand poids** you've taken a great weight off my shoulders; **3**○ fig (voler) to relieve (**de qch** of sth); **il s'est fait ~ de son portefeuille** somebody relieved him of his wallet.
II se soulager *vpr* **1**○ (satisfaire un besoin naturel) euph to relieve oneself; **2** (s'apaiser) **elle m'a raconté tout cela pour se ~** she told me the whole story to get it off her chest.

soûlant○**, ~e** /sulɑ̃, ɑ̃t/ *adj* **elle est ~e!** she makes my head spin!; **son discours était ~** his/her speech made my head spin.

soûlard●**, ~e** /sulaʀ, aʀd/ *nm,f* drunk, wino●.

soûler /sule/ [1] **I** *vtr* **1** (rendre ivre) [*personne*] to get [sb] drunk [*personne*]; [*alcool*] to make [sb] drunk [*personne*]; **ils cherchaient à la ~ au gin/à la bière** they were trying to get her drunk on gin/on beer; **2** (griser) [*odeur, parfum, grand air*] to intoxicate [*personne*]; **3**○ (étourdir) **tu nous soûles avec tes histoires/discours** you make our heads spin with your stories/speeches; **ce voyage m'a soûlée** the trip left me reeling.
II se soûler *vpr* **1** (s'enivrer) to get drunk; **se ~ à la bière** to get drunk on beer; **se ~ la gueule**● to get sloshed○, to get pissed●; **2** (se griser) **se ~ de qch** to become intoxicated with sth [*paroles, musique*]; **se ~ de travail** to get punch-drunk from work.

soûlerie○ /sulʀi/ *nf* drinking spree, bender○; **participer à une ~** to go on a bender○ ou drinking spree.

soulèvement /sulɛvmɑ̃/ *nm* (insurrection) uprising.
■ **~ de terrain** Géol upheaval of the ground.

soulever /sulve/ [16] **I** *vtr* **1** (déplacer vers le haut) [*personne*] to lift [*objet*]; [*vent, tourbillon, véhicule*] to whip up [*feuilles, poussière*]; **~ qn/qch de terre** [*personne*] to pick sb/sth up; [*vent*] to sweep sb/sth up into the air; **les vagues soulevaient le navire** the waves lifted the ship up; ▶ **montagne 2** (entraîner) to arouse [*enthousiasme, colère, dégoût*]; to stir up [*foule, peuple, opinion*] (**contre** against); to raise [*problèmes, difficultés, obstacles*]; to give rise to [*protestations, tollé, applaudissements, débats*]; **ils ont réussi à ~ l'opinion contre les syndicats** they succeeded in stirring up opinion against the unions; **3** (faire considérer) to raise [*question, problème, interrogation*]; **la nouvelle réforme soulève encore une fois la question** the new reform once again raises the issue; **4**○ (dérober) to nick○ GB, to swipe○ [*objet, portefeuille*]; **5**● (séduire) to pull○ GB, to make○ US [*fille, femme*].
II se soulever *vpr* **1** (se dresser) to raise oneself up; **il demanda au malade de se ~ un peu** he asked the patient to raise himself up a bit; **je me suis soulevé pour mieux voir** I raised myself to see better; **il s'est soulevé sur un coude** he propped himself up on his elbow; **la couverture se soulève au rythme de sa respiration** the blanket rises and falls with his/her breathing; **2** (se révolter) [*peuple, groupe*] to rise up (**contre** against).
IDIOMES **ça me soulève le cœur** or **l'estomac** (odeur, sensation) it turns my stomach; (attitude, ignominie) it makes me sick.

soulier /sulje/ *nm* shoe.
IDIOMES **être dans ses petits ~s** to feel uncomfortable.

souligner /suliɲe/ [1] *vtr* **1** (d'un trait) to underline [*mot, titre*]; to outline [*yeux*]; **~ qch en bleu** to underline sth in blue ink; **~ les mots de deux traits** underline the words twice; **2** (accentuer) to emphasize [*attitude, remarque, importance, intérêt, situation*]; to set off [*teint, éclat*]; **c'est à ~** it must be emphasized.

soûlographe○ /sulɔgʀaf/ *nmf* boozer○.

soûlographie○ /sulɔgʀafi/ *nf* drunkenness.

soumettre /sumɛtʀ/ [60] **I** *vtr* **1** (vaincre) to bring [sb/sth] to heel [*personne, groupe, région*]; to subdue [*ennemi, rebelles, armée*]; **2** (assujettir) **~ qn/qch à** to subject sb/sth to; **nous sommes soumis à un règlement/à l'impôt** we are subjected to regulations/to tax; **3** (proposer) to submit (**à** to); **~ un projet à un spécialiste/au jugement de qn** to submit a project to an expert/to sb's judgment; **~ une loi au vote** to put a law to the vote; **~ une proposition à qn** to put forward a proposal to sb; **4** (faire subir) **~ un sportif à un dur entraînement** to submit an athlete to hard training; **~ un produit à une température élevée** to submit a product to a high temperature.
II se soumettre *vpr* **1** (se rendre) [*ennemi, rebelles, région*] to submit; **2** (accepter) **se ~ à** to submit to [*règlement*].

soumis, ~e /sumi, iz/ **I** *pp* ▶ **soumettre**.
II *pp adj* submissive.

soumission /sumisjɔ̃/ *nf* **1** (assujettissement) submission (**à** to); **vivre dans la ~** to live in submission; **2** (reddition) submission (**à** to); **faire sa ~ à** to surrender to; **3** Admin, Comm tender; **~ cachetée** sealed tender; **faire une ~** to submit a tender.

soumissionnaire /sumisjɔnɛʀ/ *nmf* tenderer.

soumissionner /sumisjɔne/ [1] *vtr* to tender.

soupape /supap/ *nf* valve.
■ **~ d'admission** inlet valve; **~ d'échappement** exhaust valve; **~ de sécurité** or **sûreté** lit, fig safety valve.

soupçon /supsɔ̃/ *nm* **1** (sur l'honnêteté, authenticité) suspicion; **être au-dessus** or **à l'abri de tout ~** to be above suspicion; **éveiller les ~s de qn** to arouse (sb's) suspicion; **avoir des ~s sur qn/qch** to have one's suspicions about sb/sth; **2** (idée vague) fml **ne pas avoir ~ de qch** [*difficultés, problèmes*] to have no notion of sth; **il n'avait pas ~ que ce serait difficile** he had no idea it would be difficult; **3**○ (faible quantité) (de lait, vin) drop, spot○; (de cannelle, sel, d'herbes aromatiques) pinch.

soupçonnable /supsɔnabl/ *adj* **il n'est pas ~** he is above suspicion; **son honnêteté n'est pas ~** his/her honesty is unquestionable ou above suspicion.

soupçonner /supsɔne/ [1] *vtr* **1** (suspecter) to suspect; **~ qn de qch/d'avoir fait qch** to suspect sb of sth/of having done sth; **2** (conjecturer) to suspect [*piège, coup bas*]; **je soupçonne qu'il y a un problème/qu'il est jaloux** I suspect that there is a problem/that he is jealous; **c'est une possibilité que je ne soupçonnais pas** it's a possibility which had not entered my mind.

soupçonneusement /supsɔnøzmɑ̃/ *adv* suspiciously.

soupçonneux, -euse /supsɔnø, øz/ *adj* suspicious, mistrustful.

soupe /sup/ *nf* **1** Culin soup; **~ de légumes/aux oignons** vegetable/onion soup; **tremper la ~** to serve the soup; **à la ~**○! hum grub up○!, come and get it!; **c'est l'heure de la ~**○ it's supper time; ▶ **cheveu, gros**; **2**○ (neige) slush.
■ **~ instantanée** instant soup; **~ populaire** soup kitchen; **~ primitive** primeval soup; **~ en sachet** packet GB ou instant soup.
IDIOMES **par ici la bonne ~**○! come on, cough up○!, come on, hand over your money!; **être ~ au lait**○ to be quick-tempered; **être trempé comme une ~**○ to be soaked to the skin, to look like a drowned rat; **cracher dans la ~**○ to bite the hand that feeds you; **faire la ~ à la grimace**○ to sulk; **cette musique, c'est de la vraie ~**○! pej this music is reall vapid!; **il me mange la ~ sur la tête** he towers over me.

soupente /supɑ̃t/ *nf* **1** (sous un toit) loft, garret; **2** (sous un escalier) cupboard under the stairs.

souper /supe/ [1] **I** *nm* **1** (tard le soir) late dinner, supper; **~ aux chandelles** candle-lit dinner; **2** B, C (le soir) dinner, supper.
II *vi* **1** (tard le soir) to have late dinner; **2** B, C (le soir) to dine.
IDIOMES **en avoir soupé de qch/de faire**○ to have had it up to here with sth/with doing○.

soupeser /supəze/ [16] *vtr* **1** lit to heft, to feel the weight of [*objet*]; **2** fig to weigh up [*arguments*].

soupière /supjɛʀ/ *nf* soup tureen.

soupir /supiʀ/ *nm* **1** (expiration) sigh (**de** of); **avoir un ~** to give a sigh; **pousser un ~** to let out ou heave a sigh; **~ de soulagement** sigh of relief; **profond** or **grand ~** deep sigh; **avec** or **dans un ~** with a sigh; ▶ **rendre**; **2** liter (du vent) sighing; (d'amoureux) **~s** sighs; **3** Mus crotchet rest GB, quarter rest US; ▶ **quart**.

soupirail, *pl* **-aux** /supiʀaj, o/ *nm* cellar window.

soupirant† /supiʀɑ̃/ *nm* suitor†.

soupirer /supiʀe/ [1] *vi* [*personne, vent*] to sigh (**de** with); **'tout est fini' soupira-t-il** 'it's all over' he sighed; **~ pour qn** to pine for sb; **~ après qch** to yearn for sth.

souple /supl/ *adj* **1** (flexible) [*articulation, corps, animal*] supple; [*tige, lame*] flexible; [*cheveux, plastique, cuir, col*] soft; ▶ **disque** **2** (aisé) [*démarche, geste, style*] flowing (*épith*); [*forme, contour*] smooth; **cette voiture est très ~** this car runs smoothly; **3** (adaptable) [*caractère, règlement, gestion, horaire*] flexible.

souplesse /suplɛs/ *nf* **1** (de tige, lame, disque) flexibility; (de cheveux, plastique, cuir) softness; (de corps, d'animal) suppleness; **2** (de démarche) litheness, suppleness; (de geste) grace; (de voiture, conduite) smoothness; (de style) fluidity; **~ des formes** or **contours** smooth curves; **3** (de caractère, règlement, langue, gestion, d'esprit, horaire) flexibility; **faire qch avec ~** to show flexibility in doing sth; **en ~** smoothly; **4** Sport (en gymnastique) walkover; **~ avant/arrière** forward/backward walkover.

souquer /suke/ [1] **I** *vtr* to tighten.
II *vi* **~ ferme** Naut to pull hard (on the oars); fig to pull one's weight.

sourate /suʀat/ *nf* sura.

source /suʀs/ *nf* **1** (d'eau) spring; **capter/exploiter une ~** to tap/exploit a spring; **2** (de cours d'eau) source; **prendre sa ~ dans** or **à** to rise in, to have its source in; **remonter à la ~ d'une rivière** to follow a river to its source; **3** (origine) source; **~ de chaleur/revenus** source of heat/income; **la ~ du conflit** the source of the conflict; **être à la ~ de** to be at the source of; **être une ~ de** to be a source of [*conflits, ennuis, profits*]; **retenue à la ~** deduction at source; **4** (référence) source; **citer/vérifier ses ~s** to give/to check one's sources; **de bonne ~, de ~ sûre** [*provenir, savoir, apprendre*] from a reliable source; **de ~ bien informée** from a well-informed source; **je tiens ces renseignements de ~ sûre** my information comes from a reliable source.
IDIOMES **ça coule de ~** it's obvious; **revenir aux ~s** to return to the roots; **retour aux ~s** return to the roots.

sourcier /suʀsje/ ▶ **510** *nm* dowser, water diviner.

sourcil /suʀsi/ *nm* Anat eyebrow; **~s épais** bushy eyebrows.

sourcilier, **-ière** /suʀsilje, ɛʀ/ *adj* [*muscle*] superciliary; ▶ **arcade**.

sourciller /suʀsije/ [1] *vi* to raise one's eyebrows; **sans ~** without batting an eyelid.

sourcilleux, **-euse** /suʀsijø, øz/ *adj* **1** (exigeant) punctilious; **2** [*hautain*] supercilious.

sourd, **~e** /suʀ, suʀd/ **I** *adj* **1** Méd [*personne*] deaf; **être ~ d'une oreille** to be deaf in one ear; **arrête de hurler, je ne suis pas ~!** there's no need to shout, I'm not deaf!; **tu es ~ ou quoi?** are you deaf or what?; **2** (insensible) deaf (**à** to); **être ~ aux supplications/prières de qn** to be deaf to sb's pleas/entreaties; **être ~ à la pitié** to feel no pity; ▶ **pot**; **3** (étouffé) [*bruit, bourdonnement, craquement, explosion*] dull, muffled; [*voix*] muffled; [*plainte, gémissement, exclamation*] faint, muted; **4** (diffus) [*douleur*] dull; [*désir, tristesse, inquiétude*] gnawing, silent; [*anxiété*] nameless; **5** (secret) [*lutte, machinations, intrigues*] secret, hidden; **6** Phon voiceless, surd.
II *nm,f* deaf person; **les ~s** the deaf.
III sourde *nf* Phon voiceless consonant.
IDIOMES **faire la ~e oreille** to turn a deaf ear; **mieux vaut entendre ça que d'être ~**○! hum what stupid things you hear!; **comme un ~** [*crier, taper, frapper*] like one possessed; **il n'est pire ~ que celui qui ne veut (pas) entendre** Prov there's none so deaf as those who will not hear; **ce n'est pas tombé dans l'oreille d'un ~** it didn't fall on deaf ears.

sourdement /suʀdəmɑ̃/ *adv* **1** (avec un bruit étouffé) [*gronder*] dully; **2** (en secret) [*agir, intriguer*] in an underhand manner.

sourdine /suʀdin/ *nf* Mus mute; (de piano) soft pedal; **jouer en ~** to play softly; **écouter la radio en ~** to have the radio on quietly; **mettre une ~ à** fig to tone down [*critiques*]; **mécontentement exprimé en ~** muted discontent; **mets un peu la ~**○ keep it down (a bit)○.

sourdingue○ /suʀdɛ̃g/ **I** *adj* **être ~** to have cloth ears○, to be deaf.
II *nmf* cloth ears (+ *v sg*); **c'est une vraie ~** she's a real cloth ears.

sourd-muet, **sourde-muette**, *pl* **sourds-muets**, **sourdes-muettes** /suʀmɥɛ, suʀdmɥɛt/ **I** *adj* deaf and dumb.
II *nm,f* deaf-mute.

sourdre /suʀdʀ/ [6] *vi* liter **1** (sortir de terre) [*eau*] to seep out (**de** from); [*source*] to rise (**de** from); **2** (jaillir) [*larme*] to well up (**de** from); **3** fig [*idée, réflexion*] to take shape (**dans** in); [*émotion*] to well up (**dans** in).

souriant, **~e**, /suʀjɑ̃, ɑ̃t/ *adj* [*visage, air, personne*] smiling.

souriceau, *pl* **~x** /suʀiso/ *nm* young mouse.

souricière /suʀisjɛʀ/ *nf* **1** (pour souris) mousetrap; **2** (pour malfaiteur) trap; **tendre une ~** to set a trap.

sourire /suʀiʀ/ [68] **I** *nm* smile; **un bon/large ~** a kindly/broad smile; **avec le ~** with a smile; **un ~ de complicité** a knowing smile; **le ~ aux lèvres** with a smile on one's lips; **un ~ flottait sur leurs lèvres** a smile was playing on their lips; **se fendre d'un large ~** [*visage*] to break into a grin ou broad smile; **avoir un ~ moqueur** (d'habitude) to have a mocking smile; (en la circonstance) to give a mocking smile; **avoir toujours le ~** to be always smiling; **être tout ~** to be all smiles ou sweetness; **garder le ~** to keep smiling (through); **faire un ~ à qn** to give sb a smile; **faire des ~s à qn** (pour charmer, pour amadouer) to smile sweetly at sb; **il n'a même pas eu un ~ de remerciement** he didn't even smile in thanks; **ce n'est pas avec de beaux ~s que tu me/la convaincras** you won't get round GB ou around US me/her like that.
II *vi* **1** (adresser un sourire) to smile (**à qn** at sb); **~ timidement/avec bonté/au milieu de ses larmes** to smile shyly/kindly/through one's tears; **~ jusqu'aux oreilles** to grin from ear to ear; **faire ~ qn** to make sb smile; **2** (être agréable) liter [*destin, fortune, climat*] to smile on [*personne*]; [*idée, projet, aventure*] to appeal to [*personne*].
IDIOMES **~ aux anges** to have a silly smile on one's face.

souris /suʀi/ *nf inv* **1** Zool mouse; **gris ~** light grey GB ou gray US; ▶ **petit**; **2** Culin *piece of meat at the knuckle end of a leg of lamb*; **3** Ordinat mouse; **4**○ (femme) bird○ GB, chick○ US.
■ **~ blanche** Zool white mouse; **~ d'hôtel** (female) cat burglar.
IDIOMES **jouer au chat et à la ~** to play cat and mouse; **quand le chat n'est pas là les ~ dansent** when the cat's away, the mice will play; ▶ **montagne**.

sournois, **~e** /suʀnwa, az/ **I** *adj* [*personne, animal, air, regard*] sly; [*conduite, pensée, action*] underhand; [*douleur, mal*] insidious.
II *nm,f* sly person, underhand person; **agir en ~** to act slyly ou in an underhand way.

sournoisement /suʀnwazmɑ̃/ *adv* [*regarder, agir*] slyly; fig [*gagner, ronger*] insidiously.

sournoiserie /suʀnwazʀi/ *nf* **1** (caractère) slyness; **2** (action) underhand trick.

sous /su/ *prép*

■ **Note** Lorsque *sous* indique une position dans l'espace il se traduit généralement par *under*: *sous la table*/*un arbre* = under the table/a tree.
– On trouvera ci-dessous exemples supplémentaires et exceptions.
– Lorsque *sous* a une valeur figurée comme dans *sous le choc, sous la menace, sous prétexte etc* la traduction de *sous* sera fournie sous le deuxième élément, respectivement *choc, menace, prétexte* etc, auquel on se reportera.

1 (en dessous de) under, underneath, beneath sout; **un journal ~ le bras** a newspaper under one's arm; **se mettre un coussin ~ la tête** to put a cushion under one's head; **le jardin était ~ la neige** the garden GB ou yard US was covered in snow; **~ l'eau/la terre** under the water/the ground, underwater/underground, below water/ground; **~ la mer** under the sea; **~ la pluie** in the rain; **j'aurais voulu rentrer ~ terre** fig I wanted the ground to swallow me up; **mes jambes tremblaient ~ moi** my legs were trembling beneath me; **2** (dans un classement) under; **~ le numéro 4757/la lettre D** under number 4757/the letter D; **3** (pendant une période) during; **~ la présidence de Mitterrand** during Mitterrand's presidency; **~ l'Occupation** during the Occupation; **~ le règne de Louis XIV** under Louis XIV, during the reign of Louis XIV; **4** (avant) within; **~ quinzaine** within the ou a fortnight GB ou two weeks; **~ peu** before long; **5** (sous l'action de) **~ traitement/anesthésie** under treatment/anaesthetic; **~ antibiotiques/pilule** on antibiotics/the pill; **~ perfusion** on a drip GB ou an IV US.

sous-alimentation, *pl* **~s** /suzalimɑ̃tasjɔ̃/ *nf* malnutrition, undernourishment.

sous-alimenté, **~e**, *mpl* **~s** /suzalimɑ̃te/ *adj* undernourished, malnourished.

sous-bois /subwa/ *nm inv* undergrowth ¢.

sous-brigadier, *pl* **~s** /subʀigadje/ *nm* (dans la police) ≈ deputy sergeant.

sous-capitalisation, *pl* **~s** /sukapitalizasjɔ̃/ *nf* undercapitalization.

sous-catégorie, *pl* **~s** /sukategɔʀi/ *nf* subcategory.

sous-chef, *pl* **~s** /suʃɛf/ *nm* gén second-in-command.
■ **~ de bureau** deputy chief clerk; **~ de gare** deputy stationmaster.

sous-classe, *pl* **~s** /suklas/ *nf* subclass.

sous-comité, *pl* **~s** /sukɔmite/ *nm* subcommittee.

sous-commission, *pl* **~s** /sukɔmisjɔ̃/ *nf* subcommission.

sous-consommation, *pl* **~s** /sukɔ̃sɔmasjɔ̃/ *nf* underconsumption.

sous-continent, *pl* **~s** /sukɔ̃tinɑ̃/ *nm* Géog subcontinent.

sous-coter /sukɔte/ [1] *vtr* to underprice.

sous-couche, *pl* **~s** /sukuʃ/ *nf* (de peinture) undercoat; (de neige) underlayer.

souscripteur, **-trice** /suskʀiptœʀ, tʀis/ *nm,f* subscriber (**de** to).

souscription /suskʀipsjɔ̃/ *nf* **1** (à une publication, une œuvre charitable) subscription (**à** to); **mettre un livre en ~** to sell a book on a subscription basis (*prior to publication*); **2** Assur **~ d'un contrat d'assurances** taking out an insurance policy; **~ collective** Assur collective underwriting; **3** Fin (à un emprunt, une émission) subscription (**à** to); **~ d'actions** application for shares; **la liste des ~s est close** the subscription list is closed; **remplir une demande de ~ d'actions** to fill in a share application form; **à cause de la faible demande de ~ d'actions** because the share offer was undersubscribed; **~ dans le** or **au capital** share in the subscribed capital; **taux de ~** take-up (of a rights issue).

souscrire /suskʀiʀ/ [67] **I** *vtr* to take out [*assurance, abonnement, plan d'épargne*]; to sign [*contrat, traite*]; to subscribe [*somme*]; **~ un risque** Assur to underwrite a risk.
II souscrire à *vtr ind* **1** (en payant) **~ à** to subscribe to [*publication, emprunt, émission, œuvre charitable*]; **2** (adhérer) **~ à** to subscribe to [*propos, décision, convention*]; **j'y souscris entièrement** I subscribe to it totally.

souscrit, **~e** /suskʀi, it/ **I** *pp* ▶ **souscrire**.
II *pp adj* **1** Fin subscribed; **émission entièrement ~e** fully subscribed issue; **2** Imprim [*lettre*] subscript.

sous-culture, *pl* **~s** /sukyltyʀ/ *nf* pej subculture.

sous-cutané, **~e**, *mpl* **~s** /sukytane/ *adj* subcutaneous; **injection ~e** subcutaneous injection.

sous-développé, **~e**, *mpl* **~s** /sudevlɔpe/ *adj* [*pays, région, économie*] underdeveloped.

sous-développement, *pl* **~s** /sudevlɔpmɑ̃/ *nm* underdevelopment.

sous-directeur, **-trice**, *mpl* **~s** /sudiʀɛktœʀ, tʀis/ *nm,f* assistant manager.

sous-direction, *pl* **~s** /sudiʀɛksjɔ̃/ *nf* division; **~ des Affaires économiques et financières** economic and financial affairs division.

sous-dominante, *pl* **~s** /sudɔminɑ̃t/ *nf* Mus subdominant.

sous-effectif, *pl* **~s** /suzefɛktif/ *nm* understaffing ¢; **il y a un problème de ~s** there's a problem of understaffing; **ils sont en ~** they're understaffed.

sous-emploi /suzɑ̃plwa/ *nm* underemployment.

sous-employer /suzɑ̃plwaje/ [23] *vtr* to underemploy [*personne, ressources*].

sous-encadrement, *pl* **~s** /suzɑ̃kadʀəmɑ̃/ *nm* (d'usine, de pays) lack of trained people; (d'école, de prison) understaffing.

sous-ensemble, *pl* **~s** /suzɑ̃sɑ̃bl/ *nm* Math subset.

sous-entendre /suzɑ̃tɑ̃dʀ/ [6] *vtr* to imply.

sous-entendu, **~e**, *mpl* **~s** /suzɑ̃tɑ̃dy/ **I** *pp* ▶ **sous-entendre**.
II *pp adj* understood.
III *nm* innuendo; **assez de ~s** enough innuendos!; **un sourire plein de ~s** a smile full of innuendo.

sous-entraîné, **~e**, *mpl* **~s** /suzɑ̃tʀene/ *adj* ill-prepared.

sous-équipé, **~e**, *mpl* **~s** /suzekipe/ *adj* underequipped.

sous-équipement /suzekipmɑ̃/ *nm* lack of equipment.

sous-espèce, *pl* **~s** /suzɛspɛs/ *nf* subspecies (*sg*).

sous-estimation, *pl* **~s** /suzɛstimasjɔ̃/ *nf* underestimation.

sous-estimer /suzɛstime/ [1] *vtr* to underestimate.

sous-évaluation, *pl* **~s** /suzevalɥasjɔ̃/ *nf* underestimation.

sous-évaluer /suzevalɥe/ [1] *vtr* to underestimate [*coût, problème*]; to undervalue [*maison, terrain*].

sous-exposer /suzɛkspoze/ [1] *vtr* Phot to underexpose [*photo*].

sous-exposition /suzɛkspozisjɔ̃/ *nf* Phot underexposure.

sous-fifre○, *pl* **~s** /sufifʀ/ *nm* underling.

sous-filiale, *pl* **~s** /sufiljal/ *nf* subbranch.

sous-groupe, *pl* **~s** /sugʀup/ *nm* subgroup.

sous-homme, *pl* **~s** /suzɔm/ *nm* subhuman.

sous-humanité, *pl* **~s** /suzymanite/ *nf* subclass of humanity.

sous-informé, **~e**, *mpl* **~s** /suzɛ̃fɔʀme/ *adj* ill-informed.

sous-investissement /suzɛ̃vɛstismɑ̃/ *nm* underinvestment.

sous-jacent, **~e**, *mpl* **~s** /suʒasɑ̃, ɑ̃t/ *adj* **1** fig (latent) [*idée, problème, tension*] underlying; **2** (au-dessous) subjacent.

Sous-le-Vent /sulǝvɑ̃/ ▶ **416** *nprfpl* **les îles ~** the Leeward Islands.

sous-lieutenant, *pl* **~s** /suljøtnɑ̃/ ▶ **390** *nm* (dans l'armée de terre) ≈ second lieutenant; (dans l'aviation) ≈ pilot officer GB, ≈ second lieutenant US.

sous-littérature, *pl* **~s** /suliteʀatyʀ/ *nf* second-rate literature, pulp fiction.

sous-locataire, *pl* **~s** /sulɔkatɛʀ/ *nmf* subtenant.

sous-location, *pl* **~s** /sulɔkasjɔ̃/ *nf* **1** (action) subletting ¢, subleasing; **2** (contrat) subletting agreement, subleasing agreement.

sous-louer /sulwe/ [1] *vtr* **1** (donner en location) to sublet, to sublease [*appartement, pièce*]; **2** (prendre en location) to sublease [*appartement, pièce*].

sous-main /sumɛ̃/ **I** *nm inv* desk blotter.
II en sous-main *loc adv* under the table, secretly.

sous-marin, **~e**, *mpl* **~s** /sumaʀɛ̃, in/ **I** *adj* **1** [*relief, volcan*] submarine; [*faune, flore*] submarine, underwater; **2** [*exploration, archéologie, câble*] underwater; [*plongeur, plongée*] deep-sea.
II *nm* **1** Naut submarine; **2**○ (espion) spy; **3** C (sandwich) submarine sandwich GB, submarine US.
■ **~ de poche** Naut mini-submarine; **~ à propulsion nucléaire** nuclear-powered submarine.

sous-marinier, *pl* **~s** /sumaʀinje/ ▶ **510** *nm* submariner.

sous-marque, *pl* **~s** /sumaʀk/ *nf* Comm sub-brand.

sous-menu, *pl* **~s** /suməny/ *nm* Ordinat submenu.

sous-ministre, *pl* **~s** /suministʀ/ *nmf* Admin Pol deputy minister.

sous-multiple, *pl* **~s** /sumyltipl/ *nm* Math submultiple.

sous-nappe, *pl* **~s** /sunap/ *nf* undercloth.

sous-off○, *pl* **~s** /suzɔf/ *nm* soldiers' slang noncom○.

sous-officier, *pl* **~s** /suzɔfisje/ ▶ **390** *nm* noncommissioned officer.

sous-ordre, *pl* **~s** /suzɔʀdʀ/ *nm* **1** Sci suborder; **2** (subalterne) subordinate.

sous-partie, *pl* **~s** /supaʀti/ *nf* subsection.

sous-payer /supeje/ [21] *vtr* to underpay [*employé*].

sous-peuplé, **~e**, *mpl* **~s** /supœple/ *adj* [*pays, région*] underpopulated.

sous-peuplement /supœpləmɑ̃/ *nm* underpopulation.

sous-pied, *pl* **~s** /supje/ *nm* foot-strap.

sous-préfecture, *pl* **~s** /supʀefɛktyʀ/ *nf* Admin *administrative subdivision of a department in France*.

sous-préfet, *pl* **~s** /supʀefɛ/ *nm*: *permanent ministerial representative in a department in France*.

sous-production /supʀɔdyksjɔ̃/ *nf* underproduction.

sous-produit, *pl* **~s** /supʀɔdɥi/ *nm* **1** (produit secondaire) by-product; **2** (produit médiocre) second-rate product.

sous-programme, *pl* **~s** /supʀɔgʀam/ *nm* Ordinat subroutine.

sous-prolétaire, *pl* **~s** /supʀɔletɛʀ/ *nmf* member of the underclass.

sous-prolétariat, *pl* **~s** /supʀɔletaʀja/ *nm* underclass.

sous-pull, *pl* **~s** /supyl/ *nm* thin poloneck jumper.

sous-race, *pl* **~s** /suʀas/ *nf* **1** Anthrop subrace; **2** pej offensive inferior race.

sous-secrétaire, *pl* **~s** /sus(ə)kʀetɛʀ/ *nmf* Admin, Pol **~ d'État** Parliamentary Undersecretary of State; **~ d'État à l'Agriculture/la Défense** Parliamentary Undersecretary (of State) to the ministry of Agriculture/Defence[GB].

sous-secrétariat, *pl* **~s** /sus(ə)kʀetaʀja/ *nf* Admin, Pol *administrative subdivision of a ministerial department*.

sous-seing /susɛ̃/ *nm inv* Jur (acte) private agreement, private contract.

soussigné, **~e** /susiɲe/ **I** *adj* undersigned; **nous, ~s Pierre et Paul Martin, certifions** we, the undersigned, Pierre and Paul Martin certify; **les personnes ~es** the undersigned.
II *nm,f* **les ~s** the undersigned.

sous-sol, *pl* **~s** /susɔl/ *nm* **1** Constr basement; **garage en ~** basement garage; **2** Géol subsoil ¢.

sous-tasse, *pl* **~s** /sutas/ *nf* B saucer.

sous-tendre /sutɑ̃dʀ/ [6] *vtr* **1** fig (constituer les fondements de) to underlie, to be behind; **2** (constituer la corde de) to subtend [*arc, courbe*].

sous-titrage, *pl* **~s** /sutitʀaʒ/ *nm* subtitling; **'~: Laure Dulac'** (sur un générique de film) 'subtitles: Laure Dulac'.

sous-titre, *pl* **~s** /sutitʀ/ *nm* **1** (titre secondaire) subtitle; **2** Cin, TV, Mus (traduction) subtitle, caption.

sous-titrer /sutitʀe/ [1] *vtr* Cin, TV, Mus to subtitle [*film, opéra*]; **film en version originale sous-titrée** film in the original version with subtitles.

sous-titreur, **-euse**, *mpl* **~s** /sutitʀœʀ, øz/ **I** ▶ **510** *nm,f* subtitler.
II sous-titreuse *nf* (machine) subtitling machine; **sous-titreuse à laser** laser subtitling machine.

soustractif, **-ive** /sustʀaktif, iv/ *adj* subtractive.

soustraction /sustʀaksjɔ̃/ *nf* **1** Math (processus) subtraction ¢; (opération) subtraction; **apprendre à faire des ~s** to learn to do subtraction; **fais encore trois ~s et tu pourras aller jouer** do another three subtractions and you can go out to play; **faire une erreur de ~** to make a mistake in the subtraction; **ta ~ est fausse** your subtraction is wrong; **2** Jur (vol) removal, taking away.

soustraire /sustʀɛʀ/ [58] **I** *vtr* **1** Math to subtract (**de** from); **2** (voler) to steal (**à** from); **3** (retirer) to take away [*personne*] (**à** from); **~ qn/qch à la vue** or **aux regards de qn** to hide sb/sth from sb's view; **une enclave soustraite au contrôle de l'ennemi** an enclave free from enemy control; **4** (protéger) to shield [*personne*] (**à qch** from sth); **~ qn à la mort** to save sb from death; **~ un site aux promoteurs** to save a site from the developers.
II se soustraire *vpr* **1** (éviter) **se ~ à** to escape from [*discipline, tâche, ennui*]; **se ~ à la vue** or **aux regards de qn** to hide from sb's view; **se ~ à ses obligations** to shirk one's duties, to shy away from one's duties; **2** (échapper à) **se ~ à** to avoid [*arrestation*]; **se ~ au danger** to escape ou avoid danger; **se ~ à la justice** to escape justice.

sous-traitance, *pl* **~s** /sutʀɛtɑ̃s/ *nf* subcontracting; **travail donné en ~** work put out to contract; **travail effectué en ~** work done on a contract basis, subcontracted work.

sous-traitant, *pl* **~s** /sutʀɛtɑ̃/ *nm* subcontractor.

sous-traiter /sutʀete/ [1] **I** *vtr* **1** (donner en sous-traitance) to subcontract, to contract [sth] out [*affaire, travail*]; **2** (exécuter à titre de sous-traitant) to do [sth] as a subcontractor.
II *vi* **1** (donner en sous-traitance) [*personne, entreprise*] to subcontract work, to contract work out; **2** (exécuter à titre de sous-traitant) to do work as a subcontractor.

sous-type, *pl* **~s** /sutip/ *nm* subcategory.

sous-utiliser /suzytilize/ [1] *vtr* to underuse.

sous-ventrière, *pl* **~s** /suvɑ̃tʀijɛʀ/ *nf* (courroie) bellyband.
IDIOMES **manger à s'en faire péter la ~**○ to eat till one is fit to burst○.

sous-verre /suvɛʀ/ *nm inv* **1** (encadrement) clip-frame; **2** (image encadrée) picture (mounted under glass); **3** (objet que l'on place sous un verre) coaster.

sous-vêtement, *pl* **~s** /suvɛtmɑ̃/ *nm* underwear ¢.

sous-vireur, **-euse** /suviʀœʀ, øz/ *adj* understeering (*épith*).

soutache /sutaʃ/ *nf* braid.

soutane /sutan/ *nf* cassock; **prendre la ~** to take the cloth; **porter la ~** to be a priest; ▶ **ortie**.

soute /sut/ *nf* Naut hold; **voyager en ~** to travel in the hold.

■ **~ à bagages** Aviat baggage hold; **~ à charbon** Naut coal store; **~ à munitions** Naut ammunition store.

soutenable /sutnabl/ *adj* **1** (supportable) bearable; **pas ~** unbearable; **difficilement ~** almost unbearable; **2** (défendable) [*argument, hypothèse*] tenable.

soutenance /sutnɑ̃s/ *nf* Univ (de mémoire, dossier) viva GB, orals US; **~ de thèse** viva GB, (dissertation) defense US.

soutènement /sutɛnmɑ̃/ *nm* retaining structure; Mines props; **travaux de ~** retaining work; **mur de ~** retaining ou supporting wall.

souteneur /sutnœʀ/ *nm* pimp○, procurer.

soutenir /sutniʀ/ [36] **I** *vtr* **1** (donner son appui) to support [*personne, projet, action, candidat, gouvernement, équipe*]; **~ la majorité/une famille pauvre** to support the majority/a poor family; **~ une grève** to support a strike; **~ à bout de bras** to keep [sb/sth] afloat [*personne, projet*]; **~ qn contre qn** to side with sb against sb; **~ sa fille contre son père** to side with one's daughter against her father; **2** Écon, Fin to support [*monnaie, marché, cours, économie*]; **3** (affirmer) to maintain [*contraire*]; to defend [*paradoxe*]; to uphold [*opinion*]; **~ que** to maintain that; **~ que la récession a pris fin** to maintain that the recession has ended; **4** (servir de support) to support [*personne, toit, monnaie*]; **mur soutenu par des étais** wall supported by props; **mes jambes ne me soutiennent plus** my legs won't hold me up; **des oreillers soutenaient la tête du malade** the patient was propped up on pillows; **5** (donner des forces) to keep [sb] going [*personne*]; **un peu de café te soutiendra** a drink of coffee will keep you going; **6** (réconforter) [*personne*] to support; [*espoir*] to sustain; **tu m'as toujours soutenu** you have always supported me; **seul l'espoir me soutient** hope alone sustains me; **~ le moral de qn** to keep sb's spirits up; **il a besoin qu'on lui soutienne le moral** his morale needs boosting; **~ le moral des troupes** to encourage the troops; **7** (faire durer) to keep [sth] alive [*curiosité, intérêt*]; to keep [sth] going [*conversation*]; to keep up, to sustain [*effort, train de vie, rythme*]; **~ l'intérêt des lecteurs** to keep the readers' interest alive; **8** (résister) to withstand [*choc, siège, assaut, regard*]; to bear [*comparaison*] (**avec** with); **elle ne soutient pas la comparaison avec ta sœur** she isn't nearly as good as your sister; **il soutient la comparaison avec ton frère** he is as good as your brother; **9** Univ to defend [*thèse, mémoire*]; **~ sa thèse** to have one's viva GB ou defense US.

II se soutenir *vpr* **1** (s'entraider) to support each other; **se ~ entre collègues** to support each other as colleagues; **2** (être défendable) [*argument, hypothèse*] to be tenable; **3** (se tenir debout) [*personne*] to hold oneself up; **elle a de la peine à se ~** she can hardly hold herself up.

soutenu, **~e** /sutny/ **I** *pp* ▶ **soutenir**.

II *pp adj* (intense) [*activité, effort, croissance*] sustained; [*attention*] close; [*rythme*] steady.

III *adj* **1** gén [*marché*] firm; [*couleur*] bold; [*style, langue*] formal, elevated; **2** Mus (maintenu) [*note, ton*] sustained.

souterrain, **~e** /sutɛʀɛ̃, ɛn/ **I** *adj* **1** (sous terre) [*lac*] subterranean; [*ouvrage, explosion, câble*] underground; ▶ **passage**; **2** (secret) [*menées, accord*] secret; **économie ~e** black economy.

II *nm* underground passage, tunnel.

soutien /sutjɛ̃/ *nm* **1** (appui) support (**à** for); **j'affirme/exprime mon ~ aux travailleurs** I confirm/express my support for the workers; **le parti a proclamé/manifesté son ~ à la majorité** the party proclaimed/showed its support for the majority; **~ financier/politique** financial/political support; **~ moral/actif** moral/active support; **mesures de ~ à l'économie** measures to support the economy; **~ en physique/anglais** Scol extra help in physics/English; **2** (agent) support; **leur fils/l'armée/le parti est leur seul ~** their son/the army/the party is their sole support; **3** (de voûte, plate-forme) support.

■ **~ de famille** wage earner in a family (exempt from national service).

soutien-gorge, *pl* **soutiens-gorge** /sutjɛ̃gɔʀʒ/ *nm* bra.

■ **~ d'allaitement** nursing bra.

soutier /sutje/ *nm* **1** fig menial, drudge; **2**† Naut coal-trimmer.

soutif○ /sutif/ *nm* (soutien-gorge) bra.

soutirage /sutiʀaʒ/ *nm* racking.

soutirer /sutiʀe/ [1] *vtr* **1** (dérober) **~ qch à qn** to squeeze sth out of sb [*argent*]; to extract [sth] from sb [*aveu, promesse*]; **2** (clarifier) to rack [*vin, bière*].

souvenance /suvnɑ̃s/ *nf* fml **à ma ~** as far as I recall; **avoir ~ de qch** to remember sth.

souvenir /suvniʀ/ [36] **I** *nm* **1** (pensée du passé) memory; **garder un bon/mauvais ~ de qch** to have happy/bad ou unhappy memories of sth; **ce n'est plus qu'un mauvais ~** it's just a bad memory; **je conserve** or **garde un horrible ~ de cette année à Londres** I have very bad memories of that year in London; **le ~ que je conserve** or **garde de lui est encore très clair** I still remember him very clearly; **~s d'école/de l'armée/de captivité** memories of schooldays/of the army/of captivity; **~s de guerre** wartime memories; **~s d'enfance** childhood memories; **chercher dans ses ~s** to sift through one's memories; **avoir (le) ~ de qch** to remember sth; **ne pas avoir ~ de** to have no recollection of; **n'avoir qu'un ~ confus de qch** to remember something only dimly; **perdre le ~ de qch** to forget sth; **au ~ de** at the memory of; **2** (mémoire) memory; **s'effacer du ~ de qn** to fade from sb's memory; **rappeler qn au (bon) ~ de qn** to remember sb to sb; **envoie une carte de temps en temps pour te rappeler à leur bon ~** send them a card from time to time to keep in touch; **3** (objet) (rappelant un lieu, un événement) souvenir (**de** of); (rappelant une personne) memento (**de** from); **c'est un ~ de voyage** it's something I brought back from one of my trips; **en ~** gén as a souvenir; (avec valeur affective) as a memento; (cadeau ayant valeur affective) as a keepsake; **il me l'a donné en ~** he gave it to me as a keepsake; **boutique de ~s** souvenir shop GB ou store US; **4** (salutation) **croyez à mon bon** or **fidèle** or **meilleur ~** yours ever; **mon bon ~ à** remember me to.

II se souvenir *vpr* **se ~ de qn/qch** to remember sb/sth; **bien se ~ de qch** to remember sth well; **je m'en souviens mal** I can't remember it very well; **se ~ (d')avoir fait** to remember doing; **se ~ que** to remember that.

III *v impers* **il me souvient que** littér I recollect that; **autant qu'il m'en souvienne** if my memory serves me right.

souvent /suvɑ̃/ *adv* often; **assez ~** quite often; **très/trop ~** very/too often; **peu ~** not very often; **le plus ~** more often than not; **c'est ~ ce qui arrive** that's what often happens; **je le fais plus ~ qu'à mon tour** I do it more often than I should.

IDIOMES **on a ~ besoin d'un plus petit que soi** Prov a mouse may help a lion.

souverain, **~e** /suvʀɛ̃, ɛn/ **I** *adj* **1** (indépendant) [*État, peuple, droit, pouvoir*] sovereign; [*décision, autorité*] supreme; **l'Allemagne unifiée et ~e** a unified, sovereign Germany; **2** (suprême) [*bonheur, talent, mépris*] supreme; **faire preuve d'une indifférence ~e** to show supreme indifference; **rechercher le ~ bien** Philos to seek the sovereign good; **3** (infaillible) [*remède, potion*] sovereign; [*conseil, vertu*] sterling; **essayez ça, c'est ~ contre les maux de gorge** try this, it works wonders for sore throats; **4** (hautain) [*personne*] haughty.

II *nm,f* sovereign, monarch; **le ~ régnant/déchu** the reigning/deposed monarch; ▶ **pontife**.

III *nm* (monnaie) sovereign.

souverainement /suvʀɛnmɑ̃/ *adv* **1** (sans appel) [*décider, juger*] without appeal; **juridiction qui statue ~** jurisdiction which gives verdicts beyond appeal; **2** (suprêmement) **votre attitude me déplaît ~** I dislike your attitude intensely; **ignorer ~ un ordre/une règle** to flout an order/a rule.

souveraineté /suvʀɛnte/ *nf* sovereignty; **~ nationale** national sovereignty; **la ~ de l'État** the sovereignty of the State.

soviet /sɔvjɛt/ *nm* soviet; **Soviet suprême** Supreme Soviet.

soviétique /sɔvjetik/ ▶ **537** *adj* Hist Soviet.

Soviétique /sɔvjetik/ ▶ **537** *nmf* Hist Soviet.

soviétiser /sɔvjetize/ [1] *vtr* to sovietize.

soviétologue /sɔvjetɔlɔg/ ▶ **510** *nmf* sovietologist.

soyeux, **-euse** /swajø, øz/ **I** *adj* [*tissu, cheveux, peau*] silky.

II *nm* silk manufacturer.

SPA /ɛspea/ *nf* (*abbr* = **Société protectrice des animaux**) society for the prevention of cruelty to animals.

spacieusement /spasjøzmɑ̃/ *adv* spaciously; **être ~ logé** to have spacious accommodation.

spacieux, **-ieuse** /spasjø, øz/ *adj* spacious.

spadassin /spadasɛ̃/ *nm* **1** (duelliste) swordsman; **2** (assassin) hired killer.

spaghetti /spageti/ *nm inv* spaghetti ℭ; **des ~ bolognaise** spaghetti bolognese.

spahi /spai/ *nm* Hist Mil spahi.

sparadrap /spaʀadʀa/ *nm* **1** (bande adhésive) surgical ou adhesive tape; **2** (pansement) (sticking) plaster GB, Band-aid®.

Sparte /spaʀt/ ▶ **857** *npr* Sparta.

spartiate /spaʀsjat/ **I** *adj* lit, fig Spartan; **à la ~** in a Spartan way.

II *nmf* Spartan.

III *nf* (sandale) Roman sandal.

spasme /spasm/ *nm* spasm; **être secoué de ~s** to be shaken by spasms.

spasmodique /spasmɔdik/ *adj* lit, fig spasmodic.

spasmophile /spasmɔfil/ *adj, nmf* spasmophile.

spasmophilie /spasmɔfili/ *nf* spasmophilia.

spasmophilique /spasmɔfilik/ *adj* spasmophilic.

spath /spat/ *nm* spar.

spatial, **~e**, *mpl* **-iaux** /spasjal, o/ *adj* **1** gén, Psych [*repérage, perception, représentation*] spatial; **2** Astronaut space (*épith*); **vaisseau ~** spaceship; **capsule/navette/base/guerre ~e** space capsule/shuttle/base/war.

spatialisation /spasjalizasjɔ̃/ *nf* **1** Psych spatializing; **2** Astronaut adaptation to conditions in space.

spatialiser /spasjalize/ [1] *vtr* **1** Psych spatialize; **2** Astronaut **~ qch** to adapt sth to conditions in space.

spatiologie /spasjɔlɔʒi/ *nf* space science.

spationaute /spasjɔnot/ ▶ **510** *nmf* astronaut.

spatio-temporel, **-elle**, *mpl* **~s** /spasjotɑ̃pɔʀɛl/ *adj* spatiotemporal.

spatule /spatyl/ *nf* **1** Culin, Art spatula; (de plâtrier) filling-knife; **2** (de ski) tip; **3** Zool (poisson) paddlefish; (oiseau) spoonbill.

■ **~ blanche** Zool common spoonbill.

spatulé, **~e** /spatyle/ *adj* spatulate.

spé○ /spe/ ▶ **mathématique**.

speaker, **speakerine** /spikœʀ, spikʀin/ ▶ **510** *nm,f* announcer.

spécial, **~e**, *mpl* **-iaux** /spesjal, o/ *adj* **1** (non général) [*formation, tarif, statut*] special; **~e dernière** TV late special; **2** (adapté) [*chaussures, peigne, appareil*] special; **shampooing ~ cheveux gras** shampoo for greasy hair; **3** (bizarre) [*mentalité, personne*] odd; **il est ~** he's a bit odd.

spécialement /spesjalmɑ̃/ *adv* **1** (particulièrement) specially; **produit ~ conçu pour** a product specially developed for; **être ~ chargé de** to be specially responsible for; **2** (très) especially; **pas ~** not especially; **plus ~** more especially.

spécialisation /spesjalizasjɔ̃/ *nf* specialization.

spécialisé, **~e** /spesjalize/ **I** *pp* ▶ **spécialiser**.
II *pp adj* [*laboratoire, établissement, études*] specialized; [*librairie, magazine*] specialist (*épith*); **être ~ dans** or **en** [*personne*] to be a specialist in; [*établissement, usine*] to specialize in; **être ~ dans l'étude de** to specialize in the study of.

spécialiser: **se spécialiser** /spesjalize/ [1] *vpr* to specialize (**en, dans** in).

spécialiste /spesjalist/ *nmf* (tous contextes) specialist (**de, en** in); **médecin ~** specialist; **c'est un ~ des plaisanteries de mauvais goût** tasteless jokes are his speciality GB ou specialty US.

spécialité /spesjalite/ *nf* **1** gén speciality GB, specialty US; **~ médicale** specialized medical field; **c'est leur ~!** iron it's their speciality!; **2** Culin speciality GB, specialty US; **les ~s de la région** the specialities GB ou specialties US of the region.

spécieusement /spesjøzmɑ̃/ *adv* liter speciously.

spécieux, **-ieuse** /spesjø, øz/ *adj* specious.

spécification /spesifikasjɔ̃/ *nf* **1** Ind Tech (de produit) specification; **2** (mention) specifying; **sans ~ d'heure ni de lieu** with no time or place specified.

spécificité /spesifisite/ *nf* **1** (de produit, maladie) specificity; **2** (caractéristique) characteristic; **3** (caractère unique) uniqueness.

spécifier /spesifje/ [2] *vtr* to specify [*date, heure*]; **~ qch à qn** specifically to tell sb sth; **~ à qn de faire** specifically to tell sb what to do.

spécifique /spesifik/ *adj* specific (**de** to).

spécifiquement /spesifikmɑ̃/ *adv* specifically.

spécimen /spesimɛn/ *nm* **1** (exemple) specimen; **2** (exemplaire) (free) sample; **3**○ (personne) odd specimen○; **c'est un drôle de ~** he's an odd specimen.

spectacle /spɛktakl/ **I** *nm* **1** (vue) sight; (événement) sight; **au ~ de...** at the sight of...; **devant un tel ~** (affreux) at this awful sight; (merveilleux) at this amazing sight; **c'était un drôle de ~ de le voir habillé ainsi** he looked a real sight dressed like that; **le ~ de la vie quotidienne** the sight of people going about their daily lives; **se donner** or **s'offrir en ~** pej to make an exhibition ou a spectacle of oneself (**devant** in front of); **2** (divertissement) **le ~ est dans la rue** iron there's a free show on the streets iron; **avoir le sens du ~** (metteur en scène) to have a real sense of theatre[GB]; (politicien) to have an eye for effect; **3** Théât (représentation) show; **allons au ~** let's go to the theatre[GB]; **~ de marionnettes/de variétés/de danse** puppet/variety/dance show; **'~s'** (rubrique) 'entertainment'; **film à grand ~** spectacular; **politique à grand ~** pej showbiz○ politics; **~ son et lumière** son et lumière; **4** (activité professionnelle) **le ~, l'industrie du ~** show business; **les métiers/les gens du ~** jobs/people in show business.
II -spectacle (*in compounds*) **1** péj **politique-~** showbiz○ politics; **football-~** showy football GB ou soccer; **2** Théât **dîner-~** dinner and floor show.

spectaculaire /spɛktakylɛʀ/ *adj* spectacular.

spectateur, **-trice** /spɛktatœʀ, tʀis/ *nm,f* **1** (au théâtre, cinéma, cirque) member of the audience; (à une manifestation sportive, un défilé) spectator; **les ~s** (au théâtre) the audience (*sg*); (dans un stade, la rue) the spectators, the crowd (*sg*); **2** (curieux) onlooker; **assister à une réunion en ~** to sit in on a meeting.

spectral, **~e**, *mpl* **-aux** /spɛktʀal, o/ *adj* **1** liter (de fantôme) spectral, ghostly; **d'une pâleur ~e** deathly pale; **2** Sci spectral; **analyse ~e** spectrum analysis.

spectre /spɛktʀ/ *nm* **1** (fantôme) ghost; **n'être plus qu'un ~** to be just a shadow of one's former self; **2** (de guerre, famine, mort) spectre[GB] (**de** of); **3** Sci spectrum; **~ lumineux** spectrum of light; **~ des couleurs** colour[GB] spectrum.

spectrogramme /spɛktʀɔgʀam/ *nm* spectrogram.

spectrographe /spɛktʀɔgʀaf/ *nm* spectrograph.

spectroscope /spɛktʀɔskɔp/ *nm* spectroscope.

spectroscopie /spɛktʀɔskɔpi/ *nf* spectroscopy.

spéculateur, **-trice** /spekylatœʀ, tʀis/ *nm,f* speculator (**sur** in).

spéculatif, **-ive** /spekylatif, iv/ *adj* speculative.

spéculation /spekylasjɔ̃/ *nf* **1** Fin speculation; **~ à la hausse/baisse** bull/bear speculation; **~ sur** speculation in [*actions, valeurs, or*]; **~ boursière** speculation on the Stock Exchange; **~ foncière** speculation in land; **~ immobilière** property speculation; **2** gén, Philos speculation (**sur** on, about); speculation about [*crise, mouvement*].

spéculer /spekyle/ [1] *vi* **1** Fin to speculate; **~ à la Bourse** to speculate on the stock market; **~ à la hausse/baisse** to bull/bear; **~ sur** to speculate in [*valeurs, actions, or*]; to speculate about [*crise, mouvement*]; **2** Philos, gén to speculate (**sur** on, about).

spéculum /spekylɔm/ *nm* speculum.

spéléologie /speleɔlɔʒi/ *nf* **1** ▶ **449** (sport) potholing GB, caving, spelunking US; **faire de la ~** to go potholing GB ou caving ou spelunking US; **2** (science) speleology.

spéléologique /speleɔlɔʒik/ *adj* **1** [*exploration, découverte*] potholing GB (*épith*), caving (*épith*), spelunking US; **2** [*étude*] speleological.

spéléologue /speleɔlɔg/ *nmf* **1** (sportif) potholer GB, caver, spelunker US; **2** (scientifique) speleologist spéc.

spencer /spɛnsœʀ/ *nm* spencer (jacket).

spermaceti /spɛʀmaseti/ *nm* spermaceti.

spermatique /spɛʀmatik/ *adj* spermatic.

spermatogenèse /spɛʀmatɔʒənɛz/ *nf* spermatogenesis.

spermatozoïde /spɛʀmatɔzɔid/ *nm* spermatozoon; **des ~s** spermatozoa; **nombre de ~s** sperm count.

sperme /spɛʀm/ *nm* sperm.

spermicide /spɛʀmisid/ **I** *adj* [*gelée*] spermicidal.
II *nm* spermicide.

sphénoïde /sfenɔid/ *nm* sphenoid bone.

sphère /sfɛʀ/ *nf* **1** Math sphere; **2** (domaine) sphere; **une ~ d'influence** a sphere of influence; **les hautes ~s de la finance** the higher echelons of finance.

sphéricité /sfeʀisite/ *nf* sphericity.

sphérique /sfeʀik/ *adj* spherical.

sphincter /sfɛ̃ktɛʀ/ *nm* sphincter.

sphinx /sfɛ̃ks/ *nm* **1** Mythol, Art Sphinx; **2** (papillon) hawkmoth.
■ **~ tête de mort** death's-head moth.

spi /spi/ *nm* spinnaker.

spina-bifida /spinabifida/ *nm inv* spina bifida.

spinal, **~e**, *mpl* **-aux** /spinal, o/ *adj* spinal.

spinnaker /spinekœʀ/ *nm* spinnaker.

spiral, **~e**, *mpl* **-aux** /spiʀal, o/ **I** *adj* spiral.
II *nm* hairspring.
III spirale *nf* **1** Math spiral; **monter/descendre en ~e** to spiral up/down; **escalier en ~e** spiral staircase; **cahier à ~es** a spiral bound notebook; **2** (amplification) spiral; **la ~e des prix et des salaires** the wage-price spiral.

spiralé, **~e** /spiʀale/ *adj* spiral (*épith*).

spirante /spiʀɑ̃t/ *nf* spirant.

spire /spiʀ/ *nf* Tech, Math turn.

spirite /spiʀit/ **I** *adj* spiritualist.
II *nmf* spiritualist.

spiritisme /spiʀitism/ *nm* spiritualism.

spiritualiser /spiʀitɥalize/ [1] *vtr* to spiritualize.

spiritualisme /spiʀitɥalism/ *nm* gén, Philos spiritualism.

spiritualiste /spiʀitɥalist/ *adj*, *nmf* gén, Philos spiritualist.

spiritualité /spiʀitɥalite/ *nf* spirituality.

spirituel, **-elle** /spiʀitɥɛl/ *adj* **1** (de l'esprit) [*nature, vie, pouvoir*] spiritual; [*père, famille, héritier*] spiritual; **2** (amusant) [*plaisanterie, personne*] witty.

spirituellement /spiʀitɥɛlmɑ̃/ *adv* **1** (par l'esprit) spiritually; **2** (avec humour) wittily.

spiritueux, **-euse** /spiʀitɥø, øz/ **I** *adj* [*vin*] with a high alcohol content.
II *nm inv* spirit; **vins et ~** wines and spirits.

spiroïdal, **~e**, *mpl* **-aux** /spiʀɔidal, o/ *adj* spiroid.

spleen /splin/ *nm* spleen; **avoir le ~** to feel despondent.

splendeur /splɑ̃dœʀ/ *nf* (de paysage, site, jour) splendour[GB]; (d'époque, de règne) glory; **cette église est une ~** this church is truly magnificent; **c'est l'égoïste dans toute sa ~** he's/she's a complete and utter egoist.

splendide /splɑ̃did/ *adj* [*objet, exposition, journée, victoire*] splendid; [*villa, pays*] magnificent; [*yeux, personne*] stunningly beautiful.

splendidement /splɑ̃didmɑ̃/ *adv* liter magnificently.

spoliateur, **-trice** /spɔljatœʀ, tʀis/ fml **I** *adj* spoliatory sout, confiscatory sout.
II *nm,f* despoiler sout.

spoliation /spɔljasjɔ̃/ *nf* fml despoliation sout.

spolier /spɔlje/ [2] *vtr* fml to despoil sout [*personne*] (**de** of).

spondaïque /spɔ̃daik/ *adj* spondaic.

spondée /spɔ̃de/ *nm* spondee.

spongieux, **-ieuse** /spɔ̃ʒjø, øz/ *adj* spongy.

spongiforme /spɔ̃ʒifɔʀm/ *adj* spongiform.

sponsor /spɔnsɔʀ/ *nm* sponsor.

sponsorat /spɔ̃sɔʀa/ *nm* sponsorship.

sponsoring /spɔnsɔʀiŋ/ *nm* = **sponsorat**.

sponsoriser /spɔ̃sɔʀize/ [1] *vtr* to sponsor.

spontané, **~e** /spɔ̃tane/ *adj* spontaneous; **génération ~e** spontaneous generation; **candidature ~e** unsolicited application.

spontanéité /spɔ̃taneite/ *nf* spontaneity.

spontanément /spɔ̃tanemɑ̃/ *adv* spontaneously.

sporadicité /spɔʀadisite/ *nf* sporadic nature.

sporadique /spɔʀadik/ *adj* sporadic.

sporadiquement /spɔʀadikmɑ̃/ *adv* sporadically.

sporange /spɔʀɑ̃ʒ/ *nm* spore case, sporangium spéc.

spore /spɔʀ/ *nf* spore.

sport /spɔʀ/ *nm* (activité générale) sport; (ensemble d'activités) sports (*pl*); **aimer le ~** to like sport; **vous faites du ~?** do you do any sports?; **quel ~ faites-vous?** which sport(s) do you do?; **je ne fais plus de ~** I don't do any sport any more; **je fais un peu de ~ tous les jours** I do a little sport every day; **j'ai fait beaucoup de ~ dans ma jeunessse** I did a lot of sport in my youth.

■ **~ amateur** amateur sport; **~ automobile** motor sports, car-racing; **~ cérébral** intellectual game; **~ en chambre**○ bedroom sports (*pl*); **~ de combat** combat sport; **~ de compétition** competitive sport; **~ d'équipe** team sport; **~ d'hiver** winter sport; **aller aux ~s d'hiver** to go on a winter sports holiday GB ou vacation US; **~ individuel** individual sport; **~ de masse** popular sport; **~ professionnel** professional sport.

IDIOMES **ça c'est du ~**○! this is no picnic○!; **il va y avoir du ~**○! this is going to be fun ou interesting!; **faire qch pour le ~** or **pour l'amour du ~** to do sth for fun ou for the fun of it.

sportif, -ive /spɔʀtif, iv/ I *adj* **1** lit [*équipement, épreuve, journal, rencontre*] sports (*épith*); **je ne suis pas ~** I'm not the sporty type, I don't go in for sports; **je ne suis pas très ~** I'm not very keen on sports ou very sporty; **2** fig [*allure*] athletic, sporty○; **conduite sportive** Aut speeding; **3** (généreux) [*personne, esprit, attitude*] sporting; **faire preuve d'esprit ~** to be a good sport, to display sportsmanship.

II *nm,f* sportsman/sportswoman; **c'est un ~** he's athletic.

sportivement /spɔʀtivmɑ̃/ *adv* sportingly.

sportivité /spɔʀtivite/ *nf* sportsmanship.

spot /spɔt/ *nm* **1** (pour éclairer) spotlight, spot; **2** (séquence) **~ (publicitaire)** commercial; **un ~ radio/télévisé** a radio/TV commercial; **3** Phys spot.

spouleur /spulœʀ/ *nm* spooler.

spoutnik /sputnik/ *nm* sputnik.

sprat /spʀat/ *nm* sprat.

spray /spʀɛ/ *nm* spray; **déodorant en ~** spray-on deodorant.

sprint /spʀint/ *nm* sprint; **battre qn au ~** to beat sb in the sprint; **piquer un ~**○ to sprint.

sprinter[1] /spʀinte/ [1] *vi* to sprint.

sprinter[2], **-euse** /spʀintœʀ, øz/ *nm,f* (en athlétisme) sprinter; (en fin de course) fast finisher.

squale /skwal/ *nm* shark.

squame /skwam/ *nf* scale, squama spéc.

square /skwaʀ/ *nm* small public garden.

squash /skwaʃ/ ▶449 *nm* squash.

squat /skwat/ *nm* squat.

squatter[1] /skwatœʀ/ *nm* squatter.

squatter[2] /skwate/, [1] **squattériser** /skwateʀize/ *vtr* to squat in [*appartement*]; to take over [*escalier*].

squelette /skəlɛt/ *nm* **1** Anat skeleton; **2**○ (personne maigre) bag of bones○, skeleton; **3** (de bateau) framework; **4** (d'une œuvre, d'un article) outline.

squelettique /skəlɛtik/ *adj* [*personne, jambes*] scrawny; Méd skeletal; fig [*arbre*] skeletal; [*rapport, article*] sketchy; **des effectifs ~s** skeleton staff; **être d'une maigreur ~** to be like a skeleton.

Sri Lanka /sʀilɑ̃ka/ ▶321, 416 *nprm* Sri Lanka.

sri-lankais, ~e /sʀilɑ̃kɛ, ɛz/ ▶537 *adj* Sri Lankan.

Sri-Lankais, ~e /sʀilɑ̃kɛ, ɛz/ ▶537 *nm,f* Sri Lankan.

SRPJ /ɛsɛʀpeʒi/ *nm* (*abbr* = **Service régional de la police judiciaire**) *regional crime squad*.

SS /ɛsɛs/ I *nm* (*abbr* = **Schutzstaffel**) SS.

II *written abbr* ▶ **sécurité**.

SSII /ɛsɛsdøzi/ *nf* (*abbr* = **société de services et d'ingénierie informatiques**) software engineering company.

stabilisateur, -trice /stabilizatœʀ, tʀis/ I *adj* [*élément, agent*] stabilizing.

II *nm* stabilizer.

stabilisation /stabilizasjɔ̃/ *nf* stabilization.

stabiliser /stabilize/ [1] I *vtr* to stabilize [*prix, marché, monnaie, pays, personnes, véhicule, gaz*]; to consolidate [*accotements*]; **accotements non stabilisés** soft verges GB, soft shoulders.

II **se stabiliser** *vpr* [*chômage, prix, taux*] to stabilize; [*personne*] to become stable.

stabilité /stabilite/ *nf* stability; **~ des prix** price stability.

stable /stabl/ *adj* stable.

stabulation /stabylasjɔ̃/ *nf* **1** (procédé) animal housing, stalling; (local) animal housing facilities, shed; **~ libre** loose housing; **2** (de poissons) storing.

staccato /stakato/ *adv* staccato.

stade /stad/ *nm* **1** Sport stadium; **2** (étape) stage; **les ~s de la production** the stages of production; **à ce ~** at this stage (**de** of).

staff /staf/ *nm* **1** (plâtre) staff; **2** (personnel) staff.

Staffordshire ▶692 *nprm* **le ~** Staffordshire.

stage /staʒ/ *nm* **1** (pour obtenir diplôme, titre) professional training; **~ pédagogique** teaching practice GB, student ou practice teaching US; **2** (pendant des études) work experience ₵; **faire un ~ pratique** to do a period of work experience; **~ rémunéré/non rémunéré** paid/unpaid work experience; **3** (pour le travail, le sport, les loisirs) course; **suivre un ~** to go on a course; **~ d'initiation à l'informatique** introductory computer course; **~ intensif** intensive course; **~ de formation** training course; **4**○ (séjour) spell; **un ~ de trois jours à l'hôpital** a three-day spell in hospital GB ou in the hospital US.

stagflation /stagflasjɔ̃/ *nf* stagflation.

stagiaire /staʒjɛʀ/ *nmf* Ind Comm trainee; (enseignant) student teacher; (infirmière) student nurse.

stagnant, ~e /stagnɑ̃, ɑt/ *adj* stagnant.

stagnation /stagnasjɔ̃/ *nf* lit, fig stagnation.

stagner /stagne/ [1] *vi* lit, fig to stagnate.

stakhanovisme /stakanɔvism/ *nm* stakhanovism.

stalactite /stalaktit/ *nf* stalactite.

stalag /stalag/ *nm* stalag.

stalagmite /stalagmit/ *nf* stalagmite.

Staline /stalin/ *npr* Stalin.

stalinien, -ienne /stalinjɛ̃, ɛn/ *adj, nm,f* Stalinist.

stalinisme /stalinism/ *nm* Stalinism.

stalle /stal/ *nf* **1** (pour chevaux) stall; **2** (d'église) stall.

stance /stɑ̃s/ I† *nf* stanza.

II **stances** *nfpl*: *a verse form used mainly in lyric poetry*.

stand /stɑ̃d/ *nm* (d'exposition) stand; (de fête foraine) stall.

■ **~ de ravitaillement** Courses Aut pit; **~ de tir** (de club sportif) shooting range; (de fête foraine) shooting gallery.

standard /stɑ̃daʀ/ I *adj inv* standard.

II *nm* Télécom switchboard.

standardisation /stɑ̃daʀdizasjɔ̃/ *nf* standardization.

standardiser /stɑ̃daʀdize/ [1] *vtr* to standardize.

standardiste /stɑ̃daʀdist/ ▶510 *nmf* switchboard operator.

standing /stɑ̃diŋ/ *nm* **1** (confort) **de (grand) ~** [*appartement*] luxury (*épith*); **2** (niveau de vie) standard of living.

staphylocoque /stafilɔkɔk/ *nm* staphylococcus; **~ doré** staphylococcus aureus.

star /staʀ/ *nf* star; **jouer les ~s** to play at being a star.

starlette /staʀlɛt/ *nf* starlet.

starter /staʀtɛʀ/ *nm* **1** Aut choke; **mettre le ~** to pull out the choke; **2** Turf starter.

starting-block, *pl* **~s** /staʀtiŋblɔk/ *nm* starting block; **être dans les ~s** to be in one's starting blocks.

starting-gate, *pl* **~s** /staʀtiŋgɛt/ *nm* ou *f* starting gate.

station /stasjɔ̃/ *nf* **1** (de métro) station; **~ de métro** tube GB ou subway US station; **descendez à la ~ Saint-Ambroise** get off at Saint-Ambroise; **c'est à deux ~s de métro d'ici** it's two tube GB ou subway US stops from here; (de taxis) taxi-rank GB, taxi stand; **2** Radio station; **~ émettrice** transmitting station; **~ de radio** radio station; **3** (lieu de séjour) resort; **~ balnéaire/climatique** seaside/health resort; **~ de sports d'hiver** winter sports resort; **~ thermale** spa; **4** (lieu d'observation scientifique) station; **~ agronomique** agricultural station; **~ météorologique** meteorological ou weather station; **~ marine** marine research station; **~ orbitale** orbiting space station; **~ spatiale** space station; **5** (position) posture; **~ debout** or **verticale** upright posture or position; **la ~ debout me donne mal au dos** standing gives me backache; **6** (pause) stop, pause; **faire une longue ~ devant une vitrine** to stop ou linger for a long time in front of a shop window; **les ~s du chemin de Croix** Relig the stations of the Cross; **planète en ~** Astron stationary planet; **7**○ Aut (station-service) service station; **~ de lavage** car wash point.

■ **~ d'épuration** sewage treatment plant; **~ graphique** graphic VDU, graphic workstation; **~ au sol** ground station; **~ de travail** workstation.

stationnaire /stasjɔnɛʀ/ *adj* **1** [*planète, véhicule*] stationary; **2** [*situation, production*] stable; **être dans un état ~** [*malade*] to be in a stable condition.

stationnement /stasjɔnmɑ̃/ *nm* **1** Aut parking; **~ interdit** no parking; **~ alterné** *parking system where drivers park on alternate sides of the street every two weeks*; **~ bilatéral** parking on both sides; **~ unilatéral** parking on one side only; **~ payant** (dans la rue) metered parking; (dans un parking) pay and display parking; **~ à durée limitée** short-term parking; **'~ gênant'** 'no parking or waiting'; **une amende pour ~ gênant** a fine for causing a parking obstruction; **~ dangereux** dangerous parking; **~ illicite** unlawful parking; **~ en épi** angle parking, chevron parking; **~ en bataille** perpendicular parking; **2** C Aut (parking) car park GB, parking lot US; **3** Mil (de troupes) stationing.

stationner /stasjɔne/ [1] *vi* **1** Aut [*véhicule, automobiliste*] to park; **défense** or **interdiction de ~** no parking; **~ en double file** to double-park; **2** Mil [*person, troupes, armée*] to station.

station-service, *pl* **stations-service** /stasjɔ̃sɛʀvis/ *nf* service station, filling station.

statique /statik/ I *adj* static.

II *nf* statics (+ *v sg*).

statisticien, -ienne /statistisjɛ̃, ɛn/ ▶510 *nm,f* statistician.

statistique /statistik/ I *adj* statistical.

II *nf* (méthode) statistics (+ *v sg*); (donnée) statistic; **établir des ~s** to draw up statistics.

■ **~ lexicale** statistical linguistics (+ *v sg*).

statistiquement /statistikmɑ̃/ *adv* statistically.

stator /statɔʀ/ *nm* stator.

statoréacteur /statoʀeaktœʀ/ *nm* ramjet engine.

statuaire /statɥɛʀ/ I *adj* statuary.

II *nmf* sculptor.

III *nf* statuary.

statue /staty/ *nf* statue (**de** of).

■ **~ équestre** equestrian statue; **~ de sel** Bible pillar of salt.

IDIOMES **se changer en ~** to be frozen to the spot.

statuer /statɥe/ [1] *vi* to give a ruling (**sur** on).

statuette /statɥɛt/ *nf* statuette.

statufier /statyfje/ [2] *vtr* **1** Art to erect a statue to; **2** (paralyser) [*peur, effroi*] to transfix.

statu quo /statykwo/ *nm inv* status quo.

stature /statyʀ/ *nf* **1** lit (gabarit) stature; (sur une étiquette de vêtements) height; **être de petite ~** to be small in stature; **2** fig (envergure) calibre[GB]; **grande ~** high calibre[GB].

statut /staty/ *nm* **1** (loi, règlement) statute; **les ~s de l'association** the association's statutes; **2** (situation) status; **le ~ de fonctionnaire** civil servant status; **avoir un ~ d'immigrant** to have immigrant status.

statutaire /statytɛʀ/ *adj* statutory.

statutairement /statytɛʀmɑ̃/ *adv* statutorily.

steak /stɛk/ *nm* steak.
■ **~ haché** (cru) minced beef GB, ground beef US; (cuit) hamburger; **~ au poivre** pepper steak.

stéarine /steaʀin/ *nf* stearin.

stéatite /steatit/ *nf* soapstone.

steeple(-chase), *pl* **~s** /stipəl(tʃɛz)/ *nm* steeplechase.

stèle /stɛl/ *nf* stele.

stellaire /stelɛʀ/ *adj* stellar.

stencil /stɛnsil/ *nm* stencil.

sténo○ /steno/ I ▶510 *nmf* (personne) shorthand typist GB, stenographer US.
II *nf* (activité) shorthand GB, stenography US; **prendre un texte en ~** to take a text down in shorthand.

sténodactylo /stenodaktilo/ ▶510 I *nmf* (personne) shorthand typist GB, stenographer US.
II *nf* (activité) shorthand typing GB, stenography US.

sténodactylographie /stenodaktilɔgʀafi/ *nf* shorthand typing GB, stenography US.

sténographe /stenɔgʀaf/ ▶510 *nmf* stenographer.

sténographie /stenɔgʀafi/ *nf* shorthand GB, stenography US.

sténographier /stenɔgʀafje/ [2] *vtr* to take [sth] down in shorthand.

sténographique /stenɔgʀafik/ *adj* shorthand (*épith*).

sténopé /stenɔpe/ *nm* Phot pinhole.

sténotype /stenɔtip/ *nf* stenotype.

sténotypie /stenɔtipi/ *nf* stenotypy.

sténotypiste /stenɔtipist/ ▶510 *nmf* stenotypist.

stentor /stɑ̃tɔʀ/ *nm* **1** gén **voix de ~** stentorian voice; **2** Zool stentor.

stéphanois, **~e** /stefanwa, az/ ▶857 *adj* of Saint-Étienne.

Stéphanois, **~e** /stefanwa, az/ *nm,f* (natif) native of Saint-Étienne; (habitant) inhabitant of Saint-Étienne.

steppe /stɛp/ *nf* steppe.

stéradian /steʀadjɑ̃/ *nm* steradian.

stercoraire /stɛʀkɔʀɛʀ/ I *adj* Bot, Méd stercoraceous.
II *nm* skua.

stère /stɛʀ/ ▶866 *nm* stere.

stéréo /stereo/ I *adj inv* (*abbr* = **stéréophonique**) stereo (*épith*).
II○ *nf* stereo.

stéréophonie /steʀeɔfɔni/ *nf* stereophony; **en ~** [*enregistrer*] in stereo; [*enregistrement*] stereophonic (*épith*).

stéréophonique /steʀeɔfɔnik/ *adj* stereophonic.

stéréoscope /steʀeɔskɔp/ *nm* stereoscope.

stéréoscopie /steʀeɔskɔpi/ *nf* stereoscopy.

stéréotype /steʀeɔtip/ *nm* **1** (personne) stereotype; **2** (cliché) cliché.

stéréotypé, **~e** /steʀeɔtipe/ *adj* (convenu) stereotypical; (banal) stereotyped.

stérile /steʀil/ *adj* **1** [*personne, animal, plante*] sterile; [*mariage*] childless; [*sol*] barren; **2** [*pansement, milieu*] sterile; **3** fig [*artiste, période*] unproductive; [*imagination*] sterile; [*discussion, travail*] fruitless.

stérilet /steʀilɛ/ *nm* coil, IUD, intrauterine device spéc.

stérilisateur /steʀilizatœʀ/ *nm* **1** Méd, Tech sterilizer; **2** Culin sterilizer.

stérilisation /steʀilizasjɔ̃/ *nf* sterilization.

stériliser /steʀilize/ [1] *vtr* **1** lit to sterilize [*personne, animal*]; to sterilize [*biberon, appareil, bocal, pansement*]; to make [sth] barren [*sol*]; **2** fig to suppress [*créativité*]; to make [sb] uncreative [*artiste*].

stérilité /steʀilite/ *nf* **1** (de personne, plante, d'animal) sterility; (de sol, région) barrenness; **2** fig (d'artiste) lack of creativity; (de discussion, travail) fruitlessness; (d'imagination) sterility; **3** (de milieu) sterility.

sterling /stɛʀliŋ/ I *adj inv* sterling; **livre ~** pound sterling.
II *nm* pound (sterling).

sterne /stɛʀn/ *nf* tern.

sternum /stɛʀnɔm/ *nm* breastbone, sternum spéc.

stéthoscope /stetɔskɔp/ *nm* stethoscope.

steward /stjuwaʀd/ *nm* steward.

stick /stik/ *nm* Cosmét stick; **déodorant en ~** deodorant stick.

stigmate /stigmat/ I *nm* **1** (trace) (sur la peau) scar; fig, littér (de vice, guerre) mark; **2** Bot, Zool stigma.
II **stigmates** *nmpl* Relig stigmata.

stigmatisation /stigmatizasjɔ̃/ *nf* stigmatization.

stigmatiser /stigmatize/ [1] *vtr* (condamner) to stigmatize.

stimulant, **~e** /stimylɑ̃, ɑ̃t/ I *adj* (physiquement) [*bain*] invigorating; [*air, climat*] bracing; (mentalement) [*paroles, lecture, concurrence*] stimulating; [*résultat*] encouraging.
II *nm* **1** (physique) (fortifiant) tonic; (excitant) stimulant; **2** (mental) stimulus.

stimulateur, **-trice** /stimylatœʀ, tʀis/ *adj* stimulating.
■ **~ cardiaque** Méd Tech pacemaker.

stimulation /stimylasjɔ̃/ *nf* stimulation.

stimuler /stimyle/ [1] I *vtr* **1** Physiol to stimulate [*organe, fonction*]; **2** (motiver) to spur [sb] on.
II *vi* **1** [*air, froid*] to be bracing; **2**○ [*récompense, résultat*] to act as a spur.

stimulus, *pl* **stimuli** /stimylys, stimyli/ *nm* stimulus.

stipendier /stipɑ̃dje/ [2] *vtr* liter pej to hire [*tueur, espion*].

stipulation /stipylasjɔ̃/ *nf* **1** Jur stipulation; **2** Assur provision.

stipuler /stipyle/ [1] *vtr* to stipulate (**que** that).

STO /ɛsteo/ *nm*: *abbr* ▶ **service**.

stock /stɔk/ *nm* lit, fig stock; **avoir qch en ~** to have sth in stock; **avoir des ~s de**○ fig to have a whole stock of; ▶ **liquidation**.
■ **~ chromosomique** Biol genome.

stockage /stɔkaʒ/ *nm* **1** (mise en réserve) Comm stocking; (accumulation excessive) stockpiling; **2** (entreposage) Comm, Ordinat storage; **capacité de ~** storage capacity; **~ des données** data storage.

stock-car, *pl* **~s** /stɔkkaʀ/ *nm* **1** (voiture) stock car; **course de ~s** stock-car race; **2** (sport) stock-car racing.

stocker /stɔke/ [1] *vtr* **1** Comm to stock; (à l'excès) to stockpile; **2** Ordinat to store [*données*].

Stockholm /stɔkɔlm/ ▶857 *npr* Stockholm.

stockiste /stɔkist/ ▶510 *nm* stockist GB (**de** of), dealer (**de** in).

stoïcien, **-ienne** /stɔisjɛ̃, ɛn/ *adj, nm,f* Philos Stoic.

stoïcisme /stɔisism/ *nm* **1** Philos Stoicism; **2** fig stoicism.

stoïque /stɔik/ I *adj* stoical.
II *nmf* stoic.

stoïquement /stɔikmɑ̃/ *adv* stoically.

stomacal, **~e**, *mpl* **-aux** /stɔmakal, o/ *adj* [*douleur, pompe*] stomach.

stomatologie /stɔmatɔlɔʒi/ *nf* stomatology.

stomatologiste /stɔmatɔlɔʒist/ *nmf*, **stomatologue** /stɔmatɔlɔg/ *nmf* ▶510 stomatologist.

stop /stɔp/ I *nm* **1** Aut (panneau) stop sign; (feu arrière) brake-light; **2**○ (auto-stop) hitching○; **faire du ~** to hitch○; **faire la France en ~** to hitch○ round[GB] France; **aller travailler en ~** to hitch○ to work; **prendre qn en ~** to give sb a lift GB ou ride US; **3** (dans un télégramme) stop.
II *excl* stop!

stoppage /stɔpaʒ/ *nm* invisible mending.

stopper /stɔpe/ [1] I *vtr* **1** (arrêter) to stop [*personne, voiture, attaque*]; to halt [*maladie, évolution*]; **2** Cout to mend.
II *vi* to stop.

stoppeur○, **-euse** /stɔpœʀ, øz/ *nm,f* hitchhiker.

store /stɔʀ/ *nm* blind; (auvent) awning.
■ **~ enrouleur** roller blind GB, roller window shade US; **~ à l'italienne** awning; **~ vénitien** Venetian blind.

strabisme /stʀabism/ *nm* squint, strabismus spéc.

strangulation /stʀɑ̃gylasjɔ̃/ *nf* strangulation.

strapontin /stʀapɔ̃tɛ̃/ *nm* **1** (siège) foldaway seat; Aut Aviat jump seat; **2** fig back seat.

Strasbourg /stʀasbuʀ/ ▶857 *npr* Strasbourg.

strasbourgeois, **~e** /stʀasbuʀʒwa, az/ ▶857 *adj* of Strasbourg.

Strasbourgeois, **~e** /stʀasbuʀʒwa, az/ *nm,f* (natif) native of Strasbourg; (habitant) inhabitant of Strasbourg.

strass /stʀas/ *nm* **1** (verroterie) paste; **collier en ~** paste necklace; **2** fig, péj **un monde de ~** a world of superficial glamour.

stratagème /stʀataʒɛm/ *nm* stratagem.

strate /stʀat/ *nf* lit, fig stratum.

stratège /stʀatɛʒ/ *nm* strategist.

stratégie /stʀateʒi/ *nf* strategy.

stratégique /stʀateʒik/ *adj* strategic.

stratégiquement /stʀateʒikmɑ̃/ *adv* strategically.

Strathclyde ▶692 *nprm* **le ~** Strathclyde.

stratification /stʀatifikasjɔ̃/ *nf* stratification.

stratifié, **~e** /stʀatifje/ I *adj* **1** Biol, Sociol stratified; **2** Tech laminated.
II *nm* (matériau) **du ~** laminate; **table en ~** laminated table.

stratifier /stʀatifje/ [2] *vtr* to stratify.

stratigraphie /stʀatigʀafi/ *nf* stratigraphy.

strato-cumulus /stʀatokymylys/ *nm inv* stratocumulus.

stratosphère /stʀatɔsfɛʀ/ *nf* stratosphere.

stratus /stʀatys/ *nm inv* stratus.

streptocoque /stʀɛptɔkɔk/ *nm* streptococcus.

streptomycine /stʀɛptɔmisin/ *nf* streptomycin.

stress /stʀɛs/ *nm inv* stress.

stressant, **~e** /stʀɛsɑ̃, ɑ̃t/ *adj* [*journée*] stressful; [*incident*] upsetting; [*perspective*] worrying.

stresser /stʀese/ [1] I *vtr* [*perspective*] to put [sb] on edge; [*travail*] to put [sb] under stress; **être stressé** (tendu) to be stressed; (irritable) to be on edge; (sous pression) to be under stress; **être stressé par le travail** to be under stress from work.
II○ *vi* to get worked up; **il n'est pas du**

genre à ~ he's not the kind of person to get worked up.

stretch /stʀɛtʃ/ *nm* Tex stretch material; **velours ~** stretch velvet; **jeans en ~** stretch jeans.

stretching /stʀɛtʃiŋ/ *nm* Sport stretch; **cours de ~** stretch class.

striation /stʀijasjɔ̃/ *nf* striation.

strict, **~e** /stʀikt/ *adj* **1** (sévère) [*discipline, morale, professeur*] strict; **il est très ~ sur la propreté** he's very strict about cleanliness; **2** (complet) [*obéissance*] total; **au sens ~** in the strict sense; **c'est ton droit le plus ~** you're perfectly entitled to do so; **c'est la ~e vérité** it's the absolute truth; **le ~ nécessaire** what is strictly necessary; **le ~ minimum** the bare ou absolute minimum; **dans la plus ~e intimité** strictly in private; **3** (austère) [*tenue, robe*] severe, austere; [*coiffure*] severe.

strictement /stʀiktəmɑ̃/ *adv* strictly.

stricto sensu /stʀiktosɛ̃sy/ *loc adv* strictly speaking.

strident, **~e** /stʀidɑ̃, ɑ̃t/ *adj* **1** [*bruit*] piercing; [*voix*] strident; **2** Ling strident.

stridulant, **~e** /stʀidylɑ̃, ɑ̃t/ *adj* [*insecte*] stridulatory.

stridulation /stʀidylasjɔ̃/ *nf* stridulation.

striduler /stʀidyle/ [1] *vi* to stridulate.

strie /stʀi/ *nf* **1** (rayure) streak; **2** (sillon) gén groove; (de front, visage) furrow; Anat, Biol, Géol stria; **des ~s** striae, striation ¢.

strié, **~e** /stʀije/ *adj* **1** (de couleur) streaked (**de** with); [*muscle*] striated; **2** (de sillons) [*roche*] striated; [*colonne*] fluted; [*coquille, tige*] grooved.

strier /stʀije/ [2] *vtr* **1** (de couleur) to streak (**de** with); **2** (faire des sillons) to make grooves in; **3** Géol to striate.

string /stʀiŋ/ *nm* G-string.

strip-tease /stʀiptiz/ *nm* **1** (spectacle) striptease; **2** (cabaret) striptease club; **danseuse de ~** striptease artist.

strip-teaseur, **-euse** /stʀiptizœʀ, øz/ ▶510 *nm,f* stripper.

striure /stʀijyʀ/ *nf* (ensemble de stries) striation ¢; (de couleur) streaking ¢.

stroboscope /stʀɔbɔskɔp/ *nm* stroboscope.

stroboscopique /stʀɔbɔskɔpik/ *adj* **1** [*effet, éclairage*] strobe (*épith*); **2** Phys [*observation*] stroboscopic.

strontium /stʀɔ̃sjɔm/ *nm* strontium.

strophe /stʀɔf/ *nf* **1** (de poème) stanza, verse; **2** (dans une tragédie grecque) strophe.

structural, **~e**, *mpl* **-aux** /stʀyktyʀal, o/ *adj* structural.

structuralement /stʀyktyʀalmɑ̃/ *adv* structurally.

structuralisme /stʀyktyʀalism/ *nm* structuralism.

structuraliste /stʀyktyʀalist/ *adj, nmf* structuralist.

structuration /stʀyktyʀasjɔ̃/ *nf* structuring.

structure /stʀyktyʀ/ *nf* **1** (agencement) structure; **~ syntagmatique/profonde/de surface** Ling phrase/deep/surface structure; **2** (organisme) organization; **~ d'accueil** shelter, refuge.

■ **~ primaire** Biol, Chimie primary structure; **~s d'accueil** facilities; (pour vieillards, handicapés) day centre[GB].

structuré, **~e** /stʀyktyʀe/ *adj* structured.

structurel, **-elle** /stʀyktyʀɛl/ *adj* structural.

structurellement /stʀyktyʀɛlmɑ̃/ *adv* structurally.

structurer /stʀyktyʀe/ [1] **I** *vtr* to structure [*pays, ouvrage, parti*].

II se structurer *vpr* [*parti, entreprise*] to be structured.

strychnine /stʀiknin/ *nf* strychnine.

stuc /styk/ *nm* stucco.

studette /stydɛt/ *nf* small flat GB ou apartment.

studieusement /stydjøzmɑ̃/ *adv* studiously.

studieux, **-ieuse** /stydjø, øz/ *adj* [*élève*] studious; [*vacances*] study (*épith*); [*ambiance*] industrious.

studio /stydjo/ *nm* **1** (logement) studio flat GB, studio apartment US; **2** (atelier) studio; **3** Cin, Radio, TV (pour tourner, enregistrer) studio; Cin (salle de projection) **~ d'art et d'essai** arts cinema GB, art house US; **tourné/enregistré en ~** filmed ou shot/recorded in the studio; **~ d'enregistrement/de danse** recording/dance studio; **~s de production** or **cinéma** film studios.

stupéfaction /stypefaksjɔ̃/ *nf* stupefaction, amazement; **à ma grande ~** to my utter amazement; **muet de ~** dumbfounded.

stupéfaire /stypefɛʀ/ *vtr* to astound, to stun.

stupéfait, **~e** /stypefɛ, ɛt/ *adj* astounded, dumbfounded; **rester ~ de qch/d'apprendre** to be astounded at sth/to hear.

stupéfiant, **~e** /stypefjɑ̃, ɑ̃t/ **I** *adj* **1** (étonnant) stunning, astounding; **2** Méd stupefying.

II *nm* Pharm drug, narcotic.

stupéfier /stypefje/ [2] *vtr* **1** (étonner) to astound, to stun; **2** Méd (hébéter) to stupefy.

stupeur /stypœʀ/ *nf* **1** (étonnement) astonishment, amazement; **2** Méd (torpeur) stupor.

stupide /stypid/ *adj* stupid.

stupidement /stypidmɑ̃/ *adv* stupidly.

stupidité /stypidite/ *nf* **1** (caractère) stupidity; **il est d'une ~!** he's incredibly stupid; **2** (remarque) stupid remark; (action) **faire une ~** to do something stupid; **faire/dire des ~s** to do/to say stupid things.

stupre /stypʀ/ *nm* liter debauchery.

stups○ /styp/ *nmpl* drugs squad GB, drug squad US.

style /stil/ *nm* **1** Art, Littérat, Sport style; **~ journalistique** journalistic style, journalese péj; **~ télégraphique** telegraphic style, telegraphese péj; **~ de vie** lifestyle; **avoir du ~** to have style; **manquer de ~** to lack style; **n'achète pas ce chapeau, ce n'est vraiment pas ton ~** don't buy this hat, it's just not your style; **elle joue de la guitare dans le ~ flamenco** she plays the guitar flamenco style; **il excelle dans un comique du ~ Laurel et Hardy** he's at his best in Laurel and Hardy style comedy; **elle veut se donner le ~ Marilyn Monroe** she's trying to cultivate the Marilyn Monroe look; **ça, c'est bien (dans) ton ~!** that's you all over○!; **c'est bien (dans) ton ~ de faire** it's typical of you ou it's just like you to do; **elle est du ~ à passer une nuit blanche pour finir un article** she's the kind that would stay up all night to finish an article; **il m'a répondu qch du ~ 'on vous téléphonera'** he told me they'd phone me, or something like that; **2** (de mobilier) **meubles de ~** (anciens) period furniture; (copiés) reproduction period furniture; **mobilier de ~ Louis XV** (ancien) Louis XV furniture; (copié) reproduction Louis XV furniture; **3** Ling speech form; **~ direct/indirect** direct/indirect ou reported speech; **4** (tige de cadran solaire) style; **5** Antiq stylus.

stylé, **~e** /stile/ *adj* [*domestique*] well-trained.

stylet /stilɛ/ *nm* **1** (couteau) stiletto; **2** Méd, Tech stylet; **3** Zool (organe) style, proboscis spéc; (aiguillon) sting.

stylique /stilik/ *nf* Ind design.

stylisation /stilizasjɔ̃/ *nf* stylization.

styliser /stilize/ [1] *vtr* to stylize; **des formes stylisées** stylized shapes.

stylisme /stilism/ *nm* **1** Art, Mode fashion design; **2** Littérat, péj excessive preoccupation with style.

styliste /stilist/ *nmf* **1** ▶510 Ind, Mode fashion designer; **2** Littérat stylist.

stylisticien, **-ienne** /stilistisjɛ̃, ɛn/ ▶510 *nm,f* specialist in stylistics.

stylistique /stilistik/ **I** *adj* stylistic.

II *nf* stylistics (+ *v sg*).

stylo /stilo/ *nm* pen.

■ **~ (à) bille** ball-point pen; **~ à cartouche** cartridge pen; **~ à encre** fountain pen; **~ (à) plume** = **~ à encre**.

stylo-feutre, *pl* **stylos-feutres** /stiloføtʀ/ *nm* felt-tip pen.

stylographe† /stilɔgʀaf/ *nm* fountain pen.

Styx /stix/ *nprm* **the ~** the Styx.

su /sy/ *nm* **au ~ de qn** liter to sb's knowledge; **au vu et au ~ de tous** openly, for all to see.

suaire /sɥɛʀ/ *nm* shroud.

suant, **~e** /sɥɑ̃, ɑ̃t/ *adj* **1** (qui sue) sweaty; **2**○ (ennuyeux) deadly dull.

suave /sɥav/ *adj* liter [*parfum, musique, sourire*] sweet; [*coloris, regard*] soft; [*contours*] smooth; [*voix*] mellifluous; [*plaisir*] exquisite; [*personne, manière*] suave.

suavement /sɥavmɑ̃/ *adv* liter [*parler, chanter*] sweetly; **sourire ~** to have a sweet smile.

suavité /sɥavite/ *nf* (de voix) mellifluous quality; (de parfum, musique) sweetness; (de coloris, regard) softness; (de contours) smoothness; (de personne, manières) suaveness.

subaigu, **-uë** /sybegy/ *adj* subacute.

subalterne /sybaltɛʀn/ **I** *adj* [*poste*] junior; [*rôle*] subordinate; (au théâtre) minor; **officier ~** Mil low-ranking officer, subaltern.

II *nmf* subordinate; Mil low-ranking officer, subaltern.

subantarctique /sybɑ̃taʀktik/ *adj* subantarctic.

subaquatique /sybakwatik/ *adj* subaquatic.

subarctique /sybaʀktik/ *adj* subarctic.

subconscient, **~e** /sybkɔ̃sjɑ̃, ɑ̃t/ **I** *adj* subconscious.

II *nm* subconscious.

subculture /sybkyltyʀ/ *nf* subculture.

subdésertique /sybdezɛʀtik/ *adj* subdesert (*épith*).

subdiviser /sybdivize/ [1] **I** *vtr* to subdivide (**en** into).

II se subdiviser *vpr* to be subdivided (**en** into).

subdivision /sybdivizjɔ̃/ *nf* subdivision.

subduction /sybdyksjɔ̃/ *nf* subduction; **zone de ~** subduction zone, Benioff zone.

subéquatorial, **~e**, *mpl* **-iaux** /sybekwatɔʀjal, o/ *adj* subequatorial.

subir /sybiʀ/ [3] *vtr* **1** (être victime de) to be subjected to [*mauvais traitements, violences, pressions*]; to suffer, to sustain [*défaite, dégâts*]; to suffer [*discrimination, brimades*]; **~ le contrecoup/les conséquences de qch** to suffer the effects/the consequences of sth; **~ le même sort** to suffer the same fate; **faire ~ à qn** to subject sb to [*mauvais traitements*]; to inflict [sth] on sb [*défaite, pertes*]; **~ les effets de la concurrence/de la récession** to experience the effects of ou to be affected by competition/the recession; **2** (être soumis à) to undergo, to be subjected to [*interrogatoire*]; to take [*examen scolaire*]; to undergo [*opération chirurgicale, examens médicaux*]; **~ l'influence de qn** to be under sb's influence; **faire ~ à qn** to subject sb to [*interrogatoire*]; to make sb take [*examen scolaire*]; to make sb undergo [*examens médicaux*]; **3** (supporter) to put up with [*personne, épreuve*]; **~ la colère de qn en silence** to suffer sb's anger in silence; **4** (être l'objet de) to undergo, to go through [*changements, transformations*].

subit, **~e** /sybi, it/ *adj* sudden.

subitement /sybitmɑ̃/ *adv* suddenly, all of a sudden.

subito (presto) /sybito (pʀɛsto)/ *adv* **1**○ (tout de suite) at once; **2** Mus subito presto.

subjectif, **-ive** /sybʒɛktif, iv/ *adj* subjective.

subjectivement /sybʒɛktivmɑ̃/ *adv* subjectively.

subjectivisme /sybʒɛktivism/ *nm* **1** (système) subjectivism; **2** fml (subjectivité) péj subjectivity.

subjectiviste /sybʒɛktivist/ *adj, nmf* subjectivist.

subjectivité /sybʒɛktivite/ *nf* subjectivity.

subjonctif, -ive /sybʒɔ̃ktif, iv/ **I** *adj* subjunctive.
II *nm* subjunctive; **au ~** in the subjunctive.

subjuguer /sybʒyge/ [1] *vtr* **1** (séduire) to captivate, to enthral[GB]; **2** (asservir) liter to subjugate.

sublimation /syblimasjɔ̃/ *nf* sublimation.

sublime /syblim/ **I** *adj* [*peinture, œuvre, personne*] sublime; **~ de générosité** sublimely generous; **se montrer ~** to be sublime; **~!** wonderful!, beautiful!
II *nm* **le ~** the sublime; **le ~ de l'histoire, c'est que** hum the best part of the story is that.
■ **la Sublime Porte** Hist the Sublime Porte.

sublimé, ~e /syblime/ **I** *adj* sublimated.
II *nm* Chimie sublimate.

sublimement /syblimәmɑ̃/ *adv* sublimely.

sublimer /syblime/ [1] *vtr, vi* to sublimate.

subliminal, ~e, *mpl* **-aux** /sybliminal, o/ *adj* subliminal.

sublimité /syblimite/ *nf* liter sublimity.

sublingual, ~e, *mpl* **-aux** /syblɛ̃gwal, o/ *adj* sublingual.

submergé, ~e /sybmɛʀʒe/ **I** *pp* ▶ **submerger.**
II *pp adj* **1** [*terre, récif*] submerged; **2** fig (débordé) **~ par l'émotion/la foule** overwhelmed by emotion/the crowd; **~ d'appels/de réclamations/de candidatures** swamped with calls/with complaints/with applications; **je suis ~ de travail** I'm inundated with work.

submerger /sybmɛʀʒe/ [13] *vtr* **1** (inonder) lit to submerge [*terre, récif*]; fig to flood [*standard téléphonique, marché*] (**de** with); **une vague de nationalisme/colère a submergé le pays** a wave of nationalism/anger swept over ou through the country; **2** (dominer) [*foule, ennemi, émotion*] to overwhelm [*personne, groupe*]; **3** (accabler) **~ qn de travail/questions** to swamp sb with work/questions.

submersible /sybmɛʀsibl/ **I** *adj* **1** Géog [*terre*] liable to flooding (*après n*); **2** Tech [*machine, navire*] submersible.
II *nm* submersible.

submersion /sybmɛʀsjɔ̃/ *nf* **1** Agric irrigation by flooding; **2** Naut (de sous-marin) submersion; (naufrage) sinking; **3** Méd **asphyxie par ~** death by drowning.

subnormal, ~e, *mpl* **-aux** /sybnɔʀmal, o/ *adj* [*intelligence*] subnormal.

subodorer○ /sybɔdɔʀe/ [1] *vtr* to detect [*malhonnêteté, piège*]; **~ quelque chose de louche** to smell a rat○.

subordination /sybɔʀdinasjɔ̃/ *nf* **1** (dépendance) subordination (**à** to); **2** Ling subordination; **conjonction de ~** subordinating conjunction.

subordonné, ~e /sybɔʀdɔne/ **I** *pp* ▶ **subordonner.**
II *pp adj* **1** (dans une hiérarchie) subordinate (**à** to); **2** (dépendant) subject (**à** to); **3** Ling subordinate (**à** to).
III *nm,f* subordinate.
IV subordonnée *nf* Ling subordinate clause; **~e circonstancielle/relative** adverbial/relative clause.

subordonner /sybɔʀdɔne/ [1] *vtr* **1** (dans une hiérarchie) **être subordonné à qn** [*soldat, fonctionnaire*] to be subordinate to sb; **2** (faire dépendre) **elle subordonne tout à son travail** everything else comes second to her job; **être subordonné à qch** [*réussite, réalisation*] to be subject to ou dependent on sth.

subornation /sybɔʀnasjɔ̃/ *nf* (d'employé) bribing; Jur (de témoin) subornation.

suborner /sybɔʀne/ [1] *vtr* **1** (corrompre) to bribe [*employé, garde*]; Jur to suborn [*témoin*]; **2**† liter (séduire) to seduce.

subreptice /sybʀɛptis/ *adj* surreptitious.

subrepticement /sybʀɛptismɑ̃/ *adv* surreptitiously.

subrogation /sybʀɔgasjɔ̃/ *nf* Jur subrogation.

subrogé, ~e /sybʀɔʒe/ *adj* **1** Jur surrogate; **~ tuteur** *guardian appointed by the Family Court*; **2** Ling **langages ~s** subrogate languages.

subroger /sybʀɔʒe/ [13] *vtr* Jur to subrogate.

subsaharien, -ienne /sybsaaʀjɛ̃, ɛn/ *adj* sub-Saharan.

subséquemment /sybsekamɑ̃/ *adv* Jur or hum (par la suite) subsequently; (en conséquence) consequently; **~ à** consequent upon.

subséquent, ~e /sybsekɑ̃, ɑ̃t/ *adj* subsequent.

subside /sybsid/ *nm* (d'État, association) grant; (entre particuliers) allowance.

subsidiaire /sybzidjɛʀ/ *adj* [*moyens*] ancillary; [*motif*] subsidiary; **question ~** tiebreaker.

subsidiairement /sybzidjɛʀmɑ̃/ *adv* in addition.

subsidiarité /sybsidjaʀite/ *nf* subsidiarity; **principe de ~** principle of subsidiarity.

subsistance /sybzistɑ̃s/ **I** *nf* (de personne) subsistence; (de plante) sustenance; (moyens de survie) **(moyens de) ~** means of support, livelihood; **frais/économie de ~** subsistence allowance/economy; **avoir la ~ assurée** to have a secure livelihood; **perdre ses moyens de ~** to lose one's means of support; **assurer sa propre ~/la ~ de sa famille** to support oneself/one's family; **contribuer à la ~ du ménage** to contribute to household expenses; **tirer sa ~ d'un bout de terrain** to eke out a living from a small piece of land.
II subsistances *nfpl* Mil food supplies.

subsistant, ~e /sybzistɑ̃, ɑ̃t/ *adj* remaining.

subsister /sybziste/ [1] **I** *vi* **1** (durer) [*crainte, doute, trace*] to remain; **2** (survivre) [*personne, coutume*] to survive; **seuls deux commerces ont subsisté** only two shops GB ou stores US have survived; **3** (subvenir à ses besoins) [*personne*] to subsist; **ça leur suffit à peine pour ~** it's barely enough for them to live on.
II *v impers* **il subsistera toujours un doute** a doubt will always remain.

subsonique /sypsɔnik/ *adj* subsonic.

substance /sypstɑ̃s/ *nf* substance; **en ~** in substance; **~s végétales/toxiques** vegetable/toxic matter ¢.
■ **~ alimentaire** foodstuff; **~ blanche** Anat white material; **~ grise** Anat grey GB ou gray US matter ¢; **~ médicamenteuse** medicine.

substantialité /sypstɑ̃sjalite/ *nf* substantiality.

substantiel, -ielle /sypstɑ̃sjɛl/ *adj* **1** (nourrissant) [*repas*] substantial; fig [*lecture*] weighty; **2** (considérable) [*nombre, baisse, recette*] substantial; [*participation, progrès*] significant.

substantiellement /sypstɑ̃sjɛlmɑ̃/ *adv* substantially.

substantif, -ive /sypstɑ̃tif, iv/ **I** *adj* [*proposition*] noun; [*style*] nominal; [*emploi*] nominal, substantival.
II *nm* noun, substantive.

substantifique /sypstɑ̃tifik/ *adj* **la ~ moelle** the true substance.

substantivation /sypstɑ̃tivasjɔ̃/ *nf* substantivization.

substantivement /sypstɑ̃tivmɑ̃/ *adv* substantively; **employer un verbe/un adjectif ~** to use a verb/an adjective as a noun.

substantiver /sypstɑ̃tive/ [1] *vtr* to substantivize.

substituable /sypstitɥabl/ *adj* substitutable; **élément qui n'est pas ~ à un autre** element which may not be substituted for another; **produits ~s** substitute products.

substituer /sypstitɥe/ [1] **I** *vtr* **1 ~ A à B** to substitute A for B, to replace B by A; **2** Jur **~ un héritage** to entail an estate.
II se substituer *vpr* **se ~ à** [*personne*] (pour représenter) to deputize for, to stand in for [*personne, groupe*]; (pour remplacer) to take the place of [*personne*]; Sport to substitute for [*personne*]; [*chose*] to take the place of, to replace [*chose*].

substitut /sypstity/ *nm* **1** (magistrat) deputy public prosecutor; **2** (remplacement) substitute (**de** for); **~ maternel** substitute mother.

substitutif, -ive /sypstitytif, iv/ *adj* [*produit*] substitute; **médication substitutive** substitutive.

substitution /sypstitysjɔ̃/ *nf* **1** (remplacement) substitution (**de qn/qch à** of sb/sth for); **produit de ~ du sucre/café** sugar/coffee substitute; **peine de ~** Jur alternative to prison; **clause de ~** Jur entailment; **2** Mus **~ de doigt** refingering.
■ **~ d'enfant** Jur substitution of a baby for another.

substrat /sypstʀa/ *nm* **1** Bot, Philos substratum; **2** Chimie, Électrotech substrate; **3** Ling substrate language.

subsumer /sypsyme/ [1] *vtr* to subsume (**à, dans** within).

subterfuge /syptɛʀfyʒ/ *nm* ploy, subterfuge ¢; **user de ~s** to use subterfuge ou all sorts of ploys.

subtil, ~e /syptil/ *adj* [*personne, intelligence, argument, nuance, parfum*] subtle; [*négociateur, manœuvre*] skilful[GB].

subtilement /syptilmɑ̃/ *adv* subtly.

subtilisation /syptilizasjɔ̃/ *nf* theft (**de** of).

subtiliser /syptilize/ [1] *vtr* (dérober) **~ qch à qn** to steal sth from sb; **elle s'est fait ~ son portefeuille** she had her purse stolen.

subtilité /syptilite/ *nf* subtlety; **les ~s de la grammaire** the subtleties of grammar.

subtropical, ~e, *mpl* **-aux** /sybtʀɔpikal, o/ *adj* subtropical.

suburbain, ~e /sybyʀbɛ̃, ɛn/ *adj* suburban.

subvenir /sybvәniʀ/ [36] *vtr ind* **~ à** to meet [*dépenses*]; **~ aux besoins du pays/de la région** to meet the country's/region's needs; **~ aux besoins de sa famille** to provide for one's family.

subvention /sybvɑ̃sjɔ̃/ *nf* (allocation) grant; (pour que le public paie moins cher) subsidy.

subventionner /sybvɑ̃sjɔne/ [1] *vtr* to subsidize.

subversif, -ive /sybvɛʀsif, iv/ *adj* subversive.

subversion /sybvɛʀsjɔ̃/ *nf* subversion (**de** of).

subversivement /sybvɛʀsivmɑ̃/ *adv* subversively.

suc /syk/ *nm* **1** lit (de fruit, viande) juice; (de plante, fleur) sap; **2** fig essence (**de** of).
■ **~s digestifs** or **gastriques** Physiol gastric juices.

succédané /syksedane/ *nm* lit, fig substitute, ersatz (**de** for); Pharm succedaneum; **~ de café/thé** coffee/tea substitute; **~s alimentaires** substitute foodstuffs.

succéder /syksede/ [14] **I succéder à** *vtr ind* **1** (remplacer) **~ à** [*personne*] to succeed [*personne*] **~ à qn à la tête d'une entreprise** to succeed sb as head of a company; **~ à qn sur le trône** to succeed sb to the throne; **2** (suivre) **~ à** [*chose*] to follow, to come after [*chose*]; **à la vague de chaleur a succédé un temps variable** the heatwave gave way to changeable weather; **l'inquiétude succéda à l'espoir** hope turned to anxiety.

II **se succéder** *vpr* (venir l'un après l'autre) [*personnes*] to succeed ou follow one another; [*choses*] to follow (one another); **se ~ de père en fils** to carry on GB ou continue from father to son; **les semaines se sont succédé** week followed week; **les orages se succèdent sans interruption** there is storm after storm.

succès /syksɛ/ *nm inv* success; **une série de ~** a string of successes; **~ scolaires/universitaires** scholastic/academic success; **un nouveau ~ diplomatique pour** another diplomatic success for; **votre ~ aux élections/à l'école/en politique** your success in the elections/at school/in politics; **le ~ du mois** this month's big success ou hit; **avoir du ~, être un ~** [*produit, livre, opération, formule*] to be a success (**auprès de** with); [*disque, chanson*] to be a hit (**auprès de** with); **avoir du ~** [*artiste*] to be a success; **avoir du ~ auprès de qn** [*personne*] to be a favourite[GB] ou a hit with sb; **avoir un ~ fou** [*personne, produit*] to be a big hit (**auprès de** with); **leur proposition n'a eu aucun ~** their proposal met with no success; **connaître un grand ~** to be a great success; **remporter un ~** to score a success; **remporter des ~** to achieve success; **faire le ~ de qn/qch** to make sb/sth successful; **à ~** [*acteur, pièce, film*] successful; **auteur à ~** best-selling author; **avec ~** successfully; **avec un égal ~** equally successfully; **sans ~** unsuccessfully; **sans grand ~** without much success.

■ **~ d'estime** succès d'estime, critical though not popular acclaim.

successeur /syksesœʀ/ *nm* successor; **le ~ de qn** the successor to sb; **désigner qn comme son ~** to designate sb as one's successor.

successif, **-ive** /syksesif, iv/ *adj* successive.

succession /syksesjɔ̃/ *nf* **1** (série, suite) (de personnes, visiteurs) stream, succession; (d'événements) series (*sg*), succession; (de jours, saisons) succession; (de nombres) series; (d'accidents, de malheurs) string, succession; **2** (transmission de pouvoir) succession; **~ au trône/à la couronne** succession to the throne/to the crown; **prendre la ~ de** to succeed [*roi*]; to take over from, to succeed [*ministre, directeur*]; **3** Jur (transmission) (de biens) succession; (de patrimoine) inheritance, estate; **par voie de ~** [*transmis*] through inheritance; **léguer/recevoir qch par voie de ~** to bequeath/inherit sth.

■ **~ testamentaire** Jur testate succession.

successivement /syksesivmɑ̃/ *adv* successively.

successoral, **~e**, *mpl* **-aux** /syksesɔʀal, o/ *adj* **droit ~** law of succession.

succinct, **~e** /syksɛ̃, ɛ̃t/ *adj* [*écrit*] succinct; [*discours*] brief; **je serai ~** I'll be brief; hum [*repas*] frugal.

succinctement /syksɛ̃tmɑ̃/ *adv* [*exposer*] succinctly.

succion /syksjɔ̃/ *nf* **1** (avec appareil) suction; **2** (avec la bouche) sucking; **bruits de ~** sucking noises.

succomber /sykɔ̃be/ [1] *vi* **1** (mourir) to die; **2** (fléchir) liter to give way, to yield; **~ sous le poids** to collapse under the weight; **~ sous le nombre** to be overwhelmed by numbers; **3** (s'abandonner) **~ à** to succumb to [*charme, désespoir, fatigue*]; to yield to, to give in to [*tentation*]; **~ à l'appel du large** to answer the call of the sea.

succube /sykyb/ *nm* succubus.

succulence /sykylɑ̃s/ *nf* succulence (**de** of).

succulent, **~e** /sykylɑ̃, ɑ̃t/ *adj* **1** (savoureux) [*repas, cuisine, fruit*] delicious; **2** Bot **plante ~e** succulent.

succursale /sykyʀsal/ *nf* branch, outlet.

sucer /syse/ [12] **I** *vtr* **1** to suck; **~ son pouce** to suck one's thumb; **~ la haine/religion avec le lait** fig to learn hatred/religion at one's mother's knee; **~ les économies de qn**○ fig to milk sb of his/her savings; **2**● to suck [sb] off●.

II **se sucer** *vpr* **se ~ la poire**◑ or **la pomme**◑ to neck○.

sucette /sysɛt/ *nf* **1** (bonbon) lollipop, lolly○; **2** (tétine) dummy GB, pacifier US.

suçon○ /sysɔ̃/ *nm* lovebite, hickey○ US; **faire un ~ à qn** to give sb a lovebite.

suçoter /sysɔte/ [1] *vtr* to suck.

sucrage /sykʀaʒ/ *nm* sugaring.

sucrant, **~e** /sykʀɑ̃, ɑ̃t/ *adj* sweetening; **matière ~e** sweetener.

sucre /sykʀ/ *nm* **1** (substance) sugar; **je bois mon thé sans ~** I don't take sugar in my tea; **du chocolat noir sans ~** sugar-free dark chocolate; **ma cocotte** or **mon lapin en ~**○ my little honeybun○, my sweetie pie○; **2** (morceau) sugar; **combien de ~s dans ton café?** how many sugars in your coffee?

■ **~ de betterave** beet sugar; **~ blanc** white sugar; **~ brun** dark brown sugar; **~ candi** candy sugar; **~ de canne** cane sugar; **~ cristallisé** granulated sugar; **~ d'érable** maple sugar; **~ glace** icing sugar GB, powdered sugar US; **~ en morceaux** lump sugar; **~ d'orge** (substance) barley sugar; (bâton) stick of barley sugar, ≈ rock; **~ en poudre** caster sugar GB, superfine sugar US; **~ roux** brown sugar; **~ semoule** caster sugar GB, superfine sugar US; **~ tiré** pulled sugar; **~ vanillé** sugar containing vanilla; **~ vanilliné** vanilla-flavoured[GB] sugar.

IDIOMES **il n'est pas en ~ tout de même!** he isn't made of glass, you know; **être tout ~ tout miel** to be all sweetness and light; **casser du ~ sur le dos de qn** to run sb down, to badmouth sb○.

sucré, **~e** /sykʀe/ **I** *adj* **1** lit [*fruit, goût, vin, biscuit*] sweet; [*lait condensé, jus de fruit*] sweetened; **non ~** unsweetened; **2** fig péj [*ton*] honeyed; **je n'aime pas son air ~** I don't like his /her smarmy○ manner.

II *nm* **1** (aliments) sweet food; **je n'aime pas le ~** I don't like sweet things; **2** péj **faire le ~** to be all sweetness.

sucrer /sykʀe/ [1] **I** *vtr* **1** (rendre doux) [*personne*] to put sugar in [*café, compote*]; (en saupoudrant) to sprinkle sugar on [*fraises, framboises*]; [*miel, saccharine*] to sweeten; **je sucre avec du miel** I use honey as a sweetener; **2**◑ (supprimer) to stop [*prime, argent de poche*]; to cancel [*permission*].

II **se sucrer**◑ *vpr* **1** (prendre du sucre) to help oneself to sugar; **2** [*profiteur*] to feather one's nest.

IDIOMES **~ les fraises** to be doddery○.

sucrerie /sykʀəʀi/ **I** *nf* (usine) sugar refinery.

II **sucreries** *nfpl* sweets GB, candy US, sweet things; **les ~s leur sont interdites** they're not allowed sweet things; **aimer les ~s** to have a sweet tooth.

sucrette® /sykʀɛt/ *nf* (artificial) sweetener.

sucrier, **-ière** /sykʀije, ɛʀ/ **I** *adj* [*industrie*] sugar; [*région*] sugar-producing.

II *nm* **1** (pot) sugar bowl; **~ verseur** sugar shaker; **2** (fabricant) sugar manufacturer; (ouvrier) sugar operative.

sud /syd/ ▶621 **I** *adj inv* [*façade, versant, côté*] south; [*frontière, zone*] southern.

II *nm* **1** (point cardinal) south; **au ~ de Paris** [*être, habiter*] south of Paris; **vers le ~** [*aller, naviguer*] south, southward; **en direction du ~** in a southerly direction; **un vent du ~** a southerly wind; **exposé au ~** south-facing (*épith*); **2** (région) south; **dans le ~ de la France** [*se situer, avoir lieu, habiter, voyager*] in the south of France; [*aller, se rendre*] to the south of France; **le ~ de l'Europe/du Japon** southern Europe/Japan; **3** Géog, Pol **le Sud** the South; **vivre dans le Sud** to live in the South; **venir du Sud** to come from the South; **du Sud** [*ville, accent*] southern.

■ **le Sud Viêt Nam** Hist South Vietnam.

sud-africain, **~e**, *mpl* **~s** /sydafʀikɛ̃, ɛn/ ▶537 *adj* South African.

Sud-Africain, **~e**, *mpl* **~s** /sydafʀikɛ̃, ɛn/ ▶537 *nm,f* South African.

sud-américain, **~e**, *mpl* **~s** /sydameʀikɛ̃, ɛn/ *adj* South American.

Sud-Américain, **~e**, *mpl* **~s** /sydameʀikɛ̃, ɛn/ *nm,f* South American.

sudation /sydasjɔ̃/ *nf* sweating.

sud-coréen, **-éenne**, *mpl* **~s** /sydkɔʀeɛ̃, ɛn/ ▶537 *adj* South Korean.

Sud-Coréen, **-éenne**, *mpl* **~s** /sydkɔʀeɛ̃, ɛn/ ▶537 *nm,f* South Korean.

sud-est /sydɛst/ ▶621 **I** *adj inv* [*façade, versant*] southeast; [*frontière, zone*] southeastern.

II *nm* southeast; **vent de ~** southeasterly wind; **le Sud-Est asiatique** South East Asia.

Sudètes /sydɛt/ *nprfpl* **1** ▶692 (région) Sudeten; **2** (monts) Sudetes.

sudiste /sydist/ *adj, nmf* Hist US Confederate.

sudorifère /sydɔʀifɛʀ/ *adj* sudoriferous; **canal ~** sweat duct.

sudorifique /sydɔʀifik/ *adj, nm* sudorific.

sudoripare /sydɔʀipaʀ/ *adj* sudoriparous; **glande ~** sweat gland.

sud-ouest /sydwɛst/ ▶621 **I** *adj inv* [*façade, versant*] southwest; [*frontière, zone*] southwestern.

II *nm* southwest; **vent de ~** southwesterly wind; **le ~ de la France** the southwest of France.

sud-vietnamien, **-ienne**, *mpl* **~s** /sydvjɛtnamjɛ̃, ɛn/ *adj* Hist South Vietnamese.

Sud-Vietnamien, **-ienne**, *mpl* **~s** /sydvjɛtnamjɛ̃, ɛn/ *nm,f* Hist South Vietnamese.

suède /sɥɛd/ *nm* (peau) suede; **gants en** or **de ~** suede gloves.

Suède /sɥɛd/ ▶321 *nprf* Sweden.

suédé, **~e** /sɥede/ *adj* [*cuir*] suede (*épith*).

suédine /sɥedin/ *nf* imitation suede.

suédois, **~e** /sɥedwa, az/ ▶462, 537 **I** *adj* Swedish.

II *nm* Ling Swedish.

Suédois, **~e** /sɥedwa, az/ ▶537 *nm,f* Swede.

suée○ /sɥe/ *nf* sweat; **cette escalade m'a donné une ~** the climb really made me sweat; **cette aventure/histoire m'a fichu une de ces ~s!** that adventure/story brought me out in a cold sweat!

suer /sɥe/ [1] **I** *vtr* **1** (exsuder) [*personne, peau*] to sweat; [*mur, roche*] to ooze [*eau, humidité*]; **il suait toute l'eau de son corps** he was dripping with sweat; **~ sang et eau** fig to sweat blood and tears (**pour faire** to do; **sur qch** over sth); **2** (dégager) [*personne*] to exude [*bêtise, ennui, misère*]; **un livre/une ville qui sue l'ennui** an incredibly boring book/town.

II *vi* to sweat (**sur** over); **~ à grosses gouttes** to sweat buckets; **faire ~** (embêter)○ to bore [sb] stiff [*personne*] (**avec** with); Culin to sweat [*légumes*]; **qu'est-ce qu'on se fait ~ ici**○**!** it's deadly boring here!

sueur /sɥœʀ/ *nf* sweat; **se mettre en ~** to break into a sweat; **être trempé de ~** to be soaked in sweat; **il avait le visage ruisselant de ~** his face was streaming with sweat; **donner des ~s froides à qn** to put sb in a cold sweat; **j'en avais des ~s froides** I was in a cold sweat about it; **vivre de la ~ des autres** to live by the sweat of others; **gagner son pain à la ~ de son front** to earn one's living by the sweat of one's brow; **il avait le front/dos en ~** he had a sweaty forehead/back.

Suez /sɥɛz/ ▶857 *npr* Suez; **l'affaire de ~** the Suez crisis; **le canal de ~** the Suez canal.

suffire /syfiʀ/ [64] **I** *vi* (être suffisant) [*somme, durée, quantité*] to be enough; **quelques gouttes suffisent** a few drops are enough; **j'y suis allé une fois, ça m'a suffi!** I went there once, and that was enough!; **il est plein de bonne volonté mais ça ne suffit pas** he's very willing but that's not enough; **ma retraite suffit à mes besoins** my pension is enough to cover my needs; **un échec a suffi à** or **pour la décourager** one setback was enough to put her off; **un radiateur suffit à** or **pour chauffer la pièce** one radiator is enough ou sufficient to heat the room; **deux heures sufffisent amplement pour faire le trajet** two hours is ample time ou is easily enough for the journey; **un rien suffit à** or **pour le mettre en colère** it only takes the slightest thing to make him lose his temper; **dix minutes lui ont suffi pour réparer la télévision** it only took him ten minutes to repair the television set.
II se suffire *vpr* **se ~ (à soi-même)** [*personne, pays*] to be self-sufficient; **pas besoin de longues explications, le film se suffit à lui-même** there's no need for long explanations, the film speaks for itself.
III *v impers* **1** (être très simple) **il suffit de faire qch** all you have to do is do sth; **il suffit de qch** all you need is sth; **il suffit d'ajouter de l'eau et c'est prêt!** all you have to do is add some water and it's ready!, just add some water and it's ready!; **c'est un réactionnaire, il suffit de lire son livre pour s'en rendre compte** he's a reactionary, you only have to read his book to realize that; **il te suffit de dire un mot pour qu'elle revienne** you only have to say one word and she'll come back; **il suffit d'un coup de téléphone pour annuler son abonnement** it only takes one phone call to cancel your subscription; **il suffit qu'elle y aille** all she has to do is go there; **2** (être suffisant) **il suffit d'une lampe pour éclairer la pièce** one lamp is enough or sufficient to light the room; **il suffirait d'un peu de pluie pour sauver la récolte** a little rain would be enough to save the crop; **il suffit d'un rien pour qu'il rougisse/s'énerve** it only takes the slightest thing to make him blush/lose his temper; **il suffit d'une seconde d'inattention pour qu'un accident se produise** it only takes a second's carelessness to cause an accident; **il lui a suffi de dix minutes pour réparer la télévision** it only took him ten minutes to repair the television set; **il suffirait d'un rien pour tout faire rater** it would only take the slightest thing to ruin everything; **3** (notion de cause à effet) **il suffit que je sorte sans parapluie pour qu'il pleuve!** every time I go out without my umbrella, it's guaranteed to rain; **il suffit qu'elle ouvre la bouche pour dire une bêtise** every time she opens her mouth she says something stupid; **4** (être satisfaisant) **ça suffit (comme ça)!, il suffit†!** that's enough!; **il ne leur a pas suffi de nous cambrioler, il a fallu qu'ils saccagent la maison** they weren't satisfied with burgling GB ou burglarizing US us, they had to wreck the house as well.
IDIOMES **à chaque jour suffit sa peine** Prov sufficient unto the day (is the evil thereof).

suffisamment /syfizamɑ̃/ *adv* enough; **~ fort/intelligent/riche** strong/intelligent/rich enough; **~ intelligent pour** intelligent enough to; **nous avons ~ marché/mangé** we've walked/eaten enough; **il y a ~ à manger pour tout le monde** there's enough food for everyone; **pièce ~ chauffée/éclairée** room that is warm/light enough; **il n'a pas ~ d'argent/de temps libre pour faire** he doesn't have enough money/free time to do; **tu n'es pas ~ couvert pour sortir par ce froid!** you're not wrapped up well enough to go out in this cold!; **j'ai ~ de problèmes sans que tu m'en crées de nouveaux** I've got enough problems without you making more for me.

suffisance /syfizɑ̃s/ *nf* **1** (vanité) self-importance, arrogance; **il est plein de ~** he's very self-important; **2** (quantité adéquate) **avoir qch en ~** to have sufficient quantities of sth; **manger à sa ~** to eat one's fill.

suffisant, **~e** /syfizɑ̃, ɑ̃t/ *adj* **1** (adéquat) sufficient; **100 francs, c'est ~** 100 francs is enough ou sufficient; **deux heures, c'est ~ pour faire le trajet** two hours is enough for the journey; **l'éclairage n'est pas ~** there is inadequate lighting; **il y a à manger en quantité ~e** there's quite enough to eat; **il y met de la bonne volonté mais ce n'est pas ~** he's willing but that's not enough; **2** (vaniteux) [*personne, ton, air*] self-important; **faire le ~** to give oneself airs, to put on airs.

suffixal, **~e**, *mpl* **-aux** /syfiksal, o/ *adj* suffixal.

suffixation /syfiksasjɔ̃/ *nf* suffixation.

suffixe /syfiks/ *nm* suffix.

suffixé, **~e** /syfikse/ *adj* Ling suffixed.

suffocant, **~e** /syfɔkɑ̃, ɑ̃t/ *adj* **1** (étouffant) [*chaleur, atmosphère*] suffocating; **2** (stupéfiant) staggering.

suffocation /syfɔkasjɔ̃/ *nf* (action) suffocation; (sensation) suffocating feeling; **crise de ~** fit of choking.

Suffolk ▶ 692 *nprm* **le ~** Suffolk.

suffoquer /syfɔke/ [1] **I** *vtr* **1** (étouffer) [*chaleur, fumée*] to suffocate; **les sanglots la suffoquaient** she was choking with sobs; **2**○ (stupéfier) **son aplomb m'a suffoqué** I was staggered by his/her cheek○.
II *vi* **1** (étouffer) to suffocate; **on suffoque ici** it's suffocating in here; **2** (s'étrangler) to choke (**de** with).

suffragant /syfʀagɑ̃/ *adj m* (évêque) suffragan.

suffrage /syfʀaʒ/ *nm* **1** Pol (système) suffrage; **~ direct/indirect/restreint/universel** direct/indirect/restricted/universal suffrage; **2** Pol (voix) vote; **~s exprimés** recorded votes; **les ~s catholiques** the catholic vote; **remporter peu de ~s** to receive few votes; **3** fig (approbation) approval ¢; **recueillir tous les ~s** to meet with universal approval.

suffragette /syfʀaʒɛt/ *nf* suffragette.

suggérer /sygʒeʀe/ [14] *vtr* to suggest (**à** to); **je suggère qu'on s'en aille** I suggest (that) we go; **elle a suggéré à la commission de modifier le projet** she suggested to the commission that they should modify the project; **la solution suggérée n'a pas été retenue** the suggested solution has not been accepted.

suggestible /sygʒɛstibl/ *adj* suggestible.

suggestif, **-ive** /sygʒɛstif, iv/ *adj* [*texte, musique*] evocative; [*pose, photos*] suggestive; [*décolleté, robe*] provocative.

suggestion /sygʒɛstjɔ̃/ *nf* suggestion; **faire une ~** to make a suggestion; **faire une ~ à qn** to suggest something to sb.

suggestionner /sygʒɛstjɔne/ [1] *vtr* **~ qn** to put ideas into sb's head, to influence sb; **il se laisse trop facilement ~** he's too suggestible.

suggestivité /sygʒɛstivite/ *nf* (de texte, musique) evocativeness; (de pose, photo) suggestiveness; (de décolleté) provocativeness.

suicidaire /sɥisidɛʀ/ **I** *adj* lit, fig suicidal.
II *nmf* person with suicidal tendencies.

suicide /sɥisid/ *nm* lit, fig suicide; **c'est du** or **un ~** fig it's suicide; **mission ~** suicide mission.

suicider /sɥiside/ [1] **I**○ *vtr* hum **on l'a suicidé** they made it look like suicide.
II se suicider *vpr* to commit suicide.

suie /sɥi/ *nf* soot.
IDIOMES **noir comme de la ~** black as soot.

suif /sɥif/ *nm* **1** (de chandelle) tallow; **2** Culin suet; **~ de bœuf/mouton** beef/mutton suet.

sui generis /sɥiʒeneʀis/ *loc adj inv* sui generis; [*couleur*] distinctive; [*odeur*] characteristic.

suint /sɥɛ̃/ *nm* suint.

suintement /sɥɛ̃tmɑ̃/ *nm* **1** (d'eau) seepage; **2** (de plaie) oozing.

suinter /sɥɛ̃te/ [1] *vi* **1** [*eau*] to seep (**de** through); [*sang, sève*] to ooze (**de** from); **2** [*mur*] to sweat; [*plaie*] to ooze.

suisse /sɥis/ **I** ▶ 537 *adj* Swiss; **~ allemand/romand** Swiss German/French.
II *nm* **1** (au Vatican) Swiss Guard; (d'église) verger; **2**† (portier) porter; **3** C (écureuil) chipmunk.

Suisse /sɥis/ **I** ▶ 537 *nm,f* (habitant) Swiss; **~ allemand/romand** German-speaking/French-speaking Swiss.
II ▶ 321 *nprf* Switzerland; **~ allemande/romande** German-speaking/French-speaking Switzerland.
IDIOMES **manger/boire en ~** to eat/drink alone.

Suissesse /sɥisɛs/ *nprf* (habitante) Swiss woman.

suite /sɥit/ **I** *nf* **1** (reste) rest; **je te raconterai la ~ plus tard** I'll tell you the rest later; **la ~ des événements** (à venir) what happens next; (déjà survenue) what happened next; **on connaît la ~** we all know what happened next; **la ~ des événements montra que** subsequent events showed that; **lis la ~ pour comprendre** read on and then you'll understand; **2** (partie suivante) (de récit) continuation; (de feuilleton) next instalment[GB]; (de repas) next course; **attendre la ~** (du repas) to wait for the next course; (du spectacle) to see what comes next; (des événements) to wait and see; **~ page 10/au prochain numéro/de la première page** continued on page 10/in the next issue/from page one; **'résultats des examens (~)'** 'examination results (continued)'; **'~ et fin'** 'concluded'; **3** (nouveau film, roman) sequel (**à, de** to); (émission, article de suivi) follow-up (**à, de** to); **j'ai une idée pour une ~ au film** I have an idea for a sequel to the film; **dans une émission qui est une ~ à celle d'hier** in a follow-up to yesterday's programme[GB]; **4** (résultat) result; **les ~s** (d'acte, de décision) the consequences; (d'affaire, incident) the repercussions; (de maladie, d'opération) the after-effects; **la ~ logique/naturelle de** the logical/natural result of; **leur négligence aurait pu avoir des ~s fâcheuses** their negligence could have had serious consequences; **l'incident n'a pas eu de ~s** the incident had no repercussions; **mourir des ~s d'une chute** to die as a result of a fall; **5** (réponse produite) **donner ~ à** to follow up [*plainte, affaire*]; to pursue [*projet*]; to act on [*requête*]; to respond to, to follow up [*lettre*]; Comm to deal with [*commande*]; **ne pas donner ~ à une lettre** to take no action concerning a letter; **rester sans ~** [*demande, plainte*] not to be followed up; [*projet*] to be dropped; **ma plainte est restée sans ~** no action was taken about my complaint; **'classé sans ~'** Admin 'no action'; **6** (indiquant la position) **faire ~ à** to follow on from [*paragraphe*]; to follow upon [*incident*]; **un vote fit ~ au débat** a vote followed the debate; **la pièce qui fait ~ au bureau** the room which leads off the study; **prendre la ~ d'une affaire** to take over a business; **prendre la ~ de qn** to take over from sb; **7** (cohérence) coherence; **ça manque de ~** it's not very coherent; **marmonner des phrases sans ~** to mutter incoherently; **avoir de la ~ dans les idées** (savoir ce que l'on veut) to be single-minded; iron (être entêté) not to be easily deterred; **n'avoir aucune ~ dans les idées** to flit from one thing to another; **8** (série) (de sommets, d'incidents) series (*sg*); (de malheurs) string, series (*sg*); (de succès) run; **article sans ~** discontinued line; **9** (dans un hôtel) suite; **10** (entourage) suite; **11** Math

series (+ *v sg*); **12** Mus suite; **~ d'orchestre** orchestral suite; **13** Ling string; **14** Jeux (aux cartes) run; **~ à pique** run in spades.
II de suite *loc adv* **1** (d'affilée) in succession, in a row; **trois fois de ~** three times in succession ou a row; **il a plu trois jours de ~** it rained for three days running; **venir trois jours de ~** to come three days running; **dormir/travailler dix heures de ~** to sleep/to work for ten hours solid; **sur dix pages de ~** over ten consecutive pages; **et ainsi de ~** and so on; **incapable d'aligner deux mots de ~** incapable of stringing two words together; **2** (immédiatement) straight ou right away; **je reviens de ~** I'll be right back.
III par la suite *loc adv* (après) afterwards; (plus tard) later; **qu'a-t-il fait par la ~?** what did he do afterwards ?
IV par suite *loc adv* consequently, as a result.
V par suite de *loc prép* due to; **par ~ d'encombrement, votre appel ne peut aboutir** all lines are engaged GB ou busy, please try again later.
VI à la suite de *loc prép* **1** (en conséquence, après) following; **à la ~ d'un incident** following an incident, as a result of an incident; **2** (derrière) behind; **rangés à la ~ des autres** placed behind the others; **à leur ~ venait la fanfare** behind them came the band; **à la ~ les uns des autres, l'un à la ~ de l'autre** one after the other; **entraîner qn à sa ~** (derrière soi) to drag sb along behind one; (dans une chute) lit, fig to drag sb down with one; **se mettre à la ~ (de la file d'attente)** to join (the end of) the queue GB ou line US.
VII suite à *loc prép* **~ à ma lettre/notre conversation** further to my letter/our conversation; **~ à votre lettre** Comm with reference to your letter; **~ à l'article d'hier** Presse following yesterday's article.

suivant[1] /sɥivɑ̃/ **I** *prép* **1** (le long de) along [*axe, pointillé*]; **2** (conformément à) in accordance with [*coutume, rituel, tradition*]; **~ leur habitude** (au présent) as they usually do, as is their wont; (au passé) as they usually did, as was their wont; **procéder ~ le mode d'emploi** to follow the directions for use; **3** (en fonction de) depending on [*temps, compétence, circonstances*]; **~ le temps/ce qu'il dira** depending on the weather/what he says; **4** (selon) according to; **~ le plan/leurs instructions** according to the map/their instructions; **~ la formule consacrée** according to the standard formula.
II suivant que *loc conj* depending on whether.

suivant[2], **~e** /sɥivɑ̃, ɑ̃t/ **I** *adj* **1** (ci-après) following; **de la manière** or **façon ~e** in the following manner; **2** (d'après) (dans le temps) following, next; (dans une série) next; **il revint le lundi ~** he came back the following Monday; **mardi et les jours ~s** Tuesday and the following days; **voir le chapitre ~** see next chapter; **le témoin ~ déclara le contraire** the next witness said the opposite.
II *nm,f* **le ~** (dans le temps) the following one, the next one; (dans une série) the next one; **appelez le ~!** call in the next one!; (au) **~!** next!; **au ~ de ces messieurs**○**!** hum next customer, please!; **pas ce lundi, le ~** not this (coming) Monday, the one after; **pas le prochain arrêt, mais le ~** not the next stop, (but) the one after; **1 000 ce mois-ci, 2 000 le ~** 1,000 this month, and 2,000 the month after; **les premiers arrivés ont pu s'asseoir, mais les ~s sont restés debout** the first to arrive got seats, but those who came later had to stand.
III le suivant, la suivante *loc adj* as follows (*jamais épith*); **les résultats sont les ~s** the results are as follows; **la situation est la ~e** the situation is as follows.
IV suivante *nf* **1** Théât, Littérat lady's maid; **2**† (dame de compagnie) companion.

suiveur, -euse /sɥivœʀ, øz/ **I** *adj* Sport [*bateau, voiture*] that is following the race (*après n*).
II *nm* **1** Sport (official) follower; **2** (imitateur) imitator; **ce n'est qu'un ~** he's just an imitator; **les ~s d'un courant de pensée** people who follow a school of thought.

suivi, ~e /sɥivi/ **I** *pp* ▸ **suivre**.
II *pp adj* **1** (maintenu) [*travail, demande*] steady; [*effort*] sustained; [*correspondance*] regular; [*habitudes*] regular; [*qualité*] consistent; [*relations*] close; **2** Comm [*article*] in general production (*après n*), that is always in stock (*épith, après n*); **3** (apprécié, adopté) **la boxe est le sport le plus ~** boxing is the most popular sport; **quelle est l'émission la plus/moins ~e?** which is the most/least popular programme[GB]?; **très/peu ~** [*feuilleton*] with a (very) large/small audience (*épith, après n*); [*cours*] well/poorly attended; [*exemple, consigne*] widely/not widely followed; **c'est une mode très/peu ~e** it's a fashion which has/hasn't really caught on; **le match a été très/peu ~** TV the match drew a large/poor number of viewers; **au cours d'un procès très/peu ~** during a trial that attracted considerable/very little public interest; **4** (cohérent) [*politique*] consistent, coherent; [*argumentation*] coherent.
III *nm* (de procédure) monitoring; Comm (de commande) follow-up; **le ~ des malades/ex-prisonniers** follow-up care for patients/ex-prisoners; **le ~ budgétaire** monitoring of the budget; **travail de ~** follow-up work; **assurer le ~ des jeunes délinquants** to follow up (on) young delinquents; **assurer le ~ d'un produit** Comm to ensure the continued supply of a product.

suivisme /sɥivism/ *nm* blind conformity, herd instinct.

suiviste /sɥivist/ *adj, nmf* conformist.

suivre /sɥivʀ/ [62] **I** *vtr* **1** (aller derrière) to follow [*personne, voiture*]; (accompagner) to accompany [*personne*]; **suivez cette voiture!** follow that car!; **suivis de leur chien** followed by their dog; **j'ai l'impression qu'on me suit** I think I'm being followed; **un interprète le suit dans ses visites officielles** an interpreter accompanies him on official visits; **faire ~ qn** to have sb followed; **~ qn en exil/dans le jardin** to follow sb into exile/into the garden GB ou yard US; **~ qn de près/de loin** lit to follow sb closely/at a distance; **~ de très près la voiture de tête** Sport to be right behind the leading car; **il est mort en juin, et elle l'a suivi de près** he died in June and she followed not long after; **il me suit partout** [*chien*] he follows me everywhere; [*sac*] it goes everywhere with me; **partez sans moi, je vous suis** don't wait for me, I'll follow; **~ qn du regard** to follow sb with one's eyes; **ta réputation t'a suivi jusqu'ici** your reputation has followed you; **~ un cerf à la trace** to stalk a stag; **suivez le guide!** this way, please!; **2** (se situer après) to follow, to come after [*période, incident, dynastie*]; (succéder à) to follow; (résulter de) to follow; **le verbe suit le sujet** the verb comes after ou follows the subject; **suivit un long silence** there followed a long silence; **le film qui suivit** the film that followed; **le jour qui suivit** the next ou following day; **la répression qui suivit l'insurrection** the clampdown that followed the insurrection; **comme nous le verrons dans l'exemple qui suit** as we shall see in the following example; **lis ce qui suit** read on; **'à ~'** 'to be continued'; **3** (aller selon) [*personne*] to follow [*flèche, sentier, itinéraire*]; [*police, chien*] to follow [*piste*]; [*bateau, route*] to follow, to hug [*côte*]; [*route*] to run alongside [*voie ferrée*]; **ils ont suivi la même voie** fig they followed the same path; **indiquer (à qn) la route à ~** to give (sb) directions; **quelle est la marche à ~?** fig what is the best way to go about it?; **~ le droit chemin** fig to keep to the straight and narrow; **lire en suivant (les lignes) du doigt dans son livre** to read with a finger under the line; ▸ **bonhomme**; **4** (se conformer à) to follow [*coutume, exemple, conseil, règlement , mode, chef de file*]; to follow [*instinct, penchant*]; to obey [*caprice, impulsion*]; **~ une recette/un traitement** to follow a recipe/a course of treatment; **décider de ~ un régime** to decide to go on a diet; **il suit/ne suit pas son régime** he keeps to/doesn't keep to his diet; **le dollar a chuté et la livre a suivi** the dollar fell and the pound followed suit; **5** (être attentif à) to follow [*leçon, match, procès*]; to follow the progress of [*élève, malade*]; **~ un feuilleton à la télévision** to watch a serial on TV; **~ l'actualité** to keep up with the news; **~ les événements de très près** to keep a close eye on developments, to watch developments closely; **c'est une affaire à ~** it's something worth watching; **être suivi** or **se faire ~ par un spécialiste** Méd to be treated by a specialist; **elle ne suit jamais en classe** she never pays attention in class; **un de nos collègues, suivez mon regard**○ hum one of our colleagues, not mentioning any names; **6** (assister à) **~ un cours de cuisine** to do a cookery GB ou cooking US course; **~ un stage de formation** to be on a training course GB, to be in a training program US; **7** (comprendre) to follow [*explication, raisonnement*]; **je vous suis** I'm with you, I follow; **je ne vous suis pas très bien** I'm not quite with you, I don't quite follow; **vous me suivez?** are you with me?; **je n'arrive pas à ~ ce qu'il dit** I can't follow what he's saying; **8** fig (ne pas se laisser distancer) to keep pace with [*personne*]; **tu vas trop vite, je ne peux pas (te) ~** you're going too fast, I can't keep up; **les prix augmentent, mais les salaires ne suivent pas** prices are going up but wages are not keeping pace; **il ne suit pas bien en chimie** Scol he's struggling to keep up in chemistry; **9** Comm **~ un article** to keep a line in stock; **10** Sport to follow [sth] through [*ballon*].
II *vi* **1** Postes **faire ~ son courrier** to have one's mail forwarded; **(prière de) faire ~** please forward; **2** Jeux (au poker) **je suis** I'm in.
III se suivre *vpr* **1** (être placés dans un ordre) [*numéros, pages*] to be in order; [*cartes*] Jeux to be consecutive; **les numéros ne se suivent pas** the numbers are not consecutive ou in order; **2** (se succéder) [*incidents*] to happen one after the other; **se ~ à quelques jours d'intervalle** to happen within a few days; **les deux frères se suivent de près** the two brothers are close in age; **3** (être cohérent) [*argumentation, exposé*] to be coherent; **argumentation qui se suit en toute logique** consistently logical line of argument.
IV *v impers* **il suit** it follows (**de** from); **d'où il suit que** from which it follows that, it therefore follows that; **comme suit** as follows.
IDIOMES **~ qn comme un caniche** or **mouton** or **toutou** to trail around after sb like a little dog.

sujet, -ette /syʒɛ, ɛt/ **I** *adj* **être ~ à** to be prone to, to be subject to [*rhumes, migraine, vertige*]; to be subject to [*colère, emportement, découragement*]; **elle est sujette à la mauvaise humeur** she's subject to bad moods; **~ à caution** [*information, témoignage, honnêteté*] questionable, unreliable.
II *nm* **1** (question) subject; **traiter un ~** to deal with a subject; **un ~ de conversation** a subject for ou topic of conversation; **leur vieille voiture est un ~ de plaisanterie pour leurs amis** their friends joke about their old car; **être un ~ de plaisanterie** [*personne*] to be the butt of jokes; **un ~ d'actualité** a topical issue, an issue in the news; **un ~ brûlant/délicat/explosif** a burning/a delicate/an explosive issue; **proposer quelque chose comme ~ de réflexion** to suggest something as food for

La superficie

Pour la prononciation des nombres, voir ***les nombres*** ▶ **545**.

Équivalences

1 sq in	=	6,45 cm^2	1 acre	=	40,47 ares *ou* 0,40 ha
1 sq ft	=	929,03 cm^2	1 sq ml	=	2,59 km^2
1 sq yd	=	0,84 m^2			

dire				**dire**
one square centimetre	1 cm^2	=	0.15 sq in	*square inches*
one square metre	1 m^2	=	10.76 sq ft	*square feet*
			1.19 sq yds	*square yards*
one square kilometre	1 km^2	=	0.38 sq mls	*square miles*
one are	1 are	=	119.6 sq yds	
one hectare	1 hectare	=	2.47 acres	*acres*

Pour l'écriture, noter:

– *l'anglais utilise un point là où le français a une virgule:* 0,15 *s'écrit* 0.15, *etc.*

– *on écrit* -metre *en anglais britannique et* -meter *en anglais américain.*

– *on peut écrire* sq in *ou* in^2, sq ft *ou* ft^2, *etc.*

il y a 10 000 centimètres carrés dans un mètre carré	=	there are 10,000 square centimetres in a square metre
10 000 centimètres carrés font un mètre carré	=	10,000 square centimetres make one square metre

quelle est la superficie du jardin?	=	what is the area of the garden? *ou* how big is the garden?
combien mesure le jardin?	=	what size is the garden? *ou* what does the garden measure?
il fait 12 m^2	=	it is 12 square metres
sa surface est de 12 m^2	=	its area is 12 square metres
il a une surface de 12 m^2	=	it is 12 square metres *ou* it is 12 square metres in area
il fait 20 m sur 10 m	=	it is 20 metres by 10 metres
il fait à peu près 200 m^2	=	it is about 200 square metres
presque 200 m^2	=	almost 200 square metres
plus de 200 m^2	=	more than 200 square metres
moins de 200 m^2	=	less than 200 square metres
la superficie de A est égale à celle de B	=	A is the same area as B
A et B ont la même surface	=	A and B are the same area

Noter l'ordre des mots dans l'adjectif composé anglais, et l'utilisation du trait d'union. Noter aussi que metre, employé comme adjectif, ne prend pas la marque du pluriel.

un jardin de 200 m^2	=	a 200-square-metre garden

On peut aussi dire: a garden 200 square metres in area.

6 mètres carrés de soie	=	six square metres of silk
vendu au mètre carré	=	sold by the square metre

thought; **je n'ai rien à dire à ce ~** I've nothing to say on that subject ou matter; **un article est paru à ce ~** an article has been published on this subject; **interrogé à ce ~** when questioned on this subject ou matter; **c'est à quel ~?** what is it about?; **au ~ de** about; **2** (thème) subject; **le ~ d'un livre/tableau** the subject of a book/painting; **c'est un ~ en or** it's a marvellous[GB] subject; **cette pièce a pour ~ la solitude** the subject of this play is solitude; **3** Scol, Univ question; **un ~ d'examen** an exam question; **un ~ d'histoire/de philosophie** a history/philosophy question; **quel est ton ~ de thèse?** what's your thesis on?; **faire une dissertation sur un ~ libre** to write an essay on a subject ou topic of one's own choice; **hors ~** off the subject; **4** (raison) cause; **c'est un ~ d'étonnement/d'inquiétude/de mécontentement** this is cause ou grounds for amazement/worry/displeasure; **c'est un ~ de contestation/de dispute** this is cause for contention/dispute; **c'est un ~ de satisfaction pour moi** this gives me satisfaction; **5** (individu) **les ~s qui se sont soumis au test médical** those who have undergone the medical test; **les ~s âgés** the elderly, elderly people; **c'est un brillant ~** (étudiant) he's a brilliant student; **c'est un mauvais ~** he's a poor specimen; **6** Ling, Philos subject; **7** (ressortissant d'un royaume) subject; **8** Sci (d'expérience) subject.

sujétion /syʒesjɔ̃/ *nf* **1** (servitude) subjection (**à** to); **être tenu en ~** to be held in subjection; **vivre dans la ~** to live in a state of subjection; **2** (contrainte) constraint; **les ~s de la vie de soldat** the constraints of a soldier's life.

sulfamide /sylfamid/ *nm* sulpha[GB] drug.

sulfatage /sylfataʒ/ *nm* copper sulphate[GB] treatment.

sulfate /sylfat/ *nm* sulphate[GB]; **~ de cuivre** copper sulphate[GB].

sulfater /sylfate/ [1] *vtr* to treat [sth] with copper sulphate[GB].

sulfateuse /sylfatøz/ *nf* **1** Agric copper sulphate[GB] sprayer; **2**○ (mitraillette) submachine gun.

sulfite /sylfit/ *nm* sulphite[GB].

sulfiter /sylfite/ [1] *vtr* to sulphur[GB].

sulfure /sylfyʀ/ *nm* **1** Chimie sulphide[GB]; **~ de carbone/cuivre** carbon/copper sulphide[GB]; **2** Art (en verrerie) sulphide[GB]; (presse-papier) glass paperweight.

sulfuré, **~e** /sylfyʀe/ *adj* sulphurated[GB]; **hydrogène ~** hydrogen sulphide[GB].

sulfurer /sylfyʀe/ [1] *vtr* to sulphurize[GB].

sulfureux, **-euse** /sylfyʀø, øz/ *adj* **1** Chimie [*acide, eau, vapeur*] sulphurous[GB]; [*bain, source*] sulphur[GB] (*épith*); [*odeur*] like sulphur[GB] (*après n*); **anhydride** or **gaz ~** sulphur[GB] dioxide; **2** fig [*personne, réputation, charme*] fiendish.

sulfurique /sylfyʀik/ *adj* sulphuric[GB].

sulfurisé, **~e** /sylfyʀize/ *adj* **papier ~** greaseproof paper.

sulky /sylki/ *nm* sulky.

sultan /syltɑ̃/ *nm* sultan.

sultanat /syltana/ *nm* sultanate.

sultane /syltan/ *nf* sultana.

Sumer /symɛʀ/ *npr* Sumer.

sumérien, **-ienne** /symeʀjɛ̃, ɛn/ **I** *adj* Sumerian.

II *nm* Ling Sumerian.

Sumérien, **-ienne** /symeʀjɛ̃, ɛn/ *nm,f* Sumerian.

summum /sɔm(m)ɔm/ *nm* height.

sumo /sumo, symo/ ▶ **449** *nm inv* sumo wrestling; **lutteur de ~** sumo wrestler.

sunnite /syn(n)it/ **I** *adj* Sunni.

II *nmf* Sunnite.

sup○ /syp/ ▶ **mathématique**.

super[1] /sypɛʀ/ *préf* super.

super[2] /sypɛʀ/ **I**○ *adj inv* great○.

II *nm* **1** (essence) four-star (petrol) GB, super, high-octane gasoline US; **2** (*abbr* = **supermarché**) supermarket.

III○ *excl* great○!

superaccélérateur /sypɛʀakseleʀatœʀ/ *nm* giant particle accelerator.

superbe /sypɛʀb/ **I** *adj* [*fleurs, robe, spectacle*] superb; [*personne*] superb-looking (*épith*); [*ville, pays*] magnificent; **il a été ~ dans ce rôle** he was superb in the part; **elle a été ~ de courage** she displayed superb courage.

II *nf* liter haughtiness.

superbement /sypɛʀbəmɑ̃/ *adv* gén [*décorer, cuisiner*] superbly; [*ignorer*] haughtily.

superbénéfice /sypɛʀbenefis/ *nm* surplus profit.

superbombardier /sypɛʀbɔ̃baʀdje/ *nm* superbomber.

supercalculateur /sypɛʀkalkylatœʀ/ *nm* supercomputer.

supercanon /sypɛʀkanɔ̃/ *nm* supergun.

supercarburant /sypɛʀkaʀbyʀɑ̃/ *nm* four-star ou high-octane petrol GB, super, high-octane gasoline US.

supercherie /sypɛʀʃəʀi/ *nf* **1** (tromperie) deception; **user de ~** to use deception; **2** (acte) hoax, act of deception; (faux) fake; **monter une ~** to set up a hoax; **~ littéraire** literary hoax.

supérette /sypeʀɛt/ *nf* minimarket, superette US.

superfétatoire /sypɛʀfetatwaʀ/ *adj* liter superfluous.

superficialité /sypɛʀfisjalite/ *nf* superficiality.

superficie /sypɛʀfisi/ *nf* **1** (aire) (de terrain, pays) area; (de pièce, bâtiment) floor area; **un pré d'une ~ de 20 hectares** a field with an area of 20 hectares; **quelle est la ~ du Japon?** what's the area of Japan?; **~ cultivée/vinicole** area under cultivation/vines; **la ~ de la Terre** the surface area of the Earth; **2** (aspect superficiel) surface; **en ~** fig superficially.

superficiel, **-ielle** /sypɛʀfisjɛl/ *adj* **1** lit [*couche*] surface (*épith*); [*blessure*] superficial; **2** fig [*personne, caractère, esprit*] superficial, shallow; [*conversation, rapports, jugement*] superficial.

superficiellement /sypɛʀfisjɛlmɑ̃/ *adv* superficially.

superfin, **~e** /sypɛʀfɛ̃, in/ *adj* [*qualité*] superior; [*produit*] quality (*épith*).

superflu, **~e** /sypɛʀfly/ **I** *adj* (de trop) superfluous; (inutile) unnecessary.

II *nm* (surabondance) superfluity sout; (excédent) surplus; **s'offrir le ~** to treat oneself to luxuries.

superforteresse /sypɛʀfɔʀtəʀɛs/ *nf* flying fortress.

supergrand○ /sypɛʀgʀɑ̃/ *nm* superpower.

super-huit /sypɛʀɥit/ *adj inv, nm inv* super-8.

supérieur, **~e** /sypeʀjœʀ/ **I** *adj* **1** (situé en haut dans l'espace) [*mâchoire, membre, paupière, lèvre*] upper; [*niveau, étage*] upper, top; **la partie ~e d'un objet** the upper ou top part of an object; **le cours ~ d'un fleuve** the upper reaches of a river; **dans le coin ~ droit** in the top right-hand corner; **2** (dans une hiérarchie) [*grades, classes sociales*] upper; **les échelons ~s d'une hiérarchie** the upper echelons of a hierarchy; **il a été promu au rang ~** he was promoted to the next rank up; **elle t'est hiérarchiquement ~e** she's above you in the hierarchy; **3** (en valeur) [*température, vitesse, coût, salaire, nombre*] higher (**à** than); [*taille, dimensions*] bigger (**à** than); [*durée*] longer (**à** than); **mes notes sont ~es à la moyenne** my marks are above average; **des coûts de production supérieurs à la moyenne** higher than average production costs; **le niveau de vie est ~ à celui des pays voisins** the standard of living is much higher than in neighbouring[GB] countries; **des taux d'intérêt ~s à 10%** interest rates higher than ou above 10%; **les chiffres sont ~s de 3% aux prévisions** the figures are 3% higher than predicted; **être ~ en nombre** to be greater in number; **des températures**

~es de 4 à 5 degrés aux moyennes saisonnières temperatures between 4 and 5 degrees higher than the seasonal averages; **température ~e à 20°C** temperature above 20°C; **4** (de meilleure qualité) [*travail, qualité*] superior (**à** to); **leur aviation est ~e à celle de leur ennemi** their air force is superior to that of their enemy; **leur adversaire leur était ~** their opponent was better than them; **5** (hautain) [*air, ton, sourire*] superior; **avoir/prendre un air ~** to have/to assume a superior air; **6** Math **si a est ~ à b** if a is greater than b; **x est égal ou supérieur à y** x is equal to or greater than y; **7** Biol, Bot, Zool higher; **8** Astron superior; **9** Géol Upper; **jurassique ~** Upper Jurassic.

II *nm,f* **1** (chef) superior; **mon ~ hiérarchique** my immediate superior; **mes ~s hiérarchiques** my superiors; **2** Relig Superior; **Père ~** Father Superior; **Mère ~e** Mother Superior.

III *nm* Univ higher education.

supérieurement /syperjœrmɑ̃/ *adv* **~ intelligent/arrogant** exceptionally intelligent/arrogant.

supériorité /syperjɔrite/ *nf* superiority; **~ écrasante/numérique** overwhelming/numerical superiority; **ton/air de ~** superior tone/manner; **complexe de ~** superiority complex; **avoir un sentiment de ~** to feel superior.

superlatif, **-ive** /sypɛrlatif, iv/ **I** *adj* superlative.

II *nm* superlative; **au ~** in the superlative.

■ **~ absolu** Ling absolute superlative; **~ relatif** Ling relative superlative.

superléger /sypɛrleʒe/ *adj m, nm* Sport (amateur) light welterweight; (professionnel) junior welterweight.

supermarché /sypɛrmarʃe/ *nm* supermarket.

supernova, *pl* **-ae** /sypɛrnɔva, nɔve/ *nf* supernova.

superordinateur /sypɛrɔrdinatœr/ *nm* supercomputer.

superpétrolier /sypɛrpetrɔlje/ *nm* supertanker.

superphosphate /sypɛrfɔsfat/ *nm* superphosphate.

superplume /sypɛrplym/ *adj, nm* junior lightweight.

superposable /sypɛrpozabl/ *adj* [*dessins, cartes*] that can be superimposed (*après n*); [*casiers, tabourets*] stackable.

superposé, **~e** /sypɛrpoze/ *adj* [*cartes, dessins*] superimposed; **des lits ~s** bunk beds.

superposer /sypɛrpoze/ [1] **I** *vtr* **1** (l'un sur l'autre) to stack (up) [*casiers, tabourets*]; to stack [*caisses, briques, matelas*]; **2** (faire coïncider) to superimpose [*dessins, formes*] (**à** on (top of)); to juxtapose [*approches, théories*] (**à** with).

II se superposer *vpr* **1** [*problèmes*] to overlap; [*dessins, formes*] to be superimposed; **ils se superposent facilement** [*tabourets, casiers*] they are easy to stack; **2** Géol [*strates*] to be superimposed.

superposition /sypɛrpozisjɔ̃/ *nf* **la ~ de deux dessins** superimposing two drawings.

superproduction /sypɛrprɔdyksjɔ̃/ *nf* Cin blockbuster○, spectacular.

superprofit /sypɛrprɔfi/ *nm* vast profit.

superpuissance /sypɛrpɥisɑ̃s/ *nf* superpower.

supersonique /sypɛrsɔnik/ *adj* supersonic.

superstitieusement /sypɛrstisjøzmɑ̃/ *adv* superstitiously.

superstitieux, **-ieuse** /sypɛrstisjø, øz/ *adj* superstitious.

superstition /sypɛrstisjɔ̃/ *nf* superstition.

IDIOMES **la ~ est fille de l'ignorance** Prov superstition is born of ignorance.

superstrat /sypɛrstra/ *nm* superstratum.

superstructure /sypɛrstryktyr/ *nf* superstructure.

supertanker /sypɛrtɑ̃kœr/ *nm* supertanker.

superviser /sypɛrvize/ [1] *vtr* to supervise, to oversee [*travail*]; to supervise [*personne*].

superviseur /sypɛrvizœr/ *nm* supervisor.

supervision /sypɛrvizjɔ̃/ *nf* supervision.

superwelter /sypɛrwɛltɛr/ *adj m, nm* (amateur) light middleweight; (professionnel) junior middleweight.

supin /sypɛ̃/ *nm* supine.

supplanter /syplɑ̃te/ [1] *vtr* to supplant (**dans** in).

suppléance /sypleɑ̃s/ *nf* gén temporary replacement post; Scol supply GB ou substitute US teaching post; **être chargé d'une ~** gén to stand in ou deputize for sb GB, to fill in for sb; **elle ne fait que des ~s** gén she only does temporary jobs; Scol she only does supply GB ou substitute US teaching jobs.

suppléant, **~e** /sypleɑ̃, ɑ̃t/ **I** *adj* [*enseignant*] supply GB, substitute US; [*médecin*] replacement, stand-in; [*juge*] deputy.

II *nm,f* replacement; (de juge) deputy; (d'enseignant) supply GB ou substitute US teacher; (de médecin) locum GB, stand-in (doctor); **un poste de ~** gén temporary replacement post; Scol supply GB ou substitute US teaching job.

suppléer /syplee/ [11] **I** *vtr* **1** (remplacer) (temporairement) to stand in for GB, to deputize for GB, to fill in for [*personne, employé*]; (définitivement) to replace [*employé*]; **2** (aider) to assist, to help [*collègue*]; **3** (compléter) to make up [*somme, manque*]; **les convecteurs suppléent le chauffage central** the convector heaters supplement ou act as a back-up to the central heating.

II suppléer à *vtr ind* **~ à** to make up for, to compensate for [*carence, lacune*]; **chez lui, la qualité supplée à la quantité** what his work lacks in terms of quantity he makes up for in quality.

supplément /syplemɑ̃/ *nm* **1** (somme d'argent) gén extra ou additional charge; (en voyage, à l'hôtel) supplement; **payer un ~** to pay extra ou an additional charge; **il y a un ~ à payer pour l'excédent de bagages** you have to pay a supplement ou you have to pay extra for excess baggage; **il y a un ~ de 20 francs si vous choisissez le saumon** you pay 20 francs extra ou there is an additional charge of 20 francs if you choose the salmon; **ce plat/le vin est en ~** this dish/the wine is extra; **les vitres électriques/sièges en cuir sont en ~** the electric windows/leather seats are (an) extra; **train à ~** Rail *train on which passengers must pay a supplement*; **2** (complément) **~ d'informations** additional ou extra information; **~ de dessert** extra portion of dessert; **~ de salaire/travail** extra pay/work; **3** Presse supplement (**à** to); **le ~ emploi du mardi** Tuesday's jobs' supplement; **4** Math supplement.

supplémentaire /syplemɑ̃tɛr/ *adj* **1** (en plus) [*dépenses, impôts, crédits*] additional, extra; [*personnel, étudiants, chômeurs*] extra, additional; **la création de 500 emplois ~s** the creation of 500 extra jobs; **c'est une preuve ~ que** this is further ou additional proof that; **une raison/un obstacle ~** another reason/obstacle, an additional reason/obstacle; **ça nous a créé des problèmes ~s** this created more problems for us; **un délai ~** another extension of the deadline; **train/bus ~** relief train/bus; **2** Math supplementary.

supplétif, **-ive** /sypletif, iv/ **I** *adj* Mil auxiliary.

II *nm* auxiliary.

suppliant, **~e** /sypliјɑ̃, ɑ̃t/ **I** *adj* [*personne, voix, paroles*] pleading; [*air, regard*] imploring.

II *nm,f* supplicant.

supplication /syplikasjɔ̃/ *nf* **1** gén plea; **2** Relig supplication.

supplice /syplis/ *nm* (tous contextes) torture; **les ~s au Moyen Âge** forms of torture in the Middle Ages; **c'était un ~** fig it was torture; **subir un ~** lit to be tortured; fig to go through torture; **infliger un ~ à qn** to torture sb; **mettre qn au ~** fig to torture sb; **j'étais au ~** fig it was agony; **le dernier ~** liter the final agony, death; **marcher au ~** to go to (one's) execution; **conduire qn au ~** to lead sb to be executed.

■ **~ du bûcher** burning alive; **~ chinois** Chinese torture; **~ du collier** necklacing; **~ de la corde** hanging; **~ du fouet** flogging; **~ de la roue** breaking on the wheel.

supplicié, **~e** /syplisje/ *nm,f* torture victim.

supplicier /syplisje/ [2] *vtr* (torturer) to torture; (exécuter) to execute.

supplier /syplije/ [2] *vtr* to beg ou beseech sout ou entreat (**de faire** to do); **je t'en supplie, écoute-moi** listen to me, I beg you.

supplique /syplik/ *nf* liter petition; **présenter** or **adresser une ~ à qn** to petition sb; **céder aux ~s de qn** to give in to sb's entreaties.

support /sypɔr/ *nm* **1** (soutien) support; **servir de ~ à qch** to serve as a support for sth; **il se sert du tabouret comme ~ pour sa jambe plâtrée** he uses the stool to support the leg he has in plaster; **2** (objet) (pour des bibelots) stand; (pour des tubes à essai) rack; **3** (aide) back-up; **pour comprendre l'histoire l'enfant a besoin du ~ des images** to understand the story, the child needs the help of pictures; **utiliser des diapositives comme ~** to use slides as backup material; **4** Art support.

■ **~ audiovisuel** audio-visual aid; **~ de données** or **d'information** Ordinat data carrier; **~ magnétique** magnetic tape; **~ pédagogique** teaching aid; **~ publicitaire** advertising medium.

supportable /sypɔrtabl/ *adj* [*froid, chaleur, épreuve, douleur*] bearable; **il fait un froid difficilement ~** it's unbearably cold; **une souffrance difficilement ~** almost unbearable pain; **c'est quelqu'un de difficilement ~** he's/she's very difficult; **la température est très ~** the temperature is quite pleasant.

supporter[1] /sypɔrte/ [1] **I** *vtr* **1** (soutenir) [*structure, colonne, pilier*] to support, to bear the weight of [*toiture, édifice*]; **2** (prendre en charge) to bear [*frais, dépenses*]; **3** (endurer) to put up with, to endure [*privations, malheur*]; to put up with [*attitude, conduite, brimade, sarcasme*]; to bear, to endure [*souffrance, solitude*]; to put up with [*personne*]; **elle ne supporte plus son mari** she can't stand her husband any more; **il ne supporte pas ce genre de musique/vantardise** he can't stand this sort of music/boasting; **elle ne supporte pas d'attendre/la vue du sang** she can't stand waiting/the sight of blood; **4** (accepter) to put up with; **elle supporte tout de lui** she puts up with ou takes anything from him; **je ne supporte pas qu'elle me réponde sur ce ton** I won't stand for her taking that tone with me; **il a mal supporté tes critiques** he found your criticisms hard to take; **5** (subir sans dommages) [*plante*] to withstand [*froid, chaleur*]; [*personne*] **elle supporte bien la chaleur** she can take ou stand the heat; **elle supporte mal la chaleur** she can't take the heat, the heat doesn't agree with her; **il ne supporte pas l'aspirine®** aspirin doesn't agree with him; **il a bien supporté son opération** he came through the operation well; **il n'a pas supporté l'opération** he didn't come through the operation; **ce plat supporte la chaleur** this dish is heat-resistant; **il a bien supporté le traitement** he reacted well to the treatment; **il a bien supporté le voyage** he stood the journey well; **il ne supporterait pas le voyage** the journey would be too much for him ; **il ne fait pas très froid, mais on supporte un pull** it's not very cold but you need a sweater; **je supporterais bien un pull** I could do with a sweater.

II se supporter *vpr* **ils ne peuvent plus se ~** they can't stand each other any more.

supporter² /sypɔʀtœʀ/ *nmf* supporter.

supposé, ~e /sypoze/ **I** *pp* ▸ **supposer**.

II *pp adj* [*nombre, coût*] supposed; [*auteur, coupable, qualité*] alleged.

supposer /sypoze/ [1] *vtr* **1** (comme base d'un raisonnement) gén to suppose; Math, Philos to postulate; **~ que** to suppose that; **en supposant** or **à ~ que** supposing (that); **à ~ que ce soit possible** supposing (that) that is possible; **la chaleur est supposée constante** the heat is taken to be constant; **2** (tenir pour probable) to assume; **je suppose qu'il a réussi à partir** I assume he managed to get away; **on peut ~ que** we can assume that; **je suppose qu'elle est en bonne santé** I assume she's in good health; **3** (impliquer) to presuppose; **cela suppose que** this presupposes that.

supposition /sypozisjɔ̃/ *nf* supposition, assumption.

suppositoire /sypozitwaʀ/ *nm* suppository.

suppôt /sypo/ *nm* liter pej **un dangereux ~ de la subversion/réaction** a dangerous subversive/reactionary.

■ **~ de Satan** or **du diable** fiend.

suppression /sypʀesjɔ̃/ *nf* **1** (d'impôt) abolition; (de droit) abolition GB, revocation; (d'interdiction, de sanction, contrôle) lifting; (d'avantages, de privilèges) removal, withdrawal; (de preuves, faits) suppression; (de publicité, subvention, pension) withdrawal; (de chômage, défauts, nuisance, vibrations) elimination; (de monopole) breaking, ending; (de mot, ligne) deletion; **la ~ du train de 8 heures 50** (une fois) the cancellation of the 8.50 train; (définitivement) the discontinuation of the 8.50 service; **~s d'emplois** or **d'effectifs** job cuts; **~ d'effectif** redundancies (*pl*) GB, layoffs (*pl*); **il y a eu 20 ~s de postes** 20 posts have gone; **2** (meurtre) elimination.

supprimer /sypʀime/ [1] **I** *vtr* **1** to cut [*emploi*]; to cut out [*poste*]; to stop [*aide, crédit, vibration*]; to abolish [*impôt, rationnement, institution, peine de mort*]; to lift [*interdiction, sanction, restriction*]; to lift, to abolish [*contrôle, censure*]; to remove [*effet, cause*]; to do away with [*examen, classe*]; to put an end to [*pauvreté, discrimination*]; to remove [*obstacle, mur*]; to withdraw [*publicité, pension, permission, subvention, permis de conduire*]; to remove, to withdraw [*privilège, avantage*]; to break, to end [*monopole*]; to eliminate [*nuisance, défaut, gaspillage*]; to repeal [*loi*]; to cease to allow [*dérogation*]; to cut off [*argent de poche*]; to cut out [*sucre, sel*]; to delete [*mot, ligne*]; to take [sth] away [*liberté*]; **~ un train** (annuler) to cancel a train; (définitivement) to discontinue a service; **2** (tuer) euph to eliminate.

II se supprimer *vpr* (se suicider) to do away with oneself.

suppuration /sypyʀasjɔ̃/ *nf* suppuration.

suppurer /sypyʀe/ [1] *vi* to suppurate.

supputation /sypytasjɔ̃/ *nf* **1** (action) calculation; **2** (prédiction) prognostication.

supputer /sypyte/ liter [1] *vtr* to calculate, to work out (**que** that); **~ ses chances de réussite** to weigh up one's chances of success.

supra /sypʀa/ *adv* above; **voir ~** see above.

supraconducteur /sypʀakɔ̃dyktœʀ/ **I** *adj* superconductive.

II *nm* superconductor.

supraconductivité /sypʀakɔ̃dyktivite/ *nf* superconductivity.

supraliminaire /sypʀaliminɛʀ/ *adj* supraliminal.

supranational, ~e, *mpl* **-aux** /sypʀanasjɔnal, o/ *adj* supranational.

supranationalisme /sypʀanasjɔnalism/ *nm* supranationalism.

supranationaliste /sypʀanasjɔnalist/ *adj, nmf* supranationalist.

supranationalité /sypʀanasjɔnalite/ *nf* supranational character.

supranormal, ~e, *mpl* **-aux** /sypʀanɔʀmal, o/ *adj* paranormal.

suprasegmental, ~e, *mpl* **-aux** /sypʀasɛgmɑ̃tal, o/ *adj* suprasegmental.

suprasensible /sypʀasɑ̃sibl/ *adj* supersensible.

supraterrestre /sypʀateʀɛstʀ/ *adj, nmf* extraterrestrial.

suprématie /sypʀemasi/ *nf* supremacy (**sur** over).

suprématisme /sypʀematism/ *nm* Suprematism.

suprême /sypʀɛm/ **I** *adj* **1** (le plus élevé) [*fonction, autorité*] supreme; **2** (très grand) [*élégance, habileté*] supreme; [*insolence*] ultimate.

II *nm* Culin **~ de foie gras** *goose or duck liver pâté*.

suprêmement /sypʀɛmmɑ̃/ *adv* supremely.

sur¹ /syʀ/ *prép*

■ **Note** Lorsque *sur* indique une position dans l'espace il se traduit généralement par *on*: *sur la table*/*une chaise* = on the table/a chair; *sur la côte*/*le lac* = on the coast/the lake.
– On trouvera ci-dessous des exemples supplémentaires et exceptions.
– Lorsque *sur* a une valeur figurée comme dans *régner sur, pleurer sur, sur l'honneur, sur place* etc la traduction sera fournie dans l'article du deuxième élément, respectivement ***régner***, ***pleurer***, ***honneur***, ***place*** etc.

1 (dessus) on; **le verre est ~ la table** the glass is on the table; **prends un verre ~ la table** take a glass from the table; **appliquer la lotion ~ vos cheveux** apply the lotion to your hair; **la clé est ~ la porte** the key is in the door; **passer la main ~ une étoffe** to run one's hand over a fabric; **il doit être ~ la route** he must be on the road ou on his way by now; **2** (au-dessus, sans contact) over; **des nuages ~ les montagnes/la plaine** clouds over the mountain tops/the plain; **un pont ~ la rivière** a bridge across ou over the river; **la nuit est tombée/l'orage s'est abattu ~ la ville** night fell/the storm broke over the city; **3** (étendue, surface) **la forêt est détruite ~ 150 hectares** the forest has been destroyed over an area of 150 hectares; **une table d'un mètre ~ deux** a table (of) one metre by two; **4** (direction) **se diriger ~ Valence** to head ou make for Valence; **une voiture déboucha ~ la droite** a car pulled out on the right; **5** (support matériel) on; **~ un morceau de papier** on a piece of paper; **elle est très jolie ~ la photo** she looks very pretty in the photograph; **dessiner ~ le sable** to draw in the sand; **6** (au sujet de) [*débat, exposé, essai, chapitre, thèse*] on; [*étude, poème*] about; [*article, livre*] on; **7** (objet d'un travail) **être ~ une affaire** to be involved in a business deal; **on est ~ un gros chantier actuellement** we're currently involved in a big construction project; **8** (indique un rapport de proportion) **une personne ~ dix** one person in ou out of ten; **une semaine ~ trois** one week in three; **il a fait trois exercices ~ quatre** he did three exercises out of four; **~ 250 employés, il y a seulement 28 femmes** out of 250 employees, there are only 28 females; **un mardi ~ deux** every other Tuesday; **il y a deux chances ~ trois qu'il ne vienne pas** there are two chances out of three that he won't come; **9** (indique l'accumulation) lit upon; fig after; **entasser pierre ~ pierre** to pile stone upon stone; **faire proposition ~ proposition** to make one offer after another, to make offer after offer; **commettre erreur ~ erreur** to make one mistake after another, to make mistake after mistake; **il a eu deux accidents coup ~ coup** he had two accidents one after the other; **10** (juste après) **ils se sont quittés ~ ces mots** with these words, they parted; **~ le moment** at the time; **~ ce** or **quoi** upon which, thereupon; **~ ce, je vous laisse** with that, I must leave you; **11** (pendant) **on ne peut pas juger ~ une période aussi courte/trois jours** you can't decide over ou in such a short period/three days; **12** Radio, TV, Télécom on [*radio, chaîne, ligne téléphonique*].

sur², ~e /syʀ/ *adj* (slightly) sour.

sûr, ~e /syʀ/ **I** *adj* **1** (fiable) [*information, source, service*] reliable; [*personne*] reliable; [*jugement, avis, base, investissement*] sound; **le temps n'est pas ~** the weather is unreliable; **avoir la main ~e** to have a steady hand; **d'une main ~e** with a steady hand; **2** (sans danger) safe; **en mains ~es** in safe hands; **en lieu ~** lit in a safe place; **le voleur a été mis en lieu ~** euph the thief has been put in prison; **le plus ~ est de faire** the safest thing is to do; **c'est plus ~** it's safer; **peu ~** unsafe; **3** (garanti) certain; **rien n'est moins ~** nothing is less certain; **une chose est ~e, (c'est que) tu t'es fait avoir**○ one thing's certain ou for sure, you've been had○; **c'est loin d'être ~** that's far from certain; **ce n'est pas si ~** it's not that certain, I wouldn't be so sure; **tu viens avec nous c'est ~?** are you definitely coming with us?; **c'est ~ et certain** it's definite; **à coup ~** definitely, for sure; **la victoire est ~e** victory is assured; **4** (convaincu) sure; **être ~ de faire** to be sure of doing; **je suis ~ qu'il viendra** I'm sure he'll come; **je suis ~ d'avoir raison** I'm sure I'm right; **je n'en suis pas si ~** I'm not so sure; **j'en suis ~ et certain** I'm positive (about it), I'm absolutely sure ou certain (of it); **et je suis ~ de ce que je dis** and I'm absolutely sure of what I'm telling you; **il est ~ de lui** (qualité) he's self-confident, he's sure of himself; (ponctuellement) he's sure of it; **on n'est jamais ~ de rien** you can never be sure of anything; **être ~ de ses possibilités** to be confident of one's abilities; **être ~ de qn** to trust sb; **j'en étais ~!** I knew it!

II *adv* (sûrement) **~ que**○ you can be sure that; **~ qu'il va pleuvoir** you can be sure that it's going to rain; **bien ~ (que oui)** of course; **bien ~ que je vous aiderai** of course I'll help you; **bien ~ que non** of course not; **(pour) ~** for sure; **'il a tort'—'pas ~'** 'he's wrong'—'I'm not so sure'.

IDIOMES **être ~ de son coup**○ to be confident of success.

surabondamment /syʀabɔ̃damɑ̃/ *adv* overabundantly.

surabondance /syʀabɔ̃dɑ̃s/ *nf* overabundance.

surabondant, ~e /syʀabɔ̃dɑ̃, ɑ̃t/ *adj* [*détails, production, illustrations*] overabundant; [*végétation*] rank.

surabonder /syʀabɔ̃de/ [1] *vi* **1** (être en nombre) to abound; **les illustrations/erreurs surabondent dans le manuel** illustrations/mistakes abound in the manual; **2** (être rempli) **~ de** or **en** to have an overabundance of; **région qui surabonde de bons vins/de sites touristiques** a region with an overabundance of good wines/of tourist spots; **cette année surabonde en festivals** there is an overabundance of festivals this year.

suractivé, ~e /syʀaktive/ *adj* superactivated.

suractivité /syʀaktivite/ *nf* overactivity.

suraigu, -uë /syʀegy/ *adj* **1** [*son, voix*] very shrill; **2** [*douleur*] very sharp.

surajouter /syʀaʒute/ [1] **I** *vtr* to add on (**à** to).

II se surajouter *vpr* to be added on (**à** to).

suralimentation /syʀalimɑ̃tasjɔ̃/ *nf* **1** (de

personne) feeding up; (consommation excessive) overeating; **2** (de moteur) supercharging, boosting.

suralimenter /syʀalimɑ̃te/ [1] *vtr* **1** (soumettre à une suralimentation) to feed [sb] up; **2** Agric to fatten [*volaille, bétail*]; **3** Tech to supercharge, to boost [*moteur*].

suranné, **~e** /syʀane/ *adj* [*idées, conceptions*] outmoded; [*style, manières*] outdated.

surarmé, **~e** /syʀaʀme/ *adj* excessively armed.

surarmement /syʀaʀməmɑ̃/ *nm* **1** (armement excessif) armament on a large scale; **2** (action de surarmer) (huge) arms build-up.

surbaissé, **~e** /syʀbese/ *adj* **1** Archit [*plafond*] lowered; [*arc, voûte*] surbased; **2** Aut [*carrosserie, voiture*] low-slung.

surbaissement /syʀbɛsmɑ̃/ *nm* Archit surbasement.

surbaisser /syʀbese/ [1] *vtr* **1** Archit to lower [*plafond*]; to surbase [*arc*]; **2** Aut to undersling.

surbooking /syʀbukiŋ/ *nm* overbooking.

surboum○† /syʀbum/ *nf* rave-up○ GB, party.

surcapacité /syʀkapasite/ *nf* overcapacity.

surcapitalisation /syʀkapitalizasjɔ̃/ *nf* overcapitalization.

surcharge /syʀʃaʀʒ/ *nf* **1** (excédent de poids) excess load, overload; (fait d'être surchargé) overloading; **~ pondérale** excess weight; **une ~ de 500 kilos** an overload of 500 kilos; **elle a 20 kilos de bagages en ~** she has 20 kilos of excess baggage; **un navire/véhicule en ~** an overloaded ship/vehicle; **des voyageurs en ~** excess passengers; **rouler en ~** to drive an overloaded vehicle; **2** (excès) **une ~ de travail** an extra load of work; **une ~ de frais** extra expenses; **il faut éviter la ~ des programmes scolaires** we must avoid overloading the school syllabus; **3** (correction) correction; **écrire un mot/chiffre en ~** to write a word/figure on top of another which has been crossed out; **4** (de timbre-poste) overprint, surcharge.

surchargé, **~e** /syʀʃaʀʒe/ **I** *pp* ▶ **surcharger**.
II *pp adj* **1** (qui est trop chargé) [*personne, animal*] overloaded, overburdened; [*véhicule, ascenseur, étagère*] overloaded; **des voyageurs ~s de bagages** passengers weighed down ou overloaded with luggage; **décoration ~e** overabundant ou excessive decoration; **2** (aux activités trop nombreuses) [*personne*] overburdened; [*journée, emploi du temps*] overloaded, overfull; (aux effectifs trop nombreux) [*classe, école, université*] overcrowded; **être ~ de** to be overburdened with [*travail, impôts, demandes*]; **3** (plein de corrections) [*manuscrit*] covered with corrections; **4** (qui porte une surcharge) [*timbre-poste*] surcharged.

surcharger /syʀʃaʀʒe/ [13] *vtr* **1** (charger à l'excès) to overload; **des bagages qui surchargent dangereusement la voiture** luggage that dangerously overloads the car; **~ un texte de citations** to cram a text with quotations; **2** (accabler) to overburden (**de** with); **~ qn de travail** to overburden sb with work; **3** (écrire par-dessus) to cover [sth] with corrections [*texte*]; **4** Postes to surcharge [*timbre-poste*]; **5** Ordinat to overload.

surchauffe /syʀʃof/ *nf* **1** lit superheating; **2** fig overheating.

surchauffer /syʀʃofe/ [1] *vtr* **1** (chauffer) to overheat [*maison, pièce*]; **2** (surexciter) to bring [sth] to fever pitch [*auditoire*]; **3** Phys, Tech to superheat [*liquide*].

surchoix /syʀʃwa/ *adj inv* [*aliments*] top quality.

surclasser /syʀklase/ [1] *vtr* to outclass.

surcompensation /syʀkɔ̃pɑ̃sasjɔ̃/ *nf* overcompensation.

surcomposé, **~e** /syʀkɔ̃poze/ *adj* [*temps*] double-compound.

surcompressé, **~e** /syʀkɔ̃pʀese/ *adj* supercharged.

surcompression /syʀkɔ̃pʀesjɔ̃/ *nf* supercharging.

surcomprimer /syʀkɔ̃pʀime/ [1] *vtr* Tech to supercharge.

surconsommation /syʀkɔ̃sɔmasjɔ̃/ *nf* Écon overconsumption; **~ de médicaments** excessive drug consumption.

surcontre /syʀkɔ̃tʀ/ *nm* (au bridge) redouble; **faire un ~** to redouble.

surcoter /syʀkɔte/ [1] *vtr* to overvalue [*monnaie*].

surcoupe /syʀkup/ *nf* (aux cartes) overtrumping.

surcouper /syʀkupe/ [1] *vtr* to overtrump.

surcoût /syʀku/ *nm* additional cost.

surcroît /syʀkʀwa/ *nm* increase (**de** in); **un ~ de travail/population** extra work/people; **un ~ de prestige/d'activité** increased prestige/activity; **de ~** moreover.

surdensité /syʀdɑ̃site/ *nf* Géog high density (of population).

surdéveloppé, **~e** /syʀdevlɔpe/ *adj* overdeveloped.

surdéveloppement /syʀdevlɔpmɑ̃/ *nm* overdevelopment.

surdimensionné, **~e** /syʀdimɑ̃sjɔne/ *adj* oversize.

surdi-mutité, *pl* **~s** /syʀdimytite/ *nf* deaf-muteness.

surdiplômé, **~e** /syʀdiplome/ *adj* overqualified.

surdité /syʀdite/ *nf* deafness.

surdosage /syʀdozaʒ/ *nm* excessive dose.

surdose /syʀdoz/ *nf* (de drogue) overdose.

surdoué, **~e** /syʀdwe/ **I** *adj* [*enfant*] gifted; [*pianiste, sportif*] exceptionally gifted.
II *nm,f* (enfant) gifted child; (pianiste) exceptionally gifted pianist; **un ~ du ballon** Sport a super-talented player.

sureau, *pl* **~x** /syʀo/ *nm* elder (tree).

sureffectif /syʀefɛktif/ *nm* (personnel) excess ou surplus staff; (situation) (en usine) overmanning; (dans un bureau) overstaffing; **un ~ de 300 personnes** a surplus staff of 300 people; **personnel en ~** excess staff; **le service est en ~** the department is overstaffed; **supprimer les ~s** to end overstaffing.

surélévation /syʀelevasjɔ̃/ *nf* **1** (activité) raising the height; **2** (résultat) extra height; **maison en ~ par rapport à la route** house built above the road.

surélever /syʀelve/ [16] *vtr* to raise the height of [*maison, route*].

sûrement /syʀmɑ̃/ *adv* **1** (très probablement) most probably; **elle est ~ malade** she must be ill; **vous avez ~ vu ce film** you must have seen that film; **'tu viendras?'—'oui ~'** 'are you coming?'—'yes, most probably'; **elle sera ~ là demain** she should be there tomorrow; **2** (bien sûr) certainly; **~ pas**, **~ que non**○ certainly not; **3** (sans risque) safely.

suremploi /syʀɑ̃plwa/ *nm* Écon labour[GB] shortage.

surenchère /syʀɑ̃ʃɛʀ/ *nf* **1** (enchère supérieure) higher bid; **faire une ~ sur qn** to bid higher than sb; **faire une ~ de 500 francs** to bid 500 francs more ou higher (**sur qn** than sb; **sur qch** for sth); **2** (exagération) escalation; **une ~ de violence** an escalation of violence; **faire de la ~ dans la violence** (terroriste) to commit acts of increasing violence; (au cinéma) to make increasingly violent films; **la ~ sur les diplômes** the demand for graduates with higher and higher qualifications; **faire de la ~** to try to go one better, to try to get one up; **faire de la ~ électorale** to make more extravagant promises than one's electoral opponents; **il fait de la ~ dans le racisme/l'anticommunisme** he goes a bit overboard on racism/anticommunism.

surenchérir /syʀɑ̃ʃeʀiʀ/ [3] *vi* **1** (faire une offre plus élevée) to bid higher; **~ sur une offre/qn** to bid higher than an offer/sb, to outbid an offer/sb; **2** (promettre plus) **~ sur qn** to outbid sb; **~ sur ses adversaires politiques** to go further than ou outbid one's political opponents; **3** (ajouter) (après soi) to add; (après autrui) to chime in.

surendetté, **~e** /syʀɑ̃dete/ *adj* [*personne, pays*] deeply in debt (*après n*); [*entreprise*] overextended.

surendettement /syʀɑ̃dɛtmɑ̃/ *nm* excessive debt; **les conséquences du ~** the consequences of overborrowing.

surentraînement /syʀɑ̃tʀɛnmɑ̃/ *nm* overtraining.

surentraîner /syʀɑ̃tʀene/ [1] *vtr*, **se surentraîner** *vpr* to overtrain.

suréquipement /syʀekipmɑ̃/ *nm* (en matériel) overequipment; (d'hôtels) over-provision.

suréquiper /syʀekipe/ [1] *vtr* to overequip.

surestarie /syʀɛstaʀi/ *nf* Jur (retard) demurrage; (pénalité) demurrage fine.

surestimation /syʀɛstimasjɔ̃/ *nf* (de bien, propriété) overvaluation; (de coût, capacité, d'importance) overestimation; (de qualité, mérite) overrating.

surestimer /syʀɛstime/ [1] **I** *vtr* to overvalue [*propriété, tableau*]; to overestimate [*coût, capacités, importance*]; to overrate [*qualités, mérites*].
II se surestimer *vpr* to rate oneself too highly.

suret, **-ette** /syʀɛ, ɛt/ *adj* tart.

sûreté /syʀte/ *nf* **1** (sécurité) (d'équipement, de lieu, personne) safety; (d'investissement) soundness; (de pays) security; **~ nucléaire** nuclear safety; **pour plus de ~** for extra safety; **dispositif/système de ~** safety device/system; **conduire qn en ~** to lead sb to safety; **~ de l'État** national security; **être en ~** [*bijou, argent, objet, personne*] to be in a safe place; **être en ~ à la banque** to be in safe keeping in the bank; **il se croyait en ~** he thought he was safe; ▶ **prudence**; **2** (assurance) (de jugement) soundness; (de geste) steadiness; (d'acteur, de musicien) confidence; **3** Tech (dispositif de sécurité) (d'une arme) safety catch; (chaîne) safety chain; (serrure) safety lock.
■ **Sûreté nationale** police (+ *v pl*); **Sûreté urbaine** local police (+ *v pl*).

surévaluation /syʀevalɥasjɔ̃/ *nf* Fin overvaluation.

surévaluer /syʀevalɥe/ [1] *vtr* to overvalue [*monnaie*]; to overestimate [*coût*].

surexcitation /syʀɛksitasjɔ̃/ *nf* overexcitement.

surexciter /syʀɛksite/ [1] *vtr* to overexcite [*enfants*]; **l'approche de Noël surexcite les enfants** children get overexcited as Christmas approaches; **foule surexcitée** highly excited crowd.

surexploiter /syʀɛksplwate/ [1] *vtr* to overexploit.

surexposer /syʀɛkspoze/ [1] *vtr* to overexpose (**de** by).

surexposition /syʀɛkspozisjɔ̃/ *nf* overexposure.

surf /sœʀf/ ▶ **449** *nm* surfing; **faire du ~** to go surfing.
■ **~ des neiges** Sport snowboard; **faire du ~ des neiges** to snowboard.

surfaçage /syʀfasaʒ/ *nm* surface finishing.

surface /syʀfas/ *nf* **1** (partie externe) surface; **à la ~ de** lit, fig on the surface of; **en ~** (à l'extérieur) lit, fig on the surface; (au-dessus du sol) above ground; **de ~** lit [*navire, courrier, structure, tension*] surface; [*métro, installations*] above ground (*après n*); fig [*amabilité*] superficial; **faire ~** lit, fig to surface; **refaire ~** lit, fig to resurface; **2** ▶ **783** (aire) surface area; **d'une ~ de** with a surface area of; **en ~** in area; ▶ **grand**; **3** Sport (au

football) area; (au tennis) surface; **~ dure/rapide** hard/fast surface.
■ **~ chauffante** or **de chauffe** heating surface; **~ commerciale** shop space; **~ de contact** contact area; **~ corrigée** *amended surface area of a property used as a basis for calculating rent*; **~ d'exposition** exhibition space; **~ financière** financial standing; **~ habitable** or **d'habitation** living space; **~ irriguée** irrigated area; **~ de refroidissement** cooling surface; **~ de réparation** penalty area; **~ sensible** sensitized surface; **~ de séparation** boundary layer; **~ d'usure** wearing surface; **~ utile** (de commerce, maison) floor space; **~ de vente** sales area.

surfacer /syʀfase/ [12] *vtr* to surface.

surfaceuse /syʀfasøz/ *nf* surfacer.

surfaire /syʀfɛʀ/ [10] *vtr* to overrate [*écrivain, qualités*].

surfait, **~e** /syʀfɛ, ɛt/ I *pp* ▶ **surfaire**.
II *pp adj* [*personne, œuvre*] overrated; [*réputation*] inflated.

surfer /sœʀfe/ [1] *vi* **1** Sport to go surfing; **2** Ordinat **~ sur Internet** to surf the Internet.

surfeur, **-euse** /sœʀfœʀ, øz/ *nm,f* surfer.

surfil /syʀfil/, **surfilage** /syʀfilaʒ/ *nm* whip-stitch.

surfiler /syʀfile/ [1] *vtr* to oversew.

surfin, **~e** /syʀfɛ̃, in/ *adj* [*qualité*] superior; [*produit*] quality (*épith*).

surgélation /syʀʒelasjɔ̃/ *nf* deep-freezing.

surgelé, **~e** /syʀʒəle/ I *pp* ▶ **surgeler**.
II *pp adj* deep-frozen.
III *nm* **le ~**, **les ~s** frozen food.

surgeler /syʀʒəle/ [17] *vtr* to deep-freeze.

surgénérateur /syʀʒeneʀatœʀ/ *nm* fast-breeder reactor.

surgir /syʀʒiʀ/ [3] *vi* [*personne, animal, voiture*] to appear suddenly (**de** from); [*problème, difficulté, phénomène*] to crop up (**de** from); **faire ~** to conjure up [*idée, craintes, image*]; to create [*demande, besoin*]; **faire ~ la vérité** to bring the truth to light.

surgissement /syʀʒismɑ̃/ *nm* liter (sudden) appearance.

surhausser /syʀose/ [1] *vtr* to raise the height of [*maison*].

surhomme /syʀɔm/ *nm* superman.

surhumain, **~e** /syʀymɛ̃, ɛn/ *adj* superhuman.

surimposer /syʀɛ̃poze/ [1] *vtr* Fisc (davantage) to surtax; (excessivement) to overtax.

surimposition /syʀɛ̃pozisjɔ̃/ *nf* Fisc (surplus) surtax; (excès) overtaxation.

surimpression /syʀɛ̃pʀesjɔ̃/ *nf* Phot double exposure; **en ~** superimposed (**à** on).

surin◐ /syʀɛ̃/ *nm* thieves' slang knife; **donner un coup de ~ à qn** to knife sb.

Suriname /syʀinam/ ▶ **321** *nprm* Surinam.

surinfection /syʀɛ̃fɛksjɔ̃/ *nf* secondary infection.

surinformation /syʀɛ̃fɔʀmasjɔ̃/ *nf* surfeit of information.

surintendance /syʀɛ̃tɑ̃dɑ̃s/ *nf* **1** (charge) superintendency; **2** (résidence) superintendent's (official) residence.

surintendant /syʀɛ̃tɑ̃dɑ̃/ *nm* superintendent.

surintendante /syʀɛ̃tɑ̃dɑ̃t/ *nf* Entr ≈ welfare officer.

surintensité /syʀɛ̃tɑ̃site/ *nf* Électrotech overload.

surinvestissement /syʀɛ̃vɛstismɑ̃/ *nm* Écon Psych overinvestment.

surir /syʀiʀ/ [3] *vi* to go sour.

surjet /syʀʒɛ/ *nm* Cout oversewing.

surjeter /syʀjəte/ [20] *vtr* Cout to oversew.

sur-le-champ /syʀləʃɑ̃/ *adv* right away.

surlendemain /syʀlɑ̃d(ə)mɛ̃/ *nm* **le ~** two days later; **le ~ matin** two days later, in the morning; **le lendemain et le ~** the next day and the day after that; **remettre une visite au ~** to postpone a visit to two days later; **le ~ de l'accident** two days after the accident.

surligner /syʀliɲe/ [1] *vtr* to highlight.

surligneur /syʀliɲœʀ/ *nm* highlighter (pen).

surliure /syʀljyʀ/ *nf* Naut whipping.

surloyer /syʀlwaje/ *nm* rent supplement.

surmenage /syʀmənaʒ/ *nm* overwork; **évitez le ~** avoid overworking.

surmener /syʀmene/ [16] I *vtr* to overwork.
II **se surmener** *vpr* to push oneself too hard.

surmoi /syʀmwɑ/ *nm* superego.

surmontable /syʀmɔ̃tabl/ *adj* surmountable.

surmonter /syʀmɔ̃te/ [1] I *vtr* **1** (dépasser) to overcome [*obstacle, problème, crise, contradiction, méfiance*]; **~ l'épreuve de la séparation** to get through ou survive (the ordeal of) separation; **2** (être placé au-dessus de) **être surmonté de qch** to be topped ou surmounted by sth; **un dôme surmonte la tour** the tower is topped ou surmounted by a dome.
II **se surmonter** *vpr* (se dépasser) **les déceptions/problèmes se surmontent** disappointments/problems can be overcome.

surmortalité /syʀmɔʀtalite/ *nf* abnormally high death rate.

surmulot /syʀmylo/ *nm* common rat, brown rat.

surmultiplication /syʀmyltiplikasjɔ̃/ *nf* overdrive.

surmultiplié, **~e** /syʀmyltiplije/ I *adj* **rapport ~**, **vitesse ~e** overdrive.
II **surmultipliée** *nf* overdrive; **passer la ~e** lit to shift into overdrive; fig to go into overdrive.

surnager /syʀnaʒe/ [13] *vi* **1** lit [*pétrole, débris*] to float; **2** fig [*souvenirs*] to linger on.

surnaturel, **-elle** /syʀnatyʀɛl/ I *adj* **1** (non naturel) supernatural; **2** (extraordinaire) eerie.
II *nm* **le ~** the supernatural.

surnom /syʀnɔ̃/ *nm* nickname.

surnombre /syʀnɔ̃bʀ/ *nm* **en ~** [*objets*] surplus (*épith*); [*employé*] redundant; [*personnel*] excess (*épith*); [*passager*] extra (*épith*); **deux d'entre nous étaient en ~** there were two too many of us.

surnommer /syʀnɔme/ [1] *vtr* to nickname; **X, surnommé Y** X, known as ou dubbed Y; **comment l'ont-ils surnommée?** what nickname did they give her?

surnuméraire /syʀnymeʀɛʀ/ *adj, nmf* supernumerary.

suroffre /syʀɔfʀ/ *nf* **1** Jur (surenchère) higher offer; **2** Écon excess supplies of goods (on the market).

suroît /syʀwɑ/ *nm* **1** Météo, Naut southwester, sou'wester; **2** (chapeau) sou'wester.

surpasser /syʀpase/ [1] I *vtr* (faire mieux que) to surpass, to outdo [*adversaire, concurrent*]; **~ qn en habileté/bon sens/érudition** to surpass ou outdo sb in skill/common sense/erudition.
II **se surpasser** *vpr* to surpass oneself, to excel oneself.

surpayer /syʀpeje/ [21] *vtr* to overpay [*salarié*]; to pay too much for [*produit, service*].

surpeuplé, **~e** /syʀpœple/ *adj* [*pays, région, ville*] overpopulated; [*local, train, rue*] overcrowded.

surpeuplement /syʀpœpləmɑ̃/ *nm* (de pays, région) overpopulation; (de ville, quartier) overcrowding.

surpiquer /syʀpike/ [1] *vtr* to topstitch.

surpiqûre /syʀpikyʀ/ *nf* topstitching.

surplace /syʀplas/ *nm inv* **faire du ~** (dans un embouteillage) to be stuck; (dans un travail, une enquête) to be getting nowhere; (en cyclisme) to do a track stand; (d'hélicoptère, oiseau) to hover.

surplis /syʀpli/ *nm inv* surplice.

surplomb /syʀplɔ̃/ *nm* overhang; **falaise/balcon en ~** overhanging cliff/balcony.

surplomber /syʀplɔ̃be/ [1] I *vtr* to overhang, to jut out over.
II *vi* to overhang.

surplus /syʀply/ I *nm inv* (excédent) (de marchandises) surplus (**de** of); (d'enthousiasme, de travail) excess (**de** of); **vendre le ~ de sa récolte** to sell off one's surplus harvest; **au ~** fml moreover.
II *nmpl* Écon surpluses; **~ agricoles** agricultural surpluses.
■ **~ américains** American army surplus ¢.

surpopulation /syʀpɔpylasjɔ̃/ *nf* overpopulation.

surprenant, **~e** /syʀpʀənɑ̃, ɑ̃t/ *adj* [*aspect, nombre, qualité, lieu*] surprising; [*personne*] amazing; **n'avoir rien de ~** to be hardly surprising; **il serait ~ qu'il vienne** it would be surprising if he came; **il est ~ de voir comment/combien** it is surprising how/how much; **un problème ~ de complexité** a surprisingly complex problem; **un enfant ~ d'intelligence** an amazingly intelligent child.

surprendre /syʀpʀɑ̃dʀ/ [52] I *vtr* **1** (étonner) to surprise; **~ tout le monde** to surprise everyone; **il sait ~ son monde** he never fails to surprise; **en ~ plus d'un** to surprise more than a few; **être agréablement surpris** to be pleasantly surprised; **2** (prendre par surprise) [*personne*] to take [sb] by surprise [*victime, ennemi*]; **la guerre l'a surprise en Allemagne** the war caught her in Germany; **un orage nous a surpris** we were caught in a thunderstorm; **se laisser ~ par les événements** to be caught out by events; **se laisser ~ par la pluie** to get caught in the rain; **se laisser ~ par la marée montante** to be caught by the rising tide; **3** (prendre sur le fait) to catch [*malfaiteur*] (**à faire** or **en train de faire** doing); **4** (être témoin de) to overhear [*conversation*]; to intercept [*regard, sourire*]; to witness [*événement*].
II *vi* (étonner) [*comportement, affirmation*] to be surprising; [*spectacle*] to surprise; [*personne*] to surprise people; **une telle remarque a de quoi ~** such a comment is somewhat surprising.
III **se surprendre** *vpr* **se ~ à faire** to catch oneself doing.

surpression /syʀpʀesjɔ̃/ *nf* high pressure.

surprime /syʀpʀim/ *nf* extra premium.

surprise /syʀpʀiz/ I *nf* **1** (événement étonnant) surprise; **quelle ~!** what a surprise!; **être** or **constituer une ~** to come as a surprise; **c'est la ~ de la journée** that's a big surprise; **créer la ~** to cause a stir; **créer une grosse ~** to cause a major stir; **ne dis rien, on veut leur faire une ~** don't say anything, we want it to be a surprise; **2** (étonnement) surprise; **à ma ~** to my surprise; **il m'a fait la ~ de venir me voir** he came to see me as a surprise; **prendre qn par ~** to take sb by surprise; **ne pas dissimuler sa ~** not to hide one's surprise; **Lyon a créé la ~ (en battant Auxerre)** Lyons produced an upset (by beating Auxerre); **ma ~ a été de constater que** I was surprised to find that; **avoir la ~/la bonne ~/la mauvaise ~ d'apprendre que** to be surprised/pleasantly surprised/unpleasantly surprised to hear that; **nulle ~ à ce que tu sois déçu** no wonder you are disappointed; **discours/élection/voyage sans ~** uneventful speech/election/trip; **l'élection a été sans ~** the election went as expected; **candidat sans ~** (prévu) expected candidate; (morne) unexceptional; **gagner sans ~** to win as expected; **3** (plaisir inattendu) surprise; **quelle gentille ~!** what a lovely surprise!
II **(-)surprise** (*in compounds*) **candidat/invité/décision/visite ~** surprise candidate/guest/decision/visit; **démission/voyage ~** unexpected resignation/trip;

hausse ~ shock increase; **grève ~** lightning strike.

surprise-partie†, *pl* **surprises-parties** /syʀpʀizpaʀti/ *nf* party.

surproduction /syʀpʀɔdyksjɔ̃/ *nf* overproduction.

surpuissant, **~e** /syʀpɥisɑ̃, ɑ̃t/ *adj* [*moteur, automobile*] high-powered; [*amplificateur*] ultra-powerful.

surqualifié, **~e** /syʀkalifje/ *adj* overqualified.

surréalisme /suʀ(ʀ)ealism/ *nm* surrealism.

surréaliste /suʀ(ʀ)ealist/ **I** *adj* **1** [*œuvre, auteur*] surrealist; **2** [*décor, paysage, vision*] surreal.
II *nmf* surrealist.

surrégénérateur /syʀʀeʒeneʀatœʀ/ *nm* fast-breeder reactor.

surrégime /syʀʀeʒim/ *nm* **le moteur tourne en ~** the engine is overrevving.

surrénal, **~e**, *mpl* **-aux** /syʀ(ʀ)enal, o/ **I** *adj* suprarenal.
II surrénale *nf* suprarenal gland.

surreprésenté, **~e** /syʀʀəpʀezɑ̃te/ *adj* overrepresented.

surréservation /syʀʀezɛʀvasjɔ̃/ *nf* overbooking.

Surrey ▶692 *nprm* **le ~** Surrey.

sursalaire /syʀsalɛʀ/ *nm* bonus (payment).

sursaturé, **~e** /syʀsatyʀe/ *adj* **1** Chimie supersaturated; **2**○ fig inundated (**de** with).

sursaut /syʀso/ *nm* **1** lit (mouvement) start; **en ~** with a start; **avoir un ~** to start, to jump; **2** fig (d'énergie, enthousiasme) sudden burst (**de** of); (d'orgueil, indignation) flash (**de** of); **dans un dernier** or **ultime ~** in a final spurt of effort.

sursauter /syʀsote/ [1] *vi* to jump (**de** with), to start (**de** with); **faire ~ qn** to make sb jump.

surseoir /syʀswaʀ/ [41] *vtr ind* **~ à** to postpone [*décision, inhumation*]; to defer [*versement*]; to stay [*jugement, exécution*].

sursis /syʀsi/ *nm* **1** (délai) respite; **je bénéficie d'un ~ de trois mois pour payer** I've been given a three-month respite to pay; **c'est un mort en ~** (criminel) he's under sentence of death; (malade) he's terminally ill; **un ministre en ~** a minister who is on the way out; **2** Jur suspended sentence; **demander/obtenir un ~** to request/get a suspended sentence; **être condamné à trois mois de prison avec ~** to be given a three-month suspended (prison) sentence; **trois mois de prison dont deux avec ~** prison sentence of three months two of them suspended; **3** (report d'incorporation) deferment of military service.
■ **~ avec mise à l'épreuve** probation order; **~ à statuer** adjournment.

sursitaire /syʀsitɛʀ/ **I** *adj* Mil **un étudiant ~** *a student whose military service has been deferred.*
II *nm* Mil *man whose military service has been deferred.*

surtaxe /syʀtaks/ *nf* surcharge; **~ à l'importation** import surcharge; **~ progressive** surtax.

surtaxer /syʀtakse/ [1] *vtr* to surcharge.

surtension /syʀtɑ̃sjɔ̃/ *nf* Électrotech (transitoire) surge; (durable) overvoltage.

surtitre /syʀtitʀ/ *nm* **1** (de journal) subhead; **2** (de doublage) supertitle.

surtout /syʀtu/ **I** *nm* **1** (pièce de table) centrepiece[GB]; **2**‡ (vêtement) overcoat, surtout†.
II *adv* above all; **~ en cas d'incendie** above all in case of fire; **j'ai ~ besoin de repos** more than anything I need a rest; **c'est pratique et ~ très simple** it's practical and, above all, very simple; **j'étais content mais ~ rassuré** I was pleased but above all relieved; **~ quand/si/que** especially when/if/as; **~ pas!** certainly not!; **~ pas lui!** especially not him!, anybody but him!; **~ pas de chien dans la maison** absolutely no dogs in the house.

survaloriser /syʀvalɔʀize/ [1] *vtr* to put too much emphasis on [*études, apparence*].

surveillance /syʀvɛjɑ̃s/ *nf* **1** gén watch; (par la police) surveillance; **exercer une ~ étroite/constante sur** to keep a close/constant watch over [*personne, installation, bâtiment*]; **placer qn sous haute ~** to put a close watch on sb; **maison/individu sous la ~ de la police** house/man under (police) surveillance; **placer qn/qch sous ~ policière** to put sb/sth under police surveillance; **mission de ~** surveillance mission; **déjouer la ~ de qn** to escape detection by sb; **~ électronique** electronic surveillance ou monitoring; **2** Scol, Univ (d'examens) supervision, invigilation GB, proctoring US; (de récréation) supervision; **sous la ~ de** under the supervision of; **assurer la ~ d'épreuves** to supervise ou invigilate GB ou proctor US exams; **3** (contrôle) supervision; **médicament à prendre sous ~ médicale** drug to be taken under medical supervision; **4** Mil (de cessez-le-feu) monitoring; (de frontières, d'espace aérien) monitoring, surveillance.

surveillant, **~e** /syʀvɛjɑ̃, ɑ̃t/ ▶510 *nm,f* **1** Scol (dans une école) supervisor; (pour les examens) invigilator GB, proctor US; **2** Admin **~/~e de prison** prison warder/wardress GB, prison guard US; **3** (dans un grand magasin) store detective.
■ **~ de baignade** lifeguard; **~ d'étude** Scol study supervisor; **~ général**† Scol chief supervisor; **~ d'internat** Scol dormitory supervisor.

surveiller /syʀveje/ [1] **I** *vtr* **1** (veiller sur) to watch, to keep an eye on [*enfants, cuisson, affaires*]; to watch (over) [*prisonnier, malade*]; **~ de près** to watch [sb/sth] closely, to keep a close ou watchful eye on; **~ du coin de l'œil** to watch [sb/sth] out of the corner of one's eye; **2** (exercer une surveillance sur) to keep watch on, to keep [sb/sth] under surveillance [*adversaire, bâtiment*]; **~ les mouvements de qn** to keep watch on sb's movements; **~ un suspect** to keep a suspect under surveillance ou observation; **il surveille ses employés** he keeps a close eye on his employees; **c'est ton tour de ~** it's your turn to keep watch; **3** (contrôler) to supervise, to oversee [*travail*]; to supervise [*sortie d'école*]; to monitor, to supervise [*cessez-le-feu, finances, fonctionnement, projet*]; to man, to monitor [*machine*]; **~ les progrès d'un élève/malade** to monitor a pupil's/patient's progress; **4** Scol, Univ to supervise ou invigilate GB ou proctor US [*examen*]; to supervise [*récréation*]; **5** (veiller à) **~ son langage/sa ligne/sa tension** to watch one's language/one's figure/one's blood pressure; **~ sa santé** to take care of one's health.
II se surveiller *vpr* to watch oneself; **tu devrais te ~ si tu ne veux pas reprendre du poids** you'd better watch yourself if you don't want to put on weight again; **avec eux, il faut sans cesse se ~** with them, you have to be on your best behaviour[GB].

survenir /syʀvəniʀ/ [36] **I** *vi* [*fait, décès, changement, orage*] to occur; [*difficulté, problème, conflit*] to arise; [*personne*] to arrive unexpectedly, to turn up○.
II *v impers* **s'il survient un problème** should any problem arise; **s'il survient qn** liter should anyone arrive.

survêtement /syʀvɛtmɑ̃/ *nm* tracksuit; **veste/pantalon de ~** tracksuit top/bottoms (*pl*) ou pants (*pl*) US; **en ~** in a tracksuit.

survie /syʀvi/ *nf* **1** (maintien en vie) lit, fig survival; **une expérience de ~ en mer** an experiment in survival at sea; **assurer la ~ de qn par des soins intensifs** to maintain sb's life by intensive care; **2** (vie future) afterlife; **croyez-vous à la ~ de l'âme?** do you believe in an afterlife?; **3** Jur survivorship.

survirer /syʀviʀe/ [1] *vi* to oversteer.

survitrage /syʀvitʀaʒ/ *nm* secondary (double) glazing.

survivance /syʀvivɑ̃s/ *nf* survival; **ces danses sont une ~ des combats rituels** these dances are a survival from ritual fights; **~ de l'âme** survival of the soul.

survivant, **~e** /syʀvivɑ̃, ɑ̃t/ **I** *adj* surviving; **conjoint ~** Jur surviving spouse.
II *nm,f* survivor; **c'est l'unique ~e de la famille** she's the sole survivor ou surviving member of the family.

survivre /syʀvivʀ/ [63] **I** *vtr ind* **~ à** to survive [*événement, accident*]; **il n'a pas survécu à ses blessures** he did not survive his wounds; **~ à qn** [*personne*] to outlive sb, survive sb; [*œuvre, influence*] to outlast sb.
II *vi* to survive; **seuls trois passagers ont survécu** only three passengers survived; **son salaire lui permet tout juste de ~** he can just about survive on his salary.
III se survivre *vpr* to live on (**dans** in); **je me survivrai dans mes enfants et dans mes œuvres** I will live on in my children and in my works.

survol /syʀvɔl/ *nm* **1** Aviat flying over ₵; **effectuer le ~ d'un territoire/site** to fly over a territory/site; **interdire le ~ de la capitale** to ban flights over the capital; **2** (de sujet) synopsis (**de** of); (de magazine, livre) quick glance (**de** at); **après un bref ~ historique** after a brief synopsis of the history; **3** Ordinat browsing.

survoler /syʀvɔle/ [1] *vtr* **1** Aviat [*avion, pilote*] to fly over [*lieu*]; **~ une ville à basse altitude** to fly low over a city; **2** (voir superficiellement) [*personne*] to skim through [*livre, magazine*]; to do a quick review of [*problème*].

survoltage /syʀvɔltaʒ/ *nm* controv (transitoire) surge; (durable) overvoltage.

survolté, **~e** /syʀvɔlte/ **I** *pp* ▶ **survolter**.
II○ *pp adj* (surexcité) [*personne, groupe*] overexcited; [*ambiance, atmosphère*] highly charged.

survolter /syʀvɔlte/ [1] *vtr* to boost [*circuit*].

sus /sy(s)/ **I** *adv*‡ **courir ~ à qn** to charge at sb; **~ à l'ennemi!** after them!
II en sus *loc adv* **être en ~** to be extra; **avec en ~ une prime** with a bonus on top; **en ~ de** on top of [*somme, salaire, location*]; in addition to [*choses, conseils*].

susceptibilité /sysɛptibilite/ *nf* touchiness; **être d'une grande ~** to be very touchy, to be oversensitive; **pour ménager les ~s** so as not to upset anybody.

susceptible /sysɛptibl/ *adj* **1** (ombrageux) touchy; **2 ~ de** [*influencer, intéresser*] likely to; **c'est ~ d'être modifié** it may be changed; **force internationale ~ d'intervenir immédiatement** international force which could be brought in immediately; **remarque ~ de plusieurs interprétations** remark open to several interpretations.

susciter /sysite/ [1] *vtr* **1** (provoquer) to spark off [*réaction, trouble, débat*]; **2** (éveiller) to arouse [*sentiment, enthousiasme, intérêt*]; **3** (faire naître) to give rise to [*crainte, réticences, vocation*]; **4** (créer) to create [*problème*] (**à** for).

suscription /syskʀipsjɔ̃/ *nf* superscription.

susdit, **~e** /sysdi, it/ *adj* aforesaid.

sus-dominante /sysdɔminɑ̃t/ *nf* Mus submediant.

susmentionné, **~e** /sysmɑ̃sjɔne/ *adj* aforementioned (*épith*).

susnommé, **~e** /sysnɔme/ *adj, nm,f* aforementioned.

suspect, **~e** /syspɛ, ɛkt/ **I** *adj* [*mort, symptôme, odeur, incendie, circonstances, allure, objet, véhicule*] suspicious; [*origine, information, morale, logique*] dubious; [*aliment, honnêteté, enthousiasme*] suspect; **déceler une odeur ~e** to notice a suspicious smell; [*personne*] suspicious-looking (*épith*); **un tel enthousiasme m'a paru ~** such enthusiasm struck me as suspect; **moi, je**

trouve ça ~ personally I find it suspicious; **je la trouve ~e** she looks suspicious to me; **trouver ~ que** to find it suspicious that; **être ~ de qch** to be suspected of sth; **il est ~ de mensonge** he's suspected of lying; **elle est peu ~e de sympathie à l'égard du régime** she'd hardly be suspected of sympathizing with the regime.
II *nm,f* suspect; **le principal ~** the prime suspect; **la police a interrogé trois ~s** the police have questioned three suspects.

suspecter /syspɛkte/ [1] *vtr* to suspect [*personne, groupe, institution*] (**de** of; **de faire** of doing); **elle a été suspectée de négligence** she was suspected of negligence; **ils sont tous suspectés d'avoir émis de fausses factures** they are all suspected of having forged invoices.

suspendre /syspɑ̃dʀ/ [6] I *vtr* **1** (pendre) to hang up; **~ des vêtements/un jambon/un tableau** to hang up clothes/a ham/a picture; **~ qch à qch** to hang sth on sth; **~ un objet à un clou/au mur** to hang an object on a nail/on the wall; **~ qch/qn par** to hang sth/sb by; **2** (interrompre) to suspend [*émission, publication, relations, paiement*]; to end [*grève*]; to adjourn [*séance, réunion, enquête, procès*]; to stop [*diffusion*]; **~ toute aide économique/l'exécution des travaux/les livraisons de pétrole** to suspend all economic aid/work/oil deliveries; **la séance est suspendue** the meeting is adjourned; **~ un ordre de grève** to suspend strike action; **~ son souffle** to hold one's breath; **~ la cotation d'une action** Fin to suspend a share; **3** (destituer) to suspend [*fonctionnaire, médecin, sportif*] (**de** from); **l'athlète est suspendu de toutes les épreuves** the athlete has been suspended from all events; **~ qn pour six mois** to suspend sb for six months; **on m'a suspendu mon permis de conduire**○ my licence was suspended.
II **se suspendre** *vpr* [*personne, animal*] to hang; **se ~ à une corde/branche** to hang from a rope/branch; **se ~ par les bras/pieds** to hang by one's arms/feet.

suspendu, **~e** /syspɑ̃dy/ I *pp* ▶ **suspendre**.
II *pp adj* [*vêtements, lustre, tableau, jambon*] hanging (**à** from; **par** by); **être ~ aux lèvres de qn** to be hanging on sb's every word; **être ~ au regard de qn** to gaze into sb's eyes; **des maisons ~es au-dessus de la vallée** houses perched above the valley.

suspens: **en suspens** /ɑ̃syspɑ̃/ *loc adv* **1** (en souffrance) [*question, problème*] outstanding (*épith*); **laisser une question/un problème en ~** to leave a question/a problem unresolved; **être/rester en ~** to be/to remain unresolved; **laisser des travaux en ~** to leave work unfinished; **2** (dans l'expectative) in suspense; **tenir qn en ~** to keep sb in suspense; **3** (en suspension) [*fumée, vapeurs*] hanging in the air.

suspense /syspɛns/ *nm* suspense; **maintenir le ~** to maintain the suspense; **le ~ reste entier** everything still hangs in the balance; **film** or **roman à ~** thriller.

suspenseur /syspɑ̃sœʀ/ *nm* Bot suspensor.

suspensif, **-ive** /syspɑ̃sif, iv/ *adj* Jur [*appel, décision*] suspensive.

suspension /syspɑ̃sjɔ̃/ *nf* **1** (attache) suspension; **câble/crochet de ~** suspension cable/hook; **~ d'un pont** suspension bridge; **2** Aut, Tech suspension; **~ hydraulique/indépendante** hydraulic/independent suspension; **la ~ est bonne** the suspension is good; **3** (interruption) (d'aide, de relations, travaux) suspension ¢; (d'enquête, de séance, procès) adjournment ¢; **~ des relations diplomatiques/de l'aide économique** suspension of diplomatic relations/of financial aid; **demander la ~ de la séance** to ask for the session to be adjourned; **4** (sanction) suspension; **~ à vie** lifetime suspension; **risquer une ~ de trois ans** to be facing a three-year suspension; **être condamné à deux ans de ~ du permis de conduire** to be disqualified GB ou suspended US from driving for two years; **5** Chimie suspension; **en ~** [*particules, matières*] in suspension; **6** (éclairage) pendant.
■ **~ d'armes** Mil cease-fire; **~ d'instance** Jur arrest of judgment.

suspensoir /syspɑ̃swaʀ/ *nm* Sport athletic support GB, athletic supporter US, jockstrap○.

suspicieux, **-ieuse** /syspisjø, øz/ *adj* suspicious.

suspicion /syspisjɔ̃/ *nf* suspicion; **un climat de ~** an atmosphere of suspicion; **faire peser la ~ sur qn** to point the finger of suspicion at sb; **avec ~** suspiciously.

Sussex ▶ 692 *nprm* **l'East ~** East Sussex; **le West ~** West Sussex.

sustentation /systɑ̃tasjɔ̃/ *nf* Aviat, Phys lift; **~ magnétique** magnetic levitation; **polygone** or **base de ~** base.

sustenter /systɑ̃te/ [1] I† *vtr* to sustain [*malade*].
II **se sustenter** *vpr* hum to have a little snack.

sus-tonique, *pl* **~s** /systɔnik/ *nf* supertonic.

susurrement /sysyʀmɑ̃/ *nm* whisper.

susurrer /sysyʀe/ [1] *vtr, vi* to whisper.

susvisé, **~e** /sysvize/ *adj* aforementioned.

suture /sytyʀ/ *nf* **1** Méd suture; **point de ~** stitch; **2** Anat, Bot, Zool suture.

suturer /sytyʀe/ [1] *vtr* Méd to stitch up, to suture spéc.

suzerain, **~e** /syzʀɛ̃, ɛn/ Hist I *adj* suzerain.
II *nm,f* suzerain, overlord.

suzeraineté /syzʀɛnte/ *nf* suzerainty.

svastika /svastika/ *nm* swastika.

svelte /svɛlt/ *adj* [*personne, taille*] slender.

sveltesse /svɛltɛs/ *nf* slenderness.

SVP (*written abbr* = **s'il vous plaît**) please.

swahili /swaili/ ▶ 462 *nm* Swahili.

swazi, **~e** /swazi/ ▶ 462, 537 I *adj* Swazi.
II *nm* Ling Swazi.

Swaziland /swazilɑ̃d/ ▶ 321 *nprm* Swaziland.

sweat-shirt, *pl* **~s** /swɛtʃœʀt/ *nm* sweatshirt.

sweepstake /swipstɛk/ *nm* sweepstake.

swing /swiŋ/ *nm* Mus, Sport swing.

swinguer /swiŋge/ [1] *vi* to swing.

sybarite /sibaʀit/ *adj, nmf* sybarite.

sybaritique /sibaʀitik/ *adj* sybarite, sybaritic.

sybaritisme /sibaʀitism/ *nm* sybaritism.

sycomore /sikɔmɔʀ/ *nm* sycamore; ▶ **faux**[1].

sycophante /sikɔfɑ̃t/ *nm* informer.

syllabaire /sil(l)abɛʀ/ *nm* **1** Ling syllabary; **2**† (livre de lecture) primer.

syllabation /sil(l)abasjɔ̃/ *nf* syllabification.

syllabe /sil(l)ab/ *nf* syllable; **~ ouverte/fermée** open/closed syllable.

syllabique /sil(l)abik/ *adj* [*écriture, vers*] syllabic; **méthode ~ (d'apprentissage de la lecture)** phonics (+ *v sg*).

syllogisme /silɔʒism/ *nm* syllogism.

syllogistique /silɔʒistik/ *adj, nf* syllogistic.

sylphe /silf/ *nm* sylph.

sylphide /silfid/ *nf* sylph.

sylvestre /silvɛstʀ/ *adj* liter sylvan littér.

sylvicole /silvikɔl/ *adj* silvicultural.

sylviculteur, **-trice** /silvikyltœʀ, tʀis/ ▶ 510 *nm,f* forester, silviculturist spéc.

sylviculture /silvikyltyʀ/ *nf* forestry, silviculture spéc.

symbiose /sɛ̃bjoz/ *nf* symbiosis; **en ~** in symbiosis.

symbiotique /sɛ̃bjɔtik/ *adj* symbiotic.

symbole /sɛ̃bɔl/ I *nm* **1** gén, Ling, Sci symbol; **2** Relig creed.
II **(-)symbole** (*in compounds*) **femme ~** icon; **une figure ~ du conservatisme** a figurehead of conservatism; **New York, ville ~ du capitalisme** New York, the very symbol of capitalism.
■ **~ des Apôtres** Apostles' Creed.

symbolique /sɛ̃bɔlik/ I *adj* **1** (significatif) [*œuvre, action, portée*] symbolic; **2** (pour la forme) [*geste, salaire, augmentation*] token (*épith*); [*prix*] nominal.
II *nf* **1** (ensemble de symboles) symbolism; **2** (étude) symbology.

symboliquement /sɛ̃bɔlikmɑ̃/ *adv* symbolically.

symbolisation /sɛ̃bɔlizasjɔ̃/ *nf* symbolization.

symboliser /sɛ̃bɔlize/ [1] *vtr* to symbolize.

symbolisme /sɛ̃bɔlism/ *nm* **1** gén, Philos symbolism; **2** Littérat Symbolism.

symboliste /sɛ̃bɔlist/ I *adj* symbolist.
II *nmf* Littérat Symbolist.

symétrie /simetʀi/ *nf* symmetry (**par rapport à** in relation to); **~ axiale/plane** axial/plane symmetry; **axe de ~** axis of symmetry.

symétrique /simetʀik/ *adj* **1** (géométriquement) [*dessin, visage, points*] symmetrical; **2** (en logique, théorie des ensembles) [*relation*] symmetric; **3** (homologue) [*attitudes, aides, objectifs*] similar.

symétriquement /simetʀikmɑ̃/ *adv* symmetrically.

sympa○ /sɛ̃pa/ *adj inv* nice.

sympathie /sɛ̃pati/ *nf* **1** (amitié) **avoir** or **éprouver de la ~ pour qn** to like sb; **montrer** or **témoigner de la ~ à qn** to be friendly toward(s) sb; **elle inspire la ~** she's very likeable; **il m'a tout de suite inspiré une grande ~** I liked him straightaway; **entre nous il y a de la ~, rien d'autre** we just get on, that's all; **faire qch par ~ pour qn** to do sth because one likes sb; **2** (d'un sympathisant) sympathy; **je n'ai aucune ~ pour** I have no sympathy for; **mes ~s vont aux...** my sympathies lie with...; **3** (compassion) sympathy; **croyez à toute ma ~** you have my deepest sympathy; **témoignages de ~** expressions of sympathy.

sympathique /sɛ̃patik/ I *adj* **1** [*personne*] nice, likeable; [*endroit, habitation*] nice, pleasant; [*ambiance, soirée*] pleasant, friendly; [*idée*] nice; **2** Anat sympathetic; **3** [*encre*] invisible.
II *nm* Physiol sympathetic nervous system.

sympathisant, **~e** /sɛ̃patizɑ̃, ɑ̃t/ *nm,f* sympathizer.

sympathiser /sɛ̃patize/ [1] *vi* to get on well (**avec qn** with sb).

symphonie /sɛ̃fɔni/ *nf* symphony; **la ~ Jupiter** the Jupiter Symphony; **une ~ de couleurs** fig a symphony of colours[GB].

symphonique /sɛ̃fɔnik/ *adj* symphonic.

symphoniste /sɛ̃fɔnist/ *nmf* symphonist.

symposium /sɛ̃pozjɔm/ *nm* symposium (**sur** on).

symptomatique /sɛ̃ptɔmatik/ *adj* symptomatic (**de** of).

symptôme /sɛ̃ptom/ *nm* symptom (**de** of); **le phénomène est le ~ d'une crise** the phenomenon is symptomatic of a crisis.

synagogue /sinagɔg/ *nf* synagogue.

synapse /sinaps/ *nf* synapsis.

synarchie /sinaʀʃi/ *nf* synarchy, joint rule.

synchronie /sɛ̃kʀɔni/ *nf* synchrony.

synchronique /sɛ̃kʀɔnik/ *adj* synchronic.

synchroniquement /sɛ̃kʀɔnikmɑ̃/ *adv* synchronically.

synchronisation /sɛ̃kʀɔnizasjɔ̃/ *nf* synchronization.

synchroniser /sɛ̃kʀɔnize/ [1] *vtr* to synchronize.

synchroniseur /sɛ̃kʀɔnizœʀ/ *nm* **1** Électrotech synchronizer; **2** Aut synchromesh.

synchroniseuse /sɛ̃kʀɔnizøz/ *nf* Cin synchronizer.

synchronisme /sɛ̃kʀɔnism/ *nm* synchronism.

synclinal, **~e**, *mpl* **-aux** /sɛ̃klinal, o/ **I** *adj* synclinal.

II *nm* syncline.

syncope /sɛ̃kɔp/ *nf* **1** Méd fainting fit; **avoir une ~** to have a fainting fit; **tomber en ~** to faint; **2** Ling syncope; **3** Mus syncopation.

syncopé, **~e** /sɛ̃kɔpe/ *adj* [*rythme, musique*] syncopated.

syncrétisme /sɛ̃kʀetism/ *nm* syncretism.

syndic /sɛ̃dik/ *nm* (d'immeuble) property manager.

■ **~ de faillite** Jur official receiver.

syndical, **~e**, *mpl* **-aux** /sɛ̃dikal, o/ *adj* (trade) union (*épith*); **accord/dirigeant/mouvement/droit ~** union agreement/leader/movement/law.

syndicalisation /sɛ̃dikalizasjɔ̃/ *nf* unionization.

syndicalisme /sɛ̃dikalism/ *nm* **1** (fait social) trade unionism; **2** (activité) union activities (*pl*); **faire du ~** to be a union activist; **3** (doctrine) syndicalism.

syndicaliste /sɛ̃dikalist/ **I** *adj* (trade) union (*épith*); **dirigeant ~** union leader.

II *nmf* union activist.

syndicat /sɛ̃dika/ *nm* (d'ouvriers) trade union; (d'agriculteurs) union; (d'employeurs) association.

■ **~ agricole** farmers' union; **~ du crime** underworld; **~ financier** financial syndicate; **~ de fonctionnaires** civil service union; **~ d'initiative** tourist information office; **~ intercommunal** association of communes (*in France*); **~ ouvrier** trade union; **~ patronal** employers' association; **~ professionnel** trade association; **~ de propriétaires** association of property owners.

syndicataire /sɛ̃dikatɛʀ/ *nmf* Assur, Fin underwriter.

syndiqué, **~e** /sɛ̃dike/ **I** *pp* ▶ **syndiquer**.

II *pp adj* **1** Pol unionized; **main-d'œuvre non ~e** non-union labour[GB]; **être ~** to be a union member; **2** Fin [*prêt, titres*] syndicated.

III *nm,f* union member.

syndiquer /sɛ̃dike/ [1] **I** *vtr* to unionize.

II se syndiquer *vpr* **1** [*personne*] to join a union; **2** [*profession*] to form a trade union.

syndrome /sɛ̃dʀom/ *nm* syndrome.

■ **~ du choc toxique**, **SCT** Toxic Shock Syndrome, TSS; **~ de Down** Down's Syndrome; **~ immunodéficitaire acquis** acquired immunodeficiency syndrome.

synecdoque /sinɛkdɔk/ *nf* synecdoche.

synérèse /sineʀɛz/ *nf* syneresis.

synergie /sinɛʀʒi/ *nf* synergy (**entre** between); **des ~s économiques/industrielles** economic/industrial synergies.

synergique /sinɛʀʒik/ *adj* synergic.

synesthésie /sinɛstezi/ *nf* synaesthesia.

synode /sinɔd/ *nm* synod.

synodique /sinɔdik/ *adj* **1** Astron synodic; **2** Relig synodal.

synonyme /sinɔnim/ **I** *adj* synonymous (**de** with); **pour lui Paris est ~ de liberté** for him Paris is synonymous with freedom.

II *nm* synonym (**de** for, of); **un dictionnaire de ~s** ≈ a thesaurus.

synonymie /sinɔnimi/ *nf* synonymy.

synonymique /sinɔnimik/ *adj* synonymic.

synopsis /sinɔpsis/ *nm inv* Cin synopsis.

synoptique /sinɔptik/ *adj* synoptic.

synovial, **~e**, *mpl* **-iaux** /sinɔvjal, o/ **I** *adj* synovial.

II synoviale *nf* synovial membrane.

synovie /sinɔvi/ *nf* synovia; **avoir un épanchement de ~** to have water on the knee.

synovite /sinɔvit/ ▶ 271 *nf* synovitis.

syntactique /sɛ̃taktik/ *adj* = **syntaxique**.

syntagmatique /sɛ̃tagmatik/ *adj* phrasal, syntagmatic; **grammaire ~** phrase-structure grammar; **règle ~** phrase-structure rule.

syntagme /sɛ̃tagm/ *nm* phrase, syntagm; **~ verbal/nominal** verb/noun phrase.

syntaxe /sɛ̃taks/ *nf* syntax.

syntaxique /sɛ̃taksik/ *adj* syntactic(al).

synthé○ /sɛ̃te/ *nm* (*abbr* = **synthétiseur**) synth○.

synthèse /sɛ̃tɛz/ *nf* **1** (d'idées) synthesis; (résumé) summary; **document** or **rapport de ~** summary; **faire la ~ de plusieurs documents** to extract the essential facts from several documents; **esprit de ~** ability to synthesize; **2** Chimie synthesis; **par ~** by synthesis; **produit de ~** synthetic product; **~ des protéines** protein synthesis; **3** Ordinat **images** or **imagerie de ~** computer generated images.

synthétique /sɛ̃tetik/ **I** *adj* **1** Chimie synthetic; Tech synthetic; **2** (non analytique) [*approche, réflexion, vision*] global; [*ouvrage*] that gives a general picture (*épith, après n*); **3** Ling synthetic; **4** Mus synthetic, synthesized.

II *nm* Tex synthetic material; **c'est du ~** it's synthetic.

synthétiquement /sɛ̃tetikmɑ̃/ *adv* synthetically.

synthétiser /sɛ̃tetize/ [1] *vtr* to synthesize.

synthétiseur /sɛ̃tetizœʀ/ *nm* synthesizer.

■ **~ de parole** speech ou voice synthesizer.

syntoniseur /sɛ̃tɔnizœʀ/ *nm* Radio tuner.

syphilis /sifilis/ ▶ 271 *nf* syphilis.

syphilitique /sifilitik/ *adj, nmf* syphilitic.

Syrie /siʀi/ ▶ 321 *nprf* Syria.

syrien, **-ienne** /siʀjɛ̃, ɛn/ ▶ 537 *adj* Syrian.

Syrien, **-ienne** /siʀjɛ̃, ɛn/ ▶ 537 *nm,f* Syrian.

systématique /sistematik/ **I** *adj* **1** [*classification, recherche, contrôle, refus, opposition*] systematic; [*aide, soutien*] unconditional; **de façon ~** systematically; **travailler de façon ~** to work systematically ou in a systematic way; **2** [*personne*] systematic; péj narrow, dogmatic.

II *nf* systematics (+ *v sg*).

systématiquement /sistematikmɑ̃/ *adv* systematically.

systématisation /sistematizasjɔ̃/ *nf* systematization.

systématiser /sistematize/ [1] **I** *vtr* to systematize.

II se systématiser *vpr* to become the rule.

système /sistɛm/ *nm* **1** (ensemble organisé, doctrine) system; **~ économique/légal/pénitentiaire** economic/legal/prison system; **entrer dans le ~** to join the system; **~ de vie** way of life; **2** (dispositif, réunion d'éléments) system; **~ d'éclairage/de transmission** lighting/transmission system; **~ de miroirs/poulies** system of mirrors/pulleys; **~ de canaux** canal system ou network; **3** (plan, méthode) system, scheme; **4** (moyen) system, way; (combine) dodge○; **prenons l'avion, c'est encore le meilleur ~** let's go by plane, it's still the best way; **5** Physiol system; **troubles du ~** Méd systemic disorders; **~ cardio-vasculaire** cardiovascular system; **~ nerveux central/végétatif** central nervous/vegetative system; **~ pileux** Physiol hair; **avoir un ~ pileux fourni** to have a lot of hair; **~ digestif** digestive system; **6** Ordinat system; **analyse/conception de ~s** systems analysis/design; **~ de gestion de bases de données** database (management) system; **~ expert** expert system; **~ d'exploitation** operating system; **~ d'information pour le management** management information system; **~ informatique** information system; **~ intégré de gestion** integrated management system; **7** Astron system; **~ planétaire/solaire** planetary/solar system.

■ **~ d'alarme** burglar alarm, alarm system; **~ casuel** Ling case system; **le ~ D**○ resourcefulness; **j'ai eu un billet par le ~ D**○ I wangled○ a ticket; **~ décimal** decimal system; **~ d'encouragement** Entr incentive scheme; **~ de gestion de bases de données**, **SGBD** Ordinat database management system, DBMS; **~ métrique** metric system; **~ monétaire européen**, **SME** European Monetary System, EMS; **~ nuageux** Météo cloud system; **~ de participation (aux bénéfices)** profit-sharing scheme.

IDIOMES **taper** or **courir sur le ~ de qn**○ to get on sb's nerves ou wick○ GB.

systémique /sistemik/ **I** *adj* systematic.

II *nf* systematism.

systole /sistɔl/ *nf* systole; **~ auriculaire/ventriculaire** auricular/ventricular systole.

systolique /sistɔlik/ *adj* systolic.

syzygie /siziʒi/ *nf* syzygy.

Tt

t, T /te/ *nm inv* t, T; **en (forme de) T** T-shaped.

t' ▶ **te.**

ta ▶ **ton**[1].

tabac /taba/ **I** ▶**193** *adj inv* tobacco-coloured[GB].
II *nm* **1** Bot, Ind tobacco; **feuille de ~** tobacco leaf; **'journée sans ~'** 'no smoking day'; **2** ▶**510** Comm (magasin d'articles pour fumeurs) tobacconist's GB, smoke shop US; (magasin de cigarettes, journaux) newsagent GB; **3**○ (succès) big hit; **faire un ~** [*personne, spectacle, produit*] to be a big hit; **4** Naut **coup de ~** squall.
■ **~ blond** Virginia tobacco; **~ brun** dark tobacco; **~ à chiquer** chewing tobacco; **~ à cigarettes** cigarette tobacco; **~ à pipe** pipe tobacco; **~ à priser** snuff; **~ à rouler** rolling tobacco.
IDIOMES **passer qn à ~**○ [*voyous*] to beat sb up.

tabagie /tabaʒi/ *nf* smoky place; **c'est une vraie ~ ici!** it's really smoky in here!

tabagisme /tabaʒism/ *nm* **1** (dépendance) tobacco addiction; **2** (intoxication) nicotine poisoning.

tabar(d) /tabaʀ/ *nm* tabard.

tabassage○ /tabasaʒ/ *nm* **1** (mise à mal) beating; **il a été victime d'un ~ en règle** he was badly beaten up; **2** (bagarre) gang-fight.

tabasser○ /tabase/ [1] **I** *vtr* to give [sb] a beating; **se faire ~** to get a beating.
II se tabasser *vpr* to lay into each other○.

tabatière /tabatjɛʀ/ *nf* **1** (boîte à tabac) snuff-box; **2** Constr (lucarne) skylight.

TABDT /teabedete/ *nm* (*abbr* = **vaccin antityphoïdique et antiparatyphoïdique A et B, antidiphtérique et tétanique**) triple vaccine.

tabellion† /tabeljɔ̃/ *nm* **1** (qui rédigeait des actes) scrivener; **2** (notaire) notary (public).

tabernacle /tabɛʀnakl/ **I** *nm* tabernacle.
II○ *excl* C damn○!

tablard /tablaʀ/ *nm* H (rayon, tablette) shelf.

tablature /tablatyʀ/ *nf* tablature.

table /tabl/ *nf* **1** (meuble) table; **une ~ en** or **de chêne** an oak table; **une ~ de salle à manger/de cuisine** a dining-room/kitchen table; **2** (lieu du repas) table; **à ~** at (the) table; **mettre** or **dresser la ~** to set ou lay the table; **être/fumer à ~** to be/to smoke at the table; **bien/mal se tenir à ~** to have good/bad table manners; **rester à ~ après le repas** to remain at the table after the meal; **nous serons dix à ~ ce midi** there'll be ten of us for lunch today; **nous étions toujours à ~ quand...** we were still eating when...; **s'asseoir à ~** (pour manger) to sit down to eat; **viens t'asseoir à ~!** come and sit at the table!; **passer** or **se mettre à ~** lit to sit down at the table; (avouer)○ to spill the beans○; **sortir** or **se lever de ~** to leave the table; **réserver une ~ (pour cinq)** to book GB ou reserve a table (for five); **à ~!** dinner's ready!; **3** (nourriture) table; **avoir une bonne ~** to keep a good table; **~ remarquable** or **de roi** marvellous[GB] spread; **restaurant réputé pour sa ~ et sa cave** restaurant with a reputation for its good food and wine cellar; **4** (lieu de discussion) table; **~ des négociations/débats** negotiating/debating table; **s'asseoir autour d'une** or **de la même ~** to get round the table; **mettre un million/le double sur la ~** to put a million/twice as much on the table; **5** (tablée) table; **présider la ~** to be at the head of the table; **6** Tech (partie plane) (de fraiseuse, ponceuse) table; (de raboteuse) bed; (d'enclume) face; **7** Math table; **~ de logarithmes/de multiplication** log/multiplication table; **~ à double entrée** two-way table; **8** Minér (facette supérieure d'une pierre) table.
■ **~ analytique** analytical table; **~ d'autel** altar table; **~ basse** coffee table; **~ de billard** billiard table; **~ de bridge** bridge table; **~ de camping** camping table; **~ de chevet** bedside table GB, night stand US; **~ de cuisson** hob; **~ à dessin** drawing board; **~ d'école** school desk; **~ d'écoute** wiretapping set; **être mis sur ~ d'écoute** to have one's phone tapped; **~ de ferme** farmhouse table; **~ glaciaire** Géog glacier table; **~ d'harmonie** sounding board; **~ d'honneur** head table; **~ d'hôte** table d'hôte; **~ de jardin** garden table; **~ de jeu** Jeux card table; **~ de lancement** launching pad; **~ à langer** changing table; **~ lumineuse** (pour diapositives) slide table; **~ de massage** massage table; **~ des matières** (table of) contents; **~ de mixage** mixing console; **~ de montage** editing bench ou table; **~ de nuit** bedside table GB, nightstand US; **~ d'opération** operating table; **~ d'orientation** viewpoint diagram; **~ à ouvrage** sewing table; **~ de ping-pong**® table-tennis table; **~ pliante** folding table; **~ à rallonges** extending table; **~ de repassage** or **à repasser** ironing board; **~ ronde** lit, fig round table; **~ ronde sur l'immigration** round table (talks) on immigration; **~ roulante** trolley; **~ de soudage** welding bench; **~ de télévision** television stand; **~ de tir** range table; **~ de toilette** washstand; **~ tournante** (phénomène) table turning; **~ traçante** Ordinat graph plotter; **~ de travail** worktable; **~ de vérité** truth table; **~s gigognes** nest of tables; **Tables de la Loi** Bible Tables of the Law.
IDIOMES **mettre les pieds sous la ~** to let others wait on you; **tenir ~ ouverte** to keep open house.

tableau, *pl* **~x** /tablo/ *nm* **1** (œuvre d'art) gén picture; (peinture) painting; ▶**galerie, vieux**; **2** (description) picture; **brosser un ~ sombre de la situation** to paint a black picture of the situation; **et pour achever** or **compléter le ~** and to cap it all; **3** (spectacle) picture; **des enfants jouant dans un jardin, quel ~ charmant!** children playing in a garden, what a charming picture!; **le ~ général est plus sombre** the overall picture is more gloomy; **en plus, il était ivre, tu vois un peu le ~**○! on top of that he was drunk, you can just imagine!; **4** (présentation graphique) table, chart; **'voir ~'** 'see table'; **~ des marées** tide table; **~ des températures** temperature chart; **~ synchronique/synoptique** historical/synoptic chart; **~ à double entrée** Ordinat two-dimensional array; **présenter qch sous forme de ~** to present sth in tabular form; **5** Scol blackboard; **écrire qch au ~** to write sth on the blackboard; **passer** or **aller au ~** to go (up) to the blackboard; **6** (affichant des renseignements) board; Rail indicator board; **~ des départs/arrivées** departures/arrivals indicator; **~ horaire** timetable; **7** (support mural) board; **~ des clés** key rack; **~ pour fusibles** fuse box; **8** (liste) register GB, roll US; **9** Théât short scene.
■ **~ d'affichage** notice board; **~ d'avancement** promotion table, roster list; **~ blanc** white board; **~ de bord** Aut dashboard; Aviat, Rail instrument panel; (en gestion) performance indicators (*pl*); **~ de chasse** (de chasseur) total number of kills; (de séducteur) list of conquests; (de pilote de chasse) total number of hits; **~ clinique** patient's charts (*pl*); **~ de commande** control panel; **~ comptable** financial statement; **~ de conférence** paperboard; **~ d'honneur** honours board GB, honor roll US; **être inscrit au ~ d'honneur** to be on the honours board GB ou honor roll US; **~ de maître** Art master painting; **~ de marche** flow chart; **~ matriciel** matrix; **~ noir** blackboard; **~ papier** paperboard; **~ de prix** price list; **~ vivant** tableau vivant.
IDIOMES **jouer** or **miser sur les deux ~x** to hedge one's bets; **gagner/perdre sur tous les ~x** to win/to lose on all counts.

tableautin /tablotɛ̃/ *nm* little picture.

tablée /table/ *nf* table; **~ de journalistes** table of journalists; **repas pour une grande ~** meal for a large party.

tabler /table/ [1] *vi* **~ sur** to bank○ on.

tablette /tablɛt/ **I** *nf* **1** (de chocolat) bar; (de chewing-gum) stick; **2** (étagère) shelf; **~ de marbre** marble shelf; **3** Pharm tablet; **~ de codéine** codeine tablet; **4** Archéol tablet; **~ d'argile** clay tablet.
II tablettes *nfpl* **1** (archives) annals; **2** (agenda) diary (*sg*); **j'ai inscrit notre rendez-vous dans mes ~s** I've made a note of our meeting in my diary.
■ **~ graphique** Ordinat graphic tablet.

tableur /tablœʀ/ *nm* spreadsheet.

tablier /tablije/ *nm* **1** (vêtement) apron; **2** (de pont) roadway.
IDIOMES **rendre son ~** to give US ou give in GB one's notice.

tabloïd /tablɔid/ *adj, nm* tabloid.

tabou /tabu/ **I** *adj* **1** (frappé d'interdit) taboo; (qu'on ne peut critiquer) [*institution, personnage*] untouchable, sacred; **2** Anthrop, Relig taboo.
II *nm* taboo.

taboulé /tabule/ *nm* tabouleh, tabouli.

tabouret /tabuʀɛ/ *nm* **1** (pour s'asseoir) stool; **2** (pour les pieds) footstool.

tabulateur /tabylatœʀ/ *nm* tabulator.

tabulation /tabylasjɔ̃/ *nf* tabulation; **taquet** or **marque de ~** tab, tabulator.

tabulatrice /tabylatʀis/ *nf* tabulator.

tac /tak/ **I** *nm* **répondre du ~ au ~** to snap back.

II *excl* **et ~!** so there!

tache /taʃ/ *nf* **1** lit (salissure) stain; **~ d'encre** gén ink stain; (sur un manuscrit) ink blot; **~ de graisse/d'huile** grease/oil stain; **~ d'humidité** damp patch; **~ de sang** bloodstain; **résister aux ~s** to be stain-resistant; **tu as fait une ~ à ton pantalon** you've got a stain on your trousers; **tu as fait une ~ sur la table** you've made a mark on the table; **faire ~** fig to stick out like a sore thumb; **2** fig (souillure) stain, blot (**à** on); **sans ~** [*réputation, honnêteté*] spotless, unblemished; [*vie*] blameless; **3** (altération) (sur un fruit) mark; (sur la peau) blotch, mark; **4** (note de couleur) (petite) spot; (plus grande) patch; **les ~s du léopard** the leopard's spots; **~s de lumière/ d'ombre** patches of light/of shade; **les affiches sont les seules ~s de couleur** the posters are the only splashes of colour[GB].

■ **~ jaune** Anat yellow spot; **~ de naissance** birthmark; **~ originelle** taint of original sin; **~ solaire** Astron sunspot; **~ de vin** gén wine stain; Anat strawberry mark; **~ de vieillesse** liver spot; **~s de rousseur** or **son** freckles.

IDIOMES **faire ~ d'huile** to spread like wildfire.

tâche /tɑʃ/ *nf* task, job; **une ~ difficile/ingrate** a difficult/thankless task; **tu ne me facilites pas la ~!** you're not making my job any easier!; **mener une ~ à bien** to see a job through; **avoir pour ~ de faire qch** to have the job of doing sth; **ne pas avoir la ~ facile** not to have an easy job; **être à la hauteur de sa ~** to be up to the job; **les ~s ménagères** household chores; **être payé à la ~** to be paid by the piece; **travailler** or **être à la ~** to be on piece-work.

tachéomètre /takeɔmɛtʀ/ *nm* tachymeter, tacheometer.

tachéométrie /takeɔmetʀi/ *nf* tacheometry.

tacher /taʃe/ [1] **I** *vtr* **1** lit (salir) [*substance*] to stain; [*personne*] to get a stain on; **taché d'huile/d'encre** oil-/ink-stained; **taché de sang** bloodstained; **tu vas ~ ta robe** you'll get a stain on your dress; **j'ai taché ma cravate** I've got a stain on my tie; **2** fig (souiller) to tarnish, to stain [*réputation*]; **3** liter (colorer) to mark [*pelage, plumage*]; **pelage gris taché de blanc** grey GB or gray US fur with white markings.

II *vi* [*fruit, vin, produit*] to stain; **ça ne tache pas** it doesn't stain.

III se tacher *vpr* **1** [*personne*] to get oneself dirty; **tu t'es tachée avec de l'encre/de l'huile** you've got ink/oil on your clothes; **2** [*tissu, tapis*] to stain, to mark; **3** [*fruit*] to become blemished.

tâcher /tɑʃe/ [1] **I** *vtr* **tâchez que ce soit fini avant midi** (conseil) try and make sure it's finished before noon; (ordre) see to it that it's finished before noon.

II tâcher de *vtr ind* **~ de faire** to try to do; **je vais ~ de le joindre avant midi** I'll try and contact him before noon; **tâchez de venir** try and come; **tâchez d'arriver à l'heure** try and be on time.

tâcheron /tɑʃʀɔ̃/ *nm* **1** péj (qui fait des tâches ingrates) drudge; (qui travaille beaucoup) hack; **un ~ de la littérature** a literary hack; **un ~ de la peinture** a hack artist; **2** (petit entrepreneur) jobber.

tacheter /taʃte/ [20] *vtr* to speckle, to spot [*pelage, plumage*]; to dot [*pré*]; **plumage gris tacheté de blanc** grey plumage speckled ou flecked with white.

tachisme /taʃism/ *nm* (en peinture abstraite) action painting, tachism(e).

tachiste /taʃist/ *nmf* action painter.

Tachkent /taʃkɛnt/ ▶ **416** *npr* Tashkent.

tachycardie /takikaʀdi/ ▶ **271** *nf* tachycardia.

tachygraphe /takigʀaf/ *nm* tachograph.

tachymètre /takimɛtʀ/ *nm* tachometer.

tacite /tasit/ *adj* tacit.

Tacite /tasit/ *npr* Tacitus.

tacitement /tasitmɑ̃/ *adv* tacitly.

taciturne /tasityʀn/ *adj* taciturn.

tacon /takɔ̃/ *nm* Zool parr.

tacot○ /tako/ *nm* banger○ GB, crate○ US.

tact /takt/ *nm* **1** (délicatesse) tact; **avoir beaucoup de ~** to be very tactful; **manquer de ~** to be tactless; **avec ~** tactfully; **2** Physiol sense of touch.

tacticien, -ienne /taktisjɛ̃, ɛn/ *nm,f* gén, Mil tactician.

tactile /taktil/ *adj* **1** Biol [*sensibilité*] tactile; **2** Ordinat [*écran*] touch-sensitive.

tactique /taktik/ **I** *adj* gén, Mil tactical; **manœuvre/erreur ~** tactical manoeuvre GB ou maneuver US/error.

II *nf* **1** (*pl*) gén tactics; **il a changé de ~** he changed tactics; **2** Mil (science) tactics (+ *v sg*).

tactiquement /taktikmɑ̃/ *adv* tactically.

tadjik /tadʒik/ ▶ **462**, **537** *adj, nm* Tajik.

Tadjik, ~e /tadʒik/ ▶ **537** *nm,f* Tajik.

Tadjikistan /tadʒikistɑ̃/ ▶ **321** *nprm* Tajikistan.

tadorne /tadɔʀn/ *nm* (mâle) sheldrake; (femelle) shelduck.

taffe◐ /taf/ *nf* (bouffée) drag○.

taffetas /tafta/ *nm inv* taffeta; **robe de ~** taffeta dress.

■ **~ gommé** (sticking) plaster GB, Band-Aid®.

tag○ /tag/ *nm* **1** (graffiti) a piece of graffiti; **des ~s** graffiti; **2** (activité) writing ou spraying graffiti.

Tage /taʒ/ ▶ **357** *nprm* **le ~** the Tagus.

tagger○ = **tagueur**.

tagliatelles /taljatɛl/ *nfpl* Culin tagliatelli ¢.

tagmème /tagmɛm/ *nm* Ling tagmeme.

tagmémique /tagmemik/ *nf* tagmemics (+ *v sg*).

taguer○ /tage/ [1] *vi* to write ou spray grafitti.

tagueur○ /tagœʀ/ *nm* gén graffiti sprayer; (artiste) graffiti artist.

Tahiti /taiti/ ▶ **416** *nprf* Tahiti.

tahitien, -ienne /taisjɛ̃, ɛn/ **I** *adj* Tahitian.

II ▶ **462** *nm* Ling Tahitian.

Tahitien, -ienne /taisjɛ̃, ɛn/ *nm,f* Tahitian.

TAI /teai/ *nm: abbr* ▶ **temps**.

taïaut /tajo/ *excl* tallyho!

taie /tɛ/ *nf* **1** (enveloppe) **~ (d'oreiller)** pillowcase; **~ (de traversin)** bolstercase; **2** (sur l'œil) corneal opacity.

taïga /tajga/ *nf* taiga.

taillable /tajabl/ *adj* Hist subject to tallage; **je ne suis pas ~ et corvéable à merci** I'm not here to be at everybody's beck and call.

taillade /tajad/ *nf* **1** (dans les chairs) cut; (volontaire) slash; **2** Cout slash.

taillader /tajade/ [1] **I** *vtr* to slash [*poignets, rideaux*]; **~ une table** to make slashes on a table top.

II se taillader *vpr* **se ~ les poignets** to slash one's wrists; **se ~ les mains** to cut one's hands badly.

taille /taj/ *nf* **1** ▶ **188** (partie du corps, de vêtement) waist, waistline; **~ fine/épaisse** slim/large waist ou waistline; **avoir une ~ de guêpe** to be wasp-waisted, to have a very slim waist; **prendre qn par la ~** to put one's arm around sb's waist; **avoir la ~ bien prise dans un manteau** to wear a coat with a fitted waist; **robe à ~ haute/basse** high-/low-waisted dress; **2** (volume) size; fig (importance) size; **de grande/petite ~** [*animal, entreprise, objet*] large/small; **entreprise de ~ moyenne** medium-sized company; **de la ~ de** the size of; **société de ~ européenne** company on a European scale; **de ~** [*problème, ambition, enjeu*] considerable, sizable; [*événement, question*] very important; **à la ~ de leurs ambitions/de l'entreprise** in keeping with their ambitions/the size of the company; **un partenaire à sa ~** a suitable partner; **l'entreprise est de ~!** it's no small undertaking!; **être de ~ à faire** to be up to ou capable of doing; **il n'est pas de ~** he's not up to it; **3** (dimension de vêtement) size; **~ 42** size 42; **quelle ~ fais-tu?** what size do you take?; **ce n'est pas ma ~** or **à ma ~** it is not my size; **'~ unique'** 'one size'; **essaie la ~ au-dessus/au-dessous** try the next size up/down; **qu'avez-vous à ma ~?** what have you got in my size?; **avoir la ~ mannequin** to be a standard size; **rayon grandes ~s** outsize department; **rayon petites ~s** petite department; **4** (hauteur) height; **être de grande/petite ~** to be tall/ short; **personne de petite/grande ~** short/tall person; **personne de ~ moyenne** person of average height; **se redresser de toute sa ~** to draw oneself up to one's full height; **il a promené sa haute ~ dans toute l'Europe** his tall figure is known throughout Europe; **5** (action de tailler) (d'arbre, buisson) pruning; (de haie) clipping, trimming; (de diamant, cristal) cutting; (de bois) carving; **6** (forme obtenue) (de diamant) cut; (de haie) shape; **7** Hist **la ~** tallage; **8** (tranchant de lame) edge; **9** Mines (galerie) tunnel.

taillé, ~e /taje/ **I** *pp* ▶ **tailler**.

II *pp adj* **1** (bâti) **~ en athlète** built like an athlete; **2** (apte) **être ~ pour faire** to be cut out to do; **il est ~ pour**○ he's cut out for it; **3** (coupé) **cristal ~** cut glass.

taille-crayons /tajkʀɛjɔ̃/ *nm inv* pencil sharpener.

taille-douce, *pl* **tailles-douces** /tajdus/ *nf* copperplate engraving; **impression en ~** copperplate printing.

tailler /taje/ [1] **I** *vtr* **1** (couper) to cut [*rubis, cristal, marbre*]; to carve [*bois*]; to sharpen [*crayon*]; to prune [*arbre, buisson*]; to cut, to clip [*haie*]; to trim [*cheveux, barbe*]; **~ une armée en pièces** to hack an army to pieces; **elle l'a taillé en pièces** fig she made mincemeat of him○; **bien taillé** [*moustache, haie*] neatly trimmed; [*veste*] well-cut; **taillé en pointe** [*crayon*] sharpened to a point; [*barbe*] trimmed to a point; **buisson taillé en cône** shrub trimmed into a cone shape; **diamant taillé en rose** rose-cut diamond; **visage taillé à la serpe** craggy features (*pl*); **2** (découper) to cut [*steak*] (**dans** from); to carve [*sculpture*]; to cut out [*vêtement*]; **~ une statue dans du marbre** to carve a statue in marble; **~ une robe dans de la soie** to make a dress out of silk; **~ un costume sur mesure** to make a suit to measure; **taillé sur mesure** [*vêtement*] made-to-measure GB, custom-made; fig [*rôle*] tailor-made; **des mots taillés dans la pierre** words carved in stone.

II *vi* **1** (faire des coupes dans) **~ dans les chairs** or **le vif** to cut into the flesh; **~ dans les programmes sociaux** fig to make cuts in the social programmes[GB]; **2** (être coupé) **~ grand/petit** [*vêtements*] to be cut on the large/small side.

III se tailler *vpr* **1** (se faire) to carve out [sth] for oneself [*carri ère, empire*]; to make [sth] for oneself [*belle réputation*]; **se ~ une grande part du marché** to corner a large share of the market; **se ~ un vif succès** to be a great success; **2**◐ (s'enfuir) to beat it○; (partir) **il faut que je me taille** I've gotta go ou run○; **3** (se couper) **se ~ la moustache** to trim one's moustache GB ou mustache US.

IDIOMES **~ une pipe à qn**● to give sb a blow job●; **ils sont tous taillés sur le même modèle** they are all exactly alike.

tailleur /tajœʀ/ **I** *nm* **1** (tenue) (woman's) suit; **être en ~ rouge** to be in a red suit; **2** ▶ **510** (personne) tailor; **s'asseoir/être**

Les tailles

Les tailles britanniques et américaines données dans les tableaux ci-dessous sont parfois arrondies aux tailles immédiatement supérieures: mieux vaut un vêtement un peu trop grand qu'un peu trop petit.

Les chaussures d'homme

en France	en GB et aux US
39	6½
40	7
41	7½
42	8½
43	9
44	10
45	11
46	12

Les chaussures de femme

en France	en GB	aux US
35	3	6
36	3½	6½
37	4	7
38	5	7½
39	6	8
40	7	8½
41	8	9

Les vêtements d'homme

en France	en GB et aux US
38	28
40	30
42	32
44	34
46	36
48	38
50	40
52	42
54	44
56	46

Les vêtements de femme*

en France	en GB	aux US
34	8	4
36	10	6
38	12	8
40	12	8
42	14	10
44	16	12
46	16	12
48	18	14
50	20	16

* Ces tailles sont utilisées pour les robes, chemisiers, pantalons, etc.

Les chemises d'homme

en France	en GB et aux US
36	14
37	14½
38	15
39	15½
40	16
41	16½
42	17
43	17½
44	18

L'anglais emploie le mot size *à la fois pour les vêtements et pour les chaussures.*

quelle taille faites-vous?	= what size are you?
quelle pointure faites-vous?	= what size are you?
faire du 85 de tour de poitrine	= to have a 34-inch bust
faire du 61 de tour de taille	= to have a 24-inch waist *ou* to measure 24 inches round the waist
faire du 90 de tour de hanches	= to measure 36 inches round the hips
avez-vous une taille 40?	= have you got a size 40?
avez-vous du 7?	= have you got a size 7?
je porte du 42	= I take a size 42
je fais du 52	= my size is 52
je chausse du 40	= my shoe size is 40
je cherche un 40	= I'm looking for a shirt with a size 16 collar
une paire de chaussures en 42	= a pair of shoes size 42
une chemise taille 15	= a shirt size 15 *ou* a size 15 shirt
avez-vous ce modèle en 40?	= have you got the same thing in a 16?
avez-vous ce modèle en plus grand?	= have you got this in a larger size?
avez-vous ce modèle en plus petit?	= have you got the same thing in a smaller size?

assis en ~ to sit down/to be sitting cross-legged.

II tailleur(-) (*in compounds*) **~(-)short** shorts suit; **~(-)pantalon** trouser suit GB, pantsuit US.

■ **~ pour dames** ladies' tailor; **~ de pierre** stone-cutter; **~ de diamants** diamond-cutter.

taillis /taji/ *nm inv* (broussailles) undergrowth ¢; (sous-bois) coppice.

tain /tɛ̃/ *nm* silvering; **glace** or **miroir sans ~** two-way mirror.

taire /tɛʀ/ [59] **I** *vtr* **1** (ne pas dire) not to reveal [*nom, secret*]; to hush up [*vérité*]; **dire ce qu'on aurait dû ~** to say what would have been better left unsaid; **2** liter (cacher) to keep [sth] to oneself [*tristesse, dépit*].

II se taire *vpr* **1** (ne pas parler) [*personne*] to be silent, to say nothing; [*nature, oiseaux*] to be silent; (ne pas dire qch) to remain silent; **se ~ sur qch** to keep quiet about sth; **il souffre et se tait** he suffers in silence; **tu as perdu une belle occasion de te ~** you would have done better to have kept quiet; **2** (cesser de parler) to stop talking, to fall silent; [*oiseau*] to fall silent; (cesser de s'exprimer) [*journaliste, opposition*] to fall silent; **faire ~** to make [sb] be quiet [*élèves*]; to silence [*opposant, sceptiques*]; to silence [*média*]; to put a stop to [*rumeurs, sarcasmes*]; **faire ~ sa jalousie** to stifle one's jealousy; **fais ~ les enfants!** keep the children quiet!, shut the children up○!; **tais-toi!** (ne parle pas) be quiet!; (ne m'en parle pas) don't talk to me about that!; **3** (s'arrêter) [*bruit, musique*] to stop; [*canon, orchestre*] to fall silent.

Taiwan /tajwan/ **▶692** *nprm* Taiwan.

taiwanais, **~e** /tajwanɛ, ɛz/ **▶462**, **692** *adj* Taiwanese.

Taiwanais, **~e** /tajwanɛ, ɛz/ *nm,f* Taiwanese.

talc /talk/ *nm* **1** (poudre) talc, talcum powder; **2** (minéral) talc(um).

talé, **~e** /tale/ *adj* [*fruit*] bruised.

talent /talɑ̃/ *nm* **1** (aptitude) talent; **exercer ses ~s de linguiste** to use one's talents as a linguist; **avoir du ~** to be talented, to have talent; **de ~** talented, gifted; **2** (personne douée) **chercher de nouveaux ~s** to look for new talent; **encourager un jeune ~** to give encouragement to a talented young person; **3** Antiq (monnaie) talent.

talentueux, **-euse** /talɑ̃tɥø, øz/ *adj* talented, gifted.

taler /tale/ [1] *vtr* to bruise [*fruit*].

talion /taljɔ̃/ *nm* talion; **loi du ~** lex talionis; **appliquer la loi du ~** to demand 'an eye for an eye'.

talisman /talismɑ̃/ *nm* talisman.

talith /talit/ *nm* tallith.

talkie-walkie, *pl* **talkies-walkies** /tokiwoki/ *nm* walkie-talkie.

talle /tal/ *nf* Agric sucker.

Tallinn /talin/ **▶857** *npr* Tallinn.

Talmud /talmyd/ *nm* Talmud.

talmudique /talmydik/ *adj* Talmudic.

taloche /talɔʃ/ *nf* **1**○ (gifle) clout○; **flanquer une ~ à qn**○ to give sb a clout○, to clout○ sb; **2** (de plâtrier) wooden float.

talocher○ /talɔʃe/ [1] *vtr* (gifler) to clout○; **se faire ~** to get a thick ear○.

talon /talɔ̃/ *nm* **1** Anat heel; **j'ai mal aux ~s** my heels are hurting; **2** (de chaussette, collant, chaussure) heel; **j'ai troué ma chaussette au ~** I've got a hole in the heel of my sock; **3** (de carnet, registre) stub, counterfoil; **un ~ de chèque** a cheque GB ou check US stub; **4** Culin end; **~ de jambon/saucisson** end of ham/sausage; **5** Jeux (aux cartes) pile, talon spéc; **piocher dans le ~** to pick a card from the pile; **6** Archit talon, ogee; **7** Équit heel; **8** Naut heel.

■ **~ d'Achille** Achilles heel; **~ aiguille** stiletto heel; **~ bobine** waisted heel; **~ haut** high heel; **~ plat** flat heel; **~ pointe** Courses Aut heel-and-toe.

IDIOMES **tourner les ~s** to turn on one's heel and walk away; **être sur les ~s de qn** to be hard ou hot on sb's heels.

talonnade /talɔnad/ *nf* (au football) back heel.

talonnage /talɔnaʒ/ *nm* **1** Sport (au rugby) heeling; **2** Naut heeling, heel.

talonner /talɔne/ [1] **I** *vtr* **1** (suivre) **~ qn** to follow hot on sb's heels; **le candidat aux élections talonne ses adversaires** fig the candidate in the elections is hot on the heels of his opponents; **2** (harceler) [*personne*] to hound [*personne*]; [*faim, inquiétude*] to torment [*personne*]; **il le talonne pour obtenir le contrat** he's badgering him to get the contract; **je les ai talonnés pour qu'ils acceptent** I badgered them to accept; **3** Équit to spur [sth] on [*cheval*]; **4** Sport (au rugby) [*joueur*] to heel [*ballon*].

II *vi* Naut to touch ou scrape the bottom with the keel.

talonnette /talɔnɛt/ *nf* **1** (de chaussures) lift (in a shoe); **2** (de chaussette, bas) heelpiece; **3** Cout (extrafort) binding.

talonneur /talɔnœʀ/ *nm* (en rugby) hooker.

talonnière /talɔnjɛʀ/ *nf* Ski heelpiece.

talquer /talke/ [1] *vtr* to put talcum powder on.

talqueux, **-euse** /talkø, øz/ *adj* talcose.

talus /taly/ *nm inv* **1** (artificiel) embankment; (naturel) bank, slope; **2** Constr (inclinaison) talus; **le ~ d'une muraille** the talus of a wall.

■ **~ continental** Géog continental slope.

talweg /talvɛg/ *nm* thalweg.

tamanoir /tamanwaʀ/ *nm* anteater.

tamarin /tamaʀɛ̃/ *nm* **1** Bot tamarind; **2** Zool tamarin.

tamarinier /tamaʀinje/ *nm* tamarind (tree).

tamaris /tamaʀis/ *nm inv* tamarisk.

tambouille○ /tɑ̃buj/ *nf* grub○.

tambour /tɑ̃buʀ/ *nm* **1** **▶534** (instrument) drum; **il battait le ~** he was beating his drum; **mener qch ~ battant** fig to deal with sth briskly; **2** **▶510** (personne) drummer; **trois jeunes ~s** three little drummer boys; **3** Tech (de lave-linge, treuil, frein) drum; **4** Archit (de colonne, coupole) drum, tambour; (de porte) tambour; **5** Cout (pour broder) tambour; **broder au ~** to embroider on a tambour.

■ **~ de basque** tambourine; **~ de ville** Hist ≈ town crier.

tambourin /tɑ̃buʀɛ̃/ *nm* **1** **▶534** (instrument) (à une peau avec grelots) tambourine; (allongé à deux peaux) tambourin, tabor; **2** (danse provençale) tambourin.

tambourinaire /tɑ̃buʀinɛʀ/ **▶510** *nmf* **1** (joueur de tambourin) tambourine player; **2** (joueur de tam-tam) drum player.

tambourinement /tɑ̃buʀinmɑ̃/ *nm* (de tambour, pluie) drumming ¢; **on entendit des ~s à la porte** there was a hammering at the door.

tambouriner /tɑ̃buʀine/ [1] *vi* **1** (frapper) **~ à la porte/fenêtre de qn** to hammer on sb's door/window; **2** (tapoter) **~ sur la table** to drum one's fingers on the table; **~ d'impatience** to drum one's fingers impatiently; **la pluie tambourine contre les vitres/sur le toit** the rain is drumming on the windows/on the roof; **3** (battre le tambour) to play the drum; (battre le tambourin) to play the tambourine.

tambour-major, *pl* **tambours-majors** /tɑ̃buʀmaʒɔʀ/ *nm* drum-major.

Tamerlan /tamɛʀlɑ̃/ *npr* Tamerlane.

tamil, **~e** /tamil/ **I** *adj* Tamil.
II ▶ 462 *nm* Ling Tamil.

tamis /tami/ *nm inv* **1** (instrument) sieve; **passer qch au ~** to sieve, to sift [*farine, sable*]; **2** (cordage de raquettes) strings (*pl*).

tamisage /tamizaʒ/ *nm* (de sable, farine) sieving, sifting.

Tamise /tamiz/ ▶ 357 *nprf* **la ~** the Thames.

tamiser /tamize/ [1] *vtr* to sieve, to sift [*sable, farine*]; to filter [*lumière, couleurs*]; **farine tamisée** sifted flour; **lumières tamisées** subdued lighting.

tamoul, **~e** /tamul/ **I** *adj* Tamil.
II ▶ 462 *nm* Ling Tamil.

Tamoul, **~e** /tamul/ *nm,f* Tamil.

tampon /tɑ̃pɔ̃/ **I** *nm* **1** (de bureau) (marque) stamp; (objet gravé) stamp; (tissu encré) **~ (encreur)** (ink) pad; **mettre** or **apposer un ~ sur un document** to stamp a document; **2** (pour éponger, frotter) gén pad; Méd, Pharm swab; **3** Rail (de wagon) buffer; **4** (pour boucher) plug; **5** Mécan (calibre) plug gauge; **6** Constr (dalle) **~ (de regard)** manhole cover; (cheville) wall plug.
II (-)tampon (*in compounds*) Chimie, Ordinat, Pol buffer; **solution ~** Chimie buffer (solution); **mémoire ~** Ordinat buffer (storage); **mettre qch en mémoire ~** Ordinat to put sth in the buffer.
■ **~ hygiénique** tampon; **~ Jex**® ≈ Brillo® pad; **~ d'ouate** cotton wool ball; **~ périodique** tampon; **~ à récurer** scourer, scouring pad.
IDIOMES **servir de ~** to act as a buffer.

tampon-buvard, *pl* **tampons-buvards** /tɑ̃pɔ̃byvaʀ/ *nm* blotter.

tamponnage /tɑ̃pɔnaʒ/ *nm* Chimie, Ordinat buffering.

tamponnement /tɑ̃pɔnmɑ̃/ *nm* **1** (de véhicules) crash; **2** Méd tamponage.

tamponner /tɑ̃pɔne/ [1] **I** *vtr* **1** (éponger) to swab [*plaie*]; to mop [*front*]; (pour vernir) to dab [*surface, meuble*]; to dab at [*ecchymose*]; **2** (timbrer) to stamp [*document*]; **3** (heurter) to crash into [*véhicule*]; **4** Chimie to buffer [*solution*]; **5** Constr **~ un mur** to insert a plug in a hole in a wall.
II se tamponner *vpr* (se heurter) [*véhicules*] to crash; ▶ **coquillard**.

tamponneuse /tɑ̃pɔnøz/ *adj f* **auto ~** bumper car, dodgem.

tamponnoir /tɑ̃pɔnwaʀ/ *nm* masonry drill bit.

tam-tam, *pl* **~s** /tamtam/ *nm* **1** ▶ 534 (tambour) tomtom; **2** (tapage) hype○; **faire du ~ autour de qch** to make a lot of fuss about sth.

tan /tɑ̃/ *nm* tan, tanbark.

tancer /tɑ̃se/ [12] *vtr* liter to scold, to admonish littér; **elle s'est fait ~ vertement** or **d'importance par sa mère** she was scolded sharply by her mother.

tanche /tɑ̃ʃ/ *nf* tench.

tandem /tɑ̃dɛm/ *nm* **1** (bicyclette) tandem; **rouler en ~** to ride a tandem; **2** fig (duo) duo; **le ~ Dupont-Durand** the Dupont-Durand duo; **travailler en ~** to work in tandem.

tandis: **tandis que** /tɑ̃di(s)k(ə)/ *loc conj* **1** (pendant le temps que) while; **2** (alors qu'au contraire) while, whereas.

tanga /tɑ̃ga/ *nm* tanga briefs (*pl*).

tangage /tɑ̃gaʒ/ *nm* (de navire, d'avion) pitching; **il y a du ~** Naut the ship is pitching; **il y a eu un coup de ~** Naut the ship pitched suddenly.

Tanganyika /tɑ̃ganika/ ▶ 459 *nprm* Hist Tanganyika; **le lac ~** Lake Tanganyika.

tangence /tɑ̃ʒɑ̃s/ *nf* tangency.

tangent, **~e** /tɑ̃ʒɑ̃, ɑ̃t/ **I** *adj* **1** Math tangent, tangential; **~ à** at a tangent to; **2**○ (de justesse) **elle passe en classe supérieure, mais c'est ~** she's moving up a class GB ou grade US, but only by the skin of her teeth○.
II tangente *nf* Math tangent.
IDIOMES **prendre la ~e**○ to make oneself scarce○.

tangentiel, **-ielle** /tɑ̃ʒɑ̃sjɛl/ *adj* Math, Phys tangential.

Tanger /tɑ̃ʒe/ ▶ 857 *npr* Tangier.

tangible /tɑ̃ʒibl/ *adj* tangible.

tangiblement /tɑ̃ʒibləmɑ̃/ *adv* tangibly.

tango /tɑ̃go/ **I** ▶ 193 *adj inv* (couleur) tangerine (*épith*).
II *nm* **1** Danse tango; **danser le ~** to do the tango; **2** (boisson) *beer mixed with grenadine.*

tanguer /tɑ̃ge/ [1] *vi* **1** [*navire, avion*] to pitch; **2** [*personne*] to be unsteady on one's feet.

tanière /tanjɛʀ/ *nf* **1** (d'animal) den; **2** (retraite) lair; **3** (taudis) hovel.

tanin /tanɛ̃/ *nm* tannin.

tank /tɑ̃k/ *nm* **1** (citerne) tank; **2** (char) tank.

tanker /tɑ̃kœʀ, tɑ̃kɛʀ/ *nm* tanker.

tankiste /tɑ̃kist/ *nm* tank server.

tannage /tanaʒ/ *nm* tanning.

tannant, **~e** /tanɑ̃, ɑ̃t/ *adj* **1** Tech [*produit*] tanning; **2**○ (lassant) [*personne*] infuriating.

tanné, **~e** /tane/ **I** *pp* ▶ **tanner**.
II *pp adj* **1** Tech [*cuir, peaux*] tanned; **2** [*visage, peau*] leathery; **le visage ~ par le soleil** his/her face made leathery by the sun; **3**○ C (fatigué) exhausted.
III tannée *nf* **1** Tech spent tan; **2**○ (volée de coups) hiding○, beating.

tanner /tane/ [1] *vtr* **1** Tech to tan [*cuir, peaux*]; **2** (brunir) [*soleil*] to make [sth] leathery [*visage, peau*]; **3**○ (lasser) to badger○ [*personne*] (**avec** with); **il nous tanne avec ses questions!** he's badgering us with his questions!; **~ qn pour faire** to badger sb to do.
IDIOMES **~ le cuir à qn**○ to tan sb's hide○.

tannerie /tanʀi/ *nf* **1** (établissement) tannery; **2** (métier) tanning.

tanneur, **-euse** /tanœʀ, øz/ ▶ 510 *nm,f* tanner.

tannique /tanik/ *adj* tannic.

tant /tɑ̃/ ▶ 662 **I** *adv* **1** (modifiant un verbe) so much; (modifiant un participe passé) much; **il a ~ crié qu'il n'a plus de voix, il n'a plus de voix ~ il a crié** he's been shouting so much that he's lost his voice; **il quitta la pièce ~ il se sentait honteux** he was so ashamed that he left the room; **il a ~ insisté que j'ai fini par céder** he was so insistent that I ended up giving in; **qu'as-tu à ~ pleurer?** why are you crying so much?; **il travaille ~!** he works so much ou so hard!; **vous m'en direz ~!** you don't say!; **il y a ~ à faire qu'il ne sait pas où commencer** there's so much to be done that he doesn't know where to start; **elle m'a ~ appris!** she taught me so much!; **~ il est vrai que**... since it's a well-known fact that...; **les diamants ~ convoités** the much coveted diamonds; **le moment ~ attendu** the long-awaited moment; **le chef ~ redouté** the much dreaded boss; **2** (dans une comparaison) **son œuvre est remarquable, ~ ses films que ses romans** his works are remarkable, both his films and his novels ou his films as much as his novels; **il est odieux avec tout le monde, ~ avec ses collègues qu'avec sa famille** he's obnoxious to everybody, both to his colleagues and to his family ou as much to his colleagues as to his family; **ce n'est pas ~ une question d'argent qu'une question de principe** it's not so much a question of money as a question of principle; **n'aimer rien ~ que**... to like nothing so much as...; **il poussait ~ qu'il pouvait** he pushed as hard as he could, he pushed for all he was worth; **tu peux protester ~ que tu voudras, il ne changera pas d'avis** you can protest as much as you like, he won't change his mind; **faire qch ~ bien que mal** to do sth with great difficulty; **3** (aussi longtemps) **~ que** as long as; **je resterai ~ qu'il y aura du travail** I'll stay as long as there's work to be had; **je ne partirai pas ~ qu'il ne m'aura pas accordé un rendez-vous** I won't leave until he's given me an appointment; **profites-en ~ que tu peux** make the most of it while you can; **aide-moi donc à déplacer cette armoire ~ que tu es là** since you're here why don't you help me move the wardrobe?; **~ que tu y es, balaye aussi la cuisine** while you're at it, sweep the kitchen as well; **traite-moi de menteur ~ que tu y es**○**!** go ahead and call me a liar!; **4** (remplaçant un nombre) **gagner/dépenser ~ par mois** to earn/to spend so much a month; **votre lettre datée du ~** your letter of such- and-such a date.
II tant de *dét indéf* **1** (avec un nom dénombrable) so many; **~ de livres/d'idées** so many books/ideas; **~ de meubles** so much furniture; **Loulou, Grovagnard, Pichon et ~ d'autres** Loulou, Grovagnard, Pichon and so many others; **des petits pavillons comme on en voit ~ en banlieue** small houses of which there are so many in the suburbs; **s'il y a ~ de tickets vendus par semaine** if so many tickets are sold per week; **2** (avec un nom non dénombrable) so much; **~ d'argent/de travail/de bonheur** so much money/work/happiness; **je n'ai jamais vu ~ de monde** I've never seen so many people; **~ d'humilité force le respect** such humility commands respect; **il y avait ~ de sel dans la soupe qu'elle était immangeable** the soup was so salty, you couldn't eat it.
III (dans des locutions) **~ pis** too bad; **~ pis pour toi/lui/eux** too bad for you/him/them, that's your/his/their bad luck; **~ mieux** so much the better; **~ mieux pour toi/lui/eux** good for you/him/them; **~ et plus** gén a great deal; (avec nom comptable) a great many; **~ et si bien que** so much so that; **il a fait ~ et si bien qu'il s'est fait renvoyer** he finally managed to get himself fired; **il est un ~ soit peu arrogant** he's a bit arrogant; **s'il avait un ~ soit peu d'imagination/de bon sens** if he had the slightest bit of imagination/of common sense, if he had an ounce of imagination/of common sense; **si tu étais (un) ~ soit peu inquiet** if you were in the least bit worried; **~ s'en faut** not by a long shot; **~ qu'à faire, autant repeindre toute la pièce** we may as well repaint the whole room; **~ qu'à faire, je préférerais que ce soit lui qui l'achète** since somebody has to buy it, I'd rather it was him; **~ qu'à acheter un ordinateur, autant en acheter un bon** if you're going to buy a computer, you may as well buy a good one; **en ~ que** as; **en ~ que lexicographe** as a lexicographer; **en ~ que tel** as such; **si ~ est qu'il puisse y aller** that is if he can go at all; **~ que ça**○**?** (avec un nom comptable) that many?; (avec un nom non comptable ou un verbe) that much?; **je ne l'aime pas ~ que ça** I don't like him/her all that much; **~ qu'à moi/toi/lui**○ as for me/you/him.

tantale /tɑ̃tal/ *nm* Chimie tantalum.

Tantale /tɑ̃tal/ *npr* Mythol Tantalus; **supplice de ~** torment of Tantalus; **c'est un véritable supplice de ~** it's really tantalizing.

tante /tɑ̃t/ *nf* **1** (dans une famille) aunt; **~ Julie** aunt Julie; **chez ma ~** lit at my aunt's; (en gage) at the pawnshop; **2**◑ offensive (homosexuel) queer◑ injur, homosexual.

tantième /tɑ̃tjɛm/ *nm* percentage.

tantine /tɑ̃tin/ *nf* auntie, aunty.

tantinet○ /tɑ̃tinɛ/ *nm* **un ~** a trifle, a tiny bit; **il exagère un ~** he's exaggerating just a tiny bit; **un ~ de** (de whisky, sel, poivre) a spot of; (d'humour, appréhension) a touch of.

tantôt /tɑ̃to/ **I** *adv* **1** (parfois) sometimes; **il était ~ calme ~ brusque** he was sometimes calm (and) sometimes brusque; **~ en français ~ en arabe** sometimes in French (and) sometimes in Arabic; **2** dial (tout à l'heure) **à ~** see you (soon); **3** dial (cet après-midi) this afternoon.
II *nm* dial (après-midi) afternoon.

tantouse◑ /tɑ̃tuz/ *nf* offensive (homosexual) queer◑ injur, homosexual.

Tanzanie /tɑ̃zani/ ▶ 321 *nprf* Tanzania.

tanzanien, -ienne /tɑ̃zanjɛ̃, ɛn/ ▶ 537 *adj* Tanzanian.

Tanzanien, -ienne /tɑ̃zanjɛ̃, ɛn/ ▶ 537 *nm,f* Tanzanian.

tao /tao/ *nm* Tao.

TAO /teao/ *nf*: *abbr* ▶ **traduction**.

taoïsme /taoism/ *nm* Taoism.

taoïste /taoist/ *adj, nmf* Taoist.

taon /tɑ̃/ *nm* horsefly.

tapage /tapaʒ/ *nm* **1** (bruit) din, racket○; **faire du ~** to make a racket○; **2** (éclat) furore; **la nouvelle a fait du ~** the news caused a furore GB ou furor US; **3** (battage) hype; **~ médiatique** media hype; **il y a eu beaucoup de ~ autour de ce livre** there has been a lot of hype about the book.
■ **~ nocturne** Jur disturbance of the peace at night.

tapageur, -euse /tapaʒœʀ, øz/ *adj* **1** (bruyant) [*personne*] rowdy; **2** (outrancier) [*luxe, élégance*] showy; (retentissant) [*campagne*] hyped-up; [*propos*] ostentatious.

tapant, ~e /tapɑ̃, ɑ̃t/ *adj* **à trois heures ~es** at three o'clock sharp ou on the dot.

tape /tap/ *nf* (amicale) pat; (plus forte) slap (**dans, sur** on); **~ amicale dans le dos** friendly pat on the back; **donner une petite ~ sur le dos de qn** (pour attirer l'attention) to give sb a little tap on the back; **elle m'a donné une ~ sur la main** she slapped my hand.

tapé, ~e /tape/ *adj* **1**○ (fou) bonkers○, nuts○; **2** (trop mûr) [*pomme, poire*] overripe.

tape-à-l'œil○ /tapalœj/ **I** *adj inv* [*couleur*] loud; [*décoration, bijou, mobilier*] garish.
II *nm inv* **ils n'achètent que du ~** they only buy showy stuff○; **c'est du ~** it's all show.

tapecul○ /tapky/ *nm* **1** (balançoire) see-saw; **2** (vieux véhicule) bone-shaker○; **3** Équit sitting trot (without stirrups); **4** Naut jigger.

tapée○ /tape/ *nf* **une ~ de, des ~s de** loads (*pl*) of.

taper /tape/ [1] **I** *vtr* **1** (frapper) to hit [*personne, chien*]; **2** (dactylographier) to type [*lettre*]; **~ 60 mots à la minute** or **60 mots/min** to type 60 words a minute, to have a typing speed of 60 wpm; **pouvez-vous me ~ ce rapport?** could you type up ou out this report for me?; **une lettre tapée à la machine** a typed ou type-written letter; **3**○ (prendre) **je peux te ~ 1 franc/une cigarette?** can I scrounge○ a franc/a cigarette off you?; **il tape tout le monde** he scrounges○ off everybody.
II taper sur *vtr ind* to hit [*clou*]; **~ sur l'épaule/le bras de qn** to tap sb on the shoulder/the arm; **~ sur qn**○ lit to thump ou belt○ sb; fig (critiquer) to slag sb off◑ GB, to badmouth○ sb; **~ sur la gueule◑ de qn** to slug○ sb in the mouth; **~ sur la table** lit to bang (one's fist) on the table; **~ sur les nerfs** ou **le système**○ **de qn** fig to get on sb's nerves; **se faire ~ sur les doigts** fig to get ou have one's knuckles rapped.
III *vi* **1** (frapper) **~ des mains** (de joie) to clap one's hands; **~ des pieds** (de colère) to stamp one's feet; **~ du pied** (d'impatience) to tap one's foot; **~ à la porte** to knock at the door; **~ dans un ballon** to kick a ball around; **un boxeur qui tape**○ **dur** a boxer with a lethal punch; **le soleil tape**○ **(dur) aujourd'hui** fig the sun is beating down today; **un vin qui tape**○ fig a wine that goes to one's head; **2**○ (se servir) **~ dans ses économies** to dip into one's savings; **~ dans la caisse** to dip ou put one's hand in the till GB ou (cash) register US; **3** (dactylographier) **~ (à la machine)** to type; **apprendre à ~ à la machine** to learn how to type; **tu tapes bien?** are you a good typist?
IV se taper *vpr* **1**○ (l'un l'autre) **se ~ dessus** to knock each other about; **2** (soi-même) **je me suis tapé sur le doigt** I hit myself on the finger; **se ~ la tête contre le mur** to bang one's head against the wall; **c'est à se ~ la tête contre les murs** fig it's enough to drive you up the wall; **3◑** (consommer) to have [*glace, bière*]; **se ~ un bon repas** to have a slap-up meal; **se ~ un mec/une nana** to have it off◑ with a guy/a girl; **4**○ (s'appuyer) to get lumbered○ GB ou stuck○ with [*corvée, importun*]; **j'ai dû me ~ le trajet à pied** I had to foot it○ all the way; **je me suis tapé la route sous la pluie** I ended up having to go all the way in the rain.
IDIOMES **~ le carton**○ to play cards; **~ comme un sourd** (à la porte) to thunder on the door; (au piano) to bash○ ou thump away; **moi! l'aider? il peut (toujours) se ~◑!** me, help him? he can whistle○ for it!; **tes histoires de famille, je m'en tape◑!** I couldn't care less ou I don't give a damn○ about your family problems!; **ils se tapent sur le ventre**○ they are thick as thieves○; **je n'aime pas qu'on me tape sur le ventre**○ I don't like people being overfamiliar with me; **c'est à s'en ~ le derrière**○ or **cul◑ par terre** it's hilarious, it's a riot○; **elle m'a tapé dans l'œil** I thought she was striking; **~ à côté** to be off target.

tapette /tapɛt/ *nf* **1**○ (langue) **avoir une bonne ~** (être bavard) to be a chatterbox○; **faire marcher sa ~** to chatter away endlessly; **2◑** offensive (homosexuel) fairy○ injur, homosexual; **3** (pour tapis) carpet beater; **4** (pour tuer les mouches) fly swatter; **5** (piège à souris) mousetrap; **6** (petite tape) pat.

tapeur○**, -euse** /tapœʀ, øz/ *nm,f* scrounger○.

tapin◑ /tapɛ̃/ *nm* **faire le ~** to be on the game○.

tapiner◑ /tapine/ [1] *vi* to be on the game○ GB, to be a hooker○.

tapineuse◑ /tapinøz/ *nf* streetwalker.

tapinois: **en tapinois** /ɑ̃tapinwa/ *loc adv* furtively.

tapioca /tapjɔka/ *nm* tapioca.

tapir /tapiʀ/ [3] **I** *nm* Zool tapir.
II se tapir *vpr* [*personne, animal*] to hide; (en ramassant son corps) to crouch; **ils sont restés tapis derrière les bosquets** they lay low behind the bushes; **maison tapie dans la forêt** liter house nestling in the forest.

tapis /tapi/ *nm inv* gén carpet, rug; (plus grand) carpet; (sur un meuble) cloth; (de salle de bains, sport) mat; **un ~ d'Orient** an oriental carpet; **~ de haute laine** deep-pile rug; **~ à poil ras** short-pile rug; **un ~ de feuilles mortes** a carpet of dead leaves; **mettre qch sur le ~** fig to bring sth up; **mettre** or **envoyer qn au ~** to throw sb; **aller/être au ~** [*boxeur*] to go down/to be on the canvas.
■ **~ de baignoire** (non-slip) bathmat; **~ de bain(s)** bathmat; **~ de billard** baize; **~ mécanique** machine-made rug ou carpet; **~ de prière** prayer mat; **~ rouge** red carpet; **dérouler le ~ rouge pour qn** to roll out the red carpet for sb; **~ roulant** (pour piétons) moving walkway; (pour bagages) carousel; (pour marchandises) conveyor belt; **~ de selle** saddle cloth; **~ de sol** groundsheet; **~ de table** table cloth; **~ vert** (sur table de conférence, de jeux) green baize; **~ volant** flying carpet.

tapis-brosse, *pl* **~s** /tapibʀɔs/ *nm* doormat.

tapisser /tapise/ [1] *vtr* **1** (poser un revêtement) (avec du papier peint) to wallpaper (**de** with); (de tissu, toile) to decorate [*pièce*] (**de** with); to cover, to decorate [*mur*]; to cover, to upholster [*fauteuil, canapé*] (**de** with); Culin to line [*plat, moule*] (**de** with); **murs tapissés de** walls covered with; **2** (servir de revêtement) [*mousse, neige*] to carpet [*sol*]; to cover [*mont, ruine*]; [*cellule, muqueuse*] to line [*organe, cavité*]; [*tentures*] to line [*ville, bâtiment*]; [*photos*] to cover [*mur, pièce*]; [*résidu, pâte*] to line [*fond*].

tapisserie /tapisʀi/ *nf* **1** (tenture, broderie) tapestry; **des ~s sont accrochées au mur** tapestries hang from the wall; **sofa recouvert de ~** tapestry-covered sofa; **2** (papier peint) wallpaper; **3** (art, technique) tapestry work; **faire de la ~** to do tapestry work; **un ouvrage de ~** a tapestry project.
IDIOMES **faire ~** (au bal) to be a wallflower.

tapissier, -ière /tapisje, ɛʀ/ ▶ 510 *nm,f* **1** (pour meubles) upholsterer; **2** (artiste, fabricant) tapestry-maker.

tapotement /tapɔtmɑ̃/ *nm* tapping.

tapoter /tapɔte/ [1] *vtr* to tap [*table, objet*]; to pat [*joues, dos*].

tapuscrit /tapyskʀi/ *nm* typescript.

taquet /takɛ/ *nm* **1** Tech (coin) wedge; (arrêt) stop; **2** Naut cleat; **3** Constr working platform.
■ **~ de tabulation** tabulator, tab (stop).

taquin, ~e /takɛ̃, in/ **I** *adj* [*personne*] teasing; **il est très ~** he's a great tease.
II *nm,f* tease.

taquiner /takine/ [1] **I** *vtr* [*personne*] to tease; [*histoire, douleur*] to bother.
II se taquiner *vpr* to tease each other.
IDIOMES **~ le goujon** to do a bit of fishing; **~ la muse** to dabble in poetry.

taquinerie /takinʀi/ *nf* teasing ¢; **tes ~s incessantes** your constant teasing.

tarabiscoté, ~e /taʀabiskɔte/ *adj* [*ornement, motif*] over-ornate; [*écriture*] over-elaborate; [*esprit, raisonnement, style*] convoluted.

tarabuster /taʀabyste/ [1] *vtr* [*ennuis, question*] to bother; [*personne*] to badger; **il me tarabuste pour que je lui achète un vélo** he's badgering me to buy him a bicycle.

tarama /taʀama/ *nm* taramasalata.

Tarascon /taʀaskɔ̃/ ▶ 857 *npr* Tarascon.

tarasconnais, ~e /taʀaskɔnɛ, ɛz/ ▶ 857 *adj* of Tarascon.

Tarasconnais, ~e /taʀaskɔnɛ, ɛz/ ▶ 857 *nm,f* (natif) native of Tarascon; (habitant) inhabitant of Tarascon.

taratata○ /taʀatata/ *excl* nonsense!, rubbish○! GB.

taraud /taʀo/ *nm* screw-tap.

taraudage /taʀodaʒ/ *nm* (opération) tapping; (résultat) threaded ou tapped hole.

tarauder /taʀode/ [1] *vtr* **1** Tech to tap, to screw; **2** fig [*angoisse, soucis*] to torment [*personne*].

taraudeur, -euse /taʀodœʀ, øz/ **I** ▶ 510 *nm,f* tapper.
II taraudeuse *nf* tapping-machine.

tarbais, ~e /taʀbɛ, ɛz/ ▶ 857 *adj* of Tarbes.

Tarbais, ~e /taʀbɛ, ɛz/ ▶ 857 *nm,f* (natif) native of Tarbes; (habitant) inhabitant of Tarbes.

Tarbes /taʀb/ ▶ 857 *npr* Tarbes.

tard /taʀ/ **I** *adv* late; **plus ~** later; **bien plus/un peu plus ~** much/a little later (on); **il est ~** it's late; **il est trop ~** it's too late; **il se fait ~** it's getting late; **au plus ~** at the latest; **plus ~ dans la soirée, elle...** later in the evening ou later that evening, she...; **remettre qch à plus ~** to put sth off till later; **il est venu ~ dans la soirée/saison** he came late in the evening/season; **~ dans la nuit** in the middle of the night; **dîner ~** to have dinner late; **il est un peu ~ pour changer de tactique** it's a bit late in the day to change tactics; **pas plus ~ qu'hier/que l'année dernière** only yesterday/last year; **ce sera pour plus ~** (une autre fois) there'll be other times.

II sur le tard *loc adv* [*partir*] late; [*se marier, commencer des études*] late in life; **déclarant sur le ~ que** announcing rather late in the day that.

IDIOMES **mieux vaut ~ que jamais** Prov better late than never Prov; **il n'est jamais trop ~ pour bien faire** Prov it's never too late to do the right thing.

tarder /taʀde/ [1] **I** *vi* **1** (à agir) **~ à faire** (être lent) to take a long time doing; (différer) to put off ou delay doing; **l'économie tarde à se stabiliser** the economy is taking time to stabilize; **il a tellement tardé à le réparer que** he put off ou delayed repairing it for so long that; **trop ~ à faire qch** to wait too long to do sth, to put off doing sth for too long; **agir sans ~** to act immediately ou without delay; **sans plus ~** without further delay; **venez sans ~** (maintenant) come straightaway GB or right now; (bientôt) come as soon as you can; **ne pas ~ à faire qch** to do sth soon; **elle n'a pas tardé à faire la même chose** she lost no time in doing the same thing; **il ne tardera pas à s'en rendre compte** he'll soon realize, he won't take long to realize; **ne tardez pas!** do it soon, don't delay!; **ça ne devrait pas ~ à se faire** it should happen soon; **2** (à arriver, se manifester) **~ (à arriver)** [*saison, réaction*] to be a long time coming; [*colis, réponse*] to take a long time; **les enfants ne vont pas ~ (à arriver)** the children won't be long, the children will be here soon; **elle tarde à revenir** she's taking a long time; **ça ne va pas ~** it won't be long; **ça n'a pas tardé** it wasn't long coming; **ne tardez pas!** don't be long!; **le moment/le temps me tarde où** I'm longing for the moment/time when.

II *v impers* **il me tarde de la revoir** I'm longing to see her again; **il me tarde qu'il parte** I'm longing for him to go.

tardif, **-ive** /taʀdif, iv/ *adj* [*repas, heure, floraison, grossesse*] late; [*regret, excuses, revirement*] belated; **à une heure tardive** at a late hour; **à un âge trop ~** too late in life.

tardivement /taʀdivmɑ̃/ *adv* **1** (pas tôt) [*arriver*] late; **plus ~** later; **2** (trop tard) [*réagir, comprendre, informer*] rather belatedly; **trop ~** too late; **ne découvrir qch que ~** to discover sth only rather late in the day.

tare /taʀ/ *nf* **1** (masse) tare; **faire la ~** to determine the tare weight; **2** Méd defect; **~s héréditaires** hereditary defects; **3** (grave défaut) defect; **les ~s d'une société** the defects of society; **être accusé d'avoir toutes les ~s** to be accused of every vice in the book.

taré, **~e** /taʀe/ **I** *adj* **1** Méd [*personne, animal*] with a defect (*épith, après n*); **2**○ offensive (fou) mental○ injur, crazy; **3** Comm [*marchandises, produit*] defective; **4** fig [*société*] sick.

II○ *nm,f* offensive mental defective.

tarentelle /taʀɑ̃tɛl/ *nf* tarantella; **danser la ~** to dance the tarantella.

tarentule /taʀɑ̃tyl/ *nf* tarantula.

tarer /taʀe/ [1] *vtr* to tare.

targette /taʀʒɛt/ *nf* bolt.

targuer: **se targuer** /taʀge/ [1] *vpr* to claim (**de qch** sth; **de faire** to do), to boast (**de qch** sth); **il se targue d'avoir créé des emplois** he prides himself on having created jobs.

tarière /taʀjɛʀ/ *nf* **1** Tech (en menuiserie) gimlet; (pour le sol) ground auger; **2** Zool ovipositor.

tarif /taʀif/ *nm* **1** (prix) gén rate; (de transport) fare; (de consultation) fee; **les ~s de chemin de fer/du métro** train/underground GB ou subway US fares; **payer plein ~** gén to pay full price; Transp to pay full fare; **~ normal/réduit/spécial** Transp normal/reduced/special fare; **~ normal/économique** Postes ≈ first-class/second-class rate; **~ de nuit** Télécom night-time rate, off-peak rate; **le ~ en vigueur** the going rate; **le ~ horaire de qch** the hourly rate for sth; **~ lettres/cartes postales** letter/postcard rate; **tu connais le ~, c'est deux jours de renvoi** fig you know the penalty—two days' suspension; **2** (document) price list, tariff GB.

■ **~ douanier** Comm customs tariff; **~ de l'impôt** Fisc taxation schedule; **~ rouge** Télécom peak rate; **~ syndical** union rate; **~s postaux** postage rates.

tarifaire /taʀifɛʀ/ *adj* [*accord, barrière, politique*] tariff (*épith*).

tarifer /taʀife/ [1] *vtr* to fix the price of [*marchandises*]; **marchandises tarifées** fixed-price goods.

tarification /taʀifikasjɔ̃/ *nf* (action) price setting; (résultat) tariff (**de** of).

tarin /taʀɛ̃/ *nm* **1**◑ (nez) hooter○ GB, schnoz○ US, nose; **2** Zool siskin.

tarir /taʀiʀ/ [23] **I** *vtr* **1** [*sécheresse*] to dry up [*source, puits*]; **2** [*mesure, politique*] to stem (the tide of) [*émigration, ressources*].

II *vi* **1** (s'assécher) [*source, puits*] to dry up, to run dry; **2** (cesser) [*larmes*] to be stemmed; [*conversation*] to dry up; **3** [*personne*] **ne pas ~ sur qch/qn** to talk endlessly about sth/sb; **ne pas ~ d'éloges sur qch/qn** to be full of praise for sth/sb.

III se tarir *vpr* lit, fig to dry up, to run dry.

tarissement /taʀismɑ̃/ *nm* lit, fig drying up.

Tarn /taʀn/ ▶357, 692, 692 *nprm* (rivière, département) **le ~** the Tarn.

Tarn-et-Garonne /taʀnegaʀɔn/ ▶692 *nprm* (département) **le ~** the Tarn-et-Garonne.

tarot /taʀo/ *nm* **1** (en cartomancie) tarot; **2** ▶449 Jeux tarot (*card game*).

Tarpéienne /taʀpejɛn/ *adj f* **roche ~** Tarpeian Rock.

IDIOMES **la roche ~ est près du Capitole** the higher you rise, the harder you fall.

tarse /taʀs/ *nm* Anat, Zool tarsus.

tarsien, **-ienne** /taʀsjɛ̃, ɛn/ **I** *adj* Anat tarsal.

II *nm* Zool tarsier.

tartan /taʀtɑ̃/ *nm* **1** Tex tartan; **2** ®Sport, Tech Tartan®.

tartane /taʀtan/ *nf* Naut tartan.

tartare /taʀtaʀ/ *adj* **1** Hist Tartar; **2** Culin **sauce ~** tartare sauce; **steak ~** steak tartare.

Tartare /taʀtaʀ/ *nmf* Tartar.

tarte /taʀt/ **I**○ *adj* (niais) [*personne*] daft○ GB, daffy○ US; [*film, chanson, chapeau, robe*] ridiculous.

II *nf* **1** Culin tart; **~ aux fraises/à la rhubarbe** strawberry/rhubarb tart; **2**○ (gifle) wallop○, slap; **flanquer** or **filer une ~ à qn** to give sb a wallop○.

■ **~ à la crème** (idée banale) stereotype; (gag) custard pie, slapstick; **~ Tatin** apple tart (*with caramel topping*).

IDIOMES **c'est pas de la ~**○ it's no picnic○.

tartelette /taʀtəlɛt/ *nf* Culin tart.

Tartempion○ /taʀtɑ̃pjɔ̃/ *nm* **Monsieur et Madame ~** Mr and Mrs Whatnot; **demande donc à ~** go and ask what's-his-name○.

tartignolle○ /taʀtiɲɔl/ *adj* [*personne*] daft○ GB, daffy○ US; [*robe, chapeau*] ridiculous.

tartine /taʀtin/ *nf* **1** (pain beurré) slice of bread and butter; **il a mangé trois ~s** he's eaten three slices of bread and butter; **peux-tu me faire une ~?** could you butter me a slice of bread?; **une ~ de beurre/confiture/miel/pâté** a slice of bread and butter/jam/honey/pâté; **veux-tu une ~ avec du miel?** would you like a slice of bread and honey?; **2**○ **il en a écrit** or **mis**○ **une ~** he wrote reams about it; **il y en a une ~!** there's reams of it!

tartiner /taʀtine/ [1] *vtr* Culin to spread [*fromage, pâté, chocolat*] (**sur** on); **chocolat/fromage à ~** chocolate/cheese spread; **pâte à ~** sandwich spread, spread.

tartre /taʀtʀ/ *nm* **1** (dans une bouilloire) scale, fur GB; **2** (sur les dents) tartar; **3** Vin tartar.

tartrique /taʀtʀik/ *adj* **acide ~** tartaric acid.

tartufe /taʀtyf/ *nm* hypocrite.

tartuferie /taʀtyfʀi/ *nf* hypocrisy.

tas /tɑ/ **I** *nm inv* **1** lit heap, pile (**de** of); **un ~ de charbon/de paille** a heap ou pile of coal/of straw; **en ~** [*mettre, poser, être*] in a heap ou pile; **il y avait du linge sale en ~ dans un coin** there was some dirty laundry piled in a corner; **un ~ de fumier** a manure heap; **un ~ de bois** (ordonné) a woodpile; (désordonné) a pile of wood; **~ de ferraille** lit scrap heap; fig (vieille voiture) wreck; **2**○ fig **un ~, des ~** lots, loads○ (**de** of); **des ~ de gens** lots ou loads of people.

II dans le tas *loc adv* **taper dans le ~** to punch people indiscriminately; **tirer dans le ~** to fire into the crowd; **foncer dans le ~** [*personne*] to fling oneself into the crowd; [*police*] to charge the crowd.

III sur le tas *loc adv* **apprendre/être formé sur le ~** to learn/to be trained on the job; **formation sur le ~** on-the-job training; **grève sur le ~** sit-down strike.

■ **~ de charge** Archit springing stones (*pl*).

Tasmanie /tasmani/ ▶416, 692 *nprf* Tasmania.

tasse /tɑs/ *nf* **1** (récipient) cup; **~ en faïence/porcelaine/plastique** earthenware/china/plastic cup; **2** (contenu) cup; **boire une ~ de thé/chocolat chaud** to drink a cup of tea/hot chocolate.

■ **~ à café** coffee cup; **~ à thé** teacup.

IDIOMES **boire la ~**○ to swallow a mouthful of water when swimming.

Tasse /tas/ *npr* **le ~** Tasso.

tassé, **~e** /tɑse/ **I** *pp* ▶ **tasser**.

II *pp adj* [*terre*] firmly packed; [*boule de neige*] hard packed; **bien ~** [*cigarette*] well packed; [*boule de neige*] very hard packed; [*whisky*] stiff; **il y en a 4 kilos bien ~s**○ there's a good 4 kilos of it; **il a la cinquantaine bien ~e**○ he's well past fifty.

tassement /tɑsmɑ̃/ *nm* **1** fig (de l'emploi, des activités) contraction; (de valeur des exportations) stagnation; (à la Bourse) decline (**de** in); (de popularité) decline (**de** in); **2** lit **~ de vertèbres** compression of the vertebrae.

tasser /tɑse/ [1] **I** *vtr* to press down [*terre*]; to tamp down [*tabac*] (**dans** in); to pack down [*foin, paille*]; to pack [*habits*] (**dans** in); to cram [*bagages*] (**dans** into; **sous** under); to pack [*gens*] (**dans** into); **les passagers étaient tassés** the passengers were packed in tightly; **le sport/l'accident lui a tassé les vertèbres** sport/the accident has given him/her compression of the vertebrae.

II se tasser *vpr* **1** (s'affaisser) (avec l'âge) to shrink; (volontairement) to make oneself look smaller; **2** (se serrer) [*personnes*] to squash up, to squeeze up; **il va falloir se ~ dans la voiture** we'll have to squash ou squeeze up in the car; **3**○ (se calmer) [*histoire, rumeur, conflit*] to die down; **au bout de trois mois les choses se sont tassées** after three months things settled down.

taste-vin /tastəvɛ̃/ *nm inv* (wine-)tasting cup.

tata○ /tata/ *nf* auntie.

tatane◑ /tatan/ *nf* shoe.

tâter /tɑte/ [1] **I** *vtr* **1** (palper) to feel; **~ le sol du pied** to test the ground; **~ un melon** to feel a melon (to see if it's ripe); **~ le pouls de qn** to feel sb's pulse; **2** (sonder) **~ l'opinion** to sound out public opinion.

II tâter de○ *vtr ind* **~ de tous les métiers** to try one's hand at ou have a go at all kinds of jobs; **quand tu auras tâté de la prison** when you've had a taste of prison.

III se tâter *vpr* hum **je me tâte**○ I'm thinking about it, I'm quite tempted.

IDIOMES **~ le terrain** to put out feelers.

tatie○ /tati/ *nf* auntie.

tatillon, -onne /tatijɔ̃, ɔn/ **I** *adj* [*personne*] nit-picking, pernickety GB, persnickety US; [*administration*] nit-picking.

II *nm,f* nit-picker.

tâtonnement /tatɔnmɑ̃/ *nm* **après mes ~s dans l'obscurité** after groping around in the dark; **les ~s des chercheurs** fig tentative research; **après 10 années de ~s** fig after 10 years of trial and error.

tâtonner /tatɔne/ [1] *vi* to grope about ou around; **avancer en tâtonnant** lit, fig to grope one's way along; **on tâtonne** (dans des recherches) we're groping in the dark.

tâtons: **à tâtons** /atatɔ̃/ *loc adv* **avancer à ~** lit, fig to feel one's way along.

tatou /tatu/ *nm* armadillo.

tatouage /tatwaʒ/ *nm* **1** (dessin) tattoo; **se faire faire un ~** to have a tattoo done; **2** (procédé) tattooing.

tatouer /tatwe/ [1] *vtr* to tattoo; **se faire ~** to get tattooed; **il s'est fait ~ un aigle sur le dos** he has had an eagle tattooed on his back; **il s'est fait ~ la poitrine** he has had his chest tattooed.

tatoueur, -euse /tatwœʀ, øz/ ▶**510** *nm,f* tattooist, tattoo artist.

taudis /todi/ *nm inv* (misérable) hovel; (mal tenu) pigsty.

taulard◑, **~e** /tolaʀ, aʀd/ *nm,f* convict, con○.

taule◑ /tol/ *nf* **1** (prison) prison, nick○; **10 ans de ~** 10 years in the nick○ ou the slammer; **faire de la ~** to do time○; **2** (chambre) room, pad○.

taulier◑, **-ière** /tolje, ɛʀ/ *nm,f* hotel boss.

taupe /top/ *nf* **1** Zool mole; **2** (peau) moleskin; **en ~** moleskin (*épith*); **3**○ (femme désagréable) **c'est une vieille ~** pej she's an old bag péj; **4**○ (espion) mole; **5**○ Univ *second year preparatory class in mathematics and science for entrance to Grandes Écoles*; **6** Gén Civ tunnel borer; **7** ▶**193** (couleur) taupe.

taupin /topɛ̃/ *nm* **1** Zool click beetle; **2**○ Univ *student in second year preparatory class for entrance to Grandes Écoles*.

taupinière /topinjɛʀ/ *nf* **1** (monticule) molehill; (galeries) (mole) tunnels (*pl*); **2**○ (petite colline) hillock.

IDIOMES **faire une montagne d'une ~** to make a mountain out of a molehill.

taureau, *pl* **~x** /tɔʀo/ *nm* Zool bull; **~ de combat** fighting bull.

IDIOMES **prendre le ~ par les cornes** to take the bull by the horns.

Taureau /tɔʀo/ ▶**874** *nprm* Taurus.

taurillon /tɔʀijɔ̃/ *nm* young bull.

taurin, ~e /tɔʀɛ̃, in/ *adj* [*jeux*] bullfighting; [*culte, monde*] of bullfighting (*après n*); [*passion*] for bullfighting (*après n*).

tauromachie /tɔʀɔmaʃi/ *nf* bullfighting, tauromachy spéc.

tauromachique /tɔʀɔmaʃik/ *adj* bullfighting, tauromachian spéc.

tautologie /totɔlɔʒi/ *nf* tautology.

tautologique /totɔlɔʒik/ *adj* tautological.

taux /to/ *nm inv* **1** Fin, Stat rate; **~ fixe/mensuel/moyen** fixed/monthly/average rate; **~ de chômage/criminalité** unemployment/crime rate; **obligations à ~ variable** variable-rate bonds; **2** Méd level; **~ d'albumine/alcoolémie/de sucre** albumin/blood alcohol/blood sugar level.

■ **~ d'abstention** rate of abstention (from voting); **~ d'amortissement** depreciation rate; **~ d'audience** audience ratings (*pl*); **~ de base bancaire** minimum lending rate GB, prime rate US; **~ de change** exchange rate; **~ de compression** Tech compression ratio; **~ de croissance** growth rate; **~ d'escompte** bank rate; **~ d'exportation** level of exports; **~ de fécondité** fertility rate; **~ de flambage** burning cost; **~ de fréquentation** Théât, Cin audience figures (*pl*); **~ d'importation** level of imports; **~ d'imposition** or **de l'impôt** tax rate; **~ d'inflation** rate of inflation; **~ d'intérêt** interest rate; **~ d'invalidité** degree of disability; **~ de mortalité** mortality rate; **~ de natalité** birthrate; **~ de salaire horaire** hourly rate of pay; **~ de séropositivité** HIV rate; **~ de syndicalisation** percentage of the workforce belonging to unions.

tavelé, ~e /tavle/ *adj* [*peau*] spotted (**de** with); [*fruit*] blemished (**de** with).

taveler /tavle/ [19] **I** *vtr* to blemish [*peau, fruit*].

II se taveler *vpr* [*peau*] to become spotted; [*fruit*] to become blemished.

tavelure /tavlyʀ/ *nf* **1** (tache) mark; **2** (maladie des arbres) scab.

taverne /tavɛʀn/ *nf* tavern.

tavernier†, **-ière** /tavɛʀnje, ɛʀ/ *nm,f* taverner†.

taxable /taksabl/ *adj* taxable.

taxateur /taksatœʀ/ *nm* (**juge**) **~** taxing master.

taxation /taksasjɔ̃/ *nf* Fisc (imposition) taxation; (fixation) assessment; **la ~ de l'épargne** the taxing of savings.

taxe /taks/ *nf* **1** Comm, Écon, Fisc tax; **~ progressive** graduated tax; **une ~ de 5%** a 5% tax; **~ locale/communale/régionale** local/municipal/regional tax; **~ sur** tax on [*produit, plus-value, transaction, producteur*]; **la ~ sur le tabac/nucléaire** the tax on tobacco/nuclear energy; **les ~s sur les importations** import levies; **total hors ~s** total exclusive of tax; **boutique hors ~s** duty-free shop GB ou store US; **2 500 francs hors ~s** 2,500 francs exclusive of tax; **1 000 francs toutes ~s comprises, 1 000 francs TTC** 1,000 francs inclusive of tax; **2** Jur taxation.

■ **~ d'aéroport** airport tax; **~ d'apprentissage** ≈ training levy; **~ de douane** customs duty; **~ foncière** property tax ; **~ d'habitation** ≈ council tax (*paid by residents to cover local services*); **~ parafiscale** indirect taxation ¢; **~ postale** postage; **~ professionnelle** ≈ business rates (*pl*) GB, business taxes (*pl*) US; **~ de raccordement** connection charge; **~ de séjour** tourism tax; **~ à la valeur ajoutée** value added tax.

taxer /takse/ [1] *vtr* **1** Comm, Fisc, Écon to tax [*produit, profit, plus-value, contribuable*]; **~ qch à 10%** to tax sth at 10%; **la loi taxe à 45% les bénéfices des sociétés** the law taxes company profits at 45%; **les plus-values sont taxées à 19%** capital gains are taxed at 19%; **2** (accuser) **~ qn de laxisme/d'élitisme/de corruption** to accuse sb of being lax/elitist/corrupt; **je me suis fait ~ de jalousie** or **jaloux** I was accused of being jealous; **~ l'affection de qn de tyrannique** to call sb's affection tyranny.

taxi /taksi/ *nm* **1** (véhicule) taxi, cab; **chauffeur de ~** taxi driver, cabdriver; **station de ~s** taxi rank GB, cab stand US; **2**○ (chauffeur) taxi driver, cabby○.

taxidermie /taksidɛʀmi/ *nf* taxidermy.

taxidermiste /taksidɛʀmist/ ▶**510** *nmf* taxidermist.

taxi-girl, *pl* **~s** /taksigœʀl/ *nf* (entraîneuse) hostess.

taximètre /taksimɛtʀ/ *nm* (taxi)meter.

taxinomie /taksinɔmi/ *nf* taxonomy.

taxinomique /taksinɔmik/ *adj* taxonomic.

taxinomiste /taksinɔmist/ *nmf* taxonomist.

taxiphone® /taksifɔn/ *nm* pay phone.

taxonomie /taksɔnɔmi/ *nf* = **taxinomie**.

Tayside ▶**692** *nprm* **le ~** Tayside.

Tbilissi /tbilisi/ ▶**857** *npr* Tbilisi.

Tchad /tʃad/ ▶**459**, **321** *nprm* Chad; **le lac ~** Lake Chad.

tchadien, -ienne /tʃadjɛ̃, ɛn/ ▶**537** *adj* Chadian.

Tchadien, -ienne /tʃadjɛ̃, ɛn/ ▶**537** *nm,f* Chadian.

tchador /tʃadɔʀ/ *nm* chador.

Tchaïkovski /tʃajkɔvski/ *npr* Tchaikovsky.

tchao○ /tʃao/ *excl* bye○!, see you○!

tchécoslovaque /tʃekɔslɔvak/ *adj* Hist Czechoslovakian, Czechoslovak.

Tchécoslovaque /tʃekɔslɔvak/ *nmf* Hist Czechoslovakian, Czechoslovak.

Tchécoslovaquie /tʃekɔslɔvaki/ *nprf* Hist Czechoslovakia.

Tchekhov /tʃekɔf/ *npr* Chekhov.

tchèque /tʃɛk/ **I** ▶**537**, **321** *adj* Czech; **République ~** Czech Republic.

II ▶**462** *nm* Ling Czech.

Tchèque /tʃɛk/ ▶**537** *nmf* Czech.

Tchernobyl /tʃɛʀnɔbil/ ▶**857** *npr* Chernobyl.

tchin(-tchin)○ /tʃin(tʃin)/ *excl* cheers!

TD○ /tede/ *nmpl*: *abbr* ▶**travail**[1].

te (**t'** *before vowel or mute h*) /t(ə)/ *pron pers* **1** (objet direct) **je ~ déteste** I hate you; **s'il essaie de ~ frapper** if he tries to hit you; **je t'entends mal** I can't hear you very well; **viens, je t'invite** come on, I'll treat you; **2** (object direct) **il ne t'a pas fait mal** he didn't hurt you; **elle ne t'a pas tout dit** she didn't tell you everything; **je ~ l'offre** I'm giving it to you; **non, je ne t'en veux pas** no, I don't bear a grudge against you; **3** (pronom réfléchi) yourself; **il faut que tu ~ soignes** you must look after yourself; **tu ~ détestes pour ça?** do you hate yourself because of that?; **si tu ne ~ méfies pas** if you're not careful; **va ~ laver** go and have a wash; **va ~ laver les mains** go and wash your hands.

té /te/ *nm* (règle) T-square; **en ~** T-shaped.

TEC /teəse/ *nf*: *abbr* ▶**tonne**.

technétium /tɛknetjɔm/ *nm* technetium.

technicien, -ienne /tɛknisjɛ̃, ɛn/ **I** *adj* technological.

II ▶**510** *nm,f* **1** (professionnel) technician; **~ agricole/supérieur** agricultural/qualified technician; **2** (spécialiste) technical expert (**de** in); **c'est un très bon ~** he's technically very good; **3** (réparateur) engineer.

■ **~ de surface** cleaner.

technicité /tɛknisite/ *nf* technical nature.

technico-commercial, **~e**, *mpl* **-iaux** /teknikokɔmɛʀsjal, o/ **I** *adj* [*ingénieur*] commercial; [*secteur, filiale*] technical sales (*épith*); **agent ~** technical sales representative.

II ▶**510** *nm,f* (personne) technical sales representative.

III *nm* (secteur) technical sales (*pl*).

Technicolor® /tɛknikɔlɔʀ/ *nm* Technicolor®; **paysage en technicolor** technicolour[GB] landscape.

technique /tɛknik/ **I** *adj* (tous contextes) technical.

II *nm* technical subjects (*pl*); **les professeurs du ~** teachers of technical subjects.

III *nf* **1** (méthode) technique; **~ artisanale/de vente** craft/sales technique; **il n'a pas la (bonne) ~**○ he hasn't got the knack○ (**pour faire** of doing); **2** (maîtrise) technique; **elle manque de ~** she lacks technique; **3** Écon, Ind technology ¢; **le développement des ~s** the development of technology; **4** Audio, Radio, TV **la ~** studio production; **à la ~ Agnès Bon** studio production by Agnès Bon.

techniquement /tɛknikmɑ̃/ *adv* technically.

technocrate /tɛknɔkʀat/ *nmf* technocrat.

technocratie /tɛknɔkʀasi/ *nf* technocracy.

technocratique /tɛknɔkʀatik/ *adj* technocratic.

technologie /tɛknɔlɔʒi/ *nf* technology; **une nouvelle ~** a new technology; **les ~s**

avancées/de pointe advanced/leading-edge technology.

technologique /tɛknɔlɔʒik/ *adj* technological.

technologue /tɛknɔlɔg/ *nmf* technologist.

technopole /tɛknɔpɔl/ *nf* town centred[GB] on research and advanced technology.

technopôle /tɛknɔpol/ *nm* high-tech business zone.

technostructure /tɛknɔstʀyktyʀ/ *nf* technostructure.

teck /tɛk/ *nm* **1** (arbre) teak; **2** (bois) teak; **meubles en ~** teak furniture.

teckel /tekɛl/ *nm* dachshund.

tectonique /tɛktɔnik/ **I** *adj* tectonic.
II *nf* tectonics (+ *v sg*); **la ~ des plaques** plate tectonics.

teddy /tedi/ *nm* Mode teddy.

Te Deum /tedeɔm/ *nm inv* Mus, Relig Te Deum.

tee /ti/ *nm* tee; **placer la balle sur le ~** to tee up.

tee-shirt, *pl* **~s** /tiʃœʀt/ *nm* T-shirt.

TEF /teəɛf/ *nm*: *abbr* ▶ **transfert**.

téflon® /teflɔ̃/ *nm* Teflon®; **casserole en ~** Teflon saucepan.

tégument /tegymɑ̃/ *nm* Bot, Zool integument.

Téhéran /teeʀɑ̃/ ▶ 857 *npr* Teheran.

teigne /tɛɲ/ *nf* **1** Méd ringworm, tinea spéc; **2** (mite) moth, tineid spéc; **3** (personne hargneuse) nasty GB ou real US piece of work○.
IDIOMES **être méchant comme une ~** to be a nasty GB ou real US piece of work.

teigneux, **-euse** /tɛɲø, øz/ *adj* **1** (hargneux) cantankerous; **2** Méd suffering from ringworm.

teindre /tɛ̃dʀ/ [73] **I** *vtr* to dye [*cheveux, tissu, cuir*]; to stain [*bois, meuble*]; **~ qch en vert** to dye sth green; **la cochenille teint en rouge** cochineal dyes things red; **~ la laine** to dye wool; **ce produit teint bien** this product is a good dye.
II se teindre *vpr* **1** (avec un produit) [*personne*] to dye one's hair; **se ~ les cheveux en roux** to dye one's hair red; **cela se teint facilement** (tissu) it's easy to dye; (bois) it's easy to stain; **2** liter (changer de couleur) **se ~ de rose** [*ciel, montagne*] to be tinged (with) pink.

teint, **~e** /tɛ̃, tɛ̃t/ **I** *pp* ▶ **teindre**.
II *pp adj* [*cheveux, étoffe, cuir*] dyed; [*bois, meuble*] stained; **il est ~** (personne) he's got dyed hair.
III *nm* **1** (peau) complexion; **au ~ clair/mat** with a fair/matt complexion; **avoir un joli ~** to have a lovely complexion; **2** (lié à la santé) **avoir le ~ rose** or **frais** to have a healthy glow; **avoir le ~ jaune** to be sallow-skinned; **avoir le ~ pâle** to look pale; ▶ **bon**.
IV teinte *nf* **1** (nuance de couleur) shade; **2** (couleur) colour[GB]; **3** fig (d'envie, de supériorité) **une ~e de** a tinge of.

teinté, **~e** /tɛ̃te/ **I** *pp* ▶ **teinter**.
II *pp adj* **1** [*lunettes, verre, crème*] tinted; [*bois*] stained; **~ jaune** yellow-tinted; **2 ~ de** [*sentiment, couleur*] tinged with.

teinter /tɛ̃te/ [1] **I** *vtr* **1** to tint [*verre*]; to stain [*bois, meuble*]; to dye [*cuir*]; **~ du verre en rouge** to tint glass red, to give glass a red tint; **2** (nuancer) **~ qch de** to tinge sth with.
II se teinter *vpr* liter **se ~ de qch** [*couleur, sentiment*] to become tinged with.

teinture /tɛ̃tyʀ/ *nf* **1** (produit) (pour cheveux, tissu, cuir) dye; (pour bois) stain; Pharm tincture; **2** (procédé) (de cheveux, tissu, cuir) dyeing; (de bois) staining; **se faire une ~** to dye one's hair; **se faire faire une ~** to have one's hair dyed.
■ **~ d'iode** tincture of iodine.

teinturerie /tɛ̃tyʀʀi/ *nf* **1** ▶ 510 (boutique de nettoyage) (dry-)cleaner's; **apporter qch à la ~** to take sth to the (dry-)cleaner's; **2** (industrie) (de la teinture) dyeing; (de nettoyage) (dry-)cleaning.

teinturier, **-ière** /tɛ̃tyʀje, ɛʀ/ *nm,f* ▶ 510 **1** (qui nettoie) dry-cleaner; **2** (qui teint) dyer.

tek /tɛk/ *nm* = **teck**.

tel, **telle** /tɛl/ **I** *adj* **1** (pareil) such; **une telle conduite vous honore** such behaviour[GB] does you credit; **un ~ homme peut être dangereux** such a man can be dangerous, a man like that can be dangerous; **personne d'autre n'a un ~ rire** no-one else has a laugh like that ou laughs like that; **une telle qualité n'existe plus** such quality ou quality like that can no longer be found; **je n'ai jamais rien vu/entendu de ~** I've never seen/heard anything like it; **~ que** such as; **les bêtes féroces telles que le tigre, la panthère** fierce animals such as the tiger, the panther; **un homme ~ que lui mérite d'être pendu** a man like that deserves to be hanged; **2** (pareil à) like; **ils s'enfuirent telle une bande de moineaux** they fled like a flock of sparrows; **les poissons de mer qui, ~ le saumon, vont se reproduire en rivières** sea fish which, like salmon, spawn in rivers; **3** (ainsi) **telle est la vérité** that is the truth; **~s furent ses propos** those were his words; **~ est cet ami à qui tu faisais confiance** that's what he's really like, that friend you trusted; **il est honnête, du moins je le crois ~** he's honest, at least I believe him to be so; **comme ~, en tant que ~** as such; **ce n'est pas sa fille mais il la considère comme telle** she's not his daughter but he treats her as if she were; **c'est peut-être son meilleur livre—moi, je le tiens pour ~** it's probably his best book—I myself consider it to be so; **~ quel, ~ que**○ controv (sans modification) as it is; **ses affaires étaient restées telles quelles** his things were left as they were; **servir le saumon ~ quel** serve the salmon as it is; **tu l'avais mis sur la table, je l'ai trouvé ~ quel** you had left it on the table, I found it lying there; **~ que** (comme) as; **~ que pratiqué** as practised[GB]; **si cette maison est telle que tu le dis** if the house is as you say it is; **Marie est restée telle que je l'ai connue** Marie has stayed as I knew her; **~ que je te connais** if I know you; **~ que vous le voyez il est milliardaire/il a 80 ans** you wouldn't believe it to look at him but he's a millionaire/he's 80; **4** (pour exprimer l'intensité) **avec un ~ enthousiasme** with such enthusiasm; **il fait une telle chaleur/un ~ froid** it is so hot/so cold; **il y avait un ~ bruit** there was so much noise; **nos problèmes sont ~s que nous devons vous en parler** our problems are such that we need to discuss them with you; **de telle sorte** or **façon** or **manière que** (accidentellement) in such a way that; (délibérément) so that; **5** (un certain) **admettons qu'il arrive ~ jour, à telle heure** suppose that he arrives on such and such a day, at such and such a time; **que je prenne telle ou telle décision il critique toujours** no matter what decision I make, he criticizes it; **apprendre à se conduire de telle ou telle façon en telle ou telle circonstance** to learn to behave in such and such a manner in such and such a situation; **je me moque de ce que pense telle ou telle personne** I don't care what certain people think; **~ autre** others; **~s autres** certain others.
II *pron indéf* **~ voulait la guerre, ~ voulait la paix** some wanted war, some wanted peace; **s'il rencontrait ~ ou ~ il le leur dirait** if he were to meet anybody he would tell them; **qu'importe si ~ et ~ ne sont pas contents** what does it matter if some people aren't pleased; **~ qui se disait son ami le renie aujourd'hui** he who claimed to be his friend denies him now; ▶ **prendre**.

télé○ /tele/ **I** *adj inv* [*émission, écran*] TV.
II *nf* **1** (émissions) TV, telly○ GB; **à la ~** on TV, on telly○; **tu as le programme ~?** have you got the TV guide?; **2** (téléviseur) TV, telly○ GB; **éteinds la ~** switch off the TV; **3** (organisme) TV.

télé-achat /teleaʃa/ *nm* teleshopping.

téléboutique® /telebutik/ *nf* phone shop GB, phone store US.

télécabine /telekabin/ *nm* cable car.

télécarte /telekaʀt/ *nf* phonecard.

télécharger /teleʃaʀʒe/ [13] *vtr* Ordinat to download.

télécinéma /telesinema/ *nm* **1** (appareil) telecine; **2** (transmission) telecine transmission.

télécom○ /telekɔm/ **I** *adj* [*réseau, satellite*] telecommunications.
II télécoms *nmpl* telecommunications.

télécommande /telekɔmɑ̃d/ *nf* remote control; **~ radioélectrique** radio control.

télécommander /telekɔmɑ̃de/ [1] *vtr* **1** Tech to operate [sth] by remote control; **voiture télécommandée** remote-controlled car; **2** fig (diriger) to mastermind; **un complot télécommandé de l'étranger** a plot masterminded from abroad.

télécommunication /telekɔmynikasjɔ̃/ *nf* telecommunications (+ *v sg*); **un réseau de ~** a telecommunications network.

téléconférence /telekɔ̃feʀɑ̃s/ *nf* **1** (séance) (audioconférence) conference call; (vidéoconférence) teleconference; **2** (principe) videoconferencing.

télécopie /telekɔpi/ *nf* fax; **numéro de ~** fax number; **par ~** by fax; **annuaire de la ~** fax directory.

télécopier /telekɔpje/ [2] *vtr* to fax.

télécopieur /telekɔpjœʀ/ *nm* fax machine, fax; **~ portable** portable fax machine.

télédétection /teledetɛksjɔ̃/ *nf* remote sensing.

télédiffuser /teledifyze/ [1] *vtr* to broadcast; **un programme télédiffusé** a televised programme[GB], a telecast.

télédiffusion /teledifyzjɔ̃/ *nf* broadcasting; **la ~ par satellite** satellite broadcasting.

télédistribution /teledistʀibysjɔ̃/ *nf* wired broadcasting.

télé-enquêteur, **-trice** /teleɑ̃kɛtœʀ, tʀis/ ▶ 510 *nm,f* telemarketer.

télé-enseignement, *pl* **~s** /teleɑ̃sɛɲəmɑ̃/ *nm* distance learning.

téléfilm /telefilm/ *nm* TV film, TV movie.

télégénique /teleʒenik/ *adj* telegenic.

télégramme /telegʀam/ *nm* telegram, cable US; **~ téléphoné** telegram by telephone.

télégraphe /telegʀaf/ *nm* telegraph.

télégraphie /telegʀafi/ *nf* telegraphy.

télégraphier /telegʀafje/ [1] *vtr* to telegraph [*message*]; **je vais leur ~** I'm going to send them a telegram ou cable US.

télégraphique /telegʀafik/ *adj* **1** [*poteau, message*] telegraph; **2** [*style*] telegraphic.

télégraphiste /telegʀafist/ ▶ 510 *nmf* **1** (opérateur) telegraphist, telegrapher; **2** (coursier) telegraph delivery person.

téléguidage /telegidaʒ/ *nm* radio control.

téléguider /telegide/ [1] *vtr* **1** lit to control [sth] by radio; **voiture téléguidée** radio-controlled car; **2** fig (diriger) to mastermind.

téléimprimeur /teleɛ̃pʀimœʀ/ *nm* teleprinter, teletypewriter US.

téléinformatique /teleɛ̃fɔʀmatik/ *nf* teleprocessing.

télékinésie /telekinezi/ *nf* telekinesis.

Télémaque /telemak/ *npr* Telemachus.

télémarché /telemaʀʃe/ *nm* teleshopping by videotex®.

télématique /telematik/ **I** *adj* [*service, réseau*] viewdata GB, videotex®.
II *nf* telematics (+ *v sg*).

télémètre /telemɛtʀ/ *nm* telemeter.

télémétrie /telemetʀi/ *nf* telemetry.

télémétrique /telemetʀik/ *adj* **visée ~** telemetric viewfinding.

télénégociateur, **-trice** /telenegɔsjatœʀ, tʀis/ ▶ 510 *nm,f* telesales operator.

téléobjectif /teleɔbʒɛktif/ *nm* telephoto lens.
téléologie /teleɔlɔʒi/ *nf* teleology.
téléologique /teleɔlɔʒik/ *adj* teleological.
télépaiement /telepɛmɑ̃/ *nm* (avec carte de crédit) credit card payment; (sur écran) electronic payment system via a computer screen.
télépathe /telepat/ **I** *adj* telepathic.
II *nmf* telepath.
télépathie /telepati/ *nf* telepathy.
télépathique /telepatik/ *adj* telepathic.
téléphérique /telefeʀik/ *nm* cable car, téléphérique.
téléphone /telefɔn/ *nm* (dispositif, appareil) telephone, phone; **avoir le ~** to be on the (tele)phone GB, to have a phone; **numéro de ~** phone number; **passer** or **donner un coup de ~** to make a phone call; **~ à touches/pièces** push-button/coin-operated telephone; **~ à carte** cardphone; **~ sans fil** cordless telephone; **~ de campagne** field telephone; **j'ai eu ta mère au ~** I talked to your mother on the phone.
■ **~ arabe** (bouche-à-oreille) grapevine, bush telegraph; Jeux Chinese whispers; **~ fixe** (dans voiture) in-car phone; **~ interprète** Télécom telephone interpreting service; **~ portable** transmobile phone; **~ portatif** pocket car phone; **~ rose** erotic chat-line; **le ~ rouge** the hot-line.
téléphoner /telefɔne/ [1] **I** *vtr* **~ qch à qn** to phone ou telephone sb with sth; **~ des résultats/une nouvelle à qn** to phone sb with results/a piece of news; **il nous a téléphoné de venir** he phoned to ask us to come.
II *vi* (en général) to phone, to telephone; (une fois) to make a phone call; **je ne téléphone jamais, j'écris** I never phone, I always write; **~ à qn** to phone sb, to call sb; **~ en France** to phone France; **~ à qn en France** to phone sb in France.
III se téléphoner *vpr* to phone each other.
téléphonie /telefɔni/ *nf* telephony.
téléphonique /telefɔnik/ *adj* [*appel, cabine*] (tele)phone (*épith*).
téléphoniste /telefɔnist/ ▶**510** *nmf* telephonist GB, (telephone) operator.
téléphotographie /telefɔtɔgʀafi/ *nf* telephotography.
téléprompteur /telepʀɔ̃ptœʀ/ *nm* Autocue® GB, teleprompter.
téléprospecteur, -trice /telepʀɔspɛktœʀ, tʀis/ ▶**510** *nm,f* telemarketer.
téléprospection /telepʀɔspɛksjɔ̃/ *nf* telemarketing.
téléreportage /teleʀəpɔʀtaʒ/ *nm* **1** (activité) television reporting; **2** (film) television report.
télescopage /telɛskɔpaʒ/ *nm* **1** lit collision (**entre** between); **2** fig (de cultures, courants) overlap.
télescope /telɛskɔp/ *nm* telescope; **~ électronique/spatial** electron/space telescope.
télescoper /telɛskɔpe/ [1] **I** *vtr* [*camion*] to crush [*voiture*].
II se télescoper *vpr* **1** lit [*véhicules*] to collide; **2** fig [*notions, tendances*] to overlap.
télescopique /telɛskɔpik/ *adj* telescopic.
téléscripteur /teleskʀiptœʀ/ *nm* teleprinter GB, teletypewriter US.
télésiège /telesjɛʒ/ *nm* chair lift.
téléski /teleski/ *nm* ski tow.
télésouffleur /telesuflœʀ/ *nm* teleprompter.
téléspectateur, -trice /telespɛktatœʀ, tʀis/ *nm,f* viewer.
télésurveillance /telesyʀvɛjɑ̃s/ *nf* electronic surveillance, telesurveillance.
Télétel® /teletɛl/ *nm* viewdata GB, videotex®.
Télétex® /teletɛks/ *nm inv* Teletex®.
télétexte /teletɛkst/ *nm* teletext.
téléthon /teletɔ̃/ *nm* telethon.
télétraitement /teletʀɛtmɑ̃/ *nm* teleprocessing.
télétransmission /teletʀɑ̃smisjɔ̃/ *nf* transmission.
télétravail /teletʀavaj/ *nm* telecommuting.
télétravailleur, -euse /teletʀavajœʀ, øz/ ▶**510** *nm,f* teleworker.
télétype® /teletip/ *nm* Teletype®, teleprinter.
télévendeur, -euse /televɑ̃dœʀ, øz/ ▶**510** *nm,f* telesales operator.
télévente /televɑ̃t/ *nf* telesales.
télévisé, ~e /televize/ *adj* [*programme, publicité, jeu*] television (*épith*); [*débat, plateau, retransmission*] televised.
téléviseur /televizœʀ/ *nm* television (set), TV (set); **~ couleur/noir et blanc** colour[GB]/black and white television; **~ écran plat** flat screen television.
télévision /televizjɔ̃/ *nf* **1** (technique) television, TV; **~ par câble/satellite** cable/satellite television; **~ (à) haute définition** high-definition television; **~ à péage** pay-TV; **2** (émissions) television, TV; **passer à la ~** to be on television ou TV; **regarder la ~** to watch television ou TV; **3** (organisme) television; **travailler à la ~** to work in television; **studio/chaîne de ~** television studio/channel; **4** (téléviseur) television, TV.
télévisuel, -elle /televizɥɛl/ *adj* [*industrie, spectacle*] television (*épith*), televisual.
télex /telɛks/ *nm inv* telex; **par ~** by telex.
télexer /telɛkse/ [1] *vtr* to telex.
télexiste /telɛksist/ ▶**510** *nmf* telex operator.
tellement /tɛlmɑ̃/ ▶**662** **I** *adv* **1** (marquant l'intensité) (modifiant un adjectif ou un adverbe) so; (modifiant un verbe) so much; (modifiant un comparatif) so much; **pas ~** not much; **il est ~ gentil/bête** he's so nice/stupid; **ça va ~ vite** it goes so fast; **c'est ~ loin l'Australie** Australia is so far away; **il t'aime ~** he loves you so much; **elle déteste ~ les interviews** she hates interviews so much; **ils ont ~ grandi** they've grown so much; **ce serait ~ mieux** it'd be so much better; **c'est ~ plus facile/rapide de cette façon** it's so much easier/quicker this way; **il n'aime pas ~ lire** he doesn't like reading much; **'ça t'a plu?'—'pas ~'** 'did you like it?'—'not much'; **'il y avait beaucoup de monde?'—'pas ~'** 'were there many people?'—'not really'; **deux ans ce n'est pas ~ long** two years isn't so very long; **ce n'est pas ~ que je sois fatigué mais...** it's not so much that I'm tired but...; **cela n'a plus ~ d'importance** it doesn't really matter any more; **je n'ai plus ~ envie d'y aller** I don't really want to go any more; **elle n'a plus ~ le temps** she doesn't really have time these days; **il n'a pas ~ fait beau** the weather wasn't that good; **il n'y a pas ~ d'années**○ not many years ago; **il n'est pas ~ plus jeune que moi** he's not that much younger than me; **'tu le vois régulièrement?'—'plus ~'** 'do you see him regularly?'—'not so much anymore'; **~ drôle/faim/vite que** so funny/hungry/fast that; **c'est ~ mieux payé que je vais accepter** it's so much better paid that I'm going to accept; **il reste ~ peu de vin que** there's so little wine left that; **il y avait ~ de gens que je me suis perdu** there were so many people that I got lost; **es-tu ~ fatigué que tu ne puisses pas bouger?** liter are you so tired that you can't even move?; **2**○ (si nombreux) **nous étions ~ à cette soirée que** there were so many of us at this party that; **il y en a ~ qui aimeraient le faire** so many people would like to do it; **3** (introduisant une cause) **j'ai de la peine à suivre ~ c'est compliqué** it's so complicated that I find it hard to follow; **on ne pouvait pas respirer ~ il y avait de monde** there were so many people that you couldn't even breathe; **nous ne sommes pas sortis ~ le temps était menaçant** the weather looked so threatening that we didn't go out.
II tellement de *dét indéf* **1** (avec un nom dénombrable) so many; **il y a ~ de livres que je ne sais pas lequel choisir** there are so many books (that) I don't know which to choose; **on voit ~ de choses bizarres** you see so many strange things; **j'ai ~ de choses à faire** I've got so many things to do, I've got so much to do; **il y a ~ de choses à voir** there's so much to see; **2** (avec un nom non dénombrable) so much; **j'ai ~ de travail que je ne sais plus où donner de la tête** I've got so much to do; **2** (avec un nom non dénombrable) so much; **j'ai ~ de travail que je ne sais plus où donner de la tête** I've got so much work (that) I don't know if I'm coming or going; **il a eu ~ de chance/succès** he was so lucky/successful; **j'ai vu ~ de monde** I saw so many people.
tel-tel /tɛltɛl/ *adj, nm* wysiwyg.
téméraire /temeʀɛʀ/ *adj* [*explorateur, chef d'entreprise, projet*] reckless; [*jugement*] rash; **courageux mais pas ~** brave but not foolhardy; **il est ~ de penser que** it is foolhardy ou rash to think that.
témérité /temeʀite/ *nf* (de personne, projet) recklessness; (de paroles) rashness; **avoir la ~ de faire** to have the temerity to do.
témoignage /temwaɲaʒ/ *nm* **1** (histoire personnelle) story; (compte-rendu) account; **le ~ d'une ancienne droguée** a former drug addict's story; **recueillir les ~s des réfugiés** to get the refugees' stories; **les ~s recueillis auprès de** the accounts given by; **apporter son ~** to give one's own account; **selon les ~s de** according to (accounts given by); **rendre ~ sans prendre position** to give an objective account (of things); **un livre exceptionnel, ~ sur une époque** fig an exceptional book, a first-hand account of an era; **2** (au cours d'une enquête) evidence ¢; Jur (déposition) evidence ¢, testimony; **des ~s contradictoires/qui concordent** conflicting/corroborating evidence; **obtenir le ~ de qn** to get evidence from sb ou sb's evidence ; **s'appuyer sur les ~s des voisins** to rely on evidence from the neighbours[GB]; **selon plusieurs ~s** according to several witnesses; **entendre le ~ de qn** to hear sb's evidence ou testimony; **rendre ~** to give evidence, to testify; **porter ~ (de qch)** to bear witness (to sth); ▶**faux**; **3** fml (marque) **~ d'amitié** (cadeau) token ou mark of friendship; (geste) expression ou gesture of friendship; **les ~s de sympathie** expressions of sympathy; **en ~ de ma reconnaissance** as a mark ou token of my gratitude; **donner des ~s de son amitié** to prove one's friendship; **rendre ~ au courage de qn** to testify to sb's courage.
témoigner /temwaɲe/ [1] **I** *vtr* **1** Jur to testify (**que** that); **elle a témoigné l'avoir vu entrer/qu'elle l'avait vu entrer** she testified to having seen him go in/that she had seen him go in; **2** (montrer) **~ de la reconnaissance/de l'affection** to show gratitude/affection; **~ de l'hostilité/de l'intérêt envers** to show hostility towards GB ou to/interest in; **la confiance qu'elle m'a témoignée** the trust she placed in me; **les marques de sympathie qui leur ont été témoignées lors de...** the sympathy they received when...; **cela témoigne que** it shows that.
II témoigner de *vtr ind* **1** (prouver) **~ de** to show; **cela témoigne de leur courage** this shows their courage; **comme en témoigne leur lettre** as their letter shows; **2** (se porter garant de) **~ du courage de qn** to vouch for sb's courage.
III *vi* **1** Jur to give evidence, to testify; **~ en faveur de qn/contre qn** to give evidence in sb's favour/against sb, to testify for sb/against sb; **être appelé à ~** to be called to give evidence ou as a witness; **2** (dire) **'il était toujours poli,' témoignent les voisins** neighbours[GB] say he was always polite.

La température

Dans les pays anglophones, la température se mesure traditionnellement en degrés Fahrenheit, mais les degrés Celsius sont de plus en plus utilisés, surtout en Grande-Bretagne. Le bulletin météo à la télévision britannique n'utilise que les degrés Celsius.

Celsius (C)	Fahrenheit (F)	
100°	212°*	*boiling point* (*point d'ébullition*)
90°	194°	
80°	176°	
70°	158°	
60°	140°	
50°	122°	
40°	104°	
37°	98.4°	
30°	86°	
20°	68°	
10°	50°	
0°	32°	*freezing point* (*point de congélation*)
–10°	14°	
–273.15°	–459.67°	*absolute zero* (*zéro absolu*)

* *Pour la prononciation des nombres,* ▶ **545**.

65°F	=	65°F	(*sixty-five degrees Fahrenheit*)
–15°C	=	–15°C	(*minus fifteen degrees Celsius*)
environ 55°	=	about 55°	(*fifty-five degrees*)
presque 60°	=	almost 60°	
plus de 50°	=	above 50° *ou* over 50°	
moins de 60°	=	below 60°	

La température des choses

quelle est la température du lait? = what temperature is the milk?
à quelle température est-il? = what temperature is it?
il est à une température de 53° = it is 53°

Noter l'absence d'équivalent anglais de l'expression à une température de.

A est plus chaud que B = A is hotter than B
B est moins chaud que A = B is cooler than A
B est plus froid que A = B is colder than A
A est à la même température que B = A is the same temperature as B
A et B sont à la même température = A and B are the same temperature

Noter que l'anglais n'a pas d'équivalent de la préposition à *dans ces deux derniers exemples.*

à quelle température l'eau bout-elle? = what temperature does water boil at?
elle bout à 100° = it boils at 100°

La température du corps

quelle est sa température? = what is his temperature?
sa température est de 38°C = his temperature is 38°C
il a 38°C de fièvre = he has a temperature of 38°C
le thermomètre indique 102°F = the thermometer shows *ou* says 102°F
il a 39,5° = his temperature is 39.5°
la température du corps est d'environ 37° = body temperature is about 37°

Le temps

quelle température fait-il aujourd'hui? = what is the temperature today?
25° au-dessous de zéro = 25° below zero
il fait 12° = it is 12°
il fait 40 degrés = it is 40 degrees
il fait –15° = it is –15° (*dire* minus fifteen degrees) *ou* it is –15° (minus fifteen)
il fait plus chaud à Nice qu'à Londres = Nice is warmer than London
il fait la même température à Nice qu'à Londres = it's the same temperature in Nice as in London

témoin /temwɛ̃/ **I** *nm* **1** (sur les lieux) witness; **~ oculaire** or **direct** eyewitness; **être (le) ~ de** to witness, to be a witness to; **le seul ~ direct** the only person actually to witness the scene; **cela a eu lieu sans ~** there were no witnesses; **prendre qn à ~** to call sb to witness (**de** to, of); **2** (au tribunal) witness; **~ de l'accusation/de la défense** prosecution/defence[GB] witness; **être ~ à charge/à décharge** to be a witness for the prosecution/for the defence[GB]; **~ défaillant** missing witness; ▶ **faux**; **3** (attestant l'authenticité) witness (**à** to); (à un mariage) witness; **parler devant ~s** to speak before witnesses; **il faut signer devant ~** you have to have your signature witnessed; **4** (à un duel) second; **5** fig (d'une époque) **avoir été ~ de la naissance du troisième Reich** to have witnessed the birth of the Third Reich; **la cathédrale, ~ de l'époque où...** the cathedral, bearing witness to an age when...; **ce village, ~ de notre amour** this village where our love blossomed; **6** (preuve) **ils sont cruels, ~ le massacre de tout un village** they are (certainly) cruel, as evidenced by the massacre of an entire village; **7** Tech (voyant) indicator ou warning light; **~ d'huile** Aut oil warning light; **8** Sport baton; **9** Constr (sur une fissure) telltale; **10** Gén Civ boundary marker.
II (-)témoin (*in compounds*) control; **groupe/sujet ~** control group/subject; **son ~** Cin guide track.
■ **~ sonore** Cin sync beep; **Témoin de Jéhovah** Relig Jehovah's witness.
IDIOMES **Dieu** or **le ciel m'en est ~** as God is my witness; **Dieu m'est ~ que je dis la vérité** as God is my witness I am speaking the truth.

tempe /tɑ̃p/ *nf* temple; **appuyer un pistolet sur la ~ de qn** to hold a gun to sb's head.

tempérament /tɑ̃peʀamɑ̃/ *nm* **1** (caractère) disposition; **être calme de ~, avoir un ~ calme** to have a calm disposition; **ce n'est pas dans mon ~ de me mettre en colère** I would never lose my temper; **elle devrait aller se plaindre, mais ce n'est pas dans son ~** she should go and complain, but she's not like that; **avoir un ~ d'artiste** to have an artistic temperament; **avoir du ~** (volontaire) to have a strong character; (sensuel) to be hot-blooded; **c'est un ~** he/she is a character; **2†** (organisme) constitution; **~ lymphatique/sanguin** lymphatic/sanguine constitution; **3** Comm, Fin **à ~** by instalments[GB]; **4** Mus temperament.

tempérance /tɑ̃peʀɑ̃s/ *nf* temperance.

tempérant, ~e /tɑ̃peʀɑ̃, ɑ̃t/ *adj* liter temperate littér.

température /tɑ̃peʀatyʀ/ *nf* **1** Méd, Sci temperature; **prendre la ~ d'un malade** to take a patient's temperature; **animal à ~ constante/variable** warm-blooded/cold-blooded animal; **2** (fièvre) temperature; **avoir** or **faire de la ~** to have ou run a temperature; **3** (humeur) **prendre la ~ du public** to sound out the public's mood; **le directeur est venu prendre la ~ dans les ateliers** the manager has come to test the water on the factory floor.
■ **~ absolue** Phys absolute temperature; **~ d'ébullition** boiling point; **~ de fusion** melting point.

tempéré, ~e /tɑ̃peʀe/ **I** *pp* ▶ **tempérer**.
II *pp adj* **1** Géog temperate; **2** Mus [*gamme, intervalle*] tempered; **'le Clavier bien ~'** 'the Well-tempered Clavier'.

tempérer /tɑ̃peʀe/ [14] *vtr* liter **1** (adoucir) to temper [*chaleur, froid*]; **2** (modérer) to temper [*fougue, enthousiasme, critique*]; to moderate [*argument*]; **~ ses ardeurs** to cool one's ardour[GB].

tempête /tɑ̃pɛt/ *nf* **1** Météo (sans pluie) gale; (avec pluie) storm; **la ~ fait rage** the gale ou storm is raging; **être pris dans une ~** to be caught in a gale ou storm; **le bateau a tenu bon dans la ~** the boat weathered the storm; **essuyer une ~** to weather a storm; **une ~ de neige** a snowstorm, a blizzard; **une ~ de sable** a sandstorm; ▶ **semer**; **2** (agitation) uproar; **son discours a provoqué une ~** his/her speech provoked an uproar; **~ politique/économique** political/economic uproar; **après la ~ boursière** after the upheaval on the stock exchange; **déclencher une ~ de protestations/réactions** to trigger a wave of protest/reactions; **c'est le calme avant** or **qui précède la ~** it's the calm before the storm; **une ~ dans un verre d'eau** a storm in a teacup GB, a tempest in a teapot US.

tempêter /tɑ̃pete/ [1] *vi* to rage (**contre** against).

tempétueux, -euse /tɑ̃pɛtɥø, øz/ *adj* **1** fig [*atmosphère, réunion*] stormy; [*personne*] tempestuous; **2** lit [*mer, côte*] storm-tossed (*épith*).

temple /tɑ̃pl/ *nm* **1** (non chrétien) temple; **2** (protestant) gén church; (méthodiste, baptiste, presbytérien) church, chapel GB; **aller au ~** to go to church; **3** fig temple (**de** of).

Templier /tɑ̃plje/ *nm* (Knight) Templar.

tempo /tɛmpo/ *nm* **1** Mus tempo; **2** (de roman, film) pace.

temporaire /tɑ̃pɔʀɛʀ/ *adj* temporary; **à titre ~** [*employer, travailler*] on a temporary basis; **délivrer un permis à titre ~** to issue a temporary permit; **permis délivré à titre ~** temporary permit.

temporairement /tɑ̃pɔʀɛʀmɑ̃/ *adv* temporarily.

temporal, ~e, *mpl* **-aux** /tɑ̃pɔʀal, o/ **I** *adj* temporal.
II *nm* temporal bone.

temporalité /tɑ̃pɔʀalite/ *nf* temporality.

temporel, -elle /tɑ̃pɔʀɛl/ *adj* **1** (lié au temps) temporal; **étudier l'aspect ~ d'un roman** to study the temporal aspect of a novel; **2** Relig (séculier) temporal; **biens ~s** worldly goods; **3** (en grammaire) temporal.

temporisateur, -trice /tɑ̃pɔʀizatœʀ, tʀis/ **I** *adj* [*politique*] temporizing (*épith*).
II *nm,f* temporizer.
III *nm* Tech (appareil) timer, time switch.

temporisation /tɑ̃pɔʀizasjɔ̃/ *nf* **relais de ~** time delay relay.

temporiser /tɑ̃pɔʀize/ [1] *vi* to stall, to temporize sout.

temps /tɑ̃/ *nm inv* **1** Météo weather ¢; **un** or **du ~ gris** grey GB ou gray US weather; **un beau ~** fine weather; **quel beau/sale ~!** what lovely/awful weather!; **il faisait un ~ merveilleux/de cochon** it was marvellous[GB]/lousy weather; **le mauvais ~ nous a empêchés de sortir** the bad weather stopped us from going out; **le ~ est à la pluie/neige** it looks like rain/snow; **le ~ est à l'orage** there's going to be a storm; **le ~ se met à la pluie** the weather is turning to rain; **vu le ~ qu'il fait** (what) with the weather as it is; **quel ~ fait-il?** what's the

La mesure du temps

une seconde	=	a second
une minute	=	a minute
une heure	=	an hour*
un jour	=	a day†
une semaine	=	a week
un mois	=	a month‡
une année	=	a year
un siècle	=	a century

* Pour la façon de donner l'heure ▶ 407.
† Pour les expressions utilisant les noms de jours ▶ 750.
‡ Pour les expressions utilisant les noms de mois ▶ 521.

Les durées

Avec des verbes

combien de temps faut-il?	=	how long does it take?
il faut trois heures	=	it takes three hours
il faudra une année	=	it'll take a year
il a fallu un quart d'heure	=	it took a quarter of an hour
ça m'a pris une demi-heure	=	it took me half an hour
j'ai mis trois heures à le faire	=	it took me three hours to do it
la lettre a mis un mois pour arriver	=	the letter took a month to arrive

L'anglais traduit normalement passer *par* spend:

passer une année à Paris	=	to spend a year in Paris

Mais avec les adjectifs évaluatifs on traduira par have:

passer une bonne soirée	=	to have a good evening

Avec des prépositions

en deux minutes	=	in two minutes
en six mois	=	in six months
en un an	=	in a year
en l'espace de quelques minutes	=	within minutes

Noter aussi:

dans deux minutes	=	in two minutes

Pendant *et* pour *se traduisent par* for, *de même que* depuis *lorsqu'il exprime une durée*:

pendant une semaine	=	for a week
pendant des heures et des heures	=	for hours and hours
je suis ici pour deux semaines	=	I'm here for two weeks
il travaille depuis un an	=	he's been working for a year
depuis bientôt dix ans	=	for going on ten years

Noter aussi le temps du passé utilisé avec for. *Voir d'autres exemples à l'article* for *dans le dictionnaire.*

il y a des années qu'ils sont mariés	=	they have been married for years

Noter l'ordre des mots et l'utilisation du trait d'union dans les adjectifs composés anglais qui indiquent une durée. Pour les noms anglais dénombrables (wait, delay *etc.*) *on aura:*

une attente de six semaines	=	a six-week wait
un retard de cinquante minutes	=	a fifty-minute delay
une journée de huit heures	=	an eight-hour day

Week, month, minute, hour *etc.*, *employés comme adjectifs, ne prennent pas la marque du pluriel.*

Mais pour les noms non-dénombrables (leave, pay etc.)*, il y a deux traductions possibles*:

quatre jours de congé	=	four days' leave *ou* four days of leave
quatre semaines de salaire	=	four weeks' pay *ou* four weeks of pay
vingt-cinq ans de bonheur	=	twenty-five years' happiness *ou* twenty-five years of happiness

Un point dans le temps

Dans le passé

quand est-ce que cela s'est passé?	=	when did it happen?
la semaine dernière	=	last week
le mois dernier	=	last month
l'année dernière	=	last year
au cours des derniers mois	=	over the last few months

Noter l'ordre des mots avec ago:

il y a deux ans	=	two years ago
il y a des années	=	years ago
il y aura un mois mardi	=	it'll be a month ago on Tuesday
il y a huit jours hier	=	a week ago yesterday *ou* a week past yesterday
il y aura huit jours demain	=	a week ago tomorrow
il y a des années qu'il est mort	=	he died years ago *ou* it's years since he died
un mois auparavant	=	a month before
un mois plus tôt	=	a month earlier
l'année d'avant	=	the year before
l'année d'après	=	the year after
quelques années plus tard	=	a few years later
au bout de quatre jours	=	after four days

Dans le futur

quand est-ce que tu le verras?	=	when will you see him?
la semaine prochaine	=	next week
le mois prochain	=	next month
l'année prochaine	=	next year

Dans *se traduit souvent par* in (*comme* en; *voir ci-dessus):*

dans dix jours *ou* in ten days' time	=	in ten days
dans quelques jours	=	in a few days

Noter aussi:

dans un mois demain	=	a month tomorrow
au cours de la semaine à venir	=	this coming week
au cours des mois à venir	=	over the coming months

Les fréquences

cela arrive tous les combien?	=	how often does it happen?
tous les jeudis	=	every Thursday
toutes les semaines	=	every week
tous les deux jours	=	every other day *or* every second day
le dernier jeudi du mois	=	the last Thursday of the month
jour après jour	=	day after day
une fois tous les trois mois	=	once every three months
deux fois par an	=	twice a year
trois fois par jour	=	three times a day

Les salaires

combien est-ce que tu gagnes de l'heure?	=	how much do you get an hour?
je gagne 70 francs de l'heure	=	I get 70 francs an hour
être payé 7 000 francs par mois	=	to be paid 7,000 francs a month
190 000 francs par an	=	190,000 francs a year

Mais noter:

être payé à l'heure	=	to be paid by the hour

weather like?; **ça dépendra du ~ qu'il fera** it'll depend on the weather; **par beau/mauvais ~** in fine/bad weather, when the weather's fine/bad; **par beau ~, on peut voir la tour** on a clear day ou when the weather's fine, you can see the tower; **par un si beau ~, tu devrais sortir!** with such fine weather, you should go out!; **par ~ clair** (de jour) on a clear day; (de nuit) on a clear night; **par ~ de pluie/neige** when it rains/snows, in rainy/snowy weather; **par tous les ~** in all weathers; ▶**pluie**; **2** (notion) time; **la fuite du ~** the swift passage of time; **le ~ efface tout** everything fades with time; **oublier avec le ~** to forget in ou with time; **avec le ~, on s'y fait** you get used to it in ou with time; **le ~ arrangera les choses** time will take care of everything, it'll be all right in the end; ▶**vivre**; **3** (durée) **peu de ~ avant/après** shortly before/after; **en peu de ~** in a short time; **dans peu de ~** shortly, before long; **il y a** or **ça fait peu de ~ que le train est parti** the train left a short time ago; **d'ici** or **dans quelque ~** before long; **(pendant) quelque** or **un certain ~** (assez courte période) for a while; (période plus longue) for some time, for quite a while; **depuis quelque** or **un certain ~ il est bizarre** he has been behaving oddly for a while now ou for some time now; **il y a quelque** or **beau** or **un certain ~ qu'on ne l'a pas vue** it's been some time since anyone saw her; **pendant** or **pour un ~** for a while; **pendant tout un ~** for quite a while; **pendant ce ~(-là)** meanwhile, in the meantime; **qu'as-tu fait tout ce ~(-là)?** what have you been doing all this time?; **qu'as-tu fait pendant (tout) ce ~(-là)?** what did you do all that time?; **en un rien de ~** in next to no time, in no time at all; **la plupart** or **les trois quarts du ~** most of the time; **tout le ~** all the time; **depuis le ~ que j'en parle** all this time I've been talking about it; **depuis le ~ que ça existe, tu devrais être au courant** you should have known, it's been around for so long; **le ~ d'installation a été plus long que prévu** it took longer than expected to install; **le ~ de la fouille m'a paru interminable** the search seemed to go on forever; **le ~ d'un après-midi/d'un week-end/d'un instant** just for an afternoon/a week-end/a minute; **ils sont restés le ~ de l'élection** they stayed just for the duration of the election; **il a souri le ~ de la photo** he smiled just long enough for the photo to be taken; **un an, le ~ d'écrire un roman** a year, just long enough to write a novel; **le ~ de me retourner** or **que je me retourne, il avait disparu** by the time I turned round GB ou around, he had disappeared; **le ~ de ranger mes affaires et j'arrive** just let me put my things away and I'll be with you; **avoir/ne pas avoir le ~** to have/not to have (the) time (**pour** for; **de faire** to do) ; **je n'ai plus beaucoup de ~** I haven't got much time left; **(j'ai) pas l'~**○! not now!; **on a le ~** we've got (plenty of) time; **si tu as le ~, pourrais-tu...?** if you've got time, could you...?; **avoir juste le ~** to have just (enough) time; **avoir tout le ~** to have bags○ of time ou plenty of time; **avoir dix** or **cent fois le ~** to have all the time in the world; **je n'avais que le ~ de faire** I only had time to do; **vous avez combien de ~ pour le déjeuner?** how long do you have for lunch?; **avoir du ~ (de) libre** to have (some) free time; **nous avons du ~ devant nous** we have plenty of time, we have time to spare; **tu as vrai-**

ment du ~ devant toi! iron have you got time to kill?; **je n'ai pas le ~ matériel de faire, je n'ai matériellement pas le ~ de faire** there just aren't enough hours in the day (for me) to do; **consacrer du ~ à qn/qch** to devote time to sb/sth GB, to spend time on sb/sth; **donner** or **laisser à qn le ~ de faire** to give sb time to do; **mettre** or **prendre du ~** to take time (**à faire, pour faire** to do); **il faut du ~ pour faire** it takes time to do; **beaucoup de ~** [*mettre, prendre*] a long time; **moins de ~ que** [*falloir, mettre, prendre*] less time than; **plus de ~ que** [*falloir, mettre, prendre*] longer than; **prendre peu de ~** not to take a long time, not to take long; **ne pas prendre beaucoup de ~** not to take long; **il m'a fallu** or **cela m'a pris** or **j'ai mis beaucoup de ~** it took (me) a long time; **il t'a fallu** or **cela t'a pris** or **tu as mis combien de ~?** how long did it take you?; **ça a pris** or **mis un ~ fou**○ it took ages○; **prendre le ~ de faire** to take the time to do; **prendre son ~** to take one's time; **prendre tout son ~** to take all the time one needs; **les enfants prennent tout mon ~** the children take up all my time; **tu y as mis le ~!, tu en as mis du ~!** you (certainly) took your time!; **j'y mettrai le ~ qu'il faudra, mais je le ferai** however long it takes, I'll get it done; **le ~ que met sa lumière à nous parvenir** the time its light takes to reach us; **si tu savais le ~ que ça (m')a pris!** if you knew how long it took (me)!; **le ~ passe vite** time flies; **le ~ passe et rien n'est prêt** time's slipping by and nothing's ready; **laisser passer le ~** to let time slip by; **ça passe le ~** it passes the time; **faire passer le ~** to while away the time (**en faisant** doing); **passer (tout) son ~ à faire** to spend (all of) one's time doing; **passer le plus clair de son ~ à faire** to spend most of one's time doing; **perdre du ~** to waste time (**à qch, en qch** on sth; **à faire** doing); **perdre son ~** to waste one's time; **nous avons perdu beaucoup de ~ à discuter** or **en discussions** we've wasted a lot of time arguing; **j'ai perdu un ~ fou**○ I've wasted loads○ of time (**à faire** doing); **avoir du ~ à perdre** to have time on one's hands; **c'est du ~ perdu, c'est une perte de ~** it's a waste of time; **cette visite, c'était vraiment du ~ (de) perdu** that visit was a real waste of time; **faire qch à ~ perdu** to do sth in one's spare time; **il n'y a plus de ~/pas de ~ à perdre** there's no more time/no time to lose; **le ~ presse!** time is short!; **être pressé par le ~** to be pressed ou pushed for time; **trouver le ~ de faire** to find (the) time to do; **j'ai trouvé le ~ long** (the) time seemed to drag, time went really slowly; **être dans les ~** Sport to be within the time; **nous sommes dans les ~** we've still got time; **finir dans les ~** to finish in time; **4** (moment) time; **à ~** [*partir, terminer*] in time; **juste à ~** just in time; **de ~ en ~, de ~ à autre** from time to time, now and then; **en même ~** at the same time (**que** as); **je suis arrivé en même ~ qu'elle** I arrived at the same time as her ou as she did; **le ~ est venu de faire** the time has come to do; **il y a un ~ pour tout** there's a time for everything; **il était ~!** (marquant l'impatience) (and) about time too!; (marquant le soulagement) just in the nick of time!; **il est ~, il n'est que ~** it's about time; **il est grand ~** it's high time (**de faire** to do); **il n'est que ~ de partir** it's high time we left; **il est ~ de partir** or **que nous partions** it's time we left; **il est ~ que tu fasses** it's time you did ou for you to do; **il n'est plus ~ de faire** it's too late to do; **en ~ utile** in time; **en ~ voulu** in due course; **en ~ opportun** at the appropriate time; **en ~ et lieu** at the right time and place; **la mesure/décision a été prise en son ~** the measure/decision was taken at the right time ou when it should have been; **5** (époque) **au** or **du ~ des Grecs** in the time of the Greeks; **au** or **du ~ de mes grand-parents/de César** in my grandparents'/Caesar's time; **les ~ modernes/préhistoriques** modern/prehistoric times; **le ~ des semailles/examens** sowing/exam time; **au ~ des dinosaures/de l'exploration spatiale** in the age of the dinosaurs/of space exploration; **au** or **du ~ où** in the days when; **regretter le ~ où** to feel nostalgia for the days when; **l'échelle des ~ géologiques** the scale of geological ages; **les ~ héroïques de** the heroic days of; **le bon** or **beau ~ de l'expansion** the good old days (*pl*) of expansion; **le bon vieux ~** the good old days (*pl*); **comme au bon vieux ~** as in the good old days; **c'était le bon ~!** those were the days!; **au plus beau ~ de** in the heyday of; **au pire ~ de** in the worst days of; **l'événement le plus grand/extraordinaire de tous les ~** the greatest/most extraordinary event of all time; **les ~ sont durs** times are hard; **ces derniers ~, ces ~ derniers** recently; **ces ~-ci** lately; **en tout ~** at all times; **de mon/leur ~** in my/their day ou time; **dans le ~, j'étais sportif** in my day, I did a bit of sport; **dans le ~, on n'avait pas l'électricité** in those days, we didn't have electricity; **depuis le ~, les choses ont dû bien changer** since then things must have really changed; **il est loin le ~ où** the days are long gone when; **il n'est pas loin le ~ où tu n'étais qu'une enfant** it's not so long ago that you were but a child; **n'avoir** or **ne durer qu'un ~** to be short-lived; **en un ~ où** at a time when; **en ~ normal** or **ordinaire** usually; **en d'autres ~** at any other time; **en ~ de paix/guerre** in peacetime/wartime; **en ces ~ de pénurie/d'abondance** in these times of hardship/of plenty; **en ce ~-là** at that time; **être de son ~** to move with the times; **être en avance sur son ~** to be ahead of one's time; **être en retard sur son ~** to be behind the times; **avoir fait son ~** [*prisonnier, militaire*] to have served one's time; [*fonctionnaire, diplomate*] to have put in one's time; pej [*personne usée*] to have outlived one's usefulness, to be past it○; [*produit à la mode, appareil, voiture*] to have had its day; ▶ **mœurs**; **6** (phase) stage; **en deux ~** in two stages; **~ mort** (d'activité, de travail) slack period; **dans un premier ~** first; **dans un deuxième ~** subsequently; **dans un dernier ~** finally; ▶ **deux**; **7** Ling (de verbe) tense; **les ~ simples/composés/du passé** simple/compound/past tenses; **adverbe de ~** adverb of time; **8** Entr (de travail) time; **avoir un travail à ~ partiel/plein** to have a part-/full-time job; **travailler à ~ partiel** to work part-time; **travailler à ~ plein** or **à ~** or **à ~ complet** to work full-time; **être employé à plein ~** to be in full-time work; **je cherche un ~ partiel**○ I'm looking for a part-time job; **~ de travail** working hours (*pl*); **~ de travail quotidien** working day GB, workday US; **~ de travail hebdomadaire** working week GB, workweek US; **9** Sport time; **un excellent ~** an excellent time; **il a fait** or **réalisé le meilleur ~** he got the best time; **améliorer son ~ d'une seconde** to knock a second off one's time; **être** or **rester dans les ~** to be inside the time; **jouer les ~ d'arrêt** (au football) to play injury time; **10** Mécan (de moteur) stroke; **moteur à quatre ~** four-stroke engine; **11** Mus time; **~ de valse** waltz time; **mesure à deux/trois/quatre ~** two-four/three-four/four-four time.

■ **~ d'accès** access time; **~ d'antenne** airtime; **~ d'arrêt** Ordinat down time; **~ atomique international, TAI** international atomic time, TAI; **~ d'attente** Ordinat latency, waiting time; **~ choisi** Entr flexitime; **~ civil** Admin local time; **~ différé** Ordinat batch mode; **~ d'exploitation** operating time; **~ faible** Mus piano; **~ fort** Mus forte; fig high point; **~ d'indisponibilité** unavailable time; **~ légal** Admin local time; **~ mort** Ordinat idle time; **~ partagé** Ordinat time-sharing; **en ~ partagé** time-sharing (*épith*); **~ de pose** Phot exposure time; **~ de positionnement** Ordinat seek time; **~ primitifs** Ling principal parts of the verb; **~ de réaction** Psych reaction time; **~ de recherche** = **~ de positionnement**; **~ réel** Ordinat real time; **en ~ réel** real-time (*épith*); **~ de réponse** response time; **~ sidéral** sidereal time; **~ solaire** solar time; **~ solaire moyen/vrai** mean/true solar time; **~ universel** Greenwich Mean Time, GMT, universal time; **~ universel coordonné, TUC** universal time coordinated, UTC; **~ de vol** flying time.

IDIOMES **au ~ pour moi!** my mistake!; **il y a un ~ de se taire et un ~ de parler** there is a time to keep silence and a time to speak; **le ~ perdu ne se rattrape jamais** or **ne revient point** Prov you can't make up for lost time; **par le ~ qui court, par les ~ qui courent** with things as they are; **prendre le ~ comme il vient** to take things as they come; **prendre** or **se donner** or **se payer**○ **du bon ~** to have a whale of a time.

tenable /tənabl/ *adj* **1** (supportable) bearable, tolerable; **la situation n'est pas ~** the situation is unbearable; **2** Mil (défendable) [*position*] tenable; **3** (discipliné) **les élèves ne sont pas ~s aujourd'hui** the pupils are being impossible today.

tenace /tənas/ *adj* **1** [*tache, odeur, migraine*] stubborn; [*parfum*] long-lasting; [*brume, bronchite, toux*] persistent; **2** [*rumeur, souvenir*] persistent; [*haine, illusion, croyance, mauvaise réputation*] entrenched; **3** [*personne*] (obstiné) tenacious; (insistant) persistent; [*volonté*] tenacious.

ténacité /tenasite/ *nf* **1** (de personne) (obstination) tenacity; (insistance) persistence; **2** (de souvenir, d'illusion) persistence; **la ~ de la douleur/de l'odeur fait penser que** the fact that the pain/the smell is so persistent suggests that.

tenaille /tənɑj/ *nf* pincers (*pl*); **~s de mécanicien/de menuisier** mechanic's/carpenter's pincers.

tenailler /tənɑje/ [1] *vtr* **il était tenaillé par le remords** he was racked with remorse; **elle était tenaillée par la faim** hunger gnawed at her.

tenancier, -ière /tənɑ̃sje, ɛʀ/ **I** *nm,f* **1** (de ferme) tenant farmer; Hist feudal tenant; **2** (de café, bar) landlord/landlady; (d'hôtel, de casino) manager/manageress.
II tenancière *nf* **tenancière de maison close** madam.

tenant, ~e /tənɑ̃, ɑ̃t/ **I** *adj* **elle est ~e du titre** she's the titleholder.
II *nm,f* Jeux, Sport **~ du titre** titleholder; **~ du trophée** holder of the trophy.
III *nm* **1** (adepte) advocate; **2** (morceau) **d'un seul ~** [*jardin, pièce de tissu*] all in one piece.

IDIOMES **les ~s et les aboutissants de qch** the ins and outs of sth.

tendance /tɑ̃dɑ̃s/ *nf* **1** (propension) tendency; **~ à la rêverie/à l'étourderie/à l'exagération** tendency to daydream/to be absent-minded/to exaggerate; **une ~ naturelle/fâcheuse à faire** a natural/unfortunate tendency to do; **avoir ~ à faire** to tend to do, to have a tendency to do; **il a ~ à croire/penser que** he tends to believe/think that; **on a trop ~ à croire que** we are too inclined to believe that; **le marché a ~ à se stabiliser** the market is becoming more stable; **2** (orientation) tendency; **une coalition de ~ centriste** an alliance with centrist tendencies; **toutes ~s politiques confondues** across party lines; **3** (école) trend; **les ~s artistiques/littéraires actuelles** present-day artistic/literary trends; **plusieurs ~s se dessinent** several trends emerge; **la ~ dominante** the dominant trend; **4** (dynamique) trend; **~ à la**

baisse/hausse downward/upward trend; **la ~ reste à l'expansion** the trend is still toward(s) growth; **la ~ s'est inversée** or **renversée** the trend has been reversed; **cette ~ se poursuivra l'année prochaine** this trend will continue into next year.

tendancieusement /tɑ̃dɑ̃sjøzmɑ̃/ *adv* tendentiously.

tendancieux, **-ieuse** /tɑ̃dɑ̃sjø, øz/ *adj* [*propos, article, interprétation*] biased[GB], tendentious.

tendeur /tɑ̃dœʀ/ *nm* **1** (de tente) guy rope; **2** (de porte-bagages) bungee grip, elastic strap; (de galerie de toit) octopus GB, elastic strap; **3** (dispositif) gén tightener; Tech (pour clôture) slack adjuster; (pour l'arrimage de conteneurs) turnbuckle.

tendineux, **-euse** /tɑ̃dinø, øz/ *adj* **1** Anat tendinous; **2** (en boucherie) stringy.

tendinite /tɑ̃dinit/ **▶ 271** *nf* tendinitis.

tendon /tɑ̃dɔ̃/ *nm* tendon.

■ **~ d'Achille** Achilles tendon.

tendre /tɑ̃dʀ/ [6] **I** *adj* **1** (non dur) [*roche, bois, fibre*] soft; [*chair, peau, viande, légumes*] tender; **2** (jeune) [*pousse, herbe, bourgeon*] new; **une ~ jeune fille** a sweet young girl; **~ enfance/jeunesse** earliest childhood/youth; **3** (pâle) [*rose, vert, bleu*] soft; **des chaussettes vert ~** pale green socks; **4** (affectueux) [*personne*] loving; [*baisers, amour, sourire, paroles*] tender; [*humour, tempérament*] gentle; **un cœur ~** a loving heart; **c'est un dur au cœur ~** beneath his tough exterior he's got a soft heart; **s'aimer d'amour ~** to love each other tenderly; **poser un regard ~ sur qn** to look tenderly ou fondly at sb; **être ~ avec qn** (affectueux) to be loving toward(s) sb; (indulgent) to show leniency toward(s) sb; **ne pas être ~ avec** or **envers** or **pour qn/qch** to be hard on sb/sth; **les critiques n'ont pas été ~s avec lui/ton roman** the critics have been hard on him/your novel; **leurs propos ne sont pas ~s pour le régime** they have some harsh words to say about the regime; **5** (cher) [*époux, ami, compagne*] dear; **ma chère et ~ épouse** my dearest wife.

II *nmf* soft-hearted person; **c'est un grand ~** he's very soft-hearted.

III *vtr* **1** (étirer) to tighten [*corde, fil, câble*]; to stretch [*élastique, peau*]; to extend [*ressort*]; **~ la peau d'un tam-tam** to stretch hide over the end of a tom-tom; **~ le cou** to crane one's neck; **~ les bras** (allonger) to hold out one's arms; (étirer) to stretch one's arms out; **jambes et pointes de pied tendues** legs straight and toes pointed; **~ le bras** (pour faire signe) to put out one's arm; (pour saisir, donner) to reach out; **le sel est devant toi, tu n'as qu'à ~ le bras** the salt's right in front of you, just reach out and get it; **~ le bras à qn** (pour soutenir) to offer ou give one's arm to sb; **~ les bras à** or **vers qn** (pour accueillir) to greet ou welcome sb with open arms; **la victoire/mon lit me tend les bras** fig victory/my bed beckons; **~ la main** (pour montrer) to point; (pour saisir, donner) to reach out; (pour mendier, serrer la main à qn) to hold out one's hand; **la politique de la main tendue** policy of openness; **~ la main à qn** (pour aider) lit to hold one 's hand out to sb; fig to lend ou give sb a helping hand; **~ la bouche** or **les lèvres** to offer one' s lips for a kiss; **~ le dos** fig to brace oneself; **~ la joue** lit to offer one's cheek; **~ l'autre joue** Bible to turn the other cheek; **2** (déployer) to spread [*toile, bâche, drap*] (**sur qch** over sth); **3** (disposer) to set [*piège, collet, souricière*]; to put up [*fil à linge*]; **~ un filet** lit to put up a net; **~ un piège** or **un filet à qn** fig to set a trap for sb; **4** (tapisser) **~ un mur/une cloison/un plafond de tissu** to hang a wall/a partition/a ceiling with cloth; **corridor/bureau tendu de toile de jute** corridor/office hung with hessian; **5** (présenter) **~ qch à qn** to hold sth out to sb; **~ un crayon/livre à qn** to hold a pencil/book out to sb; **~ une cigarette/du feu à qn** to offer sb a cigarette/a light.

IV tendre à *vtr ind* **1** (viser à) **~ à un but/un idéal** to strive for a goal/an ideal; **les mesures tendent à alléger l'impôt** the measures are aimed at reducing taxes; **2** (avoir tendance à) **~ à faire** to tend to do; **la différence tend à s'accentuer** the difference tends to become more pronounced.

V *vi* **1** (s'orienter) **~ vers** to strive for; **~ vers la perfection/l'absolu** to strive for perfection/the absolute; **2** (se rapprocher) **~ vers** to approach [*valeur, chiffre*]; to tend to [*zéro, infini*].

VI se tendre *vpr* **1** (devenir tendu) [*câble, fil, corde*] to tighten; **2** (devenir conflictuel) [*relations, rapports*] to become strained.

tendrement /tɑ̃dʀəmɑ̃/ *adv* [*caresser, embrasser, se tenir la main, aimer*] tenderly; **un couple ~ uni** a loving couple.

tendresse /tɑ̃dʀɛs/ *nf* **1** (affection donnée) tenderness; (affection reçue) affection; **mots pleins de ~** words full of tenderness; **avec ~** [*regarder, embrasser, aimer*] tenderly; **avec une grande ~** very tenderly; **avoir** or **éprouver de la ~ pour qn** to have tender feelings for sb; **avoir besoin de ~** to need affection, to need a little tender loving care; **chercher un peu de ~** to be looking for affection; **n'avoir aucune ~ pour qn** to have no affection for sb; **2** (acte tendre) affectionate gesture; (parole tendre) tender word; **dire mille ~s à qn** to say sweet things to sb; **'mille ~s'** (dans une lettre) 'with all my love'.

tendreté /tɑ̃dʀəte/ *nf* (de viande) tenderness; (de bois, métal) softness.

tendron /tɑ̃dʀɔ̃/ *nm* Culin (de bœuf) plate; (de veau) flank.

tendu, **~e** /tɑ̃dy/ **I** *pp* **▶ tendre**.

II *pp adj* [*corde, courroie*] tight; **les courroies ne sont pas assez ~es** the straps are not tight enough.

III *adj* (crispé) [*personne, visage, relations, réunion*] tense; [*marché*] nervous; **on le sent ~, vulnérable** you can see he's tense and vulnerable; **dans une ambiance extrêmement ~e** in an extremely tense atmosphere; **la situation dans la capitale est très ~e** the situation in the capital is very tense; **le marché monétaire reste ~** the money market remains nervous.

ténèbres /tenɛbʀ/ *nfpl* **les ~** lit, fig darkness ¢; **les ~ de qch** fig the darkness of sth; **l'ange/le prince/l'empire des ~** Relig the Angel/the Prince/the Realm of Darkness.

ténébreux, **-euse** /tenebʀø, øz/ **I** *adj* liter **1** [*endroit*] dark; **2** (mystérieux) [*affaire, période*] obscure.

II *nm inv* **un beau ~** a broodingly handsome man.

teneur /tənœʀ/ *nf* **1** (de solide) content; (de gaz, liquide) level; **~ en sucre/quartz** sugar/quartz content; **de forte/faible ~ en quartz** with a high/low quartz content; **boisson à faible ~ en alcool** low alcohol drink, drink with a low alcohol content; **2** (de rapport, discours, d'acte juridique) import.

ténia /tenja/ *nm* tapeworm, tænia spéc.

tenir /təniʀ/ [36] **I** *vtr* **1** (serrer) to hold [*objet, personne, animal*]; **tiens-moi ça** hold this (for me); **tiens-moi** hold me; **tiens-moi la main** hold my hand; **~ qn par la main/le bras** to hold sb's hand/arm; **~ un enfant contre sa poitrine** to hold a child to one's breast; **~ qch à la main/dans ses mains** to hold sth in one's hand/in one's hands; **~ un couteau par le manche** to hold a knife by the handle; **~ la rampe** to hold onto the banister; **~ son chien** to hold one's dog; **~ fermement qch** to hold sth firmly ou tightly; **~ qch serré sous le bras** to hold sth firmly ou tightly under one's arm; **tiens!, tenez!** (voici) here you are!; (écoutez-moi) look!; **tiens! c'est pour toi** (voici un cadeau) here, it's for you; (voici une gifle) take that!; **si je le tenais!** if I could get or lay my hands on him!; **bien ~** to hold on to [*portefeuille, chien*]; **faire ~ une lettre/un message à qn†** to dispatch a letter/a message to sb; **▶ deux**; **2** (avoir sous son contrôle) to keep [sb] under control [*élèves, enfants*]; **~ sa classe** to control one's class well; **~ son cheval** Équit to keep one's horse well in hand; **il nous tient** he's got a hold on us; **3** Mil (occuper, contrôler) to hold [*colline, pont, ville*]; **~ la première place** Sport to be in first place; **4** (avoir attrapé) to hold [*animal, coupable, meurtrier*]; **je te tiens!** I've caught ou got you!; **pendant que je te tiens** fig whilst I've got you; **~ une grippe**○ to have flu GB ou the flu US; **5** (posséder) to have [*preuves, renseignements*]; **il tient le sujet de son prochain roman** he's got the subject of his next novel; **~ qch de qn** to get sth from sb [*trait physique, caractère, information*]; **il tient ses yeux bleus de son père** he gets his blue eyes from his father; **il tient ses informations d'un ami** he got his information from a friend; **je tiens cette nouvelle de Paul** I got this news from Paul; **d'où** or **de qui tenez-vous ce renseignement?** where did you get that information?; **d'où tenez-vous cette certitude?** what makes you so certain?; **elle tient ses bijoux de sa mère** she inherited her jewels from her mother; **6** (avoir la charge de) to hold [*emploi, poste, assemblée*]; to run [*café, boutique, maison, journal, municipalité*]; to be in charge of, to be on duty on [*standard, bureau d'accueil*]; **bien ~ sa maison** to keep one's house spick and span; **~ la comptabilité** to keep the books; **7** (garder) to keep; **~ qn occupé** to keep sb busy; **~ sa chambre propre** to keep one's room tidy; **~ les aliments au frais** to keep food in a cool place; **'~ hors de portée des enfants'** 'keep out of reach of children'; **~ un accord secret** to keep an agreement secret; **~ la porte fermée** to keep the door closed; **~ une note** Mus to hold a note; **~ un article†** to carry an item; **~ les cours†** Fin to maintain prices; **8** (conserver une position) **~ sa tête droite/immobile** to hold one's head upright/still; **~ les bras écartés** to hold one's arms apart; **~ les mains/les bras en l'air** to hold up one's hands/one's arms; **~ les yeux ouverts/baissés** to keep one's eyes open/lowered; **~ les poings serrés** to keep one's fists clenched; **9** (maintenir en place) to hold down [*chargement*]; to hold up [*pantalon, chaussettes*]; **~ la porte fermée avec son pied** to hold the door shut with one's foot; **10** (ne pas s'écarter de) to keep to [*trajectoire*]; to keep [*rythme*] ; **~ sa droite/sa gauche** to keep to the right/to the left; **~ le large** to stay in open waters; **11** (résister) **ne pas ~ la comparaison** not to bear comparison; **~ l'eau** to be waterproof; **~ la mer** [*navire*] to be seaworthy; **~ le coup** (physiquement, moralement) to hold out; **~ le choc** lit [*matériel, appareil, verre*] to withstand the impact; [*personne*] to stand the strain; **12** (contenir) to hold [*quantité*]; **~ vingt litres** to hold twenty litres[GB]; **ma voiture ne tient que deux personnes** there's room for only two people in my car; **13** (occuper) [*objet*] to take up [*espace, place, volume*]; [*personne*] to hold [*rôle, position*]; **~ peu de place** not to take up much room; **~ la place de deux personnes** to take up as much room as two people; **le monument tient le centre de la place** the monument stands in the centre[GB] of the square; **14** (considérer) **~ qch pour sacré** to hold sth sacred; **~ qn pour responsable** to hold sb responsible; **je le tiens pour un lâche** I consider him (to be) a coward; **je tiens mes renseignements pour exacts** I consider my information to be correct; **~ qn pour mort** to give sb up for dead; **~ pour certain que** to regard it as certain that.

II tenir à *vtr ind* **1** (avoir de l'attachement pour) **~ à** to be fond of, to like [*personne, *objet*]; **~ à sa réputation/à la vie** to value one's reputation/one's life; **il tient à son argent** he can't bear to be parted from his money; **~ à son indépendance** to like one's independence; **~ au corps** [*aliment*] to be nourishing; **2** (vouloir) **j'y tiens** I insist; **si vous y tenez** if you insist; **~ à faire** to want to do; **elle tient à vous parler** she insists on speaking to you; **je ne tiens pas à faire** I'd rather not do; **~ à ce que qn fasse** to insist that sb should do; **je ne tiens pas à ce qu'elle fasse** I'd rather she didn't do; **je tiens beaucoup à la revoir** I'd really like to see her again; **il tient à rentrer avant la nuit** he's anxious to get home before dark; **nous tenons absolument à vous avoir à dîner bientôt** you really must come to dinner soon; **ne reste pas si tu n'y tiens pas** don't stay if you don't want to; **3** (être dû à) **~ à** to be due to; **la mauvaise récolte tient au manque d'eau** the poor harvest is due to a lack of water; **tes erreurs tiennent à ton inexpérience** your mistakes are due to your lack of experience.

III tenir de *vtr ind* **1** (ressembler à) **~ de** to take after; **~ de sa mère/son père** to take after one's mother/one's father; **il a de qui ~**○ you can (just) see who he takes after ou where he gets it from; **de qui peut-elle ~ pour être si méchante?** where does she get her nastiness from?; **2** (s'apparenter à) **~ de** to border on; **~ du délire** to border on madness.

IV *vi* **1** (rester en place) [*clou, attache, corde, étagère, barrage, soufflé*] to hold; [*timbre, colle, sparadrap*] to stick; [*assemblage, bandage*] to stay in place; [*coiffure*] to stay tidy; [*mise en plis*] to stay in; **~ au mur avec de la colle/des épingles** (adhérer) to stick to the wall with glue/pins; **~ sur une jambe/un pied** to stand on one leg/one foot; **ces chaussures ne me tiennent pas aux pieds** these shoes won't stay on my feet; **2** (résister) **~ (bon)** (surmonter les conditions) [*personne, matériel*] to hold out; (refuser de capituler) gén to hang on, to hold out; Mil to hold out; (ne pas relâcher sa prise) [*personne*] to hang on; **~ sans cigarettes jusqu'à la fin de la réunion** to last ou go without cigarettes till the end of the meeting; **~ jusqu'à la fin de la réunion** to hold out until the end of the meeting; **~ économiquement** to hold ou last out in economic terms; **j'espère que ma voiture va ~ (bon)** I hope my car will last out; **on a voulu me renvoyer mais j'ai tenu (bon)** they wanted to fire me but I hung on; **je ne peux plus (y) ~** I can't stand it any longer; **il n'y a pas de télévision qui tienne**○ there's no question of watching television; **3** (durer) **le plan tient-il toujours?** is the plan still on?; **leur mariage tient encore** their marriage is still holding together; **le soleil n'a pas tenu longtemps** the sun didn't last long; **la neige tient/ne tient pas** the snow is settling/is not settling; **les fleurs n'ont pas tenu** the flowers didn't last long; **la couleur n'a pas tenu** the colour[GB] has faded; **~ au lavage** [*couleur*] not to run in the wash GB ou laundry US; **4** (rester valable) [*théorie, argument*] to hold good; **ton alibi ne tient plus** your alibi no longer stands up; **'ça tient toujours pour demain?'** 'is it still all right for tomorrow?'; **5** (être contenu) [*personnes, véhicule, meubles, objets*] to fit (**dans** into); **mes vêtements tiendront dans une valise** my clothes will fit into one suitcase; **~ à six dans une voiture** to fit six into a car; **faire ~ six personnes dans une voiture** to fit six people into a car; **mon article tient en trois pages** my article takes up only three pages; **~ en hauteur/largeur/longueur** to be short enough/narrow enough/short enough (**dans** for); **~ en hauteur dans une pièce** to fit into a room (heightwise); **ne pas ~ en hauteur/largeur/longueur** to be too tall/wide/long (**dans** for); **ne pas ~ en largeur dans un espace** to be too wide for a space.

V se tenir *vpr* **1** (soi-même) [*personne*] to hold [*tête, ventre, bras*]; **se ~ la tête de douleur** to hold one's head in pain; **se ~ la tête à deux mains** to hold one's head in one's hands; **2** (l'un l'autre) **se ~ par le bras** [*personnes*] to be arm in arm; **ils se tenaient par la taille** they had their arms around each other's waists; **se ~ par la main** [*personnes*] to hold hands; **3** (s'accrocher) to hold on; **se ~ par les pieds** to hold on with one's feet; **se ~ à une branche/à la rampe** to hold onto a branch/onto the banisters; **se ~ d'une main à qch** to hold onto sth with one hand; **tiens-toi** or **tenez-vous bien**○ fig prepare yourself for a shock; **4** (demeurer) **se ~ accroupi/allongé/penché/courbé/à genoux** to be squatting/stretched out/leaning/bent over/kneeling; **se ~ au milieu/à la porte** (debout) to be standing in the middle/at the door; **se ~ caché/sans bouger/au chaud** to stay hidden/still/in the warm; **se ~ prêt** to be ready; **se ~ tranquille** (immobile) to keep still; (silencieux) to keep quiet; (dans la légalité) to behave oneself; **se ~ immobile** (debout) to stand still; **5** (se comporter) to behave; **se ~ bien/mal** to behave well/badly; **savoir se ~** to know how to behave; **tiens-toi bien!** behave yourself!; **6** (avoir une posture) **se ~ droit** or **bien/mal** to have (a) good posture/(a) bad posture; **tiens-toi droit!** (debout) stand up straight!; (assis) sit straight!; **7** (avoir lieu) [*manifestation, exposition*] to be held; **la réunion se tiendra au Caire** the meeting will be held in Cairo; **8** (être liés) [*événements*] to fit together; **9** (être cohérent) [*exposé, raisonnement, œuvre*] to hold together; **il n'y a rien à dire, tout se tient** there's nothing to be said, it all holds together; **ça se tient** it makes sense; **10** (se considérer) **se ~ pour** to consider oneself to be; **je me tiens pour satisfait des résultats** I consider myself to be satisfied with the results; **tenez-vous le pour dit**○**!** I don't want to have to tell you again!; **11** (être fidèle) **s'en ~ à** to stand by; **je m'en tiendrai à ma promesse/notre accord/leur décision** I will stand by my promise/our agreement/their decision; **12** (se limiter) **s'en ~ à** to keep to; **s'en ~ au minimum/au sujet** to keep to a minimum/to the point; **s'en ~ aux ordres** to stick to orders; **s'en ~ là** to leave it there; **ne pas savoir à quoi s'en ~ avec qn/qch** not to know what to make of sb/sth.

VI *v impers* **il ne tient qu'à toi de partir** it's up to you to decide whether to leave; **qu'à cela ne tienne!** never mind!

VII tiens *excl* oh!; **tiens (donc), vous voilà!** oh, there you are!; **tiens, je parie que c'est ta mère!** oh! I bet it's your mother; **tiens, vous croyez?** do you think so?; **tiens, tu es invité aussi?** oh! so you've been invited as well?; **tiens, tu n'étais pas au courant?** didn't you know?; **tiens donc!** iron fancy that!; **tiens tiens (tiens)!** well, well!

IDIOMES **en ~ pour qn** to have a crush on sb.

Tennessee /tenesi/ ▶ 692 *nprm* Tennessee.

tennis /tenis/ **I** ▶ 449 *nm* (activité) tennis.
II *nm* ou *f inv* (chaussure) tennis shoe.
■ **~ de table** table tennis.

tennisman, *pl* **tennismen** /tenisman, mɛn/ *nm* controv male tennis player.

tenon /tənɔ̃/ *nm* (en menuiserie) tenon; **assemblage à ~ et mortaise** mortice and tenon joint.

ténor /tenɔʀ/ **I** *adj* Mus [*saxophone*] tenor.
II *nm* **1** ▶ 134 (chanteur, voix, instrument) tenor; **2** (personnalité) (de sport) star; (de parti, profession) leading light; **un ~ de la droite bavaroise** a leading light of the Bavarian right.

tenseur /tɑ̃sœʀ/ *adj m, nm* Anat, Math tensor.

tensiomètre /tɑ̃sjɔmɛtʀ/ *nm* **1** Tech tensiometer; **2** Méd sphygmomanometer.

tension /tɑ̃sjɔ̃/ *nf* **1** (de câble, corde, courroie) tension, tautness; (de muscle) tension; **2** Méd blood pressure; **baisse de ~** drop in blood pressure; **prendre la ~ de qn** to take sb's blood pressure; **faire** or **avoir de la ~** to have high blood pressure; **~ nerveuse** nervous tension; **~ d'esprit** mental concentration; **être sous ~** to be under stress ou pressure; **3** Électrotech tension, voltage; **une ~ de 3 000 volts** a tension of 3,000 volts; **basse/haute/moyenne ~** low/high/medium voltage; **baisse de ~** drop in voltage; **mettre un appareil sous ~** to switch on ou turn on a machine; **sous ~** [*circuit, fil*] live; [*appareil*] switched on; **4** (discorde) tension; **des ~s politiques/ethniques/raciales** political/ethnic/racial tensions; **la ~ entre les deux pays est telle que** relations between the two countries are so strained that; **5** Phys (de vapeur) pressure; (de liquide) tension; **~ superficielle** surface tension; **6** Phon (effort musculaire) tension; (phase de l'articulation) on-glide.
■ **~ artérielle** blood pressure.

tentaculaire /tɑ̃takyləʀ/ *adj* **1** [*ville*] sprawling (*épith*); [*entreprise, organisation*] with far-reaching interests (*après n*), tentacular (*épith*); [*pouvoir*] far-reaching (*épith*); **2** Zool tentacular.

tentacule /tɑ̃takyl/ *nm* tentacle; **étendre ses ~s dans une région** fig to spread its tentacles into a region.

tentant, **~e** /tɑ̃tɑ̃, ɑ̃t/ *adj* tempting.

tentateur, **-trice** /tɑ̃tatœʀ, tʀis/ **I** *adj* tempting.
II *nm,f* tempter/temptress.

tentation /tɑ̃tasjɔ̃/ *nf* temptation (**de** of; **de faire** to do); **céder/résister à la ~** to give in to/to resist temptation; **la ~ du repli sur soi est grande** there is a great temptation to turn in upon oneself; **la ~ est forte de demander plus** it's very tempting to ask for more; **dériver vers des ~s xénophobes** to succumb to the temptation of xenophobia.

tentative /tɑ̃tativ/ *nf* attempt; **faire une ~ de suicide** to make a suicide attempt; **trois ~s de suicide** three suicide attempts; **~ de meurtre** gén murder attempt; Jur attempted murder; **faire une ~ de meurtre contre qn** to attempt to murder sb; **~ de coup d'État** attempted coup; **faire une ~ de coup d'État** to attempt a coup; **faire une ~ d'évasion** to try to escape; **deux ~s d'évasion** two escape attempts; **faire une ~ auprès de qn pour obtenir qch** to try to obtain sth from sb.

tente /tɑ̃t/ *nf* tent; **~ de camping** tent; **~ familiale** frame tent; **~ dôme** dome tent; **~ canadienne** ridge tent; **dormir sous la ~** [*campeurs, soldats*] to sleep under canvas; [*nomades*] to sleep in tents.
■ **~ à oxygène** oxygen tent.

tente-abri, *pl* **tentes-abris** /tɑ̃tabʀi/ *nf* small tent.

tenter /tɑ̃te/ [1] *vtr* **1** (essayer) to attempt; **il a tenté de s'échapper** he attempted to escape; **j'ai tout tenté pour la dissuader** I've tried everything to dissuade her; **~ l'impossible** to attempt the impossible; **~ sa chance** to try one's luck, to have a go; **~ le coup** to give it a try○, to have a go○; **je vais ~ l'expérience** I'll have a go, I'll give it a try; **~ le tout pour le tout** to risk one's all; **2** (attirer) to tempt; **cela/l'idée ne la tente guère** that/the idea doesn't appeal to her very much; **ça ne me tente qu'à moitié** I'm only half tempted by it; **se laisser ~ par** to let oneself be tempted by; **laisse-toi ~!** be a devil!; **cette année, je suis tenté par l'Égypte** this year I feel like going to Egypt; **3** (éprouver) to tempt; **~ le sort** to tempt fate ou providence.

IDIOMES **~ le diable** to court disaster.

tenture /tɑ̃tyʀ/ *nf* **1** (grand rideau) curtain, drape US; **~s** (décoratif, à grands plis) draperies; **2** (tendu aux murs) fabric wall covering; **3** Art (sur un mur) **~ (murale)** (wall) hanging; **4** (de funérailles) **~s** draperies.

tenu, **~e** /təny/ **I** *pp* ▶ **tenir**.

II pp adj 1 (entretenu) bien/mal ~ [enfant] well/badly cared for; [maison] well/badly kept; [troupes] well/badly turned out; maison impeccablement ~e very well kept house; chambre bien ~/mal ~e tidy/untidy room; 2 (contrôlé) (par parents, enseignant) être très ~ par to be kept on a tight rein by; 3 (contraint) ~ de faire required to do; être ~ de dresser un inventaire mensuel to be required to draw up a monthly inventory; ~ à bound by; être ~ au secret professionnel to be bound by professional secrecy; ▸impossible; 4 (occupé) ~ par detained by; être ~ par une affaire urgente to be held up ou detained by an urgent matter; 5 Mus [note, accord] held.

III nm Sport (en basket) holding.

IV **tenue** nf 1 (organisation) confirmer la ~e prochaine d'élections libres to confirm that free elections will be held in the near future; six jours avant la ~e de la conférence six days before the opening of the conference; pendant la ~e du congrès du parti during the party conference; interdire la ~e d'une réunion to ban a meeting; 2 (gestion) ~e de la comptabilité or des comptes bookkeeping ¢; 3 (vêtements) ~e (vestimentaire) dress ¢, clothes (pl); être en ~e décontractée to wear casual clothes; ~e d'hiver/été gén winter/summer clothes (pl); (de soldat, policier) winter/summer uniform; se mettre en ~e to change; être en petite ~e to be scantily clad; être en ~e légère (peu vêtu) to be scantily dressed; (avec vêtements légers) to be in light clothing; être/se mettre en grande ~e gén to be in/to put on ceremonial dress; Mil to be in/to put on full dress uniform; en ~e [policier, fonctionnaire] uniformed; '~e correcte exigée' (à l'entrée d'un lieu public) 'appropriate clothing must be worn'; 4 (apparence extérieure) avoir une ~e impeccable/recherchée to be impeccably/elegantly dressed; avoir une ~e débraillée to be scruffily dressed; 5 (manières) avoir de la ~e to have good manners; ne pas avoir de ~e to have bad manners; avoir une bonne ~e à table to have good table manners; un peu de ~e! mind your manners!; 6 (posture) posture ¢; 7 (qualité) journal d'excellente or de haute ~e quality newspaper; 8 Fin (comportement) performance; bonne/mauvaise ~e des actions/de l'or good/poor performance of the shares/of gold; 9 Mus (d'accord, de note) holding.

■ ~e de campagne Mil battle ou field dress ¢; ~e de cérémonie gén ceremonial dress ¢; Mil mess kit; ~e camouflée Mil camouflage uniform; ~e de combat Mil battledress ¢; (de policier) riot gear ¢; ~e léopard Mil camouflage uniform; ~e de route Aut roadholding ¢; ~e de soirée Mode formal dress ¢; '~e de soirée exigée' 'black tie'; ~e de sortie Mil dress uniform; ~e de travail gén work(ing) clothes (pl); Mil fatigues (pl); ~e de ville Mode smart clothes; ~e de vol Aviat flying gear ¢.

ténu, ~e /teny/ adj 1 lit [fil, lien] weak; 2 fig [rapport, distinction] tenuous; [souvenir, son, souffle, brume] faint.

ténuité /tenɥite/ nf liter (de distinction) tenuousness; (de son, souvenir) faintness.

tenure /tənyʀ/ nf Hist tenure; ~ féodale feudal tenure.

téorbe /teɔʀb/ ▸534 nm theorbo.

TEP /teəpe/ nf: abbr ▸tonne.

tequila /tekila/ nf tequila.

■ ~ frappée tequila slammer.

ter /tɛʀ/ adv 1 (dans une adresse) ter; 15 ~ 15 ter; cf 15B; 2 (indication) three times.

tératologie /teʀatɔlɔʒi/ nf teratology.

tératologique /teʀatɔlɔʒik/ adj teratological.

tercet /tɛʀsɛ/ nm tercet.

térébenthine /teʀebɑ̃tin/ nf turpentine; (essence de) ~ turpentine.

térébinthe /teʀebɛ̃t/ nm terebinth.

tergal® /tɛʀgal/ nm Terylene®; robe en ~ Terylene dress.

tergiversation /tɛʀʒivɛʀsasjɔ̃/ nf equivocation ¢; après moult ~s after much equivocation.

tergiverser /tɛʀʒivɛʀse/ [1] vi 1 (par indécision) to dither; 2 (discuter sans résultats) to shilly-shally.

terme /tɛʀm/ I nm 1 (mot) term; ~ technique/de droit/de médecine technical/legal/medical term; au sens premier du ~ in the original sense of the word; le ~ de quota désigne the word ou term 'quota' designates; en ~s élogieux/injurieux in glowing/offensive terms; en d'autres ~s in other words; dans tous les sens/toute la force du ~ in every sense/the full sense of the word; selon les ~s du ministre as the minister put it; pardonnez-moi le ~ if you'll pardon the expression; la question se pose en ces ~s: qui est responsable? the question is this: who is responsible?; c'est en ces ~s que le ministre a décrit la situation this was how the minister described the situation; il a décrit les résultats en ces ~s he described the results thus; 2 (fin) end; mettre un ~ à qch to put an end to sth; au ~ de at the end of; au ~ de la réunion at the end of the meeting; toucher à son ~ to come to an end; toucher au ~ de ses souffrances to come to the end of one's sufferings; arriver à ~ [plan, épargne] to come to its appointed end; [période, délai, contrat] to expire; mener qch à ~ to see sth through to completion [projet, opération]; mener une grossesse à ~ to carry a pregnancy (through) to full term; naître à/avant ~ to be born at full/before term; accoucher avant ~ to give birth prematurely; enfant né avant ~ premature baby; 3 (échéance) passé ce ~ vous paierez des intérêts after this date, you will pay interest; cela risque, à ~, de poser des problèmes this may, eventually, cause problems; à court/moyen /long ~ [emprunt, problème, stratégie] short-/medium-/long-term (épith); investissement à long ~ long-term investment; à court/moyen/long ~ c'est possible it is possible in the short/medium/long term; achat/vente à ~ Fin forward buying/selling; 4 Jur (date de paiement du loyer) due date; (période de location) rental period; (montant de la location) rent; payer son ~ to pay one's rent; le jour du ~ approchait the day when the rent was due was drawing near; 5 Math term; ~s d'un polynôme/d'une fraction terms of a polynomial/of a fraction; 6 Philos (en logique) term; ~s d'un syllogisme/d'une proposition terms of a syllogism/of a proposition; trouver un moyen ~ (équilibre) to find a happy medium (entre between); (compromis) to find a compromise (entre between); 7 Art (sculpture) term.

II **termes** nmpl 1 (clauses) terms; les ~s du contrat sont très clairs the terms of the contract are very clear; aux ~s de l'article 3 in pursuance of article 3; accords aux ~s desquels les deux pays s'engagent à faire agreements according to the terms of which both countries undertake to do; ~s de l'échange terms of trade; 2 (relations) terms; être en bons/mauvais ~s avec qn to be on good/bad terms with sb; 3 (dimension) en ~s de in terms of; en ~s de profit/formation/productivité in terms of profit/training/productivity; la question se pose aussi en ~s financiers the issue is also a financial one.

terminaison /tɛʀminɛzɔ̃/ nf Ling ending.

■ ~ nerveuse Anat nerve ending.

terminal, ~e, mpl -aux /tɛʀminal, o/ I adj [année] final; classe ~e Scol final year (of secondary school); phase ~e (d'une opération) concluding phase; (d'une maladie) terminal phase; le stade ~ d'un cancer the terminal phase of cancer.

II nm 1 Aviat terminal; 2 Ind, Naut terminal; ~ pétrolier/maritime oil/shipping terminal; 3 Ordinat terminal; ~ d'ordinateur computer terminal.

III **terminale** nf Scol final year (of secondary school).

■ ~ de données Ordinat data terminal equipment, DTE; ~ point de vente, TPV point-of-sale terminal, EPOS terminal.

terminer /tɛʀmine/ [1] I vtr 1 (aller jusqu'au bout de) to finish [lettre, repas, récit, travail, études, course]; ils n'ont pas terminé leur formation they haven't finished their training; termine ton déjeuner finish your lunch; il ne termine jamais ses phrases he never finishes his sentences; 2 (conclure) to end [activités, période, discours]; le dollar a terminé la semaine à 6,18 francs the dollar ended the week at 6.18 francs; ~ sa carrière à Hongkong/en tant que consultant to end one's career in Hong Kong/as a consultant; ~ son discours par une mise en garde/sur une note optimiste/en rappelant que to end one's speech with a warning/on a happy note/by reminding the audience that; ~ le repas par une liqueur/chanson to end the meal with a liqueur/song.

II vi to finish; avez-vous terminé? have you finished?; ~ premier or à la première place to finish first; en ~ avec qch/qn to be through with sth/sb; nous avons terminé chez Maxence we ended up at Maxence's; c'est terminé, je n'irai plus jamais! that's that, I'm never going back!; pour ~ je dirai que in conclusion let me say that; l'indice a terminé en baisse/hausse Fin the index closed lower/higher; ~ en hausse de douze points à 1821 to close twelve points up at 1821.

III **se terminer** vpr 1 (dans le temps) to end; mon mandat se termine en décembre my mandate ends in December; l'été/le projet se termine summer/the project is coming to an end; se ~ par une promenade/par des licenciements to end with a walk/in dismissals; se ~ bien/mal [relation, événement] to end well/badly; [film, roman] to have a happy/sad ending; se ~ sur une note positive/comique [film, événement] to end on a positive/comic note; se ~ tragiquement [pièce] to end tragically; [excursion] to end in tragedy; être terminé to be over; le match est terminé the match is over; 2 (dans l'espace) se ~ par qch [tuyau, lame, corps] to end in; [date, numéro, prix] to end in ou with; [verbe, mot] to end in; le tuyau se termine par un coude the pipe ends in a bend; les numéros qui se terminent par cinq numbers ending in five; tous les mots se terminant par 'ment' all words ending in 'ment'; un morceau de bois terminé par un crochet en métal a piece of wood with a metal hook at the end.

terminologie /tɛʀminɔlɔʒi/ nf terminology.

terminologique /tɛʀminɔlɔʒik/ adj terminological.

terminologue /tɛʀminɔlɔg/ ▸510 nmf terminologist.

terminus /tɛʀminys/ nm inv (de train) end of the line; (de bus) terminus; '~ du train, tout le monde descend' 'all change please, the train terminates here'.

termite /tɛʀmit/ nm termite.

termitière /tɛʀmitjɛʀ/ nf termites' nest, termitarium spéc.

ternaire /tɛʀnɛʀ/ adj 1 Math, Chimie ternary; 2 Mus [rythme] compound.

terne /tɛʀn/ I adj [cheveux, poil] dull, lifeless; [couleur] drab; [blanc] dingy; [œil, regard] lifeless; [personne, vie] dull; [événement, campagne électorale] lacklustre[GB], dull.

II nm 1 Jeux (aux dés) double trey; 2 Électrotech three-phase transmission wire.

ternir /tɛʀniʀ/ [3] I vtr 1 to tarnish [métal];

to fade [*tissu*]; **2** to tarnish [*image, réputation*]; to detract from [*exploit*].

II se ternir *vpr* [*cuivre*] to tarnish.

ternissement /tɛʀnismɑ̃/ *adv* (de métal, réputation) tarnishing.

terrain /tɛʀɛ̃/ *nm* **1** (sol) ground ₵, soil ₵; (relief) ground ₵, terrain ₵; **du ~ sablonneux** sandy ground ou soil; **~s tertiaires/volcaniques** tertiary/volcanic formations; **avancer sur un ~ glissant** fig to be on slippery ground; **2** (parcelle) plot of land; **acheter un ~** to buy a plot of land; **un ~ à bâtir** a building plot; **un ~ non constructible** a plot of land not suitable for development; **3** (étendue) land ₵; **~ marécageux** marshy land; **acheter du ~** to buy land; **~ industriel/à bâtir** industrial/building land; **le prix du ~ au m²** the price of land per m²; **4** (au football, rugby) field; (au volley-ball, basket-ball) court; (au golf) course; **sortir du ~** [*joueur*] to go off the field; [*balle*] (au football) to go out of play; (au rugby) to go into touch; **disputer un match sur ~ adverse/sur son propre ~** to play an away game/a home game; **5** (sphère d'activité) **sur le ~ économique/juridique** in the field of economics/law; **nous ne vous suivrons pas sur ce ~** we won't go along with you there; **chercher/trouver un ~ d'entente** fig to seek/to find common ground; **6** (champ de recherche) field; **travailler sur le ~, faire du ~** to do fieldwork, to work in the field; **7** (état, milieu) Méd predisposing factors (*pl*); Sociol environment; **~ favorable** Méd predisposition (**à** to); Sociol favourable environment; **le ~ familial** the family background ou environment; **offrir un ~ favorable à** to provide a fertile breeding ground for [*maladie, idéologie*]; **être le ~ d'expérimentation de l'architecture moderne** to be the proving ground for modern architecture; **8** (groupe influençable) **les jeunes sont un ~ favorable** young people are easy targets; **9** Mil (lieu d'opérations) field; (en termes de relief) terrain; (en termes d'avance ou de recul) ground; **sur le ~** in the field; **connaître le ~** to know the terrain; **gagner/perdre du ~** to gain/to lose ground; **céder du ~** to give ground; **occuper le ~** to hold the field; **être en ~ connu** or **familier** fig to be on familiar territory; **être sur son ~, avoir l'avantage du ~** lit, fig to be on one's own ground; **déblayer le ~** to clear the ground; **préparer le ~** fig to pave the way; **tâter** or **sonder le ~** fig to put out feelers.

■ **~ d'atterrissage** landing strip; **~ d'aviation** airfield; **~ de basket-ball** basketball court; **~ de camping** campsite; **~ de cricket** cricket pitch; (avec les installations) cricket ground; **~ de chasse** area reserved for hunting, hunting ground littér; **~ de jeu(x)** playground ; **~ de football** soccer pitch, football pitch GB; (avec les installations) football ground; **~ de golf** golf course; **~ de manœuvre, ~ militaire** army training ground; **~ de handball** handball court; **~ de tennis** tennis court; **~ de tir** firing range; **~ de rugby** rugby pitch; (avec les installations) rugby ground; **~ de sport(s)** sports ground, playing field; **~ vague** piece of waste land; **~ de volley-ball** volleyball court.

terrasse /tɛʀas/ *nf* **1** (le long d'un bâtiment) terrace; **s'installer à la ~ d'un café** to sit at a table outside a café; **prendre un café en** or **à la ~** to have a coffee at an outside table; **prix en ~** price for service outside; **2** (toiture) flat roof; (grand balcon) large balcony; (plus grand) roof garden; **toiture en ~** flat roof; **3** Agric **culture(s) en ~s** terrace cultivation ₵; **rizières en ~s** terraced rice-fields; **cultiver le riz en ~s** to grow rice on terraces; **4** Géog **~ fluviale/rocheuse** river/rock terrace.

■ **~ vitrée** veranda GB, porch US.

terrassement /tɛʀasmɑ̃/ *nm* earthwork; **faire des travaux de ~** to carry out earthworks; **du matériel de ~** earth-moving equipment.

terrasser /tɛʀase/ [1] *vtr* **1** (jeter à terre) to knock down; **2** (priver de forces) [*maladie*] to strike down; **terrassé par** prostrated by [*chaleur, chagrin*].

terrassier /tɛʀasje/ **▶510** *nm* building labourer[GB], navvy° GB.

terre /tɛʀ/ **I** *nf* **1** (surface du sol) ground; **le cycliste était à ~** the cyclist was lying on the ground; **être jeté à ~** to be thrown to the ground; **sous ~** underground; **à 200 mètres sous ~** 200 metres[GB] underground; **ne frappez jamais un adversaire à ~** never hit a man when he's down; **mettre pied à ~** Équit to dismount; **mettre un genou à ~** to go down on one knee; **2** (matière) gén earth; Agric soil; **~ rouge/séchée** red/dried-up earth; **~ fertile/stérile** fertile/infertile soil; **l'eau, l'air, la ~ et le feu** water, air, earth and fire; **sortir de ~** lit [*plante*] to come up; [*animal*] to poke its head out of the ground; fig **une ville nouvelle est sortie de ~** a new town has sprung up; **porter** or **mettre qn en ~** liter to bury sb; **3** (campagne) **le retour à la ~** the movement back to the land; **rester attaché à la ~** to stay close to the land; **travailler la ~** to work the land; **4** (terrain) land ₵; **acheter/vendre une ~** to buy/to sell a plot of land; **des ~s** land; **elle possède des ~s en Anjou** she owns land in Anjou; **se retirer sur ses ~s** to go and live on one's estate; **vivre de ses ~s** to live off the land; **5** (région) land; **des ~s lointaines/vierges** distant/virgin lands; **une ~ inconnue** an unknown land, terra incognita littér; **en ~ chrétienne/musulmane** on Christian/Muslim land; **la ~ natale de qn** sb's native land; **la ~ de mes ancêtres** the land of my ancestors; **la ~ d'Afrique** liter the African continent; **la ~ d'Alsace** liter the Alsace region; **leur pays a toujours été une ~ d'accueil** their country has always welcomed newcomers; **6** (opposé à mer) land; **une bande/langue de ~** a strip/tongue of land; **un vent de ~** a land breeze; **aller à ~** to go ashore; **apercevoir la ~** to sight land; **'Terre!'** 'land ho!'; **être loin de toute ~** to be far from land; **s'enfoncer à l'intérieur des ~s** to go deep inland; **regagner la ~ ferme** to reach land ou terra firma littér; **7** (où vit l'humanité) earth; **être/vivre sur ~** to be/to live on earth; **quitter la ~** euph to die; **la ~ et le ciel** Relig things earthly and things heavenly; **prendre toute la ~ à témoin** to take the whole world as one's witness; **il croit que la ~ entière est contre lui** he thinks the whole world is against him; **redescends** or **reviens sur ~!** fig come back to earth!; **8** Art **de la ~ (glaise)** clay; **une statuette/pipe en ~** a clay figurine/pipe; **un pot de** or **en ~** an earthenware pot; **9** Électrotech earth GB, ground US; **relier qch à la ~** to earth GB ou ground US sth.

II terre à terre *loc adj inv* [*question*] basic; [*conversation, personne*] pedestrian.

III par terre *loc adv* (dehors) on the ground; (dedans) on the floor; **ils étaient assis/couchés par ~** they were sitting/lying on the ground ou floor; **se rouler par ~** lit to roll about on the ground ou floor; fig (de rire) to fall about laughing; **c'est à se rouler par ~** it's hilarious; **se rouler par ~ de douleur/rire** to roll on the ground with pain/laughter; **mon chapeau/le téléphone est tombé par ~** my hat/the telephone fell on the ground ou floor; **ça a fichu tous nos projets par ~**° it messed up all our plans°.

■ **~ d'asile** country of refuge; **~ battue** trodden earth; **sur ~ battue** [*tennis*] on a clay court; **~ de bruyère** Hortic peat; **~ cuite** baked clay; Art terracotta; **figurine en ~ cuite** terracotta figurine; **~ à foulon** fuller's earth; **~ glaise** clay; **~ noire** chernozem; **~ d'ombre** umber; **~ de pipe** pipeclay; **~ à poterie** or **potier** potter's clay; **~ de Sienne** sienna; **~ de Sienne brûlée** burned sienna; **~ végétale** topsoil; **~s rares** rare earths.

IDIOMES **avoir les pieds sur ~** to have one's feet firmly planted on the ground; **garder les pieds sur ~** to keep one's feet on the ground; **ne pas avoir les pieds sur ~** to be a dreamer, to have one's head in the clouds; **elle voulait rentrer sous ~** or **à cent pieds sous ~** she wished the ground would swallow her up.

Terre /tɛʀ/ *nf* Earth; **sur la ~** on Earth.

■ **la ~ Adélie** Adelie land; **la ~ de Feu** Tierra del Fuego; **la ~ promise** the Promised Land; **la ~ Sainte** the Holy Land.

terreau, *pl* **~x** /tɛʀo/ *nm* compost; **~ pour plantes d'appartement** potting compost.

■ **~ de feuilles** leaf mould.

terre-neuve /tɛʀnœv/ *nm inv* **1** Zool Newfoundland (dog); **2** fig (personne) **un vrai ~** a good Samaritan.

Terre-Neuve /tɛʀnœv/ **▶692** *nprf* Newfoundland.

terre-plein, *pl* **terres-pleins** /tɛʀplɛ̃/ *nm* **1** (de bâtiment) platform; **2** (de route) central reservation GB, median strip US; (de rond-point) central island; **3** Mil terreplein.

terrer /tɛʀe/ [1] **I** *vtr* Agric to earth up [*arbre, vigne*]; to earth over [*semis*].

II se terrer *vpr* **1** (dans son terrier) [*lapin*] to disappear into its burrow; [*renard*] to go to earth; **2** [*fugitif*] to hide, to go to ground; **on ne les voit jamais, ils se terrent chez eux** we never see them, they're holed up in their house.

terrestre /tɛʀɛstʀ/ *adj* **1** Géog (de la planète) [*diamètre, atmosphère*] of the Earth; **2** Sci [*animaux*] land (*épith*), terrestrial; **3** (au sol) [*guerre, transport*] land (*épith*); [*missile*] land- ou ground-based (*épith*); **4 les choses ~s** earthly things; **la vie ~** life on earth; **le paradis ~** heaven on earth.

terreur /tɛʀœʀ/ *nf* **1** (sentiment) terror; **paralysé par la ~** frozen by terror; **hurler de ~** to scream with terror; **une ~ irraisonnée** an irrational fear; **ma ~ de tomber malade** my fear of falling ill; **c'est ma grande ~** it's my greatest fear; **vivre dans la ~** to live in fear; **2** (comme moyen politique) terror; **3** (personne) **c'est la ~ du quartier** he's the terror of the neighbourhood[GB]; **elle était ma ~** I dreaded her; **jouer les ~s** to be a terror.

Terreur /tɛʀœʀ/ *nf* Hist **la ~** the Terror.

terreux, -euse /tɛʀø, øz/ *adj* **1** (souillé de terre) [*chaussures, mains, genoux*] muddy; [*pomme de terre*] covered in earth; [*salade*] full of dirt; (mal lavée) gritty; **2** (semblable à la terre) [*goût, consistance*] earthy; **avoir le teint ~** fig to have a grey GB ou gray US complexion.

terrible /tɛʀibl/ *adj* **1** (très intense) [*froid, chaleur, bruit, douleur, embouteillage*] terrible; [*vent, orage*] terrible, tremendous; [*soif, envie*] tremendous, terrible; [*colère*] terrible; **2** (épouvantable) [*catastrophe, maladie, accident*] terrible, dreadful; **3**° (pénible) terrible, awful; **c'est ~ d'être pingre à ce point** it's awful ou terrible being so mean; **c'est ~ de devoir tout ranger après lui** it's awful ou terrible having to put everything away after him; **il est ~, il ne veut jamais avoir tort** it's terrible the way he never wants to admit that he's wrong; **4**° (remarquable) terrific, fantastic°; **il n'est pas ~ ce restaurant/film** that's not a great restaurant/film; **il a eu un succès ~** he was a big hit°.

terriblement /tɛʀibləmɑ̃/ *adv* terribly; **~ plus fort/plus difficile** an awful lot stronger/more difficult; **il a ~ grandi** he's grown an awful lot.

terrien, -ienne /tɛʀjɛ̃, ɛn/ *adj* **propriétaire ~** landowner; **les grandes fortunes terriennes** the wealthy landowners.

Terrien, -ienne /tɛʀjɛ̃, ɛn/ *nm,f* earthman/earthwoman.

terrier /tɛʀje/ *nm* **1** (d'une bête) gén hole; **un ~ de lapin** a rabbit hole ou burrow; **un ~ de renard** a fox's earth; **un ~ de blaireau** a badger's sett; **2** (chien) terrier.

terrifiant, ~e /tɛʀifjɑ̃, ɑ̃t/ *adj* **1** (faisant peur) terrifying; **2** (hors du commun) [*bêtise, changement*] incredible.

terrifié, ~e /tɛʀifje/ **I** *pp* ▶ **terrifier**.
II *pp adj* [*personne, air*] terrified; **s'enfuir ~** to flee in terror.

terrifier /tɛʀifje/ [2] *vtr* to terrify.

terril /tɛʀi(l)/ *nm* slag heap.

terrine /tɛʀin/ *nf* **1** Culin terrine; **~ de saumon/canard** salmon/duck terrine; **2** (récipient) (allongé) terrine; (rond) earthenware bowl.

territoire /tɛʀitwaʀ/ *nm* **1** (d'un pays) territory; **le ~ national/allemand** national/German territory; **être en ~ ennemi** lit, fig to be on enemy territory; **sur l'ensemble du ~** throughout the country; **2** (chez les animaux) territory; **délimiter son ~** lit, fig to mark out one's territory; **défendre son ~** lit, fig to defend one's territory; **empiéter sur le ~ de qn** fig to encroach on sb's territory.
■ **~ de chasse** area reserved for hunting, hunting ground littér; **~ d'outre-mer, TOM** French overseas (administrative) territory; **les ~s (arabes) occupés** Pol, Géog the Occupied Territories.

Territoires du Nord-Ouest /tɛʀi twaʀdynɔʀwɛst/ ▶ **692** *nprmpl* Northwest Territories.

territorial, ~e *mpl* **-iaux** /tɛʀitɔʀjal, o/ **I** *adj* **1** (d'un État) [*intégrité, concessions, eaux*] territorial; **2** Admin [*administration*] (de subdivision) divisional; (de région) regional.
II territoriale *nf* Hist territorial army.

territorialité /tɛʀitɔʀjalite/ *nf* territoriality (**de** of).

terroir /tɛʀwaʀ/ *nm* land; **l'attachement au ~** the love of the land; **produits/vin du ~** local products/wine.

terrorisant, ~e /tɛʀɔʀizɑ̃, ɑ̃t/ *adj* terrifying.

terrorisé, ~e /tɛʀɔʀize/ **I** *pp* ▶ **terroriser**.
II *pp adj* **1** (effrayé) terrified; **2** (soumis à la terreur) terrorized.

terroriser /tɛʀɔʀize/ [1] *vtr* **1** (user de terreur) to terrorize; **2** (effrayer) [*orage, mauvais rêve, adulte*] to terrify.

terrorisme /tɛʀɔʀism/ *nm* terrorism; **le ~ d'État** State terrorism; **c'est du ~ (intellectuel)!** fig it's pure intimidation; **un acte de ~** an act of terrorism.

terroriste /tɛʀɔʀist/ **I** *adj* **1** Pol [*groupe, action, idéologie*] terrorist; **2** [*argument, attitude*] intimidatory.
II *nmf* terrorist.

tertiaire /tɛʀsjɛʀ/ **I** *adj* **1** Écon [*secteur*] service (*épith*), tertiary; [*industrie*] service; **l'emploi/l'activité ~** work/activity in the service sector; **la ville est un pôle ~** the town is a centre[GB] for the service industries; **2** Géol [*ère, plissement*] Tertiary; **3** Méd tertiary.
II *nm* **1** Écon service sector; **2** Géol Tertiary.

tertiarisation /tɛʀsjaʀizasjɔ̃/ *nf* **~ (de l'économie** or **des activités)** development of the service sector.

tertio /tɛʀsjo/ *adv* thirdly.

tertre /tɛʀtʀ/ *nm* mound; **~ funéraire** burial mound.

tes ▶ **ton**[1].

Tessin /tesɛ̃/ ▶ **692** *npr* **le (canton du) ~** the (canton of) Ticino.

tessiture /tesityʀ/ *nf* range.

tesson /tesɔ̃/ *nm* shard, fragment (**de** of); **~ de bouteille** piece of glass; **des ~s de bouteille** broken glass ₵.

test /tɛst/ **I** *nm* **1** Zool (enveloppe calcaire) test; **2** (pour évaluer) test; **~ psychologique/de sélection/de grossesse** psychological/selection/pregnancy test; **~ (de dépistage) du sida** Aids test; **faire passer des ~s à qn** (à l'école, pour recruter) to give sb tests; Méd to carry out tests on sb; **3** Chimie = **têt**.
II -test (*in compounds*) **match-~** trial match; **rencontre-~** preliminary meeting; **semaine-~** trial week; **région-~** pilot region.
■ **~ d'orientation** Scol aptitude test.

testable /tɛstabl/ *adj* [*théorie*] testable.

testament /tɛstamɑ̃/ *nm* **1** Jur will; **faire son ~** lit to make one's will; **mourir sans laisser de ~** to die intestate; **ceci est mon ~** this is my last will and testament; **2** liter (message ultime) legacy; **3** Bible, Relig **l'Ancien/le Nouveau Testament** the Old/the New Testament.
■ **~ authentique** *will drawn up by a lawyer in the presence of witnesses*; **~ mystique** *will written and signed by the testator and handed sealed to the lawyer*; **~ olographe** handwritten will, holograph will spéc; **~ public** = **~ authentique**; **~ secret** = **~ mystique**.

testamentaire /tɛstamɑ̃tɛʀ/ *adj* [*clause, disposition*] of a will (*après n*).

testateur /tɛstatœʀ/ *nm* testator.

testatrice /tɛstatʀis/ *nf* testatrix.

tester /tɛste/ [1] **I** *vtr* (tous contextes) to test (**dans** in; **sur** on; **auprès de** on); **testé en laboratoire** laboratory-tested.
II *vi* Jur to make a will.

testeur /tɛstœʀ/ *nm* tester.

testicule /tɛstikyl/ *nm* testicle, testis spéc.

testimonial, ~e, *mpl* **-aux** /tɛstimɔnjal, o/ *adj* testimonial.

testostérone /tɛstɔsteʀɔn/ *nf* testosterone.

têt /tɛ/ *nm* **~ à gaz** beehive shelf; **~ à rôtir** crucible.

tétanie /tetani/ ▶ **271** *nf* tetany; **une crise de ~** an attack of tetany.

tétanique /tetanik/ *adj* [*contraction*] tetanic; [*patient*] tetanus (*épith*); **le bacille ~** the tetanus bacillus.

tétanisation /tetanizasjɔ̃/ *nf* tetanization.

tétanisé, ~e /tetanize/ **I** *pp* ▶ **tétaniser**.
II *pp adj* **1** Méd tetanized; **2** (figé) [*personne, animal*] paralyzed.

tétaniser /tetanize/ [1] **I** *vtr* **1** Méd to tetanize [*muscle, membre*]; **2** (figer) to paralyze [*personne*].
II se tétaniser *vpr* [*muscle*] to seize up.

tétanos /tetanos/ ▶ **271** *nm inv* tetanus.

têtard /tɛtaʀ/ *nm* **1** Zool tadpole; **2** (arbre) pollard.

tête /tɛt/ ▶ **188** *nf* **1** gén (d'animal, insecte, de personne, plante) head; **bouger la ~** to move one's head; **dessiner une ~ de femme** to draw a woman's head; **statue à ~ de chien** statue with a dog's head; **en pleine ~** (right) in the head; **blessure à la ~** head injury; **frapper qn à la ~** to hit sb on the head; **la ~ la première** [*tomber, plonger*] head first; **la ~ basse** (humblement) with one's head bowed; **la ~ haute** (dignement) with one's head held high; **garder la ~ haute** fig to hold one's head high; **~ baissée** [*se lancer, foncer*] headlong; **la ~ en bas** [*être suspendu, se retrouver*] upside down; **au-dessus de nos ~s** (en l'air) overhead; **sans ~** [*corps, cadavre*] headless; **coup de ~** headbutt; **donner un coup de ~ à qn** to headbutt sb; **tomber sur la ~** lit to fall on one's head; **être tombé sur la ~**○ fig to have gone off one's rocker○; **salut, p'tite ~**○! hello, bonehead○!; ▶ **bille**, **coûter**, **donner**, **gros**; **2** (dessus du crâne) head; **se couvrir/se gratter la ~** to cover/to scratch one's head; **avoir la ~ rasée** to have a shaven head; **sortir ~ nue** or **sans rien sur la ~** to go out bareheaded; **se laver la ~** to wash one's hair; **j'ai la ~ toute mouillée** my hair's all wet; **3** (visage) face; **une bonne/sale ~** a nice/nasty face; **il a une belle ~** he's got a nice face; **si tu avais vu ta ~!** you should have seen your face!; **t'as vu la ~ qu'il a tirée**○? did you see his face?; **tu en fais une ~!** what a face you're pulling!; **ne fais pas cette ~-là!** don't pull such a face!; **faire une ~ longue comme ça**○ to look miserable; **il a fait une drôle de ~ quand il m'a vu** he pulled a face when he saw me; **quelle ~ va-t-il faire?** how's he going to react?; **faire une ~ de circonstance** to assume a suitable expression; **à cette nouvelle, il a changé de ~** on hearing this, his face fell; **il (me) fait la ~** he's sulking; **ne fais pas ta mauvaise ~** don't be so difficult; **elle fait sa mauvaise ~** she's being difficult; **il a une ~ à tricher** he looks like a cheat; **elle a une ~ à être du quartier** she looks like a local; **tu as une ~ à faire peur, aujourd'hui!** you look dreadful today!; **se faire la** or **une ~ de Pierrot** to make oneself up as (a) Pierrot; ▶ **six**; **4** (esprit) **de ~** [*citer, réciter*] from memory; [*calculer*] in one's head; **tu n'as pas de ~!** you have a mind like a sieve!; **avoir en ~ de faire** to have it in mind to do; **avoir qch en ~** to have sth in mind; **j'ai bien d'autres choses en ~ pour le moment** I've got a lot of other things on my mind at the moment; **je n'ai pas la référence en ~** I can't recall the reference; **où avais-je la ~?** whatever was I thinking of?; **ça (ne) va pas, la ~**○? are you feeling all right?; **j'ai la ~ vide** my mind is a blank; **j'avais la ~ ailleurs** I was dreaming, I was thinking of something else; **elle n'a pas la ~ à ce qu'elle fait** her mind isn't on what she's doing; **avoir la ~ pleine de projets, avoir des projets plein la ~** to have one's head full of plans; **quand il a quelque chose dans la** or **en ~, il ne l'a pas ailleurs**○ once he's got GB ou gotten US something into his head, he can't think of anything else; **n'avoir rien dans la ~** to be empty-headed, to be an airhead○; **c'est lui qui t'a mis ça dans la ~!** you got that idea from him!; **mets-lui ça dans la ~** drum it into him/her; **se mettre dans la** or **en ~ que** to get it into one's head that; **se mettre dans la** or **en ~ de faire** to take it into one's head to do; **mets-toi bien ça dans la ~!** get it into your head once and for all!; **mettez-vous dans la ~ que je ne signerai pas** get it into your head that I won't sign; **passer par la ~ de qn** [*idée*] to cross sb's mind; **on ne sait jamais ce qui leur passe par la ~** you never know what's going through their minds; **passer au-dessus de la ~ de qn** to be ou go (right) over sb's head; **sortir de la ~ de qn** to slip sb's mind; **ça m'est sorti de la ~** it slipped my mind; **cette fille lui a fait perdre la ~** he's lost his head over that girl; **monter la ~ à Pierre contre Paul** to turn Pierre against Paul; **j'ai la ~ qui tourne** my head's spinning; **ça me fait tourner la ~** it's making my head spin; **monter à la ~, faire tourner la ~ de qn** [*alcool, succès*] to go to sb's head; **elle t'a fait tourner la ~** she's turned your head; **il n'est pas bien dans sa ~**○ he isn't right in the head; **il a encore toute sa ~ (à lui)** he's still got all his faculties ou marbles○; **il n'a plus sa ~ à lui** he's no longer in possession of all his faculties, he's lost his marbles○; **n'en faire qu'à sa ~** to go one's own way; **tenir ~ à qn** to stand up to sb; **sur un coup de ~** on an impulse; ▶ **fort**; **5** (personne) face; **j'ai déjà vu cette ~-là quelque part** I've seen that face somewhere before; **voir de nouvelles ~s** to see new faces; **avoir ses ~s** to have one's favourites[GB]; **en ~ à ~** [*être, rester, dîner*] alone together; **être (en) ~ à ~ avec qn** to be alone with sb; **rencontrer qn en ~ à ~** to have a meeting with sb in private; **un dîner en ~ à ~** an intimate dinner for two; **6** (mesure de longueur) head; **avoir une ~ de plus que qn, dépasser qn d'une ~** to be a head taller than sb; **gagner d'une courte ~** [*personne*] to win by a narrow margin; [*cheval*] to win by a short head;

avoir une ~ d'avance sur qn to be a short length in front of sb; **7** (unité de troupeau) head (*inv*); **30 ~s de bétail** 30 head of cattle; **un troupeau de 500 ~s** a herd of 500 head; **8** (individu) **par ~** gén a head, each; Stat per capita; **par ~ de pipe**○ each; **ça fera 500 francs par ~** it'll be 500 francs each ou a head; **le PNB par ~** the per capita GNP; **9** (vie) head; **ma ~ est mise à prix** there's a price on my head; **vouloir la ~ de qn** (mort) to want sb's head; (disgrâce) to be after sb's head; **risquer sa ~** to risk one's neck○; **des ~s vont tomber** fig heads will roll; **10** (direction) **frapper une révolte à la ~** to go for the leaders of an uprising; **le groupe de ~** the leading group; **c'est lui la ~ pensante du projet/mouvement/gang** he's the brains behind the project/movement/gang; **être à la ~ d'un mouvement/parti** to be at the head of a movement/party; **il restera à la ~ du groupe** he will stay on as head of the group; **il a été nommé à la ~ du groupe** he was appointed head of the group; **on l'a rappelé à la ~ de l'équipe** he was called back to head up ou lead the team; **prendre la ~ du parti** to become leader of the party; **prendre la ~ des opérations** to take charge of operations; **être à la ~ d'une immense fortune** to be the possessor of a huge fortune; **11** (premières places) top; **les élèves qui forment la ~ de la classe** the pupils at the top of the class; **les candidats en ~ de liste** the candidates at the top of the list; **être en ~** (de liste, classement) to be at the top; (d'élection, de course, sondage) to be in the lead; **venir en ~** to come first; **marcher en ~** to walk at the front; **à la ~ d'un cortège** at the head of a procession; **marcher en ~ d'un cortège** to head ou lead a procession; **il est en ~ au premier tour** Pol he's in the lead after the first round; **il est en ~ dans les sondages** he's leading in the polls; **l'équipe de ~ au championnat** the leading team in the championship; **arriver en ~** [*coureur*] to come in first; [*candidat*] to come first; **le gouvernement, le premier ministre en ~, a décidé que**... the government, led by the Prime Minister, has decided that...; **des tas de gens viendront, ta femme en ~** heaps of people are coming, your wife to begin with; **en ~ de phrase** at the beginning of a sentence; **12** (extrémité) (de train) front; (de convoi, cortège) head; (d'arbre, de mât) top; (de vis, rivet, clou) head; **les wagons de ~** the front carriages GB ou cars US; **une place en ~ de train** a seat at the front of the train; **je préfère m'asseoir en ~** I prefer to sit at the front; **la ~ du convoi s'est engagée sur le pont** the head of the convoy went onto the bridge; **l'avion a rasé la ~ des arbres** the plane clipped the tops of the trees ou the treetops; **en ~ de file** first in line; ▶ **queue**; **13** Sport (au football) header; **faire une ~** to head the ball; **14** Mil (d'engin) warhead; **~ chimique/nucléaire** chemical/nuclear warhead; **missile à ~s multiples** multiple-warhead missile; **15** Électron (d'enregistrement, effacement) head; (d'électrophone) cartridge; **~ de lecture** (de magnétophone, magnétoscope) head.

■ **~ d'affiche** Cin, Théât top of the bill; **~ d'ail** Bot, Culin head of garlic; **~ en l'air** scatterbrain; **être ~ en l'air** to be scatterbrained; **~ blonde** (enfant) little one; **nos chères ~s blondes** hum our little darlings; **~ brûlée** daredevil; **~ de chapitre** chapter heading; **~ chercheuse** Mil homing device; **missile à ~ chercheuse** homing missile; **~ à claques**○ pain○; **quelle ~ à claques, ce type!** he's somebody you could cheerfully punch in the face; **~ de cochon**○ = **~ de lard**; **~ couronnée** crowned head; **~ de delco**® Aut distributor cap; **~ d'écriture** Ordinat write ou writing head; **~ d'effacement** Ordinat erase ou erasing head; **~ d'épingle** lit, fig pinhead; **~ flottante** Ordinat floating head; **~ de lard**○ péj (têtu) mule; (mauvais caractère) grouch; **~ de ligne** Transp end of the line; **~ de linotte** scatterbrain; **~ de liste** Pol chief candidate; **~ de lit** bedhead GB, headboard; **~ magnétique** magnetic head; **~ de mort** (crâne) skull; (symbole de mort) death's head; (emblème de pirates) skull and crossbones (+ *v sg*); **~ de mule**○ mule; **être une vraie ~ de mule** to be as stubborn as a mule; **~ de nègre** Culin chocolate marshmallow; **~ de nœud**● offensive prick●; **~ d'oiseau**○ péj featherbrain; **~ de pioche**○ = **~ de mule**; **~ de pont** Mil bridgehead; **~ de série** Sport seeded player; **~ de série numéro deux** number two seed; **~ de Turc**○ whipping boy; **être la ~ de Turc de qn** to be sb's whipping boy; **~ de veau** Culin calf's head.

IDIOMES **j'en mettrais ma ~ à couper** or **sur le billot** I'd put my head on the block; **en avoir par-dessus la ~** to be fed up to the back teeth○ (**de** with); **se prendre la ~ à deux mains** (pour réfléchir)○ to rack one's brains○; **prendre la ~**○, **être une (vraie) prise de ~**○ to be a drag○.

tête-à-queue /tɛtakø/ *nm inv* **faire un ~** [*voiture, automobiliste*] to slew round GB ou around; **à la suite d'un ~** after the car slewed around.

tête-à-tête /tɛtatɛt/ *nm inv* (d'amis, amants) tête-à-tête; (de politiciens) private meeting.

tête-bêche /tɛtbɛʃ/ *adv* (pour des personnes) top-to-tail; (pour des objets) head-to-tail; **on a dormi ~** we slept top-to-tail; **les deux lits étaient disposés ~** the two beds were placed head-to-tail; **timbres ~** tête-bêche stamps.

tête-de-loup, *pl* **têtes-de-loup** /tɛtdəlu/ *nf* ceiling brush.

tête-de-nègre /tɛtdənɛɡʀ/ ▶ **193** *adj inv*, *nm inv* dark brown.

tétée /tete/ *nf* **1** (action) feeding, nursing; **l'heure de la ~** feeding ou nursing time; **il m'a téléphoné pendant la ~** he phoned me while I was feeding ou nursing the baby; **2** (repas) feed; **six ~s par jour** six feeds a day.

téter /tete/ [14] **I** *vtr* [*bébé, animal*] to suck at [*sein, mamelle*]; to feed from [*biberon*]; to suck [*lait*]; **~ sa mère** to suckle, feed.

II *vi* [*bébé*] to suckle, feed; [*animal*] to suckle; **donner à ~ à** to feed, suckle littér [*bébé*]; to suckle [*animal*].

têtière /tɛtjɛʀ/ *nf* **1** (de siège) headrest; **2** Naut (sommet de voile carrée) head; (renfort de voile triangulaire) headboard; **3** Équit headpiece; **4** (de serrure) faceplate.

tétine /tetin/ *nf* **1** (de biberon) teat GB, nipple US; **2** (sucette) dummy GB, pacifier US; **3** Vét teat.

téton○ /tetɔ̃/ *nm* **1** (sein) tit◑, breast; **2** Tech lug.

tétrachlorure /tetʀaklɔʀyʀ/ *nm* tetrachloride.

tétraèdre /tetʀaɛdʀ/ *nm* tetrahedron.

tétralogie /tetʀalɔʒi/ *nf* gén tetralogy; (de romans) quartet; **la Tétralogie** Mus the Ring (of the Nibelung).

tétramètre /tetʀamɛtʀ/ *nm* tetrameter.

tétraplégie /tetʀapleʒi/ *nf* quadriplegia.

tétraplégique /tetʀapleʒik/ *adj* quadriplegic.

tétrarque /tetʀaʀk/ *nm* tetrarch.

tétras /tetʀa/ *nm inv* grouse; ▶ **grand**.

tétras-lyre, *pl* **~s** /tetʀaliʀ/ *nm* black grouse.

tétrasyllabe /tetʀasil(l)ab/ **I** *adj* tetrasyllabic.

II *nm* tetrasyllabic line.

tétrasyllabique /tetʀasil(l)abik/ *adj* tetrasyllabic.

têtu, **~e** /tety/ *adj* [*personne, animal*] stubborn; **les faits sont ~s** the facts won't go away.

IDIOMES **être ~ comme un âne** or **une mule** or **une bourrique** to be as stubborn as a mule.

teuf-teuf, *pl* **teufs-teufs** /tœftœf/ *nm* ou *f* (*also onomat*) **1** (bruit de voiture) baby talk brm brm; **2**○ (vieille voiture) rattletrap.

teuton, **-onne** /tøtɔ̃, ɔn/ *adj* **1** Hist Teutonic; **2**† offensive German.

Teuton, **-onne** /tøtɔ̃, ɔn/ *nm,f* **1** Hist Teuton; **2**† offensive German.

teutonique /tøtɔnik/ *adj* **1** Hist Teutonic; **2**† offensive German.

texan, **~e** /tɛksɑ̃, an/ *adj* Texan.

Texan, **~e** /tɛksɑ̃, an/ *nm,f* Texan.

Texas /tɛksas/ ▶ **692** *nprm* Texas.

texte /tɛkst/ *nm* **1** gén text; (livre) text; (passage) extract, text; **le ~ d'une chanson/d'un ouvrage illustré/d'un discours** the text of a song/of an illustrated book/of a speech; **faire une explication de ~** to do a commentary on a text; **~s choisis de Montaigne** selected extracts from Montaigne; **lire une œuvre étrangère dans le ~** to read a foreign work in the original; **en français dans le ~** in French in the original text; **'~ intégral'** 'unabridged text'; **2** Cin, Théât (script) script; (rôle à apprendre) lines (*pl*), part; **3** Admin, Jur, Pol (libellé) wording, text; **le ~ d'un contrat** the wording of a contract; **4** Ordinat text; **5** Imprim copy.

■ **~ de loi** (proposé) bill; (promulgué) law; **adopter un ~ de loi** to pass a law; **le ~ (de loi) entre en vigueur demain** the bill will become law tomorrow; **~ libre** Scol free composition; **les ~s sacrés** Relig the sacred texts.

texteur /tɛkstœʀ/ *nm* word processor.

textile /tɛkstil/ **I** *adj* **1** [*industrie, société, commerce*] textile; **le secteur ~** the textile industry; **2** (avant tissage) **fibres ~s** fibres[GB]; **matières ~s végétales** plant fibres[GB]; **3** (en étoffe) **les articles ~s** textiles.

II *nm* **1** (secteur industriel) textile industry; **le secteur du ~** the textile industry; **les ouvriers du ~** textile workers; **2** (avant tissage) fibre[GB]; (tissu) textile; **~s artificiels/synthétiques** artificial/synthetic fibres[GB].

texto○ /tɛksto/ *adv* [*répéter, copier*] word for word; **il m'a dit ~, 'c'est bien fait pour elle'** he told me in so many words, 'she got what she deserved'.

textuel, **-elle** /tɛkstɥɛl/ *adj* **1** (conforme) [*copie, reproduction*] exact; [*traduction*] literal; **2** (du texte) [*analyse*] textual; [*sens*] literal; [*citation, passage*] from the text.

textuellement /tɛkstɥɛlmɑ̃/ *adv* [*rapporter*] verbatim, word for word; **je ne cite pas ~** I'm not quoting word for word; **il m'a dit ~, 'je m'en moque'** he told me in so many words, 'I couldn't care less'.

texture /tɛkstyʀ/ *nf* **1** (de tissu, matériau, peinture) texture; **2** (de roman, pièce de théâtre) structure.

tézigue◑ /tezig/ *pron pers* you.

TGV /teʒeve/ *nm* (*abbr* = **train à grande vitesse**) TGV, high-speed train.

thaï, **~e** /taj/ **I** ▶ **537** *adj* Thai.

II ▶ **462** *nm* Ling Thai.

Thaï, **~e** /taj/ ▶ **537** *nm,f* Thai.

thaïlandais, **~e** /tajlɑ̃dɛ, ɛz/ ▶ **537** *adj* Thai.

Thaïlandais, **~e** /tajlɑ̃dɛ, ɛz/ ▶ **537** *nm,f* Thai.

Thaïlande /tajlɑ̃d/ ▶ **321** *nprf* Thailand.

thalamus /talamys/ *nm inv* Anat thalamus.

thalassémie /talasemi/ ▶ **271** *nf* thalassaemia.

thalassothérapie /talasoteʀapi/ *nf* thalassotherapy.

thalle /tal/ *nm* thallus.

thalweg = **talweg**.

thaumaturge /tomatyʀʒ/ *nmf* thaumaturge.

thé /te/ *nm* **1** (feuilles, infusion) tea; **~ vert/**

noir green/black tea; **~ au lait** tea with milk; **~ au citron/au jasmin/à la menthe** lemon/jasmine/mint tea; **~ à la bergamote** Earl Grey tea; **~s de Chine/de Ceylan** China/Ceylon teas; **à l'heure du ~** at teatime; **prendre le ~ chez qn** to have tea at sb's home; **être invité à prendre le ~** to be asked to tea; **2** (réunion) tea party.

théâtral, **~e**, *mpl* **-aux** /teɑtʀal, o/ *adj* **1** Théât [*œuvre, langage*] dramatic; [*représentation, adaptation*] stage (*épith*); [*saison, compagnie*] theatre[GB] (*épith*); **elle veut faire une carrière ~e** she wants to be an actress, she wants to go on the stage; **2** (exagéré) péj [*geste*] histrionic; [*ton*] melodramatic; **il s'exprime de façon très ~e** he is very melodramatic.

théâtralement /teɑtʀalmɑ̃/ *adv* lit theatrically; péj histrionically.

théâtralité /teɑtʀalite/ *nf* (de texte, décor, situation) dramatic quality (**de** of).

théâtre /teɑtʀ/ *nm* **1** littér (genre) theatre[GB]; **le ~ de l'absurde** the theatre[GB] of the absurd; **aimer le ~ classique/burlesque/expérimental** to like classical/burlesque/experimental theatre[GB]; **le ~ de Molière/de Racine** Molière's/Racine's plays; **le ~ antique** Greek classical drama; **de ~** [*acteur, directeur, billet*] theatre[GB] (*épith*); [*décor, costume, masque*] stage (*épith*); fig [*gestes*] histrionic; **c'est un homme de ~** he's a man of the theatre[GB]; **coup de ~** lit coup de théâtre; fig dramatic turn of events, coup de théâtre sout; **2** (art dramatique) **faire du ~** (comme profession) to be an actor; (à l'école) to do drama; (en amateur) to be involved in amateur dramatics; **se destiner au ~** to intend to go on stage; **adapter une nouvelle pour le ~** to adapt a short story for the stage; **faire son ~**○ fig to put on one's act; **c'est du ~** fig it's just a put-on○; **3** (lieu) theatre[GB]; **le ~ était plein** the theatre[GB] was full; **être le ~ d'affrontements/d'émeutes** fig to be the scene of fighting/of riots; **le ~ des opérations** Mil the theatre[GB] of operations.
■ **~ de Boulevard** farce; **~ antique** amphitheatre[GB]; **~ de marionnettes** puppet theatre[GB]; **~ d'ombres** shadow theatre[GB]; **~ en plein air** open-air theatre[GB]; **~ de verdure** = **~ en plein air**.

théâtreux○, **-euse** /teɑtʀø, øz/ *nm,f* pej second-rate actor/actress.

thébaïde /tebaid/ *nf* liter retreat.

thébain, **~e** /tebɛ̃, ɛn/ **▶857** *adj* Theban.

Thébain, **~e** /tebɛ̃, ɛn/ **▶857** *nm,f* Theban.

Thèbes /tɛb/ **▶857** *npr* Thebes.

théier /teje/ *nm* tea plant.

théière /tejɛʀ/ *nf* teapot.

théine /tein/ *nf* theine.

théisme /teism/ *nm* theism.

théiste /teist/ **I** *adj* [*penseur*] theist; [*pensée, œuvre*] theistic.
II *nmf* theist.

thématique /tematik/ **I** *adj* **1** (conçu par thèmes) [*ouvrage*] organized according to subject (*après n*); [*classement*] by subject (*après n*); **index ~** (dans un livre) subject index; (dans un annuaire) classification index; **de manière ~** by subject; **2** Mus, Ling, Littérat thematic.
II *nf* themes (*pl*).

thème /tɛm/ *nm* **1** (sujet) (de débat, d'émission) topic, subject; (de discours, film) theme; **~ de réflexion** topic for thought; **le débat aura pour ~ principal...** the main topic for discussion will be...; **2** (traduction) prose, translation (*into the foreign language*); **faire un ~ latin** to do a Latin prose; **3** Mus theme; **4** Ling (radical) stem; (topique) theme.
■ **~ astral** Astrol birth chart.

théocratie /teɔkʀasi/ *nf* theocracy.

théocratique /teɔkʀatik/ *adj* theocratic.

Théocrite /teɔkʀit/ *npr* Theocritus.

théodolite /teɔdɔlit/ *nm* theodolite.

théogonie /teɔgɔni/ *nf* (généalogie des dieux) theogony; (ensemble des dieux) pantheon.

théologal, **~e**, *mpl* **-aux** /teɔlɔgal, o/ *adj* **vertus ~es** theological virtues.

théologie /teɔlɔʒi/ *nf* theology; **docteur en ~** doctor of divinity; **études de ~** theological studies; **institut de ~** school of divinity.

théologien, **-ienne** /teɔlɔʒjɛ̃, ɛn/ *nm,f* theologian.

théologique /teɔlɔʒik/ *adj* theological.

Théophraste /teɔfʀast/ *npr* Theophrastus.

théorbe /teɔʀb/ **▶534** *nm* theorbo.

théorème /teɔʀɛm/ *nm* theorem; **~ d'Archimède/de Pythagore** Archimedes'/Pythagoras' theorem.

théoricien, **-ienne** /teɔʀisjɛ̃, ɛn/ *nm,f* theoretician; **ce n'est pas un ~ de la musique** he has no theoretical knowledge of music.

théorie /teɔʀi/ *nf* **1** (connaissance abstraite) theory (**de** of); **la ~ littéraire/des quanta** literary/quantum theory; **en ~** in theory; **des cours de ~** gén lessons in theory; Mus theory lessons; **2** (concept, opinion) theory (**sur** about); **savoir élaborer des ~s** pej to be good at theorizing.

théorique /teɔʀik/ *adj* theoretical; **d'un point de vue ~** theoretically (speaking), from a theoretical point of view.

théoriquement /teɔʀikmɑ̃/ *adv* **1** (en théorie) theoretically; **2** (de façon théorique) [*établir, prouver*] using theoretical methods.

théorisation /teɔʀizasjɔ̃/ *nf* fml theorizing.

théoriser /teɔʀize/ [1] **I** *vtr* **~ des observations expérimentales** to develop a theory based on experimental observations.
II *vi* to theorize (**sur** about).

théosophe /teɔzɔf/ *nmf* theosophist.

théosophie /teɔzɔfi/ *nf* theosophy.

théosophique /teozɔfik/ *adj* theosophical.

thérapeute /teʀapøt/ *nmf* therapist.

thérapeutique /teʀapøtik/ **I** *adj* gén [*effet, choix*] therapeutic; [*progrès*] in treatment (*après n*); **la prise en charge ~ de** the care and treatment of
II *nf* **1** (traitement) treatment; **2** (science) therapeutics (+ *v sg*).

thérapie /teʀapi/ *nf* **1** Méd treatment; **2** Psych therapy.
■ **~ génique** gene therapy.

thermal, **~e**, *mpl* **-aux** /tɛʀmal, o/ *adj* [*source, eaux*] thermal; **cure ~e** course of hydrotherapy, water cure; **station ~e** spa; **établissement ~** hydrotherapic establishment; **faire une cure ~e** to take the waters.

thermalisme /tɛʀmalism/ *nm* **1** Méd balneology; **2** (activité) hydrotherapy industry.

thermes /tɛʀm/ *nmpl* **1** Antiq thermae; **2** (établissement thermal) thermal baths.

thermidor /tɛʀmidɔʀ/ *nm* Thermidor (*eleventh month of the French revolutionary calendar, ≈ August*).

thermique /tɛʀmik/ *adj* thermal; **une ascendance** or **un vent ~** a thermal.

thermochimie /tɛʀmoʃimi/ *nf* thermochemistry.

thermocollage /tɛʀmokɔlaʒ/ *nm* heat-sealing.

thermocollant, **~e** /tɛʀmokɔlɑ̃, ɑ̃t/ *adj* [*tissu, ruban*] iron-on (*épith*).

thermocouple /tɛʀmokupl/ *nm* thermocouple.

thermodynamique /tɛʀmɔdinamik/ **I** *adj* thermodynamic.
II *nf* thermodynamics (+ *v sg*).

thermoélectricité /tɛʀmoelɛktʀisite/ *nf* thermoelectricity.

thermoélectrique /tɛʀmoelɛktʀik/ *adj* thermoelectric; **effet ~** Seebeck effect; **pile ~** thermoelectric couple.

thermoformage /tɛʀmɔfɔʀmaʒ/ *nm* thermoforming.

thermoformé, **~e** /tɛʀmofɔʀme/ *adj* thermally moulded.

thermogène /tɛʀmɔʒɛn/ *adj* heat-generating.

thermographe /tɛʀmɔgʀaf/ *nm* thermograph.

thermographie /tɛʀmɔgʀafi/ *nf* thermography, thermal imaging.

thermolactyl® /tɛʀmɔlaktil/ *nm* **1** Tex thermal material; **2** (vêtement) item of thermal clothing.

thermoluminescence /tɛʀmɔlyminesɑ̃s/ *nf* thermoluminescence.

thermomètre /tɛʀmɔmɛtʀ/ *nm* thermometer; **~ médical** clinical thermometer; **~ à mercure/à alcool/à gaz** mercury/alcohol/gas thermometer; **~ à maxima et minima** maximum and minimum thermometer; **le ~ indique 42 degrés** the thermometer shows 42 degrees; **le ~ va chuter pendant le week-end** temperatures will drop during the weekend; **le ~ des tensions internationales** the barometer of international tensions.

thermométrie /tɛʀmɔmetʀi/ *nf* thermometry.

thermométrique /tɛʀmɔmetʀik/ *adj* Phys thermometric; Météo temperature (*épith*).

thermonucléaire /tɛʀmɔnykleɛʀ/ *adj* thermonuclear.

thermopile /tɛʀmɔpil/ *nf* thermopile.

thermoplastique /tɛʀmɔplastik/ *adj* thermoplastic.

Thermopyles /tɛʀmɔpil/ *nprfpl* **les ~** Thermopylae; **la bataille des ~** the battle of Thermopylae.

thermorégulation /tɛʀmɔʀegylasjɔ̃/ *nf* thermoregulation, homeothermy.

thermorésistant, ~e /tɛʀmɔʀezistɑ̃, ɑ̃t/ *adj* Biol thermotolerant; Phys, Tech heat-resistant.

thermos® /tɛʀmos/ *nm* ou *f inv* Thermos®, vacuum flask GB.

thermoscope /tɛʀmɔskɔp/ *nm* thermoscope.

thermosiphon /tɛʀmɔsifɔ̃/ *nm* thermosiphon.

thermosphère /tɛʀmɔsfɛʀ/ *nf* thermosphere.

thermostat /tɛʀmɔsta/ *nm* thermostat; **cuire à four moyen, ~ 6** cook in a moderate oven, at thermostat 6.

thermothérapie /tɛʀmɔteʀapi/ *nf* Méd thermotherapy, deep heat therapy.

thésard○, **~e** /tezaʀ, aʀd/ *nm,f* PhD student.

thésaurisation /tezɔʀizasjɔ̃/ *nf* **1** (de richesses, connaissances) hoarding; **2** Écon accumulation of capital.

thésauriser /tezɔʀize/ [1] **I** *vtr* to hoard (up) [*argent, richesses, connaissances*].
II *vi* to hoard money.

thésaurus /tezɔʀys/ *nm inv* **1** (de philologie, d'archéologie) lexicon; **2** (répertoire) thesaurus.

thèse /tɛz/ *nf* **1** Univ (de doctorat) thesis GB, dissertation US (**sur qn/qch** on sb/sth); **être en ~** to be working on a thesis ou dissertation; **faire une ~** to do a thesis; **2** (point de vue) thesis, argument; **film/roman à ~** film/novel with a message; **3** (supposition) theory; **avancer/écarter la ~ de l'accident** to put forward/to discount the theory that it was an accident.

Thésée /teze/ *npr* Theseus.

Thessalie /tɛsali/ **▶692** *nprf* **la ~** Thessaly.

thessalien, **-ienne** /tɛsaljɛ̃, ɛn/ *adj* Thessalian.

Thessalonique /tɛsalɔnik/ **▶857** *npr* Salonika.

thêta /tɛta/ *nm inv* theta.

thibaude /tibod/ *nf* carpet underlay.

thomisme /tɔmism/ *nm* Thomism.

thomiste /tɔmist/ *adj, nmf* Thomist.

thon /tɔ̃/ *nm* tuna.

■ ~ **blanc** longfin tuna, albacore; ~ **rouge** bluefin tuna.
thonier, **-ière** /tɔnje, ɛʀ/ **I** *adj* tuna (*épith*). **II** *nm* tuna boat.
Thora /tɔʀa/ *nf* **la ~** the Torah.
thoracique /tɔʀasik/ *adj* thoracic; **cage ~** ribcage.
thorax /tɔʀaks/ ▶188 *nm inv* thorax.
thorium /tɔʀjɔm/ *nm* thorium.
Thrace /tʀas/ ▶692 *nprf* Thrace.
thrène /tʀɛn/ *nm* threnody.
thriller /sʀilœʀ/ *nm* thriller.
thrombocyte /tʀɔ̃bosit/ *nm* thrombocyte.
thrombose /tʀɔ̃boz/ ▶271 *nf* thrombosis.
Thulé /tyle/ *npr* Thule.
thulium /tyljɔm/ *nm* thulium.
thune° /tyn/ *nf* **des ~s** money ₵; **ne pas avoir une ~** not to have any money, to be broke°.
Thurgovie /tyʀgɔvi/ ▶692 *nprf* **la ~, le canton de ~** the canton of Thurgau.
thuriféraire /tyʀifeʀɛʀ/ *nm* **1** (admirateur) eulogist; **2** Relig thurifer.
thuya /tyja/ *nm* thuja.
thym /tɛ̃/ *nm* thyme.
thymique /timik/ *adj* thymic.
thymus /timys/ *nm inv* thymus.
thyroïde /tiʀɔid/ **I** *adj* [*cartilage, glande, corps*] thyroid. **II** *nf* thyroid (gland).
thyroïdien, **-ienne** /tiʀɔidjɛ̃, ɛn/ *adj* thyroid.
thyroxine /tiʀɔksin/ *nf* thyroxine.
thyrse /tiʀs/ *nm* thyrsus.
tian /tjɑ̃/ *nm* **1** (ustensile) tian (*earthenware dish*); **2** (mets) tian (*gratin of fish or vegetables*).
tiare /tjaʀ/ *nf* tiara; **~ pontificale** papal tiara.
IDIOMES **coiffer la ~** to ascend the throne of St Peter.
Tibère /tibɛʀ/ *npr* Tiberius.
Tibériade /tibeʀjad/ ▶459, 857 *npr* Tiberias; **le lac de ~** Lake Tiberias.
Tibet /tibɛ/ ▶692 *nprm* Tibet.
tibétain, **~e** /tibetɛ̃, ɛn/ **I** *adj* Tibetan. **II** ▶462 *nm* Ling Tibetan.
Tibétain, **~e** /tibetɛ̃, ɛn/ *nm,f* Tibetan.
tibia /tibja/ *nm* (os) shinbone, tibia spéc; (partie antérieure de la jambe) shin; **un coup de pied dans les ~s** a kick in the shins.
Tibre /tibʀ/ ▶357 *nprm* Tiber.
tic /tik/ *nm* **1** Méd tic; **prendre un ~** to develop a tic; **être plein de ~s** to be constantly twitching; **avoir le visage ravagé de ~s** to suffer from a severe facial tic; **2** (habitude) (dans les gestes) habit; (dans la parole) tic; **prendre les ~s de qn** to pick up sb else's habits; **~ de langage** verbal tic; **3** Vét (de cheval) vice.
■ **~ de l'air** wind-sucking; **~ douloureux de la face** tic douloureux, trigeminal neuralgia; **~ rongeur** crib-biting.
ticket /tikɛ/ *nm* **1** gén ticket; **2**° (10 francs) ≈ quid°.
■ **~ de caisse** Comm till receipt GB, sales slip US; **~ de métro** underground GB ou subway US ticket; **~ modérateur** Prot Soc *patient's contribution towards cost of medical treatment*; **~ de pain** bread coupon; **~ de quai** Rail platform ticket; **~ de rationnement** ration coupon.
IDIOMES **avoir un** or **le ~ avec qn**° to be well in with sb°.
ticket-repas, *pl* **tickets-repas** /tikɛ ʀəpɑ/ *nm* luncheon voucher GB, meal ticket US.
ticket-restaurant®, *pl* **tickets-restaurant** /tikɛʀɛstɔʀɑ̃/ *nm* luncheon voucher GB, meal ticket US.
tic-tac /tiktak/ *nm inv* (*also onomat*) ticktock; **faire ~** to tick.
tie-break /tajbʀɛk/ *nm* tiebreaker.
tiédasse° /tjedas/ *adj* péj lukewarm, tepid.
tiède /tjɛd/ **I** *adj* **1** lit (désagréablement) [*café, soupe*] lukewarm; [*bain*] tepid; (agréablement) [*eau, air, nuit*] warm; [*saison, température*] mild; ▶ **salade**; **2** fig (sans enthousiasme) [*sentiment, applaudissements, partisan*] lukewarm, half-hearted; [*accueil*] lukewarm.
II *nmf* péj (membre d'un parti, groupe) lukewarm ou half-hearted supporter; (adepte) half-hearted believer.
III *adv* **servez ~** serve slightly warm; **dépêche-toi ou tu vas manger ~** hurry up or your food will get cold; **il fait ~** (dehors) it's mild; (dedans) it's nice and warm.
tièdement /tjɛdmɑ̃/ *adv* [*applaudir, travailler, approuver*] half-heartedly; **je n'approuve que ~ leur projet** I'm not entirely in favour[GB] of their plan.
tiédeur /tjedœʀ/ *nf* **1** lit (agréable) (de saison) mildness; (d'air, de nuit, pièce) warmth; **les premières ~s du printemps** liter the first warm days of spring; **2** fig (de sentiment, partisan) half-heartedness.
tiédir /tjediʀ/ [3] **I** *vtr* (réchauffer) to warm up [*eau*]; (refroidir) to cool (down).
II *vi* **1** [*liquide, air*] (se réchauffer) to warm (up); (refroidir) to cool (down); **faire ~** to warm ou heat (up) [*café*]; **laisser ~** to allow [sth] to cool; **2** fig [*sentiment*] to cool; [*enthousiasme*] to wane.
tien, **tienne** /tjɛ̃, tjɛn/ **I** *adj poss* **je suis tienne** I'm yours; **une tienne connaissance** an acquaintance of yours.
II le tien, la tienne, les tiens, les tiennes *pron poss* yours; **un métier comme le ~** a job like yours; **mon mari et le ~** our husbands; **mon patron et le ~** our two bosses; **j'ai mes soucis, tu as les ~s** we each have our own worries; **à la tienne!** (à ta santé) gén cheers!; iron the best of luck!; **les ~s** (ta famille) your family (*sg*); **c'est un des ~s?** péj is he one of your lot?; **tu as encore fait des tiennes!** you've been up to mischief again!; ▶ **y**[1].
tiens /tjɛ̃/ ▶ **tenir**.
tierce ▶ **tiers** I, III.
tiercé /tjɛʀse/ ▶449 *nm* Turf system of betting on three placed horses; **jouer au ~, faire le ~** to bet on the horses; **avoir le ~ dans l'ordre** to win on the horses with the right placings; **donner un ~ dans l'ordre** (avant une course) to give a winning tip on the horses.
tierceron /tjɛʀsəʀɔ̃/ *nm* tierceron.
tiers, **tierce** /tjɛʀ, tjɛʀs/ **I** *adj* third; **un pays ~** gén another country; (par rapport à un groupe) a non-member country; **une tierce personne** gén an outsider; Jur a third party; **en main tierce** Jur in the hands of a third party.
II *nm inv* **1** Math third (**de** of); **il a fait le ~ du travail** he's done one third of the work; **j'ai rédigé les deux ~ de ma thèse** I've written two thirds of my thesis; **j'en suis aux deux ~, je suis au dernier ~** I'm two thirds of the way through; **réduire qch d'un ~** to reduce sth by one third; **la ville a été détruite aux deux ~** two thirds of the town has been destroyed; **2** (personne) (inconnu) outsider; Jur third party; **agir pour le compte d'un ~** to act on behalf of a third party; **avoir recours à un ~** to go through a third party; **3** Assur, Aut **une assurance au ~** third-party insurance; **s'assurer au ~** to take out third-party insurance.
III tierce *nf* **1** Jeux three card run, tierce; **2** Mus third; **intervalle de tierce** interval of a third; **3** Relig terce; **à tierce** at terce; **4** Imprim page proof.
■ **tierce majeure** or **à l'as** three card run ace high, tierce major; **le Tiers État** Hist the Third Estate; **~ payant** Prot Soc third-party payer (*direct payment by insurance for medical care*); **~ provisionnel** *tax payment equal to one third of annual tax.*
tiers-monde /tjɛʀmɔ̃d/ *nm* Pol Third World; **la dette/les pays du ~** Third World debt/countries.
tiers-mondisme /tjɛʀmɔ̃dism/ *nm* support for the Third World.
tiers-mondiste /tjɛʀmɔ̃dist/ **I** *adj* [*conscience, mouvement*] Third-World (*épith*); [*discours, politique*] in support of the Third World.
II *nmf* supporter of the Third World.
tifs° /tif/ *nmpl* hair ₵; **se faire couper les ~** to have one's hair cut.
tige /tiʒ/ *nf* **1** (de plante) gén stem; (plus épaisse et rigide) stalk; **~ d'asperge** asparagus spear; **une ~ de rhubarbe** a stick of rhubarb; **arbre de haute/basse ~** standard/half-standard (tree); **2** (jeune arbre) sapling; **3** Mode leg; **chaussures à ~ (basse)/à ~ haute** ankle/long boots; **4** (baguette) rod; **~ de métal** metal rod; (partie allongée) (de clé, clou, rivet) shank; **5** (de plume) shaft; **6** (en généalogie) common ancestor; **faire ~** to found a line; **7**° (cigarette) fag° GB, ciggy°.
■ **~ de culbuteur** Aut pushrod.
tignasse /tiɲas/ *nf* **1** (cheveux mal entretenus) mop of hair; **2**° (chevelure) hair.
tigre /tigʀ/ *nm* **1** Zool (animal) tiger; (peau) tigerskin; **2** (personne cruelle) monster.
■ **~ du Bengale** Bengal tiger; **~ mangeur d'hommes** man-eating tiger; **~ royal** = **~ du Bengale**; **~ de Sibérie** Siberian tiger.
IDIOMES **être jaloux comme un ~** to be insanely jealous.
Tigre /tigʀ/ ▶357 *nprm* Tigris.
tigré, **~e** /tigʀe/ *adj* **1** (rayé) striped; **~ de noir/rouge** black-/red-striped; **2** (tacheté) spotted; **~ de noir/blanc** with black/white spots.
tigresse /tigʀɛs/ *nf* Zool, fig tigress.
tigron /tigʀɔ̃/ *nm* tigon.
tilbury /tilbyʀi/ *nm* tilbury.
tilde /tilde, tild(ə)/ *nm* tilde.
tillac /tijak/ *nm* deck.
tilleul /tijœl/ *nm* **1** (arbre) limetree; (bois) limewood; **vert ~** pale green; **2** (fleur) lime-blossom; **3** (tisane) lime-blossom tea; **~ menthe** lime-blossom and mint tea.
tilt /tilt/ *nm* Jeux tilt sign; **faire ~** [*machine*] to show tilt; [*personne*] to make the machine stop.
IDIOMES **ça a fait ~ (dans mon esprit)**° the penny dropped°; **ça a fait ~ entre nous**° we clicked when we met.
timbale /tɛ̃bal/ ▶534 *nf* **1** (gobelet) (en métal) metal tumbler; (en plastique) plastic cup; **2** Mus kettledrum; **~s** timpani; **3** Culin timbale.
timbalier /tɛ̃balje/ ▶510 *nm* timpanist.
timbrage /tɛ̃bʀaʒ/ *nm* **1** Postes postmarking; **dispensé de ~** postage paid GB, post paid US; **2** (de document) stamping.
timbre /tɛ̃bʀ/ *nm* **1** (vignette) stamp; **~ tarif rapide/tarif lent** first-class/second-class stamp; **~ à cinq francs** five-franc stamp; **~ premier jour** first-day cover; **2** (marque) gén, Jur stamp; Postes postmark; **3** (instrument) stamp; **~ sec/humide** embossing/ink stamp; **4** (sonorité) gén tone; Mus timbre; (de voyelle) timbre; **voix au ~ voilé** husky voice; **~ chaud/riche** warm/rich tone; **voix sans ~** toneless voice; **5** (sonnette, sonnerie) (de porte, vélo) bell; (de réveil) ring; **6** Méd patch; **~ à la nicotine** nicotine patch; **~ tuberculinique** test square (*for tuberculin patch test*).
■ **~ dateur** date stamp; **~ fiscal** *stamp affixed to official document e.g. passport.*
timbré, **~e** /tɛ̃bʀe/ **I** *pp* ▶ **timbrer**.
II *pp adj* **1** [*enveloppe, document*] stamped; **2** [*voix*] **voix (bien) ~e** resonant voice.
III° *adj* (fou) loony°.
IV° *nm,f* loony°.
timbre-amende, *pl* **timbres-amendes** /tɛ̃bʀamɑ̃d/ *nm*: *stamp purchased in payment of a traffic fine.*
timbre-cotisation, *pl* **timbres-**

cotisations /tɛ̃bʀ(ə)kɔtizasjɔ̃/ *nm*: *stamp purchased to pay a subscription.*

timbre-escompte, *pl* **timbres-escompte** /tɛ̃bʀɛskɔ̃t/ *nm* trading stamp.

timbre-poste, *pl* **timbres-poste** /tɛ̃bʀ(ə)pɔst/ *nm* Postes postage stamp.

timbre-quittance, *pl* **timbres-quittances** /tɛ̃bʀ(ə)kitɑ̃s/ *nm* receipt stamp.

timbrer /tɛ̃bʀe/ [1] *vtr* (tous contextes) to stamp, to put a stamp on [*enveloppe, document*].

timide /timid/ **I** *adj* [*personne, animal*] shy, timid; [*critique, réforme*] timid; [*succès, résultat*] limited; **d'un air ~** shyly, timidly; **faussement ~** coy.

II *nmf* shy person; **c'est un grand ~** he's terribly shy; **il joue les ~s** he's pretending to be shy, he's being coy.

timidement /timidmɑ̃/ *adv* (avec timidité) shyly; (craintivement) timidly; (sans conviction) half-heartedly.

timidité /timidite/ *nf* shyness; **il est d'une ~ maladive** he's pathologically shy; **avec ~** shyly.

timing /tajmiŋ/ *nm* **1** (calendrier) schedule; **2** Sport timing.

timon /timɔ̃/ *nm* **1** Naut (barre de gouvernail) tiller; (gouvernail) rudder; **2** (d'attelage) shaft.

timonerie /timɔnʀi/ *nf* **1** Naut (abri) wheelhouse; (personnel) helmsmen (*pl*), quartermasters (*pl*); **2** Aut, Aviat steering and braking systems.

timonier /timɔnje/ ▶510 *nm* Naut helmsman.

timoré, **~e** /timɔʀe/ *adj* **1** (craintif) timorous; **2**† (trop scrupuleux) over-scrupulous.

tinctorial, **~e**, *mpl* **-iaux** /tɛ̃ktɔʀjal, o/ *adj* [*opération, produit*] dyeing (*épith*); **substances ~es** dyestuffs; **bois ~** dyewood; **plantes ~es** dye-producing plants.

tinette /tinɛt/ *nf* latrine bucket; (en prison) slopping-out bucket.

tintamarre /tɛ̃tamaʀ/ *nm* **1** (bruit) din; **on ne s'entend pas dans ce ~** we can't hear each other in this din; **faire du ~** to make a din; **2** (protestation) fuss; **faire du ~** to make a fuss.

tintement /tɛ̃tmɑ̃/ *nm* (de cloche) chiming; (de clochette, grelot) tinkling; (de couverts, verres, monnaie) clinking; (de sonnette) ringing; (de clés) jingling.

■ **~ d'oreilles** Méd ringing in the ears, tinnitus spéc.

tinter /tɛ̃te/ [1] *vi* [*cloche*] to chime; [*sonnette*] to ring; [*clochette, grelot*] to tinkle; [*verre, monnaie, couvert*] to clink; [*bidon*] to clang; [*clé*] to jingle; Mus [*triangle*] to ring; **faire ~** to ring [*cloche, sonnette, clochette*]; to clink [*verre, monnaie, couvert*]; to clang [*bidon*]; to jingle [*clé*]; Mus to strike [*triangle*].

IDIOMES **les oreilles me tintent** my ears are ringing.

tintin○ /tɛ̃tɛ̃/ *excl* no way○!

tintinnabuler /tɛ̃tinabyle/ [1] *vi* [*clochettes, grelots*] to tinkle.

Tintoret /tɛ̃tɔʀɛ/ *npr* **le ~** Tintoretto.

tintouin○ /tɛ̃twɛ̃/ *nm* **1** (vacarme) din, racket○; **2** (souci) lots of bother; **se donner du ~** to go to a lot of bother.

tipi /tipi/ *nm* te(e)pee.

tique /tik/ *nf* tick.

tiquer /tike/ [1] *vi* **1**○ [*personne*] to wince; **sans ~** without batting an eyelid GB ou eyelash US; **~ sur qch** to object to sth; **2** [*cheval*] to crib(-bite).

tir /tiʀ/ *nm* **1** Mil (coups de feu) fire ¢; **déclencher le ~** to open fire; **~ nourri/sporadique** heavy/sporadic fire; **2** Mil, Sport (avec des armes légères) shooting ¢; (avec des armes lourdes) gunnery ¢; **~ couché/accroupi** prone/squat shooting; **s'entraîner au ~** to practise[GB] shooting; **exercices de ~** shooting practice ¢; **exercices de ~ sur cible** target practice ¢; **3** Mil (lancement) firing ¢; **pendant le ~** during firing; **~ de grenades/missiles** grenade/missile firing; **~ continu** continuous firing; **4** Astronaut (lancement) launching ¢; **~ de fusée** rocket launching; **5** Jeux shooting; **~ forain** (stand) rifle range ; **concours de ~** shooting contest; **6** Sport (avec ballon) shot; **~ au but** (au football) shot at goal; **7** Chasse shooting; **~ aux faisans/canards** pheasant/duck shooting.

■ **~ à l'arbalète** crossbow archery; **~ à l'arc** archery; **~ d'artillerie** artillery fire ¢; **~ de balisage** marking fire ¢; **~ à balles réelles** firing ¢ with live ammunition; **~ de barrage** barrage fire ¢; fig barrage; **~ à blanc** firing ¢ with blanks; **~ à la carabine à air comprimé** air rifle shooting; **~ à la carabine petit calibre (position couchée)** small-bore rifle (prone) shooting; **~ à la carabine petit calibre (trois positions)** small-bore (three position) shooting; **~ à la cible courante** moving target shooting; **~ d'élite** marksmanship; **~ à la fosse olympique** clay pigeon trapshooting; **~ coup par coup** single shot fire ¢; **~ croisé** Mil crossfire ¢; Sport cross; **~ de fusil** gunfire ¢; **~ de harcèlement** harassing fire ¢; **~ de mitraillette** submachine-gun fire ¢; **~ de mortier** mortar fire ¢; **~ aux pigeons d'argile** clay pigeon shooting; **~ plongeant** low angle fire ¢; **~ de précision** pinpoint firing ¢; **~ au pistolet à air comprimé** air pistol shooting; **~ au pistolet libre** free pistol shooting; **~ au pistolet de ~ rapide** rapid fire pistol shooting; **~ au pistolet de ~ sportif** sport pistol shooting; **~ en rafale** burst firing ¢; **~ de ratissage** combing fire ¢; **~ de réparation** penalty; **~ de semonce** warning shots (*pl*); **~ skeet** skeet shooting; **~ tendu** flat trajectory fire ¢.

tirade /tiʀad/ *nf* **1** Littérat, Théât declamation; **2** pej (discours) tirade péj.

tirage /tiʀaʒ/ *nm* **1** Jeux **~ (au sort)** draw; **~ hebdomadaire/spécial** weekly/special draw; **désigner par ~ (au sort)** to draw [*nom, vainqueur*]; **le ~ (au sort) a désigné le Danemark contre l'Angleterre** Denmark has been drawn against England; **2** Édition, Imprim, Presse (impression, réimpression) impression; (nombre) (de livres) run; (de journaux) circulation; **troisième ~** third impression; **quotidien à grand ~** mass-circulation daily; **~ limité/numéroté** limited/numbered edition; **3** Ordinat (copie papier) hard copy; **4** Art, Cin, Phot (d'estampe, de négatif) (processus) printing ¢; (résultat) print; **un beau ~** a fine print; **5** Constr (de cheminée) draught GB, draft US; **6** (désaccord) friction ¢; **il y a du ~ entre eux** there's friction between them.

■ **~ en fac-similé** facsimile edition; **~ de luxe** de luxe edition; **~ de tête** advance issue.

tiraillement /tiʀajmɑ̃/ *nm* **1** (sur corde) pulling ¢, tugging ¢; **2** (sensation) nagging pain; **~s d'estomac** hunger pangs; **3** fig (friction) friction ¢ **(entre** between); **des ~s au sein de l'équipe** friction in the team.

tirailler /tiʀaje/ [1] **I** *vtr* **1** (tirer) to tug (at), to pull (at) [*corde, manche, barbe*]; **~ qn par le bras** to tug at sb's arm; **2** fig **être tiraillé entre son travail et sa famille/deux personnes** to be torn between one's work and one's family/two people.

II *vi* [*soldat, tireur*] (au hasard) to fire ou shoot at random; (de temps en temps) to fire intermittently; **ça tiraille de tous les côtés** there's firing on all sides.

tirailleur /tiʀajœʀ/ *nm* **1** Mil skirmisher; **en ~s** in skirmishing position; **2** Hist, Mil colonial infantryman.

■ **~ sénégalais** Senegalese infantry man.

Tirana /tiʀana/ ▶857 *npr* Tirana.

tirant /tiʀɑ̃/ *nm* **1** (de chaussure) bootstrap; **2** (de charpente) tie beam.

■ **~ d'air** Constr, Naut (de pont) vertical clearance; **~ d'eau** Naut draught GB, draft US; **avoir un ~ d'eau de six mètres** to draw six metres[GB].

tire○ /tiʀ/ *nf* (voiture) car; ▶ **vol**.

tiré, **~e** /tiʀe/ **I** *pp* ▶ **tirer**.

II *pp adj* **1** (tendu en arrière) [*cheveux*] drawn back; **avoir les cheveux ~s** to wear one's hair tied back; ▶ **cheveu**, **couteau**, **épingle**; **2** (fatigué) **avoir les traits ~s** to look drawn; **3** (fermé) [*rideau, verrou*] drawn; **4** Édition **~ à part** [*article, texte*] off-printed.

III *nm,f* (payeur) drawee.

IV *nm* **1** Édition **un ~ à part** an off-print; **2** (tir) shooting ¢.

V tirée○ *nf* (longue distance) tidy walk○.

tire-au-flanc○ /tiʀoflɑ̃/ **I** *adj inv* lazy, skiving○ GB (*épith*); **être ~** to be lazy ou a skiver○ GB.

II *nm inv* gén shirker, skiver○ GB.

tire-botte, *pl* **~s** /tiʀbɔt/ *nm* bootjack.

tire-bouchon, *pl* **~s** /tiʀbuʃɔ̃/ *nm* corkscrew; **queue en ~** curly tail; **manches/pantalon en ~** (en spirale) twisted sleeves/trousers GB ou pants US; (en accordéon) wrinkled sleeves/trousers GB ou pants US.

tire-bouchonner /tiʀbuʃɔne/ [1] *vi* (en spirale) [*manche, pantalon*] to be twisted; (en accordéon) [*manche, pantalon*] to be wrinkled; **un pantalon tire-bouchonnant** a wrinkled pair of trousers GB ou pants US.

tire-clou, *pl* **~s** /tiʀklu/ *nm* (de marteau) nail claw; (autonome) nail puller.

tire-comédon, *pl* **~s** /tiʀkɔmedɔ̃/ *nm* blackhead remover.

tire-d'aile: **à tire-d'aile** /atiʀdɛl/ *loc adv* lit in a flurry of wings; fig hurriedly.

tire-fesses○ /tiʀfɛs/ *nm inv* ski tow.

tire-fond /tiʀfɔ̃/ *nm inv* **1** (vis à bois) coach screw; **2** (écrou de maçonnerie) coach bolt.

tire-jus◑ /tiʀʒy/ *nm inv* snot-rag◑, handkerchief.

tire-laine† /tiʀlɛn/ *nm inv* thief.

tire-lait /tiʀlɛ/ *nm inv* breast pump.

tire-larigot: **à tire-larigot** /atiʀlaʀigo/ *loc adv* [*boire*] non-stop.

tire-ligne, *pl* **~s** /tiʀliŋ/ *nm* ruling pen.

tirelire /tiʀliʀ/ *nf* piggy bank; **piocher dans/casser sa ~** to raid/to break one's piggy bank.

tire-nerf, *pl* **~s** /tiʀnɛʀ/ *nm* Dent barbed broach.

tirer /tiʀe/ [1] **I** *vtr* **1** (déplacer) [*personne, animal, véhicule*] to pull [*véhicule*]; [*personne*] to pull up [*fauteuil, chaise*]; [*personne*] to pull away [*tapis*]; **~ la tête en arrière** to toss one's head back; ▶ **chapeau**, **couverture**; **2** (exercer une traction) (avec une force régulière) to pull [*cheveux*]; to pull on [*corde*]; (par à-coups) to tug at [*cordelette, manette, sonnette*]; **~ qn par le bras** to pull sb's arm; **~ les cheveux à qn** to pull sb's hair; **~ qn par la manche** to tug at sb's sleeve; **3** (tendre) **~ ses cheveux en arrière** to pull back one's hair; **~ ses bas** to pull up one's stockings; **~ sa chemise/jupe** to straighten one's shirt/skirt; ▶ **épingle**; **se faire ~ la peau**○ Cosmét to have a face-lift; **la peau/ça me tire**○ my skin/it feels tight; **4** (fermer) to draw [*verrou, rideau*]; to pull down [*store*]; to close [*porte, volet*]; **5** Mil to fire off [*balle, obus, grenade*]; to fire [*missile*]; **~ un coup de feu** to fire a shot; **~ le canon** (pour honorer) to fire a salute; **~ vingt et un coups de canon** to fire a twenty-one gun salute; **6** (propulser) to shoot [*balle, flèche*] **(sur** at); **elle lui a tiré (une balle) dans le dos** she shot him in the back; **7** (viser) **~ le canard/faisan/gibier** to shoot duck/pheasant/game; **8** Sport (de ballon) **~ un corner/penalty** to take a corner/penalty; **~ un coup franc** (au football) to take a free kick; (au handball, basket-ball) to take a free throw; **9** (choisir au hasard) **~ (au sort)** to draw [*carte, loterie, nom, gagnant, adversaire*]; to draw for [*parte-*

naire]; **~ les blancs** to draw white; **~ une bonne carte** to draw a strong card; **10** Jeux (aux cartes) **~ ses atouts** to draw trumps; **11** Astrol **~ les cartes à qn** to tell the cards for sb; **se faire ~ les cartes** to have one's fortune told with cards; **12** (prendre) to draw [*vin, bière, eau, électricité, argent*] (**de**, **sur** from); **~ de l'eau du puits** to draw water from the well; **~ de l'argent sur un compte** to draw money from an account; ▶**vin**; **13** (sortir) **~ de qch** to take [sth] out of sth [*objet*]; to pull [sb] out of sth [*personne*]; **~ un stylo de son sac/d'un tiroir** to take a pen out of one's bag/out of a drawer; **~ un enfant de l'eau/des flammes** to pull a child out of the water/out of the flames; **~ qch de sa poche** to pull sth out of one's pocket; **~ une bouffée de sa cigarette/pipe** to take a puff at ou on one's cigarette/pipe; ▶**épingle**, **marron**, **ver**; **14** (faire sortir) **~ de qch** to get [sb/sth] out of sth [*personne, pays, entreprise*]; **~ le pays de la récession** to get the country out of recession; **tire-moi de là!** get me out of this!; **~ qn d'une maladie** to pull sb through an illness; **tu l'as tirée de son silence/sa mélancolie** you drew her out of her silence/her melancholy; **15** (obtenir) **~ de qn** to get [sth] from sb [*renseignement, aveu*]; **~ de qch** to draw [sth] from sth [*force, ressources*]; to derive [sth] from sth [*orgueil, satisfaction*]; to make [sth] out of sth [*argent*]; **tu ne tireras pas grand-chose de cette voiture** (comme argent) you won't get much for this car; (comme service) you won't get much out of this car; **tu ne tireras pas grand-chose de lui** (comme argent, renseignements, preuve d'intelligence) you won't get much out of him; **~ le maximum de la situation** to make the most of the situation; **~ un son d'un instrument** to get a note out of an instrument; **16** (dériver) **~ de qch** to base [sth] on sth [*récit, film*]; to get [sth] from sth [*nom*]; **le film est tiré du roman** the film is based on the novel; **la guillotine tire son nom de son inventeur** the guillotine gets its name from its inventor; **le mot est tiré de l'anglais** the word comes from the English; **17** (extraire) **~ de qn/qch** to take [sth] from sb/sth [*texte*]; to derive [sth] from sth [*substance*]; **texte tiré de Zola/la Bible** text taken from Zola/the Bible; **le médicament est tiré d'une plante** the drug comes from a plant; **18** (faire un tirage) to print [*livre, tract, texte, négatif*]; to run off [*épreuve, exemplaire*]; **journal tiré à dix mille exemplaires** newspaper with a circulation of ten thousand; **19** (tracer) to draw [*ligne, trait*]; **~ un chèque** Fin to draw a cheque GB ou check US (**sur** on); **~ des plans** fig to draw up plans; ▶**comète**; **20**○ (passer) **plus qu'une heure/semaine à ~** only one more hour/week to go; **~ quelques années en prison** to spend a few years in prison.

II *vi* **1** (exercer une traction) to pull; **~ sur qch** (avec une force régulière) to pull on sth; (d'un coup ou par à-coups) to tug at sth; **tire fort!** pull hard!; **~ sur les rames** to pull on the oars; **~ de toutes ses forces** to heave with all one's might; **le moteur tire bien/tire mal**○ the engine is pulling well/isn't pulling properly; ▶**corde**; **2** (utiliser une arme) to shoot (**sur** at); (à feu) to fire (**sur** at); **~ à l'arc** to shoot with a bow and arrow; **~ à la carabine/à l'arbalète** to shoot with a rifle/with a crossbow; **~ pour tuer** to shoot to kill; **~ au fusil/en l'air/à balles réelles** to fire a gun/into the air/with live ammunition; **~ le premier** to fire first, to shoot first; **se faire ~ dessus** to come under fire, to be shot at; ▶**boulet**; **elle lui a tiré dans la jambe** she shot him in the leg; **3** Sport (au football) to shoot; (au handball, basket-ball) to take a shot; **~ au but** (au football) to take a shot at goal; **4** (choisir au hasard) **~ (au sort)** to draw lots; **on n'a qu'à ~** let's just draw lots; ▶**paille**; **5** (prendre) **~ sur** to draw on; **~ sur son compte/ses réserves** to draw on one's account/one's reserves; **6** (aspirer) **la cheminée tire bien/tire mal** the chimney draws well/doesn't draw well; **~ sur sa cigarette/pipe** to draw on one's cigarette/pipe; **7** Imprim, Presse **~ à mille exemplaires** [*périodique*] to have a circulation of a thousand; **à combien tire la revue?** what's the circulation of the magazine?; **8** (avoir une nuance) **~ sur le jaune/le bleu/le vert/le violet/l'orangé** to be yellowish/bluish/greenish/purplish/orangy; **être d'un bleu tirant sur le vert** to be greenish-blue; **9** (se rapprocher) **~ sur la cinquantaine** (âge) to be pushing fifty; **10** (dévier) [*voiture*] **~ à gauche/droite** to pull to the left/right; Équit **~ à la main** [*cheval*] to pull.

III se tirer *vpr* **1** (sortir) **se ~ de** to come through [*situation, difficultés*]; **se ~ de ses ennuis** to come through one's troubles; ▶**pas**; **2**○ (partir) **je me tire** I'm off○ GB, I'm splitting○; **tire-toi** get lost○; **je me suis tiré de chez lui** I cleared from his place; **je me suis tiré de chez mes parents** I left home; **je vais me ~ à Montréal** I'm going off to Montreal; **3** (se servir d'une arme) **se ~ une balle** to shoot oneself (**dans** in); **se ~ une balle dans la tête** to blow one's brains out; **se ~ dessus** (l'un l'autre) lit to shoot at one another; **4** (exercer une traction) **se ~ la moustache** to pull at one's moustache; **5**○ (se débrouiller) **s'en ~** to cope; **il s'en tire mal** (forte contrainte) he's finding it hard to cope; (travail délicat) he doesn't do very well; **comment est-ce que vous vous en tirez?** how do you cope?; **elle s'en tire mieux que lui** (épreuve de résistance) she is coping better than he is; (épreuve d'habileté) she is doing better than him; **elle s'en tire tout juste** she just gets by; **6**○ (échapper) **s'en ~** (à un accident) to escape; (à une maladie) to pull through; (à une punition) to get away with it○; **je m'en suis tiré avec quelques égratignures** I escaped with a few scratches; **son médecin pense qu'elle s'en tirera** her doctor thinks (that) she will pull through; **sans diplôme, il ne s'en tirera jamais** without a degree, he'll never get by; **il ne s'en tirera pas comme ça** he's not going to get away with it; **s'en ~ à bon prix** to get off lightly; ▶**compte**.

tiret /tiʀɛ/ *nm* Imprim, Ling dash.

tirette /tiʀɛt/ *nf* **1** Tech (rigide) pull tab; (souple) cord; **2** (de meuble) (sliding) support; **3** B (fermeture à glissière) zip GB, zipper US.

tireur, **-euse** /tiʀœʀ, øz/ **I** *nm,f* **1** Mil, Sport marksman/markswoman; **être (un) bon/mauvais ~** to be a good/poor shot; **2** (personne armée) gunman; **~ embusqué** sniper; **3** Sport (au football) striker; (aux boules) thrower; **4** Fin (émetteur) drawer; **5** Phot (opérateur) printer; **6**○ (pickpocket) pickpocket.

II tireuse *nf* **1** (robinet) spigot; **vin à la tireuse** wine from the barrel; **bière/cidre à la tireuse** draught GB ou draft US beer/cider; **2** Phot (machine) printer.

■ **~ à l'arbalète** crossbowman ; **~ à l'arc** archer; **~ de cartes** fortune teller (*using cards*); **~ d'élite** expert marksman; **tireuse d'élite** expert markswoman.

tiroir /tiʀwaʀ/ *nm* **1** (de meuble) drawer; **~ de bureau** desk drawer; **~ secret** secret drawer; **fouiller dans tous les ~s** to go through all the drawers; **traîner au fond d'un ~** to lie forgotten in the bottom of a drawer; **finir sa carrière dans le fond d'un ~** fig to end one's career in a second-rate job; **2** Mécan (soupape) slide valve; **3** (épisode) **à ~s** [*pièce, roman*] episodic, à tiroirs spéc; **problème à ~s** Math sequential problem.

IDIOMES **racler les fonds de ~** to scrape some money together.

tiroir-caisse, *pl* **tiroirs-caisses** /tiʀwaʀkɛs/ *nm* **1** lit cash register; **2** fig (dispensateur d'argent) cash dispenser.

IDIOMES **avoir la main dans le ~** to have one's hand in the till.

tisane /tizan/ *nf* herbal tea, tisane; **faire une ~** to make a cup of herbal tea; **de la ~ en sachets** herbal teabags.

tisanière /tizanjɛʀ/ *nf*: *mug for preparing herbal tea.*

tison /tizɔ̃/ *nm* (fire) brand.

IDIOMES **Noël au balcon, Pâques aux ~s** Prov when it's mild at Christmas, it's cold at Easter.

tisonner /tizɔne/ [1] *vtr* to poke.

tisonnier /tizɔnje/ *nm* poker.

tissage /tisaʒ/ *nm* **1** (fabrication) weaving ¢; **le ~ des tapis** rug-weaving; **faire du ~** to weave; **2** (texture) weave.

tissé, **~e** /tise/ **I** *pp* ▶**tisser**.

II *pp adj* **1** lit [*coton, drap, tapis*] woven; **~ à la main** hand-woven; **2** fig **récit ~ de mensonges** story riddled with lies.

tisser /tise/ [1] *vtr* **1** [*personne, machine*] to weave; **métier à ~** weaving loom; **2** [*araignée*] to spin [*toile*].

tisserand, **~e** /tisʀɑ̃, ɑ̃d/ ▶**510** *nm,f* weaver.

tisseur, **-euse** /tisœʀ, øz/ *nm,f* weaver; **~ de tapis/drap** rug/cloth weaver.

tissu /tisy/ *nm* **1** (étoffe) material, fabric; **acheter du ~** to buy some material ou fabric; **un joli ~ imprimé** a pretty printed material ou fabric; **les ~s synthétiques** synthetic materials ou fabrics; **~ de bonne qualité** good quality material ou fabric ou cloth; **revêtement mural/ceinture en ~** fabric wall-covering/belt; **c'est du ~?** is it fabric?; **2** Anat, Physiol, Bot tissue; **le ~ osseux/organique/nerveux/musculaire/cellulaire** bone/organic/nervous/muscle/cellular tissue; **3** (ensemble) (d'intrigues, de contradictions) web; (de calomnies, d'improbabilités, inepties) string; **un ~ de mensonges** a pack ou web ou tissue of lies; **un ~ d'insinuations calomnieuses** a web of slanderous insinuation ; **~ urbain/social** Sociol urban/social fabric; **~ industriel** industrial base.

■ **~ d'ameublement** upholstery fabric ou material.

tissu-éponge, *pl* **tissus-éponges** /tisyepɔ̃ʒ/ *nm* (terry) towelling[GB] ¢.

tissulaire /tisylɛʀ/ *adj* tissue (*épith*).

titan /titɑ̃/ *nm* titan; **de ~** titanic; ▶**travail**[1].

Titan /titɑ̃/ *npr* Mythol Titan.

titane /titan/ *nm* titanium.

titanesque /titanɛsk/ *adj* titanic.

Tite /tit/ *npr* Relig, Bible Titus.

Tite-Live /titliv/ *npr* Livy.

titi○ /titi/ *nm* **~ (parisien)** urchin, scamp.

Titien /tisjɛ̃/ *npr* **le ~** Titian.

titillation /titijasjɔ̃/ *nf* titillation.

titiller /titije/ [1] *vtr* **1** (taquiner) to titillate; **2** (chatouiller) to tickle [*corps*].

titisme /titism/ *nm* Titoism.

titrage /titʀaʒ/ *nm* **1** (de film, livre, chanson) titling; **2** Chimie (de solution) titration; (de minerai) assay.

titre /titʀ/ *nm* **1** (de film, livre, chanson, d'article) title; (de chapitre) heading; **page de ~** title page; **un autre ~ pour un article** another title for an article; **donner un ~ à** to give [sth] a title [*livre, article, film*]; **au ~ évocateur/de circonstance** [*film, ouvrage*] with an evocative/appropriate title; **avoir pour ~** to be entitled; **sous le ~ (de)** entitled; ▶**faux**, **rôle**, **sous**; **2** Presse headline; **les ~s de l'actualité** the headlines; **lire les gros ~s** to read the headlines; **3** (rang) title; **~ honorifique** honorary title; **~ mondial** world title; **~ nobiliaire** or **de noblesse** title; **pr étendre au ~ de...** to aspire to the title of...; **le ~ de comte/ministre/docteur/champion du monde** the title of count/minister/doctor/world champion; **défendre son ~** [*sportif*] to defend one's title; **donner à qn le ~ de** to address sb as; **elle a le ~ de docteur en linguistique** she's got a doctorate in linguis-

Les titres de politesse

On ne trouvera ici que quelques indications générales sur la façon de s'adresser à quelqu'un et de parler de quelqu'un en utilisant son titre. Pour les titres militaires, ▶ 390*, et pour les autres titres, consulter les articles du dictionnaire. Pour les titres utilisés dans les lettres, voir* **activités**.

Comment s'adresser à quelqu'un

Dans la plupart des circonstances ordinaires, l'anglais n'utilise pas d'équivalent de monsieur, madame *etc.*

bonjour, madame	=	good morning
bonsoir, mademoiselle	=	good evening
bonjour, monsieur	=	good afternoon
excusez-moi, madame	=	excuse me
pardon, monsieur, pourriez-vous me dire ...	=	excuse me, could you tell me ...

Les mots Mr, Mrs, Miss *et* Ms *sont toujours utilisés avec le nom de la personne; on ne les utilise jamais seuls.*

bonjour, madame	=	good morning, Mrs Smith
au revoir, mademoiselle	=	goodbye, Miss Smith
bonsoir, monsieur	=	good evening, Mr Smith

Attention: Ms *(dire* [mɪz] *ou* [məz]*) permet de faire référence à une femme dont on connaît le nom sans préciser sa situation de famille. Il n'y a pas d'équivalent français:*

bonjour, madame *ou* bonjour, mademoiselle	=	good morning, Ms Smith

Les anglophones utilisent les prénoms beaucoup plus volontiers que les francophones. Lorsqu'en français on dit simplement bonjour, *en anglais on précise souvent* good morning, Paul *ou* good morning, Anne *etc. De même, au début d'une lettre, un anglophone écrira facilement* Dear Anne, Dear Paul *etc., bien avant que le Français n'en vienne à utiliser le prénom.*

Les mots Madam *et* Sir *ne sont utilisés que par les vendeurs des magasins, les employés de restaurants, d'hôtels etc. Ils sont toujours utilisés sans le nom propre:*

bonjour, madame	=	good morning, Madam
bonne nuit, monsieur	=	good night, Sir

En anglais, le titre de doctor *est utilisé pour les docteurs de toutes disciplines. Mais on ne peut l'utiliser seul, sans nom propre, que pour un docteur en médecine.*

bonsoir, docteur	=	good evening, doctor (*médecin*)
bonjour, docteur	=	good morning, Doctor Smith (*en médecine ou d'une autre spécialité*)

Comment parler de quelqu'un

M Dupont est arrivé	=	Mr Dupont has arrived
Mme Dupont a téléphoné	=	Mrs Dupont phoned *ou* Ms Dupont phoned
le rabbin Lévi est malade	=	Rabbi Lévi is ill

L'anglais n'utilise pas d'article défini devant les noms de titres lorsqu'ils sont suivis du nom propre.

le roi Richard I	=	King Richard I (*dire* King Richard the first)
l'inspecteur Hervet	=	Inspector Hervet
le prince Charles	=	Prince Charles
la princesse Anne	=	Princess Anne
le pape Jean-Paul II	=	Pope John-Paul II (*dire* Pope John-Paul the second)

Mais si le titre est suivi du nom du pays, du peuple, de la ville etc., l'anglais utilise l'article défini.

le roi des Belges	=	the King of the Belgians
le prince de Galles	=	the Prince of Wales
l'évêque de Durham	=	the Bishop of Durham

tics; **le ~ d'ingénieur** the status of qualified engineer; **en ~** [*professeur, directeur*] titular; [*fournisseur*] appointed; [*maîtresse, rival*] official; [*chef d'orchestre*] resident; [*acteur, danseur*] regular; **champion du monde en ~** world title holder; **~s universitaires** (diplômes) university qualifications; **promotion sur ~** promotion on the basis of one's qualifications; **ils n'ont pas droit au ~ de réfugié(s)** they have no right to refugee status; **revendiquer le ~ de résistant** to claim the status of a resistance fighter; **4** (motif) **à juste ~** quite rightly; **à plus d'un ~** in many respects; **à ~ d'exemple/de précaution** as an example/a precaution; **à ~ expérimental/de comparaison** by way of experiment/of comparison; **à ~ définitif/provisoire** on a permanent/temporary basis; **à ~ privé** in a private capacity; **à ~ gracieux** or **gratuit** free; **à ~ onéreux** for a fee; **participer à qch à ~ officiel/personnel** to take part in sth in an official/a private capacity; **à ~ indicatif** as a rough guide; **ce prix n'est donné qu'à ~ indicatif** or **d'indication** this price is only a guideline; **à quel ~ a-t-il été invité?** why was he invited?; **au même ~ que vous** in the same capacity as yourself; **elle a, à ce ~, rencontré le président** she met the president in that capacity; **à double ~** on two counts; **au ~ de l'aide économique** in economic aid; **somme déduite au ~ de frais de représentation** sum deducted as representing entertainment expenses; **perçu au ~ de droits d'auteur** received as royalties; **5** Jur (document) deed; (subdivision de livre) title; **6** Fin (valeur) security; **~ au porteur** bearer security; **~ nominatif** registered security; **~ de placement** investment security; **7** Écon item; **~ budgétaire** budgetary item; **8** Chimie titre[GB]; **9** Vin (de vins et spiritueux) strength; **10** (de métal précieux) fineness.

■ **~ courant** Édition running title; **~ de créance** proof of debt; **~ ecclésiastique** ecclesiastical title; **~ de gloire** claim to fame; **~ participatif** non-voting share (*in public sector companies*); **~ de participation** equity share; **~ de propriété** title deed; **~ de saisie** distraining order; **~ de transport** ticket; **~ universel de paiement**, **TUP** universal payment order.

titré, ~e /titʀe/ **I** *pp* ▶ **titrer**.

II *pp adj* **1** (noble) titled; **être ~** to be titled; **2** Chimie standard.

titrer /titʀe/ [1] *vtr* **1** Presse **le journal du dimanche titrait...** the headlines in the Sunday paper read...; **le journal du dimanche titrait en gras...** banner headlines in the Sunday paper read...; **le Temps titrait sur quatre colonnes 'la fin de la démocratie'** 'the end of democracy' announced 'le Temps' in a four-column spread; **2** Chimie to titrate [*solution*]; to assay [*minerai*].

titubant, ~e /titybɑ̃, ɑ̃t/ *adj* [*personne, démarche*] unsteady.

tituber /titybe/ [1] *vi* to stagger (**de** with); **je titubais de fatigue** I was staggering with exhaustion; **il tituba, s'arrêta puis repartit** he staggered along, stopped, then set off again; **ils sont sortis du pub en titubant** they staggered out of the pub.

titulaire /titylɛʀ/ **I** *adj* **1** Admin [*enseignant*] (d'école, de lycée) who has been confirmed in his/her post (*après n*); (d'université) tenured; [*agent, personnel*] permanent; **2** Sport **joueur ~** full member of the team.

II *nmf* **1** (membre permanent) (dans une école, un lycée) teacher who has been confirmed in his/her post; (à l'université) tenured lecturer GB ou professor US; (dans un ministère, une administration) permanent staff member; **être ~ d'un poste** (d'école, de lycée) to have been confirmed in one's post; (d'université) to have tenure; (d'administration) to be a permanent staff member; **2** (possesseur) holder; **être ~ d'une licence/du permis de conduire/d'un passeport** to hold a degree/a driver's licence[GB]/a passport; **être ~ de la nationalité italienne/d'un contrat de travail** to have Italian nationality/a contract of employment; **les ~s d'un compte en banque/d'une carte de crédit** account/credit-card holders.

titularisation /titylaʀizasjɔ̃/ *nf* **1** (action) gén confirmation in a post; Univ granting of tenure; **2** (statut) gén permanent staff status; Univ tenure; **3** (de sportif) inclusion in the team.

titulariser /titylaʀize/ [1] *vtr* **1** Scol to confirm [sb] in a post [*instituteur, professeur*]; **2** Univ to grant tenure to [*professeur*]; **3** Admin to give permanent status to [*agent, personnel*]; **4** Sport to make [sb] a full member of the team [*joueur*].

TNP /teɛnpe/ *nm* (*abbr* = **Théâtre national populaire**) *state-funded theatre in France.*

TNT /teɛnte/ *nm* (*abbr* = **trinitrotoluène**) TNT.

toast /tost/ *nm* **1** (pain grillé) gén toast **C**; (très mince) Melba toast; **trois ~s** three pieces of toast; **2** (canapé) canapé; **~s au fromage/saumon** cheese/salmon canapés; **3** (célébration) toast; (discours) toast; **~ en l'honneur de** toast in honour[GB] of; **porter un ~ à qch/en l'honneur de qn** to toast sth/sb.

Tobago /tɔbago/ *nprf* Tobago; ▶ **Trinité**.

toboggan /tɔbɔgɑ̃/ *nm* **1** Jeux slide; (de piscine) waterslide; **faire du ~** to go on the slide; **2** ®Gén Civ flyover GB, overpass US; **3** Tech chute; **4** Aviat (d'évacuation) emergency chute; **5** Sport (traîneau) toboggan.

toc /tɔk/ **I**○ *adj inv* (fou) crazy○.

II○ *nmsg* (faux) fake **C**; **tes colliers, c'est du ~** your necklaces are fakes; **un bijou en ~** a piece of fake jewellery GB ou jewelry US; **sa culture, c'est du ~** his learning is bogus.

III *excl* (*also onomat*) tap!; **~! ~!—qui est là?** knock! knock!—who's there?; **tu vois, j'avais raison, et ~!** you see, I was right, so there!

tocante○ /tɔkɑ̃t/ *nf* ticker○, watch.

tocard○, **~e** /tɔkaʀ, aʀd/ **I** *adj* [*voiture, meuble, décor*] lousy, crummy○; [*mise en scène*] lousy, rotten, crummy○.

II *nm* **1** (cheval) rank outsider; **2** (personne) halfwit.

toccata /tɔkata/ *nf* Mus toccata.

tocsin /tɔksɛ̃/ *nm* alarm (bell), tocsin littér; **sonner le ~** lit to sound the alarm ou tocsin; fig to raise ou sound the alarm.

toc-toc○ /tɔktɔk/ **I** *adj inv* potty○ GB, nutty○.

II *nm* (*also onomat*) knock knock!

toge /tɔʒ/ *nf* **1** Univ gown; Jur robe; **2** Antiq toga; **~ prétexte/virile** toga pretexta/virilis.

Togo /tɔgo/ ▶ 321 *nprm* Togo.

togolais, ~e /tɔgɔlɛ, ɛz/ ▶ 537 *adj* Togolese.

Togolais, ~e /tɔgɔlɛ, ɛz/ ▶ 537 *nm,f* Togolese.

tohu-bohu○ /tɔybɔy/ *nm inv* (confusion) confusion; (tumulte) commotion, hurly-burly.

toi /twa/ *pron pers* **1** (sujet) **~ qui aimes tant le chocolat** you, who love chocolate so much; **c'est ~?** is that you?; **je sais que ce n'est pas ~** I know it wasn't you; **tes amis et ~ serez les bienvenus** you and your friends will be welcome; **~, ne dis**

rien don't say anything; **2** (dans une comparaison) **je travaille plus que ~** I work more than you ou than you do; **elle est plus âgée que ~** she's older than you ou than you are; **il les voit plus souvent que ~** (que tu ne les vois) he sees them more often than you do; (qu'il ne te voit) he sees them more often than you ou than he sees you; **3** (objet) **te frapper, ~, quelle idée!** hit YOU, what a thought!, hit YOU, the very idea!; **4** (après une préposition) you; **à cause de/autour de/après ~** because of/around/after you; **un cadeau pour ~** a present for you; **pour ~ c'est important?** is it important to you?; **elle ne pense pas à ~** she doesn't think of you; **elle n'écrit à personne sauf à ~** she doesn't write to anyone but you; **sans ~, nous n'aurions pas pu réussir** we could never have managed without you; **à ~** (en jouant) your turn; **ce sont des amis à ~** they're YOUR friends; **tu n'as pas de coin à ~ dans la maison, ça va changer** you haven't got a room of your own in the house, but that will change; **à ~, je peux dire la vérité** I can tell YOU the truth; **la tasse verte est-elle à ~?** is the green cup yours?; **c'est à ~** (appartenance) it's yours, it belongs to you; (séquence) (it's) your turn; **c'est à ~ de faire la vaisselle** it's your turn to do the dishes; **c'est à ~ de choisir** (ton tour) it's your turn to choose; (ta responsabilité) it's up to you to choose; **5** (pronom réfléchi) yourself; **libère-~ pour samedi soir** make sure you're free for Saturday evening; **reprends-~** pull yourself together; **6** (toi-même) yourself; **tu devrais prendre soin de ~** you should take care of yourself; **pense un peu à ~ aussi** think of yourself a little as well.

toile /twal/ *nf* **1** Tex cloth; **~ de lin/chanvre/coton** linen/hemp/cotton (cloth); **des vêtements de ~** (heavy) cotton clothes; **de la grosse ~** canvas; **draps de ~** linen sheets; **2** Art (support) canvas; (tableau) canvas, painting; **~ de maître** master painting; **3** Naut canvas; **réduire la ~** to reduce the canvas.
■ **~ d'amiante** asbestos cloth; **~ d'araignée** gén spider's web; (dans une maison, un grenier) cobweb; **l'araignée tisse sa ~** the spider is weaving its web; **~ d'avion** Aviat aeroplane GB ou airplane US canvas; **~ cirée** oilcloth; **~ émeri** emery cloth; **~ de fond** Théât backcloth, backdrop; fig backdrop; **~ goudronnée** tarpaulin; **~ de jute** hessian; **~ à matelas** ticking; **~ métallique** wire mesh; **~ à sac** sackcloth; **~ de tente** (tissu) canvas; (tente) tent; **~ à voiles** Naut canvas, sailcloth.
IDIOMES **se faire une ~**○ to go to see a film ou movie○ US.

toilerie /twalʀi/ *nf* **1** (fabrication) textile manufacture; **2** (commerce) textile trade.

toilettage /twalεtaʒ/ *nm* **1** (d'animal) grooming; **salon de ~** grooming parlour[GB]; **séance de ~** grooming session; **2** (de structure) cleaning up; (de loi) touching up.

toilette /twalεt/ **I** *nf* **1** (soins corporels) **faire sa ~** [*personne*] to have a wash; [*animal*] to wash itself; **faire un brin de ~** to have a quick wash; **as-tu fini ta ~?** have you washed?; **produit/savon/accessoire de ~** toilet product/soap/accessory; **'tout pour la ~ de bébé'** 'baby care products'; **faire la ~ d'un mort** to lay out a corpse ou body; **faire la ~ d'un chien/cheval** to groom a dog/horse; **2** (nettoyage de monument, ville) face-lift; **faire la ~ de la capitale** to give the capital a face-lift; **3** (vêtements) outfit; **en belle** or **grande ~** all dressed up (*jamais épith*); **4**† (meuble) (pour se laver) washstand; (coiffeuse) dressing table.
II toilettes *nfpl* (cabinet d'aisances) (chez quelqu'un) toilet (*sg*) GB, bathroom (*sg*) US; (dans un lieu public) toilets, restroom (*sg*) US; **aller/avoir envie d'aller aux ~s** to go/to need to go to the toilet GB ou bathroom US; **~s pour dames** ladies (+ *v sg*) GB, ladies' room US; **~s pour hommes** gents (+ *v sg*) GB, men's room US.
■ **~ de chat** cat's lick; **faire une ~ de chat** to have a quick wash, to give oneself a cat's lick.

toiletter /twalete/ [1] *vtr* to groom [*chien, chat, cheval*].

toiletteur, -euse /twalεtœʀ, øz/ ▶510 *nm,f* dog groomer; **aller chez un ~** to take one's pet to a grooming parlour[GB].

toi-même /twamεm/ *pron pers* yourself; **l'as-tu fait ~?** did you do it yourself?; **en ~ qu'en penses-tu?** what do you really think?; **c'est ~ qui me l'as dit** you yourself told me; **ce qui s'est passé, tu l'as vu ~** you yourself saw what happened, you saw with your own eyes what happened.

toise /twaz/ *nf* **1** (instrument) height gauge; **passer à la ~** to be measured; **2** ▶477 (unité) toise (≈ 6 1/2 ft).

toiser /twaze/ [1] **I** *vtr* to look [sb] up and down [*personne*].
II se toiser *vpr* to look each other up and down.

toison /twazɔ̃/ *nf* **1** (pelage) fleece; **2** (chevelure) mane; (poils abondants) abundant growth (of hair).
■ **la Toison d'or** the Golden Fleece.

toit /twa/ *nm* **1** gén (de maison, voiture, tunnel) roof; **un ~ en dôme/coupole/terrasse** a domed/cupolated/flat roof; **un ~ à une pente/deux pentes** a lean-to/ridge roof; **~ à 4 pans** or **pentes** hipped roof; **~ à la Mansart** mansard roof; **~ en pente** sloping roof; **habiter sous les ~s** to live in a garret; **d'ici on voit les ~s de Paris** from here you can see the rooftops of Paris; **2** fig (maison) roof; **vivre sous le même ~** to live under the same roof; **se retrouver sans ~** to find oneself without a roof over one's head.
■ **le ~ du Monde** the roof of the world; **~ ouvrant** sunroof.
IDIOMES **crier qch sur (tous) les ~s** to shout sth from the rooftops.

toit-terrasse, *pl* **toits-terrasses** /twatεʀas/ *nm* flat roof.

toiture /twatyʀ/ *nf* (structure) roof; (matériau) roofing.

Tokyo /tɔkjo/ ▶857 *npr* Tokyo.

tôle /tol/ *nf* **1** Ind (matière) sheet metal; (plaque) metal sheet ou plate; **un toit de** or **en ~** a sheet-metal roof; **la voiture n'est plus qu'un tas de ~s** the car is a wreck; **~ froissée** crumpled metal; **2**◐ (prison) = **taule 1**.
■ **~ à biscuits** baking sheet, cookie sheet US; **~ émaillée** enamelled[GB] sheet metal; **~ étamée** tin plate; **~ galvanisée** galvanized sheet metal; **~ ondulée** corrugated iron; **~ à tartes** tart tin.

tôlé, ~e /tole/ *adj* **neige ~e** crusted snow.

Tolède /tɔlεd/ ▶857 *npr* Toledo.

tolérable /tɔleʀabl/ *adj* [*attente, douleur, situation*] bearable; [*attitude, comportement*] tolerable, acceptable; **ce n'est pas ~!** it's intolerable!

tolérance /tɔleʀɑ̃s/ *nf* **1** (ouverture d'esprit) tolerance; (indulgence) indulgence (**envers, à l'égard de** toward(s)); **être d'une grande ~ avec qn** to be very tolerant with sb; **2** (dérogation) **ce n'est pas un droit c'est une ~** it isn't legal but it is tolerated; **~s grammaticales/orthographiques** permitted variations in grammar/spelling; **3** (à un médicament) tolerance (**à** of); (au bruit) tolerance (**à** of); **4** Relig tolerance, toleration.

tolérant, ~e /tɔleʀɑ̃, ɑ̃t/ *adj* [*personne, société*] tolerant (**envers** toward, towards GB).

tolérer /tɔleʀe/ [14] **I** *vtr* **1** (accepter) to tolerate, to turn a blind eye to [sth] [*infraction, écart de conduite*]; **2** Méd to tolerate [*médicament, substance*]; **3** (supporter) [*personne*] to tolerate, to put up with [sth] [*insulte, comportement*]; to tolerate [*personne, présence*]; **il ne tolère pas qu'on le contredise** he can't tolerate being contradicted; **tes parents tolèrent que tu rentres si tard?** do your parents put up with your coming home so late?
II se tolérer *vpr* to tolerate each other.

tôlerie /tolʀi/ *nf* (technique) sheet-metal working; (commerce) sheet-metal trade; (atelier) sheet-metal works (*pl*); (ensemble de tôles) metalwork; (de voiture) bodywork.

tolet /tɔlε/ *nm* Naut thole.

tôlier -ière /tolje, εʀ/ ▶510 *nm,f* **1** Ind sheet-metal worker; Aut panel beater; **2**○ (patron d'hôtel) hotel boss.

tollé /tɔle/ *nm* outcry, hue and cry; **ça a été un ~ général** there was general uproar.

Tolstoï /tɔlstɔj/ *npr* Tolstoy.

toluène /tɔlɥεn/ *nm* toluene.

TOM /tɔm/ *nm*: *abbr* ▶ **territoire**.

tomahawk /tɔmaok/ *nm* tomahawk.

tomaison /tɔmεzɔ̃/ *nf* **1** (numérotation) volume numbering; **2** (division) separation into volumes.

tomate /tɔmat/ *nf* **1** (fruit) tomato; **deux kilos de ~s** two kilos of tomatoes; **~s farcies/à la provençale** stuffed/Provençal tomatoes; **confiture de ~s vertes** green tomato jam; **2** (plante) tomato plant; **plant de ~** tomato seedling; **3** (apéritif) *pastis with a dash of grenadine*.
■ **~ cerise** cherry tomato.
IDIOMES **être rouge comme une ~** (à cause du soleil) to be as red as a lobster; (à cause de la gêne) to be as red as a beetroot.

tombal, ~e, *mpl* **-aux** /tɔ̃bal, o/ *adj* **1** (de tombe) **inscription ~e** gravestone inscription; **2** (de mort) **d'une couleur** or **pâleur ~e** deathly pale.

tombant, ~e /tɔ̃bɑ̃, ɑ̃t/ *adj* [*épaules*] sloping; [*moustaches, paupières*] drooping (*épith*); [*oreilles de chien*] floppy; [*poitrine*] pej sagging péj; ▶ **nuit**.

tombe /tɔ̃b/ *nf* (fosse) grave; (dalle) gravestone; **creuser une ~** to dig a grave; **une ~ en marbre/granite** a marble/granite gravestone; **aller sur la ~ de qn** to visit sb's grave; **mettre des fleurs sur une ~** to put flowers on a grave.
IDIOMES **se retourner dans sa ~** to turn in one's grave; **être/rester muet comme une ~** to be/remain as silent as the grave; **emporter un secret dans la ~** to carry a secret to the grave; **avoir un pied dans la ~** to have one foot in the grave; **suivre qn dans la ~** to follow sb to the grave.

tombeau, *pl* **~x** /tɔ̃bo/ *nm* **1** (monument) tomb; **mettre qn au ~** to lay sb in his/her grave; **porter qn au ~** to bear sb to his/her grave; **la mise au ~** Art the Entombment; **2** (personne discrète) **c'est un ~** he/she will keep mum○; **3** (fin) death; **le ~ de nos libertés** the death of our liberties; **vivre avec qn jusqu'au ~** to live with sb till the grave.
IDIOMES **rouler à ~ ouvert** to drive at breakneck speed.

tombée /tɔ̃be/ *nf* **à la ~ du jour** at close of day littér; **(à) la ~ de la nuit** (at) nightfall.

tomber /tɔ̃be/ [1] **I** *nm* (de vêtement, tissu) hang ¢; **ce velours a un beau ~** this velvet hangs well.
II *vtr* (+ *v avoir*) **1** Sport to throw [*lutteur*]; fig to beat [*équipe*]; **2**○ (séduire) to bed○ [*femme*]; (charmer) **il les tombe toutes** they all fall for him.
III *vi* (+ *v être*) **1** (faire une chute) gén to fall; (de sa propre hauteur) [*personne, chaise*] to fall over; [*animal*] to fall; [*arbre, mur*] to fall down; (d'une hauteur, d'un support) [*personne, vase*] to fall off; [*fruits, feuilles, bombe*] to fall; [*cheveux, dents*] to fall out; [*plâtre, revêtement*] to come off; **je me suis cassé un bras/j'ai cassé un vase en tombant** I fell and broke my arm/a vase; **~ à la mer/dans une rivière** to fall into the sea/into a river; **~ dans un trou** to fall down a hole; **~ sur** to fall on [*tapis, maison, tête*]; **~**

sur le derrière○ or **cul**◑ to land on one's backside; **~ d'un toit/de cheval** to fall off a roof/off a horse; **~ d'un arbre** [*personne*] to fall from a tree; [*fruit, feuille*] to fall off a tree; **~ du lit/de ma poche** to fall out of bed/out of my pocket; **l'assiette m'est tombée des mains** the plate fell out of my hands; **ces lunettes me tombent du nez** these glasses are slipping off my nose; **attention, tu vas me faire ~!** be careful, you'll make me fall!; **j'ai fait ~ un vase** I knocked a vase over; **j'ai fait ~ le vase de l'étagère** I knocked the vase off the shelf; **il a fait ~ son adversaire** (au rugby) he brought his opponent down; **le vent a fait ~ une tuile du toit/un arbre sur les voitures** the wind blew a tile off the roof/a tree down onto the cars; **se laisser ~ dans un fauteuil/sur un lit** to flop into an armchair/onto a bed; **laisser ~ un gâteau sur le tapis** to drop a cake on the carpet; **le skieur s'est laissé ~ pour s'arrêter** the skier dropped to the ground to stop himself; **2** (venir d'en haut) [*pluie, neige, foudre*] to fall; [*brouillard*] to come down; [*rayon, clarté*] to fall (**sur** onto); [*rideau de théâtre*] to fall, to drop; **un rayon de lumière tombait sur mon livre** a ray of light fell onto my book; **il est tombé 200 mm d'eau** or **de pluie pendant la nuit** 200 mm of rain fell during the night; **il tombe des gouttes** it's spotting with rain; **qu'est-ce que ça tombe**○**!, ça tombe dru**○**!** (pluie) it's pouring down!, it's coming down in buckets○!; **la pluie n'a pas cessé de ~ pendant tout le voyage** it rained steadily throughout the journey; **la foudre est tombée sur un arbre** the lightning struck a tree; **une faible lueur tombait de la lucarne** there was a dim light coming through the skylight; **une pâle clarté tombait de la lune** the moon cast a pale light; **3** (faiblir, baisser) [*valeur, prix, température*] to fall (**de** by; **à** to); [*ardeur, colère*] to subside; [*fièvre*] to come down; [*vent*] to drop; [*jour*] to draw to a close; [*conversation*] to die down; **le dollar est tombé au-dessous de 5 francs** the dollar has fallen to below 5 francs; **la température est tombée à/de 10°C** the temperature has fallen to/by 10°C; **leur personnel est tombé à 200 employés** their staff is down to 200 employees; **faire ~** to bring down [*prix, température*]; to dampen [*enthousiasme*]; **il est tombé bien bas** (affectivement) he's in very low spirits; (moralement) he has sunk very low; **il est tombé bien bas dans mon estime** he has gone right down in my esteem ou estimation; **je tombe de sommeil** I can't keep my eyes open; **4** (être vaincu, renversé) [*dictateur, régime, ville*] to fall; (disparaître) [*obstacle, objection*] to vanish; [*opposition*] to subside; [*préjugé*] to die out; **le roi est tombé** (aux cartes) the king has been played; **faire ~** to bring down [*régime, dictateur*]; to remove [*obstacle*]; to eradicate [*tabou*]; **faire ~ les barrières** fig to break down barriers; **5** (s'affaisser) [*poitrine*] to sag; [*épaules*] to slope; **avoir les épaules qui tombent** to have sloping shoulders; ▶**bras**; **6** (pendre) [*chevelure, mèche*] to fall; [*vêtement, rideau*] to hang; **cheveux qui tombent sur les yeux** hair that falls over one's eyes; **manteau qui tombe bien/mal** coat that hangs well/badly; **sa jupe lui tombe (jusqu')aux chevilles** her skirt comes down to her ankles; **7** (se retrouver, se placer) **~ dans un piège** lit, fig to fall into a trap; **~ en disgrâce/ruine** to fall into disgrace/ruin; **~ dans la vulgarité/sensiblerie** to lapse into vulgarity/sentimentality; **vous tombez dans le paradoxe** you are being paradoxical; **~ sous le charme de qn** to fall under sb's spell; **~ sous le coup d'une loi** Jur to fall within the provisions of a law; **~ aux mains** or **entre les mains de qn** [*document, pouvoir*] to fall into sb's hands; **la conversation est tombée sur la politique** the conversation came around to politics; ▶**Charybde, sens**; **8** (devenir) to fall; **~ malade/amoureux** to fall ill/in love; **9** (être donné) [*décision, sentence, verdict*] to be announced; [*nouvelle*] to break; [*réponse*] to be given; **~ sur les écrans** [*nouvelle*] to come through on screen; **la nouvelle nous tombe à l'instant** Radio, TV the news has just come through to us; **dès que le journal tombe des presses** as soon as the newspaper comes off the press; **les paroles qu'il a laissé ~ de sa bouche** the words that fell from his lips; ▶**sourd**; **10** (rencontrer) **~ sur** gén to come across [*inconnu, détail, objet*]; to run into [*ami, connaissance*]; (recevoir en partage) to get; (avoir de la chance dans ses recherches) **~ sur la bonne page/le bon numéro** to hit on the right page/the right number; **je suis tombé sur un sujet difficile/un examinateur sévère à l'examen** I got a difficult question/a harsh examiner in the exam; **je suis tombé par hasard sur ce que je cherchais** I found what I was looking for by chance ; **mes yeux sont tombés sur une jolie femme/une expression amusante** my eyes fell on a pretty woman/a funny expression; **si tu prends cette rue, tu tomberas sur la place** if you follow that street, you'll come to the square; **11** (survenir) gén to come; **c'est tombé juste au bon moment/comme il fallait** it came just at the right time/when it was needed; **cette réforme ne pouvait pas mieux/plus mal ~** this reform couldn't have come at a better/worse time; **tu ne pouvais pas mieux ~!** (au bon moment) you couldn't have come at a better time!; (avoir de la chance) you couldn't have done better!; **tu tombes bien/mal, j'allais partir** you're lucky/unlucky ou you've timed that well/badly, I was just about to leave; **ça tombe bien/mal, j'avais justement besoin de ce livre** that's good/bad luck, I just needed that book; **il faut toujours que ça tombe sur moi** or **que ça me tombe dessus**○**!** [*décision, choix*] why does it always have to be me?; [*mésaventure*] why does it always have to happen to me?; **~ au milieu d'une** or **en pleine réunion** [*personne*] to walk right into a meeting; [*annonce, nouvelle*] to come right in the middle of a meeting; **12** (coïncider) [*date, anniversaire, fête*] to fall on [*jour, quantième*]; **ça tombe un mercredi/le 17 avril** it falls on a Wednesday/on 17 April; **13** (abandonner) **laisser ~** to give up [*emploi, activité*]; to drop [*sujet, projet, habitude*]; **il a fallu laisser ~** I/we etc had to give up; **laisse ~!** (désintérêt, désabusement) forget it!; (irritation) give it a rest○!; **laisser ~ qn** (pour se séparer) to drop sb; (pour ne plus aider) to let sb down; **il a laissé ~ sa petite amie** he dropped his girlfriend; **ne me laisse pas ~!** don't let me down!; ▶**chaussette**; **14** (agresser) **~ sur qn** (physiquement) [*soldats, voyous*] to fall on sb, to lay○ into sb; [*pillards, police*] to descend on sb; (critiquer) to go for sb, to lay○ into sb; **ils nous sont tombés dessus à dix contre un** they fell on us, ten to one; **il s'est fait ~ dessus par des voleurs/un chien** he was set on by robbers/attacked by a dog; **15** (mourir) euph [*soldat*] to fall euph; **~ sous le feu de l'ennemi** to fall under enemy fire; **~ pour qch** to die for sth; ▶**champ**.

IDIOMES **en ~ sur le derrière**○ or **cul**◑ to be flabbergasted○.

tombereau, *pl* **~x** /tɔ̃bʀo/ *nm* **1** (charrette) tip-up cart; (contenu) cartload; **2** Gén Civ (véhicule) dumper truck GB, dumptruck US; (contenu) truckload; **3** Rail wagon GB, boxcar US; (contenu) wagonload; **4** fig (grande quantité) **des ~x de** loads○ of.

tombeur○, **-euse** /tɔ̃bœʀ/ *nm,f* **1** (séducteur) charmer; **2** (vainqueur) **le ~ de qn/d'une équipe** the one who brought sb/a team down.

tombola /tɔ̃bɔla/ *nf* tombola GB, lottery.

Tombouctou /tɔ̃buktu/ ▶**857** *npr* Timbuktu.

tome /tɔm/ **I** *nm* **1** (volume) volume; **2** (division à l'intérieur d'un ouvrage) part, book.
II *nf* = **tomme**.

tomer /tome/ [1] *vtr* **1** (diviser en parties) to divide into books; (diviser en volumes) to divide into volumes; **2** (numéroter) to mark [sth] with the volume number [*page, livre*].

tomme /tɔm/ *nf* tomme ou tome (cheese).

tommette /tɔmɛt/ *nf* hexagonal floor tile.

tomographie /tɔmɔgʀafi/ *nf* tomography.

ton[1], **ta**, *pl* **tes** /tɔ̃, ta, te/ *adj poss*

■ **Note** En anglais, on ne répète pas le possessif coordonné: *ta femme et tes enfants* = your wife and children.

your; **tes amis** your friends; **~ imbécile de mari**○ your stupid husband; **tes parents à toi**○ your parents; **c'est pour ~ bien** it's for your own good; **un de tes amis** a friend of yours; **~ gentil collègue** that nice colleague of yours; **j'ai fait tes courses** I've done the shopping for you; **à ~ arrivée/départ** when you arrived/left; **je ne suis pas ~ juge** it's not up to me to tell you what to do; **tu peux te la garder, ta voiture**○ you can keep your precious car.

ton[2] /tɔ̃/ *nm* **1** (de la voix) (hauteur) pitch; (inflexion) tone; (qualité) tone, voice; (expression) tone (of voice); **~ grave/aigu** low/high pitch; **~ criard/rauque** shrill/husky voice; **d'un ~ dédaigneux** scornfully; **d'un ~ sec** drily; **sur le ~ de la conversation** conversationally; **sur un ~ solennel** in a solemn tone; **baisser le ~** lit to lower one's voice; fig to moderate one's tone; **faire baisser le ~ à qn** fig to take sb down a peg (or two); **parle-moi sur un autre ~!** don't use that tone with me!; **eh bien, si tu le prends sur ce ~** well, if you're going to take it like that; **je le leur ai dit** or **répété sur tous les ~s** fig I've told them a thousand times; **changement de ~** (de voix) change of tone; (d'attitude) change of tune; **2** Ling tone; **langue à ~s** tone language; **~ montant/descendant** rising/falling tone; **3** (style) tone; **donner le ~** gén to set the tone; (pour une mode) to set the fashion; **être/se mettre dans le ~** to fit in; **de bon ~** in good taste, tasteful; **il est/serait de bon ~ de faire** it is/it would be good form to do; **4** Mus (hauteur des notes) pitch; (tonalité) key; (intervalle) tone; (instrument) pitch pipe; **donner le ~** to give the pitch; **~ de si bémol majeur** key of b flat major; ▶**quart**; **5** (couleur) shade, tone; **des ~s de bleu** shades of blue; **~ soutenu** deep shade; **d'un ~ un peu plus soutenu** in a slightly deeper shade; **~ sur ~** in matching tones.

tonal, **~e** /tɔnal/ *adj* Ling, Mus tonal; **hauteur ~e** pitch; **langue ~e** tone language.

tonalité /tɔnalite/ *nf* **1** Mus (ton) key; (échelle des sons) tonality; (en phonétique) (de voyelle) tone; **2** (qualité) (de voix) tone; fig (de roman, film) tone; **la ~ pessimiste d'un film** the pessimistic tone of a film; **3** (couleurs) tonality; **4** Télécom dialling[GB] tone GB, dial tone US.

tondeur, **-euse** /tɔ̃dœʀ, øz/ **I** *nm,f* **~ de chiens** dog groomer; **~ de moutons** sheep shearer.
II tondeuse *nf* **1** (pour tondre) (chiens) clippers (*pl*); (moutons) shears (*pl*); **2** (de coiffeur) clippers (*pl*); **3** (de jardin) lawnmower.
■ **tondeuse à gazon** lawnmower; **tondeuse (à gazon) électrique/à main** electric/manual lawnmower; **tondeuse sur coussin d'air** hovermower GB, air-cushion mower.

tondre /tɔ̃dʀ/ [6] *vtr* **1** (un animal) to shear [*mouton, laine*]; to clip [*chien, poils*]; ▶**laine**; **2** (une personne) (à ras) **~ qn** to shave sb's head; **3**○ (couper les cheveux à) **~ qn** to cut sb's hair; **se faire ~**○ to have one's hair cut; **il s'est fait ~** (court) he's had his hair cropped; (très court) he's been scalped hum; **4** (dans un jardin) to mow [*gazon, pelouse*]; **5**○ (voler) **~ qn** to fleece○ sb.

tondu, **~e** /tɔ̃dy/ **I** *pp* ▶ **tondre**.

II *pp adj* **1** [*mouton*] shorn; [*chien*] clipped; **2** [*cheveux*] shorn; [*crâne*] shaven GB, shaved; [*prisonnier*] (rasé) with a shaven head (*après n*).

III *nm,f* skinhead; ▶ **pelé**.

Tonga /tɔ̃ga/ ▶**321**, **416** *nprfpl* Tonga; **les îles ~** the Tonga islands.

tongs /tɔ̃g/ *nfpl* flip-flops, thongs US.

tonic /tɔnik/ *nm* tonic.

tonicité /tɔnisite/ *nf* **1** (de climat, air) bracing effect; **2** (de muscle) tone.

tonifiant, **~e** /tɔnifjɑ̃, ɑ̃t/ *adj* **1** [*climat, air*] bracing; [*promenade*] invigorating; **2** (pour les muscles, la peau) [*exercice*] toning (*épith*); **lotion ~e** Cosmét toning lotion.

tonifier /tɔnifje/ [2] *vtr* to tone up [*muscles, épiderme*]; **lotion pour ~** toning lotion; **un climat qui tonifie l'organisme** an invigorating climate.

tonique /tɔnik/ **I** *adj* **1** (stimulant) [*remède, boisson, vin*] tonic (*épith*); fig [*air, froid*] invigorating; [*lecture*] stimulating; **2** (astringent) **lotion ~** toning lotion; **3** Ling tonic.

II *nm* **1** Méd, fig tonic; **2** (lotion) toning lotion.

III *nf* Mus tonic.

tonitruant, **~e** /tɔnitʀyɑ̃, ɑ̃t/ *adj* [*rire, voix*] booming (*épith*).

tonitruer /tɔnitʀye/ [1] *vi* to thunder.

Tonkin /tɔ̃kɛ̃/ ▶**692** *nprm* Tonkin.

Tonkinois, **~e** /tɔ̃kinwa, az/ *adj, nm,f* Tonkinese.

tonnage /tɔnaʒ/ *nm* tonnage; **~ brut/net** gross/net tonnage; **cargo de fort ~** cargo ship of high tonnage.

tonnant, **~e** /tɔnɑ̃, ɑ̃t/ *adj* [*voix*] booming; [*colère*] thunderous.

tonne /tɔn/ *nf* **1** ▶**620** Mes (1 000 kg) tonne, metric ton; **un (camion de) sept ~s** a 7-tonne truck, a 7-tonner○; **2** fig (grande quantité) ton; **des ~s de choses à faire** tons ou loads of things to do; **3** (tonneau) tun; **4** (bouée) buoy.

■ **~ équivalent charbon, TEC** ton coal equivalent; **~ équivalent pétrole, TEP** ton oil equivalent, TOE.

tonneau, *pl* **~x** /tɔno/ *nm* **1** (contenant, contenu) gén barrel; (de whisky, vin, d'huile) barrel, cask; (de poudre) keg; **~ de bière** barrel of beer; **~ à bière** beer barrel; **mettre le vin en ~** to put the wine into casks ou barrels; **2** (en voiture) somersault; **faire plusieurs ~x** to turn over ou somersault several times; **3** Naut ton; **~ d'affrètement/de jauge** freight/register ton; **4** Aviat barrel roll.

IDIOMES **du même ~**○ of the same kind.

tonne-kilomètre, *pl* **tonnes-kilomètre** /tɔnkilɔmɛtʀ/ *nf* Rail ton kilometre[GB]

tonnelet /tɔnlɛ/ *nm* small barrel, keg.

tonnelier /tɔnəlje/ ▶**510** *nm* cooper.

tonnelle /tɔnɛl/ *nf* arbour[GB]; **être sous une ~** to be in an arbour[GB].

tonnellerie /tɔnɛlʀi/ *nf* cooperage.

tonner /tɔne/ [1] **I** *vi* **1** [*personne*] to thunder; **pas question! tonna-t-il** no way! he thundered; **~ contre** to inveigh against; **2** [*artillerie*] to thunder; **les canons ont tonné toute la nuit** the guns thundered away all night.

II *v impers* to thunder; **il tonne** it's thundering; **il a tonné toute la nuit** it thundered all night.

tonnerre /tɔnɛʀ/ **I** *nm* **1** Météo thunder; **un coup de ~** lit a clap of thunder; fig a thunderbolt; **la nouvelle fut un coup de ~ dans un ciel bleu** the news was a bolt from the blue; **les roulements du ~** the rumbling of the thunder; **2** (de canons, artillerie) thundering; **voix de ~** thunderous voice; **il est sorti dans** or **sous un ~ d'applaudissements** he left to thunderous applause; **3**○ (haute qualité) **du ~** fabulous; **ça marche du ~** [*appareil, entreprise*] it's going fantastically well.

II *excl* blast!; **mille ~s**† blast (it)!; **~ de Brest**† shiver my timbers†!; **~ de Dieu**◑ hellfire!

tonsure /tɔ̃syʀ/ *nf* (de clergé) tonsure.

tonsuré, **~e** /tɔ̃syʀe/ *adj* [*tête, moine*] tonsured.

tonsurer /tɔ̃syʀe/ [1] *vtr* to tonsure.

tonte /tɔ̃t/ *nf* **1** (époque, action) **~ (des moutons)** shearing; **2** (laine) fleece; **3** (dans un jardin) mowing; **la ~ du gazon a pris une heure** it took an hour to mow the lawn.

tontine /tɔ̃tin/ *nf* **1** Fin, Jur tontine; **2** Hort *protective straw* or *moss wrapping around the roots of a plant during transport*.

tonton○ /tɔ̃tɔ̃/ *nm* uncle; **~ Pierre** Uncle Pierre.

tonus /tɔnys/ *nm inv* **1** (de personne) energy, dynamism; **avoir du ~** to be dynamic, to be full of pep○; **redonner du ~ à qn** to revitalize sb; **2** (du muscle) tone, tonus.

top /tɔp/ **I** *adj*○ **~ modèle** top model; **être au ~ niveau** to be at the top of the league, to be the best; **~ secret**○ top secret.

II *nm* **1** (signal sonore) pip, beep; **'au quatrième ~ il sera exactement...'** 'at the fourth stroke the time will be...'; **donner le ~ de départ** (dans une course) to give the starting signal; **attention, ~, partez!** on your marks, get set, go!; **'attention! ~, c'est parti!'** Jeux 'Ready? Play!'; **2** (de classement) **le ~ 50** the top 50.

topaze /tɔpaz/ **I** ▶**193** *adj inv* topaz-coloured[GB]

II *nf* topaz.

toper /tɔpe/ [1] *vi* **topons là!** let's shake on it!, done!

topinambour /tɔpinɑ̃buʀ/ *nm* Jerusalem artichoke.

topique /tɔpik/ **I** *adj* **1** fml [*preuve, remarque, précision*] apposite sout; **2** Pharm topical.

II *nf* Psych schema.

topo○ /tɔpo/ *nm* (oral) short talk (**sur** on); (écrit) short piece (**sur** on); **faire un ~ sur qch** (discours) to give a short talk on sth; **c'est toujours le même ~** it's always the same old story○.

topographe /tɔpɔgʀaf/ ▶**510** *nmf* topographer.

topographie /tɔpɔgʀafi/ *nf* (science, relief) topography.

topographique /tɔpɔgʀafik/ *adj* topographical.

topologie /tɔpɔlɔʒi/ *nf* topology.

topologique /tɔpɔlɔʒik/ *adj* topological.

topométrie /tɔpɔmetʀi/ *nf* topometry.

toponyme /tɔpɔnim/ *nm* place name, toponym spéc.

toponymie /tɔpɔnimi/ *nf* **1** (science) toponomy; **2** (ensemble de noms) place names (*pl*), toponomy spéc.

toponymique /tɔpɔnimik/ *adj* toponymic.

toquade○ /tɔkad/ *nf* **1** (pour une activité, un objet) passion (**pour** for); **avoir une ~ pour qch** to go crazy about sth; **2** (amoureuse) crush○ (**pour** on), infatuation (**pour** with); **avoir une ~ pour qn** to have a crush on sb○, to be infatuated with sb.

toquante○ /tɔkɑ̃t/ *nf* ticker○, watch.

toque /tɔk/ *nf* **1** (de femme) toque; (de cuisinier) chef's hat; (de juge) hat; **~ en fourrure** fur cap; **2** (de jockey) cap.

toqué○, **~e** /tɔke/ **I** *adj* crazy○; **être ~ de qn** (amoureux) to be crazy○ about sb.

II *nm,f* nutcase○, nutter○.

toquer /tɔke/ [1] **I**○ *vi* (frapper) to knock.

II se toquer *vpr* **se ~ de qch** to go crazy about sth; **se ~ de qn** to fall for sb○, to become infatuated with sb.

torche /tɔʀʃ/ *nf* (flambeau) torch; **être transformé en ~ vivante** to become a human torch; **éclairé par des ~s** [*jardin, parcours*] torchlit; **parachute en ~** candled parachute.

■ **~ électrique** torch GB, flashlight US.

torche-cul● /tɔʀʃky/ *nm inv* toilet paper, bog paper◑; **c'est un ~** (journal) it's trash.

torchée◑ /tɔʀʃe/ *nf* thrashing.

torcher /tɔʀʃe/ [1] **I** *vtr* **1**◑ to wipe [*fesses*]; **~ un enfant** to wipe a child's bottom; **2**○ (avec torchon) to wipe; **3**○ (faire vite) to dash off○ [*article, rapport*]; (bâcler) to cobble [sth] together [*article, rapport*]; **un article bien torché** (ton admiratif) a well-written article.

II se torcher● *vpr* **se ~ (le cul**●**)** to wipe one's arse● GB ou ass◑ US; **je m'en torche** I don't give a shit◑.

torchère /tɔʀʃɛʀ/ *nf* **1** (candélabre) torchère; **2** (en pétrochimie) flare stack.

torchis /tɔʀʃi/ *nm inv* cob (*mixture of clay and straw used for walls*).

torchon /tɔʀʃɔ̃/ *nm* **1** gén cloth; (pour la vaisselle) tea towel GB, dish towel US; **donner** or **passer un coup de ~ sur** to give [sth] a wipe [*vaisselle, meuble*]; **coup de ~**○ (lutte) scrap○; (épuration) purge, clean-up○; ▶ **serviette**; **2** péj (journal) rag○; (travail mal présenté) messy piece of work; **c'est un vrai ~!** it's a mess!; **3** B (serpillière) floor cloth.

IDIOMES **le ~ brûle (entre eux)**○ it's war (between them).

tordant○, **~e** /tɔʀdɑ̃, ɑ̃t/ *adj* [*personne, histoire*] hilarious, very funny; **ce type est ~!** that guy○ is a scream○!

tord-boyaux○ /tɔʀbwajo/ *nm inv* gut-rot○.

tordre /tɔʀdʀ/ [6] **I** *vtr* **1** (tourner violemment) **~ le bras/le poignet à qn** to twist sb's arm/wrist; **~ le cou à un poulet** to wring a chicken's neck; **~ le cou à qn**○ lit, fig to wring sb's neck; **2** (déformer) to bend [*pare-chocs, clou, tige de métal, barre*]; **3** (contracter) **la douleur/peur lui tordait le visage** his face was distorted with pain/fear; **l'angoisse lui tordait l'estomac** fear was tying his stomach up in knots; **4** (enrouler) to twist [*mouchoir, laine*]; **5** (essorer) to wring out [*linge*]; **ne pas ~** do not wring.

II se tordre *vpr* **1** (se faire mal à) **se ~ le pied/la cheville/le poignet** to twist one's foot/ankle/wrist; **2** (plier) [*pare-chocs*] to bend; [*roue*] to buckle; **3** (sous l'effet d'une émotion, d'une douleur) **se ~ de douleur** to writhe in pain; **se ~ de rire** to double up laughing; **il y a de quoi se ~**○**!** it's a scream○!

tordu, **~e** /tɔʀdy/ **I** *pp* ▶ **tordre**.

II *pp adj* **1** (déformé) [*nez, jambes, barre*] crooked; [*branches, tronc*] twisted; [*ferraille*] twisted, buckled; **2** fig [*idée*] weird, strange; [*raisonnement, logique*] twisted; **inventer un coup ~** to come up with an underhand trick; **avoir l'esprit ~** to have a twisted mind; **il est complètement ~**○**!** he's off his rocker○!, he's completely mad!; **il faut être vraiment** or **avoir l'esprit ~ pour imaginer que...** you have to have a really twisted mind to imagine that...

III○ *nm,f* nutcase○, nut○.

tore /tɔʀ/ *nm* Archit, Math torus.

toréador /tɔʀeadɔʀ/ ▶**510** *nm* toreador.

toréer /tɔʀee/ [11] *vi* to fight bulls.

torero /tɔʀeʀo/ ▶**510** *nm* bullfighter, torero.

torgnole◑ /tɔʀɲɔl/ *nf* clout○, wallop○; **flanquer une ~ à qn** to give sb a clout○.

toril /tɔʀil/ *nm* bullpen.

tornade /tɔʀnad/ *nf* tornado; **entrer comme une ~** fig to sweep in like a whirlwind.

toron /tɔʀɔ̃/ *nm* strand.

torpédo /tɔʀpedo/ *nf* open tourer GB, touring car US.

torpeur /tɔʀpœʀ/ *nf* torpor.

torpide /tɔʀpid/ *adj* also Méd torpid.

torpillage /tɔʀpijaʒ/ *nm* lit, fig torpedoing (**de qch** of sth).

torpille /tɔʀpij/ *nf* torpedo.

torpiller /tɔʀpije/ [1] *vtr* lit, fig to torpedo.

torpilleur /tɔʀpijœʀ/ *nm* **1** (bateau) torpedo boat; **2** (marin) torpedo gunner.

torréfacteur /tɔʀʀefaktœʀ/ *nm* **1** ▶510 (commerçant) coffee merchant; **2** (machine) (à café, cacao) roasting machine.

torréfaction /tɔʀʀefaksjɔ̃/ *nf* (de café, cacao) roasting.

torréfier /tɔʀʀefje/ [2] *vtr* to roast [*café, cacao*]; **café torréfié** roasted coffee.

torrent /tɔʀɑ̃/ *nm* lit, fig torrent; **~ de boue/de plaisanteries** torrent of mud/jokes; **des ~s de larmes** floods of tears; **pleuvoir à ~s** to rain very heavily, to rain in torrents.

torrentiel, **-ielle** /tɔʀɑ̃sjɛl/ *adj* torrential; **des pluies torrentielles** torrential rain.

torrentueux, **-euse** /tɔʀɑ̃tɥø, øz/ *adj* torrential.

torride /tɔʀ(ʀ)id/ *adj* **1** [*climat, région*] torrid; [*soleil, été, après-midi*] scorching; **il fait une chaleur ~** it's boiling ou scorching (hot); **2** [*érotisme, scène*] torrid; [*nuit*] passionate; [*actrice*] extremely sexy.

tors, **torse**[1] /tɔʀ, tɔʀs/ *adj* Tex [*fil, soie*] twisted; [*jambes*] crooked; [*pied de lampe*] twisted.

torsade /tɔʀsad/ *nf* **1** gén twist, coil (**de** of); **2** (d'un tricot) cable stitch; **un pull à ~** a cable-knit sweater; **faire des ~s** to do cable stitch; **3** Archit cable moulding; **une colonne à ~s** Archit a cable column.

torsader /tɔʀsade/ [1] *vtr* to twist [*fils, soie*]; **un bougeoir torsadé** a twisted candlestick; **une colonne torsadée** Archit a cable column.

torse[2] /tɔʀs/ *nm* **1** ▶188 Anat, Art torso; **2** gén chest; **bomber le ~** to stick out one's chest; **avoir le ~ moulé dans un maillot** to be wearing a tight-fitting vest; **se mettre ~ nu** to strip to the waist; **il était ~ nu** he was stripped to the waist.

torsion /tɔʀsjɔ̃/ *nf* **1** gén, Tex twisting (**de** of); **2** Phys torsion.

tort /tɔʀ/ **I** *nm* **1** (défaut de raison) **avoir ~** to be wrong (**de faire** to do); **il a eu ~ de les licencier** he was wrong to fire ou dismiss them; **on aurait ~ de croire que c'est facile** it would be wrong ou a mistake to think it's easy; **il n'a pas tout à fait ~ de dire ça** he's not entirely wrong in saying that; **tu n'as pas ~ de les laisser tomber!** I don't blame you for dropping them!; **j'aurais bien ~ de m'inquiéter !** it would be silly of me to worry!; **être en ~, être dans son ~** to be in the wrong; **se mettre/mettre qn en ~** to put oneself/sb in the wrong; **donner ~ à qn** [*arbitre, juge*] to blame sb; [*faits, réalité*] to prove sb wrong; ▶**absent**; **2** (faute) fault; **les ~s sont partagés** there are faults on both sides; **tous les ~s sont de leur côté** it's all their fault, they're entirely to blame; **prendre tous les ~s à son compte** to take all the blame ou all responsibility; **reconnaître ses ~s** to acknowledge that one has done wrong; **avoir des ~s envers qn** to have wronged sb; **le jugement a été prononcé à leurs ~s** Jur the case went against them; **divorce prononcé aux ~s du mari** Jur divorce granted against the husband; **3** (erreur) mistake; **c'est un ~ de s'imaginer que...** it's a mistake to think that...; **j'ai eu le ~ de le croire** I made the mistake of believing him; **c'est le grand ~ que tu as eu** that's where you went wrong, that was your big mistake; **mon ~, c'est d'être trop impulsif** my trouble is that I am too impulsive; **4** (préjudice) wrong; **demander réparation d'un ~** to demand compensation for a wrong; **faire du** or **porter ~ à qn/qch** to harm sb/sth; **ça ne fait de ~ à personne** it doesn't do anybody any harm, it doesn't hurt anybody.

II à tort *loc adv* [*accuser*] wrongly; **à ~ ou à raison** rightly or wrongly; **à ~ et à travers** [*dépenser*] wildly; **parler à ~ et à travers** to talk a lot of nonsense.

torticolis /tɔʀtikɔli/ ▶271 *nm inv* stiff neck; **avoir un** or **le ~** to have a stiff neck.

tortillard○ /tɔʀtijaʀ/ *nm* small local train.

tortiller /tɔʀtije/ [1] **I** *vtr* to twist [*fibres*]; **~ son mouchoir/sa moustache/ses cheveux** to twiddle one's handkerchief/moustache GB ou mustache US/hair.

II○ *vi* (remuer) **~ du derrière**○ ou **des fesses**○ to wiggle one's bottom; **elle dansait en tortillant des hanches** she wiggled her hips as she danced.

III se tortiller *vpr* [*ver*] to wriggle; **se ~ d'impatience sur sa chaise** [*personne*] to be fidgeting with impatience on one's chair; **un petit ver se tortillait dans l'assiette** a little maggot was wriggling on the plate.

IDIOMES **il n'y a pas à ~**○ there's no wriggling out of it; **se ~ comme un ver/une anguille** to wriggle like a worm/an eel.

tortillon /tɔʀtijɔ̃/ *nm* (de papier, tissu) twist (**de** of); (de cheveux) wisp (**de** of).

tortionnaire /tɔʀsjɔnɛʀ/ **I** *adj* [*policier*] who carries out torture (*après n*); [*régime, gouvernement*] which practises[GB] torture (*après n*).

II *nmf* torturer.

tortue /tɔʀty/ *nf* **1** Zool (d'eau) turtle; (terrestre) tortoise, turtle US; **~ d'eau douce** freshwater turtle; **2** (personne lente) slowcoach○ GB, slowpoke○ US; **3** Zool (papillon) tortoiseshell.

■ **~ géante** giant tortoise.

IDIOMES **avancer comme une ~** to proceed at a snail's pace.

tortueusement /tɔʀtɥøzmɑ̃/ *adv* tortuously.

tortueux, **-euse** /tɔʀtɥø, øz/ *adj* **1** lit [*chemin*] tortuous; [*rue, ruisseau, escalier*] winding; **2** fig [*manœuvres, conduite*] devious; [*langage, discours*] convoluted; [*esprit, raisonnement*] tortuous; **suivre un chemin ~** fig to follow a tortuous path; **j'ai eu un cheminement politique/professionnel ~** my political/professional career has been tortuous.

torturant, **~e** /tɔʀtyʀɑ̃, ɑ̃t/ *adj* [*pensée, remords*] agonizing.

torture /tɔʀtyʀ/ *nf* **1** (physique) torture ₡; **une ~** a form of torture; **arrêter la ~** or **les ~s** to put a stop to torture; **instruments de ~** instruments of torture; **chambre** or **salle des ~s** torture chamber; **sous la ~** under torture; **infliger la ~ à qn** to torture sb; **2** (morale) agony; (de jalousie) torment; **la ~ psychologique** mental torture; **trois mois d'attente, j'étais à la ~** three months' waiting, it was torture.

torturer /tɔʀtyʀe/ [1] **I** *vtr* **1** lit [*policier, gouvernement*] to torture [*personne*]; **être torturé par la faim** to be starving; **2** fig [*pensée, sentiment*] to torment; **visage/air torturé** tormented face/look; **vision du monde/poésie torturée** tormented vision of the world/poetry; **être torturé** [*personne*] to have a tormented nature; **être torturé par** to be tormented by [*jalousie, doute, remords*]; **3** (forcer le sens de) to distort [*texte*]; **style torturé** tortured style.

II se torturer *vpr* fig to torment oneself; **se ~ l'esprit** (cherchant solution) to rack one's brains.

torve /tɔʀv/ *adj* [*œil, regard*] menacing, baleful; **il lui jeta un regard ~** he shot her a baleful glance.

toscan, **~e** /tɔskɑ̃, an/ **I** *adj* Géog Tuscan.

II ▶462 *nm* Ling Tuscan.

Toscan, **~e** /tɔskɑ̃, an/ *nm,f* Tuscan.

Toscane /tɔskan/ ▶692 *nprf* Tuscany.

tôt /to/ *adv* **1** (de bonne heure) [*commencer, se lever*] early; **~ le matin** early in the morning; **~ dans la vie/la saison** early in life/the season; **plus ~ que d'habitude** earlier than usual; **il a appris à lire très ~** he learned to read very early (on); **le plus ~ possible** as early as possible; **il est trop ~ pour déjeuner** it's too early for lunch; ▶**avenir**; **2** (bientôt, vite) soon, early; **le plus ~ possible** as soon as possible; **le plus ~ serait le mieux** the sooner the better; **si je l'avais su plus ~** if I had known sooner ou earlier; **il est trop ~ pour décider** it's too soon to decide; **trop ~ après qch** too soon after sth; **~ ou tard** sooner or later; **pour Pâques, au plus ~** by Easter, at the earliest; **tu n'étais pas plus ~ parti qu'il est arrivé** no sooner had you left than he arrived; **j'aurai ~ fait de le réparer** it won't take me long to mend it, I'll soon have it mended; **on ne m'y reprendra pas de si ~** I won't do that again in a hurry; **on ne la reverra pas de si ~** we won't see her again in a hurry, it will be a long time before we see her again; **tu as fini? ce n'est pas trop ~**○! you've finished? about time too○!

total, **~e**, *mpl* **-aux** /tɔtal, o/ **I** *adj* **1** (complet) [*contradiction, retour, contrôle, retrait*] complete, total; **l'illusion se révèle ~e** it turns out to be a complete illusion; **je suis en accord ~ avec leur déclaration** I agree with them totally; **un manque ~ d'objectivité** a complete ou total lack of objectivity; **2** (somme de plusieurs parties) [*revenu, quantité, prix, surface, budget*] total; [*hauteur, nombre*] full (*épith*).

II *nm* total; **faire le ~ des dépenses** to add up the expenditure; **il n'a pas fermé la porte à clé, ~**○**, il s'est tout fait voler** he didn't lock the door, the upshot was that he had everything stolen.

III au total *loc adv* **1** (dans un calcul) **au ~ cela fait 350 francs** altogether that comes to 350 francs; **2**○ (dans un bilan) **au ~, le problème reste entier** when all's said and done the problem remains unsolved.

IV totale○ *nf* **1** (hystérectomie) **on lui a fait une** ou **la ~e!** she had it all taken away○!, she's had a hysterectomy; **2** (indiquant une série de mésaventures) **la ~e!** total disaster!

totalement /tɔtalmɑ̃/ *adv* totally, completely.

totalisateur /tɔtalizatœʀ/ *nm* **1** Ordinat accumulator; **2** Turf totalizator.

totalisation /tɔtalizasjɔ̃/ *nf* adding up, totalling[GB] (**de** of).

totaliser /tɔtalize/ [1] *vtr* **1** (faire le total de) to total, to add up [*bénéfices, souscriptions*]; **2** (atteindre le total de) to have a total of [*points, buts, votes*]; **~ 13% des voix/7 000 francs** to total 13% of the votes/7,000 francs; **l'équipe qui totalise le plus grand nombre de points** the team with the greatest number of points.

totalitaire /tɔtalitɛʀ/ *adj* **1** (dictatorial) [*régime, État*] totalitarian; **2** Philos [*doctrine, religion*] all-embracing (*épith*).

totalitarisme /tɔtalitaʀism/ *nm* totalitarianism.

totalité /tɔtalite/ *nf* **la ~ d'un héritage/de la route/des élèves de la classe** all the ou the whole inheritance/road/class; **la ~ du personnel** all the staff, the whole staff; **la ~ des installations/activités/dépenses** all the installations/activities/expenditure; **la ~ du pouvoir** all the power; **il a dilapidé la presque ~ de sa fortune** he has almost frittered away his whole fortune; **appréhender un problème dans sa ~** to look at a problem in its entirety; **le restaurant a brûlé dans sa ~** the restaurant was totally ou completely burned down; **ils sont financés en ~ par l'État** they are entirely ou completely state-financed; **nous vous rembourserons en ~** we will refund you in full.

totem /tɔtɛm/ *nm* **1** (emblème) lit, fig totem; **2** (poteau) totem pole.

totémique /tɔtemik/ *adj* totemic.

totémisme /tɔtemism/ *nm* totemism.

toton /tɔtɔ̃/ *nm* teetotum.

touage /twaʒ/ *nm* Naut warping.

touareg /twaʀɛg/ *adj* Tuareg.

Touareg /twaʀɛg/ *nmf inv* Tuareg.

toubib○ /tubib/ *nm* doctor, quack○ GB; **elle est ~** she's a doctor.

toucan /tukɑ̃/ *nm* toucan.

touchant, **~e** /tuʃɑ̃, ɑ̃t/ *adj* [*cérémonie*] moving; [*image, histoire, sentiment, cadeau*] touching; **elle est très ~e dans ce rôle** she's very moving in the part; **c'était très ~** it was very touching; **être ~ de simplicité** [*geste, cérémonie*] to be touchingly simple; **être ~ d'innocence/de gentillesse** to be endearingly innocent/kind.

touche /tuʃ/ *nf* **1** Tech(commande manuelle) (de clavier) key; (de machine à laver, téléviseur, vidéo) button; (d'instrument à cordes) fret; **la ~ des majuscules/de retour en arrière/fonction** the shift/backspace/function key; **la ~ d'enregistrement/d'avance rapide/de rembobinage** the record/fast forward/rewind button; **ma machine à laver a une ~ 'économie'** my washing machine has got an economy cycle; **2** Art (coup de pinceau) stroke; (style) touch; (tache de peinture) dash, touch; **peindre par petites ~s** to paint in small strokes; **faire qch par petites ~s** fig to do sth bit by bit; **on reconnaît la ~ de Manet/Balzac** you can recognize Manet's/Balzac's touch; **une ~ de vert/jaune** a dash ou touch of yellow/green; **une ~ d'originalité/de fantaisie** fig a touch of originality/fantasy; **mettre la dernière ~ à qch**, **mettre la ~ finale à qch** to put ou add the finishing touches to sth; **3** Sport (**ligne de**) **~** gén sideline; (au football, rugby) sideline, touchline; **sortir en ~** to go into touch; **mettre** or **dégager le ballon en ~** to kick the ball into touch; **la ~ est pour Lille** (au football) it's a Lille throw; **remise en ~** (au football) throw-in; (au rugby) line-out; **être/rester sur la ~** to be/to stay on the sidelines; **mettre qn sur la ~** fig to push sb aside; **4** (en escrime) hit; **5** Pêche bite; **faire une ~** to get a bite; **6**◐ (rencontre) **faire une ~** to score○; **7**○ (allure) **tu as vu la ~ qu'il a avec ce chapeau!** he looks ridiculous in that hat!; **elle avait une de ces ~s!** she was a sight!; **la ~!** what a sight!

touche-à-tout /tuʃatu/ *adj inv* **être ~** [*bébé*] to be into everything; [*esprit curieux*] to be a jack of all trades.

touche-pipi○ /tuʃpipi/ *nm inv* **jouer à ~** to play doctors and nurses.

toucher /tuʃe/ [1] **I** *nm* **1** (sens) **le ~** touch, the sense of touch; **reconnaître des objets au ~** to identify objects by touch; **un tissu doux au ~** a fabric which is soft to the touch; **2** Méd digital examination; **~ rectal** digital examination of the rectum; **3** Mus (d'un pianiste) touch.

II *vtr* **1** (poser la main sur) **~** (**de la main**) to touch [*objet, surface, personne*]; **'prière de ne pas ~'** 'please do not touch'; **ne touche pas, pas touche**○**!** don't touch!; **~ le bras/l'épaule/le dos de qn** to touch sb's arm/shoulder/back, to touch sb on the arm/shoulder/back; **~ du bois** (par superstition) to touch wood; **je touche du bois, mais je ne suis jamais malade** I never get ill, touch wood!; **~ le front de qn** to feel sb's forehead; **~ qch du doigt** lit, fig to put one's finger on sth; **2** (être en contact avec) to be touching [*mur, plafond, fond*]; **~ le sol** [*animal, sauteur, avion*] to land; **3** (heurter) to hit [*adversaire, voiture, trottoir*]; **si tu recules encore tu vas ~ le mur** if you reverse any more, you'll hit the wall; **ne pas ~ une** or **la balle**○ not to get near the ball; **'touché!'** (en escrime) 'touché!'; (à la bataille navale) 'hit!'; **~ qn à la tête/poitrine** to hit sb in the head/chest; **touché dans le dos il s'est effondré** he was hit in the back and slumped down; **4** (attendrir) to touch [*personne*] ; **ça me touche beaucoup** I am very touched; **j'ai été très touchée de ta visite** or **que tu viennes me voir** I was very touched by your visit; **5** (affecter) [*événement, changement, crise, loi*] to affect [*personne, secteur, pays*]; [*intempérie*] to hit [*région, ville*]; **rien ne la touche** nothing affects her; **la récession touche tout le monde** the recession affects everybody; **le chômage touche 15% de la population active** unemployment affects 15 per cent of the working population; **la région la plus touchée par l'ouragan** the area hardest hit by the hurricane; **6** (être contigu à) [*pays*] to be next to, to border (on); [*maison, usine*] to be next to, to adjoin [*bâtiment, parc*]; **leur terrain touche le nôtre** their land is next to ou adjoins ours; **7** (encaisser) [*personne*] to get, to receive [*argent, indemnités, dividendes*]; to cash [*chèque, mandat*]; to get [*retraite*]; to win [*tiercé, loterie*]; **il a touché une grosse somme à son départ** he got a lot of money when he left; **elle ne va ~ aucune indemnité** she won't get ou receive any compensation; **ils touchent une petite retraite** they get a small pension; **8** (joindre) **~ qn** to get hold of sb; **il est difficile à ~ par téléphone** he's difficult to get hold of on the phone; **9** Presse, Radio, TV **~ trois millions d'auditeurs** or **de téléspectateurs** to have an audience of three million; **~ sept millions de lecteurs** to have a readership of seven million.

III toucher à *vtr ind* **1** (poser la main sur) **~ à** to touch [*objets*]; **ne touchez à rien** don't touch anything; **il n'a pas touché à son repas** he didn't touch his meal; **il ne touche plus à une goutte d'alcool** he doesn't touch a drop of alcohol anymore; **~ à tout** lit to be into everything; fig to be a Jack-of-all trades; **il ne touche plus à un fusil** he won't go near a rifle anymore; **'touche pas à mon pote**○**'** 'hands off my pal○'; **avec son air de ne pas y ~, c'est un malin**○ he looks as if butter wouldn't melt in his mouth, but he's a sly one; **2** (concerner) **~ à** to concern; **la réforme touche à l'emploi des jeunes** the reform concerns youth employment; **tout ce qui touche à la discipline/l'individu** anything that relates to ou that concerns discipline/the individual; **c'est un problème qui touche à l'éthique** it's a question of ethics; **3** (porter atteinte à) **~ à** to infringe on [*droit, liberté, privilège*]; to detract from [*dignité*]; **~ aux principes fondamentaux de la démocratie** to infringe on the fundamental principles of democracy; **4** (modifier) to change; **on ne peut ~ aux coutumes** tradition is sacrosanct; **5** (aborder) to get on to [*question, problème*]; **vous touchez à un sujet délicat/une question fondamentale** you're getting on to a delicate subject/a fundamental issue.

IV se toucher *vpr* **1** (se tâter) (l'un l'autre) to feel each other; (soi-même) to feel oneself; **se ~ la tête/le bras/les pieds** (l'un l'autre) to feel each other's heads/arms/feet; (soi-même) to feel one's head/arm/feet; **2**◐ (se masturber) to play with oneself○; **3** (être contigu) (maisons, jardins, immeubles) to be next to each other; **nos deux maisons se touchent** our houses are next door to each other.

touche-touche: **à touche-touche** /atuʃtuʃ/ *loc adv* **être à ~** [*voitures*] (dans un bouchon) to be nose to tail, to be bumper to bumper; [*personnes, tentes, caravanes*] to be on top of each other○.

touée /twe/ *nf* Naut (chaîne) warp; (longueur de chaîne) scope.

touer /twe/ [1] *vtr* Naut to warp.

toueur /twœʀ/ *nm* tug.

touffe /tuf/ *nf* (de cheveux, poils, d'herbe) tuft; (de violettes, myosotis, genêts, d'arbres) clump; **planter qch par ~s** to plant sth in clumps.

touffeur /tufœʀ/ *nf* liter sweltering heat.

touffu, **~e** /tufy/ *adj* **1** [*sourcils, barbe*] bushy; [*végétation, forêt*] dense; [*buisson*] thick; [*arbre*] leafy; **au poil ~** [*chien, chat*] with thick fur; **2** [*texte, discours, style*] dense.

touillage○ /tujaʒ/ *nm* gén stirring; (de salade) tossing.

touiller○ /tuje/ [1] *vtr* to stir [*sauce*]; to toss [*salade*].

toujours /tuʒuʀ/ *adv* **1** (exprimant la continuité) always; **cela a ~ existé et existera ~** it always has existed and it always will; **je t'aimerai ~** I'll always love you; **ce n'est pas ~ vrai** that is not always true; **comme ~** as always; **vouloir ~ plus** always to want more; **pour ~** forever; **ils se connaissent depuis ~** they've known each other all their lives; **j'en rêve depuis ~** I've always dreamed about it; **de ~** [*ami*] very old; [*amitié*] long-standing; **~ plus vite** faster and faster; **~ plus grand** bigger and bigger; **des frais ~ plus importants** ever-increasing costs; **2** (exprimant la répétition) always; **il est ~ en retard** he is always late; **c'est ~ pareil** it's always the same; **ce n'est pas ~ évident** it's not always obvious; **~ prêt à aider/critiquer** always ready to help/criticize; **vous serez ~ le bienvenu** you're always welcome; **3** (encore) still; **il est ~ couché?** is he still in bed?; **il n'est ~ pas levé?** is he still not up?; **c'est ~ aussi difficile** it's still just as hard; **4** (de toute façon) anyway; **viens ~** come anyway; **on peut ~ essayer** we can always try; **cela peut ~ servir** it might come in handy; **c'est ~ mieux que rien** it's still better than nothing; **c'est ~ ça de pris** or **de gagné** that's something at least; **~ est-il que** the fact remains that.

Toulon /tulɔ̃/ **▶857** *npr* Toulon.

toulonnais, **~e** /tulɔnɛ, ɛz/ **▶857** *adj* of Toulon.

Toulonnais, **~e** /tulɔnɛ, ɛz/ **▶857** *nm,f* (natif) native of Toulon; (habitant) inhabitant of Toulon.

toulousain, **~e** /tuluzɛ̃, ɛn/ **▶857** *adj* of Toulouse.

Toulousain, **~e** /tuluzɛ̃, ɛn/ **▶857** *nm,f* (natif) native of Toulouse; (habitant) inhabitant of Toulouse.

Toulouse /tuluz/ **▶857** *npr* Toulouse.

toundra /tundʀa/ *nf* tundra.

toupet /tupɛ/ *nm* **1**○ (effronterie) cheek○, nerve○; **quel ~!** what a cheek○!; **elle ne manque pas de ~!** she's got a cheek○ ou a lot of nerve○!; **avoir le ~ de faire qch** to have the cheek○ to do sth; **2** (de laine, crins) tuft; (de cheveux) (petite touffe) tuft; (sur sommet de tête) quiff GB, forelock US; (**faux**) **~** (perruque) toupee.

toupie /tupi/ *nf* **1** (jouet) top; **faire tourner une ~** to spin a top; **2** (en menuiserie) spindle moulder GB ou molder US; **3**○ (femme) pej **vieille ~** old bag○ péj.

IDIOMES **tourner comme une ~** to spin around and around.

tour /tuʀ/ **I** *nm* **1** (mouvement rotatif) gén turn; Mécan, Mes revolution; **5000 ~s** (**par**) **minute** 5,000 revolutions ou revs○ per minute; **l'essieu grince à chaque ~ de roue** the axle squeaks at every turn of the wheel; **donner un ~ de vis** to give the screw a turn; **donner un ~ de clé** to turn the key; **être à quelques ~s de roue de** to be just around the corner from; **faire un ~ de manège** to have a go on the merry-go-round; **faire un ~ de valse** to waltz around the floor; **la Terre fait un ~ sur elle-même en 24 heures** the Earth rotates once in 24 hours; **faire un ~ sur soi-même** [*danseur*] to spin around; **un** (**disque**) **33/45/78 ~s** an LP/a 45 ou single/a 78; **fermer qch à double ~** to double-lock sth; **s'enfermer à double ~** fig to lock oneself away; **à ~ de bras**○ [*frapper*] with a vengeance; [*investir, racheter*] left right and centre[GB]○; **▶quart**; **2** (mouvement autour de) **faire le ~ de qch** gén to go around sth; (en voiture) to drive around sth; **le train fait le ~ du lac en deux heures** the train takes two hours to go around the lake; **faire le ~ du monde** to go around the world; **la nouvelle a vite fait le ~ du village** the news spread rapidly through the village; **il a fait le ~ de l'Afrique en stop** he hitchhiked around Africa **faire le grand ~** fig to go the long way round GB ou around US; **en deuxième ~ de circuit** Sport on the second lap of the circuit; **faire un ~ d'honneur** to do a lap of honour[GB]; **avec plusieurs ~s de corde, ça tiendra** with the rope wound around a few times, it'll hold; **mettre trois ~s de corde** to wind the rope around three times; **donner plusieurs ~s à la pâte** Culin to fold the dough several times; ▶ **cadran**, **propriétaire**, **repartir II**, **sang**; **3** ▶ **477⌋**, **793⌋** (pourtour) (bords) edges (*pl*); (circonférence) circumference; (mensuration) measurement; (mesure standard) size; **le ~ de l'étang est couvert de jonquilles** there are daffodils all around the edges of the pond; **elle a le ~ des yeux fardé au kohl** she has kohl around her eyes; **tronc de 15 mètres de ~** trunk 15 metres[GB] in circumference ou 15 metres around; **~ de tête/cou/taille/hanches** head/neck/waist/hip measurement; **faire du 90 de ~ de poitrine** ≈ to have a 36-inch bust; ▶ **poitrine**; **4** (déplacement bref) (à pied) walk, stroll; (à bicyclette) ride; (en voiture) drive, spin; **faire un (petit) ~** (à pied) to go for a walk ou stroll; **si nous allions faire un ~?** shall we go for a walk?; **je suis allé faire un ~ à Paris/en ville** I went to Paris/into GB ou down town; **je vais faire un ~ chez des amis** I'm just going to pop round GB ou go over US to some friends; **fais un ~ à la nouvelle exposition, ça vaut le coup** go and have a look round GB ou around US the new exhibition, it's worth it; **faire des ~s et des détours** lit [*route, rivière*] to twist and turn; fig [*personne*] to beat about the bush; **5** (examen bref) look; **faire le ~ d'un problème /sujet** to have a look at a problem/subject; **faire un (rapide) ~ d'horizon** to have a quick overall look (**de** at), to make a general survey (**de** of); **faire le ~ de ses ennemis/relations** to go through one's enemies/acquaintances; **on en a vite fait le ~**○ pej (de problème, sujet, d'ouvrage) there's not much to it; (de personne) there's not much to him/her/them etc; **6** (moment d'agir) gén turn; (de compétition, tournoi, coupe) round; **à qui le ~?** whose turn is it?; **c'est ton ~** it's your turn; **chacun son ~** each one in his turn; **jouer avant son ~** to play out of turn; **à mon ~ de faire** it's my turn to do; **récompensé à mon ~** rewarded in my turn; **attendre/passer son ~** to wait/miss one's turn; **c'est au ~ de qn** it 's sb's turn; **notre équipe a été battue au second ~** our team was defeated in the second round; **la cuisine est nettoyée, maintenant c'est au ~ du salon** the kitchen is cleaned up, now for the living-room; **il perd plus souvent qu'à son ~** (il regrette) he loses more often than he would like; (je critique) he loses more often than he should; **~ à ~** (alternativement) by turns; (à la suite) in turn; **être ~ à ~ gentil et agressif** to be nice and agressive by turns; **il a été ~ à ~ patron d'entreprise, ministre et professeur d'économie** he has been in turn a company boss, a minister and an economics teacher; ▶ **rôle**; **7** Pol (consultation) ballot; **les résultats du premier/second ~** the results of the first/second ballot; **au second ~** on the second ballot; **scrutin à deux ~s** two-round ballot; **~ de scrutin** ballot, round of voting; **8** (manœuvre, ruse) trick; **jouer un bon/mauvais/sale ~ à qn** to play a good/nasty/dirty trick on sb; **ma mémoire me joue des ~s** my memory is playing tricks on me; **et le ~ est joué** that's done the trick; **un peu de peinture et le ~ est joué** a bit of paint will do the trick; **ça te jouera des ~s** it's going to get you into trouble one of these days; ▶ **pendable**, **sac**; **9** (manipulation habile) trick; **~ de cartes** card trick; **~ de prestidigitation** conjuring trick; **~ d'adresse** feat of skill; **~ de main** knack; **en un ~ de main** (habilement) deftly; (rapidement) in a flash; **~ de force** gén amazing feat; (performance) tour de force; **constituer un ~ de force** to be an amazing feat; **réussir le ~ de force de faire** to achieve the amazing feat of doing; ▶ **passe-passe**; **10** (allure, aspect) (de situation, relations) turn; (de création, mode) twist; **~ (de phrase)** Ling turn of phrase; **le ~ qu'ont pris les événements** the turn events have taken; **donner un ~ nouveau à qch** to give a new twist to sth; **c'est un ~ assez rare en français** it's a somewhat unusual turn of phrase in French; **11** Tech (machine-outil) lathe; **fait au ~**† [*jambe, corps*] shapely.

II *nf* **1** Archit tower; (immeuble) tower block GB, high rise US; **2** Jeux (d'échecs) rook, castle; **3** Hist Mil (machine de guerre) siege-tower.

■ **~ de Babel** Relig, Ling, fig Tower of Babel; **~ de chant** Art, Mus song recital; **~ de contrôle** Aviat control tower; **~ Eiffel** Eiffel Tower; **~ de forage** Tech derrick; **~ de France** (de cycliste) Tour de France; (de compagnon) *journeyman's travelling*[GB] *apprenticeship*; **~ de garde** Mil turn of duty; **~ de guet** Mil watchtower; **~ d'ivoire** fig ivory tower; **s'enfermer** or **se retrancher dans sa ~ d'ivoire** to shut oneself away in an ivory tower; **~ de Londres** Tower of London; **~ mort** Naut round turn; **~ de Pise** Leaning Tower of Pisa; **~ de potier** Art potter's wheel; **~ de refroidissement** Nucl cooling tower; **~ de rein(s)** Méd back strain; **se donner** or **attraper un ~ de rein(s)** to strain one's back; **~ de table** Fin pool; **faire un ~ de table** (à un réunion) to sound out everybody ou to go round GB ou around US the table; **après un rapide ~ de table** having gone round GB ou around US the table quickly (to see what people think).

tourbe /tuʀb/ *nf* peat; **un feu de ~** a peat fire.

tourbeux, -euse /tuʀbø, øz/ *adj* peaty.

tourbière /tuʀbjɛʀ/ *nf* peat bog.

tourbillon /tuʀbijɔ̃/ *nm* **1** Météo (masse d'air) whirlwind; **2** (masse d'eau) whirlpool; **3** (mouvement en spirale) whirl; **~ de poussière/feuilles** whirl of dust/leaves; **4** fig (de souvenirs) swirl; (de réformes) whirlwind, maelstrom; **le ~ de la vie** the merry-go-round of life.

tourbillonnement /tuʀbijɔnmɑ̃/ *nm* (de neige, feuilles) swirling, whirling; (de danseurs) twirling.

tourbillonner /tuʀbijɔne/ [1] *vi* **1** lit [*neige, feuilles*] to swirl, to whirl; [*danseurs*] to twirl; **2** fig [*idées, souvenirs*] to swirl around.

tourelle /tuʀɛl/ *nf* **1** Archit turret; **2** (de char) turret; (de sous-marin) conning tower; **3** Phot **~ d'objectifs** lens turret.

tourière /tuʀjɛʀ/ *adj f* Relig **sœur ~** sister at convent gate.

tourillon /tuʀijɔ̃/ *nm* Tech swivel pin GB, kingpin US.

tourisme /tuʀism/ *nm* **1** (activité de loisir) tourism; **faire du ~** to tour around, to go sightseeing; **ils ont fait un peu de ~** they toured around a bit, they did a bit of sightseeing; ▶ **grand**; **2** (activité économique) tourist industry; **l'industrie du ~** the tourist industry.

■ **~ vert** countryside holidays (*pl*) GB ou vacations (*pl*) US.

touriste /tuʀist/ *nmf* tourist; **j'ai séjourné à Lima en ~** I stayed in Lima as a tourist; **il suit les cours en ~** he goes to his lessons whenever he feels like it.

touristique /tuʀistik/ *adj* **1** (relatif au tourisme) [*brochure, menu, saison*] tourist (*épith*); [*afflux*] of tourists (*épith, après n*); **2** (qui attire les touristes) [*ville, circuit*] which attracts tourists (*épith, après n*), touristy○; **c'est une région très ~** the area attracts a lot of tourists.

tourment /tuʀmɑ̃/ *nm* liter **1** (douleur morale) torment; **donner des ~s à qn** to be a torment for sb; **2**‡ (supplice) torture ¢.

tourmente /tuʀmɑ̃t/ *nf* liter **1** (tempête) storm; **2** fml (trouble) turmoil.

tourmenté, ~e /tuʀmɑ̃te/ **I** *pp* ▶ **tourmenter**.

II *pp adj* **1** (très inquiet) [*personne, visage*] tormented; [*expression, âme, esprit*] tortured; **2** (très agité) [*époque, histoire*] turbulent; [*mer*] turbulent; [*vie*] turbulent; **3** (irrégulier) [*paysage*] rugged; [*forme*] contorted; **4** (tarabiscoté) [*style*] tortured; [*parcours*] tortuous.

tourmenter /tuʀmɑ̃te/ [1] **I** *vtr* **1** (inquiéter) to worry [*personne*]; **2** (faire souffrir) [*persécuteur, douleur, remords, doute*] to torment [*personne*]; **~ des animaux** to torment animals; **~ qn de reproches** to torment sb with reproaches; **3** (harceler) [*créancier*] to harass [*débiteur*].

II se tourmenter *vpr* to worry.

tourmenteur, -euse /tuʀmɑ̃tœʀ, øz/ *nm,f* liter tormenter.

tournage /tuʀnaʒ/ *nm* **1** Cin (prise de vues) shooting ¢, filming ¢; (lieu de réalisation) set; **le ~ d'un film/d'une scène** the shooting of a film/of a scene; **pendant le ~** during shooting; **les gens qui sont sur le ~** the people on set; **ils se sont rencontrés sur le ~** they met on (the) set; **le film est en cours de ~** the film is being shot; **entre deux ~s** between two films; **2** Tech turning; **~ du bois/du métal** wood-/metal-turning.

tournailler○ /tuʀnaje/ [1] *vi* **~ dans tous les sens** to wander about; **~ autour de qn** to hang around sb.

tournant, ~e /tuʀnɑ̃, ɑ̃t/ **I** *adj* **1** (qui pivote) [*siège, mécanisme*] swivel (*épith*); [*jet*] rotating; [*scène, porte*] revolving; **2** (qui fait des détours) [*mouvement*] turning (*épith*); [*service, bibliothèque*] mobile; **3** (qui alterne) [*poste, présidence*] rotating (*épith*); [*action politique, mesure*] staggered.

II *nm* **1** (virage) bend; **prendre un ~** [*conducteur, voiture*] to take a bend; **2** (événement) turning point; **marquer un ~** to mark a turning point; **~ décisif/historique** crucial/historic turning point; **3** (charnière) turn; **au ~ du siècle** at the turn of the century; **4** (orientation) change of direction; **faire prendre un ~ à qch** to make a change of direction in sth; **prendre un ~** to change tack.

IDIOMES **je t'aurai au ~**○! I'll get my own back!; **je les attends au ~**○! I'll make sure they get their just deserts!

tourné, ~e /tuʀne/ **I** *pp* ▶ **tourner**.

II *pp adj* **1** (orienté) **~ vers** [*regard, yeux, personne*] turned toward(s); [*activité, opération, politique*] oriented toward(s); [*ouverture, maison, passage*] facing (*épith, après n*); **~ vers le passé** backward-looking; **porte ~e vers la mer** gate facing the sea; **~ vers l'avenir** forward-looking; **2** (fait) **bien ~** [*compliment, lettre*] nicely phrased; [*personne, taille*] shapely; **expression bien ~e** well-turned phrase; **mal ~** [*phrase*] clumsy; [*lettre*] poorly phrased; ▶ **esprit**; **3** (façonné au tour) turned; **4** (aigri) [*lait, crème*] sour, off (*jamais épith*); [*sauce*] off (*jamais épith*).

III tournée *nf* **1** (de facteur, laitier, représentant) round; (de politicien) **~ (électorale)** election tour; (d'équipe, de chanteur, troupe) tour; **~e de promotion** promotional tour; **faire sa ~e** [*facteur*] to do one's round; **en ~e** [*orchestre, troupe*] on tour; **être/partir en ~e** to be/to go on tour; **2**○ (au café) round; **c'est ma ~e !** it's my round!; **offrir une ~e générale** to pay for drinks all round GB ou around US; **3**○ (rossée) beating; **prendre une ~e** to take a beating; **mettre une ~e à qn** to give sb a beating.

tournebouler○† /tuʀnəbule/ [1] *vtr* to upset.

tournebroche /tuʀnəbʀɔʃ/ *nm* (rotating) spit.

tourne-disque, *pl* **~s** /tuʀnədisk/ *nm* record player.

tournedos /tuʀnədo/ *nm inv* tournedos.

tournemain: **en un tournemain** /ɑ̃nɛ̃tuʀnəmɛ̃/ *loc adv* in no time.

tourner /tuʀne/ [1] **I** *vtr* **1** (faire pivoter) to turn [*volant, clé, bouton, meuble*]; **~ la tête vers** to turn to look at; **~ les yeux vers** to look at; **le bruit m'a fait ~ la tête** I looked around at the noise; ▶**bouche**, **tête**; **2** Cin to shoot [*film, scène*]; **scène tournée à Pékin** scene shot in Beijing; ▶**bout**; **3** (éluder) to get around [*difficulté, obstacle, problème, loi*]; **4** (formuler) to phrase [*lettre, compliment, critique*]; **il tourne bien ses phrases** he has a nice turn of phrase; **il tourne mal ses phrases** he doesn't have a very elegant turn of phrase; **5** Tech (façonner) to turn [*bois, pièce*]; to throw [*pot*]; **6** (transformer) **~ qn en dérision** or **ridicule** to make sb a laughing stock; **~ qch en dérision** to make a mockery of sth; **7** (orienter) to turn [*pensées, attention*] (**vers** to); to direct [*colère*] (**contre** against); **8** (envisager) **~ et retourner qch dans son esprit** to mull sth over; **~ une proposition en tous sens pour en trouver les implications** to look at a proposal from every angle to work out the implications; **9** (remuer) to stir [*sauce*]; to toss [*salade*].

II *vi* **1** (pivoter) gén [*clé, disque*] to turn; [*roue*] to turn, to revolve; [*planète, rotor, hélice*] to rotate; [*porte à gonds*] to swing; [*porte à tambour*] to revolve; (rapidement) [*toupie, étoile, particule, danseur*] to spin; **~ sur soi-même** to spin around; **faire ~** gén to turn; (rapidement) to spin; **danseur qui fait ~ sa partenaire** dancer spinning his partner around; **faire ~ les tables** (en spiritisme) to do table-turning; ▶**heure**, **œil**, **tête**; **2** (graviter) **~ autour de** gén to turn around; [*planète, étoile*] to revolve around; [*avion*] to circle; **~ au-dessus de** [*hélicoptère, oiseau*] to circle over; [*insecte*] to buzz around; **3** (aller et venir) **~ (en rond)** [*personne*] to go around and around; [*automobiliste*] to drive around and around; **~ en rond** fig [*discussion, négociations*] to go around in circles; **ça fait une heure qu'on tourne** (en voiture) we've been driving around for an hour; **il tourne dans son bureau depuis une heure** he has been pacing up and down in his office for the last hour; ▶**cage**, **pot**; **4** (virer) to turn (**vers** toward, towards GB); **tournez à gauche** turn left; **le chemin tourne entre les arbres** the path winds between the trees; ▶**chance**, **vent**; **5** (se situer) **~ autour de** [*effectifs, somme d'argent*] to be (somewhere) in the region of, to be round about○ GB, to be around; **6** (fonctionner) [*moteur, usine, entreprise*] to run; **~ rond** [*moteur*] to run smoothly; [*entreprise, affaires*] to be doing well; **l'usine tourne au tiers de sa capacité** the factory is running at one third of its capacity; **les affaires tournent (bien)** business is good; **faire ~ qch** to run sth [*entreprise*]; **il y a quelque chose qui ne tourne pas rond dans cette histoire**○ there's something fishy○ about this business; **mon frère ne tourne pas rond depuis quelque temps**○ my brother has been acting strangely for some time; **7** (évoluer) **comment ont tourné les choses?** how did things turn out?; **les choses ont bien/mal tourné pour lui** things turned out well/badly for him; **leur frère a mal tourné** their brother turned out badly; **leur réunion a mal tourné** their meeting went badly; **~ à l'avantage de qn/au désavantage de qn** to swing in sb's favour^GB/against sb; **la réunion a tourné à la bagarre /en mascarade** the meeting turned into a brawl/into a farce; **mon rhume a tourné en bronchite** my cold turned into bronchitis; **8** Cin [*réalisateur*] to shoot, to film; [*acteur*] to make a film GB ou movie US; **~ dans un film** [*acteur*] to make a film GB ou movie US; **~ en Espagne** to shoot in Spain; **elle a tourné avec les plus grands acteurs** she's worked with top actors; **silence, on tourne!** quiet everyone, we're shooting!; **9** (faire une tournée) [*représentant, spectacle*] to tour; **troupe de théâtre qui tourne en Europe** theatre^GB company touring (in) Europe; **le spectacle a tourné dans toute la France** the show went all over France on tour; **10** (fermenter) [*lait, sauce, viande*] to go off; **11** (chercher à séduire) **~ autour de qn** to hang around sb; **qu'est-ce qu'il a à me ~ autour**○**?** why doesn't he leave me alone?

III se tourner *vpr* **1** (se diriger, par intérêt ou besoin) **se ~ vers** or **du côté de qn/qch** to turn to sb/sth; **se ~ vers la botanique/un ami** to turn to botany/a friend; **se ~ du côté du mysticisme** to turn to mysticism; **ne pas savoir vers qui se ~/de quel côté se ~** not to know who to turn to/which way to turn; **de quelque côté qu'on se tourne** whichever way you turn; **2** (changer de position) **se ~ vers qn/qch** to turn toward(s) sb/sth; **tous les yeux se sont tournés vers elle** all eyes turned toward(s) her; **nous nous sommes tournés dans la direction d'où venait le bruit** we turned in the direction of the noise; **3** (faire demi-tour sur soi-même) to turn around; **tournez-vous, je me change!** turn around, I'm changing!; **tourne-toi, que je voie ta coupe de cheveux** turn around and let me see your haircut; **tourne-toi un peu plus sur la** or **à gauche** just turn a little bit more to the left; **se ~ et se retourner dans son lit** to toss and turn; ▶**pouce**.

tournesol /tuʀnəsɔl/ *nm* **1** Bot sunflower; **2** Chimie litmus; **papier ~** litmus paper.

tourneur, -euse /tuʀnœʀ, øz/ ▶**510** *nm,f* **1** Tech turner; (sur machine industrielle) lathe operator; **~ sur bois** woodturner; **atelier de ~** turnery; **2** Tex reeler.

tournevis /tuʀnəvis/ *nm inv* screwdriver.
■ **~ à cliquet** ratchet screwdriver; **~ cruciforme** Phillips® screwdriver; **~ électrique** power screwdriver.

tournicoter○ /tuʀnikɔte/ [1] *vi* **~ autour de qn/qch** to hang around sb/sth.

tourniquet /tuʀnikɛ/ *nm* **1** (barrière) turnstile; **2** (présentoir) revolving stand; **~ à cartes postales** revolving postcard stand; **3** (d'arrosage) sprinkler; **4** (de chirurgie) tourniquet; **5** (de volet) hook; **6** Naut roller.

tournis○ /tuʀni/ *nm* **avoir le ~** to feel ou be dizzy ou giddy; **donner le ~ à qn** to make sb dizzy ou giddy.

tournoi /tuʀnwa/ *nm* gén tournament; **le Tournoi des Cinq Nations** the Five Nations Championship; **~ oratoire** liter debating contest.

tournoiement /tuʀnwamɑ̃/ *nm* (de feuilles) swirling (**de** of); (de moucherons) circling (**de** of); (danseurs) whirling (**de** of).

tournoyer /tuʀnwaje/ [23] *vi* **1** [*feuilles, papiers*] to swirl around; [*vautours*] to wheel; [*moucherons*] to fly around in circles; [*cerf-volant*] to spiral; **2** [*danseurs*] to whirl; **faire ~** (en dansant) to spin [sb] around; to twirl [sth] [*baguette, jupe*]; to make [sth] spiral [*cerf-volant*]; **3** [*fumée*] to rise in spirals.

tournure /tuʀnyʀ/ *nf* **1** (aspect) turn; **la ~ des événements** the turn of events; **prendre une ~ imprévue** to take an unexpected turn; **prendre bonne ~** to take a turn for the better; **prendre une ~ fâcheuse** or **mauvaise** to go wrong; **je n'aime pas la ~ que prend la situation** I don't like the way the situation is developing; **prendre ~** [*projet*] to take shape; **cela donne à l'affaire une tout autre ~** this puts a completely different complexion on things; **2** (formulation) turn of phrase; **~ idiomatique/dialectale/familière** idiomatic/dialectal/colloquial expression.
■ **~ d'esprit** frame of mind.

touron /tuʀɔ̃/ *nm* ≈ nougat.

tour-opérateur, *pl* **~s** /tuʀɔpeʀatœʀ/ *nm* controv tour operator.

tourte /tuʀt/ *nf* pie; **~ à la viande** meat pie; **~ aux poireaux/aux abricots** leek/apricot pie.

tourteau, *pl* **~x** /tuʀto/ *nm* **1** Culin, Zool crab; **2** Agric oil cake.

tourtereau, *pl* **~x** /tuʀtəʀo/ **I** *nm* Zool young turtle dove.
II tourtereaux *nmpl* hum (personnes) lovebirds hum.

tourterelle /tuʀtəʀɛl/ *nf* turtle dove.

tourtière /tuʀtjɛʀ/ *nf* pie dish.

tous ▶**tout**.

Toussaint /tusɛ̃/ *nf* **la ~** (jour) All Saints' Day; **à la ~** (jour) on All Saints' Day; (période) at the end of October, at Halloween US; **un temps de ~** autumnal ou fall US weather.

tousser /tuse/ [1] *vi* **1** Méd to cough; **2** (pour attirer l'attention) to cough; **3** [*moteur, voiture*] to splutter.

toussotement /tusɔtmɑ̃/ *nm* **1** Méd slight cough; **2** (pour attirer l'attention) cough; **3** (d'un moteur) splutter.

toussoter /tusɔte/ [1] *vi* **1** Méd (habituellement) to have a slight cough; (ponctuellement) to cough slightly; **2** (pour attirer l'attention) to cough; **3** [*moteur, voiture*] to splutter.

tout /tu/, **~e** /tut/, *mpl* **tous** /tu *adj*, tus *pron*/, *fpl* **toutes** /tut/ **I** *pron indéf* **1 tout** (chaque chose) everything; (n'importe quoi) anything; (l'ensemble) all; **penser à ~** to think of everything; **~ est prêt** everything is ready; **le sucre, les graisses, le sel, ~ me fait mal** sugar, fat, salt, everything is bad for me; **être ~ pour qn** to be everything to sb; **~ peut arriver** anything can happen; **le chien mange (de) ~** the dog will eat anything; **~ est prétexte à querelle(s)** any pretext will do to start a quarrel; **~ n'est pas perdu** all is not lost; **~ ou rien** all or nothing; **~ ou partie de qch** all or part of sth; **~ va bien** all's well, everything's fine; **en ~** (au total) in all; (entièrement) in every respect; **en ~ et pour ~** all told; **et ~ ça parce que/pour** and all because/for; **~ bien compté** or **pesé** or **considéré** all in all; **~ est là** fig that's the whole point; **c'est ~ dire** I need say no more; **et ~ et ~**○ and all that sort of thing; **et ce n'est pas ~!** and that's not all!; **ce n'est pas ~ (que) de commencer un travail, il faut le finir** it's not enough ou it's all very well to start off a job, it's got to be finished; **avoir ~ d'un singe/assassin** to look just like a monkey/murderer; ▶**bien**, **monde**, **salaire**, **or**; **2 tous** /tus/, **toutes** (la totalité des êtres ou choses) all; (la totalité des éléments d'une catégorie, d'un groupe) all of them/us/you; **nous sommes tous des pécheurs** we are all sinners; **le film n'est pas à la portée de tous** the film is not accessible to all; **merci à tous** thank you all; **tous ensemble** all together; **ce sont tous d'anciens soldats** all of them are ou they are all former soldiers; **il les a tous cassés** he has broken all of them, he's broken them all; **il l'a dit devant nous tous** he said it in front of all of us; **leurs enfants, tous musiciens de talent** their children, all of them talented musicians; **tous ne sont pas d'accord** not all of them agree; **~es tant qu'elles sont** all of them, each and every one of them; **vous tous qui le connaissez** all of you who know him; **écoutez-moi tous** listen to me, all of you; **est-ce que ça conviendra à tous?** will it suit everybody ou everyone?

II *adj* **1** (exprimant la totalité) **bois ~ ton lait** drink all your milk, drink up your milk; **~ le reste est à jeter** everything else is to be thrown away; **manger ~ un pain** to eat a whole loaf; **~ Pompéi a été enseveli** the whole of Pompeii was buried; **~ Nice se réjouit** the whole of ou all Nice rejoiced; **il a plu ~e la journée** it rained all day (long) ou the whole day; **pendant ~e une année** for a whole year; **la semaine se passa ~e à attendre** the whole ou entire week was spent waiting; **j'ai passé ~ mon dimanche à travailler** I spent the whole of ou all Sunday working; **je ne l'ai pas vu de ~**

tout

Quand *tout* fait partie d'une locution comme *à tout hasard, de toute(s) part(s), tout compte fait, tout nu, tout neuf, tout plein, tout simplement* etc., la traduction sera donnée sous le terme principal.

Remarques sur l'adjectif

1 Lorsque *tout*, adjectif singulier, exprime la totalité, plusieurs traductions sont possibles mais non toujours interchangeables.

De manière générale:

on emploiera *all* lorsque le mot qualifié est non dénombrable

tout le vin = all the wine
tout l'argent = all the money
tout ce bruit = all that noise
tout leur talent = all their talent
c'est tout ce que je sais = that's all I know

on emploiera *whole* si *tout* peut être remplacé par *entier*

tout le gâteau = the whole cake
tout le groupe = the whole group
tout un livre = a whole book

Mais:

connaître tout Zola/le Japon = to know the whole of Zola/Japan
lire tout 'Les Misérables' = to read the whole of 'Les Misérables'
pendant tout mon séjour = for the whole of my stay

2 *throughout* (ou *all through*) signifie *du début à la fin, d'un bout à l'autre*. On l'emploie souvent pour insister sur la durée ou l'étendue devant un terme singulier ou pluriel qui désigne l'espace de temps ou l'événement pendant lequel un fait a lieu, ou encore le territoire sur lequel il a lieu:

pendant tout le match = throughout the match
pendant tous ces mois = throughout those months
la rumeur se répandit dans toute la province = the rumour spread throughout the province
faire tout le trajet debout = to stand throughout the journey *ou* to stand for the whole journey
il neige sur toute la France = it's snowing throughout France *ou* it's snowing all over France

Au pluriel, *tous, toutes* se traduiront par *all* pour exprimer la totalité, par *every* pour insister sur les composants d'un ensemble, ou encore par *any* pour indiquer l'absence de discrimination. On notera que *every* et *any* sont suivis du singulier.

l'été I haven't seen him all summer; **cet enfant est ~e ma vie** this child is my whole life; **c'est ~ le plaisir que tu y trouves?** is that all the pleasure ou the only pleasure it gives you?; **~ le problème est là** that's where the problem lies; **~ cela ne compte pas** none of that counts; **le meilleur dentiste de ~e la ville** the best dentist in town; **~ le monde** everybody; ▸ **cœur, monde, temps**; **2** (véritable) **c'est ~ un travail/événement** it's quite a job/ an event; **il a fait ~e une histoire** he made a real ou big fuss, he made quite a fuss; **c'est ~ un art** there's a whole art to it; **3 tout ce qui/que/dont** (l'ensemble) all; (toutes les choses) everything; (sans discrimination) anything; **~ ce qui compte** all that matters; **c'est ~ ce que je fais** that's all I do; **~ ce dont j'ai besoin** all I need; **j'ai acheté ~ ce qui était sur la liste** I bought everything that was on the list; **il dit ~ ce qui lui passe par la tête** he says anything that comes into his head; **~ ce qu'il dit n'est pas vrai** not all of what he says is true; **~ ce que le village compte d'enfants, ~ ce qu'il y a d'enfants dans le village** all the children in the village; **être ~ ce qu'il y a de plus serviable** to be most obliging; **c'est ~ ce qu'on fait de mieux** it's the best there is; **'tu en es sûr?'—'~ ce qu'il y a de plus sûr'** 'are you sure?'—'as sure as can be', 'absolutely sure'; **4** (n'importe quel) any; **à ~ âge** at any age; **de ~e nature** of any kind; **à ~e heure du jour ou de la nuit** at all times of the day or night; **'service à ~e heure'** '24 hour service'; **à ~ moment** (n'importe quand) at any time; (sans cesse) constantly; **~ prétexte leur est bon** they'll jump at any excuse; **~e personne qui** anyone ou anybody who; **~e autre solution serait rejetée** any other solution would be rejected; **~ autre que lui/toi aurait abandonné** anybody else would have given up; **~e publicité est interdite** all advertising is prohibited; **pour ~e réclamation, s'adresser à...** all complaints should be addressed to...; **~ billet n'est pas valable** not all tickets are valid; ▸ **vérité**; **5** (sans déterminant: total) **en ~e innocence/franchise** in all innocence/honesty; **en ~e liberté** with complete freedom; **donner ~e satisfaction** to give complete satisfaction; **c'est ~ bénéfice** it's all profit; **il aurait ~ intérêt à placer cet argent** it would be in his best interests to invest this money; **partir en ~e hâte** to leave in a great hurry; **un jardin de ~e beauté** a most beautiful garden; **être à ~e extrémité** to be close to death; ▸ **épreuve, hasard, prix, vitesse**; **6** (unique, seul) **il a souri pour ~e réponse** his only reply was a smile, he smiled by way of a reply; **on lui donne quelques légumes pour tous gages** all that he gets in the way of wages is a few vegetables; **elle a un chien pour ~e compagnie** the only company she has ou all she has for company is a dog; **7 tous, toutes** (les uns et les autres sans distinction) all, every (+ *sg*); **ceci vaut pour tous les candidats** this applies to all candidates ou to every candidate; **en tous pays** in all countries, in every country; **en ~es choses** in all things, in everything; **~es les pages sont déchirées** all the pages are torn, every page is torn; **les lettres ont ~es été signées** the letters have all been signed; **j'ai ~es les raisons de me plaindre** I have every reason to complain; **tous les hommes sont mortels** all men are mortal; **il a fait tous les métiers** he's done all sorts of jobs; **tous les prétextes leur sont bons** they'll use any excuse (**pour** to); **meubles tous budgets** furniture to suit every pocket; **tous deux se levèrent** both of them got up, they both got up; **nous irons tous les deux** both of us will go, we'll both go; **je les prends tous les trois/quatre etc** I'm taking all three/four etc (of them); **8** (chaque) **tous/toutes les** every; **à tous les coins de rue** on every street corner; **saisir ~es les occasions** to seize every opportunity; **tous les jours/mois/ans** every day/month/ year; **tous les quarts d'heure/10 mètres** every quarter of an hour/10 metres; **un cachet ~es les quatre heures** one tablet every four hours; **tous les deux jours/mois** every other day/month; **tous les combien?** how often?

III *adv* (*normally invariable, but agrees in gender and in number with feminine adjective beginning with consonant or h-aspirate*) **1** (très, extrêmement) very, quite; (entièrement) all; **~ doucement** very gently; **ils sont ~ contents** they are very happy; **elles sont ~ étonnées/~es honteuses** they are very surprised/ashamed; **être ~ excité** to be very ou all excited; **être ~ jeune/ petit** to be very young/small; **~ enfant, elle aimait déjà dessiner** as a small child she already liked to draw; **c'est ~ naturel** it's quite natural; **des yeux ~ ronds de surprise** eyes wide with surprise; **être ~ mouillé/sale** to be all wet/dirty; **~ seul dans la vie** all alone in life; **faire qch ~ seul** to do sth all by oneself; **c'est ~ autre chose, c'est une ~ autre histoire** it's a different matter altogether; **2** (devant un nom) **c'est ~ le portrait de sa mère** she's the spitting ou very image of her mother; **c'est ~ l'inverse** or **le contraire** it's the very opposite; **ça m'en a ~ l'air** it looks very much like it to me; **tu as ~ le temps d'y réfléchir** you've got plenty of time to think it over; **avec toi, c'est ~ l'un ou ~ l'autre** you see everything in black and white; **3** (tout à fait) **la ~e dernière ligne** the very last line; **les ~ premiers fruits de l'été** the very first fruits of summer; **j'habite ~ près** I live very close by ou very near; **~ près de** very close to, very near; **~ à côté de/contre/en haut** right by/against/at the top; **il les a mangés ~ crus** he ate them raw; **un gâteau ~ entier** a whole cake; **j'en sais ~ autant que lui** I know just as much as he does; **c'est ~ aussi cher** it's just as expensive; **vêtue ~ de noir, ~ de noir vêtue** dressed all in black; **maison ~ en longueur** very long and narrow house; **un jeu ~ en finesse** a very subtle game; **une semaine ~e de fatigue** a very tiring week; **une vie ~e de soucis** a life full of worry; **ils étaient ~ en sang/en sueur** they were covered in blood/bathed in sweat; **être ~ en larmes** to be in floods of tears; **la colline est ~ en fleurs** the hill is a mass of flowers; **elle est ~(e) à son travail** she's totally absorbed in her work; **4** (d'avance) **~ prêt** ready-made; **sauces/ idées ~es faites** ready-made sauces/ideas; **des légumes ~ épluchés** ready-peeled vegetables; ▸ **cuit, vu**; **5** (en même temps) while; (bien que) although; **il lisait ~ en marchant** he was reading as he walked; **elle le défendait ~ en le sachant coupable** she defended him although she knew he was guilty; ▸ **en**; **6** (marquant la concession: quoique) **~ aussi étrange que cela paraisse** however strange it may seem; **~ prudemment que l'on conduise** however carefully one drives; **~ malins qu'ils sont, ils...** clever though they may be, they..., they may be clever, but they...; **~e reine qu'elle est, elle ne peut pas faire ça** she may be a queen, but she can't do that; **7** (rien d'autre que) **être ~ énergie/muscle** to be all energy/muscle; **être ~ sourires** to be all smiles; **je suis ~ ouïe** hum I'm all ears; **veste ~ cuir/laine** all leather/wool jacket; ▸ **feu, sucre**.

IV du tout *loc adv* **pas du ~, point du ~** liter not at all; **sans savoir du ~** without knowing at all; **je ne le vois plus du ~** I don't see him at all now; **il ne m'en reste plus du ~** I have none left at all; **crois-tu qu'il m'ait remercié? du ~!** do you think he thanked me? not at all!

V *nm* (*pl* **~s**) **1** (ensemble) **former un ~** to make up ou form a whole; **mon ~** (charade) my whole, my all; **du ~ au ~** completely; **2 le ~** (la totalité) the whole lot, the lot; (l'essentiel) the main thing; **vendre le ~ pour 200 francs** to sell the (whole) lot for 200 francs; **le ~ est de réussir/qu'il réussisse** the main ou most important thing is to succeed/that he should succeed; **le Grand Tout** Relig the Great Whole; **ce n'est pas le ~**○**!** this is no good!

VI tout- (*in compounds*) **le Tout-Paris/ -Londres** the Paris/London smart set.

■ **~ à coup** suddenly; **~ d'un coup** (soudain) suddenly; (à la fois) all at once; **~ à fait** (entièrement) quite, absolutely; **ce n'est pas ~ à fait vrai/pareil** it's not quite

true/the same thing; **c'est ~ à fait vrai** it's quite ou absolutely true; **'tu es d'accord?'—'~ à fait'** 'do you agree?'—'absolutely'; **il est ~ à fait charmant** he's absolutely ou perfectly charming; **être ~ à fait pour/contre** to be totally for/against; **~ à l'heure** (bientôt) in a moment; (peu avant) a little while ago, just now; **à ~ à l'heure!** see you later!; **~ de même** (quand même) all the same, even so; (indigné) **~ de même!** really!, honestly!; (vraiment) quite; **tu aurais ~ de même pu faire attention!** all the same ou even so you might have been careful!; **c'est ~ de même un peu fort!** really ou honestly, it's a bit much!; **c'est ~ de même bizarre que** it's quite strange that; **~ de suite** at once, straight away; **ce n'est pas pour ~ de suite** (ce n'est pas pressé) there's no rush; (ce sera long) it's going to take some time.
IDIOMES **~ est bien qui finit bien** all's well that ends well; **être ~ yeux ~ oreilles** to be very attentive.

tout-à-l'égout /tutalegu/ *nm inv* main drainage; **installer le ~** to install main drainage; **avoir le ~** to be on the main drains.

Toutankhamon /tutɑ̃kamɔ̃/ *npr* Tutankhamun, Tutankhamen.

toutefois /tutfwa/ *adv* however; **il a ~ précisé que** however, he made it clear that; **sans ~ que cela nuise à l'ensemble** without this spoiling the overall effect, however; **je viendrai demain, si ~ ça ne vous dérange pas** I'll come tomorrow, as long as that doesn't put you out.

toute-puissance /tutpɥisɑ̃s/ *nf* (de Dieu, d'argent, de dictateur) omnipotence; (de pays, d'entreprise) supremacy.

toutim(e)◑ /tutim/ *nm* **le ~** the whole caboodle○, the whole lot.

toutou○ /tutu/ *nm* doggie○, dog; **un bon ~** a nice doggie○; **suivre qn comme un ~** to follow sb around like a little dog.

tout-petit, *pl* **~s** /tup(ə)ti/ *nm* (nourrisson) baby; (très jeune enfant) toddler.

tout-puissant, **toute-puissante**, *pl* **~s**, **toutes-puissantes** /tupɥisɑ̃, tut pɥisɑ̃t/ **I** *adj* all-powerful; **le ~ patron** the all-powerful boss.
II *nmpl* **les ~s de ce monde** the all-powerful of this world.

Tout-Puissant /tupɥisɑ̃/ *nm* Relig **le ~** the Almighty, God Almighty.

tout-venant /tuv(ə)nɑ̃/ *nm inv* **1** gén (personnes) all and sundry; **il n'a pas choisi, il a pris le ~** he did not make a choice, he just took whatever there was; **2** Mines run of mine, unsorted coal.

toux /tu/ *nf inv* cough; **une ~ sèche/grasse** a dry/loose cough; **médicament pour** or **contre la ~** cough medicine; **avoir une quinte de ~** to have a coughing fit.

toxémie /tɔksemi/ *nf* toxaemia[GB], blood poisoning.

toxicité /tɔksisite/ *nf* toxicity.

toxicodépendance /tɔksikodepɑ̃dɑ̃s/ *nf* drug dependency.

toxicodépendant, **~e** /tɔksikodepɑ̃dɑ̃, ɑ̃t/ *nm,f* drug addict.

toxicologie /tɔksikɔlɔʒi/ *nf* toxicology.

toxicologique /tɔksikɔlɔʒik/ *adj* toxicological.

toxicologue /tɔksikɔlɔg/ **▶510** *nmf* toxicologist.

toxicomane /tɔksikɔman/ *nmf* drug addict.

toxicomanie /tɔksikɔmani/ *nf* drug addiction.

toxicose /tɔksikoz/ *nf* toxicosis; **~ du nourrisson** or **du nouveau-né** infant toxicosis.

toxine /tɔksin/ *nf* toxin.

toxique /tɔksik/ **I** *adj* toxic, poisonous; **non ~** non toxic.
II *nm* toxin, poison.

toxoplasmose /tɔksɔplasmoz/ **▶271** *nf* toxoplasmosis.

TP /tepe/ *nm: abbr* ▶ **travail**[1]

TPV /tepeve/ *nm: abbr* ▶ **terminal**.

trac○ /tʀak/ *nm* (sur scène, devant une caméra) stage fright; (avant un examen, une conférence) nerves (*pl*); **avoir le ~** gén to feel nervous; (sur scène) to have stage fright; **donner le ~ à qn** [*situation, pensée, personne*] to put the wind up sb○, to scare sb; **tout à ~** out of the blue.

traçage /tʀasaʒ/ *nm* **1** (dessin) Ind, Naut marking out; Constr laying-out; Cout marking (**de** of); **2** Mines heading, drift; **3** Ordinat tracing.
■ **~ à la vapeur** Tech steam tracing.

traçant, **~e** /tʀasɑ̃, ɑ̃t/ *adj* **1** Ordinat **table ~e** graph plotter; **2** Mil **balle ~e** tracer (bullet); **3** Bot [*racine*] creeping.

tracas /tʀaka/ *nm inv* **1** (provoqué) trouble; **donner** or **valoir du ~ à qn** to put sb to a lot of trouble; **2** (subi) problems (*pl*); **~ quotidiens** everyday problems; **3** (inquiétude) worries (*pl*); **se faire du ~ pour** or **au sujet de qn/qch** to worry about sb/sth.

tracasser /tʀakase/ [1] **I** *vtr* [*santé, problème, attitude*] to bother [*personne*].
II se tracasser *vpr* **1** (s'inquiéter) to worry (**pour qn** about sb; **au sujet de qch, pour qch** about sth); **ne vous tracassez pas!** don't worry; **2** (être dérangé) **se ~ à faire** to have the bother of doing.

tracasserie /tʀakasʀi/ *nf* **1** (ennui) hassle○ ₡; **les ~s de la vie moderne** the hassle○ of modern life; **2** (harcèlement) harassment ₡; **les ~s administratives à l'encontre des étrangers** harassment of foreigners by the authorities.

tracassier, **-ière** /tʀakasje, ɛʀ/ *adj* [*administration, organisme*] nit-picking, full of red tape.

trace /tʀas/ *nf* **1** (piste) trail; **perdre la ~ d'un animal** to lose an animal's tracks; **retrouver la ~ d'un voleur/des tableaux volés** to pick up the trail of a thief/of the stolen paintings; **suivre qn à la ~** lit to track sb; fig to follow sb's trail; **faire la ~** (au ski) to blaze the ou a trail; **skier dans la ~ de qn** to ski in sb's tracks; **2** (empreinte) **~s** tracks; **~s d'ours/de ski** bear's/ski tracks; **~s de pneus** tyre GB ou tire US tracks; **~s de pas** footprints, footmarks; **repartir sur ses ~s** lit, fig to retrace one's steps; **marcher sur** or **suivre les ~s de qn** fig to follow in sb's footsteps; **un itinéraire touristique sur les ~s de Van Gogh** fig a tourist route following in the steps of Van Gogh; **3** (marque) (de brûlure) mark; (cicatrice) scar; (de peinture) mark; (de sang, d'humidité) trace; **~s de freinage** skidmarks; **~s de doigts** fingermarks; **~s de coups** (bleus) bruises; **l'enfant a des ~s suspectes** the child has some suspicious marks ou bruises; **~s de fatigue sur le visage** signs of tiredness on the face; **les ~s indélébiles d'une enfance malheureuse** fig the indelible scars of an unhappy childhood; **l'aventure avait laissé des ~s profondes en lui** the experience had marked him deeply; **4** (indice) (d'activité) sign; (de passage, présence) trace; **des ~s d'effraction** signs of a break-in; **il n'y avait aucune ~ du conducteur** there was no trace ou sign of the driver; **disparaître sans laisser de ~s** to disappear without a trace; **les archéologues ont trouvé de nombreuses ~s de cette civilisation** archaeologists have found many traces of this civilization; **5** (quantité infime) **des ~s de mercure** traces of mercury; **'lipides: ~s'** 'lipids: trace'; **sa déclaration ne comportait pas la moindre ~ d'humour/d'ironie** his/her pronouncement bore not the slightest trace of humour[GB]/of irony.

tracé /tʀase/ *nm* **1** (plan) (de route, ville etc) layout; **2** (parcours) (de route, ligne ferroviaire) route; (de fleuve) course; (de frontière, côte) line; **3** (de courbe, croquis) line (**de** of); **sa palette et son ~ sont extraordinaires** his/her range of colour[GB] and sense of line are extraordinary; **4** Ordinat inking.

tracer /tʀase/ [12] **I** *vtr* **1** (dessiner) to draw [*ligne, plan, rectangle, portrait*]; (sur graphique) to plot [*courbe*]; (écrire) to write [*caractères, mot*]; to plan the route of [*autoroute, oléoduc*]; **dessin tracé à l'encre/à la craie** ink/chalk drawing; **~ un trait à la règle** to draw a line with a ruler; **les patineurs traçaient des arabesques sur la glace** the skaters traced ou described arabesques on the ice; **2** (établir) **~ une frontière précise entre le légal et l'illégal** to draw the line between what is legal and what is illegal; **~ un portrait de qn** to paint a picture of sb; **~ un tableau pessimiste de qch** to paint a pessimistic picture of sth; **à 15 ans son avenir était déjà tout tracé** at 15, his future was already mapped out ; **~ les grandes lignes d'une action** to map out the main lines of action (to be taken); **~ un programme/une politique** to outline a programme/a policy; **3** (ouvrir) to open up [*piste, route*]; **~ sa propre voie** fig to make one's own way (in life); **~ le chemin à qn** fig to show sb the way.
II◑ *vi* (aller vite) to belt along○.

traceur /tʀasœʀ, øz/ **I** *adj* [*balle, substance*] tracer.
II *nm* **1** **▶510** (ouvrier) lay-out marker; **2** Sci (colorant, isotope) tracer; Chimie **~ radioactif** label; **3** Ordinat **~ de courbes** graph plotter.

trachéal, **~e**, *mpl* **-aux** /tʀakeal, o/ *adj* tracheal.

trachée /tʀaʃe/ *nf* windpipe, trachea spéc.

trachée-artère, *pl* **trachées-artères** /tʀaʃeaʀtɛʀ/ *nf* windpipe, trachea spéc.

trachéen, **-éenne** /tʀakeɛ̃, ɛn/ *adj* tracheal.

trachéite /tʀakeit/ **▶271** *nf* tracheitis ₡.

trachéo-bronchite, *pl* **~s** /tʀakeo bʀɔ̃ʃit/ **▶271** *nf* tracheobronchitis ₡.

trachéotomie /tʀakeɔtɔmi/ *nf* tracheotomy; **on lui a fait une ~** he had a tracheotomy.

trachome /tʀakom/ **▶271** *nm* trachoma.

traçoir /tʀaswaʀ/ *nm* scriber.
■ **~ à tourelle** Géog turret graver; **~ à trépied** Géog rigid tripod engraver.

tract /tʀakt/ *nm* pamphlet, tract.

tractable /tʀaktabl/ *adj* [*caravane*] which can be towed (*après n*).

tractation /tʀaktasjɔ̃/ *nf* negotiation; **en ~** under negotiation; **~s en cours** negotiations under way.

tracté, **~e** /tʀakte/ **I** *pp* ▶ **tracter**.
II *pp adj* [*remorque*] tractor-drawn.

tracter /tʀakte/ [1] *vtr* [*véhicule*] to tow [*remorque*]; [*câble, remonte-pente*] to pull up [*funiculaire, skieur*].

tracteur /tʀaktœʀ, tʀis/ *nm* tractor.

traction /tʀaksjɔ̃/ *nf* **1** (mode d'entraînement) traction; **~ animale/électrique/mécanique** animal/electric/mechanical traction; **à ~ animale** drawn by animals; **à ~ mécanique** mechanically drawn; **2** Sport **faire des ~s** (à la barre, aux anneaux) to do pull-ups; (au sol) to do press-ups GB ou push-ups; **3** Tech (effort mécanique) tension.
■ **~ arrière** Aut rear-wheel drive; **~ avant** Aut front-wheel drive.

tractus /tʀaktys/ *nm inv* tract.

tradition /tʀadisjɔ̃/ *nf* **1** (coutume) tradition; **~ familiale/orale** family/oral tradition; **un pays de ~s démocratiques/libérales** a country with democratic/liberal traditions; **la ~ veut que** tradition has it that; **être dans la ~ de qch/qn** to be in the tradition of sth/sb; **être de ~** to be traditional; **il est de ~ de** it's traditional to; **c'est la ~ que/de faire** it's traditional that/to do; **par ~** traditionally; **2** (légende) legend; **la ~ veut que la ville**... legend has it that the town...; **3** Jur handing over (of property).

traditionalisme /tʀadisjɔnalism/ *nm* traditionalism.

traditionaliste /tʀadisjɔnalist/ *adj, nmf* traditionalist.

traditionnel, **-elle** /tʀadisjɔnɛl/ *adj* [*cuisine, médecine*] traditional; **de façon traditionnelle** traditionally.

traditionnellement /tʀadisjɔnɛlmɑ̃/ *adv* traditionally.

traducteur, **-trice** /tʀadyktœʀ, tʀis/ I ▶510 *nm,f* translator; **~ littéraire/technique** literary/technical translator.
II **traductrice** *nf* (appareil) translator.

traducteur-interprète, *pl* **traducteurs-interprètes** /tradyktœʀɛ̃tɛʀpʀɛt/ ▶510 *nm* translator-interpreter.

traduction /tʀadyksjɔ̃/ *nf* **1** (action) translation; **la ~ est un exercice difficile** translation is a difficult exercise; **faire de la ~ littéraire/technique** to do literary/technical translation; **la ~ libre/littérale** free/literal translation; **diplôme/école de ~** translation diploma/school; **la ~ de ce texte m'a pris cinq heures** it took me five hours to translate this text; **la ~ en allemand** translating into German; **être en cours de ~** to be in the process of being translated; **2** (texte) translation; **~ approximative** loose translation; **~ en anglais** English translation; **faire des ~s** to do translation work; **3** fig (de sentiments, d'idées) expression.
■ **~ assistée par ordinateur**, **TAO** computer-aided translation, CAT.

traduire /tʀadɥiʀ/ [69] I *vtr* **1** (dans une langue différente) lit to translate [*texte, auteur*] (**en** into; **de** from); **un nom traduit par un verbe** a noun translated by a verb; **roman traduit de l'anglais** novel translated from the English; **2** (exprimer) [*mot, écrivain, ton, artiste, œuvre, style*] to convey; [*révolte, agitation, violence*] to be the expression of; [*hausse, cours, instabilité, marché*] to be the result of; **~ en actes** to put into practice; **3** Jur **~ qn en justice** to bring sb to justice; **~ qn en correctionnelle** to bring sb before the criminal court.
II **se traduire** *vpr* **1** (être exprimé) [*joie, angoisse, peur*] to manifest itself (**par** in); to be manifested (**par** in); **2** (avoir pour résultat) [*crise, récession, instabilité, action*] to result (**par** in); [*mécontentement*] to find expression (**par** in); **se ~ par un échec** to result in failure.

traduisible /tʀadɥizibl/ *adj* translatable.

Trafalgar /tʀafalgaʀ/ *nprm* Trafalgar; **coup de ~** disaster.

trafic /tʀafik/ *nm* **1** (commerce illicite) traffic (**de** in); **~ d'armes** arms dealing; **~ de drogue** drug trafficking; **faire du ~ de qch** to traffic ou deal in sth; **il fait du ~ d'armes** he's an armsdealer ou a gunrunner; **2** Transp **~ (routier)** traffic; **une ligne à fort ~** a line with ou carrying heavy traffic; **~ aérien/maritime/ferroviaire** air/sea/rail traffic; **~ de marchandises/voyageurs** goods/passenger traffic; **~ de transit entre** transit traffic between; **3**○ (circulation routière) traffic.
■ **~ d'influence** Jur influence peddling.
IDIOMES **qu'est-ce que c'est que ce ~**○? what's going on here?

traficotage○ /tʀafikɔtaʒ/ *nm* shady dealings (*pl*).

traficoter○ /tʀafikɔte/ [1] I *vtr* (comploter) péj to scheme (**avec qn** with sb); **qu'est-ce que tu traficotes encore**○? what are you up to?
II *vi* (vivre de petits trafics) to be a petty criminal.

trafiquant, **~e** /tʀafikɑ̃, ɑ̃t/ *nm,f* trafficker, dealer (**de** in); **~ de drogue** drugs dealer; **~ d'armes** arms dealer, gunrunner; **un petit ~** a small-time trafficker; **un petit ~ de drogue** a small-time drug dealer, a drug pusher○.

trafiquer /tʀafike/ [1] *vtr* **1** (truquer) to fiddle ou tamper with [*compteur, voiture*]; to doctor [*vin*]; **2**○ (faire) péj **je me demande ce qu'il trafique** I wonder what he's up to.

tragédie /tʀaʒedi/ *nf* (tous contextes) tragedy.

tragédien, **-ienne** /tʀaʒedjɛ̃, ɛn/ *nm,f* tragic actor, tragedian/tragedienne.

tragi-comédie, *pl* **~s** /tʀaʒikɔmedi/ *nf* tragicomedy.

tragi-comique, *pl* **~s** /tʀaʒikɔmik/ *adj* tragicomic.

tragique /tʀaʒik/ I *adj* tragic; **ce n'est pas ~** it's not the end of the world.
II *nm* **1** Littérat, Théât (auteur) tragedian; (genre) **le ~** tragedy; (caractère) tragic elements (*pl*); **2** (gravité) tragedy; **le ~ d'une situation** the tragedy of a situation; **tourner au ~** to take a tragic turn; **prendre qch au ~** to make a drama out of sth.

tragiquement /tʀaʒikmɑ̃/ *adv* tragically.

trahir /tʀaiʀ/ [3] I *vtr* **1** (manquer de fidélité à) to betray [*pays, ami, secret, cause, confiance*]; to break [*parole, serment, promesse*]; **2** (révéler) [*rougeur, voix*] to betray, to give away [*confusion, peur, impatience*]; [*écriture*] to betray, to reveal [*personnalité*]; [*paroles*] to betray, to reveal [*pensée*]; **3** (rendre infidèlement) [*traducteur, metteur en scène, mots*] to misrepresent; **4** (faire défaut) [*jambes, forces*] to fail [*person*].
II **se trahir** *vpr* (se dévoiler) to give oneself away, to betray oneself.

trahison /tʀaizɔ̃/ *nf* **1** (manquement à un engagement) treachery ¢; **il est prêt aux pires ~s** he is capable of the worst treachery; **~ de qch/qn** betrayal of sth/sb; **une ~** a betrayal, an act of treachery; **2** Mil, Pol treason ¢; **être condamné/fusillé pour ~** to be sentenced/shot for treason; **il s'agit d'une ~** it amounts to treason, it's an act of treason; **il y a eu des milliers de ~s** there were thousands of cases of treason; **haute ~** high treason; **3** (d'un texte, d'une pensée) misrepresentation (**de** of).

traille /tʀaj/ *nf* (câble) ferry cable; (bac) cable ferry.

train /tʀɛ̃/ I *nm* **1** Rail train; **prendre le ~ de 21 heures** to take the 9 pm train; **monter/être dans le ~** to get/to be on the train; **descendre du ~** to get off the train; **mettre qn dans le ~** to put sb on the train; **accompagner qn au ~** to see sb off at the station; **par le** or **en ~** [*voyager, transporter*] by train; **préférer le ~ à l'avion** to prefer train travel to flying; ▶ **marche**, **vache**; **2** (convoi) train; **~ de péniches** train of barges; **3** (série) series; **~ de mesures/d'économies** series of measures/of economies; **4** (enchaînement) train; **le ~ des événements** the train of events; **5** (allure) pace; **accélérer/ralentir le ~** to speed up/to slow down; **aller bon** or **grand ~** (marcher vite) to walk briskly; **aller bon ~** [*rumeurs*] to be flying around; [*ventes, affaires*] to be going well; [*conversation*] to flow easily; [*équipage, voiture*] to be going quite fast; **au ~ où l'on va/vont les choses** (at) the rate we're going/things are going; **aller son ~** [*affaire*] to be getting on all right; **aller son petit ~** [*personne, affaire, négociations*] to go peacefully along; **à fond de ~**○ at top speed; ▶ **mener**; **6** Zool **~ de derrière** hindquarters; **~ de devant** forequarters; **7**○ (de personne) backside○; **8** Mil **le ~** corps of transport GB, transportation corps US.
II **en train** *loc* **1** (en forme) **être en ~** to be full of energy; **ne pas être en ~** not to have much energy; **2** (en marche) **mettre qch en ~** to get [sth] started ou going [*processus, travail*]; **se mettre en ~** gén to get going; Sport to warm up; **j'ai du mal à me mettre en ~ le matin** I have a hard job getting going in the morning; **mise en ~** Sport warm-up; **la mise en ~ d'un projet** getting a project under way; **3** (en cours) **être en ~ de faire** to be doing; **j'étais en ~ de dormir/lire** I was sleeping/reading.
■ **~ arrière** Aut back axle assembly; **~ d'atterrissage** undercarriage; **sortir le** or **son ~ d'atterrissage** to lower the undercarriage; **~ avant** Aut front axle assembly; Aviat nose (landing) gear; **~ baladeur** Aut sliding gear; **~ de bois** raft; **~ électrique** (jouet simple) toy train; (modèle réduit) model train; (jeu avec accessoires) train set; **~ d'engrenages** Mécan train of gears, gear train; **~ fantôme** ghost train; **~ de laminoirs** Tech mill train; **~ de neige** Transp *train to ski resorts*; **~ d'ondes** Phys wave train; **~ de pneus** Aut set of tyres GB ou tires US; **~ roulant** Aut running gear; **~ de rouleaux** Ind roller path; **~ de roulement** Aut undercarriage; **~ routier** Transp articulated lorry GB, tractor-trailer US; **~ sanitaire** hospital train; **~ de sénateur** hum stately pace; **aller son ~ de sénateur** to go at a stately pace; **~ spatial** linked-up spacecraft (+ *v pl*); **~ de tiges** (pour forage) string; **~ de vie** lifestyle; **réduire son ~ de vie** to live more modestly.
IDIOMES **faire le petit ~** to do the conga; **un ~ peut en cacher un autre** fig be on your guard.

traînailler○ /tʀɛnɑje/ [1] *vi* = **traînasser**.

traînant, **~e** /tʀɛnɑ̃, ɑ̃t/ *adj* [*pas, démarche*] shuffling; **voix ~e** drawl.

traînard, **~e** /tʀɛnaʀ, aʀd/ I *adj* pej [*démarche*] sluggish; **accent ~** drawling accent.
II *nm,f* (personne lente) slowcoach○ GB, slowpoke○ US; (qui reste en arrière) straggler.

traînasser○ /tʀɛnase/ [1] *vi* pej **1** (perdre son temps) to loaf about; **2** (travailler lentement) to take ages (**en faisant** doing).

traîne /tʀɛn/ *nf* **1** Mode (de robe) train; **robe à ~** dress with a train; **2** Pêche seine (net); **pêcher à la ~** to seine, to seine net fish.
IDIOMES **être à la ~** [*personne, pays, système*] to lag behind; [*bateau*] to be in tow; **mettre à la ~** to tow [*bateau*].

traîneau, *pl* **~x** /tʀɛno/ *nm* **1** (véhicule) sleigh; **promenade en ~** sleigh ride; **2** (d'un aspirateur) cylinder; **aspirateur ~** cylinder vacuum cleaner; **3** Pêche seine (net); **4** Chasse dragnet.

traînée /tʀɛne/ *nf* **1** (tache allongée) streak; **~ de sang/peinture** streak of blood/paint; **2** (trace) trail; **~ lumineuse** luminous trail; **~ blanche** (d'avion) white vapour[GB] trail; ▶ **poudre**; **3**◑ offensive (femme facile) slut◑ injur; **4** (en aérodynamique) drag.

traîne-misère† /tʀɛnmizɛʀ/ *nmf inv* destitute person.

traîner /tʀɛne/ [1] I *vtr* **1** (tirer) to drag [sth] (along) [*valise*]; to drag [sth] across the floor [*chaise*]; **il traînait un grand sac derrière lui** he was dragging a big bag behind him; **~ qn par les pieds/les cheveux** to drag sb (along) by the feet/the hair; **2**○ (être encombré) (en portant) to lug○ [sth] around [*objet*]; (en tirant) to drag [sth] around [*objet*]; (en subissant) to drag [sb] along [*personne*]; **elle l'a traîné à une réunion d'affaires** she dragged him along to a business meeting; **3** (forcer à aller) to drag [sb] off [*personne*]; **~ qn chez le médecin/le coiffeur** to drag sb off to the doctor's/the hairdresser's; **~ qn devant les tribunaux** to drag sb into court; **4** (supporter longtemps) **il traîne un rhume depuis deux semaines** for two weeks now he's had a cold that he can't shake off; **elle a traîné toute sa vie des sentiments de jalousie** she has harboured[GB] feelings of jealousy all her life; **elle a traîné toute sa vie les conséquences de cette décision** the effects of this decision followed her throughout her life; **5** (utiliser avec lenteur) **~ les pieds** lit, fig to drag one's feet; **~ la voix** to drawl.
II *vi* **1** (perdre son temps) **~ dans les rues/dans les couloirs/dans les bars** to hang around in the streets/in the corridors/in bars; **~ en ville** to hang around town; **'qu'est-ce que tu as fait aujourd'hui?'—'j'ai traîné'** 'what did you do today?'—'I loafed around○'; **on a traîné à**

table (après le repas) we sat around the table for a long time after the meal; (à manger) we had a long leisurely meal; **j'ai traîné au lit** I had a lie-in GB, I slept in; **ils traînent ensemble** they hang around together doing nothing; **~ avec des gens un peu louches** to hang around with some funny people; **il y avait quelques touristes qui traînaient** there were a few tourists drifting about the place; **2** (faire lentement) to take forever (**pour faire** doing); **elle traîne une heure dans la salle de bains** she lingers in the bathroom for an hour; **ne traîne pas, on doit terminer à 4 heures** get a move on○, we've got to finish at four; **ça ne va pas ~, il aura terminé les travaux à Noël** he won't hang about, he'll be finished by Christmas; **je savais qu'il dirait une bêtise, et ça n'a pas traîné** I knew he'd say something silly, and it wasn't long in coming; **3** (aller sans hâte) to dawdle; **ne traîne pas en rentrant de l'école** don't dawdle on your way back from school; **~** (**derrière**) to lag ou trail behind, to trail along in the rear; **quelques élèves traînaient derrière** a few pupils were trailing along in the rear; **ne traînez pas derrière!** keep up there at the back!; **4** (ne pas se terminer) [*chantier, maladie*] to drag on; [*odeur*] to linger; **faire** or **laisser ~** (**les choses**) to let things drag on; **ne donne pas de réponse, fais ~** don't give an answer, let things drag on a bit; **laisser ~ qch en longueur** to let sth drag on for ages; **un film qui traîne en longueur** a long-drawn-out film; **5** (être en contact avec) **~ par terre** [*jupe*] to trail on the ground; [*rideaux*] to trail on the floor; **~ dans la boue/poussière** [*bas de jupe*] to trail in the mud/dust; **ça a traîné dans la boue** it's all muddy; **ta manche traîne dans ton assiette** your sleeve is in your plate; **6** (être tiré) **~ derrière qch** to be trailing behind sth; **7** (ne pas être rangé) [*vêtements, jouets*] to be lying about ou around; **laisser ~ qch** to leave sth lying about ou around [*chéquier, document*]; **un manteau qui traîne sur une chaise** a coat thrown over a chair; **ramasser qch qui traînait dans la boue** to pick up sth lying in the mud; **8** (être très courant) **avec ces microbes qui traînent** with all the germs (that are) around; **une explication qui traîne dans tous les livres** an explanation that is given in all the books.

III se traîner *vpr* **1** (ramper) [*blessé*] **se ~ par terre/jusqu'à la porte** to drag oneself along the ground/to the door; **se ~ aux pieds de qn** to crawl at sb's feet; **2** (aller avec effort) **se ~ jusqu'à la cuisine** to drag oneself through to the kitchen; **je n'ai pas envie de me ~ jusqu'à Paris** I don't feel like trailing off GB ou schlepping○ US to Paris; **3** (être oisif) to loaf about○; **4** (avancer lentement) [*voiture, train, escargot*] to crawl along; [*procès, négociations*] to drag on; [*chantier*] to proceed at a crawl.

IDIOMES **~ la jambe** or **la patte**○ to limp; **~ ses guêtres**○ or **ses bottes**○ to knock around○; **avoir les mains qui traînent** to be light-fingered.

traîne-savates○ /tʀɛnsavat/ *nm inv* pej good-for-nothing.

training /tʀeniŋ/ *nm* training.

■ **~ autogène** Psych autogenic training.

train(-)train○ /tʀɛ̃tʀɛ̃/ *nm inv* daily round.

traire /tʀɛʀ/ [58] *vtr* to milk [*vache, chèvre, brebis*]; to draw [*lait*]; **~ le lait d'une vache** to draw the milk from a cow; **machine à ~** milking machine.

trait /tʀɛ/ **I** *nm* **1** (ligne) gén line; (fait d'un seul mouvement) stroke; (de code Morse) dash; **remplissez-le jusqu'au ~** fill it up to the line ou mark; **souligner un mot d'un ~ rouge** to underline a word in red; **barrer qch d'un ~ rageur** to cross sth out angrily; **dessiner qch à grands ~s** to make a rough sketch of sth; **exposer la situation/décrire qch à grands ~s** to explain the situation/describe sth in broad outline; **avoir le ~ juste** to draw accurately; **avoir le ~ sûr** to have a steady hand; **au ~** [*dessin, gravure*] line (*épith*); **~ de scie** sawcut; **d'un ~ de plume** fig with a stroke of the pen; **~ pour ~** [*réplique, copie*] line for line; [*reproduire*] line by line; **être le portrait ~ pour ~ de qn** to be an exact replica of sb; **se ressembler ~ pour ~** to be like two peas in a pod; ▶**forcer**; **2** (particularité) (de chose) feature; (de personne) trait; **le ~ dominant** or **essentiel de qch** the main feature; **~ caractéristique** characteristic; **~ particulier** particular feature; **~ frappant** striking feature; **~ de caractère** or **personnalité** trait, characteristic; **c'est un ~ bien français** it's a typically French trait; **le ~ commun entre cette méthode et l'autre** what the two methods have in common; **c'est un ~ commun entre ton fils et le mien** that's something our sons have in common; **ils n'ont aucun ~ commun** they have nothing in common; **avoir des ~s communs** to be alike in some respects; **3** Ling, Phon feature; **~ distinctif/pertinent** distinctive/relevant feature; **~ sémantique/syntaxique/lexical** semantic/syntactical/lexical feature; **4** (pointe verbale) **~** (**mordant**) scathing remark; **lancer** or **décocher un ~ à qn** to say something scathing to sb; **~ cruel** cruel remark; **diriger ses ~s contre qn** to be sarcastic at sb's expense; **5** (expression) **~ d'humour** or **d'esprit** witticism; **~ de génie** stroke of genius; **6** (rapport) **avoir ~ à** to relate to; **documents ayant ~ à la retraite/sécurité** documents relating to retirement/security; **7** (fois) **d'un** (**seul**) **~** gén at one go; **lire qch d'un ~** to read sth at one sitting; **dire qch d'un ~** to say sth straight out; **boire qch d'un ~** to drink sth in one gulp; **boire à longs** or **grands ~s** to drink in long draughts GB ou drafts US; **8** (petite quantité) dash; **mettez un ~ de cognac** add a dash of cognac; **9** (traction) **de ~** [*animal*] draught GB ou draft US; **10** (lanière) trace; **11**† (projectile) dart, shaft; **arme de ~** shaft; **tomber sous les ~s de l'ennemi** to fall beneath the shafts of the enemy.

II traits *nmpl* (visage) features; **avoir des ~s grossiers/fins/creusés** to have coarse/delicate/sunken features; **avoir les ~s fatigués** or **tirés** to look drawn; **présenter/décrire qn sous les ~s de** to introduce/depict sb as.

■ **~ d'union** Ling hyphen; fig (intermédiaire) link (**avec** with; **entre** between); **s'écrire avec un ~ d'union** to be hyphenated, to have a hyphen; **ça s'écrit sans ~ d'union** it's not hyphenated.

IDIOMES **tirer un ~ sur qch** to put sth behind one; **il vaut mieux tirer un ~ sur cette affaire** we'd better put this matter behind us.

traitant /tʀɛtɑ̃/ *adj m* **médecin ~** (généraliste) doctor, GP; (spécialiste) specialist.

traite /tʀɛt/ **I** *nf* **1** Fin draft, bill; **tirer/escompter une ~** to draw/to discount a draft; **2** (commerce de personnes) **~ des êtres humains** prostitution; **la ~ des Blanches** the white slave trade; Hist **la ~ des Noirs** the slave trade; **3** Agric milking; **la ~ des vaches** milking cows; **l'heure de la ~** milking time; **la ~ mécanique** machine milking; **salle de ~** milking shed.

II d'une traite *loc adv* **d'une** (**seule**) **~** [*réciter*] in one breath; [*boire*] in one go; **faire 500 km d'une** (**seule**) **~** to do 500 km non-stop ou at a stretch.

■ **~ documentaire** documentary bill.

traité /tʀete/ *nm* **1** Jur treaty; **le ~ de Rome** the Treaty of Rome; **le ~ de Maastricht** the Maastricht Treaty; **un ~ d'amitié** a treaty of friendship; **~ de paix** peace treaty; **~ commercial** trade agreement; **2** (ouvrage) treatise (**sur, de** on).

traitement /tʀɛtmɑ̃/ *nm* **1** Méd treatment ¢; **être en ~** to be undergoing treatment; **suivre/prescrire un ~** to follow/prescribe a course of treatment; **2** (salaire) salary; **3** (comportement envers) treatment; **c'est le ~ normal des prisonniers** it's the way prisoners are normally treated; ▶**mauvais**; **4** (manière d'aborder, de régler) handling; **critiquer le ~ d'un dossier sensible** to criticize the way sensitive information was handled; **il faut accélérer le ~ des demandes** applications must be dealt with ou processed more quickly; **~ plus complet de la question** fuller treatment of the issue; **5** Ordinat processing ¢; **le ~ automatique des données** automatic data processing; **~ parallèle/(en) série/par lots** parallel/serial/batch processing; **~ informatique d'images vidéo** computer processing of video images; **~ de l'information** data processing; **~ à distance** teleprocessing; **6** Tech (de minerai, d'eaux) processing ¢; (de bois, textile) treatment; **~ des déchets industriels** processing ou treatment of industrial waste; **centre de ~ des eaux** water-processing plant.

■ **~ de faveur** preferential ou special treatment; **~ de texte** Ordinat (processus) word-processing; (logiciel) word-processing package.

traiter /tʀete/ [1] **I** *vtr* **1** (agir envers) to treat [*personne, animal, objet*]; **~ qn en malade/comme son fils** to treat sb like an invalid/like a son; **~ qn en égal** to treat sb as an equal; **être bien/mal traité** to be well/badly treated; **~ durement qn** to be hard on sb; **la critique l'a traité durement** the critics gave him a rough ride; **si tu traitais mieux ces plantes/livres** if you treated these plants/books better; **~ qn comme un chien** to treat sb very badly, to treat sb like dirt; **2** (soigner) Méd to treat [*malade, affection, symptôme*]; **être traité** or **se faire ~ pour un ulcère** to have treatment for an ulcer; **3** (développer) to deal with [*question, sujet*]; Art to treat [*thème*]; **il n'a pas traité le sujet** he hasn't dealt with the subject; **~ un mot dans un dictionnaire** to treat a word in a dictionary; **4** (régler) to deal with [*problème, dossier, scandale, affaire*]; **5** (soumettre à une opération) to treat [*bois, textile, aliment, sang, récoltes*]; to process [*eaux usées*]; **non traité** [*bois, aliment*] untreated; **6** Ordinat to process [*données, information, image*]; **7** (qualifier) **~ qn de qch** to call sb sth; **~ qn de menteur** to call sb a liar; **~ qn de paresseux** to call sb lazy; **elle m'a traité de tous les noms** she called me all sorts of names; **se faire ~ de tous les noms d'oiseaux** to get called all the names under the sun.

II traiter de *vtr ind* **~ de** to deal with [*sujet, thème*]; **l'auteur/l'œuvre traite de** the author/work deals with.

III *vi* (négocier) to negotiate, to do GB ou make a deal; **~ avec qn** to negotiate ou deal with sb; **~ d'égal à égal** (**avec qn**) to deal with sb on equal terms.

IV se traiter *vpr* **ils se sont traités de tous les noms** they called each other all sorts of names.

traiteur /tʀɛtœʀ/ **▶ 510** *nm* caterer.

traître, **traîtresse** /tʀɛtʀ, tʀɛtʀɛs/ **I** *adj* **1** [*personne, parole, temps, escalier, virage*] treacherous; **être ~ à qch** to be a traitor to sth; **2 il n'a pas compris/dit un ~ mot** he hasn't understood/didn't utter a single word.

II *nm,f* traitor (**à** to); hum traitor, scoundrel; **mon ~ de fils** my scoundrel ou traitor of a son; **en ~** in a treacherous ou underhand way; **prendre qn en ~** to take sb by surprise; **coup en ~** stab in the back.

traîtreusement /tʀɛtʀøzmɑ̃/ *adv* treacherously.

traîtrise /tʀɛtʀiz/ *nf* **1** (acte) act of treachery, (act of) betrayal; **par ~** treacherously; **agir par ~** to act out of treachery; **2** (de personne) treachery, treacherousness; (d'escalier, de virage) treacherousness.

trajectoire /tʀaʒɛktwaʀ/ *nf* **1** (de projectile)

trajectory; **2** (de planète, satellite, particule) path; **3** (carrière) career, path in life.

trajet /tʀaʒɛ/ *nm* **1** (voyage) journey; (par mer) crossing; **faire** or **effectuer un ~** to make a journey; **un ~ de cinq minutes/deux kilomètres** a `five-minute/two-kilometre[GB] journey; **2** (parcours) route; **le ~ emprunté par le Président** the President's route; **3** Anat (de veine, nerf) course.

tralala○ /tʀalala/ **I** *nm* (luxe) fuss; **se marier en grand ~** to have a posh wedding○; **...et tout le ~** ...and all the trimmings.

II *excl* ha ha!

tram○ /tʀam/ *nm* (*abbr* = **tramway**) tram GB, streetcar US.

tramail /tʀamaj/ *nm* trammel (net).

trame /tʀam/ *nf* **1** (de tissu) weft, woof; **2** (d'histoire, de spectacle) framework; (de vie) fabric.

tramer /tʀame/ [1] **I** *vtr* **1** (tisser) to weave [*tissu*]; **2** fig (ourdir) to hatch [*complot*].

II se tramer *vpr* [*complot*] to be hatched; **j'aimerais savoir ce qui se trame là-bas** I'd like to know what is being hatched over there.

tramontane /tʀamɔ̃tan/ *nf* tramontane.

tramp /tʀɑ̃p/ *nm* tramp steamer.

trampoline /tʀɑ̃pɔlin/ *nm* **1** (appareil) trampoline; **2** ▶ **449** (discipline) trampolining; **faire du ~** to do trampolining, to trampoline.

tramway /tʀamwɛ/ *nm* (voiture) tram GB, streetcar US; (système) tramway GB, streetcar line US.

tranchant, **~e** /tʀɑ̃ʃɑ̃, ɑ̃t/ **I** *adj* **1** [*couteau, lame, pierre*] sharp; **du côté ~/non ~** with the sharp/blunt edge; **2** [*personne*] forthright; [*ton*] peremptory, curt.

II *nm* **1** (de la main) side; (de couteau, lame) sharp edge, cutting edge; **du ~ de la main** with the side of one's hand; **à double ~** lit, fig double-edged; **2** (outil) (d'apiculteur) scraper; (de tanneur) fleshing knife.

tranche /tʀɑ̃ʃ/ *nf* **1** (de pain, viande, fromage) slice; (de lard, bacon) rasher; **en ~s** (pain etc) in slices; (bacon) in rashers; **couper en ~s** to slice, to cut [sth] into slices [*pain, gâteau, jambon, rosbif*]; to cut [sth] into rashers [*bacon*]; **2** (de temps) (d'opération, de travaux) phase; (dans l'emploi du temps) period, time slot; **3** (de livre, pièce de monnaie) edge; **4** (en boucherie) **~ (grasse)** silverside GB, round; **5** Fin (d'emprunt, de crédit, prêt) instalment[GB]; (d'actions) block, tranche; **6** Math group, section.

■ **~ d'âge** age bracket; **~ horaire** time slot; **~ d'imposition** tax bracket ; **~ de paiement** Fin instalment[GB]; **~ de revenu** income bracket; **~ de salaire** wage bracket; **~ de vie** slice of life.

IDIOMES **s'en payer une ~**○ to have a whale of a time○, to have lots of fun.

tranché, **~e** /tʀɑ̃ʃe/ **I** *pp* ▶ **trancher**.

II *pp adj* [*saumon*] pre-sliced.

III *adj* **1** [*opinion, position, réponse, catégories*] cut-and-dried, clear-cut; [*inégalités*] clear-cut; **2** [*couleurs*] bold, distinct; **3** [*limite, ligne, zone*] clear-cut.

IV tranchée *nf* **1** Mil trench; **2** (chemin) cutting.

V tranchées *nfpl* Méd colic ₵, gripes○ (*pl*).

■ **~es utérines** Méd afterpains.

tranchefile /tʀɑ̃ʃfil/ *nf* Imprim headband.

trancher /tʀɑ̃ʃe/ [1] **I** *vtr* **1** (couper) to slice, to cut [*pain, viande*]; to cut through, to slice through [*corde, nœud, peau*]; to cut [sth] off, to sever [*tête, membre*]; to slit [*gorge*]; **~ un doigt à qn** to cut sb's finger off, to sever sb's finger; **~ la gorge à qn** to slit sb's throat; **2** (régler) to settle, to resolve [*question, affaire, désaccord, litige*].

II *vi* **1** (contraster) [*couleur, silhouette*] to stand out (**avec** with; **sur** against); **~ avec** [*joie, état, décision*] to stand out in sharp contrast to, to contrast sharply with; **2** (décider) to come to a decision; **il est difficile de ~** it's difficult to come to a decision; **le président a tranché contre le projet de construction d'un barrage** the president decided against building the dam; **la justice a tranché en faveur de l'accusé** the court decided in favour[GB] of the accused; **~ entre** to decide between; **3** (arrêter une discussion) to break off, to stop short; **~ court/net** to break off suddenly/abruptly; **tranchons là!** let's close the matter there!

tranchet /tʀɑ̃ʃɛ/ *nm* leather knife.

tranchoir /tʀɑ̃ʃwaʀ/ *nm* **1** (couteau) chopper, cleaver; **2** (planche) chopping board; **3** Zool zanclus.

tranquille /tʀɑ̃kil/ *adj* **1** (calme) [*tempérament, voisins, classe*] quiet; [*allure, voix, assurance*] calm; **un enfant ~** a quiet ou placid child; **tiens-toi ~!** (ne bouge pas!) keep still!, stop fidgeting!; (tais-toi!) be quiet!; **2** (sans agitation) [*heure, jour*] quiet, calm; [*eau, ciel, nuit*] calm, tranquil littér; [*café, rue, vie, soirée, bonheur*] quiet; [*sommeil, vacances*] peaceful; **trouver un coin ~ pour discuter** to find a quiet corner to talk in; **il s'est tenu ~ pendant quelques mois** he behaved himself for a few months; **c'est ~, ici!** it's peaceful here!; **jouir d'un bonheur ~** to live a life of calm contentment; **se promener dans la nuit ~** to go for a walk in the calm of the night; **viens me voir à un moment plus ~** (quand nous serons seuls) come and see me when it's quieter; (quand je serai moins occupé) come and see me when I've got more time; **3** (sans souci) **être ~** to be ou feel easy in one's mind; **ne pas être ~** to be ou feel uneasy, to be worried; **sa mère n'est pas ~ quand il sort** his mother worries ou is uneasy when he goes out; **sois** ou **tu peux être ~, je ne dirai rien** don't worry, I won't say anything; **sois ~ (que) ça se retournera contre toi**○**!** iron it will backfire on you, don't you worry!; **4** (en paix) **avoir l'esprit ~** to be easy in one's mind; **avoir la conscience ~** to have a clear conscience; **j'ai la conscience ~** my conscience is clear; **laisse ton frère ~** leave your brother alone; **je te laisse ~** I leave you in peace; **laisse ma montre ~!** fig leave my watch alone!

tranquillement /tʀɑ̃kilmɑ̃/ *adv* **1** (dans le calme) **elle dort ~** she's sleeping peacefully; **peut-on se voir ~?** could we have a quiet word?; **j'aimerais pouvoir travailler ~** I wish I could work in peace and quiet; **2** (sans bruit) quietly; **elle tricotait ~** she was knitting away quietly; **il a réussi ~ à se faire un nom** without a fuss, he managed to make a name for himself; **3** (sans se presser) **nous avons marché ~** we walked along at a leisurely pace; **elle a roulé ~** she drove along unhurriedly; **je suis arrivé ~** I wandered in; **4** (sans souci) happily; **il attendait ~ de l'autre côté de la rue** he was happily waiting on the other side of the street; **nous étions ~ en train de discuter** we were chatting away happily; **5** (sereinement) calmly; **~, sans s'affoler** calmly, without panicking; **expliquer/affirmer qch ~** to explain/to state sth calmly.

tranquillisant, **~e** /tʀɑ̃kilizɑ̃, ɑ̃t/ **I** *adj* [*paroles, nouvelle, effet*] reassuring, comforting.

II *nm* tranquillizer[GB]

tranquilliser /tʀɑ̃kilize/ [1] **I** *vtr* to reassure; **ça tranquillise de savoir que** it is reassuring to know that.

II se tranquilliser *vpr* to stop worrying.

tranquillité /tʀɑ̃kilite/ *nf* **1** (de tempérament, personne) calmness, serenity (**de** of); (d'eau, de nuit) liter calmness, stillness (**de** of); (de moment, lieu) calm, quiet (**of de**); **après deux jours de ~ les combats ont repris** after two days of calm, the fighting resumed; **il m'a annoncé la nouvelle avec ~** he told me the news calmly; **pour une fois, j'ai pu travailler en toute ~** for once I was able to work without being disturbed; **2** (absence d'inquiétude) **~ (d'esprit)** peace of mind; **pour votre ~, fermez la porte à clé** for you own peace of mind, lock the door; **en toute ~** with complete peace of mind, with an easy mind; **partez en toute ~** you can leave with an easy mind; **3** (vie paisible) **aspirer à la ~** to long for peace and quiet; **je tiens à ma ~** I value my peace and quiet.

transaction /tʀɑ̃zaksjɔ̃/ *nf* **1** gén, Fin, Comm transaction (**entre X et Y** between X and Y); **faire une ~** to make a transaction; **le volume des ~s atteint**... the trading volume reaches...; **2** Jur (compromis) settlement.

transactionnel, **-elle** /tʀɑ̃zaksjɔnɛl/ *adj* Jur [*règlement*] compromise (*épith*). ▶ **analyse**.

transafricain, **~e** /tʀɑ̃zafʀikɛ̃, ɛn/ *adj* [*réseau, chemin de fer*] trans-African.

transalpin, **~e** /tʀɑ̃zalpɛ̃, in/ **I** *adj* **1** (qui traverse les Alpes) [*route, liaison*] transalpine; **2** (italien) [*presse, club, député*] Italian.

II *nm,f* Italian.

transamazonien, **-ienne** /tʀɑ̃zamazɔnjɛ̃, ɛn/ **I** *adj* trans-Amazonian.

II transamazonienne *nf* Trans-Amazonian highway.

transaméricain, **~e** /tʀɑ̃zameʀikɛ̃, ɛn/ *adj* trans-American.

transaminase /tʀɑ̃zaminɑz/ *nf* transaminase.

transat○ /tʀɑ̃zat/ **I** *nm* deckchair; (pour bébé) baby chair.

II *nf* Sport transatlantic race; **~ en solitaire** single-handed transatlantic race.

transatlantique /tʀɑ̃zatlɑ̃tik/ *adj* [*course, commerce, vol*] transatlantic.

transbahuter○ /tʀɑ̃sbayte/ [1] *vtr* to shift [*objets, meubles*]; to ferry [*gens*].

transbordement /tʀɑ̃sbɔʀdəmɑ̃/ *nm* (de marchandises) transshipment; (de passagers) transfer.

transborder /tʀɑ̃sbɔʀde/ [1] *vtr* to tranship [*marchandises*]; to transfer [*passagers*].

transbordeur /tʀɑ̃sbɔʀdœʀ/ *nm* **1** (pont) transporter bridge; **2** Rail traverser; **3** Naut ferry.

transcanadien, **-ienne** /tʀɑ̃skanadjɛ̃, ɛn/ *adj* trans-Canada.

transcendance /tʀɑ̃sɑ̃dɑ̃s/ *nf* transcendence.

transcendant, **~e** /tʀɑ̃sɑ̃dɑ̃, ɑ̃t/ *adj* **1** Philos transcendent; **2**○ (génial) wonderful; **3** Math transcendental.

transcendantal, **~e**, *mpl* **-aux** /tʀɑ̃sɑ̃dɑ̃tal, o/ *adj* transcendental.

transcender /tʀɑ̃sɑ̃de/ [1] **I** *vtr* to transcend [*personne, notion*].

II se transcender *vpr* to transcend oneself.

transcodage /tʀɑ̃skɔdaʒ/ *nm* transcoding.

transcoder /tʀɑ̃skɔde/ [1] *vtr* to transcode.

transcodeur /tʀɑ̃skɔdœʀ/ *nm* transcoder.

transconteneur /tʀɑ̃skɔ̃tənœʀ/ *nm* container ship.

transcontinental, **~e**, *mpl* **-aux** /tʀɑ̃skɔ̃tinɑ̃tal, o/ *adj* transcontinental.

transcripteur /tʀɑ̃skʀiptœʀ/ *nm* transcriber.

transcription /tʀɑ̃skʀipsjɔ̃/ *nf* **1** gén transcription; (discours transcrit) transcript; **2** Jur registration.

transcrire /tʀɑ̃skʀiʀ/ [67] *vtr* **1** gén, Ling to transcribe [*texte, mots*]; **2** fig to translate [*émotion, ambiance*]; **3** Mus, Biol to transcribe.

transducteur /tʀɑ̃sdyktœʀ/ *nm* transducer.

transduction /tʀɑ̃sdyksjɔ̃/ *nf* Biol Chimie, Tech transduction.

transe /tʀɑ̃s/ *nf* trance; **être/entrer en ~** to be in/to go into a trance; fig to get worked up

transept /tʀɑ̃sɛpt/ *nm* transept.

transférable /tʀɑ̃sfeʀabl/ *adj* transferable.

transférer /tʀɑ̃sfeʀe/ [14] *vtr* **1** gén, aussi Ordinat to transfer [*prisonnier, pouvoirs, argent, siège social, données*] (**à, dans, sur**

to); to relocate [*bureaux, usine*] (**à, dans** to); to transfer [*appel*] (**sur** to); **faire ~** to have [sth] transferred [*contrat, appels*]; **les arrêts du car ont été transférés à**... the coach GB ou bus US stops have been moved to...; **2** Jur to transfer [*biens, propriétés*] (**à** to); to convey [*droit*] (**à** to); **3** Psych to transfer (**sur** onto).

transfert /tʀɑ̃sfɛʀ/ *nm* **1** gén (de personne, pouvoirs, siège social, données, d'argent) transfer (**à, dans, sur** to); (de bureaux, d'usine) relocation (**à, dans** to); **~ de fonds/capitaux** transfer of funds/capital; **faire** or **opérer un ~ de fonds** to transfer funds; **~ de technologie** technological transfer; **il a demandé son ~ dans une autre agence** he asked for a transfer ou to be transferred to another branch; **~ de populations** mass population shift; **2** Jur (de biens, propriétés) transfer; (de droit) conveyance; **3** Psych transference (**de** of; **sur** onto).
■ **~ d'appel** Télécom call diversion; **~ de données** Ordinat data transfer; **~ électronique de fonds**, **TEF** electronic funds transfer, EFT.

transfiguration /tʀɑ̃sfigyʀasjɔ̃/ *nf* **1** Relig Transfiguration; **2** gén transformation.

transfigurer /tʀɑ̃sfigyʀe/ [1] *vtr* **1** Relig **être transfiguré** to be transfigured; **2** (transformer) to transform; **la joie l'a transfigurée** her joy has completely transformed her.

transformable /tʀɑ̃sfɔʀmabl/ *adj* **1** (adaptable) [*meuble*] convertible (**en** into); **canapé ~ en lit** sofa bed; **2** Sport [*essai*] convertible.

transformateur, **-trice** /tʀɑ̃sfɔʀmatœʀ, tʀis/ **I** *adj* transformation.
II *nm* Électrotech transformer.

transformation /tʀɑ̃sfɔʀmasjɔ̃/ *nf* **1** (modification) (de personne, pays) transformation (**en** into); (de minerai, substance, énergie) conversion (**en** into); **subir une ~** [*pays, société*] to undergo a change; (radicale) to undergo a transformation; [*produit agricole, textile*] to be processed; [*bâtiment*] to be altered; (en mieux) to be transformed; **travaux de ~** Constr alterations; **la maladie a opéré une profonde ~ en lui** the illness wrought a profound change in him; **2** Sport conversion; **3** Ling, Math transformation.

transformationnel, **-elle** /tʀɑ̃sfɔʀmasjɔnɛl/ *adj* transformational.

transformée /tʀɑ̃sfɔʀme/ *nf* Math transform.

transformer /tʀɑ̃sfɔʀme/ [1] **I** *vtr* **1** (modifier) to alter [*vêtement, façade*]; to change, to alter [*personne, attitude, paysage, société*]; (profondément, en mieux) to transform; **~ les mentalités** to alter people's thinking; (profondément) to transform people's thinking; **tout ~ dans le jardin** to change everything in the garden; **l'incendie/l'érosion a transformé le paysage** fire/erosion has completely altered the landscape; **la prospérité a transformé la région** prosperity has transformed the region; **quelques fleurs et la pièce est transformée** a few flowers make all the difference to the room; **transformée par le bonheur** transformed by happiness; **depuis qu'il ne boit plus, il est transformé** since he stopped drinking he's a different person; **2** (métamorphoser) **~ qn/qch en** gén to turn sb/sth into; (en améliorant) to transform sb/sth into; **~ la maison en chantier** fig to turn the house into a building site; **~ un handicap en atout** to turn a handicap into an asset; **~ un pays en un État modèle** to transform a country into a model state; **~ un garage en bureau** to convert a garage into an office; **~ le lait en fromage** to make milk into cheese; **3** Chimie to convert [*substance*] (**en** into); **4** Sport to convert [*essai*]; **5** Math to transform [*figure*].
II se transformer *vpr* **1** [*personne, société, pays*] to change; (profondément, en mieux) [*pays, société*] to be transformed; [*personne*] (délibérément) to transform oneself; (passivement) to be transformed; **se ~ en** gén to turn into; (radicalement, en mieux) to be transformed into; **se ~ en loup-garou/État modèle** to be transformed into a werewolf/a model state; **2** Biol [*embryon, larve, bourgeon*] to turn into; **le têtard se transforme en grenouille** the tadpole turns into a frog; **3** Chimie to be converted (**en** into).

transformisme /tʀɑ̃sfɔʀmism/ *nm* transformism.

transformiste /tʀɑ̃sfɔʀmist/ *adj, nmf* transformist.

transfrontalier, **-ière** /tʀɑ̃sfʀɔ̃talje, ɛʀ/ *adj* [*travailleur*] cross-border (*épith*); [*revue, centre culturel*] catering for communities on both sides of the borders (*après n*); [*permis, carte*] valid on both sides of the border (*après n*).

transfuge /tʀɑ̃sfyʒ/ *nmf* **1** gén, Pol defector (**de** from); **2** Mil deserter.

transfusé, **~e** /tʀɑ̃sfyze/ **I** *pp* ▶ **transfuser**.
II *pp adj* [*sang*] transfused; [*personne*] who has been given a blood transfusion (*après n*).
III *nm,f* person who has been given a blood transfusion.

transfuser /tʀɑ̃sfyze/ [1] *vtr* to give a blood transfusion to [*malade*]; **~ du sang à un malade** to give a patient a blood transfusion.

transfusion /tʀɑ̃sfyzjɔ̃/ *nf* transfusion; **~ sanguine** blood transfusion; **faire une ~ à qn** to give sb a transfusion.

transgresser /tʀɑ̃sgʀese/ [1] *vtr* to contravene [*ordre*]; to break [*loi, règle, tabou*]; to defy [*interdiction*]; to go beyond [*analyse*]; **~ les limites de la décence** to cross the bounds of decency.

transgression /tʀɑ̃sgʀɛsjɔ̃/ *nf* (d'ordre) contravention; (de tabou, règle, loi) breaking; (d'interdiction) defiance.

transhumance /tʀɑ̃zymɑ̃s/ *nf* transhumance spéc, (*seasonal migration of livestock to summer pastures*).

transhumant, **~e** /tʀɑ̃zymɑ̃, ɑ̃t/ *adj* [*troupeau*] migrant (*épith*), transhumant spéc.

transhumer /tʀɑ̃zyme/ [1] **I** *vtr* to move [sth] to summer pastures [*troupeau, bétail*].
II *vi* [*troupeau*] to move to summer pastures.

transi, **~e** /tʀɑ̃zi/ **I** *pp* ▶ **transir**.
II *pp adj* chilled; **~ de froid** chilled to the bone; **~ de peur** paralysed[GB] with fear; **être ~ jusqu'à la moelle** to be chilled to the marrow; **un amoureux ~** a bashful lover.

transiger /tʀɑ̃ziʒe/ [13] *vi* to compromise; **~ avec qn/qch** to compromise with sb/sth; **~ sur qch** to compromise on sth; **on ne transige pas sur les principes** you don't compromise on matters of principle.

transir /tʀɑ̃ziʀ/ [3] *vtr* [*froid*] to chill; [*peur*] to paralyse[GB].

transistor /tʀɑ̃zistɔʀ/ *nm* (composant, poste de radio) transistor.

transit /tʀɑ̃zit/ *nm* gén, Transp transit; **en ~** in transit; **salle/port/opérations de ~** transit lounge/port/operations; **cité de ~** temporary settlement.
■ **~ intestinal** Méd bowel movement.

transitaire /tʀɑ̃zitɛʀ/ **I** *adj* [*commerce*] transit (*épith*); **pays ~** transit point.
II *nmf* Comm forwarding agent.

transiter /tʀɑ̃zite/ [1] *vi* **~ par** [*marchandises, passagers*] to pass through ou via; **les informations transitent par son bureau** information passes through his/her office; **les pays font ~ leur pétrole par** countries send their oil via.

transitif, **-ive** /tʀɑ̃zitif, iv/ *adj* **1** Ling [*verbe*] transitive; **verbe ~ direct/indirect** direct/indirect transitive verb; **2** Math [*relation*] transitive.

transition /tʀɑ̃zisjɔ̃/ *nf* (tous contextes) transition (**entre** between; **vers** to); **sans ~** without any transition; **période de ~** transition period; **gouvernement de ~** transitional government.

transitionnel, **-elle** /tʀɑ̃zisjɔnɛl/ *adj* [*choc, objet*] transitional.

transitivement /tʀɑ̃zitivmɑ̃/ *adv* transitively.

transitivité /tʀɑ̃zitivite/ *nf* Ling, Math transitivity.

transitoire /tʀɑ̃zitwaʀ/ *adj* **1** (de transition) [*période, gouvernement, phase*] transitional; **2** (passager) [*présence*] transitory.

Transjordanie /tʀɑ̃sʒɔʀdani/ *nprf* Trans-Jordan.

Transkei /tʀɑ̃skaj/ *nprm* Transkei.

translater /tʀɑ̃slate/ [1] *vtr* Math, Phys to translate [*triangle*].

translation /tʀɑ̃slasjɔ̃/ *nf* translation.

translittération /tʀɑ̃sliteʀasjɔ̃/ *nf* transliteration.

translittérer /tʀɑ̃sliteʀe/ [14] *vtr* to transliterate.

translocation /tʀɑ̃slɔkasjɔ̃/ *nf* translocation.

translucide /tʀɑ̃slysid/ *adj* [*verre, matière*] translucent.

translucidité /tʀɑ̃slysidite/ *nf* translucence.

transmanche /tʀɑ̃smɑ̃ʃ/ *adj inv* cross-Channel.

transmetteur /tʀɑ̃smɛtœʀ/ *nm* Télécom transmitter.
■ **~ d'ordres** Naut (engine room) telegraph.

transmettre /tʀɑ̃smɛtʀ/ [60] **I** *vtr* **1** (communiquer) to pass [sth] on, to convey [*information, savoir, vœux, ordre, nouvelle*] (**à** to); **~ un dossier au tribunal** to pass a file on to the court; **~ une plainte au tribunal** to lodge a complaint with the court; **envoyez votre candidature au journal qui transmettra** send your application to the newspaper which will then forward it; **veuillez leur ~ mon meilleur souvenir** remember me to them; **transmets-leur mes félicitations/amitiés** give them my congratulations/regards; **2** Télécom to transmit [*message, image, appel, signaux, données*] (**par** by); **~ un appel par radio/des images par satellite** to transmit a call by radio/images by satellite; **3** Radio, TV (émettre) to broadcast [*nouvelles, résultats , émission*]; **cette émission est transmise en direct depuis l'Élysée** this programme[GB] is broadcast live from the Élysée; **4** (léguer) to pass [sth] on [*récit, savoir, découverte*]; to pass [sth] down, to hand [sth] down [*culture, secret, tradition, fortune*] (**à** to); to hand [sth] on [*terre, propriété*] (**à** to); **il veut ~ le récit de ses aventures à la postérité** he wants to pass on the story of his adventures to posterity; **une tradition transmise de génération en génération** a tradition passed down through generations ou from generation to generation; **5** (passer) to hand over [*pouvoir, direction*] (**à** to); **6** Méd to transmit, to pass [sth] on [*maladie, microbe*]; **7** Tech (conduire) to transmit [*son, vibration, mouvement, chaleur*].
II se transmettre *vpr* **1** (l'un l'autre) to pass [sth] on to each other [*message, information, données*]; **ils se sont transmis des informations** they passed information on to each other; **2** Télécom [*signaux, données, informations*] to be transmitted (**par** by); **3** [*tradition, secret, culture, droit*] to be handed down, to be passed down; [*récit, savoir*] to be passed on; **un titre qui se transmet de père en fils** a title which is passed ou handed down from father to son; **4** [*maladie, microbe*] to be transmitted, to be passed on; **se ~ par piqûre d'insectes/par le sang** to be transmitted ou passed on by insect bites/through the blood; **une maladie qui se transmet sexuellement** a sexually transmitted disease.

transmigration /tʀɑ̃smigʀasjɔ̃/ *nf* transmigration.

transmissibilité /tʀɑ̃smisibilite/ *nf* (tous contextes) transmissibility, transmittability.

transmissible /tʀɑ̃smisibl/ *adj* (tous contextes) transmissible, transmittable.

transmission /tʀɑ̃smisjɔ̃/ **I** *nf* **1** (communication) transmission, passing on (**de** of; **à** to); **la ~ des connaissances** the communication ou transmission of knowledge; **2** Télécom, Phys, Tech transmission (**de** of; **à** to); **la ~ d'images par satellite** the transmission of images by satellite; **3** Radio, TV broadcasting, transmission (**de** of); **la ~ d'une émission en direct de Moscou** the broadcasting ou transmission of a programme[GB] live from Moscow; **4** (de tradition, secret, culture) handing down, passing down (**de** of; **à** to); (de fortune, bien, titre, d'héritage) Jur transfer (**de** of; **à** to); **5** Aut, Mécan transmission; **une voiture à ~ automatique** a car with automatic transmission; **6** Méd transmission (**de** of; **à** to); **la ~ d'une maladie par le sang** the transmission of a disease through the blood.

II transmissions *nfpl* Mil signals; **il travaille aux ~s** he works in the signals department; **il travaille dans les ~s** he works in signals.

■ **~ de données** Ordinat data transfer; **~ de pensées** thought transference; **la ~ des pouvoirs** Jur the handover of power.

transmuer /tʀɑ̃smɥe/ [1] *vtr* to transmute [*plomb*]; **~ qch en** to transmute sth into.

transmutabilité /tʀɑ̃smytabilite/ *nf* transmutability.

transmutation /tʀɑ̃smytasjɔ̃/ *nf* Chimie, fig transmutation.

transmuter /tʀɑ̃smyte/ [1] *vtr* = **transmuer**.

transnational, **~e**, *mpl* **-aux** /tʀɑ̃s nasjɔnal, o/ *adj* transnational.

transocéanique /tʀɑ̃zɔseanik/ *adj* transoceanic.

Transpac /tʀɑ̃spak/ *nm*: *public packet network*.

transpalette /tʀɑ̃spalɛt/ *nm* forklift (truck).

transparaître /tʀɑ̃spaʀɛtʀ/ [73] *vi* [*forme, lumière, intentions*] to show through (**sur** on; **dans** in); [*angoisse, embarras*] to show (**sur** on; **dans** in); **~ à travers qch** to show through sth; **laisser ~** [*visage, propos*] to betray; [*personne*] to let [sth] show [*émotions, sentiments*].

transparence /tʀɑ̃spaʀɑ̃s/ *nf* **1** lit (de verre, diamant, tissu, cloison) transparency; (d'eau) clearness; **on voyait ses jambes par** or **en ~ à travers sa jupe** you could see her legs through her skirt; **2** (de teint, peau) translucency; (de regard, couleur) limpidity; **3** fig (de personne, d'allusions, intentions) transparency; (de gestion, transaction, débat) openness; **réclamer la ~ du financement de qch/une plus grande ~ dans le financement de qch** to demand openness about the funding of sth/a greater openness about the funding of sth; **la ~** Pol openness; **la ~ des marchés** Écon the openness of trade to scrutiny; **4** Cin back projection.

transparent, **~e** /tʀɑ̃spaʀɑ̃, ɑ̃t/ **I** *adj* **1** [*verre, diamant, tissu, cloison*] transparent; [*eau*] clear; **2** [*teint, peau*] translucent; [*regard, couleur*] limpid; **3** [*personne, allusion, intentions*] transparent; [*gestion, transaction, débat*] open.

II *nm* (pour rétroprojecteur) transparency.

transpercer /tʀɑ̃spɛʀse/ [12] *vtr* **1** [*épée, flèche, lance*] to pierce [*corps*]; [*balle*] to go through; [*personne*] (avec une épée, flèche, lance) to pierce [*corps, bras, jambe*]; to run [sb] through [*personne*]; **~ qn de son épée** or **d'un coup de son épée** to run sb through with one's sword; **~ qn du regard** fig to give sb a piercing look; **2** (passer au travers) [*pluie, produit*] to go through [*vêtement, papier*]; **3** [*douleur*] to shoot through; [*froid*] to go right through [*personne*].

transpiration /tʀɑ̃spiʀasjɔ̃/ *nf* **1** (phénomène) sweating, perspiration; **être en ~** to be perspiring ou sweating; **2** (sueur) sweat, perspiration; **3** Bot transpiration.

transpirer /tʀɑ̃spiʀe/ [1] *vi* **1** Physiol to sweat, to perspire; **je transpire des mains** my hands sweat; **~ à grosses gouttes** to be dripping ou streaming with sweat; **2**○ (travailler dur) to sweat (**sur qch** over sth); **il a beaucoup transpiré sur ce projet** he sweated a lot over this project; **faire ~ qn** to make sb sweat; **3**○ (être divulgué) [*information, secret*] to leak out; [*sentiment, opinion*] to come out; **espérons que rien ne transpirera de cette affaire** let's hope none of this business leaks out.

transplant /tʀɑ̃splɑ̃/ *nm* transplant.

transplantable /tʀɑ̃splɑ̃tabl/ *adj* Méd, Bot transplantable.

transplantation /tʀɑ̃splɑ̃tasjɔ̃/ *nf* **1** Méd transplant; **~ cardiaque/pulmonaire** heart/lung transplant; **~ d'organes** organ transplants (*pl*); **2** Bot transplantation.

transplanté, **~e** /tʀɑ̃splɑ̃te/ *nm,f* transplant patient.

transplanter /tʀɑ̃splɑ̃te/ [1] *vtr* (tous contextes) to transplant.

transport /tʀɑ̃spɔʀ/ **I** *nm* **1** Transp transport, transportation US; **le ~ de marchandises/voyageurs** the transport of goods/passengers; **réseau de ~** transport network; **mode de ~** means of transport; **frais de ~** transport costs; **~ ferroviaire et maritime** transport by rail and sea; **~ aérien** air transport; **~ par route** gén road transport; (de marchandises) road haulage; **compagnie de ~** gén transport company; (par route) haulage company GB, trucking company US; **compagnie de ~ maritime** shipping line; **le prix comprend le ~ en car** (excursion) the price includes the coach GB ou bus trip; (de l'aéroport) the price includes the coach GB ou bus transfer; **endommagé pendant le ~** damaged in transit; **au cours de mon ~ à l' hôpital** when I was being taken to hospital; **2** Mil Naut (**bâtiment de**) **~** transport (ship).

II transports *nmpl* **1** Transp transport ₵, transportation ₵ US; **~s urbains/régionaux** urban/regional transport; **2** liter (effusion) transports; **~s de joie** transports of joy.

■ **~ de fonds** Comm transfer of funds; **~ sur les lieux** Jur *visit to the scene of the crime by the examining magistrate*; **~ de troupes** Mil Naut troop transport; **~s en commun** public transport ou transportation US; **~s publics** Admin public transport ou transportation US.

transportable /tʀɑ̃spɔʀtabl/ *adj* [*objet*] transportable; **il n'est pas ~** [*blessé*] he cannot be moved.

transporter /tʀɑ̃spɔʀte/ [1] **I** *vtr* **1** (déplacer) (sur soi) to carry [*personne, objet*]; (avec un véhicule) to transport [*passagers, marchandises*]; **~ qch sur son dos/dans ses bras** to carry sth on one's back/in one's arms; **~ un million de passagers par an** to transport one million passengers a year; **marchandises transportées par rail/bateau** goods transported by rail/ship; **être transporté à l'hôpital** to be taken to hospital; **être transporté d'urgence à l'hôpital** to be rushed to hospital; **l'avion qui transportait le président à Bastia** the plane which was taking the president to Bastia; **le taxi/l'avion/le bateau transportant Madame Leroy** the taxi/the plane/the boat carrying Mrs Leroy; **avion qui peut ~ 500 passagers** plane which can carry 500 passengers; **2** (transférer) to carry [*pollen, virus, maladie*]; **3** (en imagination) to transport; **être transporté dans un monde féerique/au Moyen Âge** to be transported to a magical world/to the Middle Ages; **4** liter (ravir) **être transporté de joie/rage** to be beside oneself with joy/rage.

II se transporter *vpr* **1** fml (aller) to take oneself; **se ~ sur les lieux** [*juge d'instruction*] to visit the scene of the crime; **2** (en imagination) **transportez-vous à Venise/au Moyen Âge/200 ans en arrière** imagine you are in Venice/in the Middle Ages/200 years in the past.

transporteur /tʀɑ̃spɔʀtœʀ/ *nm* **1** ▶510 (entreprise) carrier; **~ aérien** air carrier; **~ routier** road haulier GB, road haulage contractor GB, trucking company US; **~ maritime** (de marchandises) shipping company; (de personnes) shipping line; **2** (machine) conveyor; **3** (navire) **~ de gaz** gas tanker; **~ de vrac** bulk carrier.

transposable /tʀɑ̃spozabl/ *adj* transposable.

transposer /tʀɑ̃spoze/ [1] *vtr* (tous contextes) to transpose [*mythe, image, mot*] (**dans, en** into; **sur** onto).

transposition /tʀɑ̃spozisjɔ̃/ *nf* (tous contextes) transposition.

transpyrénéen, **-éenne** /tʀɑ̃spiʀeneɛ̃, ɛn/ *adj* [*région, route*] trans-Pyrenean.

transsaharien, **-ienne** /tʀɑ̃ssaaʀjɛ̃, ɛn/ *adj* [*route, rallye*] trans-Sahara.

transsexualisme /tʀɑ̃ssɛksɥalism/ *nm* transsexualism.

transsexualité /tʀɑ̃ssɛksyalite/ *nf* transsexuality.

transsexuel, **-elle** /tʀɑ̃ssɛksɥɛl/ *adj, nm,f* transsexual.

transsibérien, **-ienne** /tʀɑ̃ssibeʀjɛ̃, ɛn/ **I** *adj* trans-Siberian.

II *nm* **le Transsibérien** the Trans-Siberian Railway.

transsonique /tʀɑ̃ssɔnik/ *adj* [*vitesse*] transonic.

transsubstantiation /tʀɑ̃ssypstɑ̃sjasjɔ̃/ *nf* transubstantiation.

transuranien, **-ienne** /tʀɑ̃syʀanjɛ̃, ɛn/ **I** *adj* transuranic.

II *nm* transuranic element.

Transvaal /tʀɑ̃sval/ *nprm* Transvaal.

transvasement /tʀɑ̃svazmɑ̃/ *nm* decanting.

transvaser /tʀɑ̃svaze/ [1] *vtr* to decant [*liquide*].

transversal, **~e**, *mpl* **-aux** /tʀɑ̃svɛʀsal, o/ **I** *adj* [*muscle, disposition*] transverse; **moteur à disposition ~e** a transversely-mounted engine; **coupe ~e** cross-section; **poutre ~e** cross-beam; **route/rue ~e** side road/street.

II transversale *nf* **1** Math transversal; **2** Transp (route) (grande) cross-country route; (petite) side road; (rue) side street.

transversalement /tʀɑ̃svɛʀsalmɑ̃/ *adv* **1** gén crosswise; **2** Aut transversely.

transverse /tʀɑ̃svɛʀs/ *adj* [*apophyse, muscle*] transverse.

transvestisme /tʀɑ̃svɛstism/ *nm* transvestism.

Transylvanie /tʀɑ̃silvani/ ▶692 *nprf* Transylvania.

trapèze /tʀapɛz/ *nm* **1** Sport trapeze; **être au ~** to be on the trapeze; **faire du ~** to perform on the trapeze; **2** Math trapezium GB, trapezoid US, **~ isocèle/rectangle** isosceles/rectangular trapezium; **3** Anat trapezium.

■ **~ volant** flying trapeze.

trapéziste /tʀapezist/ ▶510 *nmf* trapeze artist.

trapézoèdre /tʀapezɔɛdʀ/ *nm* trapezohedron.

trapézoïdal, **~e**, *mpl* **-aux** /tʀapezɔidal, o/ *adj* trapezoid.

trapézoïde /tʀapezɔid/ **I** *adj* Math trapezoid.

II *nm* Anat trapezoid.

trappe /tʀap/ *nf* **1** gén (ouverture) trap door; **2** Théât trap door; **passer à la ~** fig to be whisked off; **3** Chasse trap.

■ **~ de visite** inspection trap.

Trappe /tʀap/ *nf* **1** (ordre) Trappist order; **2** (couvent) Trappist monastery.

trappeur /tʀapœʀ/ ▶ 510 *nm* trapper.

trappiste /tʀapist/ *nm* Trappist (monk).

trappistine /tʀapistin/ *nf* Trappistine.

trapu, **~e** /tʀapy/ *adj* **1** (court et large) [*homme, silhouette*] stocky, thickset; [*monument, bâtiment*] squat; **2**○ (ardu) [*problème, question*] tough; **3**○ (calé) students' slang [*élève*] brainy○; **être ~ en** to be an ace at.

traque /tʀak/ *nf* **1** Chasse tracking; **2** fig (chasse à l'homme) hunt; **la ~ des bandits** the hunt for the criminals.

traquenard /tʀaknaʀ/ *nm* lit, fig trap; **tomber dans un ~** to fall into a trap.

traquer /tʀake/ [1] *vtr* **1** (poursuivre) to track down [sb], to hunt [sb] down; (importuner) [*photographe*] to hound [*vedette*]; **2** (contrôler) to monitor [*dépenses, surplus*]; **3** Chasse to track down, to stalk [*animal*].

traquet /tʀakɛ/ *nm* Zool **~ (motteux)** wheatear; **~ oreillard** black-eared wheatear; **~ (pâtre)** stonechat.

trauma /tʀoma/ *nm* Méd, Psych trauma.

traumatique /tʀomatik/ *adj* Méd, Psych traumatic.

traumatisant, **~e** /tʀomatizɑ̃, ɑ̃t/ *adj* Méd, Psych traumatic.

traumatiser /tʀomatize/ [1] *vtr* Psych, aussi hum to traumatize [*personne*].

traumatisme /tʀomatism/ *nm* **1** Méd traumatism; **~ crânien** cranial traumatism; **2** Psych, fig trauma.

traumatologie /tʀomatɔlɔʒi/ *nf* traumatology; **service de ~** trauma unit.

traumatologique /tʀomatɔlɔʒik/ *adj* [*chirurgie, traitement*] trauma (*épith*).

traumatologiste /tʀomatɔlɔʒist/, **traumatologue** /tʀomatɔlɔg/ *nmf* trauma consultant.

travail[1], *pl* **-aux** /tʀavaj, o/ **I** *nm* **1** (contraire de repos) work; **le ~ intellectuel** intellectual work; **le ~ scolaire** schoolwork; **ça demande des mois de ~** it requires months of work; **se mettre au ~** to get down to work, to start work; **être en plein ~** to be busy working; **2** (tâche faite, à faire) job; (ensemble des tâches, besogne) work ₵; **faire un ~** to do a job; **distribuer le ~** to allocate jobs; **ce n'est pas mon ~** it's not my job; **c'est un ~ de professionnel** (à faire) it's a job for a professional; (bien fait) it's a very professional job; **c'est un ~ d'homme** it's man's work; **commencer un ~** to start a job; **mener un ~ de recherche** to do research work; **avoir du ~** to have work to do; **j'ai un ~ fou** I'm up to my eyes in work, I've got a lot of work on; **les enfants, ça donne du ~, les enfants, c'est du ~** children make a lot of work; **les gros travaux** the heavy work; **s'occuper à de petits travaux** to do little jobs; **faire quelques travaux de jardinage** to do a few gardening jobs; **(félicitations) c'est du beau ~!** also iron you've done a great job on that; **qu'est-ce que c'est que ce ~?** what do you call this?; **et voilà le ~!** that's that done!; **3** (fait d'exercer un emploi) work; (emploi rémunéré) work ₵, job; (lieu) work; **ne me téléphone pas à mon ~** don't call me at work; **chercher du/un ~** to look for work/a job; **bien content d'avoir du/un ~** glad to be in work/to have a job; **être sans ~** to be out of work; **donner du ~ à qn** (employer) to give sb a job; **reprendre le ~** to go back to work; **cesser le ~** to stop work; **aller au ~** to go to work; **être au ~** to be at work; **que fais-tu comme ~?** what do you do?, what's your job?; **il ne fait que son ~** he's only doing his job; **le ~ en usine/de bureau** factory/office ou clerical work; **le ~ temporaire/à mi-temps** temporary/part-time work; **un ~ à mi-temps** a part-time job; **le ~ en équipe** team work; **le ~ en équipes** shiftwork; **le ~ de nuit** nightwork; **il a un ~ de nuit** he works nights; **le ~ indépendant** freelance work, self-employment; **conditions/semaine de ~** working conditions/week; **vivre de son ~** to work for one's living; ▶ **salaire**; **4** Écon, Sociol (activité, population active) labour[GB] ₵; **le capital et le ~** capital and labour[GB]; **organisation/division du ~** organization/division of labour[GB]; **force de ~** workforce; **entrer dans le monde du ~** to enter the world of work; **la psychologie du ~** industrial psychology; **5** (résultat d'un fonctionnement) (de machine, d'organe) work ₵; **le ~ du cœur** the work done by the heart; **le ~ musculaire** muscular effort, the work done by the muscles; **6** (ouvrage érudit) work (**sur** on); **publier un ~ sur la Renaissance** to publish a work on the Renaissance; **7** (façonnage) **le ~ de** working with ou in [*métal, bois, pierre*]; **le ~ de l'ivoire est difficile** working with ou in ivory is difficult; **apprendre le ~ du bois/métal** to learn woodwork/metalwork; **8** (technique, exécution) workmanship; **un ~ superbe** a superb piece of workmanship; **un coffret d'un beau ~** a beautifully made box; **une dentelle d'un ~ délicat** a delicate piece of lacework; **9** Mécan, Phys work; **10** (action) (d'eau, érosion) action (**de** of); fig (d'imagination, inconscient) workings (*pl*) (**de** of); **le ~ du temps** the work of time; **11** (altération) (de vin) fermentation, working; (de bois) warping; **12** Méd (pendant accouchement) labour[GB]; **entrer/être en ~** to go into/be in labour[GB]; **salle de ~** labour[GB] ward.

II travaux *nmpl* **1** (en chantier) work (*sg*); (sur une route) roadworks GB, roadwork ₵ US; **travaux de construction/réfection/soutènement** construction/renovation/retaining work ₵; **travaux de terrassement** earthworks; **travaux d'aménagement** (de bâtiment) alterations (**de** to), improvements (**de** to); (d'un site) redevelopment ₵ (**de** of); (d'une route) roadworks (**de** on); **faire faire des travaux dans sa maison** to have work done in one's house; **nous sommes en plein travaux** we're in the middle of having some work done; **'fermé pour travaux'** (sur une devanture) 'closed for repairs ou alterations'; **'attention, travaux'** gén 'caution, work in progress'; (sur une route) 'caution, road under repair'; **2** (recherche, études) work ₵ (**sur** on); **publier le résultat de ses travaux** to publish the results of one's work; **3** (débats) (d'assemblée, de commission) deliberations; **4** (opérations de même nature) **les travaux agricoles/de la ferme** agricultural/farm work; **travaux de couture** needlework.

■ **~ à la chaîne** assembly-line work; **~ clandestin** *work for which no earnings are declared*; **~ à domicile** working at or from home; **~ des enfants** child labour[GB]; **~ d'intérêt général** Jur community service; **~ manuel** manual work; **~ au noir**○ gén *work for which no earnings are declared*; (exercice d'un second emploi non déclaré) moonlighting; **~ aux pièces** piece work; **~ posté** shift work; **~ de Romain** Herculean task; **~ de titan** = **~ de Romain**; **travaux d'aiguille** needlework ₵; **travaux des champs** agricultural ou farm work ₵; **travaux de dame** fancywork ₵; **travaux dirigés**, **TD** Univ practical (*sg*); **travaux forcés** Jur hard labour[GB] (*sg*); fig slave labour[GB] ₵; **travaux manuels** Scol handicrafts; **travaux ménagers** housework ₵; **travaux pratiques**, **TP** Scol, Univ practical work ₵; (en laboratoire) lab work ₵; **travaux préparatoires** Jur (pour un texte de loi) preliminary documents; **travaux publics**, **TP** (travail) civil engineering ₵; (ouvrages) civil engineering works, public works; **travaux routiers** roadworks GB, roadwork ₵ US.

travail[2], *pl* **~s** /tʀavaj/ *nm* (appareil) trave.

travaillé, **~e** /tʀavaje/ **I** *pp* ▶ **travailler**.

II *pp adj* **1** (fignolé) [*bijou*] finely-worked; [*sculpture*] elaborate; [*or, argent*] wrought; [*métal*] chased; [*dessin*] elaborate, detailed; [*langue, style, article*] polished; **l'éclairage a été longuement ~** the lighting has been carefully thought out; **2** (tourmenté) [*personne*] **~ par le doute/l'inquiétude** racked with doubt/anxiety; **3** (non chômé) **heures ~es** (à faire) hours of work; (faites) hours worked; **on exige un minimum de 45 heures ~es par mois** they require a minimum of 45 hours of work per month; **le nombre d'heures ~es a diminué** the number of hours worked has decreased.

travailler /tʀavaje/ [1] **I** *vtr* **1** (pour perfectionner) to work on [*style, matière scolaire, mouvement, voix, muscles*]; to practise[GB] [*sport, instrument, chant, sonate*]; **~ son latin** to work on one's Latin; **~ le saut en longueur** to practise[GB] the long jump; **2** (manipuler) to work [*bois, métal*]; Culin to knead [*pâte*]; to stir [sth] until smooth [*sauce*]; Agric to work, to cultivate [*terre*]; to cultivate [*vigne*]; **3** Sport to train [*cheval, taureau*]; **~ une balle** to put (some) spin on a ball; **4** (préoccuper) **~ qn** [*affaire, idée*] to be ou prey on sb's mind, to bother sb; (tourmenter) [*jalousie , douleur*] to plague sb; **je ne sais pas ce qui le travaille** I don't know what's bothering him; **un doute me travaillait** I had a nagging doubt; **c'est la jalousie qui le travaille** he's plagued ou tormented by jealousy; **ce sont ses dents qui le travaillent** (parlant d'un bébé) he is out of sorts because he's teething.

II travailler à *vtr ind* **~ à** to work on [*projet, dissertation*]; to work towards [*objectif*]; **~ quatre ans à sa thèse** to work on one's thesis for four years; **~ à rétablir la paix** to endeavour[GB] to restore peace; **~ à la perte de qn** to try to engineer sb's downfall.

III *vi* **1** (faire un effort) [*personne, machine*] to work; [*muscles*] to work; **~ de ses mains** to work with one's hands; **~ sur un texte/projet** to work on a text/project; **faire ~ un élève** to make a pupil work; **faire ~ ses biceps** to use one's biceps; **faire ~ son cerveau** to apply one's mind; **ton imagination travaille trop** you have an overactive imagination; **2** (exercer un métier) to work; **~ en usine/à domicile** to work in a factory/at home; **~ dans l'édition/le textile** to work in publishing/textiles; **~ comme secrétaire** to work as a secretary; **~ en équipes/de nuit** to work shifts/nights; **~ en indépendant** to work freelance, to be self-employed; **ta mère travaille?** does your mother work?; **il a hâte de ~** he can't wait to start work; **faire ~ les enfants** to put children to work; **~ au noir** gén *to work without declaring one's earnings*; (exercer un second emploi non déclaré) to moonlight; **3** (faire des affaires) Comm [*commerçant, magasin, hôtel*] to do business; **bien ~** to do good business; **l'épicier/restaurant ne travaille pas beaucoup** the grocer/restaurant isn't doing much business; **~ avec l'étranger** to do business abroad; **~ pour l'exportation** to work in exports; **nous travaillons surtout l'été/avec les touristes** most of our trade is in the summer/with tourists; **~ à perte** [*entreprise, commerce*] to run at a loss; **4** (produire un revenu) [*argent*] to work; **faire ~ son argent** to make one's money work for one; **5** (œuvrer) **~ pour/contre qn** to work for/against sb; **nous voulons la paix et c'est dans ce sens que nous travaillons** we want peace and we are working toward(s) it; **~ pour/contre ses intérêts** to act in/against one's own interests; **6** (s'entraîner) [*athlète*] to train; [*boxeur*] to train, work out; [*musicien, danseur*] to practise[GB]; **~ aux barres parallèles** to work on the parallel bars; **7** (se modifier) [*bois*] to warp; [*vin*] to ferment; [*pâte*] to prove, to rise; **8** (se déformer) [*poutre*] to be in stress.

travailleur, **-euse** /tʀavajœʀ, øz/ **I** *adj* **1**

(appliqué) [*élève, employé*] hardworking; **2** Sociol [*classes, masses*] working.

II *nm,f* worker.

III **travailleuse** *nf* (meuble) workbox, sewing box.

■ **~ agricole** farm worker; **~ clandestin** *worker not declared by his employer*; **~ à domicile** homeworker; **~ de force** labourer[GB]; **~ frontalier** *person who crosses a border to work every day*; **~ indépendant** self-employed person, freelance (worker); **~ intellectuel** intellectual worker; **~ manuel** manual worker; **~ au noir** gén *worker who doesn't declare his earnings*; (ayant un deuxi ème emploi non déclaré) moonlighter; **~ social** social worker; **travailleuse familiale** home help.

travaillisme /tʀavajism/ *nm* Labour doctrine.

travailliste /tʀavajist/ I *adj* [*gouvernement, idée, député, parti*] Labour; **congrès ~** Labour party congress; **être ~** (membre du parti) to be a member of the Labour party; (sympathisant) to be a Labour party supporter.

II *nmf* (député) Labour MP; (votant) Labour supporter; **le candidat des ~s** the Labour candidate.

travée /tʀave/ *nf* **1** (rangée) row; **2** Tech, Constr span.

travelling /tʀavliŋ/ *nm* (méthode) tracking; (plan) tracking shot; **~ avant/arrière** tracking in/out; **~ latéral** sideways tracking.

travelo◑ /tʀavlo/ *nm* drag queen○, transvestite.

travers /tʀavɛʀ/ I *nm inv* **1** (petit défaut) foible, quirk; (erreur) mistake; **il n'a pas succombé à ce ~** he didn't make that mistake; **le film ne tombe jamais dans le ~ de la sensiblerie** the film never lapses into sentimentality; **2** Naut (côté) beam; **par le ~** abeam; **3** Culin **~ de porc** sparerib.

II **à travers** *loc* **1** (ponctuel) [*voir, regarder*] through; **il est passé à ~ tous les contrôles** he slipped through all the checks; **passer à ~ les mailles du filet** lit, fig to slip through the net; **la vitre est si sale qu'on ne voit pas à ~** the window is so dirty that you can't see through it; **sentir le froid à ~ ses gants** to feel the cold through one's gloves; **2** (dans l'espace) [*voyager, marcher*] across; **voyager à ~ l'Europe/le monde** to travel across Europe/the world; **passer** or **aller** or **couper à ~ champs** to cut across the fields; **se promener à ~ les prés** to walk through the fields; **la maladie affecte des milliers de gens à ~ le monde** the disease affects thousands of people across the world; **le mouvement s'étend à ~ le pays** the movement is spreading through ou across the country; **3** (dans le temps) through; **voyager à ~ le temps** to travel through time; **des événements qui se répètent à ~ l'histoire** events which recur through ou throughout history; **4** (par l'intermédiaire de) through; **je ne le connais qu'à ~ ses écrits** I only know him through his writing; **c'est le racisme qu'ils combattent à ~ lui** they're fighting racism through him; **à ~ ces informations** through this information.

III **au travers** *loc* **1** (en traversant) through; **passer au ~ de** fig to escape [*contrôle, inspection*]; **il y a eu des licenciements, heureusement il est passé au ~** there have been redundancies, fortunately his job wasn't affected; **2** (par l'intermédiaire de) in; **au ~ d'une série d'entretiens** in a series of interviews.

IV **de travers** *loc adv* **1** (dans une mauvaise position) askew; **il a mis son chapeau de ~** he has put his hat on askew; **ta veste est boutonnée de ~** your jacket is buttoned up wrongly; **il a le nez de ~** he has a twisted nose; **marcher de ~** to walk sideways; **se garer de ~** to park badly; **j'ai avalé de ~** lit it went down the wrong way; **regarder qn de ~** fig to give sb filthy looks, to glare at sb; **2** (de façon inexacte) wrong, wrongly; **tout va de ~ aujourd'hui** everything's going wrong today; **quand elle est de mauvaise humeur, elle prend tout de ~** when she's in a bad mood, she takes everything the wrong way; **je fais tout de ~ aujourd'hui** I can't do anything right today; **comprendre de ~** to misunderstand.

V **en travers** *loc* (en position transversale) across; **un bus était en ~ de la route** a bus was sideways, blocking the road; **se mettre en ~ de la route** [*personnes*] to stand in the middle of the road; **la voiture a dérapé et s'est mise en ~ de la route** the car skidded and ended up sideways, blocking the road; **se mettre en ~ du chemin de qn** fig to get in sb's way; **avoir un os en ~ de la gorge** to have a bone stuck in one's throat; **rester en ~ de la gorge à qn**○ fig [*attitude, arrogance*] to stick in sb's throat; [*propos, insultes*] to be hard to swallow; ▶ **long**.

traversable /tʀavɛʀsabl/ *adj* [*cours d'eau, chemin*] which can be crossed (*après n*); **rivière ~ à gué** fordable river.

traverse /tʀavɛʀs/ *nf* **1** Rail sleeper GB, tie US; **2** Constr (de fenêtre, grille, d'armoire) crosspiece, strut; (de porte) rail; **3** (rue) side street.

traversée /tʀavɛʀse/ *nf* **1** (de mer, pont, pays, d'océan) crossing; **faire une bonne ~** to have a good crossing; **faire la ~ du fleuve en pirogue** to cross the river in a dugout; **la ~ de la Chine en voiture** crossing China by car; **faire la ~ du Vercors à pied** to cross the Vercors on foot; **la ~ du désert** lit crossing the desert; fig (d'homme politique) a period in the wilderness; (entreprise) a difficult period; **2** (de ville, tunnel) **évitez la ~ de Paris aux heures de pointe** avoid going through Paris in the rush hour.

traverser /tʀavɛʀse/ [1] *vtr* **1** (passer d'un côté à l'autre) to cross [*route, pont, frontière*]; to cross, to go across [*ville, montagne, océan, pays, pièce*]; (passer à travers) to go through, to pass through [*ville, pays, forêt, tunnel*]; to make one's way through [*groupe, foule*]; **il traversa le salon pour aller dans la chambre** he went ou passed through the living-room to get to the bedroom; **l'avion traverse une zone de turbulences** the aircraft is going through a spot of turbulence; **il traversa le jardin en courant** he ran across the garden GB ou yard US; **~ le lac en bateau** to cross ou go across the lake in a boat; **~ le lac à la nage** to swim across the lake; **~ (une rivière) à gué** to ford a river; **il a traversé sans regarder** he crossed the road without looking; **maintenant, on traverse** now let's cross over; **2** (franchir) [*rivière*] to go through, to flow through [*région, plaine*]; [*route, tunnel*] to go through [*ville, région, montagne*]; [*pont, rivière*] to cross [*voie ferrée, ville*]; **3** (transpercer) [*humidité, pluie*] to come through [*vêtement, mur*]; **la balle lui a traversé le bras** the bullet went ou passed right through his arm; **4** (passer par une période) [*population, pays, entreprise*] to go through [*crise, difficulté*]; [*personne*] to live through, to go through [*guerre, occupation*]; (subsister) liter [*manuscrit, nom*] to live on through [*siècles*]; [*pratique, tradition*] to persist through [*temps, générations*]; **ils ont traversé des moments difficiles** they've gone through some difficult times; **5** fig (se présenter de manière fugitive) [*douleur*] to shoot through [*personne, membre*]; **~ l'esprit de qn** to cross sb's mind.

traversier /tʀavɛʀsje/ *nm* C (ferry) ferry.

traversière /tʀavɛʀsjɛʀ/ ▶ 534 *adj f* **flûte ~** (transverse) flute.

traversin /tʀavɛʀsɛ̃/ *nm* bolster.

travesti, **~e** /tʀavɛsti/ I *pp* ▶ **travestir**.

II *pp adj* (déguisé) in disguise; **rôle ~** role played by a member of the opposite sex.

III *nm* **1** (personne) transvestite; **2** Théât (acteur) actor playing a female role; (dans un cabaret) drag artist○, female impersonator; **3** (déguisement) fancy dress.

travestir /tʀavɛstiʀ/ [3] I *vtr* **1** (déguiser) to dress [sb] up [*personne, acteur*] (**en** as); **2** (dénaturer) to distort [*vérité, réalité*]; to misrepresent [*pensée*].

II **se travestir** *vpr* **1** (se déguiser) to dress up (**en** as); **2** (prendre l'apparence du sexe opposé) to cross-dress, to dress up as a member of the opposite sex.

travestisme /tʀavɛstism/ *nm* transvestism.

travestissement /tʀavɛstismɑ̃/ *nm* **1** (action de se déguiser) dressing-up; **2** (déguisement) fancy dress, disguise; **3** (dénaturation) distortion, travesty; **4** Psych transvestism, cross-dressing.

traviole○: **de traviole** /d(ə)tʀavjɔl/ *loc adv* [*accrocher, attacher*] skew-whiff○ GB, crooked; **le tableau est accroché de ~** the picture is hung skew-whiff○ GB ou crooked; **il marche de ~**○ he walks lopsided○; **il comprend tout de ~**○ he always gets the wrong end of the stick○.

trayeur, **-euse** /tʀɛjœʀ, øz/ I ▶ 510 *nm,f* milker/milkmaid.

II **trayeuse** *nf* (machine à traire) milking machine.

trayon /tʀɛjɔ̃/ *nm* teat, papilla spéc.

trébuchant, **~e** /tʀebyʃɑ̃, ɑ̃t/ *adj* [*démarche*] stumbling; ▶ **sonnant**.

trébucher /tʀebyʃe/ [1] *vi* **1** lit to stumble (**sur** on; **contre** against); **l'obstacle l'a fait ~** the obstacle made him stumble; **2** fig [*candidat, adversaire*] to slip up; **~ sur un mot** to stumble over a word.

trébuchet /tʀebyʃɛ/ *nm* **1** (piège) bird-trap; **2** (balance) assay balance.

tréfilage /tʀefilaʒ/ *nm* wiredrawing.

tréfiler /tʀefile/ [1] *vtr* to wiredraw.

tréfilerie /tʀefilʀi/ *nf* wireworks (+ *v sg*).

tréfileur /tʀefilœʀ/ *nm* (ouvrier) wiredrawer; (industriel) owner of a wireworks.

tréfileuse /tʀefiløz/ *nf* (machine) wiredrawer, wiredrawing machine.

trèfle /tʀɛfl/ *nm* **1** Agric, Bot clover; **~ à quatre feuilles** four-leaf clover; **2** Jeux (carte) club; (couleur) clubs (*pl*); **la dame/le dix de ~** the Queen/the ten of clubs; **jouer ~** to play clubs; **avoir du ~** to be holding clubs; **3** Aut **échangeur en ~** cloverleaf junction; **4** Archit trefoil; **5**○ (argent) dough○, bread○; **6** (symbole de l'Irlande) shamrock.

■ **~ blanc** white clover; **~ incarnat** crimson clover; **~ des prés** red clover; **~ rampant** = **~ blanc**; **~ rouge** = **~ des prés**.

tréflière /tʀeflijɛʀ/ *nf* field of clover.

tréfonds /tʀefɔ̃/ *nm inv* liter **le ~ de** the very depths of.

treillage /tʀɛjaʒ/ *nm* **1** (assemblage de lattes) trellis; **~ métallique** wire grille; **2** (clôture) lattice fence; **3** (pour vigne) trellis.

treillager /tʀɛjaʒe/ [13] *vtr* **1** to put a trellis on [*mur*]; to lattice [*window*]; **2** (clôturer) to put a lattice fence around.

treille /tʀɛj/ *nf* **1** (tonnelle) (vine) arbour[GB]; **2** (vigne) climbing vine; **le jus de la ~** the juice of the grape.

treillis /tʀɛji/ *nm inv* **1** Mil (tenue) fatigues (*pl*); **~ de combat** combat fatigues; **2** Tex canvas; **3** (assemblage de lattes) trellis; **~ métallique** wire grille; **4** (de verrière, vitrail) lattice.

treize /tʀɛz/ ▶ 545, 407, 212 I *adj inv* thirteen.

II *pron* thirteen; **vendre des œufs ~ à la douzaine** Comm to sell eggs at thirteen for the price of twelve; fig **il y en a ~ à la douzaine** they are ten a penny fig.

treizième /tʀɛzjɛm/ ▶ 545, 212 *adj* thirteenth.

■ **~ mois** *bonus equal to a month's salary*.

trekking /tʀɛkiŋ/ ▶ 449 *nm* (activité) trekking.

tréma /tʀema/ *nm* Ling diaeresis; **i ~** i diaeresis.

trémail /tʀemaj/ *nm* Pêche trammel.

tremblant, **~e** /tʀɑ̃blɑ̃, ɑ̃t/ *adj* **1** [*personne, animal, mains*] shaking (**de** with), trembling (**de** with); **être tout ~** to be shaking ou trembling all over; **~ de peur/de froid/d'émotion** shaking ou trembling with fear/with cold/with emotion; **2** [*voix*] trembling (**de** with); **d'une voix ~e de colère** his/her voice trembling with anger; **3** [*image, lueur*] flickering; [*son*] tremulous, quavering.

tremble /tʀɑ̃bl/ *nm* aspen.

tremblement /tʀɑ̃bləmɑ̃/ *nm* **1** (de personne, mains) shaking ¢, trembling ¢; (de lèvres) trembling ¢; **son corps était agité de ~s** he/she was trembling ou shaking all over; **2** (de voix) tremor, trembling ¢; (de voix âgée) quavering ¢; (de son, note) wavering ¢; [*de lueur, lumière*] flickering ¢; **parler avec des ~s dans la voix** to speak with a tremor in one's voice ou in a trembling voice; **3** (de feuilles) quivering; (de vitres) rattling ¢; **un ~** (de sol, d'immeuble) a tremor.

■ **~ de terre** earthquake.

IDIOMES **et tout le ~**○ and the whole caboodle○.

trembler /tʀɑ̃ble/ [1] *vi* **1** [*personne, mains, jambes*] to shake (**de** with), to tremble; **~ de tout son corps** ou **de tous ses membres** to shake ou tremble all over; **2** [*voix*] (de colère, joie) to tremble, to shake (**de** with); (de vieillesse) to quaver; [*son, note*] to waver; **3** [*immeuble, plancher*] to shake; **la terre a encore tremblé en Californie** (légèrement) there have been tremors again in California; (tremblement de terre) there has been another earthquake in California; **faire ~ qch** to shake sth, to make sth shake; **faire ~ les vitres** to make the windows shake ou rattle; **4** (avoir peur) to tremble (**devant** before); **~ pour qn** to fear for sb; **~ à l'idée de faire** to tremble at the thought of doing; **je tremble qu'il ne s'aperçoive de mon erreur** I'm terrified he'll notice my mistake; **faire ~ qn** to terrify sb; **5** [*lumière, flamme, image*] to flicker; **6** [*feuilles*] to quiver; (mouvement très doux) to shiver.

IDIOMES **~ comme une feuille** to shake like a leaf.

tremblotant, **~e** /tʀɑ̃blɔtɑ̃, ɑ̃t/ *adj* **1** [*personne, main*] trembling; **il était tout ~** he was shaking ou trembling all over; **2** [*voix*] (d'émotion) tremulous; (de vieillesse) quavering; [*son*] quavering; **3** [*image, flamme, lumière*] flickering.

tremblote○ /tʀɑ̃blɔt/ *nf* **avoir la ~** (à cause du froid) to have the shivers; (à cause de l'âge) to have the shakes○; (par peur, nervosité) to have the jitters○.

tremblotement /tʀɑ̃blɔtmɑ̃/ *nm* **1** (de personne, mains) trembling ¢, tremor; **les ~s de ses mains** his/her trembling hands; **2** (de voix) (émue, effrayée) tremor; (âgée) quaver; **3** (de lumière) flickering ¢.

trembloter /tʀɑ̃blɔte/ [1] *vi* **1** [*personne, mains*] to tremble slightly; **2** [*voix*] (de joie, d'émotion) to tremble; (de vieillesse) to quaver; **3** [*lumière, flamme*] to flicker.

trémie /tʀemi/ *nf* **1** Ind, Tech hopper; **2** (mangeoire) feeding box; **3** Gén Civ **~ d'accès à un passage souterrain/tunnel** underpass/tunnel approach.

trémière /tʀemjɛʀ/ *adj f* **rose ~** hollyhock.

trémolo /tʀemɔlo/ *nm* **1** (de voix) quaver; **avoir des ~s dans la voix** to have a quavering voice; **2** (d'instrument) tremolo.

trémoussement /tʀemusmɑ̃/ *nm* **1** (agitation) fidgeting ¢; **2** (danse) prancing (around) ¢.

trémousser: **se trémousser** /tʀemuse/ [1] *vpr* **1** (s'agiter) to fidget; **2** (danser) to wiggle around.

trempage /tʀɑ̃paʒ/ *nm* **1** (de linge, légumes secs) soaking; **2** (de semences) soaking; **3** Tech (d'orge) mashing, steeping; (de verre) tempering; (de papier) damping, wetting.

trempe /tʀɑ̃p/ *nf* **1** (de personne) **avoir de la ~** to be made of stern stuff; **il faudrait quelqu'un de votre ~** we need someone of your calibre[GB]; **avoir la ~ d'un dirigeant** to have the makings of a leader; **2**○ (coups) walloping○ ¢; **recevoir une bonne ~**○ to get a good walloping○; **3** (de métal) (action) tempering; (qualité) temper.

trempé, **~e** /tʀɑ̃pe/ **I** *pp* ▶ **tremper**.

II *pp adj* **1** [*personne, vêtements*] soaked (through), drenched; [*herbe*] sodden; [*linge*] soaking wet; **être ~ de sueur** to be soaked in sweat, to be dripping with sweat; **avoir les cheveux ~s** to have dripping wet hair; **2** Tech [*acier*] tempered; [*verre*] toughened; **3** [*caractère*] hardened, tough.

tremper /tʀɑ̃pe/ [1] **I** *vtr* **1** (beaucoup) [*pluie, personne*] to soak [*personne, vêtement*]; **2** (rapidement) to dip (**dans** in); **~ son biscuit dans son thé** to dunk one's biscuit GB ou cookie US in one's tea; **j'ai juste trempé mes lèvres** I just had a sip; **3** (longuement) to soak [*mains, aliment*] (**dans** in); **4** Tech to temper [*acier, verre*]; **5** (aguerrir) to strengthen [*personne*].

II *vi* **1** (être dans un liquide) [*linge, légumes secs*] to soak; **faire ~ qch** to soak sth; **mettre qch à ~** to put sth to soak; **laisser qch à ~** to leave sth to soak; **2** (être impliqué) **~ dans qch** to be mixed up in sth.

III se tremper *vpr* (dans la mer) to go for a dip; (dans un bain) to have a quick bath.

trempette○ /tʀɑ̃pɛt/ *nf* (quick) dip; **faire ~** to go for a dip.

tremplin /tʀɑ̃plɛ̃/ *nm* **1** Sport (de natation, gymnastique) springboard; (de ski) ski jump; (de ski nautique) water-ski jump; **2** fig springboard.

trémulation /tʀemylasjɔ̃/ *nf* tremor.

trentaine /tʀɑ̃tɛn/ *nf* about thirty; ▶ **cinquantaine**.

trente /tʀɑ̃t/ ▶ **545**, **212** *adj inv, pron* thirty.

trente(-)et(-)un /tʀɑ̃teœ̃/ **I** ▶ **545**, **212** *adj inv, pron* thirty-one.

II ▶ **449** *nm* Jeux **le ~** ≈ pontoon.

IDIOMES **se mettre sur son ~**○ to dress up to the nines; **être sur son ~**○ to be dressed up to the nines.

trentenaire /tʀɑ̃tənɛʀ/ *adj* **1** (qui dure trente ans) thirty-year; **2** (qui a 30 ans et plus) [*personne*] in his/her thirties; [*arbre, construction*] at least thirty years old.

trente-six /tʀɑ̃tsis/ ▶ **545**, **212** *adj inv, pron* thirty-six.

IDIOMES **(en) voir ~ chandelles**○ to see stars.

trente-trois /tʀɑ̃ttʀwa/ ▶ **545**, **212** *adj inv, pron* thirty-three; **'dites ~'** 'say ninety-nine'.

■ **~ tours** LP, album.

trentième /tʀɑ̃tjɛm/ ▶ **545** *adj* thirtieth.

trépan /tʀepɑ̃/ *nm* **1** Tech trepan; **2** Méd trephine.

trépanation /tʀepanasjɔ̃/ *nf* Méd trephination.

trépané, **~e** /tʀepane/ *nm,f* person who has been trepanned.

trépaner /tʀepane/ [1] *vtr* to trephine.

trépas† /tʀepɑ/ *nm* demise; **passer de vie à ~** to pass on GB, to pass away.

trépassé, **~e** /tʀepɑse/ **I** *pp* ▶ **trépasser**.

II *pp adj* deceased.

III *nm,f* **les ~s** the dead, the departed; **la fête des ~s** All Souls' Day.

trépasser /tʀepɑse/ [1] *vi* to pass away.

trépidant, **~e** /tʀepidɑ̃, ɑ̃t/ *adj* **1** [*moteur, machine*] vibrating; **2** [*allure, rythme*] pulsating; [*vie, activité*] hectic; [*histoire*] exciting.

trépidation /tʀepidasjɔ̃/ *nf* vibration.

trépider /tʀepide/ [1] *vi* to shake, to vibrate.

trépied /tʀepje/ *nm* gén tripod; (pour chaudron) trivet.

trépignement /tʀepiɲəmɑ̃/ *nm* (de colère, d'impatience) stamping ¢ (**de** with); (d'excitation, de joie) jumping ¢ up and down (**de** with).

trépigner /tʀepiɲe/ [1] *vi* (de colère, d'impatience) to stamp one's feet (**de** with); (de joie, d'excitation, enthousiasme) to jump up and down (**de** with).

trépointe /tʀepwɛ̃t/ *nf* welt.

tréponématose /tʀepɔnematoz/ ▶ **271** *nf* treponematosis.

tréponème /tʀepɔnɛm/ *nm* treponema.

très /tʀɛ/ *adv* **1** (modifiant un adjectif) very; **~ heureux/propre** very happy/clean; **~ avancé/connu** very advanced/well-known; **le spectacle/dîner était ~ réussi** the show/dinner went (off) very well; **~ disputé** [*match*] closely contested; **~ répandu** [*pratique*] very widespread; [*opinion*] widely held; **il est ~ aimé dans l'école/dans l'entreprise** he is very well liked at school/in the company; **être ~ amoureux** to be very much in love; **à un prix ~ inférieur** at a very much lower price; **la grève a été ~ suivie** the strike was very well supported; **2** (modifiant une expression adjectivale) very; **~ en avance/en retard/au courant/à la mode** very early/late/well-informed/fashionable; **~ homme d'affaires** very much a businessman; **3** (modifiant un adverbe) very; **~ tôt/bien/loin** very early/well/far; **je me porte ~ bien** I'm very well; **~ gentiment/volontiers** very kindly/willingly; **à ~ bientôt** see you very soon; **~ franchement, je ne sais pas** quite frankly, I don't know; **'tu vas bien?'—'non, pas ~'** 'are you well?'—'no, not terribly'; **4** (dans des locutions verbales) **j'ai ~ soif** I'm very thirsty; **j'ai ~ besoin de vacances** I really need a vacation; **elle a ~ envie de partir** she's dying to leave; **j'ai ~ envie de faire pipi**○ I'm desperate for a pee○.

trésor /tʀezɔʀ/ *nm* **1** (amas d'objets précieux) treasure ¢; **découvrir un ~** to discover a treasure trove; **chasse** or **course au ~** treasure hunt; **le ~ d'une église** a church's treasures; ▶ **chercheur**; **2** (objet précieux) treasure; **la balle rouge était un de ses ~s** the red ball was one of his/her treasures; **~s artistiques/archéologiques** artistic/archeological treasures; **les ~s du cinéma français** the gems of the French cinema; **les ~s de la mer** the riches of the sea; **3** (grande quantité) **un ~ de** a wealth of [*information, documents*]; **déployer des ~s d'inventivité/de diplomatie** to show infinite inventiveness/diplomacy; **4** Admin, Fin **le Trésor (public)** *government department in charge of public finance*; **5** (musée, chapelle) treasure house; **6** (personne) treasure; **mon ~** (terme d'affection) treasure, precious.

■ **~ de guerre** lit war chest; fig nest egg.

trésorerie /tʀezɔʀʀi/ *nf* **1** (ressources disponibles) funds (*pl*); (somme en liquide) cash ¢; **avoir des problèmes de ~** to have cash flow problems; **mouvements de ~** cash flows; **état/prévisions de ~** cash flow statement/forecast (*sg*); **de ~** [*budget, gestion, solde, opérations*] cash; **il dispose de 50000 francs en ~** or **d'une ~ de 50000 francs** he has 50,000 francs cash at his disposal; ▶ **moyen**; **2** (comptabilité) accounts (*pl*); **leur ~ est bien/mal tenue** their accounts are well/badly kept; **3** Admin, Fin **la ~** (comptabilité) government finance; (bureaux) *department in charge of public finance*; (en Grande-Bretagne) the Treasury.

trésorier, **-ière** /tʀezɔʀje, ɛʀ/ *nm,f* gén treasurer; Admin paymaster.

trésorier-payeur, *pl* **trésoriers-payeurs** /tʀezɔʀjepɛjœʀ/ *nm* **~ général** *head of the Trésor public in each French region*.

tressage /tʀɛsaʒ/ *nm* **1** (de cheveux) plaiting, braiding US; **2** (de paille, fil, corde, cuir) plaiting; (tissage) weaving; (de corbeille, d'objet) weaving.

tressaillement /tʀesajmɑ̃/ *nm* **1** (de surprise, peur) start (**de** of); (de plaisir, joie, d'espoir) quiver (**de** of); (de douleur) wince; **avoir des ~s** (de surprise, peur) to start (**de** with); (de plaisir, joie, d'espoir) to quiver (**de** with); (de douleur) to wince (**de** with); **2** (tremblement) (de personne, muscle, d'animal) twitch; (de machine, sol) vibration.

tressaillir /tʀesajiʀ/ [28] *vi* **1** (de surprise, peur) to start (**de** with); (de plaisir, joie, d'espoir) to quiver (**de** with); (de douleur) to wince (**de** with); **2** (trembler) [*personne, animal, muscle*] to twitch; [*machine, sol, chose*] to vibrate.

tressautement /tʀesotmɑ̃/ *nm* **1** (de surprise) start; **2** (de véhicule) jolt.

tressauter /tʀesote/ [1] *vi* **1** (sursauter) to start; **un cri le fit ~** a cry made him start; **2** (être secoué) [*véhicule*] to jolt; [*personne*] to be jolted; [*objets*] to jump; **faire ~ la voiture/les passagers** to jolt the car/the passengers.

tresse /tʀes/ *nf* **1** (de cheveux) plait, braid US; **2** (de fil, tissu, cuir) braid.

tresser /tʀese/ [1] *vtr* **1** to plait, braid US [*cheveux*]; **2** (pour faire un cordon) to plait [*paille, fil, corde, cuir*]; (tisser) to weave [*paille, corde, objet*]; **soulier tressé** lattice-work shoe.

IDIOMES **~ des couronnes à qn** to sing sb's praises.

tréteau, *pl* **~x** /tʀeto/ *nm* trestle.

IDIOMES **monter sur les ~x** to go on the stage.

treuil /tʀœj/ *nm* winch.

trêve /tʀɛv/ *nf* **1** Mil truce; **demander/signer une ~** to seek/to sign a truce; **respecter/violer une ~** to respect/to violate a truce; **observer une ~ de trois jours** to observe a three-day truce; **2** (moment de répit) respite; **après quelques jours de ~** after a few days' respite; **sans ~** unceasingly, without any let-up; **~ de plaisanteries/balivernes!** that's enough joking/nonsense!

■ **~ des confiseurs** Pol Christmas ou New Year truce; **~ de Dieu** Hist Truce of God.

Trèves /tʀɛv/ **▶857** *npr* Trier.

trévise /tʀeviz/ *nf* radicchio.

tri /tʀi/ *nm* **1** (pour répartir) sorting; **faire le ~ de** to sort [*courrier*]; to sort out [*documents, vêtements*]; **2** (pour choisir) sorting out, selection; **faire le ~ de** to sort [sth] out [*photos, information*]; **faire un ~ parmi des choses/gens** to select among things/people; **opérer un ~ sévère** to be very selective; **fais le ~ dans ce qu'elle dit** don't believe everything she says.

■ **~ postal** sorting; **centre de ~ (postal)** sorting office.

triacide /tʀiasid/ *nm* tribasic acid.

triade /tʀijad/ *nf* **1** (groupe de trois) triad; **2** (société secrète chinoise) Triad.

triage /tʀijaʒ/ *nm* **procéder au ~ de qch** to sort sth out; **gare de ~** marshalling[GB] yard.

trial /tʀijal/ Sport **I** *nm* (épreuve) scramble.

II *nf* (moto) trial bike GB, dirt bike US.

triangle /tʀijɑ̃gl/ *nm* **1** Math triangle; **~ isocèle/équilatéral** isosceles/equilateral triangle; **~ rectangle** right-angled triangle GB, right triangle US; **~s égaux/semblables** congruent/similar triangles; **2** (objet) triangle; **~ de soie** triangle of silk; **en ~** in a triangle; **montage (connecté) en ~** delta connection; **3** **▶534** Mus triangle; **4** (couple et amant ou maîtresse) (love) triangle.

■ **~ des Bermudes** Géog Bermuda Triangle; **~ de présignalisation** Gén Civ red warning triangle; **~ quelconque** Math triangle.

triangulaire /tʀijɑ̃gylɛʀ/ **I** *adj* **1** (en forme de triangle) triangular; **2** (entre trois personnes, pays) three-way; **élection ~** three-way election.

II○ *nf* (élection) three-way election.

triangulation /tʀijɑ̃gylasjɔ̃/ *nf* Tech triangulation.

trianguler /tʀijɑ̃gyle/ [1] *vtr* to triangulate.

trias /tʀijas/ *nm* **le ~** the Triassic.

triasique /tʀijasik/ *adj* Triassic.

triathlon /tʀiatlɔ̃/ *nm* triathlon.

triatomique /tʀiatɔmik/ *adj* triatomic.

tribal, **~e**, *mpl* **-aux** /tʀibal, o/ *adj* tribal.

tribalisme /tʀibalism/ *nm* tribalism.

triboélectricité /tʀibɔelɛktʀisite/ *nf* triboelectricity.

triboluminescence /tʀibolyminɛsɑ̃s/ *nf* triboluminescence.

tribord /tʀibɔʀ/ *nm* starboard; **côte à ~** land to starboard; **virer à ~** to bear to starboard.

tribu /tʀiby/ *nf* (tous contextes) tribe; **le chef de ~** lit, also hum the head of the tribe.

tribulations /tʀibylasjɔ̃/ *nfpl* tribulations.

tribun /tʀibœ̃/ *nm* **1** Hist tribune; **2** (orateur) great orator.

tribunal, *pl* **-aux** /tʀibynal, o/ *nm* **1** Jur (lieu, magistrats) court; **aller devant les tribunaux** [*affaire*] to be taken before the court; [*personne*] to go to court; **porter une affaire devant les tribunaux** to bring ou take a matter to court; **traîner qn devant les tribunaux** to take sb to court; **le ~ a décidé que** the court has decided that; **séance/vacation/rentrée d'un ~** court session/vacation/reopening; **2** fig **~ de l'histoire/de l'humanité** the judgment seat of history/humanity; **~ de Dieu**, **~ suprême** the judgment seat of God; **le ~ des hommes** the justice of men; **le ~ de l'opinion** the bar of public opinion; **s'ériger en ~ du goût/des mœurs** to set oneself up as an arbiter of taste/morals.

■ **~ administratif** ≈ administrative court; **~ de commerce** *court dealing with trade disputes*; **~ correctionnel** *court trying criminal cases of a fairly serious nature*; **~ ecclésiastique** ecclesiastical court; **~ d'exception** ≈ specialized court; **~ de grande instance** higher level court (*presided over by three judges dealing with cases of a fairly serious nature*); **~ incompétent** unqualified court; **~ d'instance** court of first instance (*presided over by a single judge dealing with less serious cases*); **~ militaire** military tribunal GB ou court US; **~ de police** police court (*dealing with petty offences[GB] punishable by a fine*); **~ pour enfants** juvenile court; **~ de première instance** = **~ de grande instance**; **~ révolutionnaire** revolutionary tribunal.

tribune /tʀibyn/ *nf* **1** (de stade, gymnase, champ de courses) stand; **louer une place de ~** or **aux ~s** to reserve a seat in a stand; **la ~ présidentielle** the president's stand; **la ~ officielle** ou **d'honneur** the VIP stand; **les ~s du public** the public stands; **2** (de salle de réunion, parlement) gallery; **la ~ de la presse** the press gallery; **3** (estrade) platform; (pour une seule personne) rostrum; **monter à la ~** lit, fig to take the platform; **parler à la ~** to speak from the platform; **tenir la ~** to hold the floor; **4** Presse (rubrique) comments column; (lieu de débat) forum for debate; **5** Archit (de chapelle, d'église) gallery.

■ **~ libre** non -editorial comment; **~ d'orgue** organ loft.

tribut /tʀiby/ *nm* Hist tribute; **ils ont payé un lourd ~ à la guerre/aux accidents de la route** war has/road accidents have taken a heavy toll.

tributaire /tʀibytɛʀ/ *adj* **1** gén **être ~ de qch** [*pays, personne, réalisation*] to depend ou be dependent on sth; **ils sont ~s les uns des autres** they're interdependent; **2** Géog **être ~ de qch** [*fleuve*] to be a tributary of sth, to flow into sth; **3** Hist [*personne*] **être ~ de qn/qch** to pay tribute to sb/sth.

tricentenaire /tʀisɑ̃tnɛʀ/ **I** *adj* three-hundred-year-old (*épith*); **être ~** to be three hundred years old.

II *nm* tercentenary, tricentennial.

tricéphale /tʀisefal/ *adj* three-headed (*épith*).

triceps /tʀisɛps/ *nm inv* triceps.

triche○ /tʀiʃ/ *nf* **c'est de la ~** that's cheating; **pour éviter la ~** to prevent cheating.

tricher /tʀiʃe/ [1] *vi* **1** (agir malhonnêtement) to cheat; **~ aux cartes/à un examen** to cheat at cards/in an exam; **~ avec les chiffres** to cheat with figures; **2** (mentir) **~ sur qch** to lie about sth; **~ sur son âge** to lie about one's age; **~ sur la qualité d'un produit** to cut corners on product quality; **~ sur le poids** to give short measure; **~ sur les prix** to overcharge.

tricherie /tʀiʃʀi/ *nf* **1** (action de tricher) cheating; **2** (acte trompeur) trick.

tricheur, **-euse** /tʀiʃœʀ, øz/ *nm,f* cheat.

trichinose /tʀikinoz/ *nf* trichinosis.

trichloréthylène /tʀiklɔʀetilɛn/ *nm* trichloroethylene.

trichlorure /tʀiklɔʀyʀ/ *nm* trichloride.

trichrome /tʀikʀom/ *adj* trichromatic.

trichromie /tʀikʀɔmi/ *nf* trichromatic printing.

tricolore /tʀikɔlɔʀ/ *adj* **1** (de trois couleurs) tricolour[GB], three-coloured[GB] (*épith*); **feux ~s** traffic lights; **2** (bleu, blanc, rouge) [*écharpe, ceinture, cocarde*] red, white and blue; **le drapeau ~** the tricolour[GB], the French flag; **3**○ (français) journ French; **l'équipe/l'entreprise ~** the French team/company.

tricorne /tʀikɔʀn/ *nm* tricorne.

tricot /tʀiko/ *nm* **1** (activité) knitting; **faire du ~** to knit; **~ plat** knitting (on two needles); **~ rond** knitting on four needles ou with a circular needle; **les différents points de ~** the different knitting stitches; **2** (ouvrage) knitting ¢; **mon ~** my knitting; **j'ai commencé un ~** I've started knitting something; **3** (étoffe) knitwear; **une robe en ~** a knitted dress; **4**† (pull de femme) sweater, jumper GB, jersey†; (pull d'homme) sweater, jumper GB; (cardigan) cardigan.

■ **~ de corps**† vest GB, undershirt US.

tricotage /tʀikɔtaʒ/ *nm* knitting.

tricoter /tʀikɔte/ [1] **I** *vtr* to knit [*chandail, chaussettes*]; **~ une écharpe à qn** to knit sb a scarf, to knit a scarf for sb; **~ de la laine** to knit with wool; **~ une maille/un rang** to knit a stitch/a row; **~ serré/lâche** to knit tightly/loosely; **un pull tricoté (à la) main** a handknit sweater; **robe tricotée** sweater dress, knitted dress.

II *vi* to knit; **~ à la main/machine** to knit by hand/machine; **aiguilles/machine à ~** knitting needles/machine.

IDIOMES **~ des jambes** ou **des pinceaux**○ hum to storm along.

tricoteur, **-euse** /tʀikɔtœʀ, øz/ **I** *nm,f* (personne) knitter.

II tricoteuse *nf* (machine) knitting machine.

trictrac /tʀiktʀak/ **▶449** *nm* trictrac (*early form of backgammon*).

tricycle /tʀisikl/ *nm* tricycle.

tridactyle /tʀidaktil/ *adj* tridactyl.

trident /tʀidɑ̃/ *nm* **1** Mythol trident; **2** (pour la pêche) trident; **3** (poisson) lesser forkbeard.

tridimensionnel, **-elle** /tʀidimɑ̃sjɔnɛl/ *adj* three-dimensional.

trièdre /tʀijɛdʀ/ **I** *adj* trihedral.

II *nm* trihedron.

triennal, **~e**, *mpl* **-aux** /tʀienal, o/ *adj* **1** (pour 3 ans) three-year (*épith*); **2** (tous les 3 ans) [*exposition, vote*] three-yearly (*épith*), triennial; [*assolement*] three-yearly (*épith*).

trier /tʀije/ [2] *vtr* **1** (pour répartir) to sort [*courrier*]; **2** (pour choisir) to sort [sth] out [*photos, information*]; to select [*clientèle*]; **il faut ~ dans ce qu'elle dit** you can't believe everything she says.

IDIOMES **~ sur le volet** to handpick.

trieur, **-euse** /tʀijœʀ, øz/ **I** ▶ 510⌋ *nm,f* (personne) sorter.
II *nm* Agric sorting machine, sorter.

trieur-calibreur, *pl* **trieurs-calibreurs** /tʀijœʀkalibʀœʀ/ *nm* sorting and grading machine.

trifolié, **~e** /tʀifɔlje/ *adj* trifoliate.

trifouiller○ /tʀifuje/ [1] *vi* **~ dans qch** to rummage through sth [*placard, affaires*]; to tinker with [*appareil, moteur*]; **qu'est-ce que tu trifouilles?** what are you up to?

triglyphe /tʀiglif/ *nm* triglyph.

trigonométrie /tʀigɔnometʀi/ *nf* trigonometry.

trigonométrique /tʀigɔnometʀik/ *adj* trigonometric.

trijumeau, *pl* **~x** /tʀiʒymo/ **I** *adj m* trigeminal.
II *nm* trigeminal nerve.

trilatéral, **~e**, *mpl* **-aux** /tʀilateʀal, o/ *adj* trilateral.

trilingue /tʀilɛ̃g/ *adj* [*texte, personne*] trilingual.

trille /tʀij/ *nm* **1** Mus trill; **2** (son) **les ~s d'un oiseau** the trilling of a bird.

trillion /tʀiljɔ̃/ ▶ 545⌋ *nm* trillion.

trilobé, **~e** /tʀilɔbe/ *adj* **1** Archit trefoiled; **2** Bot trifoliate.

trilogie /tʀilɔʒi/ *nf* trilogy.

trimaran /tʀimaʀɑ̃/ *nm* trimaran; **course en ~** trimaran race.

trimbal(l)age /tʀɛ̃balaʒ/, **trimbal(l)ement**○ /tʀɛ̃balmɑ̃/ *nm* lugging about.

trimbal(l)er○ /tʀɛ̃bale/ [1] **I** *vtr* to lug [sth] around [*valise, objet*]; to drag [sb] around [*personne*]; **j'ai trimbalé mon correspondant anglais dans tout Paris** I dragged my English pen-friend all over Paris; **qu'est-ce qu'il trimbale!** look at the state of him!
II se trimbal(l)er *vpr* to trail around; **elle se trimbale partout avec sa mère** she trails around everywhere with her mother; **il se trimbale tous les jours jusqu'à l'autre bout de la ville pour aller travailler** he treks across to the other side of town every day to go to work.

trimer○ /tʀime/ [1] *vi* to slave away; **faire ~ qn** to keep sb slaving away.

trimestre /tʀimɛstʀ/ *nm* **1** Univ, Scol term; **au premier/deuxième/troisième ~** in the first/second/third term; **2** Fin, Pol, Écon quarter; **3** (somme reçue) quarterly income; (somme payée) quarterly payment.

trimestriel, **-elle** /tʀimɛstʀijɛl/ *adj* **1** Univ, Scol **examen** or **contrôle ~** end-of-term exam; **recevoir son bulletin ~** to get one's end-of-term report; **2** [*revue, numéro*] quarterly; [*cotisation, réunion*] quarterly.

trimètre /tʀimɛtʀ/ *nm* trimeter.

trimoteur /tʀimɔtœʀ/ **I** *adj* three-engined.
II *nm* three-engined plane.

tringle /tʀɛ̃gl/ *nf* **1** gén rail; **~ à rideaux** curtain rail, curtain rod US; **~ à vêtements** clothes rail, hanging rail; **2** Tech rod; **3** Archit taenia.

tringler /tʀɛ̃gle/ [1] *vtr* **1** Tech to chalk a line on [*tissu, pièce de bois*]; **2**● (posséder sexuellement) to fuck●.

trinitaire /tʀinitɛʀ/ *adj, nmf* Trinitarian.

trinité /tʀinite/ *nf* (ensemble) trinity.

Trinité /tʀinite/ **I** *nf* Relig **la ~** the Trinity; (fête) Trinity Sunday; **à Pâques ou à la ~** fig when the cows come home; **il te remboursera à Pâques ou à la ~** you'll be waiting till the cows come home before he pays you back.
II *nprf* ▶ 321⌋, 416⌋ (île) Trinidad.

trinitrobenzène /tʀinitʀobɛ̃zɛn/ *nm* trinitrobenzene.

trinitrotoluène /tʀinitʀotɔlɥɛn/ *nm* trinitrotoluene.

trinôme /tʀinom/ *nm* trinomial.

trinquer /tʀɛ̃ke/ [1] *vi* **1** gén to clink glasses; **~ avec qn** lit to clink glasses with sb; fig to go drinking with sb; **~ à qch** to drink to sth; **trinquons à ta réussite!** let's drink to your success!; **2**○ (boire avec excès) to booze○; **3**○ (subir les conséquences de qch) to pay the price; (être puni) to take the rap○; **les parents boivent, les enfants trinquent** the parents drink and the children pay the price; **ils sont tous responsables mais lui seul a trinqué** they are all to blame but he took the rap○.

trinquet /tʀɛ̃kɛ/ *nm* foremast.

trinquette /tʀɛ̃kɛt/ *nf* forestaysail.

trio /tʀi(j)o/ *nm* **1** Mus (œuvre, formation) trio; **~ pour piano, violon et violoncelle** trio for piano, violin and cello; **les ~s de Haydn** Haydn's trios; **2** (groupe de trois personnes) trio (**de** of).

triode /tʀiɔd/ *nf* triode.

triolet /tʀijɔlɛ/ *nm* **1** Mus triplet; **2** Littérat triolet.

triomphal, **~e**, *mpl* **-aux** /tʀijɔ̃fal, o/ *adj* triumphant.

triomphalement /tʀijɔ̃falmɑ̃/ *adv* triumphantly, exultantly.

triomphalisme /tʀijɔ̃falism/ *nm* triumphalism.

triomphaliste /tʀijɔ̃falist/ *adj* triumphalist.

triomphant, **~e** /tʀijɔ̃fɑ̃, ɑ̃t/ *adj* triumphant.

triomphateur, **-trice** /tʀijɔ̃fatœʀ, tʀis/ **I** *adj* triumphant.
II *nm,f* triumphant victor; **leur pays a été le plus grand ~ aux jeux Olympiques** their country carried off all the medals at the Olympic Games.

triomphe /tʀijɔ̃f/ *nm* triumph (**sur** over); **un ~ électoral** an electoral triumph; **avoir un sourire/pousser un cri de ~** to wear a smile/to let out a cry of triumph; **porter qn en ~** to carry sb in triumph; **faire un ~ à qn** to give sb a triumph; **film qui remporte un ~** film which is having tremendous success; **avoir le ~ modeste** to be modest about one's success.

triompher /tʀijɔ̃fe/ [1] **I triompher de** *vtr ind* to triumph over [*adversaire*]; to overcome [*résistance, crainte*]; **la démocratie a triomphé du totalitarisme** democracy has triumphed over totalitarianism.
II *vi* **1** (réussir) [*combattant*] to triumph; [*artiste*] to have a resounding success; [*mensonge, vérité*] to prevail; **faire ~ qn/qch** to make sb/sth triumph; **2** (manifester) [*personne*] to be triumphant ou exultant.

trip○ /tʀip/ *nm* drug users' slang trip○; **c'est pas mon ~!** it's not my scene○ ou bag○ US!

tripaille○ /tʀipaj/ *nf* innards (*pl*).

tripale /tʀipal/ *adj* three-bladed.

triparti, **~e** /tʀipaʀti/ *adj* = **tripartite**.

tripartisme /tʀipaʀtism/ *nm* tripartite or three-party system.

tripartite /tʀipaʀtit/ *adj* Pol, Bot tripartite.

tripatouillage○ /tʀipatujaʒ/ *nm* **1** (de comptes, statistiques) fiddling○; **2** (d'élections) rigging ¢; **~s électoraux** vote-rigging, poll-rigging.

tripatouiller○ /tʀipatuje/ [1] *vtr* **1** (altérer) to fiddle about○ with, to tamper with [*texte*]; to fiddle○, to rig [*résultats électoraux*]; **2** (bricoler) to fiddle with○, to tinker with [*moteur, machine*]; **3** (tripoter) to fiddle with○, to toy with [*objet*]; to paw○ [*personne*].

tripe /tʀip/ **I** *nf* **1** Culin tripe ¢; **~s à la mode de Caen** tripe à la mode de Caen; **2**○ (sensibilité) **avoir la ~ patriotique/révolutionnaire** to be a dyed-in-the-wool patriot/revolutionary; **prendre** or **saisir aux ~s** to be gut-wrenching○; **chanter/jouer avec ses ~s** to sing/to act from the heart.
II tripes○ *nfpl* (entrailles) guts, innards; **mettre les ~s de qn à l'air** to rip sb's guts out○; **rendre ~s et boyaux**○ to be as sick as a dog, to spew up◑; **avoir mal aux ~s**○ to have bellyache.

triperie /tʀipʀi/ ▶ 510⌋ *nf* (boutique) tripe shop; (commerce) tripe trade.

tripette /tʀipɛt/ *nf* **ne pas valoir ~**○ not to be worth a brass farthing○ GB ou red cent○ US.

triphasé, **~e** /tʀifaze/ *adj* three-phase; **courant ~** three-phase current.

triphtongue /tʀiftɔ̃g/ *nf* triphthong.

tripier, **-ière** /tʀipje, ɛʀ/ ▶ 510⌋ *nm,f* tripe butcher.

triplace /tʀiplas/ *adj* three-seater.

triplan /tʀiplɑ̃/ *nm* triplane.

triple /tʀipl/ **I** *adj* (*before n*) [*rôle, objectif, détonation*] triple (*épith*); **l'avantage est ~** the advantages are threefold; **en ~ exemplaire** in triplicate; **avoir un livre/une photo en ~** to have three copies of a book/a photograph; **~ idiot**○**!** prize idiot○!
II *nm* **coûter le ~** to cost three times as much, to cost triple ou treble the amount; **boire/fumer le ~ de qn** to drink/to smoke three times as much as sb (does), to drink/to smoke triple the amount that sb does; **son salaire est le ~ du mien** he/she earns three times as much as I do ou treble what I do.
■ **la Triple Alliance** the Triple Alliance; **~ croche** demisemiquaver; **la Triple Entente** Hist the Triple Entente; **~ saut** triple jump.

triplé, **~e** /tʀiple/ **I** *nm* Sport hat trick; **réussir un ~** to make it a hat trick.
II *nm,f* (enfant) triplet.

triplement /tʀipləmɑ̃/ **I** *adv* (pour trois raisons) in three respects; **il s'est ~ trompé** he was wrong on three counts ou in three respects.
II *nm* trebling, tripling (**de** of); **~ des effectifs/prix** threefold increase in staff/prices.

tripler /tʀiple/ [1] **I** *vtr* **1** (multiplier par trois) to treble [*somme, quantité, prix*]; to treble, triple [*épaisseur, dimension, volume*]; **2** (refaire à nouveau) **~ une classe** Scol to repeat a class GB ou grade US again.
II *vi* [*prix, population, somme, quantité*] to treble, to increase threefold; [*épaisseur, couche*] to treble; **~ de qch** (de valeur, poids, volume, taille) to treble in sth.

triplette /tʀiplɛt/ *nf* team of three boules players.

triplex® /tʀiplɛks/ *nm inv* **1** (verre de sécurité) Triplex® GB, safety glass; **2** (appartement) three-floor maisonette GB, triplex (apartment) US.

triplicata /tʀiplikata/ *nm* third copy; **dactylographier en ~** to type in triplicate.

triplure /tʀiplyʀ/ *nf* Cout interlining.

Tripoli /tʀipɔli/ ▶ 857⌋ *npr* Tripoli.

triporteur /tʀipɔʀtœʀ/ *nm* delivery tricycle.

tripot○ /tʀipo/ *nm* **1** (maison de jeu) gambling joint○; **2** (endroit mal famé) dive○.

tripotage /tʀipɔtaʒ/ *nm* **1** (attouchements) groping ¢; **2** (intrigue) skulduggery ¢; **les ~s électoraux** electoral skulduggery.

tripotée○ /tʀipɔte/ *nf* **1** (volée de coups) (good) hiding○, beating; **2** (défaite) thrashing○, defeat; **3** (ribambelle) **une ~ de** hordes (*pl*) of, a whole slew of○ US.

tripoter /tʀipɔte/ [1] **I**○ *vtr* **1** (caresser) pej to grope○ péj [*femme, fesses*]; **se faire ~ dans les coins** to get groped in corners; **2** (manier) (nerveusement) to fiddle with [*objet, moustache*]; (distraitement) to finger; **on ne tripote pas les poires, s'il vous plaît!** please don't touch the pears!; **cesse de te ~ le nez!** stop picking your nose!
II◑ **se tripoter** *vpr* to wank● GB, to jerk off●, to masturbate.

tripoteur, **-euse** /tʀipɔtœʀ, øz/ **I**○ *adj* [*mains*] groping○; **ce qu'il est ~!** he can't keep his hands to himself○!
II *nm,f* ◑(peloteur) groper◑.

triptyque /tʀiptik/ *nm* **1** Relig triptych; **2** Littérat, Mus trilogy; **3** Admin triptyque.

triquard◑ /tʀikaʀ/ *nm* prisoners' slang *criminal prohibited from entering France or a particular area.*

trique /tʀik/ *nf* **1** (gourdin) cudgel; **battre à coups de ~** to cudgel; **recevoir un coup de ~** to be cudgelled[GB]; **enfant qui ne marche qu'à la ~** child who needs a firm hand; **2**● (érection) **avoir la ~**● to have a hard-on●; **3**◑ prisoners' slang *prohibition from entering certain areas (or whole) of France.*
IDIOMES **être maigre** or **sec comme un coup de ~** to be as thin as a rake, to be as skinny as a rail US.

triquer /tʀike/ [1] **I** *vtr* (battre) to thrash.
II● *vi* (avoir une érection) to have a hard-on●.

triréacteur /tʀiʀeaktœʀ/ *nm* tri-jet.

trirectangle /tʀiʀɛktɑ̃gl/ *adj* trirectangular.

trirème /tʀiʀɛm/ *nf* trireme.

trisaïeul, **~e** /tʀizajœl/ *nm,f* great-great-grandfather/grandmother; **~s** great-great-grandparents.

trisannuel, **-elle** /tʀizanɥɛl/ *adj* triennial.

trisecteur, **-trice** /tʀisɛktœʀ, tʀis/ *adj* trisecting.

trisection /tʀisɛksjɔ̃/ *nf* trisection.

trisomie /tʀizɔmi/ *nf* trisomy; **~ 21** Down's Syndrome, trisomy 21 spéc.

trisomique /tʀisɔmik/ **I** *adj* Méd [*enfant*] Down's syndrome (*épith*); **être ~** to have Down's syndrome.
II *nmf* Down's syndrome child, trisomic spéc.

trisser /tʀise/ [1] **I** *vtr* (bisser de nouveau) **~ qn** to make sb perform a second encore.
II *vi* **1**◑ (se sauver) to clear off○, to scoot○, to clear out○ US; **2** [*hirondelle*] to twitter.

triste /tʀist/ *adj* **1** (pas gai) [*personne, visage*] sad; [*maison, ville, région*] dreary, depressing; [*ciel, temps, journée*] gloomy; [*histoire, livre, soirée, événement*] sad, depressing; [*couleur*] drab, dreary; [*existence, enfance*] dreary; **être/se sentir ~** to be/to feel sad; **avoir l'air tout ~** to look really sad; **c'est une enfant ~** she's a sad child; **être ~ de faire** to be sad to do; **j'étais ~ de le voir partir** I was sad to see him go; **être ~ à l'idée** or **la pensée de qch/de faire** to be sad at the idea ou thought of sth/of doing; **elle est ~ que je m'en aille** she's sad that I'm leaving; **il est** or **c'est ~ de faire** it is sad to do; **il est** or **c'est ~ que** it is sad that; **avoir ~ mine** or **figure** [*personne*] to look pitiful; **mon gâteau a bien ~ mine** my cake is a sorry sight; ▶ **bonnet**; **2** (déplorable) [*résultat, fin, affaire*] dreadful; [*conséquence*] sad; [*spectacle, état*] sorry; **c'est la ~ vérité** it's the sad truth; **on l'a retrouvé dans un ~ état** he was found in a sorry state; **détenir le ~ record d'alcoolisme** to hold the record for heavy drinking, a dubious achievement; **faire la ~ expérience de qch** to have learned about sth to one's sorrow; **se lamenter sur son ~ sort** to lament one's fate; **3** (méprisable) [*personnage*] unsavoury[GB], disreputable; [*réputation*] dreadful; **un ~ imbécile** a despicable character; **un ~ sire** a disreputable character.
IDIOMES **~ comme la pluie** or **à mourir** desperately sad; **c'était pas ~**○ it was quite something.

tristement /tʀistəmɑ̃/ *adv* **1** (avec tristesse) [*sourire, regarder, se résoudre*] sadly; [*s'habiller*] in drab colours[GB]; **regarder qn ~** to look at sb sadly; **2** (de façon regrettable) [*révélateur*] all too (*épith*); **c'est ~ vrai** unfortunately, it's only too true; **une vie ~ ordinaire** a drearily ordinary life.

tristesse /tʀistɛs/ *nf* **1** (d'histoire, événement, de personne, musique) sadness; (de lieu, maison, soirée) dreariness; (de ciel, temps, journée) gloominess; **un sentiment de ~** a feeling of sadness; **un poème empreint de ~** a poem pervaded with sadness; **la ~ des banlieues** the dreariness of the suburbs; **répondre/dire avec ~** to reply/to say sadly; **c'est avec ~ que nous avons appris que** we have learned with sorrow that; **M et Mme Vernet ont la ~ de vous faire part du décès de leur fils Pierre** Mr and Mrs Vernet have to inform you of the death of their son Pierre; **2** (événement) sorrow; **les petites joies et les petites ~s de la vie** life's little ups and downs.

tristounet○, **-ette** /tʀistunɛ, ɛt/ *adj* [*personne, regard, histoire*] rather sad; [*couleur, appartement, temps*] rather dreary.

trisyllabe /tʀisil(l)ab/ **I** *adj* trisyllabic.
II *nm* trisyllable.

trisyllabique /tʀisil(l)abik/ *adj* trisyllabic.

tritium /tʀitjɔm/ *nm* tritium.

triton /tʀitɔ̃/ *nm* **1** Zool (mollusque) triton; (amphibien) newt; **2** Mus tritone.

Triton /tʀitɔ̃/ *npr* Mythol Triton.

trituration /tʀityʀasjɔ̃/ *nf* (d'aliments, de substances) grinding up, trituration spéc; (de papiers, cartons) pulping.

triturer /tʀityʀe/ [1] *vtr* **1** (tripoter) to twist [*mouchoir*]; to fiddle with [*bouton*]; to knead [*pâte*]; **2** (broyer) to grind up, triturate spéc [*aliments, substances*].
IDIOMES **se ~ la cervelle** or **les méninges**○ to rack one's brains○.

tritureuse /tʀityʀøz/ *nf* pulvimixer.

triumvir /tʀijɔmviʀ/ *nm* triumvir.

triumvirat /tʀijɔmviʀa/ *nm* triumvirate.

trivalence /tʀivalɑ̃s/ *nf* trivalency.

trivalent, **~e** /tʀivalɑ̃, ɑ̃t/ *adj* trivalent.

trivalve /tʀivalv/ *adj* trivalve.

trivial, **~e**, *mpl* **-iaux** /tʀivjal, o/ *adj* **1** (grossier) [*manières, humour*] coarse, crude; **2** (banal) [*objet*] ordinary, everyday (*épith*); [*style*] mundane péj; **3** (simpliste) [*explication, démonstration*] simplistic; **4** Math trivial.

trivialité /tʀivjalite/ *nf* **1** (caractère vulgaire) coarseness, crudeness; **2** (caractère banal) triteness, triviality; **3** (parole banale) platitude; **4** (chose banale) triviality.

troc /tʀɔk/ *nm* barter; **faire du ~** to barter (**avec** with); **faire un ~**○ to do a swap○ (**avec** with); **économie de ~** barter economy.

trochaïque /tʀɔkaik/ *adj* trochaic.

trochée /tʀɔʃe/ *nm* trochee.

troène /tʀɔɛn/ *nm* privet ¢; **une haie de ~s** a privet hedge.

troglodyte /tʀɔglɔdit/ *nm* **1** (homme) cave-dweller, troglodyte spéc; **2** (oiseau) (winter) wren.

trogne○ /tʀɔɲ/ *nf* mug○, face.

trognon /tʀɔɲɔ̃/ **I**○ *adj* [*enfants*] sweet; **ce qu'elle est ~, cette gamine!** that kid's really sweet ou cute○.
II *nm* (de pomme, poire) core; (de salade, chou) stalk; **il est pourri jusqu'au ~** fig he's rotten to the core.
IDIOMES **se faire avoir jusqu'au ~** to be well and truly had○.

Troie /tʀwa/ *npr f* Troy; **la guerre/le cheval de ~** the Trojan war/horse.

troïka /tʀɔika/ *nf* troika.

trois /tʀwa/ ▶**545**, **407**, **212** **I** *adj inv, pron, nm inv* three; ▶ **cuiller**.
II○ *adv* three, third, thirdly.
■ **les ~ coups** three knocks (*to signal the curtain is about to rise*).
IDIOMES **être haut comme ~ pommes** to be kneehigh to a grasshopper; **jamais deux sans ~** bad luck comes in threes.

trois-deux /tʀwadø/ *nm inv* Mus three-two time; **en ~** in three-two time.

trois-huit /tʀwaɥit/ **I** *nm inv* Mus three-eight time; **en ~** in three-eight time.
II *nmpl inv* Entr system (sg) of three eight-hour shifts; **je fais les ~** I work shifts.

troisième /tʀwazjɛm/ ▶**545**, **212** **I** *adj* third.
II *nf* Scol *fourth year of secondary school, age 14–15.*
■ **le ~ âge** the elderly; **club du ~ âge** old people's club; Admin senior citizens.

troisièmement /tʀwazjɛmmɑ̃/ *adv* thirdly.

trois-mâts /tʀwamɑ/ *nm inv* three-master.

trois-quarts /tʀwakaʀ/ **I** *adj inv* [*manches, veste*] three-quarter length.
II *nm inv* **1** Mode (manteau) three-quarter length coat; **2** Sport (joueur de rugby) three-quarter; **3** Mus (violon) three-quarter violin.
III de trois-quarts *loc adj* [*portrait, photo*] three-quarter (*épith*).

trois-quatre /tʀwakatʀ/ *nm inv* Mus three-four time; **en ~** in three-four time.

trolley○ /tʀɔlɛ/ *nm*: *abbr* = **trolleybus**.

trolleybus /tʀɔlɛbys/ *nm inv* trolley bus.

trombe /tʀɔ̃b/ *nf* **1** (cyclone) waterspout; **départ en ~** Sport flying start; **démarrer en ~** (coureur) to get off to a flying start; (voiture, pilote) to shoot off at high speed; fig (entreprise, économie) to get off to a flying start; **arriver en ~** to come hurtling in; **partir en ~** to go hurtling off; **traverser/passer en ~** to hurtle across/past; **2** (averse) **~s d'eau** downpour; (masse d'eau) masses of water; **des ~s d'eau se sont abattues sur nous** we were caught in a downpour ou cloudburst; **le barrage déversait des ~s d'eau** masses of water was cascading out of the dam.

trombine○ /tʀɔ̃bin/ *nf* mug○, face.

trombinoscope○ /tʀɔ̃binɔskɔp/ *nm* gén group photo; Pol *official register of French deputies including photographs.*

tromblon /tʀɔ̃blɔ̃/ *nm* **1** (arme) blunderbuss; **2** (dispositif) grenade adaptor.

trombone /tʀɔ̃bɔn/ *nm* **1** ▶**534** (instrument) trombone; **~ à coulisse/à pistons** slide/valve trombone; **2** (musicien) trombonist, trombone player; **3** (de bureau) paperclip.

tromboniste /tʀɔ̃bɔnist/ ▶**510** *nm* trombonist, trombone player.

trompe /tʀɔ̃p/ *nf* **1** Zool (d'éléphant) trunk; (d'insecte, de mollusque) proboscis; **2** ▶**534** Mus horn; **3** Aut (avertisseur) horn; **4** Archit squinch.
■ **~ de chasse** hunting horn; **~ à eau** water jet pump; **~ d'Eustache** Eustachian tube; **~ de Fallope** Fallopian tube.

trompe-la-mort /tʀɔ̃plamɔʀ/ *nmf inv* daredevil.

trompe-l'œil /tʀɔ̃plœj/ *nm inv* **1** Art trompe l'oeil; **paysage/façade en ~** trompe l'oeil landscape/façade; **2** (ce qui fait illusion) smokescreen.

tromper /tʀɔ̃pe/ [1] **I** *vtr* **1** (duper) [*personne*] to deceive; [*information*] to mislead; **être trompé par qn** to be deceived by sb; **~ l'opinion publique/les électeurs** to mislead the public/the voters; **nous avons été trompés par les bons résultats/la ressemblance** we were misled by the good results/the resemblance; **on nous a trompés sur la qualité des produits/l'état de la maison** the quality of the goods/the condition of the house was misrepresented; **il y a des signes** or **gestes qui ne trompent pas** there's no mistaking the signs; **~ l'ennemi** to deceive ou trick the enemy; **2** (faire des infidélités à) to be unfaithful to (**avec** with), to deceive, to cheat on○ [*mari, femme*]; **il la trompe** he's unfaithful to her; **un mari trompé** a deceived husband; **3** (échapper à) **~ la vigilance** or **surveillance de qn** to slip past sb's guard; **~ la défense/le gardien de but** to trick the defence[GB]/the goalkeeper; **4** (faire diversion à) to stave off [*désir, besoin*]; **~ son ennui/sa peur** to stave off one's boredom/one's fear; **~ la faim** to stave off hunger.
II se tromper *vpr* **1** (mentalement) to be mistaken (**dans** in); **se ~ dans son choix** to be mistaken in one's choice, to make the wrong choice; **se ~ sur qn** to be wrong about sb; **je me suis trompé sur leurs intentions** I misunderstood their intentions; **si je ne me trompe** if I'm not mistaken; **il**

> **trop**
>
> *trop* adverbe modifiant un verbe se traduit par *too much*. Il se traduit par *too* lorsqu'il modifie un adjectif, un adverbe. Dans le cas d'expressions comme *avoir soif/faim/chaud* traduites par *to be* + adjectif, il se traduit par *too*:
>
> *j'ai trop froid, je rentre* = I'm too cold, I'm going home
>
> Voir exemples supplémentaires et exceptions I.
>
> *trop de* déterminant indéfini se traduit par *too many* lorsqu'il est suivi d'un nom dénombrable:
>
> *trop de livres* = too many books
> *trop d'idées* = too many ideas
>
> et par *too much* lorsqu'il est suivi d'un nom non dénombrable:
>
> *trop de travail* = too much work
>
> Attention, certains mots dénombrables français ne le sont pas en anglais et réciproquement:
>
> *trop de meubles* = too much furniture
> *trop de monde* = too many people
>
> Voir exemples supplémentaires et exceptions II.

ne faut pas s'y ~, qu'on ne s'y trompe pas make no mistake about it; **le public ne s'y est pas trompé** the public got it right; **se ~ sur toute la ligne**○ to be completely wrong; **2** (concrètement) to make a mistake; **tu t'es trompé, il n'y a pas de trait d'union** you've made a mistake, there's no hyphen; **se ~ de dix francs/deux heures** to be ten francs/two hours out GB ou off US; **se ~ de rue/bus** to take the wrong street/bus; **se ~ de manteau/clé** to take the wrong coat/key; **se ~ de date/jour** to get the date/day wrong; **se ~ de numéro/bâtiment** to get the wrong number/building; **se ~ de porte** lit (dans la rue) to get the wrong house; (à l'intérieur) to get the wrong door; fig to come to the wrong place.

tromperie /tʀɔ̃pʀi/ *nf* **1** gén deceit ¢; **les ~s du gouvernement** government deception; **~s conjugales** infidelities; **il y a ~ sur la marchandise**○! I've been sold a lemon○!; **2** Jur misrepresentation ¢.

trompette /tʀɔ̃pɛt/ **I** *nm* (dans un orchestre) trumpet (player); (dans l'armée) bugler; (dans une fanfare) trumpeter.

II *nf* **1** ▶**534** Mus trumpet; **~ en si** trumpet in B; **2** Zool conch (shell).

■ **~ bouchée** muted trumpet; **~ de cavalerie** bugle; **~ à pistons** valve trumpet.

IDIOMES **sans tambour ni ~** without making a song and dance (about it).

trompette-de-la-mort, *pl* **trompettes-de-la-mort** /tʀɔ̃pɛtdəlamɔʀ/ *nf* Bot horn of plenty.

trompettiste /tʀɔ̃petist/ ▶**510** *nmf* trumpet (player).

trompeur, **-euse** /tʀɔ̃pœʀ, øz/ *adj* [*promesse, chiffre*] misleading; [*distance, apparence*] deceptive.

tronc /tʀɔ̃/ *nm* **1** (fût) (d'arbre) trunk; (de colonne) shaft; **un ~ d'arbre** a tree-trunk; **2** (partie du corps) trunk, torso; (partie de vaisseau, nerf) trunk; **3** (dans église) collection box.

■ **~ commun** (d'espèces, de langues) common origin; (de lignes de bus) joint section; (de disciplines) (common) core curriculum; **~ de prisme** truncated prism.

IDIOMES **se casser le ~**◑ to worry ou to get into a sweat○ about things; **ne te casse pas le ~ pour si peu!** it's not worth getting into a sweat○ about.

troncation /tʀɔ̃kasjɔ̃/ *nf* Ling truncation.

troncature /tʀɔ̃katyʀ/ *nf* Ordinat truncation.

tronche○ /tʀɔ̃ʃ/ *nf* mug○, face; **avoir une sale ~** to look like an ugly customer○; **faire une sale/drôle de ~** to look fed-up○/out of sorts.

tronçon /tʀɔ̃sɔ̃/ *nm* gén section; (de tube, bois) length, section; (de phrase, texte) part, section.

tronconique /tʀɔ̃kɔnik/ *adj* (shaped) like a truncated cone.

tronçonnage /tʀɔ̃sɔnaʒ/ *nm* sawing up, cutting into sections.

tronçonner /tʀɔ̃sɔne/ [1] *vtr* to cut [sth] into sections, to saw [sth] up.

tronçonneuse /tʀɔ̃sɔnøz/ *nf* **1** (scie portative) chain saw; **2** (machine-outil) power saw.

trône /tʀon/ *nm* **1** (de roi) throne; **monter sur le ~** to come to the throne; **perdre son ~** to lose one's throne; **héritier du ~** heir to the throne; **prétendant au ~** pretender to the throne; **discours du Trône** Queen's/King's speech; **descendre du ~** (abdiquer) to give up the throne; **2**○ (siège des WC) throne○ GB, can◑ US.

trôner /tʀone/ [1] *vi* **1** (être à la place d'honneur) **le professeur trônait au milieu de ses étudiants** the professor was holding court surrounded by his students; **~ sur** [*vase, photo*] to have pride of place on [*cheminée*]; **2** Pol [*roi, reine*] to sit enthroned.

tronquer /tʀɔ̃ke/ [1] *vtr* **1** (couper) to truncate [*texte, déclaration*]; to cut out [*faits, détails*]; **2** Archit **colonne tronquée** truncated column.

trop /tʀo/ ▶**662** **I** *adv* **1** (indiquant un excès) (modifiant un adjectif ou un adverbe) too; (modifiant un verbe) too much; **~ difficile/court/tôt** too difficult/short/early; **une tâche ~ difficile** too difficult a task; **une réaction ~ vive** too violent a reaction; **~ longtemps** too long; **beaucoup** or **bien ~ lourd/compliqué** far ou much too heavy/complicated; **j'ai ~ mangé/bu** I've had too much to eat/drink; **elle aime ~ son confort** she likes her comfort too much; **j'ai ~ dormi** I've slept too much; **il fait ~ chaud** it's too hot; **tu travailles ~** you work too hard; **ça c'est ~ fort!** that's (just) too much!; **nous sommes ~ nombreux** there are too many of us; **nous sommes ~ peu nombreux** there are too few of us; **un écrivain ~ peu connu** an author who is sadly little known; **12 francs c'est ~ peu** 12 francs is too little; **ce serait ~ beau** I'd/you'd/we'd be so lucky; **c'est ~ bête!** how stupid!; **~ enthousiaste** overenthusiastic; **un fromage ~ fait** an overripe cheese; **on n'est jamais ~ prudent** you can't be too careful; **j'ai parlé ~ vite** I spoke too soon; **tu en as ~ dit** (tais-toi) you've already said too much; **elle en fait (un peu) ~** she overdoes it (a bit); **c'en est ~!** that's the end!; **elle a ~ peur de tomber/se perdre** she's too scared of falling/getting lost; **~ peu de gens se rendent compte que** too few people realize that; **~ malade pour être transporté** too ill to be moved; **~ beau pour être vrai** too good to be true; **'tu aimes la viande?'—'pas ~'** 'do you like meat?'—'not too much'; **il ne faut pas ~ s'y fier** don't rely on it too much; **ce n'est pas ~ cher/tard** it's not too expensive/late; **nous ne serons pas ~ de deux** it'll take at least two of us; **je ne le connais que ~** I know him only too well; **sans ~ savoir si** without really knowing if; **faire qch sans ~ y croire** to do sth without really believing in it; **j'ai ~ à faire** I've got too much to do; **tu me demandes ~** you're expecting too much of me; **ils sont ~ dans la classe** there are too many pupils in the class; **c'est ~ pour moi** it's too much for me; **~ c'est ~!** enough is enough!; ▶**étreindre**; **2** (employé avec valeur de superlatif) **~ gentil** too kind; **~ mignon** too sweet ou cute○; **c'était ~ drôle** it was so funny; **vous êtes ~ aimable** you're too kind; **tu es ~ bonne pour moi** you're too good for me; **il est ~ sympa**○ he's so nice; **elle n'est pas ~ contente** she's none too happy; **ça ne va pas ~ mal, merci** not so bad, thanks; **je n'en sais ~ rien** I don't really know; **ça ne me dit ~ rien** I don't really feel like it; **3**○ (incroyable) **il est ~, lui!** he's too much○!; **c'est ~, ça!** that's incredible!

II trop de *dét indéf* **1** (avec nom dénombrable) too many; **il y a ~ d'accidents** there are too many accidents; **sans ~ de problèmes** without too much difficulty; **~ de fruits** too much fruit; **il y a ~ de choses à faire** there's too much to do; **2** (avec nom non dénombrable) too much; **~ de pression/d'importance** too much pressure/importance; **prends du pain, j'en ai ~** take some bread, I've got too much; **sans ~ d'espoir/de mal** without too much hope/trouble; **~ de monde** too many people.

III de trop, en trop *loc adv* **trois tomates en** or **de ~** three tomatoes too many; **il y a une assiette en ~** there's one plate too many; **j'ai dix kilos de bagages en ~** my luggage is ten kilos over; **j'ai quelques kilos en ~** I'm a few kilos overweight; **perdez vos kilos en ~** lose those extra kilos; **si tu as du tissu en ~ tu peux faire un coussin** if you have some material left over, you can make a cushion; **il y a 12 francs de ~** there's 12 francs too much; **sa remarque était de ~** his remark was uncalled for; **être /se sentir de ~** to be/to feel one is in the way; **je suis parti, je me sentais de ~** I left, I felt (as if) I was in the way; **il faut le dire si je suis de ~!** iron do tell me if I'm in the way, won't you?; **deux jours ne seraient pas de ~ pour finir** it'll take a good two days to finish.

IV par trop *loc adv* = **trop**.

trope /tʀɔp/ *nm* trope.

tropézien, **-ienne** /tʀɔpezjɛ̃, ɛn/ ▶**857** *adj* of Saint-Tropez.

Tropézien, **-ienne** /tʀɔpezjɛ̃, ɛn/ ▶**857** *nm,f* (natif) native of Saint-Tropez; (habitant) inhabitant of Saint-Tropez.

trophée /tʀɔfe/ *nm* (tous contextes) trophy; **~ sportif** sports trophy; **~ de chasse** hunting trophy.

tropical, **~e**, *mpl* **-aux** /tʀɔpikal, o/ *adj* tropical.

tropicaliser /tʀɔpikalize/ [1] *vtr* to tropicalize [*matériau, appareil*].

tropique /tʀɔpik/ **I** *nm* tropic; **~ du Cancer/Capricorne** tropic of Cancer/Capricorn.

II les ~s *nmpl* (zone) the tropics; **vivre sous les ~s** to live in the tropics.

tropisme /tʀɔpism/ *nm* tropism.

troposphère /tʀɔpɔsfɛʀ/ *nf* troposphere.

trop-perçu, *pl* **~s** /tʀopɛʀsy/ *nm* **1** (d'argent) overcharge; **2** Jur (d'impôts) overpayment of tax; **remboursement d'un ~** tax refund.

trop-plein, *pl* **~s** /tʀoplɛ̃/ *nm* **1** (excès) (de liquide) excess; (de choses, personnes) excess number; (d'affection, d'émotion) overabundance; **avoir un ~ d'énergie** to have excess energy; **un ~ de liquidités** an excess cash-flow; **2** Tech (de lavabo, baignoire) overflow.

troquer /tʀɔke/ [1] *vtr* **1** Comm to trade (**contre** for), to barter (**contre** for); **2** (échanger) **~ qch/qn contre** or **pour qch/qn** to exchange ou swap sth/sb for sth/sb.

troquet○ /tʀɔkɛ/ *nm* bar.

trot /tʀo/ *nm* Équit trot; **partir au ~** to set off at a trot; **faire du ~** to trot; **aller au ~** to trot along; **au ~!** Équit trot on!; fig at the double GB, on the double US; ▶**petit**.

■ **~ allongé** Équit extended trot; **~ assis** Équit sitting trot; **~ attelé** Équit harness race; **~ enlevé** Équit rising trot; **~ monté** Équit trotting race under saddle; **~ de travail** Équit working trot.

Trotski /tʀɔtski/ *npr* Trotsky.

trotskisme, **trotskysme** /tʀɔtskism/ *nm* Trotskyism.

trotskiste, **trotskyste** /tʀɔtskist/ *adj, nmf* Trotskyite.

trotte○ /tʀɔt/ *nf* fair walk; **ça fait une ~** it's a fair ou quite a walk.

trotte-menu /tʀɔtməny/ *adj inv* liter **la gent ~** the mouse tribe.

trotter /tʀɔte/ [1] *vi* **1** Équit [*cheval, cavalier*] to trot; **2** (aller à petits pas) [*adulte, souris*] to scurry (about); [*enfant*] to toddle; **il n'a qu'un an et trotte déjà** he's only a year old and is already toddling; **3** fig **~ dans la tête** [*pensée*] to go through one's mind; [*musique*] to go through one's head; **4** (marcher beaucoup) to be on the go; **j'ai trotté toute la matinée** I've been on the go all morning.

trotteur /tʀɔtœʀ/ *nm* **1** Équit trotter; **2** Mode (chaussure) *flat, broad-heeled shoe*.

trotteuse /tʀɔtøz/ *nf* (de montre, chronomètre) second hand.

trottinement /tʀɔtinmɑ̃/ *nm* Équit jogging **¢**.

trottiner /tʀɔtine/ [1] *vi* **1** Équit [*cheval*] to jog; **2** (aller à petits pas) [*personne, souris*] to scurry along.

trottinette /tʀɔtinɛt/ *nf* (patinette) scooter.

trottoir /tʀɔtwaʀ/ *nm* pavement GB, sidewalk US; **sur le ~ d'en face** on the pavement GB ou sidewalk US opposite; **le bord du ~** the kerb GB ou curb US.

■ **~ roulant** Transp moving pavement GB, moving sidewalk US.

IDIOMES **faire le ~**○ to be on the game○ GB, to be a hooker○.

trou /tʀu/ *nm* **1** (cavité) hole; **tomber dans un ~** to fall into a hole; **un ~ de deux mètres de profondeur** a hole two metres[GB] deep; **~ d'obus** shell hole; **2** (repaire) hole; **se réfugier dans son ~** [*lapin, renard*] to take refuge in its hole; **faire son ~**○ [*personne*] to carve out a niche for oneself; **3** (perforation) (de passoire, ceinture, filet) hole; (d'instrument à vent) finger hole; **faire un ~ dans qch** to make a hole in sth; **faire un ~ à la perçeuse** to drill a hole; **le ~ d'une aiguille** the eye of a needle; **4** (déchirure) hole; **une chemise pleine de ~s** a shirt full of holes; **avoir un ~ à sa chaussette** to have a hole in one's sock; **le ~ dans la couche d'ozone** the hole in the ozone layer; **se faire un ~ dans la tête** to gash one's head badly; **5** (lacune) gap; **j'ai un ~ dans mon emploi du temps** gén I have a gap in my timetable; Scol I have a free period; **6**○ (déficit) deficit, shortfall; **un ~ dans le budget** a budget deficit, a shortfall in the budget; **un ~ de vingt millions** a twenty million deficit; **7** (argent détourné) **il a laissé un ~ de vingt millions** when he left there was twenty million unaccounted for; **8**○ (petite localité): **~ (perdu)** dump○, godforsaken place; **il n'est jamais sorti de son ~** he's never been out of his own backyard; **9**◑ (prison) prison, nick○; **aller au ~** to go to prison, to go to the nick○; **10**◑ (prison militaire) glasshouse○ GB, military prison; **faire du ~** to be in the glasshouse○ GB, to be in a military prison; **11**◑ (tombe) **être dans le ~** to be six feet under○; **mettre qn dans le ~** to bury sb.

■ **~ d'aération** airhole; **~ d'air** Aviat air pocket; **~ de balle**◑ arsehole● GB, asshole◑ US; **~ borgne** Mécan blind hole; **~ de Botal** Anat foramen ovale; **~ du chat** Naut lubber's hole; **~ de cigarette** cigarette burn; **~ du cul**● arsehole● GB, asshole◑ US; **~ de flûte** Mus finger hole; **~ de graissage** Mécan lubrication hole; **~ d'homme** Tech manhole; **~ de mémoire** lapse of memory; **j'ai un ~ (de mémoire)** my mind has gone blank; **~ de nez**○ nostril; **~ noir** Astron black hole; **~ normand** *glass of spirits between courses to aid digestion*; **~ occipital** Anat foramen magnum; **~ d'ozone** ozone hole; **~ de serrure** keyhole; **~ du souffleur** Théât prompt box; **~ de souris** mousehole; **~ de ver** wormhole.

IDIOMES **ne pas avoir les yeux en face des ~s**○ not to be able to see straight; **faire le ~** [*coureur, cycliste*] to open up a lead.

troubadour /tʀubaduʀ/ *nm* troubadour.

troublant, **~e** /tʀublɑ̃, ɑ̃t/ *adj* **1** (déconcertant) [*problème, anecdote, circonstance*] disturbing; [*coïncidence, document, fait*] disconcerting; **leur ressemblance est ~e** their resemblance is disconcerting; **2** (qui émeut) [*décolleté*] that stirs desire (*épith, après n*).

trouble /tʀubl/ **I** *adj* **1** (pas transparent) [*eau, vin*] cloudy; [*verres, vitres*] smudgy; **2** (flou) [*image, photo*] blurred; [*contours*] vague, blurred; **j'ai la vue ~** (temporaire) my eyes are blurred; (permanent) I have blurred vision; **3** (équivoque) [*sentiment*] confused; [*relation*] equivocal; (louche) [*affaire, milieu, personnage*] shady; [*comportement*] shifty.

II *adv* **je vois ~** (temporaire) my eyes are blurred; (permanent) I have blurred vision.

III *nm* **1** (insécurité) unrest; **2** (mésentente, malaise) **semer le ~** to sow discord; **jeter le ~** to stir up trouble; **jeter le ~ dans les esprits** to sow confusion in people's minds; **3** (confusion) confusion; (gêne) embarrassment; **ton ~ était visible** (gêne) you were visibly embarrassed ou flustered; **éprouver** or **ressentir un certain ~** to feel rather confused; **dominer son ~** to overcome one's confusion; **pour apaiser** or **dissiper son ~** to put him/her at ease; **4** (émoi) emotion; **ressentir un ~** to feel an emotion; **le premier ~ amoureux** the first stirrings of love; Méd disorder; **~s digestifs/nerveux/de la vue/du sommeil** (peut-être graves) digestive/nervous/visual/sleep disorders; **de légers ~s gastriques** (pas graves) minor gastric problems; **~s de la personnalité/du comportement/du langage** personality/behavioural[GB]/speech disorders; **~ fonctionnel** functional disorder; **~s de la mémoire** memory problems.

IV *nmpl* unrest **¢**, disturbances; **de graves ~s ont éclaté** serious disturbances have broken out; **réprimer des ~s** to quell unrest; **~s ethniques** ethnic unrest.

trouble-fête /tʀubləfɛt/ *nmf inv* spoilsport; **jouer les ~** to be a spoilsport.

troubler /tʀuble/ [1] **I** *vtr* **1** (brouiller) to make [sth] cloudy, to cloud [*eau, vin*]; to blur [*vue, image*]; **~ la réception des images** to interfere with reception; **2** (déranger) to disturb [*silence, sommeil, pays, personne*]; to disrupt [*réunion, spectacle, projets*]; **~ l'ordre public** (un individu) to cause a breach of the peace; (groupe d'insurgés) to disturb the peace; **en ces temps troublés** in these troubled times; **3** (déconcerter) to disconcert [*accusé, candidat, élève*]; **être troublé** (gêné) to be flustered; **être profondément troublé par qch** [*mauvaise nouvelle, mort*] to be deeply disturbed by sth; **quelque chose me trouble** (rendre perplexe) something's bothering ou puzzling me; **4** (égarer) to affect [*jugement, raison, esprit, assurance*]; **5** liter (mettre en émoi) to disturb euph [*personne*].

II se troubler *vpr* **1** (perdre contenance) [*personne, candidat, accusé*] to become flustered; **répondre sans se ~** to answer without getting flustered; **2** (devenir trouble) [*liquide*] to become cloudy, to cloud; [*idées*] to become confused; **ma vue se troubla** my eyes became blurred.

trouduc● /tʀudyk/ *nm* offensive arsehole● GB, asshole● US injur.

troué, **~e** /tʀue/ **I** *pp* ▶ **trouer**.

II *pp adj* (avec un trou) with a hole in it (*épith, après n*); (avec plusieurs trous) with holes in it (*épith, après n*); **ta chemise est ~e** your shirt has got a hole in it, your shirt has got holes in it; **tout ~** full of holes (*après n*); **être ~ au genou/au coude/dans le dos** [*vêtement*] to have a hole in the knee/in the elbow/in the back; **ton pantalon est ~ aux fesses** you've got a hole in the seat of your trousers ou pants US; **mon seau est ~** there's a hole in my bucket; **jeans ~s** ripped jeans.

III trouée *nf* **1** (ouverture) (dans une haie, un bois) gap, opening; (dans le ciel) break in the clouds; **2** Mil breach; **3** Géog gap, pass.

trouer /tʀue/ [1] *vtr* **1** (perforer) (d'un trou) to make a hole in; (de plusieurs trous) to make holes in; **~ de balles** to riddle with bullets; **tu as troué ta chemise** you've made a hole in your shirt; **~ un drap avec une cigarette** to make ou burn a hole in a sheet with a cigarette; **j'ai troué mes chaussures** (à la longue) I've worn a hole in my shoe, I've worn holes in my shoes; **2** (former une ouverture) [*passage, porte*] to form an opening in [*muraille, mur*]; **de larges brèches trouaient la muraille** there were large openings in the wall; **3** (transpercer) [*lumière*] to pierce [*nuit, brouillard*]; [*cri*] to pierce [*silence, nuit*].

IDIOMES **~ la peau à qn**○ to put a bullet in sb○; **tu vas te faire ~ la peau**○ you 're going to get yourself shot.

troufignon◑ /tʀufiɲɔ̃/ *nm* arsehole● GB, asshole● US, anus.

troufion○ /tʀufjɔ̃/ *nm* soldier, squaddie○ GB, GI US.

trouillard◑, **~e** /tʀujaʀ, aʀd/ **I** *adj* cowardly; **il est très ~** he's very cowardly, he's a real coward ou chicken○.

II *nm,f* chicken○, coward.

trouille◑ /tʀuj/ *nf* fear; **avoir la ~** to be scared (**de qch** of sth; **de faire** of doing); **flanquer**○ or **foutre**◑ **la ~ à qn** to scare sb, to give sb a fright; **être mort de ~** to be scared stiff.

trouillomètre◑ /tʀujɔmɛtʀ/ *nm* **avoir le ~ à zéro** to be scared stiff.

troupe /tʀup/ *nf* **1** Mil troops (*pl*); **la ~** (l'armée) the troops (*pl*), the army; (les simples soldats) the rank and file, the troops; **les ~s** the troops, the army (*sg*); **les ~s de débarquement/de choc** landing/shock troops; **~s aéroportées** airborne troops; **faire intervenir la ~** to call in the troops; **lever des ~s** to raise troops; **des ~s fraîches** fresh troops; **mouvement/déploiement de ~s** troop movement/deployment; **passer les ~s en revue** to review the troops; **servir dans la ~** to serve as a soldier; **2** fig (de syndicat, parti) **les ~s** the troops; **3** Théât, Danse company; (qui voyage) troupe; **4** (groupe) (d'éléphants, de cerfs) herd; (de moutons, d'oiseaux) flock; (de touristes) troop; (d'enfants) band; **en ~** in a band ou group; **se déplacer en ~** to go about in a band ou group; **en route, mauvaise ~!** hum let's go!; **5** (chez les scouts) troop.

troupeau, *pl* **~x** /tʀupo/ *nm* **1** (de bisons, de vaches, d'éléphants, de cerfs) herd; (de moutons, de chèvres) flock; (d'oies) gaggle; **2** (de personnes) péj herd; **3** Relig flock.

troupier /tʀupje/ *nm* squaddie GB, soldier; **comique ~** (genre) barrack room humour[GB]; (comédien) ≈ stand-up comic.

IDIOMES **boire comme un ~** to drink like a fish; **fumer comme un ~** to smoke like a chimney; **jurer comme un ~** to swear like a trooper.

troussage /tʀusaʒ/ *nm* Culin trussing.

trousse /tʀus/ *nf* **1** (pochette) (little) case; **2** (contenu) kit.

■ **~ à couture** sewing kit; **~ (d'écolier)** pencil case; **~ de manucure** manicure set; **~ de maquillage** make-up bag; **~ de médecin** doctor's bag; **~ à outils** tool kit; **~ de secours** first-aid kit; **~ de toilette** toilet bag.

IDIOMES **avoir la police aux ~s** to have the police hot on one's heels; **être aux ~s de qn** to be hot on sb's heels.

trousseau, *pl* **~x** /tʀuso/ *nm* **1** (de clés) bunch; **un ~ de clés** a bunch of keys; **2** (de mariée) trousseau; (d'enfant) clothes (*pl*).

troussequin /tʀuskɛ̃/ *nm* **1** Équit cantle; **2** Tech marking gauge.

trousser /tʀuse/ [1] *vtr* **1** Culin to truss [*vo-*

laille]; **2** liter (rédiger) skilfully[GB] to dash off [*poème, compliment*]; **une biographie bien troussée** a skilfully[GB] written biography.

trousseur† /tʀusœʀ/ *nm* **~ de jupons**○ womanizer.

trou-trou, *pl* **~s** /tʀutʀu/ *nm* openwork ¢.

trouvaille /tʀuvaj/ *nf* **1** (découverte) find; (invention) invention; **faire une ~** (trouver un objet) to make a find; (apprendre qch) to discover sth new; **fais-moi voir tes ~s** show me what you've found; **tu parles d'une ~!** iron so what's new!; **2** (idée originale) innovation; **un spectacle plein de ~s** a show full of innovations.

trouvé, **~e** /tʀuve/ **I** *pp* ▶ **trouver**.
II *pp adj* [*image, métaphore, comparaison*] well-chosen; **réplique bien ~e** neat riposte; **tout ~** [*réponse, solution, prétexte*] ready-made; [*coupable, candidat*] obvious; **vous êtes la personne toute ~e pour ce travail** you're the very person we need for the job.

trouver /tʀuve/ [1] **I** *vtr* **1** (par hasard) to find [*parapluie, chat, cadavre*] (**en faisant** while doing); **où as-tu trouvé ça?** where did you find that?; **nous avons trouvé un petit hôtel charmant** we found a charming little hotel; **~ qch dans un tiroir/la rue/le bus** to find sth in a drawer/in the street/on the bus; **c'est surprenant de vous ~ ici!** I'm surprised to find you here!; **on trouve de tout ici** they have everything here; **~ qch par hasard** to come across sth; **j'ai trouvé Luc au supermarché** I ran into Luc at the supermarket; **2** (découvrir en cherchant) to find [*personne, clés, gants, numéro de téléphone, erreur*]; **il a trouvé la maison/femme de ses rêves** he found the house/woman of his dreams; **~ l'amour/la paix** to find love/peace; **j'ai trouvé quelqu'un à qui demander conseil** I've found someone to go to for advice; **elle a trouvé quelqu'un qui peut la renseigner/l'aider** she's found somebody who can give her the information/help her; **alors tu le trouves ce livre?** have you found that book yet?; **~ son chemin** to find one's way; **j'ai eu du mal à ~ leur maison** I had trouble finding their house; **tu trouveras à manger dans la cuisine** you'll find something to eat in the kitchen; **~ ce que l'on cherche** to find what one is looking for; **les médecins n'ont pas trouvé ce qu'il avait** the doctors couldn't find what was wrong with him; **ils ont trouvé qui a volé la voiture** they found the person who stole the car; **~ de quoi écrire** to find something to write with; **vous le trouverez à son bureau/chez lui** you'll find him in his office/at home; **savez-vous où je peux la ~?** do you know where I can find her?; **veuillez ~ ci-joint...** (dans une lettre) please find enclosed...; **j'ai trouvé!** I've got it!; **combien trouves-tu dans le premier exercice?** what answer did you get for the first exercise?; **tu as trouvé ça tout seul?** iron did you work that out all by yourself?; **si tu continues tu vas me ~**○**!** don't push your luck○!; **il va ~ à qui parler** he's going to be for it○; ▶ **chaussure**; **3** (se procurer) to find [*emploi, appartement, associé*]; **il ne trouve pas de travail** he can't find a job; **j'ai trouvé une amie en elle** I found a friend in her; **~ une consolation dans** to find consolation in; **~ du plaisir/une satisfaction dans qch/à faire** to get pleasure/satisfaction out of sth/out of doing; **~ un réconfort dans** to take comfort in; **il ne nous reste plus qu'à ~ le financement** all we have to do now is get financial backing; **4** (voir) to find; **~ qch dans un état lamentable** to find sth in an appalling state; **~ qch cassé/déchiré/ouvert** to find sth broken/torn/open; **~ qn debout/couché/assis** to find sb standing/lying down/sitting down; **~ qn malade/en pleurs/mort** to find sb ill/in tears/dead; **il a été trouvé mort dans son lit un matin** he was found dead in his bed one morning; **~ qn en train de faire** to find sb doing; **je les ai trouvés en train de fouiller dans mes affaires** I found them rummaging through my belongings; **ils sont tous venus me ~ après le cours** they all came to see me after the class; **je vais aller ~ le responsable du rayon** I'm going to go and see the head of the department; **5** (estimer) **~ qn gentil/adorable/pénible** to think sb is nice/adorable/tiresome; **je trouve ça bizarre/drôle/inadmissible** I think it's strange/funny/intolerable; **comment trouves-tu mon gâteau?** what do you think of my cake?; **comment trouves-tu mon ami?** what do you think of my friend?, how do you like my friend?; **~ triste de faire** to find it sad to do; **il trouve (ça) dommage de ne pas en profiter** he thinks it's a shame not to take advantage of it; **j'ai trouvé bon de vous prévenir** I thought it right to warn you; **~ un intérêt à qch/faire** to find sth interesting/find it interesting to do; **~ des qualités/défauts à qch/qn** to see good qualities/faults in sth/sb; **elle ne me trouve que des défauts** she only sees my faults; **je me demande ce qu'elle lui trouve!** I wonder what she sees in him!; **elle m'a trouvé bonne/mauvaise mine** she thought I looked well/didn't look well; **je te trouve bien calme, qu'est-ce que tu as?** you're very quiet, what's the matter?; **~ que** to think that; **tu trouves que j'ai tort/raison?** do you think I'm wrong/right?; **ils ont trouvé que j'exagérais** they thought I was going too far; **tu trouves?** do you think so?; **je ne trouve pas qu'il est** or **soit méchant** I don't think he's so bad; **6** (imaginer) to come up with [*raison, excuses, moyen, produit*]; **~ une astuce** to come up with a crafty solution; **ils ont trouvé un nouveau système** they've come up with a new system; **~ à s'amuser/s'occuper** to find sth to play with/do; **~ qch à dire sur** to find sth to say about; **~ à redire** to find fault; **~ le moyen de faire** also iron to manage to do; **il n'a rien trouvé de mieux que de le leur répéter!** iron he WOULD have to go and tell them!
II se trouver *vpr* **1** (être situé) to be; **se ~ à Rome/dans l'avion/au bord de la rivière** to be in Rome/on the plane/on the river bank; **le résumé se trouve page 11** the summary is on page 11; **se ~ incapable** or **dans l'impossibilité de faire** to be unable to do; **je me trouvais seule chez moi** I was home alone; **2** (se retrouver) [*personne*] to find oneself [*bloqué, pris, isolé*]; [*projet*] to be [*compromis, entravé*]; [*ville, région, pays*] to be [*assiégé, envahi, inondé*]; **se ~ confronté à de grosses difficultés** to have run into major problems; **3** (se sentir) to feel; **se ~ mal à l'aise quelque part** to feel uneasy somewhere; **se ~ embarrassé** to feel embarrassed; **se ~ bien quelque part** to be happy somewhere; **se ~ mal** to pass out; **j'ai failli me ~ mal** I nearly passed out; **4** (se considérer) **il se ~ beau/laid** he thinks he's good-looking/ugly; **5** (se procurer) to find oneself [*emploi, logement, voiture*]; to find [*raisons, excuses, motif*]; **trouve-toi une occupation** find yourself something to do; **elle s'est trouvé un petit ami** she's found herself a boyfriend.
III *v impers* **il se trouve que je le connais** I happen to know him; **il se trouve que nous nous connaissons** we happen to know each other; **il se trouve que je le savais** as it happens, I already knew; **il se trouve qu'elle ne leur avait rien dit** as it happened, she hadn't told them anything; **il ne s'est trouvé que dix personnes pour accepter** in the event, only ten people accepted; **ça s'est trouvé comme ça**○ it just happened that way; **si ça se trouve**○ **ça te plaira/tu les verras** you might like it/see them; **si ça se trouve**○ **il est mort/ne viendra pas** he might be dead/not come.

trouvère /tʀuvɛʀ/ *nm* trouvère (*poet in the Middle Ages in northern France*).

troyen, **-enne** /tʀwajɛ̃, ɛn/ ▶ **857** *adj* Trojan.

truand /tʀyɑ̃/ *nm* **1** (membre de la pègre) gangster, mobster; **2** (escroc) crook.

truander○ /tʀyɑ̃de/ [1] **I** *vtr* to con○ [*personne*]; **~ sur qch** to cheat on sth.
II *vi* to cheat.

trublion /tʀyblijɔ̃/ *nm* troublemaker.

truc /tʀyk/ *nm* **1**○ (procédé) knack; **trouver le ~ pour faire qch** to find the knack of doing sth; **avoir un ~ pour gagner de l'argent** to know a good way of making money; **ça y est, j'ai pigé le ~**○ that's it, I've got it; **2**○ (chose) thing; (dont on a oublié le nom) thingummy○, whatsit○; **qu'est-ce que c'est que ce ~?** what on earth is that thing○?; **il y a un tas de ~s à faire dans la maison** there are loads○ of things to do in the house; **c'est pas mal ton ~** it's not bad, that thing of yours○; **passe-moi le ~ qui est sur la table** pass me the thingummy○ ou whatsit○ on the table; **3**○ (fait quelconque) thing; **il y a un ~ qui ne va pas** there's something wrong; **ils nous ont raconté des ~s épouvantables** they told us some dreadful things; **je viens juste de penser à un ~** I've just thought of something; **le vélo, c'est pas mon ~**○ cycling's not my thing; **moi, mon ~ c'est les vacances à la campagne** what I love are holidays GB ou vacations US in the country; **c'était une maison superbe, gigantesque, au bord de la mer, tu vois le ~!** it was a fantastic house, enormous, by the sea, do you get the idea?; **4** (savoir-faire) trick; **un ~ du métier** a trick of the trade; **y'a un ~**○ there's a trick to it; **5**○ (personne) what's-his-name/what's-her-name; **6** Cin, Théât (trucage) special effect.

trucage, **truquage** /tʀykaʒ/ *nm* **1** Cin, Théât special effect; **le ~ des images** the making of special visual effects; **des ~s optiques** optical effects; **2** (de comptes, dossier) doctoring; (d'élections) rigging, fixing.

truchement /tʀyʃmɑ̃/ *nm* **1**† (interprète) interpreter; **2** (intermédiaire) liter **par le ~ de qch** through sth; **par le ~ de qn** through the intervention of sb.

trucider○ /tʀyside/ [1] *vtr* to bump off○, to kill.

truck /tʀœk/ *nm* flat truck GB, flatcar US.

trucmuche○ /tʀykmyʃ/ *nm* thingumabob○; **hé, ~!** hey, thingumabob○!

truculence /tʀykylɑ̃s/ *nf* earthiness.

truculent, **~e** /tʀykylɑ̃, ɑ̃t/ *adj* [*histoire, style, personne*] earthy.

truelle /tʀyɛl/ *nf* **1** Constr trowel; **2** Culin fish slice.

truffe /tʀyf/ *nf* **1** (champignon, chocolat) truffle; **2** (de chien) nose.

truffer /tʀyfe/ [1] *vtr* **1** Culin to stuff [sth] with truffles [*pâté, dinde*]; **2** (remplir) **il a truffé son discours de citations** he stuffed his speech with quotations; **la pièce était truffée de micros** the room was larded with bugging devices; **ta lettre est truffée de fautes** your letter is riddled with mistakes.

truffier, **-ière** /tʀyfje, ɛʀ/ **I** *adj* [*chêne*] truffle (*épith*); [*chien, porc*] truffle-sniffing (*épith*); [*région*] truffle-rich (*épith*).
II truffière *nf* truffle ground.

truie /tʀɥi/ *nf* Zool sow.

truisme /tʀɥism/ *nm* truism.

truite /tʀɥit/ *nf* Zool, Culin trout; **~ aux amandes** trout with almonds.
■ **~ arc-en-ciel** rainbow trout; **~ au bleu** *trout poached alive*; **~ de mer** sea trout; **~ de rivière** brook trout; **~ saumonée** salmon trout.

truité, **~e** /tʀɥite/ *adj* [*chien*] spotted; [*cheval*] dappled; [*poterie*] crackled.

trumeau, *pl* **~x** /tʀymo/ *nm* **1** Archit (entrefenêtre) pier; (de cheminée) overmantel; (pilier) pillar; **2** Culin shin.

truquer /tʀyke/ [1] *vtr* **1** (altérer) to fiddle○ [*comptes, résultats*]; to doctor [*dossier, déclaration*]; **2** Jeux to load [*dés*]; to mark [*cartes*];

3 (fausser) to fix, to rig [*enquête, élections, match*]; **un combat truqué** a rigged fight.
truquiste /tʀykist/ ▶510 *nmf* Cin special effects technician.
trusquin /tʀyskɛ̃/ *nm* marking gauge.
trust /tʀœst/ *nm* (groupement) trust; (entreprise puissante) trust, cartel; **loi anti-~** anti-trust law.
truster○ /tʀœste/ [1] *vtr* to bag○, to monopolize.
trypanosome /tʀipanɔzom/ *nm* trypanosome.
trypsine /tʀipsin/ *nf* trypsin.
tsar /tsaʀ/ *nm* tsar, czar.
tsarévitch /tsaʀevitʃ/ *nm* tsarevitch, czarevitch.
tsarine /tsaʀin/ *nf* tsarina, czarina.
tsariste /tsaʀist/ *adj, nmf* tsarist, czarist.
tsé-tsé /tsetse/ *nf inv* **(mouche) ~** tsetse (fly).
TSF† /teɛsɛf/ *nf* (*abbr* = **télégraphie sans fil**) **(poste de) ~** wireless†, radio.
T-shirt /tiʃœʀt/ *nm* T-shirt.
tsigane /tsigan/ = **tzigane**.
tsoin-tsoin, **tsouin-tsouin** /tswɛ̃tswɛ̃/ *excl* boom-boom!
tss-tss /tsts/ *excl* tut-tut!
tsunami /tsunami/ *nm* tsunami.
TSVP (*written abbr* = **tournez s'il vous plaît**) PTO GB, over US.
TTC /tetese/ *loc adv*: *abbr* ▶ **taxe**.
tu[1] /ty/ *pron pers* **1** gén you; **~ es en retard** you're late; **~ n'as pas peint la porte** you haven't painted the door; **crois-~ que**...? do you think that...?; **2** Relig you, thou‡.
IDIOMES **être à ~ et à toi avec qn** to be on familiar terms with sb, to be pally○ with sb.
tu[2] /ty/ *nm* **l'emploi du ~** the use of the 'tu' form; **dire ~ à qn** to address sb using the 'tu' form; **on se dit ~** let's address one another using the 'tu' form.
TU (*written abbr* = **temps universel**) UT.
tuant○, **~e** /tɥɑ̃, ɑ̃t/ *adj* [*travail, voyage*] exhausting, knackering●; [*personne*] exhausting.
tub /tœb/ *nm* (bath)tub.
tuba /tyba/ *nm* **1** ▶534 Mus tuba; **2** Sport snorkel.
tubage /tybaʒ/ *nm* **1** Méd intubation; **~ gastrique/du larynx** gastric/laryngeal intubation; **2** Mines (well) casing.
tubard●, **~e** /tybaʀ, aʀd/ **I** *adj* [*personne*] consumptive.
II *nm,f* consumptive, TB case○.
tube /tyb/ **I** *nm* **1** (objet cylindrique) tube; (tuyau) pipe; **~ de verre/de métal** glass/metal tube; **~ gradué** graduated tube; **2** (emballage) (de comprimés) tube; (de dentifrice, peinture, colle) tube; **3**○ (chanson à succès) hit; **le ~ de l'été** the hit of the summer; **4** (lampe) tube, lamp; **~ luminescent/fluorescent** luminescent/fluorescent tube.
II à pleins tubes○ *loc adv* **mettre le son à pleins ~s**○ to turn the sound right up○; **écouter un disque à pleins ~s**○ to listen to a record at full blast; **rouler à pleins ~s**○ to drive flat out; **déconner à pleins ~s**○ (faire des erreurs) to do really stupid things; (dire des bêtises) to talk a load of rubbish○.
■ **~ acoustique** speaking tube; **~ capillaire** capillary tube; **~ cathodique** cathode ray tube; **~ compte-gouttes** dropper tube; **~ criblé** sieve tube; **~ digestif** digestive tract; **~ électronique** electronic tube; **~ à essai** test tube; **~ lance-torpilles** torpedo tube; **~ au néon** neon tube; **~ pollinique** pollen tube; **~ de rouge à lèvres** lipstick.
tuber /tybe/ [1] *vtr* Mines, Tech to tube [*sondage, puits*].
tubercule /tybɛʀkyl/ *nm* **1** Bot tuber; **2** Anat tuberosity; **3** Méd tubercle.
tuberculeux, **-euse** /tybɛʀkylø, øz/ **I** *adj* **1** Méd [*patient*] tubercular; **2** Bot [*plante*] tuberous.
II *nm,f* Méd TB ou tuberculosis sufferer.
tuberculine /tybɛʀkylin/ *nf* tuberculin.
tuberculinique /tybɛʀkylinik/ *adj* [*test, réaction*] tuberculin.
tuberculose /tybɛʀkyloz/ ▶271 *nf* tuberculosis, TB; **~ pulmonaire/rénale/génitale** pulmonary/renal/genital tuberculosis.
tubéreux, **-euse** /tybeʀø, øz/ **I** *adj* [*plante*] tuberous.
II tubéreuse *nf* tuberose.
tubérosité /tybeʀozite/ *nf* **1** Bot tubercle; **2** Anat (des os) tuberosity.
tubulaire /tybylɛʀ/ *adj* tubular.
tubulé, **~e** /tybyle/ *adj* **1** Bot [*fleur*] tubular; **2** Tech tubulate.
tubuleux, **-euse** /tybylø, øz/ *adj* **1** Bot tubular; **2** Anat tubulous.
tubulure /tybylyʀ/ *nf* **1** Tech (ensemble des tubes) tubing; (orifice) connection piece, neck; **2** (conduit) neck, nozzle, pipe.
■ **~ d'admission** inlet manifold; **~ d'échappement** exhaust manifold.
TUC /tyk/ *nm* **1** (*abbr* = **travaux d'utilité collective**) paid community service (*for the young unemployed*); **2** *abbr* ▶ **temps**.
tuciste /tysist/ *nmf*: *young unemployed person on paid community service.*
tudesque /tydɛsk/ *adj* Teutonic.
tudieu‡ /tydjø/ *excl* zounds‡!
tué /tɥe/ *nm* person killed; **sept ~s, cinq blessés** seven people killed, five injured.
tue-mouches /tymuʃ/ *adj inv* **papier ~** flypaper.
tuer /tɥe/ [1] **I** *vtr* **1** (faire mourir) to kill [*personne, animal, plante*]; **trois civils ont été tués par un commando** three civilians were killed by a commando; **onze touristes ont été tués dans un accident** eleven tourists have been killed in an accident; **~ un sanglier/une poule/une vipère** to kill a boar/a hen/an adder; **~ qn en duel** to kill sb in a duel; **l'alcool tue** alcohol kills; **la route tue** cars can kill; **tu ne tueras point** Bible thou shalt not kill; **~ qn d'un coup de fusil** or **par balles** to shoot sb dead; **elle a été tuée d'une balle dans la tête** she was shot in the head and killed; **six personnes ont été tuées par balles** six people were shot dead; **~ qn à coups de bâton** to beat sb to death; **~ qn à coups de pierres** to stone sb to death; **~ qn à coups de matraque** to club sb to death; **~ qn par strangulation** to strangle sb; **~ le cochon** to kill the pig; ▶ **mère, ours, poule, veau**; **2** (détruire) to kill [*amour, initiative, petit commerce*]; **3**○ (épuiser) (physiquement) [*personne, travail*] to kill; **les enfants m'ont tuée ce matin** the children have worn me out ou run me ragged○ this morning; **tu sais, quelquefois tu me tues!** I think you'll be the death of me!
II se tuer *vpr* **1** (trouver la mort) [*personne*] to be killed; **se ~ en voiture** or **dans un accident de voiture** to be killed in a car accident; **il s'est tué en tombant du toit** he fell to his death from a roof; **2** (se suicider) to kill oneself; **il a préféré se ~** he chose to kill himself; **3**○ (s'épuiser) **se ~ au travail** or **à la tâche** to work oneself to death; **se ~ à faire** to kill oneself doing; **je me tue à te le dire** I keep on telling you.
IDIOMES **~ le temps** to kill time.
tuerie /tyʀi/ *nf* killings (*pl*).
tue-tête: **à tue-tête** /atytɛt/ *loc adv* [*chanter, crier*] at the top of one's voice.
tueur, **-euse** /tɥœʀ, øz/ **I** *adj* [*cellule*] killer.
II *nm,f* **1** (assassin) killer; **2** (chasseur) hunter; **~ d'éléphants** elephant hunter; **3** ▶510 (ouvrier d'abattoir) slaughterman/slaughterwoman.
■ **~ à gages** hired ou professional killer.
tuf /tyf/ *nm* tuff; **~ calcaire** calcareous tufa.
tuile /tɥil/ *nf* **1** Constr tile; **~ ronde** pantile; **~ plate** (flat) roofing tile; **2**○ (événement fâcheux) blow; **tu parles d'une ~!** what a blow!
■ **~ aux amandes** Culin *almond biscuit*; **~ faîtière** ridge tile; **~ mécanique** interlocking pantile; **~ romaine** pantile.
tuilerie /tɥilʀi/ *nf* **1** (industrie) tilemaking industry; **2** (usine) tile factory.
tuilier, **-ière** /tɥilje, ɛʀ/ **I** *adj* [*industrie*] tilemaking.
II ▶510 *nm,f* tilemaker.
tulipe /tylip/ *nf* **1** Bot tulip; **2** (ornement) (lampe) tulip-shaped lamp.
tulipier /tylipje/ *nm* tulip tree.
tulle /tyl/ *nm* tulle.
tuméfaction /tymefaksjɔ̃/ *nf* (phénomène, résultat) tumefaction.
tuméfier /tymefje/ [2] *vtr* to make [sth] swell up [*partie du corps*]; **avoir les paupières tuméfiées** to have swollen eyelids.
tumescence /tymɛsɑ̃s/ *nf* tumescence.
tumescent, **~e** /tymɛsɑ̃, ɑ̃t/ *adj* tumescent.
tumeur /tymœʀ/ *nf* tumour[GB]; **~ au sein/cerveau** breast/brain tumour[GB]; **~ bénigne/maligne** benign/malignant tumour[GB].
tumoral, **~e**, *mpl* **-aux** /tymɔʀal, o/ *adj* tumorous.
tumulte /tymylt/ *nm* **1** (désordre bruyant) uproar; **s'achever dans le ~** to end in uproar; **2** (agitation) turmoil.
tumultueusement /tymyltɥøzmɑ̃/ *adv* tumultuously.
tumultueux, **-euse** /tymyltɥø, øz/ *adj* [*période, séance, journée*] turbulent; [*vie, jeunesse*] turbulent, tempestuous; [*relations, entrevue*] stormy.
tumulus /tymylys/ *nm inv* burial mound, tumulus spéc.
tuner /tynɛʀ/ *nm* tuner.
tungstène /tœ̃gstɛn/ *nm* tungsten.
tunique /tynik/ *nf* **1** Antiq, Mil, Mode tunic; **2** Anat tunic, tunica spéc; **3** Relig tunic, tunicle.
Tunis /tynis/ ▶857 *npr* Tunis.
Tunisie /tynizi/ ▶321 *nprf* Tunisia.
tunisien, **-ienne** /tynizjɛ̃, ɛn/ ▶537 *adj* Tunisian.
Tunisien, **-ienne** /tynizjɛ̃, ɛn/ ▶537 *nm,f* Tunisian.
tunnel /tynɛl/ *nm* **1** Transp tunnel; **~ routier/ferroviaire** road/railway tunnel; **le ~ sous la Manche** the Channel Tunnel; **creuser un ~** to dig a tunnel; **2** Tech tunnel; **3** Phys **effet ~** tunnel effect.
■ **~ aérodynamique** wind tunnel.
IDIOMES **voir le bout du ~** to see light at the end of the tunnel; **être au bout du ~** to be at the end of the tunnel.
tunnelier /tynəlje/ *nm* rotary digger shield.
TUP /typ/ *nm* ▶ **titre**.
tuque /tyk/ *nf* C knitted cap.
turban /tyʀbɑ̃/ *nm* turban.
turbin○ /tyʀbɛ̃/ *nm* daily grind○, work; **aller au ~** to go to work.
turbine /tyʀbin/ *nf* turbine; **~ hydraulique/à vapeur/à gaz** hydraulic/steam/gas turbine; **~ à action/réaction** action/reaction turbine.
turbiner○ /tyʀbine/ [1] *vi* to slog away○, to work hard.
turbo /tyʀbo/ **I** *nm* Aut turbo; **un ~ diesel** a turbo-diesel.
II○ *nf* Aut turbo (model); **une 205 ~ diesel** a 205 turbo-diesel.
IDIOMES **mettre le ~**○ to go into overdrive.
turbocompresseur /tyʀbokɔ̃pʀesœʀ/ *nm* turbocharger.
turbomoteur /tyʀbomɔtœʀ/ *nm* turbine engine.
turbopompe /tyʀbopɔ̃p/ *nf* turbopump, turbine-pump.
turbopropulseur /tyʀbopʀɔpylsœʀ/ *nm* turbopropellor.

turboréacteur /tyʀboʀeaktœʀ/ *nm* turbojet (engine).

turbot /tyʀbo/ *nm* turbot.

turbotrain /tyʀbotʀɛ̃/ *nm* turbotrain.

turbulence /tyʀbylɑ̃s/ *nf* **1** (tourbillon) turbulence **¢**; **traverser une zone de ~s** to go through an area of turbulence; **2** (indiscipline) unruliness; (agitation) unrest **¢**; **~s boursières/politiques** stock market/political unrest.
■ ~ atmosphérique turbulence **¢**.

turbulent, **~e** /tyʀbylɑ̃, ɑ̃t/ *adj* [*enfant*] unruly; [*classe*] rowdy, unruly; [*vie*] turbulent; [*adolescent, région, ville*] rebellious; **être ~ en classe** to be disruptive in class.

turc, **turque** /tyʀk/ ▶ 462, 537 **I** *adj* Turkish; **toilettes** or **WC à la turque** hole-in-the-ground toilet; **à la turque** Mus alla turca.
II *nm* Ling Turkish.

Turc, **Turque** /tyʀk/ ▶ 537 *nm,f* Turk; ▶ **grand**, **fort**.

turf /tœʀf/ *nm* **1** (courses) **le ~** (horse) racing, the turf; (terrain)† racecourse GB, racetrack; **2**○ (travail) work; **3**◐ (prostitution) prostitution.

turfiste /tœʀfist/ *nmf* racegoer, punter○ GB.

turgescence /tyʀʒesɑ̃s/ *nf* turgescence.

turgescent, **~e** /tyʀʒesɑ̃, ɑ̃t/ *adj* turgescent.

turgide /tyʀʒid/ fml *adj* swollen, turgid sout.

turista○ /tuʀista/ ▶ 271 *nf* Montezuma's revenge○, acute attack of diarrhoea (*experienced by tourists*).

turkmène /tyʀkmɛn/ ▶ 462, 537 *adj, nm* Turkmen.

Turkmène /tyʀkmɛn/ *nmf* ▶ 537 Turkmen.

Turkménistan /tyʀkmenistɑ̃/ ▶ 321 *nprm* Turkmenistan.

turlupiner○ /tyʀlypine/ [1] *vtr* [*idée, problème*] to bother, to bug○.

turne◐ /tyʀn/ *nf* room.

turnover /tœʀnɔvœʀ/ *nm* turnover.

turpide /tyʀpid/ *adj* fml base, low.

turpitude /tyʀpityd/ *nf* **1** (caractère) turpitude sout, depravity; **2** (acte) base act; (parole) low remark.

turque ▶ **turc**.

Turquie /tyʀki/ ▶ 321 *nprf* Turkey.

turquoise /tyʀkwaz/ ▶ 193 **I** *adj inv* turquoise; **bleu ~** turquoise blue.
II *nm* (couleur) turquoise.
III *nf* Minér turquoise.

tutélaire /tytelɛʀ/ *adj* **1** (qui protège) tutelary, protecting (*épith*); **2** Jur tutelary.

tutelle /tytɛl/ *nf* **1** Jur (d'enfant, adulte) guardianship, tutelage; **placer qn sous ~** to place sb in the care of a guardian; **~ légale** legal guardianship; **2** Admin ≈ supervision; **être placé sous ~ administrative** to be placed under administrative supervision; **autorité de ~** supervision authority; **3** (en droit international) (**régime de**) **~** trusteeship; **territoire sous ~** trust territory; **4** (dépendance) supervision, domination; **sous la ~ de qn** under the domination of sb; **sous ~** under supervision; **tenir qn en ~** to hold dominion over sb; **~ politique** political domination; **5** (protection) protection; **la ~ des lois** the protection of the law; **organisme de ~** parent body.

tuteur, **-trice** /tytœʀ, tʀis/ **I** *nm,f* **1** Jur guardian; **~ légal/testamentaire** legal/testamentary guardian; **2** ▶ 510 Scol, Univ tutor.
II *nm* Bot stake, support.

tuteurage /tytœʀaʒ/ *nm* Bot staking.

tutoiement /tytwamɑ̃/ *nm* use of the form '*tu*'.

tutorat /tytɔʀa/ *nm* **1** Scol, Univ tutorial system; **2** Jur system of guardianship.

tutoyer /tytwaje/ [23] **I** *vtr* to address [sb] using the 'tu' form; fig to be on familiar terms with [*auteurs classiques*].
II se tutoyer *vpr* to address one another using the 'tu' form.

tutrice ▶ **tuteur**.

tutti frutti /tut(t)ifʀutti/ *nm inv* tutti frutti.

tutti quanti○ /tutikwɑ̃ti/ *nm* **et ~** and all the rest.

tutu /tyty/ *nm* Danse tutu.

Tuvalu /tyvaly/ ▶ 321, 416 *nprm* Tuvalu; **les îles ~** the Tuvalu Islands.

tuyau, *pl* **~x** /tɥijo/ *nm* **1** Tech pipe; **~ de** or **en cuivre/caoutchouc** copper/rubber pipe; **des ~x** pipes, piping **¢**; **2**○ (information) tip○ (**sur** about); **tu n'aurais pas un ~?** do you have any tip?; **un ~ crevé** a lousy tip; **3**○ Méd tube; **débrancher tous les ~x** to disconnect all the tubes.
■ ~ d'amenée Gén Civ feeder pipe; **~ d'arrosage** Agric hose; **~ de cheminée** Constr flue; **~ de descente** Constr downpipe GB, downspout US; **~ d'échappement** Aut exhaust; **~ d'écoulement** Constr wastepipe; **~ d'incendie** Tech fire hose; **~ d'orgue** Mus organ pipe; **~ de poêle** Tech stovepipe; ○(pantalon) drainpipes (*pl*); **~ de refroidissement** Tech coolant pipe.

tuyauter /tɥijɔte/ [1] *vtr* **1**○ (fournir des renseignements) to tip [sb] off; **se faire ~ par qn** to be tipped off by sb; **2** Cout, Mode to flute.

tuyauterie /tɥijɔtʀi/ *nf* **1** Tech piping **¢**; **une ~ défectueuse** faulty piping; **2** Mus pipes (*pl*); **3**○ hum (intestins) guts○ (*pl*), intestines (*pl*).

tuyère /tɥijɛʀ/ *nf* **1** Aviat (de moteur à réaction) exhaust nozzle; (de parachute) slot; **2** Tech (de haut-fourneau) blast pipe; **3** Agric (de pulvérisateur) delivery pipe.

TV (*written abbr* = **télévision**) TV.

TVA /tevea/ *nf* (*abbr* = **taxe à la valeur ajoutée**) VAT; **la ~ sur l'automobile** VAT on cars.

TVHD /teveaʃde/ *nf* (*abbr* = **télévision à haute définition**) HDTV.

tweed /twid/ *nm* tweed; **une veste en ~** a tweed jacket.

twist /twist/ *nm* twist.

twister /twiste/ [1] *vi* to twist, to dance the twist.

tympan /tɛ̃pɑ̃/ *nm* **1** Anat eardrum, tympanum spéc; **l'explosion lui a crevé un ~** one of his eardrums was perforated in the explosion; **un bruit à te percer le ~** an earsplitting noise; **2** Archit tympanum; **3** (d'horloge) pinion.

tympanique /tɛ̃panik/ *adj* Anat tympanic.

tympanon /tɛ̃panɔ̃/ ▶ 534 *nm* dulcimer.

Tyne ▶ 692 *nprm* **le ~ and Wear** Tyne and Wear.

type /tip/ **I** *nm* **1** (genre) type, kind; **les emplois de ce ~ sont rares** jobs of this kind are rare; **la banque propose un nouveau ~ de placement financier** the bank is offering a new type of financial investment; **il condamne ce ~ de comportement** he condemns this type of behaviour; **plusieurs accidents de ce ~ ont eu lieu** several accidents of this kind have occurred; **un climat de ~ tropical** a tropical-type climate; **la clientèle est d'un ~ nouveau** the clientele is of a new kind; **2** (représentant) (classic) example; **elle est le ~ même de la femme d'affaires** she's the classic example of a business woman; **c'est le ~ même de l'erreur impardonnable** it's a classic example of the unforgivable mistake; **3** (modèle) type, kind; **un avion d'un ~ nouveau** a new type of plane; **4** (caractères physiques) type; **il a le ~ nordique** he is a Nordic type, he has Nordic looks; **une femme de ~ méditerranéen** a woman with Mediterranean looks; **quel est ton ~ de femme?** what's your type of woman?; **ce n'est pas mon ~** he's/she's not my type; **5**○ (homme) guy○, chap○; **c'est un drôle de ~** he's an odd sort of chap; **quel sale ~!** what a swine○ ou bastard◐!; **c'est un chic ~** he's a really nice guy; **un brave ~** a nice chap; **un pauvre ~** a pathetic individual; **6** (modèle de caractère) type; (de médaille) type; **7** Tech (pièce) type; (empreinte) typeface.
II (-)type (*in compounds*) typical, classic; **l'homme d'affaires/l'intellectuel ~** the typical businessman/intellectual; **l'exemple/l'erreur ~** the typical example/mistake; **c'est l'étudiante-~** she's a typical student; **un cas ~ de schizophrénie** a classic case of schizophrenia; **le formulaire ~** the standard application form.

typé, **~e** /tipe/ **I** *pp* ▶ **typer**.
II *pp adj* **1 je crois qu'il est espagnol, en tout cas, il a un visage très ~** I think he's Spanish, anyway, he looks typically Spanish; **elle est Espagnole mais elle n'est pas très ~e** she's Spanish but she doesn't look it; **2** [*personnage*] typical; **les personnages de ses romans sont toujours bien ~s** the characters in his/her novels are always very well-drawn types.

typer /tipe/ [1] *vtr* [*auteur, dramaturge*] to portray [sb] as a type [*personnage*]; [*acteur*] to play [sb] as a type [*personnage*].

typhique /tifik/ *adj* typhic.

typhoïde /tifɔid/ ▶ 271 **I** *adj* typhoid.
II *nf* typhoid fever.

typhoïdique /tifɔidik/ *adj* typhic.

typhon /tifɔ̃/ *nm* typhoon.

typhus /tifys/ ▶ 271 *nm inv* typhus.

typique /tipik/ *adj* **1** (caractéristique) [*exemple, instrument, maison*] typical (**de** of); **l'ambiance ~ des salles de concert** the typical concert hall atmosphere; **c'est un cas ~** it's a typical case; **leur comportement est ~** their behaviour[GB] is typical; **2** (pittoresque) controv [*objet, instrument, sculpture, village*] typical; **3** Biol typical.

typiquement /tipikmɑ̃/ *adv* typically; **une famille ~ américaine** a typically American family.

typo○ /tipo/ **I** *nm* (*abbr* = **typographe**) typographer.
II *nf* (*abbr* = **typographie**) typography.

typographe /tipɔgʀaf/ ▶ 510 *nmf* typographer; **un ouvrier ~** a typographical worker.

typographie /tipɔgʀafi/ *nf* **1** (technique) letterpress (printing), typography; **2** (opérations, savoir-faire) typography.

typographique /tipɔgʀafik/ *adj* typographical; **erreur ~** typographical ou printer's error, misprint.

typographiquement /tipɔgʀafikmɑ̃/ *adv* typographically; **imprimer ~** to print by letterpress.

typologie /tipɔlɔʒi/ *nf* typology (**de** of); **classification par ~s** typological classification, classification by typology.

typologique /tipɔlɔʒik/ *adj* typological.

typomètre /tipɔmɛtʀ/ *nm* line gauge.

Tyr /tiʀ/ ▶ 857 *npr* Tyre, Tyr.

tyran /tiʀɑ̃/ *nm* (tous contextes) tyrant; **~ domestique** domestic tyrant.

tyranneau, *pl* **~x** /tiʀano/ *nm* petty tyrant.

tyrannie /tiʀani/ *nf* tyranny; **la ~ d'un patron** the tyranny of a boss; **subir la ~ de qn/qch** to be tyrannized by sb/sth.

tyrannique /tiʀanik/ *adj* tyrannical.

tyranniser /tiʀanize/ [1] *vtr* (tous contextes) to tyrannize.

tyrannosaure /tiʀanozɔʀ/ *nm* tyrannosaur.

Tyrol /tiʀɔl/ ▶ 692 *nprm* Tyrol.

tyrolien, **-ienne** /tiʀɔljɛ̃, ɛn/ **I** *adj* [*chapeau*] Tyrolean.
II tyrolienne *nf* Mus Tyrolienne.

Tyrolien, **-ienne** /tiʀɔljɛ̃, ɛn/ *nm,f* Tyrolean.

Tyrone ▶ 692 *npr* **le comté de ~** Tyrone.

tzar = **tsar**.

tzigane /dzigan, tsigan/ **I** *adj* [*musique, orchestre, origine*] gypsy.
II *nmf* gypsy.
III *nm* Ling Romany.

Uu

u, **U** /y/ *nm inv* u, U; **en (forme de) U** U-shaped.

UAL /yaɛl/ *nf* (*abbr* = **unité arithmétique et logique**) ALU.

ubac /ybak/ *nm* north-facing side, ubac spéc.

ubiquité /ybikɥite/ *nf* ubiquity sout, omnipresence sout; **je n'ai pas le don d'~!** I can't be everywhere at once!

ubuesque /ybyɛsk/ *adj* grotesque, Ubuesque littér.

UC /yse/ *nf* ▶ **unité**.

UDF /ydeɛf/ *nf* (*abbr* = **Union pour la démocratie française**) *French political party of the centre right*.

UEFA /yœfa/ *nf* (*abbr* = **Union européenne de football association**) UEFA; **la coupe de l'~** the UEFA cup.

UER /yœɛʀ/ *nf* **1** Univ *abbr* ▶ **unité**; **2** Radio, TV (*abbr* = **Union européenne de radiodiffusion**) EBU.

UFR /yɛfɛʀ/ *nf*: *abbr* ▶ **unité**.

uhlan /ylɑ̃/ *nm* uhlan.

UHT /yaʃte/ *adj* (*abbr* = **ultra-haute température**) UHT; **lait ~** UHT milk.

ukase /ykɑz/ *nm* = **oukase**.

Ukraine /ykʀɛn/ ▶ **321** *nprf* **l'~** the Ukraine.

ukrainien, **-ienne** /ykʀɛnjɛ̃, ɛn/ ▶ **537**, **462** **I** *adj* Ukrainian.
II *nm* Ling Ukrainian.

Ukrainien, **-ienne** /ykʀɛnjɛ̃, ɛn/ ▶ **537** *nm,f* Ukrainian.

ulcération /ylseʀasjɔ̃/ *nf* ulceration.

ulcère /ylsɛʀ/ ▶ **271** *nm* ulcer; **avoir un ~ à l'estomac** to have a stomach ulcer; **~ variqueux** varicose ulcer.

ulcérer /ylseʀe/ [14] **I** *vtr* **1** (outrer) [*propos, comportement*] to sicken, to revolt; **je suis ulcéré par son attitude** I am revolted by his attitude; **2** Méd to ulcerate [*tissu, organe*].
II s'ulcérer *vpr* [*plaie*] to ulcerate.

ulcéreux, **-euse** /ylseʀø, øz/ *adj* [*plaie*] ulcerated; [*état, poussée*] ulcerous; [*maladie*] ulcerative.

uléma /ylema/ *nm* ulama, ulema.

ULM /yɛlɛm/ ▶ **449** *nm inv* (*abbr* = **ultraléger motorisé**) (engin) microlight; (sport) microlighting.

ulmaire /ylmɛʀ/ *nf* meadowsweet.

Ulster /ylstœʀ/ ▶ **692** *nprm* Ulster.

ultérieur, **~e** /ylteʀjœʀ/ *adj* [*développement, œuvre, génération*] subsequent; **une date ~e** a later date.

ultérieurement /ylteʀjœʀmɑ̃/ *adv* **1** (par la suite) subsequently; **2** (plus tard) later.

ultimatum /yltimatɔm/ *nm* (tous contextes) ultimatum; **lancer** or **envoyer un ~ à un pays/à qn** to present a country/sb with an ultimatum; **rejeter/accepter un ~** to reject/accept an ultimatum.

ultime /yltim/ *adj* **1** (dernier d'une série) [*appel, concession, entraînement, épisode*] final, last; [*avertissement, délai*] final; **2** (suprême) [*plaisir, but*] ultimate; **3** Ling [*constituant*] ultimate.

ultra /yltʀa/ **I** *adj* [*groupe*] extremist.

un

Emploi et prononciation de *a* et *an*

On emploie *a* /ə/ devant les consonnes, les h aspirés et les semi-consonnes /j/, /w/ (dans *a university, a one-eyed man*), et *an* /ən/ devant les voyelles et h muets (hour, honest, heir).

***un* = pronom**

L'emploi de *un* en corrélation avec ***autre*** est traité sous *autre*. Voir aussi ***chose***, ***comme***, ainsi que les verbes avec lesquels le pronom se substitue familièrement à un groupe nominal comme ***coller*** – *en coller une*, ***placer*** – *en placer une* etc.).

***un* = adjectif numéral**

En général, *un*, adjectif numéral, se traduit indifféremment par *a* ou *one*:

j'ai un garçon et deux filles = I have a (*ou* one) boy and two girls

En revanche *un* se traduit par *one* quand on veut insister sur le nombre. Ainsi, on dira:

il ne reste qu'une pomme (pas deux) = there's only one apple left
mais: *il ne reste qu'une pomme* (pas d'autres fruits) = there's only an apple left

j'ai un frère et deux sœurs (nous sommes quatre enfants) = I have one brother and two sisters
mais: *j'ai un frère qui est informaticien* (j'ai d'autres frères) = I have a brother who is a computer scientist

ça coûte une livre = it costs a pound *ou* it costs one pound
mais: *ça coûte une livre cinquante* = it costs one pound fifty

cela a pris une heure = it took an hour *ou* it took one hour
mais: *il est une heure* = it is one o'clock

II *nmf* **1** Pol extremist; **2** Hist ultraroyalist.

ultraconfidentiel, **-ielle** /yltʀakɔ̃fidɑ̃sjɛl/ *adj* [*document, information*] top secret.

ultraconservateur, **-trice** /yltʀa kɔ̃sɛʀvatœʀ, tʀis/ *adj* ultraconservative.

ultrafin, **~e** /yltʀafɛ̃, in/ *adj* [*tranche*] wafer-thin; [*collant*] sheer; [*fibre*] ultra-fine.

ultragauche /yltʀagoʃ/ *nf* Pol **l'~** the radical leftists (*pl*).

ultraléger, **-ère** /yltʀaleʒe, ɛʀ/ *adj* [*matériau, cigarette*] ultra light; [*équipement, vêtement, tissu*] very light.

ultramicroscope /yltʀamikʀɔskɔp/ *nm* ultramicroscope.

ultramicroscopique /yltʀamikʀɔskɔpik/ *adj* ultramicroscopic.

ultramoderne /yltʀamɔdɛʀn/ *adj* [*maison, appartement*] ultramodern; [*technique, système, matériel*] state-of-the-art (*épith*).

ultramontain, **~e** /yltʀamɔ̃tɛ̃, ɛn/ *adj* ultramontanist.

ultramontanisme /yltʀamɔ̃tanism/ *nm* ultramontanism.

ultranationaliste /yltʀanasjɔnalist/ *adj, nmf* ultranationalist.

ultra-orthodoxe /yltʀaɔʀtɔdɔks/ *adj* ultra-orthodox.

ultraraffiné, **~e** /yltʀaʀafine/ *adj* [*manières, ambiance*] ultra-refined.

ultrarapide /yltʀaʀapid/ *adj* high-speed (*épith*).

ultrasecret, **-ète** /yltʀasəkʀɛ, ɛt/ *adj* top secret.

ultrasensible /yltʀasɑ̃sibl/ *adj* [*personne*] hypersensitive; [*appareil, film*] ultrasensitive; [*problème, donnée*] highly sensitive.

ultrason /yltʀasɔ̃/ *nm* ultrasound ₵; **les ~s sont utilisés en médecine** ultrasound is used in medicine.

ultrasonique /yltʀasɔnik/ *adj* ultrasonic.

ultraviolet, **-ette** /yltʀavjɔlɛ, ɛt/ **I** *adj* ultraviolet.
II *nm* ultraviolet ray; Cosmét **séance d'~s** session on a sunbed.

ululement /ylylmɑ̃/ *nm* hooting ₵.

ululer /ylyle/ [1] *vi* to hoot.

Ulysse /ylis/ *npr* Ulysses.

un, **une** /œ̃(n), yn/ ▶ **545**, **407** **I** *art indéf* (*pl* **des**) **1** (au singulier) a, an; **une pomme** an apple; **une femme vous demande** a woman is asking for you; **~ ciel couvert** an overcast sky; **avec ~ sang-froid remarquable** with remarkable self-control; **il n'a pas dit ~ mot** he didn't say a ou one word; **il n'y avait pas ~ arbre** there wasn't a single tree; **c'est ~ Paul furieux que j'ai vu sortir du bureau** it was an angry Paul that I saw coming out of the office; **leur mère était une Montagut** their mother was a Montagut; **~ chien est plus docile qu'~ chat** dogs are more docile than cats, a dog is more docile than a cat; **~ accident est vite arrivé** accidents soon happen; **~ jour, je t'en parlerai** I'll tell you about it one day; **2** (au pluriel) **il y avait des mille-pattes et des scorpions** there were millipedes and scorpions; **il y a des gens qui ne comprennent jamais rien** there are some people who never understand anything; **des invités avaient déjà défait leur cravate** some guests had already loosened their ties; **3** (en emphase) **il fait ~ froid** or **~ de ces froids!** it's so cold!; **j'ai une soif** or **une de ces soifs!** I'm so thirsty!; **elle marchait avec une grâce!** she was walking so gracefully!; **elle m'a donné une de ces gifles!** she gave me such a slap!; **il y a ~ monde aujourd'hui!** there are so many people today!; **il travaille jusqu'à des deux heures du matin** he works up until two in the morning; **il y en a des qui vont bien rire**○**!** some people are going to have a good laugh!.

II *pron* (*pl* **uns**, **unes**) gén one; **(l')~ de** or **d'entre nous** one of us; **(l')~ des meilleurs** one of the best; **~ de ces jours** or **quatre**○ one of these days; **l'~ est diplomate** one is a diplomat; **les ~s pensent que**... some think that...; **pas ~ n'a dit merci** not one of them said thank you; **~ qui sera surpris, c'est**... one person who will be surprised is...; **t'en as ~, de bateau, toi**○? have YOU got a boat?
III *adj* one, a (*devant une consonne*), an (*devant une voyelle*); **j'y suis resté ~ jour** I stayed there for a ou one day; **trente et une personnes ont été blessées** thirty-one people were injured; **ici, il pleut ~ jour sur deux** it rains every other day here.
IV *nm,f* one; **il n'en reste qu'~** there's only one left ; **il y en a ~ par personne** there's one each; **j'en ai déjà mangé ~** I've already eaten one; **les deux villes n'en font plus qu'une** the two cities have merged into one; **~ à** ou **par ~** [*cueillir, ramasser, laver*] one by one; [*arriver, entrer, partir*] one by one, one after the other; **traiter les problèmes ~ à** ou **par ~** to deal with the problems one by one.
V○ *adv* firstly, for one thing; **~, je fais ce que je veux et deux ça ne te regarde pas!** firstly, I do what I like and secondly it's none of your business!, for one thing I do what I like, for another thing it's none of your business!
VI *nm* **1** (nombre) one; **il y a trois ~s dans cent onze** there are three ones in one hundred and eleven; **~, deux, trois, partez!** one, two, three, go!; **faire un ~** (aux dés) to throw a one; **2** (valeur ordinale) **page/scène ~** page/scene one; **3** fig **elle ne faisait qu'~ avec sa machine** she and her machine were as one; **dans l'adversité ils ne font qu'~** they are united in the face of adversity.
VII **une** *nf* **la une** the front page; **être à la une** to be in the headlines, to be on the front page.
IDIOMES **tu peux me prêter 20 francs? je suis sans ~**○ could you lend me twenty francs? I'm broke○; **s'en jeter ~ (derrière la cravate)**○ to knock back a drink○; **elle est fière comme pas une** she's extremely proud; **il est menteur comme pas ~** he's the greatest liar; **c'est tout ~** it's all one to me; **~ pour tous et tous pour ~** all for one and one for all.

unanime /ynanim/ *adj* [*personnes, opinion publique, sentiment*] unanimous (**à faire** in doing); **ils sont unanimes à condamner l'attentat** they are unanimous in condemning the attack.

unanimement /ynanimmɑ̃/ *adv* **1** Pol [*voter, approuver, rejeter*] unanimously; **2** fig universally; **il est ~ célébré comme un grand écrivain** he is universally hailed as a great writer.

unanimité /ynanimite/ *nf* unanimity; **à l'~** [*élire, voter, adopter*] unanimously; **il a été élu à l'~ moins deux voix** he was elected with only two votes against; **prendre une décision à l'~** to reach a unanimous decision; **faire l'~** to have unanimous support ou backing (**parmi** from).

underground /œndœʀɡʀawnd/ *adj, nm* Art, Mus underground.

une(s) *art indéf, pron, adj* ▶ **un** I, II, III, IV, VII.

UNEF /ynɛf/ *nf* (*abbr* = **Union nationale des étudiants de France**) *French student union.*

UNESCO /ynɛsko/ *nf* (*abbr* = **United Nations Educational, Scientific and Cultural Organization**) UNESCO.

uni, **~e** /yni/ I *pp* ▶ **unir**.
II *pp adj* [*communauté, famille*] close-knit; [*amis, couple*] close; [*peuple, partisans, militants*] united (**dans** in).
III *adj* **1** (d'une teinte) [*tissu, couleur*] plain, self-coloured[GB]; **2** (sans aspérité) [*surface*] smooth, even; [*mer*] calm; **mener une vie ~e et tranquille** fig to lead a quiet, uneventful life.
IV *nm* Tex **elle porte de/préfère l'~** she wears/prefers plain colours[GB]; **acheter de l'~** to buy plain fabric; **ce modèle existe aussi en ~** this model is also available in plain colours[GB].
IDIOMES **être ~s comme les (deux) doigts de la main** to be very close.

uniate /ynjat/ *adj, nmf* Uniat.

uniatisme /ynjatism/ *nm* Uniatism.

unicaméral, **~e**, *mpl* **-aux** /ynikameʀal, o/ *adj* unicameral.

UNICEF /ynisɛf/ *nm* (*abbr* = **United Nations International Children's Emergency Fund**) UNICEF.

unicellulaire /yniselylɛʀ/ I *adj* unicellular.
II *nm* unicellular organism.

unicité /ynisite/ *nf* uniqueness.

unicolore /ynikɔlɔʀ/ *adj* plain, self-coloured[GB].

unidimensionnel, **-elle** /ynidimɑ̃sjɔnɛl/ *adj* unidimensional.

unidirectionnel, **-elle** /ynidiʀɛksjɔnɛl/ *adj* **1** Télécom [*faisceau, émetteur*] unidirectional; [*récepteur*] one-way; **2** Transp [*chaussée, rue*] one-way.

unième /ynjɛm/ ▶ **545**, **212** *adj* first; **vingt et ~** twenty-first.

unificateur, **-trice** /ynifikatœʀ, tʀis/ *adj* unifying.

unification /ynifikasjɔ̃/ *nf* unification.

unifier /ynifje/ [2] I *vtr* **1** (rassembler) to unify [*pays, forces, vues, marché*]; **l'Allemagne unifiée** unified Germany; **2** (homogénéiser) to standardize [*procédure, réseau*].
II **s'unifier** *vpr* [*pays, groupes*] to unite.

uniforme /ynifɔʀm/ I *adj* [*paysage, maisons, mobilier, mouvement*] uniform; [*augmentation, réglementation*] across-the-board (*épith*); [*existence, journées*] unchanging; **ciel d'un bleu ~** uniformly blue sky; **vitesse ~** (d'un véhicule) regular speed; (de plusieurs véhicules) uniform speed.
II *nm* (costume) uniform; **un ~ de policier** a police uniform; **porter un ~** to wear a uniform; **être en ~** to be in uniform; **être en grand ~** to be in full dress uniform; **policier en ~** uniformed policeman; **endosser/quitter l'~** to go into/to leave the army.

uniformément /ynifɔʀmemɑ̃/ *adv* [*gris, plat, vêtu*] uniformly; **mouvement ~ accéléré** Phys uniformly accelerated motion; **les jours s'écoulent ~** the days go by, each one like the one before.

uniformisation /ynifɔʀmizasjɔ̃/ *nf* (de programmes, normes) standardization.

uniformiser /ynifɔʀmize/ [1] *vtr* to standardize [*programmes, taux*]; to make [sth] uniform [*teinte*].

uniformité /ynifɔʀmite/ *nf* (de goûts, résultats, paysage) uniformity; (de vie) monotony.

unijambiste /yniʒɑ̃bist/ I *adj* one-legged (*épith*); **être ~** to have only one leg.
II *nmf* one-legged person.

unilatéral, **~e**, *mpl* **-aux** /ynilateʀal, o/ *adj* [*décision, désarmement*] unilateral; **stationnement ~** parking on one side only.

unilatéralement /ynilateʀalmɑ̃/ *adv* [*décider, accorder, annoncer*] unilaterally; [*stationner*] on one side only.

unilingue /ynilɛ̃ɡ/ *adj* unilingual, monolingual.

uniment /ynimɑ̃/ *adv* fml (de façon uniforme) uniformly; (sans façon) plainly.

uninominal, **~e**, *mpl* **-aux** /yninɔminal, o/ *adj* Pol [*scrutin*] for a single candidate (*épith, après n*).

union /ynjɔ̃/ *nf* **1** (alliance) union; **~ du corps et de l'âme** union of mind and body; **l'~ politique européenne** European political union; **2** (association) association; **~ de consommateurs** consumers' association; **~ de producteurs** association of producers; **3** (mariage) union sout, marriage; **de cette ~ allaient naître trois fils** from this union ou marriage three sons would come; **4** Math union; **'A ~ B'** 'A union B'.
■ **~ douanière** Écon, Fisc customs union; **~ économique et monétaire** Écon, Fin economic and monetary union; **~ libre** cohabitation; **~ mystique** Relig mystic union; **~ sacrée** united front; **former l'~ sacrée contre** to present a united front against; **~ sportive**, **US** sports club; **Union européenne** European Union; **Union des Républiques socialistes soviétiques** Hist Union of Soviet Socialist Republics; **Union soviétique** Hist Soviet Union.
IDIOMES **l'~ fait la force** Prov united we stand, divided we fall.

unionisme /ynjɔnism/ *nm* Unionism.

unioniste /ynjɔnist/ *nmf* Unionist.

unipare /ynipaʀ/ *adj* uniparous.

unipersonnel, **-elle** /ynipɛʀsɔnɛl/ I *adj* **1** Ling [*verbe*] impersonal; **2** Jur **entreprise unipersonnelle à responsabilité limitée** company owned by a sole proprietor.
II *nm* impersonal verb.

unipolaire /ynipɔlɛʀ/ *adj* Anat, Électrotech, Phys unipolar.

unique /ynik/ *adj* **1** (seul de son espèce) (*before n*) only; **il est l'~ témoin/candidat** he's the only witness/candidate; **c'est son ~ fille sur sept enfants** she's his only daughter out of seven children; **c'est l'~ cas où**... it's the only case where...; **c'est l'~ voie qui y mène** it's the only way to get there; ▶ **seul**; **2** (seul pour tous) single; **marché/monnaie ~** single market/currency; **parti ~** single party; **système à parti ~** one-party system; **'prix ~'** 'all at one price'; **proposer un candidat ~ aux élections** to put forward one candidate only at the elections; **3** (remarquable) unique; **c'est un cas ~ dans l'histoire des sciences** it's a unique case in the history of science; **c'est une occasion ~ de faire** it's a unique opportunity to do; **~ au monde/en Europe** [*personne, objet, fait*] unique in the world/in Europe; **~ en son genre** [*personne, objet*] most unusual; [*fait, événement*] one-off GB, one-shot (*épith*) US; **4**○ (singulier) priceless; **ce type est ~!** that guy's priceless○!; **5** (sans frère ni sœur) **être fille/fils ~** to be an only child.

uniquement /ynikmɑ̃/ *adv* **1** (exclusivement) exclusively; **programme ~ consacré à la littérature** programme[GB] devoted exclusively to literature; **salon meublé ~ avec du moderne** living room furnished exclusively in a modern style; **il pense ~ à s'amuser** all he thinks about is having fun; **il est ~ préoccupé par sa famille/son image** all he thinks about is his family/his image; **en vente ~ par correspondance/par abonnement** available by mail order/by subscription only; **2** (seulement) only; **nous ne sommes pas ici ~ pour travailler** we're not here just to work; **c'était ~ pour te faire plaisir/taquiner** it was only to please/tease you; **ce n'est pas ~ par paresse que**... laziness is not the only reason why...; **~ dans un but commercial** purely for commercial ends.

unir /yniʀ/ [3] I *vtr* **1** (rassembler) to unite [*pays, territoire*] (**à** to); [*liens, intérêts, passion*] to unite, bind [sb] together [*personnes, groupes, pays*]; **ils sont unis derrière leur chef** they're united behind their leader; **des hommes unis par les mêmes idées** men brought together by the same ideas; **2** (combiner) to combine; **méthode qui unit simplicité et efficacité** method which combines simplicity with effectiveness, method which is both simple and effective; **il faut ~ nos forces** we must join forces; **unissons nos ressources** let us combine ou pool our resources; **3** (marier) to join [sb] in matrimony sout; **le maire les a**

unis they were joined in matrimony by the mayor.

II **s'unir** *vpr* **1** (se rassembler) [*personnes, pays, peuples, régions*] to unite (**à**, **avec** with; **contre** against; **pour faire** to do); **2** (se marier) [*personnes*] to marry; **3** (se combiner) fig [*couleurs*] to blend, to go together.

unisexe /yniseks/ *adj* unisex.

unisexualité /yniseksɥalite/ *nf* unisexuality.

unisexué, **~e** /yniseksɥe/ *adj* unisexual.

unisson /ynisɔ̃/ *nm* unison; **à l'~** Mus in unison; fig in accord.

unitaire /ynitɛʀ/ **I** *adj* **1** Pol [*manifestation, rassemblement, campagne, stratégie*] common; **2** Comm [*prix, coût*] unit; **3** Phys [*champ*] unified; Math [*vecteur*] unit; **4** Relig Unitarian.

II *nmf* Relig Unitarian.

unitarien, **-ienne** /ynitaʀjɛ̃, ɛn/ *adj, nm,f* Unitarian.

unitarisme /ynitaʀism/ *nm* Unitarianism.

unité /ynite/ *nf* **1** (cohésion) also Théât unity; **il faut préserver l'~ nationale/du parti** national/party unity must be preserved; **~ d'action/de temps/de lieu** Théât unity of action/time/place; **réaliser l'~ d'un pays/parti** to unify a country/party; **un roman/film qui manque d'~** a novel/film lacking in cohesion; **il y a ~ de vues entre les deux leaders** the two leaders share the same viewpoint; **2** (élément) unit; **prix à l'~** price per unit; **20 francs l'~** 20 francs each; **vendre qch à l'~** to sell sth singly, sell sth as a separate item; **3** (dans ensemble) unit; **~ de production/fabrication** production/manufacturing unit; **4** Mes (étalon) unit; **~ de mesure/temps** unit of measurement/time; **~ monétaire** unit of currency; **5** Math unit; **la colonne des ~s** the units column; **6** Mil (troupe) unit; Mil Naut (navire) craft; **~ aéroportée/blindée/d'élite** airborne/armoured/crack unit; **7** Télécom unit; **télécarte 50 ~s** 50-unit phonecard.

■ **~ centrale (de traitement)**, **UC** Ordinat central processing unit; **~ de disque** Ordinat disk drive; **~ d'enseignement et de recherche**, **UER** university department; **~ de formation et de recherche**, **UFR** university department; **~ lexicale** Ling lexical unit; **~ de valeur**, **UV** course unit.

univalve /ynivalv/ *adj* univalve.

univers /ynivɛʀ/ *nm inv* **1** Astron universe; **la naissance de l'~** the birth of the universe; **2** (humanité) whole world; **3** (monde) world; **des ~ bien distincts** distinctly separate worlds; **l'~ de Kafka** Kafka's world; **un ~ totalement irréel** a totally unreal world.

■ **~ du discours** Ling universe of discourse.

universalisation /ynivɛʀsalizasjɔ̃/ *nf* universalization.

universaliser /ynivɛʀsalize/ [1] **I** *vtr* to universalize.

II **s'universaliser** *vpr* to become widespread.

universalisme /ynivɛʀsalism/ *nm* Philos, Relig universalism.

universaliste /ynivɛʀsalist/ *adj, nmf* Philos, Relig universalist.

universalité /ynivɛʀsalite/ *nf* universality.

universaux /ynivɛʀso/ *nmpl* Ling, Philos universals.

universel, **-elle** /ynivɛʀsɛl/ **I** *adj* [*langage, principe, thème, méthode, outillage*] universal; [*histoire*] world; [*remède*] all-purpose (*épith*); **esprit ~** polymath.

II *nm* Ling, Philos universal.

universellement /ynivɛʀsɛlmɑ̃/ *adv* universally.

universitaire /ynivɛʀsitɛʀ/ **I** *adj* [*échange, ville, cursus*] university (*épith*); [*travail, formation, niveau*] academic.

II *nmf* academic.

université /ynivɛʀsite/ *nf* **1** (établissement) university GB, college US; **l'Université de Montréal** the University of Montreal; **être à l'~** to be at university GB, to be in college US; **aller à l'~** to go to university GB, to go to college US; **2** (enseignement supérieur) higher education; **l'~ est en crise** higher education is in crisis.

■ **~ d'été** Univ summer school; Pol party conference (*assembling young members and potential members*); **~ du troisième âge** University of the Third Age (*higher education courses for Senior Citizens*).

univocité /ynivɔsite/ *nf* univocality.

univoque /ynivɔk/ *adj* **1** Ling univocal; **2** [*réalité, fait*] unequivocal; **3** Méd [*symptôme*] pathognomonic; [*remède*] specific.

uns *pron* ▶ **un** II.

Untel, **Unetelle** /œ̃tɛl, yntɛl/ *nm,f* **Monsieur ~** Mr so-and-so; **Madame Unetelle** Mrs so-and-so.

Unterwald /untœʀvald/ ▶ **692** *npr* **le canton d'~** the canton of Unterwalden.

upérisation /ypeʀizasjɔ̃/ *nf* ultra heat treatment.

uppercut /ypɛʀkyt/ *nm* uppercut.

Uranie /yʀani/ *npr* Urania.

uranifère /yʀanifɛʀ/ *adj* uranium-bearing.

uranium /yʀanjɔm/ *nm* uranium; **~ naturel/enrichi** natural/enriched uranium.

uranoscope /yʀanɔskɔp/ *nm* stargazer.

Uranus /yʀanys/ **I** *npr* Mythol Uranus.

II *nprf* Astron Uranus.

urbain, **~e** /yʀbɛ̃, ɛn/ *adj* **1** (de la ville) [*milieu, transport, tissu*] urban; **vie ~e** city life; **2** fml (civil) [*personne*] urbane.

urbanisation /yʀbanizasjɔ̃/ *nf* urbanization.

urbanisé, **~e** /yʀbanize/ **I** *pp* ▶ **urbaniser**.

II *pp adj* [*zone*] built-up (*épith*); **la zone est très ~** the area is very built up.

urbaniser /yʀbanize/ [1] **I** *vtr* to urbanize [*région*].

II **s'urbaniser** *vpr* [*zone*] to become built up; [*population*] to become urbanized.

urbanisme /yʀbanism/ *nm* town planning GB, city planning US.

urbaniste /yʀbanist/ ▶ **510** *nmf* town planner GB, city planner US.

urbanistique /yʀbanistik/ *adj* urbanistic.

urbanité /yʀbanite/ *nf* fml urbanity.

urée /yʀe/ *nf* urea.

urémie /yʀemi/ *nf* uraemia GB; **avoir de l'~** to have uraemia.

urémique /yʀemik/ *adj, nmf* uraemic.

urétéral, **~e**, *mpl* **-aux** /yʀeteʀal, o/ *adj* ureteric.

uretère /yʀtɛʀ/ *nm* ureter.

uréthane /yʀetan/ *nm* urethane.

urétral, **~e**, *mpl* **-aux** /yʀetʀal, o/ *adj* urethral.

urètre /yʀɛtʀ/ *nm* urethra.

urétrite /yʀetʀit/ ▶ **271** *nf* urethritis.

urgence /yʀʒɑ̃s/ *nf* **1** (caractère) urgency; **il y a ~** it's urgent, it's a matter of urgency; **l'~ nous a obligés à...** the urgency of the situation compelled us to...; **l'~ d'une tâche** the urgency of a task; **d'~** [*agir, se réunir*] immediately, as a matter of urgency; **de toute** or **d'extrême ~** as a matter of great urgency; **transporter qn d'~ à l'hôpital** to rush sb to (the) hospital; **convoquer qn d'~** to summon sb urgently; **appeler qn d'~** to call sb immediately; **opérer qn d'~** to give sb emergency surgery; **mesures/soins d'~** emergency measures/treatment; **en ~** as a matter of urgency, immediately; **appeler le médecin/l'ambulance en ~** to call the doctor/an ambulance as a matter of urgency, immediately; **2** (cas urgent) gén matter of urgency; Méd emergency; **le service des ~s**, **les ~s** the casualty department, casualty ¢; **où sont les ~s?** where is casualty?, where is emergency US?

urgent, **~e** /yʀʒɑ̃, ɑ̃t/ *adj* urgent; **rien d'~** nothing urgent; **il est ~ de prendre des mesures** measures must be taken immediately; **il est ~ d'envoyer des secours** help must be sent immediately.

urger○ /yʀʒe/ [13] *vi* to be urgent.

Uri /yʀi/ ▶ **692** *npr* **le canton d'~** the canton of Uri.

urinaire /yʀinɛʀ/ *adj* urinary; **appareil ~** urinary tract.

urinal, *pl* **-aux** /yʀinal, o/ *nm* urinal.

urine /yʀin/ *nf* urine ¢; **une analyse des ~s** urinalysis.

uriner /yʀine/ [1] *vi* to urinate.

urinoir /yʀinwaʀ/ *nm* **1** (lieu) public urinal; **2** (cuvette) urinal.

urique /yʀik/ *adj* uric.

urne /yʀn/ *nf* **1** (pour voter) **~ (électorale)** ballot box; **le verdict des ~s** the result of the polls; **se rendre aux ~s** to go to the polls; **bouder les ~s** to stay away from the polls; **être appelé aux ~s** to be called upon to vote; **le gouvernement sorti des ~s** the newly-elected government; **2** (vase) urn; **~ cinéraire** or **funéraire** funeral urn.

IDIOMES **bourrer les ~s**○ to rig the ballot.

urogénital, **~e**, *mpl* **-aux** /yʀoʒenital, o/ *adj* urogenital.

urographie /yʀɔgʀafi/ *nf* urography.

urologie /yʀɔlɔʒi/ *nf* urology.

urologue /yʀɔlɔg/ ▶ **510** *nmf* urologist.

URSS /yʀɛsɛs, yʀs/ *nprf* Hist (*abbr* = **Union des Républiques socialistes soviétiques**) USSR.

URSSAF /yʀsaf/ *nf* (*abbr* = **Union pour le recouvrement des cotisations de sécurité sociale et d'allocations familiales**) *body managing social security payments and funds*.

ursuline /yʀsylin/ *nf* Ursuline.

urticaire /yʀtikɛʀ/ ▶ **271** *nf* hives, urticaria spéc; **avoir de l'~** to have hives.

IDIOMES **donner de l'~ à qn**○ to get on sb's nerves.

urubu /yʀyby/ *nm* black vulture.

Uruguay /yʀygwɛ/ ▶ **321** *nprm* Uruguay.

uruguayen, **-enne** /yʀygwejɛ̃, ɛn/ ▶ **537** *adj* Uruguayan.

Uruguayen, **-enne** /yʀygwejɛ̃, ɛn/ ▶ **537** *nm,f* Uruguayan.

us /ys/ *nmpl* **les ~ et coutumes** the ways and customs.

US /yɛs/ *nf*: *abbr* ▶ **union**.

USA /yɛsa/ *nmpl* (*abbr* = **United States of America**) USA.

usage /yzaʒ/ *nm* **1** (fait d'utiliser) use; **l'~ des caméscopes se répand rapidement** the use of camcorders is spreading rapidly; **l'~ de la force/torture** the use of force/torture; **je te donne cette machine à écrire, je n'en ai plus l'~** I'm giving you this typewriter as I don't have any further use for it; **à l'~** [*rétrécir, déteindre, se distendre*] with use; **par l'~** [*sali, terni, encrassé*] with use; **en ~** in use; **disqualifié pour ~ d'anabolisants** disqualified for using anabolic steroids; **il m'a interdit l'~ de l'alcool** he told me not to drink alcohol; **connaître/apprendre l'~ de qch** to know how/to learn how to use sth; **faire ~ de** to use; **faire un ~ fréquent de qch** to use sth frequently; **faire ~ de son autorité** to exercise one's authority; **faire grand ~ de qch** to use sth a lot; **faire bon/mauvais ~ de qch** to put sth to good/bad use; **faire de l'~** [*tissu, vêtement*] to last; **2** (possibilité d'utiliser) use; **à l'~ de qn** for the use of sb; **pour leur ~ personnel** for their own use; **d'un ~ courant/limité** in common/of limited use; **'réservé à l'~ du personnel'** 'for staff use only'; **à ~ privé/militaire/industriel** for private/military/industrial use; **à ~ externe** Pharm for external use only; **à ~ interne** Pharm for internal use;

immeuble à ~ de bureaux office block; **à ~s multiples** [*appareil*] multipurpose (*épith*); **quel est l'~ de cette machine?** what's this machine used for?; **il a perdu l'~ d'un œil/de la jambe droite** he's lost the use of one eye/of his right leg; **hors d'~** [*vêtement*] unwearable; [*machine*] out of order; **tellement abasourdie qu'elle en a perdu l'~ de la parole** so amazed that she lost the power of speech; **retrouver l'~ de la vue** to recover one's eyesight; **je ne lui laisse pas l'~ de ma voiture** I don't let him use my car; **3** Ling usage; **en ~** in usage; **l'~ veut qu'on dise** usage requires that one should say; **les règles du bon ~** the rules of good usage; **expression entrée dans l'~** expression that has entered current usage; **sorti de l'~** [*mot, expression*] no longer used (*après n*); **4** (pratique courante) custom; **un ~ qui commence à se répandre/à se perdre** a custom that is beginning to spread/to die out; **entériner l'~ par des lois** to fix custom by law; **connaître les ~s d'un pays** to know the customs ou ways of a country; **l'~ est de faire** (dans la vie courante) the custom is to do; (dans la vie professionnelle) it's usual practice to do; **comme le veut l'~** as is customary; **conformément aux ~s** in accordance with custom; **politesses d'~** customary courtesies; **précautions/recommandations d'~** usual precautions/recommendations.

■ **~ de faux** Jur use of forged documents; **faux et ~ de faux** forgery and use of false documents.

usagé, **~e** /yzaʒe/ *adj* **1** (usé) [*vêtement*] well-worn; [*pneu*] worn; **2** (déjà utilisé) [*vêtement, seringue, préservatif*] used.

usager /yzaʒe/ *nm* (de service) user; (de langue) speaker; **~ de la route** road-user; **~ des transports en commun** user of public transport.

usant, **~e** /yzɑ̃, ɑ̃t/ *adj* [*travail, vie*] exhausting, wearing; [*personne*] wearing, tiresome.

usé, **~e** /yze/ **I** *pp* ▶ **user**.

II *pp adj* [*vêtement, chaussure, objet, pièce*] worn; [*personne*] worn-down; [*organisme, cœur, yeux*] worn-out; [*sujet, plaisanterie*] hackneyed; **mes chaussures sont déjà un peu ~es aux talons** the heels of my shoes are already slightly worn (down); **une veste complètement ~e** a worn-out ou threadbare jacket; **~ jusqu'à la corde** lit [*vêtement, tapis*] threadbare; [*pneu*] worn down to the tread; fig [*plaisanterie*] hackneyed; **un homme ~ par dix ans de détention** a man worn down by ten year's imprisonment; **personne ~e par le travail/l'alcool** person worn down by work/drink; ▶ **eau**.

user /yze/ [1] **I** *vtr* [*personne, temps, frottement*] to wear out [*vêtement, chaussure, objet*]; [*travail, soucis, temps*] to wear out [*personne*]; **tu vas ~ l'embrayage si tu conduis comme ça** you'll wear out the clutch if you drive like that; **les piles du poste de radio sont usées** the batteries in the radio are worn out ou have gone; **la maladie l'a usé prématurément** the illness wore him out prematurely; **~ ses vêtements jusqu'à la corde** to wear one's clothes out; **des tapis/vêtements usés jusqu'à la corde** threadbare carpets/clothes; **la mer a usé la falaise** the sea has eroded the cliff; **~ sa santé** to ruin one's health; **ça use les yeux de lire dans le noir** reading in the dark strains your eyes; **avoir les yeux usés** to have ruined one's eyesight; **j'ai usé trois crayons/paires de chaussures** I've got GB ou gotten US through three pencils/pairs of shoes.

II user de *vtr ind* to use [*stratagème, formule, termes, alcool*]; to exercise [*droit*]; to exploit [*possibilité*]; to take [*précautions*]; **~ de diplomatie** to be diplomatic; **~ et abuser de qch** to use and abuse sth; **il faut en ~ avec modération/avec prudence** it should be used in moderation/with care; **en ~ bien/mal avec qn** to treat sb well/badly; **elle en use avec lui d'une façon inacceptable** she treats him in the most appalling manner.

III s'user *vpr* **1** [*vêtement, tissu, chaussure, pièce*] to wear out; **2** [*personne*] **s'~ à la tâche** or **au travail** to wear oneself out with overwork, burn oneself out○; **s'~ la santé/les yeux** to ruin one's health/eyesight.

usinage /yzinaʒ/ *nm* **1** (fabrication avec une machine-outil) machining; **2** (fabrication industrielle) manufacture.

usine /yzin/ *nf* factory, plant; **travailler à l'~** to work in a factory; **fabriqué en ~** factory-made; **prix sortie d'~** factory(-gate) price; **c'est l'~, ici**○! fig it's like a production line here!; **c'est une ~ à diplômés** fig it churns out graduates○, it's a diploma mill○ US.

■ **~ d'armement** armaments factory; **~ automobile** car factory, automobile plant US; **~ center** factory outlet; **~ chimique** chemical plant; **~ clés en main** Ind turnkey factory; **~ d'incinération (d'ordures)** refuse-incinerating plant; **~ métallurgique** ironworks (*pl*); **~ de montage** assembly plant; **~ de retraitement (des déchets nucléaires)** Nucl nuclear reprocessing plant; **~ sidérurgique** steelworks (*pl*).

usiner /yzine/ [1] **I** *vtr* **1** (avec machine-outil) to machine; **2** (fabriquer) to manufacture.

II○ *vi* **ça usine, dans le bureau!** they're hard at it in the office○!

usinier†, **-ière** /yzinje, ɛʀ/ *adj* [*production*] factory (*épith*); [*industrie*] manufacturing (*épith*).

usité, **~e** /yzite/ *adj* [*terme, formule, temps*] commonly-used (*épith*), commonly used (*jamais épith*); **peu ~** rarely-used (*épith*), rarely used (*jamais épith*).

ustensile /ystɑ̃sil/ *nm* utensil.

■ **~ de cuisine** Culin kitchen utensil; **~ de jardinage** Hort garden tool.

usuel, **-elle** /yzɥɛl/ **I** *adj* [*objet*] everyday (*épith*); [*mot, expression, appellation*] common.

II *nm* (livre) reference book (*not for loan*).

usuellement /yzɥɛlmɑ̃/ *adv* ordinarily.

usufruit /yzyfʀɥi/ *nm* Jur usufruct; **avoir/garder l'~ de qch** to have/retain the usufruct of sth.

usufruitier, **-ière** /yzyfʀɥitje, ɛʀ/ **I** *adj* usufructuary.

II *nm,f* tenant for life, usufructuary spéc.

usuraire /yzyʀɛʀ/ *adj* usurious.

usure /yzyʀ/ *nf* **1** (détérioration) (de tissu, vêtement) wear and tear (**de** on); (de pneu, disque, machine) wear (**de** on); **résister à l'~** to wear well; **2** (affaiblissement) (de forces, d'énergie, adversaire) wearing down; (d'idéologie) declining attraction; (de régime) declining power; **l'~ du pouvoir** the erosion of power; **3** (action corrosive) **~ du temps** wearing effect of time; **~ du quotidien** wear and tear of daily life; **4** Fin, Jur usury; **prêter à ~** to lend at excessively high rates.

IDIOMES **avoir qn à l'~**○ to wear sb down.

usurier, **-ière** /yzyʀje, ɛʀ/ *nm,f* usurer, loan shark○.

usurpateur, **-trice** /yzyʀpatœʀ, tʀis/ *nm,f* usurper.

usurpation /yzyʀpasjɔ̃/ *nf* usurpation.

usurper /yzyʀpe/ [1] *vtr* to usurp [*titre, réputation*]; **une victoire non usurpée** a well-deserved success.

ut /yt/ *nm* C.

Utah /yta/ ▶ **692** *nprm* Utah.

utérin, **~e** /yteʀɛ̃, in/ *adj* Anat, Jur uterine.

utérus /yteʀys/ *nm* womb, uterus.

utile /ytil/ **I** *adj* **1** (d'utilité générale) [*objet, produit, renseignement*] useful; **2** (d'utilité ponctuelle) **être ~** [*personne, livre*] to be helpful; [*allumette, parapluie*] to come in handy; **votre canif m'a été très ~** your penknife came in very handy; **se rendre ~** to make oneself useful; **votre aide m'a été très ~** you've been most helpful; **il est ~ de signaler** it's worth pointing out; **il n'a pas jugé ~ de me prévenir** gén he didn't think it necessary to let me know; (en critiquant) he didn't see fit to let me know; **en quoi puis-je vous être ~?** how can I help you?; **ce ne sera pas ~** it won't be necessary.

II *nm* **joindre l'~ à l'agréable** to mix business with pleasure.

utilement /ytilmɑ̃/ *adv* [*combattre, intervenir*] effectively; [*s'occuper*] usefully; [*dépenser*] wisely; [*compléter*] nicely; [*se référer*] profitably.

utilisable /ytilizabl/ *adj* [*objet*] usable; **il est encore ~ chez nous** we can still make use of it.

utilisateur, **-trice** /ytilizatœʀ, tʀis/ *nm,f* user.

■ **~ final** Ordinat end user.

utilisation /ytilizasjɔ̃/ *nf* **1** (fait d'utiliser) use; **2** (utilité) use (**de** for); **une nouvelle ~ d'un produit** a new use for a product.

utiliser /ytilize/ [1] *vtr* **1** (se servir) to use [*méthode, outil, service, expression, produit*]; to make use of [*potentiel, compétence, ressources*]; **~ au mieux** to make the most of; **bien ~** to make good use of; **2** (exploiter) to use, to exploit [*personne*]; **il ne se fait des amis que pour les ~** he makes friends only in order to use them.

utilitaire /ytilitɛʀ/ **I** *adj* [*conception, époque*] utilitarian; [*préoccupation, enseignement, rôle*] practical; [*objet*] functional; [*véhicule*] commercial.

II *nm* Ordinat utility.

utilitarisme /ytilitaʀism/ *nm* utilitarianism.

utilitariste /ytilitaʀist/ *adj, nmf* utilitarian.

utilité /ytilite/ *nf* **1** (caractère utile) usefulness; **~ d'une loi/un appareil** usefulness of a law/a device; **être d'une grande ~** [*livre, appareil*] to be very useful; [*personne*] to be very helpful; **n'être d'aucune ~** [*livre, appareil*] to be of no use; **être de peu d'~** [*livre, appareil*] to be of little use; **ne pas voir l'~ de qch/de faire** not to see the point in sth/in doing; **2** (utilisation) use; **je n'en ai pas l'~** I have no use for it; **une de ses ~s** one of its uses.

■ **~ publique** Jur public benefit; **reconnu** or **déclaré d'~ publique** directed to the public benefit (*après n*).

IDIOMES **jouer les ~s** Théât to play bit parts; gén to be a menial.

utopie /ytɔpi/ *nf* **1** Philos, Pol Utopia; **2** (chimère) wishful thinking ¢.

utopique /ytɔpik/ *adj* [*projet, idée*] utopian.

utopisme /ytɔpism/ *nm* utopianism.

utopiste /ytɔpist/ *nmf* utopian.

UV /yve/ **I** *nmpl* (*abbr* = **ultraviolets**) **1** Phys ultraviolet rays; **2** Cosmét **séance d'~** session on a sunbed; **se faire des ~** to use a sunbed.

II *nf inv*: *abbr* ▶ **unité**.

uvulaire /yvylɛʀ/ *adj* uvular.

uvule /yvyl/ *nf* uvula.

v, **V** /ve/ *nm inv* **1** (lettre) v, V; **en (forme de) V** [*objet*] V-shaped; **encolure en V** V-neck; **pull en V** V-necked sweater; **faire le V de la victoire** to give the victory salute; ▶ **vitesse**; **2 V** (*written abbr* = **volt**) **120 V** 120 V.

va /va/ ▶ **aller** II.

vacance /vakɑ̃s/ **I** *nf* Admin (de charge, poste) vacancy.
II vacances *nfpl* holiday GB, vacation US; **être en ~s** to be on holiday GB ou vacation US; **partir** ou **aller en ~s** to go (away) on holiday GB ou vacation US; **prendre des ~s** to go on holiday GB, to take a vacation US; **ils ont pris trois semaines de ~s** they took a three-week holiday GB ou vacation US; **passer de bonnes ~s** to have a good holiday GB ou vacation US; **bonnes ~s!** have a good holiday GB ou vacation US!; **avoir besoin de ~s** to need a holiday GB ou vacation US; **avoir droit à cinq semaines de ~s** to be entitled to five weeks' holiday GB ou vacation US; **pendant les ~s** during the holidays GB ou vacation US; **ils vont toujours en ~s en Bretagne** they always go on holiday to Brittany GB, they always take their vacation in Brittany US; **~s d'été/de Noël** summer/Christmas holidays GB ou vacation US; **~s d'été**, **grandes ~s** Scol summer holidays GB, summer vacation US; **photos de ~s** holiday snaps GB, vacation snaps US.
■ **~s judiciaires** Jur vacation (*sg*); **~s parlementaires** Pol parliamentary recess; **~ du pouvoir** Admin, Pol power vacuum; **~s scolaires** Scol school holiday GB ou vacation US; **~ de succession** Jur abeyance of succession; **~s universitaires** Univ university vacation.

vacancier, **-ière** /vakɑ̃sje, ɛʀ/ *nm,f* holidaymaker GB, vacationer US.

vacant, **~e** /vakɑ̃, ɑ̃t/ *adj* **1** (disponible) [*logement*] vacant, empty; [*emploi, poste*] vacant; [*siège*] vacant; **2** Jur [*succession*] in abeyance (*après n*); [*biens*] unclaimed.

vacarme /vakaʀm/ *nm* din, racket○; **faire du ~** to make a din ou racket○; **dans un ~ assourdissant** with a deafening noise.

vacataire /vakatɛʀ/ **I** *adj* [*enseignant, personnel*] temporary.
II *nmf* Admin temporary employee; Scol supply teacher GB, substitute teacher US.

vacation /vakasjɔ̃/ **I** *nf* **1** Scol, Univ supply work ₵; Admin temporary work; **être payé à la ~** to be paid by the session; **2** Jur (séance de travail) session; **3** Comm (vente aux enchères) auction.
II vacations *nfpl* **1** Jur (vacances) recess (*sg*); **2** (honoraires) fees.

vaccin /vaksɛ̃/ *nm* **1** Méd vaccine; **~ contre la grippe/polio** flu/polio vaccine; **faire un ~ à qn** to vaccinate sb; **2** fig safeguard (**contre** against).
■ **~ informatique** computer vaccine.

vaccinal, **~e**, *mpl* **-aux** /vaksinal, o/ *adj* vaccinal.

vaccination /vaksinasjɔ̃/ *nf* vaccination; **~ contre la polio/variole** polio/smallpox vaccination; **il n'y a pas de ~ contre le rhume** there's no vaccination against the common cold.

vaccine /vaksin/ *nf* (maladie) cowpox, vaccinia spéc.

vacciner /vaksine/ [1] *vtr* **1** Méd, Vét to vaccinate (**contre** against); **se faire ~** to get vaccinated; **2** (endurcir) hum **~ qn contre** to put sb off; **~ qn contre le jeu/mariage** to put sb off gambling/getting married; **plus d'affaires sentimentales, je suis vacciné**○! no more romance, I've learned my lesson!
IDIOMES **il est majeur et vacciné** he's a big boy now hum, he's old enough to make his own decisions.

vachard○, **~e** /vaʃaʀ, aʀd/ *adj* mean, nasty.

vache /vaʃ/ **I**○ *adj* [*commentaire, personne*] mean, nasty; **il est ~ avec elle** he's really mean to her; **cette prof, elle est ~!** she's really mean, that teacher!; **il n'a pas été ~, il aurait pu nous coller une amende** he was nice about it, he could have given us a fine; **faire un coup ~ à qn** to pull a mean ou dirty trick on sb.
II○ **vache de** *loc adj* hell○ of; **on m'a offert un ~ de bouquin** I was given a hell of a good book.
III *nf* **1** (animal) cow; **2** (cuir) cowhide; **3**○ (personne méchante) (homme) bastard◑, son of a bitch◑; (femme) bitch◑; **ah les ~s, ils sont partis sans moi!** the bastards◑, they've gone without me!; **faire un coup en ~ à qn** to pull a mean ou dirty trick on sb; **donner des coups de pieds en ~ à qn** lit to kick sb when no-one is looking; fig to stab sb in the back; **4**○ †(police) **les ~s** the fuzz○ (+ *v pl*), the pigs○; **mort aux ~s!** kill the pigs○!
IV○ **la vache** *excl* (admiration) wow!; (commisération) **oh la ~! il a dû se faire mal!** God! that must have hurt!; (agacement, douleur) hell!
■ **~ à eau** water bottle; **~s grasses** prosperous times; **années de ~s grasses** prosperous years; **~ à lait** Agric dairy cow; fig cash cow○, money-spinner○; **~ laitière** Agric dairy cow; **~s maigres** lean times; **ann ées de ~s maigres** lean years; **~ sacrée** Relig sacred cow.
IDIOMES **parler français comme une ~ espagnole**○ to speak very bad French; **avoir l'air d'une ~ qui regarde passer un train**○ to look vacant ou gormless GB; ▶ **enragé**, **pisser**.

vachement○ /vaʃmɑ̃/ *adv* **1** (très) [*bien, beau, dur, froid*] really; **2** (beaucoup) really; **il a ~ maigri** he lost a hell of a lot○ of weight.

vacher /vaʃe/ ▶ **510** *nm* cowman.

vachère /vaʃɛʀ/ ▶ **510** *nf* cowgirl.

vacherie○ /vaʃʀi/ *nf* **1** (attitude) meanness, nastiness; **il est d'une ~ avec elle!** he's really mean to her!, he's an absolute bastard◑ to her!; **2** (propos) nasty ou bitchy○ remark; **dire des ~ à qn** to bitch◑ to sb; **3** (sale coup) dirty trick; **faire une ~ à qn** to pull a dirty trick on sb; **4** (calamité) **c'est une vraie ~ ce virus** this virus is a bloody◑ GB ou damned○ nuisance; **cette ~ de bagnole ne veut pas démarrer** this bloody◑ GB ou damned○ car won't start.

vacherin /vaʃʀɛ̃/ *nm* **1** (fromage) vacherin cheese; **2** (dessert) vacherin (*meringue with fruit and whipped cream*).

vachette /vaʃɛt/ *nf* **1** (animal) young cow; **2** (cuir) calfskin; **portefeuille en ~** calfskin wallet.

vacillant, **~e** /vasijɑ̃, ɑ̃t/ *adj* **1** (tremblant) [*jambes*] unsteady; [*personne*] unsteady on one's legs; [*lumière, flamme*] flickering; **2** (fragile) [*pouvoir, majorité*] shaky; [*santé, mémoire, raison*] failing; [*volonté*] vacillating; [*opinions*] wavering.

vacillement /vasijmɑ̃/ *nm* **1** (mouvement) (de chose) swaying ₵; (de flamme) flickering ₵; **2** (irrésolution) wavering ₵; **3** (affaiblissement) faltering ₵.

vaciller /vasije/ [1] *vi* **1** (être chancelant) [*personne*] to be unsteady on one's legs; [*jambes*] to be unsteady; **2** (osciller) [*personne, objet*] to sway; [*lumière, flamme*] to flicker; **3** (se détériorer) [*santé, mémoire, raison*] to fail; [*pouvoir, majorité*] to weaken; **4** (hésiter) [*volonté, politique*] to waver; **~ dans ses résolutions** to waver in one's resolutions.

va-comme-je-te-pousse○: **à la va-comme-je-te-pousse** /alavakɔmʃtəpus/ *loc adv* any old how○, in a slapdash way.

vacuité /vakɥite/ *nf* emptiness, vacuity sout.

vade-mecum /vademekɔm/ *nm inv* vade mecum.

vadrouille○ /vadʀuj/ *nf* stroll; **être en ~** to be wandering about; **partir en ~** to wander off.

vadrouiller○ /vadʀuje/ [1] *vi* to wander around; **elle vadrouillait dans les rues d'Oxford** she was wandering around the streets of Oxford.

va-et-vient /vaevjɛ̃/ *nm inv* **1** (allées et venues) (de personnes, véhicules) comings and goings (*pl*) (**de** of); (de dossiers, d'idées) toing and froing; **faire le ~** [*personne, bateau*] to go to and fro (**entre qch et qch** between sth and sth); [*dossier, loi*] to go backwards and forwards GB, to go back and forth; **2** (mouvement de foule) toing and froing (**de** in); **3** (balancement) toing and froing; **mouvement de ~** (horizontal) to and fro motion; (vertical) up-and-down movement; **4** Électrotech two-way switch; **5** Naut (cordage) hauling line; **6** Tech (charnière) two-way hinge; (porte) swing door.

vagabond, **~e** /vagabɔ̃, ɔ̃d/ **I** *adj* [*personne*] wandering (*épith*); [*chien*] stray (*épith*); [*existence, esprit, imagination*] roving (*épith*); [*humeur*] volatile.
II *nm,f* vagrant.

vagabondage /vagabɔ̃daʒ/ *nm* **1** (errance) (de personne) wandering; (de pensée) roving; **2** Jur vagrancy ₵.

vagabonder /vagabɔ̃de/ [1] *vi* **1** [*personne, animal*] to wander (**dans** through); **~ à travers le monde** to roam the world; **2** [*imagination*] to wander; [*pensées*] to stray.

vagin /vaʒɛ̃/ ▶ **188** *nm* vagina.

vaginal, **~e**, *mpl* **-aux** /vaʒinal, o/ *adj* vaginal.

vaginisme /vaʒinism/ ▶ **271** *nm* vaginismus.

vaginite /vaʒinit/ ▶271 *nf* vaginitis.

vagir /vaʒiʀ/ [3] *vi* [*nouveau-né*] to wail.

vagissement /vaʒismɑ̃/ *nm* wail.

vague /vag/ **I** *adj* **1** (imprécis) [*forme, bruit, impression, réponse, geste*] vague; **avoir une ~ idée de qch** to have a vague idea of sth; **2** (rêveur) [*air, regard*] vague; **d'un air ~** [*contempler*] vaguely; **3** (quelconque) **il a fait une ~ école de commerce** he went to some sort of business school; **c'est une ~ relation de travail** I know him/her vaguely through work; **ce sont de ~s parents** they're distant relatives.
II *nm* **il regardait dans le ~** he was staring into space; **ton regard était perdu dans le ~** you had a faraway look in your eyes; **il se complaisait dans le ~ de ses rêveries** he was happy in his dreamworld; **la direction est restée dans le ~ sur la question des salaires** management has remained vague on ou as to the question of wages.
III *nf* **1** lit wave; **la ~ montante/déferlante** the gathering/breaking wave; **faire des ~s** [*vent*] to make ripples; fig [*démission, scandale*] to cause a stir, to make waves; **2** fig wave; **une ~ d'arrestations/de violence** a wave of arrests/of violence; **par ~s** [*arriver, attaquer*] in waves; **la ~ montante du mécontentement** the rising tide of discontent; **la ~ montante des opposants** the rapidly increasing numbers of opponents.
■ **~ à l'âme** melancholy; **avoir du ~ à l'âme** to feel melancholic; **~ de chaleur** Météo heatwave; **~ de froid** Météo cold spell.
IDIOMES **être au creux de la ~** [*personne, entreprise*] to be at a low ebb; **le creux de la ~ est passé** the worst of the crisis is over; **surtout, pas de ~s!** above all, no scandal!

vaguelette /vaglɛt/ *nf* wavelet.

vaguement /vagmɑ̃/ *adv* [*évoquer, indiquer*] vaguely; [*honteux, embarrassé, irrité*] faintly; [*peindre*] roughly; **un roman ~ historique** a vaguely historical novel; **on avait ~ décoré la pièce pour la circonstance** they had put up a few decorations for the occasion; **j'ai ~ vu qu'il parlait à quelqu'un** I sort of saw him talking to someone; **on savait ~ qu'elle avait eu des problèmes avec la justice** there was a vague rumour[GB] that she'd had a brush with the law.

vaguemestre /vagmɛstʀ/ *nm* Mil regimental postmaster; Mil Naut postman.

vahiné /vaine/ *nf* Tahitian woman.

vaillamment /vajamɑ̃/ *adv* courageously, valiantly sout.

vaillance /vajɑ̃s/ *nf* courage; **avec ~** courageously.

vaillant, **~e** /vajɑ̃, ɑ̃t/ *adj* **1** (courageux) [*sportif, équipe, soldat*] courageous; **2** (vigoureux) [*personne*] strong; [*vieillard*] sturdy.
IDIOMES **à cœur ~ rien d'impossible** Prov where there's a will, there's a way; **ne plus avoir un sou ~** not to have got two pennies to rub together GB, to be down to one's last dime US.

vain, **~e** /vɛ̃, vɛn/ **I** *adj* **1** (inutile) [*effort, tentative*] vain, futile; [*regrets*] futile; [*démarche, discussion*] fruitless, futile; **mes efforts ont été ~s** my efforts were in vain; **avec lui, toute discussion serait ~e** talking to him would be futile; **leur sacrifice n'aura pas été ~** their sacrifice will not have been in vain; **il est ~ de faire** it is futile to do; **2** (illusoire) [*promesses*] empty; [*espoirs*] vain; **3** (superficiel) [*plaisirs, mots*] vain, empty; **le pouvoir de la presse n'est pas un ~ mot** the power of the press isn't an empty word; **4** (vaniteux) [*personne*] vain.
II en vain *loc adv* in vain; **c'est en ~ que** it was in vain that.

vaincre /vɛ̃kʀ/ [57] **I** *vtr* **1** (battre) to defeat [*adversaire, équipe, armée*]; **2** (surmonter) to overcome [*sommeil, complexe, mauvais sort, scepticisme*]; to conquer [*chômage, préjugés, maladie*].
II *vi* to win; **il leur faut ~** they have to win.

vaincu, **~e** /vɛ̃ky/ **I** *pp* ▶ **vaincre**.
II *pp adj* [*équipe, armée, nation*] defeated; **elle part ~e d'avance** she has given up before she has even started; **s'avouer ~** to admit defeat (**face à qn** to sb; **face à qch** faced with sth).
III *nm,f* loser; **les ~s** Mil the defeated (+ *v pl*).

vainement /vɛnmɑ̃/ *adv* in vain.

vainqueur /vɛ̃kœʀ/ **I** *adj m* [*pays*] victorious; **sourire ~** smile of victory; **sortir ~ de** to emerge victorious from [*guerre, match, élections*]; to emerge triumphant from [*négociations*].
II *nm* (de bataille) victor; (d'épreuve sportive, élections) winner (**de, devant** against); (de loterie, concours) prizewinner; (de désert, montagne) conqueror; **il a été le grand ~ des négociations** he was the true winner in the negotiations.

vair /vɛʀ/ *nm* Hérald, Mode vair; **la pantoufle de ~ de Cendrillon** Cinderella's glass slipper.

vairon /vɛʀɔ̃/ **I** *adj m* **yeux ~s** eyes of different colours[GB].
II *nm* Zool minnow.

vaisseau, *pl* **~x** /vɛso/ *nm* **1** Anat, Bot vessel; **2** Naut vessel; Mil, Naut warship; **3** Archit nave.
■ **~ amiral** Mil, Naut, fig flagship; **~ capillaire** Anat capillary; **~ fantôme** Flying Dutchman; **~ sanguin** Anat blood vessel; **~ spatial** Astronaut spaceship.
IDIOMES **brûler ses ~x** to burn all one's boats.

vaisselier /vɛsəlje/ *nm* dresser.

vaisselle /vɛsɛl/ *nf* **1** (plats pour manger) crockery GB, dishes (*pl*); **~ de porcelaine** china; **de la belle ~** fine china; **2** (plats à laver) dishes (*pl*); **laver** or **faire la ~** to do the dishes, to wash up GB, to do the washing-up GB; **essuyer la ~** to dry up, to do the drying up GB.

val, *pl* **~s** ou **vaux** /val, vo/ *nm* valley.
IDIOMES **être toujours par monts et par vaux** to be always on the move.

valable /valabl/ *adj* **1** (acceptable) [*explication, raison*] valid; [*solution*] viable; [*interlocuteur*] valid; **2** (non périmé) [*papier d'identité, document, offre*] valid (**jusqu'à** until); **ma proposition reste ~** my offer still holds; **3**° (intéressant) [*œuvre, projet*] worthwhile; [*personne*] pretty good°.

valablement /valabləmɑ̃/ *adv* [*soutenir*] legitimately; [*démontrer*] conclusively; **voter ~** to have a valid vote.

Valais /valɛ/ ▶692 *nprm* **le (canton de) ~** the (canton of) Valais; **habiter dans le ~** to live in Valais.

Val-de-Marne /valdəmaʀn/ ▶692 *nprm* (département) **le ~** Val-de-Marne.

valdinguer° /valdɛ̃ge/ [1] *vi* [*personne, objet*] to go flying°; **~ dans l'escalier** to go tumbling down the stairs; **envoyer ~** (faire tomber) to send [sb/sth] flying°; (éconduire) to send [sb] packing°.

Val-d'Oise /valdwaz/ ▶692 *nprm* (département) **le ~** Val d'Oise.

valence /valɑ̃s/ *nf* valency GB, valence US.

Valence /valɑ̃s/ ▶857 *npr* **1** (en France) Valence; **2** (en Espagne) Valencia.

valenciennes /valɑ̃sjɛn/ *nf inv* Valenciennes lace.

valériane /valeʀjan/ *nf* valerian.

valet /valɛ/ ▶510 *nm* **1** (serviteur) manservant; **2** Jeux jack; **~ de pique** jack of spades; **3** (de menuisier) clamp.
■ **~ de chambre** valet; **~ de comédie** Théât wily manservant; **~ d'écurie** stableman; **~ de ferme** farm hand; **~ de nuit** valet; **~ de pied** footman.
IDIOMES **les bons maîtres font les bons ~s** Prov one leads by example.

valetaille /valtaj/ *nf* pej flunkeys (*pl*).

Valette /valɛt/ ▶857 *nprf* **la ~** Valetta.

valétudinaire /valetydinɛʀ/ *adj, nmf* valetudinarian sout.

valeur /valœʀ/ *nf* **1** (prix) value; **prendre/perdre de la ~** to go up/go down in value; **acheter qch d'une ~ de 100 francs** to buy sth worth 100 francs; **d'une ~ inestimable** [*bijou, meuble*] priceless; **avoir beaucoup de ~** to be very valuable; **n'avoir aucune ~, être sans ~** to have no value, to be worth nothing; **vendre qch en dessous de sa ~** to sell sth for less than it's worth; **un vase de ~** a valuable vase; **les objets de ~** valuables; **mettre un terrain en ~** to develop a plot of land; **la mise en ~ d'une terre** the development of a piece of land; **2** (qualité) (de personne, d'artiste) worth; (d'œuvre) value, merit; (de méthode, découverte) value; **apprécier qn à sa ~** (positif) to recognize sb's worth; (négatif) to get the measure of sb; **prouver sa ~** to show one's worth; **avoir une ~ symbolique/sentimentale** to have symbolic/sentimental value; **faire la ~ de qch** to give sth value; **attacher de la ~ à qch** to value sth; **attacher une grande ~ à qch** to set great value on sth; **sans ~** worthless; **un homme de ~** (moralement) a very estimable man; **attirer des candidats de ~** (en compétence) to attract high-quality candidates; **la ~ de l'écrivain a été reconnue** the author's talent has been recognized; **le mot garde toute sa ~** the word keeps its full force; **mettre qch en ~** to emphasize, highlight [*fait, talent, qualité*]; to set off [*yeux, teint, tableau*]; **le cadre met le tableau en ~** the frame sets off the painting; **mettre qn en ~** [*couleur, maquillage*] to suit ou flatter sb; **la coupe de la robe met sa taille en ~** the cut of the dress shows off her slim waist; **se mettre en ~** [*coquette*] to make the best of oneself; [*candidat*] to show oneself to best advantage; **3** (validité) validity; **~ légale** legal validity; **avoir ~ de** to be, to constitute; **avoir ~ de norme/symbole** to be the norm/a symbol; **ceci n'a pas ~ d'engagement** this does not constitute a commitment; **je souhaite que leur action ait ~ d'exemple** I hope that their action serves as an example; **4** (principe moral) value; **les ~s morales/démocratiques/traditionnelles** moral/democratic/traditional values; **nous n'avons pas les mêmes ~s** we don't share the same values; **5** Fin (effet de commerce) bill of exchange; (en Bourse) security; **~s** securities, stock ₵, stocks and shares; **les ~s minières** mining shares ou stock ₵ ou securities; **le marché** or **la Bourse des ~s** the stock market; **date** or **jour de ~** (dans une banque) value date; **6** Compta asset; **~s disponibles/immobilisées** liquid/fixed assets; **7** (quantité) **ajouter la ~ de deux cuillerées à café** add the equivalent of two teaspoons; **8** Math value; **la ~ algébrique/absolue d'un nombre** the algebraic/absolute value of a number; **en ~ absolue/relative** fig in absolute/relative terms; **9** Jeux (de pion, carte) value; **10** Ling, Mus value; **11†** (courage) valour†[GB].
■ **~ ajoutée** added value; **~ de** or **à la casse** scrap value; **~ déclarée** value; **~ d'échange** exchange value; **~ à l'échéance** value at maturity; **~ locative** rental value; **~ marchande** market ou sale value; **~ nominale** nominal ou face value; **~ nominative** registered security; **~ or** gold value; **~ de premier ordre** Fin blue chip; **~ refuge** safe investment; **~ sûre** gilt-edged security GB, blue chip; fig safe bet; **~ d'usage** use value; **~ vedette** Fin leader, blue chip; **~ vénale** market ou sale value; **~s mobilières** securities; ▶ **taxe**.

valeureusement /valøʀøzmɑ̃/ *adv* valorously†.

valeureux, **-euse** /valøʀø, øz/ *adj* valorous†.

validation /validasjɔ̃/ *nf* Jur, Univ validation; Jeux, Transp stamping.

valide /valid/ *adj* **1** [*ticket, passeport, contrat, argument*] valid; **non ~** invalid; **2** [*personne, population*] able-bodied; [*bras*] good (*épith*); (en forme) fit; **je ne me sens pas encore bien ~** I don't feel very fit yet.

valider /valide/ [1] *vtr* to stamp [*titre de transport*]; **faire ~** to have [sth] validated [*bulletin de loto*]; to have [sth] recognized [*diplôme*].

valideuse /validøz/ *nf* stamping machine (*for lottery coupons*).

validité /validite/ *nf* validity.

valise /valiz/ *nf* (bagage) suitcase; **faire/défaire ses ~s** to pack/unpack; **s'il n'est pas content, il n'a qu'à faire ses ~s** if he doesn't like it, he can pack his bags.
■ **~ diplomatique** diplomatic bag GB, diplomatic pouch US.
IDIOMES **se faire la ~**○ to clear off○ GB, to clear out○ US; **avoir des ~s sous les yeux**○ to have bags under one's eyes; **pose tes ~s**○! get with it○!

valium /valjɔm/ *nm* valium.

vallée /vale/ *nf* valley; **la ~ du Nil** the Nile valley.
■ **~ d'effondrement** Géol rift valley; **~ glaciaire** Géog glaciated valley; **~ de larmes** vale of tears.

vallon /valɔ̃/ *nm* dale, small valley.

vallonné, **~e** /valɔne/ *adj* [*relief, paysage*] undulating; [*pays*] hilly.

vallonnement /valɔnmɑ̃/ *nm* hills and valleys (*pl*).

valoche○ /valɔʃ/ *nf* **1** (valise) suitcase; **2** (cerne) **~s** bags under the eyes.

valoir /valwaʀ/ [45] **I** *vtr* (procurer) **~ qch à qn** to earn sb [*châtiment, éloges, critiques, inimitiés*]; to win sb [*amitié, admiration*]; to bring sb [*ennuis*]; **ça ne m'a valu que des ennuis** it brought me nothing but trouble, I got nothing but trouble out of it; **ce qui lui a valu d'aller en prison** which earned ou got him/her a prison sentence; **cela lui a valu d'être élu/exclu du parti** it got him elected/expelled from the party; **tout ce que t'a valu ta baignade, c'est un bon rhume** all you got out of going swimming is a nasty cold; **que me vaut l'honneur de ta visite?** hum to what do I owe the honour[GB] (of your visit)?
II *vi* **1** (en termes monétaires) [*maison, article*] **~ une fortune/cher/encore plus cher** to be worth a fortune/a lot/even more; **ça vaut combien?** how much is it (worth), what is it worth?; **ça vaut bien 50 francs** (à peu près) it must be worth 50 francs; (largement) it's well worth 50 francs; **ça ne vaut pas grand-chose** it's not worth much; **~ de l'or** fig [*idée*] to be very valuable; [*employé*] to be worth one's weight in gold; ▶ **avertir**, **deux**; **2** (qualitativement) **que vaut ce film/vin?** what's that film/wine like?; **que vaut-il en tant que gestionnaire?** how good an administrator is he?; **il ne vaut pas mieux que son frère** he's no better than his brother; **ils ne valent pas mieux l'un que l'autre** there's nothing to choose between them; **le film ne vaut pas grand-chose** the film isn't very good ou isn't up to much○; **il ne vaut pas cher** he is a worthless individual ou a bad lot○; **ne rien ~** [*matériau, produit, roman*] to be rubbish, to be no good; [*outil, traitement, méthode*] to be useless; [*argument*] to be worthless; **il ne vaut rien comme cuisinier** he's a useless cook; **le pneu ne vaut plus rien** the tyre has had it○; **la chaleur/le climat ne me vaut rien** heat/the climate doesn't suit me; **l'alcool ne vaut rien pour le foie** alcohol doesn't do the liver much good; **le voyage ne m'a rien valu** the journey hasn't done me any good; **le film vaut surtout par la qualité du dialogue** the principal merit of the film is the quality of the dialogue[GB]; **je sais ce que je vaux** I know my own worth; **il n'y a rien qui vaille dans cette œuvre** there's nothing good about this work; **il ne me dit rien qui vaille** I've got misgivings about him; **ça ne me dit rien qui vaille** (projet, annonce) I don't like the sound of it; **elle valait mieux que cela!** she deserved better than that!; **3** (égaler) to be as good as; **ton travail vaut bien/largement le leur** your work is just as good/every bit as good as theirs; **une explication qui en vaut une autre** an explanation which is as good as any other; **rien ne vaut la soie** nothing beats silk; **tout cela ne vaut pas la Corse** it's still not as good as Corsica; **le frère vaut la sœur** iron the brother is just as bad as the sister; **4** (équivaloir à) to be worth; **un ouvrier expérimenté vaut trois débutants** an experienced worker is worth three novices; **5** (mériter) to be worth; **le musée vaut la visite** or **le déplacement/le détour** the museum is worth a visit/a detour; **la question vaut d'être posée** the question is worth asking; **ça vaut/ne vaut pas la peine** or **le coup**○ **d'y aller** it is/isn't worth going; **ça vaut la peine que tu y ailles** it's worth your going; **ça en vaut la peine, ça vaut le coup**○ it's worth it; **ça vaut le coup d'œil**○ it's worth seeing; **6** (être valable) [*règle, critique*] to apply; **la règle vaut pour tous les cas/pour tout le monde** the rule applies in all cases/to everybody; **ceci vaut surtout pour son dernier roman** this is particularly true of his/her last novel; **7** (avec faire) **faire ~** (faire fructifier) to put [sth] to work [*argent*]; to put [sth] to good use [*terrain*]; to turn [sth] to good account [*bien*]; (mettre en avant) to point out [*mérite, nécessité*]; to emphasize, highlight [*qualité, trait*]; to advance [*argument*]; to assert [*droit*]; to make [sth] known [*intention*]; **faire ~ que** to point out that, to argue that; **faire ~ la difficulté qu'il y aurait à faire qch** to point out the difficulty of doing sth; **faire ~ ses droits à la retraite** to claim one's right to retirement; **faire ~ ses relations** to mention one's connections; **se faire ~** to push oneself forward, to get oneself noticed (**auprès de qn** by sb); **8** Comm **à ~** to be deducted (**sur** from); **une somme à ~, un à ~** a sum on account.
III se valoir *vpr* [*produit, œuvres*] to be the same; **les deux candidats se valent** there's nothing to choose between the two candidates; **ça se vaut**○ it's all the same.
IV *v impers* **il vaut mieux faire**, **mieux vaut faire** it's better to do; **mieux vaut** or **il vaut mieux une dispute qu'un malentendu** an argument is better than a misunderstanding, rather an argument than a misunderstanding; **il vaut mieux que tu y ailles** you'd better go; **il aurait mieux valu qu'il se taise** he would have done better to keep quiet; **cela vaut mieux**○ it's better like that ou that way.
IDIOMES **vaille que vaille** somehow or other; **un tiens vaut mieux que deux tu l'auras**, **il vaut mieux tenir que courir** a bird in the hand is worth two in the bush.

valorisant, **~e** /valɔʀizɑ̃, ɑ̃t/ *adj* **1** (respecté) [*travail, profession, possession*] prestige (*épith*); **travail peu ~** low-grade job; **2** (gratifiant) [*travail, expérience*] fulfilling[GB]; **nous vous offrons un stage ~** we offer a training period which will help you fulfil[GB] your potential; **travail peu ~** stultifying job.

valorisation /valɔʀizasjɔ̃/ *nf* **1** Pub (promotion) promotion; **~ d'un produit** promotion of a product; **2** Écon (mise en valeur) (de région, ressources) development; **3** Fin (hausse de valeur) (de monnaie) rise; (de terrains) rise in value.

valoriser /valɔʀize/ [1] **I** *vtr* **1** (promouvoir) to promote [*produit*]; to make [sth] attractive [*travail, profession, études*]; **2** (mettre en valeur) to develop [*région, ressources*]; to put [sth] to advantage [*diplôme, savoir-faire*]; **3** Fin (faire fructifier) to put [sth] to work [*capital*].
II se valoriser *vpr* [*candidat*] to show oneself to best advantage; [*coquette*] to make the most of oneself.

valse /vals/ *nf* **1** Danse waltz; **danser la ~** to do the waltz; **2** (changement fréquent) constant succession; **~ des ministres** frequent cabinet reshuffles (*pl*); **~ des étiquettes** or **prix** continual price rises (*pl*).

valse-hésitation, *pl* **valses-hésitations** /valsezitasjɔ̃/ *nf* shilly-shallying○ ¢.

valser /valse/ [1] *vi* **1** Danse to waltz; **l'argent valse entre leurs mains**○ they spend money hand over fist; **envoyer ~ qn**○ (projeter) to send sb flying; (rembarrer) to send sb packing○; **le sac est allé ~ à l'autre bout de la pièce**○ the bag was sent flying across the room; **2**○ (changer) [*prix*] to be continually rising; [*personnel*] to be always changing; **ça valse dans le service** there's a constant turnover of staff; **faire ~ les étiquettes** to raise prices constantly; **il fait ~ les ministres** he keeps changing his ministers.

valseur, **-euse** /valsœʀ, øz/ **I** *nm,f* Danse waltzer; **les ~s** the waltzing couples.
II valseuses● *nfpl* (testicules) balls●, testicles.

valve /valv/ *nf* (tous contextes) valve.

valvulaire /valvylɛʀ/ *adj* valvular.

valvule /valvyl/ *nf* valve.
■ **~ mitrale** Anat mitral valve.

vamp○ /vɑ̃p/ *nf* vamp.

vamper○ /vape/ [1] *vtr* to vamp○.

vampire /vɑ̃piʀ/ *nm* **1** (revenant) vampire; **un film de ~s** a vampire film; **2** (personne avide) bloodsucker; **3** Zool vampire bat.

vampiriser /vɑ̃piʀize/ [1] *vtr* to suck the lifeblood from.

vampirisme /vɑ̃piʀism/ *nm* **1** lit vampirism; **2** (avidité) rapacity.

van /vɑ̃/ *nm* **1** (fourgon) (pour chevaux) horsebox GB, horse-car US; (pour marchandises) van; **2** (panier) winnowing basket.

vanadium /vanadjɔm/ *nm* vanadium.

Vancouver /vɑ̃kuvɛʀ/ ▶ **857** *npr* Vancouver; **l'île de ~** Vancouver Island.

vandale /vɑ̃dal/ *nmf* vandal.

Vandale /vɑ̃dal/ *nmf* Hist Vandal.

vandaliser /vɑ̃dalize/ [1] *vtr* to vandalize.

vandalisme /vɑ̃dalism/ *nm* vandalism.

vandoise /vɑ̃dwaz/ *nf* Zool dace.

vanesse /vanɛs/ *nf* vanessa.

vanille /vanij/ *nf* vanilla; **une gousse de ~** a vanilla pod; **de la ~ en poudre** vanilla powder; **à la ~** [*glace*] vanilla (*épith*); [*crème*] vanilla-flavoured[GB] (*épith*).

vanillé, **~e** /vanije/ *adj* [*goût*] vanilla (*épith*); [*dessert*] vanilla-flavoured[GB]; **sucre ~** sugar containing vanilla.

vanillier /vanije/ *nm* vanilla plant.

vanilliné, **~e** /vaniline/ *adj* **sucre ~** vanilla-flavoured[GB] sugar.

vanité /vanite/ *nf* **1** (orgueil) vanity; **sans ~** with all due modesty; **tirer ~ de qch** to pride oneself on sth; **blesser qn dans sa ~** to wound sb's pride; **flatter qn dans sa ~** to flatter sb's ego; **avoir la ~ de croire que** to be presumptuous enough to believe that; **2** (peu de valeur) (de richesses) emptiness; (d'efforts) futility; (de promesse) hollowness; (d'entreprise) uselessness; **3** Art vanitas.
IDIOMES **~ des ~s, tout est ~** vanity of vanities, all is vanity.

vaniteux, **-euse** /vanitø, øz/ **I** *adj* vain, conceited.
II *nm,f* vain ou conceited person.

vanity-case, *pl* **~s** /vanitikes/ *nm* vanity case.

vannage /vanaʒ/ *nm* winnowing.

vanne /van/ *nf* **1** (de barrage) gate; (d'écluse, de moulin) sluice gate; **2**○ (propos) dig○;

envoyer une ~ or **des ~s à qn** to have a dig at sb○.

■ **~ de décharge** Tech floodgate; **~ glissante** Tech slide gate; **~ levante** Tech lift gate; **~ roulante** Tech roller gate; **~ de sécurité** Ind (dans un forage pétrolier) kelly cock; **~ de vidange** sluice gate.

IDIOMES **ouvrir les ~s**○ to make funds available; **fermer les ~s**○ to cut funding.

vanneau, *pl* **~x** /vano/ *nm* lapwing.

■ **~ huppé** Northern lapwing; **~ téro** Southern lapwing.

vanner /vane/ [1] *vtr* **1** Agric to winnow; **2**○ (fatiguer) to tire [sb] out [*personne*]; **je suis vannée!** I'm tired out ou knackered○ GB ou pooped○!

vannerie /vanʀi/ *nf* basket-making; **objets en ~** wickerwork, basketwork.

vanneur, **-euse** /vanœʀ, øz/ ▶ **510** *nm,f* winnower.

vannier, **-ière** /vanje, ɛʀ/ ▶ **510** *nm,f* basket-maker.

vantail, *pl* **-aux** /vɑ̃taj, o/ *nm* (de porte) leaf; (de fenêtre) casement; (de volet) shutter; (d'armoire) door; **porte à double ~** double-door.

vantard, **~e** /vɑ̃taʀ, aʀd/ **I** *adj* boastful (*épith*); **il est ~** he's a boaster.

II *nm,f* boaster, braggart.

vantardise /vɑ̃taʀdiz/ *nf* **1** (caractère) boastfulness; **2** (parole) boast.

vanter /vɑ̃te/ [1] **I** *vtr* to praise [*qualité, vertu, talent, personne*]; **tant vanté** so highly praised; **~ les mérites de qn/qch** to speak highly of sb/sth.

II se vanter *vpr* **1** (être un vantard) to brag (**de** about); **elle se vante toujours de tes succès** she is always bragging about your achievements; **il n'y a pas de quoi se ~!** there's nothing to brag about!; **il a cassé le vase mais il ne s'en est pas vanté** he broke the vase but he kept quiet about it; **2** (s'enorgueillir) **se ~ de faire** to pride oneself on doing; **il se vante de posséder la plus belle collection au monde** he prides himself on having the finest collection in the world; **3** (prétendre) **se ~ de faire** to make out that one does; **elle se vante de tout réussir** she makes out that she makes a success of everything.

Vanuatu /vanyatu/ ▶ **321**, **416** *nprm* Vanuatu; **les îles ~** the Vanuatu Islands.

va-nu-pieds /vanypje/ *nmf inv* tramp, bum○.

vapes◐ /vap/ *nfpl* **être (complètement) dans les ~** to be in a complete daze; **tomber dans les ~** to pass out○.

vapeur /vapœʀ/ **I** *nf* **1** (d'eau) steam; **à ~** [*machine, bateau*] steam (*épith*); **aller à toute ~** to go full steam ahead; **renverser la ~** Naut to go astern; fig to backpedal; **faire cuire qch à la ~** to steam sth; **la cuisine à la ~** steam cooking; **2** Phys vapour[GB].

II vapeurs *nfpl* **1** (émanations) fumes; **des ~s d'essence** petrol fumes GB, gas fumes US; **2**† (bouffées de chaleur) **elle a des ~s!** she has a touch of the vapours[GB]†!

■ **~ atmosphérique** atmospheric vapour[GB]; **~ d'eau** steam.

vaporeux, **-euse** /vapɔʀø, øz/ *adj* **1** (léger) [*vêtement, matériau*] diaphanous; **2** fml (brumeux) [*paysage, horizon*] misty.

vaporisateur /vapɔʀizatœʀ/ *nm* **1** Cosmét spray, atomizer; **un ~ à parfum** a perfume atomizer; **2** Agric spray.

vaporisation /vapɔʀizasjɔ̃/ *nf* **1** (d'insecticide, de parfum) spraying (**de** of); **2** Phys vaporization (**de** of).

vaporiser /vapɔʀize/ [1] **I** *vtr* **1** (projeter) to spray; **lotion à ~ sur la peau** lotion to be sprayed onto the skin; **il a vaporisé de la lotion sur ses cheveux** he sprayed his hair with hair lotion; **2** Phys [*chaleur*] to vaporize [*liquide*].

II se vaporiser *vpr* Phys to vaporize.

vaquer /vake/ [1] **I** *vi* (s'arrêter) [*tribunal, assemblée*] to be in recess; [*cours*] to stop.

II vaquer à *vtr ind* **~ à ses occupations** or **affaires** to attend to one's business.

Var /vaʀ/ ▶ **357**, **692** *nprm* (fleuve, département) **le ~** the Var.

varan /vaʀɑ̃/ *nm* Zool monitor.

■ **~ de Bornéo** earless monitor.

varappe /vaʀap/ ▶ **449** *nf* rock-climbing; **faire de la ~** to go rock-climbing.

varappeur, **-euse** /vaʀapœʀ, øz/ *nm,f* rock-climber.

varech /vaʀɛk/ *nm* kelp.

vareuse /vaʀøz/ *nf* **1** Mil Naut jersey; **2** Mil uniform jacket; **3** Mode smock.

variabilité /vaʀjabilite/ *nf* variability.

variable /vaʀjabl/ **I** *adj* **1** (fluctuant) [*durée, efficacité, production, tarif, nombre*] variable; **des obligations à taux ~** Fin bonds at variable rates; **être ~ selon qch** to vary according to sth; **leurs sketches sont d'une durée ~** their sketches vary in length; **les hausses sont ~s d'un produit à l'autre** the price rises vary from product to product; **2** (changeant) [*ciel, temps*] changeable; [*humeur*] unpredictable; **vent ~ de faible à modéré** wind varying from weak to moderate; **dans des proportions ~s** in varying proportions; **ils ont des opinions ~s** they have shifting opinions; **3** (modifiable) [*hauteur, focale*] adjustable; **un siège à hauteur ~** a seat with adjustable height; ▶ **avion**; **4** Math, Ordinat [*quantité, nombre, données*] variable; **5** Ling **un mot ~** a word which inflects.

II *nf* Math, Fin, Phys, Stat variable.

■ **~ de décision** Écon operative choice; **~ visuelle** Géog visual reference point.

variance /vaʀjɑ̃s/ *nf* variance.

variante /vaʀjɑ̃t/ *nf* variant.

■ **~ combinatoire** combinatory ou conditioned variant; **~ libre** free variant.

variateur /vaʀjatœʀ/ *nm* **~ de lumière** dimmer switch; **~ de vitesse** variable speed drive.

variation /vaʀjasjɔ̃/ *nf* **1** (changement) variation (**de** in); **~ de température** variation in temperature; **~s cycliques/régulières** cyclic/regular variations; **~ à la baisse/à la hausse** downward/upward movement; **~s de l'opinion publique** changes in public opinion; **~s de l'état d'un malade** changes in a patient's condition; **~ de l'orthographe au cours des siècles** changes in spelling over the centuries; **connaître de fortes ~s** [*prix, températures*] to fluctuate considerably; **2** Mus variation; **~s pour piano** variations for piano; **le film propose une nouvelle ~ sur (le thème de) l'exil** fig the film puts forward a new variation on (the theme of) exile.

■ **~s saisonnières** Écon seasonally adjusted figures; **en données corrigées des ~s saisonnières** according to the seasonally adjusted figures.

varice /vaʀis/ *nf* varicose vein, varix spéc; **avoir des ~s** to have varicose veins.

varicelle /vaʀisɛl/ ▶ **271** *nf* chicken pox, varicella spéc.

varié, **~e** /vaʀje/ *adj* **1** (diversifié) [*menu, clientèle, programme, répertoire, échantillon, paysage*] varied; **une expérience ~e** diverse ou varied experience; **j'ai un travail ~** my work is quite varied; **plumage ~** variegated plumage; **2** (multiple) [*instruments, exercices*] various; **sous des formes ~es** in various forms; **des activités aussi ~es que** activities as varied as; **aborder les problèmes les plus ~s** to tackle a wide range of problems; **une population d'origines ~es** a population of diverse origins; **'sandwichs/desserts ~s'** 'a selection of sandwiches/desserts'.

varier /vaʀje/ [2] **I** *vtr* **1** (apporter des changements à) to vary [*menu, présentation, décoration*]; **2** (diversifier) to vary; **(faire) ~ qch en fonction de qch** to vary sth according to sth; **pour ~ les expériences j'ai fait plusieurs métiers** I've had various jobs to get different types of experience; **pour ~ les plaisirs** just for a (pleasant) change.

II *vi* **1** (changer) [*prix, température, rituel, programme, date*] to vary (**avec, en fonction de, au gré de** according to); **l'inflation varie de 4% à 6%** inflation fluctuates between 4% and 6%; **les prix varient entre 50 et 200 francs** prices vary between 50 francs and 200 francs; **l'incubation varie de cinq semaines à six mois** the incubation varies from five weeks to six months; **2** (changer d'opinion) **l'accusé ne varie pas** the accused is sticking to his story; **il ne varie jamais dans ses déclarations** he never changes his tune; **leur réponse n'a pas varié** their reply is always the same.

IDIOMES **souvent femme varie, bien fol est qui s'y fie** Prov woman is fickle.

variété /vaʀjete/ **I** *nf* **1** (diversité) variety (**de** of); **la ~ des réponses/tâches** the variety of replies/tasks; **les activités manquent de ~** the activities are lacking in variety; **aimer la ~** to like variety; **apporter de la ~** to bring variety (**dans** to); **des menus/paysages d'une grande ~** very varied menus/landscapes; **la ~ de leur jeu surprend toujours l'adversaire** Sport their opponents are always taken aback at how varied their game is; **une grande ~ de matériaux/de couleurs/d'articles** a wide range of materials/of colours[GB]/of items; **2** Bot variety; **3** (type) sort; **différentes ~s de chocolats/céréales** different sorts of chocolates/cereals; **une ~ de grippe** a strain of flu.

II variétés *nfpl* **spectacle de ~s** variety show; **la chanson de ~s** middle-of-the-road popular song; **un chanteur de ~s** (middle-of-the-road) popular singer; **musique de ~s** kitchen-sink music; **les ~s françaises/italiennes** French/Italian popular music.

variole /vaʀjɔl/ ▶ **271** *nf* smallpox, variola spéc.

variolé, **~e** /vaʀjɔle/ *adj* [*visage*] pockmarked.

variolique /vaʀjɔlik/ *adj* [*éruption*] smallpox (*épith*), variolous spéc.

variqueux, **-euse** /vaʀikø, øz/ *adj* varicose.

varlope /vaʀlɔp/ *nf* trying plane GB, plane US.

varloper /vaʀlɔpe/ [1] *vtr* to plane.

Varsovie /vaʀsɔvi/ ▶ **857** *npr* Warsaw.

vas /va/ ▶ **aller** II.

vasculaire /vaskylɛʀ/ *adj* vascular.

vascularisation /vaskylaʀizasjɔ̃/ *nf* vascularization.

vascularisé, **~e** /vaskylaʀize/ *adj* vascular.

vase /vɑz/ **I** *nm* (à fleurs, ornemental) vase.

II *nf* **1** Géol silt, sludge; **2**○ (pluie) rain.

■ **~s communicants** Phys connected vessels; **~ Dewar** Phys Dewar flask; **~ d'expansion** Tech surge tank; **~ de nuit** chamber pot; **~s sacrés** Relig sacred vessels.

IDIOMES **vivre/être élevé en ~ clos** to live/be brought up without any contact with the outside world; **c'est la goutte d'eau qui fait déborder le ~** it's the last straw.

vasectomie /vazɛktɔmi/ *nf* vasectomy.

vaseline® /vazlin/ *nf* Vaseline®.

vaseux, **-euse** /vazø, øz/ *adj* **1** (boueux) muddy; **2**○ (fatigué) **je me sens plutôt ~** I'm not really with it; **3**○ (peu cohérent) [*discours, argument*] woolly.

vasistas /vazistas/ *nm* (à lamelles) louvre[GB] window; (dans une fenêtre) opening windowpane.

vasoconstricteur, **-trice** /vazokɔ̃stʀiktœʀ, tʀis/ **I** *adj* vaso-constrictive.

II *nm* **1** Pharm vasoconstrictor; **2** Anat vasoconstrictor, vasoconstrictive nerve.

vasoconstriction /vazokɔ̃stʀiksjɔ̃/ *nf* vasoconstriction.

vasodilatateur, **-trice** /vazodilatatœʀ, tʀis/ **I** *adj* vasodilator.
II *nm* **1** Pharm vasodilator; **2** Anat vasodilator (nerve).

vasodilatation /vazodilatasjɔ̃/ *nf* vasodilatation.

vasomoteur, **-trice** /vazomɔtœʀ, tʀis/ *adj* vasomotor.

vasomotricité /vazomɔtʀisite/ *nf* vasomotivity.

vasouillard○, **~e** /vazujaʀ, aʀd/ *adj* **1** (fatigué) **je me sens ~** I'm not with it; **2** (peu cohérent) [*discours, argument*] woolly.

vasouiller○ /vazuje/ [1] *vi* [*personne*] to flounder.

vasque /vask/ *nf* **1** (de fontaine) basin; **2** (coupe) bowl.

vassal, **~e**, *mpl* **-aux** /vasal, o/ **I** *adj* **État ~** vassal state.
II *nm,f* Hist vassal; fig slave; **il se comporte en ~** he behaves like a slave.

vassaliser /vasalize/ [1] *vtr* to subjugate.

vassalité /vasalite/ *nf* vassalage.

vaste /vast/ *adj* **1** (de grande étendue) [*pièce, domaine, bâtisse, secteur, réseau*] vast; [*marché*] huge; **créer un ~ secteur industriel** to create a vast industrial sector; **la salle/le domaine n'est pas très ~** the room/the property is not very large; **le ~ monde** the wide world; **2** (nombreux) [*public, auditoire, choix, sélection, collection*] large; [*rassemblement*] huge; **3** (de grande envergure) [*programme, projet, entreprise, escroquerie*] massive; [*campagne*] extensive; [*plaisanterie*] huge; [*débat, enquête*] wide-ranging; [*mouvement, offensive*] large-scale; [*réforme*] far-reaching; [*œuvre, sujet*] wide-ranging; **une ~ opération de prévention** a massive preventative operation; **porté par un ~ élan de solidarité** carried along by a huge wave of solidarity.

va(t): **à Dieu va(t)** /adjøva(t)/ *loc excl* come what may.

va-t-en-guerre /vatɑ̃gɛʀ/ *nm inv* warmonger.

Vatican /vatikɑ̃/ **▶321** *nprm* Vatican City.

vaticination /vatisinasjɔ̃/ *nf* fml, pej soothsaying, vaticination sout.

vaticiner /vatisine/ [1] *vi* fml, pej to soothsay, to vaticinate sout.

va-tout /vatu/ *nm inv* **jouer/tenter son ~** to stake/risk everything.

Vaud /vo/ **▶692** *nprm* **le (canton de) ~** the (canton of) Vaud; **habiter dans le ~** to live in Vaud.

vaudeville /vodvil/ *nm* light comedy, vaudeville; **tourner au ~** to turn into a farce.

vaudevillesque /vodvilɛsk/ *adj* farcical.

vaudois, **~e** /vodwa, waz/ **▶692** *adj* **1** Géog [*accent, costume, firme*] from the canton of Vaud (*après n*); **2** Hist Relig Waldensian.

Vaudois, **~e** /vodwa, waz/ *nm,f* **1** Géog inhabitant of the canton of Vaud; **2** Hist Relig Waldensian; **les ~** the Waldensians ou Waldenses.

vaudou /vodu/ *adj inv, nm* voodoo.

vau-l'eau: **à vau-l'eau** /avolo/ *loc adv* **aller à ~** to be falling apart.

vaurien, **-ienne** /voʀjɛ̃, ɛn/ *nm,f* **1** (chenapan) rascal; **(espèce de) petit ~!** you little rascal!; **2** pej (crapule) lout, yobbo○ GB, hoodlum○.

Vaurien® /voʀjɛ̃/ *nm* Naut Vaurien.

vautour /votuʀ/ *nm* **1** Zool vulture; **2** (personne avide) vulture; **les ~s de la finance** the vultures in the financial world.

vautrer: **se vautrer** /votʀe/ [1] *vpr* **1** (s'étaler) to sprawl; **se ~ dans l'herbe/sur le sable** to sprawl in the grass/on the sand; **2** (s'affaler) to loll; **se ~ dans un fauteuil** to loll in an armchair; **ne reste pas vautré toute la journée** don't spend all day lolling around; **3** (se rouler) to wallow; **se ~ dans la boue/dans la débauche** to wallow in the mud/in debauchery.

vauvert: **au diable vauvert** /odjablə vovɛʀ/ *loc adv* miles from anywhere.

va-vite: **à la va-vite** /alavavit/ *loc adv* pej in a rush; **un travail fait à la ~** a rush job.

VDQS /vedekyɛs/ *nm*: *abbr* **▶ vin**.

veau, *pl* **~x** /vo/ *nm* **1** Zool calf; **2** Culin veal; **côte de ~** veal chop; **foie/pied de ~** calf's liver/foot; **3** (cuir) calfskin; **4**○ (personne amorphe) dope○; (voiture) sluggish car; (cheval) nag.
■ **~ marin** Zool seal; **~ d'or** Bible golden calf; (les richesses) Mammon.
IDIOMES **pleurer comme un ~** to cry one's eyes out; **tuer le ~ gras** to kill the fatted calf.

vécés○ /vese/ *nmpl* loo○ (*sg*) GB, toilet (*sg*).

vecteur /vɛktœʀ/ *nm* **1** (support) vehicle; **~ de** vehicle of [*agressivité, impulsion*]; vehicle for [*culture, information*]; **2** Math vector; **3** Biol (de maladie) carrier, vector spéc; **4** Mil (véhicule) carrier.

vectoriel, **-ielle** /vɛktɔʀjɛl/ *adj* [*calcul, produit*] vector (*épith*).

vécu, **~e** /veky/ **I** *pp* **▶ vivre**.
II *pp adj* **1** (authentique) [*drame, événement, histoire*] real-life (*épith*); **2** Philos (subjectif) [*durée, temps*] subjective.
III *nm* **1** (expériences) personal experiences (*pl*); **tirer son inspiration de son ~** to draw inspiration from one's own personal experiences; **2** (réalité) real life; **c'est du ~** [*film, roman*] it's real life.

vedettariat /vədetaʀja/ *nm* stardom; **accéder au ~** to rise to stardom.

vedette /vədɛt/ **I** *nf* **1** (célébrité) star; **~ de cinéma** film star, movie star US; **une ~ de la politique** a famous politician; **l'événement a fait d'elle une ~ de l'actualité** the event put her in the public eye; **avoir la ~** [*acteur, orateur*] to have top billing; **tenir la ~** [*acteur, événement*] to be in the limelight; **partager la ~ avec qn** lit to share top billing with sb; **partager la ~ avec qn/qch** fig to share the limelight with sb/sth; **se mettre en ~** to push oneself forward; **mettre qn/qch en ~** to turn the spotlight on sb/sth; **2** Naut (de police, pompiers) launch.
II (-)vedette (*in compounds*) **joueur ~** star player; **danseur ~** star; **enfant ~** child star; **mannequin ~** top model; **match ~** big match GB ou game US; **produit ~** biggest seller; **titre** or **valeur ~** Fin blue chip.
■ **~ américaine** support (act); **~ de combat** fast attack craft; **~ de croisière** cabin cruiser; **~ lance-torpilles** motor torpedo boat GB.

védique /vedik/ *adj* Vedic.

védisme /vedism/ *nm* Vedaism.

végétal, **~e**, *mpl* **-aux** /veʒetal, o/ **I** *adj* (propre aux plantes) [*cellule, tissu, anatomie, pathologie*] plant (*épith*); (venant des plantes) [*huile, teinture, origine*] vegetable (*épith*).
II *nm* vegetable, plant.

végétalien, **-ienne** /veʒetaljɛ̃, ɛn/ *adj, nm,f* vegan.

végétalisme /veʒetalism/ *nm* veganism.

végétarien, **-ienne** /veʒetaʀjɛ̃, ɛn/ *adj, nm,f* vegetarian; **être ~** to be a vegetarian.

végétarisme /veʒetaʀism/ *nm* vegetarianism.

végétatif, **-ive** /veʒetatif, iv/ *adj* Bot, Physiol vegetative; **vie végétative** vegetative life.

végétation /veʒetasjɔ̃/ **I** *nf* Bot vegetation.
II végétations *nfpl* Méd adenoids.

végéter /veʒete/ [14] *vi* [*personne*] to vegetate; [*affaires, marché, projet*] to stagnate.

véhémence /veemɑ̃s/ *nf* vehemence; **avec ~** vehemently.

véhément, **~e** /veemɑ̃, ɑ̃t/ *adj* [*personne, discours, propos*] passionate, vehement; [*orateur*] passionate.

véhiculaire /veikylɛʀ/ *adj* **langue ~** lingua franca.

véhicule /veikyl/ *nm* **1** (moyen de transport) vehicle; **~ blindé** armoured[GB] vehicle; **2** (moyen d'expression) vehicle (**de** for).
■ **~ lourd** heavy goods vehicle; **~ de tourisme** private car; **~ sanitaire** ambulance; **~ utilitaire** commercial vehicle.

véhiculer /veikyle/ [1] *vtr* (transporter) to carry, transport [*personnes, marchandises*]; (transmettre) to carry [*substance, virus, message, idée*]; **~ des rumeurs** to circulate ou spread rumours[GB]; **~ une image** to promote an image; **le cholestérol est véhiculé dans le sang** cholesterol is carried in the blood.

veille /vɛj/ *nf* **1** (jour précédent) **la ~** the day before; **la ~ au soir** the night ou evening before; **la ~ de l'examen/de notre départ** the day before the exam/before we left; **passer la ~ de Noël/du Jour de l'An** to spend Christmas/New Year's Eve; **la ~ de sa mort, il se sentait mieux** the day before he died, he was feeling better; **en cette ~ de Pâques 1951** the day before this Easter of 1951; **en cette ~ d'élections** on the eve of these elections; **à la ~ de** (juste avant) on the eve of [*guerre, élections*]; **être à la ~ de faire** to be on the verge of doing; **2** Physiol (état normal) waking; (état forcé) vigil; **une nuit de ~** an all-night vigil; **être en état de ~** to be awake; **pendant l'état** or **en période de ~, leur température augmente** while they're awake, their temperature increases; **ses longues heures de ~ l'ont épuisée** the many hours without sleep have worn her out; **3** (garde) watch; **des heures de ~** hours on watch.
■ **~ technologique** *keeping up with technological innovations*.

veillée /veje/ *nf* **1** (soirée) evening; **les longues ~s d'hiver** the long winter evenings; **à la ~** in the evening; **2** (auprès d'un malade) vigil.
■ **~ d'armes** Hist knightly vigil; fig on the eve of battle; **~ funèbre** or **mortuaire** wake.

veiller /veje/ [1] **I** *vtr* to watch over [*blessé, malade*]; to keep watch over [*mort*].
II *vtr ind* **1** (penser) **~ à** to look after; **~ au bonheur/bien-être de qn** to look after sb's happiness/well-being; **~ au bon déroulement de qch** to see to it that something goes smoothly; **~ à sa santé** to look after one's health; **veille à fermer la porte** make sure that you close the door; **~ à ce que** to make sure that, to see to it that; **veillez à ce que tout se passe bien** make sure that everything goes smoothly; **2** (protéger) **~ sur** to watch over; **~ sur un enfant** to watch over a child.
III *vi* **1** (rester éveillé) to stay up; **~ au chevet** or **auprès de qn** to sit up at sb's bedside; **2** (monter la garde) to be on watch; **3** (être vigilant) to be watchful; **heureusement, la police veille** fortunately, the police are there.
IDIOMES **~ au grain** to be on one's guard.

veilleur, **-euse** /vɛjœʀ, øz/ **I ▶510** *nm,f* (guetteur) look-out.
II veilleuse *nf* **1** (lampe) night light; **mettre une lampe en veilleuse** to dim a light; **2** (d'appareil à gaz) pilot light; **3** Aut side light GB, parking light US; **il était en veilleuses** he had his side lights on.
■ **~ de nuit** night watchman.
IDIOMES **mets-la en veilleuse**◐! put a sock in it◐! GB, can it◐! US; **mettre qch en veilleuse** to put sth on the back burner [*projet, entreprise*].

veinard○, **~e** /venaʀ, aʀd/ **I** *adj* lucky, jammy○ GB.
II *nm,f* lucky ou jammy○ GB devil○.

veine /vɛn/ *nf* **1** Anat vein; **ne pas avoir de sang dans les ~s** fig to have no guts○; **▶ saigner**; **2** Bot (nervure) vein; **les ~s** (de chou, marbre) the veining **₵**; (de bois) the grain **₵**; **3** Mines (de charbon) seam; (de métal) vein; **exploiter une ~** lit to work a seam; fig to milk a subject for all it's worth; **4** (inspiration) inspiration; **~ poétique** poetic inspiration; **de** or **dans la même ~** in the same vein; **être en ~ de générosité** to be in a generous mood; **5**○ (chance) luck; **il a de la ~** (en général) he's lucky; (cette fois) he's in luck; **il n'a pas de ~** (en général) he's unlucky; (cette fois) he's out of luck; **ne pas avoir de ~ avec qn/qch** to have no luck with sb/sth; **avoir une ~ de pendu** or **cocu**○ to have the luck of the devil○; **coup de ~** stroke of luck; **c'est bien ma ~** that's just my luck; **pas de ~**! hard luck!; **tu as de la ~/c'est une ~ qu'il soit là** you're lucky/it's lucky he's here.

■ **~ cave** vena cava; **~ coronaire** coronary vein; **~ jugulaire** jugular vein; **~ porte** portal vein; **~ pulmonaire** pulmonary vein.

veiné, **~e** /vene/ *adj* [*peau, main, marbre*] veined; [*bois*] grained; **marbre ~ de rose** pink-veined marble; **pomme ~e de rouge** apple streaked with red.

veineux, **-euse** /vɛnø, øz/ *adj* **1** Anat [*circulation, système*] venous; **2** [*bois*] grainy; [*marbre*] veined.

veinule /venyl/ *nf* Anat, Bot venule.

veinure /venyʀ/ *nf* (du bois) grain ₵; (du marbre) veining ₵.

vêlage /vɛlaʒ/ *nm* **1** Vét (de vache) calving; **2** Géog (d'iceberg) calving.

vélaire /velɛʀ/ **I** *adj* velar.

II *nf* velar consonant.

vélarisation /velaʀizasjɔ̃/ *nf* velarization.

velcro® /vɛlkʀo/ *nm* velcro®; **fermeture (par) ~** velcro fastening.

vêlement /vɛlmɑ̃/ *nm* = **vêlage**.

vêler /vɛle/ [1] *vi* [*vache*] to calve.

vélin /velɛ̃/ *nm* vellum.

véliplanchiste /veliplɑ̃ʃist/ *nmf* windsurfer.

velléitaire /vɛlleitɛʀ/ **I** *adj* [*personne, tempérament*] weak-willed.

II *nmf* waverer.

velléité /vɛlleite/ *nf* (désir vague) vague desire; (tentative) vague attempt; **avoir des ~s d'indépendance** to feel a vague desire to be independent; **juguler toute ~ d'action** to suppress any vague desire to act; **étouffer les ~s de réforme** to put down any vague attempts at reform; **il n'a pas manifesté la moindre ~ de résistance** he did not show the slightest inclination to resist; **à la moindre ~ de rébellion** at the slightest sign of rebellion.

vélo○ /velo/ *nm* **1** (bicyclette) bike○; **c'est plus facile en** or **à ~** it's easier by bike; **aller en ville en ~** to go into town by bike, to cycle into town; **faire 10 kms en ~** to cycle 10 kms; **2** ▶ **449** (sport) cycling; **faire du ~** to cycle, to go cycling.

■ **~ d'appartement** exercise bike; **~ de course** racing bike; **~ tout terrain**, **VTT** mountain bike.

véloce /velɔs/ *adj* liter [*personne*] fleet of foot littér (*jamais épith*); [*animal*] swift; [*doigts*] nimble.

vélocipède /velosipɛd/ *nm* velocipede.

vélocité /velɔsite/ *nf* (de pianiste) nimble-fingeredness; (de footballeur) speed; (d'animal) swiftness; **exercices de ~** Mus finger exercises; Tech velocity.

vélo-cross /velokʀɔs/ *nm inv* **1** ▶ **449** (sport) cyclo-cross; **faire du ~** to go cyclo-cross racing; **2** (vélo) cyclo-cross bike.

vélodrome /velodʀom/ *nm* velodrome.

vélomoteur /velomɔtœʀ/ *nm* moped.

vélomotoriste /velomɔtɔʀist/ *nmf* moped rider.

véloski /veloski/ ▶ **449** *nm* **1** (engin) skibob; **2** (sport) skibobbing.

velours /vəluʀ/ *nm* (lisse) velvet; (à côtes) corduroy, cord; **rideau en** or **de ~** velvet curtain; **avoir une peau de ~** to have a velvety skin; **yeux de ~** doe eyes; **avoir des yeux de ~** to be doe-eyed; **cette sauce/ce vin c'est du ~** this sauce/this wine is as smooth as velvet.

■ **~ côtelé** corduroy, cord.

IDIOMES **une main de fer dans un gant de ~** an iron fist in a velvet glove; **jouer sur du ~** to have it made○; **faire patte de ~** [*chat*] to draw in its claws; [*hypocrite*] to switch on the charm.

velouté, **~e** /vəlute/ **I** *adj* **1** (doux) [*peau*] velvety, velvet (*épith*); [*pêche, pelage, tissu, son*] velvety; (suave) [*sauce, vin*] smooth; [*regard*] mellow; **2** Tech **papier ~** flock wallpaper; **tissu ~** material with a raised velvet design.

II *nm* **1** Culin (sauce) velouté sauce; (potage) **~ d'asperges/de champignons** cream of asparagus/of mushroom soup; **2** (douceur) (au toucher) softness; (au goût) smoothness; **le ~ de sa peau** his/her velvety skin, his/her velvet skin.

velouter /vəlute/ [1] **I** *vtr* **1** to give a velvety softness to [*joue*]; to soften [*voix, regard*]; to make [sth] smooth [*sauce*]; **2** Tech to give a velvet finish to [*papier, tissu*].

II se velouter *vpr* [*voix*] to become mellow; [*regard*] to soften.

velouteux, **-euse** /vəlutø, øz/ *adj* velvety.

Velpeau® /vɛlpo/ *npr* **bande ~** Méd crepe bandage, Ace bandage® US.

velu, **~e** /vəly/ *adj* [*personne, animal, insecte*] hairy; [*plantes*] villous.

velum, **vélum** /velɔm/ *nm* **1** (pièce de tissu) canopy, awning; **2** (membrane) velum.

vélux® /velyks/ *nm inv* Velux® window.

venaison /vənɛzɔ̃/ *nf* game; (daim) venison.

vénal, **~e**, *mpl* **vénaux** /venal, o/ *adj* **1** (intéressé) [*personne, sentiment*] venal; [*comportement*] mercenary; **2** Comm [*valeur*] monetary.

vénalité /venalite/ *nf* venality.

vendable /vɑ̃dabl/ *adj* saleable[GB]; **cette voiture n'est pas ~** this car is impossible to sell.

vendange /vɑ̃dɑ̃ʒ/ *nf* grape harvest; **~ de médailles** fig harvest of medals; **faire la ~** or **les ~s** [*vigneron*] to harvest the grapes; [*saisonnier*] to go grape-picking; **pendant les ~s** during the grape harvest.

vendanger /vɑ̃dɑ̃ʒe/ [13] **I** *vtr* to harvest [*raisin*]; to pick the grapes from [*vigne*]; **machine à ~** mechanical grape harvester.

II *vi* Agric (cueillir) to harvest the grapes.

vendangeur, **-euse** /vɑ̃dɑ̃ʒœʀ, øz/ **I** *nm,f* grape-picker.

II vendangeuse *nf* **1** (machine) mechanical grape harvester; **2** Bot aster.

Vendée /vɑ̃de/ ▶ **692** *nprf* (région, département) **la ~** the Vendée.

vendéen, **-éenne** /vɑ̃deɛ̃, ɛn/ ▶ **692** *adj* of the Vendée.

Vendéen, **-éenne** /vɑ̃deɛ̃, ɛn/ ▶ **692** *nm,f* (natif) native of the Vendée; (habitant) inhabitant of the Vendée.

vendémiaire /vɑ̃demjɛʀ/ *nm* Vendémiaire (*first month of the French revolutionary calendar, ≈ October*).

venderesse /vɑ̃dʀɛs/ *nf* Jur vendor.

vendetta /vɑ̃dɛtta/ *nf* vendetta.

vendeur, **-euse** /vɑ̃dœʀ, øz/ *nm,f* **1** ▶ **510** (employé de magasin) shop assistant, salesclerk US, salesperson; **'recherchons ~s expérimentés'** 'experienced salespersons ou shop assistants GB wanted'; **on demande un ~ au rayon fruits, s'il vous plaît** we need an assistant at the fruit counter, please; **2** ▶ **510** Entr (responsable des ventes) salesperson, salesman/saleswoman; **c'est un excellent ~** he's an excellent salesman; **3** (dans une transaction) seller; Jur vendor; **il y a litige entre l'acheteur et le ~** there's a litigation dispute between the buyer and the seller ou vendor; **désolé mais je ne suis pas ~** sorry but I'm not selling.

■ **~ ambulant** Comm pedlar GB, peddler US; **~ de journaux** newsvendor GB, newsdealer; **~ de rêve** pedlar of dreams.

vendre /vɑ̃dʀ/ [6] **I** *vtr* **1** Comm, Écon, Fin to sell (**à** to); **~ à crédit** to sell on credit; **~ en gros** to wholesale, to sell [sth] wholesale; **~ au détail** to retail; **~ à la pièce** to sell [sth] singly; **~ au poids** to sell [sth] by weight; **~ qch par trois/quatre** to sell sth in sets of three/four ou in threes/fours; **~ à perte** to sell [sth] at a loss; **~ bon marché/cher** to sell [sth] cheaply/at a high price; **il m'a vendu sa voiture 20 000 francs** he sold me the car for 20,000 francs; **ça fait ~** it boosts sales; **~ ses charmes/faveurs** to sell one's charms/favours[GB]; **'à ~'** 'for sale'; **ma voiture n'est pas à ~** my car is not for sale; **être vendu comme neuf** to be sold as new; **être vendu comme esclave** to be sold into slavery; **2** (trahir) to betray, to shop○ GB [*personne, complice*] (**à** to); to sell [*secrets, plans*].

II se vendre *vpr* **1** (être vendu) to be sold; **ces produits ne se vendent pas en France** these products are not sold ou are not available in France; **ça se vend uniquement en pharmacie** it's only sold ou available in chemists' GB ou pharmacies; **se ~ à la pièce/au poids** to be sold singly/by the weight; **2** (trouver acquéreur) to sell; **se ~ bien/mal** to sell well/badly; **savoir se ~** fig [*personne*] to know how to sell oneself; **3** (se compromettre) to sell out (**à** to); (pour de l'argent) to sell oneself (**à** to); **se ~ à l'ennemi** to sell out to the enemy. ▶ **lentille**, **ours**.

IDIOMES **il vendrait père et mère pour arriver à ses fins** he' d give anything to get what he wants.

vendredi /vɑ̃dʀədi/ ▶ **750** *nm* Friday; **~ treize** Friday the thirteenth; **~ saint** Good Friday.

IDIOMES **tel qui rit ~ dimanche pleurera** Prov there'll be tears before long.

vendu, **~e** /vɑ̃dy/ **I** *pp* ▶ **vendre**.

II *pp adj* (corrompu) [*juge, arbitre, fonctionnaire*] bribed; **~, l'arbitre!** the referee's a traitor!

III *nm,f* traitor; **c'est un ~!** he's sold out, he's a traitor.

venelle /vənɛl/ *nf* alleyway.

vénéneux, **-euse** /venenø, øz/ *adj* [*champignon, plante*] poisonous.

vénérable /veneʀabl/ **I** *adj* (respectable) [*personne*] venerable; [*arbre, objet*] ancient; **par respect pour son âge ~** out of respect for his great age.

II *nm* **1** Relig (titre) Venerable; **2** (de loge maçonnique) Grand Master.

vénération /veneʀasjɔ̃/ *nf* veneration; **avoir** or **éprouver de la ~ pour qn** to worship ou venerate sb.

vénérer /veneʀe/ [14] *vtr* **1** Relig to venerate; **2** (respecter) to revere [*personne*]; **~ la mémoire de qn** to venerate sb's memory.

vénerie /venʀi/ *nf* hunting, venery spéc.

vénérien, **-ienne** /veneʀjɛ̃, ɛn/ *adj* venereal; **maladie vénérienne** venereal disease, VD.

vénérologie /venerɔlɔʒi/ *nf* venereology.

vénérologue /venerɔlɔg/ ▶ **510** *nmf* venereologist.

Vénétie /venesi/ ▶ **692** *nf* **la ~** Venetia.

veneur /vənœʀ/ *nm* huntsman; ▶ **grand**.

Venezuela /venezɥela/ ▶ **321** *nprm* Venezuela.

vénézuélien, **-ienne** /venezɥeljɛ̃, ɛn/ ▶ **537** *adj* Venezuelan.

Vénézuélien, **-ienne** /venezɥeljɛ̃, ɛn/ ▶ **537** *nm,f* Venezuelan.

vengeance /vɑ̃ʒɑ̃s/ *nf* **1** (concept) revenge; **par ~** out of revenge; **esprit de ~** spirit of revenge; **crier ~** to cry out for revenge; **2** (acte) revenge (**contre** against); **un acte de ~** an act of revenge; **mettre sa ~ à exécution** to get one's revenge; **ma ~ sera terrible!** my vengeance will be terrible!

IDIOMES **la ~ est un plat qui se mange**

froid Prov revenge is a dish best eaten cold Prov.

venger /vɑ̃ʒe/ [13] **I** *vtr* to avenge [*crime, injustice, personne*]; **~ l'honneur/la mort de qn** to avenge sb's honour[GB]/death.

II se venger *vpr* to get ou take one's revenge (**de qn** on sb; **en faisant** by doing); **se ~ sur qn/qch** to take it out on sb/sth; **je me vengerai!** I shall have ou get my revenge!; **se ~ de qch** to get ou take one's revenge for [*humiliation, duperie*]; **il l'a fait pour se ~** he did it in revenge.

vengeur, **vengeresse** /vɑ̃ʒœʀ, vɑ̃ʒʀɛs/ **I** *adj* [*personne, acte, propos*] vengeful; [*bras, épée*] avenging; [*lettre, communiqué*] vindictive; **pointer un index ~** to point menacingly.

II *nm,f* avenger.

véniel, **-ielle** /venjɛl/ *adj* **1** Relig [*péché*] venial; **2** (excusable) [*faute, oubli*] excusable, pardonable.

venimeux, **-euse** /vənimø, øz/ *adj* **1** [*insecte, dard, plante*] venomous, poisonous; **2** [*personne, remarque*] venomous, poisonous; [*ton, haine*] venomous.

venin /vənɛ̃/ *nm* **1** (substance) venom; **~ de serpent** snake venom; **2** (haine) venom; **cracher son ~** to speak with great venom; **répandre son ~ contre qn** to make venomous ou poisonous remarks about sb; **remarque pleine de ~** venomous ou poisonous remark.

venir /vəniʀ/ [36] **I** *v aux* **1** (marque l'occurrence) **~ aggraver la situation** to make the situation worse; **~ contribuer au chômage** to push unemployment up; **2** (marque le mouvement) **le ballon est venu rouler sous mes pieds/atterrir○ dans notre jardin** the ball rolled up to my feet/landed in our garden; **3** (marque le développement) **et si je venais à tomber malade?** what if I should fall ill GB ou get sick US?; **s'il venait à pleuvoir** if it should rain; **même s'il venait à changer d'avis** even if he were to change his mind; **s'il venait à l'apprendre** if he ever got to hear about it; **s'il venait à la quitter** if he ever left her; **quand il venait à sortir** when he happened to go out; **la maladie vint à s'aggraver** the illness became more serious; **il en vint à la détester** he came to hate her.

II *vi* **1** (dans l'espace) to come; **viens quand tu veux** come whenever you like; **je viens** or **suis venu pour m'excuser** I've come to apologize; **il est venu (droit) sur moi** he came straight up to me; **tu peux toujours ~ chez moi/dans mon bureau/à Londres/au Canada/en Irlande** you can always come to my house/to my office/to London/to Canada/to Ireland; **il vient beaucoup de gens le samedi** lots of people come on Saturdays; **la route vient jusqu'ici** the road comes this far; **l'eau leur venait aux genoux** the water came up to their knees; **~ de loin/de Hongkong** to come from far away/from Hong Kong; **allez, viens!** come on!; **d'où viens-tu?** (reproche) where have you been?; **j'en viens** I've just been there; **il est venu quelqu'un pour toi** (encore là) someone's here to see you; (reparti) someone came to see you; **je viens de sa part** he/she sent me to see you; **faire ~ qn** (demander) to send for sb, to get sb○; (obtenir) to get sb to come; (attirer) to attract sb; **faire ~ le plombier** to send for the plumber, to get the plumber in; **tu ne pourras jamais la faire ~** you'll never get her to come; **faire ~ les clients** to attract customers, to bring in the customers; **faire ~ le médecin** to call the doctor; **c'est le champagne qui le fait ~** he comes for the champagne; **pourquoi nous avoir fait ~ si tôt?** why did they get us to come here so early?; **faire ~ qch** (commander) to order sth; (par la poste) to send for sth; **faire ~ son thé du Yunnan/ses chaussures d'Italie** to get one's tea from Yunnan province/one's shoes from Italy; **je suis venu ce soir vous parler du racisme**

> **venir**
>
> ***venir de* + infinitif**
>
> *venir* verbe auxiliaire servant à former le passé immédiat:
>
> *venir de faire* = to have just done
> *elle vient (tout juste) de partir* = she's (only) just left
> *il venait de se marier* = he'd just got married
> *je viens de te le dire* = I've just told you
>
> Attention aux exceptions du genre:
>
> *vient de paraître* = (pour un livre) 'just published!' (mais pour un disque) 'new release'
>
> ***venir* + infinitif**
>
> La traduction de la construction dépend du temps:
>
> *j'ai demandé au plombier de venir vérifier la chaudière* = I asked the plumber to come and check the boiler
> *le plombier viendra vérifier la chaudière* = the plumber will come and check the boiler
> *le plombier vient vérifier la chaudière aujourd'hui* = the plumber is coming to check the boiler today
>
> *te rappelles-tu quel jour le plombier est venu vérifier la chaudière?* = can you remember which day the plumber came to check the boiler?
>
> *il était venu vérifier la chaudière et il en a profité pour réparer le robinet de l'évier* = he had come to check the boiler and took the opportunity to mend the tap on the sink
>
> *viens voir* = come and see
>
> Cependant, pour les activités sportives, on aura:
>
> *elle a décidé de venir nager* = she has decided to come swimming
> *elle a décidé de venir faire du cheval* = she has decided to come riding
>
> On pourra aussi avoir:
>
> *viens déjeuner* = come for lunch (*lunch* étant un nom)
> *venez nous voir un de ces jours* = come over sometime *ou* (*GB*) come round sometime
>
> Exemples supplémentaires et exceptions sont présentés ci-dessous aussi bien pour *venir* verbe auxiliaire **I**, que pour *venir* verbe intransitif **II**.

I've come here tonight to talk to you about racism; **plantes venues d'ailleurs** plants from far-off places; **produits venus d'ailleurs** imported products; **gens venus d'ailleurs** (étrangers) foreigners; (des extérieurs) outsiders; **le nom ne me vient pas à l'esprit** the name escapes me; **les mots ne venaient pas** he/she etc couldn't find the words; **l'inspiration ne venait pas** inspiration failed him/her etc; **ça m'est venu tout d'un coup** (une idée) it suddenly came to me; **l'idée lui vint que** the idea occurred to him/her that; **ça ne m'est jamais venu à l'idée** or **l'esprit** it never crossed my mind ou occurred to me; **il ne m'est jamais venu à l'idée** or **l'esprit de te mentir/qu'il pourrait mentir** it never occurred to me to lie to you/that he would lie; **il lui est venu une idée bizarre** he/she had a weird idea; **un sourire lui vint aux lèvres, il lui vint un sourire aux lèvres** he/she gave a smile; **2** (dans le temps) **il faut prendre les choses comme elles viennent** you must take things as they come; **ça vient, ça vient○!** it's coming!, it's on its way!; **l'année qui vient** the coming year; **dans les années à ~** in the years to come; **dans les jours à ~** in the next few days; **le moment venu** (au futur) when the time comes; (au passé) when the time came; **quand le printemps viendra** when spring comes; **(il) viendra un jour où il le regrettera** the day will come when ou there'll come a day when he'll regret it; **la nuit va bientôt ~** it'll soon be dark; **le moment du départ est venu** it's time to leave; **dans l'heure qui vient** within the hour; **les difficultés à ~** future problems; **attends, ça va ~** wait, it's coming; **je préfère laisser** or **voir ~ (les choses)** I'd rather wait and see how things turn out; **alors, ça vient○?, ça vient oui ou non○?** (une réponse) am I ever going to get an answer○?; (une personne) are you ever coming?; **comment êtes-vous venu à l'enseignement?** how did you come to take up teaching?; **~ en troisième position** to come third; **~ loin derrière** to trail a long way behind; **~ ensuite** to follow, to come next; **il est venu un moment où j'étais trop fatigué** I got to the point when I was too tired; **3** (marquant l'origine) **~ d'une famille protestante** to come from a Protestant family; **~ du grec** to come from the Greek; **de quelle école vient-il?** what school did he go to?; **cette bague me vient de ma tante** my aunt left me this ring; **le succès du roman vient de son style** the novel's success is due to its style; **ça vient du fait que la situation a changé** it stems from the fact that the situation has changed; **ça vient de ce qu'ils ne se parlent pas** it's all because they don't talk to each other; **d'où vient qu'il ne comprend jamais?** how is it that he never understands?, how come he never understands?; **d'où vient que vous êtes triste?** why are you sad?; **de là vient qu'il est toujours angoissé** hence his continual anxiety, that's why he's always anxious; **ça me vient naturellement** or **tout seul** that's just the way I am; **4** (dans une hiérarchie) **~ après/avant** to come after/before; **la famille vient avant le reste** the family comes before everything else; **5 en venir à** to come to; **j'en viens au problème qui vous préoccupe** I now come to your problem; **en ~ à abandonner ses études** to get to the point of dropping out; **s'il faut en ~ là** if it gets to that point, if it comes to that; **il en était venu à la faire suivre/vouloir se suicider** he even had her followed/considered suicide; **comment a-t-elle pu en ~ à de telles extrémités?** how could she have resorted to such desperate measures?; **ils y viendront d'eux-mêmes** (à une idée) they'll come round of their own accord; **venons-en à l'ordre du jour** let's get down to the agenda; **où veut-il en ~ (au juste)?** what's he driving at?; **en ~ aux mains** to come to blows; **ils en sont venus aux coups** they came to blows.

Venise /vəniz/ ▶ 857 *npr* Venice.

vénitien, **-ienne** /venisjɛ̃, ɛn/ **I** *adj* Venetian.

II ▶ 462 *nm* Ling Venetian dialect.

Vénitien, **-ienne** /venisjɛ̃, ɛn/ *nm,f* Venetian.

vent /vɑ̃/ *nm* **1** Météo wind; **~ d'est/du nord** east/north wind; **~ du large** seaward wind; **grand ~** strong wind; **~ de côté** crosswind; **il fait** or **il y a du ~** it's windy, there's a wind blowing; **le ~ tourne** lit, fig the wind is turning; **voir de quel côté souffle le ~** lit, fig to see which way the wind is blowing; **coup** or **rafale de ~** gust of wind; **emporté par le ~** blown away by the wind; **flotter** or **claquer au ~** to flap in the wind; **nez au ~** nose in the air; **cheveux au ~** hair flying in the wind; **exposé/ouvert à tous les ~s** exposed/open to all weathers; **en plein ~** lit exposed to the wind; (dehors) in the open; **passer en coup de ~** fig to rush through; **elle était coiffée en coup de ~** her hair was tousled; **faire du ~** (avec éventail) to create a breeze; hum (en s'activant) to flap around; ▶ **semer**, **décorner**, **quatre**; **2** Naut **~ favorable**, **bon ~** favourable[GB] wind, fair wind; **~ mauvais** unfavourable[GB] wind; **~ arrière** following wind; **~ debout** or **contraire** headwind; **naviguer (par) ~ arrière** or **sous le ~** to sail before the wind; **naviguer (par) ~ debout** or **contre le ~** to sail into the wind; **avoir le ~ en poupe** lit to sail ou run before the wind; fig to have the wind in one's sails; **~ frais** strong breeze; **coup de ~** fresh gale; **fort coup de ~** strong gale; **côté sous le ~** leeward side; **côté du ~** winward side; **3** Chasse **prendre le ~** [*chien*] to pick up the scent; [*personne*] to get the feel of things; **4** (impulsion) **un ~ de liberté/révolte** a wind of freedom/revolt; **un ~ de folie soufflait dans le pays** a wave of madness swept through the country; **le ~ du changement** the wind of change; **5** euph (flatulence) wind ₵; **lâcher un ~** to break wind; **avoir des ~s** to have wind.

■ **~ alizé** trade wind; **~ coulis** draught GB ou draft US; **~ de sable** desert wind; **~ solaire** solar wind.

IDIOMES **filer** or **aller** ou **courir comme le ~** to be as swift as the wind; **c'est du ~!** fig it's just hot air!; **du ~**○**!** (partez) get lost○!; **bon ~**○**!** good riddance!; **quel bon ~ vous amène?** to what do I ou we owe the pleasure (of your visit)?; **être dans le ~** to be trendy; **avoir ~ de qch** to get wind of sth; **contre ~s et marées** [*faire*] come hell or high water; [*avoir fait*] against all odds.

Vent /vɑ̃/ ▶ 416 *nprm* **les îles du ~** the Windward Islands.

ventail, *pl* **ventaux** /vɑ̃taj, o/ *nm* **1** Hist (de heaume) visor; **2** = **vantail**.

vente /vɑ̃t/ *nf* sale; **être en ~** to be for sale; **en ~ chez votre marchand de journaux** available ou for sale at your newsagent's; **en ~ libre** gén freely available; [*médicaments*] available over the counter, available without prescription; **mettre qch en ~** to put [sth] up for sale [*maison, commerce*]; to put [sth] for sale [*objet*]; **mise en ~** (de maison, commerce) putting up for sale; (d'objet) putting on sale; **équipe/technique/surface de ~** sales team/technique/area; **directeur/service des ~s** sales manager/department; **il s'occupe de la ~** he's in sales; **avoir l'expérience de la ~** to have sales experience.

■ **~ par correspondance**, **VPC** Comm mail order selling; **~ à découvert** Fin short sale; **~ au détail** retailing; **~ aux enchères** auction (sale); **~ forcée** hard sell; **~ en gros** wholesaling.

venté, **~e** /vɑ̃te/ *adj* windswept.

venter /vɑ̃te/ [1] *v impers* to blow; **il vente** the wind is blowing; **qu'il pleuve, qu'il neige ou qu'il vente** come rain or shine.

venteux, **-euse** /vɑ̃tø, øz/ *adj* [*journée, mois*] windy; [*région, pays*] windswept.

ventilateur /vɑ̃tilatœʀ/ *nm* gén fan; (aérateur) ventilator; (extracteur) extractor fan GB, exhaust fan US.

ventilation /vɑ̃tilasjɔ̃/ *nf* **1** (aération) ventilation; (système) ventilation (system); **2** (répartition) (de personnel) ventilation; (de tâches, matériaux) allocation; (de dépenses, déficit, résultats) Compta (action) breaking down; (résultat) breakdown (**de** of); **3** Jur separate valuation.

■ **~ pulmonaire** Méd pulmonary ventilation.

ventiler /vɑ̃tile/ [1] *vtr* **1** (aérer) to ventilate [*pièce, moteur*]; **2** Méd to ventilate [*malade*]; **3** Compta to break down [*dépenses, bénéfices*]; **4** (diviser) to divide up [*groupe, ensemble*]; (répartir) to assign [*personnel*]; to allocate [*tâches, matériaux*]; **5** Jur (dans vente globale) to value [sth] separately.

ventôse /vɑ̃toz/ *nm* Ventôse (*sixth month of the French revolutionary calendar*, ≈ *March*).

ventouse /vɑ̃tuz/ *nf* **1** (d'adhésion) suction pad GB, suction cup US; **crochet à ~** suction hook; **faire ~** to stick; **2** (pour déboucher) plunger; **faire un bruit de ~** to make a sucking noise; **3** Bot, Zool sucker; (chez la grenouille) adhesive disc; **4** Méd cupping glass; **poser des ~s à qn** to cup sb.

ventral, **~e**, *mpl* **-aux** /vɑ̃tʀal, o/ *adj* [*nageoire*] ventral; **parachute ~** lap-pack parachute; **rouleau ~** straddle roll.

ventre /vɑ̃tʀ/ ▶ 188 *nm* **1** (abdomen, estomac) stomach, tummy○, belly; **s'allonger sur le ~** to lie on one's stomach, to lie face down; **rentrer le ~** to hold in one's stomach; **avoir du ~** gén to have a fat stomach; (homme) to have a paunch; **avoir mal au ~** to have stomach-ache ou tummy-ache○; **cela me donne mal au ~ de voir ça** fig it makes me ill to see it; **avoir le ~ creux/plein** to have an empty/a full stomach; **se remplir le ~**○ (se nourrir) to fill one's belly; (trop manger) to gorge oneself péj; **le ~ de la terre** liter the bowels of the earth littér; **voyons ce que la chaudière a dans le ~** let's have a look at the inside of the boiler; **2** (d'animal) (under)belly; **le poisson flottait ~ à l'air** the fish was floating belly up; **3** (utérus) womb; **dans le ~ de sa mère** in his mother's womb; **4** (siège du courage) **ne rien avoir dans le ~** to have no guts○; **avoir la rage/la peur au ~** to feel sick with fury/fear; **je ne sais pas ce qu'il a dans le ~**○ I don't know what he's made of; **5** (partie renflée) (de marmite, bateau, d'avion) belly; **6** Tech **faire ~** [*mur*] to bulge out; [*plafond*] to sag; **7** Phys (d'onde) antinode.

■ **le ~ de Paris** *the former covered market in Paris*.

IDIOMES **courir ~ à terre** to run flat out; **tu as les yeux plus gros que le ~** your eyes are bigger than your stomach.

ventrebleu† /vɑ̃tʀəblø/ *excl* begad†!

ventrée○ /vɑ̃tʀe/ *nf* **une ~ de** a bellyful of○; **se mettre une (bonne) ~ de prunes** to stuff oneself○ with plums.

ventre-saint-gris† /vɑ̃tʀəsɛ̃gʀi/ *excl* begad†!, gadzooks†!

ventriculaire /vɑ̃tʀikylɛʀ/ *adj* ventricular.

ventricule /vɑ̃tʀikyl/ *nm* Anat **1** (de cœur, d'encéphale) ventricle; **2** (d'oiseau) ventriculus.

ventrière /vɑ̃tʀijɛʀ/ *nf* **1** (de selle) girth; **2** (de charpente) purlin; **3** (de navire) bilge block.

ventriloque /vɑ̃tʀilɔk/ ▶ 510 *nmf* ventriloquist.

ventriloquie /vɑ̃tʀilɔki/ *nf* ventriloquism.

ventripotent, **~e** /vɑ̃tʀipɔtɑ̃, ɑ̃t/ *adj* portly, fat-bellied péj.

ventru, **~e** /vɑ̃tʀy/ *adj* [*homme*] paunchy, pot-bellied; [*marmite, meuble*] rounded; [*mur*] bulging.

venu, **~e** /vəny/ **I** *pp* ▶ **venir**.

II *pp adj* **1** (à propos) **bien ~** [*plaisanterie, commentaire, critique*] apt; **mal ~** [*décision, plaisanterie*] badly timed; **être mal ~ à** or **de critiquer** [*personne*] to be the last person who should criticize; **il serait mal ~ de le leur dire** it wouldn't be a good idea to tell them; **2** (réussi) **bien ~** [*œuvre, plaisanterie*] clever.

III *nm,f* **nouveau ~** newcomer; ▶ **premier**.

IV venue *nf* visit; **la ~e du ministre** the minister's visit; **attendre la ~e du médecin** to wait for the doctor to come; **les raisons de sa ~e sont obscures** it's not clear why he/she came; **~e au monde** birth; **~e du Messie** coming of the Messiah; **lors de ta ~e, nous ferons** when you come we shall do, during your visit we shall do.

Vénus /venys/ **I** *npr* Mythol Venus; **la ~ de Milo** the Venus de Milo.

II *nprf* Astron Venus.

vêpres /vɛpʀ/ *nfpl* Relig vespers.

ver /vɛʀ/ *nm* **1** Zool worm; (dans le bois) woodworm; (dans la nourriture) maggot, grub; **être mangé par les ~s** to be worm-eaten; **2** Méd (parasite) worm; **avoir des ~s** to have worms.

■ **~ blanc** cockchafer grub; **~ luisant** glowworm; **~ plat** flatworm; **~ rond** round worm; **~ de sable** sandworm; **~ à soie** silkworm; **~ solitaire** tapeworm; **~ de terre** earthworm; **~ de vase** bloodworm.

IDIOMES **être nu comme un ~** to be stark naked; **tirer les ~s du nez à qn**○ to worm information out of sb; **le ~ est dans le fruit** the rot has already set in.

véracité /veʀasite/ *nf* truthfulness, veracity sout; **douter de la ~ de qch** to doubt the veracity of sth, to doubt whether sth is true; **être convaincu de la ~ des dires de qn** to be convinced of the veracity ou truthfulness of sb's testimony, to be sure that sb is telling the truth.

véranda /veʀɑ̃da/ *nf* veranda; **sous la ~** on the veranda.

verbal, **~e**, *mpl* **-aux** /vɛʀbal, o/ *adj* **1** (oral) [*promesse, accord, joute*] verbal; **2** (de langage) [*débordement, attaque, violence*] verbal; **3** Ling (de verbe) [*groupe, locution, adjectif*] verbal; [*catégorie, forme*] verb (*épith*); **syntagme ~** verb phrase.

verbalement /vɛʀbalmɑ̃/ *adv* verbally; **s'engager ~** to make a verbal commitment (**à faire** to do); **agresser qn ~** to be verbally aggressive with sb.

verbalisation /vɛʀbalizasjɔ̃/ *nf* **1** Psych verbalization; **2** (d'infraction) recording of an offence.

verbaliser /vɛʀbalize/ [1] **I** *vtr* Psych to verbalize [*sentiments*].

II *vi* (dresser procès-verbal) to record an offence[GB].

verbe /vɛʀb/ *nm* **1** Ling verb; **2** (langage) language; **la magie du ~** the magic of words ou language; **avoir le ~ facile** to be quick to talk; **avoir le ~ fleuri** to use flowery language; **avoir le ~ haut** to be arrogant in one's speech; **3** Relig **le Verbe** the Word.

■ **~ actif** active verb; **~ d'action** action ou dynamic verb; **~ défectif** defective verb; **~ d'état** stative verb; **~ impersonnel** impersonal verb; **~ intransitif** intransitive verb; **~ passif** passive verb; **~ pronominal** reflexive verb; **~ transitif** transitive verb.

verbeux, **-euse** /vɛʀbø, øz/ *adj* [*personne, orateur, style*] verbose; [*discours*] wordy.

verbiage /vɛʀbjaʒ/ *nm* (abondance de paroles) verbiage, verbosity.

verbosité /vɛʀbozite/ *nf* verbosity.

verdâtre /vɛʀdɑtʀ/ ▶ 193 *adj* pej greenish.

verderolle /vɛʀdəʀɔl/ *nf* (**rousserolle**) **~** marsh warbler.

verdeur /vɛʀdœʀ/ *nf* **1** (truculence) rawness; **2** (vigueur) sprightliness; **3** (acidité) tartness, acidity.

verdict /vɛʀdikt/ *nm* **1** Jur (décision de jury) verdict; **rendre un ~** to return ou announce a verdict; **~ d'acquittement** verdict of not guilty, acquittal; **~ de culpabilité** guilty verdict, verdict of guilty; **2** fig (appréciation) verdict, judgment; **le ~ des urnes/de la critique/du public** the electorate's/critics'/public's verdict; **un ~ sans appel** a verdict ou judgment without appeal.

verdier /vɛʀdje/ *nm* greenfinch.

verdir /vɛʀdiʀ/ [3] *vi* **1** (devenir vert) gén to turn green; [*cuivre*] to tarnish; **2** (pâlir) to turn pale.

verdoyant, **~e** /vɛʀdwajɑ̃, ɑ̃t/ *adj* green, verdant littér.

verdoyer /vɛʀdwaje/ [23] *vi* liter **1** (être vert) to be green ou verdant littér; **2** (devenir vert) to turn green ou verdant littér.

verdunisation /vɛʀdynizasjɔ̃/ *nf* chlorination.

verdure /vɛʀdyʀ/ *nf* **1** (végétation) greenery; **maison perdue dans la ~** house swathed in greenery; **2** (légumes verts) green vegetables (*pl*); **3** (couleurs) verdure littér, greenness.

véreux, **-euse** /veʀø, øz/ *adj* **1** (contenant des vers) [*fruit*] wormy; **2** (malhonnête) [*politicien, avocat*] bent○, crooked; [*affaire, contrat*] dodgy○ GB, shady○, dubious.

verge /vɛʀʒ/ *nf* **1** Anat penis; **2** (pour battre) switch, birch.
IDIOMES **donner des ~s pour se faire battre** to make a rod for one's own back.

vergé /vɛʀʒe/ *nm* laid paper.

vergeoise /vɛʀʒwaz/ *nf* brown sugar.

verger /vɛʀʒe/ *nm* orchard; **un ~ en fleurs** an orchard in bloom.

vergeté, **~e** /vɛʀʒəte/ *adj* [*peau*] streaked.

vergeture /vɛʀʒətyʀ/ *nf* stretch mark.

verglaçant, **~e** /vɛʀglasɑ̃, ɑ̃t/ *adj* **pluie ~e** freezing rain.

verglacé, **~e** /vɛʀglase/ *adj* icy.

verglas /vɛʀgla/ *nm* black ice; **attention aux plaques de ~** look out for patches of black ice.

vergogne: **sans vergogne** /sɑ̃vɛʀgɔɲ/ **I** *loc adv* **1** (sans honte) shamelessly; **2** (sans hésitation) straight out.
II *loc adj* (sans scrupule) unscrupulous.

vergue /vɛʀg/ *nf* Naut yard.
■ **~ de hunier** topsail yard; **~ de misaine** foreyard; **~ de perroquet** topgallant yard.

véridique /veʀidik/ *adj* [*détail, histoire, fait*] true; [*description, témoignage*] truthful; **l'anecdote est ~** the story is true.

vérifiable /veʀifjabl/ *adj* [*histoire, récit, source, méthode*] verifiable sout; **être facilement ~** to be easy to check ou verify.

vérificateur, **-trice** /veʀifikatœʀ, tʀis/ ▶ 510 *nm,f* controller.
■ **~ aux comptes** auditor.

vérification /veʀifikasjɔ̃/ *nf* (d'appareil, expérience) check (**de** on); (d'alibi, de fait) verification; **procéder à** or **effectuer des ~s** to carry out checks (**sur** on); **une ~ d'identité** an identity check; **~ faite, après ~** on checking, after checking; **après les ~s d'usage** after the usual checks.
■ **~ aux comptes** audit.

vérifier /veʀifje/ [2] **I** *vtr* **1** (tester) to check [*appareil, instrument*]; (contrôler) to check [*identité, adresse, norme, calcul*]; **~ que/si** to check that/if ou whether; **vérifie que la fenêtre est fermée** check that the window is closed; **2** (confirmer) to verify, check [*affirmation, témoignage*]; to confirm [*événement, hypothèse*]; to verify [*fait*]; **attendez, je vais ~** hold on, I'll just check; **l'information reste à ~** the information has still to be checked; **l'hypothèse n'est pas vérifiée dans les faits** the hypothesis is not borne out by the facts.
II se vérifier *vpr* [*hypothèse, théorie*] to be borne out; **se ~ dans les faits** to be borne out by the facts.

vérin /veʀɛ̃/ *nm* (screw) jack.
■ **~ hydraulique** hydraulic jack; **~ pneumatique** pneumatic jack.

véritable /veʀitabl/ *adj* **1** (authentique) [*ami*] true, genuine, real; [*sentiment, discussion*] true, real; [*artiste*] true; [*cuir*] real, genuine; [*or, argent*] real; **2** (réel) [*nom, raison, responsable*] real, actual; [*colère*] real; [*joie*] true; **voici la ~ histoire de**... this is the real ou true story of...; **sous leur jour ~** in their true light; **3** (intensif) (*before n*) real, veritable; **c'est une ~ catastrophe!** it's an absolute ou real catastrophe!; **un ~ forcené** an absolute maniac; **la pièce est une ~ fournaise/glacière** the room is like an oven/a fridge.

véritablement /veʀitabləmɑ̃/ *adv* **1** (dans la réalité) really, actually; **a-t-elle ~ du chagrin?** does she really feel any grief?; **ces mesures n'ont jamais été ~ appliquées** these measures have never really ou actually been applied; **2** (intensif) **c'est ~ un scandale!** it really is a scandal!

vérité /veʀite/ *nf* **1** gén truth; **au nom de la ~** in the name of truth; **la ~ historique** historical truth; **posséder** or **détenir la ~** to know everything; **le quart d'heure** or **la minute de ~** the moment of truth; **l'épreuve de ~** the acid test; **faire la ~ sur qch** to disclose the truth about sth; **il y a une part de ~ dans ce qu'il dit** there's some truth in what he says; **c'est la pure ~** that's the absolute truth; **à la ~** to tell the truth; **en ~, je n'en suis pas sûr** to tell the truth, I'm not sure about it; **c'est un type extraordinaire, en ~** he's an extraordinary character, that's for sure; **2** (affirmation vraie) truth; **une ~ éternelle** an eternal truth; **énoncer des ~s premières** to state the obvious; **toute ~ n'est pas bonne à dire** some things are better left unsaid; ▶ **quatre**; **3** (authenticité) (de personnage, scène, reconstitution) realism; (de sentiment, d'expression) sincerity; **4** (nature profonde) true nature; **la ~ de qn** sb's true nature; **la ~ des choses/de l'art** the true nature of things/of art.
■ **~ de La Palice** truism.
IDIOMES **à chacun sa ~** Prov each to his own; **en ~ je vous le dis** verily I say unto you; **la ~ sort de la bouche des enfants** Prov out of the mouths of (very) babes (and sucklings).

verjus /vɛʀʒy/ *nm* verjuice.

verlan /vɛʀlɑ̃/ *nm*: *French slang formed by inverting the syllables.*

vermeil, **-eille** /vɛʀmɛj/ **I** ▶ 193 *adj* **1** fml (rouge vif) bright red; **teint ~** rosy complexion; **2** Vin **vin ~** ruby wine.
II *nm* (argent doré) vermeil.

vermicelle /vɛʀmisɛl/ *nm* **des ~s** vermicelli ¢.
■ **~s chinois** rice noodles.

vermiculaire /vɛʀmikylɛʀ/ *adj* vermiform.

vermiforme /vɛʀmifɔʀm/ *adj* vermiform.

vermifuge /vɛʀmifyʒ/ **I** *adj* [*comprimé, sirop*] worm (*épith*), anthelmintic spéc.
II *nm* wormer, anthelmintic spéc.

vermillon /vɛʀmijɔ̃/ ▶ 193 **I** *adj inv* (rouge vif) bright red, vermilion.
II *nm* **1** (couleur) bright red, vermilion; **2** (sulfure de mercure) vermilion, cinnabar.

vermine /vɛʀmin/ *nf* **1** (parasites) vermin; **être rongé par la ~** to be eaten away by vermin; **2** (personnes) scum, vermin.

vermisseau, *pl* **~x** /vɛʀmiso/ *nm* small earthworm.

Vermont /vɛʀmɔ̃/ ▶ 692 *nprm* Vermont.

vermoulu, **~e** /vɛʀmuly/ *adj* **1** [*planche, mobilier*] worm-eaten, wormy US; **2** [*idéologie, institutions*] moth-eaten.

vermout(h) /vɛʀmut/ *nm* vermouth.

vernaculaire /vɛʀnakylɛʀ/ *adj, nm* vernacular.

vernal, **~e** /vɛʀnal/ *adj* Astron vernal.

verni, **~e** /vɛʀni/ **I** *pp* ▶ **vernir**.
II *pp adj* lit [*bois, peinture*] varnished; [*chaussures*] patent-leather (*épith*); [*faïence*] glazed.
III○ *adj* (chanceux) lucky; **il n'est pas ~** he's unlucky.

vernier /vɛʀnje/ *nm* vernier (scale).

vernir /vɛʀniʀ/ [3] **I** *vtr* Tech to varnish [*planche, meuble*]; to glaze [*faïence, poterie*]; to apply nail varnish GB ou nail polish to, to varnish GB ou polish [*ongles*].
II se vernir *vpr* **se ~ les ongles** to apply nail varnish GB ou nail polish to one's nails, to varnish GB ou polish one's nails.

vernis /vɛʀni/ *nm* **1** (pellicule solide) (sur bois) varnish; (sur céramique) glaze; **une couche de ~** a coat of varnish; **2** (apparence) veneer; **un ~ de culture/de modernisme** a veneer of culture/modernism; **si on gratte le ~, on s'aperçoit que**... if you scratch the surface, you'll see that...
■ **~ du Japon** lacquer ou varnish tree; **~ à ongles** nail varnish GB ou polish.

vernissage /vɛʀnisaʒ/ *nm* **1** Art preview, private view; **le ~ de l'exposition** the private view of the exhibition; **2** Tech (de bois) varnishing; (de céramique) glazing.

vernissé, **~e** /vɛʀnise/ *adj* **1** [*tuiles, carreaux*] glazed; **2** [*plumes, feuilles*] glossy.

vernisser /vɛʀnise/ [1] *vtr* to glaze.

vernisseur, **-euse** /vɛʀnisœʀ, øz/ ▶ 510 *nm,f* (de meubles) varnisher; (de poterie) glazer.

vérole /veʀɔl/ ▶ 271 *nf* **1**○ (syphilis) syphilis; **2**† (variole) pox†.

vérolé○, **~e** /veʀɔle/ *adj* **1** (par la syphilis) pox-ridden○; **2** (en mauvais état) rotten.

Vérone /veʀɔn/ ▶ 857 *npr* Verona.

véronique /veʀɔnik/ *nf* **1** (plante) speedwell, veronica spéc; **2** (en tauromachie) veronica.

verrat /veʀa/ *nm* studboar.

verre /vɛʀ/ *nm* **1** (matière) glass; **de** or **en ~** glass (*épith*); **fabriquer du ~** to make ou manufacture glass; **industrie du ~** glass industry; **travail du ~** glasswork; **des débris de ~** broken glass ¢; **2** (récipient) glass; **~ à eau/vin/cognac** water/wine/brandy glass; **~s et couverts** glassware and cutlery; **lever son ~ à la santé de qn** to raise one's glass to sb; **remplir/vider son ~** to fill/empty one's glass; ▶ **casser**; **3** (contenu) glass, glassful; **j'ai bu un grand ~ de jus de fruit** I drank a large glass(ful) of fruit juice; **un ~ d'eau/de vin** a glass of water/wine; **4** (boisson) drink; **offrir un ~ à qn** to buy sb a drink; **prendre un ~** to have a drink; **un petit ~** a quick drink; **avoir bu un ~ de trop** to have had one too many; **boire le ~ de l'amitié** to toast one's friendship; **5** (plaque) glass; **monter une gravure/photo sous ~** to mount an engraving/a photograph under glass; **changer le ~ d'un cadre** to change the glass in a frame; **mettre qch sous ~** to put sth under glass; **6** Phys (lentille) lens; **~ concave/convexe** concave/convex lens; **~s de lunettes** spectacle lenses; **~ grossissant** magnifying glass.
■ **~ antireflets** anti-glare glass; **~ armé** wired glass; **~ blanc** white glass; **~ cathédrale** cathedral glass; **en ~ consigné** returnable bottle; **~ de contact** contact lens; **~ correcteur** corrective lens; **~ à dents** toothglass; **~ dépoli** frosted glass; **~ doseur** measuring glass; **~ feuilleté** laminated glass; **~ filé** spun glass; **~ filtrant** light protective glass; **~ flotté** floatglass; **~ fumé** (pour lunettes) tinted lens; (pour vitrage) tinted glass; **~ gradué** measuring jug; **~ de lampe** lamp chimney; **~ de montre** Chimie watch-glass; **~ à moutarde** cheap glass; **~ optique** optical glass; **en ~ perdu** nonreturnable; **~ à pied** stemmed glass; **~ plat** flat glass; **~ de silice** silica ou quartz glass; **~ soufflé** blown glass; **~ textile** textile glass.

verrerie /vɛʀʀi/ *nf* **1** (fabrication) glassmaking; **2** (objets) glassware; **3** (usine) glassworks (*pl*), glass factory.

verrier, **-ière** /vɛʀje, ɛʀ/ **I** *adj* glass (*épith*).
II ▶ 510 *nm* glassmaker, glass manufacturer.
III verrière *nf* **1** (toit vitré) glass roof; **2** (grand vitrage) glass wall, glassed-in wall; **3** (de cockpit) canopy.

verroterie /vɛʀɔtʀi/ *nf* glass jewellery GB ou jewelry US.

verrou /vɛʀu/ *nm* gén bolt; (à bouton) deadbolt; (à clé) deadlock; **~ 3 points** multilock; **mettre le ~** to shoot the bolt; **pousser** or **tirer le ~** (fermer) to shoot the

bolt; (ouvrir) to draw the bolt; **fermer [qch] au ~** to bolt [*fenêtre, porte*].
■ **~ haute sécurité** high security door lock; **~ de sûreté** double security lock.
IDIOMES **être sous les ~s** to be under lock and key; **mettre** or **placer qn sous les ~s** to put ou place sb under lock and key, to lock sb up; **faire sauter un ~** to overcome an obstacle.

verrouillage /vɛʀujaʒ/ *nm* (action) bolting; (d'arme à feu) locking; (dispositif) locking mechanism.
■ **~ central** or **centralisé (des portes)** Aut central locking; **~ de fichier** Ordinat file locking; **~ radar** lock on.

verrouiller /vɛʀuje/ [1] *vtr* **1** gén to bolt [*fenêtre, porte*]; to lock [*portière, arme*]; to cordon off [*quartier*]; **~ une majorité parlementaire** to protect a parliamentary majority; **2** Ordinat to lock.

verrue /vɛʀy/ *nf* Méd wart.
■ **~ plantaire** verruca, plantar wart spéc.

verruqueux, **-euse** /vɛʀykø, øz/ *adj* wart-like, verrucose spéc.

vers[1] /vɛʀ/ *prép*

■ **Note** Lorsque *vers* indique une direction, une tendance ou une orientation, il se traduit généralement par *toward(s)*. On notera que *towards* est plus courant en anglais britannique et *toward* en anglais américain.
– Lorsque *vers* fait partie d'une expression du genre *se tourner vers, tendre vers, départ vers etc* la traduction est donnée respectivement à ***tourner, tendre, départ***.
– On trouvera ci-dessous des usages particuliers de *vers*.

1 lit (en direction de) toward(s); **il vint ~ moi** he came toward(s) me; **elle courut ~ l'enfant** she ran toward(s) the child; **il n'a même pas tourné la tête ~ elle** he didn't even look in her direction; **se déplacer de la gauche ~ la droite** to move from left to right; **des exportations ~ le Japon** exports to Japan; **des migrations ~ le sud** migration to the south; **il habite plus ~ le nord** he lives further north; **'~ les quais'** (sur un panneau) 'to trains'; **2** fig (en direction de) to, toward(s); **un premier pas ~ la négociation** a first step toward(s) negotiation; **une association tournée ~ la culture** a culture-oriented association; **3** (aux environs de) (lieu) near, around; (temps) about; (période) toward(s); **on s'arrêtera ~ Dijon pour déjeuner** we'll stop for lunch near Dijon; **c'est ~ les 3 000 m d'altitude qu'elle s'est sentie mal** she started feeling ill GB ou sick US at an altitude of about 3,000 m; **les rues sont toujours encombrées ~ le centre-ville** the streets are always congested around the town centre[GB]; **~ cinq heures/le 10 juillet/l'an 2000** about five o'clock/10 July/the year 2000; **~ le soir** toward(s) evening; **~ la fin du mois de septembre** toward(s) ou around the end of September; **il a vécu jusque ~ l'âge de 80 ans** he lived to about the age of 80; **elle est tombée malade ~ l'âge de 25 ans** she became ill GB ou sick US when she was about 25.

vers[2] /vɛʀ/ **I** *nm inv* (ligne de poésie) line (of verse); **le premier/troisième ~** the first/third line; **un ~ de douze syllabes** a line of twelve syllables; **un poème/une pièce en ~** a poem/a play in verse.
II *nmpl* (poésie) poetry **¢**; **dire/faire des ~** to recite/write poetry ou verse.
■ **~ blanc** blank verse; **~ héroïque** heroic verse; **~ libre** free verse; **~ de mirliton** doggerel **¢**.

versant /vɛʀsɑ̃/ *nm* side.

versatile /vɛʀsatil/ *adj* [*personne*] unpredictable, volatile.

versatilité /vɛʀsatilite/ *nf* unpredictability, volatility.

verse: **à verse** /avɛʀs/ *loc adv* **il pleut à ~** it's pouring down.

versé, **~e** /vɛʀse/ *adj* **très ~ en** well-versed in; **il est fort peu ~ dans l'art de flatter** he's not at all well-versed in the art of flattery.

Verseau /vɛʀso/ **▶ 874** *nprm* Aquarius.

versement /vɛʀsəmɑ̃/ *nm* **1** (de somme) payment; **~ comptant** cash payment; **le ~ de l'impôt peut s'effectuer sur place** tax can be paid in person; **2** (échelonné) instalment[GB]; **en plusieurs ~s** by instalments[GB]; **3** (dépôt) deposit; **~ en espèces** cash deposit; **faire un ~ sur son compte** to pay money into one's account; **bulletin** or **bordereau de ~** paying-in GB ou deposit US slip.

verser /vɛʀse/ [1] **I** *vtr* **1** (servir) to pour [*boisson*] (**dans** into); (transvaser) to pour [*liquide, sable, terre*]; (sans précautions) to tip [*liquide, sable, terre*]; **~ à boire à qn** to pour sb a drink; **verse-moi un peu de vin** pour me some wine; **verse du détergent sur la tache** pour some detergent on the stain; **attention, tu verses à côté** careful, you're spilling it; **▶ huile**; **2** (payer) to pay [*somme, arrhes, pension*] (**à qn** to sb; **sur** into); **on leur verse une commission** they get a commission; **il lui verse une pension alimentaire** he gives her alimony; **mon employeur verse mon salaire sur mon compte bancaire** my employer pays my salary into my bank account; **3** (répandre) to shed [*larme, sang*]; **~ le sang** to shed blood; **~ son sang pour la patrie** liter to be wounded fighting for one's country littér; **~ des larmes sur qn/qch** to shed tears over sb/sth; **4** (ajouter) to add (**à** to); **~ une pièce à un dossier** to add a document to a file; **5** Mil (affecter) to assign (**dans** to); **~ qn dans la cavalerie/l'infanterie** to assign sb to the cavalry/the infantry.
II *vi* **1** (se renverser) to overturn; **~ dans le fossé** to topple into the ditch; **2** (se laisser aller à) to lapse (**dans** into); **il verse un peu trop dans le mélodrame** he tends to be melodramatic; **3** (laisser couler) [*cruche*] to pour.

verset /vɛʀsɛ/ *nm* **1** (de la Bible, du Coran) verse; **2** (prière) versicle; **3** Littérat verset.

verseur, **-euse** /vɛʀsœʀ, øz/ *adj* pouring; **flacon ~** bottle with a pouring spout.

versificateur, **-trice** /vɛʀsifikatœʀ, tʀis/ *nm, f* (poète) poet; péj versifier.

versification /vɛʀsifikasjɔ̃/ *nf* versification.

versifier /vɛʀsifje/ [2] **I** *vtr* to put [sth] into verse [*poème, texte*].
II *vi* to versify.

version /vɛʀsjɔ̃/ *nf* **1** (traduction) translation (*into one's own language*); **une ~ latine** a latin translation; **une épreuve de ~** a translation test; **2** (interprétation) version; **j'ai entendu une toute autre ~ de l'incident** I heard a completely different version of the incident; **la ~ officielle** the official version; **3** Cin, Littérat, Mus version; **une nouvelle ~ du quatuor** a new version of the quartet; **la ~ de 1948** the 1948 version; **en ~ espagnole** in the Spanish version; **la ~ américaine d'un film français** the American version of a French film; **~ intégrale/abrégée** complete/abridged version; **4** Ind, Comm (modèle) model, version; **la ~ GTI de cette voiture** the GTI model of this car.
■ **~ doublée** Cin dubbed version; **~ longue** Cin full-length version; **~ originale**, **vo** Cin original version; **en ~ originale (sous-titrée)** in the original language (with subtitles).

verso /vɛʀso/ *nm* back, verso spéc; **voir au ~** see over(leaf); **▶ recto**.

vert, **~e** /vɛʀ, vɛʀt/ **I ▶ 193** *adj* **1** gén green; [*région, pays*] green, verdant littér; **~ foncé/clair** dark/light green; **une banlieue ~e** a leafy suburb; **être ~ de peur** to be white with fear, to look green around the gills○; **▶ mûr**; **2** (non arrivé à maturité) [*fruit, légume*] green, unripe; [*bois*] green; [*vin*] immature; **3** (vigoureux) [*vieillard*] sprightly; **elles sont loin mes ~es années!** the years of my youth are long past!; **4** (sévère) (*before n*) [*semonce, réprimande*] sharp, stiff.
II ▶ 193 *nm* green; **une robe d'un ~ hideux** a dress of a hideous green (colour[GB]); **je suis passé au (feu) ~** I went through when the light was green; **le feu est passé au ~** the light went ou turned green.
III verts *nmpl* Pol **les ~s** the environmentalists, the ecologists GB; **les Verts** the French Green party.
■ **~ amande** almond (green); **~ bouteille** bottle green; **~ d'eau** sea-green; **~ émeraude** emerald green; **~ galant** old charmer; **~ olive** olive green; **~ pistache** pistachio green; **~ pomme** apple green; **~ tilleul** sage green.
IDIOMES **en dire de ~es** to tell spicy ou risqué stories; **avoir les doigts ~s**, **avoir la main ~e** to have green fingers GB ou a green thumb US; **se mettre au ~**○ to take a break in the country.

vert-de-gris /vɛʀdəgʀi/ **I ▶ 193** *adj inv* blue-green.
II *nm* Tech verdigris.

vert-de-grisé, *pl* **vert-de-grisés** /vɛʀdəgʀize/ *adj* **1** (oxydé) covered in verdigris; **2 ▶ 193** (couleur) blue-green.

vertébral, **~e**, *mpl* **-aux** /vɛʀtebʀal, o/ *adj* vertebral.

vertèbre /vɛʀtɛbʀ/ *nf* vertebra; **les ~s cervicales/dorsales/lombaires** cervical/dorsal/lumbar vertebrae; **se déplacer une ~** to slip a disc.

vertébré, **~e** /vɛʀtebʀe/ **I** *adj* vertebrate.
II *nm* vertebrate.

vertement /vɛʀtəmɑ̃/ *adv* sharply.

vertex /vɛʀtɛks/ *nm* vertex.

vertical, **~e**, *mpl* **-aux** /vɛʀtikal, o/ **I** *adj* **1** Math, gén [*axe, plan, mouvement, position, décollage*] vertical; [*miroir, panneau*] upright; **la station ~e** standing position; **2** (selon une hiérarchie) [*intégration, organisation, croissance*] vertical.
II verticale *nf* Math, Phys vertical; **mettre qch à la ~e** to put sth upright; **le rocher se dresse à la ~e** the rock rises sheer.

verticalement /vɛʀtikalmɑ̃/ *adv* **1** gén [*se déplacer, tomber, plonger*] vertically; **2** (dans les mots croisés) down.

verticalité /vɛʀtikalite/ *nf* verticality.

vertige /vɛʀtiʒ/ *nm* **1** (sensation) dizziness, giddiness; (dû à la hauteur) vertigo; **avoir le ~** (habituellement) to suffer from vertigo; (ponctuellement) to feel dizzy ou giddy; **être pris de ~** lit, fig to become dizzy ou giddy; **donner le ~ à qn** fig, lit to make sb dizzy ou giddy; **2** (malaise) dizzy ou giddy spell, attack of vertigo; **avoir des ~s** to have dizzy ou giddy spells; **3** (exaltation) **~ de l'amour/de la gloire/du succès** intoxicating effect of love/of fame/of success.

vertigineux, **-euse** /vɛʀtiʒinø, øz/ *adj* [*hauteur*] dizzy, giddy; [*profondeur, ascension*] breathtaking; [*allure, vitesse*] breathtaking, breakneck (*épith*); [*somme, chute, augmentation, progression*] staggering.

vertu /vɛʀty/ **I** *nf* **1** (intégrité) (moral) virtue; **d'une grande ~** of great moral virtue; **2** (chasteté) virtue, honour[GB]; **perdre/protéger sa ~** to lose/protect one's virtue or honour[GB]; **de petite ~** of easy virtue; **3** (qualité) quality, virtue; **les ~s humaines** human qualities; **4** (propriété) (de plante, remède) property; (de choses abstraites) virtue; **des ~s cicatrisantes/digestives** healing/digestive properties.
II en vertu de *loc prép* Jur by virtue of, pursuant to [*article, loi, ordonnance*]; gén in accordance with [*accord, disposition, système*].
IDIOMES **faire de nécessité ~** to make a virtue of necessity.

vertueusement /vɛʀtɥøzmɑ̃/ *adv* virtuously.

vertueux, **-euse** /vɛʀtɥø, øz/ *adj* virtuous.

vertugadin /vɛʀtygadɛ̃/ *nm* farthingale.

verve /vɛʀv/ *nf* eloquence; **retrouver toute**

sa ~ to regain one's eloquence; **être très en ~** to be in sparkling form; **un livre plein de ~** an imaginative book.

verveine /vɛʀvɛn/ *nf* **1** Bot verbena; **2** (liqueur) **(liqueur de) ~** verbena liqueur; **3** (tisane) verbena tea; **boire une ~** to drink a cup of verbena tea.

vésical, ~e, *mpl* **-aux** /vezikal, o/ *adj* bladder (*épith*), vesical spéc.

vésicatoire /vezikatwaʀ/ *adj, nm* vesicant.

vésiculaire /vezikylɛʀ/ *adj* **1** Méd of the gall bladder (*après n*); **2** (en forme de vésicule) vesicular.

vésicule /vezikyl/ *nf* **1** Anat, Bot vesicle; **2** Méd (cloque) blister, vesicle spéc.

■ **~ biliaire** gall bladder; **~s séminales** Anat seminal vesicles.

vésiculeux, -euse /vezikylø, øz/ *adj* vesicular.

vespasienne /vɛspazjɛn/ *nf* public urinal.

vespéral, ~e, *mpl* **-aux** /vɛspeʀal, o/ **I** *adj* liter evening (*épith*).

II *nm* Relig vesperal.

vesse-de-loup, *pl* **vesses-de-loups** /vɛsdəlu/ *nf* puffball.

vessie /vesi/ *nf* bladder; **~ gazeuse** or **natatoire** air ou swim bladder.

IDIOMES **prendre des ~s pour des lanternes**○ to think the moon is made of green cheese; **faire prendre à qn des ~s pour des lanternes**○ to pull the wool over sb's eyes○.

vestale /vɛstal/ *nf* vestal virgin.

veste /vɛst/ *nf* jacket; **une ~ en lin/jean/cuir** a linen/denim/leather jacket; **~ à basques** jacket with basques; **tomber la ~**○ to take off one's jacket.

■ **~ de chasse** hunting jacket; **~ d'intérieur** smoking jacket; **~ de pyjama** pyjama GB ou pajama US jacket; **~ de survêtement** Sport tracksuit top.

IDIOMES **retourner sa ~**○ Pol to change sides, to sell out; **prendre une ~**○ to come a cropper○.

vestiaire /vɛstjɛʀ/ *nm* **1** (salle) (dans un stade, gymnase) changing GB ou locker room; (dans un musée, un théâtre, une discothèque) cloakroom; **dans les ~s du stade** in the stadium changing rooms GB; **demander son ~** to ask for one's coat; **laisser sa fierté/ses scrupules au ~** fig to forget one's pride/one's scruples; **laisser ses bonnes manières au ~** to leave one's good manners at home; **2** (meuble) locker.

vestibulaire /vɛstibylɛʀ/ *adj* Anat vestibular.

vestibule /vɛstibyl/ *nm* Archit **1** (d'édifice) hall; (d'hôtel, de théâtre) foyer GB, lobby; **2** Anat vestibule.

vestige /vɛstiʒ/ *nm* **1** (de construction, d'objet) relic; **les ~s d'un bâtiment/d'une ville** the remains of a building/of a town; **des ~s archéologiques** archeological remains; **l'unique ~ du château** the only relic of the castle, all that remains of the castle; **2** (d'époque, de tradition) vestige; **les ~s d'une civilisation** the vestiges of a civilization.

vestimentaire /vɛstimɑ̃tɛʀ/ *adj* **dépenses ~s** clothing expenses; **tenue ~** way of dressing; **mode ~** fashion; **règlement** or **code ~** dress code; **élégance ~** elegance in dress.

veston /vɛstɔ̃/ *nm* (man's) jacket.

Vésuve /vezyv/ *nprm* **le ~** Vesuvius.

vêtement /vɛtmɑ̃/ *nm* **1** (pièce d'habillement) item ou piece of clothing; **des ~s** clothes, clothing ¢; **~s d'été/d'hiver** summer/winter clothes; **si tu sors, prends un ~, il fait froid** put something on if you are going out, it's cold; **emporte des ~s chauds** take some warm clothes ou clothing; **~s de travail** workclothes; **ce ~ se vend très bien** this garment is selling very well; **un ~ de pluie** a raincoat; **~s du dimanche** Sunday best, Sunday clothes; **'~s pour hommes'** 'menswear', 'men's fashions'; **'~s pour dames/enfants'** 'ladies'/children's wear ou fashions'; **~s de ski** skiing clothes; **~s de sport** sportswear; **2** (secteur d'activité) clothing trade, garment industry US.

vétéran /veteʀɑ̃/ *nm* Mil, fig veteran (**de** of).

vétérinaire /veteʀinɛʀ/ **I** *adj* [*médecine, clinique*] veterinary.

II ▶**510** *nmf* vet, veterinary surgeon GB, veterinarian US.

vétille /vetij/ *nf* trifle.

vêtir /vɛtiʀ/ [33] **I** *vtr* (habiller) to dress [*personne, poupée*] (**de** in); (mettre) to put on [*vêtement, uniforme*].

II se vêtir *vpr* to dress (oneself), to get dressed (**de** in).

vétiver /vetivɛʀ/ *nm* vetiver.

veto /veto/ *nm* veto; **mettre** or **opposer son ~ à qch** to veto sth; ▶ **droit**.

vêtu, ~e /vety/ **I** *pp* ▶ **vêtir**.

II *pp adj* dressed; **être ~ de qch** to be dressed ou clad in sth, be wearing sth; **il est arrivé, tout de blanc ~** he arrived, dressed all in white; **être ~ de neuf** to be wearing brand new clothes; **à demi ~** half-dressed; **être bien/mal ~** to be well-/badly-dressed.

vétuste /vetyst/ *adj* (délabré) dilapidated, rundown; (obsolète) outdated.

vétusté /vetyste/ *nf* (délabrement) dilapidation (**de** of), run-down state (**de** of); (ancienneté) (great) age (**de** of), outdated state (**de** of).

vétyver /vetivɛʀ/ *nm* vetiver.

veuf, veuve /vœf, vœv/ **I** *adj* widowed; **être ~/veuve** to be a widower/widow; **jouer les veuves éplorées** to act the grief-stricken widow.

II *nm,f* widower/widow; **Mme Brun, veuve Dupont** Mrs Brun, the widow of Mr Dupont; ▶ **orphelin**.

III veuve *nf* **1**† ○(guillotine) guillotine; **2** (oiseau) whydah.

■ **veuve de guerre** war widow; **veuve noire** black widow (spider).

veule /vøl/ *adj* [*personne*] weak, spineless.

veulerie /vølʀi/ *nf* weakness, spinelessness.

veuvage /vœvaʒ/ *nm* **1** (perte du conjoint) loss of one's husband/wife; **2** (état de veuf) (state of) being a widower; (état de veuve) widowhood; **depuis son ~** since he/she was widowed.

veuve *adj, nf* ▶ **veuf**.

vexant, ~e /vɛksɑ̃, ɑ̃t/ *adj* (blessant) [*parole, refus*] hurtful (**pour** to); (contrariant) tiresome, vexing.

vexation /vɛksasjɔ̃/ *nf* humiliation.

vexatoire /vɛksatwaʀ/ *adj* **mesures ~s envers les immigrés** measures intended to humiliate immigrants.

vexer /vɛkse/ [1] **I** *vtr* **1** (blesser) to offend, to upset; **être vexé par qch/par qn** to be upset ou offended at sth/by sb; **2** (contrarier) to annoy.

II se vexer *vpr* to take offence[GB] (**de** at), to be upset (**de** at); **se ~ d'un rien** to take offence[GB] easily.

VHF /veaʃɛf/ *adj inv, nf* (*abbr* = **very high frequency**) VHF; **récepteur ~** VHF receiver.

VHS /veaʃɛs/ *nm* (*abbr* = **video home system**) VHS.

via /vja/ *prép* **1** (en passant par) via; **aller de Paris à Lyon ~ Dijon** to go from Paris to Lyons via Dijon; **2** (par l'intermédiaire de) via, through; **apprendre qch ~ qn/la presse** to hear about sth via ou through sb/the press.

viabilisé, ~e /vjabilize/ *adj* [*terrain*] with all mains services (*épith, après n*).

viabiliser /vjabilize/ [1] *vtr* to provide [sth] with mains services [*terrain*].

viabilité /vjabilite/ *nf* **1** (de fœtus) viability; **2** (de régime, d'entreprise) viability; **3** (de terrain) **assurer la ~ d'un terrain** to provide a building site ou plot with services; **travaux de ~** laying on GB ou installation US of services; **4** (de route) suitability for vehicles.

viable /vjabl/ *adj* **1** [*fœtus*] viable; **2** [*projet*] feasible; [*entreprise*] viable; [*situation*] bearable, tolerable; **leur collaboration n'est pas ~** their collaboration can't last.

viaduc /vjadyk/ *nm* viaduct.

viager, -ère /vjaʒe, ɛʀ/ Jur **I** *adj* [*rente, intérêt*] life (*épith*), for life (*épith, après n*); **à titre ~** for (the duration of one's) life.

II *nm* (rente) life annuity; **acheter qch en ~** to buy sth by paying a life annuity; **vendre qch en ~** to sell sth for a life annuity.

viande /vjɑ̃d/ *nf* **1** Culin meat; **~ de bœuf/mouton** beef/mutton; **2**◐ flesh; **toute cette ~ étalée sur la plage** all that bare flesh on the beach; **il va y avoir de la ~ froide**◐**!** somebody is going to get it!

■ **~ blanche** white meat; **~ des Grisons** dried beef; **~ noire** game; **~ rouge** red meat.

viander /vjɑ̃de/ [1] **I** *vi* [*cerf*] to graze.

II se viander◐ *vpr* to get smashed up○ GB, to get bunged up○ US.

viatique /vjatik/ *nm* **1** Relig viaticum; **2** comfort, support; **muni du seul ~ de** with nothing to sustain him/me etc but.

vibrant, ~e /vibʀɑ̃, ɑ̃t/ **I** *adj* **1** (animé de vibrations) [*coussin, lame*] vibrating; **2** (ému) [*voix*] resonant; [*discours*] vibrant; [*hommage*] glowing; [*plaidoyer*] impassioned; [*foule*] excited, feverish; **~ d'excitation/de colère/de joie** quivering with excitement/with anger/with joy.

II vibrante *nf* Ling vibrant; **~e battue** flap; **~e roulée** trill.

vibraphone /vibʀafɔn/ ▶**534** *nm* vibraphone, vibes○ (*pl*).

vibraphoniste /vibʀafɔnist/ ▶**510** *nmf* vibraphone player, vibes player.

vibrateur /vibʀatœʀ/ *nm* vibrator.

vibratile /vibʀatil/ *adj* **cils ~s** (vibratile) cilia.

vibration /vibʀasjɔ̃/ *nf* vibration; **ressentir/causer des ~s** to feel/cause vibrations; **~ de l'air (due à la chaleur)** shimmering of the air (in the heat); **traitement par ~s** vibromassage.

vibrato /vibʀato/ *nm* vibrato.

vibratoire /vibʀatwaʀ/ *adj* vibratory.

vibrer /vibʀe/ [1] **I** *vtr* to vibrate [*béton*].

II *vi* **1** (osciller) gén, Phys [*lame, son*] to vibrate; **2** (frémir) [*voix*] to quiver (**de** with); [*cœur*] to thrill; **elle vibrait de tout son être** liter she felt a thrill go through her; **on vibre en les écoutant** your spine tingles when you listen to them; **faire ~ l'âme/les foules** to stir the soul/the crowds; **faire ~ la corde patriotique/sociale** to rouse people's patriotism/social conscience.

vibreur /vibʀœʀ/ *nm* vibrator.

vibrion /vibʀijɔ̃/ *nm* **1** (bactérie) vibrio; **2**○ (enfant) fidget○.

vibrionner○ /vibʀijɔne/ [1] *vi* (s'agiter) to fidget○; (s'activer) to faff○ around GB, to dither.

vibrisse /vibʀis/ *nf* **1** (humaine) nostril hair; **2** (de chat) whisker, vibrissa spéc.

vibromasseur /vibʀomasœʀ/ *nm* vibromasseur.

vicaire /vikɛʀ/ *nm* curate.

■ **~ apostolique** vicar apostolic; **le ~ du Christ** the Vicar of Christ; **~ général** vicar general.

vicariat /vikaʀja/ *nm* vicariate.

vice /vis/ *nm* **1** (débauche) vice; **vivre dans le ~** to lead a dissolute life; **se lever à 4h du matin, c'est du ~** hum it's a sin to get up at 4 in the morning; **2** (mauvaise habitude) vice; **avoir tous les ~s** to have every possible vice; **mon ~, c'est le tabac** my vice is smoking; **3** (défaut physique) fault, defect.

■ **~ caché** hidden defect ou fault; **~ de**

conformation physical defect; **~ de construction** construction fault; **~ de fabrication** manufacturing fault; **~ de forme** technicality; **rejeté pour ~ de forme** dismissed on a technicality; **~ de procédure** legal irregularity.

vice-amiral, *pl* **-aux** /visamiʀal, o/ ▶ 390 *nm* ≈ rear-admiral; **~ d'escadre** ≈ vice-admiral.

vice-chancelier, *pl* **~s** /visʃɑ̃səlje/ ▶ 813 *nm* vice-chancellor.

vice-consul, *pl* **~s** /viskɔ̃syl/ *nm* vice-consul.

vicelard○, **~e** /vislaʀ, aʀd/ *adj* **1** (pervers) [*personne, regard*] depraved, corrupt; **2** (rusé) [*question, clause*] trick (*épith*); [*personne*] sly, sneaky; **c'est ~ de lui demander ça** it's not fair to ask him/her that.

vicennal, **~e**, *mpl* **-aux** /visenal, o/ *adj* Jur (qui dure 20 ans) [*loyer, plan*] twenty-year (*épith*); (qui se produit tous les 20 ans) [*événement*] occurring every 20 years (*épith, après n*).

vice-présidence, *pl* **~s** /vispʀezidɑ̃s/ *nf* (d'État) vice-presidency; (de comité, d'entreprise) vice-chairmanship, vice-presidency US.

vice-président, **~e**, *mpl* **~s** /vispʀezidɑ̃, ɑ̃t/ *nm,f* (de nation) vice-president; (de conseil, comité, d'entreprise) vice-chair(man), vice-president US.

vice-roi, *pl* **~s** /visʀwa/ ▶ 813 *nm* viceroy.

vicésimal, **~e**, *mpl* **-aux** /visezimal/ *adj* Math vicenary, in base 20 (*après n*).

vice(-)versa /visvɛʀsa/ *adv* vice versa.

vichy /viʃi/ **I** *nm* **1** (tissu) gingham; **une robe en ~** a gingham dress; **2** (eau) vichy water; **un ~ menthe** vichy water with peppermint cordial.
II *nf* (pastille) **(pastille) ~®** vichy mint.

Vichy /viʃi/ *npr* **1** ▶ 857 Géog Vichy; **2** Hist the Vichy government.

vichyssois, **~e** /viʃiswa, az/ ▶ 857 *adj* **1** of Vichy; **2** Culin **potage ~** vichyssoise.

vichyste /viʃist/ *adj* Hist **1** [*personne*] supporter of the Vichy government; **2** (relatif au gouvernement de Vichy) of the Vichy government.

vicier /visje/ [2] **I** *vtr* **1** Jur to invalidate [*élection, acte, contrat*]; **2** (altérer) to pollute [*air*]; to contaminate [*sang*].
II se vicier *vpr* [*air*] to become polluted.

vicieusement /visjøzmɑ̃/ *adv* **1** (pour tromper) deceitfully; **2** (de façon dépravée) lustfully.

vicieux, **-ieuse** /visjø, øz/ **I** *adj* **1** (dépravé) [*personne*] lecherous; **il faut être ~ pour aimer ça** you've got to be perverted to like that; **2** (sournois) [*personne*] sly; [*coup, attaque*] well-disguised; [*question*] trick (*épith*); [*argumentation*] deceitful; **3** (défectueux) [*locution, prononciation*] wrong; [*position*] abnormal; **un cercle ~** a vicious circle; **4** (indocile) [*cheval*] vicious.
II *nm,f* pervert.

vicinal, **~e**, *mpl* **-aux** /visinal, o/ *adj* Admin **chemin ~** byroad.

vicissitudes /visisityd/ *nfpl* (épreuves) trials and tribulations; (changements) vicissitudes, ups and downs○; **les ~ de la vie/l'histoire** the vicissitudes ou ups and downs of life/history; **les ~ de la mode/politique** the vagaries of fashion/politics.

vicomte /vikɔ̃t/ ▶ 813 *nm* viscount.

vicomté /vikɔ̃te/ *nf* viscountcy.

vicomtesse /vikɔ̃tɛs/ ▶ 813 *nf* viscountess.

victime /viktim/ *nf* **1** (d'accident, de désastre, phénomène) victim, casualty (**de** of); **le cyclone a fait de nombreuses ~s** the cyclone claimed many victims ou casualties; **les ~s des accidents de la route** road accident victims, road casualties; **leur entreprise fut l'une des ~s de la crise du pétrole** fig their firm was one of the casualties of the oil crisis; **être ~ de calomnies/d'une idéologie/des circonstances** fig to be a victim of slander/of an ideology/of circumstances; **être ~ d'un infarctus** to be the victim of a heart attack; **être ~ d'un complot** fig to be the victim of a conspiracy; **les ~s du cancer** cancer victims; **arrête de jouer les ~s** iron stop playing the victim iron; **le joueur, ~ d'une blessure au genou**... the player, suffering from a knee injury...; **~ d'une panne, il a abandonné la course** hit by mechanical problems, he abandoned the race; **il a été ~ de son succès/bon cœur/orgueil** his success/kindheartedness/pride has been his undoing; **2** Jur victim; **3** (créature offerte en sacrifice) sacrificial victim.

victoire /viktwaʀ/ *nf* gén victory (**sur** over; **contre** against); Sport win (**sur** over; **contre** against); **remporter une ~ écrasante** Pol, Sport to win a crushing victory; **~ aux élections** victory in the elections; **crier** or **chanter ~** to claim victory; **(remporter) une ~ sur soi-même** (to win) a personal battle.

victoria /viktɔʀja/ *nf* **1** (véhicule) victoria; **2** (plante) victoria.

Victoria /viktɔʀja/ **I** *npr* Victoria; **les chutes ~** the Victoria falls.
II ▶ 416, 459, 857 *npr* Géog (île, État, ville) Victoria; **le lac ~** Lake Victoria.

victorien, **-ienne** /viktɔʀjɛ̃, ɛn/ *adj* Victorian.

victorieusement /viktɔʀjøzmɑ̃/ *adv* triumphantly.

victorieux, **-ieuse** /viktɔʀjø, øz/ *adj* [*pays, armée*] victorious; [*athlète, équipe*] winning (*épith*), victorious; [*débuts, tir*] successful; [*sourire*] of victory (*épith, après n*); **être ~ de** to win victory over [*pays, équipe*]; to gain victory in [*compétition*].

victuailles /viktɥɑj/ *nfpl* Culin provisions, victuals.

vidage /vidaʒ/ *nm* **1** (d'une fosse, machine) emptying (**de** of); **2**○ (d'indésirables) throwing out (**de** of).

vidame /vidam/ *nm* Hist vidame.

vidange /vidɑ̃ʒ/ **I** *nf* **1** (de cuve, fosse, fossé) emptying (**de** of); **2** Aut oil change; **faire la ~** to change the oil; **huile de ~** waste oil; **3** (tuyau d'évacuation) (de baignoire) drain; (de lave-linge) waste pipe; **4** (cycle de lave-linge) emptying.
II vidanges *nfpl* **1** (matière) sewage ¢; **2** C (ramassage d'ordures) rubbish collection GB, garbage collection US.

vidanger /vidɑ̃ʒe/ [13] **I** *vtr* **1** to empty, to drain [*cuve, fosse*]; **2** to drain off [*liquide*].
II *vi* [*lave-linge*] to empty.

vidangeur /vidɑ̃ʒœʀ/ *nm* **1** (d'égout) sewage tanker driver; **2** C (éboueur) dustman GB, garbage collector US.

vidangeuse /vidɑ̃ʒøz/ *nf* sewer tanker.

vide /vid/ **I** *adj* **1** (sans contenu) [*lieu, boîte*] empty (**de** of); [*cassette, page*] blank; **ensemble ~** Math empty set; **les mains ~s** fig empty-handed; **~ de son contenu** empty of its contents; **pièce ~ de meubles** room empty of furniture; **tu l'as loué ~ ou meublé?** are you renting it unfurnished or furnished?, are you renting it empty or furnished?; **2** (dépeuplé, inoccupé) [*salle, rue, fauteuil*] empty (**de** of); [*appartement*] empty (**de** of), vacant; **la maison est ~ sans les enfants** the house seems empty without the children; **~ de tout habitant** empty of all inhabitants; **3** (sans intérêt, substance, idées) [*vie, slogan, esprit, journée*] empty; [*regard*] vacant; **se sentir ~** to feel empty; **j'ai la tête ~** my mind is a blank; **~ d'intérêt** devoid of any interest; **~ de sens** meaningless.
II *nm* **1** (espace) space; **suspendu dans le ~** dangling in space; **sauter** or **se jeter dans le ~** lit to jump into space; fig to leap into the unknown; **et au-dessous de lui, le ~** (alpiniste) and below him, a sheer drop; (acrobate) and nothing between him and the ground; **être attiré par le ~** to be drawn toward(s) the edge; **être penché au-dessus du ~** (en montagne) to be on the edge of a sheer drop; (d'une tour) to be leaning over and looking down into space; **regarder dans le ~** to stare into space; **parler dans le ~** (sans auditeur) to talk to oneself; (sans sujet) to talk at random; **promettre dans le ~** fig to make empty promises; **2** Phys vacuum; fig (absence à combler) vacuum; **~ absolu** absolute vacuum; **la nature a horreur du ~** nature abhors a vacuum; **emballé sous ~** vacuum packed; **du café sous ~** vacuum-packed coffee; **pompe à (faire le) ~** vacuum pump; **faire le ~** to create a vacuum; **faire le ~ autour de soi** fig to drive everybody away; **j'ai besoin de faire le ~ dans ma tête** I need to forget about everything; **3** (absence à combler) vacuum, void; (absence douloureuse) void; **~ politique/intellectuel** political/intellectual vacuum; **laisser/créer/combler un ~** to leave/create/fill a vacuum; **sa mort a laissé un grand ~ dans ma vie** his/her death left a great void ou emptiness in my life; **4** (vacuité) emptiness; **le ~ de l'existence/de leurs propos** the emptiness of life/of their words; **5** (trou) (entre deux objets) gap, empty space; (dans un emploi du temps) gap; **combler un** or **le ~** lit, fig to fill a gap.
III à vide *loc adv* (sans contenu) empty; (sans résultat) with no result; **la clé tourne à ~** the key is not catching; **essai à ~** no-load test; **camion à ~** truck without a load.
■ **~ juridique** gap ou lacuna in the law; **~ sanitaire** crawl space, underfloor ventilation space.

vidé, **~e** /vide/ **I** *pp* ▶ **vider**.
II○ *pp adj* (fatigué) worn out; **être ~ de son énergie** to be drained of energy.

vidéaste /videast/ ▶ 510 *nmf* video director.

vidéo /video/ **I** *adj inv* video; **équipement/jeu ~** video equipment/game.
II *nf* (équipement, film) video; **tourner un film en ~** to make a video.
■ **~ inverse** or **inversée** Ordinat reverse video.

vidéocassette /videokasɛt/ *nf* videotape, videocassette, video; **en ~** on video.

vidéoclip /videoklip/ *nm* TV (music) video.

vidéoclub /videoklœb/ *nm* video store, video shop GB.

vidéocommunication /videokɔmynikasjɔ̃/ *nf* link-up.

vidéoconférence /videokɔ̃feʀɑ̃s/ *nf* Télécom **1** (séance) video-conference; **2** (principe) video conferencing.

vidéodisque /videodisk/ *nm* videodisc.

vidéofréquence /videofʀekɑ̃s/ *nf* video frequency.

vidéogramme /videɔgʀam/ *nm* videogram.

vidéographie /videogʀafi/ *nf* videography.

vidéophone /videɔfɔn/ *nm* videophone.

vidéoprojecteur /videopʀɔʒɛktœʀ/ *nm* videoprojector.

vide-ordures /vidɔʀdyʀ/ *nm inv* rubbish GB ou garbage US chute.

vidéotex® /videɔtɛks/ *adj inv, nm inv* videotex®.

vidéothèque /videɔtɛk/ *nf* (de prêt) video library; (chez soi) video collection.

vide-poches /vidpɔʃ/ *nm inv* **1** (coupe) tidy; **2** Aut map compartment.

vide-pomme, *pl* **~s** /vidpɔm/ *nm* applecorer.

vider /vide/ [1] **I** *vtr* **1** (débarrasser) to empty [*poche, boîte, pièce, verre*]; to empty, to drain [*cuve, étang, réservoir*]; (avaler) to down [*verre*]; to go through [*paquet de biscuits*]; **~ un sac dans qch/sur une table** to empty a bag into sth/onto a table; **~ qch de son contenu** to empty sth of its contents; **~ un coffre-fort** to clean out a safe; **2** (retirer) to empty [sth] (out) [*eau, ordu-*

res] (**dans** into); **~ une bouteille dans l'évier** to empty a bottle into ou down the sink; **~ le grain d'un silo** to empty the grain out of a silo; **3** (rendre désert) to empty [*lieu*]; **la sirène a vidé les rues** the siren emptied the streets; **4**○ (expulser) to throw [sb] out○, to kick [sb] out○ [*intrus, indésirable*]; **se faire ~ de l'école** to be kicked out of school; **5** (évider) to gut [*poisson*]; to draw [*volaille*]; to core [*pomme*]; to hollow out [*tomate*]; **6** (priver) **~ qch de sa substance/son sens** to deprive sth of all substance/meaning; **7**○ (épuiser) (physiquement) to wear [sb] out; (mentalement) to drain.

II se vider *vpr* [*cuve, salle, ville*] to empty; [*canalisation, eau*] to empty (**dans** into); **en été, Paris se vide de ses habitants** in the summer all Parisians leave town.

IDIOMES **~ les lieux** or **le plancher**○ to leave.

videur○, **-euse** /vidœʀ, øz/ **▶510** *nm,f* bouncer.

vidoir /vidwaʀ/ *nm* (de vide-ordures) chute.

viduité /vidɥite/ *nf* Jur **délai de ~** *period of time before a widow or divorcee may remarry.*

vie /vi/ *nf* **1** gén, Biol life; **sauver la ~ de qn** to save sb's life; **rendre la ~ à qn** to bring sb back to life; **risquer sa ~** to risk one's life; **sacrifier** ou **donner sa ~ pour qn** to give one's life for sb; **devoir la ~ à qn** to owe sb one's life; **être en ~** to be alive; **maintenir qn en ~** to keep sb alive; **il y a laissé sa ~** that was how he lost his life; **sans ~** lifeless; **on l'a retrouvé sans ~** they found him dead; **donner la ~ à qn** to bring sb into the world; **sauver des ~s** to save lives; **~ végétale/animale/humaine** plant/animal/human life; **être entre la ~ et la mort** [*malade*] to hover between life and death; **y a-t-il une ~ après la mort?** is there life after death?; **y a-t-il de la ~ sur Mars?** is there life on Mars?; **2** (période) life; **avoir une ~ dure** to have a hard life; **pour la ~** for life; **courte/longue ~** short/long life; **sur** or **vers la fin de leur ~** toward(s) the end of their lives; **la peur/course de ma ~** the fright/race of my life; **elle a travaillé toute sa ~** she worked all her life; **je ne vous ai jamais vu de ma ~** I've never seen you in my life; **pour la première fois de ma ~** for the first time in my life; **il n'y a pas que le travail/l'amour dans la ~** there's more to life than work/love; **avoir quelqu'un dans sa ~** to have somebody in one's life; **partager la ~ de qn** to share one's life with sb; **ce n'est pas la femme de ma ~** she's not the love of my life; **que feras- tu dans la ~?** what are you going to do in life?; **faciliter la ~ à qn** to make life easier for sb; **vivre sa ~** to lead one's own life; **passer sa ~ à faire** gén to spend one's life doing; (tout le temps) to spend all one's time doing; **à ~** [*bannir, défigurer, marquer*] for life; [*bannissement, suspension*] lifetime (*épith*); [*emprisonnement, adhésion, président*] life (*épith*); **œuvre d'une ~** work of a lifetime; **c'est la chance de ta ~** it's the chance of a lifetime; **durer toute une ~** to last a lifetime; **tu as toute la ~ devant toi** you've got your whole life in front of you; **3** (activité) life; **la ~ urbaine/rurale** city/country life; **la ~ culturelle/professionnelle** cultural/professional life; **la ~ moderne/actuelle** modern/ present day life; **la ~ d'entreprise** corporate life; **mener une ~ de luxe** to lead a life of luxury; **la ~ est chère** the cost of living is high; **avoir une ~ active/sédentaire** to lead an active/a sedentary life; **mode de ~** lifestyle; **apprendre/connaître la ~** to learn/know what life is all about; **notre ~ de couple** our relationship, our life together (as a couple); **comment réussir sa ~ de couple** how to live together and make it work; **▶bâton**, **enterrer**; **4** (vitalité) life; **prendre ~** to come to life; **reprendre ~** to come back to life; **déborder de ~** to be bursting with life; **donner de la ~ à un personnage** to bring a character to life; **donner de la ~ à une fête** to liven up a party; **mettre de la vie dans qch** to liven sth up; **plein de ~** [*personne, lieu*] full of life; **manquant de ~**, **sans ~** [*personne, lieu*] lifeless; **5** (biographie) life; **écrire la ~ de qn** to write a life of sb; **la ~ de Mozart** the life of Mozart; **6** Tech (durabilité) life; **~ d'un appareil/d'une pile** life of a machine/of a battery.

■ **~ active** Sociol working life; **~ antérieure** former life; **~ chère** high cost of living; **~ éternelle** eternal life; **~ de famille** family life; **~ intérieure** inner life; **~ privée** private life; **~ quotidienne** daily life; **~ spirituelle** spiritual life.

IDIOMES **c'est la ~!** that's life!; **ça c'est la ~!**, **c'est la ~ d'artiste!** this is the life!; **ce n'est pas une ~!** it's no life!; **quelle ~!** what a life!; **ainsi va la ~** that's the way it goes; **ils ont la belle ~** they have a good life; **c'est la belle ~!** what a life!; (en ce moment) this is the life!; **une ~ de chien**○ a dog's life; **avoir la ~ dure** [*préjugés*] to be ingrained; **mener la ~ dure à qn** to make life hard for sb, to give sb a hard time; **faire la ~**○ [*enfants*] to have a wild time; [*adultes*] to live it up○; **à la ~, à la mort!** till death us do part!; **entre eux c'est à la ~ à la mort** with them it's for life.

vieil ▶ vieux.

vieillard, **~e** /vjɛjaʀ, aʀd/ *nm,f* old man, old woman; **les ~s** old people.

vieille ▶ vieux.

vieillerie /vjɛjʀi/ *nf* **1** (objet) old thing; (idée) old idea; **2**○ (état) old age.

vieillesse /vjɛjɛs/ *nf* **1** (de personne) old age; (de bâtiment, d'arbre) great age; **dans ta ~** in your old age; **mourir de ~** to die of old age; **2**○ (personnes âgées) **la ~** the old (+ *v pl*).

IDIOMES **si jeunesse savait, si ~ pouvait** Prov if the young man did but know, and the old man were but able.

vieilli, **~e** /vjɛji/ **I** *pp* **▶vieillir**.

II *pp adj* **1** (usé) [*peau, visage, tentures*] old-looking; **j'ai trouvé ta sœur très vieillie** I thought your sister had aged a lot; **2** (démodé) [*équipement*] outdated; [*expression, tournure*] dated; **3** (bonifié) **vin ~ en fût** wine matured in the cask.

vieillir /vjɛjiʀ/ [3] **I** *vtr* **1** (en apparence) [*coiffure, robe*] to make [sb] look older; **le maquillage la vieillit de 10 ans** make-up makes her look 10 years older; **2** (en estimation) **ne me vieillis pas, j'ai 59 ans!** don't make me any older than I am, I'm only 59!; **3** (physiquement) [*maladie, pauvreté*] to age.

II *vi* **1** (en âge) **je vieillis** I am getting old; **j'ai vieilli** I'm older; (en maturité) I have grown up; **je me sens ~** I feel my age; **pour bien ~, faites du sport** to stay young, take exercise; **il refuse de se voir ~** he can't accept the fact that he's not so young any more; **~ dans la fonction publique** to spend a lifetime in the civil service; **je ne veux pas ~ ici** I don't want to be here till I die; **2** (se dégrader) [*corps, bâtiment*] to show signs of age; [*personne*] to age; **elle n'a pas vieilli** she hasn't aged, she doesn't look any older; **il vieillit mal** (apparence) he's losing his looks; **elle vieillit bien** she looks good for her age; **il a vieilli de 10 ans en 6 mois** he has aged 10 years in 6 months; **3** Sociol **notre population vieillit** we have an ageing population; **4** Vin to mature, age; **5** (se démoder) [*œuvre*] to become outdated; [*institution*] to stultify; **une pièce de théâtre qui n'a pas vieilli** a play which has lasted well.

III se vieillir *vpr* **1** (en apparence) to make oneself look older; **2** (en mentant) to make oneself out to be older; **se ~ d'au moins trois ans** to put at least three years on one's age.

vieillissant, **~e** /vjɛjisɑ̃, ɑ̃t/ *adj* [*personne, objet, institution*] ageing.

vieillissement /vjɛjismɑ̃/ *nm* **1** (de personne, population, peau) ageing; **retarder le ~** to delay the ageing process; **2** (d'institution) stultification; **3** Vin ageing.

vieillot, **-otte** /vjɛjo, ɔt/ *adj* quaint; **habillée de façon vieillotte** pej quaintly dressed; **cela te donne un air ~** it gives you a charming old-fashioned air.

vielle /vjɛl/ **▶534** *nf* Mus hurdy-gurdy.

Vienne /vjɛn/ **I ▶857** *npr* **1** (ville d'Autriche) Vienna; **2** (ville de France) Vienne.

II ▶357, **692** *nprf* (rivière, département) Vienne.

viennois, **~e** /vjɛnwa, az/ **▶857** *adj* **1** (de Vienne) (en Autriche) Viennese; (en France) of Vienne; **2** Culin [*chocolat, café, pâtisserie, pain*] Viennese; **escalope ~e** Wiener schnitzel.

viennoiserie /vjɛnwazʀi/ *nf* Culin **1** (gâteau) Viennese pastry; **2** (ensemble des produits) Viennese pastries (*pl*); **3** (magasin) bakery selling Viennese pastries.

vierge /vjɛʀʒ/ **I** *adj* **1** [*personne*] virgin (*épith*); **elle est ~** she is a virgin; **rester/mourir ~** to remain/die a virgin; **2** (non utilisé) [*cassette, feuille*] blank; [*cahier, pellicule*] unused; [*casier judiciaire*] clean; [*dossier, agenda*] empty; **3** (non exploré) [*terre, domaine*] virgin; **cimes ~s** unclimbed peaks; **4** (pur) [*laine*] new; [*cire, huile d'olive*] virgin; **5** (non souillé) liter [*neige*] virgin; [*réputation, vie*] unblemished; **~ de** free from, unsullied by; **6** (non fécondé) [*œuf, génisse*] unfertilized.

II *nf* virgin.

Vierge /vjɛʀʒ/ **I** *nf* **1** Relig **la (Sainte) ~** the (Blessed) Virgin; **la ~ Marie** the Virgin Mary; **Sainte ~!** Good Heavens!; **2** Art (représentation) madonna; **une ~ de marbre** a marble madonna; **~ à l'Enfant** Madonna and Child.

II ▶874 *nprf* Astrol, Astron Virgo.

■ **~ noire** Black Madonna.

Viêt Nam /vjɛtnam/ **▶321** *nprm* Vietnam; **République socialiste du ~** Socialist Republic of Vietnam; **~ du Nord/du Sud** Hist North/South Vietnam.

vietnamien, **-ienne** /vjɛtnamjɛ̃, ɛn/ **▶537**, **462** **I** *adj* Vietnamese.

II *nm* Ling Vietnamese.

Vietnamien, **-ienne** /vjɛtnamjɛ̃, ɛn/ **▶537** *nm,f* Vietnamese; **~ du Nord/du Sud** Hist North/South Vietnamese.

vieux, (**vieil** *before vowel or mute h*), **vieille**, *mpl* **vieux** /vjø, vjɛj/ **I** *adj* **1** (d'âge avancé) [*personne, couple, animal*] old; **vieil imbécile** old fool; **être ~ avant l'âge** to be old before one's time; **je me fais vieille** I'm getting old; **pour/sur mes ~ jours** for/in my old age; **▶os**, **singe**; **2** (d'un âge relatif) **être plus ~ que qn/qch** to be older than sb/sth; **être moins ~ que qn** to be younger than sb; **être moins ~ que qch** not to be as old as sth; **la plus vieille église** the oldest church; **chatons ~ de quelques jours** kittens only a few days old; **une institution vieille de 100 ans** a 100-year-old institution; **~ de plus de 100 ans** over 100 years old; **3** (ancien) old; **dans la vieille ville** in the old town; **le ~ Nîmes** the old part of Nîmes; **le ~ continent** the old world; **une vieille connaissance** an old acquaintance; **au bon ~ temps** in the good old days; **mes bonnes vieilles pantoufles** my dear old slippers; **mon nouveau et mon ~ vélo** my new bike and my old one; **c'est un ~ rêve à moi** it has always been my dream; **c'est de la vieille histoire** that's ancient history; **une vieille amitié/rivalité** a long-standing friendship/rivalry; **il est très vieille France** he's a gentleman of the old school; **des habitudes vieille France** formal manners; **des prénoms qui font vieille France** first names which are full of old-world charm; **▶école**, **métier**.

II *nm,f* **1** (personne âgée) old person; **un petit ~** a little old man; **une petite vieille** a little old woman; **les ~** old people; **c'est un ~** he's old; **mes ~**○ (parents) my parents; **mon ~**○ (père) my old man○; **ma vieille**○ my old woman○; **2** (vétéran) **c'est une vieille, elle est ici depuis deux ans** she's an old hand, she's been here two years; **3**○ (camarade) **salut, ~!** hello, mate○! GB, hi, pal○! US; **mon pauvre ~** you poor old thing; **ça va, ma vieille?** how are you, dear?

III *adv* **vivre ~** to live to a ripe old age; **un chignon, ça fait ~** a bun makes you look old; **il s'habille ~** he dresses like an old man; **ta sœur fait ~** your sister looks old.

IV *nm* (choses anciennes) **le ~** old things (*pl*); **prendre un coup de ~** to age; **faire du neuf avec du ~** to revamp things.

■ **vieil or** old gold; **vieille barbe**○ old bore; **vieille branche**○ old thing†; **vieille fille** old maid; **vieille garde** old guard; **vieille noix**○ = **vieille branche**; **vieille peau** pej old bag○ péj; **~ beau** ageing Romeo; **~ clou**○ (véhicule) old crock○; **~ croûton**○ pej old duffer○; **~ garçon** old bachelor; **~ jeton**○ old fuddy-duddy○; **~ jeu** old-fashioned; **~ renard** old fox; **~ rose** dusty pink, old rose; **~ routier** old stager; **~ schnock**○ pej fuddy-duddy○.

IDIOMES **~ comme le monde, ~ comme Hérode** or **Mathusalem** as old as the hills; **c'est un ~ de la vieille**○ (vétéran) he's an old hand; (ami) he's a very old friend.

vif, vive[1] /vif, viv/ I *adj* **1** (brillant) [*couleur, lumière*] bright; **jaune ~** bright yellow; **2** (animé) [*personne*] lively, vivacious; [*imagination*] vivid; **avoir l'œil** or **le regard ~** to have an intelligent look in one's eyes; ▶**eau**; **3** (agressif, coléreux) [*débat, protestations*] heated; [*opposition*] fierce; **répondre d'un ton ~** to answer sharply; **de vives critiques** sharp criticism; **elle est un peu vive avec lui** (comportement) she's a bit quick-tempered with him; (ton) she's a bit sharp with him; **sa réaction a été un peu vive** he/she reacted rather strongly; **4** (net, important) [*contraste*] sharp; [*intérêt, désir*] keen; [*inquiétude*] deep; [*embarras, mécontentement, crainte, douleur*] acute; [*préoccupation*] serious; [*déception*] bitter; [*succès*] notable; **c'est avec un ~ plaisir que** it is with great pleasure that; **ressentir une vive émotion** to be deeply moved; **j'avais le ~ sentiment que** I felt strongly that; **5** (rapide) [*rythme, geste*] brisk; **marcher d'un pas ~** to walk at a brisk pace; **à vive allure** [*conduire, rouler*] at a fast speed; [*travailler, marcher*] at a brisk pace; **avoir l'esprit ~** to be very quick; **être ~ à réagir/protester** to be quick to react/protest; **6** (perçant, tranchant) [*froid, vent*] keen; [*arête*] sharp; **air ~** fresh air; **l'air est ~** the air is bracing; **cuire à feu ~** to cook over a high heat; **7** (vivant) alive; **être enterré/grillé ~** to be buried/roasted alive; **de vive voix** in person.

II *nm* **1** gén **à ~** [*chair*] bared; [*genou*] raw; [*fil électrique*] exposed; **avoir les nerfs à ~** to be on edge; **la plaie est à ~** it's an open wound; **mettre à ~** to expose [*os*]; to rub [sth] raw [*main*]; **cela me met les nerfs à ~** it puts me on edge; **piquer** or **blesser qn au ~** to sting ou cut sb to the quick; **être piqué** or **blessé au ~** to be stung ou cut to the quick; **piquer au ~ la curiosité de qn** to arouse sb's curiosity; **(pris) sur le ~** [*croquis*] thumbnail (*épith*); [*photo*] candid; [*notes*] on the spot (*jamais épith*); [*entretien*] live; **trancher** or **tailler dans le ~** lit to cut into the (living) flesh; (réduire) to make drastic cuts; (décider) to make a clear-cut decision; **nous sommes entrés tout de suite dans le ~ du sujet** or **débat** we went straight to the point; **2** Jur **entre ~s** [*donation, mutation, partage*] inter vivos.

III **vive** *nf* Zool weever.

vif-argent, *pl* **vifs-argents** /vifaʀʒɑ̃/ *nm* Chimie quicksilver.

vigie /viʒi/ *nf* **1** Naut (matelot) lookout; (poste) (sur le mât) crow's nest; (à la proue) lookout post; (balise) warning buoy; **être en ~** to be on watch; **2** Rail lookout box.

vigilance /viʒilɑ̃s/ *nf* vigilance; **avec ~** vigilantly; **échapper à la ~ de qn** (de douanier, contrôleur) to escape sb's notice; (de mère, nourrice) to escape sb's attention; **tromper la ~ de qn** to avoid detection by; **bouton/levier de ~** alarm button/switch.

vigilant, ~e /viʒilɑ̃, ɑ̃t/ *adj* [*personne*] vigilant; [*œil*] watchful; **attention ~e** great attention; **regard ~** watchful eye.

vigile /viʒil/ I *nm* **1** (veilleur de nuit) night watchman; (garde) security guard; **2** Hist watch.

II *nf* Relig vigil; **la ~ de Noël** Christmas vigil.

vigne /viɲ/ *nf* **1** (plant) vine; **10 hectares de ~(s)** 10 hectares of vines; **il cultive la ~** he's a wine grower; **2** (terrain planté) vineyard; **3** (travail) wine growing; **dans la région la ~ ne rapporte pas beaucoup** in this area wine growing doesn't bring much profit.

■ **~ mère** stock; **~ vierge** Virginia creeper.

vigneron, -onne /viɲ(ə)ʀɔ̃, ɔn/ ▶**510** *nm,f* winegrower.

vignette /viɲɛt/ *nf* **1** Prot Soc *detachable label on medicines for reimbursement by social security*; **2** Aut tax disc GB; **3** Comm label; **4** Art, Imprim (motif) vignette.

vignoble /viɲɔbl/ *nm* vineyard; **le ~ hongrois/alsacien** the vineyards of Hungary/Alsace.

vignot /viɲo/ *nm* (peri)winkle.

vigogne /vigɔɲ/ *nf* Zool (animal) vicuna; **laine de ~** vicuna wool.

vigoureusement /viguʀøzmɑ̃/ *adv* vigorously.

vigoureux, -euse /viguʀø, øz/ *adj* **1** (physiquement) [*personne, poignée de main*] vigorous; [*athlète, corps*] strong, powerful; [*plante, végétation*] sturdy; [*constitution, vieillard*] robust, sturdy; [*coup*] powerful; [*main, bras*] strong; **2** (déterminé) [*résistance, attaque, mesure, style*] vigorous; [*croissance, sentiment*] strong; [*talent*] strong, robust; [*langage*] strong, forceful; **rencontrer une vigoureuse opposition** to encounter vigorous opposition; **3** (intense) [*parfum*] strong; [*formule, effet*] powerful; **4** (net) [*dessin, contour*] strong, bold; [*coloris*] strong, striking.

vigueur /vigœʀ/ I *nf* **1** (énergie) vigour[GB]; **plein de ~** full of vigour[GB]; **un discours plein de ~** a vigorous speech; **avec ~** vigorously; **reprendre avec ~** [*lutte*] to start again with renewed vigour[GB]; **2** (force musculaire) strength; **avec ~** vigorously, with vigour[GB]; **frapper avec ~** to bang; **3** (de plante, forêt) sturdiness; **4** (de trait, forme) vigour[GB].

II **en vigueur** *loc adj* [*loi, dispositif*] in force; [*régime, conditions*] current; **actuellement en ~** currently in force; **être en ~** to be in force; **cesser d'être en ~** to cease to apply; **en ~ depuis le 1er mars** in force since 1 March; **entrer en ~** to come into force; **depuis l'entrée en ~ de la loi** since the law came into force.

VIH /veiaʃ/ *nm* (*abbr* = **virus immunodéficitaire humain**) HIV.

viking /vikiŋ/ *adj* Viking.

Viking /vikiŋ/ *nprmf* Viking.

vil, ~e /vil/ *adj* liter **1** (méprisable) [*personne, âme*] base littér; [*action*] vile, base; **le plus ~ des hommes** the basest of men; **2** (grossier) [*besogne, tâche*] base littér; **3** (sans valeur) **à ~ prix** at a giveaway price.

vilain, ~e /vilɛ̃, ɛn/ I *adj* **1** (laid) [*bâtiment, personne, animal*] ugly; **le ~ petit canard** the ugly duckling; **c'est vraiment ~ ce chapeau!** that hat looks awful!; **faire ~** [*tableau, couleurs*] to look ugly; [*construction*] to be an eyesore; **ça fait ~ dans le paysage** it's a real eyesore, it's a blot on the landscape; **2**○ (méchant) [*bête, microbe*] nasty; [*garçon, fille*] naughty; **jouer un ~ tour à qn** to play a nasty trick on sb; **ça va faire du ~, il va y avoir du ~** there's going to be big trouble○; **la discussion a tourné au ~** the discussion turned nasty○; **3** (répréhensible) [*affaire, bruits, rumeur*] nasty; [*défaut*] bad; [*mot*] dirty; **il a de ~es manières** he's got some dirty habits; **c'est très ~ de lécher son assiette** it's very rude to lick your plate; **4** (mauvais) [*temps*] awful; [*goût*] nasty; **5** (inquiétant) [*toux, blessure, abcès*] nasty.

II *nm,f* naughty boy/girl; **oh, le ~!** what a naughty boy!; **arrête de faire la ~e!** stop being naughty!

III *nm* Hist villein.

IDIOMES **jeux de mains, jeux de ~s** Prov it will end in tears; **être dans de ~s draps** to be in a nasty mess○.

vilainement /vilɛnmɑ̃/ *adv* badly, hideously; **une pièce ~ décorée** a hideously decorated room.

vilebrequin /vilbʀəkɛ̃/ *nm* **1** (outil) brace and bit; **2** (de moteur) crankshaft.

vilement /vilmɑ̃/ *adv* vilely.

vilenie /vileni/ *nf* fml **1** (bassesse) baseness (**de** of); **2** (action vile) vile ou base act; **commettre une ~** to commit a base ou vile act.

vilipender /vilipɑ̃de/ [1] *vtr* liter to revile sout.

villa /villa/ *nf* **1** (maison d'habitation) ≈ detached house; **2** (maison de plaisance) villa; **3** Antiq villa.

village /vilaʒ/ *nm* village; **un ~ de Dordogne/d'Autriche** a village in the Dordogne/in Austria.

■ **~ classé** listed GB ou landmarked US village; **~ olympique** Olympic village; **~ de toile** tent village; **~ de vacances** holiday GB ou vacation US village.

villageois, ~e /vilaʒwa, az/ I *adj* village (*épith*).

II *nm,f* villager.

ville /vil/ ▶**857** *nf* **1** (agglomération, habitants) town, (de grande importance) city; **la ~ de Brest** the town of Brest; **la ~ de Paris** the city of Paris; **la deuxième ~ du pays** the country's second city; **le meilleur restaurant de la ~** the best restaurant in town; **la vieille ~** the old town; **la ~ haute/basse/neuve** the upper/lower/new town; **~ natale/adoptive/d'attache** home/adoptive/base town; **~ industrielle/olympique** industrial/Olympic town ou city; **~ minière** mining town; **~ universitaire** university city ou town; **~ portuaire** port town; **~ côtière/de province/frontière** coastal/provincial/border town; **une ~ d'art** a town of artistic interest; **une ~ sainte** a holy city; **~ forte** or **fortifiée** fortified town; **les gens des ~s** town ou city dwellers, townees○ péj; **de ~** [*vêtements, chaussures*] town; **en ~** [*conduire, habiter*] in town; **aller en ~** to go into town; **la vie en ~** town ou city life; **2** (administration) town ou city council.

■ **~ d'eau(x)** spa town; **~ franche** free city; **~ de garnison** garrison town; **~ libre** semiautonomous city; **~ nouvelle** new town; **~ ouverte** open city; **la Ville Éternelle** the Eternal City; **la Ville Lumière** the City of Light.

ville-champignon, *pl* **villes-champignons** /vilʃɑ̃piɲɔ̃/ *nf* mushroom town, boom town.

ville-dortoir, *pl* **villes-dortoirs** /vildɔʀtwaʀ/ *nf* dormitory town GB, bedroom community US.

villégiature /vileʒjatyʀ/ *nf* (séjour) holiday GB, vacation US; **partir/être en ~** to go/be on holiday GB ou vacation US; **lieu de ~**

Les villes

Les noms de villes

Toute ville peut être désignée par les expressions the town of ... *ou* the city of ...: town *s'applique en anglais britannique à toute agglomération d'une certaine importance, et en anglais américain à toute commune, même très peu peuplée. En Grande-Bretagne* city *désigne les très grandes villes, ainsi que les villes ayant une cathédrale.*

À avec les noms de villes

À *se traduit par* to *avec les verbes de mouvement (par ex.* aller, se rendre, *etc.).*

aller à Toulouse = to go to Toulouse
se rendre à La Haye = to travel to The Hague

À *se traduit par* in *avec les autres verbes (par ex.* être, habiter *etc.).*

vivre à Toulouse = to live in Toulouse

Lorsqu'une ville est une étape sur un itinéraire, à *se traduira par* at.

s'arrêter à Dublin = to stop at Dublin

Les noms des habitants

L'anglais est moins friand que le français de noms d'habitants des villes. Pour les villes des îles britanniques, seuls quelques-uns sont assez courants, comme Londoner, Dubliner, Liverpudlian *(de Liverpool),* Glaswegian *(de Glasgow),* Mancunian *(de Manchester) etc. Pour les villes américaines, on a* New Yorker, Philadelphian *etc. Pour les autres pays,* Parisian, Berliner, Roman *etc.*

Pour traduire un nom d'habitant de ville, il est toujours possible d'utiliser inhabitants *ou* people: *par ex., pour* les Toulousains, *on peut dire* the inhabitants of Toulouse, the people of Toulouse *etc.*

De avec les noms de villes

Les expressions françaises avec de *se traduisent le plus souvent par l'emploi du nom de ville en position d'adjectif.*

l'accent de Toulouse = a Toulouse accent
l'aéroport de Toulouse = Toulouse airport
les cafés de Toulouse = Toulouse cafés
l'équipe de Toulouse = the Toulouse team
les hivers de Toulouse = Toulouse winters
les hôtels de Toulouse = Toulouse hotels
la région de Toulouse = the Toulouse area
les restaurants de Toulouse = Toulouse restaurants
la route de Toulouse = the Toulouse road
les rues de Toulouse = Toulouse streets
le train de Toulouse = the Toulouse train

Mais:

je suis de Toulouse = I come from Toulouse
une lettre de Toulouse = a letter from Toulouse
le maire de Toulouse = the Mayor of Toulouse
un plan de Toulouse = a map of Toulouse

Les adjectifs dérivés

Les adjectifs dérivés des noms de villes n'ont pas toujours d'équivalent en anglais. Plusieurs cas sont possibles mais on pourra presque toujours utiliser le nom de la ville placé avant le nom qualifié:

la région bordelaise = the Bordeaux area

Pour souligner la provenance on choisira from + *le nom de la ville:*

l'équipe bordelaise = the team from Bordeaux

Pour parler de l'environnement on optera pour of + *le nom de la ville:*

les rues bordelaises = the streets of Bordeaux

Et pour situer on utilisera in + *le nom de la ville:*

mon séjour bordelais = my stay in Bordeaux

holiday spot GB, vacation spot US; **centre de ~** holiday resort GB, resort US.

ville-satellite, *pl* **villes-satellites** /vilsatelit/ *nf* satellite town.

villeux, -euse /vilø, øz/ *adj* villous.

villosité /villozite/ *nf* **1** Anat (saillie) villus; **~s intestinales** intestinal villi; **2** Bot, Zool (surface velue) villosity.

Vilnius /vilnjys/ ▶857 *npr* Vilnius.

vin /vɛ̃/ *nm* **1** (de raisin) wine; **~ blanc/rouge/pétillant/mousseux** white/red/semi-sparkling/sparkling wine; **~ rosé** rosé (wine); **~ doux/sec/demi-sec** sweet/dry/medium-dry wine; **~ de consommation courante** ordinary wine; **grand ~** fine wine; **~ d'Alsace** Alsace wine; **~ de pays** or **de terroir** *quality wine produced in a specific region*; **sauce au ~** wine sauce; **ce ~ a du corps** this wine is full-bodied; **un ~ qui se fait** a wine which is maturing; **mettre le ~ en bouteilles** to bottle wine; **couper son ~** (mettre de l'eau) to add water to one's wine; (mettre un autre vin) to blend one's wine; **2** (d'origine végétale) wine; **~ de riz** rice wine.

■ **~ d'appellation d'origine contrôlée** appellation contrôlée (*with a guarantee of origin*); **~ bourru** *new wine still undergoing fermentation*; **~ chaud** mulled wine; **~ de coupage** blended wine; **~ cuit** *wine which has undergone heating during maturation*; **~ délimité de qualité supérieure**, **VDQS** *wine of a defined area with strict production laws*; **~ gris** very pale rosé wine; **~ d'honneur** reception; **~ de liqueur** fortified wine; **~ de messe** communion wine; **le ~ nouveau** *wine from the latest vintage*; **~ de paille** *wine made from dried grapes*; **~ de table** table wine.

IDIOMES **avoir le ~ gai/mauvais/triste** to get happy/nasty/maudlin after a drink; **être entre deux ~s** to be tipsy○; **mettre de l'eau dans son ~** to mellow; **quand le ~ est tiré, il faut le boire** Prov once you have started something, you have to see it through.

vinaigre /vinɛgʀ/ *nm* vinegar; **un assaisonnement à l'huile et au ~** an oil and vinegar dressing; **~ de vin/de Xérès** wine/sherry vinegar; **~ à l'estragon** tarragon vinegar.

IDIOMES **faire ~**○ to get a move on○; **tourner au ~** to turn sour; **on ne prend pas les mouches avec du ~** Prov it doesn't pay to take a hard line.

vinaigrer /vinegʀe/ [1] *vtr* to season [sth] with vinegar; **salade/moutarde vinaigrée** salad/mustard seasoned with vinegar; **trop vinaigré** [*sauce, cornichons*] too vinegary.

vinaigrerie /vinɛgʀəʀi/ *nf* **1** (usine) vinegar factory; **2** (industrie) vinegar production.

vinaigrette /vinɛgʀɛt/ *nf* vinaigrette, French dressing; **à la** or **en ~** in vinaigrette; **poireaux ~** leeks in vinaigrette.

vinaigrier /vinɛgʀije/ *nm* **1** (flacon) vinegar bottle; **2** ▶510 (personne) (fabricant) vinegar maker; (industriel, commerçant) vinegar dealer.

vinasse○ /vinas/ *nf* pej plonk○ péj GB, cheap wine; **un repas arrosé d'une infâme ~** a meal with awful plonk GB ou cheap wine; **tu sens la ~**! you smell of booze○!

vindicatif, -ive /vɛ̃dikatif, iv/ *adj* vindictive.

vindicte /vɛ̃dikt/ *nf* gén condemnation; Jur prosecution and conviction; **être en butte à/échapper à la ~ publique** to be exposed to/to escape public condemnation.

vineux, -euse /vinø, øz/ *adj* **1** ▶193 (couleur de vin rouge) [*teint, visage*] purplish; **rouge ~** burgundy(-coloured[GB]); **2** (rappelant le vin) [*odeur*] of wine (*après n*); [*fruit*] wine-flavoured[GB]; **3** (riche en alcool) [*vin*] full-bodied.

vingt /vɛ̃, vɛ̃t/ ▶545, 407, 212 **I** *adj inv* twenty.

II *pron* twenty; **~ sur ~** twenty out of twenty; **j'ai eu ~ sur ~ à mon devoir d'histoire** ≈ I got full marks GB ou full credit US for my history paper.

vingtaine /vɛ̃tɛn/ *nf* about twenty; ▶**cinquantaine** 1.

vingt-deux /vɛ̃tdø/ ▶545, 407, 212 **I** *adj inv, pron* twenty-two; ▶**rifle**.

II○ *excl* look out!, watch it○!; **~, v'là les flics**○! look out! it's the cops○!

vingtième /vɛ̃tjɛm/ ▶545, 212 *adj* twentieth.

vinicole /vinikɔl/ *adj* [*activité, secteur, société, région*] wine-producing (*épith*); [*cave, commerce*] wine (*épith*); [*matériel, équipement*] wine-making (*épith*).

vinification /vinifikasjɔ̃/ *nf* **1** (procédé) wine production; **méthodes de ~** wine production methods; **~ en blanc/rouge** production of white/red wine; **2** (fermentation) vinification.

vinifier /vinifje/ [2] *vtr* to make [sth] into wine [*jus de raisin*].

vinyle /vinil/ *nm* **1** (matériau) vinyl; **2** (disque) vinyl.

vinylique /vinilik/ *adj* vinyl (*épith*).

viol /vjɔl/ *nm* (de personne) rape; (de lieu, loi) violation.

violacé, ~e /vjɔlase/ **I** ▶193 *adj* purplish; **un rouge ~** a purplish red.

II violacée *nf* Bot violacea; **les ~es** Violaceae.

violacer /vjɔlase/ [12] **I** *vtr* [*froid*] to turn [sth] purple [*visage, doigts*].

II se violacer *vpr* [*peau, visage*] to turn purple; [*ciel*] to take on a purplish hue.

violateur, -trice /vjɔlatœʀ, tʀis/ *nm,f* Jur fml transgressor sout (**de** of).

violation /vjɔlasjɔ̃/ *nf* **1** (de loi, territoire, traité) violation; **2** (de secret, d'accord) breach; **~ du secret professionnel** breach of confidentiality; **en ~ d'une règle** in breach of a rule.

■ **~ de domicile** Jur forcible entry (*into a person's home*); **~ de sépulture** Jur desecration of a grave.

violâtre /vjɔlɑtʀ/ *adj* ▶193 purplish.

viole /vjɔl/ ▶534 *nf* viol.

■ **~ d'amour** viola d'amore; **~ de bras** viola da braccia ou arm viol; **~ de gambe** viola da gamba.

violemment /vjɔlamɑ̃/ *adv* violently.

violence /vjɔlɑ̃s/ *nf* **1** (de personne, événement, sentiment) violence; **la ~ de la répression/du vent** the violence of repression/of the wind; **la ~ dans les écoles/les stades** violence in schools/the stadiums; **~ armée** armed violence; **~ verbale** verbal abuse; **d'une ~ insoutenable** [*scène, film*] unbearably violent; **avec ~** [*agir, réagir*] violently; **avec une rare ~** [*agir, réagir*] with extreme violence; **par la ~** [*éprouvé, miné*] by violence; [*imposer, soumettre*] through violence; [*répondre, résister*] with violence; **répliquer à la ~ par la ~** to meet violence with violence; **sous la ~ du choc, elle s'est évanouie** the violence of the impact made her faint; **faire ~ à qn** fml to force sb (**pour qu'il fasse** to do); **se faire ~** fml to force oneself (**pour faire** to do); **se faire une douce ~** hum to force oneself hum; **2** (acte) act of violence; **commettre/subir des ~s** to commit/suffer violence ou acts of violence; **~s ethniques/policières/**

sexuelles ethnic/police/sexual violence; **inculpé de ~s à enfant** charged with child abuse; **inculpé de ~s à l'égard de qn** charged with violence against sb; **~s et voies de fait** Jur violent behaviour[GB] and common assault; **elle n'avait subi aucune ~** she hadn't suffered any assault.

violent, **~e** /vjɔlɑ̃, ɑ̃t/ **I** *adj* [*personne, réaction*] violent; [*couleur*] harsh; [*poison*] powerful; [*inquiétude*] acute; [*désir*] overwhelming; **non ~** [*mouvement, moyens*] nonviolent; [*manifestation*] peaceful, nonviolent.
II *nm,f* violent person.

violenter /vjɔlɑ̃te/ [1] *vtr* (agresser) to assault sexually; (violer) to rape.

violer /vjɔle/ [1] *vtr* **1** (agresser sexuellement) to rape [*personne*]; **se faire ~** to be raped; **2** (profaner) to desecrate [*tombe*]; to violate [*territoire, souveraineté*]; to break into [*domicile*]; **~ l'intimité de qn** fig to invade sb's privacy; **3** (enfreindre) to violate [*traité*]; to infringe, to contravene [*loi*]; **4** liter to violate [*esprits, consciences*].

violet, **-ette** /vjɔlɛ, ɛt/ ▶ **193** **I** *adj* purple; **mes mains sont violettes de froid** my hands are purple with cold.
II *nm* (couleur) purple.
III violette *nf* Bot violet; **eau de toilette à la ~** violet-scented eau de toilette.

violeur /vjɔlœʀ/ *nm* rapist.

violine /vjɔlin/ ▶ **193** *adj* deep purple.

violon /vjɔlɔ̃/ ▶ **534** *nm* **1** (instrument) violin; **jouer du ~** to play the violin; **2** (musicien) violinist, violin; **les ~s** the violins; **3**○ (prison) **au ~** in the nick○ GB, in the slammer○ US ou can○ US.
■ **~ d'Ingres** hobby.
IDIOMES **accorder ses ~s** to reach an agreement; **autant pisser dans un ~**○**!** it's just pissing◑ in the wind; **payer les ~s du bal** or **de la fête** to foot the bill○, to pick up the tab○.

violoncelle /vjɔlɔ̃sɛl/ ▶ **534** *nm* **1** (instrument) cello; **jouer du ~** to play the cello; **2** (musicien) cellist, cello.

violoncelliste /vjɔlɔ̃sɛlist/ ▶ **534**, **510** *nmf* cellist.

violoneux /vjɔlɔnø/ *nm inv* (de noce) village fiddler, fiddler.

violoniste /vjɔlɔnist/ ▶ **534**, **510** *nmf* violinist.

vioque◑ /vjɔk/ **I** *adj* pej old.
II *nmf* pej old man/old woman.

viorne /vjɔʀn/ *nf* **1** (arbrisseau) viburnum; **2** (clématite) clematis.

VIP○ /viajpi/ *nm* (*abbr* = **very important person**) VIP.

vipère /vipɛʀ/ *nf* **1** Zool viper, adder; **2** (personne médisante) viper; **avoir** or **être une langue de ~** fig to have a wicked tongue.
■ **~ aspic** asp.

vipérin, **~e** /vipeʀɛ̃, in/ **I** *adj* **1** Zool viperine; **2** fig (méchant) [*langue, regard*] venomous; [*propos*] poisonous, vicious.
II vipérine *nf* Bot viper's bugloss, blueweed US.

virage /viʀaʒ/ *nm* **1** (courbe) bend, curve; **~ dangereux** dangerous bend; **~ relevé** banked curve; **~ serré** sharp bend; **~ en épingle à cheveux** hairpin bend; **~ à droite/gauche** bend to the right/left; **'~s sur 10 km'** 'bends for 10 km'; **il prend ses ~s beaucoup trop vite** he takes bends ou goes around bends far too fast; **il ne faut pas freiner dans les ~s** you shouldn't brake when going around a bend; **prendre un ~ à la corde** to hug a bend; **prendre un ~ sur les chapeaux de roues** to go around a bend at breakneck speed; **le panneau est à l'entrée/à la sortie du ~** the signpost is before/after the bend; **rater un ~** to fail to negotiate a bend; **~ en S** S bend; **2** (changement d'orientation) change of direction; **parti qui amorce un ~ à droite** party which takes a turn to the right ou shifts toward(s) the right; **3** Phot toning; **~ à l'or/au cuivre** gold/copper toning; **4** Chimie colour[GB] change; **le ~ du rouge au violet** the turning from red to purple; **5** Sport (en ski) turn; **~ parallèle/stem** parallel/stem turn; **6** Méd **~ d'une cuti-réaction** positive reaction to a skin test.
■ **~ sur l'aile** bank; **faire un ~ sur l'aile** to bank; **~ à 180 degrés** fig U-turn.

virago /viʀago/ *nf* virago.

viral, **~e**, *mpl* **-aux** /viʀal, o/ *adj* viral.

vire /viʀ/ *nf* ledge.

viré, **~e** /viʀe/ **I**○ *adj* **être bien/mal ~** to be in a good/bad mood.
II virée○ *nf* (voyage) trip; (promenade) (en voiture) drive, ride, spin; (à vélo, moto) ride; **ils sont allés faire une ~e en Normandie le week-end dernier** they went on a trip to Normandy ou on a tour round[GB] Normandy last weekend; **~e nocturne en moto** night motorbike ride; **une ~e dans les bars de la ville** a tour of the bars in town.

virement /viʀmɑ̃/ *nm* Fin transfer; **faire un ~** to make a transfer; **~ bancaire/postal** bank/postal transfer; **~ interne** internal transfer; **j'ai fait un ~ de mon compte d'épargne sur mon compte-chèques** I transferred money from my savings account to my current account GB ou checking account US.
■ **~ automatique** standing order; **~ de bord** Naut tacking; **~ budgétaire** reallocation of funds.

virer /viʀe/ [1] **I** *vtr* **1** Fin to transfer [*argent, somme, salaire*] (**sur** to); **2**○ (licencier) to fire, to sack○ GB [*employé*]; **où qu'il travaille, il finit toujours par se faire ~** wherever he works, he always ends up getting fired ou getting the sack○ GB; **3**○ (expulser) gén to throw [sb] out [*importun*] (**de** of); (d'un cours) to send [sb] out [*élève*]; (du lycée) to expel [*élève*]; **4**○ (enlever) to remove; **on va ~ la table, ça nous fera plus de place** we'll move the table out ou get rid of the table, it'll give us more space; **vire-moi ce chapeau, tu as l'air ridicule!** take off that hat ou get rid of that hat, you look ridiculous!; **5** Phot to tone [*épreuve*]; **6** Naut to weigh [*ancre*]; to haul in [*amarres*].
II *vi* **1** (tourner sur soi) to turn around; **2** (changer de direction) [*véhicule, parti politique*] to turn; **~ à droite/gauche** [*véhicule, parti politique*] to turn ou shift to the right/left; **~ sur l'aile** to bank; **3** Naut [*navire*] to turn; **~ de bord** or **vent devant** lit to go about; **~ de bord** fig to do a U-turn, to do a flip-flop US; **~ sur les amarres** to turn at anchor; **~ au cabestan** to strain at the capstan; **~ vent arrière** to gybe GB, to jibe; **4** (changer de couleur) [*étoffes, solution*] to change colour[GB]; [*couleur*] to change; **5** Phot [*épreuve*] to tone.
III virer à *vtr ind* **~ au rouge/bleu** to turn red/blue; **~ à l'aigre** to turn sour; **le parti vire au conservatisme** the party is turning ou going conservative.
IV○ **se virer** *vpr* to beat it○; **vire-toi de là!** beat it○!, scram○!

vireux, **-euse** /viʀø, øz/ *adj* [*plante*] noxious; [*odeur*] nauseating.

virevolte /viʀvɔlt/ *nf* **1** (tour sur soi-même) twirl; **2** (revirement) about-turn GB, about-face, volte-face.

virevolter /viʀvɔlte/ [1] *vi* to twirl.

Virgile /viʀʒil/ *npr* Virgil.

virginal, **~e**, *mpl* **-aux** /viʀʒinal, o/ **I** *adj* [*innocence, regard*] virginal, maidenly littér; **blancheur ~e** virgin whiteness.
II ▶ **534** *nm* Hist Mus virginal.

Virginie /viʀʒini/ ▶ **692** *nprf* Virginia.

Virginie-Occidentale /viʀʒiniɔksidɑ̃tal/ ▶ **692** *nprf* West Virginia.

virginité /viʀʒinite/ *nf* **1** lit virginity; **garder/perdre sa ~** to keep/lose one's virginity; **2** fig purity.
IDIOMES **refaire une ~ à qn** to restore sb's clean image; **se refaire une ~** to re-establish one's good reputation.

virgule /viʀgyl/ *nf* **1** Ling comma; **mettre une ~ à une phrase** to put a comma in a sentence; **à la ~ près** down to the last comma; **sans changer une ~** without changing as much as a comma; **en ~** comma-shaped; **2** Math (decimal) point; **deux ~ vingt-cinq** two point two five; **s'arrêter deux chiffres après la ~** to stop at two decimal places.
■ **~ fixe** Ordinat fixed-point system; **~ flottante normalisée** Ordinat floating-point system.

viril, **~e** /viʀil/ *adj* [*homme, force, courage*] manly, virile; [*traits, apparence*] masculine, virile; **il est très ~** he's very masculine ou manly; **les amitiés ~es** male friendships.

virilement /viʀilmɑ̃/ *adv* in a virile ou manly manner.

virilisant /viʀilizɑ̃/ *adj* **médicament ~** drug that has a virilizing effect.

virilisation /viʀilizasjɔ̃/ *nf* virilization.

viriliser /viʀilize/ [1] *vtr* to virilize.

virilisme /viʀilism/ *nm* virilism.

virilité /viʀilite/ *nf* **1** (caractéristiques physiques) masculinity, virility; **2** (aptitude à engendrer) virility; **3** (attitude masculine) manliness; **son attitude manque de ~** his attitude is rather unmanly.

virion /viʀjɔ̃/ *nm* virion.

virole /viʀɔl/ *nf* **1** (cercle métallique) ferrule; **couteau à ~** pocket knife with a safety catch; **2** Tech (mould) collar.

viroler /viʀɔle/ [1] *vtr* **1** (renforcer d'un anneau de métal) to ferrule, to fit [sth] with a ferrule [*outil*]; **2** Tech (fabrication de monnaies) to place [sth] in a collar [*flans*].

virologie /viʀɔlɔʒi/ *nf* virology.

virologiste /viʀɔlɔʒist/, **virologue** /viʀɔlɔg/ ▶ **510** *nmf* virologist.

virtualité /viʀtɥalite/ *nf* **1** Philos virtuality; **2** (aptitude) potentiality **₵**.

virtuel, **-elle** /viʀtɥɛl/ *adj* **1** [*succès, résultat, marché*] potential; **à l'état ~** potentially; **2** Philos, Phys virtual.

virtuellement /viʀtɥɛlmɑ̃/ *adv* **1** (pratiquement) virtually; **2** (en théorie) potentially.

virtuose /viʀtɥoz/ **I** *adj* **1** Mus virtuoso (*épith*); **un violoniste ~** a virtuoso violinist; **2** (doué) [*écrivain, dessinateur*] virtuoso (*épith*); [*joueur*] master; **être ~ dans l'art de faire** to be a past master at doing.
II *nmf* **1** Mus virtuoso; **un ~ du piano/violon** a piano/violin virtuoso; **2** (personne douée) master; **un virtuose de qch** a master of sth.

virtuosité /viʀtɥozite/ *nf* **1** Mus virtuosity; **interpréter qch avec ~** to give a virtuoso performance of sth; **2** (habileté) brilliance; **faire preuve de ~ dans** to show brilliance in.

virulence /viʀylɑ̃s/ *nf* **1** Méd virulence; **2** (âpreté) virulence; **avec ~** virulently.

virulent, **~e** /viʀylɑ̃, ɑ̃t/ *adj* **1** Méd [*microbe, poison*] virulent; **2** (acerbe) [*personne, critique, propos*] virulent, scathing.

virus /viʀys/ *nm* **1** Méd virus; **le ~ du sida/de la grippe** the Aids/flu virus; **2** (manie) bug○, craze; **le ~ du cinéma/du voyage** the film/travel bug○; **3** Ordinat virus.

vis /vis/ *nf* screw; **tête/noyau de vis** head/stem of screw; **serrer/desserrer une ~** to tighten/loosen a screw; **~ à tête plate/ronde** flatheaded/roundheaded screw.
■ **~ d'Archimède** Archimedean screw; **~ autoperceuse** self-tapping screw; **~ à bois** wood screw; **~ cruciforme** Phillips® screw; **~ sans fin** worm, endless screw; **~ mère** (de tour) leading spindle; **~ à métaux** machine screw; **~ micrométrique** Sci micrometre[GB] screw; **~ platinées** Aut contact points; **~ de pressoir** Vin press screw; **~ de rappel** adjusting screw.
IDIOMES **serrer la ~ à qn** to tighten the screws on sb.

visa /viza/ *nm* **1** (sur un passeport) visa (**pour** for); **2** (sceau) stamp.

■ **~ de censure** Cin (censor's) certificate; **~ de sortie** Admin exit visa; **~ de touriste** Admin tourist visa.

visage /vizaʒ/ ▶188| *nm* lit, fig face; **~ rond/familier/défait** round/familiar/drawn face; **l'angoisse se lisait sur son ~** his distress was visible on his face; **le vrai ~ de qn/qch** the true face of sb/sth; **les ~s de qn** the faces of sb; **à ~ humain** with a human face; **à deux ~s** two-faced; **les deux ~s d'une politique/révolution** the two aspects of a policy/revolution; **le nouveau ~ de l'Allemagne/Europe/industrie** the new face of Germany/Europe/industry; **sans ~** faceless; **à ~ découvert** openly; **faire bon/mauvais ~ à qn** to give sb a warm/cool welcome; ▶ **lire**.

■ **~ pâle** Hist paleface.

visagiste® /vizaʒist/ ▶510| *nmf* ≈ beautician.

vis-à-vis /vizavi/ I *nm inv* **1** (bâtiment) **avoir la prison pour ~** to live opposite the prison; **maison sans ~** house with an open outlook; **2** (personne) (à table, dans le train) person opposite; (voisin d'en face) person who lives opposite; **j'ai demandé du feu à mon ~** I asked the person opposite for a light; **3** (position) **en ~** opposite each other; **assis en ~** sitting opposite each other; **4** Sport opponent; **5** (rencontre face-à-face) meeting, encounter; **6** (sofa) vis-à-vis, tête-à-tête.

II **vis-à-vis de** *loc prép* **1** (à l'égard de) **~ de qch** in relation to sth; **~ de qn** towards sb; **être honnête ~ de soi-même** to be honest with oneself; **2** (comparé à) **mon malheur n'est rien ~ du vôtre** my misfortune is nothing beside yours; **le dollar s'effrite ~ des monnaies européennes** the dollar is declining against European currencies.

viscéral, **~e**, *mpl* **-aux** /viseʀal, o/ *adj* **1** (instinctif) [*haine, émotion*] visceral sout, deep-rooted; **réaction ~e** gut reaction; **2** Anat visceral.

viscéralement /viseʀalmɑ̃/ *adv* **elle est ~ opposée à ce projet** she is violently ou virulently opposed to this plan; **il est ~ raciste** he is a racist to the core, he is a dyed-in-the-wool racist.

viscère /visɛʀ/ *nm* **1** Anat internal organ; **2** (de l'abdomen) **les ~s** viscera.

viscose /viskoz/ *nf* viscose.

viscosité /viskozite/ *nf* viscosity.

visée /vize/ *nf* **1** (objectif) aim; (dessein) design; **une loi ayant comme ~ de protéger les enfants** a law whose aim is to protect children; **une politique à ~ expansionniste/internationale** an expansionist/internationalist policy; **avoir des ~s sur qn/qch** to have designs on sb/sth; **la société a des ~s sur son concurrent** the company has designs on its competitor; **n'avoir aucune ~ agressive sur les États voisins** to have no aggressive intentions toward(s) neighbouring[GB] states; **ils ont des ~s sur le marché européen** they are aiming at the European market; **2** (avec un instrument) Astron, Géog sighting; Phot viewing; (avec une arme) aiming; **prendre une ~** Naut, Aviat to take a sight.

■ **~ d'arpentage** surveying shot; **~ corrigée** Lead Computer Gun Sight, LCGS; **~ reflex** reflex viewfinding; **~ télémétrique** telemetric viewfinding.

viser /vize/ [1] I *vtr* **1** (pointer son regard) to aim at [*cible*]; (vouloir atteindre) to aim for [*cœur, centre*]; **2** (aspirer à) to aim for [*poste, résultats*]; to aim at [*marché*]; **~ la première place** to aim to be first; **3** (concerner) [*loi, campagne*] to be aimed at; [*remarque, allusion*] to be meant ou intended for; **le projet de loi vise les bas salaires** the bill is aimed at the low-paid; **les employés visés par la décision** the employees to whom the ruling applies, the employees who are affected by the ruling; **se sentir visé** to feel one is being got at○; **4**○ (regarder) to get a load of○, to take a look at; **vise un peu ça!** get a load of that!; **5** Admin to stamp [*document*]; to visa GB, put a visa in US [*passeport*].

II **viser à** *vtr ind* **~ à qch/à faire** to aim at sth/to do; **émission qui vise à changer les attitudes** programme[GB] which aims to change attitudes; **le projet de loi vise à la privatisation des banques** the bill is aimed at privatizing banks, the bill aims to privatize banks.

III *vi* **1** (avec un fusil, un appareil photo) to aim; **~ juste/trop à gauche** to aim accurately/too far left; **2** fig **~ (trop) haut/bas** to set one's sights (too) high/low.

viseur /vizœʀ/ *nm* **1** Phot, Cin viewfinder; **2** (d'arme) sight.

■ **~ de bombardement** bombsight; **~ à cadre lumineux** Phot, Cin collimator viewfinder; **~ de tir aérien** = **~ de bombardement**.

visibilité /vizibilite/ *nf* visibility; **~ réduite à cause de brouillard** reduced visibility due to fog; **la ~ était mauvaise** visibility was poor; **virage sans ~** blind bend.

visible /vizibl/ *adj* **1** (perceptible) visible; **~ à l'œil nu** visible to the naked eye; **2** (manifeste) obvious; **il a fait des progrès ~s** he has made tangible ou obvious progress; **son émotion était ~** he was visibly moved, you could see that he was moved; **elle va beaucoup mieux, c'est ~** she's obviously a lot better, you can see she's a lot better; **3** (en état de recevoir) [*personne*] available; **4** (accessible au public) **les tableaux du jeune artiste sont ~s jusqu'au 17 mai** the young artist's paintings can be seen until 17 May.

visiblement /viziblǝmɑ̃/ *adv* **1** (manifestement) visibly, obviously; **2** (de façon perceptible à l'œil) visibly, perceptibly.

visière /vizjɛʀ/ *nf* **1** (de casquette, képi) peak; **2** (de casque, heaume) visor; **3** (sans couvre-chef) eyeshade, visor; **mettre la main en ~** to shade one's eyes with one's hand.

visioconférence /vizjokɔ̃feʀɑ̃s/ *nf* **1** (séance) video-conference; **2** (principe) video-conferencing.

vision /vizjɔ̃/ *nf* **1** (faculté de voir) eyesight, vision; **~ nocturne** night vision; **2** (conception) view; **il faut avoir une ~ globale du problème** we need to take a global view of the problem; **la ~ du monde des occidentaux** the western view of the world; **une ~ pessimiste des choses** a pessimistic view of things; **3** (spectacle) sight; **la scène de l'accident était une véritable ~ d'horreur** the scene of the accident was a horrible sight; **4** (apparition) vision; **avoir des ~s** to see things, have visions.

visionnaire /vizjɔnɛʀ/ *adj, nmf* visionary.

visionner /vizjɔne/ [1] *vtr* to view [*film, diapositives*].

visionneuse /vizjɔnøz/ *nf* viewer.

visiophone /vizjɔfɔn/ *nm* videophone.

Visitation /vizitasjɔ̃/ *nf* **la ~** the Visitation.

visite /vizit/ I *nf* **1** (chez un ami) visit; (rapide) call; **~ de politesse** courtesy call; **recevoir** or **avoir la ~ de qn** to have a visit from sb; **rendre ~ à qn, faire une ~ à qn** to visit sb, to pay sb a call, to call on sb; **être en ~ chez qn** to be paying sb a visit; **passer son temps en ~s** to spend one's time calling on ou visiting people; **ta ~ me ferait plaisir** I would love to see you; **tu aurais besoin d'une ~ chez le dentiste/coiffeur** you should go to the dentist's/hairdresser's; **2** (de chef d'État) visit; **en ~ officielle au Japon** on an official visit to Japan; **3** (à un prisonnier, interne, malade) visit; **heures de ~** visiting hours ou time; **4** (en touriste) visit; **elle recommande la ~ du château** she recommends visiting the castle ou a visit to the castle; **~ accompagnée** or **guidée** guided tour; **5** (pour inspecter) inspection; **faire la ~ de** to make an inspection of, to inspect [*chantier, usine*]; **la ~ d'une maison** (avant de l'acheter) viewing a house; **6** (visiteur) visitor; **attendre de la ~** to expect visitors ou company; **avoir de la ~** to have visitors ou company; **avoir des ~s/une ~** to have visitors/a visitor; **7** (chez un médecin) consultation; (à domicile) visit, call; **le médecin est en ~** or **fait ses ~s** the doctor is making his (house) calls; **8** (de représentant) visit, call.

II **visite-** (*in compounds*) **~-éclair/-surprise** lightning/surprise visit.

■ **~ de contrôle** Méd follow-up visit; **~ domiciliaire** house search; **~ du diocèse** pastoral visitation; **~ d'entretien** Aut service; **~ (médicale)** (contrôle) medical (examination); (bilan) checkup.

visiter /vizite/ [1] *vtr* **1** [*touriste, curieux*] to visit, to go round[GB] [*musée, ville, pays*]; **faire ~ un lieu à qn** to show sb around a place; **le musée le plus visité** the museum that attracts the most visitors; **2** [*client*] to view [*appartement*]; to visit [*magasin*]; **3** hum ○[*cambrioleur*] **la villa a été visitée!** they've had callers at the villa!; **4** [*médecin, prêtre*] to visit [*malade, vieillard, prisonnier*]; **5** (inspecter) to inspect [*institution, local, navire*]; **6** (se manifester) [*bonheur, paix, grâce divine*] to visit.

visiteur, **-euse** /vizitœʀ, øz/ *nm,f* **1** (ami) visitor, caller; **les ~s** Sport the visiting team (*sg*); **2** (touriste) visitor.

■ **~ médical** Comm medical rep; **~ en pharmacie** Comm pharmaceutical rep; **~ de prison** prison visitor.

vison /vizɔ̃/ *nm* **1** (animal, fourrure) mink; **2** (manteau) mink (coat).

visonnière /vizɔnjɛʀ/ *nf* mink farm, minkery.

visqueux, **-euse** /viskø, øz/ *adj* **1** [*liquide, produit, consistance*] viscous, viscid; **2** (poisseux) sticky, gooey○; **3** (mielleux) [*personne, manières*] smarmy○, unctuous.

visser /vise/ [1] I *vtr* **1** (fixer avec des vis) to screw on [*serrure, boîtier*] (**dans** into; **sur** onto); **~ qch à fond** to screw sth up tight; **2** (fermer) to screw [sth] on [*couvercle, bouchon*]; **3** (immobiliser) **être vissé sur sa chaise/devant la télé/à son bureau** to be glued to one's chair/to the TV/to one's desk.

II **se visser** *vpr* [*pièces*] to screw together; [*couvercle, bouchon*] to screw on.

visserie /visʀi/ *nf* **1** (articles) screws and bolts; **2** (fabrique) screw factory.

visu /vizy/ *nm* Ordinat VDU; ▶ **de visu**.

visualisation /vizɥalizasjɔ̃/ *nf* **1** gén visualization; **2** Aviat, Ordinat display.

visualiser /vizɥalize/ [1] *vtr* **1** (représenter) to show [*données*]; **~ une variation sous forme de courbe** to show a variation in the form of a graph; **2** (mentalement) to visualize [*image, mot*]; **3** Ordinat to display; **4** controv Cin, TV to put [sth] on screen.

visuel, **-elle** /vizɥɛl/ I *adj* (tous contextes) visual; **organes ~s** visual organs; **avoir une bonne mémoire visuelle** to have a good visual memory.

II *nm,f* person with a strong visual sense; **c'est un ~** he has a strong visual sense.

III *nm* **1** Ordinat visual display unit, VDU; **2** Presse, Pub, TV **le ~** visuals (*pl*).

visuellement /vizɥɛlmɑ̃/ *adv* **1** (au moyen de la vue) **constater qch ~** to see sth with one's own eyes; **se souvenir ~ de qch** to see sth in one's mind's eye; **2** (sur le plan visuel) [*intéressant, amélioré*] visually.

vital, **~e**, *mpl* **-aux** /vital, o/ *adj* **1** Biol, Physiol vital; **2** (primordial) essential, vital.

vitalité /vitalite/ *nf* (de personne) vitality, energy; (de marché, d'économie) vitality; **elle déborde de ~** she's bursting with energy.

vitamine /vitamin/ *nf* vitamin; **~ A/B** vitamin A/B.

vitaminé, **~e** /vitamine/ *adj* [*médicament, lait, biscuit*] with added vitamins (*épith, après n*).

vitaminique /vitaminik/ *adj* vitamin (*épith*); **carences ~s** vitamin deficiencies.

La vitesse

La vitesse des véhicules

En anglais, on mesure couramment la vitesse des trains, des avions et des automobiles en miles à l'heure, même si les compteurs indiquent aussi les kilomètres.

30 miles à l'heure valent environ 50 km/h
50 miles à l'heure valent environ 80 km/h
80 miles à l'heure valent environ 130 km/h
100 miles à l'heure valent environ 160 km/h

Noter qu'on écrit -metre en anglais britannique, et -meter en anglais américain.

50 kilomètres à l'heure	=	50 kilometres an hour *ou* 50 kilometres per hour
100 km/h	=	100 kph (*dire* kilometres an hour; p *signifie* per = par)
100 miles à l'heure	=	100 mph (*dire* miles an hour), = 160 km/h
à quelle vitesse la voiture roulait-elle?	=	what speed was the car going at? *ou* how fast was the car going?
elle roulait à 150 km/h	=	it was going at 150 kph
elle roulait à quatre-vingts à l'heure	=	it was going at fifty (*50 miles à l'heure*), it was going at 80 kph
la voiture faisait du combien?	=	what was the car doing?
elle faisait du 160 *(km/h)*	=	it was doing a hundred (mph), it was doing 160 kph
faire du 160 á l'heure	=	to do a hundred (mph) *ou* to do 160 kph
à une vitesse de 80 km/h	=	at a speed of 50 mph, at a speed of 80 kph

Noter l'absence d'équivalent anglais de la préposition française de avant le chiffre dans:

la vitesse de la voiture était de 160 km/h	=	the speed of the car was 100 mph, the speed of the car was 160 kph
à peu près 80 km/h	=	about 50 mph, about 80 kph
presque 80 km/h	=	almost 50 mph, almost 80 kph
plus de 70 km/h	=	more than 45 mph, more than 70 kph
moins de 85 km/h	=	less than 55 mph, less than 85 kph
A va plus vite que B	=	A is faster than B
B roulait moins vite que A	=	B was going slower than A
A va aussi vite que B	=	A is as fast as B
A roulait à la même vitesse que B	=	A was going at the same speed as B
A et B vont à la même vitesse	=	A and B go at the same speed

La vitesse du son et de la lumière

le son se déplace à 330 m/s	=	sound travels at 330 metres per second (*dire* three hundred and thirty metres per second)
la vitesse de la lumière est de 300 000 km/s	=	the speed of light is 186,300 miles per second

vite /vit/ *adv* **1** (rapidement) quickly; **~ et bien** quickly and well; **très/trop/un peu ~** very/too/a bit quickly; **au plus ~, le plus ~ possible** as quickly as possible; **~!** quick!; **aller ~** to be quick; **faire ~** to be quick (**de** to); **elle a eu ~ fait de répondre** she was quick to answer; **ça ira ~** [*opération, traitement*] it'll soon be over; [*procédure, réparation*] it won't take long; **puis on est passé ~ fait**○ **au sujet suivant** then we quickly went on to the next subject; **on a pris un verre/mangé ~ fait**○ we had a quick drink/snack; **je range ma chambre ~ fait bien fait**○ **et j'arrive** I'll give my room a quick tidy and I'm coming; **range ta chambre, et plus ~ que ça!**○ tidy up your room, and be quick about it!; **2** (peu après le début) soon; **il a ~ compris** he soon understood; **elle s'est ~ fatiguée d'expliquer** she soon got tired of explaining; **elle se fatigue/s'ennuie ~** she soon gets tired/bored; **c'est une affection bénigne, ça passera ~** it's only a minor trouble, it'll soon get better; **ce travail devient ~ ennuyeux/épuisant** this work soon becomes boring/exhausting; **ils se sont retrouvés ~ fait**○ **derniers du classement** they soon found themselves in last place; **3** (hâtivement) **j'ai parlé trop ~** (sans réfléchir) I spoke too hastily; (sans tenir compte de tout) I spoke too soon; **c'est ~ dit!** that's easy to say!; **c'est ~ fait d'accuser le temps** it's easy to blame the weather.

vitesse /vitɛs/ *nf* **1** (rapidité) speed; **à grande/petite ~** [*se déplacer, circuler*] at high/low speed; **à une ~ folle** at an incredible speed; **à la ~ d'un cheval au galop/de 50 km/h** at the speed of a galloping horse/at a speed of 50 km/h; **à la ~ moyenne de** at an average speed of; **prendre/perdre de la ~** to gather/lose speed; **~ de pointe** maximum speed; **~ du son/de la lumière** speed of sound/of light; **il travaille à une ~!** he works so fast!; **partir à toute ~** to rush away; **la voiture est passée à toute ~** the car flashed past; **à deux ~s** [*courrier, système, régime*] two-tier (*épith*); **faire de la ~** [*automobiliste*] to drive fast; **gagner** or **prendre qn de ~** lit, fig to outstrip sb; **en ~** (vite) quickly; (trop vite) in a rush; **passer en ~** [*personne*] to pop in○; **nous avons mangé en ~ avant de partir** we had a quick meal before leaving; **je vous écris en ~ depuis l'aéroport** I'm writing you a quick note from the airport; **range ta chambre, et en ~!** tidy up your room, and be quick about it!; **(il s'enfuit) de toute la ~ de ses petites jambes** (he ran away) as fast as his little legs would carry him; **2** Tech (engrenage, rapport) gear; **voiture à cinq ~s** car with five gears; **boîte à cinq ~s** five-speed gearbox; **il y a une cinquième ~ sur sa voiture** his car has a fifth gear; **passer les ~s** to change gear GB, to shift gear US; **passer la ~ supérieure/inférieure** to change up/down a gear; **passer ses ~s en douceur** to go smoothly through the gears; **faire grincer les ~s** to crunch the gears; **bicyclette à trois/douze ~s** three-/twelve-speed bicycle; **passer à la ~ supérieure** fig to speed things up.

■ ~ angulaire M écan angular velocity; **~ initiale** Mécan initial velocity; (de balle, obus) muzzle velocity; **~ de libération** Astronaut, Phys escape velocity; **~ de propagation** Phys velocity of propagation; **~ radiale** Astron radial velocity; **~ de réaction** Chimie, Psych speed of reaction; **~ de rotation** Mécan rotational velocity; **~ de sédimentation** Biol, Méd sedimentation rate.

IDIOMES **à la ~ grand V, en quatrième ~** at top speed; **expédier qch en petite ~** Rail to send sth by goods train.

viticole /vitikɔl/ *adj* [*industrie, cave*] wine (*épith*); [*région, pays*] wine-producing (*épith*).

viticulteur, -trice /vitikyltœʀ, tʀis/ **▶510** *nm,f* wine-grower, viticulturalist.

viticulture /vitikyltyʀ/ *nf* wine-growing, viticulture.

vitrage /vitʀaʒ/ *nm* **1** (surfaces vitrées) windows (*pl*); **poser le ~ d'une pièce** to put the windows in a room; **double ~** double glazing; **2** (châssis) gén glass panelling[GB]; (pour séparer) glass partition; (pour abriter) glass roof; **3** Tech (verres plats) plate glass; **4** (pose) glazing.

vitrail, *pl* **-aux** /vitʀaj, o/ *nm* **1** (fenêtre) stained glass window; **2** (technique, fabrication) stained glass window making; **l'art du ~** the art of stained glass.

vitre /vitʀ/ *nf* **1** (de fenêtre) pane, windowpane; (fenêtre) window; (panneau) pane of glass; **faire** or **laver les ~s** to clean the windows; **2** (de voiture, train) window; **baisse/remonte la ~ s'il te plaît** put the window down/up please.

■ ~ arrière rear window; **~ blindée** bulletproof window; **~ électrique** electric window; **~ teintée** (de voiture) tinted window; (de bâtiment) tinted (pane of) glass.

vitré, ~e /vitʀe/ **I** *pp* ▶ **vitrer**.

II *pp adj* **1** (en vitres) glass (*épith*), glazed (*épith*); **surface ~e** glass surface; **bureaux ~s** glass-walled offices; **studio de télévision ~** glass-panelled[GB] TV studio; **toiture ~e** glass roof; **2** Anat (de l'œil) vitreous.

III *nm* Anat (de l'œil) vitreous body.

vitrer /vitʀe/ [1] *vtr* to glaze [*panneau, fenêtre, serre*]; **~ une porte** to put windows in a door.

vitrerie /vitʀəʀi/ **▶510** *nf* **1** (magasin) glazier's; **2** (fabrication) glasswork; (industrie) glass industry.

vitreux, -euse /vitʀø, øz/ *adj* **1** [*regard*] glazed; **2** Minér [*éclat*] glassy; [*état, roche*] vitreous.

vitrier /vitʀije/ **▶510** *nm* glazier.

vitrification /vitʀifikasjɔ̃/ *nf* **1** (de parquet) varnishing, sealing; **2** Tech (en verrerie) vitrification; (en génie nucléaire) vitrification.

vitrifier /vitʀifje/ [2] **I** *vtr* **1** (vernir) to varnish [*parquet*]; **2** Tech (en verrerie) to vitrify; (en génie nucléaire) to vitrify.

II se vitrifier *vpr* to vitrify; **lave qui se vitrifie en refroidissant** lava that vitrifies on cooling.

vitrine /vitʀin/ *nf* **1** (de boutique) (shop ou store) window; **article en ~** item in the window; **je voudrais le modèle en ~** I'd like the one in the window; **faire les ~s** (regarder) to go window-shopping; (décorer) to dress the windows; **elle a passé la journée à lécher les ~s** she spent the whole day window-shopping; **2** (meuble) display cabinet GB, curio cabinet US; **3** (de musée) (show)-case; **4** fig (mise en valeur) showcase; **cette exposition sera la ~ de l'informatique européenne** this exhibition will be a showcase for European computer technology.

■ ~ frigorifique chill cabinet GB, refrigerated case US.

vitriol /vitʀijɔl/ *nm* vitriol; **humour/discours au ~** fig vitriolic humour[GB]/speech.

vitrioler /vitʀijɔle/ [1] *vtr* **1** (lancer du vitriol) to throw vitriol at [*personne, animal*]; **2** Tech to vitriolize, treat [sth] with vitriol [*eau, toiles*].

vitro ▶ **in vitro**.

vitrocéramique /vitʀoseʀamik/ *nf* ceramic; **table de cuisson en ~** ceramic hob.

vitupération /vitypeʀasjɔ̃/ *nf* vituperation.

vitupérer /vitypeʀe/ [14] **I** *vtr* liter to vituperate against [*comportement, défaut*].

II *vi* to rail; **~ contre** controv to rail against.

vivable /vivabl/ *adj* [*situation, atmosphère, personne*] bearable; **pas ~** unbearable; **ce n'est pas ~ ici** it is impossible to live here.

vivace[1] /vivas/ *adj* **1** Bot perennial; **plante ~** perennial; **2** (durable) [*tradition, souvenir*] enduring.

vivace[2] /vivatʃe/ *adj inv, adv* Mus vivace.

vivacité /vivasite/ *nf* **1** (fougue) (de personne) vivacity; (de sentiment, passion) intensity; **2** (promptitude) (de mouvement) vivacity; (de repartie, d'intelligence) keenness; (de réaction) swiftness; (brusquerie) brusqueness; **avec ~** (promptement) [*se mouvoir, réagir*] swiftly; (brusquement) [*répondre, répliquer*] sharply; **il est d'une surprenante ~ pour son âge** he's surprisingly sprightly for his age; **3** (de souvenir, impression, couleur) vividness; (de regard) spark; (de lueur) brightness.

vivandier, -ière /vivɑ̃dje, ɛʀ/ *nm,f* sutler, vivandiere.

vivaneau, *pl* **~x** /vivano/ *nm* red snapper.

vivant, ~e /vivɑ̃, ɑ̃t/ **I** *adj* **1** (en vie) [*personne, animal, cellule*] living; **il est ~** he is alive; **il est toujours ~** he is still alive ou living; **un homard ~** a live lobster; **transportant des animaux ~s** transporting live animals; **moi ~, jamais il ne l'épousera** he'll marry her over my dead body; **2** (en chair et en os) [*exemple, symbole*] living; **d'après le modèle ~** from life; **ta mère, c'est un dictionnaire ~!** your mother is a walking dictionary; **3** (animé) [*personne*] lively, vivacious; [*lieu, récit, style*] lively; **4** (reproduisant bien la vie) [*description, récit*] vivid; **5** (vivace) **être encore ~** [*coutume, souvenir*] to be still alive.
II *nm* **1** (être vivant) living being; **les ~s** the living; **les ~s et les morts** the living and the dead; ▶**bon**; **2** (période de vie) **de mon/leur ~** in my/their lifetime; **du ~ de mon père** while my father was alive; **3** (vie) life.

vivarium /vivaʀjɔm/ *nm* vivarium.

vivats /viva/ *nmpl* cheers.

vive I ▶**vif I, III.**
II ▶**vivre II.**

vive-eau, *pl* **vives-eaux** /vivo, *pl* vivzo/ *nf* spring tide.

vivement /vivmɑ̃/ *adv* **1** (fortement) [*encourager, critiquer, recommander, réagir*] strongly; [*inquiéter*] greatly; [*contraster, augmenter*] sharply; [*émouvoir, regretter, ressentir*] deeply; [*contester, attaquer*] fiercely; **je souhaite ~ vous rencontrer** I should very much like to meet you; **2** (rapidement) [*partir, se lever*] swiftly; **~ dimanche!** I can't wait for Sunday!; **~ qu'elle s'en aille!** I can't wait for her to go!; **3** (avec emportement) **parler ~ à qn** to speak sharply to sb.

viveur /vivœʀ/ *nm* fast liver, pleasure-seeker.

vivier /vivje/ *nm* **1** (naturel) fishpond; (artificiel) fish-tank; (sur un bateau) fish well; **2** (pépinière) breeding ground; **un ~ d'ingénieurs** a breeding ground for engineers.

vivifiant, ~e /vivifjɑ̃, ɑ̃t/ *adj* **1** (revigorant) [*air, climat*] invigorating; **2** (stimulant) [*activité, paroles*] stimulating.

vivifier /vivifje/ [2] *vtr* **1** (revigorer) [*air, climat, soleil*] to invigorate [*personne, plante*]; **2** (stimuler) to breathe new life into [*région, secteur, économie*].

vivipare /viviparʀ/ **I** *adj* viviparous.
II *nm* viviparous mammal.

viviparité /vivipaʀite/ *nf* viviparity.

vivisection /vivisɛksjɔ̃/ *nf* vivisection.

vivo ▶**in vivo**.

vivoter /vivɔte/ [1] *vi* to struggle along; **~ de qch** to scrape a living from sth.

vivre /vivʀ/ [63] **I** *vtr* **1** (connaître) to live through [*époque, période*]; to go through [*heures difficiles, cauchemar, enfer*]; to experience [*amour, passion*]; **~ son mariage comme un sacrifice** to view one's marriage as self-sacrifice; **être vécu comme un affront** to be taken as an insult; **~ une vie tranquille/agitée** to lead a quiet/hectic life; **la vie vaut d'être vécue** life is worth living; **~ sa vie** to lead one's own life; **2** (ressentir) to cope with [*divorce, échec, changement*]; **comment as-tu vécu votre séparation?** how did you cope with your separation?; **~ sa foi** to put one's faith into practice[GB]?
II *vi* **1** Biol (être vivant) [*personne, animal, plante*] to live; **~ longtemps/vieux/centenaire** to live for a long time/to a great age/to be a hundred; **cesser de ~** euph to pass away; **vive la révolution/le président!** long live the revolution/the president!; **vive(nt) les vacances!** three cheers for the holidays GB ou the vacation US!; **vive la vie!** life is wonderful!; **vive moi/nous!** three cheers for me/us!; **vive Paul!** hurray for Paul!; **2** (habiter) [*personne, animal, plante*] to live; **~ à la campagne/en démocratie** to live in the country/in a democracy; **il vit avec quelqu'un** he's living with somebody; **~ à cinq dans une chambre** to live five to a room; **être facile/difficile à ~** [*conjoint, concubin*] to be easy/difficult to live with; [*ami, collègue*] to be easy/difficult to get on with; **~ les uns sur les autres** to live on top of each other; **3** (exister) [*personne*] to live; **~ en ermite** to live like a hermit; **~ dans la crainte/pour ses enfants** to live in fear/for one's children; **~ avec son temps** to move with the times; **~ à contre-courant** to go one's own way; **~ en pyjama** to live in one's pyjamas GB ou pajamas US; **se laisser ~** to take things easy; **apprendre à qn à ~**○ to teach sb some manners○; **savoir ~** (profiter de la vie) to know how to enjoy life; (être poli) to know how things are done; **4** (survivre) [*personne*] to live; **bien ~** to live well; **~ de peu** to live on very little; **de quoi vit-elle?** what does she live on?; **avoir de quoi ~** to have enough to live on; **~ avec presque rien/sur son capital/de la charité** to live on next to nothing/on one's capital/on charity; **~ de légumes** to live on vegetables; **~ sur sa réputation** to live on one's reputation; **~ de ses rentes** to have a private income; **faire ~ qn** (matériellement) to keep sb; **~ aux dépens de qn** to live off sb; **~ d'espoir** to live in hope; **qu'est-ce qui te fait ~?** what keeps you going?; **5** (durer) [*relation, mode, idéologie*] to last; **le gouvernement ne vivra pas longtemps** the government won't last long; **avoir vécu** [*personne*] to have seen a great deal of life; hum (être usé) [*objet, idée*] to have had its day; **mes chaussures ont vécu** my shoes have had their day; **leur souvenir vivra dans nos mémoires** their memory will live on in our hearts; **6** (être animé) [*ville, rue*] to be full of life.
III se vivre *vpr* (être ressenti) **le divorce se vit souvent très mal** divorce is often very hard to cope with.
IV vivres *nmpl* **1** (nourriture) food, supplies; **2** (moyens de subsistance) **couper les ~s à qn** to cut off sb's allowance.
IDIOMES **le ~ et le couvert** board and lodging; **~ de l'air du temps** to live on air; **~ sur un grand pied** to live in great style; **qui vivra verra** what will be will be.

vivrière /vivʀijɛʀ/ *adj f* **cultures ~s** subsistence crops.

vizir /viziʀ/ *nm* vizier; **le Grand ~** the Grand Vizier.

vlan /vlɑ̃/ *excl* **et ~! encore une porte qui claque!** bang! another door slamming!; **et ~! il m'envoie un coup de poing** wham! he punches me.

vo /veo/ *nf*: *abbr* ▶**version**.

vocable /vɔkabl/ *nm* **1** (mot) term; **2** Relig **chapelle sous le ~ de** chapel dedicated to.

vocabulaire /vɔkabylɛʀ/ *nm* vocabulary; **~ actif/passif/fondamental** active/passive/basic vocabulary; **le ~ de Racine/de la botanique** the vocabulary of Racine/of botany; **'~ bilingue d'informatique'** 'a bilingual vocabulary of computer technology'; **leur ~ est ésotérique/très riche/limité** their vocabulary is esoteric/very rich/poor.

vocal, ~e, *mpl* **-aux** /vɔkal, o/ *adj* vocal.

vocalement /vɔkalmɑ̃/ *adv* vocally.

vocalique /vɔkalik/ *adj* vowel (*épith*), vocalic.

vocalisation /vɔkalizasjɔ̃/ *nf* **1** Mus singing exercise; **2** Ling vocalization.

vocalise /vɔkaliz/ *nf* singing exercise, exercise in vocalization spéc; **faire des ~s** to practise[GB] singing exercises.

vocaliser /vɔkalize/ [1] **I** *vtr* Ling to vocalize.
II *vi* Mus to practise[GB] singing exercises, vocalize spéc.
III se vocaliser *vpr* Ling to become vocalized.

vocalisme /vɔkalism/ *nm* Ling, Phon **1** (système vocalique) vowel system; **2** (d'un mot) vowel pattern; **3** (théorie) vocalism.

vocatif /vɔkatif/ *nm* Ling vocative; **au ~** in the vocative.

vocation /vɔkasjɔ̃/ *nf* **1** (de personne) vocation, calling; **~ sacerdotale** vocation for the priesthood; **~ artistique/littéraire** artistic/literary vocation; **~ contrariée** frustrated calling; **manquer sa ~** to miss one's vocation; **se sentir une ~ de médecin** to feel that medicine is one's vocation; **se sentir une ~ de comptable** to feel drawn to accountancy; **il n'a pas la ~ de l'enseignement** he's not cut out to be a teacher, teaching isn't his vocation; **2** (d'institution) purpose; **il assigne à l'école une double ~** he thinks schools should serve a dual purpose; **l'association a pour ~ d'aider les malades** or **l'aide aux malades** the association is intended to help the sick; **salles à ~ récréative** rooms intended for leisure activities; **région à ~ touristique/agricole** tourist/farming area; **école à ~ technique** technical school; **chaîne à ~ culturelle** cultural channel.

vocifération /vɔsifeʀasjɔ̃/ *nf* clamour[GB] ₵, vociferation sout; **pousser des ~s** to utter cries of rage.

vociférer /vɔsifeʀe/ [14] **I** *vtr* to shout [*insultes*].
II *vi* to shout, to vociferate sout; **~ contre** to shout angrily at.

vocodeur /vɔkɔdøʀ/ *nm* vocoder.

vodka /vɔdka/ *nf* vodka; **~ orange** vodka and orange, screwdriver.

vœu, *pl* **~x** /vø/ *nm* **1** (souhait) wish; **faire un ~** to make a wish; **mon ~ le plus cher est qu'il guérisse** my dearest wish is that he should recover; **il a exprimé** or **émis le ~ que l'école soit reconstruite** he expressed the wish that the school should be rebuilt; **les élèves doivent émettre** or **formuler des ~x d'orientation** pupils must indicate their preferred subject choices; **je fais des ~x pour que la paix revienne** I hope and pray that peace may return; **appeler qch de tous ses ~x** to hope and pray for sth; **former des ~x pour le bonheur/la réussite de qn** to wish sb every happiness/success; **former des ~x pour la santé de qn** to wish sb a speedy recovery; **'tous mes ~x t'accompagnent'** 'my best wishes go with you'; **'nos meilleurs ~x aux jeunes époux'** 'our best wishes to the bride and groom'; **2** (de Nouvel An) New Year's greetings; **recevoir les ~x du personnel** to receive New Year's greetings from the staff; **adresser ses ~x à qn** to wish sb a happy New Year; **le message de ~x du Président** Radio, TV the President's New Year address to the nation; **meilleurs ~x de bonne et heureuse année** best wishes for the New Year, Happy New Year; **3** (promesse) vow; **~x de pauvreté/chasteté** vows of poverty/chastity; **prononcer ses ~x** Relig to take one's vows; **faire ~ de pauvreté** to take a vow of poverty; **faire ~ de fidélité** to vow to remain faithful; **faire ~ de se venger** to vow to take one's revenge.
■ **~ pieux** wishful thinking ₵; **faire des ~x pieux** to indulge in wishful thinking.

vogue /vɔg/ *nf* **1** (mode) fashion, vogue; **la ~ des cheveux longs est passée/de retour** the fashion for long hair has passed/is coming back; **la ~ des Beatles** the Beatles craze○; **en ~** [*style, idée, personne*] fashionable, in vogue (*jamais épith*); [*objet,* *vêtement*] in fashion (*jamais épith*); **c'est très en ~** [*voiture, musique*] it's the latest craze○ ou thing○; [*vêtement*] it's the latest fashion; **2** (fête) dial fair.

voguer /vɔge/ [1] *vi* liter **1** [*navire*] (naviguer) to sail (**vers** toward, towards GB); **2** fig [*esprit, pensées*] to wander; **insouciant de tout, il voguait au gré des événements** oblivious to everything, he drifted with the flow of events.

IDIOMES **et vogue la galère!** come what may!

voici /vwasi/ **I** *prép* **son fils est né ~ un mois** his/her son was born a month ago; **~ quelque temps** some time ago; **~ bientôt deux mois qu'elle travaille chez nous** she's been working with us for nearly two months.

II *présentatif* **1** (pour désigner) (une chose proche) **~ ma clé/mes clés** here is my key/are my keys; (une personne proche) **~ le docteur qui arrive** here comes ou here's the doctor; **les ~** here they are, here they come; **'me ~'** 'here I am'; **2** (en guise de présentation) **~ ma fille** this is my daughter; **~ mes enfants** these are my children; **M. Bon/le ressort que ~ est**... Mr Bon/this spring here is...; **3** (en guise d'introduction) **~ l'adresse** here's the address, this is the address; **~ les résultats** here are the results, these are the results; **~ le programme/la solution** the programme[GB]/the answer is as follows; **le film raconte l'histoire que ~** the film tells the following story; **~ comment/pourquoi/où** here's ou this is how/why/where; **~ où je voulais en venir** that's the point I wanted to make; **~ ce qu'il a fait/ce dont je t'ai parlé** this is what he did/what I was telling you about; **~ qui va vous étonner/amuser** here is ou this is something that'll surprise you/that you'll find amusing; **4** (pour souligner une situation, une action, un événement) **~ enfin l'été** summer's here at last; **~ venir l'hiver/le cortège** here comes winter/the procession; **je sens que ~ venir l'instant des reproches** I feel that the moment for criticisms is approaching ou upon us hum; **'je voudrais la clé du trois'—'~, madame'** 'I'd like the key to number three'—'here you are, madam'; **tu veux des fraises? en ~** you'd like some strawberries? here you are (then); **nous y ~** (à la maison) here we are; (au cœur du sujet) now we're getting there; **~ nos amis bien perplexes/enfin au calme** now our friends are really confused/have got some quiet at last; **alors qu'on le croyait calmé, le ~ qui s'enfuit à nouveau** just when we thought he had calmed down he runs off again.

III voici que *loc conj* liter all of a sudden; **~ qu'elle disparaît sans laisser d'adresse** all of a sudden she disappeard without leaving an address; **~ qu'arrive l'armée ennemie** here come the enemy forces.

voie /vwa/ *nf* **1** fig (chemin) way; **la ~ de la paix/modernisation/sagesse** the way to peace/modernization/wisdom; **être sur la ~ d'un accord** to be on the way to an agreement; **montrer la ~ à qn** to show sb the way; **montrer la ~** [*personne, pays, entreprise*] to lead the way; **ouvrir la ~ à** to pave the way for; **la ~ est libre** the way is clear; **chercher/trouver sa ~** to look for/find one's way in life; **entreprise en ~ de devenir le cinquième groupe européen** company on its way to becoming number five in Europe; **sur** or **dans la ~ de** on the road to; **s'engager sur** or **dans une ~ dangereuse** to embark on a dangerous course; **choisir/suivre une ~ médiane** fig to choose/follow a middle course; **être sur la bonne/mauvaise ~** [*personne*] to be on the right/wrong track; **les travaux/négociations sont en bonne ~** the work is/the negotiations are progressing; **la ~ royale vers le pouvoir** the fast track to power; **les sociétés déficitaires ou en ~ de l'être** companies in deficit or (in the process of) becoming so; **en ~ de désintégration** disintegrating (*après n*); **par ~s de conséquence** consequently; **espèce en ~ d'extinction** or **de disparition** endangered species; **pays en ~ de développement** developing country; ▶ **impénétrable**; **2** (intermédiaire) channels (*pl*); **par la ~ diplomatique** through diplomatic channels; **par la ~ du référendum** by means of a referendum; **par ~ de presse** through the press; **par des ~ détournées** by roundabout means; **par ~ de tracts/d'affiches** through leaflets/posters; **par ~ de mer** by sea; **par la ~ des airs** by air; **par ~ d'action** Jur by bringing action; ▶ **concours**, **conséquence**, **scrutin**; **3** (subdivision de route) lane; (route) road; (rue) street; **route à trois ~s** three-lane road; **~ réservée aux autobus** bus lane; **~ à sens unique** (en rase campagne) one-way road; (en ville) one-way street; **~ à double sens** (en rase campagne) road for two-way traffic GB, two-way road US; (en ville) street for two-way traffic GB, two-way street US; **4** Rail (rails) track; **~ large/étroite** wide-/narrow-gauge track; **ligne à ~ unique/à double ~** single-/double-track line; **ne rien jeter sur la ~** do not throw anything onto the track; **'défense de traverser les ~s'** 'keep off the tracks'; **le train entre en gare ~ 2** the train is arriving at platform 2; **5** Pharm (mode d'administration) **par ~ injectable** by injection; **par ~ rectale** rectally; **par ~ intraveineuse** intravenously; **par ~ buccale** or **orale** orally; **par ~ nasale** nasally; ▶ **racolage**, **scandale**, **violence**.

■ **~ d'accélération** acceleration lane; **~ aérienne** Transp air route; **~ de communication** Transp transport link; **~ à contresens** contraflow lane; **~ de décélération** deceleration lane; **~ d'eau** Naut leak; **~ d'évitement** Rail siding; **~ express** expressway; **~ ferrée** Rail (infrastructure) railway track GB, railroad track US; Transp (mode de transport, ligne) railway GB, railroad US; **~ fluviale** Transp (inland) waterway; **~ de garage** Rail siding; **mettre qn sur une ~ de garage** fig to shunt sb onto the sidelines; **~ de gauche** fast lane; **~ hertzienne** Télécom Hertzian waves (*pl*); **par la ~ hertzienne** by Hertzian waves; **~ hiérarchique** Admin right channels (*pl*); **Voie lactée** Astron Milky Way; **~ maritime** Transp sea route; **~ navigable** Transp waterway; **~ privée** Admin private road; **~ publique** Jur public highway; **sur la ~ publique** on the public highway; **~ de raccordement** Rail connecting track; Gén Civ slip road; **~ rapide** expressway; **~ de recours** Jur path for appeal; **~ sans issue** Gén Civ, fig dead end; (sur panneau) no through road; **~ souterraine** underpass; **~s de fait** Jur (agression) battery (*sg*); Admin, Jur (atteinte aux droits) ≈ infringement of civil liberties; **~s nasales** Anat nasal passages; **~s respiratoires** Anat respiratory tract (*sg*); **~s urinaires** Anat urinary tract (*sg*).

voilà /vwala/ **I** *prép* **son fils est né ~ un mois** his/her son was born a month ago; **~ bientôt deux mois qu'elle travaille chez nous** she's been working with us for nearly two months.

II *présentatif* **1** (pour désigner) (en opposition à voici) **et ~ une clé/des clés** and there is a key/are keys; **le ~ encore!** there he is again!; **voici ton parapluie et ~ le mien** this is your umbrella and here's mine; **2** (même valeur que voici) here is [*clé, livre*]; here are [*clés, livres*]; **tu cherchais ton sac? le ~** were you looking for your bag? here it is; **~ ma mère** here's ou here comes my mother; **attention, la ~!** watch out, here she comes!; **me ~!** (j'arrive) I'm coming!; (je suis là) here I am!; **voici mon fils et ~ ma fille** this is my son and this is my daughter; **ah! te ~! c'est à cette heure que tu rentres?** ah, there you are! what time do you call this?; **tiens! ~ le soleil!** look! here's the sun!; **3** (pour conclure) **~ tout** that's all; **~ comment/pourquoi/ce que** that's how/why/what; **~ où je voulais en venir** that's the point I wanted to make; **~ où nous en étions** that's where we were up to; **~ ce que c'est de faire le malin/désobéir** that's what happens if you show off/disobey; **~ ce que déclare un jeune homme** so says a young man; **il est malade, ~ ce qui le tracasse** he's ill, that's what's worrying him; **je n'ai pas pu venir, ~ tout** (ne posez pas de questions) I couldn't come, that' s all there is to it; **~ qui ne va pas arranger vos affaires/ne se reproduira pas** well, that won't sort things out for you/won't happen again; **~ qui m'arrange!** that's what I need!; **~ de quoi faire réfléchir les jeunes** that's something for young people to think about; **4** (en introduction) here is, this is [*histoire, adresse*]; here are, these are [*chiffres, adresses*]; **~ le programme/la solution** the programme[GB]/the answer is as follows; **le film raconte l'histoire que ~** the film tells the following story; **~ comment/pourquoi/où** (en introduction) this is how/why/where; (en conclusion) that's how/why/where; **'seulement** or **c'est que ~,' dit-elle, 'je n'ai pas d'argent'** 'the problem ou thing is,' she said, 'I don't have any money'; **5** (pour souligner) **~ enfin l'été!** summer's here at last!; **'je voudrais la clé du trois'—'~, madame'** 'I'd like the key to number three'—'here you are, madam'; **nous y ~** (à la maison) here we are; (au cœur du sujet) now we're getting there; **~ nos amis bien perplexes/enfin au calme** now our friends are really confused/have got some quiet at last; **alors qu'on le croyait calmé, le ~ qui s'enfuit à nouveau** just when we thought he had calmed down he runs off again; **le ~ qui se remet à rire!** there he goes again laughing!; **à peine étais-je arrivé, le ~ qui vient vers moi** I'd only just arrived when there he was coming toward(s) me; **te ~ content!** now you're happy!; **te ~ revenu!** you're back again!; **vous ~ prévenus!** you've been warned!; **~ bien la manie française de tout critiquer!** that's the typical French habit of criticizing everything!; **~ bien les hommes!** that's men for you!; **~ bien ta mauvaise foi/façon exceptionnelle de conduire!** so much for your dishonesty/brilliant driving!; **ridicule, ~ le mot!** ridiculous! that's the word!

III en voilà *loc* **1** (en donnant) **tu veux des fraises? en ~** you'd like some strawberries? here you are; **vous vouliez des explications? en ~** you wanted more details! well, here you are (then); **en ~ pour dix francs** here's ten francs worth; **2** (valeur exclamative) **en ~ un mal élevé!** what a badly brought up boy!; **mon dieu! en ~ des histoires!** good Lord! what a fuss!; **en ~ assez!** that's enough!; **en ~ un qui ne recommencera pas!** there's someone who won't do it again!; **en ~ au moins un avec qui on peut parler!** there's somebody, at least, you can talk to!

IV voilà que○ *loc* **et ~ qu'une voiture arrive** and the next thing was a car arrived; **~ qu'il se met à rire** all of a sudden he started laughing; **et ~ qu'elle refuse/qu'il tombe malade** and then she had to go and refuse/he had to go and get ill GB ou sick US.

V *excl* **~! j'arrive!** (I'm) coming!, I'm on my way!; **~! ça arrive!** (it's) coming!, it's on its way!; **(et) ~! ils sont partis!** there you are, they've left!; **(et) ~! il remet ça!** there he goes again!; **ah! ~!** (je comprends) oh! that's it!, I see!; **on vit, on meurt, (et puis) ~!** you live, you die and that's it!

IDIOMES **il a de l'argent, en veux-tu en**

~! he has as much money as he could wish for!

voilage /vwalaʒ/ *nm* net curtain GB, sheer curtain US.

voile /vwal/ **I** *nm* **1** Mode, Relig (morceau d'étoffe) veil; **~ de deuil/de mariée** mourning/bridal veil; **prendre le ~** Relig to take the veil; **2** (étoffe) voile; **3** (masque abstrait) veil; **on jeta un ~ (pudique) sur l'affaire** a veil was drawn over the affair; **lever le ~ sur qch** to bring sth out in the open; **soulever un coin du ~ sur qch** to gain a glimpse into sth; **avoir un ~ sur** or **devant les yeux** to be blind to reality; **4** Tech (dans un liquide) cloud; (sur une radiographie) shadow; Phot fog; **un ~ blanchâtre opacifiait la solution** a whitish cloud was fogging the solution ; **~ de développement/de vieillissement** Phot fog in developing/from ageing; **avoir un ~ au poumon** to have a shadow on one's lung; **5** (écran) **regarder qch à travers un ~ de larmes** to look at sth through a mist of tears; **le brouillard étendait un ~ épais sur le paysage** there was a thick veil of fog over the landscape; **6** (de champignon) veil; **~ général/partiel** universal/partial veil.

II *nf* Naut **1** (toile) sail; **~ aurique/carrée/latine** fore-and-aft/square/lateen sail; **faire ~ vers** to sail toward(s); **mettre à la ~** to make way under sail; **toutes ~s dehors** lit full sail ahead; fig using every possible means; **2** (voilier) sailing boat, sailboat US; **3** (activité) sailing; **il fait de la ~ depuis deux ans** he's been going sailing for two years; **il donne des cours de ~ en été** he gives sailing lessons in the summer.

■ **~ blanc** Météo whiteout; **~ chimique** (chemical) fog; **~ d'étai** staysail; **~ islamique** yashmak; **~ noir** blackout; **~ du palais** soft palate, velum; **~ rouge** redout; **~ solaire** solar sail.

IDIOMES **être à ~ et à vapeur**○ to be AC/DC○; **mettre les ~s**○ to clear off○ GB, to clear out○ US; **avoir du vent dans les ~s**○ to be three sheets to the wind, to be drunk.

voilé, **~e** /vwale/ **I** *pp* ▸ **voiler**.

II *pp adj* **1** [*personne, objet*] veiled; **~ de noir** veiled in black; **2** (troublé) [*soleil, ciel*] hazy; [*regard, yeux*] misty; [*voix*] with a catch in it (*épith, après n*); [*photo, film*] fogged; **la lune est ~e par des nuages** the moon is veiled in cloud; **ils avaient les yeux ~s de larmes** their eyes were misted over with tears; **dit-elle, la voix légèrement ~e par l'émotion** she said with a slight catch in her voice; **3** (obscur) [*allusion, menace, critique*] veiled; **ils ont fait des allusions à peine ~es** they made thinly veiled allusions; **4** (déformé) [*roue*] buckled; [*panneau*] warped.

voilement /vwalmɑ̃/ *nm* (de roue) buckle; (de panneau) warp.

voiler /vwale/ [1] **I** *vtr* **1** (dissimuler) [*nuage, brume*] to veil [*ciel, paysage, soleil*]; [*personne, fait*] to conceal [*événement, fait*]; **~ son dépit** to conceal one's annoyance; **2** (déformer) to buckle [*roue*]; to warp [*panneau*]; **3** (troubler) [*contrariété, expression*] to mist [*regard*]; [*émotion*] to put a catch in [*voix*]; **les larmes me voilaient le regard** the tears were misting my vision; **4** (couvrir d'étoffe) to cover [*visage, nudité*]; to veil [*statue*].

II se voiler *vpr* **1** (se déformer) [*roue*] to buckle; [*panneau*] to warp; **2** (se troubler) [*ciel*] to cloud over; [*soleil, paysage*] to become hazy; [*regard*] to become misty; [*voix*] to have a catch in it; **3** (avec étoffe) [*personne*] to wear a veil; [*musulmane*] to wear the veil; **se ~ le visage** to veil one's face.

IDIOMES **se ~ la face** to look the other way.

voilerie /vwalʀi/ *nf* sail-loft.

voilette /vwalɛt/ *nf* veil; **rabattre/relever sa ~** to put the veil down/up; **une femme en ~** a woman wearing a hat with a veil.

voilier /vwalje/ *nm* **1** Naut (bateau) sailing boat GB, sailboat US; (grand navire) yacht, sailing ship; **2** Naut (fabricant, réparateur) sailmaker; **3** Zool **oiseau bon/mauvais ~** bird well/badly adapted for long distance flight.

voilure /vwalyʀ/ *nf* **1** Naut (ensemble des voiles) sails (*pl*); (surface des voiles) sail; **une ~ de 500m²** 500m² of sail; **balancer/régler la ~** to balance/adjust the rigging; **2** Aviat (d'avion) wing surface; (de parachute) canopy; **3** (courbure de déformation) (de roue) buckling; (de panneau) warping.

■ **~ tournante** Aviat rotary wing.

voir /vwaʀ/ [46] **I** *vtr* **1** (percevoir par les yeux) to see [*personne, objet*]; **dis-moi ce que tu vois** gén tell me what you see; **je ne vois rien** I can't ou don't see anything; **je n'y vois rien** I can't see a thing; **il faut le ~ pour le croire** it has to be seen to be believed; **je les ai vus de mes propres yeux** or **de mes yeux vu!** I saw them with my own eyes!; **je les ai vus comme je te vois!** I saw them as plainly as I see you standing there!; **que vois-je!** liter what's this I see?; **à la ~ si triste** when you see her so sad; **à le ~, on le prendrait pour un clochard** to look at him, you'd think he was a tramp; **faire ~ qch à qn** to show sb sth; **laisser ~ son ignorance** to show one's ignorance; **sa jupe fendue laissait ~ ses cuisses** her slit skirt showed her thighs; **~ qch en rêve** to dream about sth; ▸ **mûr**; **2** (être spectateur, témoin de) [*personne*] to see [*film, incident, événement*]; [*période, lieu, organisation*] to see [*événement, évolution, changement*]; **aller ~ un film** to go to see a film GB ou movie US; **nous voyons les prix augmenter** we see prices rising; **je les ai vus partir/qui partaient** I saw them leave/leaving; **on l'a vue entrer** she was seen going in, someone saw her go in; **la voiture qu'il a vue passer** the car he saw go by; **la ville qui l'a vue naître** her native town, the town where she was born; **le film est à ~** the film is worth seeing; **c'est triste/intéressant à ~** it' s sad/interesting to see; **c'est beau à ~** it's beautiful to look at; **ce n'est pas beau à ~** it's not a pretty sight; **il faut ~ comment**○! you should see how!; **j'aurais voulu que tu voies ça!** you should have seen it!; **je voudrais bien t'y ~!** I'd like to see how you'd get on!; **a-t-on jamais vu pareille audace!** have you ever seen such cheek!; **on n'a jamais vu ça!** it's unheard of!; **et vous n'avez encore rien vu!** you ain't seen nothing yet○! hum; **qu'est-ce qu'il ne faut pas ~, on aura tout vu!** could you ever have imagined such a thing!; **voyez-moi ça!** just look at that!; **3** (se figurer) to see; **comment vois-tu l'avenir?** how do you see the future?; **je le vois** or **verrais bien enseignant** I can just see him as a teacher; **je ne la vois pas faire ça toute sa vie** I can't see her doing it forever; **~ sa vie comme un désastre** to view one's life as a disaster; **on voit bien comment** it's easy to see how; **on ne voit guère comment, on voit mal comment** it's difficult to see how; **j'ai vu le moment où il allait m'étrangler** I thought he was about to strangle me; **je vois ça d'ici** I can just imagine; **tu vois un peu s'il arrivait maintenant!** just imagine, if he turned up now!; **4** (juger) to see; **c'est ma façon de ~ (les choses)** that's the way I see things; **je ne partage pas ta façon de ~** I see things differently from you; **~ en qn un ami** to see sb as a friend; **je ne vois pas qu'il y ait lieu d'intervenir** I don't see any reason to intervene; **c'est à toi de ~** it's up to you to decide; **~ favorablement une réforme** to be favourably[GB] disposed toward(s) a reform; **tu vas te faire mal ~ de Sophie** Sophie is going to think badly of you; **je te vois mal parti** you're heading for trouble; **5** (comprendre, déceler) to see [*cause, moyen, avantage*] (**dans** in); **je vois** I see; **je vois ce que tu veux dire** I see what you mean; **je ne vois pas qui tu veux dire** I don't know who you mean; **tu vois où elle veut en venir?** do you see what she's getting at?; **je ne vois pas où est le problème** I can't see the problem; **je ne vois pas l'intérêt d'attendre** I can't see the point of waiting; **je n'y vois aucun mal** I see no harm in it; **je ne vois aucun mal à ce qu'elle signe** I see no harm in her signing; **si tu n'y vois pas d'inconvénient** if it's all right with you, if you have no objection; **tu ne vois pas qu'il ment?** can't ou don't you see that he's lying? ; **on voit bien qu'elle n'a jamais travaillé!** you can tell ou it's obvious that she's never worked!; **je le vois à leur attitude** I can tell by their attitude; **à quoi le vois- tu?** how can you tell?; **6** (constater, découvrir) to see; **comme vous le voyez** as you can see; **à ce que je vois** from what I can see; **~ si/combien/pourquoi** to find out ou to see if/how much/why; **vois si c'est sec** see if it's dry; **vois si ça leur convient** find out ou see if it suits them; **on verra bien** well, we'll see; **'je ne paierai pas!'—'c'est ce que nous verrons!'** 'I won't pay!'—'we shall see about that!'; **c'est à ~** that remains to be seen; **j'ai fait ça pour ~** I did it to see what would happen; **essaie pour ~** try and see!; **essaie un peu/touches-y, pour ~!** (menace) you just try it/touch it!; **vous m'en voyez ravi** I am delighted about it; **7** (examiner, étudier) to see [*malade*]; to look at [*problème, dossier*]; (dans un texte) **~ page 10/le mode d'emploi** see page 10/instructions for use; **je verrai (ce que je peux faire)** I'll see (what I can do); **voyons** let's see; **8** (recevoir, se rendre chez, fréquenter) to see [*client, médecin, ami*]; **je le vois peu en ce moment** I don't see much of him at the moment; **aller ~ qn** gén to go to see sb; (à l'hôpital) to go to visit sb; **je passerai la ~ demain** I'll call on her tomorrow, I'll pop in and see her tomorrow; **9** (visiter) to see [*ville, monument*]; **~ du pays** to see the world; **10** (avoir un rapport avec) **avoir quelque chose à ~ avec** to have something to do with; **ça n'a rien à ~!** that's got nothing to do with it!; **il n'a rien à ~ là-dedans** or **à y ~** it's got nothing to do with him. ▸ **chandelle**.

II voir à *vtr ind* fml (veiller à) to see (**à** to); **voyez à ce que tout soit prêt** see to it ou make sure that everything is ready; **faudrait ~ à réserver des places**○ we ought to see about reserving ou booking GB seats; **voyez à réserver les places** make sure you reserve ou book GB the seats.

III *vi* **1** (avec les yeux) **~, y ~** to be able to see; **est-ce qu'un bébé (y) voit à la naissance?** can a baby see at birth?; **je** or **j'y vois à peine** I can hardly see; **(y) ~ double** to see double; **je vois trouble** everything is a blur; **~ loin** lit to see a long way off; **2** (par l'esprit) **(y) ~ clair dans qch** to have a clear understanding of sth; **~ loin** (être prévoyant) to look ahead; (être perspicace) to be far-sighted; **~ grand** to think big; **elle a vu juste** she was right; **il faut ~** (ça mérite réflexion) we'll have to see; (c'est incroyable) you wouldn't believe it; **3** (pour insister) **voyons ~** let's see now; **regardez ~** take a look; **dites ~** tell me; **montrez ~** show me; **4** (en incise) **vois-tu, voyez-vous** you see; **5** (rappel à l'ordre) **voyons, sois sage!** come on now, behave yourself!

IV se voir *vpr* **1** (dans la glace , en imagination) to see oneself; **elle se voyait déjà sur les planches** she could already see herself on the stage; **2** (être conscient de) to realize; **il s'est vu sombrer dans la folie** he realized he was going mad; **3** (se remarquer) [*tache, défaut*] to show; **ça se voit** it shows; **ça ne se voit pas qu'un peu**○! it sticks out a mile!; **4** (se produire) **cela se voit tous les jours** it happens all the time ou every day; **cela ne se voit pas tous les jours** it isn't something you see every day; **ça ne s'est jamais vu!** it's unheard of!; **5** (se trouver) **se ~ obligé** or **dans l'obligation de faire qch** to find oneself forced to do; **ils se sont vu ré-**

pondre que they were told that; **6** (se rencontrer, se fréquenter) to see each other; **7** (sympathiser) **ils ne peuvent pas se ~** they can't stand each other; **8** (être vu) to be seen; **la tour se voit de loin** the tower can be seen from far away; **9**○ **s'en ~** to have a hard time (**pour faire** doing).

IDIOMES **ne pas ~ plus loin que le bout de son nez** to see no further than the end of one's nose; **je préfère ~ venir** I would rather wait and see; **on t'a vu venir**○! they saw you coming○!; **je te vois venir**○ I can see what you're getting at GB ou where you're coming from○; **je ne peux pas le ~ (en peinture)**○ I can't stand him; **je t'ai assez vu** I've had enough of you; **en ~ de belles** or **de toutes les couleurs** to go through some hard times; **j'en ai vu d'autres** I've seen worse; **en faire ~ à qn** to give sb a hard time; **va te faire ~ (ailleurs)**○, **va ~ ailleurs** or **là-bas si j'y suis**○! get lost○!; **qu'il aille se faire ~**○! tell him to get lost○!; **il ferait beau ~ ça!** that would be the last straw!

voire /vwaʀ/ *adv* **1** (et même) or even, not to say; **l'épidémie tend à stagner, ~ à régresser** the epidemic has stopped spreading, or even retreated; **un changement serait prématuré, ~ dangereux** any change would be premature, not to say dangerous; **2** (marquant le doute) is this the case?

voirie /vwaʀi/ *nf* **1** (réseau) road, rail and waterways network; **2** (administration) *administration in charge of the road, rail and waterways network*.

voisé, **~e** /vwaze/ *adj* voiced.

voisement /vwazmɑ̃/ *nm* voicing.

voisin, **~e** /vwazɛ̃, in/ **I** *adj* **1** (de voisinage) [*maison, rue, pays, ville*] neighbouring[GB] (*épith*), nearby; (proche) [*forêt, lac, hôpital*] nearby; (d'à côté) [*pièce, table, maison*] next (**de** to); **dans une rue/ville ~e** in a neighbouring[GB] street/town; **dans la/une forêt ~e** in the/a nearby forest; **à la table ~e** at the next table; **dans la maison ~e** in the house next door; fig [*date, résultat, pourcentage*] close (**de** to); **les régions ~es de la Manche** the regions bordering the English Channel; **entretenir de bonnes relations avec les pays ~s** to maintain good relations with neighbouring[GB] countries; **2** (similaire) [*sentiments, idées*] similar; [*espèces*] (closely) related; **~ de** [*théorie, idée*] akin to; [*espèce*] related to.

II *nm,f* neighbour[GB]; **les ~s d'à côté** the next door neighbours[GB], the people next door; **les ~s d'en face** the people who live opposite; **les ~s de dessus/dessous** the people who live upstairs/downstairs; **ma ~e de palier** the woman across the landing; **mon ~ de table** the man ou person next to me at table; **mon ~ de droite** (à table etc) the man ou person (sitting) on my right; **'on ne copie pas sur son ~'** you mustn't copy from the person next to you; **avoir un dangereux ~ à sa frontière** to have a dangerous neighbour[GB] on one's doorstep; **venir en ~** lit to drop in ou by; fig to make an informal visit; **dire du mal du ~** fig to speak ill of others.

voisinage /vwazinaʒ/ *nm* **1** (voisins) neighbourhood[GB], neighbours[GB] (*pl*); **ameuter tout le ~** to rouse all the neighbours[GB] ou the whole neighbourhood[GB]; **entretenir des rapports de bon ~** lit, fig to maintain neighbourly[GB] relations; **des querelles de ~** neighbourhood[GB] disputes; **2** (environs) neighbourhood[GB]; **les enfants du ~** the children of the neighbourhood[GB]; **les maisons du ~** the houses in the neighbourhood[GB]; **3** (proximité) proximity; **vivre dans le ~ d'une usine/école** to live close to a factory/school.

voiture /vwatyʀ/ *nf* **1** Aut (automobile) car, automobile US; **2** Rail (wagon) carriage GB, coach GB, car US; **~ de tête/de queue** first/last carriage GB ou car US; **~ de première/seconde (classe)** first/second class carriage GB ou car US; **en ~!** all aboard!; **3** (véhicule) (pour voyageurs) carriage; (pour marchandises) cart.

■ **~ bélier** ramraiding car; **~ à bras** hand-drawn cart; **~ cellulaire** prison van GB, police wagon US; **~ à cheval** horse-drawn carriage; **~ de course** racing car; **~ école** driving-school car; **~ d'enfant** pram GB, baby carriage US; **~ d'infirme** wheelchair; **~ de location** hire car GB, rental car US; **~ de location sans chauffeur** self-drive hire car GB, rental car US; **~ particulière** private car; **~ pie** panda car GB, police car; **~ piégée** booby-trapped car; **~ de place** hired GB ou rental US chauffeur-driven limousine; **~ de poste** stage coach; **~ de sport** sports car; **~ de tourisme** saloon (car) GB, sedan US; **~ sans permis** very small car (*which can be driven without a licence*).

IDIOMES **à pied, à cheval, en ~** by whatever means of transport; **se garer** or **se ranger des ~s** to give up one's wild lifestyle.

voiture-balai, *pl* **voitures-balais** /vwatyʀbalɛ/ *nf* support vehicle.

voiture-bar, *pl* **voitures-bars** /vwatyʀbaʀ/ *nf* buffet car.

voiture-lit, *pl* **voitures-lits** /vwatyʀli/ *nf* sleeper, sleeping car US.

voiture-poste, *pl* **voitures-postes** /vwatyʀpɔst/ *nf* mail van GB, mailcar US.

voiturette /vwatyʀɛt/ *nf* very small car (*which can be driven without a licence*).

voiturier /vwatyʀje/ *nm* **1** (d'hôtel, de restaurant) (personne) valet; (service) valet-parking; **2** Jur carrier.

voix /vwa/ *nf inv* **1** Phon, Physiol voice; **d'une ~ douce/puissante/cassée** in a gentle/powerful/cracked voice; **~ de femme/d'homme** woman's/man's voice; **~ blanche** expressionless voice; **élever la ~** to raise one's voice; **~ intérieure** inner voice; **entendre des ~s** to hear voices; **à ~ haute** out loud; **à ~ basse** in a low voice; **donner de la ~** Chasse [*chien*] to give tongue; **être/rester sans ~** to be/remain speechless; **à portée de ~** within earshot; **2** (expression) voice; **la ~ de la sagesse/de la raison/du cœur** the voice of wisdom/of reason/of the heart; **c'est la ~ du sang qui parle** it's in the blood; **3** Mus voice; **~ de soprano/ténor/baryton** soprano/tenor/baritone voice; **~ de tête/poitrine** head/chest voice; **être en ~** to be in good voice; **avoir de la ~** to have a loud voice; **poser** or **placer sa ~** to place one's voice; **il a la ~ bien/mal placée** his voice is correctly/incorrectly placed; **travailler sa ~** to work on one's voice; **cantate à quatre ~** cantata for four voices; **une des plus belles ~ du monde** one of the finest voices in the world; **4** (opinion) voice; **la ~ du peuple/des opprimés** the voice of the people/of the oppressed; **faire entendre sa ~** to make oneself heard; **5** Pol vote; **par 194 ~ contre 33** by 194 votes to 33; **additionner les ~ des socialistes et celles des communistes** to count the socialists' and the communists' votes together; **avoir ~ consultative** to be present in an advisory capacity; **avoir ~ délibérative** to have the right to vote; **6** Ling voice; **à la ~ active/passive** in the active/passive voice.

■ **~ angélique** (d'orgue) vox angelica; **~ céleste** (d'orgue) voix céleste; **~ humaine** (d'orgue) vox humana; **~ off** Cin voice-over.

vol /vɔl/ **I** *nm* **1** (d'oiseau) flight (**de** of); **prendre son ~** to take wing, to fly off; **à ~ d'oiseau** as the crow flies; **2** (groupe) **un ~ de** a flight of [*canards, cigognes*]; a cloud of [*insectes*]; **de haut ~** lit [*oiseau*] high-flying (*épith*); fig [*diplomate*] high-flying (*épith*); [*cambrioleur*] big-time (*épith*); [*prostituée*] high-class (*épith*); **3** (d'avion, de fusée) flight; **le ~ pour Paris** the Paris flight; **il y a 3 heures de ~ entre** it's a three-hour flight between; **avoir 1000 heures de ~ à son actif** to have logged 1,000 flying hours; **en (plein) ~** in flight; **de ~** [*conditions*] flying; [*plan, simulateur*] flight; **4** (délit) theft (**de** of); (plus important) robbery; **commettre un ~** to commit a theft ou robbery; **c'est du ~ (manifeste)!** it's daylight robbery!; **c'est du ~ organisé!** fig it's a racket!

II au vol *loc adv* **tirer un oiseau au ~** to shoot a bird in flight; **attraper une balle au ~** to catch a ball in mid-air; **saisir des bribes de conversations au ~** to catch snatches of conversation.

■ **~ à l'arraché** Jur bag snatching; **~ avec effraction** Jur burglary; **~ à l'étalage** shoplifting; **~ habité** manned flight; **~ libre** Sport hang gliding; **faire du ~ libre** to go hang gliding; **~ à main armée** armed robbery; **~ qualifié** Jur aggravated theft GB, grand larceny US; **~ à la roulotte**○ theft from a parked vehicle; **~ sec** air travel; **~ simple** Jur theft; **~ à la tire** pickpocketing; **~ à voile** gliding; **faire du ~ à voile** to go gliding.

volage /vɔlaʒ/ *adj* fickle.

volaille /vɔlɑj/ *nf* Agric, Culin **1** (ensemble) poultry; **2** (animal) fowl; **plumer une ~** to pluck a fowl.

volailler, -ère /vɔlaje, ɛʀ/ ▶ **510** *nm,f* (éleveur) poultry farmer; (marchand) poulterer.

volant, **~e** /vɔlɑ̃, ɑ̃t/ **I** *adj* **1** (qui vole) flying; **le personnel ~** Aviat the flying staff; **2** (mobile) [*camp, pont*] flying; [*personnel*] mobile.

II *nm* **1** (de voiture) steering wheel; **être au ~** to be at the wheel; **prendre le ~** to take the wheel; **reprendre le ~** to get back behind the wheel; **un brusque coup de ~** a sharp turn of the wheel; **donner un coup de ~** to turn the wheel sharply; **un as du ~** an ace driver; **l'alcool au ~ tue** drink-driving kills; **campagne publicitaire pour la sécurité au ~** campaign promoting safe driving; **2** (de vêtement) flounce, tier; **à ~s** flounced; **3** (réserve) margin, reserve; **~ de sécurité** safety margin, reserve fund; **~ de trésorerie/main-d'œuvre** financial/labour[GB] reserves (*pl*); **4** (de badminton) shuttlecock; **faire une partie de ~** to play badminton; **5** (de carnet à souches) tear-off portion; **6** Tech (modérateur de mouvement) fly(-governor); (à main) hand-wheel.

■ **~ d'inertie** flywheel; **~ magnétique** magneto.

volapük /vɔlapyk/ ▶ **462** *nm* volapuk.

volatil, **~e**[1] /vɔlatil/ *adj* volatile.

volatile[2]† /vɔlatil/ *nm* **1** (volaille) fowl; **2** (oiseau) bird, feathered friend hum.

volatilisable /vɔlatilizabl/ *adj* volatilizable.

volatilisation /vɔlatilizasjɔ̃/ *nf* volatilization.

volatiliser /vɔlatilize/ [1] **I** *vtr* Chimie to volatilize.

II se volatiliser *vpr* **1** Chimie to volatilize; **2** (disparaître) hum to vanish into thin air, disappear.

volatilité /vɔlatilite/ *nf* volatility.

vol-au-vent /vɔlovɑ̃/ *nm inv* vol-au-vent.

volcan /vɔlkɑ̃/ *nm* **1** (relief) volcano; **~ éteint/en sommeil/en activité** extinct/dormant/active volcano; **être assis sur un ~** fig to be sitting on a volcano; **2** (personne) spitfire.

volcanique /vɔlkanik/ *adj* **1** [*activité, région, roche*] volcanic; **2** [*tempérament*] explosive.

volcanisme /vɔlkanism/ *nm* volcanism.

volcanologie /vɔlkanɔlɔʒi/ *nf* volcanology.

volcanologue /vɔlkanɔlɔg/ ▶ **510** *nm* volcanologist.

volée /vɔle/ **I** *nf* **1** (d'oiseaux) (action de voler) flight; (vol groupé) flock, flight; **d'une seule ~** [*franchir*] in a nonstop flight; **une ~ d'étourneaux** a flock ou flight of starlings; **une ~ d'enfants** fig a swarm of children; **prendre sa ~** to take wing, to fly off; **un**

acteur/écrivain de haute ~ fig a first-rate actor/writer; **2** (grêle) (de projectiles, coups) volley (**de** of); **une ~ de pierres/plombs** a volley of stones/shot; **donner** or **flanquer**○ **une (bonne) ~ à qn** lit to give sb a good thrashing; fig to thrash sb; **prendre une ~ aux échecs** fig to get thrashed at chess; **3** (ensemble de marches d'escalier) flight (of stairs); **4** (sports de raquette, volley-ball) volley; **reprendre la balle de ~** to take the ball on the volley; **saisir la balle à la ~** fig to seize the opportunity.

II à toute volée *loc adv* **lancer qch à toute ~** to hurl sth; **gifler qn à toute ~** to strike sb a resounding slap in the face; **claquer une porte à toute ~** to slam a door; **les cloches sonnaient à toute ~** to bells were pealing out.

■ **~ basse** (au tennis) low volley; **~ en coup droit** (au tennis) drive volley; **~ haute** smash; **~ de revers** backhand volley.

IDIOMES **les enfants se sont éparpillés comme une ~ de moineaux** the children scattered like flies ; **asséner une ~ de bois vert à qn** to deliver a blistering critique of sb.

voler /vɔle/ [1] **I** *vtr* **1** (dérober) to steal [*objet, secret, baiser*] (**à qn** from sb); **on lui a volé sa voiture, il s'est fait ~ sa voiture** he's had his car stolen; **il s'est fait ~ la victoire** fig he's been robbed of his victory; **tu ne l'as pas volé!** fig it serves you right, you asked for it!; **2** (léser) to rob; **~ le client** to cheat ou rob the customer; (plus fort) to rip the customer off○; **~ l'État** to steal from the State; **~ qn sur la quantité/le poids** to cheat sb over the quantity/the weight; **500 francs? tu t'es fait ~!** 500 francs? you've been ripped off!; **on se fait ~ dans ce magasin!** you get ripped off in that shop!; **on n'a pas été volés!** fig we got our money's worth!

II *vi* **1** [*insecte, avion, pilote*] to fly; fig [*poussière, plume*] to fly; **~ au vent** [*cheveux, jupe*] to blow in the wind; **2** (être lancé) lit, fig [*pierres, insultes*] to fly; **~ en éclats** [*vitre*] to shatter; fig [*certitude*] to be shattered; **faire ~ la réputation de qn en éclats** fig to shatter sb's reputation; **3** (se précipiter) **~ au secours de qn** to rush to sb's aid; fig **~ de bouche en bouche** [*nouvelle*] to spread like wildfire. ▶ **mouche**.

IDIOMES **ça vole bas!** (c'est grivois) that's a bit near the knuckle!; (c'est idiot) that's pretty mindless stuff!

volet /vɔlɛ/ *nm* **1** (contrevent) shutter; **2** (de plan, politique, problème) constituent; **le projet comporte trois/plusieurs ~s** the project has three/several constituents; **3** (de dépliant) (folding) section; **4** (de polyptique) panel; **5** Aviat flap; **sortir les ~s** to raise the flaps.

■ **~ de courbure** Aviat plain ou simple flap; **~ de courbure à fente** Aviat slotted flap; **~ roulant** roller shutter.

voleter /vɔlte/ [20] *vi* [*insecte, papier*] to flutter.

voleur, -euse /vɔlœʀ, øz/ **I** *adj* **être ~** [*chat*] to be a thief; [*enfant*] to be light-fingered; [*commerçant*] to be dishonest; **être ~ et menteur** to be a thief and a liar.

II *nm,f* (malfaiteur) thief; (tricheur) swindler; **un ~ de voiture** a car thief; **crier 'au ~!'** to shout 'stop thief!'; **jouer au gendarme et au ~** to play cops and robbers.

■ **~ à l'étalage** shoplifter; **~ de grand chemin** Hist highwayman; **~ d'enfant** child kidnapper[GB] ou abductor.

IDIOMES **être ~ comme une pie** to be a real thieving magpie; **se sauver comme un ~** to slip away like a thief in the night; **entrer/sortir comme un ~** to slip in/out.

Volga /vɔlga/ *nprf* ▶ **357** Volga.

volière /vɔljɛʀ/ *nf* aviary.

volige /vɔliʒ/ *nf* **1** (de toiture) batten; **2** (de plafond) strip of cladding; **des ~s** wood cladding.

volitif, -ive /vɔlitif, iv/ *adj* **1** Psych volitional; **2** Ling volitive.

volition /vɔlisjɔ̃/ *nf* volition.

volley(-ball) /vɔlɛ(bol)/ ▶ **449** *nm* volleyball.

volleyeur, -euse /vɔlɛjœʀ, øz/ *nm,f* (au volley) volleyball player; (au tennis) volleyer.

volontaire /vɔlɔ̃tɛʀ/ **I** *adj* **1** (délibéré) [*départ, enrôlement, contribution, travail*] voluntary; [*détérioration, abus*] deliberate; **je l'ai vexé mais ce n'était pas ~ de ma part** I've upset him, but I didn't mean to; **2** (opiniâtre) [*personne, air, comportement*] determined.

II *nmf* volunteer; **se porter ~ pour faire** to volunteer to do.

volontairement /vɔlɔ̃tɛʀmɑ̃/ *adv* [*se priver, renoncer, partir*] voluntarily; [*dissimuler, provoquer, faire mal*] deliberately.

volontariat /vɔlɔ̃taʀja/ *nm* voluntary service.

volontarisme /vɔlɔ̃taʀism/ *nm* voluntarism.

volontariste /vɔlɔ̃taʀist/ *adj* voluntarist.

volonté /vɔlɔ̃te/ **I** *nf* **1** (disposition) will; **imposer sa ~** to impose one's will (**à qn** on sb); **la ~ du peuple** the will of the people; **il a été inscrit contre sa ~** he was entered against his will; **même avec la meilleure ~ du monde** even with the best will in the world; **'que ta ~ soit faite'** Relig 'thy will be done'; **bonne/mauvaise ~** goodwill/ill-will; **faire preuve de bonne/mauvaise ~** to show goodwill/ill-will; **être plein de bonne ~** to be full of goodwill; **une personne/un geste de bonne ~** a person/an act of goodwill; **elle y met de la mauvaise ~** she's doing it with bad grace or reluctantly; **contrarier/aller contre la ~ de qn** to thwart/go against sb's wishes; **deux ~s contraires se sont exprimées** two opposing wishes were expressed; **manifester la ~ de faire** to show one's willingness to do; **leur ~ de signer les accords/refuser le compromis est claire** their willingness to sign the agreements/refuse the compromise is clear; **~ de puissance/conquête/paix/vengeance** desire for power/conquest/peace/revenge; **faire appel aux bonnes ~s** to appeal for volunteers; ▶ **dernier**, **quatre**; **2** (trait de caractère) willpower; **avoir de la ~** to have willpower; **faire preuve de ~** to show willpower; **c'est une question de ~** it's a question of willpower; **réussir à faire qch à force de ~** to succeed in doing sth by sheer willpower; **avoir une ~ de fer** to have an iron will.

II à volonté *loc adv* **1** (autant que l'on veut) **'vin/pain/crudités à ~'** 'unlimited wine/bread/salad'; ▶ **feu**; **2** (comme on veut) [*modulable*] as required.

volontiers /vɔlɔ̃tje/ *adv* **1** (avec plaisir) gladly; **je t'aiderais ~** I would gladly help you; **j'irais ~ à Paris** I'd love to go to Paris; **'tu veux un café/du vin?'—'(bien) ~'** 'would you like a coffee/some wine?'—'I'd love one/some'; **'tu me le prêtes?'—'~'** 'will you lend it to me?'—'certainly', 'I'd be delighted to'; **2** (facilement) [*imaginer, oublier*] easily; [*reconnaître, admettre*] readily; **je me passe ~ de tes services** I can easily do without your help; **je le crois ~** I'm quite ready to believe it; **on dit/croit/critique ~** people like to say/think/criticize.

volt /vɔlt/ *nm* Mes volt.

voltage /vɔltaʒ/ *nm* voltage.

voltaïque /vɔltaik/ *adj* **1** Électrotech voltaic; **2** Ling Voltaic.

voltaire /vɔltɛʀ/ *nm* (fauteuil) upright armchair.

voltampère /vɔltɑ̃pɛʀ/ *nm* volt-ampere.

volte /vɔlt/ *nf* circle; **faites une ~ de 10 mètres de diamètre** do a 10-metre[GB] circle.

volte-face /vɔlt(ə)fas/ *nf inv* **1** lit **faire ~** to turn around; **2** fig volte-face, U-turn; **faire ~** to do a U-turn.

voltige /vɔltiʒ/ *nf* **1** (au trapèze) **(haute) ~** acrobatics (+ *v pl*); **un numéro de ~** an acrobatic act; **2** Équit vaulting; **3** Aviat **~ (aérienne)** aerobatics (+ *v pl*); **4** fig **un exercice de haute ~** a very delicate operation.

voltiger /vɔltiʒe/ [13] *vi* **1** (doucement) [*papiers, rideaux, feuilles*] to flutter; **2** (violemment) [*classeur, objet*] to fly, to go flying.

voltigeur /vɔltiʒœʀ/ *nm* Hist, Mil light infantryman.

voltmètre /vɔltmɛtʀ/ *nm* voltmeter.

volubile /vɔlybil/ *adj* **1** (personne) voluble; **2** Bot twining.

volubilis /vɔlybilis/ *nm* morning glory.

volubilité /vɔlybilite/ *nf* volubility.

volucompteur® /vɔlykɔ̃tœʀ/ *nm* volumeter.

volume /vɔlym/ ▶ **866** *nm* **1** (grandeur) volume (**de** of); **~ respiratoire** Physiol respiratory volume; **le ~ d'un fleuve** the volume of a river's flow; **doubler de ~** to double in volume; **eau oxygénée à 10 ~s** 10-volume hydrogen peroxide; **donner du ~ à ses cheveux** to give one's hair body; **faire du ~** [*colis, bagages*] to be bulky; **2** Écon volume; **le ~ d'activité/d'échanges/des transactions** the volume of activity/of trade/of transactions; **3** (tome) volume; **4** (intensité) volume; **monter le ~** to turn up the volume; **~ sonore/d'enregistrement** sound/recording level.

volumétrique /vɔlymetʀik/ *adj* volumetric; **compteur ~** Tech volume counter ou meter.

volumineux, -euse /vɔlyminø, øz/ *adj* [*livre, dossier*] thick; [*documentation, correspondance*] voluminous; [*meuble, objet, bagages*] bulky; [*seins, fesses*] ample.

volumique /vɔlymik/ *adj* **masse ~** density.

volupté /vɔlypte/ *nf* **1** (sensuelle) voluptuousness; **avec ~** voluptuously; **2** (intellectuelle) exquisite pleasure.

voluptueusement /vɔlyptɥøzmɑ̃/ *adv* voluptuously.

voluptueux, -euse /vɔlyptɥø, øz/ *adj* voluptuous.

volute /vɔlyt/ *nf* **1** (de colonne) volute; (de violon) scroll; **des ~s de fumée** curls of smoke; **2** Zool volute.

volve /vɔlv/ *nf* Bot volva.

vomi○ /vɔmi/ *nm* vomit.

vomique /vɔmik/ *adj* **noix ~** nux vomica.

vomiquier /vɔmikje/ *nm* nux vomica tree.

vomir /vɔmiʀ/ [3] **I** *vtr* **1** (recracher) [*personne*] to bring up [*repas, nourriture*]; to vomit [*bile, sang*]; **il a vomi tout son biberon** he brought up all his bottle; **2** (projeter) to spew out [*lave, déchets*]; to belch [*feu, vapeur, fumée*]; **3** (abhorrer) to loathe.

II *vi* [*personne*] to be sick, to vomit; **je vais ~** I'm going to be sick; **avoir envie de ~** to feel sick; **donner envie de ~** lit to make [sb] feel sick; fig to make [sb] sick; **c'est à ~** fig it makes you sick, it makes you puke◐. ▶ **tripe**.

vomissement /vɔmismɑ̃/ *nm* (action) vomiting; (résultat) vomit; **être pris de ~s** to start to vomit.

■ **~s du matin** Physiol morning sickness.

vomissure /vɔmisyʀ/ *nf* vomit **₵**.

vomitif, -ive /vɔmitif, iv/ **I** *adj* emetic.

II *nm* emetic.

vorace /vɔʀas/ *adj* lit, fig voracious.

voracement /vɔʀasmɑ̃/ *adv* voraciously.

voracité /vɔʀasite/ *nf* voracity, voraciousness.

vortex /vɔʀtɛks/ *nm* Tech, Météo vortex.

vos ▶ **votre**.

Vosges /voʒ/ ▶ **692** *nprfpl* (région, département) **les ~** the Vosges.

Le volume

Pour les mesures en litres, décilitres, hectolitres etc. voir ***la capacité*** **▶ 117**.
Pour la prononciation des nombres, voir ***les nombres*** **▶ 545**.

Équivalences

1 cu in	=	16,38 cm^3		
1 cu ft	=	1728 cu in	=	0,03 m^3
1 cu yd	=	27 cu ft	=	0,76 m^3

dire				**dire**
one cubic centimetre	1 cm^3	=	0.061 cu in^3	*cubic inches*
one cubic decimetre	1 dm^3	=	0.035 cu ft	*cubic feet*
one cubic metre	1 m^3	=	35.315 cu ft	
		=	1.308 cu yd	*cubic yard*

Pour l'écriture, noter:
– l'anglais utilise un point là où le français a une virgule.
– on écrit -metre en anglais britannique et -meter en anglais américain.
– on peut écrire cu in *ou* in^3, cu ft *ou* ft^3, *etc.*

il y a 1 000 000 centimètres cubes dans un mètre cube	=	there are a million cubic centimetres in a cubic metre
1 000 000 centimètres cubes font un mètre cube	=	a million cubic centimetres make one cubic metre
quel est le volume de la caisse?	=	what is the volume of the box?
elle fait 2 m^3	=	it is 2 cubic metres
elle a un volume de 2 m^3	=	its volume is 2 cubic metres
à peu près 3 m^3	=	about 3 cubic metres
presque 3 m^3	=	almost 3 cubic metres
plus de 2 m^3	=	more than 2 cubic metres
moins de 3 m^3	=	less than 3 cubic metres
le volume de A est supérieur à celui de B	=	A has a greater volume than B
le volume de B est inférieur à celui de A	=	B has a smaller volume than A
A et B ont le même volume	=	A and B have the same volume
le volume de A est égal à celui de B	=	A has the same volume as B
5 m^3 de terre	=	five cubic metres of soil
vendu au mètre cube	=	sold by the cubic metre

Noter l'ordre des mots dans les adjectifs composés anglais, et l'utilisation du trait d'union. Noter aussi que metre, employé comme adjectif, ne prend pas la marque du pluriel.

un réservoir de 200 m^3 = a 200-cubic-metre tank

On peut aussi dire a tank 200 cubic metres in volume.

vosgien, -ienne /voʒjɛ̃, ɛn/ **▶ 692** *adj* of the Vosges (*après n*).

Vosgien, -ienne /voʒjɛ̃, ɛn/ **▶ 692** *nm,f* (natif) native of the Vosges; (habitant) inhabitant of the Vosges.

votant, ~e /vɔtɑ̃, ɑ̃t/ *nm,f* voter.

votation /vɔtasjɔ̃/ *nf* H voting.

vote /vɔt/ *nm* **1** (action) voting, vote (**contre** against; **en faveur de** in favour[GB] of); **droit de ~** right to vote; **~ d'un budget** voting on a budget; **~ à main levée/à bulletin secret** vote by show of hands/by secret ballot; **~ par correspondance** postal vote GB, absentee vote US; **~ par procuration** vote by proxy; **~ rural/populaire** rural/popular vote; **procéder au ~** to vote; **~ d'une loi** passing of a bill; **2** (opinion exprimée) vote; **compter les ~s** to count the votes; **3** (ensemble des votants) **le ~ républicain** the Republican voters ou vote.

■ **~ blanc** Pol blank vote; **~ de confiance** vote of confidence; **~ sanction** protest vote; **~ utile** tactical vote.

voter /vɔte/ [1] **I** *vtr* [*personne, comité*] to vote [*crédit, budget, amendement*]; to pass [*projet de loi*]; **~ la suppression/l'amnistie de qch** to vote for the suppression of/an amnesty on sth; **~ les pleins pouvoirs à qn** to vote to give sb full powers.

II *vi* to vote (**pour** for; **contre** against); **~ écologiste/socialiste** to vote for the Greens/socialists, to vote Green/socialist; **~ (pour) Durand** to vote for Durand; **~ par procuration** to vote by proxy; **~ à main levée/à bulletin secret** to vote by a show of hands/by secret ballot; **~ contre un projet de loi** to vote a bill down; **~ utile** to vote tactically; **~ blanc** to cast a blank vote.

votif, -ive /vɔtif, iv/ *adj* votive.

votre, *pl* **vos** /vɔtʀ, vo/ *adj poss*

■ **Note** En anglais, on ne répète pas le possessif coordonné: *votre nom et votre adresse* = your name and address.

your; **avez-vous tous ~ passeport?** have you all got your passports?; **c'est pour ~ bien** it's for your own good; **un de vos amis** a friend of yours; **~ gentil collègue** that nice colleague of yours; **j'ai fait vos courses** I've done the shopping for you; **à ~ arrivée présentez-vous à la réception** when you arrive go to reception; **vos nom et adresse** (une personne) your name and address; (plusieurs personnes) your names and addresses; **que Votre volonté soit faite** Thy will be done.

vôtre /votʀ/ **I** *adj poss* **mes biens sont ~s** all I have is yours; **'amicalement ~'** 'best wishes'.

II le vôtre, la vôtre, les vôtres *pron poss* yours; **une maison comme la ~** a house like yours; **ils ont des habitudes très différentes des ~s** their habits are very different from your own; **à la ~**○**!**, **à la bonne ~**○**!** (à votre santé) cheers!; iron the best of luck!; **les ~s** (votre famille) your family (*sg*); **vous et les ~s** péj you and your kind; **je ne pourrai pas être des ~s** I won't be able to join you; **vous avez encore fait des ~s!** you've been up to mischief again!; **▶ y**.

vouer /vwe/ [1] **I** *vtr* **1** (porter) **~ un sentiment à qn** to nurse a feeling for sb; **il leur voue une haine farouche/un amour profond** he nurses a deep hatred of them/a deep love for them; **~ une reconnaissance éternelle à qn** to be ou feel eternally grateful to sb; **~ un véritable culte à qn** to (hero-)worship sb; **la passion qu'ils vouent à leur ville** their passionate love for ou devotion to their town; **2** (destiner) to doom; **film voué à l'échec** film doomed to failure, film bound to fail; **jeune fille vouée au célibat** girl destined to remain unmarried; **le manque de médecins voue la population aux maladies endémiques** the lack of doctors makes endemic disease inevitable; **~ qn à la vindicte publique** to expose sb to public condemnation; **3** (consacrer) **~ sa vie/son temps à qch** to devote one's life/one's time to sth; **pays voué à l'élevage** country entirely given over to cattle-breeding; **4** (dédier) **~ qn à Dieu/un saint** to dedicate sb to God/a saint; **▶ gémonies**.

II se vouer *vpr* **1** (se consacrer) **se ~ à qch** to devote oneself to sth; **2** (se porter) **ils se vouent une haine féroce** they hate each other intensely.

IDIOMES **je ne sais plus à quel saint me ~** I don't know which way to turn.

vouloir /vulwaʀ/ [48] **I** *nm* Philos will; **bon ~** goodwill; **dépendre du bon ~ de qn** to depend on sb's goodwill; **attendre le bon ~ de qn** to wait at sb's pleasure sout.

II *vtr* **1** (exiger) to want; **je veux une voiture/une nouvelle secrétaire** I want a car/a new secretary; **elle veut partir/que tout soit fini avant 8 heures** she wants to leave/everything finished by 8 o'clock; **que voulez-vous d'elle?** what do you want from her?; **qu'est-ce qu'ils nous veulent**○ **encore?** what more do they want of us?; **il vend sa voiture, il en veut 15 000 F** he's selling his car, he wants 15,000 francs for it; **comme le veut la loi/la coutume** as the law/custom demands; **le règlement voudrait que tu portes une cravate** you're normally required to wear a tie ; **▶ fin²**; **2** (désirer, souhaiter) **que veux-tu boire/pour Noël?** what do you want to drink/for Christmas?; (plus poli) what would you like to drink/for Christmas?; **comme tu veux** or **voudras** as you wish; **je voudrais un kilo de poires/vous parler en privé** I'd like a kilo of pears/to speak to you in private; **je comprends très bien que tu ne veuilles pas répondre** I can quite understand that you may not wish to reply; **tu vois que tu y arrives quand tu (le) veux** you see you can do it when you really want to; **il ne suffit pas de ~, il faut encore pouvoir** wishing is not enough; **ce n'était pas si difficile que ça, il suffisait de ~** it wasn't that difficult, all you needed was the will to do it; **elle veut/voudrait être astronaute** she wants/would like to be an astronaut; **je ne veux pas d'elle comme secrétaire** I don't want her as a secretary; **je ne veux pas de ce tableau dans ma chambre** I don't want that picture in my room; **je n'en veux pas, de ton argent!** I don't want your money!; **elle veut ton bonheur** or **que tu sois heureux** she wants you to be happy; **je voudrais bien rester/vous aider, mais** I would like to stay/to help you, but; **ils auraient bien voulu participer à la réunion d'hier** they would have liked to have taken part in yesterday's meeting; **je voudrais bien qu'on finisse avant la nuit** I would like us to finish before tonight; **nous aurions également voulu ajouter que** we would also have liked to add that; **je voulais vous dire que** I wanted to tell you that; **on dira ce qu'on voudra, c'était moins pollué avant** they can say what they like, it was less polluted before; **tu veux que je te dise? ton guide, c'est un escroc** I hate to say it , but the guide is a crook; **je ne voudrais pas vous déranger** I don't want to put you out; **sans ~ te vexer, ton chapeau est un peu voyant** without wanting to sound rude, your hat is a bit garish; **sans le ~** [*bousculer, révéler*] by accident; [*se retrouver*] accidentally; **il m'a fait mal sans le ~** he hurt me unintentionally ou without meaning to; **viens quand tu veux** come whenever you want ou like; **fais comme tu veux, mais ne me dérange pas tout le temps!** do what you like ou want, but don't keep bothering me all the time!; **'qu'est-ce qu'on fait ce soir?'—'comme tu veux** or **voudras'** 'what shall we do tonight?'—'whatever you like, it's up to you'; **que tu le veuilles ou non** whether you like it or not; **elle fait ce qu'elle veut de son mari** she twists her husband around her little finger; **elle fait ce qu'elle veut de ses mains** she can do anything with her hands; **je ne vous veux aucun mal** I don't wish you any harm; **tu ne veux/voudrais pas me faire croire que** you're not telling/trying to tell me that;

après ce qu'il a fait, tu voudrais que je lui fasse confiance? do you expect me to trust him after what he's done?; **comment voulez-vous qu'on travaille dans ces conditions?** how do you expect people to work in these conditions?; **que veux-tu que j'y fasse?** what do you want ou expect me to do about it?; **que veux-tu que je te dise? c'est de ta faute!** what do you expect me to say? it's your fault!; **comment veux-tu qu'elle résiste?** how could she resist?; **comment veux-tu que je le sache?** how should I know?; **pourquoi voudrais-tu qu'il refuse?** why should he refuse?; **c'est la vie, que voulez-vous!** what can you do, that's life!; **que veux-tu, on n'y peut rien!** what can you do, it's hopeless!; **j'aurais voulu t'y voir**○! I'd like to have seen you in the same position!; **tu l'auras voulu!** it'll be all your own fault!; ▶**beurre**, **peau**, **voilà**; **3** (accepter) **voulez-vous (bien) fermer la fenêtre/me prêter votre stylo?** would you mind closing the window/lending me your pen?; **vous voudrez bien renvoyer le formulaire** please return the form; **tu voudras bien leur transmettre ce message** will you please give them this message; **voudriez-vous avoir l'obligeance de faire** fml would you be so kind as to do; **demander à** or **prier qn de bien ~ faire** fml to ask sb to be so kind as to do, to ask sb kindly to do sout; **on voudra bien se référer aux ouvrages suivants** please refer to the following works; **voudrais-tu aller m'acheter le journal, s'il te plaît** would you go and buy me the paper, please; **voulez-vous** or **veuillez répéter votre question, s'il vous plaît** would you repeat your question please; **veuillez patienter** (au téléphone) please hold the line; **si vous le voulez bien, nous commencerons sans lui** if you don't mind, we'll start without him; **si vous voulez bien me suivre** if you'd like to follow me; **si vous voulez bien de moi comme quatrième au bridge** if you'll have me as a fourth at bridge; **veux-tu (bien) te taire!** will you (please) be quiet!; **ils ont bien voulu nous prêter leur voiture** they were kind enough to lend us their car; **elle a bien voulu leur accorder une entrevue** she was kind enough to grant them an interview; **nous vous remercions d'avoir bien voulu faire** thank you for doing; **elle n'a pas voulu signer** she would not sign; **le bois ne veut pas brûler** the wood won't burn; **le moteur ne veut pas partir** the engine won't start; **ma blessure ne veut pas guérir** my wound won't heal; **tout le monde attendait qu'elle veuille (bien) se montrer** everyone was waiting for her to put in an appearance; **elle veut bien prendre ce poste à condition d'être mieux payée** she's happy to take the job on condition that she's paid more; **je veux bien te croire** I'm quite prepared to believe you; (plus réticent) I'd like to believe you; **si l'on veut bien admettre/se rappeler que** if one accepts/remembers that; **il était mieux informé (des faits) qu'il ne veut bien le dire** he knew more about it than he's prepared to admit; **je veux bien croire que la vie est dure, mais** I know life is hard, but; **je veux bien qu'il soit malade/qu'ils fassent grève, mais** I know he's ill/they're on strike, but; **'ça s'est bien passé?'—'si on veut'** 'did it go well?'—'so-so○'; **'ce n'est pas cher/difficile'—'si on veut!'** 'it's not expensive/difficult'—'or so you say!'; **'c'était plus confortable avant!'—'si tu veux, mais'** 'it was more comfortable before!'—'maybe, but'; **4** (signifier) **~ dire** to mean; **que veux-tu dire?** what do you mean?; **qu'est-ce que ça veut dire?** (signification) what does that mean?; (attitude) what's all this about?; **pour moi, ça ne veut rien dire** it means nothing to me; **et alors, ça veut dire quoi de bousculer les gens comme ça**○**?** hey, what do you mean by pushing people like that?; **ça veut tout simplement dire qu'on va payer plus d'impôts** it simply means we're going to pay higher taxes; **que voulez-vous dire par là?** what (exactly) do you mean by that?; **tu ne veux pas dire qu'il est médecin?** you don't mean to tell me he's a doctor?; **ça voudrait dire tout refaire** that would mean doing everything all over again; **5** (prétendre) **la légende veut que** legend has it that; **comme le veut la légende/tradition** as legend/tradition has it; **leur théorie veut que** according to their theory; **on a voulu voir en lui un pionnier de l'architecture** people tended to see him as a pioneering architect.

III en vouloir *vtr ind* **1**○ (être déterminé) to want to get on; **il réussira, il en veut!** he wants to get on, and he'll succeed!; **ce sont de bons élèves/soldats, et qui en veulent** they are good students/soldiers who want to get on; **2** (garder rancune) **en ~ à qn** to bear a grudge against sb; **je leur en veux de m'avoir trompé** I hold it against them for not being honest with me; **ne m 'en veux pas si je remets notre rendez-vous** please forgive me if I put off our meeting; **3** (avoir des vues sur) **en ~ à qch** to be after sth; **elle en veut à notre fortune** she's after our money.

IV se vouloir *vpr* **1** (prétendre être) [*personne*] to like to think of oneself as; [*ouvrage, théorie, méthode*] to be meant to be; **ils se veulent pacifistes/rassurants** they like to think of themselves as pacifists/as being reassuring; **mon livre se veut objectif/à la portée de tous** my book is meant to be objective/accessible to all; **2** (chercher à être) to try to be; **les dirigeants se sont voulus conciliants** the leaders tried to be conciliatory; **3** (se reprocher) **s'en ~** to be cross with oneself; **s'en ~ de** to regret; **je m'en veux d'avoir été si dur avec elle/de ne pas l'avoir écoutée** I really regret being so hard on her/not listening to her; **je m'en serais voulu de ne pas vous avoir prévenu** I would never have forgiven myself if I hadn't warned you; **il ne faut pas vous en ~, ce n'était pas de votre faute!** you mustn't blame yourself, it wasn't your fault!

IDIOMES **~ c'est pouvoir** Prov, **quand on veut, on peut** where there's a will there's a way; **je veux**○! you bet○!

voulu, **~e** /vuly/ **I** *pp* ▶**vouloir**.

II *pp adj* **1** (requis) **il n'a pas les compétences ~es** he hasn't got the required skills; **ils seront punis avec toute la sévérité ~e** they'll be punished with due severity; **on n'obtient jamais les renseignements ~s** you never get the information you want; **en temps ~** in time; **au moment ~** at the right time; **2** (intentionnel) **des répétitions ~es** deliberate repetition; **notre rencontre n'était pas ~e** our meeting was not planned; **il est arrivé en retard et c'était ~** he was late deliberately.

vous[1] /vu/ *pron pers* **1** (sujet) you; **~ êtes en avance** you're early; **~ n'avez pas terminé** you haven't finished; **~ êtes trop bonne** you are too kind; **je sais que ce n'est pas ~** I know it wasn't you; **c'est ~ qui avez gagné** you have won, you're the winner; **~ aussi, ~ avez l'air malade** you don't look very well either, you look ill GB ou sick US too; **~ qui connaissez bien la ville, dites-moi** you who know the town well, tell me; **2** (dans une comparaison) **elles travaillent plus que ~** they work more than you (do); **ils sont plus âgés que ~** they are older than you (are); **elle le voit plus souvent que ~** (que nous ne le voyez) she sees him more often than you do; (qu'elle ne vous voit) she sees him more often than you ou than she sees you; **3** (objet) **ils ~ ont trahis** they have betrayed you; **je ~ déteste** I hate you; **nous ne ~ entendons pas** we can't hear you; **4** (vous = à vous) **je ne veux pas ~ faire mal** I don't want to hurt you; **elle ne ~ dit pas tout** she doesn't tell you everything; **ils ~ en veulent** they bear a grudge against you; **5** (après préposition) you; **à cause de/autour de/après ~** because of/around/after you; **un cadeau pour ~** a present for you; **pour ~, ça compte?** does it matter to you?; **elle n'écrit à personne sauf à ~** she doesn't write to anyone but you; **sans ~, je n'aurais pas survécu** I wouldn't have survived without you; **ce sont des amis à ~?** are they friends of yours?; **sans voiture à ~ c'est difficile** it's difficult without a car of your own; **à ~, il a raconté une histoire très différente** he told you quite a different story; **est-ce que la voiture bleue est à ~?** is the blue car yours?; **c'est à ~** (appartenance) it's yours, it belongs to you; (séquence) it's your turn; **à ~** (dans une séquence) your turn; **à ~ de choisir** (votre tour) it's your turn to choose; (votre responsabilité) it's up to you to choose; **6** (pronom réfléchi) (singulier) yourself; (pluriel) yourselves; **reprenez-~** (à une personne) pull yourself together; (à plusieurs personnes) pull yourselves together; **allez ~ laver** go and have a wash GB, go and wash up US; **allez ~ laver les mains** go and wash your hands; **7** (vous-même) yourself; (vous-mêmes) yourselves; **prenez soin de ~** look after yourself; **pensez à ~ deux** think of yourselves.

vous[2] /vu/ *nm* **l'emploi du ~** the use of the 'vous' form; **dire ~ à qn** to address sb using the 'vous' form.

vous-même, *pl* **vous-mêmes** /vumɛm/ *pron pers* **1** (de politesse) yourself; **vous me l'avez dit ~** you told me yourself; **vous avez décidé ~ de partir** you decided yourself to go away; **ainsi vous éliminez pour ~ toute possibilité de voyage** so you're ruling out any possibility of travel for yourself; **ne vous repliez pas sur ~** don't turn in on yourself; **2** (vous tous) **allez-y ~s** go yourselves; **vous verrez par ~s** you'll see for yourselves.

vousseau, *pl* **~x** /vuso/ = **voussoir**.

voussoiement /vuswamɑ̃/ *nm* = **vouvoiement**.

voussoir /vuswaʀ/ *nm* voussoir.

voussoyer /vuswaje/ [23] *vtr* = **vouvoyer**.

voussure /vusyʀ/ *nf* **1** (de voûte) (courbure) arching; (partie courbe) arch; **2** (archivolte) archivolt.

voûte /vut/ *nf* (plafond) vault; (de porche) archway; (de grotte, tunnel) roof; fig (de feuillage) arch; (ouvrage) vaulting ₵; **~ en berceau/d'arêtes** barrel/groined vault; **~ d'ogives** or **en ogive** or **sur croisée d'ogives** ogival vault; **~ en éventail** fan vaulting; **en ~** Archit vaulted; ▶**clé**.

■ **la ~ céleste** gén the sky; liter the heavens; **~ crânienne** dome of the skull; **la ~ étoilée** liter the starry vault; **~ du palais** Anat roof of the mouth; **~ palatine** = **~ du palais**; **~ plantaire** Anat arch of the foot.

voûté, **~e** /vute/ **I** *pp* ▶**voûter**.

II *pp adj* **1** Archit vaulted, arched; ▶**cave**; **2** (courbé) [*personne*] stooping; [*dos*] bent; **il est ~** or **il a le dos ~** he has a stoop.

voûter /vute/ [1] **I** *vtr* **1** Archit to vault [*pièce*]; **2** (courber) to give [sb] a stoop [*personne*].

II se voûter *vpr* [*personne*] to develop a stoop; [*dos*] to become bent.

vouvoiement /vuvwamɑ̃/ *nm* using the 'vous' ou polite form.

vouvoyer /vuvwaje/ [23] **I** *vtr* to address [sb] using the 'vous' form.

II se vouvoyer *vpr* to address one another using the 'vous' form.

vox populi /vɔkspɔpyli/ *nf* vox populi.

voyage /vwajaʒ/ *nm* (dans son ensemble) trip; (déplacement) journey; **notre ~ à Paris/au Japon/à l'étranger** our trip to Paris/to Japan/abroad; **lors de** or **à mon troisième ~** on my third trip; **partir en ~** to go on a trip; **être en ~** to be (away) on a trip; **j'ai fait cinq ~s pour transporter mes**

livres I made five trips to move my books; **rentrer de ~** to come back from a trip ou journey; **le ~ de retour a été fatigant** the return journey was tiring; **j'ai fait le ~ aller en bateau** I made the outward journey by boat; **vous avez fait bon ~?** did you have a good journey?; **bon ~!** have a good trip ou journey!; **le ~ en train s'est mal passé** the train journey was terrible; **un ~ de 500 km** a 500 km journey; **faire un ~ en Italie/autour du monde** to go on a trip ou to travel to Italy/around the world; **aimer les ~s** to love travelling[GB]; ▶ **jeunesse**.

■ **~ d'affaires** business trip; **être en ~ d'affaires** to be on a business trip; **~ d'agrément** pleasure trip; **~ en groupe** tour; **~ d'études** study trip; **~ à forfait** inclusive tour; **~ de noces** honeymoon; **nous sommes en ~ de noces** we're on our honeymoon; **~ officiel** official trip; **~ organisé** package tour.

IDIOMES **faire le grand ~** to pass away.

voyager /vwajaʒe/ [13] *vi* to travel; **~ en train/voiture/avion** to travel by train/car/plane; **~ de nuit/de jour** to travel at night/by day; **~ pour affaires/pour son plaisir/pour une société** to travel on business/for pleasure/for a company; **ce vin ne voyage pas bien** this wine doesn't travel well; **les bagages ont voyagé par le train** the luggage went by train; **récit qui vous fait ~ dans le temps/à travers l'histoire** story that takes you on a journey through time/through history.

voyageur, **-euse** /vwajaʒœʀ, øz/ **I** *adj* liter **j'ai un frère ~** (qui aime voyager) I have a brother who likes travelling[GB]; (qui voyage beaucoup) I have a brother who travels a lot; **elle mène une existence voyageuse** she spends her life travelling[GB] around; **être d'humeur voyageuse** to have itchy feet.

II *nm,f* **1** (passager) passenger; **les ~s en transit** transit passengers; **'réservé aux ~s munis de billets'** 'ticketholders only'; **2** (aventurier) traveller[GB]; **Marco Polo fut un grand ~** Marco Polo was a great traveller[GB]; **grand ~, mon oncle a parcouru le monde entier** a great traveller[GB], my uncle went all over the world.

■ **~ de commerce** travelling[GB] salesman.

voyagiste /vwajaʒist/ ▶**510** *nmf* tour operator.

voyance /vwajɑ̃s/ *nf* clairvoyance.

voyant, **~e** /vwajɑ̃, ɑ̃t/ **I** *adj* **1** (criard) [*couleur, robe*] loud; **2** (ostentatoire) [*train de vie*] ostentatious, showy.

II *nm,f* **1** (extralucide) clairvoyant; **2** (qui y voit) sighted person; **les ~s** the sighted.

III *nm* light; **~ d'huile** oil warning light; **~s d'un tableau de bord** Aut dashboard warning lights.

voyelle /vwajɛl/ *nf* vowel; **~ ouverte/fermée** open/close vowel; **~ entravée/libre** checked/free vowel.

voyeur, **-euse** /vwajœʀ, øz/ *nm,f* voyeur.

voyeurisme /vwajœʀism/ *nm* voyeurism.

voyou /vwaju/ **I** *adj inv* [*air*] loutish.

II *nm* **1** (crapule) lout, yobbo○ GB, hoodlum○ US; **2** (chenapan) rascal.

VPC *written abbr* ▶ **vente**.

vrac: **en vrac** /ɑ̃vʀak/ *loc adv* **1** (non emballé) (au détail) loose, unpackaged; (en gros) in bulk; **2** (pêle-mêle) [*empilé*] higgledy piggledy○; **tout mettre en ~ dans un tiroir** to throw everything haphazardly into a drawer; **jeter ses idées en ~ sur le papier** to jot down one's ideas as they come.

vrai, **~e** /vʀɛ/ **I** *adj* **1** (conforme à la vérité) true; **c'est bien ~!** that's absolutely true!; **ce n'est que trop ~** it's only too true; **il n'en est pas moins ~ que...** it's nonetheless true that...; **~ de ~**○ absolutely true; **il n'y a rien de ~ dans ses déclarations** there's no truth in his statements; **c'est bien toi qui l'as pris, pas ~?** YOU took it, didn't you?; **j'ai bien le droit de plaisanter, pas ~?** I can have a joke if I like, can't I?; **son film ne montre pas le ~ Napoléon** his film doesn't show the real Napoleon; **2** (réel) true; **une histoire ~e** a true story; **ils avaient, il est ~, un avantage au départ** true, they had an advantage at the start; **aussi ~ que je vous voie maintenant** as true as I'm standing here; **la ~e raison de mon départ** the real reason for my leaving; **mais c'est pas ~!**○ I don't believe it!; **3** (authentique) real, genuine; [*jumeau*] identical; **un ~ diamant** a real diamond; **le ~ problème n'est pas là** that's not the real problem; **il n'a pas de ~s amis** he doesn't have any real friends; **un ~ Rembrandt** a genuine Rembrandt; **une ~e blonde** a natural blonde; **4** (intensif) real, veritable; **c'est un ~ miracle** it's a real ou veritable miracle; **un ~ petit Mozart** a real little Mozart; **c'est un ~ régal** it's a real delight; **c'est un ~ salaud**◐ he 's a real bastard◐; **la pièce est une ~e fournaise/glacière** the room is like an oven/a fridge; **ma vie est un ~ roman** my life is like something out of a novel; **5** (naturel) (*after n*) [*personnage, caractère*] true to life; [*sentiments, émotion*] true; **plus ~ que nature** [*tableau, scène*] larger than life (*après n*).

II *nm* truth; **il y a du ~ dans ce que tu dis** there's some truth in what you say; **on ne distingue plus le ~ du faux dans leur histoire** one can't tell fact from fiction in their story; **être dans le ~** to be in the right; **pour de ~** for real; **au ~** in truth; **à ~ dire, à dire ~** to tell the truth; **peut-être dit-il ~** he may be telling the truth; ▶ **prêcher**.

III *adv* **faire ~** to look real; **parler ~** to speak plainly; **son discours sonne ~** his speech has the ring of truth.

vraiment /vʀɛmɑ̃/ *adv* really; **il faut ~ être bête pour croire ça** one would have to be really stupid to believe that; **je ne veux pas ~ être président** I don't really want to be president; **je ne veux ~ pas être président** I really don't want to be president.

vraisemblable /vʀɛsɑ̃blabl/ **I** *adj* (qui paraît vrai) [*excuse*] convincing, plausible; [*histoire, scénario*] plausible; (probable) likely; **il est ~ que** it is likely ou probable that; **peu ~** [*excuse*] not very convincing, quite unconvincing; [*histoire*] rather implausible; **ce qui me paraît peu ~ c'est** what strikes me as very unlikely is.

II *nm* **nouvelles qui sont dans l'ordre du ~** news which is within the bounds of probability; **rester dans le ~** to keep within the bounds of credibility.

vraisemblablement /vʀɛsɑ̃blabləmɑ̃/ *adv* probably; **'viendra-t-elle?'—'~ pas'** 'will she come?'—'probably not'; **ils ne signeront ~ pas ce traité** it seems unlikely that they will sign this treaty.

vraisemblance /vʀɛsɑ̃blɑ̃s/ *nf* **1** (d'hypothèse) likelihood; (de situation, d'intrigue) plausibility; (d'explication) verisimilitude; **contre/selon toute ~** against/in all likelihood, against/in all probability; **2** Littérat, Théât verisimilitude.

vrille /vʀij/ *nf* **1** (spirale) spiral; Sport spiral; Aviat tailspin, spiral; **faire une ~ avant/arrière** Sport to do a forward/backward spiral; **se mettre en ~** [*avion*] to go into a tailspin; [*corde, ficelle*] to get twisted; **descendre en ~** [*avion*] to go into a spiral dive; **2** Bot tendril; **3** Tech gimlet.

vrillé, **~e** /vʀije/ **I** *pp* ▶ **vriller**.

II *pp adj* **1** [*tige*] tendrilled[GB]; **2** [*fil*] twisted.

vriller /vʀije/ [1] **I** *vtr* [*percer*] to bore, to pierce [*bois*].

II *vi* **1** [*avion*] to spiral; **2** [*fil*] to twist, to become twisted.

III se vriller *vpr* [*fil*] to twist.

vrillette /vʀijɛt/ *nf* furniture beetle.

vrombir /vʀɔ̃biʀ/ [3] *vi* **1** [*moteur*] (après une accélération) to roar; (en continu) to throb; **faire ~ un moteur** to rev up an engine; **2** [*mouche*] to buzz.

vrombissement /vʀɔ̃bismɑ̃/ *nm* **1** (de moteur) roar ¢; **2** (de mouche) buzzing.

vroum /vrum/ *excl* brrmmm!

VRP /veɛʀpe/ *nm* (*abbr* = **voyageur représentant placier**) representative, rep○.

VSL /veɛsɛl/ *nm* **1** (*abbr* = **véhicule sanitaire léger**) PTS ambulance, patient transport service ambulance; **2** Mil (*abbr* = **volontaire pour un service long**) *conscript who volunteers for extended military service*.

VSNA /veɛsena/ *nmf* Mil (*abbr* = **volontaire du service national actif**) *person involved in community service in lieu of military service*.

VSOP /veɛsope/ *adj, nm* (*abbr* = **very superior old pale**) VSOP.

VTT /vetete/ *nm*: *abbr* ▶ **vélo**.

vu, **~e** /vy/ **I** *pp* ▶ **voir**.

II *pp adj* **1** (considéré) **être bien ~** [*personne*] to be well thought of (**de** by); **être mal ~** [*personne*] not to be well thought of (**de** by); **c'est bien/mal ~ de faire cela** it's good/bad form to do that; **ce serait plutôt mal ~** it wouldn't go down well; **2** (jugé) **bien ~!, c'est bien ~!** good point!; **c'est tout ~** my mind is made up; **3** (compris) **~?, c'est bien ~?** got it○?

III *nm* fml **sur le ~ du dossier** from the file.

IV *prép* in view of; **~ leur âge/importance** in view of their age/importance.

V vu que *loc conj* in view of the fact that.

VI vue *nf* **1** (vision) eyesight; **les troubles de la ~e** eye trouble; **avoir une bonne/mauvaise ~e** to have good/bad eyesight; **perdre/recouvrer la ~e** to lose/regain one's sight; **don de seconde** ou **double ~e** gift of second sight; **avoir la ~e basse** or **courte** lit, fig to be short-sighted GB ou near-sighted US; **ça fatigue la ~e** it strains your eyes; **en ~e** [*personnalité*] prominent, high-profile○ (*épith*); **la côte/une solution est en ~e** the coast/a solution is in sight; **en ~e de la côte** within sight of the coast; **mettre une photo bien en ~e** to display a photo prominently; **chercher à se mettre en ~e** to try to get noticed; **c'est quelqu'un de très en ~e en ce moment** he's/she's very much in the public eye at the moment; **2** (regard) sight; **à première ~e** at first sight; **connaître qn de ~e** to know sb by sight; **ne perds pas cet enfant de ~e** don't let that child out of your sight; **perdre qn de ~e** fig to lose touch with sb; **perdre qch de ~e** fig to forget sth; **le paysage qui s'offrait à la ~e** the landscape before us; **détourner la ~e** to avert one's eyes ou gaze (**de** from); **à ~e** [*tirer*] on sight; [*dessiner*] freehand; [*atterrir, piloter*] without instruments; Fin [*retrait*] on demand; [*dépôt*] at call; **payable à ~e** payable on demand ou sight; **3** (panorama) view; **chambre avec ~e sur la mer** room with sea view; **vue imprenable** magnificent and protected view; **avoir ~e sur le square** [*pièce, personne*] to look out onto the square; **d'ici, on a une ~e plongeante sur la vallée** from here you get a bird's-eye view of the valley; **4** (spectacle) sight; **s'évanouir à la ~e du sang** to faint at the sight of blood; **à ma ~e, il s'enfuit** he took to his heels when he saw me ou on seeing me; **5** (dessin, photo) view (**de** of); **une ~e de la cathédrale** a view of the cathedral; **~e de face/de côté** front/side view; **un film de 12 ~es** Phot a 12 exposure film; ▶ **prise**; **6** (façon de voir) view; **~es** views (**sur** on); **une ~e optimiste des choses** an optimistic view of things; ▶ **échange, point**; **7** (projet) **~es** plans; (desseins) **avoir des ~es sur qn/qch** to have designs on sb/sth; **avoir qn en ~e** to have sb in mind; **j'ai un terrain en ~e** (je sais lequel conviendrait) I have a plot of land in mind; (je voudrais obtenir) I've got my eye on a piece of land; **avoir en ~e de faire qch** to have it in mind to do sth; **en ~e de qch/de faire qch** with a view to sth/to doing sth; **8** Jur (ouverture) window.

■ **~e éclatée** exploded view; **~e d'ensemble** overall view; **ce n'est qu'une ~e de l'esprit** it's entirely imaginary.

IDIOMES **ni ~ ni connu**○ no-one will know; **pas ~ pas pris** it can't hurt if nobody knows; **au ~ et au su de tous** openly and publicly; **à ~e de nez**○ at a rough guess; **à ~e d'œil** before your very eyes; **vouloir en mettre** or **en jeter plein la ~e à qn** to try to dazzle ou impress sb.

vulcain /vylkɛ̃/ *nm* Zool red admiral.

Vulcain /vylkɛ̃/ *npr* Mythol Vulcan.

vulcanisation /vylkanizasjɔ̃/ *nf* vulcanization.

vulcaniser /vylkanize/ [1] *vtr* to vulcanize.

vulcanologie /vylkanɔlɔʒi/ *nf* volcanology.

vulcanologue /vylkanɔlɔg/ ▶ **510** *nmf* volcanologist.

vulgaire /vylgɛʀ/ **I** *adj* **1** (grossier) [*personne, propos*] vulgar, coarse; **2** (banal) ordinary; **un ~ chat/balai/iris** a common-or-garden cat/broom/iris; **comme un ~ délinquant** like a common delinquent; **c'est un ~ employé** he's just a lowly employee; **3** (courant) [*plante, nom*] common; **la langue ~** the vernacular; **explication en langue ~** explanation in simple language; **4** [*esprit, opinion*] common.

II *nm* (grossièreté) vulgarity; **tomber dans le ~** to lapse into vulgarity.

vulgairement /vylgɛʀmɑ̃/ *adv* **1** (sans raffinement) [*s'habiller*] in a common way; [*s'exprimer*] coarsely; **2** (dans la langue courante) [*appeler*] commonly; **la valériane, ~ appelée herbe aux chats** valerian, commonly known as catnip.

vulgarisateur, -trice /vylgaʀizatœʀ, tʀis/ **I** *adj* [*revue*] for the general public (*après n*).

II *nm,f* popularizer.

vulgarisation /vylgaʀizasjɔ̃/ *nf* popularization; **revue de ~ scientifique** scientific review for the general public.

vulgariser /vylgaʀize/ [1] **I** *vtr* (rendre accessible) to popularize [*science, technologie*]; to bring [sth] into general use [*expression*].

II se vulgariser *vpr* [*technologie*] to become generally accessible; [*expression*] to come into general use; **la culture vulgarisée** popular culture.

vulgarisme /vylgaʀism/ *nm* vulgarism.

vulgarité /vylgaʀite/ *nf* **1** (grossièreté) vulgarity, coarseness; **2** (banalité) ordinariness.

Vulgate /vylgat/ *nf* **la ~** the Vulgate.

vulgum pecus○ /vylgɔmpekys/ *nm* pej **le ~** the hoi-polloi.

vulnérabilité /vylneʀabilite/ *nf* vulnerability.

vulnérable /vylneʀabl/ *adj* **1** (exposé) lit, fig vulnerable (**à** to); **les cyclistes sont ~s en cet endroit** cyclists are vulnerable at that spot; **être ~ aux critiques/à la pollution** to be vulnerable to criticism/to pollution; **il est ~ à la gorge** his vulnerable point is his throat; **2** (au bridge) vulnerable.

vulnéraire /vylneʀɛʀ/ *nf* kidney vetch.

vulvaire /vylvɛʀ/ **I** *adj* Anat vulvar; ▶ **fourchette**.

II *nf* Bot stinking goosefoot.

vulve /vylv/ *nf* vulva.

vulvite /vylvit/ ▶ **271** *nf* vulvitis.

Ww

w, **W** /dublәve/ *nm inv* **1** (lettre) w, W; **2 W** (*written abbr* = **watt**) **60 W** 60 W; **3 W3** WWW.

wagnérien, **-ienne** /vagneʀjɛ̃, ɛn/ *adj, nm,f* Wagnerian.

wagon /vagɔ̃/ *nm* **1** (pour matériel, animaux) wagon GB, car US; (pour personnes) carriage GB, car US; **2** (contenu) wagonload GB, carload US.

■ **~ à bestiaux** cattle truck GB, cattle car US; **~ couvert** covered goods wagon GB, freight car US; **~ de marchandises** goods wagon GB, freight car US; **~ plat** flat wagon GB, flatcar US; **~ réfrigérant** refrigeration wagon GB, refrigeration car US.

wagon-bar, *pl* **wagons-bars** /vagɔ̃baʀ/ *nm* buffet car.

wagon-citerne, *pl* **wagons-citernes** /vagɔ̃sitɛʀn/ *nm* Rail tanker.

wagon-lit, *pl* **wagons-lits** /vagɔ̃li/ *nm* sleeper, sleeping car US.

wagonnet /vagɔnɛ/ *nm* trolley GB, cart US.

wagon-poste, *pl* **wagons-postes** /vagɔ̃pɔst/ *nm* mail van GB, mail car US.

wagon-restaurant, *pl* **wagons-restaurants** /vagɔ̃ʀɛstɔʀɑ̃/ *nm* restaurant car GB, dining car US.

wahhabisme /waabism/ *nm* Wahhabism.

Wahhabites /waabit/ *nmpl* Wahhabis.

Walhalla /valala/ *nprm* Valhalla.

walkie-talkie, *pl* **walkies-talkies** /wokitoki/ *nm* walkie-talkie.

walkman® /wokman/ *nm* walkman®.

walkyrie /valkiʀi/ *nf* **1** Mythol (déesse) Valkyrie; **2** hum (femme imposante) battleaxe[GB] hum.

wallaby, *pl* **wallabies** /walabi/ *nm* wallaby.

wallon, **-onne** /walɔ̃, ɔn/ **▶ 462** **I** *adj* Walloon.

II *nm* Ling Walloon.

Wallon, **-onne** /walɔ̃, ɔn/ *nm,f* Walloon.

Wallonie /walɔni/ **▶ 692** *nprf* Walloon area of Belgium.

wapiti /wapiti/ *nm* wapiti.

warrant /vaʀɑ̃/ *nm* warehouse warrant.

Warwickshire **▶ 692** *nprm* **le ~** Warwickshire.

Washington /waʃiŋtɔn/ *npr* **1** **▶ 857** (ville) Washington DC; **2** **▶ 692** (État) **l'État de ~** Washington State.

wassingue /vasɛ̃g/ *nf* floorcloth.

wastringue /vastʀɛ̃g/ *nf* spoke shave.

water-ballast, *pl* **~s** /watɛʀbalast/ *nm* ballast tank.

water-closet, *pl* **~s** /watɛʀklɔzɛt/ *nm* water closet.

water-polo /watɛʀpɔlo/ **▶ 449** *nm* water polo.

waters○ /watɛʀ/ *nmpl* toilets.

watt /wat/ *nm* watt.

watt-heure, *pl* **watts-heures** /watœʀ/ *nm* watt-hour.

wattmètre /watmɛtʀ/ *nm* wattmeter.

WC /(dublә)vese/ *nmpl* toilet; **aller aux ~** to go to the toilet.

Wear **▶ 692** *nprm* ▶ **Tyne**.

Web /wɛb/ *nm* Web; **un site ~** a Web site.

weber /vebɛʀ/ *nm* weber.

week-end, *pl* **~s** /wikɛnd/ *nm* weekend.

welter /vɛltɛʀ/ *adj, nm* welterweight.

western /wɛstɛʀn/ *nm* western.

western-spaghetti, *pl* **westerns-spaghettis** /wɛstɛʀnspageti/ *nm* spaghetti western.

Westphalie /vɛstfali/ **▶ 692** *nprf* Westphalia.

wharf /waʀf/ *nm* wharf.

whisky, *pl* **whiskies** /wiski/ *nm* (écossais) whisky, Scotch; (irlandais, américain) whiskey.

whist /wist/ **▶ 449** *nm* whist.

white-spirit /wajtspiʀit/ *nm* white spirit.

wigwam /wigwam/ *nm* wigwam.

Wiltshire **▶ 692** *nprm* **le ~** Wiltshire.

winch /winʃ/ *nm* winch.

winchester /winʃɛstɛʀ/ *nf* (fusil) Winchester® rifle.

Wisconsin /viskɔnsin/ **▶ 692** *nprm* Wisconsin.

wishbone /wiʃbon/ *nm* Naut, Sport wishbone boom.

wisigoth, **~e** /vizigo, ɔt/ *adj* Visigothic.

Wisigoth, **~e** /vizigo, ɔt/ *nm,f* Visigoth.

wisigothique /visigɔtik/ *adj* Visigothic.

won /wɔn/ **▶ 46** *nm* won.

Worcester **▶ 692** *nprm* ▶ **Hereford**.

Worcestershire **▶ 692** *nprm* **le ~** Worcestershire.

Wyoming /wajomiŋ/ **▶ 692** *nprm* Wyoming.

x, **X** /iks/ *nm inv* **1** (lettre) x, X; ▶ **rayon**; **2** Math (inconnue) x; **j'ai fait le trajet x plus une fois** I've done the journey innumerable times; **il y a x temps que c'est fini** it's been over for ages; **3** (pour désigner un inconnu) **X, Monsieur X** X, Mr X; **porter plainte contre X** Jur to take an action against person or persons unknown; **4**○ Univ **l'X** the École Polytechnique; **un X** (élève) a graduate of the École Polytechnique; **5** Cin **film classé X** pornographic movie.

xénon /ksenɔ̃/ *nm* xenon.

xénophobe /gzenɔfɔb/ **I** *adj* xenophobic. **II** *nmf* xenophobe.

xénophobie /gzenɔfɔbi/ *nf* xenophobia.

Xénophon /gzenɔfɔ̃/ *npr* Xenophon.

xérès /kseʀɛs/ *nm* sherry.

xérophyte /kseʀɔfit/ *nf* xerophyte.

Xerxès /gzɛʀsɛs/ *npr* Xerxes.

xylographe /ksilɔgʀaf/ *nm* xylographer.

xylographie /ksilɔgʀafi/ *nf* **1** (art) xylography; **2** (œuvre) xylograph.

xylographique /ksilɔgʀafik/ *adj* xylographic.

xylophage /ksilɔfaʒ/ *adj* xylophagous.

xylophène® /ksilɔfɛn/ *nm* wood preservative.

xylophone /ksilofɔn/ ▶ **534** *nm* xylophone.

y[1], **Y** /igʀɛk/ *nm inv* (lettre) y, Y.

y[2] /i/ *pron*

■ **Note** Les expressions comme *y rester, il y a* seront traitées sous le verbe.
– Lorsque *y* met en relief un groupe exprimé, on ne le traduit pas: *tu y vas souvent, à Londres*○? = do you often go to London?; *je n'y comprends rien, moi, aux échecs*○ = I don't understand anything about chess.
– Lorsque *y* ne remplace aucun groupe identifiable, on ne le traduit pas: *c'est plus difficile qu'il n'y paraît* = it's harder than it seems; *je n'y vois rien* = I can't see a thing.

1 (à ça) **rien n'~ fait** it's no use; **elle n'~ peut rien** there's nothing she can do about it; **j'~ viens** I'm coming to that point; **tu n'~ arriveras jamais** you'll never manage; **tu ~ crois?** do you believe it?; **je vais m'~ mettre demain** I'll start tomorrow; **je n'~ comprends rien** I don't understand a thing; **il n'~ connaît rien** he knows nothing about it; **j'~ pense parfois** I sometimes think about it; **tu sais ~ jouer?** can you play?; **tu t'~ attendais?** were you expecting it?; **elle n'a rien à ~ perdre** she's got nothing to lose; **tu ~ as gagné** you got the best deal; **2** (là) there; **j'~ serai en août** I'll be there in August; **elle ~ mange parfois** she sometimes goes there to eat; **n'~ va pas** don't go; **j'~ suis allé hier** I went yesterday; **3**◑ (à lui, à elle) **dis-~** tell him/her; **parles-~** talk to him/her; **coupes-~ les cheveux** cut his/her hair; **4**◑ (il, ils) he/they; **~ vient?** is he coming?; **~ comprennent pas** they don't understand; **5**◑ (il) **c'est-~ pas dommage qu'~ pleuve?** what a pity it's raining!; **c'est-~ pas gentil!** how nice!; **6** (avec le verbe avoir) **des pommes? il n'y en a plus/pas** apples? there are none left/none; **du vin? il n'y en a plus/pas** wine? there's none left/none; **quand ~ en a plus, ~ en a encore**○ there's always more where that came from; **il n'~ a qu'à téléphoner, ~ a qu'à téléphoner**○ just phone; **'il n'~ a qu'à le repeindre!'—'~ a qu'à**○**, c'est facile à dire!'** 'all you have to do is repaint it!'—'just repaint it! easier said than done!'

IDIOMES **~ mettre du sien** to work at it.

yacht /ˈjot/ *nm* yacht.

yacht-club, *pl* **~s** /ˈjotklœb/ *nm* yacht club.

yachting /ˈjotiŋ/ **▶449** *nm* yachting; **faire du ~** to go yachting.

yachtman†, *pl* **yachtmen** /ˈjotman, mɛn/ *nm* yachtsman.

ya(c)k /ˈjak/ *nm* yak.

Yamoussoukro /ˈjamusukʀo/ **▶857** *npr* Yamoussoukro.

yang /ˈjɑ̃g/ *nm* yang.

yankee /ˈjɑ̃ki/ *adj, nmf* Yankee.

Yaoundé /ˈjaunde/ **▶857** *npr* Yaoundé.

yaourt /ˈjauʀ(t)/ *nm* yoghurt; **~ nature/aromatisé/aux fruits** natural/flavoured[GB]/fruit yoghurt.

yaourtière /ˈjauʀtjɛʀ/ *nf* yoghurt-maker.

yard /ˈjaʀd/ **▶477** *nm* yard.

yatagan /ˈjatagɑ̃/ *nm* yataghan.

yearling /ˈjœʀliŋ/ *nm* yearling.

Yémen /ˈjemɛn/ **▶321** *nprm* Yemen; **~ du Nord/Sud** Hist North/South Yemen.

yéménite /ˈjemenit/ **▶537**, **462** *adj* Yemeni.

Yéménite /ˈjemenit/ **▶537** *nmf* Yemeni.

yen /ˈjɛn/ **▶46** *nm* yen.

yéti /ˈjeti/ *nm* yeti.

yeuse /ˈjøz/ *nf* holm oak.

yeux *nmpl* ▶ **œil**.

yé-yé, *pl* **~s** /ˈjeje/ **I** *adj inv* sixties (*épith*). **II** *nm* **1** (musique) **le ~** *French version of rock 'n' roll in the 60s*; **2** (chanteur) **les ~s** French 60s rock stars.

yiddish /ˈjidiʃ/ **▶462** *adj inv, nm* Yiddish.

yin /ˈjin/ *nm* yin.

ylang-ylang /ˈilɑ̃ilɑ̃/ *nm* ylang-ylang.

yod /ˈjɔd/ *nm* Ling yod.

yodler /ˈjɔdle/ [1] *vi* to yodel.

yoga /ˈjɔga/ **▶449** *nm* yoga; **faire du ~** to do yoga.

yoghourt /ˈjɔguʀ(t)/ *nm* = **yaourt**.

yogi /ˈjɔgi/ *nm* yogi.

yole /ˈjɔl/ *nf* skiff.

Yom Kippour /ˈjɔmkipuʀ/ *nprm* Yom Kippur.

Yonne /jɔn/ **▶357**, **692** *nprf* (rivière, département) **l'~** the Yonne.

Yorkshire **▶692** *nprm* **le ~** Yorkshire; **le North/South/West ~** North/South/West Yorkshire.

yougoslave /ˈjugɔslav/ **▶537** *adj* Yugoslavian.

Yougoslave /ˈjugɔslav/ **▶537** *nmf* Yugoslav.

Yougoslavie /ˈjugɔslavi/ *nprf* Yugoslavia.

youpi○ /ˈjupi/ *excl* yippee!

youpin◑, **~e** /ˈjupɛ̃, in/ *adj, nm,f* offensive yid◑ injur.

yourte /ˈjuʀt/ *nf* yurt.

youyou /ˈjuju/ *nm* **1** (cri) ululation sout; **2** (embarcation) dinghy.

yo-yo® /ˈjojo/ *nm inv* yoyo®.

ypérite /ipeʀit/ *nf* yperite.

ytterbium /itɛʀbjɔm/ *nm* ytterbium.

yttrium /itʀijɔm/ *nm* yttrium.

yuan /ˈjuan/ **▶46** *nm* yuan.

yucca /ˈjuka/ *nm* yucca.

Yukon /ˈjykɔ̃/ **▶357**, **692** *nprm* **le ~** the Yukon; **Territoire du ~** Yukon territory.

Yvelines /ivlin/ **▶692** *nprfpl* (département) **les ~** Yvelines.

Zz

z, Z /zɛd/ *nm inv* z, Z.
z'◑ /z/ *particule de liaison* **(y) z'arrivent** they're coming.
ZAC /zak/ *nf*: *abbr* ▶ **zone.**
Zacharie /zakaʀi/ *npr* Zacharias.
ZAD /zad/ *nf*: *abbr* ▶ **zone.**
zain /zɛ̃/ *adj m* [*cheval*] whole-coloured[GB].
Zaïre /zaiʀ/ ▶ 321 *nprm* Zaïre.
zaïrois, ~e /zaiʀwa, az/ ▶ 537 *adj* Zairean.
Zaïrois, ~e /zaiʀwa, az/ ▶ 537 *nm,f* Zairean.
zakouski /zakuski/ *nmpl* zakuski.
Zambèze /zɑ̃bɛz/ ▶ 357 *nprm* **le ~** the Zambezi.
Zambie /zɑ̃bi/ ▶ 321 *nprf* Zambia.
zambien, -ienne /zɑ̃bjɛ̃, ɛn/ ▶ 537 *adj* Zambian.
Zambien, -ienne /zɑ̃bjɛ̃, ɛn/ ▶ 537 *nm,f* Zambian.
Zanzibar /zɑ̃zibaʀ/ ▶ 416 *nprf* Zanzibar.
zapper /zape/ [1] *vi* (à la télévision) to channel-flick, to flick through the channels, to change channels.
zazou /zazu/ *nm*: *eccentric young jazz lover during World War II.*
zèbre /zɛbʀ/ *nm* **1** zebra; **2**○ fig bloke○ GB, guy○ US; **un drôle de ~** an odd bloke, a weird guy.
zébré /zebʀe/ *adj* [*tissu*] zebra-striped; **~ de** streaked with; **ciel ~ d'éclairs** sky streaked with lightning.
zébrure /zebʀyʀ/ *nf* stripe.
zébu /zeby/ *nm* zebu.
Zélande /zelɑ̃d/ *nprf* Zealand.
zélateur, -trice /zelatœʀ, tʀis/ *nm,f* liter zealot; **~ de qn/qch** supporter of sb/sth.
zèle /zɛl/ *nm* zeal, enthusiasm; **avec ~** enthusiastically, with zeal ou enthusiasm; **sans faire de ~** without zeal ou enthusiasm; **faire du ~** or **de l'excès de ~** to be overzealous, to overdo it; **pousser le ~ jusqu'à faire qch** to go so far as to do sth.
zélé, ~e /zele/ *adj* enthusiastic, zealous.
zélote /zelɔt/ *nm* Hist Zealot.
zen /zɛn/ *adj inv, nm* zen.
zénana /zenana/ *nm* zenana.
zénith /zenit/ *nm* lit, fig zenith; **à son ~** [*soleil*] in the ou at its zenith; [*carrière*] at its height; **être au ~ de qch** to be at the zenith sout ou height of sth.
zénithal, ~e, *mpl* **-aux** /zenital, o/ *adj* [*distance*] zenithal; [*lumière*] of the zenith (*après n*).
zéphyr /zefiʀ/ *nm* liter zephyr.
zeppelin /zɛplɛ̃/ *nm* zeppelin.
zéro /zeʀo/ ▶ 545 **I** *adj num* **1** (avant nom) **~ heure** midnight, twenty-four hundred (hours); **il sera exactement ~ heure vingt minutes dix secondes** the time will be twelve twenty and ten seconds; **les enfants de ~ à six ans** children from nought to six years old; **j'ai eu ~ faute dans ma dictée** I didn't make a single mistake in my dictation; **'~ défaut, ~ délai, ~ stock, ~ panne'** 'zero defect, zero delay, zero stock, zero breakdown'; **2** (après nom) zero; **niveau/croissance ~** zero level/growth; **le numéro ~ d'un journal** the trial issue of a newspaper.
II *nm* **1** (chiffre) zero, nought GB; **falsifier un chiffre en ajoutant un ~** to falsify a figure by adding a nought GB ou zero; **le prix se termine par un ~** the price ends in a nought GB ou zero; **2** (sur une échelle de valeurs) zero; **croissance proche de ~** growth that is near zero; **remettre un compteur à ~** to reset a counter at ou to zero, to zero a counter; **remettre les compteurs à ~** fig to make a fresh start; **40 degrés en dessous de ~** 40 degrees below zero; **avoir le moral à ~** fig to be down in the dumps○; **croître de ~ à la valeur V** to increase from zero to value V; **tendre vers ~** to tend toward(s) zero; **3** (évaluation) zero, nought GB; **avoir un ~ en latin** to get zero ou nought in Latin; **c'est beau à regarder mais question goût c'est ~**○ it's nice to look at, but no marks for flavour[GB]; **4** (en sport) gén nil, nothing; (au tennis) love; **gagner trois (buts) à ~** to win three nil; **l'emporter par deux sets à ~** to win by two sets to love.
■ **~ absolu** absolute zero; **~ de conduite** bad mark for behaviour[GB]; **~ pointé** fail mark GB ou grade US.
IDIOMES **les avoir à ~**◑ to be scared shitless◑ ou stiff○; **partir de ~** to start from scratch; **repartir de ~** to start from scratch again, to go (right) back to square one; **tout reprendre à ~** to start all over again; **avoir la boule à ~**○ to have a shaven head.
zeste /zɛst/ *nm* **1** (écorce) zest ¢; **un ~ de citron** the zest of a lemon; **2** fig **un ~ de chance** a bit of luck; **un ~ de provocation** a touch of provocation.
zêta /dzɛta/ *nm inv* zeta.
zeugme /zøgm/ *nm* zeugma.
Zeus /zøs/ *npr* Zeus.
zézaiement /zezɛmɑ̃/ *nm* lisp.
zézayer /zezeje/ [21] *vi* to lisp.
zibeline /ziblin/ *nf* sable; **un manteau de ~** a sable coat.
zieuter○ /zjøte/ [1] *vtr* to get a load of○, take a look at.
zigomar○ /zigɔmaʀ/ *nm* pej guy○.
zigoto○ /zigɔto/ *nm* guy○; **un drôle de ~** a funny guy; **faire le ~** to clown around.
zigouiller◑ /ziguje/ [1] *vtr* to bump [sb] off○, to kill; **se faire ~** to get bumped off○.
zigue○ /zig/ *nm* guy○.
zigzag /zigzag/ *nm* zigzag; **une route en ~** a winding road; **faire des ~s** to zigzag **(parmi** through); **partir en ~s** to zigzag off.
zigzaguer /zigzage/ [1] *vi* to zigzag.
Zimbabwe /zimbabwe/ ▶ 321 *nprm* Zimbabwe.
zimbabwéen, -éenne /zimbabweɛ̃, ɛn/ ▶ 537 *adj* Zimbabwean.
Zimbabwéen, -éenne /zimbabweɛ̃, ɛn/ ▶ 537 *nm,f* Zimbabwean.
zinc /zɛ̃g/ *nm* **1** zinc; **toiture de ~** tin roofing; **2**○ (comptoir) counter, bar; **3**○ (avion) plane.
zinguer /zɛ̃ge/ [1] *vtr* to cover [sth] with zinc [*toiture*].
zingueur /zɛ̃gœʀ/ ▶ 510 *nm* roofer.
zinnia /zinja/ *nm* zinnia.
zinzin○ /zɛ̃zɛ̃/ **I** *adj inv* cracked○; **elle est un peu ~** she's a bit cracked○ ou a bit of a nut○.
II *nmf* (personne) lunatic, nut○.
III *nm* thingummy○ GB, thingamajig○.
zip /zip/ *nm* zip GB, zipper US.
zippé, ~e /zipe/ *adj* [*sac, blouson*] zip-up (*épith*).
zircon /ziʀkɔ̃/ *nm* zircon.
zirconium /ziʀkɔnjɔm/ *nm* zirconium.
zizanie /zizani/ *nf* ill-feeling, discord; **semer la ~** to stir up ill-feeling, sow discord sout.
zizi○ /zizi/ *nm* willy○ GB, wiener○ US, penis.
zloty /zlɔti/ ▶ 46 *nm* Fin zloty.
zob● /zɔb/ *nm* prick●, penis.
zodiac® /zɔdjak/ *nm* Naut inflatable dinghy.
zodiacal, ~e, *mpl* **-aux** /zɔdjakal, o/ *adj* [*lumière*] zodiacal; [*signe*] of the zodiac (*après n*).
zodiaque /zɔdjak/ *nm* zodiac.
zoé /zɔe/ *nf* zoea.
zombie /zɔ̃bi/ *nm* zombie.
zona /zona/ ▶ 271 *nm* shingles ¢, herpes zoster spéc; **avoir un ~** to have shingles.
zonage /zonaʒ/ *nm* zoning.
zonard○, **~e** /zonaʀ, aʀd/ *nm,f* pej drop-out○.
zone /zon/ *nf* **1** (secteur) zone, area; **~ de radiation/combat** radiation/combat zone; **~ de pêche** fishing zone; **~ de cultures** agricultural area; **~ de turbulences** Météo area of turbulence; **~ interdite** no-go area GB, off-limits area; (sur un panneau) no entry; **2** fig (domaine) area; **~ de recherche** area of research; **~ floue/d'ombre** blurred/shady area; **3** (banlieue pauvre) **la ~** the slum belt; **de seconde ~** second-rate.
■ **~ d'activités** business park; **~ d'aménagement concerté, ZAC** Admin integrated development zone; **~ d'aménagement différé, ZAD** Admin area set aside for development; **~ artisanale** small industrial estate GB ou park; **~ bleue** Aut restricted parking zone; **~ de chalandise** Admin, Comm catchment area; **~ de données** Ordinat data field; **~ d'environnement protégé** environmental protection zone; **~ érogène** Physiol erogenous zone; **~ d'exclusion aérienne** Mil no-fly zone; **~ franc** Fin franc area; **~ franche** Écon free zone; **~ frontière** border area; **~ industrielle** industrial estate GB ou park US; **~ d'influence** Pol sphere ou area of influence; **~ libre** Hist unoccupied France; **~ de libre-échange** Écon free-trade area; **~ monétaire** Fin monetary area; **~ occupée** Hist occupied France; **~ postale** Postes postal area ou zone GB, zone of improved postage, ZIP US; **~ sterling** Fin sterling area; **~ sensible** lit potential trouble-spot; fig potential trouble area; **~ sinistrée** Admin disaster area; **~ tampon** Mil, Pol buffer zone;

Les signes du zodiaque

		signe		personnes	date
Bélier	=	Aries	['eəri:z]	Ariens	Mar 21–Apr 20
Taureau	=	Taurus	['tɔ:rəs]	Taureans	Apr 21–May 20
Gémeaux	=	Gemini	['dʒemɪnaɪ,-nɪ:]	Geminis	May 21–Jun 21
Cancer	=	Cancer	['kænsə(r)]	Cancerians	Jun 22–July 22
Lion	=	Leo	['li:əʊ]	Leos	July 23–Aug 22
Vierge	=	Virgo	['vɜ:gəʊ]	Virgos *ou* Virgoans	Aug 23–Sept 22
Balance	=	Libra	['li:brə]	Libras	Sept 23–Oct 23
Scorpion	=	Scorpio	['skɔ:pɪəʊ]	Scorpios	Oct 24–Nov 21
Sagittaire	=	Sagittarius	[ˌsædʒ'teərɪəs]	Sagittarians	Nov 22–Dec 21
Capricorne	=	Capricorn	['kæprɪ'kɔ:n]	Capricorns	Dec 22–Jan 19
Verseau	=	Aquarius	[a'kweərɪəs]	Aquarians	Jan 20–Feb 18
Poissons	=	Pisces	['paɪsi:z]	Pisceans	Feb 19–Mar 20

Dans les expressions suivantes, Lion *est pris comme exemple; tous les autres signes s'utilisent de la même façon.*

je suis Lion	=	I'm Leo *ou* I'm a Leo
je suis Gémeaux	=	I'm a Gemini
né sous le signe du Lion	=	born under the sign of Leo *ou* born in Leo
les Lions/Cancers sont très généreux	=	Leos/Cancerians are very generous
que dit l'horoscope pour les Lions?	=	what's the horoscope for Leo?

~ à urbaniser en priorité, **ZUP** priority development area.

zoner○ /zone/ [1] *vi* to hang about○ ou around○.

zoo /zo/ *nm* zoo.

zoologie /zɔɔlɔʒi/ *nf* zoology.

zoologique /zɔɔlɔʒik/ *adj* zoological.

zoologiste /zɔɔlɔʒist/ **▶510** *nmf* zoologist.

zoom /zum/ *nm* **1** Phot (objectif) zoom lens; **2** Cin zoom; **un ~ avant/arrière** a zoom in/ out.

zootechnicien, **-ienne** /zɔɔtɛknisjɛ̃, ɛn/ **▶510** *nm,f* animal technician.

zou○ /zu/ *excl* **allez ~!** (va-t-en) go on, out!; (dépêche-toi) hurry up.

zouave /zwav/ *nm* **1**○ (clown) clown, comedian; **faire le ~** to play the fool GB, to clown around○; **2** (soldat) zouave.

Zoug /zug/ **▶692** *npr* **le canton de ~** the canton of Zug.

zouk /zuk/ *nm* zouk (*type of Caribbean music and dance*).

zouker /zuke/ *vi* to dance to zouk music.

zoulou, **~e** /zulu/ **▶462** **I** *adj* Zulu. **II** *nm* Zulu.

Zoulou /zulu/ *nm* Zulu.

zozo○ /zozo/ *nm* ninny○ GB, jerk○ US.

zozoter /zɔzɔte/ [1] *vi* to lisp.

ZUP /zyp/ *nf*: *abbr* ▶ **zone**.

Zurich /zyʀik/ *npr* **1** **▶857** (ville) Zurich; **2** **▶692** (région) **le canton de ~** (the canton of) Zurich; **le lac de ~** Lake Zurich.

zut○ /zyt/ *excl* damn○!

zyeuter○ = **zieuter**.

zygoma /zigɔma/ *nm* zygoma.

zygomatique /zigɔmatik/ *adj*, *nm* zygomatic.

IDIOMES **titiller le ~ de qn**○ to make [sb] laugh.

zygote /zigɔt/ *nm* zygote.

zyzomys /zizɔmis/ *nm* zyzomys, rock rat.

Contents

General advice on writing in French

Having good ideas isn't enough: you have to know how to get them across. This section offers some general advice on communicating clearly and effectively in French.

Presentation

The presentation of French is very similar to that of English. Just bear in mind that the paragraphs should stand out well on the page. In the case of an essay, they should all be about the same length (except for the introduction and the conclusion). Starting a new paragraph is not done in an arbitrary way, but only when moving on to a new idea. It is often advised to develop only one idea per paragraph.

Spelling

If the reader comes across too many spelling mistakes, s/he will lose the thread of the text and have difficulty in following your argument. So take care over your spelling and reread the text several times. Check systematically to see that you have not made the most common mistakes (agreement of adjectives and past participles, accents, verb endings).

Punctuation

Another very important aspect of French writing is punctuation. This makes a text easier to read and can sometimes change the meaning of a sentence completely, as we shall see later. The rules of punctuation are stricter in French than they are in English. The most straightforward punctuation marks, such as the exclamation mark and the interrogation mark, are used as in English. For the others, which are more complex and are sometimes used differently in French and in English, we give a list of the basic rules.

The stop

The stop is used:

- to indicate the end of a sentence (when it is called a full stop);
- after some abbreviations (for example, *c.v.* for *curriculum vitae*, *etc.* for *et cetera*, *p.j.* for *pièce jointe*).

Punctuation
continued

It should be noted that if an abbreviation comes at the end of a sentence, the abbreviation stop is merged with the full stop:

Veuillez joindre un c.v. à votre lettre.

Veuillez joindre un c.v.

One common fault to be avoided: *etc.* is never followed by suspension points (. . .)!

Il y avait des chats, des chiens, des oiseaux, etc.

and not

Il y avait des chats, des chiens, des oiseaux, etc. . .

WATCH OUT! Abbreviations which end with the last letter of the full word are not followed by a stop, unless they come at the end of a sentence. For example: *bd* for *boulevard*.

Suspension points

Suspension points are mainly used:

- to leave a sentence, a paragraph, etc. in suspense, inviting the reader to dream or to reflect:

  Elle fixa l'horizon et se mit à rêver. . .

- to show that a list could be continued:

  Elle avait rangé dans son tiroir les crayons, les gommes, les stylos. . .

- to indicate thought, hesitation, emotion:

  Elle irait lui parler dès ce soir . . . ou peut-être attendrait-elle demain . . . non, il fallait qu'il sache tout de suite.

- to create the effect of anticipation in the reader:

  Il essaya de la rattraper . . . mais en vain.

  À suivre. . .

- to show that some words have been left out of a quotation.

WATCH OUT! There are always three suspension points. They are merged with the full stop and the abbreviation stop. They can be used with other punctuation marks, such as the comma, the question mark, the exclamation mark, or the semi-colon.

Suspension points are also used in the form . . ./. . . in the bottom right-hand corner of a page to show that the text continues on the next page.

Suspension points are only followed by a capital if they come at the end of a sentence. One should write:

Il lui fallait des carottes, des tomates, des haricots . . . Il alla donc au marché.

but

Il avait marché des kilomètres . . . pour rien.

Punctuation
continued

The colon

The colon is used:

- to introduce a quotation, a proverb, or dialogue:

  Comme on dit souvent : tel père, tel fils.

  Elle a ajouté : «Ça m'est égal!»

- to introduce an explanation or a summary of what has just been said:

  Les arbres commençaient à roussir, les premières feuilles tombaient : l'automne était là.

- to introduce a list:

  Il vous faudra :
  – un cahier;
  – un classeur;
  – du papier à dessin.

or

Elle avait choisi ce qu'elle porterait ce soir : une robe noire, une veste rouge et des escarpins noirs.

Note that in French there is a space both before and after the colon.

WATCH OUT! After a colon and opening quotation marks, a capital letter is always used.

The semi-colon

The semi-colon is used to distinguish the subclauses in a complex sentence:

Elle savait que seul le résultat comptait; qu'il faille faire des sacrifices lui importait peu.

It is also used between clauses of similar construction when some of them contain an ellipsis:

Il était secrétaire; sa sœur, infirmière; et son jeune frère, instituteur.

The semi-colon is used to separate the different items in a list:

Il vous faudra :
– un cahier;
– un classeur;
– du papier à dessin.

It should be noted that the different items do not require a capital letter.

The comma

The comma is used between independent clauses which have a certain continuity between them:

Il s'arrêta devant la boutique, il jeta un œil dans la vitrine, il entra.

When the two clauses are joined by a co-ordinating conjunction (*et*/*ou*), the comma usually disappears:

Punctuation
continued

Il traversa la rue et il entra dans la boutique.

The comma is, however, used in front of *et/ou/mais* if one of the two clauses already contains a conjunction:

La rue était sombre et silencieuse, et elle prit peur.

With the conjunctions *mais*, *car*, *donc*, *or*, the comma is not obligatory.

Watch out when using the comma with the conjunction *ni*:

Il ne parle ni anglais ni espagnol.

but

Il ne parle aucune langue étrangère, ni l'anglais, ni l'espagnol.

and

Il ne parle ni l'anglais, ni l'espagnol, ni l'allemand.

A comma is used:

- when part of a sentence is displaced:

  Je lui ai écrit hier.

  but

  Hier, je lui ai écrit.

- when a comment clause is inserted or when calling out to someone:

  Les jeux vidéo font, paraît-il, beaucoup de tort à la lecture.

  Attends, Laurence!

- on either side of an apposition (an apposition adds details but can be removed without the sentence becoming grammatically incorrect):

  Sa collègue, une petite brune aux yeux verts, entra dans le bureau.

  Son père, lui, n'a jamais quitté le village.

When the apposition is a subordinate clause, the comma is also used:

Qu'il veuille partir, je l'admets.

WATCH OUT! If this clause is the subject there is no comma:

Qu'il veuille partir est compréhensible.

Relative clauses are separated by a comma when the pronoun (*qui/que*) is too far from the noun it relates to. One should write:

La femme que j'ai rencontrée ce matin m'a parlé de toi.

but

J'aime beaucoup le chat de la voisine, qui a de grands yeux verts.

Without the comma, one would think that it was the neighbour who had green eyes and not the cat.

In independent clauses, the comma separates items in lists. There is no comma before *et*:

Il acheta des roses, des tulipes, des lys et des œillets.

Elle m'a montré les cadeaux de son père, de sa mère, de son frère et de sa sœur.

Punctuation
continued

Les dictionnaires, les classeurs et les cahiers étaient rangés sur les étagères.

Les dictionnaires, les classeurs, les cahiers, étaient rangés sur les étagères.

Watch out when writing sums in numbers. French does not use the comma in the same way as English:

	one thousand	two point five
French	1 000	2,5
English	1,000	2.5

The dash

Dashes are used:

- to introduce replies in a dialogue:

  «Tu as vu ce film?

  – Non, jamais.»

- to distinguish between the elements of a list;
- to isolate a comment clause, including one inside a parenthesis:

  Cette hypothèse — à laquelle je ne crois pas du tout — est l'œuvre d'un journaliste.

  Le rapport donne les derniers chiffres du chômage (chômage qui sévit à travers l'Europe — même dans les pays les plus riches — et qui ne semble pas près de régresser).

Quotation marks and the presentation of dialogue

French quotation marks (« ») are used in preference to English ones (" "). Quotation marks are used:

- to emphasize a word which is going to be explained or which is being used in an improper, humorous, or ironic way;
- to show the beginning and the end of a quotation;
- for the titles of poems;
- to show the beginning and the end of a dialogue or to introduce direct speech:

  Il l'interrogea :
  «Vous êtes arrivé quand?
  – Pourquoi cette question? Je n'ai rien fait de mal!
  – C'est ce que nous allons voir!»

Here, the use of the quotation marks is not obligatory. They could have been left out. In such a case a dash would have been used in front of the first question.

Il l'interrogea :
– Vous êtes arrivé quand?
– Pourquoi cette question? Je n'ai rien fait de mal!
– C'est ce que nous allons voir!

Inverted commas are not used on either side of a break in direct speech.

«Tiens, dit-elle en ouvrant les rideaux, les voilà!»

Punctuation

continued

Capitals

The rules for the use of capitals are very complex and changeable. Here are a few leads to help you. It should be noted that the use of capitals is slightly different in French and in English.

The following require a capital letter:

- the first word of a sentence;
- the first word of a quotation, however short it may be:

  Il cria : «Non.»

- the beginning of each line of verse in a poem;
- proper names of people;
- the names of towns, countries, rivers, nationalities, and races:

  . . . à Paris . . . le Sénégal . . . la Tamise . . . les Français . . . les Blancs . . . la République d'Irlande

- titles and occupations which replace a person's name:

  . . . le Président . . . Madame la Directrice. . .

- the different forms of address in a letter:

  Cher Monsieur.

  Veuillez agréer, Madame, mes salutations distinguées.

- the names of associations, organizations, etc.:

  l'Alliance française . . . la Compagnie générale des Eaux. . .

- the names of great historical periods or events:

  . . . la Renaissance . . . la Révolution française . . . la Guerre de Cent Ans. . .

The following do not require capital letters:

- the names of days of the week and months of the year:

  C'était le début du mois de novembre. C'est vendredi.

- adjectives denoting nationality or region:

  . . . un citoyen suédois . . . une femme africaine . . . une spécialité alsacienne . . . la République italienne. . .

- nouns and adjectives referring to a language:

  . . . la grammaire française . . . Il parle anglais. L'italien est une langue latine.

- titles or qualities which precede a proper noun:

  . . . le président Chirac. . .

Capital letters in the titles of artistic works

As a general rule:

- capitalize the initial letter of the first word only, provided it is not a definite article:

  À la recherche du temps perdu

  Une vie

- capitalize the initial letters of the first two words if they are a definite article followed by a noun:

  Le Journal d'une femme de chambre

- capitalize the initial letters of the first three words if they are a definite article followed by an adjective followed by a noun:

  La Double Inconstance

Of course, if the title includes a proper name, a capital is required for the proper name as well:

L'Enfance de Bacchus

The titles of books and works of art must always be underlined or written in italics.

Style

Of course, everyone has his or her own style and there is no magic formula. One piece of advice, however: avoid sentence structures which are too complex. If you give too much information in the same sentence, you risk confusing the reader and increasing the number of mistakes in your French. The clearer the style, the easier the text is to read.

Thus, rather than:

Dans ce film, *Do the right thing*, qui a été tourné en 1989 et qui est son premier film, Spike Lee décrit les rivalités qui opposaient les noirs américains et les italo-américains à New York, dans les années 50.

it would be better to write:

Do the right thing, tourné en 1989, est le premier film de Spike Lee. Il y décrit les rivalités qui opposaient les noirs américains et les italo-américains dans le New York des années 50.

You should also consider using rhetorical questions (that is to say, questions which do not anticipate a reply and whose purpose is solely to introduce what comes next). This will make your text more lively and the style will be lighter.

For instance, instead of beginning a paragraph with the following phrase:

On peut se demander quelles sont les motivations du personnage principal.

one could write:

Quelles sont donc les motivations du personnage principal?

Once again, for reasons of clarity, repetition should be avoided as far as possible. It is much better to use **synonyms**. A thesaurus is a very useful worktool. What's more, looking for synonyms is an excellent way of increasing your vocabulary!

So if you are writing an article about *la télévision*, you should think of using words like *télé*, *petit écran*, *poste*, etc.

Reading French texts which deal with the same subject as your essay is also a good way of finding synonyms. You will find the vocabulary in context, and the nuances of meaning between different words will be more obvious. You will also notice that the more you read in French, the easier it becomes to write it.

Style
continued

French constructions will seem more natural and you will be less prone to translate English structures word for word.

Writing a text is not simply a question of putting sentences together. Your text has to come across as a coherent whole. When you are reading, you will undoubtedly notice that **link words** are used more often in French than they are in English. These allow you to emphasize the logical connections which exist in your text. The following list gives link words and phrases which you may find useful.

Link words

à l'inverse

À l'inverse, on peut se demander si ce n'est pas un choix délibéré de l'auteur. — *On the other hand*, one may wonder if it is not a deliberate choice on the author's part.

à savoir

Pendant la période d'incubation, *à savoir* deux semaines avant que la maladie ne se déclare, le sujet est très contagieux. — During the incubation period, *that is to say* for two weeks before the onset of symptoms, the subject is very infectious.

au contraire

On découvre, *au contraire*, que le personnage est coupable du crime. — *On the contrary*, we discover that the character is guilty of the crime.

aussi

aussi requires the subject to be inverted when it is not followed by a comma

Aussi faut-il tenir compte des bouleversements sociaux qu'a connus le XIXe siècle. — The social upheavals which took place during the nineteenth century must *also* be considered.

Aussi, il est intéressant de constater à quel point l'auteur est influencé par son milieu social. — It is *also* interesting to ask to what extent the author has been influenced by his social background.

autant dire que

Autant dire qu'il faut se méfier des jugements hâtifs. — *In other words* we must be wary of hasty judgements.

autrement dit

Nous sommes en 1919, *autrement dit* au lendemain de la première guerre mondiale. — It is the year 1919, *in other words*, just after the end of the First World War.

avant tout / avant toute chose

Avant toute chose, il convient de rappeler les différentes étapes de l'évolution de l'enfant. — *First*, we should recall the different stages of a child's development.

Link words
continued

cependant

Il n'est *cependant* pas considéré comme un auteur majeur.	He is not, *however*, considered to be a major author.

certes

Certes, la vengeance n'est pas la seule motivation du héros.	*Admittedly*, revenge is not the character's only motive.

d'abord

Nous verrons, *d'abord*, comment l'auteur décrit la tristesse du personnage.	We shall see, *first of all*, how the author describes the unhappiness of the character.

d'où

D'où la nécessité pour l'enfant de s'identifier à des personnages imaginaires.	*Hence* the necessity for the child to identify with imaginary characters.

donc

Nous évoquerons *donc* les poètes contemporains de Verlaine.	We will, *therefore*, consider the poets who were Verlaine's contemporaries.

du moins

C'est *du moins* l'hypothèse la plus crédible.	*At any rate* it is the most credible hypothesis.

en bref

En bref, il s'agit d'un constat d'échec.	*In short*, it is an admission of failure.

en d'autres termes

L'enfant accepte mal l'arrivée d'un nouveau-né. *En d'autres termes*, il est jaloux.	The child has difficulty in accepting the new baby. *In other words*, he is jealous.

Link words
continued

en effet

L'auteur connaissait bien le milieu bancaire. Il avait, *en effet*, travaillé pour une grande banque parisienne pendant près de dix ans.	The author was well acquainted with the world of banking. *Indeed*, he had worked for a large Parisian bank for almost ten years.

en fait

En fait, on ignore tout des liens qui les unissent.	*In fact* we know nothing about the ties which bond them.

en outre

En outre, il faut préciser que Verdi était un fervent partisan de l'unité italienne.	*Moreover*, it must be stated that Verdi was an ardent supporter of Italian unity.

en premier lieu

Nous nous attacherons, *en premier lieu*, à rappeler la situation économique du pays avant la révolution.	*In the first place*, we must consider the economic situation of the country before the revolution.

en résumé

En résumé, on peut dire que la télévision a volé une partie des spectateurs du cinéma.	*To sum up*, one can say that television has taken part of the audience away from the cinema.

en revanche

En revanche, il est peu crédible que l'auteur ait ignoré l'œuvre de Baudelaire.	*On the other hand*, it is implausible that the author was unaware of Baudelaire's work.

encore

encore used at the beginning of a sentence requires an inversion of the subject

Ces champignons ne sont, paraît-il, pas dangereux. *Encore* faut-il savoir les distinguer des autres.	These mushrooms are said not to be dangerous, but you *still* need to know how to tell them apart from the others.

enfin

Enfin, nous essaierons de souligner les points communs des deux poètes.	*Finally*, we will attempt to underline the points which the two poets have in common.

Link words
continued

ensuite	
Nous parlerons *ensuite* des problèmes d'insertion des immigrés.	We will *then* talk about the problems of integration faced by immigrants.
mais	
Mais cela ne justifie pas le recours à la violence.	*But* that does not justify resorting to violence.
malgré	
Malgré son immense succès, il est resté très simple.	*Despite* his huge success, he has remained very unpretentious.
néanmoins	
Il faut *néanmoins* préciser qu'il a grandi au sein d'une famille très pratiquante.	It must *none the less* be pointed out that he came from a very religious family.
or	
Or l'auteur est lui-même d'origine slave.	*Now* the author is himself of Slav origin.
par ailleurs	
On sait, *par ailleurs*, que le chat tient une place importante dans l'Antiquité égyptienne.	*In addition*, the cat is known to have held an important place in ancient Egypt.
par conséquent	
Il faut, *par conséquent*, tenir compte du contexte historique.	We must, *therefore*, take the historical context into account.
pour finir	
Pour finir, nous nous interrogerons sur l'avenir du livre, dans un monde où le support informatique prend chaque jour plus d'importance.	*Finally*, we will examine the future of the book in a world where the computer is becoming daily more important.
pourtant	
Le problème racial ne constitue *pourtant* pas la seule explication.	The racial problem is not, *however*, the only explanation.

Link words
continued

quoi qu'il en soit

Quoi qu'il en soit, ces mesures mettront du temps à produire leur effet.	*Be that as it may*, these measures will take time to have an effect.

seulement

Seulement, le destin en a décidé autrement.	*But* fate decided otherwise.

toutefois

Le roman n'est *toutefois* pas entièrement autobiographique.	The novel is *nevertheless* not entirely autobiographical.

The structure of the text

Whatever type of text you are writing in French (an article, an essay, a review of a meeting, a report, etc.), you should always bear in mind that the structure is very important. Even if your ideas are excellent, a French reader will be distracted if your text doesn't follow a rigorous and logical plan.

Your text should, therefore, always have an introduction, a development (usually consisting of two or three large sections), and a conclusion.

The introduction

This consists of a general sentence which introduces and arranges the subject and presents the structure of the plan.

The development

In both English and French there are many different sorts of plan. One can proceed chronologically, listing a series of events; stating the facts, the causes, and the consequences so as to describe a phenomenon; etc. In French, however, the classic plan is known as 'thesis, antithesis, synthesis'. It consists of opposing two theses, or points of view. The first part presents the reasons for agreeing with the question asked in the title; the second, the reasons for disagreeing; finally, in the last part, the pros and cons are weighed up—so a synthesis of the various ideas is made before concluding.

The conclusion

This briefly recaps the main arguments presented in the development and answers the problems or questions raised in the introduction.

Here, to help you, is a model of an article. This will show you in context the various elements which we have been dealing with so far: structuring the text, link words, etc.

Model French essay

Pour ou contre la télévision?

Depuis sa création, la télévision a connu une évolution phénoménale et a fait son entrée dans la plupart des foyers. Objet indispensable pour certains, elle n'est pour d'autres qu'une source d'abrutissement et de sous-culture. **Alors**, pour ou contre la télévision? Pour tenter de répondre à cette question, nous évoquerons **dans un premier temps** les effets négatifs de ce média. Nous nous attacherons **ensuite** à en décrire les aspects positifs.

introduction

Contrairement à bien d'autres activités, regarder la télévision est peu contraignant. Le téléspectateur n'a qu'à appuyer sur le bouton de mise en marche de son téléviseur et subir passivement les programmes qui lui sont proposés. **En bref**, il n'a aucun effort à faire. **Dans ces conditions**, il semble facile de se laisser aller à passer son temps libre à zapper du fond de son fauteuil. La télé est une présence dont on ne peut plus se passer et risque **alors** de devenir abrutissante.

On peut **aussi** reprocher à la télévision son manque d'originalité et son uniformité. La télévision est devenue un véritable enjeu commercial. La guerre des chaînes laisse **donc** peu de place à la créativité. Même le traitement de l'information se conforme aux objectifs commerciaux et perd de son objectivité. On a **ainsi** vu se développer, au cours des années, l'information-spectacle. Il faut tout montrer, avant les autres, au risque

development part 1

remember to use synonyms

link words

Model French essay
continued

d'être impudique ou de banaliser la violence.

La violence est **d'ailleurs** un autre problème important à la télévision. Qu'il s'agisse d'information ou de fiction, il est parfois difficile de mesurer l'effet de certaines images sur l'esprit des enfants ou des adolescents et de leur en faire comprendre les implications. Si la violence est présentée comme un jeu dans un dessin animé, un enfant a-t-il assez de discernement pour juger de ce qui est acceptable ou non dans la vie de tous les jours?

On ne peut nier les excès qu'entraîne la télévision. Peut-on en conclure **pour autant** qu'elle n'apporte rien de positif? Ce serait oublier qu'elle a **avant tout** été conçue comme une source de divertissement, rôle qu'elle remplit parfaitement bien. Elle est, **en outre**, une compagnie non négligeable pour les personnes seules. Elle permet de se relaxer facilement et de partager ces moments de détente en famille. **Car** on peut être devant son téléviseur sans que la communication au sein du foyer n'en souffre. Regarder une émission à plusieurs peut créer une certaine connivence entre les personnes qui la regardent. Suivre les programmes préférés de ses enfants avec eux permet de partager leur imaginaire, de leur expliquer des passages qu'ils ne comprennent pas, de leur faire découvrir de nouveaux centres d'intérêt.

La télévision est un divertissement mais elle se révèle aussi informative et éducative. **En fait**,

question used as a transition

development part 2

Model French essay
continued

on peut considérer le petit écran comme une fenêtre sur le monde. De par la diversité de ses programmes, elle peut donner envie de lire, de voir un film, de découvrir un pays. . . Bien exploité, ce média est un outil d'apprentissage très efficace et permet aux enseignants de diversifier leurs méthodes d'enseignement et de rendre leurs cours plus vivants.

Le petit écran fait **par ailleurs** partie de l'identité culturelle d'un pays. Les personnes d'une même génération ont regardé les mêmes émissions pour enfants, connaissent les mêmes programmes, les mêmes personnalités du spectacle et de la politique. Il paraît **donc** difficile de connaître parfaitement la culture d'un pays sans prendre cet aspect en compte.

En conclusion, il semble impossible de condamner la télévision d'un bloc ou d'en faire un éloge sans réserve. Au cours des années, la télévision s'est **en effet** avérée un média à facettes multiples, pouvant offrir le meilleur comme le pire. Elle fait désormais indéniablement partie du quotidien de chacun. C'est **donc** au téléspectateur qu'appartient la responsabilité de choisir les programmes qu'il regarde et de décider de l'importance qu'il accorde à son téléviseur.

conclusion

Model French essay translated

Television: for or against?

Since its creation, television has enjoyed a phenomenal success and is now found in the majority of homes. An indispensable item for some, others see it as a source of stupefaction and lowering of cultural standards. So, should we be for or against television? To try to answer this question, we shall first of all look at the negative effects of television, and we will then examine its positive aspects.

Watching television differs from many others activities in that it does not require you to do anything. All that is needed is to turn the television on and to absorb passively whatever programmes are being shown. In other words, no effort is required. In fact, it can be very easy to spend all one's free time switching channels from the comfort of the sofa. The television becomes a presence which one can no longer do without, and does, therefore, risk becoming stupefying.

It is also possible to criticise television for its lack of originality and its uniformity. Television has become a major commercial venture and the ratings war leaves little room for creativity. Even the way in which the news is treated is subject to commercial interests, and thus loses its objectivity. Because of this, the phenomenon of news events has developed over the years. Everything has to be shown before the other channels show it, even at the risk of being intrusive or of trivializing violence.

Violence is, in any case, another significant problem for television. Whether it is on the news or in a fictional story, it is sometimes difficult to assess the effect which certain images will have upon children or teenagers, or to get them to understand their implications. If violence is presented playfully in a cartoon, does a child have the ability to judge what is and what is not acceptable in everyday life?

The excesses of television cannot be denied. But, for all that, can we conclude that it has no positive aspects? It was, after all, created as a means of entertainment, a role which it fills perfectly well. What's more, it is a major source of company for people who live on their own. It helps you relax easily and it allows families to spend their leisure time together. For it is possible to watch television without conversation necessarily suffering. Watching a programme in a group can often create a sense of shared understanding among the viewers. Following one's children's favourite

Model French essay translated

continued

programmes allows one to share in the world of their imagination, to explain parts to them which they don't understand, and to help them discover new areas of interest.

Television is a form of entertainment but it can also be informative and educational. In fact, it is possible to see it as a window onto the world. The diversity of its programmes can make you want to read more about a subject, make you want to go and see a film or visit another country . . . If it is put to good use, the television is a very useful way of learning and it gives teachers more scope in their teaching methods, allowing them to make their classes much more stimulating.

What's more the small screen is a part of a country's cultural identity. People from the same generation all watched the same children's programmes, all know the same series, the same actors and the same politicians. It is difficult, therefore, really to understand the culture of a country perfectly without taking this aspect into account.

To conclude then, it would appear to be impossible to condemn television totally or to praise it unreservedly. Over the years, television has certainly shown that it has many sides, able to offer both good and bad. It has undeniably become part of daily life for everyone. It is, therefore, the viewer's own responsibility to choose which programmes he or she watches and to decide just how important television should be.

French correspondence

Business

How to address an envelope

How to lay out a letter

sender — Sandrine Pulvar
24 rue des Arts
75011 Paris

addressee — Madame Solicot
35 boulevard Voltaire
75011 Paris

date — Le 24 mars 1997

Recommandé avec A.R.

opening formula — Madame,

body of the letter —

J'ai l'honneur de vous informer que je souhaite résilier le bail à loyer signé le 4 avril 1993 pour l'appartement du 24 rue des Arts.

Je me tiens à votre disposition pour convenir d'une date de remise des clés et établir avec vous un état des lieux.

Je me permets de vous rappeler que vous disposez d'un délai maximal de trois mois après mon départ pour me restituer la somme de 3 100 francs que je vous ai versée à titre de dépôt de garantie.

closing formula — Veuillez agréer, Madame, l'assurance de mes sentiments distingués.

signature — S Pulvar

S. Pulvar

Announcing a wedding in the family

Monsieur et Madame Norbert LESOURD
Monsieur et Madame Raoul RIVIERE
Monsieur et Madame Paul AURIA

sont heureux de vous faire part du mariage
de leurs enfants et petits-enfants

BORIS et AUDE

qui sera célébré le samedi 13 septembre 1997 à 16 heures

en l'Église Notre-Dame-des-Mariniers
à Villeneuve-lès-Avignon

33, rue de la République
74000 Annecy

86, chemin du Pont de Pierre
84000 Avignon

Announcing the birth of a baby

Pierre et Marguerite partagent avec Adrien et Alice
la joie de vous annoncer la naissance de

Nathalie

Le 10 juillet 1997

Monsieur et Madame Bon
24, rue Basfroi
75011 PARIS

Visiting card

Christian et Lise Poirier

ont le regret de ne pouvoir assister au cocktail que vous organisez le 3 mai pour célébrer les 25 ans de la société Jacquet et vous félicitent pour ces nombreuses années de succès.

35 avenue des Platanes
94100 St Maur
01 43 54 63 87

Invitation to a wedding

Gérard et Jacqueline Achard
12, rue Champollion
10009 Troyes

Troyes, le 5 avril 1997

Cher ami,

J'ai le plaisir de vous annoncer que nous marions notre fille Hélène le 12 juin à Paris. Vous recevrez bientôt un faire-part et une invitation pour le lunch qui suivra, mais je tenais à vous avertir dès maintenant pour que vous puissiez retenir votre journée du samedi. Le mariage aura lieu à la mairie du 6e à 14 heures et la messe sera célébrée en l'église Saint-Germain-des-Prés à 15 h 30.

Amicalement,

Jacqueline

Congratulations on a wedding

Martigues, le 18 août 1997

Chers amis,

Nous nous réjouissons pour vous du mariage de votre fille et nous vous en félicitons de tout coeur. Paul sera certainement un excellent gendre pour vous et un beau-frère apprécié par vos enfants.

Nous vous chargeons de transmettre aux futurs époux nos meilleurs voeux de bonheur et serons enchantés de venir les embrasser le jour J.

Très amicalement,

Isobelle

Good wishes for the New Year

Éliane Debard
25, rue des Alouettes
38180 Seyssin

le 4 janvier 1997

Je vous présente mes meilleurs vœux de bonheur et de réussite pour la nouvelle année. Que 1997 vous apporte tout ce que vous souhaitez, à vous, à votre famille et à tous ceux qui vous sont chers.

Éliane Debard

Thanks for New Year wishes

Fanny Cogne
7, avenue Calade
10099 Troyes

le 6 janvier 1997

Je vous remercie de vos vœux. À notre tour, ma famille et moi vous adressons les nôtres les plus sincères.

Fanny Cogne

Condolences: formal

Jean et Eliane Pinchon
117, boulevard Lamartine
71000 Mâcon

Mâcon, le 27 novembre 1997

Monsieur,

Nous vous adressons nos condoléances les plus sincères à l'occasion de la disparition tragique de votre épouse. Sachez qu'elle restera dans notre souvenir comme une personne exceptionnelle, et que nous partageons votre peine.

Recevez, Monsieur, l'expression de notre douloureuse sympathie.

E. Pinchon

Condolences: informal

Belley, le 22 avril 1997

Chère Janine,

J'ai appris par Francette la triste nouvelle du décès de Paul.

Je te présente mes condoléances les plus sincères, et t'assure que je pense beaucoup à toi en ces moments difficiles.

Crois bien, ma chère Janine, à l'expression de ma profonde sympathie.

Richard

Thanks for condolences: formal

Bordeaux, le 25 juin 1997

Madame,

Nous avons été très touchés de la sympathie que vous nous avez témoignée lors du décès de notre mère et nous vous en remercions sincèrement. Elle nous parlait souvent de vous et avait beaucoup d'estime pour vous.

Ces moments sont difficiles à traverser et les signes d'amitié sont toujours les bienvenus. Aussi nous vous prions de croire, Madame, en nos sentiments reconnaissants.

Raoul et Suzanne Dupin

Thanks for condolences: informal

Metz, le 18 février 1997

Très chers Paul et Lucie,

C'est vraiment gentil de nous avoir écrit ce petit mot si touchant. Nous savons très bien qu'il vous était impossible d'être avec nous le jour de l'enterrement de Jacques, mais nous vous savions proches de nous par la pensée.

Il va maintenant falloir reprendre le cours de la vie et c'est avec une amitié aussi fidèle que la vôtre que nous garderons courage.

Encore un grand merci du fond du cœur et à bientôt.

Nicole

Invitation to a visit

Versailles, le 26 avril 1997

Cher Charles,

A l'occasion du pont de l'Ascension, Henri et moi invitons quelques amis dans notre maison de campagne à côté de Blois. Nous serions heureux si vous pouviez être des nôtres.

Nous attendrons tous nos invités jeudi pour le déjeuner. N'oubliez pas votre équipement de golf: nous ferons un parcours si le temps le permet.

Nous vous embrassons.

Ghislaine

Invitation to a party

Paris, le 23 juin 1997

Cher Raymond,

Nous avons eu l'idée de réunir tous les copains de fac dans notre maison de Manosque le samedi 5 juillet pour arroser la thèse de Pierre. Même Albert a promis d'être là! Ce sera à la bonne franquette.

Rendez-vous aux environs de 21 heures. A bientôt.

Amicalement

Marie

Accepting an invitation: formal

Troyes, le 17 avril 1997

Chers amis,

Je vous remercie de votre aimable invitation au mariage de votre fille le samedi 14 juin, que j'accepte avec joie. J'arriverai par le train de vendredi soir, puisqu'il n'y a plus de train le samedi.

Dans l'attente du plaisir de vous revoir, je vous adresse mes meilleures salutations.

Thomas Lemaître

Accepting an invitation: informal

Valence, le 29 juin 1997

Chers Marie et Pierre,

Super, l'idée de l'arrosage de thèse! J'accepte, bien sûr, mais j'ai un dernier rendez-vous à 20 h 15 ce jour-là, et je ne pourrai donc pas arriver avant 22 h, le temps de passer chez moi pour quitter ma blouse blanche.

En attendant, bravo à Pierre, et grosses bises.

Raymond

Invitation to a holiday together

Rueil-Malmaison, le 18 mai 1997

Chers Laurence et Alexandre,

Merci beaucoup pour votre carte de Suède. Nous avons pensé que nous pourrions profiter de votre passage en France pour faire ce tour de la Corse dont nous parlons depuis si longtemps. Nous aimerions partir le lundi 23 juin, et rester jusqu'au 17 juillet. Qu'en pensez-vous?

Dans l'attente d'une réponse de votre part, croyez, chers amis, à nos sentiments les meilleurs.

Lucien

Jacqueline

Declining an invitation

Londres, le 1er mai 1997

Ma chère Ghislaine

Votre lettre m'a fait grand plaisir, et je tiens à vous remercier d'avoir pensé à moi. Mais je dois hélas refuser votre aimable invitation: je m'étais précédemment engagé à prendre part le même jour à la célébration des noces d'or de tante Agnès et oncle Michel à Nice.

J'espère que nous aurons très bientôt l'occasion de nous revoir. Amicalement.

Marc

Thanking for hospitality

Strasbourg, le 21 juin 1997

Chère madame, cher monsieur,

Je tiens à vous remercier de m'avoir invitée aux fiançailles d'Isolde, et je vous suis particulièrement reconnaissante de m'avoir offert de passer la nuit chez vous.

La fête a été très agréable et j'ai eu grand plaisir à vous revoir dans de si heureuses circonstances.

Encore merci pour tout. Bien à vous.

Anne

Thanking for a wedding gift

Brest, le 17 août 1997

Chère Anne,

Je tenais à te remercier une fois encore pour le magnifique cadre en argent que tu nous as offert en cadeau de mariage. Nous l'avons déjà utilisé... pour exposer une photo du mariage!

Grosses bises

Isolde

Arranging an exchange visit

Dublin, le 2 avril 1997

Una et Dan Farrelly
28, Leeson Drive
Artane
Dublin 5
Irlande

Monsieur et Madame Pierre Beaufort
Chalet "Les Edelweiss"
Chemin des Rousses
74400 Chamonix

Chers Danièle et Pierre,

Nous serions très heureux d'accueillir votre fils chez nous entre le 10 et le 31 juillet et en échange d'envoyer notre fils Kilian chez vous pendant le mois d'août.

Kilian a 16 ans. Il fait du français depuis 4 ans. C'est un garçon sportif: il aime la randonnée, la natation et le tennis.

Merci de nous dire assez rapidement si cette idée vous convient afin que nous puissions réserver les places d'avion le plus tôt possible.

Croyez en nos sentiments les meilleurs.

U. Farrelly

U. Farrelly

Making travel plans

Monsieur et Madame Bernard Dubois
Villa les Etourneaux
132 bis, Passage du Réservoir
69140 Rillieux-la-Pape

Rillieux-la-Pape, le 15 mai 1997

Monsieur, Madame,

Nous avons bien reçu votre lettre nous confirmant que vous pourriez aller chercher notre fille Lucy le 12 juillet au soir à l'aéroport. Elle s'en réjouit car elle était un peu inquiète à l'idée de prendre le bus toute seule jusqu'à la gare. Nous vous communiquerons, dès que nous l'aurons, le numéro de son vol et l'heure exacte de son arrivée.

Lucy est facilement reconnaissable: elle mesure 1 m 65 et elle a les cheveux roux. Nous nous permettrons de vous appeler le soir même afin de nous assurer qu'elle est bien arrivée.

Nous vous remercions de l'accueil que vous lui réserverez et vous prions de croire, Monsieur, Madame, en nos sentiments les meilleurs.

J. Smith

J. Smith

Thanking the host family

Nantucket, le 17 septembre 1997

Chers Monsieur et Madame Robin,

Je voudrais vous remercier pour les vacances merveilleuses que j'ai passées dans votre propriété de Saint-Malo. Je n'oublierai jamais les repas où il y avait tant de bonnes choses, le bridge et les parties de pêche avec René. J'ai tant de bons souvenirs que je n'arrête pas de parler de la France à tous mes amis. J'espère que j'aurai très bientôt l'occasion de vous revoir tous.

Je vous embrasse affectueusement.

Doug

Enquiry to the tourist office

M. et Mme François Bolard
10, rue Eugène Delacroix
06200 Nice

Syndicat d'Initiative
de St-Gervais
74170 Saint-Gervais-les-Bains

Nice, le 24 mars 1997

Monsieur,

Mon mari et moi envisageons de passer nos vacances d'été à Saint-Gervais. Nous vous serions reconnaissants de bien vouloir nous faire parvenir toute la documentation dont vous disposez sur les hôtels, la station thermale ainsi que sur les activités proposées aux touristes en saison. Vous trouverez ci-joint une enveloppe timbrée pour la réponse.

Dans l'attente de vous lire, je vous prie d'agréer, Monsieur, l'expression de mes sentiments distingués.

Bolard

E. Bolard

Offering house exchange

Pierre Clément
Résidence des Lacs d'Auvergne
Chalet n° 18
63610 Besse

Madame Perrin
2 rue de la Poste
14360 Trouville-sur-Mer

Clermont, le 2 mai 1997

Chère Madame,

Vos amis, monsieur et madame Blanchet, nous ont dit que vous seriez heureuse de pouvoir échanger votre villa en Normandie contre notre chalet qui est au bord du lac des Corbeaux, en Auvergne. Nous serions intéressés par cette idée pour la seconde quinzaine d'août.

Si cette période vous convient, nous vous adresserons une photo et un descriptif détaillé du chalet.

Dans l'attente de vous lire, je vous adresse, Chère Madame, mes sentiments les meilleurs.

P. Clément

Responding to an offer of house exchange

L. Dury
Chalet des Pentes
38860 les Deux-Alpes

Madame J. Lemaire
Route de Châteauroux
36200 Argenton-sur-Creuse

le 1er mai 1997

Madame,

J'ai bien reçu votre offre d'échanger votre ferme à la campagne et notre chalet entre le 1er et le 30 juin prochains. Nous sommes désolés, mais les dates que vous proposez ne correspondent pas à celles où nous envisageons de prendre nos vacances. Peut-être l'année prochaine cela sera-t-il possible? Nous reprendrons contact avec vous en temps voulu.

Je vous souhaite bonne chance et vous adresse, Madame, mes salutations distinguées.

L. Dury

Booking a hotel room

Madame Solange Vernon
125 bis, Route Nationale
18340 Levet

Maison de Famille Le Repos
Chemin des Lys
06100 Grasse

le 22 mars 1997

Monsieur le Directeur,

J'ai bien reçu le dépliant de votre maison, ainsi que les tarifs que je vous avais demandés, et je vous en remercie.

Je souhaite réserver une chambre calme avec bains et wc, en pension complète pour la période du 27 avril au 12 mai. Je vous adresse ci-joint un chèque de 600 francs d'arrhes.

Je vous en souhaite bonne réception, et vous remerciant par avance, je vous prie de croire, Monsieur le Directeur, en mes sentiments les meilleurs.

S. Vernon

P.J.: un chèque postal de 600 francs

Booking a gîte

Claire Fauvel
36 avenue du Général de Gaulle
78400 Chatou
01 34 42 78 76

Madame Poterre
Route du Champ blanc
56630 Vernon

Le 4 février 1997

Madame,

J'ai eu votre adresse par l'intermédiaire du syndicat d'initiative de Vannes qui m'a envoyé une liste des gîtes de la région.

Mon mari et moi recherchons, pour les vacances de Pâques, une maison calme et avec un grand jardin. Nous avons trois enfants et nous souhaiterions prendre nos vacances du 5 au 12 avril. Auriez-vous l'amabilité de me faire savoir si votre gîte est disponible à ces dates? Pourriez-vous également me confirmer le tarif annoncé par le syndicat d'initiative, à savoir 1 800 francs la semaine?

Je vous remercie d'avance et vous prie d'agréer, Madame, mes salutations distinguées.

C. Fauvel

Enquiry to camp site

E. Aubin
3, bd du Maréchal Joffre
94260 Fresnes

Camping des Vagues
Bd de la Plage
44250 Saint-Brévin-les-Pins

Fresnes, le 3 avril 1997

Monsieur,

Nous avons eu votre adresse par le Syndicat d'Initiative de Saint-Brévin, et nous aimerions avoir quelques renseignements complémentaires sur votre camping.

Pourriez-vous nous préciser si les emplacements sont ombragés, si les animaux sont admis et s'il y a des commerces à proximité? Nous aimerions également connaître vos tarifs, ainsi que les délais pour réserver.

Vous remerciant par avance, je vous prie de croire, Monsieur, en mes sentiments distingués.

E. Aubin

Booking a caravan site

Monsieur C. Bonnet
235, Bd Lénine
95200 Sarcelles

Camping-Caravaning
"LES EMBRUNS"
18, allée des Capucins
22116 Moëlan-sur-Mer

Sarcelles, le 14 juin 1997

Madame,

Nous souhaitons à nouveau réserver, cette année en août, l'emplacement de caravane que nous avions loué en juillet dernier et qui se trouvait dans la partie nord du camping (numéro 12/B/224).

Acceptez-vous les animaux cette année? Nous avons un tout petit chien que nous ne pouvons laisser chez nous.

Dès que nous aurons confirmation de votre part, nous vous adresserons le montant de la réservation, que vous voudrez bien nous indiquer.

Veuillez croire, Madame, en l'expression de nos sentiments distingués.

Renting a holiday house

Monsieur C. Pernaudet
135, rue de la Gaîté-Montparnasse
75014 Paris

Agence "LES DUNES"
Promenade de l'Océan
33120 Arcachon

Paris, le 7 mai 1997

Messieurs,

Nous sommes à la recherche d'une location pour le mois d'août prochain dans votre région. Nous souhaitons trouver une maison pour 6/8 personnes avec un terrain clos et ombragé, même éloigné de la plage.

Pourriez-vous nous adresser le descriptif détaillé, avec si possible une photo et les tarifs de location, de ce que vous avez à nous proposer?

Dans l'attente de votre réponse, je vous prie d'agréer, Messieurs, l'expression de mes sentiments distingués.

Letting your house

Monsieur et Madame Léon Panisse
Résidence Le Bord de Mer
Rue des Pins
83230 Bormes-les-Mimosas

Monsieur Brun
8, place Colbert
69001 Lyon

Bormes, le 4 avril 1997

Cher Monsieur,

La maison que nous mettons en location est une villa de plain-pied, avec terrasse face à la mer et accès direct à la plage. Elle est située sur un terrain clos et boisé.

Elle se compose de deux chambres (couchage pour 6 personnes en tout), un salon-salle à manger, une kitchenette équipée, une salle de bains avec douche et un WC indépendant. Le montant de la location pour juillet est de F11 000 charges non comprises.

Souhaitant que cette offre vous convienne, je vous prie d'agréer, Cher Monsieur, l'expression de mes sentiments distingués.

L. Panisse

Postcards

Chers amis,

Juste un petit bonjour de Palma où nous passons de très agréables vacances. Il fait un temps splendide et les plages sont superbes. Merci encore d'avoir accepté de garder Félix pendant notre absence. Nous vous revaudrons cela à l'occasion.

A très bientôt!

Emmanuel et Pierline

Monsieur et Madame Pierret

78 rue du Chemin vert

54000 Nancy

FRANCE

Soleil, pistes enneigées et soirées raclette au coin du feu: on ne pouvait rêver mieux.

Notre séjour s'annonce très bien et nous espérons en profiter au maximum.

Bons baisers de Courchevel et à bientôt.

Frédéric et Josiane

Monsieur et Madame Gendre

56 rue Jean Jaurès

75018 Paris

Asking for a theatre programme listing

M. Jean Leduc
12, boulevard de la République
77300 Fontainebleau

Opéra Bastille
Service Réservations
120, rue de Lyon
75012 Paris

le 22 juin 1997

Monsieur,

Je vous serais reconnaissant de bien vouloir me faire parvenir le programme complet des représentations prévues pour la saison 1997-98, ainsi que toutes les précisions concernant les dates, les tarifs, les abonnements et les jours et heures d'ouverture de vos guichets.

Dans l'attente de vous lire, recevez, Monsieur, l'assurance de mes sentiments distingués.

Jean Leduc

J. Leduc

Cancelling a hotel booking

Frédéric Brunet
5, rue du Marché
73700 Bourg-Saint-Maurice

Hôtel des Voyageurs
9, cours Gambetta
91949 Les Ulis CEDEX

Bourg, le 15 décembre 1997

Monsieur,

Je suis au regret de devoir annuler ma réservation d'une chambre pour deux personnes pour la nuit du 24 au 25 décembre, que j'avais effectuée par téléphone le 18 novembre dernier, à mon nom.

Je vous remercie de votre compréhension et vous prie d'agréer, Monsieur, l'expression de mes sentiments distingués.

F. Brunet

Ordering theatre tickets

Monsieur J. Greiner
12, rue des Arènes
13200 Arles

Théâtre de Poche
Place du Théâtre
84100 Orange

le 24 mai 1997

Messieurs,

Suite à mon appel téléphonique de ce jour, je vous adresse un chèque de 1250 francs à l'ordre du Théâtre de Poche pour la réservation en matinée du 7 juin prochain de cinq corbeilles.

Comme convenu, je retirerai ces places le jour même, une demi-heure avant le début du spectacle.

Veuillez agréer, Messieurs, l'expression de mes sentiments distingués.

J. Greiner

P.J.: un chèque bancaire de 1250 francs

Writing to a lawyer about house purchase

Christiane Picard
Tour B, Immeuble Les Anémones
Boulevard Leclerc
95200 Sarcelles

Maître Nicaud
Notaire
22, Place de l'Eglise
13150 Tarascon

Paris, le 1er décembre 1997

Cher Maître,

Je serais intéressée par une petite propriété dans la région d'Avignon. J'ai besoin d'un bâtiment d'habitation de 6 pièces au moins, et d'un terrain attenant arboré de 5000 m² environ. Je vous serais reconnaissante si vous acceptiez de vous charger de me trouver quelque chose.

Dans l'attente de votre réponse, veuillez agréer, Cher Maître, l'expression de ma considération distinguée.

Picard C.

Writing to a future neighbour

Albert Mercier
Le Clos
22, rue du Foyer
25110 Baume-les-Dames

Madame Laurent
29, impasse des Chrysanthèmes
25000 Besançon

le 26 février 1997

Madame,

Vous avez appris que la famille Binet avait dû mettre en vente sa maison pour cause de mutation. J'en suis le nouveau propriétaire et je compte m'y installer dès que les travaux de remise en état seront terminés, c'est-à-dire au printemps prochain.

J'espère que ces travaux ne vous dérangeront pas trop, et que j'aurai le plaisir de faire votre connaissance lors de mon installation. Je crois deviner, à la vue de votre superbe jardin, que nous partageons le même goût du jardinage!

Dans l'attente de vous rencontrer, je vous adresse, Madame, mes salutations distinguées.

A. Mercier

A. Mercier

To a neighbour

Joseph Bocquet
27, rue de Verdun
25000 Besançon

M. André Delacroix
29, rue de Verdun
25000 Besançon

le 6 janvier 1997

Monsieur,

J'ai eu la grande surprise de constater au cours de mon récent séjour dans ma villa de Besançon que vous aviez fait planter deux saules pleureurs le long du mur mitoyen qui sépare nos deux propriétés. Ces arbres n'étant pas à la distance réglementaire, et dans le souci de préserver nos bonnes relations de voisinage, je vous demande de bien vouloir les faire déplacer, et vous en remercie par avance.

Recevez mes meilleurs sentiments.

J. Bocquet

J. Bocquet

Giving written notice to a landlord

Sandrine Pulvar
24 rue des Arts
75011 Paris

Madame Solicot
35 boulevard Voltaire
75011 Paris

Le 24 mars 1997

Recommandé avec A.R.

Madame,

J'ai l'honneur de vous informer que je souhaite résilier le bail à loyer signé le 4 avril 1993 pour l'appartement du 24 rue des Arts.

Je me tiens à votre disposition pour convenir d'une date de remise des clés et établir avec vous un état des lieux.

Je me permets de vous rappeler que vous disposez d'un délai maximal de trois mois après mon départ pour me restituer la somme de 3 100 francs que je vous ai versée à titre de dépôt de garantie.

Veuillez agréer, Madame, l'assurance de mes sentiments distingués.

S. Pulvar

S. Pulvar

Acknowledgement of a debt

Je, soussignée, Aline Debard, domiciliée au 39 rue des Amandiers à Nanterre, reconnais devoir à Jean-Claude Lebrun, domicilié au 45 place Verdun à Saint-Cloud, la somme de 6 000 francs qu'il a bien voulu me prêter. Je m'engage à lui rembourser cette somme dans un délai de douze mois avec un intérêt de 10 %.

Bon pour la somme de six mille francs.

Fait à Saint-Cloud le 5 avril 1997.

To a bank: disputing bank charges

Jean-François Devert
3 rue des Lilas
92100 Boulogne

Monsieur Girard
Directeur d'agence
Banque MASSON
1 place Glacière
92100 Boulogne
Le 19 mars 1997

Monsieur,

Je reçois aujourd'hui même mon relevé bancaire et je constate avec étonnement que quatre jours d'agios ont été retenus sur mon compte.

Mon compte a effectivement été à découvert du 10 au 14 mars, mais à la suite d'une erreur de la part de vos services. Le 3 mars, j'ai en effet déposé un chèque de 3 500 francs qui a été égaré. Dès que je me suis aperçu que mon compte n'avait pas été crédité du montant du chèque, je l'ai signalé à l'un de vos employés, qui m'a assuré qu'il ne serait pas tenu compte de mon découvert.

Je trouve absolument anormal d'être pénalisé pour une erreur indépendante de ma volonté et me verrais dans l'obligation de clore définitivement mon compte courant et mon compte épargne si vous ne faites pas le nécessaire pour régler la situation au plus vite.

Veuillez agréer, Monsieur, l'expression de mes sentiments distingués.

J-F Devert

J-F. Devert

To an insurance company about a claim

Monsieur Ramirez
86, rue de la Convention
75015 Paris

ASSURTOURIX
123, Rue Duranton
75449 Paris CEDEX 15

Paris, le 24 mars 1997

Lettre recommandée
Police n° 3400510F

Messieurs,

Par la police référencée ci-dessus en date du 24 janvier 1987, j'ai fait assurer mon appartement situé rue de la Convention.

A la suite des très fortes bourrasques de la nuit dernière, les stores de la terrasse nord, ainsi que les volets, ont été arrachés et ont gravement endommagé le balcon voisin. Puis-je vous demander de m'envoyer un de vos experts le plus tôt possible, afin de constater l'étendue du sinistre et de chiffrer le montant des dommages subis?

Avec mes remerciements, je vous prie de croire, Messieurs, à l'assurance de mes sentiments distingués.

A. Ramirez

To the telephone company

Mlle Elkabouri
27, rue Pierre et Marie Curie
88100 Epinal

Agence Commerciale
France Télécom
88001 Epinal

le 1er mai 1997

Objet: demande de raccordement au réseau

Monsieur,

Je désire faire installer le téléphone dans mon nouveau domicile, 27, rue Pierre et Marie Curie. L'appartement n'est actuellement pas équipé de prise de raccordement au réseau téléphonique. J'aimerais que soient installés deux postes. Je voudrais également pouvoir disposer d'un minitel.

Je vous serais reconnaissante de bien vouloir faire le nécessaire.

Veuillez agréer, Monsieur, l'assurance de mes salutations distinguées.

F. Elkabouri

F. Elkabouri

To a newspaper: asking for support

JEAN-MICHEL JOLIVET
3 BIS, CHEMIN DES ACACIAS
13260 CASSIS

Marseille, le 18 juin 1997

LA RAFALE
Le Quotidien des Bouches-du-Rhône
12, route des Calanques
13004 MARSEILLE

Messieurs,

En tant que Vice-Président du Club de Pêche des Bouches-du-Rhône, et comme chaque année, je viens solliciter votre collaboration pour l'organisation de notre kermesse d'été.

Vous avez en effet pour habitude de faire connaître, gracieusement, et par voie de presse, les dates de cette kermesse qui se déroulera cette année les 13 et 14 juillet sur le Vieux Port. Je compte sur vous pour prendre en charge, comme l'an dernier, le montage du podium ainsi que l'animation de notre tombola.

Pourriez-vous me donner une réponse rapide? Je vous remercie par avance de cette aide que vous nous apportez à tous.

Je vous prie de croire, Messieurs, en mes sentiments reconnaissants.

J Jolivet

To a television channel: approving

Madame ROSIERE
156, boulevard des Maréchaux
75013 PARIS

Paris, le 12 novembre 1997

Emission l'Echo du Passé
France 2
35, rue Cardinet
75017 PARIS

Messieurs,

Je tiens à vous féliciter chaleureusement pour votre dernière émission de l'Echo du Passé de dimanche dernier.

Si vous avez été violemment critiqués pour votre présentation de courts-métrages d'époque, je tiens à vous faire part de ma totale adhésion à votre point de vue. Il est en effet indispensable, afin de se forger une opinion personnelle objective, de pouvoir se référer à des documents authentiques même s'ils ne sont pas d'une qualité irréprochable.

Je vous encourage donc à continuer dans cette voie et vous assurant de mon soutien, je vous prie de croire en toute ma considération.

S. Rosière

To a teacher about sick child's absence

Mours-Saint-Eusèbe, le 23 mars 1997

Madame,

Je vous demande de bien vouloir excuser l'absence de mon fils Julien DUPONT, élève de cinquième B, les 19, 20, 21 et 22 mars dernier. Julien a dû rester alité en raison d'une double otite. Je vous adresse ci-joint un certificat médical.

Veuillez agréer, Madame, l'expression de mes sentiments distingués.

A. Dupont

To a school about admission

Madame H. Vannier
Lieu-dit Les Chênes Verts
1123, Route de Montluçon
18270 Culan

Monsieur le Directeur
Ecole Privée Mixte
Rue de la Gare
18200 Saint-Amand-Montrond

le 3 mars 1997

Monsieur,

A la rentrée scolaire prochaine, notre fils Robert fera son entrée en 6ème. Nous habitons une ferme isolée, et nous envisageons de le mettre en pension.

Avant de solliciter un rendez-vous avec vous, nous souhaiterions connaître les conditions d'admission dans votre école, ainsi que le règlement de l'internat et le montant des frais de pension et de scolarité.

Par avance, je vous remercie de votre réponse et vous prie de croire, Monsieur, en mes salutations distinguées.

H. Vannier

To a university about admission

Stephen Evans
3136 P Street NW
Washington, DC, 20007
USA

Washington, le 8 avril 1997

M. le Président
de l'Université Lumière
86, rue Pasteur
69365 Lyon Cedex 07

Objet : demande de renseignements

Monsieur le Président,

Je suis étudiant en latin à l'Université de Columbia où je suis en train de terminer ma Maîtrise (MA). Je vous serais reconnaissant de me faire savoir s'il est possible de m'inscrire dans votre université pour y faire un Doctorat, et de me dire quelles sont les démarches à effectuer.

Veuillez agréer, Monsieur le Président, l'expression de mes respectueuses salutations.

S. Evans

Enquiring about prices

le 18 février 1997

Association des Parents d'élèves
Groupe scolaire de la Ville basse
3, rue George Sand
87100 LIMOGES
Tél.: 05 55 22 78 04

RECREATOUR
25 avenue du Château
41000 BLOIS

Monsieur,

Nous souhaiterions organiser durant trois jours – au moment du week-end du 1er mai – une visite de la région bordelaise pour les enfants de notre établissement et leur parents.

Nous aurions besoin d'une documentation complète, et souhaiterions connaître les tarifs :

- pour le voyage en car seulement,
- pour le voyage et l'hébergement,
- pour le voyage, l'hébergement et les repas en demi-pension.

Vous remerciant par avance de votre réponse, nous vous prions de croire, Monsieur, en nos sentiments distingués.

Madame Petit
Présidente de l'Association

Enquiry to the tennis club

le 15 juin 1997

Madame P. Martinez
23, clos des Martyrs
13006 Marseille

CLUB DE TENNIS
DES GARRIGUES
Chemin des Bruyères
13260 Cassis

Messieurs,

Future habitante de Cassis, je souhaiterais connaître les conditions d'inscription à votre club, et savoir si vous proposez des cours particuliers ou des stages. Pratiquez-vous des tarifs familiaux? En effet, mon mari et mon fils aîné, joueurs classés, souhaitent un entraînement intensif alors que mes deux plus jeunes enfants souhaiteraient débuter.

Par avance, je vous remercie des informations que vous voudrez bien me fournir et vous prie de croire, Messieurs, en mes sentiments les meilleurs.

P. Martinez

To the builders: asking for an estimate

le 17 mars 1997

Monsieur et Madame Yves Laplace
Villa Mon Rêve
56, rue du Bois
59600 Maubeuge
tél.: 03 27 09 66 46

Monsieur Berthin
Entreprise Mahieux et Cie
Zone Industrielle
Bloc Q7 T23
59600 Maubeuge

Monsieur,

Nous souhaiterions faire construire à l'adresse ci-dessus une piscine chauffée et éclairée qui puisse être utilisable dès l'été prochain. Pourrions-nous convenir d'un rendez-vous ici, afin que vous puissiez vous rendre compte sur place des caractéristiques de notre propriété?

Nous vous demanderons d'apporter une documentation variée afin que nous puissions faire notre choix. Nous souhaiterions avoir un devis précis au moment des vacances de Pâques.

Nous vous adressons, Monsieur, nos salutations distinguées.

Y. Laplace

To the builders: asking for work to be undertaken

Club des Sportifs
12, allée de la Plage
14800 Deauville
Tél.: 02 35 03 12 76

Deauville, le 15 mai 1997

ENTREPRISE Roux
Route de Normandie
14001 Caen cedex

Monsieur,

Nous avons le plaisir de vous faire savoir que le devis que vous nous avez adressé pour la construction d'un tennis "Clairdal" nous convient parfaitement.

Nous souhaitons que les travaux commencent le plus tôt possible afin que tout soit terminé, y compris l'aménagement floral, pour le 18 juin prochain, les tournois commençant la semaine suivante.

Nous vous prions de croire, Monsieur, en nos sentiments les meilleurs.

Monsieur Lecarré
Gérant

To the builders: complaining about delay

le 15 juin 1997

Monsieur Guy Moreau
12, rue Henri Gorjus
69004 Lyon

Entreprise Simon Associés
69006 Lyon

Lettre avec AR

Messieurs,

Lors de notre dernier rendez-vous de chantier, je vous avais dit mon inquiétude quant au retard qu'avaient pris les travaux que nous vous avons confiés. Vous m'aviez alors assuré que tout serait terminé pour le 1er juillet.

Il est évident aujourd'hui qu'il me sera impossible d'emménager à cette date, les travaux de plomberie n'ayant même pas commencé. Je vous rappelle que j'ai promis de libérer mon logement actuel pour le 30 juin et que les frais causés par un retard de votre part seront à votre charge.

Je vous prie d'agréer, Monsieur, l'expression de mes sentiments distingués.

G. Moreau

To the builders: complaining about quality of work

Mouthe, le 7 novembre 1997

M. Brunaud
25240 Mouthe
téléphone : 03 81 82 13 27

M. Pinet
Entreprise de bâtiment
Grand rue
25970 Epeugney

Monsieur,

Je vous ai fait poser des doubles vitrages en PVC dans ma résidence de Mouthe le mois dernier. Je suis au regret de vous dire que toutes les fenêtres de l'étage présentent le même défaut d'étanchéité, qui entraîne la présence de condensation entre les deux vitres. Ces travaux étant sous garantie, je vous demanderais de faire le nécessaire dans les plus brefs délais afin qu'une solution soit apportée avant l'hiver.

Veuillez agréer, Monsieur, l'expression de mes salutations distinguées.

M. Brunaud

Looking for a placement in a computer company

Laurent PIGNON
14 bis, impasse des Aqueducs
69005 LYON
tél. : 04 78 47 98 54

Lyon, le 12 décembre 1997

Société Giudici
Z.I. des Pâquerettes
69575 DARDILLY CEDEX

à l'attention de Monsieur le Chef du Personnel

Monsieur,

Actuellement étudiant à l'Ecole d'Informatique Générale de Lyon, je dois effectuer un stage d'une durée de quatre mois dans une entreprise d'informatique afin de mettre en pratique l'enseignement qui m'est dispensé.

Connaissant bien la réputation de votre entreprise dans la région, je souhaiterais vivement pouvoir faire ce stage d'informaticien chez vous. Je me tiens à votre entière disposition si vous désirez me rencontrer.

Vous remerciant par avance de l'attention que vous voudrez bien porter à ma candidature, je vous prie, Monsieur, d'agréer l'expression de mes sentiments respectueux.

L. Pignon

p.j.: un curriculum vitae

Looking for a job

Mme Lise Martin
26, boulevard Jean Jaurès
78000 Versailles
tél.: 01 43 20 80 20

Versailles, le 7 novembre 1997

Société Design et Déco
17, rue Henri Barbusse
75014 Paris

Monsieur,

Titulaire d'un diplôme de décoratrice d'intérieur et ayant une solide expérience dans la profession, ainsi que vous pourrez le constater à la lecture du curriculum ci-joint, je vous écris pour vous proposer mes services. Ayant élevé mes deux enfants, je cherche un emploi à plein temps, mais saurai me contenter d'un mi-temps si nécessaire.

Dans l'attente de vous lire, je vous prie d'agréer, Monsieur, l'expression de mes sentiments les meilleurs.

L. Martin

P.J.: un curriculum avec photographie
un dossier de mes réalisations antérieures

Enquiring about jobs

Valérie Giraud
Les Flots
Route de Deauville
14360 Trouville-sur-Mer

Trouville, le 27 octobre 1997

A Monsieur le Directeur
Editions La Pensée Française
Paris

Monsieur,

Après un diplôme de sciences politiques (IEP Paris), j'ai entamé il y a quelques années une carrière de journaliste que je me vois contrainte d'abandonner pour des raisons familiales. J'aimerais dorénavant utiliser mes dons et mes compétences dans le domaine de l'édition ou de la traduction. Je parle trois des principales langues européennes, ainsi que l'indique le C.V. ci-joint, et je pense avoir de bonnes dispositions pour l'écriture.

Je suis prête à me rendre à un entretien si vous le jugez utile.

Recevez, Monsieur, l'expression de mes salutations distinguées.

V. Giraud

P.J. : un curriculum vitae

Replying to a job ad

JEAN-LUC MORIN
12, AVENUE D'ANGLETERRE
62107 CALAIS

Calais, le 14 février 1997

A Monsieur le Directeur
Arts et Design Gadgeteria
27, rue Victor Hugo
59001 Lille

Monsieur,

L'annonce parue en page 2 de l'édition du 12 février du Courrier Picard concernant un poste de concepteur m'a vivement intéressé. Mon contrat à durée déterminée chez Solo and Co. touche à sa fin. Je pense posséder l'expérience et les qualifications requises pour vous donner toute satisfaction dans ce poste, comme vous pourrez le constater au vu de mon CV. Je me tiens à votre disposition pour un entretien éventuel, et vous prie d'agréer, Monsieur, l'expression de mes sentiments distingués.

J.L. Morin

P.J.: un CV avec photo

Applying for a job as an au pair

Sally Kendall
5, Tackley Place
Reading RG2 6RN
England

Reading, le 17 avril 1997

Madame et Monsieur,

Vos coordonnées m'ont été communiquées par l'agence "Au Pair International", qui m'a demandé de vous écrire directement. Je suis en effet intéressée par un emploi de jeune fille au pair pour une période de six mois au moins, à partir de l'automne prochain.

J'adore les enfants, quel que soit leur âge, et j'ai une grande expérience du baby-sitting, comme vous pourrez le constater au vu du CV ci-joint.

Dans l'espoir d'une réponse favorable, je vous prie d'agréer, Madame et Monsieur, l'expression de mes respectueuses salutations.

S. Kendall

P.J.: un CV

Offering a job as an au pair

Madame E. Dulac
122, rue de la Mignonne
69009 Lyon
téléphone: 04 78 22 97 64

le 26 mai 1997

Madame,

J'ai appris par le Centre Social que votre fille de 17 ans était à la recherche d'un emploi qui lui permettrait de s'occuper de jeunes enfants. Or je cherche une jeune fille sérieuse qui puisse prendre en charge mes jumelles de cinq ans pendant le mois de juillet lorsque je serai au bureau, et qui puisse faire quelques petits travaux ménagers. Elle serait nourrie, logée, blanchie et recevrait une rémunération de 3000 F par mois.

Si cela intéresse votre fille, je lui propose de prendre contact avec moi dès que possible au numéro ci-dessus.

Je vous prie de croire, Madame, en mes sentiments les meilleurs.

E. Dulac

Asking for a reference

Craig McKenzie
15 Rowan Close
Torquay
Devon
TQ2 7QJ

Torquay, le 12 janvier 1997

Monsieur,

J'ai été votre étudiant en DEA pendant l'année 1990-1991.

Je constitue actuellement un dossier pour postuler un emploi à l'Université de St Andrews et je dois fournir deux lettres de recommandation. Accepteriez-vous d'en écrire une? Si votre réponse est oui, je vous serais très reconnaissant de faire parvenir cette lettre directement à l'université.

Avec mes remerciements, et l'expression de mes sentiments respectueux.

P.J.: description de poste
enveloppe timbrée

Giving a reference

UNIVERSITE DE CLERMONT-FERRAND 1
27, avenue Michelin
63567 Clermont-Ferrand Cedex 3
téléphone 04 73 40 60 31

Clermont-Ferrand, le 13 mars 1997

A QUI DE DROIT

Monsieur Louis Filard a été mon étudiant en classe de géométrie pendant l'année universitaire 1989–90. Bien que la classe ait été fort nombreuse, je me souviens de lui comme d'un étudiant attentif, prompt à poser des questions très souvent pertinentes, et obtenant des résultats tout à fait honorables dans ses travaux écrits. Sérieux et appliqué, il a fait montre de qualités qui laissent bien augurer de son avenir. Je ne doute pas qu'il puisse donner entièrement satisfaction dans l'emploi qu'il postule.

E. Chapier

Madame Eliane Chapier
Maître de Conférences
Faculté de Mathématiques
Université de Clermont-Ferrand

Thanking for a reference

Christian Jouanneau
12, avenue d'Angleterre
62107 Calais

le 30 mars 1997

Chère Madame,

Je tiens à vous remercier d'avoir bien voulu apporter votre soutien à ma candidature à un poste de concepteur chez Arts et Design Gadgeteria. J'ai eu un entretien avec leur directeur du personnel, et j'ai le plaisir de vous annoncer que j'ai été sélectionné. J'en suis très satisfait, d'autant plus qu'il y avait de nombreux candidats. Transmettez mon bon souvenir à mes anciens collègues.

Recevez, Chère Madame, l'expression de ma profonde gratitude.

Accepting a job

Gabriel Maréchal
11, rue Jules Ferry
85000 La Roche-sur-Yon

M. Ramirez
Ferme modèle du Grand Pré
14260 Aunay-sur-Odon

le 3 avril 1997

Monsieur,

C'est avec le plus grand plaisir que j'ai reçu votre courrier m'informant que j'avais été choisi pour le poste de pépiniériste auquel j'étais candidat. Je vous confirme par la présente que je serai en mesure de prendre ce poste à compter du 5 mai. J'arriverai dans la soirée du 4, et me présenterai à vous dès 7 heures le lendemain matin.

Je vous prie de croire, Monsieur, à mes sentiments les meilleurs.

G. Maréchal

Refusing a job

René Perrot
13, rue Lamartine
38590 Brézins

Entreprise Bideau
Electricité générale
Quartier des Balmes
01370 Saint-André-de-Corcy

le 28 mars 1997

Monsieur,

Je vous suis reconnaissant de m'avoir offert un emploi d'électricien dans votre entreprise. Toutefois, ma situation personnelle a changé depuis notre dernier entretien. En effet, ma femme qui travaille dans l'Education nationale vient d'être nommée en Haute-Vienne. Je me vois donc dans l'obligation de refuser votre offre.

J'espère que vous ne me tiendrez pas rigueur de ce désistement, et vous prie d'agréer l'expression de mes meilleurs sentiments.

R. Perrot

Resigning from a job

Manuella Viera
27 rue des Epinettes
75017 Paris

M. Benoît Gance
Directeur Général
S.R.T.I.

Recommandé avec A.R.

Le 5 juin 1997

Monsieur,

J'ai l'honneur de vous présenter ma démission du poste d'assistante de direction que j'occupe dans votre entreprise depuis le 15 septembre 1994.

Mon préavis commencera le 6 juin 1997 et s'achèvera le 6 août 1997, date après laquelle je serais libre de tout engagement envers votre entreprise.

Veuillez agréer, Monsieur, toute ma considération.

M.Viera

M Viera

Resigning from a post: waiter

Frédéric Aubert
12, avenue de la Gare
07100 Annonay

M. Bedeau
Café-Bar des Anglais
Grand Place
07440 Alboussière

Annonay, le 12 septembre 1997

Monsieur,

Par cette lettre je vous prie de prendre note de ma décision de démissionner de mon emploi de garçon de café à dater du 10 octobre prochain. Pour des raisons familiales, je me vois en effet dans l'obligation de quitter la région.

Je vous remercie de la sympathie que vous m'avez exprimée au cours des dernières semaines, qui ont été particulièrement difficiles.

Je vous prie de croire à mes sentiments les meilleurs.

F. Aubert

Attestation of employment

S.R.T.I.
48 rue St André
92800 Puteaux - La Défense

A QUI DE DROIT

Je soussigné, Benoît Gance, certifie que mademoiselle Manuella Viera a travaillé en qualité d'assistante de direction à la S.R.T.I. du 15 septembre 1994 au 6 août 1997.

Fait à Paris le 6 août 1997.

Benoît Gance

M. Benoît Gance
Directeur Général

CV: American academic

HEIDER Sarah Delores

née le 27/09/52

Nationalité américaine

Adresse

1123 Cedar Avenue
Evanston
Illinois 60989
Etats-Unis

Formation

PhD (Doctorat) en Littérature (La Poétique de Shakespeare et sa vision de la femme) soutenu en 1983 à Northwestern University, Evanston, Illinois.

Maîtrise de Littérature anglaise et américaine obtenue en 1977 à l'Université de Pennsylvanie, Philadelphie.

Licence d'Anglais de l'Université de Californie, Berkeley.

Expérience professionnelle

Depuis 1992	Professeur associée, Département d'anglais, Northwestern University.
1988 - 1992	Professeur assistante, spécialiste de la Renaissance, Département d'anglais, Northwestern University.
1983 - 1987	Professeur assistante, Département d'anglais, Université de Pennsylvanie, Philadelphie.
1980 - 1983	Attachée de recherche sous la direction du Professeur O'Leary (Féminisme et Poétique de Shakespeare), Northwestern University.
1979 - 1980	Attachée de recherche, Département d'études féministes, Northwestern University.
1977 - 1979	Assistante, spécialiste du théâtre de la Renaissance anglaise, Northwestern University.

Distinctions

Bourse de Recherche Wallenheimer en 1992 - 1993.

Poste de recherche doctorale Milton Wade en 1979 - 1980.

Bourse d'études de la Fondation Pankhurst/Amersham en 1977 - 1979.

Travaux de recherche et publications

Voir liste ci-jointe.

Divers

Présidente de la Commission "Renaissance Minds" (étude de l'idéologie de la période de la Renaissance anglaise).

Membre de l'UPCEO (Commission inter-universitaire pour la défense des droits de la femme) depuis 1984.

Conseillère auprès des éditions Virago à Londres (collection des études sur la Renaissance) en 1989 - 1990.

Conseillère auprès des éditions Pandora, New York, en 1987.

CV: French academic

Jacques Tessier
Spécialiste de Biologie Végétale
Docteur d'Etat

Né le 30 octobre 1943

Marié, deux enfants de 7 et 3 ans.

Adresse: 12, cours Fauriel, 42000 Saint-Etienne

Téléphone: +33 4 77 24 37 12

Fax: (Université): +33 4 77 19 67 23

E-mail: phyveg@ismu.univ-stet.fr

Thèse d'état soutenue en Octobre 1985 devant l'Université de Paris XII:
"Effets comparés des rayonnements Ω et r sur la croissance de *Calluna vulgaris* et *Erica vagans*"
sous la direction de Jean-Pierre Chenu, Professeur de Biologie végétale à l'Université Paris XII.
Mention : Très Honorable à l'unanimité du jury.

EXPERIENCE PROFESSIONNELLE

Depuis 1986	Maître de Conférences de Biologie Végétale à l'Université de Saint-Etienne.
1979 - 1986	Maître-assistant de Biologie Végétale à l'Université de Brest.
1978 - 1979	Détaché à l'Université de Georgetown, U.S.A., chargé d'un projet d'étude sur le comportement des plantes dicotylédones en apesanteur pour la NASA.
1973 - 1978	Assistant de Biologie Végétale à l'Université de Caen.
1971 - 1973	Professeur agrégé de Sciences Naturelles au Lycée d'Etat de Dunkerque.

RECHERCHE ET PUBLICATIONS

Trois livres et vingt-sept articles publiés à ce jour (voir liste ci-jointe).

Principaux domaines de recherche : la croissance des plantes en fonction des conditions de lumière et d'humidité, avec un intérêt particulier pour les graminées.

CV: French school-leaver

CURRICULUM VITAE

Catherine Belin
18, avenue Edouard Herriot
01000 Bourg-en-Bresse
Tél.: 04 74 50 09 13

Nationalité française

Née le 28 mai 1979 à Vienne, Isère

FORMATION ET DIPLOMES

1990 - 1994
Collège d'enseignement général Frison-Roche, Vizille, Isère.
1994 - 1997
Lycée Carriat, Bourg-en-Bresse.
Baccalauréat série A2, mention assez bien, obtenu en juillet 1997.

EXPERIENCE PROFESSIONNELLE

Caissière à l'hypermarché de Bourg-en-Bresse, juillet 1996.

Agent de bureau intérimaire à la Sécurité Sociale, caisse de Lons-le-Saunier, août 1996 et juillet-août 1997.

Grande expérience de garde d'enfants.

Cours particuliers de français et d'allemand de la Sixième à la Troisième.

DIVERS

Bon niveau en dactylographie (40 mots/minute environ).

Allemand courant (lu, parlé et écrit). Nombreux séjours courts en Allemagne.

Pratique du badminton et du ski de fond.

CV: English graduate

GRANTLEY Paul Alan

Adresse:
26 Countisbury Drive
BRIGHTON BN3 1RG
Grande-Bretagne
Tél.: 01273 53 49 50

Né le 22 mai 1974`
Célibataire
Nationalité britannique

FORMATION

1993 - 1996
King's College, Londres: B.Sc. (Licence) en Biochimie (2.1. = mention bien)

1992
A Levels (Deuxième partie du Baccalauréat) options: Biologie, Chimie, Physique et Mathématiques.

1990
O Levels (Première partie du Baccalauréat) options :

Mathématiques, Physique, Biologie, Chimie, Commerce, Anglais, Allemand et Sociologie.

1985 - 1992
Brighton College Boys' School (Lycée)

EXPERIENCE PROFESSIONNELLE

Mars 1994
une semaine comme "double" du Directeur Adjoint du Marketing chez EAA Technology (Sources d'énergie écologiques) à Didcot près d'Oxford.

Juillet 1993
deux semaines chez Alford & Wilston Ltd (Produits chimiques), Warley, Midlands de l'Ouest.

CENTRES D'INTERET

Au Lycée
Capitaine de l'équipe de rugby pendant deux ans.
Membre du club d'échecs.

A l'Université
Membre de l'équipe de rugby.
Organisateur de la Semaine de Charité (1988).
Délégué aux activités sportives dans l'association des étudiants.

DIVERS

Bonne connaissance de l'outil informatique, en particulier sur Macintosh.
Permis de conduire.
Intérêt pour les voyages : tour du monde en 1987-88, entre le Lycée et l'Université.

CV: French junior executive

Ingénieur informaticien

Hervé Maurier

né le 14 mars 1966 à Lons-le-Saunier
marié, sans enfants

25, rue Paul Doumer
54000 Nancy
Téléphone: 03 82 27 61 12

Formation

juin 1988	Diplôme d'Ingénieur.
1984 - 1988	Ecole Nationale de Chimie et Physique Industrielle de Metz, section Informatique.
1984	Baccalauréat série C à Lons-le-Saunier, Mention assez bien.

Expérience professionnelle

Depuis septembre 1991	Ingénieur chez SEIM Nancy, responsable de projet depuis janvier 1993, chargé de la conception des systèmes informatiques de l'E.D.F.
1989 - 1991	Ingénieur chez LID Informatique, Lunéville, emploi de cadre technico-commercial.
1988	Stage de trois mois chez Alsthom Nancy.
1987	Stage de deux mois chez Rhône-Poulenc, Strasbourg.

Divers

Président de l'antenne nancéenne des "Restos du cœur".

Anglais parlé courant : nombreux séjours de vacances aux Etats-Unis.

Pratique assidue de la spéléologie et du parapente.

CV: Male English senior executive

Robert Charlton STEVENSON

21 Liston Road
Clapham Old Town
LONDON SW4 0DF
Royaume-Uni

Téléphone et télécopie: 44 171 622 2467

Nationalité britannique

Né le 27 juin 1954

FORMATION ET DIPLOMES

1980	Maîtrise de Gestion (avec mention) à l'Armour Business School, Boston, Etats-Unis.
1978 - 1980	Deux années aux Etats-Unis.
1976	BSc (Licence) de Mécanique à l'Université du Dorset, Willingdon, Royaume-Uni.
1973 - 1976	Université du Dorset, Willingdon, Royaume-Uni.
1973	A level (Baccalauréat)

EXPERIENCE PROFESSIONNELLE

1992 - 1994	Directeur adjoint de Jermyn-Sawyers International, Londres.
1987 - 1992	Directeur pour l'Asie, Société Pharmaceutique Peterson, Hong Kong
1983 - 1987	Directeur, Kerry-Masterton Management Consultants (consultants en gestion des entreprises), Bonn.
1980 - 1983	Consultant, Kerry-Masterton Management Consultants, Londres.
1976 - 1978	Stagiaire en gestion des entreprises, Jamieson Matthews Ltd, Crawley, Sussex.

DIVERS

Bilingue anglais-français.

Brevet de pilote amateur.

Loisirs: ski, ski nautique, parapente, voile.

CV: Female English middle-manager

CURRICULUM VITAE

HUNT Mary Phyllis

16 Victoria Road
Brixton
LONDRES SW7 5HU
Tél.: 44 171 467 79 68

Nationalité britannique

Née le 11 mars 1963

FORMATION ET DIPLOMES

1985 - 1986
Ecole de Commerce de l'Université d'Essex: Diplôme de Troisième Cycle en Commerce-Gestion et Allemand.

1981 - 1983 et 1984 - 1985
London School of Economics (Grande Ecole de Sciences Economiques de Londres), Département Commerce: BSc (Licence)
First Class Honours (distinction réservée aux meilleurs étudiants) en Commerce et Economie.

1983 - 1984
Séjour d'une année à Bonn, Allemagne: étude de l'allemand économique en cours du soir. Divers emplois de bureau en tant qu'intérimaire.

1974 - 1981
Grammar School for Girls (Lycée de jeunes filles) : 7 disciplines pour la première partie du Baccalauréat (O levels),et 4 pour la deuxième partie (A levels): Mathématiques, Histoire, Economie et Allemand

EXPERIENCE PROFESSIONNELLE

Depuis 1992
Sous-Directrice, Retail Outlets Division (Département des Ventes au Détail), Delicatessen International, Londres.

1991 - 1992
Acheteuse adjointe, Delicatessen International, Paris

1989 - 1991
Directrice adjointe, Sainsway Foodstores plc, Faversham, Kent.

1987 - 1989
Formation de Directeur, Sainsway Foodstores plc (Grand magasin d'alimentation), Londres.

Asking for a catalogue

Thomas Lavant
3, rue des Epinettes
94170 Le Perreux

Besançon, le 13 janvier 1997

Entreprise J. Rossi SARL
Optique en gros
Z.I. des Hauts Fourneaux
25000 BESANÇON

Monsieur

Je vous serais reconnaissant de bien vouloir m'envoyer le catalogue des jumelles et longues-vues que vous commercialisez, avec la liste des prix.

Recevez, Monsieur, l'assurance de mes salutations distinguées.

T. Lavant

Sending a catalogue

AGENCE BERNARD
S.A.R.L.
85, route de l'Hippodrome
92153 SURESNES CEDEX
tél.: 01 46 26 51 22 fax: 01 46 26 44 99

Suresnes, le 6 février 1997

Madame Ménard
Résidence du Val d'Or - Appartement 2B
92800 PUTEAUX

Réf. : ML-94-127

Chère Madame,

Comme chaque année, nous vous adressons un catalogue des voyages que nous proposons à des prix très avantageux aux personnes retraitées pouvant partir en dehors des périodes d'affluence. Vous y trouverez tous les détails concernant les dates, les prix, les conditions de séjour, etc.

Que vous choisissiez le Sahara ou le Cap Nord, vous serez enchantée de votre décision. De plus, nous offrons gracieusement un superbe sac de voyage à nos premiers inscrits.

Alors, à bientôt, Madame Ménard, le plaisir de vous voir et croyez en nos sentiments très dévoués.

N Lefet

Nicole LEFET
Responsable Commerciale

P. J.: un catalogue 1997

Asking for samples

Madame Bordoni
Couturière
2, impasse du Parc
50760 Barfleur
Téléphone: 02 45 45 22 34

Filatures Fouquet
1854 route de Nantes
49300 Cholet

le 18 avril 1994

Madame, Monsieur,

J'ai bien reçu votre catalogue et je vous en remercie, mais avant de passer ma commande, je souhaiterais recevoir un lot d'échantillons des tissus qui figurent de la page 248 à la page 322.

Je vous remercie de votre compréhension et vous adresse, Madame, Monsieur, mes salutations distinguées.

G. Bordoni

Sending samples

S.A.R.L. SOFITTO
3, rue du Bois 10000 TROYES
Téléphone: 03 29 10 47 30 Télécopie: 03 29 10 51 88

Troyes, le 28 juillet 1997

Madame Isabelle Dubreuil
15, av. de la République
86000 Poitiers

Référence : 45-22-0XT

Madame,

Suite à votre demande, nous avons le plaisir de vous adresser par courrier séparé un échantillonnage complet de toutes les laines que nous pouvons vous fournir.

Vous trouverez certainement ce qui vous conviendra parmi les nombreux coloris et les diverses variétés de fil que nous vous proposons. Lorsque vous aurez fait votre choix, nous vous serions reconnaissants de nous retourner ces échantillons afin que nous puissions en faire bénéficier d'autres clientes.

Restant à votre disposition pour tout renseignement complémentaire, je vous prie de croire, Madame, en mes sentiments respectueux et dévoués.

G Durand

G. Durand
Service Commercial

Asking for an estimate

Monsieur et Madame Mercier
32, avenue des Marronniers
94500 Champigny sur Marne
Tél: 01 48 93 72 30

le 3 juin 1997

Cavanna & Fils
76, quai de la Marne
94170 Le Perreux

Messieurs,

Suite à notre conversation téléphonique de ce jour, nous vous confirmons notre requête.

Propriétaires d'un petit pavillon, nous souhaiterions procéder à quelques travaux d'agrandissement, et en particulier faire construire un jardin d'hiver dans le prolongement de la salle de séjour. Nous souhaiterions donc convenir d'un rendez-vous afin que vous puissiez établir un devis.

Dans l'attente de votre réponse, nous vous adressons nos sincères salutations.

C. Mercier

Sending an estimate

ENTREPRISE CAPRARA
56, rue A. Fourny
73100 Aix-les-Bains
téléphone: 04 79 57 88 76

le 19 mai 1997

Monsieur Villeret
22, passage de la Gare
73100 Aix-les-Bains

Référence: 94 AI 229 ADP

Monsieur,

A la suite de notre rendez-vous du 6 mai dernier, je vous adresse le devis que vous m'aviez demandé et qui comporte les différents aménagements dont nous avions parlé pour l'installation de votre piscine.

J'espère qu'il vous conviendra et vous remerciant de votre confiance, je vous prie d'agréer, Monsieur, l'expression de mes sentiments dévoués.

Philippe Barrault
Directeur Commercial

To an air-conditioning company: asking for an estimate

MODSTYLE
22 rue d'Alsace – 75010 Paris
tél +33 1 48 99 45 34 – télécopie +33 1 48 99 45 44
société anonyme au capital de 300 000F - R. C. Paris N 57668746

Responsable clientèle
SRGC
Société Régionale de
Génie Climatique
45 avenue Gallieni
93140 Bondy

Le 14 avril 1997

Monsieur,

Je dirige une petite entreprise de prêt-à-porter, dans le dixième arrondissement. Soucieux du bien-être de mes employés, je souhaiterais faire installer un nouveau système de climatisation dans nos bureaux et ateliers.

Nos locaux sont répartis sur les deux derniers étages d'un immeuble ancien et s'étendent sur une surface totale de 300 m2. Votre entreprise m'a été recommandée par l'un de nos partenaires commerciaux, la société Gallier et j'espère que vous serez en mesure d'effectuer les travaux pour nous.

Je vous serais reconnaissant de bien vouloir prendre contact avec moi et de m'envoyer dès que possible l'un de vos experts, afin qu'un devis soit établi.

Veuillez agréer, Monsieur, mes salutations distinguées.

Monsieur F. Binet
Directeur général

Sending details of availability of spare parts

Etablissements Renard
Zone Industrielle
38250 Saint-Egrève
Téléphone: 04 76 75 43 21 Télécopie: 04 76 75 88 47

Saint-Egrève, le 23 mai 1997

Madame Annick Deschamps
25, Rue du Lavoir
38740 VINAY

Référence 05-02 VLS

Madame,

En réponse à votre lettre du 16 courant, j'ai le plaisir de vous informer que nous pouvons vous fournir des pièces de rechange pour toutes les grandes marques d'appareils électroménagers fabriqués au cours des quinze dernières années. Nos prix, joints en annexe, sont donnés hors TVA (18,60 %) et port non compris. Si vous décidez de commander, il est impératif que vous nous indiquiez, outre la marque, le nom et le numéro de série de votre appareil.

Dès réception de votre commande, nous ferons le nécessaire pour que les pièces vous parviennent rapidement. Si vous en avez besoin de façon très urgente, nous pouvons vous les faire livrer par coursier (le port étant à votre charge).

Dans l'espoir que ces précisions répondront à votre attente, je vous prie d'agréer, Madame, l'expression de mes sentiments distingués.

Jean-Michel Brun
Directeur Commercial

P.J. tarif des pièces détachées robots ménagers.

Sending details of prices

Société de location "Jardin et Maison"
157, route de Genas
69500 Bron
TELEPHONE : 04 78 54 65 77 TELECOPIE : 04 78 54 22 34

Bron, le 15 juin 1997

Monsieur Girardin
Résidence Martinon
27, rue Jules Ferry
69130 Ecully

Monsieur,

Vous trouverez ci-joint nos tarifs de location pour l'outillage de jardin. Nous attirons votre attention sur nos tarifs dégressifs en cas de location de longue durée et sur nos tarifs "fidélité" en cas de location à intervalles réguliers.

Restant à votre disposition, nous vous prions de croire, Monsieur, en nos sentiments dévoués.

J.B. Roulet
Service commercial

Asking for discount

Société SOGEFOP
route de Pierrefeu
83170 Brignoles
téléphone : 04 42 27 86 13
télécopie: 04 42 27 00 01

Brignoles, le 14 novembre 1997

Confiseries du Port
2, place du Port
13500 Martigues

Messieurs,

Je souhaiterais offrir pour Noël à tout mon personnel un assortiment de fruits confits. Votre catalogue propose une présentation en paniers de 150 grammes au prix de 46F50 pièce TTC sous la réf. 18/22. Je souhaiterais pouvoir vous en commander 1580.

Etant donné l'importance de cette commande, qui pourrait se renouveler chaque année, je vous demande une remise de 10%.

Par avance, je vous remercie de votre réponse et vous prie de croire, Messieurs, en mes sentiments distingués.

Monsieur Robert Ledoux
Président-directeur général

Accepting a discount

Société Levet
128 bis, Grande Rue
76190 Yvetot
téléphone: 02 35 89 27 68
télécopie: 02 35 89 99 99

le 17 février 1997

Garage des Sapins
27, Square des Sapins
33170 Gradignan

Référence RAD 94 35/22

Monsieur,

Nous avons bien reçu votre demande de réduction sur la commande du 13 janvier dernier, et nous avons le plaisir de vous faire savoir qu'à titre exceptionnel nous vous accordons une remise de 2,5 %. Votre facture est donc ramenée à 1432550,50F.

Veuillez agréer, Monsieur, l'expression de nos salutations distinguées.

R. Dormois
Directeur Commercial

Approach about openings

FABRIQUE ARTISANALE GUYOT
12, avenue du Maréchal Joffre
42000 Saint-Etienne
tél. 04 77 45 09 87

Saint-Etienne, le 28 octobre 1997

Comité d'Entreprise de Mazza S.A.
7, Place de la République
42300 Roanne

Madame, Monsieur,

Nos chocolats, dont la réputation n'est plus à faire, sont une excellente idée de cadeau pour les fêtes de fin d'année. Aussi sommes-nous heureux de vous adresser notre catalogue ainsi que les tarifs préférentiels que nous accordons aux collectivités pour toute commande groupée d'un montant minimum de 800 F.

En outre, si nous enregistrons votre commande avant le 18 novembre, nous aurons le plaisir de vous faire bénéficier d'une remise supplémentaire de 3%.

Espérant vous compter parmi nos nouveaux clients, nous vous adressons, Madame, Monsieur, nos salutations les plus sincères.

J. M. Charlier
Directeur du Marketing

Follow-up to this approach

✱ FABRIQUE ARTISANALE GUYOT ✱
12, avenue du Maréchal Joffre
42000 Saint-Etienne
tél. 04 77 45 09 87

le 3 novembre 1997

Madame, Monsieur,

Le 28 octobre dernier, nous vous avons adressé notre catalogue ainsi que les tarifs préférentiels que nous réservons aux collectivités comme la vôtre à l'approche des fêtes de fin d'année.

Nous sommes certains que notre offre exceptionnelle a retenu toute votre attention et que votre commande est déjà prête. Nous vous rappelons que si elle nous parvient avant le 18 novembre, vous bénéficierez d'une remise supplémentaire de 3%. Il n'est pas trop tard!

Nous serons heureux de vous compter parmi nos nouveaux clients et vous assurons, Madame, Monsieur, de notre dévouement.

J.M. Charlier
Directeur du Marketing

Acknowledging delivery

le 12 décembre 1997

S. Kaoun
Société Delauney
83, avenue Charles de Gaulle
92320 Châtillon

Monsieur P. Langlois
SOTEP
76, bd de Strasbourg
77420 Champs

Réf: SK/CL57/94/09/231

Monsieur le Directeur,

Suite à ma commande du 23 septembre, j'ai bien reçu les 30 bureaux Classic 57, et je vous en remercie.

Vous trouverez ci-joint un chèque d'un montant de 10 200 francs à l'ordre de votre société qui constitue comme prévu le troisième et dernier versement.

Veuillez agréer, Monsieur le Directeur, mes sentiments distingués.

S. Kaoun

P.J.: un chèque bancaire de 10 200 francs

Complaining about delivery: late arrival

le 30 mai 1997

M. F. Lorinet
89, impasse des Cordeliers
36100 Issoudun

Société Tout pour l'Eau
92, avenue de Paris
36000 Châteauroux

Objet: Commande 94/3/5302/127/VG

Monsieur,

Voilà plus de deux mois que j'attends la baignoire réf. 5302 couleur vert d'eau que je vous ai commandée le 15 mars dernier. Vous m'aviez assuré lors de la commande qu'elle me serait livrée sous trois semaines.

Je vous serais reconnaissant de me faire savoir dans les délais les plus brefs la date exacte où cet article me sera livré, faute de quoi je me verrai contraint d'annuler ma commande.

Dans l'attente de vous lire, je vous prie de croire, Monsieur, à mes sentiments distingués.

F. Lorinet

Complaining about delivery: wrong goods

"La Maison du Sous-Vêtement"
15, rue Magenta
42000 Saint-Etienne
Tél.: 04 77 42 17 82

le 12 septembre 1997

USINES LOIRETEXTILE
Confection - Vente en gros
Z.I. des Epis
42319 Roanne CEDEX

Référence commande n° 94/08/30-ZDX

Messieurs,

J'ai bien reçu votre livraison, mais je me vois dans l'obligation de vous retourner le colis, les tailles des articles ne correspondant pas à celles indiquées sur le bon de commande.

Je vous saurais gré de bien vouloir corriger votre erreur et de me faire parvenir les articles conformes à ma commande dans les plus brefs délais.

Veuillez agréer, Messieurs, l'expression de ma considération distinguée.

A. Hébert
Gérant

Answering a complaint about delivery of wrong goods

LA PORTE ROUGE V.P.C.
Chemin des Dames
59339 TOURCOING CEDEX
tél: 03 27 98 47 75 fax: 03 27 98 51 52

le 15 mai 1997

Madame Guillot
2, place de l'Eglise
38250 CORRENCON-EN-VERCORS

Réf.: Cmde 94/fil/289

Chère cliente,

Nous avons bien reçu votre courrier du 13 mai dernier nous signalant que la livraison faite par nos services n'était pas conforme à votre commande.

En effet, la couette 240 x 220 réf. 727.372 n'étant plus disponible, nous avons pensé vous être agréable en vous adressant un article de qualité supérieure que nous vous offrons au même prix que celui que vous aviez commandé. Si toutefois vous ne souhaitez pas profiter de cette occasion exceptionnelle, vous pouvez nous retourner cet article en port dû et nous vous le rembourserons.

Nous vous prions de croire, chère cliente, en nos sentiments dévoués.

M. Constantin
Directeur des Ventes

Disputing an invoice: already paid

le 19 décembre 1997

B. Conrad
Le Manoir aux Emaux
17108 Saintes

Meubles Le Vieux Rustique
Zone artisanale des Fougères
D 939
17030 La Rochelle

Monsieur,

Par lettre du 18 décembre, vous me demandez de régler votre facture n° 721 de 47921,37 francs du 11 septembre concernant la livraison de meubles divers. Or cette facture a déjà été payée, par mandat postal daté du 7 octobre. Je vous la renvoie donc, en vous demandant de bien vouloir vérifier vos comptes.

Veuillez agréer, Monsieur, l'expression de mes salutations distinguées.

B.Conrad

P.J.: votre facture

Answering complaint about invoice: already paid

IMPRIMERIE VITFAIT
Route de Chartreuse
38500 VOIRON
Téléphone : 04 76 05 98 71

Le 18 septembre 1997

Mademoiselle Estelle Dutreuil
8, boulevard Joseph Vallier
38000 Grenoble

Objet: commande n° 94/08/21

Mademoiselle,

Nous accusons réception de votre courrier du 12 septembre dernier concernant la facture de la commande ci-dessus. Cette facture vous a en effet été adressée en double exemplaire, ce dont nous vous prions de bien vouloir nous excuser. L'erreur est due au système informatique récemment mis en place et encore mal rodé.

Nous vous remercions de ne pas tenir compte de cette relance et vous prions d'agréer, Mademoiselle, l'expression de nos sentiments distingués.

Louis Moulin
Responsable du Service Comptable

Disputing an invoice: too high

"Les Amis de la Spatule"
Association à but non lucratif Loi 1901
Téléphone 05 61 60 62 33

le 15 septembre 1997

Raoul Blanchard
Trésorier de l'Association
11, rue Juliette Lamber
24000 Périgueux

"LA MERE LEGRAS"
Hôtel Restaurant
6, rue Ampère
24200 Sarlat

Madame,

Je reçois votre facture n° 94/08/31/XYZ86 correspondant au banquet des Anciens de la Spatule du 31 août dernier et je me permets d'en contester le montant.

Nous étions convenus d'un prix d'environ 250 F par personne pour le repas, apéritifs et digestifs compris. Or votre facture fait apparaître un prix de 295 F par personne, ce qui ramène le prix du café (qui était en sus) à 45 F !

Pensant qu'il s'agit d'une erreur, je vous demanderais de bien vouloir rectifier cette facture en conséquence, et vous prie d'agréer, Madame, l'expression de mes sentiments distingués.

R. Blanchard

Answering complaint about invoice: too high

DUROUCHOUX SARL
BP 52
95300 Pontoise
téléphone: 02 33 87 29 86

Pontoise, le 11 août 1997

Monsieur Pierre Delpuech
28, Allée du Bois
77300 Fontainebleau

Objet: commande n° 94 EMB 127

Monsieur,

En réponse à votre courrier du 22 juillet 97, nous vous prions de bien vouloir ne pas tenir compte de la facture 94/999/888 qui comporte une erreur en votre défaveur.

Vous trouverez ci-joint une facture, réf. 94/888/999, qui correspond à votre commande.

Avec toutes nos excuses, recevez, Monsieur, nos salutations distinguées.

P. Boulier
Le Responsable du Service Comptabilité

Sending a cheque in payment

Monsieur Linet
Le Verger
14 ter, Chemin des Mouilles
47000 Agen
téléphone: 05 58 57 39 47

Monsieur Chartier
Pépiniériste
12, rue de la Plage
34200 Sète

Agen, le 25 février 1997

Référence: 1994-23

Monsieur,

En règlement de votre facture 129-GTX-47 du 24 février, veuillez trouver ci-joint un chèque bancaire n° 9 543 395 d'un montant de 1257,75 F.

Vous en souhaitant bonne réception, je vous prie d'agréer, Monsieur, l'expression de mes sentiments distingués.

C. Linet

P.J.: 1 chèque de la Banque Populaire d'Agen et du Sud-Ouest

Acknowledging payment received

ROBINETTERIE Durand
7, rue Pierre Gaultier
57050 METZ
TELEPHONE: 03 89 57 13 24

Le 23 juillet 1997

Monsieur Dechaux
21, route du Lac
73100 AIX-LES-BAINS

Commande n° 12 H 889

Monsieur,

Par la présente, nous accusons réception du paiement de la facture 78900HOC par chèque postal n° 0025863 du 18 juillet 1997 d'un montant de 172,89 F.

Vous remerciant pour votre règlement, nous vous prions d'agréer, Monsieur, l'expression de nos sentiments distingués.

Le Service Comptabilité

Wrong payment received

GARAGE SIMOUN
Place du Champ de Foire
91150 ETAMPES
téléphone: 03 60.14.91.49

Etampes, le 24 octobre 1994

Monsieur Dupuis
25 ter, avenue du Stade
14000 CAEN

Réf. facture 560/94/08/25789

Monsieur,

Nous avons bien reçu votre chèque bancaire n° 8 2563 114 du 19 octobre 1994 d'un montant de 1500 F.

Le montant total de la facture qui vous a été adressée étant de 1957 F 18, vous nous êtes redevable de la somme de 457,18 F que nous vous remercions par avance de bien vouloir nous régler dans les plus brefs délais.

Veuillez agréer, Monsieur, l'expression de nos sentiments distingués.

B. Fournier
Gérant

Reminder of invoice outstanding

ENTREPRISE DE BATIMENT MAZZA
289, route Nationale
35000 Châteauroux
Tél.: 03 85 04 92 78

le 18 juillet 1997

Monsieur Jean-Louis Jacquet
3, Place Albert Camus
36100 Issoudun

Facture n° 94/126B72 du 22 avril 97

Monsieur,

Nous vous rappelons que notre facture n° 94/126B72 du 22 avril 97 dont le paiement était prévu au deuxième trimestre 97 reste impayée à ce jour.

Nous vous remercions par avance de bien vouloir régulariser votre situation dans les plus brefs délais et vous prions d'agréer, Monsieur, l'expression de nos salutations distinguées.

L Bayard

Luc Bayard
Agent Comptable

Enquiring about reproduction rights and costs

Julie Collins
Service des reproductions
Sandford Publishing Co.
Dalton Street
Wantage OX12 6DP
Grande-Bretagne

Service des Archives du Film
Centre National de la Cinématographie

Le 13 février 1997

Madame, Monsieur,

Dans le cadre du centenaire du cinéma, Sandford Publishing Co s'apprête à publier un ouvrage sur le cinéma européen des origines à nos jours. Les auteurs souhaitant insérer dans le corps du texte un certain nombres de clichés appartenant à vos archives, je vous serais très reconnaissante de bien vouloir me faire parvenir une documentation sur les modalités et les coûts de reproduction.
Veuillez agréer, Madame, Monsieur, l'expression de ma considération distinguée.

Julie Collins

Julie Collins
Responsable
Service des reproductions

Sending an invoice

Simon Gillon
6 Leckford Road
London SW11 7YU
0171-455 45 78

Université de la Sorbonne
Paris IV

Le 27 novembre 1997

Note d'honoraires

Objet: notre contrat réf. 97 447 66 en date du 10 octobre 1997.

Dans le cadre du colloque "Art et Mythologie":

- conférence intitulée : 'L'héritage mythologique chez Nicolas Poussin' (16/11) **1 300 francs**

- frais de déplacement et d'hébergement, forfait **1 100 francs**

Total 2 400 francs

Avec mes remerciements,

S Gillon

S Gillon

Memorandum

NOTE DE SERVICE

Le 05/06/1997

Pour des raisons de sécurité, il est rappelé au personnel que l'accès aux locaux est strictement interdit du vendredi 22h00 au lundi 6h00, sauf autorisation spéciale délivrée par M. Fabre.

La direction

Fax: business

L.C. INFORMATIQUE
12, RUE CLAUDE BERNARD
86000 POITIERS
N° de téléphone: 05 49 41 54 67
N° de télécopie: 05 49 41 22 82

TRANSMISSION PAR TELECOPIE

Date: 12 août 1997

Veuillez remettre ce document à : Jean Briant

Numéro de télécopie : 19 44 1705 82 31 54

De la part de : Stéphanie Langlois

Nombre de pages (y compris cette page) : 1

Message : Prière de me faire parvenir de toute urgence, par Chronopost si possible, l'original de vos billets d'avion et de train pour que je puisse procéder à votre remboursement.

J'aurai aussi besoin de vos notes d'hôtel et de restaurant, mais c'est moins urgent.

Merci, et amitiés,

Langlois

S. Langlois

Si vous ne recevez pas ce document au complet, veuillez nous en aviser le plus rapidement possible par téléphone ou télécopie.

Fax: personal

DE: Guy Planais
Allée des Colibris
85110 Chantonnay
Télécopie: 02 51 72 27 32
Téléphone: 02 51 22 37 91

A: Jane Mella
896 Career Street
Ottawa K1N 6N5
Canada

Le 11 juin 1997

Chère Jane,

URGENT: J'aurais besoin des coordonnées de Sun-Yun-Lee à Hong Kong. Je n'arrive pas à les retrouver. Ce serait gentil si tu pouvais me refaxer dans la journée. Merci, et à bientôt.

Guy

Agenda of meeting

Vous êtes priés d'assister ou de vous faire représenter à

L'ASSEMBLEE GENERALE ORDINAIRE DES COPROPRIETAIRES DE LA RESIDENCE DES ACACIAS

qui aura lieu le

24 septembre 1997
à 20 heures précises

Salle de Réunion du Sous-Sol

sur l'ordre du jour suivant:

1° Remplacement de la porte principale du garage.
Comparaison des divers devis proposés.

2° Installation de compteurs d'eau froide individuels.

3° Aménagement d'un terrain de jeu pour les enfants.
Examen des emplacements possibles.

4° Question du tapage nocturne.

5° Demande de M. Chauffour d'installer une antenne panoramique sur son balcon (11ème étage).

6° Questions diverses.

G. Malet

G. Malet
Le Syndic

Circular about conference

ECOLE SUPERIEURE DES INTERPRETES ET TRADUCTEURS DE LA VILLE DE GRENOBLE

Colloque international

"La technologie au service du traducteur"

du 17 au 19 septembre 1997

Sous le haut patronage de la Ville de Grenoble et de la Région Rhône-Alpes

Avec la collaboration des sociétés FOGEP et MERLIN et de la Banque Industrielle de l'Isère

Centre International des Colloques
Cité Internationale
Grenoble, France

Programme provisoire
[...]

Comité scientifique
[...]

Comité d'organisation
[...]

Langues de travail : anglais et français

Appel à communications

Les personnes qui désirent présenter une communication sont priées de faire parvenir pour le 13 juin au plus tard à l'adresse ci-dessous un résumé (maximum deux pages format A4, interligne 1,5) à l'attention de M. René-Pierre Longjumeau, Coordonnateur du Comité Scientifique du colloque.

Pour tout renseignement, contacter le Secrétariat du Colloque "La Technologie au Service du Traducteur", 86 rue Pasteur, 38365 Grenoble Cedex 01. Tél.: 04 76 69 22 41; Télécopie: 04 76 69 51 47;
E-mail: ronal@cism.univ-greno2.fr.

Minutes of meeting

CHORALE MUNICIPALE

Association à but non lucratif - Loi 1901
2, route des Luthiers
88000 Epinal
Téléphone : 03 29 65 87 87

COMPTE-RENDU DE LA REUNION DE RENTREE DU CONSEIL

D'ADMINISTRATION

du 25 septembre 1997

Présents: Lucie Bauland, Chantal Berne, Charles Brivet, Pierre Masson, Daniel Perret, Sylvie Popelin, Cécile Thibaut, Phillippe Toupin, Valérie Quatrain.

Excusés: *Mlle Anne Rouet (Procuration à Mme Chantal Berne)*, M. Pierre Dupuis.

Absente: Mlle Valérie Gorge.

Le quorum étant atteint, la séance est ouverte à 20 h par le Président Perret et se déroule selon l'ordre du jour prévu et distribué aux membres du conseil.

1° Approbation du procès-verbal de la réunion du 21 mars 1994
Unanimité, moins une voix (Mlle Popelin).

2° Recrutements
Le Président présente les deux nouvelles recrues: une soprano, Mlle Giuseppina FURNO et un ténor, M. Jean LEGRESLE.

3° Bilan de la tournée d'été
Le Président fait le point sur la tournée d'été qui s'est déroulée en Alsace du 28 juillet au 8 août. M. Brivet pose le problème du choix du répertoire.

4° Programme de la saison 1997/1998
Conformément aux souhaits de la majorité des choristes, le programme proposé pour 1997/1998 portera exclusivement sur la musique du XVIe siècle. La proposition soumise au vote à main levée est adoptée à l'unanimité moins une voix.

5° Budget
Le Trésorier prend la parole pour présenter les comptes de la saison qui s'achève. Après un long débat, le budget est adopté à l'unanimité.

6° Elections au Bureau
Le mandat de certains membres du Bureau venant à expiration, il est procédé à des élections. Sont candidats: Mme BAULAND pour la Vice-Présidence et M. BRIVET pour le Secrétariat.
Les résultats du vote sont les suivants:
Mme BAULAND: 11 voix pour, 1 voix contre, 1 abstention ;
M. BRIVET: 9 voix pour, 4 abstentions.
Les deux candidats sont élus.
Aucun candidat n'ayant postulé pour le siège de Trésorier, le mandat du Trésorier est reconduit.

7° Questions diverses
Il est rappelé que les choristes ne doivent pas se garer sur le trottoir car ils gênent l'entrée principale de l'immeuble.
Suite à une intervention de Mlle Popelin, le Président rappelle que chacun doit avoir une présentation impeccable pour les concerts.

L'ordre du jour étant épuisé, la séance est levée à 22 h 30.

Letter announcing academic conference

UNIVERSITE DE PERPIGNAN

FACULTE DES SCIENCES HUMAINES, JURIDIQUES, ECONOMIQUES ET SOCIALES
DEPARTEMENT D'ETUDES ECONOMIQUES

55, avenue de Villefranche
66860 PERPIGNAN Cedex
Téléphone: 04 68 34 87 56 - Télécopie: 04 68 54 91 20 - Télex: 505.564.F UNIPERP

XXXIIème CONGRES DE LA S.U.E.S.

14-15-16 MAI 1997

Chère collègue, cher collègue,

Le Département d'Etudes Economiques de l'Université de Perpignan est heureux d'accueillir pour la première fois le Congrès de la S.U.E.S. les 14, 15 et 16 mai 1997. Tout sera mis en œuvre pour que cette manifestation soit une réussite.

Le thème choisi, "Les changements dans les économies des pays de l'Europe de l'Est", est d'une grande actualité et d'une grande richesse.

Nous vous communiquerons le programme détaillé de la conférence et le nom des intervenants dans notre deuxième circulaire.

Vous trouverez dans ce premier envoi:

- l'avant-programme,
- un bulletin d'inscription,
- la liste des ateliers prévus,
- la fiche de réservation hôtelière.

Dans l'attente de ce grand événement, nous vous prions d'agréer, chère collègue, cher collègue, l'expression de nos sentiments dévoués.

Pour le Comité d'Organisation

D. Huet

French advertisements

House/Apartment Sales

Immobilier

Ventes

VDS mais. F4, 3 ch., 100 m^2 env., 2 sdb, cuis. équip., gar., terr. clos, Exclus. Anse Immobilier 04 74 77 01 13

Urgt cède cse mutation F3 tt cft, t. b. état, ch. c. gaz indiv., ds résid. stand., prest. lux., px à déb., libre imméd. Tél.HR 04 72 88 63 29

Part. vd F2 + mezz. ds mais. mitoyenne, c.c. indiv. fuel, gar., jard. privat., quart. calme, 800 000F ferme, libre 1/7/97. Tél. 01 45 27 33 11

100 km nrd Lyon, autoroute Tournus, mais. bressanne, à rénov., 6 p., 350 m^2 habitables, dépendances, pré attenant 3500 m^2 convient pour chevaux, px 300 000 F. S'adres. P.LALOY, not. à Paris 01 45 05 79 88

Sologne, belle propriété XVe, cachet, 50 ha, étgs, bois, poss. chasse, dépend., mais. gard., excel. ét., px intér. Écrire Maisons de France, 18 bd du Roi, 78000 Versailles

Prox. plage, vds Sanary, villa 3/4 pers., 1 ch. + mezz., kitch. équip., ll, lv, park. et jard. privat. 28 U Écr. jrnl réf. 97zx007

A saisir, Villars les Dombes, except. terr. arb., hors lotissement, constructible, 1000m^2, calme, prox. golf. 04 74 83 65 12

Feyzin le Haut, près église, suite incendie, à vdre, épave mais. bourgeoise, 400 m^2 sur 6600 m^2 terr. av. arbres, px 595 000F, T 04 78 15 62 03

à rénov. **(à rénover)** needs modernization
à vdre **(à vendre)** for sale
c.c. **(chauffage central)** central heating (Note: also stands for charges comprises. See under Locations.)
ch. **(chambre)** bedroom
ch. c. **(chauffage central)** central heating
cse mutation **(pour cause de mutation)** because of job transfer
cuis. équip. **(cuisine équipée)** fully fitted kitchen
dépend. **(dépendances)** outbuildings
ds **(dans)** in
écr. **(écrire à)** write to
env. **(environ)** about
étgs **(étangs)** ponds
excel. ét. **(excellent état)** (in) excellent condition
except. **(exceptionnel)** exceptional
exclus. **(exclusivité)** sole agents
F4 **(appartement quatre pièces)** 3-bedroom flat
gar. **(garage)** garage
ha **(hectare)** hectare
HR **(heures des repas)** (at) meal times (between 12 and 2 or between 7 and 9 p.m.)
imméd. **(immédiatement)** (available) immediately
indiv. **(individuel)** individual
jard. privat. **(jardin privatif)** own garden
jrnl **(journal)** newspaper
kitch. équip. **(kitchenette équipée)** fully fitted kitchenette
ll **(lave-linge)** washing machine
lv **(lave-vaisselle)** dishwasher
m^2 **(mètres carrés)** square metres
mais. **(maison)** house
mais. gard. **(maison de gardien)** caretaker's house
mezz. **(mezzanine)** mezzanine floor
not. **(notaire)** notary (lawyer involved in all French property transfers)
nrd **(nord)** north
p. **(pièce)** room
p **(pour)** for
park. **(parking)** parking space
part. **(particulier)** private individual (i.e. not an agency)
pers. **(personnes)** people
poss. chasse **(possibilité de chasser)** hunting possible
prest. lux. **(prestations luxueuses)** luxuriously appointed
prox. **(à proximité de)** close to
px à déb. **(prix à débattre)** price to be discussed
px intér. **(prix intéressant)** attractive (i.e. low) price
quart. **(quartier)** neighbourhood
réf. **(référence)** reference (number)
résid. **(résidence)** apartment complex
s'adres. **(s'adresser à)** contact
sdb **(salle de bains)** bathroom
stand. **(de bon standing)** desirable
t. b. état **(très bon état)** (in) excellent condition
terr. arb. **(terrain arboré)** wooded land
terr. av. arb. **(terrain avec arbres)** wooded land
terr. clos **(terrain clos)** fenced plot
tt cft **(tout confort)** all mod cons
U **(unités)** units (1 unit = 10,000 francs)
urgt **(urgent)** urgent(ly)
vds/vd **(vends)** (I am) selling, for sale
XVe **(quinzième siècle)** 15th century

House/Apartment/Room Lets

Locations

Centr. ville Annecy, loue mais. bourg., 8 p., récept. 45 m2, gar., cave, jard. 300 m2, ch.c. fuel, quartier résid., 13 500F/mens. cc, LARAGENCE 05 56 32 48 79

Part. à part. ag. s'abst., loue F3, 2ch., sdb, ds immeuble centre Villeurbanne, esp. verts, cave, b. état, 2 500F CC, 04 78 92 13 22 p. 249 hor. bur.

Part. loue ch. meublée pour étudiant, 18 m2 dans tb villa quartier univ., calme, av. douche, poss. cuis., prise tél. et TV, entrée séparée, lib. 27 sept., loyer 1 800F cc, tél : 04 78 49 26 76

A LOUER Hte Loire, rég. Chambon sur Lignon, mais. indiv. isolée, terr. expo. Sud, tt conft, 7 pers maxi., juin juillet septembre, mois, sem., quinz. TEL HR 04 71 59 29 33

URG Dir. de Sté rech. appart. F3 à louer, env. Saverne, cuis. équip., balc., park., maxi. 3 500F/mois cc, tél. 03 85 34 37 29

Cadre sup. Sophia Antipolis ch. loc. à l'année, mais. camp. proche Nice, 4/5 pers., calme, esp. verts, même modeste. Tél 04 67 72 63 95

ag. s'abst. (agences s'abstenir) no agencies (i.e. only private individuals should apply)
appart. (appartement) apartment, flat
av. (avec) with
b. état (bon état) good condition
balc. (balcon) balcony
cadre sup. (cadre supérieur) executive
cc, CC (charges comprises) service charges included (in the rent)
centr. ville (centre ville) city centre
ch. (chambre) bedroom
ch.c. (chauffage central) central heating
ch. loc. (cherche une location) seeks rented accommodation
cuis. équip. (cuisine équipée) fully fitted kitchen
Dir. de Sté (directeur de société) company director
ds (dans) in
env. (aux environs de) in the area of, close to
esp. verts (espaces verts) green space (e.g. gardens, parkland)
expo. sud (exposé au sud) south facing
F 3 (trois pièces principales) 2-bedroom apartment
gar. (garage) garage
hor. bur. (horaires de bureau) office hours (between 8 and 12 or between 2 and 5)
HR (heures des repas) meal times (between 12 and 2 or between 7 and 9 p.m.)
Hte Loire (département de la Haute-Loire) the department (administrative district) of the Haute-Loire
jard. (jardin) garden
lib. (libre) free (from a certain date)
m² (mètres carrés) square metres
mais. bourg. (maison bourgeoise) substantial family house (also conveys idea of 'comfortable')
mais. camp. (maison de campagne) house in the country
mais. indiv. (maison individuelle) detached house
maxi (maximum) maximum
mens. (mensuels) per month
p. (pièce) room
p. 249 (poste 249) extension 249
park. (parking) parking space
part. à part (particulier à particulier) private let
pers. (personnes) people
poss. cuis. (possibilité de faire la cuisine) cooking facilities
quartier résid. (quartier résidentiel) residential area
quartier univ. (quartier universitaire) university area
quinz. (quinzaine) fortnight(ly)
récept. (réception) reception room, living room
rech. (recherche) is seeking
rég. (région) region
sdb (salle de bains) bathroom
sem. (semaine) week(ly)
tb (très beau/belle) delightful
tél. (téléphone) telephone
terr. (terrain) garden or land or plot
tt conft (tout confort) all mod cons
URG (urgent) urgent(ly)

House/Apartment holiday exchanges

Échanges vacances

Échange maison ds village Landes, 4/5 pers, sdb, cuis. équip., petit jard., avec maison ou appartement Alpes sud même caract. p. 3 sem. à part du 3 juin 1997. Tél 01 45 20 16 38

VACANCES: éch t b maison Haute-Provence (20 min. Draguignan), 6 pers., contre maison standing équiv. Sussex pour août 1997. Poss. éch. voit. Tél. 01 43 54 09 53

Échange luxueux appt Paris Avenue Foch, 2ch, 2sdb, terrasse ombragée, tv câble, a/c, parking, contre appt similaire centre Londres pour avril mai juin 1998. Tél. 01 45 27 98 12

Éch. bglw tt cft, 4/5 pers, PALAVAS LES FLOTS, contre logt équiv. Bret. sud, 14 juil/15 août. T. HR 02 98 72 41 68

La Ciotat, échange carav. Caravelair 4 pers. empl. ombragé ds camping 3 étoiles, prox. mer, centre com., animations, prise TV, contre standg ident. montagne ou camp. 1ère quinz. juil. Envoy. photo, descript. et propositions au jrnl, réf. EC 182

a/c (air conditionné) air conditioning
à part (à partir de) from (a date)
appt (appartement) flat
bglw (bungalow) holiday chalet
Bret. sud (Bretagne sud) southern Brittany
camp. (campagne) country
caract. (caractéristiques) features
carav. (caravane) caravan
centre com. (centre commercial) shopping centre
ch. (chambre) bedroom
cuis. équip. (cuisine équipée) fully fitted kitchen
descript. (description) description
ds (dans) in
éch. (échange) exchange (offered for)
empl. (emplacement) site (for caravan or tent)
envoy. (envoyer) (please) send
équiv. (équivalent) equivalent
HR (heures des repas) meal times (between 12 and 2 or between 7 and 9 p.m.)
jard. (jardin) garden
jrnl (journal) newspaper
logt équiv. (logement équivalent) equivalent accommodation
min (minutes) minutes
p (pour) for
pers. (personnes) people
poss. (possibilité) possibility
prox. mer (à proximité de la mer) close to the sea
quinz. juil. (quinzaine de juillet) fortnight in July
réf. (référence) reference number
sdb (salle de bains) bathroom
sem. (semaine) week
standg équiv. (standing équivalent) comparable standard (of accommodation, fittings, etc.)
t b (très beau/belle) delightful
tél. (téléphoner) telephone
tt cft (tout confort) all mod cons
tv (télévision) television
voit. (voiture) car

Vehicle Sales

Vente de véhicules, deux-roues, bateaux

VDS Ford Scorpio
11 cv, gris métal., août 94, ttes opts, int. cuir, TBE, 49 000 kms, sous argus, tél. dom. ap. 19 h 03 85 66 24 87

A vdre camping-car Ford ess., ann. 92, 3/4 pers., 120 000 kms, mot. ref. nf, intér. parf. ét., px à déb. Tél. b.05 57 92 13 74

VW Fourg. Diesel
95, DA, ouv s/le côté, 40 000 kms, première main, CENTRAL AUTO St Priest 04 78 21 80 52

Part. vd
Suzuki Dk 650
05/94, 1re m., 5 200 km, accessoires. Tél. 04 72 84 99 87. h.b.

Vélo femme, Peugeot 1/2 course, 10 vitesses, 2 plat., vert métal., t.b.ét., occas. à saisir, 1 500F 01 42 51 36 10 Mme Millard

Vds dériveur 505, coque alu., voiles terg., av. remorque. A voir Port Leucate les w.e. Prendre r.v. 04 67 37 90 21

1ère m. (première main) only one owner
à vdre (à vendre) for sale
alu. (aluminium) aluminium
ann. 92 (année 92) year (of manufacture) 1992
ap. (après) after
av. (avec) with
cv (chevaux) horsepower
D.A. (direction assistée) power steering
ess. (à essence) petrol engine
fourg. (fourgonnette) small van
h.b. (heures de bureau) (in) office hours (i.e. between 8 and 12 or between 2 and 5)
int.cuir. (intérieur en cuir) leather upholstery
métal. (métallisé) metallic
mot. (moteur) engine
occas. (occasion) bargain
ouv. s/le côté (ouvrant sur le côté) side door
parf. ét. (parfait état) in perfect condition
part. (particulier) private sale
pers. (personnes) people
plat. (plateaux) gear wheels
px à déb. (prix à débattre) price to be discussed
ref. nf (refait à neuf) completely reconditioned
r.v. (rendez-vous) appointment
t.b.ét., TBE (très bon état) (in) excellent condition
tél. b. (téléphoner aux heures de bureau) phone in office hours (between 8 and 12 or between 2 and 5)
tél. dom. (téléphoner au domicile) phone home number
terg. (tergal) Terylene
ttes opts (toutes options) all extras
vd, vds (vend, vends) for sale
w.e. (week-end) weekend

Articles for Sale

Ventes: divers

Tr. b. tap. persan, 125 x 230, frangé, fond bleu, impecc. 8 200F, à sais. T. 03 25 43 18 77

Cse dble empl., vds cuisinière mixte, 60 x 60, 4 feux électr., four à gaz, t. b. ét., tél. HR 02 39 50 71 23

Cède frigo Vedette 150 l, freezer 30 l, dim. 60 x 60 x 185, peu servi, intér. impecc., T 05 56 32 41 76

Offr. spéc. à sais., 1 lot de lav. ling. Miele, 5 kg, b. ét. mécan., px 50% nf, à emport. ELECTROMENAGER, 152 rte de Limonest, dim. compris

vds sèch. linge Philips, modèle réc, état nf, 3 000 F, tél 02 32 21 85 91

A vdre aspirat. Hoover traîneau, rouge, silencx, tire-fil, 220 v. tél 03 82 34 15 67

Vds fer à vap. Calor Pressing Plus, jam. servi, tél 05 58 32 14 97

A vdre chaîne hifi, dble K7, CD, 2 ampli. 25W, px à déb. T. 05 59 12 65 34

Suite cess. act. PME cède son outil inf.: ord. Philips P4000, disque mém. 120 millions, 3 écr., 1 impr. P2934/02, 1 log. compta. paie, gest. commerc., tt parf ét., val. ach. 270 000 F, px à déb 04 74 92 36 25 mat

URGT vds canapé 3 pl. + 2 chauff., imit. cuir fauv., parf. état 5 000 F tél 05 59 45 62 71

Cse dpt, cède sal. de jard. plast. blanc, 1 tble rde 6 pers. + chaises, 2 transat. et parasol assort., 3 000 F, tél. ap. 19h 01 27 36 15 89

Cause démgnt, cède 2 paires dble ridx, 235 x 120 cm, coul. crème ; 2 paires voilages ; 1 bac fleur Riviera 1m/25cm. Tél 02 51 36 47 98

125 x 230 (125 sur 230) 125 by 230 (centimetres)
à déb. (à débattre) (price) to be discussed
à emport. (à emporter) for quick sale
à sais. (à saisir) bargain
à vdre (à vendre) for sale
ampli. (amplificateurs) amplifiers
ap. (après) after
aspirat. (aspirateur) vacuum cleaner
assort. (assortis) matching
b. ét. mécan. (bon état mécanique) good mechanical condition, good working order
cess. act. (cessation d'activité) going out of business, closing down
chauff. (chauffeuses) easy chairs (Note: also stands for chauffage)
compta. (comptabilité) accounts
coul. (couleur) colour
cse dble empl. (pour cause de double emploi) surplus to requirements
cse dpt (pour cause de départ) (as) owner leaving, moving house
dble K7 (double cassette) double-cassette deck
dble ridx (doubles rideaux) curtains
démgnt (déménagement) moving house/premises
dim. (dimensions) measurements
dim. comp. (dimanches compris) including Sundays
écr. (écrans) screens, monitors
électr. (électrique) electric
fauv. (fauve) fawn (colour)
frigo (réfrigérateur) fridge
gest. commerc. (gestion commerciale) sales management
imit. (imitation) imitation
impecc. (impeccable) perfect condition, as new
impr. (imprimante) printer
inf. (informatique) computing (equipment)
intér. (intérieur) interior
jam. servi (jamais servi) never used
l (litre) litre
lav. ling. (lave-linge) washing machine
log. (logiciel) software
mat. (matin) (in the) mornings
mém. (mémoire) memory
nf (neuf) new
offr. spéc. (offre spéciale) special offer
ord. (ordinateur) computer
parf. ét. (parfait état) (in) perfect condition
pers. (personnes) people
pl. (places) seats
plast. (plastique) plastic
PME (petite et/ou moyenne entreprise) small and/or medium-sized enterprise/SME
px (prix) price
réc. (récent) recent
rte (route) road
sal. de jard. (salon de jardin) garden furniture
sèch. linge (sèche-linge) tumble dryer
silencx (silencieux) quiet
T. (téléphone) telephone
t. b. ét. (très bon état) very good condition
tap. (tapis) carpet
tble rde (table ronde) circular table
tél. HR (téléphoner aux heures des repas) phone at meal times (i.e. between 12 and 2 or between 7 and 9 p.m.)
transat (transatlantique) deckchair
tr. b. (très beau) very fine
tt (tout) all
urgt (urgent) urgent
v volt
val. ach. (valeur à l'achat) cost when new
vap. (vapeur) steam
vds (vends) for sale
W (watt) watt

Jobs

Emplois

Offre

URG fam. écossaise (avocat) rég. Glasgow, 2 enfts 3/5 ans cherche J.F. au pair, bon anglais, juil-août 97, Ecrire Mme R. Burns 5 Menzies Crescent Fintry Stirlingshire G63 0YL

Ch. f. de mén. 2x4h/sem., a.m. préfér., sér. réf. exig., Tél Mme PIERRAT 01 42 59 17 23

Centre de vac. ch. H à tt faire du 1/7/97 au 31/8/97 pr petits trvx, surveill. enfts, sér. réf. exigées, logé, nourri, blanchi + 3 500F/ms. Ecr. jrnl réf. PLM258

Ch. cple gardiens pr propriété isolée, 250 km sud Paris, petits travx jard., logt indpt, sal. intér., sér. réf. exigées. Se présent., Château du Lac 18100 Vierzon

Pr rempIt cong. mater. PME ch. hot. accueil, pet. secrét., tél., tt txte, CDD 3 mois à part. 15 oct. proch., voit. indispens., ts frs payés, possib. contr. long. dur. Ecr. jrnl PU322

Rech. un/-e trad. spécial. bio-médical ang/alld et alld/ang. pr trad. simult congrès internat. Bruxelles du14/6 au 17/6/97. Pdre cont. Mme Roux en écriv. au jrnal qui transmettra

Entr. TP ch. VRP multic., départ. 42, 74, 01. Envoy. CV + photo + prétent. à BATIDUR 285 cours Lafayette 69100 Villeurbanne

Demande

Jne F., 23 a., diplômée Ec. Sup. Com., bil. Fr/Angl, tt txte, excel. présent. ch. empl. 1/2 tps, accept. déplcts. Ecr. jrnl Réf. OEZ98

J.F. nat. française, 20 ans, aimant enfts, sér. réf., souhaite trouver fam. anglophone, suivi trav. scol. poss., dispon. juil. août 97, écr. journ. ZOL150

Etud. prépa. donne crs anglais français ts niveaux tél: 03 27 42 31 86

1/2 tps (mi-temps) half-time
2x4h/sem. (deux fois quatre heures par semaine) 4 hours twice a week
a. (ans) years (old)
à part. (à partir de) from (date)
accept. déplcts (accepte les déplacements) will travel
angl (anglais) English
alld (allemand) German
a.m. préfér. (l'après-midi de préférence) preferably afternoon
bil. Fr/Angl (bilingue français/anglais) bilingual French/English
CDD (contrat à durée déterminée) fixed-term contract
ch. (cherche) seeks
cong. mater. (congé de maternité) maternity leave
contr. long. dur. (contrat de longue durée) long-term contract
cple (couple) couple
crs (cours) lessons
départ. (départements) departments (French districts)
dispon. (disponible) available
Ec. Sup. Com. (École Supérieure de Commerce) Business School
écr. (écrire à) (please) write to
empl. (emploi) job
en écriv (en écrivant) by writing
enfts (enfants) children
entr. TP (entreprise de travaux publics) civil engineering firm
envoy. (envoyer) (please) send
étud. (étudiant(e)) student
excel. présent. (excellente présentation) very smart appearance
exig. (exigé) required, essential
f. de mén. (femme de ménage) cleaning lady
fam. (famille) family
F/ms (francs par mois) francs per month
H. à tt faire (homme à tout faire) odd-job man
h/sem. (heures par semaine) hours per week
hot. accueil (hôtesse d'accueil) receptionist
indispens. (indispensable) indispensable
internat. (international) international
J.F., Jne F (jeune fille/femme) young woman
jrnl (journal) newspaper
juil. (juillet) July
logt indpt (logement indépendant) separate accommodation
ms (mois) month
nat. (nationalité) nationality
oct. (octobre) October
pdre cont. (prendre contact avec) contact
pet. secrét. (petit secrétariat) some secretarial duties
petits trvx (petits travaux) light (manual) work
PME (petite et/ou moyenne entreprise) small and/or medium-sized enterprise, SME
poss. (possible) possible
possib. (possibilité) possibility
pr (pour) for
prépa. (classe préparatoire) post-baccalaureate class for entry to Grandes Écoles
prétent. (prétentions) salary expectation
proch. (prochain) next
rech. (recherche) seeking
réf. (référence) reference (number)
rég. (région) region
rempIt (remplacement) replacement
sal. intér. (salaire intéressant) attractive salary
se présent. (se présenter) apply in person
sér. réf. (sérieuses références) excellent references
surveill. enfts (surveillance d'enfants) looking after children
tél. (téléphone) telephone
trad. simult. (traduction simultanée) simultaneous translation
trad. spécial. (traducteur/-trice spécialisé/-e) technical translator
trav. scol. (travail scolaire) homework
travx jard. (travaux de jardinage) gardening
ts (tous) all
ts frs payés (tous frais payés) all expenses paid
tt txte (traitement de texte) word processing
URG. (urgent) urgent
vac. (vacances) holidays
voit. (voiture) car
VRP multic. (voyageur représentant placier multicartes) sales representative for several different companies

Using the telephone and the Minitel

Practical information: how to phone

■ **Within Metropolitan France**

Metropolitan France is now divided into five telephone calling zones and all French numbers consist of ten digits (instead of eight digits as until recently). The first two digits correspond to the various zones:

- all numbers for Paris/Île-de-France are prefixed by 01;
- all numbers for the North-West are prefixed by 02;
- all numbers for the North-East as prefixed by 03;
- all numbers for the South-East (including Corsica) are prefixed by 04;
- and finally, all numbers for the South-West are prefixed by 05.

■ **To the overseas departments**

Wait for the dialling tone, dial **0** + the area code + the number (six digits).

■ **To overseas territories and foreign countries**

Wait for the dialling tone, dial **00**. On hearing the new dialling tone, dial the area code (for overseas territories) or the country code plus the number (including area code).

Useful vocabulary

The phone and the calling procedures

décrocher	to pick up the phone
raccrocher	to hang up
le combiné	the receiver, the handset
un numéro de téléphone	a telephone number
un numéro de poste	an extension number
numéroter	to dial the number
composer le numéro	to dial the number
la tonalité	the dialling tone
l'indicatif (téléphonique) d'une ville/ d'un pays	the area/country code
un correspondant	a correspondent
un opérateur	an operator
un téléphone sans fil	a cordless telephone
un téléphone à fréquence vocale	a digital phone, a tone-dialling phone
un répondeur (automatique) (interrogeable à distance)	a telephone answering machine (with remote access)
un bip sonore	a tone (on a recorded message)
une messagerie vocale	a voice mail
un annuaire	a telephone directory
un bottin (colloquial)	a phone book
les pages jaunes	the yellow pages
les pages blanches	the phone book

Useful vocabulary

continued

les numéros d'appel d'urgence (15 for emergency medical assistance, 17 for the Police, 18 for the fire brigade)	the emergency telephone numbers
les numéros d'appel gratuits	toll-free phone numbers
un numéro vert	a Freefone number
un télécopieur	a fax machine
entendre la sonnerie du téléphone	to hear the phone ring
régler la sonnerie du téléphone	to set the volume
c'est occupé/ça sonne occupé	it's engaged/the line is engaged
laisser sonner 3/5/. . . fois	to leave the phone to ring 3/5/. . . times
ça ne répond pas	there's no answer

Useful vocabulary

continued

Common phrases used on the phone

Allô	Hello
Ne quittez pas	Hold the line please
Veuillez patienter	Hold the line please
Je vous le/la passe	I'll put you on to him/her
C'est de la part de qui?	Who's calling please?
Puis-je lui transmettre un message?	May I take a message?
Un instant, je vous prie	One moment, please
Est-ce que je pourrais parler à. . .	May I speak to. . .
Je rappellerai plus tard	I'll call back later
C'est personnel	It's a personal call
Monsieur Hallé est en ligne	Mr Hallé is on the phone
(C'est) Lise à l'appareil	It's Lise (speaking)
Puis-je parler à Claire, s'il vous plaît?	May I speak to Claire please?
C'est moi	Speaking

Useful vocabulary

continued

When you are not at home

une cabine (téléphonique)	a phone booth
un téléphone à pièces	a coin-operated payphone
un Publiphone/téléphone à carte	a cardphone
une Télécarte	a phonecard
un Point-phone	a coin-operated payphone available for public use in restaurants, hotels, etc.
un Publifax	a fax machine available for public use in airports, hotels, etc.
un téléphone de voiture	a car phone
un téléphone portable	a mobile phone
un Bi-Bop	a type of mobile phone (a France Télécom registered design)
un pageur	a pager

Useful vocabulary

continued

Some of the services offered by France Télécom

les dérangements	for registering complaints about a faulty line or faults in the network generally
les renseignements téléphoniques	directory enquiries, directory assistance
être sur liste rouge	to be ex-directory
l'annuaire électronique	electronic directory on Minitel
téléphoner à quelqu'un en pcv	to make a reverse-charge call to somebody or to call somebody collect
la conversation à trois	three-way calling, a service which allows a three-way conversation between the user and two correspondents
le signal d'appel	call waiting, a service which enables the user to put a call on hold in order to take a second call
la facturation détaillée	itemized billing
le transfert d'appel	call diversion, a service which enables the user to redirect her/his calls to another number
le Mémo-appel	the reminder call

Useful vocabulary

continued

The Minitel

un Minitel	a terminal linking phone users to databases
pianoter sur le Minitel	to consult the Minitel
taper (le code, etc.)	to key (the code, etc.)
l'écran	the screen
le clavier	the keyboard
les touches de fonction:	the function keys:
envoi	enter
annulation	cancel
suite	next
répétition	repeat
retour	previous
sommaire	content
correction	delete
guide	help
connexion / fin	connect/exit
3614, 3615, 3616. . .	the numbers for accessing the Minitel services. They are followed by a code, e.g. 3615 code SNCF allows users to access rail information (timetables,etc.).

Practical information: how to use the Minitel

1 Switch on the Minitel.

2 Lift the receiver and wait for the dialling tone.

3 Dial the number (3614, 3615, etc.).

4 Wait for the beep, then press **CONNEXION-FIN**.

5 Now key the access code.

Additional points

- **To return to a previous menu**
  press **RETOUR** or **SOMMAIRE**.

- **If you want to scroll forward or scroll back**
  press **SUITE** to go forward or **RETOUR** to return to a previous screen.

- **If you want to confirm your choice**
  press **ENVOI**. The **GUIDE** key provides assistance should you require any.

- **If you make a mistake**
  use the **CORRECTION** key to erase a character or the **ANNULATION** key to erase a block of keyed text.

On the phone. . .

Remember

In French, telephone numbers are given using double figures
e.g. for 01 34 67 62 12 you say:

zéro-un trente-quatre soixante-sept soixante-deux douze

(zero-one, thirty-four, sixty-seven, sixty-two, twelve).

It's also a good idea to practise spelling words in French, your surname or your first name. Here are some examples:

example 1

« – Interspace, bonjour!

– *Bonjour! Est-ce que je pourrais parler à monsieur Rossi, s'il vous plaît? C'est de la part de mademoiselle Martinez.*

– Ah, je regrette, monsieur Rossi est en réunion actuellement. Puis-je prendre un message?

– *Oui, pourriez-vous lui demander de me rappeler au 01 45 66 74 64.*

– 01 45 66 74 64, mademoiselle Martinez. C'est noté, je le lui dirai.

– *Merci beaucoup, au revoir.*

– Au revoir, mademoiselle.»

example 2

« – Renseignements, bonjour!

– *Bonjour monsieur, je cherche à obtenir le numéro de mademoiselle Salathé à Nanterre.*

– Vous pouvez m'épeler le nom de votre correspondant, s'il vous plaît?

– *Salathé, s.a.l.a.t.h.e accent aigu.*

– Vous connaissez son adresse exacte?

– *Oui, 3 rue Guy Môquet.*

– Ne quittez pas, je traite votre demande.

– . . .

– Allô? Je suis désolé, mademoiselle Salathé est sur liste rouge, je ne peux pas vous communiquer son numéro.

– *Merci quand même, au revoir.*

– Au revoir, madame.»

On the phone. . .
continued

example 3

« – Allô?

– *Allô, Hervé?*

– Non, c'est son père.

– *Oh, excusez-moi, monsieur, c'est Jean à l'appareil, est-ce qu'Hervé est là?*

– Oui, il vient de rentrer. Ne quitte pas, je l'appelle. . .»

example 4

« – Bonjour, vous êtes bien au 05 56 78 02 72. Nous ne sommes pas là pour l'instant mais laissez-nous un message après le bip sonore et nous vous rappellerons dès notre retour!

– . . . *Bip!. . .*

– Bonjour, c'est Michel, je voulais juste savoir si ça vous disait d'aller au cinéma ce soir. Rappelez-moi si vous ne rentrez pas trop tard. Sinon à plus tard. Salut!»

example 5

« – Allô?

– *Allô, bonjour madame!*

– Bonjour!

– *Pourrais-je parler à monsieur Pilard, s'il vous plaît?*

– Oui, c'est de la part de qui?

– *Mademoiselle Pierquin.*

– Je suis désolée, la ligne de monsieur Pilard est occupée, vous patientez?

– *Oui, oui.*

– . . .

– . . .

– Allô, monsieur Pilard est toujours en ligne. Je peux peut-être vous renseigner. C'est à quel sujet?

– *C'est personnel. Mais ce n'est pas urgent, je rappellerai plus tard. Merci.*

– De rien, au revoir mademoiselle!

– *Au revoir!*»

On the phone. . .
continued

example 6

« – Allô?

– *Allô, bonsoir! Je suis bien chez Monsieur et Madame Roux?*

– Oui.

– *Est-ce que je pourrais parler à madame Roux, s'il vous plaît?*

– Ah, je suis désolé, ma femme est sortie, je peux prendre un message?

– *Oui, s'il vous plaît, je suis Annie Alpardin, une de ses collègues. Je voulais juste lui dire que j'ai trouvé son agenda dans le couloir en sortant du bureau. Je ne voulais pas qu'elle le cherche.*

– C'est très aimable de votre part, je le lui dirai dès qu'elle rentrera.

– *Merci, au revoir monsieur.*

– Au revoir.»

Prefixes for the new 10-digit numbers

Paris/Île-de-France

New prefix to add	In front of number starting with	New prefix to add	In front of number starting with	New prefix to add	In front of number starting with
01	30	01	43	01	49
01	34	01	44	01	53
01	39	01	45	01	55
01	40	01	46	01	60
01	41	01	47	01	64
01	42	01	48	01	69

Province

New prefix to add	In front of number starting with	New prefix to add	In front of number starting with	New prefix to add	In front of number starting with
03	20	02	48	04	76
03	21	05	49	04	77
03	22	04	50	04	78
03	23	02	51	04	79
03	24	05	53	03	80
03	25	02	54	03	81
03	26	05	55	03	82
03	27	05	56	03	83
03	28	05	57	03	84
03	29	05	58	03	85
02	31	05	59	03	86
02	32	03	60	03	87
02	33	05	61	03	88
05	34	05	62	03	89
02	35	05	63	04	90
02	37	05	65	04	91
02	38	04	66	04	92
02	39	04	67	04	93
02	40	04	68	04	94
02	41	04	69	04	95
04	42	04	70	02	96
02	43	04	71	02	97
03	44	04	72	02	98
05	45	04	73	02	99
05	46	04	74		
02	47	04	75		

Overseas departments

Departments	10-digit numbers
Guadeloupe	0590 + 6-digit number
Guyana	0594 + 6-digit number
Martinique	0596 + 6-digit number
Reunion	0262 + 6-digit number
St Pierre and Miquelon	0508 + 6-digit number
Mayotte	0269 + 6-digit number

Overseas territories

New Caledonia	00 687
French Polynesia	00 689
Wallis and Futuna Islands	00 681

Sending an E-mail

Fichier	Edition	Vue	Texte	Message	Rattacher	Agent	Outil	Fenêtre

Adresse: fta.fiba.cc-mail.compuserve.fr
Pour: tous
c.c.:
accusé [ ]
Date: Mer 21/08/96
Heure: 15:56:27
Emission: [✓] normale [ ] basse [ ] haute
Objet: places de théâtre

Nouveau
Adresser
Envoyer
Renvoyer
Enregistrer projet
Répondre
Faire suivre
Supprimer
Message suivant
Message précédent
Supprimer suivant
Supprimer précédent
Afficher pièces jointes
Lancer pièces jointes
Renommer pièces jointes

Message interne: avis à tous! Je vends deux places de théâtre pour "La Double Inconstance" de Marivaux à la Comédie française le 30/11/96 à 20h. Prix des places: 150 francs. Si vous êtes intéressés, contactez-moi par courrier électronique (adresse: sménard@fiba.cc-mail.compuserve.fr) ou par téléphone au poste 4512.
Serge

cliquer sur «message»—clicking on "mail"

nouveau	new	message suivant	next
adresser	address	message précédent	next
envoyer	send	supprimer message suivant	delete next
renvoyer	send again	supprimer message précédent	delete previous
enregistrer projet	save new mail	afficher pièces jointes	read attachments
répondre	answer	lancer pièces jointes	attach
faire suivre	forward	renommer pièces jointes	rename attachments
supprimer	delete		

Receiving an E-mail

Fichier Edition Vue Texte Message Rattacher Agent Outil Fenêtre

Auteur: Claire Desforges (cdesforg@cyrius.CHUcréteil.fr)
Date: 24/09/96
Heure: 11:36:12
Taille du message: 295 caractères
c.c.: Sandrine Dupont
Objet: Fiche technique centrifugeuse CJ-5464

J'accuse bonne réception de la centrifugeuse modèle CJ-5464. Je constate toutefois l'absence de la fiche technique correspondante. Merci de bien vouloir me la faire parvenir de toute urgence par fax ou par modem.
C. Desforges, Responsable du matériel de recherche et d'examen, C.H.U. de Créteil.

un message électronique/ un E-mail	an E-mail
envoyer un E-mail	to send an E-mail
recevoir un E-mail	to get an E-mail
courrier arrivée	incoming mail
nouveau message	new mail
message non lu	unread message
message envoyé	message sent
objet	subject
c.c. (copie à):	c.c. (carbon copy)
accusé de réception	acknowledgement of receipt
une adresse électronique	an E-mail address
émission: normale/basse/haute	definition: normal/low/high
une boîte de dialogue	a dialog box
une feuille de message	a message window
imprimer	to print
enregistrer	to save
quitter	to exit
activé/désactivé	active/passive
ajouter des pièces jointes	to attach a document
lire un menu:	to read a menu:
fichier	file
édition	edit
vue	view
texte	text
message	mail
rattacher	attach
agent	user
outils	tools
fenêtre	window
aide	help
modifier une fenêtre:	to modify a window:
restauration	restore
déplacement	move
dimension	size
réduction	reduce
agrandissement	enlarge
fermeture	close
suivant	next

Dictionnaire anglais–français

English–French dictionary

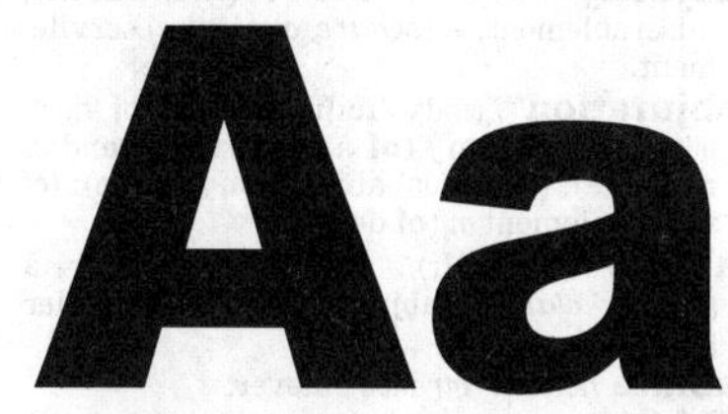

a[1], **A** /eɪ/ **n 1** (letter) a, A *m*; **from A to Z** de A à Z; **the A to Z of cooking** la cuisine de A à Z; **2 A** Mus la *m*; **3 A** (place) **how to get from A to B** comment se rendre d'un endroit à un autre; **4 a** (in house number) **47a** cf 47 bis; **5 A** GB Transp **on the A7** sur la route A7.

a[2] /eɪ, ə/ (*avant voyelle ou 'h' muet* **an** /æn, ən/) *det* un/une; ▶ **few**, **little**[1], **lot**[1], **many**.

A-1 /eɪ/†○ *adj* formidable.

AA *n* **1** GB Aut (*abrév* = **Automobile Association**) organisme *m* d'assistance pour les automobilistes; **2** *abrév* ▶ **Alcoholics Anonymous**; **3** US Univ (*abrév* = **Associate in Arts**) diplôme *m* universitaire de lettres (*de 2 ans*).

AAA *n* **1** GB (*abrév* = **Amateur Athletics Association**) *fédération d'athlétisme britannique*; **2** US Aut (*abrév* = **American Automobile Association**) association *f* américaine des automobilistes.

Aachen /ˈɑːkən/ ▶ **1818** *pr n* Aix-la-Chapelle.

AAM *n* Mil (*abrév* = **air-to-air missile**) missile *m* air-air.

Aargau ▶ **1776** *pr n* **the canton of ~** le canton d'Argovie.

AAUP *n* US (*abrév* = **American Association of University Professors**) association *f* américaine des enseignants d'université.

AB *n* **1** Naut (*abrév* = **able-bodied seaman**) matelot *m* de deuxième classe; **2** US Univ (*abrév* = **Bachelor of Arts**) diplôme *m* universitaire de lettres et sciences humaines.

ABA *n* GB (*abrév* = **Amateur Boxing Association**) fédération *f* de boxe britannique.

aback /əˈbæk/ *adv* **to be taken ~ by** être déconcerté par [*remark, proposal, experience*]; **I was somewhat/totally taken ~** j'étais un peu déconcerté/complètement abasourdi.

abacus /ˈæbəkəs/ *n* (*pl* **-cuses**) **1** (counting frame) boulier *m*; **2** Archit abaque *m*.

abaft /əˈbɑːft, US əˈbæft/ **I** *adv* sur l'arrière.
II *prep* sur l'arrière de.

abalone /ˌæbəˈləʊnɪ/ *n* ormeau *m*.

abandon /əˈbændən/ **I** *n* abandon *m*; **with gay ~** avec une belle désinvolture.
II *vtr* abandonner, délaisser [*person*]; abandonner [*animal, car, hope, game, plan, trial, town*] (**to** à); renoncer à [*activity, claim, prosecution, idea*]; arrêter [*strike*]; **to ~ the attempt to do** renoncer à faire; **~ ship!** abandonnez le navire!; **to ~ play** Sport interrompre la partie.
III *v refl* **to ~ oneself** s'abandonner (**to** à).

abandoned /əˈbændənd/ *adj* **1** [*person, animal, place*] abandonné; **2** (licentious) [*behaviour*] dévergondé; **3** (wild) [*dance, music*] frénétique.

abandonment /əˈbændənmənt/ *n* gen abandon *m*; (of strike) arrêt *m*.

abase /əˈbeɪs/ *v refl* sout **to ~ oneself** s'abaisser (**before** devant).

abasement /əˈbeɪsmənt/ *n* avilissement *m*; **self-~** abaissement *m* de soi.

abashed /əˈbæʃt/ *adj* décontenancé (**at** à; **by** par).

abate /əˈbeɪt/ **I** *vtr* sout **1** gen diminuer [*noise, pollution*]; **2** Jur (end) **to ~ a nuisance** supprimer un abus; **3** Jur (cancel) remettre [*writ, sentence*].
II *vi* [*flood, wind, fever*] baisser; [*storm, rage, shock*] diminuer.

abatement /əˈbeɪtmənt/ *n* (of storm, wind) apaisement *m*; (of fever, noise) diminution *f*; (of feelings) apaisement *m*.

abattoir /ˈæbətwɑː(r), US ˌæbəˈtwɑːr/ *n* GB abattoir *m*.

abbess /ˈæbes/ *n* abbesse *f*.

abbey /ˈæbɪ/ *n* abbaye *f*.

abbot /ˈæbət/ *n* (père *m*) abbé *m*.

abbreviate /əˈbriːvɪeɪt/ *vtr* abréger (**to** en).

abbreviation /əˌbriːvɪˈeɪʃn/ *n* **1** (short form) abréviation *f*; **2** (process) raccourcissement *m*.

ABC *n* **1** (alphabet) alphabet *m*; **2** (basics) **the ~ of** l'abc or le b.a. ba de [*cooking, photography etc*]; **3** US TV (*abrév* = **American Broadcasting Company**) *l'une des quatre grandes chaînes de télévision américaines*.
IDIOMS **as easy as ~** simple comme bonjour.

ABD *n* US Univ (*abrév* = **all but dissertation**) *étudiant ayant réussi les unités obligatoires de doctorat mais n'ayant pas encore présenté sa thèse*.

abdicate /ˈæbdɪkeɪt/ **I** *vtr* renoncer à [*power, right*]; abdiquer [*responsibility*]; **to ~ the throne** abdiquer (la couronne).
II *vi* abdiquer.

abdication /ˌæbdɪˈkeɪʃn/ *n* (royal) abdication *f*; (of responsibility) renonciation *f* (**of** à).

abdomen /ˈæbdəmən/ *n* abdomen *m*.

abdominal /æbˈdɒmɪnl/ *adj* abdominal.

abduct /əbˈdʌkt/ *vtr* enlever.

abduction /əbˈdʌkʃn/ *n* **1** (of person) enlèvement *m*; **2** (of muscles) abduction *f*.

abductor /əbˈdʌktə(r)/ *n* **1** (kidnapper) ravisseur/-euse *m/f*; **2** (also **~ muscle**) (muscle *m*) abducteur *m*.

abed† /əˈbed/ *adj* **to be ~** être couché; **to lie ~** rester couché.

Abel /ˈeɪbl/ *pr n* Abel.

Aberdonian /ˌæbəˈdəʊnɪən/ **I** *n* (native) natif/-ive *m/f* d'Aberdeen; (inhabitant) habitant/-e *m/f* d'Aberdeen.
II *adj* d'Aberdeen.

aberrant /əˈberənt/ *adj* [*behaviour, nature*] aberrant; [*result*] anormal.

aberration /ˌæbəˈreɪʃn/ *n* **1** (deviation) aberration *f*; **2** (lapse) égarement *m*; **in a moment of ~** dans un moment d'égarement.

abet /əˈbet/ *vtr* (*p prés etc* **-tt-**) être complice de [*lawbreaker, crime*]; **to aid and ~ sb in doing sth** être complice de qn pour faire qch; **to be accused of aiding and ~ting** être accusé de complicité.

abetter, **abettor** /əˈbetə(r)/ *n* complice *mf*.

abeyance /əˈbeɪəns/ *n* sout **in ~** [*matter, situation*] en suspens; [*law*] inappliqué; **to fall into ~** tomber en désuétude; **to hold sth in ~** garder qch vacant.

> **a²**
>
> The determiner or indefinite article *a* or *an* is translated by *un* + *masculine noun* and by *une* + *feminine noun*:
>
> *a tree* = un arbre
> *a chair* = une chaise
>
> There are, however, some cases where the article is not translated:
> with professions and trades:
>
> *her mother is a teacher* = sa mère est professeur
>
> with other nouns used in apposition:
>
> *he's a widower* = il est veuf
>
> with *what a*:
>
> *what a pretty house* = quelle jolie maison
>
> For translations of *a few, a little, a lot, a great many* see the entries ***few***, ***little***, ***lot***, ***many***.
>
> When expressing prices in relation to weight, the definite article *le/la* is used in French:
>
> *ten francs a kilo* = dix francs le kilo
>
> In other expressions where *a/an* means *per* the French translation is usually *par*:
>
> *50 kilometres an hour* = 50 kilomètres par heure
> *twice a day* = deux fois par jour
>
> For translations of all other expressions using the indefinite article such as *to make a noise*, *to make a fortune*, *at a blow* etc. consult the appropriate noun entry (***noise***, ***fortune***, ***blow*** etc.).

abhor /əbˈhɔː(r)/ *vtr* (*p prés etc* **-rr-**) abhorrer [*violence, injustice*]; exécrer [*person, opinion, task*].
IDIOMS **nature ~s a vacuum** la nature a horreur du vide.

abhorrence /əbˈhɒrəns, US -ˈhɔːr-/ *n* horreur *f*; **to have an ~ of** avoir horreur de; **to hold sth in ~** avoir qch en horreur.

abhorrent /əbˈhɒrənt, US -ˈhɔːr-/ *adj* odieux/-ieuse; **to be ~ to sb** être intolérable à qn.

abide /əˈbaɪd/ (*prét, pp* **abode** ou **~d**) **I** *vtr* **I can't ~ sth/doing** je ne peux pas supporter qch/de faire.
II *vi* **to ~ by** respecter [*rule, decision*]; maintenir [*statement*].

abiding /əˈbaɪdɪŋ/ *adj* [*image, memory*] qui persiste (*after n*); [*love*] durable.

ability /əˈbɪlətɪ/ **I** *n* **1** (capability) capacité *f* (**to do** de faire); (**the**) **~ to pay** Jur la solvabilité; Tax la faculté contributive; **to the best of one's ~** de son mieux; **within the limits of one's ~** [*contribute*] dans la mesure de ses moyens; **2** (talent) talent *m*; **someone of proven ~** quelqu'un au talent reconnu; **his ~ as** son talent de.
II abilities *npl* (skills) compétences *fpl*; Sch (of pupils) aptitudes *fpl*; **mental abilities** compétences intellectuelles; **musical abilities** talents musicaux.

abject /ˈæbdʒekt/ *adj* **1** [*state, conditions*] misérable; [*failure*] lamentable; **~ poverty**

misère *f*; **2** [*slave, coward*] abject; [*apology*] servile.

abjectly /ˈæbʒektlɪ/ *adv* **1** [*live, subsist*] misérablement; **2** [*behave, apologize*] servilement.

abjuration /ˌæbdʒʊˈreɪʃn/ *n* sout (of right, title) renonciation *f* (**of** à); (of claim) abandon *m* (**of** de); (of religion) abjuration *f* (**of** de); (of vice) reniement *m* (**of** de).

abjure /əbˈdʒʊə(r)/ *vtr* sout renoncer à [*rights, claims*]; abjurer [*religion*]; renier [*vice*].

ablate /æbˈleɪt/ *vtr* Med enlever.

ablation /æbˈleɪʃn/ *n* Med ablation *f*.

ablative /ˈæblətɪv/ **I** *n* ablatif *m*; **in the ~** à l'ablatif; **~ absolute** ablatif absolu.
II *adj* ablatif/-ive.

ablaze /əˈbleɪz/ *adj* **1** (alight) [*building, town*] en feu, en flammes; **to set sth ~** enflammer qch; **2** (lit up) lit, fig **to be ~ with** être illuminé de [*candles, lights, fireworks*]; être enflammé de [*rage, excitement*].

able /ˈeɪbl/ *adj*

■ **Note** *to be able to* meaning *can* is usually translated by the verb *pouvoir*: *I was not able to go* = je ne pouvais pas y aller; *I was not able to help him* = je ne pouvais pas l'aider. The main exception to this occurs when *to be able to* implies the acquiring of a skill, when *savoir* is used: *he's nine and he's still not able to read* = il a neuf ans et il ne sait toujours pas lire.
– For more examples and other uses, see the entry below.

1 (having ability to) **to be ~ to do/be** pouvoir faire/être; **he was/wasn't ~ to read it** il pouvait/ne pouvait pas le lire; **she was ~ to play the piano at the age of four** elle savait jouer du piano à quatre ans; **I'll be (better) ~ to give you more information after the meeting** je serai en mesure de or je pourrai vous donner plus de renseignements après la réunion; **2** (skilled) [*lawyer, teacher etc*] compétent; (gifted) [*child*] doué.

able: **~-bodied** *adj* robuste, fort; **~ rating** *n* matelot *m* breveté; **~ seaman** *n* (also **~-bodied seaman**) matelot *m* de deuxième classe.

ablutions /əˈbluːʃnz/ *npl* sout ablutions *fpl*; **to perform one's ~** faire ses ablutions.

ably /ˈeɪblɪ/ *adv* [*work, write*] avec compétence; **~ assisted by his colleagues** secondé par des collègues compétents.

ABM *n* Mil (*abrév* = **anti-ballistic missile**) missile *m* antimissile.

abnegate /ˈæbnɪgeɪt/ *vtr* renoncer à [*rights, privileges, pleasures*].

abnegation /ˌæbnɪˈgeɪʃn/ *n* sout **1** (of rights, privileges, pleasures) renoncement *m* (**of** à); **2** (also **self-~**) renoncement *m*, abnégation *f*.

abnormal /æbˈnɔːml/ *adj* anormal also Comput.

abnormality /ˌæbnɔːˈmælətɪ/ *n* **1** (feature) anomalie *f*; **2** (state) anormalité *f*.

abnormally /æbˈnɔːməlɪ/ *adv* [*high, low, slow, difficult*] anormalement; [*behave, react, develop*] de façon anormale.

abo /ˈæbəʊ/ *n* Austral injur aborigène *mf* (d'Australie).

aboard /əˈbɔːd/ **I** *adv* **1** gen [*take, live*] à bord; **to go** ou **climb ~** monter à bord; **all ~!** Naut tout le monde à bord!; Rail, Transp en voiture!; **2** Naut bord à bord.
II *prep* à bord de [*ship, plane*]; dans [*coach, train*]; **~ ship** à bord.

abode /əˈbəʊd/ *n* **1** (home) sout demeure *f*; **my humble ~** hum mon humble demeure; **X, of no fixed ~** sout X, sans domicile fixe; **2** Jur (residence) **his place of ~** son domicile; **the right of ~** le droit de résidence.

abolish /əˈbɒlɪʃ/ *vtr* abolir [*law, right, tax, penalty*]; supprimer [*subsidy, service, allowance*].

abolition /ˌæbəˈlɪʃn/ *n* (of law, right, tax, penalty) abolition *f*; (of subsidy, service, allowance) suppression *f*.

abolitionist /ˌæbəˈlɪʃənɪst/ *n* abolitionniste *mf* also US Hist.

abominable /əˈbɒmɪnəbl/ *adj* [*crime, practice, system, conditions*] abominable; [*food, weather, behaviour*] abominable, détestable; **the ~ snowman** l'abominable homme des neiges.

abominably /əˈbɒmɪnəblɪ/ *adv* [*treat, behave*] de manière odieuse; [*play, perform*] de manière abominable; [*rude, arrogant*] abominablement; [*hot, cold*] horriblement.

abominate /əˈbɒmɪneɪt, US -mən-/ *vtr* exécrer [*hypocrisy, terrorism*]; hum détester [*homework, vegetables*].

abomination /əˌbɒmɪˈneɪʃn, US -mən-/ *n* **1** (loathing) horreur *f* (**of** de); **2** (object) abomination *f*; **what an ~!** quelle abomination!

aboriginal /ˌæbəˈrɪdʒənl/ **I** *n* (native) indigène *mf*.
II *adj* [*inhabitant, plant, species*] aborigène.

Aboriginal /ˌæbəˈrɪdʒənl/ *n, adj* aborigène (*mf*) (d'Australie).

aborigine /ˌæbəˈrɪdʒənɪ/ *n* aborigène *mf*.

Aborigine /ˌæbəˈrɪdʒənɪ/ *n* aborigène *mf* (d'Australie).

abort /əˈbɔːt/ **I** *n* US abandon *m*.
II *vtr* **1** (terminate) faire avorter [*fœtus, pregnancy, mother*]; **2** (interrupt) interrompre [*mission, launch, plan, trial*]; **3** Comput (abandon) abandonner [*program, operation*].
III *vi* **1** [*mother, embryo, animal*] avorter; **2** [*plan, launch, mission, attack*] échouer; **3** Comput [*program*] s'arrêter.

abortifacient /əˌbɔːtɪˈfeɪʃənt/ *adj* abortif/-ive.

abortion /əˈbɔːʃn/ **I** *n* **1** (termination) avortement *m*; **back-street ~** avortement clandestin; **to perform** ou **carry out an ~ on sb** pratiquer un avortement sur qn; **~ on demand**, **~ on request** l'avortement libre; **to have an ~** se faire avorter; **2** (monstrosity) horreur *f*.
II *modif* [*law, debate*] sur l'avortement; [*rights*] à l'avortement; [*pill*] abortif/-ive.

abortionist /əˈbɔːʃənɪst/ *n* avorteur/-euse *m/f*; **back-street ~** avorteur/-euse *m/f* clandestin/-e, faiseuse *f* d'anges.

abortive /əˈbɔːtɪv/ *adj* **1** (unsuccessful) (*épith*) [*attempt, scheme, project*] avorté; [*coup, raid, attack*] manqué; **2** Med abortif/-ive.

abound /əˈbaʊnd/ *vi* abonder (**in, with** en).

about /əˈbaʊt/

■ **Note** *about* is used after certain nouns, adjectives and verbs in English (*information about, a book about, curious about, worry about etc*). For translations, consult the appropriate entries (***information***, ***book***, ***curious***, ***worry*** etc).
– *about* often appears in British English as the second element of certain verb structures (*move about, rummage about, lie about etc*). For translations, consult the relevant verb entries (***move***, ***rummage***, ***lie*** etc).

I *adj* **1** (expressing future intention) **to be ~ to do** être sur le point de faire; **2** (rejecting course of action) **I'm not ~ to do** je ne suis pas près de faire; **3** (awake) debout; **you were (up and) ~ early this morning** tu étais debout tôt ce matin.
II *adv* **1** (approximately) environ, à peu près; **it's ~ the same as yesterday** c'est à peu près pareil qu'hier; **at ~ 6 pm** à environ 18 h; **it's ~ as useful as an umbrella in a hurricane** iron c'est aussi utile qu'un parapluie dans un ouragan; ▶**round**; **2** (almost) presque; **to be (just) ~ ready** être presque prêt; **that seems ~ right** ça a l'air d'aller, ça devrait aller; **I've had just ~ enough of her!** j'en ai plus qu'assez d'elle!; **I've had ~ as much as I can take!** j'en ai plus qu'assez!; ▶**just**; **3** (in circulation) **there was no-one ~** il n'y avait personne; **there are few people ~** il y a peu de gens dans les parages; **there is a lot of food poisoning ~** il y a beaucoup d'intoxications alimentaires en ce moment, les intoxications alimentaires ne manquent pas en ce moment; **there's a lot of it ~** ça ne manque pas; **4** (in the vicinity) **to be somewhere ~** être dans les parages; **she must be somewhere ~** elle doit être dans les parages, elle doit être quelque part par là; **5** (indicating reverse position) **the other way ~** l'inverse, le contraire; ▶**put about**, **turn about**.
III *prep* **1** (concerning, regarding) **a book/film ~ sb/sth** un livre/film sur qn/qch; **to talk ~** parler de [*problem, subject*]; **what's it ~?** (of book, film etc) ça parle de quoi?; **it's ~...** il s'agit de...; **may I ask what it's ~?** pourriez-vous me dire de quoi il s'agit?; **I'm ringing ~ my results** j'appelle pour mes résultats; **it's ~ my son's report** c'est au sujet du bulletin scolaire de mon fils; **~ your overdraft**... pour ce qui est de votre découvert...; **2** (in the nature of) **there's something weird/sad ~ him** il a quelque chose de bizarre/triste; **there's something ~ the place that intrigues me** l'endroit a quelque chose qui me fascine; **what I like ~ her is** ce que j'aime chez elle c'est; **3** (bound up with) **business is ~ profit** ce qui compte dans les affaires, ce sont les bénéfices; **teaching is all ~ communication** enseigner, c'est communiquer; **that's what life is all ~** c'est la vie; **4** (occupied with) **to know what one is ~** savoir ce qu'on fait; **mind what you're ~!** GB fais attention or fais gaffe○ à ce que tu fais!; **while you're ~ it**... tant que tu y es..., par la même occasion...; **and be quick ~ it!** et fais vite!; **5** (around) **to wander/run ~ the streets** errer/courir dans les rues; **strewn ~ the floor** éparpillés sur le sol; **6** (in invitations, suggestions) **how** ou **what ~ some tea?** et si on prenait un thé?; **how ~ going into town?** et si on allait en ville?; **how ~ it?**, **how ~ you?** ça te or vous dit?; **7** (when soliciting opinions) **what ~ the transport** GB ou **transportation** US **costs?** et les frais de transport?; **what ~ us?** et nous alors?; **'what ~ the dinner?'—'what ~ it?'** 'et le repas alors?'—'quoi, le repas?'; **what ~ you?** et toi?; **what ~ Natasha?** et Natasha?; **how ~ it?** qu'est-ce que tu en penses?; **8** sout (on) **hidden ~ one's person** [*drugs, arms*] caché sur soi; ▶**wit**; **9** GB (surrounding) autour de; **there were trees ~ the house** il y avait des arbres autour de la maison.
IDIOMS **it's ~ time (that)** il serait temps que (+ *subj*); **~ time too!** il était temps!, ce n'est pas trop tôt○!; **that's ~ it** (that's all) c'est tout; (that's the situation) en gros, oui, c'est à peu près ça.

about-face, **about-turn** *n* GB Mil demi-tour *m*; fig volte-face *f inv*; **the government has done an ~** le gouvernement a fait volte-face.

above /əˈbʌv/ **I** *pron* **the ~** (person) le susdit/la susdite *m/f*; **the ~ are all witnesses** les personnes susnommées sont toutes témoins; **the ~ are all stolen vehicles** les véhicules susmentionnés sont tous volés.
II *prep* **1** (vertically higher) au-dessus de; **to live ~ a shop** habiter au-dessus d'une boutique; **your name is ~ mine on the list** ton nom est au-dessus du mien sur la liste; **the hills ~ Monte Carlo** les collines qui surplombent Monte-Carlo; **2** (north of) au nord de; **~ this latitude** au nord de cette latitude; **3** (upstream of) en amont de; **4** (morally) **she's ~ such petty behaviour** elle n'est pas capable d'un comportement aussi mesquin; **they're not ~ cheating/lying** ils sont tout à fait capables de tricher/de mentir; **he's not ~ lending us a hand** il n'hésitera pas à nous aider; **5** (in preference to) par-dessus; **to admire sth ~ all others** admirer qch par-dessus tout; **~ all else** par-dessus tout; **to value happiness ~ wealth** accorder plus d'importance au bonheur qu'à l'argent; **6** (superior in status, rank) au-dessus de; **a general is ~ a corporal** un général

est au-dessus d'un caporal; **to be ~ sb in the world rankings** être mieux placé que qn au classement mondial; **he thinks he's ~ us** il se croit supérieur à nous; **7** (greater than) au-dessus de; **~ average** au-dessus de la moyenne; **~ the limit** au-dessus de la limite; **children ~ the age of 12** les enfants âgés de plus de 12 ans; **to rise ~** dépasser [*amount, percentage, limit, average*]; ▶ **over**[1]; **8** (transcending, beyond) **~ suspicion** au-dessus de tout soupçon; **she's ~ criticism** on ne peut pas la critiquer; **~ reproach** irréprochable; **9** (too difficult for) **to be ~ sb** [*subject, book*] dépasser qn; **10** (higher in pitch) au-dessus de; **11** (over) **I couldn't hear him ~ the sound of the drill** je ne pouvais pas l'entendre à cause du bruit de la perceuse; **a shot was heard ~ the shouting** on a entendu un coup de feu par-dessus les cris.

III *adj* **the ~ names/items** les noms/articles susmentionnés fml or figurant ci-dessus.

IV *adv* **1** (higher up) **a desk with a shelf ~** un bureau avec une étagère au-dessus; **the noise from the apartment ~** le bruit qui vient de l'appartement d'au-dessus; **the view from ~** la vue d'en haut; **an order from ~** un ordre qui vient d'en haut; **ideas imposed from ~** des idées imposées d'en haut; **2** (earlier in the text) **see ~** voir ci-dessus; **as stated ~** comme indiqué ci-dessus; **3** (more) **children of 12 and ~** les enfants âgés de 12 ans et plus; **tickets at £10 and ~** des billets à partir de dix livres; **those on incomes of £18,000 and ~** ceux dont les revenus atteignent ou dépassent 18000 livres sterling; **4** (in the sky) **the sky up ~ was clear** le ciel était dégagé; **to look up at the stars ~** lever les yeux vers les étoiles; **the powers ~** les puissances célestes; **in Heaven ~** aux cieux; ▶ **cut**.

V above all *adv phr* surtout.

IDIOMS **to get ~ oneself** ne plus se sentir○.

above: **~board** *adj* régulier/-ière, correct; **~ground** *adv* au-dessus du sol, à la surface; **~-mentioned** *adj* susmentionné fml; **~-named** *adj* susnommé.

abracadabra /ˌæbrəkəˈdæbrə/ *excl* abracadabra!

abrade /əˈbreɪd/ *vtr* **1** Geol [*element*] éroder [*rock*]; **2** Tech [*sandpaper*] abraser [*wood, surface*].

abrasion /əˈbreɪʒn/ *n* **1** (on skin) écorchure *f*; **2** (from friction) (of rock) abrasion *f*; (of paint, metal) usure *f*.

abrasive /əˈbreɪsɪv/ **I** *n* abrasif *m*.

II *adj* **1** (trait) [*person, manner, style, tone*] mordant; **2** (substance) abrasif/-ive.

abrasively /əˈbreɪsɪvlɪ/ *adv* [*say, reply, write*] de façon mordante.

abrasiveness /əˈbreɪsɪvnɪs/ *n* (of remark, criticism, tone) rudesse *f*.

abreaction /ˌæbrɪˈækʃn/ *n* Psych abréaction *f*.

abreast /əˈbrest/ *adv* **1** (side by side) de front; **cycling three ~** pédalant à trois de front; **in line ~** en ligne de front; **to be/come ~ of** [*vehicle, person*] être/venir à la hauteur de; **2** (in touch with) **to keep/to keep sb ~ of** [*developments, current affairs*] se tenir/tenir qn au courant de; **to keep ~ of the times** marcher avec son temps.

abridge /əˈbrɪdʒ/ *vtr* abréger.

abridg(e)ment /əˈbrɪdʒmənt/ *n* **1** (version) version *f* abrégée; **2** (process) abrègement *m*.

abroad /əˈbrɔːd/ *adv* **1** [*be, go, live, work, travel*] à l'étranger; **imported from ~** importé de l'étranger; **news from home and ~** des nouvelles nationales et internationales; **2** (in circulation) **there is a rumour ~ that...** le bruit court selon lequel...; **there is a new spirit ~** il y a un nouvel état d'esprit général; **there is a feeling ~ that...** le sentiment général est que...; **3**† (outside) dehors.

abrogate /ˈæbrəgeɪt/ *vtr* sout abroger.

abrogation /ˌæbrəˈgeɪʃn/ *n* sout abrogation *f*.

abrupt /əˈbrʌpt/ *adj* **1** (sudden) [*end, change etc*] brusque; **to come to an ~ end** se terminer brusquement; **2** (curt) [*manner, person, tone, remark*] brusque; **3** (disjointed) [*speech, style*] haché; **4** (steep) abrupt.

abruptly /əˈbrʌptlɪ/ *adv* **1** (suddenly) [*end, change, resign, leave*] brusquement; **2** (curtly) [*speak, behave, gesture*] avec brusquerie; **3** (steeply) [*rise, fall, drop*] à pic.

abruptness /əˈbrʌptnɪs/ *n* **1** (in manner) brusquerie *f*; **2** (suddenness) soudaineté *f*.

ABS *n, adj* Aut (*abrév* = **anti-lock braking system**) ABS; **~ brakes** freins *mpl* ABS.

abscess /ˈæbses/ *n* abcès *m*.

abscond /əbˈskɒnd/ *vi* s'enfuir (**from** de; **with** avec).

absconding /əbˈskɒndɪŋ/ *n* fuite *f*.

abseil /ˈæbseɪl/ GB **I** *n* rappel *m*.

II *vi* descendre en rappel (**from** de); **to ~ down sth** descendre qch en rappel.

abseil device *n* GB descendeur *m*.

abseiling /ˈæbseɪlɪŋ/ ▶ **1282** *n* GB descente *f* en rappel; **to go ~** faire de la descente en rappel.

absence /ˈæbsəns/ *n* **1** gen, Sch (of person) absence *f*; **in/during sb's ~** en/pendant l'absence de qn; **2** (of thing) manque *m*; **in the ~ of** faute de [*alternative, cooperation, evidence, assurances etc*].

IDIOMS **~ makes the heart grow fonder** Prov l'absence attise les grandes passions; **to be conspicuous by one's ~** iron briller par son absence.

absent I /ˈæbsənt/ *adj* **1** gen, Sch (not there) [*person, thing, emotion*] absent (**from** de); **to be conspicuously ~** iron briller par son absence; **'(to) ~ friends!'** (as toast) 'aux amis absents!'; **2** Mil **to be** ou **go ~ without leave** être en absence illégale; **3** (preoccupied) [*look*] absent.

II /əbˈsent/ *v refl* sout **to ~ oneself** s'absenter (**from** de).

absentee /ˌæbsənˈtiː/ *n* gen, Sch absent/-e *m/f*.

absentee ballot *n* vote *m* par correspondance.

absenteeism /ˌæbsənˈtiːɪzəm/ *n* absentéisme *m*.

absentee: **~ landlord** *n* propriétaire *mf* absentéiste; **~ voter** *n* électeur/-trice *m/f* par correspondance.

absently /ˈæbsəntlɪ/ *adv* [*muse, stare*] d'un air absent; [*say*] distraitement.

absent: **~-minded** *adj* distrait; **~-mindedly** *adv* [*behave, speak*] distraitement; [*stare*] d'un air absent; **~-mindedness** *n* distraction *f*.

absinth(e) /ˈæbsɪnθ/ *n* absinthe *f*.

absolute /ˈæbsəluːt/ **I** *n* **1 the ~** l'absolu *m*; **2** (rule, principle) vérité *f* absolue; **rigid ~s** des vérités qui n'admettent aucune contradiction.

II *adj* **1** (complete) [*certainty, discretion, minimum, proof, right etc*] absolu; Pol [*power, monarch*] absolu; **~ majority** Pol majorité *f* absolue; **~ beginner** vrai débutant; **2** (emphatic) [*chaos, disaster, idiot, scandal*] véritable; **3** Phys, Chem [*humidity, scale*] maximum; [*alcohol, temperature, zero*] absolu; **4** Jur **decree ~** décret *m* irrévocable; **the decree was made ~** le décret a été prononcé irrévocable; **5** Ling [*ablative, construction*] absolu; **6** Philos, Math [*term, value etc*] absolu.

absolute discharge *n* GB Jur dispense *f* de peine.

absolutely /ˈæbsəluːtlɪ/ *adv* **1** (totally) [*certain, right*] absolument; [*mad*] complètement; [*refuse, believe*] absolument; Pol [*rule*] en monarque absolu; **2** (emphatic) **this hotel is ~ the most expensive I know** cet hôtel est vraiment le plus cher que je connaisse; **I ~ adore opera!** je suis fou/folle○ d'opéra!; **3** (certainly) absolument; **~ not!** pas du tout!; **4** Ling dans un sens absolu.

absolute pitch *n* Mus oreille *f* absolue.

absolution /ˌæbsəˈluːʃn/ *n* absolution *f* (**from** de).

absolutism /ˈæbsəluːtɪzəm/ *n* Pol absolutisme *m*; Relig prédestination *f*.

absolve /əbˈzɒlv/ *vtr* **1** sout (clear) **to ~ sb from** ou **of sth** décharger qn de qch; **2** Relig (forgive) absoudre (**from** de).

absorb /əbˈzɔːb/ *vtr* **1** lit absorber [*liquid, drug, oxygen, heat, sound*]; **2** fig absorber [*attention, facts, costs, profits, business, village, region, people*]; **3** (withstand) absorber [*impact, force*]; amortir [*shock, jolt*]; encaisser [*punch, blow, insult, pressure*].

absorbed /əbˈzɔːbd/ *adj* absorbé (**in** ou **by** par); **~ in a book/one's work** plongé dans un livre/son travail; **to get** ou **become ~ in sth** s'absorber dans qch.

absorbency /əbˈzɔːbənsɪ/ *n* pouvoir *m* absorbant; **a high-~ material** un tissu très absorbant.

absorbent /əbˈzɔːbənt/ *n, adj* absorbant (*m*).

absorbent cotton *n* US coton *m* absorbant.

absorbing /əbˈzɔːbɪŋ/ *adj* passionnant.

absorption /əbˈzɔːpʃn/ *n* **1** lit (of nutrients, liquid, minerals) absorption *f*; **2** fig (of people) intégration *f*; (of business, costs, profits) absorption *f*; **3** (of shock, impact) amortissement *m*; **4** (in activity, book) concentration *f* (**in** sur).

abstain /əbˈsteɪn/ *vi* **1** gen, Relig s'abstenir (**from** de; **from doing** de faire); **2** Pol s'abstenir (**from doing** de faire).

abstainer /əbˈsteɪnə(r)/ *n* **1** (teetotaller) **he's a total ~** il s'abstient complètement de boire de l'alcool; **2** Pol (in vote) abstentionniste *mf*.

abstemious /æbˈstiːmɪəs/ *adj* [*person*] sobre; [*habits, diet*] frugal; **you're being very ~!** tu es très raisonnable!

abstemiously /æbˈstiːmɪəslɪ/ *adv* [*live, eat*] frugalement.

abstemiousness /æbˈstiːmɪəsnɪs/ *n* (of person) sobriété *f*; (of habits, diet) frugalité *f*.

abstention /əbˈstenʃn/ *n* **1** Pol (from vote) abstention *f* (**from** de); **2** (abstinence) abstinence *f* (**from** de).

abstinence /ˈæbstɪnəns/ *n* abstinence *f* (**from** de).

abstinent /ˈæbstɪnənt/ *adj* [*person*] sobre; [*habits*] sobre, modéré.

abstract I /ˈæbstrækt/ *n* **1** (theoretical) **the ~** l'abstrait *m*; **in the ~** dans l'abstrait; **2** (summary) résumé *m*; **3** Fin, Jur extrait *m*; **4** Art œuvre *f* abstraite.

II /ˈæbstrækt/ *adj* **1** (theoretical) abstrait; **2** Art abstrait; **3** Ling [*noun, verb*] abstrait.

III /əbˈstrækt/ *vtr* **1** (summarize) **to ~ sth from** tirer qch de [*documents, data*]; **2** (remove) sout dérober (**from sb** à qn; **from sth** dans qch); **3** (theorize) **to ~ sth from sth** extraire qch de qch.

IV *v refl* **to ~ oneself from sth** se soustraire à qch.

abstracted /əbˈstræktɪd/ *adj* [*gaze, expression, smile*] distrait; **he seemed rather ~** il avait l'air plutôt absent.

abstractedly /əbˈstræktɪdlɪ/ *adv* d'un air absent.

abstraction /əbˈstrækʃn/ *n* **1** (idea) idée *f* abstraite, abstraction *f*; **to talk in ~s** parler de manière abstraite; **2** (abstract quality) abstraction *f*; **3** Art (tendency) abstraction *f*; (work) œuvre *f* abstraite; **4** (vagueness) distraction *f*; **an air of ~** un air distrait; **5** (of property, money) sout détournement *m* (**from** de).

abstruse /əbˈstruːs/ *adj* abstrus.

abstruseness /əbˈstruːsnɪs/ *n* caractère *m* abstrus.

absurd /əbˈsɜːd/ **I** *n* **the ~** Philos, Theat l'absurde *m*.

II *adj* [*act, appearance, idea*] ridicule; **it was ~ (of sb) to do** c'était absurde (de la part de qn) de faire; **it is ~ that** c'est absurde que (+ *subj*).

absurdity /əb'sɜːdətɪ/ *n* absurdité *f*; **the height of ~** le comble de l'absurdité; **to the point of ~** à la limite de l'absurdité.

absurdly /əb'sɜːdlɪ/ *adv* [*wealthy, expensive*] ridiculement; [*behave*] de façon ridicule.

ABTA /'æbtə/ *n* GB (*abrév* = **Association of British Travel Agents**) association *f* des agences de voyages britanniques.

Abu Dhabi /ˌɑːbuː 'dɑːbɪ/ **▶1131** *pr n* Abou-Dabi.

abundance /ə'bʌndəns/ *n* abondance *f*, profusion *f* (**of** de); **in ~** en abondance, à profusion.

abundant /ə'bʌndənt/ *adj* abondant; **to be ~ in** être riche en.

abundantly /ə'bʌndəntlɪ/ *adv* **1** (in large quantities) abondamment; **2** [*clear, obvious*] tout à fait; **to make sth ~ clear (to sb)** faire comprendre qch de manière tout à fait claire (à qn).

abuse I /ə'bjuːs/ *n* **1** (maltreatment) mauvais traitement *m*; (sexual) sévices *mpl* (sexuels); **child ~** sévices sexuels exercés sur un enfant; **2** (misuse) (of hospitality, position, power, trust) abus *m*; **drug ~** usage *m* des stupéfiants; **alcohol ~** abus d'alcool; **3** (insults) injures *fpl*; **a stream of ~** un flot d'injures; **a term of ~** une injure.

II /ə'bjuːz/ *vtr* **1** (hurt) maltraiter; (sexually) abuser de [*woman*]; exercer des sévices sexuels sur [*child*]; **2** (misuse) abuser de [*drug, hospitality, position, power, trust*]; **3** (insult) injurier.

abuser /ə'bjuːzə(r)/ *n* (also **sex ~**, **sexual ~**) personne *f* qui exerce des sévices sexuels; **child ~** personne *f* qui exerce des sévices sexuels sur les enfants.

abusive /ə'bjuːsɪv/ *adj* **1** (rude) [*person*] grossier/-ière (**to** envers); **2** (insulting) [*words*] injurieux/-ieuse; **3** (improper) [*use*] abusif/-ive.

abusively /ə'bjuːsɪvlɪ/ *adv* grossièrement.

abut /ə'bʌt/ (*p prés etc* **-tt-**) I *vtr* [*building*] être contigu à; Constr juxtaposer [*wallpaper, wood*].

II *vi* (adjoin) être contigu (**onto** à); (be supported) prendre appui (**against** sur).

abutment /ə'bʌtmənt/ *n* gen contrefort *m*; (on bridge) butée *f*.

abuzz /ə'bʌz/ *adj*, *adv* **to be ~** être en émoi (**with** à cause de; **about, over** à propos de).

abysmal /ə'bɪzml/ *adj* épouvantable.

abysmally /ə'bɪzməlɪ/ *adv* abominablement.

abyss /ə'bɪs/ *n* lit, fig abîme *m*.

Abyssinia /ˌæbɪ'sɪnjə/ **▶1131** *pr n* Hist Abyssinie *f*.

Abyssinian /ˌæbɪ'sɪnjən/ **▶1486** Hist I *n* Abyssinien/-ienne *m/f*.

II *adj* abyssinien/-ienne.

Abyssinian cat *n* chat *m* abyssin.

a/c *n* (*abrév écrite* = **account**) compte *m*.

AC *abrév* ▶ **alternating current**.

acacia /ə'keɪʃə/ *n* acacia *m*.

Acad *n*: *abrév écrite* = **Academy**.

academe /'ækədiːm/ *n* littér université *f*; **the halls** ou **groves of ~** les couloirs de l'université.

academia /ˌækə'diːmɪə/ *n* l'université *f*.

academic /ˌækə'demɪk/ I *n* universitaire *mf*.

II *adj* Univ **1** (in college, university) [*career, life, post, teaching, work*] universitaire; [*year*] académique; **~ adviser** directeur/-trice *m/f* des études; **~ freedom** liberté *f* d'enseignement; **2** (scholarly) [*achievement, background, child, reputation*] intellectuel/-elle; [*school*] bien coté; **she's not very ~** elle n'est pas très douée pour les études; **~ course** ≈ cours *m* d'enseignement général; **3** (educational) [*book*] (for school) scolaire; (for university) universitaire; **4** (theoretical) [*debate, exercise, question*] théorique; **to be a matter of ~ interest** être d'un intérêt théorique; **5** Art, Literat [*painter, writer*] académique.

academically /ˌækə'demɪklɪ/ *adv* [*qualified, minded*] intellectuellement; [*able, excellent, interesting, respectable*] sur le plan intellectuel.

academicals /ˌækə'demɪklz/ *npl* GB Univ = **academic dress**.

academic dress *n* ¢ Univ tenue *f* universitaire; **in ~** vêtu de la toge et du mortier universitaires.

academician /əˌkædə'mɪʃn, US ˌækədə'mɪʃn/ *n* académicien/-ienne *m/f*.

academy /ə'kædəmɪ/ *n* **1** Sch école *f*; **military/naval ~** école militaire/navale; **2** (training school) école *f*; **~ of music** conservatoire *m* de musique; **~ of art** académie *f* d'art; **3** (learned society) académie *f* (of de).

Academy Award *n* Cin Oscar *m*.

acanthus /ə'kænθəs/ *n* (*pl* **~es** ou **-thi**) acanthe *f*.

Acas, ACAS /'eɪkæs/ *n* GB (*abrév* = **Advisory Conciliation and Arbitration Service**) *comité qui traite des problèmes entre employeurs et employés*.

accede /ək'siːd/ *vi* sout **1** (to request, suggestion, wish) accéder (**to** à); **2** Pol (to treaty, agreement, congress) adhérer (**to** à); **3** (to post) accéder (**to** à); (to throne) monter (**to** sur).

accelerate /ək'seləreɪt/ I *vtr* fig accélérer [*decline, growth*].

II *vi* **1** Aut accélérer; **to ~ away** partir en trombe (**from** de); **to ~ from 0–60 mph** monter de 0 à 100 km/h; **2** fig [*decline, growth*] s'accélérer.

acceleration /əkˌselə'reɪʃn/ *n* (all contexts) accélération *f*; **~ time** Aut temps d'accélération.

accelerator /ək'seləreɪtə(r)/ *n* Aut, Chem, Phys, Physiol accélérateur *m*; **to step on the ~** Aut appuyer sur l'accélérateur; **to let up on the ~** Aut relâcher l'accélérateur.

accent I /'æksent, -sənt/ *n* gen, Ling, Mus, fig accent *m*; **in** ou **with a French ~** avec un accent français; **to put the ~ on sth** mettre l'accent sur qch; **with the ~ on quality** avec l'accent mis sur la qualité.

II /æk'sent/ *vtr* **1** Ling, Mus accentuer; **2** fig souligner [*issue, point*].

accented /'æksentɪd, -sənt-/ *adj* [*speech*] avec un accent; **he speaks a heavily ~ English** il parle l'anglais avec un fort accent.

accentuate /æk'sentʃʊeɪt/ *vtr* gen souligner (**by** par); Mus accentuer.

accentuation /ækˌsentʃʊ'eɪʃn/ *n* gen, Ling, Mus accentuation *f*.

accept /ək'sept/ I *vtr* **1** (take, receive) accepter [*gift, offer, suggestion, apology, candidate, money*]; **2** (resign oneself to) accepter [*fate, situation*]; **3** (tolerate) admettre [*behaviour, immigrant, new idea*]; **it is generally ~ed that** il est admis que; **4** (take on) assumer [*task, role, function*].

II accepted *pp adj* [*behaviour, fact, definition*] admis; **in the ~ sense of the word** dans le sens usuel du mot.

acceptability /əkˌseptə'bɪlətɪ/ *n* admissibilité *f*.

acceptable /ək'septəbl/ *adj* **1** (welcome) [*gift, money*] bienvenu; **2** (agreeable) [*idea, offer*] acceptable (**to** à); **3** (allowable) [*behaviour, risk*] acceptable; **to be ~ to do** être acceptable de faire; **it is ~ that** il est acceptable que (+ *subj*); **to an ~ level** à un niveau acceptable; **within ~ limits** dans des limites acceptables.

acceptably /ək'septəblɪ/ *adv* **1** [*express, introduce etc*] raisonnablement; **2** [*good, high, low etc*] suffisamment.

acceptance /ək'septəns/ *n* **1** (of offer, invitation, fate, limitations) acceptation *f* (**of** de); **a letter of ~** une lettre d'acceptation; **2** (of plan, proposal) approbation *f* (**of** de); **to meet with** ou **find ~** recevoir l'approbation; **to gain ~** gagner l'approbation; **3** Fin, Insur (of bill, policy) acceptation *f*; Comm (of goods) réception *f*.

acceptance trials *npl* Naut essais *mpl* de recette.

acceptation /ˌæksep'teɪʃn/ *n* Ling acception *f*.

acceptor /ək'septə(r)/ *n* **1** Comm accepteur *m*; **2** Phys (atome *m*) accepteur *m*.

access /'ækses/ I *n* **1** (means of entry) accès *m*; **pedestrian/wheelchair ~** accès pour les piétons/fauteuils roulants; **~ to the centre is from the street** l'accès au centre se fait par la rue; **to gain ~ to sth** accéder à qch; **'No ~'** (on signs) 'accès interdit'; **2** (ability to obtain, use) accès *m* (**to** à); **to have ~ to information/education/a database** avoir accès à des informations/l'éducation/une base de données; **open ~** libre accès; **3** Jur (right to visit) **right of ~** droit *m* de visite; **to have ~ (to one's children)** avoir un droit de visite (auprès de ses enfants); **to grant/deny ~** accorder/refuser le droit de visite; **right of ~ to prisoners** le droit de visiter les prisonniers; **4** Comput accès *m* (**to** à); **5** sout (attack) accès *m*; **an ~ of rage/remorse** un accès de colère/remords.

II *modif* **1** (entry) [*control, door, mode, point*] d'accès; **2** (visiting) [*rights*] de visite.

III *vtr* gen, Comput accéder à [*database, information, machine*].

accessary *n* = **accessory** I 2.

access course *n* GB Univ *cours permettant à des candidats d'entrer à l'Université sans les titres requis*.

accessibility /əkˌsesə'bɪlətɪ/ *n* (all contexts) accessibilité *f* (**of** de; **to** pour).

accessible /ək'sesəbl/ *adj* **1** (easy to reach) [*place, education, file, information, person*] accessible (**to** à); **2** (easy to understand) [*art, novel, writer, style*] accessible (**to** à); **3** (affordable) [*car, holiday, price etc*] abordable (**to** pour).

accession /æk'seʃn/ I *n* **1** ¢ (to power, throne, estate, title) accession *f* (**to** à); (to treaty, organization) adhésion *f* (**to** à); **2** C (book, exhibit) (nouvelle) acquisition *f*.

II *vtr* mettre au catalogue [*book, exhibit*].

accession number *n* numéro *m* d'enregistrement.

accessorize /ək'sesəraɪz/ *vtr* accessoiriser; **~ your car with...** ajoutez au confort de votre voiture avec...

accessory /ək'sesərɪ/ I *n* **1** Aut, Fashn accessoire *m*; (luxury item) Aut extra *m*; **2** Jur complice *mf* (**to** de); **~ before/after the fact** complice par instigation/après coup.

II *modif* gen, Anat accessoire; [*market*] Aut des accessoires.

access: **~ road** *n* (to building, site) route *f* d'accès; (to motorway) bretelle *f* d'accès; **~ television programme** *n* GB TV *émission permettant à des particuliers d'exprimer leurs avis ou de diffuser un programme d'intérêt particulier*; **~ time** *n* Comput temps *m* d'accès.

accidence /'æksɪdəns/ *n* morphologie *f* flexionnelle.

accident /'æksɪdənt/ I *n* **1** (mishap) accident *m* (**with** avec); **by ~** accidentellement; **car/industrial/road ~** accident de voiture/du travail/de la route; **~s in the home** accidents domestiques; **to have an ~** avoir un accident; **to meet with an ~** être victime d'un accident; **~ and emergency service** (in hospital) service des urgences; **I had an ~ with the teapot** j'ai malencontreusement cassé la théière; **I'm sorry, it was an ~** je m'excuse, c'était un accident; **~s will happen!** ce sont des choses qui arrivent!; **the baby's had a little ~** euph le petit n'a pas pu se retenir euph; **a chapter of ~s** une succession de problèmes; **2** (chance) hasard *m*; **by ~** par hasard; **it is no ~ that**... ce n'est pas un hasard que..., ce n'est pas par hasard que...; **he is rich by an ~ of birth** le hasard a voulu qu'il soit né riche; **it was more by ~ than design** c'était accidentel plutôt que délibéré.

II *modif* [*figures, statistics*] se rapportant aux accidents; [*protection*] contre les accidents; **(personal) ~ insurance** assurance *f* (individuelle) accidents; **~ prevention** (at work) prévention *f* des accidents du travail; (road) prévention *f* routière; **~ victim** accidenté/-e *m/f*.

accidental /ˌæksɪˈdentl/ I *n* Mus accident *m*. II *adj* **1** (by accident) [*death*] accidentel/-elle; **2** (by chance) [*meeting, mistake*] fortuit; **3** (incidental) [*effect*] secondaire.

accidentally /ˌæksɪˈdentəlɪ/ *adv* (by accident) accidentellement; (by chance) par hasard; **to do sth ~ on purpose** iron faire qch malencontreusement iron.

Accident and Emergency Unit *n* (service *m* des) urgences *fpl*.

accident-prone /ˌæksɪdəntˈprəʊn/ *adj* **to be ~** être sujet/-ette aux accidents.

acclaim /əˈkleɪm/ I *n* **1** (praise) louanges *fpl*; **to win ~** avoir du succès; **2** (cheering) acclamations *fpl*; **roars of ~** des cris d'enthousiasme.

II *vtr* **1** (praise) applaudir; **~ed by the critics** encensé par la critique; **~ed by the public** applaudi du public; **2** (cheer) acclamer; fig **the new system was ~ed as a technological breakthrough** le nouveau système a été acclamé comme une percée technologique; **3** (proclaim) **to ~ sb (as) sth** proclamer qn qch.

III **acclaimed** *pp adj* très applaudi.

acclamation /ˌækləˈmeɪʃn/ *n* acclamation *f*; **by/with ~** par acclamation.

acclimate /ˈæklɪmeɪt, əˈklaɪ-/ US = **acclimatize**.

acclimation /ˌæklaɪˈmeɪʃn/ US = **acclimatization**.

acclimatization /əˌklaɪmətaɪˈzeɪʃn, US -tɪˈz-/ *n* lit, fig acclimatation *f* (**to** à).

acclimatize /əˈklaɪmətaɪz/ I *vtr* acclimater (**to** à); **to get** ou **become ~d** s'acclimater.
II *vi* s'acclimater.
III *v refl* **to ~ oneself** s'acclimater (**to** à).

accolade /ˈækəleɪd, US -ˈleɪd/ *n* **1** (specific honour) honneur *m*; **the highest ~** la consécration suprême; **2** (praise) **to receive** ou **win ~s from all sides** être loué par tout le monde; **3** (on being knighted) accolade *f*.

accommodate /əˈkɒmədeɪt/ I *vtr* **1** (provide room, space for) [*person, hotel*] loger; [*vehicle, room, public building, site*] contenir; **how many cars will the car park ~?** combien de voitures est-ce que le parking peut contenir?; **I can't ~ a freezer** je n'ai pas assez de place pour un congélateur; **2** (adapt to) s'adapter à [*change, idiosyncrasy, view*]; **3** (reconcile) concilier [*objection, role*] (**with** avec); **4** (satisfy) satisfaire [*need, request, wish*]; **5** (meet request) sout **I think I can ~ you** je crois pouvoir satisfaire votre demande; **to ~ sb with sth** fournir qch à qn [*required item*]; accorder qch à qn [*loan, credit terms*].
II *v refl* **to ~ oneself to** s'adapter à [*change, different viewpoint*].

accommodating /əˈkɒmədeɪtɪŋ/ *adj* [*attitude, person*] accommodant (**to** envers).

accommodatingly /əˈkɒmədeɪtɪŋlɪ/ *adv* [*say*] d'un ton conciliant; [*act*] de façon accommodante.

accommodation /əˌkɒməˈdeɪʃn/ *n* **1** (also **~s** US) (living quarters) logement *m*; **hotel/overnight ~** logement en hôtel/pour la nuit; **living ~** logement; **private/student ~** logement privé/pour étudiants; **'~ to let'** GB 'location'; **office ~** bureaux *mpl*; **2** (adjustment) gen adaptation *f*; Physiol (of eye) accommodation *f*; **3** Fin Comm (loan) crédit *m* relais.

accommodation: **~ address** *n* GB boîte *f* à lettres; **~ bill** *n* lettre *f* de change acceptée; **~ bureau** GB, **~s bureau** US *n* agence *f* de logement; **~ ladder** *n* échelle *f* de coupée; **~ officer** GB, **~s officer** US ▶**1692**| *n* responsable *mf* de l'hébergement; **~ road** *n* voie *f* privée; **~ train** *n* US Rail omnibus *m*.

accompaniment /əˈkʌmpənɪmənt/ *n* gen, Mus accompagnement *m* (**to** à); **as an ~ to sth** pour accompagner qch; **with piano ~** Mus avec accompagnement au piano; **to the ~ of soft music** au son d'une musique douce.

accompanist /əˈkʌmpənɪst/ *n* accompagnateur/-trice *m/f*.

accompany /əˈkʌmpənɪ/ I *vtr* gen, Mus accompagner; **accompanied** accompagné (**by sb** par qn; **by sth** de qch; **on sth** Mus à qch).
II *vi* Mus être l'accompagnateur/l'accompagnatrice *m/f*.

accomplice /əˈkʌmplɪs, US əˈkɒm-/ *n* complice *mf* (**in, to** de).

accomplish /əˈkʌmplɪʃ, US əˈkɒm-/ *vtr* gen accomplir; réaliser [*objective*].

accomplished /əˈkʌmplɪʃt, US əˈkɒm-/ *adj* **1** [*performer, performance, sportsperson*] très compétent; **highly ~** consommé; **an ~ fact** un fait accompli; **2**† [*young lady*] accompli†.

accomplishment /əˈkʌmplɪʃmənt, US əˈkɒm-/ *n* **1** (act of accomplishing) accomplissement *m*; **2** (thing accomplished) réussite *f*; **that's no mean** ou **small ~!** ça n'est pas peu de chose!; **3** (skill) talent *m*.

accord /əˈkɔːd/ I *n* accord *m* (**on** sur); **in ~ with sth** en accord avec qch; **to be in ~ with sb** être d'accord avec qn; **of my own ~** de moi-même; **with one ~** d'un commun accord; **to reach an ~** se mettre d'accord.
II *vtr* accorder (**sth to sb** qch à qn).
III *vi* **to ~ with** concorder avec.

accordance /əˈkɔːdəns/: **in accordance with** *prep phr* **1** (in line with) [*act*] conformément à [*rules, wishes*]; **in ~ with your instructions, I have**... conformément à vos instructions, j'ai...; **to be in ~ with** être conforme à [*law, agreement, requirement*]; **in ~ with her principles** en accord avec ses principes; **2** (proportional to) selon; **taxes levied in ~ with the individual's ability to pay** taxes prélevées selon la capacité individuelle de paiement.

according /əˈkɔːdɪŋ/: I **according to** *prep phr* **1** (in agreement with) [*act*] selon [*law, regulations, principles*]; **~ to plan** comme prévu; **2** (by reference to) d'après [*newspaper, person, thermometer*].
II **according as** *conj phr* sout dans la mesure où.

accordingly /əˈkɔːdɪŋlɪ/ *adv* (all contexts) en conséquence.

accordion /əˈkɔːdɪən/ ▶**1481**| *n* accordéon *m*.

accordionist /əˈkɔːdɪənɪst/ ▶**1692**|, **1481**| *n* accordéoniste *mf*.

accordion pleat /əˌkɔːdɪən ˈpliːt/ *n* pli *m* accordéon.

accost /əˈkɒst/ *vtr* gen aborder; (for sexual purpose) accoster.

account /əˈkaʊnt/ I *n* **1** Accts, Fin (money held at bank) compte *m* (**at, with** à); **to open/close an ~** ouvrir/fermer un compte; **in my/his ~** sur mon/son compte; **I'd like to know the balance on my ~** j'aimerais savoir combien j'ai sur mon compte; **2** Comm (credit arrangement) compte *m*; **to have an ~ at a shop** avoir un compte dans un magasin; **an ~ with the baker** un compte chez le boulanger; **to charge sth to** ou **put sth on sb's ~** mettre qch sur le compte de qn; **on ~** (as part payment) d'acompte; **£100 on ~ and the rest in May** 100 livres sterling d'acompte et le reste en mai; **to settle an ~** (in shop) régler un compte; (in hotel) régler une note; **to settle ~s** fig régler un compte; **3** Accts, Advertg (client) budget *m* (de publicité); **the Renault ~** le budget Renault; **4** (financial record) compte *m*; **5** (bill) facture *f*; **electricity ~** facture d'électricité; **6** GB (on stock exchange) **the ~** le terme *m*; **7** (consideration) **to take sth into ~, to take ~ of sth** tenir compte de qch; **to fail to take sth into ~** omettre de tenir compte de qch; **this aspect has not been taken into ~** on n'a pas tenu compte de cet aspect, cet aspect n'est pas entré en ligne de compte; **8** (description) compte-rendu *m*; **to give an ~ of sth** faire un compte-rendu de qch; **for his ~ of what happened** pour sa version de ce qui s'est passé; **by all ~s, from all ~s** au dire de tous; **by his own ~** tel qu'il le dit lui-même; **9 to call** ou **bring sb to ~** (bring to book) demander des comptes à qn; **she was called** ou **brought to ~ for these complaints/for failing to finish the job** on lui a demandé des comptes pour ces plaintes/pour ne pas avoir fini le travail; **10** (impression) **to give a good ~ of oneself** faire bonne impression (**in** dans); **they gave a good ~ of themselves in the match** ils ont fait bonne impression dans le match; **11** (indicating reason) **on ~ of sth/sb** à cause de qch/qn; **on this** ou **that ~** pour cette raison; **on no ~** sous aucun prétexte; **on no ~ must you open the door** n'ouvrez la porte sous aucun prétexte; **on my/his ~** à cause de moi/lui; **don't change the date on my ~!** ne change pas la date à cause de moi!; **12** (advantage, benefit) **on my/his ~** exprès pour moi/lui; **don't come on my ~!** ne viens pas exprès pour moi!; **she was worried on her own ~** elle s'inquiétait pour son (propre) sort; **to act on one's own ~** agir de sa propre initiative; **to set up business on one's own ~** s'installer or se mettre à son compte; **to put** ou **turn sth to (good) ~** mettre qch à profit; **13** (importance) **to be of little ~/some ~** avoir peu d'importance/une certaine importance (**to sb** pour qn); **it's of no ~ to them whether he's alive or dead** peu leur importe qu'il soit vivant ou mort.

II **accounts** *npl* **1** Accts (records) comptabilité *f* ¢, comptes *mpl*; **to keep the ~s** tenir la comptabilité or les comptes; **the party ~s** la comptabilité du parti; **the ~s show a profit** les comptes font apparaître un bénéfice; **2** (department) (service *m*) comptabilité *f*.

III **accounts** *modif* [*staff*] comptable; [*department*] comptabilité *inv*.

IV *vtr* sout (regard as) **he was ~ed a genius** on le considérait comme un génie.

■ **account for**: **~ for [sth/sb] 1** (explain) expliquer [*events, fact, behaviour*]; justifier [*expense*] (**to sb** auprès de qn); retrouver [*missing people, vehicle*]; **2** (represent, make up) représenter [*proportion, percentage*]; **exports ~ for 10% of their trade** les exportations représentent 10% de leurs affaires; **3** (destroy, kill) détruire [*vehicle, plane*]; abattre [*animal*]; mettre [qn] hors d'état de nuire [*soldier, attacker*]; **4** Journ, Sport mettre [qn] hors-jeu.

accountability /əˌkaʊntəˈbɪlətɪ/ *n* gen, Fin responsabilité *f* (**to** devant).

accountable /əˈkaʊntəbl/ *adj* responsable; **to be ~ to sb** être responsable devant qn (**for** de); **to hold sb ~ for sth** tenir qn pour responsable de qch; **to make sb ~ to** rendre qn responsable envers.

accountancy /əˈkaʊntənsɪ/ I *n* **1** (profession) comptabilité *f*; **to go into ~** devenir comptable; **2** (studies) comptabilité *f*.
II *modif* [*course, department, degree, exam, firm, training*] de comptabilité.

accountant /əˈkaʊntənt/ ▶**1692**| *n* comptable *mf*.

account: **~ book** *n* livre *m* de comptes; **~ day** *n* Fin jour *m* de liquidation; **~ executive** *n* Advertg chef *m* de publicité; **~ holder** *n* (with bank, building society, credit company) titulaire *mf*; (with shop, business) personne *f* qui a un compte.

accounting /ə'kaʊntɪŋ/ **I** *n* comptabilité *f*.
II *modif* [*method, procedure, period, standards, year*] comptable; [*department*] comptabilité.

account number *n* numéro *m* de compte.

accoutrements /ə'ku:trəmənts/ *npl* équipement *m* also hum.

accredit /ə'kredɪt/ **I** *vtr* **1** (appoint) accréditer [*official, representative, journalist*]; **2** (approve) agréer [*institution, qualification, professional*]; **3** Pol accréditer [*ambassador*]; **4** (credit) attribuer [*quality, belief*] (**to** à); **to be ~ed with doing** se voir attribuer le mérite d'avoir fait.
II accredited *pp adj* **1** gen, Journ [*journalist, representative*] accrédité; [*professional, institution*] agréé; **2** Agric, Vet **~ed herd** troupeau *m* officiellement indemne de tuberculose.

accreditation /ə,kredɪ'teɪʃn/ *n* **1** (of official, representative, journalist) accréditation *f*; **2** (of institution, qualification, professional) agrément *m*.

accretion /ə'kri:ʃn/ *n* **1** (process) (of substance) accumulation *f*; Jur (of wealth, inheritance) accroissement *m*; **2** (substance) (soot, dirt) accumulation *f*; Biol (plants) accroissement *m*; Geol (deposits, lava) accrétion *f*.

accrual /ə'kru:əl/ *n* Fin accumulation *f*.

accrue /ə'kru:/ **I** *vi* **1** Fin s'accumuler; **the interest accruing to my account** les intérêts qui s'accumulent sur mon compte; **2** gen [*advantages*] revenir (**to** à); [*power, influence*] s'accumuler (**to sb** entre les mains de qn).
II accrued *pp adj* [*interest, dividends, charges, expenses*] cumulé; [*wealth*] amassé.

accumulate /ə'kju:mjʊleɪt/ **I** *vtr* accumuler [*possessions*]; amasser [*money, wealth*]; rassembler [*evidence, information*]; accumuler [*debts, losses*].
II *vi* (all contexts) s'accumuler.
III accumulated *pp adj* [*anger, tension, frustration*] accumulé.

accumulation /ə,kju:mjʊ'leɪʃn/ *n* (quantity, process) (of wealth, objects, detail, problems, dirt) accumulation *f*; (of rubbish) entassement *m*.

accumulative /ə'kju:mjʊlətɪv, US -leɪtɪv/ *adj* **1** [*effect, result*] cumulatif/-ive; **2** [*person, society*] porté sur l'accumulation des biens matériels; **3** Fin = **cumulative**.

accumulator /ə'kju:mjʊleɪtə(r)/ *n* **1** Elec accumulateur *m*; **2** Sport (bet) pari *m* avec report; **3** Comput registre *m* accumulateur.

accuracy /'ækjərəsɪ/ *n* (of figures, estimate, translation) justesse *f*; (of map, translator, aim) précision *f*; (of description, data, diagnosis, forecast) exactitude *f*; (of instrument, watch) justesse *f*.

accurate /'ækjərət/ *adj* [*figures, estimate, translation*] juste; [*translator, reports, aim, map*] précis; [*description, information*] exact, juste; [*watch, instrument*] juste; [*diagnosis, forecast*] exact; [*assessment*] correct.

accurately /'ækjərətlɪ/ *adv* [*calculate*] exactement; [*describe, report*] avec exactitude; [*estimate, remember, assess*] précisément; [*translate, measure*] avec précision.

accursed /ə'kɜ:sɪd/ *adj* sout [*person, exam*] satané (*before n*).

accusal /ə'kju:zl/ *n* accusation *f*.

accusation /,ækju:'zeɪʃn/ *n* accusation *f* (**of** de; **against** contre; **that** selon laquelle); **to make an ~** porter une accusation; **to reject/refute an ~** rejeter/refuter une accusation.

accusative /ə'kju:zətɪv/ Ling **I** *n* accusatif *m*.
II *adj* [*case, ending*] de l'accusatif.

accusatory /ə'kju:zətərɪ, US -tɔ:rɪ/ *adj* accusateur/-trice.

accuse /ə'kju:z/ *vtr* gen, Jur accuser (**of** de; **of doing** de faire); **he ~d me of stealing his pen** il m'a accusé d'avoir volé son stylo; **to stand ~d of sth** être accusé de qch.

accused /ə'kju:zd/ *n* Jur **the ~** (one) l'accusé/-e *m/f*; (several) les accusés/-es *m/fpl*.

accuser /ə'kju:zə(r)/ *n* accusateur/-trice *m/f*.

accusing /ə'kju:zɪŋ/ *adj* accusateur/-trice.

accusingly /ə'kju:zɪŋlɪ/ *adv* [*say*] d'un ton accusateur; [*look, point*] de façon accusatrice.

accustom /ə'kʌstəm/ **I** *vtr* **to ~ sb to sth/to doing** habituer qn à qch/à faire.
II *v refl* **to ~ oneself to sth/to doing** s'habituer à qch/à faire.

accustomed /ə'kʌstəmd/ *adj* **1 to be ~ to sth/to doing** avoir l'habitude de qch/de faire; **to become ~ to sth/to doing** s'habituer à qch/à faire; **2** [*manner, greeting, route*] habituel/-elle.

AC/DC **I** *n* (*abrév* = **alternating current/direct current**) courant *m* alternatif/courant continu.
II○ *adj* (bisexual) à voile et à vapeur○, bisexuel/-elle.

ace /eɪs/ **I** *n* **1** (in cards) as *m*; **2** fig (trump) carte *f* maîtresse; **3** (tennis) service *m* gagnant; **4** (expert) as *m*; **a flying ~** un as de l'aviation; **to be an ~ at doing sth**○ être un champion pour faire qch.
II○ *adj* (great) super○; **an ~ driver/skier** un as du volant/du ski.
IDIOMS **to have an ~ up one's sleeve** ou **in the hole** avoir un atout en réserve; **to hold all the ~s** avoir tout pouvoir; **to be within an ~ of sth** être à deux doigts de qch; **to play one's ~** jouer son atout.

Ace bandage® *n* US ≈ bande *f* Velpeau®.

acerbic /ə'sɜ:bɪk/ *adj* (all contexts) acerbe.

acerbity /ə'sɜ:bətɪ/ *n* aigreur *f*.

acetate /'æsɪteɪt/ *n* Chem, Tex acétate *m*.

acetic acid /ə,si:tɪk 'æsɪd/ *n* acide *m* acétique.

acetone /'æsɪtəʊn/ *n* acétone *f*.

acetylene /ə'setɪli:n/ *n* acétylène *m*.

acetylene: **~ lamp** *n* lampe *f* à acétylène; **~ torch**, **~ burner** *n* chalumeau *m* à acétylène.

acetylene welding *n* (process) soudage *m* à l'acétylène; (joint) soudure *f* à l'acétylène.

ache /eɪk/ **I** *n* **1** (physical) douleur *f* (**in** à); **~s and pains** douleurs *fpl*; **2** (emotional) chagrin *m*.
II *vi* **1** (physically) [*person*] avoir mal; [*limb, back*] faire mal; **to ~ all over** avoir mal partout; **2** littér (suffer emotionally) **to ~ with** mourir de [*humiliation, despair*]; **my heart ~s for the refugees** j'ai le cœur qui se serre à la pensée des réfugiés; **3** (yearn) brûler (**to do** de faire; **with** de).
IDIOMS **to laugh till one's sides ~** rire à se tenir les côtes.

achieve /ə'tʃi:v/ **I** *vtr* **1** (reach) atteindre [*aim, objective*]; atteindre à [*perfection*]; arriver à [*consensus, balance*]; **2** (obtain) obtenir [*success, result*]; remporter [*victory*]; réaliser [*ambition*]; **to ~ something in life** faire quelque chose de sa vie; **to ~ nothing** ne rien accomplir.
II *vi* réussir.

achievement /ə'tʃi:vmənt/ *n* **1 C** (accomplishment) réussite *f* (**in sth** dans le domaine de qch); **her many ~s** ses nombreuses réussites; **2 ¢** (performance) succès *mpl*; **to recognize sb for his/her ~** reconnaître les succès de qn; **3 ¢** (realisation) **the ~ of** la réalisation de [*ambition, goal*]; **a sense of ~** un sentiment de satisfaction; **what is necessary for the ~ of peace** ce qui est nécessaire pour arriver à un accord de paix.

achiever /ə'tʃi:və(r)/ *n* (also **high ~**) personne *f* qui réussit.

Achilles /ə'kɪli:z/ *pr n* Achille.

Achilles: **~ heel** *n* talon *m* d'Achille, point *m* faible; **~ tendon** *n* Anat tendon *m* d'Achille.

aching /'eɪkɪŋ/ *adj* **1** (physically) [*limb*] qui fait mal (*after n*); **2** littér [*heart*] déchiré; [*beauty, emotion*] poignant; **an ~ void** un grand vide.

achromatic /,ækrəʊ'mætɪk/ *adj* achromatique.

acid /'æsɪd/ **I** *n* **1** Chem acide *m*; **2**○ (drug) acide○ *m*.
II *modif* **~ content** teneur *f* en acide; **~ level** taux *m* d'acidité.
III *adj* **1** (sour) [*taste, rock, soil*] acide; **2** fig [*tone*] aigre; [*remark*] caustique.

acid: **~ drop** *n* bonbon *m* acidulé; **~ green** *n, adj* vert (*m*) fluo○; **~ head**◑ *n* camé/-e◑ *m/f* (*au LSD*); **~ house party** *n* GB grande boum *f* (*dans un entrepôt*).

acidic /ə'sɪdɪk/ *adj* acide.

acidification /ə,sɪdɪfɪ'keɪʃn/ *n* acidification *f*.

acidify /ə'sɪdɪfaɪ/ **I** *vtr* acidifier.
II *vi* s'acidifier.

acidity /ə'sɪdətɪ/ *n* **1** Chem acidité *f*; **2** fig (of tone, remark) causticité *f*.

acidity regulator *n* Chem correcteur *m* d'acidité.

acid: **~ radical** *n* Chem radical *m* acide; **~ rain** *n* **¢** pluies *fpl* acides; **~ rock** *n* ≈ rock *m* psychédélique; **~ stomach** *n* Med acidité *f* gastrique; **~ test** *n* fig épreuve *f* de vérité (**of** de; **for** pour).

acidulous /ə'sɪdjʊləs, US -dʒʊl-/, **acidulent** /ə'sɪdjʊlənt, US -dʒʊl-/ *adj* acidulé.

ack-ack /,æk'æk/ *n* **1** (weapons) artillerie *f* antiaérienne; **2** (weaponfire) barrage *m* antiaérien.

acknowledge /ək'nɒlɪdʒ/ **I** *vtr* **1** (admit) admettre [*fact*]; reconnaître [*error*]; **to ~ that** admettre que; **to ~ to oneself** reconnaître en son for intérieur (**that** que); **2** (recognize) reconnaître [*ability, problem, authority, claim*]; **to be ~d as** ou **to be an excellent lawyer/doctor** être connu comme un excellent avocat/médecin; **to ~ sb as leader** reconnaître qn pour chef; **this opera is ~d as** ou **to be one of his greatest works** tout le monde s'accorde à reconnaître que cet opéra est une de ses plus grandes œuvres; **3** (express thanks for) remercier [qn] de [*gift, help*]; répondre à [*applause*]; **to ~ one's sources** (in book) citer ses sources; **4** (confirm receipt of) accuser réception de [*letter, parcel*]; **5** (show recognition of) montrer qu'on a vu [qn]; **he ~d them with a wave** il leur fit un signe de la main; **she didn't even ~ me** ou **my presence** elle a fait semblant de ne pas me voir.
II acknowledged *pp adj* [*leader, champion, expert*] incontesté; [*writer, artist*] renommé, reconnu.

acknowledgement /ək'nɒlɪdʒmənt/ **I** *n* **1** (admission) (of fact, problem, authority, claim) reconnaissance *f* (**of** de; **that** que); (of error, guilt) aveu *m* (**of** de; **that** que); **in ~ that** reconnaissant que; **in ~ of sth** en reconnaissance de qch; **2** (confirmation of receipt) accusé *m* de réception; **3** (recognition of presence) signe *m* de reconnaissance.
II acknowledgements *npl* (in book etc) remerciements *mpl*.

acme /'ækmɪ/ *n* **the ~ of** le summum de.

acne /'æknɪ/ ▶ 1354 *n* acné *f*.

acolyte /'ækəlaɪt/ *n* Relig, fig acolyte *m*.

aconite /'ækənaɪt/ *n* aconit *m*.

acorn /'eɪkɔ:n/ *n* gland *m*.

acoustic /ə'ku:stɪk/ **I** *n* = **acoustics 2**.
II *adj* **1** gen [*effect, problem, instrument*] acoustique; [*tile, material*] insonorisant; **2** Mil [*detonator*] acoustique.

acoustically /ə'ku:stɪklɪ/ *adv* acoustiquement.

acoustic: **~ coupler** *n* Comput coupleur *m* acoustique; **~ guitar** ▶ 1481 *n* guitare *f* sèche; **~ hood** *n* Comput capot *m* d'insonorisation; **~ phonetics** *n* (+ *v sg*) phonétique *f* acoustique.

acoustics /ə'ku:stɪks/ *n* **1** (science) (+ *v sg*) acoustique *f*; **2** (properties) (+ *v pl*) acoustique *f*.

ACPO *n* GB (*abrév* = **Association of**

Chief Police Officers) association *f* des officiers supérieurs de la police.

acquaint /ə'kweɪnt/ **I** *vtr* **to ~ sb with sth** mettre qn au courant de qch; **to be ~ed** se connaître; **to get** ou **become ~ed with sb** faire la connaissance de qn; **to get** ou **become ~ed with sth** découvrir qch.
II *v refl* **to ~ oneself with sth** se renseigner sur qch.

acquaintance /ə'kweɪntəns/ *n* **1** (friend) connaissance *f*; **an ~ of mine** une de mes connaissances; **a French ~** un ami français/une amie française *m/f*; **2** (knowledge) connaissance *f* (**with** de); **to improve on ~** gagner à être connu; **to have a nodding** ou **passing ~ with sb/sth** connaître qn/qch vaguement; **3** (relationship) relations *fpl*, rapports *mpl*; **to make sb's ~** faire la connaissance de qn; **to renew ~ with sb** renouer avec une connaissance; **to strike up an ~ with sb** nouer des relations avec qn; **on closer** ou **further ~** tout compte fait.

acquiesce /ˌækwɪ'es/ *vi* **1** (concede, accept) acquiescer; **2** (collude) **to ~ in sth** ne pas s'opposer à qch.

acquiescence /ˌækwɪ'esns/ *n* **1** (agreement) accord *m*; **2** (collusion) **~ in sth** connivence *f* avec qch.

acquiescent /ˌækwɪ'esnt/ *adj* **1** (in agreement) d'accord; **2** (unassertive) soumis.

acquire /ə'kwaɪə(r)/ *vtr* acquérir [*skill, knowledge, experience*]; obtenir [*information*]; faire l'acquisition de [*house, painting etc*]; prendre [*meaning, nuance*]; acheter [*company, shares*]; contracter [*habit*]; iron se pourvoir de [*husband, lover*]; **to ~ a taste for sth** prendre goût à qch.

acquired /ə'kwaɪəd/ *adj* [*characteristic, knowledge*] acquis; **it's an ~ taste** c'est quelque chose qu'il faut apprendre à aimer.

acquisition /ˌækwɪ'zɪʃn/ *n* **1** gen (object bought) acquisition *f*; **2** Fin (company) achat *m*; **3** (process) acquisition *f*.

acquisitive /ə'kwɪzətɪv/ *adj* **1** [*person, society*] attaché aux biens de consommation; **2** Fin [*company, conglomerate*] qui a une politique agressive de rachat.

acquisitiveness /ə'kwɪzətɪvnɪs/ *n* soif *f* de possession.

acquit /ə'kwɪt/ (*p prés etc* **-tt-**) **I** *vtr* Jur acquitter; **to ~ sb of (doing) sth** acquitter qn accusé d'avoir fait qch; **to be ~ted of murder** ou **of murdering sb** être disculpé de l'accusation de meurtre de qn.
II *v refl* **to ~ oneself well/badly in** s'en tirer○ bien/mal à [*interview, examination*]; **she ~ted herself well in the competition** le concours s'est bien passé pour elle.

acquittal /ə'kwɪtl/ *n* Jur acquittement *m*.

acre /'eɪkə(r)/ ▶ **1771** **I** *n* Meas acre *f*, ≈ demi-hectare *m*.
II acres *npl* **~s of** des hectares *mpl* de [*woodland, grazing*]; **~s (and ~s) of room**○ énormément d'espace.

acreage /'eɪkərɪdʒ/ *n* Meas superficie *f*.

acrid /'ækrɪd/ *adj* **1** [*fumes, smell*] âcre; **2** [*remark, tone*] caustique.

acrimonious /ˌækrɪ'məʊnɪəs/ *adj* [*tone*] hargneux/-euse; [*argument, debate, divorce, dispute*] acrimonieux/-ieuse.

acrimony /'ækrɪmənɪ, US -məʊnɪ/ *n* acrimonie *f*.

acrobat /'ækrəbæt/ ▶ **1692** *n* acrobate *mf*.

acrobatic /ˌækrə'bætɪk/ *adj* [*person, feat*] acrobatique; [*skill*] d'acrobate.

acrobatics /ˌækrə'bætɪks/ *n* **1** (art) (+ *v sg*) acrobatie *f*; **2** (movements) (+ *v pl*) acrobaties *fpl*.

acronym /'ækrənɪm/ *n* acronyme *m*.

Acropolis /ə'krɒpəlɪs/ *pr n* Acropole *f*.

across /ə'krɒs/

■ **Note** *across* frequently occurs as the second element in certain verb combinations (*come across, run across, lean across etc*). For translations, look at the appropriate verb entry (*come, run, lean etc*).

I *prep* **1** (from one side to the other) **to go** ou **travel ~ sth** traverser qch; **to run/hurry ~ the room** traverser la pièce en courant/en vitesse; **to travel ~ country/town** traverser la campagne/la ville; **a journey ~ the desert** un voyage à travers le désert; **the bridge ~ the river** le pont qui traverse la rivière; **to be lying ~ the bed** être couché en travers du lit; **the line ~ the page** la ligne en travers de la page; **~ the years** à travers les années; **she leaned ~ the table** elle s'est penchée au-dessus de la table; **the scar ~ his face** la cicatrice sur sa figure; **his hair fell ~ his face** ses cheveux lui tombaient dans la figure; **he wiped his hand ~ his mouth** il a passé la main sur sa bouche; **the light flickered ~ the carpet** la lumière dansait sur la moquette; **the plane flew ~ the sky** l'avion a traversé le ciel; **2** (to, on the other side of) de l'autre côté de; **he lives ~ the street/square** il habite de l'autre côté de la rue/place; **he sat down ~ the desk/room (from me)** il s'est assis de l'autre côté du bureau/de la pièce; **the shops ~ town** les magasins de l'autre bout de la ville; **he looked ~ the lake to the boathouse** il a regardé le hangar de l'autre côté du lac; **she shouted ~ the room to them** elle leur a crié quelque chose depuis l'autre côté de la pièce; **3** (all over, covering a wide range of) **~ the world** partout dans le monde, à travers le monde; **~ the country/region** dans tout le pays/toute la région; **there is anger right ~ the industry** il y a des signes de colère dans tout le secteur; **scattered ~ the floor/the square** éparpillés sur le sol/la place; **cultural links ~ borders** fig les liens culturels au-delà des frontières.
II *adv* **1** (from one side to the other) **the lake is two miles ~** le lac fait deux miles de large; **to help sb ~** aider qn à traverser; **2** (on, to the other side) **to go ~ to sb** aller vers qn; **to look ~ at sb** regarder vers qn; **he called ~ to her** il l'a appelée.
III across from *prep phr* en face de.

across-the-board **I** *adj* **1** (affecting all levels) [*increase, cut*] général; **2** US Turf **to put on an ~ bet** jouer gagnant et placé.
II across the board *adv* (affecting all levels) à tous les niveaux.

acrostic /ə'krɒstɪk/ *n* acrostiche *m*.

acrylic /ə'krɪlɪk/ **I** *n* **1** Tex acrylique *m*; **2** Art (also **~ paint**) acrylique *m*.
II *modif* [*garment*] en acrylique.

act /ækt/ **I** *n* **1** (action, deed) acte *m*; **to be in the ~ of doing** être en train de faire; **an ~ of cruelty/kindness** un acte de cruauté/bonté; **it was the ~ of a madman** il fallait être fou pour faire ça; **2** Jur, Pol (law) (also **Act**) loi *f*; **Act of Parliament/Congress** loi votée par le Parlement/le Congrès; **3** Theat acte *m*; **a play in five ~s** une pièce en cinq actes; **4** (entertainment routine) numéro *m*; **song and dance ~** numéro *m* de chant et de danse; **to put on an ~** fig péj jouer la comédie; **it's all an ~** c'est de la frime○ or du cinéma○; **to get in on the ~** s'y mettre; **their company started the trend and now all their rivals want to get in on the ~** c'est leur entreprise qui a lancé la mode et maintenant tous leurs concurrents veulent s'y mettre aussi.
II *vtr* Theat jouer [*part, role*]; **he ~ed (the part of) the perfect host** fig il s'est comporté en hôte irréprochable.
III *vi* **1** (take action) agir; **we must ~ quickly** il nous faut agir rapidement; **she still believes she was ~ing for the best** elle persiste à penser qu'elle a fait pour le mieux; **they only ~ed out of fear** c'est la peur qui les a fait agir; **to ~ for sb, to ~ on behalf of sb** agir au nom de or pour le compte de qn; **2** (behave) agir, se comporter; **to ~ aggressively towards sb** se comporter or agir de manière agressive envers qn; **3** Theat jouer, faire du théâtre; fig (pretend) jouer la comédie, faire semblant; **she can't ~!** Theat elle joue mal!, c'est une mauvaise actrice!; **4** (take effect) [*drug, substance*] agir; **5** (serve) **to ~ as** [*person, object*] servir de; **he ~ed as their interpreter** il leur a servi d'interprète.
IDIOMS **to be caught in the ~** être pris sur le fait or en flagrant délit; **to get one's ~ together** se prendre en main; **it will be a hard ~ to follow** ça sera difficile à égaler.
■ **act on** agir conformément à [*information*]; tenir compte de [*warning*]; suivre [*advice*].
■ **act out** jouer [*role, part*]; représenter, reconstituer [*event*]; réaliser [*fantasy*]; Psych extérioriser, exprimer [*impulse, feeling*].
■ **act up**○ (misbehave) [*person*] se tenir mal; (malfunction) [*machine*] déconner◑, être détraqué.

acting /'æktɪŋ/ **I** *n* Cin, Theat (performance) jeu *m*, interprétation *f*; (occupation) métier *m* d'acteur; **have you done any ~?** est-ce que vous avez fait du théâtre?
II *modif* Cin, Theat [*style*] de jeu; [*talent, skill*] d'acteur.
III *adj* [*director, inspector etc*] intérimaire.

acting profession *n* **1** (occupation) Theat théâtre *m*; Cin cinéma *m*; **2** (actors collectively) acteurs *mpl*, comédiens *mpl*.

actinic /æk'tɪnɪk/ *adj* actinique.

actinium /æk'tɪnɪəm/ *n* actinium *m*.

action /'ækʃn/ *n* **1** ¢ gen action *f*; (to deal with situation) mesures *fpl*; **freedom of ~** liberté *f* d'action; **to take ~** agir, prendre des mesures (**against** contre); **to take ~ to do** prendre des mesures pour faire; **drastic ~** des mesures draconiennes; **the situation demands immediate ~** la situation exige des mesures immédiates; **a man of ~** un homme d'action; **day of ~** journée *f* d'action; **to push** ou **drive sb into ~** pousser qn à agir; **to put a plan/an idea into ~** mettre un projet/une idée à exécution; **to get into ~** entrer en action; **to put sth out of ~** mettre qch en panne; **his accident put him out of ~ for three months** son accident l'a mis complètement à plat○ pendant trois mois; **to be out of ~** [*machine*] être en panne; [*person*] être inactif/-ive; **you should see her in ~!** gen il faut la voir en pleine action!; iron il faut la voir à l'œuvre!; **to be back in ~** être de retour; **for ~ please** (on memo) pour exécution; **2** (deed) acte *m*; **to judge sb by their ~s** juger qn à ses actes; **he defended his ~ in sacking them** il a défendu ce qu'il avait fait en les licenciant; **~s speak louder than words** mieux vaut agir que parler; **3** (fighting) action *f*, combat *m*; **to see (some) ~** combattre; **to go into ~** aller au combat or au feu; **to be killed in ~** être tué au combat; **killed by enemy ~** tué par l'ennemi; **4** Cin, Theat action *f*; **the ~ takes place in Beirut** l'action se passe à Beyrouth; **~!** moteur!; **5**○ (excitement) **to be at the centre of the ~** être au centre de l'action; **I don't want to miss out on the ~** je ne veux pas rater ce qui se passe; **that's where the ~ is** c'est là où ça bouge○; **they want a piece of the ~** (want to be involved) ils ne veulent pas être en reste; (want some of the profits) ils veulent leur part du gâteau○; **6** Jur action *f*, procès *m*; **to bring an ~ against sb** intenter une action contre qn; **libel ~** procès en diffamation; **7** (movement) (of body) mouvement *m*; **wrist ~** mouvement *m* du poignet; **8** Tech (in machine, piano) mécanisme *m*; **9** Chem action *f*.
IDIOMS **~ stations!** Mil, fig à vos postes!

actionable /'ækʃənəbl/ *adj* [*remark, offence*] passible de poursuites.

action: **~ committee** *n* comité *m* d'action; **~ film** *n* film *m* d'action; **~ group** *n* groupe *m* de pression; **Action on Smoking and Health** *n* GB *groupe de pression anti-tabac*; **~-packed** *adj* [*film*] plein d'action; [*weekend, holiday*] bien rempli; **~ painting** *n* peinture *f* gestuelle.

action replay *n* GB TV répétition *f* d'une séquence; **to show an ~ of a goal** repasser un but au ralenti.

action shot *n* Phot instantané *m*.

activate /'æktɪveɪt/ *vtr* **1** gen, Tech faire démarrer [*machine, system*]; actionner [*button, switch*]; déclencher [*alarm, procedure*]; stimuler [*brain, memory*]; **2** Nucl rendre [qch] radioactif; **3** US Mil mettre [qch] sur pied [*unit*]; **4** Chem activer.

activated carbon *n* Chem charbon *m* activé.

activation /,æktɪ'veɪʃn/ *n* **1** gen (of machine, system) démarrage *m*; (of alarm, procedure) déclenchement *m*; (of brain, memory) stimulation *f*; **2** Nucl, Chem activation *f*; **3** US Mil mise *f* sur pied.

activator /'æktɪveɪtə(r)/ *n* Chem activateur *m*.

active/'æktɪv/ *adj* **1** gen [*person, life, mind, member, resistance*] actif/-ive; [*campaign*] énergique; [*debate*] animé; [*volcano*] en activité; **to be ~ in** être un membre actif de [*party, organization*]; **to be ~ in doing** s'employer (activement) à faire; **to play an ~ role** ou **part in sth** jouer un rôle actif dans qch; **to take an ~ interest in sth** s'intéresser activement à qch; **2** Mil [*unit*] actif/-ive; **3** Ling [*voice, verb*] actif/-ive; **4** Fin [*trading, dealing*] actif/-ive; **5** Comput [*file, window*] actif/-ive; **6** Jur [*law*] en vigueur.

active: **~ citizen** *n* GB *personne prenant une part active à la prévention criminelle*; **~ duty**, **~ service** *n* Mil service *m* actif; **~ ingredient** *n* principe *m* actif.

active list *n* Mil (liste *f* de) cadres *mpl* d'active; **to be on the ~** être cadre d'active.

actively /'æktɪvlɪ/ *adv* activement; **to be ~ considering doing** penser sérieusement à faire.

active vocabulary *n* vocabulaire *m* actif.

activism /'æktɪvɪzəm/ *n* activisme *m*.

activist /'æktɪvɪst/ *n* activiste *mf*.

activity /æk'tɪvətɪ/ *n* (all contexts) activité *f*; **business activities** activités *fpl* professionnelles; **brain ~** activité *f* cérébrale.

activity holiday *n* GB ≈ vacances *fpl* sportives.

act: **~ of contrition** *n* acte *m* de contrition; **~ of faith** *n* acte *m* de foi; **~ of God** *n* désastre *m* naturel; **~ of war** *n* acte *m* de guerre.

actor /'æktə(r)/ *n* acteur *m*, comédien *m*.

actress /'æktrɪs/ *n* actrice *f*, comédienne *f*.

Acts of the Apostles *npl* Actes *mpl* des Apôtres.

ACTT *n* GB (*abrév* = **Association of Cinematographic, Television and Allied Technicians**) syndicat *m* des techniciens de l'audiovisuel.

actual /'æktʃʊəl/ *adj* **1** (real, specific) réel/réelle; **I don't remember the ~ words/figures** je ne me rappelle pas les mots/chiffres exacts; **in ~ fact** en fait; **it has nothing to do with the ~ problem/work** cela n'a rien à voir avec le problème/ travail lui-même; **2** (genuine) même (*after n*); **this is the ~ room that Shakespeare worked in** voici la pièce même où Shakespeare travaillait; **3** (as such) à proprement parler; **he didn't give me an ~ cheque but**... il ne m'a pas donné un chèque à proprement parler mais...

actuality /,æktʃʊ'ælətɪ/ *n* réalité *f*.

actualize /'æktʃʊəlaɪz/ *vtr* **1** (make real) réaliser; **2** (represent realistically) actualiser.

actually /'æktʃʊəlɪ/ *adv* **1** (contrary to expectation) en fait; **their profits have ~ risen** en fait, leurs bénéfices ont augmenté; **he's ~ a very good driver** en fait, il est bon conducteur; **2** (in reality) vraiment; **yes, it ~ happened!** mais oui, c'est vraiment arrivé!; **they didn't ~ complain** ils ne se sont pas vraiment plaints; **3** (as sentence adv) en fait; **~, I'm not at all surprised** en fait, cela ne me surprend pas du tout; **no, she's a doctor, ~** non, en fait, elle est médecin; **~, I don't feel like it** à vrai dire je n'en ai pas envie; **4** (exactly) exactement; **what ~ happened?** qu'est-ce qui s'est passé exactement?; **what time did they ~ leave?** à quelle heure sont-ils partis exactement?; **5** (expressing indignation) carrément; **she ~ accused me of lying!** elle m'a carrément accusé de mentir!; **6** (expressing surprise) **she ~ thanked me** elle est allée jusqu'à me remercier.

actuarial /,æktʃʊ'eərɪəl/ *adj* [*calculation*] actuariel/-ielle; [*training*] d'actuaire.

actuary /'æktʃʊərɪ, US -tʃʊerɪ/ **▶ 1692** *n* Fin actuaire *mf*.

actuate /'æktʃʊeɪt/ *vtr* **1** Tech mettre [qch] en marche [*machine, system, device*]; déclencher [*alarm*]; **2** (motivate) pousser.

acuity /ə'kju:ətɪ/ *n* sout acuité *f*.

acumen /'ækjʊmən, ə'kju:mən/ *n* sagacité *f*; **business ~** sens *m* des affaires.

acupressure /'ækjʊpreʃə(r)/ *n* digipuncture *f*.

acupuncture /'ækjʊpʌŋktʃə(r)/ *n* acupuncture *f*.

acupuncturist /'ækjʊpʌŋktʃərɪst/ **▶ 1692** *n* acupuncteur/-trice *m/f*.

acute /ə'kju:t/ *adj* **1** (intense) [*anxiety, grief*] vif/vive; [*boredom, remorse*] profond; **to cause sb ~ embarrassment** beaucoup embarrasser qn; **2** Med [*condition, illness, symptom*] aigu/aiguë; **~ patient** urgence *f*; **~ care** soins *mpl* d'urgence; **~ hospital** hôpital *m* spécialisé dans les soins d'urgence; **3** (grave) [*crisis, shortage, situation*] grave; **4** (keen) [*person, mind*] pénétrant; [*intelligence*] aigu/aiguë; **to have ~ eyesight/hearing** avoir la vue/l'oreille fine; **to have an ~ sense of smell** avoir l'odorat fin.

acute: **~ accent** *n* Ling accent *m* aigu; **~ angle** *n* Math angle *m* aigu; **~-angled** *adj* Geom acutangle.

acutely /ə'kju:tlɪ/ *adv* **1** (intensely) [*suffer*] vivement; [*embarrassed, sensitive*] excessivement; **I am ~ aware of these problems** je suis extrêmement conscient de ces problèmes; **here the need for more funding is felt most ~** ici le besoin de crédits se fait sentir de façon très aiguë; **2** (shrewdly) [*observe*] avec perspicacité.

acuteness /ə'kju:tnɪs/ *n* **1** (sharpness) (of mind, judgment) finesse *f*; **2** (of pain) intensité *f*; **3** Med (of disease, condition) gravité *f*; **4** (seriousness) (of shortage, crisis) gravité *f*.

acute respiratory disease, **ARD** **▶ 1354** *n* maladie *f* aiguë de l'appareil respiratoire.

ad /æd/ *n* (*abrév* = **advertisement**) **1** Journ (also **small ~**) petite annonce *f* (**for** pour); **2** Radio, TV pub○ *f* (**for** pour).

AD (*abrév* = **Anno Domini**) ap J.-C.

A/D *adj* (*abrév* = **analogue-digital**) analogique-numérique.

adage /'ædɪdʒ/ *n* adage *m* (**that** selon lequel).

adagio /ə'dɑ:dʒɪəʊ/ **I** *n* adagio *m*.
II *modif* **~ passage** adagio *m*.
III *adv* adagio.

Adam /'ædəm/ *pr n* Adam.
IDIOMS **I don't know him from ~** je ne le connais ni d'Ève ni d'Adam.

adamant /'ædəmənt/ *adj* catégorique (**about** sur); **to be ~ that** (regarding past events) être catégorique sur le fait que; (regarding future events) insister sur le fait que; **to remain ~** rester inébranlable.

adamantly /'ædəməntlɪ/ *adv* [*opposed*] catégoriquement; [*say, oppose*] de façon catégorique.

Adam's apple *n* pomme *f* d'Adam.

adapt /ə'dæpt/ **I** *vtr* adapter (**to** à; **for** pour; **from** de).
II *vi* s'adapter (**to** à).
III *v refl* **to ~ oneself** s'adapter (**to** à).

adaptability /ə,dæptə'bɪlətɪ/ *n* **1** (of person) (flexibility) faculté *f* d'adaptation; (ability to change) adaptabilité *f* (**to** à); **2** (of book, film) adaptabilité *f* (**to** pour); (of machine, system, vehicle) adaptabilité *f* (**to** à).

adaptable /ə'dæptəbl/ *adj* [*person, organization*] capable de s'adapter; **to be ~ for** [*book, play*] pouvoir être adapté pour [*cinema, TV*]; **to be ~ to sth** [*system, machine*] pouvoir être adapté à qch.

adaptation /,ædæp'teɪʃn/ *n* (all contexts) adaptation *f*.

adapter, adaptor /ə'dæptə(r)/ *n* **1** Elec, Mech adaptateur *m*; **2** (person) adaptateur/-trice *m/f*.

adapter ring, **adapter tube** *n* Phot bague *f* d'adaptation.

ADC *n* (*abrév* = **analogue-digital converter**) convertisseur *m* analogique-numérique.

add /æd/ *vtr* **1** gen ajouter, rajouter (**onto, to** à); **to ~ that** ajouter que; **I've nothing to ~** je n'ai rien à ajouter; **2** Math (also **~ together**) additionner; **to ~ sth to** ajouter qch à [*figure, total*]; **~ the two figures (together)** additionner les deux chiffres.
■ **add in**: **~ [sth] in, ~ in [sth]** ajouter.
■ **add on**: **~ [sth] on, ~ on [sth]** ajouter; **to ~ on an extra room** agrandir une maison en ajoutant une pièce.
■ **add to**: **~ to [sth]** ajouter à [*problems, costs, income*]; accentuer [*irritation, tension, confusion*]; agrandir [*house, total*].
■ **add up**: ¶ **~ up** [*facts, figures*] s'accorder; **it doesn't ~ up** fig cela ne tient pas debout○; **it all ~s up!** lit (accumulate) tout cela s'additionne; fig (make sense) je comprends tout maintenant!; **to ~ up to** lit [*total*] s'élever à [*amount, number*]; [*factors*] contribuer à [*success, disaster, result*]; **his achievements ~ up to very little** il n'a pas accompli grand-chose; ¶ **~ up [sth], ~ [sth] up** additionner [*cost, numbers, totals*].

added /'ædɪd/ *adj* supplémentaire; **~ to which**... ajoutez à cela que...

addendum /ə'dendəm/ *n* (*pl* **-da**) addenda *m inv* (**to** à).

adder /'ædə(r)/ *n* **1** (snake) vipère *f*; **2** Comput additionneur *m*.

addict /'ædɪkt/ *n* **1** (drug-user) toxicomane *mf*; **coffee ~** accro○ *mf* du café; **2** fig (enthusiast) fana○ *mf*, accro○ *mf*; **telly ~**○ accro○ *mf* de la télé○.

addicted /ə'dɪktɪd/ *adj* **to be/become ~** lit avoir/former une dépendance (**to** à); fig être/devenir fanatique or accro○ (**to** de).

addiction /ə'dɪkʃn/ *n* **1** lit (to alcohol, drugs) dépendance *f* (**to** à); **drug ~** toxicodépendance *f*; **tobacco ~** tabagisme *m*; **2** fig (to music, chocolate) passion *f* (**to** pour).

addictive /ə'dɪktɪv/ *adj* **1** lit [*drug, substance*] qui crée une dépendance; **tobacco is ~** le tabac crée une dépendance; **2** fig **to be ~** [*chocolate, power*] être comme une drogue.

adding machine *n* machine *f* à calculer.

addition /ə'dɪʃn/ **I** *n* **1** (person or thing added) (to text, list, house) ajout *m*; (to team, range) adjonction *f*; (to corporation, company) acquisition *f*; **the latest ~ to the family** le dernier-né/la dernière-née *m/f* de la famille; **2** ¢ (process of adding) gen adjonction *f* (**of** de); Math addition *f*.
II in addition *adv phr* en plus.
III in addition to *prep phr* en plus de.

additional /ə'dɪʃənl/ *adj* supplémentaire; **~ charge** supplément *m*.

additionally /ə'dɪʃənəlɪ/ *adv* (moreover) en outre; (also) en plus; **~, there was a risk of fire** en outre, il y avait un risque d'incendie; **we ~ offer private tuition** et en plus nous offrons des cours particuliers.

additive /'ædɪtɪv/ *n* additif *m*.

addled /'ædld/ *adj* lit [*egg*] pourri; fig [*brain*] confus.

addle-headed○ /ˌædl'hedɪd/ *adj* abruti○.

add-on /'ædɒn/ **I** *n* option *f*.
II *adj* supplémentaire.

address /ə'dres, US 'ædres/ **I** *n* **1** (place of residence) adresse *f*; **to change (one's) ~** changer d'adresse; **2** (speech) discours *m* (**to** à); **to give** ou **deliver an ~** faire un discours; **3** (as etiquette) **form of ~ (for sb)** formule *f* pour s'adresser à qn; **4** Comput adresse *f*.
II *vtr* **1** (write address on) mettre l'adresse sur [*parcel, letter*]; **to ~ sth to sb** adresser qch à qn; **to be wrongly ~ed** avoir un libellé incorrect; **2** (speak to) s'adresser à [*group, person*]; **Mr X will now ~ the meeting** maintenant M. X va prendre la parole; **3** (aim) adresser [*remark, complaint*] (**to** à); **4** (tackle) aborder [*question, issue*]; s'occuper de [*problem, needs*]; **5** (use title of) **to ~ sb as sth** appeler qn par son titre de qch; **6** (in golf) s'apprêter à frapper [*ball*].
III *v refl* **to ~ oneself to sth** aborder [*question, issue*]; s'occuper de [*problem, needs*]; se mettre à [*task, job*].

address book *n* carnet *m* d'adresses.

addressee /ˌædre'siː/ *n* destinataire *mf*.

addressing /ə'dresɪŋ, US 'ædresɪŋ/ *n* Comput adressage *m*.

Addressograph® /ə'dresəʊgrɑːf, US -græf/ *n* adressographe *m*.

adduce /ə'djuːs, US ə'duːs/ *vtr* sout fournir [*evidence*]; invoquer [*reason*]; citer [*fact*].

adductor /ə'dʌktə(r)/ *n* Anat (muscle *m*) adducteur *m*.

Adelaide /'ædəleɪd/ **▶1818** *pr n* Adélaïde.

adenoidal /ædɪ'nɔɪdl, US -dən-/ *adj* nasillard.

adenoids /'ædɪnɔɪdz, US -dən-/ *npl* végétations *fpl* (adénoïdes).

adept I /'ædept/ *n* expert/-e *m/f*.
II /ə'dept/ *adj* [*cook, gardener*] expert; **to be ~ at sth/at doing** être expert en qch/en l'art de faire.

adequacy /'ædɪkwəsɪ/ *n* **1** (of sum) caractère *m* adéquat; **2** (of description, explanation, theory) adéquation *f*; **3** (of person) (for job, task) compétence *f*.

adequate /'ædɪkwət/ *adj* **1** [*funds, supply, staff, insurance, parking*] suffisant (**for** pour; **to do** pour faire); **2** [*punishment, care, arrangements*] satisfaisant; **3** [*description, explanation, performance*] correct; **an ~ range of options** une gamme de possibilités correcte; **4 to be ~** [*person*] être à la hauteur (**to** de).

adequately /'ædɪkwətlɪ/ *adv* **1** [*pay, compensate*] convenablement; [*insure*] suffisamment; **2** [*prepared, equipped, educated*] suffisamment; **this ~ meets our needs** cela nous suffit largement; **3** [*describe, explain*] convenablement; [*perform*] correctement.

adhere /əd'hɪə(r)/ *vi* **1** lit coller, adhérer (**to** à); **2** fig **to ~ to** adhérer à [*belief, ideology*]; observer [*rule, policy, plan, commitment*]; respecter, observer [*standards, deadlines*]; être d'accord avec [*opinion*].

adherence /əd'hɪərəns/ *n* (to belief, ideology) adhésion *f* (**to** à); (to rule, plan, method, policy) observation *f* (**to** de); (to deadline, commitment) respect *m* (**to** de).

adherent /əd'hɪərənt/ *n* (of party) membre *mf*; (of cult, religion) disciple *mf*; (of doctrine) adhérent/-e *m/f*; (of plan, policy) tenant/-e *m/f*.

adhesion /əd'hiːʒn/ *n* **1** lit, Med adhérence *f*; **2** fig (to belief, religion) adhésion *f* (**to** à).

adhesive /əd'hiːsɪv/ **I** *n* colle *f*, adhésif *m*.
II *adj* gen collant; [*stamp*] gommé; **~ tape** papier *m* collant, Scotch® *m*; **self-~** autocollant.

ad hoc /ˌæd 'hɒk/ **I** *adj* [*arrangement, plan*] improvisé; [*alliance, group*] temporaire; [*speech*] de circonstance *inv* (*after n*); [*committee, decision, legislation*] ad hoc *inv* (*after n*); **on an ~ basis** au coup par coup.
II *adv* [*do*] au coup par coup.

adieu† /ə'djuː, US ə'duː/ **I** *n* (*pl* **~s** ou **~x**) adieu *m*; **to bid sb ~** faire ses adieux à qn.
II *excl* adieu!

ad infinitum /ˌæd ˌɪnfɪ'naɪtəm/ *adv* [*continue*] à n'en plus finir; [*extend*] à l'infini.

ad interim /ˌæd 'ɪntərɪm/ **I** *adj* [*measure*] provisoire.
II *adv* [*arrange*] provisoirement.

adipose /'ædɪpəʊs/ *adj* adipeux/-euse.

adiposity /ˌædɪ'pɒsətɪ/ *n* adiposité *f*.

adjacent /ə'dʒeɪsnt/ *adj* **1** (touching) [*buildings, gardens, fields*] contigu/-uë; **~ to sth** attenant à qch; **2** (nearby) voisin (**to** de); **3** Math [*angle*] adjacent.

adjectival /ˌædʒək'taɪvl/ *adj* adjectival.

adjectivally /ˌædʒək'taɪvəlɪ/ *adv* [*function*] de façon adjectivale.

adjective /'ædʒɪktɪv/ *n* adjectif *m*.

adjective law *n* Jur droit *m* procédural.

adjoin /ə'dʒɔɪn/ **I** *vtr* [*room*] être contigu/-uë à; [*building, land*] être attenant à.
II *vi* [*land, buildings*] être attenant; [*rooms*] être contigu/-uë.
III adjoining *pres p adj* [*building, land*] attenant; [*room, office, state, province*] voisin.

adjourn /ə'dʒɜːn/ **I** *vtr* ajourner [*session, trial, meeting*] (**for** pour; **until** à); **to ~ sentence** Jur ajourner une sentence; **the session was ~ed** la séance a été levée.
II *vi* **1** (suspend proceedings) s'arrêter (**for** pour); Jur suspendre la séance; (close session) lever la séance; **Parliament** ou **the House ~ed** (for break) la Chambre a interrompu les débats; (at end of debate) la Chambre a levé la séance; **2** souvent hum (move on) passer (**to** à).

adjournment /ə'dʒɜːnmənt/ *n* (of trial) ajournement *m*; (of session) suspension *f*; (of debate) renvoi *m*.

adjournment debate *n* GB Pol débat *m* final (*avant les vacances parlementaires*).

adjudge /ə'dʒʌdʒ/ *vtr* Jur **1** (decree) déclarer (**that** que); **the court ~d him (to be) guilty** le tribunal l'a déclaré coupable; **to be ~d as** être déclaré comme étant; **he is ~d to have done** on a déclaré qu'il a fait; **2** (award) adjuger [*costs*]; allouer, accorder [*damages*].

adjudicate /ə'dʒuːdɪkeɪt/ **I** *vtr* gen, Jur juger [*contest*]; régler [*dispute*]; examiner [*case, claim*].
II *vi* **1** gen, Jur choisir (**between** entre); **to ~ on sth** se prononcer sur qch; **2** (in chess) analyser les positions.

adjudication /əˌdʒuːdɪ'keɪʃn/ *n* **1** (of contest) jugement *m*; **2** Jur décision *f*; **under ~** en train d'être examiné.

adjudication: **~ of bankruptcy**, **~ order** *n* Jur jugement *m* déclaratif de liquidation judiciaire; **~ panel** *n* Admin, Comm équipe *f* décisionnelle; (of contest) juges *mpl*.

adjudicator /ə'dʒuːdɪkeɪtə(r)/ *n* juge *m*.

adjunct /'ædʒʌŋkt/ **I** *n* **1** (addition) annexe *f* (**of, to** de); **2** (person) subalterne *mf* (**of, to** de); **3** US (part-time role) adjoint *m*; **4** Ling adjoint *m*.
II *adj* US [*teacher, professor*] adjoint.

adjure /ə'dʒʊə(r)/ *vtr* adjurer [*person*] (**to do** à faire).

adjust /ə'dʒʌst/ **I** *vtr* **1** gen, Tech régler [*component, control, fitting, level, position, machine, speed*]; ajuster [*amount, price, rate, timetable*]; rajuster [*clothing*]; rectifier [*figures, statistics*]; mettre au point [*terms, arrangements*]; **to ~ sth to sth** adapter qch en fonction de qch; **to ~ [sth] upwards/downwards** augmenter/diminuer [*salary, sum*]; **2** Insur régler [*claim*].
II *vi* **1** (adapt) [*person*] s'adapter (**to** à); **2** (be adaptable) [*component, fitting, machine*] s'ajuster; [*seat*] être réglable; **to ~ to sth** [*machine, component, fitment, control*] se régler sur qch.
III -adjusted (*dans composés*) **well-~ed** [*person*] équilibré.

adjustability /əˌdʒʌstə'bɪlətɪ/ *n* (of machine, appliance) réglage *m*; (of rate) ajustement *m*.

adjustable /ə'dʒʌstəbl/ *adj* **1** gen [*appliance, fitting, level, position, seat, speed*] réglable; [*timetable*] variable; [*rate*] ajustable; **tilt/height ~** Aut à inclinaison/à hauteur variable; **2** Insur [*loss, claim*] donnant droit à une indemnité (*after n*).

adjustable spanner, **adjustable wrench** *n* clé *f* à molette.

adjuster /ə'dʒʌstə(r)/ *n* Insur rédacteur/-trice *m/f* sinistre.

adjustment /ə'dʒʌstmənt/ *n* **1** Fin (of rates, charges) rajustement *m* (**of** de); **2** Tech (of control, fitting, machine) réglage *m* (**of** de); **3** gen (modification) modification *f* (**to** de); **to make ~s to** apporter des modifications à [*strategy, system, machine, arrangements, lifestyle*]; rajuster [*garment*]; **4** gen (mental, physical) adaptation *f* (**to** à); **to make the ~ to** s'adapter à [*culture, lifestyle*]; **5** Insur indemnité *f*.

adjutant /'ædʒʊtənt/ **▶1612** *n* Mil officier *m* adjoint.

adjutant bird, **adjutant stork** *n* adjudant *m*, marabout *m* chevelu.

ad-lib /ˌæd 'lɪb/ **I** *n* (on stage) improvisation *f*; (witticism) bon mot *m*.
II *adj* [*comment, line, performance*] improvisé; [*comedian*] d'improvisation.
III *adv* [*perform, speak*] en improvisant.
IV *vtr, vi* (*p prés etc* **-bb-**) improviser.

ad-libbing /ˌæd'lɪbɪŋ/ *n* ¢ improvisations *fpl*.

ad libitum /ˌæd 'lɪbɪtəm/ *adj, adv* Mus ad libitum.

adman○ /'ædmæn/ *n* publicitaire *m*.

admass /'ædmæs/ GB **I** *n* masses *fpl*.
II *modif* [*culture*] de masse; [*society*] de consommation.

admin○ /'ædmɪn/ GB **I** *n* administration *f*.
II *adj* administratif/-ive.

administer /əd'mɪnɪstə(r)/ *vtr* **1** (also **administrate**) (manage) gérer [*company, affairs, estate, policy, project, funds*]; gouverner [*territory*]; **2** (dispense) administrer [*punishment, medicine, treatment*]; exercer [*justice*]; donner [*caution*]; Relig administrer [*sacrament*].

administrate /əd'mɪnɪstreɪt/ *vtr* = **administer** 1.

administration /ədˌmɪnɪ'streɪʃn/ *n* **1** (of business, funds) gestion *f*; **2** (of hospital, school, territory) administration *f*; **3** Jur (of company) administration *f* judiciaire; **to go into ~** être placé sous administration judiciaire; **4** (of justice) exercice *m*; **5** (government) **C** gouvernement *m*; **6** (paperwork) travail *m* administratif.

administration: **~ building**, **~ block** GB *n* bâtiment *m* administratif; **~ costs**, **~ expenses** *n* Accts frais *mpl* de gestion; **~ order** *n* Jur ordonnance *f* instituant l'administration judiciaire.

administrative /əd'mɪnɪstrətɪv, US -streɪtɪv/ *adj* administratif/-ive; **~ tribunal** tribunal *m* administratif.

administratively /əd'mɪnɪstrətɪvlɪ, US -streɪtɪvlɪ/ *adv* [*complex, convenient, impossible*] du point de vue administratif.

administrator /əd'mɪnɪstreɪtə(r)/ **▶1692** *n* **1** Comm, Mgmt administrateur/-trice *m/f* (**for, of** de); **sales ~** directeur/-trice *m/f* des ventes; **2** (of hospital, school, theatre) administrateur *m*; **3** Jur, Fin administrateur *m* judiciaire.

admirable /'ædmərəbl/ *adj* admirable.

admirably /'ædmərəblɪ/ *adv* admirablement.

admiral /'ædmərəl/ *n* **1** **▶1612** Mil, Naut amiral *m*; **fleet ~** US, **~ of the fleet** GB amiral; **2** Zool nymphalidé *m*.

admiralty /ˈædmərəltɪ/ *n* **1** Mil (rank of admiral) amirauté *f*; **2** GB Hist ≈ ministère *m* de la Marine.

Admiralty Board *n* GB état-major *m* de la Marine britannique.

admiration /ˌædməˈreɪʃn/ *n* admiration *f* (**for** pour); **to be the ~ of sb** faire l'admiration de qn; **to look at sb/sth with** ou **in ~** être en admiration devant qn/qch.

admire /ədˈmaɪə(r)/ *vtr* admirer [*person, painting, quality*]; **he ~s her for her courage** il admire son courage; **to ~ sb for doing** admirer que qn fasse; **to be ~d by sb** être admiré de qn.

admirer /ədˈmaɪərə(r)/ *n* **1** admirateur/-trice *m/f*; **you have an ~!** hum t'as un admirateur!; **2** (lover) soupirant *m*.

admiring /ədˈmaɪərɪŋ/ *adj* admiratif/-ive.

admiringly /ədˈmaɪərɪŋlɪ/ *adv* [*look, say*] avec admiration.

admissibility /əˌdmɪsəˈbɪlətɪ/ *n* Jur recevabilité *f*.

admissible /ədˈmɪsəbl/ *adj* Jur, gen recevable.

admission /ədˈmɪʃn/ **I** *n* **1** (entry) entrée *f*, admission *f*; **~ to a country/an organization** entrée or admission dans un pays/une organisation; **to refuse sb ~** refuser l'entrée à qn; **to gain ~** se faire admettre (**to** dans); **'~ by ticket only'** 'entrée sur présentation d'un billet uniquement'; **no ~** entrée interdite (**to** à); **2** (fee charged) (droit *m* d') entrée *f*; **to charge £5 ~** faire payer 5 livres de droit d'entrée; **3** (confession) aveu *m*; **his ~ that**... son aveu selon lequel...; **by your/his/her etc own ~** de votre/son etc propre aveu; **an ~ of** un aveu de [*guilt, failure, weakness*].
II admissions *npl* **1** Univ inscriptions *fpl*; **2** Med admissions *fpl*.

admission: **~s office** *n* Univ service *m* d'inscriptions; **~s officer** ▶ 1692 *n* Univ agent *m* chargé des inscriptions; **~s procedure** *n* Univ procédure *f* d'inscription.

admit /ədˈmɪt/ (*p prés etc* **-tt-**) **I** *vtr* **1** (accept) reconnaître, admettre [*mistake, fact*]; **to ~ that** reconnaître que; **to ~ to** reconnaître [*error, mistake, fact*]; **he ~s to making a mistake** il reconnaît s'être trompé; **she ~s to feeling angry** elle reconnaît qu'elle était en colère; **it is annoying, I** (**must** ou **have to**) **~** c'est embêtant, je dois le reconnaître; **he would never ~ that**... il ne voudrait jamais admettre que...; **it is generally ~ted that** on s'accorde à reconnaître que; **to ~ defeat** s'avouer vaincu; **2** (confess) avouer [*crime, wrongdoing*] reconnaître [*guilt*]; **to ~ that one has done** avouer avoir fait; **to ~ to sth/doing** avouer qch/avoir fait; **3** (allow to enter) [*person, authority*] laisser entrer [*person*] (**into** dans); **this ticket ~s two** (**people**) ce billet est valable pour deux personnes; **'this ticket ~s you to the house and gardens'** 'ce billet vous donne accès au bâtiment et aux jardins'; **'dogs not ~ted'** 'entrée interdite aux chiens'; **to be ~ted to hospital** être hospitalisé; **4** (allow to become a member) admettre [*person*] (**to** à); **5** Jur **to ~ sth in evidence** admettre qch comme moyen de preuve.
II *vi* (allow) **~ of** sout admettre, permettre.

admittance /ədˈmɪtns/ *n* accès *m*, entrée *f*; **to gain ~** réussir à entrer; **to refuse sb ~** refuser l'entrée à qn; **'no ~'** 'accès interdit au public'.

admittedly /ədˈmɪtɪdlɪ/ *adv* il est vrai, il faut en convenir; **~, he did lie but**... il est vrai qu'il a menti, mais...

admixture /ædˈmɪkstʃə(r)/ *n* sout **1** (mixing) mélange *m* (**of** de); **2** (added element) part *f* (**of** de); **3** (alien ingredient) élément *m*.

admonish /ədˈmɒnɪʃ/ *vtr* sout **1** gen, Jur (reprimand) admonester fml (**for** pour; **for doing** pour avoir fait); **2** (advise) conseiller vivement à.

admonition /ˌædməˈnɪʃn/ *n* sout **1** gen, Jur (reprimand) admonition *f* fml; **2** gen, Mil (warning) avertissement *m*.

admonitory /ədˈmɒnɪtrɪ, US -tɔːrɪ/ *adj* sout **1** (warning) [*letter, speech*] d'avertissement *m*; **2** (disapproving) [*remark, tone, look*] de réprimande.

ad nauseam /ˌæd ˈnɔːzɪæm/ *adv* [*discuss, repeat, practise*] à n'en plus finir; [*hear, endure*] des centaines de fois.

adnominal /ˌædˈnɒmɪnl/ *n, adj* adnominal (*m*).

ado /əˈduː/ *n* **without more** ou **further ~** sans plus de cérémonie.
IDIOMS **much ~ about nothing** beaucoup de bruit pour rien.

adobe /əˈdəʊbɪ/ **I** *n* (brick, material) adobe *m*.
II *modif* [*house*] en pisé.

adolescence /ˌædəˈlesns/ *n* adolescence *f*; **in early/late ~** dans les premières/dernières années de l'adolescence.

adolescent /ˌædəˈlesnt/ **I** *n* adolescent/-e *m/f*.
II *adj* **1** (teenage) [*crisis, rebellion*] d'adolescent; [*problem*] des adolescents; [*years*] de l'adolescence; [*friend*] adolescent; **~ boy/girl** adolescent/-e *m/f*; **~ acne** acné *f* juvénile; **2** (childish) [*humour, behaviour*] puéril.

Adonis /əˈdəʊnɪs/ *pr n* Mythol, fig Adonis.

adopt /əˈdɒpt/ *vtr* adopter [*child, idea, method, attitude*]; prendre [*accent, tone, identity*]; choisir [*candidate, career*]; adopter [*bill, proposal, recommendation*]; **to ~ sb as candidate** Pol choisir qn comme candidat.

adopted /əˈdɒptɪd/ *adj* [*child*] adopté; [*son, daughter*] adoptif/-ive; [*name, country*] d'adoption.

adoption /əˈdɒpʃn/ **I** *n* (of child, identity) adoption *f* (**of** de; **by** par); (of idea, method, bill) adoption *f* (**of** de; **by** par); (of candidate) choix *m* (**of** de; **by** par); **French by ~** Français/-e d'adoption.
II *modif* [*papers, process*] d'adoption; [*expert*] en adoption.

adoption agency *n*: *service officiel chargé des questions d'adoption*.

adoptive /əˈdɒptɪv/ *adj* adoptif/-ive.

adorable /əˈdɔːrəbl/ *adj* adorable.

adoration /ˌædəˈreɪʃn/ *n* adoration *f* (**of** de); **his ~ for his mother** l'adoration qu'il porte à sa mère; **in ~** en adoration.

adore /əˈdɔː(r)/ *vtr* adorer (**to do, doing** faire).

adoring /əˈdɔːrɪŋ/ *adj* [*husband*] épris; [*fan*] passionné; [*look, gaze*] rempli d'adoration.

adoringly /əˈdɔːrɪŋlɪ/ *adv* avec adoration.

adorn /əˈdɔːn/ littér **I** *vtr* orner [*building, room, walls*] (**with** de); parer [*body, hair*] (**with** de).
II *v refl* **to ~ oneself** se parer (**with** de).

adornment /əˈdɔːnmənt/ *n* **1** (object) ornement *m*; **2** ¢ (art) décoration *f* (**of** de).

ADP *n* (*abrév* = **automatic data processing**) traitement *m* automatique de l'information.

adrenal /əˈdriːnl/ *adj* surrénal.

adrenal gland *n* glande *f* surrénale.

adrenalin(e) /əˈdrenəlɪn/ *n* Physiol, gen adrénaline *f*; **a rush** ou **surge of ~** une montée d'adrénaline; **to get the ~ flowing** faire monter l'adrénaline.

Adriatic (sea) /ˌeɪdrɪˈætɪk/ ▶ 1511 **I** *pr n* **the ~** la mer *f* Adriatique, l'Adriatique *f*.
II *adj* [*coast, resort*] de l'Adriatique.

adrift /əˈdrɪft/ *adj, adv* **1** (floating free) [*person, boat*] à la dérive; **to set** ou **cast ~** laisser aller à la dérive; **to be ~** aller à la dérive; **2 to go ~** [*plan*] aller à vau-l'eau; **3** (loose) **to come ~** se détacher (**of, from** de); **4** GB Sport **two goals ~ of their rivals** à deux buts de leurs rivaux.

adroit /əˈdrɔɪt/ *adj* habile (**in, at** à; **in** ou **at doing** à faire).

adroitly /əˈdrɔɪtlɪ/ *adv* habilement.

adroitness /əˈdrɔɪtnɪs/ *n* habileté *f*.

adspeak /ˈædspiːk/ *n* jargon *m* publicitaire.

aduki bean /æˈduːkɪ biːn/, **adzuki bean** /æˈdzuːkɪ biːn/ *n* Culin adzuki *m*, petite fève *f*.

adulate /ˈædjʊleɪt, US ˈædʒʊ-/ *vtr* sout aduler.

adulation /ˌædjʊˈleɪʃn, US ˌædʒʊ-/ *n* sout adulation *f* (**of** de); **in ~** avec adulation.

adult /ˈædʌlt, əˈdʌlt/ **I** *n* gen, Jur adulte *mf*; **'~s only'** 'interdit aux moins de 18 ans'.
II *adj* **1** [*smoker, driver, animal*] adulte; [*class, clothes, fiction*] pour adultes; [*population, mortality, audience, behaviour*] adulte; [*life*] d'adulte; [*son, daughter*] majeur; **2** euph (pornographic) [*film, magazine*] pour adultes.

Adult Education *n* GB formation *f* permanente.

Adult Education Centre *n* GB centre *m* de formation pour adultes.

adulterate /əˈdʌltəreɪt/ *vtr* falsifier (**with** par addition de).

adulteration /əˌdʌltəˈreɪʃn/ *n* falsification *f* (**of** de; **with** par addition de).

adulterer /əˈdʌltərə(r)/ *n* adultère *m*.

adulteress /əˈdʌltərɪs/ *n* (*pl* **~es**) adultère *f*.

adulterous /əˈdʌltərəs/ *adj* adultère.

adultery /əˈdʌltərɪ/ *n* adultère *m* (**with** avec).

adulthood /ˈædʌlthʊd/ *n* ¢ âge *m* adulte; **to survive into/reach ~** survivre à/atteindre l'âge adulte.

adult literacy *n* GB **~ classes** cours *m* d'alphabétisation pour adultes.

Adult Training Centre *n* GB centre *m* d'aide au travail.

adumbrate /ˈædʌmbreɪt/ *vtr* sout **1** (outline) ébaucher; **2** (foreshadow) préfigurer.

advance /ədˈvɑːns, US -ˈvæns/ **I** *n* **1** (forward movement) gen, Mil avance *f* (**on** sur); fig (of civilization, in science) progrès *m*; **with the ~ of old age** avec l'âge; **recent ~s in medicine** les progrès récents dans le domaine de la médecine; **a great ~ for democracy** un grand pas en avant pour la démocratie; **2** (sum of money) avance *f*, acompte *m* (**on** sur); **to ask for an ~ on one's salary** demander une avance sur son salaire; **3** (increase) **any ~ on £100?** (at auction etc) cent livres, qui dit mieux?
II advances *npl* (overtures) (sexual) avances *fpl*; (other contexts) démarches *fpl*; **to make ~s to sb** (sexually) faire des avances à qn; (other contexts) faire des démarches auprès de qn.
III in advance *adv phr* [*book, reserve, notify, know*] à l'avance; [*thank, pay, arrange, decide*] à l'avance, d'avance; **a month in ~** un mois à l'avance; **here's £30 in ~** voici 30 livres d'avance ou d'acompte; **you need to book your seats well in ~** il faut réserver vos places longtemps à l'avance; **to send on luggage in ~** envoyer des bagages à l'avance; **to send sb on in ~** envoyer qn en avant.
IV in advance of *adv phr* avant [*person*]; **she arrived half an hour in ~ of the others** elle est arrivée une demi-heure avant les autres; **a thinker in ~ of his time** un penseur en avance sur son temps or qui devance son époque.
V *vtr* **1** (move forward) faire avancer [*tape, film, clock*]; Mil avancer [*troops*]; (in chess) avancer [*piece*]; (move to earlier date) avancer [*time, date*] (**to** à); fig (improve) faire progresser, faire avancer [*career, knowledge, research*]; **2** (promote) servir [*cause, interests*]; **3** (put forward) avancer [*theory, explanation etc*]; **4** (pay up front) avancer [*sum*] (**to** à).
VI *vi* **1** (move forward) [*person*] avancer, s'avancer (**on, towards** vers); Mil [*army*] avancer (**on** sur); [*morning, evening*] avancer; **the procession ~d down the aisle** le cortège progressait le long de l'allée centrale; **2** (progress) [*person, society, civilization, knowledge, technique*] progresser, faire des progrès; **to ~ in one's career**

progresser dans sa carrière; **3** (increase) [*prices*] augmenter, être en hausse; **4** sout (be promoted) [*employee*] avoir une promotion.

advance: **~ booking** *n* réservation *f* (*faite à l'avance*); **~ booking office** *n* service *m* des réservations; **~ copy** *n* Publg exemplaire *m* témoin.

advanced /əd'vɑːnst, US -'vænst/ *adj* [*course, studies, class*] supérieur; [*student, pupil, stage*] avancé; [*level*] élevé; [*equipment, technology*] de pointe, perfectionné; [*research*] poussé; [*ideas*] avancé; **~ mathematics/physics** cours supérieur de mathématiques/de physique; **~ course in maths** cours de mathématiques pour étudiants avancés; **to be ~ in years** être d'un âge avancé; **the disease has reached an ~ stage** la maladie est parvenue à un stade avancé; **the season was well ~** la saison était bien avancée.

advanced: **~ credit** *n* US Univ équivalence *f*; **~ gas-cooled reactor**, **AGR** *n* réacteur *m* à gaz avancé or poussé, AGR *m*; **Advanced Level** *n* GB Sch = **A-level**; **~ standing** *n* US Univ équivalence *f*.

advance guard *n* Mil avant-garde *f*.

advancement /əd'vɑːnsmənt, US -'væns-/ *n* **1** (furtherance) (of cause, minority etc) promotion *f*; (of science) progrès *m*, avancement *m*; **2** sout (promotion) (of person) avancement *m*, promotion *f*; (in society) ascension *f*.

advance: **~ notice** *n* préavis *m*; **~ party** *n* Mil équipe *f* d'avant-garde; **~ payment** *n* Comm, Fin avance *f*.

advance warning *n* préavis *m*; **we were given no ~** on ne nous a pas prévenus.

advantage /əd'vɑːntɪdʒ, US -'vænt-/ **I** *n* **1** (favourable position) avantage *m*; **economic/political/psychological/competitive ~** avantage *m* en termes économiques/politiques/psychologiques/de compétition; **to have an ~ over** avoir un avantage sur [*person, system, theory, model, method*]; **to give sb an ~ over sb** donner à qn un avantage sur or par rapport à qn; **to put sb at an ~** avantager qn; **to gain the ~** prendre l'avantage; **2** (beneficial aspect) avantage *m*; **there are several ~s** il y a plusieurs avantages; **there is an ~ in doing** il y a avantage à faire; **the ~ is that**... l'avantage est que...; **the ~ that** l'avantage que; **there is some/no ~ in doing** il est intéressant/il n'est pas intéressant de faire; **3** (asset) avantage *m*; **to have the ~ of an education/of living near the sea** avoir l'avantage d'avoir fait des études/d'habiter près de la mer; **leur big ~ is to have**... leur grand avantage est qu'ils ont...; **'computing experience an ~'** (in job ad) 'expérience en information atout supplémentaire'; **4** (profit) **it is to his/their ~ to do** il est dans son/leur intérêt de faire; **to do/use sth to one's (own) ~** faire/utiliser qch à son avantage; **it's to everyone's ~ that** tout le monde profite du fait que; **to turn a situation to one's ~** transformer une situation à son avantage; **5** (best effect) **to show sth to (best) ~** montrer qch sous un jour avantageux; **6 to take ~ of** utiliser, profiter de [*situation, facility, offer, service*]; (exploit unfairly) utiliser, exploiter [*person*]; **7** (in tennis) avantage *m*; **8** Sport **France's 3-point ~** l'avantage de 3 points de la France.
II *vtr* sout avantager.

advantaged /əd'vɑːntɪdʒd, US -'vænt-/ **I** *n* **the ~** (+ *v pl*) les privilégiés *mpl*.
II *adj* privilégié.

advantageous /ˌædvən'teɪdʒəs/ *adj* avantageux/-euse (**to** pour; **to do** pour faire).

advantageously /ˌædvən'teɪdʒəslɪ/ *adv* [*act, buy, sell, invest*] au mieux de vos/ses etc intérêts; **the change worked out very ~ for us** le changement nous a été très profitable.

advent /'ædvent/ *n* (of person) arrivée *f* (**of** de); (of technique, product) apparition *f* (**of** de).

Advent /'ædvent/ Relig **I** *pr n* Avent *m*.
II *modif* [*candle, calendar, Sunday*] de l'Avent.

Adventist /'ædventɪst/ *n* adventiste *mf*.

adventitious /ˌædven'tɪʃəs/ *adj* sout fortuit.

adventure /əd'ventʃə(r)/ **I** *n* aventure *f*; **it was an ~ for me to see the pyramids** voir les pyramides représentait pour moi une véritable aventure.
II *modif* [*story, film*] d'aventures.

adventure: **~ holiday** *n* GB vacances *fpl* 'aventure'; **~ playground** *n* GB aire *f* de jeux (aménagée).

adventurer /əd'ventʃərə(r)/ *n* **1** (daring person) aventurier/-ière *m/f*; **2** péj (schemer) aventurier *m*.

adventuress /əd'ventʃərɪs/ *n* (*pl* **~es**) aventurière *f* also pej.

adventurous /əd'ventʃərəs/ *adj* [*person*] aventureux/-euse; [*person, plan, policy, tastes*] novateur/-trice; [*holiday, life*] aventureux/-euse.

adverb /'ædvɜːb/ *n* adverbe *m*.

adverbial /əd'vɜːbɪəl/ **I** *n* locution *f* adverbiale.
II *adj* adverbial.

adverbially /əd'vɜːbɪəlɪ/ *adv* adverbialement.

adversarial /ˌædvə'seərɪəl/ *adj* **1** Jur accusatoire; **2** gen antagoniste.

adversary /'ædvəsərɪ, US -serɪ/ *n* adversaire *mf*.

adversary proceeding *n* US Jur procédure *f* contradictoire.

adverse /'ædvɜːs/ *adj* [*reaction, aspect, conditions, decision, publicity*] défavorable (**to** à); [*trend, effect, consequences, influence*] négatif/-ive (**to** pour).

adversely /'ædvɜːslɪ/ *adv* **to affect/influence sb/sth ~** avoir un effet négatif/une influence négative sur qn/qch.

adversity /əd'vɜːsətɪ/ *n* **1** ¢ (misfortune) adversité *f*; **in ~** dans l'adversité; **2** (instance of misfortune) malheur *m*.

advert **I**° /'ædvɜːt/ *n* GB (in newspaper) annonce *f*; (in personal column) petite annonce *f*; (on TV) pub° *f*, spot *m* publicitaire.
II /əd'vɜːt/ *vi* sout **to ~ to sth** faire une référence à qch.

advertise /'ædvətaɪz/ **I** *vtr* **1** (for publicity) faire de la publicité pour [*product, party, group, event, service*]; annoncer [*price, rate, speaker*]; **2** (for sale) mettre or passer une annonce pour [*car, furniture, house etc*]; **I'm ringing about the car ~d in Monday's paper** j'appelle à propos de l'annonce du journal de lundi pour une voiture; **3** (for applications) mettre or passer une annonce pour [*job, vacancy*]; **the post has been ~d in the local paper/several times** le poste a fait l'objet d'une annonce dans la presse locale/à plusieurs reprises; **4** (make known) signaler [*presence*]; afficher [*contacts, losses, ignorance, weakness*]; **to ~ (the fact) that** faire savoir que; **to ~ one's presence** signaler sa présence; **we would like to ~ our willingness to**... nous aimerions faire connaître que nous sommes prêts à...
II *vi* **1** (for sales, publicity) faire de la publicité; **2** (for staff) passer une annonce; **to ~ in the newspaper/for an accountant** passer une annonce dans le journal/pour recruter un comptable.

advertisement /əd'vɜːtɪsmənt, US ˌædvər'taɪzmənt/ *n* **1** (for company, product etc) publicité (**for** pour); (for event, concert) publicité (**for** pour); **a beer ~** une publicité pour de la bière; **a good/bad ~ for** fig une bonne/mauvaise publicité pour; **2** (to sell house, car, appliance etc) annonce *f*; (in small ads) petite annonce *f*; **3** (also **job ~**) annonce *f* (**for** pour); (in small ads) petite annonce *f* (**for** pour); **4** ¢ publicité *f*; **for the purposes of ~** à des fins publicitaires.

advertiser /'ædvətaɪzə(r)/ *n* (company) agence *f* de publicité; (agent) publicitaire *mf*; (on radio, in newspaper) US annonceur *m*.

advertising /'ædvətaɪzɪŋ/ *n* ¢ **1** (activity, profession) publicité *f*; **a career in ~** une carrière dans la publicité; **to go into ~** entrer dans la publicité; **2** (advertisements) **beer/tobacco ~** la publicité pour la bière/le tabac; **TV/newspaper/roadside ~** la publicité à la TV/dans les journaux/sur les panneaux; **the power of ~** l'influence de la publicité.

advertising: **~ agency** *n* agence *f* de publicité; **~ agent** ▶ **1692** *n* publicitaire *mf*; **~ campaign** *n* campagne *f* publicitaire; **~ executive** ▶ **1692** *n* cadre *m* publicitaire; **~ industry** *n* publicité *f*; **~ man** ▶ **1692** *n* publicitaire *m*; **~ revenue** *n* recettes *fpl* publicitaires; **Advertising Standards Authority**, **ASA** *n* GB Admin, Comm bureau *m* de vérification de la publicité.

advice /əd'vaɪs/ *n* **1** ¢ (informal) conseils *mpl* (**on** sur; **about** à propos de); **his ~ to them was to keep calm/to pay** il leur a conseillé de rester calmes/de payer; **her ~ that parents should reward their children** son conseil aux parents de récompenser leurs enfants; **a word** ou **piece of ~** un conseil; **to give sb ~** donner des conseils à qn; **to take** ou **follow sb's ~** suivre les conseils de qn; **to do sth against sb's ~** faire qch malgré les recommandations de qn; **to do sth on sb's ~** faire qch sur la recommandation de qn; **it was sound/good ~** c'était un conseil judicieux/un bon conseil; **if you want my ~** (opinion) si tu veux mon avis; **2** ¢ (professional) **to seek** ou **take ~ from sb (about sth)** demander conseil à qn (à propos de qch); **to seek financial/legal/medical ~** consulter un expert financier/un avocat/un médecin; **to follow medical ~** suivre les conseils du médecin; **get expert ~** consultez un spécialiste; **I shall have to take legal ~** il faudra que je consulte un avocat; **3** Comm avis *m*; **~ of delivery** avis de réception.

advice note *n* **1** (in banking) avis *m* d'opération; **2** Comm (from sender) avis *m* d'expédition; (from receiver) avis *m* de réception.

advice of delivery *n* avis *m* de réception.

advisability /ədˌvaɪzə'bɪlətɪ/ *n* sagesse *f*; **to have doubts about the ~ of doing sth** se demander s'il serait sage de faire qch.

advisable /əd'vaɪzəbl/ *adj* recommandé; **it is ~ to do** (speaking officially) il est recommandé de faire; (less categorically, to friend) il est prudent de faire.

advise /əd'vaɪz/ **I** *vtr* **1** (give advice to) conseiller, donner des conseils à (**about** sur); (give information to) renseigner (**about** sur); **to ~ sb to do** [*person, organization*] conseiller à qn de faire; **to ~ sb against doing sth** déconseiller à qn de faire qch; **to ~ sb what to do** conseiller qn sur ce qu'il doit faire; **to ~ sb on sth** (act as advisers) conseiller qn en matière de qch; **to ~ sb of** avertir qn contre [*risk, danger*]; **you are ~d to**... il est recommandé de...; **passengers are ~d to do/not to do** il est recommandé aux passagers de faire/de ne pas faire; **ill-~d** [*course of action*] pas très malin/-igne; **you would be well-~d/ill-~d to stay at home** vous feriez bien de/vous auriez tort de rester chez vous; **2** (recommend) recommander [*rest, course of action*]; **3** sout (inform) aviser (**of** de); **to ~ sb that** aviser qn que.
II *vi* **to ~ on sth** (give advice) conseiller sur qch; (inform) renseigner sur qch; **to ~ on doing sth** conseiller sur la façon de faire qch.

advisedly /əd'vaɪzɪdlɪ/ *adv* [*use word, say*] en toute connaissance de cause.

adviser, **advisor** /əd'vaɪzə(r)/ *n* (in official capacity) conseiller/-ère *m/f* (**to** auprès de); (unofficially) collaborateur/-trice *m/f*; **she acts as an ~ to the committee** elle a un rôle de conseillère auprès du comité; **he is a financial/scientific ~** c'est un conseiller financier/scientifique; **a senior ~ for educa-**

tion un conseiller d'éducation de grade supérieur.

advisory /əd'vaɪzərɪ/ *adj* [*role*] consultatif/-ive; **~ committee** comité *m* de restructuration; **to act/do sth in an ~ capacity** agir/faire qch à titre consultatif.

advisory: **~ group** *n* comité *m* consultatif; **~ service** *n* service *m* d'aide et de conseil.

advocaat /ˌædvə'kɑː/ *n* advocaat *m*.

advocacy /'ædvəkəsɪ/ *n* **1** plaidoyer *m*; **the ~ of sth by sb** le plaidoyer de qn en faveur de qch; **2** Jur plaidoierie *f*.

advocate I /'ædvəkət/ *n* **1** ▶ 1692 Jur avocat/-e *m/f*; **2** (supporter) partisan *m*; **to be an ~ of** être partisan de.
II /'ædvəˌkeɪt/ *vtr* recommander (**doing** de faire); **the policy ~d by the director** la politique que recommande le directeur.

advt *abrév écrite* = **advertisement**.

adze, **adz** US /ædz/ *n* herminette *f*.

AEA *n* GB *abrév* ▶ **Atomic Energy Authority**.

AEC *n* US *abrév* ▶ **Atomic Energy Commission**.

Aegean /iː'dʒiːən/ ▶ 1511 I *pr n* **the ~** la mer Égée.
II *adj* égéen/-éenne.

Aegeus /'iːdʒjuːs/ *pr n* Égée.

aegis /'iːdʒɪs/ *n* **under the ~ of** sous l'égide de.

aegrotat /'iːgrəʊtæt/ *n* GB Univ attestation d'équivalence.

Aeneas /ɪ'niːəs/ *pr n* Énée.

Aeneid /ɪ'niːɪd/ *pr n* **the ~** l'Énéide *f*.

aeolian /iː'əʊlɪən/ *adj* éolien/-ienne; **~ harp** harpe *f* éolienne.

Aeolus /'iːələs, iː'əʊləs/ *pr n* Éole.

aeon, **eon** US /'iːən/ *n* **1** fig **~s ago**○ il y a une éternité; **2** Géol milliard *m* d'années.

aerate /'eəreɪt/ *vtr* **1** aérer [*soil*]; **2** (make effervescent) gazéifier [*liquid*]; **3** oxygéner [*blood*].

aerial /'eərɪəl/ I *n* antenne *f*; **TV/radio ~** antenne *f* de télévision/radio; **satellite ~** antenne *f* parabolique.
II *adj* (*avant n*) aérien/-ienne; **~ photograph/view** photo *f*/vue *f* aérienne.

aerial: **~ camera** *n* appareil *m* de photo pour prises de vues aériennes; **~ ladder** *n* US échelle *f* pivotante; **~ warfare** *n* guerre *f* aérienne.

aerie US = **eyrie**.

aerobatics /ˌeərə'bætɪks/ I *n* **1** (performance) (+ *v sg*) voltige *f* aérienne; **2** (manoeuvres) (+ *v pl*) acrobaties *fpl* aériennes.
II *modif* [*stunt, display*] d'acrobaties aériennes.

aerobic /eə'rəʊbɪk/ *adj* [*respiration, fermentation*] aérobie; [*workout*] d'aérobic.

aerobics /eə'rəʊbɪks/ ▶ 1282 I *n* (+ *v sg*) aérobic *m*.
II *modif* [*class, routine*] d'aérobic.

aerodrome /'eərədrəʊm/ *m* GB aérodrome *m*.

aerodynamic /ˌeərəʊdaɪ'næmɪk/ *adj* (all contexts) aérodynamique.

aerodynamics /ˌeərəʊdaɪ'næmɪks/ *n* **1** (science) (+ *v sg*) aérodynamique *f*; **2** (styling) (+ *v sg*) aérodynamisme *m*: **3** (forces) (+ *v pl*) forces *fpl* aérodynamiques.

aeroengine /'eərəʊendʒɪn/ *n* aéromoteur *m*.

aerogram(me) /'eərəgræm/ *n* aérogramme *m*.

aerograph /'eərəʊgrɑːf, US -græf/ *n* météographe *m*.

aerolite /'eərəlaɪt/ *n* aérolithe *m*.

aeromodelling GB, **aeromodeling** US /ˌeərəʊ'mɒdəlɪŋ/ *n* aéromodélisme *m*.

aeronaut /'eərənɔːt/ *n* aéronaute *mf*.

aeronautic(al) /ˌeərə'nɔːtɪk(l)/ *adj* [*skill*] aéronautique; [*magazine, college*] d'aéronautique.

aeronautic: **~(al) engineer** ▶ 1692 *n* ingénieur *m* en aéronautique; **~(al) engineering** *n* aéronautique *f*.

aeronautics /ˌeərə'nɔːtɪks/ I *n* (+ *v sg*) aéronautique *f*.
II *modif* [*firm, institute*] d'aéronautique; [*student*] en aéronautique.

aeroplane /'eərəpleɪn/ GB, **airplane** /'eərpleɪn/ US *n* avion *m*; **by ~** en avion.

aerosol /'eərəsɒl, US -sɔːl/ I *n* **1** (spray can) bombe *f* aérosol; **2** (system) aérosol *m*.
II *modif* [*paint, deodorant*] en aérosol.

aerospace /'eərəʊspeɪs/ I *n* (industry) industrie *f* aérospatiale.
II *modif* [*engineer, company*] de l'aérospatiale; [*project*] aérospatial.

Aeschylus /'iːskələs/ *pr n* Eschyle.

Aesop /'iːsɒp/ *pr n* Ésope.

aesthete /'iːsθiːt/, **esthete** /'esθiːt/ US *n* esthète *mf*.

aesthetic, **esthetic** US /iːs'θetɪk/ I *n* esthétique *f*.
II *adj* **1** [*sense, appeal*] esthétique; **2** [*design, arrangement*] harmonieux/-ieuse.

aesthetically /iːs'θetɪklɪ/, **esthetically** /es'θetɪklɪ/ US *adv* [*satisfying, pleasing*] esthétiquement; [*restore, improve*] avec goût.

aestheticism /iːs'θetɪsɪzəm/, **estheticism** /es'θetɪsɪzəm/ US *n* (doctrine, quality) esthétisme *m*; (taste) sens *m* du beau.

aesthetics /iːs'θetɪks/, **esthetics** /es'θetɪks/ US *n* **1** (concept) (+ *v sg*) esthétique *f*; **2** (aspects of appearance) (+ *v pl*) esthétique *f*.

aether *n* = **ether**.

AEU *n* GB (*abrév* = **Amalgamated Engineering Union**) syndicat *m* des techniciens.

af *n*: *abrév* ▶ **audio frequency**.

AFA *n* GB (*abrév* = **Amateur Football Association**) *fédération des clubs amateurs de football*.

afar /ə'fɑː(r)/ *adv* littér au loin, à distance; **from ~** de loin.

AFB *n* US (*abrév* = **Air Force Base**) base *f* aérienne.

AFDC *n* US (*abrév* = **Aid to Families with Dependent Children**) *programme fédéral d'aide aux familles monoparentales*.

affability /ˌæfə'bɪlətɪ/ *n* affabilité *f*.

affable /'æfəbl/ *adj* affable.

affably /'æfəblɪ/ *adv* affablement.

affair /ə'feə(r)/ I *n* **1** (event, incident, thing) affaire *f*; **the Haltrey ~** l'affaire Haltrey; **the wedding was a grand ~** le mariage a été une affaire prestigieuse; **the dress/cake was an extraordinary ~** la robe/le gâteau était extraordinaire; **2** (matter) affaire *f*; **at first the conflict seemed a small ~** au début, le conflit ne paraissait pas grave; **state of ~s** situation *f*; **it's a sad state of ~s** c'est lamentable; **3** (relationship) liaison *f* (**with** avec); (casual) aventure *f*; **a passionate ~** une liaison passionnée; **4** (concern) affaire *f*; **it's my ~** c'est mon affaire.
II **affairs** *npl* **1** Pol, Journ affaires *fpl*; **foreign ~s** affaires étrangères; **~s of state** affaires d'état; **they should not interfere in Egypt's (internal) ~s** ils ne devraient pas se mêler des affaires de l'Égypte; **he deals with consumer ~s** il s'occupe de la protection du consommateur; **foreign/religious ~ correspondent** Journ spécialiste *mf* de politique internationale/des questions religieuses; **2** (business) affaires *fpl*; **to put one's ~s in order** mettre de l'ordre dans ses affaires.

affect /ə'fekt/ I *n* Psych émotion *f*, affect *m*.
II *vtr* **1** (influence) [*law, decision, event, issue*] concerner [*person, group, region*]; [*problem, injustice, strike, cuts*] toucher [*person, group, region*]; [*factor, development*] avoir une incidence sur [*earnings, job, state of affairs*]; **how is it ~ing the baby?** quelles sont les conséquences pour le bébé?; **2** (emotionally) [*experience, image, music*] émouvoir; [*news, discovery, atmosphere*] affecter; **3** Med (afflict) atteindre [*person*]; toucher [*heart, liver, faculty*]; **4** sout (feign) feindre [*surprise, ignorance*] (**to do** de faire); prendre [*accent*]; **5** sout (like) affectionner.

affectation /ˌæfek'teɪʃn/ *n* (all contexts) affectation *f* (**of** de).

affected /ə'fektɪd/ *adj* **1** (influenced) (by event, change, decision) (adversely) touché (**by** par); (neutrally, positively) concerné (**by** par); **~ by the disaster** sinistré; **2** (emotionally) ému (**by** par); (adversely) affecté (**by** par); **3** Med [*part*] infecté (**by** par); [*person*] atteint (**by** de); **4** péj (mannered) affecté; **5** péj (feigned) affecté.

affectedly /ə'fektɪdlɪ/ *adv* [*behave, speak*] avec affectation.

affecting /ə'fektɪŋ/ *adj* émouvant.

affection /ə'fekʃn/ *n* affection *f* (**for sb** pour qn); **to show ~** témoigner de l'affection; **the ~s of the public** l'affection du public; **to win sb's ~s** gagner le cœur de qn.

affectionate /ə'fekʃənət/ *adj* [*child, animal*] affectueux/-euse; [*memory*] tendre; [*picture, account*] plein d'affection.

affectionately /ə'fekʃənətlɪ/ *adv* [*smile, speak, recall*] affectueusement; **yours ~** (ending letter) bien affectueusement; **~ known as** (of person) répondant au surnom affectueux de.

affective /ə'fektɪv/ *adj* Ling, Psych affectif/-ive.

affidavit /ˌæfɪ'deɪvɪt/ *n* déclaration *f* écrite sous serment; **to swear an ~** déclarer par écrit sous serment (**that** que).

affiliate /ə'fɪlɪeɪt/ I *n* filiale *f*.
II *vtr* affilier (**to, with** à).
III *vi* (combine) s'affilier (**with** à).

affiliated /ə'fɪlɪeɪtɪd/ *adj* affilié (**to, with** à); **~ member** adhérent/-e *m/f*.

affiliation /əˌfɪlɪ'eɪʃn/ *n* (process, state) affiliation *f*; (link) attaches *fpl*; **what is his political ~?** de quelle tendance politique est-il?

affiliation: **~ order** *n* Jur *assignation d'enfant à un père putatif*; **~ proceedings** *n* GB Jur *action en recherche de paternité*.

affinity /ə'fɪnətɪ/ *n* **1** (liking, attraction) attirance *f* (**with, for** pour); **2** (resemblance) ressemblance *f* (**to, with** avec); **3** (relationship) rapport *m* (**between** entre); **4** Jur parenté *f*; **5** Chem affinité *f*.

affinity: **~ (credit) card** *n*: *carte de crédit émise pour les membres d'un groupe donné*; **~ group** *n*: *groupe de personnes partageant des intérêts communs*.

affirm /ə'fɜːm/ *vtr* **1** (state positively) affirmer (**that** que); **2** (state belief in) proclamer [*right, policy*]; **3** (confirm, strengthen) confirmer [*support, popularity*]; **4** Jur déposer sans prêter serment.

affirmation /ˌæfə'meɪʃn/ *n* **1** gen affirmation *f* (**of** de); **2** Jur déposition *f* sans prestation de serment.

affirmative /ə'fɜːmətɪv/ I *n* affirmatif *m*; **to reply in the ~** répondre par l'affirmative.
II *adj* [*reply, nod, statement*] affirmatif/-ive.
III *excl* US affirmatif.

affirmative action *n*: *mesures antidiscriminatoires dans le recrutement professionnel*.

affirmatively /ə'fɜːmətɪvlɪ/ *adv* affirmativement.

affix I /'æfɪks/ *n* Ling affixe *m*.
II /ə'fɪks/ *vtr* sout coller [*stamp*]; apposer [*signature*].

afflict /ə'flɪkt/ *vtr* [*poverty, disease, recession*] frapper; [*grief*] accabler; [*illness*] toucher; **to be ~ed by** être accablé de [*grief*]; être touché par [*illness*].

affliction /ə'flɪkʃn/ *n* (illness) affection *f*; (suffering) malheur *m*; **in ~** en détresse.

affluence /'æflʊəns/ *n* **1** (wealthiness) richesse *f*; (plenty) abondance *f*; **2** (flow of people) affluence *f*.

affluent /'æflʊənt/ I *n* **1** Geog affluent *m*; **2 the ~** (+ *v pl*) les riches.
II *adj* [*person, area, society*] riche.

affluential /ˌæflʊ'enʃl/ *adj* riche et influent.

affluenza /ˌæflʊ'enzə/ *n*: *troubles psychiques affectant les nantis.*

afflux /'æflʌks/ *n* **1** Med afflux *m*; **2** sout (of people) = **affluence 2**.

afford /ə'fɔːd/ *vtr* **1** (have money for) **to be able to ~ sth** avoir les moyens d'acheter qch; **if I can ~ it, I'll buy a car** si j'ai les moyens, je vais acheter une voiture; **to be able to ~ to do sth** (as necessary expense) être en mesure de faire qch; (as chosen expense) pouvoir se permettre de faire qch; **I can't ~ to pay the rent** je ne suis pas en mesure de payer le loyer; **I can't ~ a new dress** je ne peux pas me permettre une nouvelle robe; **how can he ~ to buy such expensive clothes?** comment est-ce qu'il fait pour acheter des vêtements aussi chers?; **please give what you can ~** donnez ce que vous pouvez; **2** (spare) **to be able to ~** disposer de [*space, time*]; **3** (risk) **to be able to ~ sth/to do** se permettre qch/de faire; **the government can't ~ the risk/to lose** le gouvernement ne peut pas se permettre ce risque/de perdre; **he can ~/can ill ~ to wait** il peut/ne peut guère se permettre d'attendre; **4** sout **to ~ sb sth** offrir qch à qn [*protection, support, view*]; fournir qch à qn [*opportunity*]; procurer qch à qn [*pleasure, satisfaction*].

affordable /ə'fɔːdəbl/ *adj* [*price*] abordable; [*pleasure, luxury*] qu'on peut s'offrir; **it's ~ for students/the elderly** c'est à la portée de la bourse des étudiants/des personnes âgées; **~ for all** à la portée de toutes les bourses; **'beautiful cars at ~ prices'** 'de belles voitures à des prix abordables'.

afforest /ə'fɒrɪst, US ə'fɔːr-/ *vtr* boiser.

afforestation /əˌfɒrɪ'steɪʃn, US əˌfɔːr-/ *n* boisement *m*.

affranchise /ə'fræntʃaɪz/ *vtr* affranchir.

affray /ə'freɪ/ *n* Jur rixe *f*.

affricate /'æfrɪkət/ *n* Phon affriquée *f*.

affright‡ /ə'fraɪt/ **I** *n* effroi *m* liter, terreur *f*.
II *vtr* effrayer.

affront /ə'frʌnt/ **I** *n* offense *f*.
II *vtr* (*gén au passif*) offenser.

Afghan /'æfgæn/ **▶1486, 1402** **I** *n* **1** (also **Afghani**) (person) Afghan/-e *m/f*; **2** (also **Afghani**) (language) pachtou *m*; **3** (coat) afghan *m*.
II *adj* (also **Afghani**) afghan.

Afghan hound *n* lévrier *m* afghan.

Afghanistan /æf'gænɪstɑːn, -stæn/ **▶1131** *pr n* Afghanistan *m*.

aficionado /əˌfɪsjə'nɑːdəʊ, əˌfɪʃj-/ *n* (*pl* **~s**) passionné/-e *m/f*.

afield /ə'fiːld/: **far afield** *adv phr* loin; **further ~** plus loin; **to look/go further ~** regarder/aller plus loin; **from as far ~ as China and India** d'aussi loin que la Chine et l'Inde.

afire /ə'faɪə(r)/ litter **I** *adj* (*jamais épith*) en feu; **to be ~ with enthusiasm** déborder d'enthousiasme.
II *adv* en feu; **to set sth ~** mettre le feu à qch.

aflame /ə'fleɪm/ littér **I** *adj* (*jamais avant n*) gen en feu; [*cheek*] en feu; [*sky, countryside*] embrasé; **to be ~ with** [*desire*] brûler de; [*enthusiasm*] déborder de.
II *adv* en feu; **to set sth ~** mettre le feu à qch.

AFL-CIO *n* US (*abrév* = **American Federation of Labor and Congress of Industrial Organizations**) *le plus important des syndicats américains.*

afloat /ə'fləʊt/ *adj, adv* **1** (in water) **to stay** ou **remain ~** [*body, person, object*] rester à la surface (de l'eau); [*boat*] rester à flot; **to get a boat ~** mettre un bateau à flot; **I could see a body/an object ~ in the water** je voyais un corps/un objet qui flottait sur l'eau; **she had difficulty staying ~** elle avait du mal à se maintenir à la surface (de l'eau); **2** (financially) **to remain** ou **stay ~** se maintenir à flot; **to keep the economy ~** maintenir l'économie à flot; **3** (at sea, on the water) sur l'eau; **it's the best-equipped ship ~** c'est le navire le mieux équipé qui soit sur l'eau; **a day/week ~** une journée/semaine sur l'eau.

afoot /ə'fʊt/ *adj* (*après n*) **there is something/mischief ~** il se prépare quelque chose/un mauvais coup; **there is a plan** ou **there are plans ~ to...** on envisage de...; **there are changes ~** il y a des changements dans l'air.

aforementioned /əˌfɔː'menʃənd/ sout ou Jur **I** *n* **the ~** le/la susnommé/-e.
II *adj* [*document, incident, person*] susmentionné; **the ~ Fred Jones** le susnommé Fred Jones.

aforesaid /ə'fɔːsed/ *adj* sout ou Jur [*document, incident, person*] susmentionné; **the ~ Fred Jones** le susnommé Fred Jones.

aforethought /ə'fɔːθɔːt/: **with malice aforethought** *adv phr* Jur avec préméditation.

a fortiori /ˌeɪ ˌfɔːtɪ'ɔːraɪ/ *adv* sout a fortiori.

afoul /ə'faʊl/ *adv* sout **to run ~ of** s'attirer des ennuis avec.

afraid /ə'freɪd/ *adj* **1** (frightened) **don't be ~** n'aie pas peur; **to be ~** avoir peur (**of** de; **to do, of doing** de faire); **she's ~ of you/of the dark** elle a peur de vous/du noir; **is he ~ of flying/of getting hurt?** a-t-il peur d'aller en avion/de se faire mal?; **2** (anxious) **to be ~** craindre (**for sb/sth** pour qn/qch); **she was ~ (that) there would be an accident** elle craignait un accident; **I was ~ (that) I would get hurt** je craignais de me faire mal; **he was ~ (that) she might get hurt** il craignait qu'elle ne se fasse mal; **I'm ~ it might rain** je crains qu'il (ne) pleuve; **3** (in expressions of regret) **I'm ~ I can't come** je suis désolé mais je ne peux pas venir; **'did they win?'—'I'm ~ not'** 'ont-ils gagné?'—'hélas, non'; **4** (as polite formula) **I'm ~ the house is in a mess** excusez le désordre dans la maison; **I'm ~ I don't agree** je ne suis pas d'accord; **'are you parking here?'—'I'm ~ so'** 'vous vous garez ici?' 'oui Madame/Monsieur'.

afresh /ə'freʃ/ *adv* à nouveau; **to start ~** recommencer; (in life) repartir à zéro.

Africa /'æfrɪkə/ *pr n* Afrique *f*; **to ~** en Afrique.

African /'æfrɪkən/ **I** *n* Africain/-e *m/f*.
II *adj* africain.

African: **~ elephant** *n* éléphant *m* d'Afrique; **~ National Congress** *n* Congrès *m* National Africain; **~ violet** *n* saintpaulia *m*.

Afrikaans /ˌæfrɪ'kɑːns/ **▶1402** *n* afrikaans *m*.

Afrikaner /ˌæfrɪ'kɑːnə(r)/ **▶1486** **I** *n* Afrikaner *mf*.
II *adj* afrikaner.

Afro /'æfrəʊ/ *n* (also **~ haircut**) coiffure *f* afro.

Afro-American /ˌæfrəʊə'merɪkən/ **I** *n* Afro-américain/-e *m/f*.
II *adj* afro-américain.

Afro-Caribbean /ˌæfrəʊˌkærɪ'biːən/ *adj* antillais.

aft /ɑːft, US æft/ *adv* Naut, Aviat à l'arrière.

AFT *n* (*abrév* = **American Federation of Teachers**) *syndicat d'enseignants américains.*

after /'ɑːftə(r), US 'æftər/

■ **Note** As both adverb and preposition, *after* is translated in most contexts by *après*: *after the meal* = après le repas; *H comes after G* = H vient après G; *day after day* = jour après jour; *just after 3 pm* = juste après 15 heures; *three weeks after* = trois semaines après.
– When *after* is used as a conjunction it is translated by *après avoir (or être) + past participle* where the two verbs have the same subject: *after I've finished my book, I'll cook dinner* = après avoir fini mon livre je vais préparer le dîner; *after he had consulted Bill ou after consulting Bill, he decided to accept the offer* = après avoir consulté Bill, il a décidé d'accepter l'offre.
– When the two verbs have different subjects the translation is *après que + indicative*: *I'll lend you the book after Fred has read it* = je te prêterai le livre après que Fred l'aura lu.
– For more examples and particular usages see the entry below.
– See also the usage note on time units **▶1807**.

I *adv* **1** (following time or event) après; **before and ~** avant et après; **soon** ou **shortly** ou **not long ~** peu après; **for weeks ~** pendant des semaines après; **straight ~** GB, **right ~** US tout de suite après; **2** (following specific time) **the week/year ~** la semaine/l'année suivante ou d'après; **the day ~** le lendemain.
II *prep* **1** (later in time than) après; **~ the film** après le film; **immediately ~ the strike** aussitôt après la grève ; **~ that date** (in future) au-delà de cette date; (in past) après cette date; **shortly ~ 10 pm** peu après 22 h; **it was ~ six o'clock** il était six heures passées, il était plus de six heures; **~ that** après (cela); **the day ~ tomorrow** après-demain; **a ceremony ~ which there was a banquet** une cérémonie après laquelle il y a eu un banquet; **he had breakfast as usual, ~ which he left** il a pris son petit déjeuner comme d'habitude, après quoi il est parti; **2** (given) après; **~ my attempt at milking, I was nervous** après ma tentative de traire les vaches je n'étais pas très sûr de moi; **~ the way he behaved** après la façon dont il s'est conduit; **~ all we did for you!** après tout ce que nous avons fait pour toi!; **3** (in spite of) malgré, après ; **~ all the trouble I took labelling the package, it got lost** malgré tout le mal que je me suis donné à étiqueter le paquet, il s'est perdu; **~ what she's been through, she's still interested?** malgré or après ce qu'elle a subi, ça l'intéresse toujours?; **4** (expressing contrast) après; **the film was disappointing ~ all the hype**○ après tout le battage○ le film était décevant; **it's boring here ~ Paris** après Paris, on s'ennuie ici; **5** (behind) **to run** ou **chase ~ sb/sth** courir après qn/qch; **please shut the gate ~ you** refermez la grille derrière vous s'il vous plaît; **6** (following in sequence) après; **your name comes ~ mine on the list** ton nom vient après le mien sur la liste; **the adjective comes ~ the noun** l'adjectif vient après le nom; **7** (following in rank, precedence) après; **she's next in line ~ Bob for promotion** elle sera la prochaine après Bob à avoir une promotion; **he was placed third ~ Smith and Jones** il est arrivé troisième après Smith et Jones; **~ you!** (letting someone pass ahead) après vous!; **8** (in the direction of) **to stare ~ sb** regarder qn s'éloigner; **'don't forget!' Mimi called ~ her** 'n'oublie pas!' lui a crié Mimi; **9** (in the wake of) derrière; **I'm not tidying up ~ you!** je n'ai pas l'intention de ranger derrière toi!; **10** (in pursuit of) **to be ~ sth** chercher qch; **that's the house they're ~** c'est la maison qu'ils veulent acheter; **the police are ~ him** il est recherché par la police; **to come** ou **go ~ sb** poursuivre qn; **he'll come ~ me** il va essayer de me retrouver; **it's me he's ~** (to settle score) c'est à moi qu'il en veut; **I wonder what she's ~?** je me demande ce qu'elle veut?; **I think he's ~ my job** je pense qu'il veut (me) prendre ma place; **to be ~ sb**○ (sexually) s'intéresser à qn; **11** (beyond) après; **about 400 metres ~ the crossroads** environ 400 mètres après le carrefour; **12** (stressing continuity, repetitiveness) **day ~ day** jour après jour; **generation ~ generation** génération après génération; **time ~ time** maintes et maintes fois; **mile ~ mile of bush** des kilomètres et des kilomètres de brousse; **it was one**

disaster ~ another on a eu catastrophe sur catastrophe; **13** (about) **to ask ~ sb** demander des nouvelles de qn; **14** (in honour or memory of) **to name a child ~ sb** donner à un enfant le nom de qn; **named ~ James Joyce** [*monument, street, institution, pub*] portant le nom de James Joyce; **we called her Kate ~ my mother** nous l'avons appelée Kate comme ma mère; **15** (in the manner of) **'~ Millet'** 'd'après Millet'; **it's a painting ~ Klee** c'est un tableau fait à la manière de Klee; ▶**fashion I 1**; **16** US (past) **it's twenty ~ eleven** il est onze heures vingt.

III *conj* **1** (in sequence of events) après avoir or être (+ *pp*), après que (+ *indic*); **don't go for a swim too soon ~ eating** ne va pas nager trop tôt après avoir mangé; **~ we had left we realized that** après être partis nous nous sommes rendu compte que; **~ she had confessed to the murder, he was released** après qu'elle a avoué le meurtre, il a été relâché; **we return the bottles ~ they have been washed** nous retournons les bouteilles après qu'elles ont été lavées; **2** (given that) **~ hearing all about him we want to meet him** après tout ce que nous avons entendu sur lui nous voulons le rencontrer; **~ you explained the situation they didn't call the police** une fois que tu leur as expliqué la situation ils n'ont pas appelé la police; **3** (in spite of the fact that) **why did he do that ~ we'd warned him of the consequences?** pourquoi a-t-il fait ça alors que nous l'avions prévenu des conséquences?

IV **afters**○ *npl* GB dessert *m*; **what's for ~s?** qu'est-ce qu'il y a comme dessert?

V **after all** *adv, prep* **1** (when reinforcing point) après tout; **~ all, nobody forced you to leave** après tout personne ne t'a obligé à partir; **2** (when reassessing stance, opinion) après tout, finalement; **it wasn't such a bad idea ~ all** après tout or finalement ce n'était pas une si mauvaise idée; **he decided not to stay ~ all** finalement il a décidé de ne pas rester.

after: **~birth** *n* placenta *m*; **~care** *n* Med suivi *m* médical; **~-dinner drink** *n* digestif *m*; **~-dinner speaker** *n* orateur/-trice *m/f* invité/-e; **~-dinner speech** *n* discours *m* à la fin d'un dîner officiel; **~-effect** *n* Med contrecoup *m* (**of** de); fig répercussion *f* (**of** de); **~glow** *n* ¢ lit dernières lueurs *fpl* du jour; fig sensation *f* agréable; **~-hours drinking** *n* GB consommation *f* d'alcool après l'heure légale de la fermeture des pubs; **~life** *n* vie *f* après la mort.

aftermath /ˈɑːftəmæθ, -mɑːθ, US ˈæf-/ *n* ¢ conséquences *fpl* (**of** de); **in the ~ of** à la suite de [*war, scandal, election*].

afternoon /ˌɑːftəˈnuːn, US ˌæf-/ ▶**1096** I *n* après-midi *m* or *f inv*; **in the ~** (dans) l'après-midi; **at 2.30 in the ~** à 2h30 de l'après-midi; **in the early/late ~** en début/en fin d'après-midi; **this ~** cet après-midi; **later/earlier this ~** plus tard/plus tôt dans l'après-midi; **the following** ou **next ~** le lendemain après-midi; **the previous ~, the ~ before** l'après-midi d'avant; **every ~** tous les après-midi; **on Friday ~s** le vendredi après-midi; **every Saturday ~** tous les samedis après-midi; **to work ~s** travailler l'après-midi.

II *modif* [*shift, train*] de l'après-midi.

III *excl* (also **good ~**) bonjour!

afternoon: **~ performance** *n* matinée *f*; **~ tea** *n* thé *m* (de cinq heures).

after: **~pains** *npl* tranchées *fpl* utérines; **~-sales service** *n* service *m* après-vente; **~-shave** *n* après-rasage *m*; **~shock** *n* Geol secousse *f* secondaire; fig retombées *fpl*; **~-sun** *adj* [*lotion, cream*] après-soleil; **~taste** *n* lit, fig arrière-goût *m*; **~-tax** *adj* [*profits, earnings*] après impôts.

afterthought /ˈɑːftəθɔːt, US ˈæf-/ *n* pensée *f* après coup; **our youngest was an ~** notre dernier enfant est arrivé sur le tard; **as an ~** après coup, en y repensant; **almost as an ~** comme en y repensant.

afterwards /ˈɑːftəwədz, US ˈæf-/ GB, **afterward** /ˈɑːftəwəd, US ˈæf-/ US *adv* **1** (after) gen après; (in a sequence of events) ensuite; **soon** ou **shortly** ou **not long ~** peu après; **immediately** ou **directly ~** aussitôt après; **straight ~** GB tout de suite après; **we saw a film, went to the restaurant then went home ~** on est allé au cinéma, puis au restaurant et ensuite on est rentré; **salmon, green salad and ~ an apple tart** du saumon et une salade verte suivis d'une tarte aux pommes; **2** (later) plus tard; **I'll tell you ~** je te le dirai plus tard; **it was only ~ that I noticed** ce n'est que plus tard que je m'en suis aperçu; **3** (subsequently) par la suite; **I regretted it ~** je l'ai regretté par la suite.

afterword /ˈɑːftəwɜːd, US ˈæf-/ *n* épilogue *m*.

AG *n*: *abrév* ▶**Attorney General**.

again /əˈgeɪn, əˈgen/

■ **Note** When used with a verb, *again* is often translated by adding the prefix *re* to the verb in French: *to start again* = recommencer; *to marry again* = se remarier; *I'd like to read that book again* = j'aimerais relire ce livre; *she never saw them again* = elle ne les a jamais revus. You can check *re+* verbs by consulting the French side of the dictionary.
– For other uses of *again* and for idiomatic expressions, see below.

adv encore; **sing it ~!** chante-le encore!; **once ~** encore une fois; **yet ~ he refused** il a encore refusé; **when you are well ~** quand tu seras rétabli; **I'll never go there ~** je n'y retournerai jamais; **he never saw her ~** il ne l'a jamais revue; **never ~!** jamais plus!; **not ~!** encore!; **~ and ~** plusieurs fois, à plusieurs reprises; **time and (time) ~** maintes fois; **~, you may think that** et ici encore, vous pourriez penser que; **(and) then ~, he may not** mais il se peut aussi qu'il ne le fasse pas; **what's his name ~**○**?** il s'appelle comment déjà?

against /əˈgeɪnst, əˈgenst/ *prep*

■ **Note** *against* is translated by *contre* when it means *physically touching* or *in opposition to*: *against the wall* = contre le mur; *he's against independence* = il est contre l'indépendance; *the fight against inflation* = la lutte contre l'inflation.
– If you have any doubts about how to translate a fixed phrase or expression beginning with *against* (*against the tide, against the clock, against the grain, against all odds etc*) you should consult the appropriate noun entry (***tide***, ***grain***, ***odds*** etc).
– *against* often appears in English with certain verbs (*turn against, compete against, discriminate against, stand out against etc*). For translations you should consult the appropriate verb entry (***turn***, ***compete***, ***discriminate***, ***stand*** etc).
– *against* often appears in English after certain nouns and adjectives (*protection against, a match against, a law against, effective against etc*). For translations consult the appropriate noun or adjective entry (***protection***, ***match***, ***law***, ***effective*** etc). For particular usages see below.

1 (physically) contre; **~ the wall** contre le mur; **2** (objecting to) **I'm ~ it** je suis contre; **I have nothing ~ it** je n'ai rien contre; **100 votes for and 20 votes ~** 100 votes pour et 20 votes contre; **to be ~ the idea** s'opposer à l'idée, être contre l'idée; **to be ~ doing** ne pas être d'accord pour faire, être contre l'idée de faire; **3** (counter to) **to go** ou **be ~** aller à l'encontre de [*tradition, policy*]; **the conditions are ~ us** les conditions ne nous sont pas favorables; **the decision went ~ us** la décision ne nous a pas été favorable; **to pedal ~ the wind** pédaler contre le vent; ▶**up**; **4** (in opposition to) contre; **the war ~ sb** la guerre contre qn; **the fight ~ inflation** la lutte contre l'inflation; **Smith ~ Jones** Smith contre Jones; **5** (compared to) **the pound fell ~ the dollar** la livre a baissé par rapport au dollar; **the graph shows age ~ earnings** le graphique représente la courbe des salaires en fonction de l'âge; ▶**as**; **6** (in contrast to) sur; **the blue looks pretty ~ the yellow** le bleu est joli sur le jaune; **~ a background of** sur un fond de; **~ the light** à contre-jour; **to stand out ~** [*houses, trees etc*] se détacher sur [*sky, sunset*]; **7** (in exchange for) contre, en échange de; **~ a voucher from the airline** contre un or en échange d'un bon distribué par la compagnie aérienne.

agape /əˈgeɪp/ I *adj* (*après n*) (person) bouche bée; [*mouth*] grand ouvert.

II *adv* bouche bée.

agar-agar /ˌeɪgɑːˈeɪgɑː(r)/ *n* agar-agar *m*.

agaric /ˈægərɪk/ *n* agaric *m*.

agate /ˈægət/ *n* agate *f*.

agave /əˈgeɪvɪ/ *n* agave *m*.

age /eɪdʒ/ ▶**971** I *n* **1** (length of existence) âge *m*; **at the ~ of 14** à l'âge de 14 ans; **she's your ~** elle a ton âge; **to look one's ~** faire son âge; **to be of retirement ~** avoir l'âge de la retraite; **to be of school ~** être en âge d'aller à l'école; **she's twice/half his ~** elle a le double/la moitié de son âge; **they are of an ~** ils sont du même âge; **to be of an ~ when...** être à l'âge où...; **act** ou **be your ~!** ne fais pas l'enfant!; **you shouldn't be doing that at your ~!** tu ne devrais pas faire ça à ton âge!; **men of retirement ~** les hommes en âge de or qui ont l'âge de la retraite; **to come of ~** atteindre la majorité; **to be of ~** être majeur/-e; **to be under ~** Jur être mineur; **~ of consent** Jur âge légal (**for** pour); **to feel one's ~** se faire vieux/vieille; **2** (latter part of life) âge *m*, vieillesse *f*; **with ~** avec l'âge; **3** (era) ère *f*, époque *f* (**of** de); **the video/computer ~** l'ère de la vidéo/de l'ordinateur; **in this day and ~** à notre époque; **through the ~s** à travers les âges or les siècles; **the Age of Reason** Hist le siècle des lumières; **4**○ (long time) (*souvent pl*) **it's ~s since I've played golf** ça fait une éternité que je n'ai pas joué au golf; **we haven't been to London for ~s** nous ne sommes pas allés à Londres depuis une éternité; **it takes ~s** ou **an ~ to get it right** cela prend un temps fou pour le faire correctement; **I've been waiting for ~s** j'attends depuis des heures.

II *vtr* [*hairstyle, experiences etc*] vieillir [*person*]; **to ~ sb 10 years** vieillir qn de 10 ans.

III *vi* [*person*] vieillir; **to ~ well** bien vieillir.

age bracket *n* = **age range**.

aged I /ˈeɪdʒɪd/ *n* **the ~** (+ *v pl*) les personnes âgées.

II *adj* **1** /eɪdʒd/ (of an age) **~ between 20 and 25** âgé/-e de 20 à 25 ans; **a boy ~ 12** un garçon de 12 ans; **2** /ˈeɪdʒɪd/ (old) vieux/vieille, âgé.

age group *n* = **age range**.

ageing /ˈeɪdʒɪŋ/ I *n* vieillissement *m*; **the ~ process** le processus de vieillissement.

II *adj* [*person, filmstar, population*] vieillissant; [*vehicle, appliance, system*] vieux/vieille (*before n*); **that hairstyle is really ~** cette coiffure te vieillit.

ageism /ˈeɪdʒɪzəm/ *n* discrimination *f* en raison de l'âge.

ageist /ˈeɪdʒɪst/ *adj* [*policy, rule*] qui défavorise les personnes en raison de leur âge; [*remark, term*] qui témoigne d'un préjugé par rapport à l'âge.

ageless /ˈeɪdʒlɪs/ *adj* **1** (not appearing to age) toujours jeune; (of indeterminate age) sans âge; **2** (timeless) [*quality, mystery*] éternel/-elle.

age limit *n* limite *f* d'âge.

agency /ˈeɪdʒənsɪ/ *n* **1** (organization, office)

Age

Note that where English says to be X years old *French says* avoir X ans (to have X years).

How old?

how old are you? = quel âge as-tu?
what age is she? = quel âge a-t-elle?

The word ans (years) *is never dropped:*

he is forty years old *or* he is forty
or he is forty years of age = il a quarante ans
she's eighty = elle a quatre-vingts ans
the house is a hundred years old = la maison a cent ans
a man of fifty = un homme de cinquante ans
a child of eight and a half = un enfant de huit ans et demi
I feel sixteen = j'ai l'impression d'avoir seize ans
he looks sixteen = on lui donnerait seize ans

Note the use of de *after* âgé *and* à l'âge:

a woman aged thirty = une femme âgée de trente ans
at the age of forty = à l'âge de quarante ans
Mrs Smith, aged forty
or Mrs Smith (40) = Mme Smith, âgée de quarante ans

Do not confuse que *and* de *used with* plus *and* moins:

I'm older than you = je suis plus âgé que toi
she's younger than him = elle est plus jeune que lui
Anne's two years younger = Anne a deux ans de moins
Margot's older than Suzanne by five years = Margot a cinq ans de plus que Suzanne
Robert's younger than Thomas by six years = Robert a six ans de moins que Thomas

X-year-old

a forty-year-old = quelqu'un de quarante ans
a sixty-year-old woman = une femme de soixante ans
an eighty-year-old pensioner = un retraité de quatre-vingts ans
they've got an eight-year-old and a five-year-old = ils ont un enfant de huit ans et un autre de cinq ans

Approximate ages

Note the various ways of saying these in French:

he is about fifty = il a environ cinquante ans *or* il a une cinquantaine d'années
or (*less formally*) il a dans les cinquante ans

(*Other round numbers in* -aine *used to express age are* dizaine (*10*), vingtaine (*20*), trentaine (*30*), quarantaine (*40*), soixantaine (*60*) *and* centaine (*100*).)

she's just over sixty = elle vient d'avoir soixante ans
she's just under seventy = elle aura bientôt soixante-dix ans
she's in her sixties = elle a entre soixante et soixante-dix ans
she's in her early sixties = elle a entre soixante et soixante-cinq ans
she's in her late sixties = elle va avoir soixante-dix ans
or (*less formally*) elle va sur ses soixante-dix ans
she must be seventy = elle doit avoir soixante-dix ans
he's in his mid forties = il a entre quarante et cinquante ans
or (*less formally*) il a dans les quarante-cinq ans
he's just ten = il a tout juste dix ans
he's barely twelve = il a à peine douze ans
games for the under twelves = jeux pour les moins de douze ans
only for the over eighties = seulement pour les plus de quatre-vingts ans

agence *f*; **to get sb through an ~** trouver qn par une agence; **'no agencies'** (in advertisement) 'agences s'abstenir'; **aid ~** organisme *m* d'entraide; **2** GB Comm (representing firm) concessionnaire *m*; **to have the Peugeot ~** être le concessionnaire Peugeot; **to have the sole ~ for** avoir la représentation exclusive de [*company, product*]; **3** (influence) intermédiaire *m*; **through an outside ~** par l'intermédiaire d'un tiers; **4** Phys, Geol **by the ~ of erosion** sous l'effet de l'érosion.

agency: **~ fee** *n* commission *f* de gestion; **Agency for International Development, AID** *n* US *organisme gouvernemental d'aide aux pays en voie de développement*; **~ nurse** *n* infirmier/-ière *m/f* intérimaire; **~ staff** *n* personnel *m* intérimaire.

agenda /əˈdʒendə/ *n* **1** Admin ordre *m* du jour; **to be on the ~** être à l'ordre du jour; **2** fig (list of priorities) programme *m*; **hidden** ou **secret ~** programme secret; **unemployment is high on the political ~** l'emploi est prioritaire dans le monde politique.

agent /ˈeɪdʒənt/ *n* **1** (acting for customer, artist, firm) agent *m* (**for sb** de qn); **area/sole ~** agent régional/exclusif; **to go through an ~** passer par un intermédiaire; **to act as sb's ~, to act as ~ for sb** représenter qn; **2** Pol (spy) agent *m*; **enemy/foreign ~** agent ennemi/étranger; **3** (cause, means) agent *m*; **4** (chemical substance) agent *m*; **cleaning ~** agent nettoyant; **5** Ling agent *m*.

IDIOMS **to be a free ~** être indépendant.

agentive /ˈeɪdʒəntɪv/ **I** *n* Ling agentif *m*.
II *adj* Ling agentif/-ive.

agent: **Agent Orange** *n* agent *m* orange; **~ provocateur** *n* agent *m* provocateur; **~s procedure** *n* Univ procédure *f* d'inscription.

age-old /ˌeɪdʒˈəʊld/ *adj* ancestral, très vieux/vieille.

age range *n* tranche *f* d'âge; **people in the 25–30 ~** les personnes entre 25 et 30 ans, les personnes dans la tranche d'âge des 25–30 ans.

agglomerate I /əˈglɒmərət/*n* agglomérat *m*.
II /əˈglɒməreɪt/ *vtr* agglomérer.
III /əˈglɒməreɪt/ *vi* s'agglomérer.

agglomeration /əˌglɒməˈreɪʃn/ *n* Geol, gen agglomération *f*.

agglutinate /əˈgluːtɪneɪt/ **I** *vtr* Ling, Med, gen agglutiner.
II *vi* Ling, gen s'agglutiner; **agglutinating language** langue *f* agglutinante.

agglutination /əˌgluːtɪˈneɪʃn, US -təˈn-/ *n* agglutination *f*.

agglutinative /əˈgluːtɪnətɪv, US -təneɪtɪv/ *adj* agglutinant.

aggrandize /əˈgrændaɪz/ *vtr* sout agrandir.

aggrandizement /əˈgrændɪzmənt/ *n* sout avancement *m*.

aggravate /ˈægrəveɪt/ **I** *vtr* **1** (make worse) aggraver [*situation, illness*]; **2** (annoy) exaspérer.
II aggravated *pp adj* Jur [*burglary, offence*] qualifié, aggravé.

aggravating /ˈægrəveɪtɪŋ/ *adj* **1** Jur (worsening) aggravant; **2**° (irritating) exaspérant.

aggravation /ˌægrəˈveɪʃn/ *n* **1** ¢ (annoyance) ennuis *mpl*; **2** (irritation) contrariété *f*; **3** (worsening) aggravation *f*.

aggregate I /ˈægrɪgət/ *n* **1** gen, Econ ensemble *m*, total *m*; **in ~** dans l'ensemble; **2** Sport score *m* total; **on ~** GB au total; **3** Constr, Geol agrégat *m*.
II aggregates *npl* (also **monetary ~s**) GB Econ agrégats *mpl* monétaires.
III /ˈægrɪgət/ *adj* **1** [*amount, cost, loss, profit*] total; [*data*] d'ensemble; [*demand, supply*] global; **2** Sport total.
IV /ˈægrɪgeɪt/ *vtr* **1** (combine) rassembler [*figures, points, score*]; regrouper [*data*]; **2** (group) répartir [*people*].

aggression /əˈgreʃn/ *n* (of person) agressivité *f*; (in situation, place, group) agression *f*.

aggressive /əˈgresɪv/ *adj* **1** [*person, reaction, behaviour*] agressif/-ive; **2** Comm, Fin [*management, policy, marketing*] agressif/-ive, dynamique.

aggressively /əˈgresɪvlɪ/ *adv* **1** [*behave, react*] avec agressivité, de manière agressive; **~ frank** d'une franchise excessive; **2** Comm, Fin [*promote*] de manière agressive; [*manage*] de façon dynamique.

aggressiveness /əˈgresɪvnɪs/ *n* agressivité *f*.

aggressor /əˈgresə(r)/ *n* agresseur *m*.

aggrieved /əˈgriːvd/ **I** *n* Jur **the ~** la partie lésée.
II *adj* **1** Jur lésé; **2** (resentful) mécontent (**at** de).

aggro° /ˈægrəʊ/ *n* GB **1** (violence) violence *f*; **2** (hostility) hostilité *f*.

aghast /əˈgɑːst, US əˈgæst/ *adj* horrifié (**at** par).

agile /ˈædʒaɪl, US ˈædʒl/ *adj* [*person, movement*] agile; [*mind*] vif/vive, agile.

agility /əˈdʒɪlətɪ/ *n* (physical, mental) agilité *f*.

Agincourt /ˈædʒɪnkɔːt/ *pr n* Azincourt.

aging *n, adj* = **ageing**.

agitate /ˈædʒɪteɪt/ **I** *vtr* **1** (shake) agiter [*liquid*]; **2** [*news, situation, argument*] troubler [*person*].
II *vi* (campaign, demonstrate) faire campagne (**for** pour; **against** contre).

agitated /ˈædʒɪteɪtɪd/ *adj* agité, inquiet.

agitatedly /ˈædʒɪteɪtɪdlɪ/ *adv* d'une manière agitée.

agitation /ˌædʒɪˈteɪʃn/ *n* **1** (political) agitation *f*; **2** (anxiety) agitation *f*; **to be in a state of ~** être agité; **3** (of liquid) agitation *f*.

agitator /ˈædʒɪteɪtə(r)/ *n* **1** (person) agitateur/-trice *m/f*; **2** Tech agitateur *m*.

agitprop /ˈædʒɪtprɒp/ *n* agit-prop *f inv*.

aglow /əˈgləʊ/ *adj* [*person, face*] rayonnant (**with** de); [*sky, hills*] embrasé; [*shop window*] illuminé; **to set sth ~** embraser qch.

AGM *n*: *abrév* ▸ **Annual General Meeting**.

agnostic /ægˈnɒstɪk/ *n, adj* agnostique (*mf*).

agnosticism /ægˈnɒstɪsɪzəm/ *n* agnosticisme *f*.

ago /əˈgəʊ/ *adv* **three weeks/two years ~** il y a trois semaines/deux ans; **some time ~** il y a quelque temps; **long ~** il y a longtemps; **how long ~?** il y a combien de temps?; **not long ~** il y a peu de temps; **as long ~ as 1986** dès 1986, déjà en 1986; **they got married forty years ~ today** cela fait quarante ans aujourd'hui qu'ils sont mariés.

agog /əˈgɒg/ *adj* **1** (excited) en émoi (**at** à cause de); **2** (eager) impatient (**to do** de faire); **we were all ~ to hear the results** on brûlait d'impatience d'apprendre les résultats.

agonize /ˈægənaɪz/ *vi* se tourmenter (**over, about** à propos de).

agonized /ˈægənaɪzd/ *adj* [*cry*] déchirant; [*expression*] angoissé.

agonizing /ˈægənaɪzɪŋ/ *adj* **1** [*pain, death*] atroce; **2** [*decision, choice*] déchirant.

agony /ˈægənɪ/ *n* **1** (physical) douleur *f* atroce; **to die in ~** mourir dans des douleurs atroces; **2** (mental) angoisse *f*; **to**

prolong the ~ prolonger l'angoisse; **it was ~!** hum c'était l'horreur!; **to pile on the ~** GB dramatiser.

agony: **~ aunt** *n* GB journaliste *mf* responsable du courrier du cœur; **~ column** *n* GB courrier *m* du cœur.

agoraphobia /ˌægərəˈfəʊbɪə/ *n* agoraphobie *f*.

agoraphobic /ˌægərəˈfəʊbɪk/ *adj* agoraphobique.

AGR *n* GB *abrév* ▶ **Advanced gas-cooled reactor**.

agrammatical /ˌeɪɡrəˈmætɪkl/ *adj* agrammatical.

agraphia /əˈɡræfɪə/ *n* agraphie *f*.

agrarian /əˈɡreərɪən/ *adj* agraire.

agree /əˈɡriː/ **I** *vtr* (*prét, pp* **agreed**) **1** (concur) être d'accord (**that** sur le fait que; **with** avec); **we ~d with him that he should leave** nous étions d'accord avec lui sur le fait qu'il devait partir; **2** (admit, concede) convenir (**that** que); **I ~ it sounds unlikely** ça a l'air peu probable, j'en conviens; **it's dangerous, don't you ~?** c'est dangereux, tu ne crois pas?; **3** (consent) **to ~ to do** accepter de faire; **4** (settle on, arrange) se mettre d'accord sur, convenir de [*date, time, venue, route, method, policy, terms, fee, price*]; se mettre d'accord sur [*candidate, change, plan, solution*]; **conditions ~d with the union/between the two parties** des conditions convenues avec le syndicat/entre les deux parties; **to ~ to do** convenir de faire, se mettre d'accord pour faire; **the industrial nations have ~d to support Soviet reforms** les pays industrialisés ont convenu de soutenir les réformes soviétiques.

II *vi* (*prét, pp* **agreed**) **1** (hold same opinion) être d'accord (**with** avec; **about, on** sur); **'I ~!'** 'je suis bien d'accord!'; **I couldn't ~ more!** je suis entièrement d'accord!; **he didn't ~ with me on what was causing the pain** il n'était pas d'accord avec moi sur la cause de la douleur; **to ~ about** ou **on doing** être d'accord pour faire; **2** (reach mutual understanding) se mettre d'accord, tomber d'accord (**about, on** sur); **they failed to ~** ils n'ont pas réussi à se mettre d'accord; **the jury ~d in finding him guilty** le jury est tombé d'accord pour le déclarer coupable; **3** (consent) accepter; **to ~ to** consentir à [*plan, suggestion, terms, decision, negotiations*]; **she'll never ~ to that** elle n'y consentira jamais; **they won't ~ to her going alone** ils ne consentiront pas à ce qu'elle y aille toute seule; **4** (hold with, approve) **to ~ with** approuver [*belief, idea, practice, proposal*]; **I don't ~ with vivisection/with what they're doing** je désapprouve la vivisection/ce qu'ils font; **5** (tally) [*stories, statements, figures, totals*] concorder (**with** avec); **the two theories ~ (with each other)** les deux théories concordent; **6** (suit) **to ~ with sb** [*climate, weather*] être bon pour qn; [*food*] réussir à qn; **I ate something that didn't ~ with me** j'ai mangé quelque chose qui ne m'a pas réussi ou qui n'est pas passé; **7** Ling s'accorder (**with** avec; **in** en).

III agreed *pp adj* [*date, time, venue, amount, budget, fee, price, rate, terms, signal*] convenu; **as ~d** comme convenu; **it was ~d that there would be a wage freeze** il était convenu qu'il y aurait un gel des salaires; **to be ~d on** être d'accord sur [*decision, statement, policy*]; **are we all ~d on this?** sommes-nous tous d'accord là-dessus?; **is that ~d?** c'est bien entendu?; ▶ **damage**.

agreeable /əˈɡriːəbl/ *adj* **1** (pleasant) [*experience, surroundings, person*] agréable; **to be ~ to sb** être aimable envers qn; **2** sout (willing) **to be ~ to sth/to doing** être d'accord pour qch/pour faire; **3** sout (acceptable) **is this ~?** êtes-vous d'accord?

agreeably /əˈɡriːəblɪ/ *adv* **1** (pleasantly) agréablement; **2** (amicably) [*say, smile*] aimablement.

agreement /əˈɡriːmənt/ *n* **1** gen, Pol, Fin (settlement, contract) accord *m* (**between** entre; **with** avec; **on** sur); **EC ~** accord de la CEE; **Anglo-Irish ~** accord anglo-irlandais; **an ~ to do** un accord pour faire; **an ~ to reduce nuclear arsenals** un accord pour réduire les armements nucléaires; **to come to** ou **reach an ~** parvenir à un accord; **under an ~** en vertu d'un accord; **2** (undertaking) engagement *m* (**to do** à faire); **an ~ to repay the loan** un engagement à rembourser le prêt; **after an ~ by the union to end the strike** après que le syndicat s'est engagé à cesser la grève; **3** (mutual understanding) accord *m* (**about, on** sur); **to be in ~ with sb** être d'accord avec qn; **by ~ with sb** en accord avec qn; **to reach ~** se mettre d'accord; **there is little ~** pratiquement personne n'est d'accord; **there is general ~ that** la plupart des gens s'accordent à dire que; **to nod in ~** acquiescer d'un signe de tête; **4** Jur (contract) contrat *m*; **under the terms of the ~** selon les termes du contrat; **5** (consent) **~ to** acceptation *f* de [*reform, cease-fire, moratorium*]; **6** Ling accord *m*.

agribusiness /ˈæɡrɪbɪznɪs/ *n* ₵ agrobusiness *m*, agro-industries *fpl*.

agricultural /ˌæɡrɪˈkʌltʃərəl/ *adj* [*land, worker, production, building*] agricole; [*expert, engineer*] agronome; [*college*] d'agriculture.

agriculturalist /ˌæɡrɪˈkʌltʃərəlɪst/, **agriculturist** /ˌæɡrɪˈkʌltʃərɪst/ US ▶ **1692** *n* agronome *mf*.

agricultural show *n* (rural) ≈ comices *mpl* agricoles; (trade fair) foire *f* agricole.

agriculture /ˈæɡrɪkʌltʃə(r)/ *n* agriculture *f*.

agrochemical /ˌæɡrəʊˈkemɪkəl/ **I** *n* substance *f* agrochimique.

II agrochemicals *npl* (+ *v sg*) (industry) agrochimie *f*.

III *adj* agrochimique.

agronomist /əˈɡrɒnəmɪst/ ▶ **1692** *n* agronome *mf*.

agronomy /əˈɡrɒnəmɪ/ *n* agronomie *f*.

aground /əˈɡraʊnd/ **I** *adj* **to be ~** être échoué.

II *adv* **to run ~** s'échouer.

ague‡ /ˈeɪɡjuː/ ▶ **1354** *n* fièvre *f* paludéenne.

ah /ɑː/ *excl* ah!; **~ well!** (resignedly) eh bien voilà!

aha /ɑːˈhɑː, əˈhɑː/ *excl* ah! ah!

ahead /əˈhed/

■ **Note** *ahead* is often used after verbs in English (*go ahead, plan ahead, think ahead etc*). For translations consult the appropriate verb entry (***go***, ***plan***, ***think*** etc). For all other uses see the entry below.

I *adv* **1** (spatially) [*go on, run*] en avant; **we've sent Josephine on ~** nous avons envoyé Josephine en éclaireur; **to send one's luggage on ~** faire envoyer ses bagages; **the road (up) ~ is blocked** la rue est barrée; **can you see what is wrong ~?** est-ce que tu vois ce qui se passe (devant)?; **a few kilometres ~** à quelques kilomètres; **a road/waterfall appeared ~** une rue/chute d'eau est apparue devant nous/lui etc; **full speed ~** Naut en avant toute; ▶ **straight**; **2** (in time) **in the months/years ~** pendant les mois/années à venir; **to apply at least a year ~** envoyer sa candidature au moins un an à l'avance; **who knows what lies ~?** qui sait ce que l'avenir nous réserve?; **there are troubled times ~ for the government** une période difficile s'annonce pour le gouvernement; **3** fig (in leading position) **to be ~ in the polls** être en tête dans les sondages; **to be 30 points ~** avoir 30 points d'avance; **to be 3% ~** avoir une avance de 3%; **another goal put them ~** un autre but leur a permis de mener; **4** fig (more advanced) **to be ~ in physics/geography** [*pupil, set*] être plus avancé en physique/géographie.

II ahead of *prep phr* **1** (spatially) devant [*person, vehicle*]; **to be three metres ~ of sb** avoir trois mètres d'avance sur qn; **2** (in time) **to be three seconds ~ of the next competitor** avoir trois secondes d'avance sur le concurrent suivant; **~ of time** en avance; **our rivals are one year ~ of us** nos rivaux sont en avance d'un an par rapport à nous; **to arrive ~ of sb** arriver avant qn; **there are difficult times ~ of us** une période difficile nous attend; **3** fig (leading) **to be ~ of sb** (in polls, ratings) avoir un avantage sur qn; **4** fig (more advanced) **to be (way) ~ of the others** [*pupil, set*] être (bien) plus avancé que les autres; **to be ~ of the field** [*business*] devancer les autres; **to be ten years ~ of the field** (in research) être dix ans en avance or avoir dix ans d'avance dans le domaine.

IDIOMS **to be ~ of one's time** être en avance sur son temps.

ahoy /əˈhɔɪ/ *excl* ohé; **ship ~!** ohé du bateau!

AI *n* **1** (*abrév* = **artificial intelligence**) IA; **2** *abrév* ▶ **artificial insemination**; **3** *abrév* ▶ **Amnesty International**.

aid /eɪd/ **I** *n* **1** (help) aide *f* (**to** à); **with/without sb's ~** avec/sans l'aide de qn; **with the ~ of** à l'aide de; **to come to sb's ~** venir en aide à qn; **to go to sb's ~** aller à l'aide de qn; **he came/went to her ~** il est venu/allé à son aide; **2** (charitable or financial support) aide *f* (**from** de; **to, for** à); **3 in ~ of** au profit de [*charity etc*]; **what's all this shouting in ~ of?** GB hum c'est en quel honneur tous ces cris?; **4** (equipment) aide *f*.

II *modif* [*budget, organization, programme, scheme*] d'entraide; **~ worker** employé/-e *m/f* d'un organisme d'entraide.

III *vtr* aider [*person*] (**to do** à faire); faciliter [*digestion, recovery, development*]; **~ed by sb/by sth** aidé par qn/de qch.

IV *vi* **1 to ~ in** faciliter; **to ~ in doing sth** aider à faire; **2** Jur ou hum **to ~ and abet sb** être complice de qn; **~ed and abetted by sb** avec la complicité de qn; **charged with ~ing and abetting** Jur accusé de complicité.

AID *n* **1** (*abrév* = **Artificial Insemination by Donor**) insemination *f* artificielle par un donneur; **2** US *abrév* ▶ **Agency for International Development**.

Aida® /eɪdə/ *n* Sewing étamine *f* (à broder).

aide /eɪd/ *n* aide *mf*, assistant/-e *m/f*.

aide-de-camp /ˌeɪddəˈkɒm, US -ˈkæmp/ ▶ **1612** *n* (*pl* **aides-de-camp**) aide *m* de camp.

Aids /eɪdz/ *n* (*abrév* = **Acquired Immune Deficiency Syndrome**) sida *m*.

Aids-related /ˌeɪdz rɪˈleɪtəd/ *adj* [*disease, virus, symptom*] lié au sida; **~ infection** infection *f* opportuniste liée au sida.

Aids-related complex, **ARC** *n* ARC *m*, phase *f* 2 du sida.

aigrette /ˈeɪɡret, eɪˈɡret/ *n* aigrette *f*.

aikido /ˈaɪkɪdəʊ/ ▶ **1282** *n* aïkido *m*.

ail /eɪl/ **I** *vtr* **1** affliger [*society, economy*]; **2**‡ chagriner [*person*].

II *vi* **to be ~ing** [*person*] être souffrant; [*company*] être mal en point.

aileron /ˈeɪlərɒn/ *n* Aviat aileron *m*.

ailing /ˈeɪlɪŋ/ *adj* **1** fig [*industry, business*] mal en point *inv*; [*economy*] fragile, mal en point *inv*; **2** [*person*] souffrant; [*pet*] malade.

ailment /ˈeɪlmənt/ *n* affection *f*, maladie *f*.

aim /eɪm/ **I** *n* **1** (purpose) but *m* (**of** de; **to do, of doing** de faire); **with the ~ of doing** dans le but de faire; **2** (with weapon) **to take (careful) ~** viser (avec soin); **to take ~ at sth/sb** viser qch/qn; **to miss one's ~** manquer sa cible; **his ~ is bad** il vise mal.

II *vtr* **1 to be ~ed at sb** [*campaign, product, insult, remark*] viser qn; **to be ~ed at doing** [*effort, action*] viser à faire;

we are ~ing the campaign at the young, the campaign is ~ed at the young dans cette campagne nous visons les jeunes; **2** braquer [*gun*] (**at** sur); lancer [*ball, stone*] (**at** sur); tenter de donner [*blow, kick*] (**at** à); diriger [*vehicle*] (**at** contre); **well-~ed** [*blow, kick*] bien placé.
III *vi* **to ~ for sth, to ~ at sth** lit, fig viser qch; **to ~ at doing, to ~ to do** (try) s'efforcer de faire; (intend) avoir l'intention de faire qch; **to ~ high** fig viser haut.

aimless /ˈeɪmlɪs/ *adj* [*person, wandering*] sans but; [*argument, gathering*] vain; [*violence*] sans objet.

aimlessly /ˈeɪmlɪslɪ/ *adv* sans but.

Ain ▶1163 *pr n* Ain *m*; **in/to the ~** dans l'Ain.

ain't○ /eɪnt/ = **am not, is not, are not, has not, have not**.

air /eə(r)/ **I** *n* **1** (substance) air *m*; **in the open ~** en plein air, au grand air; **I need a change of ~** j'ai besoin de changer d'air; **to come up for ~** [*swimmer, animal*] remonter à la surface pour respirer; **to let the ~ out of a tyre/balloon** dégonfler un pneu/ballon; **2** (atmosphere, sky) air *m*; **he threw the ball up into the ~** il a jeté le ballon en l'air; **the helicopter rose up into the ~** l'hélicoptère a décollé; **the birds of the ~** les oiseaux qui volent; **the swans took to the ~** les cygnes se sont envolés or ont pris leur envol; **to send sth/to travel by ~** envoyer qch/voyager par avion; **Paris (seen) from the ~** Paris vu d'avion; **the battle was fought on the ground and in the ~** la bataille fut livrée sur terre et dans les airs; **to clear the ~** lit [*storm*] rafraîchir l'air; fig détendre l'atmosphère; **3** Radio, TV **to be/go on the ~** [*broadcaster, interviewee*] être/passer à l'antenne; **to go off the ~** quitter l'antenne; **while the programme was still on the ~** alors que l'émission était encore en cours de diffusion; **the series will be back on the ~ in January** le feuilleton reprendra en janvier; **he went on the ~ to reassure the public** il est intervenu à la radio or à la télévision pour rassurer le public; **off the ~, she confided that...** hors antenne, elle a confié que...; **the channel goes off the ~ at midnight** la chaîne cesse d'émettre à minuit; **4** (manner) (of person) air *m*; (aura, appearance) (of place) aspect *m*, air *m*; **with an ~ of innocence/indifference** d'un air innocent/indifférent; **an ~ of mystery surrounds the project** le projet est entouré de mystère; **he has a certain ~ about him** il a une certaine allure; **5** Mus air *m*; **6** littér (breeze) souffle *m* de vent.
II *vtr* **1** (dry) faire sécher; (freshen by exposing to air) aérer [*garment, room, bed*]; **don't wear that shirt, it hasn't been ~ed** ne mets pas cette chemise, elle n'est pas complètement sèche; **2** (express) exprimer, faire part de [*opinion, view*]; **to ~ one's grievances** exposer ses griefs; **to ~ one's knowledge** faire étalage de son savoir; **3** US (broadcast) diffuser.
IDIOMS **there's something in the ~** il y a quelque chose dans l'air, il y a quelque chose qui se trame; **he could sense trouble in the ~** il sentait qu'il y avait de l'orage dans l'air fig; **there's a rumour in the ~ that...** le bruit court que...; **to put on ~s, to give oneself ~s** péj se donner de grands airs; **our plans are still totally up in the ~** nos projets sont toujours très flous or vagues; **to be walking** ou **treading on ~** être aux anges; **to disappear** ou **vanish into thin ~** se volatiser; **they produced** ou **conjured these figures out of thin ~** leurs chiffres étaient complètement fantaisistes.

air: **~ alert** *n* alerte *f* aérienne; **~ ambulance** *n* avion *m* sanitaire; **~ bag** *n* Aut airbag *m*; **~ base** *n* base *f* aérienne; **~ bed** *n* GB matelas *m* pneumatique; **~ bladder** *n* vésicule *f*.

airborne /ˈeəbɔːn/ *adj* **1** Bot [*spore, seed*] porté par le vent; **2** Aviat, Mil [*troops, division*] aéroporté; **once the plane was ~** une fois que l'avion avait décollé; **the plane remained ~** l'avion est resté dans les airs.

air: **~ brake** *n* Aut, Rail frein *m* à air comprimé; Aviat aérofrein *m*, frein *m* aérodynamique; **~ brick** *n* brique *f* creuse; **~ bridge** *n* GB pont *m* aérien.

airbrush /ˈeəbrʌʃ/ **I** *n* aérographe *m*.
II *vtr* peindre [qch] à l'aérographe.

air: **~ bubble** *n* (in liquid, plastic, wallpaper) bulle *f* d'air; (in glass, metal etc) soufflure *f*; **~burst** *n* explosion *f* aérienne; **~bus** *n* airbus *m*; **~ chamber** *n* Tech cloche *f* à air; Biol chambre *f* à air; **~ chief marshal ▶1612** *n* GB général *m* de l'armée aérienne; **~ commodore ▶1612** *n* général *m* de brigade aérienne; **~-condition** *vtr* installer l'air conditionné or la climatisation dans; **~-conditioned** *adj* climatisé; **~-conditioner** *n* climatiseur *m*; **~-conditioning** *n* climatisation *f*, air *m* conditionné; **~-cooled** *adj* [*engine*] à refroidissement par air; **~ corridor** *n* couloir *m* aérien; **~craft** *n* (*pl* **~**) avion *m*, aéronef *m*; **~craft carrier** *n* porte-avions *m inv*; **~craft(s)man ▶1612** *n* GB soldat *m* de deuxième classe (de l'armée de l'air); **~craft(s)woman** *n* GB femme soldat *f* de deuxième classe dans l'armée de l'air; **~crew** *n* équipage *m* (d'un avion); **~ cushion** *n* (inflatable cushion) coussin *m* pneumatique; (of hovercraft) coussin *m* d'air; **~ cylinder** *n* cylindre *m* à air comprimé; **~ disaster** *n* catastrophe *f* aérienne; **~drome** *n* US aérodrome *m*.

airdrop /ˈeədrɒp/ **I** *n* parachutage *m*.
II *vtr* (*p prés etc* **-pp-**) parachuter.

air duct /ˈeədʌkt/ *n* conduit *m* d'air or d'aération.

Airedale (terrier) /ˈeədeɪl/ *n* airedale (terrier) *m*.

air: **~fare** *n* tarif *m* d'avion; **~field** *n* aérodrome *m*, terrain *m* d'aviation; **~flow** *n* gen, Aut, Aviat courant *m* atmosphérique; (in wind tunnel) écoulement *m* d'air; **~ force** *n* armée *f* de l'air, forces *fpl* aériennes; **~ force blue** *n* bleu *m* outremer; **~frame** *n* cellule *f* aéronautique or d'avion.

airfreight /ˈeəfreɪt/ *n* **1** (method of transport) transport *m* aérien; **by ~** par transport aérien, par avion; **2** (goods) fret *m* aérien; **3** (charge) tarif *m* aérien.

air: **~-freshener** *n* désodorisant *m* d'atmosphère; **~ gun** *n* fusil *m* or carabine *f* à air comprimé; **~head**○ *n* péj évaporé/-e *m/f*; **~ hole** *n* trou *m* d'aération; **~ hostess ▶1692** *n* hôtesse *f* de l'air.

airily /ˈeərɪlɪ/ *adv* avec désinvolture, avec insouciance.

airiness /ˈeərɪnɪs/ *n* **1** (of room, house, place) aspect *m* clair et spacieux; **2** (nonchalance) (of manner, attitude, gesture) désinvolture *f*, insouciance *f*; (of promise) légèreté *f*.

airing /ˈeərɪŋ/ *n* **1** (of linen) (drying) séchage *m*; (freshening) aération *f*; **2** fig (mention) **to give an idea/issue an ~** mettre une idée/question sur le tapis; **the issue got its first public ~ yesterday** la question a été abordée ouvertement pour la première fois hier; **3** Radio, TV diffusion *f*.

airing cupboard *n* GB *placard qui contient la chaudière et où l'on range le linge*.

air lane *n* couloir *m* aérien or de navigation aérienne.

airless /ˈeəlɪs/ *adj* [*room*] qui sent le renfermé; [*weather, evening*] lourd, étouffant.

air letter *n* aérogramme *m*.

airlift /ˈeəlɪft/ **I** *n* pont *m* aérien; **~ of refugees** évacuation *f* de réfugiés par pont aérien.
II *vtr* évacuer [qn] par pont aérien [*evacuees*]; acheminer [qch] par pont aérien [*supplies, goods*]; **to be ~ed to hospital** être transporté par hélicoptère jusqu'à l'hôpital.

airline /ˈeəlaɪn/ **I** *n* **1** Aviat (company) compagnie *f* aérienne or de transports aériens; **2** Tech, gen (source of air) tuyau *m* d'air; (diver's) voie *f* d'air.
II *modif* Aviat [*pilot, staff*] de compagnie aérienne; [*company*] aérien/-ienne, de transports aériens.

airliner /ˈeəlaɪnə(r)/ *n* avion *m* de ligne.

airlock /ˈeəlɒk/ *n* **1** (in pipe, pump etc) poche *f* or bulle *f* d'air; **2** (in spaceship) sas *m*.

airmail /ˈeəmeɪl/ **I** *n* poste *f* aérienne; **to send sth (by) ~** envoyer qch par avion.
II *vtr* envoyer [qch] par avion.

air: **~mail edition** *n* Journ *édition sur papier léger pour envoi par avion*; **~mail envelope** *n* enveloppe *f* par avion; **~mail label** *n* étiquette *f* 'par avion'; **~mail paper** *n* papier *m* pelure, papier *m* par avion; **~man** *n* gen, Mil aviateur *m*; **~man basic ▶1612** *n* US Mil Aviat soldat *m* (de l'armée de l'air américaine); **~man first class ▶1612** *n* US Mil Aviat caporal *m* (de l'armée de l'air américaine); **~ marshal ▶1612** *n* GB général *m* de corps aérien; **~ mass** *n* masse *f* d'air; **~ miles** *npl*: *système de carte de fidelité de compagnies aériennes*; **~ miss** *n* quasicollision *f* aérienne; **~mobile** *adj* US aéroporté; **~plane** *n* US avion *m*; **~ plant** *n* orchidacée *f* (*cultivée comme plante d'ornement*).

airplay *n* Radio, TV **this record gets a lot of ~** ce disque passe souvent à la radio.

air: **~ pocket** *n* (in pipe, enclosed space) poche *f* d'air; Aviat trou *m* d'air; **~ pollution** *n* pollution *f* atmosphérique.

airport /ˈeəpɔːt/ **I** *n* aéroport *m*.
II *modif* [*buildings, runways, staff*] de l'aéroport; **~ taxes** taxes *fpl* d'aéroport.

air: **~ power** *n* puissance *f* aérienne; **~ pressure** *n* pression *f* atmosphérique; **~ pump** *n* pompe *f* à air, gonfleur *m*; **~ raid** *n* attaque *f* aérienne, raid *m* (aérien); **~-raid precautions** *npl* défense *f* passive; **~-raid shelter** *n* abri *m* antiaérien; **~-raid siren** *n* sirène *f* d'alerte aérienne; **~-raid warden** *n* préposé/-e *m/f* à la défense passive; **~-raid warning** *n* alerte *f* aérienne; **~ rifle** *n* carabine *f* à air comprimé; **~screw** *n* GB hélice *f*; **~-sea base** *n* base *f* aéronavale; **~-sea rescue** *n* opération *f* de sauvetage en mer (*par hélicoptère*); **~ shaft** *n* (in mine) puits *m* d'aérage; **~ship** *n* dirigeable *m*; **~ show** *n* (flying show) meeting *m* aérien; (trade exhibition) salon *m* de l'aéronautique; **~ shuttle** *n* navette *f* aérienne.

airsick /ˈeəsɪk/ *adj* **to be ~** avoir le mal de l'air.

air: **~sickness** *n* mal *m* de l'air; **~ sock** *n* manche *f* à air; **~ space** *n* espace *m* aérien; **~speed** *n* vitesse *f* propre, vitesse *f* par rapport à l'air; **~speed indicator** *n* Aviat badin *m*; **~stream** *n* gen, Meteorol courant *m* atmosphérique; Ling colonne *f* d'air; **~strip** *n* piste *f* (d'atterrissage or de décollage); **~ suspension** *n* suspension *f* pneumatique; **~ terminal** *n* (at airport) aérogare *f*; (in town: terminus) terminal *m*; **~tight** *adj* hermétique, étanche à l'air; **~time** *n* Radio, TV temps *m* d'antenne; **~-to-air** *adj* Mil [*missile*] air-air *inv*; [*refuelling*] en vol; **~-traffic control, ATC** *n* (activity) contrôle *m* du trafic aérien; (building) tour *f* de contrôle; **~-traffic controller ▶1692** *n* contrôleur/-euse *m/f* aérien/-ienne, aiguilleur *m* du ciel; **~ valve** *n* gen soupape *f* d'air; (in central heating system) purgeur *m* d'air; **~ vent** *n* prise *f* d'air; **~ vice-marshal** *n* GB général *m* de division aérienne.

airwaves /ˈeəweɪvz/ *npl* Radio, TV ondes *fpl*; **on the ~** sur les ondes.

airway /ˈeəweɪ/ *n* **1** Aviat (route) voie *f* aérienne; **2** (airline) compagnie *f* aérienne; **3** (ventilating passage) galerie *f* d'aérage; **4** Anat voie *f* respiratoire.

air: **~worthiness** *n* navigabilité *f*; **~worthy** *adj* en état de navigation.

airy /ˈeərɪ/ *adj* **1** [*room, house*] clair/-e et spacieux/-ieuse; **2** (casual) [*manner, attitude, gesture*] désinvolte, insouciant; **~ promises** promesses *fpl* en l'air.

airy-fairy○ /ˌeərɪˈfeərɪ/ *adj* GB [*idea, scheme, person*] farfelu○.

aisle /aɪl/ *n* **1** (in church) (side passage) bas-côté *m*; (centre passage) allée *f* centrale; **2** (passageway) (in train, plane) couloir *m*; (in cinema, shop) allée *f*.
IDIOMS **the film had us rolling in the ~s**○ le film nous a fait mourir de rire; **to lead sb down the ~** hum se marier avec qn.

aisle seat *n* (in plane) (siège *m* au bord d'une) allée *f*; (in cinema, theatre) place *f* en bout de rangée.

Aisne ▶ **1163** *pr n* Aisne *m*; **in/to the ~** dans l'Aisne.

aitch /eɪtʃ/ *n*: *orthographe de la prononciation de la lettre h*; **to drop one's ~es** ne pas aspirer les 'h', avoir un accent populaire.

ajar /əˈdʒɑː(r)/ *adj, adv* entrouvert, entrebaillé.

AK US Post *abrév écrite* = **Alaska**.

aka (*abrév* = **also known as**) alias.

akimbo /əˈkɪmbəʊ/ *adj* (**with**) **arms ~** les poings sur les hanches.

akin /əˈkɪn/ *adj* **1** (similar) **to be ~ to** être semblable à; **her style is more/closely ~ to cubism** son style ressemble davantage/beaucoup au cubisme; **2** (tantamount) **to be ~ to sth/to doing** (disapproving) équivaloir à qch/à faire.

AL 1 *abrév écrite* Aut Admin = **Albania**; **2** *abrév écrite* US Post = **Alabama**.

ALA *abrév écrite* = **all letters answered**.

Alabama /ˌæləˈbæmə/ ▶ **1744** *pr n* Alabama *m*.

alabaster /ˈæləbɑːstə(r), US -bæs-/ **I** *n* albâtre *m*.
II *modif* [*statue, ashtray*] en albâtre *m*.

alacrity /əˈlækrətɪ/ *n* sout empressement *m*; **with ~** avec empressement.

Aladdin /əˈlædɪn/ *pr n* Aladin.

Aladdin's cave *n* fig caverne *f* d'Ali-baba.

Alar /ˈeɪlɑː(r)/ *n* Chem Alar®, dominozide *m*.

alarm /əˈlɑːm/ **I** *n* **1** (feeling) frayeur *f*; (concern) inquiétude *f*; **in ~** avec inquiétude; (stronger) apeuré; **I don't want to cause ~ but...** je ne veux pas vous inquiéter mais...; **there is cause for ~** il y a de bonnes raisons de s'inquiéter; **there is no cause for ~** inutile de s'inquiéter; **2** (warning signal, device) alarme *f*; **smoke ~** détecteur *m* de fumée; **to activate** ou **set off an ~** déclencher une alarme; **the ~ went off** l'alarme s'est mise en marche; **to raise the ~** lit donner l'alarme; fig sonner l'alarme; **3** = **alarm clock**.
II *vtr* **1** (worry) inquiéter; (stronger) faire peur à [*person*] (**with** avec; **by doing** en faisant); mettre [qch] en alerte [*animal*]; **2** (fit system) installer un système d'alarme sur [*car*]; **this car is ~ed** cette voiture est équipée d'un système d'alarme.

alarm bell *n* sonnette *f* d'alarme; **~s are ringing** GB fig un signal d'alarme se déclenche; **to set the ~s ringing** GB fig tirer la sonnette d'alarme.

alarm call *n* Telecom réveil *m* téléphoné.

alarm clock *n* réveille-matin *m*, réveil *m*; **to set the ~ for eight o'clock** mettre le réveil à huit heures; **the ~ went off** le réveil a sonné.

alarmed /əˈlɑːmd/ *adj* effrayé; **don't be ~!** rassurez-vous!

alarming /əˈlɑːmɪŋ/ *adj* alarmant.

alarmingly /əˈlɑːmɪŋlɪ/ *adv* [*act, behave*] de façon alarmante; **~ violent/rapid** d'une violence/rapidité alarmante; **~, we have no news of them** nous sommes alarmés de n'avoir aucune nouvelle d'eux.

alarmist /əˈlɑːmɪst/ *n, adj* alarmiste (*mf*).

alarm: **~ signal** *n* signal *m* d'alarme; **~ system** *n* système *m* d'alarme.

alas /əˈlæs/ *excl* hélas.

Alaska /əˈlæskə/ ▶ **1744** *pr n* Alaska *m*.

Alaskan /əˈlæskən/ **I** *n* habitant/-e *m/f* de l'Alaska.
II *adj* de l'Alaska.

alb /ælb/ *n* Relig aube *f*.

albacore /ˈælbəkɔː(r)/ *n* thon *m* blanc, germon *m*.

Albania /ælˈbeɪnɪə/ ▶ **1131** *pr n* Albanie *f*.

Albanian /ælˈbeɪnɪən/ ▶ **1486**, **1402** **I** *n* **1** (person) Albanais/-e *m/f*; **2** (language) albanais *m*.
II *adj* albanais.

albatross /ˈælbətrɒs, US *also* -trɔːs/ *n* albatros *m* (also in golf).
IDIOMS **to be the ~ around sb's neck** être un grave problème pour qn.

albeit /ˌɔːlˈbiːɪt/ *conj* sout quoique (+ *subj*), bien que (+ *subj*).

Alberta /ælˈbɜːtə/ *pr n* Alberta *m*.

Albigensian /ˌælbɪˈdʒensɪən/ *adj* albigeois.

albinism /ˈælbɪnɪzəm/ *n* albinisme *m*.

albino /ælˈbiːnəʊ, US -baɪ-/ *n, adj* albinos (*inv*).

Albion /ˈælbɪən/ *pr n* Albion *f*; **perfidious ~** la perfide Albion.

album /ˈælbəm/ *n* gen, Mus album *m*; **photo/stamp ~** album de photos/timbres.

albumen /ˈælbjʊmɪn, US ælˈbjuːmən/ *n* Biol, Bot albumen *m*.

albumin /ˈælbjʊmɪn, US ælˈbjuːmɪn/ *n* albumine *f*.

albuminous /ælˈbjuːmɪnəs/ *adj* albumineux/-euse.

Alcestis /ælˈsestɪs/ *pr n* Alceste.

alchemist /ˈælkəmɪst/ *n* alchimiste *mf*.

alchemy /ˈælkəmɪ/ *n* Chem, fig alchimie *f*.

alcohol /ˈælkəhɒl, US -hɔːl/ **I** *n* alcool *m*.
II *modif* [*abuse, level, consumption*] d'alcool; [*poisoning*] par l'alcool; **the ~ content of a drink** la teneur en alcool d'une boisson; **there is an ~ ban in the stadium** la vente d'alcool est interdite dans le stade.

alcohol-free /ˌælkəhɒlˈfriː, US -hɔːl-/ *adj* [*drink*] sans alcool.

alcoholic /ˌælkəˈhɒlɪk, US -hɔːl-/ **I** *n* alcoolique *mf*.
II *adj* [*drink, ingredient*] alcoolisé; [*person, stupor, haze*] alcoolique.

Alcoholics Anonymous, AA *pr n* Alcooliques Anonymes.

alcoholism /ˈælkəhɒlɪzəm, US -hɔːl-/ *n* alcoolisme *m*.

alcove /ˈælkəʊv/ *n* renfoncement *m*.

alder /ˈɔːldə(r)/ *n* (tree, wood) aulne *m*.

alderman /ˈɔːldəmən/ *n* GB formerly magistrat *m* municipal; US ≈ conseiller/-ère *m/f* municipal/-e; **board of aldermen** US ≈ conseil *m* municipal.

ale /eɪl/ *n* bière *f*; **brown/light/pale ~** bière brune/légère/blonde.

aleatory /ˈeɪlɪətərɪ/, **aleatoric** /ˌeɪlɪəˈtɒrɪk/ *adj* gen, Mus aléatoire.

alec(k) /ˈælɪk/ IDIOMS **to be a smart ~**○ être un monsieur je-sais-tout.

Aleppo /əˈlepəʊ/ ▶ **1818** *pr n* Alep.

alert /əˈlɜːt/ **I** *n* alerte *f*; **to be on the ~ for** se méfier de [*danger*]; **fire/bomb ~** alerte au feu/à la bombe; **security ~** alerte de sécurité; **to be on (red) ~** Mil être en état d'alerte (rouge); **to be on full ~** être en état d'alerte générale.
II *adj* **1** (lively) (child) éveillé; (old person) alerte; **2** (attentive) vigilant; **to be ~ to** avoir conscience de [*danger, risk, fact, possibility*].
III *vtr* **1** (contact) alerter [*army, police, hospital*]; **2** (ask for vigilance) mettre [qn/qch] en état d'alerte [*airport, customs etc*]; **3 to ~ sb to** mettre qn en garde contre [*danger*]; attirer l'attention de qn sur [*fact, situation*].

alertness /əˈlɜːtnɪs/ *n* **1** (attentiveness) vigilance *f*; **2** (liveliness of mind) vivacité *f*.

Aleutian Islands /əˈluːʃɪən/ ▶ **1381** *pr npl* **the ~** les îles *fpl* Aléoutiennes.

A-level /ˈeɪlevl/ *n* GB Sch ≈ baccalauréat *m* (*dans une matière*).

alevin /ˈælɪvɪn/ *n* alevin *m*.

alewife /ˈeɪlwaɪf/ *n* Zool alose *f*.

Alexander /ˌælɪgˈzɑːndə(r)/ *pr n* Alexandre.

Alexander technique *n* technique *f* Alexander.

Alexandria /ˌælɪgˈzɑːndrɪə/ ▶ **1818** *pr n* Alexandrie *f*.

alexandrine /ˌælɪgˈzændraɪn/ *n* alexandrin *m*; **in ~s** en alexandrins.

alfalfa /ælˈfælfə/ *n* luzerne *f*.

alfresco /ælˈfreskəʊ/ *adj, adv* en plein air.

algae /ˈældʒiː, ˈælgaɪ/ *npl* algues *fpl*.

algal /ˈælgəl/ *adj* [*scum, growth, bloom*] des algues; [*population*] d'algues.

algebra /ˈældʒɪbrə/ *n* algèbre *f*.

algebraic /ˌældʒɪˈbreɪɪk/ *adj* algébrique.

Algeria /ælˈdʒɪərɪə/ ▶ **1131** *pr n* Algérie *f*.

Algerian /ælˈdʒɪərɪən/ ▶ **1486** **I** *n* Algérien/-ienne *m/f*.
II *adj* algérien/-ienne.

Algiers /ælˈdʒɪəz/ ▶ **1818** *pr n* Alger.

ALGOL /ˈælgɒl/ *n* (*abrév* = **algorithmic oriented language**) ALGOL *m*; **to learn/use ~** apprendre/utiliser l'ALGOL.

Algonqui(a)n /ælˈgɒŋkwɪən/ ▶ **1486**, **1402** **I** *n* (*pl* **~s**, **~**) **1** (person) Algonquin/-e *m/f*, Algonkin/-e *m/f*; **2** Ling algonquin *m*, algonkin *m*.
II *adj* algonquin, algonkin.

algorithm /ˈælgərɪðəm/ *n* Math, Comput algorithme *m*.

algorithmic /ˌælgəˈrɪðmɪk/ *adj* Math, Comput algorithmique.

alias /ˈeɪlɪəs/ **I** *n* faux nom *m*; **under an ~** sous un faux nom.
II *prep* alias.

alibi /ˈælɪbaɪ/ **I** *n* **1** Jur alibi *m*; **2** (excuse) excuse *f*.
II○ *vtr* (*p prés* **alibiing**; *prét, pp* **alibied**) surtout US **they ~ed him** ils lui ont trouvé un alibi.

Alice /ˈælɪs/ *pr n* Alice; **~ in Wonderland** Alice au pays des merveilles.

Alice band *n* GB bandeau *m* pour les cheveux.

alien /ˈeɪlɪən/ **I** *n* **1** Jur (foreigner) étranger/-ère *m/f*; **2** (being from space) extraterrestre *mf*.
II *adj* **1** gen, Jur étranger/-ère (**to** à); **2** (from space) extraterrestre; **3** (atypical) **~ to sb/sth** étranger/-ère à qn/qch.

alienate /ˈeɪlɪəneɪt/ **I** *vtr* **1** (estrange) écarter [*supporters, colleagues*]; **2** Jur aliéner (**from** de); **3** (separate) séparer (**from** de).
II alienated *pp adj* [*minority, group*] exclu (**from** de).

alienation /ˌeɪlɪəˈneɪʃn/ *n* **1** gen (process) éloignement *m* (**of** de); (state) isolement *m* (**from** de); **2** Jur, Pol, Psych aliénation *f*.

alienation effect *n* Theat distanciation *f*.

alienist† /ˈeɪlɪənɪst/ *n* US Med aliéniste† *mf*.

alight /əˈlaɪt/ **I** *adj* **1** [*match, fire*] allumé; [*building, grass*] en feu; **to set sth ~** mettre le feu à qch; **2** fig **her eyes were ~ with curiosity** ses yeux brillaient de curiosité; **his face was ~ with happiness** son visage rayonnait de joie; **the goal set the stadium ~** le but a déchainé le stade.
II *vi* [*passenger*] descendre (**from** de); [*bird*] se poser (**on** sur); [*gaze, thoughts*] s'arrêter (**on** sur).

align /əˈlaɪn/ **I** *vtr* aligner (**with** sur).
II aligned *pp adj* aligné (**with** sur); **the ~ed/non-~ed nations** les pays alignés/non-alignés.

all

As a pronoun

When *all* is used to mean *everything* it is translated by *tout*:

is that all? = c'est tout?
all is well = tout va bien

When *all* is followed by a *that* clause *all that* is translated by *tout ce qui* when it is the subject of the verb and *tout ce que* when it is the object:

all that remains to be done = tout ce qui reste à faire
that was all (that) he said = c'est tout ce qu'il a dit
after all (that) we've done = après tout ce que nous avons fait
we're doing all (that) we can = nous faisons tout ce que nous pouvons
all that you need = tout ce dont tu as besoin

When *all* is used to refer to a specified group of people or objects the translation reflects the number and gender of the people or objects referred to; *tous* is used for a group of people or objects of masculine or mixed or unspecified gender and *toutes* for a group of feminine gender:

we were all delighted = nous étions tous ravis
'where are the cups?' 'they're all in the kitchen' = 'où sont les tasses?' 'elles sont toutes dans la cuisine'

For more examples and particular usages see the entry ***all***.

As a determiner

In French, determiners agree in gender and number with the noun they precede. So *all* is translated by *tout* + masculine singular noun:

all the time = tout le temps

by *toute* + feminine singular noun:

all the family = toute la famille

by *tous* + masculine or mixed gender plural noun:

all men = tous les hommes
all the books = tous les livres

and by *toutes* + feminine plural noun:

all women = toutes les femmes
all the chairs = toutes les chaises

For more examples and particular usages see the entry ***all***.

As an adverb

When *all* is used as an adverb meaning *completely* it is generally translated by *tout*:

my coat's all dirty = mon manteau est tout sale
he was all alone = il était tout seul
they were all alone = ils étaient tout seuls
the girls were all excited = les filles étaient tout excitées

However, when the adjective that follows is in the feminine and begins with a consonant the translation is *toute/toutes*:

she was all alone = elle était toute seule
the bill is all wrong = la facture est toute fausse
the girls were all alone = les filles étaient toutes seules

For more examples and particular usages see the entry ***all***. Phrases such as *all along, all but, at all, for all* and *of all* are each treated separately in the entry ***all***.

III *v refl* **to ~ oneself** gen, Pol s'aligner (**with** sur).

alignment /ə'laɪnmənt/ *n* **1** gen, Pol alignement *m* (**with** sur); **to be in ~/out of ~** être aligné/désaligné (**with** sur); **2** Comput position *f*.

alike /ə'laɪk/ **I** *adj* (identical) pareil/-eille; (similar) semblable; **to look/sound ~** se ressembler; **all men are ~** les hommes sont tous les mêmes.
II *adv* [*dress, think*] de la même façon; **for young and old ~** pour les jeunes (tout) comme pour les personnes âgées; **driver and passenger ~ are**... le conducteur tout comme le passager est...
IDIOMS **share and share ~** il faut partager.

alimentary /,ælɪ'mentərɪ/ *adj* [*system, process*] digestif/-ive; [*rules, laws*] alimentaire; **~ canal** tube *m* digestif.

alimony /'ælɪmənɪ, US -məʊnɪ/ *n* Jur pension *f* alimentaire.

alive /ə'laɪv/ *adj* **1** lit (living) vivant, en vie; **to keep sb/sth ~** maintenir qn/qch en vie [*person, animal*]; **to keep a plant ~** entretenir une plante; **to stay ~** rester en vie; **to bury sb ~** enterrer qn vivant; **to be burnt ~** être brûlé/-e vif/vive; **to be taken/captured ~** être pris/capturé vivant; **~ and well, ~ and kicking** lit, fig bien vivant; **it's good** ou **great to be ~!** il fait bon vivre!; **no man ~** personne au monde; **just ~** entre la vie et la mort; **2** (lively) [*person*] vivant; [*mind, senses*] en éveil; **to bring [sth] ~** rendre [qch] vivant [*story, account*]; animer [*party, place*]; **to come ~** [*party, place*] s'animer; [*history*] prendre vie; **3** (in existence) [*institution, art, tradition*] vivant; [*interest, faith*] vif/vive; **to keep [sth] ~** préserver [*tradition etc*]; **we shall keep his memory ~** nous perpétuerons sa mémoire; **to keep dialogue ~** Pol maintenir le dialogue; **it kept our hopes ~** cela nous faisait garder espoir; **4** (teeming) **~ with** grouillant de [*insects etc*]; **5** (aware) **~ to** conscient de [*possibility etc*].

alkali /'ælkəlaɪ/ *n* alcali *m*.

alkaline /'ælkəlaɪn/ *adj* alcalin.

alkalinity /,ælkə'lɪnətɪ/ *n* alcalinité *f*.

alkaloid /'ælkəlɔɪd/ *n* alcaloïde *m*.

alky◐ /'ælkɪ/ *n* US alcoolique *mf*, alcoolo○ *mf*.

all /ɔ:l/ **I** *pron* **1** (everything) tout; **to risk ~** tout risquer; **~ or nothing** tout ou rien; **~ is not lost** tout n'est pas perdu; **~ was well** tout allait bien; **~ will be revealed** hum vous saurez tout hum; **~ is orderly and stable** tout n'est qu'ordre et stabilité; **will that be ~?** ce sera tout?; **and that's not ~** et ce n'est pas tout; **that's ~** (all contexts) c'est tout; **speed is ~** l'essentiel, c'est la vitesse; **in ~** en tout; **500 in ~** 500 en tout; **~ in ~** somme toute; **we're doing ~ (that) we can** nous faisons tout ce que nous pouvons (**to do** pour faire); **after ~ that has happened** après tout ce qui s'est passé; **after ~ she's been through** après tout ce qu'elle a vécu; **it's not ~ (that) it should be** [*performance, service, efficiency*] ça laisse à désirer; **~ because he didn't write** tout ça parce qu'il n'a pas écrit; **and ~ for a piece of land!** et tout ça pour un lopin de terre!; **2** (the only thing) tout; **but that's ~** mais c'est tout; **that's ~ I want** c'est tout ce que je veux; **that's ~ we can suggest** c'est tout ce que nous pouvons vous conseiller; **she's ~ I have left** elle est tout ce qui me reste; **~ I know is that** tout ce que je sais c'est que; **~ you need is** tout ce qu'il te faut c'est; **that's ~ we need!** iron il ne manquait plus que ça!; **3** (everyone) tous; **~ wish to remain anonymous** tous souhaitent rester anonymes; **~ but a few were released** ils ont tous été relâchés à quelques exceptions près; **thank you, one and ~** merci à (vous) tous; **'~ welcome'** 'venez nombreux'; **~ of the employees** tous les employés, tout le personnel; **~ of us want**... nous voulons tous...; **not ~ of them came** ils ne sont pas tous venus; **we want ~ of them back** nous voulons qu'ils soient tous rendus; **4** (the whole amount) **~ of our belongings** toutes nos affaires; **~ of this land is ours** toutes ces terres sont à nous; **not ~ of the time** pas tout le temps; **5** (emphasizing unanimity or entirety) **we ~ feel that** nous avons tous l'impression que; **we are ~ disappointed** nous sommes tous déçus; **these are ~ valid points** ce sont des points qui sont tous valables; **it ~ seems so pointless** tout cela paraît si futile; **I ate it ~** j'ai tout mangé; **what's it ~ for?** (all contexts) à quoi ça sert (tout ça)?; **who ~ was there?** US qui était là?; **y'~ have a good time now!** US amusez-vous bien!
II *det* **1** (each one of) tous/toutes; **~ men are born equal** tous les hommes naissent égaux; **~ questions must be answered** il faut répondre à toutes les questions; **~ those people who** tous ces gens qui; **~ those who** tous ceux qui; **as in ~ good films** comme dans tous les bons films; **in ~ three films** dans les trois films; **2** (the whole of) tout/toute; **~ his life** toute sa vie; **~ the time** tout le temps; **~ day/evening** toute la journée/soirée; **~ year round** toute l'année; **~ the money we've spent** tout l'argent que nous avons dépensé; **in ~ his glory** dans toute sa gloire; **I had ~ the work!** c'est moi qui ai eu tout le travail!; **you are ~ the family I have!** tu es toute la famille qui me reste!; **and ~ that sort of thing** et tout ce genre de choses; **oh no! not ~ that again!** ah non! ça ne va pas recommencer!; **3** (total) **in ~ honesty/innocence** en toute franchise/innocence; **4** (any) **beyond ~ expectations** au-delà de toute attente; **to deny ~ knowledge of sth** nier avoir connaissance de qch.
III *adv* **1** (emphatic: completely) tout; **~ alone** ou **on one's own** tout seul; **to be ~ wet** être tout mouillé; **dressed ~ in white** habillé tout en blanc; **~ around the garden/along the canal** tout autour du jardin/le long du canal; **to be ~ for sth** être tout à fait pour qch; **to be ~ for sb doing** être tout à fait favorable à ce que qn fasse; **I'm ~ for women joining the army** je suis tout à fait favorable à ce que les femmes entrent dans l'armée; **it's ~ about**... c'est l'histoire de...; **tell me ~ about it!** raconte-moi tout!; **he's forgotten ~ about us!** il nous a complètement oubliés!; **she asked ~ about you** elle a demandé de tes nouvelles; **2** (emphatic: nothing but) **to be ~ legs** être tout en jambes; **to be ~ smiles** (happy) être tout souriant; (two-faced) être tout sourire; **to be ~ sweetness** iron être tout sourire; **that stew was ~ onions!** il n'y avait pratiquement que des oignons dans ce ragoût!; **3** Sport (for each party) **(they are) six ~** (il y a) six partout; **the final score is 15 ~** le score final est de 15 partout.
IV *n* **to give one's ~** tout sacrifier (**for sth** à qch; **for sb** pour qn; **to do** pour faire).
V all+ (*dans composés*) **1** (completely) **~-concrete/-glass/-metal** tout en béton/verre/métal; **~-digital/-electronic** entièrement numérique/électronique; **~-female**, **~-girl** [*band, cast, group*] composé uniquement de femmes; **~-male/-white** [*team, production, jury*] composé uniquement d'hommes/de blancs; **~-union** [*workforce*] entièrement syndiqué; **2** (in the highest degree) ▶ **all-consuming**, **all-embracing**, **all-important etc**.
VI all along *adv phr* depuis le début, toujours; **they knew it ~ along** ils le savaient depuis le début, ils l'ont toujours su.
VII all but *adv phr* pratiquement, presque.

VIII all of *adv phr* au moins; **he must be ~ of 50** il doit avoir au moins 50 ans.

IX all that *adv phr* **he's not ~ that strong** il n'est pas si fort que ça; **it's not as far as ~ that!** ce n'est pas si loin que ça!; **I don't know her ~ that well** je ne la connais pas si bien que ça.

X all the *adv phr* **~ the more** d'autant plus; **~ the more difficult/effective** d'autant plus difficile/efficace; **~ the more so because** d'autant plus que; **to laugh ~ the more** rire encore plus; **~ the better!** tant mieux!

XI all too *adv phr* [*accurate, easy, widespread*] bien trop; **it is ~ too obvious that** il n'est que trop évident que; **she saw ~ too clearly that** elle a parfaitement bien vu que; **~ too often** bien trop souvent.

XII and all *adv phr* **1 they moved furniture, books and ~** ils ont tout déménagé y compris les meubles et les livres; **2**○ GB **the journey was very tiring what with the heat and ~** le voyage était très fatigant avec la chaleur et tout ça; **it is and ~!** mais si!

XIII at all *adv phr* **not at ~!** (acknowledging thanks) de rien!; (answering query) pas du tout!; **it is not at ~ certain** ce n'est pas du tout certain; **if (it is) at ~ possible** si possible; **is it at ~ likely that...?** y a-t-il la moindre possibilité que...? (+ *subj*); **there's nothing at ~ here** il n'y a rien du tout ici; **we know nothing at ~** ou **we don't know anything at ~ about** nous ne savons rien du tout de; **if you knew anything at ~ about** si tu avais la moindre idée de; **anything at ~ will do** n'importe quoi fera l'affaire.

XIV for all *prep phr, adv phr* (despite) en dépit de; (in as much as) **for ~ I know** pour autant que je sache; **for ~ that** malgré tout, quand même; **they could be dead for ~ the difference it would make!** ils pourraient être morts, ça ne changerait rien!

XV of all *prep phr* **1** (in rank) **the easiest of ~** le plus facile; **first/last of ~** pour commencer/finir; ▶ **best, worst**; **2** (emphatic) **why today of ~ days?** pourquoi justement aujourd'hui?; **not now of ~ times!** ce n'est pas le moment!; **of ~ the nerve!** quel culot!; **of ~ the rotten luck!** quel manque de chance or de pot○!; ▶ **people, place, thing**.

IDIOMS **~'s well that ends well** tout est bien qui finit bien; **to be as mad/thrilled as ~ get out**○ US être vachement○ en colère/excité; **he's not ~ there**○ il n'a pas toute sa tête; **it's ~ go**○ **here!** GB on s'active○ ici!; **it's ~ one to me** ça m'est égal; **it's ~ up with us**○ GB nous sommes fichus○; **it was ~ I could do not to laugh** il a fallu que je me retienne pour ne pas rire; **that's ~ very well, that's ~ well and good** tout ça c'est bien beau; **speeches are ~ very well but** c'est bien beau les discours mais; **it's ~ very well to do** c'est bien beau de faire; **it's ~ very well for them to talk** ça leur va bien de parler.

Allah /'ælə/ *pr n* Allah.

all: **~-American** *n* gen [*girl, boy, hero*] typiquement américain; Sport [*record, champion*] américain; **~-around** *adj* US = **all-round**.

allay /ə'leɪ/ *vtr* sout dissiper [*fear, suspicion, doubt*].

all clear *n* **1** Mil (signal) signal *m* de fin d'alerte; **2** fig **to give sb the ~** [*committee*] donner le feu vert à qn (**to do** pour faire); [*doctors*] déclarer qn guéri.

all: **~-consuming** *adj* [*passion, ambition*] effréné; **~-day** *adj* [*event*] qui dure toute la journée.

allegation /,ælɪ'geɪʃn/ *n* gen, Jur allégation *f* (**about** sur; **against** contre; **of** de; **that** selon laquelle).

allege /ə'ledʒ/ **I** *vtr* **to ~ that** (claim) prétendre que (+ *conditional*); (publicly, in court etc) déclarer que (+ *conditional*); **X ~d that Y had phoned him/had stolen the money** X a prétendu or a déclaré que Y lui aurait téléphoné/aurait volé l'argent; **it is/was ~d that...** il est/a été dit que...

II alleged *pp adj* [*attacker, victim, conspiracy, crime, confession*] présumé; **his ~d attempt to...** la tentative qu'il aurait faite de...

allegedly /ə'ledʒɪdlɪ/ *adv* prétendument.

allegiance /ə'li:dʒəns/ *n* gen, Jur allégeance *f*; **to swear ~ to sb/sth** prêter serment *m* d'allégeance à qn/qch; **to pledge ~ to the flag** prêter serment *m* devant le drapeau.

allegoric(al) /,ælɪ'gɒrɪk(l), US -'gɔ:r-/ *adj* allégorique.

allegorically /,ælɪ'gɒrɪklɪ, US -'gɔ:r-/ *adv* allégoriquement.

allegory /'ælɪgərɪ, US -gɔ:rɪ/ *n* allégorie *f* (**of** de).

alleluia /,ælɪ'lu:jə/ *excl* alléluia.

all-embracing *adj* global.

Allen key, Allen wrench /'ælən/ *n* clé *f* Allen.

allergic /ə'lɜ:dʒɪk/ *adj* allergique (**to** à) also fig.

allergic reaction *n* réaction *f* allergique.

allergist /'ælədʒɪst/ ▶ **1692** *n* allergologue *mf*.

allergy /'ælədʒɪ/ *n* allergie *f* (**to** à) also fig.

alleviate /ə'li:vɪeɪt/ *vtr* soulager [*boredom, pain, suffering*]; réduire [*fears, overcrowding, stress, unemployment*].

alleviation /ə,li:vɪ'eɪʃn/ *n* (of boredom, suffering, pain) soulagement *m* (**of** de); (of overcrowding, stress, unemployment) réduction *f* (**of** de).

alley /'ælɪ/ *n* **1** (for pedestrians) allée *f*; (for vehicles) ruelle *f*; **2** (in park) allée *f*; **3** US (on tennis court) couloir *m*.

IDIOMS **it's right up my ~**○ c'est vraiment mon truc○.

alley cat *n* chat *m* de gouttière.

IDIOMS **to have the morals of an ~** péj coucher à droite et à gauche◐.

alleyway /'ælɪweɪ/ *n* = **alley** 1.

all: **All Fools' Day** *n* GB premier *m* avril; **~-found** *adj* logé et nourri.

alliance /ə'laɪəns/ *n* gen, Pol, Mil alliance *f* (**between** entre; **with** avec); **in ~ with** en collaboration avec; **to form an ~** former une alliance.

allied /'ælaɪd/ *adj* **1** [*country, army, party*] allié (**with** avec; **to** à); **2** [*trades, subjects*] connexe.

Allier ▶ **1163** *pr n* Allier *m*; **in/to the ~** dans l'Allier.

alligator /'ælɪgeɪtə(r)/ *n* alligator *m*.

all: **~-important** *adj* essentiel/-ielle; **~-in** *adj* GB [*fee, price*] tout compris; **~ in**○ *adj* GB crevé○, épuisé; **~-inclusive** *adj* [*fee, price*] tout compris; **~-in-one** *adj* [*garment*] d'une seule pièce; **~-in wrestling** ▶ **1282** *n* Sport catch *m*.

alliteration /ə,lɪtə'reɪʃn/ *n* allitération *f*.

alliterative /ə'lɪtrətɪv, US ə'lɪtəreɪtɪv/ *adj* allitératif/-ive.

all: **~-night** /'ɔ:lnaɪt/ *adj* [*party, meeting, session*] qui dure toute la nuit; [*service*] ouvert toute la nuit; [*radio station*] qui émet 24 heures sur 24; **~-nighter**○ *n*: *soirée* (or *film* or *concert etc*) *qui dure toute la nuit*.

allocate /'æləkeɪt/ *vtr* affecter [*funds, resources*] (**for, to** à); attribuer [*money, land*] (**to** à); accorder [*time*] (**to** à); assigner, attribuer [*tasks*] (**to** à).

allocation /,ælə'keɪʃn/ *n* **1** (amount) crédits *mpl*; **2** (process) affectation *f*.

allograph /'æləgrɑ:f, US -græf/ *n* Ling allographe *m*.

allomorph /'æləmɔ:f/ *n* Ling allomorphe *m*.

allopathic /,ælə'pæθɪk/ *adj* allopathique.

allopathy /ə'lɒpəθɪ/ *n* allopathie *f*.

allophone /'æləfəʊn/ *n* allophone *m*.

all-or-nothing *adj* [*approach, policy, judgment*] extrémiste.

allot /ə'lɒt/ **I** *vtr* (*p prés etc* **-tt-**) attribuer [*money, resources*] (**to** à); assigner [*task, job*] (**to** à).

II allotted *pp adj* [*time*] imparti; **his ~ted task** la tâche qu'on lui a assignée.

allotment /ə'lɒtmənt/ *n* **1** GB (garden) parcelle *f* de terre; **2** (allocation) attribution *f*.

all-out /'ɔ:laʊt/ **I** *adj* [*strike*] total; [*assault, attack*] en règle; [*attempt, effort*] acharné.

II all out *adv* **to go all out for success/victory** tout faire pour réussir/gagner.

allover /'ɔ:ləʊvə(r)/ *adj* [*tan*] intégral; **with an ~ pattern** [*garment*] entièrement couvert de motifs.

all over /,ɔ:l'əʊvə(r)/ **I** *adj* (finished) fini; **when it's ~** quand tout sera fini.

II *adv* **1** (everywhere) partout; **to be trembling ~** trembler de partout; **2**○ (to a T) **that's Mary ~!** c'est Mary tout craché!

III *prep* **1** lit partout dans [*room, town, country*]; **~ China** partout en Chine; **I have spots ~ my arms** j'ai des boutons partout sur les bras; ▶ **place, walk, write**; **2**○ fig (known in) **to be ~** [*news, secret*] faire le tour de [*village, office*]; **3** (fawning over) **to be ~ sb** être aux petits soins pour qn; **they were ~ each other** ils n'arrêtaient pas de se bécoter○.

allow /ə'laʊ/ **I** *vtr* **1** (authorize) permettre à, autoriser à [*person, organization*] (**to do** de faire); autoriser [*action, change*]; laisser [*choice, freedom*] (**to do** de faire); **to ~ sth to be changed/demolished** autoriser le changement/la démolition de qch; **to ~ sb home/in/out** autoriser qn à rentrer chez soi/entrer/sortir; **to ~ sb (to have) alcohol/sweets** autoriser l'alcool/les bonbons à qn; **she isn't ~ed alcohol** l'alcool lui est interdit; **visitors are not ~ed on the site** le chantier est interdit aux visiteurs; **I'm ~ed to take 20 days' annual leave** j'ai le droit de prendre 20 jours de congé par an; **he ~ed the situation to get worse** il a laissé la situation s'aggraver; **I ~ed her to bully me** je l'ai laissée me harceler; **2** (enable) **to ~ sb/sth to do** permettre à qn/qch de faire; **extra cash would ~ the company to expand** des fonds supplémentaires permettraient à la société de s'agrandir; **the bridge was too low to ~ the lorry to pass** le pont était trop bas pour permettre au camion de passer; **~ me to introduce myself** permettez-moi de me présenter; **~ me!** permettez(-moi)!; **3** (allocate) prévoir; **to ~ two days for the job** prévoir deux jours pour faire le travail; **~ extra fabric for shrinkage** prévoir du tissu supplémentaire en cas de rétrécissement; **4** (concede) [*referee*] accorder [*goal*]; [*insurer*] agréer [*claim*]; [*supplier*] accorder, consentir [*discount*]; **I'll ~ that this isn't always the case** j'admets que ce n'est pas toujours le cas; **even if we ~ that her theory might be correct...** même en admettant que sa théorie soit correcte...; **5** (admit) [*club*] admettre [*children, women*]; **'no dogs ~ed'** 'interdit aux chiens'; **6** (condone) tolérer [*rudeness, swearing*].

II *v refl* **to ~ oneself 1** (grant) s'accorder [*drink, treat*]; **I only ~ myself one cup of coffee per day** je ne me permets qu'une tasse de café par jour; **2** (allocate) prévoir; **~ yourself two days to do the job** prévois deux jours pour faire le travail; **3** (let) se laisser; **I ~ed myself to be persuaded** je me suis laissé persuader.

■ **allow for**: **~ for [sth]** tenir compte de [*delays, variations, wastage*]; **I couldn't ~ for him changing his mind** je ne pouvais pas prévoir qu'il changerait d'avis.

■ **allow of** sout: **~ of [sth]** admettre.

allowable /ə'laʊəbl/ *adj* **1** Tax déductible; **2** (permissible) admissible; **3** Jur légitime.

allowance /ə'laʊəns/ *n* **1** (grant) gen, Soc Admin allocation *f*; (from employer) indemnité *f*; **clothing/travel ~** indemnité *f* vestimentaire/de transport; **mileage ~** ≈ indemnité *f* kilométrique; **2** Tax abattement *m* fiscal; **single person's ~** abattement *m* pour personnes seules; **personal ~s** abattements sur l'impôt; **3** (spending money) (for child) argent *m* de poche; (for spouse) argent *m* (pour les dépenses courantes); (for student, teenager) argent *m* (pour vivre); (from trust) rente *f*; **she has an ~ of £5,000 a year from her parents** ses parents lui versent une pension de 5 000 livres sterling par an; **4** (entitlement) **your baggage ~ is 40 kgs** vous avez droit à 40 kg de bagages; **what is my duty-free ~?** à quelle quantité de marchandises hors taxe ai-je droit?; **5** Comm (discount) rabais *m*; US (trade-in payment) reprise *f*; **to give sb a 10% ~** accorder un rabais de 10% à qn; **6** (concession) **to make allowance(s) for** tenir compte de [*inflation, growth, variations*]; **to make ~(s) for sb** essayer de comprendre qn.

alloy I /ˈælɔɪ/ *n* alliage *m*.
II /əˈlɔɪ/ *vtr* allier; fig (spoil) altérer.

alloy: **~ steel** *n* acier *m* allié; **~ wheel** *n* roue *f* en alliage léger.

all: **~-party** *adj* [*support*] de tous les partis; [*committee*] où tous les partis sont représentés; **~-pervasive** *adj* [*odour*] pénétrant; [*power, tendency*] omniprésent; **~-points bulletin, APB** *n* US alerte *f* générale; **~-powerful** *adj* tout-puissant; **~-purpose** *adj* [*building, living area*] polyvalent; [*utensil, machine*] multi-usages.

all right, **alright** /ˌɔːlˈraɪt/ **I**○ *n* GB **he's/she's a bit of ~** c'est un beau mec○/une belle nana○.
II *adj* **1** (expressing satisfaction) [*film, trip, house, game, outfit*] pas mal○; **the interview was ~** l'entretien s'est plutôt bien passé; **she's ~** (pleasant) elle est sympa○; (attractive) elle n'est pas mal○; (competent) elle est bien; **sounds ~ to me**○! (acceptance) pourquoi pas!; **is my hair ~?** ça va mes cheveux?; **you look ~** (reassuring) tu es très bien comme ça; **2** (well) **to feel ~** aller bien; **I'm ~ thanks** ça va merci; **3** (able to manage) **will you be ~?** est-ce que ça va aller?; **don't worry, we're ~** ne t'inquiète pas, tout va bien pour nous; **to be ~ for** avoir assez de [*money, time, work*]; **4** (acceptable) **it's ~ to do** il n'y a pas de mal à faire; **is it ~ if...?** est-ce que ça va si...?; **would it be ~ to leave early?** est-ce que c'est gênant si on s'en va plus tôt?; **is that ~ with you?** ça ne te dérange pas?; **that's ~ for young people but...** ça passe encore pour les jeunes mais...; **it's ~ for you** toi tu n'as pas à t'en faire; **that's (quite) ~!** ce n'est rien du tout!
III *adv* **1** (quite well) [*work, function*] comme il faut; [*see, hear*] bien; **to manage** ou **cope ~** s'en sortir; **she's doing ~** tout va bien pour elle; **2** (without a doubt) **she knows/I'm annoyed ~!** bien sûr qu'elle sait/que je suis en colère!; **the car is ours ~** c'est bien notre voiture.
IV *particle* **1** (giving agreement) d'accord; **2** (conceding a point) d'accord; **~ ~! point taken!** ça va! j'ai compris!; **3** (seeking consensus) d'accord?, ça va?; **4** (seeking information) **~, whose idea was this?** bon d'accord, qui a eu cette idée?; **5** (introducing topic) bien; **~, let's move on to...** bien, passons à...

all-risk *adj* Insur [*policy, cover*] tous risques.

all-round /ˌɔːlˈraʊnd/ *adj* [*athlete, artist, service*] complet/-ète; [*improvement*] général; **to have ~ talent** avoir du talent dans tous les domaines.

all-rounder /ˌɔːlˈraʊndə(r)/ *n* **to be a good ~** être bon en tout.

all: **All Saints' Day** *n* GB Toussaint *f*; **~-seater stadium** *n* GB stade *m* n'ayant que des places assises; **All Souls' Day** *n* GB Jour *m* des Morts.

allspice /ˈɔːlspaɪs/ *n* piment *m* de la Jamaïque.

all square *adj* **to be ~** [*people*] être quitte; [*teams*] être à égalité; [*accounts*] être équilibré.

all-star /ˈɔːlstɑː(r)/ *adj* [*team*] de vedettes; **~ cast** Cin brillante distribution *f*.

all: **~-terrain bike, ATB** *n* vélo *m* tout-terrain, VTT *m*; **~-terrain vehicle, ATV** *n* véhicule *m* tout-terrain.

all-time /ˈɔːltaɪm/ *adj* [*record, best seller*] absolu; **the ~ greats** (people) les grands *mpl*; **~ high** record *m* absolu; **to be at an ~ low** [*person, morale*] être au plus bas; [*figures, shares*] n'avoir jamais été plus bas; **this film is one of the ~ greats** c'est l'un des plus grands films de tous les temps.

all told *adv* en tout.

allude /əˈluːd/ *vi* **to ~ to sth** faire allusion à qch.

allure /əˈlʊə(r)/ *n* attrait *m*; (sexual) attraits *mpl*.

alluring /əˈlʊərɪŋ/ *adj* **1** [*person*] enjôleur/-euse; **2** [*place, prospect*] attrayant.

allusion /əˈluːʒn/ *n* allusion *f* (**to** à).

allusive /əˈluːsɪv/ *adj* allusif/-ive.

allusively /əˈluːsɪvlɪ/ *adv* de manière allusive.

alluvial /əˈluːvɪəl/ *adj* alluvial.

alluvium /əˈluːvɪəm/ *n* (*pl* **-viums** ou **-via**) alluvion *f*.

all-weather *adj* [*pitch, track*] tous temps; **~ court** (terrain *m* en) quick® *m*.

ally /ˈælaɪ/ **I** *n* (*pl* **-ies**) **1** gen, Mil allié/-e *m/f*; **2** Mil Hist **the Allies** les Alliés.
II /əˈlaɪ/ *v refl* **to ~ oneself with** ou **to** s'allier avec or à; **to be allied with** ou **to** être allié avec or à.

all-year-round *adj* [*resort*] ouvert toute l'année; **for ~ use** utilisable toute l'année.

alma mater /ˌælmə ˈmɑːtə(r), ˈmeɪtə(r)/ *n* alma mater *f*.

almanac(k) /ˈɔːlmənæk, US *also* ˈæl-/ *n* almanach *m*.

almighty /ɔːlˈmaɪtɪ/ *adj* [*crash, row, explosion*] formidable.

Almighty /ɔːlˈmaɪtɪ/ **I** *n* Relig **the ~** le Tout-Puissant.
II *adj* **~ God** Dieu Tout-Puissant.

almond /ˈɑːmənd/ **I** *n* **1** (nut) amande *f*; **2** (also **~ tree**) amandier *m*.
II *modif* [*essence, oil, paste*] d'amande.

almond-eyed /ˌɑːmənd'aɪd/ *adj* aux yeux en amande.

almoner /ˈɑːmənə(r), US ˈælm-/ *n* GB (formerly) assistant/-e *m/f* social/-e (*d'un hôpital*).

almost /ˈɔːlməʊst/

■ **Note** When *almost* is used to mean *practically* it is translated by *presque*: *we're almost ready* = nous sommes presque prêts; *it's almost dark* = il fait presque nuit; *the room was almost empty* = la salle était presque vide.
– When *almost* is used with a verb in the past tense to describe something undesirable or unpleasant that nearly happened, it is translated using the verb *faillir* followed by an infinitive: *I almost forgot* = j'ai failli oublier; *he almost fell* = il a failli tomber.

adv **1** (practically) presque; **~ everybody** presque tout le monde; **~ any train** presque tous les trains; **we're ~ there** nous sommes presque arrivés; **she has ~ finished the letter** elle a presque fini la lettre; **2** (implying narrow escape) **he ~ died** il a failli mourir; **they ~ missed the train** ils ont failli rater le train.

alms† /ɑːmz/ *npl* aumône *f*; **to give ~** faire l'aumône.

alms: **~ box** *n* Hist tronc *m* pour les pauvres; **~house** *n* GB Hist hospice *m*.

aloe /ˈæləʊ/ *n* **1** (plant) aloès *m*; **2 aloes** (also **bitter ~s**) (+ *v sg*) aloès *m* (médicinal).

aloft /əˈlɒft, US əˈlɔːft/ *adv* **1** gen [*hold, soar*] en l'air; [*seated, perched*] en haut; **from ~** d'en haut; **2** Naut dans la mâture.

aloha /əˈləʊə/ *excl* US salut.

alone /əˈləʊn/ **I** *adj* (*épith*) **1** (on one's own) seul; **all ~** tout seul; **to be ~** être seul; **to leave sb ~** lit laisser qn seul; (in peace) laisser qn tranquille; **she needs to be left ~** elle a besoin qu'on la laisse tranquille; **leave that bike ~!** ne touche pas à ce vélo!; **to get sb ~** voir qn en privé; **2** (isolated) seul; **I feel so ~** je me sens si seul; **he, ~ of his group...** lui, le seul de son groupe...; **she is not ~ in thinking that...** elle n'est pas la seule à penser que...; **to stand ~** [*building*] être isolé; [*person*] se tenir seul; fig être sans égal.
II *adv* **1** (on one's own) [*work, arrive, travel*] seul; **to live ~** vivre seul; **2** (exclusively) **for this reason ~** rien que pour cette raison; **last month ~/on books ~ we spent** rien que le mois dernier/rien qu'en livres nous avons dépensé; **this figure ~ shows** le chiffre à lui seul montre; **she ~ can help us** elle seule peut nous aider; **the credit is yours ~** le mérite en revient à toi seul. ▶ **let**[1].
IDIOMS **to go it ~**○ faire cavalier seul; **to leave well ~** ne se mêler de rien.

along /əˈlɒŋ, US əˈlɔːŋ/

■ **Note** When *along* is used as a preposition meaning *all along* it can usually be translated by *le long de*: *there were trees along the road* = il y avait des arbres le long de la route. For particular usages see the entry below.
– *along* is often used after verbs of movement. If the addition of *along* does not change the meaning of the verb, *along* will not be translated: *as he walked along* = tout en marchant.
– However, the addition of *along* often produces a completely new meaning. This is the case in expressions like *the project is coming along, how are they getting along?*. For translations consult the appropriate verb entry (***come, get*** etc).

I *adv* **to push/pull sth ~** pousser/tirer qch; **to be walking/running ~** marcher/courir; **she'll be ~ shortly** elle sera ici d'un moment à l'autre; **you go in, I'll be ~ in a second** entrez, j'arrive tout de suite; **they're no further ~ in their research** ils n'ont pas avancé dans leurs recherches; **there'll be another bus ~ in half an hour** le prochain bus passe dans une demi-heure.
II *prep* **1** (also **~side**) (all along) le long de; **the houses ~ the riverbank** les maisons situées le long de la rivière; **~ (the side of) the path/the motorway** le long du sentier/de l'autoroute; **to run ~ the beach** [*path, railway, fence*] longer la plage; [*cable*] être enterré le long de la plage; **there were chairs ~ the wall** il y avait des chaises contre le mur; **all ~ the canal** tout le long du canal; ▶ **all**; **2** (the length of) **to walk ~ the beach/~ the road** marcher sur la plage/dans la rue; **to look ~ the shelves** chercher dans les rayons; **3** (at a point along) **to stop somewhere ~ the motorway** s'arrêter quelque part sur l'autoroute; **halfway ~ the corridor on the right** au milieu du couloir à droite; **halfway ~ the path** à mi-chemin; **somewhere ~ the way** lit quelque part en chemin; fig quelque part.
III along with *prep phr* **1** (accompanied by) accompagné de; **to arrive ~ with six friends** arriver accompagné de six amis; **2** (at same time as) en même temps que; **to be convicted ~ with two others** être déclaré coupable en même temps que deux autres.

alongside /əˈlɒŋsaɪd, US əlɔːŋˈsaɪd/ **I** *prep* **1** (all along) = **along II 1**; **2** (next to) **to draw up ~ sb** [*vehicle*] s'arrêter à côté de qn; **to learn to live ~ each other** [*groups*] apprendre à coexister; **3** Naut **to come ~ the quay/a ship** accoster le quai/un navire.
II *adv* **1** gen à côté; **the car and the motorbike ~** la voiture et la moto qui est/était à côté; **I'd like to have my father ~** j'aimerais que mon père soit à mes côtés; **2** Naut **to come ~** accoster.

aloof /əˈluːf/ *adj* **1** (remote) distant; **to remain** ou **stand ~** rester or être distant; **2** (uninvolved) **to remain** ou **stand ~ from** se tenir à l'écart de.

aloofness /əˈlu:fnɪs/ *n* réserve *f* (**from** vis-à-vis de).

alopecia /ˌæləˈpi:ʃə/ *n* alopécie *f*.

aloud /əˈlaʊd/ *adv* (audibly) [*say, read*] à haute voix; [*think, wonder*] tout haut.

alp /ælp/ *n* **1** (peak) montagne *f* (des Alpes); **2** (pasture) alpe *f*.

alpaca /ælˈpækə/ **I** *n* **1** Zool alpaga *m*; **2** Tex alpaga *m*.
II *modif* [*coat, blanket*] en alpaga.

alpenhorn /ˈælpənhɔ:n/ *n* cor *m* des Alpes.

alpenstock /ˈælpənstɒk/ *n* alpenstock *m*.

Alpes-de-Haute-Provence ▶ **1163** *pr n* Alpes-de-Haute-Provence *fpl*; **in/to the ~** dans les Alpes-de-Haute-Provence.

Alpes-Maritimes ▶ **1163** *pr n* Alpes-Maritimes *fpl*; **in/to the ~** dans les Alpes-Maritimes.

alpha /ˈælfə/ **I** *n* **1** (letter) alpha *m*; **the ~ and omega (of sth)** l'alpha et l'oméga (de qch); **2** GB Univ (grade) 20 *m* (**in** en); **to get an ~** avoir un 20.
II *modif* [*iron, particle, radiation, ray*] alpha *inv*.

alphabet /ˈælfəbet/ *n* alphabet *m*.

alphabetic /ˌælfəˈbetɪk/ *adj* alphabétique.

alphabetical /ˌælfəˈbetɪkl/ *adj* [*guide, list, index*] alphabétique; **in ~ order** par ordre alphabétique.

alphabetically /ˌælfəˈbetɪklɪ/ *adv* [*list, arrange*] par ordre alphabétique.

alphabetize /ˈælfəbətaɪz/ *vtr* classer par ordre alphabétique.

alphabet soup *n* potage *m* aux pâtes (*en forme de lettres*).

alphanumeric /ˌælfənju:ˈmerɪk, US -nu:-/ *adj* alphanumérique.

alpine /ˈælpaɪn/ **I** *n* (at high altitudes) plante *f* alpine; (at lower altitudes) plante *f* alpestre.
II *adj* **1** (also **Alpine**) gen alpin; **~ troops** Mil troupes *fpl* alpines; **2** Sport **~ skiing** ski *m* alpin.

alpinist /ˈælpɪnɪst/ *n* alpiniste *mf*.

Alps /ælps/ *pr npl* **the ~** les Alpes *fpl*; **the Swiss/French ~** les Alpes suisses/françaises.

already /ɔ:lˈredɪ/ *adv* déjà; **it's 10 o'clock ~** il est déjà 10 heures; **he's ~ left** il est déjà parti; **I've told you twice ~!** je te l'ai déjà dit deux fois!; **I can't believe it's June ~** je n'arrive pas à croire que nous sommes déjà au mois de juin; **have you finished ~?** tu as déjà fini?; **you've got too many clothes ~** tu as déjà bien assez de vêtements.
IDIOMS **so come on ~!** US (indicating irritation) dépêche-toi à la fin!; **that's enough ~!** US ça suffit à la fin!

alright = **all right**.

Alsace /ælˈsæs/ ▶ **1273** *pr n* Alsace *f*; **to live in ~** habiter en Alsace.

Alsatian /ælˈseɪʃn/ **I** *n* **1** GB (dog) berger *m* allemand; **2** (native) Alsacien/-ienne *m/f*.
II *adj* alsacien/-ienne; **~ wines** les vins d'Alsace.

also /ˈɔ:lsəʊ/ *adv* **1** (too, as well) aussi; **~ available in red** existe aussi en rouge; **he ~ likes golf** il aime aussi le golf; **it is ~ worth remembering that** il serait bon aussi de ne pas oublier que; **2** (furthermore) en plus; **~, there wasn't enough to eat** en plus il n'y avait pas assez à manger.

alt. **I** *n*: *abrév écrite* = **altitude**.
II *adj*: *abrév écrite* = **alternate**.

altar /ˈɔ:ltə(r)/ *n* autel *m*.
IDIOMS **to lead sb to the ~**† ou hum conduire qn à l'autel†; **to be sacrificed on the ~ of** être immolé sur l'autel de.

altar: **~ boy** *n* enfant *m* de chœur; **~ cloth** *n* nappe *f* d'autel; **~ piece** *n* retable *m*; **~ rail** *n* balustrade *f* d'autel.

alter /ˈɔ:ltə(r)/ **I** *vtr* **1** (change) changer [*opinion, lifestyle, person, rule, timetable*]; modifier [*judgment, amount, document*]; altérer [*speed, value, climate*]; transformer [*building*]; **that does not ~ the fact that** cela ne change rien au fait que; **to ~ the appearance of sth** changer l'aspect de qch; **2** Sewing retoucher [*dress, shirt etc*]; (radically) transformer; **to have sth ~ed** faire retoucher or faire transformer qch; **3** US euph (castrate) faire opérer euph, castrer; (spay) faire opérer euph.
II *vi* changer.

alterable /ˈɔ:ltərəbl/ *adj* modifiable.

alteration /ˌɔ:ltəˈreɪʃn/ **I** *n* **1** (act of altering) (of building) transformation *f*; (of will, document, law) modification *f*; (of timetable, route, circumstances) changement *m*; (of work, process) modification *f*; **2** (result of altering) (to will, document, law) modification *f* (**to, in** de); (to timetable, route) modification *f* (**to** de); **3** Sewing (action, result) retouche *f*; (radical) transformation *f*.
II alterations *npl* Constr **1** (result) transformations *fpl* (**to** à); **to carry out ~s** effectuer des transformations; **major ~s** transformations importantes; **minor ~s** légères transformations; **structural ~s** altérations de structure; **2** (process) travaux *mpl*.

altercation /ˌɔ:ltəˈkeɪʃn/ *n* sout altercation *f* (**about** ou **over** à propos de; **between** entre).

altered chord, **altered cord** *n* Mus accord *m* altéré.

alter ego /ˌæltər ˈegəʊ, US ˈi:gəʊ/ *n* alter ego *m*.

alternate **I** /ɔ:lˈtɜ:nət/ *n* US (stand-in) remplaçant/-e *m/f*.
II /ɔ:lˈtɜ:nət/ *adj* **1** (successive) [*chapters, colours, layers*] en alternance; **~ circles and squares** des cercles et des carrés en alternance; **2** (every other) **to count ~ lines** compter une ligne sur deux; **on ~ days/Mondays** un jour/lundi sur deux; **3** US (other) autre; **4** Bot [*leaf, branch*] alterne.
III /ˈɔ:ltəneɪt/ *vtr* **to ~ sth and** ou **with sth** alterner qch et qch.
IV /ˈɔ:ltəneɪt/ *vi* **1** (swap) [*people*] se relayer; [*colours, patterns, seasons*] alterner (**with** avec); **Paul and Simon ~ (with each other)** Paul et Simon se relaient; **to ~ with sb** relayer qn, alterner avec qn; **to ~ between hope and despair/laughing and crying** passer de l'espoir au désespoir/du rire aux larmes; **2** Electron [*current, voltage*] être redressé.

alternate angles *npl* Math angles *mpl* alternes.

alternately /ɔ:lˈtɜ:nətlɪ/ *adv* [*move, bring, ask*] alternativement; **they criticize and praise him ~** tantôt ils le critiquent, tantôt ils le félicitent.

alternate rhyme *n* rime *f* alternée.

alternating /ˈɔ:ltəneɪtɪŋ/ *adj* [*colours, layers, lines*] en alternance.

alternating: **~ current**, **AC** *n* courant *m* alternatif; **~ saw** *n* scie *f* alternative; **~ series** *npl* Math séries *fpl* alternées.

alternation /ˌɔ:ltəˈneɪʃn/ *n* **1** (change) alternance *f* (**between** entre); **the ~ of day and night** l'alternance du jour et de la nuit; **2** Philos disjonction *f*.

alternative /ɔ:lˈtɜ:nətɪv/ **I** *n* **1** (specified option) (from two) alternative *f*, autre possibilité *f*; (from several) possibilité *f*; **one ~ is**... une des possibilités serait...; **the ~ is to do** l'autre possibilité serait de faire; **the ~ is for sb to do** l'autre possibilité serait que qn fasse; **to choose/refuse the ~ of doing** choisir/refuser l'autre possibilité qui serait de faire; **there are several ~s to surgery** il y a d'autres possibilités que la chirurgie; **what is the ~ to imprisonment/pesticides?** quelle autre possibilité existe-t-il que l'emprisonnement/les pesticides?; **2** (possible option) choix *m*; **to have an/no ~** avoir/ne pas avoir le choix; **to have no ~ but to do** ne pas avoir d'autre choix que de faire; **to have the ~ of staying or leaving** avoir le choix entre rester et partir; **I chose the expensive/political ~** j'ai choisi la solution chère/politique; **as an ~ to the course on offer/to radiotherapy, you can choose**... outre le cours proposé/la radiothérapie, vous pouvez choisir...
II *adj* **1** (other) [*activity, career, date, design, flight, method, plan, route*] autre; [*accommodation, product*] de remplacement; [*solution*] de rechange; **2** (unconventional) [*comedian, culture, scene, theatre, bookshop*] alternatif/-ive; [*lifestyle, therapy*] non-conventionnel/-elle; **3** Ecol alternatif/-ive.

alternative hypothesis *n* Stat hypothèse *f* alternative.

alternatively /ɔ:lˈtɜ:nətɪvlɪ/ *adv* sinon; **or ~ we could go home** ou sinon nous pourrions rentrer.

alternative: **~ medicine** *n* ¢ médecines *fpl* parallèles or douces; **~ prospectus** *n* GB Univ *annexe au livret de l'étudiant, préparée par les étudiants*; **~ school** *n* US Sch établissement *m* scolaire non conventionnel; **~ technology**, **AT** *n* technologie *f* alternative.

alternator /ˈɔ:ltəneɪtə(r)/ *n* Elec alternateur *m*.

although /ɔ:lˈðəʊ/ *conj* **1** (in spite of the fact that) bien que (+ *subj*); **~ she was late** bien qu'elle ait été en retard, malgré son retard; **~ he claims to be shy** bien qu'il prétende être timide; **they're generous, ~ poor** ils sont généreux, quoique pauvres or bien qu'ils soient pauvres; **2** (but, however) bien que (+ *subj*), mais; **I think he's her husband, ~ I'm not sure** je crois que c'est son mari, bien que je n'en sois pas sûr; **you don't have to attend, ~ we advise it** nous ne vous obligeons pas à venir, mais nous vous le conseillons.

altimeter /ˈæltɪmi:tə(r), US ælˈtɪmətər/ *n* altimètre *m*.

altitude /ˈæltɪtju:d, US -tu:d/ **I** *n* **1** (above sea-level) altitude *f*; **at high/low ~** à haute/basse altitude; **at ~** en altitude; **2** Astron altitude *f*.
II *modif*: **~ training** entraînement *m* en altitude.

altitude sickness *n* mal *m* d'altitude.

alto /ˈæltəʊ/ **I** *n* (*pl* **-tos**) **1** ▶ **1868** (singer, voice) (female) contralto *m*; (in choir) alto *f*; (male singer) haute-contre *m*; **2** (part) **to sing ~** être alto; **3** (instrument) alto *m*.
II *modif* [*clarinet, flute, saxophone*] alto *inv*; **~ solo** (female) solo *m* de contralto; (male) solo *m* de haute-contre; **~ part** partie *f* alto.

alto clef *n* clé *f* d'ut.

altogether /ˌɔ:ltəˈgeðə(r)/ *adv* **1** (completely) [*ridiculous, impossible, different*] complètement; **not ~ true** pas complètement vrai; **he gave up ~** il a complètement abandonné; **that's another matter ~** c'est une tout autre histoire; **2** (in total) en tout; **how much is that ~?** ça fait combien en tout?; **3** (all things considered) tout compte fait; **~, it was a mistake** tout compte fait, c'était une erreur.
IDIOMS **in the ~**○ à poil○.

altruism /ˈæltru:ɪzəm/ *n* altruisme *m*.

altruist /ˈæltru:ɪst/ *n* altruiste *mf*.

altruistic /ˌæltru:ˈɪstɪk/ *adj* altruiste.

alum /ˈæləm/ *n* **1** Miner alun *m*; **2**○ US Sch, Univ *abrév* = **alumna**, **alumnus**.

alumina /əˈlu:mɪnə/ *n* oxyde *m* d'aluminium.

aluminium /ˌæljʊˈmɪnɪəm/ GB, **aluminum** /əˈlu:mɪnəm/ US **I** *n* aluminium *m*.
II *modif* [*utensil*] en aluminium; [*alloy, bronze, sulphate*] d'aluminium.

aluminium foil *n* papier *m* aluminium.

aluminize /əˈlu:mɪnaɪz/ *vtr* aluminer.

alumna /əˈlʌmnə/ *n* (*pl* **-nae**) US Sch, Univ (of school) ancienne élève *f*; (of college) ancienne étudiante *f*.

alumnus /əˈlʌmnəs/ *n* (*pl* **-ni**) US Sch, Univ (of school) ancien élève *m*; (of college) ancien étudiant *m*.

alveolar /ˌæl'vɪələ(r), ˌælvɪ'əʊlə(r)/ I *n* alvéolaire *f*.
II *adj* alvéolaire; **~ ridge** arcade *f* alvéolaire.

alveolus /ˌæl'vɪələs, ˌælvɪ'əʊləs/ *n* (*pl* **-li**) alvéole *m*.

always /'ɔːlweɪz/ *adv* toujours; **he's ~ complaining** il est toujours en train de se plaindre, il n'arrête pas de se plaindre.

alyssum /'ælɪsəm/ *n* Bot alysse *f*.

Alzheimer's disease /'æltshaɪməz/ ▶ 1354 *n* maladie *f* d'Alzheimer.

am[1] /æm/ ▶ **be**.

am[2] /æm, eɪem/ ▶ 1096 *adv* (*abrév* = **ante meridiem**) **three ~** trois heures (du matin).

AM *n* **1** Radio (*abrév* = **amplitude modulation**) MA; **2** US Univ (*abrév* = **Master of Arts**) ≈ maîtrise *f* de lettres.

AMA *n* (*abrév* = **American Medical Association**) US Association *f* médicale américaine.

amalgam /ə'mælgəm/ *n* **1** sout (blend) amalgame *m*; **2** (alloy) amalgame *m*; **dental ~** amalgame dentaire.

amalgamate /ə'mælgəmeɪt/ I *vtr* **1** (merge) fusionner [*companies, parties, posts, schools*] (**with** avec; **into** en); **they ~d several companies into one large enterprise** ils ont fusionné plusieurs sociétés en une seule grande entreprise; **2** Miner amalgamer (**with** à); **3** (blend) mélanger [*styles*].
II *vi* **1** [*company, party, trade union, school*] fusionner (**with** avec); **2** Miner s'amalgamer (**with** à).
III **amalgamated** *pp adj* [*school, association, trade union*] unifié.

amalgamation /əˌmælgə'meɪʃn/ *n* **1** (merging, merger) (of companies, posts, trade unions, schools) fusion *f* (**with** avec; **into** en); (of styles, traditions) mélange *m*; **2** Miner amalgamation *f*.

amanuensis /əˌmænjʊ'ensɪs/ *n* (*pl* **-ses**) sout copiste *mf*.

amaranth /'æmərænθ/ *n* Bot, Culin amarante *f*.

amaryllis /ˌæmə'rɪlɪs/ *n* amaryllis *f*.

amass /ə'mæs/ *vtr* accumuler [*shares, data, scores*]; amasser [*fortune, valuables*].

amateur /'æmətə(r)/ I *n* **1** Sport, gen amateur *m*; **she's still an ~** elle est encore amateur; **2** péj (dabbler) amateur *m*.
II *modif* **1** [*sportsperson, musician, enthusiast*] amateur; [*sport*] en amateur; **~ dramatics** théâtre *m* amateur; **to have an ~ interest in sth** s'intéresser à qch en amateur; **2** péj (unskilled) **it's ~ work** c'est du travail d'amateur pej.

amateurish /'æmətərɪʃ/ *adj* péj [*work, campaign, attitude*] d'amateur; **to do sth in an ~ way** faire qch malhabilement.

amateurism /'æmətərɪzəm/ *n* amateurisme *m* also pej.

amatory /'æmətərɪ, US -tɔːrɪ/ *adj* littér galant liter.

amaze /ə'meɪz/ *vtr* surprendre; (stronger) stupéfier; **to be ~d by** être stupéfié par; **you never cease to ~ me!** tu me surprendras toujours!; **'amaze your friends'** 'étonnez vos amis'.

amazed /ə'meɪzd/ *adj* [*reaction, silence, look, person*] stupéfait (**at** de; **to do** de faire); **I'm ~ (that)** ça m'étonne que (+ *subj*).

amazement /ə'meɪzmənt/ *n* stupéfaction *f*; **in** ou **with ~** avec stupéfaction; **to everyone's ~** à la stupéfaction générale; **to my/her etc ~** à ma/sa etc grande surprise; **he couldn't hide his ~ at seeing everyone again** il n'a pu cacher sa surprise en revoyant tout le monde.

amazing /ə'meɪzɪŋ/ *adj* [*performer, feat, chance, game, offer*] exceptionnel/-elle; [*person, contrast, place, experience, event, success, film*] incroyable; [*amount, cost*] exorbitant; [*number, reaction, lack, defeat*] surprenant; **it's ~ how different people can be** c'est incroyable ce que les gens peuvent être différents; **it's ~ that** c'est incroyable que (+ *subj*).

amazingly /ə'meɪzɪŋlɪ/ *adv* [*good, bad, ignorant, cheap*] incroyablement; **to be ~ honest/clever/simple/varied** être d'une franchise/intelligence/simplicité/variété étonnante; **~ (enough),...** si surprenant que cela puisse paraître,...

Amazon /'æməzən, US -zɒn/ ▶ 1644 I *pr n* **1** (river) Amazone *m*; **2** Mythol Amazone *f*; **3** fig (also **amazon**) (strong woman) virago *f* pej.
II *modif* [*basin, forest, tribe*] amazonien/-ienne.

Amazonian /ˌæmə'zəʊnɪən/ *adj* **1** Geog amazonien/-ienne; **2** Mythol **the ~ queen** la reine des Amazones.

ambassador /æm'bæsədə(r)/ ▶ 1268 *n* **1** (diplomatic) ambassadeur *m*; **the US/French Ambassador** l'ambassadeur des États-Unis/de France; **the ~ to Japan/to Greece** l'ambassadeur au Japon/en Grèce; **2** fig (representative) ambassadeur *m*.

ambassador: **~-at-large** *n* (*pl* **~s-at-large**) US ambassadeur *m* itinérant; **~ extraordinary** *n* ambassadeur *m* extraordinaire.

ambassadorial /æmˌbæsə'dɔːrɪəl/ *adj* [*post*] d'ambassadeur; [*car, residence*] de l'ambassadeur.

ambassadorship /æm'bæsədəʃɪp/ *n* **1** (post) ambassade *f*; **2** (function) fonction *f* d'ambassadeur.

ambassadress /æm'bæsədrɪs/ ▶ 1268 *n* (diplomat, diplomat's wife) ambassadrice *f* also fig.

amber /'æmbə(r)/ ▶ 1104 I *n* **1** (resin) ambre *m*; **2** GB (traffic signal) orange *m*; **at ~** à l'orange; **to change** ou **turn to ~** passer à l'orange; **3** (colour) ambre *m*.
II *modif* [*necklace, ring*] d'ambre.
III *adj* [*eyes, fruit, fabric*] couleur d'ambre; [*light, wine*] ambré.

amber gambler○ /'æmbə gæmblə(r)/ *n* GB chauffard○ *m* (*qui passe à l'orange*).

ambergris /'æmbəgriːs, US -grɪs/ *n* ambre *m* gris.

amber nectar○ /ˌæmbə 'nektə(r)/ *n* GB hum bière *f*.

ambidextrous /ˌæmbɪ'dekstrəs/ *adj* ambidextre.

ambience /'æmbɪəns/ *n* sout ambiance *f*.

ambient /'æmbɪənt/ *adj* [*temperature, noise*] ambiant.

ambiguity /ˌæmbɪ'gjuːətɪ/ *n* gen, Ling ambiguïté *f* (**about** à propos de); **some ambiguities** quelques ambiguïtés.

ambiguous /æm'bɪgjʊəs/ *adj* gen, Ling ambigu/-uë.

ambiguously /æm'bɪgjʊəslɪ/ *adv* [*state, phrase*] de façon ambiguë; **~ worded** [*statement*] tourné de façon ambiguë; [*document*] présenté de façon ambiguë.

ambit /'æmbɪt/ *n* sout **to fall** ou **lie within the ~ of** [*power, authority*] relever du domaine de; [*study, discussion, festival*] entrer dans le cadre de; **the play was staged outside the festival's ~** la pièce a été représentée en dehors du festival.

ambition /æm'bɪʃn/ *n* **1** (quality) ambition *f* (**to do** de faire); **to have ~** avoir de l'ambition; **2** (aim) rêve *m* (**to do, of doing** de faire); **it was his lifelong ~ to visit Japan** son rêve de toujours était de visiter le Japon; **3** (*gen pl*) (aspiration) ambition *f* (**to do, of doing** de faire); **political/literary ~s** ambitions politiques/littéraires; **she has leadership ~s** elle ambitionne le pouvoir.

ambitious /æm'bɪʃəs/ *adj* **1** [*person*] ambitieux/-ieuse (**for sb** pour qn); **to be ~ to do** avoir l'ambition de faire; **2** [*goal, work, scheme*] ambitieux/-ieuse.

ambitiously /ˌæm'bɪʃəslɪ/ *adv* ambitieusement.

ambivalence /æm'bɪvələns/ *n* ambivalence *f*; **to display ~ about/towards** avoir des sentiments mêlés à propos de/à l'égard de.

ambivalent /æm'bɪvələnt/ *adj* ambivalent; **to be ~ about/towards** avoir une attitude ambivalente à propos de/à l'égard de.

amble /'æmbl/ I *n* **1** (ramble) promenade *f*, balade○ *f*; **2** (pace) allure *f* tranquille; **at an ~** d'un pas tranquille; **3** Equit amble *m*.
II *vi* **1** (stroll) **to ~ off** partir tranquillement; **we ~d around the gardens** nous nous sommes promenés tranquillement dans les jardins; **2** Equit trotter l'amble.

ambrosia /æm'brəʊzɪə, US -əʊʒə/ *n* ambroisie *f* also fig.

ambulance /'æmbjʊləns/ I *n* ambulance *f*.
II *modif* [*service, station*] d'ambulances; **~ crew** équipe *f* d'ambulanciers/-ières.

ambulance: **~ chaser**○ *n* US péj avocat *m* (*racolant sa clientèle au service des urgences*); **~ driver** ▶ 1692 *n* ambulancier/-ière *m/f*; **~man** ▶ 1692 *n* ambulancier *m*; **~woman** ▶ 1692 *n* ambulancière *f*.

ambulatory /'æmbjʊlətərɪ, US -tɔːrɪ/ I *n* déambulatoire *m*.
II *adj* **1** Med **~ patient** patient/-e *m/f* d'hospitalisation de jour; **~ care** US traitement *m* ambulatoire; **2** Jur [*will*] modifiable.

ambush /'æmbʊʃ/ I *n* **1** embuscade *f*; **to lie in ~** se tenir en embuscade; **to walk** ou **fall into an ~** tomber dans une embuscade.
II *vtr* tendre une embuscade à [*soldiers, convoy*]; **to be ~ed** être pris en embuscade.

ameba US = **amoeba**.

ameliorate /ə'miːlɪəreɪt/ sout I *vtr* améliorer.
II *vi* s'améliorer.

amelioration /əˌmiːlɪə'reɪʃn/ *n* **1** sout gen amélioration *f*; **2** Ling mélioration *f*.

amen /ɑː'men, eɪ-/ *excl* amen; **to say ~ to sth** dire amen à qch; **~ to that!** assurément!

amenable /ə'miːnəbl/ *adj* **1** (obliging) souple; **2 ~ to** [*person*] sensible à [*reason etc*]; [*person, situation*] soumis à [*regulations*]; **the theory is ~ to proof** la théorie peut être prouvée.

amend /ə'mend/ I *vtr* **1** (alter) amender [*constitution, bill, law, treaty*]; modifier [*document, statement, contract, plan*]; **2** sout (correct) réformer fml [*behaviour, lifestyle*].
II *vi* sout s'amender.

amendment /ə'mendmənt/ *n* **1** (alteration) (to constitution, bill, law, treaty) amendement *m* (**to** à); (to document, statement, contract, plan) modification *f* (**to** à); **the Fifth Amendment** US Jur le cinquième amendement; **2** (altering) Jur, Pol amendement *m*; gen modification *f*; **3** sout (of behaviour) correction *f*.

amends /ə'mendz/ *npl* **1** (reparation) **to make ~ for** réparer [*damage, hurt*]; **she has rejected all their efforts to make ~** (financial) elle a rejeté toutes leurs tentatives de la dédommager; **2 to make ~** (redeem oneself) se racheter.

amenity /ə'miːnətɪ, ə'menətɪ/ I *n* sout (pleasantness) agrément *m*.
II **amenities** *npl* **1** (facilities) (of hotel, locality) équipements *mpl*; (of house, sports club) installations *fpl*; **public/recreational amenities** équipements *mpl* collectifs/de loisir; **2**† (courtesies) civilités *fpl*.

amenity bed *n* GB lit *m* d'hôpital avec supplément (*donnant droit à certains avantages*).

amenorrhea /eɪˌmenə'rɪə/ *n* aménorrhée *f*.

America /ə'merɪkə/ ▶ 1131 *pr n* Amérique *f*.

American /ə'merɪkən/ ▶ 1486, 1402 I *n* **1** (person) Américain/-e *m/f*; **2** (language) américain *m*.
II *adj* américain.

Americana /əˌmerɪ'kɑːnə/ *n*: *objets ou documents américains*.

American: ~ **cheese** *n* cheddar *m* américain; ~ **Civil War** *pr n* guerre *f* de sécession; ~ **dream** *n* rêve *m* américain; ~ **eagle** *n* (emblem) aigle *m* américain; ~ **English** *n* américain *m*; ~ **football** *n* football *m* américain.

American Indian ▶ 1486 **I** *n* Indien/-ienne *m/f* d'Amérique.
II *adj* des Indiens d'Amérique.

Americanism /əˈmerɪkənɪzəm/ *n* américanisme *m*.

Americanize /əˈmerɪkənaɪz/ *vtr* américaniser; **to become ~d** s'américaniser.

American: ~ **Legion** *n* association *f* d'anciens combattants américains; ~ **plan** *n* Tourism pension *f* complète; ~ **revolution** *n* guerre *f* d'Indépendance américaine; ~ **Standard Version** *n* version *f* américaine de la Bible.

americium /ˌæməˈrɪsɪəm/ *n* américium *m*.

Amerind /ˈæmərɪnd/ *n* = **Amerindian I**.

Amerindian /ˌæmərˈɪndɪən/ ▶ 1486 US **I** *n* Indien/-ienne *m/f* d'Amérique.
II *adj* amérindien/-ienne.

amethyst /ˈæmɪθɪst/ **I** *n* **1** (gem) améthyste *f*; **2** ▶ 1104 (colour) violet *m* d'améthyste.
II *modif* [*necklace, brooch*] d'améthyste.
III *adj* (also **~-coloured**) couleur d'améthyste *inv*.

Amex /ˈeɪmeks/ *n* (*abrév* = **American Stock Exchange**) *deuxième Bourse newyorkaise*.

amiability /ˌeɪmɪəˈbɪlətɪ/ *n* amabilité *f* (**towards** à l'égard de).

amiable /ˈeɪmɪəbl/ *adj* [*person*] aimable (**to** ou **towards** avec); [*comedy, performance, manner*] plaisant; [*chat*] amical; **in an ~ mood** d'humeur plaisante.

amiably /ˈeɪmɪəblɪ/ *adv* [*chat, smile, behave*] de façon aimable.

amicable /ˈæmɪkəbl/ *adj* **1** (friendly) [*gesture, manner, relationship*] amical; **2** Jur **an ~ settlement/solution** un arrangement/une solution à l'amiable; **to come to an ~ agreement with sb** arriver à un accord à l'amiable avec qn.

amicably /ˈæmɪkəblɪ/ *adv* **1** [*live, behave*] de façon amicale; **2** [*settle, part*] à l'amiable.

amid /əˈmɪd/, **amidst** /əˈmɪdst/ *prep* **1** (against a background of) au milieu de [*laughter, applause*]; à la suite de [*allegations, criticism, reports, rumours*]; **the search continues ~ growing concern** ou **fears for the child's safety** les recherches se poursuivent alors que l'on craint de plus en plus pour la sécurité de l'enfant; **the directors met ~ growing pressure from shareholders for their resignation** les administrateurs se sont réunis alors que les actionnaires exerçaient une pression de plus en plus forte pour obtenir leur démission; **2** (surrounded by) parmi, au milieu de [*fields, trees, wreckage*].

amidships /əˈmɪdʃɪps/ *adv* au centre du navire.

amino acid /əˌmiːnəʊ ˈæsɪd/ *n* acide *m* aminé.

amiss /əˈmɪs/ **I** *adj*: **there is something ~ (with him/them)** il y a quelque chose qui ne va pas (avec lui/eux); **there is nothing ~** tout va bien; **there is nothing ~ in doing** il n'y a rien de mal à faire.
II *adv* **to take sth ~** prendre qch de travers; **a drink wouldn't come** ou **go ~!** un verre serait le bienvenu!, un verre ne serait pas de refus.

amity /ˈæmətɪ/ *n* sout (interpersonal) concorde *f* fml; (international) (bonne) entente *f*.

ammeter /ˈæmɪtə(r)/ *n* ampèremètre *m*.

ammo○ /ˈæməʊ/ *n* ¢ (*abrév* = **ammunition**) munitions *fpl*.

ammonia /əˈməʊnɪə/ *n* **1** (gas) ammoniac *m*; **2** (solution) ammoniaque *f*.

ammoniac /əˈməʊnɪæk/ *n* gomme *f* ammoniaque.

ammonite /ˈæmənaɪt/ *n* Geol ammonite *f*.

ammonium /əˈməʊnɪəm/ **I** *n* ammonium *m*.
II *modif* [*chloride, phosphate*] d'ammonium.

ammunition /ˌæmjʊˈnɪʃn/ *n* ¢ Mil munitions *fpl*; fig armes *fpl*.

ammunition: ~ **belt** *n* (for machine gun) bande *f* chargeur; ~ **depot**, ~ **dump** *n* dépôt *m* de munitions

amnesia /æmˈniːzɪə, US -niːʒə/ *n* amnésie *f*; **period/attack of ~** période *f*/crise *f* d'amnésie; **he is suffering from ~** il est atteint d'amnésie.

amnesiac /æmˈniːzɪæk, US -ˈniːʒɪæk/ *n, adj* amnésique (*mf*).

amnesty /ˈæmnəstɪ/ **I** *n* Pol, Jur (pardon, period) amnistie *f* (**for** pour); **to grant an ~ to sb** accorder l'amnistie à qn; **under an ~** dans le cadre de l'amnistie.
II *vtr* amnistier.

Amnesty International, AI *n* Amnesty International *f*.

amniocentesis /ˌæmnɪəʊsenˈtiːsɪs/ *n* amniocentèse *f*.

amnion /ˈæmnɪən/ *n* amnios *m*.

amniotic /ˌæmnɪˈɒtɪk/ *adj* amniotique; ~ **fluid** liquide *m* amniotique; ~ **sac** poche *f* des eaux or de l'amnios spec.

amoeba /əˈmiːbə/ *n* amibe *f*.

amoebic /əˈmiːbɪk/ *adj* amibien/-ienne; ~ **dysentery** dysenterie *f* amibienne.

amok /əˈmɒk/ *adv* **to run ~** [*person, animal, crowd*] être pris de folie furieuse; [*imagination*] se débrider; [*prices*] flamber.

among /əˈmʌŋ/, **amongst** /əˈmʌŋst/ *prep* **1** (amidst) parmi; **~ the population/crowd** parmi la population/foule; **~ the trees/ruins** au milieu des arbres/ruines, parmi les arbres/ruines; **I found it ~ her papers/belongings** je l'ai trouvé parmi or dans ses papiers/affaires; **~ those present was the ambassador** parmi les personnes présentes il y avait l'ambassadeur; **your case is only one ~ many** vous n'êtes qu'un cas parmi d'autres; **I count him ~ my closest friends** je le compte parmi mes meilleurs amis; **to be ~ friends** être entre amis; **~ others** entre autres; **~ other things** entre autres choses; **many of the soldiers deserted, ~ them Tom** beaucoup des soldats ont déserté, dont Tom or entre autres Tom; **2** (affecting particular group) chez; **unemployment ~ young people/graduates** le chômage chez les jeunes/les diplômés; **this illness is commonest ~ the elderly** cette maladie se rencontre le plus fréquemment chez les personnes âgées; **3** (one of) **it is ~ the world's poorest countries** c'est un des pays les plus pauvres du monde; **this book is not ~ her most popular works** ce livre ne fait pas partie de ses œuvres les plus connues; **she was ~ those who survived** elle a été de ceux qui ont survécu, elle a fait partie des survivants; **we are hoping to be ~ the first** nous espérons être dans les premiers; **4** (between) entre; **~ ourselves/themselves** entre nous/eux/elles; **his estate was divided ~ his heirs** ses biens ont été partagés entre ses héritiers; **sort it out ~ yourselves** arrangez ça entre vous; **they can never agree ~ themselves** ils n'arrivent jamais à se mettre d'accord; **one bottle ~ five isn't enough** une bouteille pour cinq ce n'est pas assez.

amoral /ˌeɪˈmɒrəl, US ˌeɪˈmɔːrəl/ *adj* amoral.

amorality /ˌeɪməˈrælɪtɪ/ *n* amoralité *f*.

amorous /ˈæmərəs/ *adj* littér ou hum amoureux/-euse; **to make ~ advances to sb** faire des avances à qn.

amorously /ˈæmərəslɪ/ *adv* littér ou hum amoureusement.

amorphous /əˈmɔːfəs/ *adj* **1** Chem, Geol amorphe; **2** gen [*object, shape, collection*] informe; [*ideas, plans*] confus.

amortization /əˌmɔːtɪˈzeɪʃn, US ˌæmərtɪ-/ *n* amortissement *m*.

amortize /əˈmɔːtaɪz, US ˈæmərtaɪz/ *vtr* amortir.

amortizement /əˈmɔːtɪzmənt/ *n* = **amortization**.

amount /əˈmaʊnt/ *n* **1** gen (quantity) (of goods, food) quantité *f*; (of people, objects) nombre *m*; **a considerable ~ of** beaucoup de; **a fair ~ of** pas mal de○; **an enormous** ou **huge ~ of** énormément de; **a certain ~ of imagination** une certaine imagination; **I'm entitled to a certain ~ of respect** je suis en droit d'attendre qu'on me respecte; **no ~ of money could compensate this loss** aucune somme d'argent ne pourrait compenser cette perte; **no ~ of persuasion will make him change his mind** on aura beau essayer de le persuader, rien ne le fera changer d'avis; **it's doubtful whether any ~ of foreign aid can save them** il est douteux que l'aide internationale, aussi importante qu'elle soit, puisse les sauver; **they've got any ~ of money** ils ont énormément d'argent; **2** (sum of money) somme *f*; (total: of bill, expenses, damages etc) montant *m*; **for an undisclosed ~** pour une somme non dévoilée; **to charge sb for the full ~** faire payer à qn le montant total; **what is the outstanding ~?** combien reste-t-il à payer?; **debts to the ~ of £10,000** des dettes qui s'élèvent à 10 000 livres sterling; **~ paid (on account)** Comm acompte versé; **~ of turnover** Comm (montant du) chiffre d'affaires; **~ carried forward** Accts report *m* à nouveau.
■ **amount to**: **~ to [sth] 1** gen, Fin (add up to) [*cost*] s'élever à; **2** (be worth, equivalent to) équivaloir à, revenir à [*confession, betrayal, defeat, triumph etc*]; **it ~s to the same thing** cela revient au même; **it ~s to blackmail!** ce n'est rien d'autre que du chantage!; **not to ~ to much** [*accusation, report*] ne pas valoir grand-chose○; **he'll never ~ to much** il n'arrivera jamais à rien; **the rain didn't ~ to much** il n'a pas beaucoup plu.

amour /əˈmʊə(r)/ *n* littér ou hum liaison *f* (amoureuse).

amp /æmp/ *n* **1** *abrév* ▶ **ampere**; **2**○ (*abrév* = **amplifier**) ampli○ *m*.

amperage /ˈæmpərɪdʒ/ *n* intensité *f* de courant.

ampere /ˈæmpeə(r), US ˈæmpɪə(r)/ *n* ampère *m*.

ampere-hour *n* ampère-heure *m*.

ampersand /ˈæmpəsænd/ *n* esperluette *f*.

amphetamine /æmˈfetəmiːn/ *n* amphétamine *f*.

amphibia /æmˈfɪbɪə/ *npl* amphibiens *mpl*.

amphibian /æmˈfɪbɪən/ **I** *n* **1** Zool amphibie *m*; **2** Aviat appareil *m* amphibie; **3** Aut véhicule *m* amphibie; **4** Mil (tank) char *m* amphibie.
II *adj* = **amphibious**.

amphibious /æmˈfɪbɪəs/ *adj* Zool, Mil amphibie.

amphitheatre /ˈæmfɪθɪətə(r)/ *n* Antiq, Univ amphithéâtre *m*; Geol **(natural) ~** cirque *m*.

amphora /ˈæmfərə/ *n* amphore *f*.

ample /ˈæmpl/ *adj* **1** (plenty) [*provisions, resources*] largement suffisant (**for** pour); [*illustration*] ample; [*evidence*] écrasant; **there's ~ room for five people** il y a largement la place pour cinq personnes; **there is ~ parking** il y a largement assez de places de parking; **to have ~ opportunity/time to do** avoir largement la possibilité/le temps de faire; **he was given ~ warning** il a été largement prévenu; **he's been given ~ opportunity to apologize** on lui a donné toutes les chances de s'excuser; **to be more than ~** suffire plus que largement; **thank you that's more than ~!** (when offered food) merci c'est plus

qu'assez!; **2** (of generous size) [*proportions, bust*] généreux/-euse; [*garment*] large.
amplification /ˌæmplɪfɪˈkeɪʃn/ *n* **1** Audio, Elec amplification *f*; **2** (of idea, statement etc) développement *m* (**of** de).
amplifier /ˈæmplɪfaɪə(r)/ *n* amplificateur *m*, ampli○ *m*.
amplify /ˈæmplɪfaɪ/ *vtr* **1** Audio, Elec, Radio amplifier; **2** gen développer [*account, statement, concept*].
amplitude /ˈæmplɪtjuːd, US -tuːd/ *n* **1** Astron, Phys amplitude *f*; **2** sout (of resources) ampleur *f*; (of mind, vision) largeur *f*.
amplitude modulation *n* modulation *f* d'amplitude.
amply /ˈæmplɪ/ *adv* [*compensated, fulfilled*] largement; [*demonstrated*] amplement.
ampoule GB, **ampule** US /ˈæmpuːl/ *n* ampoule *f* (pour seringue).
ampulla /æmˈpʊlə/ *n* (*pl* **-lae**) Anat, Antiq ampoule *f*; Relig (for wine, water) calice *m*; (for holy oil) ampoule *f*.
amputate /ˈæmpjʊteɪt/ **I** *vtr* amputer; **to ~ sb's leg** amputer qn de la jambe.
II *vi* amputer.
amputation /ˌæmpjʊˈteɪʃn/ *n* amputation *f* (**of** de).
amputee /ˌæmpjʊˈtiː/ *n* amputé/-e *m/f*.
Amsterdam /ˌæmstəˈdæm/ **▶1818** *pr n* Amsterdam.
Amtrak /ˈæmtræk/ *n* US *société de transports ferroviaires*.
amuck /əˈmʌk/ *adv* = **amok**.
amulet /ˈæmjʊlɪt/ *n* amulette *f*.
amuse /əˈmjuːz/ **I** *vtr* **1** (cause laughter) amuser; **to be ~d at** ou **by** s'amuser de; **the shareholders were not ~d by the decision** la décision n'a pas fait sourire les actionnaires; **I'm not ~d!** je ne trouve pas ça drôle!; **2** (entertain) [*game, story*] distraire; **to keep sb ~d** distraire qn; **3** (occupy) [*activity, hobby*] occuper; **to keep oneself ~d** s'occuper.
II *v refl* **to ~ oneself** **1** (entertain) se distraire; **2** (occupy) s'occuper.
III amused *pp adj* amusé.
amusement /əˈmjuːzmənt/ *n* **1** (mirth) amusement *m* (**at** face à); **to my great ~** à mon grand amusement; **to do sth for ~** faire qch pour s'amuser; **a look of ~** un air amusé; **to conceal one's ~** dissimuler son envie de rire; **2** (diversion) distraction *f*; **to do sth for ~** faire qch pour se distraire; **3** (at fairground) (*gén pl*) attraction *f*.
amusement: **~ arcade** *n* GB salle *f* de jeux électroniques; **~ park** *n* parc *m* d'attractions.
amusing /əˈmjuːzɪŋ/ *adj* amusant.
amusingly /əˈmjuːzɪŋlɪ/ *adv* de façon amusante.
amyl alcohol *n* alcool *m* amylique.
amylase /ˈæmɪleɪz/ *n* amylase *f*.
amyl nitrate *n* nitrite *m* amylique.
an /æn, ən/ ▶ **a²**.
an. *abrév écrite* = **anno**.
Anabaptist /ˌænəˈbæptɪst/ *n, adj* anabaptiste (*mf*).
anabolic steroid /ˌænəˈbɒlɪk ˈstɪərɔɪd/ *n* stéroïde *m* anabolisant.
anachronism /əˈnækrənɪzəm/ *n* anachronisme *m*; **to be an ~** [*object, custom, institution etc*] être un anachronisme; [*person*] faire figure d'anachronisme.
anachronistic /əˌnækrəˈnɪstɪk/ *adj* anachronique.
anaconda /ˌænəˈkɒndə/ *n* anaconda *m*.
anaemia /əˈniːmɪə/ **▶1354** *n* anémie *f*.
anaemic /əˈniːmɪk/ *adj* **1** Med anémique; **to become ~** s'anémier; **2** fig péj [*character, performance, poem*] fade.
anaerobic /ˌæneəˈrəʊbɪk/ *adj* anaérobie.
anaesthesia GB, **anesthesia** US /ˌænɪsˈθiːzɪə/ *n* anesthésie *f*.
anaesthetic GB, **anesthetic** US /ˌænɪsˈθetɪk/ *n, adj* anesthésique (*m*); **to be under ~** être sous anesthésie.
anaesthetics /ˌænɪsˈθetɪks/ *n* GB (+ *v sg*) anesthésiologie *f*.
anaesthetist /əˈniːsθətɪst/ **▶1692** *n* GB (médecin) anesthésiste *mf*.
anaesthetize GB, **anesthetize** US /əˈniːsθətaɪz/ *vtr* anesthésier.
anaglyph /ˈænəglɪf/ *n* anaglyphe *m*.
anagram /ˈænəgræm/ *n* anagramme *f* (**of** de).
anal /ˈeɪnl/ *adj* Anat, Psych anal; **~ intercourse, ~ sex** coït *m* anal; **~ stage** Psych stade *m* anal.
analgesia /ˌænælˈdʒiːzɪə, US -ʒə/ *n* analgésie *f*.
analgesic /ˌænælˈdʒiːsɪk/ *n, adj* analgésique (*m*).
analog surtout US = **analogue**.
analog computer *n* calculateur *m* analogique.
analogic(al) /ˌænəˈlɒdʒɪk(l)/ *adj* analogue, analogique.
analogous /əˈnæləgəs/ *adj* analogue (**to, with** à).
analogue /ˈænəlɒg, US -lɔːg/ *n* analogue *m*.
analogue: **~ clock** *n* réveil *m* analogique; **~-digital convertor** *n* convertisseur *m* analogique-numérique; **~ watch** *n* montre *f* analogique.
analogy /əˈnælədʒɪ/ *n* analogie *f*; **by ~ with** par analogie avec; **to draw an ~** faire une analogie (**between** entre; **with** avec).
anal: **~ retention** *n* Psych rétention *f* anale; **~ retentive** *adj* Psych qui manifeste de la rétention anale.
analysand /əˈnælɪsænd/ *n* personne *f* en analyse.
analyse GB, **analyze** US /ˈænəlaɪz/ *vtr* **1** gen, Ling analyser; **2** GB Psych psychanalyser.
analysis /əˈnælɪsɪs/ *n* **1** gen, Ling analyse *f*; **in the final** ou **last ~** en fin de compte; **2** Psych psychanalyse *f*; **to be in ~** être en analyse.
analyst /ˈænəlɪst/ **▶1692** *n* **1** gen analyste *mf*; **2** Psych (psych)analyste *mf*.
analytic(al) /ˌænəˈlɪtɪk(l)/ *adj* (all contexts) analytique.
analyze *vtr* US = **analyse**.
anamorphosis /ˌænəmɔːˈfəʊsɪs/ *n* anamorphose *f*.
anap(a)est /ˈænəpiːst/ *n* anapeste *m*.
anaphora /əˈnæfərə/ *n* anaphore *f*.
anaphoric /ˌænəˈfɒrɪk/ *adj* anaphorique.
anarchic(al) /əˈnɑːkɪk(l)/ *adj* anarchique.
anarchism /ˈænəkɪzəm/ *n* anarchisme *m*.
anarchist /ˈænəkɪst/ *n, adj* anarchiste (*mf*).
anarchy /ˈænəkɪ/ *n* anarchie *f*.
anastigmatic /ˌænəstɪgˈmætɪk/ *adj* anastigmate.
anathema /əˈnæθəmə/ *n* (*pl* **~s**) Relig anathème *m*; fig abomination *f*; **history/cruelty is ~ to him** il a l'histoire/la cruauté en horreur.
anathematize /əˈnæθəmətaɪz/ *vtr* jeter l'anathème sur.
Anatolia /ˌænəˈtəʊlɪə/ *pr n* Anatolie *f*.
Anatolian /ˌænəˈtəʊlɪən/ **I** *n* Ling anatolien *m*.
II *adj* Ling anatolien/-ienne.
anatomical /ˌænəˈtɒmɪkl/ *adj* anatomique.
anatomist /əˈnætəmɪst/ *n* anatomiste *mf*.
anatomize /əˈnætəmaɪz/ *vtr* disséquer.
anatomy /əˈnætəmɪ/ **I** *n* **1** Med, Biol anatomie *f*; **2** fig (of subject, event) analyse *f* (détaillée) (**of** de).
II *modif* [*class, lesson*] d'anatomie.
ANC *n* (*abrév* = **African National Congress**) ANC *f*.
ancestor /ˈænsestə(r)/ *n* lit, fig ancêtre *mf*.
ancestral /ænˈsestrəl/ *adj* ancestral; **the ~ home** la demeure ancestrale.
ancestress /ænˈsestrɪs/ *n* ancêtre *f*, aïeule *f*.
ancestry /ˈænsestrɪ/ *n* **1** (lineage) ascendance *f*; **2** (ancestors collectively) ancêtres *mpl*, aïeux *mpl*.
anchor /ˈæŋkə(r)/ **I** *n* **1** Naut ancre *f*; **to drop** ou **cast ~** jeter l'ancre; **to raise (the) ~, to weigh** ou **up ~** lever l'ancre; **to come to ~** mouiller; **to be** ou **lie at ~** être ancré; **to ride at ~** être à l'ancre or au mouillage; **to slip ~** filer par le bout; **2** fig point *m* d'ancrage; (person) soutien *m*; **3** = **anchorman, anchorwoman**.
II *vi* [*ship*] mouiller, jeter l'ancre.
III *vtr* **1** ancrer [*ship, balloon*]; arrimer [*tent, roof etc*] (**to** à); **2** US Radio, TV présenter.
anchorage /ˈæŋkərɪdʒ/ *n* **1** Naut (place, action) ancrage *m*, mouillage *m*; fig ancrage *m*; **2** Naut (fee) droits *mpl* de mouillage.
anchorite /ˈæŋkəraɪt/ *n* anachorète *m*.
anchorman /ˈæŋkəmən/ **▶1692** *n* **1** Radio, TV présentateur *m*; (in network, organization) pivot *m*; **2** Sport relayeur *m*.
anchor ring /ˈæŋkərɪŋ/ *n* cigale *f* Tech.
anchorwoman /ˈæŋkəwʊmən/ **▶1692** *n* Radio, TV présentatrice *f*.
anchovy /ˈæntʃəvɪ, US ˈæntʃəʊvɪ/ **I** *n* anchois *m*.
II *modif* [*sauce*] aux anchois; **~ paste** beurre *m* d'anchois.
ancient /ˈeɪnʃənt/ **I** *n* gen, Antiq ancien *m*.
II *adj* **1** (dating from BC) antique; (very old) ancien/-ienne; **~ Greek** Ling grec ancien; **~ Greece/Rome** la Grèce/Rome antique; **~ history** (subject) histoire *f* ancienne; **that's ~ history!** fig c'est de l'histoire ancienne; **~ monument** monument *m* historique; **in ~ times** dans les temps anciens; **the ~ world** l'antiquité *f*, le monde antique; **2**○ [*person, car*] très vieux/vieille; **I must be getting ~** je dois me faire bien vieux.
ancillary /ænˈsɪlərɪ, US ˈænsəlerɪ/ **I** *n* **1** (office, department etc) service *m* annexe; **2** (person) auxiliaire *m*.
II *adj* [*service, staff, task, industry, equipment, role*] auxiliaire; [*cost*] accessoire; [*road*] secondaire; **to be ~ to** (complementary) être auxiliaire à; (subordinate) être subordonné à.
and /ænd, ənd, ən, n/

■ **Note** When used as a straightforward conjunction, *and* is translated by *et*: *to shout and sing* = crier et chanter; *Tom and Linda* = Tom et Linda; *my friend and colleague* = mon ami et collègue.
– *and* is sometimes used between two verbs in English to mean 'in order to' (*wait and see, go and ask, try and rest etc*). To translate these expressions, look under the appropriate verb entry (***wait***, ***go***, ***try*** etc).
– For examples and other uses, see the entry below.

---

conj **1** (joining words or clauses) et; **cups ~ plates** des tasses et des assiettes; **there'll be singing ~ dancing** on va chanter et danser; **he picked up his papers and went out** il a ramassé ses papiers et il est sorti; **2** (in numbers) **two hundred ~ sixty-two** deux cent soixante-deux; **three ~ three-quarters** trois trois-quarts; **five ~ twenty** ‡ ou littér vingt-cinq; **3** (with repetition) **more ~ more interesting** de plus en plus intéressant; **faster ~ faster** de plus en plus vite; **it got worse ~ worse** c'est devenu de pire en pire; **I waited ~ waited** j'ai attendu pendant des heures; **to talk on ~ on** parler pendant des heures; **for days ~ days** pendant des jours et des jours; **we laughed ~ laughed!** qu'est-ce qu'on a ri!; **there are friends ~ friends** il y a ami et ami; **4** (for emphasis) **it's lovely ~ warm** il fait bon; **come nice ~ early** viens tôt; AND **he didn't even say thank you** et en plus il n'a même pas dit merci; **5** (in phrases) **~ all that** et tout le reste; **~ that**○ GB et tout ça; **~ so on** et ainsi de suite; **~ how**○! et comment!; **~?** et alors?; **6** (alike)

summer ~ winter été comme hiver; **I think about you day ~ night** je pense à toi jour et nuit; **7** (with negative) **I haven't got pen ~ paper** je n'ai ni stylo ni papier; **he doesn't like singing ~ dancing** il n'aime ni chanter ni danser.

Andalucia, **Andalusia** /ˌændəluːˈsɪə/ *pr n* Andalousie *f*.

Andalucian, **Andalusian** /ˌændəluːˈsɪən/ I *n* Andalou/-ouse *m/f*.
II *adj* andalou/-ouse.

andante /ænˈdæntɪ/ *n, adj, adv* andante (*m*).

AND circuit, **AND gate** /ænd/ *n* Comput circuit *m* ET.

Andean /ænˈdɪən/ *adj* andin, des Andes; **the ~ mountains** la Cordillière des Andes.

Andes /ˈændiːz/ *pr npl* **the ~** les Andes *fpl*.

andiron /ˈændaɪən/ *n* chenet *m*.

Andorra /ænˈdɔːrə/ ▶ 1131 *pr n* Andorre *f*.

Andorran /ænˈdɔːrən/ ▶ 1486 I *n* Andorran/-ane *m/f*.
II *adj* andorran.

Andrew /ˈændruː/ *pr n* André.

androgen /ˈændrədʒən/ *n* androgène *m*.

android /ˈændrɔɪd/ *n* androïde *m*.

Andromache /ænˈdrɒməkɪ/ *pr n* Andromaque.

Andromeda /ænˈdrɒmɪdə/ *pr n* Mythol, Astron Andromède *f*; **the ~ Galaxy** la Nébuleuse d'Andromède.

androsterone /ænˈdrɒstərəʊn/ *n* androstérone *f*.

anecdotal /ˌænɪkˈdəʊtl/ *adj* [*memoirs, account*] anecdotique; [*talk, lecture*] plein d'anecdotes; **on the basis of ~ evidence...** selon des sources non confirmées...

anecdote /ˈænɪkdəʊt/ *n* anecdote *f*.

anemia *n* US = **anaemia**.

anemic *adj* US = **anaemic**.

anemometer /ˌænɪˈmɒmɪtə(r)/ *n* anémomètre *m*.

anemone /əˈnemənɪ/ *n* Bot anémone *f*.

aneroid barometer /ˌænərɔɪd bəˈrɒmɪtə(r)/ *n* baromètre *m* anéroïde.

anesthesia *n* US = **anaesthesia**.

anesthesiologist /ˌænɪsˌθiːzɪˈɒlədʒɪst/ ▶ 1692 *n* US (médecin) anesthésiste *mf*.

anesthesiology /ˌænɪsˌθiːzɪˈɒlədʒɪ/ *n* US anesthésiologie *f*.

anesthetic *n, adj* US = **anaesthetic**.

anesthetist /əˈniːsθətɪst/ ▶ 1692 *n* US infirmier/-ière *m/f* anesthésiste.

anesthetize *vtr* US = **anaesthetize**.

aneurism /ˈænjʊrɪzəm, US -nʊ-/ *n* anévrisme *m*.

anew /əˈnjuː, US əˈnuː/ *adv* (once more) encore, de nouveau; (in a new way) à nouveau; **to begin ~** recommencer.

angel /ˈeɪndʒl/ *n* **1** lit, fig ange *m*; **the ~ of death** l'Ange de la Mort; **~ of mercy** ange de miséricorde; **be an ~ and answer the phone!** si tu veux répondre au téléphone tu seras un ange!; **2**○ Comm, Theat bailleur/-eresse *m/f* de fonds.
IDIOMS **to be on the side of the ~s** avoir le droit de son côté; **to rush in where ~s fear to tread** se lancer avec le courage de l'inconscience.

angel cake *n* = **angel food cake**.

Angeleno, **Angelino** /ˌændʒəˈliːnəʊ/ *n* US habitant/-e *m/f* de Los Angeles.

angel: **~fish** *n* scalaire *m*; **~ food cake** *n* ≈ gâteau *m* de Savoie (*coloré en rose et blanc*); **~-hair pasta**, **~'s hair** *n* US vermicelles *mpl*.

angelic /ænˈdʒelɪk/ *adj* angélique.

angelica /ænˈdʒelɪkə/ *n* angélique *f*.

angelically /ænˈdʒelɪklɪ/ *adv* [*smile etc*] angéliquement; [*beautiful*] comme un ange.

Angelino *n* US = **Angeleno**.

angel: **~ shark** *n* ange *m* de mer; **~s-on-horseback** *n* GB brochette *f* d'huîtres à l'anglaise.

angelus /ˈændʒɪləs/ *n* angélus *m*.

anger /ˈæŋgə(r)/ I *n* colère *f* (**at** devant); **to feel ~ towards sb** ressentir de la colère contre qn; **in ~** sous le coup de la colère; **a fit of ~** un accès de colère.
II *vtr* [*decision, remark*] mettre [qn] en colère [*person*]; **she was ~ed by his comment** sa réflexion l'a mise en colère; **to be easily ~ed** se mettre facilement en colère.

angina (pectoris) /ænˌdʒaɪnə (ˈpektərɪs)/ ▶ 1354 *n* angine *f* de poitrine.

Angl. *abrév écrite* = **Anglican**.

angle /ˈæŋgl/ I *n* **1** gen, Math angle *m*; **at a 60° ~** à un angle de 60°; **~ of attack/of descent/of refraction** angle d'attaque/de chute/de réfraction; **camera ~** angle de vue; **to make/form an ~ with sth** faire/former un angle avec qch; **to be at an ~ to sth** [*table*] faire un angle avec [*wall*]; [*tower*] pencher par rapport à [*ground*]; **from every ~** sous tous les angles; **seen from this ~** d'ici; **at an ~** en biais; **2** (point of view) point *m* de vue (**on** sur); **to look at/see sth from sb's ~** regarder/voir qch du point de vue de qn; **from every ~** sous tous les angles; **3** (perspective, slant) **what ~ is the newspaper putting on this story?** sous quel angle est-ce que le journal présente cette histoire?; **seen from this ~** sous cet angle; **4** (corner) angle *m* (**of** de); **5** Sport gen angle *m*; (of shot, kick) angle *m* de tir; **6**○ US (advantage) bénéf○ *m*; **he never does anything unless there's an ~** il ne fait jamais rien sans qu'il y ait un bénéf○ au bout!
II *vtr* **1** (tilt) orienter [*camera, light, table*] (**towards** vers); incliner [*racket, ball*]; **to ~ sth sideways/upwards/downwards** incliner qch en oblique/vers le haut/vers le bas; **2** Sport (hit) (diagonally) jouer [qch] près des lignes [*ball, shot*]; **3** fig (slant) orienter [*programme*].
III *vi* **1** Fishg pêcher (à la ligne); **to ~ for salmon** pêcher le saumon; **2**○ fig (try to obtain) **to ~ for** chercher à obtenir [*compliments, money, tickets, work*]; **to ~ for sb's attention** chercher à attirer l'attention de qn.
IV **angled** *pp adj* [*shot, volley*] ajusté; [*serve*] à effet (*after n*); [*lamp, mirror*] incliné.

angle: **~ bracket** *n* Tech équerre *f*; **~ iron** *n* cornière *f*; **~ plate** *n* Tech équerre *f* de montage.

Anglepoise® /ˈæŋglpɔɪz/ *n* **~ (lamp)** lampe *f* d'architecte.

angler /ˈæŋglə(r)/ *n* pêcheur/-euse *m/f* (à la ligne).

angler fish *n* lotte *f* (de mer), baudroie *f*.

Anglesey /ˈæŋglsɪ/ ▶ 1381 *pr n* Anglesey *f*.

Anglican /ˈæŋglɪkən/ *n, adj* anglican/-e (*m/f*).

Anglicanism /ˈæŋglɪkənɪzəm/ *n* anglicanisme *m*.

anglicism /ˈæŋglɪsɪzəm/ *n* anglicisme *m*.

Anglicist /ˈæŋglɪsɪst/ *n* angliciste *mf*.

anglicize /ˈæŋglɪsaɪz/ *vtr* angliciser; **to become ~d** s'angliciser.

angling /ˈæŋglɪŋ/ ▶ 1282 I *n* pêche *f* (à la ligne).
II *modif* [*club, competition*] de pêche (à la ligne).

Anglo /ˈæŋgləʊ/ I *n* US Américain/-e *m/f* (*d'origine anglo-saxonne*).
II **Anglo+** (*dans composés*) anglo-.

Anglo-American /ˌæŋgləʊəˈmerɪkən/ ▶ 1486 I *n* Anglo-Américain/-e *m/f*.
II *adj* anglo-américain.

Anglo-Catholic /ˌæŋgləʊˈkæθəlɪk/ *n*: *membre du mouvement de la Haute Église anglicane proche du catholicisme*.

Anglo-Catholicism /ˌæŋgləʊkəˈθɒlɪsɪzəm/ *n*: *mouvement de la Haute Église anglicane proche du catholicisme*.

Anglo-French /ˌæŋgləʊˈfrentʃ/ ▶ 1486, 1402 I *n* Ling anglo-normand *m*.
II *adj* anglo-français, franco-britannique.

Anglo-Indian /ˌæŋgləʊˈɪndɪən/ ▶ 1486 I *n* **1** (ex-patriot) Britannique *mf* vivant en Inde; **2** (of mixed race) métis/-isse *m/f* (*de parents anglais et indien*).
II *adj* anglo-indien/-ienne.

Anglo-Irish /ˌæŋgləʊˈaɪərɪʃ/ ▶ 1486 I *npl* **the ~** les Anglo-Irlandais.
II *adj* anglo-irlandais.

Anglo-Norman /ˌæŋgləʊˈnɔːmən/ ▶ 1486, 1402 I *n* **1** (person) Anglo-Normand/-e *m/f*; **2** (language) anglo-normand *m*.
II *adj* anglo-normand.

Anglophile /ˈæŋgləʊfaɪl/ *n, adj* anglophile (*mf*).

Anglophobe /ˈæŋgləʊfəʊb/ *n* anglophobe *mf*.

Anglophobia /ˌæŋgləʊˈfəʊbɪə/ *n* anglophobie *f*.

Anglophone /ˈæŋgləʊfəʊn/ *n, adj* anglophone (*mf*).

Anglo-Saxon /ˌæŋgləʊˈsæksn/ ▶ 1486, 1402 I *n* **1** (person) Anglo-Saxon/-onne *m/f*; **2** (language) anglo-saxon *m*.
II *adj* **1** gen anglo-saxon/-onne; **2** euph [*expletive*] cru.

Angola /æŋˈgəʊlə/ ▶ 1131 *pr n* Angola *m*.

Angolan /æŋˈgəʊlən/ ▶ 1486 I *n* Angolais/-e *m/f*.
II *adj* angolais.

angora /æŋˈgɔːrə/ I *n* angora *m*.
II *modif* [*cat, rabbit*] angora *inv*; [*jumper, scarf*] en angora.

angostura /ˌæŋgəˈstjʊərə, US -ˈstʊərə/ *n* angusture *f*.

angostura bitters® *npl* Angostura®, amer *m*.

angrily /ˈæŋgrɪlɪ/ *adv* [*react, speak*] avec colère.

angry /ˈæŋgrɪ/ *adj* **1** [*person*] en colère, furieux/-ieuse; [*animal*] furieux/-ieuse; [*expression, eyes, letter, reaction, voice*] furieux/-ieuse; [*outburst, scene, words*] de colère; **to look ~** avoir l'air en colère; **to be ~ at** ou **with sb** être en colère contre qn; **to be ~ at/about sth** être en colère à cause de/à propos de qch; **to be ~ at doing sth** être en colère de faire qch; **I was ~ at having to wait** j'étais en colère d'avoir à attendre; **to get** ou **grow ~** se fâcher; **to make sb ~** exaspérer qn; **2** fig [*cloud, sea, sky*] littér menaçant; [*wound, rash*] vilain.

angry: **~-looking** *adj* [*person*] à l'air furieux (*after n*); [*sky*] à l'air menaçant (*after n*); [*wound*] vilain; **Angry Young Man** *n* GB Literat *jeune écrivain des années 50–60 qui attaque l'ordre établi*.

angstrom /ˈæŋstrəm/ *n* angström *m*.

anguish /ˈæŋgwɪʃ/ *n* **1** (mental) angoisse *f* (**about, over** face à); **to be in ~** être dans l'angoisse; **2** (physical) douleur *f*; **to cry out in ~** crier de douleur.

anguished /ˈæŋgwɪʃt/ *adj* **1** (mentally) angoissé; **2** (physically) [*suffering*] aigu/-uë.

angular /ˈæŋgjʊlə(r)/ *adj* **1** gen (bony) [*face, features, jaw, shape*] anguleux/-euse; [*person*] au physique anguleux; [*rock*] anguleux/-euse; [*building*] plein d'angles; **2** Phys angulaire.

aniline /ˈænɪliːn, US ˈænəlaɪn/ I *n* aniline *f*.
II *modif* [*dye, oil*] d'aniline.

anima /ˈænɪmə/ *n* anima *f*.

animadversion /ˌænɪmædˈvɜːʃn, US -ʒn/ *n* sout critique *f*.

animadvert /ˌænɪmædˈvɜːt/ *vi* sout **to ~ on sth** critiquer qch.

animal /ˈænɪml/ I *n* **1** lit (creature, genus) animal *m*, bête *f*; **domestic/farm ~** animal domestique/de ferme; **~, vegetable and mineral** les animaux, les végétaux, et les minéraux; **2** (brutish person) **to behave like ~s** [*people*] se conduire comme des brutes; **to bring out the ~ in sb** réveiller la bête en qn; **3** fig (entity) **man is a political ~** l'homme est un animal politique; **there's no such ~** ça n'existe pas; **the**

new company is a very different ~ la nouvelle entreprise est une chose différente.
II *modif* **1** (of animals) [*welfare*] des animaux; [*feed*] pour animaux; [*behaviour, fat, kingdom*] animal; **2** (basic) [*nature, instinct, pleasure*] animal; [*needs*] primaire; [*desires*] péj bestial.

animal: **~ activist** *n* militant/-e *m/f* pour les droits des animaux; **~ courage** *n* courage *m* instinctif; **~ cracker** *n* US *biscuit en forme d'animal*; **~ experiment** *n* expérience *f* sur les animaux; **~ husbandry** *n* élevage *m*; **~ kingdom** *n* règne *m* animal; **~ liberation front** *n* mouvement *m* pour la libération des animaux; **~ lover** *n* ami/-e *m/f* des bêtes; **~ product** *n* produit *m* d'origine animale; **~ rights** *npl* droits *mpl* des animaux; **~ sanctuary** *n* refuge *m* pour animaux; **~ (high) spirits** *npl* entrain *m*; **~ testing** *n* expérimentation *f* animale.

animate I /ˈænɪmət/ *adj* [*person*] vivant; [*object*] animé.
II /ˈænɪmeɪt/ *vtr* **1** (make active) animer [*person, cartoon*]; **2** (enliven) animer [*person*]; **~d by the thrill of the chase** tout excité par la chasse.

animated /ˈænɪmeɪtɪd/ *adj* (all contexts) animé; **an ~ film** un dessin animé.

animatedly /ˈænɪmeɪtɪdlɪ/ *adv* avec animation.

animation /ˌænɪˈmeɪʃn/ *n* animation *f*.

animator /ˈænɪmeɪtə(r)/ **▶ 1692** *n* réalisateur/-trice *m/f* de dessin animé.

animism /ˈænɪmɪzəm/ *n* animisme *m*.

animist /ˈænɪmɪst/ *n, adj* animiste (*mf*).

animosity /ˌænɪˈmɒsətɪ/ *n* animosité *f* (**between** entre; **towards** envers).

animus /ˈænɪməs/ *n* **1** sout (dislike) animosité *f* (**between** entre; **towards** envers); **2** Psych animus *m*.

anise /ˈænɪs/ *n* Bot anis *m*.

aniseed /ˈænɪsiːd/ I *n* **1** (flavour) anis *m*; **2** (seed) graine *f* d'anis.
II *modif* [*biscuit, drink, sweet*] à l'anis; **~ ball** bonbon *m* à l'anis.

Anjou /ˈɒnjuː/ **▶ 1273** *pr n* Anjou *m*.

Ankara /ˈæŋkərə/ **▶ 1818** *pr n* Ankara.

ankle /ˈæŋkl/ **▶ 1037** *n* cheville *f*; **to break/sprain/twist one's ~** se casser/se fouler/se tordre la cheville.

ankle: **~bone** *n* astragale *m*; **~ bracelet**, **~ chain** *n* chaîne *f* de cheville.

ankle-deep *adj* **the snow was ~** la neige arrivait jusqu'aux chevilles; **to be ~ in sth** avoir qch jusqu'aux chevilles.

ankle-length *adj* **an ~ dress** une robe descendant jusqu'aux chevilles.

ankle sock *n* socquette *f*.

anklet /ˈæŋklɪt/ *n* **1** (jewellery) chaîne *f* de cheville; **2** US (sock) socquette *f*.

ankylosis /ˌæŋkɪˈləʊsɪs/ *n* ankylose *f*.

annalist /ˈænəlɪst/ *n* annaliste *m*.

annals /ˈænlz/ *npl* annales *fpl*; **to go down in the ~ (of history)** figurer dans les annales.

anneal /əˈniːl/ *vtr* recuire; **~ed glass** verre recuit.

annex I /ˈæneks/ *n* (also **annexe** GB) (all contexts) annexe *f* (**to** à).
II /əˈneks/ *vtr* annexer [*territory, land, country*] (**to** à).

annexation /ˌænɪkˈseɪʃn/ *n* (action) annexion *f* (**of** de); (land annexed) territoire *m* annexé.

Annie Oakley○ /ˌænɪ ˈəʊklɪ/ *n* US billet *m* de faveur.

annihilate /əˈnaɪəleɪt/ *vtr* (all contexts) anéantir.

annihilation /əˌnaɪəˈleɪʃn/ *n* (all contexts) anéantissement *m*.

anniversary /ˌænɪˈvɜːsərɪ/ I *n* anniversaire *m* (**of** de); **wedding ~** anniversaire de mariage; **fifth ~** cinquième anniversaire.
II *modif* [*celebration, dinner, festival, reunion*] (of historical event) commémoratif/-ive; **our ~ dinner** (of wedding) un dîner pour fêter notre anniversaire de mariage.

anno Domini, **Anno Domini** /ˌænəʊ ˈdɒmɪnaɪ/ *adv* après Jésus-Christ.

annotate /ˈænəteɪt/ *vtr* annoter; **~d edition** édition annotée.

annotation /ˌænəˈteɪʃn/ *n* **1** (note) (printed in book) note *f*; (added by reader) annotation *f*; **2** (action) annotation *f*; **3** Comput commentaire *m*.

announce /əˈnaʊns/ I *vtr* annoncer (**that** que); **we are pleased to ~** nous sommes heureux d'annoncer.
II *vi* US annoncer sa candidature; **to ~ for** poser sa candidature à [*political office*]; se déclarer pour [*candidate*].

announcement /əˈnaʊnsmənt/ *n* **1** (spoken) annonce *f* (**of** de; **that** indiquant que); **to make an ~** faire une annonce; **official/public ~** annonce officielle/publique; **2** (written) avis *m*; (of birth, death) faire-part *m inv*.

announcer /əˈnaʊnsə(r)/ *n* **1** (on TV) speaker/-erine *m/f*; **radio ~** présentateur/-trice *m/f* de radio; **2** (at rail station) annonceur/-euse *m/f*.

annoy /əˈnɔɪ/ *vtr* [*person*] (by general behaviour) agacer; (by opposing wishes, plans) contrarier; [*discomfort, noise, disturbance*] gêner; **what really ~s me is that I was not informed** ce qui me contrarie, c'est que je n'ai pas été tenu au courant; **officer, this man's ~ing me** monsieur l'agent, cet homme m'embête.

annoyance /əˈnɔɪəns/ *n* **1** (crossness) agacement *m* (**at** devant); contrariété *f* (**at** à); **a look of ~** un regard agacé; **much to her ~** à son grand mécontentement; **2** (nuisance) désagrément *m*.

annoyed /əˈnɔɪd/ *adj* contrarié (**by** par); (stronger) agacé, fâché (**by** par); **to be ~ with sb** être fâché contre qn; **to get ~ with sb** se fâcher contre qn; **she was ~ with him for being late** elle était contrariée or elle n'était pas contente parce qu'il était en retard; **you're not ~ with me, are you?** tu ne m'en veux pas?; **he was ~ (that) I hadn't replied** il était contrarié parce que je n'avais pas répondu.

annoying /əˈnɔɪɪŋ/ *adj* agaçant (**to do** de faire); **the ~ thing is that**... ce qui est agaçant or fâcheux, c'est que...; **how ~!** c'est agaçant!

annoyingly /əˈnɔɪɪŋlɪ/ *adv* **the engine is ~ noisy** le moteur est bruyant au point d'en être gênant; **~, the train was late** le train était en retard, ce qui était contrariant.

annual /ˈænjʊəl/ I *n* **1** (book) album *m* (annuel); **2** (plant) plante *f* annuelle; ▶ **hardy annual**.
II *adj* annuel/-elle.

Annual General Meeting, **AGM** *n* assemblée *f* générale annuelle.

annualize /ˈænjʊəlaɪz/ *vtr* annualiser.

annualized percentage rate, **APR** *n* taux *m* d'intérêt annuel.

annually /ˈænjʊəlɪ/ *adv* [*cost, earn, pay, produce*] par an; [*award, do, hold, inspect*] tous les ans.

annual percentage rate *n* = **annualized percentage rate**.

annuity /əˈnjuːətɪ, US -ˈnuː-/ *n* rente *f*; **life(-time) ~** rente viagère; **deferred ~** rente différée; **pension ~** pension *f* de retraite par capitalisation.

annuity bond *n* titre *m* de rente perpétuelle.

annul /əˈnʌl/ *vtr* (*p prés etc* **-ll-**) annuler [*marriage, treaty, vote*]; abroger [*law*].

annular /ˈænjʊlə(r)/ *adj* [*eclipse, ligament*] annulaire.

annulment /əˈnʌlmənt/ *n* (of marriage) annulation *f*; (of legislation) abrogation *f*.

annulus /ˈænjʊləs/ *n* (*pl* **-li** ou **-luses**) Tech couronne *f*.

Annunciation /əˌnʌnsɪˈeɪʃn/ *n* Annonciation *f*.

anode /ˈænəʊd/ *n* anode *f*.

anodize /ˈænədaɪz/ *vtr* anodiser; **~d aluminium** aluminium anodisé.

anodyne /ˈænədaɪn/ I *n* **1** (painkiller) analgésique *m*; **2** fig (soothing thing) baume *m*.
II *adj* **1** (inoffensive) inoffensif/-ive; pej (bland) anodin; **2** (analgesic) analgésique.

anoint /əˈnɔɪnt/ *vtr* **1** oindre; **to ~ with oil** oindre; **2** (appoint to high office) sacrer; **to be sb's ~ed heir** fig être le protégé or l'oint fml de qn; **the ~ing of the sick** Relig l'onction *f* des malades.

anomalous /əˈnɒmələs/ *adj* (all contexts) anormal.

anomaly /əˈnɒməlɪ/ *n* (situation, law, fact) anomalie *f* (**in** dans); (person) phénomène *m* (anormal).

anomie, anomy /ˈænəmɪ/ *n* Sociol anomie *f*.

anon /əˈnɒn/ *adv* † ou hum **see you ~** à tout à l'heure; **more of that ~** (written) voir ci-après; (spoken) nous reviendrons là-dessus.

anon. /əˈnɒn/ *abrév* = **anonymous**.

anonymity /ˌænəˈnɪmətɪ/ *n* (all contexts) anonymat *m*; **to preserve one's ~** garder l'anonymat; **to preserve sb's ~** préserver l'anonymat de qn.

anonymous /əˈnɒnɪməs/ *adj* (all contexts) anonyme; **to wish to remain ~** souhaiter garder l'anonymat.

anonymously /əˈnɒnɪməslɪ/ *adv* [*buy, complain, give, write*] anonymement; [*give information, make donation*] de façon anonyme.

anorak /ˈænəræk/ *n* **1** (garment) anorak *m*; **2**○ (person) personne *f* terne.

anorexia /ˌænəˈreksɪə/ *n* **1** (also **~ nervosa**) anorexie *f* mentale; **2** (loss of appetite) anorexie *f*.

anorexic /ˌænəˈreksɪk/ *n, adj* anorexique (*mf*).

another /əˈnʌðə(r)/

■ **Note** When *another* is used as a determiner it is translated by *un autre* or *une autre* according to the gender of the noun that follows: *another ticket* = un autre billet; *another cup* = une autre tasse. However, when *another* means *an additional, encore* can also be used: *another cup of tea?* = une autre tasse de thé *or* encore une tasse de thé? For more examples and particular usages, see I below.
– When *another* is used as a pronoun it is translated by *un autre* or *une autre* according to the gender of the noun it refers to: *that cake was delicious, can I have another?* = ce gâteau était délicieux, est-ce que je peux en prendre un autre?; *I see you like the peaches—have another* = je vois que tu aimes les pêches—prends-en une autre. Note that *en* is always added in French when *un/une autre* are used as pronouns. For more examples and particular usages, see II below.

I *det* **1** (an additional) un/-e autre, encore un/-e; **would you like ~ drink?** est-ce que tu veux un autre verre?, encore un verre?; **they want to have ~ child** ils veulent avoir un autre enfant; **we have received yet ~ letter** nous avons reçu encore une nouvelle lettre; **that will cost you ~ £5** cela vous coûtera 5 livres sterling de plus; **they stayed ~ three hours** ils sont restés encore trois heures or trois heures de plus; **without ~ word** sans rien dire de plus; **in ~ five weeks** dans cinq semaines; **it was ~ ten years before they met again** dix ans se sont écoulés avant qu'ils se rencontrent de nouveau; **and ~ thing,...** et de plus,...; **not ~ programme about seals!** encore une émission sur les phoques!; **2** (a different) un/-e autre; **~ time** une autre fois; **he has ~ job/~ girlfriend now** il a un nouveau travail/une nouvelle copine mainte-

nant; **can I have ~ one?** est-ce que je peux en avoir un/-e autre?; **there's ~ way of doing it** il y a une autre façon de le faire; **to put it ~ way...** en d'autres termes...; **that's quite ~ matter** ça c'est une autre histoire or question; **3** (new) **~ Garbo** une nouvelle Garbo; **~ Vietnam** un nouveau Vietnam.
II *pron* un/-e autre; **can I have ~?** est-ce que je peux en avoir un/-e autre?; **he loved ~** littér il était amoureux d'un/-e autre, il aimait quelqu'un d'autre; **~ of the witnesses said that** un autre témoin a dit que; **one after ~** l'un/l'une après l'autre; **she tried on one hat after ~** elle a essayé tous les chapeaux les uns après les autres; **of one kind or ~** d'une sorte ou d'une autre; **for one reason or ~** pour une raison ou une autre; **in one way or ~** d'une façon ou d'une autre; **ignorance is one thing, vulgarity is quite ~** l'ignorance est une chose, mais la vulgarité en est une autre; **imagining things is one thing, creating them is quite ~** l'imagination est une chose, la création en est une autre.

A. N. Other /ˌeɪ en ˈʌðə(r)/ *n* GB ≈ monsieur Untel/madame Unetelle *m/f*.

anoxia /əˈnɒksɪə/ *n* anoxie *f*.

anoxic /əˈnɒksɪk/ *adj* anoxique.

ANSI *n* US (*abrév* = **American National Standards Institute**) institut *m* américain de normalisation.

answer /ˈɑːnsə(r), US ˈænsər/ **I** *n* **1** (reply) réponse *f* (**to** à); **to get/give an ~** obtenir/donner une réponse; **an ~ in writing** une réponse par écrit; **there's no ~** (to door) il n'y a personne; (on phone) ça ne répond pas; **in ~ to sth** en réponse à qch; **she has all the ~s, she has an ~ for everything** elle a réponse à tout, elle croit tout savoir pej; **her only ~ was to laugh** pour seule réponse elle a éclaté de rire; **I won't take no for an ~!** pas question de refuser!; **there's no ~ to that!** que voulez-vous répondre à ça?; **France's ~ to Marilyn Monroe** hum la version française de Marilyn Monroe; **2** (solution) (to difficulty, puzzle) solution *f* (**to** à); Sch, Univ réponse *f* (**to** à); **the right/wrong ~** la bonne/mauvaise réponse; **there is no easy ~ (to the problem)** c'est un problème difficile à résoudre; **it's the ~ to all our problems** c'est la solution à tous nos problèmes; **he doesn't pretend to know all the ~s** il ne prétend pas avoir réponse à tout; **3** (to criticism) réponse *f* (**to** à); **~ to a charge** Jur réfutation *f* d'une accusation.
II *vtr* **1** (reply to) répondre à [*question, invitation, letter, person*]; **to ~ that** répondre que; **to ~ the door** aller or venir ouvrir la porte; **to ~ the telephone** répondre au téléphone; **to ~ the call** lit, fig répondre à l'appel; **she ~ed him with a smile** elle lui a répondu par un sourire; **to ~ violence with violence** répondre à la violence par la violence; **our prayers have been ~ed** nos prières ont été exaucées; **2** gen, Jur (respond) répondre à [*criticism, accusation, allegation*]; **to ~ a charge** répondre d'une accusation; **he was in court to ~ charges of theft** il devait répondre d'une accusation de vol devant le tribunal; **there was no case to ~** il n'y avait pas matière à inculpation; **3** (meet) répondre à [*need, demand*]; **we saw nobody ~ing that description** nous n'avons vu personne répondant à cette description; **4** Naut **to ~ the helm** obéir à la barre.
III *vi* **1** (respond) répondre; **it's not ~ing** GB Telecom ça ne répond pas; **to ~ to the name of X** répondre au nom de X; **2** (correspond) **to ~ to** répondre or correspondre à [*description*]; **3** (account) **to ~ for sb** répondre de qn; **to ~ to sb** être responsable devant qn; **he ~s to management for any decisions he takes** il doit répondre de toutes les décisions qu'il prend devant la direction; **...or you'll have me to ~ to!** ...ou tu auras affaire à moi!
■ **answer back**: ¶ **~ back** gen, Jur répondre; ¶ **~ [sb] back** GB répondre; **don't dare ~ (me) back!** comment oses-tu (me) répondre?
■ **answer for**: **~ for [sth]** (account for) répondre de [*action, behaviour*]; **they have a lot to ~ for!** ils ont beaucoup de comptes à rendre!; **to ~ for sb's honesty** se porter garant de l'honnêteté de qn.

answerable /ˈɑːnsərəbl, US ˈæns-/ *adj* **1** (accountable) **to be ~ to sb** être responsable devant qn; **to be ~ for** être responsable de [*decision, actions*]; **they are ~ to no-one** ils n'ont de comptes à rendre à personne; **2** [*question*] à laquelle on peut répondre.

answer-back /ˈɑːnsəbæk, US ˈæns-/ **I** *n* réponse *f* (automatique).
II *modif* **~ code** indicatif *m* (d'un téléimprimeur).

answering: **~ machine** *n* répondeur *m* (téléphonique); **~ service** *n* permanence *f* téléphonique.

answerphone /ˈɑːnsəfəʊn, US ˈæns-/ *n* répondeur *m* (téléphonique).

ant /ænt/ *n* fourmi *f*; **flying ~** fourmi volante.
IDIOMS **to have ~s in one's pants**○ avoir la bougeotte○.

antacid /æntˈæsɪd/ *n, adj* alcalin (*m*).

antagonism /ænˈtæɡənɪzəm/ *n* antagonisme *m* (**between** entre); **mutual/class ~** antagonisme mutuel/de classes; **~ to** ou **towards sb/sth** hostilité *f* à l'égard de qn/qch.

antagonist /ænˈtæɡənɪst/ *n* antagoniste *mf*.

antagonistic /ænˌtæɡəˈnɪstɪk/ *adj* **1** (hostile) [*person, attitude*] hostile (**to, towards** à); **2** (mutually opposed) [*theories, forces*] antagoniste.

antagonistically /ænˌtæɡəˈnɪstɪklɪ/ *adv* [*act, glare, say*] avec hostilité.

antagonize /ænˈtæɡənaɪz/ *vtr* (annoy) contrarier (**with** avec); (stronger) éveiller l'hostilité de (**by doing** en faisant; **with** avec).

Antarctic /ænˈtɑːktɪk/ **I** *pr n* **the ~** l'Antarctique *m*.
II *adj* (also **antarctic**) antarctique.

Antarctica /ænˈtɑːktɪkə/ *pr n* Antarctique *m*.

Antarctic: **~ Circle** cercle *m* polaire antarctique; **~ Ocean** ▶ **1511** *n* océan *m* Antarctique.

ant bear *n* oryctérope *m*.

ante /ˈæntɪ/ **I** *n* première mise *f*; **to up the ~** lit, fig augmenter la mise.
II *vtr* miser.
■ **ante up**○ US casquer○.

anteater /ˈæntiːtə(r)/ *n* fourmilier *m*.

antebellum /ˌæntɪˈbeləm/ *adj* **1** US **the ~ South** *les États du Sud des États-Unis d'avant la guerre de Sécession*; **2** gen **~ Europe** l'Europe d'avant la guerre.

antecedent /ˌæntɪˈsiːdnt/ **I** *n* **1** (precedent) Ling, Math, Philos antécédent *m*; **2** (ancestor) ancêtre *m*.
II *adj* antérieur (**to** à).

antechamber /ˈæntɪtʃembə(r)/ *n* = **anteroom**.

antedate /ˌæntɪˈdeɪt/ *vtr* **1** (put earlier date on) antidater [*cheque, letter*]; **2** (predate) précéder (**by** de).

antediluvian /ˌæntɪdɪˈluːvɪən/ *adj* antédiluvien/-ienne.

antelope /ˈæntɪləʊp/ *n* antilope *f*.

antenatal /ˌæntɪˈneɪtl/ GB **I** *n* examen *m* prénatal.
II *adj* prénatal.

antenatal: **~ class** *n* GB cours *m* d'accouchement sans douleur; **~ clinic** *n* GB service *m* de consultation prénatale.

antenna /ænˈtenə/ *n* (*pl* **-ae** ou **-as**) (all contexts) antenne *f*.

antepenultimate /ˌæntɪpɪˈnʌltɪmət/ *adj* antépénultième.

ante-post /ˌæntɪˈpəʊst/ *adj* GB Turf [*favourite*] d'avant le jour de la course.

ante-post bet *n* GB Turf *pari effectué avant que les numéros des chevaux soient connus*.

anterior /ænˈtɪərɪə(r)/ *adj* antérieur.

anteroom /ˈæntɪruːm, -rʊm/ *n* antichambre *f*.

anthem /ˈænθəm/ *n* **1** (theme tune) hymne *m*; **2** Relig (motet) motet *m*; (antiphon) antienne *f*; ▶ **national anthem**.

anther /ˈænθə(r)/ *n* anthère *f*.

anthill /ˈænthɪl/, **antheap** /ˈænthiːp/ *n* fourmilière *f*.

anthologist /ænˈθɒlədʒɪst/ *n* anthologiste *mf*, auteur *m* d'anthologies.

anthology /ænˈθɒlədʒɪ/ *n* anthologie *f*.

Anthony /ˈæntənɪ/ *pr n* Antoine.

anthracite /ˈænθrəsaɪt/ *n* anthracite *m*.

anthrax /ˈænθræks/ ▶ **1354** *n* (*pl* **-thraces**) (disease) charbon *m*; (pustule) anthrax *m*.

anthropoid /ˈænθrəpɔɪd/ *n, adj* anthropoïde (*m*).

anthropoid ape *n* singe *m* anthropoïde.

anthropological /ˌænθrəpəˈlɒdʒɪkl/ *adj* anthropologique.

anthropologist /ˌænθrəˈpɒlədʒɪst/ ▶ **1692** *n* anthropologue *mf*, anthropologiste *mf*.

anthropology /ˌænθrəˈpɒlədʒɪ/ *n* anthropologie *f*.

anthropometry /ˌænθrəˈpɒmɪtrɪ/ *n* anthropométrie *f*.

anthropomorphic /ˌænθrəpəˈmɔːfɪk/ *adj* anthropomorphique.

anthropomorphism /ˌænθrəpəˈmɔːfɪzəm/ *n* anthropomorphisme *m*.

anthropomorphous /ˌænθrəpəˈmɔːfəs/ *adj* **1** (human-shaped) anthropomorphe; **2** = **anthropomorphic**.

anthropophagous /ˌænθrəˈpɒfəɡəs/ *adj* anthropophage.

anthropophagus /ˌænθrəˈpɒfəɡəs/ *n* (*pl* **-gi**) anthropophage *mf*.

anthropophagy /ˌænθrəˈpɒfədʒɪ/ *n* anthropophagie *f*.

anthroposophy /ˌænθrəˈpɒsəfɪ/ *n* anthroposophie *f*.

anti /ˈæntɪ/ **I** *prep* contre; **to be ~ (sth)** être contre (qch).
II anti+ (*dans composés*) anti-.

antiabortion /ˌæntɪəˈbɔːʃn/ *adj* contre l'avortement.

antiabortionist /ˌæntɪəˈbɔːʃənɪst/ *n* adversaire *mf* de l'avortement.

antiaircraft /ˌæntɪˈeəkrɑːft, US -kræft/ *adj* [*battery, fire, gun, missile, weapon*] antiaérien/-ienne.

antiaircraft defence *n* défense *f* contre aéronefs or avions, DCA *f*.

antiallergic /ˌæntɪəˈlerdʒɪk/ *adj* antiallergique.

antiapartheid /ˌæntɪəˈpɑːteɪt, ˌæntɪə ˈpɑːtaɪd/ *adj* anti-apartheid.

antiauthoritarian /ˌæntɪɔːθɒrɪˈteərɪən/ *adj* [*person*] contestataire; [*attitude, measures*] antiautoritaire.

antibacterial /ˈæntɪbækˈtɪərɪəl/ *adj* antibactérie.

antiballistic missile /ˌæntɪbəlɪstɪk ˈmɪsaɪl, US ˈmɪsl/ *n* missile *m* antimissile.

antibiotic /ˌæntɪbaɪˈɒtɪk/ **I** *n* antibiotique *m*; **to be on ~s** être sous antibiotiques.
II *adj* antibiotique.

antibody /ˈæntɪbɒdɪ/ *n* anticorps *m*.

Antichrist /ˈæntɪkraɪst/ *n* antéchrist *m*; **the ~** l'Antéchrist.

anticipate /ænˈtɪsɪpeɪt/ **I** *vtr* **1** (expect, foresee) prévoir, s'attendre à [*problem, trouble, delay, victory*]; **to ~ that** prévoir que; **as ~d** comme prévu; **they are anticipating large crowds** ils prévoient la venue de nombreuses personnes; **we ~ meeting him soon** nous pensons le rencontrer bientôt; **I didn't ~ him doing that** je ne

m'attendais pas à ce qu'il fasse ça; **she eagerly ~d the moment when she would tell him** elle savourait le moment où elle allait le lui dire; **2** (guess in advance) anticiper [*sb's needs, movements, wishes, reaction, result*]; **3** (preempt) devancer [*person, act*]; **he tried to lock the door but she ~d him** il a essayé de fermer la porte à clé mais elle l'a devancé; **4** (prefigure) préfigurer [*later work, invention, development*].
II *vi* anticiper; **but I'm anticipating a little** (when telling story) mais j'anticipe.
III -anticipated (*dans composés*) **much-~d** tant attendu; **long-~d** attendu depuis si longtemps.

anticipation /æn,tɪsɪ'peɪʃn/ *n* **1** (excitement) excitation *f*; (pleasure in advance) plaisir *m* anticipé; **in ~ of sth** à l'idée de qch; **she smiled in ~** elle souriait en se réjouissant d'avance; **2** (expectation) prévision *f* (**of** de); **in ~ of** en prévision de; **to show good ~** ou **a good sense of ~** (Sport) faire preuve d'un bon sens d'anticipation; **thanking you in ~** (in letter) en vous remerciant d'avance; **3** Jur (property law) jouissance *f* anticipée.

anticipatory /æn,tɪsɪ'peɪtərɪ/ *adj* **1 to take ~ measures** ou **action** prendre des mesures par anticipation; **2** Psych [*response, reaction*] d'anticipation; **3** Ling extraposé.

anticlerical /,æntɪ'klerɪkl/ **I** *n* anticlérical/-e *m/f*.
II *adj* anticlérical.

anticlericalism /,æntɪ'klerɪkəlɪzəm/ *n* anticléricalisme *m*.

anticlimax /,æntɪ'klaɪmæks/ *n* déception *f*; **what an ~!** quelle déception!; **there was a sense of ~** tout le monde était déçu.

anticline /'æntɪklaɪn/ *n* anticlinal *m*.

anticlockwise /,æntɪ'klɒkwaɪz/ *adj, adv* GB dans le sens inverse des aiguilles d'une montre.

anticoagulant /,æntɪkəʊ'ægjʊlənt/ *n, adj* anticoagulant (*m*).

anticorrosive /,æntɪkə'rəʊsɪv/ **I** *n* produit *m* anticorrosion.
II *adj* anticorrosion *inv* (*never pred*).

antics /'æntɪks/ *npl* (comical) pitreries *fpl*; pej bouffonneries *fpl*.

anticyclone /,æntɪ'saɪkləʊn/ *n* anticyclone *m*.

antidandruff /,æntɪ'dændrʌf/ *adj* antipelliculaire.

antidepressant /,æntɪdɪ'presnt/ *n, adj* antidépresseur (*m*).

antidote /'æntɪdəʊt/ *n* Med, fig antidote *m* (**to, for** contre, à).

antiestablishment /,æntɪɪs'tæblɪʃmənt/ *adj* contestataire.

antifreeze /'æntɪfri:z/ *n* antigel *m*.

antifriction metal /,æntɪfrɪkʃn 'metl/ *n* métal *m* antifriction.

antigen /'æntɪdʒən/ *n* antigène *m*.

antiglare /,æntɪ'gleə(r)/ *adj* [*screen*] antireflet *inv*.

Antigua and Barbuda /æn,ti:gə ənd bɑ:'bu:də/ ▶ **1131** *pr n* Antigua-et-Barbuda *f*.

antihero /'æntɪhɪərəʊ/ *n* antihéros *m*.

antihistamine /,æntɪ'hɪstəmɪn/ *n* antihistaminique *m*; **I need ~** j'ai besoin d'antihistaminiques.

anti-inflation /,æntɪɪn'fleɪʃn/ *adj* (*avant n*) [*policy, programme*] anti-inflation; [*rhetoric, opinion*] anti-inflationniste.

anti-inflationary /,æntɪɪn'fleɪʃənərɪ, US -nerɪ/ *adj* antiinflationniste.

anti-interference /,æntɪɪntə'fɪərəns/ *adj* antiparasite.

antiknock /'æntɪnɒk/ *n* antidétonant *m*.

antilock /'æntɪlɒk/ *adj* antiblocage.

antilogarithm /,æntɪ'lɒgərɪðəm, US -'lɔ:g-/ *n* antilogarithme *m*.

antimacassar /,æntɪmə'kæsə(r)/ *n* têtière *f*.

antimagnetic /,æntɪmæg'netɪk/ *adj* antimagnétique.

antimarket /,æntɪ'mɑ:kɪt/ *adj* GB [*MP, group, lobby*] adversaire du Marché commun; [*speech, opinion, article*] contre le Marché commun.

antimarketeer /,æntɪmɑ:kɪ'tɪə(r)/ *n* GB adversaire *mf* du Marché commun.

antimatter /'æntɪmætə(r)/ *n* antimatière *f*.

antimissile /'æntɪmɪsaɪl, US -mɪsl/ *n, adj* antimissile (*m*).

antimony /'æntɪmənɪ, US -məʊnɪ/ *n* antimoine *m*.

antinuclear /,æntɪ'nju:klɪə(r), US -nu:-/ *adj* antinucléaire.

antinuke○ /,æntɪ'nju:k, US -'nu:-/ *adj* antinucléaire.

antipathetic /,æntɪpə'θetɪk/ *adj* opposé (**to, towards** à).

antipathy /æn'tɪpəθɪ/ *n* antipathie *f* (**for, to, towards** envers; **between** entre).

antipersonnel /,æntɪ,pɜ:sə'nel/ *adj* Mil antipersonnel.

antiperspirant /,æntɪ'pɜ:spɪrənt/ **I** *n* produit *m* antitranspiration.
II *adj* antitranspiration *inv*.

antiperspirant deodorant **I** *n* produit *m* antitranspiration déodorant.
II *adj* antitranspiration déodorant.

antiphony /æn'tɪfənɪ/ *n* antienne *f*.

antipodean /æn,tɪpə'di:ən/ **I** *n*: *personne qui vient d'Australie ou de Nouvelle-Zélande*.
II *adj* [*cousin, politics*] d'Australie et Nouvelle-Zélande.

Antipodes /æn'tɪpədi:z/ *npl* GB **the ~** l'Australie et la Nouvelle-Zélande.

antiquarian /,æntɪ'kweərɪən/ ▶ **1692** **I** *n* (dealer) antiquaire *mf*; (scholar) archéologue *mf*; (collector) collectionneur/-euse *m/f* d'antiquités.
II *adj* [*history*] ancien/-ienne; **~ bookshop** librairie de livres anciens.

antiquary /'æntɪkwərɪ, US -kwerɪ/ ▶ **1692** *n* **1** (dealer) antiquaire *mf*; **2** (scholar) archéologue *mf*.

antiquated /'æntɪkweɪtɪd/ *adj* [*machinery, idea, procedure*] archaïque; [*building*] vétuste.

antique /æn'ti:k/ **I** *n* **1** (piece of furniture) meuble *m* ancien; (other object) objet *m* ancien; **genuine ~** (piece of furniture) meuble *m* d'époque; (other object) objet *m* d'époque; **2**○ péj (person) vieux fossile *m*.
II *adj* **1** [*clock, lace, silver*] ancien/-ienne; **2** (old-style) à l'ancienne; **~ oak** chêne traité à l'ancienne.
III *vtr* vieillir [*furniture*].
IV *vi* US faire les antiquaires.

antique: **~ dealer** ▶ **1692** *n* antiquaire *mf*; **~(s) fair** *n* foire *f* aux antiquités; **~ shop** ▶ **1692** *n* magasin *m* d'antiquités.

antiquity /æn'tɪkwətɪ/ *n* **1** (ancient times) antiquité *f*; **in/since ~** dans/depuis l'antiquité; **classical ~** l'antiquité grecque et romaine; **2** (great age) ancienneté *f*; **of great ~** très ancien/-ienne; **3** (relic) antiquité *f*.

antiracism /,æntɪ'reɪsɪzəm/ *n* antiracisme *m*.

antiracist /,æntɪ'reɪsɪst/ *n, adj* antiraciste (*mf*).

antireligious /,æntɪrɪ'lɪdʒəs/ *adj* [*person, views, propaganda*] antireligieux/-ieuse.

anti-riot /,æntɪ'raɪət/ *adj* [*police, squad*] antiémeutes *inv*.

anti-roll bar /,æntɪ'rəʊl bɑ:(r)/ *n* barre *f* antiroulis.

antirrhinum /,æntɪ'raɪnəm/ *n* muflier *m*.

anti-rust /,æntɪ'rʌst/ *adj* antirouille *inv*.

antisegregationist /,æntɪsegrə'geɪʃənɪst/ *n, adj* antiségrégationniste (*mf*).

anti-Semite /,æntɪ'si:maɪt, US -'semaɪt/ *n* antisémite *mf*.

anti-Semitic /,æntɪsɪ'mɪtɪk/ *adj* antisémite.

anti-Semitism /,æntɪ'semɪtɪzəm/ *n* antisémitisme *m*.

antisepsis /,æntɪ'sepsɪs/ *n* antisepsie *f*.

antiseptic /,æntɪ'septɪk/ *n, adj* antiseptique (*m*).

anti-skid /,æntɪ'skɪd/ *adj* antidérapant.

antislavery /,æntɪ'sleɪvərɪ/ *adj* antiesclavagiste.

anti-smoking /,æntɪ'sməʊkɪŋ/ *adj* antitabac.

antisocial /,æntɪ'səʊʃl/ *adj* **1 ~ behaviour** gen comportement *m* incorrect; (criminal behaviour) comportement *m* délinquant; **it is ~ to smoke in public places** fumer dans les lieux publics est un manque de considération pour les autres; **2** (reclusive) sauvage.

antispasmodic /,æntɪspæz'mɒdɪk/ *n, adj* antispasmodique (*m*).

anti-strike /,æntɪ'straɪk/ *adj* antigrève.

antisubmarine /,æntɪsʌbmə'ri:n/ *adj* anti-sous-marin.

antitank /,æntɪ'tæŋk/ *adj* antichar.

anti-terrorist /,æntɪ'terərɪst/ *adj* antiterroriste.

anti-theft /,æntɪ'θeft/ *adj* [*lock, device*] antivol; [*camera*] de surveillance; **~ steering lock** antivol de direction.

antithesis /æn'tɪθəsɪs/ *n* (*pl* **-theses**) sout **1** (opposite) contraire *m* (**of** de); (in ideas) antithèse *f* (**of** de); **2** (contrast) contraste *m* (**between** entre); **her views are in complete ~ to his** son point de vue est radicalement opposé au sien; **3** Literat, Philos antithèse *f*.

antithetic(al) /,æntɪ'θetɪk(l)/ *adj* sout [*views, opinions*] antithétique; **to be ~ to sth** aller à l'encontre de qch.

antithetically /,æntɪ'θetɪklɪ/ *adv* sout par antithèse.

antitoxic /,æntɪ'tɒksɪk/ *adj* antitoxique.

antitoxin /,æntɪ'tɒksɪn/ *n* antitoxine *f*.

antitrust /,æntɪ'trʌst/ *adj* antitrust *inv*.

antitrust law *n* US loi *f* antitrust.

anti-vivisection /,æntɪ,vɪvɪ'sekʃən/ *adj* contre la vivisection.

anti-vivisectionist /,æntɪ,vɪvɪ'sekʃənɪst/ **I** *n* militant/-e *m/f* contre la vivisection.
II *adj* = **antivivisection**.

antlers /'æntləz/ *npl* (on stag, as trophy) bois *mpl* de cerf.

Antony /'æntənɪ/ *pr n* Antoine.

antonym /'æntənɪm/ *n* antonyme *m*.

antonymy /æn'tɒnɪmɪ/ *n* antonymie *f*.

Antrim /'æntrɪm/ ▶ **1624** *pr n* comté *m* d'Antrim.

antsy○ /'æntsɪ/ *adj* US nerveux/-euse; **to feel ~** ne pas tenir en place.

Antwerp /'æntwɜ:p/ ▶ **1818** *pr n* Anvers.

anus /'eɪnəs/ *n* anus *m*.

anvil /'ænvɪl/ *n* enclume *f* also Anat.

anxiety /æŋ'zaɪətɪ/ *n* **1** (apprehension) grandes inquiétudes *fpl* (**about** à propos de; **for** pour); **she caused them great ~** elle leur a causé beaucoup de soucis; **to be in a state of high ~** être très angoissé; **2** (source of worry) souci *m*; **to be an ~ to sb** causer des soucis à qn; **3** (eagerness) désir *m* ardent (**to do** de faire); **in her ~ to get there on time she forgot her passport** elle tenait tellement à y arriver à l'heure qu'elle a oublié son passeport; **4** Psych anxiété *f*.

anxiety: **~ attack** *n* crise *f* d'angoisse; **~ neurosis** *n* Psych névrose *f* d'angoisse.

anxious /'æŋkʃəs/ *adj* **1** (worried) très inquiet/-iète (**about** à propos de; **for** pour); **to be ~ about doing** s'inquiéter de faire; **to be very** ou **extremely ~** être angoissé; **2** (causing worry) [*moment, time*] angoissant; **3** (eager) très désireux/-euse (**to do** de faire); **I am ~ for him to know** ou **that he should know** je tiens beaucoup à ce qu'il sache; **to be ~ for sth** avoir un fort désir de qch; **she is most ~ to meet you** elle a très envie de faire votre connaissance.

anxiously /'æŋkʃəslɪ/ *adv* **1** (worriedly) avec inquiétude; **2** (eagerly) avec impatience.

anxiousness /'æŋkʃəslɪ/ *n* = **anxiety** 1, 3.

any /ˈenɪ/

■ **Note** When *any* is used as a determiner in negative sentences it is not usually translated in French: *we don't have any money* = nous n'avons pas d'argent.
– When *any* is used as a determiner in questions it is translated by *du, de l', de la* or *des* according to the gender and number of the noun that follows: *is there any soap?* = y a-t-il du savon?; *is there any flour?* = y a-t-il de la farine?; *are there any questions?* = est-ce qu'il y a des questions?
– For examples and other determiner uses see I in the entry below.
– When *any* is used as a pronoun in negative sentences and in questions it is translated by *en*: *we don't have any* = nous n'en avons pas; *have you got any?* = est-ce que vous en avez?
– For more examples and other pronoun uses see II below.
– For adverbial uses such as *any more, any longer, any better etc* see III below.

I *det* **1** (with negative, implied negative) **he hasn't got ~ money/food** il n'a pas d'argent/de nourriture; **they never receive ~ letters** ils ne reçoivent jamais de lettres; **they hardly ate ~ cake** ils n'ont presque pas mangé de gâteau; **I don't want ~ breakfast/lunch** je ne veux pas de petit déjeuner/déjeuner; **I don't need ~ advice** je n'ai pas besoin de conseils; **they couldn't get ~ details** ils n'ont pas obtenu la moindre information; **he hasn't got ~ common sense** il n'a aucun bon sens; **2** (in questions, conditional sentences) **is there ~ tea/bread?** est-ce qu'il y a du thé/pain?; **have you got ~ plums?** est-ce que vous avez des prunes?; **if you have ~ doubts** si vous avez le moindre doute; **if you have ~ money** si vous avez de l'argent; **3** (no matter which) n'importe quel/quelle, tout; **~ hat/pen will do** n'importe quel chapeau/stylo fera l'affaire; **you can have ~ cup you like** vous pouvez prendre n'importe quelle tasse; **~ teacher will tell you the same thing** n'importe quel professeur te dira la même chose; **~ information would be very useful** tout renseignement serait très utile; **~ complaints should be addressed to Mr Cook** pour toute réclamation adressez-vous à M. Cook; **~ child caught smoking will be punished** tout enfant surpris à fumer sera puni; **I'm ready to help in ~ way I can** je suis prêt à faire tout ce que je peux pour aider; **I do not wish to restrict your freedom in ~ way** je n'ai pas l'intention d'entraver votre liberté de quelque façon que ce soit; **he might return at ~ time** il peut revenir d'un moment à l'autre; **if you should want to discuss this at ~ time** si à un moment ou à un autre vous souhaitez discuter de cela; **come round and see me ~ time** passe me voir quand tu veux; **~ one of you could have done it** n'importe qui d'entre vous aurait pu le faire; **I don't buy ~ one brand in particular** je n'achète aucune marque en particulier; **you can only take out £200 at ~ one time** vous ne pouvez retirer que 200 livres sterling à chaque fois; ▸**case**[1], **chance**, **event**, **means**, **minute**[1], **old**, **rate**.

II *pron* **1** (with negative, implied negative) **he hasn't got ~** il n'en a pas; **there is hardly ~ left** il n'en reste presque pas; **there aren't ~ others** il n'y en a pas d'autres; **she doesn't like ~ of them** (people) elle n'aime aucun d'entre eux/elles; (things) elle n'en aime aucun/-e; **2** (in questions, conditional sentences) **I'd like some tea, if you have ~** je voudrais du thé, si vous en avez; **have you got ~?** est-ce que vous en avez?; **have ~ of you got a car?** est-ce que l'un/-e d'entre vous a une voiture?; **are ~ of them blue?** y en a-t-il des bleus?; **we have very few blue shirts left, if ~** il doit rester très peu de chemises bleues, si toutefois il en reste; **if we have ~, they'll be over there** si nous en avons, ils/elles seront là-bas; **3** (no matter which) n'importe lequel/laquelle; **'which colour would you like?'—'~'** 'quelle couleur veux-tu?'—'n'importe laquelle'; **~ of those pens** n'importe lequel de ces stylos; **~ of them could do it** n'importe qui d'entre eux/elles pourrait le faire.

III *adv* **1** (with comparatives) **there isn't ~ better lawyer in the country** c'est le meilleur avocat du pays; **is he feeling ~ better?** est-ce qu'il se sent mieux?; **have you got ~ more of these?** est-ce que vous en avez d'autres?; **do you want ~ more wine?** voulez-vous encore du vin?; **we can't give you ~ more than £4 an hour** nous ne pouvons pas vous donner plus de 4 livres sterling de l'heure; **I can't paint pictures ~ more than I can write poetry** je ne suis pas plus capable de peindre des tableaux que d'écrire des poèmes; **I don't like him ~ more than you do** je ne l'aime guère plus que toi; **I don't know ~ more than that** c'est tout ce que je sais; **~ more of that and I'm leaving** si ça continue je m'en vais; **~ more stealing and you'll be in big trouble**○ si tu continues à voler tu vas avoir de gros problèmes; **he doesn't live here ~ more** ou **longer** il n'habite plus ici; **I won't put up with it ~ longer** ça ne peut pas continuer ainsi; **if we stay here ~ longer** si nous restons plus longtemps; **can't you walk ~ faster?** tu ne peux pas marcher plus vite?; **if it gets ~ hotter in here I shall have to leave** s'il se met à faire plus chaud il faudra que je sorte; **I can't leave ~ later than 6 o'clock** il faut que je parte à 6 heures au plus tard; **2**○ (at all) du tout; **that doesn't help me ~** ça ne m'aide pas du tout; **it didn't bother him ~** ça ne l'a pas du tout dérangé.

anybody /ˈenɪbɒdɪ/ *pron* **1** (with negative, implied negative) personne; **there wasn't ~ in the house/car** il n'y avait personne dans la maison/voiture; **there's never ~ at home** il n'y a jamais personne chez eux; **without ~ knowing** sans que personne le sache; **I didn't have ~ to talk to** il n'y avait personne avec qui j'aurais pu parler; **I don't like him and nor does ~ else** je ne l'aime pas, d'ailleurs personne ne l'aime; **hardly ~ came** il n'est venu presque personne; **2** (in questions, conditional sentences) quelqu'un; **is there ~ in the house/car?** est-ce qu'il y a quelqu'un dans la maison/voiture?; **did ~ see him?** est-ce que quelqu'un l'a vu?; **if ~ asks, tell them I've gone out** si quelqu'un me cherche, dis que je suis sorti; **if ~ can persuade him, John can** si quelqu'un peut le convaincre, c'est John; **is ~ nice/interesting coming?** y a-t-il quelqu'un de sympa○/d'intéressant qui vient?; **3** (no matter who) **~ could do it** tout le monde pourrait le faire; **~ but him/you/his wife** tout le monde sauf lui/toi/sa femme; **~ who wants to, can go** tous ceux qui le veulent, peuvent y aller; **~ but you would have given it to him** n'importe qui d'autre que toi le lui aurait donné; **~ with any intelligence would realize that** n'importe quelle personne un peu sensée se serait rendu compte que; **~ can make a mistake/break a glass** ça arrive à tout le monde de faire une erreur/casser un verre; **~ would think you were deaf** tout le monde doit croire que tu es sourd; **you can invite ~ (you like)** tu peux inviter qui tu veux; **4** (somebody unimportant) **she's not just ~, she's the boss** ce n'est pas n'importe qui, c'est la patronne; **we can't ask just ~ to do it, we need a skilled mechanic** nous ne pouvons pas demander à n'importe qui de le faire, nous avons besoin d'un vrai mécanicien; **I wouldn't give it to just ~** je ne le/la donnerais pas à n'importe qui; **5** (somebody important) **~ who was ~ was at the party** tous les gens importants étaient à la soirée; **he isn't ~ in this town** ce n'est pas quelqu'un d'important dans cette ville. ▸**guess**.

anyhow /ˈenɪhaʊ/ *adv* **1** (in any case) = **anyway**; **2** (in a careless, untidy way) n'importe comment; **there were clothes scattered around the room ~** il y avait des vêtements éparpillés partout dans la pièce; **they splashed the paint on ~** ils ont repeint n'importe comment.

anyone /ˈenɪwʌn/ *pron* = **anybody**.

anyplace○ /ˈenɪpleɪs/ *adv* US = **anywhere**.

anyroad○ /ˈenɪrəʊd/ *adv* GB dial = **anyway**.

anything /ˈenɪθɪŋ/ *pron* **1** (with negative, implied negative) rien; **she didn't say/do ~** elle n'a rien dit/fait; **they never do ~** ils ne font jamais rien; **he didn't have ~ to do** il n'avait rien à faire; **she doesn't want ~ (too) expensive/cheap** elle ne veut rien de (trop) cher/de bon marché; **there was hardly ~ left** il ne restait presque rien; **don't believe ~ he says** ne crois pas un mot de ce qu'il dit; **2** (in questions, conditional sentences) quelque chose; **is there ~ in the box?** est-ce qu'il y a quelque chose dans le carton?; **have you got ~ in blue/red?** est-ce que vous avez quelque chose en bleu/rouge?; **if ~ happens** ou **should happen to her** si quoi que ce soit lui arrive; **is there ~ to be done?** peut-on faire quelque chose?; **is there ~ in the rumour that...?** est-il vrai que...?; **is there ~ in what he says?** est-ce qu'il y a du vrai dans ce qu'il dit?; **3** (no matter what) tout; **~ is possible** tout est possible; **you can have ~ (you like)** tu peux avoir tout ce que tu veux; **she'll eat ~** elle mange tout or n'importe quoi; **I'd do** ou **give ~ to get that job** je ferais tout pour obtenir cet emploi; **they'd do ~ for you** ils sont toujours prêts à rendre service; **she likes ~ sweet/to do with football** elle aime tout ce qui est sucré/qui a rapport au football; **it could cost ~ between £50 and £100** ça peut coûter de 50 à 100 livres sterling; **he was ~ but happy/intelligent/a liar** il n'était pas du tout heureux/intelligent/menteur; **'was it interesting?'—'~ but!'** 'est-ce que c'était intéressant?'—'tout sauf ça'; **he wasn't annoyed, if ~, he was quite pleased** il n'était pas fâché, au contraire, il était content.
IDIOMS **~ goes** tout est permis; **as easy/funny as ~** facile/drôle comme tout; **to run/laugh/work like ~** courir/rire/travailler comme un fou○; **do you need a towel or ~?** as-tu besoin d'une serviette ou de quelque chose?; **it's not that I don't like you or ~** ce n'est pas que je ne t'aime pas.

anytime /ˈenɪtaɪm/ *adv* (also **any time**) **1** (no matter when) n'importe quand; **~ after 2 pm** n'importe quand à partir de 14 heures; **~ you like** quand tu veux; **if at ~ you feel lonely**... si jamais tu te sens seul...; **at ~ of the day or night** à n'importe quelle heure du jour ou de la nuit; **2** (at any moment) à tout moment; **he could arrive ~ now** il pourrait arriver d'un moment à l'autre.

anyway /ˈenɪweɪ/ *adv* **1** (in any case, besides) de toute façon; **I was planning to do that ~** j'avais l'intention de le faire de toute façon; **I don't want to go, and ~ I have to wait for Debby** je ne veux pas y aller, et de toute façon je dois attendre Debby; **why do you want to know, ~?** pourquoi est-ce que tu veux le savoir, de toute façon?; **who wants to work there, ~?** de toute façon, qui voudrait travailler là?; **2** (nevertheless) quand même; **I don't really like hats, but I'll try it on ~** je n'aime pas vraiment les chapeaux, mais je vais quand même l'essayer; **thanks ~** merci quand même; **3** (at least, at any rate) en tout cas; **we can't go out, not yet ~** nous ne pouvons pas sortir, pas pour l'instant en tout cas; **he doesn't like them, that's what he said ~** il ne les aime pas, c'est ce qu'il a dit en tout cas; **up until recently ~, people were saying that** jusqu'à récemment en tout cas, les gens disaient que; **4** (well: as sentence adverb) **~, we arrived at the station...** bon, nous sommes arrivés à la gare...; **~, I'd better go now, see you later!** bon, il faut que j'y aille, à plus tard!

anywhere /'enɪweə(r), US -hweər/ *adv* **1** (with negative, implied negative) **you can't go ~** tu ne peux aller nulle part; **there isn't ~ to sit/sleep** il n'y a pas de place pour s'asseoir/dormir; **we didn't go ~ special/interesting** nous ne sommes allés nulle part de spécial/d'intéressant; **they didn't go ~ this weekend** ils ne sont allés nulle part ce weekend; **you won't get ~ if you don't pass your exams** fig tu n'arriveras à rien si tu ne réussis pas tes examens; **crying isn't going to get you ~** fig ça ne t'avancera à rien de pleurer; **James came second but I didn't come ~** James est arrivé deuxième mais moi, je ne suis pas entré dans le classement; **2** (in questions, conditional sentences) quelque part; **have you got a radio/a comb ~?** avez-vous une radio/un peigne quelque part? ; **did you go ~ nice?** est-ce que tu es allé dans un endroit agréable?; **we're going to Spain, if ~** si on va quelque part, ce sera en Espagne; **have you seen Andrew ~?** est-ce que tu as vu Andrew quelque part?; **can you think of ~ she might be?** as-tu la moindre idée de l'endroit où elle peut être?; **3** (no matter where) **~ you like** où tu veux; **~ in the world/in England** partout dans le monde/en Angleterre; **~ except** ou **but Bournemouth** partout sauf à Bournemouth; **I'll go ~ where there's sun** j'irai n'importe où du moment qu'il y a du soleil; **~ she goes, he follows her** il la suit partout où elle va; **'where do you want to go?'—'~ exotic/hot'** 'où veux-tu aller?'—'dans un endroit exotique/où il fait chaud'; **~ between 50 and 100 people** entre 50 et 100 personnes.

Anzac /'ænzæk/ *n* **1** (*abrév* = **Australia-New Zealand Army Corps**) *bataillon de soldats australiens et néo-zélandais*; **2** Sport **the ~ team** l'équipe de joueurs australiens et néo-zélandais.

AOB *n* (*abrév* = **any other business**) tour *m* de table (*à la fin d'une réunion*).

AONB *n* GB *abrév* ▶ **Area of Outstanding Natural Beauty**.

aorist /'eərɪst/ *n* aoriste *m*.

aorta /eɪ'ɔ:tə/ *n* (*pl* **-tas, -tae**) aorte *f*.

aortic /eɪ'ɔ:tɪk/ *adj* aortique.

aortic: **~ arch** *n* crosse *f* aortique; **~ valve** *n* valvule *f* aortique.

Aosta /æ'ɒstə/ *n* Aoste.

AP *n*: *abrév* ▶ **Associated Press**.

apace /ə'peɪs/ *adv* littér **1** (quickly) rapidement; **2** (abreast) **to keep ~ with sth** marcher de front avec qch.

Apache /ə'pætʃɪ/ ▶ **1486**, **1402** *n* **1** (person) Apache *mf*; **2** Ling apache *m*.

apart /ə'pɑ:t/

■ **Note** *apart* is used after certain verbs in English (*keep apart, tell apart etc*). For translations consult the appropriate verb entry (***keep***, ***tell*** etc).

I *adj, adv* **1** (at a distance in time or space) **the trees were planted 10 metres ~** les arbres étaient plantés à 10 mètres d'intervalle; **the babies were born 2 weeks ~** les bébés sont nés à 2 semaines d'intervalle; **the houses were far ~** les maisons étaient éloignées les unes des autres; **the two farms were far ~** les deux fermes étaient éloignées l'une de l'autre; **countries as far ~ as China and Spain** des pays aussi éloignés l'un de l'autre que la Chine et l'Espagne; **he stood ~ (from the group)** il se tenait à l'écart (du groupe); **the posts need to be placed further ~** les poteaux doivent être davantage écartés; **2** (separate from each other) séparé; **we hate being ~** (of couple) nous détestons être séparés; **they need to be kept ~** il faut les garder séparés; **3** (leaving aside) à part; **dogs ~, I don't like animals** à part les chiens, je n'aime pas les animaux; **finances ~, we're quite happy** à part les problèmes d'argent, nous sommes heureux; **4** (different) **a race/a world ~** une race/un monde à part; **we are very far ~ on the subject of immigration** nous ne sommes pas du tout d'accord sur la question de l'immigration; **5** (in pieces) **he had the TV ~ on the floor** il avait démonté la télé et elle était en pièces détachées sur le sol.

II apart from *prep phr* **1** (separate from) à l'écart de; **it stands ~ from the other houses** elle est à l'écart des autres maisons; **he lives ~ from his wife** il vit séparé de sa femme; **2** (leaving aside) en dehors de, à part; **~ from Karen/the garden** en dehors de or à part Karen/le jardin; **~ from working in an office, he...** en plus de travailler dans un bureau, il...; **~ from being illegal, it's also dangerous** (mis) à part que c'est illégal, c'est aussi dangereux; **~ from anything else, I don't even like swimming** pour commencer, je n'aime pas la natation.

apartheid /ə'pɑ:theɪt, -aɪt/ *n* apartheid *m*.

apartment /ə'pɑ:tmənt/ **I** *n* (flat) appartement *m*; **executive** ou **luxury ~** appartement *m* de grand standing; **holiday ~** appartement *m* de vacances; **studio ~** studio *m*.

II apartments *npl* (suite of rooms) appartements *mpl*.

apartment: **~ block** *n* immeuble *m*; **~ house** *n* US résidence *f*.

apathetic /,æpə'θetɪk/ *adj* (by nature) amorphe; (from illness, depression) apathique; **to be ~ about sth/towards sb** être indifférent à qch/envers qn.

apathy /'æpəθɪ/ *n* apathie *f*; **there is widespread ~ among schoolchildren** l'apathie est très répandue chez les écoliers.

APB *n* US *abrév* ▶ **all points bulletin**.

ape /eɪp/ **I** *n* **1** Zool grand singe *m*; **female ~** guenon *f*; **2**○ US pej (person) brute *f*.

II *vtr* singer [*speech, behaviour, manners*].

IDIOMS to go ~◑ US (in anger) piquer une crise○; (in enthusiasm) s'emballer.

Apennines /'æpənaɪnz/ *pr npl* **the ~** les Apennins *mpl*.

aperitif /ə'perətɪf, US ə,perə'ti:f/ *n* apéritif *m*.

aperture /'æpətʃʊə(r)/ *n* **1** (in wall, door) ouverture *f*; (small) interstice *m*; **2** (in telescope, camera) ouverture *f*; **wide/narrow ~** Phot grande/petite ouverture *f*.

apeshit● /'eɪpʃɪt/ US **I** *n* connerie● *f*.

II *adj* **to go ~ over sth** s'emballer○ pour qch.

apex /'eɪpeks/ *n* (*pl* **-exes, -ices**) Math, fig sommet *m*.

APEX /'eɪpeks/ *n* (*abrév* = **Advance Purchase Excursion**) APEX *m*.

aphasia /ə'feɪzɪə, US -ʒə/ *n* aphasie *f*.

aphasic /ə'feɪzɪk/ *adj* aphasique.

aphid /'eɪfɪd/ *n* puceron *m*.

aphis /'eɪfɪs/ *n* (*pl* **-ides**) aphidé *m*, aphidien *m*.

aphonia /ə'fəʊnɪə/ *n* aphonie *f*.

aphonic /ə'fɒnɪk/ *adj* [*letter*] aphonique; [*person*] aphone.

aphorism /'æfərɪzəm/ *n* aphorisme *m*.

aphrodisiac /,æfrə'dɪzɪæk/ *n, adj* aphrodisiaque (*m*).

apiarist /'eɪpɪərɪst/ ▶ **1692** *n* apiculteur/-trice *m/f*.

apiary /'eɪpɪərɪ, US -ɪerɪ/ *n* rucher *m*.

apiece /ə'pi:s/ *adv* **1** (for each person) chacun/-e *m/f*; **he gave them an apple ~** il leur a donné une pomme chacun/-e; **2** (each one) **the melons cost one franc ~** les melons coûtent un franc la pièce.

aplenty /ə'plentɪ/ *adv* en profusion.

aplomb /ə'plɒm/ *n* aplomb *m*; **to have the ~ to do** avoir l'aplomb de faire; **with great ~** avec beaucoup d'aplomb.

apocalypse /ə'pɒkəlɪps/ *n* **1** Bible **the Apocalypse** l'Apocalypse *f*; **the four horsemen of the Apocalypse** les quatre cavaliers de l'Apocalypse; **2** (disaster, destruction) apocalypse *f*.

apocalypse watcher *n* pessimiste *mf*.

apocalyptic /ə,pɒkə'lɪptɪk/ *adj* apocalyptique.

apocopate /ə'pɒkəpeɪt/ *vtr* abréger par apocope.

apocopation /ə,pɒkə'peɪʃn/, **apocope** /ə'pɒkəpɪ/ *n* apocope *f*.

Apocrypha /ə'pɒkrɪfə/ *n* (+ *v sg ou pl*) **the ~** les apocryphes *mpl*.

apocryphal /ə'pɒkrɪfl/ *adj* (all contexts) apocryphe.

apogee /'æpədʒi:/ *n* Astron, fig apogée *m*; **to reach its ~** atteindre son apogée.

apolitical /,eɪpə'lɪtɪkl/ *adj* apolitique.

Apollo /ə'pɒləʊ/ *n* **1** Mythol Apollon *m*; fig (beautiful man) apollon *m*; **2** (spaceship) Apollo *m*.

apologetic /ə,pɒlə'dʒetɪk/ *adj* [*gesture, letter, phone call, smile*] d'excuse; **to be ~ about sth** s'excuser de qch; **to be ~ about doing** ou **for having done** s'excuser d'avoir fait; **to look/sound ~** avoir l'air contrit.

apologetically /ə,pɒlə'dʒetɪklɪ/ *adv* [*say*] d'un ton contrit; [*shrug, look at*] d'un air contrit.

apologetics /ə,pɒlə'dʒetɪks/ *n* (+ *v sg*) apologétique *f*.

apologia /,æpə'ləʊdʒɪə/ *n* apologie *f*.

apologist /ə'pɒlədʒɪst/ *n* apologiste *m*; **~ for sth/sb** défenseur de qch/qn.

apologize /ə'pɒlədʒaɪz/ *vi* s'excuser (**to sb** auprès de qn; **for sth** de qch; **for doing** d'avoir fait).

apology /ə'pɒlədʒɪ/ *n* **1** (excuse) excuses *fpl* (**for sth** pour qch; **for doing** pour avoir fait); **to make an ~** s'excuser; **to make/give one's apologies** faire/présenter ses excuses; **to send one's apologies** envoyer ses excuses; **Mrs X sends her apologies** sout Mme X vous prie d'accepter ses excuses sout; **to owe sb an ~** devoir des excuses à qn; **without ~** sans excuse; **I make no ~ for reminding you of John's contribution to the firm** je n'essaie pas de me justifier en vous rappelant la contribution de John à l'entreprise; **to publish an ~** Journ publier des excuses; **2** (poor substitute) **an ~ for sth** un semblant de qch; **3** sout (apologia) apologie *f* (**for** de).

apoplectic /,æpə'plektɪk/ *adj* **1** (furious) [*criticism, prediction*] furibond; **to be ~ (with rage)** être furibond; **2**† Med [*fit, attack*] d'apoplexie; [*patient*] apoplectique.

apoplexy /'æpəpleksɪ/ *n* **1** (rage) accès *m* de rage; **2**† Med apoplexie *f*.

apostasy /ə'pɒstəsɪ/ *n* Relig, fig apostasie *f*; **~ from** abjuration *f* de.

apostate /ə'pɒsteɪt/ **I** *n* apostat/-e *m/f* (**from** de).

II *adj* apostat.

apostatize /ə'pɒstətaɪz/ *vi* apostasier.

a posteriori /,eɪ ,pɒsterɪ'ɔ:raɪ/ *adj* [*reasoning, deduction*] a posteriori.

apostle /ə'pɒsl/ *n* Relig, fig apôtre *m* (**of** de).

Apostles' Creed *n* Symbole *m* des apôtres, Credo *m*.

apostolate /ə'pɒstələt/ *n* apostolat *m*.

apostolic /,æpə'stɒlɪk/ *adj* apostolique; **the ~ succession** le siège apostolique.

apostrophe /ə'pɒstrəfɪ/ *n* Print apostrophe *f*; Literat (address) apostrophe *f* (**to** à).

apostrophize /ə'pɒstrəfaɪz/ *vtr* lancer une apostrophe à.

apothecary‡ /ə'pɒθəkərɪ, US -kerɪ/ *n* apothicaire‡ *m*.

apotheosis /ə,pɒθɪ'əʊsɪs/ *n* (*pl* **-ses**) sout apothéose *f*.

appal GB, **appall** US /ə'pɔ:l/ *vtr* (GB *p prés etc* **-ll-**) (shock) scandaliser; (horrify, dismay) horrifier; **to be ~led at** ou **by** (shocked) être scandalisé par; (horrified) être horrifié par; **to be ~led that** être horrifié par le fait que; **he was ~led to hear that** il a été horrifié d'entendre que.

Appalachian /,æpə'leɪtʃɪən/ *adj* [*climate, wildlife*] appalachien/-ienne; **in the ~ Mountains** dans les Appalaches.

Appalachians /,æpə'leɪtʃɪənz/ *pr npl* **the ~** les Appalaches *fpl*.

appalled /ə'pɔ:ld/ *adj* (horrified, dismayed) horrifié; (shocked) scandalisé.

appalling /ə'pɔ:lɪŋ/ *adj* **1** (shocking) [*crime, conditions, bigotry*] épouvantable; [*injury*] affreux/-euse; **it's ~ that** il est révoltant que (+ *subj*); **it's ~!** c'est un scandale!; **2** (very bad) [*manners, joke, taste*] exécrable; [*noise, weather*] épouvantable; [*stupidity*] incroyable.

appallingly /ə'pɔ:lɪŋlɪ/ *adv* **1** (shockingly) [*behave, treat*] de manière épouvantable; **unemployment figures are ~ high** le taux de chômage a atteint un niveau déplorable; **2** (extremely) **an ~ difficult problem** un problème d'une épouvantable difficulté; **furnished in ~ bad taste** meublé avec un goût exécrable.

apparatchik /,æpə'rɑ:tʃɪk/ *n* (*pl* **-s, -chiki**) apparatchik *m* (also fig).

apparatus /,æpə'reɪtəs, US -'rætəs/ *n* **1** (equipment) ¢ gen équipement *m*; (in lab) instruments *mpl*; (in gym) agrès *mpl*; Phot équipement *m* photographique; **2** (for specific purpose) appareil *m*; **diving/heating ~** appareil de plongée/de chauffage; **critical ~** Literat appareil critique; **3** (organization) machine *f*; **bureaucratic ~** machine du gouvernement.

apparel /ə'pærəl/ *n* ¢ **1** GB‡, US vêtements *mpl*; **2** US **protective ~** vêtements *mpl* de protection; **women's ~** (in department store) vêtements *mpl* de femme.

apparent /ə'pærənt/ *adj* **1** (seeming) [*contradiction, success, willingness*] apparent; **2** (clear) évident; **to become ~ that** devenir évident que; **this is ~ when** ceci devient évident quand; **for no ~ reason** sans raison or cause apparente.

apparently /ə'pærəntlɪ/ *adv* apparemment.

apparition /,æpə'rɪʃn/ *n* (all contexts) apparition *f*.

appeal /ə'pi:l/ **I** *n* **1** (call) appel *m* (**for** à); **an ~ for calm** un appel au calme; **an ~ to sb to do** un appel à qn pour qu'il/qu'elle fasse; **2** (charity event) appel *m* (**for, on behalf of** en faveur de); **an ~ for** un appel au don de [*food, blankets, clothes*]; **to launch an ~** lancer un appel; **3** Sport (to umpire, referee) contestation *f* (**against** contre; **to** auprès de); **4** Jur appel *m*; **to lodge an ~** faire appel; **an ~ to the Supreme Court** un pourvoi en cassation; **5** (attraction) charme *m*; (interest) intérêt *m*; **to have ~/a certain ~** avoir du charme/un certain charme; **to have wide ~** plaire à des gens très différents; **it holds no ~ for me** ça ne m'intéresse pas.

II *vi* **1** Jur faire appel (**against** de); **the right to ~** le droit de faire appel; **to ~ to** recourir à l'arbitrage de [*council, tribunal, individual*]; faire appel à [*high court*]; **2** Sport **to ~ to** demander l'arbitrage de [*umpire, referee*]; **to ~ against** contester [*decision, call*]; **3** (call, request) **to ~ for** lancer un appel à [*order, tolerance*]; **to ~ for witnesses** faire appel à témoins; **to ~ to sb to do** (formal call) prier qn de faire; **to ~ to the public for help** demander de l'aide au public; **to ~ to sb's better nature/sense of honour** faire appel aux bons sentiments/au sens de l'honneur de qn; **4** (attract, interest) **to ~ to sb** [*idea*] tenter qn; [*person*] plaire à qn; [*place*] attirer qn; **does the idea ~?** l'idée te tente?; **Austria doesn't really ~** l'Autriche ne m'attire pas vraiment; **gardening doesn't ~ to me** le jardinage ne me dit rien.

appeal: **~(s) court** *n* cour *f* d'appel; **~ fund** *n* fonds *m* d'aide.

appealing /ə'pi:lɪŋ/ *adj* **1** (attractive) [*child, kitten*] attachant; [*plan, theory*] séduisant; [*modesty, reserve*] charmant; **2** (beseeching) [*look, eyes*] suppliant.

appealingly /ə'pi:lɪŋlɪ/ *adv* de façon attrayante.

appeal(s) judge *n* juge *m* en cour d'appel.

appear /ə'pɪə(r)/ *vi* **1** (become visible) [*person, ship, growth, symptom, ghost*] apparaître; **to ~ to sb in a vision** apparaître à qn dans une vision; **2** (turn up) arriver; **to ~ on the scene** arriver sur place; **to ~ from nowhere** apparaître; **where did she ~ from○?** hum d'où est-ce qu'elle est sortie○?; **3** (seem) **to ~ to be/to do** [*person*] avoir l'air d'être/de faire; **to ~ depressed** avoir l'air déprimé; **to ~ deserted** [*place*] sembler être désert; **to ~ to be crying** avoir l'air de pleurer; **to ~ to have forgotten** avoir l'air d'avoir oublié; **it ~s/~ed that** il semble/semblait que; **it ~s to me that** il me semble que; **there ~s to be, there would ~d to be** on dirait qu'il y a; **so it ~s, so it would ~** à ce qu'il paraît; **his parents, it ~s, were ambitious** il semble que ses parents avaient de l'ambition; **4** Journ, Publg [*book, work, article*] paraître; **5** Cin, Theat, TV (perform) **to ~ on stage** paraître en scène; **to ~ on TV** passer à la télévision; **to ~ as** jouer dans le rôle de; **to be currently ~ing in** jouer en ce moment dans; **6** Jur (be present) comparaître (**before** devant; **for** pour); **to ~ in court** comparaître devant le tribunal; **to ~ as counsel for the defence** plaider pour l'accusé; **to ~ as a witness** comparaître comme témoin; **7** (be written) [*name, score*] paraître (**on** sur; **in** dans).

appearance /ə'pɪərəns/ **I** *n* **1** (arrival) (of person, vehicle) arrivée *f*; (of development, invention, symptom) apparition *f*; **2** Cin, Theat, TV passage *m*; **to make an ~ on television/on stage** passer à la télévision/à la scène; **to make one's first screen ~** faire ses débuts à l'écran; **a rare screen ~ by X** une des rares apparitions à l'écran de X; **cast in order of ~** distribution par ordre d'entrée en scène; **3** (public, sporting) apparition *f*; **to make a public ~** faire une apparition publique; **this is his first ~ for Ireland** il fait ses débuts pour l'équipe d'Irlande; **to put in an ~** faire acte de présence; **4** Jur (in court) comparution *f* (**in, before** devant); **to enter an ~** comparaître en justice; **5** (look) (of person) apparence *f*; (of district, object) aspect *m*; **to check one's ~** vérifier sa tenue; **to be self-conscious about one's ~** être gêné par son aspect physique; **'smart ~ essential'** 'excellente présentation exigée'; **to give sth the ~ of** donner à qch l'apparence de; **to be foreign in ~** avoir l'air étranger; **6** (semblance) **to give the ~ of sth/of doing** donner l'apparence de qch/de faire; **it had all the ~s** ou **every ~ of** cela avait tout l'air de; **to maintain an ~ of objectivity** conserver un semblant d'objectivité; **7** Journ, Publg (of book, article) parution *f*.

II appearances *npl* (external show) apparences *fpl*; **to judge** ou **go by ~s** se fier aux apparences; **going by ~s...** à en juger par les apparences...; **for the sake of ~s, for ~s' sake** pour la forme; **to keep up ~s** sauvegarder les apparences; **to all ~s** apparemment; **contrary to/in spite of ~s** contrairement aux/en dépit des apparences; **~s can be deceptive** les apparences sont souvent trompeuses.

appease /ə'pi:z/ *vtr* apaiser.

appeasement /ə'pi:zmənt/ *n* apaisement *m*; **a policy of ~** une politique de conciliation.

appellant /ə'pelənt/ *n* appelant/-e *m/f*.

appellate /ə'pelət/ *adj* Jur d'appel; **~ court** cour *f* d'appel.

appellation /,æpə'leɪʃn/ *n* sout appellation *f*.

append /ə'pend/ *vtr* sout ajouter (**to** à).

appendage /ə'pendɪdʒ/ *n* appendice *m* also fig.

appendectomy /,æpen'dektəmɪ/, **appendicectomy** /ə,pendɪ'sektəmɪ/ *n* appendicectomie *f*.

appendicitis /ə,pendɪ'saɪtɪs/ **▶1354** *n* appendicite *f*; **acute ~** appendicite aiguë.

appendix /ə'pendɪks/ *n* (*pl* **-ixes, -ices**) **1** Anat appendice *m*; **to have one's ~ removed** se faire opérer de l'appendicite; **2** (to printed volume) appendice *m*; (to book, report) annexe *f*.

Appenzell **▶1776** *pr n* **the canton of ~** le canton d'Appenzell, l'Appenzell *m*.

appertain /,æpə'teɪn/ *vi* sout **to ~ to sth** (belong) appartenir à qch; (relate) se rapporter à qch.

appetite /'æpɪtaɪt/ *n* **1** (desire to eat) appétit *m*; **he has a good/poor ~** il a bon appétit/il n'a pas d'appétit; **the walk has given me an ~** la promenade m'a donné de l'appétit; **to work up an ~** se donner de l'appétit; **it'll spoil** ou **take away your ~** ça va te couper l'appétit; **2** (strong desire) appétit *m* (**for** de); **these books will whet your ~ for travel** ces livres vous donneront envie de voyager.

appetite suppressant *n* coupe-faim *m inv*.

appetizer /'æpɪtaɪzə(r)/ *n* (drink) apéritif *m*; (biscuit, olive etc) amuse-gueule *m inv*; (starter) hors-d'œuvre *m*.

appetizing /'æpɪtaɪzɪŋ/ *adj* appétissant.

Appian Way /,æpɪən 'weɪ/ *pr n* voie *f* Appienne.

applaud /ə'plɔ:d/ **I** *vtr* **1** (clap) applaudir [*play, performance*]; **2** (approve of) applaudir à [*choice, tactics, initiative*]; applaudir [*person*].

II *vi* applaudir.

applause /ə'plɔ:z/ *n* ¢ applaudissements *mpl*; **there was a ripple/burst of ~** les applaudissements crépitaient/ont éclaté; **he came on to loud/rapturous ~** il a été bruyamment/vivement applaudi.

apple /'æpl/ **I** *n* pomme *f*; **the (Big) Apple** New York.

II *modif* [*juice, peel, pip, skin*] de pomme; [*brandy, puree*] de pommes; [*fritter, tart, turnover*] aux pommes.

IDIOMS **he is the ~ of her eye** c'est la prunelle de ses yeux; **there's a bad ~ in every bunch** ou **in every barrel** il y a toujours une brebis galeuse; **to upset the ~ cart○** tout ficher par terre○.

apple: **~ blossom** *n* fleurs *fpl* de pommier; **~ brandy** *n* eau-de-vie *f* de pommes, ≈ calvados *m*; **~core** *n* trognon *m* de pomme; **~ green** **▶1104** *n* vert pomme *m inv*; **~jack** *n* US eau-de-vie *f* de pommes (*faite à partir du cidre*); **~ orchard** *n* pommeraie *f*, verger *m* de pommiers.

apple pie *n* Culin tourte *f* aux pommes.

IDIOMS **everything is in ~ order** tout est dans un ordre parfait.

apple pie bed *n* lit *m* en portefeuille.

apple polish○ US *vtr* **to ~ sb** passer la brosse à reluire à qn.

apples and pears○ *n* GB escalier *m*.

apple sauce *n* **1** Culin compote *f* de pommes; **2○** US bobards○ *mpl*.

apple tree *n* pommier *m*.

appliance /ə'plaɪəns/ *n* appareil *m*; **electrical ~** appareil électrique; **household ~** appareil électroménager.

applicability /,æplɪkə'bɪlətɪ, ə,plɪ-/ *n* validité *f* d'application (**to** à).

applicable /'æplɪkəbl, ə'plɪkəbl/ *adj* [*argument, excuse*] valable; [*law, rule, requirement*] en vigueur; **discounts where ~ are shown on the bill** les rabais éventuels figurent sur la note; **if ~** le cas échéant; **to be ~ to** s'appliquer à, concerner.

applicant /ˈæplɪkənt/ **I** *n* **1** (for job, place) candidat/-e *m/f* (**for** à); **job ~** candidat/-e *m/f*; **2** (for passport, benefit, grant, loan, visa, asylum) demandeur/-euse *m/f* (**for** de); (for citizenship) postulant/-e *m/f* (**for** à); **3** (for licence, franchise) solliciteur/-euse *m/f*; **4** (for membership) candidat/-e *m/f*; **~ for membership of** candidat à l'adhésion à; **5** (for shares) souscripteur/-trice *m/f*; **share ~** souscripteur/-trice d'actions; **6** Insur proposant/-e *m/f*; **7** Jur (for divorce, patent, bankruptcy, order) demandeur/-euse *m/f*, requérant/-e *m/f*.
II *modif* [*company, state*] demandeur/-euse (*after n*).

application /ˌæplɪˈkeɪʃn/ **I** *n* **1** (request) (for job) candidature *f* (**for** à); (for membership, admission, passport, loan, promotion, transfer) demande *f* (**for** de); (for shares) souscription *f* (**for** de); **to make an ~ for a job** ou **a job ~** poser sa candidature à un poste; **to make an ~ for a university place** faire une demande d'inscription à une université; **university ~** dossier *m* d'inscription; **a letter of ~** une lettre de candidature; **to fill out a job/passport ~** remplir un formulaire de candidature/de demande de passeport; **on ~** sur demande; **2** (spreading) application *f* (**to** à); **one ~ is sufficient** une (seule) couche suffit; **for external ~ only** réservé à l'usage externe; **3** (positioning) (of sticker) apposition *f*; (of decorations) disposition *f*; (of beads, sequins) application *f*; **4** (implementation) (of law, penalty, rule) application *f*; (of logic, theory, training) application *f*; **to put one's training into ~** mettre sa formation en pratique; **5** (use) application *f*; **to have military ~s** avoir des applications militaires; **the ~ of computers to** l'application de l'ordinateur à; **6** Comput application *f*; **7** Jur (for divorce, patent, bankruptcy, order) demande *f* (**for** de).
II *modif* (also **~s**) Comput [*package, program, programmer, software*] d'application.

application form *n* (for loan, credit card, passport) formulaire *m* de demande; (for job) formulaire *m* de candidature; (for membership, admission) demande *f* d'inscription.

applicator /ˈæplɪkeɪtə(r)/ *n* applicateur *m*.

applied /əˈplaɪd/ *adj* [*linguistics, maths, science*] appliqué.

applied psychology *n* psychotechnique *f*.

appliqué /æˈpliːkeɪ, US ˌæplɪˈkeɪ/ **I** *n* application *f*.
II *modif* [*motif, decoration*] en application.
III *vtr* appliquer [*motif*] (**on** sur); **to ~ a cushion** orner un coussin d'applications.

apply /əˈplaɪ/ **I** *vtr* **1** (spread) appliquer [*glue, make-up, paint*] (**to** sur); **2** (use) appliquer [*logic, theory, rule, standard, method, penalty, technology, heat*] (**to** à); exercer [*friction, pressure*] (**to** sur); **to ~ the (foot) brake** freiner; **to ~ the handbrake** serrer le frein à main; **3** (give) appliquer [*label, term*] (**to** à); **4** (affix) apposer [*sticker*] (**to** sur); disposer [*decoration*] (**to** sur); appliquer [*bandage, sequins*] (**to** sur).
II *vi* **1** (request) faire une demande; **to ~ for** demander [*divorce, citizenship, custody, maintenance*]; faire une demande de [*passport, loan, grant, patent, visa*]; **to ~ for shares** faire une demande (de souscription) d'actions; **to ~ to do** demander à faire; **to ~ to be transferred** demander une mutation; **2** (seek work) poser sa candidature; **to ~ for** poser sa candidature à [*job*]; **to ~ for the job of** poser sa candidature au poste de; **'~ in writing to'** 'envoyez votre candidature par lettre manuscrite à'; **'~ within'** 'adressez-vous à l'intérieur'; **3** (seek entry) (to college) faire une demande d'inscription (**to** à); (to club, society) faire une demande d'adhésion (**to** à); **to ~ for a place on a course** faire une demande d'inscription à un cours; **to ~ to join** demander à entrer dans [*army, group*]; **to ~ to become a member of** faire une demande d'adhésion à; **4** (be valid) [*definition, term*] s'appliquer (**to** à); [*ban, rule, penalty*] être en vigueur; **to ~ to** s'appliquer à; **the ban ceases to ~ from March** l'interdiction ne sera plus en vigueur à partir du mois de mars; **and that applies to you all** et ça vaut pour or s'applique à tout le monde; **5** (contact) **to ~ to** s'adresser à; **~ to the Embassy** adressez-vous à l'Ambassade.
III *v refl* **to ~ oneself** s'appliquer (**to** à; **to doing** à faire).

appoggiatura /əˌpɒdʒəˈtʊərə/ *n* appogiature *f*.

appoint /əˈpɔɪnt/ **I** *vtr* **1** (name) nommer [*person*] (**to sth** à qch; **to do** pour faire; **as** comme); fixer [*date, place*]; **he has been ~ed director** il a été nommé directeur; **newly ~ed** récemment nommé; **2** (equip) aménager [*accommodation*]; **well ~ed** bien aménagé.
II appointed *pp adj* [*time, place*] fixé.

appointee /əpɔɪnˈtiː/ *n* **1** gen candidat/-e *m/f* retenu/-e; **2** Jur bénéficiaire *mf*.

appointive /əˈpɔɪntɪv/ *adj* [*job, post*] obtenu par nomination; [*system*] pourvu par nomination.

appointment /əˈpɔɪntmənt/ *n* **1** (meeting, consultation) rendez-vous *m* (**at** chez; **with** avec; **to do** pour faire); **business ~** rendez-vous *m* d'affaires; **by ~** sur rendez-vous; **to have an ~** avoir un rendez-vous; **to make an ~** prendre rendez-vous; **to break/cancel an ~** ne pas venir à/annuler un rendez-vous; **please write/phone for an ~** veuillez écrire/téléphoner pour prendre rendez-vous; **2** Admin, Pol (nomination) nomination *f* (**as** comme; **to sth** à qch; **to do** pour faire); **'by ~ to her Majesty'** Comm 'fournisseur de Sa Majesté'; **to take up an ~ (as sth)** prendre ses fonctions (comme qch); **3** (job) poste *m* (**as** de; **of** de); **'Appointments'** (in paper) 'Offres d'emploi'.

apportion /əˈpɔːʃn/ *vtr* répartir [*blame, money, cost*] (**among** parmi; **between** entre).

apportionment /əˈpɔːʃənmənt/ *n* (dividing up) répartition *f*; US Pol (in House of Representatives), répartition *f* des sièges; US Pol (of tax revenue) répartition *f*.

apposite /ˈæpəzɪt/ *adj* sout pertinent.

appositely /ˈæpəzɪtlɪ/ *adv* sout pertinemment.

apposition /ˌæpəˈzɪʃn/ *n* apposition *f*; **in ~ to** en apposition à.

appraisal /əˈpreɪzl/ *n* évaluation *f*; **to make an ~ of sth** (estimation) évaluer qch; **to give an ~ of sth** (statement of value) donner une évaluation de qch; **job ~** entretien *m* de carrière.

appraise /əˈpreɪz/ *vtr* **1** (examine critically) juger [*painting, information, appearance*]; **2** (evaluate) estimer [*value*]; évaluer [*job performance*].

appreciable /əˈpriːʃəbl/ *adj* [*time, change, quantity*] appréciable; [*difference, reduction*] sensible.

appreciably /əˈpriːʃəblɪ/ *adv* sensiblement.

appreciate /əˈpriːʃɪeɪt/ **I** *vtr* **1** (be grateful for) être sensible à [*honour, favour*]; être reconnaissant de [*kindness, sympathy*]; apprécier [*help, comfort, effort, pleasure*]; **I'd ~ it if you could reply soon** je vous serais reconnaissant de répondre sans tarder; **an early reply would be ~d** nous vous serions reconnaissants de répondre sans tarder; **I ~ being consulted** j'aime bien qu'on me consulte; **2** (realize) se rendre (bien) compte de, être conscient de; **to ~ that** se rendre bien compte que; **I ~ (the fact) that** je me rends bien compte que; **yes, I can ~ that** oui, je m'en rends bien compte; **as you will ~** comme vous vous en rendrez bien compte; **you don't ~ how hard he has worked** vous ne mesurez pas à sa juste valeur à quel point il a travaillé dur; **to ~ sth at its true value** apprécier qch à sa juste valeur; **3** (enjoy) apprécier [*music, art, good food*].
II *vi* Fin [*object, valuables*] prendre de la valeur; [*value*] monter.

appreciation /əˌpriːʃɪˈeɪʃn/ *n* **1** (gratitude) remerciement *m* (**for** pour); **in ~ of sth** en remerciement de qch; **as a mark of ~** en guise de remerciement; **a letter of ~** une lettre de remerciements; **to show one's ~** manifester sa gratitude; **2** (awareness) compréhension *f* (**of** de); **to have some/no ~ of** mesurer/ne pas mesurer [*extent, difficulty, importance*]; **3** (enjoyment) appréciation *f* (**of** de); **ladies and gentlemen, please show your ~** mesdames, messieurs, applaudissez s'il vous plait; **4** Literat, Sch (commentary) commentaire *m*; **art ~** analyse *f* artistique; **literary ~** commentaire *m* littéraire; **5** Fin hausse *f* (**of, in** de); **~ in value** valorisation *f*.

appreciative /əˈpriːʃətɪv/ *adj* **1** (grateful) reconnaissant (**of** de); **2** (admiring) admiratif/-ive; **3** (aware) sensible (**of** à).

appreciatively /əˈpriːʃətɪvlɪ/ *adv* **1** (admiringly) admirativement; **2** (gratefully) avec reconnaissance.

apprehend /ˌæprɪˈhend/ *vtr* **1** Jur (arrest) appréhender; **2** sout (fear) appréhender; **3** sout (comprehend) saisir [*complexity, meaning*].

apprehension /ˌæprɪˈhenʃn/ *n* **1** (fear) (of sth specific) crainte *f*; (vague) inquiétude *f*; **~ about sth** inquiétude au sujet de qch; **his ~ of being seized by the police** sa crainte d'être arrêté par la police; **2** Jur (arrest) arrestation *f*.

apprehensive /ˌæprɪˈhensɪv/ *adj* [*glance, person*] craintif/-ive; **to be deeply/slightly ~** être très/légèrement inquiet/-iète; **to feel ~ about sth** (fearful) appréhender qch; (worried) avoir des inquiétudes au sujet de qch; **to be ~ about doing sth** appréhender de faire qch; **they were ~ of an enemy attack** ils craignaient une attaque ennemie; **they are ~ that he will betray them** ils craignent qu'il ne les trahisse.

apprehensively /ˌæprɪˈhensɪvlɪ/ *adv* [*wait, watch, glance*] avec appréhension.

apprentice /əˈprentɪs/ **I** *n* **1** apprenti/-e *m/f* (also fig); **to be an ~ to sb** être l'apprenti de qn; **to train as an ~ with sb** faire son apprentissage chez qn; **to work as an ~ with sb** être apprenti chez qn; **to work as an ~ for three years** faire trois ans d'apprentissage; **electrician's ~** apprenti/-e *m/f* électricien/-ienne.
II *modif* (trainee) [*baker, mechanic*] apprenti/-e (*before n*).
III *vtr* **to be ~d to sb** être en apprentissage chez qn.

apprenticeship /əˈprentɪsʃɪp/ *n* apprentissage *m* (also fig); **to serve/complete one's ~** faire/compléter son apprentissage; **to take an ~ with a firm** entrer en apprentissage dans une maison.

apprise /əˈpraɪz/ *vtr* sout **to ~ sb of sth** instruire qn de qch fml.

appro○ /ˈæprəʊ/ *n* GB Comm (*abrév* = **approval**) **on ~** à l'essai.

approach /əˈprəʊtʃ/ **I** *n* **1** (route of access) (to town, island) voie *f* d'accès; Mil approche *f*; **all the ~es to the city have been sealed off** toutes les voies d'accès de la ville ont été bouclées; **the ~ to the house** le chemin or l'allée qui mène à la maison; **2** (advance) (of person) approche *f*, arrivée *f*; (of season, old age) approche *f*; **3** (way of dealing) approche *f*; **an ~ to doing** une façon de faire; **an original ~ to the problem** une façon originale d'aborder le problème; **a new ~ to child psychology** une nouvelle façon d'aborder la psychologie de l'enfant, une nouvelle approche de la psychologie de l'enfant; **we need to try a different ~** nous devons essayer une méthode différente; **I don't care for their ~** je n'aime pas leur façon de s'y prendre; **she is very Freudian in her ~** elle a une optique très freu-

dienne; **4** (overture) démarche *f*; (proposal to buy etc) proposition *f*; **to make ~es to sb** gen, Comm faire des démarches auprès de qn; **5** (approximation) **this was the nearest ~ to a solution/a cease-fire** c'était ce qui ressemblait le plus à une solution/un cessez-le-feu; **6** Aviat = **approach path**.
II *vtr* **1** (draw near to) s'approcher de [*person, place*]; (verge on) approcher de; **it was ~ing dawn** l'aube approchait; **it was ~ing midnight** il était presque minuit; **he is ~ing sixty** il approche (de) la soixantaine; **a woman ~ing middle age/retirement** une femme approchant de la cinquantaine/de la retraite; **gales ~ing speeds of 200 km per hour** des vents qui atteignaient presque les 200 km à l'heure; **he looked at her with something ~ing admiration** il la regardait presque avec admiration; **a profit of something ~ing five million dollars** un bénéfice de près de cinq millions de dollars; **2** (deal with) aborder [*problem, topic, subject*]; **3** (make overtures to) s'adresser à [*person*]; (more formally) faire des démarches auprès de [*person, company*]; (with offer of job, remuneration) solliciter (**about** au sujet de); **she was ~ed by a man in the street** elle a été abordée par un homme dans la rue; **the company has been ~ed by several buyers** la compagnie a été contactée par plusieurs acheteurs, plusieurs acheteurs ont fait des démarches auprès de la compagnie; **he has been ~ed by several publishers** il a reçu des propositions de plusieurs maisons d'édition.
III *vi* [*person, animal, car*] (s')approcher; [*event, season, date*] approcher; **the time is fast ~ing when...** le moment est imminent où...

approachable /ə'prəʊtʃəbl/ *adj* [*person*] abordable, d'un abord facile; [*place*] accessible.

approach: **~ lights** *npl* Aviat balises *fpl*, balisage *m*; **~ path** *n* Aviat axe *m* d'approche; **~ road** *n* bretelle *f*, route *f* d'accès; **~ shot** *n* (in golf) (coup *m* d')approche *f*; **~ stage** *n* Aviat phase *f* d'approche.

approbation /ˌæprə'beɪʃn/ *n* sout approbation *f*; **with the ~ of** avec l'approbation de.

appropriate I /ə'prəʊprɪət/ *adj* **1** (suitable for occasion, situation) [*attitude, behaviour, choice, place, time, treatment*] approprié (**for** pour); [*dress, gift, style*] qui convient (*after n*) (**for** à); [*punishment*] juste (**for** à); [*remark*] de circonstance (*after n*); **~ to** approprié à [*needs, situation, circumstances*]; **it is ~ that sb should do** il est normal que qn fasse; **'delete as ~'** 'rayer la mention inutile or les mentions inutiles'; **2** (apt) [*name, date*] bien choisi; **he's chosen a most ~ name for his dog** le nom de son chien est très bien choisi; **3** (relevant) [*authority, department*] compétent.
II /ə'prəʊprɪeɪt/ *vtr* **1** (for own use) gen s'approprier; Jur affecter [*land*] (**for** à); **2** US Econ affecter [*funds*] (**for** à).

appropriately /ə'prəʊprɪətlɪ/ *adv* **1** (suitably for occasion) [*behave, dress, speak*] avec à-propos; [*dress*] convenablement; **2** (aptly) [*designed, chosen, sited*] judicieusement.

appropriateness /ə'prəʊprɪətnɪs/ *n* (of dress, behaviour) convenance *f*; (of choice, decision, occasion, remark) à-propos *m*.

appropriation /əˌprəʊprɪ'eɪʃn/ *n* **1** Jur (removal) appropriation *f*; (seized item) crédit *m*; **2** US Econ affectation *f* (**for** à).

approval /ə'pru:vl/ *n* **1** (favourable opinion) approbation *f* (**of** de); **to win sb's ~** gagner l'approbation de qn; **she nodded/smiled her ~** elle a montré son approbation d'un signe de la tête/d'un sourire; **2** Admin (authorization) gen approbation *f* (**to do** pour faire); (for institution, professional) agrément *m*; **subject to sb's ~** soumis à l'approbation de qn; **to give (one's) ~ to** donner son approbation à [*plan, scheme, reform*]; **to get/send sth on ~** recevoir/envoyer qch à l'essai; **3** Admin (certificate of authorization) **C** approbation *f*; **drug/pesticide/product ~** approbation d'un médicament/d'un pesticide/d'un produit.

approvals procedure *n* procédure *f* d'approbation.

approve /ə'pru:v/ **I** *vtr* (authorize) approuver [*product, plan, statement, list, decision*] (**for sth** pour qch); accepter [*person*]; **the motion was ~d by 20 to 3** la motion a été approuvée par 20 contre 3.
II *vi* (be in favour of) **to ~ of sth/sb** apprécier qch/qn; (**not**) **to ~ of sb doing sth** (ne pas) apprécier que qn fasse qch; **he doesn't ~ of drinking/smoking** il est contre l'alcool/le tabac.

approved school† *n* GB Soc Admin centre *m* de redressement.

approving /ə'pru:vɪŋ/ *adj* approbateur/-trice.

approvingly /ə'pru:vɪŋlɪ/ *adv* [*look, smile*] d'un air approbateur; [*speak, write*] d'un ton approbateur.

approx *abrév écrite* ▶ **approximately**.

approximate I /ə'prɒksɪmət/ *adj* [*date, idea, method*] approximatif/-ive; **~ to** proche de; **~ time of arrival, ATA** heure approximative d'arrivée.
II /ə'prɒksɪmeɪt/ *vtr* **1** (come close to) se rapprocher de [*frequency, profits, size*]; **2** (resemble) ressembler à [*idea, objective*].
III /ə'prɒksɪmeɪt/ *vi* **to ~ to** (in quantity, size etc) se rapprocher de; (in nature, quality etc) ressembler à.

approximately /ə'prɒksɪmətlɪ/ *adv* **1** (about) environ; **it holds ~ 10 litres** ou **10 litres ~** il contient environ 10 litres; **at ~ four o'clock** vers quatre heures; **2** [*equal, true, correct etc*] à peu près.

approximation /əˌprɒksɪ'meɪʃn/ *n* **1** approximation *f*; **a rough ~** une approximation grossière; **the nearest ~ to it is** ce qui s'en rapproche le plus, c'est; **2** (figure, calculation) approximation *f* (**of** de).

appurtenances /ə'pɜ:tɪnənsɪz/ *npl* **1** (trappings) sout accessoires *mpl* (**of** de); Jur (of house) appartenances *fpl* et dépendances *fpl*; **2** Jur (rights, responsibilities) droits *mpl*, privilèges *mpl* et servitudes *fpl* (**of** de).

Apr *abrév écrite* = **April**.

APR *n*: *abrév* ▶ **annualized percentage rate**.

après-ski /ˌæpreɪ'ski:/ **I** *n* détente *f* après le ski.
II *adj* [*activities*] après le ski; [*clothes*] que l'on porte après le ski.

apricot /'eɪprɪkɒt/ ▶ **1104** **I** *n* **1** (fruit) abricot *m*; **2** (tree) abricotier *m*; **3** (colour) couleur *f* abricot *inv*.
II *modif* **1** [*skin, stone*] d'abricot; [*brandy, jam*] d'abricots; [*sauce, yoghurt*] aux abricots; **2** [*blossom, wood*] d'abricotier.
III *adj* (colour) abricot *inv*.

April /'eɪprɪl/ ▶ **1472** *n* avril *m*.

April Fool /ˌeɪprɪl 'fu:l/ *n* (person) victime *f* d'un poisson d'avril; **~!** poisson d'avril!

April: **~ Fools' Day** *n* le premier avril; **~ Fools' trick** *n* poisson *m* d'avril; **~ showers** *npl* ≈ giboulées *fpl* de mars.

a priori /ˌeɪ praɪ'ɔ:raɪ/ *adj* [*reasoning, argument*] à priori; [*acceptance*] inconditionnel/-elle; **an ~ assumption** un a priori.

apron /'eɪprən/ *n* **1** (garment) tablier *m*; **butcher's ~** tablier *m* de boucher; **lead ~** tablier *m* de plomb; **2** (for vehicles, planes) aire *f* de stationnement; **3** (on machinery) tablier *m*.
IDIOMS **to be tied to sb's ~ strings** être pendu aux basques de qn.

apron stage *n* proscenium *m*.

apropos /ˌæprə'pəʊ/ **I** *adj* [*remark*] opportun.
II *adv* à propos (**of** de).

apse /æps/ *n* abside *f*.

apt[1] /æpt/ *adj* **1** (suitable) [*choice, description, comparison*] heureux/-euse; [*title, style, comment*] approprié (**to, for** à); **2** (inclined) **to be ~ to do** être enclin à faire; **this is ~ to happen** cela a tendance à se produire; **3** (clever) doué (**at doing** pour faire).

apt[2] *abrév écrite* = **apartment**.

aptitude /'æptɪtju:d, US -tu:d/ *n* aptitude *f*; **he has no ~ for this work** il n'a aucune aptitude pour ce travail; **to have an ~ for maths** être doué pour les maths.

aptitude test *n* test *m* d'aptitude.

aptly /'æptlɪ/ *adv* [*named, described*] avec justesse; [*chosen*] bien.

aptness /'æptnɪs/ *n* justesse *f*.

Apulia /ə'pju:lɪə/ *pr n* Pouilles *fpl*; **in ~** dans les Pouilles.

aquaculture /'ækwəkʌltʃə(r)/ *n* aquaculture *f*.

aqualung /'ækwəlʌŋ/ *n* scaphandre *m* autonome.

aquamarine /ˌækwəmə'ri:n/ ▶ **1104** **I** *n* (gem) aigue-marine *f*; (colour) bleu-vert *m inv*.
II *adj* bleu-vert *inv*.

aquanaut /'ækwənɔ:t/ *n* aquanaute *mf*.

aquaplane /'ækwəpleɪn/ **I** *n* aquaplane *m*.
II *vi* Sport faire de l'aquaplane; Aut GB faire de l'aquaplanage.

Aquarian /ə'kweərɪən/ ▶ **1916** **I** *n* [*person*] Verseau *m*.
II *adj* [*nature, characteristics*] (du) Verseau.

aquarium /ə'kweərɪəm/ *n* (*pl* **-iums, -ia**) aquarium *m*; **fresh-water/marine ~** aquarium *m* d'eau douce/d'eau de mer.

Aquarius /ə'kweərɪəs/ ▶ **1916** *n* Verseau *m*.

aquarobics /ˌækwə'rɒbɪks/ ▶ **1282** *n* (+ *v sg*) aquagym *f*.

aquatic /ə'kwætɪk/ *adj* [*plant, environment*] aquatique; [*sport*] nautique.

aquatint /'ækwətɪnt/ *n* aquatinte *f*.

aqueduct /'ækwɪdʌkt/ *n* aqueduc *m*.

aqueous /'eɪkwɪəs/ *adj* also Miner aqueux/-euse; **~ humour**‡ humeur *f* aqueuse.

aquiline /'ækwɪlaɪn/ *adj* [*nose, features*] aquilin.

Aquinas /ə'kwaɪnəs/ *pr n* St Thomas d'Aquin.

Aquitaine /ˌækwɪ'teɪn/ ▶ **1273** *pr n* Aquitaine *f*; **in/to ~** en Aquitaine.

AR *abrév écrite* = **Arkansas**.

Arab /'ærəb/ ▶ **1486** **I** *n* **1** [*person*] Arabe *mf*; **2** Equit cheval *m* arabe; (mare) jument *f* arabe.
II *adj* **1** [*country, customs, people*] arabe; **the ~ world** le monde arabe; **2** Equit [*sire, blood*] arabe.

arabesque /ˌærə'besk/ *n* arabesque *f*.

Arabia /ə'reɪbɪə/ *pr n* Arabie *f*.

Arabian /ə'reɪbɪən/ *adj* [*desert, landscape*] d'Arabie; **the ~ Sea** la mer d'Arabie; **the ~ Nights** les Mille et Une Nuits.

Arabic /'ærəbɪk/ ▶ **1402** **I** *n* arabe *m*; **classical/modern ~** arabe *m* classique/moderne.
II *adj* [*dialect, numerals, script*] arabe.

Arab-Israeli /ˌærəbɪz'reɪlɪ/ *adj* israélo-arabe.

Arabist /'ærəbɪst/ *n* arabisant/-e *m/f*.

arabization /ˌærəbaɪ'zeɪʃn/ *n* arabisation *f*.

arabize /'ærəbaɪz/ *vtr* arabiser.

arable /'ærəbl/ *adj* [*crop, land, sector*] arable; **~ farmer** agriculteur/-trice *m/f*; **~ farming** agriculture *f*.

Arab League *n* Ligue *f* arabe.

Araby /'ærəbɪ/ *pr n* littér Arabie *f*.

arachnid /ə'ræknɪd/ *n* arachnide *m*.

Aramaic /ˌærə'meɪɪk/ ▶ **1402** *n* araméen *m*.

Aran /'ærən/ ▶ **1381** *pr n* **the ~ Islands** les îles *fpl* Aran; **on the ~ Islands** dans les îles Aran.

Aran: **~ sweater** *n* pull *m* irlandais; **~ wool** *n* ≈ laine *f* de pays.

arbiter /'ɑ:bɪtə(r)/ *n* (spokesperson, mediator) arbitre *m*; **an ~ of taste** un arbitre du bon goût; **~s of fashion** arbitres de la mode.

arbitrarily /ˈɑːbɪtrərəlɪ, US ˈɑːrbɪtrerəlɪ/ *adv* arbitrairement.

arbitrary /ˈɑːbɪtrərɪ, US ˈɑːrbɪtrerɪ/ *adj* arbitraire; **the conclusions are extremely ~** les conclusions sont des plus arbitraires.

arbitrate /ˈɑːbɪtreɪt/ **I** *vtr* arbitrer [*dispute, wages claim*].
II *vi* arbitrer (**between** entre); **the committee ~s in such matters** c'est le comité qui joue le rôle d'arbitre pour ces questions.

arbitration /ˌɑːbɪˈtreɪʃn/ *n* arbitrage *m*; **to refer a case to ~** soumettre une affaire à l'arbitrage; **to go to ~** ≈ aller aux prud'hommes.

arbitration: **~ award** *n* sentence *f* arbitrale; **~ tribunal** *n* GB cf conseil *m* de prud'hommes.

arbitrator /ˈɑːbɪtreɪtə(r)/ *n* (mediator) médiateur/-trice *m/f* (**between** entre); (in industrial disputes) arbitre *m*; **industrial ~** (conseiller/-ère *m/f*) prud'homme *m*.

arbor *n* US = **arbour**.

Arbor Day /ˈɑːbə(r)/ *n* US Journée *f* de l'arbre.

arboreal /ɑːˈbɔːrɪəl/ *adj* arboricole.

arboretum /ˌɑːbəˈriːtəm/ *n* (*pl* **-tums, -ta**) arboretum *m*.

arboriculture /ˈɑːbərɪkʌltʃə(r)/ *n* arboriculture *f*.

arboriculturist /ˌɑːbərɪˈkʌltʃərɪst/ **▶ 1692** *n* arboriculteur *m*.

arbour GB, **arbor** US /ˈɑːbə(r)/ *n* charmille *f*.

arbutus /ɑːˈbjuːtəs/ *n* arbousier *m*.

arc /ɑːk/ **I** *n* gen, Geom arc *m*; Elec arc *m* (électrique).
II *vi* gen décrire un arc; Elec faire jaillir un arc.

ARC *n*: *abrév* ▶ **Aids-related complex**.

arcade /ɑːˈkeɪd/ *n* arcade *f*; **shopping ~** galerie *f* marchande.

Arcadia /ɑːˈkeɪdɪə/ *pr n* Geog, littér Arcadie *f*.

Arcadian /ɑːˈkeɪdɪən/ Geog, littér **I** *n* Arcadien/-ienne *m/f*.
II *adj* arcadien/-ienne.

Arcady /ˈɑːkədɪ/ *pr n* = **Arcadia**.

arcane /ɑːˈkeɪn/ *adj* **1** (incomprehensible) impénétrable; **2** (mysterious) obscur.

arch /ɑːtʃ/ **I** *n* **1** Archit (dome) voûte *f*; (archway) arche *f*; (for bridge) arche *f*; (triumphal) arc *m*; **2** Anat (of foot) voûte *f* plantaire; (of eyebrows) arc *m*; **to have fallen ~es** avoir un affaissement de la voûte plantaire.
II *adj* **1** (mischievous) [*look, manner*] malicieux/-ieuse; **2** péj (superior) [*person, voice, remark*] condescendant.
III *vtr* arquer; **to ~ one's back** [*person*] cambrer le dos; [*cat*] faire le dos rond.
IV *vi* [*branch, rainbow*] former une voûte.
V arch+ (*dans composés*) par excellence; **~-enemy** ennemi/-e *m/f* juré/-e; **~-rival** grand rival.

archaeological GB, **archeological** US /ˌɑːkɪəˈlɒdʒɪkl/ *adj* archéologique.

archaeologist GB **archeologist** US /ˌɑːkɪˈɒlədʒɪst/ **▶ 1692** *n* archéologue *mf*.

archaeology GB, **archeology** US /ˌɑːkɪˈɒlədʒɪ/ *n* archéologie *f*.

archaic /ɑːˈkeɪɪk/ *adj* archaïque.

archaism /ˈɑːkeɪɪzəm/ *n* archaïsme *m*.

archangel /ˈɑːkeɪndʒl/ *n* archange *m*.

archbishop /ˌɑːtʃˈbɪʃəp/ *n* archevêque *m*.

archbishopric /ˌɑːtʃˈbɪʃəprɪk/ *n* archevêché *m*.

archdeacon /ˌɑːtʃˈdiːkən/ *n* archidiacre *m*.

archdiocese /ˌɑːtʃˈdaɪəsɪs/ *n* archidiocèse *m*.

archduchess /ˌɑːtʃˈdʌtʃɪs/ *n* archiduchesse *f*.

archduke /ˌɑːtʃˈdjuːk, US -ˈduːk/ *n* archiduc *m*.

arched /ˈɑːtʃd/ *adj* gen voûté; [*eyebrows*] arqué.

archeology *n* = **archaeology**.

archer /ˈɑːtʃə(r)/ *n* Mil, Hist, Sport archer *m*; **the Archer** Astrol le Sagittaire.

archery /ˈɑːtʃərɪ/ **I** *n* tir *m* à l'arc.
II *modif* [*club, target, team*] de tir à l'arc.

archetypal /ˌɑːkɪˈtaɪpl/ *adj* **the** ou **an ~ hero/villain** l'archétype du héros/méchant.

archetype /ˈɑːkɪtaɪp/ *n* archétype *m*.

Archimedes /ˌɑːkɪˈmiːdiːz/ *pr n* Archimède; **~' principle/screw** le principe/la vis d'Archimède.

archipelago /ˌɑːkɪˈpeləgəʊ/ *n* archipel *m*.

architect /ˈɑːkɪtekt/ **▶ 1692** *n* **1** (as profession) architecte *mf*; **2** fig (of plan, policy) artisan *m*.

architectural /ˌɑːkɪˈtektʃərəl/ *adj* [*design, style*] architectural; [*student*] en architecture; [*studies*] d'architecture.

architecturally /ˌɑːkɪˈtektʃərəlɪ/ *adv* du point de vue de l'architecture.

architecture /ˈɑːkɪtektʃə(r)/ *n* (all contexts) architecture *f*.

architrave /ˈɑːkɪtreɪv/ *n* architrave *f*.

archive /ˈɑːkaɪv/ *n* archive *f*; **in the ~s** dans les archives; **film/radio ~** archives du cinéma/de la radio.

archivist /ˈɑːkɪvɪst/ **▶ 1692** *n* archiviste *mf*.

archly /ˈɑːtʃlɪ/ *adv* **1** (mischievously) malicieusement; **2** péj (condescendingly) avec condescendance.

archpriest /ˌɑːtʃˈpriːst/ *n* archiprêtre *m*.

arc lamp, **arc light** *n* lampe *f* à arc.

Arctic /ˈɑːktɪk/ **I** *pr n* **the ~** l'Arctique *m*; **to/in the ~** dans l'Arctique.
II *adj* **1** [*climate, animal*] arctique; **2** [*expedition, equipment*] polaire; **3** fig (icy) [*conditions, temperature*] glacial.

Arctic Circle *n* cercle *m* polaire arctique.

arctic fox *n* renard *m* polaire.

Arctic Ocean **▶ 1511** *n* océan *m* Arctique.

arc: **~ welder** *n* soudeur *m* à l'arc; **~ welding** *n* soudage *m* à l'arc.

Ardèche **▶ 1163** *pr n* Ardèche *f*; **in/to the ~** dans l'Ardèche, en Ardèche.

Ardennes /ɑːˈden/ **▶ 1163** *pr n* Ardennes *fpl*; **in/to the ~** dans les Ardennes.

ardent /ˈɑːdnt/ *adj* **1** (fervent) [*revolutionary, supporter*] fervent; [*defence, opposition*] passionné; **she was an ~ follower of the cause** elle était passionnément dévouée à la cause; **2** (passionate) [*lover, nights*] passionné.

ardently /ˈɑːdntlɪ/ *adv* [*look, worship*] ardemment; [*defend, speak, write*] avec ardeur; [*support*] passionnément.

ardour GB, **ardor** US /ˈɑːdə(r)/ *n* ardeur *f*; **with ~** avec ardeur; **to cool sb's ~** modérer l'ardeur de qn.

arduous /ˈɑːdjʊəs, US -dʒʊ-/ *adj* [*path, journey, task*] ardu; [*climate*] pénible; [*winter*] rigoureux/-euse.

arduously /ˈɑːdjʊəslɪ, US -dʒʊ-/ *adv* péniblement.

arduousness /ˈɑːdjʊəsnɪs, US -dʒʊ-/ *n* (of task, journey) difficulté *f*; (of weather, conditions) dureté *f*.

are /ɑː(r)/ ▶ **be**.

area /ˈeərɪə/ **I** *n* **1** (region) (of land) région *f*; (of sky) zone *f*; (of city) zone *f*; (district) quartier *m*; **in the London/Paris ~** dans la région de Londres/de Paris; **residential/rural/slum ~** zone *f* résidentielle/rurale/pauvre; **2** (part of building) **dining ~** coin *m* salle-à-manger; **no-smoking/smoking ~** zone *f* non-fumeurs/fumeurs; **reception ~** entrée *f*; **sleeping ~** coin *m* chambre; **waiting ~** salle *f* d'attente; **3** (sphere of knowledge) domaine *m*; (part of activity, business, economy) secteur *m*; **that's not my ~** ce n'est pas mon domaine; **~ of interest/of expertise/of responsibility** domaine d'intérêt /d'expertise/de responsabilité; **~ of doubt/of concern/of disagreement** sujet de doute/d'inquiétude/de désaccord; **4** Anat zone *f*; **5** Math (in geometry) aire *f*; (of land) superficie *f*; **the farm was 50 km² in ~** la ferme était d'une superficie de 50 km²; **6** GB (access to basement) cour *f* d'entrée en sous-sol.
II *modif* [*board, headquarters, manager, office*] régional.

area: **~ bombing** *n* Mil bombardement *m* de zone; **~ code** *n* Telecom indicatif *m* de zone; **Area of Outstanding Natural Beauty, AONB** *n* zone *f* naturelle protégée.

arena /əˈriːnə/ *n* arène *f* (also fig); **the political ~** l'arène politique.

aren't /ɑːnt/ ▶ **be**.

areola /æˈrɪələ/ *n* (*pl* **-lae** ou **-las**) aréole *f*.

Argentina /ˌɑːdʒənˈtiːnə/ **▶ 1131** *pr n* Argentine *f*.

Argentine /ˈɑːdʒəntaɪn/ **▶ 1131** **I** *n* **1** (country) l'Argentine *f*; **the ~ (Republic)** l'Argentine *f*; **2** (native, inhabitant) Argentin/-e *m/f*.
II *adj* argentin; **the ~ people** les Argentins.

Argentinian /ˌɑːdʒənˈtɪnɪən/ **▶ 1486** **I** *n* Argentin/-e *m/f*.
II *adj* argentin.

argon /ˈɑːgɒn/ *n* argon *m*.

Argonaut /ˈɑːgənɔːt/ *n* Argonaute *mf*.

argosy /ˈɑːgəsɪ/ *n* littér galion *m* (*de commerce*).

arguable /ˈɑːgjʊəbl/ *adj* discutable; **it's ~ that** on peut soutenir que; **it's ~ whether** on peut se demander si.

arguably /ˈɑːgjʊəblɪ/ *adv* sans doute.

argue /ˈɑːgjuː/ **I** *vtr* **1** (debate) discuter (de), débattre (de); **they ~d the point for hours** ils ont discuté or débattu la question pendant des heures; **to ~ one's point** argumenter son point de vue; **to ~ the case for disarmament** exposer les raisons en faveur du désarmement; **it could be ~d that** on pourrait soutenir que; **well-~d** [*case, essay*] bien argumenté; **2** (maintain) soutenir; **she/the book ~s that he was wrongly convicted** elle/le livre soutient qu'il a été injustement condamné; **3** (persuade) **to ~ sb into/out of doing sth** persuader/dissuader qn de faire qch (*à force d'argument*); **I ~d my way into this job** je suis parvenu à obtenir cet emploi à force de discussions; **4** (provide evidence of) [*action, behaviour, incident*] dénoter; [*document*] suggérer; **the evidence ~s that** tout porte à croire que.
II *vi* **1** (quarrel) se disputer (**with** avec); **they're always arguing (with each other)** ils se disputent constamment; **to ~ about** ou **over money** se disputer pour des questions d'argent; **we ~d about who should pay** nous nous sommes disputés pour savoir qui devait payer; **don't ~ (with me)!** on ne discute pas!; **2** (debate) discuter, débattre; **to ~ about** discuter de, débattre de [*case, issue, politics etc*]; **3** (put one's case) argumenter (**against** contre); **to ~ in favour of/against doing sth** exposer les raisons pour faire/pour ne pas faire qch; **to ~ for** ou **in favour of** parler en faveur de [*policy, measure*]; **4** sout (testify) témoigner; **it ~s against him that he has no alibi** le fait qu'il n'a pas d'alibi témoigne contre lui.
■ **argue out**: **~ out [sth]**, **~ [sth] out** débattre [qch] à fond [*issue, proposal etc*].

argument /ˈɑːgjʊmənt/ *n* **1** (quarrel) dispute *f* (**about** à propos de); **to have an ~** se disputer; **without ~** sans discuter; **2** (reasoned discussion) débat *m*, discussion *f* (**about** à propos de); **there is a lot of ~ about this at the moment** on en discute beaucoup or c'est un sujet très discuté en ce moment; **she won the ~** c'est elle qui a eu le dernier mot; **beyond ~** indiscutable; **it's open to ~** c'est discutable; **I'm open to ~** je suis ouvert à la discussion; **one side of the ~** une version de l'affaire; **for ~'s sake** à titre d'exemple; **3** (case) argument *m* (**for** en faveur de; **against** contre); (line of reasoning) raisonnement *m*; **I can't**

follow your ~ je n'arrive pas à suivre ton raisonnement; **his main ~ is that** son argument principal est que; **there is a strong ~ for neutrality** il y a de bonnes raisons pour rester neutre.

argumentation /ˌɑːgjʊmenˈteɪʃn/ *n* argumentation *f*.

argumentative /ˌɑːgjʊˈmentətɪv/ *adj* [*person*] ergoteur/-euse, chicanier/-ière; [*tone*] péremptoire.

argy-bargy○ /ˌɑːdʒɪˈbɑːdʒɪ/ *n* chamaillerie○ *f*.

aria /ˈɑːrɪə/ *n* (*pl* **arias**) aria *f*.

Ariadne /ˌærɪˈædnɪ/ *pr n* Ariane; **~'s web** le fil d'Ariane.

Arian /ˈeərɪən/ I *n* Arien/-ienne *m/f*.
II *adj* arien.

Arianism /ˈeərɪənɪzəm/ *n* arianisme *m*.

ARIBA *n* (*abrév* = **Associate of the Royal Institute of British Architects**) membre *m* de l'institut britannique des architectes.

arid /ˈærɪd/ *adj* aride also fig.

aridity /əˈrɪdətɪ/ *n* aridité *f* also fig.

Ariège ▶ 1163 *pr n* Ariège *f*; **in/to the ~** dans l'Ariège.

Aries /ˈeəriːz/ ▶ 1916 *n* Bélier *m*.

aright /əˈraɪt/ *adv* sout [*read, understand*] correctement; **did I hear you ~?** vous ai-je bien compris?; **to set** ou **put sth ~** mettre de l'ordre dans qch.

arise /əˈraɪz/ *vi* (*prét* **arose**, *pp* **arisen**) **1** (occur) [*problem*] survenir (**out of** du fait de); **to ~ from sth** émaner de qch; **if it ~s that** s'il se trouve que; **if the need ~s** si le besoin se fait sentir; **she solves problems as they ~** elle règle les problèmes à mesure qu'ils surviennent; **the question ~s whether** la question se pose de savoir si; **2** (be the result of) résulter (**from** de); **matters arising** questions soulevées par le rapport; **3**‡ (stand) se lever; **4**‡ (rebel) se soulever (**against** contre).

aristo○ /ˈærɪstəʊ/ *n* aristo○ *mf*.

aristocracy /ˌærɪˈstɒkrəsɪ/ *n* aristocratie *f*.

aristocrat /ˈærɪstəkræt, US əˈrɪst-/ *n* aristocrate *mf*.

aristocratic /ˌærɪstəˈkrætɪk, US əˌrɪst-/ *adj* aristocratique.

Aristophanes /ˌærɪˈstɒfəniːz/ *pr n* Aristophane.

Aristotelian /ˌærɪstəˈtiːlɪən/ *adj* aristotélicien/-ienne.

Aristotelianism /ˌærɪstəˈtiːlɪənɪzəm/ *n* aristotélisme *m*.

Aristotle /ˈærɪstɒtl/ *pr n* Aristote.

aristotype /ˈærɪstətaɪp/ *n* (papier) aristotipe *m*.

arithmetic /əˈrɪθmətɪk/ *n* (subject) arithmétique *f*; **to be good at ~** être bon/bonne en arithmétique or calcul.

arithmetical /ˌærɪθˈmetɪkl/ *adj* arithmétique.

arithmetician /əˌrɪθməˈtɪʃn/ *n* arithméticien/-ienne *m/f*.

arithmetic: **~ mean** *n* moyenne *f* arithmétique; **~ progression** *n* progression *f* arithmétique.

Arizona /ˌærɪˈzəʊnə/ ▶ 1744 *pr n* Arizona *m*.

ark /ɑːk/ *n* (boat, in synagogue) arche *f*.
IDIOMS **to be out of the ~** être vieux/vieille comme Hérode.

Ark /ɑːk/ *n* Relig **the ~ of the Covenant** l'Arche *f* de l'Alliance.

Arkansas /ˈɑːkənsɔː/ ▶ 1744 *pr n* Arkansas *m*.

arm /ɑːm/ ▶ 1037 I *n* **1** Anat, fig bras *m*; **~ in ~** bras dessus bras dessous; **to give sb one's ~** donner le bras à qn; **to take sb's ~** prendre le bras de qn; **to take/hold sb in one's ~s** prendre/tenir qn dans ses bras; **to have sth over/under one's ~** avoir qch sur/sous le bras; **to fold one's ~s** se croiser les bras; **in** ou **within ~'s reach** à portée de la main; **2** (sleeve) manche *f*; **3** (influence) **to have a long ~** avoir le bras long; **the long ~ of the law** le bras de la justice; **4** (of crane, robot, record player) bras *m*; **5** (of spectacles) branche *f*; **6** (of chair) accoudoir *m*; **7** (subsidiary) Pol branche *f*; Econ branche *f*, filiale *f*; **8** (of sea) bras *m*.
II **arms** *npl* **1** (weapons) armes *fpl*; **under ~s** sous les armes; **to take up ~s** lit prendre les armes; fig s'insurger (**against** contre); **to be up in ~s** (in revolt) être en rébellion (**against** contre); (angry) être furieux/-ieuse; **2** Herald armes *fpl*, armoiries *fpl*; **coat of ~s** armoiries *fpl*.
III *vtr* **1** (militarily) armer [*troops, rebels, missile, warhead*]; **2** (equip) **to ~ sb with sth** lit, fig fournir qch à qn [*tool, information etc*].
IV *v refl* **to ~ oneself** Mil s'armer; **to ~ oneself with** lit s'armer de [*weapon, facts, statistics*].
IDIOMS **to cost an ~ and a leg**○ coûter les yeux de la tête○; **to keep sb at ~'s length** tenir qn à distance; **a list as long as my ~** une liste qui n'en finit plus; **to twist sb's ~** faire pression sur qn, exercer des pressions sur qn; **with open ~s** à bras ouverts; **I would give my right ~ for/to do** je donnerais tout ce que j'ai pour/pour faire.

Armada /ɑːˈmɑːdə/ *n* **1** Hist **the ~** l'Invincible Armada *f*; **2** Mil (fleet) armada *f*.

armadillo /ˌɑːməˈdɪləʊ/ *n* (*pl* **~s**) tatou *m*.

Armageddon /ˌɑːməˈgedn/ *n* Bible Armageddon *m*; fig lutte *f* suprême.

Armagh /ɑːˈmɑː/ ▶ 1624 *pr n* comté *m* d'Armagh.

armament /ˈɑːməmənt/ Mil I *n* (loading of weapons) armement *m*.
II **armaments** *npl* (system) armements *mpl*.
III **armaments** *modif* [*factory, firm, manufacturer*] d'armement; [*industry*] de l'armement.

armature /ˈɑːmətʃʊə(r)/ *n* **1** Elec gen armature *f*; (in dynamo) induit *m*; **2** Art (frame) armature *f*; **3** Zool, Bot armure *f*.

armband /ˈɑːmbænd/ *n* **1** (for buoyancy) bracelet *m* de natation; **2** (for mourner) crêpe *m* de deuil; **3** (for identification) brassard *m*.

armchair /ˈɑːmtʃeə(r)/ I *n* fauteuil *m*.
II *modif* péj [*general, socialist, traveller*] de salon pej.

armed /ɑːmd/ I *adj* [*criminal, guard, raider, unit*] armé (**with** de); [*raid, robbery*] à main armée; [*missile*] muni d'une tête d'ogive.
II **-armed** (*dans composés*) **hairy-/long-~** aux bras poilus/longs.
IDIOMS **to be ~ to the teeth** être armé jusqu'aux dents.

armed forces, **armed services** *npl* forces *fpl* armées; **to be in the ~** être dans l'armée.

Armenia /ɑːˈmiːnɪə/ ▶ 1131 *pr n* Arménie *f*.

Armenian /ɑːˈmiːnɪən/ ▶ 1486, 1402 I *n* **1** (native, inhabitant) Arménien/-ienne *m/f*; **2** (language) arménien *m*; **to speak ~** parler l'arménien; **in ~** en arménien.
II *adj* arménien/-ienne.

armful /ˈɑːmfʊl/ *n* (*pl* **~s**) brassée *f*; **by the ~** [*presents, flowers*] plein *inv* les bras.

armhole /ˈɑːmhəʊl/ *n* emmanchure *f*.

armistice /ˈɑːmɪstɪs/ *n* armistice *m*.

Armistice Day *n* le onze *m* novembre.

armlet /ˈɑːmlɪt/ *n* bracelet *m*.

armor US = **armour**.

armorial /ɑːˈmɔːrɪəl/ *adj* armorial.

armour GB, **armor** US /ˈɑːmə(r)/ *n* **1** Hist (clothing) **a suit of ~** une armure *f* (complète); **2** (protective covering) (on tank, ship etc) armure *f*; Zool armure *f*; Elec (on wire, cable) gaine *f*; fig (against criticism) cuirasse *f*; **3** (tanks) (+ *v sg ou pl*) blindés *mpl*.

armour-clad /ˌɑːməˈklæd/ *adj* [*vehicle*] blindé; [*ship*] cuirassé.

armoured GB, **armored** US /ˈɑːməd/ *adj* **1** Mil [*vehicle, regiment*] blindé; **2** Zool avec une carapace.

armoured: **~ car** *n* véhicule *m* blindé; **~ personnel carrier** *n* véhicule *m* blindé de transport de troupes.

armourer GB, **armorer** US /ˈɑːmərə(r)/ *n* armurier *m*.

armour: **~-piercing** *adj* [*ammunition*] perforant; [*mine, missile*] antichar *inv*; **~ plate**, **~ plating** *n* (on tank) blindage *m*; (on ship) cuirassage *m*; **~-plated** *adj* = **armour-clad**.

armoury GB, **armory** US /ˈɑːmərɪ/ *n* **1** Mil (array, collection, store) arsenal *m*; (factory) manufacture *f* d'armes; **2** fig (store, resources) arsenal *m* (**of** de).

arm: **~pit** *n* aisselle *f*; **~rest** *n* accoudoir *m*; **~s control** *n* contrôle *m* des armements; **~s dealer** *n* négociant *m* d'armes; **~s dump** *n* dépôt *m* d'armes; **~s factory** *n* usine *f* d'armement.

arm's-length /ˌɑːmzˈlenθ/ *adj* **1** Comm [*competition*] libre; [*sale*] loyal; [*price*] de pleine concurrence; **2** (independent) [*company, inspectorate, relationship, supplier*] sans lien de dépendance.
IDIOMS **to keep sb at ~** tenir qn à distance.

arm: **~s limitation** *n* réduction *f* or contrôle *m* des armements; **~s manufacturer** *n* fabricant *m* d'armes; **~s race** *n* course *f* aux armements; **~s treaty** *n* traité *m* sur le contrôle des armements; **~-twisting** *n* pressions *fpl* directes; **~ wrestle** *vi* faire un bras de fer; **~ wrestling** ▶ 1282 *n* bras-de-fer *m*.

army /ˈɑːmɪ/ I *n* **1** Mil armée *f*; **in the ~** dans l'armée; **to go into the ~** entrer dans l'armée; **to join the ~** s'engager; **2** fig armée *f* (**of** de).
II *modif* [*discipline, life, staff, uniform*] militaire; [*wife*] de militaire; [*accommodation*] militaire.

army: **~ ant** *n* fourmi *f* soldat; **~ corps** *n* corps *m* d'armée; **Army List** *n* GB Mil annuaire *m* militaire; **~ officer** ▶ 1612 *n* officier *m* de l'armée de terre; **~ surplus store** *n* Comm, Mil surplus *m*.

aroma /əˈrəʊmə/ *n* arôme *m*.

aromatherapy /əˌrəʊməˈθerəpɪ/ *n* aromathérapie *f*.

aromatherapy: **~ lamp** *n* diffuseur *m* d'arômes; **~ oil** *n* huile *f* essentielle.

aromatic /ˌærəˈmætɪk/ I *n* aromate *m*.
II *adj* aromatique.

arose /əˈrəʊz/ *pret* ▶ **arise**.

around /əˈraʊnd/

■ **Note** *around* often appears as the second element of certain verb structures (*come around, look around, turn around etc*). For translations, consult the appropriate verb entry (***come***, ***look***, ***turn*** etc).
– *go around* and *get around* generate many idiomatic expressions. For translations see the entries ***go*** and ***get***.

I *adv* **1** (approximately) environ, à peu près; **it sells for ~ £200** ça coûte environ or à peu près 200 livres sterling; **at ~ 3 pm** vers 15 heures; **2** (in the vicinity) **to be** (**somewhere**) **~** être dans les parages; **I'll be ~** je serai dans les parages, je ne serai pas loin; **is there anyone ~?** il y a quelqu'un?; **are they ~?** est-ce qu'ils sont là?; **I just happened to be ~** je me trouvais là par hasard; **I don't want to be ~ when** je préfère ne pas être là quand (+ *future*); **3** (in circulation) **to be ~** [*product, technology, phenomenon*] exister; [*person*] être là; **to be ~ again** [*fashion, style*] revenir à la mode; **CDs have been ~ for years** ça fait des années que les CD existent; **I wish I'd been ~ 50 years ago** j'aurais aimé être là il y a 50 ans; **I'm glad I won't be ~ when** heureusement je ne serai pas là quand (+ *future*); **not to be ~ long enough to do** ne pas rester assez longtemps pour faire; **is he still ~?** est-ce qu'il est encore là?; **she's** been ~ fig elle a vécu, elle a roulé sa bosse○; **one of the most gifted musicians ~** un des musiciens les plus doués du moment; **there is far less money ~** les gens ont beaucoup moins d'argent; **there's a lot of corruption ~** il y a beaucoup de corruption; **4** (available) **to be ~** être là; **I wish you were ~ more** j'aimerais que tu sois là plus souvent; **will she be ~ next week?** est-ce qu'elle sera là la semaine prochaine?; **there are still some strawberries ~** on trouve encore des fraises; **5** (in all directions) **all ~** lit tout autour; (in general) partout; **to go all the way ~** [*fence, wall, moat*] faire tout le tour; **the only garage for miles ~** le seul garage à des kilomètres à la ronde; **we like to travel ~** nous aimons voyager; **6** (in circumference) **three metres ~** [*tree trunk*] de trois mètres de circonférence; **7** (in different, opposite direction) **a way ~** lit un chemin pour contourner [*obstacle*]; **there is no way ~ the problem** n'y a pas moyen de contourner le problème; **to go the long way ~** prendre le chemin le plus long; **to turn sth the other way ~** retourner qch; **to do it the other way ~** faire le contraire; **I didn't ask her, it was the other way ~** ce n'est pas moi qui lui ai demandé, c'est l'inverse; **the wrong/right way ~** dans le mauvais/bon sens; **to put one's skirt on the wrong way ~** mettre sa jupe à l'envers; **you're Ben and you're Tom, is that the right way ~?** tu es Ben, et toi tu es Tom, c'est bien ça?; **8** (also GB **round**) (in specific place, home) **to ask sb (to come) ~** dire à qn de passer; **she's coming ~ today** elle passe aujourd'hui; **I'll be ~ in a minute** j'arrive.

II *prep* (also GB **round**) **1** (on all sides of) autour de [*fire, table, garden, lake*]; **~ the outside of the house** autour de la maison; **a scarf ~ her head** une écharpe autour de la tête; **she put her arm ~ his shoulders** elle a mis son bras autour de ses épaules; **the villages ~ Dublin** les villages des environs de Dublin; **2** (throughout) **clothes scattered ~ the room** des vêtements éparpillés partout dans la pièce; **in several locations ~ the country** dans plusieurs endroits à travers le pays; **(all) ~ the world** partout dans le monde; **from ~ the world** venant du monde entier; **doctors ~ the world** les médecins à travers le monde; **to go ~ the world** faire le tour du monde; **to walk ~ the town** se promener dans la ville; **he'll show you ~ the castle** il vous fera visiter le château; **to go** ou **look ~ the house** faire le tour de la maison; **3** (in the vicinity of, near) **somewhere ~ the house/~ Paris** quelque part dans la maison/près de Paris; **I like having people ~ the house** ou **place** j'aime avoir des gens à la maison; **the people ~ here** les gens d'ici; **she's not from ~ here** elle n'est pas d'ici or de la région; **4** (at) vers; **~ midnight/1980** vers minuit/1980; **~ the same time we...** c'est à peu près à ce moment-là que nous...; **5** (in order to circumvent) **to go ~** éviter [*town centre*]; contourner [*obstacle*]; **there's a way ~ the problem** il y a un moyen de contourner le problème; ▶ **get round**; **6** (to the other side of) **to go ~ the corner** tourner au coin; **to go ~ a bend** prendre un virage; **~ the mountain** de l'autre côté de or derrière la montagne; **7** Meas, Sewing **he's 90 cm ~ the chest** il fait 90 de tour de poitrine.

IDIOMS **what goes ~ comes ~** on récolte ce qu'on a semé.

arousal /ə'raʊzl/ *n* **1** (excitation) excitation *f*; **(sexual) ~** excitation *f* sexuelle; **2** (awakening) excitation *f* **(of** de).

arouse /ə'raʊz/ *vtr* **1** (cause) éveiller [*interest, attention*]; exciter [*anger, jealousy*]; **the picture ~d a feeling of disgust in me** le tableau a éveillé en moi un sentiment de dégoût; **the taxes ~d the anger of the people** les impôts ont excité la colère du peuple; **2** (sexually) **to be ~d by sth** être excité par qch; **3** (waken) **to ~ sb from sleep** tirer qn du sommeil.

arpeggio /ɑː'pedʒɪəʊ/ *n* arpège *m*.

arrack /'ærək/ *n* arak *m*.

arraign /ə'reɪn/ *vtr* **1** Jur traduire en justice; **to ~ sb before the court** traduire qn en justice; **to be ~ed on a charge of murder** être inculpé de meurtre; **2** sout gen (accuse, rebuke) tancer fml.

arraignment /ə'reɪnmənt/ *n* Jur (by judge) lecture *f* de l'acte d'accusation (suivie de la question).

Arran /'ærən/ ▶ **1381** *pr n* île *f* d'Arran.

arrange /ə'reɪndʒ/ **I** *vtr* **1** (put in position) disposer [*chairs, ornaments*]; arranger [*room, hair, clothes*]; arranger, disposer [*flowers*]; **2** (organize) organiser [*party, wedding, meeting, holiday, schedule*]; fixer [*date, appointment*]; **to ~ sth with sb** fixer or organiser qch avec qn; **to ~ that** faire en sorte que (+ *subj*); **to ~ to do** s'arranger pour faire; **I'll ~ it** je ferai le nécessaire; **to ~ a marriage** arranger un mariage; **have you got anything ~d for this evening?** avez-vous quelque chose de prévu pour ce soir?; **we've ~d to go out** ou **to meet this evening** on s'est donné rendez-vous pour ce soir; **3** (bring about agreement on) convenir de [*agreement, loan, mortgage*]; fixer [*price*]; **'date: to be ~d '** (on memo) 'date: à déterminer'; **4** Mus arranger, adapter [*piece*].

II *vi* **to ~ for sth** prendre des dispositions pour qch; **to ~ for sb to do** prendre des dispositions pour que qn fasse; **to ~ for sth to be done** prendre des dispositions pour que qch soit fait; **to ~ with sb to do** décider avec qn de faire.

arranged marriage *n* mariage *m* arrangé.

arrangement /ə'reɪndʒmənt/ *n* **1** (positioning) (of hair, jewellery) arrangement *m*; (of objects, chairs) disposition *f*; (of ideas: on page) organisation *f*; (of shells, dried flowers etc) composition *f*; **seating ~s** disposition des chaises; **2** (agreement) entente *f*, accord *m* **(with sb** avec qn); **by ~ with sb** par un accord avec qn; **by ~** (par) entente préalable, sur demande; **under the ~, I will receive...** selon l'accord, je recevrai...; **to come to an ~** s'arranger; **3** (plan) dispositions *fpl*; (preparations) préparatifs *mpl*; (measures) mesures *fpl*; **to make ~s to do** s'arranger pour faire; **to make ~s with sb (for him to do)** prendre des dispositions avec qn (pour qu'il fasse); **to make ~s for sth to be done** prendre des dispositions or faire le nécessaire pour que qch soit fait; **to make ~s for doing** prendre des dispositions pour faire; **I don't need a lift, I've already made ~s** je n'ai pas besoin d'être reconduit/-e, j'ai déjà pris des dispositions; **can I leave the ~s to you?** est-ce que tu peux t'occuper de l'organisation?; **Bob is looking after all the ~s** Bob s'occupe de tout; **what are the ~s for the funeral/journey?** qu'est-ce qui est prévu pour l'enterrement/le voyage?; **economic/security/social ~s** mesures économiques/de sécurité/sociales; **parking ~s** facilités *fpl* de stationnement.

arrant /'ærənt/ *adj* littér [*liar*] fieffé (*before n*); **it's ~ nonsense!** c'est complètement absurde!

array /ə'reɪ/ **I** *n* **1** (of goods, products) gamme *f*; **2** (of weaponry) panoplie *f*; **3** (of troops, people) déploiement *m*; **battle ~** ordre *m* de bataille; **4** (of numbers) tableau *m*; **5** Comput tableau *m*; **6** littér (clothes) habits *mpl* d'apparat; **in all their ~** dans leurs plus beaux atours; **7** (of factors, problems) panoplie *f*; **8** Electron réseau *m*.

II *vtr* **1** Mil déployer [*troops*]; **2** Jur établir la liste des [*jurors*]; **3** Fashn **~ed in** paré de.

III *v refl* littér **to ~ oneself in** se parer de.

arrears /ə'rɪəz/ *npl* arriéré *m*; **my payments are in ~** ou **I am in ~ with my payments** j'ai du retard dans mes paiements; **to be 6 months in ~** avoir 6 mois de retard dans ses paiements; **to fall into ~** s'arriérer; **mortgage ~** arriérés de crédit-logement; **rent ~** arriéré de loyer; **serious ~** gros arriérés.

arrest /ə'rest/ **I** *n* Jur arrestation *f*; **to be under ~** être en état d'arrestation; **to put sb under ~** arrêter qn.

II *vtr* **1** [*police*] arrêter; **to ~ sb on a charge/on suspicion of sth** arrêter qn sur l'inculpation/sur présomption de qch; **2** (halt) arrêter [*decline, development, disease*]; enrayer [*spread*]; **~ed growth/development** Med arrêt de croissance/de développement; **3** (attract) attirer [*attention, gaze*].

arrestable /ə'restəbl/ *adj* Jur passible d'arrestation.

arresting /ə'restɪŋ/ *adj* **1** (attractive) saisissant; **2** (making an arrest) [*officer*] qui a procédé à l'arrestation.

arrest: **~ of judgment** *n* Jur suspension *f* d'exécution d'un jugement; **~ warrant** *n* mandat *m* d'arrêt.

arrhythmia /ə'rɪðmɪə/ *n* arythmie *f*.

arrival /ə'raɪvl/ *n* **1** (of person, transport) arrivée *f*; **on sb's/sth's ~** à l'arrivée de qn/qch; **2** Admin, Comm (of package) arrivage *m*; **3** (of new character or phenomenon) apparition *f*; **her ~ on the scene** son apparition sur la scène; **4** (person arriving) arrivé/-e *m/f*; **late ~** (in theatre) retardataire *mf*; **new ~** (in community) nouveau/-elle venu/-e *m/f*; (baby) nouveau-né *m*.

arrival: **~ lounge** *n* salon *m* d'arrivée; **~ platform** *n* quai *m* d'arrivée; **~s board** *n* tableau *m* d'arrivée; **~ time** *n* heure *f* d'arrivée.

arrive /ə'raɪv/ *vi* **1** (at destination) arriver **(at** à; **from** de); **'arriving Berlin 7.25 am'** (announcement) 'arrivée à Berlin 7 heures 25'; **to ~ on the scene** lit arriver (sur les lieux); fig apparaître; **2** (reach) **to ~ at** parvenir à [*decision, agreement, solution etc*]; **3** (be social success) arriver.

arrogance /'ærəgəns/ *n* arrogance *f*.

arrogant /'ærəgənt/ *adj* arrogant.

arrogantly /'ærəgəntlɪ/ *adv* avec arrogance.

arrogate /'ærəgeɪt/ *vtr* sout **to ~ sth to oneself** s'arroger qch fml.

arrow /'ærəʊ/ *n* **1** (weapon) flèche *f*; **to fire** ou **shoot an ~** décocher une flèche; **2** (symbol) flèche *f*; **marked with an ~** [*road, text*] fléché.

arrowhead /'ærəʊhed/ *n* pointe *f* de flèche.

arrowroot /'ærəʊruːt/ *n* Bot marante *f*; Culin arrow-root *m*.

arse● /ɑːs/ GB *n* cul● *m*; **get off your ~◑!** magne-toi le popotin◑!; **move your ~◑!** bouge tes fesses◑!

IDIOMS **he can't tell his ~ from his elbow** il est con◑ comme un balai.

■ **arse about◑** GB faire le con◑/la conne◑.

arsehole● /'ɑːshəʊl/ GB *n* **1** (stupid person) connard◑/connasse◑ *m/f*; **2** (anus) trou *m* du cul◑.

arselicker● /'ɑːslɪkə(r)/ *n* GB lèche-cul◑ *m inv*.

arsenal /'ɑːsənl/ *n* lit, fig arsenal *m*.

arsenic /'ɑːsnɪk/ *n* arsenic *m*; **~ poisoning** empoisonnement *m* à l'arsenic.

arsenical /ɑː'senɪkl/ *adj* [*drug, substance*] arsenical.

arsenic: **~ trioxide** *n* anhydride *m* arsénieux; **~ trisulphide** *n* orpiment *m*.

arson /'ɑːsn/ *n* incendie *m* criminel; **~ attack** incendie *m* criminel.

arsonist /'ɑːsənɪst/ *n* pyromane *mf*.

art /ɑːt/ **I** *n* **1** (creation, activity, representation) art *m*; **I'm bad at ~** je suis mauvais en dessin; **2** (skill) art *m*; **the ~ of listening/of survival** l'art d'écouter/de survivre.

II arts *npl* **1** (culture) **the ~s** les arts *mpl*; **2** Univ lettres *fpl*; **to study (the) ~s** faire des études de lettres; **3 ~s and crafts** gen artisanat *m*; (school subject) travaux *mpl* manuels.

as

When *as* is used as a preposition or a conjunction to mean *like* it is translated by *comme*:
dressed as a sailor = habillé comme un marin
as usual = comme d'habitude
as often happens = comme c'est souvent le cas

As a conjunction in time expressions, meaning *when* or *while*, *as* is translated by *comme*:
as she was coming down the stairs = comme elle descendait l'escalier

However, where a gradual process is involved, *as* is translated by *au fur et à mesure que*:
as the day went on, he became more anxious = au fur et à mesure que la journée avançait il devenait plus inquiet

As a conjunction meaning *because*, *as* is translated by *comme* or *puisque*:
as he is ill, he can't go out = comme il est malade *or* puisqu'il est malade, il ne peut pas sortir.

When used as an adverb in comparisons, *as ... as* is translated by *aussi ... que*:
he is as intelligent as his brother = il est aussi intelligent que son frère

But see category number **X** in the entry ***as*** for *as much as* and *as many as*.

Note also the standard translation used for fixed similes:
as strong as an ox = fort comme un bœuf
as rich as Croesus = riche comme Crésus

Such similes often have a cultural equivalent rather than a direct translation. To find translations for English similes, consult the entry for the second element.

When *as* is used as a preposition to indicate a person's profession or position, it is translated by *comme*:
he works as an engineer = il travaille comme ingénieur

Note that the article *a/an* is not translated.

When *as* is used with a preposition to mean *in my/his capacity as*, it is translated by *en tant que*:
as a teacher I believe that ... = en tant qu'enseignant je crois que ...

For more examples, particular usages and phrases like *as for, as from, as to* etc. see the entry ***as***.

III‡ *v* **thou ~** tu es.

IDIOMS ~ for ~'s sake l'art pour l'art.

art: **~ collection** *n* (of paintings) collection *f* de tableaux; (of other artworks) collection *f* d'œuvres d'art; **~ collector** *n* collectionneur/-euse *m/f* d'œuvres d'art; (of paintings only) collectionneur/-euse *m/f* de tableaux; **~ college** *n* école *f* des beaux-arts; **~ dealer ▶ 1692** *n* marchand/-e *m/f* d'œuvres d'art; (of paintings only) marchand/-e *m/f* de tableaux.

art deco /ˌɑːt ˈdekəʊ/ *n, adj* art déco (*m inv*).

artefact /ˈɑːtɪfækt/ *n* objet *m* (fabriqué).

arterial /ɑːˈtɪərɪəl/ *adj* (*avant n*) **1** Anat [*disease, circulation*] artériel/-ielle; **2 ~ road** grand axe *m*; **~ line** Rail grande ligne *f*.

arteriole /ɑːˈtɪərɪəʊl/ *n* artériole *f*.

arteriosclerosis /ɑːˌtɪərɪəʊskləˈrəʊsɪs/ **▶ 1354** *n* artériosclérose *f*.

artery /ˈɑːtərɪ/ *n* **1** artère *f*; **blocked arteries** artères *fpl* bouchées; **to suffer from blocked arteries** souffrir d'un rétrécissement des artères; **2** (road) artère *f*; (railway) grande ligne *f*.

artesian well /ɑːˌtiːzɪən ˈwel, US ɑːrˌtiːʒn/ *n* puits *m* artésien.

art exhibition *n* (paintings) exposition *f* de tableaux; (sculpture) exposition *f* de sculpture.

art form *n* lit forme *f* d'art; **to become an ~** devenir un art.

artful /ˈɑːtfl/ *adj* **1** [*sculpture, lighting*] ingénieux/-ieuse; **2** [*politician, speaker*] (skilful) habile; (crafty) rusé; **~ dodger** roublard/-e.

artfully /ˈɑːtfəlɪ/ *adv* [*arranged, entwined*] ingénieusement; [*expressed*] avec adresse; [*suggest, imply*] astucieusement.

art gallery *n* (museum) musée *m* d'art; (commercial) galerie *f* d'art.

arthritic /ɑːˈθrɪtɪk/ *n, adj* arthritique (*mf*).

arthritis /ɑːˈθraɪtɪs/ **▶ 1354** *n* arthrite *f*; **to suffer from** ou **have ~** avoir de l'arthrite.

arthropod /ˈɑːθrəpɒd/ *n* arthropode *m*.

Arthurian /ɑːˈθjʊrɪən/ *adj* [*legend, romance*] du roi Arthur.

artic○ /ˈɑːtɪk/ GB Transp *n* semi○ *m*.

artichoke /ˈɑːtɪtʃəʊk/ **I** *n* artichaut *m*.
II *modif* [*head, heart, leaf, stalk*] d'artichaut; [*salad, soup*] aux artichauts.

article /ˈɑːtɪkl/ **I** *n* **1** (object) objet *m*; **~ of clothing** article *m* vestimentaire; **2** Journ article *m* (**about, on** sur); **magazine/newspaper ~** article *m* de magazine/de journal; **3** Admin, Jur (clause) article *m*; **in** ou **under Article 12** à l'article 12; **~ of faith** Relig, fig article de foi; **the Thirty-nine Articles** Relig les trente-neuf articles de foi (*de l'Église Anglicane*); **4** Ling article *m*; **definite/indefinite/partitive ~** article défini/indéfini/partitif.
II articles *npl* Jur **to be in ~s** faire un stage chez un notaire.

articled clerk *n* Jur stagiaire *mf* chez un notaire.

articulate I /ɑːˈtɪkjʊlət/ *adj* **1** gen [*critic, defender, speaker*] qui s'exprime bien; [*argument, document, speech*] bien construit; **2** Anat articulé.
II /ɑːˈtɪkjʊleɪt/ *vtr* (pronounce) articuler; (express) exprimer [*views, feelings, needs*].
III /ɑːˈtɪkjʊleɪt/ *vi* (pronounce) articuler.

articulated lorry *n* GB semi-remorque *m*.

articulately /ɑːˈtɪkjʊlətlɪ/ *adv* avec aisance (et clarté).

articulation /ɑːˌtɪkjʊˈleɪʃn/ *n* **1** (expression) articulation *f*; **2** (pronunciation) prononciation *f*; **3** Anat articulation *f*.

articulatory /ɑːˌtɪkjʊˈleɪtərɪ, US -təːrɪ/ *adj* articulatoire.

articulatory phonetics *n* (+ *v sg*) phonétique *f* articulatoire.

artifact *n* = **artefact**.

artifice /ˈɑːtɪfɪs/ *n* **1** (trick) ruse *f*; **2** (cunning) astuce *f*; **3** (artificiality) artifice *m*.

artificer /ɑːˈtɪfɪsə(r)/ *n* artificier *m*.

artificial /ˌɑːtɪˈfɪʃl/ *adj* **1** [*colour, organ, ingredient, fur, lake, snow, lighting*] artificiel/-ielle; [*fertilizer*] chimique; [*eye*] de verre; [*hair*] faux/fausse; **2** fig [*person, manner, smile, atmosphere, distinction, comparison*] artificiel/-ielle.

artificial: **~ climbing** *n* escalade *f* artificielle; **~ horizon** *n* horizon *m* artificiel; **~ insemination, AI** *n* insémination *f* artificielle; **~ intelligence, AI** *n* intelligence *f* artificielle.

artificiality /ˌɑːtɪfɪʃɪˈælətɪ/ *n* pej (of person) affectation *f*, manque *m* de naturel; (of manner, emotion) affectation *f*; (of situation) côté *m* artificiel.

artificial limb *n* (appareil *m* de) prothèse *f*, membre *m* artificiel.

artificially /ˌɑːtɪfɪʃɪˈælətɪ/ *adv* artificiellement.

artificial respiration *n* respiration *f* artificielle; **to give sb ~** faire la respiration artificielle à qn.

artillery /ɑːˈtɪlərɪ/ *n* Mil (guns, regiment) artillerie *f*; **heavy ~** lit artillerie *f* lourde.

artisan /ˌɑːtɪˈzæn, US ˈɑːrtɪzn/ *n* artisan *m*.

artist /ˈɑːtɪst/ **▶ 1692** *n* **1** Art, Theat artiste *mf*; **comic ~** acteur *m* comique; **2**○ (person) **con ~**, **rip-off ~** arnaqueur/-euse◐ *m/f*; **piss ~** pilier○ *m* de bistrot.

artiste /ɑːˈtiːst/ *n* Theat artiste *mf*.

artistic /ɑːˈtɪstɪk/ *adj* [*talent, creation, activity, community*] artistique; [*temperament, person*] artiste; [*career*] d'artiste, artistique; **to be ~** avoir un talent artistique.

artistically /ɑːˈtɪstɪklɪ/ *adv* (in terms of art) artistiquement, de façon artistique; (tastefully) [*arrange, decorate*] avec goût.

artistic director ▶ 1692 *n* directeur *m* artistique.

artistry /ˈɑːtɪstrɪ/ *n* art *m*, talent *m* artistique.

artless /ˈɑːtlɪs/ *adj* [*smile*] naturel/-elle; **almost too ~** d'une naïveté étudiée.

artlessly /ˈɑːtlɪslɪ/ *adv* [*smile*] avec naturel; **his ~ appealing mannerisms** ses façons *fpl* d'un naturel charmant.

artlessness /ˈɑːtlɪsnɪs/ *n* naïveté *f*.

art nouveau /ˌɑːt ˈnuːvəʊ/ *n, adj* modern style (*m*), art (*m*) nouveau.

art: **~ school** *n* école *f* des beaux-arts; **Arts Council** *n* GB *commission subventionnant la création artistique*; **~s degree** *n* licence *f* ès lettres; **~s funding** *n* (by state) subventions *fpl* accordées aux arts; (by sponsors) mécénat *m*; **~s student** *n* étudiant/-e *m/f* en lettres; **~ student** *n* étudiant/-e *m/f* des beaux-arts; **~work** *n* travail *m* d'art.

arty○ /ˈɑːtɪ/ *adj* [*person, family*] du genre artiste; [*district*] bohème; [*clothes, decoration*] de style bohème.

arty: **~-crafty**○ GB, **artsy-craftsy**○ US *adj* péj [*décor*] de style soi-disant artisanal; **~-farty**○ GB, **artsy-fartsy**○ US *adj* péj qui affiche un intérêt à la culture.

ARV *n* US (*abrév* = **American Revised Version**) *traduction américaine de la Bible*.

Aryan /ˈeərɪən/ **I** *n* Aryen/-enne *m/f*.
II *adj* aryen/-enne.

as /æz, əz/ **I** *conj* **1** (in the manner that) comme; **~ you can see, I am very busy** comme vous le voyez, je suis très occupé; **~ you know** comme vous le savez; **~ usual** comme d'habitude; **~ is usual in such cases** comme c'est l'usage en pareil cas; **do ~ I say** fais ce que je te dis; **~ I see it** à mon avis; **~ I understand it** autant que je puisse en juger; **he likes reading, ~ I do** il aime la lecture, (tout) comme moi; **loving Paris ~ I do, I couldn't bear to live anywhere else** j'aime tellement Paris que je ne pourrais pas vivre ailleurs; **knowing you ~ I do, it didn't surprise me** je te connais tellement bien que ça ne m'a pas étonné; **the street ~ it looked in the 1930s** la rue telle qu'elle était dans les années 30; **~ often happens** comme c'est souvent le cas; **just ~ he dislikes the theatre, so too does he dislike opera** il déteste l'opéra tout autant que le théâtre; **~ he lived, so did he die** il est mort comme il a vécu; **he lives abroad, ~ does his sister** il vit à l'étranger, tout comme sa sœur; **clad ~ he was only in a towel, he did not want to answer the door** comme il n'était vêtu que d'une serviette, il ne voulait pas aller ouvrir la porte; **leave it ~ it is** laisse-le tel quel; **I'm overworked ~ it is** je suis déjà assez débordé comme ça; **we're in enough trouble ~ it is** nous avons déjà assez d'ennuis comme ça; **'~ is'** Comm 'en l'état'; **I bought the apartment ~ it was** j'ai acheté l'appartement tel quel; **~ one man to another** d'homme à homme; **~ with so many people in the 1960s, she...** comme beaucoup de personnes dans les années 60, elle...; **~ with so much in this**

country, the system needs to be modernized comme beaucoup de choses dans ce pays, le système a besoin d'être modernisé; **~ it were** pour ainsi dire; **~ you were!** Mil repos!; **two is to four ~ four is to eight** Math deux est à quatre ce que quatre est à huit; **2** (while, when) alors que; (over more gradual period of time) au fur et à mesure que; **he came in ~ she was coming down the stairs** il est entré alors qu'elle descendait l'escalier; **~ she grew older, she grew richer** au fur et à mesure qu'elle vieillissait, elle devenait plus riche; **~ a child, he...** (quand il était) enfant, il...; **3** (because, since) comme, puisque; **~ you were out, I left a note** comme or puisque vous étiez sortis, j'ai laissé un petit mot; **~ she is sick, she cannot go out** étant donné qu'elle est malade, elle ne peut pas sortir; **4** (although) **strange ~ it may seem, she never returned** aussi curieux que cela puisse paraître, elle n'est jamais revenue; **comfortable ~ the house is, it's still very expensive** aussi confortable que soit la maison, elle reste quand même très chère; **try ~ he might, he could not forget it** il avait beau essayer, il ne pouvait pas oublier; **much ~ I like you, I have to say that** je t'aime bien, mais il faut que je te dise que; **be that ~ it may** quoi qu'il en soit; **5 the same...~** le/la même...que; **I've got a jacket the same ~ yours** j'ai la même veste que toi; **the same man ~ I saw last week** le même homme que j'ai vu la semaine dernière; **the same ~ always** comme d'habitude; **he works for the same company ~ me** il travaille pour la même entreprise que moi; **6** (expressing purpose) **so ~ to do** pour faire, afin de faire; **he left early so ~ to be on time** il est parti de bonne heure afin de or pour ne pas être en retard; **she opened the door quietly so ~ not to wake him** elle a ouvert la porte doucement afin de or pour ne pas le réveiller.

II as and when *conj phr* **~ and when the passengers arrive** au fur et à mesure que les voyageurs arrivent; **~ and when the need arises** quand il le faudra, quand le besoin s'en fera sentir; **~ and when you want** à votre convenance.

III as if *conj phr* comme (si); **it' s not ~ if she hadn't been warned!** ce n'est pas comme si elle n'avait pas été prévenue !; **he looked at me ~ if to say 'I told you so'** il m'a regardé avec l'air de dire 'je te l'avais bien dit'; **it looks ~ if we've lost** on dirait que nous avons perdu; **~ if by accident/magic** comme par hasard/magie; **~ if I cared!** comme si ça me faisait quelque chose!

IV *prep* **1** (in order to appear to be) comme, en; **to be dressed ~ a sailor** être habillé comme un marin or en marin; **disguised ~ a clown** déguisé en clown; **in the book he is portrayed ~ a victim** dans ce livre on le présente comme une victime; **2** (showing function, status) comme; **he works ~ a pilot/engineer** il travaille comme pilote/ingénieur; **a job ~ a teacher** un poste d'enseignant; **she has a reputation ~ a tough businesswoman** elle a la réputation d'être dure en affaires; **speaking ~ his closest friend, I...** comme je suis son meilleur ami, je voudrais dire que je...; **I like her ~ a person, but not ~ an artist** je l'aime bien en tant que personne mais pas en tant qu'artiste; **my rights ~ a parent** mes droits en tant que parent; **film ~ an art form** le cinéma en tant qu'art; **~ a lexicographer, he has a special interest in words** en tant que lexicographe il s'intéresse tout particulièrement aux mots; **with Lauren Bacall ~ Vivien** Cin, Theat avec Lauren Bacall dans le rôle de Vivien; **3** (other uses) **to treat sb ~ an equal** traiter qn en égal; **he was quoted ~ saying that** il aurait dit que; **it came ~ a shock to learn that** ça a été un véritable choc d'apprendre que; **think of it ~ an opportunity to meet new people** dis-toi que ça va être l'occasion de faire de nouvelles connaissances.

V as against *prep phr* contre, comparé à; **75% this year ~ against 35% last year** 75% cette année contre 35% l'année dernière.

VI as for *prep phr* quant à, pour ce qui est de; **~ for the children** pour ce qui est des enfants, quant aux enfants; **~ for him, he can go to hell**◐! lui, il peut aller se faire voir◐!

VII as from, as of *prep phr* à partir de; **~ from** ou **of now/April** à partir de maintenant/du mois d'avril; **~ of yet** jusqu'ici, jusqu'à présent.

VIII as such *prep phr* en tant que tel; **he doesn't believe in religion ~ such** il ne croit pas à la religion en tant que telle; **they are your equals and should be treated ~ such** ce sont vos égaux et vous devriez les traiter comme tels or en tant que tels.

IX as to *prep phr* sur, quant à; **this gave them no clue ~ to his motives/~ to his whereabouts** cela ne leur a rien appris sur ses intentions/sur l'endroit où il se trouvait.

X *adv* **1** (expressing degree, extent) **~... ~...** aussi... que...; **he is ~ intelligent ~ you** il est aussi intelligent que toi; **he is not ~** ou **so intelligent ~ you** il n'est pas aussi intelligent que toi; **he's just ~ intelligent ~ you** il est tout aussi intelligent que toi; **she can't walk ~ fast ~ she used to** elle ne peut plus marcher aussi vite qu'avant; **~ fast ~ you can** aussi vite que possible; **~ strong ~ an ox** fort comme un bœuf; **he's twice ~ strong ~ me** il est deux fois plus fort que moi; **it's not ~ good ~ all that** ce n'est pas si bien que ça; **I paid ~ much ~ she did** j'ai payé autant qu'elle; **~ much ~ possible** autant que possible; **~ little ~ possible** le moins possible; **~ soon ~ possible** dès que possible; **not nearly ~ much ~** beaucoup moins que; **not ~ often** moins souvent; **their profits are down by ~ much ~ 30%** leurs bénéfices ont connu une baisse de 30%, ni plus ni moins; **the population may increase by ~ much ~ 20%** l'augmentation de la population risque d'atteindre 20%; **~ many ~ 10,000 people attended the demonstration** il n'y avait pas moins de 10000 personnes à la manifestation; **by day ~ well ~ by night** de jour comme de nuit; **she can play the piano ~ well ~ her sister** elle joue du piano aussi bien que sa sœur; **they have a house in Nice ~ well ~ an apartment in Paris** ils ont une maison à Nice ainsi qu'un appartement à Paris; **~ well ~ being a poet, he is a novelist** il est poète et romancier; **2** (expressing similarity) comme; **~ before, she...** comme avant, elle...; **they tried to carry on ~ before** ils essayaient de continuer comme avant; **I thought ~ much!** c'est ce qu'il me semblait!; **V ~ in Victor** V comme Victor.

ASA *n* GB **1** *abrév* ▶ **Advertising Standards Authority**; **2** (*abrév* = **Amateur Swimming Association**) fédération *f* de natation.

asap /ˈeɪsæp/ (*abrév écrite* = **as soon as possible**) dès que possible.

asbestos /əzˈbestɒs, æs-/ *n* amiante *m*.

asbestosis /ˌæzbeˈstəʊsɪs, ˌæs-/ ▶ 1354 *n* asbestose *f*.

asbestos mat *n* plaque *f* d'amiante.

ascend /əˈsend/ sout **I** *vtr* gravir [*steps, hill*]; **to ~ the throne** monter sur le trône.
II *vi* [*person*] monter; [*bird, soul, deity*] s'élever.

ascendancy /əˈsendənsɪ/ *n* ascendant *m*; **to be in the ~** avoir l'ascendant; **to have/gain the ~ over sb** avoir/prendre l'ascendant sur qn.

ascendant /əˈsendənt/ **I** *n* **1** Astrol ascendant *m*; **to be in the ~** être à l'ascendant; **2** sout (powerful position) **they are in the ~** ils ont l'ascendant.
II *adj* sout [*class, group*] dominant.

Ascension /əˈsenʃn/ *n* Relig **the ~** l'Ascension *f*.

Ascension Island ▶ 1381 *pr n* l'Île *f* de l'Ascension.

ascent /əˈsent/ *n* **1** (of smoke, gas) montée *f*; (of soul, balloon, plane) ascension *f*; **2** (in cycling) montée *f*; (in mountaineering) ascension *f*; (of path) montée *f*; **to make an ~ of the volcano** faire l'ascension du volcan; **3** sout (advancement) ascension *f*.

ascertain /ˌæsəˈteɪn/ *vtr* établir (**that** que); **to ~ what had happened** pour établir ce qui s'était passé.

ascertainable /ˌæsəˈteɪnəbl/ *adj* vérifiable.

ascetic /əˈsetɪk/ **I** *n* ascète *mf*.
II *adj* ascétique.

asceticism /əˈsetɪsɪzəm/ *n* ascétisme *m*.

ASCII /ˈæskɪ/ (*abrév* = **American Standard Code for Information Interchange**) **I** *n* ASCII *m*.
II *modif* **~ file** fichier *m* ASCII.

ascribable /əˈskraɪbəbl/ *adj* [*work of art*] attribuable (**to** à); [*mistake, accident*] (laying blame) imputable (**to** à); (morally neutral) attribuable (**to** à).

ascribe /əˈskraɪb/ *vtr* **to ~ sth to sb** attribuer qch à qn [*influence*]; attribuer qch à qn [*work, phrase*]; imputer qch à qn [*accident, mistake*]; **the accident can be ~d to human error** l'accident est attribuable à l'erreur humaine.

ascription /əˈskrɪpʃn/ *n* ascription *f*.

asdic /ˈæzdɪk/ *n* GB Hist asdic *m*.

ASEAN *n* (*abrév* = **Association of South East Asian Nations**) ASEAN *f*, Association *f* des Nations d'Asie du Sud-Est.

aseptic /ˌeɪˈseptɪk, US əˈsep-/ *adj* aseptique.

asexual /ˌeɪˈsekʃʊəl/ *adj* asexué also fig.

ash /æʃ/ **I** *n* **1** (burnt residue) cendre *f*; **to be reduced** ou **burned to ~es** être réduit en cendres; **2** (tree) frêne *m*; (wood) frêne *m*; **made of** ou **in ~** en frêne.
II ashes *npl* (remains) cendres *fpl*.
III *modif* [*bark, branch, leaf, twig*] de frêne; [*furniture, panelling, veneer*] en frêne; [*plantation, grove*] de frênes.

ASH /æʃ/ GB (*abrév* = **Action on Smoking and Health**) comité *m* de lutte contre le tabagisme.

ashamed /əˈʃeɪmd/ *adj* **to be** ou **feel ~** avoir honte (**of** de; **to do** de faire); **to be ~ that** avoir honte que (+ *subj*); **she was ~ to be seen with him** elle avait honte de se montrer avec lui; **you ought to be ~ of yourself** tu devrais avoir honte; **~ of his ignorance, he...** honteux de son ignorance, il...; **it's nothing to be ~ of** il ne faut pas en avoir honte.

ash: **~bin** *n* US poubelle *f*; **~ blond** *adj* blond cendré *inv*; **~can** *n* US poubelle *f*.

ashen /ˈæʃn/ *adj* [*complexion*] terreux/-euse.

ashen faced *adj* blême.

ashlar /ˈæʃlə(r)/ *n* pierre *f* de taille.

ashore /əˈʃɔː(r)/ *adv* **1** (towards seashore) vers le rivage; (towards lake shore, river bank) vers la rive; **he was swimming ~** il nageait vers le rivage/la rive; **the oil slick is being washed ~ by the tide** la nappe de pétrole est emportée vers le rivage par la marée; **2** (arriving on shore) **to come/go ~** débarquer; **to swim ~** gagner le rivage/la rive à la nage; **washed ~** rejeté sur le rivage; **the gas is piped ~** le gaz est acheminé au rivage par des conduits; **to put men/goods ~** débarquer des hommes/des marchandises; **3** (on land) à terre; **to spend a week ~** [*sailor*] passer une semaine à terre; [*tourist*] faire une escale d'une semaine; **whenever I'm ~** chaque fois que je suis à terre.

ash pan *n* cendrier *m* (de foyer).

ashram /ˈæʃrəm/ *n* ashram *m*.

ash: **~tray** *n* cendrier *m*; **~ tree** *n* frêne

m; **Ash Wednesday** *n* mercredi *m* des Cendres.

ashy /ˈæʃɪ/ *adj* (in colour) cendré; (covered in ash) couvert de cendres; **~ material** cendres *fpl*.

Asia /ˈeɪʃə, US ˈeɪʒə/ ▶ 1131 *pr n* Asie *f*; **Central/South-East ~** Asie centrale/du sud-est; **the communist countries of ~** les pays communistes de l'Asie.

Asia Minor /ˌeɪʃəˈmaɪnə(r), US ˌeɪʒə-/ *pr n* Asie *f* mineure.

Asian /ˈeɪʃn, US ˈeɪʒn/ **I** *n* (from Far East) Asiatique *mf*; (in UK) *personne originaire du sous-continent indien*.
II *adj* [*river, custom, politics*] asiatique.

Asian: **~ American** *n* Américain/-e *m/f* d'origine asiatique; **~ Briton** *n* GB Britannique *mf* d'origine pakistanaise/indienne etc; **~ flu** ▶ 1354 *n* grippe *f* asiatique.

Asiatic /ˌeɪʃɪˈætɪk, US ˌeɪʒɪ-/ *adj* [*peoples, nations*] asiatique.

aside /əˈsaɪd/ **I** *n* gen, Theat, Cin aparté *m*; **to say sth as** ou **in an ~** dire qch en aparté; (as digression) dire qch en passant.
II *adv* **1** (to one side) **to stand** ou **step** ou **move ~** s'écarter; **to turn ~** se détourner; **to cast** ou **throw [sth] ~** mettre [qch] au rebut [*clothes, gift*]; écarter [*idea, theory*]; **to set** ou **put** ou **lay [sth] ~** (save) mettre [qch] de côté; (in shop) réserver; **to brush** ou **sweep [sth] ~** écarter [*objections, protests, worries*]; **to lay** ou **put a book ~** mettre un livre de côté; **to push** ou **move sb ~** écarter qn; **to take sb ~** prendre qn à part; **leaving ~ all these problems** laissons de côté tous ces problèmes; **to set a verdict ~** Jur casser un jugement; **2** (apart) **money ~, let's discuss accommodation** laissons de côté la question d'argent et parlons du logement; **joking ~** blague à part○.
III aside from *prep phr* à part; **~ from political concerns** à part les inquiétudes politiques.

asinine /ˈæsɪnaɪn/ *adj* sout [*behaviour, question*] sot/sotte; **an ~ remark** une sottise.

ask /ɑːsk, US æsk/ **I** *vtr* **1** (enquire as to) demander [*name, reason*]; **to ~ a question** poser une question; **to ~ sb sth** demander qch à qn; **I ~ed him the time** je lui ai demandé l'heure; **I ~ed you a question!** je t'ai posé une question!; **there's something I'd like to ~ you** il y a quelque chose que j'aimerais te demander; **80% of those ~ed said no** 80% des personnes interrogées ont dit non; **'how?' she ~ed** 'comment?' a-t-elle demandé; **to ~ if** ou **whether/why/who** demander si/pourquoi/qui; **I ~ed her why** je lui ai demandé pourquoi; **I'm ~ing you how you did it** je veux savoir comment tu l'as fait; **I wasn't ~ing you** je ne t'ai rien demandé; **don't ~ me!** va savoir!; **2** (request) demander [*permission, tolerance*]; **to ~ sb's opinion about** demander à qn son avis sur; **it's too much to ~** c'est trop demander; **to ~ to do** demander à faire; **to ~ sb to do** demander à qn de faire; **to ~ sth of** ou **from sb** demander qch à qn; **all I ~ from you is loyalty** tout ce que je te demande c'est d'être loyal; **to ~ a price for sth** demander un prix pour qch; **what price is she ~ing for it?** combien elle le vend?; **the money is there for the ~ing** il y a de l'argent pour qui le demande; **I ~ you!** GB je te demande un peu!; **3** (invite) inviter [*person*]; **to ~ sb to** inviter qn à [*concert, party*]; **to ~ sb to dinner** inviter qn à dîner; **to ~ sb out** inviter qn à sortir; **to ~ sb in** inviter qn à entrer; **we ~ed him along** nous l'avons invité à se joindre à nous; **he ~ed her to marry him** il lui a demandé de l'épouser; **I wasn't ~ed** on ne m'a pas invité.
II *vi* **1** (request) demander; **you could have ~ed** tu aurais pu demander; **you only have to ~** tu n'as qu'à demander; **2** (make enquiries) se renseigner (**about sth** sur qch); **to ~ about sb** s'informer au sujet de qn; **I'll ~ around** je demanderai autour de moi.
III *v refl* **to ~ oneself** se demander [*reason*]; **to ~ oneself a question** se poser une question; **to ~ oneself why/who** se demander pourquoi/qui.
■ **ask after**: **~ after [sb]** demander des nouvelles de qn; **she ~ed after you** elle a demandé de tes nouvelles.
■ **ask for**: ¶ **~ for [sth]** demander [*drink, money, help, restraint*]; **he was ~ing for it**○, **he ~ed for it**○! il l'a bien cherché!; ¶ **~ for [sb]** (on telephone) demander à parler à; (from sick bed) demander à voir; **the police were here ~ing for you** la police est venue ici et a demandé à te parler; **to ~ sb for sth** demander qch à qn; **I ~ed him for the time** je lui ai demandé l'heure.

askance /əˈskæns/ *adv* **to look ~ at sb/sth** considérer qn/qch avec méfiance.

askew /əˈskjuː/ *adj, adv* de travers.

asking price *n* prix *m* demandé.

aslant /əˈslɑːnt, US əˈslænt/ **I** *adv* obliquement.
II *prep* en travers de.

asleep /əˈsliːp/ *adj* **to be ~** dormir; **be quiet he's ~** ne fais pas de bruit il dort; **to fall ~** s'endormir; **they were found ~** on les a trouvés endormis; **to be half ~** (not yet awake) être à moitié endormi; (falling asleep) dormir à moitié; **to be sound** ou **fast ~** dormir à poings fermés; **to be ~ on one's feet** dormir debout.

ASLEF /ˈæslef/ *n* GB (*abrév* = **Associated Society of Locomotive Engineers and Firemen**) syndicat *m* de cheminots.

asp /æsp/ *n* aspic *m*.

asparagus /əˈspærəgəs/ **I** *n* asperge *f*; **do you like ~?** aimez-vous les asperges?
II *modif* [*frond, shoot*] d'asperge; [*mousse, sauce, soup*] aux asperges; **an ~ plant** une asperge.

asparagus: **~ fern** *n* asparagus *m*; **~ tip** *n* pointe *f* d'asperge.

ASPCA *n* GB (*abrév* = **American Society for the Prevention of Cruelty to Animals**) société *f* pour la protection des animaux.

aspect /ˈæspekt/ *n* **1** (feature) aspect *m*; **2** (angle) point *m* de vue; **from a political ~** d'un point de vue politique; **to examine every ~ of sth** examiner qch sous tous ses aspects; **seen from this ~** vu sous cet angle; **3** (orientation) orientation *f*; **a westerly ~** une orientation ouest; **4** (view) vue *f*; **a pleasant front ~** une vue agréable sur le devant; **5** Astrol, Ling aspect *m*; **6** littér (appearance) aspect *m*; **a man of repulsive ~** un homme à l'allure repoussante.

aspen /ˈæspən/ *n* tremble *m*.

asperity /əˈsperətɪ/ *n* sout (of voice, style) aspérité *f*; (of person, comments) mordant *m*.

aspersions /əˈspɜːʃns, US -ʒnz/ *npl* sout **to cast ~ on** dénigrer [*person*]; mettre en doute [*ability, capacity*]; **are you casting ~?** vous semez le doute?

asphalt /ˈæsfælt, US -fɔːlt/ **I** *n* bitume *m*.
II *modif* [*drive, playground*] bitumé.
III *vtr* bitumer.

asphodel /ˈæsfədel/ *n* asphodèle *m*.

asphyxia /əsˈfɪksɪə, US æsˈf-/ *n* Med asphyxie *f*; **the cause of death was ~** la mort est due à l'asphyxie; **to die from ~** mourir asphyxié.

asphyxiate /əsˈfɪksɪeɪt, US æsˈf-/ **I** *vtr* asphyxier; **they were ~d by the smoke** ils ont été asphyxiés par la fumée.
II *vi* s'asphyxier.

asphyxiation /əsˌfɪksɪˈeɪʃn/ *n* Med asphyxie *f*; **to die of** ou **from ~** mourir asphyxié; **to cause death by** ou **through ~** entraîner la mort par asphyxie.

aspic /ˈæspɪk/ *n* Culin aspic *m*; **salmon in ~** aspic de saumon; **to preserve sth in ~** fig garder qch en conserve.

aspidistra /ˌæspɪˈdɪstrə/ *n* aspidistra *m*.

aspirant /əˈspaɪərənt/ **I** *n* **to be an ~ to sth** aspirer a qch.
II *adj* **these ~ actors/managers** ces gens qui aspirent à devenir acteurs/directeurs.

aspirate **I** /ˈæspərət/ *n* Phon aspirée *f*.
II /ˈæspərət/ *adj* aspiré.
III /ˈæspɪreɪt/ *vtr* (all contexts) aspirer.

aspiration /ˌæspɪˈreɪʃn/ *n* **1** (desire) aspiration *f* (**to** à); **to have ~s to do** aspirer à faire; **2** Med, Phon aspiration *f*.

aspire /əˈspaɪə(r)/ *vi* aspirer (**to** à; **to do** à faire); **it ~s to be an exclusive restaurant** cela se veut un restaurant de luxe.

aspirin /ˈæsprɪn/ *n* aspirine® *f*; **two ~(s)** deux comprimés d'aspirine; **half an ~** un demi comprimé d'aspirine.

aspiring /əˈspaɪərɪŋ/ *adj* **~ authors/journalists etc** ceux qui aspirent à devenir auteurs/journalistes etc.

ass /æs/ *n* **1** (donkey) âne *m*; **2**○ (fool) idiot/-e *m/f*; **to make an ~ of oneself** se rendre ridicule; **the law is an ~** GB la loi est absurde; **3**◑ US cul◑ *m*.
IDIOMS **to get one's ~ in gear**◑, **to get off one's ~**◑ se magner le cul◑; **get your ~ out of here**◑! fous le camp◑!; **to have sb's ~**◑ se venger; **piece of ~**◑ nana◑ *f*; **to kick (some) ~**◑ cogner○; **to kiss sb's ~**◑ lécher le cul à qn◑; **not to know one's ~ from a hole in the ground**◑ être con◑ comme un balai; **to work one's ~ off**◑ travailler dur; **your ~ is grass**◑! tu vas en baver!

assail /əˈseɪl/ *vtr* sout **1** (attack) attaquer [*person*]; **2** (plague, harass) assaillir; **to be ~ed by worries/by doubts/by questions** être assailli par les soucis/par le doute/de questions; **we are constantly ~ed by demands** on nous bombarde de demandes.

assailant /əˈseɪlənt/ *n* **1** (criminal) agresseur *m*; **2** Mil assaillant/-e *m/f*.

Assam /æˈsæm/ **I** *pr n* (province) Assam *m*.
II *n* (tea) thé *m* d'Assam.

assassin /əˈsæsɪn, US -sn/ *n* assassin *m*.

assassinate /əˈsæsɪneɪt, US -sən-/ *vtr* assassiner.

assassination /əˌsæsɪˈneɪʃn, US -səˈneɪʃn/ **I** *n* assassinat *m*.
II *modif* [*bid, attempt*] d'assassinat.

assault /əˈsɔːlt/ **I** *n* **1** Jur (on person) agression *f* (**on** sur); (sexual) agression *f* sexuelle (**on** sur); **physical ~** agression *f*; **verbal ~** injures *fpl*; **2** gen, Mil (attack) assaut *m* (**on** de); **air/ground ~** assaut aérien/terrestre; **to make an ~ on** monter à l'assaut de [*fortress, town*]; attaquer [*troops*]; **to make an ~ on a record** Sport essayer de battre un record; **3** fig (criticism) (on belief, theory, shortcoming) attaque *f* (**on** de); (on person, organisation, reputation) atteinte *f* (**on** à); **to make an ~ on** attaquer [*policy, supposition*]; **4** fig (on ears, nerves) agression *f* (**on** de).
II *modif* [*troops, weapon, ship*] d'assaut.
III *vtr* **1** Jur agresser [*person*]; **to be indecently ~ed** être victime d'une agression sexuelle; **2** Mil assaillir; **3** fig agresser [*ears, nerves*].

assault: **~ and battery** *n* Jur coups *mpl* et blessures *fpl*; **~ charge** *n* accusation *f* de coups et blessures; **~ course** *n* Mil parcours *m* du combattant; **~ craft** *n* bateau *m* d'assaut; **~ rifle** *n* fusil *m* d'assaut.

assay /əˈseɪ/ Miner, Mining **I** *n* essai *m*.
II *vtr* analyser.

ass-backwards◑ /ˌæsˈbækwədz/ US **I** *adj* sans queue ni tête.
II *adv* **he does everything ~** il fait tout à l'envers.

assegai /ˈæsəgaɪ/ *n* sagaie *f*.

assemblage /əˈsemblɪdʒ/ *n* sout **1** (collection of people, animals, objects, ideas) collection *f*; **2** Tech, Art assemblage *m*.

assemble /əˈsembl/ **I** *vtr* **1** (gather) rassembler [*data, ingredients, people*]; **2** (construct) assembler; **easy to ~** facile à monter.
II *vi* [*marchers, passengers, vehicles*] se

rassembler; [*parliament, team, family*] se réunir.

III **assembled** *pp adj* [*reporters, delegates*] rassemblé; [*family, friends*] réuni; **the ~d company** l'assistance.

assembler /ə'semblə(r)/ ▶ 1692 *n* **1** (in factory) assembleur/-euse *m/f*; **2** (company) entreprise *f* d'assemblage; **3** Comput assembleur *m*.

assembly /ə'semblɪ/ *n* **1** (of people) assemblée *f*; **2** Pol (institution) assemblée *f*; **legislative/general ~** assemblée législative/générale; **3** Sch rassemblement *m*; **4** Pol (congregating) réunion *f*; **freedom of ~** liberté *f* de réunion; **5** Ind, Tech (of components, machines) assemblage *m*; **~ instructions** instructions *fpl* de montage; **6** (of data, facts) rassemblement *m*; **7** Tech (device) assemblage *m*; **engine ~** bloc-moteur *m*; **tail ~** Aviat dérive *f*; **8** Comput assemblage *m*.

assembly: **~ hall** *n* hall *m* de réunion; **~ language** *n* Comput langage *m* assembleur.

assembly line *n* chaîne *f* de montage; **to work on the ~** travailler à la chaîne.

assembly: **~man** *n* US Pol membre *m* d'une assemblée législative; **~ plant** *n* Aut, Ind usine *f* de montage; **~ point** *n* lieu *m* de rassemblement; **~ room** *n* salle *f* de réunion; **~ shop** *n* Ind atelier *m* de montage; **~woman** *n* US membre *m* d'une assemblée législative.

assent /ə'sent/ **I** *n* assentiment *m*; **to give one's ~ to sth** donner son assentiment à qch; **he nodded his ~** il acquiesça d'un signe de tête; **by common ~** d'un commun accord.

II *vi* sout donner son assentiment (**to** à).

assert /ə'sɜːt/ **I** *vtr* **1** (state) affirmer (**that** que); (against opposition) soutenir (**that** que); **to ~ one's authority/strength** affirmer son autorité/pouvoir; **2** (demand) revendiquer [*right, claim*].

II *v refl* **to ~ oneself** s'affirmer.

assertion /ə'sɜːʃn/ *n* (statement) déclaration *f* (**that** selon laquelle); **it was an ~ of her strength/authority** c'était une manière d'affirmer son pouvoir/autorité.

assertive /ə'sɜːtɪv/ *adj* assuré.

assertiveness /ə'sɜːtɪvnɪs/ *n* Psych, Admin affirmation *f* de soi; **lack of ~** manque *m* d'assurance; **I admire your ~** j'admire votre assurance *f*.

assertiveness training *n* formation *f* à l'affirmation de soi.

assess /ə'ses/ **I** *vtr* **1** gen évaluer [*ability, effect, person, problem, result, work*]; **2** Fin, Insur, Jur estimer [*damage, loss, property, value*]; **3** Tax imposer [*person*]; fixer [*tax, amount*]; **to be ~ed for tax** être imposé; **4** Sch contrôler [*pupil*].

II *vi* évaluer.

assessable /ə'sesəbl/ *adj* imposable.

assessment /ə'sesmənt/ *n* **1** gen appréciation *f* (**of** de); **2** Fin, Insur, Jur estimation *f* (**of** de); **3** Tax (also **tax ~**) imposition *f*; **4** Sch contrôle *m*.

assessor /ə'sesə(r)/ ▶ 1692 *n* **1** Fin contrôleur *m*; **2** Insur expert *m*; **3** Jur assesseur *m*.

asset /'æset/ **I** *n* **1** Fin bien *m*; **2** fig (advantage) (quality, skill, person) atout *m*; **she is a great ~ to the team** elle est un grand atout pour l'équipe.

II **assets** *npl* (private) biens *mpl*, avoir *m* ¢; Comm, Fin, Jur actif *m* ¢; **~s and liabilities** actif et passif; **capital/property ~s** actif financier/immobilier.

asset: **~ stripper** *n* dépeceur *m*; **~ stripping** *n* dépeçage *m*.

asseverate /ə'sevəreɪt/ *vtr* sout affirmer solennellement.

asseveration /əˌsevə'reɪʃn/ *n* sout affirmation *f* solennelle.

asshole● /'æshəʊl/ *n* US connard◑/conasse◑ *m/f*.

assiduity /ˌæsɪ'djuːətɪ, US -duː-/ *n* assiduité *f*.

assiduous /ə'sɪdjʊəs, US -dʒʊəs/ *adj* assidu.

assiduously /ə'sɪdjʊəslɪ, US -dʒʊəslɪ/ *adv* assidûment.

assign /ə'saɪn/ *vtr* **1** (allocate) assigner [*funding, resources, housing, task*] (**to** à); **2** (delegate) **to ~ a task to sb, to ~ sb to a task** affecter qn à une tâche; **to ~ sb to do** désigner qn pour faire; **they were ~ed certain duties** on les a désignés pour faire certaines tâches; **3** (attribute) attribuer [*role, importance, name, value, responsibility*] (**to** à); **4** (appoint) nommer (**to** à); **5** Jur (transfer) céder; **6** (fix) assigner [*time, date, place*] (**for** à); **7** Comput **to ~ sth to a key** affecter qch à une touche.

assignation /ˌæsɪg'neɪʃn/ *n* **1** sout ou hum rendez-vous *m* (**with** avec); **2** Jur cession *f*.

assignee /ˌæsaɪ'niː/ *n* cessionnaire *mf*.

assignment /ə'saɪnmənt/ *n* **1** (professional) (diplomatic, military) poste *m*; (specific duty) mission *f*; **to be on ~ to** être en poste à; **2** (academic) devoir *m*; **3** (of duties, staff, funds) affectation *f*; **4** Jur (of rights, contract) cession *f*.

assignor /ə'saɪnə(r)/ *n* cédant *m*.

assimilate /ə'sɪmɪleɪt/ **I** *vtr* (all contexts) assimiler (**to** à).

II *vi* s'assimiler (**to** à).

assimilation /əˌsɪmɪ'leɪʃn/ *n* (all contexts) assimilation *f* (**to** à).

Assisi /ə'siːsɪ/ ▶ 1818 *pr n* Assise.

assist /ə'sɪst/ **I** *n* US Sport assistance *f*.

II *vtr* **1** (help) gen aider; (in organization, bureaucracy) assister (**to do, in doing** à faire); **to ~ sb in/out/down etc** aider qn à entrer/sortir/descendre etc; **to ~ one another** s'entraider; **to ~ sb financially** aider qn financièrement; **a man is ~ing police with their inquiries** euph un homme est interrogé par la police dans le cadre de l'enquête; **2** (facilitate) faciliter [*development, process, safety*].

III *vi* **1** (help) aider (**in doing** à faire); **to ~ in** prendre part à [*operation, rescue*]; **2** sout (attend) assister (**at** à).

IV **-assisted** (*dans composés*) **computer/operator-~ed** assisté par ordinateur/par un opérateur; **government-~ed scheme** projet financé par l'État.

assistance /ə'sɪstəns/ *n* aide *f* (**to** à); (more formal) (in organization, bureaucracy) assistance *f* (**to** à); **to come to sb's ~** venir à l'aide de qn; **to give ~ to sb** prêter assistance à qn; **with the ~ of** avec l'aide de [*person*]; à l'aide de [*device, instrument, tool etc*]; **mutual ~** entraide *f*; **financial/economic/military ~** aide *f* financière/économique/militaire; **can I be of ~?** puis-je aider or être utile?

assistant /ə'sɪstənt/ ▶ 1692 **I** *n* **1** (helper) assistant/-e *m/f*; (in bureaucratic hierarchy) adjoint/-e *m/f*; **2** GB Sch, Univ (**foreign language**) **~** (in school) assistant/-e *m/f*; (in university) lecteur/-trice *m/f*.

II *modif* [*editor, librarian, producer etc*] adjoint.

assistant: **~ manager** ▶ 1692 *n* gérant/-e *m/f* adjoint/-e; **~ professor** ▶ 1692 *n* US Univ ≈ maître assistant *m*; **~ sales manager** ▶ 1692 *n* directeur/-trice *m/f* des ventes adjoint/-e.

assistantship /ə'sɪstəntʃɪp/ *n* US Univ *poste d'assistant pour des étudiants diplômés chargés de travaux dirigés*.

assist: **~ed place** *n* GB Sch *place d'élève subventionnée par l'État dans une école privée*; **~ed reproduction** *n* procréation *f* médicalement assistée.

assizes /ə'saɪzɪz/ *npl* GB Jur assises *fpl*.

ass-kisser◑ /'æskɪsə(r)/ *n* lèche-cul◑ *mf inv*.

associate I /ə'səʊʃɪət/ *n* **1** (colleague, partner) associé/-e *m/f* also péj; **she's a business ~ of mine** c'est une de mes associées; **an ~ in crime** un/une complice; **Browns and Associates** Comm Browns et Associés; **2** (of society) associé/-e *m/f*; (of academic body) membre *m*; **3** US Univ ≈ Deug *m*.

II /ə'səʊʃɪət/ *adj* [*body, member*] associé.

III /ə'səʊʃɪeɪt/ *vtr* **1** (connect in thought, imagination) associer; **to ~ X with Y** associer X à Y; **these symptoms are ~d with old age** ces symptômes sont associés à la vieillesse; **I ~ him with Communism** je l'associe au communisme; **2** (be involved in) **to be ~d with** [*person*] faire partie de [*movement, group*]; péj être mêlé à [*shady business*]; **I don't want to be ~d with such a dishonest plan** je ne souhaite pas être mêlé à un projet si malhonnête.

IV /ə'səʊʃɪeɪt/ *vi* **to ~ with sb** fréquenter qn.

V **associated** *pp adj* **1** (linked in thought) [*concept*] associé; **2** (connected) [*member*] associé; [*benefits, expenses*] annexe; **the department and its ~d services and committees** le département et les services et comités adjoints; **the plan and its ~d issues/problems** le projet et les questions/problèmes qui en découlent.

VI /ə'səʊʃɪeɪt/ *v refl* **to ~ oneself with** s'associer à [*campaign, policy*].

associate: **~ company** société *f* liée; **~ dean** Univ vice-président/-e *m/f*; **~ director** *n* Theat directeur/-trice *m/f* associé/-e; Comm directeur/-trice *m/f* adjoint/-e; **Associated Press**, **AP** *n* Journ *une des principales agences de presse*; **~ editor** ▶ 1692 rédacteur/-trice *m/f* associé/-e; **~ judge** *n* juge *m* assesseur; **~ justice** *n* US juge *m* de la Cour Suprême; **~ member** *n* membre *m* associé; **~ membership** *n* adhésion *f* en tant que membre associé; **~ professor** ▶ 1692 *n* US Univ ≈ maître *m* de conférences.

association /əˌsəʊsɪ'eɪʃn/ *n* **1** (club, society) association *f*; **to form/join an ~** former/rejoindre une association; **2** (relationship) (between ideas) association *f*; (between organizations, people) relations *fpl* (**between** entre; **with** avec); (sexual) liaison *f* (**with** avec); **a close ~** une étroite association; **in ~ with** en association avec; **3** (mental evocation) (*gén au pl*) souvenir *m*; **to have good/bad ~s for sb** rappeler de bons/mauvais souvenirs à qn; **to have ~s with sth** évoquer qch; **the word 'feminist' has certain ~s** le mot 'féministe' a certaines connotations.

association football *n* football *m*.

associative /ə'səʊʃɪətɪv/ *adj* associatif/-ive.

associative store, associative storage *n* Comput mémoire *f* associative.

assonance /'æsənəns/ *n* assonance *f*.

assorted /ə'sɔːtɪd/ *adj* [*objects, events, colours etc*] varié; [*foodstuffs*] assorti; [*group*] hétérogène; **ill ~** mal assorti; **in ~ sizes** dans toutes les tailles.

assortment /ə'sɔːtmənt/ *n* (of objects, products, colours) assortiment *m* (**of** de); (of people) mélange *m* (**of** de); **in an ~ of colours/sizes** dans différentes couleurs/tailles.

Asst. *abrév écrite* = **assistant**.

assuage /æ'sweɪdʒ/ *vtr* littér apaiser [*sorrow, pain, fear*]; étancher [*thirst*]; assouvir [*hunger, desire*].

assume /ə'sjuːm, US ə'suːm/ *vtr* **1** (suppose) supposer (**that** que); **I ~ she knows** je suppose qu'elle sait; **we must ~ that** on doit présumer que; **I ~ him to be French** je suppose qu'il est français; **assuming that to be true** en supposant que cela soit vrai; **it is/has been ~d that** on suppose/a supposé que; **tomorrow, I ~** demain, je suppose; **it is widely ~d that she knows** il est communément admis qu'elle sait; **let's ~** ou **assuming that's correct** supposons que cela soit exact; **they just ~ (that) he can't do it** ils croient qu'il est incapable de le faire; **2** (take on) prendre [*control, identity, office, power, significance, shape*]; assumer [*duty, responsibility*]; affecter [*air, attitude, expression, ignorance, indifference*]; **under an ~d name** sous un nom d'emprunt.

assumption /ə'sʌmpʃn/ *n* **1** (supposition) supposition *f*; (belief) idée *f*; Philos, Sci hypo-

> **at**
> When *at* is used as a straightforward preposition it is translated by *à*:
> *at the airport* = à l'aéroport
> *at midnight* = à minuit
> *at the age of 50* = à l'âge de 50 ans
>
> Remember that *à + le always* becomes *au* and *à + les always* becomes *aux* (*au bureau, aux bureaux*).
>
> When *at* means *at the house, shop*, etc. *of* it is translated by *chez*:
> *at Amanda's* = chez Amanda
> *at the hairdresser's* = chez le coiffeur
>
> If you have doubts about how to translate a phrase or idiom beginning with *at* (*at the top of, at home, at a guess* etc.) you should consult the appropriate noun entry (***top, home, guess*** etc.). This dictionary contains usage notes on such topics as ***age, the clock, length measurement, games and sports*** etc. Many of these use the preposition *at*. For the index to these notes ▶ **1919**.
>
> *at* also often appears in English as the second element of a phrasal verb (*look at, aim at* etc.). For translations, look at the appropriate verb entry (***look, aim*** etc.).
>
> *at* is used after certain nouns, adjectives and verbs in English (*her surprise at, an attempt at, annoyed at* etc.). For translations, consult the appropriate noun, adjective or verb entry (***surprise, attempt, annoy*** etc.).
>
> In the entry ***at***, you will find particular usages and idiomatic expressions which do not appear elsewhere in the dictionary.

thèse *f*; **the ~ that** l'idée selon laquelle; **on the ~ that** dans l'idée que; **to work on the ~ that** présumer que; **to make an ~** faire une supposition; **a false ~** Philos, Sci une mauvaise hypothèse; **2** (of duty, power) prise *f* (**of** de).

Assumption /ə'sʌmpʃn/ *n* Relig Assomption *f*.

assurance /ə'ʃɔ:rəns, US ə'ʃʊərəns/ *n* **1** (of sth done) assurance *f*; **to give sb an** ou **every ~ that** donner à qn l'assurance que; **2** (of future action, situation) promesse *f* (**of** de); **you have my ~ that** je peux vous assurer que; **repeated ~s** des promesses réitérées; **3** (self-confidence) assurance *f*; **4** GB Insur assurance *f*; **life ~** assurance-vie *f*.

assure /ə'ʃɔ:(r), US ə'ʃʊər/ *vtr* **1** (state positively) assurer; **to ~ sb that** assurer à qn que; **I (can) ~ you** je vous assure; **to be ~d of sth** être sûr de qch; **I was ~d by the council that** la municipalité m'a assuré que; **rest ~d that** soyez assuré que; **2** (ensure) assurer [*agreement, peace, safety etc*]; **this ~s her a place in the team** cela lui assure une place dans l'équipe; **3** GB Insur assurer.

assured /ə'ʃɔ:d, US ə'ʃʊərd/ **I** *n* GB Insur **the ~** l'assuré/-e *m/f*.
II *adj* **1** (confident) [*voice, manner*] assuré; [*person*] plein d'assurance; **she is very ~** elle a beaucoup d'assurance; **2** (beyond doubt) assuré.

assuredly /ə'ʃɔ:rɪdlɪ, US -'ʃʊər-/ *adv* sout assurément.

Assyria /ə'sɪrɪə/ ▶ **1131** *pr n* Hist Assyrie *f*.

Assyrian /ə'sɪrɪən/ ▶ **1486**, **1402** **I** *n* **1** (person) Assyrien/-ienne *m/f*; **2** (language) assyrien *m*.
II *adj* assyrien/-ienne.

AST *n*: *abrév* ▶ **Atlantic Standard Time**.

astatine /'æstəti:n/ *n* astate *m*.

aster /'æstə(r)/ *n* aster *m*.

asterisk /'æstərɪsk/ **I** *n* astérisque *m*; **marked with an ~** marqué d'un astérisque.
II *vtr* marquer [qch] d'un astérisque.

astern /ə'stɜ:n/ *adv* Naut à l'arrière (**of** de); **to go ~** [*vessel*] faire machine arrière.

asteroid /'æstərɔɪd/ *n* astéroïde *m*.

asthma /'æsmə, US 'æzmə/ ▶ **1354** **I** *n* asthme *m*; **to have ~** avoir de l'asthme.
II *modif* **~ sufferer** asthmatique *mf*.

asthmatic /æs'mætɪk/ *n, adj* asthmatique (*mf*).

astigmatic /,æstɪg'mætɪk/ *n, adj* astigmate (*mf*).

astigmatism /ə'stɪgmətɪzəm/ *n* astigmatisme *m*.

astir /ə'stɜ:(r)/ *adj* **1** (up and about) debout *inv*; **2** (moving) en mouvement.

ASTMS /'æstmz/ *n* GB (*abrév* = **Association of Scientific, Technical, and Managerial Staffs**) syndicat *m* des employés de bureau et de laboratoire.

astonish /ə'stɒnɪʃ/ *vtr* surprendre, étonner; **it ~es me that** ce qui me surprend ou m'étonne c'est que; **I was ~ed by his answer** sa réponse m'a vraiment surpris ou étonné; **you ~ me!** iron tu m'étonnes!

astonished /ə'stɒnɪʃt/ *adj* surpris, étonné (**by, at** par; **to do** de faire); **to be ~ that** être vraiment étonné que (+ *subj*), trouver extraordinaire que (+ *subj*).

astonishing /ə'stɒnɪʃɪŋ/ *adj* [*ability, skill, intelligence, generosity*] étonnant; [*bargain, career, performance*] extraordinaire; [*beauty, energy, speed, success, profit*] incroyable; **it is ~ that** il est incroyable que (+ *subj*); **prices rose by an ~ 40%** les prix ont augmenté de 40%, pourcentage étonnant.

astonishingly /ə'stɒnɪʃɪŋlɪ/ *adv* incroyablement; **~ (enough), they won!** chose extraordinaire, ils ont gagné!

astonishment /ə'stɒnɪʃmənt/ *n* surprise *f*, étonnement *m*; **in** ou **with ~** avec surprise ou stupéfaction; **to my/her ~** à ma/sa grande surprise; **to look at sb/sth in ~** regarder qn/qch avec étonnement.

astound /ə'staʊnd/ *vtr* stupéfier; **to be ~ed by sth** être stupéfié par qch.

astounded /ə'staʊndɪd/ *adj* stupéfait (**at** de; **to do** de faire).

astounding /ə'staʊndɪŋ/ *adj* incroyable.

astrakhan /,æstrə'kæn, US 'æstrəkən/ **I** *n* astrakan *m*.
II *modif* [*garment*] d'astrakan.

astral /'æstrəl/ *adj* astral.

astray /ə'streɪ/ *adv* **1 to go astray** (go missing) [*object, funds*] se perdre, être perdu; [*person*] se perdre; **2 to go astray** (go wrong) [*plan etc*] être contrarié; **3** fig **to lead sb ~** (confuse) induire qn en erreur; (corrupt) détourner qn du droit chemin.

astride /ə'straɪd/ **I** *adv* lit [*be, ride, sit*] à califourchon; [*stand*] jambes écartées.
II *prep* (seated) à califourchon sur; (standing) jambes écartées au-dessus de; fig **to stand** ou **sit ~ sth** [*building, company etc*] dominer qch.

astringent /ə'strɪndʒənt/ **I** *n* astringent *m*.
II *adj* **1** Cosmet, Med astringent; **2** fig [*remark, tone*] cinglant.

astrologer /ə'strɒlədʒə(r)/ ▶ **1692** *n* astrologue *mf*.

astrological /,æstrə'lɒdʒɪkl/ *adj* astrologique.

astrologist /ə'strɒlədʒɪst/ *n* = **astrologer**.

astrology /ə'strɒlədʒɪ/ *n* astrologie *f*.

astronaut /'æstrənɔ:t/ ▶ **1692** *n* astronaute *mf*.

astronautical /,æstrə'nɔ:tɪkl/ *adj* astronautique.

astronautics /,æstrə'nɔ:tɪks/ *n* (+ *v sg*) astronautique *f*.

astronomer /ə'strɒnəmə(r)/ ▶ **1692** *n* astronome *mf*.

astronomical /,æstrə'nɒmɪkl/, **astronomic** /,æstrə'nɒmɪk/ *adj* Astron, fig astronomique.

astronomically /,æstrə'nɒmɪkəlɪ/ *adv* **prices are ~ high** les prix sont astronomiques; **~ expensive** incroyablement cher.

astronomy /ə'strɒnəmɪ/ *n* astronomie *f*.

astrophysicist /,æstrəʊ'fɪzɪsɪst/ ▶ **1692** *n* astrophysicien/-ienne *m/f*.

astrophysics /,æstrəʊ'fɪzɪks/ *n* (+ *v sg*) astrophysique *f*.

Astroturf® /'æstrəʊtɜ:f/ *n* gazon *m* artificiel.

astute /ə'stju:t, US ə'stu:t/ *adj* astucieux/-ieuse.

astutely /ə'stju:tlɪ, US ə'stu:tlɪ/ *adv* astucieusement.

astuteness /ə'stju:tnɪs, US -'stu:-/ *n* astuce *f*.

asunder /ə'sʌndə(r)/ *adv* littér **to tear sth ~** déchirer qch.

Aswan /æs'wɑ:n/ *pr n* Assouan; **~ High Dam** (haut) barrage *m* d'Assouan.

asylant /ə'saɪlənt/ *n* sout réfugié/-e *m/f*.

asylum /ə'saɪləm/ *n* **1** gen, Pol asile *m*; **to grant/give/seek ~** accorder/donner/chercher asile; **political ~** asile politique; **right of ~** droit *m* d'asile; **2†** Med péj asile *m*; **lunatic ~** asile de fous.

asylum-seeker *n* demandeur/-euse *m/f* d'asile.

asymmetric /,eɪsɪ'metrɪk/, **asymmetrical** /,eɪsɪ'metrɪkl/ *adj* asymétrique; **~ bars** Sport barres asymétriques.

asymmetry /eɪ'sɪmɪtrɪ, æ'sɪmɪtrɪ/ *n* asymétrie *f*.

asynchronous /eɪ'sɪŋkrənəs/ *adj* Comput asynchrone.

at /æt, ət/ *prep* **1** (with place, time, age etc) à; **2** (at the house etc of) chez; **3** (followed by superlative) **the garden is ~ its prettiest in June** juin est le mois où le jardin est le plus beau; **I'm ~ my best in the morning** c'est le matin que je me sens le mieux; **he was ~ his most irritating** il était particulièrement énervant; **she was ~ her best ~ 50** (of musician, artist etc) à 50 ans elle était au sommet de son art; **4○** (harassing) **he's been (on) ~ me to buy a new car** il n'arrête pas de me casser les pieds pour que j'achète une nouvelle voiture○.
IDIOMS **I don't know where he's ~○** je ne le comprends pas du tout; **while we're ~ it○** pendant qu'on y est○; **I've been (hard) ~ it all day** je n'ai pas arrêté de la journée; **they're ~ it again○!** les voilà qui recommencent!

AT *n*: *abrév* ▶ **alternative technology**.

atavism /'ætəvɪzəm/ *n* atavisme *m*.

atavistic /,ætə'vɪstɪk/ *adj* atavique.

ataxia /ə'tæksɪə/ *n* ataxie *f*.

ataxic /ə'tæksɪk/ *adj* ataxique.

ATB *n*: *abrév* ▶ **all-terrain bike**.

ATC *n* **1** *abrév* ▶ **air-traffic control**; **2** GB (*abrév* = **Air Training Corps**) unité *f* de préparation militaire pour l'armée de l'air (*jusqu'à 18 ans*).

ate /eɪt/ *prét* ▶ **eat**.

Athanasian Creed /,æθəneɪʃn 'kri:d/ *n* credo *m* de Saint Athanase.

atheism /'eɪθɪɪzəm/ *n* athéisme *m*.

atheist /'eɪθɪɪst/ *n, adj* athée (*mf*).

atheistic /,eɪθɪ'ɪstɪk/ *adj* athée.

Athena /ə'θi:nə/ *pr n* Athéna.

Athenian /ə'θi:nɪən/ **I** *n* Athénien/-ienne *m/f*.
II *adj* athénien/-ienne.

Athens /'æθɪnz/ ▶ **1818** *pr n* Athènes.

athirst /ə'θɜ:st/ *adj* littér **to be ~ for sth** être assoiffé de qch.

athlete /'æθli:t/ *n* athlète *mf*.

athlete's foot /,æθli:ts 'fʊt/ ▶ **1354** *n* mycose *f*, champignons *mpl* aux pieds; **to have ~** avoir une mycose.

athletic /æθ'letɪk/ *adj* **1** [*event, club, coach*] d'athlétisme; **2** [*person, body*] athlétique.

athletics /æθ'letɪks/ ▶ **1282** **I** *n* (+ *v sg*) GB athlétisme *m*; US sports *mpl*.
II *modif* [*club*] GB d'athlétisme; US sportif/-ive.

athletic support GB, **athletic supporter** US *n* suspensoir *m*.

atishoo /əˈtɪʃu:/ *excl* atchoum!

Atlantic /ətˈlæntɪk/ **I** ▶1511 *pr n* **the ~** l'Atlantique *m*.

II *adj* gen de l'Atlantique; [*coast, current*] atlantique.

Atlantic: **~ Charter** *n* Hist Pacte *m* atlantique; **~ Ocean** *n* océan *m* Atlantique; **~ Provinces** *npl* Provinces *fpl* atlantiques; **~ Standard Time, AST** *n* heure *f* normale de l'Atlantique.

Atlantis /ətˈlæntɪs/ *pr n* l'Atlantide *f*.

atlas /ˈætləs/ *n* atlas *m*; **road/motoring ~** atlas routier/automobile.

Atlas Mountains *pr npl* (montagnes *fpl* de l')Atlas *m*.

ATM *n*: *abrév* ▶ **automatic teller machine**.

atmosphere /ˈætməsfɪə(r)/ *n* **1** (air) gen, Phys atmosphère *f*; **the earth's ~** l'atmosphère terrestre; **2** (mood) gen ambiance *f*; (bad) atmosphère *f*; **there was a bit of an ~**○ l'atmosphère était tendue; **the film is full of ~** le film est très évocateur.

atmospheric /ˌætməsˈferɪk/ **I atmospherics** *npl* **1** Radio, TV (interference) parasites *mpl*, bruit *m* atmosphérique; Meteorol (disturbances) perturbations *fpl* atmosphériques; **2** (of song, film) ambiance *f*.

II *adj* **1** [*conditions, pressure, pollution*] atmosphérique; **2** [*film, lighting, music*] d'ambiance.

atoll /ˈætɒl/ *n* atoll *m*.

atom /ˈætəm/ *n* Phys, fig atome *m*; **hydrogen ~** atome d'hydrogène.

atom bomb *n* bombe *f* atomique.

atomic /əˈtɒmɪk/ *adj* **1** [*structure*] atomique; **2** [*weapon, explosion, power*] nucléaire, atomique.

atomic: **Atomic Energy Authority, AEA** *n* GB Commissariat *m* à l'énergie atomique; **Atomic Energy Commission, AEC** *n* US Commissariat *m* à l'énergie atomique; **~ power station** *n* centrale *f* atomique; **~ reactor** *n* réacteur *m* atomique; **~ scientist** ▶1692 *n* atomiste *mf*; **~ theory** *n* théorie *f* atomique; **~ weight** *n* masse *f* atomique.

atomize /ˈætəmaɪz/ *vtr* **1** Phys (into atoms) atomiser; **2** (into spray) atomiser; **3** (destroy) pulvériser.

atomizer /ˈætəmaɪzə(r)/ *n* atomiseur *m*.

atonal /eɪˈtəʊnl/ *adj* atonal.

atonality /ˌeɪtəʊˈnælətɪ/ *n* atonalité *f*.

atone /əˈtəʊn/ *vi* **to ~ for** expier [*sin, crime*]; racheter [*error, rudeness*].

atonement /əˈtəʊnmənt/ *n* rédemption *f*; **Day of Atonement** Grand Pardon *m*.

atonic /əˈtɒnɪk/ *adj* Med, Mus atone.

atop /əˈtɒp/ *prep* littér en haut de.

atria /ˈeɪtrɪə/ *pl* ▶ **atrium**.

atrium /ˈeɪtrɪəm/ *n* (*pl* **atria**) **1** Anat orifice *m* auriculo-ventriculaire; **2** Archit atrium *m*.

atrocious /əˈtrəʊʃəs/ *adj* **1** (horrifying) [*crime, treatment etc*] atroce; **2** (bad) [*accent, spelling, price etc*] épouvantable; [*food*] infecte.

atrociously /əˈtrəʊʃəslɪ/ *adv* de façon atroce.

atrocity /əˈtrɒsətɪ/ *n* (all contexts) atrocité *f*.

atrophied /ˈætrəfɪd/ *adj* (all contexts) atrophié.

atrophy /ˈætrəfɪ/ **I** *n* **1** (degeneration) dégénérescence *f*; **2** Med atrophie *f*.

II *vi* Med, fig s'atrophier.

attaboy○ /ˈætəbɔɪ/ *excl* US bravo!

attach /əˈtætʃ/ **I** *vtr* **1** (fasten) attacher [*objet*] (**to** à); (to letter) joindre; **2** (to organization) **to be ~ed to sth** être attaché à qch; **3** (attribute) attacher [*condition, importance*] (**to** à); **to ~ blame to sb for sth** reprocher qch à qn.

II *vi* sout **to ~ to sth** [*blame*] reposer sur qch; [*responsibility*] faire partie de qch; [*salary*] être afférent à qch.

III *v refl* **to ~ oneself to sb/sth** lit, fig s'attacher à qn/qch.

attaché /əˈtæʃeɪ, US ˌætəˈʃeɪ/ *n* attaché/-e *m/f*; **cultural/military/press ~** attaché/-e culturel/-elle/militaire/de presse.

attaché case *n* attaché-case *m*.

attached /əˈtætʃt/ *adj* **1** (fond) **~ to sb/sth** attaché à qn/qch; **to grow ~ to sb/sth** s'attacher à qn/qch; **2** [*document, photograph*] ci-joint; **3** [*outbuilding*] attenant; **a house with ~ garage** ou **with garage ~** une maison avec un garage attenant.

attachment /əˈtætʃmənt/ *n* **1** (affection) attachement *m* (**to, for** pour); **to form an ~ to sb** s'attacher à qn; **2** (device) accessoire *m*; **mixing/slicing ~** accessoire pour mixer/pour faire des tranches; **3** (placement) **to be on ~ to** être en détachement à; **4** (act of fastening) fixation *f*; **5** Jur **~ of earnings** retenue *f* sur salaire.

attack /əˈtæk/ **I** *n* **1** gen, Mil, Sport attaque *f* (**on** contre); (unprovoked, criminal) agression *f* (**against, on** contre); (terrorist) attentat *m*; **on the ~** à l'attaque; **to come under ~** Mil être attaqué (**from** par); fig être l'objet de critiques virulentes (**from** de la part de); **to leave oneself open to ~** fig s'exposer à la critique; **to feel under ~** se sentir agressé; **to mount** ou **launch an ~ on sth** lit attaquer; fig s'attaquer à qch; **2** Med (of chronic illness) crise *f* (**of** de); **to have an ~ of flu** attraper la grippe; **to have an ~ of hiccups** avoir le hoquet; **to have an ~ of giggles** être pris d'un fou rire.

II *vtr* **1** gen, Med, Mil, Sport attaquer [*person, enemy, position*]; (criminally) agresser [*victim*]; fig attaquer [*book, idea, policy*]; **2** (tackle) s'attaquer à [*task, problem*].

IDIOMS **~ is the best form of defence** l'attaque est la meilleure défense.

attacker /əˈtækə(r)/ *n* gen agresseur *m*; Mil, Sport attaquant/-e *m/f*; **sex ~** violeur *m*.

attain /əˈteɪn/ *vtr* **1** (achieve) atteindre [*position, objective*]; réaliser [*ambition*]; acquérir [*knowledge*]; parvenir à [*happiness*]; **2** (reach) atteindre [*eye*].

attainable /əˈteɪnəbl/ *adj* réalisable.

attainment /əˈteɪnmənt/ *n* **1** (achieving) (of knowledge) acquisition *f*; (of goal) réalisation *f*; **2** (success) réussite *f*.

attainment target *n* Sch cible *f* d'acquisition.

attempt /əˈtempt/ **I** *n* **1** tentative *f* (**to do** de faire); **to make an ~ to do** ou **at doing** tenter de faire; **in an ~ to do** pour essayer de faire; **on my/his first ~** dès ma/sa première tentative; **~ to escape, escape ~** tentative d'évasion; **to make an ~ on a record** tenter de battre un record; **at least she made an ~!** au moins elle a essayé!; **he made no ~ to apologize** il n'a même pas tenté de s'excuser; **good ~!** bien essayé!; **he made an ~ at a smile** il a esquissé un sourire; **it's my first ~ at a cake** c'est la première fois que je fais un gâteau; **not bad for a first ~!** ce n'est pas mal pour un premier essai!; **2** (attack) attentat *m*; **~ on sb's life** attentat contre la vie de qn; **to make an ~ on sb's life** attenter à la vie de qn.

II *vtr* tenter (**to do** de faire); s'attaquer à [*exam question*]; **to ~ suicide** tenter de se suicider; **to ~ the impossible** tenter l'impossible; **~ed robbery/murder** tentative de vol/meurtre.

attend /əˈtend/ **I** *vtr* **1** (go to, be present at) assister à [*birth, ceremony, auction, interview, meeting, performance*]; aller à [*church, school*]; suivre [*class, course*]; **the event was well/poorly ~ed** beaucoup de/peu de monde assistait à l'événement; **2** (accompany) [*courtier*] accompagner; [*consequence, danger*] fig sout accompagner; [*publicity*] fig sout entourer; **3** (take care of) soigner [*patient*].

II *vi* **1** (be present) être présent; **2** (pay attention) être attentif/-ive (**to** à); **now ~ to me, children**†! écoutez-moi bien, les enfants!

■ **attend to**: **~ to [sb/sth]** s'occuper de [*person, problem*]; **that lock/letter needs ~ing to, John** il faut s'occuper de cette serrure/lettre, John; **are you being ~ed to, madam?** est-ce que quelqu'un s'occupe de vous, madame?

attendance /əˈtendəns/ *n* **1** (presence) (at event, meeting, course) présence *f* (**at** à); (at clinic) visite *f* (**at** à); **church ~** pratique *f* religieuse; **school ~** gen fréquentation *f* scolaire; (for specific period) présence *f* à l'école; **his ~ at school has been poor** il n'a pas beaucoup fréquenté l'école; **to take ~** US Sch prendre les présences; **to be in ~** être présent; **2** (number of people present) assistance *f*; **3** (as helper, companion) **to be in ~ on** s'occuper de [*patient*]; accompagner [*dignitary*].

attendance: **~ allowance** *n* GB Soc Admin *allocation payée par l'État à quelqu'un qui s'occupe d'un proche sévèrement handicapé*; **~ centre** *n* GB Jur centre *m* de réinsertion sociale; **~ officer** ▶1692 *n* Sch inspecteur/-trice *m/f*; **~ record** *n* taux *m* de présence; **~ register** *n* Sch registre *m* des absences.

attendant /əˈtendənt/ **I** *n* **1** ▶1692 (in cloakroom, museum, car park) gardien/-ienne *m/f*; (in cinema) ouvreuse *f*; (at petrol station) pompiste *mf*; (at swimming pool) surveillant/-e *m/f*; **medical ~** membre *m* du personnel médical; **2** (for bride etc) demoiselle *f* d'honneur; **the queen and her ~s** la reine et sa suite; **3**† (servant) domestique *mf*.

II *adj* sout **1** (associated) [*cost, danger, issue, perk, problem*] associé; [*symptom*] concomitant; **2** (attending) [*aide, helper, bodyguard*] attaché à sa personne; [*nurse*] en charge.

attention /əˈtenʃn/ **I** *n* **1** (notice, interest) attention *f*; **media ~** attention des médias; **to attract (much) ~** attirer (beaucoup) l'attention; **to get/hold/have sb's ~** attirer/retenir/avoir l'attention de qn; **to be the centre** ou **focus of attention** être le centre d'attention; **to draw ~ to sth, to focus ~ on sth** attirer l'attention sur qch; **to seek** ou **demand ~** [*child*] chercher à attirer l'attention; **to give one's full ~ to sth** prêter toute son attention à qch; **to divide one's ~ between X and Y** partager son attention entre X et Y; **to turn one's ~ to sth** tourner son attention sur qch; **I wasn't paying ~** je ne faisais pas attention; **to bring sth to sb's ~** porter qch à l'attention de qn; **it has come to my ~ that** il est venu à mon attention que; **it has been drawn to my ~ that** j'ai appris que; **~ please!** votre attention s'il vous plaît!; **pay ~!** écoutez!; **2** (treatment, care) gen attention *f*; Med assistance *f*; **medical ~** assistance médicale; **his spelling needs ~** il doit faire attention à l'orthographe; **~ to detail** le souci du détail; **to give some ~ to sth** s'occuper de qch; **the car needs ~** il faut s'occuper de la voiture; **my hair needs ~** il faut que je fasse quelque chose pour mes cheveux; **I will give the matter my earliest** ou **urgent ~** sout je m'occuperai de la question dès que possible; **for the ~ of** à l'attention de; **some letters for your ~, sir** pourriez-vous regarder ces lettres monsieur?; **with proper ~ she will recover** si elle est bien suivie, elle se rétablira ; **with proper ~ the washing machine will last for years** bien entretenue, cette machine à laver marchera de nombreuses années; **3** Mil **to stand to** ou **at ~** être au garde-à-vous; **to come to ~** se mettre au garde-à-vous.

II *excl* Mil garde-à-vous!

attention-seeking **I** *n* besoin *m* d'attirer l'attention.

II *adj* [*person*] cherchant à attirer l'attention.

attention span *n* **he has a very short ~** il n'arrive pas à se concentrer très longtemps.

attentive /əˈtentɪv/ *adj* (alert) attentif/-ive; (solicitous) attentionné (**to** à).

attentively /əˈtentɪvlɪ/ *adv* (alertly) attentivement; (solicitously) avec attention.

attentiveness /əˈtentɪvnɪs/ *n* **1** (concentration) attention *f*; **2** (solicitude) prévenance *f*.

attenuate /əˈtenjʊeɪt/ **I** *adj* (also **attenuated**) atténué.
II *vtr* **1** modérer [*criticism, attack*]; **2** Med amincir.

attenuation /əˌtenjʊˈeɪʃn/ *n* **1** (of criticism, attack) modération *f*; **2** Med (of body, limb) amincissement *m*.

attest /əˈtest/ sout **I** *vtr* **1** (prove) confirmer; **an ~ed fact** un fait reconnu; **2** (declare) attester (**that** que); **3** (authenticate) légaliser [*will, signature*]; **4** Admin viser [*application, certificate*].
II *vi* **1 to ~ to** (prove) [*fact, development, skill*] témoigner de; **2** (affirm) attester; **as the figures will ~** comme les chiffres l'attesteront.

attestation /ˌæteˈsteɪʃn/ *n* attestation *f*.

attic /ˈætɪk/ *n* grenier *m*; **in the ~** au grenier.

Attica /ˈætɪkə/ *pr n* Attique *f*.

attic: **~ room** *n* mansarde *f*; **~ window** *n* lucarne *f*.

Attila /ˈætɪlə, əˈtɪlə/ *pr n* **~ the Hun** Attila, roi des Huns.

attire† /əˈtaɪə(r)/ **I** *n* gen vêtements *mpl*; hum accoutrement *m*; **in formal ~** en tenue officielle.
II *vtr* vêtir; **~d in** vêtu de.

attitude /ˈætɪtjuːd, US -tuːd/ **I** *n* **1** (way of behaving or reacting) attitude *f* (**to, towards** GB à l'égard de); **her ~ to life/the world** sa façon de voir la vie/le monde; **this will require a change in ~** ceci exigera un changement de comportement; **2** (affected pose) pose *f* affectée; **to strike an ~** prendre une pose affectée; **3**○ (assertiveness, dynamism) **to have ~** avoir de l'allure; **4** (physical position) position *f*.
II attitudes *npl* (of social group etc) comportements *mpl*.
III *modif* **to have an ~ problem** avoir des problèmes relationnels.

attitudinal /ˌætɪˈtjuːdɪnl/ *adj* [*change, problem*] d'attitude.

attitudinize /ˌætɪˈtjuːdɪnaɪz, US -ˈtuːdən-/ *vi* péj prendre une attitude affectée.

attorney /əˈtɜːnɪ/ *n* **1** ▶ **1692** US (lawyer) avocat *m*; **2 power of ~** procuration *f*; **letter of ~** procuration *f*.

Attorney General, AG *n* (*pl* **Attorneys General**) Attorney *m* General, ministre *m* de la justice des États-Unis.

attract /əˈtrækt/ *vtr* **1** gen attirer [*person, animal, students, buyers, custom, investment, criticism etc*]; **to ~ attention** attirer l'attention; **to ~ sb's attention** attirer l'attention de qn (**to** sur); **he was very ~ed to her** elle l'attirait beaucoup; **2** Fin [*account, sum*] comporter [*interest rate*].

attraction /əˈtrækʃn/ *n* **1** (favourable feature) (of proposal, place, offer) attrait *m* (**of sth** de qch; **of doing** de faire; **for** pour); **I can't see the ~ of (doing)** je ne vois pas l'intérêt de (faire); **to have** ou **hold little ~/some ~** présenter peu d'intérêt/un certain intérêt; **2** (entertainment, sight) attraction *f*; **tourist ~** attraction touristique; **the main ~** la principale attraction; **3** (instinctive or sexual allure) attirance *f* (**to** pour); **4** Phys attraction *f*; **5** Bot (to light) attirance *f*.

attractive /əˈtræktɪv/ *adj* [*person*] séduisant; [*child*] charmant; [*place, design, music, feature*] attrayant; [*offer, idea, rate*] séduisant, attrayant (**to** pour); [*plant*] joli; [*food*] appétissant; **he's/she's very ~** il/elle a beaucoup de charme.

attractively /əˈtræktɪvlɪ/ *adv* [*furnished, arranged*] de manière attrayante; [*dressed*] coquettement; **~ priced** mis en vente à un prix intéressant.

attractiveness /əˈtræktɪvnɪs/ *n* (of person, place) charme *m*; (of investment) attrait *m*; (of proposal) intérêt *m*.

attributable /əˈtrɪbjʊtəbl/ *adj* **to be ~ to** [*change, profit, success etc*] être dû à; [*error, fall, loss etc*] être imputable à.

attributable profit *n* Fin bénéfices *mpl* nets.

attribute I /ˈætrɪbjuːt/ *n* gen attribut *m*; Ling épithète *f*.
II /əˈtrɪbjuːt/ *vtr* attribuer [*blame, responsibility, crime, death, delay, profit, success*] (**to** à); imputer, attribuer [*error, failure, breakdown*] (**to** à); accorder [*features, qualities*] (**to** à); attribuer [*remark, statement, work of art*] (**to** à).

attribution /ˌætrɪˈbjuːʃn/ *n* attribution *f* (**of** de; **to** à).

attributive /əˈtrɪbjʊtɪv/ *adj* Ling épithète.

attributively /əˈtrɪbjʊtɪvlɪ/ *adv* Ling **used ~** employé comme épithète.

attrition /əˈtrɪʃn/ *n* (all contexts) usure *f*; **war of ~** guerre *f* d'usure.

attune /əˈtjuːn, US əˈtuːn/ **I** *vtr* **to be ~d to sth** être sensible à qch.
II *v refl* **to ~ oneself to sth** s'adapter à qch.

ATV *n*: *abrév* ▶ **all-terrain vehicle**.

atypical /ˌeɪˈtɪpɪkl/ *adj* atypique.

Aube ▶ **1163** *pr n* Aube *f*; **in/to the ~** dans l'Aube.

aubergine /ˈəʊbəʒiːn/ *n* GB aubergine *f*.

aubretia /ɔːˈbriːʃə/ *n* aubriétie *f*.

auburn /ˈɔːbən/ ▶ **1104** *adj* auburn *inv*.

auction /ˈɔːkʃn, ˈɒkʃn/ **I** *n* enchère *f* (*gen pl*); **at ~** aux enchères; **to put sth up for/to be up for ~** mettre qch/être aux enchères; **to sell/for sale by ~** vendre/en vente aux enchères; **to go to an ~** aller à une vente aux enchères.
II *vtr* vendre aux enchères; **they have ~ed their house** ils ont vendu leur maison aux enchères.
■ **auction off**: **~ [sth] off, ~ off [sth]** vendre qch aux enchères.

auction bridge *n* bridge *m* aux enchères.

auctioneer /ˌɔːkʃəˈnɪə(r)/ ▶ **1692** *n* commissaire-priseur *m*.

auction: **~ house** *n* US société *f* de commissaires-priseurs; **~ room(s)** *n(pl)* salle *f* de vente aux enchères; **~ sale** *n* vente *f* aux enchères.

audacious /ɔːˈdeɪʃəs/ *adj* (bold) audacieux/-ieuse; (cheeky) impudent.

audaciously /ɔːˈdeɪʃəslɪ/ *adv* audacieusement.

audacity /ɔːˈdæsətɪ/ *n* audace *f*; **to have the ~ to...** avoir l'audace de...

Aude ▶ **1163** *pr n* Aude *f*; **in/to the ~** dans l'Aude.

audibility /ˌɔːdəˈbɪlətɪ/ *n* audibilité *f*.

audible /ˈɔːdəbl/ *adj* audible.

audibly /ˈɔːdəblɪ/ *adv* distinctement.

audience /ˈɔːdɪəns/ *n* **1** (in cinema, concert, theatre) public *m*; Radio auditeurs *mpl*; TV public *m*; **to hold an ~** tenir un public; **2** (for books) lecteurs *mpl*; (for ideas) public *m*; **to reach a wider ~** atteindre un public plus large; **to lose one's ~** être abandonné par son public; **3** (meeting) sout audience *f* (**with sb** auprès de qn).

audience: **~ participation** *n* participation *f* du public; **~ ratings** *npl* indice *m* d'écoute; **~ research** *n* sondages *mpl* du public.

audio /ˈɔːdɪəʊ/ *adj* audio *inv*.

audio: **~book** *n* livre-cassette *m*; **~ cassette** *n* audiocassette *f*; **~ frequency, af** *n* audiofréquence *f*.

audiotyping /ˈɔːdɪəʊtaɪpɪŋ/ *n* audiotypie *f*.

audiotypist /ˈɔːdɪəʊtaɪpɪst/ ▶ **1692** *n* audiotypiste *mf*.

audiovisual, AV /ˌɔːdɪəʊˈvɪʒʊəl/ *adj* audiovisuel/-elle.

audit /ˈɔːdɪt/ **I** *n* audit *m*; **National Audit Office** GB ≈ Cour *f* des comptes; **to carry out** ou **do an ~** effectuer un audit.
II *vtr* auditer, vérifier.

auditing /ˈɔːdɪtɪŋ/ *n* audit *m*.

audition /ɔːˈdɪʃn/ **I** *n* audition *f* (**for** pour); **to go for an ~** passer une audition.
II *vtr, vi* auditionner (**for** pour).

auditor /ˈɔːdɪtə(r)/ ▶ **1692** *n* **1** commissaire *m* aux comptes; **internal/external ~** auditeur/-trice *m/f* interne/externe; **2** US (student) auditeur/-trice *m/f*.

auditorium /ˌɔːdɪˈtɔːrɪəm/ *n* (*pl* **-iums** ou **-ia**) **1** Theat salle *f*; **2** US (for meetings) salle *f* de conférences; Sch, Univ amphithéâtre *m*; (concert hall) salle *f* de spectacle; (stadium) stade *m*.

auditor's report *n* Accts rapport *m* d'auditeur.

auditory /ˈɔːdɪtrɪ, US -tɔːrɪ/ *adj* auditif/-ive.

auditory phonetics *n* (+ *v sg*) phonétique *f* auditive.

audit trail *n* Comput analyse *f* rétrospective.

Audubon Society /ˈɔːdəbɒn səsaɪətɪ/ *n* US *société protectrice de la nature*.

AUEW *n* GB (*abrév* = **Amalgamated Union of Engineering Workers**) syndicat *m* des ouvriers mécaniciens.

Aug *abrév écrite* = **August**.

Augean stables /ɔːˌdʒiːən ˈsteɪblz/ *npl* Mythol **the ~** les écuries *fpl* d'Augias.

auger /ˈɔːgə(r)/ *n* (for wood) vrille *f*; (for ground) foreuse *f*.

aught /ɔːt/ ‡ ou dial **for ~ I know** pour autant que je sache; **for ~ I care** pour ce que j'en ai à faire.

augment /ɔːgˈment/ **I** *vtr* gen, Mus augmenter (**with** de; **by** de; **by doing** en faisant); **~ed sixth** Mus sixième augmentée.
II *vi* augmenter.

augmentation /ˌɔːgmenˈteɪʃn/ *n* gen, Mus augmentation *f*.

augmentative /ɔːgˈmentətɪv/ *adj* Ling augmentatif/-ive.

augur /ˈɔːgə(r)/ *vi* **to ~ well/ill for sb/sth** être de bon/mauvais augure pour qn/qch.

augury /ˈɔːgjʊrɪ/ *n* littér augure *m*.

august /ɔːˈgʌst/ *adj* sout imposant, auguste fml.

August /ˈɔːgəst/ ▶ **1472** *n* août *m*.

Augustan /ɔːˈgʌstən/ *adj* Antiq, Literat d'Auguste.

Augustine I /ɔːˈgʌstiːn/ *n* (member of order) Augustin *m*.
II /əˈgʌstɪn/ *pr n* **St. ~** saint Augustin.

Augustinian /ˌɔːgəˈstɪnɪən/ *adj* [*doctrine*] augustinien/-ienne; [*friar*] de l'ordre de saint Augustin; [*order*] de saint Augustin.

Augustus /ɔːˈgʌstəs/ *pr n* Auguste.

auk /ɔːk/ *n* **great ~** grand pingouin *m*; **little ~** mergule *m* nain.

aunt /ɑːnt, US ænt/ *n* tante *f*; **Aunt Dodie** tante Dodie; **no, Aunt** non, ma tante.
IDIOMS **oh my giddy ~**○! hum mon Dieu!

auntie, aunty○ /ˈɑːntɪ, US ˈæntɪ/ *n* **1** lang enfantin tantine *f*, tatan *f*, tatie *f*, tata *f* baby talk; **2** GB (BBC) **Auntie** la BBC.

Aunt Sally /ˌɑːnt ˈsælɪ, US ˌænt-/ *n* **1** ▶ **1282** GB Sport ≈ jeu *m* de massacre; **2** fig (victim, butt) tête *f* de Turc.

au pair /ˌəʊ ˈpeə(r)/ *n* (jeune) fille *f* au pair.

aura /ˈɔːrə/ *n* (*pl* **-ras** ou **-rae**) (of place) atmosphère *f*; (of person) aura *f*.

aural /ˈɔːrəl, aʊrəl/ **I** *n* Sch exercice *m* de compréhension et d'expression orales; Mus ≈ dictée *f* musicale.
II *adj* **1** gen auditif/-ive; **2** Med auriculaire; [*test*] auditif; **3** Sch [*comprehension, test*] oral.

aureole /ˈɔːrɪəʊl/ *n* (all contexts) auréole *f*.

auricle /ˈɔːrɪkl/ *n* (of heart) oreillette *f*; (of ear) oreille *f* externe.

aurochs /ˈɔːrɒks, ˈɔːrɒks/ *n* (*pl* **~**) aurochs *m*.

aurora /ɔːˈrɔːrə/ *n* (*pl* **-ras** ou **-rae**) (all contexts) aurore *f*; **~ australis/borealis** aurore australe/boréale.

auscultate /ˈɔːskəlteɪt/ *vtr* ausculter.

auscultation /ˌɔːskəlˈteɪʃn/ *n* auscultation *f*.
auspices /ˈɔːspɪsɪz/ *n pl* auspices *mpl*; **under the ~ of** sous les auspices de.
auspicious /ɔːˈspɪʃəs/ *adj* prometteur/-euse.
auspiciously /ɔːˈspɪʃəslɪ/ *adv* de façon prometteuse.
Aussie○ /ˈɒzɪ/ **I** *n* Australien/-ienne *m/f*.
II *adj* australien/-ienne.
austere /ɒˈstɪə(r), ɔːˈstɪə(r)/ *adj* austère.
austerely /ɒˈstɪəlɪ, ɔːˈstɪəlɪ/ *adv* de façon austère.
austerity /ɒˈsterətɪ, ɔːˈsterətɪ/ **I** *n* austérité *f*.
II *modif* GB [*furniture, clothing*] *fabriqué par l'État pendant la Deuxième Guerre mondiale*.
Australasia /ˌɒstrəˈleɪʒɪə, ˌɔːs-/ *pr n* Australasie *f*.
Australasian /ˌɒstrəˈleɪʒn, ˌɔːs-/ **I** *n* natif/-ive *m/f* d'Australasie.
II *adj* d'Australasie.
Australia /ɒˈstreɪlɪə, ɔːˈs-/ ▶ **1131** *pr n* Australie *f*.
Australian /ɒˈstreɪlɪən, ɔːˈs-/ ▶ **1486** **I** *n* (person) Australien/-ienne *m/f*.
II *adj* australien/-ienne.
Australian: **~ Antarctic Territory** *n* territoire *m* de l'Antarctique australien; **~ Capital Territory** *n* Territoire *m* fédéral de Canberra.
Austria /ˈɒstrɪə, ˈɔːstrɪə/ ▶ **1131** *pr n* Autriche *f*.
Austrian /ˈɒstrɪən, ˈɔːstrɪən/ ▶ **1486** **I** *n* Autrichien/-ienne *m/f*.
II *adj* autrichien/-ienne.
Austrian blind *n* store *m* bouillonné.
Austro-Hungarian /ˌɒstrəʊ hʌŋˈgeərɪən/ *adj* austro-hongrois.
AUT *n* GB (*abrév* = **Association of University Teachers**) syndicat *m* des enseignants du supérieur.
autarchy /ˈɔːtɑːkɪ/ *n* autocratie *f*.
authentic /ɔːˈθentɪk/ *adj* **1** Art, Jur [*painting, document*] authentique; [*information*] authentique; **2** gen [*source*] sûr.
authenticate /ɔːˈθentɪkeɪt/ *vtr* authentifier.
authenticity /ˌɔːθenˈtɪsətɪ/ *n* authenticité *f*.
author /ˈɔːθə(r)/ ▶ **1692** **I** *n* **1** (of book, play, report) auteur *m*; **2** (by profession) écrivain *m*; **he's an ~** il est écrivain; **3** (of plan, scheme) auteur *m*.
II *vtr* US rédiger [*report, study*].
authoress† /ˈɔːθərɪs/ ▶ **1692** *n* femme *f* écrivain; **she is an ~** elle est écrivain.

■ Note L'usage moderne préfère *author*.

authoritarian /ɔːˌθɒrɪˈteərɪən/ **I** *n* partisan *m* de l'autorité.
II *adj* pej autoritaire.
authoritarianism /ɔːˌθɒrɪˈteərɪənɪzəm/ *n* pej autoritarisme *m*.
authoritative /ɔːˈθɒrətətɪv, US -teɪtɪv/ *adj* **1** (forceful) [*person, voice, manner*] autoritaire; **2** (reliable) [*work, report*] qui fait autorité; [*source*] bien informé.
authority /ɔːˈθɒrətɪ/ **I** *n* **1** (power) autorité *f* (**over** sur); **the ~ of the state** l'autorité de l'État; **to have the ~ to do** avoir toute autorité pour faire; **to have no ~ to do** n'avoir aucune autorité pour faire; **to be in ~** occuper un poste de responsabilité; **he will be reported to those in ~** son cas sera référé à qui de droit; **who's in ~ here?** qui commande ici?; **to do sth on sb's ~** faire qch sous les ordres de qn; **to be/act under sb's ~** être/agir sous les ordres de qn; **on one's own ~** de son propre chef; **2** (forcefulness, confidence) autorité *f*; **to speak with ~** parler avec autorité; **to lack ~** [*person, performance*] manquer d'autorité; **3** (permission) autorisation *f*; **to give sb (the) ~ to do** autoriser qn à faire, donner à qn l'autorisation de faire; **4** (organization) autorité *f*; **5** (expert) (person) autorité *f*, expert *m* (**on** en matière de); (book, film) œuvre *f* de référence; **6** (source of information) source *f*; **what is your ~ for these figures?** de quelles sources proviennent vos chiffres?; **I have it on good ~ that** je sais de source sûre que.
II authorities *npl* gen, Admin, Pol autorités *fpl*; **to report sth to the authorities** signaler qch aux autorités; **the school/hospital authorities** la direction de l'école/de l'hôpital.
authorization /ˌɔːθəraɪˈzeɪʃn/ *n* (authority, document) autorisation *f*; **to give** ou **grant ~** accorder une autorisation; **to give** ou **grant ~ to do** accorder l'autorisation de faire.
authorize /ˈɔːθəraɪz/ **I** *vtr* autoriser [*person, institution*] (**to do** à faire); autoriser [*payment, visit*].
II authorized *pp adj* [*signature, signatory, biography, version*] autorisé; [*dealer*] agréé.
Authorized Version *n* **the ~** (**of the Bible**) la Bible (anglaise) de 1611.
authorship /ˈɔːθəʃɪp/ *n* (of book, poem) paternité *f*; (profession) profession *f* d'auteur.
autism /ˈɔːtɪzəm/ *n* autisme *m*.
autistic /ɔːˈtɪstɪk/ *adj* [*person*] autiste; [*response etc*] autistique.
auto○ /ˈɔːtəʊ/ US **I** *n* auto *f*.
II *modif* [*parts, accident*] d'auto; [*industry*] automobile; [*mechanic*] automobile; [*workers*] de l'industrie automobile.
autobiographical /ˌɔːtəʊbaɪəˈgræfɪkl/ *adj* autobiographique.
autobiography /ˌɔːtəʊbaɪˈɒgrəfɪ/ *n* autobiographie *f*.
autochthon /ɔːˈtɒkθən/ *n* autochtone *mf*.
autochthonous /ɔːˈtɒkθənəs/ *adj* autochtone.
autocracy /ɔːˈtɒkrəsɪ/ *n* autocratie *f*.
autocrat /ˈɔːtəkræt/ *n* autocrate *mf*.
autocratic /ˌɔːtəˈkrætɪk/ *adj* autocratique.
autocrime /ˈɔːtəʊkraɪm/ *n*: *délits tels que les vols de voitures, d'autoradio etc*.
autocross /ˈɔːtəʊkrɒs/ *n* auto-cross *m*.
autocue /ˈɔːtəʊkjuː/ *n* TV prompteur *m*.
auto-da-fé /ˌɔːtəʊdɑːˈfeɪ/ *n* (*pl* **autos-da-fe**) autodafé *m*.
autodidact /ˈɔːtəʊˌdaɪdækt/ *n* sout autodidacte *mf*.
autogenics /ˌɔːtəʊˈdʒenɪks/ *n* (+ *v sg*) Psych *ensemble d'exercices de training autogène*.
autogenic training *n* Psych training *m* autogène.
autogiro /ˌɔːtəʊˈdʒaɪərəʊ/ *n* autogire *m*.
autograph /ˈɔːtəgrɑːf, US -græf/ **I** *n* autographe *m*.
II *modif* [*album, hunter*] d'autographes.
III *vtr* dédicacer [*book, record*]; signer [*memento*].
autoimmune /ˌɔːtəʊɪˈmjuːn/ *adj* [*disease*] auto-immun; [*system*] autoimmunitaire.
autologous /ˌɔːtəʊˈlɒgəs/ *adj* Med [*graft, transfusion*] autologue.
automat /ˈɔːtəmæt/ *n* distributeur *m* automatique.
automata /ɔːˈtɒmətə/ *pl* ▶ **automaton**.
automata theory *n* Comput théorie *f* des automates.
automate /ˈɔːtəmeɪt/ *vtr* automatiser [*factory, process*]; **fully ~d** entièrement automatisé.
automatic /ˌɔːtəˈmætɪk/ **I** *n* **1** (washing machine) machine *f* à laver automatique; **2** (car) voiture *f* (à changement de vitesse) automatique; **3** (gun) automatique *m*; **4** (setting) **to be on ~** [*machine, heating*] être en position automatique, sur automatique○; **to be in ~**○ [*person*] hum être en pilotage automatique○.
II *adj* (all contexts) automatique.
automatically /ˌɔːtəˈmætɪklɪ/ *adv* (all contexts) automatiquement.
automatic pilot *n* (device) pilote *m* automatique; (system) lit, fig pilotage *m* automatique; **to be on ~** Aviat être sur pilote automatique or en pilotage automatique; fig (person) être comme un automate.
automatic teller machine, **ATM** *n* guichet *m* automatique.
automation /ˌɔːtəˈmeɪʃn/ *n* (of process, factory) automatisation *f*; **office ~** bureautique *f*; **industrial ~** robotique *f*.
automaton /ɔːˈtɒmətən, US -tɒn/ *n* (*pl* **-s**, **automata**) (robot, person) automate *m*.
automobile /ˈɔːtəməbiːl, ˌɔːtəməˈbiːl/ *n* US, GB† automobile *f*.
automobilia /ˌɔːtəməˈbiːlɪə/ *npl* accessoires *mpl* auto (*de collection*).
automotive /ˌɔːtəˈməʊtɪv/ *adj* **1** [*design, industry, product, sales*] automobile; **2** (self-propelling) automoteur/-trice.
autonomic /ˌɔːtəˈnɒmɪk/ *adj* autonome.
autonomic nervous system *n* système *m* nerveux autonome.
autonomous /ɔːˈtɒnəməs/ *adj* (all contexts) autonome.
autonomy /ɔːˈtɒnəmɪ/ *n* (all contexts) autonomie *f*.
autopilot /ˈɔːtəʊpaɪlət/ *n* Aviat, fig pilote *m* automatique, bloc *m* de pilotage.
autopsy /ˈɔːtɒpsɪ/ *n* autopsie *f* also fig; **to do/perform an ~ on sb** faire/pratiquer l'autopsie de qn.
autosuggestion /ˌɔːtəʊ səˈdʒestʃən/ *n* autosuggestion *f*.
auto-teller /ˌɔːtəʊˈtelə(r)/ *n* distributeur *m* (automatique) de billets.
autotimer /ˈɔːtəʊtaɪmə(r)/ *n* programmateur *m*.
autumn /ˈɔːtəm/ ▶ **1671** **I** *n* surtout GB automne *m*; **in ~** en automne; **in the ~ of her years** à l'automne de sa vie.
II *modif* [*leaves, colours, fashions*] d'automne.
autumnal /ɔːˈtʌmnəl/ *adj* [*colour, light*] automnal; [*weather*] d'automne.
Auvergne /əʊˈveən/ ▶ **1273** *pr n* Auvergne *f*; **in the ~** en Auvergne.
auxiliary /ɔːgˈzɪlɪərɪ/ **I** *n* **1** (person) auxiliaire *mf*; **2** Ling (verbe *m*) auxiliaire *m*; **3** Hist (soldier) auxiliaire *m*.
II *adj* [*equipment, engine, staff, forces*] auxiliaire.
auxiliary: **~ nurse** ▶ **1692** *n* aide-soignant/-e *m/f*; **~ verb** *n* (verbe *m*) auxiliaire *m*.
AV *adj*: *abrév* ▶ **audiovisual**.
avail /əˈveɪl/ sout **I** *n* **to be of little ~** ne pas servir à grand-chose; **to be of no ~** ne servir à rien; **to no ~** **without ~** en vain.
II *v refl* **to ~ oneself of** profiter de [*opportunity*]; accepter [*offer*].
availability /əˌveɪləˈbɪlətɪ/ *n* (of option, strategy, service) existence *f*; (of drugs) présence *f* (sur le marché); **~ of credit** possibilité *f* d'obtenir des crédits; **stock ~** disponibilité *f*; Comm **subject to ~** (of holidays, hotel rooms, theatre seats etc) dans la limite des places disponibles; (of hire vehicles) dans la limite des véhicules disponibles; **demand exceeds ~** la demande est supérieure à l'offre.
available /əˈveɪləbl/ *adj* **1** [*product, room, money, credit, information*] disponible (**for** pour; **to** à); **to make sth ~ to sb** mettre qch à la disposition de qn; **to be ~ from** [*product*] être disponible dans [*shop*]; [*service*] être fourni par [*organization*]; **by every ~ means** par tous les moyens possibles; **2** (free) [*person*] (for appointment etc) disponible; (for relationship, sex) pej disponible; **to make oneself ~ for sth/sb** se libérer pour qch/qn; **she is not ~ for comment** elle se refuse à tout commentaire.
avalanche /ˈævəlɑːnʃ, US -læntʃ/ *n* avalanche *f* also fig.
avant-garde /ˌævɒŋˈgɑːd/ **I** *n* avant-garde *f*.
II *adj* d'avant-garde.
avarice /ˈævərɪs/ *n* cupidité *f*.

IDIOMS **rich beyond the dreams of ~** riche comme Crésus.

avaricious /ˌævəˈrɪʃəs/ *adj* cupide.

avdp Meas *abrév écrite* = **avoirdupois**.

Ave *abrév écrite* = **Avenue**.

Ave Maria /ˌɑːveɪ məˈrɪə/ *n* Ave Maria *m inv*.

avenge /əˈvendʒ/ **I** *vtr* venger [*person, death, defeat, honour*].
II *v refl* **to ~ oneself on sb** se venger de qn; **to ~ oneself on sb for sth** se venger de qch sur qn.

avenger /əˈvendʒə(r)/ *n* vengeur/-eresse *m/f*.

avenging /əˈvendʒɪŋ/ *adj* [*person, force, bullet, goal*] vengeur/-eresse; **~ angel** ange *m* exterminateur.

avenue /ˈævənjuː, US -nuː/ *n* **1** (street, road) avenue *f*; (path, driveway) allée *f*; **2** fig (possibility) possibilité *f*; **to explore every ~** explorer toutes les possibilités.

aver /əˈvɜː(r)/ *vtr* (*p prés etc* **-rr-**) sout affirmer (**that** que + *indic*).

average /ˈævərɪdʒ/ **I** *n* gen, Math moyenne *f* (**of** de); **national ~** moyenne nationale; **on (the) ~** en moyenne; **above/below (the) ~** au-dessus de/au-dessous de la moyenne; **at an ~ of** à une moyenne de; **to take an ~** prendre une moyenne approximative; **to work out an ~** faire une moyenne; **by the law of ~s** selon la loi des probabilités; **Mr Average** Monsieur Tout-le-Monde.
II *adj* gen, Math [*amount, cost, earnings, person, rate*] moyen/-enne; **on an ~ day I work seven hours** en moyenne, je travaille sept heures par jour; **a book suitable for an ~ 10-year-old** un livre qui convient à un enfant de 10 ans; **a very ~ writer** péj un auteur très moyen or médiocre.
III *vtr* faire en moyenne [*distance, quantity, time*]; **I ~ seven hours' work a day** en moyenne je travaille sept heures par jour; **we ~d 95 km/h on the motorway** nous avons fait une moyenne de 95 km/h sur l'autoroute.
■ **average out**: ¶ **their pay ~s out at about £10 an hour** ils gagnent en moyenne 10 livres sterling de l'heure; **their working day ~s out at seven hours** leur journée de travail fait en moyenne sept heures; ¶ **~ out [sth], ~ [sth] out** faire la moyenne de; **we ~d out the bill at £10 each** nous avons partagé la note et avons payé 10 livres sterling chacun.

averse /əˈvɜːs/ *adj* opposé (**to** à); **to be ~ to doing sth** répugner à faire qch.

aversion /əˈvɜːʃn, US əˈvɜːrʒn/ *n* aversion *f* (**to** pour); **to have an ~ to doing** avoir horreur de faire; **his pet ~** sa bête noire.

avert /əˈvɜːt/ *vtr* **1** (avoid, prevent) éviter [*disaster, crisis, liquidation, criticism*]; **2** (turn away) **to ~ one's eyes/gaze from sth** lit, fig détourner les yeux/le regard de qch.

Aveyron ▶**1163** *pr n* Aveyron *m*; **in/to the ~** dans l'Aveyron, en Aveyron.

aviary /ˈeɪvɪərɪ, US -vɪerɪ/ *n* volière *f*.

aviation /ˌeɪvɪˈeɪʃn/ *n* aviation *f*.

aviation: **~ fuel** *n* kérosène *m*; **~ industry** *n* industrie *f* aéronautique.

aviator /ˈeɪvɪeɪtə(r)/ ▶**1692** *n* aviateur/-trice *m/f*.

aviculture /ˈeɪvɪˌkʌltʃə(r)/ *n* aviculture *f*.

aviculturist /ˌeɪvɪˈkʌltʃərɪst/ ▶**1692** *n* aviculteur/-trice *m/f*.

avid /ˈævɪd/ *adj* [*collector, reader*] passionné; [*enthusiast, supporter*] fervent; **to be ~ for sth** être avide de qch.

avidity /əˈvɪdɪtɪ/ *n* avidité *f* (**for** de).

avidly /ˈævɪdlɪ/ *adv* [*read, collect*] avec avidité; [*support*] avec ferveur.

avocado /ˌævəˈkɑːdəʊ/ **I** *n* **1** (fruit) avocat *m*; **2** (tree, plant) avocatier *m*.
II *modif* [*salad, mousse*] à l'avocat.

avocet /ˈævəset/ *n* avocette *f*.

avoid /əˈvɔɪd/ *vtr* **1** (prevent) éviter [*accident, error, dispute, penalty*]; **to ~ doing** éviter de faire; **it is to be ~ed** c'est à éviter; **2** (keep away from) éviter [*person, location, nuisance*]; éviter [*gaze*]; esquiver [*issue, question*]; **3** Jur (invalidate) annuler [*contract*].

avoidable /əˈvɔɪdəbl/ *adj* évitable; **an ~ tragedy** une tragédie qui aurait pu être évitée.

avoidance /əˈvɔɪdəns/ *n* **~ of** (of injuries, expenditure, delay) prévention *f* de; (of responsibility, emotion) refus *m* de; (of issue, subject, problem) fuite *f* devant; (of person) tendance *f* à éviter; ▶**tax avoidance**.

avoirdupois /ˌævədəˈpɔɪz/ *n* avoirdupoids *m*.

Avon /ˈeɪvn/ ▶**1624** *pr n* Avon *m*.

avow /əˈvaʊ/ *vtr* sout **1** (admit) avouer; **2** (declare) affirmer.

avowal /əˈvaʊəl/ *n* sout **1** (confession) aveu *m*; **2** (declaration) affirmation *f*.

avowed /əˈvaʊd/ *adj* **1** (admitted) avoué; **2** (declared) déclaré.

avowedly /əˈvaʊɪdlɪ/ *adv* sout **1** (by admission) de son/leur etc propre aveu; **2** (by declaration) ouvertement.

avuncular /əˈvʌŋkjʊlə(r)/ *adj* (all contexts) bienveillant.

AWACS /ˈeɪwæks/ (*abrév* = **Airborne Warning and Control System**) **I** *n* AWACS *m*.
II *modif* [*plane*] AWACS.

await /əˈweɪt/ *vtr* **1** [*person*] attendre [*outcome, event, opportunity, decision, praise*]; **long-~ed** longuement attendu; **eagerly ~ed** attendu avec impatience; **in prison ~ing trial** en détention préventive; **2** [*fate, surprise, welcome*] attendre [*person*]; **her book ~s publication** son livre est en attente de publication.

awake /əˈweɪk/ **I** *adj* **1** (not yet asleep) éveillé; (after sleeping) réveillé; **wide ~** bien réveillé; **half ~** mal réveillé; **to be ~** être éveillé or réveillé; **to stay ~** rester éveillé; **to lie ~** rester au lit sans dormir; **to shake sb ~** secouer qn pour le réveiller; **I was still ~** je ne dormais pas; **the noise kept me ~** le bruit m'a empêché de dormir; **2** (aware) **to be ~ to sth** être conscient de qch.
II *vtr* (*prét* **awoke** ou **awaked** littér, *pp* **awoken** ou **awaked** littér) **1** (from sleep) réveiller; **2** fig éveiller [*fear, suspicion*]; réveiller [*memory*].
III *vi* (*prét* **awoke** ou **awaked** littér, *pp* **awoken** ou **awaked** littér) **1** (from sleep) se réveiller; **to ~ from a deep sleep** sortir d'un sommeil profond; **I awoke to find him gone** en me réveillant, je me suis rendu compte qu'il était parti; **2** (become aware) **to ~ to** prendre conscience de [*fact, responsibilities, duties*].

awaken /əˈweɪkən/ (*prét* **awoke** ou **awakened** littér, *pp* **awoken** ou **awakened** littér) **I** *vtr* **1** (from sleep) réveiller; **2** (generate) faire naître [*fear, hope, interest*]; éveiller [*suspicions*]; **3** (make aware) **to ~ sb to** rendre qn conscient de [*danger, disadvantage, problem*].
II *vi* (*prét* **awoke** ou **awakened** littér, *pp* **awoken** ou **awakened** littér) **1** (from sleep) se réveiller; **2** (become aware) **to ~ to sth** prendre conscience de qch.

awakening /əˈweɪkənɪŋ/ **I** *n* lit (from sleep) réveil *m*; fig (of emotion, interest) éveil *m* (**of** de); (of awareness) prise *f* de conscience (**to** de); **rude ~** lit réveil brutal; fig rappel *m* brutal à la réalité.
II *adj* lit qui se réveille; fig naissant.

award /əˈwɔːd/ **I** *n* **1** (prize) prix *m*; (medal, certificate) distinction *f* honorifique; **an ~ for bravery** une distinction honorifique pour votre/son etc courage; **the ~ for the best actor** le prix du meilleur acteur; **to win/present an ~** gagner/remettre un prix; **2** (grant) bourse *f*; **3** (decision to give) (of prize, grant) attribution *f*; Jur **an ~ of damages** des dommages-intérêts.
II *vtr* **1** décerner [*prize*]; attribuer [*grant*]; **2** Jur accorder [*damages*]; **3** Sport accorder [*points*]; **to ~ a penalty** accorder une pénalité.

award: **~ ceremony** *n* cérémonie *f* de remise de prix; **~ winner** *n* lauréat/-e *m/f*.

award-winning /əˈwɔːdwɪnɪŋ/ *adj* [*book, film, design*] primé; [*writer, architect etc*] lauréat.

aware /əˈweə(r)/ *adj* **1** (conscious) conscient; (informed) au courant; **to be ~ of** (realize) être conscient de [*problem, effect, importance, need, danger etc*]; (be informed about) être au courant de [*fact, circumstance, development*]; **to become ~ that** prendre conscience que; **she became ~ of noises downstairs** elle s'est rendu compte qu'il y avait des bruits venant d'en-bas; **to make sb ~ of/that** rendre qn conscient de/que; **I'm well ~ of that** j'ai bien conscience de cela; **to be ~ that** savoir que, se rendre compte que; **are they ~ (of) how late it is?** se rendent-ils compte de l'heure?; **as far/not as far as I'm ~** à ma/pas à ma connaissance; **2** (well-informed) averti; **to be politically/environmentally ~** être au courant des questions de politique/d'environnement.

awareness /əˈweənɪs/ *n* conscience *f* (**of** de; **that** que); **political ~** conscience politique; **public ~ of this problem has increased** l'opinion *f* publique a de plus en plus pris conscience de ce problème.

awareness campaign *n* campagne *f* de sensibilisation.

awash /əˈwɒʃ/ *adj* (*après v*) inondé also fig (**with** de).

away /əˈweɪ/

■ **Note** *away* often appears in English as the second element of a verb (*run away, put away, get away, look away, give away etc*). For translations, look at the appropriate verb entry (***run***, ***put***, ***get***, ***look***, ***give*** etc).
– *away* often appears after a verb in English to show that an action is continuous or intense. If *away* does not change the basic meaning of the verb only the verb is translated: *he was snoring away* = il ronflait. If *away* does change the basic meaning of the verb (*he's grinding away at his maths*), consult the appropriate verb entry.
– This dictionary contains Usage Notes on topics like distance. For the index to these Notes see ▶**1919**.

I *adj* **1** Sport [*goal, match, win*] à l'extérieur; **the ~ team** les visiteurs *mpl*; **2**° GB (drunk) **to be well ~** être parti° or soûl.
II *adv* **1** (not present, gone) **to be ~** gen, Sch être absent (**from** de); (on business trip) être en déplacement; **I'll be ~ (for) two weeks** je serai absent pendant deux semaines; **to be ~ on vacation/on business** être en vacances/en voyage d'affaires or en déplacement; **to be ~ from home** ne pas être chez soi, être absent de chez soi; **I'll have to be ~ by 10** il faut que je sois parti avant 10 heures; **she's ~ in Paris** elle est à Paris; **she's ~ at a conference** elle est partie à un congrès; ▶**fairy**; **2** (distant in space) **3 km/50 m ~** à 3 km/50 m; **10 cm ~ from the edge** à 10 cm du bord; **a weekend ~ in the country** un week-end à la campagne; **I hate to be ~ from home** je déteste ne pas être chez moi; **~ with you!** arrête de dire des bêtises!; **3** (distant in time) **London is two hours ~** Londres est à deux heures d'ici; **my birthday is two months ~** mon anniversaire est dans deux mois; **the election/the exam is only days ~** l'élection/l'examen aura lieu dans quelques jours seulement; ▶**far, get, keep, stay**; **4** (in the opposite direction) **to shuffle/crawl ~** partir en traînant les pieds/en rampant; ▶**drive, walk**; **5** (for emphasis) **~ back in 1920** en 1920; **~ over the other side of the lake** de l'autre côté du lac; **6** Sport [*play, win*] à l'extérieur.

awe /ɔː/ **I** *n* crainte *f* mêlée d'admiration;

(less fearful) respect *m*; **to watch/listen in ~** regarder/écouter impressionné.

II *vtr* **to be ~ed by sth** être impressionné par qch.

awe-inspiring /ˈɔːɪnspaɪərɪŋ/ *adj* [*person*] intimidant; [*landscape, experience*] impressionnant.

awesome /ˈɔːsəm/ *adj* redoutable.

awestruck /ˈɔːstrʌk/ *adj* impressionné.

awful /ˈɔːfl/ *adj* **1** [*book, film, food, weather*] (bad) affreux/-euse; (stronger) exécrable; **that ~ woman!** cette horrible femme!; **you are ~!** hum petit coquin!; **it was ~ to have to...** ça a été horrible d'être obligé de...; **2** (horrifying, tragic) [*news, accident, crime*] horrible, atroce; **how ~ (for you)** comme c'est atroce (pour vous); **3** (unwell) **I feel ~** je ne me sens pas bien du tout; **you look ~** tu n'as pas l'air bien du tout; **4** (guilty) ennuyé; **I felt ~ (about) leaving her alone** j'étais très ennuyé de la laisser seule; **5**○ (emphasizing) **an ~ lot (of)** énormément (de); **an ~ cheek** ou **nerve** un culot incroyable; **to be in an ~ hurry** être extrêmement pressé.

awfully /ˈɔːflɪ/ *adv* [*hot, cold, near, far, fast, difficult, boring*] terriblement; [*clever*] extrêmement; **he's ~ late/early** il est terriblement en retard/en avance; **she's ~ nice** elle est excessivement gentille; **I'm not ~ sure** je ne suis pas absolument sûr; **thanks ~** mille mercis.

awfulness /ˈɔːfəlnɪs/ *n* (of situation, place, object) atrocité *f*; (of person) caractère *m* désagréable.

awhile /əˈwaɪl/ *adv* un moment; **not yet ~** pas de sitôt.

awkward /ˈɔːkwəd/ *adj* **1** (not practical) [*tool*] peu commode; [*shape, design*] difficile; **with this toothbrush you can get at all the ~ corners** cette brosse à dents permet d'atteindre les endroits peu accessibles; **the room has ~ proportions** la pièce a un agencement bizarre; **to be sitting in an ~ position** être assis dans une position inconfortable; **2** (clumsy) [*person, movement, gesture*] maladroit; [*prose, style*] gauche; **3** (complicated, inconvenient) [*arrangement, issue*] compliqué, difficile; [*choice*] difficile; [*moment, day*] mal choisi; **at an ~ time** au mauvais moment; **to make life ~ for sb** compliquer la vie à qn; **it's a bit ~: I'm so busy** c'est difficile: je suis si occupé; **4** (embarrassing) [*question*] embarrassant; [*situation*] délicat; [*silence*] gêné; **5** (embarrassed) mal à l'aise, gêné; **to feel ~ about doing** se sentir gêné de faire; **to feel/look ~** se sentir/avoir l'air mal à l'aise; **6** (uncooperative) [*person*] difficile (**about** à propos de); **he's being ~ about the whole thing** il n'est pas très coopératif dans cette affaire; **the ~ age** l'âge ingrat; **the ~ squad**○ GB hum les empêcheurs de tourner en rond.

awkwardly /ˈɔːkwədlɪ/ *adv* **1** (inconveniently) **~ placed/designed** mal placé/conçu; **~ for me, he was only free at 10 o'clock** malheureusement pour moi, il n'était libre qu'à 10 h; **2** (clumsily) [*move, hold, express oneself*] maladroitement, avec maladresse; [*fall, land*] lourdement; **3** (with embarrassment) [*speak, apologize*] d'un ton gêné; [*behave*] d'une manière embarrassée.

awkwardness /ˈɔːkwədnɪs/ *n* **1** (clumsiness) maladresse *f*; **2** (delicacy) (of situation) côté *m* gênant; **3** (inconvenience) caractère *m* mal commode; **4** (embarrassment) malaise *m*.

awl /ɔːl/ *n* (for leather) alène *f*; (for wood etc) poinçon *m*.

awning /ˈɔːnɪŋ/ *n* (on shop) banne *f*, auvent *m*; (on tent, caravan, house, restaurant) auvent *m*; (on market stall) bâche *f*.

awoke /əˈwəʊk/ *prét* ▶ **awake**.

awoken /əˈwəʊkən/ *pp* ▶ **awake**.

AWOL /ˈeɪwɒl/ *adj, adv* Mil, hum (*abrév* = **absent without leave**) **to be** ou **go ~** Mil être en absence illégale; hum partir sans laisser d'adresse, disparaître.

awry /əˈraɪ/ **I** *adj* [*clothing, picture*] de travers *inv*; [*budget, figures*] faux/fausse.

II *adv* **to go ~** [*plan, policy*] mal tourner; [*economy, budget*] partir en déroute; **to put sth ~** désorganiser qch.

axe, **ax** US /æks/ **I** *n* **1** lit hache *f*; **2** fig **the ~ has fallen** le couperet est tombé; **to face the ~** être menacé du couperet; **to get the ~**○ (lose one's job) se faire virer○; (be cancelled) [*plan*] être abandonné; **3**○ US (instrument) instrument *m* musical; (saxophone) sax○ *m*; (guitar) guitare *f*.

II *vtr* virer○ [*employee*]; supprimer [*jobs, funding, organization*]; abandonner [*project, plan*].

IDIOMS **to have an ~ to grind** servir un intérêt; **they have no ~ to grind** ils ne servent aucun intérêt.

axial /ˈæksɪəl/ *adj* axial.

axiom /ˈæksɪəm/ *n* axiome *m* (**that** selon lequel).

axiomatic /ˌæksɪəˈmætɪk/ *adj* **1** Ling, Math, Philos axiomatique; **2** gen **it is ~ that** il est évident que; **it is ~ to do** il est obligatoire de faire.

axis /ˈæksɪs/ *n* (*pl* **axes**) **1** gen, Math axe *m*; **on the x/y ~** sur l'axe des x/des y; **~ of rotation** axe de rotation; **2** fig (line of thought) **to be on the Smith-Jones ~** se situer dans la mouvance Smith-Jones; **3** Pol Hist **the Axis Powers** les puissances de l'Axe.

axle /ˈæksl/ *n* essieu *m*; **front ~** essieu avant; **rear ~** (on front-wheel drive) essieu arrière; (on heavy vehicle, on rear-wheel drive) pont *m* arrière.

axle grease *n* graisse *f* à essieux.

ayatollah /ˌaɪəˈtɒlə/ *n* ayatollah *m*.

aye /aɪ/ **I** *particle* dial GB oui; GB Naut **~ ~ sir** à vos ordres.

II *n* (in voting) **the ~s** les oui, les voix pour.

III *adv* **to vote ~** voter oui or pour.

AYH *n* US (*abrév* = **American Youth Hostels**) Association *f* des auberges de jeunesse.

azalea /əˈzeɪlɪə/ *n* azalée *f*.

Azerbaijan /ˌæzəbaɪˈdʒɑːn/ ▶ **1131** *pr n* Azerbaïdjan *m*.

Azerbaijani /ˌæzəbaɪˈdʒɑːnɪ/ ▶ **1486**, **1402** **I** *n* **1** (person) Azéri *mf*; **2** (language) azéri *m*.

II *adj* azerbaïdjanais.

AZERTY, **azerty** /aˈzɜːtɪ/ *adj* **~ keyboard** clavier *m* azerty.

azimuth /ˈæzɪməθ/ *n* azimut *m*.

Azores /əˈzɔːz/ ▶ **1381** *pr n* **the ~** les Açores *fpl*.

AZT *n* (*abrév* = **azidothymidine**) AZT *f*.

Aztec /ˈæztek/ ▶ **1486**, **1402** **I** *n* **1** (person) Aztèque *mf*; **2** (language) aztèque *m*.

II *adj* aztèque.

azure /ˈæʒə(r), -zjə(r)/ ▶ **1104** **I** *n* azur *m*.

II *adj* [*sea, sky, eyes*] d'azur; [*fabric*] azur (*inv*).

Bb

b, **B** /biː/ *n* **1** (letter) b, B *m*; **2** **B** Mus si *m*; **3** **b** *abrév écrite* = **born**.

BA *n* (*abrév* = **Bachelor of Arts**) diplôme *m* universitaire en lettres et sciences humaines.

baa /bɑː/ **I** *n* bêlement *m*.
II *vi* (*prés* **~s**, *prét, pp* **~ed**) bêler.
III *excl* bêe!

BAA *n*: *abrév* ▶ **British Airports Authority**.

babble /ˈbæbl/ **I** *n* murmure *m* confus; (louder) clameur *f* confuse.
II *vtr* bafouiller [*words, excuse*]; **'yes, yes,' he ~d** 'oui, oui,' bafouilla-t-il.
III *vi* **1** [*baby*] babiller; [*stream*] murmurer; **2** = **~ on**; **3** US (speak in tongues) parler en langues.
■ **babble on** péj ratiociner, pérorer (**about** sur).

babbler /ˈbæblə(r)/ *n* bavard/-e *m/f*.

babbling /ˈbæblɪŋ/ *n* US (speaking in tongues) glossolalie *f*.

babe /beɪb/ *n* **1** littér bébé *m*; **a ~ in arms** lit un enfant au berceau; fig un jeunot○; **2**○ (woman) minette○ *f*; (form of address) ma belle○.

baboon /bəˈbuːn/ *n* babouin *m*.

baby /ˈbeɪbɪ/ **I** *n* **1** (child) bébé *m*; **newborn ~** nouveau-né *m*; **to have a ~** avoir un bébé; **Baby Jesus** le petit Jésus; **she's the ~ of the family** c'est la petite dernière or la benjamine; **don't be such a ~**○! ne fais pas le bébé!; **2** (youngest) (of group) benjamin/-e *m/f*; **3**○ (pet project) **the show is his ~**○ (his invention) le spectacle est sa création; (his special responsibility) il a la responsabilité du spectacle; **4**○ surtout US (girlfriend) copine *f*; (as address) chérie *f*; (boyfriend) copain *m*; (as address) chéri *m*; **5**○ US (admired object) (car, plane etc) petite merveille *f*.
II *modif* [*brother, sister*] petit; [*animal*] bébé-; [*vegetable*] nain; [*clothes, product*] pour bébés; **~ daughter** petite fille; **~ son** petit garçon; **~ bird** oisillon *m*.
III○ *vtr* péj dorloter.
IDIOMS **I was left holding the ~**○ on m'a refilé le bébé○; **to throw the ~ out with the bathwater**○ jeter le bébé avec l'eau du bain; **smooth as a ~'s bottom**○ doux/douce comme une peau de bébé.

baby blue ▶ **1104** *adj* bleu clair *inv*.

baby blues○ *npl* **1** Psych déprime○ *f* après l'accouchement; **2** US (eyes) yeux *mpl* bleus.

baby: **~ boom** *n* baby boom *m*; **~ boomer** *n* personne *f* née pendant les années du baby boom; **~ buggy** *n* GB poussette *f*; **~ carriage** *n* US landau *m*; **~ carrier** *n* porte-bébé *m inv* (dorsal); **~ death** *n* mort *f* subite du nourrisson; **~ doll pyjamas** *npl* pyjama *m* très court (*à culotte et manches courtes et bouffantes*); **~ elephant** *n* éléphanteau *m*; **~-faced** *adj* fig au visage innocent; **~ food** *n* aliments *mpl* pour bébés; **~ grand** ▶ **1481** *n* piano *m* quart de queue, piano crapaud.

Babygro® /ˈbeɪbɪgrəʊ/ *n* grenouillère *f*, pyjama *m* de bébé.

babyhood /ˈbeɪbɪhʊd/ *n* petite enfance *f*; **in** ou **during ~** pendant la petite enfance.

babyish /ˈbeɪbɪɪʃ/ *adj* enfantin; péj puéril.

Babylon /ˈbæbɪlən/ ▶ **1818** *n* lit, fig Babylone.

Babylonian /ˌbæbɪˈləʊnɪən/ **I** *n* Babylonien/-ienne *m/f*.
II *adj* babylonien/-ienne.

baby: **~ minder** *n* GB nourrice *f*; **~'s breath** *n* US Bot gypsophile *f*.

baby-sit /ˈbeɪbɪsɪt/ (*prét, pp* **-sat**) **I** *vtr* garder.
II *vi* faire du babysitting, garder des enfants.

baby-sitter /ˈbeɪbɪsɪtə(r)/ *n* baby-sitter *mf*.

baby-sitting /ˈbeɪbɪsɪtɪŋ/ *n* baby-sitting *m*; **to go** ou **do ~** faire du baby-sitting.

baby sling *n* Kangourou®, porte-bébé *m inv*.

baby snatcher *n* voleur/-euse *m/f* d'enfants; **she's a ~!** fig hum elle les prend au berceau!

baby: **~ talk** *n* langage *m* enfantin; **~ tooth**○ *n* dent *f* de lait; **~ walker** *n* trotteur *m*; **~wear** *n* vêtements *mpl* pour bébés; **~ wipe** *n* lingette *f*.

baccalaureate /ˌbækəˈlɔːrɪət/ *n* **1** US Univ (diploma) ≈ licence *f*; (speech) discours *m* de remise de diplômes; **2** Sch **European/International Baccalaureate** baccalauréat *m* européen/international.

baccarat /ˈbækərɑː/ *n* baccara *m*.

bacchanal /ˈbækənl/ *n* littér (orgy) bacchanale *f*.

bacchanalia /ˌbækəˈneɪlɪə/ *n* **1** Antiq (also **Bacchanalia**) (+ *v pl*) bacchanales *fpl*; **2** (orgy) bacchanale *f*.

bacchanalian /ˌbækəˈneɪlɪən/ *adj* bachique.

Bacchic /ˈbækɪk/ *adj* bachique.

Bacchus /ˈbækəs/ *pr n* Bacchus.

baccy○ /ˈbækɪ/ *n* GB tabac *m*.

bachelor /ˈbætʃələ(r)/ *n* **1** (single man) célibataire *m*; **a confirmed ~** un célibataire endurci; **an eligible ~** un beau parti; **to remain a ~** rester célibataire; **2** **Bachelor** Univ **Bachelor of Arts/Law etc** (degree) cf diplôme *m* universitaire de lettres/droit etc.

bachelor: **~ apartment**, **~ flat** GB *n* garçonnière *f*; **~ girl**† *n* célibataire *f*.

bachelorhood /ˈbætʃələhʊd/ *n* célibat *m*.

bachelor's degree *n* Univ cf licence *f* (**in** en).

bacillary /bəˈsɪlərɪ/ *adj* **1** (of bacilli) bacillaire; **2** = **bacilliform**.

bacilliform /bəˈsɪlɪfɔːm/ *adj* bacilliforme.

bacillus /bəˈsɪləs/ *n* (*pl* **-li**) bacille *m*.

back /bæk/ ▶ **1037** **I** *n* **1** Anat, Zool dos *m*; **to be (flat) on one's ~** lit être (à plat) sur le dos; fig être au lit; **to sleep on one's ~** dormir sur le dos; **he was lying on his ~** il était allongé sur le dos; **to travel on the ~ of a donkey** voyager à dos d'âne; **to have one's ~ to sb/sth** tourner le dos à qn/qch; **with her ~ to the door** le dos tourné vers la porte; **to turn one's ~ on sb/sth** lit, fig tourner le dos à qn/qch; **as soon as my ~ is turned** dès que j'ai le dos tourné; **to do sth behind sb's ~** lit, fig faire qch dans le dos de qn; **with one's ~ to the engine** dans le sens contraire à la marche; **to put one's ~ into it**○ travailler dur ; **put your ~ into it**○! allons, un peu de nerf○!; **he's always on my ~**○ il est toujours sur mon dos; **get off my ~**○! fiche-moi la paix○!; **I was glad to see the ~ of him** j'étais content de le voir partir; **to be at the ~ of** être à l'origine de [*conspiracy, proposal*]; **to put sb's ~ up** offenser qn; **to live off sb's ~** vivre aux crochets de qn; **2** (reverse side) (of page, cheque, card, envelope) dos *m*, verso *m*; (of fabric) envers *m*; (of medal, coin) revers *m*; **on the ~ of an envelope** au dos d'une enveloppe; **to sign the ~ of a cheque** endosser un chèque; **the ~ of the hand** le dos de la main; **3** (flat side) (of knife, fork, spoon) dos *m*; **4** (rear-facing part) (of vehicle) arrière *m*; (of electrical appliance) face *f* arrière; (of shirt, coat) dos *m*; **to hang one's coat on the ~ of the door** pendre son manteau derrière la porte; **the shelves are oak but the ~ is plywood** les étagères sont en chêne mais le fond est en contreplaqué; **a blow to the ~ of the head** un coup sur l'arrière de la tête; **a lump on the ~ of the head** une bosse derrière la tête; **the knife fell down the ~ of the fridge** le couteau est tombé derrière le réfrigérateur; **the keys were down the ~ of the sofa** les clés avaient glissé derrière les coussins du canapé; **5** (area behind building) **to be out ~**, **to be in the ~** US (in the garden) être dans le jardin; (in the yard) être dans la cour; **he's round** ou **in the ~** il est dans le jardin; **the view out ~ is lovely** la vue que l'on a à l'arrière est très jolie; **there's a small garden out ~** ou **round the ~** il y a un petit jardin derrière; **the bins are out ~** ou **round the ~** les poubelles sont derrière la maison; **the steps at the ~ of the building** l'escalier à l'arrière de l'immeuble; **6** Aut arrière *m*; **to sit in the ~** s'asseoir à l'arrière; **there are three children in the ~** il y a trois enfants à l'arrière; **to sit at the ~ of the plane/at the ~ of the bus** s'asseoir à l'arrière de l'avion/au fond du bus; **7** (furthest away area) (of cupboard, drawer, fridge) fond *m*; (of stage) fond *m*; **at** ou **in the ~ of the drawer** au fond du tiroir; **right at the ~ of the cupboard** tout au fond du placard; **at the ~ of the audience** au fond de la salle; **those at the ~ couldn't see** ceux qui étaient derrière ne pouvaient pas voir; **the ~ of the throat** l'arrière-gorge *f*; **the ~ of the mouth** la gorge *f*; **8** (of chair, sofa) dossier *m*; **9** Sport arrière *m*; **left ~** arrière gauche; **10** (end) fin *f*; **at the ~ of the book/file** à la fin du livre/fichier; **11** (book spine) dos *m*.
II *adj* **1** (at the rear) [*axle, wheel, bumper*] arrière; [*paw, leg*] arrière; [*bedroom*] du fond; [*edge*] arrière; [*page*] dernier/-ière (*before n*); [*garden, gate*] de derrière; **~ tooth** molaire *f*; **2** (isolated) [*road*] petit (*before n*); **~ alley** ou **lane** ruelle *f*; **~ country** arrière-pays *m*.
III *adv* **1** (indicating return after absence) **to be ~** être de retour; **I'll be ~ in five minutes/six weeks** je reviens dans cinq

minutes/six semaines; **to arrive** ou **come ~** rentrer (**from** de); **he's ~ at work** il a repris le travail; **she's ~ in (the) hospital** elle est retournée à l'hôpital; **it's good to be ~ home** c'est agréable de rentrer chez soi or de se retrouver à la maison; **when is he due ~?** quand doit-il rentrer?; **to go ~ to** reprendre [*work*]; retourner en [*France, China*]; retourner au [*Canada, Japan*]; retourner à [*Paris, museum, shop*]; **the mini-skirt is ~** (in fashion) les mini-jupes sont de nouveau à la mode; **2** (in return) **to call** ou **phone ~** rappeler; **I'll write ~ (to him)** je lui répondrai; **he hasn't written ~ yet** il n'a pas encore répondu; **'OK,' he shouted ~** 'OK,' a-t-il répondu en criant; **to punch sb ~** rendre son coup à qn; **to smile ~ at sb** rendre son sourire à qn; **he was rude ~** il a été aussi impoli avec moi que je l'avais été avec lui; ▶ **answer**; **3** (backwards, in a reverse direction) [*glance, jump, step, lean*] en arrière; **4** (away) **we overtook him 20 km ~** nous l'avons doublé il y a 20 km; **there's a garage 10 km ~** nous avons passé un garage à 10 km en arrière; **5** (ago) **25 years ~** il y a 25 ans; **a week/five minutes ~** il y a une semaine/cinq minutes; **6** (a long time ago) **~ in 1964/April** en 1964/avril; **~ before Easter/the revolution** avant Pâques/la révolution; **~ in the days when** du temps où; **it was obvious as far ~ as last year/1985 that** déjà l'année dernière/en 1985 il était évident que; **to go** ou **date ~ to** remonter à [*Roman times, 1700*]; **7** (once again) **she's ~ in power/control** elle a repris le pouvoir/les commandes; **Paul is ~ at the wheel** Paul a repris le volant; **to get ~ to sleep** se rendormir; **to go ~ home** rentrer chez soi; **to go ~ to bed** se recoucher; **8** (nearer the beginning) **ten lines ~** dix lignes plus haut; **ten pages ~** dix pages plus tôt or avant; **9** (indicating return to sb's possession) **to give/send sth ~** rendre/renvoyer qch (**to** à); **to put sth ~** remettre qch; **I've got my books ~** on m'a rendu mes livres; **to get one's money ~** être remboursé; **he wants his dictionary ~ now** il veut que tu lui rendes son dictionnaire tout de suite; **10** (expressing a return to a former location) **to travel to London and ~** faire l'aller-retour à Londres; **the journey to Madrid and ~** l'aller-retour à Madrid; **we walked there and took the train ~** nous y sommes allés à pied et nous avons pris le train pour rentrer; **how long will it take to drive ~?** combien de temps est-ce que ça prendra pour rentrer en voiture?; **11** (in a different location) **meanwhile, ~ in France, he...** pendant ce temps, en France, il...; **~ in the studio, recording had begun** au studio, l'enregistrement avait commencé; **I'll see you ~ at the house/in the office** je te verrai à la maison/au bureau.

IV back and forth *adv phr* **to go** ou **travel ~ and forth** (commute) [*person, bus*] faire la navette (**between** entre); **to walk** ou **go ~ and forth** faire des allées et venues (**between** entre); **to swing ~ and forth** [*pendulum*] osciller; **to sway ~ and forth** se balancer; **the film cuts** ou **moves ~ and forth between New York and Paris** le film se passe entre New York et Paris.

V *vtr* **1** (support) soutenir [*candidate, party, person, bid, bill, action*]; appuyer [*application*]; apporter son soutien à [*enterprise, project*]; **the strike is ~ed by the union** le syndicat soutient la grève; **the junta is ~ed by the militia** la junte est soutenue par la milice; **2** (finance) financer [*project, undertaking*]; **3** (endorse) garantir [*currency*]; **to ~ a bill** Comm, Fin endosser, avaliser une traite; **4** (substantiate) justifier [*argument, claim*] (**with** à l'aide de); **5** (reverse) faire reculer [*horse*]; **to ~ the car into the garage** rentrer la voiture au garage en marche arrière; **to ~ sb into/against sth** faire reculer qn dans/contre qch; **to ~ oars** ou **water** déramer; **6** (bet on) parier sur [*horse, favourite, winner*]; **to ~ a loser** [*race goer*] miser sur un cheval perdant; fig (invest ill-advisedly) mal placer son argent; (support a lost cause) soutenir une cause perdue d'avance; **to ~ the wrong horse** lit, fig miser sur le mauvais cheval; **7** (stiffen, line) consolider, renforcer [*structure*]; endosser [*book*]; renforcer, entoiler [*map*]; maroufler [*painting*]; doubler [*fabric*]; **8** Mus accompagner [*singer, performer*]; **9** Naut masquer, coiffer [*sail*].

VI *vi* **1** (reverse) faire marche arrière; **2** Naut [*wind*] changer de direction.

VII -backed (*dans composés*) **1** (of furniture) **a high-/low-~ed chair** une chaise avec un dossier haut/bas; **2** (lined, stiffened) **canvasl-/foam-~ed** doublé de toile/de mousse; **3** (supported) **UN-~ed** soutenu par l'ONU; **4** (financed) **government-~ed** financé par l'État.

IDIOMS **to break the ~ of a journey/task** faire le plus gros du voyage/travail. ▶ **beyond**, **duck**, **hand**, **own**, **scratch**, **wall**.

■ **back away** reculer; **to ~ away from** lit s'éloigner de [*person, precipice*]; fig prendre ses distances par rapport à [*issue, problem*]; chercher à éviter [*confrontation*].

■ **back down**: ¶ **~ down** (give way) céder; **you can't ~ down now** tu ne peux pas céder maintenant; **to ~ down from** chercher à éviter [*confrontation*]; **to ~ down on** ou **over** reconsidérer [*sanctions, proposal, allegations*]; ¶ **~ down [sth]** [*person*] descendre [qch] à reculons [*slope*]; [*car*] descendre [qch] en marche arrière [*drive, hill*].

■ **back off 1** (move away) reculer; **2** fig (climb down) se montrer plus coopérant; **to ~ off over** céder sur [*issue, matter*].

■ **back onto**: **~ onto [sth]** [*house*] donner sur [qch] à l'arrière [*fields, railway*].

■ **back out**: ¶ **~ out 1** (come out backwards) [*person*] sortir à reculons; [*car, driver*] sortir en marche arrière ; **to ~ out of** [*person*] sortir de [qch] en reculant [*room*]; [*car, driver*] sortir de [qch] en marche arrière [*garage, parking space*]; **2** (renege on) se désister, reculer; **to ~ out of** annuler [*deal, contract*]; [*competitor, team*] se retirer de [*event*]; ¶ **~ [sth] out** faire sortir [qch] en marche arrière [*vehicle*]; **to ~ the car out of the garage** faire sortir la voiture du garage en marche arrière.

■ **back up**: ¶ **~ up 1** (reverse) [*driver, vehicle*] reculer, faire marche arrière; **~ up a few metres** recule de quelques mètres; **2** US (block) [*drains*] s'obstruer; **3** US (tail back) [*traffic*] se bloquer; ¶ **~ [sth] up, ~ up [sth] 1** (support) [*facts, evidence*] confirmer [*claims, case, theory*]; **2** Comput sauvegarder [*data, file*]; ¶ **~ [sb] up** soutenir [*person*].

backache /'bækeɪk/ *n* mal *m* de dos; **to have ~** GB, **to have a ~** US avoir mal au dos.

back bacon *n* Culin bacon *m* maigre.

backbench /ˌbæk'bentʃ/ **I** *n* GB Pol **1** (area of the House) banc *m* des députés; **2** ¢ (MPs) députés *mpl*; **support from the ~(es)** le soutien des députés.

II *modif* [*committee, discussion, revolt etc*] des députés; **~ MP** député *m*.

back: **~bencher** *n* GB Pol député *m*; **~biting** *n* médisance *f*.

backboard /'bækbɔ:d/ *n* (in basketball) panneau *m*.

back boiler *n* chaudière *f* (*située derrière le foyer d'une cheminée*).

backbone /'bækbəʊn/ *n* **1** (spine) (of person, animal) colonne *f* vertébrale; (of fish) grande arête *f*; **2** fig (strong feature) ossature *f*; **to be the ~ of** [*people, players*] constituer l'ossature de [*group, team*]; [*person, concept*] être le pilier de [*organization, project, ideology*]; **3** fig (courage) cran○ *m*; **to have the ~ to do** avoir le cran○ de faire; **he has no ~** c'est une larve.

back-breaking *adj* éreintant.

back burner *n*: IDIOMS **to put sth on the ~** mettre qch en veilleuse [*project etc*].

back: **~chat** *n* GB insolence *f*; **~cloth** *n* Theat, fig toile *f* de fond.

backcomb /'bækkəʊm/ *vtr* crêper [*hair*]; **to ~ one's hair** se crêper les cheveux.

back: **~ copy** *n* Publg ancien numéro *m*; **~ court** *n* Sport fond *m* de court; **~ cover** *n* gen dos *m*; Publg quatrième *f* de couverture.

backdate /'bækdeɪt/ *vtr* antidater [*cheque, letter*]; **to be ~d to 1 April** être antidaté avec effet rétroactif au 1er avril; **a pay-rise** GB ou **raise** US **~d to 1 January** une augmentation de salaire avec effet rétroactif au 1er janvier.

back door *n* (of car) portière *f* arrière; (of building) porte de derrière; **to come in through the ~** fig entrer par la petite porte.

backdrop /'bækdrɒp/ *n* **1** Theat toile *f* de fond; **2** fig toile *f* de fond; **to be a ~ to** ou **for sth** servir de toile de fond à qch; **to take place against a ~ of war** se dérouler sur fond de guerre.

back-end /ˌbæk'end/ *n* **1** (rear) arrière *m*; **the ~ of the year** GB la fin de l'année; **2** Comput terminal *m*.

IDIOMS **to look like the ~ of a bus**○ péj GB être moche○.

back end processor *n* Comput ordinateur *m* principal, processeur *m* dorsal.

backer /'bækə(r)/ *n* **1** (supporter) allié/-e *m/f*; **2** Fin (of project, event) commanditaire *m*; (of business) bailleur *m* de fonds; **3** Games parieur/-ieuse *m/f*.

back-fastening *adj* [*bra*] qui s'attache derrière.

backfire /'bækfaɪə(r)/ *vi* **1** [*scheme, tactics*] avoir l'effet inverse; **to ~ on sb** se retourner contre qn; **2** [*car*] pétarader.

back: **~ flip** *n* saut *m* périlleux arrière; **~ formation** *n* Ling dérivation *f* régressive; **~gammon** ▶ **1282** *n* jaquet *m*.

background /'bækgraʊnd/ **I** *n* **1** (of person) (social) milieu *m*; (personal, family) origines *fpl*; (professional) formation *f*; **to come from a middle-class ~** être issu d'un milieu bourgeois, avoir des origines bourgeoises; **people from poor ~s** les gens issus d'un milieu pauvre; **we want someone with a scientific/computer ~** nous cherchons quelqu'un ayant une formation scientifique/d'informaticien; **a ~ in law/linguistics** une formation juridique/en linguistique; **2** (context) contexte *m*; **the economic/political ~** le contexte économique/politique; **against a ~ of violence** dans un climat de violence; **these events took place against a ~ of war** ces événements avaient pour toile de fond la guerre or se sont deroulés pendant la guerre; **what's the ~ to the situation?** qu'est-ce qui est à l'origine de la situation?; **3** (of painting, photo, scene) fond *m*, arrière-plan *m*; **that's me in the ~** me voilà à l'arrière-plan; **we could see the Alps in the ~** on voyait les Alpes au loin; **against a ~ of** sur un fond de; **on a red ~** sur un fond rouge; **4** (not upfront) **in the ~** au second plan; **to be/remain in the ~** être/rester au second plan; **to push sb/sth into the ~** reléguer qn/qch au second plan; **ill-feeling was always there in the ~** la rancune était toujours là dans l'ombre; **5** (of sound, music) **a ~ of laughter/music** des rires/de la musique en bruit de fond; **voices in the ~** des voix en bruit de fond.

II *modif* **1** [*briefing, information, knowledge, material*] concernant les origines de la situation; **2** [*music, lighting*] d'ambiance.

background: **~ noise** *n* bruit *m* de fond; **~ radiation** *n* radiation *f* naturelle; **~ reading** *n* lectures *fpl* complémentaires (*autour d'un sujet*).

backhand /'bækhænd/ **I** *n* **1** (stroke) revers *m*; **to have a strong ~** avoir un bon revers; **2** (writing) écriture *f* penchée à gauche.

II *adj* **1** Sport [*volley*] de revers; **~ drive** coup *m* droit de dos; **2** [*writing*] penché à gauche.

backhanded /ˌbækˈhændɪd/ *adj* [*compliment*] équivoque.

backhander /ˈbækhændə(r)/ *n* **1** (blow) revers *m*; **2** (bribe) pot-de-vin *m*; **3** (reproof) critique *f*.

backing /ˈbækɪŋ/ **I** *n* **1** (reverse layer) revêtement *m* intérieur; (to stiffen) support *m*; **2** Fin, fig (support) soutien *m*; **3** Mus accompagnement *m*.

II *modif* Mus [*singer, group*] d'accompagnement; **~ vocals** chœurs *mpl*, choristes *mfpl*.

backing store *n* Comput mémoire *f* auxiliaire.

back: **~ interest** *n* arriérés *mpl* d'intérêts; **~ issue** *n* Publg ancien numéro *m*; **~ kitchen** *n* arrière-cuisine *f*.

backlash /ˈbæklæʃ/ *n* réaction *f* violente (**against** contre); **nationalist/military ~** retour *m* de bâton nationaliste/militaire.

back: **~less** *adj* [*dress*] dos-nu *inv*; **~-line** *n* (in tennis) ligne *f* de fond de court; **~list** *n* Publg liste *f* des ouvrages disponibles; **~ lit** *adj* rétro-éclairé; **~ load** *n* Comm chargement *m* de retour.

backlog /ˈbæklɒg/ *n* retard *m*; **I've got a huge ~ (of work)** j'ai plein de travail en retard; **a ~ of orders** une accumulation de commandes en souffrance; **to clear one's ~** liquider le travail en retard.

back: **~ marker** *n* Sport dernier/-ière *m/f*; **~ matter** *n* Publg appendices *mpl*; **~ number** *n* Publg ancien numéro *m*; **~-of-the-envelope** *adj* [*calculation*] approximatif/-ive; **~ orders** *npl* commandes *fpl* en attente or en souffrance.

backpack /ˈbækpæk/ *n* sac *m* à dos.

backpacker /ˈbækpækə(r)/ *n* routard/-e○ *m/f*.

backpacking /ˈbækpækɪŋ/ *n* ¢ randonnée *f*; **to go ~** faire de la randonnée.

back pain ▸**1354** *n* mal *m* de dos; **to have ~** avoir mal au dos.

back: **~ passage** *n* rectum *m*; **~ pay** *n* rappel *m* de salaire.

back-pedal /ˌbækˈpedl/ *vi* (*p prés etc* **-ll-** GB, **-l-** US) lit rétropédaler; fig faire marche arrière; **he's always ~ling** il revient toujours sur ce qu'il dit.

back-pedalling /ˌbækˈpedlɪŋ/ *n* ¢ lit rétropédalage *m*; fig **no more ~!** arrête de revenir sur ce que tu dis!

back: **~ pocket** *n* poche *f* arrière; **~ projection** *n* rétro-éclairage *m*; **~ rent** *n* arriérés *mpl* de loyer; **~ rest** *n* dossier *m*.

back room **I** *n* chambre *f* du fond.

II **backroom** *modif* [*window, ceiling*] de la chambre du fond; **the ~ boys** ou **staff** les experts qui travaillent dans les coulisses.

backscratcher /ˈbækskrætʃə(r)/ *n* gratte-dos *m inv*.

back seat *n* siège *m* arrière; **to take a ~** fig s'effacer.

back: **~seat driver** *n*: *passager qui donne sans arrêt des conseils au conducteur*; **~shift** *n* GB Ind (shift) poste *m* du soir; (workers) équipe *f* du soir; **~shop** *n* arrière-boutique *f*.

backside /ˈbæksaɪd/ *n* derrière *m*, fesses *fpl*.

back: **~sight** *n* Mil crân *m* de mire; **~slang** *n* GB *argot qui consiste à prononcer les mots à l'envers*, ≈ verlan *m*; **~slapping** *n* cordialité *f* exubérante; **~slash** *n* Print barre *f* oblique inverse; **~slider** *n* récidiviste *m*; **~sliding** *n* récidive *f*.

backspace /ˈbækspeɪs/ **I** *n* Comput, Print espacement *m* arrière.

II *vi* reculer.

backspace key *n* rappel *m* arrière.

backspin /ˈbækspɪn/ *n* Sport **to put ~ on a ball** donner de l'effet à une balle.

backstage /ˈbæksteɪdʒ/ *adv* **he's ~** il est en coulisse; [*work, go*] dans les coulisses.

backstairs /ˈbæksteəz/ **I** *npl* escalier *m* de service.

II *adj* [*gossip, connivance*] de coulisses.

backstitch /ˈbækstɪtʃ/ **I** *n* point *m* arrière.

II *vi* coudre en point arrière.

backstop /ˈbækstɒp/ *n* **1** Sport (fielder) receveur *m*; (screen) grillage *m* de fond de court; **2** fig (protection) protection *f* (**against** contre).

back straight, **back stretch** *n* Sport ligne *f* droite de retour.

backstreet /ˈbækstriːt/ **I** *n* petite rue *f*; **the ~s of Naples** péj les quartiers *mpl* pauvres de Naples.

II *modif* [*loanshark, abortionist*] clandestin.

back: **~stroke** *n* dos *m* crawlé; **~swept** *adj* [*hair*] balayé en arrière; **~talk** *n* US = **backchat**; **~ tax** *n* arriérés *mpl* d'impôts.

back-to-back **I** *adj* **~ houses** maisons adossées l'une contre l'autre.

II *adv* **1** (with backs touching) **to stand ~** [*two people*] se mettre dos à dos; **2** (consecutively) **to win three tournaments ~** gagner trois tournois de suite; **to watch two episodes ~** regarder deux épisodes de suite.

back to front **I** *adj* (facing the wrong way) à l'envers; fig **you've got it all ~** tu as tout compris de travers.

II *adv* [*put on, wear*] à l'envers.

backtrack /ˈbæktræk/ *vi* **1** (retract a statement) faire marche arrière; **to ~ on a promise** revenir sur une promesse; **2** (retrace one's steps) rebrousser chemin.

back translation *n* Ling rétro-traduction *f*.

backup /ˈbækʌp/ **I** *n* **1** (support) soutien *m*; Mil renforts *mpl*; **to need ~** [*police officer, troops*] avoir besoin de renforts; **2** (replacement) **to keep a battery/car as a ~** garder une batterie/voiture de secours; **3** Comput sauvegarde *f*.

II *modif* **1** (support) [*equipment*] de renfort; **~ troops** renforts *mpl*; **~ supplies** réserves *fpl*; **2** (replacement) [*plan, system, vehicle*] de secours; **3** Comput [*file, copy*] de sauvegarde.

backup light *n* US Aut feu *m* de recul.

backward /ˈbækwəd/ **I** *adj* **1** (towards the rear) [*glance, look, step*] en arrière; **~ roll** roulade *f* arrière; **~ somersault** salto *m* arrière; **2** (primitive) [*culture, nation, society, economy*] arriéré; **to be technologically ~** souffrir d'un retard technologique; **3** Psych, Sch (handicapped) [*child*] arriéré; (slow to learn) [*pupil*] retardé; **4** (hesitant) **he wasn't ~ about accepting the free trip** il n'a pas été long à accepter le voyage gratuit; **she isn't ~ in coming forward** hum elle n'hésite pas à se mettre en avant.

II *adv* US = **backwards**.

backwardation /ˌbækwəˈdeɪʃn/ *n* Fin déport *m*.

backward-looking *adj* passéiste.

backwardness /ˈbækwədnɪs/ *n* **1** (of intellect) arriération *f*; (of culture, economy) retard *m*; **2** (shyness) timidité *f*; **3** (reticence) hésitation *f* (**in doing** à faire).

backwards /ˈbækwədz/ GB, **backward** /ˈbækwəd/ US **I** *adj* **a ~ jump/glance/step** un bond/regard/pas en arrière.

II *adv* **1** (in a reverse direction) [*walk, crawl*] à reculons; [*lean, step, fall*] en arrière; **to face ~** [*person*] tourner le dos; **to move ~** reculer; **facing ~** (in train) dans le sens contraire de la marche; **to be facing ~** avoir le dos tourné; **to travel ~ and forwards** faire la navette (**between** entre); **to walk ~ and forwards** faire des allées et venues; **to swing ~ and forwards** se balancer; ▸**bend**; **2** (starting from the end) [*count*] à rebours; [*play, wind*] à l'envers; **to say** ou **recite sth ~** dire qch en commençant par la fin; **3** (the wrong way round) **to put sth on ~** mettre qch devant-derrière or à l'envers; **to get sth ~** fig mal comprendre [*message, instructions*]; **you've got it all ~!** tu as tout mélangé!; **4** (thoroughly) **to know sth ~** connaître qch par cœur.

backwash /ˈbækwɒʃ/ *n* Naut remous *m*.

backwater /ˈbækwɔːtə(r)/ *n* **1** lit (of pool, river) eaux *fpl* mortes; **2** fig (isolated area) gen village *m* tranquille; péj trou○ *m* pej; **cultural ~** désert *m* culturel.

backwoods /ˈbækwʊdz/ *npl* US région *f* forestière inexploitée.

backwoodsman /ˈbækwʊdzmən/ *n* **1** lit rustre *m*, péquenaud○ pej; **2**○ GB Pol pair *m* qui fréquente peu la Chambre des Lords.

backyard /ˌbækˈjɑːd/ *n* **1** GB (courtyard) arrière-cour *f*; **2** US (backgarden) jardin *m* de derrière; **3** fig **in one's ~** (in a nearby area) près de chez soi; (in nearby country) près de ses frontières; **we don't want a power station in our ~** nous ne voulons pas de centrale nucléaire près de nos frontières or près de chez nous; **they consider the ex-colony to be their ~** ils veulent garder un pied dans leur ancienne colonie.

bacon /ˈbeɪkən/ **I** *n* ≈ lard *m*; **a rasher of ~** une tranche de bacon; **streaky/smoked ~** lard maigre/fumé; **~ and egg(s)** des œufs au bacon.

II *modif* [*fat, rind*] de lard.

IDIOMS **to bring home the ~**○ faire bouillir la marmite○; **to save sb's ~**○ tirer qn d'affaire○.

bacon-slicer *n* coupe-jambon *m inv*.

bacteria /bækˈtɪərɪə/ *npl* bactéries *fpl*.

bacterial /bækˈtɪərɪəl/ *adj* bactérien/-ienne.

bacteriological /bækˌtɪərɪəˈlɒdʒɪkl/ *adj* bactériologique.

bacteriologist /bækˌtɪərɪˈɒlədʒɪst/ *n* bactériologiste *mf*.

bacteriology /bækˌtɪərɪˈɒlədʒɪ/ *n* bactériologie *f*.

bacterium /bækˈtɪərɪəm/ *n* (*pl* **-ria**) bactérie *f*.

bad /bæd/ **I** *n* **1** (evil) **there is good and ~ in everyone** il y a du bon et du mauvais dans chacun; **she only sees the ~ in him** elle ne voit que ses mauvais côtés; **to go to the ~** mal tourner; **2** (unpleasantness, unfavourableness) **the good and the ~** le bon et le mauvais; **he ended up £100 to the ~** il a fini par perdre 100 livres sterling.

II *adj* (*comp* **worse**; *superl* **worst**) **1** (poor, inferior, incompetent, unacceptable) [*book, harvest, spelling, eyesight, answer, memory, cook, father, liar, management, decision, idea*] mauvais (*before n*); [*joke*] stupide; **a ~ thing** une mauvaise chose; **to have ~ hearing** ne pas très bien entendre; **to have ~ teeth/~legs** avoir de mauvaises dents/de vilaines jambes; **to be ~ at** être mauvais en [*subject*]; **to be ~ at sport** ne pas être doué pour le sport; **to be ~ at doing** (do badly) ne pas être doué pour faire; (dislike doing, do reluctantly) avoir du mal à faire; **that's ~!** (disapproving) c'est une honte!; **not ~**○ pas mauvais, pas mal○; **it wouldn't be a ~ idea to...** ce ne serait pas une mauvaise idée de...; **as bosses go she's not ~** comme patronne elle n'est pas mal○; **2** (unpleasant, unfavourable, negative) [*news, day, time, year, smell, dream, reaction, review, result, forecast, omen, sign, mood, temper*] mauvais (*before n*); **it's ~ enough having to wait, but...** c'est déjà assez pénible de devoir attendre, mais...; **it looks** ou **things look ~** cela s'annonce mal (**for** pour); **that's ~!** (it's a pity) c'est bête!; **the journey/exam wasn't ~ at all** le voyage/l'examen s'est plutôt bien passé; **too ~!** (sympathetic) pas de chance!; (hard luck) tant pis!; **3** (morally or socially unacceptable) [*person, behaviour, habit, life, manners, example, influence, reputation*] mauvais (*before n*); [*language, word*] grossier/-ière; **~ dog!** vilain!; **you ~ girl!** vilaine!; **he's been a ~ boy** il a été vilain, il n'a pas été gentil; **it is ~ to do** c'est mal de faire; **it is ~ of sb to do** ce n'est pas bien de la part de qn de faire; **it is ~ that** il est regrettable que (+ *subj*); **it will look ~** cela fera mauvais effet; **to feel ~** avoir mauvaise conscience (**about** au sujet de); **I feel ~ about leaving you on your own/being late yesterday** j'ai mauvaise conscience de te laisser tout seul/d'avoir été en retard hier; **4** (severe, serious) [*accident, attack, fracture, injury, mistake*] grave; [*case*] sérieux/-ieuse; **to have ~ toothache** avoir très mal aux dents; **a ~ cold** un gros rhume; **how ~ is it?** c'est grave?; **it looks ~** cela a l'air grave; **5** (harmful, injurious) **~ for** mauvais pour; **smoking is ~ for you** ou **your health** fumer est mauvais pour la santé; **it's ~ for you to eat that** tu ne devrais pas manger ça; **it's ~ for industry** c'est néfaste pour l'industrie; **it will be ~ for mothers** cela fera du tort aux mères; **6** (inappropriate, unsuitable) [*time, moment, place, example*] mauvais; **~ weather for skiing** mauvais temps pour faire du ski; **a ~ car for learning to drive in** une mauvaise voiture pour apprendre à conduire; **that's a ~ place to park** ce n'est pas un bon endroit pour se garer; **it's a ~ time to buy a house** ou **for buying a house** ce n'est pas le bon moment pour acheter une maison; **it's a ~ colour/shape for you** c'est une couleur/forme qui ne te va pas; **this may not be a ~ opportunity to...** ce n'est peut-être pas un mauvais moment pour...; **7** (ill, with a weakness or injury) **to have a ~ back** souffrir du dos; **to have a ~ chest** être malade des poumons; **to have a ~ heart** être cardiaque; **to have a ~ leg** avoir mal à la jambe; **that's my ~ knee!** c'est le genou qui me fait mal!; **my back is ~ today** j'ai très mal au dos aujourd'hui; **she was very ~ in the night** elle a été très malade pendant la nuit; **to feel ~** se sentir mal; **'how are you?'—'not so ~'** 'comment vas-tu?'—'pas trop mal'; **to be in a ~ way**○ filer un mauvais coton○; **you are in a ~ way, aren't you?** ça ne va pas fort, on dirait!; **8** Fin [*money, note*] faux/fausse; [*loan*] douteux/-euse; [*insurance claim*] frauduleux/-euse; **9**○ (good) terrible○; **10** (rotten) [*fruit*] pourri; **to go ~** pourrir.

II *adv*○ surtout US [*need, want*] méchamment○; **it hurts ~** ça fait sérieusement mal; **he's/she's got it ~** il/elle est vraiment mordu/-e○.

IDIOMS **to be in ~** US avoir des ennuis; **to be in ~ with sth** US être en froid avec qn; **he's ~ news** il faut se méfier de lui.

bad: **~ apple**○ *n* pourri/-e○ *m/f*; **~ ass**● *n* US fouteur/-euse *m/f* de merde●.

bad blood *n* mésentente *f*; **there is ~ between them** ils sont à couteaux tirés.

bad: **~ boy** *n* enfant *m* terrible; **~ breath** *n* mauvaise haleine *f*; **~ cheque** *n* chèque *m* sans provision or en bois○; **~ debt** *n* créance *f* douteuse.

baddie○, **baddy**○ /ˈbædɪ/ *n* méchant/-e *m/f*.

bade‡ /beɪd, bæd/ *prét* ▶ **bid** II, III.

badge /bædʒ/ *n* **1** (sew-on, pin-on, adhesive) badge *m*; **2** (coat of arms) insigne *m*; **membership ~** insigne de membre; **3** (symbol) symbole *m*, insigne *m* liter; **~ of office** insigne de fonction.

badger /ˈbædʒə(r)/ **I** *n* Zool blaireau *m*.

II *vtr* harceler; **to ~ sb to do** harceler qn pour qu'il/qu'elle fasse.

badger baiting *n*: *déterrage de blaireaux avec des chiens*.

badlands /ˈbædlændz/ *npl* US bad-lands *fpl*.

badly /ˈbædlɪ/ *adv* (*comp* **worse**; *superl* **worst**) **1** (not well) [*begin, behave, fit, sleep, teach, treat*] mal; [*cooked, educated, fed, equipped, made, managed, worded*] mal; **to go ~** [*exam, interview, meeting*] mal se passer; **to do ~** [*candidate, company*] obtenir de mauvais résultats; **to take sth ~** mal prendre qch; **he didn't do too ~** il ne s'est pas mal débrouillé○; **she hasn't done ~ for herself** elle ne s'est pas mal débrouillée○ dans la vie; **the shop hasn't done ~ out of me** je n'ai pas été un mauvais client pour le magasin; **to do ~ by sb** ne pas être correct avec qn; **to be/feel ~ done by** être/se sentir mal traité; **please don't think ~ of me** s'il vous plaît, ne m'en veuillez pas; **2** (seriously) [*suffer*] beaucoup; [*beat*] brutalement; [*disrupt, affect*] sérieusement; [*burnt, damaged*] gravement; [*hurt*] gravement, grièvement; **~ hit** durement touché; **our plans went ~ wrong** nos projets ont très mal tourné; **I was ~ mistaken** je me suis lourdement trompé; **the team was ~ beaten** l'équipe a été largement battue; **3** (urgently) **to want/need sth ~** avoir très envie de/grand besoin de qch; **to be ~ in need of help/cleaning** avoir grand besoin d'aide/d'être nettoyé; **how ~ do you need it?** en as-tu vraiment besoin?

badly behaved *adj* désobéissant.

badly off *adj* (poor) pauvre; **to be ~ for space/clothes** manquer d'espace/de vêtements.

badman /ˈbædmæn/ *n* US bandit *m*.

bad-mannered /ˌbædˈmænəd/ *adj* qui a de mauvaises manières; **she's very ~** elle a de très mauvaises manières.

badminton /ˈbædmɪntn/ ▶ **1282** *n* badminton *m*.

badmouth○ /ˈbædmaʊð/ *vtr* dire du mal de [*person*].

badness /ˈbædnɪs/ *n* **1** (moral, ethical) méchanceté *f*; **2** (of performance, film, book) médiocrité *f*.

bad-tempered /ˌbædˈtempəd/ *adj* **1** (temporarily) [*person, reply*] irrité; **2** (habitually) [*person, nature*] irritable.

baffle /ˈbæfl/ **I** *n* (also **~ board**) (for sound) baffle *m*; (for fluids) déflecteur *m*.

II *vtr* rendre [qn] perplexe, confondre.

baffled /ˈbæfld/ *pp adj* perplexe (**by** devant), confondu (**by** par).

bafflement /ˈbæflmənt/ *n* perplexité *f*, confusion *f*.

baffling /ˈbæflɪŋ/ *adj* déroutant.

BAFTA /ˈbæftə/ *n* GB (*abrév* = **British Association of Film and Television Arts**) *association qui récompense annuellement les meilleurs films et émissions de télévision*.

bag /bæg/ **I** *n* **1** (container) sac *m* (**of** de); **to put sth in a ~** mettre qch dans un sac; **20 pence a ~** 20 pence le sac; **2** (hunting) **to get a good ~** faire bonne chasse; **3**◑ péj (woman) teigne *f* péj.

II bags *npl* **1** (baggage) bagages *mpl*; **to pack one's ~s** lit faire ses bagages; fig faire ses valises; **2**○ GB (lots) **~s of** plein de [*money, time*]; **I've got ~s left** il m'en reste des tonnes○ *fpl*.

III *vtr* (*p prés etc* **-gg-**) **1**○ (save, get) retenir [*seat, table*]; empocher [*medal*]; **to ~ sth for sb, to ~ sb sth** retenir qch pour qn; **2**○ Sport marquer [*goal, point*]; tuer [*hare, bird*]; attraper [*fish*]; **3** (put in bags) = **bag up**; **4**○ US (capture) capturer.

IV *vi* (*p prés etc* **-gg-**) [*garment*] se déformer; **to ~ at the knees** pocher aux genoux.

IDIOMS **a mixed ~** un mélange hétérogène; **~s I**○, **~s me**○ GB à moi; **it's in the ~**○ c'est dans le sac or la poche○; **it's not my ~**○ US ce n'est pas mon truc○; **the whole ~ of tricks**○ tout le bataclan○; **to be left holding the ~** US payer les pots cassés○; **to have ~s under one's eyes** avoir des valises sous les yeux○.

■ **bag up**: **~ [sth] up, ~ up [sth]** mettre [qch] en sac, ensacher.

bagatelle /ˌbægəˈtel/ *n* **1** (game) billard *m* anglais; **2** Mus bagatelle *f*; **3** (trifle) littér bagatelle *f*; **a mere ~** une simple bagatelle.

bagel /ˈbeɪgl/ *n* petit pain *m* (en couronne).

bagful /ˈbægfʊl/ *n* (*pl* **~s** ou **bagsful**) sac *m* (plein) (**of** de); **four ~s** quatre sacs.

baggage /ˈbægɪdʒ/ *n* **1** (luggage) ¢ bagages *mpl*; **ideological ~** fig héritage *m* idéologique; **2** Mil équipement *m*; **3**○ †(girl) coquine *f*.

IDIOMS **bag and ~** avec armes et bagages○.

baggage: **~ allowance** *n* franchise *f* de bagages; **~ car** *n* fourgon *m*; **~ carousel** *n* tapis *m* roulant (*pour bagages*); **~ check** *n* US bulletin *m* de consigne; **~ check-in** *n* enregistrement *m* des bagages; **~ checkroom** *n* US consigne *f*; **~ hall** *n* = **baggage reclaim**; **~ handler** ▶ **1692** *n* bagagiste *mf*; **~ locker** *n* US consigne *f* automatique; **~ reclaim** *n* réception *f* des bagages; **~ room** *n* consigne *f* manuelle.

bagger /ˈbægə(r)/ *n* US Comm employé/-e *m/f* chargé/-e d'emballer les achats.

bagging /ˈbægɪŋ/ *n* Tex toile *f* à sac.

baggy /ˈbægɪ/ *adj* [*garment*] large; **to go ~ at the knees** [*garment*] faire des poches aux genoux; **his clothes are ~** il flotte dans ses vêtements.

Baghdad /ˌbægˈdæd/ ▶ **1818** *pr n* Bagdad.

bag: **~ lady**○ *n* clocharde *f* (*qui transporte tous ses biens dans des sacs en plastique*); **~man**○ *n* US, Austral intermédiaire *m* (*qui empoche des pots-de-vin*); **~ person**○ *n* clochard/-e *m/f* (*qui transporte tous ses biens dans des sacs*); **~pipes** ▶ **1481** *n* cornemuse *f*; **~ snatcher** *n* voleur/-euse *m/f* de sacs à main.

Bahamas /bəˈhɑːməz/ ▶ **1131** *pr n* **the ~** les Bahamas *fpl*.

Bahamian /bəˈhɑːmɪən/ *adj* [*native, inhabitant, climate*] des Bahamas.

Bahrain /bɑːˈreɪn/ ▶ **1131** *pr n* Bahreïn *m*.

Bahraini /bɑːˈreɪnɪ/ ▶ **1486** *n* Bahreïnien/-ienne *m/f*.

Bahrein /bɑːˈreɪn/ *pr n* = **Bahrain**.

bail /beɪl/ **I** *n* **1** Jur caution *f*; **to be (out) on ~** être libéré sous caution; **to release sb on ~ of £5,000** ou **on £5,000 ~** libérer qn contre une caution de 5 000 livres sterling; **to set ~ at...** fixer la caution à...; **to stand** ou **go ~ for sb** se porter garant pour qn; **to put up ~ for sb** payer la caution pour qn; **to request/grant ~** demander/accorder la mise en liberté sous caution; **to jump ~** ne pas comparaître (devant un tribunal); **2** Sport (in cricket) bâtonnet *m*.

II *vtr* **1** Jur mettre [qn] en liberté provisoire; **they were ~ed to appear in court next Monday** ils ont été mis en liberté provisoire jusqu'à leur comparution devant le tribunal lundi prochain; **2** Naut écoper [*water*].

■ **bail out** ¶ **1** Naut écoper; **2** (jump from plane) sauter; ¶ **~ out [sb], ~ [sb] out 1** (get out of trouble) tirer d'affaire [*person*]; Fin renflouer [*company*]; **2** Jur payer la caution pour [*person*]; ¶ **~ out [sth], ~ [sth] out** Naut écoper [*water*]; vider [*boat*].

bail: **~ bond** *n* US Jur caution *f*; **~bondsman** *n* US Jur garant *m*.

bailee /beɪˈliː/ *n* Jur dépositaire *mf*.

bailey /ˈbeɪlɪ/ *n* **1** (wall) mur *m* d'enceinte; **2** (court) cour *f* intérieure.

Bailey bridge /ˈbeɪlɪ brɪdʒ/ *n* pont *m* Bailey.

bailiff /ˈbeɪlɪf/ ▶ **1692** *n* **1** Jur (also for evictions) huissier *m*; **to send in the ~s** envoyer les huissiers; **2** GB (on estate) intendant/-e *m/f*.

bailment /ˈbeɪlmənt/ *n* dépôt *m*.

bailor /ˈbeɪlə(r)/ *n* déposant *m*.

bailout /ˈbeɪlaʊt/ *n* Fin subvention *f*.

bailsman /ˈbeɪlzmən/ *n* US = **bailbondsman**.

bairn /beən/ *n* GB dial enfant *mf*.

bait /beɪt/ **I** *n* lit, fig appât *m*; **to use sth/sb as ~** utiliser qch/qn comme appât; **to rise to** ou **swallow the ~** lit, fig mordre à l'hameçon.

II *vtr* **1** (put bait on) appâter [*trap, hook*] (**with** avec); **they ~ed the trap with her**

son fig ils se sont servis de son fils comme appât; **2** (tease) taquiner [*person*]; **3** (set dogs on) lancer des chiens contre [*bear, badger*].

baize /beɪz/ *n* (fabric) drap *m* de billard; (on billiard table) tapis *m*, drap *m* de billard.

bake /beɪk/ **I** *n* **1** (dish) **fish/vegetable ~** ≈ gratin *m* de poisson/de légumes; **2** (occasion) **cake/pancake ~** réunion *f* pour faire des gâteaux/des crêpes.
II *vtr* **1** Culin faire cuire [qch] au four [*dish, vegetable*]; faire [*bread, cake, pastry*]; **2** [*sun*] dessécher; **3** [*kiln*] cuire.
III *vi* **1** (make bread) [*person*] faire du pain; (make cakes, pastry) faire de la pâtisserie; **2** (cook) [*food*] cuire; **3** fig (in sun) [*town, land*] cuire; [*person*]○ lézarder; **the mud had ~d hard** la boue avait durci.
IV baked *pp adj* [*salmon, apple*] au four; **freshly ~d** tout chaud sorti du four; **home ~d** fait à la maison.

bake: **~d Alaska** *n* Culin omelette *f* norvégienne; **~d beans** *n* Culin haricots *mpl* blancs à la sauce tomate; **~d potato** *n* Culin pomme *f* de terre en robe des champs (au four); **~house** *n* four *m* (communal).

Bakelite® /ˈbeɪkəlaɪt/ *n* Bakélite® *f*.

bake-off *n* US concours *m* de cuisine.

baker /ˈbeɪkə(r)/ **▶1692** *n* **1** (who makes bread) boulanger/-ère *m/f*; (who makes bread and cakes) boulanger-pâtissier/boulangère-pâtissière *m/f*; **2** (shop) **~'s (shop)** boulangerie *f*, boulangerie- pâtisserie *f*.
IDIOMS **a ~'s dozen** treize à la douzaine.

bakery /ˈbeɪkərɪ/ **▶1692** *n* boulangerie *f*, boulangerie-pâtisserie *f*.

bake sale *n* vente *f* de charité (*de gâteaux*).

Bakewell tart /ˌbeɪkwel ˈtɑːt/ *n* GB *gâteau à la confiture et aux amandes*.

baking○ /ˈbeɪkɪŋ/ *adj* (hot) [*place, day*] brûlant; **I'm absolutely ~!** je crève○ de chaud!; **it's ~ today!** quelle fournaise aujourd'hui!

baking: **~ powder** *n* Culin levure *f* chimique; **~ soda** *n* Culin bicarbonate *m* de soude.

baksheesh /ˈbækʃiːʃ, bækˈʃiːʃ/ *n* (tip) pourboire *m*; (bribe) bakchich *m*.

balaclava /ˌbæləˈklɑːvə/ *n* (also **~ helmet**) cagoule *f*; (mountaineer's) passe-montagne *m*.

balalaika /ˌbæləˈlaɪkə/ **▶1481** *n* balalaïka *f*.

balance /ˈbæləns/ **I** *n* **1** (stable position) lit, fig équilibre *m* (**between** entre); **to lose one's ~** perdre l'équilibre; **to keep one's ~** garder son équilibre; **to knock sb off ~** faire perdre l'équilibre à qn; **to catch sb off ~** fig prendre qn au dépourvu; **to throw sb off ~** fig perturber qn; **ecological/racial ~** équilibre *m* écologique/racial; **to achieve a ~** parvenir à un équilibre; **to upset the ~** bouleverser l'équilibre; **to bring sth into ~** équilibrer qch; **the right ~** le juste milieu; **the ~ of nature** l'équilibre naturel; **the ~ of sb's mind** l'équilibre mental de qn; **while the ~ of his mind was disturbed** alors qu'il était en état de démence; **the ~ of interests** Pol l'équilibre des intérêts; **the ~ of power** l'équilibre des forces; **to hold the ~ of power** être en position d'inverser l'équilibre des forces; **2** (scales) lit, fig balance *f*; **to be in the ~** fig être dans la balance; **to hang in the ~** fig être en jeu; **on ~** tout compte fait; **on ~ it has been a good year** tout compte fait l'année a été bonne; **3** Accts, Comm (in account) solde *m*; **~ in hand/brought forward** le solde en caisse/reporté; **to pay the ~** verser le surplus; **4** (remainder) restant *m*; **if we pay off £100, that will leave a ~ of £50** si nous remboursons 100 livres sterling, il en restera 50 livres sterling à payer.
II *vtr* **1** fig (compensate for) (also **~ out**) compenser, équilibrer; **the losses are ~d by the profits** les pertes sont compensées par les profits; **to ~ each other (out)** s'équilibrer; **2** (counterbalance) contrebalancer [*weights, design, elements*]; **you need something to ~ the picture on that side** il vous faut quelque chose pour contrebalancer le tableau de ce côté; **3** (perch) poser or mettre [qch] en équilibre (**on** sur); **the ball was ~d on his nose** le ballon était en équilibre sur son nez; **4** (adjust) équilibrer [*diet, activity, timetable*]; **5** (weigh up, compare) peser; **to ~ the pros and cons** peser le pour et le contre; **to ~ sth against sth** mesurer qch en fonction de qch; **6** Accts, Comm équilibrer [*account, books, budget, economy*]; **7** Aut équilibrer [*wheels*].
III *vi* **1** lit [*one person*] se tenir en équilibre (**on** sur); [*one thing*] tenir en équilibre (**on** sur); [*two things, persons*] s'équilibrer; **2** fig (also **~ out**) [*benefits, drawbacks*] se compenser; **3** Accts, Comm [*books, figures, budget*] être en équilibre; **to make sth ~, to get sth to ~** équilibrer qch.
IV balanced *pp adj* [*person, behaviour, discussion, view, diet, meal, schedule, curriculum, budget*] équilibré; [*article, report*] objectif/-ive; [*decision*] réfléchi.

balance of payments *n* balance *f* des paiements; **the ~ surplus/deficit** l'excédent/le déficit de la balance des paiements.

balance: **~ of power** *n* Pol équilibre *m* des forces, rapport *m* de force; **~ of terror** *n* équilibre *m* de la terreur; **~ of trade** *n* balance *f* du commerce extérieur; **~ sheet** *n* bilan *m*; **~ wheel** *n* balancier *m*.

balancing act *n* lit numéro *m* d'équilibriste; fig tentative *f* de compromis; **to do a ~** fig tenter d'atteindre un compromis.

balcony /ˈbælkənɪ/ *n* **1** (in house, hotel) balcon *m*; **on the ~** (seen from below) au balcon; (seen from interior) sur le balcon; **2** (of theatre) deuxième balcon *m*; **in the ~** (seats) au deuxième balcon.

bald /bɔːld/ *adj* **1** [*man, head*] chauve; **to go ~** devenir chauve, se dégarnir; **he has a ~ spot** ou **patch** il a un début de calvitie; **2** [*lawn, carpet, terrain*] pelé; **3** Aut [*tyre*] lisse; **4** (blunt) [*statement, question*] abrupt; [*fact, reality*] brut; [*style*] dépouillé.

baldachin, baldaquin /ˈbɔːldəkɪn/ *n* baldaquin *m*.

bald eagle *n* aigle *m* chauve.

balderdash○† /ˈbɔːldədæʃ/ **I** *n* ¢ idioties *fpl*.
II *excl* balivernes!

bald-headed /ˌbɔːldˈhedɪd/ *adj* chauve; **a ~ man** un chauve.

balding /ˈbɔːldɪŋ/ *adj* **a ~ man** un homme à la calvitie naissante; **his ~ head** son début de calvitie; **he's slightly ~** il devient un peu chauve.

baldly /ˈbɔːldlɪ/ *adv* [*state, remark*] sans détours.

baldness /ˈbɔːldnɪs/ *n* **1** (of person) calvitie *f*; **2** (of terrain) nudité *f*; **3** (of tyres) usure *f*; **4** (of statement) brutalité *f*; (of style) dépouillement *m*.

baldy○ /ˈbɔːldɪ/ *n* injur chauve *m*.

bale /beɪl/ **I** *n* balle *f*.
II *vtr* **1** mettre [qch] en balles [*hay, cotton, paper*]; **2** GB = **bail**.
■ **bale out** GB = **bail out**.

Balearic Islands /ˌbælɪˌærɪk ˈaɪləndz/ **▶1381** *pr npl* (also **Balearics**) **the ~** les (îles) Baléares *fpl*.

baleful /ˈbeɪlfʊl/ *adj* littér [*influence, presence*] maléfique liter; [*glance, eye*] torve.

balefully /ˈbeɪlfəlɪ/ *adv* littér [*look, watch*] d'un œil torve; [*gesture*] d'un air menaçant.

balk /bɔːk/ **I** *n* **1** (beam) solive *f*; **2** US (in baseball) feinte *f*.
II *vtr* contrecarrer [*plan, intention*]; **to be ~ed of** être frustré de [*leadership, chance*].
III *vi* **1** [*person*] regarder à deux fois; **to ~ at** reculer devant [*risk, cost, prospect*]; **she ~ed at spending so much** elle rechignait à dépenser autant d'argent; **he ~ed at the idea** l'idée lui répugnait; **2** US (in baseball) faire une feinte.

Balkan /ˈbɔːlkən/ **I Balkans** *pr npl* **the ~s** les Balkans *mpl*.
II *adj* [*country, state, peninsula, peoples*] balkanique; **the ~ mountains** le mont Balkan.

balkanization, Balkanization /ˌbɔːlkənaɪˈzeɪʃn, US -nɪˈz-/ *n* balkanisation *f*.

ball /bɔːl/ **I** *n* **1** Sport, Tech (sphere) (in tennis, golf, cricket) balle *f*; (in football, rugby) ballon *m*; (in billiards, croquet) boule *f*; (for children) balle *f*, ballon *m*; Mil, Tech balle *f*; **tennis/golf ~** balle *f* de tennis/de golf; **2** (rolled-up object) (of dough, clay) boule *f* (**of** de); (of wool, string) pelote *f* (**of** de); (smaller) peloton *m* (**of** de); **a ~ of fire** lit, fig une boule de feu; **to curl up into a ~** [*person, cat*] se rouler en boule; **to knead dough into a ~** travailler de la pâte en boule; **to wind sth into a ~** pelotonner qch; **3** Anat **the ~s of one's feet** les demi-pointes *fpl* (des pieds); **the ~ of one's thumb** la base *f* charnue du pouce; **4** (dance) bal *m*.
II balls◑ *npl* **1** lit (testicles) couilles● *fpl*; **2** fig **that's a lot** ou **load of ~s** tout ça c'est des conneries◑; **to have sb by the ~s** tenir○ qn; **she's got ~s** elle en a○; **to have the ~s to do** avoir le culot○ de faire; **to break one's ~s to do** se casser le cul◑ pour faire.
III balls◑ *excl* et merde!◑
IV *vtr* **1** (clench) serrer [*fist*]; **2** US◑ (have sex with) baiser●.
V *vi* **1** [*fist*] se serrer; **2** US◑ (have sex) baiser●.
IDIOMS **the ~ is in your/his court** la balle est dans ton/son camp; **to be on the ~**○ gen être efficace; (old person) avoir toute sa tête; **to play ~**○ coopérer (**with** avec); **to set the ~ rolling** (for conversation) lancer la conversation; (for activity) démarrer; **to keep the ~ rolling** (in conversation) entretenir la conversation; (in activity) tenir le rythme; **to have a ~**○ s'amuser comme un fou/une folle; **he has the ~ at his feet** c'est à lui de jouer; **that's the way the ~ bounces!** US c'est la vie!; **to carry the ~**○ US prendre la responsabilité.
■ **balls up**◑ GB, **ball up**◑ US: **~ up [sth], ~ [sth] up** semer la merde● dans.

ballad /ˈbæləd/ **I** *n* **1** (musical poem) ballade *f*; **2** (song) romance *f*.
II *modif* [*writer, singer*] de ballades.

ball and chain *n* lit, fig boulet *m*.

ball-and-socket joint *n* **1** Anat articulation *f* mobile; **2** Tech joint *m* à rotule.

ballast /ˈbæləst/ *n* **1** (in balloon, ship) lest *m*; **in ~** Naut sur lest; **2** (on rail track, road) ballast *m*.

ball bearing *n* Tech **1** (ball) bille *f* de roulement; **2** (bearing) roulement *m* à billes.

ball: **~boy** *n* (in tennis) ramasseur *m* de balles; **~-breaker**◑, **~-buster**◑ US *n* (task) casse-cul◑ *mf*; (person) casse-couilles● *mf*; **~ cock** *n* Tech robinet *m* à flotteur; **~ control** *n* contrôle *m* du ballon; **~ dress** *n* robe *f* de bal.

ballerina /ˌbæləˈriːnə/ **▶1692** *n* danseuse *f* de ballet, ballerine *f*.

ballet /ˈbæleɪ/ **I** *n* **1** (art) ballet *m*; **classical ~** le ballet classique; **2** (amateur) danse *f* (classique); **3** (performance) ballet *m*; **to go to the ~** aller voir une représentation de ballet; **4** (also **~ company**) corps *m* de ballet; **the Kirov Ballet** le (ballet du) Kirov.
II *modif* [*company, mistress*] de ballet; [*class, school, teacher*] de danse; **~ dress** tutu *m*; **~ shoe** chausson *m* (de danse).

ballet dancer *n* danseur/-euse *m/f* de ballet.

balletomane /ˈbælɪtəʊmeɪn/ *n* ballet(t)omane *mf*.

ballgame /ˈbɔːlgeɪm/ *n* **1** gen jeu *m* de balle or ballon; **2** US match *m*.
IDIOMS **that's a whole new** ou **completely different ~**○ c'est tout une autre histoire.

ball: **~ girl** *n* (in tennis) ramasseuse *f* de balles; **~ gown** *n* robe *f* de bal.

ballistic /bəˈlɪstɪk/ *adj* balistique.

ballistic: **~ galvanometer** *n* galvanomètre *m* balistique; **~ missile** *n* missile *m* balistique.

ballistics /bəˈlɪstɪks/ *n* (+ *v sg*) balistique *f*.

ball lightning *n* éclair *m* en boule.

balloon /bəˈluːn/ **I** *n* **1** Aviat gen ballon *m*; **(hot air)** ~ montgolfière *f*; **2** (toy) ballon *m*; **to blow up a ~** gonfler un ballon; **3** (for cartoon speech) bulle *f*, phylactère *m* spec.
II *modif* [*flight*] en montgolfière; [*crash, accident*] de montgolfière.
III *vi* **1** Aviat **to go ~ing** faire de la montgolfière; **2** (also **~ out**) (swell) [*sail, skirt*] se gonfler; **3** (increase quickly) [*deficit, debt*] galoper.
IDIOMS **to go down** GB ou **go over** US **like a lead ~** tomber à plat; **when the ~ goes up** lorsque l'affaire éclatera.

balloon: **~ flask** *n* ballon *m*; **~ glass** *n* ballon *m*.

ballooning /bəˈluːnɪŋ/ ▶1282 **I** *n* **to go ~** faire de la montgolfière *f*.
II *modif* [*display, accident*] de montgolfière.

balloonist /bəˈluːnɪst/ *n* aéronaute *mf*.

balloon tyre GB, **balloon tire** US *n* pneu *m* ballon.

ballot /ˈbælət/ **I** *n* **1** (process) scrutin *m*; **secret ~** scrutin secret; **by ~** au scrutin; **the election was held by secret ~** l'élection s'est faite à bulletins secrets; **2** (vote) vote *m* (à bulletins secrets) (**of** de; **on** sur); **the first/second ~** le premier/second tour de scrutin; **strike ~** vote *m* pour décider d'une grève; **postal ~** GB vote *m* par correspondance; **to take a ~** procéder à un vote; **3** (also **~ paper**) bulletin *m* de vote; **4** US Pol (list of candidates) liste *f* des candidats concurrents.
II *vtr* consulter (par vote) (**on** sur).
III *vi* voter au scrutin (**on** sur; **to do** pour faire).

ballot box *n* **1** lit urne *f* (électorale); **2** fig (system) **the ~** les urnes *fpl*; **at the ~** aux urnes.

ballot-box stuffing *n* US fraude *f* électorale.

balloting /ˈbælətɪŋ/ *n* ¢ consultation *f* (par vote).

ballpark /ˈbɔːlpɑːk/ *n* US Sport stade *m* de baseball.
IDIOMS **to be in the ~**○ US être dans la bonne fourchette; **not to be in the ~**○ US être à côté de la plaque.

ball: **~park figure** *n* chiffre *m* approximatif; **~point (pen)** *n* stylo *m* (à) bille; **~room** *n* salle *f* de danse; **~room dancing** *n* danse *f* de salon; **~-shaped** *adj* en forme de balle; **~s-up**◑ GB, **~-up**◑ US *n* merdier◑ *m*.

ballsy◑ /bɔːlzɪ/ *adj* plein de punch○.

ball valve *n* soupape *f* à flotteur.

bally○† /ˈbælɪ/ **I** *adj* GB euph sacré○.
II *adv* [*good, stupid*] sacrément○†.

ballyhoo○ /ˌbælɪˈhuː, US ˈbælɪhuː/ **I** *n* **1** (in campaign) battage *m*; **2** (fuss) tapage *m*.
II *vtr* US faire du battage autour de [*event, product, person*].

balm /bɑːm/ *n* **1** (oily) baume *m*; **2** littér (peace) baume *m*; **it was ~ to my soul** cela m'a mis du baume au cœur; **3** Bot (also **lemon ~**) citronnelle *f*.

balmy /ˈbɑːmɪ/ *adj* **1** [*air, evening, weather*] doux/douce; **2**○ GB = **barmy**.

baloney○ /bəˈləʊnɪ/ US **I** *n* ¢ idioties *fpl*.
II *excl* balivernes!

balsa /ˈbɔːlsə/ **I** *n* **1** (also **~ wood**) balsa *m*; **2** (tree) balsa *m*.
II *modif* [*model, raft*] en balsa.

balsam /ˈbɔːlsəm/ *n* **1** (oily) baume *m*; **2** (tree) baumier *m*.

balsam fir *n* sapin *m* baumier.

Baltic /ˈbɔːltɪk/ **I** *pr n* **the ~** la Baltique.
II *adj* balte.

Baltic Republics *pr npl* **the ~** les républiques *fpl* baltes.

Baltic Sea ▶1511 *pr n* **the ~** la mer *f* Baltique.

Baltic States *pr n* **the ~** les États *mpl* baltes.

baluster /ˈbæləstə(r)/ *n* Archit balustre *m*.

balustrade /ˌbæləˈstreɪd/ *n* balustrade *f*.

bamboo /bæmˈbuː/ **I** *n* bambou *m*; **made of ~** en bambou.
II *modif* [*chair, fence, hut*] en bambou.

bamboo curtain *n* (also **Bamboo Curtain**) **the ~** le rideau de bambou.

bamboo shoot *n* pousse *f* de bambou.

bamboozle○ /bæmˈbuːzl/ *vtr* **1** (trick) embobiner○; **to ~ sb into doing** embobiner○ qn pour qu'il fasse; **to ~ sb out of** refaire○ qn de [*money*]; **2** (mystify) déboussoler○, désorienter.

ban /bæn/ **I** *n* interdiction *f* (**on sth** de qch; **on doing** de faire); **overtime/smoking ~** interdiction de faire des heures supplémentaires/de fumer; **~ on foreigners working without a permit** interdiction pour les étrangers de travailler sans permis.
II *vtr* (*p prés etc* **-nn-**) interdire [*author, group, activity, book, drug*]; suspendre [*athlete*]; **to ~ sb from** exclure qn de [*sport, event*]; **to ~ sb from driving/travelling abroad** interdire à qn de conduire/de voyager à l'étranger; **traffic is ~ned from the city centre** le centre-ville est interdit à la circulation.
III banned *pp adj* [*writer, book, group, drug*] interdit; [*athlete*] suspendu.

banal /bəˈnɑːl, US ˈbeɪnl/ *adj* banal; **~ topics** des sujets banals.

banality /bəˈnælətɪ/ *n* (quality, remark) banalité *f*.

banana /bəˈnɑːnə/ **I** *n* **1** (fruit) banane *f*; **a bunch of ~s** un régime de bananes; **2** (also **~ palm**) bananier *m*; **3**◑ US (person) **to be top ~** [*actor*] être la vedette; [*worker*] être le chef; **to be second ~** être un sous-fifre.
II *modif* [*yoghurt, ice cream*] à la banane.
IDIOMS **to go ~s**○ (get angry) piquer une crise○; (get excited) devenir dingue○.

banana: **~ boat** *n* bananier *m*; **~ republic** *n* péj république *f* bananière pej.

banana skin *n* peau *f* de banane.
IDIOMS **to slip on a ~** glisser sur une peau de banane.

banana split *n* banane *f* royale.

band /bænd/ **I** *n* **1** Mus (rock) groupe *m* (de rock); (army) clique *f*; (municipal) fanfare *f*; **brass/jazz ~** orchestre *m* de cuivres/de jazz; **2** (with common aim) groupe *m* (**of** de); **3** (of light, colour, land) bande *f*; **4** Radio bande *f*; **the 31 metre ~** la bande des 31 mètres; **5** GB (of age, income tax) tranche *f*; **6** Sch GB (level) niveau *m*; **7** (for binding) (ribbon: for hair, hat) ruban *m*; (around waist) ceinture *f*; (around neck) col *m*; (around arm) brassard *m*; (around head) bandeau *m*; **rubber** ou **elastic** GB **~** élastique *m*; **8** Tech (metal) ruban *m* (métallique); (rubber) courroie *f*; **9** (track) Mus (on record) plage *f*; Comput (on disk) piste *f*; **10** (ring) anneau *m*; **wedding ~** alliance *f*.
II *vtr* **1** GB Sch classer [qch] par niveaux; **2** (stripe) border.
■ **band together** se réunir (**to do** pour faire).

bandage /ˈbændɪdʒ/ **I** *n* bandage *m*; **he has a ~ round his head/on his leg** il a la tête/la jambe bandée.
II *vtr* bander [*head, limb, wound*]; **to have one's foot ~d** se faire bander le pied.
■ **bandage up**: **~ [sb/sth] up, ~ up [sb/sth]** bander [qn/qch] entièrement; **he was (all) ~d up** il était couvert de bandages.

Band-Aid® /ˈbændeɪd/ *n* Med (plaster) pansement *m* (adhésif); **a ~ solution** fig, péj une solution d'attente.

bandan(n)a /bænˈdænə/ *n* (foulard) bandana *m*.

B and B, b and b /ˌbiː ən ˈbiː/ *n* GB *abrév* ▶ **bed and breakfast**.

bandbox† /ˈbændbɒks/ *n* carton *m* à chapeau(x).

banding /ˈbændɪŋ/ *n* GB **1** (of tax system) assiette *f* (fiscale); **2** Sch (streaming) répartition *f* par niveaux.

bandit /ˈbændɪt/ *n* bandit *m*.

bandit country *n* pays *m* des hors-la-loi.

banditry /ˈbændɪtrɪ/ *n* banditisme *m*.

band leader *n* chef *m* d'orchestre.

bandmaster /ˈbændmɑːstə(r)/ *n* (of military band) chef *m* de musique; (of brass band) chef *m* de fanfare.

bandoleer, bandolier /ˌbændəˈlɪə(r)/ *n* cartouchière *f*.

band: **~ saw** *n* scie *f* à ruban; **~ shell** *n* US Mus conque *f* d'orchestre (*plateau en plein air à fond réverbérant*); **~sman** *n* (*pl* **-men**) gen, Mil musicien *m*; **~stand** *n* kiosque *m* (à musique).

bandwagon /ˈbændwægən/ *n* IDIOMS **to jump** ou **climb on the ~** prendre le train en marche; **accused of climbing on the socialist/feminist ~** accusé de prendre le train socialiste/des féministes en marche.

bandy /ˈbændɪ/ **I** *adj* arqué; **to have ~ legs** avoir les jambes arquées.
II *vtr* **to ~ words/blows with sb**† avoir des mots/échanger des coups avec qn; **I'm not going to ~ words with you!** je ne vais pas discuter avec vous!
■ **bandy about, bandy around**: **~ [sth] about** ou **around** avancer [*names, information, statistics*].

bandy-legged /ˌbændɪˈlegɪd/ *adj* [*person*] aux jambes arquées; **he's ~** il a les jambes arquées.

bane /beɪn/ *n* fléau *m* (**of** de); **she/it is the ~ of my life** ou **existence!** elle/ça m'empoisonne la vie or l'existence!

baneful /ˈbeɪnfl/ *adj* littér néfaste liter.

bang /bæŋ/ **I** *n* **1** (noise) (of gun, firework, bomb, burst balloon) détonation *f*, boum *m*; (of door, window) claquement *m*; **to hear a loud ~** entendre une forte détonation or un grand boum; **2** (knock) coup *m*; **my knee got a nasty ~** j'ai reçu un vilain coup sur le genou.
II bangs *npl* US frange *f*.
III *adv*○: **~ in the middle** en plein centre; **to arrive ~ on time** arriver à l'heure pile; **~ on target** lit en plein dans le mille; **production is ~ on target** on a atteint pile○ nos objectifs de production; **the technology is ~ up to date** la technologie est des plus récentes.
IV *excl* (imitating gun) pan!; (imitating explosion) boum!, bang!
V *vtr* **1** (place sth noisily) **to ~ sth down on** poser bruyamment qch sur; **to ~ down the receiver** raccrocher brutalement; **2** (causing pain) **to ~ one's head** se cogner la tête (**on** contre); **I'll ~ your heads together!** (to two children) vous allez recevoir tous les deux des claques!; **3** (strike) taper sur [*drum, saucepan*]; **to ~ one's fist on the table, to ~ the table with one's fist** taper du poing sur la table; **4** (slam) claquer [*door, window*]; **5**● (have sex with) se taper● [*woman*].
VI *vi* **1** (strike) **to ~ on** cogner à [*wall, door*]; **he ~ed on the table with his fist** il a tapé du poing sur la table; **to ~ against** se cogner contre [*table, chair*]; **2** (make noise) [*door, shutter*] claquer; **to ~ shut** se fermer en claquant; **to ~ in the wind** claquer au vent; **3**● (have sex) baiser●.
IDIOMS **~ goes**○ **my holiday/my promotion** je peux dire adieu à mes vacances/ma promotion; **to go out with a ~** finir avec un grand éclat.
■ **bang in**: **~ [sth] in, ~ in [sth]** enfoncer [*nail, peg, tack*] (**with** à coups de).
■ **bang into**: **~ into [sb/sth]** heurter.
■ **bang on about** GB: **~ on about [sth]**○ rabâcher [*subject*].

■ **bang up**: ~ [**sb**] **up**, ~ **up** [**sb**] GB (put in jail) boucler○; **to be ~ed up for five years** être bouclé pour cinq ans.

banger /ˈbæŋə(r)/ *n* **1**○ (car) guimbarde○ *f*; **old ~** vieille guimbarde; **2** (firework) pétard *m*; **to let off a ~** lancer un pétard; **3**○ GB (sausage) saucisse *f*; **~s and mash** saucisses avec de la purée.

Bangkok /ˌbæŋˈkɒk/ ▶ 1818 *pr n* Bangkok.

Bangladesh /ˌbæŋgləˈdeʃ/ ▶ 1131 *pr n* Bangladesh *m*; **in/to ~** au Bangladesh.

Bangladeshi /ˌbæŋgləˈdeʃɪ/ ▶ 1486 **I** *n* Bangladais/-e *m/f*.
II *adj* [*culture, politics*] du Bangladesh.

bangle /ˈbæŋgl/ *n* bracelet *m*, jonc *m*.

bang-on○ /ˌbæŋˈɒn/ *adj* GB [*answer, guess*] en plein dans le mille○; [*calculation*] impec○.

banish /ˈbænɪʃ/ *vtr* **1** sout (expel) bannir (**from** de); **2** littér ou hum (drive away) bannir; **to ~ all thoughts of winter** bannir toute pensée d'hiver.

banishment‡ /ˈbænɪʃmənt/ *n* sout bannissement *m*.

banister, **bannister** GB /ˈbænɪstə(r)/ *n* rampe *f* (d'escalier); **leaning on the ~s** s'appuyant à la rampe; **to slide down the ~s** glisser sur la rampe.

banjax○ /ˈbændʒæks/ **I** *vtr* bousiller○ [*machine*].
II banjaxed *pp adj* [*machine*] bousillé○; **I'm absolutely ~ed** je suis complètement lessivé○.

banjo /ˈbændʒəʊ/ ▶ 1481 **I** *n* (*pl* **-jos** ou **-joes**) banjo *m*.
II *modif* [*case, music, string*] de banjo.

bank /bæŋk/ **I** *n* **1** Fin, Games banque *f*; **the Bank of France/of England** la Banque de France/d'Angleterre; **blood ~** banque du sang; **to break the ~** Games faire sauter la banque; **it won't break the ~** fig ça ne ruinera personne; **2** (border) (of river, lake) rive *f*; (of canal) berge *f*; **the ~s of the Nile/of the Thames** les bords *mpl* du Nil/de la Tamise; **to break its ~s** [*river*] sortir de son lit; **3** (mound) (of earth, mud) talus *m*; (of snow) congère *f*; **4** (slope) (by road, railway track) talus *m*; (by racetrack) virage *m* incliné; (by mineshaft) carreau *m*; **5** (section of sea bed) banc *m*; **sand ~** banc de sable; **6** (mass) (of flowers) massif *m*; (of fog, mist) banc *m*; **a ~ of cloud** un banc de nuages; **7** Aviat virage *m* sur l'aile; **8** (series) (of switches, oars, keys, floodlights) rangée *f*; **9** Mining (face) front *m* de taille; **10** (bench for rower) banc *m* de nage.
II *modif* [*credit, debt*] bancaire; [*employee, staff*] de banque.
III *vtr* **1** Fin déposer [qch] à la banque [*cheque, money*]; **2** (border) border [*track, road*]; **to be ~ed by** être bordé par; **3** Aviat incliner [qch] sur l'aile [*plane*]; **4** (fuel) = **bank up**.
IV *vi* **1** Fin **to ~ with** avoir un compte à la; **who do you ~ with?** où as-tu ton compte?; **2** Aviat [*plane*] virer sur l'aile.
IDIOMS **to be as safe as the Bank of England** être à toute épreuve.
■ **bank on**: **~ on** [**sb/sth**] compter sur [qn/qch]; **don't ~ on it!** n'y compte pas!; **to ~ on doing** escompter faire; **to ~ on sb to do** compter sur qn pour faire.
■ **bank up**: ¶ **~ up** [*snow, earth, mud*] s'amonceler; ¶ **~** [**sth**] **up**, **~ up** [**sth**] **1** (pile up) entasser [*snow, earth, mud*]; **2** (cover with fuel) charger [*fire*]; **3** (make a slope by) surhausser [*road, racetrack*].

bankable /ˈbæŋkəbl/ *adj* **1** Fin escomptable; **2** fig (of star) **to be ~** être une valeur sûre.

bankable asset *n* Fin bien *m* escomptable.

bank: **~ acceptance** *n* Fin acceptation *f* de banque; **~ account** *n* Fin compte *m* bancaire; **~ balance** *n* Fin solde *m* bancaire; **~ bill** *n* US (note) billet *m* de banque; **~book** *n* livret *m* bancaire; **~ card** *n* carte *f* bancaire; **~ charges** *npl* Fin frais *mpl* bancaires, frais *mpl* de gestion de compte; **~ clerk** ▶ 1692 *n* employé/-e *m/f* de banque; **~ draft** *n* Fin traite *f* bancaire.

banker /ˈbæŋkə(r)/ ▶ 1692 *n* **1** Fin (owner) banquier/-ière *m/f*; (executive) cadre *mf* de banque; **2** Games banquier *m*.

banker: **~'s draft** *n* Fin traite *f* bancaire; **~'s order** *n* virement *m* bancaire; **~'s reference** *n* références *fpl* bancaires.

bank: **Bank for International Settlements**, **BIS** *n* Banque *f* des règlements internationaux, BRI; **Bank Giro Credit**, **BGC** *n* GB Fin crédit *m* par virement bancaire.

bank holiday *n* **1** GB jour *m* férié; **2** US jour *m* de fermeture des banques.

banking /ˈbæŋkɪŋ/ **I** *n* Fin **1** (business) opérations *fpl* bancaires; **2** (profession) la banque; **to study ~** faire des études bancaires; **3** Aviat virage *m* sur l'aile.
II *modif* [*group, sector, system, facilities*] bancaire; **~ business** affaires *fpl* bancaires.

banking hours *n* heures *fpl* d'ouverture des banques.

bank: **~ lending** *n* prêts *mpl* bancaires; **~ loan** *n* Fin prêt *m* bancaire; **~ manager** ▶ 1692 *n* directeur/-trice *m/f* d'agence bancaire; **~note** *n* billet *m* de banque; **~ raid** *n* hold-up *m*, attaque *f* de banque; **~ rate** *n* † GB = **minimum lending rate**; **~ robber** *n* cambrioleur/-euse *m/f* de banque; **~ robbery** *n* cambriolage *m* de banque.

bankroll /ˈbæŋkrəʊl/ **I** *n* fonds *mpl*.
II *vtr*○ financer [*person, party*].

bankrupt /ˈbæŋkrʌpt/ **I** *n* failli/-e *m/f* spec; **he's a ~** il a fait faillite.
II *adj* **1** (ruined) [*person*] ruiné; [*business, economy*] en faillite; **~ stock** articles *mpl* de saisie; **to be declared/made ~** être déclaré/mis en faillite; **to go ~** faire faillite; **2** (lacking) **to be morally ~** (person) être dépourvu de scrupules; (society) être décadent; **to be ~ of** être dépourvu de [*ideas, principles*].
III *vtr* mettre [qn/qch] en faillite [*person, company*].

bankruptcy /ˈbæŋkrʌpsɪ/ *n* **1** (financial) faillite *f*; **2** (moral, intellectual) décadence *f*.

bankruptcy: **~ court** *n* ≈ tribunal *m* de commerce; **~ proceedings** *npl* procédure *f* de faillite.

bank: **~ statement** *n* relevé *m* de compte; **~ transfer** *n* virement *m* bancaire.

banner /ˈbænə(r)/ **I** *n* **1** (in protest, festival) banderole *f*; **2** (name) bannière *f*; **under the ~ of** sous la bannière de; **3** Hist (ensign) étendard *m*.
II *adj* US [*year, performance*] record *inv*.

banner headline *n* (*souvent pl*) gros titre *m*.

bannister *n* GB = **banister**.

banns /bænz/ *npl* Relig bans *mpl*; **to read the ~** publier les bans.

banquet /ˈbæŋkwɪt/ **I** *n* banquet *m*; **medieval/official ~** banquet médiéval/officiel; **to hold a ~ in honour of sb** donner un banquet en l'honneur de qn.
II *vi* banqueter.

banquet(ing) hall *n* salle *f* de(s) banquet(s).

banshee /bænˈʃiː, US ˈbænʃiː/ *n* fée *f* (*dont les hurlements annoncent une mort prochaine*).
IDIOMS **to wail like a ~** crier comme un perdu.

bantam /ˈbæntəm/ *n* **~ cock** coq *m* nain; **~ hen** poule *f* naine; **to breed ~s** élever des poules naines.

bantamweight /ˈbæntəmweɪt/ **I** *n* **~** (**boxer**) (boxeur *m*) poids *m* coq.
II *modif* [*champion, title*] des poids coq.

banter /ˈbæntə(r)/ **I** *n* ¢ plaisanteries *fpl*.
II *vi* badiner (**with** avec).

bantering /ˈbæntərɪŋ/ *adj* badin.

banty○ = **bantam**.

banyan /ˈbænɪən/ *n* banian *m*.

BAOR *n*: *abrév* ▶ **British Army of the Rhine**.

baptism /ˈbæptɪzəm/ *n* **1** Relig baptême *m*; **2** fig (initiation) débuts *mpl*; **~ of fire** baptême *m* du feu.

baptismal /bæpˈtɪzməl/ *adj* [*name, rite*] de baptême; **~ font** fonts *mpl* baptismaux.

Baptist /ˈbæptɪst/ *n, adj* baptiste (*mf*).

baptistry /ˈbæptɪstrɪ/ *n* baptistère *m*.

baptize /bæpˈtaɪz/ *vtr* baptiser; **to be ~d a Catholic** être baptisé dans l'Église catholique.

bar /bɑː(r)/ **I** *n* **1** (strip of metal, wood) barre *f*; **2** (on cage, cell, window) barreau *m*; **to put sb/be behind ~s** mettre qn/être derrière les barreaux; **3** (place for drinking) bar *m*; (counter) comptoir *m*; **to sit at the ~** s'asseoir au comptoir; **I'll go to the ~** je vais chercher les boissons; **4** (block) (of soap, gold, chocolate) barre *f*; **5** (obstacle) obstacle *m* (**to** pour; **to doing** pour faire); **your age is not a ~** votre âge ne constitue pas un obstacle; **6** Jur (profession) **the ~** le barreau; **to study for the ~** se destiner au barreau; **to be called to the ~** entrer au barreau; **7** Jur (in court) barre *f*; **to come to the ~** venir à la barre; **the prisoner at the ~** l'accusé/-e *m/f*; **8** Sport (in gym, across goal) barre *f*; **to practise on the ~s** s'exercer aux barres; **9** Mus mesure *f*; **two beats in a/to the ~** deux temps dans une/par mesure; **10** (in electric fire) résistance *f*; **11** Mil GB (on medal) barrette *f*; US (on uniform) galon *m*; **12** Herald barre *f*.
II *prep* sauf; **all ~ one** tous sauf un seul; **~ none** sans exception.
III *vtr* (*p prés etc* **-rr-**) **1** (block) barrer [*way, path*]; **to ~ sb's way** barrer le passage à qn; **2** (ban) exclure [*person*] (**from sth** de qch); interdire [*activity*]; **journalists were ~red** l'accès était interdit aux journalistes; **to ~ sb from doing** interdire à qn de faire; **his religion ~s him from marrying** sa religion lui interdit de se marier; **3** (fasten) mettre la barre à [*gate, shutter*]; **the gate was ~red** on avait mis la barre au portail.
IV barred *pp adj* **1** [*window*] à barreaux; **2** (striped) **~red with** barré de [*colour, mud*].
V -barred (*dans composés*) **four/five-~red gate** portail à quatre/cinq barreaux.
IDIOMS **a no holds ~red contest** une lutte où tous les coups sont permis; **it was a divorce battle with no holds ~red** le divorce a été une lutte où tous les coups semblaient permis.

bar association *n* US Jur association *f* juridique.

barb /bɑːb/ **I** *n* **1** (on hook, arrow) barbe *f*; **2** fig (remark) pique *f*; **3** (on feather) barbe *f*; **4** Equit barbe *m*.
II *vtr* garnir [qch] de barbes.

Barbadian /bɑːˈbeɪdɪən/ ▶ 1486 **I** *n* Barbadien/-ienne *m/f*.
II *adj* [*person, custom, cuisine, government*] de la Barbade.

Barbados /bɑːˈbeɪdɒs/ ▶ 1131, 1381 *pr n* la Barbade *f*; **in/to ~** à la Barbade.

barbarian /bɑːˈbeərɪən/ *n, adj* barbare (*mf*) also pej.

barbaric /bɑːˈbærɪk/ *adj* (brutal, primitive) barbare.

barbarically /bɑːˈbærɪklɪ/ *adv* [*act, behave*] de façon barbare.

barbarism /ˈbɑːbərɪzəm/ *n* **1** (brutality, primitiveness) barbarie *f*; **2** littér (error) barbarisme *m*.

barbarity /bɑːˈbærətɪ/ *n* **1** (brutality, primitiveness) barbarie *f*; **2** (brutal act) atrocité *f*.

barbarize /ˈbɑːbəraɪz/ *vtr* sout massacrer [*language*]; **to ~ sb** faire de qn un vrai sauvage.

barbarous /ˈbɑːbərəs/ *adj* (all contexts) barbare.

barbarously /ˈbɑːbərəslɪ/ *adv* [*act, behave*] de façon barbare; **to be ~ rude/ignorant** être d'une impolitesse/d'une ignorance totale.

Barbary /ˈbɑːbərɪ/ *pr n* Barbarie *f*.

Barbary ape *n* magot *m*.

Barbary Coast *pr n* **the ~** la côte *f* de Barbarie.

Barbary: **~ duck** *n* canard *m* de Barbarie; **~ horse** *n* cheval *m* barbe.

barbecue /ˈbɑːbɪkjuː/ **I** *n* **1** (grill) barbecue *m*; **2** (party) barbecue *m*; **3** (food) grillade *f*.
II *vtr* **1** (on charcoal etc) faire griller [qch] au barbecue; **2** (cook in spicy sauce) faire griller [qch] façon barbecue.

barbecue sauce *n* sauce *f* barbecue.

barbed /ˈbɑːbd/ *adj* **1** [*hook, arrow*] à barbes; **2** (*tjrs épith*) [*comment, criticism*] acerbe; [*wit*] mordant.

barbed wire, **barbwire** US **I** *n* (fil *m* de fer) barbelé *m*.
II *modif* [*fence, barricade*] de (fil de fer) barbelé.

barbel /ˈbɑːbl/ *n* **1** (fish) barbeau *m*; **2** (of catfish) barbillon *m*.

barbell /ˈbɑːbel/ *n* barre *f* d'haltères.

barber /ˈbɑːbə(r)/ ▶**1692** *n* coiffeur *m* (pour hommes); **he's a ~** il est coiffeur; **to go to the ~'s** aller chez le coiffeur.

barber: **~ college** *n* US école *f* de coiffure (pour hommes); **~shop quartet** *n*: *quatuor masculin chantant a cappella*; **~'s pole** GB, **~ pole** US *n* enseigne *f* de coiffeur; **~'s shop** GB, **~shop** US ▶**1692** *n* salon *m* de coiffure (pour hommes).

barbican /ˈbɑːbɪkən/ *n* barbacane *f*.

barbital /ˈbɑːbɪtl/ US = **barbitone**.

barbitone /ˈbɑːbɪtəʊn/ *n* GB barbital *m*.

barbiturate /bɑːˈbɪtjʊrət/ *n* barbiturique *m*.

barbituric acid /ˌbɑːbɪˈtjʊərɪk/ *n* acide *m* barbiturique.

barbiturism /bɑːˈbɪtjʊrɪzəm/ *n* barbituromanie *f*.

barbs○ /bɑːbz/ *npl* US (*abrév* = **barbiturates**) barbituriques *mpl*.

barbwire *n* US = **barbed wire**.

barcarole /ˌbɑːkəˈrəʊl, -ˈrɒl/ *n* barcarolle *f*.

Barcelona /ˌbɑːsɪˈləʊnə/ ▶**1818** *pr n* Barcelone; **in/to ~** à Barcelone.

bar: **~ chart** *n* histogramme *m*; **~ code** *n* code-barres *m*; **~-coded** *adj* à code-barres; **~-code reader** *n* lecteur *m* de codes-barres.

bard /bɑːd/ **I** *n* **1** littér (poet) chantre *m*; **the Bard (of Avon)** Shakespeare; **2**‡ (minstrel) barde *m*; **3** Culin (bacon fat) barde *f* (de lard).
II *vtr* Culin barder.

bardic /ˈbɑːdɪk/ *adj* bardique.

bare /beə(r)/ **I** *adj* **1** (naked) [*body, flesh, leg*] nu; **a child with ~ feet** un enfant aux pieds nus; **to walk with ~ feet** marcher pieds nus or nu-pieds (*inv*); **to sit in the sun with one's head ~** s'asseoir au soleil la tête nue ou nu-tête (*inv*); **~ to the waist** torse nu; **with one's ~ hands** à mains nues; **2** (exposed) [*blade, boards, wall, wood*] nu; **to lay ~** dévoiler [*plan, private life, secret*]; **to lay one's soul** ou **heart ~** mettre son cœur à nu; **3** (empty) [*cupboard, house, room*] vide; **~ of** vide de [*furniture, food*]; **to strip sth ~** vider qch; **4** (stark) [*branch, mountain, rock*] nu; [*earth, landscape*] dénudé; **~ of** dépourvu de [*leaves, flowers*]; **5** (mere) **a ~ 3%/20 dollars** à peine 3%/20 dollars; **to last a ~ 30 seconds** durer à peine 30 secondes; **the ~st sign/indication of** le moindre signe/la moindre indication de; **6** (absolute) strict (*before n*); **the ~ minimum** le strict minimum; **the ~ essentials** ou **necessities** le strict nécessaire; **7** (unembellished) [*facts, statistics*] brut; **8** (in Bridge) [*ace, king*] sec/sèche.
II *vtr* **to ~ one's chest** se découvrir la poitrine; **to ~ one's teeth** montrer les dents; **to ~ one's head** se découvrir; **to ~ one's heart/soul** to ouvrir son cœur/âme à.

bare: **~-ass(ed)**◑ *adj* cul-nu◑; **~back** *adv* [*ride*] à cru; **~back rider** *n* cavalier/-ière *m/f* qui monte à cru.

bare bones /ˌbeəˈbəʊnz/ **I** *npl* **the ~** l'essentiel *m*; **the ~ of the story are** l'essentiel de l'histoire est.
II bare-bones *adj* [*account*] réduit à sa plus simple expression.

barefaced /ˈbeəfeɪst/ *adj* [*lie*] éhonté; [*cheek, nerve*] effronté.

barefoot /ˈbeəfʊt/ **I** *adj* [*person*] aux pieds nus; **to be ~** être nu-pieds.
II *adv* [*run, walk*] pieds nus.

bare: **~headed** *adj* [*person*] tête nue; **~legged** *adj* [*person*] aux jambes nues (*after n*).

barely /ˈbeəlɪ/ *adv* **1** [*audible, capable, conscious, disguised*] à peine, tout juste; **to be ~ able to walk** pouvoir à peine or tout juste marcher; **~ 12 hours later** à peine 12 heures plus tard; **~ concealed hostility** hostilité à peine dissimulée; **she had ~ finished when** elle venait juste de finir quand; **2** [*furnished*] pauvrement.

bareness /ˈbeənɪs/ *n* nudité *f*.

bar exams *n* GB ≈ certificat *m* d'aptitude à la profession d'avocat.

barf◑ /bɑːf/ **I** *n* US vomi *m*; **~!** dégueulasse○!
II *vi* dégobiller, vomir.

barfly○ /ˈbɑːflaɪ/ *n* US pilier *m* de bar○.

bargain /ˈbɑːgɪn/ **I** *n* **1** (deal) marché *m* (**between** entre); **to make** ou **strike a ~** conclure un marché; **to keep one's side of the ~** tenir sa part du marché; **to drive a hard ~** négocier ferme or serré; **into the ~** par-dessus le marché; **2** (good buy) affaire *f*; **what a ~!** quelle bonne affaire! **to get a ~** faire une affaire; **a ~ at £10** une affaire à 10 livres sterling.
II *modif* [*buy, book, house*] à prix réduit.
III *vi* **1** (for deal) négocier (**with** avec); **to ~ for** négocier [*freedom, release, increase*]; **2** (over price) marchander (**with** avec); **to ~ for a lower price** marchander un prix plus bas.
■ **bargain for**, **bargain on**: **~ for**, **~ on sth** s'attendre à qch; **we got more than we ~ed for** nous ne nous attendions pas à ça.

bargain: **~ basement** *m* coin *m* des affaires; **~ hunter** *n* personne *f* à l'affût d'une bonne affaire.

bargaining /ˈbɑːgɪnɪŋ/ **I** *n* (over pay) négociations *fpl*.
II *modif* [*framework, machinery, position, power, procedure, rights*] de négociation.

bargaining chip *n* atout *m* dans les négociations.

bargain: **~ offer** *n* promotion *f*; **~ price** *n* prix *m* avantageux.

barge /bɑːdʒ/ **I** *n* **1** (living in, freight) péniche *f*; (freight only) chaland *m*; **2** (for ceremony, pageant) barque *f* d'apparat; **3** (in navy) vedette *f*.
II *vtr* (shove) bousculer [*player, runner*].
III *vi* (move roughly) **to ~ through a crowd** se frayer un chemin dans une foule en bousculant tout le monde; **to ~ past sb** passer devant qn en le bousculant.
■ **barge in** (enter noisily) faire irruption; (interrupt) interrompre brutalement; **to ~ in on sb** faire irruption chez qn; **to ~ in on a meeting** faire irruption dans une réunion; **sorry to ~ in** désolé de vous interrompre.
■ **barge into** faire irruption dans [*room, house*]; bousculer [*person*].

bargee /bɑːˈdʒiː/ ▶**1692** *n* GB batelier *m*.

bargepole /ˈbɑːdʒpəʊl/ *n* perche *f*.
IDIOMS **I wouldn't touch him/it with a ~** je ne voudrais de lui/cela pour rien au monde.

baritone /ˈbærɪtəʊn/ ▶**1868** **I** *n* baryton *m*.
II *modif* **1** [*voice, solo*] de baryton; [*part*] baryton; **2** [*sax, oboe*] baryton *inv*.

barium /ˈbeərɪəm/ *n* baryum *m*.

barium meal *n* bouillie *f* de sulfate de baryum.

bark /bɑːk/ **I** *n* **1** (of tree) écorce *f*; **chipped ~, shredded ~** Hort copeaux *mpl* d'écorce; **2** (of dog) aboiement *m*; **3** littér (boat) barque *f*.
II *vtr* **1** (graze) [*person*] s'écorcher [*shin, elbow*]; **2** (shout) aboyer [*order*]; [*barker*] faire bruyamment la publicité pour [*wares*].
III *vi* [*dog, person*] fig aboyer (**at sb/sth** après qn/qch).
IDIOMS **his ~ is worse than his bite** il fait plus de bruit que de mal; **to be ~ing up the wrong tree** faire fausse route; **to keep a dog and ~ oneself** faire un travail qu'on pourrait déléguer à quelqu'un d'autre.
■ **bark out**: **~ out [sth]** aboyer [*order etc*].

barker /ˈbɑːkə(r)/ *n* (at fair) bonimenteur *m*.

barking /ˈbɑːkɪŋ/ **I** *n* aboiements *mpl*.
II *adj* [*dog*] qui aboie; [*cough, laugh*] aboyant.
IDIOMS **to be ~ mad**○ GB être complètement fou/folle.

barley /ˈbɑːlɪ/ *n* Agric orge *f*; Culin orge *m*.

barley: **~corn** *n* grain *m* d'orge; **~ field** *n* champ *m* d'orge; **~ sugar** *n* sucre *m* d'orge; **~ water** *n* GB sirop *m* d'orgeat; **~ wine** *n* GB bière *f* (très forte).

barm /bɑːm/ *n* GB dial levure *f*.

bar: **~maid** ▶**1692** *n* serveuse *f* de bar, barmaid *f*; **~man** ▶**1692** *n* (*pl* **~men**) barman *m*.

bar mitzvah /ˌbɑː ˈmɪtzvə/ *n* **1** (also **Bar Mitzvah**) (ceremony) bar-mitsva *f*; **2** (boy) bar-mitsva *m*.

barmy○ /ˈbɑːmɪ/ *adj* GB [*person*] maboul○; [*plan, idea, outfit*] loufoque○; **to be as ~ as they come** être complètement timbré○; **to go ~** (get angry) piquer une crise○; (get excited) devenir dingue○.

barn /bɑːn/ *n* (for crops) grange *f*; (for cattle) étable *f*; (for horses) écurie *f*; **a great ~ of a place**○ une grande bâtisse.

barnacle /ˈbɑːnəkl/ *n* bernacle *f*, anatife *m* spec.

barnacle goose *n* bernache *f* (nonnette).

barn dance *n* soirée *f* de danses villageoises.

barn door *n*: IDIOMS **it's as big as a ~** c'est gros comme une maison.

barney○ /ˈbɑːnɪ/ *n* GB accrochage *m*; **to have a ~ with sb** avoir une prise de bec○ avec qn.

barn owl *n* (chouette *f*) effraie *f*.

barnstorm /ˈbɑːnstɔːm/ *vtr, vi* US *parcourir le pays dans le cadre d'une campagne électorale*.

barnstormer /ˈbɑːnstɔːmə(r)/ *n* orateur *m* enflammé.

barnstorming /ˈbɑːnstɔːmɪŋ/ *adj* tonitruant.

barnyard /ˈbɑːnjɑːd/ *n* basse-cour *f*.

barogram /ˈbærəgræm/ *n* barogramme *m*.

barograph /ˈbærəgrɑːf, US -græf/ *n* barographe *m*.

barometer /bəˈrɒmɪtə(r)/ *n* Meteorol baromètre *m* also fig; **the ~ is rising/falling** le baromètre monte/descend; **the ~ is set fair** le baromètre est au beau.

barometric /ˌbærəˈmetrɪk/ *n* barométrique.

baron /ˈbærən/ *n* **1** (noble) baron *m*; **Baron Smith** le baron Smith; **2** (tycoon) baron *m*; **drugs ~** baron *m* de la drogue; **media ~** magnat *m* des médias; **industrial ~** gros industriel *m*; **3** Culin **~ of beef** double aloyau *m* de bœuf.

baroness /ˈbærənɪs/ *n* baronne *f*; **Baroness Smith** la baronne Smith.

baronet /ˈbærənɪt/ *n* baronnet *m*.

baronial /bəˈrəʊnɪəl/ *adj* (of a baron)

baronnial; (splendid) imposant; **~ hall** demeure seigneuriale.

barony /'bærənɪ/ *n* baronnie *f*.

baroque /bə'rɒk, US bə'rəʊk/ **I** *n* **the ~** le baroque.

II *adj* baroque.

barque *n* = **bark** *n*.

barrack /'bærək/ **I barracks** *n* (+ *v sg* ou *pl*) **1** Mil caserne *f*; **in (the) ~s** à la caserne; **2**○ péj (building) grande baraque *f*.

II *vtr* GB (heckle) conspuer.

barracking /'bærəkɪŋ/ *n* huées *fpl*.

barrack room I *n* chambrée *f*.

II *modif* péj [*joke*] de corps de garde; [*language*] grossier/-ière.

barrack: **~-room lawyer** GB, **~s lawyer** US *n* péj chicaneur/-euse *m/f*; **~s bag** *n* sac *m* (de soldat); **~ square** *n* cour *f* de caserne.

barracuda /ˌbærə'ku:də/ *n* (*pl* **~s** ou *collect* **~**) barracuda *m*.

barrage /'bærɑ:ʒ, US bə'rɑ:ʒ/ *n* **1** Civ Eng barrage *m*; **2** Mil tir *m* de barrage; **3** fig (of questions, criticism) barrage *m*; (of complaints) déluge *m*; (of publicity) mitraillage *m*.

barrage balloon *n* ballon *m* de barrage.

barrel /'bærəl/ **I** *n* **1** (container) (for beer, wine, cider, olives) tonneau *m*, fût *m*; (for herring) caque *f*; (for tar) gonne *f*; (for petroleum) baril *m*; **2** (also **~ful**) (of beer, wine, olives) tonneau *m*; (of herrings) caque *f*; (of petroleum) baril *m*; **3** (of cannon) tube *m*; (of firearm) canon *m*; **4** (of pen) manche *m*; **5** (of watch, clock) barillet *m*.

II *vtr* (*p prés etc* **-ll-**, US **-l-**) mettre [qch] en tonneau [*beer, wine*].

III○ *vi* (*p prés etc* **-ll-**, US **-l-**) **to go ~ling along** rouler en trombe.

IDIOMS **it was a ~ of laughs** ou **fun**○ iron ce n'était pas très marrant○; **both ~s** à bras raccourcis; **to have sb over a ~**○ avoir qn à sa merci; **to buy/transport sth lock, stock and ~** acheter/transporter qch dans sa totalité; **to scrape the bottom of the ~** gratter les fonds de tiroir.

barrel: **~-chested** *adj* [*person*] baraqué○; [*horse*] au poitrail puissant; **~house** *n* US (saloon) bar *m* style cowboy; Mus *style de jazz simpliste et bruyant*; **~ organ** *n* orgue *m* de Barbarie.

barren /'bærən/ *adj* **1** [*land*] aride; [*plant*] infertile; [*woman*]‡ stérile; **2** (unrewarding) [*effort, activity*] stérile; [*style*] sec/sèche; **to be ~ of sth** manquer de qch.

Barren Lands, **Barren Grounds** *npl* toundras *fpl* (*du Grand Nord canadien*).

barrenness /'bærənnɪs/ *n* (of land) aridité *f*; (of plant) infertilité *f*; (of woman)‡ stérilité *f*.

barrette /bə'ret/ *n* US barrette *f*.

barricade /ˌbærɪ'keɪd/ **I** *n* barricade *f*; **to man the ~s** monter aux barricades.

II *vtr* barricader.

III *v refl* **to ~ oneself** Mil se barricader (**in, into** dans); gen s'enfermer (**in, into** dans).

barrier /'bærɪə(r)/ *n* **1** gen, Aut, Mil barrière *f*; (**ticket**) **~** Rail guichet *m* (de quai); **2** fig (cultural, economic, medical, psychological) barrière; (to understanding, progress) obstacle *m* (**to** à); **language ~** barrière linguistique; **trade ~** barrière douanière; **to break down ~s** supprimer les barrières; **to put up ~s** Psych se fermer.

barrier: **~ cream** *n* crème *f* protectrice; **~ method** *n* Med méthode *f* de contraception locale; **~ nursing** *n* ≈ traitement *m* d'isolement préventif.

barrier reef *n* barrière *f* corallienne; **the Great Barrier Reef** la Grande Barrière.

barring /'bɑ:rɪŋ/ *prep* à moins de; **~ accidents** à moins d'un accident; **nobody, ~ a madman** personne, à moins d'être fou.

barrio /'bɑ:rɪəʊ/ *n* US quartier *m* latino-américain.

barrister /'bærɪstə(r)/ ▶1692 *n* GB avocat/-e *m/f*.

barrow /'bærəʊ/ *n* **1** Constr, Hort brouette *f*; GB (on market) voiture *f* de quatre saisons; **2** Archeol tumulus *m*; **3** (pig) castrat *m*.

barrow boy *n* GB **1** ▶1692 Comm marchand *m* de quatre saisons; **2**○ péj jeune parvenu *m* (*du monde des affaires*).

bar: **~ school** *n* institution *f* où l'on prépare le certificat d'aptitude à la profession d'avocat; **~ stool** *n* tabouret *m* de bar.

Bart. *n*: *abrév écrite* = **baronet**.

bartender /'bɑ:tendə(r)/ *n* US barman/barmaid *m/f*.

barter /'bɑ:tə(r)/ **I** *n* troc *m*.

II *vtr* troquer (**for** contre); **the Bartered Bride** Mus la Fiancée Vendue.

III *vi* **1** (by exchange) faire du troc; (one deal) faire un troc; **2** (haggle) marchander.

Bartholomew /bɑ:'θɒləmju:/ *pr n* Barthélemy *m*; **the St. ~'s Day massacre** Hist (le massacre de) la Saint-Barthélemy.

baryton /'bærɪtəʊn/ *n* (instrument) baryton *m*.

basal /'beɪsl/ *adj* Anat, Bot, Med basal.

basal: **~ anaesthesia** GB, **~ anesthesia** US *n* prémédication *f*; **~ cell carcinoma** *n* épithélioma *m* basocellulaire; **~ metabolic rate** *n* taux *m* métabolique basal; **~ metabolism** *n* métabolisme *m* basal.

basalt /'bæsɔ:lt, US 'beɪ-, bə'sɔ:lt/ *n* basalte *m*; **~ lava** lave basaltique.

bascule /'bæskju:l/ *n* bascule *f*; **~ bridge** pont à bascule.

base /beɪs/ **I** *n* **1** gen, Mil (centre of operations) base *f*; **military/naval ~** base *f* militaire/navale; **to return to ~** Mil rentrer à sa base; **2** (bottom part) (of object, spine, mountain, structure) base *f*; (of tree, cliff) pied *m*; (of tail) point *m* d'attache; (of sculpture, statue) socle *m*; (of lamp) pied *m*; **bed ~** bois *m* de lit; **3** fig (basis) (for assumption, theory) base *f*; (for research) point *m* de départ; **to have a broad ~** avoir une base solide; **4** Chem, Culin, Pharm base *f*; **5** Math (arithmetic, geometry) base *f*; **in ~ 2** en base 2; **6** Sport base *f*; **to get to first ~** atteindre la première base.

II *adj* (contemptible) [*act, motive, emotion*] ignoble.

III *vtr* **1** (take as foundation) fonder [*calculation, assumption, decision, policy, research, character*] (**on** sur); **to be ~d on** être fondé sur [*theory, policy etc*]; **the film is ~d on the novel by Henry James/a true story** le film est tiré du roman de Henry James/d'une histoire vraie; **2** (have as operations centre) (*gén au passif*) baser; **to be ~d in** ou **at London/Paris** [*person, company*] être basé à Londres/Paris.

IV -based (*dans composés*) basé sur; **computer/pupil-~d** [*method, policy*] basé sur les ordinateurs/les élèves; **London-/Paris-~d** [*person, company*] basé à Londres/Paris; **home-~d** basé à la maison.

IDIOMS **to be off ~**○ US dérailler; **to catch sb off ~**○ US prendre qn au dépourvu; **to steal a ~ on sb**○ US devancer qn; **to touch all the ~s** US penser à tous les détails; **to touch ~** (**with sb**) prendre contact (avec qn).

base: **~ball** ▶1282 *n* base-ball *m*; **~board** *n* US plinthe *f*; **~ camp** *n* lit, fig camp *m* de base; **~ coat** *n* première couche *f*; **~ form** *n* Ling base *f*; **~ jumping** ▶1282 *n* base jump *m*.

Basel /'bɑ:zl/, **Basle** /bɑ:l/ ▶1818, 1776 *pr n* (town, canton) Bâle *m*.

base lending rate *n* taux *m* de base bancaire.

baseless /'beɪslɪs/ *adj* sans fondement.

baseline /'beɪslaɪn/ *n* **1** (in tennis) ligne *f* de fond; **2** fig base *f*; **3** Advertg signature *f*.

Basel-Land ▶1776 *pr n* **the half-canton of ~** le demi-canton de Bâle-campagne.

Basel-Stadt ▶1776 *pr n* **the half-canton of ~** le demi-canton de Bâle-ville.

basely /'beɪslɪ/ *adv* littér [*betray, insult*] bassement; [*treat*] de façon indigne.

base man *n* US Sport gardien *m* de base.

basement /'beɪsmənt/ **I** *n* **1** gen sous-sol *m*; **in the ~** au sous-sol; **2** Archit (foundations) soubassement *m*.

II *modif* [*flat, apartment, kitchen*] en sous-sol.

base metal *n* métal *m* non précieux.

baseness /'beɪsnɪs/ *n* bassesse *f*.

base: **~ period** *n* Stat période *f* de base; **~ rate** *n* taux *m* de base; **~ station** *n* Telecom station *f* de base; **~ year** *n* Fin année *f* de référence.

bash○ /bæʃ/ **I** *n* (*pl* **-es**) **1** (blow) coup *m*; **2** (dent) bosse *f*; **my car has a ~ on the door** la portière de ma voiture est cabossée; **3** (attempt) tentative *f*; **to have a ~ at sth** s'essayer à qch; **to give sth a ~** s'essayer à qch; **go on, have a ~!** vas-y, essaie un coup○!; **give it a ~!** vas-y, essaie!; **4**† (party) grande fête *f*; **5** US (good time) **to have a ~** bien s'amuser.

II *vtr* **1** (hit) cogner [*person*]; rentrer dans [*tree, wall, kerb*]; **she ~ed her head on** ou **against the shelf** elle s'est cogné la tête contre l'étagère; **he ~ed my head against the wall** il m'a cogné la tête contre le mur; **to ~ sb on** ou **over the head** frapper qn à la tête; **2** (criticize) dénigrer [*group, person*].

■ **bash about**, **bash around**: **~ [sb] about** ou **around** cogner sur○ [*person*].

■ **bash in**: **~ [sth] in**, **~ in [sth]** défoncer [*door, part of car*].

■ **bash into**: **~ into [sth]** rentrer dans.

■ **bash on** persévérer; **to ~ on with sth** en mettre un coup sur qch○.

■ **bash out**: **~ out [sth]**, **~ [sth] out** expédier [*work*]; jouer [*tune*].

■ **bash up**: **~ [sb] up**, **~ up [sb]** cogner [*person*]; cabosser [*car*].

bashful /'bæʃfl/ *adj* timide; **to be ~ about doing** hésiter à faire.

bashfully /'bæʃfəlɪ/ *adv* timidement.

bashfulness /'bæʃflnɪs/ *n* timidité *f*.

bashing○ /'bæʃɪŋ/ *n* **1** (beating) raclée○ *f*; **this table has taken a ~ over the years!** cette table en a vu au cours des ans○!; **2** (defeat) raclée○ *f*; **to give sb a ~** donner une raclée○ à qn; **to take a ~** ramasser une raclée○; **3** fig (criticism) dénigration *f* systématique; **union ~** dénigration systématique des syndicats; **to take a ~** (**from**) se faire éreinter (par).

basic /'beɪsɪk/ **I basics** *npl* **the ~s** l'essentiel *m*: (of knowledge, study) principes *mpl* fondamentaux; (food) denrées *fpl* de première nécessité; **to go back to ~s** revoir les principes fondamentaux; **to get down to ~s** aborder l'essentiel.

II *adj* **1** (fundamental) [*aim, arrangement, fact, need, quality*] essentiel/-ielle; [*belief, research, problem, principle*] fondamental; [*theme*] principal; **2** (elementary) [*education, knowledge, skill, rule*] élémentaire; **3** (rudimentary) [*accommodation, meal, facilities, supplies*] de base; **the accommodation was rather ~** péj le logement était un peu rudimentaire; **4** (before additions) [*pay, wage, working hours*] de base; **5** Chem basique.

BASIC /'beɪsɪk/ *n* Comput (*abrév* = **beginners' all-purpose symbolic instruction code**) basic *m*; **in ~** en basic.

basically /'beɪsɪklɪ/ *adv* **1** (fundamentally) fondamentalement; **a ~ capitalist society** une société fondamentalement capitaliste; **2** (for emphasis) **~, I don't like him very much** en fait, je ne l'aime pas beaucoup; **~, life's been good** dans l'ensemble ou tout compte fait, on a eu de la chance.

basic: **~ law** *n* Pol, Jur ≈ Constitution *f*; **~ overhead expenditure** *n* Fin frais *mpl* généraux essentiels; **~ rate** *n* gen taux *m* de base; Tax taux *m* de base d'imposition; **~ salt** *n* sel *m* basique; **~ slag** *n* scories *fpl* de déphosphoration; **~ training** *n* Mil formation *f* militaire de base.

basil /ˈbæzl/ *n* basilic *m*.

basilica /bəˈzɪlɪkə/ *n* basilique *f*.

basilisk /ˈbæzɪlɪsk/ *n* Mythol, Zool basilic *m*.

basin /ˈbeɪsn/ *n* **1** Culin bol *m*; (large, for mixing) terrine *f*; **2** (for washing) lavabo *m*; (not plumbed) cuvette *f*; (for washing up) cuvette *f*; **wash** ou **hand ~** lavabo *m*; **3** Geog, Geol bassin *m*; **4** Naut (of port) bassin *m*; (of canal) gare *f*; **5** (of fountain) bassin *m*.

basinful /ˈbeɪsɪnfʊl/ *n* pleine cuvette *f*.
IDIOMS **to have had a ~ of sth**○ avoir eu sa dose de qch○.

basis /ˈbeɪsɪs/ *n* (*pl* **-ses**) (for action, negotiation) base *f* (**for, of** de); (of discussion) cadre *m*; (of theory) point *m* de départ; (for belief, argument) fondements *mpl* (**for** de); **on the ~ of** sur la base de [*earnings, evidence, experience, salary*]; **on the ~ that** en partant du principe que; **on that ~** ceci étant; **on the same ~** dans les mêmes conditions; **to serve as the ~ for sth** servir de base à qch.

bask /bɑːsk, US bæsk/ *vi* se prélasser; **to ~ in** se prélasser à [*sunshine, warmth*]; jouir de [*approval, affection*]; **to ~ in sb's reflected glory** tirer fierté du succès de qn.

basket /ˈbɑːskɪt, US ˈbæskɪt/ *n* **1** (with one handle) panier *m*; (with no handle or two) corbeille *f*; (carried on back) hotte *f*; (for game, fish) bourriche *f*; (on donkey) panier *m*; **sewing** ou **work ~** corbeille *f* à ouvrage; **~ of currencies** Fin panier *m* de devises; **2** Sport (in basketball) panier *m*; **to make** ou **score a ~** réussir un panier; **3** (in skiing) rondelle *f*; (in fencing) coquille *f*; **4**◑ US (male genitals) bazar *m*◑, organes *mpl* génitaux mâles.

basketball /ˈbɑːskɪtbɔːl, US ˈbæsk-/ ▶ 1282 *n* (game) basket(-ball) *m*; (ball) ballon *m* de basket.

basketball shoe *n* basket *f*.

basket case○ *n* **1** (nervous wreck) **she's a ~** c'est un paquet de nerfs; **2** (economy, country) grand/-e invalide *m/f*; **3** (car, machine, etc) tas *m* de ferraille.

basket: **~ chair** *n* fauteuil *m* en osier; **~ clause** *n* clause *f* attrape-tout.

basketful /ˈbɑːskɪtfʊl, US ˈbæsk-/ *n* panier *m* (**of** de).

basket: **~ maker** ▶ 1692 *n* vannier/-ière *m/f*; **~-making** *n* vannerie *f*; **~work** *n* (craft, objects) vannerie *f*.

basking shark /ˈbɑːskɪŋ ʃɑːk, US ˈbæsk-/ *n* (requin *m*) pèlerin *m*.

Basle /bɑːl/ ▶ 1818 *pr n* = **Basel**.

basmati rice /bəzˌmætɪ ˈraɪs/ *n* riz *m* basmati.

basque /bæsk/ *n* (on jacket etc) basques *fpl*.

Basque /bæsk, bɑːsk/ ▶ 1486, 1402 **I** *n* **1** (person) Basque *mf*; **2** (language) basque *m*.
II *adj* basque.

Basque Country *n* **the ~** le pays Basque.

bas-relief /ˈbæsrɪliːf, ˈbɑːrɪliːf/ **I** *n* bas-relief *m*; **in ~** en bas-relief.
II *adj* en bas-relief.

Bas-Rhin ▶ 1163 *pr n* Bas-Rhin *m*; **in/to the ~** dans le Bas-Rhin.

bass[1] /beɪs/ ▶ 1868, 1481 **I** *n* **1** (voice) (voix de) basse *f*; (singer) basse *f*; **he's a ~** c'est une basse; **2** (instrument) basse *f*; (in jazz) contrebasse *f*; **3** (part) (partie de) basse *f*; **to sing (the) ~** chanter la basse; **4** (frequency) basse *f*.
II *modif* **1** [*voice, range, solo*] de basse; [*aria*] pour basse; **2** [*flute, guitar, trombone, tuba*] basse; **the ~ strings** les basses; **3** [*part, line*] de basse; **4** (frequency) [*controls, sound, notes*] grave.

bass[2] /bæs/ *n* Zool (freshwater) perche *f*; (sea) Zool bar *m*; Culin loup *m* (de mer).

bass /beɪs/: **~-baritone** ▶ 1868 *n* baryton-basse *m*; **~ clef** *n* clé *f* de fa; **~ drum** ▶ 1481 *n* grosse caisse *f*.

Basse-Normandie ▶ 1273 *pr n* Basse-Normandie *f*; **in/to ~** en Basse-Normandie.

basset /ˈbæsɪt/ *n* (also **~ hound**) (chien *m*) basset *m*.

basset horn ▶ 1481 *n* cor *m* de basset.

bass horn /beɪs/ *n* serpent *m*.

bassist /ˈbeɪsɪst/ ▶ 1481 *n* bassiste *mf*.

bassoon /bəˈsuːn/ ▶ 1481 *n* basson *m*.

basso profundo /ˈbæsəʊ prəˈfʌndəʊ/ ▶ 1868 **I** *n* basse *f* profonde.
II *modif* [*voice*] de basse profonde; [*aria*] pour basse profonde.

bastard /ˈbɑːstəd, US ˈbæs-/ **I** *n* **1**◑ (term of abuse) salaud◑ *m*; **you rotten ~!** espèce de salaud◑!; **he was a real ~ to her** il était vraiment salaud◑ avec elle; **2**◑ (humorously, derisively) **poor ~!** pauvre type○!; **the silly ~!** le crétin◑!, le con◑!; **you lucky ~!** sacré veinard○!; **3**◑ (problem, task) **that was a ~ of a question!** c'était une question empoisonnante○!; **this word is a ~ to translate!** ce putain◑ de mot est impossible à traduire!; **4**† (illegitimate child) bâtard/-e *m/f*.
II *adj* **1** [*child*] bâtard; **2** fig (hybrid) bâtard, corrompu; **3** Print [*title*] faux/fausse.

bastardized /ˈbɑːstədaɪzd, US ˈbæs-/ *adj* [*language*] abâtardi; [*style of architecture*] dégradé; [*race*] dégénéré.

bastardy /ˈbɑːstədɪ, US ˈbæs-/ *n* Jur bâtardise *f*.

baste /beɪst/ *vtr* **1** Culin arroser; **2** Sewing bâtir, faufiler.

bastion /ˈbæstɪən/ *n* **1** Archit bastion *m*; **2** fig (stronghold) bastion (**of** de); (defence) rempart *m* (**against** contre).

bat /bæt/ **I** *n* **1** Sport batte *f*; **cricket/baseball ~** batte de cricket/de baseball; **table tennis ~** raquette *f* de tennis de table; **2** Zool chauve-souris *f*; **3**○ **old ~** pej vieille bique○; **4**○ (blow) coup *m*.
II *vtr* (*p prés etc* **-tt-**) frapper.
III *vi* (*p prés etc* **-tt-**) Sport (be batsman) être le batteur; (handle a bat) manier la batte.
IDIOMS **at a terrific ~**○ GB à toute allure; **to be blind as a ~** être myope comme une taupe; **to do sth off one's own ~**○ faire qch de sa propre initiative; **to go to ~ for sb**○ US appuyer○ qn; **(right) off the ~**○ US sans délai; **like a ~ out of hell**○ comme un possédé; **to play a straight ~** jouer franc jeu; **without ~ting an eyelid** GB ou **eye(-lash)** US sans sourciller; ▶ **belfry**.
■ **bat around: ~ [sth] around, ~ around [sth] 1** discuter [*idea*]; **2** Sport **we ~ted the ball around** nous avons échangé quelques balles.
■ **bat down: ~ [sth] down** US démolir [*argument, suggestion*].
■ **bat out: ~ [sth] out, ~ out [sth]** US préparer [qch] en vitesse.

batch /bætʃ/ *n* (of loaves, cakes) fournée *f*; (of cement) gâchée *f*; (of eggs, fish) arrivage *m*; (of letters) tas *m*, liasse *f*; (of books, text, goods, orders) lot *m*; (of recruits) contingent *m*; (of candidates, prisoners etc) groupe *m*; Comput lot *m*.

batch: **~ file** *n* Comput fichier *m* séquentiel; **~ mode** *n* Comput mode *m* différé; **~ processing** *n* Comput traitement *m* séquentiel or par lots.

bated /ˈbeɪtɪd/ *adj* **with ~ breath** en retenant son souffle.

bath /bɑːθ, US bæθ/ **I** *n* **1** (wash, washing water) bain *m*; **to have** ou **take** US **a ~** prendre un bain; **to run a ~** faire couler un bain; **to give sb a ~** donner un bain à qn; **give the baby his ~!** donne son bain au bébé!; **2** GB (tub) baignoire *f*; **acrylic/enamel ~** baignoire en acrylique/en émail; **sunken ~** baignoire encastrée; **I was in the ~** j'étais dans mon bain; **3** US (bathroom) salle *f* de bains; **4** Chem, Phot, Tech, Tex bain *m*; **water/dye ~** bain froid/de teinture.
II baths *npl* **1** (for swimming) piscine *f*; **2** (in spa) thermes *mpl*; **3**† (municipal) bains *mpl* publics; **4**○ US (for homosexuals) sauna *m* pour homosexuels.
III *vtr* GB baigner.
IV *vi* GB prendre un bain.
IDIOMS **to take a ~** US subir des pertes (financières); **to take an early ~**○ (in football) euph être mis sur la touche.

bath: **Bath bun** *n* GB *petit pain rond au lait et aux raisins secs*; **Bath chair**† *n* fauteuil *m* roulant; **~ cube** *n* cube *m* de bain.

bathe /beɪð/ **I** *n* GB sout bain *m*; **to go for** ou **to have a ~** aller se baigner.
II *vtr* **1** laver [*wound*] (**in** dans; **with** à); **to ~ one's feet** prendre un bain de pieds; **2** littér [*wave*] baigner [*shore*]; **3** US baigner [*child*].
III *vi* **1** (swim) [*person*] se baigner; **to go bathing** aller se baigner; **2** US (take bath) prendre un bain; **3** littér **to be ~d in** ruisseler de [*sweat*]; être inondé de [*light*]; être baigné de [*tears*].

bather /ˈbeɪðə(r)/ *n* baigneur/-euse *m/f*.

bathhouse /ˈbɑːθhaʊs/ *n* **1**‡ bains *mpl* publics; **2**○ US (for homosexuals) sauna *m* pour homosexuels; **3** US (on beach) cabine *f* (de plage).

bathing /ˈbeɪðɪŋ/ *n* baignade *f*; **'~ prohibited'** 'baignade interdite'.

bathing: **~ beauty** *n* belle baigneuse *f*; **~ cap** *n* bonnet *m* de bain; **~ costume** *n* costume *m* de bain; **~ hut** *n* cabine *f* de bain; **~ machine** *n* Hist cabine *f* de bain roulante; **~ suit**† *n* = **bathing costume**; **~ trunks**† *n* slip *m* de bain.

bath: **~ mat** *n* tapis *m* de bain; **~ oil** *n* huile *f* de bain.

bathos /ˈbeɪθɒs/ *n* bathos *m*, chute *f* du sublime au trivial.

bathrobe /ˈbɑːθrəʊb/ *n* sortie *f* de bain.

bathroom /ˈbɑːθruːm, -rʊm/ *n* **1** (for washing) salle *f* de bains; **2** US (lavatory) (public) toilettes *fpl*; (at home) salle *f* de bains; **to go to the ~** [*person*] aller aux toilettes; [*animal*] faire ses besoins.

bathroom: **~ cabinet** *n* armoire *f* de toilette; **~ fittings** *npl* accessoires *mpl* de salle de bains; **~ scales** *npl* pèse-personne *m*.

bath: **~ salts** *npl* sels *mpl* de bain; **~ soap** *n* savon *m* de bain; **~ towel** *n* serviette *f* de bain; **~tub** *n* baignoire *f*; **~water** *n* eau *f* du bain.

bathysphere /ˈbæθɪsfɪə(r)/ *n* bathysphère *f*.

batik /bəˈtiːk, bæˈtiːk/ *n* batik *m*.

batiste /bæˈtiːst, bəˈt-/ *n* Tex batiste *f*.

batman /ˈbætmən/ ▶ 1612 *n* GB Mil ordonnance *m*.

baton /ˈbætn, ˈbætɒn, US bəˈtɒn/ *n* GB (policeman's) matraque *f*; Mil, Mus baguette *f*; Sport (in relay race) témoin *m*; (used by French traffic policeman, majorette) bâton *m*; **under the ~ of** Mus sous la direction de; **to take up the ~** fig prendre la relève.

baton: **~ charge** *n* GB charge *f* à la matraque; **~ round** *n* GB balle *f* en caoutchouc; **~ twirler** *n* US majorette *f*.

bats○ /bæts/ *adj* cinglé○, toqué○.

batsman /ˈbætsmən/ *n* Sport batteur *m*.

battalion /bəˈtælɪən/ *n* Mil, fig bataillon *m*.

batten /ˈbætn/ **I** *n* **1** Constr (for door, floor) latte *f*; (in roofing) volige *f*; **2** Naut (in sail) latte *f* (de voile); (for tarpaulin) latte *f* (de fixation); **3** Theat herse *f*.
II *vtr* latter [*door*]; planchéier, latter [*floor*]; voliger [*roof*].
IDIOMS **to ~ down the hatches** Naut fermer les écoutilles; fig se préparer au pire.
■ **batten on** péj être or vivre aux crochets de [*person, family*].

batter /ˈbætə(r)/ **I** *n* **1** Culin gen pâte *f*; (for frying) pâte à frire; **pancake ~** pâte à crêpes; **fish in ~** beignets *mpl* de poisson; **2** Sport batteur *m*.
II *vtr* **1** [*person*] battre [*victim, wife, child*]; **to ~ sb to death** battre qn à mort; **2** [*storm, bombs*] ravager; [*waves*] battre.
III *vi* tambouriner (**at** à; **on** sur).

■ **batter down**: **~ [sth] down, ~ down [sth]** enfoncer [*door*].

battered /ˈbætəd/ *adj* [*kettle, hat*] cabossé; [*book, suitcase etc*] très abîmé; [*person*] (physically) battu; fig (emotionally) très éprouvé; [*economy*] très éprouvé; [*pride*] meurtri.

battered baby syndrome *n* syndrome *m* de l'enfant battu.

battering /ˈbætərɪŋ/ *n* **1** (from person) raclée○ *f*; **the problem of wife-~** le problème des maris qui battent leurs femmes; **2 to take** ou **get a ~** (from bombs, storm, waves) être ravagé (**from** par); (from opponents) Sport prendre une raclée○; (from critics) se faire descendre (**by** par); (emotionally) en prendre un coup○; **this car/table has taken a ~ over the years** cette voiture/table a souffert○ au cours des années.

battering-ram *n* bélier *m*.

battery /ˈbætərɪ/ *n* **1** Elec pile *f*; Aut batterie *f*; **2** Mil batterie *f*; **3** Agric (for hens) batterie *f*; **4** fig (large number) (of objects, tests) batterie *f*; (of questions) feu *m* nourri; **5** Jur coups *mpl* et blessures *fpl*.

battery: **~ acid** *n* solution *f* acide pour piles; **~ charger** *n* chargeur *m* de batteries; **~ chicken** *n* poulet *m* d'élevage industriel; **~ controlled** *adj* à piles; **~ farming** *n* élevage *m* en batterie; **~ fire** *n* tir *m* par salves; **~ hen** *n* = **battery chicken**; **~-lead connection** *n* cosse *f* de batterie; **~ operated, ~ powered** *adj* à piles; **~ set** *n* Radio poste *m* à piles; **~ shaver** *n* rasoir *m* à piles.

battle /ˈbætl/ **I** *n* **1** Mil bataille *f* (**for** pour, **against** contre, **between** entre); **to die in ~** mourir au combat; **to fight a ~** combattre; **to win/lose a ~** gagner/perdre une bataille; **the Battle of Waterloo** la bataille de Waterloo; **to go into ~** engager le combat; **to join ~** s'engager dans la bataille; **to do ~ with sb** se battre avec qn; **the field of ~** le champ de bataille; **2** fig lutte *f* (**for** pour, **against** contre, **over** à propos de); **political ~** lutte *f* politique; **take-over ~** Pol lutte *f* de succession; **legal ~** bataille *f* légale; **the ~ is on for/to do** la lutte est engagée pour/pour faire; **the ~ to prevent Aids** la lutte pour la prévention du sida; **it's a ~ of wills between them** c'est à qui l'emportera entre eux; **a ~ of words** un échange acerbe; **to fight one's own ~s** se défendre tout seul; **to fight sb's ~s** se battre pour le compte de qn.
II *modif* Mil [*formation, stations, zone*] de combat.
III *vtr* US lutter contre.
IV *vi* Mil, fig combattre (**with sb** contre qn); **to ~ for** se disputer [*supremacy*]; lutter pour [*life, survival*]; **to ~ to do** lutter pour faire; **to ~ one's way through** vaincre [qch] de haute lutte [*difficulties, opposition*]; **he ~d his way to a victory** il a remporté la victoire de haute lutte.
IDIOMS **that's half the ~** c'est déjà un grand pas de fait.
■ **battle on** persévérer.
■ **battle out**: **to ~ it out** lutter avec acharnement (**for** pour).

battle array /ˈbætləreɪ/ *n* **in ~** en ordre de bataille.

battle-axe /ˈbætlæks/ *n* **1**○ fig péj (woman) virago○ *f*; **2** lit hache *f* d'armes.

battle: **~ cruiser** *n* croiseur *m* cuirassé; **~ cry** *n* lit, fig cri *m* de ralliement.

battledore /ˈbætldɔ:(r)/ *n* raquette *f* pour jeu de volant; **~ and shuttlecock** ▶ **1282** jeu *m* de volant.

battle: **~dress** *n* tenue *f* de campagne; **~ drill** *n* ¢ manœuvres *fpl*; **~ fatigue** *n* US commotion *f*, état *m* de choc dû aux combats; **~field** *n* lit, fig champ *m* de bataille; **~field missile** *n* missile *m* sol-sol tactique; **~ground** *n* lit champ *m* de bataille; fig sujet *m* de discussion; **~ honour** GB, **~ honor** US *n* lit, fig distinction *f* au combat; **~ lines** *npl* Mil lignes *fpl* de combat; fig stratégie *f*.

battlements /ˈbætlmənts/ *npl* lit, fig remparts *mpl*.

battle: **~ order** *n* lit, fig ordre *m* de bataille; **~ royal** (*pl* **~s royal, ~ royals**) *n* lit mêlée *f* générale; fig bataille *f* en règle; **~-scarred** *adj* lit marqué par la guerre; fig marqué par la vie; **~ scene** *n* Cin, Theat scène *f* de bataille; **~ship** *n* cuirassé *m*; **~ships** ▶ **1282** *npl* Games touché-coulé *m*; **~ tank** *n* char *m* d'assaut.

batty○ /ˈbætɪ/ *adj* cinglé○, toqué○; **to go ~** devenir fou/folle, dérailler○.

bauble /ˈbɔ:bl/ *n* **1** (ornament) babiole *f*; pej (item of jewellery) colifichet *m*; **2** (jester's) marotte *f*.

baud /bɔ:d/ *n* Comput baud *m*.

baulk = **balk**.

bauxite /ˈbɔ:ksaɪt/ *n* bauxite *f*.

Bavaria /bəˈveərɪə/ *pr n* Bavière *f*.

Bavarian /bəˈveərɪən/ **I** *n* Bavarois/-e *m/f*.
II *adj* bavarois; **the ~ Alps** les Alpes *fpl* bavaroises; **~ cream** Culin bavaroise *f*.

bawd‡ /bɔ:d/ *n* catin† *f*.

bawdiness /ˈbɔ:dɪnɪs/ *n* (of story, song) grivoiserie *f*; (of person) paillardise *f*.

bawdy /ˈbɔ:dɪ/ *adj* [*story, song*] grivois; [*person*] paillard; **~ house**‡ bordel *m*.

bawl /bɔ:l/ **I** *vtr* brailler.
II *vi* **1** (weep) brailler; **2** (shout) hurler; **to ~ at sb/at sb to do sth** hurler sur qn/à qn de faire qch.
■ **bawl out**○: ¶ **~ [sb] out** engueuler○; ¶ **~ out [sth]** brailler.

bay /beɪ/ **I** *n* **1** Geog baie *f*; **the Bay of Biscay/of Bengal** le golfe de Gascogne/du Bengale; **the Bay of Pigs** la Baie des Cochons; **2** Hunt **to be at ~** être aux abois; **to bring to ~** acculer; **to hold** ou **keep at ~** fig tenir [qn] à distance [*attacker, opponent*]; stopper [*famine*]; enrayer [*unemployment, inflation etc*]; **3** Bot (*also* **~ tree**) laurier(-sauce) *m*; **4** (parking area) aire *f* de stationnement; **loading ~** aire de chargement; **5** Archit (section of building) travée *f*; (recess) renfoncement *m*; (window) bow-window *m*; **6** Aviat, Naut (compartment) soute *f*; ▶ **bomb bay**; **7** (horse) alezan *m*.
II *adj* [*horse*] bai.
III *vi* [*dog*] aboyer (**at** contre, après); **to ~ at the moon** hurler à la lune or à la mort; **to ~ for sb's blood** fig réclamer la tête de qn.

bay leaf *n* feuille *f* de laurier.

bayonet I /ˈbeɪənɪt/ *n* Mil, Elec baïonnette *f*; **at ~ point** à la pointe de la baïonnette; **to fix ~s** fixer la baïonnette au canon.
II /ˈbeɪənɪt, ˌbeɪəˈnet/ *vtr* (*p prés etc* **-t-** ou **-tt-**) passer à la baïonnette.

bayonet: **~ charge** *n* charge *f* à la baïonnette; **~ practice** *n* ¢ exercices *mpl* de baïonnette; **~ socket** *n* douille *f* à baïonnette.

bayou /ˈbaɪu:/ *n* US bayou *m*, marécages *mpl*.

bay: **~ rum** *n* lotion *f* capillaire (au piment de la Jamaïque); **~ window** *n* bow-window *m*; **~ wreath** *n* couronne *f* de laurier.

bazaar /bəˈzɑ:(r)/ *n* (oriental) bazar *m*; (sale of work) vente *f* de charité; (shop) bazar *m*.

bazoo○ /bəˈzu:/ *n* US gueule○ *f*.

bazooka /bəˈzu:kə/ *n* bazooka *m*, lance-roquettes *m inv* antichar.

B & B *n*: *abrév* ▶ **bed and breakfast**.

BBC (*abrév* = **British Broadcasting Corporation**) BBC *f*.

BB gun *n* US carabine *f* à air comprimé.

BBQ *n*: *abrév écrite* = **barbecue**.

BC (*abrév* = **Before Christ**) av. J.-C.

BCD *n* (*abrév* = **binary-coded decimal**) DCB *f*.

BCG *n* Pharm BCG *m*.

BD *n* (*abrév* = **Bachelor of Divinity**) diplôme *m* universitaire de théologie.

BDS *n* GB (*abrév* = **Bachelor of Dental Surgery**) diplôme *m* de chirurgie dentaire.

be /bi:, bɪ/ *vi* (*p prés* **being**; *3ᵉ pers prés* **is**, *prét* **was**, *pp* **been**) **1** gen être; **it's me, it's I** c'est moi; **he's a good pupil** c'est un bon élève; **2** (in probability) **if Henri were here** si Henri était là; **were it not that...** si ce n'était que...; **were they to know** s'ils savaient; **if I were you** à ta place; **had it not been for Frank, I'd have missed the train** sans Frank j'aurais raté le train; **3** (phrases) **so be it** d'accord; **be that as it may** quoi qu'il en soit; **as it were** pour ainsi dire; **even if it were so** même si c'était le cas; **I preferred it as it was** je l'aimais mieux avant; **leave it as it is** ne changez rien; **to be or not to be** être ou ne pas être; **let** ou **leave him be** laisse-le tranquille.

BE *n*: *abrév* ▶ **bill of exchange**.

beach /bi:tʃ/ **I** *n* plage *f*.
II *modif* [*bag, mat*] de plage; [*party*] à la plage.
III *vtr* échouer [*boat*]; **~ed whale** lit baleine *f* échouée; fig (building, object, person) mastodonte *m*.

beach: **~ ball** *n* ballon *m* de plage; **~ buggy** *n* buggy *m*; **~ bum**○ *n*: *jeune vagabond qui passe l'été sur les plages*.

beachcomber /ˈbi:tʃkəʊmə(r)/ *n* **1** (person) *personne qui récupère les objets échoués ou oubliés sur la plage*; **2** (wave) vague *f* déferlante.

beach: **~head** *n* tête *f* de pont; **~ hut** *n* cabine *f* de plage; **~robe** *n* serviette-cabine *f*; **~wear** *n* tenues *fpl* de plage.

beacon /ˈbi:kən/ *n* **1** Naut (lighthouse) phare *m*; (lantern) fanal *m*; (signalling buoy) balise *f*; fig phare *m*, flambeau *m*; **to shine like a ~** fig briller comme un phare; **2** Aviat balise *f*, phare *m*; **3** (also **radio ~**) (transmitter) radiobalise *f*, radiophare *m*; **4** (on ambulance, police car) gyrophare *m*; **5** Hist (on hill etc) feu *m* (*pour donner l'alarme*); **6** GB (hill) colline *f*.

bead /bi:d/ *n* **1** (jewellery) perle *f*; **~s, string of ~s** collier *m*; **2** Relig (rosary) grain *m*; **to say** ou **tell one's ~s**† réciter son chapelet; **3** (drop) (of sweat, dew) goutte *f*, perle *f*; **~s of perspiration had formed on his forehead** la sueur perlait sur son front; **4** Tech (on gun) guidon *m*; **to draw a ~ on sth/sb** viser qch/qn avec précision.

bead curtain *n* rideau *m* de perles.

beaded /ˈbi:dɪd/ *adj* [*dress, blouse*] garni de perles.

beadily /ˈbi:dɪlɪ/ *adj* [*look, stare*] avec des yeux de fouine pej, fixement.

beading /ˈbi:dɪŋ/ *n* **1** (wooden) baguette *f*; (decorative) chapelet *m*; **2** (on dress) garniture *f* de perles.

beadle /ˈbi:dl/ *n* **1** Relig bedeau *m*; **2** ▶ **1692** GB Univ huissier *m*, appariteur *m*.

beady /ˈbi:dɪ/ *adj* **~ eyes** yeux *mpl* de fouine pej; **I've got my ~ eye on you** GB hum je t'ai à l'œil.

beady-eyed /ˌbi:dɪˈaɪd/ *adj* aux yeux de fouine pej, aux yeux perçants.

beagle /ˈbi:gl/ **I** *n* beagle *m*.
II *vi* chasser avec des beagles.

beak /bi:k/ *n* **1** (of bird, turtle) bec *m*; **2**○ (nose) tarin○ *m*; **3**○ †GB (magistrate) magistrat *m*; (headmaster) protal○ *m*.

beaker /ˈbi:kə(r)/ *n* **1** (cup) gobelet *m*; **2** Chem vase *m* à bec.

beam /bi:m/ **I** *n* **1** (of light, torch, laser) rayon *m*; (of vehicle lights, lighthouse, searchlight) also Phys faisceau *m*; **on full ~** GB Aut, **on high ~** US Aut en (pleins) phares; **on low ~** US Aut en code; **2** Constr poutre *f*; **3** (in gymnastics) poutre *f*; **4** (central shaft) (of weighing scales) fléau *m*; Mech balancier *m*; **5** Aviat, Naut (radio or radar course) faisceau *m* de guidage; **to be off ~** GB, **to be off the ~** US être sorti du faisceau; fig être à côté de la plaque○; **6** Naut (cross-member) traverse *f*; (greatest width) largeur *f*; **on the port ~** à bâbord; **on the starboard ~** à tribord; **7** (smile) grand sourire *m*.
II *vtr* **1** [*radio, satellite*] transmettre [*pro-*

be

The direct French equivalent of the verb *to be* in subject + to be + predicate sentences is *être*:

I am tired = je suis fatigué
Caroline is French = Caroline est française
the children are in the garden = les enfants sont dans le jardin

It functions in very much the same way as *to be* does in English and it is safe to assume it will work as a translation in the great majority of cases.

Note, however, that when you are specifying a person's profession or trade, *a*/*an* is not translated:

she's a doctor = elle est médecin
Claudie is still a student = Claudie est toujours étudiante

This is true of any noun used in apposition when the subject is a person:

he's a widower = il est veuf

But

Lyons is a beautiful city = Lyon est une belle ville

For more information or expressions involving professions and trades consult the usage note ▶ 1692.

For the conjugation of the verb *être* see the French verb tables.

Grammatical functions

The passive

être is used to form the passive in French just as *to be* is used in English. Note, however, that the past participle agrees in gender and number with the subject:

the rabbit was killed by a fox = le lapin a été tué par un renard
the window had been broken = la fenêtre avait été cassée
their books will be sold = leurs livres seront vendus
our doors have been repainted red = nos portes ont été repeintes en rouge

In spoken language, French native speakers find the passive cumbersome and will avoid it where possible by using the impersonal *on* where a person or people are clearly involved: *on a repeint nos portes en rouge*.

Progressive tenses

In French the idea of something happening over a period of time cannot be expressed using the verb *être* in the way that *to be* is used as an auxiliary verb in English.

The present

French uses simply the present tense where English uses the progressive form with *to be*:

I am working = je travaille
Ben is reading a book = Ben lit un livre

In order to accentuate duration *être en train de* is used: *je suis en train de travailler*; *Ben est en train de lire un livre.*

The future

French also uses the present tense where English uses the progressive form with *to be*:

we are going to London tomorrow = nous allons à Londres demain
I'm (just) coming! = j'arrive!
I'm (just) going! = j'y vais!

The past

To express the distinction between *she read a newspaper* and *she was reading a newspaper* French uses the perfect and the imperfect tenses: *elle a lu un journal*/*elle lisait un journal*:

he wrote to his mother = il a écrit à sa mère
he was writing to his mother = il écrivait à sa mère

However, in order to accentuate the notion of describing an activity which went on over a period of time, the phrase *être en train de* (≈ *to be in the process of*) is often used:

'what was he doing when you arrived?' 'he was cooking the dinner' = 'qu'est-ce qu'il faisait quand tu es arrivé?' 'il était en train de préparer le dîner'
she was just finishing her essay when … = elle était juste en train de finir sa dissertation quand …

The compound past

Compound past tenses in the progressive form in English are generally translated by the imperfect in French:

I've been looking for you = je te cherchais

For progressive forms + *for* and *since* (*I've been waiting for an hour, I had been waiting for an hour, I've been waiting since Monday* etc.) see the entries ***for*** and ***since***.

Obligation

When *to be* is used as an auxiliary verb with another verb in the infinitive (*to be to do*) expressing obligation, a fixed arrangement or destiny, *devoir* is used:

she's to do it at once = elle doit le faire tout de suite
what am I to do? = qu'est-ce que je dois faire?
he was to arrive last Monday = il devait arriver lundi dernier
she was never to see him again = elle ne devait plus le revoir.

In tag questions

French has no direct equivalent of tag questions like *isn't he?* or *wasn't it?* There is a general tag question *n'est-ce pas?* (literally *isn't it so?*) which will work in many cases:

their house is lovely, isn't it? = leur maison est très belle, n'est-ce pas?
he's a doctor, isn't he? = il est médecin, n'est-ce pas?
it was a very good meal, wasn't it? = c'était un très bon repas, n'est-ce pas?

However, *n'est-ce pas* can very rarely be used for positive tag questions and some other way will be found to express the extra meaning contained in the tag: *par hasard* (*by any chance*) can be very useful as a translation:

'I can't find my glasses' 'they're not in the kitchen, are they?' = 'je ne trouve pas mes lunettes' 'elles ne sont pas dans la cuisine, par hasard?'
you haven't seen Gaby, have you? = tu n'as pas vu Gaby, par hasard?

In cases where an opinion is being sought, *si?* meaning more or less *or is it? or was it?* etc. can be useful:

it's not broken, is it? = ce n'est pas cassé, si?
he wasn't serious, was he? = il n'était pas sérieux, si?

In many other cases the tag question is simply not translated at all and the speaker's intonation will convey the implied question.

In short answers

Again, there is no direct equivalent for short answers like *yes I am*, *no he's not* etc. Where the answer *yes* is given to contradict a negative question or statement, the most useful translation is *si*:

'you're not going out tonight' 'yes I am!' = 'tu ne sors pas ce soir' 'si'

In reply to a standard enquiry the tag will not be translated:

'are you a doctor?' 'yes I am' = 'êtes-vous médecin?' 'oui'
'was it raining?' 'yes it was' = 'est-ce qu'il pleuvait?' 'oui'

Probability

For expressions of probability and supposition (*if I were you* etc.) see the entry ***be***.

Other functions

Expressing sensations and feelings

In expressing physical and mental sensations, the verb used in French is *avoir*:

to be cold = avoir froid
to be hot = avoir chaud
I'm cold = j'ai froid
to be thirsty = avoir soif
to be hungry = avoir faim
to be ashamed = avoir honte
my hands are cold = j'ai froid aux mains

If, however, you are in doubt as to which verb to use in such expressions, you should consult the entry for the appropriate adjective.

Discussing health and how people are

In expressions of health and polite enquiries about how people are, *aller* is used:

how are you? = comment allez-vous?
(*more informally*) comment vas-tu?
(*very informally as a greeting*) ça va?
are you well? = vous allez bien?
how is your daughter? = comment va votre fille?
my father is better today = mon père va mieux aujourd'hui

Discussing weather and temperature

In expressions of weather and temperature *faire* is generally used:

it's cold = il fait froid
it's windy = il fait du vent

If in doubt, consult the appropriate adjective entry.

Visiting somewhere

When *to be* is used in the present perfect tense to mean *go*, *visit* etc., French will generally use the verbs *venir*, *aller* etc. rather than *être*:

I've never been to Sweden = je ne suis jamais allé en Suède
have you been to the Louvre? = est-ce que tu es déjà allé au Louvre? *or* est-ce que tu as déjà visité le Louvre?
Paul has been to see us three times = Paul est venu nous voir trois fois

Note too

has the postman been? = est-ce que le facteur est passé?

For *here is*, *here are*, *there is*, *there are* see the entries ***here*** and ***there***.

The translation for an expression or idiom containing the verb *to be* will be found in the dictionary at the entry for another word in the expression: for *to be in danger* see ***danger***, for *it would be best to …* see ***best*** etc.

This dictionary contains usage notes on topics such as ***the clock***, ***time units***, ***age***, ***weight measurement***, ***days of the week***, and ***shops, trades and professions***, many of which include translations of particular uses of *to be*. For the index to these notes ▶ 1919.

gramme, signal]; **the concert was ~ed all over the world** le concert a été diffusé partout dans le monde; **2** fig **his father ~ed his congratulations** son père, rayonnant, l'a félicité.
III *vi* **1** [*sun, moon*] rayonner; **the sun ~ed down on us** le soleil rayonnait au-dessus de nous; **2** (smile) rayonner.
IDIOMS **to be broad in the ~**○ être fort des hanches.

beam: **~ balance** *n* balance *f* à fléau; **~ compass** *n* compas *m* à verge.

beam end *n* Naut flanc *m* (d'un bateau); **to be on its ~s** Naut être couché sur le flanc; **to be on one's ~s** GB fig○ être complètement fauché○.

beaming /'bi:mɪŋ/ *adj* (all contexts) rayonnant.

bean /bi:n/ **I** *n* **1** Culin, Hort haricot *m*; **green ~**, **French ~** haricot vert; **broad ~** fève *f*; **cocoa ~** fève *f* de cacao; **coffee ~** grain *m* de café; **2 old ~** GB○† mon vieux.
II *vtr* **to ~ sb**○ US donner un coup sur la tête de qn.
IDIOMS **to be full of ~s**○ GB (be lively) être en pleine forme; US (be wrong) se gourer○ complètement; **I haven't got a ~**○ je n'ai pas un radis○; **I don't know a ~** ou **~s about it**○ je n'y connais rien; **it's not worth a ~**○ ça ne vaut rien.

bean: **~ bag** *n* (seat) fauteuil *m* poire; (for throwing) sac *m* de haricots; **~ counter**○ *n* US péj gratte-papier *m inv* pej; **~ curd** *n* fromage *m* de soja; **~feast**○ *n* gueuleton○ *m*.

beano○ /'bi:nəʊ/ *n* GB fête *f*.

bean: **~pole** *n* Hort espalier *m*; fig (thin person) perche *f*; **~ salad** *n* salade *f* de haricots; **~sprout** *n* germe *m* de soja; **~stalk** *n* tige *f* de haricot; **Bean Town**○ *pr n* US Boston *m*.

bear /beə(r)/ **I** *n* **1** Zool ours *m*; **2**○ péj (man) ours *m* (mal léché); **3** Fin baissier *m*.
II *vtr* (*prét* **bore**, *pp* **borne**) **1** (carry) [*person, animal*] porter [*load*]; [*vehicle*] transporter [*load*]; **2** (bring) [*person*] apporter [*gift, message*]; [*wind, water*] porter [*seed, sound*]; **borne on the wind** porté par le vent; **3** (show visibly) [*envelope, shield*] porter; fig porter [*scar, mark*]; **envelopes ~ing the company logo** enveloppes qui portent le sigle de la société; **he still ~s the scars** fig il en reste marqué; **to ~ a resemblance to** ressembler à; **to ~ no relation to** n'avoir aucun rapport avec; **to ~ no comparison with** être sans commune mesure avec; **to ~ witness to sth/to the fact that** témoigner de qch/de ce que; **4** (have) [*person, company*] porter [*name, title*]; **5** (keep) **to ~ sth in mind** (remember) se souvenir de [*suggestion, information*]; (take into account) prendre en compte [*factors*]; **to ~ in mind that** ne pas oublier que; **~ing in mind his inexperience,...** compte tenu de son inexpérience,...; **6** (support) **to ~ the weight of** [*structure, platform*] supporter le poids de [*person, object*]; [*body part*] supporter, soutenir le poids de [*person*]; **7** fig (endure, tolerate) supporter [*illness, hardship, suspense, pressure, smell, person*]; **it's more than I can ~** c'est plus que je n'en peux supporter; **I can't ~ the thought of him going to prison** je ne supporte pas l'idée qu'il aille en prison; **she can't ~ doing the housework** elle ne supporte pas de faire le ménage; **I can't ~ his preaching to me** je ne supporte pas qu'il me fasse la morale; **I can't ~ to watch** je ne veux pas voir ça; **how can you ~ to drink it?** comment peux-tu boire ça?; **'after a long illness bravely borne'** (in obituary) 'à la suite d'une longue et cruelle maladie'; **8** fig (accept) encourir [*cost, responsibility, blame*]; **9** (stand up to) résister à [*scrutiny, inspection*]; **the plan won't ~ close scrutiny** le plan ne résistera pas à un examen approfondi; **that story/joke doesn't ~ repeating** cette histoire/plaisanterie ne vaut pas le coup d'être répétée; **the consequences don't ~ thinking about** mieux vaut ne pas penser aux conséquences; **10** (nurture) porter [*love*]; **the love she bore her father** l'amour qu'elle portait à son père; **to ~ sb ill will** en vouloir à qn; **to ~ a grudge against sb** en vouloir à qn, avoir de la rancune contre qn; **he bore her nothing but resentment** il n'éprouvait pour elle que du ressentiment; **11** (yield) [*tree, land*] donner [*fruit , blossom, crop*]; Fin [*account, investment*] rapporter [*interest*]; **to ~ fruit** [*tree*] donner des fruits; fig [*idea, investment*] porter ses fruits; **12**† ou littér (*pp actif* **borne**, *pp passif* **born**) (give birth to) [*woman*] donner naissance à; [*animal*] mettre bas; **to ~ sb a child** donner un enfant à qn.
III *vi* (*prét* **bore**, *pp* **borne**) **1 to ~ left/right** [*person*] prendre à gauche/à droite; **to ~ east/west** [*person*] aller à l'est/à l'ouest; [*road*] obliquer vers l'est/l'ouest; **2** Naut (lie) **there is land ~ing south-south-east** une côte est signalée au sud-sud-est; **3** (weigh) **to ~ heavily/hardest on sb** [*tax, price increase*] peser lourdement/le plus durement sur qn; **to bring influence/pressure to ~ on** exercer une influence/une pression sur [*person, system*]; **to bring all one's energies to ~ on sth** mettre toute son énergie à qch.
IV *v refl* (*prét* **bore**, *pp* **borne**) **to ~ oneself** (behave) se comporter; **he bore himself bravely** il s'est comporté avec courage; **~ yourself with pride** soyez digne.
■ **bear along**: **~ [sb/sth] along**, **~ along [sb/sth]** entraîner ; **borne along by the tide/his enthusiasm** entraîné par la marée/son enthousiasme.
■ **bear away**: **~ [sb/sth] away**, **~ away [sb/sth]** [*person*] enlever [*person*]; [*wind, water*] emporter [*person, boat*].
■ **bear down 1** gen appuyer fort (**on** sur); **~ down on the screw/plank** appuyez sur la vis/planche; **2** (approach aggressively) **to ~ down on** se ruer sur [*person, group*]; **3** (in childbirth) pousser.
■ **bear in**: **to ~ in with** Naut s'approcher de [*land*]; **the truth has been borne in upon us** la vérité s'est fait jour en nous; **it was finally borne in upon them that** ils ont fini par comprendre que.
■ **bear off 1** = **bear away**; **2 to ~ off from** Naut s'écarter de [*land*].
■ **bear on**: **~ on [sb/sth]** avoir un effet sur; (stronger) peser sur; **factors ~ing directly on the outcome** facteurs qui ont un effet direct sur le résultat; **the cuts would ~ hardest on the poor** c'est sur les pauvres que les diminutions pèseraient le plus lourdement.
■ **bear out**: ¶ **~ out [sth]** confirmer [*theory, claim, story*]; ¶ **~ [sb] out** appuyer; **he'll ~ me out on this** il confirmera ce que je dis.
■ **bear up**: **~ up** [*person*] tenir le coup; [*structure*] résister; **to ~ up against** faire face à [*shock, misfortune*]; **'OK?'—'I'm ~ing up'** 'ça va?'—'on fait aller'.
■ **bear upon** = **bear on**.
■ **bear with**: **~ with [sb]** être indulgent avec; **it's boring but please ~ with me** c'est ennuyeux mais je vous demanderai d'être indulgent; **please ~ with me for a minute** pardonnez-moi un instant; **to ~ with it** être patient.

bearable /'beərəbl/ *adj* supportable.

bear: **~baiting** *n* combat *m* d'ours et de chiens; **~ cub** *n* ourson *m*.

beard /'bɪəd/ **I** *n* **1** (on man) barbe *f*; **a bushy ~** une barbe touffue; **to grow a ~** se faire pousser la barbe; **to shave off one's ~** se raser la barbe; **to wear a ~** porter la barbe; **the man with the ~** le barbu; **2** (tuft, barbel) (on dog, goat) barbiche *f*; (on fish) barbes *fpl*; (on bird) barbe *f*; **3** (on wheat, barley) barbe *f*; **4** (in typography) talus *m* (de pied).
II *vtr* affronter.
IDIOMS **to ~ the lion in his den** braver le lion dans son antre.

bearded /'bɪədɪd/ *adj* barbu; **a ~ youth** un jeune barbu.

bearded: **~ lady** *n* femme *f* à barbe; **~ tit** *n* mésange *f* à moustache.

beardless /'bɪədlɪs/ *adj* imberbe.

beardless youth *n* péj blanc-bec *m* pej.

bearer /'beərə(r)/ **I** *n* **1** gen (of news, gift) porteur/-euse *m/f*; **2** (of letter, equipment) porteur *m*; **3** Fin, Jur (of note, cheque) porteur *m*; (of passport) titulaire *mf*; **4** Hort **the pear tree is still a good ~** le poirier donne encore beaucoup de fruits.

bearer: **~ bond** *n* Fin titre *m* au porteur; **~ cheque** GB, **~ check** US *n* Fin chèque *m* au porteur.

bear garden *n* fig pétaudière *f*.

bear hug /'beəhʊg/ *n* **1** (embrace) étreinte *f*; **to give sb a ~** serrer qn dans ses bras; **2** (in wrestling) immobilisation *f* des bras.

bearing /'beərɪŋ/ **I** *n* **1** (posture) allure *f*; **of soldierly ~** à l'allure martiale; **regal ~** port de roi or reine; **his dignified ~** son port digne; **2** (relevance) **to have no/little ~ on sth** n'avoir aucun rapport/avoir peu de rapport avec qch; **3** Naut relèvement *m* au compas; **the ~ is 137°** le relèvement est de 137°; **true/magnetic ~** relèvement vrai/magnétique; **to take a compass ~** faire un relevé au compas; **to take the ship's ~s** faire le point; **4** Tech palier *m*; **5** Herald meuble *m*.
II bearings *npl* **1** (orientation) **to get** ou **find one's ~s** se repérer; **to lose one's ~s** lit être désorienté; fig perdre le nord; **to take one's ~s** s'orienter; **2** Aut, Mech palier *m*.

bearish /'beərɪʃ/ *adj* **1** péj [*person, behaviour*] bourru; **2** Fin [*market*] à la baisse.

bear: **~ market** *n* Fin marché *m* à la baisse; **~ pit** *n* fosse *f* aux ours.

bearskin /'beəskɪn/ **I** *n* **1** (pelt) peau *f* d'ours; **2** Mil (hat) bonnet *m* à poil.
II *modif* [*rug*] en peau d'ours.

beast /bi:st/ *n* **1** (animal) bête *f*; **the king of the ~s** le roi des animaux; **~ of burden** bête de somme; **~ of prey** carnassier *m*; **the Beast** Bible l'antéchrist *m*, la Bête de l'Apocalypse; **2**○ pej (person) (annoying) chameau○ *m*; (brutal) brute *f*; **he's a selfish ~!** c'est un sale égoïste; **to bring out the ~ in sb** (make angry) rendre qn enragé, (make lustful, brutal) réveiller la bête qui sommeille en qn; **3**○ péj (job, task, problem) saloperie◑ *f*; **it's a ~ of a job!** c'est une vraie corvée!
IDIOMS **it's in the nature of the ~** hum c'est dans l'ordre des choses.

beastliness /'bi:stlɪnɪs/ *n* **1** (unpleasantness) (of person, behaviour, trick) méchanceté *f*, vacherie○ *f*; (of food, weather, illness) caractère *m* abominable; **2** (bestiality) bestialité *f*.

beastly○ /'bi:stlɪ/ **I** *adj* **1**† (unpleasant) [*person, behaviour*] rosse○; [*trick*] sale (*before n*); [*food*] infecte; [*weather*] moche○; [*illness*] abominable; **to be ~**○ **to sb** être rosse○ avec qn; **what a ~**○ **thing to do!** c'est vraiment moche○ d'avoir fait ça!; **2** (bestial) bestial.
II *adv* bigrement○.

beat /bi:t/ **I** *n* **1** (repeated sound) battement *m*; **the ~ of the drum/dancers' feet** le battement du tambour/des pieds des danseurs; **to the ~ of the drum** au son du tambour; **2** Mus (rhythm, tempo) rythme *m*; (in a bar) temps *m*; (in verse) accentuation *f*; **3** (pulsation) (of heart) battement *m*, pulsation *f*; **heart ~** battement du cœur; **80 ~s per minute** 80 pulsations à la minute; **his heart missed** ou **skipped a ~ when he saw her** son cœur s'est arrêté de battre quand il l'a vue; **4** Phys, Elec (pulse) battement *m*; **5** (in police force) (area) secteur *m* de surveillance; (route) ronde *f*; **her ~ covers the town centre** son secteur de surveillance couvre le centre-ville; **to patrol one's ~** faire sa ronde; **policeman on the ~** agent qui fait

la ronde; **6** Hunt (act) battue *f*; (area) terrain *m* de battue.
II *modif* [*poet, writer, philosophy*] de la Beat Generation.
III○ *adj* claqué○; **we were absolutely ~** nous étions complètement claqués.
IV *vtr* (*prét* **beat**, *pp* **beaten**) **1** (strike aggressively) [*person*] battre [*person, animal*]; **to ~ sb with a stick/whip** donner des coups de bâton/de fouet à qn; **to ~ sth into sb** inculquer qch à qn; **~ some respect into him** inculquez-lui un peu de respect; **they beat grammar into our heads** on nous a inculqué la grammaire à coups de marteau; **you'll have to ~ the truth out of him** il te faudra lui arracher la vérité; **I had my high spirits ~en out of me** on m'a fait perdre mon enthousiasme; **to ~ sb into submission** faire obéir qn par la manière forte; **to ~ sb black and blue**○ battre qn comme plâtre○, rouer qn de coups; **to be ~en about the head** recevoir des coups sur la tête; **to ~ the shit**● ou **hell**○ **out of sb** tabasser○ qn; **2** (strike with tool, fist) [*person*] marteler [*door*] (**with** avec); [*person*] battre [*metal, carpet*] (**with** de); [*bird, animal*] battre [*air, ground*] (**with** de); [*hunter*] battre [*undergrowth*]; **she beat the dust out of the rug** elle a battu le tapis pour le dépoussiérer; **to ~ sth into shape** façonner qch; **to ~ sth flat** aplatir qch; **~ the steak with a mallet** Culin aplatir le steak avec un attendrisseur; **to ~ the dents out of a car wing** marteler une aile pour la débosseler; **3** Mus, Mil (produce sound) battre [*drum, tambourine*]; marquer [*rhythm*]; **to ~ the retreat/the tattoo** Mil battre la retraite/le rappel; **to ~ time** battre la mesure; **to ~ time to the music with one's feet** rythmer la musique avec les pieds; **4** Culin (mix vigorously) battre [*mixture, eggs*]; fouetter [*cream*]; **~ the sugar and butter together** battez ensemble le sucre et le beurre; **to ~ sth into sth** incorporer qch à qch en battant; **5** (make escape) **to ~ one's way/a path through** se frayer un chemin/un passage à travers [*crowd, obstacles*]; **to ~ a retreat** gen, Mil battre en retraite; **~ it**○! fiche le camp○!; **6** (flap) **to ~ its wings** battre des ailes; **7** (defeat) battre [*opponent, team*]; vaincre [*inflation, drug abuse etc*]; surmonter [*illness*]; mettre fin à [*child abuse, rape*]; **we beat them at chess** nous les avons battus aux échecs; **to be ~en at sth** se faire battre à qch; **8** (confound) [*mystery*] avoir raison de [*person*]; **a mystery which has ~en the experts** un mystère qui a eu raison des spécialistes; **it ~s me how/why** je n'arrive pas à comprendre comment/pourquoi; **we admit to being ~en** nous nous avouons vaincus; **'why did he leave?'—'~s me**○**!'** 'pourquoi est-il parti?'—'ça me dépasse!'; **this problem's got me beat**○ ou **~en** ce problème me dépasse complètement; **9** (arrive earlier) éviter [*rush, crowds*]; devancer [*person*]; **he beat me to the meeting place** il m'a devancé au rendez-vous; **she beat me to it** elle a été plus rapide que moi; **he beat me to the door** il est arrivé le premier à la porte; **I beat my sister to the altar** je me suis mariée avant ma sœur; **~ the budget!** n'attendez pas les augmentations!; **10** gen, Sport (outdo) battre [*score*]; dépasser [*target*]; surclasser [*product*]; **his score will take some ~ing** son score sera difficile à battre; **our product ~s yours** notre produit surclasse le vôtre; **it ~s doing** c'est toujours mieux que de faire; **it ~s walking** c'est toujours mieux que de marcher; **you can't ~ Italian shoes/a nice cup of tea** rien ne vaut les chaussures italiennes/une bonne tasse de thé; **our prices are difficult to ~** nos prix sont imbattables; **this scenery takes some ~ing** ces paysages sont incomparables; **your manners take some ~ing** iron ton comportement dépasse toutes les bornes; **~ that (if you can)!** qui dit mieux!; **that ~s everything!** ça c'est le bouquet○!
V *vi* (*prét* **beat**, *pp* **beaten**) **1 to ~ against** (strike repeatedly) [*waves*] battre [*shore, cliff*]; [*rain*] fouetter [*face*]; [*rain*] battre [*window*]; **2 to ~ at** ou **on** [*person*] cogner; **3** Physiol [*heart, pulse*] battre (**with** de); **4** (make sound) [*drum*] battre; **5** (flap) [*wings*] battre; **6** Hunt battre les taillis; **7** Naut louvoyer; **to ~ to windward** louvoyer au plus près.
IDIOMS **a rod** ou **stick to ~ sb with** une arme contre qn; **if you can't ~ 'em, join 'em** il faut savoir hurler avec les loups; **to ~ the charge** US échapper à l'accusation.
■ **beat back**: **~ [sth] back, ~ back [sth]** repousser [*group, flames*].
■ **beat down**: ¶ **~ down** [*rain, hail*] tomber à verse (**on** sur); [*sun*] taper (**on** sur); ¶ **~ [sth] down, ~ down [sth] 1** (flatten) [*rain, wind*] coucher [*crop, grass*]; **2** (break open) [*person*] enfoncer [*door*]; ¶ **~ [sb] down to** faire descendre [qn] à; **I beat her down to 100 dollars** je l'ai fait descendre à 100 dollars.
■ **beat in**: **~ [sth] in, ~ in [sth]** défoncer; **he'd had his skull ~en in** on lui avait défoncé le crâne.
■ **beat off**: **~ [sb/sth] off, ~ off [sb/sth]** repousser [*attack, attackers*]; chasser [*insects*].
■ **beat out**: **~ [sth] out, ~ out [sth]** marteler [*metal*]; rythmer [*tune*]; battre [*rhythm*] (**on** sur); étouffer [*flames*].
■ **beat up**: **~ [sb] up, ~ up [sb]** tabasser○.

beaten /ˈbiːtn/ **I** *pp* ▶ **beat**.
II *adj* **1** (defeated) [*team, competitor, army*] battu; **2** (flattened) [*metal*] battu; **3** Culin [*egg*] battu.
IDIOMS **off the ~ track** dans un endroit écarté; **to go off the ~ track** quitter les sentiers battus.

beater /ˈbiːtə(r)/ *n* **1** Hunt rabatteur/-euse *m/f*; **2** Mus mailloche *f*.

beatific /ˌbɪəˈtɪfɪk/ *adj* gen béat; Relig béatifique.

beatification /bɪˌætɪfɪˈkeɪʃn/ *n* béatification *f*.

beatify /bɪˈætɪfaɪ/ *vtr* béatifier.

beating /ˈbiːtɪŋ/ *n* **1** (punishment) raclée○ *f*, correction *f*; **to get a ~** recevoir une raclée○; **to give sb a ~** flanquer une raclée à qn○; **2**○ (defeat) **they will take some ~** ils ne seront pas faciles à battre; **3**○ (rough treatment) **to give one's car a ~** en faire voir de toutes les couleurs○ à sa voiture; **to take a ~** [*speaker, politician*] être malmené; [*toy, car*] en voir de dures○; **these toys are designed to take a ~** ces jouets sont très résistants; **4** (of metal, carpet) battage *m*; **5** (sound) (of drum, heart, wings) battement *m*; **6** Hunt battue *f*.

beating up○ /ˌbiːtɪŋ ˈʌp/ *n* tabassage○ *m*; **to get a ~** se faire tabasser○; **to give sb a ~** tabasser○ qn.

beatitude /bɪˈætɪtjuːd, US -tuːd/ *n* sout gen, Bible béatitude *f*.

beatnik /ˈbiːtnɪk/ *n* beatnik *mf*.

beat-up○ /ˈbiːtʌp/ *adj* [*car*] déglingué.

beau /bəʊ/ *n* (*pl* **beaux**) **1** littér ou hum (suitor) galant *m*, soupirant *m*; **2**† (dandy) dandy *m*.

beau compass *n* compas *m* à verge.

Beaufort scale /ˌbəʊfət ˈskeɪl/ *n* échelle *f* de Beaufort.

beauteous /ˈbjuːtɪəs/ *adj* littér sublime.

beautician /bjuːˈtɪʃn/ ▶ **1692** *n* (beauty specialist) esthéticien/-ienne *m/f*; US (hairdresser) coiffeur/-euse *m/f*.

beautiful /ˈbjuːtɪfl/ *adj* **1** (aesthetically attractive) beau/belle (*before n*); **a ~ place** un bel endroit; **a ~ example** of un bel exemple de; **2** (wonderful) [*day, holiday, feeling, experience*] merveilleux/-euse; [*weather*] superbe; **3** (skilful) [*shot, goal*] superbe; **he's a ~ writer** il écrit divinement bien.

■ Note: the irregular form *bel* of the adjective *beau, belle* is used before masculine nouns beginning with a vowel or a mute 'h'.

beautifully /ˈbjuːtɪfəlɪ/ *adv* **1** (perfectly) [*play, write, behave, function*] admirablement (bien); [*written, designed etc*] admirablement; **that will do ~** cela conviendra parfaitement; **2** (attractively) [*displayed, furnished, situated*] magnifiquement; **~ dressed** habillé avec beaucoup de goût; **3** (emphatic) [*empty, quiet, soft, warm, accurate*] merveilleusement.

beautiful people *n* **the ~** le beau monde.

beautify /ˈbjuːtɪfaɪ/ **I** *vtr* embellir.
II *v refl* **to ~ oneself** se faire une beauté.

beauty /ˈbjuːtɪ/ **I** *n* **1** (quality) beauté *f*; **to spoil** ou **mar the ~ of** nuire à la beauté de; **2** (woman) beauté *f*; **3** (beautiful feature) **the beauties of** les beautés de [*nature, landscape*]; **4** (advantage) **the ~ of the system is that**... ce qu'il y a de bien dans ce système, c'est que...; **that's the ~ of it** c'est ce que cela a de bien; **5** (perfect example) **a ~ of a goal/car** un but/une voiture superbe; **that's a real ~** hum c'est un modèle du genre!
II *modif* [*contest, product, treatment*] de beauté.
IDIOMS **age before ~** ≈ c'est le bénéfice de l'âge; **~ is in the eye of the beholder** Prov rien n'est laid pour celui qui aime; **Beauty and the Beast** la Belle et la Bête.

beauty: **~ editor** *n* Journ rédacteur/-trice *m/f* de la rubrique 'beauté'; **~ parlour**†, **~ shop, ~ salon** US ▶ **1692** *n* salon *m* de beauté; **~ queen** *n* reine *f* de beauté.

beauty sleep *n* hum **to need one's ~** avoir besoin de ménager sa santé.

beauty specialist ▶ **1692** *n* esthéticien/-ienne *m/f*.

beauty spot *n* **1** (on skin) grain *m* de beauté; (fake) mouche *f*; **2** Tourism gen coin *m* superbe; (official) site *m* pittoresque.

beaver /ˈbiːvə(r)/ **I** *n* **1** (animal, fur, hat) castor *m*; **2** Hist (part of helmet) mentonnière *f*; **3**● US (female genitals) chatte● *f*; **4**● US (woman) gonzesse○ *f*.
II *modif* [*garment*] de castor; **~ lamb coat** manteau *m* en mouton doré.
IDIOMS **to work like a ~** travailler d'arrache-pied. ▶ **eager beaver**.
■ **beaver away** travailler d'arrache-pied (**at** à).

becalmed /bɪˈkɑːmd/ *adj* encalminé.

became /bɪˈkeɪm/ *prét* ▶ **become**.

because /bɪˈkɒz, US *also* -kɔːz/ **I** *conj* parce que; **don't do it just ~ you can** ne le fais pas simplement parce que tu en es capable; **just ~ you're older doesn't mean you're right** ce n'est pas parce que tu es plus âgé que tu as raison; **he was locked out ~ he'd left early and forgotten his key** il n'a pas pu entrer parce qu'il était parti tôt et qu'il avait oublié sa clé; **just ~ you're jealous**○**!** tout ça parce que tu es jaloux!; **'why?'—'(just) ~'** 'pourquoi?'—'parce que'; **all the more so ~** d'autant plus que.
II because of *prep phr* à cause de; **~ of the rain** à cause de la pluie; **don't worry, I'm not leaving ~ of you** ne t'inquiète pas, ce n'est pas à cause de toi que je m'en vais; **~ of you we're late!, we're late and it's all ~ of you!** c'est à cause de toi que nous sommes en retard!

beck /bek/ *n* **1 to be at sb's ~ and call** être à la disposition de qn; **to have sb at one's ~ and call** faire marcher qn au doigt et à l'œil; **2** GB dial (stream) ruisseau *m*.

beckon /ˈbekən/ **I** *vtr* faire signe à; **to ~ sb in** faire signe à qn d'entrer; **to ~ to sb to do** faire signe à qn de faire; **a bright future ~s you in Europe** un bel avenir t'attend en Europe.
II *vi* **1** lit (with gesture) faire signe (**to** à); **2** fig (lure) attirer; **success ~ed** le succès se profilait à l'horizon.

become /bɪˈkʌm/ (*prét* **became**; *pp* **become**) **I** *vtr* [*colour, dress, style*] aller bien à [*person*]; [*attitude, modesty*] convenir à [*person*].
II *vi* **1** (grow to be) devenir; **to ~ famous/fat/fashionable** devenir célèbre/gros/à la mode; **to ~ law** devenir loi;

to ~ ill tomber malade; to ~ aware se rendre compte; 2 (achieve position) devenir; to become queen/a doctor devenir reine/médecin.
III *v impers*: what has ~ of your brother? qu'est-ce que ton frère est devenu?; what has ~ of those photos? où sont passées ces photos?; it ill-~s you to criticize cela vous va mal de critiquer.

becoming /bɪ'kʌmɪŋ/ *adj* [*behaviour*] convenable; [*garment, hair cut etc*] seyant.

becomingly /bɪ'kʌmɪŋlɪ/ *adv* 1 (attractively) [*arranged, dressed*] de manière élégante; [*blush, smile*] de manière charmante; 2 (suitably) [*dressed*] comme il faut.

becquerel /'bekərəl/ *n* becquerel *m*.

bed /bed/ I *n* 1 (place to sleep) lit *m*; double ~ lit *m* à deux places; single ~ lit *m* à une place; to get into ~ se mettre au lit; to get out of ~ sortir du lit; to go to ~ aller au lit; it's time for ~ il est l'heure d'aller au lit or de se coucher; to send/put sb to ~ envoyer/mettre qn au lit; to be in ~ être au lit, être couché; to take to one's ~† s'aliter; a 40 ~ ward/hotel une salle/un hôtel de 40 lits; I need a ~ for the night j'ai besoin d'un lit pour la nuit; to give sb a ~ for the night héberger qn pour une nuit; to sleep in separate ~s faire lit à part; her ~ of pain littér son lit de douleur; the dog makes his ~ in the hall le chien a un coin pour dormir dans l'entrée; 2○ (sex) to go to ~ with coucher avec; what's he like in ~? au lit il est comment?; to catch sb in ~ with surprendre qn au lit avec; to get into ~ with lit coucher avec [*person*]; fig s'associer à [*company, group, lobby*]; 3 Hort (of flowers) parterre *m*; (of manure, compost) lit *m*; (of produce) carré *m*; a rose ~, a ~ of roses un parterre de roses; 4 (bottom) (of sea) fond *m*; (of river) lit *m*; the sea ~ le fond de la mer; 5 Geol couche *f*; 6 Tech (of machine tool) banc *m*; 7 Journ, Print to put a newspaper to ~ boucler un journal; 8 Aut (of car) châssis *m*; (of truck) plateau *m*; 9 Constr (of wall) lit *m*; (of road) plate-forme *f*.
II *vtr* (*p prés etc* -dd-) 1 Hort (also ~ out) repiquer [*seedlings*]; dépoter [*plants*]; 2† (sleep with) coucher avec [*person*].
IDIOMS to be brought to ~ of† accoucher de [*boy, girl*]; to get out of ~ on the wrong side se lever du pied gauche; her life is a ~ of nails sa vie est un calvaire; life is not a ~ of roses tout n'est pas rose dans la vie; you've made your ~, now you must lie in it Prov comme on fait son lit, on se couche Prov.
■ **bed down**: ¶ ~ down se coucher; ¶ ~ [sth] down, ~ down [sth] faire la litière à [*horse*].
■ **bed in**: ~ [sth] in Constr sceller [*beam*].

BEd /ˌbiː'ed/ *n* (*abrév* = bachelor of education) diplôme *m* universitaire de pédagogie.

bed and board *n* le gîte et le couvert *m*.

bed and breakfast, B and B /ˌbed ən 'brekfəst/ *n* 1 Tourism (type of accommodation) chambre *f* avec petit déjeuner, ≈ chambre *f* d'hôte; to offer ~ offrir des chambres avec petit déjeuner; 2 Tourism (building) maison *f* qui fait chambres d'hôte; to run a ~ avoir des chambres d'hôte; 3 GB Soc Admin (also ~ accommodation) logement *m* de substitution.

bed: ~ base *n* sommier *m*; ~ bath *n* toilette *f* au lit; ~bug *n* punaise *f* de lit; ~chamber† *n* chambre *f* à coucher; ~clothes *npl* couvertures *fpl*.

bedding /'bedɪŋ/ I *n* 1 (for humans) literie *f*; 2 (for animals) litière *f*.
II *modif* Hort [*fork, trowel*] à repiquage; [*plant*] annuel/-elle.

bedeck /bɪ'dek/ *vtr* orner (with de).

bedevil /bɪ'devl/ *vtr* (*p prés etc* -ll-, -l- US) (plague) tracasser [*person*]; contrarier [*plans*]; (confuse) embrouiller [*problem, situation, person*]; ~led[GB] by doubt/remorse rongé par le doute/le remords; project ~led[GB] by a lack of funds projet qui souffre de l'insuffisance des crédits.

bedfellow /'bedfeləʊ/ *n* 1 fig to make strange ~s former un tandem bizarre; 2† lit compagnon/compagne *m/f* de lit.

Bedfordshire /'bedfədʃə(r)/ ▶ 1624 *pr n* Bedfordshire *m*.

bed: ~head *n* tête *f* de lit; ~ jacket *n* liseuse *f*.

bedlam /'bedləm/ *n* 1 (chaos) chahut○ *m*; (infernal) bastringue○ *m*; it's ~ in here! quel cirque○ ici!; 2 Hist maison *f* de fous.

bed linen *n* draps *mpl*.

Bedouin /'bedʊɪn/ I *n* Bédouin/-e *m/f*.
II *adj* bédouin.

bd: ~ pad *n* alaise *f*; ~pan *n* Med bassin *m*; ~post *n* colonne *f* (*d'un lit*).

bedraggled /bɪ'drægld/ *adj* [*person, clothes*] dépenaillé; [*hair*] embroussaillé.

bedridden /'bedrɪdn/ *adj* alité, cloué au lit.

bedrock /'bedrɒk/ *n* 1 Geol substrat *m* rocheux; 2 fig (basis) fondement *m*.

bedroll /'bedrəʊl/ *n* couchage *m*.

bedroom /'bedruːm, -rʊm/ I *n* chambre *f* (à coucher); a four ~ house une maison avec quatre chambres; a two ~ flat GB ou apartment un trois-pièces.
II *modif* 1 lit [*carpet, furniture, window*] de chambre; my ~ carpet la moquette de ma chambre; 2○ (sexual) [*antics, secrets*] intime; ~ scene scène *f* d'amour.

bedroom: ~ farce *n* Theat vaudeville *m*; ~ slipper *n* pantoufle *f*; ~ suburb *n* US banlieue-dortoir *f*.

Beds *n* GB Post *abrév écrite* = Bedfordshire.

bed-settee /ˌbedsə'tiː/ *n* canapé-lit *m*.

bedside /'bedsaɪd/ I *n* chevet *m*; to be at sb's ~ être au chevet de qn.
II *modif* [*book, lamp*] de chevet.

bedside manner *n* comportement *m* envers les malades; he has a good ~ il est gentil avec les malades.

bedside: ~ rug *n* descente *f* de lit; ~ table *n* table *f* de nuit or de chevet.

bed: ~sit○, ~sitter, ~-sittingroom† *n* GB chambre *f* meublée; ~sock *n* chausson *m* de nuit; ~sore *n* escarre *f*; ~spread *n* dessus *m* de lit; ~spring *n* ressort *m* (de sommier); ~stead *n* cadre *m* de lit; ~straw *n* Bot gaillet *m*.

bedtime /'bedtaɪm/ I *n* it's ~ c'est l'heure d'aller se coucher; I have some tea at ~ je prends du thé avant de me coucher; 11 o'clock is my ~ je me couche à 11 heures; it's way past your ~ il y a longtemps que tu devrais être au lit.
II *modif* [*story, drink*] avant de s'endormir; ~ reading lecture *f* pour l'oreiller.

bed: ~warmer *n* chaufferette *f*; ~wetter *n* enfant *m* incontinent; ~wetting *n* énurésie *f*.

bee /biː/ *n* 1 (insect) abeille *f*; 2 US (meeting) réunion *f* (pour travaux en commun).
IDIOMS to think one is the ~'s knees○ se prendre pour un crack○; the birds and the ~s hum ≈ les cigognes et les choux hum; to be as busy as a ~ s'activer comme une abeille.

Beeb○ /biːb/ *n* GB hum the ~ la BBC.

beech /biːtʃ/ I *n* 1 (tree) hêtre *m*; 2 (also ~ wood) bois *m* de hêtre.
II *modif* [*hedge, forest*] de hêtres; ~ grove hêtraie *f*.

beech: ~ marten *n* martre *f*, marte *f*; ~mast *n* ¢ faines *fpl* (tombées par terre); ~nut *n* faine *f*.

bee eater *n* guêpier *m*.

beef /biːf/ I *n* 1 Culin (viande *f* de) bœuf *m*; minced ~ GB, ground ~ US viande *f* (de bœuf) hachée; roast ~ rôti *m* de bœuf, rosbif *m*; 2○ US (grievance) what's your ~○? c'est quoi ton problème?; I've got no ~ with you○ je n'ai rien contre toi.
II *vi* (also ~ on) râler○ (about à propos de).
IDIOMS put a bit of ~ into it!○ mettez-y un peu de nerf!○.
■ **beef up**: ~ up [sth] étoffer [*content, resources*]; augmenter [*budget*]; renforcer [*control*].

beef: ~burger *n* hamburger *m*; ~cake○ *n* ¢ (photos *fpl* d')hommes *mpl* musclés; ~ cattle *npl* gros bétail *m*; ~eater *n* gardien *m* de la Tour de Londres; ~ export *n* exportation *f* de bœuf; ~ farming *n* élevage *m* de bœufs; ~ market *n* marché *m* du bœuf; ~ olive *n* paupiette *f* de bœuf; ~steak *n* steak *m* (de bœuf); ~steak tomato *n* grosse tomate *f*; ~ stew *n* pot-au-feu *m*; ~ stock *n* bouillon *m* de bœuf; ~ tea *n* bouillon *m* de bœuf.

beefy /'biːfɪ/ *adj* 1 [*flavour*] de bœuf; 2○ [*man*] mastoc○.

beehive /'biːhaɪv/ *n* 1 (for bees) ruche *f*; 2 = beehive hairdo.

beehive hairdo *n* chignon *m* en hauteur.

beekeeper /'biːkiːpə(r)/ ▶ 1692 *n* apiculteur/-trice *m/f*.

beeline /'biːlaɪn/ *n*: IDIOMS to make a ~ for se diriger tout droit vers.

been /biːn, US bɪn/ *pp* ▶ be.

bee orchid *n* ophrys *m* abeille.

beep /biːp/ I *n* (of electronic device, answering machine) bip *m*; (of car) coup *m* de klaxon®; Radio top *m* sonore.
II *vtr* appeler [qn] au bip, biper.
III *vi* [*electronic device*] faire bip or bip-bip; [*car*] klaxonner.

beeper /'biːpə(r)/ *n* bip(-bip) *m*.

beer /bɪə(r)/ I *n* bière *f*.
II *modif* [*barrel, bottle*] de bière.
IDIOMS life isn't all ~ and skittles la vie n'est pas toujours rose; ▶ small.

beer: ~ belly *n* bedaine *f* (de buveur de bière); ~ bottle *n* canette *f*; ~ bust○ *n* US Univ beuverie *f* à la bière; ~ can *n* boîte *f* de bière; ~fest *n* fête *f* de la bière; ~ garden *n* gen jardin *m* de pub; (in Germany) ≈ guinguette *f*; ~ mat *n* dessous *m* de verre.

beerswilling /'bɪəswɪlɪŋ/ *adj* péj se soûlant à la bière.

beery /'bɪərɪ/ *adj* [*evening, party*] où la bière coule à flots; [*person, breath, atmosphere*] qui sent la bière; ~ face trogne *f* de soûlard.

bee: ~ sting *n* piqûre *f* d'abeille; ~swax *n* cire *f* d'abeille.

beet /biːt/ *n* betterave *f*.
IDIOMS to turn as red as a ~ US devenir rouge comme une tomate.

beetle /'biːtl/ I *n* 1 Zool (insect) scarabée *m*; (genus) coléoptère *m*; 2 Tech (tool) maillet *m*; 3○ Aut coccinelle○ *f* (*modèle de Volkswagen*).
II *vi*○ to ~ in entrer précipitamment; to ~ off filer○.

beetle: ~-browed *adj* (with thick eyebrows) aux sourcils touffus; fig (scowling) renfrogné; ~ drive *n* GB ≈ partie *f* de loto.

beetling /'biːtlɪŋ/ *adj* [*cliff*] surplombant; [*brow*] proéminent.

beetroot /'biːtruːt/ *n* GB betterave *f*.
IDIOMS to turn as red as a ~ devenir rouge comme une tomate.

beet sugar *n* sucre *m* de betterave.

befall /bɪ'fɔːl/ (*prét* befell, *pp* befallen) littér (*s'emploie uniquement à l'infinitif et à la troisième personne*) I *vtr* arriver à, échoir à; it befell that il advint que; I hope no harm will ever ~ him j'espère qu'il ne lui arrivera jamais malheur.
II *vi* advenir.

befit /bɪ'fɪt/ *vtr impers* (*p prés etc* -tt-) sout convenir à; as ~s sb/sth comme il convient à qn/qch; it ill ~s him to... il lui sied mal de...

befitting /bɪ'fɪtɪŋ/ *adj* sout [*modesty, honesty*]

before

When *before* is used as a preposition in expressions of time or order of sequence or importance it is translated by *avant*:

before the meeting = avant la réunion
she left before me = elle est partie avant moi

For more examples and particular usages, see **I 1, 2, 3** in the entry ***before***.

When *before* is used as a preposition meaning *in front of* (when you are talking about physical space) or *in the presence of* it is translated by *devant*:

before our eyes = devant nos yeux
he declared before his mother that ... = il a déclaré devant sa mère que ...

When *before* is used as an adjective after a noun it is translated by *précédent/-e*:

the time before = la fois précédente

the one before is translated by *le précédent* or *la précédente*:

no, I'm not talking about that meeting but the one before = non, je ne parle pas de cette réunion-là mais de la précédente

For particular usages see **II** in the entry ***before***.

When *before* is used as an adverb meaning *beforehand* it is translated by *avant* in statements about the present or future;

I'll try to talk to her before = j'essaierai de lui en parler avant
you could have told me before = tu aurais pu me le dire avant

When *before* means *previously* in statements about the past it is translated by *auparavant*:

I had met her two or three times before = je l'avais rencontrée deux ou trois fois auparavant

When *before* means *already* it is translated by *déjà*:

I've met her before = je l'ai déjà rencontrée
you've asked me that question before = tu m'as déjà posé cette question

In negative sentences *before* is often used in English simply to reinforce the negative. In such cases it is not translated at all:

I'd never eaten snails before = je n'avais jamais mangé d'escargots
you've never told me that before = tu ne m'as jamais dit ça

For particular usages see **III** in the entry ***before***.

When *before* is used as a conjunction, it is translated by *avant de* + infinitive where the two verbs have the same subject:

before he saw her he recognized her voice = il a reconnu sa voix avant de la voir
before I cook dinner I'm going to phone my mother = avant de préparer le dîner je vais appeler ma mère

Where the two verbs have different subjects, the translation is *avant que* + subjunctive:

Tom wants to see her before she leaves = Tom veut la voir avant qu'elle parte

Some speakers and writers add *ne* before the verb: Tom veut la voir avant qu'elle ne parte, but this is simply a slightly precious effect of style and is never obligatory. For particular usages see **IV** in the entry ***before***.

approprié; **in a style ~ a managing director** dans le style qui convient à un PDG.

befog /bɪˈfɒɡ/ *vtr* (*p prés etc* **-gg-**) embrouiller [*person, mind, issue*]; **his mind ~ged with drink** l'esprit embrumé par l'alcool.

before /bɪˈfɔ:(r)/ **I** *prep* **1** (earlier than) avant; **the day ~ yesterday** avant-hier; **the day ~ the interview** la veille de l'entretien; **I was there the week ~ last** j'y étais il y a deux semaines; **they hadn't met since ~ the war** ils ne s'étaient pas vus depuis avant la guerre; **it should have been done ~ now** ça aurait dû être fait avant; **phone if you need me ~ then** téléphonez-moi si vous avez besoin de moi avant; **six weeks ~ then** six semaines avant ou auparavant; **she became a doctor, like her mother ~ her** elle est devenue médecin comme sa mère; **~ long it will be winter** ce sera bientôt l'hiver; **~ long, he was speaking Spanish fluently** très vite, il parlait l'espagnol couramment; **not ~ time!** ce n'est pas trop tôt!; **it was long ~ your time** c'était bien avant ta naissance; **2** (in order, sequence, hierarchy) avant; **G comes ~ H in the alphabet** dans l'alphabet le G est avant le H; **your name comes ~ mine on the list** sur la liste ton nom est avant le mien; **the page ~ this one** la page précédente; **3** (in importance, priority) avant; **to put quality ~ quantity** placer la qualité avant la quantité; **for him, work comes ~ everything else** pour lui le travail passe avant tout; **should we place our needs ~ theirs?** devrions-nous accorder plus d'importance à nos besoins qu'aux leurs?; **ladies ~ gentlemen** honneur aux dames; **4** (this side of) avant; **turn left ~ the crossroads** tournez à gauche avant le carrefour; **5** ▶ 1096 US (in time expressions) **ten ~ six** six heures moins dix; **6** (in front of) devant; **she appeared ~ them** elle est apparue devant eux; **the desert stretched out ~ them** le désert s'étendait devant eux; **~ our very eyes** sous nos propres yeux; **they fled ~ the invader** ils ont fui devant l'envahisseur; **7** (in the presence of) devant; **he was brought ~ the king** on l'a amené devant le roi; **to appear ~ a court** comparaître devant un tribunal; **to put proposals ~ a committee** présenter des projets à une commission; **to bring a bill ~ parliament** présenter un projet de loi au parlement; **8** (confronting) face à; **they were powerless ~ such resistance** ils étaient impuissants face à une telle résistance; **these are the alternatives ~ us** voici les choix qui s'offrent à nous; **the task ~ us** la tâche qui nous attend.
II *adj* précédent; **the day ~** la veille; **the week/the year ~** la semaine/l'année précédente; **this page and the one ~** cette page et la précédente.
III *adv* (at an earlier time) avant; **as ~** comme avant; **~ and after** avant et après; **he had been there two months ~** il y était allé deux mois auparavant; **have you been to India ~?** est-ce que tu es déjà allé en Inde?; **I've never been there ~** je n'y suis jamais allé; **haven't we met ~?** on s'est déjà rencontré, il me semble?; **I've never seen him ~ in my life** c'est la première fois que je le vois; **it's never happened ~** c'est la première fois que ça arrive; **long ~** bien avant.
IV *conj* **1** (in time) **~ I go, I would like to say that** avant de partir, je voudrais dire que ; **~ he goes, I must remind him that** avant qu'il parte, il faut que je lui rappelle que; **it was some time ~ she was able to walk again** il lui a fallu un certain temps pour pouvoir marcher de nouveau; **~ I had time to realize what was happening, he...** avant que j'aie eu le temps de comprendre ce qui se passait, il...; **it will be years ~ I earn that much money!** je ne gagnerai pas autant d'argent avant des années!; **oh, ~ I forget, did you remember to post that letter?** avant que j'oublie, est-ce que tu as pensé à envoyer cette lettre?; **2** (rather than) plutôt que; **he would die ~ betraying that secret** il mourrait plutôt que de révéler ce secret; **3** (otherwise, or else) **get out of here ~ I call the police!** sortez d'ici ou j'appelle la police!; **4** (as necessary condition) pour que (+ *subj*); **you have to show your ticket ~ they'll let you in** il faut que tu montres ton ticket pour qu'ils te laissent entrer.
IDIOMS **~ you could say Jack Robinson** en moins de temps qu'il ne faut pour le dire, en moins de deux○; **~ you know where you are...** on n'a pas le temps de dire ouf que...

beforehand /bɪˈfɔ:hænd/ *adv* **1** (ahead of time) à l'avance; **be there one hour ~** sois là une heure à l'avance; **let me know ~** prévenez-moi; **2** (earlier) auparavant, avant; **we had seen them five minutes ~** nous les avions vus cinq minutes auparavant or plus tôt; **journalists knew ~** les journalistes le savaient déjà.

before tax *adj* [*income*] brut; [*profit*] avant impôts.

befoul /bɪˈfaʊl/ *vtr* sout lit, fig souiller.

befriend /bɪˈfrend/ *vtr* (look after) prendre [qn] sous son aile; (make friends with) se lier d'amitié avec.

befuddle /bɪˈfʌdl/ *vtr* brouiller les idées de [*person*]; embrouiller [*mind*]; **to be ~d by drink** être abruti par l'alcool.

beg /beɡ/ **I** *vtr* (*p prés etc* **-gg-**) **1** (solicit) demander [*food, money*] (**from** à); **2** (request) demander [*favour, permission*] (**from, of** à); **to ~ sb for sth** demander qch à qn; **I ~ged his forgiveness** je lui ai demandé de me pardonner; **to ~ to be chosen** demander à être choisi; **to ~ leave to do** demander la permission de faire; **I ~ your pardon** je vous demande pardon; **I ~ to differ** je ne suis pas du même avis; **3** (entreat) supplier [*person*] (**to do** de faire); **'stop, I ~ (of) you!'** 'arrêtez, je vous en supplie!'; **4** (leave unresolved) éluder [*problem, question*].
II *vi* (*p prés etc* **-gg-**) **1** (solicit) [*person*] mendier (**from** à); [*dog*] faire le beau; **to ~ for** mendier [*money, food*]; **2** (request) demander; **to ~ for** demander [*help, patience*]; **3** (entreat) implorer; **to ~ for sth** implorer qch; **to ~ to be spared/to be forgiven** implorer la clémence/le pardon.
IDIOMS **to ~ the question** laisser de côté le problème de fond; **these apples are going ~ging** personne ne veut de ces pommes.
■ **beg off** s'excuser de ne pas pouvoir venir.

began /bɪˈɡæn/ *prét* ▶ **begin**.

beget‡ /bɪˈɡet/ (*prét* **begot** /bɪˈɡɒt/ ou **begat** /bɪˈɡæt/, *pp* **begotten** /bɪˈɡɒtn/) *vtr* lit, fig engendrer.

beggar /ˈbeɡə(r)/ **I** *n* **1** (pauper) mendiant/-e *m/f*; **2**○ GB (man) **a lucky ~** un veinard○; **you lucky ~!** espèce de veinard○!; **a poor ~** un pauvre diable○; **a crazy ~** un fou.
II *vtr* **1** ruiner [*person, company*]; **2** (defy) **to ~ description** défier toute description.
IDIOMS **~s can't be choosers** Prov faute de grives on mange des merles Prov.

beggarly /ˈbeɡəlɪ/ *adj* **1** (poor) [*existence, meal*] misérable; **2** (inadequate) [*amount, wage*] dérisoire; [*thanks*] maigre (*before n*).

beggar-my-neighbour /ˌbeɡəmaɪˈneɪbə(r)/ ▶ 1282 *n* ≈ bataille *f*.

beg: **~ging bowl** *n* sébile *f*; **~ging letter** *n* lettre *f* de sollicitation.

begin /bɪˈgɪn/ **I to begin with** *adv phr* **1** (at first) au début, au départ; **I didn't understand to ~ with** au début je n'ai pas compris; **2** (firstly) d'abord, premièrement; **3** (at all) **I wish I hadn't told her to ~ with** pour commencer, je n'aurais jamais dû lui en parler.

II *vtr* (*p prés* **-nn-**; *prét* **began**; *pp* **begun**) **1** (start) commencer [*journey, list, meeting, job, game, meal*] (**with** par, avec); se lancer dans [*adventure*]; aller à [*school*]; **to ~ to do** commencer à faire; **it's ~ning to rain** il commence à pleuvoir; **to ~ doing** commencer à faire; **I began the letter (with) 'Dear Sir'** j'ai commencé la lettre par 'Monsieur'; **'well ...,' she began** 'eh bien...,' commença-t-elle; **I ~ work next week** je commence à travailler la semaine prochaine; **the builders ~ work on Tuesday** les ouvriers commencent les travaux mardi; **they began laughing** ou **to laugh again** ils ont recommencé à rire; **2** (start to use) entamer, ouvrir [*bottle, packet, jar*]; entamer [*loaf*]; commencer [*notebook, page*]; **3** (start out) débuter [*career*] (**as** comme); **I began life as a farmer's son** je suis fils de fermier; **we began married life in Scotland** quand nous étions jeunes mariés nous habitions en Écosse; **this novel began life as a short story** ce roman a d'abord vu le jour sous la forme d'une nouvelle; **4** (have slightest success) **I can't ~ to describe it** il m'est impossible de le décrire; **I don't ~ to understand** vraiment, je ne comprends pas; **I couldn't ~ to imagine how he felt** je ne pouvais vraiment pas imaginer ce qu'il éprouvait; **5** (initiate) provoquer [*debate, dispute*]; lancer [*campaign, trend*]; commencer [*tradition*]; déclencher [*war*]; fonder [*dynasty*]; **to ~ a conversation with** engager la conversation avec; **6** (come first in) marquer le commencement de [*series, collection, festival*]; **A ~s the alphabet** l'alphabet commence par A.

III *vi* (*p prés* **-nn-**; *prét* **began**; *pp* **begun**) **1** (commence) [*custom, meeting, play, problem, storm, term*] commencer; **let's ~** commençons; **to ~ with** commencer par; **to ~ by doing** commencer par faire; **a name ~ning with C** un nom qui commence par C; **the week ~ning the 25th** la semaine qui commence le 25; **to ~ in 1995/in May** commencer en 1995/en mai; **your problems have only just begun!** tes problèmes ne font que commencer!; **to ~ well/badly** bien/mal commencer; **to ~ again** recommencer; **after the war began** après le début de la guerre; **before the lecture ~s** avant le début de la conférence; **2** (have its starting point) [*river*] prendre sa source; **the road ~s in York** la route part de York; **where does the national park ~?** où commence le parc national?

■ **begin on**: **~ on [sth]** attaquer [*cake, garden*].

beginner /bɪˈgɪnə(r)/ *n* débutant/-e *m/f*; **'Spanish for ~s'** 'espagnol pour débutants'; **~s' class** cours *m* pour débutants.

IDIOMS **~'s luck!** aux innocents les mains pleines!; **'~s please!'** Theat 'en scène s'il vous plaît'.

beginning /bɪˈgɪnɪŋ/ **I** *n* (start) début *m*, commencement *m*; **in** ou **at the ~** au départ, au début; **since the ~ of March** depuis le début du mois de mars; **at the ~ of September** début septembre; **at the ~ of the month** au début du mois; **from ~ to end** du début jusqu'à la fin; **to go back to the ~** reprendre au début; **since the ~ of time** depuis la nuit des temps; **in the Beginning was the Word** au commencement était le Verbe.

II beginnings *npl* **1** (origins) (of person, business) débuts *mpl*; (of theory, movement) origines *fpl*; **his humble ~s** ses modestes débuts; **the theory has its ~s in the 19th century** l'origine de la théorie remonte au XIXe siècle; **to grow from small ~s** [*company*] s'agrandir après des débuts modestes; **2** (start) **the ~s of** le début de [*solution, trend*].

begone /bɪˈgɒn, US -ˈgɔːn/ *excl*‡ hors d'ici!

begonia /bɪˈgəʊnɪə/ *n* bégonia *m*.

begot /bɪˈgɒt/ *prét* ▶ **beget**.

begotten /bɪˈgɒtn/ *pp* ▶ **beget**.

begrimed /bɪˈgraɪmd/ *adj* noirci, crasseux/-euse.

begrudge /bɪˈgrʌdʒ/ *vtr* = **grudge** II.

beguile /bɪˈgaɪl/ *vtr* **1** (entice, trick) leurrer; **to be ~d** se laisser leurrer (**with** par); **he ~d her into doing** il l'a si bien enjôlée qu'elle a fait; **2** (charm) captiver; **3** (pass pleasantly) **to ~ the time** faire passer le temps.

beguiling /bɪˈgaɪlɪŋ/ *adj* captivant.

begum /ˈbeɪgəm/ *n* bégum *f*.

begun /bɪˈgʌn/ *pp* ▶ **begin**.

behalf /bɪˈhɑːf, US -ˈhæf/: **on ~ of** GB, **in ~ of** US *prep phr* **1** (as representative of) [*act, speak, sign, accept award etc*] au nom de, pour; [*phone, write, convey message, come*] de la part de; **2** (in the interest of) [*campaign, plead*] en faveur de, pour; [*negotiate*] pour le compte de; **don't be uneasy on my ~** ne vous inquiétez pas pour moi or à mon sujet.

behave /bɪˈheɪv/ **I** *vi* **1** (act) [*person, group, animal*] (naturally, characteristically) se comporter (**towards** envers); (in given circumstances) se conduire (**towards** avec, envers); **he's behaving like an idiot** il se conduit comme un idiot; **he ~s like a tyrant** il se comporte en tyran; **you didn't have to ~ like that!** tu n'avais pas à te conduire comme ça!; **what a way to ~!** quelle façon de se conduire!; **the supporters ~d well/badly** les supporters se sont bien/mal conduits; **he ~d badly towards her** il s'est mal conduit envers elle; **2** (function) [*machine, device, substance, system*] se comporter.

II *v refl* **to ~ oneself** [*person*] bien se comporter; **~ yourself!** tiens-toi bien!; **is the computer behaving itself?** hum est-ce que l'ordinateur marche?

behaviour GB, **behavior** US /bɪˈheɪvjə(r)/ **I** *n* **1** (of person, group, animal) gen comportement *m* (**towards** envers); (in given set of circumstances) conduite *f*; **antisocial/disruptive/model ~** comportement anti-social/perturbateur/modèle; **for good/bad ~** pour bonne/mauvaise conduite; **2** (of substance, chemical) comportement *m*; **3** (of device, machine) fonctionnement *m*.

II *modif* [*disorder, patterns*] de comportement.

IDIOMS **to be on one's best ~** bien se tenir; **try to be on your best ~** tâchez de bien vous conduire.

behavioural GB, **behavioral** US /bɪˈheɪvjərəl/ *adj* [*change, disorder, problem*] de comportement; [*theory*] du comportement.

behavioural science *n* science *f* du comportement.

behaviourism GB, **behaviorism** US /bɪˈheɪvjərɪzəm/ *n* behaviorisme *m*.

behaviourist GB, **behaviorist** US /bɪˈheɪvjərɪst/ *n, adj* behavioriste (*mf*).

behaviour therapy *n* thérapie *f* de comportement, comportementalisme *m* spec.

behead /bɪˈhed/ *vtr* décapiter.

beheld /bɪˈheld/ *pret, pp* ▶ **behold**.

behemoth /bɪˈhiːmɒθ/ *n* **1** (beast) béhémoth *m*; **2** fig (person) hippopotame *m*; (building, institution) mastodonte *m*.

behest /bɪˈhest/ *n* sout **at the ~ of sb** sur l'ordre de qn.

behind /bɪˈhaɪnd/

■ **Note** When used as a preposition to talk about the physical position of something, *behind* is translated by *derrière*: *behind the house* = derrière la maison.

– *behind* is sometimes used in verb combinations (*fall behind, lag behind etc*). For translations, consult the appropriate verb entry (***fall***, ***lag*** etc).

– For adverbial uses and figurative prepositional uses see the entry below.

I○ *n* derrière○ *m*.

II *adj* **to be ~ with** avoir du retard dans [*studies, work*]; **to be too far ~** avoir trop de retard; **to be ~ in one's research** être en retard dans ses recherches; **to be a long way ~** être franchement en retard; **I'm ~ with my rent** je n'ai pas payé mon loyer.

III *adv* [*follow on, trail*] derrière; [*look, glance*] en arrière; **the car ~** la voiture de derrière.

IV *prep* **1** (at rear of) (physically) derrière [*person, vehicle, object*]; **the mountains ~ the town** les montagnes qui se trouvent/trouvaient derrière la ville; **~ my back** lit derrière le dos; fig derrière mon dos; **2** (at other side of) derrière [*desk, counter, barrier, line*]; **to work ~ the bar** être barman/barmaid *m/f*; **3** fig (concealed) **~ the smile** derrière son sourire; **the reality ~ the façade** la réalité derrière les apparences; **the real story ~ the news** la véritable histoire que les médias n'ont pas révélée; **4** fig (less advanced than) **to be ~ the others** [*pupil*] être en retard par rapport aux autres; **5** fig (motivating) **the reasons ~ his declaration** les raisons qui motivent/motivaient etc sa déclaration; **what is ~ his actions?** qu'est-ce qui le pousse à agir ainsi?; **who is ~ this proposal?** qui est à l'origine de cette proposition?; **6** fig (supporting) **to be (solidly) ~ sb** soutenir qn (à fond); **he has no family ~ him** il n'a pas de famille pour le soutenir; **the woman ~ the man** journ la femme en coulisses; **7** fig (in past) **he has three years' experience ~ him** il a trois ans d'expérience derrière lui; **those days are ~ me now** cette période est bien loin; **I've put all that ~ me now** j'ai oublié tout ça.

behindhand /bɪˈhaɪndhænd/ *adv* **to be** ou **get ~ with** être en retard dans [*work, studies*].

behind-the-scenes I *adj* en coulisses.
II behind the scenes *adv* en coulisses.

behold /bɪˈhəʊld/ *vtr* (*prét, pp* **beheld**) littér ou hum voir; **it was a wonder to ~** c'était un spectacle merveilleux; ▶ **lo**.

beholden /bɪˈhəʊldən/ *adj* sout **to be ~ to sb** être redevable à qn (**for** de).

beholder /bɪˈhəʊldə(r)/ *n* spectateur/-trice *m/f*.

IDIOMS **beauty is in the eye of the ~** Prov ≈ ce qu'on aime est toujours beau Prov.

behove GB /bɪˈhəʊv/, **behoove** /bɪˈhuːv/ US *v impers* sout **it ~s sb to do sth** (as duty) il incombe or appartient à qn de faire qch; (for advantage) il est de l'intérêt de qn de faire qch; **it ill ~s her to...** c'est mal venu de sa part de...

beige /beɪʒ/ ▶ **1104** *n, adj* beige (*m*).

Beijing /beɪˈdʒɪŋ/ ▶ **1818** *pr n* Pékin, Beijing.

being /ˈbiːɪŋ/ *n* **1** (entity) (human) être *m*; (animal) créature *f*; **2** (soul) être *m*; **with my whole ~** de tout mon être; **3** (existence) **to bring sth into ~** faire de qch une réalité; **to be brought into ~** devenir réalité; **to come into ~** prendre naissance.

Beirut /ˈbeɪruːt, ˌbeɪˈruːt/ ▶ **1818** *pr n* Beyrouth.

bejabbers○ /bɪˈdʒæbəz/, **bejesus**○ /bɪˈdʒiːzəs/ **I** *n* **to scare the ~ out of sb** flanquer○ la trouille○ à qn.
II *excl* bon Dieu○!

bejewelled GB, **bejeweled** US /bɪˈdʒuːəld/ *adj* [*person, hand, dress*] paré de bijoux; [*object*] incrusté de joyaux.

belabour GB, **belabor** US /bɪˈleɪbə(r)/ *vtr* **1** (attack) (physically) rouer [qn] de coups; (verbally) accabler [qn] d'injures; **2** US pej insister sur [*point, issue*].

Belarus /ˌbjeləʊˈrus/ ▶ **1131** *pr n* ▶ **Byelorussia**.

belated /bɪˈleɪtɪd/ *adj* tardif/-ive.
belatedly /bɪˈleɪtɪdlɪ/ *adv* tardivement.
belay /bɪˈleɪ/ **I** *n* (in climbing) assurage *m*, assurance *f*.
II *vtr* **1** Naut amarrer; **2** (in climbing) assurer.
III *vi* **1** Naut [*rope*] être amarré; **2** (in climbing) assurer.
belaying pin *n* Naut cabillot *m* (d'amarrage).
belch /beltʃ/ **I** *n* renvoi *m*, rot *m*.
II *vi* roter○, avoir un renvoi; fig [*smoke, flames*] s'échapper.
III *vtr* = **belch out**.
■ **belch out**: ¶ **~ out** s'échapper; ¶ **~ [sth] out, ~ out [sth]** vomir, cracher [*smoke, flames*].
beleaguered /bɪˈliːɡəd/ *adj* **1** [*city, troops*] assiégé; **2** fig [*person*] débordé; [*company, programme*] menacé.
Belfast /ˌbelˈfɑːst/ ▶**1818** *pr n* Belfast.
belfry /ˈbelfrɪ/ *n* beffroi *m*, clocher *m*.
IDIOMS **to have bats in the ~**○ avoir une araignée au plafond○.
Belgian /ˈbeldʒən/ ▶**1486** **I** *n* Belge *mf*.
II *adj* [*custom, town, people etc*] belge; [*embassy, ambassador*] de Belgique.
Belgium /ˈbeldʒəm/ ▶**1131** *pr n* Belgique *f*.
Belgrade /ˌbelˈɡreɪd/ ▶**1818** *pr n* Belgrade.
belie /bɪˈlaɪ/ *vtr* **1** (show to be false) contredire [*hopes, promises, predictions*]; **his smile ~d his despair** son sourire dissimulait son désespoir; **2** (disguise) tromper sur [*appearances, feelings, facts*].
belief /bɪˈliːf/ *n* **1** (conviction, opinion) conviction *f* (**about** sur, à propos de); **political/religious ~s** convictions politiques/religieuses; **to go against sb's ~s** aller à l'encontre des convictions de qn; **in the ~ that** convaincu or persuadé que; **it's my ~ that** je suis convaincu or persuadé que; **to the best of my ~** à ma connaissance; **contrary to popular ~** contrairement à ce qu'on pense généralement; **2** (credence) **to be beyond** ou **past ~** être absolument incroyable; **wealthy/stupid beyond ~** incroyablement riche/bête; **3** (confidence, trust) confiance *f*, foi *f*; **her ~ in democracy/justice** sa foi or confiance dans la démocratie/la justice; **~ in oneself** confiance en soi; **4** Relig (faith) foi *f*; (article of faith) croyance *f*; **his ~ in God/evil** sa croyance en Dieu/dans le mal.
believable /bɪˈliːvəbl/ *adj* (conceivable) croyable; (plausible, realistic) [*character, explanation*] crédible.
believe /bɪˈliːv/ **I** *vtr* **1** (accept as true) croire [*evidence, statement, fact, person*]; **~ (you) me!** croyez-moi! **~ it or not** croyez-le ou pas; **would you ~ it?** le croiriez-vous?; **I'll ~ it when I see it** je le croirai quand je le verrai; **it has to be seen to be ~d** il faut le voir pour le croire; **I can't ~ (that) he did that** je n'arrive pas à croire qu'il ait fait cela; **I can ~ that of her!** ça ne m'étonne pas d'elle!; **don't you ~ it!** n'en croyez rien!; **I don't ~ you!** ce n'est pas vrai!; **I can well ~ it** je suis prêt à le croire; **I don't ~ a word of it!** je n'en crois pas un mot!; **if he's to be ~d** à l'en croire; **I'll ~ you, thousands wouldn't** je te crois, mais je dois bien être le seul; **I can't ~ my luck!** je n'arrive pas à le croire!; **she could hardly** ou **scarcely ~ her eyes** elle en croyait à peine ses yeux; **2** (think, be of the opinion) croire, estimer; **I ~ (that) she is right, I ~ her to be right** je crois or j'estime qu'elle a raison; **Mr Smith, I ~?** M. Smith, je crois?; **it is ~d that** on croit or estime que; **he is ~d to be dead** on le croit mort; **she is ~d to be a spy** on pense que c'est une espionne; **to ~ sth to be true/false** croire or estimer que qch est vrai/faux; **to have reason to ~ that** avoir des raisons de croire que; **I have every reason to ~ that** j'ai toutes les raisons de croire que; **to let sb ~ (that)** laisser croire à qn que; **to lead sb to ~ (that)** faire croire à qn que; **to give sb to ~ (that)** donner à qn des raisons de croire que; **I ~ so** je crois que oui; **I ~ not** je crois que non.
II *vi* **1** (have confidence, trust) **to ~ in** croire à; [*promises, discipline, exercise etc*]; **to ~ in sb** avoir confiance en qn; **to ~ in doing** croire or estimer qu'il est bon de faire; **I ~ in taking a cold shower every morning** je crois qu'il est bon de prendre une douche froide tous les matins; **to fight for what one ~s in** lutter pour ce en quoi on croit or pour ses convictions; **you have to ~ in what you do** il faut croire à or avoir foi dans ce qu'on fait; **2** Relig avoir la foi; **to ~ in God/reincarnation** croire en Dieu/à la réincarnation; **to ~ in ghosts** croire aux fantômes.
III *v refl* **to ~ oneself to be** se croire; **he ~s himself to be really clever** il se croit vraiment intelligent.
IDIOMS **seeing is believing** il faut le voir pour le croire.
believer /bɪˈliːvə(r)/ *n* Relig croyant/-e *m/f*; gen (in hard work, progress, liberty) adepte *mf* (**in** de); **to be a ~ in doing** croire or estimer qu'il est bon de faire; **she's not a ~ in ghosts/miracles** elle ne croit pas aux fantômes/miracles; **he's a great ~ in exercise** il croit aux vertus de l'exercice.
Belisha beacon /bəˌliːʃə ˈbiːkən/ *n* GB lumière *f* clignotante (*pour signaler un passage clouté*).
belittle /bɪˈlɪtl/ *vtr* rabaisser [*person, achievement, action*]; déprécier [*efforts*]; **to feel ~d** se sentir déprécié.
belittling /bɪˈlɪtlɪŋ/ *adj* [*comment*] désobligeant.
Belize /beˈliːz/ ▶**1131** *pr n* Bélize *m*.
Belizean /beˈliːzɪən/ ▶**1486** **I** *n* Bélizien/-ienne *m/f*.
II *adj* bélizien/-ienne.
bell /bel/ **I** *n* **1** (chiming) (in church) cloche *f*; (on sheep, goat) clochette *f*; (on toy, cat) grelot *m*; (on bicycle) sonnette *f*; (for servant) clochette *f*; **to ring the ~s** faire sonner les cloches; **2** (buzzer) sonnette *f*; **door ~** sonnette *f*; **to ring the ~** appuyer sur la sonnette; **I can hear the ~** j'entends sonner; **3** (warning device) sonnerie *f*; **4**○ GB (phone call) **to give sb a ~** passer un coup *m* de fil à qn; **5** Bot clochette *f*; **6** Naut coup *m* de cloche; **eight ~s** huits coups piqués; **to ring eight ~s** piquer huit coups; **7** (of stag, hound) bramement *m*; **8** Mus pavillon *m*; **9** Sport gong *m*.
II *vtr* attacher une clochette à [*goat, sheep*].
IDIOMS **that name/number rings a ~** ce nom/numéro me dit quelque chose; **with ~, book and candle** par tous les moyens; **to be as sound as a ~** être en parfaite santé; **to be saved by the ~** être sauvé par le gong; **to ~ the cat** se lancer dans une mission dangereuse.
belladonna /ˌbeləˈdɒnə/ *n* **1** Bot belladone *f*; **2** Med (atropine) atropine *f*; (hyoscyamine) hyoscyamine *f*.
bell: **~-bottomed** *adj* à pattes *fpl* d'éléphant; **~-bottoms** *npl* pantalon *m* à pattes d'éléphant; **~boy** ▶**1692** *n* US groom *m*, chasseur *m*; **~ buoy** *n* bouée *f* à cloche; **~ captain** ▶**1692** *n* US *responsable d'un groupe de grooms*.
belle /bel/ *n* belle *f*, beauté *f*; **the ~ of the ball** la reine du bal.
bell: **~ glass** *n* cloche *f* en verre; **~ heather** *n* bruyère *f* cendrée; **~hop** ▶**1692** *n* US groom *m*, chasseur *m*.
bellicose /ˈbelɪkəʊs/ *adj* sout belliqueux/-euse.
bellicosity /ˌbelɪˈkɒsətɪ/ *n* caractère *m* belliqueux, agressivité *f*.
belligerence /bɪˈlɪdʒərəns/ *n* gen agressivité *f*; Pol belligérance *f*.
belligerency /bɪˈlɪdʒərənsɪ/ *n* belligérance *f*.
belligerent /bɪˈlɪdʒərənt/ **I** *n* Pol (country) belligérant *m*.
II *adj* **1** gen agressif/-ive; **2** Pol (at war) belligérant.
bell jar *n* cloche *f* en verre.
bellow /ˈbeləʊ/ **I** *n* (of bull) mugissement *m*; (of person) hurlement *m*, beuglement○ *m*.
II *vi* [*bull*] mugir (**with** de); [*person*] hurler, beugler○ (**with** de).
III *vtr* brailler [*command*].
■ **bellow out**: **~ out [sth]** brailler [*command, song*].
bellows /ˈbeləʊz/ *npl* (for fire, in forge) soufflet *m*; (of organ) soufflerie *f*; Phot soufflet *m*; **a pair** ou **set of ~** un soufflet.
bell: **~ pepper** *n* US poivron *m*; **~-pull** *n* (handle) poignée *f* de sonnette; (rope) cordon *m* de sonnette; **~-push** *n* bouton *m* de sonnette; **~-ringer** *n* carillonneur *m*, sonneur *m*.
bell-ringing *n* **to go ~** aller carillonner.
bell: **~ rope** *n* (in church) corde *f* de cloche; (in house) cordon *m* de sonnette; **~-shaped** *adj* en forme de cloche; **Bell's palsy** ▶**1354** *n* paralysie *f* faciale; **~ tent** *n* tente *f* conique; **~ tower** *n* clocher *m*; **~wether** *n* (mouton *m*) meneur *m* du troupeau; fig chef *m* de file.
belly /ˈbelɪ/ *n* **1**○ (stomach) ventre *m*; (paunch) bedaine○ *f*; **2** (of animal) ventre *m*; **3** (abdomen) ventre *m*; **4** (curved part) (of ship, plane) ventre *m*; (of violin, cello) table *f* (d'harmonie); (of jar, vase) renflement *m*; (of sail) creux *m*; **5 ~ of pork** poitrine *f* de porc; **6**‡ (womb) entrailles *fpl*.
IDIOMS **to go ~ up**○ [*fish*] mourir; [*business*] faire faillite.
■ **belly out**: **~ out** [*sail*] se gonfler; **~ [sth] out** gonfler.
■ **belly up to**○ s'approcher tout contre.
bellyache○ /ˈbelɪeɪk/ **I** *n* **1** lit mal *m* au ventre; **to have a ~** avoir mal au ventre; **2**○ fig râlerie○ *f*.
II *vi* (*p prés* **-aching**) râler○ (**about** contre).
bellyaching○ /ˈbelɪeɪkɪŋ/ *n* râlerie○ *f*; **stop your ~!** arrête de râler○!
belly: **~band** *n* sous-ventrière *f*; **~button**○ *n* nombril *m*; **~ dance** *n* danse *f* du ventre; **~ dancer** *n* danseuse *f* du ventre; **~ flop**○ *n* (in swimming) plat *m*.
bellyful○ /ˈbelɪfʊl/ *n*: IDIOMS **to have a ~ of sth** en avoir sa claque○ de qch.
belly landing *n* atterrissage *m* sur le ventre; **to make a ~** atterrir sur le ventre.
belly: **~ laugh** *n* gros rire *m*; **~ tank** *n* réservoir *m* ventral.
belong /bɪˈlɒŋ, US -lɔːŋ/ *vi* **1** (be the property of) **to ~ to** appartenir à; **don't take what doesn't ~ to you** ne prends pas ce qui ne t'appartient pas or qui n'est pas à toi; **we ~ to each other** nous appartenons l'un à l'autre; **2** (be member of) **to ~ to** appartenir à [*family, generation, party, union*]; faire partie de [*club, society, gang, set*]; être inscrit à [*library*]; **3** (have its proper place) aller; **where do these books ~?** où vont ces livres?; **it doesn't ~ on this shelf** cela ne va pas sur cette étagère; **put it back where it ~s** remets-le à sa place; **4** (fit in) [*person*] être à sa place; **you don't ~ here** tu n'es pas à ta place ici; **everybody wants to ~** tout le monde veut avoir sa place quelque part; **I don't feel I ~ anywhere** j'ai l'impression de n'être nulle part à ma place; **to give immigrants a sense of ~ing** donner aux immigrés le sentiment de faire partie du pays; **we ~ together** nous sommes faits pour être ensemble; **5** Jur **it ~s to sb to do** il appartient à qn de faire.
belongings /bɪˈlɒŋɪŋz, US -ˈlɔːŋ-/ *npl* affaires *fpl*; **personal ~** effets *mpl* personnels.
beloved /bɪˈlʌvɪd/ **I** *n* littér ou hum bien-aimé/-e *m/f*.
II *adj* bien-aimé.
below /bɪˈləʊ/

■ **Note** When *below* is used as a preposition to talk about the physical position of something, it is most often translated by *au-dessous de*: *the*

apartment below mine = l'appartement au-dessous du mien; *below the knee* = au-dessous du genou.
– The most notable exceptions are for the expressions *below the ground* and *below the surface*, when *sous* is used: sous le sol, sous la surface.
– For other prepositional uses of *below* and for adverbial uses see the entry below.

I *prep* **1** (under) en-dessous de; **the apartment ~ mine** l'appartement au-dessous du mien; **~ the knee/the waist** au-dessous du genou/de la taille; **~ the surface** sous la surface; **~ (the) ground** sous le sol; **one kilometre ~ the surface** à un kilomètre de profondeur; **~ sea level** au-dessous du niveau de la mer; **his name was ~ mine on the list** son nom était au-dessous du or sous le mien sur la liste; **in the field ~ the castle** dans le champ en contrebas du château; **the valley/river ~ them/you etc** la vallée/rivière en contrebas; **2** (less than: in quantity, degree etc) en-dessous de, inférieur à; **~ the average/10%** en-dessous de or inférieur à la moyenne/10%; **~ the age of 12** en-dessous de 12 ans; **10° ~ (freezing)** 10° en-dessous de zéro; **~ target/expectations/inflation** inférieur aux objectifs/aux prévisions/à l'inflation; **his performance was ~ his usual standard** sa prestation était bien moins bonne que d'habitude; **your behaviour was (well) ~ the standard expected of a manager** ta conduite n'était pas (du tout) à la hauteur du poste de directeur; **3** (inferior in rank to) **the people ~ him in the department** les gens du service au-dessous de lui; **those ~ the rank of Major** Mil les militaires qui sont au-dessous du grade de major; **a lieutenant is ~ a captain** lieutenant est un grade inférieur à capitaine; **those employees ~ management level** les employés qui ne font pas partie de la direction; **the teams ~ them in the table** (Sport etc) les équipes moins bien classées qu'eux; **4** (south of) au sud de, au-dessous de; **~ Liverpool/London** au sud de Liverpool/de Londres; **5** (downstream from) en aval de; **6** (unworthy of) ▶ **beneath I 2**.
II *adv* **1** (lower down) **100 metres ~** 100 mètres plus bas; **the village/the river ~** le village/la rivière en contrebas; **the people/cars (down) ~** les gens/voitures en bas; **the apartment ~** l'appartement d'en-dessous; **seen from ~** vu d'en bas; **the miners working ~** les mineurs qui travaillent sous terre; **2** (later on page, in book etc) ci-dessous; **see ~** voir ci-dessous; **the information ~** les données ci-dessous; **3** (not in heaven) **here ~** (on earth) ici-bas; **down ~** (in hell) en enfer.

below stairs *adv* dans l'office (*des domestiques*).

belt /belt/ **I** *n* **1** Fashn ceinture *f*; **he had a gun in his ~** il avait un pistolet à la ceinture; **2** Aut, Aviat ceinture *f*; **safety** ou **seat ~** ceinture de sécurité; **3** (area) ceinture *f*; **a ~ of industry** une ceinture industrielle; **a ~ of poverty around the inner city** une zone de pauvreté autour du centre urbain; **a ~ of trees** une rangée d'arbres; **mountain/earthquake ~** zone *f* de montagnes/de séisme; **4** Meteorol zone *f*; **a ~ of rain/of low pressure** une zone de pluie/de basse pression; **5** Tech courroie *f*; **6** Sport (in boxing, judo) ceinture *f*; **to be a black ~** être ceinture noire; **the world heavyweight ~** le titre mondial des poids lourds; **7**○ (blow) beigne○ *f*, coup *m* de poing; **to give sb a ~** flanquer une beigne○ à qn; **I gave the ball a good ~** j'ai donné un grand coup de pied dans le ballon; **8** Sch (for punishing) lanière *f* de cuir.
II○ *vtr* **1**○ (hit) flanquer une beigne à○, gifler [*person*]; donner un grand coup de pied dans [*ball*]; **he ~ed him in the mouth/across the face** il lui a flanqué une beigne en plein sur la bouche/la figure; **2** Sch (as punishment) donner une correction à [qn] (*avec une lanière de cuir*); **3**○ = **belt down**.
III *vi* (go fast) **he ~ed home** il est rentré chez lui à toute vitesse; **to ~ along** ou **down** [*person*] dévaler [qch] à toute vitesse [*street*]; [*car*] filer sur [*motorway*].
IV belted *pp adj* [*coat*] avec (une) ceinture.
IDIOMS **to tighten one's ~** se serrer la ceinture; **to hit sb below the ~** donner un coup bas à qn; **that remark was a bit below the ~** cette remarque était un coup bas; **she has 15 years' experience/two tournaments under her ~** elle a 15 ans d'expérience/deux tournois à son actif; **a ~ and braces job**○ un boulot○ où deux précautions valent mieux qu'une.
■ **belt down**○: **~ down [sth], ~ [sth] down** US avaler [qch] d'un trait [*drink*].
■ **belt off**○ filer à toute vitesse.
■ **belt out**: **~ out [sth], ~ [sth] out** [*person*] chanter [qch] à pleins poumons; [*jukebox*] brailler.
■ **belt up 1** GB○(shut up) la fermer○, se taire; **~ up!** ferme-la!○; **2** Aut attacher sa ceinture de sécurité.

beltway /'beltweɪ/ *n* US Aut périphérique *m*.

belvedere /'belvɪdɪə(r)/ *n* belvédère *m*.

bemoan /bɪ'məʊn/ *vtr* sout déplorer.

bemuse /bɪ'mju:z/ *vtr* rendre [qn] perplexe.

bemused /bɪ'mju:zd/ *adj* perplexe.

ben /ben/ *n* Scot mont *m*; **Ben Nevis** Ben Nevis *m*.

bench /bentʃ/ *n* **1** gen, Sport (seat) banc *m*; **to be on the (substitute's) ~** être sur la touche; **2** GB Pol banc *m*; **to be on the opposition ~es** siéger dans l'opposition; **3** Jur (also **Bench**) (judges collectively) magistrature *f* (assise); **~ and bar** la magistrature et le barreau; **to be** ou **sit on the ~** être membre de la magistrature (assise); **4** Jur (also **Bench**) (judge or judges in one case) Cour *f*; **to thank the ~** remercier la Cour; **to approach the ~** venir à la barre; **to be on the ~ for a case** juger une affaire; **5** Tech (workbench) établi *m*; (in lab) paillasse *f*.

bencher /'bentʃə(r)/ *n* Jur (also **Bencher**) *membre établi de la magistrature britannique*.

bench lathe *n* tour *m* à banc.

benchmark /'bentʃmɑ:k/ **I** *n* **1** gen, Civ Eng point *m* de référence; **2** Fin (price) prix *m* de référence; **3** Comput test *m* de performance.
II *vtr* (compare, test) tester [*systems*].

benchmark job *n* poste-repère *m*.

bench: **~ press** *n* développé *m* couché; **~ seat** *n* banquette *f*; **~ test** *n* test *m* préliminaire; **~ warmer**○ *n* US Sport habitué/-e *m/f* de la touche; **~ warrant** *n* mandat *m* d'arrêt.

bend /bend/ **I** *n* **1** gen (in road) tournant *m*, virage *m*; (in racetrack) tournant *m*; (in pipe) coude *m*; (in river) courbe *f*; (of elbow, knee) pli *m*; **at the ~ of the road** au tournant or virage de la route; **on the ~** dans le tournant; **there's a ~ in the road** la route fait un virage; **to come around a ~** prendre un virage; **2** Naut (knot) nœud *m* de jonction.
II bends ▶ **1354** *npl* Med (+ *v sg ou pl*) maladie *f* des caissons.
III *vtr* (*prét, pp* **bent**) **1** (force into a curve) plier [*knee, arm, leg*]; courber, pencher [*head*]; pencher, plier [*body*]; courber [*back*]; faire un coude à [*pipe, bar*]; plier [*wire*]; réfracter [*light*]; infléchir [*ray*]; (by mistake) tordre [*pipe, mudguard, nail*]; **to ~ one's arm** plier le bras; **to go down on ~ed knee** se mettre à genoux; **to ~ sb to one's will** fig plier qn à sa volonté; **2** (distort) travestir [*truth, facts*]; faire une entorse à [*principle*]; **to ~ the rules** contourner le règlement; **3** (direct) **to ~ one's mind/attention to** concentrer son esprit/attention sur; **to ~ one's steps towards** littér se diriger vers.
IV *vi* (*prét, pp* **bent**) **1** (become curved) [*road, path*] tourner; [*river*] (once) s'incurver; (several times) faire des méandres; [*frame, bar*] plier; [*branch*] ployer; [*nail, mudguard*] se tordre; **my arm won't ~** je ne peux pas plier le bras; **2** (stoop) [*person*] se courber, se pencher; **to ~ forward/backwards** se pencher en avant/en arrière; **to ~ low** se courber jusqu'à terre; **to ~ double** se plier en deux; **his head was bent over a book** il était penché sur un livre; **3** (submit) **to ~ to** se plier à [*person, will*].
IDIOMS **round** GB ou **around** US **the ~**○ fou/folle; **to go (a)round the ~** devenir fou/folle; **to drive sb (a)round the ~** rendre qn fou/folle; **to ~ over backwards for sb/to do** se mettre en quatre○ pour qn/pour faire.
■ **bend back**: ¶ **~ back** [*person*] se pencher à l'arrière; **to ~ back on itself** [*road, river*] faire demi-tour; ¶ **~ [sth] back, ~ back [sth]** (to original position) redresser [*book, pin*]; (away from natural position) replier [qch] (en arrière) [*book, pin*]; **to ~ one's fingers back** plier les doigts (en arrière); **to ~ sth back into shape** redresser qch.
■ **bend down**: ¶ **~ down** [*person*] se pencher, se courber; ¶ **~ [sth] down, ~ down [sth]** faire ployer [*branch*]; replier [qch] en arrière [*flap*].
■ **bend over**: ¶ **~ over** [*person*] se pencher, se courber; ¶ **~ [sth] over, ~ over [sth]** replier.

bender /'bendə(r)/ *n* **1**○ (drinking bout) **to go on a ~** prendre une cuite○; **2** GB (shelter) abri *m* de fortune.

bend sinister *n* Herald barre *f* de bâtardise.

beneath /bɪ'ni:θ/

■ **Note** When used as a preposition (= under), *beneath* is translated by *au-dessous de*: *beneath his feet* = au-dessous de ses pieds. When used as an adverb (the trees beneath), *beneath* is translated by *en dessous*: *the trees beneath* = les arbres en dessous. For particular and figurative usages see below.

I *prep* **1** (under) sous; **~ the table** sous la table; **the valley/river ~ them/you etc** la vallée/rivière en contrebas; fig **he hid his disappointment ~ a polite smile** il a masqué sa déception derrière un sourire poli; **~ the calm exterior he...** sous ses apparences calmes, il...; **2** (unworthy of) indigne de [*person*]; **it is ~ her/you etc to do** c'est indigne d'elle/de toi etc de faire; ▶ **dignity**.
II *adv* en dessous; **the apartment/the people/the cars/the trees ~** l'appartement/les gens/les voitures/les arbres en dessous; **the valley/river ~** la vallée/rivière en contrebas.

Benedict /'benɪdɪkt/ *pr n* Benoît.

Benedictine I *n* **1** /ˌbenɪ'dɪktɪn/ Relig bénédictin/-e *m/f*; **2** /ˌbenɪ'dɪkti:n/ (liqueur) Bénédictine *f*.
II /ˌbenɪ'dɪktɪn/ *adj* bénédictin.

benediction /ˌbenɪ'dɪkʃn/ *n* **1** (blessing) Relig, fig bénédiction *f*; **in ~** en signe de bénédiction; **2** (Catholic ceremony) bénédiction *f*, salut *m*.

benefaction /ˌbenɪ'fækʃn/ *n* sout (generosity) bonté *f*; (donation) don *m*.

benefactor /'benɪfæktə(r)/ *n* bienfaiteur *m*.

benefactress /'benɪfæktrɪs/ *n* bienfaitrice *f*.

benefice /'benɪfɪs/ *n* bénéfice *m*.

beneficence /bɪ'nefɪsns/ *n* **1** ¢ (kindness) bienveillance *f*; **2** (charitable help) générosité *f*.

beneficent /bɪ'nefɪsnt/ *adj* **1** (kindly) [*concern, regime, rule*] bienveillant; **2** (generous) [*assistance, patron*] généreux/-euse; [*work*] de bienfaisance.

beneficial /ˌbenɪ'fɪʃl/ *adj* **1** (advantageous) [*effect, influence*] bénéfique; [*treatment*] efficace; [*change*] salutaire; [*outcome, result*] favorable; **to be ~ to** être bénéfique pour; **to be ~ for** être avantageux/-euse pour; **2** Jur [*interest*] d'usufruit; [*owner, use*] usufruitier/-ière.

beneficially /ˌbenɪˈfɪʃəlɪ/ *adv* [*influence*] favorablement.

beneficiary /ˌbenɪˈfɪʃərɪ, US -fɪʃɪerɪ/ *n* **1** Jur bénéficiaire *mf*; **to be the only ~ of a will** être le seul/la seule bénéficiaire testamentaire; **2** (recipient) bénéficiaire *mf*; **3** Relig bénéficier *m*.

benefit /ˈbenɪfɪt/ **I** *n* **1** ¢ (helpful effect) avantage *m* (**from** de); **to be of ~ to** profiter à [*patient, environment, industry*]; **to feel the ~ of** ressentir l'effet *m* favorable de [*change, holiday, treatment*]; **to get some ~ from** tirer profit de [*holiday, treatment*]; **to give sb the ~ of** faire profiter qn de [*experience, knowledge*]; **to give sb the ~ of one's advice** donner un bon conseil à qn; **2** Soc Admin allocation *f*; **to be on ~(s)** GB toucher les allocations; **to live off ~(s)** GB vivre sur les allocations; **3** C (advantage) avantage *m*; **the ~s of modern technology** les avantages de la technologie moderne; **to have health ~s** offrir des avantages sanitaires; **to have the ~ of** bénéficier de [*education*]; **with the ~ of hindsight** avec l'avantage du recul; **with the ~ of experience** avec le bénéfice de l'expérience; **to be to sb's ~** être à l'avantage de qn; **to reap the ~s of** récolter les bénéfices de; **4** ¢ (good) **it's for your own ~** c'est pour ton propre bien; **for the ~ of the newcomers** à l'intention des nouveaux; **he's just crying for your ~** il pleure juste pour attirer ton attention; **5** (perk) avantage *m*; **'salary £20,000 plus ~s'** 'salaire de 20 000 livres sterling plus avantages sociaux'; **~s in kind** avantages *mpl* en nature; **tax-free ~s** bénéfices *mpl* nonimposables.
II *modif* [*concert, gig, match*] de bienfaisance; [*claim*] d'allocation; [*office*] des allocations.
III *vtr* (*p prés etc* **-t-**) profiter à [*person*]; être avantageux/-euse pour [*group, nation*]; être utile à [*economy, industry*]; être bon/bonne pour [*health*]; **to do sth to ~ sb** faire qch au bénéfice de qn.
IV *vi* (*p prés etc* **-t-**) profiter; **I will ~ the most** j'en profiterai le plus; **to ~ from** ou **by** tirer profit ou profiter de; **to ~ from** ou **by doing** gagner à faire.
IDIOMS **to give sb the ~ of the doubt** accorder le bénéfice du doute à qn.

benefit: **~ association**, **~ club** *n* US société *f* de secours mutuel; **~ payment** *n* allocation *f*, prestation *f*; **~s package** *n* Mgmt avantages *mpl*.

Benelux /ˈbenɪlʌks/ **I** *n* Bénélux *m*.
II *modif* [*countries, organization*] du Bénélux.

benevolence /bɪˈnevələns/ *n* **1** (kindness) bienveillance *f*; (generosity) générosité *f*; **2** (kind deed) bienfait *m*; (gift) don *m*; **3** Hist prêt *m* obligatoire (*au roi*).

benevolent /bɪˈnevələnt/ *adj* **1** [*person, smile, gesture*] bienveillant (**to, towards** envers); [*dictator, government*] éclairé; **2** (charitable) [*organization, trust, fund*] de bienfaisance.

benevolently /bɪˈnevələntlɪ/ *adv* avec bienveillance.

BEng *n* (*abrév* = **Bachelor of Engineering**) diplôme *m* universitaire d'ingéniérie.

Bengal /beŋˈgɔːl/ *pr n* Bengale *m*.

Bengali /beŋˈgɔːlɪ/ **▶ 1486**, **1402** **I** *n* **1** (person) Bengali/-e *m/f*; **2** Ling bengali *m*, bengalais *m*.
II *adj* **1** [*custom, food, people*] bengalais; **2** Ling bengali.

Bengal: **~ light** *n* feu *m* de Bengale; **~ tiger** *n* tigre *m* du Bengale.

benighted /bɪˈnaɪtɪd/ *adj* littér arriéré, primitif/-ive.

benign /bɪˈnaɪn/ *adj* **1** gen [*person, smile, gesture*] bienveillant; [*climate*] doux/douce; [*conditions, circumstances*] propice; [*influence, effect*] bénéfique; **2** Med bénin/-igne.

Benin /beˈniːn/ **▶ 1131** *pr n* Bénin *m*.

Beninese /ˌbenɪˈniːz/ **▶ 1486** **I** *npl* Béninois *mpl*.
II *adj* béninois, du Bénin.

benison‡ /ˈbenɪzn/ *n* bénédiction *f*.

benny○ /ˈbenɪ/ *n* argot des drogués stimulant comprimé *m* de benzédrine.

bent /bent/ **I** *pret, pp* ▶ **bend**.
II *n* **1** (flair) dispositions *fpl* (**for** pour); (liking) goût *m*, penchant *m* (**for, towards** pour); **to have a ~ for maths** avoir des dispositions pour les maths; **to be of a studious ~** avoir du goût pour l'étude; **2** Bot = **bent grass**.
III *adj* **1** [*nail, wire, stick etc*] tordu; [*old person*] (stooped) courbé; **2 to be ~ on doing sth** vouloir à tout prix faire qch; **3**○ (corrupt) [*policeman etc*] véreux/-euse; **4**◑ (homosexual) injur **he's ~** il est pédé◑ offensive.
IDIOMS **to be/to get ~ out of shape**○ US être/se mettre en rogne○.

bent: **~ grass** *n* agrostis *f*; **~wood** *adj* en bois courbé.

benumb /bɪˈnʌm/ **I** *vtr* engourdir.
II benumbed *pp adj* lit, fig engourdi (**by** par).

Benzedrine® /ˈbenzədriːn/ *n* benzédrine *f*.

benzene /ˈbenziːn/ *n* benzène *m*.

benzene ring *n* noyau *m* benzénique.

benzine /ˈbenziːn/ *n* benzine *f*.

benzoin /ˈbenzəʊɪn/ *n* **1** Chem benzoïne *f*; **2** Bot (resin) benjoin *m*; (plant) styrax *m* (benjoin).

benzole /ˈbenzəʊl/ *n* benzol *m*.

bequeath /bɪˈkwiːð/ *vtr* Jur léguer (**to** à); fig léguer, transmettre [*custom, legislation, concept etc*] (**to** à).

bequest /bɪˈkwest/ *n* Jur, fig legs *m* (**to** à).

berate /bɪˈreɪt/ *vtr* sout admonester fml, réprimander (**for** pour).

Berber /ˈbɜːbə(r)/ **▶ 1402** **I** *n* **1** (person) Berbère *mf*; **2** Ling berbère *m*.
II *adj* berbère.

berberis /ˈbɜːbərɪs/ *n* épine-vinette *f*.

bereave /bɪˈriːv/ *vtr* littér **1** (*prét, pp* **bereaved**) (by death) endeuiller [*person, family*]; **2** (*prét, pp* **bereft**) (deprive) priver (**of** de).

bereaved /bɪˈriːvd/ **I** *n* **the ~** (+ *v pl*) la famille endeuillée.
II *adj* [*person, family*] endeuillé, en deuil.

bereavement /bɪˈriːvmənt/ *n* (state, event, period of mourning) deuil *m*; (sorrow) chagrin *m*.

bereft /bɪˈreft/ *adj* sout **1 ~ of** privé de [*love, friendship*]; dépourvu de [*furniture, contents, ideas*]; **~ of hope** désespéré; **2** (forlorn) [*person*] abandonné.

beret /ˈbereɪ, US bəˈreɪ/ *n* béret *m*.

berg /bɜːg/ *n* iceberg *m*.

bergamot /ˈbɜːgəmɒt/ *n* **1** (fruit) bergamote *f*; (tree) bergamotier *m*; **2** (plant) monarde *f* (fistuleuse).

bergschrund /ˈbeəkʃrʊnt/ *n* rimaye *f*.

beriberi /ˌberɪˈberɪ/ **▶ 1354** *n* béribéri *m*.

berk◑ /bɜːk/ *n* GB péj crétin○ *m*.

berkelium /bɜːˈkɪlɪəm/ *n* berkélium *m*.

Berks *n* GB Post *abrév écrite* = **Berkshire**.

berlin /bɜːˈlɪn/ *n* (carriage) berline *f*.

Berlin /bɜːˈlɪn/ **▶ 1818** *pr n* Berlin; **the ~ Wall** Hist le mur de Berlin.

Berliner /bɜːˈlɪnə(r)/ *n* Berlinois/-e *m/f*.

Bermuda /bəˈmjuːdə/ **▶ 1131** *pr n* les Bermudes *fpl*; **in ~** aux Bermudes; **the ~ Triangle** le triangle des Bermudes.

Bermudan /bəˈmjuːdən/ **▶ 1486** **I** *n* Bermudien/-ienne *m/f*.
II *adj* bermudien/-ienne, des Bermudes.

Bermudas /bəˈmjuːdəz/, **Bermuda shorts** *npl* bermuda *m*.

Bern /bɜːn/ **▶ 1818**, **1776** *pr n* Berne; **the canton of ~** le canton de Berne.

Bernese /ˈbɜːniːz/ **I** *n* Bernois/-e *m/f*.
II *adj* bernois; **the ~ Alps** ou **Oberland** l'Oberland bernois.

berry /ˈberɪ/ *n* baie *f*.
IDIOMS **to be as brown as a ~** être tout bronzé.

berserk /bəˈsɜːk/ *adj* fou furieux/folle furieuse; **to go ~** être pris/prise de folie furieuse.

berth /bɜːθ/ **I** *n* **1** Naut, Rail (for sleeping) couchette *f*; **lower/middle/upper ~** couchette du dessous/du milieu/du dessus; **a four-~ boat** un bateau à quatre places; **2** Naut (for ship) mouillage *m*; **a safe ~** un mouillage sûr; **at ~** au mouillage; **3**○ Naut, fig (job) poste *m*.
II *vtr* faire mouiller; **to be ~ed at** être mouillé à.
IDIOMS **to give sb/sth a wide ~**○ éviter qn/qch.

beryl /ˈberəl/ *n* béryl *m*.

beryllium /bəˈrɪlɪəm/ *n* béryllium *m*.

beseech /bɪˈsiːtʃ/ *vtr* (*prét, pp* **beseeched** ou **besought**) sout implorer [*forgiveness*]; solliciter [*favour*]; **to ~ sb to do** supplier qn de faire.

beseeching /bɪˈsiːtʃɪŋ/ *adj* sout implorant, suppliant.

beseechingly /bɪˈsiːtʃɪŋlɪ/ *adv* [*look*] d'un regard implorant; [*ask, write*] d'un ton implorant.

beset /bɪˈset/ *vtr* (*prét, pp* **beset**) (*gén au passif*) assaillir (**with** de); Mil assiéger; **a project ~ with problems/difficulties** un projet émaillé de problèmes/difficultés; **a country ~ by strikes** un pays en proie aux grèves.

besetting /bɪˈsetɪŋ/ *adj* [*fear, worry*] obsédant; **his ~ sin** son grand défaut.

beside /bɪˈsaɪd/ *prep* **1** (next to) à côté de; **~ him/you** à côté de lui/de toi; **~ the sea/the road/the path** au bord de la mer/de la route/du chemin; **2** (in comparison with) par rapport à; **my problems seem rather insignificant ~ yours** mes problèmes semblent assez insignifiants par rapport aux tiens or à côté des tiens; **3** (apart from) = **besides II**.
IDIOMS **to be ~ oneself (with anger)** être hors de soi; **to be ~ oneself (with excitement)** être surexcité; **to be ~ oneself with happiness** ou **joy** être fou/folle de joie.

besides /bɪˈsaɪdz/ **I** *adv* **1** (moreover) d'ailleurs; **2** (in addition) en plus, aussi; **she has a car and a motorbike ~** elle a une voiture et une moto en plus, elle a une voiture et aussi une moto; **and much else ~** et bien d'autres choses encore; **and a few more ~s** et bien d'autres encore.
II *prep* (apart from) en plus de, à part; **they need other things ~ money** ils ont besoin d'autre chose que d'argent; **~ John they're all teachers** à part John ils sont tous professeurs; **~ having a headache, I've got a temperature** à part un mal de tête, j'ai aussi de la fièvre; **~ waiting there's not a lot we can do** à part attendre, nous ne pouvons pas faire grand-chose; **~ being an artist, she also writes poetry** c'est une artiste et en plus, elle fait de la poésie; **nobody knows ~ Mary** personne n'est au courant sauf or à part Mary; **everyone ~ me/you** tout le monde sauf moi/toi; **~ which** d'ailleurs, de toute façon.

besiege /bɪˈsiːdʒ/ *vtr* **1** Mil assiéger; **2** fig assaillir [*person*]; assiéger [*place*]; **to ~ sb with** assaillir qn de [*questions etc*].

besmear /bɪˈsmɪə(r)/ *vtr* littér **1** lit barbouiller (**with** de); **2** fig souiller.

besmirch /bɪˈsmɜːtʃ/ *vtr* littér vilipender liter.

besotted /bɪˈsɒtɪd/ *adj* (infatuated) (with person) follement épris (**with** de); (with idea) obsédé (**with** par).

besought /bɪˈsɔːt/ *prét, pp* ▶ **beseech**.

bespangled /bɪˈspæŋgld/ *adj* littér émaillé liter (**with** de).

bespatter /bɪˈspætə(r)/ *vtr* éclabousser (**with** de).

bespeak /bɪˈspiːk/ *vtr* (*prét* **bespoke**, *pp*

bespoke ou **bespoken**) sout **1** (be evidence of) témoigner de; **2** (order in advance) commander [*goods*]; réserver [*room, seat*].

bespectacled /bɪˈspektəkld/ *adj* sout à lunettes.

bespoke /bɪˈspəʊk/ **I** *prét, pp* ▶ **bespeak**. **II** *adj* GB [*suit, jacket*] (fait) sur mesure; [*tailor*] à façon; Comput personnalisé.

bespoken /bɪˈspəʊkən/ *pp* ▶ **bespeak**.

besprinkle /bɪˈsprɪŋkl/ *vtr* littér (with dew) couvrir (**with** de); (with powder, sugar etc) saupoudrer (**with** de).

Bess /bes/ *pr n* **Good Queen ~** GB Hist la bonne reine Élisabeth (Première).

best /best/ **I** *n* **1** (most enjoyable, pleasant) **the ~** le/la meilleur/-e *m/f*; **it's the ~ of the stories** cette histoire, c'est la meilleure; **the North will have the ~ of the weather** c'est le nord du pays qui profitera du beau temps; **I think we've had the ~ of the day** je pense que le beau temps est fini pour aujourd'hui; **to look the ~** être le mieux; **to sound the ~** avoir le meilleur son, sonner le mieux; **to taste the ~** être le/la meilleur/-e; **to smell the ~** avoir la meilleure odeur; **2** (of the highest quality, standard) **the ~** le/la meilleur/-e *m/f*; **the ~ there is** le meilleur qui soit; **the ~ of its kind** le meilleur du genre; **it's not her ~** (of book, play) ce n'est pas le/la meilleur/-e qu'elle ait écrit/-e; **only the ~ is good enough for me/my son** pour moi/mon fils je veux ce qu'il y a de mieux; **only the ~ is good enough for him** seul le meilleur peut lui convenir; **3** (most competent) **the ~** le/la meilleur/-e *m/f*; **she's one of the ~** c'est l'une des meilleures; **to be the ~ at** être le/la meilleur/-e en [*subject, game*]; **who's the ~ at drawing/swimming?** qui dessine/nage le mieux?; **4** (most appropriate, desirable or valid) **the ~** le/la meilleur/-e *m/f*; **it's the ~ I've got** c'est le meilleur que j'aie; **it's for the ~** (recommending course of action) c'est la meilleure solution; (of something done) c'est tant mieux; **to do sth for the ~** faire qch pour le mieux; **it's not the ~ of times to do** ce n'est pas le meilleur moment pour faire; **5** (most favourable) **the ~** le mieux; **the ~ we can hope for/say** le mieux qu'on puisse espérer/dire; **at ~** au mieux; **I find it difficult to do at the ~ of times** j'ai déjà du mal à le faire; **he's a difficult man at the ~ of times** déjà en temps ordinaire il est difficile à vivre; **to make the ~ of sth** s'accommoder de qch; **6** (peak, height) **to be at its ~** [*wine, cheese*] être parfait; [*city, view, landscape*] être le/la plus beau/belle; **this is modern art at its ~** c'est ce que l'art moderne peut produire de mieux; **to be at one's ~** (physically, in mood) être au mieux de sa forme; **to be at one's ~ writing poetry/playing villains** exceller dans la poésie/dans les rôles de méchants; **this is Eliot at her ~** c'est Eliot dans ce qu'elle a fait de meilleur; **it was not in the ~ of taste** ce n'était pas du meilleur goût; **the ~ of friends** les meilleurs amis du monde; **7** (greatest personal effort) **to do one' s ~ to do** faire de son mieux or faire (tout) son possible pour faire; **is that the ~ you can/the car can do?** c'est le mieux que tu puisses/que la voiture puisse faire?; **to get the ~ out of** obtenir le meilleur de [*pupil, worker*], tirer le meilleur parti de [*gadget*]; **8** (virtues, qualities) **to bring out the ~ in sb** [*crisis, suffering*] inciter qn à donner le meilleur de lui-même; **9** (most advantageous or pleasing part) **the ~ of it is** gen le mieux, c'est que; (most amusing) le plus beau, c'est que; **to get the ~ of** avoir la part du lion dans [*deal, bargain*]; gagner dans [*arrangement*]; **10** (good clothes) **to keep sth for ~** garder or réserver qch pour les grandes occasions; ▶ **Sunday best**; **11** (good wishes) (on an occasion) meilleurs vœux *mpl*; (friendly greeting) amitiés *fpl*; **give her my ~** transmets-lui mes meilleurs vœux or amitiés; **all the ~!** (good luck) bonne chance!; (cheers) à ta santé!; **all the ~, Ellie** (in letter) amitiés, Ellie; **wishing you all the ~ on your retirement** meilleurs vœux de bonheur pour votre retraite; **12** (winning majority) **~ of three/five** au meilleur des trois/cinq; **to play (the) ~ of three** jouer au meilleur des trois; **it's the ~ of five** c'est au meilleur des cinq.
II *adj* (*superlative of good*) **1** (most excellent or pleasing) meilleur; **the ~ book I've ever read/written** le meilleur livre que j'aie jamais lu/écrit; **the ~ idea she's had all day** la meilleure idée qu'elle ait eue de la journée; **the ~ hotel in town** le meilleur hôtel de la ville; **the ~ thing about sth/about doing** ce qu'il y a de mieux dans qch/lorsqu'on fait; **one of the ~ things about sth/about doing** l'un des plus grands avantages de qch/lorsqu'on fait; **to look ~** être le mieux; **to sound ~** avoir le meilleur son, sonner le mieux; **to taste ~** être le/la meilleur/-e; **to smell ~** avoir la meilleure odeur; **this wine is ~ served chilled** ce vin est parfait si on le sert frais; **she looks ~ in black** c'est en noir qu'elle est le mieux; **she speaks the ~ French** c'est elle qui parle le mieux français; **she said it in her ~ French** elle l'a dit dans son meilleur français; **in your ~ handwriting** dans ta plus belle écriture; **my ~ dress** ma plus belle robe; **my ~ sheets** mes plus beaux draps; **'~ before end May'** 'à consommer de préférence avant fin mai'; **2** (most competent) [*teacher, poet*] meilleur; **the award for ~ actor** le prix du meilleur acteur; **who is the ~ swimmer?** qui nage le mieux?; **to be ~ at** être le/la meilleur/-e en [*subject, sport*]; être le/la meilleur/-e à [*instrument*]; **to be ~ at cooking** cuisiner le mieux; **the ~ mother you could wish for** la meilleure mère dont on puisse rêver; **may the ~ man win!** que le meilleur gagne!; **3** (most appropriate or suitable) [*tool, example, way, time, idea*] meilleur; **these ones are ~ for cutting paper** pour couper du papier ceux-ci sont le mieux; **they're ~ for cutting paper, not fabric** c'est pour couper du papier et non pas du tissu qu'ils conviennent le mieux; **it is ~ for older children** cela convient mieux aux enfants plus âgés; **the ~ person for the job** la personne qui convient le mieux pour ce travail; **the ~ thing to do** la meilleure chose à faire; **the ~ thing would be to do, it would be ~ to do** le mieux serait de faire; **it would be ~ if he did** le mieux serait qu'il fasse; **4** (most beneficial) [*exercise, food*] meilleur; **to consider what is ~ for sb** réfléchir à ce qui est le mieux pour qn.
III *adv* (*superlative of well*) le mieux; **to behave/fit/hear ~** se comporter/aller/entendre le mieux; **the ~ fed/qualified/organized** le mieux nourri/qualifié/organisé; **the ~ organized person** la personne la mieux organisée; **the ~ prepared/equipped/loved** le plus préparé/équipé/aimé; **the ~ loved woman** la femme la plus aimée; **to like sth ~** aimer qch le mieux or le plus; **to like sth ~ of all** aimer qch mieux or plus que tout; **~ of all** mieux que tout; **he works ~ on his own** c'est seul qu'il travaille le mieux; **to do ~** réussir le mieux; **who did ~?** qui a le mieux réussi?; **to do sth as ~ one can** faire qch de son mieux; **you'd ~ do**○ tu ferais mieux de faire; **such advice is ~ ignored/followed** il vaut mieux ignorer/suivre de tels conseils; **you know ~** c'est toi le meilleur juge.
IV *vtr* (defeat, outdo) (in argument) avoir le dessus sur [*person*]; (in contest, struggle) battre, vaincre [*opponent*]; **to be ~ed in an argument** avoir le dessous dans une discussion.
IDIOMS **to do sth with the ~ of them** faire qch avec tout un chacun; **it happens to the ~ of us** (mishap, failure) ça arrive à tout le monde; (death) c'est notre lot à tous.

best: **~-before date** *n* date *f* limite de consommation; **~ boy** *n* Cin assistant/-e *m/f* du chef électricien; **~ end (of neck)** *n* carré *m* d'agneau (*entre les côtes découvertes et les côtes premières*).

best friend *n* meilleur/-e ami/-e *m/f*; **man's ~** le meilleur ami de l'homme.

bestial /ˈbestɪəl, US ˈbestʃəl/ *adj* lit, fig bestial.

bestiality /ˌbestɪˈælətɪ, US ˌbestʃɪ-/ *n* lit, fig bestialité *f*.

bestiary /ˈbestɪərɪ, US -tɪerɪ/ *n* bestiaire *m*.

bestir /bɪˈstɜː(r)/ *v refl* (*p prés etc* **-rr-**) sout **to ~ oneself** s'agiter.

best man *n* témoin *m* (*de mariage*).

bestow /bɪˈstəʊ/ *vtr* sout accorder [*honour, favour*] (**on, upon** à); conférer [*title*] (**on, upon** à); octroyer [*gift*] (**on, upon** à); prodiguer [*wealth, energy, praise*] (**on, upon** à); prêter [*attention*] (**on, upon** à).

bestowal /bɪˈstəʊəl/ *n* sout octroi *m*.

bestraddle /bɪˈstrædl/ *vtr* littér enfourcher [*horse, bicycle*]; être à califourchon sur [*chair*].

bestrew /bɪˈstruː/ *vtr* (*prét* **bestrewed** /bɪˈstruːd/, *pp* **bestrewed** ou **bestrewn** /bɪˈstruːn/) littér joncher (**with** de).

bestseller /ˌbestˈselə(r)/ *n* **1** (product) (book) bestseller *m*, livre *m* à succès; **this product is our ~** ce produit est celui qui se vend le mieux; **2** (writer) auteur *m* de bestsellers, auteur *m* à succès.

best-selling /ˌbestˈselɪŋ/ *adj* **1** [*car, computer, product*] le/la plus vendu/-e; **a ~ novel/romance/book** un bestseller; **2** [*writer, author, novelist*] populaire; **the ~ novelist of 1992** le romancier qui s'est vendu le plus en 1992.

bet /bet/ **I** *n* **1** (gamble) pari *m*; **to have a ~ on a race/on a horse** parier dans une course/sur un cheval; **to place** ou **put** ou **lay a ~ on** parier or faire un pari sur [*horse, dog*]; miser sur [*number, colour*]; **to make a ~ that** faire le pari que; **to make a ~** parier or faire un pari (**with** avec); **to do sth for a ~** faire qch à la suite d'un pari; **'place your ~s!'** (in roulette) 'faites vos jeux!'; **this make of car is supposed to be a good** ou **safe ~** cette marque de voiture devrait être une valeur sûre; **your best ~ is to take the motorway** le mieux pour toi est de prendre l'autoroute; **2** (guess) **my ~ is that** moi je pense que; **3** (stake) gen pari *m*; (in casino) mise *f*.
II *vtr* (*p prés etc* **-tt-**; *prét, pp* **bet** ou **~ted**) gen parier (**on** sur); (in gambling) parier, miser; **to ~ that** parier que; **I bet you 100 dollars (that) I win** je te parie 100 dollars que je gagne; **you can ~ your ass**● ou **your life** ou **your boots**○ ou **your bottom dollar**○ **(that)** tu peux parier tout ce que tu veux or ta chemise que; **bet you can/can't!** (between children) chiche!
III *vi* (*p prés etc* **-tt-**; *prét, pp* **bet** ou **~ted**) gen parier (**on** sur) gen parier; (in casino) miser; **to ~ on a horse** parier or miser sur un cheval; **to ~ on a race** jouer or parier dans une course; **to ~ on sth happening** parier que qch va se produire; **something will go wrong, you can ~ on it** il y a forcément quelque chose qui va aller de travers, tu peux en être sûr; **I'm willing to ~ on it!** j'en mettrais ma tête à couper!; **I wouldn't ~ on it!** je n'y compterais pas trop!; **I'll ~!** (in agreement) ça se comprend!; (ironically) ben voyons○!; **you bet!** tu parles!, et comment!

beta /ˈbiːtə, US ˈbeɪtə/ *n* béta *m*.

beta: **~-blocker** *n* bétabloquant *m*; **~-blocking** *adj* bétabloquant; **~ globulin** *n* béta-globuline *f*.

betake /bɪˈteɪk/ *v refl* (*prét* **betook**, *pp* **betaken**) **to ~ oneself** s'en aller (**to** à).

beta: **~ particle** *n* particule *f* béta; **~ ray** *n* rayon *m* béta.

betcha○ /ˈbetʃə/ *excl* je te parie; **you ~!** US tu parles○!, et comment○!

betel /ˈbiːtl/ *n* bétel *m*.

betel nut *n* noix *f* d'arec *or* de bétel.

bethink‡ /bɪˈθɪŋk/ *v refl* (*prét, pp* - **thought**) **to ~ oneself of sth** considérer qch.

Bethlehem /ˈbeθlɪhem/ ▶ **1818** *pr n* Bethléem.

betide‡ /bɪˈtaɪd/ *vtr, vi* advenir.

betimes‡ /bɪˈtaɪmz/ *adv* de bonne heure.

betoken /bɪˈtəʊkən/ *vtr* sout **1** (show) indiquer; **2** (presage) laisser présager.

betook /bɪˈtʊk/ *prét* ▶ **betake**.

betray /bɪˈtreɪ/ **I** *vtr* **1** (be false to) trahir [*country, feelings, interests, person, secret, trust*]; tromper [*lover*]; manquer à [*promise*]; **to feel ~ed** se sentir trahi; **2** (reveal) révéler [*characteristic, interest, nature*]; trahir [*curiosity, presence*]; montrer [*emotion*].
II *v refl* **to ~ oneself** se trahir.

betrayal /bɪˈtreɪəl/ *n* (of country, ideal, person) trahison *f*; (of secret, plan) révélation *f*; (of fear, intention) manifestation *f*; (of facts, truth) divulgation *f*; **~ of trust** abus *m* de confiance; **a sense of ~** le sentiment d'avoir été trahi.

betroth‡ /bɪˈtrəʊð/ *vtr* fiancer (**to** à).

betrothal‡ /bɪˈtrəʊðl/ *n* fiançailles *fpl* (**to** avec).

betrothed‡ /bɪˈtrəʊðd/ **I** *n inv* (*pl* **~**) fiancé/-e *m/f*.
II *adj* **to be ~** être fiancé; **the ~ couple** les fiancés.

better[1] /ˈbetə(r)/

■ **Note** When *better* is used as an adjective it is translated by *meilleur* or *mieux* depending on the context (see below, and note that *meilleur* is the comparative form of *bon*, *mieux* the comparative form of *bien*). The choice between *meilleur* and *mieux* in the construction *to be better than* depends on whether *bon* or *bien* would be used originally with the noun. Other constructions translate as follows: *this is a better bag/car* = ce sac/cette voiture est mieux; *it is better to do* = il vaut mieux faire *or* il est mieux de faire.
– As an adverb, *better* can almost always be translated by *mieux*. For more examples and particular usages, see the entry below.

I *n* **1** (something preferable, more excellent) **the ~** le/la meilleur/-e *m/f*; **much** ou **by far the ~ of the two** de loin le/la meilleur/-e des deux; **2** (more desirable state of affairs) **to deserve/expect/hope for ~** mériter/attendre/espérer mieux; **so much the ~, all the ~** tant mieux; **a change** ou **turn for the ~** une amélioration; **to change** ou **take a turn for the ~** s'améliorer; **the weather changed, and not for the ~** le temps a changé, et pas en mieux; **3** (superior person) **one's ~s** ses supérieurs *mfpl*.
II *adj* (*comparative of good*) **1** (more pleasing, satisfactory) [*weather, day, news, joke, forecast, review, salary, price, range*] meilleur; [*party, game, book, film activity*] mieux; **playing is ~ than watching** jouer, c'est mieux que de regarder; **to get ~** s'améliorer; **the weather is no ~** le temps n'est pas meilleur or ne s'est pas amélioré; **things are getting ~** ça va mieux; **'good news?'—'it couldn't be ~!'** 'bonnes nouvelles?'—'on ne peut meilleures!'; **to look/sound ~** être/sonner mieux; **to taste/smell ~** être/sentir meilleur, avoir un/-e meilleur/-e goût/odeur; **it would taste all the ~ for some salt** ce serait meilleur avec du sel; **it looked all the ~ for it** cela n'en était que mieux; **that's ~!** voilà qui est mieux!; **2** (well, recovered) **to be ~** [*patient, cold, headache*] aller mieux; **to feel all the ~ for** se sentir mieux après [*rest, meal*]; **~ than I/it was** mieux qu'avant; **3** (happier) [*mood*] meilleur; **to feel ~** se sentir mieux; **I'd feel ~ if you did/didn't do** je me sentirais mieux si tu faisais/ne faisais pas; **if it makes you feel any ~** (less worried or awkward) si ça t'aide à te sentir mieux; (less sad) si ça peut te consoler; **to feel ~ about doing** (less nervous) se sentir à même de faire; (less worried, guilty) avoir moins de scrupules à faire; **4** (of superior quality, class) [*food, result, film, book, quality*] meilleur; [*car, carpet, district, family*] mieux; [*land, school, hotel*] meilleur, mieux; [*coat, shoes, furniture*] de meilleure qualité; **one of the ~ schools** une des meilleures écoles; **he went to a ~ school than I did** ou **than me** il est allé dans une école meilleure que la mienne; **5** (more virtuous, commendable) [*person*] mieux; [*life, influence, nature*] meilleur; **to be a ~ man/woman than** être mieux que; **you're a ~ man than I am!** tu es mieux que moi!; **to be no ~ than sb** ne pas être mieux que qn; **to be no ~ than a thief** être un voleur ni plus ni moins; **6** (more skilled) [*doctor, actor, teacher*] meilleur; **to be a ~ poet than sb** être meilleur poète que qn; **to be a ~ swimmer than sb** nager mieux que qn; **to be a ~ singer than dancer** chanter mieux que l'on ne danse; **to be a ~ father than husband** être meilleur père que mari; **to be ~ at** être meilleur en [*subject, sport*]; **to be ~ at doing** faire mieux; **he's no ~ at driving than she is** ou **than her** il ne conduit pas mieux qu'elle; **7** (more suitable, valid, appropriate) [*tune, tool, way, word, idea, example, reason, excuse, choice*] meilleur; **to be ~ for** être meilleur pour [*purpose, task*]; **to be ~ for doing** être mieux pour faire; **to be ~ than nothing** être mieux que rien; **~ a part-time job than no job** mieux vaut un travail à mi-temps que pas de travail; **the bigger/sooner the ~** le plus grand/vite possible; **the faster you work the ~** plus tu travailles vite, mieux ça vaudra; **the less said about that the ~** mieux vaut ne pas parler de ça; **who ~ to play the part?** qui mieux pourrait jouer le rôle?; **where/how ~ to do...?** quel meilleur endroit/moyen pour faire...?; **8** (more beneficial) [*exercise, food*] meilleur; **swimming is ~ for you than running** nager est meilleur pour la santé que courir; **9** (more accurate) [*description, recollection, view, understanding*] meilleur; **in order to get a ~ look** pour mieux voir; **to be a ~ likeness** être plus ressemblant.
III *adv* (*comparative of well*) **1** (more adequately or excellently) mieux; **to fit/behave ~ than** aller/se comporter mieux que; **~ made/organized than** mieux fait/organisé que; **to think ~ of sb** avoir une meilleure opinion de qn; **~ behaved/educated** plus sage/cultivé; **to be ~ tempered/mannered** avoir meilleur caractère/de meilleures manières; **to do ~** (in career, life) réussir mieux; (in exam, essay) faire mieux; (in health) aller mieux; **'could do ~'** 'pourrait or peut mieux faire'; **the ~ to see/hear** pour mieux voir/entendre; **the more she talked, the ~ I understood** plus elle parlait, mieux je comprenais; **2** (more advisably or appropriately) mieux; **it couldn't have been ~ timed** ça n'aurait pu mieux tomber; **the money would be ~ spent on** il vaudrait mieux dépenser l'argent en; **he is ~ left alone** il vaut mieux le laisser seul; **you would be ~ advised to do** tu serais mieux avisé de faire; **you would do ~ to do** tu ferais mieux de faire; **you had ~ do, you'd ~ do** (advising) tu ferais mieux de faire; (warning) tu as intérêt à faire; **I'd ~ go** je ferais mieux de m'en aller; **'will she come?'—'she'd ~!** ou **she ~**○**!'** 'est-ce qu'elle viendra?'—'elle a intérêt!'; **'will it be open?'—'it had ~ be!** ou **it ~ had be**○**!'** 'est-ce que ça sera ouvert?'—'il y a intérêt!'; **'more cake?'—'I'd ~ not'** 'encore du gâteau?'—'non merci'; **'shall I come?'—'~ not'** 'est-ce que je viens?'—'il vaut mieux pas'; **~ still,...** ou mieux,...
IV *vtr* **1** (surpass) améliorer [*score, one's performance, achievement*]; faire mieux que [*rival's performance, achievement*]; **to ~ sb's offer** offrir un meilleur prix que qn; **2** (improve) améliorer [*condition, quality*].
V *v refl* **to ~ oneself** améliorer sa condition.
IDIOMS **for ~ (or) for worse** gen advienne que pourra; (in wedding vow) pour le meilleur et pour le pire; **to get the ~ of** [*person*] triompher de, vaincre [*enemy, opponent, problem*]; **his curiosity got the ~ of him** sa curiosité a pris le dessus; **the problem got the ~ of her** le problème l'a dépassée; **to go one ~** faire encore mieux (**than** que); **to think ~ of it** changer d'avis.

better[2] /ˈbetə(r)/ *n* parieur/-ieuse *m/f*.

betterment /ˈbetəmənt/ *n* sout **1** gen amélioration *f*; **2** Jur plus-value *f*.

better off /ˌbetərˈɒf/ **I** *n* **the better-off** (+ *v pl*) les riches *mpl*.
II *adj* **1** (more wealthy) plus riche (**than** que); **their better-off neighbours** leurs voisins plus riches; **I was ~ then** j'avais plus d'argent à l'époque; **2** (having more) **to be ~ for** avoir plus de [*space, books, boyfriends*] (**than** que); **3** (in a better situation) mieux; **you'd be ~ in hospital** tu serais mieux à l'hôpital; tu seras plus à l'aise dans [*different job*]; **you'd have been ~ doing** tu aurais mieux fait de faire; **you're ~ as you are** tu es mieux comme tu es; **you're ~ without him** tu es mieux sans lui.

betting /ˈbetɪŋ/ *n* **1** (activity) paris *mpl*; **2** (odds) côte *f*; **3** (likelihood) **what's the ~ that...?** quelles sont les chances que...? (+ *subj*); **the ~ is (that) she'll win** tout laisse à penser qu'elle va gagner.

betting: **~ shop** *n* GB bureau *m* de paris; **~ slip** *n* bulletin *m* de pari individuel; **~ tax** *n* impôt *m* sur les paris.

bettor /ˈbetə(r)/ *n* US parieur/-ieuse *m/f*.

between /bɪˈtwiːn/

■ **Note** When *between* is used as a preposition expressing physical location (*between the lines*), time (*between 8 am and 11 am*), position in a range (*between 30 and 40 kilometres*), relationship (*link between, difference between*) it is translated by *entre*. For particular usages, see the entry below.

I *prep* **1** (in space) entre; **there is a wall ~ the two gardens** il y a un mur entre les deux jardins; **there are no stops ~ this station and Paris** il n'y a pas d'arrêt entre cette gare et Paris, cette gare est le dernier arrêt avant Paris; **2** (in time) entre; **~ meals** entre les repas; **~ the ages of 12 and 18** entre l'âge de 12 et 18 ans; **~ now and next year** d'ici l'année prochaine; **3** (on a scale or range) entre; **it costs ~ £10 and £20** cela coûte entre dix et vingt livres sterling; **it's ~ 50 and 60 kilometres away** c'est à environ 50 ou 60 kilomètres d'ici; **4** (to and from) entre; **flights ~ London and Amsterdam** les vols entre Londres et Amsterdam; **the train that goes ~ London and Brighton** le train qui va de Londres à Brighton or qui assure la liaison Londres-Brighton; **5** (indicating connection or relationship) entre; **the link ~ smoking and cancer** le lien entre le tabagisme et le cancer; **what's the difference ~ the two?** quelle est la différence entre les deux?; **you must settle it ~ yourselves** il faut que vous le régliez entre vous; **nothing now stands ~ us and success** rien ne peut plus faire obstacle à notre réussite maintenant; **we mustn't allow this to come ~ us** il ne faut pas que cela crée des problèmes entre nous; **it's something ~ a novel and an autobiography** cela tient à la fois du roman et de l'autobiographie; **6** (indicating sharing, division) entre; **the estate was divided ~ them** les biens ont été divisés entre eux; **they drank the whole bottle ~ (the two of) them** à eux deux, ils ont bu toute la bouteille; **they had only one suitcase ~ (the three of) them** ils n'avaient qu'une seule valise pour trois; **~ ourselves, ~ you and me (and the gatepost)** entre nous; **7** (together, in combination) **the couples have seventeen children ~ them** à eux tous, les couples ont dix-sept enfants; **~**

them, they collected £200 en tout, ils ont réuni 200 livres sterling; **they wrote the article ~ them** (two people) ils se sont mis à deux pour écrire l'article; (more than two) ils se sont mis à plusieurs pour écrire l'article; **~ (the two of) us, we earn £30,000 a year** à nous deux nous gagnons 30000 livres sterling par an; **~ housework, minding the children and studying, I never have any time to myself** entre le ménage, les enfants et les études, je n'ai pas une minute à moi.

II *adv* (also **in ~**) **1** (in space) au milieu, entre les deux; (in time) dans l'intervalle, entre les deux; **the two main roads and the streets (in) ~** les deux rues principales et les petites rues situées entre elles or et les petites rues au milieu; **she spent four years at university and two years training, with a year off (in) ~** elle a passé quatre ans à l'université et deux ans en formation, avec une année sabbatique entre les deux; **neither red nor orange but somewhere (in) ~** ni rouge ni orange mais entre les deux.

betweentimes, **betweenwhiles** /bɪˈtwiːntaɪmz, bɪˈtwiːnwaɪlz, US -hwaɪlz/ *adv* entre-temps.

betwixt /bɪˈtwɪkst/ I *adv* **~ and between** entre les deux.

II *prep* littér entre.

bevel /ˈbevl/ I *n* **1** (edge) biseau *m*; (larger) surface *f* oblique; **2** (tool) fausse équerre *f*, sauterelle *f*.

II *vtr* tailler [qch] en biseau [*mirror, edge*].

bevel: **~ edge** *n* biseau *m*; **~ gear** *n* engrenage *m* conique ou d'angle; **~led mirror** *n* glace *f* biseautée; **~ square** *n* fausse équerre *f*, sauterelle *f*.

beverage /ˈbevərɪdʒ/ *n* boisson *f*, breuvage *m* liter or hum.

bevvy○ /ˈbevɪ/ GB dial coup○ *m* (*à boire*).

bevy /ˈbevɪ/ *n* **1** fig (of girls, critics, experts) groupe *m*; **2** (of quails) volée *f*.

bewail /bɪˈweɪl/ *vtr* pleurer [*lack, loss etc*].

beware /bɪˈweə(r)/ I *excl* prenez garde!, attention!

II *vi* **2** gen se méfier (**of** de); **to ~ of doing** faire attention à ne pas faire, se garder de faire fml; **you must ~ of losing your wallet** vous devriez faire attention à ne pas perdre votre portefeuille; **you had better ~** tu ferais mieux de te méfier; **~ lest you be deceived** littér prenez garde à ne pas vous laisser berner; **2** (on sign) **~ of** attention à; **'~ of pickpockets'** 'attention aux pickpockets'; **'~ of the dog'** 'attention chien méchant'; **'~ of falling rocks'** 'attention, chute de pierres'.

bewilder /bɪˈwɪldə(r)/ *vtr* déconcerter (**with sth** avec qch; **by doing** en faisant).

bewildered /bɪˈwɪldəd/ *adj* [*person*] déconcerté (**at, by** par); [*look, curiosity*] perplexe.

bewildering /bɪˈwɪldərɪŋ/ *adj* déconcertant.

bewilderingly /bɪˈwɪldərɪŋlɪ/ *adv* **~ complex/imprecise** d'une complexité/d'une imprécision déconcertante.

bewilderment /bɪˈwɪldəmənt/ *n* stupéfaction *f*; **to her ~** à sa stupéfaction.

bewitch /bɪˈwɪtʃ/ I *vtr* **1** fig (attract) subjuguer; **2** (cast spell on) jeter un sort à.

II **bewitched** *pp adj* subjugué (**by** par).

bewitching /bɪˈwɪtʃɪŋ/ *adj* ensorcelant.

bewitchingly /bɪˈwɪtʃɪŋlɪ/ *adv* [*smile, dance*] de façon ensorcelante; **~ beautiful** d'une beauté ensorcelante.

beyond /bɪˈjɒnd/

■ **Note** *beyond* is often used with a noun to produce expressions like *beyond doubt, beyond a joke, beyond the grasp of, beyond the bounds of etc.* For translations of these and similar expressions where *beyond* means *outside the range of*, consult the appropriate noun entry (**doubt**, **joke**, **grasp**, **bounds** etc). See also I3 below.

I *prep* **1** (on the far side of) au-delà de [*border, city limits, region, mountain range*]; **~ the city walls** (but close) de l'autre côté des murs de la ville; (covering greater distance) au-delà des murs de la ville; **just ~ the tower** juste derrière la tour; **the countries ~ the Atlantic** les pays d'outre-atlantique; **2** (after a certain point in time) au-delà de; **~ 1998** au-delà de 1998; **well ~ midnight** bien au-delà de minuit; **~ the age of 11** au-delà de 11 ans; **to work ~ retirement age** travailler au-delà de l'âge de la retraite; **to go ~ a deadline** dépasser un délai; **3** (outside the range of) **~ one's means/resources/strength** au-dessus de ses moyens/ressources/forces; **~ all hope/expectation** au-delà de toute espérance/attente; **~ one's control** hors de son contrôle; **driven ~ endurance** poussé à bout; **he is ~ help** on ne peut rien faire pour lui; **to be wise ~ one's years** être très mûr pour son âge; **4** (further than) au-delà de; **to look ~ sth** voir au-delà de qch; **the world must look ~ the Gulf crisis** le monde devrait voir au-delà de la guerre du Golfe; **to move ~ sth** passer outre qch; **to go** ou **get ~ sth** aller au-delà de qch; **to go ~ being** être bien plus que; **it won't go ~ these four walls** fig ça restera entre nous; **5** (too much for, above) **to be ~ sb's ability** ou **competence** [*task, activity*] être au-dessus des capacités de qn; **it's ~ my comprehension!** ça me dépasse!; **to be ~ sb** [*activity, task, subject*] dépasser qn; **it's ~ me!** ça me dépasse!; **why they care is ~ me** ça me dépasse que ça les préoccupe (*subj*) autant; **it's ~ me how she manages** je ne sais pas comment elle s'en sort—ça me dépasse; **it's not ~ him to make the dinner!** iron il est quand même capable de préparer le repas!; **6** (other than) en dehors de, à part; **we know little about it ~ the fact that** nous savons très peu de choses là-dessus en dehors du fait que or à part que; **~ that there's not much one can do** en dehors de cela il n'y a pas grand-chose à faire; **he gets nothing ~ the basic salary** on ne lui donne rien de plus que le salaire de base.

II *adv* **1** (expressing location: further on) **in the room ~** dans la pièce d'après; **~ there was a garden** plus loin il y avait un jardin; **the canal and the trees ~** le canal et les arbres de l'autre côté; **an island in the bay ~** une île au loin dans la baie; **as far as London and ~** jusqu'à Londres et au-delà; **2** (expressing time) au-delà; **up to the year 2000 and ~** jusqu'à l'an 2000 et au-delà; **healthcare during pregnancy and ~** les précautions de santé pendant la grossesse et au-delà.

III *conj* à part (+ *infinitive*); **there was little I could do ~ reassuring him that** je ne pouvais pas faire grand-chose à part le rassurer en lui disant que.

IV *n* **the ~** l'au-delà *m*.

IDIOMS **to be in the back of ~** [*house, farm*] être au bout du monde; **to live in the back of ~** vivre dans un trou perdu○.

bezant /ˈbeznt/ *n* Archit, Herald besant *m*.

bezel /ˈbezl/ *n* **1** (of tool) biseau *m*; **2** (of gem) facette *f*, biseau *m* spec; **3** (mount for gem) chaton *m*.

bezique /bɪˈziːk/ **▶ 1282** *n* bésigue *m*.

b/f, **B/F** *abrév écrite* = **brought forward**.

B film, **B movie** *n* film *m* de série B.

BFPO *n* (*abrév* = **British Forces Post Office**) secteur *m* postal (des forces armées britanniques).

BGC *n*: *abrév* ▶ **Bank Giro Credit**.

B-girl○ *n* US entraîneuse *f*.

Bhutan /buːˈtɑːn/ **▶ 1131** *pr n* Bhoutan *m*.

Biafra /bɪˈæfrə/ *pr n* Hist Biafra *m*.

Biafran /bɪˈæfrn/ Hist I *n* Biafrais/-e *m/f*.

II *adj* biafrais, du Biafra.

biannual /baɪˈænjʊəl/ *adj* bisannuel/-elle.

bias /ˈbaɪəs/ I *n* (*pl* **-es**) **1** (prejudice) parti *m* pris (**on the part of** de la part de); **to display ~** faire preuve de parti pris; **political/media ~** parti pris politique/dans les médias; **2** (active discrimination) discrimination *f* (**against** envers); **racial/sexual ~** discrimination raciale/sexuelle; **3** (tendency) tendance *f* (**in favour of, towards** pour); **an American ~** une tendance pro-américaine; **a female ~** un préjugé favorable envers les femmes; **a left-wing ~** une tendance de gauche; **4** Sewing biais *m*; **on the ~** dans le biais; **5** Stat distorsion *f*; **6** (of steering, bowl) déviation *f*.

II *vtr* (*p prés etc* **-s-** ou **-ss-**) influer sur [*person, decision, result*]; **to ~ sb against/in favour of** prévenir qn contre/en faveur de.

bias binding, **bias tape** US *n* Sewing (ruban *m* de) biais *m*.

biased, **biassed** /ˈbaɪəst/ *adj* [*decision, judge, opinion*] partial; [*system, report*] manquant d'objectivité (*after n*); **this report is ~** ce reportage manque d'objectivité; **a politically ~ comment** un commentaire politiquement tendancieux; **he's politically ~** il a des partis *mpl* pris politiques; **to be ~against/in favour of** avoir un préjugé défavorable/favorable envers.

bias ply tyre GB, **bias ply tire** US *n* pneu *m* croisé ceinturé.

bib /bɪb/ *n* **1** (baby's) bavoir *m*; **2** (of apron, dungarees) bavette *f*.

Bible /ˈbaɪbl/ I *n* Bible *f*; **it's his ~** fig c'est sa bible.

II *modif* [*reading, study*] de la Bible.

Bible: **~ basher**○ *n* péj évangéliste *mf* à tous crins; **~ Belt** *n*: *région du sud des États-Unis caracterisée par son fondamentalisme*; **~ puncher**○, **~ thumper**○ *n* péj = **Bible basher**.

biblical /ˈbɪblɪkl/ *adj* biblique.

bibliographer /ˌbɪblɪˈɒgrəfə(r)/ **▶ 1692** *n* bibliographe *mf*.

bibliographic(al) /ˌbɪblɪəˈgræfɪk(l)/ *adj* bibliographique.

bibliography /ˌbɪblɪˈɒgrəfɪ/ *n* bibliographie *f*.

bibliophile /ˈbɪblɪəfaɪl/ *n* bibliophile *mf*.

bibulous /ˈbɪbjʊləs/ *adj* sout ou hum éthylique.

bicameral /ˌbaɪˈkæmərəl/ *adj* bicaméral.

bicameral legislature *n* (body) corps *m* législatif bicaméral; (system) bicamérisme *m*.

bicarbonate /ˌbaɪˈkɑːbənət/ *n* bicarbonate *m*.

bicarbonate of soda *n* bicarbonate *m* de soude.

bicentenary /ˌbaɪsenˈtiːnərɪ, US -ˈsentənerɪ/, **bicentennial** /ˌbaɪsenˈtenɪəl/ I *n* bicentenaire *m* (**of** de).

II *modif* [*celebration, festival, year*] du bicentenaire.

bicephalous /ˌbaɪˈsefələs/ *adj* bicéphale.

biceps /ˈbaɪseps/ *n* (*pl* **~**) biceps *m*.

bichloride /ˌbaɪˈklɔːraɪd/ *n* = **dichloride**.

bichromate /ˌbaɪˈkrəʊmeɪt/ *n* = **dichromate**.

bicker /ˈbɪkə(r)/ *vi* se chamailler (**about, over** au sujet de; **with** avec).

bickering /ˈbɪkərɪŋ/ *n* chamailleries *fpl*; **constant ~** éternelles querelles *fpl* or chamailleries.

bicuspid /ˌbaɪˈkʌspɪd/ I *n* prémolaire *f*.

II (also **bicuspidate**) *adj* bicuspide.

bicycle /ˈbaɪsɪkl/ I *n* bicyclette *f*, vélo○ *m*; **on a/by ~** à bicyclette; **to ride a ~** faire de la bicyclette; **to fall off a** ou **one's ~** tomber de bicyclette; **to get on/off a ~** monter à/descendre de vélo.

II *modif* [*clip, pump, ride, shed, tour*] à bicyclette; [*bell, chain, lamp, wheel*] de bicyclette; [*hire, repair*] de bicyclettes.

III *vi* aller à bicyclette.

bicycle: **~ lane** *n* piste *f* cyclable; **~ race** *n* course *f* cycliste; **~ rack** *n* (in yard) parc *m* à bicyclettes; (on car) galerie *f*; **~ track** *n* piste *f* cyclable.

bid /bɪd/ **I** *n* **1** (at auction) enchère *f* (**for** sur; **of** de); **the opening/closing ~** la première/dernière enchère; **to make a ~ for sth** mettre une enchère sur qch; **to raise one's ~ by £200** surenchérir de 200 livres sterling; **2** (for contract) soumission *f* (**for** pour; **of** de); (for company) offre *f* (**for** pour; **of** de); **to make a ~ for a building contract** soumissionner or faire une soumission pour un contrat de construction; **3** (attempt) tentative *f* (**to do** pour faire); **escape/suicide ~** tentative *f* d'évasion/de suicide; **in a ~ to do** afin de faire; **to make a ~ for power/the presidency** tenter d'accéder au pouvoir/à la présidence; **4** (in Bridge) (first) annonce *f*; (subsequent) enchère *f*; **to make a ~** faire une annonce or enchère; **it's your ~** c'est à toi de déclarer; **no ~** je passe.

II *vtr* (*p prés* **-dd-**; *prét* **bade** ou **bid**; *pp* **bidden** ou **bid**) **1** Comm, Fin offrir [*money*] (**for** pour); **what am I bid for this painting?** à combien est-ce que j'estime ce tableau?; **2** (say) **to ~ sb good morning/goodbye** dire bonjour/au revoir à qn; **to ~ sb farewell** faire ses adieux à qn; **to ~ sb welcome** souhaiter la bienvenue à qn; **3**† (command) **to ~ sb to do** ordonner à qn de faire; **do as you are bid** fais ce qu'on te dit; **4**‡ (ask) **to ~ sb to do** inviter qn à faire; **5** (in Bridge) annoncer.

III *vi* (*p prés* **-dd-**; *prét* **bade** ou **bid**; *pp* **bidden** ou **bid**) **1** Comm, Fin (at auction) mettre une enchère, enchérir (**for** sur); (for contract) soumissionner (**for** pour); (for company) faire une offre (**for** pour); **to ~ against sb in an auction** renchérir sur qn dans une vente aux enchères; **five other companies are ~ding against us for the contract** cinq autres sociétés font des offres pour le contrat; **2** (in Bridge) faire une annonce, parler.

■ **bid up**: **~ [sth] up** faire monter [*price*].

bid bond *n* Fin *caution de participation à une adjudication internationale.*

biddable /ˈbɪdəbl/ *adj* **1** (obedient) docile; **2** (in Bridge) [*hand, suit*] demandable.

bidden /ˈbɪdn/ *pp* ▶ **bid**.

bidder /ˈbɪdə(r)/ *n* **1** (at auction) enchérisseur/-euse *m/f* (**for** pour); **to go to the highest ~** être adjugé au plus offrant; **successful ~** adjudicataire *mf*; **2** Comm (for contract) soumissionnaire *m* (**for** pour); (for land, property) acheteur/-euse *m/f* potentiel/-ielle (**for** de); **they are ~s for the company** ils font une offre d'achat pour l'entreprise; **3** (in Bridge) demandeur *m*.

bidding /ˈbɪdɪŋ/ *n* **1** ¢ (at auction) enchères *fpl*; **the ~ opened at £1 million** les enchères ont commencé à un million de livres sterling; **the ~ closed at £50,000** l'adjudication s'est faite à 50 000 livres sterling; **2** (command) **he did my ~** il a fait ce que je lui ai dit; **he did it at my ~** il l'a fait sur mon ordre; **she needed no second ~** on n'a pas eu à le lui dire deux fois; **3** ¢ (in Bridge) annonces *fpl*.

bidding: **~ group** *n* groupe *m* acheteur potentiel; **~ prayer** *n* Relig intention *f* de prière; **~ war** *n* lutte *f* de surenchères.

biddy○ /ˈbɪdɪ/ *n* **an old ~** une vieille bonne femme.

bide /baɪd/ *vi* ‡ ou GB dial demeurer†.

IDIOMS **to ~ one's time** attendre le bon moment.

bidet /ˈbiːdeɪ, US biːˈdeɪ/ *n* bidet *m*.

bidirectional /ˌbaɪdɪˈrekʃənl, -daɪ-/ *adj* bidirectionnel.

bid price *n* Fin cours *m* or prix *m* acheteur, prix *m* offert.

biennial /baɪˈenɪəl/ **I** *n* **1** (plant) plante *f* bisannuelle; **2** (event) biennale *f*.

II *adj* [*event*] biennal; [*plant*] bisannuel/-elle.

bier /bɪə(r)/ *n* (coffin) bière *f*; (stand) catafalque *m*.

biff○ /bɪf/ **I** *n* beigne◑ *f*.

II *excl* vlan!

III *vtr* flanquer○ une beigne◑ à.

bifocal /baɪˈfəʊkl/ *adj* [*lens*] bifocal.

bifocals /baɪˈfəʊklz/ *npl* verres *mpl* à double foyer, verres *mpl* bifocaux spec.

bifurcate /ˈbaɪfəkeɪt/ *vi* sout bifurquer.

bifurcation /ˌbaɪfəˈkeɪʃn/ *n* sout bifurcation *f*.

big /bɪg/ *adj* **1** (in build) (tall) grand (*before n*); (strong) grand et fort, costaud○; euph (heavy) fort; **to get ~(ger)** (taller) grandir; (fatter) grossir; (in pregnancy) s'arrondir; **2** (in size) [*bed, room, building, garden, lake, town*] grand (*before n*); [*animal, car, boat, parcel, box*] gros/grosse (*before n*), grand (*before n*); **a ~ book** (thick) un gros livre; (large-format) un grand livre; **to have ~ hands/~ feet** avoir de grandes mains/de grands pieds; **in ~ letters** en grosses lettres; **3** (in age) grand (*before n*); **his ~ brother** son grand frère, son frère aîné; **the ~ boys** les grands; **you're a ~ girl** tu es une grande fille; **you're ~ enough to know that** tu es assez grand pour savoir que; **4** (in extent) [*family, crowd, class, party*] grand (*before n*); [*collection, organization, company*] gros/grosse (*before n*), grand (*before n*); [*meal*] copieux/-ieuse; **to be a ~ eater** manger beaucoup; **5** (important) [*question, problem, decision, change, moment, event*] grand (*before n*); **it makes a ~ difference** ça fait une grande différence; **the extra rooms make a ~ difference** ça fait une grande différence d'avoir des salles en plus; **you're making a ~ mistake** tu es en train de faire une grave erreur; **I think we're on to something ~**○ je sens que nous allons découvrir quelque chose d'important; **this may be the start of something ~** c'est peut-être le début de quelque chose d'important; **6** (emphatic) **you ~ baby!** espèce de bébé!; **~ bully!** espèce de grande brute!; **to be ~ in the music business**○ être très connu dans le monde de la musique; **to be in ~ trouble** être dans le pétrin○; **he gave me a ~ smile** il m'a fait un grand sourire; **the ~ moment** le grand moment; **a ~ thank you to**... un grand merci à...; **to do sth in a ~ way** faire qch sur une grande échelle; **to do things in a ~ way** faire les choses en grand; **he fell for her in a ~ way** il est tombé follement amoureux d'elle; **7**○ US (enthusiastic) **to be ~ on** être fanatique or fana○ de [*activity*]; **8** (generous) [*person*] généreux/-euse; **to have a ~ heart** avoir bon cœur, être très généreux; **that's ~ of you!** iron c'est trop généreux de ta part! iron; **9** gen, Pol **the Big Four/Five** les Quatre/Cinq Grands.

IDIOMS **to be** ou **go over ~**○ faire fureur, faire un tabac○ (**in** à, en); **to have a ~ head** péj avoir la grosse tête○; **to have a ~ mouth** ne pas savoir garder un secret; **why can't you keep your ~ mouth shut?** tu n'aurais pas pu la fermer○?; **to have ~ ideas, think ~**○ voir grand○; **what's the ~ idea?** qu'est-ce qui te prend?; **to look ~** US péj se donner de l'importance, frimer○; **to make it ~**○ avoir beaucoup de succès; **to talk ~**○ fanfaronner.

bigamist /ˈbɪgəmɪst/ *n* bigame *mf*.

bigamous /ˈbɪgəməs/ *adj* [*person, marriage*] bigame.

bigamy /ˈbɪgəmɪ/ *n* bigamie *f*.

big: **Big Apple** *n* New York; **~ band** *n* big band *m*.

big bang *n* **1** Astron big bang *m*; **2** GB Fin **the ~** le big bang (*la chute des valeurs à la Bourse de Londres en octobre 1986*).

big: **Big Ben** *n* Big Ben *m*; **Big Bertha** *n* Mil Hist la Grosse Berthe; **~-boned** *adj* bien charpenté.

Big Brother *n* Big Brother *m*, l'État *m* omniprésent; **~ is watching you** vous êtes sous surveillance.

big business *n* **1** ¢ les grandes entreprises *fpl*; **2 to be ~** rapporter gros.

big: **~ cat** *n* grand félin *m*; **~ cheese**○† *n* péj huile○ *f* pej, grosse légume○ *f*; **~ dipper**† *n* (at funfair) montagnes *fpl* russes; **Big Dipper** *n* US Astron Grande Ourse *f*, Grand Chariot *m*; **~ end** *n* GB Aut tête *f* de bielle.

big fish○ *n* fig gros bonnet○ *m*.

IDIOMS **to be a ~ in a small pond** GB ou **sea** US briller dans un petit groupe.

big: **~ game** *n* gros gibier *m*; **~ game hunter** *n* chasseur *m* de gros gibier; **~ game hunting** *n* chasse *f* au gros gibier.

big gun *n* **1** Mil gros canon *m*; **2**○ (important person) grand manitou○ *m*, gros bonnet○ *m*.

IDIOMS **to bring out the ~s** sortir la grosse artillerie; **to carry** ou **hold the ~s** avoir du poids, être puissant.

big: **~head**○ *n* péj crâneur/-euse○ *m/f*; **~headed**○ *adj* péj crâneur○/-euse, prétentieux/-ieuse; **~headedness**○ *n* péj vantardise *f*; **~-hearted** *adj* généreux/-euse.

bight /baɪt/ *n* **1** Geog baie *f*; **2** (in rope) boucle *f*.

big money○ *n* **to make ~**○ se faire un fric fou○, gagner gros; **there's ~ in computers**○ il y a beaucoup d'argent à faire dans les ordinateurs.

bigmouth○ /ˈbɪgmaʊθ/ *n* péj **1** (indiscreet person) **he's such a ~**○**!** il ne sait pas tenir sa langue!; **2** (loudmouth) grande gueule○ *f* pej.

bigmouthed○ /ˈbɪgmaʊðd/ *adj* péj grande gueule○ *inv*.

big name *n* (in music, art) grand nom *m*; (in film, sport) star *f*; **to be a ~** être connu (**in sth** dans le monde de qch).

big noise○ *n* gros bonnet○ *m*, huile○ *f* pej.

bigot /ˈbɪgət/ *n* gen doctrinaire *mf*; (about religion) bigot/-e *m/f*.

bigoted /ˈbɪgətɪd/ *adj* gen doctrinaire; (about religion) bigot/-te.

bigotry /ˈbɪgətrɪ/ *n* gen tendances *fpl* doctrinaires; (about religion) bigoterie *f*.

big: **~ screen** *n* grand écran *m*; **~ shot**○ *n* gros bonnet○ *m*, huile○ *f* pej; **Big Smoke**○ *n* GB hum Londres.

big stick○ *n* **the ~**○ la politique du bâton; **to carry** ou **wield the ~**○ pratiquer la politique du bâton.

big talk○ *n* ¢ fanfaronnades *fpl*; **to be full of ~** être vantard.

Big Ten *n* US Univ dix grandes universités *fpl* du centre-ouest.

big time○ /ˈbɪgtaɪm/ **I** *n* **the ~**○ la gloire *f*, la réussite *f*; **to make** ou **hit the ~**○ percer, réussir.

II big-time *modif* [*crook*] de grande envergure; **~ gambler** flambeur○ *m*; **~ industrialist** gros industriel *m*.

big: **~ toe** *n* gros orteil *m*; **~ top** *n* (tent) grand chapiteau *m*; fig (circus) cirque *m*.

big wheel *n* **1** GB (at funfair) grande roue *f*; **2**○ (important person) gros bonnet○ *m*.

bigwig○ /ˈbɪgwɪg/ *n* péj grosse légume○ *f*, huile○ *f* pej.

bijou /ˈbiːʒuː/ *adj* [*residence, apartment*] charmant; [*boutique*] chic.

bike /baɪk/ **I** *n* **1** (cycle) vélo *m*; **on a/by ~** à vélo; **can you ride a ~?** sais-tu faire du vélo?; **to get on/off a ~** monter à/descendre de vélo; **2** (motorbike) moto *f*.

II *modif* [*light, maintenance*] de vélo; [*ride, shed*] à vélo; [*hire*] de vélos. ▶ **bicycle lane**.

IDIOMS **on your ~**○**!** GB allez! du balais○!

biker○ /ˈbaɪkə(r)/ *n* motard○ *m*; **~('s) jacket** veste *f* de moto.

bikini /bɪˈkiːnɪ/ *n* bikini® *m*.

bilabial /ˌbaɪˈleɪbɪəl/ *n, adj* bilabiale (*f*).

bilateral /ˌbaɪˈlætərəl/ *adj* gen, Sci bilatéral.

bilaterally /ˌbaɪˈlætərəlɪ/ *adv* bilatéralement.

bilberry /ˈbɪlbrɪ, US -berɪ/ *n* (fruit, bush) myrtille *f*.

bile /baɪl/ *n* Physiol bile *f*; fig fiel *m*.

bile duct *n* canal *m* biliaire.

bilge /bɪldʒ/ *n* **1** Naut bouchain *m*; **2** (nonsense)○† inepties *fpl*.

bilge: **~ pump** *n* pompe *f* de cale; **~ water** *n* eau *f* de sentine.

bilharzia /ˌbɪlˈhɑːtsɪə/ ▶ 1354 *n* bilharziose *f*.

bilingual /ˌbaɪˈlɪŋgwəl/ *adj* bilingue; **she's ~ in French and German** elle est bilingue français-allemand.

bilingualism /ˌbaɪˈlɪŋgwəlɪzəm/ *n* bilinguisme *m*.

bilious /ˈbɪlɪəs/ *adj* **1** Med bilieux; **~ attack**† crise *f* de foie; **2** fig [*mood*] revêche; [*colour*] nauséeux.

biliousness /ˈbɪlɪəsnɪs/ *n* ₵ nausées *fpl*.

bilk /bɪlk/ *vtr* **1** (swindle) escroquer [*person*] (**of, out of** de); **2** (thwart) contrecarrer; **3** (elude) se dérober à.

bill /bɪl/ **I** *n* **1** Comm (for payment) (in restaurant) addition *f*; (for maintenance, electricity etc) facture *f*; (from hotel, doctor, dentist etc) note *f*; **electricity/gas/telephone ~** facture *f* or note *f* d'électricité/de gaz/de téléphone; **he gave me a ~ for £10** il m'a donné une note or facture de 10 livres; **he gave me a ~ for repairing the car** il m'a donné une note or facture pour la réparation de la voiture; **he gave me a ~ for the work/the damage** il m'a facturé le travail/les dégâts; **to pay/settle a ~** payer/régler une note or facture or addition; **to make out a ~** établir une note or facture; **put it on the ~, please** mettez-le sur ma note s'il vous plaît; **2** Jur, Pol (law) (also **Bill**) projet *m* de loi; **Education/Employment Bill** projet *m* de loi pour l'éducation/l'emploi; **to pass/defeat a ~** adopter/rejeter un projet de loi; **3** (poster) affiche *f*; **to be on the ~** être à l'affiche; **to be top of the ~, to top the ~** être en tête d'affiche; **'stick no ~s'** 'défense d'afficher'; **4** US (banknote) billet *m* (de banque); **dollar/ten dollar ~** billet *m* d'un dollar/de dix dollars; **5** Zool (beak) bec *m*; **6**† Fin (promise to pay) billet *m* à ordre; **7** Geog (promontory) promontoire *m*.
II *vtr* **1** (send demand for payment) faire une facture à [*person, company*]; **to ~ sb for sth** facturer qch à qn; **to ~ sb for doing** faire une facture à qn pour avoir fait; **he ~ed me for repairing the car** il m'a fait une facture pour la réparation de la voiture; **2** Theat, gen (advertise) **to be ~ed as...** [*event, entertainment, meeting*] être annoncé comme étant...; **the show was ~ed as a musical comedy** le spectacle était affiché comme étant une comédie musicale; **he is ~ed to appear at the Odeon/in 'Hamlet'/as Hamlet** il est à l'affiche à l'Odéon/de 'Hamlet'/dans le rôle de Hamlet.
IDIOMS **to fit** ou **fill the ~** faire l'affaire; **to give sb/sth a clean ~ of health** lit trouver qn/qch en parfait état de santé; fig blanchir qn/qch. ▶ **coo**.

billboard /ˈbɪlbɔːd/ *n* panneau *m* d'affichage.

billet /ˈbɪlɪt/ **I** *n* **1** Mil cantonnement *m*; **2** Ind billette *f*.
II *vtr* cantonner [*soldier, refugee*] (**on, with** chez).

billeting officer ▶ 1612 *n* Mil officier *m* responsable du cantonnement.

bill: **~fold** *n* US portefeuille *m*; **~ hook** *n* serpe *f*.

billiard /ˈbɪlɪəd/ ▶ 1282 **I billiards** *n* (+ *v sg*) billard *m*.
II *modif* [*ball, cue, table*] de billard.

billing /ˈbɪlɪŋ/ *n* **1** Theat (of performers) affiche *f*; **to get top ~** tenir le haut de l'affiche; **2** Comm facturation *f*; **itemized ~** facturation détaillée.
IDIOMS **~ and cooing** fig câlins *mpl* d'amoureux.

billion /ˈbɪlɪən/ ▶ 1505 **I** *n* **1** (a thousand million) milliard *m*; **2** GB (a million million) billion *m*.
II billions○ *npl* (exaggerating) des tonnes○ *fpl* (**of** de).
III *adj* **a ~ people** un milliard de personnes; **two ~ dollars** deux milliards de dollars.

billionaire /ˌbɪlɪəˈneə(r)/ *n* milliardaire *mf*.

bill: **~ of exchange**, **BE** *n* Comm, Fin lettre *f* de change; **~ of fare** *n* menu *m*; **~ of lading** *n* Comm connaissement *m*.

bill of rights *n* gen, Pol déclaration *f* des droits (d'un peuple); **Bill of Rights** US Hist Constitution *f* des États-Unis.

bill of sale *n* acte *m* de vente.

billow /ˈbɪləʊ/ **I** *n* **1** (of smoke, steam) tourbillons *mpl*; **2** littér (sea) **the ~s** les flots *mpl*.
II *vi* [*clouds, steam, smoke*] s'élever en tourbillons.
■ **billow out** [*skirt, sail*] se gonfler; [*steam*] s'élever.

billowy /ˈbɪləʊɪ/ *adj* littér [*smoke, clouds*] ondoyant; [*sea*] houleux/-euse.

billposter, **billsticker** /ˈbɪlpəʊstə(r), ˈbɪlstɪkə(r)/ ▶ 1692 *n* colleur *m* d'affiches.

billy /ˈbɪlɪ/ *n* **1** Austral, GB (also **~can**) gamelle *f*; **2** US (truncheon) matraque *f*.

billy goat *n* bouc *m*.

billy-o(h)○† /ˈbɪlɪəʊ/ *n* **to run like ~** courir comme un dératé.

bimbo○ /ˈbɪmbəʊ/ *n* péj (stupid woman) bécasse○ *f*; (pretty girl) minette○ *f*; (starlet) starlette○ *f*.

bimetallic /ˌbaɪmɪˈtælɪk/ *adj* bimétallique.

bimetallism /ˌbaɪˈmetəlɪzəm/ *n* bimétallisme *m*.

bin /bɪn/ **I** *n* **1** GB (for rubbish) poubelle *f*; **put** ou **throw it in the ~** jetez-le à la poubelle; **2** (for storage) casier *m*; (for grain) récipient *m*; Wine casier *m* (à bouteilles); **storage ~** casier *m* de rangement.
II *vtr* (*prés p etc* **-nn-**) mettre [qch] à la poubelle, jeter.

binary /ˈbaɪnərɪ/ *adj* (all contexts) [*code, number, weapon*] binaire.

binary: **~ fission** *n* fission *f* binaire; **~ star** *n* étoile *f* binaire, binaire *f*; **~ system** *n* Math, Comput numération *f* binaire, binaire *m*.

bind /baɪnd/ **I**○ *n* corvée *f*; **what a ~!** quelle corvée!; **it's a ~ having to...** c'est une vraie corvée de devoir...
II *vtr* (*prét, pp* **bound**) **1** (tie up) attacher [*hands, feet, bundle, parcel*]; ligoter [*person*]; panser [*wound*]; **they bound him to a post** ils l'ont attaché à un poteau; **2** (constrain) **to ~ sb to do** [*law, rule, contract, oath*] imposer à qn de faire; **to be bound by** [*person*] être tenu par [*law, rule, contract, oath*]; **3** (unite) (also **~ together**) unir [*people, family, community*]; **the love that ~s him to her** l'amour qui l'unit à elle; **4** Sewing poser un biais sur [*edge*]; **5** (in bookbinding) relier [*book*] (**in** en); **6** Culin lier [*mixture*] (**with** avec).
III *vi* (*prét, pp* **bound**) (cohere) Biol, Chem [*particles*] se lier (**to** à); Culin [*mixture*] lier.
IV *v refl* (*prét, pp* **bound**) **to ~ oneself** (commit oneself) (to belief, action) s'engager (**to sth** à qch); (emotionally) se lier (**to sb** à qn).
IDIOMS **to be in a ~**○ US être dans le pétrin○.
■ **bind over**: **~ [sb] over** Jur relâcher [qn] sous condition; **he was bound over to keep the peace** on l'a relâché sous condition qu'il ne récidive pas; **he was bound over to appear before the High Court** on l'a relâché sous condition pour qu'il puisse comparaître devant la cour suprême.
■ **bind up**: **~ up [sth], ~ [sth] up** bander [*wound, part of body*]; attacher [*bundle*].

binder /ˈbaɪndə(r)/ *n* **1** (for papers) classeur *m*; **2** Agric lieuse *f*; **3** Constr, Ind (for cement, paint) liant *m*.

binder twine *n* Agric ficelle *f* à lier.

bindery /ˈbaɪndərɪ/ *n* atelier *m* de reliure.

binding /ˈbaɪndɪŋ/ **I** *n* **1** (cover) (on book) reliure *f*; **cloth/leather ~** reliure *f* d'étoffe/de cuir; **2** (process) (of book) reliure *f*; **3** Sewing (bias) biais *m*; (for hem, seam) extrafort *m*; **4** (on ski) fixation *f*.
II *adj* [*agreement, contract, decision, duty, force, procedure, rule*] qui lie, qui engage; **you should know that the contract/rule is ~** vous devriez savoir que le contrat/la règle vous engage or lie; **to be ~ (up)on sb** lier qn, engager qn.

bindweed /ˈbaɪndwiːd/ *n* liseron *m*.

bin end *n* Wine bouteille *f* fin de série.

binge○ /bɪndʒ/ **I** *n* (overindulgence) gen frénésie *f*; (drinking) beuverie *f*; (festive eating) gueuleton○ *m*; **to go on a ~** (celebrating) aller faire la noce; **to have a ~** (as part of eating disorder) se bourrer de nourriture.
II *vi* (*p prés* **bingeing** ou **binging**) se bourrer de nourriture; **to ~ on** se bourrer de.

bingo /ˈbɪŋgəʊ/ ▶ 1282 **I** *n* bingo *m*.
II *modif* [*card, game, hall*] de bingo.
III *excl* (by game winner) bingo!, j'ai gagné!; gen eurêka!

bin liner *n* GB sac *m* poubelle.

binnacle /ˈbɪnəkl/ *n* Naut boîte *f* à compas.

binocular /bɪˈnɒkjʊlə(r)/ *adj* binoculaire.

binoculars /bɪˈnɒkjʊləz/ *npl* jumelles *fpl*.

binomial /ˌbaɪˈnəʊmɪəl/ **I** *n* Math, Biol binôme *m*.
II *adj* [*distribution, coefficient*] binomial.

binomial: **~ nomenclature** *n* taxinomie *f* binomiale; **~ theorem** *n* Math binôme *m* de Newton.

bint○ /bɪnt/ *n* GB gonzesse◑ *f*.

binuclear /ˌbaɪˈnjuːklɪə(r), US -ˈnuː-/ *adj* binucléaire.

biochemical /ˌbaɪəʊˈkemɪkl/ *adj* biochimique.

biochemist /ˌbaɪəʊˈkemɪst/ ▶ 1692 *n* biochimiste *mf*.

biochemistry /ˌbaɪəʊˈkemɪstrɪ/ *n* biochimie *f*.

biodegradable /ˌbaɪəʊdɪˈgreɪdəbl/ *adj* biodégradable.

biodiversity /ˌbaɪəʊdɪˈvɜːsətɪ/ *n* diversité *f* biologique.

bioengineering /ˌbaɪəʊˌendʒɪˈnɪərɪŋ/ *n* génie *m* biologique.

biofeedback /ˌbaɪəʊˈfiːdbæk/ *n* bio-feedback *m*.

biofuel /ˈbaɪəʊfjʊəl/ *n* biocarburant *m*.

biogenesis /ˌbaɪəʊˈdʒenəsɪs/ *n* biogenèse *f*.

biographer /baɪˈɒgrəfə(r)/ ▶ 1692 *n* biographe *mf*.

biographical /ˌbaɪəˈgræfɪkl/ *adj* biographique.

biography /baɪˈɒgrəfɪ/ *n* biographie *f*.

biological /ˌbaɪəˈlɒdʒɪkl/ *adj* biologique.

biological clock *n* horloge *f* biologique.

biologically /ˌbaɪəˈlɒdʒɪklɪ/ *adv* biologiquement.

biological: **~ powder** *n* lessive *f* avec enzyme; **~ shield** *n* Nucl, Ecol bouclier *m* biologique; **~ warfare** *n* guerre *f* biologique.

biologist /baɪˈɒlədʒɪst/ ▶ 1692 *n* biologiste *mf*.

biology /baɪˈɒlədʒɪ/ **I** *n* biologie *f*.
II *modif* [*teacher, lesson, laboratory*] de biologie.

biomass /ˈbaɪəʊmæs/ *n* biomasse *f*.

biome /ˈbaɪəʊm/ *n* biome *m*.

biomedical /ˌbaɪəʊˈmedɪkl/ *adj* biomédical.

biometrics /ˌbaɪəʊˈmetrɪks/ *n* (+ *v sg*) biométrie *f*.

bionic /baɪˈɒnɪk/ *adj* bionique.

bionics /baɪˈɒnɪks/ *n* (+ *v sg*) bionique *f*.

biophysicist /ˌbaɪəʊˈfɪzɪsɪst/ ▶ 1692 *n* biophysicien/-ienne *m/f*.

biophysics /ˌbaɪəʊˈfɪzɪks/ *n* (+ *v sg*) biophysique *f*.

biopic○ /ˈbaɪˈɒpɪk/ *n* Cin biographie *f* romancée.

biopsy /ˈbaɪɒpsɪ/ *n* biopsie *f*.

biorhythm /ˈbaɪəʊrɪðəm/ *n* biorythme *m.*

biosphere /ˈbaɪəʊsfɪə(r)/ *n* biosphère *f.*

biosynthesis /ˌbaɪəʊˈsɪnθəsɪs/ *n* biosynthèse *f.*

biota /baɪˈəʊtə/ *npl* biote *m.*

biotechnology /ˌbaɪəʊtekˈnɒlədʒɪ/ *n* biotechnologie *f.*

biotic /baɪˈɒtɪk/ *adj* biotique.

biowarfare /ˌbaɪəʊˈwɔːfeə(r)/ *n* guerre *f* biologique.

bipartisan /ˌbaɪpɑːtɪˈzæn, baɪˈpɑːtɪzn/ *adj* Pol [*government, agreement*] bipartite.

bipartite /baɪˈpɑːtaɪt/ *adj* bipartite.

biped /ˈbaɪped/ *n, adj* bipède (*m*).

biplane /ˈbaɪpleɪn/ *n* biplan *m.*

bipolar /baɪˈpəʊlə(r)/ *adj* [*transistor, planet*] bipolaire.

bipolarization /baɪˌpəʊləraɪˈzeɪʃn, US -rɪˈz-/ *n* (magnetic) bipolarisation *f.*

bipolarize /baɪˈpəʊləraɪz/ *vtr* bipolariser [*metal*].

birch /bɜːtʃ/ **I** *n* **1** (also **~ tree**) bouleau *m*; **2** (also **~ wood**) (bois *m* de) bouleau *m*; **3** (also **~ rod**) Hist fouet *m*; **to get the ~** recevoir le fouet.
II *vtr* Hist fouetter [*offender*].

birching /ˈbɜːtʃɪŋ/ *n* Hist (peine *f* du) fouet *m.*

bird /bɜːd/ *n* **1** Zool oiseau *m*; **2**○ GB (girl) nana○ *f*; **to pull the ~s** draguer les nanas○; **3**○ (person) **a funny** ou **queer old ~** un drôle d'oiseau○.
IDIOMS **a little ~ told me**○ mon petit doigt m'a dit; **as free as a ~** libre comme l'air; **the ~s and the bees** le b-a ba de la vie; **to sing like a ~** chanter comme un oiseau; **to tell sb about the ~s and the bees** expliquer à qn comment naissent les enfants; **the ~ has flown** l'oiseau s'est envolé; **to do ~**○ faire de la taule○; **to get the ~**○ se faire siffler; **to give** ou **flip sb the ~**○ US envoyer paître qn○; **to kill two ~s with one stone** faire d'une pierre deux coups; **(strictly) for the ~s** fait pour les imbéciles. ▶ **feather.**

bird: **~ bath** *n* vasque *f* pour oiseaux; **~-brain**○ *n* cervelle *f* d'oiseau○; **~cage** *n* cage *f* à oiseaux; **~ call** *n* cri *m* d'oiseau; **~-fancier** *n* amateur/-trice *m/f* d'oiseaux; **~-feeder** *n* trémie *f.*

birdie /ˈbɜːdɪ/ **I** *n* **1** (in golf) birdie *m*; **2**○ (bird) zoziau○ *m.*
II *vtr* (in golf) marquer un birdie à [*hole*].
IDIOMS **watch the ~**○! Phot le petit oiseau va sortir!

bird: **~ life** *n* oiseaux *mpl*; **~like** *adj* semblable à un oiseau; **~lime** *n* glu *f*; **~ man**○ *n* ornithologue *mf*; **~ of paradise** *n* oiseau *m* de paradis; **~ of prey** *n* oiseau *m* de proie; **~ sanctuary** *n* réserve *f* ornithologique; **~seed** *n* graines *fpl* (pour les oiseaux); **~'s eye view** *n* vue *f* d'ensemble; **~'s foot trefoil** *n* Bot trèfle *m* en patte d'oiseau; **~'s nest** *n* nid *m* d'oiseau.

bird's-nesting *n* **to go ~** aller ramasser les œufs dans les nids.

bird: **~'s nest soup** *n* soupe *f* aux nids d'hirondelle; **~song** *n* chant *m* des oiseaux; **~ species** *n* espèce *f* d'oiseau; **~table** *n* perchoir *m*; **~watcher** *n* ornithologue *mf* amateur/-trice.

bird-watching /ˈbɜːdwɒtʃɪŋ/ *n* observation *f* de la vie des oiseaux; **to go ~** observer les oiseaux.

biretta /bɪˈretə/ *n* barrette *f.*

birling /ˈbɜːlɪŋ/ ▶ **1282** *n* US birling *m*, bûche *f* roulante.

biro® /ˈbaɪərəʊ/ *n* GB (*pl* **~s**) stylo-bille *m*, bic®; **in ~** au stylo-bille.

birth /bɜːθ/ *n* gen, lit, fig naissance *f* (**of** de); Med (process of giving birth) accouchement *m*; **to give ~** [*person*] accoucher (**to** de); **to give ~ to** [*animal*] mettre bas [*young*]; **a difficult/easy ~** un accouchement difficile/facile; **at ~** à la naissance; **by ~** de naissance; **French/Catholic by ~** français/catholique de naissance; **from ~ he had lived in Paris** depuis sa naissance il avait vécu à Paris; **blind from ~** aveugle de naissance; **of high ~** de haute naissance; **of low ~** d'origine *f* modeste; **of French ~** né/née français/-e; **date/place of ~** date *f*/lieu *m* de naissance; **the ~ of Christianity/Marxism** la naissance du Christianisme/du Marxisme.

birth certificate *n* certificat *m* de naissance.

birth control **I** *n* (in society) contrôle *m* des naissances; (by couple) contraception *f*; **to practise ~** [*couple*] utiliser une méthode de contraception.
II *modif* [*method, device*] de contraception, contraceptif/-ive; [*advice*] en matière de contraception.

birthday /ˈbɜːθdeɪ/ **I** *n* anniversaire *m*; **Happy Birthday!** Bon or Joyeux Anniversaire!; **to wish sb (a) happy ~** souhaiter à qn un bon or joyeux anniversaire; **on my/his ~** (pour) le jour de mon/son anniversaire; **on his tenth ~** pour son dixième anniversaire; **to celebrate sb's ~** fêter l'anniversaire de qn.
II *modif* [*cake, card, drink, entertainment, greetings, guest, present*] d'anniversaire.
IDIOMS **in one's ~ suit**○ hum, euph en costume d'Adam or d'Ève○ hum.

birthday: **~ boy** *n* vedette *f* du jour; **~ girl** *n* vedette *f* du jour; **Birthday Honours list** *n* GB *liste des distinctions honorifiques accordées par le souverain le jour de son anniversaire*; **~ party** *n* (for child) goûter d'anniversaire; (for adult) soirée *f* d'anniversaire.

birth: **~ defect** *n* infirmité *f* de naissance; **~ing pool** *n* Med piscine *f* d'accouchement; **~ing stool** *n* Med chaise *f* d'accouchement; **~mark** *n* tache *f* de naissance; **~ mother** *n* mère *f* biologique; **~ pangs** *npl* fig affres *fpl* de l'accouchement (**of** de); **~place** *n* lit lieu *m* de naissance; fig berceau *m* (**of** de); **~rate** *n* taux *m* de natalité; **~ register** *n* registre *m* des naissances; **~right** *n* gen droit *m* (acquis à la naissance); (of first-born) droit *m* d'aînesse; **~s column** *n* Journ rubrique *f* des naissances; **~ sign** *n* signe *m* du zodiaque; **~s, marriages, and deaths** *npl* Journ carnet *m* du jour; **~stone** *n* pierre *f* porte-bonheur; **~ weight** *n* poids *m* à la naissance.

BIS *n*: *abrév* ▶ **Bank for International Settlements.**

biscuit /ˈbɪskɪt/ **I** *n* **1** GB (thin cake) biscuit *m*, petit gâteau *m*; **plain/sweet ~s** petits gâteaux secs/sucrés; **2** US (soft bread) pain *m* au lait; **3** (also **~ ware**) biscuit *m* de porcelaine.
II ▶ **1104** *adj* (also **~-coloured**) de couleur bise *inv.*
IDIOMS **to take the ~** [*person*] avoir le pompon; [*event*] être le pompon.

biscuit: **~ barrel** *n* boîte *f* à biscuits; **~ factory** *n* biscuiterie *f*; **~ firing** *n* Ind cuisson *f* au four sans glaçure; **~ tin** *n* boîte *f* à biscuits.

bisect /baɪˈsekt/ *vtr* diviser [qch] en deux parties égales.

bisection /baɪˈsekʃn/ *n* bissection *f.*

bisector /baɪˈsektə(r)/ *n* (line) (droite *f*) bissectrice *f*; (plane) plan *m* bissecteur.

bisexual /baɪˈsekʃʊəl/ *n, adj* bisexuel/-elle *m/f.*

bishop /ˈbɪʃəp/ *n* **1** Relig évêque *m*; **2** (in chess) fou *m.*

bishopric /ˈbɪʃəprɪk/ *n* évêché *m.*

bismuth /ˈbɪzməθ/ *n* bismuth *m.*

bison /ˈbaɪsn/ *n* (*pl* **~**) bison *m.*

bisque /bɪsk/ *n* **1** Culin bisque *f*; **lobster ~** bisque de homard; **2** (earthenware) biscuit *m* de faïence; **3** Sport point *m* de handicap.

bissextile /bɪˈsekstaɪl/ *adj* [*year*] bissextile.

bistable /baɪˈsteɪbl/ *adj* bistable.

bistoury /ˈbɪstərɪ/ *n* bistouri *m.*

bistre /ˈbɪstə(r)/ ▶ **1104** *n, adj* bistre (*m*).

bistro /ˈbiːstrəʊ/ *n* ≈ bistrot *m.*

bit /bɪt/ **I** *prét* ▶ **bite.**
II *n* **1** (small piece) (of food, substance, wood) morceau *m* (**of** de); (of paper, string, garden, land) bout *m* (**of** de); **a ~ of cheese/coal** un morceau de fromage/charbon; **a ~ of news** une nouvelle; **every ~ of dirt** la moindre petite saleté; **a food processor and all its ~s**○ un robot et tous ses accessoires *mpl*; **every ~ of her wanted to say yes** elle voulait dire oui de tout son cœur; **to take sth to ~s** démonter qch; **to come/fall to ~s** s'en aller/tomber en morceaux; **2**○ (small amount) **a ~** un peu; **a little ~** un petit peu; **three and a ~** trois et des poussières○; **and a ~ over** et des poussières○; **would you like a ~ more?** tu en veux encore?; **a ~ of** un peu de [*time, peace, sun, butter, money etc*]; **a ~ of everything** un peu de tout; **a ~ of difficulty/information** quelques difficultés/informations; **a ~ of advice** un petit conseil; **with a ~ of luck** avec un peu de chance; **to have a ~ of bad luck** ne pas avoir de chance; **to do a ~ of shopping** faire quelques courses *fpl*; **it won't do a ~ of good** ça ne servira à rien; **it isn't a ~ of use asking** cela ne sert à rien de demander; **that corkscrew isn't a ~ of use** ce tire-bouchon est bon à jeter; **wait a ~!** attends un peu!; **after a ~** un peu après; **quite a ~ of, a good ~ of** pas mal de [*time, money, resentment etc*]; **quite a ~** ou **a good ~ further/bigger** bien plus loin/grand; **3**○ (section) passage *m*; **listen, this ~ is brilliant!** écoute, ce passage est génial○!; **the next ~ is even better** ce qui suit est encore mieux; **the ~ where Hamlet dies** le moment où Hamlet meurt; **4** Comput bit *m*, élément *m* binaire; **a 16-~ model** un modèle de 16 bits; **5**† (coin) pièce *f*; **6** Equit mors *m*; **standard ~** mors *m* normal; **7** Tech (also **drill ~**) mèche *f.*
III○ **a ~** *adv phr* (rather) un peu; **a ~ deaf/cold/surprising** un peu sourd/froid/surprenant; **a ~ early** un peu trop tôt; **a ~ like me** un peu comme moi; **move back a ~** recule un peu; **it's asking a ~ much** c'est un peu trop demander; **she isn't a ~ like me** elle ne me ressemble pas du tout; **it's a ~ of a surprise/a mess** c'est un peu surprenant/en désordre; **he's a ~ of a brute/a Tory** il a un côté brute/Conservateur; **for a ~ of a change** pour changer un peu; **a ~ of a disappointment** un peu décevant; **to have a ~ of a headache** avoir un peu mal à la tête; **a ~ of a problem** un petit problème; **it was a ~ of a shock to me** ça m'a un peu choqué; **it was a ~ of a joke** ce n'était pas très sérieux; **we had a ~ of a giggle** nous avons bien ri.
IDIOMS **a ~ of this and a ~ of that** un peu de tout; **a ~ of stuff**○ une gonzesse○; **~ by ~** petit à petit; **~s and bobs**○ affaires *fpl*; **~s and pieces** (fragments) morceaux *mpl*; (belongings) affaires *fpl*; **every ~ as good/clever** tout aussi bon/intelligent; **he's every ~ a lawyer** c'est le type même de l'avocat; **not a ~!** de rien!; **not a ~ of it**○! pas du tout!; **that's a ~ off**○! c'est pas très réglo○!; **to do one's ~** faire sa part (de boulot○); **to have/take the ~ between one's teeth** avoir/prendre le mors aux dents; ▶ **bite.**

bitch /bɪtʃ/ **I** *n* **1** Zool chienne *f*; **a labrador ~** une chienne labrador; **2**◐ (as insult) garce◐ *f*, salope◐ *f*; **you son of a ~**◐! espèce de salaud◐!; **3**○ (malicious woman) **to be a ~** être vache○; **don't be a ~!** sois pas vache○!; **4**○ [*aggravation*] **a ~ of a job** un sale boulot○; **life's a ~** la vie n'est pas un cadeau○.
II○ *vi* **1** (gossip spitefully) dire du mal (**about** de); **2** US (complain) pester○ (**about** contre).

bitchy○ /ˈbɪtʃɪ/ *adj* **1** (malicious) [*person, comment*] malveillant; **to be ~ about sb**

débiner○ qn; **2** US (aggressive) hargneux/-euse.

bite /baɪt/ **I** *n* **1** (mouthful) bouchée *f*; **in one ~** en une bouchée; **to have** ou **take a ~ of sth** prendre une bouchée de qch; **to take a ~ out of sth** fig faire un trou dans qch; **that will take a big ~ out of our budget/profits** cela va faire un grand trou dans notre budget/marge bénéficiaire; **2**○ (snack) morceau *m* (à manger); **to have a ~ (to eat)** manger un morceau; **to have** ou **grab a quick ~ (to eat)** manger un morceau en vitesse; **3** fig (impact, keen edge) (of wind, cold) morsure *f*; (of food) piquant *m*; (of argument, performance, style, film) mordant *m*; **his speech/film has ~** son discours/film a du mordant; **4** (from insect) piqûre *f*; (from dog, snake) morsure *f*; **insect ~** piqûre *f* d'insecte; **5** Fishg touche *f*; **to have a ~** lit avoir une touche; fig trouver amateur; **the house is up for sale but we haven't had any ~s yet** la maison est en vente mais nous n'avons pas encore trouvé amateur; **6** Dent occlusion *f*.
II *vtr* (*prét* **bit**, *pp* **bitten**) [*person, animal*] mordre; [*insect*] piquer; **to ~ sth in two** couper [qch] en deux d'un coup de dent; **to ~ one's nails** se ronger les ongles.
III *vi* (*prét* **bit**, *pp* **bitten**) **1** (take effect) [*measure, policy, rule, new rates, strike, shortage*] se faire sentir; **2** Fishg [*fish*] mordre.
IDIOMS **he/she won't ~ you**○! il/elle ne va pas te manger○!; **to ~ one's lip** se mordre les lèvres; **to ~ the hand that feeds you** cracher dans la soupe; **the biter bit** tel est pris qui croyait prendre; **to be bitten by the DIY/health food bug**○ attraper le virus○ du bricolage/de la diététique; ▸**bullet**.
■ **bite back**: **~ back [sth]** ravaler [*rude comment, reply*].
■ **bite into**: **~ into [sth]** lit mordre dans [*fruit, sandwich etc*]; fig (affect) avoir un effet sur [*economy, finances*] .
■ **bite off**: **~ off [sth]**, **~ [sth] off** arracher [qch] d'un coup de dent.
■ **bite on**: **~ on [sth]** mordre sur.
■ **bite through**: **~ through [sth]** [*person, animal*] percer [qch] avec ses dents.

bite mark *n* marque *f* de morsure.

bite-sized /ˈbaɪtsaɪzd/ *adj* de la taille d'une bouchée; **~ chunks** ou **pieces of chicken** des bouchées de poulet.

biting /ˈbaɪtɪŋ/ *adj* **1** (penetrating) [*wind*] cinglant; [*cold*] pénétrant; **2** fig [*comment, irony, sarcasm, satire, wit*] mordant; **3** (capable of biting) [*insect*] qui pique.

bitingly /ˈbaɪtɪŋlɪ/ *adv* d'un ton mordant.

bit: **~ part** *n* Theat petit rôle *m*; **~ slice (micro)processor** *n* Comput (micro)processeur *m* en tranches; **~ slicing** *n* Comput découpage *m* bit par bit.

bitten /ˈbɪtn/ *pp* ▸**bite** IDIOMS **once ~ twice shy** Prov chat échaudé craint l'eau froide Prov.

bitter /ˈbɪtə(r)/ **I** *n* GB (beer) bière *f* (*au fort pourcentage de houblon, légèrement amère*).
II bitters *npl* bitter *m*.
III *adj* **1** (sour) amer/-ère; **2** (resentful) [*person, tone, memory, comment*] amer/-ère; **she felt ~ about the way they had treated her/about his accusation** la façon dont ils l'avaient traitée/son accusation la remplissait d'amertume; **3** (fierce) [*critic*] acerbe; [*hatred*] profond; [*opposition, rivalry*] farouche; [*attack, battle*] féroce; [*argument, feud*] violent; **they are ~ enemies** ils se haïssent farouchement; **4** (very cold) [*weather, wind*] glacial; **5** (hard to accept) [*disappointment, truth*] cruel/-elle; [*legacy*] littér lourd; [*harvest*] littér dur; [*blow*] dur; **the result was a ~ blow to the party** le résultat a porté un coup dur au parti; **I know from ~ experience that** ma triste expérience m'a appris que.
IDIOMS **it's a ~ pill to swallow** la pilule est dure à avaler; **to fight/carry on to the ~ end** lutter/aller jusqu'au bout.

bitter: **~ almond** *n* amande *f* amère; **~ aloes** *n* aloès *m* médicinal; **~ lemon** *n* Schweppes® *m* (citron).

bitterly /ˈbɪtəlɪ/ *adv* **1** (resentfully) [*complain, resent, laugh, speak*] amèrement; **2** (intensely) [*unhappy, angry*] extrêmement; [*criticized, disappointed*] cruellement; [*regret*] profondément; [*fight, contest*] farouchement; [*weep*] amèrement; **a ~ divided party** un parti profondément divisé; **a ~ cold wind** un vent glacial; **it's ~ cold** il fait un froid terrible.

bittern /ˈbɪtən/ *n* butor *m*.

bitterness /ˈbɪtənɪs/ *n* lit, fig amertume *f*.

bitter orange *n* Bot, Culin bigarade *f*.

bittersweet /ˌbɪtəˈswiːt/ **I** *n* Bot douce-amère *f*.
II *adj* lit aigre-doux/aigre-douce; fig doux-amer/douce-amère.

bitty /ˈbɪtɪ/ *adj* **1** (scrappy) [*account*] fragmentaire; **2**○ (tiny) (also **little ~, itty ~**) **a little ~ baby** un petit bout de chou○; **a little ~ piece of** un petit bout de.

bitumen /ˈbɪtjʊmɪn, US bəˈtuːmən/ *n* bitume *m*.

bituminous /bɪˈtjuːmɪnəs, US -ˈtuː-/ *adj* bitumineux/-euse.

bivalent /baɪˈveɪlənt/ *n, adj* bivalent (*m*).

bivalve /ˈbaɪvælv/ *n, adj* bivalve (*m*).

bivouac /ˈbɪvʊæk/ **I** *n* bivouac *m*.
II *vi* (*p prés etc* **-ck-**) bivouaquer.

biweekly /baɪˈwiːklɪ/ **I** *adj* [*publication*] (twice weekly) bihebdomadaire; (every two weeks) bimensuel/-elle.
II *adv* [*appear*] (twice weekly) deux fois par semaine; (every two weeks) toutes les deux semaines.

biz○ /bɪz/ *n* = **business**.
IDIOMS **to be just the ~**○ être au quart de poil○.

bizarre /bɪˈzɑː(r)/ *adj* bizarre.

bizarrely /bɪˈzɑːlɪ/ *adv* bizarrement.

blab○ /blæb/ (*p prés etc* **-bb-**) **I** *vtr* = **blab out**.
II *vi* **1** (reveal secret) vendre la mèche○, parler; **2** US (talk idly) jacasser (**about** sur).
■ **blab out**: **~ out [sth]**, **~ [sth] out** aller raconter [*secret*].

blabbermouth○ /ˈblæbəmaʊθ/ *n* péj pipelette○ *f*.

black /blæk/ ▸**1104** **I** *n* **1** (colour) noir *m*; **in ~** en noir; **to wear ~** gen porter du noir, s'habiller en noir; (in mourning) porter le deuil; **2** (also **Black**) (person) Noir/-e *m/f*; **3** Fin **to be in the ~** être créditeur/-trice; **to stay in the ~** maintenir un solde créditeur; **to put sb back in the ~** permettre à qn de sortir du rouge; **4** Games (in chess, draughts) noirs *mpl*; (in roulette) noir *m*; **I'll be ~** je prends les noirs; **5** (snooker or pool ball) (bille *f*) noire *f*.
II *adj* **1** (dark) [*car, cloud, hair, paint*] noir; [*night*] obscur; **to paint/dye sth ~** peindre/teindre qch en noir; **to go** ou **turn ~** devenir noir, noircir; **2** (African, Afro-Caribbean) (also **Black**) [*skin, community, culture, president*] noir; [*school*] pour les Noirs; **a ~ man/woman** un Noir/une Noire; **3** (without milk) [*coffee*] noir; [*tea*] nature; **4** (dirty) [*face, mark, towel*] noir; **5** (macabre) [*comedy, humour*] noir; **6** (gloomy) [*mood, picture, thoughts*] noir; [*despair*] profond; [*future, prospect*] sombre; [*news, day, week*] mauvais; **it was a ~ day for us when he left** le jour où il est parti a été un mauvais jour pour nous; **she's in one of her ~ moods** elle est d'humeur noire; **things are looking ~ for us** les choses se présentent mal pour nous; **Black Monday** Fin Lundi noir; **7** (angry) [*look*] meurtrier/-ière; [*mood*] massacrant; **his face was as ~ as thunder** on lisait dans ses yeux une colère noire; **8** (evil) [*deed, heart, magic, thought*] noir; ▸**black and white**.
III *vtr* **1** (put black onto) noircir [*sb's face, hands*]; cirer [*boots*]; **to ~ one's face/hands** se noircir le visage/les mains; **2** GB (bruise) **to ~ sb's eye** faire un œil au beurre noir à qn; **3** GB (boycott) boycotter.
IDIOMS **as ~ as coal/soot** noir comme du charbon/de la suie. ▸**blue**.
■ **black out**: ¶ **~ out** [*person*] s'évanouir; ¶ **~ [sth] out, ~ out [sth]** **1** (hide all lights) faire le black-out dans [*house*]; faire l'obscurité sur [*stage*]; **2** (cut power) couper le courant dans [*area*]; **3** (suspend broadcasting) interrompre la diffusion de [*programme*]; **4** (obliterate) rayer (d'un gros trait noir) [*name, word*].
■ **black up** [*actor*] se noircir le visage.

black: **Black Africa** *pr n* Geog Afrique *f* noire; **~ American** *n* noir/-e *m/f* américain/-e.

blackamoor‡ /ˈblækəmɔː(r), -mʊə(r)/ *n* péj nègre *m* pej.

black and white ▸**1104** **I** *n* **1** Cin, Phot noir et blanc *m*; **in ~** en noir et blanc; **2** (in writing) **here it is in ~** le voici écrit noir sur blanc.
II *adj* **1** Cin, Phot, TV [*TV, camera film*] noir et blanc (*inv*); [*movie, print, photo, photography*] (en) noir et blanc (*inv*); **2** (clear-cut) [*matter, situation*] nettement défini.
IDIOMS **he sees everything in ~** pour lui c'est tout noir ou tout blanc.

black: **~ arts** *npl* sciences *fpl* occultes; **~ball** *vtr* blackbouler (**from** de); **~ bass** *n* Fishg black-bass *m*; **~ bear** *n* ours *m* noir d'Amérique; **~ beetle** *n* Zool cafard *m*.

black belt *n* ceinture *f* noire (**in** de); **to be a ~** être ceinture noire.

blackberry /ˈblækbrɪ, -berɪ/ **I** *n* mûre *f*.
II *modif* [*tart, pie*] aux mûres; [*juice, jam*] de mûres.

blackberry bush *n* Bot ronce *f*.

blackberrying /ˈblækberɪɪŋ/ *n* cueillette *f* des mûres; **to go ~** aller cueillir des mûres.

blackbird /ˈblækbɜːd/ *n* merle *m*.

blackboard /ˈblækbɔːd/ *n* tableau *m* (noir); **on the ~** au tableau.

black: **~board duster** *n* (cloth) chiffon *m*; (brush) brosse *f*; **~board jungle** *n* GB Sch enfer *m* scolaire.

black book *n* fig liste *f* noire; **to be in sb's ~** ou **~s** ne pas être dans les petits papiers de qn, ne pas avoir la cote auprès de qn.

black: **~ box** *n* Aviat, Comput boîte *f* noire; **~bread** *n* pain *m* de seigle; **~ cab** *n* grand taxi *m* noir; **~cap** *n* fauvette *f* à tête noire; **~cock** *n* coq *m* de bruyère, tétras *m* lyre; **Black Country** *pr n* Black Country *m* (*nom donné à la région industrielle d'Angleterre située au nord-ouest de Birmingham*).

blackcurrant /ˌblækˈkʌrənt/ Bot, Culin **I** *n* cassis *m*.
II *modif* [*tart*] aux cassis; [*drink, sweet, yoghurt*] au cassis; [*jam, bush*] de cassis.

black: **Black Death** *n* peste *f* noire; **~ economy** *n* économie *f* parallèle.

blacken /ˈblækən/ **I** *vtr* **1** [*actor, soldier*] se barbouiller [qch] de noir [*face*]; [*smoke*] noircir [*brick, wood*]; [*disease, frost*] brûler [*plant*]; [*dirt*] salir [*towel*]; **the ~ed remains of** les restes calcinés de [*car, roast*]; **2** (diminish) ternir [*reputation, name*]; noircir [*person*]; **3** US (bruise) **to ~ sb's eye** faire un œil au beurre noir à qn.
II *vi* **1** (grow darker) [*sky, stove*] noircir; **2** [*mood*] s'assombrir.

black eye /ˌblækˈaɪ/ *n* œil *m* poché, œil *m* au beurre noir○; **to give sb a ~** pocher l'œil à qn; **to get a ~** se faire pocher l'œil.

blackfly /ˈblækflaɪ/ *n* **1** (aphid) puceron *m*; **2** (bloodsucker) simulie *f*.

black: **Black Forest** *pr n* Geog Forêt-Noire *f*; **Black Forest gateau** GB, **Black Forest cake** US *n* Culin gâteau *m* de la Forêt-Noire; **Black Friar** *n* Relig dominicain *m*, Frère *m* prêcheur; **~ frost** *n* gel *m* noir; **~ gold**○ *n* or *m* noir○, pétrole *m*;

~ grouse *n* petit coq *m* de bruyère, tétraslyre *m*.

blackguard /ˈblægɑːd/ *n* ‡ ou hum canaille *f*.

black: **~head** *n* Med point *m* noir, comédon *m* spec; **~-headed gull** *n* mouette *f* rieuse; **~-hearted** *adj* littér mauvais, vil; **~ hole** *n* Astron trou *m* noir; **~ ice** *n* verglas *m*.

blacking /ˈblækɪŋ/ *n* **1** GB (boycotting) boycottage *m* (**of** de); **2**† (polish) cirage *m* noir.

blackish /ˈblækɪʃ/ ▶ 1104 *adj* [*shade, hair*] qui tire sur le noir (*after n*); [*stain, substance*] noirâtre.

blackjack /ˈblækdʒæk/ *n* **1** ▶ 1282 Games black jack *m*; **2** US (club) matraque *f*; **3** Miner blende *f*, sphalérite *f*.

blacklead /ˈblækled/ **I** *n* (for stove) mine *f* de plomb; (in pencil) graphite *m*.
II *vtr* frotter [qch] à la mine de plomb.

blackleg○ /ˈblækleg/ GB **I** *n* péj jaune○ *m* pej, briseur/-euse *m/f* de grève.
II *vi* (*p prés etc* **-gg-**) briser la grève.

blacklist /ˈblæklɪst/ **I** *n* liste *f* noire; **to put sb on a ~** mettre qn sur une liste noire or à l'index.
II *vtr* mettre [qn] à l'index.

blackly /ˈblæklɪ/ *adv* [*glower, stare*] d'un air furieux.

black magic *n* magie *f* noire.

blackmail /ˈblækmeɪl/ **I** *n* chantage *m*.
II *vtr* faire chanter; **to ~ sb into doing** lit faire chanter qn pour qu'il/elle fasse; fig, hum soudoyer qn pour qu'il/elle fasse.

blackmailer /ˈblækmeɪlə(r)/ *n* maître-chanteur *m*.

black: **Black Maria**○ *n* GB panier *m* à salade○, voiture *f* cellulaire; **~ mark** *n* fig mauvais point *m*.

black market **I** *n* marché *m* noir; **on the ~** au marché noir.
II *modif* [*price, goods*] du marché noir; [*goods, trade, trader*] au noir.

black: **~ marketeer** *n* personne *f* qui vend au marché noir; **~ mass** *n* messe *f* noire; **Black Monk** *n* dominicain *m*; **Black Muslim** *n* US Relig Black Muslim *mf*, membre *m* de la Nation d'Islam.

blackness /ˈblæknɪs/ *n* **1** (darkness, night) obscurité *f*; **2** (dark colour) (of hair, ink) noir *m*; (of water, clouds) couleur *f* noire; **3** (gloominess) (of outlook, thoughts) caractère *m* sombre; **4** (evilness) (of heart, thoughts) noirceur *f*; (of deeds) atrocité *f*.

blackout /ˈblækaʊt/ *n* **1** (in wartime) black-out *m*; **2** (power cut) panne *f* de courant; **3** Radio, TV interruption *f* des émissions; **4** Journ black-out *m*; **to impose a news ~** imposer le black-out aux organes de presse; **5** (faint) étourdissement *m*; **6** (loss of memory) trou *m* de mémoire.

black: **Black Panthers** *npl* US Pol Black Panthers *mpl* (*groupe de libération des Noirs revendiquant le partage du pouvoir blanc*); **~ pepper** *n* poivre *m* noir; **Black Power** (**movement**) *n* US Pol Black Power *m* (*mouvement politique des Noirs américains se battant pour l'égalité avec les Blancs*); **~ pudding** *n* GB Culin boudin *m* noir; **Black Rod** *n* GB Pol *huissier de la Chambre des Lords*; **Black Sea** *pr n* Geog mer *f* Noire; **~ sheep** *n* fig brebis *f* galeuse; **Blackshirt** *n* Hist Chemise *f* noire; **~smith** ▶ 1692 *n* forgeron *m*.

blackspot /ˈblækspɒt/ *n* fig point *m* noir; **unemployment/accident ~** endroit *m* connu pour son taux élevé de chômage/d'accidents.

black: **Black Studies** *npl* études *fpl* afro-américaines; **~ swan** *n* Zool cygne *m* noir, cygne *m* d'Australie; **~ taxi** *n* = **black cab**; **~thorn** *n* prunellier *m*.

black tie **I** *n* (on invitation) **'~'** 'tenue de soirée'.
II *modif* [*dinner, function*] en tenue de soirée.

black: **Black velvet** *n* cocktail *m* de stout et de champagne; **~water fever** ▶ 1354 *n* fièvre *f* bilieuse hémoglobinurique; **~ widow** (**spider**) *n* Zool veuve *f* noire.

bladder /ˈblædə(r)/ *n* **1** Anat vessie *f*; **2** (in ball) vessie *f*; **3** Bot vésicule *f*.

bladder: **~wort** *n* utriculaire *f*; **~wrack** *n* fucus *m* vésiculeux.

blade /bleɪd/ *n* **1** (cutting edge) (of knife, sword, axe) lame *f*; **2** (for propulsion) (of fan, propeller, oar) pale *f*; (of turbine) aube *f*; (of windscreen wiper) balai *m*; **3** Bot (of grass) brin *m*; **4** Sport (oar) pale *f*; **5** littér (sword) lame *f*; **6** Phon (of tongue) plat *m*; **7**† (man) gaillard *m*.

blah○ /blɑː/ **I** *n* also onomat **~ ~ ~** blablabla *m*.
II US **blahs** *npl* **the ~s** le cafard○ *m*.

blamable /ˈbleɪməbl/ *adj* = **blameworthy**.

blame /bleɪm/ **I** *n* **1** (responsibility) responsabilité *f* (**for** de); **to accept/share the ~** accepter/partager la responsabilité; **to take the ~, to bear the ~** sout prendre or assumer la responsabilité; **to put** ou **place** ou **lay the ~ for sth on sb** attribuer la responsabilité de qch à qn; **the ~ lies with the government** la faute en revient au gouvernement; **don't put the ~ on me** ne m'accuse pas; **he got the ~ for the broken vase/for leaking the information** on l'a accusé d'avoir cassé le vase/d'avoir divulgué l'information; **why do I always get the ~?** pourquoi est-ce toujours moi qu'on accuse?; **she did it but I got the ~** c'est elle qui l'a fait mais c'est moi qui ai payé les pots cassés○; **2** (criticism) reproches *mpl*; **to deserve some of the ~** mériter des reproches; **to be free from ~** n'avoir rien à se reprocher; **without ~** irréprochable.
II *vtr* en vouloir à [*person, group*]; accuser [*weather, recession, system*]; **she has always ~d me** elle m'en a toujours voulu; **he has resigned and who can ~ him?** il a démissionné et on ne peut pas lui en vouloir; **to ~ sb for sth** reprocher qch à qn; **I ~d her for the accident** je lui ai reproché l'accident; **to ~ sth on sb** attribuer la responsabilité de qch à qn; **she ~d her tiredness on the heat** elle a mis sa fatigue sur le compte de la chaleur; **to be to ~ for** être responsable de [*accident, crisis, problem*].
III *v refl* **to ~ oneself** s'en vouloir; **to ~ oneself for** se sentir responsable de [*tragedy, outcome*]; **you mustn't ~ yourself** tu n'as rien à te reprocher; **you've only yourself to ~** tu ne peux t'en prendre qu'à toi-même.

blameless /ˈbleɪmlɪs/ *adj* [*person*] innocent; [*activity, life*] irréprochable; **the government is not entirely ~** le gouvernement n'est pas entièrement innocent.

blamelessly /ˈbleɪmlɪslɪ/ *adv* [*act, behave*] de façon irréprochable.

blameworthy /ˈbleɪmwɜːðɪ/ *adj* **1** (responsible) [*person*] responsable; **2** (reprehensible) [*action, conduct*] répréhensible.

blanch /blɑːntʃ, US blæntʃ/ **I** *vtr* (all contexts) blanchir.
II *vi* [*person*] blêmir.

blanched almonds *npl* amandes *fpl* blanchies.

blancmange /bləˈmɒnʒ/ *n* blanc-manger *m*.

bland /blænd/ *adj* [*food, flavour, diet*] fade; [*person, character*] terne; [*account, interview*] insipide; [*intonation*] sans relief.

blandish† /ˈblændɪʃ/ *vtr* enjôler.

blandishment† /ˈblændɪʃmənt/ *n* flatterie *f*.

blandly /ˈblændlɪ/ *adv* platement.

blandness /ˈblændnɪs/ *n* platitude *f*.

blank /blæŋk/ **I** *n* **1** (empty space) blanc *m*; **to fill in the ~s** remplir les blancs; **leave a ~ if you don't know the answer** laisse un blanc si tu ne sais pas la réponse; **my mind's a ~** j'ai la tête vide; **2** US (clean form) fiche *f* vierge; **3** (dummy bullet) balle *f* à blanc; **to fire ~s** lit tirer à blanc; fig hum être stérile; **4** Ind pièce *f* brute.
II *adj* **1** (without writing, pictures) [*paper, page*] blanc/blanche; [*wall*] nu; [*screen*] vide; [*form, canvas*] vierge; **a ~ piece of paper** une feuille blanche; **2** (unused) [*cassette, disk*] vierge; **3** (expressionless) **a ~ look** un air absent; **a row of ~ faces** des visages *mpl* à l'air absent; **4** (uncomprehending) [*look, expression*] ébahi; **to look ~** avoir l'air ébahi; **he gave me a ~ look** il m'a lancé un regard ébahi; **5** (without memory) **my mind went ~** j'ai eu un trou de mémoire; **6** (imitation) [*door, window*] faux/fausse; **7** (absolute) [*refusal, rejection*] catégorique; [*astonishment*] absolu.
III *vtr* US Sport **we ~ed the opposition** nous n'avons pas laissé l'équipe adverse marquer un point.
IDIOMS **to draw a ~** faire chou blanc.
■ **blank out**: ¶ **~ out** [*person*] avoir un trou de mémoire; ¶ **~ [sth] out, ~ out [sth]** effacer [*word*]; fig rayer [qch] de sa mémoire [*memory, event*].

blank cheque GB, **blank check** US *n* **1** Fin chèque *m* en blanc; **2** fig carte *f* blanche; **to give/write sb a ~** donner/laisser carte blanche à qn; **I've got a ~ to reorganize the factory** j'ai reçu carte blanche pour réorganiser l'usine.

blanket /ˈblæŋkɪt/ **I** *n* **1** (bedcover) couverture *f*; **electric ~** couverture chauffante; **2** (layer) (of snow, ash) couche *f*; (of cloud, fog) nappe *f*; (of smoke) nuage *m*; (of flowers, weeds) tapis *m*; **3** Nucl couche *f* fertile.
II *modif* (global) [*ban, condemnation, policy*] global; [*use*] excessif/-ive.
III *vtr* **1** Naut déventer; **2** (cover) couvrir; **the fields were ~ed in fog** les champs étaient couverts de brouillard.
IDIOMS **to be a wet ~** être un rabat-joie; **to be born on the wrong side of the ~**† euph être un enfant illégitime.

blanket: **~ bath** *n* toilette *f* couchée; **~ box, ~ chest** *n* GB coffre *m* à linge; **~ clause** *n* Jur, Insur condition *f* générale; **~ cover** *n* Insur couverture *f* globale; **~ coverage** *n* Journ reportage *m* intégral; **~ finish** *n* Sport arrivée *f* serrée; **~ insurance** *n* assurance *f* globale; **~ rate** *n* taux *m* forfaitaire; **~ stitch** *n* point *m* de feston.

blankety-blank○ /ˌblæŋkətɪˈblæŋk/ *adj* hum euph US (damned) **that ~ dog!** ce fichu chien!

blankly /ˈblæŋklɪ/ *adv* **1** (uncomprehendingly) [*stare, look*] d'un air ébahi; **2** (without expression) [*stare, look*] d'un air absent.

blankness /ˈblæŋknɪs/ *n* (puzzled look) air *m* décontenancé; (lack of expression) vacuité *f*.

blank: **~ space** *n* blanc *m*; **~ verse** *n* Literat vers *mpl* blancs or non rimés.

blare /bleə(r)/ **I** *n* beuglement *m*.
II *vi* = **blare out**.
■ **blare out**: ¶ **~ out** [*music, radio*] jouer à plein volume; **the music was blaring out from his bedroom** de sa chambre on entendait la radio qui jouait à plein volume; ¶ **~ out [sth]** déverser [*music, advertising*].

blarney○ /ˈblɑːnɪ/ **I** *n* baratin○ *m*.
II *vtr, vi* baratiner○.
IDIOMS **to have kissed the ~ stone** avoir la parole facile.

blasé /ˈblɑːzeɪ, US blɑːˈzeɪ/ *adj* blasé (**about** sur).

blaspheme /blæsˈfiːm/ *vtr, vi* blasphémer.

blasphemer /blæsˈfiːmə(r)/ *n* blasphémateur/-trice *m/f*.

blasphemous /ˈblæsfəməs/ *adj* [*person*] blasphémateur/-trice; [*statement*] blasphématoire.

blasphemously /ˈblæsfəməslɪ/ *adv* de façon blasphématoire.

blasphemy /ˈblæsfəmɪ/ *n* blasphème *m* (**against** contre); **it is ~ to say** c'est un blasphème de dire; **~ law** loi *f* contre le blasphème.

blast /blɑːst, US blæst/ **I** *n* **1** (explosion) explosion *f*; **2** (gust) rafale *f*; **a ~ of wind** une rafale de vent; **3** (air current from explosion) souffle *m* (**from** dégagé par); **4** (noise) (on trumpet) sonnerie *f*; (on whistle, car horn) coup *m*; **to give a ~ on** faire sonner [*trumpet*]; donner un coup de [*whistle, carhorn*]; **a ~ of pop music** un morceau de musique pop à plein volume; **he plays his records at full ~** il met ses disques à plein volume; **the radio is on at full ~** la radio est à fond; **5**○ (fun) **to have a ~** bien se marrer○; **the party was a ~** on s'est bien marré à la fête.
II *excl* zut!○
III *vtr* **1** (blow up) faire sauter [*building*]; dynamiter [*rockface*]; **to ~ a hole in a wall** percer un mur à l'explosif; **2** (damage) [*wind*] endommager [*tree*]; [*frost, disease*] détruire [*plant, crop*]; **3**○ (criticize) [*article, review*] descendre [qn/qch] en flammes○ [*person, performance, work*]; **4** (strike hard) [*golfer, soccer player*] frapper [qch] de toutes ses forces [*ball*]; **5** Tech = **sandblast**.
IV *vi* **1** Mining utiliser des explosifs; **we ~ed through the rock wall** nous avons fait sauter la paroi rocheuse à l'explosif; **2** (make a noise) [*trumpets*] retentir.
IDIOMS **the song was a ~ from the past**○ **for me** cette chanson me replongeait dans le passé; **to ~ sb/sth out of the water**○ fig descendre qn/qch en flammes○.
■ **blast away**: **~ away** (with gun) mitrailler; **to ~ away at** mitrailler [*person, target*].
■ **blast off**: ¶ **~ off** [*rocket*] décoller; ¶ **~ [sth] off, ~ off [sth] 1** (fire) [*gunman*] tirer avec [*rifle*]; **2** (lift off) [*explosion*] faire sauter [*roof*].
■ **blast out**: ¶ **~ out** [*music*] retentir; ¶ **~ [sth] out, ~ out [sth]** [*radio, speaker*] cracher○ [*music*].

blasted /ˈblɑːstɪd, US ˈblæst-/ *adj* **1** (withered) [*foliage*] flétri; [*crop*] endommagé; **2**○ (for emphasis) fichu; **where's the ~ screwdriver?** où est ce fichu tournevis?; **some ~ idiot locked the door!** il y a une espèce d'idiot qui a fermé la porte à clé!

blast: **~ furnace** *n* haut-fourneau *m*; **~ furnaceman** ▶ **1692** *n* ouvrier *m* des hauts-fourneaux.

blasting /ˈblɑːstɪŋ, US ˈblæst-/ *n* **1** Mining travail *m* à l'explosif; **2** Audio distortion *f*.

blast injection *n* Mech injection *f* sous pression.

blastoderm /ˈblɑːstədɜːm, US ˈblæst-/ *n* blastoderme *m*.

blast-off /ˈblɑːstɒf, US ˈblæst-/ *n* lancement *m*; **three, two, one, ~!** trois, deux, un, feu!

blatancy /ˈbleɪtnsɪ/ *n* (of advertising, attitude) caractère *m* éhonté.

blatant /ˈbleɪtnt/ *adj* [*lie, bias, disregard*] éhonté; [*example, abuse*] flagrant; **to be ~ about** [*person*] être direct à propos de.

blatantly /ˈbleɪtntlɪ/ *adv* [*copy, disregard*] ouvertement; **to be ~ obvious** être l'évidence même.

blather○ /ˈblæðə(r)/ **I** *n* bêtises *fpl*.
II *vtr* raconter [*idiocies*].
III *vi* dire n'importe quoi.

blaze /bleɪz/ **I** *n* **1** (fire) (in hearth) feu *m*, flambée *f*; (accidental) incendie *m*; **firemen got the ~ under control** les pompiers ont maîtrisé l'incendie; **2** (sudden burst) (of flames) embrasement *m*; **the garden is a ~ of colour** le jardin est éclatant de couleurs; **there was a sudden ~ of colour in the sky** le ciel a brusquement changé de couleur; **she left in a ~ of glory/in a ~ of publicity** fig elle est partie couronnée de gloire/sous les feux des médias; **3** Equit liste *f*; **4** (cut in tree) encoche *f*, griffe *f*.
II blazes○ *npl* (hell) **what the ~s are you up to?** qu'est-ce que tu fabriques○?; **how the ~s did he do it?** comment diable a-t-il fait ça?; **to run like ~s** courir comme un dératé/une dératée; **go to ~s!** allez au diable!
III *vtr* **1** (mark) griffer, marquer [*tree*]; **to ~ a trail** lit baliser une voie; fig faire œuvre de pionnier; **2** (spread) **to ~ sth abroad** sout crier qch sur tous les toits.
IV *vi* **1** (also **~ away**) (burn furiously) [*fire*] brûler, flamber; [*house, car*] brûler; **2** (also **~ away**) (give out light) [*lights*] briller; **3** (shoot) [*gun, cannon*] pétarader; **the troops advanced, all guns blazing** lit les troupes avançaient en tirant; **she went into the meeting all guns blazing** fig elle est entrée dans la réunion tout feu tout flamme.
V blazing *pres p adj* **1** (violent) [*argument*] violent; [*heat*] accablant; [*fire*] ronflant; [*building, car*] embrasé; [*sun, sunshine*] plein (*before n*); **2**○ (furious) furax○ *inv*, fou/folle de rage; **she was blazing (mad)** elle était furax○.
■ **blaze down** [*sun*] taper (**on** sur).
■ **blaze up** [*fat, fire*] s'embraser.

blazer /ˈbleɪzə(r)/ *n* blazer *m*.

blazon /ˈbleɪzn/ **I** *n* Herald blason *m*.
II *vtr* **1** Herald blasonner; **2** gen claironner [*details, news*]; arborer [*name, slogan*].
■ **blazon forth, blazon out**: **~ forth [sth], ~ [sth] forth** claironner.

bleach /bliːtʃ/ **I** *n* **1** (also **household ~**) (liquid) ≈ eau *f* de javel; (powder, cream) agent *m* blanchissant et désinfectant; **2** (for hair) décolorant *m*.
II *vtr* décolorer [*hair*]; blanchir [*linen*]; **~ed hair** cheveux décolorés; **to ~ one's hair** se décolorer les cheveux.
■ **bleach out**: **~ [sth] out, ~ out [sth]** effacer [*image*]; faire disparaître [*colour, stain*].

bleachers /ˈbliːtʃəz/ *npl* gradins *mpl* (découverts).

bleak /bliːk/ **I** *n* (fish) ablette *f*.
II *adj* **1** (cold, raw) [*landscape, region*] désolé; [*weather, season*] maussade; **2** (miserable, discouraging) [*prospect, outlook, future*] sombre; [*existence, world, surroundings*] sinistre; **to paint a ~ picture of** peindre un sombre tableau de.

bleakly /ˈbliːklɪ/ *adv* **1** [*stare, say*] sombrement; **2** [*snow, blow*] lugubrement.

bleakness /ˈbliːknɪs/ *n* **1** (of weather, landscape, surroundings) sévérité *f*; **2** (of prospects, future) noirceur *f*.

bleary /ˈblɪərɪ/ *adj* [*eyes*] bouffi; **to be ~-eyed** avoir les yeux bouffis; **to feel ~** se sentir vaseux/-euse.

bleat /bliːt/ **I** *n* **1** (of sheep, goat) bêlement *m*; **2** péj (of person) jérémiades *fpl*.
II *vi* **1** [*sheep, goat*] bêler; **2** péj [*person*] se lamenter (**about** sur).

bleb /bleb/ *n* **1** (on skin) cloque *f*; **2** (on water, glass) bulle *f*.

bled /bled/ *pp* ▶ **bleed**.

bleed /bliːd/ (*prét, pp* **bled**) **I** *vtr* **1** Med saigner; **2** fig **to ~ sb for sth** soutirer qch à qn; **to ~ sb white** ou **dry** saigner qn à blanc; **3** Tech purger [*radiator*]; **4** Print faire déborder.
II *vi* **1** saigner; **my finger's ~ing** j'ai le doigt qui saigne; **he was ~ing from the head** il saignait d'une blessure à la tête; **is my nose ~ing?** est-ce que je saigne du nez?; **to stop sth ~ing** arrêter qch de saigner; **he was ~ing to death** il perdait tout son sang; **he bled to death** il est mort d'une hémorragie; **2** fig **to ~ for one's country** verser son sang pour sa patrie; **my heart ~s for the baby's mother** mon cœur saigne pour la mère du bébé; **my heart ~s!** iron ça me fend le cœur!; **3** [*tree, plant*] pleurer; **4** [*colour, dye*] déteindre; **5** Print déborder.

bleeder /ˈbliːdə(r)/ *n* **1**◑ GB bougre○ *m*; (in anger) salaud◑ *m*; **lucky ~!** sacré veinard○!; **2**○ (hemophiliac) hémophile *mf*.

bleeding /ˈbliːdɪŋ/ **I** *n* **1** ¢ saignement *m*; (heavy) hémorragie *f*; **to stop the ~** arrêter le saignement or l'hémorragie; **2** (deliberate) saignée *f*.
II *adj* **1** [*wound*] saignant; [*corpse, victim*] ensanglanté; [*hand, leg etc*] qui saigne; **2**◑ GB **this ~ car!** cette foutue◑ voiture!; **~ idiot!** bougre de con◑!
III◑ GB *adv* sacrément.

bleeding heart I *n* **1** Bot cœur-de-Jeannette *m*, cœur-de-Marie *m*; **2** fig péj cœur *m* sensible péj.
II *modif* US **a ~ liberal** péj libéral/-e *m/f* au cœur sensible.

bleed valve *n* robinet *m* de purge.

bleep /bliːp/ **I** *n* **1** (signal) bip *m*, bip-bip *m*; Radio, TV top *m*; **2** GB = **bleeper**.
II *vtr* **1** GB **to ~ sb** appeler qn (au bip), biper qn; **2** Radio, TV censurer par un bip [*word, person*].
III *vi* émettre un signal sonore or des signaux sonores.
IV *excl* US euph zut!

bleeper /ˈbliːpə(r)/ *n* GB bip *m* (*appareil*).

bleeping○ /ˈbliːpɪŋ/ *adj* US euph sacré○ (*before n*).

blemish /ˈblemɪʃ/ **I** *n* **1** lit gen imperfection *f*; (on fruit) tache *f*; (pimple) bouton *m*; défaut *m* (**on** dans); (on reputation) tache *f* (**on** à); **2** fig (on beauty, happiness) ombre *f*.
II *vtr* tacher [*fruit*]; ternir [*beauty, happiness*]; entacher [*reputation*].

blench /blentʃ/ *vi* **1** (quail) frémir (de peur); **2** (pale) blêmir.

blend /blend/ **I** *n* **1** (fusion) (of sounds, smells) mélange *m* (**of** de); (of styles, colours, ideas) mariage *m* (**of** de); (of qualities, skills) combinaison *f* (**of** de); **2** (mixture) (of coffees, teas, whiskies) mélange *m*; (of wines) coupage *m* (**of** de); **our own special ~** notre mélange maison; **3** (fabric) **cotton ~** coton *m* mélangé.
II *vtr* mélanger, marier [*foods, colours, styles, sounds, tastes*]; allier [*qualities, ideas*] (**with** à); **~ all the ingredients together** mélanger tous les ingrédients.
III *vi* **to ~ (together)** [*colours, tastes, styles*] se fondre ensemble; **to ~ with** [*colours, tastes, sounds*] se marier à; [*smells, visual effects*] se mêler à; [*buildings, styles, ideas*] s'accorder à.
■ **blend in**: ¶ **~ in** [*colour, building*] s'harmoniser (**with** avec); ¶ **~ in [sth], ~ [sth] in** incorporer.
■ **blend into**: **~ into sth** se fondre dans [*setting, landscape*]; **to ~ into the background** se fondre dans le paysage.

blended whisky *n* whisky *m* (*mélange de malts et de whisky de grains*).

blender /ˈblendə(r)/ *n* **1** mixeur *m*, mixer *m*; **2** (person) (of coffee) torréfacteur *m*; **3** Constr (brush) brosse *f* plate.

blending /ˈblendɪŋ/ *n* (of coffees) torréfaction *f*; (of wines) coupage *m*; (of whiskies) mélange *m*.

blenny /ˈblenɪ/ *n* blennie *f*.

bless /bles/ **I** *vtr* **1** Relig bénir [*building, congregation, food, marriage, person, sacrament*]; **God ~ America/the Queen** que Dieu bénisse l'Amérique/la Reine; **God ~ you** que Dieu vous bénisse; **we ~ you for your great mercy** nous vous rendons grâce pour votre grande miséricorde; **goodbye, God ~!** au revoir!; **2**○ (affectionately) **~ her** ou **~ her heart!** c'est un ange!; **~ you!** (after sneeze) à vos souhaits!; **3**○ †(in surprise) **~ me!** ou **~ my soul!** ou **well I'm ~ed!** ça alors!; **4** (favour) **to ~ sb with** doter qn de; **to be ~ed with** jouir de [*health, luck, skill, intelligence, beauty*]; **we were never ~ed with children** le ciel a voulu que nous n'ayons jamais eu d'enfants; **to be ~ed with six children** avoir le bonheur d'avoir eu six enfants; **5** (be grateful to) **~ you for answering so quickly** merci d'avoir répondu si vite; **you paid the bill? ~ you!** tu as réglé la facture? tu es un ange!
II *v refl* **to ~ oneself** se signer.
IDIOMS **(I'm) ~ed if I know** je ne sais abso-

lument pas; **(I'm) ~ed if I can remember** je ne m'en souviens absolument pas.

blessed /'blesɪd/ **I** *n* Relig **the ~** (+ *v pl*) les bienheureux.
II *adj* **1** (holy) [*place*] béni; **the Blessed Sacrament** le saint sacrement; **the Blessed Virgin** la Sainte Vierge; **our Blessed Lord** Notre Seigneur; **of ~ memory** d'heureuse mémoire; **2** (beatified) bienheureux/-euse (*before n*); **~ are the poor** Bible heureux les pauvres; **3** (welcome) [*warmth, quiet*] bienfaisant; [*relief*] heureux/-euse; **4**○ (damned) fichu◑; **every ~ day** tous les jours que Dieu fait; **the whole ~ day** toute la sainte journée.

blessedly /'blesɪdlɪ/ *adv* **~ warm/quiet** délicieusement chaud/calme; **~, everything was working properly** par bonheur, tout marchait bien.

blessedness /'blesɪdnɪs/ *n* **1** Relig béatitude *f*; **2** (good fortune) bonheur *m*; **single ~** célibat *m*.

blessing /'blesɪŋ/ *n* **1** (asset, favour) bienfait *m*; **it is a ~ (for him) that he is healthy** heureusement, il est en bonne santé; **dishwashers are a ~ for busy people** les lave-vaisselle sont une bénédiction pour les personnes actives; **a mixed ~** un bienfait relatif; **a ~ in disguise** un bienfait caché; **count your ~s!** estime-toi heureux!; **2** (relief) soulagement *m*; **it is a ~ to know (that) he's safe** c'est un soulagement de savoir qu'il est sauf; **3** (approval) **with the ~ of sb**, **with sb's ~** avec la bénédiction de qn; **to give one's ~ to sth** approuver qch sans réserve; **4** Relig bénédiction *f*; **to give sb one's ~** donner sa bénédiction à qn; **to say a ~ over sth** bénir qch; **to ask God's ~ on sth/sb** demander à Dieu de bénir qch/qn; **a service of ~** un office de bénédiction.

blether /'bleðə(r)/ *n, vi* = **blather**.

blew /blu:/ *prét* ▶ **blow** II, III.

blewits /'blu:ɪts/ *n* (+ *v sg*) pied-bleu *m*.

blight /blaɪt/ **I** *n* **1** Bot (of cereals, roses) rouille *f*; **potato ~** mildiou *m* (de la pomme de terre); **2** fig (on society) plaie *f* (**on** de); **urban ~, inner city ~** délabrement *m* urbain; **planning ~** nuisance *f* (*produite par les excès de l'urbanisme*); **to cast a ~ on sth** gâcher qch.
II *vtr* attaquer [*crop*]; fig briser [*marriage*]; gâcher [*childhood*]; compromettre [*chances*]; faire s'envoler [*hopes*].

blighter†○ /'blaɪtə(r)/ *n* GB andouille○ *f*; **poor ~** pauvre andouille○; **you lucky ~!** sacré veinard○!; **little ~!** petite peste○!

Blighty† /'blaɪtɪ/ *n* GB argot des militaires l'Angleterre *f*, 'le pays'.

blimey○ /'blaɪmɪ/ *excl* GB mince alors!○

blimp /blɪmp/ *n* **1**○ GB pej **Colonel Blimp** vieux réactionnaire *m* bougon; **2** Aviat dirigeable *m*; **3** Cin blindage *m* insonorisant; **4**○ US (fat person) gros lard○ *m*.

blimpish /'blɪmpɪʃ/ *adj* GB péj réactionnaire.

blind /blaɪnd/ **I** *n* **1 the ~** (+ *v pl*) les aveugles *mpl* voir note; **school for the ~** école pour aveugles or non-voyants *mpl*; **2** (at window) store *m*; **3** (front) façade *f*; (subterfuge) feinte *f*; **it was just a ~** ce n'était qu'une façade; **4** US (hide) affût *m*.
II *adj* **1** lit [*person*] aveugle voir note; **a ~ man/woman** un/-e aveugle; **to go ~** perdre la vue; **to be ~ in one eye** être borgne; **are you ~○?** tu es aveugle ou quoi○?; **2** (unaware) [*person, panic, rage, acceptance, obedience*] aveugle; **to be ~ to** être aveugle à [*fault, defect*]; être insensible à [*quality, virtue*]; être inconscient de [*risk, danger*]; **3** (from which one can't see) [*corner, brow of hill*] sans visibilité; **on my ~ side** dans mon angle mort; **~ entrance** entrée dérobée; **4** (without looking) [*tasting*] en aveugle; **5** (blank) [*wall, facade*] aveugle; **6** Aviat [*landing*] sans visibilité; **7**○ (slightest) **he doesn't know a ~ thing about it** il n'y connaît strictement rien.
III *adv* **1** (without seeing) [*fly, land*] sans visibilité; [*taste*] en aveugle; **2** Culin [*bake*] à blanc; ▶ **rob, swear**.
IV *vtr* **1** lit [*injury, accident*] rendre aveugle [*person*]; **to be ~ed in an accident** perdre la vue dans un accident; **to be ~ed in one eye** perdre un œil; **2** (dazzle) [*sun, light*] éblouir [*person*]; **3** (mislead, overwhelm) [*pride, love*] aveugler; **to be ~ed by** être aveuglé par [*passion, love*].
V *vi* GB ▶ **eff**.
IDIOMS **love is ~** l'amour est aveugle; **it's a case of the ~ leading the ~** ils n'en savent pas plus long l'un que l'autre; **to turn a ~ eye** fermer les yeux (**to** sur); ▶ **bat**.

■ Note Ce mot peut être perçu comme injurieux dans cette acception. Lui préférer *visually handicapped* ou *visually impaired*.

blind alley *n* lit, fig voie *f* sans issue; **to lead up a ~** ne mener nulle part.

blind date *n* **1** (meeting) rendez-vous *m* avec un/-e inconnu/-e; **to go on a ~** avoir rendez-vous avec un/-e inconnu/-e; **2** (person) inconnu/-e *m/f* avec qui l'on a rendez-vous.

blind drunk○ *adj* complètement bourré○.

blinder /'blaɪndə(r)/ *n* **1**○ GB Sport coup *m* fumant○; **2** US (for horse) œillère *f*.

blindfold /'blaɪndfəʊld/ **I** *n* bandeau *m*.
II *adj* (also **~ed**) [*person*] aux yeux bandés; **to be ~** avoir les yeux bandés.
III *adv* (also **~ed**) [*find way*] les yeux fermés.
IV *vtr* bander les yeux à [*person*].

blinding /'blaɪndɪŋ/ *adj* [*intensity, light, flash*] aveuglant; [*headache, pain*] atroce; **the solution came to me in a ~ flash** fig la solution m'est apparue dans un éclair de lucidité.

blindingly /'blaɪndɪŋlɪ/ *adv* [*shine*] d'un éclat aveuglant; **to be ~ obvious** sauter aux yeux.

blindly /'blaɪndlɪ/ *adv* **1** fig [*obey, follow*] aveuglément; **2** lit [*advance, grope*] à l'aveuglette.

blind man's buff ▶ **1282** *n* Games colin-maillard *m*.

blindness /'blaɪndnɪs/ *n* **1** Med, lit cécité *f*; **2** fig aveuglement *m*.

blind spot *n* **1** Med (in eye) point *m* aveugle; **2** (in car, on hill) angle *m* mort; **to be in sb's ~** être dans l'angle mort de qn; **3** fig (point of ignorance) ignorance *f* ¢; **to have a ~ as far as sth is concerned** ne rien comprendre à qch.

blind: **~ test** *n* Comm test *m* en aveugle, blind-test *m*; **~worm** /'blaɪndwɜ:m/ *n* orvet *m*.

blink /blɪŋk/ **I** *n* (of eye) battement *m* des paupières; **without a ~** fig sans ciller.
II *vtr* **to ~ one's eyes** cligner des yeux.
III *vi* [*person*] cligner des yeux; [*light*] clignoter; **without ~ing** sans ciller also fig.
IDIOMS **in the ~ of an eye** en un clin d'œil; **it's (gone) on the ~○** c'est détraqué○.
■ **blink away**: **to ~ away one's tears** battre des paupières pour s'arrêter de pleurer.
■ **blink at**: **~ at [sth]** **1** (overlook) fermer les yeux sur; **2** (be taken aback) **he ~ed at the size of the bill** il a tiqué en voyant la note○.
■ **blink back**: **to ~ back one's tears** retenir ses larmes en clignant des yeux.

blinker /'blɪŋkə(r)/ **I** *n* **1** Aut clignotant *m*; (emergency light) gyrophare *m*; US (at crossing) (feu *m*) clignotant *m*; **2** (on horse) *gen pl* œillère *f*; **to wear ~s** avoir des œillères also fig.
II *vtr* mettre des œillères à [*horse*].
III blinkered *pp adj* [*attitude, approach*] borné.

blinking /'blɪŋkɪŋ/ **I** *n* ¢ (of eye) battement *m* des paupières; (of light) clignotement *m*.
II○ GB *adj* sacré (*before n*); **~ idiot** idiot *m* de première○.
III○ GB *adv* **you'll ~ well do it now!** c'est maintenant, et plus vite que ça○!; **no I ~ well won't!** ça sûrement pas!

blinty /'blɪntɪ/ *n* US crêpe *f*.

blip /blɪp/ *n* **1** (on screen) spot *m*; (on graph, line) accident *m* (d'une courbe); **2** (sound) bip *m*; **3** (hitch) contretemps *m*; **4** Econ, Fin (drop) fléchissement *m*.

bliss /blɪs/ *n* **1** Relig, liter béatitude *f*; **2**○ fig délice *m*; **what ~!** quel délice!; **wedded ~, domestic ~** sérénité *f* conjugale.

blissful /'blɪsfl/ *adj* **1** (wonderful) délicieux/-ieuse; **~ ignorance** une douce ignorance; **2** Relig bienheureux/-euse.

blissfully /'blɪsfəlɪ/ *adv* voluptueusement; **to be ~ happy** être au comble du bonheur; **a ~ happy month** un mois de bonheur parfait; **to be ~ unaware of/that** être à cent lieues de se douter de/que; **~ ignorant** dans la plus parfaite ignorance.

blister /'blɪstə(r)/ **I** *n* (on skin) ampoule *f*; (on paint) cloque *f*; (in glass, on metal) soufflure *f*.
II *vtr* faire peler [*skin*]; faire cloquer [*paint*]; **relief for ~ed feet** un remède pour les ampoules aux pieds; **~ed paint** peinture cloquée; **~ed glass** verre à soufflures.
III *vi* [*skin, paint*] cloquer; [*person*] peler; **my feet ~ easily** j'ai facilement des ampoules aux pieds.

blistering /'blɪstərɪŋ/ **I** *n* (of skin) formation *f* d'ampoules; (of paint) formation *f* de cloques; **it helps to avoid ~** ça permet d'éviter les ampoules or les cloques.
II *adj* [*heat*] caniculaire; [*sun*] torride; [*attack, criticism*] féroce; [*tongue*] acéré; [*reply*] cinglant; **at a ~ speed** ou **pace** à une allure foudroyante.

blisteringly /'blɪstərɪŋlɪ/ *adv* **~ hot** torride; **~ sarcastic** extrêmement cinglant; **~ fast** à une allure foudroyante.

blister pack **I** *n* blister *m*, habillage *m* transparent.
II *vtr* mettre [qch] sous blister or sous habillage transparent.

blithe /blaɪð/ *adj* (nonchalant) insouciant; (cheerful) allègre.

blithely /'blaɪðlɪ/ *adv* (nonchalantly) avec insouciance; (cheerfully) allègrement; **~ ignorant of sth** parfaitement inconscient de qch.

blithering○ /'blɪðərɪŋ/ *adj* **a ~ idiot** un/-e idiot/-e *m/f* de première○; **you ~ idiot!** espèce d'idiot!

blithesome /'blɪðəsəm/ *adj* liter béat.

blitz /blɪts/ **I** *n* **1** Mil Aviat bombardement *m* aérien; **the Blitz** GB Hist le Blitz; **2** fig vaste campagne *f*; **to have a ~ on sth** s'attaquer à qch.
II *vtr* lit, fig bombarder; **to ~ sb with questions** bombarder qn de questions.

blitzed○ /blɪtst/ *adj* (drunk) bourré○.

blitzkrieg /'blɪtskri:g/ *n* (war) guerre *f* éclair *inv*; (attack) attaque *f* éclair.

blizzard /'blɪzəd/ *n* tempête *f* de neige; (in Arctic regions) blizzard *m*.

bloat /bləʊt/ *n* Vet ballonnement *m*.

bloated /'bləʊtɪd/ *adj* **1** lit [*face, body*] bouffi; [*stomach*] ballonné; **to feel ~** se sentir ballonné; **2** fig [*estimate, imagery*] gonflé; [*style*] ampoulé; [*bureaucracy, sector*] surgonflé; [*capitalist*] bouffi.

bloater /'bləʊtə(r)/ *n* ≈ hareng *m* saur.

blob /blɒb/ *n* **1** (of paint, cream etc) grosse goutte *f*; **2** (indistinct shape) forme *f* floue.

bloc /blɒk/ *n* Pol bloc *m*; **en ~** en bloc.

block /blɒk/ **I** *n* **1** (slab) bloc *m*; **a ~ of ice/marble** un bloc de glace/marbre; **a ~ of ice cream** une glace *f* (au litre); **2** (building) **~ of flats** immeuble *m* (d'habitation); **office/residential ~** immeuble de bureaux/d'habitation; **administration ~** bâtiment *m* administratif; **science ~** bloc *m* scientifique; **3** (group of buildings) pâté *m* de maisons; **to drive round the ~** faire le tour du pâté de maisons; **he lives three ~s away** US il habite à trois rues d'ici; **the bank is two ~s south** US la banque est à deux rues d'ici au sud; **4** (for butcher, executioner) billot *m*; **to put** ou **lay one's head on the ~** fig donner sa tête à couper; **5** (group) (of seats, tickets) groupe *m*; (of stamps) bloc *m*; (of shares) paquet *m*, tranche *f*; **a ~ of three lessons** trois cours d'affilée; **6** (obstruction) **to be a ~ to** être un obstacle à [*reform, agreement*]; **to be a ~ to progress** être une entrave au progrès; **to put a ~ on** bloquer [*price, sale*]; entraver [*initiative*]; **7** Print cliché *m*; **8** Comput bloc *m*; **9** Tech (housing pulleys) palan *m*; **10**○ (head) caboche○ *f*, tête *f*; **I'll knock your ~ off**◑ je vais te casser la figure○; **11** Rail canton *m*; **12** Sport obstruction *f*.

II **blocks** *npl* Dance chaussons *mpl* à pointes.

III *vtr* **1** (obstruct) bloquer [*exit, road, pass*]; boucher [*drain, gutter, hole, artery*]; gêner [*traffic*]; **to ~ sb's way** ou **path** barrer le passage à qn; **to have a ~ed nose** avoir le nez bouché; **2** (impede) bloquer [*market, project*]; faire obstacle à [*advance, escape, progress*]; faire opposition à [*bill*]; **you're ~ing my light** tu me caches la lumière; **you're ~ing my view** tu me bouches la vue; **3** Fin bloquer [*assets, currency, funds*]; **4** Sport bloquer [*ball, opponent, rope*].

■ **block in**: **~ [sb/sth] in** **1** (when parking) bloquer [*car, driver*]; **2** Art colorer [*area, figure*].

■ **block off**: **~ [sth] off, ~ off [sth]** **1** (seal off) barrer [*road, path*]; **2** Phot (mask) masquer [*negative*].

■ **block out**: **~ out [sth], ~ [sth] out** **1** (hide) boucher [*view*]; cacher [*light, sun*]; **2** (suppress) refouler [*memory, problem*].

■ **block up**: **~ up [sth], ~ [sth] up** boucher [*artery, drain, gutter, hole, street*].

blockade /blɒˈkeɪd/ **I** *n* Mil blocus *m*.

II *vtr* bloquer, faire le blocus de [*port*].

blockade runner *n* Mil briseur *m* de blocus.

blockage /ˈblɒkɪdʒ/ *n* (in artery) obstruction *f*; (in pipe, drain, distribution) blocage *m*; (in river) engorgement *m*; **intestinal ~** occlusion *f* intestinale.

block: **~ and tackle** *n* Tech moufle *f*; **~board** *n* latté *m*; **~book** *vtr* louer [qch] en groupe [*seats, rooms*]; **~-booking** *n* location *f* de groupe.

blockbuster○ /ˈblɒkbʌstə(r)/ **1** (book) livre *m* à succès, bestseller *m*; **2** (film) superproduction *f*; **3** Mil bombe *f* de très grande puissance.

block capital *n* Print majuscule *f* d'imprimerie; **in ~s** (on form) en caractères *mpl* or capitales *fpl* d'imprimerie.

block diagram *n* **1** Comput, Electron schéma *m* fonctionnel; **2** Geol, Geog blocdiagramme *m*.

block: **~ grant** *n* GB Admin subvention *f* gouvernementale (*aux autorités locales pour assurer les services publics*); **~head**○ *n* péj âne○ *m*, imbécile○ *mf*.

blockhouse /ˈblɒkhaʊs/ *n* **1** Mil blockhaus *m*; **2** US Hist (fort) fortin *m*; **3** Aerosp poste *m* de lancement.

block: **~lava** *n* Geol lave *f* pétrifiée; **~ letter** *n* = **block capital**; **~ printing** *n* Print impression *f* sur cliché bois; **~ release course** *n* cours *m* de formation continue; **~ tin** *n* lingot *m* d'étain; **~ vote** *n* Pol vote *m* groupé; **~ voting** *n* Pol système *m* du vote groupé.

bloke○ /bləʊk/ *n* GB type○ *m*, mec○ *m*.

blond /blɒnd/ ▶ **1104** *adj* [*person, hair*] blond; [*wood*] clair.

blonde /blɒnd/ ▶ **1104** **I** *n* blonde *f*.

II *adj* blond.

blood /blʌd/ **I** *n* **1** Biol, Physiol sang *m*; **to give ~** donner son sang; **the ~ rushed to his cheeks** il a rougi; **the ~ rushed to my head** le sang m'est monté au visage; **the sound made my ~ run cold** le bruit m'a glacé le sang; **to kill sb in cold ~** tuer qn de sang-froid; **to have sb's ~ on one's hands** fig avoir la mort de qn sur la conscience; **to draw first ~** faire couler le premier sang; **to do ~s** faire des analyses de sang; **2** (breeding) sang; **royal ~** sang royal; **there is Danish ~ on his mother's side** il y a du sang danois du côté de sa mère; **music is in her ~** elle a la musique dans le sang; **a prince of the ~** un prince de sang; **~ tells** bon sang ne saurait mentir; **3** (anger) **his ~ is up** il est furieux; **my ~ was boiling** je bouillais de rage; **it makes my ~ boil!** ça me fait bouillir!; **4** (vigour) **new** ou **fresh** ou **young ~** sang neuf.

II *vtr* Hunt barbouiller le visage de [qn] de sang de renard tué [*hunter*]; donner le goût du sang à [*hound*].

IDIOMS **~ is thicker than water** la voix du sang est la plus forte; **he's after my ~!**○ il veut ma peau!○; **it's like getting ~ out of a stone** (making someone speak) autant essayer de faire parler un muet; (making someone pay) autant faire pleurer les pierres, il/elle est tellement radin/-e○!

blood: **~-and-thunder**† *adj* [*novel, film*] d'aventures; **~ bank** *n* banque *f* du sang; **~bath** *n* bain *m* de sang; **~ blister** *n* pinçon *m*; **~ brother** *n* frère *m* de sang; **~ cell** *n* globule *m* (du sang); **~-cholesterol** *n* taux *m* de cholestérol du sang; **~ clot** *n* caillot *m* de sang; **~ clotting agent** *n* agent *m* coagulant du sang; **~ corpuscle** *n* globule *m* (du sang); **~ count** *n* Med numération *f* globulaire.

bloodcurdling /ˈblʌdkɜːdlɪŋ/ *n* **a ~ scream** un cri à vous figer le sang dans les veines.

blood: **~ donor** *n* donneur/-euse *m/f* de sang; **~ feud** *n* lutte *f* à mort; **~ flow** *n* débit *m* sanguin; **~ group** *n* groupe *m* sanguin; **~ heat** *n* température *f* du sang; **~hound** *n* limier *m*.

bloodless /ˈblʌdlɪs/ *adj* **1** (peaceful) [*revolution, coup*] sans effusion de sang; **2** (pale) blême; **3** (drained of blood) exsangue.

bloodletting /ˈblʌdletɪŋ/ *n* **1** Med saignée *f*; **2** (killing) massacre *m*.

blood: **~line** *n* lignée *f*; **~ lust** *n* soif *f* de sang; **~mobile** *n* US Med centre *m* mobile de collecte du sang; **~ money** *n* argent *m* versé pour un meurtre; **~ orange** *n* orange *f* sanguine; **~ plasma** *n* plasma *m* sanguin; **~ poisoning** *n* septicémie *f*.

blood pressure *n* Med tension *f* artérielle; **high ~** hypertension *f*; **low ~** hypotension *f*; **my ~ rose/fell** ma tension a monté/baissé.

blood: **~ product** *n* Med produit *m* sanguin; **~ pudding** *n* Culin boudin *m* noir; **~red** *n, adj* rouge (*m*) sang (*inv*); **~ relation, ~ relative** *n* parent/-e *m/f* par le sang; **~root** *n* Bot sanguinaire *f*; **~ sausage** *n* US = **blood pudding**; **~ serum** *n* sérum *m* sanguin; **~shed** *n* effusion *f* de sang; **~shot** *adj* injecté de sang; **~-soaked** *adj* trempé de sang; **~ sport** *n* Hunt sport *m* sanguinaire; **~stain** *n* tache *f* de sang; **~stained** *adj* taché de sang; **~stock** *n* Equit (+ *v sg ou pl*) bêtes *fpl* de race; **~stone** *n* Miner jaspe *m* sanguin; **~stream** *n* Med courant *m* sanguin; **~sucker** *n* lit, fig sangsue *f*; **~ sugar** *n* glucide *m*; **~ test** *n* Med analyse *f* de sang; **~thirstiness** *n* soif *f* de sang.

bloodthirsty /ˈblʌdθɜːstɪ/ *adj* **1** [*murderer, tiger*] assoiffé de sang; **2** [*film, novel*] sanguinaire.

blood: **~ ties** *npl* liens *mpl* de sang; **~ transfusion** *n* transfusion *f* sanguine; **~ type** *n* groupe *m* sanguin; **~ vessel** *n* vaisseau *m* sanguin; **~worm** *n* Zool ver *m* de vase.

bloody /ˈblʌdɪ/ **I** *adj* **1** (covered in blood) [*hand, sword, rag*] ensanglanté; **to have a ~ nose** avoir le nez en sang; **to give sb a ~ nose** lit faire saigner le nez de qn; fig faire souffrir qn; **2** (violent) [*battle, deed*] sanglant; [*regime, tyrant*] sanguinaire; **3**◑ GB (expressing anger, frustration) sacré○; **this ~ car!** cette sacrée○ voiture!; **what a ~ miracle!** c'est un sacré○ miracle!; **you ~ fool!** espèce d'idiot○!; **you've got a ~ nerve!** tu as un sacré culot○!; **~ hell!** merde◑!; **what the ~ hell are you doing here?** qu'est-ce que tu fous là?◑; **4**○ (unpleasant) **the interview was ~** l'entretien a été atroce; **he was perfectly ~ to me** il a été parfaitement dégueulasse◑ avec moi○; **5** (red) rouge sang (*inv*).

II◑ *adv* GB (for emphasis) [*dangerous, difficult, expensive*] sacrément○; **she sings ~ well** elle chante sacrément○ bien; **the film was ~ awful** le film était absolument nul○; **a ~ good film** un super○ film; **what a ~ stupid idea!** quelle idée débile○!; **don't be so ~ stupid!** arrête tes conneries◑!; **it's ~ ridiculous!** c'est vraiment con◑!; **you had ~ well better do** tu as intérêt à faire.

IDIOMS **~ but unbowed** le corps meurtri mais la tête haute.

Bloody Mary *n* vodka *f* avec du jus de tomate.

bloody-minded /ˌblʌdɪˈmaɪndɪd/ *adj* GB **don't be so ~** ne fais pas ta tête de mule; **he's just being ~** il fait ça pour embêter le monde.

blooey○ /ˈbluːɪ/ *adv* US **to go ~** foirer○.

bloom /bluːm/ **I** *n* **1** (flower) fleur *f*; **2** (flowering) floraison *f*; **in ~** en fleur; **in full ~** en pleine floraison; **to come into ~** fleurir; **3** (on skin, fruit) velouté *m*; **4** fig **in the ~ of youth** dans la fleur de l'âge; fig **to take the ~ off sth** jeter une ombre sur qch.

II *vi* (be in flower) être fleuri; (come into flower) fleurir.

bloomer /ˈbluːmə(r)/ *n* **1**○† GB bévue *f*; **2** (plant) **late/early ~** plante *f* à floraison tardive/précoce; **3** GB Culin gros pain *m*.

bloomers /ˈbluːməz/ *npl* culotte *f* bouffante (*portée autrefois par les femmes*).

blooming /ˈbluːmɪŋ/ **I** *adj* **1** (healthy) [*person*] resplendissant; [*plant*] magnifique; [*friendship*] florissant; **~ with health** resplendissant de santé; **~ period** floraison *f*; **2**○ GB fichu○; **~ idiot!** espèce d'idiot○!

II○ GB *adv* **it ~ well isn't!** sûrement pas!

Bloomsbury group /ˈbluːmzbrɪ gruːp/ *n*: *cercle d'artistes et d'écrivains londoniens* (*dont Virginia Woolf et Duncan Grant*) *entre 1907 et 1930*.

blooper○ /ˈbluːpə(r)/ *n* US gaffe○ *f*.

blossom /ˈblɒsəm/ **I** *n* **1** (flowers) fleurs *fpl*; **in ~** en fleur(s); **in full ~** en pleine floraison; **the valley is full of ~** la vallée est pleine d'arbres en fleur; **to come into ~** fleurir; **~ time** floraison *f*; **2** (flower) fleur *f*.

II *vi* fleurir; fig **to ~ (out)** s'épanouir; **she is ~ing into a lovely woman** elle devient une très belle femme.

blot /blɒt/ **I** *n* gen tache *f*; (of ink) pâté *m*; fig ombre *f*.

II *vtr* (*p prés etc* **-tt-**) **1** (dry) sécher [qch] au buvard [*writing*]; **to ~ one's lipstick** enlever le rouge à lèvres superflu; **2** (stain) tacher; fig ternir; **3** = **blot out**.

IDIOMS **to ~ one's copybook** se faire mal voir; **to be a ~ on the escutcheon** ternir le blason de qn; **to be a ~ on the landscape** lit gâter le paysage; fig faire une ombre au tableau.

■ **blot out**: **~ out [sth]** [*person*] effacer; [*mist, rain*] masquer.

■ **blot up**: **~ up [sth], ~ [sth] up** éponger.

blotch /blɒtʃ/ **I** *n* **1** (on skin) plaque *f* rouge; **2** (of ink, colour) grosse tache *f*.

II *vtr* barbouiller [*paper, face*].

III *vi* [*pen*] faire des taches.

blotchy /ˈblɒtʃɪ/ *adj* [*complexion*] marbré; [*leaf, paper etc*] tacheté.

blotter /'blɒtə(r)/ *n* **1** (for ink) (small) tampon *m* buvard; (on desk) sous-main *m inv*; **2** US (police, commercial) registre *m*.

blotting paper *n* papier *m* buvard.

blotto○ /'blɒtəʊ/ *adj* cuité○.

blouse /blaʊz, US blaʊs/ ▶**1703** *n* **1** (woman's) chemisier *m*; **2** US Mil vareuse *f*.

blouson /'blu:zɒn/ *n* blouson *m*.

blow /bləʊ/ **I** *n* **1** (stroke) coup *m*; **killed by a ~ to the back of the head** tué d'un coup derrière la tête; **to fell sb with a ~** (with fist) abattre qn d'un coup de poing; (with stick) abattre qn d'un coup de bâton; **to exchange ~s** échanger des coups; **to come to ~s** en venir aux mains (**over** au sujet de); **to strike a ~ for** fig frapper un grand coup pour [*freedom, rights*]; **2** fig (shock, knock) coup *m*; **to deal sb a savage ~** porter un très mauvais coup à qn; **the ~ fell** le coup est tombé; **to be a ~** être un coup terrible (**to sth** porté à qch; **to, for sb** pour qn); **3** (of nose) **to give one's nose a ~** se moucher; **give your nose a good ~** mouche-toi un bon coup; **4**○ GB (marijuana) herbe○ *f*; **5** (cocaine) blanche○ *f*, cocaïne *f*.
II *vtr* (*prét* **blew**; *pp* **blown**) **1** [*wind*] **to ~ sth out of** faire voler qch par [*window*]; **the wind blew the door open/shut** un coup de vent a ouvert/fermé la porte; **to be blown off course/onto the rocks** être dévié/poussé sur les rochers par le vent; **it's ~ing a gale** il y a de la tempête; **2** [*person*] faire [*bubble, smoke ring*]; **to ~ smoke in sb's face** envoyer or souffler la fumée dans la figure de qn; **to ~ an egg** vider un œuf (en soufflant dedans); **to ~ glass** souffler du verre; **to ~ sb a kiss** envoyer un baiser à qn; **3 to ~ one's nose** se moucher; **4** gen, Mus souffler dans [*trumpet, whistle, flute*]; **to ~ the whistle for half-time** siffler la mi-temps; **5** [*explosion*] provoquer [*hole*] (**in** dans); **to be blown to pieces** ou **bits by** être réduit en poussière par; **to ~ a safe** faire sauter un coffre-fort; **6** Elec, Mech faire sauter [*fuse, gasket*]; griller [*lightbulb*]; **7**○ (spend) claquer○ [*money*] (**on** dans); **8**○ (expose) faire tomber [*cover*]; découvrir [*operation*]; **9**○ (make a mess of) **to ~ it** tout ficher en l'air○; **to ~ one's chances** ficher ses chances en l'air○; **to ~ one's lines** se mélanger les pinceaux○; **that's really blown it**○! c'est fichu○ cette fois!; **10**○ † (*pp* **blowed**) **~ it!** zut○!; **~ him!** qu'il aille au diable; **well, ~ me down** ou **I'll be ~ed!** mince alors○!; **I'll be ~ed if I'll pay!** pas question que je paye!○; **11**○ US **to ~ town** se tirer○ vite fait; **12** US (exaggerate) ▶**blow up**; **13**○ (drugs slang) **to ~ grass** fumer (de l'herbe); **14**● (fellate) tailler une pipe à●.
III *vi* (*prét* **blew**; *pp* **blown**) **1** [*wind*] souffler; **the wind's ~ing from the north** le vent vient or souffle du nord; **it's ~ing hard tonight** le vent souffle fort ce soir; **2** (move with wind) **to ~ in the wind** [*leaves, clothes*] voler au vent; **3** [*person*] souffler (**into** dans; **on** sur); **4** (sound) [*whistle*] retentir; [*trumpet*] sonner, retentir; [*foghorn*] rugir; **when the whistle ~s** au coup de sifflet; **5** [*whale*] souffler; **6** (break, explode) [*fuse, gasket*] sauter; [*bulb*] griller; [*tyre*] éclater; **7**○ (leave quickly) filer○.
IDIOMS **to ~ a fuse**○ ou **a gasket**○ ou **one's lid**○ ou **one's stack**○ ou **one' s top**○ piquer une crise○; **it really blew my mind**○ ou **blew me away!**○ (with admiration, astonishment) j'en suis resté baba○.
■ **blow around, blow about** GB: ¶ **~ around** [*leaves, papers, litter*] voler dans tous les sens; ¶ **~ [sth] around, ~ around [sth]** faire voler [qch] dans tous les sens.
■ **blow away**: ¶ **~ away** [*object, hat, paper*] s'envoler; ¶ **~ [sth] away, ~ away [sth]** [*wind*] emporter [*object*]; [*explosion*] souffler [*roof*]; **to ~ the dust away** souffler sur la poussière; ¶ **~ [sb] away**○ (kill) descendre○ [*person*].
■ **blow down**: ¶ **~ down** [*tree, fence, house*] tomber (à cause du vent); ¶ **~ [sth] down, ~ down [sth]** [*wind*] faire tomber [*chimney, tree, house*].
■ **blow in**: ¶ **~ in 1** [*snow, rain*] entrer; **2** (in explosion) [*door, window*] être enfoncé; ¶ **~ [sth] in, ~ in [sth] 1** [*wind*] faire entrer [*snow, rain*]; **2** [*explosion*] enfoncer [*door, window*].
■ **blow off**: ¶ **~ off 1** [*hat*] s'envoler; **2** (gush out) [*gas, liquid*] s'échapper; ¶ **~ [sth] off, ~ off [sth]** [*wind*] emporter [*hat*]; [*explosion*] emporter [*hand, limb, roof*]; **to ~ sb's head off** faire sauter la tête de qn; **he had his leg blown off** il a perdu sa jambe; **to ~ the leaves off the trees** [*wind*] faire tomber les feuilles des arbres; **to ~ the dust off sth** [*person*] enlever la poussière de qch en soufflant dessus.
■ **blow out**: ¶ **~ out 1** [*candle, flame*] s'éteindre; **2** [*oil well*] laisser échapper du pétrole; [*gas well*] laisser échapper du gaz; ¶ **~ [sth] out, ~ out [sth] 1** (extinguish) souffler [*candle*]; éteindre [*flames*]; **2** (inflate) **to ~ one's cheeks out** gonfler les or ses joues; **to ~ itself out** [*gale, storm*] tomber.
■ **blow over**: ¶ **~ over 1** (pass, die down) [*storm*] tomber; [*affair*] être oublié; [*discontent, protest*] se calmer; [*anger*] passer, tomber; **2** (topple) [*fence, tree*] tomber (à cause du vent); ¶ **~ [sb/sth] over** [*wind*] renverser [*person, tree, fence*].
■ **blow up**: ¶ **~ up 1** (in explosion) [*building*] sauter; [*bomb*] exploser; **2** [*wind, storm*] se lever; **3** [*trouble, problem, affair*] éclater; **4**○ (become angry) [*person*] s'emporter; **to ~ up at sb** s'emporter après qn, engueuler○ qn; **5** (inflate) **it ~s up** c'est gonflable; **it won't ~ up!** je n'arrive pas à le/la gonfler!; ¶ **~ [sth/sb] up, ~ up [sb/sth]** (in explosion) faire sauter [*building, person*]; faire exploser [*bomb*]; ¶ **~ [sth] up, ~ up [sth] 1** (inflate) gonfler [*tyre, balloon*]; **2** Phot (enlarge) agrandir; **3** (exaggerate) exagérer; **the story has been blown (up) out of all proportion** l'histoire a été exagérément grossie.

blow: **~-by-blow** *adj* [*account*] par le menu; **~down** *n* Nucl dépressurisation *f*.

blow-dry /'bləʊdraɪ/ **I** *n* brushing *m*; **a cut and ~** une coupe avec brushing.
II *vtr* **to ~ sb's hair** faire un brushing à qn; **to ~ one's hair** se faire un brushing.

blower○† /'bləʊə(r)/ *n* (telephone) téléphone *m*; **to get on the ~** passer un coup de fil○ (**to** à).

blow: **~fly** *n* mouche *f* bleue; **~gun** *n* US sarbacane *f*; **~hard**○ *n* US vantard/-e *m/f*.

blowhole /'bləʊhəʊl/ *n* **1** Zool (of whale) évent *m*; **2** (in ice) trou *m* d'air.

blow job● /'bləʊdʒɒb/ *n* **to give sb a ~** tailler une pipe à qn●.

blowlamp /'bləʊlæmp/ *n* GB = **blowtorch**.

blown /bləʊn/ **I** *pp* ▶**blow II, III**.
II *adj* [*rose*] épanoui.

blowout /'bləʊaʊt/ *n* **1** Elec court-circuit *m*; **2** Aut (of tyre) crevaison *f*; **3** Mining (in oil or gas well) jaillissement *m*; **4** Aviat (of jet engine) panne *f*; **to have a ~** tomber en panne; **5**○ (meal) gueuleton○ *m*; **to have a ~** faire un gueuleton○.

blowpipe /'bləʊpaɪp/ *n* **1** GB (for darts) sarbacane *f*; **2** (of blowtorch) chalumeau *m*; **3** (in glassmaking) tube *m* de soufflage.

blowtorch /'bləʊtɔ:tʃ/ *n* lampe *f* à souder.

blow-up /'bləʊʌp/ **I** *n* **1** Phot agrandissement *m*; **2**○ (argument) engueulade◑ *f*.
II *adj* (inflatable) [*doll, toy, dinghy*] gonflable.

blowy○ /'bləʊɪ/ *adj* venteux/-euse, venté.

blowzy /'blaʊzɪ/ *adj* péj [*woman*] à l'aspect négligé.

blub○ /blʌb/ *vi* (*p prés etc* **-bb-**) GB chialer○.

blubber /'blʌbə(r)/ **I** *n* (of whale) graisse *f* de baleine; ○fig hum (of person) graisse *f*, lard○ *m*; **~-faced** au visage boursouflé; **~-lipped** lippu.
II○ *vi* pleurer comme un veau.

blubbery /'blʌbərɪ/ *adj* adipeux/-euse; **to have ~ lips** être lippu.

bludgeon /'blʌdʒən/ **I** *n* matraque *f*.
II *vtr* matraquer; **to ~ sb to death** tuer qn à coups de matraque; **she ~ed him into doing it** fig elle l'a harcelé pour qu'il le fasse.

blue /blu:/ ▶**1104** **I** *n* **1** (colour) bleu *m*; **to go** ou **turn ~** bleuir, devenir bleu; **2** (sky) littér **the ~** l'azur *m* liter; **3** GB Univ (honour) **to be/get an Oxford/Cambridge ~** être/devenir membre d'une équipe sportive d'Oxford/de Cambridge; **4**○ GB Pol **a true ~** un partisan ardent du parti Conservateur; **5** US Hist (in civil war) nordiste *mf*.
II blues *npl* **1** Mus **the ~s** le blues *m*; **to sing/play the ~s** chanter/jouer du blues; **2**○ (depression) **the ~s** le cafard; **to have the ~s** avoir le cafard○.
III blues *modif* Mus [*music, musician, fan, festival*] de blues.
IV *adj* **1** (in colour) bleu; fig **to be ~ from** ou **with the cold** être bleu de froid; **2** (depressed) **to feel ~** avoir le cafard○; **to look ~** avoir l'air déprimé; **3**○ (smutty) [*film*] porno○; [*joke*] osé, cochon/-onne○; **4**○ GB Pol conservateur/-trice.
V *vtr*○ GB (squander) **to ~ (all) one's money on sth** dépenser tout son fric sur qch○.
IDIOMS **to say sth out of the ~** dire qch à brûle-pourpoint; **to appear/happen out of the ~** apparaître/se passer à l'improviste; **to go off into the ~** partir à l'aventure; **to vanish into the ~** s'évanouir dans la nature; **the air was ~!** les gros mots fusaient!; **black and ~** couvert de bleus; **to beat sb black and ~**○ battre qn comme plâtre○; **to throw a ~ fit** piquer une crise○; **to tell sb sth/repeat sth (to sb) until one is ~ in the face** se tuer à dire qch à qn/à répéter qch (à qn); **you can shout until you're ~ in the face, I'm going anyway!** cause toujours, j'y vais quand même○!; ▶**moon, murder**.

blue: **~ baby** *n* enfant *m* bleu; **~ baby syndrome** *n* maladie *f* bleue; **Bluebeard** *pr n* Mythol, fig Barbe-bleue *m*.

bluebell /'blu:bel/ *n* Bot **1** (wood hyacinth) jacinthe *f* des bois; **2** (harebell) campanule *f*.

blue: **~berry** *n* US Bot myrtille *f*; **~bird** *n* rouge-gorge *m* bleu; **~-black** ▶**1104** *n, adj* [*hair*] noir (*m*) à reflets bleus; [*material*] bleu (*m*) foncé *inv*; **~ blood** *n* sang *m* bleu or noble; **~-blooded** *adj* de sang bleu or noble.

blue book *n* **1** Pol livre *m* blanc; **2** US Sch cahier *m* bleu (*utilisé pour les examens*); **3** US (society listing) ≈ bottin *m* mondain.

bluebottle /'blu:bɒtl/ *n* **1** Zool mouche *f* bleue; **2** Bot bleuet *m*; **3**○ †GB flic○ *m*.

blue: **~ cheese** *n* (fromage *m*) bleu *m*; **~ cheese dressing, ~ cheese sauce** *n* sauce *f* salade au fromage bleu.

blue chip **I** *n* **1** Fin valeur *f* vedette; **2** Games (in poker) jeton *m* de grande valeur.
II *modif* Fin [*company, customer*] de premier ordre; **~ (share)** valeur *f* de premier ordre; **~ investment** placement *m* sûr or de tout repos.

blue collar *adj* **~ worker** ouvrier *m*, col *m* bleu; **~ union** syndicat *m* ouvrier; **~ vote** vote *m* des cols bleus.

blue-eyed /'blu:aɪd/ *adj* aux yeux bleus.

blue-eyed boy○ *n* GB fig (of public, media, teacher) chouchou *m*○, chéri *m*○; (of influential person) protégé *m*.

bluegrass /'blu:grɑ:s, US -græs/ *n* **1** Bot pâturin *m*; **2** Mus blue grass *m* (*musique folklorique du Kentucky*).

blue: **~-green** ▶**1104** *n, adj* turquoise (*m*) *inv*; **Blue Helmets, Blue Berets** *npl* Mil Casques *mpl* bleus; **~ jay** *n* geai *m* bleu; **~ jeans** *npl* jean *m*; **~ law** *n* US

Jur *loi limitant les activités publiques le dimanche*; **~ light** *n* (on emergency vehicles) gyrophare *m*; **~ mould** GB, **~ mold** US *n* pénicillium *m*.

blueness /ˈbluːnɪs/ *n* bleu *m* ¢.

blue: **~nose**○ *n* péj bien-pensant/-e *m/f* pej; **~ note** *n* (in jazz) blue note *f*.

blue pencil I *n* **to go through sth with the ~** (edit) corriger qch; (censor) censurer qch.
II **blue-pencil** *vtr* (*p prés etc* GB **-ll-**, US **-l-**) (edit) corriger [*text*]; (censor) censurer [*film, book*].

Blue Peter /ˌbluːˈpiːtə(r)/ *n* Naut pavillon *m* de partance.

blueprint /ˈbluːprɪnt/ *n* **1** Archit, Tech bleu *m*; **2** fig (plan) projet *m*, propositions *fpl* (**for** pour; **for doing** pour faire); **it's a ~ for success/disaster** cela mène tout droit au succès/à la catastrophe; **monetarist/industrial ~** politique *f* monétariste/industrielle.

blue ribbon I *n* premier prix *m*.
II *modif* **1** US Jur [*jury, panel*] d'experts; **2** (premier) [*event*] grand (*before n*).

blue: **~ rinse** *n* Cosmet rinçage *m* à reflets argents; **~ rinse brigade** *n* GB hum péj vieilles bourgeoises *fpl* bien-pensantes pej; **~ shark** *n* requin *m* bleu; **~stocking** *n* péj bas-bleu *m* pej.

blue streak○ *n* US **to talk a ~** parler à toute vitesse; **to run a ~** courir comme une flèche.

bluesy /ˈbluːzɪ/ *adj* Mus inspiré du blues.

blue: **~ tit** *n* mésange *f* bleue; **~ whale** *n* baleine *f* bleue.

bluff /blʌf/ I *n* **1** (ruse) bluff *m* (also in cards); **2** (bank) escarpement *m*; (cliff) falaise *f*.
II *adj* [*person, manner*] carré.
III *vtr* bluffer○; **to ~ sb into thinking sth** faire croire qch à qn; **to ~ one's way out of a situation** se tirer d'une situation en bluffant.
IV *vi* bluffer (also in cards); **he's (only) ~ing** il bluffe.
IDIOMS **to call sb's ~** prendre qn au mot (*sachant qu'il bluffe*); **it's time we called his ~** il est temps qu'on le mette au pied du mur; **to ~ it (out)** s'en tirer en bluffant or au bluff.

bluffer /ˈblʌfə(r)/ *n* bluffeur/-euse *m/f*.

bluish /ˈbluːɪʃ/ ▶ 1104 *adj* bleuté.

blunder /ˈblʌndə(r)/ I *n* bourde *f*.
II *vi* **1** (make mistake) faire une bourde; **~ badly** faire une grosse bourde; **2** (move clumsily) **he ~ed into the table** il s'est cogné à la table.
■ **blunder about**: **she ~ed about in the dark** elle avançait dans l'obscurité en se cognant.
■ **blunder on**: **~ on [sth]** découvrir qch sans le vouloir.

blunderbuss /ˈblʌndəbʌs/ *n* tromblon *m*.

blunderer /ˈblʌndərə(r)/ *n* balourd *m*.

blundering /ˈblʌndərɪŋ/ I *n* balourdise *f*.
II *adj* balourd; **~ idiot!** triple idiot!

blunt /blʌnt/ I *adj* **1** [*knife, scissors*] émoussé; [*pencil*] mal taillé; [*needle*] épointé; **this knife is ~** ce couteau ne coupe plus; **a ~ instrument** un instrument contondant; **2** (frank) [*person, manner*] abrupt; [*refusal, reply*] catégorique; [*criticism*] direct; **to be ~ with you** pour être tout à fait franc avec toi.
II *vtr* émousser [*knife, scissors*]; épointer [*pencil, needle*]; couper [*appetite*]; endurcir [*feeling*]; émousser [*intelligence*]; tempérer [*enthusiasm*].

blunt cut I *n* US (hairstyle) coupe *f* carrée.
II *vtr* couper [qch] au carré [*hair*].

bluntly /ˈblʌntlɪ/ *adv* franchement; **to put it ~** pour parler franchement.

bluntness /ˈblʌntnɪs/ *n* (of person) francparler *m*; (of manner, answer) rudesse *f*.

blur /blɜː(r)/ I *n* image *f* floue; **the writing was just a ~ to me** l'écriture me semblait brouillée; **after that it all became a ~** ensuite les choses se sont un peu brouillées; **her memories are just a ~** ses souvenirs sont extrêmement confus.
II *vtr* (*p prés etc* **-rr-**) brouiller; **to ~ the distinction between X and Y** confondre X et Y.
III *vi* (*p prés etc* **-rr-**) se brouiller.

blurb /blɜːb/ I *n* gen descriptif *m* (promotionnel); (on book cover) texte *m* de présentation (*sur la couverture*); péj baratin *m*.
II *vtr* décrire.

blurred /blɜːd/ *adj* indistinct; [*image, photo, idea*] flou; [*memory*] confus; **to have ~ vision** avoir des troubles de la vue; **to become ~** [*eyes*] se voiler.

blurt /blɜːt/ *vtr* ▶ **blurt out**.
■ **blurt out**: **~ [sth] out, ~ out [sth]** laisser échapper; **he ~ed everything out** il a craché le morceau○.

blush /blʌʃ/ I *n* **1** (flush) rougeur *f*; **without a ~** sans scrupules; **to spare sb's ~es** ménager (la modestie de) qn; **at first ~** sout à première vue; **to hide one's ~es** dissimuler son embarras; **2** US = **blusher**.
II *vi* rougir (**at** devant; **with** de); **to ~ for sb** avoir honte pour qn; **I ~ to admit it** j'ai honte de le dire.

blusher /ˈblʌʃə(r)/ *n* Cosmet fard *m* à joues.

blushing /ˈblʌʃɪŋ/ I *n* rougissement *m*.
II *adj* [*person*] rougissant.

bluster /ˈblʌstə(r)/ I *n* **1** (of wind) bourrasque *f*; **2** fig (angry) fulminations *fpl*; (boasting) fanfaronnades *fpl*.
II *vi* **1** [*wind*] souffler en bourrasques; (violently) souffler en tempête; **2** fig [*person*] (angrily) fulminer (**at sb** contre qn); (boastfully) fanfaronner.

blusterer /ˈblʌstərə(r)/ *n* (boastful person) fanfaron/-onne *m/f*; (angry) braillard/-e *m/f*.

blustering /ˈblʌstərɪŋ/ I *n* ¢ (boasting) fanfaronnades *fpl*; (rage) fulminations *fpl*.
II *adj* (boastful) fanfaron/-onne; (angry) braillard.

blustery /ˈblʌstərɪ/ *adj* **~ wind** bourrasque *f*; **it's a ~ day** le vent souffle en bourrasques.

blu-tak® /ˈbluːtæk/ *n* patafix® *m*.

BM *n* **1** *abrév* ▶ **British Museum**; **2** (*abrév* = **Bachelor of Medicine**) diplôme *m* universitaire de médecine; **3**○ US *abrév* ▶ **bowel movement**.

BMA *n* (*abrév* = **British Medical Association**) association *f* britannique des médecins.

B movie /biː muːvɪ/ *n* film *m* de série B.

BMus (*abrév* = **Bachelor of Music**) diplôme *m* universitaire d'études musicales.

BO *n* **1**○ (*abrév* = **body odour**) odeur *f* corporelle; **he's got ~** il sent○; **2** US *abrév* ▶ **box office**.

boa /ˈbəʊə/ *n* **1** Zool boa *m*; **2** (**feather**) **~** boa *m*.

boa constrictor *n* (boa) constricteur *m*.

Boadicea /ˌbəʊədɪˈsiːə/ *pr n* Boadicée.

boar /bɔː(r)/ *n* **1** (wild) sanglier *m*; **young (wild) ~** marcassin *m*; Culin **~'s head** hure *f* (de sanglier); **2** (male pig) verrat *m*.

board /bɔːd/ I *n* **1** (plank) planche *f*; **2** Admin conseil *m*; **~ of directors** conseil d'administration; **to sit** ou **be on the board (of directors)** siéger au conseil d'administration; **disciplinary ~** conseil de discipline; **~ of inquiry** commission *f* d'enquête; **~ of editors** comité *m* de rédaction; **~ of examiners** jury *m* d'examen; **~ of governors** Sch comité *m* de gestion d'une école; **3** Games (playing surface) tableau *m*; (in poker) tapis *m* de jeu; **4** Sch tableau *m* (noir); **5** (notice board) (for information) panneau *m* d'affichage; (to advertise) panneau *m*; **6** Comput, Electron plaquette *f*; **7** (accommodation) **full ~** pension *f* complète; **half ~** demi-pension *f*; **to pay £30 a week ~** payer 30 livres par semaine pour sa pension; **~ and lodging, room and ~** le gîte et le couvert.
II **boards** *npl* **1** (floor) plancher *m*; **bare ~s** plancher nu; **2** Print plats *mpl*; **limp ~s** cartonnage *m* souple; **in paper ~s** cartonné; **3** Theat estrade *f*; **to tread the ~s** faire du théâtre; **4** US (+ *v sg*) (entrance exam) examen *m* d'entrée; (final exam) examen *m* de fin d'année.
III *modif* Admin [*meeting, member*] du conseil d'administration.
IV **on board** *adv phr* **to be on ~** ou **on ~ ship** être à bord; **to go on ~** embarquer, monter à bord; **to get on ~** monter dans [*bus, train*]; monter à bord de [*plane, ship*]; **there were 200 passengers on ~ the ship/plane** il y avait 200 passagers à bord du bateau/de l'avion; **to take sth on ~** lit embarquer [*cargo, passengers*]; fig prendre [qch] en compte [*changes, facts*]; adopter [*proposal*]; assumer [*problem*].
V *vtr* **1** (get on) monter à bord de [*boat, plane*]; monter dans [*bus, train*]; **she ~ed the ship at Athens** elle est montée à bord du navire à Athènes; **2** Naut [*customs officer*] arraisonner [*vessel*]; [*pirates, marines*] aborder [*vessel*].
VI *vi* être en pension (**with** chez); Sch [*pupil*] être interne.
IDIOMS **above ~** légal; **across the ~** à tous les niveaux; **to go by the ~** tomber à l'eau; **to sweep the ~** tout gagner, tout rafler○.
■ **board over**: **~ [sth] over, ~ over [sth]** boucher [qch] avec des planches [*hole, shaft*].
■ **board out**: **~ [sb] out, ~ out [sb]** mettre [qn] en pension [*child*].
■ **board up**: **~ [sth] up, ~ up [sth]** boucher [qch] avec des planches [*door, window*]; barricader [qch] avec des planches [*house, shop*].

boarder /ˈbɔːdə(r)/ *n* **1** (lodger) pensionnaire *m*; **2** Sch interne *mf*.

board game ▶ 1282 *n* jeu *m* de société (à damier).

boarding /ˈbɔːdɪŋ/ *n* **1** Aviat, Naut embarquement *m*; **2** Naut (by customs officer) arraisonnement *m*; **3** Mil abordage *m*.

boarding: **~ card** *n* Aviat, Naut carte *f* d'embarquement; **~ house** *n* pension *f*; **~ party** *n* Naut, Mil groupe *m* d'abordage; **~ school** *n* école *f* privée avec internat.

boardroom /ˈbɔːdruːm, -rʊm/ *n* (room) salle *f* du conseil; **everyone from shopfloor to ~** tous, des ouvriers jusqu'à la direction.

board: **~ sailing** ▶ 1282 *n* Sport planche *f* à voile; **~walk** *n* US chemin *m* fait de planches.

boarhound /ˈbɔːhaʊnd/ *n* vautre *m*; **pack of ~s** vautrait *m*.

boar hunting /ˈbɔːhʌntɪŋ/ *n* chasse *f* au sanglier.

boast /bəʊst/ I *n* **1** vantardise *f*; **it is his ~ that he is never late** il se vante de ne jamais être en retard; **it was an empty** ou **idle ~** c'était du bluff; **it is our proud ~ that...** nous sommes fiers que...; **2** Sport (in squash) double-mur *m*.
II *vtr*: **the town ~s a beautiful church** la ville s'enorgueillit d'une belle église; **the computer ~s two floppy disk drives** l'ordinateur est équipé de deux lecteurs de disquettes; **'I have six medals', she ~ed** 'j'ai six médailles', dit-elle en fanfaronnant.
III *vi* **1** se vanter (**about** de); **to ~ of being** se vanter d'être; **she said it quite without ~ing** elle l'a dit sans vouloir se vanter; **without ~ing** sans vouloir me/se etc vanter; **nothing to ~ about** (sth good) rien de bien extraordinaire; (sth bad) pas de quoi se vanter; **2** (in squash) faire un boast.

boaster /ˈbəʊstə(r)/ *n* vantard/-e *m/f*.

boastful /ˈbəʊstfl/ *adj* [*person*] vantard; **without being ~** sans se vanter; **to make ~ remarks** faire de l'épate.

boastfully /ˈbəʊstfəlɪ/ *adv* [*speak*] en fanfaronnant; [*write*] en se vantant.

boastfulness /ˈbəʊstflnɪs/ *n* vantardise *f*.

The human body

When it is clear who owns the part of the body mentioned, French tends to use the definite article, where English uses a possessive adjective:

he raised his hand = il a levé la main
she closed her eyes = elle a fermé les yeux

Note, for instance, the use of la *and* mon *here:*

she ran her hand over my forehead = elle a passé la main sur mon front

For expressions such as he hurt his foot *or* she hit her head on the beam, *where the owner of the body part is the subject of the verb, i.e. the person doing the action, use a reflexive verb in French:*

she has broken her leg = elle s'est cassé la jambe

(*literally* she has broken to herself the leg – *there is no past participle agreement because the preceding reflexive pronoun* se *is the indirect object*).

he was rubbing his hands = il se frottait les mains
she was holding her head = elle se tenait la tête

Note also the following:

she broke his leg = elle lui a cassé la jambe (*literally* she broke to him the leg)
the stone split his lip = le caillou lui a fendu la lèvre (*literally* the stone split to him the lip)

Describing people

For ways of saying how tall someone is, ▶ 1412, *of stating someone's weight,* ▶ 1883, *and of talking about the colour of hair and eyes,* ▶ 1104.

Here are some ways of describing people in French:

his hair is long = il a les cheveux longs
he has long hair = il a les cheveux longs
a boy with long hair = un garçon aux cheveux longs
a long-haired boy = un garçon aux cheveux longs
the boy with long hair = le garçon aux cheveux longs
her eyes are blue = elle a les yeux bleus
she has blue eyes = elle a les yeux bleus
she is blue-eyed = elle a les yeux bleus
the girl with blue eyes = la fille aux yeux bleus
a blue-eyed girl = une fille aux yeux bleus
his nose is red = il a le nez rouge
he has a red nose = il a le nez rouge
a man with a red nose = un homme au nez rouge
a red-nosed man = un homme au nez rouge

When referring to a temporary state, the following phrases are useful:

his leg is broken = il a la jambe cassée
the man with the broken leg = l'homme à la jambe cassée

but note

a man with a broken leg = un homme avec une jambe cassée

For other expressions with body part terms, ▶ 1354.

boasting /ˈbəʊstɪŋ/ *n* vantardise *f*.

boat /bəʊt/ **I** *n* **1** (vessel) bateau *m*; (sailing) voilier *m*; (rowing) barque *f*; (liner) paquebot *m*; **he crossed the lake in a ~** il a traversé le lac en bateau; **2** (ferry) bateau *m*; **by ~** en bateau.
II *modif* [*journey, trip*] en bateau; [*building, builder, hire*] de bateaux.
IDIOMS **to be in the same ~**○ être tous dans la même galère; **to miss the ~** manquer le coche; **to push the ~ out**○ GB faire les choses en grand; **to rock the ~**○ jouer les trouble-fête○; **don't rock the ~**○! ne fais pas de vagues○!

boat deck *n* pont *m* des embarcations.

boater /ˈbəʊtə(r)/ *n* **1** (hat) canotier *m*; **2** US (person) canoteur *m*.

boat: **~hook** *n* Naut gaffe *f*; **~house** *n* abri *m* à bateaux.

boating /ˈbəʊtɪŋ/ **I** *n* gen navigation *f* de plaisance; (in rowing boat) canotage *m*.
II *modif* [*accident, enthusiast, gear*] de bateau; [*holiday, trip*] en bateau.

boatload /ˈbəʊtləʊd/ *n* (of goods) cargaison *f*; **~s of tourists** des bateaux pleins de touristes.

boat: **~man** *n* (on ferry) batelier *m*; (hiring) loueur *m* de bateaux; **~ neck** *n* col *m* bateau; **~ people** *npl* boat people *mpl*; **Boat Race** *n* GB course *f* d'aviron (*entre les universités d'Oxford et de Cambridge*).

boatswain /ˈbəʊsn/ *n* maître *m* d'équipage.

boat: **~ train** *n*: *train faisant correspondance avec le bateau*; **~yard** *n* chantier *m* de construction de bateaux.

bob /bɒb/ **I** *n* **1** (haircut) coupe *f* au carré; **2** (nod) **a ~ of the head** un signe de tête; **3** (curtsy) petite révérence *f*; **4** (weight) (on plumb line) plomb *m*; (on pendulum) poids *m*; (on fishing line) bouchon *m*; **5** (tail) queue *f* écourtée; **6**○ GB (money) (*pl* **~**) shilling *m*; **I bet that costs a ~ or two** je parie que cela coûte une fortune; **he's not short of a ~ or two** il n'est pas à quelques francs près; **7** Sport (also **bobsleigh**) bobsleigh *m*.
II *vtr* (*p prés etc* **-bb-**) **1** (cut) couper [qch] au carré [*hair*]; couper [qch] court [*tail*]; **2** (nod) **to ~ one's head** faire un signe de tête; **3 to ~ a curtsy** faire une petite révérence (**to** à).
III *vi* (*p prés etc* **-bb-**) **1** (move) [*boat, float*] danser; **to ~ down** [*person*] se baisser subitement; **to ~ up** [*person, float*] refaire surface; **to ~ up and down** [*person, boat*] s'agiter; [*heads*] apparaître et disparaître; **2** Games **to ~ for apples**: *chercher à saisir avec les dents des pommes flottant dans un baquet d'eau*.
IV bobbed *pp adj* [*hair, tail*] coupé court.

bob-a-job /ˈbɒbədʒɒb/ *n* GB *système par lequel les scouts gagnent de l'argent en faisant de petits travaux*.

bobbin /ˈbɒbɪn/ *n* bobine *f*; (for lace-making) fuseau *m*.

bobbin lace *n* dentelle *f* au fuseau.

bobble /ˈbɒbl/ **I** *n* **1** (on hat etc) pompon *m*; **2** US (blunder) bévue *f*.
II *vtr* US mal attraper [*ball*].
III *vi* US commettre une bévue.

bobble hat *n* bonnet *m* à pompon.

bobby○† /ˈbɒbɪ/ GB *n* agent *m* (de police).

bobby: **~ pin** US *n* barrette *f*, pince *f* à cheveux; **~ socks**, **~ sox** *npl* socquettes *fpl*.

bobbysoxer○ /ˈbɒbɪsɒksə(r)/ *n* US péj minette○ *f*, jeune fille *f*.

bobcat /ˈbɒbkæt/ *n* lynx *m* roux.

bobsled /ˈbɒbsled/ *n* = **bobsleigh**.

bobsleigh /ˈbɒbsleɪ/ ▶ 1282 **I** *n* bobsleigh *m*.
II *vi* faire du bobsleigh.

bobtail /ˈbɒbteɪl/ *n* **1** (tail) queue *f* écourtée; **2** (dog) bobtail *m*; **3** (horse) cheval *m* à la queue écourtée.

Boche○† /bɒʃ/ *npl* injur **the ~** les boches○ *mpl*○† offensive.

bock /bɒk/ *n* bière *f* brune.

bod○ /bɒd/ *n* **1** GB (person) type○ *m*, mec○ *m*; **2** US (body) corps *m*.

bode /bəʊd/ *vi* littér **to ~ well/ill** être de bon/mauvais augure (**for** pour).

bodega /bəʊˈdiːgə/ *n* **1** (storehouse) *entrepôt de vins espagnols*; **2** US (grocery) épicerie *f* (hispano-américaine).

bodge GB = **botch**.

bodice /ˈbɒdɪs/ *n* (of dress) corsage *m*; **fitted ~** corsage *m* ajusté.

bodice ripper *n* hum roman *m* de cape et d'épée.

bodily /ˈbɒdɪlɪ/ **I** *adj* [*function*] physiologique; [*fluid*] organique; [*need, welfare, well-being*] physique; [*injury*] corporel/-elle.
II *adv* [*carry, pick up*] à bras-le-corps; **to throw sb out ~** prendre qn à bras-le-corps et le/la jeter dehors.

bodkin /ˈbɒdkɪn/ *n* (for threading tape etc) passe-lacet *m*; (for making holes) poinçon *m*.

body /ˈbɒdɪ/ **I** *n* **1** (of person, animal) corps *m*; **~ and soul** corps et âme; **to have just enough to keep ~ and soul together** avoir juste assez pour survivre; **to sell one's ~** se prostituer; **all he wants is your ~**○ tout ce qu'il veut, c'est coucher avec toi○; **2** (corpse) corps *m*, cadavre *m*; **a dead ~** un cadavre; **3** (main section) (of car) carrosserie *f*; (of boat) coque *f*; (of aircraft) fuselage *m*; (of camera) boîtier *m*; (of violin, guitar) caisse *f* de résonance; (of text, type) corps *m*; (of dress) corsage *m*; **the ~ of the church** la nef; **4** (large quantity) (of water) étendue *f*; (of laws) recueil *m* or corps *m* (de lois); **a large ~ of evidence** un vaste faisceau de preuves; **there is a ~ of opinion in favour of** l'ensemble *m* de l'opinion est en faveur de; **the ~ of support for her is growing** le soutien en sa faveur va croissant; **5** (group) (of troops, students) corps *m*; **the student ~** la masse des étudiants; **the main ~ of demonstrators** le gros des manifestants; **in a ~** en masse; **6** (organization) organisme *m*; **advisory/official ~** organisme consultatif/officiel; **disciplinary ~** commission *f* disciplinaire; **7** Phys corps *m*; **8** (fullness) (of wine) corps *m*; (of hair) volume *m*; **9** Fashn (garment) body *m*; **10**○ †(person) bonhomme○/bonne femme○ *m/f*.
II *modif* **1** Cosmet [*lotion, scrub*] pour le corps; [*care, paint*] corporel/-elle; **2** Aut [*repair*] de carrosserie.
IDIOMS **over my dead ~**! plutôt mourir!; **you'll do that over my dead ~**! plutôt mourir que te laisser faire ça!

body: **~ armour** GB, **~ armor** US *n* tenue *f* pare-balles; **~ bag** *n* housse *f* mortuaire; **~ belt** *n* ceinture *f* d'haltérophilie.

body blow *n* lit coup *m* porté au corps; **to deal a ~ to** fig porter un coup sérieux à.

bodybuilder /ˈbɒdɪbɪldə(r)/ *n* **1** Sport culturiste *mf*; **2** ▶ 1692 Aut carrossier *m*.

body-building /ˈbɒdɪbɪldɪŋ/ ▶ 1282 **I** *n* culturisme *m*.
II *adj* [*exercise*] musculaire; [*food*] énergétique.

body cavity *n* cavité *f* corporelle.

bodycheck /ˈbɒdɪtʃek/ **I** *n* (in ice-hockey) interception *f*.
II *vtr* intercepter [*opponent*].

body: **~ clock** *n* horloge *f* corporelle; **~ corporate** *n* Jur personne *f* morale; **~ count** *n* décompte *m* des morts; **~ double** *n* Cin doublure *f* érotique; **~ fat** *n* tissus *mpl* adipeux; **~ filler** *n* Aut mastic *m* de finition; **~ fluids** *npl* fluides *mpl* organiques.

bodyguard /ˈbɒdɪgɑːd/ *n* **1** (individual) garde *m* du corps; **2** (group) protection *f* rapprochée.

body: **~ hair** *n* poils *mpl*; **~ heat** *n* chaleur *f* corporelle; **~ image** *n* schéma *m* corporel; **~ language** *n* langage *m* corporel; **~ mike**○ *n* micro○ *m* portatif; **~ odour** GB, **~ odor** US, **BO**○ *n* odeur *f* corporelle; **~ piercing** *n* piercing *m*; **~ politic** *n* corps *m* social; **~ scan** *n* examen *m* corporel au scanner; **~-scanner** *n* scanner *m*.

body search I *n* fouille *f* corporelle; **intimate ~** fouille *f* intime.
II *vtr* fouiller.

body: **~ shell** *n* Aut coque *f*; **~ shop** *n* Aut atelier *m* de carrosserie.

body snatching *n* **1** (of corpses) vol *m* de cadavres; **2**○ Mgmt *recrutement de candidats par chasseur de têtes.*

body: **~ stocking**, **~ suit** *n* body *m*, justaucorps *m*; **~ surfing** *n* surf *m* sans planche; **~ type** *n* Print caractère *m* principal; **~ warmer** *n* gilet *m* matelassé; **~ weight** *n* poids *m*; **~work** *n* carrosserie *f*.

Boer /bɔ:(r)/ *n* Boer *mf*; **the ~ War** la guerre des Boers.

boffin○ /ˈbɒfɪn/ *n* GB expert *m*; **computer ~** expert *m* en informatique.

boffo◑ /ˈbɒfəʊ/ *adj* US [*play, movie*] à succès.

bog /bɒg/ *n* **1** (marshy ground) marais *m*; **2** (also **peat ~**) tourbière *f*; **3**◑ GB (toilet) chiottes◑ *fpl*.
IDIOMS **to get ~ged down in sth** s'enliser dans qch.

bogey /ˈbəʊgɪ/ I *n* **1** (evil spirit) croquemitaine *m*; **2** (imagined fear) spectre *m*; (to frighten people) épouvantail *m*; **3** (in golf) bogey *m*; **to make** ou **take a ~** faire un au dessus du par, faire un bogey; **4**◑ GB (in nose) crotte○ *f* de nez.
II *vtr* (in golf) **to ~ the 2nd hole** faire un au dessus du par au 2ème.

bogeyman /ˈbəʊgɪmæn/ *n* croquemitaine *m*.

boggle /ˈbɒgl/ I *vtr* **it ~s the mind** ça dépasse l'imagination.
II *vi* **the mind ~s!** c'est époustouflant!; **the mind** ou **imagination ~s at the idea** on a du mal à imaginer ça; **mind-boggling** époustouflant.

boggy /ˈbɒgɪ/ *adj* [*ground*] (swampy) marécageux/-euse; (muddy) bourbeux/-euse; (peaty) [*soil*] tourbeux/-euse.

bogie /ˈbəʊgɪ/ *n* **1** GB Rail bog(g)ie *m*; **2** = **bogey**.

bog: **~ oak** *n* chêne *m* de tourbière; **~ roll**◑ *n* GB papier-chiottes◑ *m*; **~ standard**◑ *adj* ordinaire.

bogus /ˈbəʊgəs/ *adj* [*official, doctor, invoice*] faux/fausse (*before n*); [*claim*] bidon; [*company*] factice.

bogyman *n* = **bogeyman**.

bohemia /bəʊˈhi:mɪə/ *n* (community) bohème *f*; (district) quartier *m* bohème.

Bohemia /bəʊˈhi:mɪə/ **▶ 1131** *pr n* Geog Bohême *f*.

bohemian /bəʊˈhi:mɪən/ I *n* bohémien/-ienne *m/f*.
II *adj* [*lifestyle*] de bohème; [*person*] bohème *inv*.

Bohemian /bəʊˈhi:mɪən/ **▶ 1486** I *n* Geog Bohémien/-ienne *m/f*.
II *adj* Geog bohémien/-ienne.

bohemianism /bəʊˈhi:mɪənɪzəm/ *n* vie *f* de bohème.

boil /bɔɪl/ I *n* **1 to be on the ~** GB lit, fig être en ébullition; **to bring sth to the ~** porter qch à ébullition; **to come to the ~** commencer à bouillir; **to go off the ~** GB [*water*] cesser de bouillir; [*person*] baisser; [*performance*] baisser en qualité; **to be off the ~** [*water*] avoir cessé de bouillir; [*project*] être au ralenti; [*situation*] être moins tendu; **2** Med furoncle *m*.
II *vtr* **1** (also **~ up**) faire bouillir, porter [qch] à ébullition [*liquid*]; **to ~ the kettle** faire bouillir l'eau dans la bouilloire; **2** (cook) faire bouillir, faire cuire [qch] à l'eau; **to ~ an egg** faire cuire un œuf; **3** (also **~-wash**) faire bouillir [*linen*].
III *vi* **1** [*water, vegetables etc*] bouillir; **the kettle is ~ing** l'eau bout (dans la bouilloire); **wait for the kettle to ~** attends que l'eau bouille (dans la bouilloire); **the saucepan ~ed dry** toute l'eau de la casserole s'est évaporée; **2** fig [*sea*] bouillonner; [*person*] bouillir (**with** de); **to make sb's blood ~** faire sortir qn de ses gonds.
IV **boiled** *pp adj* Culin **~ed chicken** poule *f* au pot; **~ed egg** œuf *m* à la coque; **~ed fish** poisson *m* au court-bouillon; **~ed ham** jambon *m* cuit à l'eau; **~ed potatoes** pommes *fpl* de terre à l'anglaise; **~ed sweet**† GB bonbon *m* à sucer.
■ **boil away 1** (go on boiling) bouillir à gros bouillons; **2** (evaporate) s'évaporer.
■ **boil down**: ¶ **~ down** Culin se réaliser (par ébullition); ¶ **~ down to** se ramener or se résumer à; ¶ **~ down [sth]**, **~ [sth] down 1** faire réduire [qch] (par ébullition) [*liquid, sauce*]; **2** (condense) réduire [*text*] (**to** à).
■ **boil over 1** lit [*water*] déborder; [*milk*] déborder, se sauver○; **2** fig [*anger, tension, excitement*] déborder.
■ **boil up**: ¶ **~ up** lit, fig monter; ¶ **~ up [sth]**, **~ [sth] up** faire bouillir.

boiler /ˈbɔɪlə(r)/ *n* **1** Tech (in central heating system, steam generator, locomotive) chaudière *f*; (for storing hot water) chauffe-eau *m inv*; **2** (for laundry) GB lessiveuse *f*; **3** Culin (chicken) poule *f* (*à faire au pot*); **4** (saucepan) casserole *f*.

boiler: **~ house** *n* bâtiment *m* des chaudières; **~maker ▶ 1692** *n* chaudronnier *m*; **~making** *n* chaudronnerie *f*; **~man ▶ 1692** *n* chauffeur *m*; **~ room** *n* salle *f* des chaudières, chaufferie *f*; **~ suit** *n* GB (workman's) bleu *m* de travail or de chauffe; (woman's) combinaison *f*.

boiling /ˈbɔɪlɪŋ/ *adj* **1** (at boiling point) [*water, milk, oil*] bouillant; **2**○ fig **it's ~ in here**○! il fait une chaleur infernale ici!; **I'm ~**○! je crève de chaud○!, je meurs de chaleur○!; **to be ~ with rage** bouillir de rage; **3** (for cooking) (*épith*) [*fowl*] à faire au pot; [*beef*] pour pot-au-feu; [*bacon*] à faire bouillir.

boiling hot○ *adj* [*day*] torride; **to be ~ hot** lit être tout bouillant○; fig crever de chaud○.

boiling point *n* lit point *m* d'ébullition; fig point *m* limite.

boisterous /ˈbɔɪstərəs/ *adj* **1** [*adult*] bruyant; [*child*] turbulent; [*crowd*] exubérant; [*meeting, game*] bruyant; **2** (tempestuous) [*wind*] violent; [*sea*] houleux/-euse.

boisterously /ˈbɔɪstərəslɪ/ *adv* [*laugh, play*] bruyamment.

bold /bəʊld/ I *n* GB Print (also **boldface** US) caractères *mpl* gras; **in ~** en (caractères) gras.
II *adj* **1** (daring) [*person*] intrépide; [*attempt, decision, plan, step*] audacieux/-ieuse; **2** (cheeky) [*person, look, stare*] effronté; [*behaviour*] hardi; **if I may make so ~ as to suggest...** sout si je peux me permettre de proposer...; **3** US, Ir (naughty) [*child*] vilain, méchant; **4** (strong) [*colour*] vif/vive; [*design*] voyant; [*handwriting, signature*] assuré; [*outline*] net/nette; **to paint with ~ strokes of the brush** peindre à grands coups de pinceau; **5** Print gras/grasse.
IDIOMS **to be as ~ as brass** avoir un culot monstre○; **to put on** ou **up a ~ front** faire front bravement.

boldly /ˈbəʊldlɪ/ *adv* **1** (daringly) hardiment; (cheekily) avec effronterie; **2** [*designed*] de manière voyante; [*outlined*] nettement; **~ coloured** aux couleurs vives.

boldness /ˈbəʊldnɪs/ *n* **1** (intrepidity) hardiesse *f*; (cheek) effronterie *f*; **2** (of design, colour) netteté *f*.

bole /bəʊl/ *n* Bot tronc *m*.

bolero /bəˈleərəʊ Mus/, /ˈbɒlərəʊ Fashn/ *n* (*pl* **~s**) Mus, Fashn boléro *m*.

boletus /bəʊˈli:təs/ *n* (*pl* **-tuses** ou **-ti**) bolet *m*.

bolide /ˈbəʊlaɪd/ *n* Astron bolide *m*.

Bolivia /bəˈlɪvɪə/ **▶ 1131** *pr n* Bolivie *f*.

Bolivian /bəˈlɪvɪən/ **▶ 1486** I *n* Bolivien/-ienne *m/f*.
II *adj* bolivien/-ienne.

boll /bəʊl/ *n* (of flax, cotton) capsule *f*.

bollard /ˈbɒlɑ:d/ *n* **1** Naut (on quay, ship) bollard *m*; **2** GB (in road etc) balise *f*.

bollix◑ /ˈbɒlɪks/ *vtr* US (also **~ up**) bâcler○.

bollocking● GB /ˈbɒləkɪŋ/ *n* engueulade○ *f*; **to give sb a ~** engueuler qn○; **to get a ~** se faire engueuler○.

bollocks● GB /ˈbɒləks/ I *n* (rubbish) ¢ conneries● *fpl*; **it's a load of ~!** rien que des conneries●; **oh ~!** et mon cul●!
II *npl* (testicles) couilles● *fpl*.

boll weevil *n* charançon *m* du cotonnier.

Bologna /bəˈləʊnjə/ **▶ 1818** *pr n* Bologne.

Bolognese /ˌbɒləˈneɪz/ I *n* (*pl* **~**) Bolognais/-aise *m/f*.
II *adj* **~ sauce** sauce *f* bolognaise; **spaghetti ~** spaghettis *mpl* (à la) bolognaise.

boloney○ /bəˈləʊnɪ/ *n* ¢ balivernes *fpl*.

Bolshevik /ˈbɒlʃəvɪk, US *also* ˈbəʊl-/ I *n* bolchevique *mf*.
II *adj* bolchevique.

Bolshevism /ˈbɒlʃəvɪzəm/ *n* bolchevisme *m*.

Bolshevist /ˈbɒlʃəvɪst/ *n*, *adj* bolcheviste (*mf*).

bolshy○ GB /ˈbɒlʃɪ/ *adj* **1** (on one occasion) [*child*] buté; [*adult*] pas commode; **to get ~** se braquer; **2** (by temperament) **he's/she's ~** c'est un râleur○/une râleuse○.

bolster /ˈbəʊlstə(r)/ I *n* traversin *m*.
II *vtr* (also **~ up**) **1** (boost) renforcer [*confidence*]; **to ~ sb's ego** donner de l'assurance à qn; **2** (shore up) soutenir [*economy*]; appuyer [*argument*].

bolt /bəʊlt/ I *n* **1** (lock) verrou *m*; **2** (screw) boulon *m*; **3 ~ of lightning** coup *m* de foudre; **4** (of cloth) rouleau *m* (de tissu); **5** (for crossbow) carreau *m*; **6** (for rifle) culasse *f* mobile; **7** (in mountaineering) (also **expansion ~**) piton *m* à expansion; **8** (dash) départ *m* précipité; **to make a ~ for it** décamper○; **to make a ~ for the door/the garden** foncer○ vers la porte/le jardin.
II **bolt upright** *adj phr* droit comme un i.
III *vtr* **1** (lock) verrouiller [*window, door*]; **to be ~ed shut** être fermé au verrou; **2** Constr boulonner [*plate, girder, section*]; **3** (also **~ down**) (swallow) engloutir [*food*]; **4** US (abandon) lâcher [*political party, candidate*].
IV *vi* **1** (flee) [*horse*] s'emballer; [*rabbit*] détaler; [*person*] décamper○, détaler○; **to ~ in/out/off** entrer/sortir/partir à toute allure; **2** Hort [*plant*] monter en graine.
IDIOMS **a ~ from** ou **out of the blue** un coup de tonnerre; **to have shot one's ~**○ avoir brûlé ses dernières cartouches.

bolt hole *n* GB lit, fig refuge *m*.

bolus /ˈbəʊləs/ *n* (*pl* **-luses**) Physiol bol *m* alimentaire.

bomb /bɒm/ I *n* **1** (explosive device) bombe *f*; **the Bomb** la bombe atomique; **this room looks like a ~'s hit it**○ cette pièce ressemble à un champ de bataille; **2**○ GB (large amount of money) **to cost/spend a ~** coûter/dépenser un argent fou○; **3**○ (flop) (of play, film) fiasco *m*.
II *vtr* bombarder [*town, house*].
III *vi* **1**○ GB (move fast) filer○; **to ~ up/down the road** remonter/descendre la rue à fond de train○; **2**○ (fail) échouer.
■ **bomb out**: **~ [sb/sth] out**, **~ out [sb/sth]** détruire la maison de [*person*]; ravager [qch] par des bombardements [*building, street*]; **we were ~ed out** nous avons été forcés de quitter notre maison à cause des bombardements.

bomb: **~ aimer** *n* Mil, Aviat bombardier *m*; **~ alert** *n* alerte *f* à la bombe.
bombard /bɒm'bɑ:d/ *vtr* **1** Mil, Phys bombarder (**with** de); **2** fig assaillir [*person*] (**with** de).
bombardier /ˌbɒmbə'dɪə(r)/ ▶1612 *n* GB brigadier-chef *m*; US bombardier *m*.
bombardment /bɒm'bɑ:dmənt/ *n* Mil, Phys bombardement *m* (**with** de).
bombast /'bɒmbæst/ *n* grandiloquence *f*.
bombastic /ˌbɒm'bæstɪk/ *adj* ampoulé, grandiloquent.
bombastically /ˌbɒm'bæstɪklɪ/ *adv* avec grandiloquence.
bomb attack *n* attentat *m* à la bombe.
Bombay duck /ˌbɒmbeɪ 'dʌk/ *n*: *poisson salé qui peut accompagner un curry*.
bombazine /'bɒmbəzi:n/ *n* alépine *f*.
bomb: **~ bay** *n* soute *f* à bombes; **~ blast** *n* explosion *f*; **~ crater** *n* cratère *m* causé par une bombe; **~ disposal** *n* déminage *m*; **~ disposal expert** ▶1692 *n* démineur *m*; **~ disposal squad**, **~ disposal unit** *n* équipe *f* de déminage.
bombed○ /bɒmd/ *adj* US bourré○, soûl.
bomber /'bɒmə(r)/ **I** *n* **1** Mil, Aviat bombardier *m*; **2** (terrorist) poseur/-euse *m/f* de bombes.
II *modif* Mil, Aviat [*crew, pilot*] de bombardier; [*raid, squadron*] de bombardiers.
bomber: **~ command** *n* commandement *m* tactique aérien; **~ jacket** *n* blouson *m* d'aviateur.
bombing /'bɒmɪŋ/ **I** *n* **1** Mil bombardement *m*; **2** (by terrorists) attentat *m* à la bombe.
II *modif* **1** Mil [*raid, mission, campaign*] de bombardement; **2** (by terrorists) [*campaign*] d'attentats à la bombe.
bomb: **~proof** *adj* à l'épreuve des bombes; **~ scare** *n* alerte *f* à la bombe.
bombshell /'bɒmʃel/ *n* **1** fig (shock) bombe *f*; **to drop a ~** fig lâcher une bombe; **2**○ (woman) **a blonde ~** une blonde explosive○.
bomb: **~ shelter** *n* abri *m* antiaérien; **~sight** *n* viseur *m* de bombardement.
bombsite /'bɒmsaɪt/ *n* **1** lit zone *f* touchée par une explosion; **2** fig (mess) champ *m* de bataille.
Bomb Squad /'bɒmskwɒd/ *n* brigade *f* antiterroriste.
bona fide /ˌbəʊnə 'faɪdɪ/ *adj* [*attempt*] sincère; [*member, refugee*] vrai (*before n*); [*offer*] sérieux/-ieuse; [*agreement, contract*] de bonne foi.
bona fides /ˌbəʊnə 'faɪdi:z/ *n* (+ *v sg ou pl*) bonne foi *f*.
bonanza /bə'nænzə/ **I** *n* **1** (windfall) pactole *f*, filon *m*; **2** (performance, festival etc) événement *m* exceptionnel; **3** Mining riche filon *m*.
II *modif*: **a ~ year** une année en or.
bonbon /'bɒnbɒn/ *n* bonbon *m* (fondant).
bond /bɒnd/ **I** *n* **1** (link) lien(s) *m(pl)* (**of** de; **between** entre); **the experience forged a ~ between them** l'expérience a créé un lien entre eux; **to strengthen a ~** resserrer des liens; **to feel a strong ~ with sb** se sentir très proche de qn; **2** (fetter) lit lien *m*; fig chaîne *f* (**of** de); **to break the ~s of routine** rompre les chaînes de la routine; **3** Fin obligation *f*; **government ~** obligation d'État; **savings/treasury ~** bon *m* d'épargne/du trésor; **4** (adhesion) adhérence *f*; **5** Chem liaison *f*; **6** Jur (guarantee) engagement *m* écrit; (deposit) caution *f*; **to set ~ at** fixer la caution à; **my word is my ~** je n'ai qu'une parole; **7** Constr appareil *m*; **8** (at customs) **in ~** en dépôt de douane; **9** = **bonded paper**.
II *modif* [*market, prices*] des obligations; [*dealer*] en obligations.
III *vtr* **1** (also **~ together**) [*glue, adhesive*] faire adhérer [*materials, surfaces*]; Constr enlier [*bricks, timber*]; **2** (also **~ together**) [*experience, suffering*] créer des liens entre [*people*]; **3** (at customs) entreposer (en douane) [*goods*].
IV *vi* **1** gen, Psych s'attacher (**with** à); **the mother and baby ~ quickly** les liens maternels se créent rapidement; **2** [*materials*] adhérer (**with** à); **3** Chem [*atoms*] s'associer (**with** à).
bondage /'bɒndɪdʒ/ *n* **1** (slavery) lit, fig esclavage *m*; (serfdom) servage *m*; **to be in ~ to sb/sth** être l'esclave de qn/qch; **2** (sexual practice) *pratique sexuelle où l'on ligote son partenaire*.
bond: **~ed paper** *n* papier *m* à lettres de luxe; **~ed warehouse** *n* entrepôt *m* en douane; **~holder** *n* porteur *m* d'obligations, obligataire *m*.
bonding /'bɒndɪŋ/ *n* **1** (between mother and baby) (process) formation *f* des liens maternels; (resulting bond) liens *mpl* maternels; **2** (between people) (process) formation *f* du lien affectif (**between** entre); (resulting bond) lien *m* affectif; **male ~** amitié *f* virile; **3** (adhesion) collage *m*; **4** Chem, Constr liaison *f*; **5** (of goods at customs) entreposage *m*.
bond: **~sman** *n* (serf) serf *m*; (slave) esclave *m*; **~swoman** *n* (serf) serve *f*; (slave) esclave *f*.
bone /bəʊn/ **I** *n* **1** (of human, animal) os *m*; (of fish) arête *f*; **made of ~** en os; **chicken on/off the ~** poulet à l'os/désossé; **to break a ~** casser un os; **to break every ~ in one's body** se rompre les os; **I'll break every ~ in his body!** je vais lui tordre le cou!; **no ~s broken** rien de cassé; **he hasn't got a romantic/jealous ~ in his body** il n'a pas une once de romantisme/jalousie; **2** (in corset etc) baleine *f*; **3**○ (trombone) trombone *m*.
II bones *npl* **1** (animal skeleton) ossements *mpl*; **2** (human remains) (in archeology) ossements *mpl* humains; **to lay sb's ~s to rest** enterrer la dépouille de qn; **my old ~s**○ mes vieux os○; **he'll never make old ~s** il ne fera pas de vieux os; **3** (dice) dés *mpl*.
III *modif* [*handle, button*] en os.
IV *vtr* **1** Culin désosser [*joint, chicken*]; enlever les arêtes de [*fish*]; **2** (reinforce) consolider [*corset, bodice*].
IDIOMS **~ of contention** sujet *m* de dispute, pomme *f* de discorde; **close to the ~** (wounding) blessant; (racy) osé; **to be a bag of ~s** être un sac d'os○; **to cut sth to the ~** réduire qch au minimum; **to feel sth in one's ~s** avoir le pressentiment de qch; **to have a ~ to pick with sb** avoir un compte à régler avec qn; **to make no ~s about sth** ne pas cacher qch; **sticks and stones may break my ~s (but words will never harm me)** Prov ≈ les chiens aboient, la caravane passe Prov; **to work one's fingers to the ~** se crever à la tâche○.
■ **bone up on**○: **~ up on [sth]** potasser○ [*subject*].
bone: **~ china** *n* porcelaine *f* tendre or à l'os; **~-crunching**○ *adj* fracassant.
boned /bəʊnd/ **I** *adj* **1** [*joint, leg, chicken*] désossé; [*fish*] sans arête; **2** [*corset, bodice*] à armature.
II -boned (*dans composés*) **fine/strong-~** à la charpente délicate/robuste.
bone: **~ dry** *adj* complètement desséché; **~head**○ *n* abruti/-e○ *m/f*; **~headed**○ *adj* débile○; **~ idle**○ *adj* flemmard○.
boneless /'bəʊnlɪs/ *adj* [*chicken breast, joint*] sans os; [*fish fillet*] sans arête.
bone: **~ marrow** *n* moelle *f* osseuse; **~-marrow transplant** *n* greffe *f* de moelle osseuse.
bonemeal /'bəʊnmi:l/ *n* **1** (fertilizer) engrais *m* phosphaté; **2** (feed) fourrage *m* phosphaté (*de cendres d'os*).
boner /'bəʊnə(r)/ *n* US **1**○ (blunder) gaffe *f*; **to pull a ~** faire une gaffe; **2**● (erection) **to have a ~** triquer●.
bone scan *n* scintigraphie *f* osseuse.
bone shaker○ *n* **1** (old vehicle) (vieille) caisse○ *f*; **2** (bicycle) (vieux) biclou◑ *m*.
bone: **~ structure** *n* structure *f* du visage; **~yard**○ US *n* cimetière *m*.
bonfire /'bɒnfaɪə(r)/ *n* (of rubbish) feu *m* de jardin; (for celebration) feu *m* de joie.
Bonfire Night *n* GB la soirée du 5 novembre (*fêtée avec feux de joie et feux d'artifice*).
bongo /'bɒŋgəʊ/ ▶1481 *n* (*pl* **~s** ou **~**) (also **~ drum**) bongo *m*.
bonhomie /ˌbɒnə'mi:/ *n* bonhomie *f*; **false ~** fausse bonhomie *f*.
bonk /bɒŋk/ **I** *n* **1**○ (blow) coup *m*; **2**● hum GB **to have a ~** baiser●.
II *vtr* **1**○ (hit) cogner; **to ~ one's head against sth** se cogner la tête contre qch; **2**● hum GB (have sex with) baiser●.
III *vi*● hum GB (have sex) baiser●.
bonkers○ /'bɒŋkəz/ *adj* dingue○.
bonnet /'bɒnɪt/ *n* **1** (hat) bonnet *m*; **2** GB Aut capot *m*; **3** Naut bonnette *f*.
IDIOMS **to have a bee in one's ~** avoir une idée fixe (**about** à propos de).
bonny /'bɒnɪ/ *adj* Scot beau/belle.
bonsai /'bɒnsaɪ/ *n* (art) art *m* du bonsaï; (plant) bonsaï *m*; **a ~ garden** un jardin bonsaï.
bonus /'bəʊnəs/ *n* **1** Comm, Fin (payment) prime *f*; **Christmas/productivity ~** prime *f* de Noël/de productivité; **no claims ~** GB Insur bonus *m*; **cash ~** prime *f*; **2** (advantage) avantage *m* (**of being** d'être).
bonus issue *n* GB Fin émission *f* d'actions gratuites.
bonus point *n* (in quiz, sports) bonus *m* d'un point; **five ~s** un bonus de cinq points.
bony /'bəʊnɪ/ *adj* **1** [*person, body, shoulders, face, features*] anguleux/-euse; [*finger, arm, knee*] osseux/-euse; **2** [*fish*] plein d'arêtes; **3** [*substance*] osseux/-euse.
bony fish *n* Zool poisson *m* osseux.
boo /bu:/ **I** *n* (jeer) huée *f*.
II *excl* (to give sb a fright) hou!; (to jeer) hou! hou!
III *vtr* (*3e pers prés* **boos**, *prét, pp* **booed**) heur [*actor, speaker*]; **to be ~ed off the stage quitter la scène sous les huées.**
IV *vi* (*3e pers prés* **boos**, *prét, pp* **booed**) pousser des huées.
IDIOMS **he wouldn't say ~ to a goose** c'est un grand timide; **he didn't say ~ (about it)** US il n'a pas pipé mot.
boob○ /bu:b/ **I** *n* **1** GB (mistake) bêtise *f*; **2** (breast) nichon○ *m*; **3**○ US (idiot) nigaud/-e *m/f*.
II *vi* GB faire une bêtise.
boo-boo○ /'bu:bu:/ *n* (mistake) boulette○ *f*; **to make a ~** faire une boulette.
boob tube○ /'bu:btju:b, US -tu:b/ *n* **1** (television) US télé○ *f*; **2** (garment) bustier *m*.
booby /'bu:bɪ/ *n* **1**† ○(silly person) nigaud/-e *m/f*; **2** Zool (gannet) fou *m*; **3**○ US = **boob I 2**.
booby: **~ hatch**○ *n* US cabanon○ *m*; **~ prize** *n* prix *m* de consolation (*décerné au dernier*).
booby trap I *n* **1** Mil mécanisme *m* piégé; **2** (joke) traquenard *m*.
II *modif* [*bomb*] piégé.
III *vtr* (*p prés etc* **-pp-**) Mil piéger [*car, bodies, building*].
boodle○ /'bu:dl/ *n* US (money) oseille○ *f*.
boogie○ /'bu:gɪ/ *vi* danser.
boogie-woogie /ˌbu:gɪ'wu:gɪ, US -'wʊgɪ/ *n* boogie-woogie *m*.
boogy board *n* (in surfing) body *m*.
boohoo /ˌbu:'hu:/ *excl* ouin!
booing /'bu:ɪŋ/ *n* ¢ huées *fpl*; **loud ~** des huées *fpl* stridentes.
book /bʊk/ **I** *n* **1** (reading matter) livre *m*, bouquin○ *m* (**about** sur); **history ~** livre d'histoire; **a ~ of** un recueil de [*quotations, poems, proverbs*]; **'Carlton Books'** (title of firm) 'Éditions *fpl* Carlton'; **2** (division, part) (of novel, trilogy) livre *m*, tome *m*; (of poem, epic, bible) livre *m*; **the Book of Genesis/of Kings** le livre de la Genèse/des Rois; **3** Fin

(for recording deposits, withdrawals) livret *m* bancaire; **4** Sch (exercise book) cahier *m*; **drawing ~** cahier de dessin; **5** (of cheques, tickets, vouchers, stamps) carnet *m*; **~ of matches** pochette *f* d'allumettes; **~ of needles** porte-aiguilles *m*; **6** (in betting) **to keep a ~ on** prendre des paris sur; **to open** ou **start a ~ on** ouvrir les paris sur; **7** (directory) annuaire *m*; **our number's** ou **we're in the ~** on est dans l'annuaire; **8** (rulebook) règlement *m*; **to do things by the ~** fig suivre le règlement; **9** (opera libretto) livret *m*.
II **books** *npl* **1** Accts, Comm livres *mpl* de comptes, comptabilité *f* ¢; **to keep the firm's ~s** tenir les livres or les comptes de l'entreprise, s'occuper de la comptabilité de l'entreprise; **2** Admin (records) registre *m*; **to be on the ~s of** être inscrit à [*club, organization*]; **we have many small businesses on our ~s** nous avons beaucoup de petites entreprises dans nos fichiers.
III *vtr* **1** (reserve) réserver, retenir [*table, seat, room, cabin, ticket*]; faire les réservations pour [*holiday*]; réserver [*taxi*]; engager [*babysitter, driver, entertainer*]; **to ~ sth for sb**, **to ~ sb sth** réserver qch pour qn; **to ~ sb into a hotel** réserver une chambre dans un hôtel pour qn; **I've ~ed him a room, I've ~ed him into a hotel** je lui ai reservé une chambre (dans un hôtel); **to be fully ~ed** être complet/-ète; **Saturday's performance is fully ~ed** c'est complet pour samedi soir, on joue à guichets fermés samedi soir; **my Tuesday afternoons are ~ed** je suis pris le mardi après-midi; **I'm fully ~ed this week** je suis pris tous les jours cette semaine; **2** (charge) [*policeman*] dresser un procès-verbal or un P.V.○ à [*motorist, offender*]; US (arrest) arrêter [*suspect*]; **he was ~ed for speeding** il a été poursuivi pour excès de vitesse; **3** GB Sport [*referee*] donner un carton jaune à [*player*]; **two players were ~ed** deux joueurs ont reçu un carton jaune; **4** Comm, Fin inscrire [*order*]; **to ~ goods to sb's account** mettre des marchandises sur le compte de qn.
IV *vi* réserver; **you are advised to ~** il est conseillé de réserver.
IDIOMS **I can read her like a ~, she is (like) an open ~ to me** elle ne peut rien me cacher; **his past is an open ~** il n'a rien à cacher sur son passé; **economics is a closed ~ to me** je ne connais rien à l'économie; **she is a closed ~ to me** je n'arrive pas à la comprendre; **to throw the ~ at sb** (reprimand) passer un savon○ à qn; (accuse) n'omettre aucun chef d'accusation (*quand on arrête qn*); (punish or sentence) donner le maximum à qn; **to be in sb's good ~s** être dans les petits papiers de qn○; **to be in sb's bad ~s** ne pas avoir la cote avec qn; **in my ~**○ **it's a crime** à mon avis or d'après moi c'est un crime; **to bring sb to ~** demander des comptes à qn, faire rendre des comptes à qn (**for** pour); **here's one for the ~!** on s'en souviendra!; **you shouldn't judge a ~ by its cover** ≈ l'habit ne fait pas le moine.
■ **book in**: ¶ **~ in** GB (at hotel) (check in) se présenter à la réception; (make reservation) réserver une chambre; **we ~ed into the hotel at 3 o'clock** nous sommes arrivés à l'hôtel à trois heures; ¶ **~ [sb] in** réserver une chambre pour.
■ **book up**: **tourists have ~ed up all the rooms** avec les touristes, il n'y a plus une chambre de libre; **to be ~ed up** être complet/-ète; **the hotel is ~ed up until next month** l'hôtel est complet jusqu'au mois prochain; **I'm ~ed up every evening next week** je suis pris tous les soirs la semaine prochaine.

bookable /ˈbʊkəbl/ *adj* [*seat*] qu'on peut retenir or réserver; **all seats ~ in advance** possibilité de réserver ses places à l'avance.

book: **~binder** ▶1692 *n* relieur/-euse *m/f*; **~binding** *n* reliure *f*; **~-burning** *n* autodafé *m*; **~case** *n* bibliothèque *f*; **~ club** *n* club *m* du livre; **~-club edition** *n* édition *f* club (*d'un livre*).

bookend /ˈbʊkend/ *n* serre-livres *m*; **two ~s** deux serre-livres.

book fair *n* salon *m* du livre.

bookie○ /ˈbʊkɪ/ *n* bookmaker *m*.

booking /ˈbʊkɪŋ/ *n* **1** GB (reservation) réservation *f*; **to make a ~** faire une réservation; **2** (engagement for performance) engagement *m*; **3** GB Sport (from referee) **to get a ~** recevoir un carton jaune; **there were two ~s** l'arbitre a donné deux cartons jaunes.

booking: **~ clerk** ▶1692 *n* GB préposé/-e *m/f* aux réservations; **~ form** *n* GB bon *m* de réservation; **~ office** *n* GB bureau *m* de location.

bookish /ˈbʊkɪʃ/ *adj* [*person*] studieux/-ieuse.

bookishness /ˈbʊkɪʃnɪs/ *n* (of person) côté *m* studieux.

book: **~ jacket** *n* jaquette *f*; **~keeper** ▶1692 *n* comptable *mf*; **~keeping** *n* comptabilité *f*; **~-learning** *n* ¢ connaissances *fpl* livresques.

booklet /ˈbʊklɪt/ *n* brochure *f*.

book: **~list** *n* liste *f* de livres; **~ lover** *n* bibliophile *mf*; **~maker** ▶1692 *n* bookmaker *m*; **~making** *n* activité *f* de bookmaker (*qui consiste à prendre des paris*); **~man** *n* homme *m* de lettres; **~mark** *n* marque-pages *m*, signet *m*; **~mobile** *n* US bibliobus *m*; **~plate** *n* ex-libris *m*; **~rest** *n* lutrin *m*; **~seller** ▶1692 *n* (person) libraire *mf*; (shop) librairie *f*; **~selling** *n* commerce *m* de livres; **~shelf** *n* (*pl* **-shelves**) (single) étagère *f*; (in bookcase) rayon *m*; **~shop** ▶1692 *n* librairie *f*; **~stall** *n* (in street market) étalage *m* de livres; GB (at airport, station) kiosque *m* à journaux; **~store** ▶1692 *n* US librairie *f*; **~ token** *n* GB chèque-livre *m*; **~ value** *n* valeur *f* comptable.

bookworm /ˈbʊkwɜːm/ *n* **1**○ (person) mordu/-e○ *m/f* de la lecture; **he's a real ~** il adore la lecture, il a toujours le nez dans un livre○; **2** (insect) pou *m* des livres.

Boolean /ˈbuːlɪən/ *adj* booléen/-éenne.

boom /buːm/ I *n* **1** (noise) (of voices, cannon, thunder) grondement *m*; (of waves) mugissement *m*; (of organ) ronflement *m*; (of drum) boum *m*; (of explosion) détonation *f*; **2** (onomat) badaboum!; **3** Econ, Fin (period of prosperity) boom *m*, période *f* de forte expansion; (in demand, prices, sales etc) explosion *f* (**in** de); **baby ~** baby-boom *m*; **export/consumer ~** boom des exportations/de la consommation; **property/credit ~** boom immobilier/du crédit; **a ~ and bust economy** une économie *f* en dents de scie; **4** (increase in popularity) boom *m* (**in de**); **5** Naut (spar) bôme *f*; (barrage) estacade *f*; **6** (on crane) gui *m*; **7** Cin, Radio, TV perche *f*.
II *modif* [*economy, industry, sector, town*] en pleine expansion; [*period, year*] de croissance; [*share*] à la hausse.
III *vtr* **1** US (cause to grow) donner un coup de fouet à; **2** US (publicize, push) pousser; **3** (shout) **'welcome!' he ~ed** 'bienvenue!' dit-il d'une voix de stentor.
IV *vi* **1** (make a noise) [*cannon, thunder*] gronder; [*bell, voice*] retentir; [*organ*] ronfler; [*sea*] mugir; **2** (prosper) [*economy, trade*] prospérer; [*exports, prices, sales*] monter en flèche; [*industry*] être en plein essor; [*hobby, sport*] être en plein boom; **business is ~ing** les affaires vont bien.
IDIOMS **to lower the ~ on sb**○ US serrer la vis à qn.
■ **boom out**: ¶ **~ out** [*music, sound*] retentir; ¶ **~ [sth] out**, **~ out [sth]** [*person*] brailler [*speech*]; [*loudspeaker*] faire retentir [*announcement*]; [*drum*] faire retentir [*rhythm*].

boom: **~ baby** *n* bébé *m* du baby boom; **~box**○ *n* (grand) radiocassette *m* portatif.

boomerang /ˈbuːməræŋ/ I *n* boomerang *m*.
II *modif* [*effect*] boomerang.
III *vi* (backfire) [*plan, campaign*] faire boomerang; **to ~ on sb** se retourner contre qn.

booming /ˈbuːmɪŋ/ *adj* **1** (loud) [*echo, sound*] retentissant; [*laugh, voice*] tonitruant; **2** (flourishing) [*economy, industry, market, town*] en plein essor; [*demand, exports, market, sales*] en forte progression.

boom microphone *n* micro *m* à perche.

boon /buːn/ *n* **1** (advantage) avantage *m*; **2** (invaluable asset) aide *f* précieuse (**to** à); **to be a great ~ to sb** apporter une aide précieuse à qn; **central heating is a ~ in winter** le chauffage central est (quelque chose de) précieux en hiver; **3** (stroke of luck) aubaine *f* (**for** pour).

boon companion *n* ami/-e *m/f* inséparable.

boondocks /ˈbuːndɒks/ *npl* US **1** (rural area) **the ~** la cambrousse○; **out in the ~** en pleine cambrousse○; **2** (rough country) maquis *m*.

boondoggle○ /ˈbuːndɒgl/ US I *n* projet *m* futile (*généralement gaspillant des fonds publics*).
II *vi* gaspiller des fonds publics (*en projets futiles*).

boonies○ /ˈbuːniːz/ *npl* US **the ~** la cambrousse○.

boor /ˈbʊə(r), bɔː(r)/ *n* grossier personnage *m*; (man only) malotru *m*.

boorish /ˈbʊərɪʃ, bɔː-/ *adj* grossier/-ière.

boorishly /ˈbʊərɪʃlɪ, bɔː-/ *adv* [*behave*] grossièrement.

boorishness /ˈbʊərɪʃnɪs, bɔː-/ *n* manque *m* d'éducation.

boost /buːst/ I *n* **1** (stimulus) coup *m* de fouet (**to** à); **to give sth a ~** stimuler qch; **2** (encouragement) encouragement *m* (**to sb** pour qn; **to sth** à qch; **to do** à faire); **to give sb a ~** encourager qn; **3** (publicity) publicité *f*; **to give sth a ~** faire du battage pour qch; **4** (upward push) **to give sb a ~** soulever qn (**up to** jusqu'à).
II *vtr* **1** (stimulate) stimuler [*aid, economy, efficiency, exports, productivity, sales*]; encourager [*investment, lending*]; augmenter [*capacity, intake, number, pay, profit, value*]; relancer [*interest*]; **to ~ sb's confidence** redonner confiance à qn; **to ~ morale** remonter le moral; **2** (enhance) améliorer [*image, performance*]; **3** Advertg faire la promotion de, promouvoir [*product*]; **4** Electron, Telecom amplifier [*signal, voltage*]; **5** Aut augmenter [*vitesse*]; rendre [qch] plus puissant [*engine*]; **6** (push up) soulever [*person*]; **7** Aerosp propulser [*rocket*].

booster /ˈbuːstə(r)/ I *n* **1** Radio, Telecom amplificateur *m*; **2** Electron survolteur *m*; **3** Aut compresseur *m*; **4** Med vaccin *m* de rappel; **5** Aerosp fusée *f* d'appoint; **6**○ US (fan) fan *m/f*.
II *modif* [*dose, injection*] de rappel.

booster cushion *n* Aut réhausseur *m*.

boosterism /ˈbuːstərɪzəm/ *n* US promotion *f* d'une ville.

booster: **~ rocket** *n* Aerosp fusée *f* d'appoint; **~ station** *n* Radio, Telecom station *f* d'amplification.

boot /buːt/ ▶1703 I *n* **1** (footwear) botte *f*; (for workman, soldier) brodequin *m*; **ankle ~** bottine *f*; **calf-length ~** demi-botte *f*; **thigh ~** cuissarde *f*; **climbing/hiking ~** chaussure *f* de montagne/randonnée; **football/rugby ~** GB chaussure *f* de football/rugby; **to put the ~ in** lit rouer qn de coups de pied; fig y aller fort; **a ~ up the backside** un bon coup de pied au derrière also fig; **2** GB Aut coffre *m*; **3**○ (dismissal) **to get the ~** se faire virer; **to give sb the ~** virer qn; **4**○ (kick) coup *m* de pied; **to give sth a ~** donner un coup de pied dans qch; **5** US Aut (wheel clamp) sabot *m* de Denver; **6** US (puncture patch) rustine® *f*; **7**○ US (recruit) bleu○ *m*, recrue *f*.
II *vtr* **1**○ (kick) envoyer un coup de pied à

[*person*]; donner un coup de pied dans [*ball*]; **2** Comput = **boot up**.

IDIOMS **as tough as old ~s** [*meat*] dur comme la semelle (de facteur); **the ~ is on the other foot** GB les rôles sont renversés; **to be/get too big for one's ~s** GB avoir/prendre la grosse tête; **to ~** par dessus le marché; **to lick sb's ~s** lécher les bottes à qn; **you can bet your ~s that** je te parie tout ce que tu veux que.

■ **boot out**: **~** [**sb**] **out**, **~ out** [**sb**] (from club, institution) renvoyer; (from company, house) mettre à la porte.

■ **boot up** Comput: **~** [**sth**] **up**, **~ up** [**sth**] amorcer [*computer, system*].

boot: **~black** *n* cireur *m* de chaussures; **~ camp** *n* US Mil Naut camp *m* d'entraînement; **~ device**, **~ drive** *n* Comput unité *f* d'initialisation.

bootee /buːˈtiː/ *n* **1** (knitted) chausson *m*; **2** (leather) bottine *f*.

booth /buːð, US buːθ/ *n* (in language lab) cabine *f*; (in restaurant) alcôve *f*; (at fairground) baraque *f*; **polling** or **voting ~** isoloir *m*; **telephone ~** cabine *f* (téléphonique).

boot: **~jack** *n* tire-botte *m*; **~lace** *n* lacet *m* (de chaussure); **~legger** *n* US bootlegger *m*.

bootless‡ /ˈbuːtlɪs/ *adj* [*attempt, search*] vain; [*cry*] inutile.

boot: **~licker** *n* lèche-bottes *mf inv*; **~maker** ▶ **1692** *n* bottier *m*; **~ polish** *n* cirage *m*; **~ scraper** *n* décrottoir *m*.

bootstrap /ˈbuːtstræp/ *n* **1** (on boot) tirant *m* de botte; **2** Comput programme *m* d'amorce.

IDIOMS **to pull oneself up by one's ~s** se faire tout seul.

bootstrap: **~ loader** *n* Comput chargeur *m* d'instructions initiales; **~ program** *n* Comput programme *m* d'amorçage.

booty /ˈbuːtɪ/ *n* butin *m*.

booze○ /buːz/ **I** *n* bibine○ *f*; (wine only) pinard○ *m*; **to be on the ~** picoler○; **he's off the ~**○ il a cessé de picoler.

II *vi* picoler○.

boozed○ /buːzd/ *adj* bourré○.

boozer○ /ˈbuːzə(r)/ *n* (person) poivrot/-ote○ *m/f*; (pub) GB pub○ *m*, bistrot† *m*; **he's a bit of a ~** il aime bien picoler.

booze-up○ /ˈbuːzʌp/ *n* GB beuverie *f*.

boozy○ /ˈbuːzɪ/ *adj* [*meal*] bien arrosé; [*laughter*] aviné; **we had a ~ evening/weekend** on a passé la soirée/le weekend à picoler○; **his ~ uncle** son oncle poivrot.

bop /bɒp/ **I** *n* **1**○ (blow) coup *m*; **2** (dance form) bebop *m*; **3**○ (disco-dancing) **to go for a ~** aller en boîte○.

II *vtr* (*p prés etc* **-pp-**) **1**○ (hit) cogner; **2**◑ US (have sex with) baiser◑.

III *vi* (*p prés etc* **-pp-**) **1**○ GB (dance) aller en boîte○; **2**○ US (walk) se pavaner; (go) faire un saut○; **3**◑ US (have sex) baiser◑.

boracic /bəˈræsɪk/ *adj* borique.

borage /ˈbɒrɪdʒ, US ˈbɔːrɪdʒ/ *n* bourrache *f*.

borax /ˈbɔːræks/ *n* borax *m*.

Bordeaux /bɔːˈdəʊ/ ▶ **1818** *n* **1** (town) Bordeaux; **2** (wine) bordeaux *m*.

bordello /bɔːˈdeləʊ/ *n* maison *f* close.

border /ˈbɔːdə(r)/ ▶ **1624** **I** *n* **1** (frontier) frontière *f* (**between** entre); **France's ~ with Spain** la frontière entre la France et l'Espagne; **on the Swiss ~** sur la frontière suisse; **to have ~s with six countries** avoir une frontière commune avec six pays; **to cross the ~** passer la frontière; **to escape over** ou **across the ~** s'échapper en passant la frontière; **our allies across the ~** nos alliés de l'autre côté de la frontière; **north of the ~** gen au nord de la frontière; (when in England) en Écosse; (when in Ireland) en Irlande du Nord; **south of the ~** gen au sud de la frontière; (when in Scotland) en Angleterre; (when in Northern Ireland) en République d'Irlande; (when in US) au Mexique; **2** (outer edge) (of forest) lisière *f*; (of estate, lake, road) bord *m*; **3** (decorative edge) (on crockery, paper) liseré *m*; (on dress, picture, cloth) bordure *f*; **4** Hort plate-bande *f*; **5** (hypothetical limit) frontière *f* (**between** entre); **to cross the ~ into bad taste** franchir la limite du bon goût; **6** Comput (of window) bordure *f*.

II Borders *pr npl* (also **Borders Region**) (in Scotland) les Borders *mpl*.

III *modif* [*control*] aux frontières; [*crossing, patrol, state*] frontalier/-ière; [*area, post, town, zone*] frontière (*after n, inv*) ; [*police*] des frontières.

IV *vtr* **1** (lie alongside) [*road, land*] longer [*lake, forest*]; [*country*] border [*ocean*]; **France ~s Italy** la France a une frontière commune avec l'Italie; **to be ~ed by** avoir une frontière commune avec; **2** (surround) border; **to be ~ed on three sides by trees** être bordé d'arbres sur trois côtés; **to be ~ed with lace** être bordé de dentelle.

■ **border on**: **~ on** [**sth**] **1** (have a frontier with) [*country*] avoir une frontière commune avec; [*garden, land*] toucher; **2** (verge on) friser [*rudeness, madness*]; **the accusation ~s on the absurd** l'accusation frise l'absurde.

border: **Border collie** *n* colley *m* écossais; **~ dispute** *n* différend *m* frontalier; **~ guard** *n* garde-frontière *m*; **~ incident** *n* incident *m* de frontière; **~land** *n* région *f* frontalière.

borderline /ˈbɔːdəlaɪn/ **I** *n* frontière *f*, limite *f* (**between** entre); **on the ~** à la frontière.

II *modif* [*case*] limite (*after n*); **he's a ~ schizophrenic** c'est un cas limite de schizophrénie; **to be a ~ fail/pass** être juste en dessous de/au-dessus de la moyenne.

border raid *n* incursion *f* armée.

bore /bɔː(r)/ **I** *prét* ▶ **bear**.

II *n* **1** (person) raseur○/-euse *m/f*; **wine/cricket ~** raseur qui ne parle que de vin/de cricket; **he's such a ~** quel raseur○; **2** (situation) barbe *f*; **what a ~!** quelle barbe!; **it's an awful ~ having to wait** quelle barbe de devoir attendre; **3** (also **~hole**) trou *m* de forage; **4** (diameter) (of gun barrel, pipe) calibre *m*; **small-~ rifle** carabine *f* de petit calibre; **12-~ shotgun** fusil *m* de calibre 12; **5** (wave) mascaret *m*.

III *vtr* **1** (annoy) ennuyer (**with** avec); **2** (drill) [*person, machine, insect*] percer [*hole*]; creuser [*well, tunnel*].

IV *vi* **to ~ into/through** [*person, machine, insect*] forer dans/à travers; **her eyes ~d into me** elle me perçait de son regard.

IDIOMS **to ~ sb stiff** ou **to death** ou **to tears** faire mourir qn d'ennui; **to ~ the pants off sb**○ faire mourir qn d'ennui.

bored /bɔːd/ *adj* [*person*] qui s'ennuie; [*expression, glance, voice*] ennuyé; **to get** ou **be ~** s'ennuyer (**with** de; **with doing** de faire); **to look ~** avoir l'air de s'ennuyer; **I'm so ~!** qu'est-ce que je m'ennuie!

boredom /ˈbɔːdəm/ *n* **1** (feeling) ennui *m* (**with** devant); **the ~ of having to wait** l'ennui d'avoir à attendre; **2** (of activity, job, lifestyle) monotonie *f*.

borer /ˈbɔːrə(r)/ *n* **1** (tool) (for wood) vrille *f*; (for shaft, tunnel) foret *m*; (for metal cylinders) alésoir *m*; **2** (worker) foreur *m*, perceur *m*; **3** (insect) insecte *m* térébrant.

boric /ˈbɔːrɪk/ *adj* borique.

boring /ˈbɔːrɪŋ/ **I** *n* (drilling) (in wood) perforation *f*; (in rock) forage *m*.

II *adj* [*person, place, activity, event*] ennuyeux/-euse; [*colour, food*] fade; **it's ~ being/doing** c'est assommant d'être/de faire.

boringly /ˈbɔːrɪŋlɪ/ *adv* [*predictable, practical*] platement; [*arranged, presented*] de façon peu intéressante.

born /bɔːn/ **I** *adj* [*person, animal*] né (**of** de; **to do** pour faire; **with** avec); **to be ~** naître; **she was ~ in Paris/in 1976** elle est née à Paris/en 1976; **when the baby is ~** quand le bébé sera né; **~ a Catholic** d'origine catholique; **she was ~ into a Jewish family** elle est née d'une famille juive; **to be ~ deaf/blind** être sourd/aveugle de naissance; **the children ~ to them** les enfants qu'ils auront (or qu'ils ont eus); **to be a ~ leader** être un chef né; **a ~ liar** un parfait menteur; **she's a ~ loser** elle est née perdante; **I wish I'd never been ~!** je voudrais ne jamais être né!; **to be ~ out of one's time** se tromper d'époque; **to be ~ (out) of sth** fig [*emotion, idea, group etc*] naître de qch.

II -born (*dans composés*) **London-/Irish-~** né à Londres/en Irlande, originaire de Londres/d'Irlande.

IDIOMS **in all my ~ days**○ de toute ma vie; **I wasn't ~ yesterday**○ je ne suis pas né de la dernière pluie; **she hasn't got the sense she was ~ with**○ elle est sosotte○; **there's one ~ every minute**○**!** quel idiot/quelle idiote!

born-again /ˌbɔːnəˈgeɪn/ *adj* **1** [*Christian*] régénéré; **2** hum nouvellement converti.

borne /bɔːn/ *pp* ▶ **bear**.

Borneo /ˈbɔːnɪəʊ/ ▶ **1381** *pr n* Bornéo *m*.

boron /ˈbɔːrɒn/ *n* bore *m*.

borough /ˈbʌrə, US -rəʊ/ *n* (in London, New York) arrondissement *m* urbain; **county ~** GB *municipalité qui est administrativement indépendante du comté*.

borough: **~ council** *n* GB conseil *m* municipal; **~ president** *n* US maire *m* d'arrondissement (*à New York*).

borrow /ˈbɒrəʊ/ **I** *vtr* emprunter [*object, money, idea, word*] (**from** à).

II *vi* Fin faire un emprunt (**from** à); **to ~ against** emprunter en fonction de [*income*].

IDIOMS **he/she is living on ~ed time** ses jours sont comptés.

borrower /ˈbɒrəʊə(r)/ *n* emprunteur/-euse *m/f*.

IDIOMS **neither a ~ nor a lender be** Prov il ne faut ni emprunter ni prêter.

borrowing /ˈbɒrəʊɪŋ/ *n* **1** Fin ¢ emprunt *m*; **certain aspects of ~** certains aspects de l'emprunt; **increase in ~** augmentation des emprunts; **~ costs** le coût de l'emprunt; **2** Ling, Literat emprunt *m* (**from** à).

borrowing: **~ requirements** *npl* besoins *mpl* d'emprunts; **~ rights** *npl* droit *m* à l'emprunt.

borstal† /ˈbɔːstəl/ *n* GB maison *f* de correction.

borzoi /ˈbɔːzɔɪ/ *n* barzoï *m*.

bosh○ /bɒʃ/ *n* n'importe quoi○.

bos'n *n* = **boatswain**.

Bosnia-Herzegovina /ˌbɒznɪəˌhɜːtsəgəʊˈviːnə/ ▶ **1131** *pr n* Bosnie-Herzégovine *f*.

Bosnian /ˈbɒznɪən/ ▶ **1486** **I** *n* Bosniaque *mf*.

II *adj* bosniaque.

bosom /ˈbʊzəm/ *n* littér **1** (chest) poitrine *f*; **to hug sb to one's ~** serrer qn contre sa poitrine; **2** (breasts) **to have a large ~** avoir beaucoup de poitrine; **an ample ~** une poitrine opulente; **3** fig (heart, soul) cœur *m*; **to be in the ~ of one's family/of the community** être au sein de sa famille/de la communauté; **to take sb to one's ~** se prendre d'affection pour qn.

bosom buddy○, **bosom friend** *n* ami/-e *m/f* intime.

Bosphorus /ˈbɒspərəs/ *pr n* **the ~** le Bosphore.

boss /bɒs/ **I** *n* **1**○ (person in charge) gen patron/-onne *m/f*; (in politics, underworld) chef *m*; **go ahead, you're the ~** iron vas-y, c'est toi le patron; **she's the ~ in the house** c'est elle qui porte la culotte○; **we'll show them who's ~** on va leur montrer qui commande ici; **2** (stud) (on shield) umbo *m*; (on ceiling) bossage *m*; (on wheel) tourteau *m*; (on propeller) moyeu *m*.

II○ *adj* US beau/belle; **this work is ~** c'est du beau boulot○.

■ **boss about**○, **boss around**○: **~** [**sb**] **about** mener [qn] par le bout du nez.

BOSS /bɒs/ *n* (*abrév* = **Bureau of State Security**) *branche des services de sécurité sud-africains.*

boss-eyed○ /ˈbɒsaɪd/ *adj* GB qui louche; **to be ~** avoir un œil qui dit zut à l'autre○.

bossiness○ /ˈbɒsɪnɪs/ *n* caractère *m* autoritaire.

bossy○ /ˈbɒsɪ/ *adj* autoritaire.

Boston baked beans US *npl* haricots *mpl* blancs (*à la sauce tomate*).

Bostonian /bɒsˈtəʊnɪən/ *n* Bostonien/-ienne *m/f*.

bosun *n* = **boatswain**.

botanic(al) /bəˈtænɪk(l)/ *adj* [*studies, drawing, term*] botanique; [*name*] latin; **~ gardens** jardin *m* botanique.

botanist /ˈbɒtənɪst/ **▶ 1692** *n* botaniste *mf*.

botanize /ˈbɒtənaɪz/ *vi* herboriser.

botany /ˈbɒtənɪ/ *n* botanique *f*.

botany wool *n* laine *f* mérinos.

botch○ /bɒtʃ/ **I** *n* (also **~-up**) **to make a ~ of sth** saboter qch; **it was a real ~** c'était complètement bâclé.
II *vtr* bâcler.

botched /bɒtʃt/ *adj* [*legislation, reform*] mal conçu; [*attempt*] raté; [*translation*] mal fait; **a ~ job** (repair, piece of work) un travail bâclé; (legislation, reform etc) un gâchis.

both /bəʊθ/ **I** *adj* **~ sides of the road** les deux côtés de la rue; **~ her eyes/parents** ses deux yeux/parents; **~ their faces/lives** leurs visages/vies; **~ children came** les enfants sont venus tous les deux; **I like ~ brothers** j'aime les deux frères; **to hold sth in ~ hands** tenir qch entre ses mains.
II *conj* **~ you and I saw him** tu l'as vu comme moi; **~ here and abroad** ici comme à l'étranger; **to show ~ firmness and tact** faire preuve à la fois de fermeté et de tact; **to act ~ wisely and swiftly** agir sagement et rapidement à la fois; **~ Paris and London have their advantages** aussi bien Paris que Londres a ses avantages.
III *pron* (+ *v pl*) (of things) les deux; (of people) tous les deux; **let's do ~** faisons les deux; **French, or German, or ~** français, allemand, ou les deux; **'which do you want?'—'~'** 'lequel veux-tu?'—'les deux'; **I know them ~** je les connais tous les deux; **~ are young, they are ~ young** ils sont jeunes tous les deux; **we ~ won something** nous avons tous les deux gagné quelque chose.
IV both of *pron phr* (+ *v pl*) **let's take ~ of them** prenons les deux; **~ of you are wrong** vous avez tort tous les deux; **~ of us think that** nous pensons tous les deux que.

bother /ˈbɒðə(r)/ **I** *n* **1** (inconvenience) ennui *m*, embêtement○ *m*; **to do sth without any ~** faire qch sans aucune difficulté; **it's too much ~** c'est trop de tracas; **to have the ~ of doing** avoir le tracas de faire; **it saves me the ~ of doing** cela m'évite le tracas de faire; **to go to the ~ of doing** se donner le mal de faire; **don't go to too much ~** ne te donne pas trop de mal; **it's no ~** ce n'est pas un problème; **2**○ ¢ GB (trouble) ennuis *mpl*; **a bit ou a spot of ~** des embêtements○ *mpl*; **to be in a bit ou spot of ~** avoir des ennuis; **3** (person) casse-pieds○ *mf inv*, enquiquineur/-euse○ *m/f*; **he's no ~ at all** il ne dérange pas du tout.
II○ *excl* zut alors!
III *vtr* **1** (worry) tracasser; **what's ~ing you?** qu'est-ce qui te tracasse?; **it doesn't ~ me in the least** ça ne me tracasse pas le moins du monde; **don't let it ~ you** ne te tracasse pas avec ça; **to be ~ed by noise** être dérangé par le bruit; **it ~s me that** cela m'ennuie que (+ *subj*); **they won't be ~ing you again** ils ne t'embêteront plus; **2** (inconvenience) déranger; **does it ~ you if I smoke?** cela vous dérange-t-il que je fume (*subj*)?; **I'm sorry to ~ you** je suis désolé de vous déranger; **oh stop ~ing me!**○ mais arrête de m'embêter à la fin!○; **to ~ sb with** ennuyer qn avec [*details, problems, questions*]; **3** (hurt) faire souffrir; **her knee is still ~ing her** son genou la fait encore souffrir; **4**○ †GB **~ the money/the neighbours!** au diable l'argent/les voisins○†!
IV *vi* **1** (take trouble) s'en faire; **please don't ~** s'il te plaît, ne te dérange pas; **why ~?** pourquoi se tracasser?; **I don't think I'll ~** je ne vais pas m'embêter avec ça; **I wouldn't ~** ce n'est pas la peine; **to ~ doing ou to do** prendre la peine de faire; **he doesn't ~ voting ou to vote** il ne prend pas la peine de voter; **don't ou you needn't ~ doing** ce n'est pas la peine de faire; **I won't ~ with a hat** ce n'est pas la peine de prendre un chapeau; **to ~ about** se tracasser au sujet de; **it's not worth ~ing about the details** ça ne vaut pas la peine de s'embêter avec des détails; **I don't know why I ~** je ne sais pas pourquoi je me tracasse; **'I want to apologize'—'don't ~!'** 'il faut que je m'excuse'—'ce n'est pas la peine!'; **don't ou you needn't ~ coming back!** ce n'est pas la peine de revenir!; **2** (worry) **to ~ about** se soucier de; **it's/he's not worth ~ing about** ça/il ne vaut pas la peine qu'on s'en occupe; **don't ~ about me, I'll be fine** ne t'inquiète pas pour moi, tout ira bien.
V bothered *pp adj* (concerned) **to be ~ed that** être ennuyé que (+ *subj*); **to be ~ed with** s'embêter avec [*detail, problem*]; **he's not ~ed about money ou about having money** ça ne l'intéresse pas d'avoir de l'argent; **I'm not ~ed** GB ça m'est égal; **I can't be ~ed** je m'en fiche○ complètement; **you just couldn't be ~ed to turn up!** tu ne t'es même pas donné la peine de venir!
VI *v refl* **to ~ oneself about** se tracasser avec [*problem*]; **▶ hot**.

botheration○† /ˌbɒðəˈreɪʃn/ *excl* la barbe!

bothersome /ˈbɒðəsəm/ *adj* ennuyeux/-euse.

Bothnia /ˈbɒθnɪə/ *pr n* **the Gulf of ~** le golfe de Botnie.

Botswana /bɒtˈswɑːnə/ **▶ 1131** *pr n* Botswana *m*.

bottle /ˈbɒtl/ **I** *n* **1** (container) (for drinks) bouteille *f*; (for perfume, medicine, tablets) flacon *m*; (for baby) biberon *m*; (for gas) bouteille *f*; **milk/whisky ~** bouteille *f* de lait/de whisky; **a ~ of wine** une bouteille de vin; **'bring a ~'** (to party) 'prière d'apporter une bouteille'; **2**○ fig (alcohol) **to hit the ~** caresser la bouteille○; **to be on the ~** caresser la bouteille○; **to go back on the ~** se remettre à boire; **to take to the ~** se mettre à boire or à picoler○; **3**○ GB (courage) courage *m*, cran○ *m*; **to lose one's ~** se dégonfler○; **have you lost your ~?** alors, tu te dégonfles○?
II *vtr* **1** (put in bottles) embouteiller, mettre [qch] en bouteilles [*milk, wine*]; **2** GB (preserve) mettre [qch] en bocal or en conserve [*fruit*].
III bottled *pp adj* [*beer, gas*] en bouteille; [*fruit*] conservé en bocaux; **~d water** eau *f* minérale.
■ **bottle out**○ GB se dégonfler○.
■ **bottle up**: **~ [sth] up, ~ up [sth] 1** (hide) étouffer [*anger, despair, grief*]; **you shouldn't ~ things ou your feelings up** tu devrais exprimer tes sentiments; **2** Mil Naut embouteiller [*fleet*].

bottle: **~ bank** *n* réceptacle *m* à verre; **~brush** *n* goupillon *m*; **~-fed** *adj* nourri au biberon; **~ feed** *vtr* nourrir [qn] au biberon; **~ feeding** *n* alimentation *f* au biberon; **~ glass** *n* verre *m* de bouteille; **~ green ▶ 1104** *n, adj* vert (*m*) bouteille *inv*.

bottleneck /ˈbɒtlnek/ *n* **1** (traffic jam) embouteillage *m*; **2** (narrow part of road) rétrécissement *m* de la chaussée; **3** (hold-up) goulet *m* d'étranglement (**in** dans).

bottle: **~-opener** *n* décapsuleur *m*; **~ party** *n* soirée *f* (*à laquelle chacun apporte une bouteille*); **~ rack** *n* casier *m* à bouteilles; **~ top** *n* capsule *f* (de bouteille).

bottlewasher /ˈbɒtlwɒʃə(r)/ *n* **chief cook and ~** hum factotum *m*.

bottom /ˈbɒtəm/ **I** *n* **1** (base) (of hill, pile, steps, wall) pied *m*; (of page) bas *m*; (of bag, bottle, hole, river, sea) fond *m*; **at the ~ of the page** en bas de la page; **to touch ~** toucher le fond; **to sink ou go to the ~** [*ship*] couler; **from the ~ of one's heart** du fond du cœur; **to knock the ~ out of** défoncer [*box*]; démolir [*argument*]; **the ~ has fallen ou dropped out of the market** le marché s'est effondré; **2** (underside) (of boat) œuvres *fpl* vives, carène *f*; (of vase, box) dessous *m*; **3** (lowest position) (of list) bas *m*; (of league) dernière place *f*; (of hierarchy) dernier rang *m*, bas *m*; **at the ~ of the list** en bas de la liste; **to be at the ~ of the heap ou pile** fig être au bas de l'échelle; **to be ou come ~ of the class** être dernier/-ière de la classe; **I started at the ~ of the company** j'ai débuté dans cette entreprise au bas de l'échelle; **to hit rock ~** fig toucher le fond; **4** (far end) (of garden, field) fond *m*; (of street) bout *m*; **5**○ (buttocks) derrière○ *m*, fesses *fpl*; **6** fig (root) fond *m*; **to get to the ~ of a mystery/of a matter** découvrir le fin fond d'un mystère/d'une affaire; **at ~, he's not reliable** dans le fond, on ne peut pas lui faire confiance; **to be ou lie at the ~ of sth** être à l'origine de qch; **7** Comm, Naut navire *m*.
II○ **bottoms** *npl* **pyjama/tracksuit ~s** pantalon *m* de pyjama/de survêtement; **bikini ~s** bas *m* de maillot de bain.
III *adj* **1** (lowest) [*layer, rung, shelf*] du bas; [*sheet*] de dessous; [*apartment*] du rez-de-chaussée; [*bunk*] inférieur; [*division, half, part*] dernier/-ière; **~ of the range** bas de gamme; **2** (last) [*place, pupil, team*] dernier/-ière; [*score*] le plus bas.
IDIOMS **~s up**○! (drink up) cul sec○!; (cheers) santé!
■ **bottom out** [*recession*] atteindre son point le plus bas.

bottom drawer *n* lit tiroir *m* du bas; fig trousseau *m* de mariée.

bottom end *n* **1** lit (far end) (of street) bout *m*; **2** fig (of league, division) partie *f* inférieure; (of market) bas *m* de gamme.

bottom: **~ gear** *n* GB Aut première *f*; **~land** *n* US Geog basses terres *fpl*.

bottomless /ˈbɒtəmlɪs/ *adj* [*chasm, well*] sans fond; **a ~ pit** lit, fig un gouffre sans fond.

bottom line **I** *n* **1** Accts, Fin lit dernière ligne *f* du bilan; (results) résultats *mpl*; **2** (decisive factor) **the ~ is that** la vérité c'est que; **that's the ~** ça c'est le vrai problème.
II *modif* [*cost, loss*] définitif/-ive.

bottom: **~most** *adj* tout/-e dernier/-ière (*before n*); **~ry** *n* Fin, Naut prêt *m* à la grosse.

bottom-up /ˌbɒtəmˈʌp/ *adj* (*tjrs épith*) **1** Comput [*design, development*] ascendant; **2** gen [*approach, methods*] ≈ consultatif/-ive (*du bas vers le haut dans une hiérarchie*).

botulism /ˈbɒtjʊlɪzəm/ **▶ 1354** *n* botulisme *m*.

Bouches-du-Rhône *pr n* Bouches-du-Rhône *fpl*; **in/to the ~** dans les Bouches-du-Rhône.

bouclé /ˈbuːkleɪ/ **I** *n* (tissu *m*) bouclette *f*.
II *adj* Tex en bouclette; **a ~ wool coat** un manteau en bouclette; **~ knitting wool** laine *f* bouclette.

boudoir /ˈbuːdwɑː(r)/ *n* boudoir *m*, petit salon *m*.

bouffant /ˈbuːfɑːn/ *adj* [*hair, hairstyle*] crêpé; [*sleeve*] bouffant.

bougainvillea /ˌbuːgənˈvɪlɪə/ *n* bougainvillier *m*.

bough /baʊ/ *n* branche *f*.
bought /bɔːt/ *prét, pp* ▶ **buy**.
bouillon /ˈbuːjɒn/ *n* bouillon *m*.
boulder /ˈbəʊldə(r)/ *n* rocher *m*.
boulder clay *n* Geol dépôt *m* argileux erratique.
boulevard /ˈbuːləvɑːd, US ˈbʊl-/ *n* boulevard *m*.
bounce /baʊns/ I *n* **1** (rebound of ball) rebond *m*; **2** (of mattress, ball, material) élasticité *f*; (of hair) souplesse *f*; **3** fig (vigour) allant *m*.
II *vtr* **1** faire rebondir [*ball*]; retransmettre [*signal, radiowave*]; **to ~ a baby on one's knee** faire sauter un bébé sur ses genoux; **2**○ **to ~ a cheque** [*bank*] GB refuser d'honorer un chèque; [*person*] US faire un chèque sans provision; **3**○ (hurry) **to ~ sb into sth/into doing sth** pousser qn dans qch/à faire qch; **4**○ (eject) vider○ [*person*].
III *vi* **1** [*ball, object*] rebondir (**off** sur; **over** au dessus de); [*person*] (on trampoline, bed) faire des bonds, sauter; **the ball ~d down the steps** la balle a descendu les marches en rebondissant; **to ~ up and down on sth** faire des bonds or sauter sur qch; **the car ~d along the track** la voiture rebondissait sur le chemin; **2** fig (move energetically) **to ~ in/along** entrer/marcher avec énergie; **3**○ [*cheque*] être sans provision.
IDIOMS **to give sb the ~**○ US [*employer*] virer○ qn; **to get the ~**○ US [*employee*] être viré○.
■ **bounce back** [*person*] (after illness) se remettre; (after lapse in career) faire un retour en force; [*currency*] remonter.
bouncer○ /ˈbaʊnsə(r)/ *n* videur *m*.
bouncing baby *n* beau bébé *m* (en pleine santé).
bouncy /ˈbaʊnsɪ/ *adj* **1** [*ball*] qui rebondit bien; [*mattress*] élastique; [*pitch, turf*] souple; [*stride, walk*] sautillant; **2** fig [*person*] dynamique.
bouncy castle *n* château *m* gonflable (*pour enfants*).
bound /baʊnd/ I *prét, pp* ▶ **bind**.
II *n* bond *m*; **in a ~, with one ~** d'un bond.
III **bounds** *npl* lit, fig limites *fpl*; **to be out of ~s** Mil, Sch [*place*] être interdit d'accès; Sport être hors du terrain; **this area is out of ~s to civilians** l'accès de cette zone est interdit aux civils; **to be within/beyond the ~s of sth** fig rester dans/dépasser les limites de qch; **it's not beyond the ~s of possibility** ce n'est pas impossible; **to keep sth within ~s** maintenir qch dans des limites acceptables; **there are no ~s to her curiosity** il n'y a pas de limites à sa curiosité; **his folly knew no ~s** sa bêtise était sans bornes; **her fury knew no ~s** elle était hors d'elle.
IV *adj* **1** (certain) **to be ~ to do sth** aller sûrement faire qch; **they're ~ to ask** ils vont sûrement demander; **she's ~ to know** elle doit sûrement savoir; **it was ~ to happen** cela devait arriver; **2** (obliged) (by promise, conditions, rules, terms) tenu (**by** par; **to do** de faire); **I am ~ to say I think it's unlikely** je dois dire que cela me semble peu probable; **he's up to no good, I'll be ~** il prépare un mauvais coup, j'en suis sûr; **3** [*book*] relié; **cloth-/leather-~** relié en toile/en cuir; **4** (heading for) **~ for** [*person, bus, train*] en route pour; [*aeroplane*] à destination de; **5** (connected) **to be ~ up with sth** être lié à qch; **her problems are ~ up with her illness** ses problèmes sont liés à sa maladie; **she is so ~ up with her family that she never goes out** sa famille lui prend tellement de temps qu'elle ne sort jamais.
V *vtr* (border) borner; **~ed by** lit, fig borné par.
VI *vi* bondir; **she ~ed into the room** elle est entrée dans la pièce en coup de vent.
VII **-bound** *dans composés* **1** (heading for) **to be London-/Paris-~** être à destination de Londres/Paris; **homeward-~** sur le chemin du retour; **outward-~** en partance; **2** (confined) immobilisé; **wheelchair-~** immobilisé sur une chaise roulante; **fog-/strike-~** immobilisé par le brouillard/la grève.
boundary /ˈbaʊndrɪ/ I *n* **1** gen, Geog limite *f* (**between** entre); **city ~** limites de la ville; **national ~** frontières *fpl* du pays; **2** fig (defining) limite *f*; (dividing) ligne *f*; **3** Sport limites *fpl* du terrain.
II *modif* [*fence, post*] qui marque la limite.
boundary: **Boundary Commission** *n* GB commission *f* qui décide du redécoupage électoral; **~ line** *n* gen frontière *f*; (in basketball) ligne *f* de touche.
bounden† /ˈbaʊndən/ *adj* **~ duty** devoir *m* impérieux.
bounder† /ˈbaʊndə(r)/ *n* GB goujat *m*.
boundless /ˈbaʊndlɪs/ *adj* [*terrain, space*] infini; [*enthusiasm, energy, ambition, generosity*] sans bornes.
bounteous /ˈbaʊntɪəs/ *adj* littér **1** (generous) généreux/-euse; **2** (abundant) abondant.
bountiful /ˈbaʊntɪfl/ *adj* littér **1** (ample) abondant; **2** (generous) généreux/-euse.
bounty /ˈbaʊntɪ/ *n* **1** (generosity) générosité *f*; **food from Nature's ~** de la nourriture qui vient de la nature généreuse; **2** (gift) don *m*; **3** (reward) prime *f*.
bounty hunter *n* chasseur *m* de primes.
bouquet /bʊˈkeɪ/ *n* (all contexts) bouquet *m*.
bourbon /ˈbɜːbən/ *n* bourbon *m*.
bourgeois /ˈbɔːʒwɑː, US ˌbʊərˈʒwɑː/ I *n* bourgeois/-e *m/f*.
II *adj* bourgeois; **a ~ woman** une bourgeoise.
bourgeoisie /ˌbɔːʒwɑːˈziː, US ˌbʊəʒwɑːˈziː/ *n* bourgeoisie *f*.
bout /baʊt/ *n* **1** (attack) (of fever, malaria) accès *m*; **a ~ of insomnia** une crise d'insomnie; **a ~ of coughing** une quinte de toux; **to have** ou **go on a drinking ~** se livrer à des excès de boisson; **during one of his drinking ~s** pendant une de ses soûleries○; **to have a ~ of flu/nausea** avoir une grippe/des nausées; **to have a ~ of depression** faire une dépression; **2** Sport combat *m*; **3** (outbreak) crise *f*; **4** (period of activity) période *f*.
boutique /buːˈtiːk/ ▶ **1692** *n* boutique *f*; **fashion ~** boutique de mode.
bovine /ˈbəʊvaɪn/ *adj* lit, fig bovin.
bovver○ /ˈbɒvə(r)/ *n* ¢ GB **1** (fighting) bagarre *f*; **2** (problems) ennuis *mpl*.
bovver: **~ boot**○ *n* Fashn ranger *m*; **~ boy**○ *n* voyou *m*.
bow[1] /bəʊ/ I *n* **1** (weapon) arc *m*; **2** Mus archet *m*; **3** (knot) nœud *m*; **to tie a ~** faire un nœud.
II *vi* manier l'archet.
IDIOMS **to have more than one string** ou **several strings to one's ~** avoir plus d'une corde or plusieurs cordes à son arc.
bow[2] /baʊ/ I *n* **1** (forward movement) salut *m*; **to make a ~** faire un salut; **to take a ~** Theat saluer; **to make one's ~** fig faire ses débuts; **2** Naut avant *m*, proue *f*; **on the starboard ~** par tribord devant; **to go down by the ~s** sombrer par l'avant; **3** Sport rameur/-euse *m/f* avant.
II *vtr* baisser [*head*]; courber [*branch*]; incliner [*tree*]; **to ~ the knee** fig se soumettre (**to** à); **to ~ one's head in prayer** prier les yeux baissés.
III *vi* **1** (bend forward) saluer; **to ~ to** saluer; **2** (give way) **to ~ to** s'incliner devant [*wisdom, knowledge, necessity, majority*]; **to ~ to pressure** céder à la pression; **to ~ to sb's opinion** se ranger à l'avis de qn; **3** (sag) [*plant, shelf*] se courber (**under** sous).
IV **bowed** *pp adj* [*head*] penché; [*back*] courbé.
IDIOMS **to ~ and scrape** fig faire des courbettes (**to** devant); **there was a lot of ~ing and scraping** il y a eu beaucoup de courbettes; **to fire a shot across sb's ~s** fig tirer un coup de semonce à qn.
■ **bow down**: ¶ **~ down** lit se prosterner (**before** devant); fig se soumettre (**before** devant); ¶ **~ [sb/sth] down** [*wind*] courber [*tree*]; [*weight*] plier, courber [*person*]; **to be ~ed down by** être plié or courbé sous [*weight, load*]; **they were ~ed down by the burden of debt** le fardeau des dettes les écrasait.
■ **bow out** (resign) prendre congé, tirer sa révérence○.
Bow bells /ˌbəʊ ˈbelz/ *npl* GB **to be born within the sound of ~** *naître en plein quartier cockney*.
bow compass /bəʊ/ *n* compas *m* à balustre.
bowdlerization /ˌbaʊdləraɪˈzeɪʃn, US -rɪˈz-/ *n* Literat expurgation *f*.
bowdlerize /ˈbaʊdləraɪz/ *vtr* Literat expurger.
bow doors /baʊ/ *npl* porte *f* d'étrave.
bowel /ˈbaʊəl/ I *n* Med intestin *m*.
II **bowels** *npl* **1** Med intestins *mpl*; **to have upset ~s** avoir les intestins détraqués; **to move one's ~s** aller à la selle; **2** fig (inner depths) profondeurs *fpl*.
III *modif* [*cancer, disease*] de l'intestin.
bowel movement *n* selles *fpl*; **to have a ~** aller à la selle.
bower /ˈbaʊə(r)/ *n* **1** (in garden) tonnelle *f*; **2** litér (chamber) boudoir *m*.
bowery /ˈbaʊərɪ/ *n* US quartier *m* fréquenté par des clochards.
bow-front(ed) /bəʊ/ *adj* [*house*] à la façade bombée; [*cabinet, chest*] bombé.
bowing /ˈbəʊɪŋ/ *n* Mus coup *m* d'archet.
bowl /bəʊl/ I *n* **1** (basin) (for food) bol *m*; (large) saladier *m*; (for soup) assiette *f* creuse; (for washing) cuvette *f*; (of lavatory) cuvette *f*; (of lamp) globe *m*; **a ~(ful) of milk** un bol de lait; **a ~(ful) of water** une cuvette d'eau; **2** (hollow part) (of pipe) fourneau *m*; (of spoon) creux *m*; **3** Sport boule *f* (en bois).
II *vtr* **1** (roll) faire rouler [*hoop, ball*]; **2** (throw) lancer [*ball*]; **3** GB Sport = **bowl out**.
III *vi* **1** Sport lancer; **to ~ to sb** lancer la balle à qn; **2** US (go bowling) aller au bowling; **3** (move fast) **to ~ along** [*person*] filer à toute allure; [*vehicle*] rouler à toute vitesse.
■ **bowl out**: **~ [sb] out** mettre [qn] hors jeu.
■ **bowl over**: **~ [sb] over** **1** (knock down) renverser [*person*]; **2** (impress) stupéfier [*person*]; **she was totally ~ed over** elle était sidérée.
bowlegged /ˌbəʊˈlegɪd/ *adj* [*person*] aux jambes arquées; **to be ~** avoir les jambes arquées.
bowlegs /ˌbəʊˈlegz/ *npl* jambes *fpl* arquées.
bowler /ˈbəʊlə(r)/ *n* **1** Sport (in cricket) lanceur *m*; (in bowls) joueur/-euse *m/f* de boules (*sur gazon*); **2** Fashn = **bowler hat**.
bowler hat *n* chapeau *m* melon.
bowline /ˈbəʊlɪn/ *n* **1** (rope) bouline *f*; **2** (knot) nœud *m* de chaise.
bowling /ˈbəʊlɪŋ/ ▶ **1282** *n* Sport **1** (ten-pin) bowling *m*; **2** (on grass) jeu *m* de boules (*sur gazon*); **3** (in cricket) service *m*.
bowling: **~ alley** *n* (building) bowling *m*; (lane) piste *f* de bowling; **~ green** *n* terrain *m* de boules (*sur gazon*).
bowls /bəʊlz/ ▶ **1282** I *n* (+ *v sg*) jeu *m* de boules (*sur gazon*).
II *modif* [*club, tournament*] de boules (*sur gazon*).
bowman /ˈbəʊmən/ *n* archer *m*.
bowsprit /ˈbəʊsprɪt/ *n* beaupré *m*.
bow /bəʊ/: **~string** *n* corde *f* d'arc; **~ tie** *n* nœud-papillon *m*.
bow-wave /baʊ/ *n* vague *f* de proue.
bow window /bəʊ/ *n* bow-window *m*.
bow-wow /ˌbaʊˈwaʊ/ *n* **1** lang enfantin (dog) toutou *m* baby talk; **2** onomat ouah! ouah!
box /bɒks/ I *n* **1** (small, cardboard) boîte *f*;

(larger, crate) caisse *f*; **~ of matches/of chocolates** boîte d'allumettes/de chocolats; **to sell apples by the ~** vendre des pommes par caisses; **it comes in a ~** cela se vend en boîte; **2** (on page) case *f*; **put a tick in the ~** cocher la case; **3** (seating area) Theat loge *f*; Sport tribune *f*; **4** (in stable) box *m*; **5** GB Sport (for protection) coquille *f*; **6**○ (television) **the ~** la télé; **7** Sport (in soccer) surface *f* de réparation; (in baseball) emplacement *m*; **8** (in gymnastics) cheval *m* de saut; **9** Post (also **Box**) boîte *f* postale; **Box 20** BP 20; **10** Aut (for gears, steering, axle) boîte *f*; **11** (slap) **a ~ on the ear** une gifle; **12** Bot buis *m*; **13** GB Transp = **box junction**; **14**○ (dilemma) impasse *f*; **15**○ Comput machine *f*.
II *modif* [*hedge, furniture*] en buis.
III *vtr* **1** (pack) ▶**box up**; **2** (fight) boxer [*opponent*]; **3** (strike) **to ~ sb's ears** gifler qn; **4** Naut **to ~ the compass** réciter la rose des vents.
IV *vi* Sport boxer.
V boxed *pp adj* [*note, information*] en encadré; **~ed set** coffret *m*; **~ed advert** encadré *m*.
■ **box in**: **~ in [sth/sb], ~ [sth/sb] in** coincer○ [*runner, car*]; **to be ~ed in** [*person*] être coincé○; [*yard, area*] être encaissé or encadré; **to feel ~ed in** se sentir enfermé.
■ **box off**: **~ off [sth], ~ [sth] off** cloisonner [*space*].
■ **box up**: **~ up [sth], ~ [sth] up** mettre [qch] en caisse, encaisser.

box: **~board** *n* carton *m* d'emballage; **~ calf** *n* box *m*, box-calf *m*; **~ camera** *n* appareil-photo *m* box; **~car** *n* US wagon *m* de marchandises.

boxer /ˈbɒksə(r)/ ▶**1692** *n* **1** Sport boxeur *m*; **2** (dog) boxer *m*.

boxer shorts *npl* caleçon *m* (court).

box: **~ful** *n* pleine boîte *f* (**of** de); **~ girder** *n* poutre-caisson *f*.

boxing /ˈbɒksɪŋ/ ▶**1282** **I** *n* boxe *f*; **to take up ~** se mettre à la boxe.
II *modif* [*champion, fan, glove, match, promoter*] de boxe.

Boxing Day /ˈbɒksɪŋ deɪ/ *n* GB lendemain *m* de Noël.

boxing ring *n* ring *m*.

box: **~ junction** *n* GB Transp milieu *m* d'intersection (*délimité par des bandes jaunes*); **~ kite** *n* cerf-volant *m* cellulaire; **~ lunch** *n* US panier-repas *m*; **~ number** *n* numéro *m* de boîte postale.

box office **I** *n* Cin, Theat **1** (ticket office) guichet *m*; **2** fig **to do well/badly at the ~** être bien/mal accueilli au box office; **to be good ~** [*show*] faire recette; [*person*] attirer les foules.
II *modif* **a ~ success/failure** un succès/échec au box office; **~ takings** recettes *fpl* des guichets; **to be a ~ attraction** attirer les foules.

box: **~ pleat** *n* pli *m* creux; **~ room** *n* GB petite chambre *f* (*servant de débarras*).

box spring *n* **1** GB (bed spring) ressort *m* de sommier; **2** US (bed base, set of springs) sommier *m* à ressorts.

box stall *n* US box *m*.

boxwood /ˈbɒkswʊd/ **I** *n* (bois *m* de) buis *m*.
II *modif* [*hedge, furniture*] en buis.

boy /bɔɪ/ **I** *n* **1** (young male) garçon *m*; **the ~s' toilet** les toilettes des garçons; **a ~'s bike** un vélo pour garçon; **come here ~!** viens ici, mon garçon; **be polite ~s!** soyez polis, les garçons!; **when I was a ~** quand j'étais petit; **the big ~s** les grands; **a new ~** gen, Sch un nouveau; **there's a good ~!** voilà, c'est bien mon petit!; **look ~s and girls** regardez, les enfants; **~s will be ~s!** il faut que jeunesse se passe!; **2** (son) fils *m*; **the Smith ~** le fils Smith; **3**○ GB (man) gars○ *m*; **to be a local ~** être un gars du coin○; **to be one of the ~s** faire partie de la bande; **to have a drink with the ~s** boire un coup avec les copains○; **an old ~** Sch un ancien élève *m*; (old man) un vieillard *m*; **the old ~**○ le vieux○ *m*; **how are you old ~?** comment ça va mon vieux?; **my dear ~** mon cher; **4**† (colonial servant) boy *m*; **5** (male animal) **down ~!** doucement, mon vieux!; **easy ~!** tout doux, mon vieux!; **6**○ US injur (black man) nègre *m* offensive.
II○ **boys** *npl* **1** (experts) gars○ *mpl*; **the legal ~s** les gars○ du service juridique; **2** (soldiers) gars○ *mpl*; **our brave ~s at the front** nos braves gars au front.
III *modif* [*detective, genius, soprano*] jeune (*before n*).
IV○ *excl* **~, it's cold here!** bon sang! ce qu'il fait froid ici!; **~ oh ~, was I scared!** eh ben○ mon vieux, ce que j'avais peur!
IDIOMS **to sort out the men from the ~s** décider des plus forts et des plus faibles; **the ~s in blue**○ GB la police; **the ~s uptown**○ US les caïds *mpl*.

boycott /ˈbɔɪkɒt/ **I** *n* boycottage *m*, boycott *m* (**against, of, on** de).
II *vtr* boycotter.

boyfriend /ˈbɔɪfrend/ *n* (petit) copain *m* or ami *m*.

boyhood /ˈbɔɪhʊd/ **I** *n* enfance *f*.
II *modif* [*dream, experience, friend*] d'enfance.

boyish /ˈbɔɪɪʃ/ *adj* **1** (youthful) [*figure, looks*] d'adolescent; **to look ~** avoir l'air d'un adolescent; **her ~ figure/looks** sa silhouette/son air de garçon; **2** (endearingly young) [*grin, charm, enthusiasm*] enfantin.

boy: **~-meets-girl** *adj* [*film, story*] du genre rencontre romantique (*after n*); **~ scout** *n* scout *m*.

bozo○ /ˈbəʊzəʊ/ *n* US rigolo *m*.

Br *adj* (*abrév écrite* = **British**) britannique.

BR *n*: *abrév* ▶**British Rail**.

bra /brɑː/ ▶**1703** *n* soutien-gorge *m*.

brace /breɪs/ **I** *n* **1** (for teeth) appareil *m* dentaire; **to wear a ~** avoir un appareil dentaire; **2** Med (for broken limb) attelle *f*; (permanent support) appareil *m* orthopédique; **3** Constr support *m*; **4** (pair) (of birds, animals) couple *m* (**of** de); (of pistols) paire *f* (**of** de); **5** (tool) vilebrequin *m*; **6** (symbol) accolade *f*.
II *vtr* **1** [*person*] arc-bouter [*body, back*] (**against** contre); **to ~ one's legs/feet against sth** appuyer les jambes/pieds contre qch; **2** Constr renforcer, consolider [*wall, structure*].
III braces *npl* GB Fashn bretelles *fpl*.
IV *vi* **1** fig **to ~ for sth** [*person, organization*] se préparer à qch; **2** lit (for crash) se recroqueviller.
V *v refl* **to ~ oneself** (physically) s'arcbouter (**for** en prévision de); fig se préparer (**for** à; **to do** à faire); **~ yourself!** préparetoi!
VI braced *pp adj* [*wall, structure*] renforcé, consolidé (**with** avec); **to be ~ for sth/to do** [*person*] être préparé à qch/à faire.
■ **brace up**: ¶ **~ up** se ressaisir; ¶ **~ up [sb], ~ [sb] up** réconforter qn.

bracelet /ˈbreɪslɪt/ *n* **1** (jewellery) bracelet *m*; **2** (watchstrap) bracelet *m* (de montre).

bracer○ /ˈbreɪsə(r)/ *n* remontant *m*.

brachycephalic /ˌbrækɪsɪˈfælɪk/ *adj* brachycéphale.

bracing /ˈbreɪsɪŋ/ *adj* vivifiant, tonifiant.

bracken /ˈbrækən/ *n* fougère *f*.

bracket /ˈbrækɪt/ **I** *n* **1** (in typography) (round) parenthèse *f*; (square) crochet *m*; **in ~s** entre parenthèses or crochets; **2** (support) (for shelf) équerre *f*; (for lamp) applique *f*; **3** Archit saillie *f*; **4** (category) tranche *f*, catégorie *f*; **age/income/tax ~** tranche d'âge/de revenus/d'impôts; **price ~** catégorie de prix.
II *vtr* **1** (put in brackets) (round) mettre [qch] entre parenthèses [*word, phrase*]; (square) mettre [qch] entre crochets [*word, phrase*]; **2** (put in category) (also **~ together**) accoler [*names, items*]; mettre [qn] dans le même groupe [*people*]; **to ~ sb/sth with** assimiler qn/qch à; **3** Mil encadrer [*target*].

brackish /ˈbrækɪʃ/ *adj* saumâtre.

bract /brækt/ *n* Bot bractée *f*.

brad /bræd/ *n* pointe *f* à tête perdue.

bradawl /ˈbrædɔːl/ *n* poinçon *m*.

brae /breɪ/ *n* Scot versant *m*.

brag /bræg/ **I** *n* **1** (boast) fanfaronnade *f*; **2** (card game) ≈ poker *m*.
II *vi* (*p prés etc* **-gg-**) se vanter (**to** auprès de; **about** de; **about doing** de faire).

braggart† /ˈbrægət/ *n* fanfaron/-onne *m/f*.

bragging /ˈbrægɪŋ/ *n* fanfaronnade *f* (**about** au sujet de).

Brahma /ˈbrɑːmə/ *pr n* Relig Brahma.

Brahman /ˈbrɑːmən/ *n* Relig brahmane *m*.

Brahmaputra /ˌbrɑːməˈpuːtrə/ ▶**1644** *pr n* Brahmapoutre *m*.

Brahmin /ˈbrɑːmɪn/ *n* **1** Relig brahmane *m*; **2** (cultural snob) souvent péj mandarin *m* pej.

braid /breɪd/ **I** *n* **1** US (of hair) tresse *f*, natte *f*; **2** ¢ (trimming) galon *m*; **gold ~** galon doré.
II *vtr* **1** US tresser [*hair*]; **2** galonner [*cushion, uniform*].
III braided /ˈbreɪdɪd/ *pp adj* [*cushion etc*] galonné; [*rug*] tressé.

Braille /breɪl/ **I** *n* braille *m*.
II *modif* [*alphabet*] braille; [*book*] en braille.

brain /breɪn/ **I** *n* **1** Anat (living organ) cerveau *m*; **2** (also **~s**) (substance) **~s** cervelle *f*; **to blow one's ~s out**○ se faire sauter la cervelle○; **3** Culin cervelle *f*; **calves' ~s** cervelle de veau; **4** (mind) **to have a good ~** être intelligent; **to have football on the ~**○ ne penser qu'au football; **5**○ (intelligent person) tête○ *f*.
II brains *npl* (intelligence) intelligence *f*; **to have ~s** être intelligent; **he's the ~s of the family** c'est lui le cerveau de la famille; **to use one's ~s** faire marcher ses cellules grises; **she was the ~s behind the operation** c'était elle le cerveau de l'affaire.
III *modif* [*cell, tissue*] du cerveau, cérébral; [*tumour*] au cerveau; [*haemorrhage*] cérébral.
IV○ *vtr* (knock out) assommer, estourbir○.
IDIOMS **to dance/study one's ~s out**○ US danser/travailler jusqu'à épuisement; **to beat sb's ~s out** défoncer le crâne de qn○; **to pick sb's ~s** avoir recours aux lumières de qn; **I need to pick your ~s** j'ai besoin de vos lumières; ▶**rack**.

brain: **~box**○ *n* grosse tête○ *f*; **~child** *n* grande idée *f*; **~ damage** *n* ¢ lésions *fpl* cérébrales; **~-damaged** *adj* qui a des lésions cérébrales.

brain dead /ˈbreɪnded/ *adj* **1** Med dans un coma dépassé; **2**○ fig péj abruti.

brain: **~ death** *n* mort *f* cérébrale; **~ drain** *n* fuite *f* des cerveaux; **~ fever** *n* fièvre *f* cérébrale.

brainless /ˈbreɪnlɪs/ *adj* [*person, scheme*] idiot; **he's completely ~** il n'a rien dans la tête.

brain: **~pan** *n* crâne *m*; **~ scan** *n* scanographie *f* du cerveau; **~ scanner** *n* scanographe *m*.

brainstorm /ˈbreɪnstɔːm/ *n* **1** Med, fig coup *m* de folie; **2**○ = **brainwave**.

brain: **~storming** *n* brainstorming *m*, remue-méninges *m inv*; **~s trust** GB, **~ trust** US *n* (all contexts) brain-trust *m*; comité *m* d'experts; **~ surgeon** *n* ▶**1692** neurochirurgien/-ienne *m/f*; **~ surgery** *n* neurochirurgie *f*; **~ teaser**○ *n* casse-tête *m inv*.

brainwash /ˈbreɪnwɒʃ/ *vtr* faire subir un lavage de cerveau à; **they were ~ed into thinking that**... on a fini par leur faire croire que...

brainwashing /ˈbreɪnwɒʃɪŋ/ *n* (of prisoners) lavage *m* de cerveau; fig péj (of public, consumers etc) bourrage○ *m* de crâne.

brainwave /ˈbreɪnweɪv/ *n* **1**○ (inspiration) idée *f* géniale, illumination *f*; **2** Med onde *f* cérébrale.

brainwork /ˈbreɪnwɜːk/ *n* travail *m* intellectuel.

brainy○ /ˈbreɪnɪ/ *adj* doué.

braise /breɪz/ *vtr* braiser; **braising beef** bœuf *m* à braiser.

brake /breɪk/ **I** *n* **1** Aut, Transp frein *m*; **to apply the ~(s)** freiner; **2** fig (curb) frein *m*; **to put a ~ on price rises** freiner la hausse des prix; **3** GB Hist (carriage) break *m*; **4** (thicket) fourré *m*.
II *vi* lit, fig freiner.

brake: **~ block** *n* patin *m* de frein; **~ disc** *n* disque *m* de frein; **~ drum** *n* tambour *m* de frein; **~ fluid** *n* liquide *m* de frein; **~ horsepower** *n* puissance *f* au frein; **~ lever** *n* levier *m* de frein à main; **~ light** *n* feu *m* stop; **~ lining** *n* garniture *f* de frein.

brakeman /ˈbreɪkmən/ *n* **1** Sport freineur *m*; **2** US Rail chef *m* de train.

brake: **~ pad** *n* plaquette *f* de frein; **~ pedal** *n* pédale *f* de frein; **~ shoe** *n* segment *m* de frein.

braking /ˈbreɪkɪŋ/ *n* freinage *m*.

braking: **~ distance** *n* distance *f* de freinage; **~ power** *n* puissance *f* de freinage; **~ system** *n* système *m* de freinage.

bramble /ˈbræmbl/ **I** *n* **1** (plant) ronce *f*; **2** GB (berry) mûre *f*.
II *modif* GB [*jam, jelly*] de mûres; [*tart*] aux mûres.

brambling /ˈbræmblɪŋ/ *n* pinson *m* du Nord.

bran /bræn/ *n* Bot, Culin son *m*.

branch /brɑːntʃ, US bræntʃ/ **I** *n* **1** (of tree) branche *f*; fig (of pipe, road, railway) embranchement *m*; (of river) bras *m*; (of candlestick, lamp) branche *f*; (of antlers) ramure *f*; (of family, language) rameau *m*; (of study, subject) domaine *m*; **2** Comm, Ind, Admin (of shop) succursale *f*; (of bank) agence *f*; (of company) filiale *f*; (of organization) division *f*, secteur *m*; (of union) section *f*; (of library) antenne *f*; **main ~** (of company) maison *f* mère; **3** US (stream) ruisseau *m*; **4** Comput branchement *m*.
II *vi* [*tree, river, nerve*] se ramifier; [*road, railway*] se diviser.
■ **branch off**: ¶ **~ off** [*road, river, railway*] bifurquer; ¶ **~ off (from)** se séparer de, s'embrancher sur [*road, railway*]; fig dévier de [*topic*].
■ **branch out**: **~ out** [*business*] se diversifier; **to ~ out into** [*business, person*] se lancer dans [*new area*]; **to ~ out on one's own** se mettre à son compte.

branch: **~ed candlestick** *n* chandelier *m* à plusieurs branches; **~ed chain** *n* Chem chaîne *f* ramifiée.

branching /ˈbrɑːntʃɪŋ, US ˈbræntʃ-/ *n* Ling ramification *f*.

branch: **~ line** *n* ligne *f* secondaire; **~ manager** *n* (of shop) directeur *m* de succursale; (of company) directeur *m* de filiale; (of bank) directeur *m* d'agence; **~ office** *n* agence *f*; **~ water** *n* US (from stream) eau *f* du ruisseau; (from tap) eau *f* du robinet.

brand /brænd/ **I** *n* **1** (make) marque *f*; **a well-known ~ of whisky** une grande marque de whisky; **own ~ products** produits à la marque de la maison; **2** (type) (of humour) type *m*; (of belief) conception *f*; (of art, of music) genre *m*; **3** (for identification) (on animal) marque *f* (au fer rouge); (on prisoner) marque *f*; fig (stigma) stigmates *mpl*; **4** littér (in fire) tison *m*; **5** littér (torch) torche *f*.
II *vtr* **1** (mark) lit marquer (au fer) [*animal*]; **2** fig marquer [*person*]; **to ~ sb as sth** désigner qn comme qch; **3** fig graver [*name, experience*]; **the experience is ~ed in my memory** l'expérience est gravée dans ma mémoire.

brand: **~ acceptance** *n* accueil *m* (réservé à une marque); **~ awareness** *n* notoriété *f* (d'une marque).

branded /ˈbrændɪd/ *adj* [*article, goods*] de marque *inv*.

brand: **~ identification** *n* identification *f* de la marque; **~ image** *n* Advertg, Comm image *f* de marque; **~ing iron** *n* fer *m* à marquer.

brandish /ˈbrændɪʃ/ *vtr* brandir.

brand: **~ leader** *n* Advertg, Comm leader *m* du marché; **~ loyalty** *n* fidélité *f* (à une marque); **~ management** *n* gestion *f* d'une marque, structure *f* par marque; **~ manager** *n* chef *m* de marque; **~ name** *n* marque *f* déposée; **~ name recall** *n* (spontaneous) notoriété *f* spontanée; (with prompting) notoriété *f* assistée; **~-new** *adj* tout neuf/toute neuve; **~ recognition** *n* identification *f* (d'une marque); **~ switching** *n* passage *m* d'une marque à une autre, zapping○ *m*.

brandy /ˈbrændɪ/ *n* **1** (grape) cognac *m*; **2** (other fruit) eau-de-vie *f*; **plum/peach ~** eau-de-vie de prune/pêche.

brandy: **~ glass** *n* verre *m* à cognac; **~ snap** *n* Culin ≈ cigarette *f* russe.

bran: **~ loaf** *n* pain *m* au son; **~ tub** *n*: *jeu où l'on pêche à la main un cadeau dans un tonneau*.

brash /bræʃ/ *adj* **1** (self-confident) [*person, manner, tone*] bravache; **2** (garish) [*colour, decor, design*] tape-à-l'œil (*inv*); **3** (harsh) [*music, sound*] agressif/-ive.

brashly /ˈbræʃlɪ/ *adv* [*behave, speak*] de façon impudente.

brashness /ˈbræʃnɪs/ *n* **1** (self-confidence) bravacherie *f*; **2** (garishness) (aspect) tape-à-l'œil *m inv*; **3** (harshness) agressivité *f*.

Brasilia /brəˈzɪljə/ ▶ **1818** *pr n* Brasilia.

brass /brɑːs, US bræs/ **I** *n* **1** (metal) laiton *m*, cuivre *m* jaune; **2** (fittings, objects) cuivres *mpl*; **3** Mus (also **brass section**) cuivres *mpl*; **4** (in church) plaque *f* commémorative; **5**○ (nerve) culot○ *m*; **6**○ (money) GB pognon○ *m*; **7**○ Mil (+ *v pl*) **the top ~** les galonnés; fig les huiles○.
II *modif* [*button, candlestick, plaque*] en cuivre jaune.
IDIOMS **to get down to ~ tacks** passer aux choses sérieuses; **it's not worth a ~ farthing** ça ne vaut pas un clou; **to be as bold as ~** avoir un drôle de culot○.
■ **brass off**○ GB: **~ [sb] off** casser les pieds à qn○; **to be ~ed off with** en avoir ras le bol de○.

brass: **~ band** *n* orchestre *m* de cuivres, fanfare *f*; **~ foundry** *n* fonderie *f* de cuivre; **~ hat**○ *n* argot des militaires officier *m* de haut rang.

brassica /ˈbræsɪkə/ *n* brassicacée *f*.

brassière† /ˈbræzɪə(r), US brəˈzɪər/ *n* soutien-gorge *m*.

brass: **~ instrument** ▶ **1481** *n* Mus cuivre *m*; **~ knuckles** *npl* US coup-de-poing *m* américain.

brass monkey *n* singe *m* en cuivre jaune.
IDIOMS **it's ~ weather outside**◑ on se les gèle dehors◑.

brass: **~ neck**○ *n* GB culot○ *m*; **~-necked**○ *adj* GB [*person*] culotté○; [*cheek, impudence*] suprême; **~ rubbing** *n* Art (activity) estampage *m* de plaques en laiton; (impression) estampe *f* d'une plaque en laiton; **~ware** *n* objets *mpl* en cuivre jaune; **~work** *n* travail *m* du cuivre.

brassy /ˈbrɑːsɪ, US ˈbræsɪ/ *adj* **1** ▶ **1104** (shiny yellow) cuivré; **2** [*sound*] (harsh) agressif/-ive; (musical) cuivré; **3** péj [*appearance, woman*] provocant.

bra strap *n* bretelle *f* (de soutien-gorge).

brat○ /bræt/ *n* péj marmot○ *m*, môme○ *mf*; **you little ~!** sale marmot!

Bratislava /ˌbrætɪˈslɑːvə/ ▶ **1818** *pr n* Bratislava.

brat pack○ *n*: *groupe d'artistes ou de sportifs jeunes et brillants*.

bravado /brəˈvɑːdəʊ/ *n* bravade *f*.

brave /breɪv/ **I** *n* **1** (Indian warrior) brave *m*; **2** **the ~** (+ *v pl*) les courageux; **none but the ~** littér seuls les courageux.
II *adj* **1** (courageous) [*person, effort*] courageux/-euse; [*smile*] brave; **be ~!** courage!; **he was very ~ about it** il a été très courageux; **it was ~ of her to do it** c'était courageux de sa part de le faire; **2** (fine) littér [*sight*] beau/belle (*before n*); **in a ~ new world** iron dans le meilleur des mondes.
III *vtr* (all contexts) braver.
IDIOMS **to put on a ~ face, to put a ~ face on things** faire bonne contenance; **to put a ~ face on [sth]** faire bonne contenance devant [*report, rumour*]; **to be as ~ as a lion** être courageux comme un lion.

bravely /ˈbreɪvlɪ/ *adv* courageusement; hum vaillamment.

bravery /ˈbreɪvərɪ/ *n* courage *m*, bravoure *f*.

bravery award *n* médaille *f* du courage.

bravo /ˌbrɑːˈvəʊ/ *excl* bravo!

bravura /brəˈvʊərə/ **I** *n* bravoure *f*.
II *modif* [*passage*] de bravoure; [*performance*] plein de bravoure.

brawl /brɔːl/ **I** *n* bagarre *f*.
II *vi* se bagarrer (**with** avec).

brawn /brɔːn/ *n* **1** GB Culin fromage *m* de tête; **2** (muscle) muscles *mpl*.
IDIOMS **all ~ no brains** tout dans les muscles, rien dans la tête.

brawny /ˈbrɔːnɪ/ *adj* musclé.

bray /breɪ/ **I** *n* (of donkey) braiment *m*; péj (of person) braillement *m*.
II *vi* [*donkey*] braire; péj [*person*] brailler; **to ~ with laughter** hurler de rire.

braze /breɪz/ *vtr* braser.

brazen /ˈbreɪzn/ *adj* **1** (shameless) éhonté; **a ~ hussy**○ une dévergondée; **2** (of brass) d'airain.
■ **brazen out**: **~ it out** payer d'audace.

brazenly /ˈbreɪznlɪ/ *adv* de façon éhontée.

brazier /ˈbreɪzɪə(r)/ *n* **1** (container) brasero *m*; **2** ▶ **1692** (worker) chaudronnier *m*.

Brazil /brəˈzɪl/ ▶ **1131** *pr n* Brésil *m*.

Brazilian /brəˈzɪljən/ ▶ **1486** **I** *n* (person) Brésilien/-ienne *m/f*.
II *adj* brésilien/-ienne.

Brazil nut *n* noix *f* du Brésil.

breach /briːtʃ/ **I** *n* **1** gen, Jur (infringement) (by breaking rule) infraction *f* (**of** à); (by failure to comply) manquement *m* (**of** à); (of copyright, privilege) violation *f*; **security ~** (of safety) manquement *m* aux règles de sécurité; (of official secret) atteinte *f* à la sûreté nationale; (of industrial secret) violation *f* du secret professionnel; **a ~ of good manners** une inconvenance; **to be in ~ of** enfreindre [*law*]; violer [*agreement*]; **2** Mil brèche *f* also fig; **3** (in relationship) rupture *f*.
II *vtr* **1** faire une brèche dans [*wall, defence*]; **2** fig ne pas respecter [*law, rule, protocol*].
IDIOMS **to be honoured in the ~** ne pas être respecté; **to step into the ~** faire un remplacement au pied levé.

breach: **~ of contract** *n* Jur rupture *f* de contrat; **~ of duty** *n* Jur manquement *m* au devoir professionnel; **~ of promise** *n* Jur (by fiancé) rupture *f* de promesse de mariage; **~ of the peace** *n* Jur atteinte *f* à l'ordre public; **~ of trust** *n* Jur abus *m* de confiance.

bread /bred/ **I** *n* **1** Culin pain *m*; **a loaf/slice of ~** une miche/tranche de pain; **to be on ~ and water** être au pain sec et à l'eau; **2**○ (money) fric○ *m*, argent *m*; **3** (livelihood) **to earn one's (daily) ~** gagner sa vie.
II *modif* [*oven, plate*] à pain; [*sauce*] au pain.
III *vtr* Culin paner [*cutlet, fish, etc*]; **~ed cutlets** côtelettes panées.
IDIOMS **to break ~ with sb** partager un repas avec qn; **to cast one's ~ upon the waters** se comporter de façon altruiste; **to know which side one's ~ is buttered on** savoir où est son intérêt; **to put ~ on the table** faire bouillir la marmite; **to put jam on the ~** mettre du beurre dans les épinards; **to take the ~ out of sb's mouth**

retirer le pain de la bouche de qn; **the best thing since sliced ~** hum l'invention la plus géniale de ces dernières années.

bread and butter I *n* tartine *f* de pain beurré; fig gagne-pain *m inv*.
II **bread-and-butter** *adj* (*tjrs épith*) [*job, issue, routine, work*] de tous les jours; [*letter*] de château; **~ pudding** ≈ pudding *m* au pain.

breadbasket /ˈbredbɑːskɪt/ *n* **1** lit corbeille *f* à pain; **2** fig (granary) grenier *m*; **3**○ (belly) ventre *m*.

bread: **~bin** *n* GB boîte *f* à pain, huche *f* à pain; **~board** *n* planche *f* à pain; **~box** *n* huche *f* à pain.

breadcrumb /ˈbredkrʌm/ I *n* miette *f* de pain.
II **breadcrumbs** *npl* Culin chapelure *f*; **to coat sth in ~s** passer qch à la chapelure; **escalopes coated in ~s** escalopes panées.

breadfruit /ˈbredfruːt/ *n* Bot, Culin **1** (fruit) fruit *m* de l'arbre à pain; **2** (also **~ tree**) arbre *m* à pain.

breadknife /ˈbrednaɪf/ *n* couteau *m* à pain.

breadline /ˈbredlaɪn/ *n* **to be on the ~** être au seuil de l'indigence; **to live above/below the ~** vivre au-dessus/au-dessous du seuil de la pauvreté.

bread: **~ roll** *n* Culin petit pain *m*; **~stick** *n* gressin *m*, longuet *m*.

breadth /bretθ/ ▶ **1412** *n* **1** Meas largeur *f*; **the length and ~ of** d'un bout à l'autre de; **2** fig (of experience, knowledge, provisions, regulations) étendue *f* (**of** de); (of mind, opinions, vision) largeur *f* (**of** de); **the course has great ~** le cours offre un large éventail de matières.
IDIOMS **to be** ou **come within a hair's ~ of** être à deux doigts de; **to search the length and ~ of the country for sb/sth** parcourir le pays à la recherche de qn/qch.

breadwinner /ˈbredwɪnə(r)/ *n* soutien *m* de famille.

break /breɪk/ I *n* **1** (fracture) fracture *f*; **2** (crack) (in plate, plank, surface) fêlure *f*; **3** (gap) (in fence, wall) brèche *f*; (in row, line) espace *m*; (in circuit, chain, sequence) rupture *f*; (in conversation, match) pause *f*; (in performance) entracte *m*; (in traffic, procession) trou *m*, espace *m*; **a ~ in the clouds** une éclaircie; **a ~ in transmission** une interruption dans la retransmission; **4** Radio, TV (also **commercial ~**) page *f* de publicité; **we're going to take a ~ now** tout de suite, une page de publicité; **5** (pause) gen pause *f*; Sch récréation *f*; **to take a ~** faire une pause; **I walked/worked for six hours without a ~** j'ai marché/travaillé pendant six heures sans m'arrêter; **to have a ~ from work** arrêter de travailler; **to take** ou **have a ~ from working/driving** ne plus travailler/conduire pendant un temps; **to take** ou **have a ~ from nursing/teaching** arrêter le métier d'infirmière/d'enseignant pendant un temps; **I often give her a ~ from looking after the kids** je m'occupe souvent des enfants pour qu'elle se repose; **give us a ~**○**!** fiche-nous la paix○!; **6** (holiday) vacances *fpl*; **the Christmas ~** les vacances de Noël; **a weekend ~ in Milan** un week-end à Milan; **7** fig (departure) rupture *f* (**with** avec); **a ~ with tradition/the past** une rupture avec la tradition/le passé; **it's time to make a** ou **the ~** (from family) il est temps de voler de ses propres ailes; (from job) il est temps de passer à autre chose; **8**○ (opportunity) chance *f*; **her big ~ came in 1973** 1973 a été l'année de sa veine○; **he gave me a ~** il m'a donné ma chance; **a lucky ~** un coup de veine○; **a bad ~** des déboires *mpl*; **to give sb an even ~** donner sa chance à qn; **9** (dawn) **at the ~ of day** au lever du jour, à l'aube *f*; **10** (escape bid) **to make a ~ for it**○ (from prison) se faire la belle○; **to make a ~ for the door/the trees** se précipiter vers la porte/les arbres; **11** Print **line ~** fin *f* d'alinéa; **page ~** changement *m* de page; **paragraph ~** fin *f* de paragraphe; **12** (in tennis) (also **service ~**) break *m*; **13** (in snooker, pool) (first shot) **it's your ~** c'est à toi de casser; (series of shots) **to make a 50 point ~** marquer une série de 50 points; **14** Mus (in jazz) break *m*.
II *vtr* (*prét* **broke**; *pp* **broken**) **1** (damage) casser [*chair, eggs, rope, stick, toy*]; casser, briser [*glass, plate, window*]; casser [*machine*]; **to ~ a tooth/a nail/a bone** se casser une dent/un ongle/un os; **to ~ one's leg/arm** se casser la jambe/le bras; **to ~ one's back** lit se casser la colonne vertébrale; **I nearly broke my back moving the piano** fig j'ai failli me briser les reins en déplaçant le piano; **to ~ one's neck** lit avoir une rupture des vertèbres cervicales; **somebody is going to ~ their neck on those steps** fig quelqu'un va se casser la figure sur ces marches○; **she broke the bottle over his head** elle lui a cassé la bouteille sur la tête; **2** (split, rupture) briser [*seal*]; couper [*sentence, word*]; **the skin is not broken** il n'y a pas de plaie; **not a ripple broke the surface of the water** pas une ride ne troublait la surface de l'eau; **to ~ surface** [*diver, submarine*] remonter à la surface; **the river broke its banks** la rivière a débordé; **3** (interrupt) [*person*] rompre [*silence*]; [*shout, siren*] déchirer [*silence*]; couper [*circuit, current*]; rompre [*monotony, spell*]; rompre [*ties, links*] (**with** avec); **to ~ one's silence** sortir de son silence (**on** à propos de); **to ~ sb's concentration** déconcentrer qn; **we broke our journey in Milan** nous avons fait un arrêt à Milan; **the tower ~s the line of the roof/of the horizon** la tour rompt la ligne du toit/de l'horizon; **to ~ step** rompre le pas; **4** (disobey) enfreindre [*law*]; ne pas respecter [*embargo, blockade, conditions, terms*]; violer [*treaty*]; désobéir à [*commandment, rule*]; briser [*strike*]; rompre [*vow*]; manquer [*appointment*]; **he broke his word/promise** il a manqué à sa parole/promesse; **5** (exceed, surpass) dépasser [*speed limit, bounds*]; battre [*record, opponent*]; franchir [*speed barrier*]; briser [*class barrier*]; **6** (lessen the impact of) couper [*wind*]; [*branches*] freiner [*fall*]; [*hay*] amortir [*fall*]; **7** fig (destroy) [*troops*] briser [*rebellion*]; briser [*person, resistance, determination, will*]; **to ~ sb's spirit** saper le moral de qn; **to ~ sb's hold over sb** débarrasser qn de l'emprise de qn; **discussions which aim to ~ this deadlock** des discussions qui visent à nous sortir de cette impasse; **to ~ a habit** se défaire d'une habitude; **8** (ruin) ruiner [*person*]; **this contract will make or ~ the company** (financially) ce contrat fera la fortune ou la ruine de l'entreprise; **this decision will make or ~ me** (personally) cette décision sera mon salut ou ma perte; **9** Equit débourrer [*young horse*]; **10** (in tennis) **to ~ sb's serve** faire le break; **11** Mil casser [*officer*]; **12** (decipher) déchiffrer [*cipher, code*]; **13** (leave) **to ~ camp** lever le camp; **14** (announce) annoncer [*news*]; révéler [*truth*]; **to ~ the news to sb** apprendre la nouvelle à qn; **~ it to her gently** annonce-lui la nouvelle avec douceur.
III *vi* (*prét* **broke**; *pp* **broken**) **1** (be damaged) [*branch, chair, egg, handle, tooth, string*] se casser; [*plate, glass, window*] se briser; [*arm, bone, leg*] se fracturer; [*bag*] se déchirer; **china ~s easily** la porcelaine se casse facilement; **the vase broke in two/into a thousand pieces** le vase s'est brisé en deux/en mille morceaux; **the sound of ~ing glass** le bruit de verre brisé; **2** (separate) [*clouds*] se disperser; [*waves*] se briser (**against** contre; **on, over** sur); **3** Sport [*boxers*] se séparer; **'~!'** (referee 's command) 'break!'; **4** (stop for a rest) faire une pause; **5** (change) [*good weather*] se gâter; [*drought, heatwave*] cesser; [*luck*] tourner; **6** (begin) [*day*] se lever; [*storm*] éclater; [*scandal, news story*] éclater; **7** (discontinue) **to ~ with sb** rompre les relations avec qn; **to ~ with a party/the church** quitter un parti/l'église; **to ~ with tradition/convention** rompre avec la tradition/les conventions; **8** (weaken) **their spirit never broke** leur moral n'a jamais faibli; **to ~ under torture/interrogation** céder sous la torture/l'interrogation; **9** (change tone) [*boy's voice*] muer; **her voice ~s on the high notes** sa voix s'éraille dans les aigus; **in a voice ~ing with emotion** d'une voix brisée par l'émotion; **10** (in snooker, pool) casser.

■ **break away**: ¶ **~ away 1** (become detached) [*island, shell*] se détacher (**from** de); **to ~ away from** [*group, person*] rompre avec [*family, party, organization*]; [*state*] se séparer de [*union*]; [*animal*] se détacher de [*herd*]; [*boat*] rompre [*moorings*]; **2** (escape) échapper (**from** à); **3** Sport [*runner, cyclist*] se détacher (**from** de); ¶ **~ away** [**sth**], **~** [**sth**] **away** enlever [*outer shell, casing*].

■ **break down**: ¶ **~ down 1** (stop functioning) [*car, elevator, machine*] tomber en panne; **we broke down on the main street** nous sommes tombés en panne sur la grand-rue; **2** (collapse) fig [*alliance, coalition*] éclater; [*negotiations*] échouer; [*contact, communication*] cesser; [*law and order*] se dégrader; [*argument*] ne pas tenir debout; [*system*] s'effondrer; [*person*] s'effondrer, craquer; **he broke down under the strain** il a craqué sous la pression; **3** (cry) fondre en larmes; **4** (be classified) [*cost findings, statistics*] se décomposer (**into** en); **the cost of the repair ~s down as follows** le prix de la réparation se décompose ainsi; **5** (decompose) [*compound*] se décomposer (**en** into); **6** (confess) (under interrogation) céder; ¶ **~** [**sth**] **down**, **~ down** [**sth**] **1** (demolish) lit enfoncer [*door*]; démolir [*fence, wall*]; fig faire tomber [*barriers*]; vaincre [*opposition, resistance, shyness*]; **2** (analyse) ventiler [*budget, cost, expenses, statistics*]; décomposer [*word*] (**into** en); décomposer [*data, findings*] (**into** par); décomposer [*argument*]; **3** (cause to decompose) décomposer [*compound, gas*] (**into** en); [*enzyme, catalyst*] dissoudre [*protein, starch*]; [*gastric juices*] dissoudre [*food*].

■ **break even** Fin rentrer dans ses frais.

■ **break forth** littér [*sun, water*] jaillir (**from** de).

■ **break free**: **~ free** [*prisoner*] s'évader; **to ~ free of** se couper de [*family*]; échapper à [*captor*].

■ **break in** ¶ **1** (enter forcibly) [*thief*] entrer (par effraction); [*police*] entrer de force; **the burglar broke in through a window** le cambrioleur est entré par une fenêtre; **2** (interrupt) interrompre; **'I don't want to go,' he broke in** 'je ne veux pas y aller,' a-t-il interrompu; **to ~ in on sb/sth** interrompre qn/qch; ¶ **~** [**sth**] **in** débourrer [*young horse*]; assouplir [*shoe*]; **to ~ in one's glasses** s'habituer à ses lunettes; ¶ **~** [**sb**] **in** accoutumer [qn] au travail [*recruit, newcomer*]; **to ~ sb in gently** donner le temps à qn de s'accoutumer au travail.

■ **break into**: **~ into** [**sth**] **1** (enter by force) entrer dans [qch] (par effraction) [*building*]; forcer la portière de [*car*]; forcer [*safe, till*]; **her car was broken into** sa voiture a été cambriolée; **2** (start to use) entamer [*new packet, new bottle, banknote, savings*]; **3** (encroach on) empiéter sur [*leisure time, working day*]; couper [*morning, day*]; **4** (begin to do) **to ~ into song/cheers** se mettre à chanter/acclamer; **to ~ into peals of laughter** éclater de rire; **to ~ into a run/gallop** se mettre à courir/au galop; **5** (make headway) [*company*] s'implanter sur [*market*]; [*person*] s'introduire dans [*job market*]; [*person*] percer dans [*show business*].

■ **break loose** [*dog, horse*] s'échapper (**from** de).

■ **break off**: ¶ **~ off 1** (snap off) [*end, mast, tip*] se casser; [*handle, piece*] se détacher; **2** (stop speaking) s'interrompre; **she broke off to answer the phone** elle s'est interrompue pour répondre au téléphone; **3** (pause) faire une pause, s'arrêter; ¶ **~ off [sth]**, **~ [sth] off** **1** (snap) casser [*branch, piece, segment, mast*]; **2** (terminate) rompre [*engagement, relationship, contact, negotiations, ties*]; interrompre [*conversation*]; **they decided to ~ it off** (relationship, engagement) ils ont décidé de rompre; **to ~ off doing** arrêter de faire.

■ **break out**: **~ out** **1** (erupt) [*epidemic, fire*] se déclarer; [*fight, panic, riot, storm*] éclater; [*rash*] apparaître; **to ~ out in a rash** ou **in spots** [*person*] avoir une éruption de boutons; [*face*] se couvrir de boutons; **to ~ out in a sweat** se mettre à transpirer; **2** (escape) [*prisoner*] s'évader; **to ~ out of** s'échapper de [*cage, prison*]; sortir de [*routine, vicious circle*]; se libérer de [*chains, straitjacket*].

■ **break through**: ¶ **~ through** [*army*] faire une percée; ¶ **~ through [sth]** percer [*defences, reserve*]; franchir [*barrier, cordon*]; se frayer un passage à travers [*crowd*]; traverser [*mur*]; [*sun*] percer [*clouds*].

■ **break up**: ¶ **~ up** **1** (disintegrate) lit [*wreck*] se désagréger; fig [*empire*] s'effondrer; [*alliance*] éclater; [*group, family, couple*] se séparer; **their marriage/relationship is ~ing up** leur mariage/relation va mal; **2** (disperse) [*crowd*] se disperser; [*cloud, slick*] se disperser; [*meeting*] se terminer; **3** GB Sch **schools ~ up on Friday** les cours finissent vendredi; **we ~ up for Christmas on Tuesday** pour Noël, nous finissons mardi; ¶ **~ [sth] up**, **~ up [sth]** (split up) disperser [*demonstrators*]; démanteler [*spy ring, drugs ring*]; séparer [*team, couple*]; désunir [*family*]; briser [*alliance, marriage*]; démembrer [*empire*]; diviser [*sentence, word*] (**into** en); morceler [*land*]; [*diagrams*] aérer [*text*]; mettre fin à [*party, fight, demonstration*]; **~ it up!** (stop fighting) ça suffit maintenant!

breakable /ˈbreɪkəbl/ **I breakables** *npl* objets *mpl* fragiles.
II *adj* fragile.

breakage /ˈbreɪkɪdʒ/ *n* **1** ¢ (damage) gen casse *f*; **to prevent ~** pour éviter la casse; **2 C** (damaged item) article *m* cassé; **'~s must be paid for'** (in shop) 'tout article cassé doit être payé'.

breakaway /ˈbreɪkəweɪ/ **I** *n* **1** (separation) (from organization) séparation *f* (**from** de); (from person, family) rupture *f* (**from** avec); **2** Sport échappée *f*; **to make a ~** faire une échappée.
II *modif* Pol (*épith*) [*faction, group, state*] séparatiste.

break dance I *n* smurf *m*.
II *vi* smurfer.

break: **~ dancer** *n* smurfeur/-euse *m/f*; **~ dancing** *n* smurf *m*.

breakdown /ˈbreɪkdaʊn/ **I** *n* **1** Aut, Mech, Tech panne *f* (**in, of** de); **in the event of a ~** en cas de panne; **he had a ~ on the motorway** il est tombé en panne sur l'autoroute; **2** (collapse) (of communications, negotiations) rupture *f*; (of discipline, order) dégradation *f*; (of alliance, coalition) éclatement *m*; (of plan) échec *m*; **3** Med dépression *f*; **to have a (nervous) ~** faire une dépression (nerveuse); **to be on the verge of a ~** être au bord de la dépression; **it's enough to give you a nervous ~!** hum il y a de quoi faire une dépression!; **4** (detailed account) (of figures, statistics, costs, budget) ventilation *f*; (of argument) décomposition *f*; (by sex, age, nationality) **a ~ of the voters according to sex/age** une répartition de l'ensemble des votants par sexe/tranche d'âge; **a ~ of how I spent the week** un emploi du temps détaillé de ma semaine passée; **5** Biol, Chem décomposition *f*.
II *modif* [*vehicle, truck*] de dépannage.

breakdown of marriage *n* Jur non-respect *m* des clauses matrimoniales.

breaker /ˈbreɪkə(r)/ *n* **1** (wave) brisant *m*; **2** ▶ **1692** (scrap merchant) casseur *m*; **3** (CB radio user) cibiste *mf*.

breaker's yard *n* Aut casse *f*.

break: **~-even** *n* Accts seuil *m* de rentabilité; **~-even point** *n* Accts point *m* mort; **~-even price** *n* Comm, Accts prix *m* de revient.

breakfast /ˈbrekfəst/ **I** *n* petit déjeuner *m*; **to have** ou **eat ~** prendre le petit déjeuner; **a ~ of cereal and toast** un petit déjeuner composé de céréales et de toasts.
II *vi* prendre le petit déjeuner.
IDIOMS **she eats men like you for ~**○ les hommes comme toi elle n'en fait qu'une bouchée○.

breakfast: **~ bar** *n* bar *m* de cuisine; **~ bowl** *n* assiette *f* creuse; **~ cereals** *npl* céréales *fpl* (pour le petit déjeuner); **~ meeting** *n* réunion *f* tôt le matin; **~ room** *n* petite salle *f* à manger; **~ television** *n* télévision *f* à l'heure du petit déjeuner; **~ time** *n* heure *f* du petit déjeuner.

break-in /ˈbreɪkɪn/ *n* cambriolage *m*.

breaking /ˈbreɪkɪŋ/ *n* **1** (smashing) lit (of bone) fracture *f*; (of rope, chain) rupture *f*; (of glass) bris *m*; (of seal) bris *m*; fig (of waves) déferlement *m*; **2** (break) (of promise) manquement *m* (**of** à); (of law, treaty) violation *f* (**of** de); (of contract) rupture *f* (**of** de); (of link, sequence, tie) rupture *f* (**of** de); **3** Ling diphtongaison *f*; **4** Equit débourrage *m*; **5** Relig **the ~ of the bread** le partage du pain; **6** Med (of voice) mue *f*.

breaking and entering *n* Jur effraction *f*.

breaking point *n* **1** Tech point *m* de rupture; **2** fig (collapse) **to be at ~** [*person*] être à bout; **to be close to ~** [*person*] être sur le point de craquer; **my patience had reached ~** ma patience était à bout.

breaking: **~ strength** *n* Tech résistance *f* à la rupture; **~ stress** *n* Tech charge *f* de rupture.

break: **~neck** *adj* [*pace, speed*] fou/folle, insensé; **~-out** *n* évasion *f*; **~point** *n* Comput point *m* d'interruption; Sport balle *f* de break.

breakthrough /ˈbreɪkθruː/ *n* Mil percée *f*; (in science, medicine) percée *f*; (in negotiations, investigation) progrès *m*; (in career, competition) percée *f*.

break-up /ˈbreɪkʌp/ **I** *n* (of empire) démembrement *m*; (of alliance, relationship) rupture *f*; (of political party, family, group) éclatement *m*; (of marriage) échec *m*; (of a company) morcellement *m*.
II *modif* Fin [*price, value*] de liquidation.

breakwater /ˈbreɪkwɑːtə(r)/ *n* (in harbour) brise-lames *m inv*; (on coastline) brise-mer *m inv*.

bream /briːm/ *n* (*pl* **~**) **1** (freshwater) brème *f*; **2** (also **sea ~**) daurade *f*.

breast /brest/ **I** *n* **1** Anat (woman's) sein *m*; **a baby at the** ou **her ~** un enfant au sein; **large ~s** une grosse poitrine; **small ~s** une poitrine plate; **2** (of poultry) blanc *m*; (in shop) filet *m*; **3** (of lamb) poitrine *f*; (of veal) tendron *m*; (of duck, pigeon) filet *m*; **4** (chest) littér poitrine *f*; **5** (heart) littér cœur *m*; **6** Mining front *m* de taille.
II *vtr* affronter [*wave*]; atteindre le sommet de [*hill*]; Sport franchir [*tape*].
III -breasted (*dans composés*) **1** (woman) **small-/large-~ed** avec une poitrine plate/une forte poitrine; **2** (coat) **double-~ed** croisé; **single-~ed** droit.
IDIOMS **to beat one's ~** faire son mea-culpa; **to make a clean ~ of sth** soulager sa conscience en avouant qch.

breast: **~-beating** *n* mea-culpa *mpl*; **~ bone** *n* sternum *m*; **~ cancer** ▶ **1354** *n* cancer *m* du sein.

breast-feed /ˈbrestfiːd/ (*prét, pp* **-fed**) **I** *vtr* allaiter; **a breast-fed baby** un bébé nourri au sein.
II *vi* allaiter.

breast: **~-feeding** *n* allaitement *m* maternel; **~-plate** *n* plastron *m* (d'une cuirasse); **~ pocket** *n* poche *f* de poitrine; **~ stroke** *n* brasse *f*; **~work** *n* Archit parapet *m*.

breath /breθ/ *n* **1** (air taken into lungs) souffle *m*; **to stop** ou **pause for ~** s'arrêter pour reprendre son souffle; **to get one's ~ back** reprendre son souffle; **out of ~** à bout de souffle; **to be short of ~** avoir le souffle court; **to catch one's ~** (breathe) reprendre souffle; (gasp) retenir son souffle; **to hold one's ~** lit retenir sa respiration; fig retenir son souffle; **to draw ~** reprendre (son) souffle; **he's as kind a man as ever drew ~** il n'y a pas plus gentil que lui; **as long as I have ~ in my body** ou **as I draw ~** tant que je vivrai; **2** (air in or leaving mouth) (with smell) haleine *f*; (visible) respiration *f*; **sb's hot ~** le souffle chaud de qn; **to have bad ~** avoir (une) mauvaise haleine; **his ~ smells of beer** son haleine sent la bière; **I could smell alcohol on his ~** je sentais à son haleine qu'il avait bu; **3** (single act) respiration *f*; **to take a deep ~** respirer profondément or à fond; **take a deep ~!** fig assieds-toi○!; **in a single ~** sans respirer; **in the same ~** dans la foulée; **with one's last** ou **dying ~** dans son dernier soupir; **to draw one's last ~** rendre son dernier soupir; **4** (of air, wind) **a ~ of** un souffle de; **to go out for a ~ of (fresh) air** sortir prendre l'air; **sb/sth is like a ~ of fresh air** qn/qch est une vraie bouffée de fraîcheur; **the first ~ of spring** le premier signe du printemps; **5** (word) **a ~ of** un soupçon de [*complaint, opposition, scandal*].
IDIOMS **don't hold your ~**○! ce n'est pas demain la veille○!; **to take sb's ~ away** couper le souffle à qn; **save your ~**○, **don't waste your ~**○ ne gaspille pas ta salive○; **it's the ~ of life to him** c'est toute sa vie; **to say sth under one's ~** dire qch à voix basse; **to laugh under one's ~** rire sous cape.

breathalyse GB, **breathalyze** US /ˈbreθəlaɪz/ *vtr* faire subir un alcootest à [*driver*]; **to be ~d** subir un alcootest.

Breathalyzer® /ˈbreθəlaɪzə(r)/ *n* alcootest *m*.

breathe /briːð/ **I** *vtr* **1** (inhale, respire) respirer [*air, oxygen, gas, scent*]; **to ~ one's last** lit rendre son dernier soupir; **to ~ its last** fig dire son dernier mot; **2** (exhale, blow) souffler [*air, smoke, germs*] (**on** sur); cracher [*fire, vapour*]; **3** (whisper) murmurer (**to** à); **I won't ~ a word** je n'en soufflerai pas un mot; **don't ~ a word!** pas un mot!; **4** (inspire with) **to ~ hope into sb** redonner de l'espoir à qn; **to ~ (some) life into sth** animer qch; **to ~ life into** [*God*] insuffler la vie dans; **to ~ new life into sth** donner un second souffle à qch.
II *vi* **1** (respire) respirer; **to ~ hard** ou **heavily** souffler fort, haleter; **to ~ easily** or **freely** lit respirer librement; **to ~ more easily** fig respirer; **2** (exhale, blow) **to ~ over sb/on sth** souffler sur qn/sur qch; **3** (wine) s'aérer.
IDIOMS **to ~ down sb's neck**○ (watch closely) être sur le dos de qn○; (be close behind) être sur les talons de qn○; **to ~ fire** fulminer; **to live and ~ sth** ne vivre que pour qch.

■ **breathe in**: ¶ **~ in** inspirer; ¶ **~ in [sth]**, **~ [sth] in** inhaler [*gas, fumes*].

■ **breathe out**: ¶ **~ out** expirer; ¶ **~ out [sth]**, **~ [sth] out** exhaler.

breather /ˈbriːðə(r)/ *n* **1** (from work) pause *f*; **to have** ou **take a ~** faire une pause; **2** (from pressure) répit *m*.

breathing /ˈbriːðɪŋ/ **I** *n* **1** (respiration) respiration *f*; **2** Ling (diacritic) esprit *m*; **rough/smooth ~** esprit rude/doux.
II *modif* [*difficulty, exercise*] respiratoire, de respiration.

breathing apparatus *n* masque *m* à oxygène.

breathing space *n* **1** (respite) répit *m*; **to give sb/to give oneself a ~** donner à qn/s'accorder un répit; **2** (postponement) délai *m* (**in which to do** pour faire).

breathless /ˈbreθlɪs/ *adj* **1** (out of breath) [*person, runner*] à bout de souffle; [*patient, asthmatic*] haletant; **to make** ou **leave sb ~** essouffler qn; **to be ~ from sth/from doing** être essoufflé par qch/après avoir fait; **2** (excited) [*hush, fascination*] extasié; [*enthusiasm*] extatique; **to be ~ with** avoir le souffle coupé par; **it left them ~** cela leur a coupé le souffle; **3** (fast) **at a ~ pace** à toute allure; **with ~ haste** en toute hâte; **4** littér [*day, night*] sans un souffle d'air; [*air*] immobile.

breathlessly /ˈbreθlɪslɪ/ *adv* **1** (out of breath) [*speak*] d'une voix haletante; [*collapse*] à bout de souffle; **2** (excitedly) [*explain, gabble*] précipitamment.

breathlessness /ˈbreθlɪsnɪs/ *n* essoufflement *m*.

breathtaking /ˈbreθteɪkɪŋ/ *adj* [*audacity, feat, pace, skill*] stupéfiant; [*scenery, view*] à vous couper le souffle.

breathtakingly /ˈbreθteɪkɪŋlɪ/ *adv* **~ beautiful** d'une beauté à vous couper le souffle; **~ audacious** d'une audace stupéfiante.

breath test **I** *n* alcootest *m*.
II *vtr* faire subir un alcootest à [*driver*]; **to be ~ed** subir un alcootest.

breath testing *n* alcootest *m*.

breathy /ˈbreθɪ/ *adj* voilé.

Brechtian /ˈbrektɪən/ *n, adj* brechtien/-ienne (*m/f*).

bred /bred/ *prét, pp* ▶ **breed**.

breech /bri:tʃ/ **I** *n* **1** Med (also **~ delivery**) accouchement *m* par le siège; **2** (of gun) culasse *f*.
II *modif* [*birth, delivery, presentation*] par le siège.
III *vtr* munir [qch] d'une culasse [*gun*].

breechblock /ˈbri:tʃblɒk/ *n* bloc *m* de culasse.

breeches /ˈbrɪtʃɪz/ *npl* **1** (also **knee ~**) culotte *f*; **a pair of ~** une culotte; **2** (also **riding ~**) culotte *f* (de cheval); **3**○ US pantalon *m*.
IDIOMS **to be too big for one's ~** avoir la grosse tête.

breeches buoy /ˈbri:tʃɪzbɔɪ/ *n* bouée-culotte *f*.

breechloading /ˈbri:tʃləʊdɪŋ/ *adj* chargé par la culasse.

breed /bri:d/ **I** *n* **1** Zool race *f*; **2** (type of person, thing) génération *f*.
II *vtr* (*prét, pp* **bred**) **1** Agric, Zool élever [*animals*]; produire [*plants*]; **2** fig engendrer [*disease, feeling, rumours, unrest*]; produire [*person*].
III *vi* (*prét, pp* **bred**) [*animals, people*] se reproduire; [*microorganisms*] se multiplier.
IV -bred *pp adj* **ill-/well-~** mal/bien élevé; **country-/city-~** élevé à la campagne/en ville.
IDIOMS **he was born and bred in Oxford, he's Oxford born and bred** il est né à Oxford et il y a grandi.
■ **breed out**: **~ out [sth], ~ [sth] out** éliminer [qch] par la sélection.

breeder /ˈbri:də(r)/ *n* **1** Agric, Zool (of animals) éleveur *m*; (of plants) producteur *m*; **2** (also **~ reactor**) Nucl surgénérateur *m*.

breeding /ˈbri:dɪŋ/ **I** *n* **1** Agric, Hort, Zool reproduction *f*; **2** (good manners) bonnes manières *fpl*; **a man of ~** un homme bien élevé; **3** Nucl surrégénération *f*.
II *adj* Zool reproducteur/-trice.

breeding ground *n* **1** Zool lieu *m* de reproduction (**for** de); **2** fig foyer *m* (**for** de).

breeding: **~ period, ~ season** *n* saison *f* de reproduction; **~ stock** *n* Agric ¢ reproducteurs *mpl*.

breeze /bri:z/ **I** *n* **1** Meteorol brise *f*; **sea ~** brise de mer; **in the ~** dans la brise; **a stiff/light ~** une forte/légère brise; **2**○ **it's a ~** c'est un jeu d'enfant; **3** Constr fraisil *m*.
II *vi* **to ~ in/out** entrer/sortir d'un air dégagé; **to ~ through life** traverser la vie avec insouciance; **to ~ through an exam** réussir un examen sans difficulté.
IDIOMS **to shoot the ~** US papoter.

breeze block /ˈbri:zblɒk/ *n* GB parpaing *m*, moellon *m*.

breezeway /ˈbri:zweɪ/ *n* US abri *m* (*entre maison et garage*).

breezily /ˈbri:zɪlɪ/ *adv* **1** (casually) de façon désinvolte; **2** (cheerfully) jovialement; **3** (confidently) avec assurance.

breezy /ˈbri:zɪ/ *adj* **1** Meteorol **it will be ~** il y aura de la brise; **it's a ~ morning** il y a une bonne brise ce matin; **2** [*place*] exposé au vent; **3** (cheerful) jovial; (confident) qui a de l'aplomb; **bright and ~** enjoué.

brekkie○, **brekky**○ /ˈbrekɪ/ *n* GB petit déj'○ *m*, petit déjeuner *m*.

Bremen /ˈbreɪmən/ ▶ **1818** *pr n* Brême.

Bren /bren/ *n* (also **~ gun**) fusil-mitrailleur *m*.

Bren (gun) carrier *n* chenillette *f*.

Brent crude /ˈbrent kru:d/ *n* Ind, Econ Brent *m*.

brent goose *n* (*pl* **brent geese**) bernache *f* cravant.

brethren /ˈbreðrən/ *npl* **1** Hist, Relig, hum frères *mpl*; **2** (in trades union) hum camarades *mpl*.

Breton /ˈbretən/ ▶ **1402** **I** *n* **1** (person) Breton/-onne *m/f*; **2** Ling breton *m*.
II *adj* breton/-onne.

Breton-speaking /ˌbretənˈspi:kɪŋ/ *adj* bretonnant.

breve /bri:v/ *n* **1** Mus double ronde *f*; **2** Ling brève *f*.

brevet /ˈbrevɪt/ *n* ≈ lettre *f* de service.

breviary /ˈbri:vɪərɪ, US -ɪerɪ/ *n* bréviaire *m*.

brevity /ˈbrevətɪ/ *n* (of event) brièveté *f*; (of speech) concision *f*; (of reply) laconisme *m*.
IDIOMS **~ is the soul of wit** Prov les plaisanteries les plus courtes sont toujours les meilleures.

brew /bru:/ **I** *n* **1** (beer) bière *f*; **special ~** cuvée *f* spéciale; ▶ **home brew**; **2** (tea) thé *m*, infusion *f*; **3** (unpleasant mixture) mixture *f*; **4** fig (of ideas, styles) mélange *m*.
II *vtr* brasser [*beer*]; préparer [*tea, mixture*]; fig préparer, mijoter○ [*plot, scandal*]; **home ~ed beer** bière brassée à la maison; **freshly ~ed coffee** café fraîchement passé.
III *vi* **1** [*beer*] fermenter; [*tea*] infuser; [*brewer*] brasser; **2** fig [*storm, crisis*] se préparer; [*quarrel, revolt*] se tramer; **there's something ~ing** il y a quelque chose qui se trame; **there's trouble ~ing** il y a de l'orage dans l'air.
■ **brew up** GB faire du thé.

brewer /ˈbru:ə(r)/ ▶ **1692** *n* brasseur *m*.

brewer: **~'s droop**○ *n* GB hum impuissance *f* sexuelle passagère (due à l'alcool); **~'s yeast** *n* levure *f* de bière.

brewery /ˈbru:ərɪ/ *n* brasserie *f*.

brewing /ˈbru:ɪŋ/ **I** *n* brasserie *f*.
II *modif* [*group, company*] qui fabrique de la bière; [*business, industry, magnate*] de la bière; [*method*] de brassage; [*equipment*] pour la fabrication de la bière.

brew-up○ /ˈbru:ʌp/ *n* GB thé *m*; **to have a ~** prendre le thé.

briar /ˈbraɪə(r)/ **I** *n* **1** (also **~ rose**) églantier *m*; **2** (heather) bruyère *f*; **3** (also **~ pipe**) pipe *f* en bruyère.
II briars *npl* (thorns) ronces *fpl*.

bribe /braɪb/ **I** *n* pot-de-vin *m*; **to offer sb a ~ to do sth** proposer un pot-de-vin à qn pour qu'il/elle fasse qch; **to give sb a ~** graisser la patte○ à qn; **to offer/accept a ~** offrir/accepter un pot-de-vin; **he was accused of taking ~s** il a été accusé de corruption.
II *vtr* **1** (large-scale) soudoyer [*police, person in authority*] (**with** avec; **to do** de faire); suborner [*witness*] (**to do** de faire); acheter [*voter*]; **2** (small-scale) graisser la patte à○ [*official*] (**to do** pour faire); **to ~ one's way into somewhere/past sb** graisser la patte à qn pour entrer quelque part/pour passer qn.

bribery /ˈbraɪbərɪ/ *n* corruption *f*; **to be open to ~** être ouvert à la corruption; **~ and corruption** tentative *f* de corruption.

bric-à-brac /ˈbrɪkəbræk/ *n* bric-à-brac *m*; **~ stall** éventaire *m* de brocanteur.

brick /brɪk/ **I** *n* **1** Constr brique *f*; **made of ~** en brique; **2** GB (child's toy) cube *m*; **3**○ †(kind person) type○/fille *m/f* sympa○; **you're a ~!** t'es un amour○!
II *modif* [*wall*] de briques; [*building*] en briques.
IDIOMS **it's like banging one's head against** ou **talking to a ~ wall** autant parler à un mur; **to ~ it**◑, **to shit ~s**◑ avoir les jetons◑; **to put one's money into ~s and mortar** investir dans la pierre; **to run up against** ou **run into a ~ wall** se heurter à un mur; **to be thick as a ~**○ être bête comme ses pieds.
■ **brick up**: **~ [sth] up, ~ up [sth]** murer [*fireplace, window*]; boucher [*hole*].

brick ~bat *n* fig violente critique *f*; **~-built** *adj* en briques; **~ cheese** *n* US fromage *m* à pâte dure.

brickie○ /ˈbrɪkɪ/ ▶ **1692** *n* GB maçon *m*.

brick: **~ kiln** *n* four *m* à briques; **~layer** ▶ **1692** *n* maçon *m*; **~laying** *n* maçonnerie *f*; **~ red** ▶ **1104** *n, adj* rouge (*m*) brique *inv*; **~work** *n* briquetage *m*; **~works** *n* briqueterie *f*; **~yard** *n* fabrique-entrepôt *f* de briques.

bridal /ˈbraɪdl/ *adj* [*dress etc*] de mariée; [*car, procession, bed, chamber*] des mariés; [*feast*] de noce.

bridal: **~ gown** *n* robe *f* de mariée; **~ party** *n* (+ *v sg ou pl*) proches *mpl* de la mariée; **~ suite** *n* suite *f* nuptiale; **~ wear** *n* robes *fpl* de mariée.

bride /braɪd/ *n* **1** (jeune) mariée *f*; **his ~** (during, after wedding) son épouse *f*; (before wedding) sa future épouse *f*; **the ~ and (bride)groom** les (jeunes) mariés *mpl*; **the Bride of Christ** l'épouse *f* du Christ; **2** (also **~-to-be**) future mariée *f*.

bridegroom /ˈbraɪdgru:m, -grʊm/ *n* **1** jeune marié *m*; **2** (also **~-to-be**) futur marié *m*.

bridesmaid /ˈbraɪdzmeɪd/ *n* demoiselle *f* d'honneur.
IDIOMS **always the ~ never the bride** l'éternel/-elle second/-e *m/f*.

bridge /brɪdʒ/ **I** *n* **1** Constr pont *m* (**over** sur; **across** au-dessus de); **2** fig (link) rapprochement *m*; **to build ~s** établir des relations (**between** entre); **3** (intermediate stage) (transitional) passerelle *f* (**between** entre); (springboard) tremplin *m* (**to** vers); **a ~ between school and university** une passerelle entre l'école et l'université; **a ~ to a new career** un tremplin vers une nouvelle carrière; **4** (on ship) passerelle *f*; **5** (of nose) arête *f*; **6** (of spectacles) arcade *f*; **7** (on guitar, violin) chevalet *m*; **8** Dent bridge *m*; **9** ▶ **1282** Games bridge *m*; **10** Mus (link) couplet *m*.
II *modif* [*game, player*] de bridge.
III *vtr* **1** lit construire un pont sur [*river*]; **2** fig **to ~ the gap between two countries/adversaries** effectuer un rapprochement entre ou rapprocher deux pays/adversaires; **to ~ the gap between the two lifestyles/levels** réduire l'écart entre les deux modes de vie/niveaux; **a snack ~s the gap between lunch and dinner** un goûter comble l'attente entre le déjeuner et le dîner; **to ~ a gap in [sth]** combler un vide dans [*conversation*]; combler un trou dans [*budget*]; combler une lacune dans [*knowledge*]; **3** (span) enjamber [*two eras*]; se maintenir tout au long de [*several periods*].
IDIOMS **a lot of water has flowed under**

the ~ beaucoup d'eau a coulé sous les ponts; **it's all water under the ~** c'est du passé; **don't cross your ~s before you come to them** Prov chaque chose en son temps Prov; **we'll cross that ~ when we come to it** on s'occupera de ce problème en temps voulu.

bridge: **~-builder** *n* Mil pontonnier *m*; fig (mediator) médiateur/-trice *m/f* (**between** entre); **~-building** *n* Mil installation *f* de ponts provisoires; fig médiation *f* (**between** entre); **~head** *n* Mil tête *f* de pont; **~ loan** *n* US Fin prêt *m* relais; **Bridge of Sighs** *pr n* Pont *m* des Soupirs; **~ party** *n* soirée *f* de bridge; **~ roll** *n* petit pain *m* brioché; **~work** *n* Dent bridge *m*.

bridging /ˈbrɪdʒɪŋ/ *n* (when climbing) opposition *f*.

bridging: **~ course** *n* GB Univ cours *m* de mise à niveau; **~ loan** *n* GB Fin prêt *m* relais.

bridle /ˈbraɪdl/ **I** *n* **1** Equit bride *f*; **2** fig frein *m*; **to put a ~ on** brider [*power, emotions*].
II *vtr* **1** (restrain) brider [*emotions, temper*]; **to ~ one's tongue** tenir sa langue; **2** Equit brider.
III *vi* (in anger) se cabrer (**at** contre; **with** sous l'effet de).

bridle path, **bridle track**, **bridleway** *n* piste *f* cavalière.

brief /briːf/ **▶ 1703** **I** *n* **1** GB gen (remit) attributions *fpl*; (role) tâche *f*; **it is your ~** ou **your ~ is to do** votre tâche consiste à faire; **with a ~ for** chargé de [*environment, immigration*]; **with a ~ to do** dont la tâche consiste à faire; **to fall within/to exceed sb's ~** faire partie des/dépasser les attributions de qn; **2** Jur dossier *m*; **to take** ou **accept a ~** accepter un dossier; **3** GB (instructions) directives *fpl*; **designer's ~** directives du concepteur; **to prepare a ~** préparer un dossier (**for** pour); **to work to a ~** suivre des directives.
II briefs *npl* (undergarment) slip *m*; **a pair of ~s** un slip.
III *adj* **1** (concise) [*account, event, summary, speech*] bref/brève; [*reply*] laconique; **to be ~, I will be ~** je serai bref; **the news in ~** les brèves; **2** (short) [*skirt*] court; [*swimwear*] minuscule; **3** (abrupt) [*manner, reply*] brusque (**with** avec).
IV in brief *adv phr* en bref.
V *vtr* **1** gen, Mil informer [*journalist, politician, worker*] (**on** de); donner des instructions à [*police, troops*] (**on** sur); donner des directives à [*artist, designer*] (**on** sur); **to be well ~ed** être bien au courant; **2** Jur confier une cause à [*lawyer*]; **to ~ sb to do** engager qn pour faire.
VI *v refl* **to ~ oneself on sth** se renseigner sur qch.
IDIOMS **to hold a watching ~ on sb** tenir qn à l'œil; **to hold no ~ for sb** ne pas se faire l'avocat de qn.

briefcase /ˈbriːfkeɪs/ *n* (with handle) serviette *f*; (without handle) porte-documents *m inv*.

briefing /ˈbriːfɪŋ/ **I** *n* **1** (meeting) briefing *m* (**on** sur), réunion *f* d'information (**on** sur); **press ~** briefing *m* de presse; **2** (information) (*sans pl*) informations *fpl*; **to give sb a ~ on sth** mettre qn au courant de qch.
II *modif* [*document, session*] d'information; [*officer*] chargé de l'information.

briefly /ˈbriːflɪ/ *adv* **1** (concisely) [*describe, speak*] brièvement; [*reply, say*] laconiquement; **2** (for short time) [*affect, look, pause*] un bref instant; [*work, meet*] brièvement; **3** (in short) en bref.

brier *n* = **briar**.

brig /brɪɡ/ *n* **1** Naut brick *m*; **2** US Naut (prison) cale *f*; **3**○ US argot des militaires (prison) taule◑ *f*.

Brig /brɪɡ/ **▶ 1268** (*abrév écrite* = **Brigadier**) **~ M. Sands** le général M. Sands.

brigade /brɪˈɡeɪd/ *n* **1** (+ *v sg ou pl*) brigade *f* also hum, pej; **cavalry ~** brigade de cavalerie; **the anti-smoking ~** la brigade antitabac; **he is one of the old ~** hum il fait partie de la vieille garde; **2** (team) équipe *f*.

brigadier /ˌbrɪɡəˈdɪə(r)/ **▶ 1612** *n* général *m* de brigade.

brigand‡ /ˈbrɪɡənd/ *n* brigand *m*.

brigandage‡ /ˈbrɪɡəndɪdʒ/ *n* brigandage *m*.

bright /braɪt/ **I** *adj* **1** (vivid) [*colour, blue, red*] vif/vive; [*garment, carpet, wallpaper*] (of one colour) de couleur vive; (of several colours) aux couleurs vives; **he went ~ red** il est devenu tout rouge; **2** (clear) [*sun, sunshine*] éclatant; [*room, location, day*] clair; [*weather*] radieux/-ieuse; [*sky*] lumineux/-euse; **~ spell** éclaircie *f*; **it will become ~er later** le temps doit s'éclaircir plus tard; **3** (shiny) [*star, moon, eye, coin, metal*] brillant; [*jewel*] étincelant; **4** (clever) intelligent; **that wasn't very ~ (of you)** ce n'était pas très malin (de ta part); **a ~ idea** une idée lumineuse; **5** (cheerful) [*person, mood*] joyeux/-euse; [*smile, face*] radieux/-ieuse; [*greeting*] chaleureux/-euse; **to look on the ~ side** voir le bon côté des choses; **6** (promising) [*future, prospect, outlook, picture*] brillant (*never pred*) ; **one of our ~est hopes in athletics** l'un de nos meilleurs espoirs en athlétisme; **in ~er days** en des jours meilleurs.
II brights○ *npl* US Aut pleins phares *mpl*.
III *adv* [*shine, burn*] d'un vif éclat.
IV bright and early *adv phr* [*get up, set off*] de bonne heure.

brighten /ˈbraɪtn/ *vtr, vi* ▶ **brighten up**.
■ **brighten up**: ¶ **~ up 1** (become cheerful) [*person, mood*] s'égayer (**at** à); [*face, expression*] s'illuminer (**at** à); [*eyes*] s'allumer (**at** à; **with** de); **2** (improve) [*prospect, outlook, situation*] s'améliorer; [*weather, sky*] s'éclaircir; ¶ **~ up [sth], ~ [sth] up 1** (make colourful, cheerful) égayer [*room, home, atmosphere, day, life*]; **2** (illuminate) [*sun, light*] éclairer; **3** (improve) rendre [qch] plus réjouissant [*prospects, future*].

bright-eyed /ˌbraɪtˈaɪd/ *adj* aux yeux brillants.
IDIOMS **~ and bushy-tailed** frais et dispos.

bright lights *npl* fig **the ~** les lumières *fpl* de la ville.

brightly /ˈbraɪtlɪ/ *adv* **1** (vividly) [*dressed*] de couleurs vives; **~ coloured** (several colours) aux couleurs vives; (of one colour) de couleur vive; **a ~ painted mural** une peinture murale aux couleurs vives; **2** (of sun, fire) [*shine, burn*] d'un éclat vif; (of eyes, metal) [*shine, sparkle, twinkle*] intensément; **3** (intensely) [*lit, illuminated*] brillamment; **4** (cheerfully) [*smile, say, greet*] joyeusement.

brightness /ˈbraɪtnɪs/ *n* **1** (of colour, light, sunshine, star, sky, smile) éclat *m*; **2** (of room, place) clarté *f*; **3** (of metal, eyes) brillant *m*; **4** (cheerfulness) vivacité *f*; **5** TV luminosité *f*; **to adjust the ~** régler la luminosité.

Bright's disease /ˈbraɪts dɪziːz/ **▶ 1354** *n* néphrite *f* chronique.

bright spark○ *n* GB petit/-e futé/-e○ *m/f*; **some ~** iron un petit malin/une petite maligne *m/f*.

bright young thing *n* GB **to be a ~** faire partie de la jeunesse dorée; **the ~s** la jeunesse dorée.

brill /brɪl/ **I** *n* Zool barbue *f*.
II○ *adj, excl* GB (*abrév* = **brilliant**) super○.

brilliance /ˈbrɪlɪəns/ *n* (of light, poetry, music) éclat *m*; (of person) génie *m*.

brilliant /ˈbrɪlɪənt/ **I** *n* (diamond) brillant *m*.
II *adj* **1** (clever, successful) [*student, mind, invention, career, success*] brillant; **2** (bright) [*colour, jewel, plumage*] éclatant; **3** GB ○(fantastic) [*holiday, party, evening*] génial○; [*person*] super○; **we had a ~ time** c'était génial; **to be ~ at sth** être douée en qch; **to be ~ at doing** avoir le don de faire.
III *excl* super○! also iron.

brilliantine /ˈbrɪlɪəntiːn/ *n* brillantine *f*.

brilliantly /ˈbrɪlɪəntlɪ/ *adv* **1** (very well) [*write, perform, argue*] brillamment; **2** (particularly) [*witty, clever, inventive*] extrêmement; **3** (very brightly) [*shine, sparkle*] avec éclat; [*lit, illuminated*] vivement; **~ coloured, ~ colourful** aux couleurs éclatantes.

Brillo pad® /ˈbrɪləʊ pæd/ *n* tampon *m* Jex®.

brim /brɪm/ **I** *n* (all contexts) bord *m*; **a wide-brimmed hat** un chapeau à large bord; **to fill sth to the ~** remplir qch à ras bord; **filled to the ~ with** rempli jusqu'au bord de [*liquid, objects*]; plein à craquer de [*people*].
II *vi* (*p prés etc* **-mm-**) **to ~ with** lit [*receptacle*] être plein à ras bord de; fig déborder de; **~ming with** débordant de; **his eyes ~med with tears** ses yeux se remplirent de larmes.
■ **brim over** lit, fig déborder (**with** de).

brimful /ˈbrɪmfʊl/ *adj* **1** [*cup, pan, bath*] plein à déborder; **2** fig **~ of** débordant de.

brimstone /ˈbrɪmstəʊn/ *n* **1**‡ (sulphur) soufre *m*; **2** Zool (butterfly) citron *m*.

brindled /ˈbrɪndld/ *adj* tacheté.

brine /braɪn/ *n* **1** (sea water) eau *f* de mer; **2** Culin saumure *f*; **3** liter (sea) mer *f*.

bring /brɪŋ/ (*prét, pp* **brought**) **I** *vtr* **1** (convey, carry) apporter [*present, powers, supplies, message, news, rain, destruction, change, happiness, consolation, hope*]; **have you brought your camera?** as-tu pris or apporté ton appareil-photo?; **wait and see what tomorrow ~s** attends de voir ce que demain nous apportera; **to ~ sth with one** apporter qch; **to ~ sb flowers/a cake** apporter des fleurs/un gâteau à qn; **the case has brought him publicity** l'affaire lui a fait de la publicité; **to ~ sb wealth/fame** rendre qn riche/célèbre; **to ~ sth to** (contribute) apporter qch à [*school, work, area*]; **it has brought prosperity to the region** cela a rendu la région prospère; **to ~ one's talents to sth** apporter son talent à qch; **to ~ one's experience to sth** faire bénéficier qch de son expérience; **that ~s the total to 100** cela fait un total de 100; **to ~ a smile to sb's face** faire sourire qn; **to ~ a blush to sb's cheeks** faire rougir qn; **to ~ sth to a halt** arrêter qch; **to ~ the conversation round** ou **around to** amener la conversation à; **to ~ sth into** faire entrer qch dans [*house, room*]; introduire qch dans [*conversation, story*]; **to ~ sth into existence** créer qch; **to ~ sth upstairs** monter qch; **the wind brought the tree down** le vent a fait tomber l'arbre; **don't forget to ~ it home** n'oublie pas de le rapporter; **to ~ shame/disgrace on sb** attirer la honte/le déshonneur sur qn; **to ~ sth on** ou **upon oneself** attirer qch; **you brought it on yourself** tu l'as cherché; **her remarks brought gasps of surprise from the audience** ses propos ont provoqué l'étonnement dans le public; **his novel brought praise from the critics** son roman lui a valu les louanges de la critique; **2** (come with) amener [*friend, relative, dog*]; **to ~ sb with one** amener qn (avec soi); **to ~ sb to** amener qn à [*wedding, party, office*]; **3** (lead, draw) **the path ~s you to the church** le chemin te conduit jusqu'à l'église; **the Games brought people to the city** les Jeux ont attiré du monde vers la ville; **the noise brought them to the window** le bruit les a attirés à la fenêtre; **I brought him to the ground** je l'ai fait tomber; **that ~s me to the question de**; ceci m'amène à la question de; **to ~ sb to himself/herself** ramener qn à la réalité; **what ~s you here?** qu'est-ce qui t'amène?; **to ~ sb to do sth** faire faire qch à qn; **I couldn't ~ him to accept** je n'ai pas pu lui faire accepter; **to ~ sb/a dog into the country** faire entrer or introduire qn/un chien dans le pays; **to ~ sb into the room** faire entrer qn dans la pièce; **to ~ sb into contact with sth** faire connaître qch à qn; **to ~ sb into contact with sb** mettre qn en contact avec qn; **to ~ sb**

home (transport home) raccompagner qn, ramener qn; (to meet family) amener qn à la maison; **4** TV, Radio **the game will be brought to you live from Sydney** le match sera retransmis en direct de Sydney; **modern technology ~s the war into your living room** la technologie moderne fait entrer la guerre jusque chez vous; **we ~ you all the latest news** on vous donne les dernières nouvelles; **'brought to you by Sudso Soap'** 'qui vous est offert par Sudso Soap' **5** Jur, Admin **to ~ a case/a dispute before the court** porter une affaire/un litige devant le tribunal; **to ~ sb before the court** faire comparaître qn devant le tribunal; **to ~ a matter before the committee/a bill before parliament** soumettre une question au comité/un projet de loi au parlement.

II *v refl* **to ~ oneself to do** se décider à faire; **I couldn't ~ myself to get up/to tell him** je n'ai pas pu me lever/le lui dire.

■ **bring about**: **~ about [sth], ~ [sth] about** provoquer [*change, reform, war, disaster, death*]; amener [*settlement, reconciliation*]; entraîner [*success, failure, defeat*].

■ **bring along**: ¶ **~ along [sth], ~ [sth] along** apporter [*object*]; ¶ **~ along [sb], ~ [sb] along** amener, venir avec [*friend, partner*].

■ **bring back**: **~ back [sth], ~ [sth] back 1** (return with) rapporter [*souvenir, gift*] (**from** de); **to ~ sb back sth** rapporter qch à qn; **2** (restore) redonner [*colour, shine*]; **to ~ sb's memory/sight back** rendre la mémoire/vue à qn; **3** (reintroduce) rétablir [*currency, custom*]; restaurer [*monarchy, democracy*]; **4** (restore memory of) rappeler [*night, time, occasion*]; **seeing her brought it all back to me** tout m'est revenu lorsque je l'ai vue; **to ~ back memories** ranimer des souvenirs; **to ~ back memories of sth** ranimer le souvenir de qch.

■ **bring down**: ¶ **~ down [sth], ~ [sth] down 1** (cause collapse of) renverser [*government, dictator*]; **2** (reduce) réduire [*inflation, unemployment, expenditure*]; faire baisser [*rate, level, price, temperature*]; diminuer [*cost of living, swelling*]; **3** (shoot down) abattre [*plane, grouse, tiger*]; **4** (cause to hit) **to ~ [sth] down on sb/sth** abattre [qch] sur qn/qch [*cane, hammer*]; **to ~ sb's wrath down on sb** littér ou hum attirer la colère de qn sur qn; ¶ **~ [sb] down**○ déprimer [*person*].

■ **bring forth**: **~ forth [sth], ~ [sth] forth 1** (provoke) susciter [*question, protest, scorn*]; **2** littér (produce) produire [*object, fruit, blossom*]; faire jaillir [*water*]; **3** littér donner naissance à [*child*].

■ **bring forward**: **~ forward [sth], ~ [sth] forward 1** (make sooner) avancer [*meeting, wedding, election*] (**by** de); **2** (propose) avancer [*proposals, plan*]; proposer [*bill, amendment, motion*]; **3** Accts reporter [*total, balance, deficit*]; **balance brought forward: £354.90** report: £354.90; **4** (bring in) présenter [*witness, person*].

■ **bring in**: ¶ **~ in [sth]** rapporter [*amount, money, interest*]; introduire [*custom*]; ¶ **~ in [sth], ~ [sth] in 1** (introduce) introduire [*legislation, measure, reference, new character*]; **2** Agric rentrer [*crop, harvest*]; récolter [*wheat, corn, fruit*]; ¶ **~ in [sb], ~ [sb] in 1** (involve) faire appel à [*consultant, expert, reinforcements, police, army*] (**from** de; **as** pour être); **if I could ~ in Mrs Cox at this point**... j'aimerais faire intervenir Mme Cox sur ce point...; **2** (to police station) amener [qn] (au poste) [*suspect*]; **to be brought in for questioning** être amené au poste pour être interrogé.

■ **bring into**: **~ [sb] into** faire participer [qn] à [*conversation, organization*]; **don't ~ my mother into this!** laisse ma mère en dehors de ça!

■ **bring off**: **~ off [sth], ~ [sth] off** réussir [*feat, performance*]; conclure [*deal*]; décrocher [*victory*].

■ **bring on**: ¶ **~ on [sth], ~ [sth] on 1** (provoke) provoquer [*attack, migraine, fit, labour*]; être à l'origine de [*bronchitis, rheumatism, pneumonia*]; **what brought that on?** (to someone) qu'est-ce qui t'a pris?; **2** (encourage) accélérer la pousse de [*plant, crop*]; ¶ **~ on [sb], ~ [sb] on 1** (to stage, field) faire entrer [*dancer, substitute*]; **2** (encourage) pousser [*player, child*].

■ **bring out**: ¶ **~ out [sth], ~ [sth] out 1** sortir [*gun, handkerchief etc*]; **2** Comm sortir [*edition, volume, new model*]; **3** (highlight) faire ressortir [*detail, colour, melody, flavour, meaning, instinct, spirit*]; **to ~ out the artist/the child in sb** faire ressortir l'artiste/l'enfant en qn; ¶ **~ out [sb], ~ [sb] out 1** (draw out) faire parler [*guest, interviewee*]; **2** (on strike) mettre [qn] en grève [*workers*]; **3 to ~ sb out in spots** donner des boutons à qn.

■ **bring round**: **~ [sb] round 1** (revive) faire revenir [qn] à soi; **2** (convince) convaincre; **to ~ sb round to one's way of thinking** amener qn à partager ses vues.

■ **bring to** = **bring round**.

■ **bring together**: **~ together [sth/sb], ~ [sth/sb] together 1** (assemble) réunir [*family, experts, sides, themes*]; **2** (create bond between) rapprocher [*couple, lovers, siblings*]; **it brought us closer together** cela nous a rapprochés.

■ **bring up**: ¶ **~ up [sth], ~ [sth] up 1** (mention) aborder, parler de [*question, subject*]; **2** (vomit) vomir, rendre [*food*]; ¶ **~ up [sb], ~ [sb] up** élever; **to ~ sb up to do** apprendre à [qn] à faire; **to be brought up by sb/in China** être élevé par qn/en Chine; **to be brought up as a Catholic** recevoir une éducation catholique; **to be brought up on stories of war** être nourri de récits de guerre; **it's the way I was brought up** c'est comme ça que j'ai été élevé; **well/badly brought up** bien/mal élevé.

bring and buy sale *n* GB vente *f* de charité.

brink /brɪŋk/ *n* lit, fig (edge) bord *m*; **on the ~ of doing** sur le point de faire; **on the ~ of disaster/success** à deux doigts du désastre/succès; **to bring sb to the ~ of sth** conduire qn au bord de qch; **to pull back from the ~ of war** renoncer à la guerre au dernier moment.

brinkmanship /ˈbrɪŋkmənʃɪp/ *n* art *m* d'aller jusqu'aux limites du possible.

briny /ˈbraɪnɪ/ **I** *n* **the ~**○† hum la grande bleue *f*.

II *adj* saumâtre.

brio /ˈbriːəʊ/ *n* brio *m*.

briquet(te) /brɪˈket/ *n* briquette *f*.

brisk /brɪsk/ *adj* **1** (efficient) [*manner, tone, gesture*] vif/vive; [*person*] efficace; **2** (energetic) [*pace, trot, movements*] rapide; [*debate*] animé; **to go for a ~ walk/swim** faire une bonne marche/quelques longueurs; **they were walking/working at a ~ pace** ils marchaient/travaillaient à vive allure; **3** (good) [*business, sales, trade*] florissant; **~ trading on the stock exchange** un marché actif à la Bourse; **business/betting was ~** les affaires/les paris marchaient bien; **the hamburger stall is doing a ~ trade** le stand des hamburgers marche bien; **we've been doing a ~ trade in suitcases** nos valises se sont bien vendues; **4** (invigorating) [*air, climate*] vivifiant; [*wind*] vif/vive; **a ~ March morning** un frais matin de mars.

brisket /ˈbrɪskɪt/ *n* Culin poitrine *f*.

briskly /ˈbrɪsklɪ/ *adv* **1** (efficiently) [*say, ask, reply*] vivement, avec vivacité; [*work*] rapidement; **she moved ~ on to the next point** elle s'est attaquée sans tarder au point suivant; **to deal ~ with a problem** résoudre un problème de façon efficace; **2** (quickly) [*walk*] d'un bon pas, à vive allure; **3** (well) [*sell*] très vite, très bien.

briskness /ˈbrɪsknɪs/ *n* (in manner, tone) vivacité *f*; (in activity, movements) dynamisme *m*.

brisling /ˈbrɪzlɪŋ/ *n* sprat *m*.

bristle /ˈbrɪsl/ **I** *n* **1** (single hair) (on brush, chin, animal, plant) poil *m*; (on pig) soie *f*; **2** (material) (on brush, mat) (real) soies *fpl*; (synthetic) poils *mpl*.

II *vi* **1** lit [*fur*] se hérisser; [*hairs*] se dresser; **2** (react angrily) se hérisser (**at** à; **with** de).

■ **bristle with**: **~ with [sth]** être hérissé de [*spikes, arms, pins, problems*]; grouiller de [*police, soldiers*].

bristly /ˈbrɪslɪ/ *adj* [*hair, beard, fibres*] dru; [*skin, surface*] couvert de poils durs; **Daddy, you're all ~!** Papa, tu piques!

Bristol board *n* bristol *m*.

bristols○ /ˈbrɪstlz/ *npl* GB nichons◑ *mpl*, seins *mpl*.

Brit○ /brɪt/ *n* Britannique *mf*.

Britain /ˈbrɪtn/ *pr n* (also **Great ~**) Grande-Bretagne *f*.

Britannia /brɪˈtænjə/ *pr n* Britannia.

Britannia metal *n* métal *m* anglais.

Britannic /brɪˈtænɪk/ *adj* britannique; **His/Her ~ Majesty** Sa Majesté britannique.

britches○ *n* US = **breeches** 3.

Briticism /ˈbrɪtɪsɪzəm/ *n* anglicisme *m*.

British /ˈbrɪtɪʃ/ ▶ 1486 **I** *npl* **the ~** les Britanniques *mpl*.

II *adj* britannique; **the ~ embassy/ambassador** l'ambassade *f*/l'ambassadeur *m* de Grande-Bretagne.

IDIOMS **the best of ~ (luck)**○! GB bonne chance!

British: **~ Airports Authority, BAA** *n* administration *f* des aéroports britanniques; **~ Antarctic Territory** *n* Territoire *m* britannique de l'Antarctique; **~ Army of the Rhine, BAOR** *n* GB Mil forces *fpl* britanniques en Allemagne; **~ Broadcasting Corporation, BBC** *n* BBC *f*; **~ Columbia, BC** *n* Colombie *f* britannique; **~ disease** *n* mal *m* britannique; **~ English** *n, adj* anglais (*m*) britannique.

Britisher /ˈbrɪtɪʃə(r)/ *n* US Britannique *mf*.

British: **~ Gas** *n* GB société *f* de distribution de gaz britannique; **~ Isles** *npl* îles *fpl* Britanniques; **~ Legion** *n* association *f* britannique d'anciens militaires; **~ Museum, BM** *n* British Museum *m*; **~ Rail, BR** *n* société *f* nationale des chemins de fer britanniques; **~ Telecom, BT** *n* GB société *f* britannique de télécommunications.

Briton /ˈbrɪtn/ *n* Britannique *mf*; Hist Breton/-onne *m/f* (*anciens habitants de la Grande-Bretagne*).

Brittany /ˈbrɪtənɪ/ ▶ 1273 *pr n* Bretagne *f*; **in ~** en Bretagne.

brittle /ˈbrɪtl/ **I** *n* (sweet) praline *f*.

II *adj* **1** lit [*twig*] cassant; [*fingernails, hair*] fragile; **2** fig [*relationship, confidence*] fragile; [*personality*] brusque; [*tone, laughter*] cassant.

brittle bones, brittle-bone disease *n* décalcification *f*.

bro /brəʊ/ **I** *n*○† (*abrév* = **brother**) frère *m*.

II Bro *n* Relig *abrév écrite* = **Brother**.

broach /brəʊtʃ/ **I** *n* **1** Tech foret *m*; **2** Culin broche *f*.

II *vtr* aborder [*subject*]; entamer [*bottle etc*].

broad /brɔːd/ ▶ 1412 **I** *n* **1**○ US (woman) grosse○ *f*, femme *f*; **2** Anat **the ~ of the back** le haut *m* du dos.

II *adj* **1** (wide) [*chest, face, grin, ribbon, river, street*] large; **to have a ~ back** lit, fig avoir le dos large; **to be ~ in the hips** être large de hanches; **to grow ~er** s'élargir; **2** (extensive) [*area, expanse, plain*] vaste; **3** (wide-ranging) [*choice, range*] grand; [*introduction, invitation, syllabus, consensus, feeling, implication*] général; [*alliance, coalition, movement*] large; **there is ~ support for the law** la loi a été largement approuvée; **4** (general) [*interpretation, meaning, term*] large; [*aim, base, notion, option, outline, principle*] général; **5** (liberal) [*opinion, view*]

large; **to have a ~ mind** avoir l'esprit large; **6** (unsubtle) [*wink*] bien visible; **to drop ~ hints about** faire des allusions évidentes à; **to drop sb a ~ hint that** faire comprendre à qn que; **7** (pronounced) [*accent*] fort (*before n*); **to speak with** ou **in a ~ Welsh accent** parler avec un fort accent gallois; **a poem in ~ Scots** une poésie en dialecte écossais; **8** (complete) **in ~ daylight** en plein jour; **9** (vulgar) [*joke, humour*] grossier/-ière; **10** Ling [*transcription*] phonétique.
IDIOMS **it's as ~ as it's long** c'est du pareil au même○.

B road *n* GB Transp route *f* secondaire.

broad-based /ˌbrɔːd'beɪst/ *adj* [*approach, campaign*] global; [*education*] généralisé; [*coalition*] d'origine très variée; [*consensus*] général; **the party has a ~ membership** les membres du parti sont d'origine très variée.

broad: **~ bean** *n* Bot, Culin fève *f*; **~brush** *adj* [*approach, sketch, survey*] sommaire.

broadcast /'brɔːdkɑːst, US -kæst/ **I** *n* émission *f*; **TV/radio ~** émission télévisée/radiophonique; **sports/live ~** émission sportive/en direct; **news ~** bulletin *m* d'informations; **the ~ of sth** la diffusion de qch; **sb's ~ to the nation** l'allocution radiotélévisée de qn à la nation.
II *vtr* (*prét, pp* **~** ou **~ed**) **1** [*station, person*] diffuser [*programme, message*] (**to** à); **2** (tell) péj raconter; **there's no need to ~ it!** ce n'est pas la peine de le crier sur les toits!; **3** Agric disséminer [*seeds*].
III *vi* (*prét, pp* **~** ou **~ed**) **1** [*station, channel*] émettre (**on** sur); **2** [*person*] faire une émission; **to ~ on the radio/on gardening** faire des émissions à la radio/sur le jardinage.
IV *adv* Agric [*sow*] en dispersion.
V *pp adj* (on TV) télévisé; (on radio) radiodiffusé; (on both) radiotélévisé.

broadcaster /'brɔːdkɑːstə(r), US -kæst-/ ▶ **1692** *n* animateur/-trice *m/f*; **news ~** journaliste *mf* de radio or télévision; **a ~ on opera** un animateur spécialiste d'opéra.

broadcasting /brɔːdkɑːstɪŋ, US -kæst-/ **I** *n* (field) communication *f* audiovisuelle; **to work in ~** travailler dans l'audiovisuel; (action) diffusion *f*; **religious/children's ~** programmes *mpl* religieux/pour les enfants.
II *modif* [*authorities, executive, legislation, restriction, service, technology, union*] de la communication audiovisuelle.

broadcasting: **~ ban** *n* interdiction *f* d'antenne; **Broadcasting Standards Council** *n* GB *organisme responsable du maintien de certaines normes dans l'audiovisuel*; ≈ CSA.

broad: **~-chested** *adj* au torse large; **Broad Church** *n* lit *groupe de l'église anglicane défendant la liberté d'interprétation de la doctrine*; **~cloth** *n* Tex drap *m* fin.

broaden /'brɔːdn/ **I** *vtr* **1** (extend) étendre [*appeal, experience, scope*]; élargir [*horizons, knowledge, outlook*]; **travel ~s the mind** les voyages ouvrent l'esprit; **2** (widen) élargir [*path, road*].
II *vi* **1** (expand) [*appeal, horizons, outlook, scope*] s'élargir; **2** (widen) [*river, road, pipe, smile*] s'élargir; [*skirt*] s'évaser.
■ **broaden out** [*river, road, pipe*] s'élargir; [*conversation*] s'étendre; **to ~ out into** [*river*] s'élargir en; [*conversation*] s'étendre à.

broad: **~ jump** *n* US Sport saut *m* en longueur; **~-leaved** *adj* Bot feuillu; **~ left** *n* GB Pol coalition *f* de gauche; **~loom** *n* (also **~loom carpet**) tapis *m* en grande largeur.

broadly /'brɔːdlɪ/ *adv* **1** (in general) [*agree, conform, correspond*] en gros; [*compatible, similar, true*] globalement; **~ speaking** en règle générale; **2** (widely) [*grin, smile*] largement.

broadly-based *adj* = **broad-based**.

broadminded /ˌbrɔːd'maɪndɪd/ *adj* [*person*] large d'esprit; [*attitude*] libéral.

broadness /'brɔːdnɪs/ *n* (width) largeur *f*; **the ~ of her mind** sa largeur d'esprit.

broad: **~sheet** *n* journal *m* de grand format; **~-shouldered** *adj* large d'épaules.

broadside /'brɔːdsaɪd/ **I** *n* **1** (criticism) attaque *f* cinglante; **to aim** ou **deliver a ~ at** lancer une attaque cinglante contre; **2** Naut (of ship) flanc *m*; (enemy fire) bordée *f*; **to deliver a ~** lâcher une bordée.
II *adv* (also **~ on**) par le travers; **a ship seen ~** un bateau vu de flanc.

broadsword /'brɔːdsɔːd/ *n* épée *f* de chevalerie.

Broadway /'brɔːdweɪ/ *pr n* Theat Broadway; **on ~** à Broadway; **an off-~ production** *pièce donnée dans une salle à proximité de Broadway.*

brocade /brə'keɪd/ **I** *n* brocart *m*.
II *modif* [*curtain, cushion*] de brocart; [*sofa*] recouvert de brocart.
III *vtr* brocher.

broccoli /'brɒkəlɪ/ *n* ȼ Bot brocoli *m*; Culin brocolis *mpl*.

brochure /'brəʊʃə(r), US brəʊ'ʃʊər/ *n* gen, Tourism, Comm (booklet) brochure *f*; (larger) catalogue *m*; (leaflet) dépliant *m*; (for hotel) prospectus *m*.

brogue /brəʊg/ *n* **1** (shoe) richelieu *m*; **2** (accent) accent *m* du terroir; **Irish ~** accent irlandais.

broil /brɔɪl/ **I** *vtr* **1** US Culin faire griller [*meat*]; [*barbecue*] griller [*meat*]; **2** fig [*sun, heat*] griller○.
II *vi* Culin, fig griller.

broiler /'brɔɪlə(r)/ *n* **1** (also **~ chicken**) poulet *m* d'élevage; **2** US (grill) gril *m*; **3**○ (hot day) journée *f* torride.

broiler: **~ house** *n* éleveuse *f*; **~ pan** *n* US gril *m*.

broiling /'brɔɪlɪŋ/ *adj* [*heat, weather*] étouffant.

broke /brəʊk/ **I** *prét* ▶ **break**.
II○ *adj* (insolvent) [*person*] fauché○; [*company, Treasury*] insolvable; **to go ~** [*company*] faire faillite.
IDIOMS **to go for ~** jouer le tout pour le tout.

broken /'brəʊkən/ **I** *pp* ▶ **break**.
II *adj* **1** (damaged) [*glass, window*] brisé; [*fingernail, tooth, bone, leg*] cassé; [*bottle, chair, handle, hinge, toy*] cassé; [*radio, washing machine*] détraqué; **'do not use on ~ skin'** (of skin product) 'ne pas utiliser en cas de plaies ouvertes'; **2** (interrupted) [*circle, line*] brisé; [*voice*] brisé; **a warm day with ~ cloud** un temps chaud, couvert avec éclaircies; **3** (irregular) [*coastline*] découpé; [*ground*] accidenté; **4** (depressed) [*man, woman*] brisé; [*spirit*] abattu; **5** (not honoured) [*contract, engagement, promise, vow*] rompu; [*appointment*] manqué; **6** (flawed) (*épith*) [*French*] mauvais (*before n*); [*sentence*] maladroit.

broken: **~ amount** *n* Fin paquet *m* d'actions hors quotité; **~ chord** *n* Mus accord *m* arpégé.

broken-down /ˌbrəʊkən'daʊn/ *adj* (*épith*) **1** (non-functional) [*vehicle, machine*] en panne; **2** (damaged) [*building, wall*] délabré; [*shoe*] éculé.

broken heart /ˌbrəʊkən 'hɑːt/ *n* cœur *m* brisé; **she has a ~** elle a le cœur brisé; **to die of a ~** mourir de chagrin.

broken-hearted /ˌbrəʊkən'hɑːtɪd/ *adj* [*person*] au cœur brisé; **to be ~** avoir le cœur brisé.

broken: **~ home** *n* Sociol famille *f* désunie; **~ lot** *n* Fin = **broken amount**.

brokenly /'brəʊkənlɪ/ *adv* [*say*] d'une voix brisée.

broken marriage *n* foyer *m* désuni.

broken reed *n* fig **to be a ~** [*person*] être incapable.

broken: **~ vowel** *n* Ling diphtongue *f*; **~ wind** *n* Vet pousse *f*; **~-winded** *adj* Vet poussif/-ive.

broker /'brəʊkə(r)/ ▶ **1692** **I** *n* Fin, Comm courtier *m*; (on stock exchange) courtier *m* en Bourse; Naut courtier *m* maritime; **commodity ~** courtier *m* de marchandises; **foreign exchange ~** cambiste *mf*; **insurance ~** courtier *m* d'assurance; **note ~** US opérateur/-trice *m/f* sur effets de commerce; **real-estate ~** US agent *m* immobilier; **power ~** négociateur/-trice *m/f* influent/-e; **an honest ~** fig un médiateur sincère.
II *vtr* Pol négocier.
III *vi* agir en médiateur (**between** entre).

brokerage /'brəʊkərɪdʒ/ **I** *n* (fee, business) courtage *m*.
II *modif* [*company*] de courtage.

broking /'brəʊkɪŋ/ GB, **brokering** /'brəʊkərɪŋ/ US *n* courtage *m*; **commodity/insurance ~** courtage *m* de marchandises/en assurance.

brolly○ /'brɒlɪ/ *n* GB pépin○ *m*, parapluie *m*.

bromide /'brəʊmaɪd/ **I** *n* **1** Pharm bromure *m*; **potassium ~** bromure de potassium; **2** fig (comment) platitude *f* (lénifiante); **3** Phot gélatino-bromure *m* d'argent; **4** Print bromure *m*.
II *modif* [*printer, paper, printing*] au gélatino-bromure d'argent.

bromine /'brəʊmiːn/ **I** *n* brome *m*.
II *modif* [*fumes, atom*] de brome; [*compound*] du brome.

bronchi /'brɒnkaɪ/ *npl* bronches *fpl*.

bronchial /'brɒŋkɪəl/ *adj* [*infection*] des bronches; [*asthma*] bronchique; [*wheeze, cough*] bronchitique; **~ tubes** bronches *fpl*; **~ pneumonia** broncho-pneumonie *f*.

bronchiole /'brɒŋkɪəʊl/ *n* bronchiole *f*.

bronchitis /brɒŋ'kaɪtɪs/ ▶ **1354** **I** *n* bronchite *f*; **to have ~** avoir une bronchite; **an attack of ~** une bronchite.
II *modif* **~ sufferer** bronchitique *mf*.

bronchopneumonia /ˌbrɒŋkəʊnjuː'məʊnɪə, US -nuː-/ ▶ **1354** *n* bronchopneumonie *f*.

bronco /'brɒŋkəʊ/ *n* (*pl* **-cos**) cheval *m* semi-sauvage (*de l'Ouest des États-Unis*).

broncobuster /'brɒŋkəʊbʌstə(r)/ *n*: *cowboy qui dompte les chevaux sauvages*.

brontosaurus /ˌbrɒntə'sɔːrəs/ *n* (*pl* **-ruses** ou **-ri**) brontosaure *m*.

Bronx cheer /ˌbrɒŋks 'tʃɪə(r)/ *n* US **to give a ~** ≈ faire pouah.

bronze /brɒnz/ **I** *n* **1** (statue, metal) bronze *m*; **2** (colour) (couleur *f* de) bronze *m*; **3** = **bronze medal**.
II *modif* [*coin, ornament*] en bronze.
III *vtr, vi* (all contexts) bronzer.

Bronze Age **I** *n* âge *m* du bronze.
II *modif* [*tool, settlement*] de l'âge du bronze.

bronze-coloured GB, **bronze-colored** US /'brɒnzkʌləd/ ▶ **1104** *adj* [*object*] couleur de bronze *inv*.

bronzed /brɒnzd/ *adj* (all contexts) bronzé.

bronze medal *n* médaille *f* de bronze.

bronzer /'brɒnzə(r)/ *n* Cosmet brunissant *m*.

brooch /brəʊtʃ/ *n* broche *f*.

brood /bruːd/ **I** *n* **1** Zool (of birds) couvée *f*, nichée *f*; (of mammals) nichée *f*; **2** hum (of children) nichée *f*, progéniture *f* hum.
II *vi* **1** (ponder) broyer du noir; **to ~ about** ou **on** ou **over** ressasser, ruminer [*problem, event, disappointment*]; **there's no point (in) ~ing about things** ça ne sert à rien de ressasser toutes ces choses; **2** Zool [*bird*] couver.

broodiness /'bruːdɪnɪs/ *n* **1**○ GB (of women) désir *m* d'avoir un enfant; **2** (moodiness) mélancolie *f*.

brooding /'bruːdɪŋ/ **I** *n* **all this ~ is pointless** ça ne sert à rien de ressasser or de ruminer tout ça.
II *adj* [*atmosphere, presence, landscape*]

menaçant; [*person, figure, face*] sombre; [*unease, menace*] pesant.

brood mare *n* (jument *f*) poulinière *f*.

broody /ˈbruːdɪ/ *adj* **1** (depressed) mélancolique, cafardeux/-euse°; **2** Agric **a ~ hen** une poule qui cherche à couver; **3**° GB **to feel** ou **be ~** [*woman*] désirer avoir un enfant.

brook /brʊk/ **I** *n* ruisseau *m*.
II *vtr* sout tolérer [*argument, refusal*].

brooklet /ˈbrʊklɪt/ *n* littér ruisselet *m*.

broom /bruːm, brʊm/ **I** *n* **1** (for sweeping) balai *m*; **2** Bot genêt *m*.
II *modif* [*flower, petal*] de genêt.
IDIOMS **a new ~ sweeps clean** Prov nouveau chef, nouvelles méthodes.

broom: **~ cupboard** *n* GB lit cagibi° *m*; **~ handle** *n* GB manche *m* à balai; **~stick** *n* manche *m* à balai.

Bros. *npl* Comm (*abrév écrite* = **Brothers**) Frères.

broth /brɒθ, US brɔːθ/ *n* bouillon *m*; **chicken ~** bouillon *m* de poule.
IDIOMS **too many cooks spoil the ~** Prov on n'arrive à rien quand tout le monde s'en mêle.

brothel /ˈbrɒθl/ *n* maison *f* close.

brothel: **~-creepers** *n* GB chaussures *fpl* à semelles de crêpe; **~-keeper** *n* tenancier/-ière *m/f* de maison close.

brother /ˈbrʌðə(r)/ **I** *n* **1** (relative) frère *m*; **a younger/older ~** un frère cadet/plus âgé; **my eldest ~** mon frère aîné; **the Kennedy ~s** les frères Kennedy; **2** (trade unionist) camarade *m*; **3** (fellow man) frère *m*; **~s in arms** frères d'armes; **a ~ officer** un compagnon d'armes; **4**° **'hey brother!'** 'hé camarade!'; **5** Relig frère *m*; **Brother Richard** Frère Richard.
II° *excl* **oh ~!** oh bon sang!

brotherhood /ˈbrʌðəhʊd/ *n* **1** (bond) fraternité *f*; **2** (organization) gen, US Rail corporation *f*; (of idealists) confrérie *f*; (trade-union) association *f*; **3** (of monks) communauté *f*; **4** (of freemasons) **the Brotherhood** la franc-maçonnerie.

brother-in-law (*pl* **brothers-in-law**) beau-frère *m*.

brotherly /ˈbrʌðəlɪ/ *adj* (all contexts) fraternel/-elle.

brougham /ˈbruːəm/ *n* coupé *m*.

brought /brɔːt/ *prét, pp* ▶ **bring**.

brouhaha /ˈbruːhɑːhɑː, US bruːˈhɑːhɑː/ *n* brouhaha *m*.

brow /braʊ/ *n* **1** (forehead) front *m*; **2** (eyebrow) sourcil *m*; **to knit** ou **furrow one's ~s** froncer les sourcils; **3** (of hill) sommet *m*.

browbeat /ˈbraʊbiːt/ **I** (*prét* **-beat**; *pp* **-beaten**) *vtr* intimider; **to ~ sb into doing** forcer qn à faire; **to ~ sb into submission** forcer qn à se soumettre; **to ~ sb into silence** réduire qn au silence.
II browbeaten *pp adj* tyrannisé.

brown /braʊn/ ▶ **1104** **I** *n* **1** (colour) (of object) marron *m*; (of hair, skin, eyes) brun *m*; **I don't like ~** je n'aime pas le marron; **in ~** en marron; **to be a deep ~** être d'un marron foncé; **2** Sport (in snooker) bille *f* marron.
II *adj* **1** (in colour) [*suit, shoes, leaves, paint, sofa, car, eyes*] marron *inv*; [*hair*] brun, châtain; **to go** ou **turn ~** [*leaf, paint*] devenir marron; **to paint/dye sth ~** peindre/teindre qch en marron; **to turn the water ~** rendre l'eau marron; **dark** ou **deep ~** marron foncé *inv*; **light** ou **pale ~** marron clair *inv*; **2** (tanned) [*person, skin*] bronzé, bruni; **to be very ~** être très bronzé; **to go ~** bronzer; **to go ~ easily** bronzer facilement; **3** (as racial feature) [*skin, face, person, race*] basané.
III *vtr* **1** Culin (in cooking) faire roussir [*sauce, gravy*]; faire dorer [*meat, onion, potato*]; **to ~ sth under the grill** faire dorer qch au gril; **2** (tan) brunir [*skin, face, body*]; **~ed by the sun** bruni or bronzé par le soleil.
IV *vi* [*meat, potatoes*] dorer; **leave to ~ in the oven** faire dorer au four.

brown ale *n* GB bière *f* brune.

brownbag° /ˈbraʊnbæg/ IDIOMS **to ~ it** (bring lunch) apporter son casse-croûte dans un sac en papier; (bring drink) *apporter une bouteille d'alcool dans un restaurant*.

brown: **~ bear** *n* ours *m* brun; **~ bread** *n* pain *m* complet; **~ coal** *n* lignite *m*.

browned-off° /ˌbraʊndˈɒf/ *adj* GB **to be ~** en avoir marre° (**with, about** de; **with doing, about doing** de faire).

brown: **~ envelope** *n* enveloppe *f* kraft; **~ fat** *n* graisse *f* brune.

Brownian motion, Brownian movement /ˈbraʊnɪən/ *n* Phys mouvement *m* brownien.

brownie /ˈbraʊnɪ/ **I** *n* **1** US (cake) brownie *m* (*petit gâteau au chocolat et aux noix*); **2** (elf) lutin *m*.
II Brownie *n* jeannette *f*.
III Brownie *modif* [*pack, leader*] des jeannettes.

brownie point° *n* hum bon point *m*.

browning /ˈbraʊnɪŋ/ *n* GB colorant *m* brun (pour les sauces).

brownish /ˈbraʊnɪʃ/ ▶ **1104** *adj* brunâtre.

brown-nose° /ˈbraʊnnəʊz/ US **I** *n* lèche-cul◑ *mf inv*, lèche-bottes° *mf inv*.
II *vtr* lécher les bottes° de.

brown: **~out** *n* US black-out *m* partiel; **~ owl** *n* chat-huant *m*; **~ paper** *n* papier *m* kraft; **~ paper bag** *n* sac *m* en papier kraft; **~ rice** *n* riz *m* complet; **Brownshirt** *n* Hist Chemise *f* brune; **~-skinned** *adj* basané, brun de peau.

brownstone /ˈbraʊnstəʊn/ *n* **1** (sandstone) grès *m* rouge; **2** US (house) maison *f* à façade de grès rouge.

brown study† *n* **to be in a ~** être plongé dans ses pensées.

brown: **~ sugar** *n* Culin sucre *m* brun, cassonade *f*; **~ trout** *n* truite *f* de mer.

browse /braʊz/ **I** *n* **to have a ~ in a bookshop** flâner dans une librairie; **to have a ~ through a book** feuilleter un livre.
II *vtr* Comput parcourir, survoler.
III *vi* **1** (potter, stroll around) flâner; (look at objects in shop) regarder; **2** (graze) brouter.
■ **browse through**: **~ through [sth]** feuilleter [*book*]; faire [*market stall, shop*].

brucellosis /ˌbruːsəˈləʊsɪs/ ▶ **1354** **I** *n* brucellose *f*.
II *modif* [*epidemic*] de brucellose; [*vaccine*] contre la brucellose.

bruise /bruːz/ **I** *n* (on skin) bleu *m*, ecchymose *f* spec (**on** sur); (on fruit) tache *f*, talure *f* (**on** sur); **covered in ~s** [*skin, limb*] couvert de bleus; **to suffer cuts and ~s** avoir des blessures légères.
II *vtr* **1** meurtrir [*person*]; **to ~ one's knee/arm** se meurtrir le genou/bras; **his fingers were badly ~d** il avait les doigts sérieusement meurtris; **he ~d my arm** il m'a meurtri le bras; **2** (damage) taler [*fruit*]; **3** (emotionally) meurtrir, blesser.
III *vi* [*person*] se faire facilement des bleus; [*arm, lips, skin*] se meurtrir; [*fruit*] se taler facilement.
IV *v refl* **to ~ oneself** (in one spot) se faire un bleu; (extensively) se meurtrir.

bruised /bruːzd/ *adj* **1** (physically) [*arm, leg, knee, elbow, shin*] contusionné; [*eye, cheek, ribs, back, muscle*] meurtri; [*fruit*] talé; **he was badly ~** il était sérieusement contusionné; **2** (emotionally) [*ego, spirit*] blessé; [*heart*] meurtri, blessé; **I feel a bit ~** je me sens un peu fragile.

bruiser° /ˈbruːzə(r)/ *n* **1** (burly man) malabar° *m*, balèze° *m*; **2** (boxer) cogneur *m*.

bruising /ˈbruːzɪŋ/ **I** *n* contusions *fpl*, ecchymoses *fpl* (**on** sur); **there is some ~ to the throat** il y a quelques contusions à la gorge.
II *adj* **1** (emotionally) [*row, battle, campaign, encounter*] violent; [*remark*] blessant; [*defeat*] écrasant; **2** (physically) [*game, encounter*] acharné.
IDIOMS **to be cruising for a ~**° US chercher une raclée°.

Brum° /brʌm/ *n* GB (*abrév* = **Birmingham**) Birmingham.

Brummie° /ˈbrʌmɪ/ GB **I** *n* (resident) habitant/-e *m/f* de Birmingham; (native) originaire *mf* de Birmingham.
II *modif* [*accent, girl*] de Birmingham.

brunch /brʌntʃ/ *n* brunch *m* (*petit déjeuner tardif et copieux remplaçant le déjeuner*).

Brunei /bruːˈnaɪ/ ▶ **1131** *pr n* Brunei *m*.

brunette /bruːˈnet/ **I** *n* (person) brune *f*.
II ▶ **1104** *adj* [*hair*] brun.

brunt /brʌnt/ *n* **to bear** ou **take the ~ of** être le plus touché par [*disaster, unemployment*]; subir le plus fort de [*fighting*]; subir tout le poids de [*anger*].

brush /brʌʃ/ **I** *n* **1** (implement) (for hair, clothes, shoes etc) brosse *f*; (small, for sweeping up) balayette *f*; (broom) balai *m*; (for paint) pinceau *m*; (chimney sweep's) hérisson *m*; **to clean sth with a ~** nettoyer qch à la brosse; **soft/hard/wire ~** brosse souple/dure/métallique; **2** (act of brushing) coup *m* de brosse; **to give one's teeth a quick ~** se brosser rapidement les dents; **3** (encounter) (confrontation with person) accrochage *m* (**with** avec); (contact with person, celebrity) contact *m* (**with** avec); **to have a ~ with the police/with the authorities** avoir affaire à la police/aux autorités; **to have a ~ with death** frôler la mort; **4** (light touch) frôlement *m*; **I felt the ~ of a bird's wing** j'ai senti un oiseau m'effleurer de son aile; **5** (vegetation or twigs) broussailles *fpl*; **6** (fox's tail) queue *f* de renard; **7** Elec (in motor) balai *m*.
II *vtr* **1** (sweep, clean) brosser [*carpet, clothes, shoes*]; **to ~ one's hair/teeth** se brosser les cheveux/les dents; **to ~ sb's hair/teeth** brosser les cheveux/les dents de qn; **to ~ sth off/into sth** (with brush or hand) brosser qch de/dans qch; **to ~ the knots out of one's hair** se démêler les cheveux; **2** (touch lightly) effleurer [*person, part of body, object*] (**with** avec); **her skirt ~ed the floor** sa jupe balayait le sol; **3** Culin **to ~ sth with** badigeonner qch avec [*water, milk, egg, oil*].
III *vi* **to ~ against** frôler [*person, part of body, object*]; **to ~ past sb** frôler qn en passant; **he ~ed past me into/out of the room** il m'a frôlé en entrant dans/en quittant la pièce.
IV brushed *pp adj* Tex [*cotton, denim, nylon*] gratté.
■ **brush aside**: **~ aside [sth/sb]**, **~ [sb/sth] aside** **1** (dismiss) balayer, repousser [*idea, thought, feeling*]; repousser [*argument, criticism, person*]; **2** (move away) écarter [*cobweb, branch, curtain*]; **3** (beat) balayer, écraser [*team, opponent, defences*].
■ **brush away**: **~ away [sth]**, **~ [sth] away** brosser, enlever [*crumbs, dirt*]; essuyer [*tear*]; écarter [*hand*].
■ **brush back**: **~ back [sth]**, **~ [sth] back** brosser [qch] en arrière [*hair*].
■ **brush down**: **~ down [sth]**, **~ [sth] down** brosser [*coat, skirt, suit, horse*].
■ **brush off**: **~ off [sth/sb]**, **~ [sth/sb] off** repousser [*person, offer, allegation, challenge*]; écarter [*threat, incident, disagreement*].
■ **brush up (on)**: **~ up (on) [sth]**, **~ [sth] up** se remettre à [*language, skill, subject*]; **I must ~ up on it** ou **~ it up** je dois m'y remettre.

brush discharge *n* Elec (décharge *f* en) aigrette *f*.

brush-off° /ˈbrʌʃɒf/ *n* **to give sb the ~** rembarrer° qn; **to get the ~** se faire rembarrer°.

brushstroke /ˈbrʌʃstrəʊk/ *n* coup *m* de pinceau.

brushup /ˈbrʌʃʌp/ *n* GB **1 to have a (wash and) ~** se rafraîchir; **2 to give one's French/piano-playing a ~** se remettre au français/à étudier le piano.

brushwood /ˈbrʌʃwʊd/ *n* **1** (firewood) brindilles *fpl*; **2** (brush) broussailles *fpl*.

brushwork /ˈbrʌʃwɜːk/ *n* Art facture *f*.

brusque /bruːsk, US brʌsk/ *adj* brusque (**with** avec).

brusquely /ˈbruːsklɪ, US ˈbrʌsklɪ/ *adv* avec brusquerie, avec rudesse.

brusqueness /ˈbruːsknɪs, US ˈbrʌsk-/ *n* brusquerie *f*, rudesse *f*.

Brussels /ˈbrʌslz/ **▶ 1818** *pr n* Bruxelles.

Brussels sprout *n* chou *m* de Bruxelles.

brutal /ˈbruːtl/ *adj* [*dictator, honesty, reply, image*] brutal; [*murderer, act, treatment, régime*] cruel/-elle; [*attack, murder*] sauvage; [*film, scene*] violent.

brutality /bruːˈtælətɪ/ *n* brutalité *f* (**of** de).

brutalize /ˈbruːtəlaɪz/ *vtr* **1** (make brutal) rendre [qn] brutal; **2** (treat brutally) brutaliser.

brutally /ˈbruːtəlɪ/ *adv* [*murder, torture, treat*] sauvagement; [*say, reply*] brutalement; **~ honest/frank** d'une honnêteté/franchise brutale; **to be ~ honest** pour être honnête.

brute /bruːt/ **I** *n* **1** (man) brute *f*; **2** (animal) bête *f*.
II *adj* **1** (physical) [*strength*] simple (*before n*); **by (sheer) ~ force** par la force; **2** (animal-like) [*instinct, passion*] bestial; **3** (simple) [*fact, question*] simple (*before n*).

brutish /ˈbruːtɪʃ/ *adj* bestial.

BS *n* **1** GB Comm (*abrév* = **British Standard**) norme *f* britannique; cf NF *f*; **2** US Univ (*abrév* = **Bachelor of Science**) ≈ (degree) diplôme *m* universitaire de sciences; (person) diplômé/-e *m/f* en sciences; **3**◑ US *abrév* ▶ **bullshit**.

BSA *n* **1** US (*abrév* = **Boy Scouts of America**) Association *f* des scouts américains; **2** GB (*abrév* = **Building Societies Association**) association *f* britannique des sociétés de crédit immobilier.

BSc *n* GB Univ (*abrév* = **Bachelor of Science**) diplôme *m* universitaire en sciences.

B-school○ *n* US école *f* commerciale.

BSE *n* Vet (*abrév* = **Bovine Spongiform Encephalopathy**) ESB *f*, encéphalopathie *f* spongiforme bovine.

BSI *n* GB Comm (*abrév* = **British Standards Institution**) *organisme britannique fixant les critères d'agrément des produits industriels*; cf AFNOR *f*.

B side /ˈbiːsaɪd/ *n* Audio face *f* B.

BST *n* (*abrév* = **British Summer Time**) *heure d'été britannique*.

BT *n*: *abrév* ▶ **British Telecom**.

BTech *n* GB Univ (*abrév* = **Bachelor of Technology**) ≈ BTS *m*.

Btu GB, **Bthu** GB, **BTU** US *n* Meas (*abrév* = **British thermal unit**) unité *f* calorifique.

bub◑ /bʌb/ *n* US mec○ *m*.

bubble /ˈbʌbl/ **I** *n* **1** (in air, liquid, glass) bulle *f* (**in** dans); (in paintwork) boursouflure *f*; **air ~, ~ of air** bulle *f* d'air; **to blow ~s** faire des bulles; **2** Fin, Comm prix *m* gonflé; **the house price ~** les prix gonflés de l'immobilier; **3** (germ-free chamber) chambre *f* stérile; **4** (sound) glouglou *m*.
II *vi* **1** (form bubbles) gen faire des bulles; [*fizzy drink*] pétiller; [*boiling liquid*] bouillonner; **to ~ out of the ground** jaillir du sol à gros bouillons; **2** fig (boil) **to ~ beneath the surface** bouillonner sous la surface; **to keep the issue bubbling** alimenter l'affaire; **3** (be lively, happy) être en effervescence; **to ~ with** déborder de [*enthusiasm, ideas*]; **4** (make bubbling sound) glouglouter.
IDIOMS **I'm waiting for the ~ to burst** je pense que c'est trop beau pour durer.
■ **bubble over** déborder (**with** de).
■ **bubble up** [*boiling liquid*] bouillonner; [*spring water*] jaillir en bouillonnant.

bubble: **~ and squeak** *n* GB *restes de chou et de purée de pommes de terre cuits à la poêle avec de l'oignon*; **~ bath** *n* bain *m* moussant; **~ car** *n* GB œuf○ *m* (*voiture monoplace des années 60*); **~ chamber** *n* chambre *f* à bulles; **~gum** *n* bubble-gum *m*; **~head**○ *n* US tête *f* de linotte○; **~ memory** *n* mémoire *f* à bulles; **~ pack** *n* GB (for small item) blister *m*; (for pills) emballage *m* pelliculé; **~ sort** *n* tri *m* par permutation; **~wrap** *n* bulle-pack® *m*.

bubbling /ˈbʌblɪŋ/ **I** *n* (sound) glouglou *m*, gargouillis *m*.
II *adj* **1** [*stream, source*] glougloutant; [*boiling liquid*] bouillonnant; **2** [*person*] débordant; [*city, atmosphere*] effervescent.

bubbly /ˈbʌblɪ/ **I** *n*○ (champagne) champagne *m*; (sparkling wine) mousseux○ *m*.
II *adj* **1** [*personality*] pétillant de vitalité; **2** [*liquid*] pétillant.

bubonic plague /bjuːˌbɒnɪk ˈpleɪɡ/ **▶ 1354** *n* peste *f* bubonique.

buccaneer /ˌbʌkəˈnɪə(r)/ *n* **1** (pirate) boucanier *m*; **2** (unscrupulous businessman) requin *m* fig.

buccaneering /ˌbʌkəˈnɪərɪŋ/ *adj* fig [*businessman, venture*] aventureux/-euse.

Bucharest /ˌbjuːkəˈrest/ **▶ 1818** *pr n* Bucarest.

buck /bʌk/ **I** *n* **1** US○ (dollar) dollar *m*; **2**○ (money) fric○ *m*; **to make a fast** *or* **quick ~** se faire du fric facile○; **to make a few ~s** se faire un peu de fric○; **3** Zool mâle *m*; **4** Equit ruade *f*; **to give a ~** lancer une ruade; **5**○ (man) **a young ~** un jeune.
II *modif* [*antelope, hare, rabbit*] mâle.
III *adj* US Mil [*private, sergeant*] simple (*before n*).
IV *vtr* **1** (throw) [*horse*] désarçonner [*rider*]; **2** (go against) aller contre [*trend, market*]; **to ~ the system** lutter contre l'ordre établi.
V *vi* **1** Equit ruer; **2** (oppose) **to ~ at** *ou* **against sth** regimber devant *or* contre [*changes, rule*].
IDIOMS **to ~ up one's ideas** se secouer○; **the ~ stops here/with the president** c'est moi/c'est le président qui hérite de la responsabilité; **to pass the ~** refiler la responsabilité à quelqu'un d'autre.
■ **buck up**: ¶ **~ up 1**○ (cheer up) se dérider; **~ up!** courage!; **2**○ (hurry up) se grouiller○; ¶ **~ [sb] up** (cheer up) [*news, person*] remonter le moral à [*person*].

bucked○ /bʌkt/ *adj* tout content.

bucket /ˈbʌkɪt/ **I** *n* **1** gen seau *m* (**of** de); **2** Tech (of scoop, dredger, waterwheel) godet *m*; (of pump) piston *m*.
II○ **buckets** *npl* **to rain ~s** pleuvoir à seaux; **to cry ~s** pleurer comme une Madeleine○; **to sweat ~s** suer à grosses gouttes.
III○ *vi* GB (also **~ down**) pleuvoir à seaux.
IDIOMS **to kick the ~** mourir, casser sa pipe○.

bucket: **~ dredge(r)** *n* drague *f* à godets; **~ elevator** *n* élévateur *m* à godets.

bucketful /ˈbʌkɪtfʊl/ *n* seau *m* (**of** de).

bucket seat *n* Aut, Aviat siège-baquet *m*.

bucket shop○ *n* **1** GB Tourism agence *f* de voyage (*proposant des billets d'avion à prix réduit*); **2** Fin société *f* frauduleuse d'agents de change.

buckeye /ˈbʌkaɪ/ *n* **1** (tree) marronnier *m* d'Inde; **2** (fruit) marron *m* (d'Inde).

Buck House○ *n* GB hum *résidence de la reine à Londres*.

bucking bronco /ˌbʌkɪŋ ˈbrɒŋkəʊ/ *n* **1** (animal) cheval *m* de rodéo; **2** Sport appareil *m* d'entraînement au rodéo.

Buckinghamshire /ˈbʌkɪŋəmʃə(r)/ **▶ 1624** *pr n* Buckinghamshire *m*.

buckle /ˈbʌkl/ **I** *n* **1** (clasp) boucle *f*; **2** (dent) (in metal) gondolage *m*; (in wheel) voilure *f*.
II *vtr* **1** (fasten) attacher, boucler [*belt, shoe, strap*]; **~ed** bien attaché; **to ~ sb into sth** attacher qn dans qch; **safely ~d in** bien attaché; **2** (damage) gondoler [*material, surface*].
III *vi* **1** (give way) lit [*metal, surface*] se gondoler; [*wheel*] se voiler; [*pillar, wall*] se déformer; [*knees, legs*] céder; fig [*person*] céder; **2** (fasten) [*belt, shoe, strap*] s'attacher, se boucler.
■ **buckle down** se mettre au boulot○; **to ~ down to sth** s'atteler à qch.
■ **buckle on**: **~ on [sth], ~ [sth] on** ceindre [*sword*]; attacher [*holster*]; revêtir [*armour*].
■ **buckle to** s'y mettre.

buck-passing /ˈbʌkpɑːsɪŋ/ *n* transfert *m* de responsabilité.

buckra○ /ˈbʌkrə/ *n* US injur Blanc *m*.

buckram /ˈbʌkrəm/ *n* bougran *m*.

Bucks *n* GB Post *abrév écrite* ▶ **Buckinghamshire**.

buck's fizz /ˌbʌks ˈfɪz/ *n* GB cocktail *m* au champagne et jus d'orange.

buckshee○ /ˌbʌkˈʃiː/ *adj, adv* GB gratis *inv*.

buckshot /ˈbʌkʃɒt/ *n* chevrotine *f*.

buckskin /ˈbʌkskɪn/ **I** *n* daim *m*.
II *modif* [*shoes, trousers*] en daim.

buck: **~'s night, ~'s party** *n* Austral *soirée pour enterrer une vie de garçon*; **~ teeth** *npl* péj dents *fpl* de lapin pej.

buckthorn /ˈbʌkθɔːn/ *n* Bot nerprun *m* purgatif.

buckwheat /ˈbʌkwiːt, US -hwiːt/ *n* sarrasin *m*, blé *m* noir.

bucolic /bjuːˈkɒlɪk/ *n, adj* bucolique (*f*).

bud /bʌd/ **I** *n* **1** Bot (of leaf) bourgeon *m*; (of flower) bouton *m*; **in ~** [*leaf*] en bourgeon; [*flower*] en bouton; **2** Biol bourgeon *m*; **3**○ US mec○ *m*.
II *vtr* (*p prés etc* **-dd-**) Hort (graft) greffer [*plant*].
III *vi* (*p prés etc* **-dd-**) **1** Bot (develop leaf buds) bourgeonner; (develop flower buds) boutonner; **2** (develop) [*leaf, flower, breast, horns*] pointer.
IDIOMS **to nip sth in the ~** tuer qch dans l'œuf.

Budapest /ˌbjuːdəˈpest/ **▶ 1818** *pr n* Budapest.

Buddha /ˈbʊdə/ **I** *pr n* (god) Bouddha *m*.
II *n* (representation) bouddha *m*.

Buddhism /ˈbʊdɪzəm/ *n* bouddhisme *m*.

Buddhist /ˈbʊdɪst/ **I** *n* bouddhiste *mf*.
II *adj* [*monk, temple, country*] bouddhiste; [*art, civilization*] bouddhique.

budding /ˈbʌdɪŋ/ *adj* **1** Bot (into leaf) bourgeonnant; (into flower) boutonnant; **2** fig [*athlete, poet, champion*] en herbe; [*talent, career, romance, interest, industry*] naissant.

buddleia /ˈbʌdlɪə/ *n* buddleia *m*.

buddy○ /ˈbʌdɪ/ **I** *n* **1** (friend) copain *m*, pote○ *m*; **2** US (form of address) mec○ *m*; **3** (in Aids care) volontaire *mf* (*attaché à un sidéen*).
II *vi* US aider les autres.

buddy: **~ buddy**○ *adj* copain-copain *inv*; **~ movie** *n* film *m* d'amitié virile; **~ system** *n* US Mil, gen organisation *f* en équipe de deux (*pour l'aide mutuelle dans des situations dangereuses*).

budge /bʌdʒ/ **I** *vtr* **1** lit bouger; **2** fig faire changer d'avis à.
II *vi* lit bouger (**from, off** de); fig changer d'avis (**on** sur); **he won't ~ from his position** fig il ne changera pas d'avis; **she will not ~ an inch** fig elle ne changera pas son opinion d'un iota (**on** sur).
■ **budge over**○, **budge up**○ se pousser.

budgerigar /ˈbʌdʒərɪɡɑː(r)/ *n* perruche *f*.

budget /ˈbʌdʒɪt/ **I** *n* **1** (personal, commercial) budget *m* (**for** pour); **annual/education ~** budget annuel/de l'éducation; **to go over/stay within ~** dépasser/ne pas dépasser le budget; **to be/operate on a tight ~** avoir/gérer un petit budget; **to balance a ~** équilibrer un budget; **a family on a ~ cannot afford luxuries** une

famille au budget serré ne peut pas se permettre des extras; **2** GB Pol (also **Budget**) Budget *m*; **in the Budget** dans le Budget.
II *modif* **1** [*cut, deficit*] budgétaire; [*target, estimate, constraints, increase*] du budget; **2** (cheap) [*holiday, offer, price*] pour petits budgets; **a low-/high-~ film** un film au petit budget/au budget énorme.
III *vtr* budgétiser [*money*] (**for** pour); US budgétiser [*time*] (**for** pour).
IV *vi* **to ~ for** [*company, government*] budgétiser ses dépenses en fonction de [*increase, needs*]; **I hadn't ~ed for a new car** je n'avais pas prévu d'acheter une nouvelle voiture.

budget account *n* GB (with bank, shop) compte-crédit *m*.

budgetary /ˈbʌdʒɪtərɪ, US -terɪ/ *adj* [*policy, control, priority*] budgétaire.

budget: **~ day** *n* GB Pol jour *m* de la présentation du Budget; **~ debate** *n* Pol débat *m* autour du Budget; **~ director** ▶1692 *n* US responsable *mf* du budget; **~ forecast** *n* prévisions *fpl* du budget; **~ heading** *n* Fin, Comm poste *m* budgétaire.

budgeting /ˈbʌdʒɪtɪŋ/ *n* budget *m*; **as a result of careful ~, I have paid off my debts** en planifiant soigneusement mon budget, j'ai remboursé mes dettes.

Budget speech *n* GB Pol discours *m* de présentation du Budget.

budgie○ /ˈbʌdʒɪ/ *n* = **budgerigar**.

Buenos Aires /ˌbwenəs ˈeərɪz/ ▶1818 *pr n* Buenos Aires.

buff /bʌf/ I *n* **1**○ (enthusiast) mordu/-e *m/f*; **he's a film ~** c'est un mordu du cinéma; **2** (colour) chamois *m inv*; **3** (leather) peau *m* de buffle; **4**○ hum (nakedness) **in the ~** à poil○; **to strip down to the ~** se mettre à poil○; **5** Tech polissoir *m*.
II *adj* chamois.
III *vtr* lustrer [*shoes*]; polir [*fingernails, metal*].

buffalo /ˈbʌfələʊ/ *n* (*pl* **-oes** or *collect* **~**) buffle *m*; US bison *m*.

buffalo grass *n* herbe *f* de prairie.

buff-coloured GB, **buff-colored** US /ˈbʌfkələd/ ▶1104 *adj* couleur *f* chamois *inv*.

buffer /ˈbʌfə(r)/ I *n* **1** fig (protection) tampon *m* (**against** contre; **between** entre); **2** Rail (on line) butoir *m*; (on train) tampon *m*; **3**○ GB **old ~** vieux bonhomme *m*; **4** Comput (also **~ memory**) mémoire-tampon *f*; **5** (for polishing) polissoir *m*; **6** (for massage) brosse *f* de massage.
II *vtr* Chem tamponner [*solution*].
IDIOMS **to run into the ~s** finir en queue de poisson.

buffer: **~ solution** *n* Chem solution *f* tampon; **~ state** *n* État *m* tampon; **~ stock** *n* Comm stock *m* régulateur; **~ store** *n* Comput mémoire *f* tampon; **~ zone** *n* zone *f* tampon.

buffet[1] /ˈbʊfeɪ, US bəˈfeɪ/ *n* (all contexts) buffet *m*; **~ lunch/dinner/supper** buffet *m*.

buffet[2] /bʌfɪt/ I *vtr* **1** lit [*wind, sea*] secouer; **2** fig [*misfortune*] frapper.
II *vi* **to ~ against sth** battre contre qch.

buffet car /ˈbʊfeɪ/ *n* GB Rail voiture-buffet *f*.

buffeting /ˈbʌfɪtɪŋ/ I *n* (of waves, sea) déferlement *m*; (of wind) rafales *fpl*.
II *adj* violent.

buffing /ˈbʌfɪŋ/ *n* (of leather) lustrage *m*; (of fingernails, metal) polissage *m*.

buffoon /bəˈfuːn/ *n* bouffon/-onne *m/f*.

buffoonery /bəˈfuːnərɪ/ *n* bouffonnerie *f*.

bug /bʌg/ I *n* **1**○ (any insect) bestiole○ *f*; **2** (bedbug) punaise *f*; **3**○ (also **stomach ~** ou **tummy ~**) ennuis *mpl* gastriques; **4** (germ) microbe *m*; **5** (fault) gen défaut *m*; Comput bogue *f*, bug *m*; **6** (hidden microphone) micro *m* caché; **7**○ (craze) virus *m*, manie *f*; **to be bitten by the golf ~** attraper le virus du golf; **8**○ US (enthusiast) mordu/-e *m/f*; **a jogging ~** un mordu du jogging.
II *vtr* (*p prés etc* **-gg-**) **1** (hide microphones in) poser des micros dans [*room, building*]; **the room is ~ged** il y a un micro (caché) dans la pièce; **2**○ (annoy) embêter○ [*person*].
■ **bug off**◑ US foutre le camp◑.
■ **bug out**○ US **her eyes ~ out** elle a les yeux exorbités.

bugaboo /ˈbʌgəbuː/ *n* (*pl* **~s**) croquemitaine *m*.

bugbear /ˈbʌgbeə(r)/ *n* (problem, annoyance) plaie○ *f*; **to be a ~ for sb** être une plaie pour qn.

bug-eyed /ˈbʌgaɪd/ *adj* aux yeux exorbités.

bugger /ˈbʌgə(r)/ I *n* **1**◑ GB (person) pej con/conne◑ *m/f*; hum couillon○ *m*; (sympathetic) bougre *m*○; **2**○ GB (difficult or annoying thing) galère○ *f*; **what a ~!** (situation) quelle merde●!; **3** Jur, gen (sodomite) sodomite *m*.
II◑ *excl* GB merde alors◑!
III *vtr* **1**◑ (expressing surprise) **~ me!** merde◑!; **I'll be ~ed!** merde alors◑!; (expressing lack of importance) **~ that!** des clous○!; **~ him/her!** qu'il/elle aille se faire voir!; **I'm ~ed if I'm going to do that!** je serais bien con◑ de faire ça!◑; **I'm ~ed if I know!** je n'en ai aucune idée!; **2** (have anal sex with) sodomiser.
IDIOMS **to play silly ~s**◑ GB faire le con◑, faire l'idiot.
■ **bugger about**◑ GB: ¶ **~ about** déconner○; ¶ **~ [sb] about** emmerder◑.
■ **bugger off**◑ GB se casser◑.
■ **bugger up**: **~ [sth] up, ~ up [sth]** bousiller○.

bugger all◑ GB /ˌbʌgər ˈɔːl/ I *pron* que dalle◑, rien.
II *adj* **he's got ~ qualifications** il a que dalle○ comme diplômes.

buggered◑ /ˈbʌgəd/ *adj* (*jamais épith*) GB **1** (broken) foutu◑, cassé; **2** (tired) canné◑, fatigué.

buggery /ˈbʌgərɪ/ *n* sodomie *f*.

bugging /ˈbʌgɪŋ/ *n* pose *f* de micros.

bugging device *n* micro *m* d'écoute.

buggy /ˈbʌgɪ/ *n* **1** GB (pushchair) poussette *f*; **2** US (pram) landau *m*; **3** Hist (carriage) boghei *m*; **4**○ †(car) bagnole○ *f*.

bugle /ˈbjuːgl/ ▶1481 *n* clairon *m* (*instrument*).

bugler /ˈbjuːglə(r)/ *n* clairon *m* (*joueur*).

build /bɪld/ I *n* carrure *f*; **a man of stocky/average ~** un homme carré/de carrure moyenne; **he has the ~ of an athlete** il a la carrure d'un athlète; **she is slender in ~** elle est mince.
II *vtr* (*prét, pp* **built**) **1** (construct) construire [*factory, city, railway*]; édifier [*church, monument*]; construire [*nest*]; **to ~ sb a house, to ~ a house for sb** construire une maison pour qn; **to ~ a wall from** ou **out of bricks** construire un mur en briques; **to ~ a nest out of twigs** construire un nid avec des brindilles; **to ~ an extension onto a house** agrandir une maison; **2** (assemble) construire [*car, engine, ship*]; **3** Comput construire [*monitor*]; créer [*software, interface*]; **4** (establish) bâtir [*career, future*]; établir [*relations, relationship*]; fonder [*empire*]; créer [*prosperity*]; former [*team*]; **to ~ a new China** bâtir une Chine nouvelle; **to ~ a future for our country/our children** bâtir un avenir pour notre pays/nos enfants; **to ~ one's hopes on sth** fonder ses espoirs sur qch; **to ~ a presence in the European market** faire sentir sa présence sur le marché européen; **5** Games former [*sequence, set, word*].
III *vi* (*prét, pp* **built**) **1** (construct) construire; **2** fig (use as a foundation) **to ~ on** tirer parti de [*popularity, success*]; **to ~ on the excitement generated by the first film** tirer parti de l'enthousiasme suscité par le premier film; **the scheme would ~ on the existing system** le projet se fonderait sur le système existant; **the company wishes to ~ on its Asian base** la société souhaite se développer à partir de sa base en Asie.
■ **build in**: **~ [sth] in, ~ in [sth]** **1** (construct) encastrer [*mirror, bookcase*]; **to ~ a wardrobe into a wall** encastrer une penderie dans un mur; **2** (incorporate) introduire [*clause, provision, guarantee*]; **to ~ a safeguard into a contract** introduire une garantie dans un contrat.
■ **build up**: ¶ **~ up** [*gas, silt, deposits*] s'accumuler; [*traffic*] s'intensifier; [*business, trade*] se développer; [*tension, pressure, excitement*] monter; ¶ **~ up [sth], ~ [sth] up** **1** (accumulate) accumuler [*weapons, wealth*]; **2** (boost) établir [*self-confidence, trust*]; gonfler [*morale*]; **don't ~ your hopes up too high** ne te fais pas d'illusions; **3** (establish) constituer [*collection*]; créer [*business, organization*]; constituer [*army*]; établir [*picture, profile*]; créer [*database*]; se faire [*reputation*]; **the college built up a large library** le collège s'est constitué une importante bibliothèque; ¶ **~ [sth/sb] up, ~ up [sth/sb]** **1** (through eating, exercise) affermir [*muscles*]; **to ~ up one's forearms** se muscler les avant-bras; **to ~ oneself up, to ~ up one's strength** prendre des forces; **2** (promote) **they built him up to be a star** ils l'ont lancé pour en faire une star.

builder /ˈbɪldə(r)/ ▶1692 *n* (contractor) entrepreneur *m* en bâtiment; (worker) ouvrier/-ière *m/f* du bâtiment; **a firm of ~s** une entreprise de bâtiment; **house/road ~** entrepreneur *m* immobilier/des ponts et chaussées.

builder: **~'s labourer** ▶1692 *n* ouvrier/-ière *m/f* du bâtiment; **~'s merchant** ▶1692 *n* fournisseur *m* de matériaux de construction; **~'s yard** *n* dépôt *m* de matériaux de construction.

building /ˈbɪldɪŋ/ *n* **1** (structure) bâtiment *m*; (with offices, apartments) immeuble *m*; (palace, church) édifice *m*; **school ~** bâtiment *m* d'école; **a ~ improvement scheme** un programme de rénovation du bâtiment; **2** (industry) bâtiment *m*; **the ~ industry** le bâtiment; **3** (action) construction *f*; **the ~ of new homes** la construction de nouvelles maisons.

building block *n* **1** (child's toy) cube *m*; **a set of ~s** un jeu de cubes; **2** fig (basic element) élément *m* de base.

building: **~ contractor** ▶1692 *n* entrepreneur *m* en bâtiment; **~ costs** *npl* frais *mpl* de construction; **~ land** *n* terrain *m* à bâtir; **~ materials** *npl* matériaux *mpl* de construction; **~ permit** *n* permis *m* de construire; **~ plot** *n* terrain *m* à bâtir; **~ site** *n* lit, fig chantier *m* (de construction); **~ society** *n* GB société *f* d'investissement et de crédit immobilier; **~ surveyor** ▶1692 *n* expert *m* géomètre; **~ trade** *n* bâtiment *m*; **~ worker** ▶1692 *n* GB ouvrier/-ière *m/f* du bâtiment.

build-up /ˈbɪldʌp/ *n* **1** (increase) (in tartar, deposits) accumulation *f* (**of** de); (in traffic) intensification *f* (**of** de); (in weapons, stocks) accumulation *f* (**of** de); (in tension, excitement) accroissement *m* (**of** de); **a ~ of carbon dioxide** une augmentation du taux de bioxide de carbone; **a military ~** une concentration de troupes; **a ~ of pressures within the government** une intensification des pressions à l'intérieur du gouvernement; **2** (publicity) ¢ préparatifs *mpl*; **the ~ to sth** les préparatifs de qch; **to give sth a good ~** faire du battage○ autour de qch.

built /bɪlt/ I *prét, pp* ▶ **build**.
II *adj* **1** (made) **he's powerfully ~** il a une puissante carrure; **he's slightly ~** il est frêle; **he's ~ for hard work** il est bâti pour les gros travaux; **2** (designed) **to be ~ for** [*car, equipment*] être conçu pour [*efficiency, speed*]; **these houses were ~ to last** ces maisons sont construites pour durer; **3** Archit **the ~ environment** la zone bâtie.
III **-built** (*dans composés*) **a Russian-~ car/factory** une voiture/usine de construc-

tion russe; **a stone-~ house** une maison en pierre.

built-in /ˌbɪlt'ɪn/ *adj* **1** [*wardrobe, shelves*] encastré; **2** [*guarantee, clause*] intégré; [*bias, racism*] inhérent; **~ obsolescence** obsolescence *f* planifiée.

built-up /ˌbɪlt'ʌp/ *adj* **1** [*region*] urbanisé; **the centre of the town has become very ~** on a beaucoup construit dans le centre de la ville; **~ area** agglomération *f*; **2** [*shoes, heels*] à semelles compensées; **a ~ nose** Theat un nez en latex.

bulb /bʌlb/ *n* **1** Elec ampoule *f* (électrique); **2** Bot bulbe *m*; **3** (of thermometer, test-tube) réservoir *m*.

bulbous /'bʌlbəs/ *adj* **1** (fat) [*nose, head*] gros/grosse; **2** Bot [*plant*] bulbeux/-euse.

Bulgaria /bʌl'geərɪə/ ▶ **1131** *pr n* Bulgarie *f*.

Bulgarian /bʌl'geərɪən/ ▶ **1486**, **1402** **I** *n* **1** (person) Bulgare *mf*; **2** Ling bulgare *m*.
II *adj* bulgare.

bulge /bʌldʒ/ **I** *n* **1** (swelling) (in clothing, carpet) bosse *f*; (in vase, column) renflement *m*; (in pipe, tube) bombement *m*; (in tyre) hernie *f*; (in plaster) boursouflure *f*; (in cheek) bosse *f*; (in stomach) **the ~ of his belly**○ son gros ventre; **2** Stat poussée *f*; **a demographic/statistical ~** une poussée démographique/statistique; **3** (increase) augmentation *f* (**in** de); **a ~ in the birth/unemployment rate** une augmentation du taux de natalité/chômage; **4** Mil saillant *m*; **the battle of the Bulge** Hist, Mil la bataille des Ardennes; fig hum la bataille contre les kilos superflus; **5**○ US (advantage) avantage *m*, dessus○ *m*.
II *vi* [*bag, pocket*] être gonflé; [*wallet*] être bourré; [*surface*] se boursoufler; [*stomach*] ballonner; [*cheeks*] être gonflé; **his eyes were bulging out of their sockets** ses yeux sortaient de leurs orbites; **to be bulging with** [*bag, vehicle, wardrobe*] être bourré de; [*book, building*] être rempli de.

bulging /'bʌldʒɪŋ/ *adj* [*eye*] exorbité; [*cheek, stomach, vein*] gonflé; [*chest, muscle*] saillant; [*surface, wall*] bombé; [*bag, file, wallet*] plein à craquer○ (*after n*).

bulgur (wheat) /'bʌlgu:(r)/ *n* bulgur *m*.

bulimia (nervosa) /bju:'lɪmɪə nɜ:'vəʊsə/ *n* boulimie *f*.

bulimic /bju:'lɪmɪk/ *n, adj* boulimique (*mf*).

bulk /bʌlk/ **I** *n* **1** (large size) (of package, correspondence, writings) volume *m*; (of building, vehicle) masse *f*; **2** (large body) corps *m* imposant; **3** (large quantity) **in ~** [*buy, sell*] en gros; [*transport, ship*] en vrac; **4** (majority) **the ~ of** la majeure partie de [*imports, research, fortune, applications*]; le plus gros de [*forces, army, workforce*]; la plupart de [*nationals, workers, voters*]; **5** (dietary fibre) fibre *f*.
II *modif* **1** Comm [*delivery, export, order, purchase, sale, supplies, supplier*] en gros; [*mailing*] en nombre: **2** Naut [*cargo, shipment, transport*] en vrac.
III *vi* **to ~ large in** occuper une place importante dans.

bulk: **~-buy** *vtr, vi* [*individual*] acheter en grosses quantités; [*company*] acheter en gros; **~-buying** *n* (by individual) achat *m* en grosses quantités; (by company) achat *m* en gros; **~ carrier** *n* cargo *m*, vraquier *m*.

bulkhead /'bʌlkhed/ *n* Naut, Aviat cloison *f*.

bulk-loading system *n* système *m* de chargement de gros.

bulky /'bʌlkɪ/ *adj* [*person*] corpulent; [*package, equipment, item*] volumineux/-euse; [*book*] épais/-aisse.

bull /bʊl/ **I** *n* **1** Zool taureau *m*; **2** (large man) mâle *m*; **3** Astrol **the Bull** le Taureau; **4** Relig bulle *f*; **5** Fin spéculateur *m* à la hausse, haussier *m*; **6**◑ *abrév* = **bullshit**◑; **7** GB *abrév* ▶ **bull's-eye 1**.
II *modif* [*elephant, whale*] mâle *m*.
III *adj* Fin [*market*] à la hausse.
IV *vtr*○ = **bullshit III**.
V *vi* **1** Fin [*speculator*] spéculer à la hausse; [*shares, stock*] être en hausse; **2**◑ = **bullshit IV**.
IDIOMS **to shoot the ~**◑ US tailler une bavette○, causer; **to go at sb/sth like a ~ at a gate** foncer tête baissée sur qn/qch; ▶ **china**.

bull: **~-bar** *n* Aut pare-buffles *m inv*; **~ calf** *n* jeune taureau *m*, taurillon *m*; **~ campaign** *n* Fin campagne *f* de spéculation à la hausse.

bulldog /'bʊldɒg/ **I** *n* bouledogue *m*.
II *modif* fig [*spirit, determination*] opiniâtre.

bulldog: **~ clip** *n* pince *f* à dessin; **~ edition** *n* US première édition *f* matinale (*d'un journal*).

bulldoze /'bʊldəʊz/ *vtr* **1** lit (knock down) détruire [qch] au bulldozer [*building, wall, forest*]; (move) nettoyer [qch] au bulldozer [*earth, rubble*]; **the village was ~d to the ground** le village a été rasé au bulldozer; **they ~d a track through the forest** ils ont percé un chemin au bulldozer dans la forêt; **2** fig (force) forcer (**into doing** à faire); **to ~ (one's way) through a crowd** se frayer un chemin dans la foule; **the government is trying to ~ the bill through parliament** le gouvernement essaie de faire passer la loi au forcing○.

bulldozer /'bʊldəʊzə(r)/ **I** *n* bulldozer *m*, bouteur *m*.
II○ *vtr* = **bulldoze**.

bullet /'bʊlɪt/ **I** *n* balle *f*; **plastic/rubber ~** balle en plastique/en caoutchouc; **to put a ~ in sb/in sb's head**○ tirer une balle sur qn/dans la tête de qn.
II *modif* [*wound*] par balle; [*hole, mark*] de balle; **a door riddled with ~ holes** une porte criblée de balles.
IDIOMS **to bite (on) the ~** y passer.

bullet-headed /ˌbʊlɪt'hedɪd/ *adj* au crâne en forme d'obus.

bulletin /'bʊlətɪn/ *n* (all contexts) bulletin *m*; **news/sports ~** bulletin d'informations/sportif; **weather ~** bulletin météorologique.

bulletin board *n* **1** US (noticeboard) tableau *m* d'affichage; **2** Comput messagerie *f*.

bulletproof /'bʊlɪtpru:f/ **I** *adj* [*glass, vehicle*] blindé; **~ vest** ou **jacket** gilet *m* pare-balles *inv*.
II *vtr* blinder [*glass, vehicle*].

bullet train *n* train *m* à grande vitesse (japonais).

bull: **~fight** *n* corrida *f*; **~fighter** ▶ **1692** *n* torero *m*; **~fighting** *n* gen corridas *fpl*; (art) tauromachie *f*.

bullfinch /'bʊlfɪntʃ/ *n* bouvreuil *m*.

bull: **~frog** *n* grenouille *f* taureau; **~horn** *n* US mégaphone *m*.

bullion /'bʊlɪən/ *n* ¢ **1** gen lingots *mpl*; **gold/silver ~ (bars)** lingots d'or/d'argent; **2** Fin **gold ~** or *m* monétaire; **~ reserve** réserve *f* métallique; **3** Tex (braid) frange *f* de cannetille.

bullish /'bʊlɪʃ/ *adj* **1** Fin [*market, shares, stocks*] en hausse, haussier/-ière; [*trend*] à la hausse; **2** (optimistic) franchement optimiste.

bull: **~ neck** *n* cou *m* de taureau; **~-necked** *adj* avec un cou de taureau; **~ note** *n* Fin obligation *f* à la hausse.

bullock /'bʊlək/ **I** *n* (young) bouvillon *m*; (mature) bœuf *m*.
II *modif* **~ cart** char *m* à bœufs.

bull: **~ position** *n* Fin position *f* à la hausse; **~ring** *n* (arena) arène *f*; (building) arènes *fpl*; **~ run** *n* Fin marché *m* à la hausse; **~ session**○ *n* US causerie *f* entre hommes○.

bull's-eye /'bʊlzaɪ/ *n* **1** (on a target) mille *m*; **to hit the ~** lit, fig taper en plein dans le mille; **to score a ~** lit, fig mettre dans le mille; **2** (sweet) *gros bonbon à la menthe* ≈ berlingot *m*; **3** Archit œil-de-bœuf *m*.

bull's-eye glass *n* verre *m* en cul de bouteille.

bullshit◑ /'bʊlʃɪt/ **I** *n* conneries◑ *fpl*, bêtises *fpl*; **to talk ~** déconner◑, dire des bêtises.
II *excl* des conneries◑ tout ça!
III *vtr* (*p prés etc* **-tt-**) rouler○, berner [*person*]; **to ~ one's way out of a tricky situation** se tirer d'une situation en bluffant.
IV *vi* (*p prés etc* **-tt-**) déconner◑, dire des bêtises.

bull: **~shitter**◑ *n* baratineur○ *m*, menteur *m*; **~ terrier** *n* bull-terrier *m*.

bully /'bʊlɪ/ **I** *n* **1** (child) petite brute *f*; (adult) tyran *m*; **the class ~** la terreur *f* de la classe; **2**○ † (also **~ beef**) singe◑ *m*.
II○ †*adj* épatant.
III○ *excl* **~ for you!** tant mieux pour toi!
IV *vtr* [*person, child*] maltraiter; [*country*] intimider; **to ~ sb into doing sth** forcer qn à faire qch; **I won't be bullied!** je ne me laisserai pas intimider!
V *vi* jouer les tyrans.
■ **bully off** Sport donner le coup d'envoi.

bully boy○ pej **I** *n* (aggressive male) dur *m*; (paid) homme *m* de main.
II *modif* **~ tactics** manœuvres *fpl* d'intimidation.

bullying /'bʊlɪɪŋ/ **I** *n* (of person, child) mauvais traitements *mpl*; (of country) intimidation *f*.
II *adj* [*person, behaviour*] brutal; [*tactics*] d'intimidation.

bully-off /'bʊlɪɒf/ *n* Sport coup *m* d'envoi.

bulrush /'bʊlrʌʃ/ *n* jonc *m* (des chaisiers).

bulwark /'bʊlwək/ *n* Mil, fig rempart *m* (**against** contre); Naut bastingage *m*; (breakwater) brise-lames *m inv*.

bum○ /bʌm/ **I** *n* **1** GB (buttocks) derrière *m*; **2** esp US (vagrant) clodo○ *m*, clochard *m*; **3** (lazy person) fainéant/-e *m/f*; **4** US **to be on the ~** vivre de la manche○.
II *adj* **1** US (bad) nase○; **~ rap** accusation *f* mensongère; **to get a ~ deal** se faire rouler dans la gadoue; **to give sb a ~ steer** donner un mauvais tuyau à qn; **2** US (injured) blessé.
III *vtr* (*p prés etc* **-mm-**) (scrounge) taper○ [*cigarette, money*] (**off, from** à); **to ~ a ride, to ~ a lift** se faire emmener en voiture.
IV *vi* (*p prés etc* **-mm-**) vivre de la manche○.
IDIOMS **to give sb/to get the ~'s rush** vider qn/être vidé à coups de pied aux fesses○; **to put ~s on seats** GB attirer les gens.
■ **bum around 1** (travel aimlessly) vadrouiller○; **2** (be lazy) traînasser.

bumbag /'bʌmbæg/ *n* GB (sacoche *f*) banane *f*.

bumbershoot○ /'bʌmbəʃu:t/ *n* US riflard○ *m*.

bumble /'bʌmbl/ *vi* **1** (also **~ on**) (mumble) marmonner; **to ~ (on) about sth** radoter à propos de qch; **2** (move) **to ~ around**, **to ~ about** déambuler.

bumblebee /'bʌmblbi:/ *n* bourdon *m*.

bumbler○ /'bʌmblə(r)/ *n* cafouilleur/-euse○ *m/f*.

bumbling○ /'bʌmblɪŋ/ *adj* **1** (incompetent) [*person*] empoté○; [*behaviour, attempt*] maladroit; **2** (mumbling) [*person*] radoteur/-euse; [*speech*] cafouilleux/-euse○.

bumboat /'bʌmbəʊt/ *n* canot *m* d'approvisionnement.

bumf○, **bumph**○ /bʌmf/ *n* GB (documents) paperasserie○ *f*; (toilet paper) PQ○, papier *m* hygiénique.

bumfreezer○ /'bʌmfri:zə(r)/ *n* GB blouson *m* court.

bummer◑ /'bʌmə(r)/ *n* **1** (useless thing) nullité○ *f*; (annoying) **this job's a real ~!** ce boulot est vraiment chiant◑!; **what a ~!** quelle poisse○!; **2** argot des drogués (trip) **to be on a ~** flipper○.

bump /bʌmp/ **I** *n* **1** (lump) (on body) bosse *f* (**on** à); (on road surface) bosse *f* (**on, in** sur); **2** (jolt) secousse *f*; **to come down with a ~**

fig dégringoler○; **3** (sound of fall) bruit *m* sourd; **4** onomat boum; **to go ~** faire boum; **5** euph hum (of pregnant woman) ventre *m*; **6**○ (of stripper) **~s and grinds** déhanchements *mpl* érotiques.
II *vtr* **1** (knock) cogner (**against, on** contre); **to ~ one's head** se cogner la tête; **to ~ sb off** ou **from** faire tomber qn de [*wall, seat*]; **2**○ US (remove) **to ~ sb from** virer○ qn de [*passenger list, job*]; **3**○ US Sport déloger (**out of, from** de); **4**○ US (promote) **to ~ sb to** catapulter○ qn au poste de [*manager, professor*]; **5**○ US (raise) = **bump up**.
III *vi* **1** (knock) **to ~ against** buter contre; **2** (move jerkily) **to ~ along** [*vehicle*] brinquebaler sur [*road*]; **to ~ over** [*vehicle*] cahoter sur [*road*]; **to ~ up and down in** [*person*] se faire secouer dans [*vehicle*].
IDIOMS **to come down to earth with a ~** revenir sur terre; **to feel** ou **read sb's ~s** interpréter les bosses crâniennes de qn; **things that go ~ in the night** les bruits effrayants de la nuit.
■ **bump into**: ¶ **~ into [sb/sth]** (collide) rentrer dans [*person, object*]; **he ~ed into me** il m'est rentré dedans; ¶ **to ~ into [sb]**○ (meet) tomber sur○.
■ **bump off**○: **~ off [sb], ~ [sb] off** liquider○.
■ **bump up**○: **~ up [sth]** **1** (increase) faire grimper○ [*price, tax, wage*] (**from** de, **to** à); **2** (exaggerate) gonfler○ [*real number*].

bumper /ˈbʌmpə(r)/ **I** *n* **1** Aut pare-chocs *m inv*; **~ to ~** pare-chocs contre pare-chocs; **2** US Rail butoir *m*; **3** (tankard) plein verre *m*.
II *adj* (*épith*) (large) [*crop, sales, year*] record *inv*; [*crowd, edition*] exceptionnel/-elle.

bumper: **~ car** *n* auto *f* tamponneuse; **~ sticker** *n* autocollant *m*.

bumph *n* = **bumf**.

bumpkin○ /ˈbʌmpkɪn/ *n* pej (also **country ~**) péquenaud/-e○ *m/f*, plouc○ *m/f*.

bumptious /ˈbʌmpʃəs/ *adj* guindé.

bumpy /ˈbʌmpɪ/ *adj* lit [*road surface*] accidenté; [*wall, ceiling*] irrégulier/-ière; [*journey, flight, landing*] agité.
IDIOMS **to be in for a ~ ride** entrer dans une mauvaise passe.

bun /bʌn/ **I** *n* **1** Culin (bread roll) petit pain *m*; (cake) petit cake *m*; **currant ~** ≈ brioche *f* au raisin; **2** (hairstyle) chignon *m*; **to put/wear one's hair in a ~** se faire/avoir un chignon.
II buns○ *npl* US miches◑ *fpl*, fesses *fpl*.
IDIOMS **to have a ~ in the oven**○ euph hum avoir un polichinelle dans le tiroir, être enceinte.

bunch /bʌntʃ/ **I** *n* **1**○ (of people) groupe *m*; pej bande *f*; **a ~ of friends** un groupe d'amis; **a ~ of idiots** une bande d'imbéciles; **a mixed ~** un groupe de gens différents; **a great ~** des gens sympas○; **2** (of flowers) bouquet *m* (**of** de); **3** (of vegetables) botte *f*; (of bananas) régime *m*; **to tie [sth] in a ~** attacher [qch] en botte [*onions, carrots, radishes*]; **4** (of objects) **a ~ of feathers** une touffe de plumes; **a ~ of keys** un trousseau de clés; **a ~ of wires** un faisceau de fils; **a ~ of twigs** un fagot de brindilles; **5**○ (lot) tas○ *m* (**of** de); **a whole ~ of things** tout un tas○ de choses; **the best** ou **pick of the ~** le meilleur du lot; **6** GB (of hair) couette *f*; **to wear one's hair in ~es** porter des couettes; **7** Sport peloton *m*.
II *vtr* **1** (put in bunches) mettre [qch] en bottes [*vegetables*]; mettre [qch] en bouquets [*flowers*]; **2** Aviat, Transp faire partir [qch] à la queue leu leu [*aircraft, buses*].
III *vi* [*fabric, skirt*] faire des plis, plisser.
IV bunched *pp adj* [*skirt, fabric*] plissé; [*people*] entassé; [*buses*] à la queue leu leu.
■ **bunch together** [*people*] s'entasser; **to be all ~ed together** être entassés.
■ **bunch up**: ¶ **~ up** [*people*] s'entasser; [*fabric, garment*] plisser; ¶ **~ up [sth], ~ [sth] up** plisser [*fabric, garment*]; **to be all ~ed up** [*skirt*] faire des plis; **to stay ~ed up** [*runners*] rester groupés.

bunco○ /ˈbʊŋkəʊ/ US **I** *n* (*pl* **~s**) arnaque○ *f*, escroquerie *f*.
II *modif* **~ thief** arnaqueur○ *m*; **~ trick** arnaque○ *f*; **~ card game** partie *f* d'entourloupe○.
III *vtr* (*3ᵉ pers prés* **~s**; *prét, pp* **~ed**) arnaquer○; **to ~ sb out of sth** arnaquer qn de qch.

buncombe *n* US = **bunkum**.

bundle /ˈbʌndl/ **I** *n* **1** (collection) (of objects) ballot *m*; (of clothes, cloth) balluchon *m*; (of papers, letters, banknotes) liasse *f*; (of books) paquet *m*; (of straw) botte *f*; **a ~ of sticks** un fagot de branches; **2** (baby, person) paquet *m*; **~ of joy** petit ange *m*; iron petit trésor *m*; **~ of fun** gen, iron marrant/-e○ *m/f*; **~ of nerves** boule *f* de nerfs; **to be a ~ of mischief** être malin comme un singe○.
II○ *vtr* **1 to ~ sb into** fourrer○ qn dans [*plane, aircraft*]; **to ~ sth into** fourrer qch dans [*container, drawer*]; **to ~ sb outside** ou **through the door** pousser qn dehors sans ménagement; **2** = **bundle up**; **3** Comput offrir (**with** avec).
III○ *vi* **to ~ into a car** (hurry) se ruer dans une voiture; (cram) s'entasser dans une voiture.
IDIOMS **I don't go a ~ on him/on jazz** GB il/le jazz ne me botte pas○; **to cost/to make a ~**○ coûter/gagner un paquet○.
■ **bundle off**: **~ [sb] off** (remove) faire sortir [qn] sans ménagement; [*police, secret service*] embarquer○; **to ~ sb off to school/to sb's house** expédier qn à l'école/chez qn.
■ **bundle up**: ¶ **~ [sth] up, ~ up [sth]** mettre [qch] en paquet [*letters, newspapers*]; mettre [qch] en fagot [*sticks, wood*]; faire un ballot de [*clothes, knitting*]; mettre [qch] en liasse [*banknotes*]; ¶ **~ [sb] up** emmitoufler (**in** dans); **to ~ oneself up** s'emmitoufler (**in** dans).

bunfight○ /ˈbʌnfaɪt/ *n* GB hum pot○ *m*, pince-fesses◑ *m inv*.

bung /bʌŋ/ **I** *n* tampon *m*, bouchon *m*.
II *vtr* **1** (stop up) boucher [*hole, barrel, bottle*]; **2**○ GB (put, throw) balancer○.
■ **bung in**○ GB: **~ [sth] in, ~ in [sth]** donner [qch] en prime [*free gift, extra*]; glisser [*question, remark*]; envoyer [*application*].
■ **bung out**○ GB: **~ [sth] out, ~ out [sth]** balancer○.
■ **bung up**○ GB: **~ [sth] up, ~ up [sth]** (block) boucher [*sink, drain, nose*]; (raise) augmenter [*prices, interest rates*].

bungalow /ˈbʌŋgələʊ/ *n* gen pavillon *m* (sans étage); (in India) bungalow *m*.

bungee jumping /ˈbʌndʒiː dʒʌmpɪŋ/ ▶ 1282 *n* saut *m* à l'élastique.

bunghole /ˈbʌŋhəʊl/ *n* bonde *f*.

bungle /ˈbʌŋgl/ **I** *n* gaffe *f*.
II *vtr* rater○ [*attempt, opportunity, burglary, investigation*]; **the whole job was ~d** tout le travail a été fait en dépit du bon sens; **he ~d it** il a fait ça en dépit du bon sens.
III *vi* rater son coup○.
IV bungled *pp adj* raté○.

bungler○ /ˈbʌŋglə(r)/ *n* manche○ *m*, maladroit/-e *m/f*.

bungling /ˈbʌŋglɪŋ/ **I** *n* maladresse *f*.
II *adj* maladroit; **you ~ idiot!** espèce de maladroit!

bunion /ˈbʌnjən/ *n* Med oignon *m*.

bunk /bʌŋk/ **I** *n* **1** Naut, Rail couchette *f*; **2** gen (also **~ bed**) (whole unit) lits *mpl* superposés; **the top/lower ~** le lit du haut/du bas; **3**○ = **bunkum**.
II○ *vi* (also **~ down**) dormir.
IDIOMS **to do a ~**○ prendre le large○.
■ **bunk off**○ gen s'éclipser; **to ~ off school** sécher l'école.

bunk bed *n* = **bunk** I 2.

bunker /ˈbʌŋkə(r)/ **I** *n* **1** Mil, gen (shelter) (for commander) bunker *m*; (for gun) blockhaus *m*; (beneath building) abri *m*; **command ~** bunker *m* du PC; **2** (in golf) bunker *m*; **3** (container) Naut, gen soute *f*.
II *vtr* **1** (in golf) lancer [qch] dans un bunker [*ball*]; (of person) **to be ~ed** se trouver dans un bunker; **2** Naut mettre [qch] en soute [*coal, oil*].

bunker mentality *n* attitude *f* défensive obsessionnelle.

bunkhouse /ˈbʌŋkhaʊs/ *n* US Agric ≈ dortoir *m*.

bunkum○ /ˈbʌŋkəm/ *n* fadaises *fpl*; **to talk ~** dire des fadaises.

bunk up *n* GB courte échelle *f*; **to give sb a ~** faire la courte échelle à qn.

bunny /ˈbʌnɪ/ *n* **1** (also **~ rabbit**) lang enfantin (Jeannot) lapin *m*; **2** (also **~ girl**) hôtesse *f* (*du club Playboy®, déguisée en lapin*).

Bunsen (burner) /ˈbʌnsn/ *n* (bec *m*) Bunsen *m*.

bunting /ˈbʌntɪŋ/ *n* **1** (flags) guirlandes *fpl*; (material) étamine *f*; **2** Zool bruant *m*.

buoy /bɔɪ/ **I** *n* gen bouée *f*; (for marking) balise *f* (flottante).
II *vtr* **1** (also **~ up**) (make cheerful) revigorer [*person, team, morale*] (**by** par); **2** (also **~ up**) Fin stimuler [*share prices, sales levels, results*] (**by** par); **3** (also **~ up**) lit (keep afloat) maintenir à flot [*person, raft, object*]; **4** Naut (mark out) baliser [*channel, rocks*].

buoyancy /ˈbɔɪənsɪ/ *n* **1** lit (of floating object) flottabilité *f*; (of supporting medium) poussée *f*; **2** fig (cheerfulness) entrain *m*; **3** Fin (of exports, market, demand) fermeté *f*.

buoyancy aid *n* bouée *f*.

buoyant /ˈbɔɪənt/ *adj* **1** [*object*] qui flotte; [*supporting medium*] qui porte; **sea water is more ~ than fresh water** l'eau de mer porte davantage que l'eau douce; **2** (cheerful) [*person, personality*] vif/vive; [*mood, spirits*] enjoué; [*tread, step*] allègre; [*effect*] revigorant; **3** Fin [*market, demand, currency*] soutenu; [*economy*] en expansion; [*prices, profits, sales*] soutenu.

buoyantly /ˈbɔɪəntlɪ/ *adv* **1** (cheerfully) [*speak*] avec enjouement; [*walk*] d'un pas allègre; **2** (lightly) [*rise, float*] vivement.

buoy rope *n* orin *m*.

BUPA /ˈbuːpə/ *n* GB (*abrév* = **British United Provident Association**) *organisme d'assurance médicale privée*.

bur *n* = **burr** I 1, 3, 4.

burble /ˈbɜːbl/ **I** *n* = **burbling**.
II *vi* **1** [*stream, water*] glouglouter; **2** (also **~ on**) marmonner; **to ~ (on) about sth** radoter à propos de qch.

burbling /ˈbɜːblɪŋ/ **I** *n* **1** (of stream, voices) gargouillis *m*; **2** (rambling talk) galimatias *m*.
II *adj* **1** [*stream, voice*] qui gargouille; **2** (rambling) [*speech, speaker*] cafouilleux/-euse.

burbot /ˈbɜːbət/ *n* lotte *f* (de rivière).

burbs○ /bɜːbz/ *n* US banlieue *f*.

burden /ˈbɜːdn/ **I** *n* **1** (responsibility) fardeau *m* (**to sb** pour qn); **the ~ of guilt/responsibility** le poids de la culpabilité/responsabilité; **the ~ of taxation** la pression fiscale; **the Third World's debt ~** le poids de la dette du Tiers-Monde; **to ease the ~ on sb** alléger le fardeau qui pèse sur qn; **this law imposes an extra ~ on mothers** cette loi constitue un fardeau supplémentaire pour les mères; **the ~ of proof** Jur la charge de la preuve; **2** lit (load) fardeau *m*; **3** (central theme) **the ~ of** la substance de [*argument etc*]; **4** Mus refrain *m*; **5** Naut jauge *f*.
II *vtr* (also **~ down**) **1** fig accabler (**with** de); **2** lit surcharger (**with** de).
III burdened *pp adj* **1** fig accablé (**with** de); **2** lit surchargé (**with** de).
IV *v refl* **to ~ oneself with sth** se charger de qch.

burdensome /ˈbɜːdnsəm/ *adj* pesant.

burdock /ˈbɜːdɒk/ *n* bardane *f*.

bureau /ˈbjʊərəʊ, US -ˈrəʊ/ *n* (*pl* **~s** ou **~x**) **1** (agency) agence *f*; (local office) bureau *m*; **information ~** bureau *m* de renseignements; **2** surtout US (government department) service *m*; **immigration/census ~** service de l'immigration/du recensement; **3** GB (writing desk) secrétaire *m*; **4** US (chest of drawers) commode *f*.

bureaucracy /bjʊəˈrɒkrəsɪ/ *n* bureaucratie *f*.

bureaucrat /ˈbjʊərəkræt/ *n* bureaucrate *mf*.

bureaucratic /ˌbjʊərəˈkrætɪk/ *adj* bureaucratique.

bureaucratically /ˌbjʊərəˈkrætɪklɪ/ *adv* bureaucratiquement.

bureaucratization /bjʊəˌrɒkrətaɪˈzeɪʃn, US -tɪˈz-/ *n* bureaucratisation *f*.

bureaucratize /bjʊəˈrɒkrətaɪz/ *vtr* bureaucratiser.

burette /bjʊəˈret/ *n* Chem burette *f*.

burg○ /bɜːg/ *n* US patelin○ *m*.

burgeon /ˈbɜːdʒən/ *vi* sout **1** fig (grow) [*talent, love, industry, crime*] croître; (multiply) [*population*] se multiplier; [*projects, industries*] voir le jour; **2** fig (flourish) [*talent, love, industry, crime*] fleurir; [*population*] être prospère; **3** lit [*plant, flower*] bourgeonner.

burgeoning /ˈbɜːdʒənɪŋ/ *adj* **1** fig (growing) [*talent, love, industry, crime*] croissant; (multiplying) [*population, projects, industries*] en plein essor; **2** fig (flourishing) [*talent, love, industry, crime*] florissant; [*population*] prospère; **3** lit [*plant, flower*] bourgeonnant.

burger /ˈbɜːgə(r)/ *n* (also **hamburger**) hamburger *m*; **beef~** beefburger *m*.

burger bar *n* fast-food *m*.

burgher‡ /ˈbɜːgə(r)/ *n* Hist ou hum bourgeois *m*.

burglar /ˈbɜːglə(r)/ *n* cambrioleur/-euse *m/f*.

burglar alarm *n* sonnerie *f* d'alarme.

burglarize /ˈbɜːgləraɪz/ *vtr* US cambrioler.

burglar-proof /ˈbɜːgləpruːf/ *adj* [*house*] protégé contre les cambrioleurs; [*safe*] inviolable; [*lock*] incrochetable.

burglary /ˈbɜːglərɪ/ *n* gen cambriolage *m*; Jur vol *m* avec effraction.

burgle /ˈbɜːgl/ *vtr* cambrioler.

burgomaster /ˈbɜːgəmɑːstə(r)/ *n* bourgmestre *m*.

Burgundian /bɜːˈgʌndɪən/ **I** *n* Bourguignon/-onne *m/f*.
II *adj* bourguignon/-onne.

Burgundy /ˈbɜːgəndɪ/ ▶ **1273** **I** *n* **1** Geog Bourgogne *f*; **in ~** en Bourgogne; **2** (wine) bourgogne *m*, vin *m* de Bourgogne; **3** ▶ **1104** (colour) (couleur *f*) bordeaux *m*.
II *adj* **1** Geog de Bourgogne; **2** (colour) bordeaux.

burial /ˈberɪəl/ **I** *n* **1** Relig (ceremony) enterrement *m*; **~ at sea** funérailles *fpl* en mer; **2** (placing in ground) (of body) inhumation *f*; (of object, waste) ensevelissement *m*.
II *modif* [*site*] de sépulture; [*service*] funèbre; [*rites*] funéraire.

burial: **~ chamber** *n* tombeau *m*; **~ ground** *n* cimetière *m*; **~ mound** *n* tumulus *m*; **~ vault** *n* caveau *m*.

burin /ˈbjʊərɪn/ *n* burin *m* de graveur.

Burkina Faso /ˌbɜːkɪnə ˈfæsəʊ/ ▶ **1131** *pr n* Burkina *m*.

burlap /ˈbɜːlæp/ *n* toile *f* à sac.

burlesque /bɜːˈlesk/ **I** *n* **1** Literat (piece of writing) parodie *f*; (genre) (genre *m*) burlesque *m*; **2** (sham) parodie *f*; **3**† US (comedy show) burlesque *m*.
II *adj* **1** [*style, show, performer*] burlesque; **2** (sham) [*ceremony, speech*] caricatural.
III *vtr* parodier.

burly /ˈbɜːlɪ/ *adj* [*person*] solidement charpenté; [*build*] imposant.

Burma /ˈbɜːmə/ ▶ **1131** *pr n* Birmanie *f*.

Burman /ˈbɜːmən/ *n* = **Burmese** I.

Burmese /bɜːˈmiːz/ ▶ **1486**, **1402** **I** *n* **1** (person) Birman/-e *m/f*; **2** (language) birman *m*.
II *adj* birman; **~ cat** chat *m* birman.

burn /bɜːn/ **I** *n* **1** gen, Med brûlure *f*; **cigarette ~s** brûlures de cigarette; **2** Aerosp combustion *f*; **3** dial (stream) ruisseau *m*.
II *vtr* (*prét, pp* **burned** ou **burnt** GB) **1** (damage by heat or fire) brûler [*papers, rubbish*]; incendier, faire brûler [*building, city*]; [*sun*] brûler [*person, skin*]; [*acid*] ronger, brûler [*surface, substance*]; [*alcohol, food*] brûler [*mouth*]; **to be ~ed to the ground** ou **to ashes** être détruit par le feu; **to be ~ed alive** être brûlé vif; **to be ~ed to death** mourir carbonisé; **to ~ one's finger/arm** se brûler le doigt/le bras; **to ~ a hole in sth** faire un trou dans qch; **2** (use) **to ~ coal/gas** [*boiler*] chauffer or marcher au charbon/au gaz; **the system ~s too much oil** le système consomme trop de mazout; **3** Culin laisser brûler [*food*]; brûler [*pan*]; **4**○ US (electrocute) électrocuter; **5**○ US (swindle) escroquer.
III *vi* (*prét, pp* **burned** ou **burnt** GB) **1** (be consumed by fire) brûler; **to ~ to a cinder** être carbonisé; **the house ~ed to the ground** la maison a complètement brûlé or a été réduite en cendres; **2** (be turned on) [*light*] être allumé; **3** (be painful) [*blister, wound*] cuire; (from sun) [*skin, part of body*] brûler; **he has the kind of skin that ~s easily** il attrape facilement des coups de soleil; **my throat is ~ing!** la gorge me brûle!; **his cheeks were ~ing (with embarrassment)** il était rouge de honte; **4** Culin [*toast, meat*] brûler; [*sauce*] prendre au fond; **5** fig (be eager) **to be ~ing to do** [*person*] brûler d'envie de faire; **to be ~ing with desire/with impatience** brûler de désir/d'impatience; **6** Aerosp brûler.
IV *v refl* (*prét, pp* **burned** ou **burnt** GB) **to ~ oneself** se brûler.
IDIOMS **to ~ one's boats** brûler ses vaisseaux.
■ **burn away** [*candle, log*] se consumer.
■ **burn down**: ¶ **~ down 1** [*house*] brûler complètement, être réduit en cendres; **2** [*candle, fire*] baisser; ¶ **~ down [sth], ~ [sth] down** incendier, réduire [qch] en cendres [*house etc*].
■ **burn off**: ¶ **~ off** [*alcohol*] s'évaporer; ¶ **~ off [sth], ~ [sth] off** décaper [qch] au chalumeau [*paint, varnish*]; Med cautériser [*wart*]; Ind faire brûler [*unwanted gas*]; fig dépenser [*energy*].
■ **burn out**: ¶ **~ out** [*candle, fire*] s'éteindre; [*light bulb*] griller; [*fuse*] sauter; fig [*person*] (through overwork) s'user; **at the rate he's working, he'll ~himself out** il va s'user à force de travailler à ce rythme; ¶ **~ out [sth], ~ [sth] out** (destroy by fire) incendier [*building, vehicle*]; Aut, Mech faire griller [*clutch, engine, motor*]; ¶ **~ out [sb], ~ [sb] out** gen, Mil forcer [qn] à sortir par l'incendie [*besieged citizens, troops*].
■ **burn up**: ¶ **~ up 1** [*fire, flames*] flamber; **2** Aerosp [*satellite, meteorite*] se volatiliser; **3**○ US (get angry) se mettre en rogne; **4** (get feverish) [*child*] brûler; ¶ **~ up [sth], ~ [sth] up** brûler [*calories, fuel, waste*]; [*sun*] griller [*lawn, vegetation*]; **she ~s up all her energy worrying** elle dépense toute son énergie à se faire du souci; **to be ~ed up with hatred/with envy** fig être dévoré de haine/d'envie; ¶ **~ up [sb], ~ [sb] up**○ US (make angry) mettre [qn] en rogne.

burned-out *adj* = **burnt-out**.

burner /ˈbɜːnə(r)/ *n* (on gas cooker) brûleur *m*; (of lamp) bec *m* (de gaz).
IDIOMS **to put sth on the back ~** mettre qch en veilleuse or en attente [*question, issue*].

burning /ˈbɜːnɪŋ/ **I** *n* **1 there's a smell of ~** ça sent le brûlé; **I can smell ~!** je sens une odeur de brûlé!; **2** (setting on fire) (of building, town) incendie *m*; ▶ **book-burning**.
II *adj* **1** (on fire) [*building, vehicle, town, forest*] en flammes, en feu; (alight) [*candle, lamp, fire*] allumé; [*ember, coal*] embrasé, ardent; fig (very hot) [*heat*] brûlant, torride; [*sun*] brûlant; **a ~ feeling** ou **sensation** une sensation de brûlure; **2** fig (intense) [*fever, thirst, desire*] brûlant; [*passion, enthusiasm*] ardent; **a ~ question** ou **issue** une question brûlante.

burning: **~ bush** *n* Bible buisson *m* ardent; **~ glass** *n* loupe *f* (*pour enflammer du papier, du bois*).

burnish /ˈbɜːnɪʃ/ littér **I** *vtr* brunir.
II burnished *pp adj* [*copper, skin, leaves*] bruni.

burnisher /ˈbɜːnɪʃə(r)/ *n* (tool) brunissoir *m*.

burnous /bɜːˈnuːs/ *n* burnous *m*.

burn-out /ˈbɜːnaʊt/ *n* **1** (of worker, staff) surmenage *m*, épuisement *m*; **2** Aerosp phase *f* finale de combustion.

burns unit *n* Med service *m* des grands brûlés.

burnt /bɜːnt/ **I** *prét, pp* ▶ **burn**.
II *adj* gen brûlé; [*smell, taste*] de brûlé, de roussi.

burnt: **~ almond** *n* amande *f* grillée, praline *f*; **~ lime** *n* chaux *f* vive; **~ offering** *n* holocauste *m*; hum (burnt meal) repas *m* brûlé; **~ orange** ▶ **1104** *n* orange *m* foncé *inv*; **~-out** *adj* lit [*building, car*] calciné; fig [*person*] usé (par le travail); **~ sacrifice** *n* = **burnt offering**; **~ sienna** ▶ **1104** *n* terre *f* de Sienne brûlée; **~ sugar** *n* caramel *m*; **~ umber** ▶ **1104** *n* terre *f* d'ombre brûlée.

burp○ /bɜːp/ **I** *n* rot○ *m*, renvoi *m*.
II *vtr* faire faire un rot○ à [*baby*].
III *vi* [*person*] roter○; [*baby*] faire son rot○.

burp gun○ *n* US (pistol) revolver *m* à répétition; (rifle) fusil *m* à répétition.

burr /bɜː(r)/ **I** *n* **1** Bot *partie de certaines plantes qui s'accroche aux vêtements, au pelage des animaux*; **2** (sound) (of machine) ronronnement *m*; (of phone, car) bruit *m* assourdi; Ling grasseyement *m* spec; **3** (of tree) loupe *f* (*d'arbre*); **4** Tech ébarboir *m*.
II *vtr* Tech ébarber.
III *vi* [*machine*] ronronner; [*phone*] sonner sourdement.

burrito /bʊˈriːtəʊ/ *n* tortilla *f*.

burro /ˈbʊrəʊ/ *n* US petit âne *m*.

burrow /ˈbʌrəʊ/ **I** *n* terrier *m*.
II *vtr* [*animal*] creuser [*hole, tunnel*]; **to ~ one's way into sth** [*animal, person*] se creuser un chemin dans qch.
III *vi* [*animal*] creuser un terrier; **to ~ into/under sth** (in ground) creuser dans/sous qch; (in blankets) se blottir dans/sous qch.

burr walnut *n* ronce *f* de noyer.

bursa /ˈbɜːsə/ *n* (*pl* **~s** ou **~ae**) Anat bourse *f*.

bursar /ˈbɜːsə(r)/ ▶ **1692** *n* (administrator) Sch, Univ intendant/-e *m/f*.

bursary /ˈbɜːsərɪ/ *n* GB Sch, Univ **1** (grant) bourse *f* (d'études); **2** (office) bureau *m* de l'intendant.

bursitis /bɜːˈsaɪtɪs/ ▶ **1354** *n* hygroma *m*.

burst /bɜːst/ **I** *n* (of flame) jaillissement *m*, jet *m*; (of bomb, shell) éclatement *m*; (of gunfire) rafale *f*; (of activity, energy, enthusiasm) accès *m*; **a ~ of growth** une poussée; **a ~ of weeping** une crise de larmes; **a ~ of laughter** un éclat de rire; **a ~ of anger** un accès de colère; **a ~ of applause** un tonnerre d'applaudissements; **a ~ of colour** une explosion de couleurs; **a ~ of inspiration** un éclat de génie; **there has been a ~ of interest in the 1920s/in her work** il y a eu un regain d'intérêt subit pour les années 20/pour son œuvre; **to put on a ~ of speed** Aut faire une pointe de vitesse.
II *vtr* (*prét, pp* **burst**) crever [*balloon, bubble, tyre*]; **to ~ a blood vessel** Med rompre un vaisseau sanguin; **the river burst its banks** le fleuve a rompu ses digues; **a burst pipe** un tuyau qui a éclaté.
III *vi* (*prét, pp* **burst**) **1** [*balloon, bubble, tyre*] crever; [*abscess*] crever, percer; [*pipe, boiler*] éclater; [*dam*] rompre; [*bomb, shell, firework*] éclater; **to be ~ing at the seams, to be full to ~ing point** [*bag, room, building*] être plein à craquer; hum [*person*] (from too much food) n'en pouvoir

plus, être plein comme une outre; **to be laughing fit to ~** se tordre de rire; **to be ~ing to do** mourir d'envie de faire; **to be ~ing (for the toilet)**○ avoir besoin de faire pipi○; **to be ~ing with health/enthusiasm/pride** déborder de santé/d'enthousiasme/de fierté; **2** (emerge suddenly) [*people*] surgir; [*water etc*] jaillir; **the sun burst through the clouds** le soleil a percé les nuages; **soldiers burst from behind the hedgerows** des soldats ont surgi brusquement de derrière les haies; **they burst onto the rock scene in 1982** ils ont fait irruption dans le monde du rock en 1982.

■ **burst forth** littér [*buds, blossom*] éclore liter; [*sun*] surgir.

■ **burst in**: **~ in** faire irruption, entrer en trombe; **to ~ in on a meeting/conversation** interrompre brusquement une réunion/conversation.

■ **burst into**: **~ into [sth] 1** entrer dans [qch] en trombe, faire irruption dans [*room, building, meeting*]; **2 to ~ into blossom** ou **bloom** s'épanouir; **to ~ into leaf** se couvrir de feuilles; **to ~ into flames** s'enflammer; **to ~ into song** se mettre à chanter; **to ~ into tears** fondre en larmes; **to ~ into laughter** éclater de rire.

■ **burst open**: ¶ **~ open** [*door*] s'ouvrir violemment or brusquement; [*bag, sack*] éclater; ¶ **~ open [sth], ~ [sth] open** ouvrir [qch] violemment.

■ **burst out 1** (come out) **to ~ out of a room/building** sortir en trombe d'une pièce/d'un immeuble; **he was ~ing out of his waistcoat** fig il était boudiné dans son gilet; **the straw was ~ing out of the mattress** la paille sortait du matelas éventré; **2** (start) **to ~ out laughing** éclater de rire; **to ~ out crying** fondre en larmes; **to ~ out singing** se mettre (tout d'un coup) à chanter; **3** (exclaim) s'écrier, s'exclamer; **'you're lying!' he ~ out angrily** 'tu mens!' s'écria-t-il en colère.

■ **burst through**: **~ through [sth]** rompre [*barricade, road block*]; **she ~ through the door** elle est entrée violemment or brusquement.

burster /ˈbɜːstə(r)/ *n* Comput, Print rupteur *m*.

burthen ‡ = **burden**.

burton /ˈbɜːtn/ *n* GB **to go for a ~**○† [*plan, enterprise*] tomber à l'eau○; [*person*] (be killed) casser sa pipe○; (fall over) prendre un gadin○.

Burundi /bəˈrʊndɪ/ ▶ 1131 *pr n* Burundi *m*.

bury /ˈberɪ/ *vtr* **1** (after death) enterrer, inhumer [*person*]; enterrer [*animal*]; **2** [*avalanche etc*] ensevelir [*person, building, town*]; **to be buried alive** être enterré vivant; **3** (hide) enterrer, enfouir [*treasure, valuable, bone*]; **to ~ oneself in the countryside** aller s'enterrer à la campagne; **village buried deep in the countryside** village perdu dans la campagne; **to ~ one's face in one's hands** se cacher le visage dans ses mains; **4** (suppress) enterrer [*differences, hatred, memories*]; **5** (engross) (*gén au passif*) **to be buried in** être plongé dans [*book, work, thoughts*]; **to ~ oneself in one's work** se plonger dans son travail; **6** (plunge) enfoncer [*dagger, teeth*] (**into** dans) ; **to ~ one's hands in one's pockets** plonger ses mains dans ses poches.

IDIOMS **let the dead ~ the dead** il faut laisser les morts ensevelir les morts.

bus /bʌs/ **I** *n* (*pl* **buses**) **1** (vehicle) autobus *m*, bus *m*; (long-distance) autocar *m*, car *m*; **by ~** [*come, go, travel*] en (auto)bus, par le bus; **on the ~** dans le bus; **2** Comput (also **~bar**) bus *m*; **address/data/memory ~** bus *m* d'adresses/de données/de mémoire; **input/output ~** bus *m* des entrées/sorties.

II *modif* [*depot, service, stop, ticket*] d'autobus.

III *vtr* (*p prés etc* **-ss-** GB, **-s-** US) acheminer [qn] par or en bus.

IV *vi* (*p prés etc* **-ss-** GB, **-s-** US) **1**○ (travel) **to ~ back/to work** revenir/aller au travail en bus; **2** (in restaurant) travailler comme aide-serveur.

IDIOMS **we'll have to ~ it** il faudra y aller en bus.

busboy /ˈbʌsbɔɪ/ *n* US aide-serveur *m*.

busby /ˈbʌzbɪ/ *n* bonnet *m* à poil (*de soldat*).

bus: **~ conductor** ▶ 1692 *n* receveur *m* d'autobus; **~ conductress** ▶ 1692 *n* receveuse *f* d'autobus; **~ driver** ▶ 1692 *n* conducteur/-trice *m/f* d'autobus.

bush /bʊʃ/ *n* **1** (shrub) buisson *m*; **a ~ of hair** fig une épaisse tignasse; **2** (in Australia, Africa) **the ~** la brousse *f*; **3** (fox's brush) queue *f*; **4** Tech bague *f*.

IDIOMS **he doesn't beat about the ~** il n'y va pas par quatre chemins; **don't beat about the ~** cessez de tourner autour du pot; **a bird in the hand is worth two in the ~** Prov un tiens vaut mieux que deux tu l'auras Prov.

bush baby *n* galago *m*.

bushed○ /bʊʃt/ *adj* (tired) crevé○, vanné○.

bushel /ˈbʊʃl/ *n* boisseau *m*; **~s of**○ US des quantités de.

IDIOMS **to hide one's light under a ~** ne pas se mettre en valeur.

bush: **~fighter** *n* Mil combattant/-e *m/f* de brousse; **~fighting** *n* Mil combat *m* de brousse; **~fire** *n* feu *m* de brousse.

bushing /ˈbʊʃɪŋ/ *n* Tech (in engine, machine) bagne *f*; (for tubes, pipes) manchon *m*.

bush jacket *n* saharienne *f*.

bush league○ US **I** *n* pej dernière division *f* (*en baseball*).

II *adj* pej médiocre.

bush: **~ leaguer**○ *n* US Sport joueur *m* de dernière division; fig, pej minable *mf*; **~man** *n* (*pl* **-men**) Austral broussard *m*; **Bushman** *n* (*pl* **Bushmen**) Boschiman *m*; **~ranger** *n* US (backwoodsman) broussard/-e *m/f*; **~ telegraph** *n* lit téléphone *m* de brousse; fig hum téléphone *m* arabe.

bushwhack /ˈbʊʃwæk/ US, Austral **I** *vtr* tendre une embuscade à.

II *vi* **1** (beat path) se frayer un chemin à travers la brousse; **2** (live in the bush) vivre dans la brousse; **3** Mil faire la guérilla.

bushwhacker /ˈbʊʃwækə(r)/ *n* **1** US, Austral broussard/-e *m/f*; (outlaw) hors-la-loi *m inv*; **2** Mil (guerilla) guérillero *m*; **3** Austral pej (boor) rustre *m*.

bushy /ˈbʊʃɪ/ *adj* **1** [*hair*] touffu; [*beard*] épais/-aisse; [*eyebrows*] broussailleux/-euse; [*tail*] touffu; **2** [*land, garden*] broussailleux/-euse.

busies○ /ˈbɪzɪz/ *npl* GB dial (police) flics○ *mpl*.

busily /ˈbɪzɪlɪ/ *adv* **~ working/writing** activement occupé à travailler/à écrire.

business /ˈbɪznɪs/ **I** *n* **1** ¢ (commerce) affaires *fpl*; **to be in ~** être dans les affaires; **to go into ~** se lancer dans les affaires; **they made a lot of money in ~** ils ont gagné beaucoup d'argent dans les affaires; **to be honest in ~** être toujours honnête en affaires; **to set up in ~** s'établir à son compte; **she went into** ou **set up in ~ as a translator** elle s'est établie comme traductrice; **the firm is no longer in ~** l'entreprise a fermé; **to do ~ with sb** traiter avec qn, faire des affaires avec qn; **they do a lot of ~ with Germany** ils font beaucoup d'affaires avec l'Allemagne; **they're in ~ together** ils sont associés; **he is a man I can do ~ with** c'est un homme avec qui je peux travailler; **to go out of ~** faire faillite; **they're back in ~** Comm ils ont repris leurs activités; **she's gone to Brussels on ~** elle est allée à Bruxelles pour affaires or en voyage d'affaires; **he's away on ~ at the moment** en ce moment il est en déplacement pour affaires; **the recession has put them out of ~** la récession les a obligés à cesser leurs activités; **it's good/bad for ~** ça fait marcher/ne fait pas marcher les affaires; **to talk ~** parler affaires; **now we're talking ~!** fig maintenant on commence à parler sérieusement!; **are you in London for ~ or pleasure?** êtes-vous à Londres pour affaires ou pour le plaisir?; **to mix ~ with pleasure** joindre l'utile à l'agréable; **~ is ~** les affaires sont les affaires; **'~ as usual'** (on shop window) 'nous restons ouverts pendant les travaux'; **it is/it was ~ as usual** fig c'est/c'était comme à l'habitude; **2** (custom, trade) **to lose ~** perdre de la clientèle; **how's ~** comment vont les affaires?; **~ is slow at the moment** les affaires marchent au ralenti or ne vont pas fort en ce moment; **most of our ~ comes from tourists** la plupart de nos clients sont des touristes; **we are doing twice as much ~ as last summer** notre chiffre d'affaires a doublé par rapport à l'été dernier; **3** (trade, profession) métier *m*; **what's your line of ~?, what (line of) ~ are you in?** vous travaillez dans quelle branche?, qu'est-ce que vous faites dans la vie?; **he's in the hotel/insurance ~** il travaille dans l'hôtellerie/les assurances; **he's the best comedian/chef in the ~**○ fig c'est le meilleur comique/chef qui existe; **4** (company, firm) affaire *f*, entreprise *f*; (shop) commerce *m*, boutique *f*; **small ~es** les petites entreprises; **she runs a small dressmaking/mail-order ~** elle dirige une petite affaire de confection/de vente par correspondance; **5** ¢ (important matters) questions *fpl* importantes; (duties, tasks) devoirs *mpl*, occupations *fpl*; **let's get down to ~** passons aux choses sérieuses; **the ~ before a meeting** Admin l'ordre *m* du jour; **we got through a lot of ~ at the meeting** on a réglé beaucoup de questions au cours de la réunion; **can we get down to ~?** on peut s'y mettre?; **to go about one's ~** vaquer à ses occupations; **to deal with daily ~** expédier les affaires courantes; **we still have some unfinished ~ to discuss** nous avons encore des choses à discuter; **he got on with the ~ of tidying up/letterwriting** il s'est mis à faire le rangement/la correspondance; **'any other ~'** (on agenda) 'questions diverses'; **6** (concern) **that's her ~** ça la regarde, c'est son affaire; **it's none of your ~!** ça ne te regarde pas!, ce n'est pas ton affaire!; **it's no ~ of yours what he does in his private life** sa vie privée ne te regarde pas; **to make it one's ~ to find out** se charger de découvrir la vérité; **mind your own ~**○! occupe-toi or mêle-toi de tes affaires○!; **he had no ~ telling her!** ce n'était pas à lui de le lui dire!; **she had no ~ to be there** elle n'avait rien à faire là-bas; **there I was minding my own ~ when** ... j'étais là tranquille dans mon coin, quand ...; **7** (affair) histoire *f*, affaire *f*; **it's a bad** ou **sorry ~** c'est une triste affaire; **the newspapers are full of this murder/drugs ~** les journaux ne parlent que de cette histoire de meurtre/de drogue; **what a dreadful ~!** quelle histoire horrible!; **no funny ~!** et pas d'histoires!; **a nasty ~** une sale affaire; **I'm fed up with the whole ~** j'en ai ras le bol○; **8** (bother, nuisance) histoire *f*; **moving house is quite a ~!** c'est toute une histoire de déménager!; **what a ~!** quelle histoire!; **9**○ euph **to do its ~** [*animal*] faire ses besoins.

II *modif* [*address, law, letter, transaction*] commercial; [*pages*] affaires; [*meeting, travel, consortium*] d'affaires; **~ people** hommes *mpl* d'affaires; **the ~ community** le monde des affaires.

IDIOMS **now we're in ~!** maintenant nous sommes prêts!, maintenant on peut y aller!; **to be in the ~ of doing** avoir pour habitude de faire; **she can sing/play the piano like nobody's ~**○ elle chante/joue du piano comme personne; **to work like nobody's ~**○ travailler d'arrache-pied; **that's the ~**○! c'est super○!; **she means ~!** elle ne plaisante pas!; **to send sb about his ~** envoyer promener qn○; **to give sb the ~**○ US en faire voir de toutes les couleurs à qn○.

business: **~ account** *n* compte *m* professionnel; **~ accounting** *n* comptabilité *f* d'entreprise; **~ activity** *n* activité *f* industrielle et commerciale; **~ administration** *n* administration *f* commerciale or industrielle; **~ agent** *n* gen agent *m* d'affaires; US (union leader) délégué/-e *m/f* syndical/-e; **~ analyst** ▶1692 *n* analyste *mf* financier/-ière; **~ associate** *n* associé/-e *m/f*; **~ call** *n* (visit) visite *f* d'affaires; (phone call) communication *f* d'affaires; **~ card** *n* carte *f* de visite; **~ centre** GB, **~ center** US *n* centre *m* d'affaires.

business class *n* Aviat classe *f* affaires; **to travel ~** voyager en classe affaires.

business: **~ college** *n* école *f* de commerce; **~ contact** *n* relation *f* d'affaires; **~ cycle** *n* cycle *m* économique; **~ deal** *n* affaire *f*; **~ economics** *n* (+ *v sg*) économie *f* de l'entreprise; **~ end** *n* hum (of firearm) côté *m* opérant; (of knife) côté *m* coupant; **~ ethics** *npl* déontologie *f* commerciale; **~ expenses** *npl* frais *mpl* professionnels; **~ failures** *npl* faillites *fpl* d'entreprises; **~ hours** *npl* gen heures *fpl* ouvrables; (in office) heures *fpl* de bureau; (of shop) heures *fpl* d'ouverture.

businesslike /ˈbɪznɪslaɪk/ *adj* [*person, manner*] sérieux/-ieuse; [*transaction*] régulier/-ière, sérieux/-ieuse; fig hum [*knife, tool*] sérieux/-ieuse; **her approach was extremely ~** sa façon de s'y prendre était très sérieuse or efficace.

business: **~ lunch** *n* déjeuner *m* d'affaires; **~ machine** *n* machine *f* de bureau.

businessman /ˈbɪznɪsmən/ ▶1692 *n* (*pl* **-men**) homme *m* d'affaires; **big ~** brasseur *m* d'affaires, affairiste *m* pej; **he's a good ~** il a le sens des affaires.

business: **~ manager** ▶1692 *n* Comm, Ind directeur commercial/directrice commerciale *m/f*; (in showbusiness) agent *m*; **~ park** *n* parc *m* d'affaires or d'activités; **~ plan** *n* projet *m* commercial; **~ premises** *npl* locaux *mpl* commerciaux; **~ proposition** *n* proposition *f*; **~ rate** *n* GB taxe *f* professionnelle; **~ reply envelope** *n* enveloppe *f* pré-affranchie, enveloppe-réponse *f*; **~ reply service** *n* service *m* de pré-affranchissement d'enveloppes-réponses; **~ school** *n* école *f* de commerce.

business sense *n* **to have ~** avoir le sens des affaires; **this decision makes good ~** sur le plan commercial c'est une bonne décision.

business: **~ services** *npl* services *mpl* aux entreprises; **~ software** *n* logiciel *m* de gestion; **~ studies** *npl* études *fpl* commerciales or de commerce; **~ suit** *n* costume *m* de ville, complet *m*; **~ trip** *n* voyage *m* d'affaires; **~ unit** *n* local *m* à usage commercial; **~woman** *n* femme *f* d'affaires.

bus(s)ing /ˈbʌsɪŋ/ *n* US ramassage *m* scolaire (*surtout pour abolir la ségrégation raciale aux États-Unis*).

busk /bʌsk/ *vi* GB [*musician*] jouer dans la rue; [*singer*] chanter dans la rue.

busker /ˈbʌskə(r)/ *n* GB (musician) musicien/-ienne *m/f* ambulant/-e; (singer) chanteur/-euse *m/f* ambulant/-e.

bus lane *n* couloir *m* d'autobus.

busload /ˈbʌsləʊd/ *n* car *m*; **a ~ of tourists** un car plein de voyageurs; **by the ~, by ~s** par cars entiers.

busman /ˈbʌsmən/ *n* employé *m* des autobus.

IDIOMS **a ~'s holiday** GB vacances *fpl* qui n'en sont pas vraiment.

bus: **~ pass** *n* carte *f* de bus; **~ route** *n* ligne *f* d'autobus; **~ shelter** *n* abribus® *m*; **~ station** *n* gare *f* routière.

bust /bʌst/ **I** *n* **1** (breasts) poitrine *f*; **2** Art buste *m*; **3**○ US (binge) **to go on the ~** faire la bringue○; **beer ~** boum○ *f*; **4**○ US (failure) (person) raté/-e *m/f*; (business, career) échec *m*; Econ effondrement *m*; **5**○ (police raid) rafle *f*; (arrest) arrestation *f*; **6**○ US (punch) coup *m*.

II *modif*: **~ size, ~ measurement** tour *m* de poitrine.

III *adj*○ **1** (broken) fichu○, foutu◑; **2** (bankrupt) **to go ~** faire faillite; **to be ~** être à sec○.

IV○ *vtr* (*prét, pp* **~** ou **~ed**) **1** (break) bousiller○ [*machine, object*]; **2** [*police*] (break up) démanteler [*organization, drugs ring etc*]; (raid) faire une descente dans [*premises*]; (arrest) épingler○ [*suspect*]; **3** (financially) ruiner [*person, firm*]; **4**○ US (demote) rétrograder [*soldier, policeman*] (**to** au rang de); **5** surt US (hit) flanquer○ un coup (or des coups) à; **6** US dresser [*horse*]; **7**○ = **burst II**.

V○ *vi* (*prét, pp* **~** ou **~ed**) **1 Brighton or ~!** c'est parti pour Brighton, quoi qu'il arrive!; **2** = **burst III**.

IDIOMS **to ~ a gut doing sth**○ se donner un mal de chien○ pour faire qch; **to ~ one's ass doing sth**◑ se casser le cul◑ pour faire qch.

■ **bust up**○: ¶ **~ up** [*couple*] rompre; [*friends*] se brouiller; ¶ **~ [sth] up, ~ up [sth]** flanquer en l'air○ [*meeting, party, relationship*].

bustard /ˈbʌstəd/ *n* outarde *f*.

buster○ /ˈbʌstə(r)/ *n* US **move over, ~!** pousse-toi de là, mon pote○!

bus terminus *n* GB terminus *m* des bus.

bustier /ˈbʌstɪeɪ/ *n* bustier *m*.

bustle /ˈbʌsl/ **I** *n* **1** (activity) effervescence *f* (of de); **hustle and ~** effervescence *f*; **2** Hist Fashn faux cul○ *m*, tournure *f*.

II *vi* [*person, crowd*] (also **~ about**) s'affairer; **to ~ in/out** entrer/sortir d'un air affairé; **to ~ with activity** être plein d'animation.

bustling /ˈbʌslɪŋ/ *adj* [*street, shop, town*] animé; [*person*] affairé.

bust-up○ /ˈbʌstʌp/ *n* engueulade○ *f*; **to have a ~ with sb** avoir une engueulade avec qn.

busty○ /ˈbʌstɪ/ *adj* à la poitrine plantureuse.

busy /ˈbɪzɪ/ **I** *adj* **1** [*person*] occupé (**with** avec; **doing** à faire); **to look ~** avoir l'air occupé; **to be too ~ to do** être trop occupé pour faire; **to keep oneself/sb ~** trouver de quoi s'occuper/occuper qn; **I try to keep ~** je tâche de trouver de quoi m'occuper; **that should keep them ~!** cela devrait les occuper!; **to get ~**○ s'y mettre○; **get ~!** allez, au travail!; **2** [*shop, office, airport, junction*] actif/-ive; [*square, street, town*] animé; [*day, week*] chargé; **to lead a ~ life** mener une vie très active; **the busiest time of year** c'est la période la plus active de l'année; **were the shops ~?** est-ce qu' il y avait beaucoup de monde dans les magasins?; **3** (engaged) [*line, photocopier*] occupé; **4** (overelaborate) [*design, wallpaper*] chargé; **5** US (prying) indiscret/-ète.

II *v refl* **to ~ oneself doing sth** faire qch pour se donner une contenance.

busy bee US **I** *n* (person) personne *f* débordant d'activité, mouche *f* du coche pej.

II busy bees *npl* (gossip) cancans *mpl*.

busy: **~body**○ *n* **he's a real ~** il se mêle de tout; **~ Lizzie** *n* GB impatiente *f*; **~ signal** *n* US Telecom tonalité *f* 'occupé'; **~ work** *n* US Sch ¢ activité *f* (*dont le but est d'occuper les élèves*).

but /bʌt, bət/ **I** *adv* (only, just) **if I had ~ known** si seulement j'avais su; **if I could ~ remember his name** si seulement je pouvais me rappeler son nom; **these are ~ two of the possibilities** ce ne sont que deux possibilités; **he's ~ a child** ce n'est qu'un enfant; **I can ~ try** je peux toujours essayer; **one can't help ~ admire her** on ne peut pas s'empêcher de l'admirer; **he couldn't help ~ feel sad** il ne pouvait s'empêcher d'être triste.

II *prep* **anything ~ that** tout, sauf ça; **anybody ~ him** n'importe qui sauf lui; **anywhere ~ Australia** n'importe où sauf en Australie; **everybody ~ Paul will be there** tout le monde sera là sauf Paul; **nobody ~ me knows how to do it** personne d'autre que moi ne sait le faire, il n'y a que moi qui sache le faire; **it's nothing ~ an insult** ce n'est qu'une insulte; **he's nothing ~ a coward** ce n'est qu'un lâche; **to do nothing ~ disturb people** ne rien faire d'autre que déranger les gens; **there's nothing for it ~ to leave** il n'y a plus qu'une solution, c'est de partir; **where ~ in France?** où sinon en France?; **who could do it ~ you?** qui pourrait le faire sinon toi?; **and whom should I meet in town ~ Steven!** et devine qui j'ai rencontré en ville, Steven!; **the last ~ one** l'avant-dernier; **the next road ~ one** la deuxième rue; ▶ **all**.

III but for *prep phr* sans; **~ for you, I would have died** sans toi je serais mort; **we would have married ~ for the war** sans la guerre or s'il n'y avait pas eu la guerre, nous nous serions mariés; **I'd have won ~ for him** sans lui or s'il n'avait pas été là, j'aurais gagné; **he would have gone ~ for me** si je n'avais pas été là il serait parti.

IV *conj* **1** (expressing contrast, contradiction) mais; **it's not an asset ~ a disadvantage** ce n'est pas un atout mais un désavantage; **I'll do it, ~ not yet** je le ferai, mais pas tout de suite; **I agree, ~ I may be wrong** je suis d'accord, mais j'ai peut-être tort; **2** (yet) mais; **cheap ~ nourishing** bon marché mais nourrissant; **he's about your height ~ fatter** il est à peu près de ta taille mais plus gros; **3** (expressing reluctance, protest, surprise) **~ that's ridiculous/wonderful!** mais c'est ridicule/formidable!; **~ we can't afford it!** mais nous n'avons pas les moyens!; **4** (except that) **never a day passes ~ she visits him** il n'y a pas de jour qu'elle ne lui rende visite; **there's no doubt ~ he'll come** il ne fait aucun doute qu'il viendra; **5** (in apologies) mais; **excuse me, ~** excusez-moi, mais; **I may be old-fashioned, ~** je suis peut-être vieux-jeu, mais; **6** (for emphasis) **not twice, ~ three times** pas deux mais trois fois; **I've searched everywhere, ~ everywhere** j'ai cherché absolument partout; **nothing, ~ nothing will persuade him to leave** il n'y a absolument rien qui puisse le persuader de partir; **7** (adding to the discussion) **~ to continue...** mais, pour continuer...; **~ first, let's consider the advantages** mais voyons tout d'abord les avantages.

IDIOMS **no ~s (about it)** il n'y a pas de 'mais' qui tienne, pas de discussion; ▶ **if**.

butane /ˈbjuːteɪn/ *n* butane *m*.

butch○ /bʊtʃ/ *adj* [*woman, appearance, manner*] offensive hommasse○; [*man*] macho○.

butcher /ˈbʊtʃə(r)/ ▶1692 **I** *n* **1** (person) lit, fig boucher *m*; **~'s (shop)** boucherie *f*; **~'s boy** GB garçon *m* boucher; **~'s meat** viande *f* de boucherie; **2** US (candy-seller) vendeur *m* ambulant.

II *vtr* **1** abattre [*animal*]; débiter [*meat*]; fig (all contexts) massacrer; **2** US vendre [*sweets, candy*].

IDIOMS **to have** ou **take a ~'s (hook) at sth/sb**○ GB jeter un œil○ à qch/qn.

butchery /ˈbʊtʃərɪ/ *n* **1** (of meat) découpage *m*; (trade) boucherie *f*; **2**† GB (shop) boucherie *f*; **3** (of people) (slaughter) massacre *m*.

butler /ˈbʌtlə(r)/ ▶1692 *n* maître *m* d'hôtel, majordome *m*; **~'s pantry** office *m*.

butt /bʌt/ **I** *n* **1** (end) gen bout *m*; (of rifle) crosse *f*; (of cigarette) mégot○ *m*; **2**○ surt US (buttocks) derrière○ *m*; **get off your ~**○! remue tes fesses○!; **3** (barrel) (gros) tonneau *m*; **4** (person: target) **to be the ~ of sb's jokes/of criticism** être la cible des blagues de qn/des critiques; **5** (on shooting range) (mound) butte *f* (de tir); (target) cible *f*; **the ~s** le champ de tir; **6** (blow) (by person)

by
When *by* is used with a passive verb it is translated by *par*:
he was killed by a tiger = il a été tué par un tigre
she was horrified by the news = elle a été horrifiée par la nouvelle
For particular usages, see the entry **by**.

When *by* is used with a present participle to mean *by means of* it is translated by *en*:
she learned French by listening to the radio = elle a appris le français en écoutant la radio
For particular usages, see the entry **by**.

When *by* is used with a noun to mean *by means of* or *using* it is translated by *par*:
by telephone = par téléphone
to hold something by the handle = tenir quelque chose par la poignée
Note, however:
to travel by bus/train/plane = voyager en bus/train/avion

In time expressions *by* is translated by *avant*:
it must be finished by Friday = il faut que ce soit fini avant vendredi
For particular usages, see the entry **by**.

by often appears as the second element in phrasal verbs (*get by*, *put by*, *stand by* etc.).
For translations, consult the appropriate verb entry (***get***, ***put***, ***stand*** etc.).

For translations of fixed phrases and expressions such as *to learn something by heart*, *to deliver something by hand* etc. consult the appropriate noun entry (***heart***, ***hand*** etc.).

For all other uses of *by* see the entry **by**.

coup *m* de tête; (by goat, ram etc) coup *m* de corne.
II *vtr* **1** [*person*] donner un coup de tête à; [*goat, ram etc*] donner un coup de corne à; **to ~ one's way through sth** se frayer un chemin à travers qch; **2** Constr abouter.
■ **butt in** (on conversation) interrompre; (during meeting) intervenir; **he kept ~ing in on our conversation** il n'arrêtait pas de mettre son grain de sel○; **there's no need for you to ~ in** tu n'as pas besoin de t'en mêler; **sorry to ~ in but** navré de vous interrompre mais; **to ~ into sb's business** US se mêler des affaires de qn.
■ **butt out**○ US **~ out!** occupe-toi de tes oignons!

butter /ˈbʌtə(r)/ **I** *n* beurre *m*.
II *vtr* beurrer [*bread*]; mettre du beurre dans [*vegetables*].
IDIOMS **it's her bread and ~** c'est son gagne-pain; **(she looks as if) ~ wouldn't melt in her mouth** on lui donnerait le bon Dieu sans confession; **to go through sth like a knife through ~** rentrer dans qch comme dans du beurre.
■ **butter up**○: **~ [sb] up, ~ up [sb]** passer de la pommade à○.

butterball /ˈbʌtəbɔːl/ *n* **1** Culin coquille *f* de beurre; **2**○ US rondouillard/-e○ *m/f*.

butter: **~bean** *n* haricot *m* de Lima, pois *m* de sept ans; **~cup** *n* Bot bouton *m* d'or; **~ dish** *n* beurrier *m*; **~fingered** *adj* maladroit, empoté; **~fingers** *n* empoté/-e *m/f*.

butterfly /ˈbʌtəflaɪ/ *n* **1** Zool papillon *m* (*pl* **-ies**); **she's a bit of a social ~** elle papillonne en société; **2** Sport = **butterfly stroke**.
IDIOMS **to have butterflies (in one's stomach)** avoir le trac○.

butterfly: **~ kiss** *n* baiser *m* de papillon; **~ net** *n* filet *m* à papillons; **~ nut** *n* papillon *m*, écrou *m* à ailettes; **~ stroke** *n* brasse *f* papillon; **~ valve** *n* soupape *f* à papillon.

butter: **~head lettuce** *n* US laitue *f*; **~ knife** *n* couteau *m* à beurre; **~milk** *n* babeurre *m*; **~ muslin** *n* étamine *f*.

butterscotch /ˈbʌtəskɒtʃ/ **I** *n* (sweet) caramel *m* dur; (flavour) caramel *m*.
II *modif* [*ice cream, sauce*] au caramel.

butterwort /ˈbʌtəwɜːt/ *n* Bot grassette *f*.

buttery /ˈbʌtərɪ/ **I** *n* **1** GB Univ ≈ cafétéria *m*; **2** (teashop) salon *m* de thé; **3** (storeroom) dépense *f*.
II *adj* [*taste*] de beurre; [*cake*] au goût de beurre; [*fingers*] plein de beurre.

buttock /ˈbʌtək/ *n* fesse *f*.

button /ˈbʌtn/ **I** *n* **1** (on coat, bell, switch, sword) bouton *m*; **to do up/to undo a ~** boutonner/déboutonner un bouton; **chocolate ~s** pastilles *fpl* de chocolat; **2**○ US (chin) pointe *f* du menton; **3** US (badge) insigne *m*, badge *m*.
II *vtr* = **button up**.
III *vi* [*dress etc*] se boutonner.
IDIOMS **as bright as a ~** vif/vive d'esprit; **he's a ~ short**○ il lui manque une case○; **on the ~**○ (exactly) au petit poil○; (on time) à l'heure pile○; **to have all one's ~s**○ avoir toute sa tête.
■ **button up**: **~ [sth] up, ~ up [sth]** boutonner [*garment*]; **~ (up) your lip!**○ la ferme!○; **the deal is all ~ed up!**○ l'affaire est dans le sac○!

button: **~-down** *adj* [*collar*] à pointes boutonnées; [*shirt*] avec col à pointes boutonnées; **~ed up** *adj* [*person*] coincé○.

buttonhole /ˈbʌtnhəʊl/ **I** *n* **1** Fashn boutonnière *f*; **2** GB (flower) fleur *f* (*portée à la boutonnière*).
II *vtr* **1** Sewing border [qch] au point de boutonnière; **2**○ (accost) accrocher○.

button: **~holer** *n* pied *m* de biche pour boutonnières; **~hole stitch** *n* point *m* de boutonnière; **~hook** *n* tire-bouton *m*; **~ mushroom** *n* champignon *m* de Paris.

Buttons† /ˈbʌtnz/ *pr n* GB groom† *m*.

button-through /ˌbʌtnˈθruː/ *adj* GB [*dress*] toute boutonnée; [*skirt*] boutonnée.

buttress /ˈbʌtrɪs/ **I** *n* **1** gen contrefort *m*; fig soutien *m*; **2** (also **flying ~**) arc-boutant *m*.
II *vtr* lit, fig étayer.

butty /ˈbʌtɪ/ *n* GB dial sandwich *m*.

buxom /ˈbʌksəm/ *adj* plantureux/-euse.

buy /baɪ/ **I** *n* **1** (bargain) **a good/bad buy** une bonne/mauvaise affaire; **2** (purchase) acquisition *f*; **sb's latest ~** l'acquisition la plus récente de qn.
II *vtr* (*prét, pp* **bought**) **1** (purchase) acheter [*food, car, shares, house*] **(from sb** à qn); **to ~ sth from the supermarket/from the baker's/from Buymore** acheter qch au supermarché/chez le boulanger/chez Buymore; **to ~ sth for sb** acheter qch pour qn; **to ~ sb sth** acheter qch à qn; **the best that money can ~** ce qui se fait de mieux; **the best car that money can ~** la meilleure voiture qui soit; **2** (obtain with money) acheter [*fame, freedom, friends*]; **happiness can't be bought** le bonheur ne s'achète pas; **we managed to ~ some time** nous avons réussi à gagner du temps; **3** (bribe) acheter [*loyalty, silence, person*]; **she can't be bought** elle est incorruptible; **4**○ (believe) avaler○, croire [*story, excuse*]; **I'm not ~ing that!** on ne me fera pas avaler ça○!; **she bought it** elle a marché○.
III *v refl* (*prét, pp* **bought**) **to ~ oneself sth** s'acheter qch.
IDIOMS **to ~ it**○ (die) casser sa pipe○.
■ **buy in** GB: **~ [sth] in, ~ in [sth]** s'approvisionner en [*food, coal*].
■ **buy into**: **~ into [sth]** Comm acheter or acquérir une part dans [*firm, partnership*].
■ **buy off**: **~ [sb] off, ~ off [sb]** acheter [*person, witness*].
■ **buy out**: **~ [sb] out, ~ out [sb]** Comm racheter la part de [*co-owner*]; Mil racheter [*soldier*]; **to ~ oneself out of** racheter son engagement dans [*army*].
■ **buy up**: **~ up [sth], ~ [sth] up** acheter systématiquement [*shares, property*].

buyback /ˈbaɪbæk/ *n* rachat *m*.

buyer /ˈbaɪə(r)/ *n* **▶ 1692** **1** (purchaser) acquéreur *m*, acheteur/-euse *m/f*; **~'s market** marché *m* d'acheteurs, marché *m* où la demande est faible; **2** (profession) acheteur/-euse *m/f*.

buying /ˈbaɪɪŋ/ *n* achat *m*.

buying power *n* Comm pouvoir *m* d'achat.

buyout /ˈbaɪaʊt/ *n* Comm rachat *m* d'entreprise; **▶ leveraged buyout**.

buzz /bʌz/ **I** *n* **1** (of insect, conversation) bourdonnement *m*; **2**○ (phone call) coup *m* de fil; **to give sb a ~** passer un coup de fil à qn; **3**○ (thrill) **I get a ~ from it, it gives me a ~** (from alcohol) ça me fait planer○; (atmosphere) **a party with a real ~** une fête vraiment pleine d'entrain; **to get a ~ out of doing** prendre son pied○ en faisant; **4**○ (rumour, news) **the ~ is that...** à ce qu'on raconte...; **what's the ~?** alors, quoi de neuf?
II *vtr* **1** (call) **to ~ sb** appeler qn au bip, biper; **2** [*plane*] raser [*crowd, building*]; frôler [*other plane*].
III *vi* **1** [*bee*] bourdonner; [*fly*] vrombir; [*buzzer*] sonner; **~ if you know the answer** appuyez sur la sonnette si vous connaissez la réponse; **2** [*head*] **her head ~ed with thoughts** les idées se bousculaient dans son esprit; **3** [*place*] **the house was ~ing with activity** tout le monde s'affairait dans la maison; **the town ~ed with rumours** la ville bourdonnait de rumeurs.
■ **buzz off**○ s'en aller; **~ off!** dégage○!

buzzard /ˈbʌzəd/ *n* **1** Zool buse *f*; **2**† péj (person) sale bougre○ *m* pej.

buzz bomb○ /ˈbʌzbɒm/ *n* V1 *m*.

buzzer /ˈbʌzə(r)/ *n* gen sonnerie *f*; (on pocket, etc) bip *m*.

buzzing /ˈbʌzɪŋ/ **I** *n* (of insects) bourdonnement *m*; (of buzzer) vibration *f*; **to have a ~ in one's ears** avoir les oreilles qui bourdonnent.
II○ *adj* (lively) [*town*] animé; [*party, atmosphere*] planant○.

buzz: **~ saw** *n* scie *f* circulaire; **~word**○ *n* mot *m* à la mode.

BVDs® /biːviːˈdiːz/ *npl* US sous-vêtements *mpl* masculins.

BVM *n* (*abrév* = **Blessed Virgin Mary**) **the ~** la Sainte Vierge *f*.

by /baɪ/ **I** *prep* **1** (showing agent, result) par; **he was bitten ~ a snake** il a été mordu par un serpent; **the house was designed by an architect** la maison a été conçue par un architecte; **a building destroyed ~ fire** un bâtiment détruit par le feu; **we were overwhelmed ~ the news** nous avons été bouleversés par la nouvelle; **~ working extra hours, he was able to earn more money** en faisant des heures supplémentaires, il a pu gagner plus d'argent; **~ selling some valuables, she was able to raise some money** en vendant quelques objets de valeur, elle a pu rassembler des fonds; **to begin ~ saying that** commencer par dire que; **any money paid ~ you will be reimbursed** tout ce que vous avez payé vous sera remboursé; **2** (through the means of) **to travel ~ bus/train** voyager en bus/train; **~ bicycle** à bicyclette, en vélo; **to pay ~ cheque** payer par chèque; **you**

can reach me ~ phone vous pouvez me contacter par téléphone; **~ candlelight** [*dine*] aux chandelles; [*read*] à la bougie; **I know her ~ sight** je la connais de vue; **I took him ~ the hand** je l'ai pris par la main; **he grabbed me ~ the hair** il m'a attrapé par les cheveux; **she was holding it ~ the handle** elle le tenait par le manche; **he has two children ~ his first wife** il a deux enfants de sa première femme; **3** (according to, from evidence of) à; **~ my watch it is three o'clock** à ma montre, il est trois heures; **I could tell ~ the look on her face that she was angry** rien qu'à la regarder je savais qu'elle était fâchée; **what did you understand ~ her remarks?** comment est-ce que tu as compris ses remarques?; **I knew him ~ his walk** je l'ai reconnu à sa démarche; **it's all right ~ me** ça me va; **4** (via, passing through) par; **we entered ~ the back door** nous sommes entrés par la porte de derrière; **we'll get there quicker if we go ~ Birmingham** nous y arriverons plus rapidement si nous passons par Birmingham; **we travelled to Rome ~ Venice and Florence** nous sommes allés à Rome en passant par Venise et Florence; **5** (near, beside) à côté de, près de; **~ the bed/the window** à côté du lit/de la fenêtre; **~ the sea** au bord de la mer; **come and sit ~ me** viens t'asseoir à côté de moi; **6** (past) **to go** ou **pass ~ sb** passer devant qn; **she walked ~ me** elle est passée devant moi; **they passed us ~ in their car** ils nous ont dépassés dans leur voiture; **please let us get ~** s'il vous plaît, laissez-nous passer; **7** (showing authorship) de; **a film ~ Claude Chabrol** un film de Claude Chabrol; **a novel ~ Virginia Woolf** un roman de Virginia Woolf; **who is it ~?** c'est de qui?; **8** (before, not later than) avant; **it must be done ~ four o'clock/next Thursday** il faut que ce soit fait avant quatre heures/jeudi prochain; **~ this time next week** d'ici la semaine prochaine; **~ the time she had got downstairs he was gone** le temps qu'elle descende, il était parti; **he ought to be here ~ now** il devrait être déjà là; **~ now it was clear that they were going to win** à ce moment-là il était clair qu'ils allaient gagner; **but ~ then it was too late** mais il était déjà trop tard; **9** (during) **~ day as well as ~ night** de jour comme de nuit; **~ daylight** au jour; **~ moonlight** au clair de lune; **10** (according to) **forbidden ~ law** interdit par la loi; **to play ~ the rules** jouer selon les règles; **it seems primitive ~ western standards** cela a l'air primitif selon or d'après les critères occidentaux; **11** (to the extent or degree of) de; **prices have risen ~ 20%** les prix ont augmenté de 20%; **he's taller than me ~ two centimetres** il fait deux centimètres de plus que moi, il est plus grand que moi de deux centimètres; **~ far** de loin; **she is ~ far the cleverest/the youngest** elle est de loin la plus intelligente/la plus jeune; **it's better ~ far** c'est beaucoup mieux; **12** (in measurements) sur; **a room 20 metres ~ 10 metres** une pièce de 20 mètres sur 10; **13** Math (in multiplication, division) par; **10 multiplied ~ 5 is 50** 10 multiplié par 5 égale 50; **14** (showing rate, quantity) à; **to be paid ~ the hour** être payé à l'heure; **~ the dozen** à la douzaine; **15** (in successive degrees, units) **little ~ little** peu à peu; **day ~ day** jour après jour; **one ~ one** un par un, un à un; **16** (with regard to) de; **he is an architect ~ profession** ou **trade** il est architecte de son métier; **~ birth** de naissance; **17** (as a result of) par; **~ accident/mistake** par accident/erreur; **~ chance** par hasard; **18** (used with reflexive pronouns) **he did it all ~ himself** il l'a fait tout seul; **she was sitting ~ herself** elle était assise toute seule; **19** (in promises, oaths) **~ God, I could kill him!** je le jure, je pourrais le tuer!; **I swear ~ heaven** je jure devant Dieu; **20** Naut (in compass directions) quart; **south ~ south-west** sud quart sud-ouest.

II *adv* **1** (past) **to go ~** passer; **the people walking ~** les gens *mpl* qui passent/passaient, les passants *mpl*; **he walked on ~ without stopping** il est passé sans s'arrêter; **a lot of time has gone ~ since then** il s'est écoulé beaucoup de temps depuis lors; **as time goes ~** avec le temps; **2** (near) près; **he lives close ~** il habite tout près; **3** (aside, in reserve) **to put money ~** mettre de l'argent de côté; **4** (to one's house) **come ~ for a drink** passe prendre un verre; **she called ~ during the week** elle est passée dans la semaine.

IDIOMS **~ and ~** bientôt; **~ the ~, ~ the bye** à propos; **but that's ~ the ~** mais ça c'est un détail, mais ça c'est autre chose.

bye /baɪ/ **I** *n* **1** GB Sport **to have** ou **get a ~** gagner par défaut.

II° *excl* au revoir!; **~ for now!** à bientôt!

bye-bye° /ˈbaɪbaɪ, bəˈbaɪ/ **I** *excl* au revoir!

II *adv* lang enfantin **to go ~** US partir; **to go ~s** GB aller au lit.

byelaw *n* = **bylaw**.

by(e)-election /ˈbaɪɪlekʃn/ *n* GB élection *f* partielle.

Byelorussia /ˌbjeləʊˈrʊʃə/ ▶ **1131** *pr n* Biélorussie *f*.

bygone /ˈbaɪɡɒn/ **I bygones** *npl* (mementos) objets *mpl* du passé.

II *adj* [*days, years, scene, etc*] d'antan; **a ~ age** ou **era** une époque révolue.

IDIOMS **to let ~s be ~s** enterrer le passé.

bylaw /ˈbaɪlɔː/ *n* **1** (of local authority) arrêté *m* municipal; **2** Comm règlement *m* intérieur.

by-line /ˈbaɪlaɪn/ *n* **1** Journ nom *m* de journaliste (*en tête d'un article*); **2** Sport ligne *f* de touche.

bypass /ˈbaɪpɑːs/ **I** *n* **1** Aut rocade *f*; **2** (pipe, channel) by-pass *m inv*; **3** Elec dérivation *f*; **4** Med pontage *m*.

II *vtr* Aut contourner [*town, city*]; fig éviter [*issue, question*]; contourner [*law, procedure*]; éviter de passer par [*manager, chief*]; **we ~ed France on our way to Italy** nous sommes allés en Italie sans passer par la France.

bypass operation *n* Med pontage *m*; **he had a ~** on lui a fait un pontage.

bypass surgery *n* pontage *m*.

by: **~play** *n* Theat action *f* secondaire; **~-product** *n* Biol, Ind dérivé *m*; fig effet *m* secondaire.

byre /ˈbaɪə(r)/ *n* GB étable *f*.

by: **~road** *n* petite route *f*, petit chemin *m*; **~stander** *n* passant *m*.

byte /baɪt/ *n* Comput octet *m*.

byway /ˈbaɪweɪ/ *n* lit petite route *f*, petit chemin *m*; fig (of history, literature etc) périphérie *f*.

byword /ˈbaɪwɜːd/ *n* **the party is a ~ for fanaticism** le parti est synonyme de fanatisme; **caution is his ~** sa devise, c'est la prudence.

by-your-leave *n* **without so much as a ~** sans même demander la permission.

Byzantine /baɪˈzæntaɪn, ˈbɪzəntaɪn/ **I** *n* Byzantin/-e *m/f*.

II *adj* [*art, civilization, empire*] byzantin also fig; [*emperor*] de Byzance.

Byzantium /bɪˈzæntɪəm/ *pr n* Hist Byzance.

Cc

c, **C** /siː/ *n* **1** (letter) c, C *m*; **2** **C** Mus do *m*, ut *m*; **3** (*abrév écrite* = **century**) **c19th**, **C19th** XIXe siècle; **4** **c** (*abrév écrite* = **circa**) vers; **c1890** vers 1890; **5** **c** *abrév écrite* = **carat**; **6** **c** US *abrév écrite* = **cent(s)**; **7** **C** GB Sch (grade) ≈ note *f* de 12 sur 20; **8** **C** *abrév* = **Celsius**, **centigrade**.

CA **1** US Post *abrév écrite* = **California**; **2** *abrév* ▸ **Central America**; **3** GB Fin *abrév* ▸ **chartered accountant**.

C/A **1** Fin *abrév* ▸ **capital account**; **2** Fin *abrév* ▸ **credit account**; **3** Fin *abrév* ▸ **current account**.

CAA *n* GB *abrév* ▸ **Civil Aviation Authority**.

cab /kæb/ *n* **1** (taxi) taxi *m*; (horse-drawn) fiacre *m*; **2** (driver's compartment) cabine *f*.

CAB **1** GB *abrév* ▸ **Citizens' Advice Bureau**; **2** US *abrév* ▸ **Civil Aeronautics Board**.

cabal /kəˈbæl/ *n* (all contexts) cabale *f*.

cabana /kəˈbɑːnə/ *n* US (tent) tente *f* de plage; (hut) cabine *f* de plage.

cabaret /ˈkæbəreɪ, US ˌkæbəˈreɪ/ **I** *n* **1** (genre) cabaret *m*; **to do ~** faire du cabaret; **2** (show) spectacle *m* de cabaret; **3** (nightclub, restaurant) cabaret *m*.
II *modif* [*performance, number*] de cabaret.

cabbage /ˈkæbɪdʒ/ *n* **1** Bot, Culin chou *m*; **2**○ GB injur (brain-damaged person) *personne réduite à l'état végétatif*; **3**○ GB (dull person) légume○ *m*.

cabbage: **~ lettuce** *n* GB laitue *f* pommée; **~ rose** *n* grande rose *f*; **~ white (butterfly)** *n* piéride *f* du chou.

cabbala /kəˈbɑːlə/ *n* lit kabbale *f*; fig cabale *f*.

cabbalistic /ˌkæbəˈlɪstɪk/ *adj* lit cabalistique; **~ signs** des signes cabalistiques.

cabby○ /ˈkæbɪ/ *n* **1** (taxi driver) chauffeur *m* de taxi; **2** Hist (coachman) cocher *m* de fiacre.

cab-driver /ˈkæbdraɪvə(r)/ *n* (taxi-driver) chauffeur *m* de taxi; Hist (coachman) cocher *m* de fiacre.

caber /ˈkeɪbə(r)/ *n* tronc *m*; **to toss the ~** lancer le tronc (*jeu écossais*).

cabin /ˈkæbɪn/ *n* **1** (hut) cabane *f*; (in holiday camp etc) chalet *m*; **2** Naut cabine *f*; **3** Aviat (containing passengers, crew) cabine *f*; (cockpit) cabine *f* de pilotage; (for cargo) soute *f*; **4** Aerosp habitacle *m*; **5** GB Rail (signal box) cabine *f* d'aiguillage; **6** GB (driver's compartment) cabine *f*.

cabin: **~ boy** *n* Hist mousse *m*; **~ class** *n*: *classe intermédiaire entre première et touriste sur les bateaux*; **~ crew** *n* Aviat personnel *m* de bord, navigants *mpl* commerciaux; **~ cruiser** *n* cruiser *m*.

cabinet /ˈkæbɪnɪt/ **I** *n* **1** (cupboard) petit placard *m*; (glass-fronted) vitrine *f*; (decorative, on legs) cabinet *m*; **cocktail** ou **drinks ~** meuble *m* bar; **display ~** vitrine *f*; **television ~** meuble *m* télévision; **2** GB Pol cabinet *m*; cf Conseil *m* des ministres.
II *modif* Pol [*crisis, decision, post*] ministériel/-ielle.

cabinet: **~maker** ▸ **1692** *n* ébéniste *m*; **~making** *n* ébénisterie *f*; **~ meeting** *n* GB cf Conseil des ministres; **~ minister** *n* GB ministre *m* (*faisant partie du Cabinet du premier ministre*); **~ reshuffle** *n* GB remaniement *m* ministériel; **~work** *n* ébénisterie *f*.

cabin trunk *n* malle *f* de voyage.

cable /ˈkeɪbl/ **I** *n* **1** (rope) câble *m*; **anchor/steel/suspension ~** câble d'ancre/d'acier/de suspension; **accelerator/brake ~** câble d'accélérateur/de frein; **2** (electric) câble *m*; **to lay a ~** poser un câble; **fibre-optic ~** GB, **fiber-optic ~** US câble en fibres optiques; **high-voltage ~** câble à haute tension; **overhead/power ~** câble aérien/électrique; **3** (television) câble *m*; **4** (telegram) câble *m*.
II *vtr* **1** (telegraph) câbler (**that** que + *indic*); **to ~ sb sth, to ~ sth to sb** câbler qch à qn; **2** (provide with cables) câbler [*house, area*].
III *modif* [*channel, network*] câblé.

cable: **~ car** *n* téléphérique *m*; **~gram** *n* câblogramme *m*; **~-knit** *adj* [*sweater*] à torsades; **~ layer** ▸ **1692** *n* câblier *m*; **~ railway** *n* funiculaire *m*; **~ release** *n* déclencheur *m* souple.

cable stitch *n* point *m* torsade; **a ~ sweater** un tricot à torsades.

cable: **~ television**, **~ TV** *n* télévision *f* par câble; **~ tray** *n* Comput, Elec chemin *m* de câbles; **~way** *n* téléphérique *m*.

caboodle○ /kəˈbuːdl/ *n* **the whole (kit and) ~** tout le bazar○, tout le bataclan○.

caboose /kəˈbuːs/ *n* **1** GB Naut coquerie *f*; **2** US Rail fourgon *m* de queue.

cab-rank, **cabstand** *n* station *f* de taxis.

ca'canny strike /kɑːˌkænɪ ˈstraɪk/ *n* GB grève *f* perlée.

cacao (tree) /kəˈkɑːəʊ, kəˈkeɪəʊ/ *n* cacaoyer *m*, cacaotier *m*.

cache /kæʃ/ **I** *n* **1** (hoard) cache *f*; **an arms ~, a ~ of arms** une cache d'armes; **2** (place) cachette *f*.
II *vtr* cacher.

cachet /ˈkæʃeɪ, US kæˈʃeɪ/ *n* (all contexts) cachet *m*.

cack-handed○ /ˌkækˈhændɪd/ *adj* GB maladroit, gauche.

cackle /ˈkækl/ **I** *n* (of hen) caquet *m*; (of person) **a ~ of amusement** un ricanement; **cut the ~**○**!** arrêtez de jacasser!
II *vi* [*hen*] caqueter; [*person*] (talk) caqueter; (laugh) ricaner.

cackling /ˈkæklɪŋ/ *n* ¢ (of hens) caquetage *m* also fig; (laughter) péj ricanements *mpl*.

cacophonous /kəˈkɒfənəs/ *adj* sout cacophonique.

cacophony /kəˈkɒfənɪ/ *n* sout cacophonie *f*.

cactus /ˈkæktəs/ *n* (*pl* **-ti**) cactus *m*.

cad○† /kæd/ *n* GB goujat *m*, malotru† *m*.

Cad○ /kæd/, **Caddy**○ /ˈkædɪ/ *n* US (*abrév* = **Cadillac**) Cad○ *f*, Cadillac *f*.

CAD *n*: *abrév* ▸ **computer-aided design**.

cadaver /kəˈdɑːvə(r), -ˈdeɪv-, US kəˈdævər/ *n* sout cadavre *m*.

cadaverous /kəˈdævərəs/ *adj* [*face, figure*] cadavérique.

CADCAM /ˈkædkæm/ *n* Comput (*abrév* = **computer-aided design and computer-aided manufacture**) CFAO *f*.

caddie, **caddy** /ˈkædɪ/ **I** *n* caddie *m*.
II *vi* **to ~ for sb** être le caddie de qn.

caddie car(t) *n* Golf chariot *m*.

caddish○† /ˈkædɪʃ/ *adj* GB mufle.

caddy /ˈkædɪ/ **I** *n* **1** US (shopping trolley) chariot *m*, caddie® *m*; **2** GB (also **tea ~**) boîte *f* à thé; **3** Sport = **caddie I**.
II *vi* Sport = **caddie II**.

cadence /ˈkeɪdns/ *n* (intonation) inflexion *f*; (rhythm) cadence *f*, rythme *m*; Mus cadence *f*.

cadenza /kəˈdenzə/ *n* Mus cadence *f*.

cadet /kəˈdet/ *n* Mil (also **officer ~**) élève *mf* officier; (in police force) élève *mf* agent de police.

cadet: **~ corps** *n* Mil unité *f* de préparation militaire (*jusqu'à 18 ans*); **~ school** *n* école *f* militaire.

cadetship /kəˈdetʃɪp/ *n*: *bourse pour faire une préparation militaire*.

cadge○ /kædʒ/ *vtr* péj **to ~ sth off** ou **from sb** taper○ qn de qch [*sum*]; taper○ qch à qn [*cigarette, money*]; **to ~ a meal/a lift** se faire inviter/emmener en voiture; **can I ~ a lift?** je peux profiter de la voiture?

cadger○ /ˈkædʒə(r)/ *n* pej gen parasite *m*; (of money) tapeur/-euse○ *m/f*; (of meals) pique-assiette○ *mf inv*.

Cadiz /kəˈdɪz/ ▸ **1818** *pr n* Cadix.

cadmium /ˈkædmɪəm/ *n* cadmium *m*.

cadre /ˈkɑːdə(r), US ˈkædrɪ/ *n* **1** (group) Mil cadre *m*; Admin, Pol noyau *m* (d'hommes); **2** Pol (person) cadre *m*.

CAE *n* Comput (*abrév* = **computer-aided engineering**) IAO *f*.

caecum GB, **cecum** US /ˈsiːkəm/ *n* cæcum *m*.

Caesar /ˈsiːzə(r)/ *pr n* César.
IDIOMS **render unto ~ what is ~'s** rendez à César ce qui est à César.

Caesarea /ˌsiːzəˈrɪə/ ▸ **1818** *pr n* Césarée *f*.

Caesarean, **Caesarian** /sɪˈzeərɪən/ *n* Med (also **~ section**) césarienne *f*.

caesium GB, **cesium** US /ˈsiːzɪəm/ *n* césium *m*.

caesura /sɪˈzjʊərə, US sɪˈʒʊərə/ *n* (*pl* **-ras**, **-rae**) césure *f*.

CAF *abrév* ▸ **cost and freight**.

café /ˈkæfeɪ, US kæˈfeɪ/ *n* **1** gen ≈ snack-bar *m* (*ne vendant pas de boissons alcoolisées*); **pavement ~** GB, **sidewalk ~** US café *m*; **2** US (restaurant) bistro *m*.

café: **~ curtains** *npl* brise-bise *m inv*; **~ society** *n* le beau monde.

cafeteria /ˌkæfəˈtɪərɪə/ *n* gen cafétéria *f*; Sch cantine *f*; Univ restaurant *m* universitaire.

cafetière /kafˈtjɛː/ *n* cafetière *f* à piston.

caff○† /kæf/ GB *n* ≈ snack-bar *m*.

caffein(e) /ˈkæfiːn/ *n* caféine *f*; **~-free** décaféiné.

caftan /ˈkæftæn/ *n* caftan *m*.

cage /keɪdʒ/ **I** *n* **1** (for bird, animal) cage *f*; (of lift) cabine *f*; (in mine) cage *f*; (in prison) cellule *f*; **2**○ Sport (basketball) panier *m*; (ice-hockey) cage *f* (de buts).
II *vtr* mettre en cage [*bird, animal*]; **a ~d animal** un animal en cage; **to pace up and**

down like a ~d animal tourner comme un animal en cage.
■ **cage in**: **~ [sb] in, ~ in [sb]** encager; **to feel ~d in** étouffer.

cagebird /ˈkeɪdʒbɜːd/ *n* oiseau *m* d'appartement or d'agrément.

cagey○, **cagy**○ /ˈkeɪdʒɪ/ *adj* **1** (wary) méfiant; **to be ~ about doing** hésiter à faire; **she's very ~ about her family** elle n'aime pas beaucoup parler de sa famille; **2** US (shrewd) astucieux/-ieuse, malin/-igne.

cagily○ /ˈkeɪdʒɪlɪ/ *adv* **1** (warily) avec méfiance; **2** US (shrewdly) astucieusement.

caginess○ /ˈkeɪdʒɪnɪs/ *n* **1** (wariness) réticence *f* (**about** à l'égard de); **2** US (shrewdness) astuce *f*.

cagoule /kəˈguːl/ *n* GB K-way® *m*.

cahoots○ /kəˈhuːts/ *npl* **to be in ~** être de mèche○ (**with** avec).

caiman *n* = **cayman**.

Cain /keɪn/ *pr n* Caïn.
IDIOMS **to raise ~**○ (make a noise) faire du boucan○; (get angry) piquer une crise○.

caïque /kaɪˈiːk/ *n* caïque *m*.

cairn /keən/ *n* **1** (of stones) cairn *m*; **2** (also **~ terrier**) cairn-terrier *m*.

cairngorm /ˈkeəngɔːm/ **I** *n* Miner quartz *m* fumé.
II *pr n* **the Cairngorms** les monts *mpl* Cairngorm.

Cairo /ˈkaɪərəʊ/ ▶**1818** *pr n* Le Caire.

caisson /ˈkeɪsn/ *n* Mil, Naut, Constr caisson *m*.

cajole /kəˈdʒəʊl/ *vtr* cajoler; **to ~ sb into doing sth** amener qn à faire qch par la cajolerie; **'give him half,' she ~d** 'donne-lui la moitié' dit-elle d'un ton cajoleur.

cajolery /kəˈdʒəʊlərɪ/ *n* ¢ cajoleries *fpl*.

Cajun /ˈkeɪdʒən/ ▶**1486**, **1402** **I** *n* **1** (person) Acadien/-ienne *m/f*; **2** (language) acadien *m*.
II *adj* acadien/-ienne.

cake /keɪk/ **I** *n* **1** Culin gâteau *m*; (sponge) génoise *f*; **2** (of soap, wax) pain *m*; **3** (of fish, potato) croquette *f*.
II *vtr* [*mud, blood*] former une croûte sur [*clothes, person*].
III *vi* [*mud, blood*] former une croûte (**on** sur).
IV caked *pp adj* [*mud, blood*] qui forme une croûte; **~d in mud** couvert de boue séchée.
IDIOMS **it's a piece of ~**○ c'est du gâteau○; **to get a** ou **one's slice** ou **share of the ~** avoir sa part du gâteau; **you can't have your ~ and eat it** on ne peut pas tout avoir, on ne peut pas avoir le beurre et l'argent du beurre; **that takes the ~**○**!** ça c'est le pompon!; ▶**hot cake**.

cake: **~ decoration** *n* décoration *f* pour gâteau; **~ flour** *n* farine *f* à gâteaux; **~ mix** *n* préparation *f* or mélange *m* pour gâteau; **~ pan** *n* US = **cake tin** 1; **~ shop** *n* ≈ pâtisserie *f*; **~ stand** *n* plat *m* à gâteaux; **~ tin** *n* (for baking) moule *m* à gâteaux; (for storing) boîte *f* à gâteaux.

cakewalk /ˈkeɪkwɔːk/ *n* cake-walk *m*.
IDIOMS **it's a ~**○**!** US c'est du gâteau○!

CAL *n*: *abrév* ▶**computer-aided learning**.

calabash /ˈkæləbæʃ/ *n* (fruit) calebasse *f*; (tree) calebassier *m*.

calaboose○ /ˌkæləˈbuːs/ *n* US taule○ *f*.

calabrese /ˌkæləˈbreɪzɪ/ *n* broccoli *m*.

Calabria /kəˈlæbrɪə/ *pr n* Calabre *f*.

Calabrian /kəˈlæbrɪən/ *adj* calabrais.

calamine /ˈkæləmaɪn/ *n* calamine *f*.

calamine lotion *n* lotion *f* calmante à la calamine.

calamitous /kəˈlæmɪtəs/ *adj* catastrophique, désastreux/-euse.

calamity /kəˈlæmətɪ/ *n* calamité *f*.

calcareous /kælˈkeərɪəs/ *adj* calcaire; **~ clay** marne *f*.

calcification /ˌkælsɪfɪˈkeɪʃn/ *n* calcification *f*.

calcify /ˈkælsɪfaɪ/ **I** *vtr* calcifier.
II *vi* se calcifier.

calcination /ˌkælsɪˈneɪʃn/ *n* calcination *f*.

calcine /ˈkælsɪn/ **I** *vtr* calciner.
II *vi* se calciner.

calcium /ˈkælsɪəm/ **I** *n* calcium *m*.
II *modif* [*carbonate, chloride, hydroxide*] de calcium.

calculable /ˈkælkjʊləbl/ *adj* calculable.

calculate /ˈkælkjʊleɪt/ *vtr* **1** (work out) calculer [*cost, distance, price, size*]; **to ~ that** calculer que; **2** (estimate) évaluer [*consequences, effect, probability, rise*]; **to ~ that** estimer que; **3** (intend) **to be ~d to do** avoir été conçu pour faire.

calculated /ˈkælkjʊleɪtɪd/ *adj* [*crime*] prémédité; [*attempt, decision, insult, malice*] délibéré; [*risk*] calculé.

calculating /ˈkælkjʊleɪtɪŋ/ *adj* **1** (scheming) [*manner, cheat, killer, politician*] calculateur/-trice; **2** (shrewd) [*approach, policy*] prudent.

calculating machine *n* machine *f* à calculer.

calculation /ˌkælkjʊˈleɪʃn/ *n* **1** (operation) calcul *m*; **to make** ou **do ~s** faire des calculs; **by my ~s** d'après mes calculs; **to get one's ~s wrong** se tromper dans ses calculs; **2** (process) calculs *mpl*; **after much ~** après de nombreux calculs; **3** (scheming) préméditation *f*.

calculator /ˈkælkjʊleɪtə(r)/ *n* calculatrice *f*, calculette *f*; (larger) machine *f* à calculer; **pocket ~** calculatrice *f* de poche, calculette *f*.

calculus /ˈkælkjʊləs/ *n* Math, Med calcul *m*.

Calcutta /kælˈkʌtə/ ▶**1818** *pr n* Calcutta.

calendar /ˈkælɪndə(r)/ *n* **1** gen calendrier *m*; **a major event in the sporting/social ~** un grand événement de la saison sportive/au chapitre des mondanités; **2** Jur (list) rôle *m*.

calendar: **~ month** *n* mois *m* calendaire; **~ year** *n* année *f* civile.

calf /kɑːf, US kæf/ *n* (*pl* **calves**) **1** Zool (cow) veau *m*; (deer) faon *m*; (buffalo) buffletin *m*; (elephant) éléphanteau *m*; (whale) baleineau *m*; **to be in ~** être pleine; **calves' liver** Culin foie *m* de veau; **2** (leather) vachette *f*; **3** Anat mollet *m*.
IDIOMS **to kill the fatted ~** tuer le veau gras.

calf: **~ love** *n* amour *m* juvénile; **~skin** *n* vachette *f*.

caliber *n* US = **calibre**.

calibrate /ˈkælɪbreɪt/ *vtr* étalonner [*scales*]; calibrer [*instrument, tube, gun*].

calibration /ˌkælɪˈbreɪʃn/ *n* (process) (of instrument, tube, gun) calibrage *m*; (of measure, scales) étalonnage *m*.

calibre GB, **caliber** US /ˈkælɪbə(r)/ *n* (all contexts) calibre *m*; **of exceptional ~** d'un calibre exceptionnel.

calico /ˈkælɪkəʊ/ **I** *n* GB calicot *m*; US indienne *f*.
II *modif* [*garment*] en calicot, en indienne.
III *adj* US tacheté.

Calif /ˈkeɪlɪf/ *n* calife *m*.

California /ˌkælɪˈfɔːnɪə/ ▶**1744** *pr n* Californie *f*.

Californian /ˌkælɪˈfɔːnɪən/ **I** *n* Californien/-ienne *m/f*.
II *adj* californien/-ienne.

caliper *n* US = **calliper**.

Caliph *n* = **Calif**.

calisthenics *n* = **callisthenics**.

calk /cælk/ *vtr* Art, Tech décalquer.

call /kɔːl/ **I** *n* **1** Telecom appel *m* (téléphonique) (**from** de); **business ~** appel professionnel; **private** ou **personal ~** appel privé; **(tele)phone ~** appel *m* (téléphonique); **I have a ~ for you** j'ai un appel pour vous; **to make a ~** appeler, téléphoner; **to make a ~ to Italy** appeler l'Italie, téléphoner en Italie; **to receive/take a ~** recevoir/prendre un appel; **to give sb a ~** appeler qn; **to return sb's ~** rappeler qn; **to put a ~ through to sb** passer un appel à qn; **2** (audible cry) (human) appel *m* (**for** à); (animal) cri *m*; **to give sb a ~** appeler qn; **3** (summons) appel *m*, **this is the last ~ for passengers to Berlin** Aviat ceci est le dernier appel pour les passagers à destination de Berlin; **this is your ten minute ~** Theat en scène dans dix minutes; **to put out a ~ for sb** (over public address) faire appeler qn; (over radio) lancer un appel à qn; **the Red Cross has put out a ~ for blankets** la Croix Rouge a lancé un appel pour obtenir des couvertures; **4** (visit) visite *f*; **social ~** visite *f* de courtoisie; **to make** ou **pay a ~** lit rendre visite (**on** à); **to pay a ~** euph aller aux toilettes; **to return sb's ~** rendre sa visite à qn; **5** (demand) demande *f*; **the strikers' ~ for a pay rise** la demande d'augmentation de salaire de la part des grévistes; **there were ~s for his resignation** sa démission a été réclamée; **a ~ for reform** une demande de réforme; **she has many ~s on her time** elle est très sollicitée; **there's no ~ for it** Comm il n'y a pas de demande (pour cet article); **we don't get much ~ for that** nous n'avons guère de demande pour cela; **to have first ~ on sth** avoir la priorité sur qch; **6** (need) **there's no ~ for sth/to do** il n'y a pas de raison pour qch/de faire; **there was no ~ for her to say that** elle n'avait aucune raison or aucun besoin de dire cela; **7** (allure) (of mountains, sea, the unknown) appel *m* (**of** de); **8** Sport décision *f*; **9** Fin (for repayment of loan) demande *f* de remboursement; (request) appel *m*; (right to buy) option *f* d'achat; **money at** ou **on ~** argent à court terme or au jour le jour; **on three months' ~** à trois mois; **payable at ~** remboursable sur présentation or à vue; **a ~ for capital/tenders** un appel de fonds/d'offres; **10** (duty) **to be on ~** [*doctor*] être de garde; [*engineer*] être de service; **11** Relig (vocation) vocation *f*.
II *vtr* **1** (say loudly) (also **~ out**) appeler [*name, number*]; crier [*answer, instructions*]; annoncer [*result*]; Games parier [*heads, tails*]; annoncer [*flight*]; **to ~ the register** Sch faire l'appel; **he ~ed (out) 'Goodbye'** il a crié 'au revoir'; **2** (summon) appeler [*lift*]; (by shouting) appeler [*person, animal, witness*]; (by phone) appeler [*person, police, taxi*]; (by letter) convoquer [*applicant, candidate*]; **he was ~ed before the committee** il a été convoqué devant la commission; **the boss ~ed me into his office** le chef m'a fait venir dans son bureau; **the police were ~ed to the scene** la police a été appelée sur les lieux; **I've ~ed you a taxi** je vous ai appelé un taxi; **come when you're ~ed** venez quand on vous appelle; **~ the next witness** appelez le témoin suivant; **you may be ~ed to give evidence** il se peut que vous soyez convoqué pour témoigner; **3** (telephone) (also **~ up**) appeler [*person, institution, number*] (**at** à; **from** de); **don't ~ us, we'll ~ you** hum (n'appelez pas) nous vous appellerons; **4** (give a name) appeler [*person, baby, animal, place, product*] (**by** par); intituler [*book, film, music, play*]; **she prefers to be ~ed by her maiden name** elle préfère qu'on l'appelle par son nom de jeune fille; **5** (arrange) organiser [*strike*]; convoquer [*conference, meeting, rehearsal*]; fixer [*election*]; **6** (waken) réveiller [*person*]; **what time shall I ~ you in the morning?** à quelle heure voulez-vous que je vous réveille?; **7** (describe as) **to ~ sb stupid/a liar** traiter qn d'imbécile/de menteur/-euse; **I wouldn't ~ it spacious/beautiful** je ne dirais pas que c'est vaste/beau; **do you ~ that plate clean?** tu appelles ça une assiette propre?; **it's not what you'd ~ an exciting film** on ne peut pas dire que ce film soit passionnant; **it's what you might ~ a delicate situation** c'est ce qui s'appelle une situation délicate; **~ that a garden**○**!** tu appelles ça un jardin!; **~ it what you will** appelle ça comme tu veux; **parapsychology or whatever they** ou **you ~ it**○ la métapsy-

chologie ou quelque chose dans ce goût-là○; (**let's**) **~ it £5** disons cinq livres sterling; **he hasn't a place to ~ his own** il n'a pas de chez-soi; **8** Sport [*referee, linesman*] déclarer; **the linesman ~ed the ball in** le juge de ligne a déclaré que la balle était bonne; **9** Fin demander le remboursement de [*loan*]; **10** Comput appeler [*file, program*].

III *vi* **1** (cry out) (also **~ out**) [*person, animal*] appeler; (louder) crier; [*bird*] crier; **London ~ing** Radio ici Londres; **2** (telephone) appeler; **where are you ~ing from?** d'où appelez-vous?; **I'm ~ing about your advertisement** j'appelle au sujet de votre annonce; **thank you for ~ing** merci d'avoir appelé; **please ~ back in an hour** rappelez dans une heure s'il vous plaît, veuillez rappeler dans une heure fml; **to ~ home** appeler chez soi or à la maison; **who's ~ing?** qui est à l'appareil?; **3** (visit) passer; **to ~ at** [*person*] passer chez [*person, shop*]; [*person*] passer à [*bank, library, town*]; [*train*] s'arrêter à [*town, station*]; [*boat*] faire escale à [*port*]; **the London train ~ing at Reading and Slough** le train à destination de Londres desservant les gares de Reading et Slough; **4** (tossing coins, racquet) parier; **you ~, heads or tails?** à toi de parier, pile ou face?

IV *v refl* **to ~ oneself** se faire appeler [*Smith, Bob*]; (claim to be) se dire, se prétendre [*poet , designer*]; **he ~s himself a writer but...** il se dit or se prétend écrivain mais...; **~ yourself a sailor**○**?** et tu te prétends marin?; **I am proud to ~ myself European** je suis fier d'être européen.

IDIOMS **it was a close ~** c'était de justesse.

■ **call away**: **~ [sb] away** appeler; **to be ~ed away** être obligé de s'absenter.

■ **call back**: ¶ **~ back 1** (on phone) rappeler; **2** (return) repasser; ¶ **~ [sb] back 1** (summon by shouting, phone back) rappeler [*person*]; **2** (recall) rappeler [*representative, diplomat*].

■ **call by** passer.

■ **call down**: ¶ **~ down** (shout from above) appeler; ¶ **~ down [sth], ~ [sth] down** appeler [*blessing, curse, vengeance*] (**on** sur).

■ **call for**: **~ for [sth] 1** (shout) appeler à [*help*]; appeler [*ambulance, doctor*]; **2** (demand) [*person*] demander [*food, drink, equipment, tool*]; [*report, article, politician, protesters*] réclamer [*changes, improvements*]; **they are ~ing for talks to be extended** ils réclament la prolongation des négociations; **3** (require) [*situation, problem, conditions*] exiger [*treatment, skill, action, understanding*]; nécessiter [*change, intervention, improvements*]; **this ~s for a celebration!** ça se fête!; **that was not ~ed for** c'était déplacé; **4** (collect) passer prendre [*person*]; passer chercher [*object*].

■ **call forth** littér: **~ forth [sth], ~ [sth] forth** susciter.

■ **call in**: ¶ **~ in 1** (visit) passer; **2** (telephone) appeler; **to ~ in sick** [*employee*] appeler pour dire qu'on est malade; ¶ **~ in [sb], ~ [sb] in 1** lit (summon inside) faire rentrer [*person, animal*]; faire entrer [*candidate, client, patient*]; **2** (send for) faire appel à [*expert, police, engineer*]; ¶ **~ in [sth], ~ [sth] in 1** (recall) demander le retour de [*library book, ticket, surplus, supplies*]; retirer [qch] de la circulation [*currency*]; retirer [qch] du commerce [*product*]; **2** Fin demander le remboursement de [*loan*].

■ **call off**: **~ off [sth], ~ [sth] off 1** lit rappeler [*dog , attacker*]; **2** fig (halt) interrompre [*arrangement, deal, plan, search, investigation, strike*]; (cancel) annuler [*show, meeting, wedding*]; **to ~ off one's engagement** rompre ses fiançailles; **to ~ off a strike** annuler un ordre de grève; **let's ~ the whole thing off** laissons tomber.

■ **call on**: **~ on [sb/sth] 1** (visit) (also **~ in on**) rendre visite à [*relative, friend*]; visiter [*patient, client*]; **2** (invite) demander à [*speaker, lecturer*] (**to do** de faire); **3** (urge) demander à (**to do** de faire); (stronger) enjoindre fml (**to do** de faire); **he ~ed on his colleagues to oppose it** il a demandé à ses collègues de s'y opposer; **4** (appeal to, resort to) s'adresser à [*person*]; avoir recours à [*services*]; faire appel à [*moral quality*]; **neighbours she can ~ on** des voisins à qui elle peut s'adresser; **we will ~ on your services** nous aurons recours à vos services; **you will have to ~ on all your patience and courage** il faudra faire appel à toute ta patience et tout ton courage.

■ **call out**: ¶ **~ out** (cry aloud) appeler; (louder) crier; ¶ **~ out [sb], ~ [sb] out 1** (summon outside) appeler; **the teacher ~ed me out to the front of the class** le professeur m'a fait venir devant le reste de la classe; **2** (send for) appeler [*expert, doctor, emergency service, repairman, troops*]; **3** Ind [*union*] lancer un ordre de grève à [*members*]; **to ~ sb out on strike** lancer un ordre de grève à qn; ¶ **~ [sth] out, ~ out [sth]** appeler [*name, number*].

■ **call over**: ¶ **~ over to [sb]** appeler; ¶ **~ [sb] over** appeler.

■ **call round** (visit) venir.

■ **call up**: ¶ **~ up** appeler; ¶ **~ up [sb/sth], ~ [sb/sth] up 1** (on phone) appeler; **2** (summon) appeler [*reserves, reinforcements*]; appeler [qn] sous les drapeaux [*soldier*]; invoquer [*ghost, spirit*]; **3** (evoke) rappeler [*memory, past event, scene*]; **4** Comput appeler (à l'écran), afficher [*data, file, menu*]; **5** Sport sélectionner [*player*].

■ **call upon** = **call on**.

CALL *n*: *abrév* ▶ **computer-aided language learning**.

callable /ˈkɔːləbl/ *adj* Fin [*bond, stock*] remboursable par anticipation; [*capital*] exigible; [*loan*] révocable.

Callanetics /ˌkælənˈetɪks/ *n* (+ *v sg*) *méthode de gymnastique basée sur les micromouvements musculaires*.

callback facility *n* Telecom rappel *m* automatique.

call box *n* GB cabine *f* téléphonique; US poste *m* téléphonique.

call boy *n* (in hotel) chasseur *m*; (in theatre) régisseur *m*.

call: **~ button** *n* (for lift) bouton *m* d'appel; **~ charge** *n* montant *m* de la communication téléphonique.

caller /ˈkɔːlə(r)/ *n* **1** Telecom personne *f* qui appelle; **we've had 15 ~s today** nous avons reçu 15 appels aujourd'hui; **2** (visitor) visiteur/-euse *m/f*; **3** (in country dance) meneur *m* de jeu.

call girl *n* call-girl *f*.

calligrapher /kəˈlɪɡrəfə(r)/, **calligraphist** /kəˈlɪɡrəfɪst/ ▶ **1692** *n* calligraphe *mf*.

calligraphic /ˌkælɪˈɡræfɪk/ *adj* calligraphique.

calligraphist /kəˈlɪɡrəfɪst/ *n* = **calligrapher**.

calligraphy /kəˈlɪɡrəfɪ/ *n* calligraphie *f*.

call-in (programme) /ˈkɔːlɪn/ *n* US, Radio émission *f* avec appels en direct.

calling /ˈkɔːlɪŋ/ *n* (vocation) vocation *f*; (profession) métier *m*.

calling card *n* carte *f* de visite.

calliper GB, **caliper** US /ˈkælɪpə(r)/ **1** Med (leg support) appareil *m* orthopédique; **2 callipers** *npl* (for measuring) compas *m* d'épaisseur.

callisthenics /ˌkælɪsˈθenɪks/ *n* (+ *v sg*) gymnastique *f* suédoise.

call: **~ letters** *npl* US Radio = **call sign**; **~ loan** *n* prêt *m* remboursable sur demande; **~ money** *n* Fin argent *m* au jour le jour; **~ option** *n* Fin option *f* d'achat.

callosity /kəˈlɒsətɪ/ *n* callosité *f*.

callous /ˈkæləs/ *adj* [*person*] inhumain, insensible; [*attitude, brutality, crime*] inhumain.

callously /ˈkæləslɪ/ *adv* [*act, speak*] durement; [*suggest*] cyniquement.

callousness /ˈkæləsnɪs/ *n* (of person) dureté *f*; (of attitude) inhumanité *f*.

call: **~-out** *n* (from repairman) dépannage *m*; **~-out charge** *n* frais *mpl* de déplacement.

callow /ˈkæləʊ/ *adj* gauche; **a ~ youth** un jeune homme encore gauche.

call: **~ queuing** *n* Telecom mise *f* en file d'attente des appels; **~ sign** *n* Radio indicatif *m*; **~ slip** *n* (in library) (to consult) fiche *f* de consultation; (to borrow) fiche *f* de prêt; **~-up** *n* Mil (general) appel *m*; (of reservists) rappel *m*; **~-up papers** *npl* Mil ordre *m* d'appel.

callus /ˈkæləs/ *n* cal *m*.

callused /ˈkæləst/ *adj* [*hands*] calleux/-euse; **to have ~ feet** avoir des durillons aux pieds.

calm /kɑːm, US *also* kɑːlm/ **I** *n* **1** (of place, atmosphere) tranquillité *f*, calme *m*; **2** (of person) calme *m*; (in adversity) sang-froid *m*; **to keep one's ~** garder son sang-froid; **3** Naut calme *m*.

II *adj* calme; **keep ~!** du calme!

III *vtr* (all contexts) calmer.

IDIOMS **the ~ before the storm** le calme avant la tempête.

■ **calm down**: ¶ **~ down** [*person, situation*] se calmer; **~ down!** du calme!, calmez-vous!; ¶ **~ [sth/sb] down, ~ down [sth/sb]** calmer [*crowd, situation*].

calming /ˈkɑːmɪŋ, US *also* ˈkɑːlm-/ *adj* [*environment, influence, sound, speech*] apaisant; [*sensation*] d'apaisement.

calmly /ˈkɑːmlɪ, US *also* ˈkɑːlmlɪ/ *adv* **1** (quietly) [*act, behave, react, speak*] calmement; [*sleep, smoke, read, wait*] tranquillement; **she took the news ~** elle a pris la nouvelle avec calme; **2** (brazenly) tranquillement.

calmness /ˈkɑːmnɪs, US *also* ˈkɑːlm-/ *n* **1** (of person) gen calme *m*; (in adversity) sang-froid *m*; **2** (of place, sea, weather) calme *m*.

Calor gas® /ˈkælə ɡæs/ *n* GB butane *m*; **~ container, ~ bottle** bouteille *f* de butane.

caloric /ˈkælərɪk/ *adj* thermique.

calorie /ˈkælərɪ/ *n* calorie *f*; **low-~ diet/drink** régime/boisson à basses calories; **to count ~s** compter les calories; **to be ~-conscious** faire attention aux calories.

calorific /ˌkæləˈrɪfɪk/ *adj* calorifique; **~ value** valeur *f* calorifique.

calque /kælk/ *n* Ling calque *m*.

CALT *n*: *abrév* ▶ **computer-aided language teaching**.

calumniate /kəˈlʌmnɪeɪt/ *vtr* sout calomnier.

calumny /ˈkæləmnɪ/ *n* sout calomnie *f*.

Calvados /ˈkælvədɒs/ ▶ **1273** *pr n* Calvados *m*; **in/to ~** dans le Calvados.

calvary /ˈkælvərɪ/ **I** *n* (all contexts) calvaire *m*.

II Calvary *pr n* le Calvaire.

calve /kɑːv, US kæv/ *vi* mettre bas.

calves /kɑːvz/ *npl* ▶ **calf**.

Calvin /ˈkælvɪn/ *pr n* Calvin.

Calvinism /ˈkælvɪnɪzəm/ *n* calvinisme *m*.

Calvinist /ˈkælvɪnɪst/ *n, adj* calviniste (*mf*).

Calvinistic /ˌkælvɪˈnɪstɪk/ *adj* calviniste.

calypso /kəˈlɪpsəʊ/ *n* calypso *m*.

calyx /ˈkeɪlɪks/ *n* (*pl* **-xes** ou **-ces**) calice *m*.

cam /kæm/ *n* Tech came *f*.

CAM *n*: *abrév* ▶ **computer-aided manufacturing**.

camaraderie /ˌkæməˈrɑːdərɪ, US -ˈræd-/ *n* camaraderie *f*.

camber /ˈkæmbə(r)/ **I** *n* (of road) bombement *m*; (of ship's deck) tonture *f*; (of beam) contreflèche *f*; (of wheels) carrossage *m*.

II *vtr* bomber [*road*]; cintrer [*beam*].

Cambodia /kæmˈbəʊdɪə/ ▶ **1131** *pr n* Cambodge *m*.

Cambodian /kæm'bəʊdɪən/ ▶1486 **I** *n* Cambodgien/-ienne *m/f*.
II *adj* cambodgien/-ienne.

Cambrian /'kæmbrɪən/ Geol **I** *n* **the ~** le cambrien *m*.
II *adj* cambrien/-ienne.

cambric /'keɪmbrɪk/ *n* batiste *f*.

Cambridgeshire /'keɪmbrɪdʒʃə(r)/ ▶1624 *pr n* Cambridgeshire *m*.

Cambs *n* GB Post *abrév écrite* = **Cambridgeshire**.

camcorder /'kæmkɔ:də(r)/ *n* caméscope® *m*.

came /keɪm/ *prét* ▶ **come**.

camel /'kæml/ ▶1104 **I** *n* **1** chameau *m*; (female) chamelle *f*; (for racing) méhari *m*; **2** (colour) couleur *f* caramel.
II *modif* **~ train** caravane *f* de chameaux; **~ driver** chamelier *m*.
III *adj* [*coat, dress*] couleur caramel *inv*.
IDIOMS **that was the straw that broke the ~'s back** c'est la goutte d'eau qui a fait déborder le vase.

camel hair I *n* poil *m* de chameau.
II *modif* [*coat, jacket*] en poil de chameau.

camellia /kə'mi:lɪə/ *n* camélia *m*.

Camelot /'kæmɪlɒt/ *pr n* **1** Mythol *capitale légendaire du Roi Arthur en Angleterre*; **2** US Pol *l'administration de John F. Kennedy*.

camembert /'kæməmbeə(r)/ *n* camembert *m*.

cameo /'kæmɪəʊ/ *n* **1** camée *m*; **~ brooch** camée monté en broche; **2** Theat, Cin **a ~ role** un camée.

camera /'kæmərə/ *n* **1** Phot appareil *m* photo; Cin, TV caméra *f*; **2** Jur **in ~** à huis clos.

camera bag *n* gen sac *m* photo; (professional) sac *m* de photographe.

camera: **~ case** *n* étui *m* (d'appareil photo); **~ crew** *n* équipe *f* de télévision; **~man** ▶1692 *n* (*pl* **-men**) cadreur *m*, cameraman *m*; **~ obscura** *n* chambre *f* noire, chambre *f* obscure; **~-ready copy**, **CRC** *n* document *m* prêt pour la photogravure.

camera-shy /'kæmərəʃaɪ/ *adj* **she's ~** elle n'aime pas qu'on la prenne en photo.

camerawork /'kæmərəwɜ:k/ *n* prise *f* de vues.

Cameroon /,kæmə'ru:n/ ▶1131 *pr n* Cameroun *m*.

Cameroonian /,kæmə'ru:nɪən/ ▶1486 **I** *n* Camerounais/-aise *m/f*.
II *adj* camerounais.

camiknickers /'kæmɪnɪkəz/ *npl* GB chemise-culotte *f*.

camisole /'kæmɪsəʊl/ *n* caraco *m*.

camomile /'kæməmaɪl/ *n* camomille *f*; **~ tea** infusion *f* de camomille.

camouflage /'kæməflɑ:ʒ/ **I** *n* (all contexts) camouflage *m*.
II *modif* [*gear, jacket, netting*] de camouflage.
III *vtr* (all contexts) camoufler (**with** avec).
IV *v refl* **to ~ oneself** se camoufler.

camp /kæmp/ **I** *n* **1** gen (of tents, buildings etc) camp *m*; (of nomads) campement *m*; **to make** ou **pitch ~** planter son camp; **to strike ~** lever le camp; **to go to ~** [*scout etc*] partir en camp; **2** fig (group) camp *m*, parti *m*; **to go over to the other ~** changer de camp; **3**○ péj (mannered style etc) cabotinage○ *m*; **it's high ~** c'est du pur cabotinage○.
II *adj* péj **1** (exaggerated) [*person*] cabotin○; [*gesture, performance*] théâtral; **2** (effeminate) efféminé; **3** (in bad taste) kitsch.
III *vi* camper; **to go ~ing** faire du camping.
IDIOMS **to have a foot in both ~s** avoir un pied dans chaque camp; **to ~ it up**○ (overact) cabotiner○; (act effeminately) forcer dans le genre efféminé.
■ **camp on** Telecom effectuer un rappel automatique.
■ **camp out** dormir sous la tente; **he's ~ing out in the lounge** il campe dans le salon.

campaign /kæm'peɪn/ **I** *n* (all contexts) campagne *f* (**for** pour; **against** contre); **to mount** ou **launch a ~** lancer une campagne.
II *vi* faire campagne (**for** pour; **against** contre); **after ten years of ~ing** au bout de dix ans de campagne.

campaigner /kæm'peɪnə(r)/ *n* gen militant/-e *m/f* (**for** pour; **against** contre); Pol candidat/-e *m/f* en campagne (électorale); **animal rights ~** militant pour les droits de l'animal; **old ~** Mil vétéran *m*.

campaign: **~ headquarters** *n* GB Pol (+ *v sg ou pl*) état-major *m*; **~ literature** *n* ¢ tracts *mpl*; **~ medal** *n* médaille *f* militaire.

campaign trail *n* **on the ~** en tournée électorale.

campaign worker *n* GB Pol membre *m* de l'état-major.

campanile /,kæmpə'ni:lɪ/ *n* campanile *m*.

camp: **~ bed** *n* lit *m* de camp; **~ chair** *n* US chaise *f* pliante; **~ commandant** *n* commandant *m* de camp.

camper /'kæmpə(r)/ *n* **1** (person) campeur/-euse *m/f*; **2** (also **~ van**) camping-car *m*; **3** US (folding caravan) caravane *f* pliante.

campfire /'kæmpfaɪə(r)/ *n* feu *m* de camp.

camp follower *n* **1** Mil civil *m* (*qui suit une armée*); (prostitute) prostituée *f*; **2** (sympathizer) sympathisant/-e *m/f*.

camphor /'kæmfə(r)/ *n* camphre *m*.

camphorated oil /,kæmfəreɪtɪd 'ɔɪl/ *n* huile *f* camphrée.

camping /'kæmpɪŋ/ *n* camping *m*; **to go ~** faire du camping.

camping: **~ equipment** *n* matériel *m* de camping; **~ gas** *n* camping-gaz® *m*; **~ ground** *n* = **campsite**; **~ holiday** *n* vacances *fpl* sous la tente; **~ stool** *n* GB pliant *m*; **~ stove** *n* réchaud *m*.

campion /'kæmpɪən/ *n* Bot lychnis *m*.

camp: **~ meeting** *n* US Relig camp *m* biblique; **~ on** *n* GB Telecom rappel *m* automatique; **~site**, **~ing site** *n* (official) terrain *m* de camping, camping *m*; **~ stool** *n* US pliant *m*.

campus /'kæmpəs/ (*pl* **-puses** /'kæmpəsɪz/) **I** *n* campus *m*; **to live on/off ~** vivre sur le/en dehors du campus.
II *modif* [*life*] de campus; [*facilities*] du campus; **~ police** US vigiles *mpl*; **a ~ university** université *f* bâtie autour d'un campus.

CAMRA /'kæmrə/ *n* GB (*abrév* = **Campaign for Real Ale**) *campagne pour l'amélioration de la qualité de la bière*.

camshaft /'kæmʃɑ:ft, US -ʃæft/ *n* arbre *m* à cames.

> **can¹**
>
> *can* and *could* are usually translated by the verb *pouvoir*. For the conjugation of *pouvoir*, see the French verb tables.
>
> | | |
> |---|---|
> | *he can wait until tomorrow* | = il peut attendre jusqu'à demain |
> | *you can go out now* | = vous pouvez sortir maintenant. |
>
> The two notable exceptions to this are as follows:
> When *can* or *could* is used to mean *know how to*, the verb *savoir* is used:
>
> | | |
> |---|---|
> | *she can speak French* | = elle sait parler français |
> | *he could read at the age of four* | = à l'âge de quatre ans il savait lire |
>
> When *can* or *could* is used with a verb of perception such as *see*, *hear* or *feel* it is not translated at all:
>
> | | |
> |---|---|
> | *I can't see her* | = je ne la vois pas |
> | *she couldn't feel anything* | = elle ne sentait rien |
>
> In requests *can* is translated by the present tense of *pouvoir* and the more polite *could* by the conditional tense of *pouvoir*.
>
> | | |
> |---|---|
> | *can you help me?* | = peux-tu m'aider? |
> | *could you help me?* | = pourrais-tu m'aider? |
>
> For particular usages of *could* when it is not simply the preterite or conditional of *can* see **13, 15, 16** in the entry ***can¹***.
> See also the entry ***able***.

can¹ /kæn, kən/ *modal aux* (*prét, cond* **could**; *nég au prés* **cannot**, **can't**) **1** (expressing possibility) **we ~ rent a house** nous pouvons louer une maison; **anyone ~ enrol** n'importe qui peut s'inscrire; **they can't** ou **cannot afford to fly** ils ne peuvent pas se permettre de prendre l'avion; **it ~ also be used to dry clothes** on peut aussi s'en servir pour faire sécher le linge; **how ~ one know in advance?** comment peut-on savoir à l'avance?; **we are confident that the job ~ be completed in time** nous sommes convaincus que le travail peut être fini à temps; **you can't have forgotten!** tu ne peux pas avoir oublié!; **it ~ be described as** on peut le décrire comme étant; **it cannot be explained logically** ça n'a pas d'explication logique; **it could be that**... il se peut que... (+ *subj*); **could be**○ peut-être; **they could be dead** ils sont peut-être morts; **it could be a trap** c'est peut-être un piège, ça pourrait être un piège; **I could be wrong** je me trompe peut-être, il se peut que j'aie tort; **this could be our most important match** c'est peut-être ou ça pourrait être le match le plus important pour nous; **the engine could explode** le moteur pourrait exploser; **it could be seen as an insult** ça pourrait être considéré comme une insulte; **it could be argued that** on pourrait dire que; **could it have something to do with the delay?** est-ce que ça pourrait avoir un rapport avec le retard?; **you could have been electrocuted!** tu aurais pu t'électrocuter!; **'did she know?'—'no, how could she?'** 'est-ce qu'elle était au courant?'—'non, comment est-ce qu'elle aurait pu l'être?'; **the computer couldn't** ou **can't have made an error** l'ordinateur n'a pas pu faire d'erreur, il est impossible que l'ordinateur ait fait une erreur; **they couldn't** ou **can't have found out so soon** ils ne peuvent pas avoir compris si vite, il est impossible qu'ils aient compris si vite; **nothing could be simpler** il n'y a rien de plus simple; **2** (expressing permission) **you ~ turn right here** vous pouvez tourner à droite ici; **I can't leave yet** je ne peux pas partir pour le moment; **we cannot allow dogs in the café** nous ne pouvons pas autoriser les chiens dans le café; **~ we park here?** est-ce que nous pouvons nous garer ici?; **people could travel without a passport** on pouvait voyager sans passeport; **we could only go out at weekends** nous ne pouvions sortir ou nous n'avions le droit de sortir que le week-end; **could I interrupt?** puis-je vous interrompre?; **3** (when making requests) **~ you leave us a message?** est-ce que tu peux nous laisser un message?; **~ you do me a favour?** est-ce que tu peux me rendre un service?; **~ I ask you a question?** puis-

je poser une question?; **can't you get home earlier?** est-ce que tu ne peux pas rentrer plus tôt ?; **could I speak to Annie?** est-ce que je pourrais parler à Annie?, puis-je parler à Annie?; **could she spend the night with you?** est-ce qu'elle pourrait dormir chez toi?; **you couldn't come earlier, could you?** est-ce que tu pourrais venir un peu plus tôt?; **couldn't you give us another chance?** est-ce que vous ne pourriez pas nous donner une autre chance?; **4** (when making an offer) **~ I give you a hand?** est-ce que je peux te donner un coup de main?; **what ~ I do for you?** qu'est-ce que je peux faire pour vous aider?; **you ~ borrow it if you like** tu peux l'emprunter si tu veux; **5** (when making suggestions) **you ~ always exchange it** tu peux toujours l'échanger; **I ~ call round later if you prefer** je peux passer plus tard si ça t'arrange; **we could try and phone him** nous pourrions essayer de lui téléphoner; **couldn't they go camping instead?** est-ce qu'ils ne pourraient pas faire du camping à la place?; **6** (have skill, knowledge to) **she can't drive yet** elle ne sait pas encore conduire; **~ he type?** est-ce qu'il sait taper à la machine?; **few people could read or write** peu de gens savaient lire ou écrire; **she never told us she could speak Chinese** elle ne nous a jamais dit qu'elle savait parler chinois; **7** (have ability, power to) **computers ~ process data rapidly** les ordinateurs peuvent traiter rapidement les données; **to do all one ~** faire tout ce qu'on peut or tout son possible; **he couldn't sleep for weeks** il n'a pas pu dormir pendant des semaines; **if only we could stay** si seulement nous pouvions rester; **I wish I could have been there** j'aurais aimé (pouvoir) être là; **I wish I could go to Japan** j'aimerais (pouvoir) visiter le Japon; **I can't** ou **cannot understand why** je ne comprends pas pourquoi, je n'arrive pas à comprendre pourquoi; **8** (have ability, using senses, to) **~ you see it?** est-ce que tu le vois?; **I can't hear anything** je n'entends rien; **we could hear them laughing** on les entendait rire; **I could feel my heart beating** je sentais mon cœur battre; **9** (indicating capability, tendency) **she could be quite abrupt** elle pouvait être assez brusque; **it ~ make life difficult** ça peut rendre la vie difficile; **Italy ~ be very warm at that time of year** il peut faire très chaud en Italie à cette période de l'année; **10** (expressing likelihood, assumption) **the cease-fire can't last** le cessez-le-feu ne peut pas durer; **it can't be as bad as that!** ça ne peut pas être aussi terrible que ça!; **it can't have been easy for her** ça n'a pas dû être facile pour elle; **he couldn't be more than 10 years old** il ne peut pas avoir plus de 10 ans; **11** (expressing willingness to act) **I cannot give up work** je ne peux pas laisser tomber le travail; **we ~ take you home** nous pouvons te déposer chez toi; **I couldn't leave the children** (didn't want to) je ne pouvais pas laisser les enfants; (wouldn't want to) je ne pourrais pas laisser les enfants; **12** (be in a position to) **one ~ hardly blame her** on peut difficilement le lui reprocher; **they ~ hardly refuse to listen** ils peuvent difficilement refuser d'écouter; **I can't say I agree** je ne peux pas dire que je suis d'accord; **I couldn't possibly accept the money** je ne peux vraiment pas accepter cet argent; **13** (expressing a reproach) **they could have warned us** ils auraient pu nous prévenir; **you could at least say sorry!** tu pourrais au moins t'excuser!; **how could you!** comment as-tu pu faire une chose pareille!; **14** (expressing surprise) **what ~ she possibly want from me?** qu'est-ce qu'elle peut bien me vouloir?; **who could it be?** qui est-ce que ça peut bien être?; **where could they have hidden it?** où est-ce qu'ils ont bien pu le cacher?; **you can't** ou **cannot be serious!** tu veux rire○!; **~ you believe it!** tu te rends compte?; **15** (for emphasis) **I couldn't agree more!** je suis entièrement d'accord!; **they couldn't have been nicer** ils ont été extrêmement gentils; **you couldn't be more mistaken** tu te trompes complètement; **16** (expressing exasperation) **I was so mad I could have screamed!** j'aurais crié tellement j'étais en colère!; **I could murder him○!** je le tuerais○!; **17** (expressing obligation) **if she wants it she ~ ask me herself** si elle le veut elle peut venir me le demander elle-même; **you ~ get lost○!** tu peux toujours courir○!; **if you want to chat, you ~ leave** si vous voulez bavarder allez faire ça dehors; **if he doesn't like it he ~ lump it○** même si ça ne lui plaît pas il va falloir qu'il fasse avec○; **18** (avoiding repetition of verb) **'~ we borrow it?'—'you ~'** 'est-ce que nous pouvons l'emprunter?'—'bien sûr'; **leave as soon as you ~** partez dès que vous pourrez; **'~ anyone give me a lift home?'—'we ~'** 'est-ce que quelqu'un peut me déposer chez moi?'—'oui, nous'.
IDIOMS **as happy/excited as ~** ou **could be** très heureux/excité; **no ~ do○** non, je ne peux pas.

can² /kæn/ **I** *n* **1** (of tinned food) boîte *f*; (aerosol) bombe *f*; (for petrol) bidon *m*; (of drink) cannette *f*; **2**◑ (lavatory) chiottes◑ *fpl*, toilettes *fpl*; **3**○ (prison) taule○ *f*; **4**○ US (rump) fesses *fpl*; **to kick sb in the ~** botter les fesses à qn○; **5**○ US Naut destroyer *m*.
II *vtr* (*p prés etc* **-nn-**) **1** Culin mettre [qch] en conserve [*fruit, vegetables*]; **2**○ **~ it! I'm trying to sleep** ferme-la○, j'essaie de dormir!; **3**○ US (dismiss) virer○.
III canned *pp adj* **1** [*food*] en boîte; **2**○ [*music, laughter, applause*] enregistré; **3**○ (drunk) bourré○.
IDIOMS **a ~ of worms** une affaire dans laquelle il vaut mieux ne pas trop fouiller; **in the ~**○ Cin (of film) dans la boîte; (of negotiations) dans la poche; **to carry the ~ for sb**○ porter le chapeau à la place de qn○.

Canada /ˈkænədə/ ▶1131 *pr n* Canada *m*.

Canada goose *n* (*pl* **Canada geese**) bernache *f* du Canada.

Canadian /kəˈneɪdɪən/ ▶1486 **I** *n* Canadien/-ienne *m/f*.
II *adj* canadien/-ienne; **to speak ~ French/English** parler le français/l'anglais du Canada; **~ bacon** US bacon *m*.

canal /kəˈnæl/ *n* **1** (waterway) canal *m*; **2** Anat (in ear) conduit *m*; **alimentary ~** tube *m* digestif; **central** ou **spinal ~** canal *m* médullaire.

canal: **~ boat**, **~ barge** *n* péniche *f*; **~ holiday** *n* GB croisière *f* en péniche.

canalization /ˌkænəlaɪˈzeɪʃn, US -lɪˈz-/ *n* (of river) canalisation *f*; (of region) construction *f* de canaux d'irrigation.

canalize /ˈkænəlaɪz/ *vtr* (all contexts) canaliser.

canapé /ˈkænəpɪ, US ˌkænəˈpeɪ/ *n* canapé *m*.

canard /kæˈnɑːd, ˈkænɑːd/ *n* (rumour) canard○ *m*.

Canaries /kəˈneərɪz/ ▶1381 *pr npl* (also **Canary Islands**) **the ~** les Canaries *fpl*.

canary /kəˈneərɪ/ *n* **1** Zool canari *m*, serin *m*; **2** = **Canary wine**.

canary: **Canary wine** *n* vin *m* des Canaries; **~ yellow** ▶1104 *n, adj* jaune (*m*) canari *inv*.

canasta /kəˈnæstə/ ▶1282 *n* canasta *f*.

can bank /kæn/ *n* (benne *f* de) dépôt *m* de cannettes.

Canberra /ˈkænbərə/ ▶1818 *pr n* Canberra.

cancan /ˈkænkæn/ *n* French-cancan *m*.

cancel /ˈkænsl/ (*p prés etc* **-ll-**, **-l-** US) **I** *vtr* **1** (call off) annuler [*event, order, booking, train, flight*]; **2** Fin, Insur (nullify) résilier [*contract, policy*]; annuler [*loan, debt, invoice*]; mettre une opposition à [*cheque, credit card*]; **3** Jur lever [*order*]; révoquer [*decree, will*]; **4** Math = **cancel out**; **5** Post oblitérer [*stamp*].
II *vi* **1** (from meal, function, meeting) se décommander; (after booking) annuler; **2** Math = **cancel out**.
■ **cancel out**: ¶ **~ out** [*figures*] s'annuler; [*arguments, views*] s'annuler; ¶ **~ out [sth]** **1** gen neutraliser [*emotion , effect, trend, gain*]; **the arguments ~ each other out** les arguments se neutralisent; **2** Math éliminer [*equation*].

cancellation /ˌkænsəˈleɪʃn/ *n* **1** (of event, order, booking, train, flight) annulation *f*; **we have three ~s** nous avons trois annulations; **2** Fin, Insur (of contract, policy) résiliation *f*; (of debt, loan, invoice) annulation *f*; **3** Jur (of will) révocation *f*; (of order, decree) levée *f*.

cancellation charge *n* frais *mpl* d'annulation.

cancer /ˈkænsə(r)/ ▶1354 **I** *n* Med, fig cancer *m*; **to have ~** avoir un cancer; **to have lung/stomach ~** avoir un cancer du poumon/de l'estomac; **a ~ sufferer** un/-e cancéreux/-euse *m/f*.
II *modif* [*risk*] de cancer; [*treatment*] du cancer.

Cancer /ˈkænsə(r)/ ▶1916 *n* **1** Astrol Cancer *m*; **2** Geog **tropic of ~** tropique *m* du Cancer.

cancer: **~-causing** *adj* cancérigène; **~ hospital** *n* centre *m* anticancéreux.

cancerous /ˈkænsərəs/ *adj* cancéreux/-euse.

cancer: **~ patient** *n* cancéreux/-euse *m/f*; **~ research** *n* cancérologie *f*; **~ screening** *n* dépistage *m* du cancer; **~ specialist** ▶1692 *n* cancérologue *mf*; **~ stick**◑ *n* GB cigarette *f*; **~ ward** *n* service *m* de cancérologie.

candelabra /ˌkændɪˈlɑːbrə/ *n* (*pl* **~** ou **~s**) candélabre *m*.

candid /ˈkændɪd/ *adj* franc/franche; **a ~ biography** une biographie qui ne cache rien; **~ camera** caméra *f* invisible.

candidacy /ˈkændɪdəsɪ/, **candidature** /ˈkændɪdətʃə/ *n* GB candidature *f*.

candidate /ˈkændɪdət, US -deɪt/ *n* **1** Pol candidat/-e *m/f*; **the ~ for mayor/for Oxford** le candidat à la mairie/pour Oxford; **a ~ for the presidency, a presidential ~** un candidat à la présidence; **parliamentary ~** candidat au parlement; **the Conservative ~** le candidat du parti conservateur; **to stand as a ~ (in an election)** se porter candidat (à une élection); **a strong/weak ~** un candidat bien/mal placé; **2** (for job) candidat/-e *m/f*, postulant/-e *m/f*; **to be a likely ~ (for the job)** être bien placé (pour obtenir le poste); **the successful ~ will have a university degree** (in ad) le candidat retenu devra avoir un diplôme universitaire; **3** Sch, Univ (in exam, for admission) candidat/-e *m/f*; **4** Sport (for selection, title) candidat/-e *m/f*; **5** fig **the sector is a ~ for restructuring/privatization** le secteur est bien placé pour être restructuré/privatisé.

candidature /ˈkændɪdətʃə/ *n* GB = **candidacy**.

candidly /ˈkændɪdlɪ/ *adv* franchement.

candidness /ˈkændɪdnɪs/ *n* franchise *f*; **with perfect ~** en toute franchise.

candied /ˈkændɪd/ *adj* (cooked in sugar) confit; (covered in sugar) enrobé de sucre; **~ peel** écorce *f* d'orange et de citron confite.

candle /ˈkændl/ *n* bougie *f*; (in church) cierge *m*; **household ~s** bougies *fpl* de ménage.
IDIOMS **to burn the ~ at both ends** brûler la chandelle par les deux bouts; **the game's not worth the ~** le jeu n'en vaut pas la chandelle; **he can't hold a ~ to his sister** il n'arrive pas à la cheville de sa sœur.

candle grease *n* (wax) cire *f*; (tallow) suif *m*.

candlelight /ˈkændllaɪt/ *n* lueur *f* de bougie; **by ~** à la lueur d'une bougie or des bougies.

candlelit dinner /ˌkændllɪt ˈdɪnə(r)/ *n* dîner *m* aux chandelles.

Candlemas /ˈkændlməs/ *n* la Chandeleur.

candle: **~ pin** *n* quille *f*; **~ pins** *n* jeu

m de quilles; **~power** *n* puissance *f* lumineuse; **~stick** *n* bougeoir *m*; (more ornate) chandelier *m*; **~tree** *n* Bot arbre *m* à cire.

candlewick /ˈkændlwɪk/ *n* tuft *m*; **~ bedspread** couvre-lit *m* en tuft.

candour GB, **candor** US /ˈkændə(r)/ *n* = **candidness**.

candy /ˈkændɪ/ **I** *n* US **1** (confectionery) confiserie *f*; **a piece of ~** un bonbon; **2** (sweet) bonbon *m*.
II *vtr* (cook in sugar) confire; (cover with sugar) enrober [qch] de sucre.
III *vi* être confit.

candy: **~ass**° *n* US couille-molle° *f*; **~ bar** *n* US barre *f* (de confiserie); **~ floss** *n* GB barbe *f* à papa; **~ store** *n* US confiserie *f* (*souvent avec bureau de tabac*); **~ striped** *adj* (pink) à rayures rose bonbon; (blue) à rayures bleu pâle; **~ striper** *n* US jeune fille *f* travaillant bénévolement dans un hôpital.

cane /keɪn/ **I** *n* **1** (material) rotin *m*; **a ~-backed chair** une chaise au dossier canné; **2** (of sugar, bamboo) canne *f*; **3** (for walking) canne *f*; (plant support) tuteur *m*; (officer's) badine *f*; GB Sch (for punishment) badine *f*.
II *modif* [*basket, blind, furniture*] en rotin.
III *vtr* **1** canner [*chair*]; **2** GB **to ~ a pupil** punir un élève en lui donnant des coups de badine.

cane sugar *n* sucre *m* de canne.

canine /ˈkeɪnaɪn/ **I** *n* **1** (tooth) canine *f*; **2** (animal) canidé *m*.
II *adj* **1** [*species*] canin; **2** Dent **a ~ tooth** une canine; **3** (using dogs) **~ corps** (in army, police) corps *m* des maîtres chiens.

caning /ˈkeɪnɪŋ/ *n* GB châtiment *m* corporel (à l'école).

canister /ˈkænɪstə(r)/ *n* boîte *f* métallique; **a ~ of tear gas, a tear gas ~** une bombe lacrymogène.

canker /ˈkæŋkə(r)/ *n* **1** Bot, Med, fig chancre *m*; **2** Vet otite *f* externe; (of horses) crapaud *m*.

cankered /ˈkæŋkəd/, **cankerous** /ˈkæŋkərəs/ *adj* Bot nécrosé; fig corrompu.

cannabis /ˈkænəbɪs/ *n* cannabis *m*; **~ resin** résine *f* de cannabis.

cannelloni /ˌkænɪˈləʊnɪ/ *n* ¢ canelloni *mpl*.

cannery /ˈkænərɪ/ *n* conserverie *f*.

cannibal /ˈkænɪbl/ *n* cannibale *mf*, anthropophage *mf*.

cannibalism /ˈkænɪbəlɪzəm/ *n* cannibalisme *m*, anthropophagie *f*.

cannibalization /ˌkænɪbəlaɪˈzeɪʃn/ *n* cannibalisation *f*.

cannibalize /ˈkænɪbəlaɪz/ *vtr* piller [*text, film etc*]; **to ~ a vehicle** enlever des pièces à un véhicule pour les utiliser ailleurs.

canning /ˈkænɪŋ/ **I** *n* mise *f* en conserve.
II *modif* [*industry*] de la conserve; [*process*] de mise en conserve.

canning factory *n* conserverie *f*.

cannon /ˈkænən/ **I** *n* **1** (*pl* **~** ou **~s**) Mil Hist canon *m*; (on aircraft) canon *m*; **2** Tech douille *f*; **3** GB Billiards carambolage *m*.
II *vtr* GB Billiards caramboler.
III *vi* **1** GB Billiards caramboler; **2** (collide) **to ~ into sb/sth** se heurter contre qn/qch.

cannonade /ˌkænəˈneɪd/ **I** *n* canonnade *f*.
II *vtr* canonner.

cannonball /ˈkænənbɑːl/ *n* **1** (missile) boulet *m* de canon; **2** (dive) **to do a ~** faire la bombe; **3** (also **~ serve**) (in tennis) service *m* canon.

cannon: **~ bone** *n* canon *m*; **~ fodder** *n* chair *f* à canon.

cannot /ˈkænɒt/ ▶ **can**[1].

canny /ˈkænɪ/ *adj* futé, malin/-igne.

canoe /kəˈnuː/ ▶ **1282** **I** *n* gen canoë *m*; (African) pirogue *f*; Sport canoë-kayac *m*.
II *vi* faire du canoë; **they ~d down the river** ils ont descendu la rivière en canoë.
IDIOMS **to paddle one's own ~** se débrouiller tout seul.

canoeing /kəˈnuːɪŋ/ ▶ **1282** *n* **to go ~** faire du canoë-kayac; **she loves ~** elle adore faire du canoë-kayac.

canoeist /kəˈnuːɪst/ *n* canoéiste *mf*.

canon /ˈkænən/ ▶ **1268** *n* **1** (rule) gen critère *m*; (of church) canon *m*; **2** Relig (priest) chanoine *m*; **Canon Foy** le chanoine Foy; **good morning, Canon Foy** bonjour, mon Père; **3** Literat (complete works) œuvre *m*; **4** Mus canon *m*; **in ~** en canon.

canonical /kəˈnɒnɪkl/ **I** **canonicals** *npl* Relig vêtements *mpl* sacerdotaux.
II *adj* canonique.

canonization /ˌkænənaɪˈzeɪʃn, US -nɪˈz-/ *n* canonisation *f*.

canonize /ˈkænənaɪz/ *vtr* canoniser.

canon law *n* droit *m* canon.

canoodle° /kəˈnuːdl/ *vi* se faire des mamours°.

can-opener /kæn/ *n* ouvre-boîtes *m inv*.

canopied /ˈkænəpɪd/ *adj* [*bed*] à baldaquin; [*throne*] surmonté d'un dais; [*entrance, balcony*] surmonté d'un auvent.

canopy /ˈkænəpɪ/ *n* **1** (for bed) baldaquin *m*; (for throne, altar, procession) dais *m*; (for hammock) toit *m*; (of glass) verrière *f*; **2** Aviat (cockpit) verrière *f*; (for parachute) voilure *f*; fig littér (sky, leaves) voûte *f*; **3** Ecol canopée *f*; **4** Mil **air ~** couverture aérienne serrée.

cant /kænt/ **I** *n* **1** (false words) paroles *fpl* creuses; (ideas) notions *fpl* creuses; **2** (prisoners', thieves') argot *m*; (lawyers') jargon *m*; **3** (sloping surface) (of road) déclivité *f*; (of rails) dévers *m*; **4** Naut gîte *f*.
II *modif* [*phrase, expression*] tout fait.
III *vtr* **1** (bevel) biseauter; **the corner was ~ed off** l'angle était taillé en biseau; **2** (tip) basculer.
IV *vi* **1** gen (tip) basculer; **2** [*ship*] (tilt) gîter.

can't /kɑːnt/ *abrév* = **cannot**.

Cantab. /ˈkæntæb/ *adj* GB Univ (*abrév écrite* = **Cantabrigiensis**) de Cambridge.

Cantal ▶ **1163** *pr n* Cantal *m*; **in/to ~** dans le Cantal.

cantaloup(e) /ˈkæntəluːp/ *n* (melon *m*) cantaloup *m*.

cantankerous /kænˈtæŋkərəs/ *adj* acariâtre.

cantata /kænˈtɑːtə/ *n* cantate *f*.

canteen /kænˈtiːn/ *n* **1** GB (dining room) cantine *f*; **in the ~** à la cantine; **a mobile ~** une cantine ambulante; **2** Mil (flask) bidon *m*; (mess tin) gamelle *f*; **3 a ~ of cutlery** une ménagère.

canter /ˈkæntə(r)/ **I** *n* gen petit galop *m*; Turf canter *m* d'entraînement; **at a ~** au petit galop; **to go for a ~** aller faire une promenade au galop; **to win at a ~** fig gagner haut-la-main.
II *vtr* mettre [qch] au petit galop.
III *vi* [*rider*] faire un petit galop; [*horse*] galoper.

canterbury /ˈkæntəbərɪ/ *n* porte-journaux *m*.

Canterbury /ˈkæntəbərɪ/ ▶ **1818** *pr n* Cantorbéry; **the ~ Tales** les Contes de Cantorbéry.

Canterbury bell *n* Bot campanule *f*.

canticle /ˈkæntɪkl/ *n* cantique *m*.

cantilever /ˈkæntɪliːvə(r)/ **I** *n* cantilever *m*, porte-à-faux *m inv*.
II *modif* [*beam*] en porte-à-faux; [*bridge, suspension*] cantilever *inv*; [*chair*] à piètement traîneau.

cantilevered /ˈkæntɪliːvəd/ *adj* en cantilever.

canting /ˈkæntɪŋ/ *adj* **~ talk** paroles *fpl* creuses.

canto /ˈkæntəʊ/ *n* Literat chant *m*.

canton /ˈkæntɒn/ *n* canton *m*.

cantonal /ˈkæntənl, kænˈtɒnl/ *adj* cantonal.

Cantonese /ˌkæntəˈniːz/ ▶ **1486**, **1402** **I** *n* **1** (*pl* **~**) (person) Cantonais/-e *m/f*; **2** (language) cantonais *m*.
II *adj* cantonais.

cantonment /kænˈtuːnmənt, US -təʊn-/ *n* cantonnement *m*.

cantor /ˈkæntɔː(r)/ *n* chantre *m*.

Cantuar. *n* (*abrév écrite* = **Cantuarensis**) de Cantorbéry.

Canuck° /kəˈnʌk/ *n* injur Canadien/-ienne *m/f* (français).

Canute /kəˈnjuːt/ *pr n* Canut.

canvas /ˈkænvəs/ **I** *n* **1** (fabric) toile *f*; (for tapestry) canevas *m*; **under ~** (in a tent) sous la tente; (under sail) sous voiles; **2** Art toile *f*; **3** fig **a broad (historical) ~** un panorama (historique); **to work/operate on a broader** ou **wider ~** travailler/agir sur une plus grande échelle; **4** (in boxing) tapis *m*.
II *modif* [*shoes, bag, chair*] en toile.

canvasback /ˈkænvəsbæk/ *n* Zool morillon *m* à dos blanc.

canvass /ˈkænvəs/ **I** *n* **1** (for votes) tournée *f* électorale; **2** (of opinion) sondage *m*; **3** Comm prospection *f*.
II *vtr* **1** Pol **to ~ voters/an area** faire du démarchage électoral auprès des électeurs/dans une région; **to ~ people for their votes/support** solliciter les voix/le soutien des électeurs; **2** (in survey) sonder [*public*] (**for, to get** pour savoir); **to ~ opinion** ou **views on sth** sonder l'opinion au sujet de qch; **3** (discuss) débattre [*idea, proposal*]; **4** Comm prospecter [*area*] (**to do** pour faire; **for** pour); **to ~ door to door** faire du démarchage.
III *vi* **1** Pol faire du démarchage électoral (**for** pour); **2** Comm faire du démarchage (**for** pour).

canvasser /ˈkænvəsə(r)/ *n* (for party) agent *m* électoral.

canvassing /ˈkænvəsɪŋ/ *n* **1** (door to door) démarchage *m*; **~ for votes/business** démarchage électoral/commercial; **2 ~ of opinion** sondage *m* d'opinion.

canyon /ˈkænjən/ *n* cañon *m*.

cap /kæp/ **I** *n* **1** (headgear) (of nurse) coiffe *f*; (of schoolboy) casquette *f*; (of uniformed official, soldier) képi *m*; (of jockey) toque *f*; **baseball ~** casquette de baseball; **2** GB Sport **he's got his Scottish ~** il a été selectionné pour l'équipe écossaise; **he's an England ~** il joue pour l'Angleterre; **3** (cover) (of pen, valve) capuchon *m*; (of bottle) capsule *f*; (for camera lens) bouchon *m*; **4** (of mushroom) chapeau *m*; **5** (for toy gun) amorce *f*; **6** Dent couronne *f*; **7** GB (also **Dutch ~**) diaphragme *m* (contraceptif); **to be fitted for a ~** se faire poser un diaphragme; **8** Archit chapiteau *m*; **9** (bird's plumage) capuchon *m*.
II *vtr* (*p prés etc* **-pp-**) **1** Admin, Fin [*government*] imposer une limite budgétaire à [*local authority*]; plafonner [*budget*]; **2** Dent couronner [*tooth*]; **3** GB Sport sélectionner [qn] pour l'équipe nationale [*footballer*]; **to be ~ped for Wales** être sélectionné pour l'équipe galloise; **4** (cover) couronner; **the hills were ~ped with snow** les collines étaient couronnées de neige.
IDIOMS **to ~ it all** pour couronner le tout; **to go to sb ~ in hand** se présenter à qn chapeau bas; **to set one's ~ at** GB ou **for** US **sb**† jeter son dévolu sur qn; **if the ~ fits, wear it!** qui se sent morveux se mouche!

cap. /kæp/ *n* (*abrév* = **capital letter**) maj.

CAP *n*: *abrév* ▶ **Common Agricultural Policy**.

capability /ˌkeɪpəˈbɪlətɪ/ *n* **1** (capacity) (of intellect, machine, system) capacité *f* (**to do** de faire); **intellectual/load ~** capacité intellectuelle/de chargement; **2** (potential strength) capacité *f* (**to do** de faire); **nuclear/military ~** capacité nucléaire/militaire; **3** (aptitude) aptitude *f* (**for** à); **management ~** aptitude à la gestion; **within/outside my capabilities** dans/au-dessus de mes moyens.

capable /ˈkeɪpəbl/ *adj* **1** (competent) compétent; **in the ~ hands of** dans les mains compétentes de; **2** (able) [*person*] capable (**of**

Capacity measurement

For cubic measurements, **▶ 1869**.

British liquid measurements

20 fl oz	= 0,57 ℓ (*litre*)	1 qt	= 1,13 ℓ* (*litres*)
1 pt	= 0,57 ℓ	1 gal	= 4,54 ℓ

* *There are three ways of saying 1,13 ℓ, and other measurements like it:* un virgule treize litres, *or (less formally)* un litre virgule treize, *or* un litre treize. *For more details on how to say numbers,* **▶ 1505**.

American liquid measurements

16 fl oz	= 0,47 ℓ	1 qt	= 0,94 ℓ
1 pt	= 0,47 ℓ	1 gal	= 3,78 ℓ

Phrases

what does the tank hold?	= combien le réservoir contient-il?
what's its capacity?	= quelle est sa contenance?
it's 200 litres	= il fait 200 litres
its capacity is 200 litres	= il fait 200 litres
my car does 28 miles to the gallon	= ma voiture fait dix litres aux cent† *or* ma voiture fait du dix litres aux cent
they use 20,000 litres a day	= ils utilisent 20 000 litres par jour

† *Note that the French calculate petrol consumption in litres per 100 km. To convert miles per gallon to litres per 100 km and vice versa simply divide the factor 280 by the known figure.*

A holds more than B	= A contient plus que B
B holds less than A	= B contient moins que A
A has a greater capacity than B	= A a une plus grande contenance que B
B has a smaller capacity than A	= B a une moins grande contenance que A
A and B have the same capacity	= A et B ont la même contenance
20 litres of wine	= 20 litres de vin
it's sold by the litre	= cela se vend au litre

Note the French construction with de*, coming after the noun it describes:*

a 200-litre tank	= un réservoir de 200 litres

de); **to be ~ of doing** (have potential to) être capable de faire; (be in danger of) risquer de faire; **~ of a better result** capable d'un meilleur résultat; **the bomb is ~ of exploding** la bombe risque d'exploser.

capably /ˈkeɪpəblɪ/ *adv* avec compétence.

capacious /kəˈpeɪʃəs/ *adj* [*pocket, car boot*] vaste; [*appetite*] énorme.

capacitance /kəˈpæsɪtəns/ *n* Elec capacitance *f*.

capacitor /kəˈpæsɪtə(r)/ *n* Elec condensateur *m*.

capacity /kəˈpæsətɪ/ *n* **1** (ability to hold) (of box, bottle) contenance *f*; (of barrel) capacité *f* (**of** de); (of concert, theatre building) capacité *f* d'accueil; (of road) capacité *f*; **the theatre has a ~ of 500** le théâtre peut accueillir 500 personnes; **seating/storage ~** capacité d'accueil/de stockage; **the theatre was packed** ou **full to ~** le théâtre était comble; **to have a great ~ for alcohol** hum avoir une bonne descente○; **2** (ability to produce) capacité *f*; **processing ~** capacité de traitement; **manufacturing** ou **production ~** capacité de production; **to operate at full ~** opérer au maximum de ses capacités; **the plant is stretched to ~** l'usine tourne au maximum de ses capacités; **3** (role) **in my ~ as a doctor** en ma qualité de médecin; **she was employed in an advisory/in a private ~** elle était employée à titre consultatif/à titre privé; **I have been employed in various capacities** j'ai été employé à divers titres; **4** (ability) **to have a ~ for** avoir un don pour [*learning, maths*]; **a ~ for doing** une aptitude à faire; **she has a great ~ for friendship/hard work** elle a une grande aptitude à se faire des amis/bien travailler; **to have the ~ to do** avoir les moyens de faire; **he has the ~ to do well** il a les moyens de bien faire; **the task/exam is well within your capacities** ce travail/examen est tout à fait à votre portée; **5** Aut cylindrée *f*; **6** Electron capacité *f*; **7** Jur capacité *f*.

cap: **~ and bells** *n* costume *m* de bouffon; **~ and gown** *n* Univ costume *m* universitaire.

caparison /kəˈpærɪsn/ Hist **I** *n* caparaçon *m*. **II** *vtr* caparaçonner.

cape /keɪp/ *n* **1** (for cyclist, fisherman, fashion) cape *f*; (for child, policeman) pèlerine *f*; **2** Geog promontoire *m*.

cape: **Cape Coloureds** *npl* (in South Africa) métis *mpl* sud-africains; **Cape Horn** *n* le cap Horn *m*; **Cape Kennedy** *pr n* cap *m* Kennedy; **Cape of Good Hope** *pr n* cap *m* de Bonne-Espérance; **Cape Province** *n* province *f* du Cap.

caper /ˈkeɪpə(r)/ **I** *n* **1** (playful leap) cabriole *f*; **to cut a ~**† faire des cabrioles; **2**○ (funny film) comédie *f*; **romantic/cop ~** comédie romantique/policière; **3**○ (dishonest scheme) combine○ *f*; **4** Bot, Culin (tree) câprier *m*; (berry) câpre *f*; **5**○ GB (hassle) **what a ~!** quel bazar○!; **you have to fill out forms and all that ~** tu dois remplir des formulaires et tout le bazar○.
II capers *npl* (antics) aventures *fpl*; **cartoon ~s with Mickey Mouse** les aventures de Mickey en bande dessinée; **the comic ~s of two teenagers** les aventures comiques de deux adolescents; **his classroom ~s amuse his friends** ses pitreries en classe amusent ses camarades.
III *vi* gambader.
■ **caper about, caper around 1** (leap around) gambader; **2**○ (act foolishly) faire le pitre.

capercaillie /ˌkæpəˈkeɪlɪ/ *n* (also **capercailzie**) grand tétras *m*.

Capernaum /kəˈpɜːnjəm/ **▶ 1818** *pr n* Capharnaüm.

capeskin /ˈkeɪpskɪn/ *n* peau *f* souple (*d'agneau ou de chevreau*).

cape: **Cape Town ▶ 1818** *pr n* Le Cap; **Cape Verde Islands ▶ 1381, 1131** *npl* Cap-Vert *m*.

cap: **~ful** *n* (contenu *m* d'un) bouchon *m*; **~ gun** *n* pistolet *m* à amorces.

capillary /kəˈpɪlərɪ, US ˈkæpɪlərɪ/ *n, adj* (all contexts) capillaire (*m*).

capital /ˈkæpɪtl/ **I** *n* **1** (letter) majuscule *f*; **2** (also **~ city**) capitale *f*; **fashion ~ of the world** capitale mondiale de la mode; **3** ¢ gen, Comm, Fin (wealth) capital *m*; (funds) capitaux *mpl*, capital *m*; **with a ~ of £500,000** au capital de 500 000 livres sterling; **to make ~ out of sth** fig tirer profit de qch; **to make political ~ out of sth** tirer profit de qch dans un but politique; **4** (capitalist interests) capital *m*; **~ and labour** le capital et le travail; **5** Archit chapiteau *m*.
II *modif* [*amount, base, loss, outlay, turnover*] de capital.
III *adj* **1** [*letter*] majuscule; **~ A** A majuscule; **crazy with a ~ C**○ dingue avec un D majuscule or un grand D○; **2** Jur [*offence, crime, sentence*] capital; **~ charge** accusation *f* entraînant la peine capitale; **~ murder** meurtre *m* passible de la peine capitale; **3** (essential) capital; **to be of ~ importance** être d'une importance capitale; **4**○† GB (excellent) épatant.

capital: **~ account**, **C/A** *n* compte *m* capital; **~ adequacy** *n* adéquation *f* du capital; **~ allowances** *npl* déduction *f* fiscale pour amortissement; **~ assets** *n* capitaux *mpl* fixes; **~ bonds** *n* bons *mpl* de capitalisation; **~ budget** *n* budget *m* d'investissement; **~ city** *n* capitale *f*; **~ cost** *n* coût *m* d'investissement; **~ equipment** *n* équipement *m*; **~ expenditure** *n* Fin dépenses *fpl* d'investissement; (personal) apport *m* personnel (en capital); **~ gain** *n* revenu *m* des capitaux; **~ gains tax** *n* impôt *m* sur les revenus des capitaux; **~ goods** *n* biens *mpl* d'équipement; **~-intensive industry** *n* industrie *f* de capitaux; **~ investment** *n* dépenses *fpl* d'investissement.

capitalism /ˈkæpɪtəlɪzəm/ *n* capitalisme *m*; **under ~** en régime capitaliste.

capitalist /ˈkæpɪtəlɪst/ *n, adj* capitaliste (*m*) also pej.

capitalistic /ˌkæpɪtəˈlɪstɪk/ *adj* capitaliste.

capitalization /ˌkæpɪtəlaɪˈzeɪʃn, US -lɪˈz-/ *n* **1** Fin (market value) capitalisation *f*; (par value) capital *m* nominal; **2** Ling emploi *m* de lettres majuscules.

capitalize /ˈkæpɪtəlaɪz/ **I** *vtr* **1** Fin capitaliser [*assets*]; **over-/under-~d** sur-/sous-capitalisé; **2** Ling écrire [qch] en majuscules.
II *vi* **to ~ on** tirer parti de [*situation, advantage*].

capital: **~ levy** *n* impôt *m* sur le capital; **~ market** *n* marché *m* financier; **~ outlay** *n* = **capital expenditure**; **~ punishment** *n* peine *f* capitale; **~ reserves** *npl* réserves *fpl* de capitaux; **~ ship** *n* bâtiment *m* de guerre; **~ spending** *n* dépenses *fpl* d'investissement; **~ stock** *n* (of firm, industry) capital *m* social; **~ structure** *n* composition *f* du capital; **~ sum** *n* gen capital *m*; (of loan) principal *m*; **~ taxation** *n* impôt *m* sur le capital; **~ transfer tax** *n* droits *mpl* de mutation.

capitation /ˌkæpɪˈteɪʃn/ *n* Tax capitation *f*.

capitation: **~-based payment** *n* système *m* de paiement par tête; **~ fee** *n* Sch dotation *f* forfaitaire par élève.

Capitol /ˈkæpɪtl/ *pr n* **the ~** US Admin, Antiq le Capitole.

Capitol Hill *n* US **1** (hill) colline *f* du Capitole; **2** (congress) congrès *m* américain.

capitulate /kəˈpɪtʃʊleɪt/ *vi* gen, Mil capituler (**to** devant).

capitulation /kəˌpɪtʃʊˈleɪʃn/ *n* gen, Mil capitulation *f* (**to** devant).

capo /ˈkæpəʊ/ *n* **1** (in Mafia) capo *m*, chef *m* de la mafia; **2** Mus (also **~ tasto**) capodastre *m*.

capon /ˈkeɪpən, -ɒn/ *n* chapon *m*.

cappuccino /ˌkæpʊˈtʃiːnəʊ/ *n* cappuccino *m*.

caprice /kəˈpriːs/ *n* **1** (whim) caprice *m*; **2** Mus capriccio *m*.

capricious /kəˈprɪʃəs/ *adj* [*person, weather, fortune*] capricieux/-ieuse; [*whim, decision*] extravagant.

capriciously /kəˈprɪʃəslɪ/ *adv* [*behave, decide*] capricieusement.

Capricorn /ˈkæprɪkɔːn/ **▶ 1916** *n* **1** Astrol Capricorne *m*; **2** Geog **tropic of ~** tropique *m* du Capricorne.

caps (*abrév* = **capital letters**) majuscules *fpl*.

capsicum /ˈkæpsɪkəm/ *n* poivron *m*.

capsize /kæpˈsaɪz, US ˈkæpsaɪz/ **I** *vtr* faire chavirer [*boat*].
II *vi* chavirer.

cap sleeve *n* Fashn mancheron *m*.

caps lock *n* (*abrév* = **capitals lock**) verr *m* maj.

capstan /ˈkæpstən/ *n* **1** Naut cabestan *m*; **2** Tech galet *m* d'entraînement.

capstan lathe *n* Ind tour *m* revolver.

capsule /ˈkæpsjuːl, US ˈkæpsl/ *n* (all contexts) capsule *f*.

Capt Mil *abrév écrite* = **Captain**.

captain /ˈkæptɪn/ **▶ 1612** I *n* gen, Mil, Sport capitaine *m*; US (precinct commander) (in police) commissaire *m* de quartier; (in fire service) capitaine *m* des pompiers; **naval/army ~** capitaine de vaisseau/de l'armée de terre; **~ of industry** fig capitaine d'industrie; **this is your ~ speaking** (on plane) ici votre commandant de bord.
II *vtr* être le capitaine de [*team*]; commander [*ship, platoon*].

captaincy /ˈkæptɪnsɪ/ *n* **1** Mil (rank) grade *m* de capitaine; **2** Sport poste *m* de capitaine; **to get ~ of the side** Sport être désigné comme capitaine; **under the ~ of X** avec X comme capitaine.

caption /ˈkæpʃn/ I *n* **1** Journ légende *f* (**to, for** accompagnant); **2** TV, Cin (sub-title) sous-titre *m*; **3** Jur *mention en tête d'acte de l'origine, du lieu et de la date*.
II *vtr* **1 to be ~ed 'ode to joy'** avoir pour légende 'ode à la joie'; **he ~ed the photo 'souvenirs'** il mit comme légende à la photo 'souvenirs'; **2** Cin, TV sous-titrer [*film*].

captious /ˈkæpʃəs/ *adj* sout [*person*] ergoteur/-euse; **~ remark** ergotage *m*.

captivate /ˈkæptɪveɪt/ *vtr* captiver, fasciner; **he was ~d by her** elle le fascinait.

captivating /ˈkæptɪveɪtɪŋ/ *adj* fascinant.

captive /ˈkæptɪv/ I *n* captif/-ive *m/f*; **to hold sb ~** garder qn en captivité; **to take sb ~** faire qn prisonnier.
II *adj* captif/-ive; **~ audience/market** public/marché captif.

captivity /kæpˈtɪvətɪ/ *n* captivité *f*; **in ~** en captivité.

captor /ˈkæptə(r)/ *n* (of person) ravisseur/-euse *m/f*; **the lion attacked its ~** le lion a attaqué celui qui l'avait capturé.

capture /ˈkæptʃə(r)/ I *n* **1** gen (of person, animal) capture *f*; (of stronghold) prise *f*; **2** Phys, Geog capture *f*.
II *vtr* **1** lit capturer [*person, animal*]; prendre [*stronghold, chess piece*]; **to ~ the market** Comm s'emparer du marché; **2** fig saisir [*moment, likeness*]; rendre [*feeling, essence, beauty*]; **to ~ sth on film** rendre qch à l'écran.

capuchin /ˈkæpjuːtʃɪn/ I *n* **1** (monkey) capucin *m*; **2** Relig capucin *m*; **3** (cape) cape *f* avec capuche.
II *adj* [*monastery*] de capucins; [*monk*] capucin.

car /kɑː(r)/ I *n* **1** Aut voiture *f*; **2** Rail wagon *m*, voiture *f*; **restaurant ~** wagon-restaurant *m*; **3** US (also **street~**) tramway *m*; **4** (compartment) (of lift) cabine *f*; (of hot-air balloon) nacelle *f*.
II *modif* Aut [*industry, loan, insurance*] automobile; [*journey, chase*] en voiture; [*accident, phone*] de voiture; [*maintenance, emissions*] des voitures.

carafe /kəˈræf/ *n* carafe *f*.

car allowance *n* indemnité *f* de déplacement.

caramel /ˈkærəmel/ I *n* (toffee, sugar) caramel *m*.
II *modif* [*dessert, cake*] au caramel.

caramelize /ˈkærəməlaɪz/ I *vtr* caraméliser [*sugar, sauce*].
II *vi* se caraméliser.

carapace /ˈkærəpeɪs/ *n* carapace *f* also fig.

carat /ˈkærət/ I *n* carat *m*.
II *modif* **18/24 ~ gold** or *m* 18/24 carats.

caravan /ˈkærəvæn/ I *n* gen caravane *f*; (for circus, gypsies) roulotte *f*; **desert ~** caravane du désert; **holiday ~** GB caravane *f* de vacances.
II *modif* GB [*holiday*] en caravane; [*site, park*] pour caravanes; [*company*] (selling) de vente de caravanes; (manufacturing) de fabrication de caravanes.
III *vi* (*p prés etc* **-nn-**) **to go ~ning** GB faire du caravanage.

caravanette /ˌkærəvæˈnet/ *n* GB camping-car *m*, auto-caravane *f*.

caravel /ˈkærəvel/ *n* (also **carvel**) Hist caravelle *f*.

caraway /ˈkærəweɪ/ I *n* (plant) carvi *m*.
II *modif* [*seed*] de carvi.

carbide /ˈkɑːbaɪd/ *n* carbure *m*.

carbine /ˈkɑːbaɪn/ *n* **1** Mil Hist carabine *f* (à canon court); **2** (modern rifle) carabine *f* automatique.

carbohydrate /ˌkɑːbəˈhaɪdreɪt/ I *n* hydrate *m* de carbone.
II *modif* **low-/high-~ diet** alimentation *f* pauvre/riche en hydrates de carbone.

carbolic /kɑːˈbɒlɪk/ *adj* phéniqué.

carbolic: **~ acid** *n* phénol *m*; **~ soap** *n* savon *m* phéniqué.

car bomb *n* bombe *f* dissimulée dans une voiture.

carbon /ˈkɑːbən/ I *n* carbone *m*.
II *modif* [*atom, compound*] de carbone.

carbonaceous /ˌkɑːbəˈneɪʃəs/ *adj* carboné.

carbonade /ˌkɑːbəˈneɪd/ *adj* (*après n*) à la carbonnade.

carbon arc lamp *n* lampe *f* à arc.

carbonate /ˈkɑːbəneɪt/ I *n* carbonate *m*.
II *vtr* carbonater.

carbonated /ˈkɑːbəneɪtɪd/ *adj* [*drink*] gazéifié.

carbonation /ˌkɑːbəˈneɪʃn/ *n* (of drinks) gazéification *f*.

carbon: **~ black** *n* noir *m* de carbone; **~ brakes** *npl* freins *mpl* au carbone; **~ copy** *n* Print copie *f* carbone; fig réplique *f* exacte; **~ cycle** *n* cycle *m* du carbone; **~-date** *vtr* dater [qch] au carbone 14; **~ dating** *n* datation *f* au carbone 14; **~ dioxide** *n* dioxyde *m* de carbone; **~ disulphide** *n* bisulfure *m* de carbone; **~ fibre** GB, **~ fiber** US *n* fibre *f* de carbone; **~ filter** *n* filtre *m* au carbone.

carbonic /kɑːˈbɒnɪk/ *adj* carbonique.

carboniferous /ˌkɑːbəˈnɪfərəs/ *adj* carbonifère; **~ period** carbonifère *m*.

carbonization /ˌkɑːbənaɪˈzeɪʃn, US -nɪˈz-/ *n* carbonisation *f*.

carbonize /ˈkɑːbənaɪz/ *vtr* **1** carboniser also hum; **2** (also **carburize**) carburer [*iron*].

carbon microphone *n* microphone *m* à charbon.

carbon monoxide /ˌkɑːbən mənˈɒksaɪd/ I *n* monoxyde *m* de carbone.
II *modif* [*poisoning*] au monoxyde de carbone; [*monitor*] du taux de monoxyde de carbone.

carbon: **~ paper** *n* (papier *m*) carbone *m*; **~ snow** *n* neige *f* carbonique; **~ steel** *n* acier *m* au carbone; **~ tetrachloride** *n* tétrachlorure *m* de carbone.

car boot sale *n* GB brocante *f* (*d'objets apportés dans le coffre de sa voiture*).

Carborundum® /ˌkɑːbəˈrʌndəm/ I *n* carbure *m* de silicium, carborundum® *m*.
II *modif* [*wheel*] en carborundum®.

carboy /ˈkɑːbɔɪ/ *n* bonbonne *f*.

carbuncle /ˈkɑːbʌŋkl/ *n* **1** Med anthrax *m*; **2** (gem) escarboucle *f*.

carburation /ˌkɑːbjʊˈreɪʃn/ *n* carburation *f*.

carburettor /ˌkɑːbəˈretə(r)/ GB, **carburetor** /ˈkɑːrbəreɪtər/ US *n* carburateur *m*.

carcass /ˈkɑːkəs/ *n* carcasse *f* also hum; **move your ~** hum pousse ta carcasse de là.

car chase *n* poursuite *f* en voiture.

carcinogen /kɑːˈsɪnədʒən/ *n* substance *f* cancérigène.

carcinogenic /ˌkɑːsɪnəˈdʒenɪk/ *adj* cancérigène.

carcinoma /ˌkɑːsɪˈnəʊmə/ *n* carcinome *m*.

card /kɑːd/ I *n* **1** (for correspondence, greetings, business etc) carte *f*; (for indexing) fiche *f*; Sport (at races) programme *m*; (in golf) carte *f* (de parcours); **membership/library ~** carte *f* de membre/de bibliothèque; **Christmas/birthday ~** carte *f* de Noël/d'anniversaire; **▶ postcard, business card etc**; **2** Games carte *f* (à jouer); **to play ~s** jouer aux cartes; **a pack of ~s** un jeu de cartes; **one's last ~** fig sa dernière carte; **one's strongest ~** fig sa carte maîtresse; **to play the race/law and order ~** fig jouer la carte raciale/de la loi et de l'ordre; **3**○† GB (person) original/-e *m/f*; **4** Tex (comb) peigne *m*.
II *vtr* Tex carder.
IDIOMS **a ~ up one's sleeve** un atout dans sa manche; **it is on** GB ou **in** US **the ~s that** il est bien possible que (+ *subj*); **they think an election is on** ou **in the ~s** ils pensent qu'il va y avoir une élection, ils pensent qu'il y a une élection dans l'air; **to get** ou **be given one's ~s**○† GB être renvoyé; **to hold all the ~s** avoir tous les atouts; **to play one's ~s right** bien se débrouiller○.

cardamom /ˈkɑːdəməm/, **cardamon** /-mən/ I *n* cardamome *f*.
II *modif* [*seed*] de cardamome.

cardboard /ˈkɑːdbɔːd/ I *n* carton *m*.
II *modif* [*box, cut-out*] en carton; **~ box** (boîte *f* en) carton *m*; [*character*] fig de carton-pâte.

card: **~board city** *n*: *zone urbaine où les sans-abri logent dans des cartons*; **~-carrying** *adj* [*member etc*] militant; **~ catalogue**, **~ catalog** US *n* fichier *m*.

carder /ˈkɑːdə(r)/ *n* cardeuse *f*.

card file *n* = **card index**.

card game *n* **1** (type of game) jeu *m* de cartes; **2** (as activity) partie *f* de cartes.

card hopper *n* Comput magasin *m* d'alimentation.

cardiac /ˈkɑːdɪæk/ *adj* cardiaque.

cardiac arrest *n* arrêt *m* du cœur.

cardie○ /ˈkɑːdɪ/ *n* **▶ cardy**.

cardigan /ˈkɑːdɪgən/ **▶ 1703** *n* cardigan *m*.

cardinal /ˈkɑːdɪnl/ I *n* Relig cardinal *m*; **Cardinal Wolsey** le cardinal Wolsey.
II *adj* [*sin, principle*] capital.

cardinal: **~ number** *n* nombre *m* cardinal; **~ point** *n* point *m* cardinal; **~ red ▶ 1104** *n* rouge *m* cardinal; **~ virtue** *n* vertu *f* cardinale; **~ vowel** *n* voyelle *f* cardinale.

card index I *n* fichier *m*.
II **card-index** *vtr* mettre [qch] sur fiche.

cardiofunk /ˈkɑːdɪəʊfʌŋk/ *n* danse *f* aérobique.

cardiogram /ˈkɑːdɪəʊgræm/ *n* cardiogramme *m*.

cardiograph /ˈkɑːdɪəʊgrɑːf, US -græf/ *n* cardiographe *m*.

cardiography /ˌkɑːdɪˈɒgrəfɪ/ I *n* cardiographie *f*.
II *modif* **~ department** service *m* de cardiographie.

cardiological /ˌkɑːdɪəˈlɒdʒɪkl/ *adj* cardiologique.

cardiologist /ˌkɑːdɪˈɒlədʒɪst/ **▶ 1692** *n* cardiologue *mf*.

cardiology /ˌkɑːdɪˈɒlədʒɪ/ *n* cardiologie *f*.

cardiopulmonary /ˌkɑːdɪəʊˈpʌlmənərɪ/ *adj* cardio-pulmonaire.

cardiovascular /ˌkɑːdɪəʊˈvæskjʊlə(r)/ *adj* cardio-vasculaire.

card: **~ key** *n* carte *f* magnétique; **~phone** *n* téléphone *m* à carte; **~ punch** *n* perforatrice *f* de cartes; **~ reader** *n* lecteur *m* de cartes perforées; **~sharp(er)** *n* tricheur/-euse *m/f* (professionnel/-elle); **~ stacker** *n* Comput récepteur *m* de cartes; **~ table** *n* table *f* de jeu; **~ trick** *n* tour *m* de cartes; **~ vote** *n* GB *vote par le biais de représentants*.

cardy○ /ˈkɑːdɪ/ *n* GB cardigan *m*.

care /keə(r)/ I *n* **1** (attention) attention *f*, soin *m*; **to take ~ to do** prendre soin de faire;

to take ~ not to do faire attention de ne pas faire; **to take ~ when doing** faire attention en faisant; **to take ~ that** faire attention que (+ *subj*); **he took (great) ~ over** ou **with his work** il a pris (grand) soin de son travail; **to take ~ in doing** mettre soin à faire; **she always takes (great) ~ in choosing the wine/preparing to go out** elle met (le plus grand) soin à choisir le vin/à se préparer pour sortir; **'take ~!'** 'fais attention!'; (expression of farewell) 'à bientôt!'; **with ~** avec soin, en faisant attention; **'handle with ~'** 'fragile'; **have a ~!** GB, **give a ~!** US fais attention!; **to exercise due** ou **proper ~** Admin, Jur prendre les précautions nécessaires; **2** (looking after) (of person, animal) soins *mpl*; (of car, plant, house, clothes) entretien *m* (**of** de); **to take ~ of** (deal with) gen s'occuper de [*child, client*]; Med soigner [*patient, invalid*]; (be responsible for) s'occuper de [*house, garden, details, tickets, arrangements*]; (be careful with) prendre soin de [*machine, car*]; (keep in good condition) entretenir [*machine, car, teeth*]; (look after for safe-keeping) garder [*shop, watch*]; **to take good ~ of sb/sth** prendre soin de qn/qch; **customer ~** service *m* auprès des clients; **to put** ou **leave sb/sth in sb's ~** confier qn/qch à qn; **in his/your ~** à sa/ta garde; **the pupils/patients in my ~** les élèves/malades dont j'ai la responsabilité; **in the ~ of his father/teacher** à la garde de son père/professeur; **John Smith, ~ of Mr and Mrs L. Smith** (on letter) John Smith, chez or aux bons soins de M et Mme L. Smith; **to take ~ of oneself** (look after oneself) prendre soin de soi; (cope) se débrouiller tout seul; (defend oneself) se défendre; **that takes ~ of that** c'est réglé; **3** Med, Psych soins *mpl*; **a policy of ~ in the community** une politique de soins en dehors du milieu hospitalier; **medical ~** soins *mpl* médicaux; **patient ~** soins *mpl*; **preventive ~** soins *mpl* préventifs; **4** GB Soc Admin **to be in ~** être à l'assistance publique; **to take** ou **put a child into ~** mettre un enfant à l'assistance publique; **5** (worry) souci *m*; **without a ~ in the world** parfaitement insouciant.

II *vtr* **I don't ~ to do** cela ne me plaît pas de faire, cela ne me dit rien de faire; **if you ~ to examine the report, you'll find that...** iron si vous voulez avoir l'obligeance d'examiner le rapport, vous constaterez que...; (as polite formula) **would you ~ to sit down?** voulez-vous vous asseoir?; **he has more money than he ~s to admit** il a plus d'argent qu'il ne veut bien le dire.

III *vi* **1** (feel concerned) **she really ~s** elle prend ça à cœur; **to ~ about** s'intéresser à [*art, culture, money, environment*]; se soucier du bien-être de [*staff, pupils, the elderly*]; se soucier de [*injustice, inequality*]; **I don't ~!** ça m'est égal!, je m'en moque!; **what do I ~ if...?** qu'est-ce que ça peut me faire que... (+ *subj*)?; **as if I/he ~d!** comme si ça me/lui faisait quelque chose!; **I/he couldn't ~ less!** ça m'est/ça lui est complètement égal!; **she couldn't ~ less about...** elle se moque or se fiche○ complètement de...; **I couldn't ~ less who wins/what happened** je me moque or me fiche○ de savoir qui va gagner/ce qui s'est passé; **they could all have died, for all he ~d** ils auraient pu mourir tous, cela lui était égal; **I don't ~ who he marries** il peut épouser qui il veut, ça m'est égal; **I'm past caring** ça m'est égal; **who ~s?** qu'est-ce que ça peut faire?; **2** (love) **to ~ about sb** aimer qn; **show him that you ~** montre-lui que tu l'aimes; **I didn't know you ~d!** hum je ne connaissais pas tes sentiments! hum.

IDIOMS **he doesn't ~ a fig** ou **a damn**○ il s'en fiche○ complètement.

■ **care for: ~ for [sb/sth] 1** (like) aimer [*person*]; **I don't ~ for chocolate/whisky** je n'aime pas le chocolat/le whisky; (as polite formula) **would you ~ for a drink?** voulez-vous boire quelque chose?; **2** (look after) s'occuper de [*child, elderly person, animal*]; soigner [*patient, wounded animal*]; **3** (maintain) entretenir [*car, garden, house*]; prendre soin de [*hair, teeth, skin, plant*].

care: **~ assistant** ▶1692 *n* GB Med aide-soignant/-e *m/f*; **~ attendant** ▶1692 *n* GB Soc Admin aide *f* familiale.

careen /kəˈriːn/ **I** *vtr* abattre [qch] en carène [*boat*].
II *vi* [*boat*] se coucher sur le côté.

career /kəˈrɪə(r)/ **I** *n* carrière *f*; **political/musical ~** carrière politique/musicale; **a ~ in television/in teaching** une carrière à la télévision/dans l'enseignement; **a ~ as a journalist** une carrière de journaliste; **~s in the media** les métiers de l'information; **throughout his school ~** pendant toute sa scolarité.
II *modif* **1** [*choice, move, opportunity, prospect*] de carrière; **2** [*diplomat, railwayman*] de carrière; [*soldier*] de métier.
III *vi* **to ~ in/out** entrer/sortir à toute vitesse; **to ~ off the road** sortir de la route à toute vitesse, foncer dans le décor○; **to ~ out of control** s'emballer.

career: **~break** *n* interruption *f* de carrière; **~ girl** *n* = **career woman**.

careerism /kəˈrɪərɪzəm/ *n* carriérisme *m*.

careerist /kəˈrɪərɪst/ *n* carriériste *mf*.

career: **~ move** *n* pas *m* en avant dans son évolution professionnelle; **~s adviser** GB, **~ advisor** US ▶1692 *n* conseiller/-ère *m/f* d'orientation; **~s guidance** *n* orientation *f* professionnelle; **~s library** *n* centre *m* d'information et d'orientation professionnelle; **~s master** ▶1692 *n* GB Sch conseiller *m* d'orientation; **~s mistress** ▶1692 *n* GB Sch conseillère *f* d'orientation; **~s office** *n* service *m* d'orientation professionnelle; **~s officer** *n* GB = **careers adviser**; **~s service** GB, **~ service** US *n* service *m* d'orientation professionnelle; **~ woman** *n* femme *f* qui se consacre à sa vie professionnelle.

carefree /ˈkeəfriː/ *adj* [*person, smile, life*] insouciant; [*feeling*] d'insouciance.

careful /ˈkeəfl/ *adj* **1** (prudent) [*person, driving*] prudent; (meticulous) [*planning, preparation*] minutieux/-ieuse; [*work, research, monitoring, examination*] méticuleux/-euse; **this chemical/equipment needs ~ handling** ce produit chimique/cet appareil est à manipuler avec soin; **this matter needs ~ handling** cette affaire doit être conduite avec soin; **to be ~ to do** ou **about doing** faire attention de faire; **to be ~ that** faire attention que (+ *subj*), faire en sorte que (+ *subj*); **to be ~ of sth** faire attention à qch; **to be ~ with sth** faire attention à qch; **to be ~ (when) doing** faire attention en faisant; **to be ~ how/where** faire attention comment/où; **to be ~ what one says** faire attention à ce qu'on dit; **'be ~!'** '(fais) attention!'; **'you can't be too ~!'** 'on n'est jamais trop prudent!'; **2** (thrifty) (*jamais épith*) [*person*] prudent; **to be ~ with money** euph, péj faire attention à l'argent.

carefully /ˈkeəfəlɪ/ *adv* [*go, walk, drive*] prudemment; [*open, remove, handle*] prudemment, avec précaution; [*say, reply*] prudemment; [*write, choose words, phrase*] soigneusement, avec soin; [*plan, organize, choose, wash, place*] soigneusement, avec soin; [*arranged, controlled, chosen, built*] soigneusement; [*listen, read, look*] attentivement; [*designed, made*] méticuleusement; **drive ~!** soyez prudent!; **go ~!** soyez prudent!; **listen/think ~!** écoutez/réfléchissez bien!

carefulness /ˈkeəflnɪs/ *n* (of person, work) soin *m*; (of driving) prudence *f*; **the ~ of his work** le soin avec lequel il travaille.

care label *n* (on clothing etc) conseils *mpl* d'entretien.

careless /ˈkeəlɪs/ *adj* **1** (negligent) [*person*] négligent, imprudent; [*work, workmanship*] bâclé; [*writing*] négligé; [*driving, handling*] négligent; [*talk*] imprudent; **~ mistake** faute d'étourderie or d'inattention; **his spelling is ~** quand il écrit il fait des fautes d'étourderie; **that was ~ of her** ce qu'elle est négligente!; **it was ~ of me to do** c'était de la négligence de ma part de faire; **to be ~ about sth/about doing** négliger qch/de faire; **to be ~ with sth** ne pas faire attention à qch; **to be ~ in sth** être négligent dans qch; **to be ~ in doing** ne pas faire attention en faisant; **to be ~ of one's appearance** ne pas se soigner; **2** (carefree) [*smile, wave, reply*] insouciant; [*gesture*] dégagé; [*grace, elegance*] naturel/-elle; **to do sth ~ of the risks** faire qch sans se soucier des risques.

carelessly /ˈkeəlɪslɪ/ *adv* **1** (negligently) [*do, act*] avec négligence; [*make, repair, write*] sans soin, à la va-vite; [*drive*] avec imprudence; [*break, drop, lose, spill*] par manque d'attention; [*dressed, arranged*] avec négligence, négligemment; **2** (in carefree way) [*walk, dance, say, wave*] avec insouciance.

carelessness /ˈkeəlɪsnɪs/ *n* **1** (negligence) négligence *f*; **2** (carefree attitude) insouciance *f*, nonchalance *f*.

care order *n* GB ordre *m* de placement à l'assistance publique.

carer /ˈkeərə(r)/ ▶1692 *n* GB **1** (relative or friend) *personne ayant un parent handicapé ou malade à charge*; **2** Soc Admin (professional) aide *f* familiale.

caress /kəˈres/ **I** *n* caresse *f*.
II *vtr* caresser.

caret /ˈkærət/ *n* (also **~ sign**) lambda *m*, signe *m* d'insertion.

caretaker /ˈkeəteɪkə(r)/ ▶1692 **I** *n* GB (at school, club) concierge *mf*; (in apartments) gardien/-ienne *m/f*, concierge *mf*; (of building while owner absent) gardien/-ienne *m/f*.
II *modif* [*government, administration*] intérimaire; [*president, prime minister, manager*] par intérim.

care worker ▶1692 *n* GB Soc Admin assistant/-e *m/f* social/-e.

careworn /ˈkeəwɔːn/ *adj* [*face*] marqué (par les soucis); **to look ~, to have a ~ expression** avoir l'air d'avoir beaucoup souffert.

car: **~fare** *n* US prix *m* du trajet; **~ ferry** *n* ferry *m*.

cargo /ˈkɑːgəʊ/ **I** *n* (*pl* **~es** ou **~s**) gen chargement *m* (**of** de); Naut cargaison *f*, chargement *m* (**of** de).
II *modif* [*bay, handler*] de chargement; [*inspection*] du chargement.

cargo: **~ plane** *n* avion *m* cargo; **~ ship** *n* cargo *m*.

car: **~ hire** *n* location *f* de voitures; **~ hire company** *n* société *f* de location de voitures; **~hop** /ˈkɑːhɒp/ ▶1692 *n* US serveur/-euse *m/f* de drive-in.

Caribbean /ˌkærɪˈbiːən/ ▶1511 **I** *n* **1** (sea) mer *f* des Antilles; **2** (person) habitant/-e *m/f* des Caraïbes.
II *modif* [*climate, cookery*] des Caraïbes; [*carnival*] des Antilles.

Caribbean Islands ▶1381 *pr npl* petites Antilles *fpl*.

caribou /ˈkærɪbuː/ *n* caribou *m*.

caricatural /ˈkærɪkətʃʊərəl/ *adj* caricatural.

caricature /ˈkærɪkətʃʊə(r)/ **I** *n* caricature *f*.
II *vtr* caricaturer.

caricaturist /ˈkærɪkətʃʊərɪst/ ▶1692 *n* caricaturiste *mf*.

caries /ˈkeəriːz/ *n* (*pl* **~**) carie *f*.

carillon /kəˈrɪljən, US ˈkærəlɒn/ ▶1481 **I** *n* (all contexts) carillon *m*.
II *vi* (*p prés etc* **-nn-**) carillonner.

caring /ˈkeərɪŋ/ **I** *n* travail *m* social.
II *modif* Med, Soc Admin [*profession, service*] paramédical; **~ professionals** le personnel paramédical.
III *adj* **1** (loving) [*parent, husband, wife*] affectueux/-euse; [*atmosphere, environment, home*] chaleureux/-euse; **2** (compassionate) [*person, approach, attitude*] compréhensif/

-ive; [*party, government, company, society*] humain.

carious /ˈkeərɪəs/ *adj* carié.

carjacking /ˈkɑːdʒækɪŋ/ *n* vol *m* de voiture (avec agression du conducteur).

carload /ˈkɑːləʊd/ *n* **we moved his things in two ~s** on a déménagé ses affaires en deux voitures; **a ~ of people/boxes** une voiture pleine de gens/de cartons.

Carmelite /ˈkɑːməlaɪt/ **I** *n* (monk) carme *m*; (nun) carmélite *f*.
II *modif* [*monastery*] de carmes; [*convent*] de carmélites; **~ order** (of monks) ordre *m* des carmes; (of nuns) ordre *m* des carmélites.

carmine /ˈkɑːmaɪn/ **▶1104** **I** *n* carmin *m*.
II *adj* [*point*] carmin *inv*.

carnage /ˈkɑːnɪdʒ/ *n* carnage *m* also fig.

carnal /ˈkɑːnl/ *adj* [*pleasure, desire*] charnel/-elle; **to have ~ knowledge of sb** Bible, sout connaître qn; hum connaître qn bibliquement.

carnation /kɑːˈneɪʃn/ *n* œillet *m*.

carnation: **~ pink** **▶1104** *n* rose *m* incarnat; **~ red** **▶1104** *n* rouge *m* incarnat.

carnet /ˈkɑːneɪ/ *n* GB **1** Tax, Admin (for goods) passavant *m*; **2** Tourism (for campsite entry) autorisation *f* d'entrée; **3** (of coupons) carnet *m*.

carnival /ˈkɑːnɪvl/ **I** *n* **1** GB (festive procession) carnaval *m*; **street/charity ~** carnaval de rue/de bienfaisance; **2** (funfair) fête *f* foraine.
II *modif* GB [*parade, atmosphere, float*] de carnaval.

carnivora /ˈkɑːnɪvɔːrə/ *npl* carnivores *mpl*.

carnivore /ˈkɑːnɪvɔː(r)/ *n* carnivore *m*.

carnivorous /kɑːˈnɪvərəs/ *adj* carnivore.

carny◐ /ˈkɑːnɪ/ *n* (also **carney**) US **1** (funfair) fête *f* foraine; **2** (person) forain *m*.

carob /ˈkærəb/ **I** *n* **1** (tree) caroubier *m*; **2** (pod) caroube *f*.
II *modif* Culin [*bar, powder*] de caroube.

carol /ˈkærəl/ **I** *n* chant de Noël.
II *vi* (*p prés etc* **-ll-**) littér [*choirsingers*] chanter joyeusement; [*bird*] gazouiller; [*flute, piccolo*] siffler.

caroller† /ˈkærələ(r)/ *n* chanteur/-euse *m/f* de chants de Noël.

carol: **~ service** *n* célébration *f* de Noël; **~ singer** *n* chanteur/-euse *m/f* de chants de Noël.

carom /ˈkærəm/ US (in billiards) **I** *n* carambolage *m*.
II *vi* [*ball*] faire un carambolage; [*player*] caramboler.

carotene /ˈkærətiːn/, **carotin** /ˈkærətɪn/ *n* carotène *m*.

carotid /kəˈrɒtɪd/ **I** *n* carotide *f*.
II *adj* [*artery*] carotidien/-ienne.

carousal /kəˈraʊzl/ *n* sout beuverie *f*.

carouse /kəˈraʊz/ *vi* sout faire la noce; **carousing businessmen** hommes d'affaires qui font la noce.

carousel /ˌkærəˈsel/ *n* **1** US (merry-go-round) manège *m*; **2** (for luggage) carrousel *m*; **3** Phot (for slides) carrousel *m*; **4** Hist (tournament) carrousel *m*.

carp /kɑːp/ **I** *n* (fish) carpe *f*.
II○ *vi* maugréer (**about** contre).

carpal /ˈkɑːpl/ **I** *n* carpe *m*.
II *adj* [*bone*] carpien/-ienne.

car park /ˈkɑːpɑːk/ *n* GB parc *m* de stationnement.

Carpathians /kɑːˈpeɪθjəns/ *pr npl* Carpates *fpl*.

carpel /ˈkɑːpl/ *n* carpelle *m*.

Carpentaria /ˌkɑːpənˈteərɪə/ **▶1511** *pr n* **Gulf of ~** golfe *m* de Carpentarie.

carpenter /ˈkɑːpəntə(r)/ **▶1692** *n* (joiner) menuisier *m*; (on building site) charpentier *m*.

carpentry /ˈkɑːpəntrɪ/ **I** *n* gen menuiserie *f*; (structural) charpenterie *f*.
II *modif* [*tool*] de menuisier, de charpentier; [*course*] de menuiserie, de charpenterie.

carpet /ˈkɑːpɪt/ **I** *n* **1** (fitted) moquette *f*; (loose) tapis *m*; **2** fig tapis *m*; **~ of flowers/snow** tapis de fleurs/neige.
II *modif* [*beater*] à tapis; [*sale, showroom*] de tapis; [*shampoo*] pour tapis.
III *vtr* **1** lit mettre de la moquette dans [*room*]; **to ~ the living-room floor** mettre de la moquette dans le séjour; **~ed with flowers** fig, littér tapissé de fleurs; **2** fig (reprimand) passer un savon à [*employee*].
IDIOMS **to be on the ~**○ être sur la sellette; **to brush** ou **push** ou **sweep sth under the ~** enterrer or étouffer qch.

carpetbag /ˈkɑːpɪtbæg/ *n* sac *m* de voyage.

carpetbagger /ˈkɑːpɪtbægə(r)/ *n* **1** US Hist profiteur *m* nordiste (*après la guerre civile*); **2** Pol candidat *m* parachuté.

carpet: **~ beetle** *n* anthrène *m*; **~ bombing** *n* Mil Hist technique *f* du tapis de bombes; **~ bowls** **▶1282** *npl* jeu *m* de boules sur tapis; **~ fitter** **▶1692** *n* poseur *m* de moquette.

carpeting /ˈkɑːpɪtɪŋ/ *n* moquette *f*.

carpet: **~ slipper** *n* charentaise *f*; **~ sweeper** *n* balai *m* mécanique; **~ tile** *n* dalle *f* de moquette.

car: **~phone** *n* radiotéléphone *m* de voiture; **~ phone** *n* téléphone *m* de voiture.

carping /ˈkɑːpɪŋ/ **I** *n* ¢ chicaneries *fpl*.
II *adj* [*criticism, person*] malveillant.

car pool *n* **to be in a ~** *s'arranger entre parents, collègues etc pour faire les trajets quotidiens avec une seule voiture*.

carport /ˈkɑːpɔːt/ *n* auvent *m* pour voitures.

carpus /ˈkɑːpəs/ *n* (*pl* **-pi**) Anat carpe *m*.

car radio *n* autoradio *m*.

carrageen, **carragheen** /ˈkærəgiːn/ *n* carragheen *m*.

car rental *n* **▶ car hire**.

carriage /ˈkærɪdʒ/ *n* **1** (vehicle) (ceremonial) carrosse *m*; (for transport) attelage *m*; **2** (of train) wagon *m*, voiture *f*; **3** ¢ (of goods, passenger) transport *m* (**by** par); **~ free/forward** port *m* gratuit/dû; **~ paid** port *m* payé; **4** Tech (of typewriter) chariot *m*; **▶ gun carriage**; **5** (person's bearing) maintien *m*; (of head) port *m*.

carriage: **~ clock** *n* pendulette *f*; **~way** *n* chaussée *f*.

carrier /ˈkærɪə(r)/ *n* **1** (transport company) transporteur *m*; (airline) compagnie *f* aérienne; **to send sth by ~** expédier qch; **2** (of disease) porteur/-euse *m/f*; **3** GB (also **~ bag**) sac *m* (*en papier ou en plastique*). **▶ troop carrier etc.**

carrier pigeon *n* pigeon *m* voyageur.

carrion /ˈkærɪən/ *n* (also **~ flesh**) charogne *f*.

carrion: **~ crow** *n* corneille *f* noire; **~ feeder** *n* charognard *m*.

carrot /ˈkærət/ *n* carotte *f* also fig.

carrot: **~ and stick** *adj* fig [*approach, tactics*] de la carotte et du bâton; **~ cake** *n* gâteau *m* à la carotte; **~ top**○ *n* hum ou péj poil *m* de carotte.

carroty○ /ˈkærətɪ/ *adj* [*hair*] rouquin○; **to have ~ hair** être rouquin○.

carry /ˈkærɪ/ **I** *n* (range) portée *f*.
II *vtr* **1** [*person, animal*] porter [*bag, shopping, load, news, message*] (**in** dans; **on** sur); **to ~ sth up/down** porter qch en haut/en bas; **to ~ sth in/out** apporter/emporter qch; **to ~ the bags over the road** traverser la route en portant les bagages; **to ~ the child across the river** porter l'enfant pour traverser la rivière; **to ~ cash/a gun** avoir de l'argent liquide/un revolver sur soi; **to ~ a memory/a picture in one's mind** avoir un sentiment/une image toujours en tête; **to ~ sth too far** fig pousser qch trop loin; **we can't afford to ~ anyone** fig nous ne pouvons pas nous permettre de traîner des poids morts; **2** [*vehicle, pipe, wire, vein*] transporter; [*wind, tide, current, stream*] emporter; **licensed to ~ passengers** autorisé à transporter des passagers; **to be carried on the wind** être porté or transporté par le vent; **to be carried along by the tide** être poussé par la marée; **the wind carried the ash towards the town** le vent a transporté les cendres vers la ville; **to ~ sth off** ou **away** emporter qch; **to ~ sb off** ou **away** emmener qn; **to ~ sth/sb back** ramener qch/qn; **to ~ one's audience with one** avoir son public derrière soi; **his quest carried him to India** sa quête l'a amené en Inde; **her talent will ~ her a long way** son talent la mènera loin; **to be carried along with the general enthusiasm** être emporté par l'enthousiasme général; **3** (feature) comporter [*warning, guarantee, review, report*]; porter [*symbol, label*]; **'The Gazette' will ~ the ad** 'La Gazette' publiera l'annonce; **4** (entail) comporter [*risk, danger, responsibility*]; être passible de [*penalty, fine*]; **to ~ conviction** être convaincant; **5** (bear, support) [*bridge, road*] supporter [*weight, load, traffic*]; **the field will not ~ that herd/crop** le champ ne convient pas à ce troupeau/cette culture; **6** Mil, Pol (win) l'emporter dans [*state, region, constituency*]; remporter [*battle, match*]; faire voter [*bill, amendment*]; **the motion was carried by 20 votes to 13** la motion l'a emporté par 20 votes contre 13; **to ~ all before one/it** [*person, argument*] l'emporter haut la main; **7** Med être porteur/-euse de [*disease*]; **she is ~ing the HIV virus** elle est porteuse du virus VIH; **8** (be pregnant with) [*woman*] être enceinte de [*boy, girl, twins*]; [*female animal*] porter [*young*]; **she is ~ing a child** elle est enceinte; **I am ~ing his child** je porte son enfant; **9** Comm (stock, sell) faire [*item, brand*]; **we ~ a wide range of** nous offrons un grand choix de; **10** (hold, bear) (permanently) porter [*tail, head*]; **he was ~ing his arm awkwardly** il se tenait le bras de façon curieuse; **11** Math retenir [*one, two*].
III *vi* [*sound, voice*] porter; **to ~ well** porter bien; **the noise carried (for) several kilometres** le bruit a porté à plusieurs kilomètres.
IV *v refl* **to ~ oneself** se tenir (**like** comme; **with** avec).
IDIOMS **to be carried away by sth** être emballé○ par qch; **to get carried away**○ s'emballer○, se laisser emporter.

■ **carry back**: ¶ **~ back [sth]**, **~ [sth] back** Tax reporter [qch] en arrière [*sum, loss*]; ¶ **~ [sb] back** (in memory) ramener [*person*] (**to** à).

■ **carry forward**: **~ forward [sth]**, **~ [sth] forward** **1** Accts reporter [*balance, total, sum*]; **2** Tax reporter [qch] en avant [*sum, loss*].

■ **carry off**: ¶ **~ off [sth]** remporter [*prize, medal*]; **to ~ it off**○ (succeed) réussir, y arriver; ¶ **~ off [sb]**, **~ [sb] off** [*illness, disease*] emporter [*person, animal*].

■ **carry on**: ¶ **~ on 1** (continue) continuer (**doing** à faire) ; **~ on!** continue!; **to ~ on down** ou **along the road** (in car) continuer la route; (on foot) poursuivre son chemin; **if it carries on like this** si ça continue comme ça; **to ~ on as if nothing had happened** continuer comme si de rien n'était; **to ~ on with sth** continuer or poursuivre qch; **2**○ (behave) se conduire; **that's no way to ~ on** ce n'est pas une façon de se conduire; **to ~ on as if** se conduire comme si; **3**○ (have affair) fricoter○, avoir une liaison (**with** avec); **4**○ (talk, go on) jacasser○; **to ~ on about sth** déblatérer○ sur qch; ¶ **~ on [sth] 1** (conduct) conduire [*business, trade*]; entretenir [*correspondence*]; mener [*conversation, negotiations, normal life*]; **2** (continue) maintenir [*tradition, custom*]; reprendre [*family firm*]; poursuivre [*activity, discussion*].

■ **carry out**: **~ out [sth]**, **~ [sth] out** réaliser [*plan, experiment, study, audit, reform, robbery*]; effectuer [*raid, attack, operation, repairs*]; exécuter [*orders, punish-*

ment, recommendations, restoration]; mener [*investigation, campaign*]; accomplir [*execution, killing*]; remplir [*duties, function, mission*]; mettre [qch] à exécution [*threat*]; tenir [*promise*].

■ **carry over**: ¶ **~ over into** [*problem, attitude, rivalry*] s'étendre à [*area of activity, personal life*]; ¶ **~ sth over into** transférer qch dans [*private life, area of activity, adulthood*]; ¶ **~ over [sth], ~ [sth] over 1** gen **to be carried over from** [*custom, habit, feeling*] remonter à [*period, childhood*]; **an item carried over from the last meeting** un point laissé en attente à la dernière réunion; **2** Fin (on stock exchange) reporter [*debt*]; **3** Accts, Tax = **carry forward**.

■ **carry through**: ¶ **~ through [sth], ~ [sth] through** mener [qch] à bien [*reform, policy, task*]; ¶ **~ [sb] through** [*humour, courage*] soutenir [*person*]; [*instincts*] guider [*person*].

carry: **~all** *n* US fourre-tout *m inv*; **~-back** *n* Accts report *m* en arrière; **~cot** *n* GB porte-bébé *m*; **~-forward** *n* Accts report *m* en avant; **~ing-on**○ *n* (*pl* **carryings-on**) incartade *f*; **~-on**○ *n* cirque○ *m*.

carryout /'kærɪaʊt/ GB *n* **1** (food) repas *m* à emporter; **2** Scot dial (alcohol) alcool *m* à emporter.

carry-over /'kærɪəʊvə(r)/ *n* Fin report *m*.

car seat *n* siège-auto *m*.

carsick /'kɑːsɪk/ *adj* **to be ~** avoir le mal de la route.

car sickness ▶ **1354** *n* mal *m* de la route.

cart /kɑːt/ **I** *n* (for hay, goods) charrette *f*; (two-wheel, for passengers) carriole *f*.

II *vtr* **1** (also **~ around, ~ about**)○ (drag, lug) trimballer○ [*luggage, shopping*]; **to ~ sth up/down the stairs** trimballer qch en haut/en bas de l'escalier; **2** Agric charrier [*hay, turnips*].

IDIOMS **to put the ~ before the horse** mettre la charrue avant les bœufs.

■ **cart off**○: **~ [sb] off** emmener [qn] de force.

cartage /'kɑːtɪdʒ/ *n* charroi *m*.

carte blanche /ˌkɑːt 'blɑːnʃ/ *n* carte *f* blanche; **to have/be given ~ to do** avoir/recevoir carte blanche pour faire.

cartel /kɑː'tel/ *n* (all contexts) cartel *m*; **drug/price ~** cartel *m* de la drogue/des prix.

carter /'kɑːtə(r)/ ▶ **1692** *n* charretier/-ière *m/f*.

Cartesian /kɑː'tiːzjən/ *n, adj* cartésien/-ienne (*m/f*).

Cartesianism /kɑː'tiːzjənɪzəm/ *n* cartésianisme *m*.

cartful /'kɑːtfʊl/ *n* charretée *f*.

Carthage /'kɑːθɪdʒ/ ▶ **1818** *pr n* Carthage.

Carthaginian /ˌkɑːθə'dʒɪnɪən/ **I** *n* Carthaginois/-e *m/f*.

II *adj* carthaginois.

carthorse /'kɑːthɔːs/ *n* cheval *m* de trait.

Carthusian /kɑː'θjuːzjən/ Relig **I** *n* chartreux/-euse *m/f*.

II *modif* [*monk, nun*] chartreux/-euse; [*monastery*] de chartreux.

cartilage /'kɑːtɪlɪdʒ/ **I** *n* cartilage *m*.

II *modif* [*operation*] du cartilage; [*problems*] de cartilage.

cartload /'kɑːtləʊd/ *n* charretée *f*.

cartographer /kɑː'tɒɡrəfə(r)/ ▶ **1692** *n* cartographe *mf*.

cartography /kɑː'tɒɡrəfɪ/ *n* cartographie *f*.

cartomancy /'kɑːtəmænsɪ/ *n* cartomancie *f*.

carton /'kɑːtn/ **I** *n* gen (small) boîte *f*; US (for house removals) carton *m*; (of yoghurt, cream) pot *m*; (of juice, milk, ice cream) carton *m*, brique *f*; (of cigarettes) cartouche *f*.

II *vtr* US (pack up) mettre [qch] dans des cartons [*belongings*].

cartoon /kɑː'tuːn/ **I** *n* **1** Cin dessin *m* animé, film *m* d'animation; **2** (drawing) dessin *m* humoristique; (in comic) (also **strip ~**) bande *f* dessinée; **3** Art (sketch) carton *m*.

II *modif* [*character*] de dessin animé; [*adventure, series*] de dessins animés.

cartoonist /kɑː'tuːnɪst/ ▶ **1692** *n* **1** Cin dessinateur/-trice *m/f* de films d'animation; **2** Journ dessinateur/-trice *m/f* humoristique; (of strip cartoons) dessinateur/-trice *m/f* de bandes dessinées.

car transporter *n* camion *m* à plateforme.

cartridge /'kɑːtrɪdʒ/ *n* **1** (for pen, gun) cartouche *f*; **2** Audio, Elec (for video, typewriter etc) cartouche *f*; (for stylus) cellule *f*; **3** Phot (for camera) chargeur *m*.

cartridge: **~ belt** *n* Hunt cartouchière *f*; **~ clip** *n* (for gun) chargeur *m* (d'arme à feu); **~ drive** *n* Comput porte-disquette *m*; **~ paper** *n* Art papier *m* à dessin; Print papier *m* fort; **~ pen** *n* stylo *m* à cartouche.

cart-track /'kɑːttræk/ *n* chemin *m* charretier.

cartwheel /'kɑːtwiːl, US -hwiːl/ *n* **1** (in gymnastics) roue *f*; **to do** ou **turn a ~** faire la roue; **2** lit roue *f* de charrette.

carve /kɑːv/ **I** *vtr* **1** (shape, sculpt) tailler, sculpter [*wood, stone, figure*]; creuser [*channel*] (**out of, from** dans); **to ~ sth into** tailler qch en forme de [*motif, figure*]; **2** (inscribe) graver [*letters, name, motif*] (**onto** sur; **in** dans); **3** Culin découper [*meat, joint*]; **to ~ a slice off the joint** découper une tranche dans le rôti; **4** (create) = **carve out**.

II *vi* découper; **will you ~?** voulez-vous découper la viande?

III carved *pp adj* [*figure, mantelpiece, wood*] sculpté.

■ **carve out**: **~ out [sth], ~ [sth] out 1** fig se faire [*niche, name*]; se tailler [*reputation, market*]; se construire [*career*]; **2** lit creuser [*gorge, channel*].

■ **carve up**: ¶ **~ up [sth], ~ [sth] up 1**○ péj (share) partager [*territory, market, industry, spoils*]; **2** Culin découper [*meat*]; ¶ **~ up [sb]**○ **1** (with knife, razor) taillader le visage à; **2** Aut faire une queue de poisson à.

carvers /'kɑːvəz/ *npl* service *m* à découper.

carvery /'kɑːvərɪ/ *n* GB buffet *m* (de viandes rôties).

carve-up○ /'kɑːvʌp/ *n* GB péj partage *m*.

carving /'kɑːvɪŋ/ *n* **1** (figure, sculpture) sculpture *f*; **2** (technique) gravure *f*; **3** Culin découpage *m*; **who'll do the ~?** qui va découper?

carving knife *n* couteau *m* à découper.

car: **~ wash** *n* lavage *m* automatique; **~ worker** ▶ **1692** *n* ouvrier/-ière *m/f* de l'industrie automobile.

caryatid /ˌkærɪ'ætɪd/ *n* caryatide *f*.

cascade /kæ'skeɪd/ **I** *n* **1** (of water, fireworks) cascade *f*; (of hair, silk, music) flot *m*; **2** Comput cascade *f*.

II *vi* tomber en cascade.

cascading /ˌkæs'keɪdɪŋ/ *adj* Comput [*window*] en cascade; **~ menu** menus *mpl* en cascade.

cascara /kæs'kɑːrə/ *n* Pharm cascara *f*.

case[1] /keɪs/ **I** *n* **1** (instance, example) cas *m*; **in several ~s** dans plusieurs cas; **a ~ of mistaken identity** un cas d'erreur sur la personne; **on a ~ by ~ basis** au cas par cas; **in which ~, in that ~** en ce cas, dans ce cas-là; **in such** ou **these ~s** dans un cas pareil; **in 7 out of 10 ~s** 7 fois sur 10, dans 7 cas sur 10; **a ~ in point** un cas d'espèce, un exemple typique; **it was a ~ of making a quick decision** il s'agissait de prendre une décision rapide; **it's a ~ of substituting X for Y** il s'agit de substituer X à Y; **it's simply a ~ of waiting** il n'y a plus qu'à attendre; **2** (state of affairs, situation) cas *m*; **that's not the ~ here** ce n'est pas le cas ici; **such** ou **this being the ~** en ce cas, dans ce cas-là; **is it the ~ that...?** est-il vrai que...?; **as** ou **whatever the ~ may be** selon le(s) cas; **should this be the ~** ou **if this is the ~, contact your doctor** si c'est le cas, consultez votre médecin; **in no ~ will customers be refunded** en aucun cas les clients ne pourront être remboursés; **3** (legal arguments) **the ~ for the Crown** GB, **the ~ for the State** US l'accusation *f*; **the ~ for the defence** la défense; **to state the ~** exposer les faits; **to put the ~ for the prosecution** représenter le ministère public; **to put the ~ for the defence** assurer la défense du prévenu; **the ~ against Foster** les faits qui sont reprochés à Foster; **there is a ~ to answer** il y a assez de preuves; **the ~ is closed** Jur, fig l'affaire or la cause est entendue; ▶ **rest**; **4** (convincing argument) arguments *mpl*; **to put the ~ for sth** trouver des arguments en faveur de qch; **to make a good ~ for sth** donner des arguments convaincants en faveur de qch; **to argue the ~ for privatization** donner des arguments en faveur de la privatisation; **there's a strong ~ against it** il y a beaucoup d'arguments contre cela; **there's a strong ~ for/against doing** il y a de bonnes raisons pour/pour ne pas faire; **5** (trial) affaire *f*, procès *m*; **criminal/civil ~** affaire criminelle/civile; **divorce ~** procès en divorce; **murder ~** procès pour meurtre; **to win one's ~** gagner son procès, avoir gain de cause; **to lose/plead a ~** plaider/perdre une cause; **the ~ before the court** l'affaire en jugement; **his ~ comes up next week** il passe en jugement la semaine prochaine; **to decide a ~** rendre un jugement; **famous ~s** causes *fpl* célèbres; **6** (criminal investigation) **the Burgess ~** l'affaire Burgess; **to work** ou **be on a ~** enquêter sur une affaire; **a murder/blackmail ~** une affaire de meurtre/de chantage; **the ~s of Sherlock Holmes** les enquêtes de Sherlock Holmes; **7** Med (instance of disease) cas *m*; (patient) malade *mf*; **30 ~s of chickenpox** 30 cas de varicelle; **he's a psychiatric ~** c'est un malade mental; **8** Soc Admin (client) cas *m*; **to deal with a lot of difficult ~s** avoir affaire à des cas difficiles; **a problem ~** un cas à problème; **9**○ (person) **he's a real ~!** c'est vraiment un cas!; **a hopeless ~** un cas désespéré; **a hard ~** un dur; ▶ **head case**; **10** Ling cas *m*; **in the accusative ~** à l'accusatif.

II in any case *adv phr* (besides, anyway) de toute façon; (at any rate) en tout cas; **and in any ~, I've no intention of staying** et de toute façon, je n'ai pas l'intention de rester; **the effect of the recession, or in any ~ of high inflation, is that...** l'effet de la récession, ou en tout cas de la forte inflation, est que...

III in case *conj phr* au cas où (+ *conditional*); **in ~ it rains** au cas où il pleuvrait; **take the street map just in ~** prends le plan au cas où; **your report, in ~ you've forgotten, was due yesterday** votre rapport, au cas où vous l'auriez oublié, était pour hier.

IV in case of *prep phr* **in ~ of fire/emergency** en cas d'incendie/d'urgence.

IDIOMS **get off my ~**○! fiche-moi la paix○!

case[2] /keɪs/ **I** *n* **1** (suitcase) valise *f*; **2** (crate, chest) caisse *f*; **to buy wine by the ~** acheter du vin par la caisse; **3** (display cabinet) vitrine *f*; **to display sth in a ~** exposer qch dans une vitrine; **4** (protective container) (for spectacles, binoculars, cartridge, weapon) étui *m*; (for jewels) écrin *m*; (of camera, watch) boîtier *m*; (of piano, clock) caisse *f*; **5** Print casse *f*; ▶ **lower case, upper case**; **6** (book-cover) couverture *f*.

II○ *vtr* (reconnoitre) **to ~ the joint** [*thief*] faire du repérage.

CASE /keɪs/ *n* (*abrév* = **computer-aided software engineering**) CPAO *f*.

case: **~book** *n* Jur, Med dossiers *mpl*; (of essays, articles) recueil *m*; **~ conference** *n*: *réunion de professionnels pour parler d'un cas social*; **~ file** *n* dossier *m*; **~ grammar** *n* grammaire *f* des cas.

case-harden I *vtr* Ind cémenter [*steel*]; fig endurcir [*person*].
II **case-hardened** *pp adj* Ind cémenté; fig endurci.

case history *n* **1** Med antécédents *mpl*; **2** (exemplary study) = **case study**.

case knife *n* US couteau *m* à gaine.

case law *n* droit *m* jurisprudentiel.

caseload /ˈkeɪsləʊd/ *n* clientèle *f*; **to have a heavy ~** avoir une clientèle nombreuse.

casement /ˈkeɪsmənt/ *n* littér fenêtre *f*, croisée *f* liter.

casement window *n* fenêtre *f* à battants.

case: **~ notes** *npl* dossier *m*; **~ study** *n* étude *f* de cas.

case system *n* Ling système *m* casuel.

casework /ˈkeɪswɜːk/ *n* **to be involved in** ou **to do ~** s'occuper des cas sociaux.

caseworker /ˈkeɪswɜːkə(r)/ ▶ **1692** *n* ≈ assistant/-e *m/f* social/-e.

cash /kæʃ/ I *n* **1** (notes and coins) espèces *fpl*, argent *m* liquide; **to pay in ~** payer en espèces; **£3,000 (in) ~** 3 000 livres sterling en espèces; **to be paid ~ in hand** être payé en espèces; **I haven't got any ~ on me** je n'ai pas d'argent liquide; **2** (money in general) argent *m*; **to be short of ~** être à court d'argent; **3** (immediate payment) comptant *m*; **will it be ~ or credit?** est-ce que vous payez (au) comptant ou à crédit?; **discount for ~** remise *f* pour paiement comptant; **£50 ~ in hand** ou **~ down** 50 livres sterling en liquide.
II *modif* [*advance, book, float*] de caisse; [*bid, offer, sale, terms, discount, transaction*] au comptant; [*allowance, alternative, compensation, deposit, grant, sum, refund, prize*] en espèces; [*price*] comptant.
III *vtr* encaisser [*cheque*].
■ **cash in**: ¶ **~ in** en profiter; **to ~ in on** tirer profit de, profiter de [*popularity, publicity, event, death*]; ¶ **~ in [sth], ~ [sth] in** se faire rembourser, réaliser [*bond, token, insurance policy*]; US encaisser [*check*]; encaisser [*gambling chips*].
■ **cash up** faire la caisse.

cashable /ˈkæʃəbl/ *adj* encaissable.

cash-and-carry /ˌkæʃənˈkærɪ/ I *n* libre-service *m* de vente en gros.
II *adj* [*store, warehouse*] de vente en gros; [*price*] de grossiste.

cash: **~ assets** *n* Fin avoirs *mpl* en caisse; **~ box** *n* caisse *f*; **~ buyer** *n* acheteur/-euse *m/f* qui paye comptant; **~ card** *n* carte *f* de retrait; **~ contribution** *n* Fin apport *m* en numéraire; **~ cow** *n* Comm, fig vache *f* à lait; **~ crop** *n* culture *f* commerciale or de rente; **~ deficit** *n* déficit *m* de trésorerie; **~ desk** *n* caisse *f*; **~ dispenser** *n* distributeur *m* automatique de billets de banque, billetterie *f*.

cashew /ˈkæʃuː/ *n* (also **~ nut**) cajou *m*.

cash flow I *n* marge *f* brute d'autofinancement, MBA *f*, cash flow *m*.
II *modif* [*analysis, crisis, forecast, problem*] de cash-flow, de MBA; **I've got a bit of a ~ problem!** hum j'ai des petits problèmes de finance!

cashier /kæˈʃɪə(r)/ ▶ **1692** I *n* caissier/-ière *m/f*.
II *vtr* Mil casser [*officer*]; gen congédier [*employee*].

cash: **~ inflow** *n* recettes *fpl*, rentrée *f* de fonds; **~ injection** *n* injection *f* de capitaux.

cashless /ˈkæʃlɪs/ *adj* [*transaction, pay*] par virement; [*society*] sans argent liquide.

cash limit *n* limite *f* budgétaire.

cashmere /ˌkæʃˈmɪə(r)/ I *n* (lainage *m* en) cachemire *m*.
II *modif* [*sweater, material*] en cachemire.

cash: **~ offer** *n* offre *f* d'achat au comptant; **~ on delivery, COD** *n* envoi *m* contre remboursement; **~ outflow** *n* dépenses *fpl*, sortie *f* de fonds; **~point** *n* = **cash dispenser**; **~point card** *n* = **cash card**; **~ ratio** *n* coéfficient *m* de trésorerie; **~ register** *n* caisse *f* enregistreuse; **~ reserves** *npl* trésorerie *f*; **~ squeeze** *n* restriction *f* de crédit; **~ with order, c.w.o.** *n* règlement *m* à la commande.

casing /ˈkeɪsɪŋ/ *n* **1** (outer shell) (of bomb, cylinder, turbine, machinery) revêtement *m*; (of gearbox) carter *m*; (of tyre) enveloppe *f* extérieure; (of cable, telephone) boîtier *m*; **2** (of shaft, chimney) cuvelage *m*; **3** (of window, door) chambranle *m*; **4** (sausage skin) boyau *m*; **5** Print emboîtage *m*.

casino /kəˈsiːnəʊ/ *n* casino *m*.

cask /kɑːsk, US kæsk/ *n* fût *m*, tonneau *m*; **wine from the ~** vin au tonneau.

casket /ˈkɑːskɪt, US ˈkæskɪt/ *n* **1** (jewel box) coffret *m*; **2** (coffin) cercueil *m*.

Caspian Sea /ˌkæspɪən ˈsiː/ ▶ **1511** *pr n* **the ~** la (mer) Caspienne.

Cassandra /kəˈsændrə/ *pr n* Mythol, fig Cassandre.

cassava /kəˈsɑːvə/ *n* Bot manioc *m*; Culin farine *f* de manioc.

casserole /ˈkæsərəʊl/ I *n* Culin **1** (container) daubière *f*, cocotte *f*; **2** GB (food) ragoût *m* cuit au four.
II *vtr* cuire [qch] à four doux.

cassette /kəˈset/ *n* Audio, Video cassette *f*; **to record on ~** enregistrer sur cassette; **to sell/be available on ~** vendre/être disponible en cassette.

cassette: **~ deck** *n* platine *f* à cassettes; **~ player** *n* lecteur *m* de cassettes; **~ recorder** *n* magnétophone *m* à cassettes; **~ recording** *n* enregistrement *m* sur cassette; **~ tape** *n* cassette *f* audio.

cassock /ˈkæsək/ *n* soutane *f*.

cassowary /ˈkæsəweərɪ/ *n* casoar *m*.

cast /kɑːst, US kæst/ I *n* **1** Cin, Theat, TV (list of actors) distribution *f*; (actors) acteurs *mpl*; **the members of the ~** les acteurs; **~ and credits** générique *m*; **~ of characters** (in play, novel) liste *f* des personnages; **Bogart and Bacall head a strong ~** Bogart et Bacall apparaissent en tête d'une brillante distribution; **the film has an all-star ~** il n'y a que des vedettes or des acteurs très connus dans ce film; **she was in the ~ of 'The Birds'** elle a joué dans 'Les Oiseaux'; **2** Art, Tech (mould) moule *m*; (moulded object) moulage *m*; **3** (arrangement) **~ of features** traits *mpl* du visage, physionomie *f*; **~ of mind** tournure *f* d'esprit; **4** (act of throwing) (of dice, net) coup *m*; (of stone) jet *m*; Fishg lancer *m*; **5** Med (squint) strabisme *m*; **to have a ~ in one eye** avoir un œil qui louche, loucher d'un œil; **6** Med (also **plaster ~**) plâtre *m*; **to have one's arm in a ~** avoir un bras dans le plâtre; **7** Zool (skin of snake, insect) dépouille *f*; (owl pellet) boulette *f* (de déchets régurgités); (of worm) déjections *fpl*; **8** (colour, tinge) nuance *f*; **with a greenish ~** tirant sur le vert.
II *vtr* (*prét, pp* **cast**) **1** (throw) jeter, lancer [*stone, net, fishing line*]; jeter [*dice*]; projeter [*light, shadow*]; **to be cast into prison** être jeté en prison; **to ~ doubt on** émettre des doutes sur; **to ~ light on** éclairer; **to ~ (a) new light on** éclairer [qch] d'un jour nouveau; **to ~ a spell on** jeter un sort à; **2** (direct) jeter [*glance, look*] (**at** sur); **her eyes were cast downwards** elle avait les yeux baissés; **to ~ one's eyes around the room/over a letter** parcourir la pièce/une lettre des yeux; **to ~ a glance over one's shoulder** jeter un coup d'œil par-dessus son épaule; **to ~ one's mind back over sth** se remémorer qch; **if you ~ your mind back to last week** si tu te rappelles ce qui s'est passé la semaine dernière; **3** Cin, Theat, TV distribuer les rôles de [*play, film*]; **she was cast in the role of** ou **as Blanche** on lui a donné le rôle de Blanche, elle a joué Blanche; **4** (shed) se dépouiller de [*leaves, feathers*]; **the snake ~s its skin** le serpent mue; **the horse cast a shoe** le cheval a perdu un fer; **5** Art, Tech couler [*plaster*]; couler, fondre [*metal*]; **statue cast in bronze** statue coulée dans le bronze; **6** Pol **to ~ one's vote** voter; **7** Astrol **to ~ sb's horoscope** faire l'horoscope de qn.
III *vi* (*prét, pp* **cast**) Fishg lancer sa ligne.
■ **cast about** GB, **cast around**: **~ about for** chercher [*excuse, remark*].
■ **cast aside**: **~ aside [sth/sb], ~ [sth/sb] aside** rejeter [*object*]; se défaire de [*anxieties, doubts, inhibitions*]; répudier, rejeter [*spouse, lover*].
■ **cast away**: **~ away [sth], ~ [sth] away** mettre [qch] au rebut [*old clothes, objects*]; se débarrasser de [*cares, inhibitions*]; **to be cast away** (shipwrecked) être naufragé.
■ **cast down**: **~ down [sth], ~ [sth] down 1** lit jeter [qch] par terre [*object*]; déposer [*weapons*]; baisser [*eyes, head*]; **2** fig faire tomber [*tyrant*]; **to be cast down** (depressed) littér être abattu.
■ **cast off**: ¶ **~ off 1** Naut larguer les amarres; **2** (in knitting) rabattre les mailles restantes; ¶ **~ off [sth], ~ [sth] off 1** (discard) ôter, enlever [*garment*]; se libérer de [*chains*]; abandonner, rejeter [*lover, friend*]; **2** Naut larguer les amarres de; **3** (in knitting) rabattre [*stitches*].
■ **cast on**: ¶ **~ on** (in knitting) monter les mailles; ¶ **~ on [sth]** monter [*stitch*].
■ **cast out**: **~ out [sth/sb], ~ [sth/sb] out** littér chasser.
■ **cast up**: **~ up [sth], ~ [sth] up 1** [*tide, sea*] rejeter [*body, flotsam*]; **2** (in air) lancer [qch] en l'air [*ball*]; **to ~ one's eyes up (to heaven)** lever les yeux au ciel; **to ~ sth up at sb** ressortir qch à qn [*accusation, misdeed*].

castanets /ˌkæstəˈnets/ ▶ **1481** *npl* castagnettes *fpl*.

castaway /ˈkɑstəweɪ, US ˈkæst-/ *n* naufragé/-e *m/f*.

caste /kɑːst/ *n* caste *f*; **the ~ system** le système des castes; **to lose ~** fig déroger.

castellated /ˈkæstəleɪtɪd/ *adj* Archit, gen crénelé.

caster /ˈkɑːstə(r), US ˈkæstər/ *n* **1** (shaker) saupoudreuse *f*; **2** (wheel) roulette *f*; **3** US (cruet) flacon *m* à condiments; **4** US (cruet stand) ménagère *f*, plateau *m* à condiments.

caster sugar GB *n* sucre *m* en poudre.

castigate /ˈkæstɪgeɪt/ *vtr* sout fustiger fml (**for sth** pour qch; **for doing** pour avoir fait).

castigation /ˌkæstɪˈgeɪʃn/ *n* sout critique *f* sévère (**of** de).

Castile /kæˈstiːl/ *pr n* Castille *f*.

Castilian /kəˈstɪlɪən/ I *n* Castillan/-e *m/f*.
II *adj* castillan.

casting /ˈkɑːstɪŋ, US ˈkæst-/ *n* **1** (throwing) lancement *m*, jet *m*; Fishg pêche *f* au lancer; **2** (in metallurgy) (act) coulée *f*, moulage *m*; (object) pièce *f*; Art moulage *m*; **3** Cin, Theat, TV distribution *f*.

casting: **~ agent** ▶ **1692** *n* responsable *mf* de la distribution; **~ couch** *n* Cin ≈ droit *m* de cuissage (*du directeur de distribution*); **~ director** ▶ **1692** *n* directeur/-trice *m/f* de la distribution.

casting vote *n* voix *f* prépondérante; **to have a** ou **the ~** avoir voix prépondérante.

cast iron I *n* fonte *f*.
II **cast-iron** *modif* **1** lit [*object*] de or en fonte; **2** fig [*alibi, excuse, guarantee*] en béton○.

castle /ˈkɑːsl, US ˈkæsl/ I *n* **1** gen, Archit château *m*; **2** (in chess) tour *f*.
II *modif* [*grounds, keep*] du château.
III *vi* (in chess) roquer.
IDIOMS **an Englishman's** GB ou **a man's** US **home is his ~** charbonnier est maître chez lui; **~s in the air** ou **in Spain** US des châteaux en Espagne.

castling /ˈkɑːslɪŋ, US ˈkæslɪŋ/ *n* (in chess) roque *m*.

cast-off /ˈkɑːstɒf, US ˈkæst-/ **I cast-offs** *npl* (clothes) vêtements *mpl* dont on n'a plus besoin, vieux vêtements; **society's ~s** fig les laissés *mpl* pour compte de la société.
II *adj* [*object, garment*] mis au rebut.

castor /ˈkɑːstə(r), US ˈkæs-/ *n* **1** Pharm castoréum *m*; **2** (wheel) (also **caster**) roulette *f*.

castor: **~ oil** *n* huile *f* de ricin; **~ oil plant** *n* ricin *m*.

castrate /kæˈstreɪt, US ˈkæstreɪt/ *vtr* castrer [*man, animal*]; fig expurger [*book, article*].

castration /kæˈstreɪʃn/ *n* castration *f*.

castrato /kæˈstrɑːtəʊ/ *n* castrat *m*.

casual /ˈkæʒʊəl/ **I** *n* (temporary worker) travailleur/-euse *m/f* temporaire; (occasional worker) travailleur/-euse *m/f* occasionnel/-elle.
II casuals *npl* (clothes) vêtements *mpl* sport; (shoes) chaussures *fpl* sport.
III *adj* **1** (informal) [*clothes, dress, person, manner, greeting*] décontracté; **to have a ~ chat** bavarder, causer○; **to come up in ~ conversation** surgir par hasard dans la conversation; **2** (occasional) [*acquaintance, relationship*] de passage; **~ sex** relations *fpl* sexuelles non suivies; **~ drug users** drogués *mpl* occasionnels; **3** (nonchalant) [*attitude, gesture, mention, approach, tone*] désinvolte; **to make a question sound ~** poser une question d'un ton détaché; **4** péj [*racism, cruelty, violence*] ordinaire; [*remark, assumption, insult*] désinvolte; **her ~ treatment of me** sa désinvolture à mon égard; **5** [*inspection, glance, onlooker*] superficiel/-ielle; **to the ~ eye it seems that** l'observateur superficiel dirait que; **6** (chance) [*encounter, error*] fortuit; **7** [*worker, labour*] (temporary) temporaire; (occasional) occasionnel/-elle; **8** Biol adventice.

casual contract **I** *n* contrat *m* temporaire.
II *modif* (temporary) temporaire; (occasional) occasionnel/-elle.

casualize /ˈkæʒʊəlaɪz/ *vtr* **to ~ labour** précariser l'emploi.

casually /ˈkæʒʊəlɪ/ *adv* **1** [*inquire, remark*] d'un air détaché; [*stroll, greet*] nonchalamment; [*glance*] superficiellement; **2** [*dressed*] simplement; **3** [*hurt, condemn*] sans y penser; **4** [*employed*] temporairement.

casualness /ˈkæʒʊəlnɪs/ *n* **1** (of manner, tone) désinvolture *f*; **2** (of clothes) décontraction *f*.

casualty /ˈkæʒʊəltɪ/ **I** *n* **1** gen (person) victime *f*; **2** (part of hospital) urgences *fpl*; **in ~** aux urgences; **3** fig (person, plan) victime *f*; **to be a ~ of sth** être victime de qch.
II casualties *npl* (soldiers) pertes *fpl*; (civilians) victimes *fpl*; **there were heavy/light casualties** Mil il y a eu de lourdes pertes/des pertes légères.
III *modif* [*department, nurse* GB] des urgences; [*ward* GB] d'urgence; Mil [*list, figures*] des victimes; **~ insurance** US assurance *f* risques divers.

casuist /ˈkæʒjʊɪst/ *n* Relig, fig casuiste *mf*.

casuistry /ˈkæzjʊɪstrɪ/ *n* Relig, fig casuistique *f*.

cat /kæt/ **I** *n* **1** (domestic) chat *m*; (female) chatte *f*; **2** (feline) félin *m*; **big ~** grand félin; **3**○ péj (woman) chipie *f*; **4**○† (guy) type○ *m*; **5**○ *abrév* ▶ **catalytic converter**.
II *modif* [*basket*] pour chat; [*litter, food*] pour chats; **the ~ family** les félins *mpl*.
IDIOMS **it was enough to make a ~ laugh**○ c'était à se tordre○; **there are more ways than one to kill** ou **skin a ~** il y a plus d'une façon de s'y prendre; **to be like a ~ on a hot tin roof** ou **on hot bricks** être sur des charbons ardents; **to fight like ~ and dog** se battre comme des chiffonniers; **to grin like a Cheshire ~** avoir un sourire fendu jusqu'aux oreilles; **to let the ~ out of the bag** vendre la mèche; **the cat's out of the bag** ce n'est plus un secret pour personne; **to look like something the ~ brought** ou **dragged in** être en piteux état; **to rain ~s and dogs** pleuvoir des cordes; **there's hardly enough room to swing a ~** il y a à peine la place de se retourner; **to think one is the ~'s whiskers** GB ou **pajamas** US ou **meow** US se croire sorti de la cuisse de Jupiter; **to (wait and) see which way the ~ jumps** attendre de voir d'où vient le vent; **when the ~'s away, the mice will play** quand le chat n'est pas là, les souris dansent; **to play ~ and mouse with sb** jouer au chat et à la souris avec qn.
■ **cat around**○ US draguer○.

cat. *abrév* = **catalogue**.

CAT *n* **1** GB (*abrév* = **College of Advanced Technology**) cf IUT; **2** Comput (*abrév* = **computer-assisted teaching**) enseignement *m* assisté par ordinateur; **3** Comput (*abrév* = **computer-assisted testing**) essais *mpl* assistés par ordinateur; **4** Comput (*abrév* = **computer-assisted training**) formation *f* assistée par ordinateur; **5** Med (*abrév* = **computerized axial tomography**) scannographie *f*.

cataclysm /ˈkætəklɪzəm/ *n* Geol, fig cataclysme *m*.

cataclysmic /ˌkætəˈklɪzmɪk/ *adj* cataclysmique.

catacombs /ˈkætəkuːmz, US -kəʊmz/ *npl* catacombes *fpl*.

catafalque /ˈkætəfælk/ *n* catafalque *m*.

Catalan /ˈkætəlæn/ ▶ **1486**, **1402** *n, adj* catalan (*m*).

catalepsy /ˈkætəlepsɪ/ *n* catalepsie *f*.

cataleptic /ˌkætəˈleptɪk/ *adj* cataleptique.

catalogue, **catalog** US /ˈkætəlɒg, US -lɔːg/ **I** *n* **1** (of goods, books) catalogue *m*; **2** (series) **a ~ of disasters/complaints** une série de catastrophes/plaintes; **3** (also **catalog**) US Univ brochure *f* (universitaire).
II *modif* [*number, price*] de catalogue.
III *vtr* dresser un catalogue de.

Catalonia /ˌkætəˈləʊnɪə/ *pr n* Catalogne *f*.

catalysis /kəˈtæləsɪs/ *n* (*pl* **-lyses**) catalyse *f*.

catalyst /ˈkætəlɪst/ *n* **1** Chem, fig catalyseur *m*; **2** = **catalytic converter**.

catalytic /ˌkætəˈlɪtɪk/ *adj* catalytique.

catalytic: **~ converter** *n* pot *m* catalytique; **~ cracker** *n* craqueur *m* catalytique.

catamaran /ˌkætəməˈræn/ *n* **1** (boat) catamaran *m*; **2** (raft) radeau *m*.

catamite /ˈkætəmaɪt/ *n* littér giton *m*.

cataphora /kəˈtæfərə/ *n* anaphore *f*.

cataphoric /ˌkætəˈfɒrɪk/ *adj* anaphorique.

catapult /ˈkætəpʌlt/ **I** *n* **1** GB lance-pierres *m inv*; **2** Mil, Aviat (also **~ launcher**) catapulte *f*; **3** Mil, Hist catapulte *f*.
II *vtr* **1** [*force, explosion*] projeter; **2** fig **to be ~ed to** être catapulté vers [*success, power*].

cataract /ˈkætərækt/ *n* **1** Med cataracte *f*; **2** (waterfall) cataracte *f*.

catarrh /kəˈtɑː(r)/ *n* catarrhe *m*.

catarrhal /kəˈtɑːrəl/ *adj* catarrheux/-euse.

catastrophe /kəˈtæstrəfɪ/ *n* catastrophe *f*.

catastrophe theory *n* théorie *f* des catastrophes.

catastrophic /ˌkætəˈstrɒfɪk/ *adj* catastrophique.

catastrophically /ˌkætəˈstrɒfɪklɪ/ *adv* [*fail*] de façon catastrophique; **~ bad** catastrophique.

catatonia /ˌkætəˈtəʊnɪə/ *n* Med catatonie *f*.

catatonic /ˌkætəˈtɒnɪk/ *adj* Med catatonique.

catbird /ˈkætbɜːd/ *n* US **to be in the ~ seat**○ trôner.

cat burglar *n* GB monte-en-l'air *m inv*.

catcall /ˈkætkɔːl/ **I** *n* sifflet *m*.
II *vi* siffler.

catch /kætʃ/ **I** *n* **1** (fastening) (on purse, brooch) fermoir *m*, fermeture *f*; (on window, door) fermeture *f*; **2** (drawback) piège *m* fig; **what's the ~?** où est le piège?; **3** (break in voice) **with a ~ in his voice** d'une voix émue; **4** (act of catching) prise *f*; **to take a ~** GB, **to make a ~** US Sport prendre la balle; **to play ~** jouer à la balle; **5** Fishg (haul) pêche *f*; (one fish) prise *f*; **to have a good ~** avoir une belle pêche; **6** Mus Hist *chanson grivoise en canon*; **7** (marriage partner) **to be a good ~** être un beau parti.
II *vtr* (*prét, pp* **caught**) **1** (hold and retain) [*person*] attraper [*ball, fish, mouse*]; [*container*] recueillir [*water, dust*]; (by running) [*person*] attraper [*person*]; **I managed to ~ her in** (at home) j'ai réussi à la trouver; **2** (take by surprise) prendre, attraper [*person, thief*]; **to ~ sb doing** surprendre qn en train de faire; **to be** ou **get caught** se faire prendre; **to ~ sb in the act**, **to ~ sb at it**○ prendre qn sur le fait; **you wouldn't ~ me smoking/arriving late!** ce n'est pas moi qui fumerais/arriverais en retard!; **you won't ~ me at it again!** on ne m'y reprendra plus!; **we got caught in the rain/in the storm** nous avons été surpris par la pluie/par la tempête; **you've caught me at an awkward moment** vous tombez mal; ▶ **balance**, **foot**, **short**, **unawares**; **3** (be in time for) attraper, prendre [*bus, train, plane*]; **to ~ the last post** ou **mail** avoir la dernière levée; **4** (manage to see) regarder [*programme*]; aller voir [*show, play*]; **5** (grasp) prendre [*hand, arm*]; agripper [*branch, rope*]; captiver, éveiller [*interest, imagination*]; **to ~ hold of sth** attraper qch; **to ~ sb's attention** ou **eye** attirer l'attention de qn; **to ~ the Speaker's eye** GB Pol obtenir la parole; **to ~ the chairman's eye** Admin obtenir la parole; **to ~ some sleep**○ dormir un peu; **6** (hear) saisir○, comprendre [*word, name*]; **do you ~ my meaning?** tu comprends ce que je veux dire?; **7** (perceive) sentir [*smell*]; discerner [*sound*]; surprendre [*look*]; **to ~ sight of sb/sth** apercevoir qn/qch; **8** (get stuck) **to ~ one's fingers/foot in** se prendre les doigts/le pied dans [*drawer, door*]; **to ~ one's shirt/sleeve on** accrocher sa chemise/manche à [*nail*]; **to get one's head/hand caught** se coincer la tête/main (**in** dans; **between** entre); **to get one's shirt/sweater caught** accrocher sa chemise/son pull-over (**on** à); **to get caught in** [*person*] se prendre dans [*net, thorns, barbed wire*]; **9** Med attraper [*disease, virus, flu*]; ▶ **cold**, **chill**; **10** (hit) heurter [*object, person*]; **the ball/stone caught him on the head** la balle/pierre l'a heurté à la tête; **to ~ sth with** heurter qch avec [*elbow, broom handle*]; **to ~ sb (with) a blow** donner un coup à qn; **11** (have an effect on) [*sun, light*] faire briller [*object, raindrops*]; [*wind*] emporter [*paper, bag*]; **to ~ one's breath** retenir son souffle; **12** (be affected by) **to ~ the sun** prendre le soleil; **to ~ fire** ou **light** prendre feu, s'enflammer; **to ~ the light** refléter la lumière; **13** (capture) rendre [*atmosphere, mood, spirit*]; **to ~ sth on film** filmer qch; **14** Sport ▶ **catch out**; **15** (trick) ▶ **catch out**; **16** (manage to reach) ▶ **catch up**.
III *vi* (*prét, pp* **caught**) **1** (become stuck) **to ~ on sth** [*shirt, sleeve*] s'accrocher à qch; [*wheel*] frotter contre [*frame*]; **2** (start to burn) [*wood, coal, fire*] prendre.
IDIOMS **you'll ~ it**○! tu vas en prendre une○!
■ **catch on** **1** (become popular) [*fashion, song, TV programme, activity, idea*] devenir populaire (**with** auprès de); **2** (understand) comprendre, saisir; **to ~ on to sth** comprendre or saisir qch.
■ **catch out**: **~ [sb] out** **1** (take by surprise) prendre [qn] de court; (doing something wrong) prendre [qn] sur le fait; **2** (trick) attraper, jouer un tour à; **3** (in cricket, baseball) éliminer [*batsman*].
■ **catch up**: ¶ **~ up** (in race) regagner du terrain; (in work) rattraper son retard; **to ~ up with** rattraper [*person, vehicle*]; **to ~ up on** rattraper [*work, sleep*]; se remettre au courant de [*news, gossip*]; ¶ **~ [sb/sth] up** **1** (manage to reach) rattraper; **2** (pick up) attra-

per [*bag, child*] (**in** dans); ¶ **~ [sth] up in** (tangle) prendre [qch] dans [*barbed wire, thorns, chain*]; **to get one's feet caught up in sth** se prendre les pieds dans qch; **I got my skirt caught up in the thorns** j'ai pris ma jupe dans les ronces; **to get caught up in** se laisser entraîner par [*enthusiasm, excitement*]; se trouver pris dans [*traffic*]; se trouver pris au milieu de [*war, bombing*]; se trouver mêlé à [*scandal, fight, argument*].

catch-22 situation *n* situation *f* inextricable.

catch-all /ˈkætʃɔːl/ **I** *n* expression *f* passe-partout.
II *modif* [*term, word, expression*] passe-partout *inv*; [*clause*] couvrant tous les cas de figure; [*category, list*] exhaustif/-ive.

catch: **~-as-catch-can** ▶ 1282 *n* catch *m*; **~ crop** *n* Agric (planted consecutively) culture *f* dérobée; (planted in same season) culture *f* intercalaire.

catcher /ˈkætʃə(r)/ *n* Sport receveur *m*.

catchfly /ˈkætʃflaɪ/ *n* Bot silène *m*.

catching /ˈkætʃɪŋ/ *adj* Med, fig contagieux/-ieuse.

catchment /ˈkætʃmənt/ *n* **1** (collecting of water) captage *m*; **2** (body of water collected) réserve *f* d'eau.

catchment area *n* **1** Geog (of river, basin) bassin *m* hydrographique; **2** Admin, Sch secteur *m*.

catchpenny /ˈkætʃpenɪ/ *adj* péj racoleur/-euse pej.

catch: **~phrase** *n* formule *f* favorite, rengaine *f*; **~up** *n* = **ketchup**.

catch-up /ˈkætʃʌp/ *n*: IDIOMS **to be playing ~** avoir du retard à rattraper.

catch-up: **~ demand** *n* rattrapage *m* de la demande; **~ effect** *n* effet *m* de rattrapage.

catchword /ˈkætʃwɜːd/ *n* **1** (popular word) mot *m* d'ordre; **2** Print mot-vedette *m*; **3** Theat mot-clé *m*.

catchy /ˈkætʃɪ/ *adj* [*jingle, tune*] entraînant; [*slogan*] accrocheur/-euse.

catechism /ˈkætəkɪzəm/ *n* catéchisme *m*.

catechist /ˈkætəkɪst/ *n* catéchiste *mf*.

catechize /ˈkætəkaɪz/ *vtr* catéchiser.

categorical /ˌkætəˈɡɒrɪkl, US -ˈɡɔːr-/, **categoric** /ˌkætəˈɡɒrɪk, US -ˈɡɔːr-/ *adj* catégorique.

categorical imperative *n* Philos impératif *m* catégorique.

categorically /ˌkætəˈɡɒrɪklɪ, US -ˈɡɔːr-/ *adv* catégoriquement.

categorize /ˈkætəɡəraɪz/ *vtr* classer [*book, person*] (**by, according to** d'après); **he has been ~d as a surrealist** on l'a rangé parmi les surréalistes.

category /ˈkætəɡərɪ, US -ɡɔːrɪ/ *n* catégorie *f*.

cater /ˈkeɪtə(r)/ **I** *vtr* US fournir la nourriture pour.
II *vi* **1** (cook) préparer des repas (**for** pour); **2 to ~ for** GB ou **to** US (accommodate) accueillir [*children, guests*]; (aim at) [*newspaper, programme*] s'adresser à; **to ~ for the needs/tastes of** pourvoir aux besoins/goûts de; **we ~ for private parties** nous assurons l'organisation de soirées privées; **3** (fulfil) **to ~ to** satisfaire [*whim, taste*].

cater-corner(ed) /ˌkeɪtəˈkɔːnəd/ *adj, adv* US = **catty-corner(ed)**.

caterer /ˈkeɪtərə(r)/ ▶ 1692 *n* traiteur *m*.

catering /ˈkeɪtərɪŋ/ **I** *n* (provision) approvisionnement *m*; (trade, career) restauration *f*.
II *modif* [*industry, company, staff*] de restauration; **~ course** études *fpl* spécialisées dans la restauration; **~ worker** employé/-e *m/f* travaillant dans la restauration.

caterpillar /ˈkætəpɪlə(r)/ *n* **1** Zool chenille *f*; **2** Tech (also **~ track**) chenille *f*.

Caterpillar® /ˈkætəpɪlə(r)/ *n* engin *m* à chenilles.

caterwaul /ˈkætəwɔːl/ **I** *n* miaulement *m*.
II *vi* miauler.

caterwauling /ˈkætəwɔːlɪŋ/ *n* ¢ miaulements *mpl*.

cat: **~ fight**○ *n* US crêpage *m* de chignon○; **~fish** *n* poisson-chat *m*; **~flap** *n* chattière *f*; **~ food** *n* aliments *mpl* pour chats; **~gut** *n* boyau *m* (de chat), catgut *m*.

Cathar /ˈkæθə(r)/ **I** *n* Cathare *mf*.
II *adj* cathare.

catharsis /kəˈθɑːsɪs/ *n* catharsis *f*.

cathartic /kəˈθɑːtɪk/ **I** *n* Med cathartique *m*.
II *adj* (all contexts) cathartique.

Cathay /kæˈθeɪ/ *pr n* littér Cathay liter *m*, Chine *f*.

cathedral /kəˈθiːdrəl/ *n* cathédrale *f*.

cathedral: **~ choir** *n* chœur *m* de cathédrale; **~ city** *n* siège *m* d'un évêché; **~ school** *n* école *f* (*de la maîtrise d'une cathédrale*).

Catherine wheel /ˈkæθrɪn wiːl, US -hwiːl/ *n* soleil *m* (*feu d'artifice*).

catheter /ˈkæθɪtə(r)/ *n* cathéter *m*.

catheterize /ˈkæθɪtəraɪz/ *vtr* introduire une sonde dans [*bladder*].

cathode /ˈkæθəʊd/ *n* sonde *f*, cathode *f*.

cathode: **~ ray** *n* rayon *m* cathodique; **~-ray tube** *n* tube *m* cathodique.

catholic /ˈkæθəlɪk/ *adj* éclectique.

Catholic /ˈkæθəlɪk/ *n, adj* catholique (*mf*).

Catholicism /kəˈθɒlɪsɪzəm/ *n* catholicisme *m*.

cathouse○ /ˈkæthaʊs/ *n* US maison *f* de passe○.

cation /ˈkætaɪən/ *n* cation *m*.

catkin /ˈkætkɪn/ *n* chaton *m*.

catlick /ˈkætlɪk/ *n* GB toilette *f* de chat.

catlike /ˈkætlaɪk/ **I** *adj* félin.
II *adv* [*walk, stalk*] comme un chat.

cat: **~ litter** *n* litière *f* pour chats; **~mint** *n* GB herbe-aux-chats *f*, chataire *f* spéc.

catnap /ˈkætnæp/ **I** *n* somme *m*.
II *vi* (*p prés etc* **-pp-**) faire un somme, sommeiller.

catnip /ˈkætnɪp/ *n* US = **catmint**.

Cato /ˈkeɪtəʊ/ *pr n* Caton.

cat-o'-nine-tails /kætəˈnaɪnˌteɪlz/ *n* (*pl* **~**) martinet *m*.

CAT scan /ˈkæt skæn/*n* Med scanner *m*; **to have a ~** passer un scanner.

cat: **~'s cradle** *n* jeu *m* de ficelle; **~'s-eye** *n* (gem) œil-de-chat *m*; **Catseye**® *n* GB Aut plot *m* rétroréfléchissant; **~'s paw** *n* dupe *f*; **~suit** *n* combinaison-pantalon *f*.

catsup /ˈkætsəp/ *n* US = **ketchup**.

cat's whisker *n* Radio chercheur *m* de détecteur à galène.

cattery /ˈkætərɪ/ *n* pension *f* pour chats.

cattiness /ˈkætɪnɪs/ *n* méchanceté *f*.

cattle /ˈkætl/ **I** *n* (+ *v pl*) bovins *mpl*.
II *modif* [*breeder, raising, rustler*] de bétail.

cattle: **~ call**○ *n* US Theat audition *f*; **~ grid** GB, **~ guard** US *n* grille *f* (*au sol qui empêche le passage du bétail*).

cattleman /ˈkætlmən/ ▶ 1692 **1** GB (herdsman) vacher *m*; **2** US (breeder) (grand) éleveur *m* de bétail.

cattle: **~ market** *n* lit marché *m* aux bestiaux; fig○ (for sexual encounters) lieu *m* de drague○; **~ shed** *n* étable *f*; **~ truck** *n* Aut fourgon *m* à bestiaux.

catty /ˈkætɪ/ *adj* méchant (**about** envers).

catty-corner(ed) /ˌkætɪˈkɔːnəd/ US **I** *adj* diagonal.
II *adv* en diagonale.

Catullus /kəˈtʌləs/ *pr n* Catulle.

catwalk /ˈkætwɔːk/ **I** *n* **1** (narrow walkway) passerelle *f*; **2** (at fashion show) podium *m*.
II *modif* [*model, show*] de mode.

Caucasian /kɔːˈkeɪʒn, -ˈkeɪzɪən/ **I** *n* **1** (white person) personne *f* de race blanche; **2** Geog (inhabitant) Caucasien/-ienne *m/f*.
II *adj* **1** [*race, man*] blanc/blanche; **2** Geog caucasien/-ienne.

Caucasus /ˈkɔːkəsəs/ *pr n* **the ~** le Caucase.

caucus /ˈkɔːkəs/ **I** *n* (*pl* **-es**) **1** (meeting) réunion *f* des instances dirigeantes; **2** (faction) groupe *m*.
II *vi* se réunir.

caudal /ˈkɔːdl/ *adj* Zool caudal.

caught /kɔːt/ *prét, pp* ▶ **catch**.

caul /kɔːl/ *n* **1** (of uterus) coiffe *f*; **2** (of stomach) grand épiploon *m*; **3** Culin crépine *f*.

cauldron /ˈkɔːldrən/ *n* chaudron *m*.

cauliflower /ˈkɒlɪflaʊə(r), US ˈkɔːlɪ-/ **I** *n* Bot, Culin chou-fleur *m*; **to have a ~ ear**○ fig avoir l'oreille en chou-fleur○.
II *modif* [*leaf, stalk*] de chou-fleur.

cauliflower cheese US *n* gratin *m* de chou-fleur.

caulk /kɔːk/ **I** *n* mastic *m*.
II *vtr* gen mastiquer; Naut calfater.

causal /ˈkɔːzl/ *adj* gen, Ling causal.

causality /kɔːˈzælətɪ/ *n* causalité *f*.

causation /kɔːˈzeɪʃn/ *n* causalité *f*.

causative /ˈkɔːzətɪv/ **I** *n* Ling causatif *m*, mot *m* causal.
II *adj* **1** gen causal; **2** Ling [*verb*] causatif/-ive, [*conjunction*] causatif/-ive, causal; [*phrase*] causal.

cause /kɔːz/ **I** *n* **1** (reason) cause *f*, raison *f* (**of** de); **there is/he has ~ for concern/optimism/alarm/complaint** il y a/il a des raisons de s'inquiéter/d'être optimiste/de s'alarmer/de se plaindre; **to give sb ~ to do** donner à qn des raisons de faire; **to have ~ to do** avoir des raisons de faire; **to give ~ for concern** susciter des inquiétudes; **the immediate/root ~** la cause directe/première; **with good ~** pour cause, à juste titre; **without good ~** sans motif valable; **2** (objective) cause *f*; **a lost ~** une cause perdue; **for a good ~** pour une bonne cause; **all in a good ~** pour la bonne cause; **in the ~ of equality/freedom** pour la cause de l'égalité/la liberté; **to make common ~ with sb** faire cause commune avec qn; **3** Jur (grounds) cause *f*; **a challenge for/without ~** une récusation pour/sans motif déterminé; **contributory ~** cause accessoire; **primary ~** cause première; **to show ~** exposer ses raisons; **4** Jur (court action) action *f*; **~ of action** motif *m* d'action en justice; **matrimonial ~s** affaires *fpl* matrimoniales.
II *vtr* causer, occasionner [*damage, flooding, grief, problem*]; provoquer [*chaos, delay, controversy, reaction*]; susciter [*excitement, surprise*]; entraîner [*suffering*]; amener [*dismay, confusion*]; **to ~ sb to cry/leave** faire pleurer/partir qn; **to ~ sb problems/anxiety** causer des problèmes/de l'inquiétude à qn; **to ~ trouble** créer des problèmes; **to ~ cancer/migraine** donner or provoquer un cancer/la migraine.

cause célèbre *n* cause *f* célèbre.

causeway /ˈkɔːzweɪ/ *n* chaussée *f* (*vers une île*).

caustic /ˈkɔːstɪk/ *adj* Chem, fig caustique.

caustic: **~ potash** *n* hydroxyde *m* de potassium; **~ soda** *n* soude *f* caustique.

cauterize /ˈkɔːtəraɪz/ *vtr* cautériser.

cautery /ˈkɔːtərɪ/ *n* **1** (instrument) cautère *m*; **2** (process) cautérisation *f*.

caution /ˈkɔːʃn/ **I** *n* **1** (care) prudence *f*; **to drive/proceed with ~** conduire/avancer avec prudence; **to err on the side of ~** pécher par excès de prudence; **great ~ should be exercised** la prudence est de mise; **2** (wariness) circonspection *f*; **the reports should be treated with some ~** les reportages devraient être traités avec beaucoup de circonspection; **3** (warning) avertissement *m*; **a word of ~** un petit conseil; **'Caution! Drive slowly!'** 'Attention! Conduire lentement!'; **4** GB Jur (given to suspect) **to be under ~** faire l'objet d'une mise en garde; **5** Jur (admonition) avertissement *m*; **to issue** ou **administer a ~** donner un avertissement; **to get off** ou **be**

let off with a ~ s'en tirer avec un avertissement; 6○† (funny person) she's a ~! c'est un sacré numéro○!

II vtr 1 (warn) avertir (that que); 'he's dangerous,' she ~ed 'il est dangereux,' a-t-elle dit en guise de mise en garde; to ~ sb against doing avertir qn de ne pas faire; to ~ sb against ou about mettre qn en garde contre [*danger, risk, problem*]; 2 Jur [*policeman*] informer [qn] de ses droits [*suspect*]; 3 Jur (admonish) réprimander; to be ~ed for speeding être réprimandé pour excès de vitesse; 4 Sport (by referee) donner un avertissement à [*player*].

IDIOMS to throw ou cast ~ to the wind(s) oublier toute prudence.

cautionary /ˈkɔːʃənərɪ, US -nerɪ/ *adj* (*épith*) [*look, gesture*] d'avertissement; a ~ word ou comment un avertissement; she gave me some ~ advice elle m'a donné un conseil en guise d'avertissement; to end on a ~ note [*speech, analysis*] se terminer par un avertissement; a ~ tale un conte moral.

caution money *n* GB caution *f*.

cautious /ˈkɔːʃəs/ *adj* 1 (careful) [*person, attitude, approach, action*] prudent; he's ~ about spending money il est prudent en ce qui concerne les dépenses; to be ~ in one's dealings with sb être prudent quand on traite avec qn; 2 (wary) [*person, welcome, reception, response, agreement, statement*] réservé; [*optimism*] prudent; to be ~ about doing ne pas aimer faire; he's ~ about committing himself il n'aime pas se prononcer.

cautiously /ˈkɔːʃəslɪ/ *adv* 1 (carefully) [*act, approach, say, move*] prudemment; 2 (warily) [*react, welcome, respond, state*] avec circonspection; [*optimistic, confident*] raisonnablement.

cautiousness /ˈkɔːʃəsnɪs/ *n* 1 (care) prudence *f* habituelle; 2 (wariness) circonspection *f*.

cavalcade /ˌkævlˈkeɪd/ *n* (on horseback) cavalcade *f*; (motorized) cortège *m*.

cavalier /ˌkævəˈlɪə(r)/ I Cavalier *pr n* GB Hist cavalier *m* (*partisan de Charles Premier*).
II *adj* cavalier/-ière.

cavalierly /ˌkævəˈlɪəlɪ/ *adv* de façon cavalière.

cavalry /ˈkævlrɪ/ I *n* cavalerie *f*.
II *modif* [*charge*] de la cavalerie; [*officer, regiment*] de cavalerie.

cavalryman /ˈkævlrɪmən/ *n* cavalier *m*.

cavalry twill /ˌkævlrɪ ˈtwɪl/ I *n* (fabric) sergé *m*.
II cavalry twills *npl* pantalon *m* en sergé.

cave /keɪv/ I *n* grotte *f*; underwater ~s grottes sous-marines.
II *vi* faire de la spéléologie.
■ **cave in**: ¶ ~ in 1 lit [*tunnel, roof, building*] s'effondrer; [*beam*] s'infléchir; his ribs ~d in under the impact il a eu les côtes enfoncées par l'impact; 2 fig [*person*] céder; ¶ ~ [sth] in, ~ in [sth] défoncer [*roof*]; enfoncer [*skull, rib cage*].

caveat /ˈkævɪæt, US ˈkeɪvɪæt/ *n* 1 gen mise *f* en garde; 2 Jur notification *f* d'opposition.

cave: ~ dweller *n* troglodyte *m*; ~-in *n* effondrement *m*.

caveman /ˈkeɪvmæn/ *n* (*pl* -men) 1 Archeol homme *m* des cavernes; 2○ (boor) rustre *m*.

cave painting *n* peinture *f* rupestre.

caver /ˈkeɪvə(r)/ *n* spéléologue *mf*.

cavern /ˈkævən/ *n* caverne *f*.

cavernous /ˈkævənəs/ *adj* 1 fig [*groan, voice, room*] caverneux/-euse; [*mouth, yawn*] profond; [*eyes*] cave; 2 [*cliffs*] riche en cavernes *fpl*.

caviar(e) /ˈkævɪɑː(r), ˌkævɪˈɑː(r)/ *n* caviar *m*.
IDIOMS to be ~ to the general être réservé à l'élite.

cavil /ˈkævl/ I *n* point *m* de détail.
II *vi* (*p prés etc* -ll-, -l- US) ergoter (about, at sur).

caving /ˈkeɪvɪŋ/ *n* spéléologie *f*; to go ~ faire de la spéléologie.

cavity /ˈkævətɪ/ *n* gen, Dent, Med cavité *f*; the chest/nasal ~ la cavité pulmonaire/nasale.

cavity: ~ block *n* GB Constr moellon *m* creux; ~ brick *n* GB brique *f* creuse; ~ wall *n* mur *m* creux; ~ wall insulation *n* isolation *f* des murs creux.

cavort /kəˈvɔːt/ *vi* (also ~ about, ~ around) hum faire des cabrioles *fpl*.

cavy /ˈkeɪvɪ/ *n* Zool cobaye *m*.

caw /kɔː/ I *n* 1 (noise) croassement *m*; 2 (cry) croa!
II *vi* croasser.

cawing /ˈkɔːɪŋ/ *n* (of crow, rook) croassement *m*.

cay /keɪ/ *n* = key I 9.

cayenne (pepper) /keɪˈen/ *n* poivre *m* de Cayenne.

Cayenne /keɪˈen/ ▶1818 *pr n* Cayenne.

cayman /ˈkeɪmən/ *n* Zool caïman *m*.

Cayman Islands /ˈkeɪmən aɪləndz/ ▶1381 *pr npl* the ~ les îles *fpl* Caïmans.

CB (*abrév* = Citizens' Band) I *n* bande *f* banalisée, bande *f* publique, bande *f* CB.
II *modif* [*equipment, radio, wavelength*] CB; ~ user cibiste *mf*.

CBE *n* GB (*abrév* = Commander of the Order of the British Empire) commandeur de l'ordre de l'empire britannique.

CBer○ /ˌsiːˈbɪə(r)/ *n* US cibiste *mf*.

CBI *n* GB (*abrév* = Confederation of British Industry) patronat *m* britannique; cf CNPF.

CBS *n* US (*abrév* = Columbia Broadcasting System) *réseau de télévision américain*.

cc ▶1869 *n* (*abrév* = cubic centimeter) cm^3; a 500 ~ engine un moteur de 500 cm^3.

CC *n* GB *abrév* ▶ County Council.

CD *n* 1 (*abrév* = compact disc) (disque *m*) compact *m*; on ~ sur (disque) compact; 2 (*abrév* = corps diplomatique) CD; 3 Mil *abrév* ▶ Civil Defence; 4 US *abrév* ▶ Congressional District; 5 US Fin *abrév* ▶ Certificate of Deposit.

CDI *n* (*abrév* = compact disc interactive) CD-I *m*, disque *m* compact interactif.

CD: ~ plate *n* ≈ immatriculation *f* diplomatique; ~ player, ~ system *n* platine *f* laser.

Cdr *n* Mil (*abrév écrite* = Commander) cf capitaine *m* de frégate.

CD-ROM /ˌsiːdiːˈrɒm/ *n* Comput disque *m* optique compact, CD-ROM *m*; on ~ sur CD-ROM.

CDT *n* US *abrév* ▶ Central Daylight Time.

cease /siːs/ I *n* without ~ sans cesse.
II *vtr* cesser; to ~ doing cesser de faire; to ~ to do cesser de faire; you never ~ to amaze me! tu m'étonneras toujours!; to ~ fire cesser le feu.
III *vi* cesser.
IDIOMS wonders ou miracles will never ~ comme quoi, il ne faut jamais désespérer.

cease-fire /ˈsiːsfaɪə(r)/ I *n* cessez-le-feu *m inv*.
II *modif* [*agreement, negotiations*] de cessez-le-feu; [*call*] au cessez-le-feu.

ceaseless /ˈsiːslɪs/ *adj* incessant.

ceaselessly /ˈsiːslɪslɪ/ *adv* [*labour, talk*] sans cesse; [*active, vigilant*] continuellement.

cecum /ˈsiːkəm/ *n* (*pl* -ca) cæcum *m*.

cedar /ˈsiːdə(r)/ I *n* 1 (also ~ tree) cèdre *m*; 2 (also ~wood) (bois *m* de) cèdre *m*.
II *modif* [*forest*] de cèdres *mpl*; [*box, chest*] en (bois *m* de) cèdre.

cede /siːd/ I *vtr* 1 gen, Jur céder [*control, land, rights*] (to à); 2 Sport concéder [*goal, match, point*] (to à).
II *vi* céder (to à).

cedilla /sɪˈdɪlə/ *n* cédille *f*.

Ceefax® /ˈsiːfæks/ *n* TV GB *messagerie électronique de la BBC accessible sur le téléviseur*; cf Antiope.

ceilidh /ˈkeɪlɪ/ *n*: *en Écosse et Irlande, rassemblement autour de musique et danse traditionnelles*.

ceiling /ˈsiːlɪŋ/ *n* 1 Aviat, Constr, Meteorol plafond *m*; a high-~ed room une pièce avec un haut plafond; 2 (upper limit) plafond *m*; to set a ~ of 10% on wage rises fixer un plafond de 10% d'augmentation des salaires; to set a ~ on the number of shareholders imposer une limite sur le nombre d'actionnaires.
IDIOMS to hit the ~ US sortir de ses gonds.

ceiling: ~ joist *n* Constr solive *f* de plafond; ~ light *n* plafonnier *m*; ~ price *n* Comm, Econ prix *m* plafond.

ceiling rate *n* gen taux *m* plafond; (of currency) cours *m* maximum.

celandine /ˈseləndaɪn/ *n* greater ~ chélidoine *f*; lesser ~ ficaire *f*.

celeb○ /ˈseleb/ *n* US célébrité *f*, personne *f* célèbre.

celebrant /ˈselɪbrənt/ *n* Relig 1 (participant) participant/-e *m/f*; 2 (officiating priest) célébrant *m*, officiant *m*.

celebrate /ˈselɪbreɪt/ I *vtr* 1 fêter [*occasion*]; (more formally) célébrer; there's nothing/there's something to ~ il n'y a pas de quoi/il y a de quoi se réjouir; 2 Relig célébrer [*mass*]; to ~ Easter célébrer Pâques; 3 (pay tribute to) célébrer [*person, life, love*].
II *vi* faire la fête; let's ~! il faut fêter ça!

celebrated /ˈselɪbreɪtɪd/ *adj* célèbre (as comme; for pour).

celebration /ˌselɪˈbreɪʃn/ I *n* 1 ¢ (action of celebrating) célébration *f*; 2 (party) fête *f*; to have a ~ faire une fête; his wife's birthday ~s les festivités à l'occasion de l'anniversaire de sa femme; 3 (public festivities) ~s cérémonies *fpl*; 4 (tribute) hommage *m* (of à); 5 Relig (of mass, marriage) célébration *f*.
II *modif* [*dinner, fireworks*] (small-scale) de fête; (public) commémoratif/-ive.

celebratory /ˌselɪˈbreɪtərɪ, US -tɔːrɪ/ *adj* [*air, mood*] de fête; to have a ~ drink after the match boire un verre pour fêter le résultat du match.

celebrity /sɪˈlebrətɪ/ I *n* (all contexts) célébrité *f*.
II *modif* [*guest*] célèbre; [*panel*] de célébrités; [*golf, match*] joué par des célébrités.

celeriac /sɪˈlerɪæk/ *n* Bot, Culin céleri-rave *m*.

celerity /sɪˈlerətɪ/ *n* sout célérité *f*.

celery /ˈselərɪ/ I *n* Bot, Culin céleri *m*; a stick/head of ~ une côte/un pied de céleri; braised ~ céleris *mpl* braisés.
II *modif* [*salad, salt, seeds*] de céleri.

celestial /sɪˈlestɪəl/ *adj* céleste.

celiac *n, adj* US = coeliac.

celibacy /ˈselɪbəsɪ/ *n* (being unmarried) célibat *m*; (abstaining from sex) chasteté *f*; a vow of ~ un vœu de chasteté.

celibate /ˈselɪbət/ I *n* (unmarried) célibataire *mf*; (abstaining from sex) personne *f* chaste.
II *adj* (unmarried) célibataire; (abstaining from sex) chaste.

cell /sel/ *n* 1 (for prisoner, monk) cellule *f*; 2 Biol, Bot cellule *f*; 3 (in honeycomb) alvéole *m*; 4 Elec, Chem élément *m*; 5 Pol cellule *f*.

cellar /ˈselə(r)/ *n* (all contexts) cave *f*.

cell: ~ biologist ▶1692 *n* cytobiologiste *mf*; ~block *n* bloc *m* cellulaire; ~ culture *n* culture *f* de tissus; ~ division *n* division *f* cellulaire; ~ formation *n* formation *f* des cellules.

cellist /ˈtʃelɪst/ ▶1692, 1481 *n* violoncelliste *mf*.

cellmate /ˈselmeɪt/ *n* compagnon/compagne *m/f* de cellule.

cello /ˈtʃeləʊ/ ▶1481 *n* violoncelle *m*.

Cellophane® /ˈseləʊfeɪn/ *n* cellophane® *f*.

cellphone /ˈselfəʊn/ *n* radiotéléphone *m*.
cellular /ˈseljʊlə(r)/ *adj* Biol cellulaire.
cellular: **~ blanket** *n* couverture *f* en maille aérée; **~ network** *n* réseau *m* cellulaire; **~ phone**, **~ telephone** *n* radiotéléphone *m*.
cellulite /ˈseljʊlaɪt/ *n* cellulite *f*, peau *f* d'orange○.
cellulitis /ˌseljʊˈlaɪtɪs/ **▶ 1354** *n* Med cellulite *f*.
celluloid® /ˈseljʊlɔɪd/ **I** *n* celluloïd® *m*.
II *modif* **1** [*sheet, object*] en celluloïd; **2** Cin [*heroine, world*] du cinéma.
cellulose /ˈseljʊləʊs/ **I** *n* cellulose *f*.
II *modif* [*paint, varnish*] cellulosique; [*acetate, nitrate*] de cellulose.
cell wall *n* Biol paroi *f* cellulaire.
Celsius /ˈselsɪəs/ *adj* Celsius *inv*.
Celt /kelt, US selt/ *n* Celte *mf*.
Celtic /ˈkeltɪk, US ˈseltɪk/ *adj* celtique, celte; **~ cross** croix *f* celtique.
cembalo /ˈtʃembələʊ/ **▶ 1481** *n* clavecin *m*.
cement /sɪˈment/ **I** *n* **1** Constr gen ciment *m*; (for tiles) mastic *m*; **2** Dent amalgame *m*; **3** Anat = **cementum**; **4** fig ciment *m*.
II *modif* [*slab, floor, step*] en ciment.
III *vtr* **1** Constr cimenter; **2** Dent obturer; **3** fig cimenter [*alliance, relations, deal*].
cementation /ˌsiːmenˈteɪʃn/ *n* cémentation *f*.
cementite /sɪˈmentaɪt/ *n* cémentite *f*.
cement mixer *n* bétonnière *f*.
cementum /sɪˈmentəm/ *n* Anat cément *m*.
cemetery /ˈsemətrɪ, US -terɪ/ *n* cimetière *m*.
cenotaph /ˈsenətɑːf, US -tæf/ *n* cénotaphe *m*.
censer /ˈsensə(r)/ *n* encensoir *m*.
censor /ˈsensə(r)/ **I** *n* (all contexts) censeur *mf*; **to act as a ~** agir en censeur.
II *vtr* (all contexts) censurer.
censorious /senˈsɔːrɪəs/ *adj* sévère (**of, about** envers).
censorship /ˈsensəʃɪp/ *n* (all contexts) censure *f*; **to exercise/lift ~** pratiquer/lever la censure.
censurable /ˈsenʃərəbl/ *adj* censurable.
censure /ˈsenʃə(r)/ **I** *n* sout ou Pol censure *f*; **vote of ~** vote *m* de censure.
II *vtr* critiquer.
census /ˈsensəs/ *n* recensement *m*; **traffic ~** étude *f* chiffrée de la circulation.
cent /sent/ **▶ 1143** *n* cent *m*; **I haven't got a ~** je n'ai pas un sou.
centaur /ˈsentɔː(r)/ *n* centaure *m*.
centenarian /ˌsentɪˈneərɪən/ *n, adj* centenaire (*mf*).
centenary /senˈtiːnərɪ/ **I** *n* centenaire *m*.
II *modif* [*year, celebration*] du centenaire.
centennial /senˈtenɪəl/ **I** *n* US centenaire *m*.
II *adj* (every 100 years) séculaire; (lasting 100 years) centenaire.
center *n* US = **centre**.
centesimal /senˈtesɪml/ *adj* centésimal.
centigrade /ˈsentɪgreɪd/ *adj* [*thermometer*] Celcius; **in degrees ~** en degrés Celsius.
centigram(me) /ˈsentɪgræm/ **▶ 1883** *n* centigramme *m*.
centilitre GB, **centiliter** US /ˈsentɪliːtə(r)/ **▶ 1869** *n* centilitre *m*.
centimetre GB, **centimeter** US /ˈsentɪmiːtə(r)/ **▶ 1412** *n* centimètre *m*.
centipede /ˈsentɪpiːd/ *n* mille-pattes *m inv*, scolopendre *f* spec.
CENTO /ˈsentəʊ/ *n* (*abrév* = **Central Treaty Organization**) CENTO *f*.
central /ˈsentrəl/ **I Central** *pr n* (also **Central Region**) (in Scotland) la région Central.
II *adj* **1** (in the middle) [*area, courtyard, district*] central; **in ~ London** dans le centre de Londres; **2** (in the town centre) [*house, apartment etc*] situé en centre-ville; **we need a ~ location for the office** il nous faut un bureau situé au centre-ville; **3** (key) [*argument, feature, message, role*] principal; **to be ~ to sth** être essentiel à qch; **4** Admin, Pol [*control, management, government, funding, planning*] central.
central: **Central African Republic ▶ 1131** *pr n* République *f* centrafricaine; **Central America** *pr n* Amérique *f* centrale; **Central American** *adj* d'Amérique centrale; **Central Asia** *pr n* Asie *f* centrale; **~ bank** *n* Fin banque *f* centrale; **~ city** *n* US quartiers *mpl* du centre; **Central Committee** *n* Pol comité *m* central; **Central Europe** *n* Europe *f* centrale; **Central European** *adj* d'Europe centrale; **Central European Time**, **CET** *n*: *heure des pays d'Europe centrale*; **~ heating** *n* chauffage *m* central.
centralism /ˈsentrəlɪzəm/ *n* centralisme *m*.
centralist /ˈsentrəlɪst/ **I** *n* centraliste *mf*.
II *adj* centralisateur/-trice.
centralization /ˌsentrəlaɪˈzeɪʃn, US -lɪˈz-/ *n* centralisation *f*.
centralize /ˈsentrəlaɪz/ *vtr* centraliser.
central locking *n* Aut verrouillage *m* central or centralisé.
centrally /ˈsentrəlɪ/ *adv* [*live, work*] en centre-ville; [*situated*] en centre-ville; [*funded, managed*] de façon centralisée; **~ heated** [*flat*] avec chauffage central; **a ~ planned economy** une économie à planification centralisée.
central: **~ nervous system** *n* système *m* nerveux central; **~ office** *n* Comm (of company) siège *m* (social); **~ processing unit**, **CPU**, **~ processor** *n* Comput unité *f* centrale; **~ reservation** *n* GB Transp terre-plein *m* central; **Central Standard Time**, **CST** *n* US heure *f* légale des États du Centre des États-Unis; **~ vowel** *n* Ling voyelle *f* centrale.
centre GB, **center** US /ˈsentə(r)/ **I** *n* **1** (middle) centre *m* (**of** de); **in the ~** au centre; **I live near the ~ of London** j'habite près du centre de Londres; **town ~, city ~** centre-ville *m*; **sweets with soft ~s** bonbons *mpl* fourrés; **2** (focus) centre *m*; **to be at the ~ of a campaign/row** être au centre d'une campagne/dispute; **to be the ~ of attention** être le centre de l'attention; **3** (seat) siège *m*; **the ~ of power/government** le siège du pouvoir/gouvernement; **4** (designated area) centre *m*; **business ~** quartier *m* des affaires; **shopping/sports/leisure ~** centre *m* commercial/sportif/de loisirs; **5** Pol centre *m*; **to be left/right of ~** [*person, politics*] être à gauche/à droite du centre; **a ~-left party** un parti du centre gauche; **6** Sport (player) centre *m*; **▶ left**.
II *modif* [*aisle, lane, line, section*] central; [*parting*] au milieu.
III *vtr, vi* Comput, Sport, Tech centrer.
IV -centred (*dans composés*) centré sur; **child-~d education** enseignement *m* centré sur l'enfant.
■ **centre around**: ¶ **~ around [sth]** [*activities, person*] se concentrer sur; [*people, industry*] se situer autour de [*town*]; [*life, plans, thoughts*] être centré sur [*holidays, person, work*]; [*demands*] viser [*conditions, pay*]; ¶ **~ [sth] around [person]** concentrer [qch] sur [*feelings, thoughts*].
■ **centre on, centre upon**: **~ on [sth]** [*activities, feelings, thoughts, work*] se concentrer sur [*person, problem, subject*].
Centre ▶ 1273 *pr n* Centre *m*; **in the ~** dans le Centre.
centre: **~ bit** *n* mèche *f* à bois; **~board** *n* dérive *f*; **Centre Court** *n* (in tennis) court *m* central.
centre-fold /ˈsentəfəʊld/ *n* **1** Print feuillet *m* central; **2** (pin-up) (picture) photo *f* de pin-up (sur double page); **3** (model) pin-up *f*.
centre-forward /ˌsentəˈfɔːwəd/ *n* Sport avant-centre *m*.
centre ground *n* Pol centre *m*; **to occupy the ~ of French politics** être au centre dans la politique française.
centre-half /ˌsentəˈhɑːf, US -ˈhæf/ *n* Sport demi-centre *m*.
centre-hung window *n* (vertical) fenêtre *f* pivotante; (horizontal) fenêtre *f* basculante.
centre of gravity GB, **center of gravity** US, **cg** *n* centre *m* de gravité.
centre-piece /ˈsentəpiːs/ *n* (of table) décoration *f* centrale; (of exhibition) clou *m*.
centre spread *n* Journ double page *f* du milieu.
centre-stage /ˌsentəˈsteɪdʒ/ **I** *n* **1** Theat centre *m* de la scène; **2** fig (prime position) **to take/occupy ~** devenir/être le point de mire.
II *adv* **to stand ~** se tenir au centre de la scène.
centre three-quarter *n* Sport trois-quarts *m inv* centre.
centrifugal /ˌsentrɪˈfjuːgl, senˈtrɪfjʊgl/ *adj* centrifuge.
centrifuge /ˈsentrɪfjuːdʒ/ *n* centrifugeuse *f*.
centring /ˈsentrɪŋ/ *n* **1** Archit cintre *m*; **2** Tech centrage *m*.
centripetal /ˌsentrɪˈpiːtl, senˈtrɪpɪtl/ *adj* centripète.
centrism /ˈsentrɪzəm/ *n* centrisme *m*.
centrist /ˈsentrɪst/ *n, adj* centriste (*mf*).
centurion /senˈtjʊərɪən, US -tʊər-/ *n* centurion *m*.
century /ˈsentʃərɪ/ **▶ 1807** *n* **1** gen siècle *m*; **in the 20th ~** au XXe siècle; **at the turn of the ~** au début du siècle; **through the centuries** à travers les siècles; **half a ~** un demi-siècle; **centuries-old** séculaire; **2** (in cricket) score *m* de cent (*au cricket*).
CEO *n*: *abrév* **▶ Chief Executive Officer**.
cephalic /sɪˈfælɪk/ *adj* céphalique.
ceramic /sɪˈræmɪk/ **I** *n* (all contexts) céramique *f*.
II *adj* [*tile, pot*] en céramique; [*hob*] en vitrocéramique; [*design, art*] de la céramique.
ceramicist /sɪˈræmɪsɪst/ **▶ 1692** *n* céramiste *mf*.
ceramics /sɪˈræmɪks/ *n* **1** (+ *v sg*) (study) la céramique *f*; **2** (+ *v pl*) (artefacts) céramiques *fpl*.
ceramist /ˈserəmɪst/ *n* = **ceramicist**.
Cerberus /ˈsɜːbərəs/ *pr n* Cerbère.
IDIOMS **it's a sop to ~** cela les fera patienter.
cereal /ˈsɪərɪəl/ **I** *n* céréale *f*; (for breakfast) céréales *fpl*; **breakfast ~** céréales pour le petit déjeuner.
II *adj* [*harvest, imports*] de céréales; [*crop, production*] céréalier/-ière.
cerebellum /ˌserɪˈbeləm/ *n* cervelet *m*.
cerebral /ˈserɪbrəl, US səˈriːbrəl/ *adj* Med cérébral; [*person, writing, music*] intellectuel/-elle.
cerebral palsy /ˌserɪbrəl ˈpɔːlzɪ, US səˈriːbrəl/ **▶ 1354** *n* paralysie *f* motrice centrale.
cerebration /ˌserɪˈbreɪʃn/ *n* sout cogitation *f*.
cerebrum /ˈserɪbrəm/ *n* (*pl* **-brums** ou **-bra**) Med cerveau *m*.
ceremonial /ˌserɪˈməʊnɪəl/ **I** *n* gen cérémonial *m*; (religious) rites *mpl*.
II *adj* **1** [*dress*] de cérémonie; **2** (ritual) cérémoniel/-ielle; (solemn) solennel/-elle; (official) officiel/-ielle.
ceremonially /ˌserɪˈməʊnɪəlɪ/ *adv* selon le cérémonial d'usage.
ceremonious /ˌserɪˈməʊnɪəs/ *adj* [*event*] solennel/-elle; [*behaviour*] cérémonieux/-ieuse.
ceremoniously /ˌserɪˈməʊnɪəslɪ/ *adv* avec cérémonie.
ceremony /ˈserɪmənɪ, US -məʊnɪ/ *n* **1** (formal event) cérémonie *f*; **marriage ~** cérémonie *f* du mariage; **2** ¢ (protocol) cérémonies *fpl*; **to stand on ~** faire des cérémonies.
cerise /səˈriːz, -riːs/ **I** *n* rouge *m inv* cerise.
II *adj* cerise *inv*.

cerium /ˈsɪərɪəm/ *n* cérium *m*.

CERN /sɜːn/ *n* (*abrév* = **Conseil Européen pour la Recherche Nucléaire**) CERN *m*.

cert○ /sɜːt/ *n* GB **it's a (dead) ~○!** ça ne fait pas un pli○!; **he's a (dead) ~○ for the next race!** il va gagner la prochaine course, ça ne fait pas un pli!

certain /ˈsɜːtn/ **I** *pron* **~ of our members/friends** certains de nos adhérents/amis.
II *adj* **1** (sure, definite) certain, sûr (**about, of** de); **I'm ~ of it** ou **that** j'en suis certain or sûr; **of that you can be ~** tu peux en être sûr; **absolutely ~** sûr et certain; **I'm ~ that I checked** je suis sûr d'avoir vérifié; **I'm ~ that he refused** je suis sûr qu'il a refusé; **I feel ~ that he'll come** je suis certain qu'il viendra; **she's not ~ that you'll be able to do it** elle n'est pas sûre que tu sois capable de le faire; **to make ~** s'en assurer, vérifier; **to make ~ of** s'assurer de [*cooperation, trust, support*]; vérifier [*facts, time, details*]; **to make ~ to do** faire bien attention de faire; **to make ~ that** (ascertain) vérifier que, s'assurer que; (ensure) faire en sorte que (+ *subj*); **as soon as I leave the phone is ~ to ring** dès que je m'en vais, je peux être sûr que le téléphone va sonner; **he's ~ to be there** il y sera certainement or sûrement; **the strike seems ~ to continue** il est presque certain que la grève continuera; **the committee is ~ to approve the measure** il est certain que le comité approuvera la mesure; **I know for ~ that** je sais de façon sûre que; **be ~ to tell him that** n'oublie pas de lui dire que; **nobody knows for ~** personne ne sait au juste; **it isn't known for ~ if he's dead** on ne sait pas au juste s'il est mort ou non; **I can't say for ~** je ne sais pas au juste; **it will be ready tomorrow, for ~** ce sera prêt demain, sans faute; **2** (assured, guaranteed) [*death, defeat, success*] certain (*after n*); [*guarantee*] sûr; **to be ~ of doing** être sûr or certain de faire; **it is ~ that** il est certain que; **this method is ~ to work** cette méthode est efficace à 100%; **he's ~ to agree** il sera d'accord, il n'y a aucun doute là-dessus; **the changes are ~ to provoke anger** ces changements provoqueront sûrement des réactions violentes; **nothing could be more ~ to offend him** c'est vraiment ce qui peut le vexer le plus facilement; **one thing is ~, you'll never succeed** une chose est sûre, tu ne réussiras jamais; **to my ~ knowledge** à ma connaissance; **I let him do it in the ~ knowledge that he would fail** je l'ai laissé faire tout en sachant très bien qu'il allait échouer; **go early to be ~ of a seat** arrivez de bonne heure pour être sûr d'avoir une place assise; **3** (specific) [*amount, number, quantity, sum*] certain (*before n*); **on ~ conditions** à certaines conditions; **~ people** certains *mpl*; **4** (slight) [*coldness, confusion, shyness, difficulty*] certain (*before n*); **to a ~ extent** ou **degree** dans une certaine mesure; **a ~ amount of time** un certain temps; **a ~ amount of frivolity/confusion/introspection** une certaine frivolité/confusion/introspection; **5** (named but not known) **a ~ Mr Cassels** un certain M. Cassels.

certainly /ˈsɜːtnlɪ/ *adv* (without doubt) certainement; (indicating assent) certainement, bien sûr; **~ not!** certainement pas!; **it's ~ possible that** il est tout à fait possible que (+ *subj*); **'may I borrow your pen?'—'~'** 'je peux vous emprunter votre stylo?'—'bien sûr'; **this exercise is ~ very difficult** cet exercice est vraiment très difficile; **we shall ~ attend the meeting** nous serons à la réunion sans faute; **~ sir/madam** (mais) certainement, monsieur/madame; **she was almost ~ innocent** elle était presque certainement innocente; **he ~ got his revenge!** iron c'est sûr qu'il a pris sa revanche!; **it is ~ true that they treated him unfairly** c'est bien vrai qu'il a été injustement traité; **'are you annoyed?'—'I most ~ am!'** 'tu es fâché?'—'ah! ça, oui alors!'

certainty /ˈsɜːtntɪ/ *n* **1** (sure thing) certitude *f* (**about** quant à); **moral certainties** certitudes morales; **for a ~** à coup sûr; **it's by no means a ~** ce n'est pas du tout sûr (**that** que + *subj*); **this candidate is a ~ for election** ce candidat est sûr d'être élu, ce candidat est une valeur sûre pour les élections; **she is a ~ to play at next weeks's concert** elle est sûre de jouer au concert la semaine prochaine; **2** ¢ (guarantee) certitude *f* (**of** de); **we have no ~ of success** nous ne sommes pas certains de réussir; **we cannot say with any ~ whether he will recover** nous ne pouvons dire avec certitude s'il va se rétablir.

certifiable /ˌsɜːtɪˈfaɪəbl/ *adj* **1** (mad) [*person*] dont l'état justifie l'internement; hum fou/folle à lier; **2** (verifiable) [*statement, evidence*] vérifiable.

certificate I /səˈtɪfɪkət/ *n* **1** (academic) certificat *m*; (more advanced) diplôme *m*; **2** (for electrician, instructor, first-aider etc) brevet *m*; **3** (of child's proficiency in sth) brevet *m*; **4** (of safety, building standards etc) certificat *m*; **test ~, MOT ~** GB certificat *m* de contrôle technique; **5** Admin (of birth, death, marriage) acte *m*; **6** Comm (of authenticity, quality) certificat *m*; **7** Cin **18-~ film** film interdit aux moins de 18 ans.
II /səˈtɪfɪkeɪt/ *vtr* certifier.

certificated /səˈtɪfɪkeɪtɪd/ *adj* diplômé.

certificate: **Certificate in Education** *n* Univ certificat *m* d'aptitude au professorat de l'enseignement du second degré; **~ of deposit, CD** *n* US Fin certificat *m* de dépôt; **Certificate of Incorporation** *n* Comm Jur acte *m* constitutif; **Certificate of Secondary Education, CSE** *n* GB Sch (avant 1988) ≈ brevet *m* des collèges.

certification /ˌsɜːtɪfɪˈkeɪʃn/ *n* **1** Jur (of document) authentification *f*; (of ship) certification *f*; (of ownership) certificat *m*; **2** (document) certificat *m*; **3** (of mental patient) mandat *m* d'internement psychiatrique.

certified: **~ bankrupt** *n* débiteur *m* (failli); **~ public accountant, CPA** *n* US Accts expert-comptable *m* agréé.

certify /ˈsɜːtɪfaɪ/ **I** *vtr* **1** Jur, Med (confirm) certifier, constater [*death*]; **to ~ sth a true copy** certifier qch pour copie conforme; **to ~ sb insane** certifier que qn est atteint d'aliénation mentale; **2** (authenticate) authentifier [*document, objet d'art*]; **3** (issue certificate to) délivrer un certificat d'aptitude professionnelle à; **4** Comm garantir [*goods*].
II *vi* **to ~ as to** attester [*authenticity, truth*].
III certified *pp adj* certifié; [*teacher*] US Sch qualifié; **to send by certified mail** US Post envoyer en recommandé.

certitude /ˈsɜːtɪtjuːd, US -tuːd/ *n* certitude *f*, conviction *f*.

cerulean /səˈruːlɪən/ *adj* littér ceruléen/-éenne liter.

cerumen /səˈruːmen/ *n* cérumen *m*.

ceruminous /sɪˈruːmɪnəs/ *adj* cérumineux/-euse.

cervical /ˈsɜːvɪkl/ *adj* cervical.

cervical: **~ cancer** ▶ **1354** *n* cancer *m* du col de l'utérus; **~ smear** *n* frottis *m* vaginal.

cervix /ˈsɜːvɪks/ *n* col *m* de l'utérus.

cesium *n* US = **caesium**.

cessation /seˈseɪʃn/ *n* sout cessation *f*; **~ of hostilities** cessation des hostilités; **without ~** sans interruption.

cession /ˈseʃn/ *n* Jur (act, process) cession *f*; (item ceded) bien *m* acquis par cession.

cessionary /ˈseʃənərɪ/ **I** *n* cessionnaire *mf*.
II *adj* de cession.

cesspit /ˈsespɪt/, **cesspool** /ˈsespuːl/ *n* lit fosse *f* d'aisances; fig cloaque *m*.

CET *n*: *abrév* ▶ **Central European Time**.

cetacean /sɪˈteɪʃn/ *n* cétacé *m*.

Ceylon /sɪˈlɒn/ **I** *pr n* Hist Ceylan *m*.
II *modif* **~ tea** thé *m* de Ceylan.

cf (*abrév* = **confer**) cf.

c/f Accts (*abrév* = **carried forward**) à reporter.

CFC *n* Ecol (*abrév* = **chlorofluorocarbon**) CFC *m*; **'contains no ~s'** 'sans CFC'.

CFE *n* **1** GB (*abrév* = **College of Further Education**) ≈ centre *m* de formation continue; **2** *abrév* ▶ **Conventional Forces in Europe**.

cg 1 (*abrév* = **centigram**) cg; **2** *abrév* ▶ **centre of gravity**.

CGA *n* Comput *abrév* ▶ **colour graphics adaptor**.

ch. *abrév écrite* = **chapter**.

CH *n* **1** Aut (*abrév* = **Confédération Hélvétique**) CH; **2** GB (*abrév* = **Companion of Honour**) ≈ chevalier *m* (*membre d'un ordre honorifique*).

cha-cha /ˈtʃɑː tʃɑː/ **I** *n* cha-cha-cha *m*.
II *vi* danser le cha-cha-cha.

chad /tʃæd/ *n* Comput confetti *m*.

Chad /tʃæd/ ▶ **1131** *pr n* Tchad *m*; **Lake ~** le lac Tchad.

Chadian /ˈtʃædɪən/ ▶ **1486** **I** *n* Tchadien/-ienne *m/f*.
II *adj* tchadien/-ienne.

chador /tʃʌdə(r)/ *n* tchador *m*.

chafe /tʃeɪf/ **I** *vtr* (rub) irriter; (breaking skin) entamer; (to restore circulation) frictionner.
II *vi* **1** (rub) frotter (**on, against** sur); **2** (feel irritated) [*person*] s'irriter (**at** de).
IDIOMS **to ~ at the bit** ronger son frein.

chaff /tʃɑːf, tʃæf, US tʃæf/ **I** *n* **1** Agric (husks) balle *f*; (fodder) menue paille *f*; **2** Aviat leurres *mpl* passifs, chaffs *mpl*; **to drop ~** larguer des leurres.
II *vtr* plaisanter (**about** sur).

chaffinch /ˈtʃæfɪntʃ/ *n* pinson *m*.

chafing-dish /ˈtʃeɪfɪŋ dɪʃ/ *n* réchaud *m* de table.

chafing-plate /ˈtʃeɪfɪŋ pleɪt/ *n* plaque *f* de friction.

chagrin /ˈʃægrɪn, US ʃəˈgriːn/ *n* dépit *m*; **(much) to his ~** à son grand dépit.

chagrined /ˈʃægrɪnd, US ʃəˈgriːnd/ *adj* sout désappointé (**at, by** par).

chain /tʃeɪn/ **I** *n* **1** (metal links) chaîne *f*; **a length of ~** une chaîne; **a gold ~** une chaîne en or; **to put** ou **keep sb in ~s** enchaîner qn; **to keep a dog on a ~** tenir un chien à la chaîne; **to break free of** ou **from one's ~s** fig rompre ses chaînes; **2** (on lavatory) chasse *f* (d'eau); **to pull the ~** tirer la chasse; **3** (on door) chaîne *f* de sûreté; **to put the ~ on (the door)** mettre la chaîne de sûreté (à la porte); **4** Comm chaîne *f* (**of** de); **supermarket/hotel ~** chaîne *f* de supermarchés/d'hôtels; **5** (series) (of events) série *f*; (of ideas) enchaînement *m*; **~ of causation** rapport *m* or relation *f* de cause à effet; **he's only a link in the ~** il n'est qu'un maillon de la chaîne; **to make** ou **form a (human) ~** faire la chaîne, faire une chaîne humaine; **6** Biol, Geog, Phys chaîne *f*; **7** Meas = 20,12 m.
II *vtr* enchaîner [*person*]; **to ~ sb's legs/wrists** attacher les jambes/poignets de qn avec des chaînes; **to ~ two people together** enchaîner deux personnes l'une à l'autre; **to ~ a dog/a bicycle to sth** attacher un chien/une bicyclette à qch avec une chaîne.
III chained *pp adj* enchaîné; **to keep sb ~ed** tenir qn enchaîné; **to be ~ed to one's desk/the kitchen sink** fig être esclave de son bureau/ses casseroles.
■ **chain down**: **~ down [sth/sb], ~ [sth/sb] down** fixer [qch] avec une chaîne [*object*]; attacher [qch] avec une chaîne [*animal*]; enchaîner [*person*] (**to** à).
■ **chain up**: **~ up [sth/sb], ~ [sth/sb] up** attacher [qch] avec une chaîne [*animal, bicycle*]; enchaîner [*person*].

chain: **~ bridge** *n* pont *m* suspendu à chaînes; **~ drive** *n* transmission *f* par chaîne; **~ gang** *n* chaîne *f* de forçats; **~ guard** *n* carter *m* (de bicyclette); **~ letter** *n* (lettre *f* de) chaîne *f*; **~ mail** *n* cotte *f* de mailles; **~man** ▶1692 *n* arpenteur *m*; **~ of command** *n* hiérarchie *f*; **~ of office** *n*: *chaîne portée par le maire pour les fonctions officielles*; **~ reaction** *n* réaction *f* en chaîne; **~ saw** *n* tronçonneuse *f*.

chain-smoke /'tʃeɪnsməʊk/ **I** *vtr* **to ~ cigarettes** fumer des cigarettes les unes après les autres.
II *vi* fumer comme un sapeur○, fumer sans arrêt.

chain: **~-smoker** *n* gros fumeur/grosse fumeuse *m/f*; **~ stitch** *n* point *m* de chaînette.

chain store **I** *n* (single shop) magasin *m* faisant partie d'une chaîne; (retail group) magasin *m* à succursales multiples.
II *modif* [*garment*] de confection.

chair /tʃeə(r)/ **I** *n* **1** (seat) (wooden) chaise *f*; (upholstered) fauteuil *m*; **dentist's ~** fauteuil de dentiste; **to take a ~** s'asseoir; **2** (chairperson) président/-e *m/f*; **to take** ou **be in the ~** présider; **Chair! Chair!** Messieurs s'il vous plaît!; **to address one's remarks to** ou **through the ~** adresser ses remarques au président; **3** Univ (professorship) chaire *f* (**of, in** de); **to hold the ~ of**... être titulaire de la chaire de...; **4** US (also **electric ~**) **to go to the ~** passer sur la chaise électrique.
II *vtr* **1** présider [*meeting*]; **2** GB porter [qn] en triomphe [*hero*].

chairbound /'tʃeəbaʊnd/ *adj* **to be ~** être dans un fauteuil roulant.

■ Note L'usage moderne préfère *in a wheelchair*.

chair lift *n* (in skiing) télésiège *m*.

chairman /'tʃeəmən/ ▶1268 *n* (all contexts) président/-e *m/f*; **Chairman Mao** le président Mao; **Mr Chairman** monsieur le Président; **Madam Chairman** madame la Présidente; **the ~'s report** le rapport annuel.

■ Note L'usage moderne préfère *chairperson*.

chairmanship /'tʃeəmənʃɪp/ *n* présidence *f*.

chairperson /'tʃeəpɜːsn/ *n* président/-e *m/f*.

chairwarmer○ /'tʃeəwɔːmə(r)/ *n* US péj rond-de-cuir *m* pej.

chairwoman /'tʃeəwʊmən/ ▶1268 *n* présidente *f*.

chaise /ʃeɪz/ *n* cabriolet *m*.

chaise longue /ˌʃeɪz 'lɒŋ, US 'lɔːŋ/ *n* (*pl* **chaise(s) longues**) chaise *f* longue.

chalcedony /kæl'sedənɪ/ *n* calcédoine *f*.

chalet /'ʃæleɪ/ *n* (mountain) chalet *m*; (in holiday camp) bungalow *m*.

chalet: **~ girl** ▶1692 *n* responsable *f* de chalet (*jeune fille qui fait la cuisine et le ménage dans un chalet loué par des skieurs*); **~ style** *adj* style chalet (*after n*).

chalice /'tʃælɪs/ *n* calice *m*.

chalk /tʃɔːk/ **I** *n* gen, Miner craie *f*; **a stick** ou **piece of ~** un bâton de craie; **on ~** Hort sur un sol crayeux.
II *modif* **1** gen, Art [*drawing*] à la craie; **~ mark** (on blackboard) trace de craie; Sewing repère à la craie; **2** [*cliff, landscape*] de craie; **3** Geol [*layer, period*] crétacé.
III *vtr* **1** (write) écrire [qch] à la craie; **2** (apply chalk to) frotter [qch] avec de la craie.
IDIOMS **not by a long ~**○! loin de là○!; **not to be able to tell ~ from cheese** ne pas savoir reconnaître un chat d'un chien; **to be as different as ~ and cheese** être comme le jour et la nuit; **to be as white as ~** être blanc comme un linge.
■ **chalk out**: **~ out [sth]**, **~ [sth] out** tracer [qch] à la craie [*line, map*].
■ **chalk up**: **~ [sth] up**, **~ up [sth]** lit, fig marquer [*score, points*]; **~ them up to me, barman**○ marquez-les sur mon compte, barman○; **~ it up to experience** la prochaine fois vous saurez.

chalk and talk **I** *n* GB Sch cours *m* magistral.
II *modif* **to use the ~ method** ne faire que des cours magistraux.

chalkboard /'tʃɔːkbɔːd/ *n* US tableau *m* (noir).

chalkface *n* GB Sch hum **at the ~** dans la classe.

chalkiness /'tʃɔːkɪnɪs/ *n* état *m* crayeux.

chalkpit /'tʃɔːkpɪt/ *n* carrière *f* de craie.

chalky /'tʃɔːkɪ/ *adj* [*soil, water, complexion, white*] crayeux/-euse; [*hands, clothing*] couvert de craie.

challenge /'tʃælɪndʒ/ **I** *n* **1** (provocation) défi *m*; **to put out** ou **issue a ~** lancer un défi; **to take up** ou **respond to a ~** relever un défi; **2** (demanding situation or opportunity) (considered stimulating) challenge *m*; (considered difficult) épreuve *f*; **to present a ~** représenter un challenge; **to rise to** ou **meet the ~** relever le challenge; **the ~ of doing** ou **to do** le challenge de faire; **to face a ~** affronter une épreuve; **unemployment is a ~ for us** le chômage nous met à l'épreuve; **I'm looking for a ~** je cherche un défi à relever; **the ~ of new ideas** la stimulation des idées nouvelles; **3** (contest) **to make a ~ for** [*competitor*] essayer de s'emparer de [*title*]; [*candidate*] entrer dans la course à [*presidency etc*]; **leadership ~** Pol tentative *f* pour s'emparer de la direction du parti; **4** (questioning) (of claim, authority) contestation *f* (**to** de); (by sentry) sommation *f*; **5** Jur récusation *f*; **6** Sport attaque *f*.
II *vtr* **1** (invite to contest or justify) défier [*person*] (**to** à; **to do** de faire); **she ~d him to prove it** elle l'a défié de le prouver; **to ~ sb to a duel** provoquer qn en duel; **'I ~ you to a duel'** 'je demande réparation'; **2** (question) débattre [*ideas*]; contester [*statement, authority*]; [*sentry*] faire une sommation à; **he ~d me on what I said** il a contesté ce que j'ai dit; **I was ~d at the gate** j'ai été interpellé au portail; **3** (test) (by proving difficult) mettre à l'épreuve [*skill, endurance, person*]; (by stimulating) stimuler [*person*]; **4** Jur récuser [*jury, witness*]; contester [*authority*].

challenge cup *n* Sport trophée *m*.

challenger /'tʃælɪndʒə(r)/ *n* Sport, Pol challenger *m* (**for** de).

challenging /'tʃælɪndʒɪŋ/ *adj* **1** (stimulating) [*ideas, career*] stimulant; [*task, role*] qui représente un challenge; [*work*] difficile mais motivant; [*book*] d'un abord difficile; **2** (confrontational) [*statement, look*] provocateur/-trice.

chamber /'tʃeɪmbə(r)/ **I** *n* **1** (room) chambre *f*; **council ~** GB salle *f* de réunion; **2** GB Pol **the upper/lower ~** la Chambre des lords/des communes; **3** Anat (of heart) cavité *f*; (of eye) chambre *f*; **4** (in caving) salle *f*; **5** Tech chambre *f*.
II chambers *npl* Jur cabinet *m*; **to hear a case in ~s** juger une affaire en cabinet.

chamberlain /'tʃeɪmbəlɪn/ *n* chambellan *m*.

chamber: **~maid** ▶1692 *n* femme *f* de chambre; **~ music** *n* musique *f* de chambre; **Chamber of Commerce**, **C of C** *n* Comm chambre *f* de commerce et d'industrie; **Chamber of Deputies** *n* Chambre *f* des Députés; **Chamber of Horrors** *n* Chambre *f* des Horreurs; **Chamber of Trade** *n* assemblée *f* permanente des Chambres de commerce et d'industrie; **~ orchestra** *n* orchestre *m* de chambre; **~ pot** *n* pot *m* de chambre.

chambray /'ʃæmbreɪ/ *n* chambray *m*.

chameleon /kə'miːlɪən/ *n* caméléon *m* also fig.

chamfer /'tʃæmfə(r)/ **I** *n* chanfrein *m*.
II *vtr* chanfreiner.

chamois /'ʃæmwɑː, US 'ʃæmɪ/ *n* (*pl* **~**) Zool chamois *m*.

chamois: **~ cloth** *n* US = **chamois leather**; **~ leather**, **shammy leather** *n* peau *f* de chamois.

champ /tʃæmp/ **I**○ *n* champion *m*.
II *vtr* mâchonner.
III *vi* **to be ~ing to do** brûler (d'impatience) de faire; **to ~ at the bit** [*horse*] piaffer d'impatience; [*person*] fig ronger son frein.

champagne /ʃæm'peɪn/ **I** *n* Wine champagne *m*; **a glass of ~** une coupe or une flûte de champagne; **pink ~** champagne rosé.
II ▶1104 *adj* (colour) champagne *inv*.

Champagne /ʃæm'peɪn/ ▶1273 *pr n* Champagne *f*; **in/to ~** en Champagne.

champagne: **~ cocktail** *n* cocktail *m* champagne brandy; **~-coloured** *adj* champagne *inv*; **~-cup** *n* coupe *f* au champagne; **~ glass** *n* (tall) flûte *f* à champagne; (open) coupe *f* à champagne.

champers○ /'ʃæmpəz/ *n* GB champ'○ *m*, champagne *m*.

champion /'tʃæmpɪən/ **I** *n* (all contexts) champion/-ionne *m/f*; **reigning ~** champion/-ionne *m/f* en titre; **world ~** champion/-ionne *m/f* du monde; **~ boxer**, **boxing ~** champion *m* de boxe.
II○ *adj* GB dial super○.
III *vtr* se faire le champion de [*cause*]; prendre fait et cause pour [*person*].

championship /'tʃæmpɪənʃɪp/ *n* championnat *m*; (over several rounds) tournoi *m*; **the swimming ~s** (one competition) le championnat de natation.

chance /tʃɑːns, US tʃæns/ **I** *n* **1** (opportunity) occasion *f*; **to have** ou **get the ~ to do** avoir l'occasion de faire; **I had the ~ of a job in China** on m'a offert la possibilité de travailler en Chine; **this was the ~ (that) she was waiting for** c'était l'occasion qu'elle attendait; **to give sb a** ou **the ~ to do** donner à qn l'occasion de faire; **the trip gave me a ~ to speak Greek** le voyage m'a donné l'occasion de parler grec; **give me a ~ to explain** laisse-moi t'expliquer; **give the tablets a ~ to work** laisse aux cachets le temps d'agir; **to take one's ~** saisir l'occasion; **you've missed your ~** tu as laissé passer l'occasion; **now's your ~!** c'est l'occasion ou jamais!; **I haven't had a ~ yet** je n'en ai pas encore eu l'occasion; **this is your last ~** c'est ta dernière chance; **this is your big ~** c'est l'occasion ou jamais; **if you get a ~** si tu en as la possibilité; **when you get a** ou **the ~, can you...?** quand tu auras le temps est-ce que tu pourras...?; **'can you do it?' 'yes, given a** ou **the ~'** 'est-ce que tu peux le faire?' 'oui, si on me laisse essayer'; **2** (likelihood) chance *f*; **there's little ~ of sb doing** il y a peu de chances que qn fasse; **there's little ~ of winning** il y a peu de chances de gagner; **the ~s of catching the thief are slim** il y a peu de chances qu'on attrape le voleur; **there is a ~ that sb will do** il y a des chances que qn fasse; **the ~s are that** il y a de grandes chances que (+ *subj*); **the ~s of sb doing are poor** il y a peu de chances que qn fasse; **she has a good ~** elle a de bonnes chances; **I have no ~** je n'ai aucune chance; **what are his ~s of recovery?** a-t-il des chances de s'en tirer?; **what are my ~s?** quelles sont mes chances?; **any ~ of a coffee**○**?** est-ce que c'est possible d'avoir un café?; **3** (luck) hasard *m*; **a game of ~** un jeu de hasard; **it happened by ~** ça s'est produit par hasard; **by a lucky ~** comme par hasard; **as ~ would have it** par coïncidence; **4** (risk) risque *m*; **to take a ~** prendre un risque; **to take a ~ on doing** prendre le risque de faire; **I'm taking no ~s** je ne prends pas de risques; **it's a ~ I'm willing to take** c'est un risque à prendre; **5** (possibility) chance *f*; **not to stand a ~** n'avoir aucune chance (**of doing** de faire); **to be still in with a ~ of doing** avoir encore une chance de faire; **are you by any ~ Juliet West?** seriez-vous, par hasard, Juliet

West?; **do you have his address by any ~?** auriez-vous, par hasard, son adresse?
II *modif* [*encounter, occurrence*] fortuit; [*discovery*] accidentel/-elle; **a ~ acquaintance** une personne rencontrée par hasard.
III *vtr* **1** (risk) **to ~ doing** courir le risque de faire; **to ~ one's luck** ou **arm** tenter sa chance; **we'll just have to ~ it** il faudra tenter notre chance or le coup; **I shouldn't ~ it if I were you** à ta place je ne risquerais pas le coup; **2** sout (happen to do) **I ~d to see it** je l'ai vu par hasard; **if you should ~ to do** si tu venais à faire.
IDIOMS **no ~**○! (I won't do it) pas question○!; (it can't be done) impossible!
■ **chance upon**, **chance on**: ¶ **~ upon [sb]** rencontrer [qn] par hasard; ¶ **~ upon [sth]** trouver [qch] par hasard.

chancel /ˈtʃɑːnsl, US tʃænsl/ *n* chœur *m*; **~ screen** clôture *f* de chœur.

chancellery /ˈtʃɑːnsələrɪ, US ˈtʃæns-/ *n* chancellerie *f*.

chancellor /ˈtʃɑːnsələ(r), US ˈtʃæns-/ *n* **1** (head of government) chancelier *m*; **2** Univ ≈ président *m*; **3** GB Jur **the Lord Chancellor** grand chancelier *m*, ministre *m* de la Justice.

Chancellor of the Exchequer *n* GB Pol Chancelier *m* de l'Échiquier.

chancellorship /ˈtʃɑːnsələʃɪp/ *n* fonction *f* de chancelier.

chancer○ /ˈtʃɑːnsə(r)/ *n* profiteur/-euse *m/f*.

chancery /ˈtʃɑːnsərɪ, US ˈtʃæns-/ *n* **1** GB Jur cour *f* de la chancellerie; **ward in ~** pupille *mf* sous tutelle judiciaire; **2** US Jur cour *f* d'équité.

chancre /ˈʃæŋkə(r)/ *n* Med chancre *m*.

chancy○ /ˈtʃɑːnsɪ, US ˈtʃænsɪ/ *adj* [*method*] aléatoire; [*project, plan*] risqué; **it's a ~ business** c'est une entreprise risquée.

chandelier /ˌʃændəˈlɪə(r)/ *n* lustre *m*.

chandler /ˈtʃɑːndlə(r), US ˈtʃæn-/ ▶ 1692 *n* (also **ship's ~**) vendeur *m* de matériel pour bateaux.

change /tʃeɪndʒ/ **I** *n* **1** (alteration) (by replacement) changement *m*; (by adjustment) modification *f*; **the ~ in the schedule** la modification du programme; **~ of air/of diet** changement d'air/de régime; **~ of direction** changement de direction; **~ of plan** changement de programme; **a ~ for the better/worse** un changement en mieux/pire; **a time of economic/social ~** une époque de changements économiques/sociaux; **to make a ~ in sth** changer qch; **to make a small/big ~ in sth** faire un petit/grand changement dans qch; **to make ~s in** apporter des changements à [*text*]; faire des changements dans [*room, company*]; **there will have to be a ~ in your attitude** il va falloir que vous changiez d'attitude; **people opposed to ~** les personnes qui sont contre le progrès; **2** (substitution, replacement) changement *m* (**of** de); **costume/scene ~** Theat changement de costume/scène; **~ of leader/government** Pol changement de dirigeant/gouvernement; **3** (fresh, different experience) changement *m*; **the ~ will do you good** le changement vous fera du bien; **it makes** ou **is a ~ from television/from staying at home** cela change un peu de la télévision/de rester chez soi; **to make a ~** pour changer un peu; **that makes a nice** ou **refreshing ~** ça change agréablement; **she needs a ~** elle a besoin de se changer les idées; **to need a ~ of air** fig avoir besoin de changer d'air; **for a ~** (for variety, as improvement) pour changer; **the train was late, for a ~** iron pour changer, le train était en retard; **4** (of clothes) vêtements *mpl* de rechange; **a ~ of socks** des chaussettes de rechange; **a ~ of suit** un costume de rechange; **take a ~ of clothes** emportez des vêtements de rechange; **5** (cash) monnaie *f*; **small ~** petite monnaie; **she gave me 6p ~** elle m'a rendu 6 pence; **don't forget your ~!** n'oubliez pas votre monnaie!; **have you got ~ for £10?** pouvez-vous me changer un billet de 10 livres?; **have you any ~ for the meter?** as-tu de la monnaie pour le parcmètre?; **60p in ~** 60 pence en petite monnaie; **'no ~ given'** (on machine) 'ne rend pas la monnaie'; **keep the ~!** gardez la monnaie; **'exact ~ please'** (on bus) 'faites l'appoint, s'il vous plaît'; **you won't get much ~ out of £20**○ tu vas payer près de 20 livres; **6** (in bell-ringing) **to ring the ~s** lit carillonner; fig introduire des changements; **7**‡ Fin la Bourse.
II *vtr* **1** (alter) (completely) changer; (in part) modifier; **the baby has ~d my life** le bébé a changé ma vie; **we have ~d the shape of the lawn/the look of the town** nous avons modifié la forme de la pelouse/l'aspect de la ville; **to ~ X into Y** transformer X en Y; **the road has been ~d from a quiet street into a motorway** d'une rue calme la route a été transformée en autoroute; **to ~ one's mind** changer d'avis (**about** à propos de); **to ~ one's mind about doing** abandonner l'idée de faire; **to ~ sb's mind** faire changer qn d'avis; **to ~ one's ways** changer de mode de vie; **that won't ~ anything** ça n'y changera rien; **2** (exchange for sth different) gen changer de [*clothes, name, car*]; (in shop) échanger [*faulty item, unsuitable purchase*] (**for** pour); **can I ~ it for a size 12?** est-ce que je peux l'échanger contre une taille 12?; **if it's too big, we'll ~ it for you** s'il est trop grand, nous vous l'échangerons; **to ~ colour** changer de couleur; **he ~d the colour** il a changé la couleur; **hurry up and get ~d!** dépêche-toi de te changer!; **to ~ sth from X to Y** (of numbers, letters, words) remplacer X par Y; (of building, area etc) transformer X en Y; **to ~ X for Y** (in shop) échanger X contre Y; **they ~d their car for a smaller one** ils ont remplacé leur voiture par un modèle plus petit; **3** (replace sth dirty, old, broken) changer [*battery, bulb, fuse, linen, accessory, wheel*]; **to ~ a bed** changer les draps; **4** (exchange with sb) échanger [*clothes, seats*]; **she ~d hats with her sister** sa sœur et elle ont échangé leurs chapeaux; **to ~ places** changer de place (**with** avec); fig (roles) intervertir les rôles; **I wouldn't ~ places with the Queen** je ne voudrais pas être à la place de la Reine; **to ~ ends** Sport changer de côté; **5** (actively switch) changer de [*course, side, job, direction, transport, TV channel, hands, feet, doctor, dentist, agent, supplier*]; **I'm tired, I have to ~ hands/feet** je suis fatigué, il me faut changer de main/pied; **to ~ hands** fig changer de propriétaire; **the hotel has ~d hands** l'hôtel a changé de propriétaire; **no money ~d hands** il n'y a pas eu d'échange d'argent; **she ~d her bag from her left hand to her right** elle a fait passer son sac de la main gauche à la main droite; **6** (alter character) changer; **to ~ sb/sth into** changer qn/qch en [*frog, prince*]; **sugar is ~d into alcohol** le sucre se transforme en alcool; **the accident ~d him from an active young man into an invalid** l'accident a transformé le jeune homme actif qu'il était en invalide; **7** (replace nappy of) changer [*baby*]; **8** Fin changer [*cheque, currency*] (**into, for** en); **to ~ some money** changer de l'argent; **9** Comput modifier.
III *vi* **1** (alter) gen changer; [*wind*] tourner; **the price hasn't ~d much** le prix a peu changé; **times ~** les temps changent; **some things never ~** il y a des choses qui ne changent jamais; **to ~ from X (in)to Y** passer de X à Y; Chem virer de X à Y; **the lights ~d from red to orange** les feux sont passés du rouge à l'orange; **she ~d from a friendly child into a sullen adolescent** l'enfant aimable qu'elle était s'est transformée en adolescente maussade; **2** (into different clothes) se changer; **he went upstairs to ~ for dinner** il monta se changer pour le dîner; **to ~ into** passer [*different garment*]; **I'm going to ~ into my jeans** je vais passer un jean; **to ~ out of** ôter, enlever [*garment*]; **3** (from bus, train) changer; **you must ~ at Sheffield** vous devez changer à Sheffield; **do I have to ~?** est-ce qu'il y a un changement?; **'~ at Tours for Paris'** (over loudspeaker) 'correspondance à Tours pour Paris'; **we ~d from a train to a bus** après un voyage en train nous avons pris le car; **all ~!** tout le monde descend!; **4** (become transformed) [*person, face, Europe*] se métamorphoser (**from** de; **into** en).
IV changed *pp adj* [*man, woman, child, animal*] autre (*before n*).
IDIOMS **you'll get no ~ out of him/her**○ c'est peine perdue.
■ **change around** = **change round**.
■ **change down** GB Aut rétrograder.
■ **change over**: ¶ **~ over** (swap) [*drivers*] changer; **I don't like my part, let's ~ over!** je n'aime pas mon rôle, échangeons!; **to ~ over from sth to sth** passer de qch à qch; **we ~d over from gas to electric heating** nous sommes passés du gaz à l'électricité pour le chauffage; ¶ **~ over [sth/sb], ~ [sth/sb] over** intervertir [*sequence, roles, people*].
■ **change round** GB ¶ changer de place; ¶ **~ [sth/sb] round, ~ round [sth/sb]** déplacer [*furniture, large objects*]; changer [qn/qch] de place [*employers, workers, small objects, words, letters*]; **she's ~d the pictures round** elle a changé les tableaux de place.
■ **change up** GB Aut passer à une vitesse supérieure.

changeability /ˌtʃeɪndʒəˈbɪlətɪ/ *n* variabilité *f*.

changeable /ˈtʃeɪndʒəbl/ *adj* [*circumstances, condition, behaviour, character, colour, situation, opinion, weather*] changeant; [*price, rate, size, speed*] variable; **her ~ moods** ses sautes *fpl* d'humeur.

changeless /ˈtʃeɪndʒlɪs/ *adj* [*law, rite, routine, passion*] immuable; [*appearance, image*] inaltérable; [*character*] constant.

changelessness /ˈtʃeɪndʒlɪsnɪs/ *n* immuabilité *f*.

changeling (child) /ˈtʃeɪndʒlɪŋ/ *n* enfant *mf* substitué/-e (*à un autre par des fées*).

change machine *n* distributeur *m* de monnaie.

change of address I *n* Admin changement *m* d'adresse.
II *modif* [*card*] de changement d'adresse; [*details*] de son/votre etc changement d'adresse.

change of life *n* retour *m* d'âge.

changeover /ˈtʃeɪndʒəʊvə(r)/ *n* **1** (time period) phase *f* de changement; **2** (transition) passage *m*; **the ~ to computers** le passage à l'informatique; **3** gen, Pol (of leaders) remaniement *m*; (of employees, guards) relève *f*; **4** Sport (of ends) changement *m*; (in relay) passage *m* du témoin; **after the half-time ~** après le changement à la mi-temps.

change: **~ purse** *n* US porte-monnaie *m inv*, bourse *f*; **~-ringing** *n* carillon *m*.

changing /ˈtʃeɪndʒɪŋ/ **I** *n* changement *m*.
II *adj* [*colours, environment*] changeant; [*attitude, world*] en évolution.

changing room /ˈtʃeɪndʒɪŋ ruːm, rʊm/ *n* Sport vestiaire *m*; US (fitting room) cabine *f* d'essayage.

channel /ˈtʃænl/ **I** *n* **1** (passage cut by or for liquid) canal *m*; **to cut a ~** creuser un canal (**in** à travers); **2** (deep, navigable part of water) chenal *m*; **3** fig (diplomatic, commercial) canal *m*; **distribution ~s** canaux *mpl* de distribution; **to do sth through the proper** ou **usual** ou **normal ~s** faire qch par la voie normale; **to go through official ~s** passer par la voie officielle; **diplomatic/legal ~s** voie *f* diplomatique/légale; **to open ~s of communication** ouvrir un réseau de communication; **4** TV chaîne *f*; **to change ~s** changer de chaîne; **to flick ~s**○ zapper; **~ one/two** la première/deuxième chaîne; **5** Radio canal *m*; **6** Archit (flute) canne-

lure *f*; **7** Tech (groove) rainure *f*; **8** Comput canal *m*, voie *f* de transmission.
II *vtr* (*p prés etc* **-ll-**, **-l-** US) **1** (carry) acheminer, canaliser [*water, liquid*] (**to, into** dans; **through** par l'intermédiaire de); **2** fig (direct) concentrer, canaliser [*efforts, energy*] (**into** dans; **into doing** pour faire); affecter [*funds, capital*] (**into** à); **to ~ funds into doing** débloquer des crédits pour faire; **to ~ aid through official bodies** canaliser l'aide par l'intermédiaire d'organismes officiels; **to ~ sth towards** canaliser qch vers [*industry, business*]; **3** (cut) creuser [*groove, gorge*] (**in** dans); **4** Archit canneler [*column*].
■ **channel off**: **~ off [sth]**, **~ [sth] off** canaliser [*liquid, energy*] (**into** dans); affecter [*funds, resources*] (**into** à).

Channel /'tʃænl/ ▶1511 I *pr n* (also **English ~**) **the ~** la Manche.
II *modif* [*crossing, port*] de la Manche.

channel: **~ bar** *n* fer *m* en U; **~ capacity** *n* capacité *f* de transmission or de débit; **~ ferry** *n* ferry *m* trans-Manche; **~-flick**○ *vi* zapper; **~ iron** *n* fer *m* en U; **Channel Islander** *n* habitant/-e *m/f* des îles Anglo-Normandes; **Channel Islands** ▶1381 *pr npl* îles *fpl* Anglo-Normandes; **~ selector** *n* sélecteur *m* de canal or de voie; **Channel Tunnel** *pr n* tunnel *m* sous la Manche.

chant /tʃɑ:nt, US tʃænt/ I *n* **1** gen chant *m* scandé; **a victory ~** un chant de victoire; **2** Mus, Relig mélopée *f*; **Gregorian ~** chant *m* grégorien.
II *vtr* **1** scander [*name, slogan*]; **2** Mus, Relig chanter [*psalm*]; psalmodier [*prayer, liturgy, schoolwork*].
III *vi* [*crowd*] scander des slogans; Mus, Relig psalmodier.

chantey /'ʃæntɪ/ *n* US = **shanty**.

chantry /'tʃɑ:ntrɪ, US 'tʃæntrɪ/ *n* petite chapelle *f*.

chaos /'keɪɒs/ *n* **1** gen, journ (on roads, at home, at work) pagaille○ *f*; (political) confusion *f*, désordre *m*; (economic) chaos *m*; **in a state of ~** [*house, room*] sens dessus dessous; (country) en plein chaos; **to cause ~** semer la pagaille; **2** littér (cosmic) chaos *m*.

chaos theory *n* théorie *f* du chaos.

chaotic /keɪ'ɒtɪk/ *adj* [*life*] désordonné; [*place, arrangements*] désordonné; **it's absolutely ~**○ c'est la pagaille○.

chap /tʃæp/ I○ *n* GB gen type○ *m*; (boy) garçon *m*; (young man) gars○ *m*; **a nice ~** un chouette type; **an old ~** un vieux; **I say old ~...** dis donc mon vieux...; **come on ~s!** allez les gars!
II *vtr* (*p prés etc* **-pp-**) gercer; (deeply) crevasser; **~ped lips** lèvres gercées.
III *vi* (*p prés etc* **-pp-**) se gercer; (deeply) se crevasser.

chap. *abrév écrite* = **chapter**.

chapatti /tʃə'pɑ:tɪ/ *n* chapati *m*.

chapel /'tʃæpl/ *n* **1** Relig (building) chapelle *f*; (service) culte *m*; **lady ~** chapelle de la Sainte Vierge; **to be church or ~** GB être anglican ou nonconformiste; **2** Journ syndicat *m* national des journalistes.

chaperone /'ʃæpərəʊn/ I *n* chaperon *m*; **to be a ~ to sb** servir de chaperon à qn.
II *vtr* chaperonner.

chaplain /'tʃæplɪn/ *n* gen aumônier *m*; (to a person) chapelain *m*.

chaplaincy /'tʃæplɪnsɪ/ *n* gen aumônerie *f* (also building); (to a person) chapellenie *f*.

chaplet† /'tʃæplɪt/ *n* **1** littér (wreath) couronne *f* de fleurs; **2** (beads) chapelet *m*.

chappie○, **chappy**○ /'tʃæpɪ/ *n* GB = **chap**.

chaps /tʃæps, ʃæps/ *npl* jambières *fpl* de cuir (*portées par les cowboys*).

Chap Stick® /'tʃæpstɪk/ *n* baume *m* pour les lèvres.

chapter /'tʃæptə(r)/ *n* **1** (in book) chapitre *m*; **in ~ 3** au chapitre 3; **2** fig (stage) chapitre *m*; **a new ~ in** un nouveau chapitre de; **3** (of association, union) section *f*; **4** Relig (also **~ house**) chapitre *m*; **5** US Fin Jur **to go ~ 11** faire faillite (*avec délai de grâce pour redresser la situation*).
IDIOMS **a ~ of accidents** une série d'accidents; **to give ~ and verse** donner la référence exacte.

char /tʃɑ:(r)/ I *n* **1**○ GB (cleaner) femme *f* de ménage; **2**†○GB (tea) thé *m*; **3** Zool omble *m* chevalier.
II *vtr* (*p prés etc* **-rr-**) carboniser; **the ~red remains** les restes carbonisés.
III *vi* (*p prés etc* **-rr-**) **1**○ GB (clean) faire des ménages; **2** (scorch) se carboniser.

charabanc† /'ʃærəbæŋ/ *n* ≈ omnibus *m*.

character /'kærəktə(r)/ I *n* **1** (personality) caractère *m*; **to have a pleasant ~** être d'un caractère agréable; **a house with ~** une maison qui a du caractère; **to act in/out of ~** agir de façon habituelle/surprenante; **his remarks are totally in ~/out of ~** ces remarques ne me surprennent pas/me surprennent de sa part; **2** (reputation) réputation *f*; **a person of good/bad ~** une personne d'une bonne/mauvaise réputation; **3** (nature) caractère *m*; **4** Literat, Theat, TV personnage *m* (**from** de); **to play the ~ of Romeo** jouer le rôle *m* de Roméo; **I hardly recognize her in ~** je la reconnais à peine sous son rôle; **5** (person) (in general) individu *m*; (appreciative) numéro○ *m*; **a real ~** un sacré numéro○; **a local ~** une figure *f* locale; **6** (moral strength) caractère *m*; **strength of ~** force *f* de caractère; **7** Comput, Print caractère *m*.
II *modif* Comput [*density, generator, reader, recognition, string*] de caractères.

character: **~ actor** *n* acteur *m* de genre; **~ actress** *n* actrice *f* de genre; **~ assassination** *n* dénigrement *m*.

characteristic /ˌkærəktə'rɪstɪk/ I *n* **1** (trait) (of person) trait *m* de caractère; (of place, theory, work) caractéristique *f*; **family ~** trait *m* héréditaire; **2** Math caractéristique *f*.
II *adj* caractéristique; **~ of** [*style, quality*] caractéristique de [*person, artist*]; **it was ~ of them to do** c'était typique de leur part de faire.

characteristically /ˌkærəktə'rɪstɪklɪ/ *adv* [*calm, helpful, mean, selfish*] typiquement; **~, he said nothing** comme d'habitude il n'a rien dit.

characterization /ˌkærəktəraɪ'zeɪʃn/ *n* **1** (character portrait) (by dramatist) représentation *f* des personnages; (by writer) peinture *f* des personnages; (by actor) interprétation *f*; **2** (depiction) peinture *f*.

characterize /'kærəktəraɪz/ *vtr* **1** Literat [*artist, writer, work*] dépeindre [*era, place, person*]; **to ~ sb as** dépeindre qn comme; **2** (typify) caractériser; **to be ~d by** se caractériser par; **3** (sum up) représenter [*era, place*]; faire le portrait de [*person*].

characterless /'kærəktəlɪs/ *adj* sans caractère.

character: **~ part** *n* Theat rôle *m* de composition; **~ reference** *n* références *fpl*; **~ set** *n* Comput, Print police *f* de caractères; **~ sketch** *n* portrait *m* rapide; **~ type** *n* Psych type *m* de caractère.

charade /ʃə'rɑ:d, US ʃə'reɪd/ *n* **1** (in game) charade *f* mimée; **to play ~s** jouer aux charades; **2** pej (pretence) comédie *f*.

charbroiled /'tʃɑ:brɔɪld/ *adj* US = **char-grilled**.

charcoal /'tʃɑ:kəʊl/ I *n* **1** (fuel) charbon *m* de bois; **2** Art fusain *m*; **a stick of ~** un morceau de fusain; **3** (colour) gris *m* anthracite.
II ▶1104 *adj* (colour) (also **~ grey**) (gris) anthracite *inv*.
III *modif* [*drawing, portrait*] au fusain; [*filter*] à charbon; **~ test** essai *m* sur le charbon.

charcoal burner *n* **1** ▶1692 (person) charbonnier *m*; **2** (for cooking) réchaud *m* à charbon de bois; (for heating) poêle *m* à charbon de bois.

Charente ▶1163 *pr n* Charente *f*; **in/to ~** en Charente.

Charente-Maritime ▶1163 *pr n* Charente-Maritime *f*; **in/to ~** en Charente-Maritime.

charge /tʃɑ:dʒ/ I *n* **1** (fee) frais *mpl*; **delivery/handling ~** frais de livraison/manutention; **electricity/telephone ~s** prix *mpl* d'électricité/du téléphone; **additional ~** supplément *m*; **small** ou **token ~** participation *f*; **there's a ~ of £2 for postage** il y a 2 livres de frais de port; **there's no ~ for installation** l'installation est gratuite; **free of ~** gratuitement; **at no extra ~** sans supplément; **2** Jur inculpation *f*; **murder/robbery ~** inculpation d'assassinat/de vol; **to be arrested on a ~ of sth** être arrêté sous l'inculpation de qch; **criminal ~s** poursuites *fpl* criminelles; **to bring ~s** porter plainte; **to prefer** ou **press ~s against sth** engager des poursuites contre qch; **to drop the ~s** abandonner les poursuites; **all ~s against him have been dropped** on a abandonné toutes les poursuites lancées contre lui; **to put sb on a ~ for theft** Mil accuser qn de vol; **3** (accusation) accusation *f* (**of** de); **this leaves you open to ~s of** cela laisse la porte ouverte aux accusations de [*nepotism, cynicism*]; **4** Mil (attack) charge *f* (**against** contre); **5** Comm (credit account) **is it cash or ~?** vous payez en liquide ou je le mets sur votre compte?; **6** (control) **to be in ~** gen être responsable; Mil commander; **the person in ~** le/la responsable; **the officer in ~ of the enquiry** l'officier responsable de l'enquête; **to be in ~ of doing** être responsable de faire; **to put sb in ~ of sth** confier la charge de qch à qn [*company, plane, project*]; confier qch à qn [*transport, training*]; **to take ~ of** assumer la charge de; **to have ~ of** être chargé de; **the pupils in my ~** les élèves à ma charge; **to take ~** prendre les choses en main; **I've left Paul in ~** c'est Paul qui sera responsable; **7** (person in one's care) (child) enfant *m* dont on s'occupe; (pupil) élève *mf*; (patient) malade *mf*; **8** (explosive) charge *f*; **9** Elec, Phys charge *f*; **10** (burden) fardeau *m* (**on** pour); **11** Relig cure *f*.
II *vtr* **1** Comm, Fin faire payer [*customer*]; prélever [*commission*]; percevoir [*interest*] (**on** sur); **to ~ sb for sth** faire payer qch à qn [*postage, call*]; **we ~ postage to the customer** nous facturons les frais d'envois au client; **how much do you ~?** vous prenez combien?; **I ~ £20 an hour** je prends 20 livres de l'heure; **my agent ~s 10% commission** mon agent prélève 10% de commission; **interest is ~d at 2% a month** l'intérêt perçu sera de 2% par mois; **labour is ~d at £25 per hour** il faut compter 25 livres de l'heure pour la main-d'œuvre; **what do you ~ for doing...?** combien faut-il compter pour faire...?; **to ~ sb extra** faire payer un supplément à qn; **I ~ double at weekends** le week-end je fais payer le double; **2** (pay on account) **to ~ sth to** mettre qch sur [*account*]; **I ~ everything** je mets tout sur mon compte; **3** Jur [*police*] inculper [*suspect*]; **to ~ sb with** inculper qn de [*crime*]; **to ~ sb with doing** inculper qn pour avoir fait; **4** (accuse) accuser (**with** de); **to ~ sb with doing** accuser qn de faire; **5** (rush at) charger [*enemy, gates*]; [*bull*] foncer sur [*person*]; **6** Elec, Phys charger [*battery, particle*]; **7** sout (order) **to ~ sb to do** ordonner à qn de faire; **to ~ sb with doing** charger qn de faire.
III *vi* **1** (demand payment) **to ~ for** faire payer [*delivery, admission*]; **I don't ~ for that** je ne fais pas payer ça; **2** (rush at) **to ~ at** [*troops*] charger [*enemy, gates*]; [*bull*] foncer sur [*person*]; **~!** à l'attaque!; **3** (run) se précipiter (**into** dans; **out of** de); **to ~ across** ou **through** traverser [qch] à toute vitesse [*room, garden*]; **to ~ up/down**

monter/descendre [qch] à toute vitesse [*stairs, road*].

chargeable /ˈtʃɑːdʒəbl/ *adj* **1** (payable) **a fee of 20 dollars is ~** un supplément de 20 dollars sera perçu; **tax is ~ at 25%** le taux des impôts à régler est de 25%; **2** Admin **to be a ~ expense** être aux frais de la société; **business travel is ~ to the company** le paiement des frais de déplacement sont pris en charge par la société.

charge: **~ account** *n* US Comm compte-client *m*; **~-cap** *vtr* GB Pol imposer une limite budgétaire à [*local authority*]; **~ card** *n* (credit card) carte *f* de crédit; (store card) carte *f* d'achat; **~-coupled device** *n* dispositif *m* à couplage de charge.

charged /tʃɑːdʒd/ *adj* **1** Phys [*battery, particle*] chargé; **a negatively ~ particle** une particule chargée négativement; **2** (intense) **a highly ~ atmosphere** une atmosphère très tendue; **a highly ~ meeting** une réunion très tendue; **an emotionally ~ scene** une scène chargée d'émotion.

chargé d'affaires /ˌʃɑːʒeɪ dæˈfeə(r)/ ▶ 1692 *n* Admin chargé *m* d'affaires.

charge: **~ hand** ▶ 1692 *n* sous-chef *m* d'équipe; **~ nurse** ▶ 1692 *n* infirmier/-ière *m/f* en chef.

charger /ˈtʃɑːdʒə(r)/ *n* **1** Electron chargeur *m*; **2**† Equit Hist cheval *m* de bataille.

charge sheet *n* GB Jur acte *m* d'accusation.

char-grilled /ˈtʃɑːgrɪld/ *adj* [*steak, burger*] grillé au charbon de bois.

charily /ˈtʃeərɪlɪ/ *adv* avec méfiance.

chariot /ˈtʃærɪət/ *n* char *m*.

charioteer /ˌtʃærɪəˈtɪə(r)/ *n* aurige *m*.

chariot race *n* course *f* de chars.

charisma /kəˈrɪzmə/ *n* gen, Relig charisme *m*.

charismatic /ˌkærɪzˈmætɪk/ **I** *n* chrétien/-ienne *m/f* faisant partie du mouvement charismatique.
II *adj* gen, Relig charismatique.

charitable /ˈtʃærɪtəbl/ *adj* [*person, act, explanation*] charitable (**to** envers); [*organization*] caritatif/-ive; **a company having ~ status** Tax ≈ une association reconnue d'utilité publique; **~ trust** Fin fondation *f* d'utilité publique; **~ work** bonnes œuvres *fpl*.

charitably /ˈtʃærɪtəblɪ/ *adv* charitablement.

charity /ˈtʃærətɪ/ **I** *n* **1** (virtue) charité *f*; **to do sth out of ~** faire qch par charité; **2** (aid, aid organizations) bénévolat *m*; **to give to/collect money for ~** donner à/collecter des fonds pour des œuvres de bienfaisance; **to accept/refuse ~** accepter/refuser l'aumône *f*; **3** (individual organization) organisation *f* caritative.
II *modif* [*sale, event*] au profit d'œuvres de bienfaisance.
IDIOMS **~ begins at home** charité bien ordonnée commence par soi-même.

charity: **~ box** *n* (in church) tronc *m*; **Charity Commissioners** *npl* GB fonctionnaires *mpl* chargés du contrôle des organisations caritatives; **~ shop** *n* magasin *m* d'articles d'occasion (*vendus au profit d'une œuvre de bienfaisance*); **~ work** *n* travail *m* bénévole (*au profit d'une œuvre de bienfaisance*); **~ worker** ▶ 1692 *n* bénévole *mf*.

charivari /ˌʃɑːrɪˈvɑːrɪ/ *n* charivari *m*.

charlady† /ˈtʃɑːleɪdɪ/ ▶ 1692 *n* GB femme *f* de ménage.

charlatan /ˈʃɑːlətən/ *n* charlatan *m*.

Charles /tʃɑːlz/ *pr n* Charles.

charleston /ˈtʃɑːlstən/ *n* charleston *m*.

charley horse○ /ˈtʃɑːlɪ hɔːs/ *n* US courbature *f* (*dans les muscles des jambes*).

charlie○ /ˈtʃɑːlɪ/ *n* **1** GB (fool) imbécile *mf*; **to look/feel a right ~** avoir l'air/se sentir ridicule; **2** US **a good-time ~** péj fêtard *m*; **3**○ (cocaine) argot des drogués cocaïne *f*.

charlotte /ˈʃɑːlɒt/ *n* Culin charlotte *f*; **strawberry ~** charlotte aux fraises.

charm /tʃɑːm/ **I** *n* **1** (capacity to please) charme *m*; **a man/town of great ~** un homme/une ville d'un grand charme; **susceptible to her ~s** sensible à ses charmes; **to use all one's ~** user de tout son charme; **to turn on the ~** péj se mettre à faire du charme; **2** (jewellery) amulette *f*; **~ bracelet** bracelet *m* à breloques; **lucky ~** porte-bonheur *m inv*; **3** (magic words) charme *m*.
II *vtr* charmer; **he ~ed his way into Head Office** il usa de tout son charme pour parvenir jusqu'à la direction; **she ~ed him into signing** elle a su si bien l'enjôler qu'il a fini par signer.
III charmed /tʃɑːmd/ *pp adj* charmé; **the ~ed (inner) circle** les initiés *mpl*.
IDIOMS **to be able to ~ the birds from the trees** être un/une véritable ensorceleur/-euse *m/f*; **to lead a ~ed life** être béni des dieux; **to work like a ~** faire merveille.

charmer /ˈtʃɑːmə(r)/ *n* **he is a real ~** il est adorable.

charming /ˈtʃɑːmɪŋ/ *adj* [*person, place, book*] charmant; [*clothing, poem*] ravissant; [*child, animal*] adorable; [*manners*] engageant; **~!** iron mais c'est gentil ça!

charmingly /ˈtʃɑːmɪŋlɪ/ *adv* [*decorate, speak, sing, behave*] de façon charmante; **~ simple** d'une simplicité charmante.

charm school *n*: *école où les jeunes filles vont apprendre l'étiquette*.

charnel house /ˈtʃɑːnl haʊs/ *n* charnier *m*.

charr *n* ▶ **char** I 3.

chart /tʃɑːt/ **I** *n* **1** (graph) graphique *m*; **temperature ~** Med feuille *f* de température; **2** (table) tableau *m*; **3** (map) carte *f*; **weather ~** carte du temps; **4** Mus **the ~s** le hit-parade; **to be number one in the ~s** être numéro un au hit-parade.
II *vtr* **1** (on map) porter [qch] sur la carte [*geographical feature*]; tracer [*route*]; **2** enregistrer [*changes, progress*].

charter /ˈtʃɑːtə(r)/ **I** *n* **1** gen, Pol charte *f*; (for company) acte *m* constitutif; **to be granted a ~** bénéficier d'une charte; **2** Comm (hiring) affrètement *m*; **on ~ to** sous contrat d'affrètement avec.
II *vtr* **1** affréter [*plane, coach etc*]; **2** Jur, Admin accorder une charte à [*corporation*].
III chartered *pp adj* [*professional*] agréé; [*corporation*] à charte.

charter: **~ed accountant**, **CA** ▶ 1692 *n* GB ≈ expert-comptable *m*; **~ed bank** *n* GB banque *f* privilégié/-e; **~ed surveyor** ▶ 1692 *n* GB expert *m* immobilier; **~ flight** *n* GB vol *m* charter; **~ plane** *n* GB charter *m*.

chartist /ˈtʃɑːtɪst/ *n* US Fin chartiste *mf*.

Chartist /ˈtʃɑːtɪst/ *n* Hist chartiste *mf*.

charwoman† /ˈtʃɑːwʊmən/ ▶ 1692 *n* femme *f* de ménage.

chary /ˈtʃeərɪ/ *adj* méfiant; **to be ~** se méfier (**of** de; **of doing** de faire).

chase /tʃeɪs/ **I** *n* **1** (pursuit) poursuite *f* (**after** de); **car/police ~** poursuite *f* en voiture/par la police; **to give ~ to sb** se lancer à la poursuite de qn; **2** fig (race) course *f* (**for** à); **the ~ for the prize/jobs** la course au prix/aux emplois; **3** Equit = **steeplechase**; **4** Hunt chasse *f*; **5** GB (deer park) chasse *f*.
II *vtr* **1** (also **~ after**) (pursue) pourchasser [*person, animal*]; courir après [*contract, job, success*]; **to ~ sb/sth up** ou **down the street** courir après qn/qch dans la rue; **2** (also **~ after**) (make advances) courir après [*man, girl*]; **3**○ (also **~ after**) (try to win) viser [*target, title*]; **4** (remove) **to ~ sb/sth from** chasser qn/qch de [*room, field etc*]; **5** (engrave) ciseler [*metal*]; **~ed silver dish** plat en argent ciselé.
III *vi* = **chase about**, **chase around**.
IDIOMS **to ~ one's (own) tail** tourner en rond.

■ **chase about**, **chase around**: ¶ **~ about** courir en tous sens; ¶ **~ around**○ [sth] parcourir [qch] dans tous les sens [*building, town*]; **we ~d all around the library looking for the book** on a parcouru la bibliothèque dans tous les sens pour trouver le livre; ¶ **~ [sb] around** poursuivre qn.

■ **chase away**: **~ [sb/sth] away**, **~ away [sb/sth]** chasser [*intruder, predator*]; fig chasser [*anxiety, fear*].

■ **chase down** US = **chase up**.

■ **chase off**: **~ [sb/sth] off**, **~ off [sb/sth]** chasser [*animal, person*].

■ **chase up** GB: ¶ **~ [sth] up**, **~ up [sth]** retrouver [*details, statistics*]; ¶ **~ [sb] up**, **~ up [sb]** activer [*person*].

chaser○ /ˈtʃeɪsə(r)/ *n* (between beers) petit coup *m* entre deux verres○; (between spirits) verre *m* entre deux petits coups○.

chasm /ˈkæzəm/ *n* **1** gouffre *m*; (deeper) abîme *m*; **2** fig abîme *m* (**between** entre).

chassis /ˈʃæsɪ/ *n* (*pl* **~**) **1** Aut, Radio, TV châssis *m*; Aviat train *m* d'atterrissage; **2**○ US (body) **she's got quite a ~** c'est un beau châssis●.

chaste /tʃeɪst/ *adj* **1** (celibate) chaste; **2** (innocent) [*relationship*] innocent; [*kiss*] chaste; **3** (sober) [*style*] sobre.

chastely /ˈtʃeɪstlɪ/ *adv* **1** (in celibacy) chastement; **2** [*written, decorated*] avec sobriété.

chasten /ˈtʃeɪsn/ **I**† *vtr* réprimander.
II chastened *pp adj* assagi; **they were suitably ~ed** comme il se doit cela les a fait réfléchir; **~ed and subdued** assagi et moins expansif.

chasteness /ˈtʃeɪstnɪs/ *n* sout **1** (celibacy) chasteté *f*; **2** (faithfulness) fidélité *f*; **3** (innocence) innocence *f*; **4** (of style, playing) sobriété *f*.

chastening /ˈtʃeɪstnɪŋ/ *adj* **to have a ~ effect on sb** faire réfléchir qn.

chastise /tʃæˈstaɪz/ *vtr* sout (physically) châtier liter; (verbally) admonester liter; **to ~ sb for sth/for doing** (verbally) admonester qn pour qch/pour avoir fait.

chastisement† /tʃæˈstaɪzmənt/ *n* (physical) châtiment *m* liter; (verbal) admonition *f* liter.

chastity /ˈtʃæstətɪ/ *n* chasteté *f*.

chastity belt *n* ceinture *f* de chasteté.

chasuble /ˈtʃæzjʊbl/ *n* chasuble *f*.

chat /tʃæt/ **I** *n* conversation *f*; **to have a ~** bavarder (**with** avec; **about** sur); **we had a ~ on the phone** on a bavardé au téléphone; **I must have a ~ with her about her work** il faut que je lui parle de son travail.
II *vi* (*p prés etc* **-tt**) bavarder (**with, to** avec).

■ **chat up**○: **~ up [sb]**, **~ [sb] up** GB (flirtatiously) draguer○; (to obtain sth) baratiner○.

chat: **~line** *n* GB gen réseau *m* téléphonique; (for sexual encounters etc) cf téléphone *m* rose; **~ show** *n* GB talk-show *m*.

chattel /ˈtʃætl/ *n* Jur bien *m*, possession *f*; **he treats his wife/child as a ~** il traite sa femme/son enfant comme si elle/s'il était sa propriété; **goods and ~s** biens et effets.

chattel mortgage *n* US gage *m*, nantissement *m*.

chatter /ˈtʃætə(r)/ **I** *n* (of person) bavardage *m*; (of crowd, audience) bourdonnement *m*; (of birds) gen gazouillis *m*; (of magpies) jacassement *m*; (of machine) cliquetis *m*.
II *vi* (also **~ away**, **~ on**) [*person*] bavarder; [*birds*] gazouiller; [*magpies*] jacasser; [*machine*] cliqueter; **her teeth were ~ing** elle claquait des dents; **his teeth were ~ing with the cold** le froid le faisait claquer des dents.

chatterbox /ˈtʃætəbɒks/ *n* moulin *m* à paroles○.

chatterer /ˈtʃætərə(r)/ *n* moulin *m* à paroles○.

chattering /ˈtʃætərɪŋ/ **I** *n* bavardage *m*.
II *adj* [*person*] qui bavarde.

chattering classes *npl* péj bourgeois *mpl* de gauche pej.

chatty /ˈtʃætɪ/ *adj* [*person*] ouvert; [*letter, style*] vivant.

Chaucerian /tʃɔːˈsɪərɪən/ *adj* de Chaucer.

chauffeur /ˈʃəʊfə(r), US ʃəʊˈfɜːr/ ▶ 1692 I *n* chauffeur *m*; **a ~-driven car** une voiture avec chauffeur.
II *vtr* conduire.

chauvinism /ˈʃəʊvɪnɪzəm/ *n* **1** gen chauvinisme *m*; **2** (also **male ~**) machisme *m*.

chauvinist /ˈʃəʊvɪnɪst/ *n, adj* **1** gen chauvin/-e (*m/f*); **2** (also **male ~**) macho○ (*m*).

chauvinistic /ˌʃəʊvɪˈnɪstɪk/ *adj* chauvin.

ChB *n* GB (*abrév* = **chirurgiae baccalaureus**) (person) *diplômé en chirurgie*; (diploma) *diplôme en chirurgie*.

cheap /tʃiːp/ I *adj* **1** [*article, meal, cut of meat, flight, service*] bon marché *inv*; **to be ~** être bon marché *inv*, ne pas coûter cher *inv*; **quality doesn't come ~** la qualité se paye; **it's ~ to produce** cela ne revient pas cher de le/la produire; **it works out ~er to take the train** cela revient moins cher de prendre le train; **the ~ seats** les places moins chères; **at a ~ rate** à bas prix; **it's ~ at the price** c'est une occasion à ce prix-là; **victory was ~ at the price** la victoire aurait pu coûter plus cher; **~ and cheerful** sans prétentions; **life is ~** la vie est sans importance; **to hold sth ~** ne pas respecter qch; **2** Econ [*labour, money*] bon marché; **3** péj (shoddy) [*furniture, shoe, wine*] de mauvaise qualité; [*jewellery*] de pacotille; **it's ~ and nasty** c'est de la camelote; **4** (easy) péj [*success, joke, jibe, laugh, gimmick, stunt, woman*] facile; **a ~ thrill** une sensation forte; **talk is ~** bavarder est facile; **5** péj (mean) [*trick, crook, liar*] sale (*before n*); **a ~ shot** un coup bas; **6** (with money) avare.
II *adv*○ [*buy, get, sell*] pour rien; **he can do the job ~** il peut faire le boulot pour pas grand-chose○; **they're going ~** ils sont au rabais.
III **on the cheap** *adv phr* [*buy, sell*] au rabais; **to do sth on the ~** péj y aller à l'économie.

cheapen /ˈtʃiːpən/ I *vtr* **1** (make less expensive) rendre [qch] moins cher [*process*]; faire baisser [*production costs*]; **2** (make less valuable) dévaloriser [*life, liberty*]; **3** (degrade) rabaisser [*person*].
II *v refl* **to ~ oneself** se rabaisser.

cheapie○ /ˈtʃiːpɪ/ I *n* **1** GB (bargain) occasion *f*; **2** US (mean person) radin○ *m*.
II *adj* US pas cher/chère○.

cheapjack /ˈtʃiːpdʒæk/ I *n* camelot† *m*.
II *adj* **~ goods** camelote *f*.

cheaply /ˈtʃiːplɪ/ *adv* [*produce, do, provide, sell*] à bas prix; [*available, accessible*] à un prix raisonnable; [*borrow*] à un faible taux d'intérêt; **to eat/live ~** manger/vivre pour pas cher; **two can live as ~ as one** vivre à deux ne coûte pas plus cher que de vivre tout seul.

cheapness /ˈtʃiːpnɪs/ *n* **1** (of article, plan, system) bas prix *m*; **2** (of joke, jibe, trick) bassesse *f*; **3** (of borrowing) faible taux *m* d'intérêt.

cheapo○ /ˈtʃiːpəʊ/ *adj* pas cher/chère○.

cheap rate *adj, adv* Telecom à tarif réduit; **to cost 25 pence a minute ~** coûter 25 pence la minute au tarif réduit.

cheapskate○ /ˈtʃiːpskeɪt/ *n* radin○ *m*.

cheat /tʃiːt/ I *n* **1** (person) tricheur/-euse *m/f*; **2** (dishonest action) tricherie *f*.
II *vtr* tromper [*person, company*]; **to feel ~ed** se sentir lésé; **to ~ sb (out) of** dépouiller qn de.
III *vi* tricher; **to ~ in** tricher à [*exam, test*]; **to ~ at cards** tricher aux cartes; **to ~ on** tromper [*person*].
IDIOMS **to ~ death** frôler la mort.

cheating /ˈtʃiːtɪŋ/ I *n* tricherie *f*; **to accuse sb of ~** accuser qn de tricher; (in past) accuser qn d'avoir triché.
II *adj* [*player*] tricheur/-euse; [*shopkeeper*] escroc *inv*.

check /tʃek/ I *n* **1** (inspection) (for quality, security) contrôle *m* (**on** sur); **security ~** contrôle de sécurité; **to carry out ~s** exercer des contrôles; **to give sth a ~** vérifier qch; **to keep a (close) ~ on sb/sth** surveiller qn/qch (de près); **2** Med examen *m*; **eye/breast ~** examen des yeux/des seins; **3** (restraint) frein *m* (**on** à); **to put** ou **place a ~ on** mettre un frein à [*immigration, production, growth*]; **to hold** ou **keep sb/sth in ~** contrôler qn/qch; **to hold oneself in ~** se maîtriser; **4** (in chess) **in ~** en échec; **to put the King in ~** faire échec au roi; **your king is in ~** échec au roi; **5** Tex (fabric) tissu *m* à carreaux; (pattern) carreaux *mpl*; (square) carreau *m*; **6** US (cheque) chèque *m*; **7** US (bill) addition *f*; **to pick up the ~** payer l'addition; **8** US (receipt) ticket *m*; **9** US (tick) croix *f* (*pour cocher*).
II *modif* [*fabric, garment etc*] à carreaux.
III *vtr* **1** (for security) vérifier [*vehicle, mechanism, fuse*]; contrôler [*person, baggage, product, ticket, passport, area*]; **to ~ that/ whether** vérifier que/si; **to ~ the toys for potential dangers** vérifier que les jouets ne sont pas dangereux; **they ~ed the hotel for bombs/gas leaks** ils se sont assurés qu'il n'y avait pas de bombe/fuite de gaz dans l'hôtel; **2** (for accuracy, reliability) vérifier [*bill, data, statement, terms, signature, banknote*]; contrôler [*accounts, invoice, output, work*]; corriger [*proofs, spelling, translation*]; **to ~ sth for accuracy** vérifier l'exactitude de qch; **to ~ sth for defects** contrôler la qualité de qch; **to ~ that/whether** vérifier que/si; **to ~ sth against** collationner qch avec [*original document*]; vérifier qch par rapport à [*recorded data, inventory*]; comparer qch avec [*signature*]; **3** (for health, progress) prendre [*temperature, blood pressure*]; tester [*reflexes*]; examiner [*eyesight*]; **to ~ that/whether** vérifier que/si; **to ~ sb's progress** vérifier les progrès de qn; **4** (inspect) examiner [*watch, map, pocket, wallet*]; **5** (find out) vérifier [*times, details, information*]; **to ~ if** ou **whether** vérifier si; **to ~ the availability of sth** vérifier si qch est disponible; **I need to ~ how cold it is/where the station is** je dois vérifier s'il fait froid/où se trouve la gare; **to ~ with sb that** demander à qn si; **I had to ~ with him that it was OK** j'ai dû lui demander si ça ne posait pas de problèmes; **6** (curb) contrôler [*price rises, inflation*]; freiner [*increase, growth, progress*]; réduire [*abuse, emigration, influence*]; démentir [*rumour*]; déjouer [*plans*]; **7** (restrain, keep in) maîtriser [*emotions*]; retenir [*tears, exclamation*]; **she ~ed an impulse to laugh** elle s'est retenue pour ne pas rire; **8** (stop) arrêter [*person, animal, enemy advance, rebellion*]; **9** (in chess) faire échec à [*player, chesspiece*]; **10** Comput cocher; **11** (in hockey) bloquer [*shot*]; **12** US (for safekeeping) mettre [qch] au vestiaire [*coat*]; mettre [qch] à la consigne [*baggage*]; **13** US (register) enregistrer [*baggage*]; **14** US (tick) = **check off**.
IV *vi* **1** (verify) vérifier (**whether, if** si); **to ~ with sb** demander à qn; **2** (examine) **to ~ for** dépister [*problems, disease, defects*]; chercher [*leaks, flaws, danger signs*]; **3** (register) **to ~ into** arriver à [*hotel*]; **4** US (tally) [*accounts*] être exact; **5** (in poker) passer.
V *v refl* **1** (restrain) **to ~ oneself** se retenir; **2** (inspect) **to ~ oneself in the mirror** se regarder dans la glace.
VI *excl* **1** (in chess) **~!** échec au roi!; **2**○ US (expressing agreement) d'ac○, d'accord.
VII **checked** *pp adj* **1** Tex [*fabric, pattern, garment*] à carreaux; **2** Ling [*vowel, syllable*] entravé.

■ **check in**: ¶ **~ in** (at airport) enregistrer; (at hotel) remplir la fiche (**at** à); US (clock in) pointer (à l'entrée); ¶ **~ [sb/sth] in, ~ in [sb/sth]** **1** Aviat, Tourism enregistrer [*baggage, passengers*]; accueillir [*hotel guest*]; **2** US (for safekeeping) (give) mettre [qch] à la consigne [*baggage*]; mettre [qch] au vestiaire [*coat*]; (take) [*attendant*] prendre [qch] en consigne [*baggage*]; prendre [qch] au vestiaire [*coat*].

■ **check off**: **~ off [sth], ~ [sth] off** cocher [*items, names*].

■ **check on**: **~ on [sb/sth]** **1** (observe) surveiller [*person*]; **to ~ on sb's progress** vérifier les progrès de qn; **2** (investigate) faire une enquête sur [*person*]; vérifier [*information*]; **to ~ on how/whether** voir comment/si.

■ **check out**: ¶ **~ out 1** (leave) partir; **to ~ out of** quitter [*hotel etc*]; **2** (be correct) [*information, story*] être correct; [*figures, details*] correspondre; **3** US (clock out) pointer (à la sortie); **4**○ euph (die) mourir, casser sa pipe○; ¶ **~ out [sth], ~ [sth] out 1** (investigate) vérifier [*information*]; examiner [*package, area, building*]; prendre [*blood pressure*]; se renseigner sur [*club, scheme*]; **2**○ (try) essayer [*place, food*]; **3** US (remove) (from library) emprunter (**from** de); (from cloakroom, left luggage) retirer (**from** de); ¶ **~ [sb] out, ~ out [sb]** **1** (screen) faire une enquête sur [*person*]; **he's been ~ed out** il a fait l'objet d'une enquête; **2** (from hotel) **to ~ out the guests** s'occuper des formalités de départ des clients; **3** US (at supermarket) s'occuper de [*customer*]; **4**○ US (take a look at) regarder, viser○; **~ him out!** vise un peu○!

■ **check over**: ¶ **~ [sth] over** vérifier [*document, wiring, machine*]; ¶ **~ [sb] over** Med faire un examen médical à [*person*].

■ **check through**: **~ [sth] through 1** vérifier [*data, work*]; **2** US Aviat enregistrer [*luggage*]; **I've ~ed her luggage through to Chicago** j'ai enregistré ses bagages pour Chicago.

■ **check up**: ¶ **~ up** vérifier (**that** que); ¶ **~ up [sth]** vérifier [*story*]; contrôler [*accounts*].

■ **check up on**: ¶ **~ up on [sb]** (observe) surveiller [*person*]; (investigate) faire une enquête sur [*person*]; ¶ **~ up on [sth]** vérifier [*story, details*].

checkbook /ˈtʃekbʊk/ *n* US carnet *m* de chèques, chéquier *m*.

checker /ˈtʃekə(r)/ ▶ 1692 I *n* **1** (employee) vérificateur/-trice *m/f*; **2** US (cashier) caissier/-ière *m/f*; **3** US (in fabric) carreau *m*; **4** US (attendant) (in left-luggage) préposé/-e *m/f* à la consigne; (in cloakroom) préposé/-e *m/f* au vestiaire; **5** US Games (piece) pion *m*.
II **checkers** *npl* ▶ 1282 jeu *m* de dames; **to play ~s** jouer aux dames.

checkerboard /ˈtʃekəbɔːd/ *n* US damier *m*.

checkered *adj* US = **chequered**.

check-in /ˈtʃekɪn/ I *n* **1** (also **~ desk**) enregistrement *m*; **2** (procedure) enregistrement *m*.
II *modif* [*point, counter*] d'enregistrement; **~ time** enregistrement *m*.

checking /ˈtʃekɪŋ/ *n* vérification *f*.

checking account *n* US compte *m* courant.

checklist /ˈtʃeklɪst/ *n* liste *f* de contrôle.

checkmate /ˈtʃekmeɪt/ I *n* échec *m* et mat; fig échec *m*.
II *excl* **~!** échec et mat!
III *vtr* faire échec à [*opponent*]; fig battre [qn] à plates coutures○.

check-off /ˈtʃekɒf/ *n* prélèvement *m* des contributions syndicales à la source.

checkout /ˈtʃekaʊt/ I *n* (also **~ counter**) caisse *f*; **on the ~** à la caisse.
II *modif* [*procedure*] de caisse; [*queue*] à la caisse.

checkout assistant, checkout operator ▶ 1692 *n* GB caissier/-ière *m/f*.

checkpoint /ˈtʃekpɔɪnt/ *n* poste *m* de contrôle; **army/police ~** contrôle *m* militaire/de police.

checkroom /ˈtʃekruːm, -rʊm/ *n* US **1** (cloakroom) vestiaire *m*; **2** (for baggage) consigne *f*.

checks and balances *npl* garde-fous *mpl*.

checkup /ˈtʃekʌp/ *n* **1** Med examen *m* médical, bilan *m* de santé; **to go for/have a ~** passer/se faire faire un examen médical; **to give sb a ~** faire un examen médical à qn; **2** Dent visite *f* de routine (chez le dentiste).

cheddar /ˈtʃedə(r)/ *n* cheddar *m* (*fromage*).

cheek /tʃiːk/ **I** *n* **1** (of face) joue *f*; **to dance ~ to ~** danser joue contre joue; **2**○ (buttock) fesse *f*; **3** (impudence) culot○ *f*; **to have the ~ to do** avoir le culot○ de faire; **what a ~!** quel culot○!; **she's got a (bit of a) ~** elle a un sacré○ culot○.
II *vtr*○ GB être insolent envers [*person*].
IDIOMS to turn the other ~ tendre l'autre joue.

cheekbone /ˈtʃiːkbəʊn/ *n* pommette *f*.

cheekily /ˈtʃiːkɪlɪ/ *adv* [*ask, say*] effrontément; [*arranged, perched*] crânement.

cheekiness /ˈtʃiːkɪnɪs/ *n* insolence *f* (**to, with** envers).

cheek: **~piece** *n* Equit montant *m* de bride; **~ pouch** *n* Zool abajoue *f*.

cheeky /ˈtʃiːkɪ/ *adj* **1** (impudent) [*person*] effronté, insolent; [*question*] impoli; **2** (pert) [*outfit, grin*] espiègle, coquin.

cheep /tʃiːp/ **I** *n* piaulement *m*.
II *vi* piauler.

cheer /ˈtʃɪə(r)/ **I** *n* **1** (shout of joy, praise) acclamation *f*; **to give a ~** pousser une acclamation or un hourra; **to get a big ~** être vigoureusement acclamé; **there were ~s when** il y a eu des acclamations quand; **to give three ~s for** faire un ban à; **three ~s!** un ban!, hourra!; **2** (happiness) réjouissance *f*, liesse† *f*; **be of good ~**‡! prenez espoir or courage!
II cheers *excl* **1** (toast) à la vôtre○!; (to close friend) à la tienne○!; **2**○ GB (thanks) merci!; **3**○ GB (goodbye) salut!
III *vtr* **1** (applaud) acclamer, applaudir [*person, team*]; **to be loudly ~ed** être accueilli par de vives acclamations; **2** (hearten) réjouir, remonter le moral à [*person*].
IV *vi* applaudir, lancer des acclamations; **to ~ for** acclamer, applaudir.
■ **cheer on**: **~ on [sb], ~ [sb] on** encourager [qn] (par des acclamations) [*person, team*].
■ **cheer up**: ¶ **~ up** reprendre courage, se ressaisir; **~ up!** courage!; ¶ **~ up [sb], ~ [sb] up** remonter le moral à [*person*]; ¶ **~ up [sth], ~ [sth] up** égayer [*room*].

cheerful /ˈtʃɪəfl/ *adj* [*person, smile, mood, music*] joyeux/-euse; [*news, prospect*] réconfortant, réjouissant; [*fire*] réconfortant; [*remark, tone*] enjoué; [*colour, room, curtains*] gai; [*belief, conviction, optimism*] inébranlable; **to be ~ about** se réjouir de.

cheerfully /ˈtʃɪəfəlɪ/ *adv* **1** (joyfully) joyeusement; **2** (blithely) [*admit, confess, declare*] allégrement.

cheerfulness /ˈtʃɪəflnɪs/ *n* gaieté *f*.

cheerily /ˈtʃɪərɪlɪ/ *adv* joyeusement, gaiement.

cheering /ˈtʃɪərɪŋ/ **I** *n* ¢ acclamations *fpl*.
II *adj* **1** [*message, news, words*] réconfortant, réjouissant; **2 ~ crowds** des foules en délire.

cheerio○ /ˌtʃɪərɪˈəʊ/ *excl* **1** (goodbye) salut○; **2** (when drinking) à la vôtre○; (to close friend) à la tienne○.

cheerleader /ˈtʃɪəliːdə(r)/ *n* majorette *f* (*qui encourage une équipe sportive sur le terrain*).

cheerless /ˈtʃɪəlɪs/ *adj* [*room, place, landscape*] triste, morne; [*outlook, prospect*] sombre.

cheery /ˈtʃɪərɪ/ *adj* joyeux/-euse, gai.

cheese /tʃiːz/ **I** *n* (substance, variety) fromage *m*.
II *modif* [*sandwich, soufflé*] au fromage.
IDIOMS to be a big ~○ être un gros bonnet (**in** dans le domaine de); **they are as different as chalk and ~** c'est le jour et la nuit; **say ~!** (for photo) souriez!
■ **cheese off**○: **~ [sb] off, ~ off [sb]** faire suer○; **to be ~d off with** en avoir marre○ de.

cheese: **~board** *n* (object) plateau *m* à fromage; (selection) plateau *m* de fromages; **~burger** *n* hamburger *m* au fromage.

cheesecake /ˈtʃiːzkeɪk/ **I** *n* **1** Culin cheesecake *m*; **2**○ US nana○ *f*.
II○ *modif* US [*photo, ad*] aiguicheur/-euse.

cheese: **~cloth** *n* étamine *f*; **~ counter** *n* fromagerie *f*, rayon *m* fromagerie; **~paring** *n* économies *fpl* de bouts de chandelle; **~ spread** *n* fromage *m* à tartiner; **~ straw** *n* allumette *f* au fromage; **~ wire** *n* fil *m* à fromage.

cheesy /ˈtʃiːzɪ/ *adj* **1** [*taste, smell*] de fromage; **2** [*grin*] large; **3**○ US (tacky) louche.

cheetah /ˈtʃiːtə/ *n* guépard *m*.

chef /ʃef/ ▶1692 *n* chef *m* cuisinier.

chef-d'œuvre /ʃeˈdɜːvrə/ *n* (*pl* **chefs d'œuvre**) chef-d'œuvre *m*.

Chekhov /ˈtʃekɒf/ *pr n* Tchekhov.

Chelsea bun /ˌtʃelsɪ ˈbʌn/ *n* GB petit pain *m* aux raisins.

chemical /ˈkemɪkl/ **I** *n* produit *m* chimique.
II *adj* [*process, reaction, industry, substance, formula*] chimique; [*equipment, experiment*] de chimie.

chemical: **~ engineer** ▶1692 *n* ingénieur *m* chimiste; **~ engineering** *n* génie *m* chimique.

chemically /ˈkemɪklɪ/ *adv* (all contexts) chimiquement.

chemical: **~ warfare** *n* guerre *f* chimique; **~ waste** *n* déchets *mpl* chimiques; **~ weapon** *n* arme *f* chimique.

chemise /ʃəˈmiːz/ *n* **1** (dress) robe-combinaison *f*; **2** Hist (undergarment) chemise *f*.

chemist /ˈkemɪst/ ▶1692, 1692 *n* **1** GB (person) pharmacien/-ienne *m/f*; **~'s (shop)** pharmacie *f*; **2** (scientist) chimiste *mf*.

chemistry /ˈkemɪstrɪ/ *n* **1** (science, subject) chimie *f*; **2** (structure, properties) propriétés *fpl* chimiques; **3** fig (rapport) affinités *fpl*; **sexual ~** attirance *f* sexuelle.

chemistry set *n* coffret *m* de jeune chimiste.

chemotherapy /ˌkiːməʊˈθerəpɪ/ *n* chimiothérapie *f*; **a course of ~** un traitement de chimiothérapie.

chenille /ʃəˈniːl/ *n* Tex chenille *f*.

cheque GB, **check** US /tʃek/ *n* chèque *m*; **by ~** par chèque; **to make out** ou **write a ~ for £20** faire un chèque de 20 livres sterling; **to cash a ~** encaisser un chèque; **to stop a ~** faire opposition à un chèque.
IDIOMS to give sb a blank ~ fig donner carte blanche à qn.

cheque: **~book** GB, **checkbook** US *n* chéquier *m*, carnet *m* de chèques; **~book journalism** *n* péj journalisme *m* à sensation (*payant à prix d'or des exclusivités*); **~ card** *n* carte *f* de garantie bancaire.

chequer GB, **checker** US /ˈtʃekə(r)/ *n* **1** Games pion *m*; **2** (square) carreau *m*; (pattern of squares) damier *m*.

chequered GB, **checkered** US /ˈtʃekəd/ *adj* **1** (with pattern of squares) à damiers; **2** fig [*career, history*] en dents de scie.

chequered flag *n* Sport drapeau *m* à damiers.

chequers GB, **checkers** US /ˈtʃekəz/ ▶1282 *n* (+ *v sg*) dames *fpl*.

cheque stub *n* talon *m* de chèque.

Cher ▶1163 *pr n* Cher *m*; **in/to the ~** dans le Cher.

cherish /ˈtʃerɪʃ/ *vtr* **1** (nurture) caresser [*hope, ambition*]; chérir [*memory, idea*]; **her most ~ed ambition** son ambition la plus chère; **2**† (treasure, love) chérir [*person*].

Chernobyl /tʃɜˈnəʊbl, *also* tʃeəˈnɒbl/ ▶1818 *pr n* Tchernobyl.

cheroot /ʃəˈruːt/ *n* cigare *m*.

cherry /ˈtʃerɪ/ **I** *n* **1** (fruit) cerise *f*; **2** (tree, wood) cerisier *m*; **3** (colour) rouge *m* cerise.
II *adj* (also **~-red**) rouge cerise *inv*.
IDIOMS life is not a bowl of cherries la vie n'est pas rose; **to get the first bite of the ~** avoir priorité; **to get two bites at the ~** pouvoir retenter sa chance; **to lose one's ~**○ perdre sa virginité.

cherry: **~ blossom** *n* ¢ fleurs *fpl* de cerisier; **~ bomb** *n* US pétard *m*; **~ brandy** *n* cherry *m*; **~ laurel** *n* laurier *m* cerise; **~ orchard** *n* cerisaie *f*.

cherry-pick /ˈtʃerɪpɪk/ *vtr* sélectionner.

cherry-picker /ˈtʃerɪpɪkə(r)/ *n* (machine) nacelle *f* élévatrice; (person) cueilleur/-euse *m/f* de cerises.

cherrypie /ˌtʃerɪˈpaɪ/ *n* **1** (flower) héliotrope *m* du Pérou; **2** (tart) tarte *f* aux cerises.

cherry: **~ plum** *n* prunier *m*, myrobolan *m*; **~ stone** *n* US Zool clam *m*; **~ tomato** *n* tomate *f* cerise; **~ tree** *n* cerisier *m*.

cherub /ˈtʃerəb/ *n* **1** Relig, Art chérubin *m*; **2** (pretty child) angelot *m*.

cherubic /tʃɪˈruːbɪk/ *adj* [*face, smile*] de chérubin; [*child*] angélique.

chervil /ˈtʃɜːvɪl/ *n* cerfeuil *m*.

Cheshire /ˈtʃeʃə(r)/ ▶1624 *pr n* Cheshire *m*.

chess /tʃes/ ▶1282 *n* échecs *mpl*; **a game of ~** une partie d'échecs.

chess: **~board** *n* échiquier *m*; **~man, ~piece** *n* pièce *f* (de jeu d'échecs); **~player** *n* joueur/-euse *m/f* d'échecs; **~ set** *n* jeu *m* d'échecs.

chest /tʃest/ **I** *n* **1** Anat poitrine *f*; **2** (container) (furniture) coffre *m*; (for packing) caisse *f*; **3** Fin (fund) caisse *f*.
II *modif* Med [*pains*] de poitrine; [*infection, specialist*] des voies respiratoires; [*X-ray*] des poumons.
IDIOMS to get something off one's ~○ vider son sac○; **to hold** or **keep one's cards close to one's ~** ne pas jouer cartes sur table.

chest cold ▶1354 *n* rhume *m* (*accompagné de toux*).

chesterfield /ˈtʃestəfiːld/ *n* canapé *m*.

chest: **~ expander** *n* extenseur *m*; **~ freezer** *n* congélateur *m* coffre; **~ measurement** ▶1703 *n* tour *m* de poitrine.

chestnut /ˈtʃesnʌt/ **I** *n* **1** (also **~ tree**) (horse) marronnier *m* (d'Inde); (sweet) châtaignier *m*; **2** (wood) châtaignier *m*; **3** (nut) (edible) marron *m*, châtaigne *f*; (conker) marron *m* d'Inde; **4** (horse) alezan *m*; **5** fig (joke) **an old ~** une plaisanterie éculée.
II *modif* [*cream, puree*] de marrons; [*stuffing*] aux marrons.
III *adj* [*hair*] châtain; **a ~ horse** un (cheval) alezan.

chest of drawers *n* commode *f*.

chesty○ /ˈtʃestɪ/ *adj* [*person*] fragile des bronches; [*cough*] de poitrine.

cheval glass /ʃəˈvæl glɑːs/ *n* psyché *f*.

chevron /ˈʃevrən/ **I** *n* chevron *m*.
II *modif* [*pattern, paving*] en chevrons.

chew /tʃuː/ **I** *n* **1** (act) mâchement *m*; **2** (sweet) bonbon *m*; **3** (of tobacco) chique *f*.
II *vtr* **1** [*person*] mâcher [*food, chewing gum*]; ronger [*fingernails*]; mordiller [*pencil etc*]; **to ~ tobacco** chiquer; **to ~ one's lip** se mordiller les lèvres; **to ~ a hole in sth** faire un trou dans qch (en rongeant); **2** [*animal*] ronger [*bone*]; mordiller [*carpet*].
III *vi* mâcher.
IDIOMS to bite off more than one can ~ s'exagérer son talent or ses capacités; **to ~ the fat**○ tailler une bavette○.
■ **chew on**: **~ on [sth]** mâcher [*food*]; ronger [*bone*]; fig○ cogiter sur○ [*problem*].
■ **chew out**○: **~ [sb] out**○ US passer un savon à○.
■ **chew over**○: **~ over [sth], ~ [sth] over**○ cogiter sur○ [*problem*].
■ **chew up**: **~ up [sth], ~ [sth] up** (bien) mâcher [*food*].

chewable /ˈtʃuːəbl/ *adj* [*tablet*] à croquer.

chew: **~ing gum** *n* chewing-gum *m*; **~ing tobacco** *n* tabac *m* à chiquer.

chewy /ˈtʃuːɪ/ *adj* difficile à mâcher; **a ~ toffee** un caramel mou.
chiaroscuro /kɪˌɑːrəˈskʊərəʊ/ **I** *n* clair-obscur *m*.
II *adj* [*effect*] de clair-obscur; [*lighting*] en clair-obscur.
chiasma /kaɪˈæzmə/ *n* (*pl* **-mata**) Anat chiasma *m*.
chiasmus /kaɪˈæzməs/ *n* Literat chiasme *m*.
chic /ʃiːk/ **I** *n* chic *m*; **to have ~** avoir du chic.
II *adj* chic *inv*.
chicanery /ʃɪˈkeməri/ *n* chicane *f*.
Chicano /tʃɪˈkɑːnəʊ/ *n* chicano *mf* (*citoyen américain d'origine mexicaine*).
chichi○ /ˈʃiːʃiː/ *adj* chochotte○.
chick /tʃɪk/ *n* **1** (fledgling) oisillon *m*; (of fowl) poussin *m*; **2**○ (young woman) nana○ *f*, gonzesse◑ *f*.
chickadee /ˈtʃɪkədiː/ *n* US mésange *f*.
chicken /ˈtʃɪkɪn/ **I** *n* **1** Agric, Zool (fowl) poulet *m*, poule *f*; **to keep ~s** élever des poules; **2** Culin (also **~ meat**) poulet *m*; **3**○ (coward) trouillard/-e○ *m/f*, poule *f* mouillée; **4** (game) **to play ~** jouer au premier qui se dégonfle○.
II *modif* [*wing, salad, stock*] de poulet; [*sandwich, soup*] au poulet.
III○ *adj* trouillard○, froussard○.
IDIOMS **it's a ~ and egg situation** c'est l'histoire de l'œuf et de la poule; **to count one's ~s (before they are hatched)** vendre la peau de l'ours avant de l'avoir tué; **he/she is no spring ~**○ il/elle n'est plus de la première jeunesse.
■ **chicken out**○ se dégonfler○; **he ~ed out of his dental appointment** il s'est dégonflé○ et il n'est pas allé chez le dentiste.
chicken: **~ breast** *n* filet *m* de poulet; **~ casserole** *n* poulet *m* à la cocotte; **~ curry** *n* poulet *m* au curry; **~ drumstick** *n* pilon *m*; **~ farmer** ▶**1692** *n* éleveur *m* de volailles; **~ farming** *n* élevage *m* de volailles.
chicken feed *n* ¢ **1** Agric nourriture *f* pour volaille; **2**○ (paltry sum) bagatelle *f*, somme *f* dérisoire; **it's ~** c'est une bagatelle.
chicken: **~-fried steak** *n* US steak *m* pané; **~-hearted** *adj* peureux/-euse; **~ livers** *npl* foies *mpl* de volaille; **~ noodle soup** *n* soupe *f* de poulet au vermicelle; **~ pox** ▶**1354** *n* varicelle *f*; **~ run** *n* basse-cour *f*.
chickenshit◑ /ˈtʃɪkɪnʃɪt/ US péj **I** *n* **1** (coward) trouillard/-e○ *m/f*, poule *f* mouillée; **2** (petty details) tracasseries *fpl*.
II *adj* **1** (cowardly) trouillard; **2** (worthless, petty) merdique◑.
chicken: **~ thigh** *n* cuisse *f* de poulet; **~ wire** *n* grillage *m* (à mailles fines).
chick: **~pea** *n* pois *m* chiche; **~weed** *n* mouron *m* blanc, mouron *m* des oiseaux.
chicory /ˈtʃɪkəri/ **I** *n* **1** (vegetable) endive *f*; **2** (in coffee) chicorée *f*.
II *modif* [*soup, salad*] aux endives.
chide† /tʃaɪd/ *vtr* réprimander (**for** pour; **for doing** pour avoir fait).
chief /tʃiːf/ **I** *n* **1** (leader) gen chef *m*; **party ~** Pol dirigeant/-e *m/f* de parti; **defence ~s** Pol responsables *mpl* de la défense; **2**○ (boss) chef○ *m*, patron○ *m*.
II *modif* **1** (primary) [*reason*] principal; **2** (highest in rank) [*editor*] en chef.
III in chief *adv phr* (chiefly) notamment, surtout.
IV -in-chief (*dans composés*) en chef; **commander-in-~** commandant en chef.
IDIOMS **too many ~s and not enough indians** trop de têtes et pas assez de bras.
chief: **~ accountant** *n* chef comptable *m*; **~ administrator** *n* administrateur/-trice *m/f* principal/-e; **~ assistant** *n* premier/-ière *m/f* adjoint/-e; **~ constable** *n* GB ≈ directeur *m* de police; **~ education officer** *n* ≈ recteur/-trice *m/f* d'académie; **~ engineer** *n* ingénieur *m* en chef.
chief executive *n* **1** Admin, Comm directeur *m* général; **2** US Pol Chef *m* de l'Exécutif (*le Président des États-Unis*).
chief: **~ executive officer**, **CEO** *n* directeur *m* général; **~ inspector** *n* gen inspecteur/-trice *m/f* principal/-e; GB (of police) inspecteur *m* de police divisionnaire; **~ justice** *n* US Président *m* de la Cour Suprême; GB Président *m* de la Cour Supérieure de Justice.
chiefly /ˈtʃiːfli/ *adv* notamment, surtout.
chief: **~ master sergeant** ▶**1612** *n* US major *m*; **~ of police** *n* ≈ préfet *m* de police; **Chief of Staff**, **C of S** ▶**1612** *n* Mil chef *m* d'état-major; (of White House) secrétaire *m* général; **~ of state** *n* US chef *m* d'État; **~ petty officer**, **CPO** ▶**1612** *n* premier maître *m*; **Chief Rabbi** *n* Grand Rabbin *m*; **~ secretary (to the Treasury)** *n* GB ministre *m* délégué au budget; **~ superintendent** *n* GB ≈ commissaire *m* divisionnaire.
chieftain /ˈtʃiːftən/ *n* chef *m* (*de clan* ou *tribu*).
chief: **~ technician** ▶**1612** *n* sergent *m*; **~ warrant officer**, **c.w.o** ▶**1612** *n* adjudant-chef *m*; **~ whip** *n* GB Pol député *m* principal parmi les whips (*députés chargés d'assurer la discipline de vote*).
chiffchaff /ˈtʃɪftʃæf/ *n* pouillot *m* véloce.
chiffon /ˈʃɪfɒn, US ʃɪˈfɒn/ **I** *n* mousseline *f*.
II *modif* [*dress, scarf*] en mousseline.
chiffonnier /ˈʃɪfɒnɪə(r), US ʃɪˈfɒnɪər/ *n* (sideboard) chiffonnier *m*.
chignon /ˈʃiːnjɒn/ *n* chignon *m*.
chihuahua /tʃɪˈwɑːwɑː/ *n* chihuahua *m*.
chilblain /ˈtʃɪlbleɪn/ *n* engelure *f*.
child /tʃaɪld/ **I** *n* (*pl* **children**) **1** (non-adult) enfant *mf*; **when I was a ~** quand j'étais enfant; **to be with ~**‡ porter un enfant (en son sein)†; **2** fig (product) **a ~ of the 60s/of nature** un enfant des années soixante/de la nature.
II *modif* **~ star/prodigy** enfant *mf* vedette/prodige.
IDIOMS **it's ~'s play** c'est un jeu d'enfant; **the ~ is father to the man** Prov l'enfant fait l'homme Prov.
child abuse *n* gen mauvais traitements *mpl* infligés à un enfant; (sexual) sévices *mpl* sexuels exercés sur l'enfant.
childbearing /ˈtʃaɪldbeərɪŋ/ *n* maternité *f*; **of ~ age** en âge d'avoir des enfants, nubile; **constant ~** grossesses *fpl* répétées; **to have ~ hips** hum avoir les hanches larges.
child benefit *n* GB ≈ allocations *fpl* familiales.
childbirth /ˈtʃaɪldbɜːθ/ *n* accouchement *m*; **to die in ~** mourir en couches.
child: **~care** *n* (nurseries etc) structures *fpl* d'accueil pour les enfants d'âge préscolaire; (bringing up children) éducation *f* des enfants; **~care facilities** *npl* crèche *f*; **~ guidance** *n* GB Soc Admin assistance *f* socio-psychologique de l'enfance.
childhood /ˈtʃaɪldhʊd/ **I** *n* enfance *f*; **in (his) early ~** dans sa prime enfance; **in (his) late ~** tard dans son enfance.
II *modif* [*home, friend, memory*] d'enfance; [*illness*] infantile; [*event, experience*] survenu dans mon/son etc enfance.
childish /ˈtʃaɪldɪʃ/ *adj* **1** (of child) d'enfant; **2** péj (immature) puéril.
childishly /ˈtsaɪldɪʃlɪ/ *adv* [*behave, say*] de façon puérile; [*simple, naïve*] comme un enfant.
childishness /ˈtʃaɪldɪʃnɪs/ *n* puérilité *f*.
child labour *n* travail *m* des enfants.
childless /ˈtʃaɪldlɪs/ *adj* sans enfants.
childlike /ˈtʃaɪldlaɪk/ *adj* enfantin.
child: **~minder** ▶**1692** *n* GB nourrice *f*; **~ molester** *n* agresseur *m* d'enfants; **~-proof** *adj* [*container, lock*] de sécurité (*à l'épreuve des enfants*); **~ protection register** *n* GB Soc Admin *registre des enfants qui selon les services sociaux risquent de subir des violences*.
children /ˈtʃɪldrən/ *pl* ▶ **child**.
children's home *n* maison *f* d'enfants.
Chile /ˈtʃɪlɪ/ ▶**1131** *pr n* Chili *m*.
Chilean /ˈtʃɪlɪən/ ▶**1486** **I** *n* Chilien/-ienne *m/f*.
II *adj* [*wine, customs, refugee etc*] chilien/-ienne.
Chile: **~ nitre** *n* salpêtre *m* du Chili; **~ pine** *n* araucaria *m*; **~ saltpetre** = **Chile nitre**.
chill /tʃɪl/ **I** *n* **1** (coldness) fraîcheur *f*; **there is a ~ in the air** le fond de l'air est frais; **2** (illness) coup *m* de froid; **to catch a ~** prendre or attraper un coup de froid; **3** fig frisson *m*; **to send a ~ through sb** ou **down sb's spine** donner des frissons à qn; **4** (in foundry) coquille *f*.
II *adj* **1** [*wind, air*] frais/fraîche; **2** fig (causing fear) [*reminder, words*] brutal.
III *vtr* **1** Culin (make cool) mettre [qch] à refroidir [*dessert, soup*]; rafraîchir [*wine*]; (keep cool) réfrigérer [*meat, fish*]; **2** [*wind*] refroidir [*air, atmosphere*]; faire frissonner [*person*]; **3** fig (cause to fear) faire frissonner [*person*]; **to ~ sb's** ou **the blood** glacer le sang à qn; **4** Tech refroidir [*casting*].
IV *vi* [*dessert*] refroidir; [*wine*] rafraîchir.
V chilled *pp adj* (cool) [*wine*] bien frais; [*soup*] froid; (refrigerated) [*food*] réfrigéré.
■ **chill out**○ décompresser○; **~ out!** laisse faire!
chill cabinet *n* GB rayonnage *m* réfrigéré.
chill casting *n* Tech **1** (process) coulée *f* en coquille; **2** (object) pièce *f* coulée en coquille.
chiller○ /ˈtʃɪlə(r)/ *n* Cin film *m* d'épouvante.
chilli, **chili** /ˈtʃɪlɪ/ *n* **1** (pod) piment *m* rouge; (powder, substance) chili *m*; **2** (also **~ con carne**) chili *m* con carne.
chilli con carne /ˌtʃɪlɪ kɒn ˈkɑːnɪ/ *n* chili *m* con carne.
chilliness = **chillness**.
chilling /ˈtʃɪlɪŋ/ **I** *n* Tech trempe *f*.
II *adj* [*story, thought, look*] effrayant.
chillingly /ˈtʃɪlɪŋlɪ/ *adv* [*speak, remind*] d'une manière terrifiante; [*obvious*] effroyablement.
chilli: **~ pepper** *n* piment *m* rouge; **~ powder** *n* chili *m* (en poudre); **~ sauce** *n* sauce *f* au chili.
chillness /ˈtʃɪlnɪs/ *n* **1** lit (of wind, air, house) fraîcheur *f*; **2** fig (of welcome, words, look) froideur *f*.
chilly /ˈtʃɪlɪ/ *adj* **1** lit froid; **it's ~ today** il fait froid aujourd'hui; **2** fig [*look, response, smile*] froid.
chime /tʃaɪm/ **I** *n* (of clock, church bell) carillon *m*; **the ~s of the clock** (sound) le carillon de l'horloge; (set of bells) carillon *m*.
II chimes *npl* (doorbell, mobile) carillon *m*.
III *vi* **1** (strike) sonner; (play a tune) carillonner; **the clock ~d three** la pendule a sonné trois heures; **2 to ~ with** [*viewpoint, experience*] s'accorder avec.
■ **chime in** interrompre.
chimera /kaɪˈmɪərə/ *n* littér (beast, idea) chimère *f*.
chimeric /kaɪˈmerɪk/ *adj* **1** gen chimérique; **2** Biol [*gene, DNA*] chimère.
chimney /ˈtʃɪmnɪ/ *n* (*pl* **-neys**) cheminée *f*; (on oil lamp) verre *m* (de lampe); (in mountaineering) cheminée *f*; **in the ~ corner** au coin du feu.
chimney: **~breast** *n* manteau *m* de cheminée; **~ corner** *n* coin *m* du feu; **~ fire** *n* incendie *m* de cheminée; **~piece** *n* tablette *f* de cheminée; **~pot** *n* mitron *m* (*sur cheminée*); **~stack** *n* cheminée *f*; **~ sweep** ▶**1692** *n* ramoneur *m*.
chimp○ /tʃɪmp/ *n* = **chimpanzee**.
chimpanzee /ˌtʃɪmpənˈziː, ˌtʃɪmpænˈziː/ *n* chimpanzé *m*; **female ~** chimpanzé *m* femelle.
chin /tʃɪn/ **I** *n* menton *m*; **double ~** double menton; **weak ~** menton fuyant.

II *vtr* (*p prés etc* **-nn-**) **1** (gym) **to ~ the bar** mettre le menton au niveau de la barre; **2**○ **to ~ sb** frapper qn au menton.
III *vi*○ (*p prés etc* **-nn-**) US bavarder.
IDIOMS **to keep one's ~ up**○ tenir le coup○; **~ up!** tiens bon!; **to take it on the ~**○ encaisser○ bravement.

china /'tʃaɪnə/ **I** *n* ¢ porcelaine *f*; **a piece of ~** une porcelaine; **rare ~** porcelaines *fpl* rares.
II *modif* [*cup, plate*] en porcelaine.
IDIOMS **like a bull in a ~ shop** comme un éléphant dans un magasin de porcelaine.

China /'tʃaɪnə/ **▶ 1131** *pr n* Chine *f*; **red ~** Chine communiste.
IDIOMS **not for all the tea in ~** pour rien au monde.

china: **~ cabinet** *n* vitrine *f* (*meuble*); **~ clay** *n* kaolin *m*; **~ closet** *n* US = **china cabinet, china cupboard**; **~ cupboard** *n* placard *m* à vaisselle.

China: **~man** *n* ‡ ou péj Chinois *m*; **~ Sea** *pr n* mer *f* de Chine; **~ tea** *n* thé *m* de Chine; **~town** *n* le quartier chinois.

chinaware /'tʃaɪnəweə(r)/ *n* objets *mpl* en porcelaine.

chinchilla /tʃɪn'tʃɪlə/ *n* (animal, fur) chinchilla *m*; **a ~ (coat)** un manteau de chinchilla.

chin-chin /ˌtʃɪn'tʃɪn/ *excl* tchin-tchin!

chine /tʃaɪn/ *n* **1** (cut of meat) échine *f*; **2** (ridge) crête *f*; **3** Naut bouchain *m*.

Chinese /tʃaɪ'niːz/ **▶ 1486**, **1402** **I** *n* **1** (native, inhabitant) Chinois/-oise *m/f*; **2** (language) chinois *m*; **to speak ~** parler le chinois; **in ~** en chinois; **to translate into ~** traduire en chinois; **3**○ GB (meal) repas *m* chinois.
II *adj* chinois/-oise; **to eat ~** manger chinois.

Chinese: **~ cabbage** *n* US = **Chinese leaves**; **~ gooseberry** *n* kiwi *m*.

Chinese lantern *n* **1** (light) lanterne *f* vénitienne; **2** Bot physalis *m*.

Chinese: **~ leaves** *npl* GB chou *m* de Chine; **~ puzzle** *n* lit, fig casse-tête *m* *inv* chinois.

chink /tʃɪŋk/ **I** *n* **1** (slit) (in wall) fente *f*; (in door, curtain) entrebâillement *m*; **2** (sound) tintement *m*.
II *vtr* faire tinter [*glasses, coins*].
III *vi* [*glasses, coins*] tinter.
IDIOMS **it's the ~ in his armour** c'est le défaut de sa cuirasse.

Chink○ /tʃɪŋk/ *n* injur Chinetoque○ *mf* offensive.

chinless /'tʃɪnlɪs/ *adj* **1** (weak-chinned) au menton fuyant; **2**○ GB (weak) mollasson○/-onne; **a ~ wonder** un abruti○ *m* du beau monde.

chinoiserie /ʃiːn'wɑːzərɪ/ *n* ¢ (style) chinoiserie *f*; (objects) chinoiseries *fpl*.

chinos /'tʃiːnəʊs/ *npl* pantalon *m* kaki.

chinstrap /'tʃɪnstræp/ *n* jugulaire *f*.

chintz /tʃɪnts/ *n* chintz *m*.

chintzy /'tʃɪntsɪ/ *adj* **1** [*room, curtains*] en chintz; [*furniture*] recouvert de chintz; **2** [*style*] (rustic) GB rustique; (fussy) chichi *inv*; (gaudy) US toc *inv*; **3** US (mean) radin○.

chin-up /'tʃɪnʌp/ *n* traction *f* (à la barre).

chin-wag /'tʃɪnwæg/ **I** *n* causette○ *f*; **to have a ~** faire la causette.
II *vi* (*p prés etc* **-gg-**) faire la causette.

chip /tʃɪp/ **I** *n* **1** (fragment) gen fragment *m* (**of** de); (of wood) copeau *m*; (of glass) éclat *m*; **2** (mark, flaw) (in wood, china, glass) ébréchure *f*; **this cup has a ~ in it** cette tasse est ébréchée; **3** GB Culin (fried potato) frite *f*; **4** US (potato crisp) chips *f*; **a packet of ~s** un paquet de chips; **5** Comput puce *f* (électronique); **6** Sport (in golf) coup *m* d'approche; (in football) chandelle *f*; **to play a ~** (in golf) faire une approche; **7** Games (in gambling) plaque *f*; (smaller) jeton *m*; **to cash in one's ~s** lit encaisser ses plaques; fig ramasser ses billes○.
II *vtr* (*p prés etc* **-pp-**) **1** (damage) ébrécher [*glass, cup, plate*]; écorner [*precious stone*]; écailler [*paint*]; **to ~ a tooth/bone** se casser une dent/un os; **a ~ped cup** une tasse ébréchée; **2** (carve) tailler [*wood, stone*]; **3** Culin couper [*potatoes*].
III *vi* (*p prés etc* **-pp-**) **1** (damage) [*plate, glass*] s'ébrécher; [*paint, varnish*] s'écailler; [*tooth*] se casser; [*precious stone*] s'écorner; **2** Sport (in golf) faire une approche.
IDIOMS **to have a ~ on one's shoulder** être amer/-ère; **he's got a ~ on his shoulder about not having gone to university** il n'est jamais allé à l'université et il en veut à tout le monde à cause de cela; **to be a ~ off the old block** être bien le fils de son père/la fille de sa mère; **when the ~s are down** dans les moments difficiles; **he's had his ~s**○ GB il est cuit○.
■ **chip away**: ¶ **~ away** [*paint, plaster*] s'écailler; **to ~ away at** (carve) tailler [*marble, rock*]; fig affaiblir [qch] progressivement [*power, authority*]; miner [*confidence*]; ¶ **~ away [sth], ~ [sth] away** enlever [qch] petit à petit [*paint, plaster*].
■ **chip in** GB○ **1** (in conversation) gen interrompre; (officiously) mettre son grain de sel○; **2** (contribute money) donner un peu d'argent; **she ~ped in with £5** elle a mis cinq livres de sa poche.
■ **chip off**: ¶ **~ off** [*paint, plaster*] s'écailler; ¶ **~ off [sth], ~ [sth] off** écailler [*plaster*] (**from** de); **he ~ped a piece off** il a enlevé un éclat; **to ~ a piece off a tooth** ébrécher une dent.

chip: **~ basket** *n* panier *m* à frites; **~board** *n* aggloméré *m*.

chipmunk /'tʃɪpmʌŋk/ *n* tamia *m*.

chipolata /ˌtʃɪpə'lɑːtə/ *n* GB chipolata *f*.

chip: **~ pan** *n* friteuse *f*; **~ped potatoes** *npl* frites *fpl*.

Chippendale /'tʃɪpəndeɪl/ *adj* chippendale *inv*.

chipper○† /'tʃɪpə(r)/ *adj* en pleine forme.

chippings /'tʃɪpɪŋz/ *npl* gravillons *mpl*; **'loose ~!'** 'danger: gravillons!'

chippy○ /'tʃɪpɪ/ *n* GB friterie *f*.

chip shop **▶ 1692** *n* marchand *m* de frites.

chiromancer /'kaɪərəʊmænsə(r)/ **▶ 1692** *n* chiromancien/-ienne *m/f*.

chiromancy /'kaɪərəʊmænsɪ/ *n* chiromancie *f*.

chiropodist /kɪ'rɒpədɪst/ **▶ 1692** *n* pédicure *mf*.

chiropody /kɪ'rɒpədɪ/ *n* podologie *f*.

chiropractic /ˌkaɪərəʊ'præktɪk/ *n* chiropraxie *f*.

chiropractor /'kaɪərəʊpræktə(r)/ **▶ 1692** *n* chiropraticien/-ienne *m/f*, chiropracteur *m*.

chirp /tʃɜːp/ **I** *n* pépiement *m*; **to give a ~** lancer un pépiement.
II *vi* [*bird*] pépier.

chirpily /tʃɜːpɪlɪ/ *adv* avec une gaieté pétillante.

chirpy○ /'tʃɜːpɪ/ *adj* pétillant.

chirrup /'tʃɪrəp/ **I** *n* (of bird) pépiement *m*.
II *vi* [*cricket, grasshopper*] chanter; [*bird*] pépier.

chisel /'tʃɪzl/ **I** *n* ciseau *m*.
II *vtr* **1** (*p prés etc* **-ll-**, US **-l-**) (shape) tailler au ciseau; (finely) ciseler; **to ~ a figure out of a piece of wood** tailler une silhouette dans un morceau de bois; [*sculptor*] sculpter une silhouette dans un morceau de bois; **~led features** fig traits burinés; **finely ~led features** fig traits finement ciselés; **2**○ US rouler○ (**out of** de).
■ **chisel in**○ US **~ in on sb** tomber sur qn○.

chiseler○ /'tʃɪzlə(r)/ *n* US (cheat) escroc *m*.

chit /tʃɪt/ *n* **1** GB (voucher) bon *m*; (bill, note, emo) note *f*; **2**○ péj **a ~ of a girl** une gamine.

chitchat○ /'tʃɪttʃæt/ *n* bavardage *m*; **to spend one's time in idle ~** perdre son temps en bavardages.

chitterlings /'tʃɪtəlɪŋz/ *npl* tripes *fpl* (*de porc*).

chivalric /'ʃɪvəlrɪk/ *adj* littér chevaleresque.

chivalrous /'ʃɪvəlrəs/ *adj* **1** (heroic) [*deeds, conduct*] chevaleresque; **2** (polite) galant.

chivalrously /'ʃɪvəlrəslɪ/ *adv* galamment.

chivalry /'ʃɪvəlrɪ/ *n* **1** ¢ (qualities, system of values) chevalerie *f*; **the age of ~** l'âge de la chevalerie; **the age of ~ is not dead** hum la galanterie n'est pas morte; **2** (courtesy) galanterie *f*; **3** (knights) la chevalerie.

chive /tʃaɪv/ **I** *n* (*gén pl*) ciboulette *f*.
II *modif* [*dressing*] à la ciboulette.

chivvy○, US **chivy**○ /'tʃɪvɪ/ *vtr* harceler; **to ~ sb into doing** harceler qn jusqu'à ce qu'il fasse.

chlamydia /klə'mɪdɪə/ *n* Med chlamydia *f*.

chloral /'klɔːrəl/ *n* chloral *m*.

chlorate /'klɔːreɪt/ *n* chlorate *m*.

chloric /'klɔːrɪk/ *adj* chlorique.

chloric acid *n* acide *m* chlorique.

chloride /'klɔːraɪd/ *n* chlorure *m*.

chlorinate /'klɔːrɪneɪt/ *vtr* **1** Chem chlorer; **2** (disinfect) javelliser [*water, swimming pool*].

chlorination /ˌklɔːrɪ'neɪʃn/ *n* **1** Chem chloration *f*; **2** (disinfection) javellisation *f*.

chlorine /'klɔːriːn/ *n* chlore *m*.

chlorofluorocarbon, CFC /ˌklɔːrəˌflʊəʊkɑː'bən/ *n* chlorofluorocarbone *m*, CFC *m*.

chloroform /'klɒrəfɔːm, US 'klɔːr-/ **I** *n* chloroforme *m*.
II *vtr* chloroformer.

chlorophyll /'klɒrəfɪl/ **I** *n* chlorophylle *f*.
II *modif* [*colouring, toothpaste*] à la chlorophylle.

ChM *n* GB (*abrév* = **Master of surgery**) (qualification) diplôme *m* supérieur de chirurgie.

choc○ /tʃɒk/ *n* GB chocolat *m*.

chocaholic○ /ˌtʃɒkə'hɒlɪk/ *n* grand/-e mangeur/-euse *m/f* de chocolat.

choc-ice /'tsɒkaɪs/ *n* GB esquimau *m*.

chock /tʃɒk/ **I** *n* (for boat, plane, vehicle) cale *f*; **to put a ~ under sth** mettre une cale sous qch; **to put sth on ~s** mettre qch sur cales; **~s away!** enlevez les cales!
II *vtr* caler [*wheel*]; Naut mettre en cale.

chock-a-block /ˌtʃɒkə'blɒk/ *adj* (*après v*) plein à craquer (**with** de).

chock-full /ˌtʃɒk'fʊl/ *adj* (*après v*) archiplein (**of** de).

chocolate /'tʃɒklət/ **▶ 1104** **I** *n* **1** (substance) chocolat *m*; **cooking ~** chocolat *m* de ménage; **plain** ou **dark ~** chocolat *m* noir; **milk ~** chocolat *m* au lait; **a bar of ~** une tablette de chocolat; **2** (sweet) chocolat *m*; **3** (drink) chocolat *m*; **drinking ~** chocolat *m*; **hot ~** chocolat *m* chaud; **4** (colour) chocolat *inv*; **dark ~** tête-de-nègre *inv*.
II *modif* [*eggs, sweets*] en chocolat; [*biscuit, cake, eclair, ice cream, sauce*] au chocolat.

chocolate: **~ chip cookie** *n* cookie *m* (*biscuit avec pépites de chocolat*); **~-coated**, **~-covered** *adj* enrobé de chocolat.

choice /tʃɔɪs/ **I** *n* **1** (selection) choix *m*; **to make a ~** faire un choix, choisir; **it was my ~ to do** c'est moi qui ai choisi de faire; **it's your ~** c'est à toi de choisir; **2** ¢ (right to select) choix *m*; **to have the ~** avoir le choix; **to have a free ~** être libre de choisir; **3** (option) choix *m* (**between, of** entre); **you have a ~ of three colours** tu as le choix entre trois couleurs; **to have no ~ but to do** se voir contraint de faire; **you have two ~s open to you** vous avez deux possibilités; **4** (range of options) choix *m*; **a wide ~** un grand choix; **a narrow ~** un choix limité; **to be spoilt for ~** avoir l'embarras du choix; **5** ¢ (preference) choix *m*; **I approve of your ~** j'approuve ton choix; **a car of my ~** une voiture de mon

choix; **out of** ou **from ~** par choix; **to be the people's ~** être choisi par le peuple; **my first ~ would be a Rolls Royce** en premier je choisirais une Rolls Royce.
II *adj* **1** (quality) [*cut, example, steak*] de choix; **2** (well-chosen) [*phrase, word*] bien choisi; **~ language** euph langage de charretier.
IDIOMS **you pays your money and you takes your ~**○ hum c'est à vous de voir.

choir /ˈkwaɪə(r)/ *n* **1** Mus (of church, school) chorale *f*; (professional) chœur *m*; (of boys at cathedral) maîtrise *f*; **to be** ou **sing in the church/school ~** faire partie de la chorale de l'église/de l'école; **2** Archit chœur *m*.

choir: **~boy** *n* petit chanteur *m*, jeune choriste *m*; **~ festival** *n* festival *m* de chant choral; **~girl** *n* jeune choriste *f*; **~master** *n* gen chef *m* des chœurs; (in church) maître *m* de chapelle; **~ organ** *n* positif *m*; **~ practice** *n* répétition *f* de la chorale; **~ school** *n* GB maîtrise *f*, manécanterie *f*; **~ screen** *n* grille *f* de chœur; **~stall** *n* stalle *f*.

choke /tʃəʊk/ I *n* **1** Aut starter *m*; **to pull out/use the ~** tirer/mettre le starter; **2** (sound) étouffement *m*; **3** (of emotion) **with a ~ in one's voice** la voix étranglée.
II *vtr* **1** (throttle) étrangler [*person*]; **to ~ sb to death** étrangler qn; **2** (impede breathing) [*fumes, smoke*] étouffer; **3** (render speechless) **~d with** [*voice*] étranglé par [*emotion*]; **4** (block) = **choke up**.
III *vi* **1** (be unable to breathe) s'étouffer; **to ~ on a fish bone/on a drink** s'étouffer avec une arête/en buvant; **to ~ to death** mourir étouffé; **2** (become speechless) **to ~ with** étouffer de [*rage, emotion*]; **3**○ US (tense up) [*athlete, player*] craquer○.
IV **choked**○ *pp adj* **1** (angry) furieux/-ieuse (**about** au sujet de); **2** (upset) affecté (**over, about** par).
■ **choke back**: **~ back [sth]** étouffer [*cough, sob*]; **to ~ back one's tears** retenir ses larmes; **to ~ back one's anger** ravaler sa colère.
■ **choke off**: **~ off [sth]** stopper [*buying, lending, growth, supplies*]; faire taire [*opposition, protest*].
■ **choke up**: **~ [sth] up, ~ up [sth]** (block) boucher [*drain, road, town centre*]; [*weeds*] étouffer [*garden*]; [*plants*] envahir [*pond*]; **the town/street was ~d up with traffic** la ville/rue était embouteillée.

choker /ˈtʃəʊkə(r)/ *n* collier *m* ras de cou; **a pearl ~** un collier de perles ras de cou.

choking /ˈtʃəʊkɪŋ/ I *n* étouffement *m*.
II *adj* [*gas, fumes*] asphyxiant; [*sensation*] d'étouffement; [*sound*] de suffocation.

cholera /ˈkɒlərə/ ▶ 1354 I *n* choléra *m*.
II *modif* [*victim, epidemic*] de choléra; [*vaccination*] contre le choléra.

choleric /ˈkɒlərɪk/ *adj* colérique, coléreux/-euse.

cholesterol /kəˈlestərɒl/ *n* cholestérol *m*.

cholesterol: **~ count, ~ level** *n* taux *m* de cholestérol; **~ screening** *n* dépistage *m* du cholestérol; **~ test** *n* analyse *f* de sang pour déterminer le taux de cholestérol.

chomp○ /tʃɒmp/ I *vtr* mâcher bruyamment.
II *vi* mâcher bruyamment; **to ~ on sth** ronger qch.

Chomskyan /ˈtʃɒmskɪən/ *adj* chomskyien/-ienne.

choo-choo /ˈtʃuːtʃuː/ *n* lang enfantin teuf-teuf *m* baby talk, train *m*.

choose /tʃuːz/ I *vtr* (*prét* **chose**, *pp* **chosen**) **1** (select) choisir [*book, career, person, option*] (**from** parmi); **to ~ which car/hat one wants** choisir quelle voiture/quel chapeau on veut; **to ~ sb as** choisir qn comme [*adviser, friend, manager*]; élire qn [*leader*]; **we chose him as our representative** nous l'avons choisi comme délégué; **we cannot ~ but do** nous n'avons pas d'autre choix que de faire; **2** (decide) **to ~ to do** décider de faire; **to ~ when/how/whether** décider quand/comment/si.
II *vi* (*prét* **chose**, *pp* **chosen**) **1** (select) choisir (**between** entre; **between doing** entre faire); **there are many models to ~ from** il y a un grand choix de modèles; **there's not much to ~ from** il y a très peu de choix; **there's nothing to ~ between X and Y** il y a très peu de différence entre X et Y; **2** (prefer) vouloir; **whenever you ~** quand tu voudras; **to do as one ~s** faire ce qu'on veut; **to ~ to do** préférer faire; **if you (so) ~** si telle est votre décision.
■ **choose up**○ US: **~ up [sb]** choisir [*team members*].

choosy /ˈtʃuːzɪ/ *adj* difficile (**about** en ce qui concerne); **I can't afford to be ~** je ne peux pas me permettre d'être difficile.

chop /tʃɒp/ I *n* **1** (blow with axe, tool, hand) coup *m*; **to cut sth off with one ~** trancher qch d'un seul coup; **2** Culin côtelette *f*; **pork ~** côtelette *f* de porc; **3**○ GB fig (axe) **to get the ~** [*person*] se faire sacquer○; [*scheme, service, programme*] être supprimé; **he's afraid of the ~** il a peur de se faire sacquer○; **4** (in table tennis) revers *m* coupé.
II **chops**○ *npl* gueule◑ *f*; **a slap across the ~s** une baffe dans la gueule◑; **to lick one's ~s** (at food) se lécher les babines; (at idea) se frotter les mains.
III *vtr* (*p prés etc* **-pp-**) **1** (cut up) couper [*wood, log*]; couper, émincer [*vegetable, meat*]; hacher [*parsley, onion*]; **to ~ sth into cubes/rounds** couper qch en cubes/rondelles; **to ~ sth to pieces** ou **bits** couper qch en morceaux; **to ~ sth finely** hacher qch; **2** fig (cut, reduce) réduire [*service, deficit, subsidy*]; (cut out) couper [*quote, footage*]; **3** Sport (give chopping blow to) frapper [qn] du tranchant de la main [*person*]; couper [*ball*].
IV **chopped** *pp adj* [*parsley, nuts, meat*] haché.
IDIOMS **~ ~**○**!** GB et que ça saute○!; **to ~ and change** [*person*] changer d'avis comme de chemise; [*situation*] évoluer par à-coups.
■ **chop down**: **~ down [sth], ~ [sth] down** abattre.
■ **chop off**: **~ off [sth], ~ [sth] off** couper [*branch, end*]; trancher [*head, hand, finger*].
■ **chop through**: **~ through [sth]** trancher [*bone, cable*]; **to ~ one's way through** se frayer un passage à la hache à travers [*undergrowth, forest*].
■ **chop up**: **~ up [sth], ~ [sth] up** couper [*wood, log*]; émincer [*meat, onion*] (**into** en).

chophouse /ˈtʃɒphaʊs/ *n* grill *m*.

chopped liver○ *n* US **1** Culin foie *m* haché; **2**○ fig **to be ~** compter pour du beurre○; **she's not ~** elle n'est pas mal; **to make ~ of sb** (beat up) mettre qn en bouilli○.

chopper /ˈtʃɒpə(r)/ I *n* **1** (axe) hache *f*; (for kitchen) hachoir *m*; **2**○ (helicopter) hélico○ *m*; **3** Elec interrupteur *m* périodique; **4**○ (motorbike) chopper○ *m*; **5**● GB (penis) pine● *f*, pénis *m*.
II **choppers**○ *npl* (real) dents *fpl*; (false) râtelier○ *m*, dentier *m*; **a set of ~s** un râtelier○.

Chopper® /ˈtʃɒpə(r)/ *n* GB vélo *m* à guidon haut.

chopping block *n* billot *m*.
IDIOMS **to be on the ~** [*business, service*] être menacé de suppression; **to put one's head on the ~** prendre des risques.

chop: **~ping board** *n* planche *f* à découper; **~ping knife** *n* couteau *m* de cuisine.

choppy /ˈtʃɒpɪ/ *adj* [*sea, water*] agité; [*wind*] instable.

chopstick /ˈtʃɒpstɪk/ *n* baguette *f* (chinoise).

chop suey /tʃɒpˈsuːɪ/ *n* Culin chop suey *m*.

choral /ˈkɔːrəl/ *adj* choral.

chorale /kəˈrɑːl/ *n* **1** (hymn, tune) choral *m*; **2** US (choir) chorale *f*, chœur *m*.

choral: **~ society** *n* chorale *f*; **~ symphony** *n* symphonie *f* pour chœur.

chord /kɔːd/ *n* **1** Mus accord *m*; **2** fig (emotional response) **it struck a ~ in** ou **with him/his listeners** cela a trouvé un écho en lui/chez ses auditeurs; **to strike** ou **touch the right ~** toucher la corde sensible; **3** Math corde *f*; **4** (of harp) corde *f*.

chore /tʃɔː(r)/ *n* **1** (routine task) tâche *f*; **the (household) ~s** les tâches ménagères; **to do the/one's ~s** faire le/son ménage; **2** (unpleasant task) corvée *f*; **shopping is such a ~!** les courses sont une vraie corvée!; **it's a real ~ having to...** c'est une vraie corvée de devoir...

choreograph /ˈkɒrɪəgrɑːf, -græf, US -græf/ *vtr* lit chorégraphier; fig orchestrer.

choreographer /ˌkɒrɪˈɒgrəfə(r)/ ▶ 1692 *n* chorégraphe *mf*.

choreographic /ˌkɒrɪəˈgræfɪk/ *adj* chorégraphique.

choreography /ˌkɒrɪˈɒgrəfɪ/ *n* chorégraphie *f*.

chorister /ˈkɒrɪstə(r), US ˈkɔːr-/ *n* choriste *mf*.

chortle /ˈtʃɔːtl/ I *n* gloussement *m*.
II *vi* glousser, rire; **to ~ at** ou **about** ou **over sth** rire de qch; **to ~ with pleasure** glousser de plaisir.

chortling /ˈtʃɔːtlɪŋ/ *n* gloussements *mpl*.

chorus /ˈkɔːrəs/ I *n* **1** (people) (supporting singers) chœur *m*; (dancers, actors) troupe *f*; (of town, village etc) chorale *f*; **2** (piece of music) chœur *m*; **3** (refrain) refrain *m*; (in jazz) chorus *m*; **to join in the ~** (one person) reprendre le refrain; (several people) reprendre le refrain en chœur; **4** (of birdsong, yells) concert *m*; **the usual ~ of protest** l'habituelle tempête de protestations; **in ~** en chœur; **5** Theat chœur *m*.
II *vtr* (utter in unison) crier [qch] à l'unisson.

chorus: **~ girl** *n* danseuse *f* de revue; **~ line** *n* troupe *f* de danseurs (*de comédie musicale*).

chose /tʃəʊz/ *pret* ▶ **choose**.

chosen /ˈtʃəʊzn/ I *pp* ▶ **choose**.
II *adj* élu; **the ~ few** les privilégiés; **I was not one of the ~ few** iron je ne faisais pas partie des heureux élus; **the Chosen One** Bible l'Élu; **the Chosen People** Bible le peuple élu.

chough /tʃʌf/ *n* crave *m*.

choux pastry /ˌʃuː ˈpeɪstrɪ/ *n* pâte *f* à choux.

chow /tʃaʊ/ *n* **1**†○ (food) rata○ *m*; **2** (dog) chow-chow *m*.

chowder /ˈtʃaʊdə(r)/ *n*: *soupe épaisse à base de fruits de mer et de légumes*.

chow mein /ˌtʃaʊ ˈmeɪn/ *n* ¢ nouilles *fpl* frites.

chrism /ˈkrɪzəm/ *n* chrême *m*.

Christ /kraɪst/ I *n* le Christ, Jésus-Christ.
II◑ *excl* bon Dieu (de bon Dieu)○, bon sang (de bon sang or de bonsoir)○.

Christadelphian /ˌkrɪstəˈdelfɪən/ *n, adj* christadelphe (*mf*).

Christ child *n* **the ~** l'enfant *m* Jésus.

christen /ˈkrɪsn/ *vtr* **1** Relig, Naut baptiser; fig (name, nickname) baptiser, nommer [*person, pet, place*]; **I was ~ed John, but everybody calls me Jack** mon nom de baptême est John, mais tout le monde m'appelle Jack; **they ~ed the dog Max** ils ont baptisé le chien du nom de Max; **2** hum (use for the first time) inaugurer [*glasses, car, dance hall*]; (soil for the first time) baptiser [*tablecloth, dress*].

Christendom /ˈkrɪsndəm/ *n* chrétienté *f*.

christening /ˈkrɪsnɪŋ/ *n* baptême *m*.

Christian /ˈkrɪstʃən/ I *n* chrétien/-ienne *m/f*; **to become a ~** se faire chrétien.
II *adj* **1** Relig chrétien/-ienne; **early ~** paléochrétien/-ienne; **2** [*attitude*] charitable; **a ~ burial** un enterrement convenable.

Christian: **~ Brother** *n* frère *m* des Écoles chrétiennes; **~ era** *n* ère *f* chrétienne.

christiania /ˌkrɪstɪˈɑːnə/ *n* christiania *m*.

Christianity /ˌkrɪstɪˈænətɪ/ *n* **1** (religion) christianisme *m*; **2** (fact of being a Christian) fait *m* d'être chrétien, qualité *f* de chrétien.

Christianize /ˈkrɪstʃənaɪz/ *vtr* christianiser.

Christian: **~ name** *n* nom *m* de baptême; **~ Science** *n* science *f* chrétienne; **~ Scientist** *n* scientiste *mf* chrétien/-ienne.

Christlike /ˈkraɪstlaɪk/ *adj* évocateur/-trice du Christ; **he was ~ in his humility** il évoquait le Christ par son humilité.

Christmas /ˈkrɪsməs/ **I** *n* (day) Noël *m*; (period) période *f* de Noël; **at ~** à Noël; **over ~** pendant la période de Noël; **to spend ~ at home/away** passer Noël chez soi/partir pour Noël; **Merry ~, Happy ~!** Joyeux Noël!
II *modif* [*cake, card, holiday, party, present, shopping*] de Noël.

Christmas: **~ bonus** *n* prime *f* de fin d'année; **~ box** *n* GB étrennes *fpl*; **~ cactus** *n* épiphyllum *m*; **~ carol** *n* (song) chant *m* de Noël; Relig cantique *m* de Noël; **~ cracker** *n* GB diablotin *m*; **~ day** *n* jour *m* de Noël; **~ dinner** *n* repas *m* de Noël; **~ eve** *n* veille *f* de Noël; **~ pudding** *n* GB pudding *m* de Noël (*dessert à base de fruits secs et d'épices*); **~ rose** *n* rose *f* de Noël; **~ stocking** *n* bas *m* de Noël (*contenant de petits cadeaux*).

Christmassy○ /ˈkrɪsməsɪ/ *adj* typique de Noël; **I'm not feeling very ~** je ne suis pas (vraiment) d'humeur à fêter Noël.

Christmastime /ˈkrɪsməstaɪm/ *n* période *f* de Noël.

Christmas tree *n* sapin *m* de Noël.
IDIOMS **to be lit up like a ~**◑ (drunk) être rond comme une queue de pelle◑.

Christopher /ˈkrɪstəfə(r)/ *pr n* Christophe.

chromatic /krəʊˈmætɪk/ *adj* Phys, Art, Mus chromatique.

chromatic printing *n* Print impression *f* polychrome.

chromatics /krəˈmætɪks/ *n* (+ *v sg*) science *f* des couleurs.

chromatic scale *n* Mus échelle *f* or gamme *f* chromatique.

chromatography /ˌkrəʊməˈtɒgrəfɪ/ *n* chromatographie *f*.

chromatology /ˌkrəʊməˈtɒlədʒɪ/ *n* = **chromatics**.

chrome /krəʊm/ **I** *n* chrome *m*.
II *modif* [*article*] chromé, en chrome.

chrome: **~ steel** *n* acier *m* chromé, chromé *m*; **~ yellow** *n* jaune *m* de chrome.

chromium /ˈkrəʊmɪəm/ *n* chrome *m*.

chromium: **~-plated** *adj* chromé, en chrome; **~ plating** *n* (process) chromage *m*; (coating) couche *f* de chrome.

chromosome /ˈkrəʊməsəʊm/ *n* chromosome *m*; **~ map** carte *f* chromosomique.

chronic /ˈkrɒnɪk/ *adj* **1** Med [*illness, state*] chronique; **2** fig [*liar*] invétéré; [*problem, situation*] chronique; [*shortage*] chronique, permanent; **3**○ GB (bad) nul/nulle○.

chronically /ˈkrɒnɪklɪ/ *adv* **1** Med **to be ~ ill** souffrir d'une maladie chronique; **the ~ sick** ceux qui sont atteints d'une affection chronique; **2** fig [*jealous, stupid, underfunded, overloaded*] extrêmement; **the country is ~ short of...** le pays souffre d'un manque chronique de...

chronicle /ˈkrɒnɪkl/ **I** *n* (tale) chronique *f*; **a ~ of misfortunes/misunderstandings** fig une suite de mésaventures/malentendus.
II Chronicles *npl* Bible (also **the Book of Chronicles**) le Livre des Chroniques.
III *vtr* [*person*] écrire une chronique de; [*book*] être une chronique de [*event, period*]; **to ~ events** [*historian*] faire la chronique des événements; [*diarist*] noter les événements (au jour le jour); **to ~ the growth of feminism/the life of Marx** retracer l'évolution du féminisme/de la vie de Marx.

chronicler /ˈkrɒnɪklə(r)/ **▶ 1692** *n* chroniqueur/-euse *m/f*.

chronological /ˌkrɒnəˈlɒdʒɪkl/ *adj* chronologique.

chronologically /ˌkrɒnəˈlɒdʒɪklɪ/ *adv* chronologiquement, par ordre chronologique.

chronology /krəˈnɒlədʒɪ/ *n* chronologie *f*.

chronometer /krəˈnɒmɪtə(r)/ *n* chronomètre *m*.

chrysalis /ˈkrɪsəlɪs/ *n* chrysalide *f*.

chrysanth○ /krɪˈsænθ/ *n* = **chrysanthemum**.

chrysanthemum /krɪˈsænθəməm/ *n* chrysanthème *m*.

chub /tʃʌb/ *n* chevenne *m*.

chubby /ˈtʃʌbɪ/ *adj* [*child, finger*] potelé; [*cheek*] rebondi; [*face, cherub*] joufflu; [*adult*] rondelet/-ette.

chubby-cheeked, **chubby-faced** *adj* joufflu, aux joues rebondies.

chuck /tʃʌk/ **I** *n* **1** (stroke) caresse *f* (sous le menton); **2** Culin (also **~ steak**) macreuse *f*; **3** Tech mandrin *m*.
II *vtr* **1**○ (throw) balancer○, jeter [*ball, book*] (to à); **~ me the newspaper** balance-moi le journal; **2**○ (get rid of) larguer○ [*boyfriend, girlfriend*]; **3** (stroke) **to ~ sb under the chin** caresser qn sous le menton; **4**○ (give up) = **chuck in**.
■ **chuck away**○: **~ [sth] away, ~ away [sth] 1** (discard) balancer○, jeter [*food, papers*]; **2** (squander) gâcher [*chance, life*]; gaspiller [*money*].
■ **chuck down**○: **it's ~ing it down** il pleut à verse.
■ **chuck in**○: **~ [sth] in, ~ in [sth]** laisser tomber [*job, studies*].
■ **chuck out**○: ¶ **~ [sth] out, ~ out [sth]** balancer○, jeter [*rubbish, clothes*]; ¶ **~ [sb] out, ~ out [sb]** vider, éjecter; **to be ~ed out of** se faire vider de [*college, club*].
■ **chuck up**◑: ¶ **~ up** dégueuler◑, vomir; ¶ **~ [sth] up, ~ up [sth]** dégueuler◑, vomir [*meal, food*].

chuck: **~er-out**○ *n* (*pl* **chuckers-out**) GB videur *m*; **~ing-out time**○ *n* GB heure *f* de fermeture (*d'un pub, club etc*); **~ key** *n* Tech clé *f* de mandrin.

chuckle /ˈtʃʌkl/ **I** *n* gloussement *m*, petit rire *m*.
II *vi* [*person*] glousser, rire; **to ~ at** ou **over sth** rire de qch; **to ~ with pleasure** glousser or rire de plaisir; **to ~ to oneself** rire sous cape.

chuck wagon *n* US cantine *f* ambulante (*dans un ranch*).

chuffed○ /tʃʌft/ *adj* GB vachement○ or super○ content (**about, at, with** de).

chug /tʃʌg/ **I** *n* halètement *m*, teuf-teuf *m*.
II *vi* (*p prés etc* **-gg-**) **1** (make noise) [*train*] haleter, faire teuf-teuf; **the train ~ged into/out of the station** le train est entré en gare/est sorti de la gare en haletant; **2** US○ = **chug-a-lug**.
■ **chug along** [*train, car*] avancer en haletant or en faisant teuf-teuf; **the project is ~ging along nicely** fig le projet suit son cours.

chug-a-lug○ /ˈtʃʌgəlʌg/ *vtr* US descendre○ [qch] d'un (seul) trait [*beer*].

chukka /ˈtʃʌkə/ *n* Sport temps *m* de jeu (*au polo*).

chum○† /tʃʌm/ *n* copain/copine○ *m/f*, pote○ *m*; **watch it, ~!** fais gaffe, mon vieux○!
■ **chum up**○† copiner○, faire équipe (**with** avec).

chummy○† /ˈtʃʌmɪ/ *adj* [*person*] sociable; pej familier/-ière; **to be ~ with sb** être intime or très lié avec qn; **they're very ~** ils sont très copain copain○.

chump /tʃʌmp/ *n* **1**○† idiot/-e *m/f*; **2** Culin selle *f* d'agneau; **3** (log) tronçon *m* (de bois).
IDIOMS **to be off one's ~**○† GB avoir perdu la boule○.

chump chop *n* tranche *f* de selle.

chunk /tʃʌŋk/ *n* **1** (piece) (of meat, fruit) morceau *m*; (of wood) tronçon *m*; (of bread) quignon *m*; **pineapple ~s** ananas *m* en morceaux; **2** (portion) (of population, text, day) partie *f*; **a fair ~** une bonne partie.

chunkily /ˈtʃʌŋkɪlɪ/ *adv* **~ built** solidement bâti, costaud○.

chunky /ˈtʃʌŋkɪ/ *adj* **1** [*soup, stew*] riche en morceaux; **2** (bulky) [*sweater, jewellery*] gros/grosse; [*person*] costaud○, trapu.

Chunnel○ /ˈtʃʌnl/ *n* GB tunnel *m* sous la Manche.

church /tʃɜːtʃ/ **I** *n* (*pl* **~es**) **1** (building) (Catholic, Anglican) Église *f*; (Protestant) temple *m*; **2** (also **Church**) (religious body) Église *f*; **the Orthodox ~** l'Église orthodoxe; **the Church of England** l'Église d'Angleterre; **to go into the ~** entrer dans les ordres; **3** (service) (in general) office *m*; (Catholic) messe *f*; **to go to ~** (in general) aller à l'office; (Catholic) aller à la messe.
II *modif* [*bell, choir, clock, steeple*] d'église; [*land*] ecclésiastique; [*fête*] paroissial; [*wedding*] religieux/-ieuse.
IDIOMS **as poor as a ~ mouse** pauvre comme Job.

church: **Church Army** *pr n* Relig *organisation anglicane joignant le zèle évangélique à l'action charitable et sociale*; **Church Commissioners** *npl* Relig *conseil de clercs et de laïcs chargé d'administrer les biens de l'Église d'Angleterre*; **Church Fathers** *npl* Relig Pères *mpl* de l'Église; **~goer** *n* Relig pratiquant/-e *m/f*; **~going** *adj* pratiquant; **~ hall** *n* salle *f* paroissiale.

Churchillian /tʃəˈtʃɪlɪən/ *adj* churchillien/-ienne.

church leader *n* Relig chef *m* d'une Église.

churchman /ˈtʃɜːtʃmən/ *n* (*pl* **-men**) **1** (clergyman) homme *m* d'église; **2** (churchgoer) pratiquant *m*.

church: **~ school** *n* école *f* religieuse; **~ service** *n* gen office *m*; (Catholic) messe *f*; **~warden** *n* marguillier *m*; **~woman** *n* pratiquante *f*.

churchy○ /ˈtʃɜːtʃɪ/ *adj* péj bigot.

churchyard /ˈtʃɜːtʃjɑːd/ *n* cimetière *m* (*autour d'une église*).

churl† /tʃɜːl/ *n* goujat† *m*.

churlish /ˈtʃɜːlɪʃ/ *adj* (surly) revêche; (rude) grossier/-ière.

churlishly /ˈtʃɜːlɪʃlɪ/ *adv* (impolitely) grossièrement; (surlily) d'un ton bourru.

churlishness /ˈtʃɜːlɪʃnɪs/ *n* (impoliteness) impolitesse *f*; (surliness) attitude *f* désagréable.

churn /tʃɜːn/ **I** *n* **1** (for butter) baratte *f*; **2** GB (container) (small) bidon *m*; (large) tank *m* à lait.
II *vtr* **1 to ~ butter** baratter; **2** fig faire tourbillonner [*water, air*].
III *vi* [*ideas*] tourbillonner; [*engine*] tourner sur place; **my stomach was ~ing** (with nausea) mon cœur se soulevait; (with nerves) j'avais l'estomac noué.
■ **churn out**: **~ [sth] out, ~ out [sth]** débiter [*speeches*]; pondre [qch] en série [*plays, novels, ideas, publicity, legislation*]; produire [qch] en série [*goods*].
■ **churn up**: **~ [sth] up, ~ up [sth]** faire des remous dans [*water*]; labourer [*earth*].

chute /ʃuːt/ *n* **1** (slide) (in plane, swimming pool, playground) toboggan *m*; **2** (channel) (for rubbish) vide-ordures *m inv*; (for coal) trémie *f*; **3** Sport (for toboggan) piste *f* de toboggan; **4**○ (parachute) pépin○ *m*, parachute *m*; **5** Geog rapide *m*.

chutney /ˈtʃʌtnɪ/ *n* condiment *m* aigre-doux; **tomato ~** condiment à la tomate.

chutzpa, **chutzpah** /ˈhʊtspə/ *n* culot○ *m*, toupet *m*.

chyme /kaɪm/ *n* chyme *m*.

CI *n*: *abrév écrite* ▶ **Channel Islands**.

CIA *n* (*abrév* = **Central Intelligence Agency**) CIA *f*.

ciao /tʃaʊ/ *excl* tchao.

cicada /sɪ'kɑːdə, US -'keɪdə/ *n* cigale *f*.

cicatrix /'sɪkətrɪks/ *n* (*pl* **-trices**) spéc cicatrice *f*.

Cicero /'sɪsərəʊ/ *pr n* Cicéron.

cicerone /ˌtʃɪtʃə'rəʊnɪ/ *n* littér cicérone *m*.

CID *n* GB (*abrév* = **Criminal Investigation Department**) police *f* criminelle.

cider /'saɪdə(r)/ *n* cidre *m*.

cider: ~ **apple** *n* pomme *f* à cidre; ~ **press** *n* pressoir *m* à cidre or à pommes; ~ **vinegar** *n* vinaigre *m* de cidre.

CIF *n* (*abrév* = **cost, insurance, and freight**) CAF.

cigar /sɪ'gɑː(r)/ **I** *n* cigare *m*.
II *modif* [*box, case*] à cigares; [*smoker*] de cigares.

cigar cutter *n* coupe-cigare *m*.

cigarette /ˌsɪgə'ret, US 'sɪgərət/ **I** *n* cigarette *f*.
II *modif* [*ash, smoke*] de cigarette; [*case, paper*] à cigarettes; [*smoker*] de cigarettes.

cigarette: ~ **butt**, ~ **end** *n* mégot *m*; ~ **card** *n*: *image offerte dans les paquets de cigarettes*; ~ **holder** *n* fume-cigarette *m inv*; ~ **lighter** *n* (portable) briquet *m*; (in car) allume-cigares *m inv*; ~ **packet** GB, ~ **pack** US *n* paquet *m* de cigarettes.

cigar: ~ **holder** *n* fume-cigare *m inv*; **~-shaped** *adj* oblong/-longue.

ciggie○, **ciggy**○ /'sɪgɪ/ *n* clope○ *f*.

cilium /'sɪlɪəm/ *n* (*pl* **cilia**) cil *m*.

CIM *n* (*abrév* = **computer-integrated manufacturing**) FIO *f*.

C-in-C /ˌsiː ɪn 'siː/ *n* (*abrév* = **Commander in Chief**) commandant *m* en chef.

cinch○ /sɪntʃ/ **I** *n* **1** (easy task) **sth/doing sth was a ~** qch/faire qch a été facile comme bonjour; **it's a ~** c'est du gâteau○; **2** (certainty) **to be a ~ to do** être sûr de faire; **that horse is a ~ to win** ce cheval va gagner la course à coup sûr; **3** US Equit sangle *f* (de selle).
II *vtr* Equit US sangler [*horse*]; attacher [qch] par une sangle [*saddle*].

cinder /'sɪndə(r)/ *n* (glowing) braise *f*; (ash) cendre *f*; (in volcano) scorie *f*; **to burn sth to a ~** réduire qch en cendres.

cinder block *n* US parpaing *m*.

Cinderella /ˌsɪndə'relə/ *pr n* Cendrillon.

cinder track *n* (piste *f*) cendrée *f*.

cineaste /'sɪnɪæst/ *n* cinéphile *mf*.

cine: **~camera** *n* caméra *f* (d'amateur); ~ **club** *n* ciné-club *m*; ~ **film** *n* pellicule *f* cinématographique.

cinema /'sɪnəmɑː, 'sɪnəmə/ *n* (all contexts) cinéma *m*; **to go to the ~** aller au cinéma; **to be interested in (the) ~** s'intéresser au cinéma; **a wonderful piece of ~** un merveilleux moment de cinéma.

cinema: ~ **complex** *n* complexe *m* multisalles; **~goer** *n* (regular) cinéphile *mf*, amateur/-trice *m/f* de cinéma; (spectator) spectateur/-trice *m/f*.

Cinemascope® /'sɪnəməskəʊp/ *n* Cinémascope® *m*.

cinematic /ˌsɪnə'mætɪk/ *adj* [*technique, work*] cinématographique; [*genius*] du cinéma; [*scene, novel, beauty*] fait pour le cinéma.

cinematographer /ˌsɪnəmə'tɒgrəfə(r)/ **▶ 1692** *n* directeur *m* de la photo, cameraman *m*.

cinematographic /ˌsɪnəˌmætə'græfɪk/ *adj* cinématographique.

cinematography /ˌsɪnəmə'tɒgrəfɪ/ *n* technique *f* cinématographique; **the ~ is superb** le film est merveilleusement photographié.

cinema-vérité /ˌsɪnəmə'verɪteɪ/ *n* cinéma-vérité *m*.

cinerary urn /ˌsɪnərərɪ 'ɜːn/ *n* urne *f* cinéraire.

cinnabar /'sɪnəbɑː(r)/ *n* cinabre *m*.

cinnamon /'sɪnəmən/ **I** *n* **1** Culin cannelle *f*; **2** (tree) cannelier *m*; **3 ▶ 1104** (colour) (couleur *f*) cannelle *f*.
II *adj* **1** Culin [*cake, cookie*] à la cannelle; [*stick*] de cannelle; **2** (colour) cannelle *inv*.

cipher /'saɪfə(r)/ **I** *n* **1** (code) chiffre *m*; **in ~** en chiffre, en code; **to write a message in ~** chiffrer or coder un message; **2** (nonentity) pantin *m*; **3** Math, Comput zéro *m*; **4** (Arabic numeral) chiffre *m* (arabe); **5** (monogram) chiffre *m*.
II *vtr* chiffrer, coder.

circa /'sɜːkə/ *prep* environ.

circadian /sɜː'keɪdɪən/ *adj* circadien/-ienne.

circle /'sɜːkl/ **I** *n* **1** (shape) cercle *m*; (of spectators, trees, chairs, flowers) cercle *m*; (of fabric, paper, colour) rond *m*; **to form a ~** [*objects*] former un cercle; [*people*] faire un cercle (**around** autour de); **to sit in a ~** s'asseoir en cercle; **to move/swim in ~s** tourner/nager en rond; **to go round in ~s** lit, fig tourner en rond; **2** (group) cercle *m*, groupe *m* (**of** de); **to be in sb's ~** faire partie du cercle de qn; **his ~ of friends** le cercle de ses amis; **in business/theatrical ~s** dans les milieux d'affaires/du théâtre; **literary ~s** le monde littéraire; **to move in fashionable ~s** fréquenter le beau monde; **3** Theat balcon *m*; **to sit in the ~** être au balcon.
II *vtr* **1** (move round) [*plane, helicopter*] tourner autour de [*airport, tower*]; [*satellite*] graviter autour de [*planet*]; [*person, animal, vehicle*] faire le tour de [*square, building*]; tourner autour de [*person, animal*]; **they ~d each other** ils se tournaient autour; **2** (encircle) encercler [*word, mistake, answer*].
III *vi* [*helicopter, plane, vulture*] décrire des cercles (**above, over** au-dessus de); [*predator, vehicle, horseman*] tourner en rond (**around** autour de); **as we walked along, the helicopter ~d overhead** on marchait, et l'hélicoptère décrivait des cercles au-dessus de nous.
IDIOMS **to come full ~** [*person*] boucler la boucle; [*situation*] revenir à son point de départ; **the wheel has come** ou **turned full ~** la boucle est bouclée; **to have ~s under one's eyes** avoir les yeux cernés; **to square the ~** résoudre (le problème de) la quadrature du cercle.

circlet /'sɜːklɪt/ *n* **1** (wreath) bandeau *m*; **2** (circle) petit cercle *m*.

circuit /'sɜːkɪt/ **I** *n* **1** (race track) (for vehicles) circuit *m*; (for athletes) piste *f*; **2** (lap) tour *m*; **to do 15 ~s of the track** faire 15 tours de circuit; **3** (regular round) circuit *m*; **the cabaret/tennis ~** le circuit de boîtes de nuit○/du tennis; **he's well-known on the ~** il est connu dans le circuit; **4** (round trip) circuit *m*; **5** Jur (periodic journey) tournée *f*; **to be on the ~** être en tournée; **6** US Jur (district) circonscription *f* judiciaire; **7** Electron circuit *m*; **to complete/break the ~** fermer/ouvrir le circuit.
II *vtr* faire le circuit de [*course, town*].

circuit: ~ **board** *n* carte *f* de circuit imprimé; ~ **breaker** *n* disjoncteur *m*; ~ **court** *n* Jur tribunal *m* itinérant (*qui siège à divers endroits de sa circonscription*); ~ **diagram** *n* schéma *m* de circuit; ~ **judge ▶ 1692** *n* Jur juge *m* itinérant.

circuitous /sɜː'kjuːɪtəs/ *adj* [*route, means, method*] indirect; [*argument*] tortueux/-euse, alambiqué; [*procedure*] compliqué.

circuitously /sɜː'kjuːɪtəslɪ/ *adv* [*proceed*] par des voies détournées; [*argue*] indirectement, de manière compliquée.

circuitry /'sɜːkɪtrɪ/ *n* ensemble *m* de circuits.

circuit training *n* série *f* d'exercices physiques (*pour l'entraînement sportif*).

circular /'sɜːkjʊlə(r)/ **I** *n* (newsletter) circulaire *f*; (advertisement) prospectus *m*.
II *adj* **1** gen [*object*] rond; [*argument, route*] circulaire; **2** Biol [*DNA*] circulaire.

circularity /ˌsɜːkjʊ'lærətɪ/ *n* circularité *f*.

circular: ~ **letter** *n* circulaire *f*; ~ **saw** *n* scie *f* circulaire.

circulate /'sɜːkjʊleɪt/ **I** *vtr* **1** (spread) (to limited circle) faire circuler; (widely) diffuser [*list, documents, information*] (**to** entre); **the report was ~d to the members** le rapport a été transmis aux membres; **2** GB (inform) mettre [qn] au courant [*members, staff*]; **3** faire circuler [*blood, water etc*].
II *vi* **1** [*water, air, rumour, pamphlet, banknote*] circuler; **2** (at party) **let's ~** on va aller faire connaissance.

circulating decimal *n* fraction *f* périodique.

circulating library *n* **1** (mobile) (in hospitals, schools) bibliothèque *f* (mobile); **2** US (lending library) bibliothèque *f* de prêt.

circulating medium *n* capital *m* de roulement.

circulation /ˌsɜːkjʊ'leɪʃn/ *n* **1** (of blood, air, water, fuel) circulation *f*; **to have good/bad ~** avoir une bonne/mauvaise circulation; **2** (distribution) (of newspaper) tirage *m*; **a ~ of 2 million** un tirage de 2 millions d'exemplaires; **3** (of coins, books) circulation *f*; **in ~** en circulation; **to withdraw from ~** retirer de la circulation; **4** (of document, information) circulation *f*; (to wide public) diffusion *f*; **for ~ to** (on document) à transmettre à; **5** (use) **a word which has entered ~** un mot qui est passé dans l'usage; **6** (social group) **she's back in ~** elle est de nouveau dans le circuit.

circulation area *n* **1** (of newspaper) zone *f* de circulation; **2** (in railway station) salle *f* des pas perdus.

circulation: ~ **department** *n* Journ service *m* de circulation; ~ **figures** *npl* chiffres *mpl* de tirage; ~ **manager** *n* responsable *mf* du service de distribution.

circulatory /ˌsɜːkjʊ'leɪtərɪ, US 'sɜːkjələtɔːrɪ/ *adj* circulatoire; ~ **system** appareil *m* circulatoire.

circumcise /'sɜːkəmsaɪz/ *vtr* circoncire [*boy*]; exciser [*girl*].

circumcision /ˌsɜːkəm'sɪʒn/ *n* (of boy) circoncision *f*; (of girl) excision *f*.

circumference /sə'kʌmfərəns/ *n* circonférence *f*; **to be 4 km in ~** avoir une circonférence de 4 km.

circumflex /'sɜːkəmfleks/ **I** *n* (also ~ **accent**) accent *m* circonflexe (**on, over** sur).
II *adj* circonflexe; **e ~** e accent circonflexe.

circumlocution /ˌsɜːkəmlə'kjuːʃn/ *n* circonlocution *f*, périphrase *f*.

circumlocutory /ˌsɜːkəm'lɒkjʊtərɪ/ *adj* périphrastique.

circumlunar /ˌsɜːkəm'luːnə(r)/ *adj* circumlunaire.

circumnavigate /ˌsɜːkəm'nævɪgeɪt/ *vtr* faire le tour de [*world*]; faire la circumnavigation de [*continent*]; passer [qch] au large [*cape*].

circumnavigation /ˌsɜːkəmˌnævɪ'geɪʃn/ *n* circumnavigation *f*.

circumpolar /ˌsɜːkəm'pəʊlə(r)/ *adj* circumpolaire.

circumscribe /'sɜːkəmskraɪb/ *vtr* **1** gen (define) circonscrire; (limit) limiter; **2** Math circonscrire.

circumspect /'sɜːkəmspekt/ *adj* sout circonspect; **to be ~ about** être circonspect quant à [*likelihood, chance*]; **to be ~ about predicting/making a commitment** ne pas vouloir prédire/s'engager.

circumspection /ˌsɜːkəm'spekʃn/ *n* sout circonspection *f*.

circumspectly /'sɜːkəmspektlɪ/ *adv* sout avec circonspection.

circumstance /'sɜːkəmstəns/ **I** *n* (event)

circonstance *f*; **a strange ~** un événement étrange.

II **circumstances** *npl* **1** (state of affairs) circonstances *fpl*; **in** ou **under the ~s** dans ces circonstances; **under no ~s** en aucun cas; **if ~s permit** si les circonstances le permettent; **due to ~s beyond our control** pour des raisons indépendantes de notre volonté; **2** (conditions of life) situation *f*; **their ~s do not permit them to travel** leurs moyens ne leur permettent pas de voyager; **in easy ~s** dans l'aisance; **in poor ~s** dans la gêne.

circumstantial /ˌsɜːkəmˈstænʃl/ *adj* **1** Jur [*evidence*] indirect; **2** (detailed) circonstancié.

circumstantiate /ˌsɜːkəmˈstænʃɪeɪt/ *vtr* sout corroborer [*statement*]; donner des détails circonstanciés sur [*incident*].

circumvent /ˌsɜːkəmˈvent/ *vtr* sout **1** (avoid) contourner [*law, problem, embargo, sanctions*]; circonvenir [*official*]; **2** (frustrate) déjouer, faire échec à [*plot*]; faire échec à [*adversary*].

circus /ˈsɜːkəs/ **I** *n* (all contexts) cirque *m*.

II *modif* [*tent, performer*] de cirque; **~ atmosphere** ambiance *f* de fête foraine.

cirque /sɜːk/ *n* cirque *m*.

cirrhosis /sɪˈrəʊsɪs/ ▶ **1354** *n* cirrhose *f*.

cirrus /ˈsɪrəs/ *n* (*pl* **cirri**) cirrus *m*.

CIS *n* (*abrév* = **Commonwealth of Independent States**) CEI *f*.

cissy *n, adj* = **sissy**.

Cistercian /sɪˈstɜːʃn/ *n, adj* cistercien/-ienne (*m/f*).

cistern /ˈsɪstən/ *n* (of lavatory) réservoir *m* de chasse d'eau; (in loft or underground) citerne *f*.

citadel /ˈsɪtədəl/ *n* citadelle *f*.

citation /saɪˈteɪʃn/ *n* (all contexts) citation *f*.

cite /saɪt/ *vtr* **1** (quote) citer; (adduce) avancer; **2** Mil (commend) citer (**for** pour); **3** Jur citer; **to be ~d in divorce proceedings** être cité dans une procédure de divorce.

citizen /ˈsɪtɪzn/ *n* **1** (of state) gen citoyen/-enne *m/f*; (when abroad) ressortissant/-e *m/f*; **~ Robespierre** le citoyen Robespierre; **a British ~** un ressortissant britannique; **2** (of town) habitant/-e *m/f*.

citizenry /ˈsɪtɪznrɪ/ *n* communauté *f*, ensemble *m* des habitants.

citizen: **Citizens' Advice Bureau**, **CAB** *n* service *m* bénévole d'assistance sur des problèmes juridiques; **~'s arrest** *n* arrestation *f* par un particulier; **~'s band**, **CB** *n* Radio bande *f* banalisée, bande *f* CB, bande *f* publique, citizen's band *f*.

citizenship /ˈsɪtɪznʃɪp/ **I** *n* nationalité *f*.

II *modif* [*papers*] de naturalisation.

citrate /ˈsaɪtreɪt/ *n* citrate *m*.

citric /ˈsɪtrɪk/ *adj* citrique.

citric acid *n* acide *m* citrique.

citron /ˈsɪtrən/ *n* citron *m*, citrus *m* medica.

citrus /ˈsɪtrəs/ **I** *n* (*pl* **-ruses**) (tree) citrus *m*; (fruit) agrume *m*.

II *adj* [*colour*] acidulé; **~ trees** les citrus *mpl*.

citrus fruit *n* (individual) agrume *m*; (collectively) les agrumes *mpl*.

city /ˈsɪtɪ/ **I** *n* **1** (town) (grande) ville *f*; **the medieval ~** la cité médiévale; **~ streets/people** rues/gens de la ville; **~ life** vie citadine; **2** GB **the City** la City (*centre des affaires à Londres*); **3** (population) ville *f*.

II *modif* [*street, people*] de la ville; [*life*] citadin.

city: **City and Guilds certificate** *n* ≈ certificat *m* d'aptitude professionnelle; **~ centre** GB, **~ center** US *n* centre-ville *m*; **~ college** *n* US université *f* (*financée par la municipalité*); **~ council** *n* conseil *m* municipal; **~ councillor** *n* GB conseiller/-ère *m/f* municipal/-e; **~ councilman**, **~ councilwoman** *n* US = **city councillor**.

city desk *n* Journ **1** US service *m* chargé de la chronique locale; **2** GB service *m* chargé de la chronique financière.

city dweller *n* citadin/-e *m/f*.

city editor *n* Journ **1** US rédacteur/-trice *m/f* chargé/-e de la chronique locale; **2** GB rédacteur/-trice *m/f* chargé/-e de la chronique financière.

city fathers *npl* édiles *mpl*.

city hall *n* US **1** (building) (in large town) hôtel *m* de ville; (in small town) mairie *f*; **2** Admin administration *f* municipale.

IDIOMS **you can't fight ~**○ on ne peut rien faire contre une bureaucratie mesquine.

city: **~ limits** *npl* limites *fpl* de la ville; **~ manager** *n* US personne *f* chargée d'administrer une municipalité; **~ news** *n* GB rubrique *f* financière; **~ planner** ▶ **1692** *n* urbaniste *mf*; **~ planning** *n* urbanisme *m*; **~scape** *n* paysage *m* urbain; **~ slicker**○ *n* citadin/-e *m/f* branché/-e; **~ state** *n* Hist cité *f*; **~ technology college**, **CTC** *n* ≈ collège *m* technique.

civet /ˈsɪvɪt/ *n* Zool civette *f*.

civic /ˈsɪvɪk/ *adj* [*administration, official*] municipal; [*pride, responsibility*] civique.

civic centre GB, **civic center** US *n* centre *m* municipal (culturel et administratif).

civics /ˈsɪvɪks/ *n* (+ *v sg*) instruction *f* civique.

civies *npl* US = **civvies**.

civil /ˈsɪvl/ *adj* **1** (civic, not military) [*affairs, aviation, disorder, wedding*] civil; **2** Jur [*case, court, offence*] civil; [*claim*] au civil; **3** (polite) [*person*] courtois; **it was ~ of him to do that** c'était aimable de sa part de faire cela.

IDIOMS **to keep a ~ tongue in one's head** mesurer ses paroles.

civil: **Civil Aeronautics Board**, **CAB** *n* US administration *f* de l'aviation civile; **Civil Aviation Authority**, **CAA** *n* GB administration *f* de l'aviation civile.

civil defence, **civil defense** US, **CD** **I** *n* défense *f* passive.

II *modif* [*authority, grant, measures, team*] de défense passive.

civil disobedience **I** *n* résistance *f* passive.

II *modif* [*campaign*] de résistance passive.

civil: **~ engineer** ▶ **1692** *n* ingénieur *m* des travaux publics; **~ engineering** *n* génie *m* civil.

civilian /sɪˈvɪlɪən/ **I** *n* civil/-e *m/f*.

II *adj* civil.

civility /sɪˈvɪlətɪ/ *n* **1** (manners) courtoisie *f*, politesse *f* (**to**, **towards** à l'égard de, envers); **2** (forms) civilité *f*, politesse *f*; **the usual civilities** les civilités or politesses d'usage.

civilization /ˌsɪvəlaɪˈzeɪʃn, US -əlɪˈz-/ *n* civilisation *f*.

civilize /ˈsɪvəlaɪz/ *vtr* civiliser, rendre [qch/qn] plus civilisé [*manners, person*].

civilized /ˈsɪvəlaɪzd/ *adj* civilisé; **to become ~** se civiliser.

civilizing /ˈsɪvəlaɪzɪŋ/ *adj* civilisateur/-trice; **she is a ~ influence on him** il s'est civilisé sous son influence.

civil: **~ law** *n* droit *m* civil; **~ liability** *n* Jur responsabilité *f* civile.

civil liberty **I** *n* libertés *fpl* individuelles.

II *modif* [*campaign, group, lawyer*] de libertés individuelles.

civil list *n* GB liste *f* civile.

civilly /ˈsɪvəlɪ/ *adv* poliment, courtoisement.

civil marriage *n* mariage *m* civil.

civil rights **I** *npl* droits *mpl* civils.

II *modif* [*campaign, march, activist*] pour les droits civils.

civil servant ▶ **1692** *n* fonctionnaire *mf*.

civil service **I** *n* fonction *f* publique.

II *modif* [*department*] de la fonction publique; [*post*] dans la fonction publique; [*recruitment*] de fonctionnaires.

civil: **Civil Service Commission**, **CSC** *n* GB commission *f* de recrutement dans la fonction publique; **~ service examination** *n* GB concours *m* d'entrée dans la fonction publique; **~ war** *n* guerre *f* civile; **~ wedding** *n* mariage *m* civil.

civvies○ /ˈsɪvɪz/ *npl* vêtements *mpl* civils; **to be in ~** être en civil.

civvy○ /ˈsɪvɪ/ *n* civil/-e *m/f*.

civvy street○ *n* vie *f* civile; **in ~** dans le civil.

CJD *n* Med *abrév* ▶ **Creutzfeld-Jakob disease**.

cl *n* (*abrév écrite* = **centilitre(s)**) cl.

clack /klæk/ **I** *n* cliquetis *m*.

II *vi* [*machine*] cliqueter; [*tongue*] claquer; **tongues were ~ing** les gens ont commencé à jacasser.

clad /klæd/ **I** *adj* **~ in** habillé en, vêtu de.

II **-clad** (*dans composés*) **black-~** habillé en or vêtu de noir.

cladding /ˈklædɪŋ/ *n* Constr revêtement *m*.

claim /kleɪm/ **I** *n* **1** (demand) revendication *f*; **to make ~s** ou **lay ~ to** revendiquer [*land, share*]; prétendre à [*throne*]; revendiquer [*right, title*]; **rival** ou **competing ~s** revendications *fpl* rivales; **wage ~** revendications *fpl* salariales; **to make a wage ~** faire connaître ses revendications salariales; **she has no ~ to the throne** elle n'a aucune prétention au trône; **there are too many ~s on her generosity** on abuse de sa générosité; **there are many ~s on my time** je suis très pris; **I've got first ~ on the money** c'est moi qui ai la priorité sur l'argent; **2** Insur (against a person) réclamation *f*; (for fire, theft) demande *f* d'indemnisation; **to make** ou **lodge** ou **put in a ~** faire une demande d'indemnisation; **a ~ for damages** une réclamation pour dommages et intérêts; **they settled their ~s out of court** ils ont convenu d'un règlement à l'amiable; **3** Soc Admin demande *f* d'allocation; **to make** ou **put in a ~** faire une demande d'allocation; **a ~ for unemployment benefit** une demande d'allocation de chômage; **4** Admin (refund request) demande *f* de remboursement; **travel ~** demande *f* de remboursement des frais de déplacement; **5** (allegation, assertion) affirmation *f* (**about** au sujet de; **by** de la part de; **of** de); **his ~ that he is innocent**, **his ~s of innocence**, **his ~s to be innocent** ses protestations d'innocence; **her ~(s) to be able to do** ses affirmations selon lesquelles elle peut faire; **some extraordinary ~s have been made for this drug** on a affirmé des choses extraordinaires sur ce médicament; **my ~ to fame** ma prétention à la gloire; **6** (piece of land) concession *f*.

II *vtr* **1** (assert) **to ~ to be able to do** prétendre pouvoir faire; **to ~ to be innocent/sincere** prétendre être innocent/sincère; **I don't ~ to be an expert** je ne prétends pas être un expert; **she ~s to know nothing about it** elle prétend n'être au courant de rien; **to ~ innocence** affirmer son innocence; **to ~ ignorance of the law** affirmer ignorer la loi; **to ~ responsibility for an attack** revendiquer un attentat; **to ~ acquaintance with sb** prétendre connaître qn; **I can ~ some credit for the success of the dictionary** je suis en droit de dire que j'ai contribué au succès du dictionnaire; **2** (assert right to) revendiquer [*money, land, property*]; **to ~ sth as a right**, **to ~ the right to sth** revendiquer le droit à qch; **she ~ed that the land was hers**, **she ~ed the land as hers** elle a prétendu que le terrain lui appartenait; **3** (apply for) faire une demande de [*free dental care, unemployment benefit*]; faire une demande de remboursement de [*expenses*]; **4** (cause) **the accident ~ed 50 lives** l'accident a fait 50 victimes or morts; **5** (require) demander [*attention*].

III *vi* **1** Insur **to ~ for damages** faire une demande pour dommages et intérêts; **2** Soc

Admin (apply for benefit) faire une demande d'allocation.

■ **claim back**: **~ back [sth]**, **~ [sth] back** se faire rembourser [*cost, expenses*]; **you should ~ your money back** vous devriez demander à être remboursé; **to ~ sth back on the insurance** se faire rembourser qch par la compagnie d'assurances; **to ~ sth back on expenses** faire passer qch sur sa note de frais.

claimant /ˈkleɪmənt/ *n* **1** Admin (for benefit, grant) demandeur/-euse *m/f* (**to** à); **2** Jur (to title, estate) prétendant/-e *m/f* (**to** à); (for compensation) demandeur/-euse *m/f*.

claim: **~ form** *n* Insur déclaration *f* de sinistre; **~s department** *n* Insur service *m* des sinistres.

clairvoyance /kleəˈvɔɪəns/ *n* voyance *f*, don *m* de seconde vue.

clairvoyant /kleəˈvɔɪənt/ **I** *n* voyant/-e *m/f*, extralucide *mf*.
II *adj* [*person*] doué de seconde vue; [*powers*] de voyance, de seconde vue.

clam /klæm/ **I** *n* **1** Zool, Culin palourde *f*; **2**○† US dollar *m*.
II *modif* [*fishing, sauce*] aux palourdes.
III *vi* US (*p prés etc* **-mm-**) aller à la pêche aux palourdes.
IDIOMS **as happy as a ~** heureux comme un poisson dans l'eau; **to shut up like a ~** ne plus piper○ mot.
■ **clam up** ne plus piper mot (**on sb** à qn).

clambake /ˈklæmbeɪk/ *n* US **1** (outdoor party) pique-nique *m* (*composé de fruits de mer au barbecue*); **2** (noisy party) fête *f*, bringue○ *f*.

clamber /ˈklæmbə(r)/ **I** *n* (up) escalade *f*; (down) descente *f*.
II *vi* grimper, se hisser (péniblement) (**into** dans; **out of** hors de); **to ~ over/up/across** escalader; **to ~ down the cliff** descendre la falaise en s'aidant de ses mains.

clam chowder /ˌklæm ˈtʃaʊdə(r)/ *n* soupe *f* aux palourdes.

clammy /ˈklæmɪ/ *adj* [*skin, hand*] moite (**with** de); [*surface, fish, cloth*] collant; [*weather*] moite.

clamorous /ˈklæmərəs/ *adj* **1** (loud) [*voice*] sonore, retentissant; [*crowd*] vociférant; **2** (demanding) [*protest*] violent, bruyant; [*demand*] impérieux/-ieuse.

clamour GB, **clamor** US /ˈklæmə(r)/ **I** *n* **1** (loud shouting) clameur *f*; **2** (demands) réclamations *fpl*.
II *vtr* (shout) **to ~ that** hurler que.
III *vi* **1** (demand) **to ~ for sth** réclamer qch; **to ~ for sb to do sth** réclamer à qn de faire qch; **2** (rush, fight) **to ~ to do sth** se bousculer pour faire qch; **to ~ for sth** se bousculer pour avoir qch; **3** (shout together) pousser des cris (**about**, **over** au sujet de); (talk noisily) vociférer.

clamp /klæmp/ **I** *n* **1** Tech (on bench) valet *m*; (unattached) presse *f*; Chem pince *f*; (for lid) système *m* d'attache (*pour fermer hermétiquement un couvercle*); **2** fig frein *m* (**on** à); **a ~ on public spending** un frein à la dépense publique; **3** Aut (also **wheel~**) sabot *m* de Denver; **4** GB Agric silo *m*; **5** US (heavy footstep) pas *m* lourd.
II *vtr* **1** Tech cramponner [*two parts*]; (at bench) fixer [qch] à l'aide d'un valet (**onto** à); **2** (clench) serrer [*jaw, teeth*]; **a pipe ~ed between his teeth** une pipe serrée entre les dents; **his jaws were ~ed shut** il serrait les mâchoires; **3** Aut (also **wheel~**) mettre un sabot de Denver à [*car*]; **4** US (tread heavily) marcher d'un pas lourd.
■ **clamp down**: **~ down** prendre des mesures; **to ~ down on** faire de la répression contre [*crime, drugs, criminals*]; mettre un frein à [*extravagance*].
■ **clamp on**: **~ on [sth]**, **~ [sth] on** **1** lit fermer [*lid*]; **2** fig imposer [*curfew, restriction, sanction*].

clampdown /ˈklæmpdaʊn/ *n* mesures *fpl* de répression (**on sb** contre qn; **on sth** de qch).

clan /klæn/ *n* lit, fig clan *m*.

clandestine /klænˈdestɪn/ *adj* clandestin.

clang /ˈklæŋ/ **I** *n* fracas *m*, bruit *m* métallique.
II *vtr* faire sonner [qch] à toute volée [*bell*]; refermer [qch] bruyamment [*door*].
III *vi* [*gate*] claquer avec un son métallique; [*bell*] retentir (avec fracas); **to ~ shut** se refermer avec fracas.

clanger○ /ˈklæŋə(r)/ *n* GB boulette○ *f*, gaffe *f*.

clanging /ˈklæŋɪŋ/ *n* bruit *m* métallique, fracas *m*.

clangour GB, **clangor** US /ˈklæŋgə(r)/ *n* littér bruit *m* métallique, fracas *m*.

clank /klæŋk/ **I** *n* bruit *m* métallique.
II *vtr* faire cliqueter [*heavy object*]; entrechoquer [*chains*].
III *vi* [*heavy object*] cliqueter; [*chains*] s'entrechoquer; **to ~ along** avancer avec un grincement métallique.

clanking /ˈklæŋkɪŋ/ **I** *n* bruit *m* métallique.
II *adj* [*chains*] qui s'entrechoquent (*after n*).

clannish /ˈklænɪʃ/ *adj* péj [*family, profession*] fermé; [*person*] qui a l'esprit de clan.

clansman /ˈklænzmən/ *n* (*pl* **-men**) membre *m* d'un clan.

clap /klæp/ **I** *n* **1** (of hands) battement *m* de mains; (round of applause) applaudissements *mpl*; (friendly slap) tape *f*; **to get a ~** être applaudi; **to give sb a ~** applaudir qn; **a ~ of thunder** un coup de tonnerre; **2**◑ (venereal disease) chtouille◑ *f*; **to get a dose of the ~** ramasser la chtouille◑.
II *vtr* (*p prés etc* **-pp-**) **1** **to ~ one's hands** battre or taper des mains, frapper dans ses mains; **~ your hands!** tapez dans vos mains!; **to ~ one's hands over one's ears** se mettre or se plaquer les mains sur les oreilles; **to ~ one's hand over sb's mouth** mettre or plaquer la main sur la bouche de qn; **to ~ sb on the back** taper qn dans le dos; **to ~ sth shut** fermer qch d'un coup sec; **2** (applaud) applaudir [*actor, performance*]; **3**○ (set) **to ~ sb in irons/in jail** mettre qn aux fers/en prison.
III *vi* (*p prés etc* **-pp-**) applaudir.
IDIOMS **to ~ eyes on** voir, poser les yeux sur; **I've never ~ped eyes on her before** c'est la première fois que je la vois.
■ **clap along** battre des mains en mesure (**to** avec).
■ **clap on**: **to ~ on one's hat** enfoncer son chapeau sur sa tête; **to ~ on the brakes**○ Aut freiner brusquement, piler○; **to ~ on sail** Naut mettre toutes voiles dehors.

clapboard /ˈklæpbɔːd/ **I** *n* planche *f* en clin.
II *modif* [*house*] en bois.

clapped-out○ /ˌklæptˈaʊt/ *adj* [*car*] pourri; [*machine*] mort○, foutu◑; [*idea*] complètement dépassé; [*economy*] sur les genoux (*jamais épith*); [*horse*] claqué; [*person*] (exhausted) crevé○; (past it) fichu○, fini.

clapper /ˈklæpə(r)/ *n* battant *m*.
IDIOMS **to run/go like the ~s**○ GB aller à fond de train.

clapperboard /ˈklæpəbɔːd/ *n* GB Cin clap *m*.

clapping /ˈklæpɪŋ/ *n* ¢ applaudissements *mpl*.

claptrap○ /ˈklæptræp/ *n* ¢ âneries *fpl*.

claque /klæk, klɑːk/ *n* claque *f*.

claret /ˈklærət/ **▶ 1104** **I** *n* **1** (wine) bordeaux *m* (rouge); **2** (colour) bordeaux *m*.
II *adj* (also **~-coloured**) bordeaux *inv*.

clarification /ˌklærɪfɪˈkeɪʃn/ *n* **1** (explanation) éclaircissement *m*, clarification *f*; **2** Culin (of butter, stock) clarification *f*; (of wine) collage *m*.

clarify /ˈklærɪfaɪ/ **I** *vtr* **1** (explain) éclaircir, clarifier [*point*]; **a ~ing statement** une mise au point; **to become clarified** s'éclaircir; **2** Culin clarifier [*butter, stock*]; coller [*wine*].
II *vi* [*person*] s'expliquer.

clarinet /ˌklærəˈnet/ **▶ 1481** *n* clarinette *f*.

clarinettist /ˌklærəˈnetɪst/ **▶ 1481**, **1692** *n* clarinettiste *mf*.

clarion /ˈklærɪən/ **I** *n* clairon *m*.
II *vtr* littér claironner.

clarion call *n* lit appel *m* de clairon; fig appel *m* à l'action.

clarity /ˈklærətɪ/ *n* (of sound) clarté *f*; (of vision, thought) clarté *f*, précision *f*.

clash /klæʃ/ **I** *n* **1** (confrontation) affrontement *m* (**between** entre; **with** avec); fig (disagreement) querelle *f* (**between** entre; **with** avec); **2** Sport (contest) affrontement *m* (**between** entre; **with** avec); **3** (contradiction) conflit *m*, incompatibilité *f* (**between** entre); **a ~ of beliefs/cultures/interests** un conflit de croyances/de cultures/d'intérêts; **a personality ~** un conflit de personnalités; **a ~ of wills** un conflit; **4** (inconvenient coincidence) **there's a ~ of meetings/classes** les réunions/cours ont lieu en même temps; **5** (noise) (of swords) cliquetis *m*; **a ~ of cymbals** un coup *m* de cymbales.
II *vtr* (bang) (also **~ together**) entrechoquer [*dustbin lids*]; frapper [*cymbals*].
III *vi* **1** (meet and fight) [*armies, rival groups*] s'affronter; fig (disagree) [*ministers, leaders*] s'affronter; **to ~ with sb** (fight) se heurter à qn; (disagree) se quereller avec qn (**on, over** au sujet de); **2** (be in conflict) [*interests, beliefs, wishes*] être incompatibles; **3** (coincide inconveniently) [*meetings, concerts, parties*] avoir lieu en même temps; **to ~ with sth** avoir lieu en même temps que qch; **4** (not match) [*colours*] jurer (**with** avec); **5** (bang) (also **~ together**) [*dustbin lids*] s'entrechoquer.

clasp /klɑːsp, US klæsp/ **I** *n* **1** (on bracelet, bag, purse) fermoir *m*; (on belt) boucle *f*; **2** (grip) étreinte *f*.
II *vtr* **1** (hold tightly) serrer [qch] dans la main [*purse, knife*]; **he ~ed her hand** il lui a serré la main; **to ~ sth to one's breast** serrer qch contre sa poitrine; **to ~ one's hands around one's knees** prendre ses genoux dans les mains; **2** (embrace) étreindre; **to ~ sb to one's breast** prendre qn dans ses bras; **3** (fasten) **to ~ a handbag shut** refermer un sac à main.

clasp knife *n* couteau *m* à virole.

class /klɑːs, US klæs/ **I** *n* **1** Sociol classe *f*; **the working ~es** la classe ouvrière; **2** Sch, Univ (group of students) classe *f*; (lesson) cours *m* (**in** de); **in ~** en cours or classe; **to give a ~** assurer un cours; **to take a ~** GB assurer un cours; US suivre un cours; **3** US Sch, Univ (year group) promotion *f*, classe *f*; **4** (category) gen classe *f*, catégorie *f*; Jur (of offence) type *m*; (of vehicle) catégorie *f*; Naut (of ship, submarine) classe *f*; **to be in a ~ of one's own** or **by oneself** être hors catégorie; **she's in a different ~ from** il n'y a aucune comparaison possible entre elle et; **he's not in the same ~ as** il n'arrive pas à la cheville de; **5**○ (elegance) classe *f*; **to have ~** avoir de la classe; **to add a touch of ~ to sth** donner un peu de distinction à qch; **6** Tourism classe *f*; **to travel first/second ~** voyager en première/deuxième classe; **a first/second ~ seat** une place de première/deuxième classe; **7** GB Univ ≈ mention *f*; **what was the ~ of your degree?** ≈ est-ce que vous avez eu votre licence avec mention?; **a first-/second-~ degree** ≈ licence avec mention très bien/bien; **8** Biol, Math classe *f*.
II○ *adj* (excellent) de classe.
III *vtr* **to ~ sb/sth among/with** classer qn/qch parmi/ avec; **to ~ sb/ sth as** assimiler qn/qch à.

class: **~ action** *n* Jur action *f* collective; **~ conscious** *adj* gen soucieux/-ieuse des distinctions sociales; (in Marxist discourse) conscient; **~ consciousness** *n* gen sentiment *m* de classe; (in Marxist discourse) conscience *f* de classe; **~ distinction** *n* distinction *f* sociale; **~ divisions** *npl* divisions *fpl* entre les classes.

classic /ˈklæsɪk/ **I** *n* **1** (literary, sporting)

classique *m*; **the ~s** Literat, Cin les classiques; **2**○ (hilarious example) **it was a real ~!** (of gaffe, blunder) c'était un chef-d'œuvre du genre!; (of error) c'était une vraie perle!; (of comment, situation) c'était trop drôle!

II *adj* (all contexts) classique.

classical /ˈklæsɪkl/ *adj* [*author, dance, beauty*] classique; **~ scholar** philologue *mf*.

classically /ˈklæsɪklɪ/ *adv* [*dress, design*] dans un style classique; **~ elegant** d'une élégance classique; **~ proportioned** aux proportions classiques; **~ trained** de formation classique.

classical music *n* classique *m*, musique *f* classique.

classicism /ˈklæsɪsɪzəm/ *n* classicisme *m*.

classicist /ˈklæsɪsɪst/ *n* (student) étudiant/-e *m/f* en lettres classiques; (teacher) professeur *m* de lettres classiques; (scholar) spécialiste *mf* de lettres classiques, philologue *mf*.

classics /ˈklæsɪks/ *n* (+ *v sg*) lettres *fpl* classiques.

classifiable /ˈklæsɪfaɪəbl/ *adj* classifiable.

classification /ˌklæsɪfɪˈkeɪʃn/ *n* **1** (category) classification *f*, catégorie *f*; **2** (categorization) classement *m*.

classified /ˈklæsɪfaɪd/ **I** *n* (also **~ ad**) petite annonce *f*.

II *adj* **1** (categorized) classifié; **2** (secret) confidentiel/-ielle.

classified: **~ ad** *n* petite annonce *f*; **~ results** *npl* GB Sport résultats *mpl* complets; **~ section** *n* rubrique *f* des petites annonces.

classify /ˈklæsɪfaɪ/ *vtr* **1** (file) classer; **to ~ sth under 'personal'** classer qch sous la rubrique 'personnel'; **2** (declare secret) classer confidentiel/-ielle.

classless /ˈklɑːslɪs, US ˈklæs-/ *adj* [*society*] sans classes; [*person*] d'une classe sociale indéfinissable; [*accent*] neutre.

class: **~ list** *n* Sch liste *f* des élèves d'une classe; **~ mark** *n* cote *f* (*d'un ouvrage en bibliothèque*); **~mate** *n* camarade *mf* de classe; **~ number** *n* = **class mark**; **~ president** *n* US chef *m* de classe; **~ rank** *n* US Sch classement *m*; Univ rang *m*; **~-ridden** *adj* marqué par les divisions entre classes; **~room** *n* salle *f* de classe; **~ structure** *n* structure *f* de classes; **~ struggle** *n* lutte *f* des classes; **~ system** *n* système *m* de classes; **~ teacher** *n* GB professeur *m* principal; **~ war(fare)** *n* guerre *f* des classes.

classy○ /ˈklɑːsɪ, US ˈklæsɪ/ *adj* [*person, dress*] qui a de la classe; [*car, hotel*] de luxe; [*actor, performance*] de grande classe; **she's really ~** elle a vraiment de la classe○.

clatter /ˈklætə(r)/ **I** *n* cliquetis *m*; (loud) fracas *m*; **a ~ of dishes** un cliquetis de vaisselle.

II *vtr* entrechoquer; **stop ~ing those dishes!** arrête ce fracas avec la vaisselle!

III *vi* [*typewriter*] cliqueter; [*dishes*] s'entrechoquer; [*vehicle*] rouler avec fracas; **to ~ in/out/down etc** entrer/sortir/descendre etc avec fracas.

clause /klɔːz/ *n* **1** Ling proposition *f*; **2** Jur, Pol clause *f*; (in will, act of Parliament) disposition *f*.

claustrophobia /ˌklɔːstrəˈfəʊbɪə/ *n* claustrophobie *f*.

claustrophobic /ˌklɔːstrəˈfəʊbɪk/ **I** *n* claustrophobe *mf*.

II *adj* [*person*] claustrophobe; [*feeling*] de claustrophobie; **it's ~ in here** il y a une atmosphère oppressante ici; **to get ~** avoir une sensation de claustrophobie, faire de la claustrophobie○.

clavichord /ˈklævɪkɔːd/ **▶ 1481** *n* clavicorde *m*.

clavicle /ˈklævɪkl/ *n* clavicule *f*.

claw /klɔː/ **I** *n* **1** Zool (of animal) griffe *f*; (of bird of prey) serre *f*; (of crab, lobster) pince *f*; **2**○ fig (hand) patte○ *f*; **to get one's ~s into sb** mettre le grappin○ sur qn; **3** (on hammer) arrache-clou *m*, pied-de-biche *m*.

II *vtr* **1** (scratch) griffer; **2** (tear) [*animal*] déchirer [qch] avec ses griffes; [*bird of prey*] déchirer [qch] avec ses serres; **3** fig **to ~ sb's eyes out** arracher les yeux de qn; **he ~ed his way to the top** il est arrivé en employant tous les moyens; **she ~ed her way out of the slums** elle s'est sortie de son milieu misérable à la force du poignet.

■ **claw at**: **~ at [sth/sb]** [*animal*] essayer de griffer [*person*]; essayer d'agripper [*person*].

■ **claw back**: **~ [sth] back, ~ back [sth] 1** GB Pol, Econ, Tax récupérer [*allowance, benefit*] (*reprendre une somme allouée par un moyen indirect*); récupérer [*investment*]; **2** Comm, Sport regagner péniblement [*position*].

clawback /ˈklɔːbæk/ *n* GB *récupération totale ou partielle par des moyens indirects d'une somme allouée*; **the ~ represents 2% of the excess income** la somme récupérée représente 2% de l'excès de revenu.

claw hammer *n* marteau *m* à panne fendue.

clay /kleɪ/ **I** *n* **1** (for sculpture) argile *f*, terre *f* glaise; **2** (soil) argile *f*; **3** (in tennis) terre *f* battue.

II *modif* **1** [*pot*] en terre; **2** Sport [*court*] en terre battue.

IDIOMS **to have feet of ~** avoir des pieds d'argile.

clayey /ˈkleɪɪ/ *adj* argileux/-euse.

clay: **~more** *n* claymore *f* (*épée écossaise à deux tranchants*); **~ pigeon** *n* pigeon *m* d'argile or de ball-trap; **~ pigeon shooting** **▶ 1282** *n* ball-trap *m*, tir *m* aux pigeons d'argile; **~ pipe** *n* pipe *f* en terre; **~ pit** *n* argilière *f*, glaisière *f*.

clean /kliːn/ **I** *n* **to give sth a ~** nettoyer qch.

II *adj* **1** (not dirty) [*clothes, dishes, floor, window, habits*] propre; [*air, water*] pur; [*wound, syringe*] désinfecté; **it is not very ~ to do** ce n'est pas très propre de faire; **she keeps her house ~** elle tient propre sa maison; **my hands are ~** lit, fig j'ai les mains propres; **~ and tidy** impeccable de propreté; **a ~ sheet of paper** une feuille blanche; **to rinse/wash sth ~** rincer/laver qch; **to lick one's plate ~** [*person*] fig ne pas en laisser une miette; [*animal*] nettoyer son assiette; **keep your shoes ~** ne salis pas tes chaussures; **2** (with no pollution) [*bomb, environment, fuel, process*] propre; **3** (not obscene) [*joke*] anodin; [*comedian*] jamais vulgaire; **keep it** ou **the conversation ~!** restons décents!; **4** (unsullied) [*reputation*] sans tache; [*record, driving licence*] vierge; **I've checked him out, he's ~**○ je me suis renseigné sur lui, il est réglo○; **5** (no longer addicted) désintoxiqué; **6**○ (without illicit property) argot des policiers **he's ~** gen il n'a rien; (no gun) il n'a pas d'arme; **the car/room is ~** on n'a rien trouvé dans la voiture/pièce; **7** Sport [*match*] sans débordements; [*tackle*] sans faute; [*player*] fair-play *inv*; [*serve, hit, throw*] précis; [*jump*] sans toucher l'obstacle; **keep it ~** (in match) pas de bavures; **8** (elegant, neat) [*lines, profile*] pur; [*edge*] net/nette; **~ break** Med fracture *f* simple; **to make a ~ break with the past** fig rompre définitivement avec le passé.

III *adv* littéralement; **the bullet went ~ through his shoulder** la balle lui a littéralement traversé l'épaule; **to jump ~ over the wall** sauter par-dessus le mur sans le toucher; **we're ~ out of bread** on n'a plus une miette de pain.

IV *vtr* **1** nettoyer [*room, shoes, gun*]; **to ~ sth from** ou **off** enlever qch de [*hands, wall, car*]; **to ~ the blackboard** effacer le tableau; **to have sth ~ed** donner qch à nettoyer; **to ~ one's teeth** se brosser les dents; **2** Culin vider [*chicken, fish*]; laver [*vegetables*].

V *vi* **1** (do housework) [*person*] faire le ménage; **I've been ~ing all morning** j'ai fait le ménage toute la matinée; **2** (become cleansed) **these handles ~ easily** ces poignées se nettoient facilement.

VI *v refl* **to ~ itself** [*animal*] faire sa toilette.

IDIOMS **to ~ up one's act** [*person*] devenir plus sérieux; **to come ~**○ **about sth** avouer qch; **I'll have to come ~**○ il va falloir que je dise la vérité; **to make a ~ sweep of sth** gagner qch haut la main.

■ **clean down**: **~ [sth] down, ~ down [sth]** nettoyer [qch] à fond.

■ **clean off**: ¶ **~ off** [*stain*] partir; **this mark won't ~ off** cette tache ne part pas; ¶ **~ [sth] off, ~ off [sth]** effacer [*chalk mark*]; enlever [*stain, graffiti*]; **to ~ sth off** effacer qch de [*blackboard*]; enlever qch de [*car, wall*].

■ **clean out**: ¶ **~ [sth] out, ~ out [sth]** (cleanse thoroughly) nettoyer [qch] à fond [*cupboard, stable, toilets*]; **you should ~ out your ears**○ tu devrais te déboucher les oreilles; ¶ **~ [sb/sth] out, ~ out [sb/sth]** (leave empty, penniless) [*thief*] mettre [qch] à sac [*house*]; [*thief, shopping trip, holiday*] mettre [qn] à sec [*person*]; **'another game?'—'no, I'm ~ed out**○**'** 'encore une partie?'—'non, je suis nettoyé'○; ¶ **~ [sb] out of** délester qn de [*jewellery, money*].

■ **clean up**: ¶ **~ up 1** (remove dirt) tout nettoyer; **2** (tidy) tout remettre en ordre (**after sb** derrière qn); **3** (wash oneself) se débarbouiller; **4**○ (make profit) [*dealer*] faire son beurre○ (**on** avec); [*gambler*] rafler la mise○; ¶ **~ [sb] up** faire la toilette de [*patient*]; **come and let me ~ you up** (to child) viens que je te fasse un brin de toilette; ¶ **~ [sth] up, ~ up [sth] 1** (remove dirt) nettoyer [*mess, rubbish, area, spillage*]; **~ that rubbish up off** ou **from the floor** débarrasse le sol de ces saletés; **2** fig (remove crime) nettoyer○ [*street, city*]; (make less obscene) expurger [*TV programme, comedy act*].

clean: **Clean Air Act** *n* Pol loi *f* antipollution; **~ and jerk** *n* Sport (in weight-lifting) épaulé-jeté *m*; **~-cut** *adj* [*image, person*] soigné.

cleaner /ˈkliːnə(r)/ **▶ 1692** *n* **1** (person) (in workplace) agent *m* de nettoyage; (in home) (woman) femme *f* de ménage; (man) agent *m* de nettoyage; **office ~** agent *m* de nettoyage; **2** (machine) nettoyeur *m*; **air ~** purificateur *m* d'air; **carpet ~** shampouineuse *f* (de tapis); **3** (detergent) produit *m* de nettoyage; **fabric/suede ~** produit *m* pour nettoyer les tissus/le daim; **biodegradable ~** produit *m* d'entretien biodégradable; **liquid ~** produit *m* d'entretien liquide; **cream ~** crème *f* de nettoyage liquide; **4** (shop) (also **cleaner's**) pressing *m*.

IDIOMS **to take sb to the ~s**○ (swindle) plumer qn○; (defeat) **Scotland took England to the ~s**○ l'Écosse a battu l'Angleterre à plate couture; (in divorce cases) **his wife took him to the ~s**○ il s'est fait nettoyer par son ex-femme○.

cleaning /ˈkliːnɪŋ/ *n* (domestic) ménage *m*; (commercial) nettoyage *m*, entretien *m*; **to do the ~** faire le ménage.

cleaning: **~ cloth** *n* chiffon *m*; **~ lady** **▶ 1692** *n* femme *f* de ménage; **~ product** *n* produit *m* d'entretien.

cleanliness /ˈklenlɪnɪs/ *n* propreté *f*.

IDIOMS **~ is next to godliness** Prov le chemin de la sainteté passe par la propreté.

clean-living /ˌkliːnˈlɪvɪŋ/ **I** *n* vie *f* saine.

II *adj* [*person, community*] aux habitudes saines.

cleanly[1] /ˈklenlɪ/ *adj* littér propre.

cleanly[2] /ˈkliːnlɪ/ *adv* [*cut*] bien, franchement; [*catch, hit*] avec précision; **to break off ~** se casser net; **she hits the notes ~** ses attaques sont justes.

cleanness /ˈkliːnnɪs/ *n* propreté *f*.

clean-out○ /ˈkliːnaʊt/ *n* nettoyage *m* à fond.

cleanse /klenz/ *vtr* **1** lit nettoyer [*skin*]; nettoyer, laver [*wound*]; épurer [*blood*]; **2** fig littér laver, purifier [*person, mind*] (**of** de); nettoyer [*society*] (**of** de).

cleanser /ˈklenzə(r)/ *n* **1** Cosmet démaquillant *m*; **2** (household) produit *m* d'entretien.

clean-shaven /ˌkliːnˈʃeɪvn/ *adj* [*features*] glabre; **he's ~** il n'a ni barbe ni moustache.

clean sheet *n* fig (record) casier *m* vierge; **to have kept a ~** gen avoir un casier vierge; Sport [*goalkeeper*] n'avoir encaissé aucun but.

cleansing /ˈklenzɪŋ/ **I** *n* nettoyage *m*.
II *adj* **1** Cosmet [*product*] démaquillant; **2** [*action*] lit nettoyant; fig purifiant.

cleansing department *n* GB Admin (service *m* de la) voirie *f*.

cleanup /ˈkliːnʌp/ *n* **1** gen nettoyage *m*; **to give sth a ~**○ nettoyer qch; **2** US (profit) joli coup *m*; **to make a ~**○ ramasser un paquet○.

cleanup campaign *n* (of city) campagne *f* de nettoyage; (of internal politics) campagne *f* d'épuration.

clear /klɪə(r)/ **I** *n* **1** (also **~ text**) Comput, Mil **in ~** en clair; **2** Sport (in football) dégagement *m*.
II *adj* **1** (transparent) [*glass, liquid*] transparent; [*blue*] limpide; [*lens, varnish*] incolore; **2** (distinct) [*image, outline, impression*] net/nette; [*writing*] lisible; [*sound, voice*] clair; **I didn't get a ~ look at the car** je n'ai pas bien vu la voiture; **he had a ~ view of the man** il voyait très bien l'homme; **3** (comprehensibly plain) [*description, instruction, text*] clair; **to make sth ~ to sb** faire comprendre qch à qn; **he made it ~ to her that he disapproved** il lui a bien fait comprendre qu'il désapprouvait; **I wish to make it ~ that** je tiens à préciser que; **is that ~?, do I make myself ~?** est-ce que c'est clair?; **to make one's views/intentions ~** exprimer clairement ses opinions/intentions; **let's get this ~** que les choses soient claires; **4** (obvious) [*lack, need, sign*] évident; [*advantage, lead*] net/nette; [*example*] beau (*before n*); [*majority*] large (*before n*); **it is ~ that** il est clair que; **it's a ~ case of fraud** il est clair qu'il s'agit d'une fraude; **5** (not confused) [*idea, memory*] clair; [*plan*] précis; **to have a ~ picture in one's mind of sth** avoir une idée très claire de qch; **to have/keep a ~ head** avoir/garder les idées claires; **we need someone with a ~ head** on a besoin de quelqu'un qui a les idées claires; **a ~ thinker** un esprit lucide; **I'm not ~ what to do/how to start** je ne sais pas très bien quoi faire/par où commencer; **I have no ~ idea how it happened** je ne sais pas très bien comment ça s'est passé; **he had a ~ understanding of the problem** il comprenait très bien le problème; **she's quite ~ about what the job involves** elle sait exactement en quoi consiste le travail; **6** (empty) [*road, view, area*] dégagé; [*table*] débarrassé; [*space*] libre; **the road is ~ of obstacles/snow** il n'y a plus d'obstacles/de neige sur la route; **7** (not guilty) [*conscience*] tranquille; **8** (unblemished) [*skin, complexion*] net/nette; **9** Med [*X-ray, scan*] normal; **10** (cloudless) [*sky*] sans nuage, clair (*after n*); [*day, night*] clair; **on a ~ day** par temps clair; **11** (frank) [*gaze, look*] franc/franche; **12** (pure) [*sound, tone, voice*] clair; **13** Culin [*honey*] liquide; **~ soup** consommé *m*; **14** (exempt from) **to be ~ of** être libre de [*debt*]; être exempt de [*blame*]; être lavé de [*suspicion*]; **15** (free) [*day, diary*] libre; **keep the 24th ~, I'm having a party** ne prévois rien d'autre le 24, je fais une fête; **16** (whole) [*week, day*] entier/-ière; **you must allow three ~ days** il faut compter trois jours entiers; **17** (net) [*gain, profit*] net *inv* (*after n*); **18** Ling clair.
III *adv* (away from) **to jump ~** sauter sur le côté; **to jump ~ of** (jump out of) sauter hors de [*vehicle*]; (avoid) **he leapt ~ of the car/rock** il a évité la voiture/pierre en sautant sur le côté; **to pull sb ~ of** extraire qn de [*wreckage*]; **to stay** ou **steer ~ of** éviter [*town centre, rocks*]; éviter [*alcohol, trouble, troublemakers*]; **he kept the boat ~ of the rocks** il a gardé le bateau au large des rochers; **stand ~ of the gates!** éloignez-vous des portes!; **to get ~ of** sortir de [*traffic, town*].
IV *vtr* **1** (remove) abattre [*trees*]; arracher [*weeds*]; enlever [*debris, papers, mines*]; dégager [*snow*] (**from, off** de); **to ~ demonstrators from the streets, to ~ the streets of demonstrators** débarrasser les rues des manifestants; **2** (free from obstruction) déboucher [*drains*]; dégager [*road*]; débarrasser [*table, surface*]; déblayer [*site*]; défricher [*land*]; **to ~ the road of snow/obstacles** dégager la neige/les obstacles de la route; **to ~ sth out of the way** (from table, seat) enlever qch; (from floor) enlever qch du passsage; **to ~ the way for sth/sb** lit libérer le passage pour qch/qn; fig ouvrir la voie pour [*developments*]; fig laisser la place à [*person*]; **3** (freshen) **to ~ the air** lit aérer; fig apaiser les tensions; **4** (empty) vider [*desk, drawer*] (**of** de); débarrasser [*room, surface*] (**of** de); lever [*post box*]; évacuer [*area, building*]; **the judge ~ed the court** le juge a fait évacuer la salle; **to ~ the office of furniture** débarrasser le bureau de tous ses meubles; **you're fired, ~ your desk** vous êtes renvoyé, débarrassez votre bureau; **his singing ~ed the room** la pièce se vida au son de sa voix; **5** (create) faire [*space*]; **to ~ a path through sth** se frayer un chemin à travers qch; **6** (disperse) dissiper [*fog, smoke*]; disperser [*crowd*]; **7** (unblock) dégager [*nose*]; **to ~ one's throat** se racler la gorge; **the fresh air will ~ your head** un peu d'air frais t'éclaircira les idées; **8** Cosmet faire disparaître [*dandruff, spots*]; **9** Wine clarifier; **10** (destroy) détruire [*building*]; **11** Comput effacer [*screen, data*]; **12** (dispose of) liquider [*stock*]; **to ~ the backlog** rattraper le retard sur le travail; **'reduced to ~'** 'solde'; **13** (pay off) s'acquitter de [*debt*]; rembourser [*loan*]; purger [*mortgage*]; **14** Fin [*bank*] compenser [*cheque*]; **15** (make) se faire [*profit*]; **16** (free from blame) [*jury*] innocenter [*accused*] (**of** de); **to be ~ed of suspicion** être lavé de tout soupçon; **to ~ one's name/reputation** blanchir son nom/sa réputation; **17** Admin, Mil (vet) mener une enquête administrative sur [*employee*]; **I've been ~ed** j'ai fait l'objet d'une enquête administrative; **she's been ~ed to see the documents** elle a été déclarée apte à consulter les documents; **18** (officially approve) approuver [*proposal, request*]; dédouaner [*goods*]; **to ~ sth with sb** obtenir l'accord de qn pour qch; **to be ~ed for take-off/landing** recevoir l'autorisation de décoller/atterrir; **19** (jump over) franchir [*fence, hurdle, wall*]; **she ~ed 2 m at the high jump** elle a réussi 2 m au saut en hauteur; **20** (pass through) passer sous [*bridge*]; passer entre [*gateposts*]; **to ~ customs** passer à la douane; **21** Sport dégager [*ball*].
V *vi* **1** (become transparent, unclouded) [*liquid, sky*] s'éclaircir; **2** (disappear) [*smoke, fog, cloud*] se dissiper; **3** (become pure) [*air*] se purifier; **4** (go away) [*rash, pimples*] disparaître; [*skin*] devenir net/nette; **5** Fin [*cheque*] être compensé.
IDIOMS **the coast is ~** fig le champ est libre; **to be in the ~** (safe) être hors de danger; (free from suspicion) être lavé de tout soupçon.
■ **clear away**: ¶ **~ away** débarrasser; ¶ **~ [sth] away, ~ away [sth]** balayer [*snow, leaves*]; enlever [*debris, rubbish*]; ranger [*papers, toys*].
■ **clear off**: ¶ **~ off**○ GB **1** (run away) filer○, se sauver; **2** (go away) ficher le camp○; **~ off, I'm busy** fiche le camp○, je suis occupé; **~ off!** fichez le camp○!; ¶ **~ off [sth]** US débarrasser [*table*].
■ **clear out**: ¶ **~ out** (run away) filer○, se sauver; ¶ **~ [sth] out, ~ out [sth]** **1** (tidy) ranger [*room*]; faire le tri dans [*drawer, cupboard*]; **2** (empty) vider [*room, house*]; **3** (throw away) jeter [*old clothes, newspapers*].
■ **clear up**: ¶ **~ up 1** (tidy up) faire du rangement; **they must ~ up after themselves** ils doivent tout ranger derrière eux; **2** (improve) [*weather*] s'éclaircir; [*rash, infection*] disparaître; ¶ **~ up [sth], ~ [sth] up 1** (tidy) ranger [*mess, toys, papers*]; ramasser [*litter, broken glass*]; ranger [*room*]; nettoyer [*beach, garden*]; **2** (resolve) résoudre [*problem, difficulty*]; dissiper [*misunderstanding*]; tirer [qch] au clair [*mystery*].

clearance /ˈklɪərəns/ **I** *n* **1** (permission) autorisation *f*; **flight ~** autorisation de vol; **to have ~ for take-off** [*plane*] avoir l'autorisation de décoller; **you need ~ for your plans** tu as besoin d'une autorisation pour ton projet; **to have ~ to do** être autorisé à faire; **2** (customs certificate) déclaration *f* en douane; **~ inwards/outwards** manifeste *m* d'entrée/de sortie; **3** Admin Mil habilitation *f* sécuritaire; **4** (removal) (of trees) abattage *m*; (of buildings) démolition *f*; (of vegetation) défrichage *m*; **land ~, site ~** défrichement *m* du terrain; **5** Comm liquidation *f*; **stock ~** liquidation de stock; **6** (gap) (below a bridge, barrier) hauteur *f* (libre); (between two objects) espace *m*; **a 10 cm ~ between the van and the wall** un espace de 10 cm entre le fourgon et le mur; **the bridge has a 4 metre ~** l'arche du pont fait 4 mètres de haut; **7** Fin compensation *f*; **8** Sport (in football, rugby) dégagement *m*; (in snooker, pool) sans faute *m*.
II Clearances *npl* Scot Hist *expulsion des habitants des Highlands en Écosse aux XVIII*[e] *et XIX*[e] *siècles pour faciliter l'élevage des moutons*.

clearance: **~ order** *n* Admin permis *m* de démolition; **~ sale** *n* Comm (total) liquidation *f*; (partial) soldes *mpl*.

clear-cut /ˌklɪəˈkʌt/ *adj* [*category, division*] précis; [*distinction, difference, outline*] net/nette; [*question, problem, rule*] clair; [*idea, plan, example*] précis; **~ features** traits bien dessinés; **the matter is not so ~** l'affaire n'est pas si simple.

clear: **~-headed** *adj* lucide; **~-headedly** *adv* avec lucidité; **~-headedness** *n* lucidité *f*.

clearing /ˈklɪərɪŋ/ *n* **1** (glade) clairière *f*; **2** (removal) (of obstacles) enlèvement *m*; (of road, mines, debris) déblaiement *m*; **3** (levelling) (of forest) abattage *m*; (of buildings) démolition *f*; (of land) défrichage *m*; **4** (eradication) (of pimples, toxins) suppression *f*; **5** Fin compensation *f*.

clearing: **~ bank** *n* GB Fin banque *f* affiliée à une chambre de compensation; **~ house** *n* Fin chambre *f* de compensation; Admin bureau *m* central.

clearing-up *n* rangement *m*; **I've got some ~ to do** je dois faire du rangement.

clearly /ˈklɪəlɪ/ *adv* **1** (distinctly) [*speak, hear, remember, write*] clairement; [*audible*] nettement; [*visible*] bien; [*see*] lit bien; fig clairement; [*labelled, signposted*] clairement; **2** (intelligibly) [*describe, explain*] clairement; **3** (lucidly) [*think*] clairement; **4** (obviously) [*drunk, worried, wrong*] manifestement; [*believe, hope, love, want*] manifestement.

clearness /ˈklɪənɪs/ *n* **1** (transparency) (of glass, water, varnish) transparence *f*; **2** Meteorol (of day, sky) clarté *f*; **3** (purity) (of air) pureté *f*; (of note, voice) clarté *f*; (of skin) pureté *f*; **4** (brightness) (of colour) clarté *f*; **5** (distinctness) (of outline, image, writing) netteté *f*; (of memory) précision *f*; **6** (candour) (of gaze, eyes) innocence *f*; **7** (intelligibility) (of style, message) clarté *f*.

clear-out○ /ˈklɪəraʊt/ *n* GB **to have a ~** faire du rangement; **to give sth a ~** faire du rangement dans qch.

clear: **~ round** *n* Equit parcours *m* sans faute; **~-sighted** *adj* perspicace; **~-sightedly** *adv* avec perspicacité;

~-sightedness *n* perspicacité *f*; **~way** *n* GB Transp route *f* à stationnement interdit.

cleat /kliːt/ *n* **1** (on sole) striure *f*, rainure *f*; **2** (shoe) chaussure *f* à crampons; **3** Naut taquet *m*; **4** (in carpentry) tasseau *m*.

cleated /ˈkliːtɪd/ *adj* [*sole*] cranté.

cleavage /ˈkliːvɪdʒ/ *n* **1** (of breasts) décolleté *m*; **to show a lot of ~** avoir un décolleté plongeant; **2** (of opinion) clivage *m*, division *f* (**between** entre).

cleave /kliːv/ **I** *vtr* (*prét* **clove** ou **cleaved**; *pp* **cleft** ou **cleaved**) **1** littér fendre; **to ~ sth in two** fendre qch en deux; **2** Geol cliver [*stone*].
II *vi* littér **1** (*prét* **cleaved** ou **clave**†; *pp* **cleaved**) **to ~ to** (be loyal to) être foncièrement attaché à; (stick to) adhérer à; **2** (split) se fendre.

cleaver /ˈkliːvə(r)/ *n* fendoir *m*.

clef /klef/ *n* clef *f*; **in the treble ~** en clef de fa.

cleft /kleft/ **I** *pp* ▶ **cleave**.
II *n* fente *f*.
III *adj* [*chin*] marqué d'un sillon.
IDIOMS **to be in a ~ stick** être pris dans un dilemme, être pris entre le marteau et l'enclume.

cleft palate *n* palais *m* fendu.

clematis /ˈklemətɪs, kləˈmeɪtɪs/ *n* clématite *f*.

clemency /ˈklemənsɪ/ *n* **1** (mercy) clémence *f* (**towards** envers, à l'égard de); **2** (of weather) clémence *f*.

clement /ˈklemənt/ *adj* [*weather, judge*] clément.

clementine /ˈkleməntiːn/ *n* clémentine *f*.

clench /klentʃ/ *vtr* serrer; **to ~ one's fist** serrer le poing; **to ~ one's teeth/jaws** serrer les dents/mâchoires; **to ~ sth between one's teeth** serrer qch entre les dents; **to say sth between ~ed teeth** dire qch sans desserrer les dents; **~ed-fist salute** salut *m* le poing levé.

Cleopatra /ˌkliːəˈpætrə/ *pr n* Cléopâtre.

clerestory /ˈklɪəstɔːrɪ/ *n* claire-voie *f*.

clergy /ˈklɜːdʒɪ/ *n* clergé *m*.

clergyman /ˈklɜːdʒɪmən/ ▶ **1692** *n* (*pl* **-men**) gen ecclésiastique *m*; (Protestant) pasteur *m*; (Catholic) prêtre *m*.

cleric /ˈklerɪk/ *n* ecclésiastique *m*.

clerical /ˈklerɪkl/ *adj* (*avant n*) **1** Relig [*matters, faction*] clérical; [*control, influence*] du clergé; [*manner*] d'ecclésiastique; **2** [*staff, employee*] de bureau; **~ work** travail *m* de bureau; **she has a ~ post** elle est employée dans un bureau.

clerical assistant ▶ **1692** *n* commis *m*.

clerical collar *n* (Catholic) col *m* romain; (Protestant) col *m* de clergyman.

clerical error *n* erreur *f* d'écriture (*dans les comptes*).

clericalism /ˈklerɪkəlɪzəm/ *n* cléricalisme *m*.

clerical: **~ student** *n* séminariste *m*; **~ worker** ▶ **1692** *n* employé/-e *m/f* de bureau.

clerihew /ˈklerɪhjuː/ *n* petit poème *m* humoristique (*sur une personne connue*).

clerk /klɑːk, US klɜːrk/ ▶ **1692** **I** *n* **1** (in office, bank etc) employé/-e *m/f*; **bank ~** employé/-e *m/f* de banque; **booking ~** employé/-e *m/f* aux réservations; **head ~** Admin chef *m* de bureau; Comm premier commis *m*; **2** (in UK) (to lawyer) ≈ clerc *m*; (in court) greffier/-ière *m/f*; **3** US (in hotel) réceptionniste *mf*; (in shop) vendeur/-euse *m/f*.
II *vi* **1** US Jur **to ~ for a judge** être stagiaire d'un juge; **2** US (in shop) travailler comme vendeur/-euse *m/f*.

clerk: **~ of the course** *n* GB Turf commissaire *m* des courses; (in motor-racing) directeur/-trice *m/f* des courses; **~ of the court** *n* GB Jur greffier *m*; **~ of the House of Commons** *n* GB greffier/-ière *m/f* de la chambre des communes; **~ of the works** *n* GB conducteur/-trice *m/f* de travaux; **~ to the justices** *n* GB conseil *m* attaché aux magistrats.

Cleveland /ˈkliːvlənd/ ▶ **1624** *pr n* Cleveland *m*.

clever /ˈklevə(r)/ *adj* **1** (intelligent) [*person*] intelligent; [*mind*] agile; **to be ~ at sth/at doing** être doué pour qch/pour faire; **to be ~ with figures** être doué pour le calcul; **that wasn't very ~!** ce n'était pas malin!; **2** (ingenious) [*solution, gadget, plot*] astucieux/-ieuse; [*person*] astucieux/-ieuse, futé; **how ~ of you!** félicitations!; **how ~ of you to find the solution** je te félicite d'avoir trouvé la solution; **3** (shrewd) astucieux/-ieuse; **4** (skilful) [*player, workman*] habile, adroit; [*manoeuvre, kick*] adroit; **to be ~ at doing** être habile à faire; **he's ~ with his hands** il est adroit de ses mains; **~ workmanship** travail fait avec beaucoup d'adresse; **5** péj (persuasive) [*argument, advertisement*] astucieux/-ieuse; [*lawyer, salesperson*] malin/-igne; **6** GB péj (cunning) **to be too ~ for sb** être trop malin/-igne pour qn; **to be too ~ by half** être beaucoup trop intelligent.

clever: **~-clever**○ *adj* GB péj [*person*] malin/-igne; [*ideas*] un peu trop ingénieux/-ieuse; **~ clogs**○, **~ dick**○ *n* GB péj gros malin *m*.

cleverly /ˈklevəlɪ/ *adv* (intelligently) intelligemment; (astutely, cunningly) astucieusement; (dextrously) adroitement; **he ~ avoided doing** il s'est bien débrouillé pour ne pas faire.

cleverness /ˈklevənɪs/ *n* (intelligence) intelligence *f*; (ingenuity) ingéniosité *f*; (quick-wittedness) vivacité *f* d'esprit; (dexterity) adresse *f*, habileté *f*; **the ~ of his replies** ses réponses futées○ ou malignes○.

cliché /ˈkliːʃeɪ, US kliːˈʃeɪ/ *n* cliché *m*, lieu *m* commun; **the car chase is a cinema ~** la course poursuite est un poncif cinématographique; **to become a ~** devenir parfaitement banal.

clichéd /ˈkliːʃeɪd, US kliːˈʃeɪd/ *adj* [*expression*] rebattu; [*idea, technique*] éculé; [*art, music*] bourré○ de clichés.

click /klɪk/ **I** *n* (of wood, metal, china) petit bruit *m* sec; (of mechanism) déclic *m*; (of fingers, heels, tongue) claquement *m*; Ling clic *m*; **with a ~ of her fingers/heels** d'un claquement de doigts/de talons.
II *vtr* **1** (make sound) **to ~ one's fingers/tongue** faire claquer ses doigts/sa langue; **to ~ one's heels** claquer des talons; **2 to ~ sth open/shut** ouvrir/fermer qch avec un bruit sec.
III *vi* **1** [*camera, lock*] faire un déclic; [*door*] faire un petit bruit sec; **I heard the cameras ~ing all at once** j'ai entendu les appareils photo se déclencher tous ensemble; **2**○ (become clear) **suddenly something ~ed** tout d'un coup ça a fait tilt○; **3** (work out perfectly) **everything ~ed for them** tout a bien marché pour eux○; **4**○ (strike a rapport) **we just ~ed** (as friends) on a sympathisé du premier coup; (sexually) on s'est plu du premier coup; **5** Comput cliquer (**on** sur).

clickety-click /ˌklɪkətɪˈklɪk/ *n* **1 to go ~** [*machine*] cliqueter; **2** GB (in bingo) soixante-six.

clicking /ˈklɪkɪŋ/ **I** *n* (of machine, cameras) cliquetis *m*.
II *adj* [*machine*] qui fait un cliquetis; **~ noise** cliquetis *m*.

click language *n* langue *f* à clics.

client /ˈklaɪənt/ *n* (all contexts) client/-e *m/f*.

clientele /ˌkliːɒnˈtel, US ˌklaɪənˈtel/ *n* clientèle *f*.

client: **~ group** *n* segment *m* de clientèle; **~ state** *n* pays *m* satellite.

cliff /klɪf/ *n* (by sea) falaise *f*; (inland) escarpement *m*; **sandstone/chalk ~s** (by sea) falaises *fpl* de grès/de craie; **steep ~s, vertical ~s** (by sea) falaises *fpl* à pic; (inland) escarpements *mpl* abrupts.

cliffhanger○ /ˈklɪfhæŋə(r)/ *n* (film) film *m* à suspense; (story) récit *m* à suspense; (situation) situation *f* à suspense; (moment) moment *m* d'angoisse; **the match was a real ~** le match a été un véritable suspense.

cliff: **~side** *n* paroi *f* d'une or de la falaise; **~top** *n* sommet *m* d'une or de la falaise.

climacteric /klaɪˈmæktərɪk/ *n* **1** Physiol climatère *m*; **2** fig point *m* crucial.

climactic /klaɪˈmæktɪk/ *adj* [*event, moment*] crucial.

climate /ˈklaɪmɪt/ *n* **1** Meteorol climat *m*; **2** fig (surroundings) atmosphère *f*; **3** Econ, Pol climat *m*.

climatic /klaɪˈmætɪk/ *adj* climatique.

climatology /ˌklaɪməˈtɒlədʒɪ/ *n* climatologie *f*.

climax /ˈklaɪmæks/ **I** *n* **1** (culmination, end) (of career) apogée *m*; (of war, frenzy, conflict) paroxysme *m*; (of plot, speech, play) point *m* culminant; **to reach its ~** [*argument, crisis, battle*] atteindre son paroxysme; [*contest*] atteindre son point culminant; [*symphony, performance*] atteindre son grand moment; **it's a fitting ~ to a long career** c'est le couronnement d'une longue carrière; **the exciting ~ of the tournament** la finale passionnante du tournoi; **2** (orgasm) orgasme *m*; **3** (in rhetoric) gradation *f*.
II *vtr* être l'apothéose de [*festival, match, week*].
III *vi* **1** (reach a high point) atteindre son grand moment; **2** (sexually) jouir.

climb /klaɪm/ **I** *n* **1** (ascent) (of hill) escalade *f* (**up** de; **to** jusqu'à); (of tower) montée *f*; (of mountain, rockface) ascension *f* (**up** de; **to** jusqu'à); **it's a steep ~ to the top of the tower** il y a une montée raide jusqu'en haut de la tour; **2** (steep hill) montée *f*; **to stall on the ~** caler dans la montée; **3** Aviat montée *f*; **4** fig (rise) ascension *f* (**from** de, **to** à).
II *vtr* **1** [*car, person*] grimper [*hill, slope*]; faire l'ascension de [*cliff, mountain*]; [*person*] escalader [*lamppost, mast, wall*]; grimper à [*ladder, rope, tree*]; monter [*steps, staircase*]; **2** Bot [*plant*] grimper à [*trellis, wall*].
III *vi* **1** (scale) gen grimper (**along** le long de, **to** jusqu'à); Sport faire de l'escalade; **to ~ down** descendre [*rockface*]; **to ~ into** monter dans [*car*]; **to ~ into bed** se mettre au lit; **to ~ over** (step over) enjamber [*log, stile*]; (clamber over) passer par-dessus [*fence, wall*]; escalader [*debris, rocks*]; **to ~ up** grimper à [*ladder, tree*]; monter [*steps*]; **2** (rise) [*sun*] se lever; [*aircraft*] monter; **3** (slope up) [*path, road*] monter; **4** (increase) [*birthrate, currency, price, temperature*] monter; [*profits*] augmenter.
IDIOMS **to ~ the wall** US grimper au mur○.
■ **climb down** revenir sur sa décision; **to ~ down over** céder sur [*issue, plan, matter*].

climb-down /ˈklaɪmdaʊn/ *n* reculade *f* (**over** sur).

climber /ˈklaɪmə(r)/ *n* **1** (mountaineer) grimpeur/-euse *m/f*, alpiniste *mf*; (rock-climber) varappeur/-euse *m/f*; **2** (plant) plante *f* grimpante.

climbing /ˈklaɪmɪŋ/ ▶ **1282** **I** *n* escalade *f*; ▶ **mountain climbing**, **rock climbing**.
II *adj* **1** Bot [*ivy, rose*] grimpant; **2** Zool grimpeur/-euse.

climbing: **~ boot** *n* chaussure *f* de randonnée; **~ expedition** *n* expédition *f* en montagne; **~ frame** *n* (in playground) cage *f* à poules; **~ irons** *npl* crampons *mpl*; **~ shoe** *n* chausson *m* d'escalade; **~ speed** *n* vitesse *f* ascensionnelle; **~ wall** *n* mur *m* d'escalade.

clime /klaɪm/ *n* littér cieux *mpl*; **in sunnier ~s** sous des cieux plus ensoleillés.

clinch /klɪntʃ/ **I** *n* **1** (in boxing) corps-à-corps *m*; **2**○ (embrace) **to be in a ~** être enlacés; **3** (nail) rivet *m*; (part of nail) pointe *f* de clou rabattue.

II *vtr* **1** Fin, Comm, Pol (secure) décrocher [*funding, holding, loan, market, order*]; **to ~ a deal** Comm conclure une affaire; Pol conclure un accord; **2** (resolve) décider de [*argument, discussion*]; **the ~ing argument** l'argument décisif; **what ~ed it was...** ce qui a été décisif c'est...; **3** Sport décrocher○ [*promotion, victory*].
III *vi* Sport combattre corps-à-corps.

clincher○ /ˈklɪntʃə(r)/ *n* (act, remark) facteur *m* décisif; (argument) argument *m* décisif; **as a ~ they offered him a company car** pour le décider ils lui ont offert une voiture de fonction.

cline /klaɪn/ *n* cline *m*.

cling /klɪŋ/ (*prét, pp* **clung**) *vi* **1** (physically) **to ~ (on) to** se cramponner à [*person, rail, raft etc*]; **to ~ together** se cramponner l'un à l'autre; **to ~ on to sth for dear life** se cramponner de toutes ses forces à qch; **2** (emotionally) **to ~ to** se cramponner à [*parent, beliefs, myth, hope, habit, lifestyle, power*]; **he ~s to me all the time** c'est un vrai crampon; **she ~s to people for support** elle s'appuie sur les autres; **3** (adhere) [*leaf, moss*] coller (**to** à); [*smell*] résister; **the road clung to the mountain** la route s'accrochait au flanc de la montagne.
■ **cling on** [*custom, myth*] survivre obstinément; **to ~ on to sth** se cramponner à qch.

clingfilm /ˈklɪŋfɪlm/ *n* GB scellofrais® *m*.

clinging /ˈklɪŋɪŋ/ *adj* [*plant*] à crampons; [*person*] fig collant.

cling peaches GB, **clingstone peaches** US *npl* pêches *fpl* jaunes.

clinic /ˈklɪnɪk/ *n* **1** (treatment centre) centre *m* médical; **Dr X's ~** le service *m* du Dr X; **2** GB (nursing-home) clinique *f*; **3** (advice or teaching session) clinique *f*.

clinical /ˈklɪnɪkl/ *adj* **1** Med [*research, test, judgment*] clinique; **2** fig (scientific) [*approach*] objectif/-ive; [*efficiency*] irréprochable; [*precision*] clinique; **3** péj (unfeeling) froid.

clinically /ˈklɪnɪklɪ/ *adv* **1** (medically) cliniquement, d'un point de vue clinique; **~ dead** cliniquement mort; **~ depressed** dépressif/-ive au sens médical du terme; **2** (unemotionally) avec une précision clinique.

clinical: **~ psychologist** ▶ **1692** *n* psychologue *mf* clinicien/-ienne; **~ psychology** *n* psychologie *f* clinique; **~ thermometer** *n* thermomètre *m* médical.

clinician /klɪˈnɪʃn/ ▶ **1692** *n* praticien/-ienne *m/f*, clinicien/-ienne *m/f*.

clink /klɪŋk/ **I** *n* **1** (noise) tintement *m*; **2**○ (prison) taule○ *f*, trou○ *m*; **in the ~** en taule○, au trou○.
II *vtr* faire tinter [*glass, keys*]; **to ~ glasses with** trinquer avec.
III *vi* [*glass, keys*] tinter.

clinker /ˈklɪŋkə(r)/ *n* **1** ¢ (ash) scories *fpl*, mâchefer *m*; **2** GB (brick) brique *f* vitrifiée; **3**○ US (blunder) bourde○ *f*, gaffe *f*; (wrong note) couac○ *m*, fausse note *f*; (failed film) bide○ *m*, navet○ *m*; (failed play) four *m*.

clip /klɪp/ **I** *n* **1** (spring-loaded) (in surgery, on clipboard etc) pince *f*; (on earring) clip *m*; **2** (grip) (for hair) barrette *f*; (on pen) agrafe *f*; (on bow tie) clip *m*; (jewellery) clip(s) *m*; **3** Elec (for wire) cavalier *m*; **4** TV, Cin (excerpt) extrait *m* (**from** de); **5** Mil (also **cartridge ~**) chargeur *m*; **6** Agric (wool) tonte *f*; **7** (notch) encoche *f*; **8** Ling forme *f* tronquée.
II *vtr* (*p prés etc* **-pp-**) **1** (cut, trim) tailler [*hedge, grass verge*]; couper [*cigar, fingernails, hair, moustache*]; tondre [*dog, sheep*]; rogner [*coin*]; rogner [*bird's wing*]; **to ~ an article out of the paper** découper un article dans un journal; **2** (by hooking) accrocher [*pen, microphone*] (**to** à); (by securing) fixer [*electric wire, brooch*] (**to** à); **there was a bill ~ped to the letter** il y avait une facture attachée à la lettre (avec un trombone); **3** GB poinçonner [*ticket*]; **4 to ~ one's speech** parler d'une manière hachée; **5** Ling tronquer; **6**○ US (swindle) arnaquer; **7** (hit, glance off) heurter.
III *vi* (*p prés etc* **-pp-**) (by hooking on) [*pen, personal stereo etc*] s'accrocher (**to** à); (by fastening on) [*lamp, brooch etc*] se fixer (**to** à).
IDIOMS **to ~ sb's wings** rogner les ailes à qn; **to give sb a ~ on the ear**○ flanquer une taloche à qn○; **to travel at a fair** ou **a brisk ~** aller à une bonne vitesse.

clip: **~board** *n* gen porte-bloc *m inv* à pince; Comput presse-papiers *m*; **~-clop** *n* bruit *m* de sabots; **~ frame** *n* sous-verre *m*.

clip joint○ *n boîte de nuit qui exploite la clientèle*.

clip-on /ˈklɪpɒn/ **I clip-ons** *npl* (earrings) clips *mpl*; (sunglasses) faces *fpl* additives.
II *adj* [*bow tie*] agrafable; [*lamp*] à fixation par pince(-étau); [*cover*] amovible.

clip-on microphone *n* micro-cravate *m*.

clipped /klɪpt/ *adj* [*speech*] haché.

clipper /ˈklɪpə(r)/ **I** *n* Aviat, Naut clipper *m*.
II **clippers** *npl* (for nails) coupe-ongles *m inv*; (for hair, hedge) tondeuse *f*.

clipping /ˈklɪpɪŋ/ **I** *n* (from newspaper etc) coupure *f* de presse.
II **clippings** *npl* (trimmings) (hair) cheveux *mpl* coupés; (nails) bouts *mpl* d'ongles; (hedge) branches *fpl* coupées; (of fabric) tombées *fpl*.

clippings library *n* bureau *m* qui recense les coupures de presse.

clippity-clop /ˌklɪpətɪˈklɒp/ *n* = **clip-clop**.

clique /kliːk/ *n* clique *f* pej, bande *f*.

cliquey, **cliquish** /ˈkliːkɪ/ *adj* [*profession, group*] fermé; [*atmosphere*] exclusif/-ive; **the office is very ~** (exclusive) l'esprit de clan est très fort dans le bureau; (divided) il y a beaucoup de clans dans le bureau.

cliquishness /ˈkliːkɪʃnɪs/ *n* esprit *m* de clan or de chapelle.

clitoral /ˈklɪtərəl/ *adj* clitoridien/-ienne.

clitoridectomy /ˌklɪtɔːrɪˈdektəmɪ/ *n* clitoridectomie *f*.

clitoris /ˈklɪtərɪs/ *n* (*pl* **-rides**) clitoris *m*.

Cllr GB *abrév écrite* = **councillor**.

cloaca /kləʊˈeɪkə/ *n* (*pl* **~e**) cloaque *m*.

cloak /kləʊk/ **I** *n* **1** (garment) cape *f*; (long, worn by men) houppelande *f*; **2** fig (front, cover) **to be a ~ for** servir de couverture à [*operation etc*]; **a ~ of respectability** un voile de respectabilité.
II *vtr* **1** (surround) **to ~ sth in** ou **with** entourer qch de [*anonymity, secrecy, humour*]; **to ~ sth in respectability** jeter un voile de respectabilité sur qch; **~ed in** enveloppé dans [*darkness*]; enrobé de [*language, style*]; enveloppé de [*ambiguity, secrecy*]; **2** (hide, disguise) masquer [*belief, intentions*].

cloak-and-dagger *adj* [*story, thriller*] d'espionnage; [*affair, tactics, operation*] clandestin; **the ~ brigade**○ GB hum les services *mpl* secrets.

cloakroom /ˈkləʊkrʊm/ *n* **1** (for coats) vestiaire *m*; **2** GB (lavatory) toilettes *fpl*.

cloak: **~room attendant** ▶ **1692** *n* (in hotel) préposé/-e *m/f* au vestiaire; GB (at toilets) préposé/-e *m/f* à l'entretien des toilettes; **~room ticket** *n* ticket *m* de vestiaire; **~s cupboard** *n* GB placard *m* (à habits).

clobber○ /ˈklɒbə(r)/ **I** *n* GB (gear) attirail○ *m*, barda○ *m*.
II *vtr* **1** (hit) tabasser○; **2** (penalize) [*police, law*] porter un coup dur à, tomber à bras raccourcis sur○; **3** (defeat) démolir○, enfoncer○ [*opponent*].

cloche /klɒʃ/ *n* **1** Hort cloche *f*; **2** (also **~ hat**) chapeau *m* cloche.

clock /klɒk/ ▶ **1096** **I** *n* **1** (timepiece) (large) horloge *f*; (small) pendule *f*; **what time does the ~ say?** quelle heure indique l'horloge or la pendule?; **to set a ~** mettre une pendule à l'heure; **to put the ~s forward/back one hour** avancer/reculer les pendules d'une heure; **he does everything by the ~** tout est minuté chez lui; **to work/watch sb around the ~** travailler/surveiller qn 24 heures sur 24; **to work against the ~** faire une course contre la montre; **the biological ~** l'horloge biologique; **the twenty-four hour ~** l'horloge de vingt-quatre heures; **2** (timer) (in computer) horloge *f* (interne); (for central heating system) horloge *f* (incorporée); **3**○ Aut compteur *m*; **a car with 40,000 kilometers on the ~** une voiture qui a 40 000 kilomètres au compteur; **4** Ind (in workplace) pointeuse *f*; **to punch the ~** pointer; **5** Sport chronomètre *m*; **to complete the course against the ~** Equit finir la course dans le temps limite; **to beat the ~** (in games) jouer dans les temps; **a race against the ~** une course contre la montre.
II *vtr* **1** Sport **he ~ed 9.6 seconds in the 100 metres** il a fait le 100 mètres en 9,6 secondes; **to ~ 5 minutes 2.987 seconds** faire un temps de 5 minutes et 2,987 secondes; **2**○ GB (hit) **to ~ sb (one)** flanquer un marron○ à qn; **3** (catch) **the police ~ed him doing 150 km an hour** la police l'a arrêté alors qu'il roulait à 150 km à l'heure; **4**○ GB Aut trafiquer le compteur de [*car*].
IDIOMS **they want to turn** ou **put the ~ back 600 years** ils veulent revenir 600 ans en arrière.
■ **clock in** GB pointer.
■ **clock off** GB = **clock out**.
■ **clock on** GB = **clock in**.
■ **clock out** pointer (à la sortie).
■ **clock up**: **~ up [sth]** **1** [*driver, car*] faire [*30,000 km*]; **2** [*worker*] travailler [*hours*].

clock face *n* cadran *m*.

clocking-in /ˌklɒkɪŋˈɪn/ *n* pointage *m*.

clock: **~ing-in time** *n* heure *f* de pointage (à l'arrivée); **~maker** ▶ **1692** *n* horloger/-ère *m/f*; **~ patience** ▶ **1282** *n* réussite *f*, patience *f*; **~ radio** *n* radio-réveil *m*; **~ tower** *n* beffroi *m*; **~-watch** *vi* regarder tout le temps l'heure.

clock-watcher /ˈklɒkwɒtʃə(r)/ *n* **to be a ~** regarder tout le temps l'heure.

clockwise /ˈklɒkwaɪz/ **I** *adj* **in a ~ direction** dans le sens des aiguilles d'une montre; **the ~ carriageway** GB Transp la chaussée sur laquelle on circule dans le sens des aiguilles d'une montre.
II *adv* dans le sens des aiguilles d'une montre.

clockwork /ˈklɒkwɜːk/ **I** *n* (in clock) mécanisme *m* or mouvement *m* d'horloge; (in toy) mécanisme *m*.
II *adj* [*toy*] mécanique; **with ~ precision** (on time) avec une précision or une exactitude d'horloge.
IDIOMS **to be as regular as ~** être réglé comme une horloge; **to go like ~** aller comme sur des roulettes.

clod /klɒd/ *n* **1** (of earth) motte *f* (de terre); **2**○ (fool) plouc○ *m*.

clodhopper○ /ˈklɒdhɒpə(r)/ *n* **1** (person) balourd/-e *m/f*, empoté/-e○ *m/f*; **2** (shoe) croquenot○ *m*.

clog /klɒg/ **I** *n* sabot *m*.
II *vtr, vi* (*p prés etc* **-gg-**) = **clog up**.
IDIOMS **to pop one's ~s**○ casser sa pipe○.
■ **clog up**: ¶ **~ up** [*drain*] se boucher; [*machinery, pores*] se boucher, s'encrasser; **the roads ~ up with traffic** des bouchons se forment sur les routes; ¶ **~ up [sth]**, **~ [sth] up** boucher [*drain*]; boucher, encrasser [*machinery, pores*]; **to be ~ged up with traffic** être paralysé par la circulation, être embouteillé.

cloister /ˈklɔɪstə(r)/ **I** *n* cloître *m*.
II *vtr* isoler, cloîtrer; **to lead a ~ed existence** mener une vie très protégée.
III *v refl* **to ~ oneself up** ou **away** se cloîtrer, s'enfermer.

clone /kləʊn/ **I** *n* Biol, Comput, fig clone *m*.
II *vtr* cloner.

The clock

What time is it?

It is ...	Il est ...	say ...
4 o'clock	4 heures *or* 4 h	quatre heures
4 o'clock in the morning *or* 4 am	4 h 00	quatre heures du matin
4 o'clock in the afternoon *or* 4 pm	16 h 00	quatre heures de l'après-midi *or* seize heures*
0400	4 h 00	quatre heures
4.02	4 h 02	quatre heures deux
two minutes past four	4 h 02	*or* quatre heures deux minutes†
4.05	4 h 05	quatre heures cinq
five past four	4 h 05	quatre heures cinq
4.10	4 h 10	quatre heures dix
ten past four	4 h 10	quatre heures dix
4.15	4 h 15	quatre heures quinze‡
a quarter past four	4 h 15	quatre heures et quart‡
4.20	4 h 20	quatre heures vingt
4.25	4 h 25	quatre heures vingt-cinq
4.30	4 h 30	quatre heures trente‡
half past four	4 h 30	quatre heures et demie‡§
4.35	4 h 35	quatre heures trente-cinq
twenty-five to five	4 h 35	cinq heures mois vingt-cinq
4.37	4 h 37	quatre heures trente-sept
twenty-three minutes to five	4 h 37	cinq heures moins vingt-trois
4.40	4 h 40	quatre heures quarante
twenty to five	4 h 40	cinq heures moins vingt
4.45	4 h 45	cinq heures moins le quart
4.50	4 h 50	quatre heures cinquante
ten to five	4 h 50	cinq heures moins dix
4.55	4 h 55	quatre heures cinquante cinq
five to five	4 h 55	cinq heures moins cinq
5 o'clock	5 h	cinq heures
16.15	16 h 15	seize heures quinze
16.25	16 h 25	seize heures vingt-cinq
8 o'clock in the evening	8 h du soir	huit heures du soir
8 pm	20 h 00	vingt heures
12.00	12 h 00	douze heures
noon *or* 12 noon	12 h 00	midi
midnight *or* 12 midnight	24 h 00	minuit

* *In timetables etc., the twenty-four hour clock is used, so that* 4 pm *is* seize heures. *In ordinary usage, one says* quatre heures (de l'après-midi).

what time is it? = quelle heure est-il?
my watch says five o'clock = il est cinq heures à ma montre
could you tell me the time? = pouvez-vous me donner l'heure?
it's exactly four o'clock = il est quatre heures juste *or* il est exactement quatre heures
it's about four = il est environ quatre heures
it's almost three o'clock = il est presque trois heures
it's just before six o'clock = il va être six heures
it's just after five o'clock = il est à peine plus de cinq heures
it's gone five = il est cinq heures passées

When?

French never drops the word heures: at five *is* à cinq heures *and so on.*

French always uses à, *whether or not English includes the word* at. *The only exception is when there is another preposition present, as in* vers cinq heures (*towards five o'clock*), avant cinq heures (*before five o'clock*) *etc.*

what time did it happen? = à quelle heure cela s'est-il passé?
what time will he come at? = à quelle heure va-t-il venir?
it happened at two o'clock = c'est arrivé à deux heures
he'll come at four = il viendra à quatre heures
at ten past four = à quatre heures dix
at half past eight = à huit heures et demie
at three o'clock exactly = à trois heures précises
at about five = vers cinq heures *or* à cinq heures environ
at five at the latest = à cinq heures au plus tard
a little after nine = un peu après neuf heures
it must be ready by ten = il faut que ce soit prêt avant dix heures
I'll be here until 6 pm = je serai là jusqu'à six heures du soir
I won't be here until 6 pm = je ne serai pas là avant six heures du soir
it lasts from seven till nine = cela dure de sept à neuf heures
closed from 1 to 2 pm = fermé entre treize et quatorze heures
every hour on the hour = toutes les heures à l'heure juste
at ten past every hour = toutes les heures à dix

† *This fuller form is possible in all similar cases in this list. It is used only in 'official' styles.*

‡ Quatre heures et quart *sounds less official than* quatre heures quinze (*and similarly* et demie *and* moins le quart *are the less official forms). The* demie *and* quart *forms are not used with the 24-hour clock.*

§ Demi *agrees when it follows its noun, but not when it comes before the noun to which it is hyphenated, e.g.* quatre heures et demie *but* les demi-heures *etc. Note that* midi *and* minuit *are masculine, so* midi et demi *and* minuit et demi.

cloning /ˈkləʊnɪŋ/ *n* clonage *m*.

close¹ /kləʊs/ **I** *n* **1** (road) passage *m*; **2** (of cathedral) enceinte *f*.

II *adj* **1** (with close links) [*relative*] proche; [*resemblance*] frappant; **to bear a ~ resemblance to sb/sth** ressembler beaucoup à qn/qch; **~ links with** Pol liens étroits avec [*country*]; liens d'amitié avec [*group, twinned town etc*]; **to work in ~ collaboration with sb** collaborer étroitement avec qn; **in ~ contact with** en contact permanent avec [*government department etc*]; en contact avec [*friend etc*]; **in ~ harmony** Mus dans une tessiture rapprochée; **2** (intimate) [*friend, adviser*] proche (**to** de); **they have a ~ friendship** ils sont très bons amis; **3** (almost equal) [*contest, finish, result, vote*] serré; **'is it the same?'—'no but it's ~'** 'c'est le même?'—'non mais c'est proche'; **a ~ copy of his signature** une imitation presque parfaite de sa signature; **it's a ~ match** (of colour, hairpiece) c'est presque la même couleur; **4** (careful, rigorous) [*scrutiny, examination, study*] minutieux/-ieuse; [*supervision*] étroit; **to pay ~ attention to sth** faire une attention toute particulière à qch; **to keep a ~ watch** ou **eye on sb/sth** surveiller étroitement qn/qch; **5** (compactly aligned) [*texture, grain*] dense; [*print, military formation*] serré; [*handwriting*] ramassé; **6** (stuffy) [*weather*] lourd; **it's ~** il fait lourd; **7**○ (secretive) **she's been very ~ about it** elle n'a rien voulu dire.

III *adv* **1** (nearby) **to live/work quite ~ (by)** habiter/travailler tout près; **they look ~er than they are** ils semblent plus près qu'ils ne le sont; **how ~ is the town?** est-ce que la ville est loin?; **it's ~, I can hear it** il ne doit pas être loin, je l'entends; **the closer he came** plus il approchait; **to bring sth closer** approcher qch; **to follow ~ behind** suivre de près; **to hold sb ~** serrer qn; **~ together** serrés les uns contre les autres; **to come closer together** se rapprocher; ▶**draw**; **2** (close temporally) **the time is ~ when** dans peu de temps; **how ~ are they in age?** combien ont-ils de différence d'âge?; **Christmas is ~** Noël approche; ▶**draw**; **3** (almost) **that's closer (to) the truth** ça c'est plus proche de la vérité; **'is the answer three?'—'~!'** 'est-ce que la réponse est trois?'—'tu y es presque'.

IV close enough *adv phr* **1** (sufficiently near) **that's ~ enough** (no nearer) tu es assez près; (acceptable as answer) ça ira; **to be/come ~ enough to do** être assez près/s'approcher suffisamment pour faire; **2** (approximately) **there were 20 yachts or ~ enough** il y avait à peu près 20 yachts.

V close to *prep phr, adv phr* **1** lit près de [*place, person, object*]; **~ to where** près de l'endroit où; **closer to** plus près de; **how ~ are we to...?** à quelle distance sommes-nous de...?; **2** (on point of) au bord de [*tears, hysteria, collapse*]; **to be ~ to doing** être sur le point de faire; **3** (almost at) **closer to 30 than 40** plus proche or plus près de 40 ans que de 30; **to come closest to** s'approcher le plus de [*ideal, conception*]; **to come ~ to doing** faillir faire; **he came ~ to giving up** il a failli abandonner; **how ~ are you to completing...?** est-ce que vous êtes sur le point de finir...?; **~ to the time when** à peu près au moment où; **it's coming ~ to the time when we must decide** l'heure de nous décider approche; **4** (also **~ on**○) (approximately) **~ to** ou **on**○ **60 people** près de or presque 60 personnes; **~ to** ou **on**○ **a century ago** il y a près d'un siècle.

VI close by *prep phr, adv phr* près de [*wall, bridge*]; **the ambulance is ~ by** l'ambulance n'est pas loin.

IDIOMS **(from) ~ to**○, **(from) ~ up** de près; **it was a ~ call**○ ou **shave**○ ou **thing** je l'ai/tu l'as etc échappé belle.

close² /kləʊz/ **I** *n* **1** gen, Sport fin *f*; **to bring sth to a ~** mettre fin à qch; **to draw to a ~** tirer à sa fin; **to come to a ~** se terminer; **at the ~ of day** littér à la tombée du jour liter; **2** Fin **~ (of trading)** clôture *f*; **at the ~** à la clôture.

II *vtr* **1** (shut) fermer [*container, door, window, eyes, mouth, mind, book, file, museum, office, shop*]; **2** (block) fermer [*border, port, airport*]; boucher [*pipe, opening*]; barrer [*road*]; interdire l'accès à [*area of town*]; **3** = **close down**; **4** (bring to an end) mettre fin à [*meeting, discussion, investigation, case*]; fermer [*account*]; **to ~ the meeting, we have** pour clore la réunion nous avons; **the subject is now ~d** le sujet est clos; **'this correspondence is now ~d'** journ 'cette rubrique est interrompue'; **5** (reduce) **to ~ the gap** fig réduire l'écart (**between** entre); **to ~ the gap on sb/sth** lit, fig rattraper qn/qch; **to ~ the gaps** (improve fault) remédier aux lacunes (**in** dans); **6** (agree) conclure [*deal, contract, sale*]; **7** Elec fermer [*circuit*].

III *vi* **1** (shut) [*airport, factory, office, polls, shop, station*] fermer (**for** pour); [*door, window, container, lid, eyes, mouth*] se fermer; [*hand, arms*] se (re)fermer (**around** sur); **the museum has ~d** le musée est fermé au public; **2** (cease to operate) [*business, factory, mine, institution*] fermer définitivement; **3** (end) [*meeting, enquiry, play, concert, season*] prendre fin; **to ~ with** se terminer par [*scene, event, song*]; **4** Fin [*currency, index, shares, market*] clôturer (**at** à); **the market ~d down/up** le marché a clôturé en baisse/en hausse; **the pound ~d up against the franc** la livre (sterling) a clôturé en hausse contre le franc; **5** (get smaller) se réduire; **the gap is closing between X**

and Y fig l'écart entre X et Y se réduit; lit la distance entre X et Y se réduit; **6** (get closer) [*pursuer, enemy*] se rapprocher (**on** de); **7** (heal) [*wound*] se refermer.

IV closed *pp adj* **1** (shut) [*door, window, container, business, public building, shop*] fermé; [*fist, mouth, eyes*] fermé; **'~d'** (sign in shop) 'fermé'; (in theatre) 'relâche'; **'~d for lunch/for repairs'** 'fermé pour le déjeuner/pour cause de réparations'; **'road ~d'** 'route barrée'; **'~d to the public'** 'interdit au public'; **'~d to traffic'** 'circulation interdite'; **behind ~d doors** fig à huis clos; **2** (restricted) [*community, circle, meeting, organization, economy*] fermé; **to have a ~d mind** avoir l'esprit fermé; **3** Math [*set*] fermé; **4** Ling [*syllable*] fermé.

■ **close down**: ¶ **~ down** [*shop , business, club, institution*] fermer définitivement; GB, Radio, TV **we are now closing down** nos émissions sont terminées pour ce soir; ¶ **~ down [sth], ~ [sth] down** fermer [qch] définitivement [*business, factory*].

■ **close in** [*pursuers, enemy*] se rapprocher (**on** de); [*winter, night*] approcher; [*darkness, fog*] descendre (**on** sur); [*jungle, forest*] se refermer; **the nights are closing in** les jours commencent à raccourcir.

■ **close off**: **~ off [sth], ~ [sth] off** fermer [qch] au public [*district, street, wing*].

■ **close out**: **~ out [sth], ~ [sth] out** US Comm liquider [*stock*]; vendre [*part of business*].

■ **close up**: ¶ **~ up 1** [*flower, petals, wound*] se refermer; [*group*] se serrer; [*troops*] serrer les rangs; **2** [*shopkeeper, caretaker*] fermer; **3 he just ~s up** il refuse d'en parler; ¶ **~ up [sth], ~ [sth] up 1** fermer [*bank, office, shop*]; **2** boucher [*hole, entrance, pipe*].

■ **close with**: ¶ **~ with [sb] 1** Comm tomber d'accord avec [*dealer, trader*] (**for** pour); **2** Mil engager le combat avec [*enemy*]; ¶ **~ with [sth]** Fin accepter [*deal, offer*].

close /kləʊs/: **~ combat** *n* corps-à-corps *m*; **~ company, ~ corporation** *n* Comm *société contrôlée par un maximum de cinq actionnaires et à régime fiscal particulier*; **~-cropped** *adj* [*hair*] coupé ras; [*grass*] ras *inv*.

closed-circuit television /kləʊzd/ *n* télévision *f* en circuit fermé.

closedown /kləʊzdaʊn/ *n* **1** Comm, Ind fermeture *f* (définitive); **2** GB Radio, TV fin *f* des émissions.

closed primary /kləʊzd/ *n* US Pol élection *f* primaire réservée aux électeurs déclarés des partis.

closed scholarship /kləʊzd/ *n* bourse *f* réservée à une certaine catégorie d'étudiants.

closed season /kləʊzd/ *n* période *f* de fermeture de la chasse et de la pêche.

closed shop /kləʊzd/ *n* Mgmt *industrie employant exclusivement les membres des syndicats*.

close /kləʊs/: **~-fitting** *adj* [*garment*] ajusté, près du corps; **~-grained** *adj* [*texture*] dense.

close-hauled /ˌkləʊsˈhɔːld/ *adj* Naut **to be ~** lofer, venir au lof.

close-knit /ˌkləʊsˈnɪt/ *adj* fig [*family, group*] très uni.

closely /ˈkləʊslɪ/ *adv* **1** (in close proximity) [*follow, look*] lit, fig de près; **crowded ~ around the painting** assemblés tout autour de la peinture; **to work ~ together** travailler en étroite collaboration; **~ written** écrit très serré; **the script was so ~ typed that** les caractères étaient si serrés que; **to be ~ packed** [*people, boxed items*] être entassés; **the houses were ~ spaced** il y avait très peu d'espace entre les maisons; **2** (not distantly) [*resemble*] beaucoup; [*identify*] tellement; [*conform*] tout à fait; [*integrated, coordinated*] bien; **the more ~ you look, the more ~ it seems to resemble him** plus on regarde, plus on trouve que la ressemblance est frappante; **which photo fits the rapist most ~?** quelle photo ressemble le plus au violeur?; **her description ~ fits that of the thief** sa description correspond parfaitement à celle du voleur; **to be ~ akin to sth** ressembler beaucoup à qch; **to be ~ related** gen être étroitement lié (**to** à); (of people) être proches parents; **3** (rigorously, in detail) [*study, monitor, observe*] de près; [*listen*] attentivement; [*question*] avec attention; **4** (evenly) **~ contested** ou **fought** serré; **to be so ~ matched that** [*competitors*] se suivre de si près que; **5** (near to body) [*shaven*] de près; **to fit ~** [*garment*] être très ajusté; **he held her ~ to him** il l'a serrée fort; **~ guarded secret** fig secret bien gardé.

close-mouthed /kləʊs/ *adj* taciturne.

closeness /ˈkləʊsnɪs/ *n* **1** (emotionally) intimité *f*; **2** (in mutual understanding) (of peoples) bonnes relations *fpl*; **the ~ of their alliance** les liens étroits qui les unissent/unissaient etc; **3** (rapport) rapport *m* (**to** à); **~ to nature** rapport à la nature; **4** (proximity) (of place) proximité *f*; (of event) approche *f*; **5** (of atmosphere) (inside) manque *m* d'air; (outside) **the ~ of the weather** le temps lourd; **6** (accuracy, similarity) (of copy) fidélité *f*; **the ~ of the resemblance** la ressemblance frappante.

close /kləʊs/: **~-run** *adj* [*race, contest*] très serré; **~-set** *adj* [*eyes, buildings*] très rapproché; **~stool** *n* Hist chaise *f* percée.

closet /ˈklɒzɪt/ **I** *n* **1** (cupboard) placard *m*; (for clothes) penderie *f*; **linen ~** placard *m* à linge; **2** (room) cabinet *m*; **3**† (lavatory) cabinet *m*.

II *modif* (secret) [*alcoholic, fascist*] inavoué, qui s'en cache.

III *vtr* enfermer; **to be ~ed with sb** être en tête-à-tête avec qn; **a ~ed world** un univers clos.

IDIOMS **to come out of the ~** [*homosexual*] déclarer publiquement son homosexualité; gen se révéler sous son propre jour.

closet drama *n*: *pièce écrite pour être lue plutôt que jouée*.

close-up /ˈkləʊsʌp/ **I** *n* gros plan *m*; **in ~** en gros plan.

II close up /ˌkləʊsˈʌp/ *adv* (**from**) **~** de près.

closing /ˈkləʊzɪŋ/ **I** *n* fermeture *f*; **Sunday ~** fermeture *f* dominicale (des magasins); **a ~ of ranks** fig un resserrement des rangs.

II *adj* [*minutes, months, days, words*] dernier/-ière; [*scene, pages, stage*] final; [*speech*] de clôture.

closing: **~ bid** *n* Fin dernière enchère *f*; **~ date** *n* date *f* limite (**for** de); **~-down sale, ~-out sale** US *n* liquidation *f*; **~ price** *n* Fin prix *m* de clôture.

closing time *n* heure *f* de fermeture; **'~!'** 'on ferme!'

closure /ˈkləʊʒə(r)/ *n* **1** (of road, lane, factory) fermeture *f*; **2** Pol clôture *f*; **to move the ~** demander la clôture; **3** (fastening) fermeture *f*; (lid) couvercle *m*; (strip) lien *m*; **4** Ling occlusion *f*.

clot /klɒt/ **I** *n* **1** (in blood, milk) caillot *m*; **~ in an artery** caillot obstruant une artère; **~ on the lung/on the brain** embolie *f* pulmonaire/cérébrale; **2**○ GB (idiot) balourd/-e *m/f*, empoté/-e○ *m/f*.

II *vtr* (*p prés etc* **-tt-**) coaguler, cailler.

III *vi* (*p prés etc* **-tt-**) (se) coaguler, (se) cailler.

cloth /klɒθ, US klɔːθ/ **I** *n* **1** (fabric) tissu *m*; **wool/silk/cotton ~** tissu *m* de laine/de soie/de coton; **2** (piece of fabric) (for polishing, dusting) chiffon *m*; (for floor) serpillière *f*; (for drying dishes) torchon *m*; (for table) nappe *f*; **altar ~** nappe *f* d'autel; **damp ~** (for cleaning) chiffon *m* humide; (for ironing) pattemouille *f*; **dish ~** (for washing dishes) chiffon *m* pour la vaisselle; **wrap it in a damp ~** enveloppez-le dans un linge humide; **3** Relig **the ~** l'habit *m* ecclésiastique; **a man of the ~** un ecclésiastique.

II *modif* [*cover, blind etc*] en tissu; **hey ~ ears**○! alors, tu es sourd?

IDIOMS **to cut one's coat according to one's ~** GB vivre selon ses moyens.

cloth: **~backed, ~bound** *adj* [*book*] relié toile; **~ cap** *n* GB lit casquette *f* de drap; fig casquette *f* (*qui symbolise la classe ouvrière*).

clothe /kləʊð/ **I** *vtr* habiller, vêtir; **to feed and ~** nourrir et habiller ou vêtir [*family, refugees*]; **to be ~d in** être habillé en ou vêtu de; **fully ~d** tout habillé.

II *v refl* **to ~ oneself** s'habiller, se vêtir.

cloth-eared○ *adj* bouché○, sourd.

clothes /kləʊðz, US kləʊz/ **▶ 1703** **I** *npl* **1** (garments) vêtements *mpl*; **children's/work ~** vêtements *mpl* d'enfants/de travail; **to put on/take off one's ~** s'habiller/se déshabiller; **to change one's ~** se changer; **without any ~ on** tout nu; **to make one's own ~** faire ses vêtements; **2** (washing) linge *m*.

II *modif* [*basket, line, peg, pin*] à linge.

IDIOMS **with only the ~ he stood up in** sans rien d'autre que les vêtements qu'il avait sur le dos.

clothes: **~ airer** *n* séchoir *m* à linge; **~ brush** *n* brosse *f* à habits; **~ drier** *n* (machine) sèche-linge *m inv*; (airer) séchoir *m* à linge; **~hanger** *n* cintre *m*; **~ horse** *n* lit séchoir *m* à linge; fig péj○ (fashionable person) minet/minette○ *m/f*; **~ moth** *n* mite *f*; **~ prop** *n* béquille *f* de corde à linge; **~ shop** *n* GB magasin *m* de vêtements; **~ tree** *n* US portemanteau *m*.

clothier† /ˈkləʊðɪə(r)/ **▶ 1692** *n* (seller) confectionneur *m*; (designer) habilleur/-euse *m/f*.

clothing /ˈkləʊðɪŋ/ *n* ¢ vêtements *mpl*; **an item** ou **article of ~** un vêtement.

clothing: **~ allowance** *n* (worker's) indemnité *f* vestimentaire; (child's) allocation *f* vêtements; **~ industry, ~ trade** *n* habillement *m*, confection *f*.

clotted cream *n* GB ≈ crème *f* fraîche épaisse.

cloture /ˈkləʊtʃə(r)/ *n* US Pol = **closure** 2.

cloud /klaʊd/ **I** *n* **1 C** (in sky) nuage *m*, nuée *f* liter; **2** ¢ Meteorol (also **~ mass**) nuages *mpl*; **some patches of ~** quelques nuages; **there's a lot of ~ about** il fait un temps très nuageux; **3** (mass) (of smoke, dust, gas) nuage *m*; (of ash, insects) nuage *m*, nuée *f*; **4** fig (negative feature) **a ~ of gloom/uncertainty** un voile de tristesse/d'incertitude; **to cast a ~ over sth** jeter une ombre sur qch; **5** (blur) (in liquid, marble, gem) nuage *m*; (in glass, on mirror) buée *f*.

II *vtr* **1** (blur) [*steam, breath*] embuer [*mirror*]; [*substance*] rendre [qch] trouble [*liquid*]; [*tears*] brouiller [*vision*]; **~ed with tears** [*eyes*] voilé or brouillé de larmes; **2** (confuse) obscurcir [*judgment*]; brouiller [*memory*]; **to ~ the issue** brouiller les cartes; **3** (blight) assombrir [*atmosphere, occasion etc*].

III *vi* = **cloud over**.

IDIOMS **to be living in ~-cuckoo-land** croire au père Noël; **to have one's head in the ~s** avoir la tête dans les nuages; **to be on ~ nine**○ être aux anges; **to be/leave under a ~** être/partir en état de disgrâce.

■ **cloud over** [*sky*] se couvrir (de nuages); [*face*] s'assombrir.

cloud: **~berry** *n* (fruit) mûre *f* rose; (plant) faux-mûrier *m*; **~burst** *n* violente averse *f*; **~ chamber** *n* Phys chambre *f* de Wilson, chambre *f* à bulles; **~ cover** *n* couverture *f* nuageuse.

clouded /ˈklaʊdɪd/ *adj* **1** [*sky, weather*] couvert, nuageux/-euse; **2** fig [*eyes, expression*] attristé, assombri.

cloudiness /ˈklaʊdɪnɪs/ *n* **1** (of sky) aspect *m* nuageux; **2** (of liquid, glass) aspect *m* terne.

cloudless /ˈklaʊdlɪs/ *adj* sans nuages, limpide.

cloudy /ˈklaʊdɪ/ *adj* **1** [*weather*] couvert;

it's ~ le temps est couvert; **2** [*liquid*] trouble; [*glass*] (misted) embué; (opaque) terni.

clout /klaʊt/ **I** *n* **1** (blow) claque *f*, coup *m*; **to give sth a ~** frapper qch; **to give sb a ~** donner un coup or une claque à qn; **2** fig (weight) influence *f* (**with** auprès de, sur); **to have** ou **carry a great deal of ~** avoir beaucoup d'influence, avoir du poids; **to have emotional ~** [*play, film*] avoir un impact emotionnel; **3** dial (cloth) chiffon *m*.
II○ *vtr* donner un coup or une claque à [*person*]; taper dans○, frapper [*ball*].
IDIOMS **ne'er cast a ~ till May be out** Prov ≈ en avril ne te découvre pas d'un fil, en mai fais ce qu'il te plaît.

clove /kləʊv/ **I** *pret* ▸ **cleave**.
II *n* Culin **1** (spice) clou *m* de girofle; **oil of ~s** essence *f* de girofle; **2** (of garlic) gousse *f*.

clove hitch *n* demi-clé *f*.

cloven /'kləʊvn/ *pp* ▸ **cleave**.

cloven foot, **cloven hoof** *n* (of animal) sabot *m* fendu; (of devil) pied *m* fourchu.

clover /'kləʊvə(r)/ *n* trèfle *m*.
IDIOMS **to be/live in ~, to be/live like a pig in ~** être/vivre comme un coq en pâte.

clover: **~leaf** *n* feuille *f* de trèfle; **~leaf junction** *n* Transp (croisement *m* en) trèfle *m*.

clown /klaʊn/ **I** *n* **1** (in circus) clown *m*; (jester) bouffon *m*; **2** péj (fool) clown *m*, pitre *m*.
II *vi* **1** = **clown around**; **2** (perform) **he taught me how to ~** il m'a appris le métier de clown.
■ **clown around** GB faire le clown or le pitre.

clowning /'klaʊnɪŋ/ *n* **1** (professional) métier *m* de clown; **2** (fooling) clowneries *fpl*, pitreries *fpl*.

cloy /klɔɪ/ *vi* [*pleasure, food*] finir par lasser; [*pleasure, fame*] perdre son charme.

cloying /'klɔɪɪŋ/ *adj* mièvre, mielleux/-euse.

club /klʌb/ **I** *n* ▸ **1282** **1** (society) (+ *v sg ou pl*) club *m*; **chess/tennis ~** club *m* d'échecs/de tennis; **book/record ~** club *m* de livres/de disques; **to be in a ~** faire partie d'un club; **2**○ (nightclub) boîte *f* de nuit○; **3** Sport club *m*; **football ~** club *m* de football; **4** (stick, weapon) massue *f*; (for golf) club *m*; **5** (at cards) trèfle *m*; **the Ace of ~s** l'as de trèfle; **to play a low/high ~** jouer un petit/gros trèfle; **two tricks in ~s, two ~ tricks** deux levées à trèfle.
II *modif* [*captain, committee, coach, member, official, rules*] du club; [*DJ, aficionado, atmosphere*] de boîte de nuit○; **on the ~ scene** dans les boîtes de nuit○; **the London ~ scene** les boîtes de nuit○ de Londres.
III *vtr* (*p prés etc* **-bb-**) frapper [qn/qch] à coups de massue; assommer [*seal*]; **to ~ sb with a brick/spade** frapper qn avec une brique/bêche; **to ~ sb with a truncheon** matraquer qn; **to ~ sb to death** tuer qn à coups de massue.
IDIOMS **join the ~**○**!, welcome to the ~**○**!** tu n'es pas le seul/la seule!; **to be in the ~**○ GB être enceinte.
■ **club together** cotiser (**for** pour; **to do** pour faire).

clubbable /'klʌbəbl/ *adj* sociable.

clubber○ /'klʌbə(r)/ *n* habitué/-e *m/f* des boîtes○.

clubbing○ /'klʌbɪŋ/ *n* **to go ~** faire la tournée des boîtes○.

club: **~ car** *n* US wagon-bar *m* de première classe; **~ chair** *n* US fauteuil *m* club.

club class *n* classe *f* club or affaires; **to fly ~** voyager en classe club or affaires.

club foot *n* pied *m* bot; **to have a ~** être pied-bot.

club: **~-footed** *adj* pied-bot *inv*; **~goer**○ *n* habitué/-e *m/f* des boîtes○; **~house** *n* (for changing) US vestiaire *m*; (for socializing) maison *f* de club, club-house *m*.

clubland /'klʌblænd/ *n* **1** (nightclubs) quartier *m* des boîtes de nuit○; **2** (gentlemen's clubs) quartier *m* des clubs.

club: **~ sandwich** *n* sandwich *m* mixte, club sandwich *m*; **~ soda** *n* US eau *f* de seltz; **~ steak** *n* US petit bifteck *m* (*coupé dans la queue du filet*); **~ subscription** *n* cotisation *f*.

cluck /klʌk/ **I** *n* gloussement *m*; **to give a ~** glousser; **the hen goes ~! ~!** la poule fait cot! cot!
II *vtr* **to ~ one's tongue** claquer de la langue.
III *vi* **1** [*hen*] glousser; **a ~ing sound** un gloussement; **2** fig **to ~ over** (fuss) s'affairer comme une mère poule autour de; (in annoyance) faire des petits bruits d'agacement devant.

clucking /'klʌkɪŋ/ *n* gloussements *mpl*.

clue /klu:/ **I** *n* **1** (in investigation) indice *m* (**to** quant à); **to provide sb with a ~ (as) to where/how etc** permettre à qn d'établir où/comment etc; **2** (hint, suggestion) indication *f* (**to, as to** quant à); **I'll give you a ~** je vais vous mettre sur la piste; **come on, give me a ~** allons, aide-moi; **3**○ (idea, notion) **I haven't (got) a ~** je n'ai aucune idée; **they haven't (got) a ~** (incompetent) ils n'(en) ont pas la moindre idée; (unsuspecting) ils ne se doutent de rien; **he hasn't (got) a ~ about history** il ne connaît rien de rien à l'histoire; **4** (to crossword) définition *f*.
II *vtr* US **to ~ sb to sth** permettre à qn d'établir qch.

clued-up○ /ˌklu:d'ʌp/ GB *adj* calé○ (**about** sur).

clueless /'klu:lɪs/ *adj* GB nul/nulle○ (**about** en).

clump /klʌmp/ **I** *n* **1** (of flowers, grass) touffe *f*; (of trees) massif *m*; (of earth) motte *f*; **2** (thud) bruit *m* sourd.
II *vtr* (also **~ together**) planter [qch] en groupes [*plants*].
III *vi* (thud) tomber avec fracas (**on** sur); **to ~ upstairs/downstairs** monter/descendre l'escalier d'un pas lourd.
■ **clump about**, **clump around** marcher d'un pas lourd.

clumsily /'klʌmzɪlɪ/ *adv* [*move*] gauchement; [*break sth*] par maladresse; [*painted, expressed*] de façon maladroite.

clumsiness /'klʌmzɪnɪs/ *n* (carelessness) maladresse *f*; (awkwardness) gaucherie *f*; (of style) lourdeur *f*; (of device, system) côté *m* peu pratique.

clumsy /'klʌmzɪ/ *adj* [*person, attempt, effort*] maladroit; [*body, limbs*] gauche; [*object*] grossier/-ière; [*animal*] pataud; [*tool*] peu maniable; [*style*] lourd; **to be ~ at sports/drawing** ne pas être très adroit en sport/dessin; **to be ~ at tennis/volleyball** ne pas être très adroit au tennis/volley; **to be ~ with one's hands/a knife** ne pas être très adroit de ses mains/avec un couteau dans les mains; **how ~ of me!** que je suis maladroit!

clung /klʌŋ/ *pret, pp* ▸ **cling**.

clunk○ /klʌŋk/ **I** *n* **1** (sound) (*aussi onomat*) bruit *m* sourd; **2**○ US (idiot) imbécile *mf*.
II *vi* faire un bruit sourd.

clunker○ /'klʌŋkə(r)/ *n* US **1** (car, machine) épave○ *f*; **2** (book, play etc) nullité○ *f*.

clunky○ /'klʌŋkɪ/ *adj* **1** (clumsy) maladroit; **2** (shabby) minable○; **3** (clunking) [*bangles etc*] qui s'entrechoquent.

cluster /'klʌstə(r)/ **I** *n* **1** (group) (of flowers, grapes, berries) grappe *f*; (of people, islands, insects, trees) groupe *m*; (of flowers) touffe *f*; (of houses) ensemble *m*; (of ideas) ensemble *m*; (of diamonds) entourage *m*; **2** Astron amas *m*; **3** Stat grappe *f*; **4** Ling (**consonant**) **~** agglomérat *m*.
II *vi* [*people*] se rassembler (**around** autour de); **they (were) ~ed in front of the shop window** ils s'agglutinaient devant la vitrine; **the trees were ~ed around the church** les arbres étaient groupés tout autour de l'église.

cluster bomb *n* bombe *f* à fragmentation.

clutch /klʌtʃ/ **I** *n* **1** Aut (mechanism) embrayage *m*; (pedal) (pédale *f* d')embrayage *m*; **to let in** ou **disengage the ~** débrayer; **to let out** ou **engage the ~** embrayer; **to release the ~** embrayer; **2** (cluster) (of eggs, chicks) couvée *f*; fig (of books, awards, companies) ensemble *m*; (of people) groupe *m*; **3** (grab) **to make a ~ at sth** tenter d'attraper qch; **4** US (tight situation) moment *m* difficile; **5** US (bag) pochette *f*.
II clutches *npl* (power) **to be in sb's ~es** être tombé sous les griffes de qn; **to fall into the ~es of** tomber sous les griffes or la patte○ de.
III *vtr* **1** (hold tightly) tenir fermement [*object, child*] (**in** dans); **to ~ sb/sth to** serrer qn/qch contre [*chest, body, oneself*]; **2** (grab at) = **clutch at**.
■ **clutch at**: **~ at [sth/sb]** tenter d'attraper [*branch, lifebelt, rail, person*]; fig s'accrocher à [*hope*]; sauter sur [*opportunity, excuse*]; **she ~ed at my arm** elle m'a saisi le bras. ▸ **straw**.

clutch: **~ bag** *n* pochette *f*; **~ cable** *n* câble *m* de commande d'embrayage; **~ disc** *n* disque *m* d'embrayage; **~ linkage** *n* embrayage *m*; **~ linkage play**, **~ pedal play** *n* garde *f* d'embrayage.

clutter /'klʌtə(r)/ **I** *n* **1** (jumbled objects) fatras *m*; **in a ~** en désordre; **2** ¢ (on radar) échos *mpl* fixes or parasites.
II *vtr* = **clutter up**.
■ **clutter up**: **~ up [sth]**, **~ [sth] up** encombrer.

cluttered /'klʌtəd/ *adj* [*room, desk, mind*] encombré (**with** de); **the presentation is ~** la présentation est fouillis (*inv*).

Clwyd /'klu:ɪd/ ▸ **1624** *pr n* Clwyd *m*.

Clyt(a)emnestra /ˌklaɪtɪm'nestrə/ *pr n* Clytemnestre.

cm (*abrév écrite* = **centimetre**) cm.

Cmdr *n* Mil *abrév écrite* = **Commander**.

CNAA *n* (*abrév* = **Council for National Academic Awards**) *organisme chargé jusqu'en 1992 du contrôle des établissements d'enseignement supérieur (non universitaires)*.

CND *n* (*abrév* = **Campaign for Nuclear Disarmament**) mouvement *m* pour le désarmement nucléaire.

c/o Post (*abrév écrite* = **care of**) chez.

Co *n* **1** Comm (*abrév* = **company**) Cie; **...and co** ...et Cie; hum et compagnie; **2** Geog (*abrév* = **county**) comté *m*.

CO *n* **1** Mil *abrév* ▸ **commanding officer**; **2** US Post *abrév écrite* = **Colorado**; **3** *abrév* ▸ **conscientious objector**.

coach /kəʊtʃ/ **I** *n* **1** (bus) (auto)car *m*; **to go by ~, to go on the ~** aller en (auto)car; **2** GB (of train) wagon *m*; **3** Sport entraîneur/-euse *m/f*; **4** (for drama, voice) répétiteur/-trice *m/f*; **5** (tutor) professeur *m* particulier; **6** (horse-drawn) (for royalty) carrosse *m*; (for passengers) diligence *f*; **7** US Aviat classe *f* touriste.
II *modif* [*holiday, journey, travel*] en (auto)car.
III *vtr* **1** Sport entraîner [*team*]; être entraîneur/-euse de [*sport*]; **2** (teach) **to ~ sb** donner des leçons particulières à qn (**in** en); **to ~ sb for an exam/for a rôle** préparer qn à un examen/pour un rôle; **to ~ sb in what to say** faire répéter à qn ce qu'il/elle doit dire.
IDIOMS **to drive a ~ and horses through sth** démolir qch.

coach: **~builder** ▸ **1692** *n* GB carrossier *m*; **~building** *n* GB carrosserie *f* (*fabrication*); **~ driver** ▸ **1692** *n* GB chauffeur *m* d'autocar.

coaching /'kəʊtʃɪŋ/ *n* ¢ **1** (in sport) entraînement *m*; **to receive ~** recevoir un entraînement; **2** (lessons) cours *mpl* particuliers.

coach: **~load** *n* GB car *m* (**of** de);

~man *n* cocher *m*; **~ operator** *n* GB compagnie *f* d'autocars; **~ park** *n* GB parking *m* réservé aux autocars (de tourisme); **~ party** *n* GB groupe *m* voyageant en autocar; **~ station** *n* GB gare *f* routière; **~ terminus** *n* GB terminus *m* (des cars); **~ trip** *n* excursion *f* en autocar; **~work** *n* GB carrosserie *f* (*caisse d'automobile*).

coagulant /kəʊˈægjʊlənt/ *n, adj* coagulant (*m*).

coagulate /kəʊˈægjʊleɪt/ **I** *vtr* coaguler.
II *vi* coaguler.

coagulation /ˌkəʊægjʊˈleɪʃn/ *n* coagulation *f*.

coal /kəʊl/ **I** *n* **1** ¢ (mineral) charbon *m*; **a piece** ou **lump of ~** un morceau de charbon; **2** (individual piece) charbon *m*; **hot** ou **live ~s** charbons *mpl* ardents; **brown ~** lignite *m*; **soft ~** houille *f* grasse; **hard ~** anthracite *m*.
II *modif* [*cellar, shed, shovel*] à charbon.
III *vtr* ravitailler [qch] en charbon.
IV *vi* [*ship*] être ravitaillé en charbon.
IDIOMS **as black as ~** noir comme du charbon; **to carry ~s to Newcastle** porter de l'eau à la rivière; **to haul sb over the ~s**○ passer un savon à qn○.

coal: **~-based** *adj* à base de charbon; **~ basin** *n* bassin *m* houiller; **~-black** *adj* noir comme du charbon; **~ box** *n* coffre *m* à charbon; **~ bunker** *n* réserve *f* à charbon; **~-burning** *adj* à charbon.

coal cutter *n* **1** (man) haveur *m*; **2** (machine) haveuse *f* à charbon.

coal: **~ deposit** *n* gisement *m* houiller; **~ depot** *n* dépôt *m* de charbon; **~ dust** *n* poussière *f* de charbon.

coalesce /ˌkəʊəˈles/ *vi* [*groups of people, ideas*] fusionner; [*substances*] se mélanger.

coalescence /ˌkəʊəˈlesns/ *n* fusion *f*.

coalface /ˈkəʊlfeɪs/ *n* front *m* de taille or d'abattage; **at the ~** lit au front de taille or d'abattage; fig au front.

coal: **~field** *n* bassin *m* houiller; **~ fire** *n* GB cheminée *f* (*où brûle un feu de charbon*); **~-fired** *adj* à charbon; **~ gas** *n* gas *m* de houille; **~ hole**○ *n* GB cave *f* à charbon; **~ industry** *n* industrie *f* minière.

coalition /ˌkəʊəˈlɪʃn/ **I** *n* **1** Pol coalition *f* (**between** entre; **with** avec); **2** gen mélange *m*.
II *modif* [*government, party, partner*] de coalition.

coal man, coal merchant ▶ **1692** *n* charbonnier *m*, marchand *m* de charbon.

Coal Measures *n* Geol **the ~** (beds) gisements *mpl* huiliers; (sub-system) le Houiller, le Silésien.

coal: **~mine** *n* mine *f* de charbon; **~miner** ▶ **1692** *n* mineur *m*.

coalmining /ˈkəʊlmaɪnɪŋ/ **I** *n* extraction *f* du charbon.
II *modif* [*family, region, town*] de mineurs.

coal oil *n* **1** US (kerosene) kérosène *m*; **2** (from coal) huile *f* lourde de houille.

coal: **~ pit** *n* mine *f* de charbon; **~ scuttle** *n* seau *m* à charbon; **~ seam** *n* gisement *m* houiller; **~ tar** *n* coaltar *m*; **~ tit** *n* Zool mésange *f* noire; **~ yard** *n* dépôt *m* de charbon.

coarse /kɔːs/ *adj* **1** [*texture, linen, wool*] grossier/-ière; [*skin*] épais/-aisse; [*hair, grass*] dru; [*sand, salt*] gros/grosse (*before n*); [*sandpaper*] à gros grains; [*paper*] rugueux/-euse; **2** (not refined) [*laugh, manners*] grossier/-ière; [*accent*] vulgaire; **~ features** des traits grossiers; **3** (indecent) [*language, joke*] cru; **4** [*food, wine*] ordinaire; **5** Geol [*sediment*] grossier/-ière.

coarse: **~ fishing** *n* GB pêche *f* à la ligne (*de poissons d'eau douce, sauf le saumon et la truite*); **~-grained** *adj* (of texture) à gros grains; (of person) grossier/-ière.

coarsely /ˈkɔːslɪ/ *adv* [*speak*] grossièrement; **~ woven** à tissage grossier; **~ ground** à grosse mouture.

coarsen /ˈkɔːsn/ **I** *vtr* rendre [qch] rêche [*skin*]; rendre [qn] grossier [*person*].
II *vi* [*person*] devenir vulgaire; [*speech, manners*] se dégrader; [*skin*] devenir rêche; [*features*] devenir lourd.

coarseness /ˈkɔːsnɪs/ *n* **1** (of manners) grossièreté *f*; **2** (of sand, salt) grosseur *f*; (of cloth) grossièreté *f*; (of features) grosseur *f*.

coast /kəʊst/ **I** *n* **1** côte *f*; **off the ~** près de la côte; **the east/west ~** la côte est/ouest; **from ~ to ~** dans tout le pays; **the ~ is clear** fig la voie est libre; **2** US **the Coast** la côte pacifique.
II *modif* [*road, path*] côtier/-ière.
III *vi* **1** (freewheel) **to ~ downhill** [*car, bicycle*] descendre en roue libre; **2** (travel effortlessly) **to ~ along at 50 mph** rouler à une vitesse de croisière de 80 km/h; **they ~ed home** fig ils ont gagné facilement; **to ~ through an exam** être reçu à un examen sans effort; **3** Naut caboter.

coastal /ˈkəʊstl/ *adj* côtier/-ière.

coaster /ˈkəʊstə(r)/ *n* **1** (mat) dessous-de-verre *m inv*; **2** (for decanter) présentoir *m*; **3** (boat) caboteur *m*; **4** US (sledge) luge *f*; (roller coaster) montagnes *fpl* russes.

coastguard /ˈkəʊstgɑːd/ ▶ **1692** *n* **1** (organization) gendarmerie *f* maritime; **2** (person) garde-côte *m*.

coastguard: **~ station** *n* poste *m* de la gendarmerie maritime; **~ vessel** *n* (vedette *f*) garde-côte *m*.

coast: **~line** *n* littoral *m*; **~-to-coast** *adj* [*broadcast*] national; [*search*] sur tout le territoire.

coat /kəʊt/ ▶ **1703** **I** *n* **1** (garment) (full-length) manteau *m*; (for men) pardessus *m*; (jacket) veste *f*; **three-quarter length ~** trois-quarts *m*; **2** Zool (of dog) poil *m*, pelage *m*; (of cat) fourrure *f*, pelage *m*; (of horse, ox, leopard) robe *f*; **3** (layer) (of paint, varnish, polish, dust, frost) couche *f*; (of bitumen) enduit *m*; **a ~ of icing** un glaçage.
II *modif* [*button, pocket etc*] de manteau.
III *vtr* **1** gen, Tech (cover) **to ~ sth with** enduire qch de [*paint, tar, adhesive, varnish*]; badigeonner qch de [*whitewash*]; revêtir qch de [*rubber*]; couvrir qch de [*dust, silt, oil, frost*]; **2** Culin **to ~ sth in** ou **with** enrober qch de [*breadcrumbs, batter, chocolate, sauce*]; dorer qch à [*egg*]; **~ed with sugar, sugar-~ed** [*sweet*] glacé; [*pill*] dragéifié.

coatdress /ˈkəʊtdres/ *n* robe-manteau *f*.

coated /ˈkəʊtɪd/ *adj* **1** Med [*tongue*] chargé; **2** Print [*paper*] couché.

coated lens *n* Phot objectif *m* bleuté or traité.

coat hanger *n* cintre *m*.

coating /ˈkəʊtɪŋ/ *n* **1** (edible) enrobage *m* (**of** de); **2** Constr, Tech, Ind (covering) revêtement *m*; **protective ~** enduit *m* protecteur.

coat: **~ of arms** *n* blason *m*, armoiries *fpl*; **~ of mail** *n* Hist cotte *f* de mailles; **~rack** *n* portemanteau *m*; **~room** *n* US vestiaire *m*.

coat-tails /ˈkəʊtteɪlz/ *npl* queue *f* d'un habit.
IDIOMS **to be always hanging on sb's ~** être toujours pendu aux basques de qn○; **to ride on sb's ~** gen profiter des efforts de qn; péj Pol se faire élire à la traîne de qn.

coat tree *n* US portemanteau *m*.

co-author /ˌkəʊˈɔːθə(r)/ **I** *n* coauteur *m*.
II *vtr* coproduire.

coax /kəʊks/ *vtr* cajoler [*person*]; attirer [qch] par la ruse [*animal*]; **to ~ sb to do** ou **into doing sth** persuader qn (gentiment) de faire qch; **to ~ sth out of sb** réussir à tirer qch de qn; **to ~ sb out of a bad mood** parvenir à dérider qn à force de cajoleries; **to ~ a car into starting** bichonner une voiture pour qu'elle démarre; **'do come,' he ~ed** 'allez, viens,' dit-il d'une manière câline.

coaxial /kəʊˈæksɪəl/ *adj* coaxial.

coaxing /ˈkəʊksɪŋ/ **I** *n* efforts *mpl* de persuasion; **no amount of ~ would make him drink it** aucun effort de persuasion ne l'amènerait à le boire.
II *adj* câlin.

coaxingly /ˈkəʊksɪŋlɪ/ *adv* d'une manière câline.

cob /kɒb/ *n* **1** (horse) cob *m*; **2** (swan) cygne *m* mâle; **3** GB (loaf) miche *f*; **4** (of maize) épi *m* de maïs; **5** GB (nut) noisette *f*; **6** GB Constr torchis *m*.

cobalt /ˈkəʊbɔːlt/ *n* cobalt *m*; **~ 60** cobalt 60.

cobalt: **~ blue** *n* bleu *m* de cobalt; **~ bomb** *n* Med, Mil bombe *f* au cobalt.

cobber○ /ˈkɒbə(r)/ *n* Austral copain○ *m*.

cobble /ˈkɒbl/ **I cobbles** *npl* pavés *mpl*.
II *vtr* **1** paver [*road*]; **2** faire [*shoes*].
III *vi* (make) faire des chaussures; (mend) réparer des chaussures.
■ **cobble together**: **~ [sth] together, ~ together [sth]** concocter [qch] à la hâte [*statement, excuse, plan*].

cobbled /ˈkɒbld/ *adj* pavé.

cobbler /ˈkɒblə(r)/ ▶ **1692** *n* **1** (shoemaker) cordonnier *m*; **2** Culin (pie) ≈ tourte *f*; (punch) punch *m* glacé.

cobblers○ /ˈkɒbləz/ *n* GB âneries *fpl*; **'and ~ to them!'** 'et merde pour eux◑!'

cobblestones /ˈkɒblstəʊnz/ *npl* pavés *mpl*.

cobnut /ˈkɒbnʌt/ *n* noisette *f*.

COBOL /ˈkəʊbɒl/ *n* (*abrév* = **common business oriented language**) COBOL *m*.

cobra /ˈkəʊbrə/ *n* cobra *m*; (Indian) serpent *m* à lunettes.

cobweb /ˈkɒbweb/ *n* toile *f* d'araignée; **that will blow away the ~s** fig ça me/te etc rafraîchira les idées.

cobwebbed /ˈkɒbwebd/, **cobwebby** /ˈkɒbwebɪ/ *adj* couvert de toiles d'araignée.

coca /ˈkəʊkə/ *n* coca *f*.

Coca-Cola® /ˌkəʊkəˈkəʊlə/ coca-cola® *m*; **two ~s please** deux cocas s'il vous plaît.

cocaine /kəʊˈkeɪn/ **I** *n* cocaïne *f*.
II *modif* [*dealer, dealing*] de cocaïne; **~ addict** cocaïnomane *mf*; **~ addiction** cocaïnomanie *f*.

coccus /ˈkɒkəs/ *n* (*pl* **-ci**) coccidie *f*.

coccyx /ˈkɒksɪks/ *n* (*pl* **-yxes** ou **-yges**) coccyx *m*.

cochair /ˈkəʊtʃeə(r)/ **I** *n* coprésident/-e *m/f*.
II *vtr* coprésider.

cochairman /ˈkəʊtʃeəmən/ *n* (*pl* **-men**) coprésident *m*.

cochairmanship /ˈkəʊtʃeəmənʃɪp/ *n* coprésidence *f*.

Cochin China /ˌkəʊtʃɪn ˈtʃaɪnə/ *pr n* Cochinchine *f*.

cochineal /ˌkɒtʃɪˈniːl/ *n* **1** Culin carmin *m*; **2** Zool cochenille *f*.

cochlea /ˈkɒklɪə/ *n* (*pl* **-leae**) cochlée *f*.

cochlear /ˈkɒklɪə(r)/ *adj* cochléaire.

cock /kɒk/ **I** *n* **1** (rooster) coq *m*; **2** Zool (male bird) (oiseau *m*) mâle *m*; **3**● (penis) bitte● *f*, pénis *m*; **4**◑ GB (nonsense) foutaises◑ *fpl*, âneries *fpl*; **that's a load of old ~** c'est de la foutaise◑; **5**◑ GB dial (term of address) **well, old ~?** alors mon vieux○?; **6** (of hay, straw) meulon *m*; **7** (weathervane) girouette *f*; **8** (of gun) chien *m* de fusil; **at full/half ~** [*pistol, gun*] armé/au cran de repos.
II *modif* [*pheasant, sparrow*] mâle ; **~ bird** mâle *m*.
III *vtr* **1** (raise) **to ~ an eyebrow** hausser les sourcils; **the dog ~ed its leg** le chien a levé la patte; **to ~ an ear** dresser l'oreille; **to keep an ear ~ed** dresser l'oreille; **he ~ed an eye at the clock** il a jeté un coup d'œil à l'horloge; **2** (tilt) pencher [*head*]; mettre [qch] sur le côté [*hat*]; **3** Mil armer [*gun*].
IDIOMS **to be ~ of the walk** péj être le roi de la basse-cour; **to go off at half ~**○ (be hasty) être impulsif/-ive; (be disappointing) partir en eau de boudin; **to live like fighting ~s** vivre comme des coqs en pâte.

■ **cock up**◑ GB: ¶ **~ up** cafouiller○; ¶ **~ [sth] up, ~ up [sth]** faire foirer◑ [*plan, schedule, assignment*]; **to ~ things up** tout faire foirer◑.

cockade /kɒˈkeɪd/ *n* cocarde *f*.

cock-a-doodle-doo /ˌkɒkəˌduːdlˈduː/ *n* cocorico *m*; **to go ~** pousser son cocorico.

cock-a-hoop○ /ˌkɒkəˈhuːp/ *adj* fier/fière comme Artaban.

Cockaigne /kɒˈkeɪn/ *pr n* pays *m* de cocagne.

cock a leekie soup /ˈkɒkəliːkɪ/ *n* GB *soupe écossaise au poulet et aux poireaux*.

cockamamie○, **cockamamy**○ /ˌkɒkəˈmæmɪ/ *adj* farfelu○.

cock-and-bull story *n* histoire *f* abracadabrante or à dormir debout; **they told some ~ about being burgled** ils ont raconté une histoire abracadabrante selon laquelle ils avaient été cambriolés.

cockatoo /ˌkɒkəˈtuː/ *n* cacatoès *m*.

cockchafer /ˈkɒktʃeɪfə(r)/ *n* hanneton *m*.

cockcrow /ˈkɒkkrəʊ/ *n* **at ~** au chant du coq.

cocked hat *n* (two points) bicorne *m*; (three points) tricorne *m*.
IDIOMS **to knock sb/sth into a ~**○ (defeat) enfoncer○ qn/qch; US (ruin) mettre en l'air○ [*case etc*].

cocker (spaniel) /ˈkɒkə(r)/ *n* cocker *m*.

cockerel /ˈkɒkərəl/ *n* jeune coq *m*.

cock: **~eyed**○ *adj* [*plans, ideas*] tordu; **~fight** *n* combat *m* de coqs; **~fighting** *n* combats *mpl* de coqs.

cockily /ˈkɒkɪlɪ/ *adv* effrontément.

cockiness /ˈkɒkɪnɪs/ *n* impudence *f*.

cockle /ˈkɒkl/ *n* (mollusc) coque *f*.
IDIOMS **it warmed the ~s of my heart to hear it** ça m'a réjoui le cœur de l'entendre; **this brandy will warm the ~s of your heart!** ce cognac va te réchauffer l'âme!

cockleshell /ˈkɒklʃel/ *n* **1** (shell) coquille *f* de coque; **2** (boat) coquille *f* de noix○.

cock lobster *n* homard *m* mâle.

cockney /ˈkɒknɪ/ **I** *n* cockney *mf* (*habitant de l'Est londonien à l'accent typique*).
II *adj* cockney *inv*.

cock: **~pit** *n* Aviat cockpit *m*, poste *m* de pilotage; Naut, Aut cockpit *m*; **~roach** *n* cafard *m*.

cockscomb /ˈkɒkskəʊm/ *n* **1** Bot crête-de-coq *f*; **2** = **coxcomb**.

cocksucker● /ˈkɒksʌkə(r)/ *n* injur salaud◑ *m*.

cocksure /ˌkɒkˈʃɔː(r), US ˌkɒkˈʃʊər/ *adj* péj [*person, manner, attitude*] présomptueux/-euse; **she's far too ~** elle est beaucoup trop sûre d'elle-même; **to be ~ about** être trop sûr de soi quant à [*abilities, prospects*].

cocktail /ˈkɒkteɪl/ *n* **1** (drink) cocktail *m*; **gin ~** cocktail à base de gin; **to mix a ~** préparer un cocktail; **to have ~s** prendre l'apéritif; **2** (mixture) **fruit ~** salade *f* de fruits; **seafood ~** cocktail de fruits de mer; **3** fig (of elements, ideas, drugs) cocktail *m*.

cocktail bar *n* **1** (also **~ lounge**) bar *m*; **2** (chic bar) bar *m* américain.

cocktail: **~ biscuit** *n* biscuit *m* pour l'apéritif; **~ cabinet** *n* GB bar *m* (*meuble*); **~ dress** *n* robe *f* de cocktail; **~ hour** *n* heure *f* des cocktails; **~ party** *n* cocktail *m*; **~ sausage** *n* petite saucisse *f* (à apéritif); **~ shaker** *n* shaker *m*; **~ stick** *n* pique *f* (à apéritif); **~ table** *n* US table *f* basse; **~ waitress** ▶ **1692** *n* barmaid *f* (*sachant préparer les cocktails*).

cocktease(r)● /ˈkɒktiːzə(r)/ *n* injur allumeuse○ *f* offensive.

cock-up◑ /ˈkɒkʌp/ *n* GB cafouillage○ *m*; **what a ~!** quel cafouillage○!; **a complete ~** un foutoir◑ absolu; **to make a ~ of sth** faire foirer◑ qch; **you made a real ~ of that!** t'as tout fait foirer◑!

cocky /ˈkɒkɪ/ *adj* impudent.

cocoa /ˈkəʊkəʊ/ **I** *n* **1** (substance) cacao *m*; **2** (drink) chocolat *m*.
II *modif* **~ powder** cacao en poudre; **~ butter** beurre *m* de cacao.

coconut /ˈkəʊkənʌt/ **I** *n* noix *f* de coco; **desiccated ~** noix de coco râpée; **creamed ~** crème *f* de coco.
II *modif* [*milk, oil, butter*] de coco; [*ice cream, yogurt, cake*] à la noix de coco.

coconut: **~ ice** *n* confiserie *f* à la noix de coco; **~ matting** *n* natte *f* en coco; **~ palm** *n* cocotier *m*; **~ pyramid** *n* GB congolais *m*; **~ shy** *n* GB jeu *m* de massacre.

cocoon /kəˈkuːn/ **I** *n* Zool, fig cocon *m*; **wrapped in a ~ of blankets** enfoui douillettement sous des couvertures.
II *vtr* envelopper douillettement; **a ~ed existence** une existence surprotégée.

cod /kɒd/ **I** *n* **1** Zool (also **~fish**) (*pl* **~**) morue *f*; **2** Culin cabillaud *m*; **3**○ (nonsense) balivernes *fpl*.
II *adj* péj [*psychology, sociology etc*] de cuisine; [*music, theatre*] de second ordre.

COD (*abrév* = **cash on delivery**, **collect on delivery** US) envoi *m* contre remboursement.

coda /ˈkəʊdə/ *n* Mus coda *f*; (to book) épilogue *m*.

coddle /ˈkɒdl/ *vtr* dorloter; **~d eggs** œufs *mpl* mollets.

code /kəʊd/ **I** *n* **1** (laws, rules) code *m*; **safety ~** règlement *m* de sécurité; **penal ~** code *m* pénal; **~ of practice** Med déontologie *f* (médicale); (in advertising) code *m* de bonne conduite; (in banking) conditions *fpl* générales; **~ of ethics** Psych, Sociol moralité *f*; **2** (of behaviour) code *m* de conduite; **to break the ~** enfreindre les règles de la bonne conduite; **~ of honour** code *m* d'honneur; **3** (cipher, message) code *m*; **to break** ou **crack the ~** déchiffrer le code; **it's in ~** c'est en code; **4** Fin **branch (sorting) ~** code *m* de succursale; **5** Telecom **(dialling) ~** indicatif *m*; **area/country ~** indicatif de zone/de pays; **6** Comput code *m*.
II *vtr* gen, Comput coder.
III *vi* (in genetics) **to ~ for** déterminer le code de.

code: **~ area** *n* Comput zone-code *f*; **~ book** *n* dictionnaire *m* chiffré.

coded /ˈkəʊdɪd/ *adj* **1** [*message*] lit codé; fig caché; [*criticism*] déguisé; **2** Comput codé; **~ decimal** décimal *m* codé binaire.

codeine /ˈkəʊdiːn/ *n* Pharm codéine *f*.

code name I *n* nom *m* de code.
II *vtr* donner un nom de code à; **the operation was ~ed Neptune** l'opération était baptisée Neptune.

code: **~ number** *n* Telecom indicatif *m*; **~ of conduct** *n* code *m* de conduite.

coder /ˈkəʊdə(r)/ *n* Comput, Electron codeur *m*.

codeword /ˈkəʊdwɜːd/ *n* lit (name) nom *m* de code; (password) mot *m* de passe; fig expression *f* codifiée.

codger○ /ˈkɒdʒə(r)/ *n* **old ~** vieux bonhomme *m*.

codicil /ˈkəʊdɪsɪl, US ˈkɒdəsl/ *n* Jur codicille *m*.

codify /ˈkəʊdɪfaɪ, US ˈkɒd-/ *vtr* codifier [*laws*]; faire un code de [*procedures*]; établir [*rules of game*].

coding /ˈkəʊdɪŋ/ *n* (of message) codage *m*; Comput codage *m* (d'un programme).

coding sheet *n* Comput feuille *f* de programmation.

cod-liver oil *n* huile *f* de foie de morue.

codpiece /ˈkɒdpiːs/ *n* Hist braguette *f*, brayette *f*.

co-driver /kəʊˈdraɪvə(r)/ *n* copilote *mf*.

codswallop○ /ˈkɒdzwɒləp/ *n* GB âneries *fpl*.

Co Durham *n* GB Post *abrév écrite* ▶ **County Durham**.

coed (*abrév* = **coeducational**) /ˌkəʊˈed/ **I** *n* US Univ étudiante *f*.
II *adj* Sch, Univ mixte; **to go ~** devenir mixte.

coedit /kəʊˈedɪt/ *vtr* [*scholar, writer*] coéditer.

coeditor /kəʊˈedɪtə(r)/ *n* (scholar, writer) coéditeur/-trice *m/f*.

coeducation /ˌkəʊedʒuːˈkeɪʃn/ *n* enseignement *m* mixte.

coeducational /ˌkəʊedʒuːˈkeɪʃənl/ *adj* mixte.

coefficient /ˌkəʊɪˈfɪʃnt/ *n* Math, Phys coefficient *m*.

coelacanth /ˈsiːləkænθ/ *n* cœlacanthe *m*.

coeliac, celiac US /ˈsiːlɪæk/ **I** *n* (sufferer) personne *f* atteinte de la maladie coeliaque.
II *adj* coeliaque; **~ disease** maladie *f* coeliaque.

coequal /kəʊˈiːkwl/ *n, adj* égal/-e (*m/f*).

coerce /kəʊˈɜːs/ *vtr* exercer des pressions sur [*person, group*]; **to ~ sb into doing sth** contraindre qn à faire qch.

coercion /kəʊˈɜːʃn, US -ʒn/ *n* coercition *f*.

coercive /kəʊˈɜːsɪv/ *adj* coercitif/-ive.

coeval /ˌkəʊˈiːvl/ sout **I** *n* contemporain/-e *m/f*.
II *adj* contemporain (**with** de).

coexist /ˌkəʊɪgˈzɪst/ *vi* coexister (**with** avec).

coexistence /ˌkəʊɪgˈzɪstəns/ *n* coexistence *f*.

coexistent /ˌkəʊɪgˈzɪstənt/ *adj* coexistant.

C of C *abrév* ▶ **Chamber of Commerce**.

C of E (*abrév* = **Church of England**) Église *f* d'Angleterre.

coffee /ˈkɒfɪ, US ˈkɔːfɪ/ **I** *n* **1** (commodity, liquid) café *m*; **a cup of ~** une tasse de café; **2** (cup of coffee) café *m*; **three ~s, please** trois cafés, s'il vous plaît; **to have a ~** prendre un café; **a black/white ~** un café (noir)/au lait.
II *modif* [*cake, ice cream, dessert*] au café; [*crop, drinker, grower, plantation*] de café; [*cup, filter, grinder, spoon*] à café.

coffee: **~ bag** *n* sachet *m* de café moulu; **~ bar** *n* café *m*.

coffee bean *n* grain *m* de café; **a kilo of ~s** un kilo de café en grains.

coffee: **~ break** *n* pause(-)café *f*; **~cake** *n* US gâteau *m* au café; **~-coloured** GB, **~-colored** US *adj* café-au-lait (*inv*); **~ grounds** *n* marc *m* de café; **~ house** *n* café *m*; **~ klatsch** *n* US *réunion entre amies pour boire le café et discuter*.

coffee machine *n* (in café) percolateur *m*; (domestic) cafetière *f* électrique; (vending machine) machine *f* à café.

coffee maker, **coffee percolator** *n* (electric) cafetière *f* électrique; (on stove) cafetière *f*.

coffee: **~ morning** *n* GB *réunion entre amies pour boire le café et discuter*; **~ pot** *n* cafetière *f*; **~ service**, **~ set** service *m* à café.

coffee shop ▶ **1692** *n* **1** (merchant's) brûlerie *f*; **2** (café) café *m*.

coffee: **~ table** *n* table *f* basse; **~-table book** *n* beau livre *m* (*sorti en grand format*); **~ tree** *n* caféier *m*.

coffer /ˈkɒfə(r)/ *n* **1** coffre *m*, caisse *f*; **the nation's ~s** les coffres du pays; **2** Archit caisson *m*.

cofferdam /ˈkɒfədæm/ *n* bâtardeau *m*.

coffered /ˈkɒfəd/ *adj* [*ceiling*] à caissons.

coffin /ˈkɒfɪn/ *n* cercueil *m*.
IDIOMS **that's another nail in their ~** cela va encore plus les enfoncer.

coffin nail○ *n* (cigarette) sèche○ *f*.

C of I (*abrév* = **Church of Ireland**) Église *f* d'Irlande.

C of S 1 (*abrév* = **Church of Scotland**) Église *f* d'Écosse; **2** *abrév* ▶ **Chief of Staff**.

cog /kɒg/ *n* Tech (tooth) dent *f* d'engrenage; (wheel) pignon *m*; **a (tiny) ~ in the machine** fig un (simple) rouage de la machine.

cogency /ˈkəʊdʒənsɪ/ *n* puissance *f*.

cogent /ˈkəʊdʒənt/ *adj* convaincant.

cogently /kəʊdʒəntlɪ/ *adv* de façon convaincante.

cogitate /ˈkɒdʒɪteɪt/ *vi* réfléchir (**about, on** à).

cogitation /ˌkɒdʒɪˈteɪʃn/ *n* réflexion *f*.

cognac /ˈkɒnjæk/ *n* cognac *m*.

cognate /ˈkɒgneɪt/ **I** *n* **1** Ling mot *m* apparenté; **2** Jur cognat *m*.
II *adj* apparenté.

cognition /kɒgˈnɪʃn/ *n* **1** gen connaissance *f*; **2** Psych, Philos cognition *f*.

cognitive /ˈkɒgnɪtɪv/ *adj* cognitif/-ive.

cognizance /ˈkɒgnɪzəns/ *n* **1** gen sout connaissance *f*; **to take ~ of sth** prendre connaissance de qch; **2** Jur compétence *f*.

cognizant /ˈkɒgnɪzənt/ *adj* gen, Jur instruit (**of** de).

cognomen /kɒgˈnəʊmen/ *n* Antiq nom *m* de famille.

cognoscenti /ˌkɒgnəˈʃentɪ/ *npl* connaisseurs *mpl*.

cog: **~ railway** *n* train *m* à crémaillère; **~wheel** *n* Tech pignon *m*.

cohabit /kəʊˈhæbɪt/ *vi* cohabiter (**with** avec).

cohabitation /ˌkəʊhæbɪˈteɪʃn/ *n* union *f* libre.

cohabitee /ˌkəʊhæbɪˈtiː/ *n* concubin/-e *m/f*.

coheir /kəʊˈeə(r)/ *n* cohéritier/-ière *m/f*.

cohere /kəʊˈhɪə(r)/ *vi* [*substance*] adhérer; [*reasoning*] être cohérent.

coherence /kəʊˈhɪərəns/ *n* (of thought) cohérence *f*; (of artistic approach) harmonie *f*; **to give ~ to sth** apporter une cohérence à qch.

coherent /kəʊˈhɪərənt/ *adj* [*argument, plan*] cohérent; **he was barely ~** (through fatigue, alcohol) on avait peine à le comprendre.

coherently /kəʊˈhɪərəntlɪ/ *adv* de façon cohérente.

cohesion /kəʊˈhiːʒn/ *n* cohésion *f*.

cohesive /kəʊˈhiːsɪv/ *adj* [*group*] uni; [*force*] cohésif/-ive.

cohort /ˈkəʊhɔːt/ *n* Antiq, fig cohorte *f*.

COHSE, **Cohse** /ˈkəʊzə/ GB (*abrév* = **Confederation of Health Service Employees**) *syndicat des employés de la santé publique*.

COI GB (*abrév* = **Central Office of Information**) *service d'information gouvernemental*.

coif /kɔɪf/ **I** *n* **1** (cap) coiffe *f*; **2**○ (hairstyle) coiffure *f*.
II○ *vtr* (*p prés etc* **-ff-**) coiffer.

coiffure /kwɑːˈfʊə(r)/ *n* coiffure *f*.

coil /kɔɪl/ **I** *n* **1** (of rope, barbed wire) rouleau *m*; (of electric wire) bobine *f*; (of smoke) volute *f*; (of hair) boucle *f*; (of snake) anneau *m*; **2** (of petrol engine) bobine *f*; **3** (contraceptive) stérilet *m*; **to have a ~ fitted** se faire poser un stérilet.
II *vtr* enrouler [*hair, rope, wire*].
III *vi* [*river, procession*] serpenter; **to ~ upwards** [*smoke*] monter en volutes.
IV *v refl* **to ~ itself** s'enrouler (**round** autour de).
■ **coil up**: ¶ **~ up** [*snake*] se lover; ¶ **~ [sth] up**, **~ up [sth]** enrouler [*rope, hosepipe, wire*].

coil spring *n* ressort *m* hélicoïdal.

coin /kɔɪn/ **I** *n* **1** pièce *f* (de monnaie); **a gold/nickel ~** une pièce d'or/de nickel; **a pound ~** une pièce d'une livre; **2** ¢ (coinage) monnaie *f*; **£5 in ~** 5 livres sterling en pièces.
II *vtr* **1** frapper [*coins*]; **she's really ~ing it** ou **money**○ elle fait des affaires en or○; **2** fig forger [*word, term*]; **money isn't everything, to ~ a phrase** l'argent ne fait pas le bonheur, comme on dit.
IDIOMS **to pay sb back in their own ~** rendre à qn la monnaie de sa pièce; **two sides of the same ~** les deux facettes d'un même problème; **the other side of the ~ is that** (sth negative) le revers de la médaille, c'est que; (sth positive) le bon côté de la chose, c'est que.

coinage /ˈkɔɪnɪdʒ/ *n* **1** ¢ (coins, currency) monnaie *f*; (making coins) frappe *f*; **2** (word, phrase) création *f*; **a recent ~** un néologisme.

coin box *n* (pay phone) cabine *f* (téléphonique) à pièces; (money box) (on pay phone, in laundromat) caisse *f*.

coincide /ˌkəʊɪnˈsaɪd/ *vi* coïncider (**with** avec).

coincidence /kəʊˈɪnsɪdəns/ *n* **1** (chance) coïncidence *f*, hasard *m*; **it is/was a ~ that** c'est/c'était par coïncidence que; **it was quite a ~** cela a été vraiment une coïncidence; **a happy ~** un heureux hasard; **by ~** par hasard; **by sheer ~** par pure coïncidence; **what a ~!** quelle coïncidence!; **2** sout (co-occurrence) coïncidence *f*.

coincident /kəʊˈɪnsɪdənt/ *adj* sout coïncident; **to be ~ with sth** coïncider avec qch.

coincidental /kəʊˌɪnsɪˈdentl/ *adj* fortuit; **any similarity is purely ~** toute ressemblance est purement fortuite.

coincidentally /kəʊˌɪnsɪˈdentəlɪ/ *adv* tout à fait par hasard.

coin: **~-op**○ *n* laverie *f* automatique; **~operated** *adj* qui marche avec des pièces.

coinsurance /ˌkəʊɪnˈʃɔːrəns/ *n* coassurance *f*.

coir /ˈkɔɪə(r)/ **I** *n* fibre *f* de coco.
II *modif* **~ matting** natte *f* en coco.

coitus /ˈkəʊɪtəs/ *n* coït *m*; **~ interruptus** coït interrompu.

coke /kəʊk/ *n* **1** (fuel) coke *m*; **2**○ (cocaine) coke○ *f*, cocaïne *f*.

Coke® /kəʊk/ *n* coca *m*.

Col *abrév écrite* = **Colonel**; **Col X** (on envelope) le Colonel X.

cola /ˈkəʊlə/ *n* **1** Bot cola *f*, colatier *m*; **2** (drink) coca *m*.

colander /ˈkʌləndə(r)/ *n* passoire *f*.

cola nut *n* noix *f* de cola.

cold /kəʊld/ **I** *n* **1** ¢ (chilliness) froid *m*; **to feel the ~** être sensible au froid, être frileux/-euse; **to be out in the ~** lit être dehors dans le froid; **to come in from** ou **out of the ~** lit se mettre à l'abri du froid; fig rentrer en grâce; **to be left out in the ~** fig être isolé; **he was trembling with ~** il grelottait de froid; **2** C Med rhume *m*; **to have a ~** être enrhumé, avoir un rhume; **to catch** ou **get a ~** attraper un rhume; **a bad ~** un gros rhume; **a ~ in the head** un rhume de cerveau.
II *adj* **1** (chilly) froid; fig [*colour, light*] froid; **to be** ou **feel ~** [*person*] avoir froid; **the room was** ou **felt ~** il faisait froid dans la pièce; **the wind is** ou **feels ~** le vent est froid; **it's ~ outside** il fait froid dehors; **it's** ou **the weather's ~** il fait froid; **it's** ou **the weather's getting ~er** le temps se refroidit; **to go ~** [*food, tea, water*] se refroidir; **don't let the baby get ~** ne laisse pas le bébé prendre froid; **to keep sth ~** tenir [qch] au frais [*food*]; **2** (unemotional) [*expression, manner, smile, heart, logic etc*] froid; **to be ~ to** ou **towards sb** être froid avec qn; **to leave sb ~** laisser qn froid; **pop music/golf leaves me ~** la musique pop/le golf me laisse froid; **3** (not recent) [*news*] déjà dépassé; **the trail has gone ~** la piste s'est effacée; **4** (unconscious) **to be out ~** être sans connaissance; **to knock** ou **lay sb out ~** assommer qn, mettre qn KO○.
III *adv* **1**○ (without preparation) [*speak, perform*] à froid○; **2** US (thoroughly) [*learn, know*] par cœur; **to turn sb down ~** envoyer qn promener○.
IDIOMS **~ hands, warm heart** mains froides, cœur chaud; **to have** ou **get ~ feet** avoir les jetons○; **in ~ blood** de sang-froid; **my blood runs ~** fig mon sang se fige; **in the ~ light of day** à tête reposée; **to be as ~ as ice** [*person, part of body*] être gelé; [*room*] être glacial; **to pour** ou **throw ~ water on sth** descendre qch en flammes○; **you're getting ~er!** Games tu refroidis!

cold-blooded /ˌkəʊldˈblʌdɪd/ *adj* **1** lit [*animal*] à sang froid; **2** fig [*criminal, killer*] sans pitié; [*crime, massacre, attack*] commis de sang-froid; [*account, description*] sans émotion.

cold: **~-bloodedly** *adv* de sang-froid; **~-bloodedness** *n* sang-froid *m*; **~ call** *n* Comm visite *f* sans préavis or d'un démarcheur; Telecom appel *m* d'un démarcheur; **~ calling** *n* Comm démarchage *m* par téléphone; **~ chisel** *n* ciseau *m* à froid; **~ comfort** *n* piètre consolation *f* (**for** pour); **~ cream** *n* cold-cream *m*; **~ cuts** *npl* assiette *f* anglaise; **~ fish**○ *n* péj pisse-froid○ *m*; **~ frame** *n* Hort châssis *m*; **~ front** *n* front *m* froid; **~-hearted** *adj* impitoyable.

coldly /ˈkəʊldlɪ/ *adv* [*enquire, reply, say*] froidement; [*receive, stare*] avec froideur; **~ polite** d'une politesse glaciale; **~ classical** d'un classicisme froid.

coldness /ˈkəʊldnɪs/ *n* lit, fig froideur *f*.

cold: **~-pressed** *adj* Culin [*oil*] pressé à froid; **~ remedy** *n* médicament *m* pour le rhume; **~ room** *n* Culin chambre *f* froide; **~ sell** *n* Comm vente *f* sans préavis.

cold shoulder **I** *n* **to give sb the ~** snober qn, battre froid à qn; **to get the ~** se faire snober.
II *vtr* snober, battre froid à.

cold: **~ snap** *n* brève vague *f* de froid; **~ sore** *n* bouton *m* de fièvre; **~ start** *n* Aut démarrage *m* à froid; **~ steel** *n* ¢ armes *fpl* blanches.

cold storage *n* **1** (process) gen conservation *f* par le froid; Chem conservation *f* cryogénique; **2** (place) chambre *f* froide or frigorifique; **to put sth into ~** lit mettre qch en chambre froide; fig mettre qch de côté.

cold store *n* chambre *f* froide or frigorifique.

cold sweat *n* sueurs *fpl* froides; **to be in a ~ about sth** avoir des sueurs froides à propos de qch; **to bring sb out in a ~** donner des sueurs froides à qn.

cold: **~ table** *n* Culin buffet *m* froid; **~ tap** *n* robinet *m* d'eau froide.

cold turkey○ *n* (treatment) sevrage *m*; (reaction) réaction *f* de manque; **to go ~** s'abstenir (**on** de); **to be ~** être en manque.

Cold War **I** *n* guerre *f* froide.
II *modif* [*era, mentality, politics*] de la guerre froide.

cold warrior *n* partisan/-e *m/f* de la guerre froide.

coleslaw /ˈkəʊlslɔː/ *n* salade *f* à base de chou cru.

coley /ˈkəʊlɪ/ *n* GB lieu noir *m*.

colic /ˈkɒlɪk/ *n* ¢ coliques *fpl*.

colicky /ˈkɒlɪkɪ/ *adj* [*baby*] qui souffre de coliques; [*pain*] provoqué par des coliques.

Coliseum /ˌkɒlɪˈsɪəm/ *n* **1 the ~** le Colisée; **2** US (exhibition hall) hall *m* d'exposition; **3** US (stadium) stade *m*.

colitis /kəˈlaɪtɪs/ ▶ **1354** *n* colite *f*.

collaborate /kəˈlæbəreɪt/ *vi* collaborer (**on, in** à; **with** avec); **they ~d with him in producing the film** ils ont collaboré avec lui à la production du film.

collaboration /kəˌlæbəˈreɪʃn/ *n* collaboration *f* (**between** entre; **with** avec; **in sth** à qch).

collaborative /kəˈlæbərətɪv/ *adj* [*project, task*] en collaboration; [*approach*] de collaboration.

collaborator /kəˈlæbəreɪtə(r)/ *n* (all contexts) collaborateur/-trice *m/f*.

collage /ˈkɒlɑːʒ, US kəˈlɑːʒ/ *n* **1** Art collage *m*; **2** (film) montage *m*; (book) mélange *m*.

collapse /kəˈlæps/ **I** *n* **1** (of regime, system, empire, bank, front, price, currency, economy, market, hopes) effondrement *m* (**of, in** de); **to be on the point** ou **brink of ~** être sur le point de s'effondrer; **2** (of deals, talks, relationship) échec *m* (**of** de); **3** (of company, newspaper) faillite *f* (**of** de); **4** (of person) (physical) écroulement *m*; (mental) effondrement *m*; **to be close to ~** être sur le point de s'écrouler; **to be on the verge** ou **brink** ou **point of ~** être sur le point de s'effondrer; **5** (of building, bridge) effondrement *m*; (of tunnel, wall, roof) écroulement *m*; (of chair, bed) affaissement *m*; **6** Med (of lung) collapsus *m*; **7** (of balloon) dégonflement *m*.

II *vtr* **1** (fold) plier [*bike, umbrella*]; **2** (combine) synthétiser [*ideas, paragraphs*]; **3** Comput réduire.

III *vi* **1** (founder) [*regime, system, empire, bank, currency, economy, hopes, plan*] s'effondrer; [*case, trial, prosecution*] échouer; [*deal, talks*] échouer; **to ~ in chaos** finir dans le chaos; **2** (go bankrupt) [*company, business*] faire faillite (**through** à cause de); **3** (slump) [*person*] s'écrouler (**due to** à cause de; **under** sous); **to ~ onto the bed/into sb's arms** s'effondrer sur le lit/dans les bras de qn; **to ~ and die** mourir subitement; **to ~ in tears** s'effondrer en larmes; **to ~ into giggles** avoir le fou-rire; **4** (fall down) [*building, bridge*] s'effondrer (**on, on top of** sur); [*tunnel, roof, wall*] s'écrouler (**on, on top of** sur); [*chair, bed*] s'affaisser (**under** sous); **5** (deflate) [*balloon*] se dégonfler; [*soufflé, pastry*] tomber; **6** Med [*lung*] se dégonfler; **a ~d lung** un collapsus pulmonaire; **7** (fold) [*bike, umbrella*] se plier.

collapsible /kə'læpsəbl/ *adj* pliant.

collar /'kɒlə(r)/ ▶1703 I *n* **1** (on garment) col *m*; **soft/stiff/wing ~** col souple/dur/cassé; **blue-/white-~ workers** les cols bleus/blancs; **to grab sb by the ~** prendre qn au collet; **2** (for dog, cat, horse) collier *m*; **3** (cut of meat) collier *m*; **4** Mech (ring) bague *f* d'arrêt; (bearing seat) collet *m*.

II○ *vtr* alpaguer◑ [*thief, runaway*]; (detain in conversation) coincer○.

IDIOMS **to get hot under the ~** se mettre en rogne○; **to have one's ~ felt** hum être pris au collet.

collarbone /'kɒləbəʊn/ *n* clavicule *f*.

collar size ▶1703 *n* encolure *f*; **his ~ is 15** il fait 39 de tour de cou; **what's your ~?** quelle encolure faites-vous?

collar stud *n* bouton *m* de col.

collate /kə'leɪt/ *vtr* collationner.

collateral /kə'lætərəl/ I *n* **1** Fin (security) nantissement *m*; **to put up ~ for a loan** offrir une garantie supplémentaire pour obtenir un prêt; **2** Jur (relation) collatéral *m*.

II *adj* **1** Jur (relative) collatéral; (subordinate) secondaire; **2** Mil **~ damage** dégâts *mpl* parmi la population civile; **3** [*species, branch of family*] collatéral; **4** Fin **~ loan** prêt *m* nanti; **~ security** nantissement *m* subsidiaire; **5** Med collatéral.

collation /kə'leɪʃn/ *n* **1** (of evidence) collation *f*; **2** sout (meal) collation *f*.

colleague /'kɒli:g/ *n* gen collègue *mf*; (among doctors, lawyers) (of man) confrère *m*; (of woman) consœur *f*.

collect /kə'lekt/ I *n* Relig collecte *f* (*prière*).

II *adv* US Telecom **to call sb ~** appeler qn en PCV.

III *vtr* **1** (gather) ramasser [*wood, leaves, litter, eggs*]; rassembler [*information, facts, evidence, documents*]; recueillir [*signatures*]; **she ~ed (up) her belongings** elle a ramassé ses affaires; **to ~ one's wits** rassembler ses esprits; **to ~ one's strength** rassembler or ramasser ses forces; **to ~ one's thoughts** se recueillir; **2** (as hobby) collectionner, faire collection de [*stamps, coins, antiques*]; **she ~s artists/stray cats** hum elle collectionne les artistes/les chats perdus; **3** (receive, contain) (intentionally) recueillir [*rain water, drips*]; (accidentally) [*objects*] prendre, ramasser [*dust*]; **4** (obtain) percevoir, encaisser [*rent*]; encaisser [*fares, money*]; recouvrer [*debt*]; toucher [*pension*]; recevoir [*degree, diploma*]; Admin percevoir [*tax, fine*]; **to ~ money for charity** collecter de l'argent pour les bonnes œuvres; **the winner ~s £2,000** le gagnant remporte 2 000 livres sterling; **5** (take away) ramasser [*tickets, empty bottles, rubbish*]; faire la levée de [*mail, post*]; **I arranged to have the parcel ~ed** j'ai pris des dispositions pour qu'on aille chercher le paquet; **what time is the post ~ed?** à quelle heure est la levée (du courrier)?; **'buyer ~s'** (in small ad) 'à venir chercher sur place'; **6** (pick up) aller chercher, passer prendre [*person*]; récupérer [*keys, book etc*]; **I have to ~ the children from school** il faut que j'aille chercher or que je passe prendre les enfants à l'école; **she ~ed the keys from a neighbour** elle a récupéré les clés chez un voisin; **to ~ a suit from the cleaners** passer prendre un costume chez le teinturier.

IV *vi* **1** (accumulate, gather) [*substance, dust, leaves*] s'accumuler; [*crowd*] se rassembler, se réunir; **2** (raise money) **to ~ for charity/famine victims** faire la quête pour des bonnes œuvres/les victimes de la famine.

V **collected** *pp adj* **1** [*person*] calme; **she remained cool, calm and ~ed** elle a gardé son sang-froid; **2** (assembled) **the ~ed works of Dickens** les œuvres complètes de Dickens; **the ~ed poems of W. B. Yeats** la collection complète des poèmes de W. B. Yeats.

VI *v refl* **to ~ oneself** se reprendre.

collectable /kə'lektəbl/ *adj* **to be very ~** [*rare objects*] être très prisé par les collectionneurs.

collectables /kə'lektəblz/ *npl* objets *mpl* de collection; **'antiques and ~'** 'antiquités et brocante'.

collect call *n* US Telecom appel *m* en PCV.

collection /kə'lekʃn/ *n* **1** ¢ (collecting) (of objects) ramassage *m*; (of old clothes, newspapers etc) collecte *f*; (of information, facts, evidence, data) rassemblement *m*; (of rent) encaissement *m*; (of debt) recouvrement *m*; (of tax) perception *f*; Post levée *f*; **the ~ of money** la collecte; **your suit/bicycle is ready for ~** votre costume/vélo est prêt; **refuse ~** ramassage *m* des ordures; **2** (set of collected items) (of coins, stamps, books, records etc) collection *f*; (anthology) recueil *m*; **art ~** collection *f* (de tableaux); **an odd ~ of people** un mélange curieux de gens; **autumn/spring ~** Fashn collection d'automne/de printemps; **3** (sum of money collected) gen collecte *f* (**for** pour); (in church) quête *f*; (for charity) quête *f*, collecte *f* (**for** au profit de); **to make** ou **organize a ~** faire la quête, organiser une collecte.

collection: **~ plate** *n* plat *m* de quête; **~ point** *n* (for parcels) guichet *m* de retrait des paquets; (for goods) guichet *m* de retrait des marchandises; (for donations, recycling) dépôt *m* (**for** de).

collective /kə'lektɪv/ I *n* entreprise *f* collective.

II *adj* (all contexts) collectif/-ive.

collective: **~ agreement** *n* convention *f* collective; **~ bargaining** *n* ¢ *négociations entre le syndicat et le patronat*; **~ farm** *n* ferme *f* collective.

collectively /kə'lektɪvlɪ/ *adv* collectivement; **~ owned** en copropriété; **they're known ~ as...** ils sont connus sous le nom de...

collective: **~ noun** *n* Ling (nom *m*) collectif *m*; **~ ownership** *n* copropriété *f*; **~ security** *n* sécurité *f* collective; **~ unconscious** *n* inconscient *m* collectif.

collectivism /kə'lektɪvɪzəm/ *n* collectivisme *m*.

collectivist /kə'lektɪvɪst/ *n, adj* collectiviste (*mf*).

collectivize /kə'lektɪvaɪz/ *vtr* collectiviser.

collector /kə'lektə(r)/ *n* **1** (of coins, stamps, antiques etc) collectionneur/-euse *m/f*; **to be a stamp ~** collectionner les timbres; **2** (official) (of taxes) percepteur *m*; (of rates) receveur *m*; (of rent, debts) encaisseur *m*; (of funds) quêteur/-euse *m/f*; **3** Elec, Radio collecteur *m*.

collector's item *n* pièce *f* de collection.

colleen† /'kɒli:n/ *n* jeune Irlandaise *f*.

college /'kɒlɪdʒ/ I *n* **1** Sch, Univ (place of tertiary education) établissement *m* d'enseignement supérieur; (school, part of university) collège *m*; US Univ faculté *f*; **to live in/out of ~** GB vivre au/hors du collège; **to go to ~, to be at** ou **in** US **~** faire des études supérieures; **to enter/leave ~** commencer/terminer ses études supérieures; **to put a child through ~** payer des études supérieures à un enfant; **to drop out of ~, to be a ~ dropout** abandonner ses études; **2** (professional body) (of arms, cardinals) collège *m*; (of doctors, surgeons) académie *f*; (of midwives, nurses) association *f*; **3**○ US (prison) prison *f*.

II *modif* [*governor, servant*] du collège; [*building*] de collège.

IDIOMS **to give sth the old ~ try** US essayer de tout son cœur.

college-bound /ˌkɒlɪdʒ'baʊnd/ *adj* US Sch [*student*] qui se destine aux études universitaires; [*program*] de préparation aux études universitaires.

college education *n* études *fpl* supérieures; **to have a ~** faire des études supérieures.

college: **~ fellow** *n* GB membre *m* du personnel académique (*dans un collège*); **~ of advanced technology, CAT** *n* GB ≈ Institut *m* Universitaire de Technologie; **~ of agriculture** *n* institut *m* agronomique; **~ of education** *n* GB ≈ École *f* normale; **~ of further education, CFE** *n* GB *école ouverte aux adultes et aux jeunes pour terminer un cycle d'études secondaires*; **~ staff** *n* (+ *v sg* ou *pl*) corps *m* académique; **~ student** *n* étudiant/-e *m/f*.

collegiate /kə'li:dʒət/ *adj* [*life*] de collège; [*university*] composé de plusieurs collèges; [*church*] collégial.

collide /kə'laɪd/ *vi* **1** [*vehicle, plane, ship*] entrer en collision (**with** avec); **I ~d with a tree** j'ai heurté un arbre; **we ~d (with each other) in the corridor** nous nous sommes heurtés dans le couloir; **2** (disagree) se heurter (**over** à propos de).

collie /'kɒlɪ/ *n* colley *m*.

collier /'kɒlɪə(r)/ ▶1692 *n* (worker) mineur *m*; (ship) charbonnier *m*.

colliery /'kɒlɪərɪ/ *n* houillère *f*.

collision /kə'lɪʒn/ *n* **1** (crash) collision *f*; **to come into ~ with** entrer en collision avec; **head-on ~** collision frontale; **mid-air ~** collision en plein ciel; **2** (clash) affrontement *m* (**between** entre).

collision course *n* **1** Naut, Aviat **the planes were on a ~** les avions allaient se percuter; **2** fig **to be on a ~** [*people, groups*] aller droit à l'affrontement.

collision damage waiver *n* Insur prime-collision *f* sans franchise.

collocate /'kɒləkeɪt/ Ling I *n* collocation *f*.

II *vi* **to ~ with sth** être une collocation de qch.

collocation /ˌkɒlə'keɪʃn/ *n* Ling **1** ¢ (combining) cooccurrence *f*; **2** (phrase) locution *f*.

colloquial /kə'ləʊkwɪəl/ *adj* familier/-ière; **~ English** anglais parlé.

colloquialism /kə'ləʊkwɪəlɪzəm/ *n* expression *f* familière.

colloquially /kə'ləʊkwɪəlɪ/ *adv* familièrement.

colloquium /kə'ləʊkwɪəm/ *n* (*pl* **-quiums** ou **-quia**) colloque *m* (**on** sur).

colloquy /'kɒləkwɪ/ *n* sout colloque *m*, entretien *m*.

collude /kə'lu:d/ *vi* comploter (**with** avec).

collusion /kə'lu:ʒn/ *n* ¢ connivence *f*; **to act in ~ with sb to do sth** agir de connivence avec qn pour faire qch.

collywobbles○ /ˈkɒlɪwɒblz/ *npl* **1** (nerves) **to have** or **get the ~** avoir la frousse; **2** (indigestion) coliques *fpl*.

cologne /kəˈləʊn/ *n* eau *f* de Cologne.

Colombia /kəˈlɒmbɪə/ ▶ 1131 *pr n* Colombie *f*.

Colombian /kəˈlɒmbɪən/ ▶ 1486 **I** *n* (person) Colombien/-ienne *m/f*.
II *adj* colombien/-ienne.

colon /ˈkəʊlən/ *n* **1** Anat côlon *m*; **2** Ling deux points *mpl*.

colonel /ˈkɜːnl/ ▶ 1612 *n* colonel *m*.

colonial /kəˈləʊnɪəl/ **I** *n* colonial/-e *m/f*.
II *adj* colonial; US Archit en style colonial.

colonialism /kəˈləʊnɪəlɪzəm/ *n* colonialisme *m*.

colonialist /kəˈləʊnɪəlɪst/ *n, adj* colonialiste (*mf*).

colonic /kəˈlɒnɪk/ *adj* du côlon; **~ irrigation** lavement *m*.

colonist /ˈkɒlənɪst/ *n* colon *m*.

colonization /ˌkɒlənaɪˈzeɪʃn, US -nɪˈz-/ *n* colonisation *f*.

colonize /ˈkɒlənaɪz/ *vtr* coloniser also fig.

colonizer /ˈkɒlənaɪzə(r)/ *n* colon *m*.

colonnade /ˌkɒləˈneɪd/ *n* colonnade *f*.

colonnaded /ˌkɒləˈneɪdɪd/ *adj* à colonnade.

colony /ˈkɒlənɪ/ *n* (all contexts) colonie *f*; **the colonies** GB Pol Hist les colonies.

color US *n, vtr, vi* = **colour**.

Colorado /ˌkɒləˈrɑːdəʊ/ ▶ 1744, 1644 *pr n* Colorado *m*.

Colorado beetle *n* doryphore *m*.

colorant /ˈkʌlərənt/ *n* colorant *m*.

coloration /ˌkʌləˈreɪʃn/ *n* coloration *f*, coloris *m*.

coloratura /ˌkɒlərəˈtʊərə/ *n* (cadenza) colorature *f*; (singer) soprano *f* colorature.

colorize /ˈkʌləraɪz/ *vtr* Cin coloriser.

color line *n* US discrimination *f* raciale.

colossal /kəˈlɒsl/ *adj* colossal.

Colossians /kəˈlɒʃnz/ *n* (+ *v sg*) les Colossiens *mpl*.

colossus /kəˈlɒsəs/ *n* (*pl* **-ssi** ou **-ssuses**) colosse *m*.

colostomy /kəˈlɒstəmɪ/ **I** *n* colostomie *f*.
II *modif* **~ bag** poche *f*.

colostrum /kəˈlɒstrəm/ *n* colostrum *m*.

colour GB, **color** US /ˈkʌlə(r)/ ▶ 1104 **I** *n* **1** (hue) couleur *f*; **what ~ is it?** de quelle couleur est-il?; **do you have it in a different ~?** est-ce que vous l'avez dans une autre couleur?; **the sky was the ~ of lead** le ciel était de la couleur du plomb; **in ~** Cin, TV en couleur; **the artist's use of ~** l'usage que l'artiste fait de la couleur; **the garden was a mass of ~** le jardin était une symphonie de couleurs; **to take the ~ out of sth** décolorer qch; **to give** ou **lend ~ to sth** colorer qch; **to paint sth in glowing ~s** fig brosser un tableau brillant de qch; **'available in 12 ~s'** 'existe en 12 coloris'; **2** (vividness) (in writing, description) couleur *f*; **period ~** couleur *f* d'époque; **a work full of ~** une œuvre haute en couleur; **3** (dye) (for food) colorant *m*; (for hair) teinture *f*; (shampoo) shampooing *m* colorant; **4** Cosmet **cheek ~** fard *m* à joues; **eye ~** fard *m* à paupières; **lip ~** rouge *m* à lèvres; **5** (racial pigmentation) couleur *f* de peau; **people of all races and ~s** des gens de toutes races et de toutes couleurs; **6** (complexion) couleur *f*; **to change ~** changer de couleur; **to lose (one's) ~** perdre ses couleurs; **to put ~ into sb's cheeks** redonner des couleurs à qn; **that should put a bit of ~ into her cheeks!** cela devrait lui redonner un peu de couleur!; **to have a high ~** (naturally) être rubicond; (from illness or embarrassment) être très rouge; **her face was drained of ~** son visage était livide; **her ~ rose** elle a rougi; **he's getting his ~ back at last** il reprend enfin des couleurs.
II colours *npl* Mil, Sport, Turf couleurs *fpl*; Naut pavillon *m*; **racing ~s** Turf couleurs de l'écurie; **the ~s of the regiment** les couleurs du régiment; **he's playing in England's ~s** il porte les couleurs de l'Angleterre; **under false ~s** Naut sous un faux pavillon; fig sous un faux jour; **to get one's tennis/football ~s** GB Sport être sélectionné pour l'équipe de tennis/football; **a scarf in the club ~s** une écharpe aux couleurs du club.
III *modif* **1** Phot, TV [*picture, photo, photography, slide*] (en) couleur; [*copier, printer*] couleur; **~ film** (for camera) pellicule *f* couleur; Cin film *m* en couleur; **2** Sociol [*prejudice, problem*] racial.
IV *vtr* **1** lit (with paints, crayons) colorier; (with commercial paints) peindre; (with food dye) colorer; (with hair dye) teindre; **to ~ sth blue** colorier or colorer or peindre or teindre qch en bleu; **2** fig (prejudice) fausser [*attitude, judgment, opinion*]; **3** fig (enhance) péj enjoliver pej [*account, story*].
V *vi* [*plant, fruit*] changer de couleur; [*person*] (also **~ up**) rougir; **to ~ (up) with** devenir rouge de [*anger, embarrassment*].
IDIOMS **let's see the ~ of your money** voyons un peu la couleur de ton argent; **to be off ~** ne pas être en forme; **to pass with flying ~s** réussir haut la main; **to show one's true ~s** se montrer sous son vrai jour.

colour: **~ analyst** ▶ 1692 *n* Fashn analyste *mf* des couleurs; **~ bar** *n* GB discrimination *f* raciale; **~ blind** *adj* daltonien/-ienne; **~ blindness** *n* daltonisme *m*.

colour code GB, **color code** US **I** *n* système *m* de classement par couleurs.
II *vtr* classer [qch] par couleurs [*files*]; identifier [qch] par des couleurs [*wires, switches*].
III colour-coded *pp adj* [*wire, switch, file*] identifié par une couleur; **each file/wire is colour-coded** chaque dossier/fil est identifié par une couleur.

coloured GB, **colored** US /ˈkʌləd/ **I** *n* injur GB, US personne *f* de couleur; (in South Africa) métis/-isse *m/f*.
II coloureds *npl* (laundry) couleurs *fpl*; **'wash ~s separately'** 'laver les couleurs séparément'.
III *adj* **1** lit [*pen, chalk, ink, paper, label, bead*] de couleur; [*picture, drawing, page*] en couleur; [*light, glass, icing*] coloré; **a brightly ~ shirt** une chemise aux couleurs vives; **2** Sociol (non-white) injur GB, US de couleur; (in South Africa) métis/-isse.
IV -coloured (*dans composés*) **a raspberry-~ dress** une robe (couleur) framboise; **copper-~ hair** des cheveux couleur cuivre; **a highly-~ account** fig un récit très enjolivé.

colour: **~-fast** *adj* grand teint *inv*; **~ filter** *n* Phot filtre *m* coloré.

colourful GB, **colorful** US /ˈkʌləfl/ *adj* **1** lit aux couleurs vives; **2** fig [*story, career, life*] haut en couleur; [*character, person*] pittoresque.

colourfully GB, **colorfully** US /ˈkʌləfəlɪ/ *adv* [*painted, dressed*] en couleurs vives.

colour graphics adaptor, **CGA** *n* Comput adapteur *m* de graphique couleur.

colouring GB, **coloring** US /ˈkʌlərɪŋ/ *n* **1** (hue) (of plant, animal) couleurs *fpl*; (of pattern) combinaison *f* des couleurs; (complexion) teint *m*; **2** ¢ Art coloriage *m*; **3** (dye) (for food) colorant *m*; (for hair) teinture *f*; **artificial ~** Culin colorant *m* artificiel.

colouring book *n* album *m* à colorier.

colourless GB, **colorless** US /ˈkʌləlɪs/ *adj* **1** lit [*liquid, substance, gas*] incolore; [*face, cheeks, hands*] blanc/blanche; **2** fig (bland) [*personality, description, life, voice*] terne.

colour: **~ magazine** *n* Journ revue *f* en couleur; **~ reproduction** *n* Art reproduction *f* en couleur; **~ scheme** *n* couleurs *fpl*, coloris *m*; **~ sense** *n* sens *m* des couleurs; **~ sergeant** ▶ 1612 *n* GB sergent-chef *m*; **~ set** *n* TV appareil *m* (en) couleur; **~ supplement** *n* Journ supplément *m* illustré; **~ television** *n* télévision *f* (en) couleur; **~ therapist** ▶ 1692 *n* Psych thérapeute *mf* spécialiste de l'influence des couleurs; **~way** *n* coloris *m*.

colt /kəʊlt/ *n* **1** Zool poulain *m*; **2** (boy) jeunot *m*; GB Sport poulain *m*.

Colt® /kəʊlt/ *n* (pistol) colt *m*.

coltish /ˈkəʊltɪʃ/ *adj* [*person*] folâtre.

coltsfoot /ˈkəʊltsfʊt/ *n* pas-d'âne *m inv*.

Columbia‡ /kəˈlʌmbɪə/ *n* Hist *nom poétique des États-Unis*.

columbine /ˈkɒləmbaɪn/ **I** *n* Bot ancolie *f*.
II Columbine *pr n* Theat Colombine.

Columbus /kəˈlʌmbəs/ *pr n* Christophe Colomb.

column /ˈkɒləm/ *n* **1** gen colonne *f*; **2** Journ rubrique *f*; **sports/political ~** rubrique sportive/politique; **letters ~** le courrier *m* des lecteurs.

column inch *n* Print, Journ cf millimètre *m* colonne.

columnist /ˈkɒləmnɪst/ *n* journaliste *mf*; **political ~** journaliste politique.

coma /ˈkəʊmə/ *n* coma *m*; **in a ~** dans le coma; **to go into a ~** entrer dans le coma.

comatose /ˈkəʊmətəʊs/ *adj* **1** Med comateux/-euse; **2** fig (with alcohol, apathy) abruti.

comb /kəʊm/ **I** *n* **1** (for hair) peigne *m*; **to run a ~ through one's hair**, **to give one's hair a (quick) ~** se donner un coup de peigne; **2** Tex carde *f*; **3** (honeycomb) rayon *m*; **4** (cock's crest) crête *f*.
II *vtr* **1 to ~ sb's hair** peigner qn; **to ~ one's hair** se peigner; **2** (search) **to ~ a place (looking) for sth** passer un lieu au peigne fin à la recherche de qch; **3** Tex carder [*wool, textile*].
■ **comb out**: **~ out [sth]**, **~ [sth] out** démêler [*knots, hair*]; **to ~ fleas/lice out of a dog** épucer/épouiller un chien.
■ **comb through**: **~ through [sth]** passer [qch] au peigne fin [*book, article*] (**for sth, looking for sth** à la recherche de qch).

combat /ˈkɒmbæt/ **I** *n* Mil combat *m*; **in ~** au combat; **to send sb into ~** envoyer qn au combat; **close/single ~** combat rapproché/singulier.
II *modif* [*aircraft, helmet, troops, zone*] de combat.
III *vtr* (*p prés etc* **-tt-**) combattre [*violence, racism, crime, inflation*]; lutter contre [*hunger, disease, poverty, fear*].

combatant /ˈkɒmbətənt/ **I** *n* combattant/-e *m/f*.
II *adj* combattant.

combative /ˈkɒmbətɪv/ *adj* combatif/-ive.

combat: **~ jacket** *n* veste *f* de treillis; **~ mission** *n* mission *f* commandée; **~ police** *n* GB brigade *f* mobile d'arrondissement.

combe *n* GB = **coomb**.

combination /ˌkɒmbɪˈneɪʃn/ **I** *n* **1** (mixture, blend) gen combinaison *f* (**of** de); (of factors, events) conjonction *f*; **for a ~ of reasons** pour de multiples raisons; **2** (mixing) mélange *m* (**of** de; **with** avec); **in ~ with** en association avec; **3** (of numbers, chemicals) combinaison *f*; **4** GB Aut side-car *m*.
II† **combinations** *npl* GB combinaison-caleçon *f*.

combination lock *n* serrure *f* à combinaison.

combine I /ˈkɒmbaɪn/ *n* **1** Comm groupe *m*; **2** Agric = **combine harvester**.
II /kəmˈbaɪn/ *vtr* **1** (pair up, link) combiner [*activities, colours, components, items, qualities, elements*] (**with** avec); associer [*ideas, aims*] (**with** à); **to ~ two companies** regrouper deux sociétés; **to ~ fantasy with realism** allier la fantaisie au réalisme; **to ~ forces** [*countries, people*] (merge) s'allier; (cooperate) collaborer; **2** Culin mélanger (**with** avec); **3** Chem combiner (**with** avec);

Colours

Not all English colour terms have a single exact equivalent in French: for instance, in some circumstances brown *is* marron, *in others* brun. *If in doubt, look the word up in the dictionary.*

Colour terms

what colour is it?	= c'est de quelle couleur? *or* (*more formally*) de quelle couleur est-il?
it's green	= il est vert *or* elle est verte
to paint sth green	= peindre qch en vert
to dye sth green	= teindre qch en vert
to wear green	= porter du vert
dressed in green	= habillé de vert

Colour nouns are all masculine in French:

I like green	= j'aime le vert
I prefer blue	= je préfère le bleu
red suits her	= le rouge lui va bien
it's a pretty yellow!	= c'est un joli jaune!
have you got it in white?	= est-ce que vous l'avez en blanc?
a pretty shade of blue	= un joli ton de bleu
it was a dreadful green	= c'était un vert affreux
a range of greens	= une gamme de verts

Most adjectives of colour agree with the noun they modify:

a blue coat	= un manteau bleu
a blue dress	= une robe bleue
blue clothes	= des vêtements bleus

Some that don't agree are explained below.

Words that are not true adjectives

Some words that translate English adjectives are really nouns in French, and so don't show agreement:

a brown shoe	= une chaussure marron
orange tablecloths	= des nappes *fpl* orange
hazel eyes	= des yeux *mpl* noisette

Other French words like this include: cerise (*cherry-red*), chocolat (*chocolate-brown*) *and* émeraude (*emerald-green*).

Shades of colour

Expressions like pale blue, dark green *or* light yellow *are also invariable in French and show no agreement:*

a pale blue shirt	= une chemise bleu pâle
dark green blankets	= des couvertures *fpl* vert foncé
a light yellow tie	= une cravate jaune clair
bright yellow socks	= des chaussettes *fpl* jaune vif

French can also use the colour nouns here: instead of une chemise bleu pâle *you could say* une chemise d'un bleu pâle; *and similarly* des couvertures d'un vert foncé (etc). *The nouns in French are normally used to translate English adjectives of this type ending in* -er *and* -est:

a darker blue	= un bleu plus foncé
the dress was a darker blue	= la robe était d'un bleu plus foncé

Similarly:

a lighter blue	= un bleu plus clair (*etc*)

In the following examples, blue *stands for most basic colour terms:*

pale blue	= bleu pâle
light blue	= bleu clair
bright blue	= bleu vif
dark blue	= bleu foncé
deep blue	= bleu profond
strong blue	= bleu soutenu

Other types of compound in French are also invariable, and do not agree with their nouns:

a navy-blue jacket	= une veste bleu marine

These compounds include: bleu ciel (*sky-blue*), vert pomme (*apple-green*), bleu nuit (*midnight-blue*), rouge sang (*blood-red*) *etc. However, all English compounds do not translate directly into French. If in doubt, check in the dictionary.*

French compounds consisting of two colour terms linked with a hyphen are also invariable:

a blue-black material	= une étoffe bleu-noir
a greenish-blue cup	= une tasse bleu-vert
a greeny-yellow dress	= une robe vert-jaune

English uses the ending -ish, *or sometimes* -y, *to show that something is approximately a certain colour, e.g.* a reddish hat *or* a greenish paint. *The French equivalent is* -âtre:

blue-ish	= bleuâtre
greenish *or* greeny	= verdâtre
greyish	= grisâtre
reddish	= rougeâtre
yellowish *or* yellowy	= jaunâtre
etc.	

Other similar French words are rosâtre, noirâtre *and* blanchâtre. *Note however that these words are often rather negative in French. It is better not to use them if you want to be complimentary about something. Use instead* tirant sur le rouge/jaune *etc.*

To describe a special colour, English can add -coloured *to a noun such as* raspberry (*framboise*) *or* flesh (*chair*). *Note how this is said in French, where the two-word compound with* couleur *is invariable, and, unlike English, never has a hyphen:*

a chocolate-coloured skirt	= une jupe couleur chocolat
raspberry-coloured fabric	= du tissu couleur framboise
flesh-coloured tights	= un collant couleur chair

Colour verbs

English makes some colour verbs by adding -en (*e.g.* blacken). *Similarly French has some verbs in* -ir *made from colour terms:*

to blacken	= noircir
to redden	= rougir
to whiten	= blanchir

The other French colour terms that behave like this are: bleu (bleuir), jaune (jaunir), rose (rosir) *and* vert (verdir). *It is always safe, however, to use* devenir, *thus:*

to turn purple	= devenir violet

Describing people ▶ 1037

Note the use of the definite article in the following:

to have black hair	= avoir les cheveux noirs
to have blue eyes	= avoir les yeux bleus

Note the use of à *in the following:*

a girl with blue eyes	= une jeune fille aux yeux bleus
the man with black hair	= l'homme aux cheveux noirs

Not all colours have direct equivalents in French. The following words are used for describing the colour of someone's hair (*note that* les cheveux *is plural in French*):

fair	= blond
dark	= brun
blonde *or* blond	= blond
brown	= châtain *inv*
red	= roux
black	= noir
grey	= gris
white	= blanc

Check other terms such as yellow, ginger, auburn, mousey *etc. in the dictionary.*

Note these nouns in French:

a fair-haired man	= un blond
a fair-haired woman	= une blonde
a dark-haired man	= un brun
a dark-haired woman	= une brune

The following words are useful for describing the colour of someone's eyes:

blue	= bleu
light blue	= bleu clair *inv*
light brown	= marron clair *inv*
brown	= marron *inv*
hazel	= noisette *inv*
green	= vert
grey	= gris
greyish-green	= gris-vert *inv*
dark	= noir

4 /ˈkɒmbaɪn/ Agric moissonner, battre [*crops*].
III /kəmˈbaɪn/ *vi* **1** (go together) [*activities, colours, styles, factors, events*] se combiner (**with** avec; **to do** pour faire); **to ~ well with** se combiner bien avec; **2** (join) [*people, groups*] s'associer (**against** contre; **to do** pour faire; **into** en); [*institutions, firms*] fusionner (**into** en); **3** Chem se combiner (**with** avec; **to do** pour faire); **to ~ easily** se combiner facilement.

combined /kəmˈbaɪnd/ *adj* **1** (joint) **~ operation** gen collaboration *f*; Mil opération *f* interarmées; **a ~ effort** une collaboration; **their ~ strength wasn't enough to move it** même en alliant leurs forces ils n'ont pas pu le déplacer; **2** (total) [*loss, salary, age, capacity, population*] total; **two men whose ~ age is 150** deux hommes ayant à eux deux 150 ans; **3** (put together) [*effects*] combiné; [*forces*] conjoint; **~ with** combiné avec; **more than all the rest ~** plus que tous les autres réunis.

combined: **~ honours** *n* GB Univ (+ *v sg ou pl*) double licence *f*; **~ pill** *n* pilule *f* combinée.

combine harvester *n* moissonneuse-batteuse *f*.

combo○ /ˈkɒmbəʊ/ *n* **1** Mus petit groupe *m*; **jazz ~** petit groupe *m* de jazz; **2** US (menu) *menu composé de deux plats au choix.*

combustible /kəmˈbʌstəbl/ *adj* [*substance*] combustible; fig [*temperament*] explosif/-ive.

combustion /kəmˈbʌstʃn/ **I** *n* combustion *f*; **internal ~ engine** moteur *m* à combustion interne.

II *modif* [*chamber, temperature, pressure*] de combustion.

come /kʌm/ **I**◐ *n* sperme *m*.

II *excl* (reassuringly) **~ (now)!** allons!; **~, ~!** (in warning, reproach) allons, allons!

III *vtr* (*prét* **came**; *pp* **come**) **1** (travel) faire; **to ~ 100 km to see** faire 100 km pour voir; **2**○ GB (act) **don't ~ the innocent with me** ne fais pas l'innocent; **to ~ the heavy-handed father** jouer les pères autoritaires.

IV *vi* (*prét* **came**; *pp* **come**) **1** (arrive) [*person, day, success, fame*] venir; [*bus, letter, news, results, rains, winter, war*] arriver; **the letter came on Monday** la lettre est arrivée lundi; **your turn will ~** ton tour arrivera; **to ~ after sb** (chase) poursuivre qn; **to ~ by** (take) prendre [*bus, taxi, plane*]; **I came on foot/by bike** je suis venu à pied/à bicyclette; **to ~ down** descendre [*stairs, street*]; **to ~ up** monter [*stairs, street*]; **to ~ down from Scotland/from Alaska** venir d'Écosse/de l'Alaska; **to ~ from** venir de [*airport, hospital*]; **to ~ into** entrer dans [*house, room*]; **the train came into the station** le train est entré en gare; **to ~ past** [*car, person*] passer; **to ~ through** [*person*] passer par [*town centre, tunnel*]; [*water, object*] traverser [*window etc*]; **to ~ to** venir à [*school, telephone*]; **to ~ to the door** venir ouvrir; **to ~ to the surface** remonter à la surface; **to ~ to the company as** entrer dans l'entreprise comme [*apprentice, consultant*]; **to ~ to do** venir faire; **to ~ running** arriver en courant; **to ~ limping down the street** descendre la rue en boitant; **to ~ crashing to the ground** [*structure*] s'écraser au sol; **to ~ streaming through the window** [*light*] entrer à flots par la fenêtre; **lunch is ready, ~ and get it!** le déjeuner est prêt, à table!; **when the time ~s** lorsque le moment sera venu; **the time has come to do** le moment est venu de faire; **I'm coming!** j'arrive!; **~ to mummy** viens voir maman; **to ~ and go** aller et venir; **you can ~ and go as you please** tu es libre de tes mouvements; **fashions ~ and go** les modes vont et viennent; **~ next week/year** la semaine/l'année prochaine; **~ Christmas/Summer** à Noël/en été; **there may ~ a time** ou **day when you regret it** tu pourrais le regretter un jour; **for some time to ~** encore quelque temps; **there's still the meal/speech to ~** il y a encore le repas/discours; **2** (approach) s'approcher; **to ~ and see/help sb** venir voir/aider qn; **to ~ to sb for** venir demander [qch] à qn [*money, advice*]; **I could see it coming** (of accident) je le voyais venir; **don't ~ any closer** ne vous approchez pas (plus); **he came to the job with preconceived ideas** quand il a commencé ce travail il avait des idées préconçues; **to ~ close** ou **near to doing** faillir faire; **3** (call, visit) [*dustman, postman*] passer; [*cleaner*] venir; **I've come to do** je viens faire; **I've come about** je viens au sujet de; **I've come for** je viens chercher; **my brother is coming for me at 10 am** mon frère passe me prendre à 10 heures; **they're coming for the weekend** ils viennent pour le weekend; **I've got six people coming to dinner** j'ai six personnes à dîner; **my sister is coming to stay with us** ma sœur vient passer quelques jours chez nous; **4** (attend) venir; **I can't** ou **won't be able to ~** je ne pourrai pas venir; **~ as you are** venez comme vous êtes; **to ~ to** venir à [*meeting, party, wedding*]; **to ~ with sb** venir avec qn, accompagner qn; **do you want to ~ fishing?** est-ce que tu veux venir à la pêche?; **5** (reach) **to ~ to, to ~ up/down to** [*water*] venir jusqu'à; [*dress, carpet, curtain*] arriver à; **I've just come to the chapter where...** j'en suis juste au chapitre où...; **6** (happen) **how did you ~ to do?** comment as-tu fait pour faire?; **that's what ~s of doing/not doing** voilà ce qui arrive quand on fait/ne fait pas; **how ~?** comment ça se fait?; **how ~ you lost?** comment ça se fait que tu aies perdu?; **~ what may** advienne que pourra; **to take things as they ~** prendre les choses comme elles viennent; **when you ~ to think of it** à la réflexion; **~ to think of it, you're right** en fait, tu as raison; **7** (begin) **to ~ to believe/hate/understand** finir par croire/détester/comprendre; **8** (originate) **to ~ from** [*person*] être originaire de, venir de [*city, country etc*]; [*word, song, legend*] venir de [*country, language*]; [*substance, food*] provenir de [*raw material*]; [*coins, stamps*] provenir de [*place, collection*]; [*smell, sound*] venir de [*place*]; **to ~ from France** [*fruit, painting*] provenir de France; [*person*] être français/-e; **to ~ from a long line of artists** être issu d'une longue lignée d'artistes; **9** (be available) **to ~ in** exister en [*sizes, colours*]; **to ~ with a radio/sunroof** être livré avec radio/toit ouvrant; **to ~ with chips** être servi avec des frites; **to ~ with matching napkins** être vendu avec les serviettes assorties; **calculators don't ~ smaller/cheaper than this** il n'existe pas de calculatrice plus petite/moins chère que celle-là; **10** (tackle) **to ~ to** aborder [*problem, subject*]; **I'll ~ to that in a moment** je reviendrai sur ce point dans un moment; **to ~ to sth** ou **to doing sth late in life** se mettre à faire qch sur le tard; **11** (develop) **it ~s with practice/experience** cela s'apprend avec la pratique/l'expérience; **wisdom ~s with age** la sagesse vient en vieillissant; **12** (be situated) venir; **to ~ after** suivre, venir après; **to ~ before** (in time, list, queue) précéder; (in importance) passer avant; **to ~ within** faire partie de [*terms*]; **to ~ first/last** [*athlete, horse*] arriver premier/dernier; **where did you ~?** tu es arrivé combien○?, tu es arrivé à quelle place?; **my family ~s first** ma famille passe avant tout; **nothing can ~ between us** rien ne peut nous séparer; **don't let this ~ between us** on ne va pas se fâcher pour ça; **to try to ~ between two people** essayer de s'interposer entre deux personnes; **nothing ~s between me and my football!** pour moi le foot c'est sacré!; **13** (be due) **the house ~s to me when they die** la maison me reviendra quand ils mourront; **death/old age ~s to us all** tout le monde meurt/vieillit; **he had it coming (to him)**○ ça lui pendait au nez; **they got what was coming to them**○ ils ont fini par avoir ce qu'ils méritaient; **14** (be a question of) **when it ~s to sth/to doing** lorsqu'il s'agit de qch/de faire; **15**○ (have orgasm) jouir.

IDIOMS **~ again**○**?** pardon?; **I don't know if I'm coming or going** je ne sais plus où j'en suis; **'how do you like your tea?'—'as it ~s'** 'tu le prends comment ton thé?'—'ça m'est égal'; **he's as stupid/honest as they ~** il n'y a pas plus stupide/honnête que lui; **~ to that** ou **if it ~s to that, you may be right** en fait, tu as peut-être raison; **to ~ as a shock/a surprise** être un choc/une surprise.

■ **come about 1** (happen) [*problems, reforms*] survenir; [*situation, change*] se produire; **the discovery came about by accident** on a fait la découverte par hasard; **2** Naut virer de bord.

■ **come across**: ¶ **~ across** (be conveyed) [*meaning, message*] passer; [*feelings*] transparaître; **the message of the film ~s across clearly** le message du film est clair; **his love of animals ~s across strongly** on sent bien qu'il adore les animaux; **she ~s across well on TV** elle passe bien à la télé; **~ across as** donner l'impression d'être [*liar, expert*]; paraître [*enthusiastic, honest*]; ¶ **~ across [sth]** tomber sur [*article, reference, example*]; découvrir [qch] par hasard [*village*]; **we rarely ~ across cases of** nous avons rarement affaire à des cas de; ¶ **~ across [sb]** rencontrer [*person*]; **one of the nicest people I've ever come across** une des personnes les plus sympathiques que j'aie jamais rencontrées.

■ **come along 1** (arrive) [*bus, person*] arriver; [*opportunity*] se présenter; **to wait for the right person to ~ along** attendre que la personne idéale se présente; **2** (hurry up) **~ along!** dépêche-toi!; **3** (attend) venir; **why don't you ~ along?** tu veux venir?; **to ~ along to** venir à [*lecture, party*]; **to ~ along with sb** venir avec qn, accompagner qn; **4** (make progress) [*pupil, trainee*] faire des progrès; [*book, building work, project*] avancer; [*painting, tennis*] progresser; [*plant, seedling*] pousser; **your Spanish is coming along** votre espagnol a progressé; **how's the thesis coming along?** est-ce que ta thèse avance?

■ **come apart 1** (accidentally) [*book, parcel, box*] se déchirer; [*shoes*] craquer; [*toy, camera*] se casser; **the toy just came apart in my hands** le jouet m'est resté dans les mains; **2** (intentionally) [*sections, components*] se séparer; [*machine, equipment*] se démonter.

■ **come around** US = **come round**.

■ **come at**: **~ at [sb] 1** (attack) [*person*] attaquer (**with** avec); [*bull, rhino*] foncer sur; **2** fig **there were criticisms/questions coming at me from all sides** j'étais assailli de critiques/questions.

■ **come away 1** (leave) lit partir; **to ~ away from** quitter [*cinema, match, show*]; sortir de [*interview, meeting*]; fig **to ~ away from the match/from the meeting disappointed/satisfied** sortir déçu/satisfait du stade/de la réunion; **to ~ away with the feeling that** rester sur l'impression que; **2** (move away) s'éloigner; **~ away!** (said by parent) pousse-toi de là!; (said by official) circulez!; **~ away from the edge** éloigne-toi du bord; **3** (become detached) [*handle, plaster, cover*] se détacher (**from** de).

■ **come back 1** (return) gen [*letter, person, memories, feeling, good weather*] revenir (**from** de; **to** à); (to one's house) rentrer ; **to ~ running back** revenir en courant; **the memories came flooding back** les souvenirs me sont revenus d'un seul coup; **to ~ back to** revenir à [*topic, problem*]; retourner auprès de [*spouse, lover*]; **to ~ back with sb** raccompagner qn; **to ~ back with** (return) revenir avec [*present, idea, flu*]; (reply) répondre par [*offer, suggestion*]; **can I ~ back to you on that tomorrow?** est-ce que nous pourrions en reparler demain?; **it's all coming back to me now** tout me revient maintenant; **the name will ~ back to me** le nom me reviendra; **to ~ back to what you were saying** pour en revenir à ce que tu disais; **2** (become popular) [*law, system*] être rétabli; [*trend, method, hairstyle*] revenir à la mode; **to ~ back into fashion** revenir à la mode.

■ **come by**: ¶ **~ by** [*person*] passer; **you must ~ by and see us** passez donc nous voir; ¶ **~ by [sth]** trouver [*book, job, money*].

■ **come down 1** (move lower) [*person*] descendre (**from** de); [*lift, barrier, blind*] descendre; [*curtain*] tomber; **to ~ down by parachute** descendre en parachute; **to ~ down in the lift** prendre l'ascenseur pour descendre; **he's really come down in the world** fig il est vraiment tombé bas; **his trousers barely came down to his ankles** son pantalon lui arrivait à peine aux chevilles; **2** (drop) [*price, inflation, unemployment, temperature*] baisser (**from** de; **to** à); [*cost*] diminuer; **cars are coming down in price** le prix des voitures baisse; **3** Meteorol [*snow, rain*] tomber; **the fog came down overnight** le brouillard est apparu pendant la nuit; **4** (land) [*helicopter*] se poser; [*aircraft*] atterrir; **5** (crash) [*plane*] s'écraser; **6** (fall) [*ceiling, wall*] s'écrouler; [*curtain rail*] tomber; [*hem*] se défaire; **7** fig (be resumed by) se ramener à [*question, problem, fact*]; **it all really ~s down to the fact that** ça se ramène au fait que.

■ **come forward 1** (step forward) s'avancer; **2** (volunteer) se présenter (**to do** pour faire); **to ~ forward with** présenter [*proof, proposal*]; offrir [*help, money, suggestions*]; **to ask witnesses to ~ forward** lancer un appel à témoins.

■ **come in 1** (enter) [*person, rain*] entrer (**through** par); **2** (return) rentrer (**from** de); **she ~s in from work at five** elle rentre du travail à cinq heures; **3** (come inland) [*tide*] monter; **a wind coming in from the sea** un vent soufflant de la mer; **4** (arrive) [*plane, train, bill, complaint, delivery, letter*] arriver; **which horse came in first?** quel cheval est arrivé premier?; **we've got £2,000 a month coming in** nous avons une rentrée de 2 000 livres sterling par mois; **5** (become current) [*trend, invention, style*] faire son apparition; [*habit, practice*] commencer à se répandre; **6** (interject) intervenir; **to ~ in with an opinion** exprimer son opinion; **7** Radio, Telecom (in radio transmission) **~ in, Delta Bravo!** c'est à vous, Delta Bravo!; **8** (participate) **to ~ in with sb** s'associer à qn; **to ~ in on the deal** participer à l'affaire; **9** (serve a particular purpose) **where do I ~ in?** à quel moment est-ce que j'interviens?; **where does the extra money ~ in?** à quel moment est-ce qu'on introduira l'argent en plus?; **to ~ in useful** ou **handy** [*box, compass, string etc*] être utile, servir; [*skill, qualification*] être utile; **10** (receive) **to ~ in for criticism** [*person*] être critiqué; [*plan*] faire l'objet de nombreuses critiques; **to ~ in for praise** recevoir des éloges.

■ **come into**: **~ into [sth] 1** (inherit) hériter de [*money*]; entrer en possession de [*inheritance*]; **2** (be relevant) **to ~ into it** [*age, experience*] entrer en ligne de compte, jouer; **luck/skill doesn't ~ into it** ce n'est pas une question de hasard/d'habileté.

■ **come off**: ¶ **~ off 1** (become detached) (accidentally) [*button, label, handle*] se détacher; [*lid*] s'enlever; [*paint*] s'écailler; [*wallpaper*] se décoller; (intentionally) [*handle, panel, lid*] s'enlever; **the knob came off in my hand** la poignée m'est restée dans la main; **the lid won't ~ off** je n'arrive pas à enlever le couvercle; **2** (fall) [*rider*] tomber; **3** (wash, rub off) [*ink*] s'effacer; [*stain*] partir; **the mark won't ~ off** la tache ne part pas; **4** (take place) [*deal*] se réaliser; [*merger, trip*] avoir lieu; **5** (succeed) [*plan, trick, project*] réussir; [*parody*] être réussi; **6** Theat, TV (be taken off) [*play*] être retiré de l'affiche; [*TV show*] être déprogrammé; **7** (fare) **she came off well** (in deal) elle s'en est très bien tirée; **who came off worst?** (in fight) lequel des deux a été le plus touché?; ¶ **~ off [sth] 1** (stop using) arrêter [*pill, tablet, heroin*]; **2** (fall off) tomber de [*bicycle, horse*]; **3** (get off) descendre de [*wall*]; **~ off the lawn!** sors de la pelouse!

■ **come on 1** (follow) **I'll ~ on later** je vous rejoindrai plus tard; **2** (exhortation) (encouraging) **~ on, try it!** allez, essaie!; **~ on, follow me!** allez, suivez-moi!; (impatient) **~ on, hurry up!** allez, dépêche-toi!; (wearily) **~ on, somebody must know the answer!** enfin, il y a sûrement quelqu'un qui connaît la réponse!; **~ on, you don't expect me to believe that!** non mais franchement, tu ne t'attends pas à ce que je croie ça!; **3** (make progress) [*person , player, patient*] faire des progrès; [*bridge, road, novel*] avancer; [*plant*] pousser; **how are the recruits coming on?** est-ce que les recrues font des progrès?; **her tennis is coming on well** elle fait des progrès en tennis; **4** (begin) [*asthma, attack, headache*] commencer; [*winter*] arriver; [*programme, film*] commencer; [*rain*] se mettre à tomber; **it came on to snow** il s'est mis à neiger; **5** (start to work) [*light*] s'allumer; [*heating, fan*] se mettre en route; **the power came on again at 11** le courant est revenu à 11 heures; **6** Theat [*actor*] entrer en scène.

■ **come out 1** (emerge) [*person, animal, vehicle*] sortir (**of** de); [*star*] apparaître; [*sun, moon*] se montrer; [*flowers, bulbs*] sortir de terre; [*spot, rash*] apparaître; **~ out with your hands up!** sortez les mains en l'air; **when does he ~ out?** (of prison, hospital) quand est-ce qu'il sort?; **he came out of it rather well** fig il ne s'en est pas mal tiré; **2** (originate) **to ~ out of** [*person*] être originaire de; [*song*] venir de; [*news report*] provenir de; **the money will have to ~ out of your savings** il faudra prendre l'argent sur tes économies; **3** (result) **to ~ out of** [*breakthrough*] sortir de; **something good came out of the disaster** il est sorti quelque chose de bon du désastre; **4** (strike) faire la grève; **to ~ out on strike** faire la grève; **5** [*homosexual*] déclarer publiquement son homosexualité; **6** (fall out) [*contact lens, tooth, key, screw, nail*] tomber; [*electrical plug*] se débrancher; [*sink plug*] sortir; [*contents, stuffing*] sortir; [*cork*] s'enlever; **his hair is coming out** il commence à perdre ses cheveux; **7** (be emitted) [*water, air, smoke*] sortir (**through** par); **the water ~s out of this hole** l'eau sort par ce trou; **8** (wash out) [*stain, ink, grease*] s'en aller, partir (**of** de); **it won't ~ out** ça ne part pas; **9** (be deleted) [*reference, sentence*] être éliminé; **10** (be published, issued) [*magazine, novel*] paraître; [*album, film, model, product*] sortir; **11** (become known) [*feelings*] se manifester; [*message, meaning*] ressortir; [*details, facts, full story*] être révélé; [*results*] être connu; [*secret*] être divulgué; **it came out that** on a appris que; **if it ever ~s out that it was my fault** si on découvre un jour que c'était de ma faute; **the truth is bound to ~ out** la vérité finira forcément par se savoir; **so that's what you think—it's all coming out now!** c'est ça que tu penses—tu finis par l'avouer!; **12** Phot, Print [*photo, photocopy*] être réussi; **the photos didn't ~ out (well)** les photos ne sont pas réussies; **red ink won't ~ out on the photocopy** l'encre rouge ne donnera rien sur la photocopie; **13** (end up) **to ~ out at 200 dollars** [*cost, bill*] s'élever à 200 dollars; **the jumper came out too big** le pull était trop grand; **the total always ~s out the same** le total est toujours le même; **14** (say) **to ~ out with** sortir [*excuse*]; raconter [*nonsense, rubbish*]; **I knew what I wanted to say but it came out wrong** je savais ce que je voulais dire mais je me suis mal exprimé; **whatever will she ~ out with next?** qu'est-ce qu'elle va encore nous sortir○?; **to ~ straight out with it** le dire franchement; **15** (enter society) faire ses débuts dans le monde.

■ **come over**: ¶ **~ over 1** (drop in) venir; **~ over for a drink** venez prendre un verre; **to ~ over to do** venir faire; **2** (travel) venir; **they came over on the ferry** ils sont venus en ferry; **she's coming over on the 10 am flight** elle arrive par l'avion de 10 heures; **she often ~s over to France** elle vient souvent en France; **their ancestors came over with the Normans** leurs ancêtres sont venus ici au temps des Normands; **3** (convey impression) [*message, meaning*] passer; [*feelings, love*] transparaître; **to make one's feelings ~ over** exprimer ses sentiments; **to ~ over very well** [*person*] donner une très bonne impression; **to ~ over as** donner l'impression d'être [*lazy, honest*]; **4**○ (suddenly become) **to ~ over all embarrassed** se sentir gêné tout à coup; **to ~ over all shivery** se sentir fiévreux/-euse tout à coup; **to ~ over all faint** être pris de vertige tout d'un coup; ¶ **~ over [sb]** [*feeling*] envahir; **what's come over you?** qu'est-ce qui te prend?; **I don't know what came over me** je ne sais pas ce qui m'a pris.

■ **come round** GB, **come around** US **1** (regain consciousness) reprendre connaissance; **2** (make a detour) faire un détour (**by** par); **3** (circulate) [*steward, waitress*] passer; **4** (visit) venir; **to ~ round and do** venir faire; **to ~ round for dinner/drinks** venir dîner/prendre un verre; **5** (occur) [*event*] avoir lieu; **the elections are coming round again** les élections auront bientôt lieu; **by the time Christmas ~s round** à Noël; **6** (change one's mind) changer d'avis; **to ~ round to an idea/to my way of thinking** se faire à une idée/à ma façon de voir les choses; **7** Naut [*boat*] venir au vent.

■ **come through**: ¶ **~ through 1** (survive) s'en tirer; **2** (penetrate) [*heat, ink*] traverser; [*light*] passer; **3** (arrive) **the fax/the call came through at midday** nous avons reçu le fax/l'appel à midi; **my posting has just come through** je viens de recevoir ma mutation; **she's still waiting for her visa/her results to ~ through** elle n'a toujours pas reçu son visa/ses résultats; **4** (emerge) [*personality, qualities*] apparaître; ¶ **~ through [sth] 1** (survive) se tirer de [*crisis*]; se sortir de [*recession*]; survivre à [*operation, ordeal, war*]; **2** (penetrate) [*ink, dye*] traverser [*paper, cloth*]; [*light*] passer au travers de [*curtains*].

■ **come to**: ¶ **~ to** (regain consciousness) (from faint) reprendre connaissance; (from trance) se réveiller; ¶ **~ to [sth] 1** (total) [*shopping*] revenir à; [*bill, expenditure, total*] s'élever à; **both columns should ~ to the same figure** les deux colonnes devraient donner le même total; **that ~s to £40** cela fait 40 livres sterling; **2** (result in) aboutir à; **if it ~s to a fight** si on en vient à se battre; **all her plans came to nothing** aucun de ses projets ne s'est réalisé; **did the plans ~ to anything?** est-ce que les projets ont abouti?; **all our efforts came to nothing** tous nos efforts ont été vains; **I never thought it would ~ to this** je n'aurais jamais imaginé que les choses en arriveraient là; **it may not ~ to that** ce ne sera peut-être pas nécessaire.

■ **come under**: **~ under [sth] 1** (be subjected to) **to ~ under scrutiny** faire l'objet d'un examen minutieux; **to ~ under suspicion** être soupçonné; **to ~ under threat** être menacé; **we're coming under pressure to do** on fait pression sur nous pour faire; **2** (be classified under) (in library, shop) être classé dans le rayon [*reference, history*]; **Dali ~s under Surrealism** Dali fait partie des surréalistes.

■ **come up**: **~ up 1** (arise) [*problem, issue, matter*] être soulevé; [*name*] être mentionné; **to ~ up in conversation** [*subject*] être abordé dans la conversation; **this type of question may ~ up** c'est le genre de question qui pourrait être posée; **2** (be due, eligible) **to ~ up for re-election** se représenter aux élections; **my salary ~s up for review in April** mon salaire sera révisé en avril; **the car is coming up for its annual service** la voiture va avoir sa révision annuelle; **3** (occur) [*opportunity*] se présenter; **something urgent has come up** j'ai quelque chose d'urgent à faire; **a vacancy has come up** une place s'est libérée; **4** (rise) [*sun, moon*] sortir; [*tide*] monter; [*bulb, seeds*] germer; [*daffodils, beans*] sortir; **5** Jur [*case, hearing*] passer au tribunal; **to ~ up before** [*case*] passer devant; [*person*] comparaître devant.

■ **come up against**: **~ up against [sth]** se heurter à [*problem, prejudice, opposition*].

■ **come up with**: **~ up with [sth]** trouver [*answer, idea, money*].

■ **come upon**: ¶ **~ upon [sth]** tomber sur [*book, reference*]; trouver [*idea*]; ¶ **~ upon [sb]** rencontrer, tomber○ sur [*friend*].

comeback /ˈkʌmbæk/ **I** *n* **1** (bid for success) (of musician, actor, boxer) come-back *m*; (of politician) rentrée *f*; **to make** ou **stage a ~** faire un come-back or une rentrée; **miniskirts are making a ~** les mini-jupes reviennent à la mode; **2** (redress) recours *m*; **to have no ~** n'avoir aucun recours; **3** (retort) réplique *f*; **4** (repercussions) répercussions *fpl*.

II *modif* [*album*] de come-back; [*campaign*] de rentrée; **~ bid** (of singer, actor) come-back *m*; (of politician) rentrée *f*.

Comecon /ˈkɒmɪkɒn/ *n* Comecon *m*.
comedian /kəˈmiːdɪən/ ▶ 1692 *n* **1** (actor) (male) comique *m*; (female) actrice *f* comique; **2** (joker) pitre *m*; **he/she is a bit of a ~** il/elle est assez pitre.
comedienne /kəˌmiːdɪˈen/ ▶ 1692 *n* actrice *f* comique.
comedown○ /ˈkʌmdaʊn/ *n* **1** (decline in status) claque○ *f*, déchéance *f*; **it's quite a ~ for her to have to do** elle trouve humiliant d'avoir à faire; **2** (disappointment) déception *f*; **it was rather a ~ for her** elle a été assez déçue.
comedy /ˈkɒmədɪ/ *n* **1** (genre) comédie *f*; **black/light ~** comédie *f* macabre/légère; **2** (play) comédie *f*; **situation ~** comédie *f* d'intrigues; (on TV) sitcom *f*; **3** (funny aspect) comique *m*; **moments of high ~** des moments de haut comique.
come-hither○ /ˌkʌmˈhɪðə(r)/ *adj* [*look*] aguichant.
comeliness /ˈkʌmlɪnɪs/ *n* littér beauté *f*.
comely /ˈkʌmlɪ/ *adj* littér beau/belle.
come-on○ /ˈkʌmɒn/ *n* **1** (sexual) **to give sb the ~** draguer qn; **2** (in sales jargon) (produit) produit *m* d'appel; (claim) accroche *f*.
comer /ˈkʌmə(r)/ *n* (arrival) arrivant/-e *m/f*; **to take on all ~s** [*champion, boxer*] se battre contre tous les challengeurs; **the contest is open to all ~s** le concours est ouvert à tout le monde.
comestible /kəˈmestəbl/ *adj* sout comestible.
comestibles /kəˈmestəblz/ *npl* sout comestibles *mpl*.
comet /ˈkɒmɪt/ *n* comète *f*.
comeuppance○ /kʌmˈʌpəns/ *n* **to get one's ~** avoir ce qu'on mérite.
comfit† /ˈkʌmfɪt/ *n* dragée *f*.
comfort /ˈkʌmfət/ **I** *n* **1** (well-being) confort *m*; (emphasizing wealth) aisance *f*; **to live in ~** vivre dans l'aisance; **he likes his ~** il aime son confort; **2** (amenity) confort *m*; **every modern ~** tout le confort moderne; **home ~s** le confort du foyer; **the ~s of civilization** les conforts or agréments *mpl* de la civilisation; **3** (consolation) réconfort *m*, consolation *f*; (relief from pain) soulagement *m*; **it's a ~ to know that** il est consolant de savoir que; **to be a great ~ to sb** [*person*] être un grand réconfort pour qn; [*knowledge, belief*] apporter beaucoup de réconfort à qn; **to take ~ from** trouver un réconfort dans; **we can take ~ from the fact that** nous pouvons nous consoler à l'idée que; **to give** ou **bring ~ to** (emotionally) procurer du réconfort à; (physically) procurer du soulagement à; **if it's any ~ to you** si cela peut vous réconforter or consoler; **to be small ~ for sb** n'être qu'une maigre consolation pour qn.
II *vtr* consoler; (stronger) réconforter; **to be ~ed by sb** se faire consoler par qn; **to be ~ed by the thought that** être réconforté à l'idée que.
IDIOMS **it's (a bit) too close for ~** (of where sb is, lives) ça fait un peu trop près; (of fighting, war) c'est dangereusement proche, ça devient inquiétant.
comfortable /ˈkʌmftəbl, US -fərt-/ *adj* **1** [*room, house, chair, bed, shoes, clothes, journey*] confortable; [*temperature*] agréable; **2** (relaxed) [*person*] à l'aise; **to make oneself ~** (in chair) s'installer confortablement; (at ease) se mettre à son aise; **are you ~ in that chair?** est-ce que vous êtes bien dans cette chaise?; **she made everybody feel ~** elle mettait tout le monde à l'aise; **the patient's condition is described as ~** l'état du malade est jugé satisfaisant; **the patient had a ~ night** le malade a passé une bonne nuit; **3** (financially) [*person, family*] aisé; [*income*] conséquent; **4** (reassuring) [*idea, thought, belief*] sécurisant; [*victory, majority, lead*] confortable; **to live at a ~ distance from** (far enough) habiter à bonne distance or assez loin de; **5** (happy) **I don't feel ~ doing** ça m'embête○ de faire; **I would feel more ~ about leaving if...** je partirais plus volontiers si...
comfortably /ˈkʌmftəblɪ, US -fərt-/ *adv* **1** (physically) [*sit*] confortablement; [*rest*] tranquillement; [*dressed, furnished*] confortablement; **2** (financially) **you can live ~ on that** cela est suffisant pour vivre confortablement; **to be ~ off** être à l'aise; **3** (easily) [*win, reach*] facilement, aisément.
comforter /ˈkʌmfətə(r)/ *n* **1** (scarf) cache-nez *m inv*; **2** (person) consolateur/-trice *m/f*; **3** US (quilt) édredon *m*.
comforting /ˈkʌmfətɪŋ/ *adj* [*sight, news, thought*] réconfortant; **it is ~ to know that** il est réconfortant de savoir que.
comfortless /ˈkʌmfətlɪs/ *adj* [*room*] sans confort, peu confortable; [*thought*] triste; [*person*] démuni.
comfort station *n* US toilettes *fpl*.
comfy○ /ˈkʌmfɪ/ *adj* confortable.
comic /ˈkɒmɪk/ ▶ 1692 **I** *n* **1** (man) comique *m*; (woman) actrice *f* comique; **2** (magazine etc) bande *f* dessinée.
II *adj* [*event, actor, appearance*] comique.
comical /ˈkɒmɪkl/ *adj* [*situation, clothes, expression*] cocasse, comique.
comically /ˈkɒmɪklɪ/ *adj* de manière comique.
comic: **~ book** *n* bande *f* dessinée; **~ opera** *n* opéra *m* comique.
comic relief *n* **to provide some ~** Theat, fig détendre l'atmosphère.
comic strip *n* bande *f* dessinée.
coming /ˈkʌmɪŋ/ **I** *n* **1** (arrival) arrivée *f*; **~ and going** va-et-vient *m inv*; **~s and goings** allées et venues *fpl*; **2** (approach) (of winter, old age) approche *f*; (of new era, event) arrivée *f*; **3** Relig avènement *m*.
II *pres p adj* [*election, event*] prochain (*before n*); [*strike*] qui s'annonce (*after n*); [*war, campaign*] qui se prépare (*after n*); [*months, weeks*] à venir (*after n*); **I leave this ~ Monday** je pars (ce) lundi.
coming-out /ˌkʌmɪŋˈaʊt/ *n* **1** (of homosexual) déclaration *f* publique de son homosexualité; **2**† (of debutante) débuts *mpl* (dans la société).
Comintern /ˈkɒmɪntɜːn/ *n* Komintern *m*.
comity /ˈkɒmətɪ/ *n* sout courtoisie *f*; **the ~ of nations** la courtoisie internationale.
comma /ˈkɒmə/ *n* (in punctuation) virgule *f*.
command /kəˈmɑːnd, US -ˈmænd/ **I** *n* **1** (order) ordre *m*; **to carry out/give a ~** exécuter/donner un ordre; **I did it at his ~** j'ai agi sur son ordre; **at the ~ 'shoot' fire at the enemy!** tirez sur l'ennemi au commandement 'feu'!; **2** (military control) commandement *m*; **to have/take ~ of a regiment** avoir/prendre le commandement d'un régiment; **to give sb ~ of sth** confier le commandement de qch à qn; **to be in ~** commander; **to be under the ~ of sb** [*person*] être sous les ordres de qn; [*regiment*] être sous les ordres or sous le commandement de qn; **I'm in ~ of the troops** les troupes sont sous mes ordres; **the enemy has ~ of the air** l'ennemi a la maîtrise du ciel; **3** (mastery) (control) maîtrise *f*; **to have full ~ of one's emotions/faculties** maîtriser parfaitement ses émotions/facultés; **to have an excellent ~ of Russian** avoir une excellente maîtrise du russe; **to be in ~ of events/the situation** avoir les événements/la situation en main; **to have sth at one's ~** avoir qch à sa disposition; **to be in ~ of oneself** être maître/maîtresse *m/f* de soi; **4** Mil (group of officers) commandement *m*; (group of soldiers) unité *f* commandée; (section of the forces) commandement *m*; (district) région *f* militaire; **air ~** commandement *m* aérien; **5** Comput commande *f*.
II *modif* Comput de commande.
III *vtr* **1** (order) ordonner à [*person*]; **to ~ sb to do** ordonner à qn de faire; **to ~ that** ordonner que (+ *subj*); **I ~ed the release of the prisoner** j'ai ordonné la libération du prisonnier; **'stop,' he ~ed** 'arrêtez,' ordonna-t-il; **2** (obtain as one's due) inspirer [*affection, obedience, respect*]; forcer [*admiration*]; **to ~ a good price** se vendre cher; **3** (dispose of) disposer de [*funds, resources, support, majority*]; **4** (dominate) [*fortress*] dominer [*valley*]; (overlook) [*place, house*] avoir vue sur; **to ~ a view of** avoir vue sur; **5** Mil commander [*regiment*]; fig [*nation, army*] maîtriser [*air, sea*].
IV *vi* commander.
commandant /ˌkɒmənˈdænt/ *n* Mil commandant *m*.
command economy *n* économie *f* dirigiste.
commandeer /ˌkɒmənˈdɪə(r)/ *vtr* Mil réquisitionner.
commander /kəˈmɑːndə(r), US -mæn-/ ▶ 1612 *n* **1** gen chef *m*; Mil commandant *m*; Mil Naut cf capitaine *m* de frégate; **~ in chief** commandant en chef; **tank ~** chef *m* de char; **2** GB (in police) *officier responsable d'un secteur de la police londonienne*; cf commissaire *m* divisionnaire.
command file *n* Comput fichier *m* de commandes.
commanding /kəˈmɑːndɪŋ, US -ˈmæn-/ *adj* **1** (authoritative) [*look, manner, voice*] impérieux/-ieuse; [*presence*] imposant; **2** (dominant) [*position*] dominant; **to have a ~ lead in the polls** être en tête des sondages; **3** (elevated) [*position*] surélevé; **the house has a ~ view over the lake** la maison domine le lac.
commanding officer, **CO** ▶ 1612 *n* commandant *m*.
commandment /kəˈmɑːndmənt, US -ˈmæn-/ *n* **1** (order) injonction *f*; **2** Relig (also **Commandment**) commandement *m*; **the Ten Commandments** les dix commandements; **to keep the ~s** observer les commandements.
command module *n* Aerosp module *m* de commande.
commando /kəˈmɑːndəʊ, US -ˈmæn-/ **I** *n* (*pl* **-os, -oes**) **1** (unit) commando *m*; **a ~ raid** une opération commando; **2** (member) (membre *m* d'un) commando *m*.
II *modif* [*operation*] commando.
command: **~ performance** *n* GB Theat représentation *f* de gala (*donnée en présence d'un membre de la famille royale*); **~ post, CP** *n* Mil poste *m* de commandement; **~ structure** *n* structure *f* hiérarchique.
commemorate /kəˈmeməreɪt/ *vtr* commémorer.
commemoration /kəˌmeməˈreɪʃn/ **I** *n* commémoration *f* (**of, for** de); **in ~ of** en commémoration de.
II *modif* [*ceremony, service*] commémoratif/-ive.
commemorative /kəˈmemərətɪv, US -ˈmeməreɪt-/ *adj* commémoratif/-ive.
commence /kəˈmens/ sout **I** *vtr* commencer [*story, proceedings*]; **'well,' he ~d** 'eh bien,' commença-t-il; **to ~ doing** commencer à faire.
II *vi* commencer; **to ~ with a song** commencer par une chanson.
commencement /kəˈmensmənt/ *n* **1** sout (start) commencement *m*; **2** US Univ (ceremony) *cérémonie de remise des diplômes*; (day) *jour de remise des diplômes*.
commend /kəˈmend/ **I** *vtr* **1** (praise) louer (**for, on** pour); **she was ~ed for bravery** on l'a louée pour son courage; **'highly ~ed'** 'louangé'; **2** (recommend) sout recommander (**sb/sth to sb** qn/qch à qn); **to have much to ~ it** avoir de grandes qualités; **3** (entrust) confier; **to ~ one's soul to God** recommander son âme à Dieu; **4**† (give regards to) sout **~ me to him** rappelez-moi à son bon souvenir.
II *v refl* **to ~ itself** (be acceptable) être acceptable (**to** à).

commendable /kə'mendəbl/ *adj* louable; **highly ~** très louable.

commendably /kə'mendəblɪ/ *adv* **~ quick/restrained** avec une louable promptitude/retenue.

commendation /ˌkɒmen'deɪʃn/ *n* **1** (praise, award) éloge *m*; **with the ~ of** avec les éloges de; **2** Mil (medal, citation) citation *f*; **3** (recommendation) approbation *f*.

commensurable /kə'menʃərəbl/ *adj* commensurable.

commensurate /kə'menʃərət/ *adj* **1** sout (proportionate) proportionné (**with** à); **2** sout (appropriate) **to be ~ with** être à la mesure de; **3** Math commensurable.

comment /'kɒment/ **I** *n* **1** (remark) (public) commentaire *m* (**on** sur); (in conversation) remarque *f* (**on** sur); (written) annotation *f*; **to make ~s** faire des commentaires (**about** au sujet de); **2** ¢ (discussion) commentaires *mpl* (**about** portant sur); **without ~** [*act, listen*] sans commentaire; [*occur, pass*] sans susciter des commentaires; **to be open to ~** être ouvert aux suggestions; **he was unavailable for ~** il s'est refusé à toute déclaration; **'no ~'** 'je n'ai pas de déclaration à faire'; **what she said was fair ~** ses remarques étaient justifiées; **3** (unfavourable image) **to be a ~ on** [*situation*] être une critique de [*society etc*].

II *vtr* (orally) remarquer (**that** que); (in writing) constater, observer (**that** que).

III *vi* **1** (remark) faire des commentaires; **to ~ on sth/sb** (neutrally) faire des commentaires sur qch/qn; (negatively) faire des observations sur qch/qn; **2** (discuss) **to ~ on** commenter [*text etc*].

commentary /'kɒməntrɪ, US -terɪ/ *n* **1** gen, Radio, TV (description) commentaire *m* (**on** de); **a running ~** un commentaire détaillé; **2** Journ (analysis) analyse *f* (**on** de); **3** Literat (criticism) commentaire *m* (**on** de); **'notes and ~ by...'** 'annoté et commenté par...'

commentary box *n* cabine *f* de reportage.

commentate /'kɒmənteɪt/ **I** *vtr* commenter.

II *vi* faire le commentaire; **to ~ on** commenter [*sporting event*].

commentator /'kɒmənteɪtə(r)/ ▶1692 *n* **1** (sports) commentateur/-trice *m/f*; **football ~** GB commentateur spécialiste de football; **2** (current affairs) journaliste *mf*; **political ~** journaliste politique; **3** (scholar) commentateur/-trice *m/f*.

commerce /'kɒmɜːs/ *n* commerce *m*; **to be** ou **work in ~** être dans les affaires.

commercial /kə'mɜːʃl/ **I** *n* annonce *f* publicitaire; **television/radio ~** annonce publicitaire à la télévision/à la radio; **beer/car ~** annonce publicitaire pour de la bière/pour une voiture.

II *adj* **1** [*airline, bank, sector, organization*] commercial; **2** (profitable) commercial pej; qui se vend bien; **3** (large-scale) [*agriculture, production*] industriel/-ielle; **4** (for the public) [*product, use*] commercial; **5** [*TV, radio*] commercial.

commercial: **~ art** *n* arts *mpl* graphiques appliqués; **~ artist** *n* graphiste *mf*; **~ break** *n* publicité *f*.

commercialism /kə'mɜːʃəlɪzəm/ *n* **1** péj mercantilisme *m* pej; **2** (principles of commerce) esprit *m* commercial.

commercialization /kəˌmɜːʃəlaɪ'zeɪʃn, US -lɪ'z-/ *n* péj commercialisation *f*.

commercialize /kə'mɜːʃəlaɪz/ *vtr* souvent péj commercialiser.

commercialized /kə'mɜːʃəlaɪzd/ *adj* péj commercialisé.

commercial law *n* droit *m* commercial.

commercially /kə'mɜːʃəlɪ/ *adv* commercialement; **~ available** disponible en commerce.

commercial: **~ traveller** ▶1692 *n* voyageur *m* de commerce; **~ vehicle** *n* véhicule *m* utilitaire.

commie° /'kɒmɪ/ *n, adj* coco° (*mf*), communiste (*mf*).

commiserate /kə'mɪzəreɪt/ **I** *vtr* **'how awful,' she ~d** 'c'est affreux,' dit-elle, compatissante.

II *vi* compatir (**with** avec; **about, over** à propos de).

commiseration /kəˌmɪzə'reɪʃn/ *n* commisération *f* fml, compassion *f*; **a look of ~** un air compatissant.

commissar /'kɒmɪsɑː(r)/ *n* Pol Hist (in USSR) commissaire *m*.

commissariat /ˌkɒmɪ'seərɪət/ *n* **1** Mil intendance *f*; **2** Pol Hist (in USSR) commissariat *m*.

commissary /'kɒmɪsərɪ/ *n* **1** US Mil (shop) magasin *m* (*dans une base militaire, une prison etc*); (officer) officier *m* d'intendance; **2** US Cin restaurant *m* de studio.

commission /kə'mɪʃn/ **I** *n* **1** (payment for goods sold) commission *f*; **to get a 5% ~ on each item** recevoir or toucher une commission de 5% sur chaque article vendu; **to work on a ~ basis** ou **on ~** travailler à la commission; **2** (professional fee) commission *f*; **we charge 1% ~ on travellers' cheques** nous prenons 1% de commission sur les chèques de voyage; **3** (advance order) commande *f* (**for** de); **to give a painter a ~** passer une commande à un peintre; **to work to ~** travailler sur commande; **4** (committee) commission *f* (**on** sur); **~ of inquiry** commission d'enquête; **5** Mil ≈ brevet *m*; **to get one's ~** être nommé officier; **to resign one's ~** démissionner; **6** sout (carrying out) (of crime, sin) perpétration *f*; **7** (authority to act) mandat *m* (**to do** pour faire); **8** (mission) mission *f*; **I have a ~ to begin negotiations** j'ai pour mission de commencer les négociations; **9** (operation) **to be in ~** [*ship*] être en service; **to be out of ~** [*ship*] être désarmé; [*machine*] être hors service; **to put a boat out of ~** désarmer un bateau; **he'll be out of ~ for the World Cup** il ne participera pas à la Coupe du Monde.

II *vtr* **1** (order) commander [*opera, portrait, report*] (**from** à); **to ~ an author to write a novel** commander un roman à un écrivain; **to ~ an artist to paint a portrait** commander un portrait à un peintre; **a ~ed portrait** un portrait sur commande; **2** (instruct) **to ~ sb to do** charger qn de faire; **3** Mil nommer [qn] à un commandment [*officer*]; **to be ~ed (as) an officer** être nommé officier; **a ~ed officer** un **officier; 4** (prepare for service) armer [*ship*]; mettre [qch] en service [*plane, equipment, weapon system*]; **the power station is ~ed for next March** la centrale entrera en service en mars prochain.

commission agent ▶1692 *n* GB **1** Comm commissionnaire *mf*; **2** (bookmaker) bookmaker *m*.

commissionaire /kəˌmɪʃə'neə(r)/ ▶1692 *n* GB portier *m*.

commissioner /kə'mɪʃənə(r)/ *n* **1** Admin membre *m* d'une commission; **2** (in police) GB ≈ préfet *m* de police; **3** (also **Commissioner**) (in the EC Commission) membre *m* de la Commission européenne; **4** US Sport *président d'une fédération sportive*.

commissioner: **Commissioner for Local Administration** *n* GB Admin *commissaire chargé d'enquêter sur les décisions prises par l'administration locale*; **Commissioner for Oaths** *n* GB Jur *officier habilité à enregistrer les déclarations sous serment*; **Commissioner of Customs and Excise** *n* GB Admin *commissaire chargé de percevoir les droits de douane et de TVA*; **Commissioner of Inland Revenue** *n* GB Tax ≈ Percepteur *m* des Impôts.

Commission for Racial Equality, CRE *n* GB organisation *f* gouvernementale contre la discrimination raciale.

commissioning editor ▶1692 *n* **1** Publg directeur/-trice *m/f* éditorial/-e; **2** TV programmateur *m*, responsable *mf* d'une unité de programme.

commission: **~ing parent** *n* parent *m* qui a recours à une mère porteuse; **~ merchant** ▶1692 *n* Comm intermédiaire *mf* à la commission; **~ sale** *n* Comm vente *f* à la commission.

commit /kə'mɪt/ (*p prés etc* **-tt-**) **I** *vtr* **1** (perpetrate) commettre [*crime, offence, sin, sacrilege, error*]; **to ~ adultery** commettre un adultère; **to ~ perjury** se parjurer; **2** (engage, promise) engager [*person*] (**to do** à faire); **this doesn't ~ you to anything** cela ne vous engage à rien; **3** (assign) consacrer [*money, time*] (**to** à); **all our funds are already ~ted** tous nos fonds sont déjà attribués; **4** Jur **to ~ sb for trial** mettre qn en accusation; **to ~ sb to a court for trial** renvoyer qn devant un tribunal; **to ~ sb to jail/to a psychiatric hospital** faire incarcérer/interner qn; **to have sb ~ted** faire interner qn; **5** (consign) sout confier (**to** à; **to sb's care** à la garde de qn); **to ~ sth to the flames** livrer qch aux flammes; **to ~ sth to paper** consigner qch; **to ~ sth to memory** confier qch à la mémoire; **to ~ sb's body to the deep** livrer le corps de qn à la mer; **6** Pol renvoyer en commission [*bill*].

II *v refl* **to ~ oneself** s'engager (**to sth** à qch; **to do** à faire); **I can't** ou **I won't ~ myself** je ne peux rien promettre (**as to** quant à); **to ~ oneself to sb** se vouer à qn.

commitment /kə'mɪtmənt/ *n* **1** (obligation) engagement *m* (**to do** à faire); **a previous/financial ~** un engagement antérieur/financier; **to meet one's ~s** honorer ses engagements; **to give a firm ~ that** s'engager fermement à ce que (+ *subj*); **to take on a ~** prendre un engagement; **absent due to family ~s** absent en raison d'obligations familiales; **2** (sense of duty) attachement *m* (**to** à); **to have a strong ~ to doing** être particulièrement attaché à faire; **the job demands complete ~** ce travail exige un total don de soi; **3** Jur = **committal**.

committal /kə'mɪtl/ *n* **1** Jur (to prison) incarcération *f*; (to psychiatric hospital) internement *m*; (to court) renvoi *m* devant un tribunal; **2** sout (consigning) **the ~ of X to Y's care** la remise *f* de X aux soins de Y; **the ~ of sb's body to the deep** l'immersion *f* du corps de qn.

committal: **~ for trial** *n* Jur renvoi *m* devant un tribunal; **~ order** *n* Jur condamnation *f* pour outrage à magistrat; **~ proceedings** *npl* Jur audience *f* préliminaire.

committed /kə'mɪtɪd/ *adj* **1** (devoted) [*parent, carer, teacher*] dévoué; [*Christian, Socialist*] fervent; **to be ~ to/to doing** se consacrer à/à faire; **to be politically/emotionally ~** être engagé politiquement/affectivement; **2** (with commitments) pris (**to doing** pour faire); **I am heavily ~** (timewise) je suis très pris; (financially) j'ai de lourds engagements; **3** [*funds, time*] attribué.

committee /kə'mɪtɪ/ *n* gen comité *m*; (to investigate, report) commission *f*; **in ~** en comité.

committee: **~man** *n* US Pol conseiller *m* municipal; **~ meeting** *n* réunion *f* du comité; **~ of the whole** *n* US comité *m* plénier; **~ stage** *n*: *phase pendant laquelle une commission discute un projet de loi*; **~woman** *n* US Pol conseillère *f* municipale.

commode /kə'məʊd/ *n* **1** (chest of drawers) commode *f*; **2** (chair) chaise *f* percée; **3** US (toilet) toilettes *fpl*.

commodious /kə'məʊdɪəs/ *adj* sout

[lodgings, bed, cupboard] spacieux/-ieuse; *[chair]* grand.

commodities broker /kəˈmɒdətɪz/ ▶1692 *n* ≈ courtier/-ière *m/f* en matières premières.

commodities market /kəˈmɒdətɪz/ *n* Fin marché *m* des matières premières.

commodity /kəˈmɒdətɪ/ *n* **1** Comm, gen article *m*; (of food) denrée *f*; **household commodities** articles *mpl* de ménage; **a rare ~** fig une denrée rare; **2** Fin matière *f* première.

commodity dollar *n* US dollar *m* marchandise.

commodore /ˈkɒmədɔ:(r)/ ▶1612 *n* **1** (in navy) contre-amiral *m*; **2** (of yacht club) président *m*.

common /ˈkɒmən/ **I** *n* (public land) terrain *m* communal; **Clapham Common** le terrain communal de Clapham.
II commons *npl* **1** (the people) **the ~s** le peuple; **2** Pol (also **Commons**) **the ~s** les Communes *fpl*; **3** US Univ (refectory) réfectoire *m*.
III *adj* **1** (often encountered) *[crime, illness, mistake, name, problem, reaction]* courant, fréquent; **in ~ use** d'un usage courant; **in ~ parlance** dans le langage courant; **it is ~ for sb to do** il est courant que qn fasse; **to be ~ among** être répandu chez *[children, mammals etc]*; **2** (shared) *[aim, approach, attributes, border, enemy, language, interest, ownership]* commun (**to** à); **for the ~ good** pour le bien commun; **by ~ agreement** d'un commun accord; **it is ~ property** c'est la propriété de tous; **it is ~ knowledge** c'est de notoriété publique; **3** (ordinary) *[man, woman]* du peuple (*after n*); **the ~ people** le peuple; **a ~ soldier** un simple soldat; **the ~ herd** péj la masse; **a ~ criminal** péj un criminel ordinaire; **4** péj (low-class) commun; **it looks/sounds ~** ça fait commun; **5** (minimum expected) *[courtesy, decency, humanity]* le/la plus élémentaire; **6** Zool, Bot *[frog, daisy, algae]* commun; **a ~ variety** une variété commune; **7** Math *[denominator, factor, multiple]* commun.
IV in common *adv phr* en commun; **to have sth in ~** avoir qch en commun; **to hold sth in ~** Jur posséder qch en commun.
IDIOMS **to be as ~ as muck** ou **dirt**○ (vulgar) être d'une vulgarité crasse○; **they are as ~ as muck**○ (widespread) on en ramasse à la pelle; **to be on short ~s** GB être rationné, faire maigre hum; **to have the ~ touch** avoir de la simplicité.

common: **Common Agricultural Policy, CAP** *n* politique *f* agricole commune; **~ assault** *n* Jur coups *mpl* et blessures *fpl*; **~ carrier** *n* US entreprise *f* de transport public; **~ chord** *n* accord *m* parfait; **~ cold** ▶1354 *n* rhume *m* de cerveau; **~ core** *n* Sch disciplines *fpl* de base.

common currency *n* **1** Fin monnaie *f* commune; **2** fig **to make sth ~** (widely used) banaliser qch; **given ~** (widely accepted) *[opinion, fact]* généralement accepté.

Common Entrance (examination) *n* GB Sch *examen d'entrée dans l'enseignement secondaire privé*.

commoner /ˈkɒmənə(r)/ *n* **1** (non-aristocrat) roturier/-ière *m/f*; **2** Hist Jur personne *f* qui a le droit de vaine pâture.

common: **~ fraction** *n* fraction *f*; **~ gender** *modif [noun]* épicène; **~ ground** *n* fig terrain *m* d'entente.

common law *n* droit *m* coutumier; **at ~** selon le droit coutumier.

common: **~-law husband** *n* concubin *m*; **~-law marriage** *n* concubinage *m*; **~-law wife** *n* concubine *f*.

commonly /ˈkɒmənlɪ/ *adv* communément; **~ known as** communément appelé.

common market, Common Market *n* Marché *m* commun.

commonness /ˈkɒmənnɪs/ *n* (widespread occurrence) fréquence *f*.

common: **~ noun** *n* nom *m* commun; **~-or-garden** *adj [variety, plant, animal]* commun; *[event, item, object]* ordinaire.

commonplace /ˈkɒmənpleɪs/ **I** *n* lieu *m* commun; **it is a ~ that** c'est un lieu commun de dire que.
II *adj* (widespread) commun; (banal, trite) banal.

commonplace book *n* recueil *m* personnel de citations.

common: **~ prostitute** *n* Jur prostituée *f*; **~ room** *n* foyer *m*, salle *f* de détente; **~ salt** *n* sel *m* ordinaire.

common sense **I** *n* bon sens *m*, sens *m* commun.
II commonsense *adj* (also **commonsensical**)○ *[attitude, approach, action]* plein de bon sens.

common: **~ share** *n* US Fin action *f* ordinaire; **~ stock** *n* US ¢ Fin actions *fpl* ordinaires; **~ time** *n* Mus mesure *f* à quatre temps.

Commonwealth /ˈkɒmənwelθ/ **I** *n* **1** GB Pol **the (British) ~ (of Nations)** le Commonwealth *m*; **2** GB Hist **the ~** le Commonwealth *m*, la République *f* de Cromwell; **3** Geog **the ~ of Australia** le Commonwealth *m* d'Australie; **the ~ of Kentucky/of Virginia** l'État *m* du Kentucky/de la Virginie; **the ~ of Puerto Rico** l'État *m* libre associé de Porto Rico.
II *modif [country]* du Commonwealth; *[leader, head of State]* d'un pays du Commonwealth; *[summit]* des pays du Commonwealth.

Commonwealth: **~ Day** *n* fête *f* du Commonwealth (*24 mai*); **~ Games** *npl* Jeux *mpl* du Commonwealth; **~ of Independent States** *pr n* Communauté *f* des États indépendants.

common year *n* année *f* non bissextile.

commotion /kəˈməʊʃn/ *n* **1** (noise) vacarme *m*, brouhaha *m*; **to make a ~** faire du vacarme; **what's all this ~?** que signifie tout ce vacarme?; **2** (upheaval, disturbance) émoi *m*, agitation *f*; **to cause a ~** causer un grand émoi; **to be in a state of ~** *[crowd]* être agité; *[town]* être en émoi.

communal /ˈkɒmjʊnl, kəˈmju:nl/ *adj* **1** (shared in common) *[property, area, room, showers]* commun; *[garden]* collectif/-ive; *[facilities]* commun, collectif/-ive; **~ ownership** copropriété *f*; **2** (done collectively) *[prayer]* collectif/-ive; **3** (of a community) *[life]* communautaire; **4** (within a community) **~ violence** ou **clashes** affrontements *mpl* communautaires.

communally /ˈkɒmjʊnəlɪ, kəˈmju:nəlɪ/ *adv* en commun, collectivement.

commune I /ˈkɒmju:n/ *n* **1** (group of people) communauté *f*; **to live in a ~** vivre en communauté; **2** Admin (in continental Europe) commune *f*; **3** Hist **the Commune** la Commune.
II /kəˈmju:n/ *vi* **1** (relate to) **to ~ with** communier avec, être en communion avec *[nature]*; s'unir à [qn] par la prière *[God]*; converser intimement avec *[person]*; **2**† Relig communier.

communicable /kəˈmju:nɪkəbl/ *adj* **1** *[idea, concept, emotion]* communicable; **2** Med *[disease, virus]* contagieux/-ieuse.

communicant /kəˈmju:nɪkənt/ *n* **1** Relig communiant/-e *m/f*; **2** (informant) sout informateur/-trice *m/f*.

communicate /kəˈmju:nɪkeɪt/ **I** *vtr* **1** (convey) communiquer *[ideas, feelings]* (**to** à); transmettre *[instructions, news, information, values]* (**to** à); **his anxiety ~s itself to others** son angoisse est communicative; **to ~ one's displeasure to sb** faire part de son mécontentement à qn; **2** (transmit) transmettre *[disease, virus]*.
II *vi* **1** (relate) communiquer (**with** avec); **how do they ~ (with each other)?** comment communiquent-ils?; **to ~ through dance/by gestures** communiquer au moyen de la danse/par des gestes; **2** (be in contact) communiquer (**with** avec); **to ~ by radio** communiquer par radio; **we no longer ~ with each other** nous avons perdu tout contact; **3** (connect) **to ~ with** communiquer avec *[room, apartment]*; **4** Relig communier.

communicating door *n* porte *f* de communication.

communication /kəˌmju:nɪˈkeɪʃn/ **I** *n* **1** (of information) transmission *f*; (of ideas, feelings) communication *f*; **a means/system of ~** un moyen/système de communication; **2** (contact) communication *f* (**between** entre); **a lack of ~** un manque de communication; **the lines of ~** les voies *fpl* de communication; **to be in ~ with sb** être en communication or en contact avec qn; **she's been in radio/telephone ~ with them** elle a communiqué avec eux par radio/téléphone; **3** (message) communication *f*.
II communications *npl* **1** Telecom, Transp (infrastructure) communications *fpl*; **a breakdown in ~s** une rupture des communications; **radio/telephone ~s** les communications radiophoniques/téléphoniques; **to have good ~s with** avoir de bonnes communications avec *[port, city]*; **2** Mil communications *fpl*, liaison *f*.
III *modif [channel, problem, system]* de communication; **~ skills** gen la communication; (in job ad) **'good ~ skills required'** 'le candidat aura le sens de la communication'.

communication: **~ cord** *n* GB sonnette *f* d'alarme; **~ interface** *n* interface *f* de communication; **~ line** *n* ligne *f* de communication; **~ science** *n* sciences *fpl* de la communication; **~s company** *n* société *f* de communications; **~s crossroads** *n* carrefour *m* de communications.

communications director ▶1692 *n* Pol *consultant en communication attaché à un parti politique*.

communication: **~s industry** *n* industrie *f* des communications; **~s link** *n* liaison *f*; **~s network** *n* réseau *m* de communications; **~s satellite** *n* satellite *m* de communication; **~ studies** *n* études *fpl* en communication.

communicative /kəˈmju:nɪkətɪv, US -keɪtɪv/ *adj* **1** (talkative) expansif/-ive (**about, on the subject of** au sujet de); **2** *[abilities, problems, skills]* de communication; **3** Ling, Sch *[approach, skills]* de communication.

communicator /kəˈmju:nɪkeɪtə(r)/ *n* **to be a good ~** avoir le sens de la communication.

communion /kəˈmju:nɪən/ *n* **1** Relig **the Anglican/Roman ~** la communion de l'Église anglicane/romaine; **the ~ of saints** la communion des saints; **2** littér (with nature, fellow man etc) communion *f*.

Communion /kəˈmju:nɪən/ *n* (also **Holy ~**) (sainte) communion *f*, Eucharistie *f*; **to make one's First ~** faire sa première communion; **to go to/take ~** aller à/recevoir la communion.

Communion: **~ cup** *n* calice *m*; **~ rail** *n* sainte table *f*; **~ service** *n* eucharistie *f*, office *m*; **~ table** *n* autel *m*; **~ wine** *n* vin *m* de messe.

communiqué /kəˈmju:nɪkeɪ, US kəˌmju:nəˈkeɪ/ *n* communiqué *m*.

Communism, communism /ˈkɒmjʊnɪzəm/ *n* communisme *m*.

Communist, communist /ˈkɒmjʊnɪst/ *n, adj* communiste (*mf*).

communistic /ˌkɒmjʊˈnɪstɪk/ *adj* communisant.

Communist Party, CP *n* parti *m* communiste.

community /kəˈmju:nətɪ/ **I** *n* **1** (social, cultural grouping) communauté *f*; **the**

student/Italian ~ la communauté estudiantine/italienne; **the business ~** le monde des affaires; **research ~** communauté *f* des chercheurs; **relations between the police and the ~** (at local level) les relations entre la police et les habitants; (at national level) les relations entre la police et le public; **in the ~ interest** dans l'intérêt de la communauté; **sense of ~** esprit *m* communautaire; **2** Relig (**religious**) **~** communauté *f* (religieuse); **3** Jur communauté *f*; **~ of goods/interests** communauté de biens/d'intérêts.
II Community *pr n* **the** (**European**) **C~** la Communauté (Européenne).
III Community *modif* [*budget, body, regulation*] communautaire, de la Communauté.

community: **~ care** *n*: *soins en dehors du milieu hospitalier*; **~ centre** *n* centre *m* de loisirs; **~ charge** *n* GB Hist impôt *m* local; **~ chest** *n* US fonds *m* de secours; **~ college** *n* US centre *m* universitaire (de premier cycle); **~ education** *n* GB *cours ouverts à tous organisés par la municipalité*; **~ health centre** *n* centre *m* médico-social; **~ home** *n* établissement *m* d'éducation surveillée; **~ life** *n* vie *f* associative; **~ medicine** *n* médecine *f* générale; **~ policeman ▸1692** *n* ≈ îlotier *m*; **~ policing** *n* ≈ îlotage *m*; **~ property** *n* US Jur communauté *f* de biens entre époux; **~ school** *n*: *établissement scolaire utilisé en dehors des heures de cours pour les activités proposées par la municipalité*; **~ service** *n* Jur travail *m* d'intérêt public; **~ singing** *n* chants *mpl* populaires (*repris en chœur par l'assistance*); **~ spirit** *n* esprit *m* communautaire; **~ worker** *n* animateur/-trice *m/f* socio-culturel/-elle.

communize /ˈkɒmjʊnaɪz/ *vtr* collectiviser [*property*]; imposer le communisme à [*people*].

commutable /kəˈmjuːtəbl/ *adj* [*pension*] convertible; [*sentence*] commuable (**into** en).

commutation /ˌkɒmjuːˈteɪʃn/ *n* **1** (replacement) Fin convertissement *m*; Jur, Ling commutation *f*; **2** US (journey) trajet *m* journalier.

commutation ticket *n* US carte *f* d'abonnement.

commutative /kəˈmjuːtətɪv/ *adj* Math commutatif/-ive.

commute /kəˈmjuːt/ **I** *n* US trajet *m* journalier.
II *vtr* Fin convertir; Jur commuer (**to** en).
III *vi* **to ~ between Oxford and London** faire le trajet entre Oxford et Londres tous les jours; **she ~s to Glasgow** elle se rend à Glasgow tous les jours; **he didn't want to ~** il ne voulait pas travailler loin de chez lui.

commuter /kəˈmjuːtə(r)/ *n* navetteur/-euse *m/f*, migrant/-e *m/f* journalier/-ière.

commuter: **~ belt** *n* grande banlieue *f*; **~ train** *n* train *m* de banlieue.

commuting /kəˈmjuːtɪŋ/ *n* trajets *mpl* quotidiens pour se rendre au travail, migrations *fpl* quotidiennes.

Comoros /ˈkɒmərəʊz/ **▸1131** *pr n* (îles *fpl*) Comores *fpl*.

comp° /kɒmp/ US *n* (free ticket) billet *m* gratuit; (person) invité/-e *m/f*; (free gift) cadeau *m*.

compact I /ˈkɒmpækt/ *n* **1** (agreement) (written) accord *m*, contrat *m*, convention *f*; (verbal) entente *f*; **2** Cosmet poudrier *m*; **3** US Aut (voiture *f*) compacte *f*, voiture *f* de faible encombrement.
II /kəmˈpækt/ *adj* **1** (compressed) [*snow, mass*] compact, dense; [*style, sentence*] concis, ramassé; **2** (neatly constructed) [*kitchen, house*] sans espace perdu, compact; [*camera, equipment, kit*] compact; **of ~ build** [*man*] râblé, trapu; [*woman*] bien fait.
III /kəmˈpækt/ *vtr* comprimer [*waste, rubbish*]; tasser [*soil, snow*].

compact: **~ disc** *n* disque *m* compact; **~ disc player** *n* platine *f* laser; **~ fluorescent light** *n* lampe *f* fluorescente compacte.

compactly /kəmˈpæktlɪ/ *adj* [*written, expressed*] dans un style concis, d'une manière concise; **~ built** [*person*] trapu; **~ designed** compact.

compactness /kəmˈpæktnɪs/ *n* (of design) compacité *f*, caractère *m* compact; (of style) concision *f*; **the ~ of his build** son corps trapu.

compactor /kəmˈpæktə(r)/ *n* US ≈ broyeur *m* d'ordures.

Companies Act /ˈkʌmpənɪz/ *n* GB Jur loi *f* sur les sociétés.

Companies House /ˈkʌmpənɪz/ *n* GB Comm Jur ≈ greffe *m* du tribunal de commerce.

companion /kəmˈpænɪən/ *n* **1** (friend) compagnon/compagne *m/f*; **to be sb's constant ~** [*hunger, fear*] être le perpétuel compagnon de qn; **a ~ in arms** un compagnon d'armes; **2** (also **paid ~**) dame *f* de compagnie; **3** (item of matching pair) pendant *m* (**to** de); **4** Literat, Publg guide *m*; **the fisherman's ~** le guide du pêcheur; **5** Naut capot *m*.

companionable /kəmˈpænɪənəbl/ *adj* [*person*] sociable; [*chat, meal*] amical; [*silence, smile*] sympathique.

companion: **~ hatch** *n* Naut panneau *m* de descente; **~ ladder** *n* Naut descente *f*; **~ piece** *n* morceau *m* d'accompagnement.

companionship /kəmˈpænɪənʃɪp/ *n* compagnie *f*; **I have a dog for ~** j'ai un chien pour me tenir compagnie.

companion: **~ volume** *n* Publg pendant *m*; **~way** *n* Naut escalier *m*.

company /ˈkʌmpənɪ/ **I** *n* **1** Comm, Jur société *f*; **airline ~** compagnie *f* aérienne; **2** Mus, Theat troupe *f*, compagnie *f*; **theatre ~** troupe *f* de théâtre, compagnie *f* théâtrale; **3** Mil compagnie *f*; **4** (companionship) compagnie *f*; **to keep sb ~** tenir compagnie à qn; **to enjoy sb's ~** apprécier la compagnie de qn; **to be good ~** être d'une compagnie agréable; **I have a cat for ~** j'ai un chat pour me tenir compagnie; **to be seen in sb's ~** ou **in ~ with sb** être vu en compagnie de qn; **to part ~ with** [*person*] gen, hum se séparer de [*person, bike, horse*]; **on political matters they part ~** en ce qui concerne la politique, ils divergent complètement; **to keep bad ~** avoir de mauvaises fréquentations; **5** (visitors) visiteurs *mpl*; **to have/expect ~** avoir/attendre du monde; **6** (society) **in ~** en société; **in mixed ~** quand les dames sont présentes; **to be fit ~ for sb** être une fréquentation pour qn; **to keep ~ with sb** fréquenter qn; **Lisa and ~** souvent péj Lisa et compagnie°; **7** (similar circumstances) **to be in good ~** ne pas être le seul/la seule; **don't worry, you're in good ~** ne t'inquiète pas, tu n'es pas le seul; **Marie, in ~ with many others, complained** Marie, ainsi que bien d'autres, s'est plainte; **8** (gathering) compagnie *f*; **the assembled ~** l'assemblée; **9** Naut équipage *m*; **10**° euph (CIA) **the Company** la CIA.
II *modif* (of all businesses) [*earnings, profits, records*] des sociétés; (of a particular business) [*accountant, car park, headquarters, newsletter*] de la société.

company: **~ car** *n* voiture *f* de fonction; **~ commander ▸1612** *n* Mil commandant *m* de compagnie; **~ director** *n* directeur/-trice *m/f* général/-e.

company doctor ▸1692 *n* **1** Med médecin *m* d'entreprise; **2** (business analyst) redresseur *m* d'entreprise.

company: **~ headquarters** *npl* Mil compagnie *f* de commandement et des services; **~ law** *n* GB Jur droit *m* des sociétés.

company lawyer ▸1692 *n* GB Jur **1** (attached to a firm) avocat/-e *m/f* d'entreprise; **2** (business law expert) juriste *mf* d'entreprise.

company: **~ man** *n* employé *m* dévoué (*à son entreprise*); **~ meeting** *n* assemblée *f* des actionnaires; **~ name** *n* Jur raison *f* sociale; **~ officer** *n* dirigeant *m* d'entreprise; **~ pension scheme** *n* régime *m* de retraite de l'entreprise.

company policy *n* ¢ politique *f* de l'entreprise; **it is/is not ~ to do** c'est/ce n'est pas dans la politique de l'entreprise de faire.

company: **~ promoter** *n* lanceur *m* d'entreprise; **~ secretary ▸1692** *n* Admin secrétaire *mf* général/-e; **~ sergeant major**, **CSM ▸1612** *n* Mil adjudant *m* de compagnie; **~ tax** *n* surtout GB impôt *m* sur les sociétés; **~ union** *n* US syndicat *m* d'entreprise.

comparability /ˌkɒmpərəˈbɪlətɪ/ *n* **1** (comparison) comparabilité *f*; **2** (equivalence) harmonisation *f*; **pay ~** harmonisation des salaires.

comparable /ˈkɒmpərəbl/ *adj* **1** (similar) [*pay, quantity, skill*] comparable (**to, with** à); **2** (equivalent) comparable (**to, with** à).

comparative /kəmˈpærətɪv/ **I** *n* Ling comparatif *m*; **in the ~** au comparatif.
II *adj* **1** Ling comparatif/-ive; **2** (relative) relatif/-ive; **in ~ terms** en termes relatifs; **he's a ~ stranger to me** je le connais à peine; **3** (based on comparison) [*method, study*] comparatif/-ive; [*linguistics, religion*] comparé.

comparative: **Comparative Cost Principle** *n* Econ théorie *f* des coûts comparatifs; **~ literature** *n* littérature *f* comparée.

comparatively /kəmˈpærətɪvlɪ/ *adv* **1** (relatively) [*safe, small, recent, young*] relativement; **~ speaking** en termes relatifs; **2** (by comparison) [*analyse, examine, judge*] comparativement.

compare /kəmˈpeə(r)/ **I** *n* **a beauty/leader beyond ~** une beauté/un chef incomparable; **to be brave beyond ~** être incomparablement courageux/-euse.
II *vtr* **1** (contrast) comparer; **to ~ sb/sth with** ou **to** comparer qn/qch à or avec; **to ~ notes with sb** fig échanger ses impressions avec qn; **2** (liken) comparer (**to** à); **3** Ling former les degrés de comparaison de [*adjective, adverb*].
III compared with *prep phr* **~d with sb/sth** par rapport à qn/qch.
IV *vi* être comparable (**with** à); **the two televisions ~ well for price** les deux téléviseurs sont comparables du point de vue du prix; **to ~ favourably/unfavourably with sth** soutenir/ne pas soutenir la comparaison avec qch; **how do they ~?** et si on les compare?; **how does this job ~ with your last one?** comment trouvez-vous cet emploi par rapport au précédent?
V *v refl* **to ~ oneself with** ou **to** se comparer à.

comparison /kəmˈpærɪsn/ *n* **1** (likening) comparaison *f* (**between** entre); **beyond ~** sans comparaison; **the ~ of sth to sth** la comparaison entre qch et qch; **to draw a ~ between sth and sth** comparer qch avec qch; **to stand ~** soutenir la comparaison (**with** avec); **2** (contrast) comparaison *f*; **for ~** à titre de comparaison; **in** ou **by ~ with** par rapport à; **3** Ling comparaison *f*; **the rules of ~** les règles de formation du comparatif.

comparison test *n* test *m* comparatif.

compartment /kəmˈpɑːtmənt/ *n* (all contexts) compartiment *m*.

compartmentalize /ˌkɒmpɑːtˈmentəlaɪz/ *vtr* lit, fig compartimenter.

compass /ˈkʌmpəs/ **I** *n* **1** gen boussole *f*; Naut compas *m*; **the points of the ~** les points *mpl* cardinaux; **2** (extent) étendue *f*; (range, scope) portée *f*, rayon *m*; **within the narrow ~ of our research** dans le champ restreint de nos recherches; **within the ~ of this article/the law** dans les limites de cet article/la loi; **the concept is beyond the ~ of most minds** le concept dépasse la portée de la plupart des esprits; **3** Mus étendue *f*.

II compasses *npl* **a pair of ~es** un compas.
III *vtr* littér **1** (encircle) encercler, entourer; **2** (comprehend) saisir, appréhender; **3‡** (go around) faire le tour de [*earth, oceans*].

compass: **~ bearing** *n* relèvement *m* au compas; **~ card** *n* rose *f* des vents; **~ course** *n* route *f* magnétique.

compassion /kəm'pæʃn/ *n* compassion *f* (**for** pour).

compassionate /kəm'pæʃənət/ *adj* [*person, act*] compatissant; **on ~ grounds** pour raisons familiales.

compassionate leave *n* gen congé *m* exceptionnel (*pour décès familial*); Mil permission *f* exceptionnelle (*pour décès familial*).

compassionately /kəm'pæʃənətlı/ *adv* [*act, treat*] avec compassion.

compass rose *n* rose *f* des vents.

compatibility /kəm,pætə'bılətı/ *n* gen, Comput compatibilité *f*.

compatible /kəm'pætəbl/ **I** *n* Comput compatible *m*.
II *adj* compatible (**with** avec); **X-~** Comput compatible X.

compatriot /kəm'pætrıət, US -'peıt-/ *n* sout compatriote *mf*.

compel /kəm'pel/ *vtr* (*p prés etc* **-ll-**) **1** (force) contraindre (**to do** à faire), obliger (**to do** de faire); **to feel ~led to do** se sentir obligé de faire; **2** (win) **to ~ sb's respect** imposer le respect à qn; **to ~ sb's attention** retenir l'attention de qn.

compelling /kəm'pelıŋ/ *adj* [*reason, argument*] indiscutable; [*performance, film, speaker, novel*] fascinant.

compellingly /kəm'pelıŋlı/ *adv* [*argue*] de façon convaincante; [*speak, write*] de manière fascinante.

compendium /kəm'pendıəm/ *n* (*pl* **-diums** ou **-dia**) **1** (handbook) manuel *m*; (encyclopedia) petite encyclopédie *f*; **2** GB (box of games) mallette *f* de jeux.

compensate /'kɒmpenseıt/ **I** *vtr* **1** (financially) indemniser [*person, loss*]; **to ~ sb for** indemniser or compenser qn de; **I will be ~d for** on m'indemnisera de; **2** (offset) compenser [*imbalance, change*].
II *vi* compenser; **to ~ for** compenser [*loss, difficulty*].

compensation /,kɒmpen'seıʃn/ *n* **1** gen compensation *f*; **to be no ~ for sth** ne pas compenser qch; **in** ou **as** ou **by way of ~** en compensation (**for** de); **2** Jur indemnisation *f*; **to award ~** accorder une indemnisation; **she was awarded £3,000 ~** on lui accorda 3 000 livres d'indemnisation.

compensatory /,kɒmpen'seıtərı, US kəm'pensətɔ:rı/ *adj* compensatoire.

compère /'kɒmpeə(r)/ *n* GB **I** *n* animateur/-trice *m/f*.
II *vtr* présenter.

compete /kəm'pi:t/ **I** *vi* **1** (for prominence, job, prize) [*person, voices, smells*] rivaliser; **to ~ against** ou **with** rivaliser avec (**for** pour obtenir); **they were competing (with each other) for the same job** ils se disputaient le même emploi; **I just can't ~ (with her)** je ne peux pas lui faire concurrence; **2** Comm [*companies*] se faire concurrence; **to ~ against** ou **with** faire concurrence à (**for** pour obtenir); **to ~ in the European market** se faire concurrence sur le marché européen; **we can't ~ with multinationals** nous ne pouvons pas entrer en concurrence avec les multinationales; **3** Sport être en compétition (**with** avec); **to ~ against** être en compétition avec; **to ~ in the 100 metres/the Olympics** participer aux 100 mètres/aux jeux Olympiques; **there were 12 horses competing** il y avait 12 chevaux en compétition.
II competing *pres p adj* rival; **competing shops** des magasins rivaux.

competence /'kɒmpıtəns/ *n* **1** (ability) compétence *f*; **to have the ~ to do** avoir la compétence voulue pour faire; **I doubt his ~ to do the work/lead the team** je doute qu'il soit capable de faire le travail/diriger l'équipe; **to require professional/scientific ~** [*task*] nécessiter une compétence professionnelle/scientifique; **2** (skill) compétences *fpl*; **her ~ as an accountant is not in question** on ne remet pas en cause ses compétences de comptable; **I don't doubt his ~ as a sailor** je ne doute pas de ses compétences de marin; **~ in word-processing is necessary for this job** il est nécessaire d'avoir des connaissances en traitement de texte pour ce travail; **we require ~ in Spanish** une bonne connaissance de l'espagnol est exigée; **3** Jur compétence *f* (**to do** pour faire); **to be within the ~ of the court** relever de la compétence du tribunal; **4** Ling compétence *f*; **5** (means) revenu *m* suffisant, aisance *f*.

competent /'kɒmpıtənt/ *adj* **1** (capable, efficient) [*teacher, swimmer, player*] compétent, capable; (trained) qualifié; **to be ~ to do** être compétent or qualifié pour faire, être capable de faire; **2** (adequate, satisfactory) [*performance, piece of work*] honorable; [*knowledge*] suffisant; [*answer*] satisfaisant; **3** Jur [*court*] compétent (**to do** pour faire); [*person*] compétent, habile (**to do** à faire).

competently /'kɒmpıtəntlı/ *adv* avec compétence, d'une manière compétente.

competition /,kɒmpə'tıʃn/ *n* **1** ¢ gen, Comm concurrence *f*, compétition *f* (**between** entre); **in ~ with** en concurrence or compétition avec (**for** pour); **unfair/keen ~** concurrence déloyale/acharnée; **2** C (contest) (for medal, prize, award, job) concours *m*; (race) compétition *f*; **3** (competitors) concurrence *f*, compétition *f*; **what's the ~ like?** à quoi ressemblent nos concurrents?

competition car *n* Sport voiture *f* de course.

competitive /kəm'petıtıv/ *adj* **1** (enjoying rivalry) [*person, personality*] qui a l'esprit de compétition; [*environment*] compétitif/-ive; **2** Comm [*company, price, product, market*] compétitif/-ive; [*advantage, disadvantage*] concurrentiel/-ielle; **~ edge** avantage *m* concurrentiel; **~ tender** appel *m* d'offres; **3** (decided by competition) [*sport*] de compétition; **by ~ examination** sur concours.

competitively /kəm'petıtıvlı/ *adv* **1** (in spirit of rivalry) [*play, behave*] dans un esprit de compétition; **2** Comm [*operate*] compétitivement; **~ priced** à des prix compétitifs.

competitiveness /kəm'petıtıvnıs/ *n* **1** (of person) esprit *m* de compétition; **2** Comm (of product, price, salary, company) compétitivité *f*.

competitor /kəm'petıtə(r)/ *n* (all contexts) concurrent/-e *m/f*.

compilation /,kɒmpı'leıʃn/ *n* **1** (collection on record, video) compilation *f*; **2** (act of compiling) (of reference book) rédaction *f*; (of dossier) constitution *f*; **3** Comput compilation *f*.

compile /kəm'paıl/ *vtr* **1** (draw up) dresser [*list, index, catalogue*]; établir [*report*]; rédiger [*reference book, entry*]; **2** Comput compiler.

compiler /kəm'paılə(r)/ *n* **1** gen compilateur/-trice *m/f*; **2** Comput compilateur *m*.

complacency /kəm'pleısnsı/ *n* suffisance *f*, assurance *f* excessive; **there is no room for ~** se sentir trop confiant serait une grave erreur.

complacent /kəm'pleısnt/ *adj* suffisant, trop confiant; **to be ~ about** être trop confiant de [*success, future*]; **to grow ~ about** perdre sa vigilance en ce qui concerne [*danger, threat*].

complacently /kəm'pleısntlı/ *adv* avec suffisance, avec une confiance excessive.

complain /kəm'pleın/ *vi* (informally) se plaindre (**to** à; **about** de); (officially) se plaindre (**to** auprès de), faire une réclamation (**to** à); (of pain, illness, symptom) se plaindre (**of** de); **to ~ that** se plaindre parce que; **I ~ed that the water was cold** je me suis plaint parce que l'eau était froide; **stop ~ing!** arrête de te plaindre; **to ~ to the police about sth** porter plainte à la police au sujet de qch; **'how's life?'—'oh, I can't ~'** 'comment ça va?'—'oh, je n'ai pas à me plaindre'.

complainant /kəm'pleınənt/ *n* Jur plaignant/-e *m/f*, demandeur/demanderesse *m/f*.

complaint /kəm'pleınt/ *n* **1** (protest, objection) gen plainte *f* (**about** concernant, au sujet de); (official) réclamation *f* (**about** concernant, au sujet de); **there have been ~s about the noise** on s'est plaint du bruit; **there have been ~s of nepotism/discrimination** on s'est plaint de népotisme/discrimination; **I have received a written ~ about your behaviour** on m'a écrit pour se plaindre de votre conduite; **there have been ~s that the service is slow** on a reproché au service d'être lent, on s'est plaint de la lenteur du service; **tiredness is a common ~** les gens se plaignent souvent de fatigue; **the workers' ~s that they are badly paid are justified** les réclamations des travailleurs concernant leur basse rémunération sont justifiées; **the canteen was closed after** ou **following ~ about poor hygiene** la cantine a été fermée suite à des plaintes concernant le manque d'hygiène; **in case of ~, contact the management** en cas de réclamation, adressez-vous à la direction; **to have grounds** ou **cause for ~** avoir lieu de se plaindre, avoir des motifs de plainte; **to lay** ou **lodge** ou **file a ~ against sb** déposer une plainte or porter plainte contre qn; **to make a ~** se plaindre, faire une réclamation; **to make** ou **submit a ~ to sb** adresser une réclamation à qn; **I've no ~s** je n'ai rien à redire; **I've no ~s about the service** je n'ai pas à me plaindre du service; **2** Med maladie *f*; **skin ~** maladie de peau; **nervous ~** maladie nerveuse; **common ~s** maladies ordinaires.

complaints procedure *n* procédure *f* de réclamation.

complaisant /kəm'pleızənt/ *adj* littér complaisant.

-complected /kəm'plektıd/ US (*dans composés*) = **-complexioned**.

complement /'kɒmplımənt/ **I** *n* **1** gen, Math, Ling complément *m* (**to** à); **2** (quota) effectif *m*; **with a full ~ of staff** avec le personnel au complet.
II *vtr* compléter; **to ~ one another** se compléter; **wine ~s cheese** le vin accompagne bien le fromage.

complementary /,kɒmplı'mentrı/ *adj* (all contexts) complémentaire (**to** de).

complementary: **~ distribution** *n* distribution *f* complémentaire; **~ medicine** *n* médecine *f* parallèle.

complete /kəm'pli:t/ **I** *adj* **1** (total, utter) (*épith*) [*abolition, chaos, darkness, freedom, rejection*] complet/-ète, total; **he's a ~ fool** il est complètement idiot; **it's the ~ opposite** c'est tout à fait le contraire; **with ~ accuracy/confidence** avec une précision/confiance totale; **~ and utter** [*despair, disaster*] total; **it's ~ and utter rubbish** c'est complètement absurde; **2** (finished) achevé; **far from/not yet ~** loin d'être/pas encore achevé; **3** (entire, full) [*collection, edition, works, record, set*] complet/-ète; **~ with** avec; **~ with batteries/instructions** avec piles/mode d'emploi; **to make my happiness ~** pour que rien ne manque à mon bonheur; **4** (consummate) [*artist, star*] complet/-ète; [*gentleman, sportsman*] parfait (*before n*).
II *vtr* **1** (finish) terminer [*building, investigation, degree course, exercise*]; achever [*task, journey*]; **to ~ a jail sentence** finir de purger une peine; **2** (make whole) compléter [*collection, trilogy, group, victory, grand slam*]; compléter [*outfit*]; compléter [*quotation, phrase*]; **to ~ an outfit with a beret** mettre un beret pour compléter une tenue; **3** (fill in) remplir [*form, questionnaire*].

III completed *pp adj* [*creation, project*] achevé; **the recently/newly ~d office building** les bureaux terminés récemment/depuis peu; **half ~d** inachevé.

completely /kəm'pliːtlɪ/ *adv* [*changed, different, forgotten, free, mad, rebuilt, unexpected*] complètement; [*failed, understandable*] totalement; [*convincing, honest*] tout à fait.

completeness /kəm'pliːtnɪs/ *n* état *m* complet (**of** de); **to ensure the ~ of your information** pour être sûr que vos informations sont complètes.

completion /kəm'pliːʃn/ *n* **1** (finishing) achèvement *m* (**of** de); **it is due for ~ by the summer** l'achèvement est prévu pour l'été; **on ~ (of the works)** à l'achèvement des travaux; **nearing ~** près d'être achevé; **2** Jur (of house sale) signature *f* de la vente; **on ~** à la signature de la vente.

completion date *n* **1** (for works) date *f* d'achèvement; **2** (for contract, sale, order) date *f* d'exécution; **3** (for house purchase) date *f* de signature de la vente.

complex /'kɒmpleks, US kəm'pleks/ **I** *n* **1** (building development) complexe *m*; **leisure ~** complexe *m* de loisirs; **housing ~** complexe *m* résidentiel; **sports ~** complexe *m* sportif; **2** Psych complexe *m*; **persecution ~** complexe *m* de persécution; **he's got a ~ about his weight** son poids lui donne un complexe; **3** Med complexe *m*.
II *adj* complexe.

complexion /kəm'plekʃn/ *n* **1** (skin colour) teint *m*; **to have a clear/bad ~** avoir une peau nette/à problèmes; **to have a fair/dark ~** avoir un teint clair/mat; **2** (nature) aspect *m*; **to change the ~ of sth, to put a new ~ on sth** présenter qch sous un jour nouveau; **of a different ~** d'une autre nature.

-complexioned /kəm'plekʃnd/ (*dans composés*) **light/dark-~** au teint clair/mat.

complexity /kəm'pleksətɪ/ *n* complexité *f*.

compliance /kəm'plaɪəns/ *n* **1** (conformity) (with ruling, standard, wishes) conformité *f* (**with** à); **to do sth in ~ with procedure/the law** faire qch conformément à la procédure/la loi; **to bring sth into ~ with** mettre qch en conformité avec; **2** (yielding disposition) caractère *m* conciliant.

compliance costs *npl* frais *mpl* de mise en conformité.

compliant /kəm'plaɪənt/ *adj* conciliant (**with, to** envers).

complicate /'kɒmplɪkeɪt/ *vtr* compliquer; **to ~ matters** ou **life** compliquer les choses.

complicated /'kɒmplɪkeɪtɪd/ *adj* compliqué.

complication /ˌkɒmplɪ'keɪʃn/ *n* **1** (problem) inconvénient *m*; **there is a further ~** il y a un autre problème; **to make ~s** compliquer les choses; **2** Med complication *f*.

complicit /kəm'plɪsɪt/ *adj* complice (**in** de).

complicity /kəm'plɪsətɪ/ *n* complicité *f*.

compliment /'kɒmplɪmənt/ **I** *n* compliment *m*; **to pay sb a ~** faire un compliment à qn; **to return the ~** lit retourner le compliment; fig répondre de la même façon; **coming from him, that's quite a ~** venant de lui c'est un beau compliment.
II compliments *npl* **1** (in expressions of praise) compliments *mpl*; **to give sb one's ~s** faire ses compliments à qn; **my ~s to the chef** mes compliments au chef; **2** (in expressions of politeness) **'with ~s'** (on transmission slip) 'avec tous nos compliments'; **'with the ~s of the management'** 'avec les compliments de la direction'; **'with the ~s of the author'** 'avec les hommages de l'auteur'; **3** (in greetings) **'with the ~s of the season'** (on Christmas cards) 'meilleurs vœux'; **my ~s to your wife** sout mes hommages à votre femme.
III *vtr* complimenter (**on** sur), faire des compliments à (**on** sur).

complimentary /ˌkɒmplɪ'mentrɪ/ *adj* **1** (flattering) [*remark, letter, review*] flatteur/-euse; **he wasn't very ~ about my poems** il s'est montré plutôt critique à l'égard de mes poèmes; **she was very ~ about my work** elle m'a fait des compliments sur mon travail; **2** (free) gratuit, à titre gracieux.

complimentary: **~ close** *n* US (in letter writing) formule *f* de politesse; **~ copy** *n* Publg exemplaire *m* donné en hommage; **~ ticket** *n* billet *m* gratuit.

compliments slip *n* carte *f* avec les compliments de l'expéditeur.

compline /'kɒmplɪn/ *n* complies *fpl*.

comply /kəm'plaɪ/ *vi* s'exécuter, obtempérer Jur; **to ~ with** se plier à [*sb's wishes*]; accéder à, Jur faire droit à [*request*]; se conformer à [*directive, orders, instructions, regulations, criteria, standards*]; respecter, observer [*rules*]; **failure to ~ with the rules may result in prosecution** le non-respect des règles pourrait entraîner des poursuites.

component /kəm'pəʊnənt/ *n* gen, Math composante *f*; Aut, Tech pièce *f*; Electron composant *m*; Chem constituant *m*.

componential /ˌkɒmpə'nenʃl/ *adj* componentiel/-ielle; **~ analysis** Ling analyse *f* componentielle.

component: **~ part** *n* élément *m* (**of** de); **~s factory** *n* usine *f* de pièces détachées.

comport /kəm'pɔːt/ *v refl* sout **to ~ oneself** se conduire.

comportment /kəm'pɔːtmənt/ *n* sout conduite *f* (**towards** envers).

compose /kəm'pəʊz/ **I** *vtr* **1** (write) gen, Litterat, Mus composer; **2** (arrange) composer [*painting, still-life, salad*]; agencer [*elements of work*]; **3** (order) composer [*features, face*]; rassembler [*thoughts, ideas*]; **4** (constitute) composer [*whole*]; **to be ~d of** être composé de; **5** Print composer.
II *vi* **1** Mus, Print composer; **2** Jur venir à composition, composer.
III *v refl* **to ~ oneself** se ressaisir; **to ~ oneself for sleep** se préparer au sommeil.

composed /kəm'pəʊzd/ *adj* [*person, features, appearance*] calme.

composedly /kəm'pəʊzɪdlɪ/ *adv* [*act, react, speak*] calmement.

composer /kəm'pəʊzə(r)/ **▶ 1692** *n* Mus compositeur/-trice *m/f* (**of** de).

composite /'kɒmpəzɪt/ **I** *n* **1** (substance) composite *m*; **a ceramic/a metallic ~** une céramique/un métal composite; **2** (character, photo, word) composite *m* (**of** de); **3** Comm entreprise *f* diversifiée; **4** Archit (also **~ order**) (ordre *m*) composite *m*; **5** Bot composée *f*.
II *adj* **1** gen, Archit, Chem, Phot composite; **2** Bot, Math composé; **3** Comm [*company, group*] diversifié.

composite: **~ rate (of) tax** *n* GB taux *m* de prélèvement à la source (*sur les dépôts bancaires*); **~ school** *n* école *f* polyvalente (*au Canada*).

composition /ˌkɒmpə'zɪʃn/ *n* **1** (make-up) composition *f* (**of** de); **metallic/similar in ~** d'une composition métallique/similaire; **the racial/religious ~ of a jury** la composition raciale/religieuse d'un jury; **2** Mus, Littér composition *f* (**of** de); **this is my own ~** cela est ma propre composition; **of my/her own ~** de ma/sa composition; **3** Sch rédaction *f* (**about, on** sur); **to get good marks for ~** avoir de bonnes notes en rédaction; **4** Print composition *f*; **5** Art composition *f*; **6** Jur accommodement *m*, composition *f*; **to come to ~** venir à composition, composer.

compositor /kəm'pɒzɪtə(r)/ **▶ 1692** *n* Print compositeur/-trice *m/f*.

compos mentis /ˌkɒmpəs 'mentɪs/ *adj* **to be ~** être en possession de toutes ses facultés.

compost /'kɒmpɒst/ Hort **I** *n* compost *m*.
II *vtr* faire du compost avec.

compost heap *n* terreau *m*.

composure /kəm'pəʊʒə(r)/ *n* calme *m*; **to lose/regain one's ~** perdre/retrouver son calme.

compote /'kɒmpəʊt, -pɒt/ *n* **1** (dessert) compote *f*; **2** US (plate) compotier *m*.

compound **I** /'kɒmpaʊnd/ *n* **1** (enclosure) enceinte *f*; **diplomatic/industrial/military/prison ~** enceinte *f* diplomatique/industrielle/militaire/de prison; **workers'/miners' ~** quartier *m* de travailleurs/de mineurs; **2** Chem composé *m* (**of** de); **carbon ~s** les composés du carbone; **3** (word) mot *m* composé; **4** (mixture) composé *m* (**of** de).
II /'kɒmpaʊnd/ *adj* **1** gen, Biol, Bot, Chem [*leaf, flower, eye, substance*] composé; **2** Ling [*tense, noun, adjective*] composé; [*sentence*] complexe; **3** Med [*fracture*] multiple.
III /kəm'paʊnd/ *vtr* **1** (exacerbate) aggraver [*difficulty, error, offence, problem, damage, anxiety*] (**by** par; **by doing** en faisant); **to ~ misfortune with error** ajouter l'erreur au malheur; **2** (combine) combiner (**with** à); **~ed of** composé de; **3** Jur **to ~ a debt** transiger sur une dette; **to ~ an offence** ou **a felony** accepter de ne pas porter plainte en contrepartie d'un dédommagement.
IV /kəm'paʊnd/ *vi* Jur (come to terms) composer (*avec ses créanciers*).

compounding /ˌkəm'paʊndɪŋ/ *n* composition *f*.

compound: **~ interest** *n* intérêt *m* composé; **~ meter** *n* US mesure *f* ternaire; **~ microscope** *n* microscope *m* composé; **~ time** *n* GB mesure *f* ternaire.

comprehend /ˌkɒmprɪ'hend/ *vtr* **1** (understand) comprendre, saisir; **2** (include, comprise) sout comprendre, englober.

comprehensible /ˌkɒmprɪ'hensəbl/ *adj* compréhensible, intelligible.

comprehension /ˌkɒmprɪ'henʃn/ *n* **1** (understanding) compréhension *f*, entendement *m*; **that is beyond my ~** cela dépasse mon entendement; **he has no ~ of the real nature of politics** il n'entend rien à la nature réelle de la politique; **2** Sch, Univ exercice *m* de compréhension.

comprehensive /ˌkɒmprɪ'hensɪv/ **I** *n* GB Sch école *f* (publique) secondaire.
II comprehensives *npl* US Univ examens *mpl* de fin d'études.
III *adj* **1** (all-embracing) [*report, survey, list*] complet/-ète, détaillé; [*knowledge*] vaste, étendu; [*planning*] global; [*coverage, training*] complet/-ète; [*measures*] d'ensemble; [*rule*] détaillé; **~ insurance policy** assurance *f* tous risques; **2** GB Sch [*education, school*] secondaire; **the ~ system** le système scolaire secondaire nonsélectif; **to go ~** abandonner la sélection à l'entrée en sixième; **3** US Sch [*examination*] de fin d'études.

compress **I** /'kɒmpres/ *n* compresse *f*.
II /kəm'pres/ *vtr* **1** (condense) comprimer [*object, substance*]; **~ed air** air comprimé; **2 to ~ one's lips** pincer les lèvres; **3** fig (shorten) condenser [*text, style*]; réduire [*period of time*].

compression /kəm'preʃn/ *n* **1** gen, Phys compression *f*; **2** (condensing) (of book, chapters) réduction *f*; **3** (concision) (of style) concision *f*; **4** Comput (of data) condensation *f*, compression *f*.

compression ratio *n* taux *m* de compression.

compressor /kəm'presə(r)/ *n* compresseur *m*.

comprise /kəm'praɪz/ *vtr* **1** (include) comprendre; (consist of) être composé de; **the apartment ~s...** l'appartement comprend...; **2** (compose) composer; **to be ~d of** être composé de.

compromise /'kɒmprəmaɪz/ **I** *n* compromis *m*; **to come to** ou **reach a ~** arriver or aboutir à un compromis; **to agree to a ~**

accepter un compromis; **to have a liking for ~** avoir l'esprit du compromis.
II *modif* [*agreement, solution, decision*] de compromis.
III *vtr* **1** (threaten) compromettre [*person*]; compromettre, mettre [qch] en péril or en danger [*principles, negotiations, reputation, chances*]; **2** US (settle) régler [*disagreement*].
IV *vi* transiger, arriver à un compromis; **to ~ on sth** trouver un compromis sur qch.
V *v refl* **to ~ oneself** se compromettre.

compromising /ˈkɒmprəmaɪzɪŋ/ *adj* compromettant.

comptroller /kənˈtrəʊlə(r)/ ▶ 1692 *n* contrôleur/-euse *m/f* des finances.

Comptroller General *n* US président *m* de la cour des comptes.

compulsion /kəmˈpʌlʃn/ *n* **1** (urge) compulsion *f*; **to feel a ~ to do** avoir une envie irrésistible de faire; **2** (force) force *f*; **there is no ~ on you to do** tu n'es pas obligé de faire; **to act under ~** agir sous la contrainte.

compulsive /kəmˈpʌlsɪv/ *adj* **1** [*liar, gambler*] gen (inveterate) invétéré; Psych compulsif/-ive; **~ eater** boulimique *mf*; **~ gardener** maniaque *m* du jardinage; **2** (fascinating) [*book, story*] fascinant; **to be ~ viewing** être fascinant.

compulsively /kəmˈpʌlsɪvlɪ/ *adv* **1** Psych [*lie, gamble, wash*] de façon compulsive; **2 to be ~ readable** être d'un intérêt irrésistible.

compulsories /kəmˈpʌlsərɪz/ *npl* Sport (in skating) figures *fpl* imposées.

compulsorily /kəmˈpʌlsərɪlɪ/ *adv* [*purchased, retired, made redundant*] d'office.

compulsory /kəmˈpʌlsərɪ/ *adj* **1** (enforced) [*subject, games, attendance, education, military service*] obligatoire; [*loan*] obligatoire, forcé; [*redundancy, retirement*] d'office; [*liquidation*] forcé; **to be forced to take ~ redundancy/retirement** être mis au chômage/à la retraite d'office; **2** (absolute) [*powers, authority, regulations*] coercitif/-ive.

compulsory: **~ purchase** *n* GB expropriation *f* (*pour cause d'utilité publique*); **~ purchase order** *n* GB ordre *m* d'expropriation (*pour cause d'utilité publique*).

compunction /kəmˈpʌŋkʃn/ *n* ⊄ scrupule *m*; **to have no ~ in** ou **about doing** n'avoir aucun scrupule à faire; **without the slightest ~** sans le moindre scrupule.

computation /ˌkɒmpjuːˈteɪʃn/ *n* calcul *m*.

computational /ˌkɒmpjuːˈteɪʃənl/ *adj* Math, Stat quantificatif/-ive; Comput sur ordinateur.

computational linguistics *n* (+ *v sg*) linguistique *f* computationnelle.

compute /kəmˈpjuːt/ *vtr* calculer.

computer /kəmˈpjuːtə(r)/ *n* ordinateur *m*; **to do sth by ~/on a ~** faire qch par ordinateur/sur ordinateur; **to have sth on ~** avoir qch sur ordinateur; **to put sth on ~** mettre qch sur ordinateur; **the ~ is up/down** l'ordinateur fonctionne/est en panne.

computer: **~-aided** *adj* assisté par ordinateur; **~-aided design, CAD** *n* conception *f* assistée par ordinateur, CAO *f*; **~-aided language learning, CALL** *n* apprentissage *m* des langues assisté par ordinateur; **~-aided language teaching, CALT** *n* enseignement *m* des langues assisté par ordinateur; **~-aided learning, CAL** *n* enseignement *m* assisté par ordinateur, EAO *m*; **~-aided manufacturing, CAM** *n* production *f* assistée par ordinateur, PAO *f*, fabrication *f* assistée par ordinateur, FAO *f*.

computerate /kəmˈpjuːtərət/ *adj* ayant des notions d'informatique.

computer: **~ code** *n* code *m* informatique; **~ dating** *n* organisation *f* de rencontres (*en utilisant un ordinateur*); **~ dating service** *n* club *m* de rencontres (*utilisant un ordinateur*); **~ engineer** ▶ 1692 *n* technicien/-ienne *m/f* en informatique; **~ error** *n* erreur *f* informatique.

computerese /kəmpjuːtəriːz/ *n* jargon *m* informatique.

computer: **~ game** *n* jeu *m* informatique; **~ graphics** *n* (+ *v sg*) infographie *f*; **~ hacker** *n* (illegal) pirate *m* informatique; (legal) passionné/-e *m/f* d'informatique; **~ hacking** *n* piratage *m* informatique; **~-integrated manufacturing** *n* fabrication *f* intégrée par ordinateur.

computerization /kəmˌpjuːtəraɪˈzeɪʃn, US -rɪˈz-/ *n* (of records, accounts) mise *f* sur ordinateur; (of work, workplace) informatisation *f*.

computerize /kəmˈpjuːtəraɪz/ *vtr* **1** (store) mettre [qch] sur ordinateur [*records, accounts*]; **2** (treat by computer) informatiser [*list, system*].

computer: **~ keyboard** *n* clavier *m* d'ordinateur; **~ keyboarder** ▶ 1692 *n* claviste *mf*, opérateur/-trice *m/f* de saisie; **~ language** *n* langage *m* de programmation; **~ literacy** *n* notions *fpl* d'informatique; **~ literate** *adj* ayant des notions d'informatique; **~ operator** ▶ 1692 *n* opérateur/-trice *m/f* sur ordinateur; **~ program** *n* Comput programme *m* informatique; **~ programmer** ▶ 1692 *n* programmeur/-euse *m/f*; **~ programming** *n* programmation *f*; **~ science** *n* informatique *f*; **~ scientist** ▶ 1692 *n* informaticien/-ienne *m/f*; **~ studies** *n* Sch, Univ informatique *f*; **~ typesetting** *n* Comput composition *f* automatique; **~ virus** *n* Comput virus *m* informatique.

computing /kəmˈpjuːtɪŋ/ *n* informatique *f*.

comrade /ˈkɒmreɪd, US -ræd/ *n* † ou Pol camarade *mf*; **~-in-arms** compagnon *m* d'armes.

comradeship /ˈkɒmreɪdʃɪp, US -ræd-/ *n* camaraderie *f*.

comsat /ˈkɒmsæt/ *n* US *abrév* = **communications satellite**.

con /kɒn/ **I** *n* **1**○ (swindle) escroquerie *f*, arnaque◑ *f*; **it was all a ~** c'était une escroquerie; **2**○ (convict) taulard○ *m*; **3** (disadvantage) désavantage *m*; ▶ **pro**.
II○ *vtr* (*p prés etc* **-nn-**) (trick) rouler○, escroquer; **to ~ sb into doing sth**○ amener qn à faire qch en abusant de sa crédulité; **to ~ sb out of sth**○ obtenir qch de qn par la ruse; **I was ~ned out of £5** on m'a eu○ de 5 livres sterling.
III‡ *vi* (*p prés etc* **-nn-**) étudier.

Con. *n* GB Pol *abrév* ▶ **Conservative**.

con artist /kɒn/ *n* = **con man**.

concatenation /kənˌkætɪˈneɪʃn/ *n* gen (of ideas, events) enchaînement *m*; Philos, Comput concaténation *f*.

concave /ˈkɒŋkeɪv/ *adj* concave.

concavity /kɒnˈkævətɪ/ *n* concavité *f*.

conceal /kənˈsiːl/ **I** *vtr* dissimuler [*object, building, fact, emotion*] (**from** à).
II concealed *pp adj* [*entrance, turning, camera*] caché.

concealment /kənˈsiːlmənt/ *n* gen, Jur dissimulation *f*; **place of ~** cache *f*.

concede /kənˈsiːd/ **I** *vtr* **1** (admit) concéder [*point*]; **to ~ that** reconnaître que; **'perhaps,' he ~d** 'peut-être,' a-t-il reconnu; **2** (surrender) accorder [*liberty, right*] (**to** à); céder [*territory*] (**to** à); **3** Sport concéder [*point, goal*] (**to** à); **to ~ the match** abandonner le match par forfait; **4** Pol **to ~ an election** concéder la victoire électorale (**to** à).
II *vi* **1** gen céder; **2** Pol reconnaître une défaite électorale; **he ~d at 2 am** il a reconnu sa défaite à 2 heures du matin.

conceit /kənˈsiːt/ *n* **1** (vanity) suffisance *f*; **2** (affectation) afféterie *f* liter; **3** (literary figure) métaphore *f* élaborée; (poem) compliment *m*.

conceited /kənˈsiːtɪd/ *adj* [*person*] vaniteux/-euse; [*remark*] suffisant; **a ~ expression** une expression de suffisance.

conceitedly /kənˈsiːtɪdlɪ/ *adv* avec vanité.

conceivable /kənˈsiːvəbl/ *adj* concevable, imaginable; **it is ~ that** il est concevable que (+ *subj*).

conceivably /kənˈsiːvəblɪ/ *adv* **I suppose it might just ~ cost more than £100** je suppose qu'il est concevable que cela coûte plus de 100 livres; **it could ~ be true/a fake** il est concevable que ce soit vrai/un faux; **they could ~ win** il est concevable qu'ils puissent gagner; **could he ~ have finished?** est-il vraisemblable qu'il ait fini?; **~, I might arrive before 10 am** il se pourrait que j'arrive avant 10 heures; **women (and ~ men) can be selected** les femmes (et en principe les hommes) peuvent être sélectionnés; **I can't ~ eat all that** je ne vois pas comment je pourrai manger tout ça; **you can't ~ expect me to do it now** tu ne peux vraiment pas t'attendre à ce que je le fasse maintenant.

conceive /kənˈsiːv/ **I** *vtr* **1** concevoir [*child*]; **2** (develop) concevoir [*hatred, idea, passion, method*]; **to ~ a hatred for sb/sth** concevoir de la haine pour qn/qch; **3** (believe) concevoir; **I cannot ~ that he would leave without saying goodbye** je ne peux concevoir qu'il parte sans dire au revoir.
II *vi* **1** (become pregnant) concevoir, devenir enceinte; **2** (imagine) **to ~ of sth** imaginer or concevoir qch; **I cannot ~ of any better solution** je ne peux pas imaginer de meilleure solution.

concentrate /ˈkɒnsntreɪt/ **I** *n* Chem, Culin concentré *m*; **orange/tomato ~** concentré d'oranges/de tomates.
II *vtr* **1** (focus) concentrer [*effort*] (**on** sur; **on doing** pour faire); employer [*resources*] (**on** sur; **on doing** à faire); centrer [*attention*] (**on** sur); **fear/pain ~s the mind** la peur/douleur fait réfléchir; **2** Chem, Culin concentrer.
III *vi* **1** (pay attention) [*person*] se concentrer (**on** sur); **to ~ on doing** s'appliquer à faire; **2** (focus) **to ~ on** [*film, report, journalist*] s'intéresser surtout à; **3** (congregate) [*animals, people*] se concentrer; **to be ~d** [*ownership, power, industry, population*] être concentré; **power is ~d in the hands of the wealthy** le pouvoir est concentré dans les mains des riches.

concentrated /ˈkɒnsntreɪtɪd/ *adj* **1** Chem, Culin concentré; **2** fig [*effort, emotion*] intense.

concentration /ˌkɒnsnˈtreɪʃn/ *n* **1** (attention) concentration *f* (**on** sur); **with great ~** avec une grande concentration; **my powers of ~** mon pouvoir de concentration; **to lose one's ~** se déconcentrer; **2** (specialization) spécialisation *f*; **~ on sales/on electrical goods** spécialisation dans le domaine de la vente/en appareillage électrique; **3** Chem concentration *f*; **high/low ~** forte/faible concentration; **4** (accumulation) concentration *f*; **the ~ of troops/power** la concentration de troupes/du pouvoir.

concentration camp *n* camp *m* de concentration.

concentric /kənˈsentrɪk/ *adj* concentrique.

concept /ˈkɒnsept/ *n* concept *m*.

conception /kənˈsepʃn/ *n* Med, fig conception *f* (**of** de); **you can have no ~ of** tu ne peux pas imaginer.

conceptual /kənˈseptʃʊəl/ *adj* conceptuel/-elle.

conceptual art *n* art *m* conceptuel.

conceptualism /kənˈseptʃʊəlɪzəm/ *n* conceptualisme *m*.

conceptualize /kənˈseptʃʊəlaɪz/ *vtr* conceptualiser.

conceptually /kənˈseptʃʊəlɪ/ *adv* [*simple, difficult*] conceptuellement.

concern /kənˈsɜːn/ **I** *n* **1** (worry) inquiétude *f* (**about, over** à propos de); **there is growing ~ about crime** la criminalité suscite de plus en plus d'inquiétude; **there is ~**

for her safety on s'inquiète pour sa sécurité; **to give rise to** ou **cause ~** être inquiétant; **there is no cause for ~** il n'y a pas lieu d'être inquiet; **there is cause for ~** il y a des raisons d'être inquiet; **he expressed ~ at my results/for my health** il m'a fait part de son inquiétude quant à mes résultats/ma santé; **my ~ that he might be in danger** mon inquiétude à l'idée qu'il puisse être en danger; **an expression of ~** (on face) une expression inquiète; **2** (preoccupation) préoccupation *f*; **environmental/petty ~s** des préoccupations écologiques/mesquines; **our main ~ is to do** notre principal souci est de faire; **3** (care) (for person) prévenance *f*; **I did it out of ~ for him** je l'ai fait par égard pour lui; **you have no ~ for safety** tu ne te préoccupes pas de la sécurité; **4** (company) entreprise *f*; **a going ~** une affaire rentable; **5** (personal business) **that's her ~** cela la regarde; **your private life is no ~ of mine** ta vie privée ne me regarde pas; **it's none of your ~, it's of no ~ to you** cela ne te regarde pas; **what ~ is it of yours?** en quoi est-ce que cela te regarde?; **6** Fin intérêts *mpl* (**in** dans).

II *vtr* **1** (worry) inquiéter [*parent, public*]; **2** (affect, interest) concerner, intéresser; **to whom it may ~** à qui de droit; **the matter doesn't ~ you** l'affaire ne te concerne pas; **as far as I'm ~ed it's a waste of time** pour moi, c'est du temps perdu; **as far as the pay is ~ed, I'm happy** en ce qui concerne le salaire, je suis satisfait; **3** (involve) **to be ~ed with** s'occuper de [*security, publicity*]; **to be ~ed in** être impliqué dans [*scandal*]; **4** (be about) [*book, programme*] traiter de; [*fax, letter*] concerner; **a book ~ed with** ou **concerning gardening** un livre qui traite de jardinage.

III *v refl* **to ~ oneself with sth/with doing** s'occuper de qch/de faire.

concerned /kən'sɜːnd/ *adj* **1** (anxious) inquiet/-ète (**about** à propos de); **I was ~ by** ou **at the decision** la décision m'inquiétait; **to be ~ at the news** trouver la nouvelle inquiétante; **to be ~ to hear that** apprendre avec inquiétude que; **to be ~ that sb may** ou **might do** être inquiet/-iète à l'idée que qn fasse; **to be ~ for sb** se faire du souci pour qn; **2** (involved) (*tjrs épith, après n*) concerné; **all (those) ~** toutes les personnes concernées.

concerning /kən'sɜːnɪŋ/ *prep* concernant.

concert /'kɒnsət/ **I** *n* **1** Mus concert *m* (**for** en faveur de); **a Madonna ~** un concert de Madonna; **in ~ at/with** en concert à/avec; **2** sout (cooperation) concert *m*; **a ~ of praise** un concert de louanges; **to act in ~** agir de concert ou d'un commun accord; **in ~ with** de concert avec.

II *modif* [*music, ticket, pianist*] de concert.

concerted /kən'sɜːtɪd/ *adj* [*action, campaign*] concerté; **to make a ~ effort to do** faire un sérieux effort pour faire.

concert: **~goer** *n* habitué/-e *m/f* des concerts; **~ grand** ▶1481 *n* piano *m* de concert; **~ hall** *n* salle *f* de concert.

concertina /ˌkɒnsə'tiːnə/ ▶1481 **I** *n* concertina *m*.

II *vi* GB [*vehicle, part of vehicle*] se plier en accordéon; **three carriages had ~ed (together)** trois wagons s'étaient télescopés.

concertmaster /'kɒnsətmɑːstə(r)/ *n* US premier violon *m*.

concerto /kən'tʃeətəʊ, -'tʃɜːt-/ *n* (*pl* **-tos** ou **-tia**) concerto *m*; **piano/violin ~** concerto pour piano/violon.

concert: **~ party** *n* Jur Fin alliance *f* occulte (*en vue d'une prise de contrôle*); **~ performance** *n* concert *m*; **~ performer** *n* concertiste *mf*; **~ pitch** *n* Mus diapason *m*; **~ tour** *n* tournée *f*.

concession /kən'seʃn/ *n* **1** (compromise) concession *f* (**on** sur); **as a ~** à titre de concession; **to make ~s** faire des concessions (**to** à); **her sole ~ to fashion** sa seule concession à la mode; **to make no ~s to** ne pas céder aux exigeances de [*tourism, comfort*]; **2** ¢ (yielding) concession *f*; **3** (discount) réduction *f*; **'~s'** 'tarif réduit'; **tax ~** dégrèvement *m*; **travel ~s** participation *f* aux frais de transport; **4** Mining (property rights) concession *f*; **mining/oil ~** concession *f* minière/pétrolière; **5** Comm (marketing rights) **to run a perfume ~** être concessionnaire de parfumerie.

concessionaire /kənˌseʃə'neə(r)/ *n* concessionnaire *mf*.

concessional /kən'seʃənl/ *adj* **on ~ terms** [*sell, supply*] à tarif préférentiel.

concessionary /kən'seʃənərɪ/ *adj* [*fare, price, rate*] réduit.

concessive /kən'sesɪv/ *adj* Ling concessif/-ive.

conch /kɒŋk, kɒntʃ/ *n* **1** (shell, creature) conque *f*; **2** Archit abside *f* voûtée en cul-de-four.

concha /'kɒŋkə/ *n* (*pl* **-ae**) Anat conque *f*.

conchology /kɒŋ'kɒlədʒɪ/ *n* conchyliologie *f*.

conciliate /kən'sɪlɪeɪt/ *vtr* apaiser.

conciliation /kənˌsɪlɪ'eɪʃn/ **I** *n* (all contexts) conciliation *f*.

II *modif* Ind [*board, meeting, scheme*] de conciliation; **~ service** commission *f* de conciliation.

conciliator /kən'sɪlɪeɪtə(r)/ *n* médiateur/-trice *m/f*.

conciliatory /kən'sɪlɪətərɪ, US -tɔːrɪ/ *adj* [*attitude, gesture, mood, terms*] conciliant; [*measures, policy, speech*] conciliatoire.

concise /kən'saɪs/ *adj* **1** (succinct) concis; **2** (abridged) **A Concise History of Celtic Art** Précis *m* d'histoire de l'art celte.

concisely /kən'saɪslɪ/ *adv* [*answer, analyse, write*] avec concision.

conciseness /kən'saɪsnɪs/, **concision** /kən'sɪʒn/ *n* concision *f*.

conclave /'kɒnkleɪv/ *n* **1** (private meeting) réunion *f* à huis clos; **2** Relig conclave *m*; **to be in ~** tenir conclave.

conclude /kən'kluːd/ **I** *vtr* **1** (finish, end) conclure, terminer [*discussion, chapter, performance*]; **'finally...,' he ~d** 'enfin...,' dit-il pour conclure; **'to be ~d'** TV 'suite et fin au prochain épisode'; Journ 'suite et fin au prochain numéro'; **2** (settle) conclure [*treaty, deal, agreement*]; **3** (deduce) conclure (**from** de; **that** que); **to ~ that sb is innocent** Jur conclure à l'innocence de qn.

II *vi* [*story, event*] se terminer (**with** par, sur), s'achever (**with** sur, par); [*speaker*] conclure (**with** par); **to ~,...** pour conclure,...; **he ~d by saying that** il a conclu en disant que.

concluding /kən'kluːdɪŋ/ *adj* final.

conclusion /kən'kluːʒn/ *n* **1** (end) (of event, book, performance) fin *f*; **in ~** en conclusion, pour terminer; **2** (opinion, resolution) conclusion *f*; **to come to** ou **to reach a ~** arriver à une conclusion; **to draw a ~ from sth** tirer une conclusion de qch; **I don't think we can draw any ~s from this** je ne pense pas que l'on puisse en conclure quoi que ce soit; **this leads us to the ~ that** ceci nous amène à conclure que; **he jumped** ou **leapt to the ~ that she was dead** il en a conclu un peu trop hâtivement qu'elle était morte; **don't jump** ou **leap to ~s!** ne tire pas de conclusions hâtives!; **3** (of agreement, deal, treaty) conclusion *f*; **4** gen, Philos (outcome) conclusion *f*; **taken to its logical ~, this would mean that** poussé à l'extrême, ceci signifierait que.

conclusive /kən'kluːsɪv/ *adj* [*argument, evidence, proof*] concluant.

conclusively /kən'kluːsɪvlɪ/ *adv* de façon concluante.

concoct /kən'kɒkt/ *vtr* (all contexts) concocter.

concoction /kən'kɒkʃn/ *n* **1 C** lit (drink, tonic) breuvage *m*; (dish) mélange *m* (**of** de); **2** fig (style, effect) mélange *m* (**of** de); **3 ¢** lit, fig (preparation) élaboration *f*.

concomitant /kən'kɒmɪtənt/ sout **I** *n* élément *m* (**of** qui coïncide avec).

II *adj* [*change, problem*] concomitant fml; **to be ~ with** aller de pair avec, être concomitant avec fml.

concord /'kɒŋkɔːd/ *n* **1** sout (harmony) concorde *f*; **2** Ling accord *m*; **3** Mus accord *m*.

concordance /kən'kɔːdəns/ *n* **1** sout (agreement) accord *m*; **to be in ~ with** s'accorder avec; **2** (index) concordance *f*.

concordancing programme *n* Comput, Ling logiciel *m* d'indexation or de concordances.

concordant /kən'kɔːdənt/ *adj* concordant; **to be ~ with** concorder avec.

concordat /kən'kɔːdæt/ *n* concordat *m*.

Concorde /'kɒŋkɔːd/ *pr n* Concorde *m*.

concourse /'kɒŋkɔːs/ *n* **1** Archit, Rail (large interior area) hall *m*; **2** sout (gathering) assemblée *f*.

concrete /'kɒŋkriːt/ **I** *n* béton *m*.

II *adj* **1** Constr [*block*] de béton; [*base*] en béton; **2** fig (all contexts) concret/-ète; **in ~ terms** en termes concrets, concrètement.

III *vtr* = **concrete over**.

■ **concrete over**: **~ over [sth]** recouvrir [qch] de béton, bétonner [*road, lawn*].

concrete: **~ jungle** *n* pej univers *m* de béton; **~ mixer** *n* bétonnière *f*.

concretion /kən'kriːʃn/ *n* Geol concrétion *f*.

concubine /'kɒŋkjʊbaɪn/ *n* (of potentate) concubine *f*.

concupiscence /kən'kjuːpɪsns/ *n* concupiscence *f*.

concupiscent /kən'kjuːpɪsnt/ *adj* concupiscent.

concur /kən'kɜː(r)/ (*p prés etc* **-rr-**) **I** *vtr* convenir (**that** que).

II *vi* **1** (agree) être d'accord (**with** avec); **2** (act together) **to ~ in** participer à [*action, measure, decision*]; **to ~ with sb in condemning** se joindre à qn pour condamner; **3** (tally) [*data, results, views*] concorder (**with** avec); **4** (combine) **to ~ to do** contribuer à faire; **everything ~red to make the show a success** tout a contribué à faire du spectacle un succès.

concurrence /kən'kʌrəns/ *n* **1** sout (agreement) accord *m*, agrément *m* fml; **in ~ with** en accord avec; **2** (combination) **~ of events** concours *m* de circonstances.

concurrent /kən'kʌrənt/ *adj* **1** (simultaneous) gen simultané; **to be given two ~ sentences of six months** Jur être condamné à deux fois six mois avec confusion des peines; **2** sout (in agreement) **to be ~ with** [*views*] concorder avec; **3** Math [*lines*] concourant.

concurrently /kən'kʌrəntlɪ/ *adv* gen simultanément; **the sentences to run ~** Jur avec confusion des peines.

concuss /kən'kʌs/ *vtr* **to be ~ed** être commotionné.

concussion /kən'kʌʃn/ *n* Med commotion *f* cérébrale.

condemn /kən'dem/ **I** *vtr* **1** (censure) condamner (**for doing** pour avoir fait); **~ed for human rights abuses** condamné pour le non respect des droits de l'homme; **to ~ sth as pointless/provocative** condamner la futilité/l'aspect provocateur de qch; **to ~ sb as an opportunist** dénoncer l'opportunisme de qn; **2** Jur (sentence) **to ~ sb to death/life imprisonment** condamner qn à mort/à perpétuité; **3** (doom) **to be ~ed to do** être condamné à faire; **to ~ sb to** condamner qn à [*isolation, poverty*]; **4** (declare unsafe) déclarer [qch] inhabitable [*building*]; déclarer [qch] impropre à la consommation [*meat*]; **5** (betray) condamner.

II condemned *pp adj* **1** [*cell*] des condamnés à mort; **~ed man/woman** condamné/-e *m/f* à mort; **2** [*building*] déclaré inhabitable.

condemnation /ˌkɒndemˈneɪʃn/ *n* **1** ¢ (censure) condamnation *f* (**of** de); **2** (indictment) **to be a ~ of sb/sth** remettre qn/qch en question; **3** C (declaration) condamnation *f*.

condemnatory /ˌkɒndemˈneɪtərɪ/ *adj* dénonciateur/-trice.

condensation /ˌkɒndenˈseɪʃn/ *n* **1** (droplets) (on walls) condensation *f*; (on windows) buée *f*; **2** Chem (process) condensation *f*; **3** (abridged version) version *f* condensée.

condense /kənˈdens/ **I** *vtr* **1** (compress) condenser (**into** en); **2** Chem condenser.
II *vi* Chem se condenser.

condensed /kənˈdenst/ *adj* (*épith*) condensé.

condensed: **~ milk** *n* lait *m* concentré sucré or condensé; **~ type** *n* Print caractère *m* étroit.

condenser /kənˈdensə(r)/ *n* Chem, Elec, Phys condenseur *m*.

condescend /ˌkɒndɪˈsend/ **I** *vtr* (deign) **to ~ to do** condescendre à faire.
II *vi* (patronize) **to ~ to sb** être condescendant envers qn.

condescending /ˌkɒndɪˈsendɪŋ/ *adj* condescendant.

condescendingly /ˌkɒndɪˈsendɪŋlɪ/ *adv* [*reply, smile*] avec condescendance.

condescension /ˌkɒndɪˈsenʃn/ *n* condescendance *f*.

condiment /ˈkɒndɪmənt/ *n* condiment *m*.

condition /kənˈdɪʃn/ **I** *n* **1** (stipulation) condition *f*; **what are the ~s of the contract/loan?** quelles sont les conditions du contrat/prêt?; **to fulfil** ou **meet** ou **satisfy the ~s** remplir les conditions; **the offer had several ~s attached to it** l'offre était soumise à plusieurs conditions; **I'll sell it under certain ~s** je le vendrai sous certaines conditions; **on ~ that** à condition que (+ *subj*); **I lent it to her on ~ that she return it on Tuesday** je le lui ai prêté à condition qu'elle me le rende mardi; **it is a ~ of the contract that you work 37 hours per week** votre contrat stipule que vous devez travailler 37 heures par semaine; **investment is an essential ~ for economic growth** l'investissement est une condition essentielle de la croissance économique; **I agree, on one ~, namely that you pay in cash** je suis d'accord, mais à une condition, que vous payiez en liquide; **general ~s** conditions générales; **~ subsequent/precedent** Jur condition suspensive/préalable; **2** (state) état *m*, condition *f*; **to be in good/bad ~** [*house, car, manuscript etc*] être en bon/mauvais état; **to keep sth in good ~** maintenir qch en bon état; **your hair is in poor ~** tes cheveux sont abîmés; **he's in good ~ for a man of 80** il est en bonne santé pour un homme de 80 ans; **to be in a stable/critical ~** être dans un état stable/critique; **her ~ is serious** elle est dans un état grave; **to be in no ~ to do** ne pas être en état de faire; **to be in an interesting ~**† euph être enceinte; **3** (disease) maladie *f*; **a heart/skin ~** une maladie cardiaque/de la peau; **a fatal/an incurable ~** une maladie mortelle/incurable; **4** (fitness) forme *f*; **to be out of ~** ne pas être en forme; **to get one's body into ~** se mettre en forme; **5** (situation) condition *f*; **the feminine/human ~** la condition féminine/humaine; **6** (in philosophy, logic) condition *f*.
II conditions *npl* (circumstances) conditions *fpl*; **to work under difficult ~s** travailler dans des conditions difficiles; **housing/living/working ~s** conditions de logement/vie/travail; **weather ~s** conditions météorologiques.
III *vtr* **1** gen, Psych conditionner; **~ed reflex** ou **response** lit, fig réflexe *m* conditionné; **people are ~ed into believing that** les gens sont conditionnés à croire que; **she argues that women are ~ed to be altruistic** elle soutient que de par leur éducation les femmes sont amenées à se comporter de façon altruiste; **2** (treat) traiter [*skin, hair*]; **this shampoo ~s the hair** ce shampooing contient un après-shampooing.

conditional /kənˈdɪʃənl/ **I** *n* Ling conditionnel *m*; **in the ~** au conditionnel.
II *adj* **1** [*agreement, acceptance, approval, support*] conditionnel/-elle; **the offer is ~ on** ou **upon the name of the donor remaining secret** l'offre a pour condition que le nom du donateur demeure (*subj*) secret; **to make sth ~ on** ou **upon sth** faire dépendre qch de qch; **the sale is ~ on** ou **upon signing the contract** la vente n'est effective qu'à la signature du contrat; **economic aid is ~ on** ou **upon democratic reform** l'aide économique ne sera accordée qu'en cas de réforme démocratique; **2** Ling [*clause, sentence*] conditionnel/-elle; **in the ~ tense** au conditionnel; **3** (in logic) [*proposition*] conditionnel/-elle.

conditional: **~ bail** *n* GB Jur mise *f* en liberté sous caution; **~ discharge** *n* GB Jur sursis *m* simple.

conditionality /ˌkəndɪʃəˈnælətɪ/ *n* Econ, Fin conditionnalité *f*.

conditionally /kənˈdɪʃənəlɪ/ *adv* **1** (with stipulations) [*agree, accept, propose*] sous conditions; **2** Jur **to be ~ discharged** bénéficier d'une libération conditionnelle.

conditional sale *n* Comm vente *f* soumise à certaines conditions.

conditioner /kənˈdɪʃənə(r)/ *n* (for hair) après-shampooing *m*, démêlant *m*; (for laundry) assouplisseur *m*; (for leather) crème *f* nourrissante.

conditioning /kənˈdɪʃənɪŋ/ **I** *n* **1** Psych conditionnement *m*; **2** Cosmet (of hair) traitement *m*.
II *pres p adj* Cosmet [*shampoo, lotion etc*] démêlant.

condo○ /ˈkɒndəʊ/ *n* US *abrév* = **condominium** 1.

condole /kənˈdəʊl/ *vi* **to ~ with sb** présenter ses condoléances à qn.

condolence /kənˈdəʊləns/ **I** *n* **letter of ~** lettre *f* de condoléance.
II condolences *npl* condoléances *fpl*.

condom /ˈkɒndɒm/ *n* préservatif *m*.

condominium /ˌkɒndəˈmɪnɪəm/ *n* **1** US (also **~ unit**) appartement *m* (dans une copropriété); **2** US (complex) (immeuble *m* en) copropriété *f*; **3** Pol (joint territory) condominium *m*.

condone /kənˈdəʊn/ *vtr* tolérer [*behaviour, exploitation, use of violence*].

condor /ˈkɒndɔː(r)/ *n* condor *m*.

conduce /kənˈdjuːs, US -ˈduː-/ *vi* sout **to ~ to** conduire à.

conducive /kənˈdjuːsɪv, US -ˈduː-/ *adj* **to be ~ to** être favorable à.

conduct **I** /ˈkɒndʌkt/ *n* **1** (behaviour) conduite *f* (**towards** envers); **2** (handling) (of campaign, business) conduite *f* (**of** de).
II /kənˈdʌkt/ *vtr* **1** (lead) conduire [*visitor, group*]; **she ~ed us around the house** elle nous a fait faire le tour de la maison; **~ed tour** ou **visit** visite guidée; **2** (manage) mener [*life, business, campaign, election*]; **to ~ sb's defence** Jur assurer la défense de qn; **3** (carry out) mener [*experiment, research*]; faire [*poll*]; célébrer [*religious ceremony*]; **to ~ an inquiry** mener une enquête (**into** sur); **4** Mus diriger [*orchestra, choir, concert*]; **5** Elec, Phys conduire, être conducteur/-trice de.
III /kənˈdʌkt/ *vi* Mus diriger.
IV /kənˈdʌkt/ *v refl* **to ~ oneself** se comporter.

conductance /kənˈdʌktəns/ *n* conductance *f*.

conduction /kənˈdʌkʃn/ *n* conduction *f*.

conductive /kənˈdʌktɪv/ *adj* conducteur/-trice.

conductivity /ˌkɒndʌkˈtɪvətɪ/ *n* conductibilité *f*.

conduct mark *n* Sch note *f* de conduite.

conductor /kənˈdʌktə(r)/ ▶ **1692** *n* **1** Mus chef *m* d'orchestre; **2** Transp (on bus) receveur *m*; Rail chef *m* de train; **3** Elec, Phys conducteur *m*.

conductress /kənˈdʌktrɪs/ ▶ **1692** *n* Transp (on bus) receveuse *f*.

conduct sheet *n* Mil, Naut feuille *f* de note.

conduit /ˈkɒndɪt, ˈkɒndjuːɪt, US ˈkɒndwɪt/ *n* **1** (pipe) conduit *m*; **2** Elec gaine *f* électrique.

condyle /ˈkɒndɪl/ *n* Anat condyle *m*.

cone /kəʊn/ *n* **1** Math, gen cône *m*; **~-shaped** en forme de cône; **paper ~** cornet *m* (en papier); **2** Bot (of conifer) cône *m*; **3** (also **ice-cream ~**) cornet *m*; **4** Aut (for traffic) balise *f*; **5** Geol (of volcano) cône *m*; **6** Anat (in retina) cône *m*; **7** Zool cône *m*.
■ **cone off**: **~ [sth] off, ~ off [sth]** baliser [*road, route*].

coney = **cony**.

confab○ /ˈkɒnfæb/ *n* **to have a ~ about sth** discuter de qch.

confabulate /kənˈfæbjʊleɪt/ *vi* **1** sout converser; **2** Psych confabuler.

confection /kənˈfekʃn/ *n* **1** Culin (cake) pâtisserie *f*, gâteau *m*; (sweetmeat) confiserie *f*; (dessert) dessert *m*; **2** hum (dress etc) robe *f*; **3** (combination) **a ~ of** une savante combinaison de; **4** (act, process) confection *f*.

confectioner /kənˈfekʃənə(r)/ ▶ **1692** *n* (making sweets) confiseur/-euse *m/f*; (making cakes) pâtissier-confiseur *m*; **~'s custard** crème *f* pâtissière; **~'s (shop)** pâtisserie-confiserie *f*; **~'s sugar** US sucre *m* glace.

confectionery /kənˈfekʃənərɪ, US -ʃənerɪ/ *n* ¢ (sweets) gen sucreries *fpl*; (high quality) confiserie *f*; (cakes) pâtisserie *f*.

confederacy /kənˈfedərəsɪ/ *n* **1** Pol confédération *f*; **the (Southern) Confederacy** US Hist les États confédérés (d'Amérique); **2** (conspiracy) conspiration *f*.

confederate **I** /kənˈfedərət/ *n* **1** (in conspiracy) complice *mf*; **2** Pol confédéré/-e *m/f*.
II /kənˈfedərət/ *adj* Pol confédéré.
III /kənˈfedəreɪt/ *vtr* confédérer.
IV /kənˈfedəreɪt/ *vi* **1** (unite) se confédérer (**with** avec); **2** (conspire) conspirer (**with** avec; **against** contre).

Confederate /kənˈfedərət/ *n, adj* Confédéré (*m*).

confederation /kənˌfedəˈreɪʃn/ *n* confédération *f*.

confer /kənˈfɜː(r)/ **I** *vtr* (*p prés etc* **-rr-**) conférer [*right, status, honour, degree*] (**on, upon** à).
II *vi* (*p prés etc* **-rr-**) conférer; **to ~ with sb about sth** conférer de qch avec qn.

conference /ˈkɒnfərəns/ **I** *n* **1** (meeting, symposium) conférence *f*; Pol congrès *m*; **to be in ~** être en conférence (**with** avec); **a ~ on** (concerning) une conférence sur; (to promote) une conférence pour; **peace/disarmament ~** conférence pour la paix/le désarmement; **(the) ~ voted to reject the motion** les participants ont rejeté la proposition; **2** US Sport groupe *m* sportif inter-universités.
II *modif* [*room, centre*] de conférences; **~ member** participant/-e *m/f*.

conference: **~ call** *n* téléconférence *f*; **~ committee** *n* US Pol *commission chargée de l'uniformisation des lois auprès du Sénat et de la Chambre des représentants*; **~ table** *n* lit table *f* de conférence; fig table *f* de négociation.

conferment /kənˈfɜːmənt/ *n* (of title) octroi *m*; Univ remise *f*.

confess /kənˈfes/ **I** *vtr* **1** avouer, confesser [*crime, truth, mistake*]; avouer, reconnaître [*desire, liking, weakness*]; **to ~ that** avouer que; **I must ~ I don't like him** j'avoue qu'il ne me plaît pas; **2** Relig [*penitent*] confesser, se confesser de [*sins*]; [*heretic etc*] confesser [*faith, belief*]; [*priest*] (hear confession of) confesser.
II *vi* **1** (admit) avouer; **to ~ to a crime** avouer (avoir commis) un crime; **to ~ to a**

liking for sth avouer avoir un faible pour qch; **2** Relig se confesser.

confessedly /kən'fesɪdlɪ/ *adv* (by one's own admission) de son propre aveu; (by general admission) de l'aveu de tous.

confession /kən'feʃn/ *n* **1** gen, Jur aveu *m* (**of** de); **to make a full ~** faire des aveux complets; **2** (in title) **'Confessions of...'** 'Les confessions de...'; **3** Relig confession *f*; **to go to ~** aller se confesser; **to make one's ~** se confesser; **to hear sb's ~** confesser qn.

confessional /kən'feʃənl/ **I** *n* **1** (in church) confessionnal *m*; **the seal of the ~** le secret de la confession; **2** (book) livre *m* de prières pénitentielles.
II *adj* **1** Relig pénitentiel/-ielle; **2** [*writing*] autobiographique.

confessor /kən'fesə(r)/ *n* confesseur *m*.

confetti /kən'fetɪ/ *n* ¢ confettis *mpl*.

confidant /ˌkɒnfɪ'dænt/ *n* confident *m*.

confidante /ˌkɒnfɪ'dænt/ *n* confidente *f*.

confide /kən'faɪd/ **I** *vtr* **1** (entrust) confier (**to** à); **to ~ sth/sb to sb's care** confier qch/qn aux soins de qn; **2** (tell) confier [*secret, hope, fear*] (**to** à).
II *vi* **to ~ in** se confier à [*person*].

confidence /'kɒnfɪdəns/ *n* **1** (faith) confiance *f* (**in** en); **to have (every) ~ in sb/sth** avoir (pleine) confiance en qn/qch; **to put one's ~ in sb** mettre sa confiance en qn; **2** Pol **vote of ~** vote *m* de confiance; **to pass a vote of ~** voter la confiance; **motion of no ~** motion *f* de censure; **to pass a vote of no ~** voter la censure or une motion de censure (**in** à l'égard de); **3** (self-assurance) assurance *f*, confiance *f* en soi; **he lacks ~** il manque d'assurance, il n'est pas sûr de lui; **4** (certainty) assurance *f*; **in the full ~ that** avec la certitude que; **I have every ~ that she will succeed** je suis sûr or persuadé qu'elle réussira; **I can say with ~ that** je suis sûr or certain or convaincu que; **5** (confidentiality) **to take sb into one's ~** se confier à qn; **to tell sb sth in (strict) ~** dire qch à qn (tout à fait) confidentiellement; **write in strictest ~ to...** écrivez-nous—nous vous promettons de respecter l'anonymat; **6** (secret) confidence *f*.

confidence: **~ game** *n* US = **confidence trick**; **~ interval** *n* intervalle *m* de confiance; **~ level** *n* Stat niveau *m* de confiance; **~ man**, **~ trickster**† *n* GB escroc *m*; **~ trick** *n* escroquerie *f*.

confident /'kɒnfɪdənt/ *adj* **1** (sure) sûr, confiant; **to be ~ that** être sûr or persuadé que; **to be ~ of success** ou **of succeeding** avoir la certitude de réussir; **she felt ~ about the future** elle avait confiance en l'avenir; **2** (self-assured) assuré, sûr de soi.

confidential /ˌkɒnfɪ'denʃl/ *adj* **1** [*advice, agreement, information, matter, document, service*] confidentiel/-ielle *m/f*; **~ secretary** secrétaire *mf* privé/-e; **private and ~** privé et confidentiel; **2** (confiding) [*tone, voice*] confidentiel/-ielle; **he became very ~ with me** il s'est ouvert tout entier à moi.

confidentiality /ˌkɒnfɪdenʃɪ'ælətɪ/ *n* confidentialité *f*.

confidentially /ˌkɒnfɪ'denʃəlɪ/ *adv* confidentiellement.

confidently /'kɒnfɪdəntlɪ/ *adv* [*speak, behave*] avec assurance; [*expect, predict*] en toute confiance.

confiding /kɒn'faɪdɪŋ/ *adj* confiant.

confidingly /kən'faɪdɪŋlɪ/ *adv* [*say*] d'un ton confiant; [*look*] d'un air confiant.

configuration /kənˌfɪgə'reɪʃn, US -ˌfɪgjʊ'reɪʃn/ *n* (all contexts) configuration *f*.

confine /kən'faɪn/ **I** *vtr* **1** (in room, cell, prison, ghetto) confiner [*person*] (**in, to** dans); interner [*mental patient*] (**in, to** dans); enfermer [*animal*] (**in** dans); **to be ~d to bed** être alité; **to be ~d to the house** être obligé de rester à la maison; **to be ~d to barracks** Mil être consigné au quartier; **2** (limit) limiter [*comments etc*] (**to** à); **the problem is not ~d to old people** le problème ne concerne pas uniquement les personnes âgées; **3**† Med **to be ~d** être en couches.
II *v refl* **to ~ oneself to/to doing** se contenter de/de faire.

confined /kən'faɪnd/ *adj* [*atmosphere, area*] confiné; [*space*] restreint.

confinement /kən'faɪnmənt/ *n* **1** (detention) (in cell, prison) détention *f* (**in, to** dans); Jur réclusion *f*; (in institution) internement *m* (**in, to** dans); **~ to barracks** Mil consigne *f*; **2**† Med (labour) couches *fpl*; (birth) accouchement *m*.

confines /'kɒnfaɪnz/ *npl* **1** (constraints) contraintes *fpl*; **2 within the ~ of** dans le cadre de [*situation, regulations*]; dans l'enceinte de [*building*].

confirm /kən'fɜ:m/ *vtr* **1** (state as true, validate) confirmer [*statement, event, identity, booking, belief, fear*]; **to ~ that** confirmer que; **two people were ~ed dead** on a confirmé que deux personnes ont trouvé la mort; **to ~ receipt of** Comm accuser réception de [*cheque, goods*]; **2** Admin approuver [*appointment*]; **to ~ sb as** confirmer qn dans son rôle de [*director etc*]; **to be ~ed in one's post** être confirmé dans ses fonctions; **3** (justify) **to ~ sb in** conforter qn dans [*belief, opinion*]; **4** Jur homologuer [*decree*]; **5** Relig confirmer.

confirmation /ˌkɒnfə'meɪʃn/ *n* **1** (of belief, statement, theory, news, suspicion, fear) confirmation *f* (**of** de; **that** que); (official) (of appointment, booking) confirmation *f* (**of** de; **that** que); **2** Jur entérinement *m*; **3** Admin, Pol (of appointment) approbation *f*; **4** Relig confirmation *f*.

confirmed /kən'fɜ:md/ *adj* [*alcoholic, smoker, liar, habit*] invétéré; [*bachelor, sinner*] endurci; [*admirer*] inconditionnel/-elle.

confiscate /'kɒnfɪskeɪt/ *vtr* confisquer (**from** à).

confiscation /ˌkɒnfɪ'skeɪʃn/ *n* confiscation *f*.

conflagration /ˌkɒnflə'greɪʃn/ *n* conflagration *f*.

conflate /kən'fleɪt/ *vtr* regrouper.

conflation /kən'fleɪʃən/ *n* regroupement *m*.

conflict **I** /'kɒnflɪkt/ *n* **1** Mil conflit *m*; **armed ~** conflit armé; **the Middle East ~** le conflit au Proche Orient; **to be in/come into ~** lit, fig être/entrer en conflit (**with** avec); **2** (dispute) conflit *m* (**between** entre); **his campaign brought him into ~ with the party** il est entré en conflit avec le parti à cause de sa campagne; **3** (dilemma) conflit *m* (**between** entre); **~ of interests** conflit d'intérêts; **to have a ~ of loyalties** être déchiré par des loyautés contradictoires.
II /kən'flɪkt/ *vi* (contradict) [*statement, feeling, attitude*] être en contradiction (**with** avec); (clash) [*events, programme*] tomber au même moment (**with** que).

conflicting /kən'flɪktɪŋ/ *adj* **1** (incompatible) [*views, feelings, interests*] contradictoire; **2** (coinciding) **I have two ~ engagements for 7 July** le 7 juillet j'ai deux rendez-vous qui tombent en même temps.

confluence /'kɒnflʊəns/ *n* **1** (of rivers) confluent *m*; **2** (of ideas, people) confluence *f*.

conform /kən'fɔ:m/ **I** *vtr* conformer (**to** à).
II *vi* **1** (to rules, conventions, standards) [*person*] se conformer (**with, to** à); [*model, machine etc*] être conforme (**with, to** à); **she has always ~ed** elle s'est toujours conformée aux règles; **to ~ to type** se conformer à la norme; **2** (correspond) [*ideas, beliefs*] se conformer (**with, to** à); [*situation*] être conforme (**with, to** à); **3** Relig faire acte de soumission à la religion d'État.

conformable /kən'fɔ:məbl/ *adj* sout (compatible, in agreement) conforme (**to, with** à); **to be ~ to sb's will** respecter la volonté de qn.

conformation /ˌkɒnfɔ:'meɪʃn/ *n* **1** gen, Anat, Geol conformation *f*; **2** Chem conformation *f* (moléculaire).

conformist /kən'fɔ:mɪst/ *n, adj* gen, Relig conformiste (*mf*).

conformity /kən'fɔ:mətɪ/ *n* **1** conformité *f* (**to** à); **in ~ with** conformément à; **2** Relig conformisme *m*.

confound /kən'faʊnd/ *vtr* **1** (perplex) déconcerter; **2** (mix up) confondre (**with** avec); **3** (discredit) démentir [*rumours*]; donner tort à, confondre† [*arguments, critics*]; **4** littér (defeat) confondre [*enemy*]; déjouer [*plans*]; **5**○† **~ it!** la barbe○!; **~ him!** qu'il aille au diable○!; **that ~ed dog** ce maudit chien○.

confront /kən'frʌnt/ *vtr* **1** (face) affronter [*danger, enemy*]; faire face à [*problem*]; **to ~ the truth** voir la réalité en face; **to be ~ed by sth** être confronté à qch; **a new problem ~ed us** nous étions confrontés à un nouveau problème; **to be ~ed by the police** se retrouver face à la police; **the cases that ~ lawyers** les affaires dont les juristes doivent se charger; **the task which ~ed us** le travail qui se présentait à nous; **2** (bring together) **to ~ sb with sth/sb** mettre qn en présence de qch/qn.

confrontation /ˌkɒnfrʌn'teɪʃn/ *n* **1** (violent encounter) affrontement *m* (**between** entre; **with** avec); **2** (dispute) affrontement *m*; **we had a ~ with our teachers** nous nous sommes disputés avec nos professeurs; **3** (encounter) **it was my first ~ with the truth** c'était la première fois que j'étais confronté à la vérité.

confrontational /ˌkɒnfrən'teɪʃənəl/ *adj* provocateur/-trice.

Confucian /kən'fju:ʃn/ **I** *n* Confucianiste *mf*.
II *adj* confucianiste.

Confucianism /kən'fju:ʃənɪzəm/ *n* confucianisme *m*.

Confucius /kən'fju:ʃəs/ *pr n* Confucius.

confuse /kən'fju:z/ **I** *vtr* **1** (bewilder) troubler [*person*]; **to ~ the enemy troops** semer la confusion dans les troupes ennemies; **2** (fail to distinguish) confondre (**with** avec); **3** (complicate) compliquer [*argument, explanation*]; **to ~ the issue** compliquer les choses; **to ~ matters even more...** pour rendre les choses encore plus compliquées...
II *vi* rendre perplexe.

confused /kən'fju:zd/ *adj* **1** [*person*] troublé; [*thoughts, mind*] confus; **to get ~** s'embrouiller; **he was ~ about the instructions** il ne comprenait pas bien le mode d'emploi; **I'm ~ about what to do** je ne sais pas trop ce que je dois faire; **2** (muddled) [*account, reasoning*] confus; [*memories, sounds*] confus; [*voices*] indistinct; [*impression*] vague.

confusedly /kən'fju:zɪdlɪ/ *adv* **1** (in bewilderment) confusément; **2** (unclearly) [*think, understand*] confusément; **he spoke ~ of his plans** il parla de ses projets de façon confuse; **3** (in embarrassment) [*blush*] de confusion; **he took the money ~** il prit l'argent l'air confus.

confusing /kən'fju:zɪŋ/ *adj* **1** (perplexing) déroutant; **2** (complicated) [*account, instructions*] peu clair.

confusion /kən'fju:ʒn/ *n* **1** (in idea, in sb's mind) confusion *f*; **to create ~** jeter la confusion (dans les esprits); **I was in a state of total ~** j'étais complètement embrouillé; **2** (lack of distinction) confusion *f*; **because of the ~ between the two names** parce qu'on avait confondu les deux noms; **to avoid ~** pour éviter toute confusion; **3** (chaos) confusion *f*; **to throw sb/sth into ~** plonger qn/qch dans la confusion; **the meeting broke up in ~** la réunion s'est terminée dans la confusion la plus totale; **4** (embarrassment) confusion *f*.

confute /kən'fju:t/ *vtr* sout réfuter.

conga /ˈkɒŋɡə/ *n* conga *f*.

con game /kɒn/ *n* escroquerie *f*.

congeal /kənˈdʒiːl/ **I** *vtr* figer [*oil, fat*]; cailler [*milk*]; coaguler [*blood*].
II *vi* [*oil, fat*] se figer; [*milk*] cailler; [*blood*] se coaguler.

congenial /kənˈdʒiːnɪəl/ *adj* [*person, company*] sympathique, agréable; [*surroundings, arrangement*] agréable.

congenital /kənˈdʒenɪtl/ *adj* **1** Med congénital; **2** fig [*fear, dislike*] congénital; [*liar*] invétéré.

congenitally /kənˈdʒenɪtəlɪ/ *adv* **1** Med **to be ~ deformed** avoir une malformation congénitale; **2** fig [*dishonest, lazy*] congénitalement.

conger /ˈkɒŋɡə(r)/ *n* congre *m*.

congested /kənˈdʒestɪd/ *adj* **1** [*road*] embouteillé; [*pavement, passage*] encombré; [*district*] surpeuplé; **2** Med congestionné.

congestion /kənˈdʒestʃn/ *n* **1** (of district) surpeuplement *m*; (of road, street) encombrement *m*; **traffic ~** embouteillages *mpl*; **2** Med congestion *f*.

conglomerate **I** /kənˈglɒmərət/ *n* (all contexts) conglomérat *m*.
II /kənˈglɒmərət/ *adj* aggloméré.
III /kənˈglɒməreɪt/ *vtr* conglomérer.
IV /kənˈglɒməreɪt/ *vi* s'agglomérer.

conglomeration /kənˌglɒməˈreɪʃn/ *n* **1** péj (jumble) fatras *m*; **2** Comm (process) conglomération *f*; (association) conglomérat *m*.

Congo /ˈkɒŋɡəʊ/ **▶ 1131, 1644** *pr n* Congo *m*.

Congolese /ˌkɒŋɡəˈliːz/ **▶ 1486** **I** *n* Congolais/-e *m/f*.
II *adj* congolais.

congratulate /kənˈɡrætʃʊleɪt/ **I** *vtr* féliciter (**on** de; **on doing** d'avoir fait); **may we ~ you on your success/engagement?** permettez-nous de vous féliciter de votre succès/à l'occasion de vos fiançailles.
II *v refl* **to ~ oneself** se féliciter (**on** de; **on doing** d'avoir fait).

congratulation /kənˌɡrætʃʊˈleɪʃn/ **I** *n* **letter of ~** lettre *f* de félicitations.
II congratulations *npl* félicitations *fpl*; **~s!** félicitations!; **~s on your success/on the birth of your new baby** (toutes mes or nos) félicitations pour votre succès/à l'occasion de la naissance de votre bébé; **to offer one's ~s to sb** adresser ses félicitations à qn.

congratulatory /kənˈɡrætʃʊlətərɪ, US -tɔːrɪ/ *adj* [*letter, telegram, speech*] de félicitations.

congregate /ˈkɒŋɡrɪɡeɪt/ **I** *vtr* rassembler.
II *vi* se rassembler (**around** autour de).

congregation /ˌkɒŋɡrɪˈɡeɪʃn/ *n* (+ *v sg ou pl*) **1** Relig (in church) assemblée *f* des fidèles; (in parish) paroissiens *mpl*; (of cardinals, ecclesiastics) congrégation *f*; **2** GB Univ assemblée *f* générale des professeurs.

congregational /ˌkɒŋɡrɪˈɡeɪʃənl/ *adj* [*prayer, singing*] des fidèles; **the Congregational Church** l'Église congrégationaliste.

Congregationalist /ˌkɒŋɡrɪˈɡeɪʃənəlɪst/ **I** *n* Congrégationaliste *mf*.
II *adj* congrégationaliste.

congress /ˈkɒŋɡres, US ˈkɒŋɡrəs/ *n* (conference) congrès *m* (**on** sur); **party ~** congrès *m* d'un parti politique.

Congress /ˈkɒŋɡres, US ˈkɒŋɡrəs/ *n* Pol **1** US Congrès *m*; **in ~** au Congrès; **she has been criticized in ~** elle a été critiquée par les membres du Congrès; **2** (in India) Congrès *m*.

Congressional /kənˈɡreʃənl/ *adj* US [*candidate*] au Congrès; [*committee*] du Congrès.

Congressional District, CD *n* US circonscription *f* d'un membre du Congrès.

congress: ~man *n* (*pl* **-men**) US membre *m* du Congrès; **~person** *n* US membre *m* du Congrès; **~woman** *n* (*pl* **-women**) US membre *m* du Congrès.

congruent /ˈkɒŋɡrʊənt/ *adj* **1** sout adéquat; **to be ~ with** être en harmonie avec; **the two theories are not ~** les deux théories ne sont pas en harmonie; **2** Math, gen congru (**to** à); (in geometry) [*triangles*] isométriques.

congruity /kəŋˈɡruːətɪ/ *n* sout **1** (correspondence) conformité *f* (**between** entre); **2** (aptness) pertinence *f*.

congruous /ˈkɒŋɡrʊəs/ *adj* sout adéquat; **to be ~ with** être en harmonie avec.

conical /ˈkɒnɪkl/ *adj* conique.

conifer /ˈkɒnɪfə(r), ˈkəʊn-/ *n* conifère *m*.

coniferous /kəˈnɪfərəs, US kəʊˈn-/ *adj* [*tree*] conifère; [*forest*] de conifères.

conjectural /kənˈdʒektʃərəl/ *adj* conjectural, hypothétique.

conjecture /kənˈdʒektʃə(r)/ **I** *n* hypothèse *f*; **to be a matter for ~** être hypothétique.
II *vtr* supposer; **to ~ sb/sth to be** émettre l'hypothèse que qn/qch est.
III *vi* faire des conjectures (**about** sur).

conjoin /kənˈdʒɔɪn/ sout **I** *vtr* lier (**with** à).
II *vi* s'unir.

conjoint /kənˈdʒɔɪnt/ *adj* sout conjoint.

conjointly /kənˈdʒɔɪntlɪ/ *adv* sout conjointement.

conjugal /ˈkɒndʒʊɡl/ *adj* conjugal.

conjugate /ˈkɒndʒʊɡeɪt/ **I** *vtr* conjuguer.
II *vi* **1** Ling se conjuguer; **2** Biol se reproduire.

conjugation /ˌkɒndʒʊˈɡeɪʃn/ *n* Ling, Biol conjugaison *f*.

conjunct /kənˈdʒʌŋkt/ *adj* conjoint.

conjunction /kənˈdʒʌŋkʃn/ *n* **1** (of circumstances, events) concours *m*; **in ~** ensemble; **in ~ with** conjointement avec; **2** Astron, Ling conjonction *f*.

conjunctiva /ˌkɒndʒʌŋkˈtaɪvə, kənˈdʒʌŋktɪvə/ *n* (*pl* **-vas, -vae**) conjonctive *f*.

conjunctive /kənˈdʒʌŋktɪv/ *adj* Anat, Ling conjonctif/-ive.

conjunctivitis /kənˌdʒʌŋktɪˈvaɪtɪs/ **▶ 1354** *n* conjonctivite *f*.

conjure /ˈkʌndʒə(r)/ **I** *vtr* **1** (by magic) faire apparaître (en faisant de la prestidigitation) [*rabbit, spirits*]; **he ~d a dinner out of thin air** fig il a préparé un dîner comme par magie à partir de rien; **a name to ~ with** fig un nom qu'on évoque avec respect; **2** /kənˈdʒʊə(r)/ (implore) **to ~ sb to do** sout conjurer qn de faire fml.
II *vi* faire des tours de prestidigitation.
■ **conjure away**: **~ away [sth]**, **~ [sth] away** faire disparaître [qch] comme par magie.
■ **conjure up**: **~ up [sth]** faire apparaître [qch] comme par magie; **to ~ up an image of sth** évoquer qch.

conjurer /ˈkʌndʒərə(r)/ *n* prestidigitateur/-trice *m/f*.

conjuring /ˈkʌndʒərɪŋ/ *n* prestidigitation *f*.

conjuring trick *n* tour *m* de prestidigitation.

conjuror = **conjurer**.

conk° /kɒŋk/ **I** *n* **1** GB (nose) pif◑ *m*; **2** US coiffure *f* décrêpée.
II *vtr* **1** frapper; **2** US décrêper [*hair*].
■ **conk out**° [*person*] s'endormir; [*car, machine*] tomber en panne.

conker° /ˈkɒŋkə(r)/ *n* GB **1** marron *m*; **2 conkers** *jeu de marrons*.

con man /kɒn/ *n* arnaqueur◑ *m*, escroc *m*.

connect /kəˈnekt/ **I** *vtr* **1** (attach) raccorder [*end, object, hose, tap*] (**to** à); accrocher [*wagon, coach*] (**to** à); **to ~ two tubes** raccorder deux tubes; **2** (link) [*road, bridge, railway*] relier [*place, road*] (**to, with** à); **I always ~ rain with Oxford** j'associe toujours la pluie à Oxford; **to ~ sb with a crime/a person** faire la connexion entre qn et un crime/une personne; **3** (to mains) brancher [*appliance*] (**to** à); brancher [qch] sur le secteur [*household, town*]; **we will ~ you on Monday** (electrically) vous aurez l'électricité lundi; (to gas) vous aurez le gaz lundi; **4** Telecom raccorder [*phone*]; **we will ~ you on Monday** nous vous raccorderons lundi; **to ~ sb to** passer [qch] à qn [*reception, department*]; **her telephone ~s her to the White House** son téléphone est relié à la Maison Blanche; **'trying to ~ you'** 'ne quittez pas'; **5** (wire up, link technically) = **connect up**.
II *vi* **1** [*room*] communiquer (**with** avec); **2** Transp [*service, bus, plane*] assurer la correspondance (**with** avec); **do the flights ~?** y a-t-il correspondance entre les vols?; **3**° (work smoothly) [*service, system*] bien marcher; **4** US Sport frapper un bon coup; **5**° US **to ~ with** (feel rapport) avoir des affinités avec; **6**° US (buy drugs) se procurer de la drogue.
■ **connect up**: **~ up [sth]**, **~ [sth] up** faire les branchements de [*video, computer*]; **to ~ sth up to** brancher qch sur; **to ~ two machines up** connecter deux machines.

connected /kəˈnektɪd/ *adj* **1** (related) [*matter, idea, event*] lié (**to, with** à); **the events are ~** les événements sont liés; **everything ~ with music** tout ce qui se rapporte à la musique; **2** (in family) apparenté (**to** à); **~ by marriage** apparenté par le mariage; **to be well ~** (through family) être de bonne famille; (having influence) avoir des relations; **3** (joined, linked) [*road, town*] relié (**to, with** à); [*pipe*] raccordé (**to, with** à); **4** (electrically) branché.

Connecticut /kəˈnetɪkət/ **▶ 1744** *pr n* Connecticut *m*.

connecting /kəˈnektɪŋ/ *adj* **1** [*flight*] de correspondance; **2** [*room*] attenant.

connecting rod *n* Aut bielle *f*.

connection, connexion† GB /kəˈnekʃn/ *n* **1** (logical link) rapport *m* (**between** entre; **with** avec); **to have a** ou **some ~ with** avoir un rapport avec; **to have no ~ with** n'avoir aucun rapport or n'avoir rien à voir avec; **is there any ~?** existe-t-il un rapport?; **to make the ~** faire le rapprochement (**between** entre); **in ~ with** au sujet de, à propos de; **in this ~...** à ce sujet...; **2** (personal link) lien *m* (**between** entre; **with** avec); **to have close ~s with** avoir des liens étroits avec [*town, country, family*]; **3** (person) (contact) relation *f*; (relative) parent *m*; **to have useful ~s** avoir des relations; **to have ~s in high places** avoir des relations haut placées; **4** (connecting up) (to mains) branchement *m*; (of pipes, tubes) raccord *m*; (of wheels) embrayage *m*; (of wires) câblage *m*; **5** Telecom (of household to network) raccordement *m*; (of caller to number) mise *f* en communication (**to** avec); **to get a ~** avoir une ligne; **bad ~** mauvaise communication *f*; **6** Transp correspondance *f*; **to miss one's ~** rater sa correspondance; **7**° US argot des drogués (dealer) dealer° *m*; (transaction) échange *m* entre dealer° et client.

connection charge *n* Telecom taxe *f* de raccordement.

connective /kəˈnektɪv/ **I** *n* conjonction *f*.
II *adj* [*tissue*] conjonctif/-ive.

conning tower /ˈkɒnɪŋ taʊə(r)/ *n* Naut kiosque *m*.

conniption° /kəˈnɪpʃn/ *n* US accès *m* de colère; **to go into ~s** se mettre en rogne°.

connivance /kəˈnaɪvəns/ *n* connivence *f*; **with the ~ of sb** avec la connivence de qn; **in ~ with sb** en connivence avec qn.

connive /kəˈnaɪv/ **I** *vi* **1 to ~ at** contribuer délibérément à [*theft, betrayal, escape*]; **2** (participate) **to ~ (with sb) to do sth** être de connivence or de mèche° (avec qn) pour faire qch.
II conniving *pres p adj* [*person*] fourbe; **a conniving glance** un regard de connivence.

connoisseur /ˌkɒnəˈsɜː(r)/ *n* connaisseur/-euse *m/f* (**of** de).

connotation /ˌkɒnəˈteɪʃn/ *n* connotation *f* (**of** de).

connotative /ˈkɒnəteɪtɪv/ *adj* connotatif/-ive.

connote /kəˈnəʊt/ *vtr* **1** (summon up) évoquer; **2** Ling connoter.

connubial /kəˈnjuːbɪəl, US -ˈnuː-/ *adj* sout conjugal.

conquer /ˈkɒŋkə(r)/ **I** *vtr* conquérir [*territory, people, outer space*]; vaincre [*enemy, unemployment, disease*]; surmonter [*habit, fear, jealousy*]; maîtriser [*skill, technology*]; surmonter [*deficit*]; **to ~ the world** fig conquérir le monde entier.
II conquered *pp adj* vaincu.
III conquering *pres p adj* victorieux/-ieuse.

conqueror /ˈkɒŋkərə(r)/ *n* gen vainqueur *m*; Sport gagnant/-e *m/f*; Mil conquérant/-e *m/f*; **William the Conqueror** Guillaume le Conquérant.

conquest /ˈkɒŋkwest/ *n* **1** ¢ (of country, mountain) conquête *f*; (of disease) éradication *f*; (of person) fig hum conquête *f*; **2** (territory) terre *f* conquise; (person) fig hum conquête *f*.

consanguinity /ˌkɒnsæŋˈgwɪnətɪ/ *n* consanguinité *f*.

conscience /ˈkɒnʃəns/ *n* conscience *f*; **it's a matter for your own ~** c'est à toi de décider en ton âme et conscience; **in all ~** en mon/son etc âme et conscience; **they have no ~** ils n'ont aucun sens moral; **he is the ~ of the nation** c'est la voix de la conscience nationale; **to have sth on one's ~** avoir qch sur la conscience; **to have a guilty** ou **bad ~** avoir mauvaise conscience; **to have a clear ~** avoir la conscience tranquille; **to do sth with a clear ~** faire qch la conscience tranquille; **they will have to live with their ~s** ils devront vivre avec un poids sur la conscience.

conscience: **~ clause** *n* clause *f* de conscience; **~ money** *n*: *argent donné pour avoir bonne conscience*; **~-stricken** *adj* bourrelé de remords.

conscientious /ˌkɒnʃɪˈenʃəs/ *adj* (all contexts) consciencieux/-ieuse.

conscientiously /ˌkɒnʃɪˈenʃəslɪ/ *adv* consciencieusement.

conscientiousness /ˌkɒnʃɪˈenʃəsnɪs/ *n* application *f*, soin *m*.

conscientious: **~ objection** *n* objection *f* de conscience; **~ objector**, **CO** *n* objecteur *m* de conscience.

conscious /ˈkɒnʃəs/ **I** *n* Psych **the ~** le conscient *m*.
II *adj* **1** (aware) conscient (**of** de; **that** du fait que); **I wasn't ~ of having hurt their feelings** je ne savais pas que je les avais offensés; **to be politically ~** être politisé; **to be environmentally/socially ~** avoir une conscience écologique/sociale; **2** (deliberate) [*decision*] réfléchi; [*effort*] consciencieux; **3** Med conscient; **I wasn't fully ~** je n'étais qu'en partie conscient; **4** Psych conscient.
III -conscious (*dans composés*) **art-~** amateur/-trice d'art; **health-~** soucieux/-ieuse de sa santé; **class-~** conscient de la hiérarchie sociale.

consciously /ˈkɒnʃəslɪ/ *adv* consciemment.

consciousness /ˈkɒnʃəsnɪs/ *n* **1** (awareness) conscience *f* (**of** de); (undefined) sentiment *m* (**of** de); **the ~ that** le sentiment que; **class ~** conscience *f* de classe; **the truth dawned upon my ~** j'ai commencé à entrevoir la vérité; **the idea penetrated public ~** l'idée a fait son chemin dans la conscience des gens; **safety ~** souci *m* en matière de sécurité; **2** (shared beliefs) conscience *f* collective; **3** Med **to lose/regain ~** perdre/reprendre connaissance.

consciousness raising *n* sensibilisation *f*.

conscript I /ˈkɒnskrɪpt/ *n* appelé *m*, conscrit† *m*.
II /ˈkɒnskrɪpt/ *modif* [*army*] de conscription; **~ soldier** appelé *m*.
III /kənˈskrɪpt/ *vtr* appeler [*soldier*]; enrôler [qn] de force [*worker*].

conscription /kənˈskrɪpʃn/ *n* **1** (system) conscription *f*; **2** (process) incorporation *f* (**into** dans).

consecrate /ˈkɒnsɪkreɪt/ *vtr* consacrer [*church, bishop*]; **~d ground** terre *f* consacrée; **a day ~d to their memory** une journée dédiée à leur souvenir.

consecration /ˌkɒnsɪˈkreɪʃn/ *n* **1** (of church, bishop) consécration *f*; **2** (Catholicism) **the Consecration** la Consécration.

consecutive /kənˈsekjʊtɪv/ *adj* consécutif/-ive; **her tenth ~ win** sa dixième victoire consécutive; **~ clause** Ling clause *f* consécutive.

consecutively /kənˈsekjʊtɪvlɪ/ *adv* consécutivement; **the sentences to run ~** Jur peines à purger consécutivement.

consensual /kənˈsensjʊəl, -ˈsenʃʊəl/ *adj* **1** Jur [*sex, act, crime*] où les deux parties sont consentantes; **2** (of consensus) [*politics, approach*] consensuel/-elle.

consensus /kənˈsensəs/ *n* consensus *m* (**among** au sein de; **about, as to** quant à; **for** en faveur de; **of** de; **on** sur; **that** selon lequel; **to do** pour faire); **a broad ~** un large consensus; **what's the ~?** quelle est l'opinion générale?; **the ~ is that** tout le monde est d'accord pour reconnaître que; **to reach a ~** parvenir à un consensus.

consensus politics *n* politique *f* de consensus.

consent /kənˈsent/ **I** *n* **1** (permission) (by person in authority) consentement *m*; (other) accord *m*; **without the owner's ~** Jur sans l'accord du propriétaire; **age of ~** âge *m* légal; **2** (agreement) **by common/mutual ~ we left** d'un commun accord nous avons tous/tous les deux décidé de partir.
II *vi* consentir; **to ~ to sth** consentir à qch; **to ~ to sb doing sth** consentir à ce que qn fasse qch; **between ~ing adults** entre adultes consentants.
III *vtr* **to ~ to do** consentir à faire.

consent form *n* GB autorisation *f*.

consequence /ˈkɒnsɪkwəns, US -kwens/ *n* **1** (result) conséquence *f*; **as a ~ of** du fait de [*change, process, system*]; à la suite de [*event*]; **in ~** par conséquent; **to take/face the ~s** accepter les conséquences; **to suffer the ~s** subir les conséquences; **2** (importance) sout importance *f*; **it's a matter of some ~** cela est très important; **he is a man of no ~** c'est quelqu'un sans importance; **he's a man of ~** c'est quelqu'un d'important; **it's of no ~ to me** cela m'est complètement indifférent.

consequent /ˈkɒnsɪkwənt, US -kwent/ *adj* **1** (resulting) **the strike and the ~ redundancies** la grève et les licenciements qu'elle a entraînés; **2 ~ upon** sout (because of) en raison de; **to be ~ upon sth** (the result of) être la conséquence de qch; **the rise in prices ~ upon the fall in the dollar** l'augmentation des prix entraînée par la baisse du dollar.

consequential /ˌkɒnsɪˈkwenʃl/ *adj* sout **1** (significant) important; **2** (self-important) péj suffisant; **3**‡ = **consequent**.

consequential loss *n* perte *f* indirecte.

consequently /ˈkɒnsɪkwentlɪ/ *adv* par conséquent.

conservancy /kənˈsɜːvənsɪ/ *n* protection *f*.

conservation /ˌkɒnsəˈveɪʃn/ **I** *n* **1** (of nature, natural resources) protection *f* (**of** de); **energy ~** maîtrise *f* de l'énergie; **2** (of heritage) conservation *f*; **3** Phys conservation *f*.
II *modif* [*group, issue, measure*] de protection.

conservation area *n* zone *f* protégée.

conservationist /ˌkɒnsəˈveɪʃənɪst/ **I** *n* défenseur *m* des ressources naturelles.
II *adj* de la défense des ressources naturelles.

conservation: **~ officer** ▶ **1692** *n* GB ≈ conservateur/-trice *m/f* des monuments historiques; **~ site** *n* site *m* protégé.

conservatism /kənˈsɜːvətɪzəm/ *n* gen, Pol conservatisme *m*.

conservative /kənˈsɜːvətɪv/ **I** *n* Pol conservateur/-trice *m/f*.
II *adj* **1** Pol [*person, society, policy*] conservateur/-trice; **2** (cautious) [*attitude*] prudent; [*estimate*] minimal; **at a ~ estimate** au bas mot; **3** [*taste, dress, style*] classique.

Conservative /kənˈsɜːvətɪv/ GB Pol **I** *n* Conservateur/-trice *m/f*.
II *adj* conservateur/-trice; **the ~ Party** le parti conservateur; **~ MP** député *m* conservateur; **to vote ~** voter pour le parti conservateur.

conservatoire /kənˈsɜːvətwɑː(r)/ *n* conservatoire *m*.

conservator /ˈkɒnsəveɪtə(r)/ ▶ **1692** *n* **1** (in museum) conservateur/-trice *m/f*; **2** US Jur tuteur/tutrice *m/f*.

conservatorship /ˈkɒnsəveɪtəʃɪp/ *n* US tutelle *f*.

conservatory /kənˈsɜːvətrɪ, US -tɔːrɪ/ *n* **1** (for plants) jardin *m* d'hiver; **2** US Mus conservatoire *m*.

conserve /kənˈsɜːv/ **I** *n* (jam) confiture *f*.
II *vtr* **1** (protect) protéger [*landscape, forest*]; sauvegarder [*wildlife*]; conserver [*remains, ruins*]; **2** (save up) économiser [*natural resources*]; garder [*moisture*]; ménager [*strength, energy*]; **3** Fin économiser [*cash, stocks*].

consider /kənˈsɪdə(r)/ **I** *vtr* **1** (give thought to, study) considérer [*alternatives, options, facts, proposal, question, beauty*]; examiner [*case, evidence, letter, problem*]; étudier [*offer*]; **to ~ how** réfléchir à la façon dont; **to ~ why** examiner les raisons pour lesquelles; **to ~ whether** décider si; **~ this** sachez que; **the jury is ~ing its verdict** le jury délibère; **2** (take into account, bear in mind) prendre [qch] en considération [*risk, cost, difficulty, matter*]; songer à [*person*]; faire attention à [*person's feelings, wishes*]; **when you ~ that** quand on songe que; **all things ~ed** tout compte fait; **3** (envisage, contemplate) envisager [*course of action, purchase*]; **to ~ doing** envisager de faire; **to ~ sb for a role** penser à qn pour un rôle; **she ~ed me for second prize** elle a pensé à moi pour le deuxième prix; **to ~ sb/sth as sth** penser à qn/qch comme qch; **4** (regard) **I ~ her (to be) a good teacher/choice** je pense que c'est un bon professeur/choix; **to ~ that** considérer or estimer que; **I ~ it my duty to warn him** j'estime de mon devoir de le prévenir; **to ~ sb/sth favourably** voir qn/qch sous un jour favorable; **~ the matter closed** considérez que l'affaire est close; **~ it done/forgotten/a deal** tiens-le pour fait/oublié/affaire conclue.
II *vi* réfléchir; **I need some time to ~** j'ai besoin d'un peu de temps pour réfléchir.
III considered *pp adj* [*answer, view, manner*] réfléchi; **it is my ~ed opinion that** c'est ma conviction que; **in my ~ed opinion** selon ma conviction.
IV *v refl* **to ~ oneself (to be) a writer/genius** se prendre pour pej or se considérer comme un écrivain/génie.

considerable /kənˈsɪdərəbl/ *adj* considérable; **at ~ expense** à un prix considérable; **to a ~ degree** ou **extent** dans une large mesure.

considerably /kənˈsɪdərəblɪ/ *adv* [*improve, vary, less, more*] considérablement.

considerate /kənˈsɪdərət/ *adj* [*person, nature*] attentionné; [*remark, behaviour, driver, motorist*] courtois; **to be ~ of sb's position/feelings/point of view** respecter la position/les sensibilités/les opinions de qn; **to be ~ towards sb** avoir des égards pour qn; **it was ~ of you to wait** c'était aimable à vous d'avoir attendu.

considerately /kənˈsɪdərətlɪ/ *adv* [*act, behave*] de manière attentionnée; **he ~ saved me a seat** il m'a aimablement gardé une place; **to behave ~ towards sb** avoir des égards pour qn.

consideration /kənˌsɪdə'reɪʃn/ *n* **1** (thought, deliberation) considération *f*, réflexion *f*; **after careful ~** après mûre réflexion; **to give ~ to sth** réfléchir à qch; **to give sth careful/serious ~** réfléchir longuement/sérieusement à qch; **to submit sth for sb's ~** soumettre qch à l'examen de qn; **~ is being given to...** on examine actuellement...; **further ~ will be given to...** on examinera de plus près...; **to take sth into ~** prendre qch en considération; **in ~ of** en considération de fml, compte tenu de; **to be under ~** [*matter*] être à l'étude; **she's under ~ for the job** on est en train d'étudier sa candidature; **2** (thoughtfulness, care) considération *f* (**for** envers); **to show ~** montrer de la considération; **to do sth out of ~** faire qch par considération; **with no ~ for others** sans aucune considération envers les autres; **3** (factor, thing to be considered) considération *f*; (concern) (objet *m* de) souci *m*; **commercial/political ~s** considérations commerciales/politiques; **it outweighs any ~ of cost/risk** cela l'emporte sur toute considération de coût/risque; **safety is the overriding ~** la sécurité constitue le souci dominant; **my family is my only ~** je ne me soucie que de ma famille; **4** (fee) **for a ~** moyennant finance; **for a small ~** moyennant une petite somme en contrepartie.

considering /kən'sɪdərɪŋ/ **I** *prep, conj* étant donné, compte tenu de; **it's not bad, ~ the price/how cheap it was** ce n'est pas mal, étant donné le prix/le peu que ça a coûté; **he did well, ~ (that) he was tired** étant donné sa fatigue, il s'en est bien sorti.
II○ *adv* tout compte fait; **it wasn't bad, ~** tout compte fait, ce n'était pas mal; **you did well, ~** tout compte fait, tu t'en es bien sorti.

consign /kən'saɪn/ *vtr* **1** (get rid of) reléguer (**to** à); **to ~ sth to the flames** livrer qch aux flammes; **2** (entrust) **to ~ sth to sb's care** confier qch aux soins de qn; **3** Comm (send) expédier [*goods*] (**to** à).

consignee /ˌkɒnsaɪ'niː/ *n* Comm, gen (of goods on consignment) dépositaire *mf*, destinataire *mf*.

consignment /kən'saɪnmənt/ *n* Comm (sending) expédition *f*; (goods) lot *m*, livraison *f*; **~ note** bordereau *m* d'expédition; **for ~** à expédier; **on ~** en dépôt.

consignor /'kən'saɪnə(r)/ *n* Comm expéditeur/-trice *m/f*.

consist /kən'sɪst/ *vi* **to ~ of** se composer de; **to ~ in** résider dans; **to ~ in doing** consister à faire.

consistency /kən'sɪstənsɪ/ *n* **1** (texture) consistance *f*; **2** (of view, policy) cohérence *f*; (of achievement) qualité *f* suivie.

consistent /kən'sɪstənt/ *adj* **1** [*growth, level, quality*] régulier/-ière; [*kindness, help, criticism etc*] constant; [*performance, recording*] homogène; [*sportsman, playing*] régulier/-ière; **2** (repeated) [*attempts, demands etc*] répété; **3** (logical) [*argument, position*] cohérent; [*basis, method*] systématique; **4 ~ with** en accord avec [*account, belief, decision etc*]; **she had injuries ~ with a fall** elle avait des blessures correspondant à une chute.

consistently /kən'sɪstəntlɪ/ *adv* (invariably) systématiquement, invariablement; (repeatedly) à maintes reprises.

consistory /kən'sɪstərɪ, US -tɔːrɪ/ *n* consistoire *m*.

consolation /ˌkɒnsə'leɪʃn/ *n* consolation *f* (**to** à); **~ prize** lit, fig prix *m* de consolation; **it's no ~ that the car is intact** ce n'est pas une consolation que la voiture soit intacte.

consolatory /kən'sɒlətərɪ, US -tɔːrɪ/ *adj* consolant; **a ~ offer** une offre en guise de consolation.

console I /'kɒnsəʊl/ *n* **1** (controls) (all contexts) console *f*; **2** (cabinet) meuble *m* (hi-fi, vidéo etc); **3** (table) console *f* also Archit.
II /kən'səʊl/ *vtr* consoler (**with** avec); **to ~ sb on** ou **for sth** consoler qn de qch.
III /kən'səʊl/ *v refl* **to ~ oneself** se consoler.

consolidate /kən'sɒlɪdeɪt/ **I** *vtr* **1** consolider [*knowledge, position*]; **2** US Sch regrouper [*schools*]; **3** Comm, Fin réunir [*resources*]; fusionner [*companies*].
II *vi* **1** (become stronger) s'affermir; **2** (unite) [*companies*] fusionner.
III consolidated *pp adj* **1** Fin consolidé; **~d fund** fonds *m* d'amortissement de la dette publique; **2** Jur **~d laws** codification *f* des lois; **3** US Sch **~d school** *école régionale regroupant les élèves des alentours*.

consolidation /kənˌsɒlɪ'deɪʃn/ *n* **1** (of knowledge, position) consolidation *f*; **2** Fin, Comm (of companies) fusion *f*.

consoling /kən'səʊlɪŋ/ *adj* consolant.

consols /'kɒnsəlz/ *npl* GB Fin consolidés *mpl*.

consommé /kən'sɒmeɪ/ *n* consommé *m*.

consonance /'kɒnsənəns/ *n* **1** sout (agreement) accord *m*; **in ~ with** en accord avec; **2** Literat, Mus consonance *f*.

consonant /'kɒnsənənt/ **I** *n* Ling consonne *f*.
II *adj* sout **1** (in agreement) en accord (**with** avec); **2** Mus harmonieux/-ieuse.

consonantal /ˌkɒnsə'næntl/ *adj* consonantique.

consonant shift *n* Ling mutation *f* consonantique.

consort I /'kɒnsɔːt/ *n* **1** (queen's) époux *m*; **the prince ~** le prince consort; **2**† (spouse) époux/épouse *m/f*; **3** Mus petit ensemble *m*.
II /kən'sɔːt/ *vi* sout **1** (socially) **to ~ with** fréquenter; **2** (be in keeping) **to ~ with** s'accorder avec.

consortium /kən'sɔːtɪəm/ *n* (*pl* **-tiums** ou **-tia**) Fin consortium *m*.

conspicuous /kən'spɪkjʊəs/ *adj* **1** (to the eye) [*feature, sign*] visible; [*garment*] voyant; **~ consumption** consommations *fpl* ostentatoires; **to be ~** se remarquer (**for** à cause de); **to make oneself ~** se faire remarquer; **to feel ~** avoir l'impression de détonner; **to be ~ by one's absence** iron briller par son absence; **in a ~ position** bien en évidence; **2** (unusual) [*success, gallantry*] remarquable; [*failure*] flagrant; **to be ~ for** être remarquable pour [*bravery, honesty, precision*]; **she was ~ for being** elle était remarquable par le fait qu'elle était; **a ~ lack of** iron un manque total de.

conspicuously /kən'spɪkjʊəslɪ/ *adv* [*placed*] bien en évidence; [*dressed*] de façon voyante; [*silent, empty, nervous*] remarquablement; **to be ~ absent** iron briller par son absence.

conspiracy /kən'spɪrəsɪ/ *n* conspiration *f* (**against** contre); **a ~ to do sth** une conspiration en vue de faire qch; **to enter into a ~** participer à or tremper dans une conspiration; **they are charged with ~ to murder** ils sont inculpés de complot pour meurtre; **a ~ of silence** une conspiration du silence.

conspirator /kən'spɪrətə(r)/ *n* conspirateur/-trice *m/f*.

conspiratorial /kənˌspɪrə'tɔːrɪəl/ *adj* [*glance, whisper, air*] entendu; [*meeting, discussion*] entre conspirateurs.

conspire /kən'spaɪə(r)/ *vi* **1** (plot) conspirer (**against** contre; **with** avec); **to ~ to do** conspirer en vue de faire; **2** (combine) **to ~ to do** [*circumstances*] conspirer à faire.

constable /'kʌnstəbl, US 'kɒn-/ ▶**1268** *n* GB Police (urban) agent *m* (de police); (rural) gendarme *m*.

constabulary /kən'stæbjʊlərɪ, US -lerɪ/ *n* GB police *f*.

constancy /'kɒnstənsɪ/ *n* (to person) constance *f* (**to** envers); (of will, belief) fermeté *f*.

constant /'kɒnstənt/ **I** *n* **1** gen facteur *m* constant (**in** de); **2** Math, Phys constante *f*.
II *adj* [*source, pressure, problem, protection, reminder, temptation, fear, threat*] permanent; [*care, growth, improvement, speed, temperature*] constant; [*demands, disputes, questions*] incessant; [*attempts, visits*] répété; [*companion*] éternel/-elle.

constantly /'kɒnstəntlɪ/ *adv* constamment.

constellation /ˌkɒnstə'leɪʃn/ *n* **1** Astron constellation *f*; **2** fig, littér (of celebrities) pléiade *f*.

consternation /ˌkɒnstə'neɪʃn/ *n* consternation *f*; **in ~** frappé de consternation; **to my/his etc ~** à ma/sa etc grande consternation.

constipate /'kɒnstɪpeɪt/ *vtr* constiper.

constipated /'kɒnstɪpeɪtɪd/ *adj* constipé.

constipation /ˌkɒnstɪ'peɪʃn/ ▶**1354** *n* constipation *f*; **to have ~** être constipé.

constituency /kən'stɪtjʊənsɪ/ *n* **1** Pol (district) circonscription *f* électorale; (voters) électeurs *mpl*; **~ party** GB section *f* locale du parti; **2** US Pol (supporters) groupe *m* de supporters.

constituent /kən'stɪtjʊənt/ **I** *n* **1** Pol électeur/-trice *m/f*; **2** gen (element) (of character) trait *m*; (of event, work of art) élément *m*; **3** Chem composant *m*; **4** Ling **~ analysis** analyse *f* en constituants.
II *adj* [*element, part*] constitutif/-ive; Pol [*assembly, member, power*] constituant.

constitute /'kɒnstɪtjuːt/ *vtr* **1** (represent) constituer [*threat, challenge, offence, revolution*]; **2** (make up) constituer [*percentage, figure*]; **3** (set up) créer [*committee, body*]; **4** (elect) nommer [*person*].

constitution /ˌkɒnstɪ'tjuːʃn, US -'tuːʃn/ *n* (all contexts) Constitution *f*; **a written ~** une Constitution écrite.

constitutional /ˌkɒnstɪ'tjuːʃənl, US -'tuː-/ **I**† *n* promenade *f*.
II *adj* **1** Pol [*amendment, law, crisis, reform, right, monarchy*] constitutionnel/-elle; [*action*] conforme à la loi; **2** (innate) [*physical characteristic*] constitutionnel/-elle; [*tendency, inability*] inné.

constitutionality /ˌkɒnstɪˌtjuːʃə'nælətɪ, US -tuː-/ *n* Jur constitutionnalité *f*.

constitutionally /ˌkɒnstɪ'tjuːʃənəlɪ, US -'tuː-/ *adv* **1** Pol (legally) constitutionnellement; **2** gen (physically) physiquement; (psychologically) par nature.

constitutive /'kɒnstɪtjuːtɪv, US -tuː-/ *adj* **1** Admin constituant; **2** Biol [*gene, mutation*] constitutif/-ive.

constrain /kən'streɪn/ sout **I** *vtr* **1** (compel) contraindre (**to do** à faire); **I am ~ed to ask you to do** je me vois dans l'obligation de vous demander de faire; **2** (limit) entraver [*research, development*].
II constrained *pp adj* [*smile*] contraint; [*silence, air*] gêné; [*atmosphere*] de gêne.

constraint /kən'streɪnt/ *n* sout **1** (compulsion) contrainte *f*; **to put a ~ on** imposer une contrainte à; **under ~** sous la contrainte; **you are under no ~** vous n'êtes en rien obligé; **2** (uneasiness) contrainte *f*.

constrict /kən'strɪkt/ **I** *vtr* **1** comprimer [*flow, blood vessel*]; gêner [*breathing, movement*]; **2** fig être une entrave pour [*person*].
II constricted *pp adj* [*voice*] étranglé; [*breathing*] gêné; [*space*] restreint; [*life*] étriqué.

constricting /kən'strɪktɪŋ/ *adj* [*garment*] serré; [*attitude*] restrictif/-ive; [*job, lifestyle*] contraignant.

constriction /kən'strɪkʃn/ *n* **1** (constraint) (of job, lifestyle etc) contrainte *f*; **a feeling of ~** un sentiment d'étouffement; **2** (of chest, throat) resserrement *m*; (of blood vessel) constriction *f*; **3** (by snake) étranglement *m*.

construct I /'kɒnstrʌkt/ *n* **1** sout, gen construction *f*; **2** Psych concept *m*.
II /kən'strʌkt/ *vtr* construire (**of** avec; **in** en).

construction /kən'strʌkʃn/ **I** *n* **1** (composition) construction *f*; **under ~** en construction; **of simple ~** construit de façon simple; **2** ¢ (also **~ industry**) bâtiment *m*; **to work in ~** ou **in the ~ industry**

travailler dans le bâtiment; **3** C (structure) construction *f*; **4** (interpretation) **to put a ~ on sth** donner une interprétation de qch; **5** Ling construction *f*.
II *modif* [*work, equipment, toy*] de construction.

constructional /kənˈstrʌkʃənl/ *adj* [*fault*] de construction.

construction: **~ engineer** ▶1692 *n* ingénieur *m* en génie civil; **~ paper** *n* papier *m* canson®; **~ site** *n* chantier *m*; **~ worker** ▶1692 *n* ouvrier/-ière *m/f* du bâtiment.

constructive /kənˈstrʌktɪv/ *n* **1** gen constructif/-ive; **2** Ind, Jur Admin **~ dismissal** fausse démission *f*, licenciement *m* implicite.

constructively /kənˈstrʌktɪvlɪ/ *adv* [*criticize, act*] de manière constructive.

constructor /kənˈstrʌktə(r)/ ▶1692 *n* constructeur/-trice *m/f*.

construe /kənˈstruː/ *vtr* **1** (interpret) interpréter [*remark, reaction, phrase*] (**as sth** comme qch); **wrongly ~d** mal interprété; **2**‡ Sch faire une analyse grammaticale de [*sentence*].

consul /ˈkɒnsl/ *n* Antiq, Pol consul *m*; **~ general** consul général; **the French ~** le consul de France.

consular /ˈkɒnsjʊlə(r), US -səl-/ *adj* consulaire.

consulate /ˈkɒnsjʊlət, US -səl-/ *n* consulat *m*.

consulship /ˈkɒnslʃɪp/ *n* consulat *m*.

consult /kənˈsʌlt/ **I** *vtr* **1** (refer to) consulter [*expert, document, dictionary*] (**about** sur); **2** (take account of) consulter [*person*]; **to ~ sb's interests** sout prendre en considération les intérêts de qn.
II *vi* (also **~ together**) s'entretenir (**about** sur); **to ~ with sb** s'entretenir avec qn.
III consulting *pres p adj* [*fees, service, work*] de conseil.

consultancy /kənˈsʌltənsɪ/ **I** *n* **1** Admin (also **~ firm**) cabinet-conseil *m*; **2** ¢ Admin (advice) conseils *mpl*; **to work in ~** travailler comme consultant; **3** GB Med (job) poste *m* de spécialiste (*dans un hôpital*).
II *modif* [*fees, service, work*] de conseil.

consultant /kənˈsʌltənt/ ▶1692 **I** *n* **1** gen, Admin (expert) consultant/-e *m/f*, conseiller/-ère *m/f* (**on, in** en; **to** de); **careers ~** conseiller/-ère *m/f* d'orientation professionnelle; **beauty ~** esthéticienne-conseil *f*; **legal ~** avocat-conseil/avocate-conseil *m/f*; **2** GB Med spécialiste *mf* (*attaché à un hôpital*).
II *modif* GB Med **~ obstetrician/psychiatrist** chef *m* du service d'obstétrique/de psychiatrie.

consultation /ˌkɒnslˈteɪʃn/ *n* **1** (meeting) (for advice) consultation *f* (**about** sur); (for discussion) entretien *m* (**about** sur); **to have a ~** ou **~s with sb** (for advice) conférer avec qn; (for discussion) s'entretenir avec qn; **2** ¢ (process) consultation *f* (**of** de); **after ~ with sb** après avoir consulté qn.

consultative /kənˈsʌltətɪv/ *adj* [*role, committee*] consultatif/-ive; **in a ~ capacity** à titre consultatif.

consult: **~ing engineer** ▶1692 *n* ingénieur-conseil *m*; **~ing hours** *npl* Med heures *fpl* de consultation; **~ing room** *n* Med cabinet *m*.

consumables /kənˈsjuːməblz, US -ˈsuːm-/ *npl* Comm consommables *mpl*.

consume /kənˈsjuːm, US -ˈsuːm-/ *vtr* **1** manger [*food*]; boire [*drink*]; [*animal*] dévorer [*prey*]; **2** (use up) consommer [*fuel, food, drink*]; absorber [*time*]; **this testing ~s a major share of the resources** une majeure partie des ressources est consacrée à ces tests; **3** (destroy) [*flames*] consumer [*building etc*]; [*illness*] ronger [*person*]; **4** (overwhelm) **to be ~d by** ou **with** être dévoré par [*envy*]; brûler de [*desire*]; être rongé par [*guilt*].

consumer /kənˈsjuːmə(r), US -ˈsuːm-/ *n* gen consommateur/-trice *m/f*; (of electricity, gas, etc) abonné/-e *m/f*.

consumer: **~ advice** *n* conseils *mpl* au consommateurs; **~ advice centre** *n* GB bureau *m* de défense du consommateur; **~ credit** *n* crédit *m* à la consommation; **~ demand** *n* demande *f* des consommateurs; **~ durables** *npl* biens *mpl* durables; **~ electronics** *npl* électronique *f* grand public; **~ goods** *npl* biens *mpl* de consommation; **~ group** *n* association *f* de consommateurs.

consumerism /kənˈsjuːmərɪzəm, US -ˈsuːm-/ *n* consumérisme *m*; **the excesses of ~** les excès de la société de consommation.

consumerist /kənˈsjuːmərɪst, US -ˈsuːm-/ péj *adj* [*society, culture*] de consommation.

consumer: **Consumer Price Index**, **CPI** *n* indice *m* des prix à la consommation; **~ products** *npl* produits *mpl* de consommation; **~ protection** *n* défense *f* du consommateur; **~ society** *n* société *f* de consommation; **~ spending** *n* dépenses *fpl* des ménages.

consuming /kənˈsjuːmɪŋ, US -suːm-/ *adj* [*passion*] dévorant; [*urge, desire*] brûlant; [*hatred*] insatiable.

consummate **I** /kənˈsʌmət/ *adj* sout parfait.
II /ˈkɒnsəmeɪt/ *vtr* sout consommer fml [*marriage*].

consummation /ˌkɒnsəˈmeɪʃn/ *n* sout (of marriage) consommation *f* fml; (of efforts) aboutissement *m*; (of desire) accomplissement *m*.

consumption /kənˈsʌmpʃn/ ▶1354 *n* **1** (of food, alcohol, fuel, goods) consommation *f*; **electricity ~**, **~ of electricity** la consommation d'électricité; **unfit for human ~** impropre à la consommation; **2**‡ Med (tuberculosis) tuberculose *f* (pulmonaire), consomption† *f*.

consumptive‡ /kənˈsʌmptɪv/ *n, adj* tuberculeux/-euse (*m/f*).

cont. *abrév écrite* = **continued**.

contact **I** /ˈkɒntækt/ *n* **1** (touch) lit or fig contact *m* (**between** entre; **with** avec); **direct ~** contact direct; **to be in/come in(to)/make ~** être en/entrer en/se mettre en contact; **to get in(to) ~** prendre contact; **to maintain/lose ~** garder/perdre contact; **to explode on ~** exploser au contact (**with** de); **to be in constant ~** être en rapports constants; **diplomatic/sporting/secret ~s** relations *fpl* diplomatiques/sportives/secrètes; **2** (by radar, radio) contact *m*; **to make/lose ~** établir/perdre contact; **to be in ~** être en contact; **3** (acquaintance) gen connaissance *f*; (professional) contact *m*; (for drugs, spy) contact *m*; **4** Elec contact *m*; **5** = **contact lens**; **6** Phot = **contact print**; **7** Med *personne ayant approché un malade contagieux*; **sexual ~** partenaire *mf* sexuel/-elle.
II /kənˈtækt, ˈkɒntækt/ *vtr* contacter, se mettre en rapport avec (**by** par); **he could not be ~ed** on n'a pas pu le contacter or se mettre en rapport avec lui.

contactable /kənˈtæktəbl, ˈkɒn-/ *adj* **she is not ~ by phone/at the moment** on ne peut pas la joindre par téléphone/en ce moment.

contact: **~ adhesive** *n* adhésif *m* de contact; **~ breaker** *n* disjoncteur *m*; **~ lens** *n* lentille *f* or verre *m* de contact; **~ print** *n* épreuve *f* par contact, planche *f* contact *inv*; **~ sport** *n* sport *m* de contact.

contagion /kənˈteɪdʒən/ *n* lit, fig contagion *f*.

contagious /kənˈteɪdʒəs/ *adj* Med, fig contagieux/-ieuse.

contain /kənˈteɪn/ **I** *vtr* **1** (hold) contenir [*amount, ingredients*]; contenir, comporter [*information, mistakes*]; **2** (curb) maîtriser [*blaze*]; enrayer [*epidemic*]; limiter [*costs, problem*]; canaliser [*strike, terrorism*]; **3** (within boundary) endiguer [*river*]; retenir [*flood*]; **4** (control) contenir [*grief, joy etc*]; **5** Mil contenir [*enemy, offensive*]; **6** Math être un multiple de.
II *v refl* **to ~ oneself** se contenir.

container /kənˈteɪnə(r)/ *n* **1** gen (for food, liquids) récipient *m*; (for plants) bac *m*; (skip, for waste) conteneur *m*; **plastic/glass ~** récipient *m* en plastique/en verre; **water ~** récipient *m* à eau; **2** Transp conteneur *m*.

container depot *n* entrepôt *m* de conteneurs.

containerization /kənˌteɪnəraɪˈzeɪʃn/ *n* (loading into containers) mise *f* en conteneur; (method of transport) conteneurisation *f*.

containerize /kənˈteɪnəraɪz/ *vtr* conteneuriser.

container: **~ lorry** *n* = **container truck**; **~ port** *n* terminal *m* à conteneurs; **~ ship** *n* porte-conteneurs *m inv*; **~ terminal** *n* terminal *m* à conteneurs; **~ transport** *n* transport *m* par conteneurs; **~ truck** *n* porte-conteneur *m*.

containment /kənˈteɪnmənt/ *n* US Pol Hist *politique de limitation de l'expansion du communisme*.

contaminate /kənˈtæmɪneɪt/ **I** *vtr* contaminer.
II contaminated *pp adj* contaminé.

contamination /kənˌtæmɪˈneɪʃn/ *n* gen, Ling contamination *f*.

contd *abrév écrite* = **continued**.

contemplate /ˈkɒntəmpleɪt/ **I** *vtr* **1** (consider deeply) réfléchir sur, contempler [*situation*]; **to ~ the day's events** réfléchir sur les événements de la journée; **2** (envisage) envisager [*option, prospect*]; **to ~ doing** envisager de faire; **it's too awful to ~** je préfère ne pas y penser; **3** (look at) contempler [*picture, scene*].
II *vi* méditer.

contemplation /ˌkɒntemˈpleɪʃn/ *n* **1** (deep thought) contemplation *f*; **to be deep** ou **lost in ~** être plongé dans ses pensées; **2** (looking) contemplation *f* (**of** de); **3** (expectation) **in ~ of the imminent disaster** en prévision du désastre imminent.

contemplative /kənˈtemplətɪv, ˈkɒntempleɪtɪv/ **I** *n* contemplatif/-ive *m/f*.
II *adj* [*person, mood*] songeur/-euse; Relig [*life, vocation, order*] contemplatif/-ive.

contemporaneity /kənˌtempərəˈniːətɪ/ *n* sout contemporanéité *f*.

contemporaneous /kənˌtempəˈreɪnɪəs/ *adj* contemporain (**with** de).

contemporaneously /kənˌtempəˈreɪnɪəslɪ/ *adv* en même temps (**with** que).

contemporary /kənˈtemprərɪ, US -pərerɪ/ **I** *n* contemporain/-e *m/f*; **he was a ~ of mine at university** nous étions à l'université à la même époque; **our contemporaries** les gens de notre âge.
II *adj* **1** (present-day) [*history, music, artist*] contemporain; (up-to-date) moderne; **2** (of same period) [*witness, style, documents*] de l'époque; [*account*] de la même époque; **to be ~ with** [*event*] coïncider avec.

contempt /kənˈtempt/ *n* mépris *m*; **to feel ~ for sb** éprouver du mépris pour qn; **his ~ for truth** son mépris de la vérité; **to hold sb/sth in ~** mépriser qn/qch, avoir du mépris pour qn/qch; **to be beneath ~** être en-dessous de tout.

contemptible /kənˈtemptəbl/ *adj* [*cowardice, person*] méprisable; **it was a really ~ thing to do** c'était en-dessous de tout que de faire cela.

contempt: **~ of congress** *n* US Pol outrage *m* au Congrès; **~ of court** *n* Jur outrage *m* à magistrat.

contemptuous /kənˈtemptjʊəs/ *adj* méprisant; **to be ~ of sth/sb** mépriser qch/qn.

contemptuously /kənˈtemptjʊəslɪ/ *adv* [*smile, say, treat*] avec mépris; [*behave*] de façon méprisante.

contend /kənˈtend/ **I** *vtr* soutenir (**that** que); **'to succeed,' she ~ed, 'we must…'** 'pour réussir,' affirma-t-elle, 'nous devons…'.

II *vi* **1 to ~ with** affronter; **he's got a lot/enough to ~ with** il a beaucoup/assez de problèmes; **2** (compete) **she was ~ing with him for first place** elle lui disputait la première place; **two teams are ~ing for the cup** deux équipes se disputent la coupe.

contender /kən'tendə(r)/ *n* **1** Sport concurrent/-e *m/f*; **the top ~** le favori/la favorite *m/f*; **the main ~s** les principaux concurrents; **she's a ~ for first place** elle est bien placée pour gagner; **there are three ~s for first place** trois personnes se disputent la première place; **2** (for job, political post) candidat/-e *m/f* (**for** à); **is he a serious ~?** est-ce que c'est un candidat sérieux?

content I *n* **1** /'kɒntent/ (relative quantity) teneur *f*; **the fat/vitamin ~** la teneur en matières grasses/en vitamines; **low/high lead ~** (in soil, metal etc) faible/forte teneur en plomb; **to have a low/high fat ~** être pauvre/riche en matières grasses; **2** /'kɒntent/ (meaning) (of essay, article) fond *m*, matière *f*; **form and ~** Literat le fond et la forme; **3** /kən'tent/ (happiness) contentement *m*.
II contents /'kɒntents/ *npl* **1** (of jar, bag) contenu *m*; (of house, for insurance) biens *mpl* mobiliers; **he emptied the drawer of its ~s** il a vidé le tiroir de tout ce qu'il contenait; **2** (of book, file) **list** ou **table of ~s** table *f* des matières; **what were the ~s of the letter?** que contenait cette lettre?
III /kən'tent/ *adj* satisfait (**with** de); **to be ~ to do** se contenter de faire; **not ~ with doing** non content de faire; **she's ~ with her life** sa vie lui convient; **he's ~ with what he has** il se contente de ce qu'il a; **I'm quite ~ here** je suis bien ici.
IV /kən'tent/ *vtr* (please) contenter; **to be easily ~ed** se contenter de peu.
V /kən'tent/ *v refl* **to ~ oneself with sth/with doing** se contenter de qch/de faire.
IDIOMS **to do sth to one's heart's ~** faire qch autant que l'on veut.

contented /kən'tentɪd/ *adj* [*person*] content (**with** de); [*feeling*] de bien-être; **he gave a ~ sigh** il a poussé un soupir de bien-être; **he's a ~ child** c'est un enfant heureux.

contentedly /kən'tentɪdlɪ/ *adv* [*sigh, smile*] de bien-être; [*read*] d'un air content.

contention /kən'tenʃn/ *n* sout **1** (opinion) assertion *f*; **it is my ~ that** je soutiens que; **2** (dispute) dispute *f*, différend *m* (**about** au sujet de); **matter** ou **point of ~** sujet *m* de dispute; **3** gen, Sport (competition) compétition *f*; **to be in ~** être en compétition.

contentious /kən'tenʃəs/ *adj* **1** [*issue, subject*] controversé; **to hold ~ views on sth** avoir des vues discutables sur qch; **2** [*person, group*] sout discuteur/-euse.

contentment /kən'tentmənt/ *n* contentement *m*; **with ~** [*sigh, smile*] de bien-être; **there was a look of ~ on his face** il avait l'air satisfait.

conterminous /kɒn'tɜːmɪnəs/ *adj* sout [*country, state*] limitrophe (**with** de); [*boundaries*] qui coïncident.

contest I /'kɒntest/ *n* **1** (competition) concours *m*; **fishing ~** concours *m* de pêche; **sports ~** rencontre *f* sportive; **to enter/hold a ~** prendre part à/organiser un concours; **it's no ~** c'est couru○ d'avance; **2** (struggle) lutte *f* (**with** avec; **between** entre); **3** (in election) **the presidential ~** la course à la présidence.
II /kən'test/ *vtr* **1** (object to) contester [*decision, point, result*]; Jur contester [*will*]; Jur attaquer [*decision*]; **2** (compete for) Sport disputer [*match*]; **a strongly ~ed seat** Pol un siège âprement disputé; **to ~ an election** Pol se présenter à une élection.

contestant /kən'testənt/ *n* (in competition, game) concurrent/-e *m/f*; (in fight) adversaire *mf*; (for job, in election) candidat/-e *m/f*.

contestation /ˌkɒntes'teɪʃn/ *n* sout contestation *f*.

context /'kɒntekst/ *n* gen, Ling contexte *m*; **in ~** [*study, understand*] dans son contexte; **out of ~** [*quote, examine*] hors contexte; **to put sth into ~** replacer qch dans son contexte.

contextual /kən'tekstʃʊəl/ *adj* contextuel/-elle.

contiguous /kən'tɪgjʊəs/ *adj* sout contigu/-uë (**to, with** à).

continence /'kɒntɪnəns/ *n* sout continence *f* fml.

continent /'kɒntɪnənt/ **I** *n* (land mass) continent *m*; **the Continent** GB l'Europe *f* continentale; **on the Continent** GB en Europe continentale.
II *adj* **1** Med ne souffrant pas d'incontinence; **2** (sexually) sout continent fml.

continental /ˌkɒntɪ'nentl/ **I** *n* Européen/-éenne *m/f* du continent.
II *modif* **1** Geog [*vegetation, climate*] continental; **2** GB [*universities, philosophy*] d'Europe continentale; **~ car** voiture *f* fabriquée en Europe continentale; **~ holiday** vacances *fpl* en Europe continentale.
IDIOMS **it's not worth a ~○** US ça ne vaut pas un sou.

continental: **~ breakfast** *n* petit déjeuner *m* (*avec café, pain, beurre et confiture*); **Continental Divide** *n* US ligne *f* de partage des eaux (dans les montagnes Rocheuses); **~ drift** *n* dérive *f* des continents; **Continental Europe** *pr n* Europe *f* continentale; **~ quilt** GB *n* couette *f*; **~ shelf** *n* plateau *m* continental.

contingency /kən'tɪndʒənsɪ/ *n* **1** gen imprévu *m*; **to provide for** ou **be prepared for contingencies** parer d'avance aux imprévus; **to cover the same contingencies** Insur couvrir les mêmes risques; **2** Philos contingence *f*.

contingency: **~ fund** *n* fonds *m* de secours; **~ plan** *n* plan *m* de réserve; **~ planning** *n* établissement *m* de plans de réserve; **~ reserve** *n* Fin réserves *fpl* de secours.

contingent /kən'tɪndʒənt/ **I** *n* gen, Mil, Philos contingent *m*.
II *adj* **1** (fortuitous) contingent; **2** sout **to be ~ on** ou **upon** dépendre de.

continual /kən'tɪnjʊəl/ *adj* continuel/-elle.

continually /kən'tɪnjʊəlɪ/ *adv* continuellement.

continuance /kən'tɪnjʊəns/ *n* **1** (of war, regime) continuation *f*; **2** (of species) continuité *f*; **3** US Jur ajournement *m*.

continuant /kən'tɪnjʊənt/ *adj* continu.

continuation /kənˌtɪnjʊ'eɪʃn/ *n* **1** (of situation, process) continuation *f*; **2** (resumption) continuation *f*, reprise *f*; **3** (in book) suite *f*; (of contract) prolongation *f*; (of route) prolongement *m*; **4** GB Fin report *m*.

continue /kən'tɪnjuː/ **I** *vtr* **1** continuer, poursuivre [*career, studies, enquiry, TV series*]; **2** (resume) continuer; **'to be ~d'** (in film) 'à suivre'; **'~d overleaf'** 'suite page suivante'; **'if I may ~'** iron 'si vous me permettez de continuer'; **'what's more,' she ~d** 'de plus,' reprit-elle; **3** continuer, poursuivre [*journey*]; **4** (preserve) maintenir [*tradition, culture, measures, standards*].
II *vi* **1** [*noise, weather, debate, strike, film*] se poursuivre; **the trial ~s** le procès se poursuit; **repair work is continuing on** les travaux se poursuivent sur; **2** (keep on) continuer (**doing, to do** à or de faire); **it ~d raining** ou **to rain** il a continué à or de pleuvoir; **3** [*person, route*] continuer; **he ~d across/down the street** il a continué de traverser/descendre la rue; **4** (in career, role) rester (**in** dans); **she will ~ as minister** elle restera ministre; **5** (in speech) poursuivre; **he ~d by citing** (in debate) il a poursuivi en citant; **6 to ~ with** continuer, poursuivre [*task, duties, treatment*]; **to ~ with the ironing** continuer de repasser.
III continuing *pres p adj* [*advance, trend, effort, debate*] continuel/-elle; **on a continuing basis** de façon permanente.

continuity /ˌkɒntɪ'njuːɪtɪ/ *n* **1** continuité *f*; **to provide ~ of services** assurer la continuité des services; **2** Cin, TV (flow) continuité *f*; **3** Cin (continuous projection) projection *f* permanente.

continuity: **~ announcer** ▶ **1692** *n* speaker/speakerine *m/f*; **~ girl** ▶ **1692** *n* scripte *f*; **~ man** ▶ **1692** *n* scripte *m*.

continuo /kən'tɪnjʊəʊ/ *n* (*pl* **-os**) Mus continuo *m*.

continuous /kən'tɪnjʊəs/ *adj* **1** [*growth, flow, decline*] continu; [*love, care*] constant; [*line, surface*] ininterrompu; [*noise*] continu; **~ assessment** GB Sch, Univ contrôle *m* continu; **~ performance** Cin cinéma *m* permanent; **2** Ling [*tense*] progressif/-ive; **it's in the present ~** c'est à la forme progressive du présent; **3** Biol [*gene*] continu.

continuously /kən'tɪnjʊəslɪ/ *adv* **1** (without a break) [*sing, talk*] sans interruption; [*breathe*] de façon continue; **2** (repeatedly) continuellement.

continuum /kən'tɪnjʊəm/ *n* (*pl* **-nuums** ou **-nua**) continuum *m*; **time-space ~** continuum espace-temps.

contort /kən'tɔːt/ **I** *vtr* **1** tordre [*limbs*]; **to ~ one's body** se contortionner; **his features were ~ed with rage** son visage était déformé par la colère; **2** (distort) déformer [*message, truth*].
II *vi* [*face, features, mouth*] se crisper.

contortion /kən'tɔːʃn/ *n* contorsion *f*.

contortionist /kən'tɔːʃənɪst/ *n* contorsionniste *m*.

contour /'kɒntʊə(r)/ *n* **1** (outline) contour *m*; **2** Geog = **contour line**.

contour: **~ line** *n* courbe *f* hypsométrique or de niveau; **~ map** *n* carte *f* hypsométrique.

contra /'kɒntrə/ **I** *n* (soldier) Contra *m*.
II *modif* **~ rebels** Contras *mpl*; **the ~ army** la Contra.

contraband /'kɒntrəbænd/ **I** *n* contrebande *f*.
II *modif* [*perfume, petrol*] de contrebande.

contrabass /ˌkɒntrə'beɪs/ ▶ **1481** *n* Mus contrebasse *f*.

contrabassoon /ˌkɒntrəbə'suːn/ ▶ **1481** *n* Mus contrebasson *m*.

contraception /ˌkɒntrə'sepʃn/ *n* contraception *f*; **to practise ~** employer un moyen de contraception.

contraceptive /ˌkɒntrə'septɪv/ **I** *n* contraceptif *m*.
II *adj* [*method*] contraceptif/-ive; **~ device** contraceptif *m*.

contract I /'kɒntrækt/ *n* **1** Admin, Jur (agreement) contrat *m* (**for** pour; **with** avec); **employment ~**, **~ of employment** contrat *m* de travail; **a two-year ~** un contrat de deux ans; **to enter into a ~ with** passer un contrat avec; **to be on a ~** être sous contrat; **to be under ~ with** être sous contrat avec; **to be under ~ to** travailler sous contrat avec; **to be out of ~** être libre de tout contrat; **2** Comm (tender) contrat *m*; **to win/lose a ~** remporter/perdre un contrat; **to award a ~ to** octroyer un contrat à; **to place a ~ for sth with** octroyer un contrat pour qch à; **a ~ to maintain** ou **for the maintenance of** un contrat d'entretien de; **to do work under ~** faire un travail par or sur contrat; **to put work out to ~** donner un travail en sous-traitance; **3○** (for assassination) **to put out a ~ on** payer un tueur à gages pour abattre [*person*]; **there's a ~ out on him** un tueur a été engagé pour l'abattre; **4** Games (in bridge) contrat *m*.
II /'kɒntrækt/ *modif* [*labour, worker*] contractuel/-elle; **the work is done on a ~ basis** le travail est effectué en sous-traitance.
III /kən'trækt/ *vtr* **1** Med (develop) contracter [*virus, disease*] (**from** par le contact avec); **2** Jur (arrange) contracter [*marriage, alliance, debt, duty, loan*]; **3** Comm, Jur **to be ~ed to**

do être tenu par contrat de faire; **4** (tighten) contracter [*muscles*].

IV /kən'trækt/ *vi* **1** Comm, Jur (undertake) **to ~ to do** s'engager par contrat à faire; **to ~ with sb to do** passer un contrat avec qn pour faire; **2** (shrink) [*wood, metal*] se contracter; [*power, influence, support, funds, market*] diminuer; **3** Med, Physiol se contracter.

■ **contract into** GB: **~ into** [**sth**] souscrire à [*group, scheme*].

■ **contract out** GB: ¶ **~ out** Fin, Jur renoncer par contrat; **to ~ out of** se retirer de [*scheme*]; ¶ **~ out** [**sth**], **~** [**sth**] **out** donner [qch] en sous-traitance [*building maintenance, work*] (**to** à).

contract: **~ agreement** *n* contrat *m*; **~ bridge** ▶ 1282 *n* Games bridge *m* contrat; **~ cleaners** *npl* entreprise *f* de nettoyage.

contractile /kən'træktaɪl, US -tl/ *adj* contractile.

contraction /kən'trækʃn/ *n* **1** (shrinkage) (of metal, wood) contraction *f*; (of industry, market, sector) réduction *f*; **2** Med, Physiol (muscular) contraction *f*; **the ~s have started** les contractions ont commencé; **3** Ling contraction *f*.

contract killer *n* tueur/-euse *m/f* à gages.

contractor /kən'træktə(r)/ ▶ 1692 *n* **1** (business) (from private sector) entrepreneur/-euse *m/f*; **defence ~** fournisseur *m* de l'armée; **2** (worker) contractuel/-elle *m/f*; **3** Jur (party) partie *f* contractante; **4** Games (in bridge) demandeur/-euse *m/f*.

contractual /kən'træktʃʊəl/ *adj* contractuel/-elle.

contractually /kən'træktʃʊəlɪ/ *adv* contractuellement; **to be ~ bound to do** être obligé par contrat de faire.

contract: **~ work** *n* prestation *f* de service; **~ worker** *n* contractuel/-elle *m/f*.

contradict /ˌkɒntrə'dɪkt/ **I** *vtr* contredire [*statement, person*]; **all the reports ~ each other** tous les rapports se contredisent.

II *vi* contredire; **don't ~!** ne me contredis pas!

contradiction /ˌkɒntrə'dɪkʃn/ *n* contradiction *f* (**between** entre); **to be in ~ with** être en contradiction avec; **it's a ~ in terms!** c'est une contradiction criante!

contradictory /ˌkɒntrə'dɪktərɪ/ *adj* [*statement, ideas, wishes*] (intrinsically) contradictoire; [*idea, wishes*] (to something else) opposé (**to** à).

contradistinction /ˌkɒntrədɪ'stɪŋkʃn/ *n* sout distinction *f*; **in ~ to** en contraste avec.

contraflow /'kɒntrəfləʊ/ GB **I** *n* circulation *f* à sens alterné.

II *modif* [*lane, traffic*] à sens alterné; **~ system** système *m* de circulation à sens alterné.

contraindicated /ˌkɒntrə'ɪndɪkeɪtɪd/ *adj* contre-indiqué.

contraindication /ˌkɒntrəɪndɪ'keɪʃn/ *n* contre-indication *f* (**against** à).

contralto /kən'træltəʊ/ ▶ 1868 **I** *n* (*pl* **-tos** ou **-ti**) **1** (voice) contralto *m*; **2** (singer) contralto *mf*.

II *adj* [*voice*] de contralto; [*solo*] pour contralto.

contraption○ /kən'træpʃn/ *n* péj ou hum (machine) engin○ *m*; (device) machin○ *m*.

contrapuntal /ˌkɒntrə'pʌntl/ *adj* [*style, piece*] en contrepoint.

contrarily /'kɒntreərɪlɪ/ *adv* [*behave, act, say*] par esprit de contradiction.

contrariness /'kɒntreərɪnɪs/ *n* esprit *m* de contrariété; **out of sheer ~** par pur esprit de contrariété.

contrariwise /'kɒntrərɪwaɪz, US -trerɪ/ *adv* **1** (conversely) inversement; **2** (in the opposite direction) en sens inverse.

contrary /'kɒntrərɪ, US -trerɪ/ **I** *n* contraire *m*; **the ~ is the case** c'est le contraire qui est vrai; **quite the ~** bien au contraire; **on the ~** (bien) au contraire; **despite views/claims to the ~** contrairement à ce que certains pensent/disent; **unless there is evidence to the ~** à moins qu'il n'y ait une preuve du contraire; **no-one said anything to the ~** personne n'a dit le contraire; **unless you hear anything to the ~** sauf contrordre.

II *adj* **1** [*idea, view*] contraire; **to be ~ to** [*activity, proposal, opinion, measure*] être contraire à; **2** [*direction, movement*] contraire (**to** à); **3** /kən'treərɪ/ [*person*] contrariant.

III contrary to *prep phr* contrairement à; **~ to popular belief/to rumours** (in spite of) contrairement à ce que l'on peut croire/à la rumeur; **~ to expectations** contre toute attente.

contrast I /'kɒntrɑːst, US -træst/ *n* **1** (difference) contraste *m* (**between** entre; **with** avec); **in ~ to sth, by ~ with sth** par contraste avec qch; **in ~ to sb** à la différence de qn; **to be a ~ to** ou **with** présenter un contraste avec [*thing, event*]; **by** ou **in ~** par contre; **2** (opposition) contraste *m* (**between** entre; **with sth** avec qch); **in ~ to** par opposition à; **3** Phot, TV contraste *m*.

II /kən'trɑːst, US -'træst/ *vtr* **to ~ X with Y** faire ressortir le contraste (qui existe) entre X et Y.

III *vi* contraster (**with** avec).

IV contrasting *adj* [*examples*] opposé; [*colour, material*] contrasté; [*view, landscape*] riche en contrastes; [*views, opinions*] très différents.

contrastive /kən'trɑːstɪv, US -'træst-/ *adj* contrastif/-ive.

contravene /ˌkɒntrə'viːn/ *vtr* sout **1** enfreindre [*law, ban*]; **to ~ article 15** enfreindre les termes de l'article 15; **2** contredire [*theory, argument*].

contravention /ˌkɒntrə'venʃn/ *n* sout infraction *f* (**of** à); **in ~ of** en violation de [*rule, law*].

contribute /kən'trɪbjuːt/ **I** *vtr* **1** Insur, Tax verser [*sum, bonus, percentage of salary*] (**to** à); financer [*costs, expenses*]; **2** (to gift, charity) donner (**to** à; **towards** pour); **3** Comm, Fin contribuer; **to ~ £5m** contribuer pour 5 millions de livres; **4** (to project, undertaking) apporter [*ideas, experience*] (**to** à); **he ~s nothing to discussions** il n'apporte rien aux discussions; **they have much to ~** ils peuvent beaucoup apporter; **5** Journ, Radio écrire [*article, column*] (**to** pour).

II *vi* **1** (be a factor in) **to ~ to** ou **towards** contribuer à [*change, awareness, productivity, decline, well-being*]; **2** (to community life, company expansion, research) participer (**to** à); **an opportunity to ~** une occasion pour participer; **3** Insur, Tax **to ~ to** participer financièrement à [*maintenance of facilities, services*]; cotiser à [*pension fund, insurance scheme*]; **4** (to charity, gift) donner (de l'argent) (**to** à); (to campaign, orchestra) participer financièrement (**to** à); **would you like to ~?** (for gift) voulez-vous participer?; **5** Journ, Radio collaborer (**to** à).

contribution /ˌkɒntrɪ'bjuːʃn/ *n* **1** (to tax, pension) contribution *f* (**towards** à); Insur cotisation *f* (**towards, to** auprès de); **we'd like you to make some ~** (payment) nous aimerions que vous participiez financièrement; **2** (to charity, campaign) don *m*; **to make a ~** faire un don (**to** à); **'all ~s gratefully received'** 'merci d'avance pour vos dons'; **3** (role played) **sb's ~ to** le rôle que qn a joué dans [*success, undertaking, decline, expansion*]; ce que qn a apporté à [*science, sport, art form*]; **you have a ~ to make** vous avez un rôle à jouer; **his outstanding ~ to politics** sa participation marquante à la vie politique; **a pathetic ~** (by team, performer) une prestation lamentable; **4** Comm (to profits, costs) contribution *f*; **5** Radio, TV participation *f*; Journ article *m*; **with ~s from** avec la collaboration de.

contributor /kən'trɪbjʊtə(r)/ *n* **1** (to charity) donateur/-trice *m/f*; **2** (in discussion) participant/-e *m/f*; **3** (to magazine, book) collaborateur/-trice *m/f*; **4** (cause) facteur *m* (**to** de).

contributory /kən'trɪbjʊtərɪ, US -tɔːrɪ/ *adj* **1 to be ~ to** [*success, failure*] contribuer à; **to be a ~ cause** être partiellement responsable (**of** de); **~ negligence** Jur *faute de la victime entraînant un partage de la responsabilité*; **a ~ factor in** un facteur de; **2 ~ pension scheme** GB ou **plan** US plan *m* de retraite (*fondé sur la participation des employés*).

con trick /kɒn/ *n* escroquerie *f*, duperie *f*.

contrite /'kɒntraɪt/ *adj* sout [*person, expression*] contrit.

contritely /kən'traɪtlɪ/ *adv* d'un air contrit.

contrition /kən'trɪʃn/ *n* sout **1** (remorse) remords *m*; **2** Relig contrition *f*.

contrivance /kən'traɪvəns/ *n* sout **1** (contraption) engin *m*; **2** (ploy) stratagème *m*; **3** (ingenuity) ingéniosité *f*.

contrive /kən'traɪv/ *vtr* **1** (arrange) organiser [*meeting, event*]; **to ~ to do sth** sout parvenir à faire qch; hum trouver moyen de faire qch hum; **2** (invent) fabriquer (avec ingéniosité) [*machine, device*]; inventer [*play, plot*]; créer [*costume, dress*].

contrived /kən'traɪvd/ *adj* pej **1** [*incident, meeting*] manigancé; **2** (forced) [*plot, ending*] tiré par les cheveux; **3** (artificial) [*style, effect, behaviour*] étudié.

control /kən'trəʊl/ **I** *n* **1** ¢ (domination) (of animals, children, crowd, country, organization, party, situation) contrôle *m* (**of** de); (of investigation, operation, project) direction *f* (**of** de); (of others' behaviour) influence *f* (**over** sur); (of life, fate) maîtrise *f* (**of, over** de); (of disease, pests, social problem) lutte *f* (**of** contre); **state ~** contrôle *m* de l'État; **to be in ~ of** contrôler [*territory, town*]; diriger [*operation, organization, project*]; maîtriser [*problem*]; **to have ~ over** contrôler [*territory, town*]; avoir du pouvoir sur [*animals, crowd, children, others' behaviour*]; maîtriser [*fate, life*]; **to take ~ of** prendre le contrôle de [*territory, town*]; prendre la direction de [*operation, organization, project*]; prendre [qch] en main [*situation*]; **to be under sb's ~, to be under the ~ of sb** [*person*] être sous la direction de qn; [*army, government, organization, party*] être sous le contrôle de qn; **to be under ~** [*fire, problem, riot, situation*] être maîtrisé; **is the situation under ~?** est-ce que nous maîtrisons la situation?; **everything's under ~** tout va bien; **to bring** ou **get** ou **keep** [**sth**] **under ~** maîtriser [*animals, crowd, fire, problem, riot*]; discipliner [*hair*]; **to be out of ~** [*animals, children, crowd, riot*] être déchaîné; [*fire*] ne plus être maîtrisable; **the situation is out of ~** la situation est devenue incontrôlable; **to let sth get out of ~, to lose ~ of sth** perdre le contrôle de qch; **to be beyond** ou **outside sb's ~** [*animal, child*] échapper au contrôle de qn; **the situation is beyond ~** la situation échappe à tout contrôle; **due to circumstances beyond our ~** pour des raisons indépendantes de notre volonté; **2** ¢ (restraint) (of self, appetite, bodily function, emotion, urge) maîtrise *f*; **to have** ou **exercise ~ over sth** maîtriser qch; **to keep ~ of oneself, to be in ~ of oneself** se maîtriser; **to lose ~ (of oneself)** perdre le contrôle (de soi); **3** ¢ (physical mastery) (of vehicle, machine, ball) contrôle *m*; (of body, process, system) maîtrise *f*; **to be in ~ of** avoir le contrôle de; **to keep/lose ~ of a car** garder/perdre le contrôle d'une voiture; **to take ~** (of car) prendre le volant; (of plane) prendre les commandes; **his car went out of ~** il a perdu le contrôle de son véhicule; **4** (lever, switch etc) (*souvent pl*) (on vehicle, equipment) commande *f*; (on TV) bouton *m* de réglage; **brightness/volume ~** TV bouton *m* de réglage de luminosité/du son; **to be at the ~s** être aux commandes; **5** Admin, Econ (regulation) contrôle *m* (**on** de); **cost/immi-**

gration ~ contrôle *m* des coûts/de l'immigration; **6** Sci (in experiment) contrôle *m*.
II *modif* [*button, knob, switch*] de commande.
III *vtr* (*p prés etc* **-ll-**) **1** (dominate) dominer [*council, government, market, organization, situation*]; contrôler [*territory, town*]; diriger [*air traffic, investigation, operation, project*]; régler [*road traffic*]; s'emparer de [*mind*]; Fin [*shareholder*] être majoritaire dans [*company*]; **2** (discipline) maîtriser [*person, animal, crowd, urge, bodily function, temper, voice, pain, inflation, unemployment, riot, fire, pests*]; endiguer [*disease, epidemic*]; dominer [*emotion, nerves, impulse*]; retenir [*laughter, tears*]; commander à [*limbs*]; discipliner [*hair*]; **3** (operate) commander [*machine, equipment, lever, cursor, movement, process, system*]; manœuvrer [*boat, vehicle*]; piloter [*plane*]; contrôler [*ball*]; **4** (regulate) régler [*speed, pressure, intensity, volume, temperature*]; réglementer [*trade, import, export*]; contrôler [*immigration, prices, wages*]; régulariser [*blood pressure*]; **5** (check) contrôler [*quality*]; vérifier [*accounts*]; **6** Sci comparer [*experimental material*] (**against** à).
IV *v refl* (*p prés etc* **-ll-**) **to ~ oneself** se contrôler.

control: **~ column** *n* Aviat manche *m* à balai; **~ experiment** *n* test *m* de contrôle; **~ group** *n* groupe *m* témoin; **~ key** *n* Comput touche *f* de contrôle.

controllable /kən'trəʊləbl/ *adj* contrôlable; [*vehicle*] manœuvrable.

controlled /kən'trəʊld/ I *adj* lit [*explosion, landing, skid*] contrôlé; [*person, expression*] impassible; [*voice*] calme; [*economy*] dirigé; [*performance*] maîtrisé; **manually/electronically ~** contrôlé manuellement/électroniquement; **under ~ conditions** Sci sous contrôle; **~ drug** Pharm ≈ médicament inscrit au tableau B.
II **-controlled** (*dans composés*) **Conservative/Labour-~** dominé par les Conservateurs/les Travaillistes; **computer-~** commandé par ordinateur.

controller /kən'trəʊlə(r)/ *n* **1** gen, Radio, TV directeur/-trice *m/f*; **2** Comm, Fin planificateur/-trice *m/f*; **3** (machine) contrôleur *m*.

controlling /kən'trəʊlɪŋ/ *adj* **1** [*authority, group, organization*] de contrôle; [*factor*] décisif/-ive; **~ power** contrôle *m*; **2** Fin **~ interest**, **~ share**, **~ stake** majorité *f* de contrôle.

control: **~ menu** *n* Comput menu *m* système; **~ panel** *n* (for plane, car) tableau *m* de bord; (on machine) tableau *m* de contrôle; (on television) (panneau *m* de) commandes *fpl*; **~ point** *n* Sport point *m* de contrôle; **~ room** *n* poste *m* de commande; Radio, TV (salle *f* de) régie *f*; **~ tower** *n* Aviat tour *f* de contrôle.

controversial /ˌkɒntrə'vɜːʃl/ *adj* **1** [*area, decision, plan, law, film*] (criticized) controversé; (open to criticism) discutable; **2** [*person, group*] (much discussed) controversé; (dubious) douteux/-euse.

controversially /ˌkɒntrə'vɜːʃəlɪ/ *adv* de façon controversée.

controversy /'kɒntrəvɜːsɪ, kən'trɒvəsɪ/ *n* controverse *f* (**about**, **over** sur; **between** entre); **the extradition ~** la controverse sur l'extradition; **to arouse bitter ~** provoquer une vive controverse; **to be the subject of much ~** soulever beaucoup de controverses.

controvert /ˌkɒntrə'vɜːt/ *vtr* sout **1** réfuter [*theory, findings*]; **2** mettre en question [*point of view*].

contusion /kən'tjuːʒn, US -'tuː-/ *n* Med contusion *f* (**to** à).

conundrum /kə'nʌndrəm/ *n* énigme *f*.

conurbation /ˌkɒnɜː'beɪʃn/ *n* conurbation *f*.

convalesce /ˌkɒnvə'les/ *vi* se remettre; **he's convalescing** il est en convalescence.

convalescence /ˌkɒnvə'lesns/ *n* (**period of**) **~** convalescence *f*.

convalescent /ˌkɒnvə'lesnt/ I *n* convalescent/-e *m/f*.
II *modif* [*leave, home*] de convalescence; [*ward*] des convalescents; **during his ~ stay** pendant sa convalescence.
III *adj* [*person*] convalescent.

convection /kən'vekʃn/ I *n* convection *f*.
II *modif* [*current*] de convection; [*heating*] par convecteurs; **~ heater** convecteur *m*.

convector (**heater**) /kən'vektə hiːtə(r)/ *n* convecteur *m*.

convene /kən'viːn/ I *vtr* organiser [*meeting*]; convoquer [*group*].
II *vi* se réunir.

convener /kən'viːnə(r)/ *n* **1** (organizer) organisateur/-trice *m/f* (d'une réunion); (chairperson) président/-e *m/f*; **2** GB Mgmt délégué/-e *m/f* syndical/-e.

convenience /kən'viːnɪəns/ *n* **1** ¢ (advantage) avantage *m* (**of doing** de faire); **the ~ of** les avantages de [*lifestyle, work, practice, method of payment*]; la commodité de [*instant food, electrical device, local shop, garment*]; **the comfort and ~ of modern tourism** le confort et les avantages du tourisme moderne; **for** (**the sake of**) **~** pour raisons de commodité; **for his/our etc ~** pour sa/notre etc convenance; **at your ~** (when it suits) quand cela vous conviendra; **at your earliest ~** Comm dès que cela vous sera possible; **2** (practical feature, device) avantage *m*; **'modern ~s'** (in ad) 'tout confort'; **3** GB sout (toilet) toilettes *fpl*.

convenience foods *npl* plats *mpl* (tout) préparés; (frozen) surgelés *mpl*; (tinned) conserves *fpl*.

convenience store *n* épicerie *f* (*ouverte tard le soir*).

convenient /kən'viːnɪənt/ *adj* **1** (suitable) [*place, date, time, arrangement*] commode; **now is not a very ~ time** ce n'est pas vraiment le moment maintenant; **to be ~ for sb** convenir à qn; **I hope this is ~ (for you)** j'espère que cela ne vous dérange pas; **to be ~ for sb to do** convenir à qn de faire; **when would be ~ for you to come?** quand est-ce que cela vous conviendrait de venir?; **if it's more ~ for her to do** si ça l'arrange de faire; **a ~ place for sth** un endroit approprié pour qch; **2** (useful, practical) [*tool, system, method etc*] pratique, commode; **it is ~** c'est pratique or commode (**that** que + *subj*; **to do** de faire); **a ~ way to do** ou **of doing** un moyen pratique de faire; **3** (in location) [*shops, amenities*] situé tout près; [*chair, table*] à portée de main; **to be ~ for** GB, **to be ~ to** US être commode pour [*station, shops, facilities*]; **4** iron péj (expedient) [*excuse, explanation, target*] commode; **it's ~ for them to ignore the facts** ça les arrange de ne pas reconnaître les faits; **how** ou **very ~!** comme c'est commode!

conveniently /kən'viːnɪəntlɪ/ *adv* **1** (in practical terms) [*arrange, borrow, repay*] de façon pratique or commode; [*arrive, leave*] opportunément, au bon moment; [*arranged, planned*] de façon pratique or commode; **the conference was ~ timed to coincide with** la date de la conférence était bien choisie pour coïncider avec; **2** (in location) **~ situated**, **~ located** bien situé, bien placé; **~ placed** bien placé; **it's ~ near the beach** c'est bien placé, près de la plage; **3** iron péj (expediently) comme par hasard.

convenor = **convener**.

convent /'kɒnvənt, US -vent/ *n* couvent *m*; **to enter a ~** entrer au couvent.

conventicle /kən'ventɪkl/ *n* **1** (meeting) assemblée *f* religieuse secrète; **2** (meeting house) lieu *m* où se tient une assemblée religieuse secrète.

convention /kən'venʃn/ *n* **1** (meeting) (of party, profession, union) convention *f*, congrès *m*; (of society, fans) assemblée *f*; **2** ¢ (social norms) convenances *fpl*, conventions *fpl*; **to flout** ou **defy ~** braver les convenances; **3** (usual practice) convention *f*; **a literary/theatrical ~** une convention littéraire/du théâtre; **4** (agreement) convention *f* (**on** sur).

conventional /kən'venʃənl/ *adj* **1** (conformist) [*person*] conformiste; [*idea, remark, belief, role*] conventionnel/-elle; [*clothes*] classique; **2** (traditionally accepted) [*approach, means, method, practice*] conventionnel/-elle; [*medicine, agriculture*] traditionnel/-elle; **the ~ wisdom about sth** ce qui est communément admis au sujet de qch; **3** Mil [*arms, weapons, war*] conventionnel/-elle.

Conventional Forces in Europe, **CFE** *n* Mil forces *fpl* conventionnelles en Europe.

conventionality /ˌkənvenʃə'nælətɪ/ *n* conformisme *m*.

conventionally /kən'venʃənəlɪ/ *adv* [*dress, behave*] de façon conventionnelle; [*measure, divide, consider*] par convention; **a ~ armed missile** Mil un missile conventionnel.

convention centre GB, **convention center** US *n* centre *m* de congrès.

conventioneer /kənˌvenʃə'nɪə(r)/ *n* US délégué/-e *m/f*.

convent school *n* école *f* de religieuses.

converge /kən'vɜːdʒ/ *vi* converger (**at** à); **to ~ on** [*people*] converger sur [*place*]; [*rays, paths etc*] converger vers [*point*].

convergence /kən'vɜːdʒəns/ *n* convergence *f*.

convergent /kən'vɜːdʒənt/ *adj* (all contexts) convergent.

convergent: **~ evolution** *n* évolution *f* convergente; **~ lens** *n* lentille *f* convergente; **~ thinking** *n* pensée *f* convergente.

conversant /kən'vɜːsnt/ *adj* **to be ~ with sth** être versé dans qch.

conversation /ˌkɒnvə'seɪʃn/ *n* conversation *f* (**about** sur, au sujet de); **to have** ou **hold a ~** avoir une conversation; **to strike up/break off a ~** engager/interrompre la conversation; **to make ~** faire la conversation; (**deep**) **in ~** en (grande) conversation.

conversational /ˌkɒnvə'seɪʃənl/ *adj* [*ability, skill, class, exercise*] de conversation; **in a ~ tone** sur le ton de la conversation.

conversationalist /ˌkɒnvə'seɪʃənəlɪst/ *n* personne *f* qui excelle dans l'art de la conversation.

conversationally /ˌkɒnvə'seɪʃənəlɪ/ *adv* [*say, observe*] sur le ton de la conversation.

conversational mode *n* Comput mode *m* dialogué.

conversation piece *n* **1 to be a ~** susciter des remarques; **2** Theat *pièce de théâtre comportant essentiellement des dialogues*.

converse I /'kɒnvɜːs/ *n* **1** gen contraire *m*; **2** Math, Philos converse *f*.
II /'kɒnvɜːs/ *adj* [*opinion, statement*] contraire; [*proposition*] inverse.
III /kən'vɜːs/ *vi* converser (**with** avec; **in** en).

conversely /'kɒnvɜːslɪ/ *adv* inversement.

conversion /kən'vɜːʃn, US kən'vɜːrʒn/ *n* **1** (of salt water, raw material, land, vehicle, object) transformation *f* (**from** de; **to, into** en); (of energy, fuel) transformation *f* (**from** de; **to, into** en); (in reactor) conversion *f*; **2** Math, Comput (of currency, measurement, weight) conversion *f* (**from** de; **into** en); **3** (of building) aménagement *m* (**to, into** en); **barn ~** grange *f* aménagée; **4** Relig, Pol conversion *f* (**from** de; **to** à); **to undergo a ~** se convertir; **5** Sport (in rugby) transformation *f*.

conversion: **~ course** *n* programme *m* de transition; **~ disorder**, **~ hysteria**† *n* hystérie *f* de conversion; **~ rate** *n* Fin taux *m* de change; **~ table** *n* table *f* de conversion.

convert I /'kɒnvɜːt/ *n* converti/-e *m/f* (**to** à); **to become a ~** se convertir; **to win/make ~s** faire des adeptes.
II /kən'vɜːt/ *vtr* **1** gen (change into sth else)

transformer; **2** (modify) adapter [*car, cooker, product*]; **3** Math, Comput convertir [*currency, measurement*] (**from** de; **to, into** en); **4** Archit aménager, reconvertir [*building, loft*] (**to, into** en); **5** Relig, Pol etc convertir [*person*] (**to** à; **from** de); **6** Sport (in rugby) transformer [*try*].
III /kən'vɜːt/ *vi* **1** gen (change) **to ~ to sth** passer à qch; **I've ~ed to unleaded (petrol)** je suis passé au sans plomb; **2** (be convertible) [*sofa, object*] être convertible (**into** en); **3** Relig, Pol etc se convertir (**to** à; **from** de); **4** Sport (in rugby) transformer.
IDIOMS **to preach to the ~** prêcher un converti ou des convertis.

converter /kən'vɜːtə(r)/ *n* **1** Elec, gen convertisseur *m*; (AC to DC) redresseur *m*; **2** Radio changeur *m* de fréquence; **3** Ind, Comput convertisseur *m*.

convertibility /kən,vɜːtə'bɪlətɪ/ *n* gen adaptabilité *f* (**to, into** à); (of currency) convertibilité *f* (**to, into** en).

convertible /kən'vɜːtəbl/ **I** *n* Aut décapotable *f*.
II *adj* **1** [*sofa, divan*] convertible; **2** Fin [*bond, currency, stock*] convertible; **3** [*car*] décapotable.

convertor /kən'vɜːtə(r)/ *n* = **converter**.

convex /'kɒnveks/ *adj* convexe.

convexity /kɒn'veksətɪ/ *n* convexité *f*.

convey /kən'veɪ/ *vtr* **1** (transmit) [*person*] transmettre [*order, message, news, information*] (**to**) à); exprimer [*opinion, judgment, feeling, idea*] (**to** à); transmettre [*regards, thanks, congratulations, condolences*] (**to** à); **to ~ to sb that/how** faire savoir à qn que/comment; **to ~ the impression of/that** donner l'impression de/que; **2** (communicate) [*words, images, gestures, music*] traduire [*mood, emotion, impression*]; **to ~ a sense** ou **feeling of** traduire une sensation or un sentiment de; **3** (transport) [*vehicle*] transporter, acheminer [*people, goods*] (**from** de; **to** à); [*pipes, network*] amener [*water*] (**to** à); [*postal system*] acheminer [*mail*] (**to** à); [*person*] transmettre [*letter, message*] (**to** à); **4** Jur transmettre [*property, legal title*] (**to** à).

conveyance /kən'veɪəns/ *n* **1** (of goods, passengers) transport *m*, acheminement *m*; **2**† (vehicle) véhicule *m*, moyen *m* de transport; **3** Jur (transfer of property, title) transfert *m*, cession *f*; **4** Jur (document) (**deed of**) ~ acte *m* de cession or de propriété.

conveyancer /kən'veɪənsə(r)/ **▶ 1692** *n* notaire *m* rédacteur des actes de cession or de propriété.

conveyancing /kən'veɪənsɪŋ/ *n* rédaction *f* des actes de cession or de propriété; **to carry out ~ for sb** rédiger un acte de cession pour qn.

conveyor /kən'veɪə(r)/ *n* **1** (also **~ belt**) (in factory) transporteur *m* à bande or à courroie; (for luggage) tapis *m* roulant; **2** (of goods, persons) transporteur *m*.

convict **I** /'kɒnvɪkt/ *n* (imprisoned criminal) détenu/-e *m/f*; (deported criminal) bagnard *m*; **ex-~** ancien détenu; **escaped ~** détenu évadé.
II /kən'vɪkt/ *vtr* **1** [*jury, court*] reconnaître or déclarer [qn] coupable (**of** de; **of doing** d'avoir fait); **to be ~ed on a charge of sth** être reconnu or déclaré coupable de qch; **a ~ed murderer/drug dealer** (in prison) un condamné pour meurtre/trafic de drogue; (now released) un ancien condamné pour meurtre/trafic de drogue; **2** [*evidence*] condamner.

conviction /kən'vɪkʃn/ *n* **1** Jur condamnation *f* (**for** pour); **to obtain/quash/uphold a ~** obtenir/annuler/maintenir une condamnation; **~ on fraud charges** condamnation pour fraude; **2** (belief) conviction *f* (**that** que); **to lack ~** manquer de conviction.

conviction: **~ politician** *n* politicien/-ienne *m/f* ayant de fortes convictions; **~ politics** *n* politique *f* basée sur des convictions.

convince /kən'vɪns/ **I** *vtr* **1** (gain credibility of) convaincre [*person, jury, reader*] (**of** de; **that** que; **about** au sujet de); **the story fails to ~** ou **does not ~** l'histoire ne convainc personne; **2** (persuade) persuader [*voter, consumer*] (**to do** de faire).
II *v refl* **to ~ oneself** se convaincre.

convinced /kən'vɪnst/ *adj* convaincu, persuadé.

convincing /kən'vɪnsɪŋ/ *adj* [*account, evidence, proof, theory*] convaincant; [*victory, lead, win*] indiscutable.

convincingly /kən'vɪnsɪŋlɪ/ *adv* [*argue, claim, demonstrate, portray*] de façon convaincante; [*win, beat*] de façon indiscutable.

convivial /kən'vɪvɪəl/ *adj* **1** [*atmosphere, evening*] cordial; **2** [*person*] chaleureux/-euse.

conviviality /kən,vɪvɪ'ælətɪ/ *n* **1** (of atmosphere, evening) cordialité *f*; **2** (of person) caractère *m* chaleureux.

convocation /,kɒnvə'keɪʃn/ *n* **1** GB Relig convocation *f* (*convention nationale du clergé anglican*); **2** GB Univ conseil *m* des anciens étudiants; **3** (convoking) convocation *f*; **4** US Univ *assemblée de membres d'une université réunie à l'occasion d'une cérémonie*.

convoke /kən'vəʊk/ *vtr* convoquer.

convoluted /'kɒnvəluːtɪd/ *adj* **1** [*argument, speech, sentence, style*] alambiqué; **2** [*vine, tendril*] convoluté; [*design, pattern*] vrillé.

convolution /,kɒnvə'luːʃn/ *n* circonvolution *f*; fig méandre *m*.

convolvulus /kən'vɒlvjʊləs/ *n* (*pl* **-luses** ou **-li**) liseron *m*.

convoy /'kɒnvɔɪ/ **I** *n* convoi *m* (**of** de); **in ~** en convoi; **under ~** sous escorte.
II *vtr* convoyer [*ship*]; escorter [*person*].

convulsant /kən'vʌlsənt/ **I** *n* **1** Med médicament *m* convulsivant; **2** (drug) drogue *f* convulsivante.
II *adj* qui provoque des convulsions, convulsivant spec.

convulse /kən'vʌls/ *vtr* **1** [*pain, sobs, grief, laughter*] convulser [*person, body*]; [*joke, comic*] faire tordre de rire [*person*]; **~d with pain** convulsé de douleur; **2** [*riots, unrest*] secouer [*country*].

convulsion /kən'vʌlʃn/ *n* convulsion *f*; **to go into ~s** entrer en convulsions; **to be in ~s** fig se tordre de rire.

convulsive /kən'vʌlsɪv/ *adj* **1** [*movement, spasm*] convulsif/-ive; **2** [*change, disturbance, riot*] perturbateur/-trice.

convulsively /kən'vʌlsɪvlɪ/ *adv* convulsivement.

cony, coney /'kəʊnɪ/ *n* **1** (fur) peau *f* de lapin; **2**‡ lapin *m*.

coo /kuː/ **I** *n* (of dove) roucoulement *m*.
II†○ *excl* GB ça alors!○
III *vtr* murmurer.
IV *vi* [*lover, dove*] roucouler; **to ~ over a baby** s'extasier devant un bébé.
IDIOMS **to bill and ~** roucouler.

co-occur /,kəʊə'kɜː(r)/ *vi* être cooccurrent.

co-occurrence /,kəʊə'kʌrəns/ *n* cooccurrence *f*.

cooing /'kuːɪŋ/ **I** *n* roucoulement *m*, roucoulade *f*.
II *adj* **a ~ voice** un roucoulement.

cook /kʊk/ **▶ 1692** **I** *n* cuisinier/-ière *m/f*; **he's a good ~** c'est un bon cuisinier.
II *vtr* **1** Culin faire cuire [*vegetables, pasta, eggs*]; préparer [*meal, meat, fish*] (**for** pour); **~ for 10 minutes** faire cuire pendant 10 minutes; **2**○ (falsify) trafiquer○, falsifier [*data, evidence, figures*]; **to ~ the books** trafiquer○ la comptabilité; **3**○ US gâcher [*chances*].
III *vi* **1** [*person*] cuisiner, faire la cuisine; **2** [*vegetable, meat, meal*] cuire; **the carrots are ~ing** les carottes sont en train de cuire; **3**○ (happen) **to be ~ing** se mijoter○; **there's something ~ing** il y a quelque chose qui se mijote○.
IV cooked *pp adj* [*food*] cuit; **to be lightly/well ~ed** être à peine/bien cuit.
■ **cook up**○: **~ up [sth]** préparer [*dish, meal*]; inventer [*excuse, story*]; mijoter○ [*plan, scheme*].

cook: **~book** *n* livre *m* de cuisine; **~-chill foods** *npl* plats *mpl* préparés; **~ed ham** *n* jambon *m* blanc or de Paris; **~ed meats** *npl* ≈ charcuterie *f*.

cooker /'kʊkə(r)/ *n* **1** GB (appliance) cuisinière *f*; **gas/electric ~** cuisinière à gaz/électrique; **2**○ (apple) pomme *f* à cuire.

cookery /'kʊkərɪ/ **I** GB *n* cuisine *f*.
II *modif* [*book, lesson, teacher*] de cuisine.

cookhouse /'kʊkhaʊs/ *n* Mil cuisine *f*.

cookie /'kʊkɪ/ *n* **1** US (biscuit) gâteau *m* sec, biscuit *m* (sec); **2**○ (person) **tough ~** dur/-e *m/f* à cuire; **smart ~** petit malin/petite maligne *m/f*; **3**○ US (woman) jolie fille *f*.
IDIOMS **that's the way the ~ crumbles**○ c'est la vie!; **to toss** ou **shoot one's ~s**● US dégueuler●.

cookie cutter US **I** *n* Culin forme *f* à biscuits.
II *adj* [*plan, project*] sans originalité.

cookie sheet *n* US Culin plaque *f* à biscuits.

cooking /'kʊkɪŋ/ **I** *n* (all contexts) cuisine *f*; **to do the ~** faire la cuisine; **to be good at ~** bien cuisiner; **Chinese/plain ~** cuisine chinoise/bourgeoise.
II *modif* [*oil, wine*] de cuisine.

cooking: **~ apple** *n* pomme *f* à cuire; **~ chocolate** *n* chocolat *m* pâtissier; **~ foil** *n* papier *m* aluminium; **~ salt** *n* gros sel *m*.

cook: **~-off** *n* US concours *m* de cuisine; **~out** *n* US barbecue *m*; **~top** *n* US table *f* de cuisson; **~ware** *n* ustensiles *mpl* de cuisine.

cool /kuːl/ **I** *n* **1** (coldness) fraîcheur *f*; **2**○ (calm) sang-froid *m*; **to keep one's ~** (stay calm) garder son sang-froid; (not get angry) ne pas s'énerver; **to lose one's ~** (get angry) s'énerver; (panic) perdre son sang-froid.
II *adj* **1** [*breeze, day, drink, water, weather*] frais/fraîche; [*fabric, dress*] léger/-ère; [*colour*] froid; **it's ~ today** il fait frais aujourd'hui; **the fan keeps the room ~** le ventilateur maintient la pièce fraîche; **to feel ~** [*surface, wine*] être frais/fraîche; **I feel ~er now** j'ai moins chaud maintenant; **your brow is ~er** ton front est un peu moins chaud; **it's getting ~, let's go in** il commence à faire frais, rentrons; **2** (calm) [*approach, handling*] calme; **to stay ~** garder son sang-froid; **to keep a ~ head** garder la tête froide; **keep ~!** reste calme; **3** (unemotional) [*manner*] détaché; [*logic, reasoning, response*] froid; **4** (unfriendly) [*reception, welcome*] froid; **to be ~ with** ou **towards sb** être froid avec qn; **5** (casual) [*person*] décontracté, cool○; [*attitude*] sans gêne; **she went up to him as ~ as you please and slapped him** elle s'est approchée de lui totalement décontractée et l'a giflé; **he's a ~ customer** il n'a pas froid aux yeux; **6** (for emphasis) **a ~ million dollars** la coquette somme d'un million de dollars○; **7**○ (sophisticated) [*clothes, car*] branché○; [*person*] branché○; **he thinks it's ~ to smoke** il pense que ça fait bien de fumer; **it's not ~ to wear a tie** ça fait nul○ de porter une cravate; **~, man**○**!** génial!; **8**○ US (great) **that's a ~ idea!** c'est une super idée○!; **that's ~!** super○!; **9**○ Mus [*jazz*] cool○ *inv*.
III *vtr* **1** (lower the temperature of) refroidir [*soup, pan*]; rafraîchir [*wine*]; [*fan*] rafraîchir [*room*]; [*air-conditioning*] refroidir [*building*]; **to ~ one's hands** se rafraîchir les mains; **2** fig calmer [*anger, ardour, passion*].
IV *vi* **1** (get colder) [*air, iron, soup, water*] refroidir; **to leave sth to ~** laisser qch refroidir; **2** (subside) [*passion*] tiédir; [*enthusiasm*] faiblir; [*friendship*] se dégrader; **rela-**

tions between them have ~ed ils sont moins proches qu'avant; **wait until tempers have ~ed** attends que les esprits se calment.
V **-cooled** *dans composés* **air-/water-~ed** Tech à refroidissement à air/eau.
IDIOMS **~ it**○! (stay calm) ne t'énerve pas!; **OK guys, ~ it**○! (stop fighting) ça suffit les gars, on se calme○!; **to play it ~**○ rester calme.
■ **cool down**: ¶ **~ down 1** (grow cold) [*engine, iron, water*] refroidir; **2** fig [*person, situation*] se calmer; ¶ **~ [sth] down** refroidir [*mixture*]; rafraîchir [*wine*]; ¶ **~ [sb] down 1** (make colder) rafraîchir [*person*]; **2** fig calmer [*person*].
■ **cool off** [*person*] (get colder) se rafraîchir; fig (calm down) [*person*] se calmer.

coolant /'ku:lənt/ *n* Tech fluide *m* caloporteur, liquide *m* de refroidissement.

cool: **~ bag** *n* GB sac *m* isotherme; **~ box** *n* GB glacière *f*.

cooler○ /'ku:lə(r)/ *n* (prison) taule○ *f*, prison *f*; **he got five years in the ~** il a pris cinq ans de taule.

cool-headed /ˌku:l'hedɪd/ *adj* [*person*] qui garde la tête froide; [*decision, approach*] réfléchi.

coolie† /'ku:lɪ/ *n* injur coolie *m*.

cooling /'ku:lɪŋ/ I *n* refroidissement *m*.
II *pres p adj* [*drink, swim*] rafraîchissant; [*breeze*] frais/fraîche; [*agent*] réfrigérant.

cool: **~ing-off period** *n* (in industrial relations) délai *m* de conciliation; Comm, Insur délai *m* de réflexion; **~ing rack** *n* Culin grille *f* pour faire refroidir les gâteaux; **~ing system** *n* système *m* de refroidissement; **~ing tower** *n* tour *f* de refroidissement.

coolly /'ku:llɪ/ *adv* **1** (lightly) [*dressed*] légèrement; **2** (without warmth) [*greet, react, say*] froidement; **3** (calmly) calmement; **4** (boldly) [*announce, demand*] sans la moindre gêne.

coolness /'ku:lnɪs/ *n* **1** (coldness) fraîcheur *f*; **2** (unfriendliness) froideur *f* (**between** entre); **3** (calmness) calme *m*.

coomb /ku:m/ *n* GB combe *f*.

coon /ku:n/ *n* **1**○ US, Zool raton laveur *m*; **2**● injur nègre/négresse *m/f* offensive.
IDIOMS **a ~'s age** US un bail○.

coonskin /'ku:nskɪn/ *n* US peau *f* de raton laveur.

coop /ku:p/ I *n* (also **chicken ~**, **hen ~**) poulailler *m*.
II *vtr* mettre [qch] dans le poulailler [*hen*].
IDIOMS **to fly the ~**○ prendre la clé des champs.
■ **coop up**: **~ [sb/sth] up** enfermer, cloîtrer; **to keep sb/sth ~ed up** garder qn/qch enfermé.

co-op /'kəʊɒp/ *n* **1**○ (*abrév* = **cooperative**) coopé○ *f*; **2** US (apartment) appartement *m* en copropriété; (building) immeuble *m* en copropriété; **to go ~** être mis en copropriété.

cooper /'ku:pə(r)/ ▶1692 *n* tonnelier *m*.

cooperage /'ku:pərɪdʒ/ *n* tonnellerie *f*.

cooperate /kəʊ'ɒpəreɪt/ *vi* coopérer (**with** avec; **in** à; **in doing** pour faire).

cooperation /kəʊˌɒpə'reɪʃn/ *n* coopération *f* (**on** à); **in (close) ~** en (étroite) coopération; **he promised full ~** il a promis son entière coopération.

cooperative /kəʊ'ɒpərətɪv/ I *n* **1** (organisation) coopérative *f*; **workers' ~** coopérative ouvrière; **2** US (apartment house) immeuble *m* en copropriété.
II *adj* **1** (joint) [*venture, effort*] conjoint; **to take ~ action** agir conjointement; **2** (helpful) [*person*] coopératif/-ive (**with** avec); **to organize sth along ~ lines** organiser qch dans un cadre coopératif; **3** Comm, Pol [*movement, society*] coopératif/-ive; **4** US [*apartment, building*] en copropriété.

cooperative: **~ bank** *n* US ≈ société *f* de crédit immobilier; **~ farm** *n* (collective farm) exploitation *f* (agricole) collective.

cooperatively /kəʊ'ɒpərətɪvlɪ/ *adv* [*work*] en coopération; **to act ~** se montrer coopératif/-ive.

cooperative: **Cooperative Party** *n* GB Pol parti *m* coopératiste; **~ society** *n* coopérative *f*.

co-opt /ˌkəʊ'ɒpt/ *vtr* **1** (onto committee) coopter [*person*] (**onto** dans); **2** (commandeer) s'emparer de [*celebrity*] (**to** pour soutenir); **3** Pol rallier [*person, group, country*] (**to** à); récupérer [*opinion, issue*].

co-option /ˌkəʊ'ɒpʃn/ *n* **1** (onto committee) cooptation *f*; **2** Pol (of group) ralliement *m*; (of opinion, issue) récupération *f*.

coordinate I /ˌkəʊ'ɔ:dɪnət/ *n* (on graph, map) coordonnée *f*.
II **coordinates** *npl* Fashn ensemble *m*.
III **coordinating** *pres p adj* **1** [*clothes, garment*] assorti, coordonné; **2** [*authority, committee*] de coordination.
IV /ˌkəʊ'ɔ:dɪneɪt/ *vtr* coordonner [*movements, effort, action, policy, response*] (**with** avec).
V /ˌkəʊ'ɔ:dɪneɪt/ *vi* agir en coordination (**with** avec).

coordinate clause *n* (proposition *f*) coordonnée *f*.

coordinated /ˌkəʊ'ɔ:dɪneɪtɪd/ *adj* [*response, policy, clothes, garment*] coordonné; **he's very ~** ses mouvements sont très coordonnés.

coordinate geometry *n* géométrie *f* analytique.

coordinating conjunction *n* conjonction *f* de coordination.

coordination /ˌkəʊ'ɔ:dɪ'neɪʃn/ *n* (all contexts) coordination *f*; **in ~** en coordination.

coordinator /ˌkəʊ'ɔ:dɪneɪtə(r)/ *n* coordinateur/-trice *m/f*.

coot /ku:t/ *n* **1** Zool foulque *f*; **2**○ idiot/-e *m/f*.
IDIOMS **as bald as a ~**○ chauve comme une boule de billard○.

co-owner /kəʊ'əʊnə(r)/ *n* copropriétaire *mf*.

cop /kɒp/ I *n* **1**○ (police officer) flic○ *m*; **traffic ~** flic○, agent *m* de la circulation; **motor cycle ~** motard *m*; **to play ~s and robbers** jouer aux gendarmes et aux voleurs; **2**○ GB (arrest) **it's a fair ~**! bien joué, je me rends○!; **3**○ GB (use) **to be not much ~** ne pas valoir grand-chose; **4** Tex canette *f*.
II *vtr* (*p prés etc* **-pp-**) **1**○ (arrest) pincer○ [*person*]; **to get ~ped doing** se faire pincer en train de faire○; **2**○ (receive) écoper de○ [*punch, punishment*]; **3**○ GB (be punished) **to ~ it** trinquer○; **4**○ (also **~ hold of**) (catch) attraper; **~ hold of the rope** attrape la corde; **5**○ (listen) écouter; **~ a load of this!** écoute-moi ça!; **6** Jur (plead guilty) **to ~ a plea** plaider coupable (*pour une charge mineure afin d'en éviter une plus grave*).
IDIOMS **to ~ a feel**○ US peloter○; **to ~ some Z's**○ US piquer un roupillon○.
■ **cop out**○ se dégonfler○; **to ~ out on a promise** manquer à une promesse; **to ~ out of doing** se défiler○ au moment de faire.

copacetic○† /ˌkəʊpə'setɪk, -'si:tɪk/ *adj* US génial○.

copartner /ˌkəʊ'pɑ:tnə(r)/ *n* associé/-e *m/f*, coassocié/-e *m/f*.

copartnership /ˌkəʊ'pɑ:tnəʃɪp/ *n* **1** (co-ownership) participation *f*; **2** (partnership) association *f*.

cope /kəʊp/ I *n* (cloak) chape *f*.
II *vtr* Constr chaperonner [*wall*].
III *vi* **1** (manage practically) [*person*] s'en sortir○, se débrouiller; [*government, police, services, system*] faire face; **to ~ with** [*person*] s'occuper de [*person, correspondence, work*]; [*government, police, industry, system*] faire face à [*demand, disaster, inflation, inquiries*]; **to learn to ~ alone** apprendre à se débrouiller tout seul; **how do you ~, with all those kids?** comment t'en sors-tu, avec tous ces gosses○?; **it's more than I can ~ with** je ne m'en sors plus; **the organization can't ~** l'organisation ne s'en sort plus or ne peut pas faire face; **2** (manage financially) s'en sortir; **to ~ on £60 a week** s'en sortir avec 60 livres sterling par semaine; **to ~ with a loan/mortgage** arriver à rembourser un prêt/prêt immobilier; **3** (manage emotionally) **to ~ with** supporter [*bereavement, depression*]; **to ~ with sb** supporter qn; **if you left me, I couldn't ~** si tu me quittais, je ne pourrais pas le supporter.

copeck *n* = **kopeck**.

Copenhagen /ˌkəʊpn'heɪgən/ ▶1818 *pr n* Copenhague.

Copernican /kə'pɜ:nɪkən/ *adj* copernicien/-ienne.

Copernicus /kə'pɜ:nɪkəs/ *pr n* Copernic.

copestone /'kəʊpstəʊn/ *n* **1** (coping stone) pierre *f* de chaperon; **2** (top stone, capstone) pierre *f* de couronnement.

copier /'kɒpɪə(r)/ *n* **1** (photocopier) photocopieuse *f*; **2** (imitator) imitateur/-trice *m/f*.

co-pilot /ˌkəʊ'paɪlət/ *n* copilote *mf*.

coping /'kəʊpɪŋ/ *n* Archit chaperon *m*.

coping stone *n* pierre *f* de chaperon.

copious /'kəʊpɪəs/ *adj* **1** (plentiful) [*crop, supply, tears*] abondant; **~ notes/data** une quantité abondante de notes/données; **2** (generous) [*quantity, serving*] copieux/-ieuse.

copiously /'kəʊpɪəslɪ/ *adv* abondamment; **to weep ~** pleurer à chaudes larmes.

cop-out○ /'kɒpaʊt/ *n* (excuse) excuse *f* bidon○; (evasive act) échappatoire *f*.

copper /'kɒpə(r)/ ▶1104 I *n* **1** Chem cuivre *m*; **2**○ (policeman) flic○ *m*; **3**○ GB (coin) petite monnaie *f* ₵; **to save a few ~s** économiser quelques sous; **4** GB Hist (for washing) lessiveuse *f*; **5** (colour) couleur *f* cuivre.
II *modif* [*alloy, deposit, mine, miner, ore*] de cuivre; [*bracelet, coin, nail, dome, pipe, wire*] de or en cuivre; [*kettle, pan*] en cuivre.
III *adj* [*hair, leaf, lipstick*] couleur cuivre *inv*.

copper beech *n* hêtre *m* pourpre.

Copper Belt /'kɒpəbelt/ *pr n* Copper Belt *f*, Ceinture *f* de cuivre.

copper: **~-bottomed** *adj* sûr; **~-coloured** GB, **-colored** US ▶1104 *adj* [*hair*] cuivré; [*leaf, lipstick, metal*] couleur cuivre *inv*; **~head** *n* mocassin *m* à tête cuivrée.

copperplate /'kɒpəpleɪt/ *n* **1** cuivre *m*; **2** (also **~ handwriting**) écriture *f* ronde.

copper: **~-rich** *adj* riche en cuivre; **~smith** ▶1692 *n* chaudronnier *m*; **~'s nark**○† *n* GB mouchard/-e○ *m/f*; **~ sulphate** *n* sulfate *m* de cuivre; **~ware** *n* cuivres *mpl*.

coppery /'kɒpərɪ/ ▶1104 *adj* [*colour*] cuivré.

coppice /'kɒpɪs/ *n* taillis *m*.

copra /'kɒprə/ *n* copra(h) *m*.

co-presidency /kəʊ'prezɪdənsɪ/ *n* coprésidence *f*.

co-president /kəʊ'prezɪdənt/ *n* coprésident/-e *m/f*.

co-property /kəʊ'prɒpətɪ/ *n* copropriété *f*.

copse /kɒps/ *n* taillis *m*.

cop-shop○ /'kɒpʃɒp/ *n* GB poste *m* de police.

Copt /kɒpt/ *n* Relig Copte *mf*.

copter○ /'kɒptə(r)/ *n* (*abrév* = **helicopter**) hélico○ *m*.

Coptic /'kɒptɪk/ *adj* [*church, tradition*] copté.

copula /'kɒpjʊlə/ *n* (*pl* **-las** ou **-lae**) copule *f*.

copulate /'kɒpjʊleɪt/ *vi* s'accoupler, copuler (**with** avec).

copulation /ˌkɒpjʊ'leɪʃn/ *n* copulation *f*.

copulative /'kɒpjʊlətɪv, US -leɪtɪv/ I *n* terme *m* copulatif.

II *adj* copulatif/-ive.

copy /ˈkɒpɪ/ **I** *n* **1** (reproduction, imitation) copie *f* (**of** de); **to make a ~** faire une copie; **certified ~** copie *f* certifiée conforme; **2** (issue, edition) (of book, newspaper, record, report) exemplaire *m*; **3** (journalist's, advertiser's text) copie *f*; **to be** ou **make good ~** être un bon sujet d'article; **to file (one's) ~** présenter sa copie or son papier○ journ.
II *vtr* **1** (imitate) copier [*person, style, design, system*] (**from** sur); **2** (duplicate) copier [*document, letter, disk, file*]; **to ~ sth onto a disk** copier qch sur disquette; **to ~ onto paper** sortir qch sur papier; **to have sth copied** faire faire une copie de qch; **3** (write out by hand) recopier [*exercise, answers, inscription, text*] (**from** sur); **to ~ sth into one's book** recopier qch sur son cahier.
III *vi* [*person, candidate, pupil*] copier (**from** sur); **to ~ in a test** copier à un examen.
■ **copy down**: **~ down [sth], ~ [sth] down** recopier (**from** sur; **into** sur).
■ **copy out**: **~ out [sth], ~ [sth] out** recopier.

copybook /ˈkɒpɪbʊk/ **I** *n* cahier *m* d'écriture.
II *modif* **1** (model) [*answer, solution*] modèle (*after n*); **~ perfect** impeccable; **2** US (trite) banal.
IDIOMS **to blot one's ~** faire des bêtises.

copycat○ /ˈkɒpɪkæt/ **I** *n* péj copieur/-ieuse *m/f*.
II *adj* [*crime, murder*] inspiré par un autre (*after n*); **a wave of ~ crimes** une épidémie de crimes similaires.

copy: **~ desk** *n* service *m* de correction; **~ edit** *vtr* Journ corriger (*pour la publication*); **~ editor** *n* Journ secrétaire *mf* de rédaction.

copyholder /ˈkɒpɪhəʊldə(r)/ *n* Print **1** (device) porte-copie *m*; **2** (person) aide-correcteur *mf*.

copy: **~ing ink** *n* encre *f* à copier; **~ing machine** *n* photocopieuse *f*.

copyist /ˈkɒpɪɪst/ *n* **1** (of old texts) copiste *mf*; **2** (imitator) imitateur/-trice *m/f*, plagiaire *mf*; **3** (forger of paintings etc) faussaire *mf*.

copy platform *n* Advertg base *f* de campagne.

copyread /ˈkɒpɪri:d/ *vtr* (*prét, pp* **-read**) US Journ corriger (*pour la publication*).

copyreader /ˈkɒpɪri:də(r)/ ▶ 1692 *n* US Journ correcteur/-trice *m/f*.

copyright /ˈkɒpɪraɪt/ **I** *n* copyright *m*, droit *m* d'auteur; **to have** ou **hold the ~** détenir le copyright or les droits; **the ~ of** ou **on sth** le copyright de qch, les droits sur qch; **to be in ~** être protégé par copyright; **to be out of ~** être tombé dans le domaine public.
II *adj* [*book, work*] protégé par un copyright.
III *vtr* déposer [*work*].

copy: **~ typist** ▶ 1692 *n* dactylo *mf*; **~writer** ▶ 1692 *n* rédacteur/-trice *m/f* publicitaire.

coquetry /ˈkɒkɪtrɪ/ *n* coquetterie *f*.

coquette /kɒˈket/ *n* coquette *f*.

coquettish /kɒˈketɪʃ/ *adj* [*person*] coquet/-ette; [*smile, look, manner*] aguichant.

coquettishly /kɒˈketɪʃlɪ/ *adv* de façon aguichante.

cor○ /kɔ:(r)/ *excl* GB ça alors○; **~ blimey**○! mince alors○!

coracle /ˈkɒrəkl/ *n* coracle *m*.

coral /ˈkɒrəl, US ˈkɔ:rəl/ **I** *n* corail *m*.
II *modif* [*earring, necklace, paperweight*] de or en corail.
III *adj* ▶ 1104 (colour) corail *inv*.

coral: **~ atoll** *n* atoll *m*; **~-coloured** ▶ 1104 *adj* (couleur) corail *inv*; **~ island** *n* île *f* corallienne; **~ pink** ▶ 1104 *n, adj* (rouge *m*) corail (*m*); **~ reef** *n* récif *m* corallien or de corail; **Coral Sea** *pr n* mer *f* de Corail; **~ snake** *n* serpent *m* corail.

cor anglais /ˌkɔ:r ˈɒŋgleɪ/ ▶ 1481 *n* cor *m* anglais.

corbel /ˈkɔ:bl/ *n* Constr corbeau *m*.

cord /kɔ:d/ **I** *n* **1** (of pyjamas, dressing gown, light switch, curtains etc) cordon *m*; **sash ~** corde *f* (de fenêtre à guillotine); **2** Elec fil *m*, cordon *m*; **3**○ (*abrév* = **corduroy**) velours *m* côtelé; **4** (umbilical) cordon *m*.
II *npl* **cords**○ pantalon *m* en velours (côtelé).
III○ *modif* [*garment*] en or de velours côtelé.

cordage /ˈkɔ:dɪdʒ/ *n* ¢ cordages *mpl*.

corded /ˈkɔ:dɪd/ *adj* [*fabric*] côtelé.

cordial /ˈkɔ:dɪəl, US ˈkɔ:rdʒəl/ **I** *n* **1** (fruit) sirop *m* de fruits; **2** US (liqueur) liqueur *m*.
II *adj* cordial (**to, with** avec).

cordiality /ˌkɔ:dɪˈælətɪ, US ˌkɔ:rdʒɪ-/ *n* cordialité *f*.

cordially /ˈkɔ:dɪəlɪ, US -dʒəlɪ/ *adv* cordialement.

cordite /ˈkɔ:daɪt/ *n* cordite *f*.

cordless /ˈkɔ:dlɪs/ *adj* sans fil, sans cordon; **~ telephone** téléphone *m* sans fil, poste *m* téléphonique sans cordon.

cordon /ˈkɔ:dn/ **I** *n* (all contexts) cordon *m*; **police ~** cordon *m* de police.
II *vtr* = **cordon off**.
■ **cordon off**: **~ off [sth], ~ [sth] off** boucler [*street, area*]; contenir [*crowd*].

cordon: **~ bleu** *n, adj* cordon-bleu (*m*); **~ sanitaire** *n* cordon *m* sanitaire.

Cordova /ˈkɔ:dəvə/, **Cordoba** /ˈkɔ:dəbə/ ▶ 1818 *pr n* Cordoue.

corduroy /ˈkɔ:dərɔɪ/ **I** *n* velours *m* côtelé; **~s** un pantalon *m* en velours côtelé.
II *modif* [*garment*] en velours côtelé.

corduroy road *n* US route *f* de rondins.

core /kɔ:(r)/ **I** *n* **1** (of apple, pear) trognon *m*; **2** fig (of problem, issue) cœur *m*; **3** (inner being) **rotten to the ~** pourri jusqu'à l'os; **selfish to the ~** foncièrement égoïste; **English to the ~** anglais jusqu'au bout des ongles; **it shook me to the ~** cela m'a remué jusqu'au fond de l'âme; **4** (of magnet) noyau *m*; **5** (of cable) âme *f*; **6** (of planet) noyau *m*; **7** Nucl cœur *m*; **8** Ind (in casting) noyau *m*; **9** Comput tore *m* magnétique; **10** (small group) noyau *m*.
II *modif* [*vocabulary*] de base; [*issue, concept, principle*] fondamental; [*activity*] principal.
III *vtr* Culin évider [*apple*]; enlever le cœur de [*apple segment*].

CORE *n* US (*abrév* = **Congress of Racial Equality**) *organisation pour la défense des droits des minorités ethniques*.

core curriculum /ˌkɔ:kəˈrɪkjʊləm/ *n* Sch, Univ tronc *m* commun.

co-religionist /ˌkəʊrɪˈlɪdʒənɪst/ *n* coreligionnaire *mf*.

coreopsis /ˌkɒrɪˈɒpsɪs/ *n* coréopsis *m*.

corer /ˈkɔ:rə(r)/ *n* (also **apple ~**) vide-pomme *m*.

core: **~ sample** *n* Geol carotte *f*; **~ skill** *n* compétences *fpl* de base.

co-respondent /ˌkəʊrɪˈspɒndənt/ *n* Jur complice *mf* d'adultère.

core: **~ subject** *n* Sch, Univ matière *f* du tronc commun; **~ time** *n* plage *f* horaire fixe.

Corfu /kɔ:ˈfu:/ ▶ 1381 *pr n* Corfou *f*.

corgi /ˈkɔ:gɪ/ *n* corgi *m*.

coriander /ˌkɒrɪˈændə(r), US ˌkɔ:r-/ *n* coriandre *f*.

Corinth /ˈkɒrɪnθ/ ▶ 1818 *pr n* Corinthe; **~ Canal** canal *m* de Corinthe; **Gulf of ~** golfe *m* de Corinthe.

Corinthian /kəˈrɪnθɪən/ **I** *n* Corinthien/-ienne *m/f*.
II **Corinthians** *npl* Bible l'Épitre *f* aux Corinthiens.
III *adj* gen, Archit corinthien/-ienne.

Coriolanus /ˌkɒrɪəˈleɪnəs/ *pr n* Coriolan.

cork /kɔ:k/ **I** *n* **1** (substance) liège *m*; **2** (of bottle) also Fishg bouchon *m*.
II *modif* [*tile, table-mat*] en liège.
III *vtr* boucher [*bottle*].
IDIOMS **to blow one's ~**○ US se mettre en rogne○.
■ **cork up**: **~ [sth] up, ~ up [sth]** boucher [*bottle*]; fig refouler [*feelings*].

corkage /ˈkɔ:kɪdʒ/ *n* droit *m* de bouchon.

corked /kɔ:kt/ *adj* **1** [*wine*] bouchonné; **2**○ GB (drunk) bourré○, ivre.

corker○† /ˈkɔ:kə(r)/ *n* GB (story) histoire *f* épatante○; (stroke, shot) coup *m* de maître; **she's a real ~!** c'est un beau brin de fille○!

corking○† /ˈkɔ:kɪŋ/ *adj* GB épatant○.

cork: **~ oak** *n* chêne-liège *m*; **~screw** *n* tire-bouchon *m*; **~screw curls** *npl* anglaises *fpl*.

corm /kɔ:m/ *n* Bot bulbe *m*.

cormorant /ˈkɔ:mərənt/ *n* cormoran *m*.

corn /kɔ:n/ *n* **1** (wheat) blé *m*; **2** US (maize) maïs *m*; **3** (seed) grain *m* (*de céréale*); **4** Med (on foot) cor *m*; **5**○ pej (in book, film etc) mièvrerie *f*.
IDIOMS **to tread on sb's ~s** froisser qn.

cornball○ /ˈkɔ:nbɔ:l/ US péj **I** *n* sensiblard/-e○ *m/f*.
II *adj* = **corny**.

corn: **Corn Belt** *n* US *région céréalière des plaines du centre des États-Unis*; **~ bread** *n* US pain *m* à base de farine de maïs; **~ bunting** *n* proyer *m*; **~cob** *n* épi *m* de maïs; **~cob pipe** *n* pipe *f* en rafle de maïs; **~crake** *n* râle *m* des genêts; **~crib** *n* US séchoir *m* à maïs; **~ dog** *n* US *saucisse enrobée de farine de maïs frite*; **~ dolly** GB *n* poupée *f* de paille.

cornea /ˈkɔ:nɪə/ *n* (*pl* **~s** ou **-neae**) cornée *f*.

corneal /ˈkɔ:nɪəl/ *adj* cornéen/-éenne.

corned beef *n* corned-beef *m*.

cornelian /kɔ:ˈni:lɪən/ *n* cornaline *f*.

corner /ˈkɔ:nə(r)/ **I** *n* **1** lit (in geometry) angle *m*; (of street, building) angle *m*, coin *m*; (of table, box, page, fabric, field, room) coin *m*; Aut (bend) virage *m*; **the house on the ~** la maison qui fait l'angle; **at the ~ of the street** au coin de la rue; **to turn** ou **go round the ~** tourner au coin de la rue; **to put a child in the ~** Sch mettre un enfant au coin; **she wiped her eyes with a ~ of her apron** elle s'est essuyé les yeux avec un coin or le bord de son tablier; **to fold sth from ~ to ~** plier qch en diagonale; **to turn down the ~ of a page** corner une page; **the car took the ~ too fast** la voiture a pris le virage trop vite; **he lives around the ~ from me** (nearby) il habite tout près de chez moi; **the post office is just around the ~** (around the bend) la poste est juste au coin; **she disappeared round the ~** elle a disparu au coin de la rue; **Christmas is just around the ~** Noël approche; **you never know what's around the ~** on ne sait jamais ce qui peut arriver; **2** (side) (of eye, mouth) coin *m*; **to watch/see sb out of the ~ of one's eye** regarder/voir qn du coin de l'œil; **3** (remote place) coin *m*; fig (of mind) coin *m*, recoin *m*; **a quiet ~ of Brittany/the office** un coin tranquille de Bretagne/du bureau; **in a remote ~ of India** dans une région reculée de l'Inde; **I searched every ~ of the house** j'ai cherché partout dans la maison; **from all four ~s of the world** des quatre coins du monde; **4** Sport (in boxing) coin *m* (de repos); (in football, hockey) corner *m*; **to take a ~** tirer un corner; **5** (column) coin *m*; **kids'/collectors' ~** le coin des enfants/des collectionneurs.
II *modif* [*cupboard, shelf, table*] de coin; **a ~ seat** (on a train) un coin fenêtre.
III *vtr* **1** (trap) lit acculer [*animal, enemy*]; fig coincer○ [*person*]; **2** (monopolize) accaparer [*supply, best seats*]; **she's ~ed the market in fashion jewellery** elle a accaparé le marché du bijou fantaisie.
IV *vi* Aut [*car*] prendre un virage; **this car ~s well** cette voiture prend bien les virages.
V **-cornered** *dans composés* **three-/four-~ed** à trois/quatre coins.

IDIOMS **to be in a tight ~** être dans une impasse; **to hold** ou **fight one's ~** se défendre; **to paint** ou **box oneself into a ~** se mettre dans une impasse; **to cut ~s** (financially) faire des économies; (in a procedure) simplifier les choses.

corner: **~ cupboard** *n* encoignure *f*; **~ flag** *n* Sport piquet *m* de coin.

cornering /ˈkɔːnərɪŋ/ *n* Aut tenue *f* de route (dans les virages).

corner: **~ shop** *n* petite épicerie *f*; **~stone** *n* Archit, fig pierre *f* angulaire; **~ways**, **~wise** *adj, adv* en diagonale.

cornet /ˈkɔːnɪt/ ▶1481 *n* **1** Mus cornet *m* (à pistons); **2** GB (for ice cream, sweets) cornet *m*.

cornetist, **cornettist** /kɔːˈnetɪst/ ▶1692, 1481 *n* cornettiste *mf*.

corn exchange *n* GB halle *f* aux grains.

cornfed /ˈkɔːnfed/ *adj* [*livestock*] nourri de maïs; **~ chicken** poulet *m* de grain.

corn: **~field** *n* GB champ *m* de blé; US champ *m* de maïs; **~flakes** *npl* corn flakes *mpl*; **~flour** *n* farine *f* de maïs; **~flower** *n* bleuet *m*, barbeau *m*; **~flower blue** ▶1104 *n* bleu *m* barbeau; **~husking** *n* US *fête qui suit la récolte du maïs*.

cornice /ˈkɔːnɪs/ *n* (all contexts) corniche *f*.

Cornish /ˈkɔːnɪʃ/ ▶1402 **I** *n* **1** Ling cornique *m*; **2 the ~** (+ *v pl*) les habitants *mpl* de Cornouailles.

II *adj* de Cornouailles, cornique.

Cornish pasty *n*: *petit pâté de viande et légumes*.

corn: **~meal** *n* farine *f* de maïs; **~ oil** *n* huile *f* de maïs; **~ on the cob** *n* maïs *m* en épi; **~ picker** *n* US moissonneuse-batteuse *f*; **~ plaster** *n* pansement *m* pour cors; **~ pone** *n* US pain *m* de maïs; **~ poppy** *n* coquelicot *m*; **~row** *n* (hairstyle) tresses *fpl* plaquées; **~ salad** *n* mâche *f*; **~ shock** *n* GB gerbe *f* de blé; **~ shuck** *n* US enveloppe *f* d'un épi de maïs; **~ starch** *n* US = **cornflour**; **~ syrup** *n* US sirop *m* de maïs.

cornucopia /ˌkɔːnjʊˈkəʊpɪə/ *n* littér lit, fig corne *f* d'abondance.

Cornwall /ˈkɔːnwɔːl/ ▶1624 *pr n* (comté *m* de) Cornouailles *f*.

corn whisk(e)y /ˈkɔːn wɪskɪ, US hwɪskɪ/ *n* bourbon *m*.

corny○ /ˈkɔːnɪ/ *adj* péj [*joke*] (old) éculé; (feeble) faiblard○; [*film, story*] à la guimauve.

corolla /kəˈrɒlə/ *n* corolle *f*.

corollary /kəˈrɒlərɪ, US ˈkɒrəlerɪ/ *n* corollaire *m* (**of, to** de).

corona /kəˈrəʊnə/ *n* **1** Astron, Anat, Archit, Bot couronne *f*; **2** Phys (also **~ discharge**) effet *m* couronne; **3** (cigar) corona *m*.

coronary /ˈkɒrənrɪ, US ˈkɔːrənerɪ/ **I** *n* Med infarctus *m*.

II *adj* [*vein, artery*] coronaire.

coronary: **~ care unit** *n* unité *f* de soins intensifs cardiologiques; **~ thrombosis** *n* infarctus *m* du myocarde.

coronation /ˌkɒrəˈneɪʃn, US ˌkɔːr-/ **I** *n* couronnement *m*.

II *modif* [*ceremony, day, robe*] du couronnement.

coroner /ˈkɒrənə(r), US ˈkɔːr-/ *n* coroner *m* (*officier de police judiciaire chargé d'enquêter sur les décès suspects*); **~'s inquest** enquête *f* judiciaire (*confiée à un coroner*).

coronet /ˈkɒrənet, US ˈkɔːr-/ *n* (for prince, nobleman etc) (petite) couronne *f*; (woman's) diadème *m*; (of flowers) couronne *f*.

corp *n* **1** *abrév* ▶ **corporal**; **2** US *abrév* ▶ **corporation**.

corporal /ˈkɔːpərəl/ ▶1612 **I** *n* (in infantry, air force) caporal-chef *m*; (in cavalry, artillery) brigadier-chef *m*.

II *adj* sout corporel/-elle.

corporal punishment *n* châtiment *m* corporel.

corporate /ˈkɔːpərət/ *adj* **1** Comm, Fin [*accounts, funds*] appartenant à une société; [*clients, employees*] d'une société (or de sociétés); **~ assets** actif *m* social; **2** (collective) [*action*] commun; [*ownership*] en commun; [*decision, responsibility, existence*] collectif/-ive.

corporate: **~ advertising** *n* publicité *f* institutionnelle; **~ body** *n* personne *f* morale; **~ culture** *n* culture *f* d'entreprise; **~ identity**, **~ image** *n* image *f* de marque (d'une société); **~ law** *n* US Jur droit *m* des sociétés; **~ lawyer** *n* US Jur (attached to firm) avocat/-e *m/f* d'entreprise; (business law expert) juriste *mf* d'entreprise.

corporately /ˈkɔːpərətlɪ/ *adv* collectivement.

corporate: **~ name** *n* raison *f* sociale; **~ planning** *n* planification *f* d'entreprise; **~ raider** *n* Fin raider *m* (*organisateur d'OPA*); **~ state** *n* Pol *État fondé sur les principes du corporatisme d'État*; **~ tax** *n* impôt *m* sur les sociétés.

corporation /ˌkɔːpəˈreɪʃn/ **I** *n* **1** Comm (grande) société *f*; **2** GB (town council) conseil *m* municipal; **3**○ GB hum (paunch) bedaine○ *f*.

II *modif* [*services, property*] municipal.

corporation: **~ lawyer** ▶1692 *n* avocat/-e *m/f* d'entreprise; **~ tax** *n* GB impôt *m* sur les sociétés.

corporatism /ˈkɔːpərətɪzəm/ *n* corporatisme *m*.

corporatist /ˈkɔːpərətɪst/ *n* corporatiste *mf*.

corporeal /kɔːˈpɔːrɪəl/ *adj* sout (bodily) corporel/-elle; (not spiritual) matériel/-ielle.

corporeal hereditaments *npl* Jur biens *mpl* corporels transmissibles par héritage.

corps /kɔː(r)/ *n* gen, Mil corps *m*; (technical branch) service *m*; **~ de ballet** corps de ballet.

corpse /kɔːps/ *n* cadavre *m*.

corpulence /ˈkɔːpjʊləns/ *n* sout corpulence *f*.

corpulent /ˈkɔːpjʊlənt/ *adj* sout corpulent.

corpus /ˈkɔːpəs/ *n* (*pl* **-pora**) **1** Literat, Ling corpus *m*; **2** Fin capital *m*.

Corpus Christi /ˌkɔːpəs ˈkrɪstɪ/ *n* la Fête-Dieu.

corpuscle /ˈkɔːpʌsl/ *n* **1** Anat, Biol (**blood**) **~** globule *m* sanguin; **red/white** (**blood**) **~** globule *m* rouge/blanc; **2** Anat (nerve ending) corpuscule *m*; **3** Phys particule *f*.

corral /kəˈrɑːl, US -ˈræl/ **I** *n* US (enclosure) corral *m*.

II *vtr* parquer [*cattle, horses*]; (surround) cerner [*demonstrator*].

correct /kəˈrekt/ **I** *adj* **1** (right) [*amount, answer*] correct, bon/bonne; [*figure*] exact; [*decision, method, order, number*] bon/bonne; **that is ~** c'est exact; **the ~ time** l'heure exacte; **to be ~ in every detail** être exact jusque dans le moindre détail; **you are quite ~** tu as parfaitement raison; **you are quite ~ in what you say** ce que tu dis est tout à fait juste; **would I be ~ in thinking that...?** aurais-je raison de croire que...?; **her suspicions proved ~** ses soupçons se sont avérés exacts or justes; **2** (proper) [*behaviour, manner, dress, person*] correct, convenable; **according to the ~ procedures** selon l'usage.

II *vtr* **1** [*teacher, proofreader*] corriger [*text, spelling, pronunciation*]; rectifier, corriger [*error*]; **2** (put right) corriger, reprendre [*person*]; corriger [*false impression*]; **~ me if I'm wrong, but...** arrêtez-moi si je me trompe, mais...; **I stand ~ed** je reconnais mon erreur; **3** Med corriger [*eyesight*]; **4** sout (punish) corriger, châtier.

III *v refl* **to ~ oneself** se reprendre.

correcting fluid *n* correcteur *m* liquide.

correction /kəˈrekʃn/ *n* **1** (act) (of text, pronunciation) correction *f*; (of error) correction *f*, rectification *f*; **2** (on manuscript) correction *f*; (in dictation) rectification *f*; **to make a ~** faire une correction; **3** sout (punishment) correction *f*, châtiment *m*; **house of ~**† maison *f* de correction†.

correction fluid *n* liquide *m* correcteur.

corrective /kəˈrektɪv/ **I** *n* correctif *m*, rectificatif *m*; **this is a ~ to the idea that** ceci apporte un démenti à l'idée que.

II *adj* **1** gen [*action*] correcteur/-trice; [*measure*] de redressement; **2** Med [*treatment*] curatif/-ive; [*shoe, lens*] correcteur/-trice; **~ surgery** chirurgie *f* réparatrice.

correctly /kəˈrektlɪ/ *adv* (all contexts) correctement.

correctness /kəˈrektnɪs/ *n* correction *f*.

Correggio /kəˈredʒɪəʊ/ *pr n* le Corrège.

correlate /ˈkɒrəleɪt, US ˈkɔːr-/ **I** *vtr* corréler, mettre en corrélation (**with** avec).

II *vi* être en corrélation (**with** avec).

correlation /ˌkɒrəˈleɪʃn/ *n* corrélation *f* (**between** entre; **with** avec); **a high/poor ~** une corrélation étroite/faible.

correlative /kɒˈrelətɪv/ **I** *n* corrélatif *m*.

II *adj* corrélatif/-ive.

correspond /ˌkɒrɪˈspɒnd, US ˌkɔːr-/ *vi* **1** (match up) concorder, correspondre (**with** à); **to ~ to sample** Comm être conforme à l'échantillon; **2** (be equivalent) être équivalent (**to** à); **they roughly ~** ils sont à peu près équivalents; **3** (exchange letters) correspondre (**with** avec; **about** au sujet de).

correspondence /ˌkɒrɪˈspɒndəns, US ˌkɔːr-/ *n* **1** (match) concordance *f* (**between** entre); **2** (relationship) correspondance *f* (**between** entre); **3** (similarity) similitude *f* (**with** avec); **4** (exchange of letters) correspondance *f*; **to be in ~ with sb** correspondre avec qn (**about** au sujet de); **to enter into ~** engager une correspondance (**about** au sujet de).

correspondence: **~ clerk**† ▶1692 *n* Comm secrétaire *mf*; **~ college** *n* établissement *m* d'enseignement par correspondance; **~ column** *n* Journ courrier *m* des lecteurs; **~ course** *n* cours *m* par correspondance.

correspondent /ˌkɒrɪˈspɒndənt, US ˌkɔːr-/ ▶1692 *n* **1** (journalist) gen journaliste *mf*; (abroad) correspondant/-e *m/f*; **political/sports ~** journaliste *mf* politique/sportif/-ive; **2** (letter writer) correspondant/-e *m/f*.

corresponding /ˌkɒrɪˈspɒndɪŋ, US ˌkɔːr-/ *adj* **1** (matching) correspondant; **on the ~ day last season** le même jour la saison dernière; **2** (similar) équivalent.

correspondingly /ˌkɒrɪˈspɒndɪŋlɪ, US ˌkɔːr-/ *adv* **1** (consequently) par conséquent; **2** (proportionately) proportionnellement.

Corrèze ▶1163 *pr n* Corrèze *f*; **in/to ~** en Corrèze.

corrida /kɔːˈriːdə/ *n* corrida *f*.

corridor /ˈkɒrɪdɔː(r), US ˈkɔːr-/ *n* **1** (in building, train) couloir *m*; **the ~s of power** fig les hautes sphères *fpl* du pouvoir; **2** Geog, Pol corridor *m*.

corridor train *n* GB train *m* à compartiments.

corrigendum /ˌkɒrɪˈgendəm, US ˌkɔːr-/ *n* (*pl* **-da**) erratum *m*.

corroborate /kəˈrɒbəreɪt/ *vtr* corroborer.

corroboration /kəˌrɒbəˈreɪʃn/ *n* corroboration *f* (**of** de).

corroborative /kəˈrɒbərətɪv, US -reɪtɪv/ *adj* corroborant.

corrode /kəˈrəʊd/ **I** *vtr* lit, fig corroder.

II *vi* se corroder.

corrosion /kəˈrəʊʒn/ *n* corrosion *f*.

corrosive /kəˈrəʊsɪv/ **I** *n* corrosif *m*.

II *adj* lit, fig corrosif/-ive.

corrugated /ˈkɒrəgeɪtɪd, US ˈkɔːr-/ *adj* [*roof*] de tôle ondulée; [*road, surface*] ondulé; [*brow, surface of lake etc*] plissé.

corrugated: **~ iron** *n* tôle *f* ondulée; **~ paper** *n* carton *m* ondulé.

corrugation /ˌkɒrəˈgeɪʃn, US ˌkɔːr-/ *n* ondulation *f*.

corrupt /kəˈrʌpt/ **I** *adj* **1** (immoral) gen [*person, behaviour, system*] corrompu; (sexually) dépravé, corrompu; **~ practices** malversations *fpl*; **2** [*text, manuscript,*

language] corrompu; Comput [*data*] corrompu; **3**† (decomposed) corrompu†.
II *vtr* **1** (pervert) pervertir; (through bribery) corrompre; **to ~ sb's morals** dépraver qn; **2** (alter) altérer [*text, manuscript*]; **3**† (decompose) corrompre†.
III *vi* **1** [*book, film, lifestyle*] corrompre; **power ~s** le pouvoir corrompt; **2**† (decompose) se décomposer.

corruptible /kə'rʌptəbl/ *adj* corruptible.

corruption /kə'rʌpʃn/ *n* **1** (immorality) gen corruption *f*; (sexual) corruption *f*, dépravation *f*; **2** (act of corrupting) corruption *f*; **~ of a minor** Jur détournement *m* de mineur; **3** (of text) altération *f*; (of computer data) altération *f*; **4**† (decay) corruption *f*.

corsage /kɔː'sɑːʒ/ *n* **1** (flowers) petit bouquet *m* de fleurs (*porté au corsage*); **2** (bodice) corsage *m*.

corsair /'kɔːseə(r)/ *n* corsaire *m*.

Corse-du-Sud ▶ 1163 *pr n* Corse-du-Sud *f*; **in/to ~** en Corse-du-Sud.

corselet /'kɔːslɪt/ *n* corselet *m*.

corset /'kɔːsɪt/ *n* corset *m*; Med corset *m* orthopédique.

Corsica /'kɔːsɪkə/ ▶ 1381, 1273 *pr n* Corse *f*; **in ~** en Corse.

Corsican /'kɔːsɪkən/ **I** *n* Corse *mf*.
II *adj* corse.

cortege /kɔː'teɪʒ/ *n* cortège *m*.

cortex /'kɔːteks/ *n* (*pl* **-tices**) Anat, Bot cortex *m*.

cortical /'kɔːtɪkl/ *adj* Anat, Bot cortical.

corticoid /'kɔːtɪkɔɪd/, **corticosteroid** /ˌkɔːtɪ'kɒstərɔɪd/ *n* corticoïde *m*.

cortisone /'kɔːtɪzəʊn/ *n* cortisone *f*.

corundum /kə'rʌndəm/ *n* corindon *m*.

coruscate /'kɒrəskeɪt, US 'kɔːr-/ *vi* sout étinceler.

coruscating /'kɒrəskeɪtɪŋ, US 'kɔːr-/ *adj* sout étincelant.

corvette /kɔː'vet/ *n* corvette *f*.

cos *n* **1** /kɒz/ (*abrév* = **cosine**) cos *m*; **2** /kɒz/ = **cos lettuce**; **3**○ /kəz/ *abrév* = **because**.

cosec /'kəʊsek/ *n* (*abrév* = **cosecant**) cosec *f*.

cosecant /ˌkəʊ'siːkənt/ *n* cosécante *f*.

cosh /kɒʃ/ GB **I** *n* matraque *f*.
II *vtr* matraquer.

cosign /ˌkəʊ'saɪn/ *vtr* Fin, Pol cosigner.

cosignatory /ˌkəʊ'sɪgnətərɪ, US -tɔːrɪ/ *n* cosignataire *mf* (**to, of** de).

cosily /'kəʊzɪlɪ/ *adv* [*sit, lie*] confortablement; [*warm*] agréablement.

cosine /'kəʊsaɪn/ *n* cosinus *m*.

cosiness /'kəʊzɪnɪs/ *n* **1** (comfort) (of room) atmosphère *f* douillette; (of clothing, chair) confort *m*; **2** (intimacy) (of conversation, gathering) intimité *f*.

cos lettuce /ˌkɒz 'letɪs/ *n* (salade *f*) romaine *f*.

cosmetic /kɒz'metɪk/ **I** *n* produit *m* de beauté.
II *adj* **1** lit cosmétique; **2** fig péj [*change, reform etc*] superficiel/-ielle.

cosmetician /ˌkɒzme'tɪʃn/ ▶ 1692 *n* cosmétologue *mf*.

cosmetic surgery *n* chirurgie *f* esthétique.

cosmic /'kɒzmɪk/ *adj* **1** lit cosmique; **2** fig (vast) [*event, struggle, battle etc*] prodigieux/-ieuse; **3**○ (wonderful) super○.

cosmic: **~ dust** *n* poussière *f* interstellaire; **~ rays** *npl* rayons *mpl* cosmiques.

cosmogony /kɒz'mɒgənɪ/ *n* cosmogonie *f*.

cosmographer /kɒz'mɒgrəfə(r)/ ▶ 1692 *n* cosmographe *mf*.

cosmography /kɒz'mɒgrəfɪ/ *n* cosmographie *f*.

cosmology /kɒz'mɒlədʒɪ/ *n* cosmologie *f*.

cosmonaut /'kɒzmənɔːt/ ▶ 1692 *n* cosmonaute *mf*.

cosmopolitan /ˌkɒzmə'pɒlɪtn/ *n, adj* cosmopolite (*mf*).

cosmos /'kɒzmɒs/ *n* cosmos *m*.

Cossack /'kɒsæk/ *n, adj* cosaque (*m*).

cosset /'kɒsɪt/ *vtr* choyer [*person*]; protéger [*industry, group*].

cossie○ /'kɒzɪ/ *n* GB maillot *m* de bain.

cost /kɒst, US kɔːst/ **I** *n* **1** (price) coût *m*, prix *m* (**of** de); **the total ~ comes to £500** le coût total revient à 500 livres; **at a ~ of £100** au prix de 100 livres; **at ~** au prix coûtant; **you must bear the ~ of any repairs** tous les frais de réparation sont à votre charge; **the ~ of renovating a house is high** la rénovation d'une maison coûte or revient cher; **at his own ~** à ses frais; **at no ~ to the taxpayer** sans que les contribuables aient à payer; **at no extra ~** sans frais supplémentaires; **at great ~** à grands frais; **he studied abroad, at great ~ to his parents** il a étudié à l'étranger, ce qui a coûté très cher à ses parents; **to count the ~ of sth** estimer le coût des dégâts causés par [*flood, earthquake*]; mesurer les conséquences de [*decision*]; **2** fig prix *m*; **at all ~s** à tout prix; **at the ~ of her own life** au prix de sa propre vie; **she's been very successful but at what ~ to her health?** elle a eu beaucoup de succès mais à quel prix pour sa santé?; **I'll do it, but not at any ~** je le ferai, mais pas à n'importe quel prix; **he knows to his ~ that** il a appris à ses dépens que; **we can generate power at little ~ to the environment** on peut produire de l'énergie sans nuire à l'environnement; **the ~ in human lives was great** beaucoup de vies ont été perdues; **whatever the ~** coûte que coûte.
II costs *npl* **1** Jur frais *mpl* de l'instance; **to pay ~s** être condamné aux dépens; **to be awarded ~s** se voir accorder le remboursement des frais; **2** Comm, Fin frais *mpl*; **transport/labour ~s** frais *mpl* de transport/de main-d'œuvre; **production ~s** coûts *mpl* de production; **to cut ~s** réduire les frais généraux; **to cover ~s** couvrir les frais.
III *vtr* **1** (*prét, pp* **cost**) coûter; **the camera ~s £250** cet appareil photo coûte 250 livres; **how much does it ~?** combien ça coûte?; **the tickets ~ too much** les billets coûtent trop cher; **silver ~s less than gold** l'argent coûte moins cher que l'or; **the meal cost us £40** le repas nous a coûté 40 livres; **the TV will ~ £100 to repair** cela coûtera 100 livres de faire réparer la télé; **a good wine ~s money** un bon vin coûte cher; **I can mend it but it will ~ you**○ je peux le réparer mais cela vous coûtera cher; **2** (*prét, pp* **cost**) fig **that decision cost him his job** cette décision lui a coûté son travail; **high inflation cost us the election** le fort taux d'inflation nous a fait perdre les élections; **politeness ~s nothing** ça ne coûte rien d'être poli; **3** (*prét, pp* **~ed**) Accts, Fin (also **~ out**) calculer le prix de revient de [*product*]; calculer le coût de [*project, work*]; **the project was ~ed at £3 million** le coût du projet a été évalué à 3 millions de livres.

cost: **~ accountant** ▶ 1692 *n* Accts analyste *mf* des coûts; **~-accounting** *n* Accts comptabilité *f* analytique; **~ and freight, CAF** *n* coût *m* et fret *m*.

co-star /'kəʊstɑː(r)/ Cin, Theat **I** *n* co-vedette *f*.
II *vtr* **a film ~ring X and Y** un film avec X et Y.
III *vi* (*p prés etc* **-rr-**) **to ~ with sb** partager la vedette avec qn.

Costa Rica /ˌkɒstə'riːkə/ ▶ 1131 *pr n* Costa Rica *m*.

Costa Rican /ˌkɒstə'riːkən/ ▶ 1486 **I** *n* Costaricain/-e *m/f*.
II *adj* costaricain.

cost: **~-benefit analysis** *n* Accts, Comm analyse *f* coût-bénéfice; **~ centre** *n* Accts centre *m* de coûts.

cost-cutting /'kɒstkʌtɪŋ, US 'kɔːst-/ **I** *n* réduction *f* des frais.
II *modif* [*exercise, strategy*] de réduction des frais; [*measures*] pour réduire les frais; **we've got rid of the fax machine as a ~ exercise** on s'est débarrassé du télécopieur pour réduire les frais.

cost: **~-effective** *adj* Mgmt rentable; **~-effectiveness** *n* rentabilité *f*.

costermonger‡ /'kɒstəmʌŋgə(r), US 'kɔːst-/ ▶ 1692 *n* (also **coster**) GB marchand/-e *m/f* des quatre saisons.

costing /'kɒstɪŋ, US 'kɔːstɪŋ/ **I** *n* **1** (discipline) comptabilité *f* analytique or d'exploitation; **2** (process) (for project) établissement *m* des coûts; (for product) établissement *m* des coûts de production.
II costings *npl* (projected figures) évaluation *f* des coûts (**for** de).

costive /'kɒstɪv, US 'kɔːstɪv/ *adj* **1** Med (constipated) constipé; **2** sout (sluggish) empoté.

costliness /'kɒstlɪnɪs, US 'kɔːst-/ *n* prix *m* élevé.

costly /'kɒstlɪ, US 'kɔːstlɪ/ *adj* **1** (expensive) [*scheme, exercise*] coûteux/-euse; [*error*] coûteux/-euse; [*taste, habit*] de luxe; **the decision proved to be ~** la décision lui/leur etc a coûté beaucoup; **2** (valuable) [*jewellery*] précieux/-ieuse.

cost: **~ of living** *n* Econ, Fin coût *m* de la vie; **~ of living adjustment** *n* indexation *f* des salaires; **~ of living allowance** *n* indemnité *f* de vie chère; **~ of living bonus** *n* prime *f* de vie chère; **~ of living index** *n* indice *m* du coût de la vie; **~ of money** *n* Fin loyer *m* de l'argent; **~ overrun** *n* Accts, Fin dépassement *m* du budget, surcoût *m*; **~-plus** *n* coût *m* majoré.

cost price *n* Comm (for producer) prix *m* de revient; (for consumer) prix *m* coûtant; **at ~** au prix coûtant.

cost-push inflation *n* Fin inflation *f* par les coûts.

costume /'kɒstjuːm, US -tuːm/ **I** *n* **1** (outfit) costume *m*; **national/period ~** costume national/d'époque; **in ~** costumé; **2**† GB (also **swimming ~**) maillot *m* de bain; **3**† (woman's suit) tailleur *m*.
II *modif* [*designer, collection, change*] de costumes.
III *vtr* costumer.

costume: **~ ball** *n* bal *m* costumé; **~ drama** *n* pièce *f* en costume d'époque; **~ jewellery** *n* ¢ bijoux *mpl* fantaisie.

costumier /kɒ'stjuːmɪə(r), US -'stuː-/ ▶ 1692 *n* costumier/-ière *m/f*.

cosy GB, **cozy** US /'kəʊzɪ/ **I** *n* (also **tea-~**) couvre-théière *m*.
II *adj* **1** (comfortable) [*chair, room, atmosphere*] douillet/-ette; [*clothing*] confortable; **to feel ~** [*person*] être confortablement installé; [*room, blanket*] être douillet/-ette; **it's ~ here** on est bien ici; **2** (intimate) [*chat, evening, meeting*] intime; **3** fig [*situation, belief*] rassurant; [*world*] protégé.
IDIOMS **to play it ~**○ US agir en douceur.
■ **cosy up**○ GB, **cozy up**○ US [*person*] se mettre bien (**to** avec).

cot /kɒt/ *n* **1** GB (for baby) lit *m* de bébé; **2** US (camp bed) lit *m* de camp; **3** (on ship) couchette *f*.

cotangent /kəʊ'tændʒənt/ *n* cotangente *f*.

cot death *n* GB mort *f* subite du nourrisson.

Côte d'Ivoire /ˌkəut dɪ'vwɑː(r)/ ▶ 1131 *pr n* Côte d'Ivoire *f*.

Côte-d'Or /ˌkəut'dɔː(r)/ ▶ 1273 *pr n* Côte-d'Or *f*; **in/to ~** en Côte-d'Or.

cotenant /ˌkəʊ'tenənt/ *n* colocataire *mf*.

coterie /'kəʊtərɪ/ *n* cercle *m*; pej coterie *f*.

coterminous /ˌkəʊ'tɜːmɪnəs/ *adj* sout mitoyen/-enne (**with** avec).

Côtes-d'Armor /ˌkəutdɑː'mɔː(r)/ ▶ 1273 *pr n* Côtes-d'Armor *fpl*; **in/to ~** dans les Côtes-d'Armor.

cotillion /kəˈtɪlɪən/ *n* cotillon *m*; US quadrille *m*.

cottage /ˈkɒtɪdʒ/ *n* petite maison *f*, maisonnette *f*; (thatched) chaumière *f*; **weekend ~** maison *f* de campagne.

cottage: **~ cheese** *n* cottage cheese *m*; **~ hospital** *n* GB ≈ polyclinique *f*; **~ industry** *n* travail *m* artisanal à domicile; **~ loaf** *n* GB miche *f* de pain; **~ piano** *n* (petit) piano *m* droit; **~ pie** *n* GB hachis *m* Parmentier.

cottager /ˈkɒtɪdʒə(r)/ *n* **1** villageois/-e *m/f*; **2** US (vacationer) vacancier/-ière *m/f* en location.

cottaging /ˈkɒtɪdʒɪŋ/ *n* drague○ *f* homosexuelle dans les WC publics.

cotter /ˈkɒtə(r)/ *n* **1** Hist (also **cottier**) valet *m* de ferme; **2** Scot (also **cottar**) paysan/-anne *m/f*; **3** Tech (also **~ pin**) goupille *f* fendue.

cotton /ˈkɒtn/ **I** *n* **1** Bot, Tex coton *m*; **2** (thread) fil *m* de coton.
II *modif* [*clothing, fabric, field*] de coton; [*industry, town*] cotonnier/-ière.
■ **cotton on**○ piger○; **to ~ on to sth** piger○ qch, saisir qch.
■ **cotton to**○ US **1** (take a liking to) s'emballer pour; **2** (approve) approuver [*plan, idea*].
■ **cotton up**○ US essayer de se mettre bien (**to** avec).

cotton: **~ batting** *n* US = **cotton wool**; **~ belt** *n* US Cotton Belt *m* (*région cotonnière des États-Unis*); **~ bud** *n* Coton-Tige® *m*; **~ cake** *n* tourteau *m* de graines de coton; **~ candy** *n* US barbe *f* à papa.

cotton drill **I** *n* Tex coutil *m*.
II *modif* [*clothing*] en coutil.

cotton: **~ gin** *n* égreneuse *f* de coton; **~ grass** *n* linaigrette *f*; **~ mill** *n* filature *f* de coton.

cotton picker ▶1692 *n* **1** (machine) ramasseuse *f* de coton; **2** (person) cueilleur/-euse *m/f* de coton.

cotton-picking○ *adj* US péj sale○ (*before n*), sacré○ (*before n*).

cotton: **~ reel** *n* bobine *f* de coton; **~seed** *n* graine *f* de coton; **~seed cake** *n* = **cotton cake**; **~seed oil** *n* huile *f* de coton; **~tail** *n* US lapin *m* de garenne; **~ waste** *n* gen étoupe *f* de coton; (for cleaning) coton *m* d'essuyage.

cotton wool *n* ouate *f* (de coton); **absorbent ~** ouate hydrophile.
IDIOMS **to wrap sb in ~** élever qn dans du coton.

cotton worker ▶1692 *n* cotonnier/-ière *m/f*.

cotyledon /ˌkɒtɪˈliːdn/ *n* cotylédon *m*.

couch /kaʊtʃ/ **I** *n* **1** (sofa) canapé *m*; **2** (doctor's) lit *m*; (psychoanalyst's) divan *m*; **to be on the ~** US être en analyse; **3** littér (bed) couche *f*; **4** Bot = **couch grass**.
II *vtr* formuler [*idea, response*]; **a reply ~ed in conciliatory terms** une réponse formulée en termes conciliants.
III *vi* littér [*animal*] être couché.

couchant /ˈkaʊtʃənt/ *adj* Herald couché.

couchette /kuːˈʃet/ *n* couchette *f*.

couch: **~ grass** /ˈkaʊtʃgrɑːs, ˈkuːtʃ, US -græs/ *n* chiendent *m*; **~ potato**○ *n* péj pantouflard/-e○ *m/f* (*qui passe son temps devant la télévision*).

cougar /ˈkuːgə(r)/ *n* puma *m*.

cough /kɒf, US kɔːf/ **I** *n* toux *f*; **dry/smoker's ~** toux sèche/de fumeur; **to have a ~** tousser; **she has a bad ~** elle a une mauvaise toux.
II *vi* tousser.
■ **cough up**: **~ up [sth]** **1** lit cracher [*blood*]; **2**○ fig cracher○ [*information*]; **to ~ up (the money)** cracher○.

cough drop, **cough lozenge** *n* pastille *f* pour la toux.

coughing /ˈkɒfɪŋ, US ˈkɔːfɪŋ/ *n* toux *f*; **~ fit** accès *m* de toux.

cough mixture, **cough syrup** *n* (sirop *m*) antitussif *m*.

could /kʊd, kəd/ ▶ **can**[1].

couldn't /ˈkʊdnt/ = **could not**.

could've /ˈkʊdəv/ = **could have**.

coulee /ˈkuːliː/ *n* US **1** (ravine) ravine *f*; **2** (stream) ruisseau *m* intermittent.

couloir /ˈkuːlwɑː(r)/ *n* Geog couloir *m*.

council /ˈkaʊnsl/ **I** *n* conseil *m*; **parish/city/international ~** conseil paroissial/municipal/international; **the Council of Europe** le Conseil de l'Europe; **in ~** en assemblée.
II *modif* [*employee, workman*] municipal; [*grant*] de la municipalité.

council: **~ chamber** *n* salle *f* du conseil; **~ estate** *n* lotissement *m* de logements sociaux; **~ flat** *n* appartement *m* à loyer modéré; **~ house** *n* habitation *f* à loyer modéré; **~ housing** *n* logements *mpl* sociaux.

councillor /ˈkaʊnsələ(r)/ *n* conseiller/-ère *m/f*; **Councillor Brown** Monsieur le conseiller/Madame la conseillère Brown.

council: **~man** *n* US conseiller *m* municipal; **~ tax** *n* ≈ impôts *mpl* locaux; **~ tenant** *n* habitant *m* de logement social; **~woman** *n* US conseillère *f* municipale.

counsel /ˈkaʊnsl/ **I** *n* **1** sout (advice) conseil *m*; **to keep one's own ~** garder ses intentions pour soi; **to take ~ (together)** se consulter; **2** Jur avocat/-e *m/f*; **~ for the defence** avocat/-e *m/f* de la défense; **~ for the prosecution** procureur *m*.
II *vtr* **1** (give advice to) conseiller [*person, family*] (**about, on** sur); **2** sout (recommend) conseiller [*caution, silence*]; **to ~ sb to do** conseiller à qn de faire.

counselling, **counseling** US /ˈkaʊnsəlɪŋ/ **I** *n* **1** (psychological advice) aide *f* psychosociale; **bereavement ~** aide psychosociale aux personnes endeuillées; **2** (practical advice) assistance *f*; **debt ~** assistance aux personnes endettées; **careers ~** orientation *f* professionnelle; **3** Sch orientation *f* scolaire.
II *modif* [*group, centre, service*] d'aide psychosociale, d'assistance.

counselling service *n* US Sch service *m* d'aide aux élèves.

counsellor, **counselor** US /ˈkaʊnsələ(r)/ ▶1692 *n* **1** (adviser) conseiller/-ère *m/f*; **trained ~** conseiller/-ère qualifié/-e; **2** US Sch conseiller/-ère *m/f* d'éducation; **3** US Jur (also **~-at-law**) avocat/-e *m/f*; **4** US (in holiday camp) moniteur/-trice *m/f*.

count /kaʊnt/ ▶1268 **I** *n* **1** (numerical record) gen décompte *m*; Pol (at election) dépouillement *m*; **to make a ~ of sth** compter qch; **there were 60 guests at the last ~** il y avait 60 invités au dernier décompte; **to keep (a) ~ of** tenir compte de qch; **to lose ~** se perdre dans ses comptes; **I've lost ~** je ne sais plus où j'en suis; **I've lost ~ of the number of times I've tried** j'ai essayé je ne sais combien de fois; **I've lost ~ of the number of complaints I've received** je ne compte plus le nombre de plaintes que j'ai reçues; **2** (level) taux *m*; **bacteria/cholesterol ~** taux de bactéries/de cholestérol; **3** (figure) chiffre *m*; **the official ~ was three million unemployed** le chiffre officiel était de trois millions de chômeurs; **4** (call) **on the ~ of three, fire!** à trois, tirez!; **I'll give you a ~ of 50** je compterai jusqu'à 50; **5** Jur chef *m* d'accusation; **he was convicted on three ~s** on l'a condamné pour trois chefs d'accusation; **6** (point) **you're wrong on both ~s** vous avez tort sur les deux points; **we're satisfied on all three ~s** les trois points qui posaient problème sont maintenant éclaircis; **7** Sport (in boxing) **to be out for the ~**○ être KO○ also fig; **8** (also **Count**) (nobleman) comte *m*.
II *vtr* **1** (add up) compter [*points, people, words, mistakes, objects*]; vérifier [*one's change*]; énumérer [*reasons, causes*]; **to ~ how much one has spent** calculer combien on a dépensé; **to ~ the votes** Pol dépouiller le scrutin; gen compter les votes; **I'm ~ing the days until Christmas** je compte les jours jusqu'à Noël; **the teacher ~ed heads** le professeur a compté les présents; **55 people, ~ing the children** 55 personnes en comptant les enfants; **20, not ~ing my sister** 20, sans compter ma sœur; **to ~ the cost of sth** fig faire le bilan de qch; **2** (consider) **to ~ sb as sth** considérer qn comme qch; **children over 15 are ~ed as adults** on considère les enfants de plus de 15 ans comme des adultes.
III *vi* **1** gen, Math compter; **to ~ (up) to 50** compter jusqu'à 50; **to ~ in fives** compter de cinq en cinq; **I've had six drinks, but who's ~ing?** j'ai bu six verres, et alors?; **2** (be relevant) compter; **this ~s towards your final mark** cela compte pour votre note finale; **3** (be of importance) compter; **qualifications ~ for little** les qualifications ne comptent guère; **all my work ~s for nothing** mon travail ne compte pour rien; **every second ~s** chaque seconde compte; **4** (be considered) **children over 15 ~ as adults** les enfants de plus de 15 ans sont considérés comme des adultes; **handbags don't ~ as luggage** les sacs à main ne sont pas considérés comme des bagages.
IDIOMS **to ~ sheep** compter les moutons; **to ~ the pennies** regarder à la dépense; **to ~ oneself lucky** ou **fortunate** s'estimer heureux; **~ yourself lucky (that) you only got a fine** estime-toi heureux de n'avoir eu qu'une amende; **it's the thought that ~s** c'est l'intention qui compte; **to stand up and be ~ed** se faire entendre.
■ **count against**: **~ against [sb]** [*criminal record, past*] être un handicap pour; [*age, background, mistakes*] jouer contre.
■ **count down** déclencher le compte à rebours (**to** avant).
■ **count in**: **~ [sb] in 1** (include) **if you're organizing an outing, ~ me in!** si tu organises une sortie, j'en suis!; **we're going on strike, can we ~ you in?** on fait la grève, est-ce qu'on peut compter sur vous?; **2** Mus faire entrer [qn] en mesure.
■ **count on**, **count upon**: **~ on [sb/sth]** compter sur [*person, event*]; **don't ~ on it!** ne comptez pas (trop) dessus!; **I was ~ing on the train being late** je comptais sur le retard du train; **I'm ~ing on you to help me** je compte sur toi pour m'aider.
■ **count out**: ¶ **~ out [sth]** compter [*money, cards*]; **he ~ed out the money** il a compté l'argent (pièce par pièce or billet par billet): ¶ **~ [sb] out 1** (exclude) **if it's dangerous you can ~ me out!** si c'est dangereux ne comptez pas sur moi!; **~ me out, I'm not interested** ne compte pas sur moi, ça ne m'intéresse pas; **~ [sb] out of** exclure [qn] de [*plans, calculations*]; **2** Sport **to be ~ed out** [*boxer*] aller au tapis.
■ **count up**: **~ up [sth]** calculer [*cost*]; compter [*money, boxes*]; **~ up how many hours you spend on the work** calculez le temps que vous aurez passé sur ce travail.

countability /ˌkaʊntəˈbɪlətɪ/ *n* Ling fait *m* d'être comptable.

countable /ˈkaʊntəbl/ *adj* **1** Ling dénombrable, comptable; **2** (quantifiable) dénombrable.

countdown /ˈkaʊntdaʊn/ *n* lit, fig compte *m* à rebours (**to** avant).

countenance /ˈkaʊntənəns/ **I** *n* littér (face) visage *m*; (expression) expression *f*.
II *vtr* sout (tolerate) admettre [*misuse, slander*]; **to ~ sb doing** admettre que qn fasse.
IDIOMS **to keep one's ~** ne pas se laisser décontenancer; **to put sb out of ~** décontenancer qn.

counter /ˈkaʊntə(r)/ **I** *n* **1** (service area) (in shop, snack bar) comptoir *m*; (in bank, post office) guichet *m*; (in pub, bar) bar *m*; **he works behind the ~** (in bank etc) il travaille au guichet; (in shop, bar) il est derrière le comptoir; **the man/girl behind**

the ~ (in shop) le vendeur/la vendeuse; (in bank, post office) le caissier/la caissière; **this medicine is available over the ~** ce médicament est vendu sans ordonnance; **guns are not sold over the ~** les armes ne sont pas en vente libre; **to buy shares over the ~** acheter des actions hors cote; **these magazines are sold under the ~** on vend ces magazines en sous-main; **to do a deal under the ~** conclure un accord en sous-main; **2** (section of a shop) rayon *m*; **perfume/glove ~** rayon parfumerie/ganterie; **cheese ~** fromagerie *f*, rayon *m* fromagerie; **3** Games pion *m*; **4** (token) jeton *m*; **5** (counting device) compteur *m*; **6** (on shoe) contrefort *m*.
II **counter to** *prep phr* [*be, go, run*] à l'encontre de; [*act, behave*] contrairement à; **this trend runs ~ to forecasts** cette tendance va à l'encontre des prévisions.
III *vtr* répondre à [*accusation, claim*]; réagir à [*threat, attack*]; s'opposer à [*trend*]; neutraliser [*effet*]; parer [*blow*]; enrayer [*inflation, increase*].
IV *vi* (retaliate) riposter; **I ~ed by accusing him of theft** j'ai riposté or répondu en l'accusant de vol; **she ~ed with a new proposal** elle a répondu par une nouvelle proposition; **he ~ed with a left hook** il a riposté par un crochet du gauche.
V **counter+** (*dans composés*) contre-.

counteract /ˌkaʊntəˈrækt/ *vtr* **1** (work against) contrer [*decision, influence, effects*]; **2** (thwart) contrecarrer [*strike, negative publicity*]; **3** (counterbalance) contrebalancer [*tendency*].

counter-argument /ˌkaʊntərˈɑːgjʊmənt/ *n* contre-argument *m*.

counter-attack /ˈkaʊntərətæk/ I *n* contre-attaque *f* (**against** sur).
II *vtr, vi* contre-attaquer.

counter-attraction /ˌkaʊntərəˈtrækʃn/ *n* attraction *f* concurrente (**to** de).

counterbalance I /ˈkaʊntəbæləns/ *n* contrepoids *m* (**to** à).
II /ˌkaʊntəˈbæləns/ *vtr* contrebalancer.

counter-bid /ˈkaʊntəbɪd/ *n* contre-offre *f*.

counterblast /ˈkaʊntəblɑːst, US -blæst/ *n* riposte *f* énergique (**to** à).

counter-charge I /ˈkaʊntətʃɑːdʒ/ *n* **1** Jur contre-accusation *f*; **2** Mil contre-offensive *f*.
II /ˌkaʊntəˈtʃɑːdʒ/ *vtr* **1** Jur riposter à [*accuser*]; **2** Mil **to ~ the enemy** lancer une contre-offensive.

countercheck I /ˈkaʊntətʃek/ *n* (double check) deuxième vérification *f*.
II /ˌkaʊntəˈtʃek/ *vtr* revérifier.

counter cheque GB, **counter check** US *n* chèque-guichet *m*.

counter-claim /ˈkaʊntəkleɪm/ *n* gen rétorsion *f*; Jur demande *f* reconventionnelle.

counter clerk ▶1692 *n* US Fin, Post caissier/-ière *m/f*.

counter-clockwise /ˌkaʊntəˈklɒkwaɪz/ *adj, adv* US dans le sens inverse des aiguilles d'une montre.

counter-culture /ˈkaʊntəkʌltʃə(r)/ *n* contre-culture *f*.

counter-current /ˈkaʊntəkʌrənt/ *n* contre-courant *m*.

counter-espionage /ˌkaʊntərˈespɪənɑːʒ/ *n* contre-espionnage *m*.

counter-example /ˈkaʊntərɪgzɑːmpl, US -zæmpl/ *n* contre-exemple *m*.

counterfeit /ˈkaʊntəfɪt/ I *n* contrefaçon *f*.
II *adj* [*signature, note*] contrefait; **~ money** fausse monnaie *f*.
III *vtr* contrefaire.

counterfeiter /ˈkaʊntəfɪtə(r)/ *n* faussaire *mf*.

counterfoil /ˈkaʊntəfɔɪl/ *n* talon *m*, souche *f*.

counter-inflationary /ˌkaʊntərɪnˈfleɪʃnrɪ, US -nerɪ/ *adj* anti-inflationniste.

counter-insurgency /ˌkaʊntərɪnˈsɜːdʒənsɪ/ *n* contre-insurrection *f*.

counter-insurgent /ˌkaʊntərɪnˈsɜːdʒənt/ *n* contre-insurgé/-e *m/f*.

counter-intelligence /ˌkaʊntərɪnˈtelɪdʒəns/ I *n* contre-espionnage *m*.
II *modif* [*activity, personnel, agency*] de contre-espionnage.

counter-intuitive /ˌkaʊntərɪnˈtjuːɪtɪv, US -ˈtuː-/ *adj* paradoxal.

counter-irritant /ˌkaʊntərˈɪrɪtənt/ *n* révulsif *m*.

countermand /ˌkaʊntəˈmɑːnd, US -ˈmænd/ *vtr* annuler [*order, decision*]; **unless ~ed** sauf contrordre.

countermarch /ˈkaʊntəmɑːtʃ/ Mil I *n* défilé *m* en sens inverse.
II *vi* défiler en sens inverse.

counter-measure /ˈkaʊntəmeʒə(r)/ *n* contre-mesure *f*.

counter-move /ˈkaʊntəmuːv/ *n* mouvement *m* contraire.

counter-offensive /ˌkaʊntərəˈfensɪv/ *n* contre-offensive *f* (**against** sur).

counter-offer /ˈkaʊntərɒfə(r)/ *n* contre-proposition *f*.

counterpane† /ˈkaʊntəpeɪn/ *n* couvre-lit *m*.

counterpart /ˈkaʊntəpɑːt/ *n* (of person) homologue *mf*; (of company, institution etc) équivalent *m* (**of, to** de); (of document) double *m*.

counterpoint /ˈkaʊntəpɔɪnt/ I *n* (all contexts) contrepoint *m*.
II *vtr* fournir un contrepoint à.

counterpoise /ˈkaʊntəpɔɪz/ I *n* **1** (weight) contrepoids *m* (**to** à); **2** (equilibrium) équilibre *m*.
II *vtr* **1** (oppose) faire contrepoids à; **2** (balance) rééquilibrer.

counter-productive /ˌkaʊntəprəˈdʌktɪv/ *adj* contre-productif/-ive.

counter-productiveness /ˌkaʊntəprəˈdʌktɪvnɪs/ *n* contre-productivité *f*.

counter-proposal /ˌkaʊntəprəˈpəʊzl/ *n* contre-proposition *f*.

counter punch I *n* contre *m*.
II **counter-punch** *vtr, vi* contrer.

Counter-Reformation /ˌkaʊntəˌrefəˈmeɪʃn/ *n* Hist Contre-Réforme *f*.

counter-revolution /ˌkaʊntəˌrevəˈluːʃn/ *n* contre-révolution *f*.

counter-revolutionary /ˌkaʊntəˌrevəˈluːʃənərɪ, US -nerɪ/ *n, adj* contre-révolutionnaire (*mf*).

countersign /ˈkaʊntəsaɪn/ I *n* Mil mot *m* de passe.
II *vtr* contresigner.

countersink /ˈkaʊntəsɪŋk/ *vtr* fraiser [*hole*]; noyer [*screw, bolt*].

counter staff *n* Fin, Post caissiers/-ières *mpl/fpl*.

counter-summit /ˈkaʊntəsʌmɪt/ *n* sommet *m* parallèle.

counter-tenor /ˌkaʊntəˈtenə(r)/ ▶1868 *n* (person) haute-contre *m*; (voice) haute-contre *f*.

counter-terrorism /ˌkaʊntəˈterərɪzəm/ *n* contre-terrorisme *m*.

counter-terrorist /ˌkaʊntəˈterərɪst/ *n, adj* contre-terroriste (*mf*).

countervailing /ˈkaʊntəveɪlɪŋ/ *adj* sout compensatoire.

counterweight /ˈkaʊntəweɪt/ *n* contrepoids *m* (**to** à).

countess /ˈkaʊntɪs/ ▶1268 *n* (also **Countess**) comtesse *f*.

counting /ˈkaʊntɪŋ/ I *n* gen calcul *m*; (of votes) dépouillement *m*; **the ~ of votes** le dépouillement du scrutin.
II *modif* [*game, rhyme, song*] pour apprendre à compter.

counting house† *n* GB bureau *m* des comptables.

countless /ˈkaʊntlɪs/ *adj* **~ cars/letters** un nombre incalculable de voitures/de lettres; **he has forgotten his key on ~ occasions** il a oublié sa clé je ne sais combien de fois; **~ millions of** des millions et des millions de.

count noun *n* Ling nom *m* comptable.

countrified /ˈkʌntrɪfaɪd/ *adj* rustique; pej rustaud.

country /ˈkʌntrɪ/ I *n* **1** (nation, people) pays *m*; **developing/Third World ~** pays en voie de développement/du tiers-monde; **to go to the ~** GB Pol appeler le pays aux urnes; **2** (native land) patrie *f*; **to die for one's ~** mourir pour sa patrie; **the old ~** le pays natal; **3** (also **~side**) (out of town) campagne *f*; **across ~** à travers la campagne; **in the ~** à la campagne; **open ~** rase campagne; **4** (area) région *f*; **fish-ing/walking ~** une région bonne pour la pêche/la marche; **cattle ~** une région d'élevage de bétail; **Brontë ~** le pays des Brontë; **cowboy ~** la terre des cowboys; **5** (also **~ music**) country (music) *f*.
II *modif* **1** [*person, road, life*] de campagne; [*scene*] campagnard; **2** Mus (also **~ and western**) [*music, singer*] de country (music).
IDIOMS **it's a free ~!** on est en république!, on est libre de faire ce qu'on veut!; **it's my line of ~** ça me connaît; **it's not really my line of ~** ce n'est pas vraiment mon fort.

country and western I *n* musique *f* country et western.
II *modif* [*singer*] de musique country et western.

country: **~ blues** *n* country blues *m*; **~-bred** *adj* élevé à la campagne; **~ bumpkin** *n* péj plouc° *mf*; **~ club** *n* club *m* de loisirs (*à la campagne*); **~ cousin** *n* péj ou hum personne *f* qui débarque de la campagne; **~ dance** *n* danse *f* folklorique; **~ dancer** *n* danseur/-euse *m/f* de danses folkloriques.

country dancing *n* danse *f* folklorique; **to go ~** danser des danses folkloriques.

country: **~ gentleman** *n* gentilhomme *m* campagnard; **~ house** *n* manoir *m*.

countryman /ˈkʌntrɪmən/ *n* (*pl* **-men**) **1** (also **fellow ~**) compatriote *m*; **2** (living out of town) campagnard *m*.

country mile° *n* longue distance *f*; **it's a ~!** c'est bien plus loin qu'un mile!

country: **~ music** *n* country music *f*; **~ park** *n* parc *m* régional; **~ rock** *n* Geol roche *f* encaissante; Mus country rock *m*; **~ seat** *n* domaine *m*.

countryside /ˈkʌntrɪsaɪd/ *n* campagne *f*; **there is some lovely ~ around here** il y a de beaux paysages par ici.

country: **Countryside Commission** *n* GB commission *f* des espaces naturels; **~wide** *adj, adv* dans tout le pays.

countrywoman /ˈkʌntrɪwʊmən/ *n* (*pl* **-women**) **1** (also **fellow ~**) compatriote *f*; **2** (living out of town) campagnarde *f*.

county /ˈkaʊntɪ/ I *n* comté *m*.
II *modif* GB [*boundary, team, agent, jail*] du comté.
III° *adj* GB péj [*accent*] ≈ d'aristocrate; **he's very ~** il fait très gentleman-farmer.

county: **~ agent** ▶1692 *n* US conseiller *m* en agriculture; **~ council, CC** *n* GB Pol ≈ conseil *m* régional; **~ councillor** *n* GB Pol ≈ conseiller/-ère *m/f* régional/-e; **~ court** *n* GB Jur ≈ tribunal *m* d'instance.

County Durham /ˌkaʊntɪ ˈdʌrəm/ ▶1624 *pr n* Comté *m* de Durham.

county: **~ seat** *n* US chef-lieu *m* de comté; **~ town** *n* GB chef-lieu *m* de comté.

coup /kuː/ I *n* **1** (also **~ d'état**) coup *m* d'État; **2** (successful move) beau coup *m*; **to pull off/score a ~** réussir/faire un beau coup.
II *modif* [*attempt*] de coup (d'État).

coup: **~ de foudre** *n* coup *m* de tonnerre; **~ de grâce** *n* coup *m* de grâce; **~ d'état** *n* coup *m* d'État.

Countries and continents

Most countries and all continents are used with the definite article in French:

France is a beautiful country	=	la France est un beau pays
I like Canada	=	j'aime le Canada
to visit the United States	=	visiter les États-Unis
to know Iran	=	connaître l'Iran

A very few countries do not:

to visit Israel	=	visiter Israël

When in doubt, check in the dictionary.

All the continent names are feminine in French. Most names of countries are feminine e.g. la France, *but some are masculine e.g.* le Canada.

Most names of countries are singular in French, but some are plural (usually, but not always, those that are plural in English) e.g. les États-Unis *mpl* (the United States), *and* les Philippines *fpl* (the Philippines). *Note, however, the plural verb* sont:

the Philippines is a lovely country	=	les Philippines sont un beau pays

In, to and from somewhere

With continent names, feminine singular names of countries and masculine singular names of countries beginning with a vowel, for in *and* to *use* en, *and for* from *use* de:

to live in Europe	=	vivre en Europe
to go to Europe	=	aller en Europe
to come from Europe	=	venir d'Europe
to live in France	=	vivre en France
to go to France	=	aller en France
to come from France	=	venir de France
to live in Afghanistan	=	vivre en Afghanistan
to go to Afghanistan	=	aller en Afghanistan
to come from Afghanistan	=	venir d'Afghanistan

Note that names of countries and continents that include North, South, East, *or* West *work in the same way:*

to live in North Korea	=	vivre en Corée du Nord
to go to North Korea	=	aller en Corée du Nord
to come from North Korea	=	venir de Corée du Nord

With masculine countries beginning with a consonant, and with plurals, use au *or* aux *for* in *and* to, *and* du *or* des *for* from:

to live in Canada	=	vivre au Canada
to go to Canada	=	aller au Canada
to come from Canada	=	venir du Canada
to live in the United States	=	vivre aux États-Unis
to go to the United States	=	aller aux États-Unis
to come from the United States	=	venir des États-Unis
to live in the Philippines	=	vivre aux Philippines
to go to the Philippines	=	aller aux Philippines
to come from the Philippines	=	venir des Philippines

Adjective uses: *français or de France or de la France?*

For French, *the translation* français *is usually safe; here are some typical examples:*

the French army	=	l'armée française
the French coast	=	la côte française
French cooking	=	la cuisine française
French currency	=	la monnaie française
the French Customs	=	la douane française
the French government	=	le gouvernement français
the French language	=	la langue française
French literature	=	la littérature française
French money	=	l'argent français
the French nation	=	le peuple français
French politics	=	la politique française
a French town	=	une ville française
French traditions	=	les traditions françaises

Some nouns, however, occur more commonly with de France *(usually, but not always, their English equivalents can have* of France *as well as* French):

the Ambassador of France *or* the French Ambassador	=	l'ambassadeur de France
the French Embassy	=	l'ambassade de France
the history of France *or* French history	=	l'histoire de France
the King of France *or* the French king	=	le roi de France
the rivers of France	=	les fleuves et rivières de France
the French team	=	l'équipe de France

but note:

the capital of France *or* the French capital	=	la capitale de la France

Note that many geopolitical adjectives like French *can also refer to nationality, e.g.* a French tourist ▶ 1486, *or to the language, e.g.* a French word ▶ 1402.

coupé /ˈkuːpeɪ/ *n* coupé *m*.

couple /ˈkʌpl/ **I** *n* **1** gen, Phys, Sport (pair) couple *m*; **young (married) ~** jeune couple; **2 a ~ of** (two) deux [*people, objects*]; (a few) deux ou trois; **a ~ of times** deux ou trois fois.
II *vtr* **1** coupler [*circuits, wheels*]; Rail atteler [*coaches*]; **2** fig (associate) associer [*names, ideas*]; **~d with** s'ajoutant à.
III *vi* [*person, animal*] s'accoupler.

coupler /ˈkʌplə(r)/ *n* (all contexts) coupleur *m*.

couplet /ˈkʌplɪt/ *n* distique *m*.

coupling /ˈkʌplɪŋ/ *n* **1** gen accouplement *m*; **2** Rail attelage *m*; **3** Elec couplage *m*.

coupon /ˈkuːpɒn/ *n* **1** (for goods) bon *m*; **petrol/clothes ~** bon d'essence/de vêtements; **2** (form) coupon *m*; **reply ~** coupon-réponse *m*; **entry ~** (for competition) bulletin *m* de participation; **3** Fin coupon *m*; **4** (in football) grille *f* de paris.

courage /ˈkʌrɪdʒ/ *n* courage *m* (**to do** de faire); **to have/lack the ~ of one's convictions** avoir/ne pas avoir le courage de ses opinions; **to pluck up the ~ to do** trouver le courage de faire; **to show ~** faire preuve de courage; **to take one's ~ in both hands** prendre son courage à deux mains; **it takes ~ to do** il faut du courage pour faire; **to take ~ from sth** être encouragé par qch.

courageous /kəˈreɪdʒəs/ *adj* courageux/-euse; **it is/was ~ of him to do it** c'est/c'était courageux de sa part de le faire.

courageously /kəˈreɪdʒəslɪ/ *adv* courageusement.

courageousness /kəˈreɪdʒəsnɪs/ *n* courage *m*, bravoure *f*.

courgette /kɔːˈʒet/ *n* courgette *f*.

courier /ˈkʊrɪə(r)/ ▶ 1692 *n* **1** (also **travel ~**) guide *m*; **2** (for parcels, documents) coursier *m*; (for drugs) transporteur *m*.

courier company *n* Comm messagerie *f* (rapide).

course /kɔːs/ **I** *n* **1** (progression) (of time, event, history, nature) cours *m* (**of** de); **in the ~ of** au cours de; **in the ~ of time** avec le temps; **in the normal** ou **ordinary ~ of things** ou **events** normalement; **in the ~ of doing** en faisant; **in the ~ of construction/development** en cours de construction/développement; **to take its ~** se mettre en train; **to run** ou **follow its ~** suivre son cours; **in due ~** en temps utile; **to change the ~ of sth** changer le cours de qch; **2** (route) (of river, road, planet, star) cours *m*; (of boat, plane) cap *m*; **to be on** ou **hold** ou **steer a ~** Aviat, Naut tenir un cap; **to be on ~ for** lit être en route pour; fig aller vers; **the economy is back on ~** l'économie s'est restabilisée; **to be** ou **go off ~** faire fausse route; **to change ~** gen, lit changer de direction; Aviat, Naut changer de cap; fig changer d'avis; **to set (a) ~ for** Aviat, Naut mettre le cap sur; **~ of action** moyen *m* d'action, parti *m*; **to take a ~ of action** prendre un parti; **this is the only ~ open to us** c'est le seul parti qui s'offre à nous; **3** Sch, Univ cours *m* (**in** en; **of** de); **art/French ~** cours *m* d'art/de français; **beginners' ~** cours *m* pour débutants; **introductory/advanced ~** cours *m* inaugural/avancé; **a ~ of study** Sch programme *m* scolaire; Univ cursus *m* universitaire; **to go on a ~** (aller) suivre un cours; **to be on a ~** suivre un cours; **4** Med, Vet (of drug) traitement *m*; (of injections) série *f*; **a ~ of treatment** un traitement; **5** Sport (in golf, athletics) parcours *m*; Turf cours *m*; **to stay the ~** lit finir la course; fig tenir bon; **6** (part of meal) plat *m*; **second/third ~** deuxième/troisième plat *m*; **the fish ~** le plat de poisson; **the cheese ~** le plateau de fromages; **7** Constr assise *f*.
II *vtr* Hunt [*dog*] courir [*quarry*]; [*person*] faire courir [*hounds*].
III *vi* **1** (rush) couler; **the tears ~d down her cheeks** les larmes coulaient sur ses joues; **the blood was coursing through** ou **in her veins** le sang coulait dans ses veines; **ideas were coursing through his mind** les idées se bousculaient dans son esprit; **2** Sport [*dogs*] courir le lièvre; [*person*] chasser.
IV -course (*dans composés*) **three/five-~** [*meal*] de trois/cinq plats.
V of course *adv phr* bien sûr, évidemment; **of ~ I do!** bien sûr que oui!; **of ~ he doesn't!** bien sûr que non!; **'did you lock the door?'—'of ~ I did!'** 'tu as fermé la porte à clé?'—'mais oui, enfin!'; **'you didn't believe him?'—'of ~ not!'** 'tu ne l'as pas cru?'—'mais non, voyons!'; **it might rain/it's too expensive, of ~** évidemment il pourrait pleuvoir/c'est trop cher; **you'll stay for dinner, of ~?** vous allez bien rester dîner?

course book *n* méthode *f*.

courser /ˈkɔːsə(r)/ *n* **1** Hunt (person) chasseur *m*; (dog) chien *m* courant; **2†** (horse) littér coursier *m* liter.

coursework /ˈkɔːswɜːk/ *n* Sch, Univ devoirs *mpl* (de contrôle continu).

coursing /ˈkɔːsɪŋ/ *n* chasse *f* (*où les chiens utilisent leur vue plutôt que leur flair*).

court /kɔːt/ **I** *n* **1** Jur cour *f*, tribunal *m*; **to appear in ~** comparaître devant un tribunal; **to say in ~ that** dire au tribunal que; **to bring sth to ~** amener qch devant le tribunal; **to go to ~** aller devant les tribunaux or en justice (**over** pour); **to take sb to ~** poursuivre qn en justice; **to rule sth out of ~** décreter que qch est irrecevable; **to settle sth out of ~** régler qch à l'amiable; **in open ~** en audience publique; **in closed ~** à huis clos; **2** Sport (for tennis, squash) court *m*; (for basketball) terrain *m*; **X is on ~ at the moment** X joue en ce moment; **3** (of sovereign) cour *f*; **to**

hold ~ fig tenir cour; **4** (also **~yard**) cour *f*.

II *modif* Jur [*case, action*] judiciaire; [*decision, hearing, ruling*] du tribunal; **~ appearance** comparution *f* en justice.

III *vtr* **1**† ou fig (try to gain love of) courtiser [*woman, voters, customers*]; **2** (seek) rechercher [*affection, favour, controversy*]; courir à [*failure, disaster*]; chercher [*trouble*].

IV† *vi* [*couple*] se fréquenter; **he's ~ing** il a une petite amie; **a ~ing couple** un couple d'amoureux; **in our ~ing days** avant notre mariage.

IDIOMS **to get laughed out of ~** se rendre complètement ridicule; **to laugh sb out of ~** tourner qn en ridicule; **to pay ~ to sb**† faire la cour à qn.

court: **~ card** *n* GB Games figure *f* (*aux cartes*); **~ circular** *n* bulletin *m* quotidien de la cour; **~ dress** *n* ¢ habit *m* de cour.

Courtelle® /kɔː'tel/ *n* Courtelle® *f*.

courteous /'kɜːtɪəs/ *adj* courtois (**to** envers); **it is/was ~ of them to do it** c'est/c'était courtois de leur part de le faire.

courteously /'kɜːtɪəslɪ/ *adv* courtoisement.

courtesan /ˌkɔːtɪ'zæn, US 'kɔːtɪzn/ *n* courtisane *f*.

courtesy /'kɜːtəsɪ/ *n* **1** courtoisie *f*; **to have the ~ to do** avoir la courtoisie de faire; **it is only common ~ to do** c'est la moindre des politesses de faire; **to do sb the ~ of doing** iron faire à qn le plaisir de faire; **to exchange courtesies** faire des échanges de politesse; **2** (**by**) **~ of** (with permission from) avec la gracieuse permission de [*rightful owner*]; (with funds from) grâce à la générosité de [*sponsor*]; (through the good offices of) grâce à [*colleagues, police, employer*]; **a free trip/flight ~ of the airline** un voyage/vol gratuit offert par la compagnie aérienne.

courtesy call *n* visite *f* de courtoisie.

courtesy car *n* voiture *f* (mise à la disposition de qn); **to give sb a ~** mettre une voiture à la disposition de qn.

courtesy: **~ coach** *n* navette *f* gratuite; **~ delay** *n* Aut plafonnier *m* à extinction différée; **~ light** *n* Aut plafonnier *m*; **~ title** *n* titre *m* de courtoisie; **~ visit** = **courtesy call**.

courthouse /'kɔːthaʊs/ *n* **1** Jur palais *m* de justice; **2** US Admin ≈ préfecture *f* (*d'un comté*).

courtier /'kɔːtɪə(r)/ *n* courtisan/dame de cour *m/f*.

courtly /'kɔːtlɪ/ *adj* **1** (polite) [*person, act, behaviour*] courtois; **2** (of a royal court) [*custom, ceremony*] de la cour.

courtly love *n* Literat amour *m* courtois.

court-martial /ˌkɔːt'mɑːʃl/ Mil, Jur **I** *n* (*pl* **courts-martial**) cour *f* martiale; **to be tried by ~** passer en cour martiale.

II *vtr* (*p prés etc* **-ll-**) faire passer [qn] en cour martiale [*soldier*]; **to be ~led** passer en cour martiale.

court: **~ of appeal** GB, **court of appeals** US *n* Jur cour *f* d'appel; **Court of Auditors** *n* (in EC) Cour *f* des comptes; **~ of domestic relations** *n* US Jur = **family court**; **~ of first instance** *n* Jur tribunal *m* de première instance; **~ of honour** GB, **~ of honor** US *n* Mil, Jur tribunal *m* d'honneur.

court of inquiry *n* **1** Mil tribunal *m* militaire; **2** gen (into accident, disaster) commission *f* d'enquête.

court: **~ of law** *n* Jur cour *f* de justice; **Court of Session** *n* GB Jur cour *f* de cassation (*en Écosse*); **Court of St James** *n* cour *f* de Saint James; **~ order** *n* Jur décision *f* judiciaire; **~ reporter** ▸ 1692 *n* Jur ≈ greffier/-ière *m/f* sténotypiste; **~room** *n* Jur salle *f* d'audience.

courtship /'kɔːtʃɪp/ *n* **1** (period of courting) fréquentation *f*; **2** (act of courting) cour *f*; **Tom's ~ of Sara** la cour que Tom fait à Sara.

court: **~ shoe** *n* escarpin *m*; **~yard** *n* cour *f*.

cousin /'kʌzn/ *n* cousin/-e *m/f*.

cove /kəʊv/ *n* **1** (bay) anse *f*; **2** US (pass) gorge *f*; **3** (also **coving**) voussure *f*; **4**○† (man) type○ *m*.

coven /'kʌvn/ *n* bande *f* de sorcières.

covenant /'kʌvənənt/ **I** *n* **1** (agreement) convention *f*; **2** Jur (payment agreement) engagement *m*; **3** Bible alliance *f*.

II *vtr* **1** (agree) sout **to ~ to do sth** convenir de faire qch; **2** Jur s'engager à verser [*money*] (**to** à).

covenanter /'kʌvənəntə(r)/ *n* Jur partie *f* contractante.

Coventry /'kɒvəntrɪ/ *pr n*: IDIOMS **to send sb to ~** mettre qn en quarantaine.

cover /'kʌvə(r)/ **I** *n* **1** (protective lid, sheath) couverture *f*; (for duvet, cushion, birdcage) housse *f*; (for table, furniture) protection *f*; (for umbrella, blade, knife) fourreau *m*; (for typewriter, record player, pan, bowl) couvercle *m*; **2** (blanket) couverture *f*; **3** (of book, magazine) couverture *f*; (of record) pochette *f*; **on the ~** (of book) sur la couverture; (of magazine) en couverture; **she's made the ~ of 'Time'** elle a fait la couverture de 'Time'; **from ~ to ~** de la première à la dernière page; **4** (shelter) abri *m*; **to provide ~** servir d'abri (**for** à); **to take ~** se mettre à l'abri; **to run for ~** courir se mettre à l'abri; **take ~!** aux abris!; **to break ~** quitter son abri; **under ~** à l'abri; **under ~ of darkness** à la faveur de la nuit; **under ~ of the confusion he escaped** il a profité de la confusion pour s'évader; **open land with no ~** terrain découvert sans abri possible; **5** (for spy, agent, operation, crime) couverture *f* (**for** pour); **that's her ~** c'est sa couverture; **to work under ~** travailler sous une identité d'emprunt; **under ~ of sth** sous le couvert de qch; **under ~ of doing** sous prétexte de faire; **to blow sb's ~**○ griller○ qn; **6** Mil couverture *f*; **air ~** couverture aérienne; **to give sb ~** couvrir qn; **I gave ~ as he advanced** je l'ai couvert tandis qu'il avançait; **7** (replacement) (for teacher, doctor) remplacement *m*; **to provide emergency ~** parer aux urgences; **8** GB Insur assurance *f* (**for** pour; **against** contre); **to give** or **provide ~ against** garantir contre; **she has ~ for fire and theft** elle est couverte contre l'incendie et le vol; **9** Fin (collateral) provision *f*; **10** (table setting) couvert *m*; **11** Mus = **cover version**.

II *modif* [*design, illustration, text*] de couverture.

III *vtr* **1** (to conceal or protect) couvrir [*table, bed, pan, legs, wound*] (**with** avec); recouvrir [*cushion, sofa, corpse*] (**with** de); boucher [*hole*] (**with** avec); **we had the sofa ~ed** on a fait recouvrir le canapé; **~ your mouth when you yawn** mets la main devant la bouche quand tu bâilles; **~ one eye and read the chart** cachez un œil et lisez le tableau; **to ~ one's ears** se boucher les oreilles; **2** (coat) [*person, dust, snow, water, layer*] recouvrir [*ground, surface, person, cake*] (**with** de); **the ground was ~ed with snow**, **snow ~ed the ground** le sol était recouvert de neige, la neige recouvrait le sol; **everything got ~ed with** ou **in sand** tout a été recouvert de sable; **the animal is ~ed in scales** l'animal est couvert d'écailles; **to ~ one's face with cream** s'enduire le visage de crème; **to be ~ed in glory** être couvert de gloire; **3** (be strewn over) [*litter, graffiti, blossom, bruises, scratches*] couvrir; **the tree was ~ed with blossom**, **blossom ~ed the tree** l'arbre était couvert de fleurs; **to ~ sb's face with kisses** couvrir le visage de qn de baisers; **4** (travel over) parcourir [*distance, area*]; (extend over) s'étendre sur [*distance, area*]; **we ~ed a lot of miles on holiday** nous avons fait beaucoup de kilomètres pendant les vacances; **5** (deal with, include) [*article, book, speaker*] traiter [*subject, field*]; [*word, term, item*] englober [*meaning, aspect*]; [*teacher*] faire [*chapter*]; [*rule, law*] s'appliquer à [*situation, person, organization*]; [*department, office*] s'occuper de [*area, region, activity*]; [*rep*] couvrir [*area*]; **that price ~s everything** le prix comprend tout, tout est inclus dans le prix; **we will ~ half the syllabus this term** nous ferons or couvrirons la moitié du programme ce trimestre; **6** (report on) [*journalist, reporter, station*] couvrir [*event, angle, story, subject, match*]; **the game will be ~ed live on BBC1** le match sera diffusé en direct par BBC1; **7** (pay for) [*amount, salary, company, person*] couvrir [*costs, outgoings*]; combler [*loss, deficit*]; **£20 should ~ it**○ 20 livres sterling devraient suffire; **to ~ one's costs** rentrer dans ses frais; **8** Insur assurer, couvrir [*person, possession*] (**for, against** contre; **for doing** pour faire); [*guarantee*] couvrir [*costs, parts*]; **are you adequately ~ed?** est-ce que vous êtes suffisamment assuré?; **9** Mil, Sport (protect) couvrir [*person, advance, retreat, exit, area of pitch*]; **I'll ~ you** je te couvre; **I've got you ~ed!** (threat) ne bougez pas ou je tire!; **keep him ~ed** tenez-le en joue; **to ~ one's back** fig se couvrir; **10** (conceal) cacher [*emotion, ignorance*]; couvrir [*noise*]; masquer [*smell*]; **11** Mus (make version of) faire sa version de [*song*]; **12** Zool (mate with) couvrir, saillir.

IV *v refl* **to ~ oneself** se protéger (**against** contre; **by doing** en faisant); **to ~ oneself with** se couvrir de [*glory, praise, shame*].

V **-covered** (*dans composés*) **snow-/scrub-~ed** couvert de neige/de broussailles; **chocolate-~ed** enrobé de chocolat.

VI **covered** *pp adj* [*porch, passage, courtyard*] couvert; [*dish, pan*] à couvercle.

■ **cover for**: **~ for [sb]** **1** (replace) remplacer, faire un remplacement pour [*colleague, employee*]; **2** (protect) couvrir [*person*]; **'I'm going to be late, ~ for me!'** 'je vais être en retard, trouve-moi une excuse!'

■ **cover in** = **cover over**.

■ **cover over**: **~ over [sth]**, **~ [sth] over** couvrir [*passage, yard, area, pool*] (**with** avec); recouvrir [*painting, mark, stain*] (**with** de).

■ **cover up**: ¶ **~ up** **1** (put clothes on) se couvrir; **2 to ~ oneself up** se couvrir (**with** de); **3** (conceal truth) étouffer une affaire; **to ~ up for** couvrir [*colleague, friend, mistakes*]; **they're ~ing up for each other** ils se couvrent l'un l'autre; ¶ **~ up [sth]**, **~ [sth] up** **1** lit recouvrir [*window, body, footprints*] (**with** avec); cacher [*answers*] (**with** avec); **2** fig dissimuler [*mistake, loss, crime, affair, truth*]; cacher [*emotion*]; étouffer [*scandal*].

coverage /'kʌvərɪdʒ/ *n* **1** (in media) couverture *f*; **television/newspaper ~** couverture par la télévision/les journaux; **they don't give much ~ to** ou **have much ~ of foreign news** ils donnent peu de nouvelles de l'étranger; **there will be live ~ of the elections** il y aura une émission en direct sur les élections; **sport gets too much TV ~** on consacre trop de temps au sport à la télé; **2** (in book, dictionary, programme) traitement *m*; **its ~ of technical terms is good/poor** il couvre bien/mal l'ensemble des termes techniques; **the programme's ~ of modern music is good** la musique moderne est bien représentée dans le programme; **3** Insur = **cover I 8**; **4** (scope of company, service, radar, radio station) couverture *f*.

cover: **~alls** *npl* US (for worker) bleu *m* de travail; (for child) salopette *f*; **~ charge** *n* prix *m* de couvert; **~ed market** *n* marché *m* couvert; **~ed wagon** *n* chariot *m* bâché; **~ girl** *n* cover-girl *f*.

covering /'kʌvərɪŋ/ *n* **1** (for wall, floor) revêtement *m*; (wrapping) enveloppe *f*; **you'll need some sort of ~ for your head** il faudra vous couvrir la tête; **2** (layer of snow, dust, moss etc) couche *f*.

covering: **~ fire** *n* tir *m* de couverture; **~ letter** *n* lettre *f* explicative.

coverlet /ˈkʌvəlɪt/ *n* couvre-lit *m*.

cover: **~ letter** *n* US lettre *f* explicative; **~ note** *n* GB Insur attestation *f* d'assurance.

cover story *n* **1** Journ article *m* annoncé en couverture; **2** (in espionage) couverture *f*; **3** fig (excuse) prétexte *m*.

covert I /ˈkʌvə(r)/ *n* (thicket) fourré *m*.

II /ˈkʌvət, US ˈkəʊvɜːrt/ *adj* [*operation, activity*] secret/-ète; [*payment*] clandestin; [*glance*] furtif/-ive; [*threat*] voilé.

covert coat *n* Hunt paletot *m*.

covertly /ˈkʌvətlɪ, US ˈkəʊvɜːrtlɪ/ *adv* secrètement.

cover: **~-up** *n* opération *f* de camouflage; **~ version** *n* Mus version *f*.

covet /ˈkʌvɪt/ *vtr* convoiter.

covetous /ˈkʌvɪtəs/ *adj* cupide; **to be ~ of sth** convoiter qch.

covetously /ˈkʌvɪtəslɪ/ *adv* avec convoitise.

covetousness /ˈkʌvɪtəsnɪs/ *n* convoitise *f*.

covey /ˈkʌvɪ/ *n* lit volée *f* (de perdrix); fig groupe *m*.

cow /kaʊ/ I *n* **1** (cattle family) vache *f*; (other animals) femelle *f*; **2**○ (woman) péj grognasse○ *f*, vache○ *f*.

II *vtr* intimider; **a ~ed look** un air de chien battu.

IDIOMS **till the ~s come home** jusqu'à la saint-glinglin○.

coward /ˈkaʊəd/ *n* lâche *mf*.

cowardice /ˈkaʊədɪs/ *n* lâcheté *f*.

cowardliness /ˈkaʊədlɪnɪs/ *n* = **cowardice**.

cowardly /ˈkaʊədlɪ/ *adj* lâche; **it was ~ of you to do it** c'était lâche de ta part de le faire.

cowbell *n* sonnaille *f*.

cowboy /ˈkaʊbɔɪ/ I *n* **1** ▶ **1692** US cowboy *m*; **to play ~s and indians** jouer aux cowboys et aux indiens; **2** (incompetent worker) péj fumiste *m*.

II *modif* **1** [*boots, hat, film*] de cowboy; **2** péj [*workman*] fumiste; [*practices*] nonprofessionnel/-elle; [*company, outfit*] pas sérieux/-ieuse.

cowcatcher /ˈkaʊkætʃə(r)/ *n* US Rail chasse-pierres *m inv*.

cower /ˈkaʊə(r)/ *vi* se recroqueviller (de peur) (**behind** derrière); **to ~ away from sb** trembler de peur devant qn.

cow: **~girl** ▶ **1692** *n* vachère *f*; **~hand**, **~herd** ▶ **1692** *n* vacher/-ère *m/f*; **~hide** *n* (leather) peau *f* de vache; US (whip) fouet *m* à lanière(s) de cuir.

cowl /kaʊl/ *n* **1** (hood) capuchon *m*; **2** (also **chimney ~**) capuchon *m*.

cowlick○ /ˈkaʊlɪk/ *n* US mèche *f* (de cheveux).

cowl neck /ˌkaʊl ˈnek/ *n* col *m* boule.

cowman /ˈkaʊmæn/ ▶ **1692** *n* vacher *m*.

co-worker /kəʊˈwɜːkə(r)/ *n* collègue *mf*.

cow: **~ parsley** *n* cerfeuil *m* sauvage; **~pat** *n* bouse *f* de vache; **~pea** *n* dolique *m*; **~poke**○ *n* US cowboy *m*; **~pox** *n* variole *f* des bovidés; **~puncher**○ *n* cowboy *m*.

cowrie, **cowry** /ˈkaʊrɪ/ *n* cauri *m*.

cow: **~shed** *n* étable *f*; **~slip** *n* Bot coucou *m*.

cox /kɒks/ Sport I *n* barreur *m*.

II *vtr*, *vi* barrer; **~ed pairs/fours** deux/quatre avec barreur.

coxcomb‡ /ˈkɒkskəʊm/ *n* plastronneur *m*.

Cox's Orange Pippin /ˌkɒksɪz ɒrɪndʒ ˈpɪpɪn/ *n* (pomme *f*) reinette *f*.

coxswain /ˈkɒksn/ *n* gen capitaine *m*; (in rowing) barreur *m*.

coy /kɔɪ/ *adj* **1** (bashful) [*person*] faussement modeste; [*smile, look*] de fausse modestie; **2** (reticent) réservé (**about** à propos de).

coyly /ˈkɔɪlɪ/ *adv* avec fausse modestie.

coyness /ˈkɔɪnɪs/ *n* **1** (shyness) fausse modestie *f*; **2** (reticence) réserve *f* (**about** à propos de).

coyote /kɔɪˈəʊtɪ, US ˈkaɪəʊt/ *n* (*pl* **~s** ou **~**) Zool coyote *m*.

coypu /ˈkɔɪpuː/ *n* (*pl* **~s** ou **~**) ragondin *m*.

cozy *adj* US = **cosy**.

CP *n* **1** Pol (*abrév* = **Communist Party**) PC *m*; **2** Mil *abrév* ▶ **command post**.

CPA *n* US *abrév* ▶ **certified public accountant**.

cpd *n*: *abrév écrite*= **compound** I 2, 3.

CPI *n* Fin *abrév* ▶ **Consumer Price Index**.

Cpl *abrév écrite* = **corporal** I.

CPO *n*: *abrév* ▶ **chief petty officer**.

cps Phys *abrév écrite* = **cycles per second**.

CPS *n* GB Jur *abrév* ▶ **Crown Prosecution Service**.

CPSA *n* GB (*abrév* = **Civil and Public Servants' Association**) *association des employés du secteur public*.

CPU *n* Comput *abrév* ▶ **central processing unit**.

cr Fin **1** *abrév écrite* = **credit** I 3; **2** *abrév écrite* = **creditor**.

crab /kræb/ I *n* **1** Zool, Culin crabe *m*; **dressed ~** crabe farci; **2** (in zodiac) **the Crab** le Cancer; **3** (louse) = **crab louse**; **4** Tech (hoist) chariot *m*.

II **crabs** *npl* Publg invendus *mpl*.

III *vtr* (*p prés etc* **-bb-**) **1** Aviat faire voler [qch] en crabe [*plane*]; **2**○ US gâcher; **to ~ sb's act** gâcher les effets de qn.

IV *vi* (*p prés etc* **-bb-**) **1**○ (complain) rouspéter (**about** sur); **2** Naut [*boat*] progresser en crabe.

IDIOMS **to catch a ~** (in rowing) plonger la rame trop profond, aller à la pêche○.

crab apple *n* (tree) pommier *m* sauvage; (fruit) pomme *f* sauvage.

crabbed /ˈkræbɪd/ *adj* **1** (surly) grincheux/-euse; **2** [*handwriting*] en pattes de mouche.

crabbing /ˈkræbɪŋ/ *n* pêche *f* aux crabes; **to go ~** aller à la pêche aux crabes.

crabby○ /ˈkræbɪ/ *adj* grincheux/-euse.

crab: **~ louse** *n* pou *m* du pubis, morpion◑ *m*; **Crab Nebula** *pr n* Astron le Crabe.

crack /kræk/ I *n* **1** (part of fine network in paint, varnish, cup, ground) craquelure *f* (**in** dans); (single marked line in wall, cup, mirror, ground, bone) fêlure *f* (**in** dans); **~s are appearing in the policy/the relationship** on commence à déceler des fêlures dans la politique/leurs relations; **2** (narrow opening) (in door) entrebâillement *m*; (in curtains) fente *f*; (in rock, wall) fissure *f*; **to open the door a ~** entrebâiller la porte; **leave the door open a ~** laisse la porte entrebâillée; **3** (drug) (also **~ cocaine**) crack *m*; **4** (sharp noise of twig, bone, whip, shot) craquement *m*; **5**○ (attempt) essai *m*, tentative *f*; **to have a ~ at doing** essayer de faire; **to have a ~ at** essayer de remporter [*title*]; essayer de battre [*record*]; tenter [*gold medal*]; **to have a ~ at (playing) Hamlet** s'essayer à jouer Hamlet; **she wants (to have) a ~ at the champion** elle veut se mesurer au champion; **it's his third ~ at the title** c'est sa troisième tentative de remporter le titre; **6**○ (jibe) moquerie *f* (**about** à propos de); (joke) plaisanterie *f* (**about** à propos de); **a cheap ~** une plaisanterie facile; **to have a ~ at sb** se moquer de qn; **7**○ GB dial (laugh, good time) rigolade *f*○.

II *adj* (*toujours épith*) [*player*] de première; [*troops, regiment, shot*] d'élite.

III *vtr* **1** (make a crack in) fêler [*mirror, bone, wall, cup*]; (make fine cracks in) fendiller, faire craqueler [*paint, varnish, cup*]; **2** (break) casser [*nut, egg, casing*]; **to ~ a safe** cambrioler un coffre-fort; **to ~ sth open** ouvrir qch; **let's ~ open a bottle of wine** ouvrons une bouteille de vin; **to ~ one's head open**○ se fendre le crâne; **she didn't ~ a book for that class**○ US elle n'a même pas ouvert un livre pour cette matière; **to ~ the market** percer sur le marché; **3** (solve) résoudre [*problem, case*]; **to ~ a code** déchiffrer un code; **to ~ a spy/crime network** démanteler un réseau d'espions/criminel; **I think I've ~ed it**○ je crois que j'ai pigé○ or compris; **4** (make cracking sound with) faire claquer [*whip*]; faire craquer [*knuckles, joints, twig*]; **to ~ sth over sb's head, to ~ sb on the head with sth** asséner un coup sur la tête de qn avec qch; **to ~ one's head on sth** se cogner la tête sur qch; **to ~ the whip** fig agiter le fouet; **5** (overcome) faire craquer [*resistance, defences, opposition*]; **6 to ~ a joke** sortir une blague○; **7** Chem craquer [*oil*].

IV *vi* **1** (develop crack(s)) [*bone, mirror, cup, wall, ice*] se fêler; [*paint, varnish*] se craqueler; [*skin*] se crevasser; [*ground*] (slightly) se fendiller; (severely) se fendre; **the earth ~ed in the heat** la terre s'est fendillée sous l'effet de la chaleur; **2** (cease to resist) [*person, opposition*] craquer; **to ~ under interrogation** craquer à la suite d'un interrogatoire; **he tends to ~ under pressure** il a tendance à craquer quand la pression monte; **3** (make sharp sound) [*knuckles, joint, twig*] craquer; [*whip*] claquer; **4** [*voice*] se casser; **her voice ~ed with emotion** sa voix s'est cassée tellement elle était émue; **5 her face ~ed into a smile** elle a souri jusqu'aux oreilles.

IDIOMS **not all** ou **not as good as it's ~ed up to be** pas aussi bon qu'on le prétend; **to get ~ing** s'y mettre; **go on, get ~ing!** vas-y, remue-toi!; **to get ~ing on** ou **with a job** se mettre au travail; **to have a fair ~ of the whip** avoir sa chance; **to give sb a fair ~ of the whip** donner sa chance à qn.

■ **crack down** prendre des mesures énergiques, sévir (**on** contre).

■ **crack up**○: ¶ **~ up 1** (have breakdown) craquer; **2** (laugh) rire; **3** argot des drogués **to ~ (it) up** fumer du crack; ¶ **~ [sb] up** faire rire.

crack-brained○ /ˈkrækbreɪnd/ *adj* saugrenu.

crackdown /ˈkrækdaʊn/ *n* mesure *f* sévère (**on** contre); **the police ~ on drug-dealing** les mesures sévères prises par la police contre le trafic des stupéfiants.

cracked /krækt/ *adj* **1** [*varnish, paint, leather, pavement*] craquelé; [*bone, kneecap, basin*] fêlé; [*skin*] crevassé; [*egg, shell*] fendu; **2**○ (mad) cinglé○.

cracked: **~ olive** *n* olive *f* cassée; **~ wheat** *n* blé *m* concassé.

cracker /ˈkrækə(r)/ *n* **1** (biscuit) cracker *m*, biscuit *m* salé; **2** (firework) pétard *m*; **3** (for Christmas) diablotin *m*; **4** US injur pauvre Blanc/Blanche *m/f*; **5**○ GB (beauty) **she's a ~!, what a ~!** c'est un canon○!

cracker: **~-barrel** *adj* US [*philosopher*] de bistrot; **~jack**† *adj* US de premier ordre.

crackers○ /ˈkrækəz/ *adj* GB cinglé○.

crack factory *n* laboratoire *m* clandestin de fabrication de crack.

crackhead○ /ˈkrækhed/ *n* drogué/-e *m/f* au crack; **they're ~s** ils se droguent au crack.

crack house○ *n* endroit *m* où l'on peut se procurer du crack.

cracking /ˈkrækɪŋ/ I *n* **1** Chem craquage *m*, cracking *m*; **2** (in varnish, paint, plaster) craquelures *fpl*.

II○ *adj* GB [*game, goal, start*] excellent; **at a ~ pace** à toute vitesse.

III○ *adv* GB **a ~ good shot** un coup formidablement bien joué; **it was a ~ good lunch** on a formidablement bien déjeuné.

crackle /ˈkrækl/ I *n* **1** (sound) crépitement *m*; **2** (in pottery) (crazing) craquelure *f*.

II *vtr* faire crisser [*foil, paper*]; faire des craquelures à [*pottery*].

III *vi* [*twig, fire, radio*] crépiter; [*hot fat, burning wood*] grésiller.

crackleware /ˈkræklweə(r)/ *n* vaisselle *f* en porcelaine craquelée.

crackling /ˈkræklɪŋ/ *n* **1** (sound) (of fire) crépitement *m*; (of foil, cellophane) crissement *m*; (on radio) friture○ *f*; **2** Culin (crisp pork) couenne *f* grillée.

cracknel /ˈkræknl/ *n* **1** (biscuit) craquelin *m*; **2** ¢ US Culin morceaux *mpl* de porc frit.

crack: **~ pipe** *n* pipe *f* à crack; **~pot**○ *n, adj* cinglé/-e○ (*m/f*).

Cracow /ˈkrækɒv/ ▶1818 *pr n* Cracovie.

cradle /ˈkreɪdl/ **I** *n* **1** (for baby) berceau *m* also fig; **from the ~** depuis le berceau; **from the ~ to the grave** du berceau à la tombe; **2** (framework) Naut ber *m*; Med (under bedclothes) arceau *m*; **3** (telephone rest) fourche *f* de combiné; **4** (hoistable platform) nacelle *f* suspendue.
II *vtr* bercer [*baby*]; tenir [qch] délicatement [*object*]; **to ~ sth in one's arms** tenir qch dans ses bras.
IDIOMS **the hand that rocks the ~ rules the world** qui mène la jeunesse dirige le monde; **to rob the ~** les prendre au berceau○.

cradlesnatcher○ /ˈkreɪdlsnætʃə(r)/ *n* **he's/she's a ~** il/elle les prend au berceau○.

cradlesong /ˈkreɪdlsɒŋ/ *n* berceuse *f*.

craft /krɑːft, US kræft/ **I** *n* **1** (skill) (art-related) art *m*; (job-related) métier *m*; **the potter's ~** l'art du potier; **the journalist's ~** ≈ le métier du journaliste; **2** (handiwork) artisanat *m*; **arts and ~s** artisanat (d'art); **3** (cunning) ruse *f*; **4** (boat) embarcation *f*; **5** Aerosp (also **space ~**) vaisseau *m* spatial.
II *modif* [*exhibition, guild*] artisanal.
III *vtr* faire [qch] à la main.

craftily /ˈkrɑːftɪlɪ, US ˈkræftɪlɪ/ *adv* astucieusement.

craftiness /ˈkrɑːftɪnɪs, US ˈkræftɪnɪs/ *n* astuce *f*.

craft: **~sman** *n* (skilled manually) artisan *m*; (skilled artistically) artiste *m*; **~smanship** *n* (manual) dextérité *f*; (artistic) art *m*; **~swoman** *n* (skilled manually) artisane *f*; (skilled artistically) artiste *f*; **~ union** *n* syndicat *m* professionnel; **~work** *n* artisanat *m*.

crafty /ˈkrɑːftɪ, US ˈkræftɪ/ *adj* astucieux/-ieuse; **it was ~ of you to do it** c'était astucieux de ta part de le faire.

crag /kræg/ *n* rocher *m* escarpé.

craggy /ˈkrægɪ/ *adj* **1** [*coastline, mountain*] escarpé; **2** [*face, features*] taillé à coups de serpe.

cram /kræm/ (*p prés etc* **-mm-**) **I** *vtr* **1** (pack) **to ~ sth into** enfoncer or fourrer○ qch dans [*case, bag, drawer, car*]; **to ~ sb into** entasser qn dans [*room, vehicle*]; **to ~ sth into one's mouth** se fourrer qch dans la bouche, enfourner qch; **they were 60 people ~med into one room** il y avait 60 personnes entassées dans une seule pièce; **to ~ a lot into one day** réussir à faire beaucoup de choses dans une seule journée; **to ~ three meetings into a morning** caser○ trois rendez-vous dans la matinée; **2** (fill) bourrer [*room, car*] (**with** de); **to be ~med full of furniture** être plein à craquer de or bourré de meubles.
II *vi* **1** (pack) **to ~ into** s'empiler or s'entasser dans [*bus, car, room*]; **2**† Sch bachoter (**for** pour).
III *v refl* **to ~ oneself with** se bourrer de [*sweets, chips*].
IV **crammed** *pp adj* [*room, closet*] plein à craquer; [*timetable*] surchargé.

crammer○ /ˈkræmə(r)/ *n* GB (school) ≈ boîte *f* à bac○.

cramp /kræmp/ **I** *n* **1** (pain) crampe *f*; **to have ~** GB, **to have a ~** US avoir une crampe; **a ~ in one's foot/leg** une crampe dans le pied/à la jambe; **writer's ~** crampe de l'écrivain; **2** (*souvent pl*) **stomach ~s** crampes *fpl* d'estomac; **3** (also **~ iron**) crampon *m* coudé; **4** = **clamp**.
II *vtr* gêner [*progress, development*].
IDIOMS **to ~ sb's style**○ faire perdre ses moyens à qn.

cramped /kræmpt/ *pp adj* **1** [*cell, house, office*] exigu/-uë; **~ conditions** conditions d'exiguïté; **to be ~ for space** être à l'étroit; **we're very ~ in here** nous sommes très à l'étroit ici; **2** [*handwriting*] en pattes de mouche.

crampon /ˈkræmpən/ *n* Sport crampon *m*.

cranberry /ˈkrænbərɪ, US -berɪ/ *n* Bot canneberge *f*.

cranberry: **~ jelly** *n* gelée *f* de canneberge; **~ sauce** *n* sauce *f* à la canneberge.

crane /kreɪn/ **I** *n* Constr, Cin, Zool grue *f*.
II *vtr* **to ~ one's neck** tendre le cou.
■ **crane forward** tendre le cou.

crane: **~ driver** ▶1692 *n* conducteur/-trice *m/f* de grue, grutier/-ière *mf*; **~ fly** *n* tipule *f*; **~ operator** ▶1692 *n* conducteur/-trice *m/f* de grue; **~sbill** *n* géranium *m* (sauvage).

crania /ˈkreɪnɪə/ *pl* ▶ **cranium**.

cranial /ˈkreɪnɪəl/ *adj* Anat crânien/-ienne.

cranial: **~ index** *n* indice *m* crânien; **~ nerve** *n* nerf *m* crânien.

cranium /ˈkreɪnɪəm/ *n* (*pl* **~s**, **-ia**) crâne *m*, boîte *f* crânienne.

crank /kræŋk/ **I** *n* **1**○ péj (freak) fanatique *mf*, fana○ *mf*; **a health-food ~** un/une fanatique or fana○ d'aliments naturels; **2** Tech manivelle *f*; **3**○ US (grouch) grincheux/-euse *m/f*.
II *vtr* faire démarrer [qch] à la manivelle [*car, engine*]; remonter [qch] (à la manivelle) [*gramophone*].
■ **crank out**: **~ out [sth], ~ [sth] out** produire [*essay, novel, film*].
■ **crank up**: **~ up [sth], ~ [sth] up** lit remonter (à la manivelle); fig mettre en marche.

crank: **~case** *n* carter *m*; **~shaft** *n* vilebrequin *m*.

cranky○ /ˈkræŋkɪ/ *adj* **1** (grumpy) grincheux/-euse; **2** (eccentric) loufoque○; **3** [*machine*] en mauvais état.

cranny /ˈkrænɪ/ *n* petite fente *f*. ▶ **nook**.

crap◑ /kræp/ **I** *n* ¢ **1** (nonsense) conneries● *fpl*; **to talk a load of ~** débiter des conneries●; **2** (of film, book, food etc) foutaise◑ *f*; **this film is ~!** c'est de la foutaise ce film!; **3** (faeces) merde● *f*; **to have a ~** chier●.
II *adj* merdique◑, nul/nulle○; **to be ~ at chemistry** être nul en chimie.
III *vtr* (*p prés etc* **-pp-**) US débiter des conneries● à.
IV *vi* (*p prés etc* **-pp-**) chier●.

crape /kreɪp/ *n* crêpe *m* (de deuil).

crappy◑ /ˈkræpɪ/ *adj* merdique◑, nul○/nulle.

craps /kræps/ *n* craps *m*; **to shoot ~** jouer au craps.

crapulent /ˈkræpjʊlənt/, **crapulous** /ˈkræpjʊləs/ *adj* sout **1** (given to drink) intempérant sout; **2** (drunk) ivre.

crash /kræʃ/ **I** *n* **1** (noise) fracas *m*; **the ~ of thunder** le fracas du tonnerre; **a ~ of breaking glass** un fracas de verre brisé; **to hit the ground with a ~** se fracasser sur le sol; **2** Aut, Aviat, Rail (accident) accident *m*; **car ~** accident de voiture; **train/air ~** catastrophe *f* ferroviaire/aérienne; **to have a ~** avoir un accident; **3** Fin (of stock market) krach *m*; (of company) faillite *f* (**of** de).
II *vtr* **1** (involve in accident) **he ~ed the car** il a eu un accident de voiture; **to ~ a car into a bus** rentrer dans ou percuter un bus; **he's ~ed the car twice already** il a déjà eu deux accidents avec la voiture; **2**○ (gatecrash) **to ~ a party** s'introduire dans une fête sans y être invité.
III *vi* **1** (have accident) [*car, plane*] s'écraser; (collide) [*vehicles, planes*] se rentrer dedans, se percuter; **to ~ into sth** rentrer dans or percuter qch; **I thought we were going to ~** Aut je croyais qu'on allait avoir un accident; Aviat je croyais que l'avion allait s'écraser; **2** Fin [*firm, company*] faire faillite; [*share prices*] s'effondrer; **3** (move loudly) **I could hear him ~ing around downstairs** je l'ai entendu faire du boucan○ en bas; **the shells ~ed all around me** les obus éclataient tout autour de moi; **to ~ through the undergrowth** s'enfoncer bruyamment dans la broussaille; **4** (fall) **to ~ to the ground** [*cup, tray, picture*] se fracasser sur le sol; [*tree*] s'abattre; **5**○ Comput [*computer, system*] se planter○; **6**○ (go to sleep) = **crash out**.
■ **crash out**○ (go to sleep) pioncer◑; (collapse) s'écrouler○.

crash barrier *n* **1** (on road) glissière *f* de sécurité; **2** (for crowd control) barrière *f*.

crash course *n* cours *m* intensif; **to take a ~ in Latin** suivre un cours intensif de latin.

crash: **~ diet** *n* régime *m* d'amaigrissement intensif; **~ helmet** *n* casque *m*.

crashing○† /ˈkræʃɪŋ/ *adj* **to be a ~ bore** [*person*] être un/une sacré/-e raseur/-euse○ *m/f*; [*event*] être barbant○ à mourir.

crash-land /ˌkræʃˈlænd/ **I** *vtr* **to ~ a plane** poser un avion en catastrophe.
II *vi* atterrir en catastrophe.

crash: **~ landing** *n* atterrissage *m* en catastrophe; **~ pad**○ *n* US piaule○ *f*.

crass /kræs/ *adj* gen grossier/-ière; **~ ignorance** ignorance *f* crasse.

crassly /ˈkræslɪ/ *adv* [*say, ask*] de façon grossière; [*insensitive*] grossièrement.

crate /kreɪt/ **I** *n* **1** (for bottles, china) caisse *f*; (for fruit, vegetables) cageot *m*; **2**○ (car) caisse○ *f*; (plane) zinc○ *m*.
II *vtr* mettre [qch] en caisse [*bottles*]; mettre [qch] en cageot [*fruit*].

crater /ˈkreɪtə(r)/ *n* **1** Astron, Geol cratère *m*; **2** (caused by explosion) entonnoir *m*.

cravat /krəˈvæt/ *n* foulard *m* (pour homme).

crave /kreɪv/ *vtr* **1** (also **~ for**) avoir un besoin maladif de [*drug*]; avoir soif de [*affection, change, fame*]; [*pregnant woman*] avoir envie de [*food*]; **2** fml implorer [*pardon, mercy*]; solliciter [*attention, permission*].

craven /ˈkreɪvn/ *adj* sout lâche.

craving /ˈkreɪvɪŋ/ *n* (for drug) besoin *m* maladif (**for** de); (for fame, love, freedom) soif *f* (**for** de); (for food) envie *f* (**for** de).

craw /krɔː/ *n* **1** (crop of bird, insect) jabot *m*; **2** (stomach of animal) estomac *m*.
IDIOMS **it sticks in my ~** ça me reste en travers de la gorge.

crawfish /ˈkrɔːfɪʃ/ **I** *n* = **crayfish**.
II *vi*○ US se dégonfler○.

crawl /krɔːl/ **I** *n* **1** Sport crawl *m*; **to do/swim the ~** faire/nager le crawl; **2** (slow pace) **at a ~** au pas; **to slow/be reduced to a ~** [*vehicle*] ralentir jusqu'à rouler au pas; [*growth*] ralentir; [*output*] être presque stagnant.
II *vi* **1** [*insect, snake, person*] ramper; **to ~ in/out** entrer/sortir en rampant; **to ~ out from under sth** sortir de sous qch; **to ~ into bed** se traîner au lit; **to ~ to the door** se traîner jusqu'à la porte; **to ~ into a hole** se glisser dans un trou; **2** (on all fours) marcher à quatre pattes; **she can ~ now** (baby) elle marche à quatre pattes maintenant; **3** (move slowly) [*vehicle*] rouler au pas; **to ~ along/in** avancer/entrer au pas; **to ~ down/up sth** descendre/monter lentement qch; **4** (pass slowly) [*time, days*] se traîner; **5**○ (seethe) **to be ~ing with** grouiller○ de [*insects, tourists, reporters*]; **6**○ (flatter, creep) faire du lèche-bottes○ (**to** à); **don't come ~ing to me** inutile de venir pleurer auprès de moi.
IDIOMS **to make sb's skin** or **flesh ~** donner la chair de poule à qn○.

crawler○ /ˈkrɔːlə(r)/ *n* **1** GB (person) lèche-bottes○ *mf*; **2** (slow vehicle) tortue○ *f*; **3**○ US (earthworm) ver *m* de terre.

crawler lane *n* GB voie *f* pour véhicules lents.

crawl space *n* Constr (under house) vide *m* sanitaire; (under large building) galerie *f* technique.

crayfish /'kreɪfɪʃ/ *n* **1** (freshwater) écrevisse *f*; **2** (spiny lobster) langouste *f*.

crayon /'kreɪən/ **I** *n* **1** (also **wax ~**) craie *f* grasse; **in ~s** à la craie grasse; **2** (also **pencil ~**) crayon *m* de couleur.
II *vtr* colorier; **to ~ sth red** colorier qch en rouge.

craze /kreɪz/ **I** *n* vogue *f*; **the ~ for sports cars, the sports car ~** la vogue des voitures de sport; **to be the latest ~** faire fureur; **it's just a ~** c'est une toquade or une folie.
II *vi* (also **~ over**) [*china, glaze*] se craqueler; [*glass*] s'étoiler.

crazed /kreɪzd/ *adj* **1** (mad) [*animal, person*] fou/folle; **power-~** ivre de pouvoir; **2** (cracked) [*china, glaze, varnish*] craquelé; [*glass*] étoilé.

crazily /'kreɪzɪlɪ/ *adv* **1** (madly) [*act*] d'une manière insensée; [*drive, run, shout*] comme un fou/une folle; **2** (at an angle) [*lean, tilt*] dangereusement.

crazy○ /'kreɪzɪ/ **I** *adj* **1** (insane) [*person, scheme*] fou/folle; [*behaviour, idea*] insensé; **to go ~** devenir fou/folle; **he/it would be ~ to do** il/ce serait fou de faire; **~ with** fou/folle de [*grief, worry*]; **you must be ~!** t'es complètement fou○!; **2** (infatuated) **to be ~ about** être fou/folle de [*person*]; être passionné de [*activity*]; **3** (startling) [*height, price, speed*] fou/folle; **to be at a ~ angle** pencher dangereusement; **4**○ US (excellent) formidable.
II○ **like crazy** *adv phr* [*shout, laugh, run*] comme un fou/une folle; **they used to fight like ~** ils n'arrêtaient pas de se battre.

crazy: **~ bone** *n* US petit juif *m* (*os sensible du coude*); **~ golf** ▶1282 *n* GB mini-golf *m*; **~ golf course** *n* GB parcours *m* de mini-golf; **~ paving** *n* GB *pavage avec des pierres de forme irrégulière*; **~ quilt** *n* US Sewing édredon *m* en patchwork; fig patchwork *m*.

CRC *n*: *abrév* ▶ **camera-ready copy**.

CRE *n* GB *abrév* ▶ **Commission for Racial Equality**.

creak /kri:k/ **I** *n* (of hinge, gate, door) grincement *m*; (of wood, floorboard, bone) craquement *m*; (of leather) crissement *m*.
II *vi* [*hinge, gate, door*] grincer; [*floorboard, bone, joint*] craquer; [*leather*] crisser; fig [*régime, organization*] craquer; **the door ~ed open** la porte s'ouvrit en grinçant.

creaking /'kri:kɪŋ/ **I** *n* = **creak I**.
II *adj* (*épith*) **1** lit [*hinge, gate, door*] grinçant; [*chair, floorboard, bone*] qui craque; [*leather*] qui crisse; **2** fig [*regime, structure*] déliquescent, qui commence à craquer.

creaky /'kri:kɪ/ *adj* **1** [*door, hinge*] grinçant; [*leather*] qui crisse; [*joint, bone, floorboard*] qui craque; **2** fig [*alibi, policy*] bancal○.

cream /kri:m/ ▶1104 **I** *n* **1** (dairy product) crème *f*; **strawberries and ~** fraises *fpl* à la crème; **2** fig **the ~ of** la crème de [*students, graduates etc*]; **the ~ of society** fig la crème or la fine fleur de la société; **3** Cosmet crème *f*; **sun ~** crème solaire; **4** (soup) **~ of** crème *f* or velouté *m* de [*mushroom, chicken, asparagus*]; **5** (chocolate) chocolat *m* fourré; (biscuit) biscuit *m* fourré; **orange ~** chocolat or biscuit fourré à l'orange; **6** (colour) (couleur *f*) crème *m*; **7** (polish) crème *f*; **shoe ~** crème à chaussures.
II *modif* Culin [*cake, bun*] à la crème.
III *adj* (colour) crème *inv*.
IV *vtr* **1** Culin travailler; **~ the butter and sugar** travailler le beurre et le sucre en pâte lisse; **~ed potatoes** purée *f* de pommes de terre; **2** (skim) écrémer [*milk*]; **3**○ US (thrash) battre [qn] à plates coutures○, écraser [*opponents*].
V● *vi* US (climax) jouir; (become excited) [*woman*] mouiller●.
IDIOMS **to look like the cat that's got the ~** avoir l'air très content de soi.
■ **cream off**: **~ off [sth]**, **~ [sth] off** garder [qch] pour soi [*best pupils, profits*]; (illegally) détourner [*funds, profits*].

cream: **~ cheese** *n* fromage *m* à tartiner; **~ cleaner** *n* crème *f* de nettoyage liquide; **~ cracker** *n* GB cracker *m*.

creamer /'kri:mə(r)/ *n* **1** (for separating cream) écrémeuse *f*; **2** US (jug) pot *m* à crème; **3** (coffee whitener) succédané *m* de crème.

creamery /'kri:mərɪ/ *n* **1** (dairy, factory) laiterie *f*; **2** (shop) crémerie *f*.

cream: **~ jug** *n* GB pot *m* à crème; **~ of tartar** *n* crème *f* de tartre, tartre *m* blanc; **~ pitcher** *n* US = **creamer** 2.

cream puff *n* **1** Culin chou *m* à la crème; **2**○ US péj (weakling) lavette○ *f* pej; **3**○ US (secondhand bargain) excellente occase○ *f*.

cream: **~ soda** *n* soda *m* parfumé à la vanille; **~ tea** *n* GB thé *m* complet (*accompagné de scones avec de la crème fraîche et de la confiture*).

creamy /'kri:mɪ/ *adj* [*texture, taste*] crémeux/-euse; [*colour*] (couleur) crème *inv*; **to have a ~ complexion** avoir un teint laiteux.

crease /kri:s/ **I** *n* **1** (in cloth, paper) (regular) pli *m*; (irregular: with iron) faux pli *m*; **to put a ~ in a pair of trousers** marquer les plis d'un pantalon; **2** (in face) pli *m*; (in palm) ligne *f*; **3** Sport *ligne qui marque la position du batteur ou du lanceur au cricket*; **to be at the ~** être batteur.
II *vtr* (crumple) froisser [*paper, cloth*].
III *vi* **1** [*cloth*] se froisser; **2** [*face*] se plisser.
■ **crease up**○: ¶ **~ up** (in amusement) plier○ (de rire); ¶ **~ [sb] up** faire plier○ (de rire).

creased /kri:st/ *adj* [*cloth, paper*] froissé; [*face, brow*] plissé.

crease-resistant /'kri:srɪsɪstənt/ *adj* [*fabric*] infroissable.

create /kri:'eɪt/ **I** *vtr* **1** (make) créer [*character, product, precedent, job, system, work of art*]; lancer [*fashion*]; **2** (cause) provoquer [*disorder, crisis, interest, scandal, repercussion*]; poser [*problem*]; **to ~ a good/bad impression** faire (une) bonne/mauvaise impression; **3** (appoint) nommer.
II○ *vi* GB faire une scène.

creation /kri:'eɪʃn/ *n* (all contexts) création *f*; **job/wealth ~** création d'emplois/de richesses; **her latest ~** sa dernière création; **the Creation** la Création.

creationism /kri:'eɪʃənɪzəm/ *n* créationnisme *m*.

creationist /ˌkri:'eɪʃnɪst/ *n* créationniste *mf*.

creative /kri:'eɪtɪv/ *adj* **1** (inventive) [*person, solution, cookery, use*] créatif/-ive; **2** (which creates) [*process, act, energy, imagination*] créateur/-trice.

creative accountancy, creative accounting *n* manipulations *fpl* comptables.

creatively /kri:'eɪtɪvlɪ/ *adv* de façon créative.

creative writing *n* (school subject) ≈ composition *f*; (general) création *f* littéraire.

creativity /ˌkri:eɪ'tɪvətɪ/ *n* créativité *f*.

creator /kri:'eɪtə(r)/ *n* créateur/-trice *m/f* (**of** de); **the Creator** le Créateur.

creature /'kri:tʃə(r)/ *n* **1** (living being) créature *f*; **2** (animal) animal *m*; **sea/water ~** animal marin/aquatique; **~ from outer space** créature (qui vient) du cosmos; **3**† (person) **charming ~** charmante créature; **(the) poor ~!** le/la pauvre!; **4** (creation) littér **a ~ of his times** une créature de son époque; **to be sb's ~** péj être la créature de qn.

creature comforts *n* confort *m* matériel ¢; **to like one's ~** aimer ses aises.

crèche /kreʃ, kreɪʃ/ *n* **1** GB (nursery) crèche *f*; (in hotel, shop etc) garderie *f*; **workplace ~, company ~** crèche *f* d'entreprise; **2** (Christmas crib) crèche *f*.

cred○ /kred/ *n*: *abrév* = **credibility**. ▶ **street cred**.

credence /'kri:dns/ *n* sout crédit *m*; **to give ~ to sth** (believe) accorder du crédit à qch; (make believable) donner du crédit à qch; **to lend ~ to sth** donner du crédit à qch; **to gain ~** acquérir du crédit; **letters of ~** Pol Admin lettres de créance.

credentials /krɪ'denʃlz/ *npl* **1** (qualifications) qualifications *fpl*; **to establish one's ~ as a writer** s'affirmer comme un écrivain; **2** gen pièce *f* d'identité; (of ambassador) lettres *fpl* de créance.

credibility /ˌkredə'bɪlətɪ/ *n* crédibilité *f* (**as** comme); **to retain/lose one's ~** conserver/perdre sa crédibilité.

credibility gap *n* écart *m* entre les apparences et la réalité.

credible /'kredəbl/ *adj* (all contexts) crédible.

credit /'kredɪt/ **I** *n* **1** (approval) mérite *m* (**for** de); **to get the ~ for sth/for doing** se voir attribuer le mérite de qch/d'avoir fait; **to give sb (the) ~ for sth/for doing** attribuer à qn le mérite de qch/d'avoir fait; **to take the ~ for sth/for doing** s'attribuer le mérite de qch/d'avoir fait; **to be a ~ to sb/sth** faire honneur à qn/qch; **to do sb ~, to do ~ to sb** être tout à l'honneur de qn; **it is to your ~ that** c'est tout à votre honneur que; **to her ~, she admitted her mistake** c'est tout à son honneur d'avoir reconnu sa faute; **she has two medals to her ~** elle a deux médailles à son actif; **he is more intelligent than he is given ~ for** il est plus intelligent qu'on ne le croit; **~ where ~ is due, they have managed to score 20 points** il faut mettre à leur crédit qu'ils ont réussi à marquer 20 points; **2** (credence) crédit *m*; **to gain ~** acquérir du crédit; **to place ~ in sth** ajouter foi à qch; **3** Comm, Fin (borrowing) crédit *m*; **to buy sth on ~** acheter qch à crédit; **to live on ~** vivre de crédits; **to give sb ~** faire crédit à qn; **her ~ is good** elle a une réputation de bonne payeuse; **4** Fin (positive balance) crédit *m*; **to be in ~** être créditeur; **to be £25 in ~** avoir un crédit de 25 livres sterling, être créditeur de 25 livres sterling; **5** US Univ unité *f* de valeur.
II credits *npl* Cin, TV générique *m*; **to roll the ~s** faire défiler le générique.
III *vtr* **1** (attribute) **to ~ sb with** attribuer [qch] à qn [*discovery, power, achievement*]; **to ~ sb with intelligence/honesty** croire or supposer qn intelligent/honnête; **to ~ sb with doing** reconnaître que qn a fait; **2** Fin créditer [*account*] (**with** de); **to ~ sth to an account** porter qch sur un compte; **3** (believe) croire, ajouter foi à [*story, assertion*]; **would you ~ it!** le croirais-tu!

creditable /'kredɪtəbl/ *adj* (all contexts) honorable.

creditably /'kredɪtəblɪ/ *adv* d'une manière honorable.

credit: **~ account, C/A** *n* Comm, Fin compte *m* personnel; **~ agency** *n* Comm, Fin agence *f* de renseignements commerciaux; **~ arrangements** *npl* Fin crédits *mpl*; **~ balance** *n* Accts solde *m* créditeur; **~ broker** ▶1692 *n* Fin établissement *m* de crédit; **~ bureau** *n* US Fin = **credit agency**; **~ card** *n* Comm, Fin carte *f* de crédit; **~ control** *n* encadrement *m* du crédit; **~ entry** *n* inscription *f* au crédit; **~ facilities** *npl* facilités *fpl* de crédit; **~ freeze** *n* Econ gel *m* des crédits; **~ hour** *n* US Univ heure *f* de cours comptabilisée pour l'obtention d'un diplôme; **~ limit** *n* Fin autorisation *f* de découvert.

credit line *n* **1** Cin, TV mention *f* au générique; **2** Fin ligne *f* de crédit.

credit: **~ money** *n* argent *m* fiduciaire; **~ note** *n* Comm avoir *m*.

creditor /ˈkredɪtə(r)/ *n* Comm, Fin créancier/-ière *m/f*.

credit: **~ rating** *n* Fin réputation *f* de solvabilité; **~ reference agency** *n* agence *f* de renseignements commerciaux; **~ sale** *n* Comm vente *f* à crédit.

credit side *n* **1** Accts actif *m*, crédit *m*; **2** fig bon côté *m*; **on the ~...** le bon côté des choses, c'est que...

credit: **~ squeeze** *n* Econ restrictions *fpl* de crédits; **~ standing**, **~ status** *n* Fin réputation *f* de solvabilité; **~ terms** *npl* Comm, Fin conditions *fpl* de crédit; **~ transfer** *n* Fin virement *m*; **~ union** *n* Fin association *f* coopérative d'épargne et de crédit.

creditworthiness /ˈkredɪtwɜːðɪnɪs/ *n* Fin solvabilité *f*.

creditworthy /ˈkredɪtwɜːðɪ/ *adj* Fin solvable.

credo /ˈkreɪdəʊ, ˈkriː-/ *n* credo *m*.

credulity /krɪˈdjuːlətɪ, US -ˈduː-/ *n* crédulité *f*; **to strain** ou **stretch sb's ~** aller trop loin.

credulous /ˈkredjʊləs, US -dʒə-/ *adj* crédule, naïf/naïve.

credulously /ˈkredjʊləslɪ, US -dʒə-/ *adv* [*believe, accept*] avec crédulité.

creed /kriːd/ *n* **1** (religious persuasion) croyance *f*; **2** (opinions) principes *mpl*; **political ~** credo *m* politique; **3** Relig (prayer) symbole *m*.

creek /kriːk, US *also* krɪk/ *n* **1** GB (inlet) (from sea) bras *m* de mer; (from river) bras *m* mort; **2** US, Austral (stream) ruisseau *m*.
IDIOMS **to be up the ~ (without a paddle)**○ être mal barré◑; **to be up shit ~●** être dans la merde●.

creel /kriːl/ *n* panier *m* de pêche, bourriche *f*.

creep /kriːp/ **I** *n*○ **1** GB (flatterer) lèche-bottes○ *mf inv*; **2** (repellent person) raclure *f*; **he's a ~** c'est une raclure.
II *vi* (*prét, pp* **crept**) **1** (furtively) **to ~ in/out** entrer/sortir à pas de loup; **to ~ behind/under sth** se glisser derrière/sous qch; **2** fig **a threatening tone had crept into his voice** petit à petit il avait pris un ton menaçant; **a blush crept over her face** le rouge lui est monté au visage; **3** (slowly) **to ~ forward** ou **along** [*vehicle*] avancer lentement; **4** [*insect*] grimper; [*cat*] ramper; **5** [*plant*] (horizontally) ramper; (climb) grimper; **6**○ GB faire du lèche-bottes○ (**to sb** à qn).
IDIOMS **to give sb the ~s**○ donner la chair de poule à qn○.
■ **creep in 1** [*wrong note, error, influence*] se glisser; **2** [*feeling, prejudice*] intervenir.
■ **creep over**: **~ over** [**sb**] [*feeling*] gagner.
■ **creep through**: ¶ **~ through** [**sb**] s'insinuer en; ¶ **~ through** [**sth**] s'insinuer dans.
■ **creep up**: **~ up** [*inflation, debt, unemployment*] grimper; **to ~ up on sb** lit s'approcher de qn à pas de loup; fig prendre qn par surprise.

creeper /ˈkriːpə(r)/ **I** *n* **1** (in jungle) liane *f*; **2** (creeping plant) plante *f* rampante; (climbing plant) plante *f* grimpante; **3** US Tech (wheeled frame) (also **floor ~**) chariot *m* de visite.
II creepers *npl* US (babysuit) grenouillère *f*, pyjama *m* de bébé.

creeping /ˈkriːpɪŋ/ *adj* **1** [*change, menace, resurgence*] insidieux/-ieuse; **2** [*plant, animal*] rampant.

creeping buttercup *n* renoncule *f* terrestre.

creepy○ /ˈkriːpɪ/ *adj* **1** [*film, feeling*] qui donne la chair de poule○; **2** [*person*] affreux/-euse○.

creepy-crawly○ /ˌkriːpɪˈkrɔːlɪ/ *n* bestiole *f*.

cremate /krɪˈmeɪt/ *vtr* incinérer.

cremation /krɪˈmeɪʃn/ *n* (ceremony) crémation *f*; (practice) incinération *f*.

crematorium /ˌkreməˈtɔːrɪəm/ GB, **crematory** /ˈkremətərɪ, US -tɔːrɪ/ US *n* (*pl* **-oria** ou **-oriums**) (building) crématorium *m*; (oven) four *m* crématoire.

crenellated /ˈkrenəleɪtɪd/ *adj* à créneaux; crénelé.

crenellation /ˌkrenəˈleɪʃən/ *n* Archit créneau *m*.

Creole /ˈkriːəʊl/ **I** ▶**1402**⌋ *n* (person) Créole *mf*; (language) créole *m*.
II *adj* Culin, Ling créole.

creosote /ˈkriːəsəʊt/ **I** *n* créosote *f*.
II *vtr* créosoter.

crepe, **crêpe** /kreɪp/ **I** *n* **1** Tex crêpe *m*; **wool/silk ~** crêpe de laine/de soie; **2** (for soles) (also **~ rubber**) crêpe *m*; **3** Culin crêpe *f*.
II *modif* [*dress*] en crêpe; [*sole*] (de) crêpe.

crepe: **~ bandage** *n* bande *f* Velpeau®; **~ de Chine** *n* crêpe *m* de Chine; **~hanger**, **crapehanger** *n* US pessimiste *mf*; **~ paper** *n* papier *m* crépon.

crept /krept/ *pret, pp* ▶ **creep**.

crepuscular /krɪˈpʌskjʊlə(r)/ *adj* crépusculaire.

crescendo /krɪˈʃendəʊ/ **I** *n* **1** Mus crescendo *m inv*; **2** fig **to reach a ~** [*campaign*] atteindre son apogée; [*noise, violence, protest*] atteindre son paroxysme.
II *adj, adv* Mus crescendo *inv*.
III *vi* Mus faire un crescendo.

crescent /ˈkresnt/ *n* **1** (shape) croissant *m*; Relig **the Crescent** le Croissant; **2** *rangée de maisons en arc de cercle*.

crescent moon *n* croissant *m* de (la) lune.

cress /kres/ *n* Bot, Culin cresson *m*.

crest /krest/ **I** *n* **1** gen, Zool crête *f*; **2** Herald (coat of arms) armoiries *fpl*; (above coat of arms) timbre *m*.
II *vtr* franchir la crête de [*hill, wave*].
III *vi* US atteindre son niveau maximum.
IV crested *pp adj* [*bird*] huppé; [*stationery*] armorié.
IDIOMS **to be on the ~ of a wave** être en période de réussite.

crestfallen /ˈkrestfɔːlən/ *adj* déconfit.

cretaceous /krɪˈteɪʃəs/ *adj* Geol crétacé; **the Cretaceous period** le crétacé.

Cretan /ˈkriːtn/ **I** *n* Crétois/-e *m/f*.
II *adj* crétois.

Crete /kriːt/ ▶**1381**⌋ *pr n* Crète *f*; **in** ou **on ~** en Crète.

cretin /ˈkretɪn, US ˈkriːtn/ *n* Med, pej crétin/-e *m/f*.

cretinism /ˈkretɪnɪzəm, US ˈkriːt-/ *n* crétinisme *m*.

cretinous /ˈkretɪnəs, US ˈkriːt-/ *adj* Med, péj crétin.

cretonne /ˈkretɒn/ *n* cretonne *f*.

Creuse ▶**1163**⌋ *pr n* Creuse *f*; **in/to ~** dans la Creuse.

Creutzfeld-Jakob disease, **CJD** /ˌkrɔɪtsfeldˈjækɒb/ ▶**1354**⌋ *n* Med maladie *f* de Creutzfeld-Jakob.

crevasse /krɪˈvæs/ *n* crevasse *f*.

crevice /ˈkrevɪs/ *n* fissure *f*.

crew /kruː/ **I** *pret* ▶ **crow**.
II *n* **1** Aviat, Naut équipage *m*; **2** (in rowing) équipe *f*; **3** Cin, Radio, Rail, TV équipe *f*; **fire ~** équipe des pompiers; **4**○ (gang) péj ou hum bande *f*.
III *vtr* Naut être membre de l'équipage de [*boat*].
IV *vi* Naut **to ~ for sb** être l'équipier de qn.

crewcut *n* coupe *f* (de cheveux) en brosse.

crewel work /ˈkruːəlwɜːk/ *n* tapisserie *f* sur canevas.

crew: **~man** *n* (*pl* **-men**) équipier *m*; **~ neck** *n* ras-de-cou *m inv*; **~ neck sweater** *n* pull *m* ras du cou.

crib /krɪb/ **I** *n* **1** lit *m* d'enfant; **2** GB (Nativity) crèche *f*; **3** Agric râtelier *m*; **4** (borrowing) emprunt *m*; **5** Sch, Univ (illicit aid) antisèche○ *f*; (translation) traduction *f*; **6** *abrév* ▶ **cribbage**.
II *vtr* (*p prés etc* **-bb-**) copier.
III *vi* (*p prés etc* **-bb-**) gen faire des emprunts; Sch, Univ copier (**from** sur).

cribbage /ˈkrɪbɪdʒ/ *n*: *jeu de cartes pour deux personnes*.

crib death *n* US Med = **cot death**.

crick /krɪk/ **I** *n* **a ~ in one's back** un tour de reins; **a ~ in one's neck** un torticolis.
II *vtr* **to ~ one's back** se faire un tour de reins; **to ~ one's neck** attraper un torticolis.

cricket /ˈkrɪkɪt/ ▶**1282**⌋ **I** *n* **1** Zool grillon *m*; **2** Sport cricket *m*.
II *modif* Sport [*equipment, ground, match*] de cricket.
IDIOMS **it's not ~**† ou hum ce n'est pas franc-jeu.

cricketer /ˈkrɪkɪtə(r)/ *n* joueur *m* de cricket.

crikey†○ /ˈkraɪkɪ/ *excl* mince alors○.

crime /kraɪm/ **I** *n* **1** (offence) (minor) délit *m*; (serious) crime *m* (**against** contre); **the ~ of murder/theft** le meurtre/vol; **a ~ of violence** un crime violent; **~s against property/the person** atteintes à la propriété/la personne; **2** ¢ (criminal activity) criminalité *f*; **drug ~** criminalité *f* liée à la drogue; **car ~** vol *m* de voiture; **computer ~** piratage *m* informatique; **~ doesn't pay** le crime ne paie pas; **3** fig (immoral act) crime *m*; **it's a ~ to waste food** c'est un crime de gaspiller la nourriture.
II *modif* [*fiction, novel, writing*] policier/-ière; [*wave, rate*] de criminalité.

Crimea /kraɪˈmɪə/ *pr n* Crimée *f*.

Crimean /kraɪˈmɪən/ *adj* de Crimée.

crime: **~ buster**○ *n* = **crime fighter**; **~-busting**○ *adj* = **crime fighting**; **~ correspondent** ▶**1692**⌋ *n* journaliste *mf* spécialisé/-e dans les affaires criminelles; **~ desk** *n* bureau *m* des affaires criminelles; **~ fighter** *n* (police officer) policier *m* (chargé de la lutte contre le crime); **~ fighting** *adj* [*body, detective*] chargé de la lutte contre le crime; [*career, days*] de lutte contre le crime; **~ figures** *npl* statistiques *fpl* de la criminalité et de la délinquance; **~ of passion** *n* crime *m* passionnel.

crime prevention I *n* lutte *f* contre le crime.
II *modif* [*campaign, effort, poster*] pour lutter contre le crime.

crime: **~ prevention officer** *n* commissaire *m* (*chargé de la lutte contre le crime*); **~ squad** *n* brigade *f* criminelle; **~ writer** ▶**1692**⌋ *n* auteur *m* de romans policiers.

criminal /ˈkrɪmɪnl/ **I** *n* criminel/-elle *m/f*.
II *adj* **1** [*activity, behaviour, history, tendency*] criminel/-elle; **the ~ element in society** la minorité criminelle dans la société; **2** fig **it's ~ to do** c'est un crime de faire.

criminal: **~ act** *n* infraction *f*; **~ assault** *n* agression *f* criminelle; **~ bankruptcy** *n* faillite *f* frauduleuse; **~ bankruptcy order** *n*: *jugement du tribunal correctionnel à l'encontre d'une personne ayant fait banqueroute*; **~ case** *n* affaire *f* criminelle.

criminal charges *npl* charges *fpl*; **to press/drop ~ (against sb)** produire/abandonner les charges (contre qn); **to face ~** être sous le coup d'une inculpation.

criminal: **~ code** *n* code *m* pénal; **~ conspiracy** *n* association *f* de malfaiteurs; **~ conversation** *n* adultère *m*; **~ conviction** *n* condamnation *f*; **~ court** *n* cour *f* d'assises; **~ damage** *n* dégradations *fpl*, dommages *mpl*; **~ injuries compensation** *n* GB *dommages et intérêts versés par l'État*; **~ inquiry** *n* enquête *f* criminelle; **~ intent** *n* intention *f* criminelle; **~ investigation** *n* = **criminal**

inquiry; **Criminal Investigation Department**, **CID** *n* GB ≈ police *f* judiciaire.

criminality /ˌkrɪmɪˈnælətɪ/ *n* criminalité *f*.

criminalization /ˌkrɪmɪnəlaɪˈzeɪʃn, US -lɪˈz-/ *n* criminalisation *f*.

criminalize /ˈkrɪmɪnəlaɪz/ *vtr* criminaliser.

criminal: **~ justice** *n* justice *f* pénale; **~ justice system** *n* système *m* de justice pénale; **~ law** *n* droit *m* pénal; **~ lawyer** ▶ 1692 *n* avocat/-e *m/f* spécialisé/-e en matière pénale, pénaliste *mf* spec; **~ liability** *n* responsabilité *f* pénale; **~ libel** *n* diffamation *f*.

criminally /ˈkrɪmɪnəlɪ/ *adv* gen Jur **a ~ motivated act** un acte commis avec l'intention de nuire; **a ~ motivated minority** un petit groupe de gens décidé à commettre un crime; **to be ~ negligent** Jur être coupable de négligence criminelle.

criminally insane *adj* dément; **to be ~** être en état de démence.

criminal: **~ negligence** *n* négligence *f* criminelle; **~ offence** *n* délit *m*; **~ procedure** *n* procédure *f* pénale; **~ proceedings** *npl* poursuites *fpl* judiciaires.

criminal record *n* casier *m* judiciaire; **to have no ~** avoir un casier judiciaire vierge.

Criminal Records Office *n* GB Jur service *m* d'identité judiciaire.

criminologist /ˌkrɪmɪˈnɒlədʒɪst/ ▶ 1692 *n* criminologue *mf*.

criminology /ˌkrɪmɪˈnɒlədʒɪ/ *n* criminologie *f*.

crimp /krɪmp/ *vtr* friser [*hair*]; pincer [*pastry*]; plisser [*fabric*].

IDIOMS **to put a ~ in sth**○ US mettre des bâtons dans les roues de qch.

Crimplene® /ˈkrɪmpliːn/ *n*: *tissu synthétique infroissable*.

crimson /ˈkrɪmzn/ ▶ 1104 I *n* cramoisi *m*.
II *adj* [*lips, nails*] pourpre; [*fabric, flower, fruit*] cramoisi; **to go** ou **blush ~** devenir cramoisi.

cringe /krɪndʒ/ I *vi* **1** (physically) avoir un mouvement de recul; **to make sb ~** provoquer un mouvement de recul chez qn; **2** (in embarrassment) avoir envie de rentrer sous terre; **to make sb ~** donner envie à qn de rentrer sous terre; **3** (grovel) se comporter de manière servile; **4** (in disgust) **it makes me ~** ça me hérisse.
II **cringing** *pres p adj* servile.

crinkle /ˈkrɪŋkl/ I *n* (in skin) ride *f*; (in fabric, paper) pli *m*.
II *vtr* gaufrer [*paper, material*]; plisser [*eyes*].
III *vi* [*leaf*] se froisser; [*face, paper*] se plisser.

crinkle-cut /ˈkrɪŋklkʌt/ *adj* [*chips*] coupe ondulée.

crinkly /ˈkrɪŋklɪ/ *adj* [*hair*] frisé; [*paper, material*] gaufré.

crinoline /ˈkrɪnəlɪn/ *n* crinoline *f*.

cripple /ˈkrɪpl/ I *n* **1** (lame) offensive impotent/-e *m/f*; **2** (inadequate) **emotional ~** personne *f* bloquée sur le plan émotionnel; **social ~** handicapé/-e *m/f* social/-e.
II *vtr* **1** (physically) estropier; (emotionally) traumatiser; **~d for life** infirme à vie; **2** fig paralyser [*country, industry, economy*]; désemparer [*ship*]; mettre [qch] hors d'usage [*vehicle, equipment*]; [*debt, burden*] écraser [*person, company*].

crippled /ˈkrɪpld/ *adj* **1** (physically) [*person*] impotent; **to be ~ with sth** être perclus de qch; **2** fig [*person*] (by debt) écrasé (**by** par); (by emotion) effondré (**by** de); [*country, industry, economy*] paralysé (**by** par); [*vehicle*] hors d'usage; [*ship*] désemparé.

crippling /ˈkrɪplɪŋ/ *adj* **1** lit [*disease*] invalidant; **2** fig [*taxes, debts, burden*] écrasant; [*emotion, inability, strike, effect*] paralysant.

crisis /ˈkraɪsɪs/ *n* (*pl* **-ses**) crise *f* (**in** dans; **over** à cause de); **cabinet/managerial ~** crise au sein du gouvernement/de la direction; **domestic ~** Pol crise interne; **housing ~** crise du logement; **cash ~** gen, Fin crise de trésorerie; **energy ~** crise d'énergie; **the Gulf ~** la crise du Golfe; **midlife ~** crise des cinquante ans; **personal** ou **emotional ~** crise émotionnelle; **to be in ~** être en crise; **to reach a ~** devenir critique; **to be at/to reach ~ point** être à/atteindre un point critique; **~ of confidence** crise de confiance; **to be at ~ level** [*stocks etc*] être à un niveau critique.

crisis centre GB, **crisis center** US *n* (after disaster) cellule *f* de crise; (for alcoholics, battered wives etc) association *f* d'entraide.

crisis: **~ intervention** *n* Soc Admin intervention *f* d'urgence; **~ management** *n* Pol gestion *f* de crise.

crisp /krɪsp/ I *n* GB (also **potato ~**) chip *f*; **smoky bacon ~s** chips goût bacon fumé.
II *adj* **1** [*batter, biscuit, chips, pastry*] croustillant; [*fruit, vegetable*] croquant; **'to keep biscuits ~'** 'pour conserver aux biscuits leur croustillant'; **2** [*fabric, garment*] frais/fraîche; [*banknote, paper, snow*] craquant; **3** [*air*] vif/vive; [*morning*] froid et piquant; **4** fig (concise) [*order, words*] bref/brève; [*manner*] brusque; [*design*] net/nette; [*musical performance*] enlevé.
IDIOMS **to be burnt to a ~**○ être carbonisé.
■ **crisp up**: ¶ **~ up** devenir croustillant; ¶ **~ up [sth]**, **~ [sth] up** réchauffer (pour rendre croustillant).

crispbread /ˈkrɪspbred/ *n* GB pain *m* grillé suédois.

crisper /ˈkrɪspə(r)/ *n* US compartiment *m* à légumes.

crisply /ˈkrɪsplɪ/ *adv* [*ironed*] fraîchement; [*reply, speak*] brusquement.

crispness /ˈkrɪspnɪs/ *n* (of biscuits) croustillant *m*; (of vegetables, fabric) fraîcheur *f*; (of air, weather) froid *m* piquant; (of design) netteté *f*; (of speech) brièveté *f*.

crispy /ˈkrɪspɪ/ *adj* croustillant; **~ noodles** nouilles *fpl* sautées.

crisscross /ˈkrɪskrɒs, US -krɔːs/ I *n* (of streets) enchevêtrement *m*.
II *adj* [*design, pattern*] en croisillons.
III *adv* en croisillons; **the streets run ~** les rues s'entrecroisent.
IV *vtr* sillonner; **to ~ sth with sth** sillonner qch de qch.
V *vi* s'entrecroiser.

crit○ /krɪt/ *n* GB papier○ *m*, critique *f*.

criteria /kraɪˈtɪərɪə/ *npl* ▶ **criterion**.

criterion /kraɪˈtɪərɪən/ *n* (*pl* **-ia**) critère *m* (**for** de); **to meet a ~** répondre à un critère.

critic /ˈkrɪtɪk/ ▶ 1692 *n* **1** (reviewer, analyst) critique *m*; **2** (opponent) détracteur/-trice *m/f*.

critical /ˈkrɪtɪkl/ *adj* **1** (crucial) [*moment*] décisif/-ive; [*point*] critique; [*stage*] crucial; **to be ~ to** être essentiel/-ielle pour assurer [*future, success*]; **2** (acute) [*condition*] critique; **3** (disapproving) critique; **to be ~ of sb/sth** critiquer qn/qch; **4** (analytical) [*approach, angle, study, theory*] critique; **5** (of reviewers) [*acclaim*] de la critique; **the film was a ~ success** le film a été acclamé par les critiques; **6** (discriminating) [*reader, viewer*] critique; **to take a ~ look at sth** examiner qch d'un œil critique; **7** Nucl, Phys critique.

critically /ˈkrɪtɪklɪ/ *adv* **1** (using judgment) [*evaluate, examine*] d'un œil critique; **2** (with disapproval) [*view*] sévèrement; [*speak*] avec animosité; **3** (seriously) [*ill, injured*] grièvement, très gravement; **~ important** capital.

critical: **~ path** *n* chemin *m* critique; **~ path analysis** *n* analyse *f* du chemin critique.

criticism /ˈkrɪtɪsɪzəm/ *n* **1** (remark, evaluation) critique *f*; **2** (study) étude *f* critique (**of** sur); **3** (analysis) critique *f*; **literary ~** critique *f* littéraire.

criticize /ˈkrɪtɪsaɪz/ *vtr* **1** (find fault with) critiquer; **to ~ sb for sth** reprocher qch à qn; **to ~ sb for doing** reprocher à qn de faire; **2** (analyse) critiquer.

critique /krɪˈtiːk/ I *n* critique *f*.
II *vtr* US (analyse) critiquer.

critter○ /ˈkrɪtə(r)/ *n* US (animal) créature *f*; (person) personne *f*.

croak /krəʊk/ I *n* (of frog) coassement *m*; (of crow) croassement *m*; (of person) voix *f* rauque.
II *vtr* dire [qch] d'une voix rauque; **to ~ a reply** répondre d'une voix rauque.
III *vi* **1** (frog) coasser; (person) parler d'une voix rauque; **2**◑ (die) crever◑.

croaker○ /ˈkrəʊkə(r)/ *n* US toubib○ *m*.

Croat /ˈkrəʊæt/ *n* Croate *mf*.

Croatia /krəʊˈeɪʃə/ ▶ 1131 *pr n* Croatie *f*.

Croatian /krəʊˈeɪʃn/ ▶ 1486 *adj* croate.

crochet /ˈkrəʊʃeɪ, US krəʊˈʃeɪ/ I *n* (art) crochet *m*; (work) ouvrage *m* au crochet.
II *vtr* faire [qch] au crochet; **a ~ed sweater** un pull au crochet.
III *vi* faire du crochet.

crochet hook *n* crochet *m*.

crock /krɒk/ I *n* **1**○ (car) tacot○ *m*; (person) croulant/-e○ *m/f*; **2**† (pot) pot *m*; **3** Hort (shard) tesson *m*; **4**◑ US conneries◑ *fpl*.
II **crocks** *npl* vaisselle *f*.

crocked○ /krɒkt/ *adj* US bourré○.

crockery /ˈkrɒkərɪ/ *n* vaisselle *f*.

crocodile /ˈkrɒkədaɪl/ I *n* **1** (animal, leather) crocodile *m*; **2** GB (line) rang *m* par deux.
II *modif* [*shoes, bag*] en crocodile, en croco○; **~ clip** pince *f* crocodile.
IDIOMS **to shed ~ tears** verser des larmes de crocodile.

crocus /ˈkrəʊkəs/ *n* (*pl* **-uses** ou **-i**) crocus *m*.

Croesus /ˈkriːsəs/ *pr n* Crésus.
IDIOMS **as rich as ~** riche comme Crésus.

croft /krɒft, US krɔːft/ *n* petite ferme *f* (*en Écosse*).

crofter /ˈkrɒftə(r), US ˈkrɔːft-/ *n* petit/-e fermier/-ière *m/f* (*en Écosse*).

cromlech /ˈkrɒmlek/ *n* cromlech *m*.

Cromwellian /krɒmˈwelɪən/ *adj* de Cromwell.

crone /krəʊn/ *n* péj vieille bique *f* pej.

crony /ˈkrəʊnɪ/ *n* souvent péj (petit/-e) copain/copine *m/f*.

cronyism /ˈkrəʊnɪɪzəm/ *n* Pol copinage *m*.

crook /krʊk/ I *n* **1** (rogue) escroc *m*; **2** (of road, river) courbe *f*; (of arm) creux *m*; **3** (shepherd's) houlette *f*; (bishop's) crosse *f*; **4** Mus (of horn) ton *m* de rechange.
II○ *adj* Austral [*person*] mal fichu○; [*food*] mauvais.
III *vtr* recourber [*finger*]; plier [*arm*]; **to ~ one's little finger** lever le petit doigt.
IDIOMS **by hook or by ~** coûte que coûte.

crooked /ˈkrʊkɪd/ I *adj* **1** (with a bend) [*line*] brisé; [*limb*] tors; [*back, person*] difforme; [*stick, finger*] crochu; [*path*] tortueux/-euse; **a ~ smile** un sourire en coin; **2** (off-centre) de travers; [*house*] de guingois *inv*; **3**○ (dishonest) malhonnête.
II *adv* de travers.

crookedly /ˈkrʊkɪdlɪ/ *adv* de travers.

croon /kruːn/ *vtr, vi* chantonner.

crooner /ˈkruːnə(r)/ *n* crooner *m*.

crop /krɒp/ I *n* **1** (type of produce) culture *f*; **export/cereal ~** culture d'exportation/céréalière; **2** (growing in field) (*souvent pl*) culture *f*; **the ~s have been trampled/will fail** les cultures ont été piétinées/seront perdues; **3** (harvest) (of fruit, vegetables) récolte *f*; (of cereals) récolte *f*, moisson *f*; **bumper ~** récolte exceptionnelle; **second ~** deuxième récolte; **the oat/rice ~** la récolte d'avoine/de riz; **4** fig (collection of prizes, medals) moisson *f*; (of people, novels, films) cuvée *f*; **this year's ~ of graduates** la cuvée des diplômés de cette année; **they are the cream of the ~** ce sont les meilleurs du lot; **5** fig, souvent hum (of weeds, spots) paquet○ *m*; **6** (short haircut) coupe *f* courte; **7** (of bird) jabot *m*; **8** (whip) cravache *f*.

II *vtr* (*p prés etc* **-pp-**) **1** (cut short) couper [qch] court [*hair*]; tailler [*tail, ears*]; **2** [*animal*] brouter [*grass, field*]; **3** Phot rogner [*photograph*]; **4** (harvest) récolter [*cereal, vegetable, fruit*]; moissonner [*wheat, corn*]; cueillir [*cherries, strawberries*]; **5** (grow produce on) cultiver [*land*]; **6** (grow) cultiver [*vegetable, cereal*].

III *vi* (*p prés etc* **-pp-**) [*produce, plant*] produire une récolte; **this variety ~s late** c'est une variété tardive.

■ **crop out** [*rock*] affleurer.

■ **crop up** [*matter, subject*] surgir; [*person, name*] être mentionné; [*problem, difficulty*] surgir; [*opportunity*] se présenter; **something's ~ped up** il y a un contretemps; **she's always ~ping up in the papers** on ne voit qu'elle dans les journaux.

crop: **~ circle** *n* cercle *m* dans les cultures (*souvent attribué à une intervention extra-terrestre*); **~ duster** *n* = **crop sprayer**; **~ dusting** *n* = **crop spraying**; **~land** *n* terre *f* en culture.

cropped /krɒpt/ *adj* **1** [*hair, curl*] coupé court; [*grass, lawn*] taillé; **2** Fashn [*jacket, top*] court; **3** [*photograph*] rogné.

cropper /ˈkrɒpə(r)/ *n* variété *f*; **late/early ~** variété tardive/précoce.

IDIOMS **to come a ~**○ GB se casser la figure○.

crop: **~ rotation** *n* rotation *f* des cultures; **~ spray** *n* pesticide *m*.

crop sprayer *n* **1** (machine) pulvérisateur *m* de pesticides; **2** (plane) avion *m* de pulvérisation de pesticides.

crop: **~ spraying** *n* pulvérisation *f* de pesticides; **~-spraying helicopter** *n* hélicoptère *m* de pulvérisation de pesticides; **~ top** *n* Fashn brassière *f*.

croquet /ˈkrəʊkeɪ, US krəʊˈkeɪ/ **▶ 1282** **I** *n* croquet *m*.

II *modif* [*equipment, game*] de croquet.

croquette /krəˈket/ *n* croquette *f*; **potato ~s**, **~ potatoes** croquettes de pommes de terre.

crosier /ˈkrəʊzɪə(r), US ˈkrəʊʒər/ *n* crosse *f*.

cross /krɒs, US krɔːs/ **I** *n* **1** (shape) croix *f*; **the Cross** Relig la Croix; **to put a ~ against** cocher [*name, item*]; **'put a ~ in the box'** 'faites une croix dans la case', 'cochez la case'; **2** Biol, Bot, Zool (hybrid) croisement *m* (**between** entre); **a ~ between Hitler and Napoleon/Biarritz and Brighton** fig un mélange d'Hitler et de Napoléon/de Biarritz et de Brighton; **3** Sewing biais *m*; **to cut sth on the ~** couper qch dans le biais; **4** Sport (in football) centre *m*.

II *adj* **1** (angry) fâché; **to be ~ with sb** être fâché contre qn; **to be ~ about sth** être agacé par qch; **to get ~** se fâcher (**with** contre); **to make sb ~** mettre qn en colère, agacer qn; **we've never had a ~ word (in 20 years)** nous ne nous sommes jamais disputés (en 20 ans); **2** (transverse) [*timber*] transversal; **3** (contrary to general direction) [*breeze, swell*] contraire.

III *vtr* **1** (go across) lit traverser [*road, country, room, sea*]; traverser, passer [*river*]; franchir [*border, line, threshold, mountains, ditch*]; [*bridge*] franchir, enjamber [*river, road*]; [*road, railway line, river*] traverser [*garden, country, desert*]; [*line*] barrer [*page*]; fig dépasser [*limit, boundary*]; **it ~ed his mind that** il lui est venu à l'esprit or l'idée que; **the thought had ~ed my mind** l'idée m'avait traversé l'esprit (**that** que); **a slight frown ~ed her features** une expression renfrognée est passée sur son visage; **to ~ the class/race divide** surmonter la barrière des classes/races; **the programme ~ed the bounds of decency** l'émission a dépassé les limites de la décence; **2** (meet) [*road, path, railway line, river*] couper [*road, path, railway line, river*]; **to ~ each other** se couper; **3** (place in shape of a cross) croiser [*spoons, knives, ropes*]; **to ~ one's legs/arms** croiser les jambes/bras; **4** Biol, Bot, Zool croiser [*plants, animals, species*]; **to ~ sth with sth** croiser qch avec qch; **5** (oppose) contrarier [*person*]; **to be ~ed in love** avoir une déception amoureuse; **6** (draw line across) barrer; **to ~ a 't'** barrer un 't'; **to ~ a cheque** GB barrer un chèque; **7** (mark to indicate) [*teacher*] ≈ souligner [qch] en rouge [*answer*]; (to indicate choice) cocher [*box*]; **8** Sport (in football) centrer [*ball*].

IV *vi* **1** (also **~ over**) (go across) traverser; **to ~ into Italy/Austria** passer en Italie/Autriche; **2** (meet) [*roads, railway lines, cars, trains*] se croiser; [*lines*] se couper; [*letters*] se croiser; **to ~ with sth** [*letter*] croiser qch; **3** (lie in shape of cross) [*straps, ropes, beams, bars*] se croiser.

V *v refl* **to ~ oneself** Relig se signer, faire le signe de la croix.

VI crossed *pp adj* Telecom [*line*] brouillé.

IDIOMS **we seem to have got our wires** ou **lines ~ed** il semble y avoir un malentendu (quelque part); **X and Y have got their wires** ou **lines ~ed** X et Y ne se sont pas compris; **to have a** ou **one's ~ to bear** porter sa croix; **▶ heart**.

■ **cross off**: **~ [sth/sb] off**, **~ off [sth/sb]** barrer, rayer [*name, thing*]; radier [*person*]; **to ~ sb's name off a list** rayer qn d'une liste.

■ **cross out**: **~ out [sth]**, **~ [sth] out** rayer, barrer [qch].

■ **cross over 1** (go across) traverser; **to ~ over to sth** (change allegiance) passer à qch [*party*]; se convertir à [*religion*]; **2** (be placed across) [*straps*] se croiser.

■ **cross through**: **~ through [sth]** rayer, barrer [qch].

cross: **~ action** *n* Jur action *f* reconventionnelle; **~bar** *n* gen barre *f*; (in football, rugby) barre *f* transversale; **~beam** *n* Constr traverse *f*; **~-bench** *n* (*gén pl*) GB Pol banc *m* d'un député noninscrit; **~-bencher** *n* député *m* noninscrit; **~bill** *n* Zool bec-croisé *m*; **~bones** *npl* **▶ skull**; **~-border** *adj* transfrontalier/-ière; **~bow** *n* arbalète *f*; **~bred** *n, adj* hybride (*m*).

crossbreed /ˈkrɒsbriːd, US ˈkrɔːs-/ **I** *n* (animal) hybride *m*; (person) injur métis/-isse *m/f*.

II *vtr* (*prét, pp* **-bred**) croiser [*animals*]; hybrider [*plants*]; **to ~ sth with** croiser qch avec [*animal*]; hybrider qch avec [*plant*].

III *vi* (*prét, pp* **-bred**) **to ~ with sth** se croiser avec qch.

cross: **~breeding** *n* (of animal) croisement *m*; (of plant) hybridation *f*; **~-Channel** *adj* trans-Manche.

cross-check **I** /ˈkrɒstʃek, US ˈkrɔːs-/ *n* recoupement *m*.

II /ˌkrɒsˈtʃek, US ˌkrɔːs-/ *vtr* vérifier [qch] par recoupement.

III *vi* faire des recoupements.

cross: **~-compiler** *n* Comput compilateur *m* croisé; **~-correlation** *n* Stat corrélation *f* croisée.

cross-country /ˌkrɒsˈkʌntrɪ, US ˌkrɔːs-/ **I** **▶ 1282** *n* Sport (in running) cross *m*; (in skiing) ski *m* de fond.

II *adj* **1** Sport (in running) [*race, champion, event*] de cross; [*runner*] de fond; (skiing) [*skier*] de fond; **~ skiing** ski *m* de fond; **2** gen (by way of fields etc) [*trip, walk, hike, run*] à travers champs; **3** (across a country) [*railway, road, route*] qui traverse le pays (*d'est en ouest*).

III *adv* [*run, walk, hike*] à travers champs.

cross: **~-court** *adj* Sport [*shot, volley*] droit croisé; **~-cultural** *adj* inter-culturel/-elle; **~current** *n* Lit, fig contre-courant *m*; **~-curricular** *adj* multidisciplinaire.

crosscut /ˈkrɒskʌt, US ˈkrɔːs-/ **I** *n* Tech coupe *f* en travers.

II *adj* Tech en travers.

cross: **~cut file** *n* Tech lime *f* à double taille; **~cut saw** *n* Tech scie *f* de travers; **~-disciplinary** *adj* Sch, Univ [*course, syllabus*] pluridisciplinaire; **~-dress** *vi* [*man*] s'habiller en femme; [*woman*] s'habiller en homme; **~-dresser** *n* travesti/-e *m/f*; **~-dressing** *n* travestissement *m*.

crosse /krɒs/ *n* Sport crosse *f* (*au jeu de lacrosse*).

cross-examination /ˌkrɒsɪɡˌzæmɪˈneɪʃn, US ˌkrɔːs-/ *n* Jur, gen contre-interrogatoire *m*.

cross-examine /ˌkrɒsɪɡˈzæmɪn, US ˌkrɔːs-/ *vtr* **1** Jur faire subir un contre-interrogatoire à [*person*]; **2** gen interroger, harceler [qn] de questions.

cross-eye /ˈkrɒsaɪ, US ˈkrɔːs-/ *n* Med strabisme *m*.

cross-eyed /ˈkrɒsaɪd, US ˈkrɔːs-/ *adj* [*person*] atteint de strabisme, qui louche; **to be ~** loucher, avoir un strabisme; **to make sb ~** faire loucher qn.

cross-fertilization /ˌkrɒsˌfɜːtəlaɪˈzeɪʃn, US ˌkrɔːs-/ *n* Bot hybridation *f*.

cross-fertilize /ˌkrɒsˈfɜːtɪlaɪz, US ˌkrɔːs-/ **I** *vtr* Bot hybrider.

II *vi* Bot s'hybrider.

crossfire /ˈkrɒsfaɪə(r), US ˈkrɔːs-/ *n* Mil, fig feux *mpl* croisés; **to be** ou **get caught in the ~** lit, fig être pris entre deux feux; **to be** ou **get caught in the ~ of questions/criticism** fig être pris sous les feux croisés des questions/de la critique.

cross: **~-grained** *adj* [*wood, timber*] aux fibres irrégulières; **~ hairs** *npl* réticule *m*; **~hatch** *vtr* hachurer (*en croisillons*).

crosshatching /ˈkrɒshætʃɪŋ, US ˈkrɔːs-/ *n* **1** (act) hachurage *m* (*croisé*); **2** (pattern) hachures *fpl* (*croisées*).

cross-index /ˌkrɒsˈɪndeks, US ˌkrɔːs-/ *vtr* faire référence à, renvoyer à.

crossing /ˈkrɒsɪŋ, US ˈkrɔːsɪŋ/ *n* **1** (journey) (over sea, lake) traversée *f*; (over border) passage *m*; **2** (for pedestrians) passage *m* (pour) piétons, passage *m* clouté; Rail (also **level ~**) passage *m* à niveau; **3** Rail, Transp (junction) croisement *m*; **4** Biol, Bot, Zool croisement *m*.

crossing-out /ˌkrɒsɪŋˈaʊt, US ˌkrɔːs-/ *n* (*pl* **~s-out**) rature *f*.

cross-legged /ˌkrɒsˈleɡɪd, US ˌkrɔːs-/ **I** *adj* assis en tailleur.

II *adv* [*sit*] en tailleur.

crossly /ˈkrɒslɪ, US ˈkrɔːslɪ/ *adv* avec humeur.

crossover /ˈkrɒsəʊvə(r), US ˈkrɔːs-/ **I** *n* **1** Mus mélange *m* de genres; **2** Rail voie *f* de croisement.

II *adj* Fashn [*bodice, straps*] croisé.

cross: **~over network** *n* Electron pont *m* diviseur; **~-party** *adj* Pol [*amendment, approach, initiative*] commun à plusieurs partis; [*group*] comprenant des membres de différents partis; [*support*] de différents partis; **~patch**○ *n* grognon○ *mf*; **~piece** *n* traverse *f*.

crossply /ˈkrɒsplaɪ, US ˈkrɔːs-/ **I** *n* Aut pneu *m* à carcasse croisée.

II *adj* Aut à carcasse croisée.

cross-pollinate /ˌkrɒsˈpɒlɪneɪt, US ˌkrɔːs-/ **I** *vtr* Bot féconder [qch] par pollinisation croisée.

II *vi* subir une pollinisation croisée.

cross-pollination /ˌkrɒspɒlɪˈneɪʃn, US ˌkrɔːs-/ *n* Bot pollinisation *f* croisée.

cross-purposes /ˌkrɒsˈpɜːpəsɪz, US ˌkrɔːs-/ *npl* **we are at ~ (with each other)** (misunderstanding) il y a un malentendu (entre nous); (disagreement) nous sommes en désaccord; **to talk at ~** se comprendre mal.

cross-question /ˌkrɒsˈkwestʃən, US ˌkrɔːs-/ *vtr* faire subir un interrogatoire à [*person*].

cross-refer /ˌkrɒsrɪˈfɜː(r), US ˌkrɔːs-/ *vtr* renvoyer [*person*] (**to** à); **to ~ sth to sth** mettre un renvoi à qch sous qch.

cross-reference /ˌkrɒsˈrefrəns, US ˌkrɔːs-/ **I** *n* renvoi *m* (**to** à).

II *vtr* faire les renvois de [*book, dictionary*]; mettre un renvoi sous [*entry, item*] (**to** à).

crossroads /'krɒsrəʊdz, US 'krɔːs-/ *n* (*pl* **~**) lit carrefour *m*; fig carrefour *m*, moment *m* décisif.

cross-section /ˌkrɒs'sekʃn, US ˌkrɔːs-/ *n* **1** lit coupe *f* transversale; **in ~** en coupe transversale; **2** fig (selection) échantillon *m* (**of** de).

cross-shaped /'krɒsʃeɪpt, US 'krɔːs-/ *adj* en forme de croix.

cross-stitch /'krɒsstɪtʃ, US 'krɔːs-/ **I** *n* point *m* de croix.
II *vtr, vi* broder au point de croix.

crosstalk /'krɒstɔːk, US 'krɔːs-/ *n* **1** Radio, Telecom diaphonie *f*; **2** GB (repartee) joutes *fpl* oratoires.

cross: **~tie** *n* US, Rail traverse *f* (de voie); **~-town** *adj* US qui traverse la ville; **~tree** *n* Naut barre *f* de flèche; **~walk** *n* US passage *m* (pour) piétons; **~way** *n* US croisement *m*; **~wind** *n* vent *m* de travers.

crosswise /'krɒswaɪz, US 'krɔːs-/ **I** *adj* **1** (diagonal) en diagonale; **2** (transverse) transversal.
II *adv* **1** (diagonally) en diagonale; **2** (transversely) transversalement.

crossword /'krɒswɜːd, US 'krɔːs-/ **I** *n* (also **~ puzzle**) (grille *f* de) mots *mpl* croisés; **to do the ~** faire les mots croisés.
II *modif* [*competition, book*] de mots croisés.

crotch /krɒtʃ/ *n* **1** Anat entrecuisse *m*; **2** (in trousers) entrejambe *m*; **too tight in the ~** trop serré à l'entrejambe.

crotchet /'krɒtʃɪt/ *n* GB Mus noire *f*.

crotchet rest *n* GB Mus soupir *m*.

crotchety /'krɒtʃɪtɪ/ *adj* grincheux/-euse.

crouch /kraʊtʃ/ **I** *n* position *f* accroupie.
II *vi* (also **~ down**) [*person*] s'accroupir; [*person, animal*] (in order to hide) se tapir; (for attack) se ramasser.

croup /kruːp/ *n* **1** Med croup *m*; **2** (of horse) croupe *f*.

croupier /'kruːpɪə(r)/ **▶ 1692** *n* croupier *m*.

crouton /'kruːtɒn/ *n* croûton *m*.

crow /krəʊ/ **I** *n* **1** (bird) corbeau *m*; **hooded ~** corneille *f* mantelée; **2** (cock's cry) chant *m* du coq.
II *vi* **1** (exult) exulter; **2** [*baby*] gazouiller; **3** (*prét* **crowed** ou **crew**†) [*cock*] chanter.
IDIOMS **as the ~ flies** à vol d'oiseau; **to make sb eat ~**○ US faire rentrer à qn ses mots dans la gorge; **stone the ~s**○! eh bien ça alors!
■ **crow about**: **~ about [sth]** se vanter de.
■ **crow over**: ¶ **~ over [sb]** crier victoire sur; ¶ **~ over [sth]** se vanter de.

crowbar /'krəʊbɑː(r)/ *n* pince-monseigneur *f*.

crowd /kraʊd/ **I** *n* **1** (mass of people) gen foule *f*; Sport spectateurs *mpl*; (audience) public *m*; **a ~ of 10,000** gen une foule de 10 000 personnes; Sport une foule de 10 000 spectateurs; **~s of people** une foule de gens; **to draw** ou **attract a ~** attirer la foule; **a ~ gathered at the scene** un attroupement s'est formé sur les lieux; **we are hoping for a big ~ at the concert** nous espérons que le public viendra nombreux au concert; **the president waved to the ~(s)** le président a salué la foule; **we ski in Norway to avoid the ~s** nous skions en Norvège pour éviter la foule; **people came in ~s to hear him** les gens sont venus l'écouter en masse; **it's not very good, but it'll pass in a ~**○ ce n'est pas terrible○, mais ça peut passer si on ne regarde pas de trop près; **to follow** ou **go** ou **move with the ~** suivre la foule; **to stand out from the ~** sortir du commun; **2**○ (group) bande *f*; **'who's coming?—'the usual ~'** 'qui est-ce qui vient?'—'toujours la même bande'; **the ~ from the office** les copains○ du bureau; **they're a friendly ~** ils sont tous très sympa○.
II *modif* [*behaviour, reaction*] de masse.
III *vtr* **1** (fill) se presser sur [*pavement, platform, road*]; s'entasser sur [*beach*]; **tourists ~ed the bars/trains** les bars/trains étaient pleins de touristes; **the roads were ~ed with cars** la circulation était très dense; **2** (squash) entasser [*people, animals, cars, furniture*] (**into** dans) ; **they have ~ed as many lines as possible onto the page** ils ont fait tenir un maximum de lignes dans la page; **they have ~ed a lot of information into this brochure** cette brochure est bourrée○ d'informations; **she ~s too much detail into her pictures** elle surcharge ses tableaux d'une foule de détails; **we always try to ~ as much as possible into our visits to Paris** nous essayons toujours de voir le plus de choses possible quand nous allons à Paris; **3** (fill to excess) remplir [*room, house, mind*] (**with** de); surcharger [*design, page*] (**with** de); **the house was ~ed with furniture/paintings** la maison était encombrée de meubles/tableaux; **4** (jostle) serrer, bousculer [*person, animal*]; serrer [*vehicle, boat*]; **5**○ (put pressure on) tanner○; **stop ~ing me! let me think!** arrête de me tanner○! laisse-moi réfléchir!
IV *vi* **1** lit **to ~ into** s'entasser dans [*room, lift, vehicle*]; **to ~ onto** s'entasser dans [*bus, train*]; **to ~ through** passer en foule par [*door, gates*]; **to ~ up/down sth** monter/descendre qch en foule [*stairs*]; **to ~ (up) against** se presser contre [*barrier*]; **2** fig **to ~ into** [*thoughts, memories, ideas*] se presser dans [*mind, memory*].
■ **crowd around, crowd round** ¶ s'attrouper; ¶ **~ around [sth]** se presser autour de; **don't ~ around the entrance** ne bloquez pas l'entrée.
■ **crowd in**: ¶ **~ in** [*people, animals*] s'entasser; **to ~ in on sb** lit [*people*] encercler qn; fig [*hills, walls*] oppresser qn; fig [*thoughts, memories*] assaillir qn; ¶ **~ in [sth/sb], ~ [sth/sb] in** entasser [*people, animals, furniture*]; accumuler [*words, lines, illustrations*].
■ **crowd out**: **~ out [sth/sb], ~ [sth/sb] out** évincer [*person, business*].
■ **crowd together**: ¶ **~ together** se serrer; ¶ **~ [sth] together, ~ together [sth]** entasser.

crowd: **~ control** *n* contrôle *m* de la foule; **~ control barrier** *n* barrière *f* de contrôle.

crowded /'kraʊdɪd/ *adj* **1** (full of people) [*train, hall, restaurant, shop*] bondé; [*private room, house*] plein à craquer; [*beach, park, street, pavement*] noir de monde; [*church*] plein; [*area, town*] plein de monde; **to be ~ with** être plein de [*people*]; **2** (cluttered) [*house, room, area, surface, table*] encombré (**with** de); [*car park*] plein (**with** de); [*display, arrangement, design*] surchargé (**with** de); **3** (busy) [*diary, holiday, life, day, week*] rempli (**with** de); [*timetable*] chargé.

crowd: **~-puller** *n* (event) grosse attraction *f*; (person) vedette *f*; **~-pulling** *adj* à succès; **~ safety** *n* sécurité *f* du public; **~ scene** *n* Cin, Theat scène *f* de foule; **~ trouble** *n* agitation *f* dans la foule.

crowfoot /'krəʊfʊt/ *n* renoncule *f* aquatique.

crowing /krəʊɪŋ/ *n* **1** (of cock) cocoricos *mpl*; **2** (boasting) vantardises *fpl*.

crown /kraʊn/ **I** *n* **1** (of monarch) couronne *f*; **a ~ of flowers/of thorns** une couronne de fleurs/d'épines; **the Crown** la Couronne *f*; **2** GB Jur ministère *m* public; **a witness for the Crown** un témoin à charge; **3** Sport championnat *m*; **4** (top) (of hill) crête *f*; (of tree) cime *f*; (of hat) fond *m*; (of road) sommet *m*; **5** (head) crâne *m*; **6** Dent couronne *f*; **7** Bot (of tree) couronne *f*; **8** GB (old coin) *ancienne pièce de monnaie*; **9** Naut diamant *m*; **10** Archit (of bridge) clé *f* d'arc; (of arch) clé *f* de voûte.
II *vtr* **1** couronner [*queen, champion*]; **to ~ sb emperor/champion** couronner qn empereur/champion; **2** (bring to worthy end) couronner; **the prize ~ed her career** le prix a couronné sa carrière; **her efforts were ~ed by success** ses efforts furent couronnés de succès; **to ~ it all, I won/the car broke down** pour couronner le tout, j'ai gagné/la voiture est tombée en panne; **3**○ (hit) taper [*person*]; **4** Dent couronner [*tooth*]; **5** Culin couronner [*cake*] (**with** de); **6** Games (in draughts) damer [*pièce*].
III○ *v refl* **to ~ oneself** se cogner violemment (**on** contre).

crown: **Crown Agents** *npl* GB Pol *organisme d'aide financière et commerciale d'échelle internationale*; **~ cap** *n* capsule *f*; **~ colony** *n* GB Pol colonie *f* britannique; **Crown court** *n* GB Jur ≈ cour *f* d'assises; **~ed head** *n* Pol tête *f* couronnée; **~ green bowling ▶ 1282** *n* GB Sport *jeu de boules sur terrain légèrement bosselé*.

crowning /'kraʊnɪŋ/ **I** *n* couronnement *m*.
II *adj* [*touch*] final; [*irony*] suprême; [*moment*] grand; [*success, victory*] définitif/-ive; **the ~ achievement of his career** le couronnement de sa carrière.

crowning glory *n* **1** (achievement) couronnement *m*; **2** (hair) **her hair is her ~** sa chevelure la rend resplendissante.

crown: **~ jewels** *npl* joyaux *mpl* de la Couronne; **Crown land** *n* GB Jur terre *f* appartenant à la Couronne; **~ prince** *n* prince *m* héritier.

crown princess *n* **1** (heir) princesse *f* héritière; **2** (wife of heir) épouse *f* du prince héritier.

crown: **Crown Prosecution Service, CPS** *n* GB Jur *organisme chargé de décider si un dossier criminel doit passer devant le tribunal*; ≈ Ministère *m* Public; **Crown prosecutor** *n* GB Jur procureur *m*; **~ roast** *n* Culin côtes *fpl* de bœuf (*disposées en forme de couronne*); **Crown servant** *n* GB Admin fonctionnaire *mf*.

crown wheel *n* **1** (in clock) roue *f* de couronne; **2** Mech couronne *f*; **~ and pinion** couple *m* conique.

crow: **~'s feet** *npl* (on face) pattes-d'oie *fpl*; **~'s nest** *n* nid *m* de pie.

crozier *n* = **crosier**.

crucial /'kruːʃl/ *adj* **1** [*role, importance, moment*] crucial; [*witness*] capital (**to, for** pour); **it is ~ that** il est essentiel que (+ *subj*); **2**○ GB (great) super○.

crucially /'kruːʃəlɪ/ *adv* **~ important** d'une importance cruciale; **~, he was there** fait décisif, il était là.

crucible /'kruːsɪbl/ *n* **1** lit creuset *m*; **2** fig épreuve *f*.

crucifix /'kruːsɪfɪks/ *n* crucifix *m*.

crucifixion /ˌkruːsɪ'fɪkʃn/ *n* crucifixion *f*; **the Crucifixion** la Crucifixion.

cruciform /'kruːsɪfɔːm/ *adj* cruciforme.

crucify /'kruːsɪfaɪ/ *vtr* **1** (execute) crucifier; **2**○ (criticize, defeat, punish) démolir○.

crud◐ /krʌd/ *n* **1** ¢ (dirt) saletés *fpl*; **2** US (illness) crève○ *f*; **3** US péj (contemptible person) minable○ *mf* pej.

crude /kruːd/ **I** *n* (oil) pétrole *m* brut.
II *adj* **1** (rough) [*tool, method*] rudimentaire; [*estimate*] approximatif/-ive; **2** (unsophisticated) [*person, manners*] fruste; [*attempt, belief, metaphor, expression*] grossier/-ière; **3** (vulgar, rude) [*laughter, language, joke*] grossier/-ière; [*person*] vulgaire; **4** (raw, unprocessed) [*rubber, ore, data, statistic*] brut; **~ oil** pétrole *m* brut; **~ birth rate** taux *m* brut de natalité.

crudely /'kruːdlɪ/ *adv* **1** (simply) [*describe, express*] de manière schématique; **~ speaking,...** grosso modo...; **2** (roughly) [*painted, made*] grossièrement; [*assembled*] sommairement; **3** (vulgarly) [*behave*] de façon grossière; [*speak*] crûment.

crudeness /'kruːdnɪs/ *n* = **crudity**.

crudity /'kruːdɪtɪ/ *n* **1** (vulgarity) grossièreté

f; **2** (of method) caractère *m* rudimentaire; **3** (of metaphor) crudité *f*.

cruel /'kroəl/ *adj* [*person, fate, treatment, world*] cruel/-elle (**to** envers); [*joke, irony*] cruel/-elle; [*winter, climate*] rigoureux/-euse; **a ~ blow** un coup très dur.

IDIOMS **you have to be ~ to be kind** Prov qui aime bien châtie bien.

cruelly /'kroəlı/ *adv* cruellement.

cruelty /'kroəltı/ *n* **1** (of person, fate, treatment) cruauté *f* (**to** envers); **2** (cruel act) cruauté *f*.

cruet /'kru:ıt/ *n* **1** GB (also **~ stand**) service *m* à condiments; **2** US (small bottle) flacon *m* (*d'huile ou de vinaigre*); **3** Relig burette *f*.

cruise /kru:z/ **I** *n* **1** Naut croisière *f*; **to be on a/to go on a ~** être en/faire une croisière; **2** Mil = **cruise missile**.

II *vtr* **1 to ~ a sea/a river** [*ship, liner*] croiser en mer/sur un fleuve; [*tourist, sailor*] être en croisière en mer/sur un fleuve; **2** [*car, driver, taxi*] parcourir [*street, city*]; **3**○ [*homosexual*] aller draguer○ dans [*place*].

III *vi* **1** [*liner, tourist*] faire une croisière (**in** en; **on** sur; **along** le long de; **around** aux abords de; **into** vers); **2** [*plane*] voler à sa vitesse de croisière; **to ~ at 10,000 metres/at 500 km/h** voler à une altitude de croisière de 10 000 mètres/à une vitesse de croisière de 500 km/h; **3** [*car*] rouler à sa vitesse de croisière; **to ~ at 80 km/h** rouler à une vitesse de croisière de 80 km/h; **4**○ [*competitor, team, candidate*] **to ~ to victory/into first place** se diriger sans problème vers la victoire/vers la première place; **to ~ through an exam** passer un examen sans problème; **5**○ [*taxi, police, car*] être en maraude; [*homosexual, teenager*] draguer○; **a cruising taxi** un taxi en maraude.

IDIOMS **to be cruising for a bruising**○ US [*child, troublemaker*] chercher des noises○.

cruise: **~ control** *n* Aut limiteur *m* de vitesse; **~ liner** *n* paquebot *m*; **~ missile** *n* missile *m* de croisière.

cruiser /'kru:zə(r)/ *n* **1** Mil croiseur *m*; **2** (cabin-cruiser) petit bateau *m* de croisière; **3** US (police car) voiture *f* de police.

cruiserweight /'kru:zəweıt/ *n* Sport poids *m* lourd (*mais pesant moins de 86,2 kg*).

cruising: **~ range** *n* Aviat autonomie *f* de vol; **~ speed** *n* vitesse *f* de croisière; **~ yacht** *n* yacht *m* (de croisière).

cruller /'krʌlə(r)/ *n* US ≈ beignet *m* (*torsadé*).

crumb /krʌm/ *n* **1** (of food) miette *f*; **2** (tiny amount) **a ~ of** une bribe de [*information, conversation*]; **a ~ of comfort** une maigre consolation; **3**○ (person) péj minable○ *mf* pej; **4** (also **~ rubber**) caoutchouc *m* pulvérisé pour recyclage.

crumble /'krʌmbl/ **I** *n* GB **apple ~** crumble *m* aux pommes.

II *vtr* (also **~ up**) émietter [*bread*]; écraser [*cheese, biscuit etc*]; réduire [qch] en poussière [*soil*].

III *vi* **1** lit [*bread*] s'émietter; [*soil, facade*] s'effriter; [*building*] se délabrer; [*cliff*] s'ébouler; **2** fig [*relationship, economy*] se désagréger; [*empire*] s'écrouler; [*opposition, hope, determination*] s'effondrer.

crumbling /'krʌmblıŋ/ **I** *n* effondrement *m*.

II *adj* **1** lit [*building*] délabré; [*facade, concrete*] qui s'effrite; [*cliff*] prêt à s'effondrer; **2** [*economy, empire*] prêt à s'effondrer.

crumbly /'krʌmblı/ **I** *n*○ (old person) injur croulant/-e○ *m/f*.

II *adj* [*bread, cheese*] qui s'émiette facilement; [*pastry, earth*] friable.

crumbs○† /krʌmz/ *excl* mince○!

crummy○ /'krʌmı/ *adj* péj **1** (seedy, substandard) minable○ pej; **2** US (unwell) **to feel ~** se sentir patraque○.

crump /krʌmp/ *n* **1** onomat boum; **2** US argot des militaires obus *m*.

crumpet /'krʌmpıt/ *n* **1** Culin *petite galette épaisse à griller*; **2**○ ¢ GB hum **a bit of ~** une belle nana○ *f*; **the thinking woman's ~** hum le mâle pour intellectuelle.

crumple /'krʌmpl/ **I** *vtr* froisser [*paper*]; écraser [*can*]; **to ~ sth into a ball** rouler qch en boule.

II *vi* **1** (crush up) [*paper, garment*] se froisser; **his face ~d** ses traits se sont décomposés; **the car ~s on impact** la voiture se plie sous le choc; **2** (collapse) [*opposition, resistance*] s'effondrer; **he ~d onto the floor** il s'affaissa au sol.

■ **crumple up** : **~ [sth] up, ~ up [sth]** froisser.

crumpled /'krʌmpld/ *adj* [*dress, page*] froissé; [*car*] écrasé; **to get ~** se froisser.

crunch /krʌntʃ/ **I** *n* **1** (sound) (of gravel, snow) crissement *m*; (of gears, broken wood, bone, glass) craquement *m*; **2** Econ, Fin (squeeze) crise *f*; **credit ~** crise *f* du crédit; **energy ~** crise *f* de l'énergie; **housing ~** crise *f* du logement.

II *vtr* **1** (eat) croquer [*apple, toast, biscuit*]; [*animal*] broyer [*bone*]; **2** (crush) craquer [*nuts*]; **3** (making noise) **she ~ed her way across the gravel** le gravier crissait sous ses pas; **4** Aut **to ~ the gears**○ faire craquer les vitesses○; **5**○ Comput traiter [*data*].

III *vi* [*snow, gravel, glass*] crisser; **his shoes ~ed on the gravel** le gravier crissait sous ses chaussures.

IV crunching *pres p adj* **a ~ing sound** ou **noise** (of gravel, snow, glass) un crissement; (of wood, bone, gears) un craquement.

IDIOMS **when** ou **if it comes to the ~** au moment critique; **the ~ came when** le moment critique est arrivé lorsque; **when it came to the ~ I...** quand je me suis retrouvé au pied du mur, je...

■ **crunch up**: **~ up [sth]** broyer [*glass, stones, metal*] (**into** en).

crunchy /'krʌntʃı/ *adj* [*vegetables, biscuits*] croquant; [*snow*] qui craque sous les pieds; [*gravel*] qui crisse sous les pieds.

crupper /'krʌpə(r)/ *n* Equit **1** (strap) croupière *f*; **2** (horse's rump) croupe *f*.

crusade /kru:'seıd/ **I** *n* **1** (also **Crusade**) Hist croisade *f*; **to go/be on a ~** partir/être en croisade; **2** (campaign) croisade *f* (**for** pour; **against** contre).

II *vi* (campaign) être en croisade (**against** contre; **for** pour).

crusader /kru:'seıdə(r)/ *n* **1** (also **Crusader**) Hist croisé *m*; **2** (campaigner) militant/-e *m/f* (**against** contre, **for** pour); **moral ~** moralisateur/-trice *m/f* militant/-e.

crusading /kru:'seıdıŋ/ *adj* combatif/-ive.

crush /krʌʃ/ **I** *n* **1** (crowd) bousculade *f*; **in the ~** dans la bousculade; **it was a ~**○ **in the car** on était à l'étroit dans la voiture; **2**○ (infatuation) toquade *f*; **to have a ~ on sb** avoir une toquade pour qn, avoir le cœur qui bat pour qn; **3** GB (drink) **orange/lemon ~** boisson *f* à l'orange/au citron.

II *vtr* **1** fig (by force, argument) écraser [*enemy, protester, uprising*]; étouffer [*protest*]; anéantir [*hopes*]; (by ridicule) anéantir [*person*]; **to be ~ed by** être accablé par [*ill-treatment, sorrow, tragedy*]; **2** (squash) (deliberately) écraser [*can, fruit, vegetable*]; concasser [*stone*]; piler [*ice*]; (in accident) écraser [*person, vehicle*] (**against** contre); broyer [*part of body*]; **to ~ sth to a powder** réduire qch en poudre; **to be ~ed to death** (by vehicle) se faire écraser; (by masonry) être écrasé sous les décombres; **3** (crease) chiffonner [*garment, fabric*]; **4** (clasp) serrer; **he ~ed her to him** il l'a serrée contre lui.

III *vi* **1 to ~ forward** se ruer en foule; **to ~ together** se serrer les uns contre les autres; **to ~ into** s'entasser dans [*room, vehicle*]; **2** [*fabrics, garments*] se froisser.

■ **crush out**: **~ [sth] out, ~ out [sth]** extraire [*juice*].

■ **crush up**: **~ [sth] up, ~ up [sth]** écraser [*biscuits*]; concasser [*rock*].

crush: **~ bar** *n* GB bar *m* (*de théâtre*); **~ barrier** *n* GB barrière *f* de sécurité; **~ed velvet** *n* velours *m* frappé.

crushing /'krʌʃıŋ/ *adj* **1** (overpowering) [*defeat, majority, weight*] écrasant; [*blow*] percutant; [*news*] accablant; **2** (humiliating) [*remark, criticism*] percutant; [*look*] écrasant de supériorité.

crushingly /'krʌʃıŋlı/ *adv* [*say*] d'un ton percutant; [*look*] d'un air écrasant de supériorité.

crushproof /'krʌʃpru:f/ *adj* [*fabric*] infroissable; [*packing*] rigide.

crust /krʌst/ *n* **1** (on bread, pie) croûte *f*; **a ~ of bread** lit, fig une croûte de pain; **to earn one's ~**○ GB gagner sa croûte○; **he'd share his last ~** il donnerait sa chemise; **2** (of mud, blood, snow) croûte *f*; **to form a ~** former une croûte; **the earth's ~** l'écorce *f* terrestre; **3** (of wine, port) dépôt *m* (de cristaux de tartre); **4**○ US culot○ *m*; **to have the ~ to do**○ avoir le culot○ de faire.

crustacean /krʌ'steıʃn/ *n* crustacé *m*.

crusty /'krʌstı/ *adj* **1** [*bread*] croustillant; **2** (irritable) grincheux/-euse.

crutch /krʌtʃ/ *n* **1** Med béquille *f*; **to walk** ou **be on ~es** marcher avec des béquilles; **2** fig (prop) béquille *f*; **religion is a ~ for** ou **to her** la religion lui sert de béquille; **3** GB (crotch) Anat entrecuisse *m*; (in trousers) entrejambe *m*; **4** Naut (for oar) dame *f* de nage.

crux /krʌks/ *n* point *m* essentiel; **the ~ of the matter** l'essentiel *m*.

cry /kraı/ **I** *n* **1** (shout, call) (of person, bird) cri *m*; **a great ~ went up** un grand cri s'est élevé; **to utter a ~** pousser un cri; **nobody heard his cries for help** personne ne l'a entendu crier au secours; **a ~ for help** fig un appel à l'aide; **there were cries of 'shame!'** les gens criaient au scandale; **there have been cries for reprisals** on a réclamé des représailles; **2** (weep) **to have a good ~**○ pleurer un bon coup○; **3** (slogan) slogan *m*; **their ~ was 'we shall overcome!'** leur slogan était 'nous vaincrons!'; **4** Hunt (of hounds) aboiements *mpl*; **to be in full ~** [*pack*] donner de la voix; **the crowd/press were in full ~ against them** GB fig la foule/presse s'acharnait contre eux.

II *vtr* **1** (shout) **'look out!' he cried** 'attention!' cria-t-il; **2** (weep) **to ~ bitter tears/tears of joy** pleurer à chaudes larmes/de joie; **how many tears I have cried over you!** combien de larmes j'ai versées à cause de toi!

III *vi* **1** (weep) pleurer (**about** à cause de); **to ~ for joy** pleurer de joie; **don't ~ about that!** ne pleure pas pour ça!; **he was ~ing for his mother** il réclamait sa mère en pleurant; **to ~ with laughter** rire aux larmes; **that'll give you something to ~ about**○! maintenant tu sauras pourquoi tu pleures!; **2** (call out) = **cry out**.

IDIOMS **for ~ing out loud!** mais ce n'est pas vrai, nom de Dieu○! ; **it's a far ~ from the days when** il est loin le temps où; **it's a far ~ from the luxury to which they were accustomed** on est loin du luxe auquel ils étaient habitués; **this small house is a far ~ from the palace where she was born** cette maisonnette est sans comparaison avec le palais dans lequel elle est née; **to ~ one's eyes** ou **heart out** pleurer à chaudes larmes.

■ **cry down** GB: **~ down [sth]** tourner [qch] en dérision [*opposition, view*].

■ **cry off** GB: (cancel appointment) se décommander; (retract promise) se dédire; **they cried off at the last minute** ils se sont décommandés au dernier moment; **to ~ off from** s'excuser de [*meeting*].

■ **cry out** (with pain, grief etc) pousser un cri or des cris; (call) crier, s'écrier; **to ~ out in anguish** pousser un cri d'angoisse; **to ~ out to sb** interpeller qn, appeler qn à haute voix; **to ~ out for** (beg for) implorer [*mercy*]; réclamer [*attention, assistance*];

(need desperately) avoir grand besoin de [*help, reforms, renovation*]; **the country is ~ing out for aid** le pays a grand besoin d'aide; **these windows are ~ing out to be cleaned** hum ces fenêtres ont grand besoin d'être nettoyées.

crybaby○ /ˈkraɪbeɪbɪ/ *n* pleurnicheur/-euse○ *m/f*.

crying /ˈkraɪɪŋ/ **I** *n* ¢ pleurs *mpl*.
II *adj* **1** (blatant) [*injustice*] criant; [*need*] urgent; **it's a ~ shame!** c'est une honte!; **2** (weeping) [*person*] en pleurs.

cryobiology /ˌkraɪəʊbaɪˈɒlədʒɪ/ *n* cryobiologie *f*.

cryogenics /ˌkraɪəˈdʒenɪks/ *n* Biol (+ *v sg*) cryogénie *f*.

cryonics /ˌkraɪˈɒnɪks/ *n* Med (+ *v sg*) cryoconservation *f*.

cryosurgery /ˌkraɪəˈsɜːdʒərɪ/ *n* Med cryochirurgie *f*.

cryotherapy /ˌkraɪəˈθerəpɪ/ *n* Med cryothérapie *f*.

crypt /krɪpt/ *n* crypte *f*.

cryptic /ˈkrɪptɪk/ *adj* **1** gen [*remark, allusion*] énigmatique; [*code, message*] sybillin; **2** Games [*crossword, clue*] crypté.

cryptically /ˈkrɪptɪklɪ/ *adv* [*say, speak*] de façon énigmatique; **~ worded** en termes sibyllins.

crypto+ (*dans composés*) crypto-.

cryptogram /ˈkrɪptəgræm/ *n* cryptogramme *m*.

cryptographer /ˌkrɪpˈtɒgrəfə(r)/ ▶1692 *n* cryptographe *mf*.

cryptographic(al) /ˌkrɪptəʊˈgræfɪk(l)/ *adj* cryptographique.

cryptography /ˌkrɪpˈtɒgrəfɪ/ *n* cryptographie *f*.

crystal /ˈkrɪstl/ **I** *n* **1** Chem cristal *m*; **wine ~s** cristaux *mpl* de tartre; **2** Miner cristal *m*; **rock ~** cristal de roche; **3** (glass) cristal *m*; **made of ~** en cristal; **4** (on watch) verre *m*.
II *modif* **1** [*chandelier, carafe*] en cristal; [*jewellery*] en cristal de roche; **2** [*water*] cristallin.
IDIOMS **as clear as ~** [*water, sound*] cristallin; [*explanation*] clair comme de l'eau de roche.

crystal ball *n* boule *f* de cristal; **to look into one's ~** fig essayer de deviner l'avenir.

crystal clear *adj* **1** [*water, acoustics*] cristallin; **2** [*explanation*] clair comme de l'eau de roche; **let me make it ~** je vais être complètement clair là-dessus.

crystal: **~ gazing** *n* tentatives *fpl* pour prévoir l'avenir; **~ lattice** *n* réseau *m* cristallin.

crystalline /ˈkrɪstəlaɪn/ *adj* (all contexts) cristallin.

crystalline lens *n* cristallin *m*.

crystallize /ˈkrɪstəlaɪz/ **I** *vtr* **1** fig concrétiser [*views, ideas*]; cristalliser [*identity, divisions*]; **2** lit cristalliser [*syrup, solution, molten rock*].
II *vi* **1** [*ideas*] se concrétiser (**around** autour de); **2** [*solution, molten rock*] se cristalliser.
III crystallized *pp adj* [*fruit, ginger*] confit.

crystallography /ˌkrɪstəˈlɒgrəfɪ/ *n* cristallographie *f*.

crystal: **~ set** *n* poste *m* à galène; **~ structure** *n* système *m* cristallin.

CSC *n* GB *abrév* ▶ **Civil Service Commission**.

CSE *n* GB (*abrév* = **Certificate of Secondary Education**) certificat *m* d'études secondaires (*passé à 16 ans*).

CSEU *n* GB (*abrév* = **Confederation of Shipbuilding and Engineering Unions**) *confédération des syndicats de la construction navale*.

CS gas *n* GB gaz *m* lacrymogène.

CSM *n*: *abrév* ▶ **company sergeant major**.

CST *n*: *abrév écrite* = **Central Standard Time**.

CSU *n* GB (*abrév* = **Civil Service Union**) syndicat *m* de fonctionnaires.

ct *abrév écrite* = **carat**.

CT US Post *abrév écrite* = **Connecticut**.

CTC *n* GB (*abrév* = **City Technology College**) ≈ collège *m* technique.

cub /kʌb/ *n* **1** Zool petit *m*; **2** (also **Cub scout**) louveteau *m*.

Cuba /ˈkjuːbə/ ▶1131 *pr n* Cuba *f*.

Cuban /ˈkjuːbən/ ▶1486 **I** *n* Cubain/-e *m/f*.
II *adj* cubain.

Cuban heel *n* talon *m* biseauté.

cubby-hole○ /ˈkʌbɪhəʊl/ *n* **1** (cramped space) réduit *m*; (snug room) piaule○ *f*; **2** (storage space) cagibi○ *m*; **3** (in desk) casier *m*.

cube /kjuːb/ **I** *n* **1** gen, Math cube *m*; **2** Culin (of meat, stock) cube *m*; (of sugar) morceau *m*; **ice ~** glaçon *m*.
II *vtr* **1** Math mettre [qch] au cube; **what is five ~d?** quel est le cube de cinq?; **2** Culin couper [qch] en cubes.

cube root *n* racine *f* cubique (**of** de).

cubic /ˈkjuːbɪk/ ▶1869, 1068 *adj* **1** gen, Math [*form*] cubique; **2** (measurement) [*metre, centimetre*] cube *inv*; **two ~ metres** deux mètres cube; **3** Math [*equation, expression*] du troisième degré.

cubic capacity *n* (of container) volume *m*; (of engine) cylindrée *f*.

cubicle /ˈkjuːbɪkl/ *n* (in changing room) cabine *f*; (in public toilets) cabinet *m*; (in dormitory) box *m*; (in library, office) US box *m*.

cubic measure *n* mesure *f* de volume.

cubism /ˈkjuːbɪzəm/ *n* cubisme *m*.

cubist /ˈkjuːbɪst/ *n, adj* cubiste (*mf*).

cub: **Cub pack** *n* meute *f* (en scoutisme); **~ reporter** ▶1692 *n* journaliste *mf* stagiaire.

cuckold‡ /ˈkʌkəʊld/ **I** *n* mari *m* trompé.
II *vtr* tromper.

cuckoo /ˈkʊkuː/ **I** *n* coucou *m*; **he's the ~ in the nest** fig, pej c'est un parasite.
II○ *adj* hum (mad) maboul○.

cuckoo: **~ clock** *n* pendule *f* à coucou; **~ pint** *n* Bot arum *m* d'Italie.

cucumber /ˈkjuːkʌmbə(r)/ **I** *n* Hort, Culin concombre *m*.
II *modif* [*sandwich*] au concombre; [*salad*] de concombre.
IDIOMS **to be as cool as a ~** être d'un calme olympien.

cud /kʌd/ *n* **to chew the ~** lit, fig ruminer.

cuddle /ˈkʌdl/ **I** *n* câlin *m*; **to have a ~** se faire un câlin; **to give sb a ~** faire un câlin à qn.
II *vtr* câliner.
III *vi* se câliner.
■ **cuddle up** se blottir (**against** contre); **to ~ up for warmth** se blottir l'un contre l'autre pour se réchauffer.

cuddly /ˈkʌdlɪ/ *adj* **1** (huggable) (sweet) adorable; (soft) doux/douce; (plump) potelé; **he's very ~** on a vraiment envie de le câliner; **2** (fond of hugging) câlin.

cuddly toy *n* GB peluche *f*.

cudgel† /ˈkʌdʒl/ **I** *n* gourdin *m*.
II *vtr* (*p prés etc* **-ll-**, **-l-** US) matraquer.
IDIOMS **to ~ one's brains**○ se creuser la tête○ (**for, to** pour); **to take up the ~s for** ou **on behalf of sb/sth** se battre pour défendre qn/qch.

cue /kjuː/ **I** *n* **1** lit Theat (line) réplique *f*; (action) signal *m*; Mus signal *m* d'entrée; TV, Radio, Cin signal *m*; **on ~** (after word) après la réplique; (after action) après le signal; **to come in on ~** [*instrument*] faire son entrée au signal; **to give sb the ~ to enter** donner la réplique à qn afin qu'il/elle fasse son entrée; **2** fig (signal) signal *m*; **to be sb's ~ to do** être le signal pour que qn fasse; **to take one's ~ from sb** faire comme qn; **as if on ~** iron comme par hasard; **right on ~** à ce moment précis; (**that's a**) **~ for a song!** le moment est venu pour une chanson; **3** Sport queue *f* de billard.
II *vtr* **1** Sport frapper [*ball*]; **2** = **cue in**.
■ **cue in**: **~ [sb] in**, **~ in [sb]** TV, Cin, Radio donner le signal à.

cue: **~ ball** *n* Sport bille *f* à jouer; **~ card** *n* TV prompteur *m*.

cuesta /ˈkwestə/ *n* Geog, Geol cuesta *f*.

cuff /kʌf/ **I** *n* **1** (at wrist) gen poignet *m*; (turned back) revers *m*; (on shirt) poignet *m*; **2** US (on trousers) revers *m*; **3** Med (for blood-pressure) manchon *m* (de tensiomètre); **4** (blow) tape *f*; **5**○ (handcuff) menotte *f*.
II *vtr* **1** (strike) donner une tape à; (on head) calotter○; **2**○ (handcuff) mettre les menottes à.
IDIOMS **to speak off the ~** faire un discours au pied levé; **an off the ~ remark/discussion** une remarque/discussion impromptue; **to buy on the ~**○ US acheter à crédit.

cuff link *n* bouton *m* de manchette.

cuisine /kwɪˈziːn/ *n* cuisine *f*; **haute ~** la grande cuisine.

cul-de-sac /ˈkʌldəsæk/ *n* (street) impasse *f*, cul-de-sac *m*; (on roadsign) voie *f* sans issue.

culinary /ˈkʌlɪnərɪ, US -nerɪ/ *adj* culinaire.

cull /kʌl/ **I** *n* **1** Agric (for livestock) réforme *f*; (of foxes) battue *f*; **2** Hunt (for skin, meat) massacre *m*; **3** (animals killed) prise *f* de chasse.
II *modif* [*animal, cow, sow*] de réforme.
III *vtr* **1** Agric réformer [*livestock*]; faire une battue à [*fox*]; **2** Hunt massacrer [*seal, whale*]; **3** (gather) puiser [*information, details*] (**from sth** dans qch).

culminate /ˈkʌlmɪneɪt/ *vtr* aboutir (**in** à).

culmination /ˌkʌlmɪˈneɪʃn/ *n* **1** (outcome) résultat *m* (**of** de); **2** (high point: of work, career) couronnement *m* (**of** de); **3** Astron point *m* culminant.

culottes /kjuːˈlɒts/ *npl* jupe-culotte *f*; **a pair of ~** une jupe-culotte.

culpability /ˌkʌlpəˈbɪlətɪ/ *n* culpabilité *f*.

culpable /ˈkʌlpəbl/ *adj* coupable (**for** de).

culpable: **~ homicide** *n* Jur homicide *m* volontaire; **~ negligence** *n* Jur négligence *f* coupable, faute *f* grave.

culprit /ˈkʌlprɪt/ *n* **1** (guilty person) coupable *mf*; **2** (main cause) principal responsable.

cult /kʌlt/ **I** *n* **1** Relig (primitive) culte *m*; (contemporary) secte *f*; **2** ¢ (worship) culte *m* (**of** de); **~ of personality** culte de la personnalité; **3** (craze) culte *m*.
II *modif* **a ~ band/film** un groupe-/film-culte; **to be a ~ figure** faire l'objet d'un culte.

cultivable /ˈkʌltɪvəbl/ *adj* cultivable.

cultivar /ˈkʌltɪvɑː(r)/ *n* cultivar *m*.

cultivate /ˈkʌltɪveɪt/ *vtr* **1** cultiver [*land, soil*]; **2** (develop) **to ~ one's image/memory** cultiver son image/sa mémoire; **to ~ one's mind** se cultiver l'esprit; **to ~ the right people** cultiver de bonnes relations.

cultivation /ˌkʌltɪˈveɪʃn/ *n* **1** Agric, Hort culture *f*; **under ~** en culture; **2** (development): **he considered the ~ of certain mannerisms essential to his image** il considérait que cultiver certains tics était essentiel à son image.

cultivator /ˈkʌltɪveɪtə(r)/ ▶1692 *n* **1** (mechanical) cultivateur *m*; (motorized) motoculteur *m*; **2** (person) cultivateur/-trice *m/f*.

cultural /ˈkʌltʃərəl/ *adj* culturel/-elle.

cultural attaché ▶1692 *n* attaché/-e *m/f* culturel/-elle.

culturally /ˈkʌltʃərəlɪ/ *adv* [*similar, different*] culturellement; **a ~ diverse country** un pays qui présente une variété de cultures; **~ (speaking)** du point de vue culturel; **to be ~ determined** être lié à la culture.

Cultural Revolution *n* Hist Révolution *f* culturelle.

culture /ˈkʌltʃə(r)/ **I** *n* **1** ¢ (art and thought) culture *f*; **high/popular ~** culture classique/populaire; **to bring ~ to the masses** mettre la culture à la portée de tous; **2** (way of life) culture *f*; **minority/dominant ~s** cultures minoritaires/dominantes; **street ~** culture qui vient de la rue; **drug ~** l'univers *m* de la drogue; **3** (cultivation) culture *f*; **sand ~** la culture dans le sable; **olive ~** la culture des olives; **4** Biol (of bacteria) culture *f* bactérienne; **tissue ~** la culture des tissus; **5** Sport **physical ~** culture *f* physique.
II *vtr* Biol faire une culture de [*bacteria, tissue*].

culture-bound /ˈkʌltʃəbaʊnd/ *adj* **1** [*test*] qui favorise un groupe culturel; **2** Ling [*term*] spécifique à une culture.

cultured /ˈkʌltʃəd/ *adj* cultivé.

cultured pearl *n* perle *f* de culture.

culture: **~-fair** *adj* US [*test, method, approach*] qui ne défavorise aucun groupe culturel; **~ medium** *n* Biol bouillon *m* de culture; **~ shock** *n* choc *m* culturel; **~-specific** *adj* spécifique à une culture; **~ vulture**○ *n* fana *mf* de culture○.

culvert /ˈkʌlvət/ *n* buse *f*, passage *m* hydraulique.

cum◑ /kʌm/ *n* sperme *m*.

-cum- /kʌm/ (*dans composés*) **garage~workshop** garage-atelier *m*; **gardener~handyman** jardinier-homme *m* à tout faire.

cumbersome /ˈkʌmbəsəm/ *adj* [*luggage, furniture*] encombrant; [*method, phrase*] lourd.

Cumbria /ˈkʌmbrɪə/ ▶ **1624** *pr n* Cumbria *m*.

cumbrous /ˈkʌmbrəs/ *adj* littér pesant.

cumin /ˈkʌmɪn/ *n* cumin *m*.

cum laude /ˌkʌm ˈlɔːdɪ, ˌkʊm ˈlaʊdeɪ/ *adv* US Univ avec mention.

cummerbund /ˈkʌməbʌnd/ *n* large ceinture *f* (*d'habit de soirée ou de costume hindou*).

cumulative /ˈkjuːmjʊlətɪv, US -leɪtɪv/ *adj* cumulatif/-ive.

cumulative: **~ action** *n* Med accumulation *f*; **~ evidence** *n* témoignages *mpl* concordants.

cumulatively /ˈkjuːmjʊlətɪvlɪ, US -leɪtɪvlɪ/ *adv* de façon cumulative.

cumulative voting *n* vote *m* multiple et cumulatif.

cumulonimbus /ˈkjuːmjʊləʊnɪmbəs/ *n* (*pl* **-bi** ou **-buses**) cumulo-nimbus *m*.

cumulus /ˈkjuːmjʊləs/ *n* cumulus *m*.

cuneiform /ˈkjuːnɪfɔːm, US kjuˈəˈnɪəfɔːrm/ **I** *n* écriture *f* cunéiforme.
II *adj* cunéiforme.

cunnilingus /ˌkʌnɪˈlɪŋgəs/ *n* cunnilingus *m*.

cunning /ˈkʌnɪŋ/ **I** *n* **1** péj (of person) ruse *f*; (nastier) fourberie *f*; (of animal) ruse *f*; **he had a reputation for ~** il avait la réputation d'être fourbe.
II *adj* **1** péj [*person*] rusé; (nastier) fourbe; [*animal*] rusé; [*look, smile*] sournois; **he's a ~ old fox** c'est un vieux renard; **2** (clever) [*trick, plot*] habile; [*device*] astucieux/-ieuse.

cunningly /ˈkʌnɪŋlɪ/ *adv* **1** [*disguised, concealed*] habilement; [*devised*] astucieusement; **2** [*look, smile, say*] d'un air rusé; pej d'un air sournois.

cunt● /kʌnt/ *n* **1** (person) con◑/conne◑ *m/f*, connard●/connasse● *m/f*; **2** (female genitals) con● *m*.

cup /kʌp/ **I** *n* **1** (container) tasse *f*; **a ~ and saucer** une tasse et une soucoupe; **2** (cupful) tasse *f*; **a ~ of tea** une tasse de thé; **two ~s of flour** deux tasses de farine; **3** Sport coupe *f*; **to win a ~ for swimming/golf** remporter une coupe en natation/en golf; **4** (in bra) bonnet *m*; **to be a B ~** prendre un bonnet B; **5** (of flower) corolle *f*; (of acorn) cupule *f*; **6** (drink) cocktail *m*; **cider ~** cocktail *m* au cidre; **7** Relig (for communion) calice *m*.
II *vtr* (*p prés etc* **-pp-**) **to ~ sth in one's hands** prendre qch dans le creux de ses mains [*butterfly, water*]; prendre qch dans les mains [*chin*]; **to ~ one's hands around** entourer [qch] de ses mains [*insect*]; mettre ses mains en paravent autour de [*flame, match*]; **to ~ one's hands around one's mouth** mettre ses mains en porte-voix; **to ~ one's hand over** couvrir [qch] de sa main [*receiver*].
III cupped *pp adj* **in one's ~ped hand** dans le creux de sa main.
IDIOMS **to be in one's ~s**† être dans les vignes du Seigneur†.

cupbearer /ˈkʌpbeərə(r)/ *n* échanson *m* (**to** de).

cupboard /ˈkʌbəd/ *n* placard *m*.
IDIOMS **the ~ is bare** les caisses sont vides.

cupboard: **~ love** *n* GB hum amour *m* intéressé; **~ space** *n* espace *m* de rangement.

cupcake /ˈkʌpkeɪk/ *n* **1** Culin petite génoise *f* individuelle; **2**○ US (girl) beau morceau *m*○.

cupful /ˈkʌpfʊl/ *n* tasse *f*; **three ~s of milk** trois tasses de lait.

cupid /ˈkjuːpɪd/ *n* Art amour *m*.

Cupid /ˈkjuːpɪd/ *pr n* Cupidon; **~'s darts, ~'s arrows** les flèches *fpl* de Cupidon.

cupidity /kjuːˈpɪdətɪ/ *n* sout cupidité *f*.

cupola /ˈkjuːpələ/ *n* **1** Archit (domed roof) coupole *f*; (lantern) lanternon *m*; **2** Mil, Mil Naut coupole *f*; **3** Ind (furnace) cubilot *m*.

cuppa○ /ˈkʌpə/ *n* GB tasse *f* de thé; **let's have a ~** on se prend un thé○.

cupping glass *n* Med ventouse *f*.

cupric /ˈkjuːprɪk/ *adj* cuivrique.

cupronickel /ˌkjuːprəʊˈnɪkl/ *n* cupronickel *m*.

cup tie *n* GB match *m* de coupe.

cur /kɜː(r)/ *n* littér, péj **1** (dog) corniaud *m*; **2** (person) (cowardly) pleutre *m*; (worthless) misérable *m*.

curable /ˈkjʊərəbl/ *adj* guérissable.

curaçao /ˌkjʊərəˈsəʊ, US -ˈsaʊ/ *n* curaçao *m*.

curare /kjʊˈrɑːrɪ/ *n* curare *m*.

curate /ˈkjʊərət/ **I** *n* vicaire *m*.
II *vtr* organiser [*exhibition*].
IDIOMS **it's like the ~'s egg** tout n'est pas mauvais.

curative /ˈkjʊərətɪv/ *adj* curatif/-ive.

curator /kjʊəˈreɪtə(r), US *also* ˈkjʊərətər/ ▶ **1692** *n* (of museum, gallery) conservateur/-trice *m/f*.

curb /kɜːb/ **I** *n* **1** (control) restriction *f* (**on** à); **2** US (sidewalk) bord *m* du trottoir; **3** Equit (chain) gourmette *f*; (bit) mors *m*.
II *vtr* **1** (control) refréner [*desires*]; limiter [*powers, influence*]; juguler [*spending*]; restreindre [*consumption*]; **to ~ one's temper** se dominer; **2** Equit mettre un mors à; **3** US **~ your dog!** apprenez le caniveau à votre chien!

curb: **~ bit** *n* mors *m* de bride; **~ service** *n* US service *m* au volant; **~stone** *n* US pierre *f* (*de bord du trottoir*); **~ weight** *n* US Aut poids *m* à vide.

curd /kɜːd/ **I** *n* = **curds**; ▶ **bean curd**.
II curds *npl* lait *m* caillé.

curd cheese *n* fromage *m* blanc (*lait caillé égoutté*).

curdle /ˈkɜːdl/ **I** *vtr* faire cailler [*milk*]; faire tourner [*sauce*].
II *vi* [*milk*] se cailler; [*sauce*] tourner.

cure /ˈkjʊə(r)/ **I** *n* **1** Med, Pharm (remedy) remède *m* (**for** contre); **2** Med (recovery) guérison *f*; **to effect a ~** sout amener une guérison; **beyond ~** [*patient*] incurable; [*condition*] désespéré; **3** fig (solution) remède *m* (**for** pour); **the situation is beyond ~** la situation est irrémédiable; **4** Med (at spa etc) cure *f*; **to take a ~** faire une cure; **5** Relig (also **~ of souls**) cure *f*.
II *vtr* **1** Med guérir [*disease, patient*] (**of** de); **2** fig guérir [*bad habit, person*] (**of** de); remédier à [*unemployment, inflation, shortage*]; **the economy is ~d of inflation** l'économie est débarrassée de l'inflation; **3** Culin (dry) sécher; (salt) saler; (smoke) fumer; **4** (treat) saler [*hide*]; traiter [*tobacco*].

cure-all /ˈkjʊərɔːl/ *n* panacée *f* (**for** contre).

curettage /ˌkjʊərɪˈtɑːʒ/ *n* curetage *m*.

curfew /ˈkɜːfjuː/ *n* couvre-feu *m*; **to impose a (ten o'clock) ~** imposer le couvre-feu (à partir de dix heures); **to lift the ~** lever le couvre-feu.

curie /ˈkjʊərɪ/ *n* curie *m*.

curing /ˈkjʊərɪŋ/ *n* Culin (drying) séchage *m*; (salting) salaison *f*; (smoking) fumage *m*.

curio /ˈkjʊərɪəʊ/ *n* curiosité *f*, objet *m* rare.

curiosity /ˌkjʊərɪˈɒsətɪ/ *n* **1** (desire to know) curiosité *f* (**about** sur, au sujet de); **to arouse/satisfy sb's ~** piquer/satisfaire la curiosité de qn; **out of (idle) ~** par (simple) curiosité; **2** (nosiness) curiosité *f*; **3** (object, text) curiosité *f*; **4** (person) original/-e *m/f*.
IDIOMS **~ killed the cat** Prov la curiosité est un vilain défaut.

curious /ˈkjʊərɪəs/ *adj* **1** (interested) curieux/-ieuse; **~ to know how/why** curieux de savoir comment/pourquoi; **to be ~ about sth** éprouver de la curiosité au sujet de qch; **I'm just ~!** j'aurais aimé savoir, c'est tout!; **2** pej (nosy) curieux/-ieuse; **3** (odd) [*person, case, effect*] curieux/-ieuse; [*place, phenomenon*] étrange; **a ~ mixture** un curieux mélange.

curiously /ˈkjʊərɪəslɪ/ *adv* **1** (oddly) [*silent, detached*] étrangement; **~ shaped** d'une forme bizarre; **~ enough,...** chose assez curieuse,...; **2** [*ask*] avec curiosité.

curl /kɜːl/ **I** *n* **1** (of hair) boucle *f*; **to wear one's hair in ~s** avoir les cheveux bouclés; **2** (of wood) copeau *m*; (of smoke) volute *f*; **with a ~ of one's lip** avec une moue dédaigneuse.
II *vtr* **1** friser [*hair*]; **2** (wind, coil) [*person, animal*] **to ~ one's fingers around sth** saisir qch; **to ~ one's toes around sth** saisir qch avec ses orteils; **to ~ oneself** ou **one's body around sth** [*person, cat*] se pelotonner contre qch; **to ~ itself around sth** [*snake, caterpillar*] s'enrouler autour de qch; **to ~ one's legs under oneself** replier les jambes sous soi; **to ~ one's lip** [*person*] faire une moue dédaigneuse; [*dog*] retrousser ses babines.
III *vi* [*hair*] friser; [*paper*] (se) gondoler; [*edges, corner, leaf*] se racornir; **to ~ around sth** s'enrouler autour de qch; **smoke ~ed upwards** la fumée montait en volutes; **his lip ~ed** il fit une moue dédaigneuse.
IDIOMS **to ~ up and die**○ rentrer dans un trou de souris○; **to make sb's hair ~**○ (in shock) faire dresser les cheveux sur la tête de qn.
■ **curl up**: ¶ **~ up** [*person*] se pelotonner; [*cat, dog*] se mettre en rond; [*paper*] (se) gondoler; [*edges, corner, leaf*] se racornir; **to ~ up in bed/in a chair** se blottir dans son lit/dans un fauteuil; **to be ~ed up on the sofa** être blotti sur le canapé; **to ~ up into a ball** [*person*] se recroqueviller; [*hedgehog*] se mettre en boule; **to ~ up with laughter**○ se tordre de rire○; **to ~ up at the edges** [*photo, paper*] (se) gondoler; ¶ **~ up [sth], ~ [sth] up** [*heat, moisture*] gondoler [*paper, leaf*]; racornir [*edges, corner*]; **to ~ oneself up** se recroqueviller.

curler /ˈkɜːlə(r)/ *n* **1** (roller) bigoudi *m*; **to be in ~s, to have one's hair in ~s** avoir des bigoudis dans les cheveux; **to put one's ~s in** se mettre des bigoudis; **2** Sport joueur/-euse *m/f* de curling.

curlew /ˈkɜːljuː/ *n* courlis *m*.

curlicue /ˈkɜːlɪkjuː/ *n* fioriture *f*.

curling /ˈkɜːlɪŋ/ ▶ **1282** *n* Sport curling *m*.

Currencies and money

(*For how to say numbers in French,* ▶ 1505)

French money

write	say
25 c	vingt-cinq centimes
1 F*	un franc
1,50† F	un franc cinquante *or* un franc cinquante centimes
2 F	deux francs
2,75 F	deux francs soixante-quinze
20 F	vingt francs
100 F	cent francs
1 000 F	mille francs
1 000 000 F	un million de francs‡

* *Note that French normally puts the abbreviation after the amount, unlike British (£1) or American ($1) English. However in some official documents amounts may be given as* "FF 2 000 000 *etc.*

† *French uses a comma to separate units (e.g. 2,75 F), where English normally has a period (e.g. £5.50).*

‡ *The franc was revalued in the 1960s, when 100 old francs became 1 new franc. However, French people who were accustomed to counting in old francs still sometimes use these when referring to very large sums (e.g. the price of houses or cars), so* deux millions de francs *might very well mean* 20 000 *new francs instead of* 2 000 000 francs.

there are 100 centimes in one franc	=	il y a 100 centimes dans un franc
a hundred-franc note	=	un billet de cent francs
a twenty-franc note	=	un billet de vingt francs
a ten-franc coin	=	une pièce de dix francs
a 50-centime piece	=	une pièce de cinquante centimes

British money

write	say
1p	un penny [pɛnɪ]
25p	vingt-cinq pence [pɛns] *or* vingt-cinq pennies [pɛnɪ]
50p	cinquante pence or cinquante pennies
£1	une livre
£1.50	une livre cinquante *or* une livre cinquante pence
£2.00	deux livres

a five-pound note	=	un billet de cinq livres
a pound coin	=	une pièce d'une livre
a 50p piece	=	une pièce de cinquante pence

American money

write	say
12c	douze cents [sɛnts]
$1	un dollar
$1.50	un dollar cinquante *or* un dollar cinquante cents

a ten-dollar bill	=	un billet de dix dollars
a dollar bill	=	un billet d'un dollar
a dollar coin	=	une pièce d'un dollar

How much?

how much is it? *or* how much does it cost?	=	combien est-ce que cela coûte?
it's 15 francs	=	cela coûte 15 francs
the price of the book is 200 francs	=	le prix du livre est de§ 200 francs
the car costs 150,000 francs	=	la voiture coûte 150 000 francs
it costs over 500 francs	=	ça coute plus de 500 francs
just under 1,000 francs	=	un peu moins de 1 000 francs
more than 200 francs	=	plus de 200 francs
less than 200 francs	=	moins de 200 francs
it costs 100 francs a metre	=	cela coûte 100 francs le mètre

§ *The* de *is obligatory here.*

In the following examples, note the use of à *in French to introduce the amount that something costs:*

a two-franc stamp	=	un timbre à deux francs
a £10 ticket	=	un billet à 10 livres

and the use of de *to introduce the amount that something consists of:*

a £500 cheque	=	un chèque de 500 livres
a two-thousand-pound grant	=	une bourse de deux mille livres

Handling money

500 francs in cash	=	500 francs en liquide
a cheque for 500 francs	=	un chèque de 500 francs
to change a 100-franc note	=	faire la monnaie d'un billet de 100 francs
a dollar travelers' check	=	un chèque de voyage en dollars
a sterling travellers' cheque	=	un chèque de voyage en livres
a £100 travellers' cheque	=	un chèque de voyage de 100 livres
there are 6 francs to the dollar	=	le dollar vaut 6 francs

curling: **~ irons** *npl* fer *m* à friser; **~ rink** *n* piste *f* de curling; **~ tongs** *npl* fer *m* à friser.

curlpaper /ˈkɜːlpeɪpə(r)/ *n* papillote *f* (*pour les cheveux*).

curly /ˈkɜːlɪ/ *adj* [*hair*] (tight curls) frisé; (loose curls) bouclé; [*moustache*] frisé; [*tail, edge, eyelashes*] recourbé.

curly-haired /ˌkɜːlɪˈheəd/, **curly-headed** /ˌkɜːlɪˈhedɪd/ *adj* (tight curls) frisé; (loose curls) bouclé.

curly: **~ kale** *n* chou *m* frisé; **~ lettuce** *n* frisée *f*.

curmudgeonly† /kɜːˈmʌdʒənlɪ/ *adj* pej grincheux/-euse.

currant /ˈkʌrənt/ **I** *n* raisin *m* de Corinthe.
II *modif*: **~ bun** ≈ brioche *f* aux raisins; **~ loaf** ≈ pain *m* brioché aux raisins.

currency /ˈkʌrənsɪ/ ▶ 1143 *n* **1** Fin monnaie *f*, devise *f*; **what is the ~ of Poland?** quelle est la monnaie polonaise?; **to buy foreign ~** acheter des devises étrangères; **have you any German ~?** avez-vous de l'argent allemand?; **2** (of word, term) fréquence *f*; (of idea, opinion) crédibilité *f*; **to gain ~** [*word, term*] devenir courant; [*idea, opinion*] se répandre; **to give ~ to sth** accréditer qch.

currency: **~ devaluation** *n* dévaluation *f* de la monnaie; **~ market** *n* marché *m* monétaire; **~ unit** *n* unité *f* monétaire.

current /ˈkʌrənt/ **I** *n* **1** lit (of electricity, water) courant *m*; (of air) flux *m*; **2** fig (trend) tendance *f*; **a ~ of opinion** un courant d'opinion.
II *adj* **1** (present) [*leader, situation, policy, value*] actuel/-elle; [*developments, crisis, year, research*] en cours; [*estimate*] présent; **2** (in common use) [*term, word*] usité; **in ~ use** usité.

current account, **C/A** *n* **1** GB Fin compte *m* courant; **2** Econ balance *f* des paiements.

current: **~ account deficit** *n* balance *f* des paiements déficitaire; **~ account surplus** *n* balance *f* des paiements excédentaire; **~ affairs** *n* (+ *v sg*) actualité *f*; **~ assets** *npl* actifs *mpl* de roulement; **~ liabilities** *npl* passif *m* exigible.

currently /ˈkʌrəntlɪ/ *adv* actuellement, en ce moment.

curriculum /kəˈrɪkjʊləm/ *n* (*pl* **-lums** ou **-la**) Sch programme *m*; **in the ~** au programme.

curriculum: **~ development** *n* Sch développement *m* des programmes; **~ vitae, CV** *n* curriculum vitae *m*, CV *m*.

curry /ˈkʌrɪ/ **I** *n* **1** (dish) curry *m*; **chicken/prawn ~** curry de poulet/de crevettes; **hot/mild ~** curry épicé/peu épicé; **2** (also **~ powder**) curry *m*.
II *vtr* **1** faire un curry de [*chicken, meat*]; **curried chicken** poulet au curry; **2** (groom) étriller [*horse*]; **3** corroyer [*leather*].
IDIOMS **to ~ favour** chercher à se faire bien voir (**with sb** de qn).

curry: **~ comb** *n* étrille *f*; **~ powder** *n* curry *m*.

curse /kɜːs/ **I** *n* **1** (problem) fléau *m*; **the ~ of poverty** le fléau de la misère; **that car is a ~!** cette voiture est une vraie plaie!; **2** (swearword) juron *m*; **~s!** diable†!; **3** (spell) malédiction *f*; **to put a ~ on** appeler la malédiction sur; **a ~ on them!** maudits soient-ils!; **4**† GB euph **to have the ~** être indisposée euph.
II *vtr* maudire; **~d be the day that...**† maudit soit le jour où...
III *vi* jurer (**at** après); **to ~ and swear** jurer comme un charretier.
IV cursed *pp adj* **1** /ˈkɜːsɪd, kɜːst/ [*man, car*] maudit; **2** /kɜːst/ **to be ~d with** gen, iron être affligé de [*bad eyes, perfect hearing*].

cursive /ˈkɜːsɪv/ **I** *n* cursive *f*.
II *adj* cursif/-ive; **in ~ script** en cursive.

cursor /ˈkɜːsə(r)/ *n* curseur *m*.

cursorily /ˈkɜːsərəlɪ/ *adv* rapidement; **to glance ~ at** jeter un coup d'œil rapide à.

cursory /ˈkɜːsərɪ/ *adj* [*glance, inspection*] rapide; **to give sth a ~ glance** jeter un coup d'œil rapide à qch.

curt /kɜːt/ *adj* [*person*] sec/sèche (**with** avec); [*manner, greeting, tone*] sec/sèche.

curtail /kɜːˈteɪl/ *vtr* **1** (restrict) mettre une entrave à [*freedom, right*]; **2** (cut back) réduire [*service, expenditure*]; **3** (cut short) écourter [*holiday*].

curtailment /kɜːˈteɪlmənt/ *n* **1** (of rights, freedom) limitation *f*; **2** (of expenditure, service) réduction *f*; **3** (of holiday) interruption *f*.

curtain /ˈkɜːtn/ **I** *n* **1** (drape) rideau *m*; **a pair of ~s** des rideaux; **to open/draw the ~s** ouvrir/tirer les rideaux; **a ~ of rain** un rideau de pluie; **2** Theat rideau *m*; **after the final ~** après la chute du rideau; **the ~ has fallen on** fig c'est la fin de [*career, era*].
II *modif* [*hook, ring*] de rideau; [*rail*] à rideaux.
III *vtr* mettre des rideaux à [*room, window*]; installer des rideaux dans [*house*].
IDIOMS **it will be ~s**○ ce sera la fin (**for** de); **to bring down the ~ on** mettre fin à.
■ **curtain off**: **~ [sth] off, ~ off [sth]** fermer [qch] par un rideau; **to be ~ed off from sth** être séparé de qch par un rideau.

curtain: **~ call** *n* Theat rappel *m*; **~ pole** *n* tringle *f* (à rideaux); **~ raiser** *n* lit, fig lever *m* de rideau; **~ tape** *n* ruban *m* fronceur; **~ wall** *n* Mil courtine *f*; Archit mur *m* rideau.

curtly /ˈkɜːtlɪ/ *adv* sèchement.

curtness /ˈkɜːtnɪs/ *n* (all contexts) sécheresse *f*.

curtsey /ˈkɜːtsɪ/ **I** *n* (*pl* **-eys** or **-ies**) révérence *f*; **to make** ou **drop a ~** faire une révérence.
II *vi* (*prét, pp* **-seyed** or **-sied**) faire la révérence (**to** à).

curvaceous /kɜːˈveɪʃəs/ *adj* surtout hum [*woman*] bien roulée○, bien faite.

curvature /ˈkɜːvətʃə(r), US -tʃʊər/ *n* gen, Phys courbure *f*; **~ of the spine** Med déviation *f* de la colonne vertébrale, scoliose *f* spec.

curve /kɜːv/ **I** *n* (in line, graph) courbe *f*; (of arch) voussure *f*; (of beam) cambrure *f*; (in road) (gentle) courbe *f*; (sharper) virage *m*; (of landscape, cheek, hips) courbe *f*; **learning ~** courbe *f* d'apprentissage; **price ~** Econ courbe *f* des prix.
II *vtr* gen courber; Tech cintrer.
III *vi* [*line, wall, arch*] s'incurver; [*edge*] se recourber; [*road, railway*] faire une courbe; **the road ~s down to the sea** le chemin descend en courbe vers la mer; **the stream ~s through the valley** le ruisseau décrit une courbe à travers la vallée.

curved /kɜːvd/ *adj* [*line, surface*] courbe, incurvé; [*wall, flowerbed*] courbe; [*staircase*] incurvé; [*chairback, table edge*] arrondi; [*brim, blade*] incurvé; [*arch*] cintré; [*nose*] busqué; [*eyebrows*] arqué; [*beak*] crochu.

curvet /kɜːˈvet/ Equit **I** *n* saut-de-mouton *m*.
II *vi* (*p prés etc* **-tt-**) faire un saut-de-mouton/des sauts-de-mouton.

curvilinear /ˌkɜːvɪˈlɪnɪə(r)/ *adj* curviligne.

curvy /ˈkɜːvɪ/ *adj* [*woman*] bien roulé.

cushion /ˈkʊʃn/ **I** *n* lit **1** coussin *m*; **a ~ of air** un coussin d'air; **2** fig (protection, reserve) garantie *f* (**against** contre); **3** (in snooker) bande *f*; **to play off the ~** jouer (par) la bande.
II *vtr* amortir [*blow, impact, costs, effects*]; **to ~ sb against sth** protéger qn contre qch; **to ~ sb's fall** amortir la chute de qn.
III cushioned *pp adj* **1** (padded) matelassé; (covered in cushions) couvert de coussins; **2** fig [*youth, era*] hyperprotégé.

cushion cover *n* housse *f* de coussin.

cushy○ /ˈkʊʃɪ/ *adj* peinard○; **a ~ number** GB (job) un boulot peinard○.

cusp /kʌsp/ *n* **1** Math sommet *m*; **2** Astron corne *f*; **3** Astrol conjonction *f*; **4** Dent cuspide *f*.

cuspidor /ˈkʌspɪdɔː(r)/ *n* US crachoir *m*.

cuss○† /kʌs/ **I** *n* **1** (oath) juron *m*; **2** (person) **a queer old ~** un vieux bonhomme bizarre.
II *vi* jurer.

cussed○† /ˈkʌsɪd/ *adj* **1** (obstinate) entêté; **2** (damned) sale○, sacré○.

cussedness○† /ˈkʌsɪdnɪs/ *n* esprit *m* de contradiction.

cussword /ˈkʌswɜːd/ *n* US gros mot *m*.

custard /ˈkʌstəd/ *n* GB (creamy) ≈ crème *f* anglaise; (set, baked) flan *m*.
IDIOMS **cowardy ~**○ poule *f* mouillée.

custard: **~ cream** *n* GB biscuit *m* fourré; **~ pie** *n* tarte *f* à la crème; **~ pie humour** *n* humour *m* tarte à la crème; **~ powder** *n* GB préparation *f* pour crème anglaise; **~ tart** *n* tarte *f* à la crème.

custodial /kʌˈstəʊdɪəl/ *adj* **1 ~ sentence** Jur peine *f* de prison; **non-~ sentence** peine *f* non privative de liberté; **to be put in ~ care** [*child*] être placé dans une maison d'enfants; **2** (in museum etc) **~ staff** personnel *m* de surveillance.

custodian /kʌˈstəʊdɪən/ **▶1692** *n* (of building, collection) gardien/-ienne *m/f*; (in museum) conservateur/-trice *m/f*; (of morals, tradition etc) gardien/-ienne *m/f*.

custody /ˈkʌstədɪ/ *n* **1** Jur (detention) détention *f*; **in ~** en détention; **to take sb into ~** arrêter qn; **to be remanded in ~** être détenu; **to escape from ~** s'évader de prison; **2** Jur (of minor) garde *f*; **in the ~ of** sous la garde de; **3** sout (keeping) garde *f*; **in the ~ of** à la garde de; **in safe ~** en mains sûres.

custom /ˈkʌstəm/ **I** *n* **1** (personal habit) coutume *f*, habitude *f*; **it is/was her ~ to do** elle a/avait l'habitude de faire; **as is/was his ~** selon sa coutume; **2** (convention) coutume *f*, usage *m*; **it is/was the ~ to do** il est/était d'usage de faire; **~ requires that** l'usage veut que (+ *subj*); **3** Comm (patronage) clientèle *f*; **they've lost a lot of ~** ils ont perdu beaucoup de clients; **I shall take my ~ elsewhere** j'irai me faire servir ailleurs; **4** Jur coutume *f*.
II *adj* [*article, equipment, system*] personnalisé.

customarily /ˈkʌstəmərəlɪ, US ˌkʌstəˈmerəlɪ/ *adv* généralement, habituellement.

customary /ˈkʌstəmərɪ, US -merɪ/ *adj* **1** gen habituel/-elle; (more formal) coutumier/-ière; **it is/was ~ for sb to do sth** la coutume veut/voulait que qn fasse qch; **as is/was ~** comme de coutume; **2** Jur coutumier; **~ law** droit coutumier.

custom-built /ˌkʌstəmˈbɪlt/ *adj* [*car*] fabriqué sur commande; [*house*] fait sur plans.

custom: **~ car** *n* voiture *f* personnalisée; **~-designed** *adj* personnalisé.

customer /ˈkʌstəmə(r)/ *n* **1** Comm client/-e *m/f*; **'~ services'** 'service *m* clientèle'; **2**○ (person) type○ *m*; **a nasty ~** un sale type○; **she's a difficult ~** elle n'est pas facile à vivre; **he's an odd ~** c'est un drôle d'oiseau○.

customize /ˈkʌstəmaɪz/ *vtr* personnaliser; **~d holidays** GB, **~d vacation** US vacances *fpl* à la carte; **~d software** logiciel *m* personnalisé.

custom-made /ˌkʌstəmˈmeɪd/ *adj* personnalisé.

customs /ˈkʌstəmz/ *n* (+ *v pl ou sg*) (authority, place) douane *f*; **at ~** à la douane; **to go through ~** passer à la douane.

customs: **Customs and Excise** *n* GB douane *f* (britannique); **~ border patrol** *n* brigade *f* volante des services de la douane; **~ clearance** *n* dédouanement *m*; **~ declaration** *n* déclaration *f* en douane; **~ duties** *npl* droits *mpl* de douane; **~ hall** *n* douane *f*; **~ house** *n* bureau *m* de douane; **~ inspection** *n* contrôle *m* douanier; **~ officer**, **~ official** **▶1692** *n* douanier/-ière *m/f*; **~ post** *n* poste *m* de douane; **~ service** *n* administration *f* des douanes; **~ shed** *n* poste *m* de douane; **~ union** *n* union *f* douanière.

cut /kʌt/ **I** *n* **1** (incision) gen entaille *f*; (in surgery) incision *f*; **to make a ~ in** faire une entaille dans [*cloth, wood*]; [*surgeon*] faire une incision dans [*flesh*]; **2** (wound) coupure *f*; **to get a ~ from sth** se couper sur qch; **3** (hairstyle) coupe *f*; **a ~ and blow-dry** une coupe-brushing; **4**○ (share) part *f*; **a ~ of the profits/takings** une part des bénéfices/recettes; **she takes a 25% ~ of the total sum** elle prend 25% de la somme globale; **5** (reduction) réduction *f* (**in** de); **a ~ in prices**, **a price ~** une baisse des prix; **a ~ in the interest/unemployment rate** une baisse du taux d'intérêt/de chômage; **job ~s** suppression *f* d'emplois; **he agreed to take a ~ in salary** il a accepté qu'on lui diminue son salaire; **6** (trim) **to give [sth] a ~** couper [*hair, grass*]; **7** Culin morceau *m*; **fillet is the most tender ~** le filet est le morceau le plus tendre; **8** (shape) (of gem) taille *f*; (of suit, jacket) coupe *f*; **9** Cin (removal of footage) coupure *f*; (shot) plan *m* de raccord (**from** de; **to** à); **final ~** final cut *m*; **10** (in editing) coupure *f*; **to make ~s in** faire des coupures dans [*article, story*]; **11** (shorter route) raccourci *m*; **12** Art, Print cliché *m*, gravure *f*; **13** Sport coup *m* tranchant; **14**○ Mus (track) morceau *m*; **classic ~s from the 60's** des morceaux classiques des années 60.
II *vtr* (*p prés* **-tt-**; *prét, pp* **cut**) **1** (slice) couper [*bread, fabric, metal, paper, slice, wood*]; faire [*hole, slit*]; **to ~ sth out of** couper qch dans [*fabric*]; découper qch dans [*magazine*]; **to ~ sth in half** ou **in two** couper qch en deux; **to ~ sth into quarters/slices/pieces** couper qch en quartiers/tranches/morceaux; **to ~ sth to shreds** ou **ribbons** mettre [qch] en pièces [*fabric, document*]; **my hands were cut to shreds** mes mains étaient tout abîmées; **2** (sever) couper [*rope, ribbon, throat, wire*]; ouvrir [*vein*]; couper [*flower, stem*]; faucher, couper [*wheat*]; fig rompre [*ties, links*]; **3** (carve out) faire [*notch*]; creuser [*channel, tunnel*]; graver [*initials*] (**in** dans); **to ~ sth open** ouvrir [*packet, sack*]; [*surgeon*] ouvrir [*chest, stomach*]; **to ~ one's way through** se frayer un chemin dans [*undergrowth*]; **4** (wound) lit (once) blesser [*victim*]; (repeatedly) taillader [*victim*]; fig [*remark*] blesser [*person*]; **to ~ one's finger/lip** se couper le doigt/la lèvre; **the rocks cut their feet** les rochers leur ont tailladé les pieds; **the wind cut me like a knife** le vent était mordant; **5** (trim) couper [*grass, hair*]; tailler [*hedge*]; **to ~ one's fringe/finger nails** se couper la frange/les ongles; **to have one's hair cut** se faire couper les cheveux; **6** (shape , fashion) tailler [*gem, marble, wood*]; découper [*pastry*]; tailler [*suit*]; [*locksmith*] refaire [*key*]; **to ~ sth into triangles/strips** couper qch en triangles/bandes; **to ~ sth into the shape of a bird** découper qch en forme d'oiseau; **7** (liberate) **to ~ sb from sth** dégager qn de [*wreckage*]; **to ~ sb/sth free** ou **loose** libérer qn/qch (**from** de); **8** (edit) couper [*article, film*]; supprimer [*scene*]; **we cut the film to 90 minutes** nous avons réduit le film à 90 minutes; **I cut the article from 3,000 to 2,000 words** j'ai réduit l'article de 3000 à 2000 mots; **9** (reduce) baisser [*price, rate*]; réduire [*cost, expenditure, inflation, list, number, staff, wages*] (**by** de); diminuer [*length, size, working day, salary*]; comprimer [*budget*]; **we've cut prices by 10%** on a baissé les prix de 10%; **we've cut the amount of time we spend on the phone** nous passons moins de temps au téléphone; **10** (grow) **to ~ a tooth** percer une dent; **to ~ one's teeth** faire ses dents; **11** (switch off) éteindre [*headlights*]; **12** (record) faire, graver [*album*]; tracer [*track*]; **13** Comput couper [*paragraph, section*]; **~ and paste** couper-coller; **~ the first paragraph and paste it in at the end** coupez le premier paragraphe et collez-le à la fin; **14** Games couper [*cards, deck*]; **15** (dilute) couper [*drink, drugs*] (**with** avec); **16** (intersect) [*line*] couper [*circle*]; [*track*] couper [*road*]; **17**○ (stop) **~ the chatter** arrêtez de jacasser; **~ the flattery/sarcasm!** assez de flatteries/sarcasme!; **~ the crap**●! arrête de déconner●!; **18**○ (fail to attend) sécher○ [*class, lesson*]; ne pas aller à [*meeting, conference*]; **19** (snub) ignorer, snober [*person*]; **she cut me dead in the street** elle m'a complètement ignoré dans la rue; **20** Cin (splice) monter.
III *vi* (*p prés* **-tt-**; *prét, pp* **cut**) **1** (slice, make an incision) couper; **this knife ~s well** ce couteau coupe bien; **cardboard ~s easily** le carton est facile à couper; **~ along the dotted line** coupez suivant les pointillés; **will the cake ~ into six?** tu crois que le gâteau fera pour six?; **to ~ into** entamer [*cake, pie*]; couper [*fabric, paper*]; inciser [*flesh, organ*]; **2** (move, go) **to ~ across the park** couper à travers le parc; **our route ~s across Belgium** notre itinéraire traverse la Belgique; **the lorry cut across my path** le camion m'a coupé la route; **to ~ down a sidestreet** couper par une petite rue; **to ~ in front of sb** (in a queue) passer devant qn; (in a car) faire une queue de poisson à qn; **3** Cin **the camera cut to the president** la caméra s'est braquée sans transition sur le président; **to ~ from the street to the courtroom** [*camera*] passer de la rue à la salle d'audience; **4** Games couper; **to ~ for the deal** couper les cartes pour déterminer qui va donner; **5** fig **to ~ into** (impinge on) empiéter sur [*leisure time, working day*].
IV *v refl* (*p prés* **-tt-**; *prét, pp* **cut**) **to ~ oneself** se couper; **to ~ oneself on the foot/chin** se couper au pied/menton; **to ~ oneself on broken glass** se couper avec un morceau de verre; **to ~ oneself a slice of meat** se couper une tranche de viande; **~ yourself some cake** coupe-toi un morceau de gâteau.
V cut *pp adj* **1** (sliced, sawn) [*fabric, rope,*

pages, timber] coupé; **ready-cut slices** tranches prédécoupées; **2** (shaped) [*gem, stone*] taillé; **a well-cut jacket** une veste bien coupée; **the trousers are cut wide** le pantalon est coupé large; **3** (injured) [*lip*] coupé; **to have a cut finger/knee** avoir une coupure au doigt/genou; **4** Agric, Hort [*hay*] fauché; [*grass, flowers*] coupé; **5** (edited) [*film, text*] avec coupures (*after n*).

IDIOMS **to be a ~ above sb/sth** être supérieur à qn/qch; **to ~ and run** fig fuir, partir en courant; **to ~ both ways** [*argument, measure*] être à double tranchant; **to have one's work cut out to do** avoir du mal à faire.

■ **cut across**: ¶ **~ across [sth] 1** (bisect) [*path*] traverser [*field*]; **2** (transcend) [*issue, disease*] ne pas tenir compte de [*class barriers, boundaries, distinctions*]; ¶ **~ across [sb]** interrompre.

■ **cut along** se dépêcher.

■ **cut at**: **~ at [sth]** attaquer [*trunk, branches*]; taillader [*rope*]; tailler dans [*hair, stone*].

■ **cut away**: **~ away [sth]** enlever [*dead wood, diseased tissue*].

■ **cut back**: ¶ **~ back** faire des économies (**on** de); ¶ **~ back [sth], ~ [sth] back 1** (reduce) réduire [*production, spending, staffing levels*] (**to** à); limiter [*expansion*] (**to** à); **2** (prune) tailler.

■ **cut down**: ¶ **~ down** réduire sa consommation; **'would you like a cigarette?'—'no, I'm trying to ~ down'** 'veux-tu une cigarette?'—'non merci, j'essaie de fumer moins'; **to ~ down on** réduire sa consommation de [*alcohol, fatty foods*]; ¶ **~ down [sth], ~ [sth] down 1** (chop down) abattre [*forest, tree*]; **2** (reduce) réduire [*consumption, spending, number, time, scale*] (**from** de, **to** à); **3** (trim) couper [*carpet, curtains*]; couper [*article, film*]; ¶ **~ [sb] down** littér [*disease*] emporter liter [*person*]; **to ~ sb down to size** rabattre le caquet à qn.

■ **cut in**: ¶ **~ in 1** (interrupt) (in conversation) intervenir; (in dancing) s'interposer; **'what about me?' he cut in** 'et moi, alors?' dit-il en interrompant la discussion; **'may I ~ in?'** (on dance floor) 'vous permettez (que je danse avec madame)?'; **to ~ in on sb** (in conversation) interrompre qn; **2** (in vehicle) **the taxi cut in in front of me** le taxi m'a fait une queue de poisson; ¶ **~ [sb] in** mettre qn dans le coup; **they cut me in on the deal** ils m'ont mis dans le coup.

■ **cut off**: ¶ **~ off [sth], ~ [sth] off 1** (remove) couper [*hair, piece, slice, top, corner*]; enlever [*excess, crusts*]; **to ~ off one's finger** se couper le doigt; **to ~ off sb's head/fingers** couper la tête/les doigts à qn; **she had all her hair cut off** elle s'est fait couper les cheveux très court; **2** (reduce) **to ~ 1% off inflation** réduire l'inflation de 1%; **they've cut 10% off their prices** ils ont baissé leurs prix de 10%; **it cut 20 minutes off the journey** cela a raccourci le trajet de 20 minutes; **she cut ten seconds off the world record** elle a amélioré le record mondial de dix secondes; **3** (disconnect) couper [*gas, power, telephone, water, supply lines*]; ¶ **~ off [sth] 1** (suspend) supprimer [*allowance, grant*]; suspendre [*financial aid*]; **2** (isolate) [*tide, army*] couper [*area, town*]; **3** (block) bloquer [*retreat, escape route*]; ¶ **~ [sb] off 1** Telecom couper qn; **2** (disinherit) déshériter qn; **he cut me off without a penny** il ne m'a pas laissé un sou; **3** (interrupt) interrompre qn; **she cut me off in mid-phrase** elle m'a interrompu en plein milieu d'une phrase; ¶ **~ [sb] off, ~ off [sb]** (isolate) [*group, person*] couper [*person*]; **to be cut off by the tide** se faire surprendre par la marée; **to feel cut off** se sentir coupé; **to ~ oneself off** se couper (**from** de).

■ **cut out**: ¶ **~ out** [*engine, fan*] s'arrêter; ¶ **~ out [sth]** supprimer [*alcohol, fatty food*]; ¶ **~ [sth] out, ~ out [sth] 1** (snip out) découper [*article, piece, shape*] (**from** dans); **2** (remove) enlever [*tumour*] (**from** de); couper [*reference, sentence*]; supprimer [*scene, chapter*]; **3** (block out) boucher [*view*]; éliminer [*draught, noise, vibration*]; **4**○ (stop) **~ the noise out!** arrêtez de faire du bruit! **~ out the laughing/fighting!** arrêtez de rire/de vous disputer!; **~ it out!** ça suffit!; ¶ **~ [sb] out 1** (isolate) exclure qn; **to ~ sb out of one's will** déshériter qn; **2 to be cut out for teaching/nursing** être fait pour être professeur/infirmière; **he's not cut out to be a teacher** il n'est pas fait pour être professeur.

■ **cut short**: ¶ **~ short [sth], ~ [sth] short** abréger [*holiday, visit, discussion*]; **to ~ the conversation short** couper court; ¶ **~ [sb] short** interrompre.

■ **cut through**: **~ through [sth]** [*knife, scissors*] couper [*cardboard, plastic*]; [*detergent*] attaquer [*grease*]; [*whip*] fendre [*air*]; [*boat*] fendre [*water*]; [*person*] éviter [*red tape*]; [*voice*] traverser [*noise*].

■ **cut up**: ¶ **~ up**○ US chahuter; ¶ **~ [sth] up, ~ up [sth]** couper [*food, meat, onions*]; disséquer [*specimen*]; [*murderer*] couper [qch] en morceaux [*corpse*]; **to ~ sth up into strips/pieces** couper qch en bandes/morceaux; ¶ **~ [sb] up 1** (wound) [*gangster*] taillader [*victim*]; **2** (upset) **to be very cut up** être très affecté (**about, by** par); **3**○ Aut faire une queue de poisson à.

cut-and-dried *adj* [*procedure, formula*] fixe; [*idea, opinion*] arrêté; [*answer, solution*] tout fait; **a ~ case** une affaire simple; **I like everything to be ~** j'aime que tout soit fin prêt.

cut and thrust *n* **the ~ of debate** les échanges animés du débat; **the ~ of professional sport** l'esprit compétitif du sport professionnel.

cutaneous /kjuːˈteɪnɪəs/ *adj* cutané.

cutaway /ˈkʌtəweɪ/ **I** *n* **1** Archit, Tech écorché *m*; **2** Cin plan *m* de coupe.

II *modif* [*diagram, drawing*] en écorché.

cutback /ˈkʌtbæk/ *n* **1** Econ réduction *f*; **~s in** réductions dans le budget de [*defence, health, education*]; réductions de [*credit, production*]; **government ~s** réductions budgétaires du gouvernement; **2** US Cin retour *m* en arrière.

cute○ /kjuːt/ *adj* surtout US **1** (sweet, attractive) mignon/-onne; pej mièvre; **2** (clever) précoce; pej malin/-igne; **to get ~** faire le malin; **to get ~ with sb** répondre avec insolence à qn.

cutely /ˈkjuːtlɪ/ *adv* **1** pej (sweetly) avec une grâce étudiée; **to smile ~** faire un mignon sourire; **2** (cleverly) avec astuce.

cutesy○ /ˈkjuːtsɪ/ *adj* mièvre.

cut glass I *n* verre *m* taillé.

II cut-glass *modif* lit [*decanter, fruit bowl*] en verre taillé; fig○ [*accent*] raffiné, distingué.

cuticle /ˈkjuːtɪkl/ *n* Anat, Bot cuticule *f*.

cuticle remover *n* crème *f* émolliente.

cutie○ /ˈkjuːtɪ/, **cutie-pie**○ /ˈkjuːtɪpaɪ/ US *n* (attractive child) enfant *mf* mignon/-onne; (clever child) malin/–igne *m/f*.

cutlass /ˈkʌtləs/ *n* sabre *m* d'abordage.

cutler /ˈkʌtlə(r)/ **▶ 1692** *n* coutelier/-ière *m/f*.

cutlery /ˈkʌtlərɪ/ *n* **¢** couverts *mpl*; **a set of ~** (for one) un couvert; (complete suite) ménagère *f*.

cutlet /ˈkʌtlɪt/ *n* (meat) côtelette *f*; (fish) darne *f*, tranche *f*; **a lamb ~** une côtelette d'agneau.

cut-off /ˈkʌtɒf/ **I** *n* **1** (upper limit) limite *f*; **2** (automatic switch) (for power) coupe-circuit *m inv*; (for water-flow) robinet *m*; **3** US (shorter route) raccourci *m*.

II cut-offs *npl* jean *m* coupé.

cut: **~-off date** *n* date-limite *f*; **~-off point** *n* gen limite *f*; Fin, Tax plafond *m*.

cut-out /ˈkʌtaʊt/ **I** *n* **1** (outline) silhouette *f*; **cardboard ~** silhouette *f* en carton; **2** Electron coupe-circuit *m inv*.

II *adj* [*doll, character, drawing*] découpé.

cut-price /ˌkʌtˈpraɪs/ **I** *adj* GB à prix réduit (*after n*).

II *adv* [*offer, sell*] à prix réduit.

cut-rate *adj* US = **cut-price**.

cutter /ˈkʌtə(r)/ *n* **1** (sharp tool) (for mining) haveuse *f*; (for lino, carpet) couteau *m*, cutter *m*; **glass-~** coupe-verre *m*; **tile-~** coupe-carrelage *m*; **2** Naut cotre *m*; **3** Sewing tailleur/-euse *m/f*.

cutter bar *n* Agric, Hort barre *f* de coupe.

cut-throat /ˈkʌtθrəʊt/ **I**† *n* coupe-jarret† *m*, assassin *m*.

II *adj* **1** (ruthless) [*battle, competition, rivalry*] acharné; [*world*] dur; **a ~ business** un milieu très dur; **2** Sport **a ~ game** un match à trois personnes.

cut-throat razor *n* GB rasoir *m* (à lame), coupe-choux○ *m inv*.

cutting /ˈkʌtɪŋ/ **I** *n* **1** (newspaper extract) coupure *f* (**from** de); **2** Hort bouture *f*; **to take a ~** faire une bouture; **3** Rail tranchée *f*; **4** (shaping) (of gem, glass) taille *f*; **5** (digging) (of a tunnel) perçage *m*; **6** (slicing) (of cake, meat) découpage *m*; **7** Cin montage *m*; **8** Comput **~ and pasting** coupé-collé *m*.

II cuttings *npl* (of wood, metal) copeaux *mpl*; **grass ~s** herbe *f* coupée.

III *adj* **1** (sharp) [*pain*] aigu/-uë; [*wind*] cinglant; **to deal sb a ~ blow** lit asséner un coup violent à qn; fig descendre qn en flèche; **2** (hurtful) [*remark*] désobligeant.

cutting: **~ board** *n* (for food) planche *f* à découper; (for sewing, crafts) planche *f* de travail; **~ disc** *n* (on saw) disque *m*; (on food processor) disque *m*.

cutting edge I *n* **1** (blade) tranchant *m*; **2** fig avant-garde *f*; **to be at the ~ of** être à l'avant-garde de [*technology, fashion*].

II *modif* [*film, industry, technology*] d'avant-garde.

cutting equipment *n* matériel *m* de désincarcération.

cuttingly /ˈkʌtɪŋlɪ/ *adv* [*say, speak, reply*] d'un ton cassant.

cutting room *n* Cin salle *f* de montage; **to end up on the ~ floor** être coupé au montage.

cutting: **~s library**, **~s service** *n* Journ *bureau qui recense les coupures de presse*; **~ table** *n* Cin table *f* de montage.

cuttlefish /ˈkʌtlfɪʃ/ *n* (*pl* **~** ou **-fishes**) seiche *f*.

CV, cv (*abrév* = **curriculum vitae**) cv, CV.

c.w.o., CWO 1 *abrév* ▶ **cash with order**; **2** US Mil *abrév* ▶ **chief warrant officer**.

cwt *abrév écrite* = **hundredweight**.

cyan /ˈsaɪæn/ *n* cyan *m*.

cyanide /ˈsaɪənaɪd/ *n* cyanure *m*.

cybercafé /ˈsaɪbəˌkæfeɪ/ *n* cybercafé *m*, café *m* Internet.

cybernetics /ˌsaɪbəˈnetɪks/ *n* (+ *v sg*) cybernétique *f*.

cyberspace /ˈsaɪbəspeɪs/ *n* Comput cyberespace *m*.

cyclamen /ˈsɪkləmən, US ˈsaɪk-/ *n* cyclamen *m*.

cycle /ˈsaɪkl/ **I** *n* **1** (movement, series) cycle *m*; **washing ~** cycle *m* de lavage; **2** (bicycle) vélo *m*, bicyclette *f*.

II *vi* aller à vélo; **to go cycling** faire du vélo; **she ~s to work** elle va au travail à vélo.

III *vtr* **to ~ 15 miles** parcourir or faire 24 km à vélo.

cycle: **~ clip** *n* pince *f* à vélo; **~ lane** *n* piste *f* cyclable; **~ race** *n* course *f* cycliste; **~ rack** *n* garage *m* à vélos; **~ shed** *n* garage *m* à vélos; **~ shop** *n* magasin *m* de vélos; **~ track** *n* piste *f* cyclable.

cyclic(al) /ˈsaɪklɪk(l)/ *adj* cyclique.

cycling /ˈsaɪklɪŋ/ **▶ 1282** *n* cyclisme *m*.

cycling holiday GB *n* vacances *fpl* à vélo; **to go on a ~** faire du cyclotourisme.

Cycling Proficiency Test GB *n* brevet *m* de jeune cycliste.

cycling shorts *npl* Sport cuissard *m*; Fashn (short *m* de) cycliste *m*.

cycling: **~ tour** *n* randonnée *f* à vélo; **~ track** *n* (professional) vélodrome *m*; **~ vacation** US = **cycling holiday**.

cyclist /ˈsaɪklɪst/ *n* gen cycliste *mf*; Sport coureur/-euse *m/f* cycliste.

cyclo-cross /ˈsaɪkləkrɒs/ ▶ 1282 *n* cyclo-cross *m*.

cyclone /ˈsaɪkləʊn/ *n* cyclone *m*; **~ fence** US barrière *f* en grillage.

cyclonic /saɪˈklɒnɪk/ *adj* cyclonal.

Cyclops /ˈsaɪklɒps/ *pr n* Cyclope.

cyclorama /ˌsaɪkləˈrɑːmə/ *n* cyclorama *m*.

cyclothymia /ˌsaɪkləʊˈθaɪmɪə/ *n* Psych cyclothymie *f*.

cyclotron /ˈsaɪklətrɒn/ *n* cyclotron *m*.

cygnet /ˈsɪgnɪt/ *n* jeune cygne *m*.

cylinder /ˈsɪlɪndə(r)/ *n* **1** Aut, Math, Tech, Print cylindre *m*; **a four-~ engine** un moteur à quatre cylindres; **2** (of revolver, watch, lock) barillet *m*; **3** GB (also **hot water ~**) ballon *m* d'eau chaude.

IDIOMS **to be firing** ou **working on all ~s**○ être au meilleur de sa forme.

cylinder: **~ block** *n* bloc-cylindres *m*; **~ capacity** *n* cylindrée *f*; **~ desk** *n* bureau *m* à cylindre; **~ head** *n* culasse *f*; **~ head gasket** *n* joint *m* de culasse.

cylindrical /sɪˈlɪndrɪkl/ *adj* cylindrique.

cymbal /ˈsɪmbl/ ▶ 1481 *n* cymbale *f*; **antique ~s** crotales *mpl*; **finger ~s** cymbales à doigts.

cynic /ˈsɪnɪk/ **I** *n* **1** gen cynique *mf*; **2 Cynic** Philos Cynique *mf*.
II *adj* (all contexts) cynique.

cynical /ˈsɪnɪkl/ *adj* cynique (**about** en ce qui concerne).

cynically /ˈsɪnɪklɪ/ *adv* cyniquement.

cynicism /ˈsɪnɪsɪzəm/ *n* (attitude) cynisme *m* also Philos; (remark) remarque *f* cynique.

cynosure /ˈsaɪnəzjʊə(r), US ˈsaɪnəʃʊər/ *n* **to be the ~ of all eyes** attirer tous les regards.

cypher *n*, *vtr* = **cipher**.

cypress (tree) /ˈsaɪprəs/ *n* cyprès *m*.

Cypriot /ˈsɪprɪət/ ▶ 1486 **I** *n* Chypriote *mf*; **a Greek ~** un/une Chypriote grec/grecque.
II *adj* chypriote.

Cyprus /ˈsaɪprəs/ ▶ 1381, 1131 *pr n* Chypre *f*.

Cyrillic /sɪˈrɪlɪk/ *adj* cyrillique.

cyst /sɪst/ *n* Med, Biol kyste *m*.

cystic fibrosis /ˌsɪstɪk faɪˈbrəʊsɪs/ ▶ 1354 *n* mucoviscidose *f*.

cystitis /sɪˈstaɪtɪs/ ▶ 1354 *n* cystite *f*; **to have ~** avoir une cystite.

cytological /ˌsaɪtəˈlɒdʒɪkl/ *adj* cytologique.

cytologist /saɪˈtɒlədʒɪst/ *n* cytologiste *mf*.

cytology /saɪˈtɒlədʒɪ/ *n* cytologie *f*.

czar, **Czar** /zɑː(r)/ ▶ 1268 *n* tsar *m*; **Czar Nicolas** le tsar Nicolas.

czarevitch /ˈzɑːrɪvɪtʃ/ *n* tsarévitch *m*.

czarina /zɑːˈriːnə/ ▶ 1268 *n* tsarine *f*.

czarist /ˈzɑːrɪst/ *n*, *adj* tsariste (*mf*).

Czech /tʃek/ ▶ 1486, 1402 **I** *n* **1** (person) Tchèque *mf*; **2** (language) tchèque *m*.
II *adj* tchèque.

Czechoslovak(ian) /ˌtʃekəˈsləʊvæk, ˌtʃekəsləˈvækɪən/ ▶ 1486, 1402 **I** *n* Tchécoslovaque *mf*.
II *adj* tchécoslovaque.

Czechoslovakia /ˌtʃekəsləʊˈvækɪə/ ▶ 1131 *pr n* Hist Tchécoslovaquie *f*.

Czech Republic ▶ 1131 *pr n* République *f* tchèque.

Dd

d, D /diː/ *n* **1** (letter) d, D *m*; **2 D** Mus ré *m*; **3 d** GB† *abrév écrite* = **penny**; **4 d** *abrév écrite* = **died.**

DA *n* US Jur *abrév* ▶ **District Attorney**.

dab /dæb/ **I** *n* **1** touche *f*; **a ~ of** une touche de [*paint, powder*]; une goutte de [*glue*]; un petit morceau de [*butter*]; **2** (fish) limande *f*; **3** (blow) petit coup *m*.
II dabs○ *npl* GB (fingerprints) empreintes *fpl* digitales.
III *vtr* se tamponner [*one's eyes, mouth*]; tamponner [*wound*]; **to ~ sth on sth** appliquer qch à qch par petites touches; **to ~ sth with sth** tamponner qch de qch.
IDIOMS **to be a ~ hand**○ **at (doing) sth** GB être doué pour (faire) qch.
■ **dab at**: **~ at [sth]** se tamponner [*eyes*]; tamponner [*stains, wound*].
■ **dab on**: **~ on [sth]**, **~ [sth] on** appliquer [qch] par touches légères [*paint, ointment*]; s'appliquer [*perfume*].
■ **dab off**: **~ off [sth]**, **~ [sth] off** enlever [qch] en tamponnant.

dabble /ˈdæbl/ **I** *vtr* **to ~ one's fingers/toes in sth** tremper ses doigts/ses orteils dans qch.
II *vi* = **dabble in**.
■ **dabble in**: **~ in [sth]** faire [qch] en amateur [*painting, writing, politics*]; flirter avec [*ideology*]; **painting? I just ~ in** la peinture? j'en fais un peu; **to ~ in the Stock Exchange** boursicoter○.

dabbler /ˈdæblə(r)/ *n* dilettante *mf*.

dabchick /ˈdæbtʃɪk/ *n* grèbe *m* castagneux.

Dacca /ˈdæka/ ▶ **1818** *pr n* Dacca.

dace /deɪs/ *n* (*pl* **~** ou **~s**) vandoise *f*.

dacha /ˈdætʃə/ *n* datcha *f*.

dachshund /ˈdækshʊnd/ *n* teckel *m*.

Dacron® /ˈdækrɒn, ˈdeɪkrɒn/ *n* dacron® *m*.

dactyl /ˈdæktɪl/ *n* dactyle *m*.

dactylic /dækˈtɪlɪk/ *adj* dactylique.

dad○, **Dad**○ /dæd/ *n* (child speaker) papa *m*; (adult speaker) père *m*; (old man) hum pépé○ *m*.

Dada /ˈdɑːdɑː/ Art **I** *n* Dada *m*.
II *adj* dada *inv*.

dadaism /ˈdɑːdəɪzəm/ *n* Art dadaïsme *m*.

dadaist /ˈdɑːdəɪst/ Art **I** *n* dadaïste *mf*.
II *adj* dada *inv*, dadaïste.

daddy○, **Daddy**○ /ˈdædɪ/ *n* papa○ *m*.

daddy-long-legs /ˌdædɪˈlɒŋlegz/ *n* (*pl* **~**) GB tipule *f*; US faucheux *m*.

dado /ˈdeɪdəʊ/ *n* (*pl* **-does** ou **-dos**) (wainscot) lambris *m* d'appui; (rail) cimaise *f*.

Dad's army○ *n* GB Mil, hum milice *f* populaire (*formée pendant la guerre de 1939-44*).

Daedalus /ˈdiːdələs/ *pr n* Dédale.

daff○ /dæf/ *n* GB *abrév* ▶ **daffodil**.

daffodil /ˈdæfədɪl/ **I** *n* jonquille *f*.
II *modif* [*bulb*] de jonquille.

daffodil yellow *n, adj* jonquille (*m*) (*inv*).

daffy○ /ˈdæfɪ/ *adj* farfelu○.

daft○ /dɑːft, US dæft/ **I** *adj* **1** (silly) bête; **2 to be ~ about sth/sb** être toqué○ de qch/qn.
II *adv* **to talk ~** dire des bêtises.
IDIOMS **~ as a brush**○ GB givré○, cinglé○.

dagger /ˈdægə(r)/ *n* **1** (weapon) (narrow) dague *f*; (wider) poignard *m*; **2** Print croix *f*.
IDIOMS **to be at ~s drawn** être à couteaux tirés (**with** avec); **to look ~s at sb** fusiller qn du regard.

dago● /ˈdeɪgəʊ/ *n* injur métèque *m* offensive.

daguerreotype /dəˈgerətaɪp/ *n* daguerréotype *m*.

dahlia /ˈdeɪlɪə, US ˈdælɪə/ *n* dahlia *m*.

Dáil Éireann /dɔɪl ˈeɪrən/ *n* Pol ≈ Chambre *f* des Députés (*du parlement irlandais*).

daily /ˈdeɪlɪ/ **I** *n* (*pl* **dailies**) **1** (newspaper) quotidien *m*; **the national dailies** les grands quotidiens; **2**○ GB (also **~ help**, **~ maid**) femme *f* de ménage.
II *adj* [*routine, visit, journey, delivery*] quotidien/-ienne; [*wage, rate, intake*] journalier/-ière; [*sight, phenomenon*] quotidien/-ienne, de tous les jours; **~ newspaper** (journal *m*) quotidien *m*; **on a ~ basis** gen tous les jours; **to be paid on a ~ basis** être payé à la journée; **to earn one's ~ bread** gagner son pain quotidien; **the ~ grind** le labeur quotidien; **the ~ round** le train-train de la vie quotidienne.
III *adv* quotidiennement, tous les jours; **to be taken twice ~** à prendre deux fois par jour; **he is expected ~** sout on l'attend d'un jour à l'autre.

daintily /ˈdeɪntɪlɪ/ *adv* délicatement.

daintiness /ˈdeɪntɪnɪs/ *n* délicatesse *f*, finesse *f*.

dainty /ˈdeɪntɪ/ **I** *n* mets *m* délicat.
II *adj* **1** [*porcelain, handkerchief*] délicat; [*shoe, hat, hand, foot*] mignon/-onne; [*figure*] menu; [*movement*] délicat; **2** [*dish, cake*] délicat; **a ~ morsel** un morceau de choix.

daiquiri /ˈdækərɪ, ˈdaɪ-/ *n* daiquiri *m*.

dairy /ˈdeərɪ/ *n* **1** (on farm etc) laiterie *f*; (shop) crémerie *f*; **2** Comm (company) société *f* laitière.

dairy: **~ butter** *n* beurre *m* fermier; **~ cattle** *n* (+ *v pl*) vaches *fpl* laitières; **~ cow** *n* vache *f* laitière; **~ cream** *n* ≈ crème *f* fraîche; **~ farm** *n* exploitation *f* laitière; **~ farming** *n* élevage *m* de vaches laitières; **~ ice cream** *n* glace *f* faite à la crème; **~maid** *n* fille *f* de ferme (qui s'occupe de la laiterie).

dairyman /ˈdeərɪmən/ *n* (on farm etc) ouvrier *m* de laiterie; (in shop) crémier *m*; US (farmer) éleveur *m* de vaches laitières.

dairy produce, **dairy products** *n* produits *mpl* laitiers.

dais /ˈdeɪs/ *n* estrade *f*.

daisy /ˈdeɪzɪ/ *n* (common) pâquerette *f*; (garden) marguerite *f*.
IDIOMS **to be as fresh as a ~** être frais/fraîche comme une rose; **to be pushing up (the) daisies**○ manger les pissenlits par la racine○.

daisy chain *n* guirlande *f* de pâquerettes.

daisy wheel **I** *n* Comput, Print marguerite *f*.
II *modif* [*printer, terminal*] à marguerite.

Dalai Lama /ˌdælaɪ ˈlɑːmə/ *pr n* dalaï-lama *m*.

dale /deɪl/ *n* vallée *f*, val *m* liter.
IDIOMS **up hill and down ~** GB, **over hill and ~** US par monts et par vaux.

dalliance /ˈdælɪəns/ *n* littér badinage *m* (galant); fig (with idea, political party) flirt *m*.

dally /ˈdælɪ/ *vi* **1 to ~ with**† flirter avec [*person*]; **2 to ~ with** fig caresser, jouer avec [*idea, plan*]; flirter avec [*political party*]; **3** (linger) traîner (**over** sur).

dalmatian, **Dalmatian** /dælˈmeɪʃn/ *n* (dog) dalmatien *m*.

dalmatic /dælˈmætɪk/ *n* dalmatique *f*.

dam /dæm/ **I** *n* **1** (construction) barrage *m*; (to prevent flooding) digue *f*; **2** (body of water) lac *m* de barrage, (lac *m* de) retenue *f*; **3** (animal) mère *f*.
II○ *adj, adv* = **damn**.
III *vtr* Constr construire un barrage sur [*river, lake*]; (to prevent flooding) endiguer.
■ **dam up**: **~ up [sth]**, **~ [sth] up 1** = **dam III**; **2** (block up) bloquer, obstruer [*river, canal*]; étouffer [*feelings*]; endiguer [*flow of words, money, supplies*].

damage /ˈdæmɪdʒ/ **I** *n* ₵ **1** (physical) (to building, machine, goods, environment) dégâts *mpl* (**to** causés à; **from** causés par); **to do** ou **cause ~** causer des dégâts; **not much ~ was done to the car** la voiture n'a pas été très endommagée; **~ of £300 was done to the car** la voiture a subi pour 300 livres sterling de dégâts; **storm ~** dégâts dûs aux intempéries; **water/frost ~** dégâts des eaux/du gel; **criminal ~** Jur (actes de) vandalisme; **~ to property** Jur dégâts matériels; **~ or loss** Insur dégâts et pertes; **2** (medical) lésions *fpl*; **to cause ~ to** abîmer [*health, part of body*]; **(irreversible) brain ~** lésions *fpl* cérébrales (irréversibles); **psychological ~** traumatisme *m* psychologique; **3** fig **to do ~ to** porter atteinte à [*cause, relationship, reputation, self-confidence, trade*]; **political ~** dommage *m* politique; **(a lot of) ~ was done to sth** qch a été (sérieusement) atteint; **it's too late, the ~ is done** trop tard, le mal est fait.
II damages *npl* Jur dommages-interêts *mpl*, dommages *mpl* et intérêts *mpl*; **to claim for ~s** réclamer des dommages-intérêts (**against sb** à qn); **a claim for ~** une demande de dommages-intérêts; **he paid £700 (in) ~s** il a payé 700 livres sterling de dommages-intérêts; **~s for loss of earnings** dommages-intérêts pour manque à gagner; **agreed ~s** dommages-intérêts fixés ; **to be liable for ~s** être civilement responsable.
III *vtr* **1** (physically) endommager [*building, machine, furniture*]; abîmer [*health, part of body*]; nuire à [*environment, crop*]; **2** fig porter atteinte à [*reputation, career, relationship, confidence, organization, negotiations*]; **~d child** Psych enfant traumatisé.
IDIOMS **what's the ~**○**?** à combien se monte la douloureuse○?

damageable /ˈdæmɪdʒəbl/ *adj* Insur dommageable.

damaging /ˈdæmɪdʒɪŋ/ *adj* **1** (to reputation, career, person) préjudiciable (**to** à, pour); [*effect*] préjudiciable; [*consequences*] désastreux/-euse; **2** (to health, environment) nuisible (**to** pour).

damagingly /ˈdæmɪdʒɪŋlɪ/ *adv* **1** [*harsh, lax*] regrettablement; **2** [*do, say*] de façon regrettable.

Damascus /də'mæskəs/ ▶1818 *pr n* Damas; **the road to ~** le chemin de Damas.

damask /'dæməsk/ **I** *n* **1** Tex damas *m*; **2** Hist (metal) acier *m* damassé; **3** (colour) vieux rose *m inv*.
II *modif* [*cloth, robe*] damassé.
III *adj* (colour) vieux rose *inv*.

damask rose *n* rose *f* de Damas.

Dam Busters /'dæmbʌstəz/ *npl* GB Mil Hist **the ~** les briseurs *mpl* de barrage (*aviateurs britanniques chargés d'une mission de bombardement en Allemagne pendant la deuxième guerre mondiale*).

dame /deɪm/ *n* **1**‡ GB dame *f*; **the ~** Theat la vieille dame (*rôle bouffon joué par un homme dans les farces traditionnelles*); **~ Fortune** Dame Fortune; **2 Dame** GB *titre octroyé à une femme décorée d'un ordre de chevalerie*; **3**○ US gonzesse○ *f*.

dame school *n* école *f* enfantine (*tenue autrefois par une dame à son domicile*).

damfool†○ /'dæmfu:l/ *adj* idiot.

dammit○ /'dæmɪt/ *excl* zut○!, merde●!; **(or) as near as ~**○ GB (ou) c'est tout comme○.

damn /dæm/ **I**○ *n* **not to give a ~** s'en ficher○; **not to give a ~ about sb/sth** se ficher de qn/qch; **it's not worth a ~**○ ça ne vaut pas un clou○; **he can't sing worth a ~** US il chante comme un pied○.
II○ *adj* **1** [*object*] fichu○; **your ~ husband** ton fichu○ mari; **you ~ lunatic!** espèce de fou○!; **I can't see a ~ thing** je n'y vois que dalle●.
III○ *adv* sacrément○; **a ~ good film/meal** un super○ film/repas; **it's just ~ stupid/unfair** c'est vraiment idiot/injuste; **I should ~ well hope so!** j'espère bien!
IV○ **damn near** *adv phr* **he ~ near killed me/ran me over** il a bien failli me tuer/m'écraser.
V○ *excl* merde●!, zut○!
VI *vtr* **1**○ (curse) **~ you!** tu m'énerves!; **~ the weather/car!** saleté de temps/de voiture○!; **homework be ~ed, I'm going out!** au diable les devoirs, je sors!; **~ the consequences/the expense** les conséquences/la dépense on s'en moque; **I 'll be ~ed!** ça alors!, je suis scié○!; **I'll be** ou **I'm ~ed if I'm going to pay!** pas question de payer!; **I'm ~ed if I know!** comme si je savais!; **~ it!** merde●!; **2** Relig damner [*sinner, soul*]; **3** (condemn) condamner [*person, action, behaviour*] **(for** pour); **to ~ sb for doing** blâmer qn d'avoir fait; **to ~ sb with faint praise** faire des critiques à qn sous forme d'éloges.

damnable /'dæmnəbl/ *adj* **1** (disgraceful) condamnable; **2**†○(awful) [*weather, person*] fichu○ (*before n*).

damnably /'dæmnəblɪ/ *adv* **1** (disgracefully) **~ cruel/wicked** d'une cruauté/d'une méchanceté condamnable; **2**†○ (extremely) sacrément○.

damnation /dæm'neɪʃn/ **I** *n* Relig damnation *f*.
II *excl*○ merde●!, zut○!

damned /dæmd/ **I** *n* (+ *v pl*) **the ~** les damnés *mpl*.
II *adj* **1** Relig damné; **2**○ ▶**damn** II.
III *adv* ▶**damn** III.

damnedest○ /'dæmdɪst/ *n* **1** (hardest) **to do** ou **try one's ~ (to do/for sb)** faire tout son possible (pour faire/pour qn); **2** (surprising) **the ~ thing happened yesterday** quelque chose d'incroyable s'est produit hier; **it was the ~ thing** c'était incroyable.

damning /'dæmɪŋ/ *adj* accablant.

Damocles /'dæməkli:z/ *pr n* Damoclès; **the Sword of ~** l'épée de Damoclès.

damp /dæmp/ **I** *n* **1** (atmosphere, conditions) humidité *f*; **2** Mining (also **fire ~**) grisou *m*; **3** Mining (also **black ~**) mofette *f*.
II *adj* [*atmosphere, building, cloth, clothes etc*] humide; [*skin*] moite.
III *vtr* **1** = **dampen**; **2** = **damp down**; **3** Mus étouffer.
■ **damp down**: **~ [sth] down, ~ down [sth]** couvrir [*fire*]; étouffer [*flames*]; apaiser [*anger*]; dédramatiser [*crisis, situation*].

damp(-proof) course *n* barrière *f* d'étanchéité.

dampen /'dæmpən/ *vtr* **1** humecter [*cloth, sponge, ironing*]; **2** fig refroidir [*enthusiasm, optimism, ardour*]; amenuiser [*hopes, resolve*]; **to ~ sb's spirits** décourager qn.

dampener *n* US = **damper** 4.

damper /'dæmpə(r)/ *n* **1** (in fireplace, stove) registre *m*; **2** Mus étouffoir *m*; **3** Audio, Electron, Mech amortisseur *m*; **4** (for stamps, ironing) mouilleur *m*.
IDIOMS **the news put a ~ on the evening**○ la nouvelle a jeté un froid dans l'assistance; **he always puts a ~ on everything**○ c'est un rabat-joie.

dampness /'dæmpnɪs/ *n* (of climate, ground, room, clothes etc) humidité *f*; (of skin) moiteur *f*.

damp: **~-proof** *adj* imperméable, hydrofuge spec; **~ squib** *n* fig pétard *m* mouillé.

damsel /'dæmzl/ *n* littér demoiselle *f*; **a ~ in distress** hum une demoiselle en détresse.

damselfly /'dæmzlflaɪ/ *n* demoiselle *f*, libellule *f*.

damson /'dæmzn/ *n* **1** (fruit) prune *f* de Damas; **2** (tree) prunier *m* de Damas.

dan /dæn/ *n* dan *m*.

dance /dɑ:ns, US dæns/ **I** *n* **1** (movement) danse *f*; (art form) ¢ la danse; **modern ~** la danse moderne; **to ask sb for a ~** inviter qn à danser; **may I have the next ~?** voulez-vous m'accorder la prochaine danse?; **the Dance of Death** la danse macabre; **2** (social occasion) soirée *f* dansante; **to give** ou **hold a ~** donner une soirée dansante.
II *modif* [*band, company, floor, music, shoes, step, studio, wear*] de danse.
III *vtr* **1** danser [*steps, dance*]; **he ~d her away** il l'a emmenée en dansant; **2** (dandle) faire danser.
IV *vi* lit, fig danser **(with** avec); **to ~ for joy** danser de joie; **to ~ with rage** trépigner de rage; **to ~ to music** danser sur de la musique.
IDIOMS **to ~ the night away** passer la nuit à danser; **to lead sb a merry ~** donner du fil à retordre à qn.
■ **dance about, dance up and down** sautiller sur place.

dance: **~ hall** *n* dancing *m*; **~ notation** *n* notation *f* chorégraphique; **~ programme** *n* carnet *m* de bal.

dancer /'dɑ:nsə(r), US 'dænsər/ *n* danseur/-euse *m/f*.

dancing /'dɑ:nsɪŋ, US 'dænsɪŋ/ **I** ▶1282 *n* danse *f*; **will there be ~?** est-ce qu'on dansera?
II *modif* [*class, school, shoes, teacher*] de danse.
III *pres p adj* littér [*waves, sunbeams*] dansant; [*eyes*] pétillant.

dancing: **~ girl** *n* danseuse *f*; **~ partner** *n* cavalier/-ière *m/f*.

D and C *n* Med (*abrév* = **dilation and curettage**) curetage *m*.

dandelion /'dændɪlaɪən/ *n* pissenlit *m*.

dander○ /'dændə(r)/ *n* **to get sb's ~ up** faire sortir qn de ses gonds○; **to get one's ~ up** se mettre en boule○ **(over, about** à cause de).

dandified /'dændɪfaɪd/ *adj* [*person*] vêtu comme un dandy; [*appearance*] de dandy.

dandle /'dændl/ *vtr* **1 to ~ a baby on one's knee** faire sauter un bébé sur ses genoux; **2** (fondle) câliner.

dandruff /'dændrʌf/ *n* ¢ pellicules *fpl*; **to have ~** avoir des pellicules; **anti-~ shampoo** shampooing *m* antipelliculaire.

dandy /'dændɪ/ **I** *n* dandy *m*.
II○ *adj* chouette○, au poil○.
IDIOMS **that's all fine and ~** c'est parfait.

Dane /deɪn/ ▶1486 *n* Danois/-e *m/f*.

dang /dæŋ/ *adj, adv, excl* US ▶**darn** II, III, IV.

danger /'deɪndʒə(r)/ *n* danger *m* **(of** de; **to** pour); (from different sources) dangers *mpl*; **to be in ~ of doing sth** risquer de faire qch; **there is no ~ in doing sth** il n'y a pas de danger à faire qch; **the ~ is that** le danger est que (+ *subj*); **there is a ~ that** il y a un risque que (+ *subj*); **there is a ~/no ~ that he will come** il risque/ne risque pas de venir; **to put sb in ~** mettre qn en danger; **the road is a ~ to children** la rue constitue un danger pour les enfants; **out of ~** hors de danger; **~!** danger!

danger area *n* zone *f* dangereuse.

danger list *n* **on the ~** Med dans un état critique.

danger money *n* prime *f* de risque.

dangerous /'deɪndʒərəs/ *adj* dangereux/-euse **(for** pour; **to do** de faire); **~ driving** Aut conduite *f* dangereuse.
IDIOMS **to be on ~ ground** être sur un terrain miné.

dangerously /'deɪndʒərəslɪ/ *adv* gen dangereusement; [*ill*] gravement; **to live ~** prendre des risques.

danger: **~ signal** *n* lit, fig signal *m* de danger; **~ zone** *n* = **danger area**.

dangle /'dæŋgl/ **I** *vi* [*puppet, keys, rope etc*] se balancer **(from** à); [*earrings*] pendiller; **with legs dangling** les jambes ballantes; **to keep sb dangling**○ tenir qn en suspens.
II *vtr* balancer [*puppet, keys etc*]; laisser pendre [*legs*]; fig faire miroiter [*prospect, reward*] **(before, in front of** à).

Danish /'deɪnɪʃ/ ▶1486, 1402 **I** *n* **1** Ling danois *m*; **2** US Culin = **Danish pastry**.
II *adj* danois.

Danish: **~ blue (cheese)** *n* bleu *m* du Danemark, danablu *m*; **~ pastry** *n* feuilleté *m* sucré (aux fruits).

dank /dæŋk/ *adj* froid et humide.

Dante /'dæntɪ/ *pr n* Dante.

Dantean /'dæntɪən/, **Dantesque** /,dæn'tiest/ *adj* dantesque.

Danube /'dænju:b/ ▶1644 *pr n* Danube *m*; **the Blue ~** Mus le (Beau) Danube Bleu.

daphne /'dæfnɪ/ *n* Bot daphné *m*.

daphnia /'dæfnɪə/ *n* daphnie *f*.

dapper /'dæpə(r)/ *adj* soigné.

dapple /'dæpl/ **I** *vtr* tacheter.
II dappled *pp adj* [*horse*] (grey) pommelé; (bay) miroité; [*cow*] moucheté; [*sky*] pommelé; [*shade, surface*] tacheté de lumière.

dapple-grey GB, **dapple-gray** US /,dæpl'greɪ/ **I** *n* cheval *m* gris-pommelé.
II *adj* gris-pommelé.

DAR US (*abrév* = **Daughters of the American Revolution**) *association patriotique composée des descendantes des combattants de la Révolution américaine*.

Darby and Joan /,dɑ:bɪ ən 'dʒəʊn/ **I** *n* **like ~** = comme Philémon et Baucis.
II *modif* **~ Club** GB club *m* du troisième âge.

Dardanelles /,dɑ:də'nelz/ *pr npl* **the ~** les Dardanelles *fpl*.

dare /deə(r)/ **I** *n* défi *m*; **to do sth for a ~** faire qch pour répondre à un défi.
II *modal aux* **1** (to have the courage to) oser **(do, to do** faire); **few ~ (to) speak out** peu de personnes osent s'exprimer; **nobody ~d ask** personne n'a osé demander; **the article ~s to criticize** l'article n'hésite pas à critiquer; **I'd never ~ say it to her** je n'oserais jamais le lui dire; **we wanted to watch but didn't ~** nous aurions voulu regarder mais n'avons pas osé; **they don't ~** ou **daren't** GB **take the risk** ils n'osent pas prendre le risque; **read on if you ~** hum continuez, si vous l'osez; **~ we follow their example?** sout aurons-nous le courage de suivre leur exemple?; **~ I say it** il faut bien le dire; **I ~ say, I daresay** GB je pense

(**that** que); **2** (expressing anger, indignation) oser (**do** faire); **they wouldn't ~!** (rejecting suggestion) ils n'oseraient pas!; **he wouldn't ~ show his face here!** il n'oserait pas se pointer ici○!; **don't (you) ~ speak to me like that!** je t'interdis de me parler sur ce ton!; **don't you ~!** (warning) ne t'avise pas de faire ça!; **how ~ you suggest that** comment oses-tu insinuer que; **how ~ you!** comment tu oses!, comment osez-vous!
III *vtr* **to ~ sb to do** défier qn de faire; **I ~ you to say it to her!** chiche que tu le lui dises○!; **go on, I ~ you!** chiche que tu y vas○!
IDIOMS **who ~s wins** la fortune appartient aux audacieux Prov.

daredevil /ˈdeədevl/ *n, adj* casse-cou (*mf*) *inv*.

daren't = **dare not**.

daresay GB ▶ **dare** II 1.

daring /ˈdeərɪŋ/ I *n* audace *f*.
II *adj* **1** (courageous) audacieux/-ieuse; **it was ~ of her to do it** elle a fait preuve d'audace en faisant cela; **2** (innovative) audacieux/-ieuse; **3** (shocking) [*suggestion, dress*] osé.

daringly /ˈdeərɪŋlɪ/ *adv* [*suggest, adapt*] de manière audacieuse.

dark /dɑːk/ I *n* **the ~** le noir, l'obscurité *f*; **in the ~** dans le noir or l'obscurité; **before/until ~** avant/jusqu'à la (tombée de la) nuit; **after ~** après la tombée de la nuit.
II *adj* **1** (lacking in light) [*room, alley, forest, day, sky*] sombre; **it is getting** ou **growing ~** il commence à faire noir or nuit; **it's ~** il fait noir or nuit; **it's very ~ in here** c'est très sombre ici; **the sky went ~** le ciel s'est assombri; **the ~ side of the moon** la face cachée de la lune; **in ~est Africa** au fin fond de l'Afrique; **2** (in colour) [*colour, suit, liquid*] sombre; **~ blue/green** bleu/vert foncé *inv*; **~ grey socks** des chaussettes gris foncé; **3** (physically) [*hair, eyes*] brun; [*skin, complexion*] brun; **she's ~** elle est brune, elle a les cheveux bruns; **his hair is getting ~er** ses cheveux ont foncé; **a small ~** ou **~-skinned woman** une petite femme à la peau brune; **4** (gloomy) [*period, mood*] sombre; **the ~ days of the recession** les sombres jours de la récession; **to look on the ~ side** voir les choses en noir; **5** (sinister) [*secret, thought, prejudice*] noir (*before n*); [*influence, threat, warning*] sombre; **the ~ side of** le côté sinistre de [*person, regime*]; **6** (evil) [*influence, force, power*] maléfique; **7** (angry) [*look*] noir; **I got a ~ look from him** il m'a jeté un regard noir; **8** Ling **~ l** l dur.
IDIOMS **to be in the ~** être dans le noir (**about** à propos de); **I was completely in the ~** j'étais dans le noir le plus complet; **to leave sb in the ~** laisser qn dans l'ignorance; **to keep sb in the ~ about sth** cacher qch à qn; **keep it ~** garde ça pour toi○; **to take a leap** ou **shot in the ~** (guess) deviner à tout hasard; (risk) prendre un grand risque; **to work in the ~** GB progresser à tâtons.

dark: **~ age** *n* fig période *f* sombre; **Dark Ages** *n* Hist Haut Moyen-Âge *m*; **~ chocolate** *n* US chocolat *m* noir; **~-complexioned** *adj* basané; **Dark Continent**† *n* continent *m* Noir.

darken /ˈdɑːkən/ I *vtr* **1** (reduce light in) obscurcir [*sky, landscape*]; assombrir [*house, room*]; **2** (in colour) foncer [*liquid, colour*]; brunir [*skin, complexion*]; **3** (cloud) assombrir [*atmosphere, future*].
II *vi* **1** (lose light) [*sky, room*] s'obscurcir; **2** (in colour) [*liquid*] foncer; [*skin, hair*] brunir; **3** (show anger) [*eyes, face*] se rembrunir; **4** (become gloomy) [*atmosphere, mood, outlook*] s'assombrir.
III **darkened** *pp adj* [*room, house*] obscur, sombre.
IV **darkening** *pres p adj* [*sky, wood*] gagné par l'obscurité; **the ~ing evenings** les soirées où la nuit tombe vite.
IDIOMS **don't ever ~ my door again!** hum ne remettez plus les pieds ici!

dark-eyed /ˌdɑːkˈaɪd/ *adj* [*person*] aux yeux sombres or noirs; **she was pale and ~** elle était pâle et avait les yeux noirs.

dark glasses *npl* lunettes *fpl* noires.

dark horse *n* **1**○ GB (enigmatic person) mystère *m*; **you're a bit of a ~**○**!** tu es vraiment énigmatique!; **2** (in sports) outsider *m*; **3** US Pol candidat-surprise/candidate-surprise *m/f*.

darkly /ˈdɑːklɪ/ *adv* **1** (grimly) [*mutter, say, hint*] sombrement; **~ humorous** d'un humour noir; **2** (in tones) **~ coloured** de couleur foncée; **3** (ominously) [*eye, watch*] d'un air sombre.

darkness /ˈdɑːknɪs/ *n* **1** (blackness) obscurité *f*; **to be in/to be plunged into ~** être dans/être plongé dans l'obscurité; **as ~ fell** à la tombée de la nuit; **in/out of the ~** dans/de l'obscurité; **2** (evil) **the forces of ~** les puissances *fpl* des ténèbres.

dark: **~room** /ˈdɑːkruːm, -rʊm/ *n* chambre *f* noire; **~-skinned** *adj* [*person*] à peau noire.

darky○, **darkey**○ /ˈdɑːkɪ/ *n* injur noir/-e *m/f*.

darling /ˈdɑːlɪŋ/ I *n* **1** (term of address) (to loved one) chéri/-e *m/f*; (to child) mon chou○; (affectedly: to acquaintance) mon cher/ma chère *m/f*; **you poor ~** (to adult) mon/ma pauvre *m/f*; (to child) mon pauvre chou○; **~ Rosie** ma Rosie chérie; **2** (kind, lovable person) amour *m*, ange *m*; **her father is a ~** son père est un amour; **the children have been little ~s** les enfants ont été des anges; **be a ~ and pour me a drink** sois un ange et sers-moi à boire; **3** (favourite) (of circle, public) coqueluche *f*; (of family, parent, teacher) chouchou/-te *m/f*.
II *adj* **1** (expressing attachment) [*child, husband*] chéri; **2** (expressing approval, admiration) **a ~ little baby/kitten** un amour de bébé/chaton; **what a ~ little house!** quelle petite maison adorable!

darn /dɑːn/ I *n* reprise *f*, raccommodage *m* (**in** à).
II○ *adj* (also **darned**) sacré○ (*before n*).
III *adv* sacrément○; **~ good** super○.
IV *excl* zut○!
V *vtr* repriser, raccommoder.

darnel /ˈdɑːnl/ *n* ivraie *f*, ray-grass *m*.

darning /ˈdɑːnɪŋ/ I *n* (all contexts) raccommodage *m*.
II *modif* [*wool, needle, egg*] à repriser; [*stitch*] de reprise.

dart /dɑːt/ I *n* **1** ▶ **1282** Sport fléchette *f*; **(game of) ~s** partie *f* de fléchettes; **to play ~s** jouer aux fléchettes; **2** (arrow) flèche *f* (courte); fig flèche *f*; **poisoned ~** flèche empoisonnée; **3** (movement) **to make a ~ for/at sth** se précipiter vers/sur qch; **4** Sewing pince *f*.
II *vi* s'élancer comme une flèche (**at** sur); **to ~ in/out/away** entrer/sortir/filer comme une flèche.
III *vtr* décocher [*glance*]; darder [*tongue, rays*].

dartboard /ˈdɑːtbɔːd/ *n* cible *f*.

darting /ˈdɑːtɪŋ/ *adj* [*glance, movement*] vif/vive.

Darwinian /dɑːˈwɪnɪən/ *adj* darwinien/-ienne.

Darwinism /ˈdɑːwɪnɪzəm/ *n* darwinisme *m*.

DASD *n*: *abrév* ▶ **direct access storage device**.

dash /dæʃ/ I *n* **1** (rush) course *f* folle; **it has been a mad ~ to do** on a dû se presser ou foncer○ pour faire; **to make a ~ for it** (run off) s'enfuir; **shall we make a ~ for it?** (to shelter) on y va?; **to make a ~ for the train** courir pour attraper le train; **2** (small amount) (of liquid) goutte *f* (**of** de); (of pepper, powder) pincée *f* (**of** de); (of colour) touche *f* (**of** de); **a ~ of humour** un rien d'humour; **3** (flair) panache *m*; **to have ~** avoir du panache; **4** (punctuation mark) tiret *m*; **5** (in morse code) trait *m*; **dot dot ~** point point trait; **6**○ Aut (dashboard) tableau *m* de bord; **7**† Sport **the 100 yard ~** le 100 mètres.
II† *excl* (exasperated) zut○!; **~ it all!** (indignant) après tout!
III *vtr* **1** (smash) **to ~ sb/sth against** [*sea, person*] projeter qn/qch contre [*rocks*]; **to ~ sth to the ground** lancer violemment qch par terre; **to ~ sb's brains out against sth** éclater la tête de qn contre qch; **2** fig (crush) anéantir [*hope*]; **hopes of success were ~ed when** tout espoir de succès a été anéanti lorsque.
IV *vi* (hurry) se précipiter, foncer○; **to ~ into** se précipiter dans; **to ~ out of** sortir en courant de; **to ~ for cover** courir se mettre à l'abri; **to ~ around** ou **about** courir de tous les côtés, courir un peu partout; **I must ~!** je me sauve!
IDIOMS **to cut a ~** avoir grande allure.
■ **dash off**: ¶ **~ off** se sauver; ¶ **~ off [sth], ~ [sth] off** écrire [qch] en vitesse [*letter, essay*].

dashboard /ˈdæʃbɔːd/ *n* tableau *m* de bord.

dashed○† /dæʃt/ *adj* sacré.

dashiki /ˈdɑːʃɪkɪ/ *n* tunique *f* africaine.

dashing /ˈdæʃɪŋ/ *adj* [*person*] fringant; [*outfit*] superbe.

dastardly /ˈdæstədlɪ/ littér *adj* infâme.

DAT /dat/ *n*: *abrév* ▶ **digital audio tape**.

data /ˈdeɪtə/ *npl* gen, Comput données *fpl*.

data: **~ acquisition** *n* acquisition *f* de données; **~ analysis** *n* analyse *f* de données; **~ bank** *n* banque *f* de données; **~base** *n* base *f* de données; **~base management system**, **DBMS** *n* système *m* de gestion de données, SGBD; **~ capture** *n* saisie *f* de données; **~ carrier** *n* support *m* d'information; **~ collection** *n* collecte *f* de données; **~ communications** *npl* transmission *f* de données; **~ corruption** *n* altération *f* de données; **~ dictionary** *n* dictionnaire *m* de données; **~ directory** *n* répertoire *m* de données; **~ disk** *n* disque *m* enregistré; **~ encryption** *n* chiffrement *m* de données; **~ entry** *n* introduction *f* de données; **~ file** *n* fichier *m* de données; **~ handling** *n* manipulation *f* de données; **~ input** *n* introduction *f* de données; **~ item** *n* donnée *f* élémentaire; **~ link** *n* liaison *f* de données; **~ management** *n* gestion *f* de données.

Datapost /ˈdeɪtəpəʊst/ *n* GB Post cf Chronopost *m*; **by ~** par Chronopost.

data preparation *n* préparation *f* des données.

data processing *n* (procedure) traitement *m* des données; (career) informatique *f*; (department) service *m* informatique.

data processing manager *n* chef *m* du service informatique.

data processor *n* (machine) machine *f* de traitement de l'information, ordinateur *m*; (worker) informaticien/-ienne *m/f*.

data: **~ protection** *n* protection *f* de l'information; **~ protection act** *n* Jur loi *f* sur l'informatique et les libertés; **~ retrieval** *n* extraction *f* de données; **~ security** *n* sécurité *f* des données.

data storage *n* (process) stockage *m* des données; (medium) support *m* d'information.

data: **~ structure** *n* structure *f* de données; **~ transmission**, **DT** *n* transmission *f* de données; **~ type** *n* type *m* de données.

date /deɪt/ ▶ **1150** I *n* **1** (day of the month) date *f*; **~ of birth** date de naissance; **~ of delivery/of expiry** date de livraison/d'expiration; **what ~ is your birthday?** quelle est la date de ton anniversaire?; **what ~ is it today?, what's the ~ today?** on est le combien aujourd'hui?; **today's ~ is May 2** aujourd'hui nous sommes le 2 mai; **there's no ~ on the letter** la lettre n'est pas datée; **'~ as postmark'** 'date: voir cachet de la poste'; **to fix** ou **set a ~** fixer une

Date

Where English has several ways of writing dates, such as May 10, 10 May, 10th May *etc. French has only one generally accepted way:* le 10 mai, (*say* le dix mai). *However, as in English, dates in French may be written informally:* 10.5.68 *or* 31/7/65 *etc.*

The general pattern in French is:

le	*cardinal number*	*month*	*year*
le	10	mai	1901

But if the date is the first of the month, use premier, abbreviated as 1er:

May 1st 1901 = le 1er mai 1901

Note that French does not use capital letters for months, or for days of the week, ▶ **1472** *and* ▶ **1883**; *also French does not usually abbreviate the names of the months:*

Sept 10 = le 10 septembre *etc.*

If the day of the week is included, put it after the le:

Monday, May 1st 1901 = le lundi 1er mai
Monday the 25th = lundi 25 (*say* lundi vingt-cinq)

Saying and writing dates

what's the date? = quel jour sommes-nous?
it's the tenth = nous sommes le dix *or* (*less formally*) on est le dix
it's the tenth of May = nous sommes le dix mai *or* (*less formally*) on est le dix mai

	Write	**Say**
May 1	le 1er mai	le premier mai
May 2	le 2 mai	le deux mai
May 11	le 11 mai	le onze mai
May 21	le 21 mai	le vingt et un mai
May 30	le 30 mai	le trente mai
May 6 1968	le 6 mai 1968	le six mai mille neuf cent soixante-huit[1]
Monday May 6 1968	le lundi 6 mai 1968	le lundi six mai mille neuf cent soixante-huit[1]
16.5.68 *GB or* 5.16.68 *US*	16.5.68	le seize cinq soixante-huit
AD 230	230 apr. J.-C.	deux cent trente après Jésus-Christ
2500 BC	2500 av. J.-C.	deux mille cinq cents ans avant Jésus-Christ*
the 16th century	le XVIe siècle†	le seizième siècle

* (i) *There are two ways of saying hundreds and thousands in dates:*
1968 = mille neuf cent soixante-huit or *dix-neuf cent soixante-huit*

(ii) *The spelling* mil *is used in legal French, otherwise* mille *is used in dates, except when a round number of thousands is involved, in which case the words* l'an *are added:*
1900 = mille neuf cents
2000 = l'an deux mille

† *French prefers Roman numerals for centuries:*
the 16th century = le XVIe

Saying *on*

French uses only the definite article, without any word for on:

it happened on 6th March = c'est arrivé le 6 mars (*say* le six mars)
he came on the 21st = il est arrivé le 21 (*say* le vingt et un)
see you on the 6th = on se voit le 6 (*say* le six))
on the 2nd of every month = le 2 de chaque mois (*say* le deux ...)
he'll be here on the 3rd = il sera là le 3 (*say* le trois)

Saying *in*

French normally uses en *for years but prefers* en l'an *for out-of-the-ordinary dates:*

in 1968 = en 1968 (*say* en mille neuf cent soixante-huit *or* en dix-neuf cent ...)
in 1896 = en 1896 (*say* en mille huit cent quatre-vingt-seize *or* en dix-huit cent ...)
in the year 2000 = en l'an deux mille
in AD 27 = en l'an 27 (*say* l'an vingt-sept) de notre ère
in 132 BC = en l'an 132 (*say* l'an cent trente-deux) avant Jésus-Christ

With names of months, in *is translated by* en *or* au mois de:

in May 1970 = en mai mille neuf cent soixante-dix *or* au mois de mai mille neuf cent soixante-dix

With centuries, French uses au:

in the seventeenth century = au dix-septième siècle

The word siècle *is often omitted in colloquial French:*

in the eighteenth century = au dix-huitième siècle *or* (*less formally*) au dix-huitième

Note also:

in the early 12th century = au début du XIIe siècle (*say* du douzième siècle)
in the late 14th century = à *or* vers la fin du XIVe siècle (*say* du quatorzième siècle)

Phrases

Remember that the date in French always has the definite article, so, in combined forms, au *and* du *are required:*

from the 10th onwards = à partir du 10 (*say* du dix)
stay until the 14th = reste jusqu'au 14 (*say* au quatorze)
from 21st to 30th May = du 21 au 30 mai (*say* du vingt et un au trente mai)
around 16th May = le 16 mai environ/vers le 16 mai (*say* le seize mai) *or* aux environs du seize mai (*say* du seize mai)
not until 1999 = pas avant 1999 (*say* mille neuf cent quatre-vingt-dix-neuf)
Shakespeare (1564–1616) = Shakespeare (1564–1616) (*say* Shakespeare, quinze cent soixante-quatre – seize cent seize)
Shakespeare b. 1564 d.1616 = Shakespeare, né en 1564, mort en 1616 (*say* Shakespeare, né en quinze cent soixante-quatre, mort en seize cent seize). *Note that French has no abbreviations for* né *and* mort.
in May '45 = en mai 45 (*say* en mai quarante-cinq)
in the 1980s = dans les années 80 (*say* dans les années quatre-vingts)
in the early sixties = au début des années 60 (*say* des années soixante)
in the late seventies = à la fin des années 70 (*say* des années soixante-dix)
the riots of '68 = les émeutes de 68 (*say* de soixante-huit)
the 14–18 war = la guerre de 14 *or* de 14–18 (*say* de quatorze *or* de quatorze-dix-huit)
the 1912 uprising = le soulèvement de 1912 (*say* de mille neuf cent douze)

---

date; **let's set a ~ now** prenons date maintenant; **the ~ of the next meeting is**... la prochaine réunion est fixée au...; **the ~ for the match is June 5** le match aura lieu le 5 juin; **at a later ~** à une date ultérieure, plus tard; (in past tense) plus tard, par la suite; **at a** ou **some future ~** plus tard; **of recent ~** récent; **2** (year: of event) date *f*; (on coin) millésime *m*; **3** (meeting) rendez-vous *m*; **he has a ~ with Jane tonight** il sort avec Jane ce soir; **on our first ~** la première fois que nous sommes sortis ensemble; **I have a lunch ~ on Friday** je suis pris à déjeuner vendredi; **to make a ~ for Monday** prendre rendez-vous pour lundi; **4** (person one is going out with) **John is her ~ for the party** c'est John qui l'emmène à la soirée; **who's your ~ for tonight?** avec qui sors-tu ce soir?; **5** (pop concert) date *f*; **they're playing five ~s in Britain** ils font cinq dates en Grande-Bretagne; **6** (fruit) datte *f*; **7** (tree) (also **~ palm**) (palmier-)dattier *m*.

II to date *adv phr* à ce jour, jusqu'ici.

III *vtr* **1** (mark with date) [*person*] dater [*letter, cheque*]; [*machine*] imprimer la date sur [*envelope, document*]; **a cheque/letter ~d March 21st** un cheque daté/une lettre datée du 21 mars; **a statuette ~d 1875** une statuette portant la date 1875; **2** (identify age of) dater [*skeleton, building, object*]; **scientists have ~d the skeleton at 300 BC** d'après les scientifiques le squelette date de 300 ans avant J.-C.; **3** (reveal age of) **the style of clothing ~s the film** le style vestimentaire trahit l'âge du film; **4** (go out with) sortir avec [*person*].

IV *vi* **1** (originate) **to ~ from, to ~ back to** dater de, remonter à; **the church ~s from** ou **back to the 17th century** l'église date du XVIIe siècle; **her problems ~ from** ou **back to the accident** ses problèmes datent du jour or remontent au jour de l'accident; **these customs ~ from** ou **back to the Middle Ages** ces coutumes remontent à l'époque médiévale; **their friendship ~s from** ou **back to childhood** leur amitié remonte à l'enfance; **2** (become dated) [*clothes, style, slang*] se démoder. ▶ **out-of-date, up-to-date**.

dated /ˈdeɪtɪd/ *adj* [*clothes, style*] démodé; [*idea, convention, custom*] dépassé; [*word, expression, language*] vieilli; **the book/film seems** ou **looks rather ~ now** le livre/film a mal vieilli; **this style is becoming ~** ce style commence à dater.

dateline /ˈdeɪtlaɪn/ *n* **1** (on document, newspaper article) *lieu et date en tête d'article, de dépêche etc*; **2** Geog (also **date line**) ligne *f* de changement de date.

date: **~ palm** *n* (palmier-)dattier *m*; **~ rape** *n* viol *m* après une sortie en tête-à-tête à deux.

date stamp I *n* **1** (device) timbre *m* dateur; **2** (mark) cachet *m*, tampon *m*.

II date-stamp *vtr* dater, apposer la date sur [qch] (avec un timbre dateur) [*bill, envelope, receipt*]; (in post office) apposer le cachet de la poste sur [*envelope, letter*].

dating agency *n* club *m* de rencontres.

dative /ˈdeɪtɪv/ **I** *n* datif *m*; **in the ~** au datif.

II *adj* [*case*] datif/-ive; [*ending, noun*] au datif.

daub /dɔːb/ **I**○ *n* péj (painting) croûte○ *f* péj.

II *vtr* **to ~ sth on a wall, to ~ a wall with sth** couvrir or barbouiller○ un mur de qch; **she had ~ed makeup on her face, she had ~ed her face with makeup** péj elle s'était peinturlurée.

daughter /ˈdɔːtə(r)/ *n* lit, fig fille *f*.

daughter: **~board** *n* Comput carte-fille *f*; **~ cell** *n* Biol cellule *f* fille; **~ chromatide** *n* Biol chromatide *f* fille; **~ chromosome** *n* Biol chromosome *m* fils; **~-in-law** *n* (*pl* **daughters-in-law**) belle-fille *f*, bru *f*; **~ language** *n* Ling langue *f* fille.

daughterly /ˈdɔːtəlɪ/ *adj* filial.

daughter nucleus *n* Biol noyau-fils *m*.

daunt /dɔːnt/ *vtr* décourager; **to be ~ed by sth** être découragé par qch; **not to be ~ed by sth** ne pas se laisser décourager or démonter par qch; **nothing ~ed, she continued on her way** elle a continué sans se laisser démonter or abattre.

daunting /ˈdɔːntɪŋ/ *adj* [*task, prospect*] décourageant; [*person*] intimidant; **it is ~ to think/read** c'est affolant de penser/lire; **starting a new job/leaving home can be (quite) ~** c'est un pas difficile de commencer un nouveau travail/partir de chez soi; **they were faced with a ~ amount of work/range of possibilities** ils étaient découragés par tout le travail à faire/toutes les possibilités qui s'offraient à eux.

dauntless /ˈdɔːntlɪs/ *adj* intrépide, hardi.

dauntlessly /ˈdɔːntlɪslɪ/ *adv* avec intrépidité.

davenport /ˈdævnpɔːt/ *n* **1** GB (desk) secrétaire *m*; **2** US (sofa) canapé-lit *m*.

David /ˈdeɪvɪd/ *pr n* David.
IDIOMS **to be like ~ and Jonathan** être comme les deux doigts de la main.

davit /ˈdævɪt/ *n* Naut bossoir *m*.

Davy Jones's Locker /ˌdeɪvɪ dʒəʊnzɪz ˈlɒkə(r)/ *n* fig, hum **to go to ~** boire la grande tasse†○, se noyer.

Davy lamp /ˈdeɪvɪ læmp/ *n* lampe *f* Davy, lampe *f* de sûreté (*des mineurs*).

dawdle /ˈdɔːdl/ *vi* **1** (waste time) traîner, traînasser○; **he ~d over breakfast/his homework** il a traîné en prenant son petit déjeuner/en faisant ses devoirs; **2** (amble along) flâner; **he ~d along the road/around the streets** il a flâné sur la route/dans les rues; **she ~d back to the house/up the hill** elle est rentrée à la maison/a remonté la colline en flânant.

dawdler /ˈdɔːdlə(r)/ *n* traînard/-e *m/f*.

dawdling /ˈdɔːdlɪŋ/ *n* **no ~ on the way home!** ne traînez ou traînassez○ pas sur le chemin de retour!

dawn /dɔːn/ **I** *n* **1** lit aube *f*, aurore *f* liter; **at ~** à l'aube; **before** ou **by ~** avant l'aube; **at the crack of ~** lit, fig à l'aube; **~ broke** le jour se leva; **(I have to work) from ~ to** ou **till dusk** (je dois travailler) toute la sainte journée or du matin au soir; **2** fig (beginning) aube *f*; **the ~ of a new era/of a new century** l'aube d'une époque nouvelle/d'un nouveau siècle; **the ~ of socialism/Thatcherism** la naissance du socialisme/thatchérisme; **the ~ of a revolution** l'aube d'une révolution; **a new ~ in computer technology/in Europe** le début d'une nouvelle ère pour la technologie informatique/pour l'Europe; **the change in government was a false ~** le remaniement ministériel n'était porteur que de faux espoirs; **since the ~ of time** depuis la nuit des temps.
II *vi* **1** (become light) [*day*] se lever; **the day ~ed sunny and warm** le jour s'annonçait chaud et ensoleillé; **the day will ~ when** fig un jour viendra où; **a new age has ~ed** une nouvelle ère a vu le jour; **hope ~ed on the horizon** l'espoir commençait à poindre; **2** (become apparent) **it ~ed on me/him etc that** je me suis/il s'est etc rendu compte que; **it suddenly ~ed on him why/how** il a compris soudain pourquoi/comment.

dawn chorus *n* concert *m* matinal des oiseaux.

dawning /ˈdɔːnɪŋ/ **I** *n* fig naissance *f* fig.
II *adj* naissant.

dawn raid *n* descente *f* de police très tôt le matin.

day /deɪ/ ▶ **1807** **I** *n* **1** (24-hour period) jour *m*; **one summer's ~** un jour d'été; **what ~ is it today?** quel jour sommes-nous aujourd'hui? **~ after ~, ~ in ~ out** jour après jour; **every ~** tous les jours; **every other ~** tous les deux jours; **from ~ to ~** d'un jour à l'autre; **from one ~ to the next** d'un jour à l'autre; **from that ~ to this** depuis ce jour-là; **any ~ now** d'un jour à l'autre; **on a ~ to ~ basis** au jour le jour; **one ~, some ~** un jour; **one fine ~** fig un beau jour; **within ~s** en quelques jours; **it's not every ~ that...** ce n'est pas tous les jours que...; **the ~ when** ou **that** le jour où; **it's ~s since I've seen him** ça fait des jours que je ne l'ai pas vu, je ne l'ai pas vu depuis des jours; **it's 15 years to the ~ since...** ça fait 15 ans jour pour jour que...; **to come on the wrong ~** se tromper de jour; **it had to happen today of all ~s!** il fallait que cela arrive or que ça tombe○ aujourd'hui; **to this ~** aujourd'hui encore; **all ~ and every ~** sans arrêt tous les jours; **the ~ after** le lendemain; **the ~ before** la veille; **the ~ before yesterday** avant-hier; **the ~ after tomorrow** après-demain; **two ~s after/two ~s before the wedding** le surlendemain/l'avant-veille du mariage; **from that ~ onwards** dès lors; **from this ~ forth** littér désormais; **she becomes more proficient by the ~** elle devient chaque jour plus compétente; **2** (until evening) journée *f*; **working/school ~** journée de travail/scolaire; **a hard/busy ~** une journée difficile/occupée; **a ~ at the seaside/shops** une journée à la mer/dans les magasins; **an enjoyable ~'s tennis/golf** une agréable journée de tennis/golf; **all ~** toute la journée; **all that ~** tout le long de cette journée; **before the ~ was out** avant la fin de la journée; **during/for the ~** pendant/pour la journée; **to be paid by the ~** être payé à la journée; **to spend the ~ doing** passer la journée à faire; **to take all ~ doing** mettre la journée à faire; **pleased with their ~'s work** contents de leur journée; **we haven't got all ~!** nous n'avons pas la journée devant nous!; **it was a hot ~** il faisait chaud; **have a nice ~!** bonne journée!; **what a ~!** quelle journée!; **3** (as opposed to night) jour *m*; **it's almost ~** il fait presque jour; **the ~s are getting longer/shorter** les jours s'allongent/raccourcissent; **to be on** ou **to work ~s** être ou travailler de jour; **we rested by ~** nous nous reposions de jour; **at close of ~** littér à la tombée du jour; **4** (specific) jour *m*; **Independence/Ascension Day** jour de l'Indépendance/de l'Ascension; **Tuesday is my shopping ~** le mardi est mon jour de courses; **decision ~ for the government** le jour décisif pour le gouvernement; **the ~ of judgment** le jour du jugement dernier; **to her dying ~** jusqu'à son dernier jour; **I might forget my lines on the ~** j'oublierai peut-être mon texte, le jour venu; **it's not your ~ is it?** décidément c'est ton jour! iron; **I never thought I'd see the ~ when sb would do** je n'aurais jamais cru qu'il me serait donné de voir un jour quelqu'un faire; **5** (as historical period) (*gén pl*) époque *f*; **the ~s of rationing** l'époque du rationnement; **in those ~s** à cette époque; **of his ~** de son époque; **in his/their ~** (at that time) à son/leur époque; (at height of success, vitality) à son/leur heure; **in her younger ~s** dans sa jeunesse; **his early ~s as...** ses débuts en tant que...; **his fighting/dancing ~s** sa carrière de boxeur/de danseur; **these ~s** ces temps-ci; **to date from the ~s before sth** dater d'avant qch.
II *modif* [*job, nurse*] de jour.
IDIOMS **in ~s gone by** autrefois; **it's all in a ~'s work** c'est du quotidien; **not to give sb the time of ~** ne pas se donner la peine de saluer qn; **to pass the time of ~ with sb** échanger quelques mots avec qn; **it's one of those ~s!** il y a des jours comme ça!; **those were the ~s** c'était le bon temps; **to be a bit late in the ~** être un peu tard; **that'll be the ~!** je voudrais voir ça!; **to call it a ~** s'arrêter là; **to carry** ou **win/to lose the ~** avoir le dessus/dessous; **to have an off ~** ne pas être soi-même; **to have had its ~** avoir fait son temps; **to have seen better ~s** avoir connu des jours meilleurs; **he's 50 if he's a ~** il a 50 ans bien tassés○!; **to make a ~ of it** profiter de la journée; **to save the ~** sauver la situation; **to see the light of ~** apparaître au grand jour; **to take one ~ at a time** prendre les choses comme elles se présentent; **your ~ will come** ton heure arrivera. ▶ **week**.

day: **~bed** *n* Med (in hospital) lit *m* de jour; **~book** *n* Comm livre *m* de caisse; **~boy** *n* GB Sch externe *m*; **~break** *n* aube *f*.

day-care /ˌdeɪˈkeə(r)/ **I** *n* Soc Admin **1** (for infirm) (in centre) assistance *f* (sociale) de jour; (in own home) aide *f* familiale; **2** (for young children) service *m* de garderie.
II *adj* [*services*] d'assistance sociale.

day centre GB, **day center** US *n* centre *m* d'accueil.

daydream /ˈdeɪdriːm/ **I** *n* rêves *mpl*; **she was lost in a ~** elle était perdue dans ses rêves.
II *vi* rêver (**about** de; **about doing** de faire); pej rêvasser.

day: **~dreamer** *n* rêveur/-euse *m/f*; **~girl** *n* Sch externe *f*; **~ labourer** GB, **~ laborer** US *n* journalier *m*.

daylight /ˈdeɪlaɪt/ **I** *n* **1** (light) jour *m*, lumière *f* du jour; **it was still ~** il faisait encore jour; **we have two hours of ~ left** on a encore deux heures avant la tombée de la nuit; **in (the) ~** (by day) de jour; (in natural light) à la lumière du jour; **2** (dawn) lever *m* du jour, point *m* du jour; **they left before ~** ils sont partis avant le lever du jour.
II *modif* [*attack, bombing, raid*] de jour; **during ~ hours** pendant qu'il fait jour.
IDIOMS **to see ~** (understand) y voir clair; (finish) voir le bout du tunnel; **to beat** ou **knock the living ~s out of sb**○ tabasser○ qn; **I'll beat** ou **knock the living ~s out of you**○! je vais te flanquer une (bonne) raclée○!

daylight robbery○ *n* **it's ~!** c'est de l'arnaque○!, c'est du vol manifeste!

daylight saving time, **DST** *n* heure *f* d'été.

day: **~ nursery** *n* garderie *f*; **~ pass** *n* (in skiing) forfait *m* pour la journée.

day release **I** *n* **on ~** en formation.
II **day-release** *modif* **day-release course** stage *m* de formation en alternance.

day: **~ return (ticket)** *n* GB Rail aller-retour *m* valable une journée; **~room** *n* foyer *m*; **~ school** *n* externat *m*.

day shift *n* **1** (time period) service *m* de jour; **to be on ~** être de jour; **2** (team) équipe *f* de jour.

daytime /ˈdeɪtaɪm/ **I** *n* journée *f*; **during** ou **in the ~** pendant la journée.
II *modif* [*hours, supervision, activity*] de jour.

day-to-day /ˌdeɪtəˈdeɪ/ *adj* quotidien/-ienne; **on a ~ basis** au jour le jour.

day: **~-trip** /ˈdeɪtrɪp/ *n* excursion *f* pour la journée; **~-tripper** *n* excursionniste *mf*.

daze /deɪz/ **I** *n* **in a ~** (from blow) étourdi; (from drug) hébété; (from news) ahuri; **I am in a complete ~ this morning** je suis dans le brouillard ce matin; **to be going around in a ~** (after bad news) avoir l'air un peu secoué; (after good news) avoir l'air aux anges.
II *vtr* **to be ~d by** être étourdi par [*fall*]; être ahuri or abasourdi par [*news*].

dazed /deɪzd/ *adj* (by blow) hébété; (by news) ahuri; **he looks a bit ~** il a l'air tout étourdi.

dazzle /ˈdæzl/ **I** *n* (of sth shiny) éclat *m*; (of sunlight, torch) lumière *f* aveuglante.
II *vtr* [*sun, torch*] éblouir, aveugler; [*skill, beauty, wealth*] éblouir; **my eyes were** ou **I was ~d by the sun** j'étais ébloui or aveuglé par la lumière du soleil; **to ~ sb with** fig éblouir qn par.

dazzling /ˈdæzlɪŋ/ *adj* [*beauty, achievement, performance*] éblouissant; [*sun, light*] aveuglant, éblouissant.

dazzlingly /ˈdæzlɪŋlɪ/ *adv* **~ beautiful/white** d'une beauté/blancheur éblouissante; **a ~ successful career** une carrière éblouissante.

dB (*abrév écrite* = **decibel**) dB.

DBMS *n* Comput *abrév* ▶**database management system**.

DBS *n* TV *abrév* ▶**direct broadcasting by satellite**.

DC 1 Elec *abrév* ▶**direct current**; **2** Geog *abrév* ▶**District of Columbia**; **3** Mus (*abrév écrite* = **da capo**) DC.

dd Comm **1** *abrév écrite* ▶**direct debit**; **2** *abrév écrite* ▶**demand deposit**.

DD *n* Univ *abrév* ▶**Doctor of Divinity**.

D-day /ˈdi: deɪ/ *n* **1** (important day) jour *m* J; **2** Mil Hist le 6 juin 1944 (*jour du débarquement des Alliés en Normandie*).

DDP *n*: *abrév* ▶**distributed data processing**.

DDT *n* Chem DDT *m*.

DE US Post *abrév écrite* = **Delaware**.

DEA *n* US (*abrév* = **Drug Enforcement Agency**) *organisme de répression du trafic de drogue* ≈ Brigade des stupéfiants.

deacon /ˈdi:kən/ *n* diacre *m*.

deaconess /ˌdi:kəˈnes, ˈdi:kənɪs/ *n* (female deacon) femme *f* diacre; (in early church) diaconesse *f*.

dead /ded/ **I** *n* **1 the ~** (+ *v pl*) (people) les morts *mpl*; **a monument to the ~** un monument aux morts; **2** (death) **to rise/be raised from the ~** ressusciter/être ressuscité d'entre les morts; **3** fig (depths) **at ~ of night, in the ~ of night** en pleine nuit, au cœur de la nuit; **in the ~ of winter** en plein hiver, au cœur de l'hiver.
II *adj* **1** (no longer living) [*person*] mort, décédé; [*animal, tree, flower, leaf, skin*] mort; **the ~ man/woman** le mort/la morte; **a ~ body** un cadavre; **to drop (down) ~** tomber raide mort; **to play ~** faire le mort/la morte; **drop ~**○**!** va te faire voir○!; **to shoot sb ~** abattre qn; **~ and buried** lit, fig mort et enterré; **they're all ~ and gone now** ils nous ont tous quittés maintenant; **more ~ than alive** plus mort que vif; **'wanted, ~ or alive'** 'recherché, mort ou vif'; **to leave sb for ~** laisser qn pour mort; **to give sb up for ~** tenir qn pour mort; **I'm absolutely ~**○ **after that walk!** (exhausted) je suis absolument mort○ après cette marche!; **2** (extinct) [*language*] mort; [*custom, law*] désuet/-ète, tombé en désuétude; [*issue, debate*] dépassé; [*cigarette*] éteint; [*fire*] éteint, mort; [*match*] usagé; **are these glasses ~?** GB avez-vous fini avec ces verres?; **3** (dull, not lively) [*place*] mort; [*audience*] apathique; **the ~ season** la morte-saison; **4** (not functioning, idle) [*battery*] à plat; [*bank account*] dormant; [*capital, money*] improductif/-ive, inactif/-ive; [*file*] qu'on ne consulte plus; **the phone went ~** tout d'un coup il n'y avait plus de tonalité (sur la ligne); **5** (impervious) **to be ~ to sth** être insensible à qch; **6** (numb) [*limb*] engourdi; **my arm has gone ~** mon bras s'est engourdi; **7** (absolute) **a ~ calm** un calme plat; **~ silence** silence de mort; **to be a ~ shot**○ être un tireur d'élite; **to come to a ~ stop** s'arrêter net; **she hit the target in the ~ centre** elle a atteint la cible en plein milieu.
III *adv* surtout GB (absolutely, completely) absolument; **are you ~ certain?** est-ce que tu es absolument sûr?, est-ce que tu es sûr et certain?; **he was staring ~ ahead** il regardait droit devant lui; **sail ~ ahead** navigue droit devant; **~ in the middle of the street** en plein milieu de la rue; **to be ~ level** être parfaitement plat; **to be ~ on time** être pile○ à l'heure; **I left (at) ~ on six o'clock** je suis parti à six heures pile○ or sonnantes; **it's ~ easy**○**!** c'est simple comme bonjour○!; **his shot was ~ on target** son coup était en plein dans le mille; **they were ~ lucky**○ **not to get caught!** ils ont eu du pot○ de ne pas se faire prendre!; **~ drunk**○ ivre mort; **~ tired**○ crevé○, claqué○; **I was ~ scared**○**!** j'avais une trouille bleue○!; **you're ~ right**○**!** tu as parfaitement raison!; **~ good!** génial○!; **'~ slow'** Aut 'roulez au pas'; **to drive ~ slow** rouler au pas; **~ straight** absolument or tout à fait droit; **to be ~ against** être totalement opposé à [*idea, plan*]; **to be ~ set on doing** être tout à fait décidé à faire; **he's ~ on**○ **for that job** US il est sûr de décrocher ce poste; **you're ~ on**○**!** US tu as tout à fait raison!; **to stop ~** s'arrêter net; **to cut sb ~** snober qn.
IDIOMS **to be ~ to the world** dormir comme une souche, être dans les bras de Morphée liter; **I wouldn't be seen ~ wearing that hat!** je ne porterais ce chapeau pour rien au monde!; **I wouldn't be seen ~ in a place like that!** pour rien au monde je ne voudrais être vu dans un endroit pareil!; **the affair is ~ but it won't lie down** l'affaire est loin d'être enterrée; **~ men tell no tales** Prov les morts ne parlent pas; **the only good traitor is a ~ traitor** un bon traître est un traître mort; **you do that and you're ~ meat**○**!** US tu fais ça et je te tue!

dead: **~ air** *n* ¢ Radio, TV blancs *mpl*; **~-and-alive** *adj* GB péj [*place*] mort; **~ ball** *n* ballon *m* sorti; **~-ball line** *n* (in rugby) ligne *f* du ballon mort; **~beat**○ *n* fainéant/-e *m/f*; **~-beat**○ *adj* éreinté, claqué○; **~bolt** *n* verrou *m* à bouton; **~ centre** *n* Tech point *m* mort.

dead duck○ *n* GB **to be a ~** [*scheme, proposal, person*] être fichu○.

deaden /ˈdedn/ *vtr* calmer, endormir [*pain*]; amortir [*blow, shock*]; assourdir [*sound*]; émousser [*enthusiasm, passion*]; [*anaesthetic*] endormir [*nerve*].

dead end /ˌdedˈend/ **I** *n* lit, fig impasse *f*; **to come to a ~** aboutir à une impasse.
II dead-end /ˈdedend/ *adj* [*job etc*] sans perspectives.

deadening /ˈdednɪŋ/ **I** *n* (of blow) amortissement *m*; (of sound) assourdissement *m*.
II *adj* Med [*effect*] anesthésiant; **the ~ effect of television on the imagination** l'effet abrutissant de la télévision sur l'imagination.

dead hand *n* péj **the ~ of bureaucracy/of the past** le poids de la bureaucratie/du passé.

deadhead /ˈdedhed/ **I** *n* **1** GB péj (stupid person) nullité *f*; **2** US (hippy) hippie *mf*; **3** US (person with free ticket) personne *f* munie d'un billet gratuit; **4** US Transp (truck) camion *m* roulant à vide; (train) train *m* roulant à vide.
II *vtr* enlever les fleurs fanées de [*plant*].

dead heat *n* (in athletics) arrivée *f* ex-aequo; (in horseracing) dead-heat *m inv*; **it was a ~** ils ont fini ex-aequo.

dead letter *n* Post lettre *f* au rebut; **to become a ~** fig [*law, custom, rule etc*] tomber en désuétude, devenir lettre morte.

dead: **~ letter box, ~ letter drop** *n* boîte *f* aux lettres; **~-letter office** *n* Post bureau *m* des rebuts.

deadline /ˈdedlaɪn/ *n* date *f* or heure *f* limite, délai *m*; **to meet a ~** respecter un délai; **to miss a ~** dépasser la date or l'heure limite, dépasser les délais; **I have a 10 o'clock ~ for this article** je dois avoir fini cet article pour dix heures; **applicants must be able to meet ~s** les candidats doivent être capables de travailler dans des délais très courts; **they have to work to very tight ~s** ils doivent travailler dans des délais très serrés; **the ~ for applications is the 15th** les candidatures doivent être déposées avant le 15.

deadliness /ˈdedlɪnɪs/ *n* (of poison, disease, blow) caractère *m* mortel; (of weapon) caractère *m* meurtrier.

deadlock /ˈdedlɒk/ **I** *n* **1** (impasse) impasse *f*; **to reach (a) ~** aboutir à une impasse; **to be at (a) ~** être dans une impasse; **to break the ~ between management and unions** sortir la direction et les syndicats de l'impasse; **2** (lock) verrou *m* haute sécurité.
II deadlocked *pp adj* [*negotiations, situation*] dans l'impasse.

dead loss *n* **1**○ pej (person) zéro○ *m*, bon à rien *m*; **the film was a ~** le film ne valait rien, le film était nul○; **these scissors are a ~!** ces ciseaux ne valent rien!; **2** Comm perte *f* sèche.

deadly /ˈdedlɪ/ **I** *adj* **1** (lethal) [*poison, disease, attack*] mortel/-elle; [*weapon*] meurtrier/-ière; fig [*enemy*] mortel/-elle; [*hatred*] meurtrier/-ière; [*rivalry*] acharné; [*insult*] dévastateur/-trice; **his aim is ~** [*gunman*] il tire avec une précision mortelle; [*sports player*] ses coups sont extrêmement précis; **the cold was ~** il faisait terriblement froid; **2** (absolute, extreme) **in ~ earnest** avec le plus grand sérieux; **with ~ accuracy** avec la plus grande précision; **3**○ (dull, boring) [*person, event*] mortel/-elle○, rasant○; **4** (deathlike) [*pallor, silence*] de mort.
II *adv* [*dull, boring*] mortellement, terriblement; **~ pale** pâle comme la mort; **to be ~ serious** être des plus sérieux.

deadly nightshade *n* belladone *f*.

deadly sin *n* péché *m* capital; **the seven ~ sins** les sept péchés capitaux.

dead: **~ man's fingers** *n* (+ *v sg*) (coral) alcyon *m*; **~ man's handle** *n* Tech poignée *f* de sécurité; Rail manette *f*; **~ matter** *n* matière *f* inanimée or inerte; **~ men**○ *npl* GB (empty bottles) bouteilles *fpl* vides, cadavres○ *mpl*.

deadness /ˈdednɪs/ *n* (of place) tristesse *f*, caractère *m* morne; (of expression, eyes) tristesse *f*.

dead: **~nettle** *n* ortie *f* blanche; **~ on arrival, DOA** *adj* Med mort avant d'arriver à l'hôpital.

deadpan /ˈdedpæn/ **I** *adj* [*humour*] pince-sans-rire *inv*; [*expression, face*] de marbre.
II *adv* d'un air pince-sans-rire.

dead reckoning *n* Naut estime *f*; **by ~** à l'estime.

dead ringer○ *n* **to be a ~ for sb** être le sosie de qn.

dead: **Dead Sea** *pr n* mer *f* Morte; **Dead Sea Scrolls** *npl* manuscrits *mpl* de la mer Morte.

dead set *n* GB **to make a ~ at sb** chercher à mettre le grappin sur qn○; **to make a ~ at sth** s'acharner comme un fou pour obtenir qch.

dead stock *n* ¢ **1** Comm invendus *mpl*; **2** Agric bâtiments *mpl* et matériel *m*.

dead weight *n* **1** gen lit poids *m* mort; fig (burden) poids *m*; **2** Naut charge *f* en lourd; **3** US fig (unproductive staff) personnel *m* inutile.

dead wood *n* lit bois *m* mort; GB fig personnel *m* inutile.

deaf /def/ **I** *n* **the ~** (+ *v pl*) les sourds *mpl*, les malentendants *mpl* voir note.
II *adj* **1** [*person, animal*] sourd voir note; **to go ~** devenir sourd; **to be ~ in one ear** être sourd d'une oreille; **that's his ~ ear** il n'entend pas de cette oreille, il est sourd de cette oreille; **2** fig **to be ~ to** être sourd à; **to turn a ~ ear to** faire la sourde oreille à, rester sourd à; **to fall on ~ ears** [*request, advice*] ne pas trouver d'écho.
IDIOMS **to be as ~ as a post**○ être sourd comme un pot○; **there are none so ~ as**

those who will not hear Prov il n'est pire sourd que celui qui ne veut pas entendre Prov.

■ Note Ce mot peut être perçu comme injurieux dans cette acception. Lui préférer *hearing-impaired*.

deaf: **~ aid** *n* GB prothèse *f* auditive, appareil *m* de correction auditive; **~-and-dumb** *n, adj* injur = **deaf without speech**.

deafen /'defn/ *vtr* assourdir, rendre [qn] sourd.

deafening /'defnɪŋ/ *adj* assourdissant.

deafeningly /'defnɪŋlɪ/ *adv* **~ loud** assourdissant.

deaf-mute /ˌdef'mju:t/ *n, adj* sourd-muet/sourde-muette (*m/f*).

deafness /'defnɪs/ *n* surdité *f*.

deaf without speech **I** *n (+ v pl)* **the ~** les sourds-muets *mpl*.
II *adj* sourd-muet/sourde-muette.

deal /di:l/ **I** *n* **1** (agreement) gen accord *m*; (in commerce, finance) affaire *f*; (with friend, criminal) marché *m*; **the pay/OPEC ~** l'accord salarial/de l'OPEC; **to make** ou **strike a ~ with sb** gen passer un accord avec qn; (in business) conclure une affaire avec qn; **to do a ~ with** faire un marché avec [*friend, kidnapper, criminal*]; négocier une affaire avec [*client, company*]; **to do a ~** (in business) conclure une affaire; (with friend, colleague) s'arranger; (with criminal) faire un marché; **to pull off a ~** mener à bien une affaire; **it's a ~!** marché conclu!; **the ~'s off** le marché est rompu; **it's no ~!** pas question!; **a good ~** une bonne affaire; **to get the best of a ~** se tirer au mieux d'une affaire; **it's all part of the ~** (part of the arrangement) ça fait partie du marché; (part of the price, package) c'est inclus dans le reste; **to be in on the ~** être dans le coup○; **2** (sale) vente *f*; **cash/credit ~** vente au comptant/à crédit; **property/arms ~** vente immobilière/d'armes; **3** (special offer, bargain) **for the best ~(s) in** ou **on electrical goods come to Electrotech** pour les meilleurs prix or les prix les plus bas en électroménager venez à Electrotech; **I got a good ~ on a used Fiat** j'ai fait une bonne affaire en achetant une Fiat d'occasion; **4** (amount) **a great** ou **good ~** beaucoup (**of** de); **he's a good ~ older than me** il est beaucoup plus âgé que moi; **they have a great ~ in common** ils ont beaucoup de choses en commun; **she travels a great ~** elle voyage beaucoup; **she means a great ~ to me** je l'aime beaucoup; **this job means a great ~ to me** ce travail est très important pour moi; **5** (treatment) **to get a good/bad ~ (from sb)** être bien/mal traité (par qn); **to give sb a fair ~** agir loyalement envers qn; **he got a raw** ou **rotten ~** il n'a vraiment pas eu de chance; **6** Games (in cards) donne *f*; **it's my ~** c'est à moi de donner; **7** (timber) bois *m* blanc.
II *vtr* (*prét, pp* **dealt**) **1** gen **to ~ a blow to sb/sth** ou **to ~ sb/sth a blow** lit, fig porter un coup à qn/qch (**with** avec); **2** Games (also **~ out**) distribuer [*cards*]; donner [*hand*].
III *vi* (*prét, pp* **dealt**) Comm, Fin (carry on business) [*person,firm*] être en activité; (operate on stock exchange) faire des opérations boursières; **to ~ in** être dans le commerce de [*commodity, product, shares*]; **we ~ in software** noussommes dans le commerce des logiciels; **we don't ~ in blackmail** fig le chantage n'est pas notre affaire.
IDIOMS **big ~**○! iron la belle affaire! iron; **it's no big ~**○ (modestly) il n'y a pas de quoi en faire un plat○; **if I lose it's no big ~**○ si je perds ce n'est pas dramatique; **to make a big ~ out of sth** faire tout un plat○ de qch.
■ **deal out**: **~ out [sth], ~ [sth] out** **1** (distribute) distribuer [*money, profit, cards*]; **2** (mete out) administrer [*punishment, fine*].
■ **deal with**: ¶ **~ with [sth]** **1** (sort out) s'occuper de [*complaint, emergency, matter, request, situation, work*]; faire face à [*social problem*]; **leave it to James, he'll ~ with it** laisse ça à James, il s'en occupera; **new measures to ~ with vandalism** de nouvelles mesures pour faire face au vandalisme; **2** (consider, discuss) traiter de [*topic, question, issue*]; ¶ **~ with [sb]** **1** (attend to, handle) s'occuper de [*client, customer, patient, public, troublemaker*]; **she's a difficult person to ~ with** elle est difficile (à vivre), elle n'est pas commode; **he did not ~ fairly with us** il n'a pas été correct avec nous; **2** (do business with) traiter avec [*person, company, terrorist organization*]; [*supplier*] vendre à [*public*]; [*customer*] se fournir chez [*stockist*].

dealer /'di:lə(r)/ ▶ **1692** *n* **1** Comm marchand/-e *m/f*; (on a large scale) négociant/-e *m/f*; (for a specific make of car, product) concessionnaire *m*; **art/carpet ~** marchand/-e *m/f* de tableaux/tapis; **authorized ~, licensed ~** revendeur *m* agréé; **second-hand car ~** marchand/-e *m/f* de voitures d'occasion; **2** (trafficker) gen trafiquant/-e *m/f*; **arms ~** trafiquant/-e d'armes; **3** (on stock exchange) opérateur/-trice *m/f*; **4** Games donneur/-euse *m/f*; **5** (drug pusher) revendeur/-euse *m/f* de drogue, dealer○ *m*.

dealership /'di:ləʃɪp/ *n* Comm concession *f* (**for** de).

dealing /'di:lɪŋ/ **I** *n* **1** Comm vente *f*; (on stock exchange) opération *f*; **foreign exchange ~** les opérations de change; **~ resumed this morning** les transactions ont repris ce matin; **~ is slow on the London Stock Exchange** la Bourse de Londres est calme; **there's heavy ~ in oil shares** les actions pétrolières sont très actives; **share ~** transactions *fpl* boursières; **the company has a reputation for fair ~** la compagnie a la réputation d'être honnête en affaires; **~ in luxury goods is profitable** le commerce de luxe est rentable; **2** Games donne *f*; **3** (trafficking) trafic *m*; **arms/drugs ~** le trafic d'armes/de drogue.
II dealings *npl* gen relations *fpl* (**with** avec) ; Comm relations *fpl* commerciales (**with** avec); **to have ~s with sb** traiter avec qn; **we've had business ~s with him for five years** nous traitons avec lui depuis cinq ans; **I don't want any further ~s with her** je ne veux plus rien avoir à faire avec elle.
III *modif* [*cost, firm, service*] commercial.

dealing room *n* Fin salle *f* des opérations.

dealmaker /'di:lmeɪkə(r)/ *n* opérateur/-trice *m/f*.

dealt /delt/ *prét, pp* ▶ **deal**.

dean /di:n/ *n* Univ, Relig doyen *m*.

deanery /'di:nərɪ/ *n* Relig (residence) doyenné *m*, presbytère *m*; (jurisdiction) doyenné *m*; (duties) décanat *m*.

deanship /'di:nʃɪp/ *n* **1** Univ poste *m* de doyen; **2** Relig décanat *m*.

dear /dɪə(r)/ **I** *n* (term of address) (affectionate) mon chéri/ma chérie *m/f*; (more formal, old-fashioned) mon cher/ma chère *m/f*; **Anne ~,...** (affectionate) Anne chérie...; (less close) ma chère Anne...; **that's 50 pence, ~**○ c'est 50 pence ma petite dame○; **you poor ~** (to child) mon pauvre chou○; (to adult) mon/ma pauvre; **all the old ~s**○ toutes les petites vieilles○; **our uncle is a ~** notre oncle est adorable; **be a ~ and answer the phone** sois gentil or (more affectionate) sois un amour, réponds au téléphone.
II *adj* **1** (expressing attachment) [*friend, mother*] cher/chère; **my ~** ou **~est girl/Anne** (patronizing) ma fille/ma chère Anne; **my ~ fellow** (insisting) cher ami; **she's a very ~ friend of mine** c'est une très bonne amie à moi; **he's my ~est friend** c'est mon meilleur ami; **~ old Richard** ce bon vieux Richard; **to hold sb/sth very ~** être très attaché à or chérir qn/qch; **their niece/freedom is very ~ to them** leur nièce/la liberté leur est très chère; **the project is ~ to his heart** le projet lui tient vraiment à cœur; **her ~est wish is to do** son vœu le plus cher est de faire; **2** (expressing admiration) [*dress, house*] mignon/-onne; [*puppy*] adorable; **a ~ old lady** une vieille dame adorable; **she's a ~ child** (in appearance) elle est mignonne; (in behaviour) c'est un amour d'enfant; **3** (in letter) cher/chère; **Dear Sir/Madam** Monsieur/Madame; **Dear Sirs** Messieurs; **Dear Mr Jones** Cher Monsieur; **Dear Mr and Mrs Jones** Cher Monsieur, Chère Madame; **Dear Anne** Chère Anne; **Dear Anne and Paul** Chère Anne, cher Paul or Chers Anne et Paul; **My ~ Catherine** Ma chère Catherine; **Dearest Robert** Mon très cher Robert; **4** (expensive) [*article, shop, workman*] cher/chère; **to get ~er** augmenter.
III *adv* lit, fig [*buy, cost*] cher.
IV *excl* **oh ~!** (dismay, surprise) oh mon Dieu!; (less serious) aïe!, oh là là!; **~ me** ou **~ ~, what a mess!** oh là là, quel désordre!; **~ me, no!** certainement pas!

dear heart *n* mon chéri/ma chérie *m/f*.

dearie○ /'dɪərɪ/ **I** *n* (term of address) (to friend) mon chéri/ma chérie *m/f*; (to customer) ma petite dame○.
II *excl* **~ me**†! or hum oh là là!

Dear John letter *n* lettre *f* de rupture.

dearly /'dɪəlɪ/ *adv* **1** (very much) **to love sb ~** aimer tendrement qn; **to love sth ~** être très attaché à qch; **they would ~ love to see you** ils seraient ravis de te voir; **I would ~ love to know** je payerais cher pour savoir; **our ~ beloved son** fml notre fils bien-aimé; **'~ beloved,...'** Relig 'mes bien chers frères,...'; **2** fig [*pay, buy*] chèrement; **~ bought** chèrement payé.
IDIOMS **to sell one's life ~** vendre chèrement sa vie.

dearth /dɜ:θ/ *n* (of books, young people, ideas) manque *m*, pénurie *f* (**of** de); **there is a ~ of funds** ce sont les fonds qui manquent.

deary○ *n, excl* = **dearie**.

death /deθ/ *n* (of person) mort *f*, décès *m*; (of animal) mort *f*; fig (of hopes, plans, dreams, civilization, democracy) anéantissement *m*; **at (the time of) his ~** à sa mort; **a ~ in the family** un décès dans la famille; **~ by hanging/drowning** mort par pendaison/noyade; **to starve/freeze to ~** mourir de faim/de froid; **to burn to ~** mourir carbonisé; **to put sb to ~** exécuter qn; **to sentence sb to ~** Jur condamner qn à mort; **~ to the king!** mort au roi!; **a fight to the ~** un combat à mort; **they fought to the ~** ils se sont battus à mort; **to drink oneself to ~** se tuer en buvant; **to work oneself to ~** se tuer au travail or à la tâche; **she's working herself to ~!** elle se tue au travail!; **she fell to her ~** elle s'est tuée en tombant; **she jumped to her ~** elle s'est tuée en sautant dans le vide; **he met his ~ in a skiing accident** il a trouvé la mort dans un accident de ski; **to come close to ~** friser la mort; **he remains a controversial figure in ~ as in life** il reste un personnage controversé aussi bien mort que vivant; **to die a violent ~** mourir de mort violente; **to do sb to ~** assassiner qn; **that excuse/joke has been done to ~** fig cette excuse/blague est éculée or est vieille comme le monde; **that play has been done to ~** cette pièce a été jouée tant de fois qu'on finit par s'en lasser; **they were united in ~** ils ont été unis dans la mort; **till ~ do us part** jusqu'à ce que la mort nous sépare; **'Deaths'** Journ 'Rubrique Nécrologique'; **a fall would mean** ou **spell ~** une chute serait fatale; **this means** ou **spells the ~ of the old industries** cela va être la mort des vieilles industries.
IDIOMS **to die a** ou **the ~** [*fashion*] disparaître complètement; [*entertainer, play*] faire un bide○; **he died the ~** il aurait voulu rentrer sous terre; **those children will be the ~ of me!** ces enfants me tueront!; **that thesis/car will be the ~ of her!** cette

thèse/voiture la tuera!; **don't tell him, it will be the ~ of him** ne le lui dis pas, ça l'achèvera; **it's a matter of life or ~** c'est une question de vie ou de mort; **to look like ~ warmed up** avoir l'air d'un cadavre ambulant; **I feel like ~ (warmed up)!** je ne me sens pas bien du tout!; **to be at ~'s door** être à (l'article de) la mort; **to be worried to ~**○ se ronger les sangs (**about** au sujet de) ; **to be frightened to ~**○ être mort de peur; **to frighten** ou **scare sb to ~** faire une peur bleue à qn○; **to be bored to ~**○ s'ennuyer à mourir; **I'm sick** ou **tired to ~**○ **of this!** j'en ai par-dessus la tête!, j'en ai ras le bol○!; **you'll catch your ~ (of cold)**○ tu vas crever○ or mourir de froid; ▶ **thousand**.

deathbed /ˈdeθbed/ **I** *n* lit *m* de mort; **on one's ~** sur son lit de mort.
II *modif* **to make a ~ conversion/confession** se convertir/se confesser sur son lit de mort; **~ scene** Cin, Theat scène *f* de l'agonie.

death benefit *n* GB capital décès *m*.

death blow *n* lit, fig coup *m* de grâce; **to deal sb/sth a ~** lit, fig donner le coup de grâce à qn/qch.

death: **~ camp** *n* camp *m* de la mort; **~ cell** *n* cellule *f* de condamné à mort; **~ certificate** *n* Jur acte *m* de décès; **~ duties** *npl* droits *mpl* de succession; **~ duty** *n* GB = **death duties**; **~ grant** *n* GB allocation *f* de décès; **~house** *n* US quartier *m* des condamnés à mort.

death knell /ˈdeθnel/ *n* lit, fig glas *m*; **to sound** ou **toll the ~ for** ou **of** fig sonner le glas de [*democracy, régime*].

deathless /ˈdeθlɪs/ *adj* immortel/-elle; **~ prose** iron prose *f* inoubliable.

death: **~like** *adj* = **deathly** I; **~ list** *n* liste *f* noire.

deathly /ˈdeθlɪ/ **I** *adj* [*pallor*] cadavérique; [*calm, silence*] de mort.
II *adv* **~ pale** d'une pâleur cadavérique, pâle comme la mort; **the house was ~ quiet** il y avait un silence de mort dans la maison.

death: **Death March** *n* Mus marche *f* funèbre; **~ mask** *n* masque *m* mortuaire or funéraire; **~ penalty** *n* peine *f* de mort; **~ rate** *n* taux *m* de mortalité; **~ rattle** *n* râle *m* d'agonie; **~ ray** *n* rayon *m* mortel; **~ roll** *n* liste *f* des morts.

death row *n* US quartier *m* des condamnés à mort; **to be on ~** être dans le quartier des condamnés à mort.

death sentence *n* lit, fig condamnation *f* à mort; **to pass a ~** prononcer une condamnation à mort.

death: **~'s head** *n* tête *f* de mort; **~'s head moth** *n* Zool sphinx *m* tête-de-mort; **~ squad** *n* escadron *m* de la mort; **~ threat** *n* menaces *fpl* de mort.

death throes *npl* lit, fig agonie *f*; **in one's ~** à l'agonie.

death toll *n* nombre *m* de morts; **the ~ has risen to thirty** le nombre de morts est passé à trente.

death trap *n* **to be a ~** être très dangereux.

death warrant *n* ordre *m* d'exécution; **to sign one's own ~** fig signer son propre arrêt de mort.

death watch beetle *n* vrillette *f*.

death wish *n* gen, Psych pulsion *f* de mort; **to have a ~** fig [*government, organization*] courir à sa perte.

deb○ /deb/ *n* = **debutante**.

debacle /deɪˈbɑːkl/ *n* fiasco *m*, débâcle *f*.

debag○ /ˌdiːˈbæg/ *vtr* GB déculotter.

debar /dɪˈbɑː(r)/ (*p prés etc* **-rr-**) *vtr* **to ~ sb from** exclure qn de [*club, ceremony, race*]; **to be ~red from voting** ne pas avoir le droit de voter.

debark /dɪˈbɑːk/ *vtr, vi* débarquer.

debarkation /ˌdiːbɑːˈkeɪʃn/ *n* débarquement *m*.

debase /dɪˈbeɪs/ **I** *vtr* **1** (lower value, quality of) dégrader [*emotion, ideal*]; abâtardir [*word*]; déprécier [*metal, currency*]; **2** (degrade) rabaisser [*person*].
II debased *pp adj* [*language*] appauvri; [*version*] appauvri, dégradé.
III *v refl* **to ~ oneself** se rabaisser (**by doing** en faisant).

debasement /dɪˈbeɪsmənt/ *n* **1** (of person, emotion) rabaissement *m*; (of word) abâtardissement *m*; **2** (of metal, currency) dépréciation *f*.

debatable /dɪˈbeɪtəbl/ *adj* discutable; **that's ~!** cela se discute!; **it is ~ whether** on peut se demander si.

debate /dɪˈbeɪt/ **I** *n* (formal) débat *m* (**on, about** sur); (more informal) discussion *f* (**about** à propos de); **parliamentary ~** débats *mpl* parlementaires; **the abortion ~** le débat sur l'avortement; **to hold a ~** organiser un débat; **to hold a ~ on** débattre de [*issue, proposal*]; **after (a) lengthy ~** après avoir longuement discuté; **to be open to ~** être discutable; **the plan is still under ~** on discute encore du plan.
II *vtr* gen, Pol (formally) débattre de [*issue, proposal, bill*]; (more informally) discuter de [*question*] (**with** avec); **I am debating whether to leave** je me demande si je dois partir; **a much ~d issue** un sujet très controversé.
III *vi* **to ~ about sth** discuter de qch (**with** avec).

debater /dɪˈbeɪtə(r)/ *n* débatteur/-euse *m/f*; **she's a good ~** elle excelle dans les débats.

debating /dɪˈbeɪtɪŋ/ *n* art *m* du débat.

debating: **~ point** *n* argument *m*; **~ society** *n* association *f* qui organise des débats.

debauch /dɪˈbɔːtʃ/ **I** *n* partie *f* de débauche.
II *vtr* dépraver.

debauched /dɪˈbɔːtʃt/ *adj* [*person*] débauché; **a ~ life** une vie de débauché.

debauchery /dɪˈbɔːtʃərɪ/ *n* débauche *f*.

debenture /dɪˈbentʃə(r)/ *n* **1** Fin obligation *f*; **2** Comm (also **customs ~**) autorisation *f* de perfectionnement actif.

debenture: **~ bond** *n* certificat *m* d'obligation; **~ holder** *n* obligataire *mf*; **~ stock** *n* obligations *fpl* non garanties.

debilitate /dɪˈbɪlɪteɪt/ *vtr* **1** (physically) débiliter; **2** (morally) démoraliser.

debilitating /dɪˈbɪlɪteɪtɪŋ/ *adj* **1** [*disease*] débilitant; **2** [*economic conditions, wrangling*] démoralisant.

debility /dɪˈbɪlətɪ/ *n* Med débilité *f* (physique).

debit /ˈdebɪt/ Accts, Fin **I** *n* débit *m*.
II *modif* [*account, balance*] débiteur/-trice; **~ entries** sommes *fpl* inscrites au débit; **on the ~ side** Accts au débit; **on the ~ side...** fig l'inconvénient c'est que...
III *vtr* débiter; **to ~ a sum to sb's account, to ~ sb** ou **sb's account with a sum** débiter le compte de qn d'une somme.

debit card *n* GB ≈ carte *f* bancaire (*sans paiement différé*).

debonair /ˌdebəˈneə(r)/ *adj* [*person*] élégant et plein d'assurance; [*manner*] insouciant.

debouch /dɪˈbaʊtʃ/ *vi* **1** Geog déboucher (**into** dans); **2** Mil déboucher (**into** dans, sur).

debrief /ˌdiːˈbriːf/ *vtr* interroger; **to be ~ed** [*diplomat, agent*] rendre compte (oralement) d'une mission; [*defector, freed hostage*] être interrogé.

debriefing /ˌdiːˈbriːfɪŋ/ *n* **1** ₵ (of freed hostage, defector) critique *f*; **the soldiers will remain here for ~** les soldats resteront ici pour rendre compte de leur mission; **2** C (report) compte rendu *m* (oral), critique *f*.

debris /ˈdeɪbriː, ˈde-, US dəˈbriː/ *n* ₵ **1** (remains) (of plane) débris *mpl*; (of building) décombres *mpl*; hum (of meal) décombres *mpl*; **2** Geol dépôts *mpl* clastiques; **3** (waste) déchets *mpl*.

debt /det/ **I** *n* **1** Fin dette *f* (**to** envers); **bad ~s** créances *fpl* douteuses; **to cancel a ~** annuler une créance; **Third World ~** la dette du tiers monde; **to run up a ~** ou **~s** faire des dettes; **to get into ~** s'endetter; **to be in ~** avoir des dettes; **she is $2,000 in ~** elle a 2 000 dollars de dettes; **to be in ~ to sb** devoir de l'argent à qn; **I'm in ~ (to the bank) to the tune of £7,000** je dois 7 000 livres sterling à la banque; **to get out of ~** acquitter ses dettes; **to pay off one's ~s** rembourser ses dettes; **2** (obligation) dette *f* (**to** envers); **a ~ of honour** une dette d'honneur; **to pay one's ~ to society** payer sa dette envers la société; **to acknowledge one's ~ to sb** reconnaître qu'on doit beaucoup à qn; **I'm forever in your ~** je vous suis infiniment reconnaissant.
II *modif* Fin [*collection, recovery, relief*] des créances; [*burden, interest, payment*] de la dette; [*capacity, level, ratio*] d'endettement; [*crisis*] de l'endettement.

debt: **~ collector** *n* agent *m* de recouvrement; **~-laden** *adj* [*country, company*] lourdement endetté; [*person*] couvert de dettes.

debtor /ˈdetə(r)/ Fin **I** *n* débiteur/-trice *m/f*.
II *modif* [*country, nation*] débiteur/-trice, endetté.

debt-ridden /ˈdetrɪdn/ *adj* criblé de dettes.

debug /ˌdiːˈbʌg/ *vtr* (*p prés etc* **-gg-**) **1** Comput déboguer; **2** Telecom enlever les micros cachés dans [*room, building*].

debugging /ˌdiːˈbʌgɪŋ/ *n* Comput débogage *m*.

debunk /ˌdiːˈbʌŋk/ *vtr* démystifier [*theory, tradition*]; briser [*myth*].

debut /ˈdeɪbjuː, US dɪˈbjuː/ **I** *n* **1** (artistic, sporting) débuts *mpl*; **to make one's screen ~** faire ses débuts à l'écran; **to make one's ~ as** faire ses débuts comme [*musician, director, politician, player*]; [*actor, opera singer*] débuter dans le rôle de; **2** (social) entrée *f* or débuts *mpl* dans le monde.
II *modif* [*album, concert, role*] premier/-ière (*before n*).
III *vi* [*film*] passer pour la première fois; **to ~ as** faire ses débuts comme.

debutant /ˈdebjuːtɑːnt/ *n* débutant *m*.

debutante /ˈdebjuːtɑːnt/ *n* débutante *f*.

Dec *abrév écrite* = **December**.

decade /ˈdekeɪd, dɪˈkeɪd, US dɪˈkeɪd/ *n* **1** (period) décennie *f*; **a ~ ago** il y a dix ans; **2** Relig (of rosary) dizaine *f*.

decadence /ˈdekədəns/ *n* décadence *f*.

decadent /ˈdekədənt/ **I Decadent** *n* Literat décadent/-e *m/f*.
II *adj* **1** décadent; **2** also **Decadent** Literat décadent.

decaf○ /ˈdiːkæf/ *n* déca○ *m*.

decaffeinated /ˌdiːˈkæfɪneɪtɪd/ *adj* décaféiné.

decal /ˈdiːkæl/ *n* surtout US décalcomanie *f*.

decalcification /diːˌkælsɪfɪˈkeɪʃn/ *n* décalcification *f*.

decalcify /diːˈkælsɪfaɪ/ *vtr* décalcifier.

decalitre GB, **decaliter** US /ˈdekəliːtə(r)/ ▶ **1068** *n* décalitre *m*.

Decalogue /ˈdekəlɒg/ *n* Décalogue *m*.

decametre GB, **decameter** US /ˈdekəmiːtə(r)/ ▶ **1412** *n* décamètre *m*.

decamp /dɪˈkæmp/ *vi* **1** (leave) partir; (furtively) filer; **to ~ with sth** s'éclipser en emportant qch; **2** Mil lever le camp.

decant /dɪˈkænt/ *vtr* **1** lit décanter [*wine*]; transvaser [*other liquid*]; **2** fig transbahuter○ [*people*].

decanter /dɪˈkæntə(r)/ *n* (for wine, port) carafe *f* (à décanter); (for whisky) flacon *m* à whisky.

decapitate /dɪˈkæpɪteɪt/ *vtr* décapiter.

decapitation /dɪˌkæpɪˈteɪʃn/ *n* décapitation *f.*

decapod /ˈdekəpɒd/ *n* Zool décapode *m.*

decarbonization /diːˌkɑːbənaɪˈzeɪʃn, US -nɪˈz-/ *n* Aut décalaminage *m.*

decarbonize /diːˈkɑːbənaɪz/ *vtr* Aut décalaminer.

decarburization /diːˌkɑːbjʊraɪˈzeɪʃn, US -rɪˈz-/ *n* Tech décarburation *f.*

decarburize /ˌdiːˈkɑːbjʊraɪz/ *vtr* Tech décarburer.

decathlete /dɪˈkæθliːt/ *n* décathlonien *m.*

decathlon /dɪˈkæθlɒn/ *n* décathlon *m.*

decay /dɪˈkeɪ/ **I** *n* **1** (rot) (of timber, meat, vegetation) pourriture *f*; (of building, area, façade) délabrement *m*; **to fall into ~** [*building*] se délabrer; **2** Dent carie *f*; **tooth** ou **dental ~** la carie dentaire; **to have ~** avoir des caries; **to prevent ~** éviter les caries; **3** Geol décomposition *f*; **4** Phys désintégration *f*; **5** fig (of society, culture) déclin *m*; (of economy, institution, industry) délabrement *m*, déclin *m*; (of nation, civilization) décadence *f*, déchéance *f*; **moral ~** déchéance morale.
II *vtr* pourrir, faire pourrir [*timber*]; gâter, carier [*teeth*].
III *vi* **1** (rot) [*timber, vegetation, food*] pourrir; [*corpse*] se décomposer, se putréfier; [*tooth*] se gâter, se carier; [*bone*] se détériorer, se carier spec; **2** (disintegrate) [*statue, façade*] se dégrader; [*building*] se détériorer, se délabrer; **3** fig (decline) [*civilization, institution*] décliner; [*beauty*] se faner; **4** Geol se décomposer; **5** Phys se désintégrer.

decayed /dɪˈkeɪd/ *adj* **1** [*timber, vegetation*] pourri; [*flesh*] décomposé, pourri; [*tooth*] carié; [*building*] délabré; **2** fig [*society*] en déclin; [*beauty*] fané; **3** Phys désintégré; **4** Geol décomposé.

decaying /dɪˈkeɪɪŋ/ *adj* **1** [*timber, vegetation*] en train de pourrir; [*tooth*] en train de se carier or se gâter; [*corpse, carcass*] en décomposition, en train de pourrir; Med [*bone*] en train de se détériorer or se carier spec; **2** [*building, street, suburb*] qui se dégrade, qui se détériore; **3** [*civilization, order, nation*] en déclin.

decease /dɪˈsiːs/ *n* décès *m.*

deceased /dɪˈsiːst/ **I** *n* **the ~** (dead person) le défunt/la défunte *m/f*; (the dead collectively) (+ *v pl*) les défunts *mpl.*
II *adj* décédé, défunt (*never predic*); **Anne Jones, ~** feue Anne Jones.

deceit /dɪˈsiːt/ *n* **1** (deceitfulness) mensonge *m*, fausseté *f*; **2** (act) tromperie *f*; **3** Jur fraude *f.*

deceitful /dɪˈsiːtfl/ *adj* [*person*] menteur/-euse; [*word*] mensonger/-ère; [*behaviour*] malhonnête; **it was ~ of him** c'était malhonnête de sa part.

deceitfully /dɪˈsiːtfəlɪ/ *adv* [*speak*] de façon malhonnête.

deceitfulness /dɪˈsiːtflnɪs/ *n* fausseté *f.*

deceive /dɪˈsiːv/ **I** *vtr* **1** (lie to and mislead) tromper, duper [*parent, friend*]; **to ~ sb into doing** amener qn à faire qch par la ruse; **to ~ sb into thinking that** faire croire à qn que; **to be ~d** (fooled) être dupe; (disappointed) être déçu; **to be ~d in sb** se tromper sur le compte de qn; **don't be ~d** ne te laisse pas avoir; **don't be ~d by his mildness/good-humour** ne te laisse pas abuser par sa douceur/bonne humeur; **don't be ~d by appearances** ne vous fiez pas aux apparences; **do my eyes ~ me?** est-ce que j'ai la berlue○?; **I thought my ears were deceiving me** j'ai cru que j'avais mal entendu; **2** (be unfaithful to) tromper [*spouse, lover*] (**with** avec).
II *vi* **he likes to ~** il aime tromper les gens; **with intent to ~** avec l'intention de tromper les gens; **appearances often ~** les apparences sont souvent trompeuses.
III *v refl* **to ~ oneself** se faire des illusions; **to ~ oneself into believing that** se convaincre à tort que.

deceiver /dɪˈsiːvə(r)/ *n* trompeur/-euse *m/f.*

decelerate /diːˈseləreɪt/ *vi* **1** Aut, Mech ralentir, décélérer spec; **2** fig [*economic growth*] ralentir.

deceleration /diːˌseləˈreɪʃn/ *n* Aut, Mech ralentissement *m*, décélération *f* spec; fig (of economic growth) ralentissement *m.*

December /dɪˈsembə(r)/ **▶ 1472** *n* décembre *m.*

decency /ˈdiːsnsɪ/ *n* **1** (good manners) politesse *f*; **common ~** la simple politesse; **they might have had the ~ to thank us** ils auraient pu avoir la politesse or la correction de nous remercier; **you can't in all ~ ask him to pay** tu ne peux décemment pas lui demander de payer; **2** (morality) **he hasn't an ounce of ~** il n'a pas le moindre sens moral; **3** (propriety) convenances *fpl*; (in sexual matters) décence *f*; **he has no sense of ~** il n'a aucun sens des convenances; **for the sake of ~** par souci or respect des convenances; **to observe the decencies** fml observer or respecter les convenances.

decent /ˈdiːsnt/ *adj* **1** (respectable) [*family, man, woman*] comme il faut, bien *inv*; **no ~ person would do a thing like that** quelqu'un de correct ne ferait jamais une chose pareille; **she wanted to give him a ~ burial** (not cheap) elle voulait qu'il ait un enterrement convenable; (with due respect) elle voulait qu'il soit enterré comme il se doit; **after a ~ interval, he remarried** par souci des convenances il a laissé écouler un certain temps avant de se remarier; **he did the ~ thing and resigned** il a fait ce qu'on attendait de lui en démissionnant; **try to persuade him to do the ~ thing** essaye de le persuader de faire ce que tout le monde attend de lui; **2** (pleasant) sympathique, bien○ *inv*; **he's a ~ sort of chap**○ c'est un type bien○; **it's ~ of him to help you** c'est très sympathique de sa part de t'aider; **3** (adequate) [*housing, wages, facilities*] convenable, décent; [*standard, level*] bon/bonne (*before n*); **4** (not shabby) [*garment, shoes*] correct; **I've nothing ~ to wear** je n'ai rien de mettable; **5** (good) [*camera, choice, education, food, holiday, score, result*] bon/bonne (*before n*); [*profit*] appréciable; **to make a ~ living** bien gagner sa vie; **I need a ~ night's sleep** j'ai besoin d'une bonne nuit de sommeil; **they do a ~ fish soup at the Nautilus** la soupe de poisson n'est pas mauvaise au Nautilus; **he serves a ~ claret** son bordeaux (rouge) n'est pas mauvais; **6** (not indecent) [*clothes, behaviour, language*] décent, correct; **are you ~?** es-tu habillé?

decently /ˈdiːsntlɪ/ *adv* **1** (fairly) [*paid, treated, housed*] convenablement, correctement; **2** (respectably) [*behave, treat*] convenablement; [*dress*] (discreetly) décemment; (presentably) correctement; **we left as soon as we ~ could** nous sommes partis aussi tôt que la décence le permettait; **we'll leave as soon as ~ possible** nous partirons dès que ce sera décemment possible; **she was ~ brought up** elle a reçu une bonne éducation.

decentralization /diːˌsentrəlaɪˈzeɪʃn, US -lɪˈz-/ *n* décentralisation *f.*

decentralize /diːˈsentrəlaɪz/ **I** *vtr* décentraliser.
II *vi* se décentraliser.

decent-sized *adj* assez grand.

deception /dɪˈsepʃn/ *n* **1** ¢ (deceiving) gen tromperie *f*, duperie *f*; Jur fraude *f*, tromperie *f*; **is she capable of such ~?** est-elle capable d'une telle duplicité?; **to obtain sth by ~** obtenir qch par fraude; **2** (trick) supercherie *f*; (to gain money, property etc) escroquerie *f.*

deceptive /dɪˈseptɪv/ *adj* [*appearance, impression*] trompeur/-euse; **her mild manner is ~** sa douceur est trompeuse; **appearances can be ~** les apparences sont parfois trompeuses, il ne faut pas se fier aux apparences.

deceptively /dɪˈseptɪvlɪ/ *adv* **1** gen **it's ~ easy** c'est plus difficile que ça ne paraît; **2** Advertg **the house is ~ spacious** la maison est plus spacieuse qu'elle ne paraît.

decibel /ˈdesɪbel/ *n* décibel *m.*

decide /dɪˈsaɪd/ **I** *vtr* **1** (reach a decision) **to ~ to do** décider de faire; (after much thought) se décider à faire; **I ~d that I would leave** j'ai décidé de partir; **I ~d that he should leave** j'ai décidé qu'il devait partir; **to ~ how to do** décider comment faire; **to ~ where/when** décider où/quand; **he hasn't ~d whether to resign/sign** il n'a pas encore décidé s'il va démissionner/signer; **it was ~d to wait** on a décidé d'attendre; **have you ~d what you're going to do?** est-ce que tu as décidé ce que tu vas faire?; **nothing has been ~d yet** rien n'a encore été décidé; **2** (settle) régler [*dispute, matter*]; décider de [*fate, outcome*]; [*goal, penalty*] être décisif/-ive pour l'issue de [*match*]; **to ~ a case** [*jury*] statuer sur une affaire; **3** (persuade) **to ~ sb to do** décider qn à faire; **what finally ~d you to buy it?** qu'est-ce qui t'a décidé à l'acheter?; **it was his selfishness that finally ~d me to leave** c'est à cause de son égoïsme que je me suis décidée à partir; **that's what ~d him against moving house** c'est pour cela qu'il a décidé de ne pas déménager.
II *vi* décider; **let her ~** laisse-la décider or prendre la décision; **it's up to him to ~** c'est à lui de décider; **I can't ~** je n'arrive pas à me décider; **fate ~d otherwise** le hasard en a décidé autrement; **have you ~d?** as-tu pris une décision?; **to ~ against doing** décider de ne pas faire; **to ~ against** ne pas adopter [*plan, idea*]; rejeter [*candidate*]; **to ~ against the red dress** (choose not to buy) décider de ne pas acheter la robe rouge; (choose not to wear) décider de ne pas mettre la robe rouge; **to ~ between** choisir, faire un choix entre [*applicants, books*]; **to ~ in favour of doing** décider de faire; **to ~ in favour of** [*jury, judge*] se prononcer pour [*plaintiff*]; [*panel, judges*] choisir [*candidate, applicant*].
■ **decide on**: ¶ **~ on [sth] 1** (choose) se décider pour [*hat, wallpaper, holiday*]; fixer [*date*]; **to ~ on a career in medicine/law** se diriger vers la médecine/le droit; **2** (come to a decision on) décider de [*measure, policy, course of action, size, budget*]; ¶ **~ on [sb]** choisir [*member, applicant*]; sélectionner [*team*].

decided /dɪˈsaɪdɪd/ *adj* **1** (noticeable) [*change*] incontestable; [*increase, drop*] net/nette; [*tendency*] net/nette, marqué; [*interest, effort*] réel/réelle; **2** (determined) [*manner, tone*] décidé, résolu; [*views*] arrêté; **to be quite ~ about doing** être bien décidé à faire.

decidedly /dɪˈsaɪdɪdlɪ/ *adv* **1** (distinctly) [*smaller, better, happier*] nettement; [*unwell, violent, odd*] vraiment, franchement; **2** (resolutely) [*say, declare*] résolument.

decider /dɪˈsaɪdə(r)/ *n* (point) point *m* décisif; (race) course *f* décisive; (goal) but *m* décisif; **the ~** (game) la belle.

deciding /dɪˈsaɪdɪŋ/ *adj* [*factor, goal, race*] décisif/-ive.

deciduous /dɪˈsɪdjʊəs, dɪˈsɪdʒʊəs/ *adj* [*tree*] à feuilles caduques; [*forest*] d'arbres à feuilles caduques; [*antlers, teeth, leaves*] caduc/caduque.

decigram(me) /ˈdesɪgræm/ **▶ 1883** *n* décigramme *m.*

decilitre GB, **deciliter** US /ˈdesɪliːtə(r)/ **▶ 1068** *n* décilitre *m.*

decimal /ˈdesɪml/ **I** *n* décimale *f*; **▶ circulating decimal etc.**
II *adj* [*system, currency, number*] décimal; **~ coinage** les pièces *fpl* du système décimal; **~ fraction** fraction *f* décimale; **~ point** virgule *f*; **to calculate to two ~ places** calculer à deux décimales; **to go ~** adopter le système décimal.

decimalization /ˌdesɪməlaɪˈzeɪʃn, US -lɪˈz-/

n (of currency, unit) décimalisation *f*; Math (of number) conversion *f* en fraction décimale.

decimalize /ˈdesɪməlaɪz/ *vtr* décimaliser [*currency, system*]; (convert to decimal system) transposer [qch] dans le système décimal [*unit*]; Math convertir [qch] en fraction décimale.

decimate /ˈdesɪmeɪt/ *vtr* lit, fig décimer.

decimation /ˌdesɪˈmeɪʃn/ *n* lit, fig décimation *f*.

decimetre GB, **decimeter** US /ˈdesɪmiːtə(r)/ ▶ **1412** *n* décimètre *m*.

decipher /dɪˈsaɪfə(r)/ *vtr* déchiffrer [*code, writing, message*].

decipherable /dɪˈsaɪfrəbl/ *adj* (all contexts) déchiffrable.

decision /dɪˈsɪʒn/ *n* (all contexts) décision *f*; **my ~ to leave** la décision que j'ai prise de partir; **to make** ou **take a ~** prendre une décision; **to reach** or **come to a ~** se décider; **the right/wrong ~** la bonne/mauvaise décision; **the judges' ~ is final** la décision du jury est sans appel; **a woman of ~** une femme qui sait ce qu'elle veut.

decision-maker *n* décideur/-euse *m/f*.

decision-making **I** *n* **to be good/bad at ~** savoir/ne pas savoir prendre des décisions.
II *modif* **~ skills** compétences *fpl* en matière de décision; **the ~ processes** les processus décisionnels.

decision table *n* Comput table *f* de décision.

decisive /dɪˈsaɪsɪv/ *adj* **1** (firm) [*manner*] très ferme, résolu; [*tone, reply*] catégorique; **he is not ~ enough** il n'a pas l'esprit de décision, il est trop indécis; **a more ~ leader** un dirigeant plus ferme; **2** (conclusive) [*battle, factor, influence*] décisif/-ive; [*argument*] concluant; **it was ~ in forcing** ou **persuading him to resign** cela l'a décidé à démissionner.

decisively /dɪˈsaɪsɪvlɪ/ *adv* [*speak*] fermement, d'un ton catégorique; [*act*] de manière résolue, avec fermeté.

decisiveness /dɪˈsaɪsɪvnɪs/ *n* (of character) esprit *m* de décision, capacité *f* à prendre des décisions; (of approach) attitude *f* tranchée, air *m* décidé; (of answer, gesture) fermeté *f*.

deck /dek/ **I** *n* **1** Naut (on ship) pont *m*; **upper/car ~** pont supérieur/des voitures; **on ~** sur le pont; **to go (up** ou **out) on ~** monter sur le pont; **below ~(s)** sur le pont inférieur; **2** US (terrace) terrasse *f*; **3** (on bus, plane) étage *m*; **upper/lower ~** étage supérieur/inférieur; **4** Audio (for records) platine *f* tourne-disque; (for cassettes) platine *f* cassettes; **5** Games **~ of cards** jeu *m* de cartes; **6**° US argot des drogués petite dose *f* d'heroïne.
II *vtr* **1** (decorate) orner [*building, room, table*] **(with** de) ; décorer [*tree*] **(with** de); **2** (dress up) parer [*person*] **(with, in** de); **3**° US (floor) envoyer [qn] par terre.
IDIOMS **all hands on ~!** Naut tout le monde sur le pont!; gen tout le monde à la rescousse!; **to clear the ~s** déblayer le terrain; **to hit the ~**° tomber par terre; **he's not playing with a full ~**° il est simplet.
■ **deck out**: ¶ **~ [sth] out, ~ out [sth]** décorer [*place*] **(with, in** de); ¶ **~ [sb] out** parer **(in** de); **he was ~ed out in his best suit** il s'était vêtu de son plus beau costume.

deck: **~chair** *n* transatlantique *m*, transat° *m*; **~hand** *n* matelot *m*; **~house** *n* rouf *m*.

deckle-edged /ˌdeklˈedʒd/ *adj* Print non affranchi.

declaim /dɪˈkleɪm/ **I** *vtr* déclamer.
II *vi* **1** (speak aloud) déclamer; **2** (protest) **to ~ against sth** (in speech) déclamer contre qch; (in writing) écrire une diatribe contre qch.

declamation /ˌdekləˈmeɪʃn/ *n* **1** (protest) diatribe *f*, tirade *f* **(against** contre); **2** (rhetorical style) déclamation *f*.

declamatory /dɪˈklæmətərɪ, US -tɔːrɪ/ *adj* déclamatoire, emphatique.

declarable /dɪˈkleərəbl/ *adj* (*avant n*) [*goods, duty*] à déclarer; [*income*] imposable.

declaration /ˌdekləˈreɪʃn/ *n* **1** (proclamation) déclaration *f*; **the Declaration of Independence** la Déclaration d'indépendance des États-Unis d'Amérique; **their ~s of innocence** leurs protestations d'innocence; **the ~ of the poll** la proclamation des résultats; **2** (formal statement) déclaration *f*; **a ~ of income** Tax une déclaration de revenus or d'impôts; **to make a false ~** Jur faire une fausse déclaration; **a customs ~** une déclaration en douane; **3** (in cards) déclaration *f*.

declaration: **~ of association** *n* acte *m* déclaratif d'association; **~ of bankruptcy** *n* jugement *m* déclaratif de faillite; **~ of intent** *n* déclaration *f* de principe; **~ of solvency** *n* déclaration *f* de solvabilité.

declarative /dɪˈklærətɪv/ *adj* Ling assertif/-ive, déclaratif/-ive.

declaratory /dɪˈklærətrɪ, US -tɔːrɪ/ *adj* Jur [*act, judgment*] déclaratif/-ive.

declare /dɪˈkleə(r)/ **I** *vtr* **1** (state firmly) déclarer **(that** que); (state openly) annoncer [*intention, support*]; (in cards) annoncer [*trumps*]; **2** (proclaim) déclarer [*war*]; proclamer [*independence, siege*]; **to ~ war on a country** déclarer la guerre à un pays; **to ~ a state of emergency** déclarer l'état d'urgence; **to ~ sb the winner/guilty** déclarer qn vainqueur/coupable; **I ~ the meeting closed** je clôture la séance; Wine **to ~ a vintage** déclarer un millésime; **3** Tax, Jur, Fin déclarer [*income*]; communiquer [*dividend*]; **nothing to ~** rien à déclarer; **to ~ one's interest in a company** déclarer ses intérêts dans une compagnie.
II *vi* **1** (make choice) se déclarer **(for** pour; **against** contre); **2** US Pol annoncer sa candidature (à la présidence); **3** Games (in cards) annoncer.
III *v refl* **to ~ oneself** se déclarer; **they ~d themselves (to be) supporters of the rebels** ils ont déclaré leur soutien pour les rebelles.
IV declared *pp adj* [*enemy, atheist*] déclaré; [*intention*] avoué, déclaré.
IDIOMS **well, I ~!** eh bien, dites donc!

declaredly /dɪˈkleərɪdlɪ/ *adv* ouvertement.

declarer /dɪˈkleərə(r)/ *n* Games demandeur *m*.

declassification /ˌdiːˌklæsɪfɪˈkeɪʃn/ *n* Admin levée *f* du secret **(of** à propos de); Mil déclassification *f*.

declassify /ˌdiːˈklæsɪfaɪ/ *vtr* Admin rendre [qch] communicable or accessible [*document, information*]; Mil déclassifier.

declension /dɪˈklenʃn/ *n* déclinaison *f*.

declinable /dɪˈklaɪnəbl/ *adj* déclinable.

declination /ˌdeklɪˈneɪʃn/ *n* **1** Geog déclinaison *f* magnétique; **2** Astron déclinaison *f*.

decline /dɪˈklaɪn/ **I** *n* **1** (of empire, civilization, economy, industry, party, politician) déclin *m* **(of** de); **to be in ~** être sur le déclin; **to go into** ou **fall into ~** tomber en déclin; **there has been a ~ in the popularity of sth** qch a perdu de sa popularité; **there has been a ~ in support for the party** le parti a perdu une partie de son électorat; **2** (of trade, demand, support) baisse *f* **(in, of** de); **to be on the** ou **in ~** être en baisse; **a 5% ~ to 175** une baisse de 5% pour atteindre 175; **to go/fall into ~** tomber en déclin; **3** (of health, condition, person) déclin *m* **(in, of** de); **to go/fall into (a) ~** dépérir; **his ~ into madness** sa chute dans la folie.
II *vtr* **1** (refuse) décliner [*offer, honour*]; **to ~ to do** refuser de faire; **2** Ling décliner.
III *vi* **1** (drop) [*number, rate, demand, sales, quality*] baisser **(by** de); [*support*] être en baisse; [*business, trade*] ralentir; **2** (wane) [*influence, empire, status, career, team*] être sur le déclin; **3** (refuse) refuser; **4** Ling se décliner; **5** littér [*sun*] se coucher.
IV declining *pres p adj* **1** (getting fewer, less) **a declining birth/inflation rate** un taux de natalité/d'inflation en baisse; **declining sales** la baisse des ventes; **the declining interest in sth** le désintérêt croissant pour qch; **2** (in decline) [*empire, industry, influence etc*] en déclin; **in her declining years** au déclin de sa vie; **3** (getting worse) [*health, quality*] déclinant.

declivity /dɪˈklɪvətɪ/ *n* déclivité *f*.

declutch /ˌdiːˈklʌtʃ/ *vi* GB débrayer.

decoction /dɪˈkɒkʃn/ *n* décoction *f*.

decode /ˌdiːˈkəʊd/ *vtr* décoder [*code, message, signal*]; déchiffrer [*handwriting, text*].

decoder /ˌdiːˈkəʊdə(r)/ *n* (all contexts) décodeur *m*.

decoding /ˌdiːˈkəʊdɪŋ/ *n* (all contexts) décodage *m*.

decoke /ˌdiːˈkəʊk/ GB Aut *vtr* décalaminer.

decollate /dɪˈkɒleɪt/ *vtr* déliasser.

décolleté /deɪˈkɒlteɪ, US -kɒlˈteɪ/ *n, adj* décolleté (*m*).

decolonize /diːˈkɒlənaɪz/ *vtr* décoloniser.

decompartmentalization /ˌdiːkɒmpɑːtˌmentəlaɪˈzeɪʃn, US -lɪˈz-/ *n* Admin décloisonnement *m*.

decompartmentalize /ˌdiːkɒmpɑːtˈmentəlaɪz/ *vtr* Admin décloisonner.

decompose /ˌdiːkəmˈpəʊz/ **I** *vtr* **1** décomposer, faire pourrir [*leaves, wood*]; décomposer, putréfier [*corpse*]; **2** Phys, Chem décomposer **(into** en).
II *vi* se décomposer.

decomposition /ˌdiːkɒmpəˈzɪʃn/ *n* décomposition *f*.

decompression /ˌdiːkəmˈpreʃn/ *n* décompression *f*.

decompression: **~ chamber** *n* caisson *m* de décompression, caisson *m* hyperbare; **~ sickness** *n* maladie *f* des caissons.

decongestant /ˌdiːkənˈdʒestənt/ **I** *n* décongestif *m*.
II *adj* décongestionnant.

decontaminate /ˌdiːkənˈtæmɪneɪt/ *vtr* décontaminer.

decontamination /ˌdiːkənˌtæmɪˈneɪʃn/ *n* décontamination *f*.

decontrol /ˌdiːkənˈtrəʊl/ **I** *n* Econ, Fin déréglementation *f*.
II *vtr* (*p prés etc* **-ll-**) Econ, Fin déréglementer.

decor /ˈdeɪkɔː(r), US deɪˈkɔːr/ *n* (specific style) décoration *f*, décor *m*; (of house) décoration *f*; Theat décor *m*.

decorate /ˈdekəreɪt/ **I** *vtr* **1** (adorn) décorer [*room, street, Christmas tree, cake*] **(with** de, avec); **2** (paint and paper) gen refaire; (paint only) peindre; (paper only) tapisser; **the whole house needs to be ~d** il faudra refaire toute la décoration de la maison; **decorating the kitchen will be our next task** (with paint) refaire les peintures dans la cuisine sera notre prochaine tâche; (with paper) tapisser la cuisine sera notre prochaine tâche; **3** Mil décorer **(for** pour); **the soldier was ~d for bravery** le soldat a été décoré pour son acte de bravoure; **they were ~d for their services to industry** ils ont été décorés pour services rendus à l'industrie; **to be ~d with** être décoré de, recevoir [*medal*].
II *vi* (in house) faire des travaux de décoration.

decorating /ˈdekəreɪtɪŋ/ *n* (of room, house) travaux *mpl* de décoration; **'painting and ~'** 'peinture-décoration'.

decoration /ˌdekəˈreɪʃn/ *n* **1** (for festivities) décoration *f*; (on garment) ornement *m*; **to put up/take down ~s** mettre/enlever les décorations; **2** (act or result) (for festivities) décoration *f*; (by painter) travaux *mpl* de décoration; **he helped us with the ~ of the study** il nous a aidés à refaire les peintures dans le bureau; **the fireplace is only for ~** la cheminée est purement ornementale; **3** Mil décoration *f*.

decorative /ˈdekərətɪv, US ˈdekəreɪtɪv/ *adj* [*border, frill*] décoratif/-ive; [*sculpture, design*] ornemental.

decorator /ˈdekəreɪtə(r)/ *n* peintre *m*, décorateur/-trice *m/f*; **'John Brown, painter and ~'** 'John Brown, peintre-décorateur or peinture-décoration'.

decorous /ˈdekərəs/ *adj* [*behaviour*] convenable; [*language, manners*] bienséant, correct.

decorously /ˈdekərəslɪ/ *adv* [*behave*] convenablement; [*dress*] strictement.

decorum /dɪˈkɔːrəm/ *n* **with ~** avec bienséance, en respectant les convenances; **a sense of ~** un sens des convenances or du décorum.

decoy **I** /ˈdiːkɔɪ/ *n* **1** gen, Mil (person, vehicle etc) leurre *m*; **2** Hunt appeau *m*.
II /dɪˈkɔɪ/ *vtr* **1** gen, Mil attirer [qn] dans un piège; **2** Hunt attirer [qch] avec un appeau.

decrease **I** /ˈdiːkriːs/ *n* gen diminution *f* (**in** de); (in price) baisse *f* (**in** de); **~ in spending** baisse de la consommation; **~ in strength** affaiblissement *m*.
II /dɪˈkriːs/ *vtr* diminuer, réduire.
III /dɪˈkriːs/ *vi* [*size, weight, population*] diminuer; [*price, cost*] baisser; [*popularity, rate*] baisser, diminuer.

decreasing /dɪˈkriːsɪŋ/ *adj* [*size, amount, population*] décroissant; [*strength*] déclinant, diminuant; [*temperature, price*] en baisse.

decreasingly /dɪˈkriːsɪŋlɪ/ *adv* de moins en moins.

decree /dɪˈkriː/ **I** *n* **1** (order) décret *m*; **by royal ~** par décret du roi; **2** (judgment) jugement *m*, arrêt *m*; **~ absolute/nisi** (in divorce) jugement définitif/provisoire (de divorce).
II *vtr* **1** gen (order, announce) décréter [*amnesty, punishment*]; **to ~ that** décréter que (+ *indic*); **2** Jur ordonner (**that** que + *subj*).
IDIOMS **fate had ~d otherwise** le sort en avait décidé autrement.

decrepit /dɪˈkrepɪt/ *adj* [*chair, table*] en mauvais état; [*building*] délabré; [*horse, old person*] décrépit.

decrepitude /dɪˈkrepɪtjuːd, US -tuːd/ *n* (of object) vétusté *f*; (of building) délabrement *m*; (of horse, old person) décrépitude *f*.

decretal /dɪˈkriːtl/ *n* Relig décrétale *f*.

decriminalization /dɪˌkrɪmɪnəlaɪˈzeɪʃn, US -lɪˈz-/ *n* décriminalisation *f*, légalisation *f*.

decriminalize /dɪˈkrɪmɪnəlaɪz/ *vtr* décriminaliser, légaliser.

decry /dɪˈkraɪ/ *vtr* décrier.

dedicate /ˈdedɪkeɪt/ **I** *vtr* **1** (devote) consacrer, dédier [*life, time*] (**to** à); dédier [*book, performance, film*] (**to** à); **she ~d her life to helping the poor** elle a consacré sa vie or elle s'est consacrée aux pauvres; **2** Relig consacrer [*church, shrine*] (**to** à).
II *v refl* **to ~ oneself to sth** se consacrer à qch; **to ~ oneself to doing** consacrer sa vie or son temps à faire.

dedicated /ˈdedɪkeɪtɪd/ *adj* **1** (keen, devoted) [*teacher, mother, doctor, fan*] dévoué; [*worker, secretary, minister*] zélé; [*disciple*] enthousiaste; [*socialist, opponent*] convaincu; [*musician, student, attitude*] sérieux/-ieuse; **we only take on people who are really ~** nous n'embauchons que des gens sérieux; **she is ~ to looking after her old parents** elle est entièrement dévouée à ses parents âgés; **he is ~ to social reform** il consacre tous ses efforts aux réformes sociales; **2** Comput, Electron spécialisé, dédié; **3** (personalized) [*copy*] dédicacé; [*area, zone*] réservé.

dedication /ˌdedɪˈkeɪʃn/ *n* **1** (devoted attitude) dévouement *m* (**to** à); **thanks to the ~ of the surgeon who performed the operation** grâce au dévouement du chirurgien qui a fait l'opération; **her ~ to duty** son attachement à son devoir, son sens du devoir; **2** (in a book, on music programme) dédicace *f*; **there are several ~s for this record** ce disque est dédié à plusieurs auditeurs; **3** (act of dedicating) (of book, performance) dédicace *f*; **4** Relig consécration *f*, dédicace *f*.

deduce /dɪˈdjuːs, US -ˈdus/ *vtr* déduire (**from** de; **that** que).

deducible /dɪˈdjuːsəbl, US -ˈduːs-/ *adj* [*conclusion, theory*] qui peut se déduire; **this theory is not ~ from the limited evidence that we have** on ne peut déduire cette théorie des quelques faits qui sont à notre disposition.

deduct /dɪˈdʌkt/ *vtr* prélever [*subscription*] (**from** sur); déduire [*sum, expenses*] (**from** de); **income tax is ~ed at source** les impôts sont prélevés à la source.

deductible /dɪˈdʌktəbl/ **I** *n* US Fin franchise *f*.
II *adj* Fin, Comm déductible.

deduction /dɪˈdʌkʃn/ *n* **1** Fin, Econ (on wages) retenue *f*; (on bill) déduction *f*; **after ~s** une fois les retenues effectuées; **to make a ~ from** faire or effectuer une retenue or une déduction sur; Tax faire un prélèvement sur; **I made a ~ of 10% from the invoice** je vous ai fait une déduction de 10% sur la facture; **2** (conclusion) déduction *f*, conclusion *f*; **to make a ~** tirer une conclusion (**from** de); **3** (reasoning) déduction *f*; **by ~** par déduction.

deductive /dɪˈdʌktɪv/ *adj* déductif/-ive.

deed /diːd/ **I** *n* **1** (action) acte *m*; **a brave ~** un acte de courage; **to do one's good ~ for the day** faire sa bonne action or sa B.A.○; **2** littér (heroic feat) exploit *m*; **3** Jur (document) gen acte *m* notarié; (for property) acte *m* de propriété.
II *vtr* US Jur transférer [qch] par acte notarié.
IDIOMS **in word and ~** en parole et en fait; **in ~ if not in name** de fait sinon en titre.

deed: **~ box** *n* coffre *m* à documents; **~ of covenant** *n* Jur acte *m* de donation; **~ of partnership** *n* Comm Jur contrat *m* de société.

deed poll *n* (*pl* **deeds poll**) Jur acte *m* unilatéral; **to change one's name by ~** changer légalement son nom.

deejay○ /ˈdiːdʒeɪ/ *n* disc-jockey *m*, animateur/-trice *m/f* (*de radio, de discothèque*).

deem /diːm/ *vtr* considérer, estimer (**that** que); **your essay was ~ed the best** votre dissertation a été considérée comme or jugée la meilleure; **we ~ed her worthy** nous l'avons estimée digne; **it was ~ed necessary/advisable to do** on a jugé nécessaire/préférable de faire.

deep /diːp/ ▶ **1412** **I** *n* littér (sea) **the ~** l'océan *m*.
II *adj* **1** (vertically) [*hole, ditch, water, wound, wrinkle, breath, sigh, curtsey, armchair*] profond; [*mud, snow, carpet*] épais/épaisse; [*container, drawer, saucepan, grass*] haut; **~ roots** Bot racines *fpl* profondes; fig bases *fpl*; **~ cleansing** Cosmet nettoyage en profondeur; **a ~-pile carpet** une moquette de haute laine; **how ~ is the river/wound?** quelle est la profondeur de la rivière/blessure?; **the lake is 13 m ~** le lac a 13 m de profondeur; **a hole 5 cm ~, a 5 cm ~ hole** un trou de 5 cm; **the floor was 10 cm ~ in water** le sol se trouvait sous 10 cm d'eau; **the sound/spring came from a source ~ in the earth** le son/la fontaine provenait des profondeurs de la terre; **2** (horizontally) [*border, band, strip*] large; [*shelf, drawer, cupboard, alcove, stage*] profond; **a shelf 30 cm ~** une étagère de 30 cm de profondeur; **people were standing six ~** les gens étaient debout sur six rangées; **cars were parked three ~** les voitures étaient garées sur trois files; **3** fig (intense) [*admiration, concern, depression, dismay, love, faith, impression, sorrow*] profond; [*interest, regret, shame*] profond, grand; [*desire, need, pleasure*] grand; [*difficulty, trouble*] gros/grosse; Physiol [*coma, sleep*] profond; **my ~est sympathy** parfois hum toutes mes condoléances; **4** (impenetrable) [*darkness, forest, jungle, mystery*] profond; [*secret*] grand; [*person*] réservé; **they live in ~est Wales** hum ils habitent au fin fond du pays de Galles; **you're a ~ one**○! tu caches bien ton jeu○!; **5** (intellectually profound) [*idea, insight, meaning, truth, book, thinker*] profond; [*knowledge, discussion*] approfondi; [*thought*] (concentrated) profond; (intimate) intime; **at a ~er level** plus en profondeur; **6** (dark) [*colour*] intense; [*tan*] prononcé; **~ blue eyes** des yeux d'un bleu intense; **7** (low) [*voice*] profond; [*note, sound*] grave; **8** (involved, absorbed) **to be ~ in** être absorbé dans [*thought, entertainment*]; être plongé dans [*book, conversation, work*]; **to be ~ in debt** être endetté jusqu'au cou; **9** [*shot, serve*] en profondeur.
III *adv* **1** (a long way down) [*dig, bury, cut*] profondément; **he thrust his hands ~ into his pockets/the snow** il a enfoncé ses mains dans ses poches/la neige; **she dived ~ into the lake** elle a plongé dans les profondeurs du lac; **he plunged the knife ~ into her body** il lui a planté le couteau dans le corps; **~ in the cellars** tout au fond des caves; **~ beneath the sea/the earth's surface** à une grande profondeur sous la mer/la surface de la terre; **to sink/dig ~er** s'enfoncer/creuser plus profondément; **to dig ~er into an affair** fig creuser (plus loin) une affaire; **to sink ~er into debt** fig s'endetter davantage; **he drank ~ of the wine** littér il a bu une large rasade de vin; **2** (a long way in) **~ in** ou **into** au cœur de; **~ in the forest, all was still** au cœur de la forêt, le silence régnait; **to go ~ into the woods** s'enfoncer au cœur des bois; **~ in the heart of the maquis/of Texas** au cœur du maquis/du Texas; **~ in space** loin dans l'espace; **~ in my heart** tout au fond de mon cœur; **to be ~ in thought/discussion** être plongé dans ses pensées/dans une discussion; **to work/talk ~ into the night** travailler/causer jusque tard dans la nuit; **he gazed ~ into my eyes** littér il s'est noyé dans mon regard; **3** fig (emotionally, in psyche) **~ down** ou **inside** dans mon/ton etc for intérieur; **~ down she was frightened** dans son for intérieur elle avait peur; **~ down she's a nice woman** elle a un bon fond; **to go ~** [*faith, emotion, loyalty, instinct*] être profond; **his problems go ~er than that** ses problèmes sont bien plus graves que cela; **to run ~** [*belief, feeling, prejudice*] être bien enraciné; **4** Sport [*hit, kick, serve*] en profondeur.
IDIOMS **to be in ~**○ y être jusqu'au cou○; **to be in ~ water** être dans de beaux draps○.

deep-dyed /ˌdiːpˈdaɪd/ *adj* **1** Tex grand teint *inv*; **2** fig [*villain*] irrécupérable.

deepen /ˈdiːpən/ **I** *vtr* **1** (dig out) creuser [*channel, hollow*]; **2** fig (intensify) augmenter [*admiration, concern, dismay, interest, love, shame*]; approfondir [*knowledge, awareness, understanding*]; **3** (make lower) rendre [qch] plus grave [*voice, pitch, tone*]; **4** (make darker) foncer [*colour*]; améliorer [*tan*].
II *vi* **1** [*river, water*] devenir plus profond; [*snow, mud*] s'épaissir; [*wrinkle, line*] se creuser; **2** fig (intensify) [*admiration, concern, dismay, interest, love, shame*] augmenter; [*knowledge, awareness, understanding*] s'approfondir; [*crisis, difficulties*] s'aggraver; [*mystery*] s'épaissir; [*silence*] se faire plus profond; [*rift, gap*] s'élargir; **3** (grow lower) [*voice, pitch, tone*] devenir plus grave; **4** (grow darker) [*colour*] foncer; [*tan*] devenir de plus en plus foncé; [*darkness, night*] s'épaissir.
III deepening *p pres adj* **1** fig (intensifying) [*darkness, emotion, interest, mystery, need,*

rift] croissant; [*crisis*] de plus en plus grave; [*awareness, understanding*] de plus en plus approfondi; [*confusion*] de plus en plus grand; [*conviction*] de plus en plus profond; **2** lit [*water*] de plus en plus haut; [*snow, mud*] de plus en plus épais/épaisse; **3** (becoming lower) [*pitch, tone*] de plus en plus grave; **4** (becoming darker) [*colour*] de plus en plus foncé.

deep end /ˈdiːpend/ *n* grand bassin *m*.
IDIOMS **to go off at the ~**○ sortir de ses gonds○; **to go** ou **jump in at the ~** fig prendre le taureau par les cornes; **to throw sb in at the ~** fig forcer qn à prendre le taureau par les cornes.

deep-felt /ˌdiːpˈfelt/ *adj* [*admiration*] sincère; [*hatred*] profond.

deep-freeze /ˌdiːpˈfriːz/ **I** *n* congélateur *m*.
II *vtr* (*prét* **-froze**, *pp* **-frozen**) congeler.

deep: **~-fried** *adj* [*meat, vegetable*] frit; **~-frozen** *adj* congelé; **~-fry** *vtr* faire frire; **~-(fat-)fryer** *n* friteuse *f*; **~-laid** *adj* [*plan*] habilement ourdi.

deeply /ˈdiːplɪ/ *adv* **1** fig (intensely) [*felt, moving*] profondément; [*involved, committed*] à fond; **our most ~ held convictions** nos convictions les plus solides; **2** (analytically) [*think, reflect*] profondément; [*discuss, examine, study*] en profondeur; **to go ~ into sth** analyser qch en profondeur; **~ meaningful** très significatif/-ive; **3** [*breathe, sigh, sleep*] profondément; **4** [*dig, cut, thrust*] profondément; [*drink*] à grands traits; [*blush*] intensément; [*tanned*] extrêmement.

deep: **~-rooted** *adj* [*fear, problem, belief, custom*] profondément enraciné; [*loyalty, affection*] profond; [*habit*] ancré; **~-sea** *adj* [*animal, plant*] de haute mer (*after n*); [*current, exploration*] sous-marin; **~-sea diver** ▶ **1692** *n* plongeur/-euse *m/f* sous-marin/-e; **~-sea diving** *n* plongée *f* sous-marine; **~-sea fisherman** ▶ **1692** *n* hauturier *m*; **~-sea fishing** *n* pêche *f* hauturière; **~-seated** *adj* = **deep-rooted**; **~-set** *adj* (très) enfoncé; **~-six**, **~-6** *vtr* US Journ enterrer [*document etc*]; **~ South** *n* US Sud *m* profond; **~ space** *n* espace *m* lointain; **~ structure** *n* Ling structure *f* profonde; **~ therapy** *n* Med radiothérapie *f* profonde.

deer /dɪə(r)/ **I** *n* (*pl* **~**) **1** (species, male of species) (red) cerf *m*; (roe) chevreuil *m*; (fallow) daim *m*; **2** (female of all species) biche *f*.
II *modif* **the ~ family** la famille des cervidés, les cervidés *mpl*.

deer: **~hound** *n* limier *m*; **~skin** *n* peau *f* de daim; **~stalker** *n* (person) chasseur *m* (de cerfs); (hat) casquette *f* à la Sherlock Holmes; **~stalking** *n* chasse *f* au cerf (*à pied*).

de-escalate /ˌdiːˈeskəleɪt/ **I** *vtr* faire baisser [*tension, violence*]; désamorcer [*crisis*]; faire entrer [qch] dans la phase de désescalade [*war*]; enrayer l'escalade de [*arms race*].
II *vi* [*tension, violence*] baisser; [*arms race*] ralentir; [*crisis*] se désamorcer; [*war*] entrer en phase de désescalade.

de-escalation /diːˌeskəˈleɪʃn/ *n* désescalade *f*.

deface /dɪˈfeɪs/ *vtr* **1** (damage) abîmer [*wall, door, furniture*]; dégrader, couvrir [qch] d'inscriptions [*painting, monument, poster*]; **do not ~ the book by writing in the margins** n'abîmez pas le livre en écrivant dans la marge; **to ~ sth with** barbouiller qch de, couvrir qch de [*graffiti, slogans*]; (scratch) abîmer qch avec [*penknife*]; **2** (make illegible) barbouiller.

defacement /dɪˈfeɪsmənt/ *n* (of monument, painting) dégradation *f*; (of inscription) barbouillage *m*.

de facto /ˌdeɪ ˈfæktəʊ/ *adj, adv* de facto.

defamation /ˌdefəˈmeɪʃn/ *n* Jur diffamation *f*; **~ of character** diffamation *f*.

defamatory /dɪˈfæmətrɪ, US -tɔːrɪ/ *adj* diffamatoire, diffamant.

defame /dɪˈfeɪm/ *vtr* diffamer.

default /dɪˈfɔːlt/ **I** *n* **1** (failure to keep up payments on mortgage, loan) non-remboursement *m* (**on** de); (failure to pay fine, debt) non-paiement *m* (**on** de); **your home is at risk in the event of a ~** votre habitation est menacée en cas de non-paiement; **to be in ~ of payment** être en cessation de paiement; **the company is in ~** la compagnie manque à ses engagements; **2** Jur (nonappearance in court) non-comparution *f*.
II *modif* [*attribute, case, option, position, value*] implicite.
III *vi* **1** (fail to make payments) ne pas régler ses échéances; **to ~ on payments** ou **on a loan** ne pas régler les échéances d'un emprunt; **to ~ on a fine** ne pas payer une amende; **to ~ on one's obligations** manquer à ses engagements; **to ~ on a promise** ne pas tenir une promesse; **2** Jur (fail to appear in court) ne pas comparaître.
IV by default *adv phr* (automatically) [*choose, select*] par défaut; **to win by ~** gagner par forfait; **to be elected by ~** être élu en l'absence de tout autre candidat.
V in default of *prep phr* en l'absence de.

defaulter /dɪˈfɔːltə(r)/ *n* **1** (nonpayer) personne *f* qui n'acquitte pas ses dettes; **mortgage/fine ~** personne qui ne règle pas les échéances de son prêt immobilier/qui ne paie pas ses amendes; **2** (nonattender) partie *f* défaillante.

defaulting /dɪˈfɔːltɪŋ/ *adj* **1** [*mortgagor, ratepayer, party*] qui n'acquitte pas ses dettes; **2** [*party, defendant, witness*] défaillant; [*team, player*] qui déclare forfait.

defeat /dɪˈfiːt/ **I** *n* **1** (in battle, election, contest) défaite *f*; **to suffer a ~**, **to meet with ~** essuyer une défaite; **to accept ~** accepter la défaite; **to concede** ou **admit ~** [*team, troops*] concéder la défaite; [*person*] avouer son échec; **England's 3–2 ~ at the hands of** ou **by Italy** la défaite de l'Angleterre 2–3 contre l'Italie; **election ~** défaite électorale; **an air of ~** un air défait; **an admission of ~** un aveu d'échec; **a personal ~** un échec personnel; **2** (of proposal, bill) rejet *m* (**of** de).
II *vtr* **1** (beat) vaincre [*enemy, army*]; battre [*team, opposition, candidate*]; faire subir une défaite à [*government*]; **he has been ~ed by the republican candidate** il a été battu par le candidat républicain; **the government was ~ed by a majority of 20** le gouvernement a été mis en échec par une majorité de 20 voix; **don't let yourself be ~ed** ne te laisse pas abattre; **2** (reject) rejeter [*bill, proposal*]; **3** (thwart) faire échouer [*attempt, plan, take-over bid*]; mettre fin à [*ambitions*]; vaincre [*inflation*]; **that ~s the whole purpose of doing** cela va à l'encontre du but recherché en faisant; **he was ~ed in his attempts to win** toutes ses tentatitves pour gagner ont échoué; **4** (seem incomprehensible to) **it's a problem that has ~ed many great minds** c'est un problème qui a tenu en échec de nombreux savants; **it ~s me** ça me dépasse.

defeated /dɪˈfiːtɪd/ *adj* [*troops*] vaincu; [*party, candidate, competitor*] vaincu, perdant; **to look ~** avoir l'air vaincu.

defeatism /dɪˈfiːtɪzəm/ *n* défaitisme *m*.

defeatist /dɪˈfiːtɪst/ **I** *n* défaitiste *mf*; **don't be such a ~!** ne sois pas si défaitiste!
II *adj* défaitiste.

defecate /ˈdefəkeɪt/ *vi* sout déféquer.

defecation /ˌdefəˈkeɪʃn/ *n* sout défécation *f*.

defect **I** /ˈdiːfekt/ *n* **1** (flaw) défaut *m*; (minor) imperfection *f*; **character ~** défaut (de caractère); **mechanical ~** faute *f* mécanique; **structural ~** vice *m* de construction; **2** (disability) **a hearing/sight/speech ~** un défaut de l'ouïe/de la vue/d'élocution; **birth ~**, **congenital ~** malformation *f* congénitale.
II /dɪˈfekt/ *vi* faire défection; **to ~ from** abandonner [*cause, party*]; s'enfuir de [*country*]; **to ~ to the West/to the republican side** passer à l'Ouest/dans le camp des républicains.

defection /dɪˈfekʃn/ *n* défection *f* (**from** de); **after her ~ to the West** après son passage à l'Ouest.

defective /dɪˈfektɪv/ **I** *n* (person) péj débile (mental) *mf* pej.
II *adj* **1** (faulty) [*reasoning, part, structure, work, method*] défectueux/-euse; [*sight, hearing, intelligence*] déficient; **a breakdown caused by ~ workmanship** une panne provoquée par des défauts de fabrication; **the building is structurally ~** le bâtiment présente des vices de construction; **2** péj (mentally deficient) débile pej; **3** Ling défectif/-ive.

defector /dɪˈfektə(r)/ *n* transfuge *mf* (**from** de).

defence GB, **defense** US /dɪˈfens/ **I** *n* **1** (act of protecting) défense *f* (**against** contre; **from, of** de); **to come to sb's ~** lit (help) venir à l'aide de qn; fig (support) prendre la défense de qn; **to put up a spirited ~** [*competitor, troops*] se défendre vaillamment; **the cat uses its claws for ~** le chat utilise ses griffes pour se défendre; **he has begun his ~ of his Wimbledon title** il a commencé à défendre son titre de Wimbledon; **they marched in ~ of the right to strike** ils ont manifesté pour défendre leur droit de grève; **in the ~ of freedom** pour défendre la liberté; **to die in the ~ of one's country** donner sa vie pour sa patrie; **2** (means of protection) défense *f* (**against** contre); **a line of ~** une ligne de défense; **a means of ~** gen un moyen de défense; Psych, Zool un mécanisme de défense; **a ~ against** un moyen de lutter contre [*anxiety, boredom, cheating*]; **3** (support) défense *f*; **I have nothing to say in his ~** je n'ai rien à dire pour sa défense; **she spoke in his ~** elle a parlé en sa défense; **in my own ~ I must say that** je dois dire pour ma propre défense que; **an article in ~of monetarism** un article défendant ou faisant l'apologie du monétarisme; **to come to sb's ~** prendre la défense de qn; **4** Jur **the ~** (representatives of the accused) la défense *f*; (case, argument) la défense *f*; **the case for the ~** la défense; **to conduct one's own ~** assurer sa propre défense; **the ~ argued that** la défense a argumenté que; **her ~ was that she was provoked** pour sa défense elle a dit qu'elle avait été provoquée; **in her ~** à sa décharge; **counsel for the ~** avocat de la défense; **witness for the ~** témoin à décharge; **to give evidence for the ~** témoigner ou déposer pour la défense; **5** Sport défense *f*; **to play in ~** jouer en défense; **6** Univ soutenance *f* (de thèse).
II defences *npl* **1** Mil défenses *fpl*; **air ~s** défenses aériennes; **2** Biol, Psych défenses *fpl*; **the body's natural ~s** les défenses naturelles du corps; **to break down sb's ~s** faire tomber les défenses de qn.
III *modif* **1** Mil [*adviser, chief, budget, expenditure, industry*] de la défense; [*contract*] pour la défense; [*electronics, policy, forces*] de défense; [*cuts*] dans la défense; **2** Jur [*counsel, lawyer*] pour la défense; [*witness*] à décharge.

Defence Department GB, **Defense Ministry** US *n* ≈ Ministère *m* de la Défense nationale.

defenceless GB, **defenseless** US /dɪˈfenslɪs/ *adj* [*person, animal*] sans défense; [*town, country*] sans défenses.

defencelessness GB, **defenselessness** US /dɪˈfenslɪsnɪs/ *n* (of person, animal) vulnérabilité *f*, incapacité *f* à se défendre; (of town, country) vulnérabilité *f*, absence *f* de défenses.

defence: **~ mechanism** GB, **defense mechanism** US *n* (of body) système *m* immunitaire; Psych mécanisme *m* de défense; **Defence minister** GB, **Defense Secretary** US *n* ≈ Ministre *m* de la défense nationale.

defend /dɪˈfend/ I *vtr* 1 (guard, protect) défendre [*fort, town, country*] (**against** contre; **from** de); défendre [*freedom, interests, rights*]; [*lawyer*] défendre [*client*]; **the government must ~ its majority** le gouvernement doit tout faire pour conserver sa majorité; 2 (justify) défendre [*argument, belief, doctrine, opinion*]; justifier [*actions, behaviour, decision*]; 3 Sport défendre [*title, record*]; 4 Univ **to ~ a thesis** soutenir une thèse.
II *vi* Sport défendre.
III *v refl* **to ~ oneself** 1 (protect oneself) lit, fig se défendre; 2 Jur [*accused*] assurer sa propre défense.
IV **defending** *pres p adj* [*counsel*] de la défense; **the ~ champion** le tenant du titre.

defendant /dɪˈfendənt/ *n* gen défendeur/-eresse *m/f*; (in an appeal court) intimé/-e *m/f*; (in criminal court) prévenu/-e *m/f*; (in assize court) accusé/-e *m/f*.

defender /dɪˈfendə(r)/ *n* gen, Sport défenseur *m*; **Defender of the Faith** Défenseur de la foi.

defense *n* US = **defence**.

defensible /dɪˈfensəbl/ *adj* défendable.

defensive /dɪˈfensɪv/ I *n* gen, Sport, Mil défensive *f*; **to be on the ~** être or se tenir sur la défensive; **to put sb on the ~** mettre qn sur la défensive.
II *adj* [*barrier, weapon, alliance*] défensif/-ive; [*movement, reaction, behaviour*] de défense; [*person*] sur la défensive (*after v*); **they were very ~ about the new proposals** ces nouvelles propositions les ont mis sur la défensive.

defer /dɪˈfɜː(r)/ I *vtr* (*p prés etc* **-rr-**) (postpone) reporter [*decision, meeting, match, publication date*] (**until** à); suspendre [*judgment*] (**until** jusqu'à); remettre [qch] à plus tard [*departure, journey*]; différer [*payment*]; **to ~ selling the house** remettre la vente de la maison à plus tard; **to ~ making a decision** remettre une décision à plus tard; **to ~ sentence** Jur accorder une peine assortie du sursis avec mise à l'épreuve; **to ~ sb's military service** mettre qn en sursis d'incorporation.
II *vi* (*p prés etc* **-rr-**) **to ~ to sb** s'incliner devant qn; **to ~ to sb's judgment/experience** s'en remettre au jugement/à l'expérience de qn; **to ~ to sb's will** ou **wishes** s'incliner devant la volonté de qn.
III **deferred** *pp adj* 1 gen [*departure, closure, purchase*] différé; 2 Fin [*annuity, interest*] différé; [*sale*] à tempérament, à crédit; **~red payment** (postponed) paiement *m* différé; (staggered) paiement *m* par versements échelonnés; **~red payment plan** contrat *m* de vente à tempérament ou à crédit; **a two-year ~red loan** un prêt avec franchise de deux ans; **~red share** action *f* à dividende différé; **~red sentence** peine *f* assortie du sursis avec mise à l'épreuve.

deference /ˈdefərəns/ *n* déférence *f*; **in ~ to, out of ~ to** ou **for** par déférence pour; **with all due ~ to X** n'en déplaise à X.

deferential /ˌdefəˈrenʃl/ *adj* [*person*] déférent (**to** à l'égard de); [*behaviour*] déférent, de déférence.

deferentially /ˌdefəˈrenʃəlɪ/ *adv* avec déférence.

deferment /dɪˈfɜːmənt/, **deferral** /dɪˈfɜːrəl/ *n* 1 (postponement) (of meeting, journey) report *m*; (of decision) report *m*; (judgment) suspension *f*; **~ of a debt** sursis *m* de paiement d'une dette; 2 US Mil **~ of draft** sursis *m* d'incorporation; **to apply for ~** demander un sursis d'incorporation.

defiance /dɪˈfaɪəns/ *n* ¢ défi *m* (**of** à); **their ~ of danger** leur mépris du danger; **their ~ of orders** leur refus d'obéir aux ordres; **in ~ of sth/sb** au mépris de qch/qn; **a gesture/act of ~** un geste/acte de défi; **in ~** [*look, say*] avec défi.

defiant /dɪˈfaɪənt/ *adj* [*person*] arrogant; [*behaviour*] provocant.

defiantly /dɪˈfaɪəntlɪ/ *adv* [*say*] avec défi; [*stare*] d'un air de défi; **she slammed the door ~** elle a claqué la porte d'un air de défi.

deficiency /dɪˈfɪʃənsɪ/ *n* 1 (shortage) (of funds, resources etc) manque *m*, insuffisance *f* (**of, in** de); Med carence *f* (**of** en); **iron/vitamin ~** carence en fer/vitamines; **~ disease** maladie de or par carence; 2 (weakness) (of argument, answer) faiblesse *f*; **his deficiencies as a poet** ses faiblesses en tant que poète; 3 Med (defect) défaut *m*; **a hearing ~** un défaut de l'ouïe; **liver/heart ~** insuffisance *f* hépatique/cardiaque.

deficient /dɪˈfɪʃnt/ *adj* (inadequate) insuffisant; (faulty, flawed) déficient; **~ in sth** pauvre or déficient en qch; **a ~ service** un service qui n'est pas à la hauteur.

deficit /ˈdefɪsɪt/ *n* Comm, Fin déficit *m*; **in ~** en déficit, déficitaire; **budget ~** déficit *m* budgétaire.

deficit spending *n* financement *m* par l'emprunt.

defile I /ˈdiːfaɪl/ *n* 1 (valley) défilé *m*; 2 (procession) file *f*.
II /dɪˈfaɪl/ *vtr* 1 (pollute) lit, fig souiller; 2 Relig profaner.

defilement /dɪˈfaɪlmənt/ *n* littér 1 (pollution) lit, fig souillure *f*; 2 Relig profanation *f*.

definable /dɪˈfaɪnəbl/ *adj* définissable.

define /dɪˈfaɪn/ *vtr* 1 (give definition of) définir [*term, concept*] (**as** comme); 2 (specify) définir, déterminer [*limits*]; définir, délimiter [*duties, powers*]; **clearly ~d responsibilities** des responsabilités bien définies; 3 (express clearly) déterminer [*problem*]; **I can't ~ how I feel about him** je ne saurais dire exactement ce que je ressens pour lui; 4 **to be ~d against** (stand out) (tree, building etc) se détacher nettement sur [*sky, background*].

definite /ˈdefɪnɪt/ *adj* 1 (not vague) [*view, plan, criteria*] précis; [*result*] sans équivoque; [*amount, sum, boundary*] précis, bien déterminé; **a ~ answer** une réponse claire et nette; **~ evidence** preuves *fpl* formelles; **to have a ~ feeling that** avoir la nette impression que; **it is ~ that** il est certain que; **there's nothing ~ yet, nothing is ~ yet** rien n'est encore sûr; 2 (firm) [*contract, offer*] ferme, définitif/-ive; [*agreement, decision*] formel/-elle, ferme; [*intention*] ferme; [*refusal*] formel/-elle, catégorique; 3 (obvious) (*before n*) [*change, improvement, increase*] net/nette; [*advantage*] certain (*after n*), évident; [*smell*] très net/nette; 4 (decided) (*before n*) [*manner, tone*] résolu; **5 to be ~** [*person*] (sure) être certain (**about** de); (firm) être formel/-elle (**about** sur).

definite: **~ article** *n* Ling article *m* défini; **~ integral** *n* Math intégrale *f* définie.

definitely /ˈdefɪnɪtlɪ/ *adv* 1 (certainly) sans aucun doute; **he ~ said he wasn't coming** il a bien dit qu'il ne viendrait pas; **she's ~ not there** elle n'est pas là, c'est sûr; **I'm ~ not going** c'est décidé, je n'y vais pas; **is she ~ going to be there?** est-ce que c'est sûr qu'elle y sera?; **it's ~ colder today** il fait nettement plus froid aujourd'hui; **this one is ~ the best/cheapest etc** celui-ci est sans conteste le meilleur/le moins cher etc; **this ~ isn't going to work** manifestement ça ne va pas marcher; **he's ~ not my type** ce n'est vraiment pas mon genre; **'do you support them?'—'~!'** 'vous leur donnez votre soutien?'—'absolument!'; 2 (categorically) [*answer*] d'une manière formelle or bien déterminée; [*commit oneself, arrange*] formellement, de manière définitive; **she stated her opinion most** ou **very ~** elle a donné son opinion de la manière la plus catégorique.

definition /ˌdefɪˈnɪʃn/ *n* 1 (of word) définition *f*; (of feeling, quality) analyse *f*; (of role, duties) clarification *f*; **by ~** par définition; 2 TV, Comput, Phot définition *f*; **a photo with good/bad ~** une photo nette/floue; 3 (of telescope) pouvoir *m* de résolution.

definitive /dɪˈfɪnətɪv/ *adj* 1 gen [*statement, version, answer, solution etc*] définitif/-ive; [*decision*] irrévocable; [*interpretation*] de référence, insurpassable; 2 Post [*stamp*] ordinaire; [*issue*] de timbres ordinaires.

definitively /dɪˈfɪnətɪvlɪ/ *adv* [*decide*] irrévocablement; [*solve, eradicate*] définitivement; [*answer*] de manière définitive.

deflate /dɪˈfleɪt/ I *vtr* 1 lit dégonfler [*tyre, balloon, ball, airbed*]; 2 fig saper [*confidence, reputation*]; rabattre [*conceit*]; dégonfler [*importance*]; démonter [*person*]; mettre fin à [*hopes*]; 3 Econ faire baisser [*prices*]; **to ~ the economy** pratiquer une politique déflationniste.
II *vi* [*tyre, balloon etc*] se dégonfler.
III **deflated** *pp adj* 1 lit [*tyre, balloon etc*] dégonflé; 2 fig [*person*] déprimé.

deflation /dɪˈfleɪʃn/ *n* 1 Econ déflation *f*; 2 lit (of tyre, balloon etc) dégonflement *m*; 3 fig **a feeling of ~** une sensation d'abattement.

deflationary /ˌdiːˈfleɪʃənərɪ, US -nerɪ/ *adj* déflationniste.

deflationist /dɪˈfleɪʃənɪst/ I *n* partisan *m* d'une politique de déflation.
II *adj* favorable à une politique de déflation.

deflect /dɪˈflekt/ I *vtr* 1 défléchir, dévier [*missile*]; détourner [*water, air*]; dévier [*light*]; **the ball was ~ed into the goal** la balle a rebondi jusque dans le but; 2 fig détourner [*blame, criticism, attention*]; 3 (dissuade) **to ~ sb from** détourner qn de [*aim, action*]; **to ~ sb from doing** dissuader qn de faire.
II *vi* [*missile, indicator, needle*] dévier (**from** de).

deflection /dɪˈflekʃn/ *n* (of missile) déviation *f*; (of river) détournement *m*, dérivation *f*; (of indicator needle) déviation *f*; (of angle) déclinaison *f*; Phys (of air) déflexion *f*; (of light) déviation *f*.

deflector /dɪˈflektə(r)/ *n* déflecteur *m*.

deflower /ˌdiːˈflaʊə(r)/ *vtr* littér déflorer [*girl*]; flétrir [*beauty*].

defoliant /ˌdiːˈfəʊlɪənt/ *n* défoliant *m*.

defoliate /ˌdiːˈfəʊlɪeɪt/ *vtr* défolier.

defoliation /ˌdiːfəʊlɪˈeɪʃn/ *n* défoliation *f*.

deforest /ˌdiːˈfɒrɪst/ *vtr* déboiser.

deforestation /ˌdiːfɒrɪˈsteɪʃn/ *n* déboisement *m*.

deform /dɪˈfɔːm/ I *vtr* (all contexts) déformer.
II *vi* (by arthritis etc) se déformer.
III **deformed** *pp adj* 1 Med déformé; (from birth) difforme; 2 [*metal, structure*] déformé.

deformation /ˌdiːfɔːˈmeɪʃn/ *n* 1 Med (by arthritis etc) déformation *f*; (congenital) malformation *f*; 2 (of metal, structure) déformation *f*.

deformity /dɪˈfɔːmətɪ/ *n* Med difformité *f*.

defraud /dɪˈfrɔːd/ *vtr* escroquer [*client, employer*]; frauder [*tax authority*]; **to ~ sb of sth** escroquer qch à qn; **to ~ the taxman of £20,000** escroquer 20 000 livres sterling au fisc.

defrauder /dɪˈfrɔːdə(r)/ *n* (professional) escroc *m*; (amateur) fraudeur/-euse *m/f*.

defray /dɪˈfreɪ/ *vtr* couvrir [*expenses*]; rembourser [*cost*].

defrayal /dɪˈfreɪəl/, **defrayment** /dɪˈfreɪmənt/ *n* remboursement *m*.

defrock /ˌdiːˈfrɒk/ *vtr* défroquer.

defrost /ˌdiːˈfrɒst/ I *vtr* décongeler [*food*]; dégivrer [*refrigerator, window*].
II *vi* [*refrigerator*] dégivrer; [*food*] décongeler.
III *v refl* **to ~ itself** [*freezer*] se dégivrer.

defroster /ˌdiːˈfrɒstə(r)/ *n* dégivreur *m*.

deft /deft/ *adj* adroit de ses mains, habile; **to be ~ at sth/at doing** être doué pour qch/pour faire.

deftly /ˈdeftlɪ/ *adv* adroitement.

deftness /ˈdeftnɪs/ *n* dextérité *f*.

defunct /dɪˈfʌŋkt/ *adj* [*organization, person*] défunt; [*practice*] révolu.

defuse /ˌdiːˈfjuːz/ *vtr* lit, fig désamorcer.

defy /dɪˈfaɪ/ *vtr* 1 (disobey) défier [*authority,*

law, person]; ne pas tenir compte de [*advice*]; faire mentir [*expectations, predictions*]; défier [*death, gravity, reality*]; **2** (challenge) [*person*] jeter un défi à [*person*]; braver [*danger*]; **to ~ sb to do** mettre qn au défi de faire; **3** (elude, resist) défier [*description, logic, analysis*] échapper à [*categorization*]; **to ~ sb's efforts/attempts to do** résister à tous les efforts/toutes les tentatives de qn à faire.

degeneracy /dɪˈdʒenərəsɪ/ *n* (of society) dégénérescence *f*; (of person, way of life) décadence *f*.

degenerate I /dɪˈdʒenərət/ *n* dégénéré/-e *m/f*.
II /dɪˈdʒenərət/ *adj* **1** [*person*] dégénéré; [*society*] dégénéré, complètement décadent; [*life*] dépravé; **2** Biol, Phys dégénéré.
III /dɪˈdʒənəreɪt/ *vi* [*race, morals, intellect*] dégénérer; [*health, quality*] se dégrader; **to ~ into** dégénérer en [*chaos, war*]; **the debate ~d into a bitter argument** le débat a dégénéré en violente querelle; **to ~ into farce** tourner à la farce.

degeneration /dɪˌdʒenəˈreɪʃn/ *n* **1** (of quality of life, goods, economy) dégradation *f*; (of health) déclin *m*; **2** Biol dégénérescence *f*.

degenerative /dɪˈdʒenərətɪv/ *adj* Med dégénératif/-ive.

degradation /ˌdegrəˈdeɪʃn/ *n* **1** (humiliation) humiliation *f* (**of** de; **of doing** de faire); **2** (debasement) (of person) (imposed) déchéance *f*; (voluntary) avilissement *m*; (of culture, knowledge, work) dégradation *f*; **3** (of environment, facilities) dégradation *f* (**of** de); **4** (squalor) misère *f*; **5** Biol, Chem, Geol dégradation *f*.

degrade /dɪˈgreɪd/ I *vtr* **1** (humiliate) humilier [*person*]; **2** (debase) être dégradant pour [*person, person's body, culture, artist*]; **films which ~ women** les films qui donnent une image dégradante de la femme; **3** (demote) dégrader [*person*]; **4** Ecol dégrader [*environment*].
II *vi* Biol, Chem, Geol se dégrader.

degrading /dɪˈgreɪdɪŋ/ *adj* [*portrayal, conditions, film etc*] dégradant (**to** pour); [*job, work*] avilissant; [*treatment, punishment*] humiliant; (stronger) dégradant.

degree /dɪˈgriː/ *n* **1** Geog, Math, Meas degré *m*; **at an angle of 40 ~s to the vertical** à un angle de 40 degrés par rapport à la verticale; **turn the knob through 180 ~s** tournez le bouton de 180 degrés; **ten ~s of latitude/longitude** 10 degrés de latitude/longitude; **20 ~s south of the equator** par 20 degrés au sud de l'équateur; **2** Meteorol, Phys degré *m*; **30 ~s Celsius** ou **centigrade** 30 degrés Celsius or centigrades; **it was 40 ~s in the shade** il faisait 40 (degrés) à l'ombre; **I had a temperature of 104 ~s** j'avais 39 de fièvre; **3** Univ diplôme *m* universitaire; **first** ou **bachelor's ~** ≈ licence *f*; **higher ~** (master's) ≈ maîtrise *f*; (doctorate) doctorat *m*; **to take/get a ~** préparer/obtenir un diplôme (universitaire); **to have a ~** être diplômé; **4** (amount) degré *m*; **this gives me a ~ of control** cela me procure un certain degré de contrôle; **a high ~ of efficiency** beaucoup de compétence; **the exact ~ of his influence is unknown** on ignore à quel point il est influent; **to such a ~ that** à un tel point que; **an alarming ~ of ignorance** un degré d'ignorance inquiétant; **to a ~, to some ~** dans une certaine mesure; **to a lesser ~** dans une moindre mesure; **I enjoy a** ou **some ~ of autonomy** je jouis d'une certaine autonomie; **I was not in the slightest ~ anxious** je n'étais pas le moins du monde inquiet; **by ~s** petit à petit; **with varying ~s of accuracy/success** avec une précision/ un succès variable; **5** US Jur **murder in the first ~** homicide *m* volontaire avec préméditation; **6** Math, Mus degré *m*; **7** Ling degré *m*; **the ~s of comparison** les degrés de la comparaison; **8**† (rank) extraction *f*; **a man of high/low ~** un homme de haute/basse extraction.

degree: **~ ceremony** *n* GB Univ cérémonie *f* de remise des diplômes; **~ certificate** *n* GB Univ diplôme *m*; **~ course** *n* GB Univ programme *m* d'études universitaires; **~ examinations** *npl* GB Univ examens *mpl* de fin d'études universitaires; **~ factory**○ GB, **~-mill**○ US *n* péj boîte○ *f* à diplômes.

dehumanization /ˌdiːhjuːmənaɪˈzeɪʃn, US -nɪˈz-/ *n* déshumanisation *f*.

dehumanize /ˌdiːˈhjuːmənaɪz/ *vtr* déshumaniser.

dehumidifier /ˌdiːˈhjuːmɪdɪfaɪə(r)/ *n* déshumidificateur *m*.

dehumidify /ˌdiːˈhjuːmɪdɪfaɪ/ *vtr* déshumidifier.

dehydrate /ˌdiːˈhaɪdreɪt/ I *vtr* déshydrater.
II *vi* se déshydrater.

dehydrated /ˌdiːˈhaɪdreɪtɪd/ *adj* **1** (dried) [*food*] déshydraté; [*powdered*] en poudre; **2** (lacking fluids) [*person*] déshydraté; **to become ~** se déshydrater; **to feel ~** être déshydraté.

dehydration /ˌdiːhaɪˈdreɪʃn/ *n* **1** (of food) déshydratation *f*; **2** Med déshydratation *f*.

de-ice /ˌdiːˈaɪs/ *vtr* dégivrer.

de-icer /ˌdiːˈaɪsə(r)/ *n* **1** Aut dégivrant *m*; **2** Aviat dégivreur *m*.

de-icing /ˌdiːˈaɪsɪŋ/ I *n* dégivrage *m*.
II *modif* [*product*] dégivrant; [*device, process*] de dégivrage.

deictic /ˈdeɪktɪk/ *n, adj* déictique (*m*).

deification /ˌdiːˈfɪˈkeɪʃn/ *n* déification *f*.

deify /ˈdiːɪfaɪ/ *vtr* déifier.

deign /deɪn/ *vtr* **to ~ to do** condescendre à faire, daigner faire.

deism /ˈdiːɪzəm/ *n* déisme *m*.

deist /ˈdiːɪst/ *n* déiste *mf*.

deistic /ˈdiːɪstɪk/ *adj* déiste.

deity /ˈdiːətɪ/ *n* divinité *f*, déité *f* liter; **the Deity** Dieu.

deixis /ˈdeɪksɪs/ *n* déixis *f*.

déjà vu /ˌdeɪʒɑː ˈvjuː/ *n* déjà-vu *m*; **a feeling of ~** une impression de déjà-vu.

dejected /dɪˈdʒektɪd/ *adj* déprimé, abattu, découragé; **to become** ou **get ~** se laisser abattre, se décourager; **to look ~** avoir l'air abattu or déprimé.

dejectedly /dɪˈdʒektɪdlɪ/ *adv* [*look, stare*] avec découragement, d'un air découragé; [*say*] d'un ton découragé, avec découragement.

de jure /ˌdeɪ ˈdʒʊərɪ/ *adj, adv* de jure.

dekko○ /ˈdekəʊ/ *n* GB coup *m* d'œil; **to have** ou **take a ~** jeter un coup d'œil (**at** à).

Delaware /ˈdeləweə(r)/ **▶ 1744** *pr n* Delaware *m*.

delay /dɪˈleɪ/ I *n* **1** (of train, plane, post) retard *m* (**of** de; **to, on** sur); (in traffic) ralentissement *m* (**of** de); **~ in taking off** retard au décollage; **we apologize for the ~** nous vous prions de nous excuser pour ce retard; **2** (slowness) **without (further) ~** sans (plus) tarder; **to apologize for one's ~ in replying** s'excuser d'avoir tardé à répondre; **the government's inexcusable ~ in publishing the report** le retard inexcusable du gouvernement à publier le rapport; **there's no time for ~** il n'y a pas de temps à perdre; **3** (time lapse) délai *m* (**of** de; **between** entre); **a few minutes' ~** un délai de quelques minutes.
II *vtr* **1** (postpone , put off) différer [*decision, publication, departure*] (**until, to** jusqu'à); **to ~ doing** attendre pour faire; **2** (hold up) retarder [*train, arrival, post, change, process*]; ralentir [*traffic*]; **bad weather ~ed us, we were ~ed by bad weather** le mauvais temps nous a retardés; **flights were ~ed by up to 12 hours** les vols ont eu jusqu'à 12 heures de retard.
III *vi* s'attarder; **don't ~!** fais vite!
IV **delayed** *pp adj* [*flight, train*] qui a été retardé; [*passenger*] en retard; **to have a ~ed reaction** réagir après coup (**to** à); **to have a ~ed effect** agir après un certain délai.
V **delaying** *pres p adj* [*action, tactic*] dilatoire.

delayed action *adj* [*shutter, fuse*] à retardement.

dele /diːlɪ/ *n* deleatur *m*.

delectable /dɪˈlektəbl/ *adj* [*meal, dish, drink*] délicieux/-ieuse; [*dress, room, child*] délicieux/-ieuse.

delectation /ˌdiːlekˈteɪʃn/ *n* délectation *f*, délice *m*; **for the ~ of** pour le plus grand plaisir de.

delegate I /ˈdelɪgət/ *n* **1** (to conference, meeting) délégué/-e *m/f*; **2** US Pol **~ (to the Convention)** délégué/-e *m/f*.
II /ˈdelɪgeɪt/ *vtr* déléguer [*power, responsibility, task*] (**to** à; **to do** pour faire); **you've been ~d to make the tea** hum nous avons décidé que c'est toi qui auras l'honneur de faire le thé.
III /ˈdelɪgeɪt/ *vi* déléguer ses responsabilités.

delegation /ˌdelɪˈgeɪʃn/ *n* (all contexts) délégation *f*.

delete /dɪˈliːt/ *vtr* gen supprimer (**from** de); (with pen) rayer, barrer; Comput supprimer, effacer [*character, file*]; **~ where inapplicable** rayer les mentions inutiles.

delete key *n* Comput touche *f* effacement.

deleterious /ˌdelɪˈtɪərɪəs/ *adj* sout [*effect, influence*] délétère liter, nuisible; **to be ~ to sth** nuire à qch.

deletion /dɪˈliːʃn/ *n* **1** (act) suppression *f*; **2** (word, line taken out) suppression *f*; (word, line crossed out) rature *f*.

delft /delft/ *n* faïence *f* de Delft.

deli○ /delɪ/ *n* **1** (shop) épicerie *f* fine; **2** US (eating place) restaurant-traiteur *m*.

deliberate I /dɪˈlɪbərət/ *adj* **1** (intentional) [*act, attempt, choice, cruelty, decision, policy, provocation etc*] délibéré; [*aggression*] réfléchi, délibéré; [*vandalism, violation*] intentionnel/-elle, délibéré; **it's ~** c'est fait exprès; **it wasn't ~** ce n'était pas fait exprès; **2** (measured) [*manner, movement etc*] mesuré.
II /dɪˈlɪbəreɪt/ *vtr* **1** (discuss) délibérer sur; **2** (consider) considérer, réfléchir sur.
III /dɪˈlɪbəreɪt/ *vi* **1** (discuss) délibérer; **2** (reflect) réfléchir, délibérer (**over, about** sur).

deliberately /dɪˈlɪbərətlɪ/ *adv* **1** (intentionally) [*do, say*] exprès, à dessein, délibérément; [*sarcastic, provocative etc*] délibérément; **I ~ addressed her by her first name** c'est exprès que je l'ai appelée par son prénom; **2** (slowly and carefully) [*speak*] posément; [*walk*] délibérément.

deliberation /dɪˌlɪbəˈreɪʃn/ *n* **1** (reflection) réflexion *f*, délibération *f*; **after careful/long ~** après mûre réflexion/une longue délibération; **2** (discussion, debate) gen délibération *f*, débat *m*; Jur délibération *f*; **3** (slowness) mesure *f*, manière *f* posée; **with ~** posément, avec mesure.

deliberative /dɪˈlɪbərətɪv/ *adj* **1** [*assembly, council*] délibérant; **2** [*conclusion, decision, speech*] mûrement réfléchi.

delicacy /ˈdelɪkəsɪ/ *n* **1** (of features) finesse *f*; (of beauty, china) délicatesse *f*, fragilité *f*; (of colour, design, craftsmanship, touch) délicatesse *f*; **2** (of health) délicatesse *f*, fragilité *f*; **3** (of mechanism, instrument) sensibilité *f*; **4** (awkwardness) (of situation, subject) délicatesse *f*; **a matter of great ~** une affaire qui demande beaucoup de tact; **5** (tact) (of person) délicatesse *f*, tact *m*; **6** Culin (savoury) mets *m* raffiné or délicat; (sweet) friandise *f*; **caviar is a great ~** le caviar est un mets très raffiné.

delicate /ˈdelɪkət/ I *adj* **1** (fine) [*features, hands*] fin; [*patterning*] délicat; (subtle) [*shade, perfume*] délicat; [*gesture*] gracieux/-ieuse; [*touch*] léger; **2** (easily damaged) [*china*] fragile; [*fabric*] délicat; **3** (finely tuned) [*mechanism*] délicat; [*balance*] précaire; **4** (not robust) [*health, stomach*] fragile, délicat; **I feel a bit ~ this morning** je me sens un peu patraque○ ce matin; **5** (requiring skill or tact) [*operation, problem, moment, situation,*

subject] délicat; **her ~ handling of the problem** sa manière habile de traiter le problème.
II **delicates** *npl* (fabrics) linge *m* délicat.

delicately /ˈdelɪkətlɪ/ *adv* **1** [*crafted, embroidered, flavoured*] délicatement; **2** [*handle, treat*] avec délicatesse; [*phrase*] avec tact, avec délicatesse.

delicatessen /ˌdelɪkəˈtesn/ *n* **1** (shop) épicerie *f* fine; **2** US (eating-place) restaurant-traiteur *m*.

delicious /dɪˈlɪʃəs/ *adj* **1** [*meal, smell*] délicieux/-ieuse, exquis; **2** [*feeling, person, story*] délicieux/-ieuse.

deliciously /dɪˈlɪʃəslɪ/ *adv* délicieusement; **the water was ~ cool** l'eau était délicieusement fraîche or d'une fraîcheur exquise.

delight /dɪˈlaɪt/ **I** *n* joie *f*, plaisir *m*; **to take ~ in sth/in doing** prendre plaisir à qch/à faire; **to take ~ in tormenting sb** se faire un plaisir de tourmenter qn; **her ~ at sth/at doing** son plaisir pour qch/à faire; **a cry of ~** un cri de joie; **to laugh in sheer ~** rire de plaisir; **it is a ~ to do** c'est un plaisir (que) de faire; **it gives me great ~ to do** c'est un grand plaisir pour moi de faire; **(much) to my ~** à ma plus grande joie; **he is his mother's ~** il est la plus grande joie de sa mère; **it's a gardener's/gastronomic ~** c'est un plaisir pour l'œil du jardinier/pour le palais; **it's a ~ to the senses** c'est un régal pour les sens; **the ~s of camping/of Paris** les joies du camping/de Paris.
II *vtr* ravir [*person*] **(with** par) ; **it ~s me that** je suis ravi que (+ *subj*).
III *vi* **to ~ in sth/in doing** prendre plaisir à qch/à faire; **I ~ed in his failure** son échec m'a ravi.

delighted /dɪˈlaɪtɪd/ *adj* [*smile, expression, person*] ravi **(about, at, by, with** de; **at doing, to do** de faire); **to be ~ that** être ravi que (+ *subj*); **to be ~ with sb** être très content de qn; **I'm ~ for you** j'en suis ravi pour toi; **(I should be) ~!** j'en serais ravi!; **~ to meet you** enchanté.

delightedly /dɪˈlaɪtɪdlɪ/ *adv* [*announce, agree, smile*] d'un air ravi; [*laugh, applaud, shriek*] avec ravissement.

delightful /dɪˈlaɪtfl/ *adj* **1** [*house, hotel, village, expression, laugh, story, party*] charmant; [*atmosphere, setting, weather, countryside, meal*] agréable; [*idea, sight, book, ballet*] merveilleux/-euse; **it is ~ to do, it is ~ doing** c'est agréable de faire; **2** [*person, personality, smile*] charmant.

delightfully /dɪˈlaɪtfəlɪ/ *adv* [*warm, peaceful*] agréablement; [*sing, play*] à merveille; **he is ~ eccentric/shy** il est délicieusement excentrique/timide.

Delilah /dɪˈlaɪlə/ *pr n* Bible Dalila.

delimit /ˌdiːˈlɪmɪt/ *vtr* délimiter.

delimitation /ˌdiːlɪmɪˈteɪʃn/ *n* délimitation *f*.

delineate /dɪˈlɪnɪeɪt/ *vtr* **1** (determine, specify) déterminer [*concerns, strategy, terms, subject, area*]; décrire [*aspects, features, character*]; **2** (mark boundaries of) lit, fig délimiter [*area, space*].

delineation /dɪˌlɪnɪˈeɪʃn/ *n* sout (of problem, plan) présentation *f*; Literat (of character) portrait *m* (psychologique); (of line, picture) tracé *m*.

delinquency /dɪˈlɪŋkwənsɪ/ *n* **1** (behaviour) délinquance *f*; **2** (offence) délit *m*; **3** US Fin défaut *m* de paiement.

delinquent /dɪˈlɪŋkwənt/ **I** *n* délinquant/-e *m/f*.
II *adj* **1** [*behaviour, child, youth*] délinquant; [*act*] de délinquance; **2** US Fin [*tax*] non payé; [*debtor*] défaillant.

deliquesce /ˌdelɪˈkwes/ *vi* tomber en déliquescence.

deliquescence /ˌdelɪˈkwesns/ *n* déliquescence *f*.

deliquescent /ˌdelɪˈkwesnt/ *adj* déliquescent.

delirious /dɪˈlɪrɪəs/ *adj* **1** Med délirant; **to become ~** être pris de délire; **to be ~** délirer; **2** fig [*crowd*] délirant, en délire; [*fan*] hystérique; **~ with joy** délirant de joie; **the crowd grew ~ with excitement** l'excitation de la foule tournait au délire.

deliriously /dɪˈlɪrɪəslɪ/ *adv* fig follement, frénétiquement; **~ happy** ivre de joie, follement heureux/-euse.

delirium /dɪˈlɪrɪəm/ *n* Med, fig délire *m*.

delirium tremens /dɪˌlɪrɪəm ˈtriːmenz/ *n* delirium tremens *m*.

deliver /dɪˈlɪvə(r)/ **I** *vtr* **1** (take to address) livrer [*goods, milk, groceries*] **(to** à); (to several houses) distribuer [*newspaper, mail*]; (to an individual) apporter [*newspaper, mail*] **(to** à); remettre [*note, written message*]; transmettre [*oral message*]; **'~ed to your door'** 'livraison à domicile'; **2** Med [*doctor, midwife*] mettre au monde [*baby*]; [*vet*] délivrer [*baby animal*]; **to be ~ed** [*baby*] être né; **she was ~ed of a son**† elle a accouché d'un garçon; **3** (utter) faire, prononcer [*speech, lecture, sermon*]; faire [*reprimand, rebuke*]; donner [*ultimatum, decision*]; rendre [*verdict, ruling*]; réciter [*line, speech in play*]; lancer [*verbal attack, joke*]; **4** (hand over) céder [*property, money, goods*] **(over to, up to** à); livrer [*town, ship*] **(over to, up to** à); **to ~ sth/sb into sb's care** confier qch/qn à qn; **5** (give, strike) asséner [*blow, punch*]; donner [*knife thrust*]; tirer [*bullets, round*]; fournir [*voltage*] **(to** à); **to ~ the final blow to sth** fig porter le coup fatal à qch; **6** (rescue) délivrer [*person*] **(from** de); **'~ us from evil'** 'délivrez-nous du mal'.
II *vi* **1** [*tradesman, company*] livrer; **the postman doesn't ~ on Sundays** le facteur ne distribue pas le courrier le dimanche; **2**○ tenir ses engagements **(on** quant à); **ultimately, the film doesn't ~** au bout du compte, le film déçoit.
III *v refl* **to ~ oneself of** sout émettre [*opinion*].
IDIOMS **stand and ~!** la bourse ou la vie!; **to ~ the goods**○ tenir ses engagements.

deliverance /dɪˈlɪvərəns/ *n* délivrance *f*.

deliverer /dɪˈlɪvərə(r)/ *n* **1** (of goods, groceries) (person) livreur/-euse *m/f*; (company) service *m* de livraison; **2** (saviour) libérateur/-trice *m/f*.

delivery /dɪˈlɪvərɪ/ **I** *n* **1** (of goods, milk) livraison *f*; (of mail, newspaper) (to several houses) distribution *f*; (to individual) livraison *f*; **to take ~ of sth** prendre livraison de qch; **on ~** à la livraison; **2** (way of speaking) élocution *f*; (speed of speaking) débit *m*; **3** (pronouncement) (of judgment, ruling) énonciation *f*; **4** (of baby) accouchement *m*; **5** Sport lancer *m*; **6** (handing over of property) remise *f*.
II *modif* [*cost, date, delay, lorry, note, order, schedule, service, time, vehicle*] de livraison.

delivery: **~ address** *n* adresse *f* du destinataire; **~ boy** *n* garçon *m* de courses; **~ charge** *n* (frais *mpl* de) port *m*; **~ girl** *n* livreuse *f*; **~ man** *n* livreur *m*; **~ room** *n* Med salle *f* d'accouchement; **~ suite** *n* GB Med salles *fpl* d'accouchement; **~ woman** *n* livreuse *f*.

dell /del/ *n* littér vallon *m* boisé.

delouse /ˌdiːˈlaʊs/ *vtr* épouiller.

Delphi /ˈdelfɪ/ *pr n* Delphes.

Delphic /ˈdelfɪk/ *adj* **1** Mythol de Delphes; **~ oracle** oracle *m* de Delphes; **2** (mysterious) sibyllin.

delphinium /delˈfɪnɪəm/ *n* delphinium *m*.

delta /ˈdeltə/ *n* **1** (Greek letter) delta *m* also Math; **2** Geog delta *m*; **3** GB Univ *note la plus basse*.

delta wing *n* aile *f* delta.

deltoid /ˈdeltɔɪd/ **I** *n* (also **~ muscle**) deltoïde *m*.
II *adj* deltoïde.

delude /dɪˈluːd/ **I** *vtr* tromper **(with** par); **he ~d them into believing that...** il a réussi à leur faire croire que...
II *v refl* **to ~ oneself** se faire des illusions; **to ~ oneself into believing that...** se persuader que...
III deluded *pp adj* **to be ~d** se tromper; **a ~d person** un naïf/une naïve *m/f*.

deluge /ˈdeljuːdʒ/ **I** *n* lit, fig déluge *m*.
II *vtr* lit, fig submerger **(with** de); **to be ~d with** être submergé par.

delusion /dɪˈluːʒn/ *n* gen illusion *f*; Psych délire *m*; **to be under the ~ that...** s'imaginer que...; **to be under a ~** se faire des illusions; **to suffer from ~s** Psych souffrir de crises de délire; **~s of grandeur** la folie des grandeurs.

delusive /dɪˈluːsɪv/ *adj* trompeur/-euse.

de luxe /dəˈlʌks, ˈlʊks/ *adj* [*model, version, edition*] de luxe; [*accommodation*] luxueux/-euse.

delve /delv/ *vi* **1 to ~ into** fouiller dans [*pocket, records, memory, subject, past*]; examiner [*motive*]; **he ~d into the book for some quotations** il a cherché dans le livre pour trouver des citations; **to ~ further** ou **deeper into** fouiller un peu [*records, subject etc*]; étudier d'un peu plus près [*book*]; **2** GB littér (dig) creuser **(into** dans).

Dem US *abrév écrite* = **Democrat, Democratic**.

demagnetize /diːˈmægnɪtaɪz/ *vtr* démagnétiser.

demagogic /ˌdeməˈgɒgɪk/ *adj* [*person*] démagogue; [*speech, manner*] démagogique.

demagogue /ˈdeməgɒg/ *n* démagogue *mf*.

demagogy /ˈdeməgɒgɪ/ *n* démagogie *f*.

de-man /ˌdiːˈmæn/ *vtr* GB réduire la main-d'œuvre de.

demand /dɪˈmɑːnd, US dɪˈmænd/ **I** *n* **1** (request) demande *f*; **there have been many ~s for his resignation** un grand nombre de personnes ont demandé sa démission; **on ~** [*divorce, abortion, access*] à la demande; Fin [*payable, available*] à vue; **2** (pressure) exigence *f*; **the ~s of** les exigences de; **I have many ~s on my time** mon temps est très pris; **the purchase will make extra ~s on our finances** cet achat va entamer encore plus nos finances; **3** Econ demande *f* **(for** de); **supply and ~** l'offre et la demande; **4** (favour) **to be in ~** être très demandé; **he's in great ~ as a singer** c'est un chanteur très demandé.
II *vtr* **1** (request) demander [*reform, release*]; (very forcefully) exiger [*payment, attention, ransom*]; **to ~ an inquiry** réclamer une enquête; **to ~ one's money back** exiger d'être remboursé; **to ~ sth from sb** exiger qch de qn; **I ~ to know the truth** je demande à savoir la vérité; (stronger) j'exige de savoir la vérité; **to ~ to see sb's licence** demander à voir le permis de qn; **she ~ed to be let in** elle a exigé qu'on la laisse entrer; **to ~ that sb do** exiger que qn fasse; **we ~ that we be included** nous demandons à être inclus; **2** (require) [*work, situation, employer*] demander [*patience, skill, time*] **(of sb** de qn); (more imperatively) exiger [*punctuality, qualities*]; **to ~ of sb that** exiger de qn que (+ *subj*).

demand: **~ deposit** *n* dépôt *m* à vue; **~ feeding** *n* allaitement *m* à la demande.

demanding /dɪˈmɑːndɪŋ, US -ˈmænd-/ *adj* **1** [*person*] exigeant; **2** [*work, course*] ardu; [*schedule*] chargé.

demand note *n* **1** GB demande *f* de paiement; **2** US effet *m* à vue.

demand-pull inflation *n* inflation *f* par la demande.

demanning /ˌdiːˈmænɪŋ/ *n* GB réduction *f* de main-d'œuvre, dégraissage○ *m*.

demarcate /ˈdiːmɑːkeɪt/ *vtr* délimiter [*space, scope*]; tracer [*boundary*].

demarcation /ˌdiːmɑːˈkeɪʃn/ *n* **1** (physical) (action, boundary) démarcation *f*; **2** Jur, Admin délimitation *f*.

demarcation dispute *n* querelle *f* de compétence (*entre syndicats*).

démarche /ˈdeɪmɑːʃ/ *n* démarche *f*.

demean /dɪˈmiːn/ *v refl* **to ~ oneself** s'abaisser (**to do** à faire).

demeaning /dɪˈmiːnɪŋ/ *adj* humiliant.

demeanour GB, **demeanor** US /dɪˈmiːnə(r)/ *n* sout (behaviour) comportement *m*; (bearing) maintien *m*.

demented /dɪˈmentɪd/ *adj* fou/folle; **to drive sb ~**○ rendre qn fou.

dementedly /dɪˈmentɪdlɪ/ *adv* comme un fou/une folle.

dementia /dɪˈmenʃə/ *n* démence *f*.

demerara (sugar) /ˌdeməˈreərə/ *n* sucre *m* roux cristallisé.

demerge /diːˈmɜːdʒ/ **I** *vtr* scinder.

II *vi* se scinder.

demerger /diːˈmɜːdʒə(r)/ *n* scission *f*.

demerit /ˌdiːˈmerɪt/ *n* **1** gen démérite fml *m*; **2** US Sch (also **~ point**) avertissement *m*.

demi+ /demɪ-/ (*dans composés*) demi-.

demigod /ˈdemɪgɒd/ *n* demi-dieu *m*.

demijohn /ˈdemɪdʒɒn/ *n* dame-jeanne *f*, bonbonne *f*.

demilitarization /diːˌmɪlɪtəraɪˈzeɪʃn, US -rɪˈz-/ *n* démilitarisation *f*.

demilitarize /ˌdiːˈmɪlɪtəraɪz/ *vtr* démilitariser; **~d zone** zone *f* démilitarisée.

demise /dɪˈmaɪz/ sout **I** *n* **1** (of institution, system, movement) disparition *f*; (of aspirations) mort *f*; **her political ~** sa disparition de la scène politique; **2** euph, hum (death) disparition *f*; **3** Jur (lease) cession *f* à bail, affermage *m*; (by inheritance) legs *m*, transmission *f*; **~ of the crown** Pol transmission de la couronne (*lors de la mort ou de la déposition du souverain*).

II *vtr* **1** Jur (by lease) céder à bail; (by will) transmettre; **2** Pol transmettre [*sovereignty, the Crown*].

demisemiquaver /ˌdemɪˈsemɪkweɪvə(r)/ *n* GB triple croche *f*.

demist /ˌdiːˈmɪst/ GB *vtr* désembuer.

demister /ˌdiːˈmɪstə(r)/ GB *n* dispositif *m* antibuée.

demo○ /ˈdeməʊ/ **I** *n* (*pl* **-mos**) (*abrév* = **demonstration**) **1** Pol manif○ *f*; **2** Aut modèle *m* de démonstration.

II *modif* [*tape, disk, cassette*] de démonstration.

demob○ /ˌdiːˈmɒb/ GB **I** *n* démobilisation *f*.

II *vtr* (*p prés etc* **-bb-**) démobiliser.

demobilization /diːˌməʊbɪlaɪˈzeɪʃn, US -lɪˈz-/ *n* démobilisation *f*.

demobilize /diːˈməʊbɪlaɪz/ *vtr* démobiliser.

democracy /dɪˈmɒkrəsɪ/ *n* démocratie *f*.

democrat /ˈdeməkræt/ *n* démocrate *mf*.

Democrat /ˈdeməkræt/ **I** *pr n* GB, US Pol Démocrate *mf*.

II *modif* [*politician*] du parti démocrate.

democratic /ˌdeməˈkrætɪk/ *adj* **1** [*institution, country*] démocratique; **2** (believing in freedom) démocrate.

Democratic /ˌdeməˈkrætɪk/ *adj* US Pol **the ~ party** le parti démocrate.

democratically /ˌdeməˈkrætɪklɪ/ *adv* démocratiquement.

democratization /dɪˌmɒkrətaɪˈzeɪʃn, US -tɪˈz-/ *n* démocratisation *f*.

democratize /dɪˈmɒkrətaɪz/ *vtr* démocratiser.

demographer /dɪˈmɒgrəfə(r)/ *n* démographe *mf*.

demographic /ˌdeməˈgræfɪk/ *adj* démographique.

demography /dɪˈmɒgrəfɪ/ *n* démographie *f*.

demolish /dɪˈmɒlɪʃ/ *vtr* **1** démolir [*building, argument, person*]; **2**○ hum engloutir [*food*]; **3**○ Sport battre [qn] à plates coutures.

demolition /ˌdeməˈlɪʃn/ **I** *n* lit, fig démolition *f*.

II *modif* [*area, squad, work*] de démolition; **~ worker** démolisseur *m*.

demon /ˈdiːmən/ **I** *n* Relig, fig démon *m*; **the ~ drink** le démon de l'alcool; **the ~ of inflation** le démon inflation.

II *modif* [*drummer, sportsman etc*] diabolique.

demonetization /diːˌmʌnɪtaɪˈzeɪʃn, US -tɪˈz-/ *n* démonétisation *f*.

demonetize /ˌdiːˈmʌnɪtaɪz/ *vtr* démonétiser.

demoniac /dɪˈməʊnɪæk/ **I** *n* diable *m*.

II *adj* = **demonic**.

demonic /dɪˈmɒnɪk/ *adj* [*aspect, person, power, etc*] diabolique; [*music, noise*] infernal.

demonology /ˌdiːməˈnɒlədʒɪ/ *n* démonologie *f*.

demonstrable /ˈdemɒnstrəbl, US dɪˈmɒnstrəbl/ *adj* démontrable; **the candidate will have ~ organizing skills** le candidat saura faire preuve d'un sens de l'organisation.

demonstrably /ˈdemɒnstrəblɪ, dɪˈmɒnstrəblɪ/ *adv* (obviously) manifestement.

demonstrate /ˈdemənstreɪt/ **I** *vtr* **1** (illustrate, prove) démontrer [*theory, principle, truth*]; **to ~ that** démontrer que; **to ~ the principle/concept that** démontrer le principe/concept selon lequel; **as ~d by this experiment** comme le démontre cette expérience; **2** (show, reveal) manifester [*emotion, concern, support*]; montrer [*skill*]; **to ~ one's concern/one's support for sth** manifester son intérêt pour/son soutien à qch; **as ~d by...** ainsi qu'en atteste...; **3** (display) faire la démonstration de [*machine, gadget, product*]; **to ~ how to do** montrer comment faire; **to ~ how sth works** montrer comment marche or fonctionne qch.

II *vi* Pol manifester (**for** en faveur de; **against** contre).

demonstration /ˌdemənˈstreɪʃn/ **I** *n* **1** Pol manifestation *f* (**against** contre; **for** en faveur de); **to stage a ~** organiser une manifestation; **2** (of emotion, support) manifestation *f*; **3** (of machine, gadget etc) démonstration *f*; **cookery ~** démonstration culinaire; **to give a ~** faire une démonstration; **4** (of theory, principle) démonstration *f*.

II *modif* [*model, match, sport*] de démonstration.

demonstrative /dɪˈmɒnstrətɪv/ **I** *n* Ling démonstratif *m*.

II *adj* **1** [*person, behaviour*] démonstratif/-ive; **2** sout **to be ~ of** être significatif/-ive de [*belief, attitude, state of mind*]; **3** Ling démonstratif/-ive.

demonstrator /ˈdemənstreɪtə(r)/ *n* **1** Pol manifestant/-e *m/f*; **2** Comm démonstrateur/-trice *m/f*; **3** GB Univ préparateur/-trice *m/f*; **4**○ Aut voiture *f* de démonstration.

demoralization /dɪˌmɒrəlaɪˈzeɪʃn, US dɪˌmɔːrəlɪˈzeɪʃn/ *n* démoralisation *f*.

demoralize /dɪˈmɒrəlaɪz, US -ˈmɔːr-/ *vtr* démoraliser; **to become ~d** se démoraliser.

demoralizing /dɪˈmɒrəlaɪzɪŋ, US -ˈmɔːr-/ *adj* démoralisant.

demote /ˌdiːˈməʊt/ *vtr* rétrograder [*person*]; ramener [qch] au deuxième plan [*idea, principle, policy etc*]; reléguer [qn] dans la division inférieure [*football team*].

demotic /dɪˈmɒtɪk/ *adj* **1** sout (of the populace) populaire; **2** Ling démotique.

demotion /dɪˈməʊʃn/ *n* (of person) rétrogradation *f*; (of idea, principle, policy) relégation *f*; (of football team) relégation *f*.

demur /dɪˈmɜː(r)/ sout **I** *n* **without ~** sans objection(s).

II *vi* (*p prés etc* **-rr-**) **1** (disagree) soulever des objections (**at** contre); **2** (complain) rechigner (**at doing** à faire).

demure /dɪˈmjʊə(r)/ *adj* **1** [*behaviour, dress*] discret/-ète; [*girl*] sage et modeste; **2** pej (coy) faussement modeste.

demurely /dɪˈmjʊəlɪ/ *adv* **1** (modestly) de façon modeste; **2** pej (coyly) avec une fausse modestie.

demureness /dɪˈmjʊənɪs/ *n* **1** (modesty) modestie *f*; **2** pej (coyness) fausse modestie *f*.

demurrage /dɪˈmʌrɪdʒ/ *n* Comm Jur surestarie *f*.

demystification /diːˌmɪstɪfɪˈkeɪʃn/ *n* démystification *f*.

demystify /ˌdiːˈmɪstɪfaɪ/ *vtr* démystifier.

demythologize /ˌdiːmɪˈθɒlədʒaɪz/ *vtr* démythifier.

den /den/ *n* **1** (of lion) antre *m*; (of fox) tanière *f*; **2** fig pej (of thieves, gamblers etc) repaire *m*; **~ of vice** ou **iniquity** lieu *m* de débauche; **drugs ~** haut-lieu *m* de la drogue; **3** fig (room) tanière *f*.

denationalization /diːˌnæʃənəlaɪˈzeɪʃn, US -lɪˈz-/ *n* dénationalisation *f*.

denationalize /ˌdiːˈnæʃənəlaɪz/ *vtr* dénationaliser.

denaturalization /diːˌnætʃərəlaɪˈzeɪʃn, US -lɪˈz-/ *n* dénaturalisation *f*.

denaturalize /ˌdiːˈnætʃərəlaɪz/ *vtr* dénaturaliser.

denature /ˌdiːˈneɪtʃə(r)/ *vtr* dénaturer.

dengue /ˈdeŋgɪ/ *n* dengue *f*.

denial /dɪˈnaɪəl/ *n* **1** (of accusation, rumour) démenti *m*; (of guilt) négation *f*; (of doctrine, rights, freedom) négation *f*; (of request) rejet *m*; **he issued a ~ of his involvement in the scandal** il a démenti être impliqué dans le scandale; **despite her ~ that she had met him** bien qu'elle ait nié l'avoir rencontré; **Peter's ~ of Christ** Bible le reniement du Christ par St Pierre; **2** Psych dénégation *f*; **3** = **self-denial**.

denial of justice *n* Jur déni *m* (de justice).

denier /ˈdenɪə(r)/ *n* Tex denier *m*; **15 ~ tights** GB, **15 ~ pantyhose** US collant *m* de 15 deniers.

denigrate /ˈdenɪgreɪt/ *vtr* dénigrer.

denigration /ˌdenɪˈgreɪʃn/ *n* dénigrement *m* (**of** de).

denim /ˈdenɪm/ **I** *n* (material) jean *m*.

II *modif* [*jacket, shirt*] en jean; **~ jeans** jean *m*.

III denims /ˈdenɪmz/ *npl* (trousers) jean *m*; (suit) ensemble *m* en jean; (overalls) bleu *m* de travail.

denizen /ˈdenɪzn/ *n* **1** (inhabitant) (person) habitant/-e *m/f*; (animal) habitant *m*; **2** (naturalized) (animal) animal *m* acclimaté; (plant) plante *f* acclimatée; **3** Jur titulaire *mf* d'une naturalisation à effets juridiques restreints.

Denmark /ˈdenmɑːk/ ▶ 1131 *pr n* Danemark *m*.

denominate /dɪˈnɒmɪneɪt/ *vtr* **1** gen dénommer; **2** Fin libeller; **~d in** libellé en [*dollars, ecus*].

denomination /dɪˌnɒmɪˈneɪʃn/ *n* **1** gen dénomination *f*; **2** Relig confession *f*; **3** Fin valeur *f*; **high/low ~ coin** pièce de forte/faible valeur; **high/low ~ banknote** grosse/petite coupure.

denominational /dɪˌnɒmɪˈneɪʃənl/ *adj* [*school*] confessionnel/-elle.

denominative /dɪˈnɒmɪnətɪv/ **I** *n* Ling dénominatif *m*.

II *adj* Ling, gen dénominatif/-ive.

denominator /dɪˈnɒmɪneɪtə(r)/ *n* dénominateur *m*.

denotation /ˌdiːnəʊˈteɪʃn/ *n* **1** Ling dénotation *f*; **2** gen (symbol used) représentation *f*; (process) dénotation *f*.

denotative /dɪˈnəʊtətɪv/ *adj* Ling dénotatif/-ive.

denote /dɪˈnəʊt/ *vtr* **1** (stand for) [*written symbol*] (on map etc) indiquer; Math désigner; [*word, phrase, notice, picture*] signifier; **2** (show proof of) dénoter [*taste, intelligence etc*].

denouement /ˌdeɪˈnuːmɒn, US ˌdeɪnuːˈmɔːŋ/ *n* dénouement *m*.

denounce /dɪˈnaʊns/ *vtr* **1** (inform on) dénoncer (**to** à); **2** (criticize) dénoncer; **3** (accuse) accuser (**for doing** d'avoir fait); **to be ~d as a traitor/thief** être accusé de trahison/vol.

denouncer /dɪˈnaʊnsə(r)/ *n* dénonciateur/-trice *m/f*.

French departments

The names of French departments usually have the definite article, except when used after the preposition en.

In, to and from somewhere

For in *and* to *use* dans le *or* dans les *for masculine and plural names of departments:*

to live in the Loiret	= vivre dans le Loiret
to go to the Loiret	= aller dans le Loiret
to live in the Landes	= vivre dans les Landes
to go to the Landes	= aller dans les Landes
to live in the Loir-et-Cher	= vivre dans le Loir-et-Cher
to go to the Loir-et-Cher	= aller dans le Loir-et-Cher

For in *and* to *use* en *for feminine names of departments:*

to live in Savoy	= vivre en Savoie
to go to Savoy	= aller en Savoie
to live in Seine-et-Marne	= vivre en Seine-et-Marne
to go to Seine-et-Marne	= aller en Seine-et-Marne

For from *use* du *(or* de l' *before a vowel) for masculine and* des *for plural names of departments:*

to come from the Loiret	= venir du Loiret
to come from the Landes	= venir des Landes
to come from the Loir-et-Cher	= venir du Loir-et-Cher

For from *use* de *without the definite article for feminine names of departments:*

to come from Savoy	= venir de Savoie
to come from Seine-et-Marne	= venir de Seine-et-Marne

Uses with nouns

Use de *with the definite article in most cases:*

a Cantal accent	= un accent du Cantal
the Var area	= la région du Var
the Creuse countryside	= les paysages de la Creuse
Loiret people	= les gens du Loiret
Yonne representatives	= les représentants de l'Yonne
Landes restaurants	= les restaurants des Landes
the Calvados team	= l'équipe du Calvados
Ardennes towns	= les villes des Ardennes

but use de *without the definite article with feminine names that include* et:

Seine-et-Marne hotels	= les hôtels de Seine-et-Marne

Some cases are undecided:

Savoy roads	= les routes de Savoie *or* de la Savoie

dense /dens/ *adj* **1** gen, Phys dense; **2** fig [*style*] dense; **3**○ (stupid) bouché○, obtus; **4** US [*book, statement*] profond.

densely /'densli/ *adv* **~ populated/wooded** très peuplé/boisé.

denseness /'densnis/ *n* **1** = **density**; **2**○ bêtise *f*.

densimeter /den'simitə(r)/ *n* densimètre *m*.

densitometer /ˌdensi'tɒmitə(r)/ *n* Phot densitomètre *m*.

density /'densəti/ *n* **1** Phys, Comput, Electron densité *f*; **2** (of housing, population) densité *f*; **high/low ~ housing** habitat *m* à forte/faible densité.

dent /dent/ **I** *n* (in wood) entaille *f*; (in metal) bosse *f*; **to make a ~ in** faire une entaille dans [*wood*]; cabosser, bosseler [*car*]; fig○ faire un trou dans○ [*savings*].

II *vtr* faire une entaille dans [*wood*]; cabosser, bosseler [*car*]; entamer [*pride*].

dental /'dentl/ **I** *n* Ling dentale *f*.

II *adj* **1** [*treatment, record, hygiene, decay*] dentaire; [*problem*] de dents; **2** Ling [*consonant*] dental.

dental: **~ appointment** *n* rendez-vous *m* chez le dentiste; **~ clinic** *n* centre *m* de soins dentaires; **~ floss** *n* fil *m* dentaire; **~ hygienist** ▶1692 *n* auxiliaire *mf* dentaire; **~ nurse** ▶1692 *n* assistant/-e *m/f* dentaire; **~ plate** *n* dentier *m*; **~ receptionist** ▶1692 *n* réceptionniste *mf* de cabinet dentaire; **~ school** *n*: *école de médecine pour les futurs dentistes*; **~ surgeon** ▶1692 *n* chirurgien-dentiste *m*; **~ surgery** *n* GB (premises) cabinet *m* dentaire; (treatment) chirurgie *f* dentaire; **~ technician** ▶1692 *n* mécanicien-dentiste *m*.

dentifrice /'dentifris/ *n* dentifrice *m*.

dentin(e) /'denti:n/ *n* dentine *f*.

dentist /'dentist/ ▶1692 *n* dentiste *mf*; **to go to the ~'s** aller chez le dentiste.

dentistry /'dentistri/ *n* médecine *f* dentaire, dentisterie *f* spec; **to study ~** faire des études dentaires.

dentition /ˌden'tiʃn/ *n* dentition *f*, denture *f* spec.

denture /'dentʃə(r)/ **I** *n* (prosthesis) prothèse *f* dentaire;

II dentures *npl* dentier *m*.

denude /di'nju:d, US -'nu:d/ *vtr* **1** lit dénuder [*land, tree*] (**of** de); **2** fig **~d of** privé de.

denunciation /diˌnʌnsi'eiʃn/ *n* dénonciation *f* (**of** de).

deny /di'nai/ *vtr* **1** démentir [*rumour, report*]; nier [*charge, accusation*]; **to ~ that** nier que; **she denies that this is true** elle nie que cela soit vrai; **to ~ the rumour/news that** démentir la rumeur/nouvelle selon laquelle; **to ~ doing** ou **having done** nier avoir fait; **to ~ all knowledge of sth** nier savoir quoi que ce soit de qch; **there's no ~ing his popularity** nul ne peut nier sa popularité; **2** (refuse) **to ~ sb sth** refuser qch à qn; **to ~ sb admittance to a building/club** refuser l'accès d'un bâtiment/club à qn; **to ~ oneself sth** se priver de qch; **he was denied bail** Jur on a rejeté sa demande de mise en liberté sous caution; **3** (renounce) renier [*God, religion*]; **4** Comm **to ~ a signature** contester une signature.

deodorant /di:'əudərənt/ **I** *n* (personal) déodorant *m*; (for room) déodorisant *m*; **underarm/foot ~** déodorant pour les aisselles/les pieds; **roll-on/spray ~** déodorant à bille/en bombe.

II *adj* déodorant.

deodorize /di:'əudəraiz/ *vtr* désodoriser.

deontology /ˌdi:ɒn'tɒlədʒi/ *n* déontologie *f*.

deoxidize /di:'ɒksidaiz/ *vtr* désoxygéner.

deoxyribonucleic acid /diˌɒksiˌraibəu nju:ˌkleiik 'æsid, US -nu:-/ *n* acide *m* désoxyribonucléique.

depart /di'pɑ:t/ **I** *vtr* **to ~ this life** littér quitter ce monde.

II *vi* **1** sout [*person, train, bus*] partir (**from** de; **for** pour); **the train for London is about to ~** le train à destination de Londres va partir; **the train now ~ing from platform one** le train au départ du quai un; **2** (deviate) **to ~ from** s'éloigner de [*attitude, position, truth*]; abandonner [*practice*].

departed /di'pɑ:tid/ **I** *n* **the ~** euph (dead person) le/la défunt/-e *m/f*; (dead people) les défunts *mpl*.

II *adj* **1** (dead) euph défunt; **2** littér (vanished) [*glory, youth*] passé.

departing /di'pɑ:tiŋ/ *adj* [*chairman, government*] sortant; [*guest*] s'apprêtant à partir.

department /di'pɑ:tmənt/ *n* **1** Comm, Fin (section) service *m*; **personnel ~** service *m* du personnel; **2** Admin Pol (governmental) ministère *m*; (administrative) service *m*; **social services ~** les services sociaux; **3** Comm (in store) rayon *m*; **electrical ~** rayon *m* électricité; **4** (in hospital) service *m*; **casualty ~** GB service *m* des urgences; **X ray ~** radiologie *f*; **5** (in university) département *m*; cf UFR *f*; **French ~** département de français; **6** Sch section *f* (*dans les écoles secondaires, regroupement des professeurs par matière sous la responsabilité d'un enseignant*); **7** Admin, Geog (district) département *m*; **8**○ (area) domaine *m*; **that's not my ~!** ce n'est pas mon domaine or rayon○!

departmental /ˌdi:pɑ:t'mentl/ *adj* (*épith*) **1** Pol (ministerial) [*colleague, committee, meeting*] de ministère; **her ~ colleagues** ses collègues du ministère; **2** Admin (of organization, business) [*chief, head, meeting*] de service, de département.

departmentalization /ˌdi:pɑ:tˌmentəlai'zeiʃn, US -li'z-/ *n* départementalisation *f*.

departmentalize /ˌdi:pɑ:t'mentəlaiz/ *vtr* départementaliser.

department head *n* **1** Admin, Comm chef *m* de service, directeur/-trice *m/f* du service; **2** Univ directeur/-trice *m/f* de département.

department manager *n* **1** (of business) chef *m* de service, directeur/-trice *m/f* du service; **2** (of store) chef *m* de rayon.

department: **Department of Defense**, **DOD** *n* US Ministère *m* de la défense; **Department of Education and Science**, **DES** *n* GB gen Ministère *m* de l'enseignement et de la science; **Department of Energy**, **DOE** *n* US Ministère *m* de l'Énergie; **Department of Health**, **DOH**, GB **Department of Health and Human Services** US *n* Ministère *m* de la santé; **Department of Social Security**, **DSS** *n* GB Ministère *m* des Affaires sociales; **Department of the Environment**, **DOE** *n* GB Ministère *m* de l'environnement; **Department of Trade and Industry**, **DTI** *n* GB Ministère *m* du commerce et de l'industrie; **~ store** *n* grand magasin *m*.

departure /di'pɑ:tʃə(r)/ **I** *n* **1** (of person, bus, train) départ *m* (**from** de; **for** pour); (from job, office) départ *m*; **2** fig (start) **this marks a new ~ in physics** ceci marque un nouveau départ en physique; **3** (from truth, regulation) entorse *f* (**from** à); (from policy, tradition etc) rupture *f* (**from** par rapport à); **this technique is a total ~ from traditional methods** cette technique s'éloigne totalement des méthodes traditionnelles; **in a ~ from standard practice...** contrairement aux usages établis...; **because of her frequent ~s from the truth** parce qu'elle s'éloigne/s'éloignait souvent de la vérité.

II *modif* [*date, time*] de départ.

departure: **~ gate** *n* porte *f* de départ; **~ lounge** *n* salle *f* d'embarquement; **~ platform** *n* Rail quai *m* de départ; **~s board** *n* tableau *m* des départs; **~s tax** *n* taxes *fpl* d'aéroport.

depend /di'pend/ *vi* **1** (rely) **to depend on sb/sth** dépendre de qn/qch, compter sur qn/qch (**for** pour); **to ~ on sb/sth to do** compter sur qn/qch pour faire; **you can ~ on him to spoil the evening** tu peux compter sur lui pour gâcher la soirée; **you can't ~ on the bus arriving on time** tu ne peux pas être sûr que le bus sera à l'heure; **you can ~ on it!** tu peux compter là dessus!; **you choose, ~ing on how much you can afford** tu as le choix, ça dépend du prix que tu veux y mettre; **the temperature varies ~ing on the season** la température varie suivant la saison; **that ~s** cela dépend; **2** (be financially dependent on) **to ~ on sb** vivre à la charge de qn.

dependability /dɪˌpendəˈbɪlətɪ/ *n* **1** (of equipment) fiabilité *f*; **2** (of person) **~ is important in an employee** il est important de pouvoir compter sur un employé.

dependable /dɪˈpendəbl/ *adj* [*person*] digne de confiance; [*car, machine*] fiable; [*forecast, news, source*] sûr.

dependant /dɪˈpendənt/ *n* Jur, Soc Admin personne *f* à charge.

dependence, **dependance** US /dɪˈpendəns/ *n* **1** (reliance) dépendance *f* (**on** vis-à-vis de); **2** (addiction) dépendance *f* (**on** à); **alcohol ~** alcoolisme *m*; **drug ~** toxicomanie *f*.

dependency /dɪˈpendənsɪ/ *n* **1** Pol (territory) territoire *m* dépendant; **2** (reliance) dépendance *f*; **his ~ on his mother/on heroin** sa dépendance vis-à-vis de sa mère/à l'héroïne; **alcohol/drug ~** dépendance à l'alcool/à la drogue.

dependency: **~ culture** *n* société *f* d'assistés; **~ grammar** *n* Ling grammaire *f* de dépendance; **~ leave** *n* GB Soc Admin *congé permettant de s'occuper d'une personne à charge.*

dependent /dɪˈpendənt/ *adj* **1** (reliant) [*relative*] à charge; **to be ~ on** ou **upon sb/sth** gen dépendre de qn/qch; (financially) vivre à la charge de qn; **a drug-~ patient** un malade ayant un traitement à vie; **an insulin-~ patient** un malade sous insuline; **2** Ling [*clause*] subordonné; **3** Math [*variable*] dépendant.

depersonalize /ˌdiːˈpɜːsənəlaɪz/ *vtr* dépersonnaliser.

depict /dɪˈpɪkt/ *vtr* (visually) représenter (**as** comme); (in writing) dépeindre (**as** comme).

depiction /dɪˈpɪkʃn/ *n* peinture *f*, représentation *f*.

depilate /ˈdepɪleɪt/ *vtr* épiler.

depilatory /dɪˈpɪlətrɪ, US -tɔːrɪ/ **I** *n* dépilatoire *m*.
II *adj* dépilatoire; **~ wax** cire *f* à épiler.

deplane /ˌdiːˈpleɪn/ *vi* US quitter l'avion.

deplete /dɪˈpliːt/ *vtr* réduire [*reserves, resources, funds, numbers*]; **a population ~d by war** une population dont l'effectif a été réduit par la guerre; **reservoirs ~d of water** des reservoirs qui sont presque à sec; **a lake ~d of fish** un lac devenu pauvre en poissons.

depletion /dɪˈpliːʃn/ *n* (of resources, funds, stock) baisse *f*, diminution *f*.

deplorable /dɪˈplɔːrəbl/ *adj* déplorable.

deplorably /dɪˈplɔːrəblɪ/ *adv* [*treat, behave*] de façon déplorable; [*late, negligent*] affreusement.

deplore /dɪˈplɔː(r)/ *vtr* déplorer; **to ~ the fact that** déplorer le fait que (+ *subj*).

deploy /dɪˈplɔɪ/ *vtr* gen, Mil déployer.

deployment /dɪˈplɔɪmənt/ *n* Admin, Mil déploiement *m*.

depolarization /diːˌpəʊləraɪˈzeɪʃn, US -rɪˈz-/ *n* **1** Pol compromis *m*; **2** Med, Phys dépolarisation *f*.

depolarize /diːˈpəʊləraɪz/ **I** *vtr* **1** Mgmt, Pol rapprocher [*attitudes, parties*]; débloquer [*discussion*]; **2** Med, Phys dépolariser.
II *vi* Pol rechercher un compromis.

deponent /dɪˈpəʊnənt/ *n, adj* déponent (*m*).

depopulate /ˌdiːˈpɒpjʊleɪt/ *vtr* dépeupler.

depopulation /diːˌpɒpjʊˈleɪʃn/ *n* dépeuplement *m*.

deport /dɪˈpɔːt/ **I** *vtr* Jur expulser [*immigrant, criminal*] (**to** vers); Hist déporter [*slaves*].
II *v refl* sout **to ~ oneself** se comporter.

deportation /ˌdiːpɔːˈteɪʃn/ *n* Jur (of immigrant, criminal) expulsion *f*; Hist (of slaves) déportation *f*.

deportation order *n* arrêté *m* d'expulsion.

deportee /ˌdiːpɔːˈtiː/ *n* déporté/-e *m/f*.

deportment /dɪˈpɔːtmənt/ *n* **1** (posture) sout maintien *m*; **2‡** (behaviour) conduite *f*.

depose /dɪˈpəʊz/ **I** *vtr* Pol, Jur (all contexts) déposer.
II *vi* Jur faire une déposition.

deposit /dɪˈpɒzɪt/ **I** *n* **1** (to bank account) dépôt *m*; **to make a ~** faire or effectuer un dépôt; **on ~** en dépôt; **2** (part payment) (on house, hire purchase goods) versement *m* initial; (on holiday, goods) acompte *m*; **to put down a ~ on a house** effectuer un versement initial sur une maison; **to leave a ~ on sth** verser des arrhes ou un acompte sur qch; **3** (to secure goods, hotel room) arrhes *fpl*, acompte *m*; **'a small ~ will secure any item'** 'vous pouvez réserver un article en versant des arrhes ou un acompte'; **4** (against damage) caution *f*; **5** (on bottle) consigne *f*; **6** GB Pol cautionnement *m*; **to lose one's ~** perdre son cautionnement; **7** Geol, Geog (of silt, mud) dépôt *m*; (of coal, mineral) gisement *m*; **8** Chem, Wine (sediment) dépôt *m*.
II *vtr* **1** (put down) déposer [*object*]; **2** (entrust) déposer [*money, valuables*]; **to ~ sth with the bank/solicitor** déposer qch à la banque/auprès de l'avocat; **to ~ sth with sb** confier qch à qn.

deposit account *n* GB Fin compte *m* de dépôt.

depositary /dɪˈpɒzɪtərɪ/ *n* **1** Jur dépositaire *mf*; **2** = **depository**.

deposition /ˌdepəˈzɪʃn/ *n* (all contexts) déposition *f*.

depositor /dɪˈpɒzɪtə(r)/ *n* Fin déposant/-e *m/f*.

depository /dɪˈpɒzɪtrɪ, US -tɔːrɪ/ *n* entrepôt *m*.

deposit slip *n* bordereau *m* de versement.

depot /ˈdepəʊ, US ˈdiːpəʊ/ *n* **1** Comm, Mil (for storage) dépôt *m*; **2** Transp, Rail **bus/railway ~** dépôt *m* d'autobus/de chemin de fer; **3** US Transp (bus station) gare *f* routière; Rail gare *f* ferroviaire.

deprave /dɪˈpreɪv/ *vtr* dépraver.

depraved /dɪˈpreɪvd/ *adj* dépravé.

depravity /dɪˈprævətɪ/ *n* dépravation *f*.

deprecate /ˈdeprɪkeɪt/ *vtr* sout (disapprove of) désapprouver.

deprecating /ˈdeprɪkeɪtɪŋ/ *adj* (disapproving) désapprobateur/-trice; (disparaging) controv réprobateur/-trice.

deprecatingly /ˈdeprɪkeɪtɪŋlɪ/ *adv* [*smile, speak*] (about oneself) avec modestie; (about sb else) avec condescendance.

deprecatory /ˌdeprɪˈkeɪtərɪ, US -tɔːrɪ/ *adj* **1** (disapproving) désapprobateur/-trice; **2** (apologetic) d'excuse.

depreciate /dɪˈpriːʃɪeɪt/ *vi* se déprécier (**against** par rapport à).

depreciation /dɪˌpriːʃɪˈeɪʃn/ *n* dépréciation *f*.

depredation /ˌdeprəˈdeɪʃn/ *n* déprédation *f*.

depress /dɪˈpres/ *vtr* **1** gen, Psych déprimer [*person*]; **2** Comm, Fin faire baisser [*profits, investment, prices, currency*]; affaiblir [*trading, stock market*]; **3** (press) abaisser [*lever*]; appuyer sur [*button, switch*].

depressant /dɪˈpresənt/ *n, adj* Med dépresseur *m*.

depressed /dɪˈprest/ *adj* **1** [*person, mood*] déprimé; **to be** ou **get ~** être déprimé; **I got very ~ about it** cela m'a beaucoup déprimé; **2** Econ, Comm [*region, district, trade, industry, sector*] en déclin; [*sales, prices*] très bas/basse; [*market*] en déclin, en crise.

depressing /dɪˈpresɪŋ/ *adj* déprimant; **that's what I find ~** c'est ce qui me déprime.

depressingly /dɪˈpresɪŋlɪ/ *adv* [*talk, describe*] de manière déprimante; **~ slow** d'une lenteur déprimante.

depression /dɪˈpreʃn/ *n* **1** Med, Psych dépression *f*; **to suffer from ~** (permanently) être dépressif/-ive; (temporarily) avoir une dépression nerveuse; **2** Econ (slump) récession *f*, crise *f* (**in** de); **the** (**Great**) **Depression** Hist la grande dépression; **3** (hollow) gen creux *m*; Geol dépression *f*; **4** Meteorol dépression *f*.

depressive /dɪˈpresɪv/ **I** *n* dépressif/-ive *m/f*.
II *adj* **1** Med dépressif/-ive; **a ~ illness** une dépression; **2** Econ [*effect, policy*] dépressif/-ive.

depressurization /diːˌpreʃəraɪˈzeɪʃn, US -rɪˈz-/ *n* dépressurisation *f*.

depressurize /ˌdiːˈpreʃəraɪz/ **I** *vtr* dépressuriser [*aircraft, container, machine*]; décompresser [*gas, liquid*].
II *vi* [*aircraft, machine*] se dépressuriser.

deprivation /ˌdeprɪˈveɪʃn/ *n* **1** (poverty) (of person) privations *fpl*; (of society) dénuement *m*; **2** Psych carence *f* affective; **3** (removal) (of right, privilege) privation *f*.

deprive /dɪˈpraɪv/ **I** *vtr* priver (**of** de); **to be ~d of** être privé de.
II deprived *pp adj* [*area, child, family*] démuni; [*childhood, existence*] malheureux/-euse.

dept *abrév écrite* = **department**.

depth /depθ/ **I** *n* **1** (measurement) (of hole, box, water) profondeur *f*; (of layer) épaisseur *f*; **to dive/dig to a ~ of 10 m** plonger/creuser à une profondeur de 10 m; **at a ~ of 30 m** à 30 m de profondeur; **12 m in ~** profond de 12 m; **to be out of one's ~** (in water) ne plus avoir pied; fig être complètement perdu; **2** (degree of intensity) (of colour) intensité *f*; (of crisis, recession) gravité *f*; (of ignorance) étendue *f*; (of emotion) intensité *f*; (of despair) fond *m*; **to be in the ~s of despair** toucher le fond du désespoir; **with ~ of feeling** avec émotion; **3** (complexity) (of knowledge) étendue *f*; (of analysis, hero, novel, work) profondeur *f*; **to examine/study sth in ~** examiner/étudier qch en détail; **4** (lowness of pitch) gravité *f*; **5** Cin, Phot **~ of focus** distance *f* focale; **~ of field** profondeur *f* de champ.
II depths *npl* (remote part) **the ~s of the sea** les profondeurs *fpl* de la mer; **in the ~s of the countryside** en pleine campagne; **in the ~s of the woods** au milieu des bois; **in the ~s of his consciousness** au fond de lui-même; **in the ~s of winter** au plus profond de l'hiver.

depth charge *n* Mil grenade *f* sous-marine.

deputation /ˌdepjʊˈteɪʃn/ *n* délégation *f*.

depute /dɪˈpjuːt/ *vtr* sout **1** charger [*person*] (**for** de; **to do** de faire); **2** assigner [*task*] (**to** à).

deputize /ˈdepjʊtaɪz/ *vi* **to ~ for sb** remplacer qn.

deputy /ˈdepjʊtɪ/ **I** *n* **1** (aide) adjoint/-e *m/f* (**to sb** de qn); (replacement) remplaçant/-e *m/f*; **to act as (a) ~ for sb** remplacer qn; **to be appointed as a ~ for sb** être nommé pour remplacer qn; **2** (politician) député *m*; **3** US (also **~ sheriff**) shérif *m* adjoint.
II *modif* [*chief executive, director, editor, head, manager, mayor*] adjoint.

deputy: **~ chairman** *n* vice-président *m*; **~ chief constable** *n* GB Police ≈ commissaire *m* divisionnaire adjoint; **~ judge** *n* Jur juge *m* suppléant; **~ leader** *n* GB Pol vice-président *m*; **~ premier**, **~ prime minister** *n* Pol vice-premier ministre *m*; **~ president** *n* Pol, Mgmt vice-président *m*; **Deputy Speaker** *n* GB Pol Vice-président/-e *m/f* des Communes.

derail /dɪˈreɪl/ **I** *vtr* faire dérailler; **the train has been ~ed** (unintentionally) le train a déraillé.
II *vi* dérailler.

derailleur gears /dəˈreɪljə(r)/ *npl* dérailleur *m*.

derailment /dɪˈreɪlmənt/ *n* déraillement *m*.

derange /dɪˈreɪndʒ/ **I** *vtr* (all contexts) déranger.
II deranged *pp adj* dérangé also hum.

derangement /dɪˈreɪndʒmənt/ *n* Psych déséquilibre *m* (mental).

derby /ˈdɑːbɪ, US ˈdɜːrbɪ/ *n* **1** (hat) chapeau

m melon; **2** Turf (competition) course *f* de chevaux; **3 the Derby** GB le derby *m* (d'Epsom).

Derbyshire /ˈdɑːbɪʃə(r)/ ▶ **1624** *pr n* Derbyshire *m*.

derecognition /ˌdiːrekəgˈnɪʃn/ *n* GB (of body, union) retrait *m* du droit de représentativité.

derecognize /ˌdiːˈrekəgnaɪz/ *vtr* GB retirer le droit de représentativité de [*body, union*].

deregulate /ˌdiːˈregjʊleɪt/ *vtr* **1** Fin libérer [*prices*]; déréguler [*trade, market*]; **2** Jur déréglementer.

deregulation /diːˌregjʊˈleɪʃn/ *n* **1** Fin (of prices) libération *f*; (of trade, market) dérégulation *f*; **2** Jur déréglementation *f*.

derelict /ˈderəlɪkt/ **I** *n* **1** (tramp) clochard/-e *m/f*; **2** Naut épave *f*.
II *adj* [*building*] (abandoned) abandonné; (ruined) en ruines; **to let sth go ~** laisser qch à l'abandon.

dereliction /ˌderɪˈlɪkʃn/ *n* abandon *m*; **~ of duty** Jur manquement *m* au devoir.

derestrict /ˌdiːrɪˈstrɪkt/ *vtr* déréglementer; **~ed road** GB Aut route sans limitation de vitesse.

deride /dɪˈraɪd/ *vtr* ridiculiser.

de rigueur /də rɪˈgɜː(r)/ *adj* (as etiquette) de rigueur; (as fashion) très à la mode.

derision /dɪˈrɪʒn/ *n* moqueries *fpl*.

derisive /dɪˈraɪsɪv/ *adj* moqueur/-euse.

derisively /dɪˈraɪsɪvlɪ/ *adv* [*speak, write*] sur un ton moqueur; **to laugh/smile ~** avoir un rire/sourire moqueur.

derisory /dɪˈraɪsərɪ/ *adj* dérisoire.

derivation /ˌderɪˈveɪʃn/ *n* **1** (source) origine *f*; **2** (process) dérivation *f*.

derivative /dəˈrɪvətɪv/ **I** *n* Chem, Ling dérivé *m*; Math dérivée *f*.
II *adj* **1** Chem, Ling, Math dérivé; **2** pej [*style*] sans originalité.

derive /dɪˈraɪv/ **I** *vtr* tirer [*benefit, income, amount*] (**from** de); retirer [*satisfaction, pleasure*] (**from** de); **to be ~d from** [*name, word*] dériver or être un dérivé de; [*enzyme, vitamin*] être un dérivé de; [*rock, data*] provenir de.
II *vi* **to ~ from** [*value, right, power*] découler de; [*idea, custom*] provenir de; [*word*] dériver de.

dermatitis /ˌdɜːməˈtaɪtɪs/ ▶ **1354** *n* dermatite *f*; **to have ~** avoir une dermatite.

dermatologist /ˌdɜːməˈtɒlədʒɪst/ ▶ **1692** *n* dermatologue *mf*.

dermatology /ˌdɜːməˈtɒlədʒɪ/ *n* dermatologie *f*.

dermis /ˈdɜːmɪs/ *n* derme *m*.

derogate /ˈderəgeɪt/ *vi* sout **to ~ from** (detract from) porter atteinte à; (deviate from) se soustraire à.

derogatory /dɪˈrɒgətrɪ, US -tɔːrɪ/ *adj* [*remark, review, person*] désobligeant (**about** envers); [*term*] péjoratif/-ive.

derrick /ˈderɪk/ *n* (crane) mât *m* de charge; (on oil-well) tour *f* de forage.

derring-do‡ /ˌderɪŋˈduː/ *n* bravoure *f*.

derringer /ˈderɪndʒə(r)/ *n* pistolet *m* (*de poche*).

derris /ˈderɪs/ *n* Hort roténone *f*.

Derry /ˈderɪ/ ▶ **1624** *pr n* (county) comté *m* de Derry; (town) Derry.

derv /dɜːv/ *n* GB Aut gazole *m*.

dervish /ˈdɜːvɪʃ/ *n* derviche *m*.

DES *n* GB *abrév* ▶ **Department of Education and Science**.

desalinate /ˌdiːˈsælmeɪt/ *vtr* dessaler.

desalination /diːˌsælɪˈneɪʃn/ **I** *n* dessalement *m*.
II *modif* [*equipment, plant*] de dessalement.

desalt /ˌdiːˈsɔːlt/ *vtr* dessaler.

descale /ˌdiːˈskeɪl/ *vtr* GB détartrer.

descaler /ˌdiːˈskeɪlə(r)/ GB *n* détartrant *m*.

descant /ˈdeskænt/ *n* déchant *m*.

descant recorder *n* flûte *f* à bec soprano.

descend /dɪˈsend/ **I** *vtr* descendre [*steps, slope, path*].
II *vi* **1** (go down) [*person, path, plane*] descendre (**from** de); **in ~ing order of importance** en or par ordre décroissant d'importance; **2** (fall) [*darkness, rain, mist*] tomber (**on, over** sur); **3** (be felt) [*gloom, chill, exhaustion*] s'abattre (**on** sur); [*calm, peace*] s'étendre (**on** sur); **4** (arrive) [*tourists, family*] arriver, débarquer○; **to ~ on sb/Oxford/the village** débarquer chez qn/à Oxford/dans le village; **to ~ on the enemy** fondre sur l'ennemi; **5** (be related to) **to ~ from, to be ~ed from** [*person, family*] descendre de; **6** (sink) **to ~ to doing** s'abaisser à faire; **to ~ so low** ou **far as to do** s'abaisser jusqu'à faire; **to ~ into** s'enfoncer dans [*chaos, sentimentality*]; sombrer dans [*alcoholism, crime*].

descendant /dɪˈsendənt/ *n* descendant/-e *m/f* (**of** de).

descent /dɪˈsent/ *n* **1** (downward motion) descente *f* (**on, upon** sur); **to make one's ~** faire sa descente; **the aircraft began its ~** l'avion a commencé sa descente; **his ~ into crime/alcoholism started in 1964** c'est en 1964 qu'il a versé dans la criminalité/qu'il a sombré dans l'alcoolisme; **2** (extraction) descendance *f*; **of Irish ~** de descendance or d'origine irlandaise; **to claim ~ from** prétendre descendre de; **a British citizen by ~** un citoyen britannique par filiation; **to trace one's line of ~ back to Henry VIII** faire remonter sa généalogie jusqu'à Henri VIII.

descramble /ˌdiːˈskræmbl/ *vtr* Telecom, TV désembrouiller.

descrambler /ˌdiːˈskræmblə(r)/ *n* Telecom, TV désembrouilleur *m*.

descrambling /ˌdiːˈskræmblɪŋ/ *n* Telecom, TV désembrouillage *m*.

describe /dɪˈskraɪb/ *vtr* **1** (give details of) décrire [*person, event, object*]; **police ~ him as...** la police le décrit comme étant...; **2** (characterize) qualifier; **to ~ sb as an idiot/sth as useless** qualifier qn d'idiot/qch d'inutile; **he's ~d as generous/as a recluse** on dit de lui qu'il est généreux/que c'est un reclus; **I wouldn't ~ him as an artist** je ne le décrirais pas comme un artiste; **it could be ~d as pretty** on pourrait dire que c'est joli; **3** Math, Tech décrire [*circle, curve*].

description /dɪˈskrɪpʃn/ *n* **1** (of person, event, object) description *f* (**of** de; **as** comme étant); (for police) signalement *m* (**of** de); **to be beyond ~** être indescriptible; **2** (type, kind) genre *m*; **of every ~, of all ~s** de toutes sortes; **items of a similar ~** articles du même genre; **I need a table of some ~** j'ai besoin de quelque chose qui puisse faire office de table. ▶ **job description**.

descriptive /dɪˈskrɪptɪv/ *adj* descriptif/-ive.

descriptive: **~ geometry** *n* géométrie *f* descriptive; **~ linguistics** *n* (+ *v sg*) linguistique *f* descriptive.

descriptivism /dɪˈskrɪptɪvɪzəm/ *n* descriptivisme *m*.

descriptivist /dɪˈskrɪptɪvɪst/ *adj* descriptiviste.

descry‡ /dɪˈskraɪ/ *vtr* apercevoir.

desecrate /ˈdesɪkreɪt/ *vtr* **1** gen défigurer [*area, landscape*]; **2** Relig profaner [*altar, shrine*].

desecration /ˌdesɪˈkreɪʃn/ *n* **1** gen (of area, landscape) enlaidissement *m*; **2** Relig (of altar, shrine) profanation *f*.

deseed /ˌdiːˈsiːd/ *vtr* épépiner.

desegregate /ˌdiːˈsegrɪgeɪt/ *vtr* **to ~ a school/beach/neighbourhood** abolir la ségrégation dans une école/sur une plage/dans un quartier.

desegregation /diːˌsegrɪˈgeɪʃn/ *n* déségrégation *f*.

deselect /ˌdiːsɪˈlekt/ *vtr* **1** GB Pol retirer l'investiture de [*person*]; **to be ~ed** perdre l'investiture du parti; **2** Comput désélectionner.

deselection /ˌdiːsɪˈlekʃn/ *n* GB retrait *m* de l'investiture.

desensitize /ˌdiːˈsensɪtaɪz/ *vtr* (all contexts) désensibiliser (**to** à).

desert I /ˈdezət/ *n* (all contexts) désert *m*.
II /ˈdezət/ *modif* [*region*] désertique; [*flora, fauna*] du désert.
III /dɪˈzɜːt/ *vtr* abandonner [*person, group, place*] (**for** pour); déserter [*cause*]; Mil abandonner [*post*]; **our luck ~ed us** la chance nous a abandonnés; **his appetite ~ed him** il a perdu l'appétit; **has she ~ed you again?** hum elle t'a encore abandonné? hum.
IV /dɪˈzɜːt/ *vi* [*soldier*] déserter; [*politician*] faire défection; **to ~ to the enemy camp** passer à l'ennemi.

desert: **~ boot** *n* pataugas® *m*; **~ campaign** *n* campagne *f* menée dans le désert; **~ crossing** *n* traversée *f* du désert.

deserted /dɪˈzɜːtɪd/ *adj* **1** (empty) désert; **2** Soc Admin [*person*] abandonné.

deserter /dɪˈzɜːtə(r)/ *n* déserteur *m* (**from** de).

desertification /dɪˌzɜːtɪfɪˈkeɪʃn/ *n* désertification *f*.

desertion /dɪˈzɜːʃn/ *n* **1** gen, Mil désertion *f*; **2** Jur abandon *m* du domicile conjugal; **to sue for divorce on the grounds of ~** demander le divorce pour cause d'abandon du domicile conjugal.

desert: **~ island** *n* île *f* déserte; **~ rat** *n* Zool gerboise *f*; **Desert Rat** *n* GB Mil Rat *m* du désert (*soldat britannique combattant dans le désert*).

deserts /dɪˈzɜːts/ *npl* **to get one's (just) ~** avoir ce qu'on mérite; **he got his just ~** il a eu ce qu'il méritait.

deserve /dɪˈzɜːv/ **I** *vtr* mériter (**to do** de faire); **to ~ well/ill of sb** sout mériter/ne pas mériter d'être bien traité par qn; **she ~s to be remembered as...** elle mérite que l'on se souvienne d'elle comme...; **you ~ better than this!** tu mérites mieux que ça!; **they only got what they ~d, it was no more than they ~d** ils n'ont eu que ce qu'ils méritaient; **what did we do to ~ this?** qu'avons-nous fait pour mériter cela?
II deserved *pp adj* [*victory, reward, success*] mérité; **richly ~d** largement mérité.

deservedly /dɪˈzɜːvɪdlɪ/ *adv* à juste titre.

deserving /dɪˈzɜːvɪŋ/ *adj* **1** [*winner*] méritant; [*cause, charity*] louable, méritoire; **2 to be ~ of** sout être digne de [*respect, consideration*].

desiccant /ˈdesɪkənt/ *n* dessiccatif *m*.

desiccate /ˈdesɪkeɪt/ **I** *vtr* **1** sécher [*food*]; **2** dessécher [*skin*].
II *vi* se dessécher.

desiccated /ˈdesɪkeɪtɪd/ *adj* **1** [*food stuff*] séché; **2** péj (dried up) desséché.

desiccation /ˌdesɪˈkeɪʃn/ *n* dessiccation *f*.

desiderata /dɪˌzɪdəˈrɑːtə/ *npl* desiderata *mpl*.

design /dɪˈzaɪn/ **I** *n* **1** (idea, conception) conception *f*; **of faulty ~** de conception défectueuse; **2** (planning, development) (of object, appliance) conception *f*; (of building, room) agencement *m*; (of clothing) création *f*; **3** (drawing, plan) (detailed) plan *m* (**for** de); (sketch) croquis *m* (**for** de); (for dress) croquis *m*; **4** (model, completed object) modèle *m*; **this car is a very modern ~** cette voiture est un modèle très moderne; **this season's new ~s** les nouveaux modèles de cette saison; **an exclusive ~ by Nino** Fashn une création originale de Nino; **5** (art of designing) gen design *m*; (fashion) stylisme *m*; **to study ~** étudier le design; ▶ **interior design etc**; **6** (decorative pattern) motif *m*; **cup with a leaf ~** tasse avec un motif de feuilles; **7** (intention) dessein *m* (**to do** de faire); **by ~** à dessein; **to have ~s on** avoir des vues *fpl*

or des visées *fpl* sur [*job, title, car*]; **to have (evil) ~s on sb/sth** avoir des vues (mal intentionnées) sur qn/qch.
II *vtr* **1** (conceive, plan out) concevoir [*object, appliance, building, garment, experiment, course*]; **well/badly ~ed** bien/mal conçu; **2** (intend) **to be ~ed for sth/to do** (destined for) être destiné à qch/à faire; (made for) être conçu pour qch/pour faire; **a course ~ed for foreign students** un cours conçu pour or destiné aux étudiants étrangers; **a track ~ed for the use of cyclists** une piste destinée aux cyclistes; **a bowl ~ed to hold four litres/for the microwave** un bol prévu or fait pour contenir quatre litres/pour le micro-onde; **to be ~ed as** (for particular purpose) être prévu or conçu comme; (in the style of) représenter, être conçu comme; **3** (draw plan for) [*draughtsman*] dessiner le patron de [*garment*]; [*designer, stylist*] créer [*costume, garment, wardrobe*]; dessiner or faire les plans de [*building, bridge, object, appliance*].

designate I /ˈdezɪgneɪt, -nət/ *adj* [*president, director, chairperson*] en titre.
II /ˈdezɪgneɪt/ *vtr* [*word*] désigner; **to ~ sb (as) sth** désigner qn (comme) qch; **to ~ sth (as) sth** classer qch (comme) qch; **they ~d the area (as) a nature reserve** on a classé la région comme réserve naturelle; **a room ~d (as) a nonsmoking area** une salle destinée aux non-fumeurs; **to ~ sth for sb/sth** destiner qch à qn/qch; **the funds ~d for this project** les fonds destinés à ce projet; **to ~ sb to do** désigner qn pour faire.

designation /ˌdezɪgˈneɪʃn/ *n* désignation *f*, dénomination *f*; **the ~ of sth as** le classement de qch comme [*national park, nonsmoking area*]; **his ~ as ambassador** sa nomination au poste d'ambassadeur.

design: **~ award** *n* (for finished product) prix *m* de la meilleure réalisation or conception; (for idea) prix *m* du meilleur projet; **~ centre** *n* (for exhibiting) salon *m* permanent; (for planning, conception) bureau *m* d'études; **~ consultant** *n* conseiller/-ère *m/f* en aménagement; **~ department** *n* Ind bureau *m* d'études; Theat scénographie *f*; **~ engineering** *n* étude *f* de conception.

designer /dɪˈzaɪnə(r)/ **▶ 1692** I *n* gen concepteur/-trice *m/f*, designer *m*; (of cars) concepteur/-trice *m/f*; (of computers, software) créateur/-trice *m/f*, concepteur/-trice *m/f*; (of furniture) créateur/-trice *m/f*; (of sets) décorateur/-trice *m/f*; (in fashion) couturier/-ière *m/f*; **hat ~** (for women) modiste *f*; (for men) chapelier *m*; **costume ~** Theat, Cin costumier/-ière *m/f*; **▶ interior designer etc**.
II *modif* [*drink, cocktail, hi-fi, sunglasses*] de dernière mode; **~ clothes, ~ labels** (made to order) vêtements *mpl* de haute couture; (available in various outlets) vêtements *mpl* griffés; **~ jeans** jean *m* couture; **~ label** griffe *f*; **~ stubble** hum barbe *f* de deux jours (*volontairement négligée*).

designer drug *n* stupéfiant *m* à formule modifiée (*conçu pour contourner les mesures contre l'usage des stupéfiants*).

design: **~ fault** *n* faute *f* de conception, vice *m* caché; **~ feature** *n* caractéristique *f* (nominale).

designing /dɪˈzaɪnɪŋ/ *adj* péj intrigant.

design: **~ specification** *n* spécification *f* du modèle; **~ student** *n* étudiant/-e *m/f* en arts appliqués.

desirability /dɪˌzaɪərəˈbɪlətɪ/ *n* ¢ **1** (of plan, option, apartment, property) avantages *mpl*; **2** (sexual) attraits *mpl*, charmes *mpl*.

desirable /dɪˈzaɪərəbl/ *adj* **1** [*outcome, course of action, solution*] souhaitable; [*area, position*] convoité; [*job, gift*] séduisant, tentant; **it is ~ that** il est souhaitable que (+ *subj*); **it was ~ to do** c'était souhaitable de faire; **~ residence, ~ property** (in ad) maison *f* de standing; **2** (sexually) désirable.

desire /dɪˈzaɪə(r)/ I *n* **1** gen désir *m* (**for** de; **to do** de faire); **to have no ~ to do** n'avoir aucune envie de faire; **it is my earnest ~ that** mon plus vif désir est que (+ *subj*); **her heart's ~** littér son plus cher désir; **2** (sexual) désir *m*.
II *vtr* gen avoir envie de, désirer [*object, reward*]; (sexually) désirer; **to ~ to do** désirer faire; **to ~ sb to do sth**, **to ~ that sb (should) do sth** désirer que qn fasse qch; **if you so ~** sout si tel est votre désir; **it leaves a lot to be ~d** cela laisse beaucoup à désirer; **to obtain the ~d effect** obtenir l'effet désiré.

desirous /dɪˈzaɪərəs/ *adj* sout désireux/-euse (**of** de).

desist /dɪˈzɪst/ *vi* sout cesser (**from doing** de faire); **to ~ from sth** cesser qch.

desk /desk/ I *n* **1** (furniture) bureau *m*; Mus pupitre *m*; **writing ~** secrétaire *m*; **2** (in classroom) (pupil's) table *f*; (old-fashioned) pupitre *m*; (teacher's) bureau *m*; **3** (in public building) **reception ~** réception *f*; **information/advice ~** bureau *m* de renseignements/d'assistance; **cash ~** caisse *f*; **4** (in newspaper office) **the ~** la rédaction; **picture/sports ~** service *m* photos/des sports; **news ~** service *m* des informations; **5** (in organization, government office) (department) département *m*; **he has a ~ at the Foreign Office** (post) il travaille au ministère des Affaires étrangères.
II *modif* [*accessories, calendar, lamp, diary, job*] de bureau; **~ pad** (blotter) sous-main *m*; (notebook) bloc-notes *m*.

deskbound /ˈdeskbaʊnd/ *adj* [*job*] sédentaire; **we are ~ all week** nous ne bougeons pas de nos bureaux de toute la semaine.

desk clerk *n* US réceptionniste *mf*.

deskill /ˌdiːˈskɪl/ *vtr* automatiser [*job, process*]; déqualifier [*person*].

deskilling /ˌdiːˈskɪlɪŋ/ *n* (of workforce) baisse *f* de qualifications; (of job, process) automatisation *f*.

desk research *n* étude *f* sur documents.

desktop /ˈdesktɒp/ I *n* **1** (dessus *m* de) bureau *m*; **2** (also **~ computer**, **~ PC**) ordinateur *m* de bureau.
II *modif* [*model*] de bureau.

desk: **~top computer**, **~top PC** *n* ordinateur *m* de bureau; **~top publishing**, **DTP** *n* micro-édition *f*, publication *f* assistée par ordinateur, PAO.

desolate I /ˈdesələt/ *adj* **1** (deserted) [*place, landscape*] désolé, désert; [*house*] abandonné; **2** (devastated) [*building, city*] dévasté; **3** (forlorn) [*person, life*] désespérément triste; [*cry*] désolé; **4** (grief-stricken) accablé de chagrin, affligé.
II /ˈdesəleɪt/ *vtr* dévaster, ravager [*town, country*]; affliger, accabler de chagrin [*person*].

desolately /ˈdesələtlɪ/ *adv* [*say, look*] d'un air accablé.

desolation /ˌdesəˈleɪʃn/ *n* **1** (loneliness, bareness) (of place, landscape) aspect *m* désolé or désert; (of person, life) désolation *f*; **a scene of utter ~** une scène de profonde désolation; **2** (grief, misery) affliction *f*; **3** (devastation) (of city, country) dévastation *f*.

despair /dɪˈspeə(r)/ I *n* **1** (emotion) désespoir *m*; **to be in ~ about** ou **over sth** être désespéré par qch; **to do sth in** ou **out of ~** faire qch par désespoir; **in ~ he phoned her** désespéré, il lui a téléphoné; **to be in the depths of ~** être au désespoir; **to drive sb to ~** réduire qn au désespoir; **2** [*person*] **to be the ~ of sb** faire le désespoir de qn.
II *vi* désespérer (**of** de; **of doing** de faire); **don't ~** ne désespérez pas!

despairing /dɪˈspeərɪŋ/ *adj* désespéré.

despairingly /dɪˈspeərɪŋlɪ/ *adv* [*look*] d'un air désespéré; [*say*] d'un ton désespéré.

despatch = **dispatch**.

desperado /ˌdespəˈrɑːdəʊ/ *n* desperado *m*.

desperate /ˈdespərət/ *adj* **1** [*person, act, attempt, measure, plea, situation*] désespéré; [*criminal*] prêt à tout; **to be ~ to do** avoir très envie de faire; **to be ~ for** avoir désespérément besoin de [*affection, money, help, trade*]; attendre désespérément [*news*]; **the refugees are ~** les réfugiés sont à bout; **a ~ case** un cas désespéré; **to do something ~** commettre un acte de désespoir; **2**○ (terrible) affreux/-euse, terrible.

desperately /ˈdespərətlɪ/ *adv* **1** [*plead, struggle, fight*] désespérément; [*look*] d'un air désespéré, désespérément; [*love*] éperdument; **to need/want sth ~** avoir très besoin/très envie de qch; **2** (as intensifier) [*poor, hungry, anxious*] terriblement; [*ill*] très gravement; **~ in love** éperdument amoureux/-euse.

desperation /ˌdespəˈreɪʃn/ *n* désespoir *m*; **in (sheer) ~ she phoned the police** en désespoir de cause elle a appelé la police; **to act out of ~** agir par désespoir; **her ~ to win/for another victory** son désir intense de gagner/de remporter une nouvelle victoire; **to drive sb to ~** réduire qn au désespoir.

despicable /dɪˈspɪkəbl, ˈdespɪkəbl/ *adj* méprisable.

despicably /dɪˈspɪkəblɪ, ˈdespɪkəblɪ/ *adv* ignoblement.

despise /dɪˈspaɪz/ *vtr* mépriser (**for** pour; **for doing** pour avoir fait).

despite /dɪˈspaɪt/ *prep* malgré, en dépit de; **~ the fact that** bien que (+ *subj*); **~ oneself** malgré soi.

despoil /dɪˈspɔɪl/ *vtr* sout littér dévaster [*area, country*].

despondency /dɪˈspɒndənsɪ/, **despondence** /dɪˈspɒndəns/ *n* abattement *m*, découragement *m*.

despondent /dɪˈspɒndənt/ *adj* abattu, déprimé, découragé; **she is ~ about her results** elle est déprimée par ses résultats.

despondently /dɪˈspɒndəntlɪ/ *adv* [*say, look, walk*] d'un air abattu or découragé.

despot /ˈdespɒt/ *n* despote *m*.

despotic /deˈspɒtɪk/ *adj* despotique.

despotically /deˈspɒtɪklɪ/ *adv* [*act, behave*] en despote.

despotism /ˈdespətɪzəm/ *n* despotisme *m*.

des res○ /ˌdez ˈrez/ *n* (in ad) maison *f* de standing.

dessert /dɪˈzɜːt/ I *n* dessert *m*.
II *modif* [*fork, plate etc*] à dessert.

dessert: **~ apple** *n* pomme *f* à couteau; **~ chocolate** *n* chocolat *m* à croquer; **~spoon** *n* cuillère *f* à dessert; **~ wine** *n* vin *m* doux.

destabilization /ˌdiːsteɪbəlaɪˈzeɪʃn, US -lɪˈz-/ *n* déstabilisation *f*.

destabilize /ˌdiːˈsteɪbəlaɪz/ *vtr* déstabiliser.

destalinization /diːˌstɑːlɪnaɪˈzeɪʃn, US -nɪˈz-/ *n* déstalinisation *f*.

destalinize /diːˈstɑːlɪnaɪz/ *vtr* déstaliniser.

destination /ˌdestɪˈneɪʃn/ *n* destination *f*; **we reached our ~ at 3 o'clock** nous sommes arrivés à destination à 3 heures.

destine /ˈdestɪn/ *vtr* destiner (**for** à).

destined /ˈdestɪnd/ *adj* **1** (preordained) destiné (**for, to** à; **to do** à faire); **it was ~ that** il était écrit que; **they were ~ never to meet again** ils n'étaient pas destinés à se revoir; **it was ~ to happen** cela devait arriver; **to be ~ for higher things** être destiné à un grand avenir; **2** [*plane, train, traveller, letter etc*] **~ for Paris** à destination de Paris, pour Paris.

destiny /ˈdestɪnɪ/ *n* (past events) destin *m*; (future events) destinée *f*; **it was her ~ to become queen** son destin était de devenir reine; **nobody knows her/his ~** personne ne connaît sa destinée; **a man of ~** (saviour) un envoyé du destin; (full of promise) un homme destiné à un grand avenir; **Destiny had decreed that...** le destin avait décrété que...

destitute /ˈdestɪtjuːt, US -tuːt/ I *n* **the ~** (+ *v pl*) les indigents *mpl*.

II *adj* **1** [*person, family, community*] sans ressources; **to leave sb ~** laisser qn dans le dénuement; **2** sout **to be ~ of** être dénué de [*feeling, common sense, funds*].

destitution /ˌdestɪˈtjuːʃn, US -tuːt-/ *n* misère *f* extrême, indigence *f*.

destroy /dɪˈstrɔɪ/ *vtr* **1** détruire [*building, town, landscape, data, letter, evidence, bacteria*]; détruire, mettre fin à [*hopes, happiness, love, relationship, reputation, career*]; anéantir [*person*]; faire exploser [*bomb, suspicious package*]; **brain/ozone-~ing** qui détruit le cerveau/la couche d'ozone; **2** (kill) abattre [*animal*]; détruire, anéantir [*population, enemy*]; **3**° Sport écraser [*opponent*].

destroyer /dɪˈstrɔɪə(r)/ *n* **1** Naut contre-torpilleur *m*, destroyer *m*; **2** (person) destructeur/-trice *m/f*; (killer) meurtrier/-ière *m/f*; **3** (fire, flood, earthquake) fléau *m*.

destruct /dɪˈstrʌkt/ **I** *n* autodestruction *f*.
II *modif* [*mechanism*] d'autodestruction; **~ button** télécommande *f* de destruction.
III *vtr* détruire, faire s'autodétruire.
IV *vi* s'autodétruire.

destructible /dɪˈstrʌktəbl/ *adj* destructible.

destruction /dɪˈstrʌkʃn/ *n* (of building, town, environment, letter, evidence) destruction *f*; (of hopes, happiness, reputation, career) ruine *f*, anéantissement *m*; (of enemy, population) destruction *f*; **the gales caused widespread ~** la tempête a fait des dégâts considérables.

destructive /dɪˈstrʌktɪv/ *adj* **1** (causing destruction) [*force, behaviour, policy, method*] destructeur/-trice; [*storm, fire*] destructeur/-trice, dévastateur/-trice; **to be ~ of** ou **to sth** être nuisible à qch; **a ~ child** un brise-fer; **2** (having potential to destroy) [*weapon, capacity*] destructif/-ive; [*urge, emotion, criticism*] destructeur/-trice.

destructively /dɪˈstrʌktɪvlɪ/ *adv* [*behave*] de façon destructrice.

destructiveness /dɪˈstrʌktɪvnɪs/ *n* (of storm, weapon, emotion, behaviour) effet *m* destructeur; (of child) penchant *m* destructeur; (of argument, régime, theory) caractère *m* destructeur.

destructor /dɪˈstrʌktə(r)/ *n* **1** GB (incinerator) gen incinérateur *m* à ordures; Ind incinérateur *m* de déchets; **2** Mil charge *f* d'autodestruction.

desuetude /dɪˈsjuːɪtjuːd, US -tuːd/ *n* sout désuétude *f*.

desultory /ˈdesəltrɪ, US -tɔːrɪ/ *adj* [*conversation*] décousu; [*attempt, effort*] sporadique; [*reading*] superficiel/-ielle; [*friendship, contact*] épisodique; **she wandered about in a ~ fashion** elle se promenait au hasard.

Det *abrév écrite* = **Detective**.

detach /dɪˈtætʃ/ **I** *vtr* gen, Mil détacher (**from** de).
II *v refl* **to ~ oneself** se détacher (**from** de).

detachable /dɪˈtætʃəbl/ *adj* [*coupon, portion of bill, section of form, strap*] détachable; [*handle, lever, collar, cuff, lining*] amovible; Phot [*lens*] mobile.

detached /dɪˈtætʃt/ *adj* **1** (separate) détaché, séparé; **2** (emotionally, intellectually) [*person, view*] détaché; [*attitude, manner*] détaché, dégagé; [*observer*] indépendant.

detached: **~ garage** *n* garage *m* indépendant; **~ house** *n* maison *f* (individuelle), pavillon *m*; **~ retina** *n* Med rétine *f* décollée.

detachment /dɪˈtætʃmənt/ *n* **1** (separation) séparation *f* (**from** de); **~ of the retina** Med décollement *m* de la rétine; **2** (emotional, intellectual) détachement *m*; **3** Mil (unit) détachement *m*.

detail /ˈdiːteɪl, US dɪˈteɪl/ **I** *n* **1** (of story, account etc) détail *m*; (decorative) détail *m*; (insignificant) (point *m* de) détail *m*; **point of ~** point *m* de détail; **in (some) ~** en détail; **in more** ou **greater ~** plus en détail; **in great** ou **minute ~** dans les moindres détails; **to go into ~s** entrer dans les détails (**about** au sujet de); **to have an eye for ~**, **to show attention to ~** prêter attention aux détails; **I'll spare you the ~s** je vous fais grâce des détails; **2** Art détail *m*; **3** Mil détachement *m*.
II details *npl* (information) renseignements *mpl*; **for further ~s...** Comm pour de plus amples renseignements...
III *vtr* **1** (list) exposer [qch] en détail [*plans, changes*]; énumérer [*items*]; **2 to ~ sb to sth** affecter qn à qch.

detail drawing *n* épure *f*.

detailed /ˈdiːteɪld, US dɪˈteɪld/ *adj* détaillé.

detain /dɪˈteɪn/ *vtr* **1** (delay) retenir; **I won't ~ you any longer** je ne vous retiendrai pas plus longtemps; **2** (keep in custody) placer [qn] en détention [*prisoner*]; **to be ~ed for questioning** être placé en garde à vue pour être interrogé; **3** (in hospital) garder.

detainee /ˌdiːteɪˈniː/ *n* (general) détenu/-e *m/f*; (political) prisonnier/-ière *m/f* (politique).

detect /dɪˈtekt/ *vtr* **1** (find, locate) découvrir [*error*]; déceler [*traces, trend, change, evidence*]; détecter [*crime, disease, leak, enemy plane*]; **2** (sense) détecter [*sound, smell*]; sentir [*mood*]; **I ~ed a note of impatience in her voice** j'ai perçu une note d'impatience dans sa voix.

detectable /dɪˈtektəbl/ *adj* discernable.

detection /dɪˈtekʃn/ **I** *n* (of crime, disease, error) détection *f*; **the ~ of crime, crime ~** la lutte contre la criminalité; **to escape ~** [*criminal*] ne pas être découvert; [*error*] ne pas être décelé; **radar ~** détection *f* radar; **submarine ~** détection *f* sous-marine.
II *modif* **(crime) ~ rate** taux *m* d'arrestations de criminels.

detective /dɪˈtektɪv/ *n* ≈ inspecteur/-trice *m/f* (de police); (private) détective *m*; **store ~** inspecteur/-trice *m/f*.

detective: **~ constable** *n* GB ≈ enquêteur *m*; **~ inspector**, **DI** *n* GB ≈ inspecteur *m* principal; **~ sergeant** *n* GB ≈ inspecteur *m* de police; **~ story** *n* roman *m* policier, polar° *m*; **~ superintendent** *n* GB ≈ commissaire *m* de police judiciaire; **~ work** *n* enquêtes *fpl* also fig.

detector /dɪˈtektə(r)/ *n* détecteur *m*.

detente /ˌdeɪˈtɑːnt/ *n* Pol détente *f*.

detention /dɪˈtenʃn/ *n* **1** (confinement) détention *f*; **to be/die in ~** être/mourir en détention; **2** (prison sentence) détention *f* criminelle; (awaiting trial) détention *f* provisoire; **3** Sch retenue *f*, colle° *f*.

detention centre GB, **detention home** US *n* centre *m* de détention pour mineurs.

deter /dɪˈtɜː(r)/ *vtr* (*p prés etc* **-rr-**) **1** (dissuade) dissuader; **a scheme to ~ burglars/vandalism** un projet pour décourager les cambrioleurs/le vandalisme; **nothing will ~ her** rien ne la fera reculer; **2** (prevent) empêcher (**from doing** de faire).

detergent /dɪˈtɜːdʒənt/ *n, adj* détergent (*m*), détersif (*m*) spec.

deteriorate /dɪˈtɪərɪəreɪt/ *vi* [*weather*] se gâter; [*health, relationship, situation*] se détériorer; [*economy, market, sales*] décliner; [*work, building, area*] se dégrader; [*leather, wood*] se détériorer; **to ~ into** [*discussion, debate etc*] dégénérer en.

deterioration /dɪˌtɪərɪəˈreɪʃn/ *n* (in weather) dégradation *f* (**in** de); (in health, situation, relationship) détérioration *f* (**in** de); (in work, performance) baisse *f* de qualité (**in** de); (of building, area) dégradation *f*; (of leather, wood) détérioration *f*; **~ in living standards** baisse *f* du niveau de vie.

determinable /dɪˈtɜːmɪnəbl/ *adj* **1** [*amount, fact*] déterminable; **2** Jur [*contract, right*] résoluble.

determinant /dɪˈtɜːmɪnənt/ *n, adj* gen, Math déterminant (*m*).

determination /dɪˌtɜːmɪˈneɪʃn/ *n* **1** (quality) détermination *f* (**to do** à faire); **2** (of amount, date etc) détermination *f*; **3** Jur, Admin (ruling) décision *f*.

determine /dɪˈtɜːmɪn/ *vtr* **1** (find out) déterminer [*cause, fact*]; **to ~ how/when etc** établir comment/quand etc; **2** (decide) déterminer, fixer [*date, price*]; **to ~ to do** résoudre de faire; **to ~ that/when etc** décider que/quand etc; **to ~ (up)on sth** se résoudre à qch; **it was ~ed that** il a été établi que; **3** (control) [*factor*] déterminer [*outcome, progress*].

determined /dɪˈtɜːmɪnd/ *adj* [*person*] fermement décidé (**to do** à faire); [*air, expression*] résolu; [*attempt, approach*] ferme; **to be ~ that** être résolu à ce que (+ *subj*).

determiner /dɪˈtɜːmɪnə(r)/ *n* Ling déterminant *m*.

determining /dɪˈtɜːmɪnɪŋ/ *adj* (*épith*) déterminant.

determinism /dɪˈtɜːmɪnɪzəm/ *n* déterminisme *m*.

determinist /dɪˈtɜːmɪnɪst/ *n, adj* déterministe (*mf*).

deterrent /dɪˈterənt, US -ˈtɜː-/ **I** *n* gen moyen *m* de dissuasion; Mil force *f* de dissuasion; **to be a ~ to sb** dissuader qn; **to act as a ~** Mil jouer un rôle de dissuasion.
II *adj* [*effect*] dissuasif/-ive; [*measure*] de dissuasion.

detest /dɪˈtest/ *vtr* détester (**doing** faire).

detestable /dɪˈtestəbl/ *adj* détestable; (stronger) odieux/-ieuse.

detestably /dɪˈtestəblɪ/ *adv* détestablement.

detestation /ˌdiːteˈsteɪʃn/ *n* **1** (hatred) haine *f*; **2** (object of hatred) objet *m* de haine.

dethrone /ˌdiːˈθrəʊn/ *vtr* détrôner.

dethronement /ˌdiːˈθrəʊnmənt/ *n* déposition *f*.

detonate /ˈdetəneɪt/ **I** *vtr* faire exploser.
II *vi* exploser.

detonation /ˌdetəˈneɪʃn/ *n* détonation *f*, explosion *f*.

detonator /ˈdetəneɪtə(r)/ *n* détonateur *m*.

detour /ˈdiːtʊə(r), US dɪˈtʊər/ **I** *n* détour *m*; **it's worth a** ou **the ~** lit, fig ça vaut le détour.
II *vtr* US **1** (redirect) dévier, détourner [*traffic*]; **2** (bypass) contourner.
III *vi* faire un détour.

detox /ˌdiːˈtɒks/ = **detoxify**, **detoxi(fi)cation**.

detoxicate /ˌdiːˈtɒksɪkeɪt/ *vtr* désintoxiquer.

detoxi(fi)cation /ˌdiːˌtɒksɪ(fɪ)ˈkeɪʃn/ **I** *n* désintoxication *f*; **to be in ~** être en cure de désintoxication.
II *modif* [*centre, treatment*] de désintoxication.

detoxify /ˌdiːˈtɒksɪfaɪ/ *vtr* désintoxiquer.

detract /dɪˈtrækt/ *vi* **to ~ from** porter atteinte à [*achievement, success, support, value*]; nuire à, porter atteinte à [*harmony, image, publicity*]; diminuer [*pleasure, happiness*].

detraction /dɪˈtrækʃn/ *n* dénigrement *m*.

detractor /dɪˈtræktə(r)/ *n* détracteur/-trice *m/f*.

detrain /ˌdiːˈtreɪn/ Mil **I** *vtr* faire descendre [qn] d'un train [*troops*].
II *vi* descendre d'un train.

detriment /ˈdetrɪmənt/ *n* **to the ~ of** au détriment de; **to their ~** à leur détriment; **to the great ~ of sth** au grand dommage de qch; **without ~ to** sans dommage pour.

detrimental /ˌdetrɪˈmentl/ *adj* nuisible (**to** à); **to be ~ to, to have a ~ effect on** nuire à, être nuisible à [*person, environment, wildlife*].

detritus /dɪˈtraɪtəs/ *n* ¢ **1** gen détritus *mpl* (**of** de); **2** Geol dépôts *mpl* détritiques.

deuce /djuːs, US duːs/ *n* **1** (in tennis) **~!** égalité!; **2** (in cards) deux *m*; **3**°† **what/where the ~?** que/où diable°?

deuced°† /ˈdjuːsɪd, djuːst, US duːst/ **I** *adj* satané (*before n*).

II *adv* diablement.

Deuteronomy /ˌdjuːtəˈrɒnəmɪ, US ˌduː-/ *pr n* Deutéronome *m*.

Deux-Sèvres ▶ 1163 *pr n* Deux-Sèvres *fpl*; **in/to ~** dans les Deux-Sèvres.

devaluate /ˌdiːˈvæljʊeɪt/ *vtr* = **devalue**.

devaluation /ˌdiːvæljʊˈeɪʃn/ *n* **1** Econ, Fin (of currency) dévaluation *f*; (of shares) baisse *f*; **a 12% ~** une dévaluation de 12%; **2** gen dévalorisation *f*.

devalue /ˌdiːˈvæljuː/ **I** *vtr* **1** Econ, Fin dévaluer (**against** contre); **to be ~d by 6%** être dévalué de 6%; **2** gen (underestimate) dévaloriser.
II *vi* Econ, Fin [*currency*] être dévalué (**against** par rapport à); [*property*] baisser; [*shares*] dévaloriser; [*government, country*] dévaluer.

devastate /ˈdevəsteɪt/ **I** *vtr* **1** lit ravager [*land, town*]; **2** fig anéantir [*person*].
II devastated *pp adj* **1** lit ravagé; **2** [*person*] anéanti (**by** par).

devastating /ˈdevəsteɪtɪŋ/ *adj* **1** lit [*attack, power, effect, storm*] dévastateur/-trice; fig [*beauty, charm*] ravageur/-euse; **2** (crushing) [*news, loss, grief*] accablant; [*comment, criticism, reply*] cinglant; [*argument*] écrasant; **to be ~ about sb/sth** fustiger qn/qch.

devastatingly /ˌdevəsteɪtɪŋlɪ/ *adv* terriblement.

devastation /ˌdevəˈsteɪʃn/ *n* **1** (of land, town) dévastation *f*; **2** (of person) anéantissement *m*.

develop /dɪˈveləp/ **I** *vtr* **1** (acquire) acquérir [*skill, knowledge*]; attraper [*illness*]; prendre [*habit*]; présenter [*symptom*]; **to ~ an awareness of sth** prendre conscience de qch; **to ~ a taste** ou **liking for sth** prendre goût à qch; **to ~ cancer** développer un cancer; **the engine ~ed a fault** le moteur a commencé à mal fonctionner; **2** (evolve) élaborer [*plan, project*]; mettre au point [*techniques, procedures, invention*]; exposer [*theory, idea*]; développer [*argument*]; **3** Comm, Ind (create) créer [*market*]; établir [*close ties, links*]; **4** (expand, build up) développer [*mind, physique*]; Comm développer [*business, market*]; **5** (improve) mettre en valeur [*land, site etc*]; aménager [*city centre*]; **6** Phot développer.
II *vi* **1** (evolve) [*child, seed, embryo*] se développer; [*intelligence*] s'épanouir; [*skills*] s'améliorer; [*society, country, region*] se développer; [*plot, play*] se développer; **to ~ into** devenir; **2** (come into being) [*friendship*] naître; [*trouble, difficulty*] naître; [*crack, hole*] se former; [*illness, symptom*] se déclarer; **3** (progress, advance) [*friendship*] se développer; [*difficulty*] s'aggraver; [*crack, fault*] s'accentuer; [*war, illness*] s'aggraver; [*game, story*] se dérouler; **4** (in size, extent) [*town, business*] se développer.

developed /dɪˈveləpt/ *adj* [*country, economy*] développé.

developer /dɪˈveləpə(r)/ *n* **1** (also **property ~**) promoteur *m* (immobilier); **2** Phot révélateur *m*; **3** Psych, Sch **early ~** enfant *m* précoce; **late ~** individu *m* qui se développe tard.

developing /dɪˈveləpɪŋ/ *adj* [*area, economy*] en expansion.

developing: **~ bath** *n* Phot bain *m* révélateur; **~ country** *n* pays *m* en voie de développement; **~ tank** *n* Phot cuve *f* à développement.

development /dɪˈveləpmənt/ *n* **1** (creation) (of commercial product) mise *f* au point; (of new housing, industry etc) création *f*; **new ~** nouveauté *f*; **2** (evolution, growth) (human, economic, industrial etc) développement *m*; **3** (fostering) (of links) développement *m*; (of the arts, sport, industry) développement *m*; **4** (of land) mise *f* en valeur; (of site, city centre etc) aménagement *m*; **5** (land etc developed) **housing ~** ensemble *m* d'habitation; (individual houses) lotissement *m*; **office ~** immeuble *m* de bureaux; **commercial ~** (ensemble de) commerces et bureaux à bâtir; **6** (innovation) progrès *m*; **major ~s in surgery** des découvertes *fpl* majeures dans le domaine de la chirurgie; **7** (event) changement *m*; **recent ~s in Europe/in the pay dispute** les derniers événements en Europe/dans le conflit salarial; **the latest ~s** les dernières nouvelles *fpl*; **to await ~s** attendre la suite des événements; **8** (of idea, theme etc) développement *m*.

developmental /dɪˌveləpˈmentl/ *adj* Psych du développement.

development: **~ area** *n* zone *f* d'aménagement; **~ bank** *n* banque *f* de développement; **~ company** *n* groupe *m* immobilier; **~ costs** *npl* coûts *mpl* de développement; **~ period** *n* période *f* de démarrage; **~ planning** *n* planification *f* d'aménagement.

deviance /ˈdiːvɪəns/, **deviancy** /ˈdiːvɪənsɪ/ *n* déviance *f*.

deviant /ˈdiːvɪənt/ **I** *n* déviant/-e *m/f*.
II *adj* déviant.

deviate /ˈdiːvɪeɪt/ *vi* **1** (from principles, intentions, norm) s'écarter (**from** de); **2** [*ship, plane, missile*] dévier (**from** de).

deviation /ˌdiːvɪˈeɪʃn/ *n* **1** (from course, route) déviation *f* (**from** par rapport à); **2** (from norm, custom) écart *m*, déviation *f* (**from** par rapport à); Pol déviation *f* (**from** par rapport à); **3** (sexual) déviance *f*; **4** (of compass needle) déviation *f*, écart *m*; **5** Stat écart *m*; **standard ~** écart *m* type.

deviationism /ˌdiːvɪˈeɪʃənɪzəm/ *n* Pol déviationnisme *m*.

deviationist /ˌdiːvɪˈeɪʃənɪst/ *n, adj* Pol déviationniste (*mf*).

device /dɪˈvaɪs/ *n* **1** (household) appareil *m*; **labour-saving ~** appareil *m* électroménager; **2** Tech dispositif *m*; **a ~ for measuring/to measure** un dispositif pour mesurer; **3** (system) système *m*; **security ~** système *m* or dispositif *m* de sécurité; **4** Comput périphérique *m*; **5** (also **explosive ~, incendiary ~**) (bomb) engin *m* explosif; **6** fig (means) gen moyen *m* (**for doing, to do** de or pour faire); Econ mesure *f* (**for doing, to do** pour faire); **7** Literat procédé *m*; **8** Herald emblème *m*.
IDIOMS **to be left to one's own ~s** être laissé à soi-même; **to leave sb to their own ~s** laisser qn se débrouiller tout seul.

devil /ˈdevl/ **I** *n* **1** (also **Devil**) Relig (Satan) **the ~** le Diable; **2** (evil spirit) démon *m*; **possessed by ~s** possédé du démon; **3**○ (for emphasis) **what the ~ do you mean?** que diable veux-tu dire?; **why the ~ do you think I invited her?** pourquoi diable est-ce-que tu crois que je l'ai invitée?; **I wondered what the ~ he was talking about/why the ~ he had come** je me demandais de quoi il pouvait bien parler/pourquoi donc il était venu; **how the ~ should I know?** comment veux-tu que je le sache?; **we'll have a ~ of a job cleaning the house** ça va être sacrément○ dur de nettoyer la maison; **4**○ (expressing affection, sympathy) **a lucky ~** un sacré○ veinard○; **he's a handsome/cheeky ~** il est sacrément○ beau/effronté; **the poor ~** le pauvre diable; **that child is a little ~** cet enfant est un vrai petit diable; **some poor ~ of a soldier** un pauvre (diable de) soldat; **5**○† (nuisance) **to be a ~ for doing** avoir la manie de faire; **she's a ~ for contradicting people** elle a la manie de contredire les autres; **these pans are a ~ to clean** ces casseroles sont une vraie plaie○ à nettoyer; **he's a ~ for gambling** c'est un joueur invétéré; **6** GB Jur *avocat stagiaire non rémunéré*.
II *vi* (*pp etc* **-ll-**) GB Jur **to ~ for sb** travailler comme avocat stagiaire pour qn.
III devilled GB, **deviled** US *adj* Culin à la diable.
IDIOMS **be a ~**○! allez, laisse-toi tenter!; **the ~ you know is better than the ~ you don't** un danger connu est préférable à un danger inconnu; **to be caught between the ~ and the deep blue sea** être pris entre l'enclume et le marteau; **we won—the ~ looks after his own** hum on a gagné—on a eu une sacrée veine○; **the ~ only knows where/why etc** Dieu seul sait où/pourquoi etc; **to have the luck of the ~**○ GB avoir une veine de cocu○ or de pendu○; **like the ~**○ [*scream, run*] comme un fou/une folle○; **speak of the ~!** quand on parle du loup (on en voit la queue)○!; **there will be the ~ to pay when he finds out!** ça va barder○ quand il l'apprendra!; **go to the ~**○**!** va au diable○!; **the ~ you did**○**!** sans blague○!; **to give the ~ his due...** il faut quand même l'admettre...

devilfish /ˈdevlfɪʃ/ *n* **1** (octopus) poulpe *m*; **2** US (manta) mante *f*.

devilish /ˈdevəlɪʃ/ **I** *adj* **1** (heinous) [*crime, act, plan*] diabolique; **2** fig [*smile, cunning*] diabolique; [*good looks*] insolent.
II○† *adv* GB = **devilishly 2**.

devilishly /ˈdevəlɪʃlɪ/ *adv* **1** (horribly) **~ cruel** d'une cruauté diabolique; **2**○ [*clever, cunning, handsome*] sacrément○; **it's ~ hard work** c'est un travail sacrément○ difficile; **it was ~ hot** il faisait une chaleur infernale.

devil-may-care /ˌdevlmeɪˈkeə(r)/ *adj* insouciant.

devilment /ˈdevlmənt/ *n* GB malice *f*; **out of sheer ~** par pure malice; **they're up to some ~ or other** ils mijotent○ quelque chose.

devilry /ˈdevlrɪ/, **deviltry** /ˈdevltrɪ/ US *n* malice *f*.

devil's advocate *n* avocat *m* du diable; **to play ~** se faire l'avocat du diable.

devil: **~'s food cake** *n* US gâteau *m* au chocolat; **~ worship** *n* satanisme *m*; **~ worshipper** *n* pratiquant/-e *m/f* du satanisme.

devious /ˈdiːvɪəs/ *adj* **1** (sly) [*person, mind, plan*] retors; [*method*] détourné; **2** (winding) [*road, path*] tortueux/-euse.

deviously /ˈdiːvɪəslɪ/ *adv* de façon retorse.

deviousness /ˈdiːvɪəsnɪs/ *n* **1** (of person, plan) caractère *m* retors; **2** (of route) complexité *f*.

devise /dɪˈvaɪz/ **I** *n* Jur legs *m*.
II *vtr* **1** (invent) concevoir [*scheme, course*]; inventer [*product, machine*]; **his problems are (entirely) of his own devising** c'est lui qui crée ses propres problèmes; **2** Jur léguer [*land, property*]; **3** Theat écrire [qch] en groupe.

devisee /ˌdɪvaɪˈziː/ *n* Jur légataire *mf*.

deviser /dɪˈvaɪzə(r)/ *n* inventeur *m*.

devisor /dɪˈvaɪzə(r)/ *n* Jur testateur/-trice *m/f*.

devitalization /ˌdiːˌvaɪtəlaɪˈzeɪʃn, US -lɪˈz-/ *n* affaiblissement *m*.

devitalize /ˌdiːˈvaɪtəlaɪz/ *vtr* affaiblir.

devocalization /ˌdiːˌvəʊkəlaɪˈzeɪʃn, US -lɪˈz-/ *n* dévocalisation *f*.

devocalize /ˌdiːˈvəʊkəlaɪz/ *vtr* dévocaliser.

devoice /dɪˈvɔɪs/ *vtr* dévoiser.

devoicing /dɪˈvɔɪsɪŋ/ *n* dévoisement *m*.

devoid /dɪˈvɔɪd/: **devoid of** *prep phr* dépourvu de [*talent, compassion*]; sans [*vanity, self-interest*].

devolution /ˌdiːvəˈluːʃn, US ˌdev-/ *n* **1** (transfer) transfert *m* (**from** de; **to** à); **2** Pol régionalisation *f*; **3** Jur dévolution *f*; **4** Biol dégénérescence *f*.

devolve /dɪˈvɒlv/ **I** *vtr* déléguer; **to ~ sth to** ou **on sb/sth** transmettre qch à qn/qch.
II *vi* **1** (be the responsibility of) [*responsibility, duty*] incomber (**on** à); **it ~s on sb to do** il incombe à qn de faire; **2** Jur passer (**on, to** à); **3** Biol dégénérer.
III devolved *pp adj* décentralisé.

Devon /ˈdevn/ ▶ 1624 *pr n* Devon *m*.

Devonian /dɪˈvəʊnɪən/ *adj* dévonien/-ienne.

devote /dɪˈvəʊt/ **I** *vtr* consacrer (**to** à; **to**

doing à faire); **a chapter ~d to**... un chapitre consacré à...
II *v refl* **to ~ oneself** se consacrer (**to** à; **to doing** à faire).

devoted /dɪˈvəʊtɪd/ *adj* [*person, animal*] dévoué (**to** à); [*friendship, service*] loyal; [*fan, following*] fervent; [*couple*] très uni; **they're ~ to each other** ils sont très attachés l'un à l'autre.

devotedly /dɪˈvəʊtɪdlɪ/ *adv* avec dévouement.

devotee /ˌdevəˈtiː/ *n* (of music, sport etc) passionné/-e *m/f* (**of** de); (of political cause) partisan/-e *m/f* (**of** de); (of person) admirateur/-trice *m/f* (**of** de); (of religious sect) adepte *mf*.

devotion /dɪˈvəʊʃn/ **I** *n* (to person, work, homeland) dévouement *m* (**to** à); (to doctrine, cause) attachement *m* (**to** à); (to God) dévotion *f* (**to** à); **her ~ to duty/to detail** son attachement au devoir/aux détails; **his ~ to the arts** (love) son amour des arts; (support) son soutien des arts.
II devotions *npl* dévotions *fpl*.

devotional /dɪˈvəʊʃənl/ *adj* [*activity, attitude*] pieux/-ieuse; [*writings*] de piété.

devour /dɪˈvaʊə(r)/ *vtr* **1** (consume) lit, fig dévorer [*food, book*]; consommer beaucoup de [*petrol, resources*]; **to be ~ed by** être dévoré par [*passion, jealousy*]; **to ~ sb with one's eyes** dévorer qn des yeux; **2** (destroy) [*fire*] dévorer [*house, forest*].

devourer /dɪˈvaʊərə(r)/ *n* lit, fig dévoreur/-euse *m/f*.

devout /dɪˈvaʊt/ *adj* **1** Relig [*Catholic, prayer*] fervent; [*act, person*] pieux/pieuse; **a ~ believer** un fervent croyant; **2** (sincere) [*hope, wish*] ardent; **it is my ~ hope/wish that** c'est mon espoir/vœu le plus ardent que (+ *subj*).

devoutly /dɪˈvaʊtlɪ/ *adv* **1** Relig [*pray, kneel*] pieusement; **2** (sincerely) [*wish, hope*] ardemment.

devoutness /dɪˈvaʊtnɪs/ *n* dévotion *f*.

dew /djuː, US duː/ *n* rosée *f*.

DEW *n* US Mil (*abrév* = **distant early warning**) **~ line** couverture *f* radar (*de l'Arctique*).

Dewar flask /ˌdjuːə(r), US ˌduː-/ *n* vase *m* de Dewar.

dew: **~claw** *n* ergot *m*; **~drop** *n* goutte *f* de rosée.

Dewey decimal system /ˈdjuːɪ, US ˈduː-/ *n* système *m* de classification décimale (*pour le classement des livres*).

dew: **~fall** *n* formation *f* de rosée; **~lap** *n* fanon *m*; **~ point** *n* point *m* de rosée; **~ pond** *n* mare *f* artificielle.

dewy /ˈdjuːɪ, US ˈduː-/ *adj* humide de rosée.

dewy-eyed /ˌdjuːɪˈaɪd, US ˌduː-/ *adj* **1** (emotional) ému; **2** (naive) ingénu.

Dexedrine® /ˈdeksədriːn/ *n* Dexédrine® *f*.

dexie○ /ˈdeksɪ/ *n* argot des drogués comprimé *m* de Dexédrine®.

dexter /ˈdekstə(r)/ *adj* Herald dextre.

dexterity /dekˈsterətɪ/ *n* dextérité *f* (**at** ou **in sth** pour qch; **at doing** à faire).

dexterous /ˈdekstrəs/ *adj* [*person, movement*] adroit; [*hand*] habile; [*mind*] agile; [*politician, manager*] habile (**at doing** pour faire); **he's ~ with a needle/brush** il manie bien l'aiguille/le pinceau.

dexterously /ˈdekstrəslɪ/ *adv* [*move*] (of person) adroitement; (of animal) agilement; [*think, manage*] habilement.

dextrin(e) /ˈdekstrɪn/ *n* dextrine *f*.

dextrose /ˈdekstrəʊs, -əʊz/ *n* dextrose *m*.

dextrous *adj* ▶ **dexterous**.

dextrously *adv* ▶ **dexterously**.

DFC *n* GB Mil (*abrév* = **Distinguished Flying Cross**) *décoration décernée par l'armée de l'air britannique*.

DFM *n* GB Mil (*abrév* = **Distinguished Flying Medal**) *médaille décernée par l'armée de l'air britannique*.

dg *n* (*abrév écrite* = **decigram**) dg *m*.

DG *n*: *abrév* ▶ **director general**.

dharma /ˈdɑːmə/ *n* dharma *m*.

dhoti /ˈdəʊtɪ/ *n* dhoti *m*.

dhow /daʊ/ *n* boutre *m*.

DI *n* GB *abrév* ▶ **Detective Inspector**.

diabetes /ˌdaɪəˈbiːtiːz/ **▶ 1354** *n* diabète *m*.

diabetic /ˌdaɪəˈbetɪk/ **I** *n* diabétique *mf*.
II *adj* [*person, symptom*] diabétique; [*chocolate, jam*] pour diabétiques.

diabolic /ˌdaɪəˈbɒlɪk/ *adj* diabolique.

diabolical /ˌdaɪəˈbɒlɪkl/ *adj* **1**○ (terrible) [*food, weather*] infect; [*result, behaviour*] lamentable; **it is ~ that** il est scandaleux que (+ *subj*); **2** (evil) [*cruelty, crime, lie*] diabolique; **3**○ (as intensifier) sacré○ (*before n*).

diabolically /ˌdaɪəˈbɒlɪklɪ/ *adv* **1** (badly) [*sing, perform*] de façon épouvantable; [*behave*] de façon odieuse; **2** (wickedly) [*laugh*] de façon diabolique; **~ cruel** d'une cruauté diabolique.

diabolo /dɪˈæbələʊ, daɪ-/ *n* diabolo *m*.

diachronic /ˌdaɪəˈkrɒnɪk/ *adj* diachronique.

diachronically /ˌdaɪəˈkrɒnɪklɪ/ *adv* diachroniquement.

diacid /ˌdaɪˈæsɪd/ *n, adj* diacide (*m*).

diacritic /ˌdaɪəˈkrɪtɪk/ **I** *n* Ling (also **diacritical mark**) signe *m* diacritique.
II *adj* (also **diacritical**) **1** Ling diacritique; **2** gen distinctif/-ive.

diadem /ˈdaɪədem/ *n* diadème *m*.

diaeresis GB, **dieresis** US /daɪˈerəsɪs/ *n* (*pl* **-ses**) **1** (phenomenon) diérèse *f*; **2** (mark) tréma *m*.

diagnose /ˈdaɪəgnəʊz, US ˌdaɪəgˈnəʊs/ *vtr* **1** Med diagnostiquer [*illness*]; **the illness was ~d as cancer** les médecins ont diagnostiqué un cancer; **he was ~ed (as a) diabetic/as having Aids** on a découvert qu'il était diabétique/qu'il avait le sida; **to ~ that** diagnostiquer que; **2** gen identifier [*problem, fault*].

diagnosis /ˌdaɪəgˈnəʊsɪs/ *n* (*pl* **-ses**) **1** Med, gen diagnostic *m*; **2** Bot diagnose *f*.

diagnostic /ˌdaɪəgˈnɒstɪk/ *adj* diagnostique.

diagnostician /ˌdaɪəgnɒˈstɪʃn/ *n* diagnosticien/-ienne *m/f*.

diagnostics /ˌdaɪəgˈnɒstɪks/ *n* **1** Med diagnose *f*; **2** Comput (+ *v pl*) diagnostic *m*.

diagonal /daɪˈægənl/ **I** *n* (all contexts) diagonale *f*.
II *adj* [*line, stripe*] diagonal; **our street is ~ to the main road** notre rue part en biais de la rue principale; **a ~ path across a field** un chemin qui coupe le champ en diagonale.

diagonally /daɪˈægənəlɪ/ *adv* (all contexts) en diagonale (**to** par rapport à).

diagram /ˈdaɪəgræm/ **I** *n* **1** gen schéma *m*; **in the ~** sur le schéma; **2** Math figure *f*; **3** Stat diagramme *m*.
II *vtr* (*p prés etc* **-mm-** ou **-m-**) US présenter [qch] sous forme de schéma.

diagrammatic /ˌdaɪəgrəˈmætɪk/ *adj* schématique.

diagrammatically /ˌdaɪəgrəˈmætɪklɪ/ *adv* schématiquement.

dial /ˈdaɪəl/ **I** *n* cadran *m*.
II *vtr* (*p prés etc* **-ll-** GB, **-l-** US) faire; (more formal) composer [*number*]; appeler [*person, city, country*]; **she ~led 73-35-49** elle a fait le 73-35-49; **to ~ 999** ≈ (for police, ambulance) appeler police secours; (for fire brigade) appeler les pompiers; **to ~ the wrong number** faire un faux ou mauvais numéro.
III dial+ (*dans composés*) **~-a-disc/-a-recipe** (service) disque/recette du jour par téléphone.

dialect /ˈdaɪəlekt/ **I** *n* dialecte *m*; **to speak ~** parler en dialecte.
II *modif* [*word, form*] dialectal; [*atlas, geography*] linguistique.

dialectal /ˌdaɪəˈlektl/ *adj* dialectal.

dialectic /ˌdaɪəˈlektɪk/ *n, adj* dialectique (*f*).

dialectical /ˌdaɪəˈlektɪkl/ *adj* dialectique.

dialectically /ˌdaɪəˈlektɪklɪ/ *adv* [*interpret*] dialectiquement; [*proceed, argue*] par la méthode dialectique.

dialectical: **~ materialism** *n* matérialisme *m* dialectique; **~ materialist** *n* matérialiste *mf* dialectique.

dialectician /ˌdaɪəlekˈtɪʃn/ *n* dialecticien/-ienne *m/f*.

dialectics /ˌdaɪəˈlektɪks/ *n* (+ *v sg*) dialectique *f*.

dialectologist /ˌdaɪəlekˈtɒlədʒɪst/ *n* dialectologue *mf*.

dialectology /ˌdaɪəlekˈtɒlədʒɪ/ *n* dialectologie *f*.

dialling GB, **dialing** US /ˈdaɪəlɪŋ/ *n* **abbreviated ~** utilisation *f* de numéros abrégés; **direct ~** appel *m* direct.

dialling: **~ code** *n* GB indicatif *m*; **~ tone** *n* GB tonalité *f*.

dialogue /ˈdaɪəlɒg, US -lɔːg/ **I** *n* (all contexts) dialogue *m* (**between** entre; **with** avec).
II *vi* dialoguer (**with** avec).

dialogue box *n* Comput boîte *f* de dialogue.

dial: **~ tone** *n* US = **dialling tone**; **~-up** *adj* [*line, network*] commuté.

dialysis /ˌdaɪˈæləsɪs/ *n* (*pl* **-lyses**) dialyse *f*; **to undergo kidney ~** se faire faire une dialyse.

dialysis machine *n* Med rein *m* artificiel.

diamagnetic /ˌdaɪəmægˈnetɪk/ *adj* diamagnétique.

diamagnetism /ˌdaɪəˈmægnɪtɪzəm/ *n* diamagnétisme *m*.

diamanté /ˌdaɪəˈmæntɪ, dɪəˈmɒnteɪ/ **I** *n* (decorative trim, jewellery, material) strass *m*; (fabric) tissu *m* pailleté.
II *modif* [*earrings*] en strass; [*fabric*] pailleté.

diameter /daɪˈæmɪtə(r)/ *n* Math diamètre *m*; **the circle is 2 m in ~** le cercle a 2 m de diamètre; **a circle with a ~ of 2 m** un cercle de 2 m de diamètre; **to magnify 15 ~s** Sci grossir 15 fois.

diametric(al) /ˌdaɪəˈmetrɪkl/ *adj* gen, Math diamétral.

diametrically /ˌdaɪəˈmetrɪklɪ/ *adv* (all contexts) diamétralement; fig **~ opposed to** diamétralement opposé à.

diamond /ˈdaɪəmənd/ **▶ 1282** **I** *n* **1** (stone) diamant *m*; **industrial ~** diamant *m* industriel; **2** (shape) losange *m*; **3** (in cards) carreau *m*; **the five of ~s** le cinq de carreau; **to play a ~** jouer carreau; **4** (in baseball) terrain *m* (de baseball).
II *modif* [*ring, brooch*] de diamants; [*dust, mine*] de diamant; **~ necklace** rivière *f* de diamants.

diamond: **~back (rattlesnake)** *n* diamantin *m*; **~ cutter** *n* tailleur *m* de diamants; **~ jubilee** *n* soixantenaire *m*, soixantième anniversaire *m*; **~ merchant** *n* diamantaire *m*; **~-shaped** *adj* en (forme de) losange; **~ wedding (anniversary)** *n* noces *fpl* de diamant.

Diana /daɪˈænə/ *pr n* Diane.

diapason /ˌdaɪəˈpeɪsn/ *n* diapason *m*; **open/stopped ~** diapason large/étroit.

diaper /ˈdaɪəpə(r), US ˈdaɪpər/ US **I** *n* couche *f* (*pour bébé*).
II *vtr* changer la couche de [*baby*].

diaphanous /daɪˈæfənəs/ *adj* diaphane.

diaphoretic /ˌdaɪəfəˈretɪk/ *n, adj* diaphorétique (*m*).

diaphragm /ˈdaɪəfræm/ *n* (all contexts) diaphragme *m*.

diarist /ˈdaɪərɪst/ *n* **1** (author) auteur *m* d'un journal (intime); **2** Journ (journalist) chroniqueur/-euse *m/f*.

diarrhoea GB, **diarrhea** US /ˌdaɪəˈrɪə/ *n* diarrhée *f*; **to have ~** avoir la diarrhée.

diarrhoeal GB, **diarrheal** US /ˌdaɪəˈrɪəl/ *adj* diarrhéique.

diary /ˈdaɪərɪ/ *n* **1** (for appointments) agenda

m; **to put sth in one's ~** noter qch dans son agenda; **my ~ is full** je suis très pris; **2** (journal) journal *m* intime; **to keep a ~** tenir un journal (intime); **3** Journ chronique *f*; **sports ~** chronique sportive.

diaspora /daɪˈæspərə/ *n* gen diaspora *f*; Relig, Hist **the Diaspora** la Diaspora.

diastase /ˈdaɪəsteɪz/ *n* diastase *f*.

diastole /daɪˈæstəlɪ/ *n* diastole *f*.

diatom /ˈdaɪətəm, US -tɒm/ *n* diatomée *f*.

diatomic /ˌdaɪəˈtɒmɪk/ *adj* diatomique.

diatonic /ˌdaɪəˈtɒnɪk/ *adj* diatonique.

diatribe /ˈdaɪətraɪb/ *n* diatribe *f* (**against** contre).

diazepam /daɪˈæzɪpæm/ *n* diazépam *m*.

dibasic /daɪˈbeɪsɪk/ *adj* dibasique.

dibber /ˈdɪbə(r)/ *n* Hort plantoir *m*.

dibble /ˈdɪbl/ **I** *n* = **dibber**.
II *vtr* repiquer (au plantoir).
III *vi* faire un trou au plantoir.

dibs○ /dɪbz/ US *npl* lang enfantin **~ on the potato crisps** à moi les chips.

dice /daɪs/ **I** *n* (*pl* **~**) Games (object) dé *m*; (game) dés *mpl*; **to throw/roll the ~** jeter/lancer le dé or les dés; **no ~**○! (refusal) pas question!; (no luck) pas de chance.
II *vtr* Culin couper [qch] en cubes.
IDIOMS **to ~ with death** risquer sa vie; **the ~ are loaded** les dés sont pipés.

dicey○ /ˈdaɪsɪ/ *adj* **1** (risky) risqué; **it's a ~ business** c'est risqué; **2** (uncertain, unreliable) douteux/-euse.

dichloride /daɪˈklɔːraɪd/ *n* bichlorure *m*.

dichotomy /daɪˈkɒtəmɪ/ *n* dichotomie *f*.

dichromate /daɪˈkrəʊmeɪt/ *n* bichromate *m*.

dichromatic /ˌdaɪkrəʊˈmætɪk/ *adj* dichromatique.

dick /dɪk/ **I** *n* **1**● (penis) bite● *f*, pénis *m*; **2**○ US (detective) détective *m*; **3**● US = **dickhead**●.
II◑ *vi* US (also **~ around**) faire le con◑.
III● *vtr* baiser●.

dickens○† /ˈdɪkɪnz/ *n* **where/who/what the ~...?** où/qui/que diable○†...? **to have the ~ of a time doing sth** avoir un mal fou à faire qch.

Dickensian /dɪˈkenzɪən/ *adj* [*character, world*] à la Dickens; [*evening*] en costume du XIXe; pej [*conditions, buildings*] insalubre.

dicker○ /ˈdɪkə(r)/ *vi* marchander.

dickhead● /ˈdɪkhed/ *n* couillon◑ *m*, abruti *m*.

dicky /ˈdɪkɪ/ **I** *n* faux plastron *m*.
II○ *adj* GB [*heart*] qui flanche; [*condition*] précaire.

dicky-bird○ /ˈdɪkɪbɜːd/ *n* **1** (bird) lang enfantin zoziau *m* baby talk; **2** hum **not a ~** que dalle○, pas un mot.

dicta /ˈdɪktə/ *pl* ▶ **dictum**.

Dictaphone® /ˈdɪktəfəʊn/ *n* dictaphone® *m*.

dictate I /ˈdɪkteɪt/ *n* (decree) ordre *m*; **to follow the ~s of one's conscience** suivre ce que dicte sa conscience.
II /dɪkˈteɪt, US ˈdɪkteɪt/ *vtr* **1** dicter [*text, letter*] (**to** à); **2** (prescribe) imposer [*terms, choices*] (**to** à); décider de, déterminer [*outcome*]; régenter [*economy, policy*] (**to** à); **to ~ that** imposer que (+ *subj*); **to ~ how** prescrire comment.
III /dɪkˈteɪt, US ˈdɪkteɪt/ *vi* **1** (out loud) **to ~ to one's secretary/into a machine** dicter une lettre (or un texte etc) à sa secrétaire/à une machine; **2** (boss sb around) **to ~ to sb** imposer sa volonté à qn; **I won't be ~d to (by someone like him)!** je n'ai pas d'ordres à recevoir (de quelqu'un comme lui)!

dictating machine *n* machine *f* à dicter.

dictation /dɪkˈteɪʃn/ *n* **1** Sch, Comm dictée *f*; **to take ~** Comm écrire sous la dictée; **2** sout (authority) autorité *f*.

dictator /dɪkˈteɪtə(r), US ˈdɪkteɪtər/ *n* Pol dictateur *m*; fig tyran *m*.

dictatorial /ˌdɪktəˈtɔːrɪəl/ *adj* [*person*] tyrannique; [*regime, powers*] dictatorial.

dictatorially /ˌdɪktəˈtɔːrɪəlɪ/ *adv* de façon dictatoriale.

dictatorship /dɪkˈteɪtəʃɪp, US ˈdɪkt-/ *n* Pol dictature *f*; fig tyrannie *f*.

diction /ˈdɪkʃn/ *n* (articulation) diction *f*; (choice of words) langage *m*; **poetic ~** langage poétique.

dictionary /ˈdɪkʃənrɪ, US -nerɪ/ **I** *n* dictionnaire *m*; **to look up sth in a ~** chercher qch dans un dictionnaire; **English ~** dictionnaire *m* d'anglais.
II *modif* [*definition, page*] de dictionnaire; [*publisher*] de dictionnaires; **~ entry** entrée *f* or article *m* de dictionnaire.

dictum /ˈdɪktəm/ *n* (*pl* **-ums** ou **-a**) **1** gen (saying) phrase *f* célèbre; **2** Jur ▶ **obiter dicta**.

did /dɪd/ *prét* ▶ **do**.

didactic /daɪˈdæktɪk, dɪ-/ *adj* didactique.

diddle○ /ˈdɪdl/ *vtr* **1** (swindle) rouler○, escroquer [*person, company*]; **to ~ sb out of sth, to ~ sth out of sb** extorquer or carotter○ qch à qn; **2** US (dawdle) traînasser○.

diddly○ /ˈdɪdlɪ/ *n* US (also **~ squat**○)
IDIOMS **to know ~** savoir que dalle◑, ne rien savoir (**about** au sujet de).

didgeridoo /ˌdɪdʒərɪˈduː/ ▶ **1481** *n* Mus didsheridou *m*.

didn't /ˈdɪdnt/ = **did not**.

Dido /ˈdaɪdəʊ/ *pr n* Didon.

die /daɪ/ **I** *n* **1** Games (*pl* **dice**) dé *m* à jouer; **2** Tech (for stamping metal) étampe *f*; **3** Tech (for screw threads) lunette *f* à fileter.
II *vtr* (*p prés* **dying**; *prét, pp* **died**) **to ~ a slow/natural/violent death** mourir de mort lente/naturelle/violente; **to ~ a noble death** mourir d'une mort noble; **to ~ a hero's/soldier's death** mourir en héros/en soldat.
III *vi* (*p prés* **dying**, *prét, pp* **died**) **1** (expire, end one's life) [*person, animal*] mourir; [*person*] décéder fml; **he was dying** il était en train de mourir; **when I ~** quand je mourrai; **she ~d a year ago** elle est morte il y a un an; **as she lay dying** alors qu'elle se mourait; **to be left to ~** être abandonné à la mort; **to ~ in one's sleep/bed** mourir dans son sommeil/lit; **to ~ young/happy** mourir jeune/heureux; **to ~ a hero** mourir en héros; **to ~ a pauper** mourir pauvre; **I'll ~ a happy man** je mourrai heureux; **to ~ without doing** mourir sans avoir fait; **to ~ of** ou **from** mourir de [*starvation, disease*]; **to ~ of natural causes** mourir de causes naturelles; **to ~ of a broken heart** mourir de chagrin; **nobody ever ~d of hard work** le travail n'a jamais tué personne; **2** (be killed) périr (**doing** en faisant); **to ~ in the attempt** périr dans cette tentative; **to ~ in action** mourir au combat; **he'd sooner** ou **rather ~ than do** il mourrait plutôt que de faire; **I'd sooner ~!** plutôt périr!; **to ~ by one's own hand** littér périr de sa propre main; **to ~ for** mourir pour [*beliefs, country, person*]; **3** (wither) [*plant, crop*] crever; **4** fig (of boredom, shame, fright) mourir (of de); **we nearly ~d!** on a failli mourir!; **I'll ~ if I have to go there!** j'en mourrai si je dois y aller!; **I wanted to ~** ou **I could have ~d when** je ne savais plus où me mettre quand; **I thought I'd/he'd ~ of shock** j'ai cru mourir/qu'il allait mourir sous l'effet du choc; **I nearly** ou **could have ~d laughing** j'ai failli mourir de rire; **5**○ (long) **to be dying to do** mourir d'envie de faire; **to be dying for** avoir une envie folle de [*coffee, break, change*]; **to be dying for sb/sth to do** souhaiter désespérément que qn/qch fasse; **6** (go out) [*light, flame, spark*] s'éteindre; **7** (fade) [*love, hatred, resentment, memory, knowledge, glory, fame*] s'éteindre; [*enthusiasm*] tomber; **the secret ~d with her** elle a emporté son secret dans la tombe; **8** hum (cease functioning) [*machine, engine*] s'arrêter; **the car suddenly ~d on me** la voiture m'a soudain lâché; **9**○ (on stage) [*comedian, entertainer*] faire un bide○.
IDIOMS **never say ~!** il ne faut jamais baisser les bras!; **the ~ is cast** le sort en est jeté; **to be as straight as a ~** fig être foncièrement honnête; **to ~ hard** avoir la vie dure.
■ **die away** [*sounds*] disparaître; [*applause, wind, rain*] s'arrêter.
■ **die back** [*plant, flower*] se flétrir; [*leaves*] se dessécher.
■ **die down 1** (in intensity) [*emotion, row*] s'apaiser; [*scandal, rumours, opposition, publicity*] disparaître; [*fighting*] s'achever; [*tremors, storm, wind*] se calmer; [*pain, swelling*] diminuer; **when all the fuss ~s down** quand tout le tapage se sera apaisé; **2** (in volume) [*noise, laughter, chatter*] diminuer; [*applause, cheers*] se calmer; **3** Bot, Hort se flétrir.
■ **die off** [*people*] mourir peu à peu; [*plant, bacteria*] mourir.
■ **die out 1** (become extinct) [*family, species, tradition, practice, language, skill*] disparaître; **2** (ease off) [*showers, rain*] s'arrêter.

die: **~-cast** *adj* moulé sous pression; **~-casting** *n* moulage *m* sous pression.

diehard /ˈdaɪhɑːd/ **I** *n* **1** Pol (in party) réactionnaire *mf*; **2** péj (conservative) ultra-conservateur/-trice *m/f*; **3** (stubborn person) irréductible *mf*.
II *adj* **1** Pol (in party) réactionnaire; **2** péj (conservative) rétrograde; **3** (stubborn) buté.

dielectric /ˌdaɪɪˈlektrɪk/ *n, adj* Phys diélectrique (*m*).

dieresis /daɪˈerəsɪs/ *n* (*pl* **-ses**) **1** (phenomenon) diérèse *f*; **2** (mark) tréma *m*.

diesel /ˈdiːzl/ *n* **1** (also **~ fuel**, **~ oil**) gazole *m*; **2** (also **~ car**) diesel *m*.

diesel: **~-electric** *adj* diesel-électrique; **~ engine** *n* Tech (in train) motrice *f* Diesel; (in car) moteur *m* Diesel; **~ train** *n* train *m* Diesel.

die: **~sinker** *n* graveur *m* de matrices; **~ stamping** *n* estampage *m*; **~stock** *n* filière *f*.

diet /ˈdaɪət/ **I** *n* **1** (food habits) (of person) alimentation *f* (**of** à base de); (of animal) nourriture *f* (**of** à base de); **~ is very important** il est très important de bien se nourrir; **2** Med (limiting food) régime *m*; **3** fig cure *f* (**of** de); **4** Hist, Pol diète *f*.
II *modif* [*biscuit, drink*] de régime; [*pill*] pour maigrir.
III *vi* être au régime.

dietary /ˈdaɪətrɪ, US -terɪ/ *adj* [*need, problem, habit*] alimentaire; [*method*] diététique.

dietary: **~ fibre** GB, **~ fiber** US *n* fibres *fpl* alimentaires; **~ supplement** *n* complément *m* vitaminique.

diet doctor ▶ **1692** *n* US nutritionniste *mf*.

dietetic /ˌdaɪəˈtetɪk/ *adj* diététique.

dietetics /ˌdaɪəˈtetɪks/ *n* (+ *v sg*) diététique *f*.

dietician, **dietitian** /ˌdaɪəˈtɪʃn/ ▶ **1692** *n* diététicien/-ienne *m/f*.

diff○ /dɪf/ *n* US (*abrév* = **difference**) **what's the ~?** quelle est la différence?

differ /ˈdɪfə(r)/ *vi* **1** (be different) différer (**from** de; **in** par; **in that** en ce que); **to ~ widely** ou **markedly** être complètement différent; **tastes ~** tous les goûts sont dans la nature; **2** (disagree) différer (d'opinion) (**on sth** sur qch; **from sb** de qn; **with sb** avec qn); **I beg to ~** permettez-moi d'être d'un avis différent; **we must agree to ~** nous devrons accepter nos différences d'opinion.

difference /ˈdɪfrəns/ *n* **1** (dissimilarity) différence *f* (**between** entre; **in, of** de); **age ~** différence d'âge; **what's the ~ between...?** quelle est la différence entre...?; **what's the ~?** (it doesn't matter) qu'est-ce que ça change?; **to tell the ~ between** faire la différence entre; **I can't tell** ou **see the ~** je ne vois pas la différence; **to make a ~** changer quelque chose; **it makes no ~ what I do** quoi que je fasse ça ne change rien; **it makes all the** ou **a world of ~** ça change tout; **what a ~ that makes!** comme c'est différent avec ça!; **it makes no ~ to me** cela m'est égal; **what ~ does it make if...?** qu'est-ce que ça change si...?; **as near as makes no ~** peu s'en faut; **a vacation with a ~** des vacances pas comme les autres; **2** (disagreement) différend *m* (**between** entre; **over** à propos de; **with** avec); **to settle one ~s** régler ses différends; **a ~ of opinion** une divergence *f* d'opinion; **~s within sth** divergences dans qch.

different /ˈdɪfrənt/ *adj* **1** (dissimilar) différent (**from, to** GB, **than** US de); **they are ~ in this respect/in their views** ils diffèrent à cet égard/dans leurs opinions; **it's very ~** c'est complètement différent; **you're no ~ from them** tu es pareil qu'eux○; **but I know ~**○ mais je sais que ce n'est pas vrai; **2** (other) autre; **to be/feel a ~ person** être/se sentir une tout autre personne; **that's ~** c'est autre chose; **that's a ~ matter** c'est tout autre chose; **it would have been a ~ story if...** cela aurait été tout autre chose si...; **it's a ~ world!** c'est un autre monde!; **3** (distinct) différent; **I've visited many ~ countries** j'ai visité beaucoup de pays différents; **4** (unusual) différent; **it's certainly ~!** c'est vraiment original!; **he always has to be ~** il faut toujours qu'il se distingue.

differential /ˌdɪfəˈrenʃl/ **I** *n* **1** (in price, rate, pay) écart *m*; **pay** ou **wage ~s** écart des salaires; **tax ~ between two products** écart entre les taux de taxation de deux produits; **2** Math différentielle *f*; **3** Aut différentiel *m*.
II *adj* (all contexts) différentiel/-ielle.

differential: **~ calculus** *n* calcul *m* différentiel; **~ equation** *n* équation *f* différentielle; **~ gear** *n* engrenage *m* différentiel.

differentially /ˌdɪfəˈrenʃəlɪ/ *adv* [*affect, benefit*] différentiellement; **to tax sth ~** appliquer une taxe à taux différentiel à qch.

differential: **~ operator** *n* opérateur *m* différentiel; **~ pricing** *n* différenciation *f* des prix.

differentiate /ˌdɪfəˈrenʃɪeɪt/ **I** *vtr* **1** (tell the difference) différencier (**from** de); **2** (make the difference) différencier (**from** de); **to be ~d by sth** se différencier par qch; **3** Math calculer la différentielle de.
II *vi* **1** (tell the difference) faire la différence (**between** entre); **2** (show the difference) [*person, analyst*] faire la distinction (**between** entre); **3** (discriminate) faire des différences (**between** entre).
III differentiated *pp adj* [*product*] distinct; **the characters are clearly ~d** les personnages sont nettement distincts.

differentiation /ˌdɪfərenʃɪˈeɪʃn/ *n* **1** (distinction) différenciation *f* (**of** de; **between** entre); **product ~** Comm différenciation du produit; **2** Math différentiation *f*.

differently /ˈdɪfrəntlɪ/ *adv* **1** (in another way) autrement (**from** que); **I'd have done it ~** je l'aurais fait autrement; **when you're older you'll think ~** quand tu seras plus âgé tu penseras autrement; **2** (in different ways) différemment (**from** de); **it affects men and women ~** cela touche les hommes et les femmes différemment; **we all see this ~** nous voyons tous cela différemment.

difficult /ˈdɪfɪkəlt/ *adj* **1** (hard, not easy to do) [*task, choice, question, puzzle*] difficile; **it is ~ to learn Russian** il est difficile d'apprendre le russe; **Russian is ~ to learn** le russe est difficile à apprendre; **it will be ~ to decide** il sera difficile de décider; **it will be ~ for me to decide** il me sera difficile de décider; **to find it ~ to do** avoir du mal à faire; **it's ~ to accept that** on a du mal à accepter que (+ *subj*); **2** (complex, inaccessible) [*author, novel, piece, concept*] difficile; **3** (awkward) [*period, age, position, personality, client, case*] difficile; **to make life ~ for** rendre la vie difficile à; **it's a ~ area** (of law, policy, ethics) c'est un sujet délicat; **~ to live with**, **~ to get on with** difficile à vivre.

difficulty /ˈdɪfɪkəltɪ/ *n* **1** (of task, activity, situation) difficulté *f*; **the ~ of doing** la difficulté de faire; **to have ~ (in) doing sth** avoir du mal à faire qch; **to have great ~ (in) doing** avoir beaucoup de mal à faire; **to have ~ with one's eyesight** avoir des problèmes de vue; **I have ~ with that idea** cette idée me pose un problème; **2** (problem) difficulté *f*, problème *m*; **the difficulties of forming a government/of living here** les difficultés de la formation d'un gouvernement/de la vie ici; **the ~ is that** le problème est que; **to run into difficulties** se heurter à des difficultés; **I can't see any ~ in doing** je ne vois aucune difficulté à faire; **3** (of puzzle, author, style) difficulté *f* (**of** de); **4** (trouble) **in ~** en difficulté.

diffidence /ˈdɪfɪdəns/ *n* manque *m* d'assurance; **~ about doing** hésitation *f* à faire.

diffident /ˈdɪfɪdənt/ *adj* [*person*] qui manque d'assurance or de confiance; [*smile, gesture*] timide; **to be ~ about doing** hésiter à faire.

diffidently /ˈdɪfɪdəntlɪ/ *adv* [*do*] d'un air mal assuré; [*speak, say*] d'un ton mal assuré.

diffract /dɪˈfrækt/ *vtr* diffracter.

diffraction /dɪˈfrækʃn/ *n* diffraction *f*.

diffraction grating *n* réseau *m* de diffraction.

diffuse I /dɪˈfjuːs/ *adj* (all contexts) diffus.
II /dɪˈfjuːz/ *vtr* diffuser (**in** dans).
III /dɪˈfjuːz/ *vi* se diffuser (**into** dans).
IV diffused *pp adj* [*light, lighting*] diffus.

diffusely /dɪˈfjuːslɪ/ *adv* de façon diffuse.

diffuseness /dɪˈfjuːsnɪs/ *n* **1** (of argument) prolixité *f*; **2** (of organization) éparpillement *m*.

diffuser /dɪˈfjuːzə(r)/ *n* réflecteur *m*.

diffusion /dɪˈfjuːʒn/ *n* diffusion *f*.

dig /dɪg/ **I** *n* **1** (poke) (with elbow) coup *m* de coude (**in** dans); (with fist) coup *m* de poing (**in** dans); **to give sb a ~ in the ribs** donner à qn un coup de coude dans les côtes; **2**○ (jibe) pique○ *f* (**at** à); **to take** ou **get in a ~ at sb** lancer une pique○ à qn; **that was a ~ at you** tu étais visé par cette remarque; **3** Archeol fouilles *fpl*; **go on a ~** aller faire des fouilles; **4** Hort coup *m* de bêche; **to give the garden a ~** donner un coup de bêche au jardin.
II digs *npl* GB (lodgings) chambre *f* (meublée) (*chez des particuliers*); **to live in ~s** habiter dans une chambre (meublée).
III *vtr* (*p prés* **-gg-**, *pp* **dug**) **1** (excavate) creuser [*ditch, tunnel, grave, trench*] (**in** dans); **to ~ a path through the snow** creuser un chemin dans la neige; **to ~ one's way** ou **oneself out of sth** se creuser un chemin pour sortir de qch; **2** Hort bêcher [*garden, plot*]; fouiller [*site*]; **3** (extract) arracher [*potatoes, root crops*]; extraire [*coal, turf*] (**out of** de); **4** (embed) enfoncer, planter [*knife, needle etc*] (**into** dans); **you're ~ging your nails into my arm!** tu m'enfonces tes ongles dans le bras!; **5**○ surtout US (like) **she really ~s that guy** ce mec la botte○; **I don 't ~ westerns** je n'adore pas les westerns; **6**○† US (look at) viser○, regarder; **~ that tie!** vise un peu la cravate○!
IV *vi* (*p prés* **-gg-**, *pp* **dug**) **1** (excavate) gen creuser (**into** dans); Hort bêcher; [*animal, bird*] fouir (**for** pour trouver); Archeol fouiller, faire des fouilles (**into** dans); **to ~ for** creuser pour trouver [*ore, treasure, remains*]; **to ~ into one's reserves** piocher○ dans ses réserves; **2** (search) **to ~ in** ou **into** fouiller dans [*pockets, bag, records*]; **she dug into her bag for the ticket** elle a fouillé dans son sac pour trouver le billet; **to ~ into sb's past** fouiller dans le passé de qn; **3 to ~ into** (uncomfortably) [*springs, thorns*] s'enfoncer dans [*body part*].
■ **dig in** ¶ **1** Mil, fig se retrancher; **2**○ (eat) attaquer○ un repas; **~ in everybody!** (at meal) servez-vous!; ¶ **~ in [sth]**, **~ [sth] in** Hort enterrer [*compost etc*]; (embed) enfoncer [*teeth, weapon, stake*]; **to ~ oneself in** Mil, fig se retrancher.
■ **dig into**: **~ into [sth] 1** fouiller dans [*bag, pockets*]; **2** fig fouiller dans [*sb's past*]; **3**○ (eat) attaquer○ [*meal, cake*].
■ **dig out**: **~ out [sth]**, **~ [sth] out** lit déterrer [*animal*] (**of** de); arracher [*root, weed*] (**of** de); enlever [*splinter, nail*] (**of** de); dégager [*body*] (**of** de); fig dénicher○ [*book, facts, information*] (**of** dans).
■ **dig up**: **~ up [sth]**, **~ [sth] up** (unearth) déterrer [*body, ruin, treasure*]; arracher [*roots, crops, plant*]; excaver [*road*]; (turn over) retourner [*ground, soil*]; bêcher [*garden*]; fig (discover) dénicher○ [*information, facts*]; déterrer [*scandal*].

digest I /ˈdaɪdʒest/ *n* **1** (periodical) digest *m*, revue *f*; **2** (summary) résumé *m*.
II /daɪˈdʒest, dɪ-/ *vtr* digérer [*food*]; assimiler [*information*].
III /daɪˈdʒest, dɪ-/ *vi* [*food*] se digérer.

digestible /dɪˈdʒestəbl/ *adj* [*food*] digeste; [*information*] assimilable, digeste.

digestion /daɪˈdʒestʃn, dɪ-/ *n* (of food) digestion *f*; (of information) assimilation *f*.

digestive /dɪˈdʒestɪv, daɪ-/ **I** *n* GB (also **~ biscuit**) ≈ biscuit *m* (sablé).
II *adj* digestif/-ive.

digestive: **~ system** *n* système *m* digestif; **~ tract** *n* appareil *m* digestif.

digger /ˈdɪgə(r)/ *n* **1** (excavator) excavateur *m*; **2** (worker) terrassier *m*; **3**○ (also **Digger**) (Australian) Australien *m*.

digging /ˈdɪgɪŋ/ **I** *n* **1** (in garden) bêchage *m*; **to do some ~** bêcher; **2** Civ Eng, Constr creusement *m*, terrassement *m*; **it will require several days' ~** il faudra creuser pendant plusieurs jours; **3** Mining forage *m* (**for** pour trouver); **4** Archeol fouilles *fpl*.
II diggings *npl* (material) Archeol fouilles *fpl*; Mining déblais *mpl*.

digit /ˈdɪdʒɪt/ *n* **1** (number) chiffre *m*; **a two-~ number** un nombre à deux chiffres; **2** Anat (finger) doigt *m*; (toe) orteil *m*.

digital /ˈdɪdʒɪtl/ *adj* **1** Comput [*display, recording*] numérique; [*clock, watch*] à affichage numérique; **2** Anat digital.

digital: **~ access lock**, **~ lock** *n* digicode® *m*; **~ audio tape**, **DAT** *n* cassette *f* audionumérique, DAT *f*; **~ computer** *n* calculateur *m* numérique.

digitalin /ˌdɪdʒɪˈteɪlɪn/ *n* Chem digitaline *f*.

digitalis /ˌdɪdʒɪˈteɪlɪs/ *n* **1** Bot digitale *f*; **2** Pharm digitaline *f*.

digitize /ˈdɪdʒɪtaɪz/ *vtr* Comput numériser.

digitizer /ˈdɪdʒɪtaɪzə(r)/ *n* Comput numériseur *m*, convertisseur *m* analogique or numérique.

diglossia /daɪˈglɒsɪə/ *n* Ling diglossie *f*.

dignified /ˈdɪgnɪfaɪd/ *adj* [*person, status*] digne; [*manner*] empreint de dignité.

dignify /ˈdɪgnɪfaɪ/ *vtr* donner du faste à [*occasion, building*]; **I wouldn't ~ that painting by calling it art** je n'honorerais pas cette toile du nom d'art.

dignitary /ˈdɪgnɪtərɪ/ *n* dignitaire *m*.

dignity /ˈdɪgnətɪ/ *n* **1** (of person, occasion) dignité *f*; **to be beneath sb's ~** être une atteinte à la dignité de qn; **to stand on one's ~** prendre de grands airs; **2** (title) titre *m*, dignité *f*.

digraph /ˈdaɪgrɑːf, US -græf/ *n* Ling digramme *m*.

digress /daɪˈgres/ *vi* faire une digression; **to ~ from** s'écarter de [*subject*].

digression /daɪˈgreʃn/ *n* digression *f*.

digressive /daɪˈgresɪv/ *adj* [*writer, speaker*] enclin à la digression; [*style*] riche en digressions.

dihedral /daɪˈhiːdrəl/ *n, adj* Math dièdre (*m*).
dike *n* ▶ **dyke** 1, 3.
diktat /ˈdɪktæt/ *n* diktat *m*.
dilapidated /dɪˈlæpɪdeɪtɪd/ *adj* délabré.
dilapidation /dɪˌlæpɪˈdeɪʃn/ *n* délabrement *m*.
dilate /daɪˈleɪt/ **I** *vtr* dilater.
II *vi* **1** (widen) se dilater; **2** (discuss at length) **to ~ on a subject** s'étendre sur un sujet.
III dilated *pp adj* [*pupils, nostrils*] dilaté; **to be 5 cm ~d** (in labour) être dilaté de 5 cm.
dilation /daɪˈleɪʃn/ *n* dilatation *f*.
dilatoriness /ˈdɪlətərɪnɪs, US -tɔːrɪ-/ *n* sout lenteur *f* (**in doing** à faire).
dilatory /ˈdɪlətərɪ, US -tɔːrɪ/ *adj* sout **1** (slow) lent; **2** (time-wasting) dilatoire also Jur.
dilatory plea *n* Jur exception *f* dilatoire.
dildo /ˈdɪldəʊ/ *n* **1** (object) godemiché *m*; **2**◐ (idiot) con/conne◐ *m/f*, imbécile *mf*.
dilemma /daɪˈlemə, dɪ-/ *n* dilemme *m* (**about, over** à propos de); **in a ~** devant un dilemme.
IDIOMS **to be on the horns of a ~** se trouver confronté à un dilemme.
dilettante /ˌdɪlɪˈtæntɪ/ **I** *n* dilettante *mf*.
II *adj* [*person*] dilettante; [*attitude*] de dilettante.
dilettantism /ˌdɪlɪˈtæntɪzəm/ *n* dilettantisme *m*.
diligence /ˈdɪlɪdʒəns/ *n* **1** gen zèle *m*, diligence *f* sout (**in** dans; **in doing** à faire); **2** Jur **to exercise due ~** éviter des actes de négligence.
diligent /ˈdɪlɪdʒənt/ *adj* appliqué; **to be ~ in doing sth** faire qch avec application.
diligently /ˈdɪlɪdʒəntlɪ/ *adv* [*work*] avec zèle.
dill /dɪl/ *n* aneth *m*.
dill pickle *n* concombres *mpl* au vinaigre et à l'aneth.
dilly○ /ˈdɪlɪ/ *n* US (person) personne *f* sensass○; (thing) chose *f* sensass○; **a ~ of an earthquake** un sacré○ tremblement de terre.
dillydally○ /ˈdɪlɪdælɪ/ *vi* **1** (dawdle) lambiner○; **2** (be indecisive) tergiverser.
dillydallying○ /ˈdɪlɪdælɪɪŋ/ *n* ₵ hésitations *fpl*.
dilute /daɪˈljuːt, US -ˈluːt/ **I** *adj* dilué.
II *vtr* **1** lit diluer [*liquid*] (**with** avec); éclaircir [*colour*]; **2** fig diluer.
III diluted *pp adj* lit, fig dilué (**with** avec).
diluted shares *npl* Fin actions *fpl* émises.
diluter /daɪˈljuːtə(r), US -ˈluːt-/ *n* diluant *m*.
dilution /daɪˈljuːʃn, US -ˈluːt-/ *n* **1** lit, fig dilution *f* (**of** de); **2** Fin **~ of equity** dilution *f* d'action.
dim /dɪm/ **I** *adj* **1** (badly lit) [*office, room, interior*] sombre; **2** (weak) [*light, flame, eye, eyesight*] faible; **to grow ~** s'affaiblir; **3** (hard to see) [*shape, figure*] vague; **4** (vague) [*recollection, appreciation*] vague (*before n*); **to have a ~ memory of** avoir un vague souvenir de; **5**○ (stupid) [*person, remark*] bouché○; **6** (not favourable) [*prospect, future*] sombre.
II *vtr* (*p prés etc* **-mm-**) **1** (turn down) baisser [*light*]; mettre [qch] en veilleuse [*oil lamp*]; **2** (cause to fade) ternir [*beauty, colour*]; **3** US baisser [*headlights*].
III *vi* (*p prés etc* **-mm-**) **1** [*lights, lamp*] baisser; **2** [*memory*] s'estomper; **3** [*eyes, sight*] s'affaiblir; **4** [*colour, beauty, hope*] se ternir.
IDIOMS **to take a ~ view of sth/of people doing** n'apprécier guère qch/que les gens fassent.
dime /daɪm/ *n* US (pièce *f* de) dix cents *mpl*.
IDIOMS **I haven't got a ~** je n'ai pas un sou; **they're a ~ a dozen**○ on en trouve à la pelle○; **it isn't worth a ~**○ ça ne vaut pas un clou○; **to stop on a ~**○ s'arrêter pile.
dime: **~ bag**○ *n* US sachet *m* de drogue (*à 10 dollars*); **~ novel** US *n* roman *m* à quatre sous.
dimension /dɪˈmenʃn/ **I** *n* **1** (aspect) dimension *f*; **to take on a whole new ~** prendre une toute autre dimension; **to bring** ou **add a new ~ to** donner une nouvelle dimension à [*discussion, problem*]; **2** (measurement) gen dimension *f*; Archit, Math, Tech cote *f*; **of huge ~s** aux dimensions énormes.
II dimensions *npl* (scope) étendue *f* ₵ (**of** de).
-dimensional /-dɪmenʃənl/ (*dans composés*) **two/three~** à deux/trois dimensions; ▶ **one-dimensional**.
dime store US *n* bazar *m*.
diminish /dɪˈmɪnɪʃ/ **I** *vtr* **1** (reduce) diminuer [*numbers, popularity, quantity, resources*]; **2** (weaken) amoindrir [*authority, influence, strength*]; diminuer [*emotion*]; **3** (denigrate) dénigrer; **4** Mus diminuer.
II *vi* **1** (decrease) [*funds, resources, numbers*] diminuer; **2** (weaken) [*emotion*] s'amenuiser; [*authority, influence, strength*] s'amoindrir.
III diminished *pp adj* **1** [*amount, enthusiasm, income, force, level, rate*] réduit; [*awareness, support*] amoindri; **to feel ~ed** se sentir rabaissé; **2** Jur **on grounds of ~ed responsibility** pour raisons de responsabilité atténuée; **3** Mus diminué.
IV diminishing *pres p adj* [*number*] de moins en moins élevé; [*funds, resources, group*] de moins en moins important; [*influence*] de moins en moins fort; **the law of ~ing returns** la loi des rendements décroissants.
diminuendo /dɪˌmɪnjʊˈendəʊ/ *n, adv* diminuendo (*m*).
diminution /ˌdɪmɪˈnjuːʃn, US -ˈnuːʃn/ *n* (of size, quantity, wages) diminution *f* (**in, of** de); (of level, intensity, power, role) affaiblissement *m* (**in, of** de).
diminutive /dɪˈmɪnjʊtɪv/ **I** *n* Ling diminutif *m*.
II *adj* [*object*] minuscule; [*person*] tout petit.
dimity /ˈdɪmətɪ/ *n* basin *m*.
dimly /ˈdɪmlɪ/ *adv* **1** [*lit*] faiblement; **2** [*perceive, make out*] vaguement; **~ visible** à peine visible; **3** [*recall, register, sense*] vaguement; **to be ~ aware of** avoir vaguement conscience de.
dimmer /ˈdɪmə(r)/ *n* (also **~ switch**) variateur *m* d'ambiance.
dimming /ˈdɪmɪŋ/ *n* **1** (of lights) atténuation *f*; **2** (of hope, glory) ternissement *m*.
dimness /ˈdɪmnɪs/ *n* **1** (of interior) obscurité *f*; (of light, lamp) faiblesse *f*; **2** (of recollection, figure, outline) imprécision *f*.
dimorphism /daɪˈmɔːfɪzəm/ *n* Biol, Chem dimorphisme *m*.
dimple /ˈdɪmpl/ **I** *n* (in flesh) fossette *f*; (on water) ride *f*.
II *vtr* [*smile*] faire apparaître des fossettes dans [*cheeks*]; [*wind*] rider [*water*].
III *vi* [*flesh*] former des fossettes; [*water*] se rider.
IV dimpled *pp adj* [*cheek, chin*] à fossette(s); [*limb*] potelé; [*surface*] bosselé; [*water*] ridé; [*glass*] dépoli.
dim: **~wit**○ *n* andouille○ *f*, imbécile○ *mf*; **~-witted**○ *adj* bouché○, obtus.
din /dɪn/ *n* (of machines) vacarme *m*; (of people) chahut *m*.
IDIOMS **to ~ sth into sb**○ enfoncer qch dans la tête de qn○.
dine /daɪn/ **I** *vtr* ▶ **wine III**.
II *vi* dîner; ▶ **wine IV**.
■ **dine in** dîner à la maison.
■ **dine off**, **dine on**: **~ off [sth]** dîner de qch.
■ **dine out** dîner dehors; **to ~ out on** resservir [*story, anecdote*].
diner /ˈdaɪnə(r)/ *n* **1** (person) dîneur/-euse *m/f*; **2** US (restaurant) café-restaurant *m*; **3** (in train) wagon-restaurant *m*.
dinero○ /ˈdaməræʊ/ *n* US fric○ *m*.
dinette /daɪˈnet/ *n* US **1** (room) coin-repas *m*; **2** (also **~ set**) mobilier *m* de cuisine.
dingaling /ˌdɪŋəˈlɪŋ/ *n* **1** onomat dring dring; **2**○ US (fool) benêt○ *m*.
dingbat○ /ˈdɪŋbæt/ *n* (idiot) andouille○ *f*, imbécile *mf*.
dingdong /ˈdɪŋdɒŋ/ **I**○ *n* **1** GB (quarrel) échange *m* vif de mots; **2** onomat ding dong; **3 DingDong**® US Culin *gâteau au chocolat fourré à la crème*.
II *adj* GB **a ~ argument** une dispute en règle.
dinge◐ /dɪndʒ/ *n* US injur nègre *m* offensive.
dinghy /ˈdɪŋgɪ/ *n* **1** (also **sailing ~**) dériveur *m*; **2** (inflatable) canot *m*.
dingo /ˈdɪŋgəʊ/ *n* dingo *m*.
dingus○ /ˈdɪŋgəs/ *n* US truc○ *m*.
dingy /ˈdɪndʒɪ/ *adj* [*colour, surroundings*] défraîchi; [*street, building, room*] minable.
dining: **~ car** *n* wagon-restaurant *m*; **~ chair** *n* chaise *f* de salle à manger; **~ hall** *n* (private) salle *f* à manger; (in institution) réfectoire *m*.
dining room **I** *n* (in house) salle *f* à manger; (in hotel) salle *f* de restaurant.
II *modif* [*furniture*] de salle à manger.
dining table *n* table *f* de salle à manger.
dink /dɪŋk/ *n* Sport amorti *m*.
dinky○ /ˈdɪŋkɪ/ *adj* **1** GB (sweet) mignon/-onne; **2** (small) petit.
DINKY○ /ˈdɪŋkɪ/ *n* (*abrév* = **dual income no kids**) *homme ou femme qui vit en couple, sans enfants, et qui gagne bien sa vie*.
dinner /ˈdɪnə(r)/ *n* **1** (meal) (evening) dîner *m*; (midday) déjeuner *m*; **at ~** au dîner or déjeuner; **to have friends to ~** avoir des amis à dîner; **to go out/be invited out to ~** dîner/être invité à dîner dehors; **to be invited to ~ at sb's** être invité à dîner chez qn; **to have ~** dîner; **we'll be ten for ~** nous serons dix à dîner; **we're having chicken for ~** on va manger du poulet au dîner; **to give the dog its ~** donner à manger au chien; **'~!'** 'à table!'; **2** (banquet) dîner *m* (**for sb** en l'honneur de qn); **3** (baby food) aliment *m* pour bébé; **vegetable ~** aliment pour bébé à base de légumes.
IDIOMS **he's had more affairs/problems than you've had hot ~s**○ des histoires amoureuses/des ennuis, il en a eu à la pelle○.
dinner: **~ bell** *n* (in house) sonnerie *f* du dîner; (in school) sonnerie *f* du déjeuner; **~ dance** *n* dîner-dansant *m*; **~ duty** *n* GB Sch surveillance *f* au réfectoire; **~ fork** *n* grande fourchette *f*; **~ hour** *n* GB Sch heure *f* du déjeuner; **~ jacket, DJ** *n* smoking *m*; **~ knife** *n* grand couteau *m*; **~ lady** *n* GB Sch femme *f* de service (à la cantine); **~ money** *n* GB Sch argent *m* pour la cantine; **~ party** *n* dîner *m*; **~ party conversation** *n* conversation *f* de salon; **~ plate** *n* grande assiette *f*; **~ roll** *n* petit pain *m*; **~ service**, **~ set** *n* service *m* de table.
dinner table *n* **at the ~** [*discuss, tell*] à table.
dinner: **~ theater** *n* US ≈ cabaret *m* (*où sont données des pièces de théâtre*); **~time** *n* heure *f* du dîner; **~ware** *n* US vaisselle *f*.
dinosaur /ˈdaɪnəsɔː(r)/ *n* lit, fig dinosaure *m*.
dint /dɪnt/: **by dint of** *prep phr* grâce à [*effort, wit, support*].
diocesan /daɪˈɒsɪsn/ *n, adj* diocésain (*m*).
diocese /ˈdaɪəsɪs/ *n* diocèse *m*.
diode /ˈdaɪəʊd/ *n* diode *f*.
dioptre, diopter US /daɪˈɒptə(r)/ *n* dioptrie *f*.
diorama /ˌdaɪəˈrɑːmə/ *n* diorama *m*.
dioxide /daɪˈɒksaɪd/ *n* dioxyde *m*.
dioxin /daɪˈɒksɪn/ *n* dioxine *f*.
dip /dɪp/ **I** *n* **1** (bathe) trempette *f*; **to go for** ou **have a quick ~** faire trempette; **2** (hollow) (in ground, road) déclivité *f*; **3** (downward movement) (of plane, head) inclinaison *f*; **4** fig (in prices, rate, sales) (mouvement *m* de) baisse *f* (**in** dans); **5** Culin sauce *f* froide (*pour*

crudités); **6** Agric (also **sheep ~**) bain *m* parasiticide; **7** Geol (of stratum) pendage *m*; **8** Phys (also **angle of ~**, **magnetic ~**) inclinaison *f* magnétique.
II *vtr* (*p prés etc* **-pp-**) **1** (put partially) tremper [*finger, toe, stick, brush*] (**in, into** dans); **2** (immerse) plonger [*garment*] (**in, into** dans); tremper [*food*] (**in, into** dans); Agric baigner [*sheep*]; **3** (bend) **to ~ one's head/knee** plier la tête/le genou; **4** GB Aut **to ~ one's headlights** baisser les phares; **~ped headlights** codes *mpl*, feux *mpl* de croisement; **to drive with ~ped headlights** rouler en code; **5** Tech (galvanize) tremper [*metal*].
III *vi* (*p prés etc* **-pp-**) **1** (move downwards) [*bird, plane*] piquer; **to ~ below the horizon** [*sun*] disparaître derrière l'horizon; **2** (slope downwards) [*land, field, road*] être en pente; **3** fig (decrease) [*price, value, exchange rate*] descendre, baisser; [*speed, rate*] descendre; **4** (put hand) **to ~ into one's bag for sth** chercher qch dans son sac; fig **to ~ into the till/one's savings for sth** puiser dans la caisse/ses économies pour qch; **5** (read a little) **to ~ into** parcourir [*book, report*].

Dip *n*: *abrév écrite* = **diploma**.

DIP /dɪp/ *n* Comput (*abrév* = **dual in-line package**) boîtier *m* à double rangée de connexions.

diphtheria /dɪfˈθɪərɪə/ ▶**1354** *n* diphtérie *f*.

diphthong /ˈdɪfθɒŋ, US -θɔːŋ/ *n* diphtongue *f*.

diphthongize /ˈdɪfθɒŋaɪz, US -θɔːŋ-/ **I** *vtr* diphtonguer.
II *vi* se diphtonguer.

diploid /ˈdɪplɔɪd/ Biol **I** *n* diploïdie *f*.
II *adj* diploïde.

diploma /dɪˈpləʊmə/ *n* diplôme *m* (**in** en).

diplomacy /dɪpˈləʊməsɪ/ *n* gen, Pol diplomatie *f*.

diploma mill○ *n* US péj *école supérieure peu cotée distribuant des diplômes sans valeur.*

diplomat /ˈdɪpləmæt/ ▶**1692** *n* gen, Pol diplomate *mf*.

diplomatic /ˌdɪpləˈmætɪk/ *adj* **1** Pol diplomatique; **a ~ presence** une représentation diplomatique; **through ~ channels** par voies diplomatiques; **2** (astute) [*person*] diplomate; [*behaviour*] diplomatique; **3** (tactful) [*remark, person*] plein de tact; **to be ~** avoir du tact.

diplomatically /ˌdɪpləˈmætɪklɪ/ *adv* (all contexts) diplomatiquement; **~ embarrassing** gênant du point de vue diplomatique.

diplomatic: **~ bag** *n* GB valise *f* diplomatique; **~ corps** *n* corps *m* diplomatique; **~ immunity** *n* immunité *f* diplomatique; **~ pouch** *n* US valise *f* diplomatique; **~ relations** *npl* relations *fpl* diplomatiques (**with** avec).

diplomatist /dɪˈpləʊmətɪst/ *n* diplomate *mf*.

dip needle *n* Phys aiguille *f* aimantée.

dipole /ˈdaɪpəʊl/ *n* **1** Elec, Phys dipôle *m*; **2** (also **~ aerial**) antenne *f* dipôle.

dipper /ˈdɪpə(r)/ *n* **1** Zool cincle *m*; **2** US (ladle) louche *f*; **3** US Astron ▶**Big Dipper**, **Little Dipper**.

dippy○ /ˈdɪpɪ/ *adj* farfelu○.

dipso○ /ˈdɪpsəʊ/ *n* péj (*abrév* = **dipsomaniac**) soûlard/-e○ *m/f*.

dipsomania /ˌdɪpsəˈmeɪnɪə/ *n* dipsomanie *f*.

dipsomaniac /ˌdɪpsəˈmeɪnɪæk/ *n* dipsomane *mf*.

dipstick /ˈdɪpstɪk/ *n* **1** Aut jauge *f* de niveau d'huile; **2**○ (idiot) cloche *f*.

dip switch *n* interrupteur *m* à positions multiples.

diptera /ˈdɪptərə/ *npl* diptères *mpl*.

dipterous /ˈdɪptərəs/ *adj* **1** Zool diptère; **2** Bot ailé.

diptych /ˈdɪptɪk/ *n* diptyque *m*.

dire /ˈdaɪə(r)/ *adj* **1** (terrible) [*consequence*] terrible; [*situation*] désespéré; [*poverty*] extrême; [*warning*] sinistre; **to be in ~ need of** avoir un besoin urgent de; **in ~ straits** dans une situation désespérée; **2**○ (awful) [*food, performance*] affreux/-euse.

direct /daɪˈrekt, dɪ-/ **I** *adj* **1** (without intermediary) [*appeal, aid, control, link, participation, talks*] direct; **in ~ contact with** (touching) en contact direct avec; (communicating) directement en contact avec; **to keep sth away from ~ heat/sunlight** ne pas exposer qch directement à la chaleur/la lumière; **2** (without detour) [*access, route, flight, train*] direct; **to be a ~ descendant of** descendre en droite ligne de; **3** (clear) [*cause, comparison, impact, influence, reference, result, threat*] direct; [*contrast, evidence*] flagrant; **to be the ~ opposite of** être tout le contraire de; **to be of no ~ value** ne pas avoir de valeur évidente; **to be in no ~ danger** ne pas être directement en danger; **4** (straightforward) [*approach, answer, method, question, response*] direct; [*person*] franc/franche; **to be ~ with sb** être franc/franche avec qn.
II *adv* **1** (without intermediary) [*deal, negotiate, speak, write, dial*] directement; **available ~ from the manufacturer** disponible directement chez le fabricant; **to pay sth ~ into sb's account** créditer qch à qn par virement automatique; **2** (without detour) [*come, go*] directement (**from** de); **to fly ~** prendre un vol direct.
III *vtr* **1** fig (address, aim) adresser [*appeal, criticism, protest, remark*] (**at** à; **against** contre); cibler [*campaign*] (**at** sur); orienter [*effort, resource*] (**to, towards** vers); **to ~ one's attention to** concentrer son attention sur; **to ~ sb's attention to** attirer l'attention de qn sur; **2** (control) diriger [*company, operation, project*]; régler [*traffic*]; **3** lit (point, aim) diriger [*attack, light, car, look, steps*] (**at** vers); pointer [*gun*] (**at** sur); **4** Cin, Radio, TV réaliser [*film, play, drama*]; Theat mettre [qch] en scène [*play*]; diriger [*actor, cameraman, musician, opera*]; **~ed by Hitchcock** réalisé par Hitchcock; **5** (instruct) **to ~ sb to do** gen ordonner à qn de faire; Jur imposer à qn de faire; **to ~ that sth (should) be done** ordonner que qch soit fait; **he ~ed that the money be repaid** il a ordonné le remboursement de l'argent; **he did it as ~ed** il l'a fait comme on lui avait indiqué; **'to be taken as ~ed'** Pharm 'à consommer selon la prescription médicale'; **6** (show route) **to ~ sb to sth** indiquer le chemin de qch à qn; **can you ~ me to the station?** pouvez-vous m'indiquer le chemin de la gare?.
IV *vi* Cin, Radio, TV faire de la réalisation; Theat faire de la mise en scène; **Lee ~ed** Lee a fait la réalisation.

direct: **~ access** *n* Comput accès *m* direct; **~ access device** *n* unité *f* à accès direct; **~ access file** *n* fichier *m* à accès direct; **~ access storage device**, **DASD** *n* unité *f* de stockage à accès direct; **~ action** *n* action *f* directe; **~ broadcasting by satellite**, **DBS** *n* TV télévision *f* directe par satellite; **~ current**, **DC** *n* Elec courant *m* continu.

direct debit *n* prélèvement *m* automatique; **by ~** par prélèvement automatique.

direct: **~ discourse** *n* US = **direct speech**; **~ election** *n* élection *f* directe; **~ grant school** *n* GB établissement *m* scolaire privé en contrat avec l'État.

direct hit *n* Mil coup *m* au but; (in archery, game) tir *m* au but; **to make a ~** Mil atteindre son objectif; **the hospital received** ou **sustained a ~** une bombe est tombée sur l'hôpital.

direction /daɪˈrekʃn, dɪ-/ **I** *n* **1** (left, right, north, south) direction *f*; **in the ~ of** en direction de; **to gesture in sb's ~** faire un geste dans la direction de qn; **in the right/wrong ~** dans la bonne/mauvaise direction; **in this** ou **that ~** dans cette direction; **to go in the opposite ~** aller en sens inverse; **in the opposite ~ to me** dans le sens opposé au mien; **from all ~s** de tous les côtés *mpl*; **a step in the right ~** fig un pas dans la bonne direction; **2** (taken by company, government, career) orientation *f*; **a change of ~** un changement d'orientation; **the right/wrong ~ for sb** la bonne/mauvaise option pour qn; **we have taken different ~s** nous avons pris des chemins différents; **to lack ~** manquer d'objectifs; **3** Cin, Radio, TV réalisation *f*; Theat mise *f* en scène; Mus direction *f*; **under the ~ of** [*orchestra*] sous la direction de; **4** (control) direction *f*; (guidance) conseils *mpl*.
II directions *npl* **1** (for route) indications *fpl*; **to give sb ~s** donner des indications à qn; **to ask for ~s** demander son chemin (**from** à); **2** (for use) instructions *fpl* (**as to, about** sur); **~s for use** mode *m* d'emploi.

> **Street directions**
>
> **How do I get there?**
>
> En sortant de la gare, allez tout droit, traversez la place où attendent les taxis, puis le parking. Vous déboucherez dans la Grand-Rue. Continuez dans la même direction sur plusieurs centaines de mètres. Vous passerez trois feux rouges. Tournez à droite au troisième, et vous vous trouverez dans la rue Maginot. Prenez la troisième rue à gauche (il y a une banque qui fait l'angle) et continuez jusqu'au bout de cette rue. Vous verrez le théâtre en face de vous. Empruntez le passage à gauche du théâtre, descendez les escaliers et vous vous retrouverez dans l'avenue des Marronniers. Prenez-la sur votre gauche en marchant sur le trottoir de gauche. Vous verrez une boucherie chevaline sur la droite de la rue juste avant le deuxième carrefour. Traversez le carrefour en diagonale. Vous apercevrez une sorte de terrain vague sur votre droite après le carrefour. Le dernier magasin, juste avant le terrain vague, est celui d'un tailleur, et il y a un café dans une cour derrière. Je vous y attendrai avec la valise et toutes les instructions. Mais attention: pas un mot à qui que ce soit!

directional /daɪˈrekʃənl, dɪ-/ *adj* directionnel/-elle.

direction finder *n* radiogoniomètre *m*.

directive /daɪˈrektɪv, dɪ-/ **I** *n* **1** Admin directive *f* (**on** relative à); **an EC ~** une directive de la CE; **2** Comput directive *f*.
II *adj* directif/-ive.

direct labour GB, **direct labor** US *n* main-d'œuvre *f* directe.

directly /daɪˈrektlɪ, dɪ-/ **I** *adv* **1** (without a detour) [*connect, contact, challenge, come, go, negotiate, quote, refer*] directement; [*aim, point*] droit; [*move*] tout droit; **to look ~ at** regarder directement; **to look ~ at sb** regarder qn droit dans les yeux; **to be ~ descended from** descendre en droite ligne de; **2** (exactly) [*above, behind, opposite*] juste; [*compare, contradict*] totalement; **to be ~ proportional to** être directement proportionnel/-elle à; **3** (at once) aussitôt; **~ after** aussitôt après; **~ before** juste avant; **4** (very soon) d'ici peu; **he'll be back ~** il va revenir d'ici peu; **5** (frankly) [*speak*] franchement; [*refuse, deny*] catégoriquement.
II *conj* GB (as soon as) dès que; **~ he saw me he stopped** dès qu'il m'a vu il s'est arrêté.

direct: **~ mail** *n* mailing *m*, publipostage *m*; **~ marketing** *n* marketing *m* direct; **~ memory access**, **DMA** *n* accès *m* direct mémoire; **~ method** *n* méthode *f* directe.

directness /daɪˈrektnɪs, dɪ-/ *n* **1** (of person, attitude) franchise *f*; **2** (of play, work, writing) authenticité *f*.

direct object *n* objet *m* direct.

director /daɪˈrektə(r), dɪ-/ *n* **1** Admin, Comm (of company, organization, programme) (solely in control) directeur/-trice *m/f*; (one of board) administrateur/-trice *m/f*; **~ of Education/of Social Services** GB Soc Admin responsable *mf* régional/-e de l'Enseignement/des Services Sociaux; **2** gen (of project, investigation) responsable *mf*; **3** Cin, TV, Radio (of film) réalisateur/-trice *m/f*, metteur *m* en scène; (of play) metteur *m* en scène; (of orchestra) chef *m* d'orchestre; (of choir) chef *m* des chœurs; **artistic ~** directeur/-trice *m/f* artistique; **~ of programmes** TV directeur/-trice *m/f* des programmes télévisés; **4** Sch, Univ **~ of studies** directeur/-trice *m/f* des études; **~ of admissions** responsable *mf* du service des inscriptions.

directorate /daɪ'rektərət, dɪ-/ *n* (board) conseil *m* d'administration; **member of the social security ~** membre de la direction de la sécurité sociale.

director general, **DG** *n* directeur *m* général.

directorial /ˌdaɪrek'tɔːrɪəl, ˌdɪ-/ *adj* **1** Admin [*duties*] de directeur/-trice; **2** Cin, Theat [*debut*] de metteur en scène; [*style*] de direction.

director: **Director of Public Prosecutions**, **DPP** *n* GB ≈ procureur *m* général; **~'s chair** *n* fauteuil *m* de metteur en scène.

directorship /daɪ'rektəʃɪp, dɪ-/ *n* (in organization, institution) direction *f*; (in company) poste *m* d'administrateur; **to hold a ~** occuper le poste d'administrateur.

directors' report *n* rapport *m* annuel.

directory /daɪ'rektərɪ, dɪ-/ *n* **1** Telecom annuaire *m*; **local ~** annuaire local; **2** Comm répertoire *m* d'adresses; **street ~** répertoire *m* des rues; **3** Comput répertoire *m*.

directory assistance *n* US = **directory enquiries**.

directory enquiries *npl* GB (service *m* des) renseignements *mpl*; **to call ~** appeler les renseignements.

direct: **~ primary** *n* US élection *f* primaire directe; **~ question** *n* Ling question *f* au style direct; **~ rule** *n* Pol gouvernement *m* direct; **~ sales** *n* vente *f* directe; **~ speech** *n* style *m* direct; **~ tax** *n* impôt *m* direct; **~ taxation** *n* imposition *f* directe; **~ transfer** *n* virement *m* automatique.

dirge /dɜːdʒ/ *n* **1** Mus, Literat hymne *m* funèbre; **2** (mournful song) chant *m* lugubre; **3** hum péj (lengthy complaint) chanson *f* lugubre.

dirigible /'dɪrɪdʒəbl/ *n* dirigeable *m*.

dirndl /'dɜːndl/ *n* **1** (costume) robe *f* tyrolienne; **2** (also **~ skirt**) jupe *f* paysanne.

dirt /dɜːt/ *n* **1** (mess) (on clothing, in room) saleté *f*; (on body, cooker) crasse *f*; (in carpet, engine, filter) saletés *fpl*; **wash the ~ off your face!** décrasse-toi la figure!; **to show the ~** être salissant; **2** (soil) terre *f*; (mud) boue *f*; **3**○ péj (gossip) ragots *mpl*; **to dig up ~ on** dénicher des ragots sur; **to dish the ~ on** ou **about** répandre des ragots sur; **4** euph (obscenity) obscénités *fpl*; (excrement) excréments *mpl*; **dog ~** crottes *fpl* de chien.

IDIOMS **to make sb eat ~**○ US faire mordre la poussière à qn○; **to treat sb like ~** traiter qn comme un moins que rien○.

dirtbike /'dɜːtbaɪk/ *n* moto *f* tous terrains, ≈ enduro *f*.

dirt cheap○ **I** *adj* [*item*] donné○.
II *adv* [*get, buy*] pour trois fois rien.

dirt farmer *n* US petit fermier *m*.

dirtiness /'dɜːtɪnɪs/ *n* **1** (of person, conditions, surroundings) saleté *f*; **2** (obscenity) grossièreté *f*.

dirt road *n* chemin *m* de terre battue.

dirt track *n* **1** Sport cendrée *f*; **2** (road) = **dirt road**.

dirty /dɜːtɪ/ **I** *adj* **1** (messy, soiled) [*face, clothing, dish, carpet, mark, nappy, car, street, beach*] sale; [*work, job*] salissant; **to get ~** se salir; **to get** ou **make sth ~** salir qch; **to get one's hands ~** fig mettre la main à la pâte; **2** Med (not sterile) [*needle*] qui a déjà servi; [*wound*] infecté; **3**○ (obscene) [*book, joke, idea, word*] cochon/-onne○; [*mind*] mal tourné; **to have a ~ mind** ne penser qu'à ça○; **4** (unhygienic, disgusting) [*habit, child*] sale; **you ~ pig**○**!** cochon/-onne○! *m/f*; **5**○ (dishonest) [*contest, election, fighter, player*] déloyal; [*cheat, liar, rascal*] sale (*before n*); [*lie*] grossier/-ière; **you ~ rat!** sale type○!; **that was a ~ trick** c'était un sale coup; **it's a ~ business** c'est une affaire louche; **6** [*colour*] sale, terne; **~ green/white** vert/blanc sale or terne; **7** (stormy) [*weather, night*] sale○ (*before n*).
II○ *adv* **1** (dishonestly) **to play** ou **fight ~** donner des coups en traître; **2** (obscenely) [*talk*] grossièrement; **to think ~** avoir des pensées obscènes; **3** (as intensifier) **a ~ great dog** un chien vachement○ gros.
III *vtr* lit, fig salir [*carpet, nappy*]; **to ~ one's hands doing** fig se salir les mains en faisant.
IDIOMS **his name seems to be a ~ word around here** son nom semble être un mot tabou ici; **to do the ~ on**○ faire une crasse○ à; **to give sb a ~ look**○ regarder qn d'un sale œil; **to send sb to do one's ~ work**○ faire faire le sale boulot○ à qn; **do your own ~ work**○**!** fais ton sale boulot○ toi-même.

dirty: **~-minded**○ *adj* à l'esprit mal tourné; **~ old man**○ *n* vieux cochon○ *m*; **~ protest** *n* GB *manifestation où les détenus marquent leur mécontentement en souillant leur cellule*; **~ tricks** *npl* Pol diffamation *f*; **~ tricks campaign** *n* campagne *f* diffamatoire; **~ war** *n* guerre *f* sale; **~ weekend**○ *n* week-end *m* de débauche.

disability /ˌdɪsə'bɪlətɪ/ **I** *n* **1** Med (handicap) infirmité *f*; **multiple disabilities** multiples infirmités *fpl*; **mental/physical ~** handicap *m* mental/physique; **partial/total ~** incapacité *f* partielle/totale; **~ for work** incapacité de travail; **2** fig (disadvantage) handicap *m*; **3** Jur (disqualification) incapacité *f*.
II *modif* [*benefit, pension*] d'invalidité.

disability cover *n* Insur assurance *f* invalidité.

disable /dɪs'eɪbl/ **I** *vtr* **1** Med [*accident, sudden illness*] rendre [qn] infirme; [*chronic illness, permanent handicap*] handicaper; **to be ~d by arthritis** être handicapé par l'arthrite; **2** (render useless) immobiliser [*machine*]; avarier [*ship*]; **3** Mil mettre [qch] hors d'action [*weapon, ship, vehicle*]; **4** Comput désactiver; **5** Jur (disqualify) **to be ~d from doing** être incapable de faire.
II disabling *pres p adj* [*illness, defect*] invalidant.

disabled /dɪs'eɪbld/ **I** *n* **the ~** (+ *v pl*) les handicapés *mpl*.
II *adj* **1** Med handicapé; **severely ~** gravement handicapé; **to be mentally ~** être handicapé mental; **2** Soc Admin (*épith*) [*facility, equipment*] pour handicapés; **~ access** voie *f* d'accès pour handicapés.

disabled: **~ driver** *n* conducteur/-trice *m/f* invalide; **~ list** *n* US Sport liste *f* des joueurs blessés; **~ person** *n* invalide *mf*.

disablement /dɪs'eɪblmənt/ **I** *n* **1** gen, Med invalidité *f*; **2** Jur incapacité *f*.
II *modif* [*benefit, pension*] d'invalidité.

disabuse /ˌdɪsə'bjuːz/ *vtr* sout détromper (**of** de).

disaccharide /daɪ'sækəraɪd/ *n* disaccharide *m*.

disadvantage /ˌdɪsəd'vɑːntɪdʒ, US -'væn-/ **I** *n* **1** (drawback) inconvénient *m*; **the ~ is that** l'inconvénient, c'est que; **2** (position of weakness) **to be at a ~** être désavantagé; **to put sb at a ~** désavantager qn; **to catch sb at a ~** prendre qn au dépourvu; **to get sb at a ~** avoir l'avantage sur qn; **to my/his ~** à mon/son désavantage; **to sell at a ~** vendre à perte; **3** (discrimination) inégalité *f*.
II *vtr* désavantager.

disadvantaged /ˌdɪsəd'vɑːntɪdʒd, US -'væn-/ **I** *n* **the ~** (+ *v pl*) les déshérités *mpl*.
II *adj* défavorisé.

disadvantageous /dɪsˌædvɑː'nteɪdʒəs, US -væn-/ *adj* défavorable (**to** à).

disaffected /ˌdɪsə'fektɪd/ *adj* mécontent (**with** de).

disaffection /ˌdɪsə'fekʃn/ *n* mécontentement *m* (**with** à propos de).

disagree /ˌdɪsə'griː/ *vi* **1** (differ) ne pas être d'accord (**with** avec; **on, about** sur); **I ~ completely** je ne suis pas du tout d'accord; **to ~ about what time to leave/which was the best restaurant** ne pas être d'accord sur l'heure du départ/le meilleur restaurant; **we often ~** nous avons souvent des avis différents; **to agree to ~** [*two people*] accepter ses désaccords; [*group*] accepter de ne pas faire l'unanimité; **2** (oppose) **to ~ with** s'opposer à [*plan, proposal*]; **3** (conflict) [*facts, results, statistics*] être en désaccord, ne pas concorder (**with** avec); **4 to ~ with sb** (upset) [*food*] ne pas réussir à qn; [*weather*] ne pas convenir à qn; **work ~s with me** hum je ne suis pas fait pour le travail.

disagreeable /ˌdɪsə'griːəbl/ *adj* [*person, reaction*] désagréable; [*remark*] désobligeant; [*appearance*] désagréable, déplaisant.

disagreeableness /ˌdɪsə'griːəblnɪs/ *n* (of task) nature *f* désagréable; (of person) manières *fpl* désagréables; (of remark) caractère *m* désagréable.

disagreeably /ˌdɪsə'griːəblɪ/ *adv* désagréablement.

disagreement /ˌdɪsə'griːmənt/ *n* **1** (difference of opinion) désaccord *m* (**about, on** sur; **as to** quant à); **to be in total ~ with sb** être en total désaccord avec qn; **there was a ~ about who was to be leader/about what method to use** il y avait un désaccord sur le dirigeant à désigner/sur la méthode à employer; **there was (serious) ~ among the participants** les participants étaient en (sérieux) désaccord; **there is some/no ~ as to the aims of the project** les avis divergent/convergent quant aux objectifs du projet; **2** (argument) différend *m* (**about, over** sur); **3** (inconsistency) divergence *f* (**between** entre).

disallow /ˌdɪsə'laʊ/ *vtr* **1** Sport refuser [*goal*]; **2** gen, Admin, Jur rejeter [*appeal, claim, decision*].

disambiguate /ˌdɪsæm'bɪgjʊeɪt/ *vtr* désambiguïser.

disappear /ˌdɪsə'pɪə(r)/ **I** *vtr* Pol euph faire disparaître [*dissident*].
II *vi* (all contexts) disparaître; **to ~ from view** disparaître de la vue; **to ~ without trace** disparaître sans laisser de trace; **to be fast ~ing** être en voie de disparition.
IDIOMS **to do a ~ing act** se volatiliser.

disappearance /ˌdɪsə'pɪərəns/ *n* disparition *f* (**of** de).

disappeared /ˌdɪsə'pɪəd/ *npl* Pol euph **the ~** (+ *v pl*) les personnes *fpl* disparues.

disappoint /ˌdɪsə'pɔɪnt/ *vtr* **1** (let down) décevoir [*person*]; **2** (upset) décevoir [*hopes, dream*]; contrecarrer [*plan*].

disappointed /ˌdɪsə'pɔɪntɪd/ *adj* **1** (let down) déçu (**about, at, by, with sth** par qch); **to be ~ that** être déçu que (+ *subj*); **to be ~ to see that** être déçu de voir que; **I am ~ in you** tu me déçois; **2** (unfulfilled) déçu.

disappointing /ˌdɪsə'pɔɪntɪŋ/ *adj* décevant; **it is ~ that** c'est décevant que (+ *subj*); **how ~!** quelle déception!

disappointment /ˌdɪsə'pɔɪntmənt/ *n* **1** (feeling) déception *f*; **to sb's ~** à la grande déception de qn; **there was general ~ at the results** à l'annonce des résultats tout le monde a été déçu; **2** (source of upset) **to be a ~ to sb** décevoir qn; **he is a real ~ to us** il nous a vraiment déçus.

disapprobation /dɪsˌæprəˈbeɪʃn/ *n* sout désapprobation *f*.

disapproval /ˌdɪsəˈpruːvl/ *n* désapprobation *f* (**of** de).

disapprove /ˌdɪsəˈpruːv/ *vi* ne pas être d'accord; **to ~ of** désapprouver [*person, behaviour, lifestyle*]; être contre [*smoking, hunting*]; **to ~ of sb doing** désapprouver or ne pas être d'accord que qn fasse.

disapproving /ˌdɪsəˈpruːvɪŋ/ *adj* [*look, gesture*] désapprobateur/-trice; **to be ~** ne pas être d'accord.

disapprovingly /ˌdɪsəˈpruːvɪŋlɪ/ *adv* [*frown, look, say*] avec désapprobation.

disarm /dɪsˈɑːm/ **I** *vtr* **1** désarmer [*criminal*]; démilitariser [*country*]; **2** fig désarmer [*critic, opponent*].
II *vi* [*country*] désarmer.

disarmament /dɪsˈɑːməmənt/ **I** *n* désarmement *m*.
II *modif* [*conference*] sur le désarmement; [*proposals*] de désarmement.

disarming /dɪsˈɑːmɪŋ/ **I** *n* désarmement *m*.
II *adj* [*smile, frankness*] désarmant.

disarmingly /dɪsˈɑːmɪŋlɪ/ *adv* [*smile, apologize*] d'une manière désarmante; **~ frank** d'une franchise désarmante.

disarrange /ˌdɪsəˈreɪndʒ/ *vtr* déranger.

disarranged /ˌdɪsəˈreɪndʒd/ *adj* défait.

disarray /ˌdɪsəˈreɪ/ *n* **1** (confusion) confusion *f*; **in complete ~** en pleine confusion; **in total ~** dans une confusion totale; **2** (disorder) désordre *m*; **in ~** en désordre.

disassemble /ˌdɪsəˈsembl/ *vtr* démonter [*gun, engine*].

disassociate /ˌdɪsəˈsəʊʃɪeɪt/ *vtr, vi* = **dissociate**.

disassociation /ˌdɪsəˌsəʊʃɪˈeɪʃn/ *n* = **dissociation**.

disaster /dɪˈzɑːstə(r), US -zæs-/ *n* gen catastrophe *f* also fig; (long-term) désastre *m*; **environmental ~** désastre écologique; **air/rail ~** catastrophe aérienne/ferroviaire; **financial ~** désastre financier; **to be heading for ~** courir à la catastrophe; **the maths teacher is a ~**○ le prof de math est une catastrophe○; **~ struck** le malheur a frappé.

disaster: **~ area** *n* lit région *f* sinistrée; fig catastrophe *f*; **~ fund** *n* fonds *m* de soutien; **~ movie** *n* film *m* catastrophe; **~ victim** *n* sinistré/-e *m/f*.

disastrous /dɪˈzɑːstrəs, US -zæs-/ *adj* désastreux/-euse, catastrophique.

disastrously /dɪˈzɑːstrəslɪ, US -zæs-/ *adv* [*end, turn out*] d'une manière désastreuse; [*fail*] lamentablement; [*expensive, extravagant etc*] terriblement; **to go ~ wrong** tourner à la catastrophe.

disavow /ˌdɪsəˈvaʊ/ *vtr* sout renier [*opinion, commitment*]; désavouer, nier [*connection*].

disavowal /ˌdɪsəˈvaʊəl/ *n* désaveu *m*.

disband /dɪsˈbænd/ **I** *vtr* gen dissoudre [*group*]; Mil licencier [*regiment, unit*].
II *vi* se disperser.

disbanding /dɪsˈbændɪŋ/ *n* (of group) dissolution *f* (**of** de); (of troops) licenciement *m* (**of** de).

disbar /dɪsˈbɑː(r)/ *vtr* (*p prés etc* **-rr-**) Jur radier.

disbarment /dɪsˈbɑːmənt/ *n* radiation *f* (du barreau).

disbelief /ˌdɪsbɪˈliːf/ *n* incrédulité *f*; **in ~** avec incrédulité.

disbelieve /ˌdɪsbɪˈliːv/ *vtr* sout ne pas croire.

disbeliever /ˌdɪsbɪˈliːvə(r)/ *n* incrédule *mf*.

disbelieving /ˌdɪsbɪˈliːvɪŋ/ *adj* incrédule.

disbud /dɪsˈbʌd/ *vtr* ébourgeonner.

disburse /dɪsˈbɜːs/ *vtr* sout débourser.

disbursement /dɪsˈbɜːsmənt/ *n* sout **1** (sum) débours *m*; **2** (act) déboursement *m*.

disc /dɪsk/ *n* **1** gen, Mus disque *m*; **on ~** sur disque; **2** Anat disque *m* (intervertébral); **to have a slipped ~** avoir une hernie discale; **3** gen, Mil **identity ~** plaque *f* d'identité; **4** Aut **tax ~** vignette *f* (automobile).

discard /dɪsˈkɑːd/ **I** *n* (in cards) défausse *f*; (cast-off garment, item) objet *m* mis au rebut.
II *vtr* **1** (get rid of) se débarrasser de [*clothes, possessions*]; jeter [qch] par terre [*litter*]; Culin jeter [*stalks, bones etc*]; mettre [*qch*] au rebut [*appliance, furniture*]; **2** (drop) abandonner [*idea, plan, policy*]; laisser tomber [*person*]; **3** (take off) enlever [*garment*]; **4** (in cards) se défausser de.
III *vi* (in cards) se défausser (d'une carte).

disc brakes *npl* Aut freins *mpl* à disques.

discern /dɪˈsɜːn/ *vtr* sout discerner [*object*]; percevoir [*meaning, truth, intention*].

discernible /dɪˈsɜːnəbl/ *adj* perceptible.

discernibly /dɪˈsɜːnəblɪ/ *adv* sensiblement.

discerning /dɪˈsɜːnɪŋ/ *adj* perspicace.

discernment /dɪˈsɜːnmənt/ *n* discernement *m*.

discharge I /ˈdɪstʃɑːdʒ/ *n* **1** (release) (of soldiers) libération *f*; (of patient) autorisation *f* de sortie; **to get one's ~** être libéré; **2** (pouring out) (of gas, liquid) déversement *m*; (of waste) déchargement *m*; Med suppuration *f*; **3** (substance released) (waste) déchets *fpl*; Med (from eye, wound etc) sécrétions *fpl*; **4** Jur relaxe *f*; **5** (repayment) règlement *m*; **in ~ of a debt** en règlement d'une dette; **6** Elec décharge *f*; **7** (performance) exercice *m*; **the ~ of his duties as manager** l'exercice de ses fonctions de directeur; **8** (firing) décharge *f*; **9** (unloading) déchargement *m*; **10** (termination) (of bankrupt) réhabilitation *f*; (of contract) annulation *f*; **a ~d bankrupt** une faillite réhabilitée.
II /dɪsˈtʃɑːdʒ/ *vtr* **1** (release) renvoyer [*patient*]; donner son congé à [*soldier*]; décharger [*accused*]; **to be ~d from hospital** être autorisé à quitter l'hôpital; **to be ~d from the army** être libéré de l'armée; **2** (dismiss) renvoyer [*employee*]; **to ~ sb from his duties** démettre qn de ses fonctions; **3** (give off) émettre [*gas, smoke*]; déverser [*sewage, water*]; décharger [*waste*]; **4** Med **to ~ pus** ou **fluid** suppurer; **to ~ blood** saigner; **5** Fin s'acquitter de [*debt*]; réhabiliter [*bankrupt*]; **6** (perform) s'acquitter de [*duty*]; remplir [*obligation*]; **to ~ one's responsibilities** assumer ses responsabilités; **7** (unload) décharger [*cargo*]; débarquer [*passengers*]; **8** Electron, Phys [*battery*] émettre [*current*]; **9** (fire) décharger [*rifle*].
III /dɪsˈtʃɑːdʒ/ *vi* [*wound*] suppurer.
IV /dɪsˈtʃɑːdʒ/ *v refl* **to ~ oneself (from hospital)** [*patient*] quitter l'hôpital.

disc harrow *n* Agric pulvériseur *m*.

disciple /dɪˈsaɪpl/ *n* gen, Bible disciple *mf*.

disciplinarian /ˌdɪsɪplɪˈneərɪən/ *n* partisan/-e *m/f* d'une discipline stricte; **to be a ~** être strict en matière de discipline.

disciplinary /ˈdɪsɪplɪnərɪ, US -nerɪ/ *adj* [*action, measure*] disciplinaire; [*problem*] concernant la discipline.

discipline /ˈdɪsɪplɪn/ **I** *n* **1** (controlled behaviour) discipline *f*; **2** (punishment) punitions *fpl*; **3** (academic subject) discipline *f*.
II *vtr* (control) discipliner; (punish) punir.
III *v refl* **to ~ oneself** se discipliner.

disciplined /ˈdɪsɪplɪnd/ *adj* [*person, group, manner*] discipliné; [*approach*] méthodique.

disc jockey ▶ 1692 *n* disc jockey *m*.

disclaim /dɪsˈkleɪm/ *vtr* nier.

disclaimer /dɪsˈkleɪmə(r)/ *n* démenti *m*; **to issue a ~** publier un démenti.

disclose /dɪsˈkləʊz/ *vtr* laisser voir [*sight, scene*]; révéler [*information, secret*]; **disclosing tablets** Dent comprimés *mpl* révélateurs de plaque dentaire.

disclosure /dɪsˈkləʊʒə(r)/ *n* révélation *f* (**of** de).

disco /ˈdɪskəʊ/ **I** *n* (event) soirée *f* disco; (club) discothèque *f*; (music) disco *m*.
II *vi* danser.

discography /dɪsˈkɒɡrəfɪ/ *n* discographie *f*.

discoloration /ˌdɪskʌləˈreɪʃn/ *n* gen décoloration *f*; (of teeth) jaunissement *m*.

discolour GB, **discolor** US /dɪsˈkʌlə(r)/ **I** *vtr* gen décolorer; jaunir [*teeth*].
II *vi* se décolorer.

discombobulate /ˌdɪskəmˈbɒbjʊleɪt/ *vtr* hum bouleverser.

discomfit /dɪsˈkʌmfɪt/ *vtr* littér déconcerter, décontenancer (**by** par).

discomfiture /dɪsˈkʌmfɪtʃə(r)/ *n* littér embarras *m*.

discomfort /dɪsˈkʌmfət/ *n* **1** (physical) sensation *f* de gêne; **2** (embarrassment) sentiment *m* de gêne.

discomposure /ˌdɪskəmˈpəʊʒə(r)/ *n* littér confusion *f*.

disconcert /ˌdɪskənˈsɜːt/ *vtr* décontenancer.

disconcerting /ˌdɪskənˈsɜːtɪŋ/ *adj* (worrying) troublant; (unnerving) déconcertant.

disconcertingly /ˌdɪskənˈsɜːtɪŋlɪ/ *adv* [*behave*] d'une manière déconcertante; **to be ~ frank/self-assured** être d'une franchise/assurance déconcertante.

disconnect /ˌdɪskəˈnekt/ *vtr* débrancher [*pipe, flex, appliance*]; couper [*telephone, gas, electricity*]; décrocher [*carriage*]; **to have** ou **get sth ~ed** faire couper qch; **I've been ~ed** (on telephone) j'ai été coupé; (because of nonpayment of bill etc) on m'a coupé le téléphone.

disconnected /ˌdɪskəˈnektɪd/ *adj* [*remarks*] décousu.

disconsolate /dɪsˈkɒnsələt/ *adj* **1** (depressed) désespéré; **2** littér (inconsolable) inconsolable.

disconsolately /dɪsˈkɒnsələtlɪ/ *adv* d'un air désespéré.

discontent /ˌdɪskənˈtent/ *n* mécontentement *m*; **the winter of ~** *hiver de grèves en 1978–79 en Grande-Bretagne*.

discontented /ˌdɪskənˈtentɪd/ *adj* mécontent (**with** de).

discontentment /ˌdɪskənˈtentmənt/ *n* mécontentement *m*.

discontinuation /ˌdɪskəntɪnjʊˈeɪʃn/ *n* sout (of service) suppression *f*; (of product) arrêt *m* (de production).

discontinue /ˌdɪskənˈtɪnjuː/ *vtr* supprimer [*service*]; arrêter [*production*]; cesser [*visits*]; **'~d line'** Comm fin *f* de série.

discontinuity /dɪsˌkɒntɪˈnjuːətɪ/ *n* sout (incoherence) discontinuité *f*; (interruption) interruption *f*.

discontinuous /ˌdɪskənˈtɪnjʊəs/ *adj* sout discontinu.

discord /ˈdɪskɔːd/ *n* **1** ¢ dissensions *fpl*; **a note of ~** une note de discorde; **2** Mus discordance *f*.
IDIOMS **apple of ~** pomme *f* de discorde.

discordant /dɪˈskɔːdənt/ *adj* gen, Mus discordant; **to strike a ~ note** produire un effet discordant.

discotheque /ˈdɪskətek/ *n* discothèque *f*.

discount I /ˈdɪskaʊnt/ *n* Comm remise *f* (**on** sur); (on minor purchase) rabais *m* (**on** sur); Fin escompte *m*; **to give sb a ~** faire une remise à qn; **I got a ~ on the chairs** on m'a fait une remise sur les chaises; **~ for cash** escompte de caisse (pour paiement au comptant); **to buy sth at a ~** acheter qch au rabais; **to be sold at a ~** Fin [*shares*] être vendu avec une décote.
II /dɪsˈkaʊnt, US ˈdɪskaʊnt/ *vtr* **1** (reject) écarter [*idea, theory, claim, possibility*], ne pas tenir compte de [*advice, report*]; **2** /ˈdɪskaʊnt/ Comm solder [*goods*]; faire une remise de [*sum of money*].

discount flight *n* vol *m* à tarif réduit.

discount house *n* **1** GB Fin banque *f* d'escompte; **2** US = **discount store**.

discount: **~ rate** *n* taux *m* d'escompte; **~ store** *n* solderie *f*.

discourage /dɪˈskʌrɪdʒ/ *vtr* **1** (dishearten) décourager; **to become ~d** se décourager; **don't be ~d!** ne te laisse pas décourager!;

2 (deter) décourager (**from** de; **from doing** de faire).

discouragement /dɪˈskʌrɪdʒmənt/ *n* **1** (despondency) découragement *m*; **2** (disincentive) **it's more of a ~ than an incentive** cela décourage plutôt que cela ne motive; **3** (disapproval) désapprobation *f*.

discouraging /dɪˈskʌrɪdʒɪŋ/ *adj* décourageant.

discourse sout **I** /ˈdɪskɔːs/ *n* (speech) discours *m* also Ling; (conversation) conversation *f*.
II /dɪˈskɔːs/ *vi* discourir (**on** sur; **about** à propos de).

discourse analysis *n* Ling analyse *f* du discours.

discourteous /dɪsˈkɜːtɪəs/ *adj* peu courtois.

discourteously /dɪsˈkɜːtɪəslɪ/ *adv* d'une manière peu courtoise.

discourtesy /dɪsˈkɜːtəsɪ/ *n* **1** ¢ (rudeness) manque *m* de courtoisie; **2** (rude remark or act) impolitesse *f*.

discover /dɪsˈkʌvə(r)/ *vtr* (all contexts) découvrir.

discoverer /dɪsˈkʌvərə(r)/ *n* **1** (of process, phenomenon) **the ~ of sth** celui/celle *m/f* qui a découvert qch; **2** (of new land) découvreur *m*.

discovery /dɪˈskʌvərɪ/ *n* **1** gen découverte *f*; **a voyage of ~** un voyage d'exploration; **she's a real ~** elle est une vraie révélation; **2** Jur communication *f* des pièces.

discredit /dɪsˈkredɪt/ **I** *n* discrédit *m*; **to bring ~ on sb** jeter le discrédit sur qn; **to his ~** à sa défaveur.
II *vtr* discréditer [*person, organization*]; mettre en doute [*idea, report, theory*]; **he ~ed the theory** il a mis en doute la théorie.

discreditable /dɪsˈkredɪtəbl/ *adj* [*behaviour*] indigne.

discreet /dɪˈskriːt/ *adj* [*action, behaviour*] discret/-ète; [*colour, elegance*] sobre.

discreetly /dɪˈskriːtlɪ/ *adv* [*act, behave*] discrètement; [*dress*] sobrement; [*make up*] d'une façon discrète.

discrepancy /dɪsˈkrepənsɪ/ *n* divergence *f* (**in** dans; **between** entre).

discrete /dɪˈskriːt/ *adj* gen distinct; Math, Phys, Ling discret/-ète.

discretion /dɪˈskreʃn/ *n* **1** (authority) discrétion *f*; **in** ou **at my/his ~** à ma/sa discrétion; **in** ou **at the committee's ~** à la discrétion du comité; **to use one's ~** agir à sa discrétion; **absolute ~** discrétion absolue; **I have ~ over that decision** cette décision est à ma discrétion; **the age of ~** l'âge de raison; **2** (tact) discrétion *f*; **the soul of ~** la discrétion même.

discretionary /dɪˈskreʃənərɪ, US -nerɪ/ *adj* discrétionnaire.

discriminate /dɪˈskrɪmɪneɪt/ *vi* **1** (act with prejudice) établir une discrimination (**against** envers; **in favour of** en faveur de); **2** (distinguish) **to ~ between X and Y** faire une or la distinction entre X et Y.

discriminating /dɪˈskrɪmɪneɪtɪŋ/ *adj* plein de discernement.

discrimination /dɪˌskrɪmɪˈneɪʃn/ *n* **1** souvent péj (prejudice) discrimination *f* (**against** envers; **in favour of** en faveur de); **positive ~** discrimination positive; **racial/sexual ~** discrimination raciale/sexuelle; **tax ~** discrimination par l'impôt; **2** (taste) discernement *m*; **3** (ability to differentiate) capacité *f* d'établir des distinctions.

discriminatory /dɪˈskrɪmɪnətərɪ, US -tɔːrɪ/ *adj* discriminatoire.

discursive /dɪˈskɜːsɪv/ *adj* discursif/-ive.

discus /ˈdɪskəs/ *n* (object) disque *m*; (event) lancer *m* du disque.

discuss /dɪˈskʌs/ **I** *vtr* (talk about) discuter de; (in book, article, lecture) examiner; **we'll have to ~ it** il faut qu'on en discute; **there's nothing to ~** il n'y a rien à dire.
II *vi* discuter.

discussant /dɪˈskʌsənt/ *n* intervenant/-e *m/f*.

discussion /dɪˈskʌʃn/ *n* gen discussion *f*; (in public) débat *m* (**on, about** sur; **of** de); (in lecture, book, article) analyse *f* (**of** de); **to be under ~** être en discussion; **to bring sth up for ~** soumettre qch à la discussion; **the plans are coming up for ~** les projets vont être discutés bientôt; **to be open to ~** être à discuter.

discussion: **~ document**, **~ paper** *n* avant-projet *m*; **~ group** *n* groupe *m* de discussion.

discus thrower *n* lanceur *m* de disque.

disdain /dɪsˈdeɪn/ **I** *n* dédain *m* (**for** pour).
II *vtr* dédaigner; **to ~ to do sth** ne pas daigner faire qch.

disdainful /dɪsˈdeɪnfl/ *adj* dédaigneux/-euse (**to** envers; **of** de).

disdainfully /dɪsˈdeɪnfəlɪ/ *adv* dédaigneusement.

disease /dɪˈziːz/ *n* Hort, Med **1** (specific illness) maladie *f*; **2** ¢ (range of infections) maladies *fpl*; **to spread ~** propager les maladies.

diseased /dɪˈziːzd/ *adj* lit, fig malade.

disembark /ˌdɪsɪmˈbɑːk/ *vtr, vi* débarquer.

disembarkation /dɪsˌembɑːˈkeɪʃn/ *n* débarquement *m*.

disembodied /ˌdɪsɪmˈbɒdɪd/ *adj* désincarné.

disembowel /ˌdɪsɪmˈbaʊəl/ *vtr* (*p prés etc* **-ll-** GB, **-l-** US) éviscérer.

disenchanted /ˌdɪsɪnˈtʃɑːntɪd, US -ˈtʃænt-/ *adj* désabusé; **to become ~ with sth** perdre ses illusions sur qch.

disenchantment /ˌdɪsɪnˈtʃɑːntmənt, US -ˈtʃænt-/ *n* désenchantement *m*.

disenfranchise /ˌdɪsɪnˈfræntʃaɪz/ *vtr* **to ~ sb** priver qn du droit électoral.

disengage /ˌdɪsɪnˈgeɪdʒ/ **I** *vtr* gen dégager (**from** de); **to ~ the clutch** Aut débrayer.
II *vi* **1** Mil cesser le combat; **2** gen, Mil **to ~ from sth** se retirer de qch.
III *v refl* **to ~ oneself** se dégager (**from** de).
IV disengaged *pp adj* sout libre.

disengagement /ˌdɪsɪnˈgeɪdʒmənt/ *n* Mil, Pol désengagement *m*.

disentangle /ˌdɪsɪnˈtæŋgl/ *vtr* lit, fig démêler (**from** de).

disequilibrium /ˌdɪsiːkwɪˈlɪbrɪəm/ *n* déséquilibre *m*.

disestablish /ˌdɪsɪˈstæblɪʃ/ *vtr* **to ~ the Church** séparer l'Église de l'État.

disestablishment /ˌdɪsɪˈstæblɪʃmənt/ *n* séparation *f* de l'Église et de l'État.

disfavour GB, **disfavor** US /dɪsˈfeɪvə(r)/ sout **I** *n* **1** (disapproval) désapprobation *f*; **to look on sb/sth with ~** considérer qn/qch avec désapprobation; **2 to be in ~** être mal vu (**with** de); **to fall into ~** tomber en disgrâce.
II *vtr* désapprouver.

disfigure /dɪsˈfɪgə(r), US dɪsˈfɪgjər/ **I** *vtr* lit, fig défigurer.
II disfigured *pp adj* défiguré (**by** par).

disfigurement /dɪsˈfɪgəmənt, US dɪsˈfɪgjə-/ *n* (all contexts) défigurement *m*.

disfranchise *vtr* = **disenfranchise**.

disgorge /dɪsˈgɔːdʒ/ **I** *vtr* déverser [*crowd, liquid*]; Med rendre [*obstruction*].
II *v refl* **to ~ itself** [*river*] se déverser.

disgrace /dɪsˈgreɪs/ **I** *n* **1** (shame) honte *f* (**of doing** de faire); **to bring ~ on sb** déshonorer qn; **to be in ~** (officially) être en disgrâce; hum ne pas être en odeur de sainteté; **there's no ~ in that** il n'y a pas de honte à cela; **2** (scandal) honte *f*; **it's a ~ that** c'est une honte que (+ *subj*); **he's a ~ to the school** il est la honte de l'école; **it's a ~!** c'est une honte!; **it's an absolute ~!** c'est scandaleux!
II *vtr* déshonorer [*team, family*].
III disgraced *pp adj* [*leader, player*] disgracié.
IV *v refl* **to ~ oneself** (dishonour oneself) se déshonorer; (behave badly) se conduire mal; **he ~d himself** il s'est mal conduit.

disgraceful /dɪsˈgreɪsfl/ *adj* [*conduct, situation*] scandaleux/-euse; **it's ~** (shameful) c'est une honte; (intolerable) c'est un scandale.

disgracefully /dɪsˈgreɪsfəlɪ/ *adv* scandaleusement.

disgruntled /dɪsˈgrʌntld/ *adj* mécontent.

disguise /dɪsˈgaɪz/ **I** *n* (costume) déguisement *m*; **in ~** lit, fig déguisé; **a master of ~** un maître du déguisement.
II *vtr* déguiser [*person, voice*]; camoufler [*blemish*]; cacher [*emotion, fact*]; **~d as a priest** déguisé en prêtre; **there's no ~sing the fact that...** on ne peut pas cacher le fait que...
III *v refl* **to ~ oneself** se déguiser (**as** en).
IDIOMS **it was a blessing in ~ for her** elle a eu de la chance dans son malheur.

disgust /dɪsˈgʌst/ **I** *n* (physical) dégoût *m*; (moral) écœurement *m* (**at** devant); **in ~** dégoûté, écœuré; **to his ~** à son grand écœurement.
II *vtr* (physically) dégoûter; (morally) écœurer.
III disgusted *pp adj* (physically) dégoûté; (morally) écœuré (**at, by, with** par); **I am ~ed with him for cheating** je suis écœuré qu'il ait triché.

disgustedly /dɪsˈgʌstɪdlɪ/ *adv* d'un air dégoûté.

disgusting /dɪsˈgʌstɪŋ/ *adj* (morally) écœurant; (physically) répugnant.

disgustingly /dɪsˈgʌstɪŋlɪ/ *adv* **1** lit **to be ~ dirty/fat** être sale/gros et répugnant; **to be ~ smelly** puer de façon répugnante; **2**○ fig **he is ~ rich** il est tellement riche que c'en est écœurant.

dish /dɪʃ/ **I** *n* **1** (plate) (for eating) assiette *f*; (for serving) plat *m*; **meat/vegetable ~** plat à viande/à légumes; **a set of ~es** un service *m*; **2** Culin (food) plat *m*; **chicken/fish ~** plat de poulet/de poisson; **side ~** garniture *f*; **3** TV (also **satellite ~**) antenne *f* parabolique; **4**○ (good-looking person) (male) beau mec○ *m*, (female) belle fille *f*.
II dishes *npl* vaisselle *f*; **to do the ~es** faire la vaisselle.
III○ *vtr* **1**† (ruin) flanquer [qch] en l'air○ [*hopes, plans*]; **2** (gossip) **to ~ the dirt on sb** répandre des ragots sur qn.
IV○ *vi* US causer○.
IDIOMS **this is just my ~**○ US c'est tout à fait mon truc○.
■ **dish out**: **~ out [sth]** distribuer [*advice, compliments, money, punishments, rebukes, rewards, supplies*]; servir [*food*]; **she knows how to ~ it out**○ elle est bonne pour critiquer.
■ **dish up**: **~ up [sth]** servir [*meal*].

disharmony /dɪsˈhɑːmənɪ/ *n* désaccord *m*.

dishcloth /ˈdɪʃklɒθ/ *n* (for washing) lavette *f*; (for drying) torchon *m* (à vaisselle).

dishearten /dɪsˈhɑːtn/ *vtr* démoraliser; **don't be ~ed!** ne te démoralise pas!

disheartening /dɪsˈhɑːtnɪŋ/ *adj* démoralisant.

dishevelled /dɪˈʃevld/ *adj* [*person*] débraillé; [*hair*] décoiffé; [*clothes*] en désordre.

dishonest /dɪsˈɒnɪst/ *adj* malhonnête.

dishonestly /dɪsˈɒnɪstlɪ/ *adv* malhonnêtement.

dishonesty /dɪsˈɒnɪstɪ/ *n* (financial) malhonnêteté *f*; (moral, intellectual) mauvaise foi *f*; Jur escroquerie *f*.

dishonour GB, **dishonor** US /dɪsˈɒnə(r)/ **I** *n* déshonneur *m*; **to bring ~ on sb** déshonorer qn.
II *vtr* **1** déshonorer [*memory, person*]; **2** Fin ne pas honorer [*cheque etc*].

dishonourable GB, **dishonorable** US /dɪsˈɒnərəbl/ *adj* [*act, behaviour*] déshonorant.

dishonourable discharge *n* exclusion *f* de l'armée (*pour conduite déshonorante*).

dishonourably GB, **dishonorably** US /dɪsˈɒnərəblɪ/ *adv* [*behave, act*] de façon déshonorante.

dish: **~pan** *n* US cuvette *f*; **~rag** *n* US lavette *f*; **~towel** *n* torchon *m*; **~washer** *n* (machine) lave-vaisselle *m inv*; (person) plongeur/-euse *m/f*; **~washer powder** *n* poudre *f* pour lave-vaisselle; **~washer salt** *n* sel *m* pour lave-vaisselle.

dishwater /ˈdɪʃwɔːtə(r)/ *n* lit eau *f* de vaisselle; fig (weak drink) péj lavasse○ *f* pej; **as dull as ~** US ennuyeux/-euse comme la pluie.

dishy○ /ˈdɪʃɪ/ *adj* GB séduisant, beau/belle (*before n*).

disillusion /ˌdɪsɪˈluːʒn/ **I** *n* désillusion *f* (**with** de).
II *vtr* **to ~ sb** faire perdre à qn ses illusions; **I hate to ~ you, but**... je ne voudrais pas te décevoir, mais...

disillusioned /ˌdɪsɪˈluːʒnd/ *adj* désabusé; **to be ~ with sth/sb** perdre ses illusions sur qch/qn.

disillusionment /ˌdɪsɪˈluːʒnmənt/ *n* désillusion *f* (**with** de).

disincentive /ˌdɪsɪnˈsentɪv/ *n* démotivation *f*; **it acts as** ou **is a ~ to work/to investment** cela n'incite pas à travailler/à l'investissement.

disinclination /ˌdɪsɪnklɪˈneɪʃn/ *n* sout **a ~ to do** un manque d'enthousiasme pour faire.

disinclined /ˌdɪsɪnˈklaɪnd/ *adj* sout **~ to do** peu disposé à faire.

disinfect /ˌdɪsɪnˈfekt/ *vtr* désinfecter.

disinfectant /ˌdɪsɪnˈfektənt/ *n* désinfectant *m*.

disinfection /ˌdɪsɪnˈfekʃn/ *n* désinfection *f*.

disinflation /ˌdɪsɪnˈfleɪʃn/ *n* déflation *f*.

disinflationary /ˌdɪsɪnˈfleɪʃənərɪ, US -nerɪ/ *adj* déflationniste.

disinformation /ˌdɪsɪnfəˈmeɪʃn/ *n* désinformation *f*.

disingenuous /ˌdɪsɪnˈdʒenjʊəs/ *adj* [*comment, reply*] peu sincère; [*smile*] faux/fausse; **you're being ~** vous ne dites pas toute la vérité.

disingenuously /ˌdɪsɪnˈdʒenjʊəslɪ/ *adv* sout [*say, answer*] de manière peu sincère.

disingenuousness /ˌdɪsɪnˈdʒenjʊəsnɪs/ *n* sout manque *m* de sincérité.

disinherit /ˌdɪsɪnˈherɪt/ *vtr* déshériter.

disintegrate /dɪsˈɪntɪgreɪt/ *vi* **1** [*aircraft*] se désintégrer; [*cloth, paper, wood*] se désagréger; **2** [*power, organization, relationship, mind*] se désagréger.

disintegration /dɪsˌɪntɪˈgreɪʃn/ *n* **1** (of aircraft) désintégration *f*; (of cloth, wood) désagrégation *f*; **2** (of organization, relationship) désintégration *f*, désagrégation *f*.

disinter /ˌdɪsɪnˈtɜː(r)/ *vtr* (*p prés etc* **-rr-**) exhumer.

disinterested /dɪsˈɪntrəstɪd/ *adj* **1** (impartial) [*observer, party, stance, advice*] impartial; **2** (uninterested) usage critiqué: voir note indifférent (**in** à).

■ Note Dans ce sens, utiliser de préférence *uninterested*.

disinterment /ˌdɪsɪnˈtɜːmənt/ *n* exhumation *f*.

disjoint /dɪsˈdʒɔɪnt/ *adj* disjoint.

disjointed /dɪsˈdʒɔɪntɪd/ *adj* [*programme, speech, report*] décousu; [*organization, effort*] incohérent.

disjunction /dɪsˈdʒʌŋkʃn/ *n* sout disjonction *f*.

disk /dɪsk/ *n* **1** Comput disque *m*; **on ~** sur disque; **2** US = **disc**.

disk: **~ directory** *n* répertoire *m* disques; **~ drive (unit)** *n* unité *f* de disques.

diskette /dɪˈsket/ *n* disquette *f*.

disk: **~ management** *n* gestion *f* disques; **~ operating system**, **DOS** *n* système *m* d'exploitation à disques, DOS *m*; **~ player** *n* lecteur *m* de disques; **~ space** *n* espace *m* disque.

dislike /dɪsˈlaɪk/ **I** *n* aversion *f*; **her ~ of sb/sth** l'aversion qu'elle ressent (or ressentait) pour qn/qch; **to take a ~ to sb/sth** prendre qn/qch en grippe, (stronger) prendre qn/qch en aversion; **I took an instant ~ to him** il m'a déplu tout de suite; **one's likes and ~s** ce que l'on aime et ce que l'on n'aime pas; **we all have our likes and ~s** on a tous nos préférences.
II *vtr* ne pas aimer; **to ~ doing** ne pas aimer faire; **I have always ~d him** je ne l'ai jamais aimé; **I ~ her intensely** je la déteste cordialement; **I don't ~ city life** je n'ai rien contre la vie urbaine.

dislocate /ˈdɪsləkeɪt, US ˈdɪsləʊkeɪt/ **I** *vtr* **1** Med **to ~ one's shoulder/hip** se démettre l'épaule/la hanche; **2** sout (disrupt) désorganiser [*transport, system*]; bouleverser [*economy, social structure*]; disperser [*population*].
II dislocated *pp adj* Med démis.

dislocation /ˌdɪsləˈkeɪʃn, US ˌdɪsləʊˈkeɪʃn/ *n* **1** (of hip, knee) luxation *f*; **2** sout (disruption) (of transport) désorganisation *f*; (of economy, social structure) bouleversement *m*; (of population) dispersion *f*.

dislodge /dɪsˈlɒdʒ/ *vtr* déplacer [*rock, tile, obstacle*] (**from** de); déloger [*foreign body*] (**from** de); déloger [*dictator, sniper*] (**from** de).

disloyal /dɪsˈlɔɪəl/ *adj* déloyal (**to** envers).

disloyalty /dɪsˈlɔɪəltɪ/ *n* déloyauté *f* (**to** envers).

dismal /ˈdɪzməl/ *adj* **1** [*place, sight*] lugubre; **2**○ [*failure, attempt*] lamentable.

dismally /ˈdɪzməlɪ/ *adv* **1** [*stare, wander*] d'un air lugubre; **2** [*fail*] lamentablement; **they failed ~ to attract investment** ils ont échoué lamentablement dans leurs efforts pour attirer les investissements; **to perform ~** [*business*] faire un chiffre d'affaires exécrable.

dismantle /dɪsˈmæntl/ *vtr* **1** (take apart) démonter [*construction, machine, missile*]; **2** (phase out) démanteler [*structure, organization, service*].

dismantling /dɪsˈmæntlɪŋ/ *n* **1** (of machine, construction) démontage *m*; **2** (of organization, system) démantèlement *m*.

dismast /dɪsˈmɑːst, US -ˈmæst/ *vtr* démâter.

dismay /dɪsˈmeɪ/ **I** *n* consternation *f* (**at** devant); **with ~** avec consternation; **to my/her ~** à ma/sa (grande) consternation; **'No!', he said in ~** 'Non!' dit-il, consterné.
II *vtr* consterner.

dismayed /dɪsˈmeɪd/ *adj* consterné (**at sth** devant qch; **to do** de faire); **~ that** consterné que (+ *subj*).

dismember /dɪsˈmembə(r)/ **I** *vtr* **1** démembrer [*corpse*]; **it ~s its prey** il met sa proie en pièces; **2** fig démembrer [*country*]; démanteler [*organization*].
II dismembered /dɪsˈmembəd/ *pp adj* [*corpse*] démembré.

dismemberment /dɪsˈmembəmənt/ *n* lit démembrement *m*; fig (of organization) démantèlement *m*.

dismiss /dɪsˈmɪs/ *vtr* **1** (reject) écarter [*idea, suggestion*]; exclure [*possibility*]; **to ~ sth as insignificant** écarter qch d'emblée; **2** (put out of mind) chasser [*thought, worry*]; **3** (sack) licencier [*employee, worker*] (**for** pour; **for doing** pour avoir fait); renvoyer [*servant*] (**for** pour; **for doing** pour avoir fait); révoquer [*civil servant*] (**for** pour; **for doing** pour avoir fait); démettre [qn] de ses fonctions [*director, official*]; **to be ~ed as head of**... être démis de ses fonctions de chef de...; **4** (end interview with) congédier [*person*]; (send out) [*teacher*] laisser sortir [*class*]; **5** Jur rejeter [*appeal, claim*]; **the charges against him were ~ed** les charges qui pesaient contre lui ont été rejetées; **the case was ~ed** il y a eu non-lieu; **6** (in cricket) sortir [*team, player*].

dismissal /dɪsˈmɪsl/ *n* **1** (of employee, worker) licenciement *m*; (of servant) révocation *f*; (of civil servant) révocation *f*; (of manager, director, minister) destitution *f*; **unfair ~**, **wrongful ~** licenciement abusif; **2** (of idea, threat) refus *m* de prendre [qch] en considération; **3** Jur (of appeal, claim) rejet *m*.

dismissive /dɪsˈmɪsɪv/ *adj* [*person, attitude*] dédaigneux/-euse; [*gesture*] de dédain; **to be ~ of** faire peu de cas de.

dismissively /dɪsˈmɪsɪvlɪ/ *adv* [*say, shrug*] d'un air dédaigneux; [*speak*] d'un ton dédaigneux; [*describe, label*] de façon dédaigneuse.

dismount /dɪsˈmaʊnt/ **I** *vtr* démonter [*gun*].
II *vi* mettre pied à terre; **to ~ from** descendre de [*horse, bicycle*].

disobedience /ˌdɪsəˈbiːdɪəns/ *n* désobéissance *f*.

disobedient /ˌdɪsəˈbiːdɪənt/ *adj* [*child*] désobéissant (**to** à); **if they were ~, he**... s'ils ne lui obéissaient pas, il...

disobey /ˌdɪsəˈbeɪ/ **I** *vtr* désobéir à [*person*]; enfreindre [*law, order, rule*].
II *vi* désobéir.

disobliging /ˌdɪsəˈblaɪdʒɪŋ/ *adj* désobligeant.

disorder /dɪsˈɔːdə(r)/ **I** *n* **1** ¢ (lack of order) désordre *m*; **in ~** en désordre; **to retreat in ~** Mil être en déroute; **2** ¢ gen, Pol (disturbances) émeutes *fpl*; **civil ~** émeutes *fpl*; **the march ended in ~** la manifestation s'est terminée en émeute; **3** C Med, Psych (malfunction) troubles *mpl*; (disease) maladie *f*; **blood/lung ~** maladie *f* du sang/des poumons; **eating ~** troubles *mpl* de l'alimentation; **mental/personality ~** troubles *mpl* psychiques/de la personnalité.
II *vtr* Med, Psych troubler.

disordered /dɪsˈɔːdəd/ *adj* [*life*] désordonné; Med [*mind, brain*] déséquilibré.

disorderly /dɪsˈɔːdəlɪ/ *adj* **1** (untidy) [*room*] en désordre; **2** (disorganized) [*person, arrangement, existence*] désordonné; Mil [*retreat*] désordonné; **3** (unruly) [*crowd, demonstration, meeting*] turbulent; fig [*imagination*] débridé.

disorderly: **~ behaviour**, **~ conduct** *n* Jur perturbation *f* de l'ordre public; **~ house** *n* Jur (brothel) maison *f* close; (gaming house) maison *f* de jeu.

disorganization /dɪsˌɔːgənaɪˈzeɪʃn, US -nɪˈz-/ *n* désorganisation *f*.

disorganize /dɪsˈɔːgənaɪz/ *vtr* désorganiser.

disorganized /dɪsˈɔːgənaɪzd/ *adj* désorganisé.

disorient = **disorientate**.

disorientate /dɪsˈɔːrɪənteɪt/ **I** *vtr* désorienter.
II disorientated *pp adj* désorienté.

disown /dɪsˈəʊn/ *vtr* **1** renier [*person*]; désavouer [*politician*]; **2** désavouer [*document, article, play*].

disparage /dɪˈspærɪdʒ/ *vtr* sout dénigrer.

disparagement /dɪˈspærɪdʒmənt/ *n* sout dénigrement *m*.

disparaging /dɪˈspærɪdʒɪŋ/ *adj* désobligeant (**about** à propos de).

disparagingly /dɪˈspærɪdʒɪŋlɪ/ *adv* [*say, comment*] de façon désobligeante; **she referred to them ~ as amateurs** elle a parlé d'eux en termes désobligeants, disant qu'ils étaient des amateurs.

disparate /ˈdɪspərət/ *adj* **1** (very different) complètement différent; **a ~ group** un groupe hétérogène; **2** (incompatible) incompatible.

disparity /dɪˈspærətɪ/ *n* disparité *f* (**between** entre).

dispassionate /dɪˈspæʃənət/ *adj* **1** (impartial) objectif/-ive (**about** au sujet de); **2** (unemotional) froid.

dispassionately /dɪˈspæʃənətlɪ/ *adv* **1** [*observe, assess, react*] objectivement; **2** (unemotionally) froidement.

dispatch /dɪˈspætʃ/ **I** *n* **1** (report) dépêche *f*; **mentioned in ~es** Mil cité à l'ordre du jour; **2** (sending) expédition *f*; **date of ~**

date d'expédition; **3** (speed) promptitude *f*; **with ~** avec promptitude.

II *vtr* **1** (send) envoyer [*person, troops*] (**to** à); expédier [*letter, parcel*] (**to** à); **2** (consume) hum expédier [*plateful*]; descendre [*drink*]; **3** (complete) expédier [*work*]; régler [*problem*]; **4** euph (kill) expédier [qn] six pieds sous terre.

dispatch box *n* **1** valise *f* diplomatique; **2 Dispatch Box** GB Pol tribune *f* (*d'où parlent les membres du gouvernement*).

dispatch rider *n* **1** Mil estafette *f*; **2** Comm dispatcher *m*.

dispel /dɪˈspel/ *vtr* (*p prés etc* **-ll-**) **1** chasser [*doubt, fear, rumour*]; dissiper [*illusion, myth, notion*]; **2** sout dissiper [*mist, cloud*].

dispensable /dɪˈspensəbl/ *adj* [*person, thing*] dont on peut se passer; **to be ~** [*thing, idea*] être superflu; [*person*] être une quantité négligeable.

dispensary /dɪˈspensərɪ/ *n* **1** (clinic) dispensaire *m*; **2** GB (in hospital) pharmacie *f*; (in chemist's) officine *f*.

dispensation /ˌdɪspenˈseɪʃn/ *n* sout **1** (dispensing) (of justice) exercice *m*; (of alms) distribution *f*; (of funds) attribution *f*; **2** (permission) Jur, Relig dispense *f*; **3** (system) Pol, Relig système *m*.

dispense /dɪˈspens/ *vtr* **1** [*machine*] distribuer [*food, drinks, money*]; **2** sout exercer [*justice*]; faire [*charity*]; prodiguer [*advice*]; attribuer [*funds*]; **3** Pharm préparer [*medicine, prescription*]; **4** (exempt) gen, Relig dispenser (**from** de).

■ **dispense with** (manage without) se passer de [*services, formalities*]; (get rid of) abandonner [*policy, regulations etc*]; (make unnecessary) rendre inutile [*resource, facility*]; **this ~s with the need for a dictionary** grâce à cela, on peut se passer du dictionnaire.

dispenser /dɪˈspensə(r)/ *n* distributeur *m*.

dispensing: **~ chemist** *n* GB pharmacien/-ienne *m/f*; **~ optician** *n* opticien/-ienne *m/f*.

dispersal /dɪˈspɜːsl/ *n* **1** (scattering) (of people, birds, fumes) dispersion *f*; (of seeds) dissémination *f*; **2** (spread) (of industry, factories, installations) dissémination *f*.

dispersant /dɪˈspɜːsənt/ *n* dispersant *m*.

disperse /dɪˈspɜːs/ **I** *vtr* **1** (scatter) disperser [*crowd, seeds, fumes*]; **2** (distribute) disséminer [*agents, troops, factories*]; **3** Chem décomposer [*particle*].

II *vi* **1** [*crowd*] se disperser; **2** [*fumes, pollution, mist*] se dissiper; **3** Chem se décomposer.

dispersion /dɪˈspɜːʃn, US dɪˈspɜːrʒn/ *n* **1** (of light) décomposition *f*; **2** (of radiation) dispersion *f*; **3** sout (of people) dispersion *f*; **4** Stat dispersion *f*.

dispirit /dɪˈspɪrɪt/ *vtr* décourager.

dispirited /dɪˈspɪrɪtɪd/ *adj* [*look, air*] découragé; [*mood*] abattu.

dispiritedly /dɪˈspɪrɪtɪdlɪ/ *adv* [*speak, sigh, trudge*] avec découragement.

dispiriting /dɪˈspɪrɪtɪŋ/ *adj* [*results, progress, remark*] décourageant (**to do** de faire); [*attitude*] déprimant.

displace /dɪsˈpleɪs/ *vtr* **1** (replace) supplanter [*competitor, leader*]; déplacer [*worker*]; **2** (expel) chasser [*person, population*]; **3** Naut, Phys déplacer.

displaced person *n* réfugié/-e *m/f*.

displacement /dɪsˈpleɪsmənt/ *n* **1** (of workers, jobs) déplacement *m*; **2** (of population) déplacement *m*; **3** Naut, Phys déplacement *m*; **4** Psych transfert *m*.

displacement: **~ activity** *n* déplacement *m*; **~ tonnage** *n* déplacement *m*.

display /dɪˈspleɪ/ **I** *n* **1** Comm (for sale) (of food, small objects) étalage *m*; (of furniture, equipment, vehicles) exposition *f*; **window ~** vitrine *f*; **to be on ~** être exposé; **on ~ in the window** exposé en vitrine; **to put sth on ~** exposer qch; **'for ~ purposes'** Comm (book) 'exemplaire *m* de présentation'; (object) 'article *m* de présentation'; **2** (for decoration, to look at) (showing) exposition *f*; **to be** ou **go on ~** être exposé; **to put sth on ~** exposer qch; **what a lovely ~ of flowers** quel bel arrangement de fleurs; **'do not touch the ~'** 'prière de ne pas toucher'; **3** (demonstration) (of art, craft, skill) démonstration *f*; (of dance, sport) exhibition *f*; **to put on** ou **mount a ~ of** organiser une démonstration or une exhibition de; **air ~** fête *f* aéronautique; **4** (of emotion, failing, quality) démonstration *f*; (of strength, wealth) déploiement *m*; **in a ~ of** dans un geste de [*anger, impatience*]; **in a ~ of solidarity/affection** pour manifester sa solidarité/son affection; **to make a ~ of** péj faire étalage de [*wealth, knowledge*]; **5** Aut, Aviat, Comput écran *m*, affichage *m*; **digital ~** affichage numérique; **6** Print, Journ **full page ~** page *f* entière de publicité; **7** Zool parade *f*.

II *vtr* **1** gen, Comm, Comput (show, set out) afficher [*information, notice, price, times, poster*]; exposer [*object*]; **the total is ~ed here** le total s'affiche ici; **2** (reveal) faire preuve de [*enthusiasm, intelligence, interest, skill*]; révéler [*emotion, ignorance, vice, virtue, strength*]; **3** péj (flaunt) faire étalage de [*beauty, knowledge, wealth*]; exhiber [*legs, chest*].

III *vi* Zool parader; [*peacock*] faire la roue.

display: **~ advertisement** *n* grande annonce *f*; **~ artist** ▶ 1692 *n* Comm étalagiste *mf*; **~ cabinet**, **~ case** *n* (in house) vitrine *f*; (in museum) vitrine *f* d'exposition; **~ panel** *n* écran *m* d'affichage; **~ rack** *n* Comm présentoir *m*; **~ type** *n* caractères *mpl* vedettes.

display unit *n* **1** Comput écran *m* de visualisation; **2** Comm = **display rack**.

display window *n* vitrine *f*.

displease /dɪsˈpliːz/ *vtr* mécontenter.

displeased /dɪsˈpliːzd/ *adj* mécontent (**with, at** de; **to do** de faire).

displeasing /dɪsˈpliːzɪŋ/ *adj* déplaisant; **to be ~ to sb/sth** déplaire à qn/qch.

displeasure /dɪsˈpleʒə(r)/ *n* mécontentement *m* (**at** causé par); **to my great ~** à mon grand mécontentement; **much to the ~ of** au grand mécontentement de.

disport /dɪˈspɔːt/ *v refl* littér, hum **to ~ oneself** s'ébattre.

disposable /dɪˈspəʊzəbl/ **I disposables** *npl* articles *mpl* jetables.

II *adj* **1** (throwaway) [*lighter, nappy, plate, razor*] jetable; **2** (available) disponible.

disposable: **~ income** *n* revenu *m* disponible; **~ load** *n* Aviat charge *f* utilisable.

disposal /dɪˈspəʊzl/ *n* **1** (removal) (of waste product) élimination *f*; **waste ~** élimination des déchets; **for ~** à jeter; **2** (sale) (of company, property) vente *f*; (of deeds, securities) cession *f*; **3** (completion) exécution *f*; **4** (for use, access) **to be at sb's ~** être à la disposition de qn; **to put** ou **place sth at sb's ~** mettre qch à la disposition de qn; **to have sth at one's ~** avoir qch à sa disposition; **all the means at my ~** tous les moyens dont je dispose; **5** (arrangement) disposition *f*.

disposal value *n* Fin valeur *f* de cession.

dispose /dɪˈspəʊz/ **I** *vtr* **1** (arrange) disposer [*furniture, ornaments, troops*]; **2** (encourage) **to ~ sb to sth/to do** disposer qn à qch/à faire.

II disposed *pp adj* **to be ~d to sth/to do** être disposé à qch/à faire; **ill-/well-~d** mal/bien disposé; **should you feel so ~d** sout si vous en avez envie.

■ **dispose of**: **~ of [sth/sb]** **1** (get rid of) se débarrasser de [*body, rival, rubbish, victim, waste*]; détruire [*evidence*]; désarmer [*bomb*]; **2** Comm écouler [*stock*]; (sell) vendre [*car, house, shares*]; **3** (deal with speedily) expédier [*business, problem, theory*].

disposer /dɪˈspəʊzə(r)/ *n* US broyeur *m* d'ordures.

disposition /ˌdɪspəˈzɪʃn/ *n* **1** (temperament) tempérament *m*; **a friendly/irritable ~** un tempérament amical/irritable; **to be of a nervous ~** avoir un tempérament nerveux; **to have a cheerful ~** être d'un naturel gai, être épanoui; **2** (tendency) tendance *f*; **to have a ~ to be/to do** avoir tendance à être/à faire; **3** (arrangement) disposition *f*; **4** Jur disposition *f*.

dispossess /ˌdɪspəˈzes/ *vtr* **1** Jur **to ~ sb of** déposséder qn de [*land, property*]; exproprier qn de [*house*]; **2** (in football) **to ~ sb** déposséder qn du ballon; **to be ~ed** perdre le ballon.

dispossessed /ˌdɪspəˈzest/ **I** *n* **the ~** (+ *v pl*) les déshérités *mpl*.

II *adj* (*tjrs épith*) [*family*] exproprié; [*son*] déshérité; **a ~ people** (poor) un peuple déshérité; (politically) un peuple dépossédé de sa terre.

dispossession /ˌdɪspəˈzeʃn/ *n* expropriation *f*.

disproportion /ˌdɪsprəˈpɔːʃn/ *n* disproportion *f* (**between** entre).

disproportionate /ˌdɪsprəˈpɔːʃənət/ *adj* disproportionné (**to** par rapport à).

disproportionately /ˌdɪsprəˈpɔːʃənətlɪ/ *adv* **~ high** [*costs, expectations*] disproportionné; **he had ~ long legs** ses jambes étaient d'une longueur disproportionnée; **the city's population is ~ young** la ville compte un nombre disproportionné de jeunes; **ethnic minorities are ~ affected by...** les minorités ethniques sont touchées de façon disproportionnée par...

disprove /dɪsˈpruːv/ *vtr* réfuter.

disputant /dɪˈspjuːtənt, ˈdɪspjʊtənt/ *n* sout discuteur/-euse *m/f*.

disputation /ˌdɪspjuːˈteɪʃn/ *n* sout débat *m*.

dispute /dɪˈspjuːt/ **I** *n* **1** (quarrel) (between individuals) dispute *f* (**between** entre; **with** avec); (between groups) conflit *m* (**over, about** à propos de; **between** entre; **with** avec); **border/pay ~** conflit frontalier/salarial; **to be in ~ with** être en conflit avec; **to have a ~ with** se disputer avec; **to enter into a ~ with** entrer en conflit avec; **2** ¢ (controversy) controverse *f* (**over, about** sur); **to be/not to be in ~** [*cause, fact, problem*] être/ne pas être controversé; **beyond ~** incontestable; **without ~** sans conteste; **there is some ~ about the cause** la cause est controversée; **it is a matter of ~** c'est une question controversée; **to be open to ~** être matière à discussion; **it is open to ~ whether this solution would work** l'efficacité de cette solution est discutable.

II *vtr* **1** (question truth of) contester [*claim, figures, result, theory*]; **I ~ that!** je m'inscris en faux!; **2** (claim possession of) se disputer [*property, territory, title*].

III *vi* débattre; **to ~ with sb about** se disputer avec qn à propos de.

IV disputed *pp adj* [*fact, theory, territory*] contesté; Jur litigieux/-ieuse.

disqualification /dɪsˌkwɒlɪfɪˈkeɪʃn/ *n* **1** gen (from post, career) exclusion *f* (**from** de); **2** Sport disqualification *f* (**from** de; **for doing** pour avoir fait); **3** GB Jur suspension *f*; **a six months' ~ for sth** une suspension de six mois pour qch; **4** Aut, Jur **~ from driving** (also **driving ~**) retrait *m* du permis de conduire; **5** (thing which disqualifies) **his lack of experience is not a ~ for the post** son manque d'expérience ne l'exclut pas du poste.

disqualify /dɪsˈkwɒlɪfaɪ/ *vtr* **1** gen (from post, career) exclure (**from** de); **to ~ sb from doing** interdire à qn de faire; **your age disqualifies you from this post** votre âge ne vous permet pas d'accéder à ce poste; **2** Sport [*regulation*] (before event) interdire (**from** de; **from doing** de faire); (after event) disqualifier (**from** de); [*physical condition*] empêcher (**from doing** de faire); **he was disqualified for taking drugs** il a été disqualifié pour avoir pris de la drogue; **3** GB Aut, Jur **to ~ sb from driving** retirer à qn son permis de conduire; **he's been disqualified for six months** on lui a retiré son permis de conduire pour six mois; **driving while disqualified** conduite *f* sans permis.

disquiet /dɪsˈkwaɪət/ sout **I** *n* inquiétude *f* (**about, over** au sujet de); **public ~** les craintes *fpl* de la population.
II *vtr* troubler.

disquieting /dɪsˈkwaɪətɪŋ/ *adj* sout troublant.

disquietingly /dɪsˈkwaɪətɪŋlɪ/ *adv* sout étrangement.

disquisition /ˌdɪskwɪˈzɪʃn/ *n* sout (oral) discours *m* (**on** sur); (written) dissertation *f* (**on** sur).

disregard /ˌdɪsrɪˈɡɑːd/ **I** *n* (for problem, feelings, person) indifférence *f* (**for sth** à qch; **for sb** envers qn); (for danger, convention, human life, law, right) mépris *m* (**for** de); **to show ~** faire preuve d'indifférence or de mépris (**for** à l'égard de).
II *vtr* **1** (discount) ne pas tenir compte de [*irrelevance, trivia, problem, evidence, remark*]; fermer les yeux sur [*wrongdoing*]; mépriser [*danger*]; **2** (disobey) ne pas respecter [*law, instruction*].

disrepair /ˌdɪsrɪˈpeə(r)/ *n* délabrement *m*; **in (a state of) ~** dans un état de délabrement avancé; **to fall into ~** [*building, machinery*] se délabrer.

disreputable /dɪsˈrepjʊtəbl/ *adj* **1** (unsavoury) [*person*] peu recommandable; [*district, establishment*] mal famé; [*behaviour*] déshonorant; **2** (tatty) [*clothes, appearance*] miteux/-euse; **3** (discredited) [*method*] douteux/-euse.

disreputably /dɪsˈrepjʊtəblɪ/ *adv* [*behave*] de manière peu honorable.

disrepute /ˌdɪsrɪˈpjuːt/ *n* **to be held in ~** [*person, work, method*] être discrédité; **to bring sb/sth into ~** jeter le discrédit sur qn/qch; **to be brought into ~** tomber dans le discrédit.

disrespect /ˌdɪsrɪˈspekt/ *n* manque *m* de respect (**for** envers); **to show ~ to** ou **towards sb** manquer de respect envers qn; **he meant no ~** il n'avait pas l'intention de manquer de respect; **no ~ (to you)** sauf votre respect; **no ~ (to him/her)** avec tout le respect que je lui dois.

disrespectful /ˌdɪsrɪˈspektfl/ *adj* [*person*] irrespectueux/-euse (**to, towards** envers); [*remark, behaviour*] irrévérencieux/-ieuse (**to, towards** envers); **it was most ~ of her to do** c'était très irrévérencieux de sa part de faire.

disrespectfully /ˌdɪsrɪˈspektfəlɪ/ *adv* [*behave, act*] de manière irrespectueuse; [*speak*] avec insolence.

disrobe /dɪsˈrəʊb/ *vi* [*official, monarch*] retirer ses vêtements de cérémonie; hum (undress) se dévêtir.

disrupt /dɪsˈrʌpt/ *vtr* perturber [*communications, traffic, trade, meeting*]; bouleverser [*lifestyle, schedule, routine, plan*]; interrompre [*electricity supply*].

disruption /dɪsˈrʌpʃn/ *n* **1** ₵ (disorder) perturbations *fpl* (**in** dans); **to cause ~ to sth** perturber qch; **2** (disrupting) (of service, trade, meeting) perturbation *f*; (of schedule, routine, plan) bouleversement *m*; (of electricity supply) interruption *f*; **3** (upheaval) bouleversement *m*.

disruptive /dɪsˈrʌptɪv/ *adj* **1** gen perturbateur/-trice; **a ~ influence** un élément perturbateur; **2** Elec **~ discharge** décharge *f* disruptive.

disruptively /dɪsˈrʌptɪvlɪ/ *adv* [*behave*] de manière perturbatrice.

disruptiveness /dɪsˈrʌptɪvnɪs/ *n* indiscipline *f*.

dissatisfaction /dɪˌsætɪsˈfækʃn/ *n* (discontent) mécontentement *m* (**with** vis-à-vis de); (milder) frustration *f*.

dissatisfied /dɪˈsætɪsfaɪd/ *adj* mécontent (**with, at** de; **that** que + *subj*).

dissect /dɪˈsekt/ **I** *vtr* **1** (cut up) disséquer [*cadaver, animal, plant*]; décomposer [*molecule, gene*]; **2** (analyse) péj disséquer [*performance, relationship, system*]; éplucher [*book, play*].
II dissected *pp adj* Bot, Geol découpé.

dissection /dɪˈsekʃn/ *n* (all contexts) dissection *f*.

dissemble /dɪˈsembl/ *vtr, vi* sout dissimuler.

disseminate /dɪˈsemɪneɪt/ *vtr* diffuser [*information, products*]; propager [*ideas, views*].

dissemination /dɪˌsemɪˈneɪʃn/ *n* (of information, products) diffusion *f*; (of ideas) propagation *f*.

dissension /dɪˈsenʃn/ *n* (discord) discorde *f*, dissensions *fpl* (**among** entre).

dissent /dɪˈsent/ **I** *n* ₵ **1** gen, Pol contestation *f*, dissensions *fpl* sout; Sport contestation *f*; **~ from** désaccord *m* avec [*policy, decision, opinion*]; **2** Relig désaccord *m*; **3** (also **~ing opinion**) US Jur dissentiment *m*.
II *vi* **1** gen, Jur (disagree) contester; **to ~ from sth** contester qch; **2** Relig **to ~ from sth** s'écarter de qch.
III dissenting *pres p adj* **1** gen, Pol [*group, opinion, voice*] contestataire; **2** GB Hist Relig non conformiste.

dissenter /dɪˈsentə(r)/ *n* contestataire *mf*.

Dissenter /dɪˈsentə(r)/ *n* GB Hist Relig non conformiste *mf*.

dissentient /dɪˈsenʃənt/ *n* sout Pol dissident/-e *m/f*.

dissertation /ˌdɪsəˈteɪʃn/ *n* **1** GB Univ mémoire *m* (**on** sur); **2** US Univ thèse *f* (**on** sur); **3** sout (treatise) traité *m* (**on** sur).

disservice /dɪsˈsɜːvɪs/ *n* **to do a ~ to sb, to do sb a ~** rendre un mauvais service à qn; **to do a ~ to** desservir fml [*country, cause, ideal*].

dissidence /ˈdɪsɪdəns/ *n* dissidence *f*.

dissident /ˈdɪsɪdənt/ **I** *n* dissident/-e *m/f*.
II *adj* dissident.

dissimilar /dɪˈsɪmɪlə(r)/ *adj* dissemblable; **~ to** différent de; **a painter not ~ in style to**... un peintre dont le style rappelle...

dissimilarity /ˌdɪsɪmɪˈlærətɪ/ *n* **1** ₵ (lack of similarity) dissemblance *f* (**in** de; **between** entre); **2** (difference) différence *f* (**in** de; **between** entre).

dissimulate /dɪˈsɪmjʊleɪt/ *vtr, vi* sout dissimuler.

dissimulation /dɪˌsɪmjʊˈleɪʃn/ *n* sout dissimulation *f*.

dissipate /ˈdɪsɪpeɪt/ sout **I** *vtr* dissiper [*fear, anger, mist*]; anéantir [*hope, enthusiasm*]; gaspiller [*fortune, advantage, energy, talent*].
II *vi* (all contexts) se dissiper.

dissipated /ˈdɪsɪpeɪtɪd/ *adj* [*person, behaviour*] dissolu; **to lead a ~ life** mener une vie de débauche.

dissipation /ˌdɪsɪˈpeɪʃn/ *n* sout **1** (of fears, anger, mist) dissipation *f*; (of hopes) anéantissement *m*; (of energy, wealth) gaspillage *m*; **2** (debauchery) débauche *f*.

dissociate /dɪˈsəʊʃɪeɪt/ **I** *vtr* gen, Chem dissocier (**from** de).
II *vi* Chem se dissocier.
III *v refl* **to ~ oneself** se dissocier (**from** de).

dissociation /dɪˌsəʊʃɪˈeɪʃn/ *n* **1** gen, Chem dissociation *f* (**from** de); **2** Psych dissociation *f* (mentale).

dissolute /ˈdɪsəluːt/ *adj* [*lifestyle*] dissolu; **a ~ man** un débauché; **she was denounced as ~** elle a été dénoncée comme une débauchée; **to lead a ~ life** mener une vie dissolue or de débauche.

dissolution /ˌdɪsəˈluːʃn/ *n* **1** (of Parliament, assembly, partnership, marriage) dissolution *f*; **the Dissolution (of the Monasteries)** GB Hist la dissolution des monastères; **2** (disappearance) dissolution *f*; **3** (dissoluteness) dissolution *f* (des mœurs).

dissolve /dɪˈzɒlv/ **I** *n* Cin fondu *m* enchaîné.
II *vtr* **1** [*acid, water*] dissoudre [*solid, grease, dirt, powder*]; **2** [*person*] faire dissoudre [*tablet, sugar, powder*] (**in** dans); **3** (break up) dissoudre [*assembly, parliament, partnership, marriage*].
III *vi* **1** (liquefy) se dissoudre (**in** dans; **into** en); **2** (fade) [*hope, feeling, opposition*] s'évanouir; [*outline, image*] disparaître; **one scene ~s into another** Cin les scènes se succèdent par fondu enchaîné; **3** (collapse) **to ~ into tears** fondre en larmes; **to ~ into giggles** ou **laughter** avoir le fou rire; **4** (break up) [*assembly, party, organization*] être dissous/-oute.

dissonance /ˈdɪsənəns/ *n* **1** Mus dissonance *f*; **2** sout (of sounds, colours, beliefs etc) discordance *f*.

dissonant /ˈdɪsənənt/ *adj* **1** Mus dissonant; **2** sout [*sounds, colours, beliefs etc*] discordant.

dissuade /dɪˈsweɪd/ *vtr* dissuader (**from doing** de faire).

dissuasion /dɪˈsweɪʒn/ *n* dissuasion *f*.

dissuasive /dɪˈsweɪsɪv/ *adj* dissuasif/-ive.

distaff /ˈdɪstɑːf, US ˈdɪstæf/ *n* quenouille *f*.
IDIOMS **on the ~ side** du côté maternel.

distance /ˈdɪstəns/ ▶1412 **I** *n* lit, fig distance *f* (**between** entre; **from** de; **to** à); **a ~ of** une distance de; **at a ~ of 50 metres** à (une distance de) 50 mètres; **at a** ou **some ~ from** à bonne distance de; **at** ou **from this ~** à cette distance; **at a safe ~** à bonne distance; **at an equal ~** à égale distance; **a long/short ~ away** loin/pas loin; **to keep sb at a ~** tenir qn à distance; **to keep one's ~** lit, fig garder ses distances (**from** avec); **to go the ~** Sport, fig tenir la distance; **to put some ~ between oneself and Paris/the border** s'éloigner de Paris/de la frontière; **from a ~** de loin; **in the ~** au loin; **it's no ~** c'est tout près ; **it's within walking ~** on peut y aller à pied; **call him, he's within shouting ~** appelle-le, il est assez près pour pouvoir t'entendre; **'free delivery, ~ no object'** 'livraison gratuite, toutes destinations'; **at a ~ it's easy to see that I made mistakes** avec du recul je vois très bien que j'ai commis des erreurs.
II *modif* [*runner, race*] de fond.
III *vtr* **1** créer une distance entre [*two people*]; **to ~ sb from sb/sth** (emotionally) créer une distance entre qn et qn/qch; **to become ~d from sb** se détacher de qn; **to ~ sb's remarks from the government view** distancier les observations de qn de l'optique gouvernementale; **2** (outdistance) distancier [*runner, rival*].
IV *v refl* **to ~ oneself** (dissociate oneself) se distancier (**from** de); (stand back) prendre du recul (**from** par rapport à).

distance learning *n* Sch, Univ enseignement *m* à distance.

distant /ˈdɪstənt/ *adj* **1** (remote) [*land, spire, hill, star*] lointain, éloigné; [*cry, voice, gunfire, bell*] éloigné, dans le lointain (*after n*); **the ~ shape/sound of sth** la forme/le bruit de qch dans le lointain; **~ from** loin de; **40 km ~ from** à 40 km de; **in the ~ past/future** dans un passé/avenir lointain; **in the dim and ~ past** dans un passé lointain; **in the not too ~ future** dans un avenir assez proche; **2** (faint) [*memory, prospect, hope, possibility*] lointain, éloigné; [*connection, concept, similarity*] lointain, vague; **~ from** éloigné de; **3** (far removed) [*relative, cousin, descendant*] éloigné; **4** (cool) [*person, manner*] distant.

distantly /ˈdɪstəntlɪ/ *adv* [*remembered, connected*] vaguement; [*say, look, greet, act*] (coolly) d'un air distant; (vaguely) d'un air vague; **to be ~ related to sb** être vaguement apparenté à qn, être un parent éloigné de qn; **they're ~ related** ils sont vaguement parents.

distaste /dɪsˈteɪst/ *n* aussi euph (slight) déplaisir *m*; (marked) dégoût *m*; **~ for** répugnance *f* pour [*person, regime, activity, idea*].

distasteful /dɪsˈteɪstfl/ *adj* aussi euph déplaisant; (markedly) répugnant; **to be ~ to sb** [*idea, incident, sight*] déplaire à qn; [*person*] être désagréable à qn; **I find the remark ~** je trouve cette réflexion de mauvais goût.

distemper /dɪˈstempə(r)/ **I** *n* **1** Vet, Zool (in dogs) maladie *f* de Carré; (in horses) angine *f* des chevaux; **2** (paint) détrempe *f*; **3** Art (technique) peinture *f* à la détrempe.
II *vtr* peindre à la détrempe.

distend /dɪˈstend/ **I** *vtr* distendre.
II *vi* se distendre.
III distended *pp adj* **~ed stomach** ventre ballonné; **~ed bladder** vessie distendue.

distension, **distention** US /dɪˈstenʃn/ *n* Med distension *f*.

distich /ˈdɪstɪk/ *n* distique *m*.

distil GB, **distill** US /dɪˈstɪl/ **I** *vtr* (*p prés etc* **-ll-** GB) **1** (purify) distiller [*liquid*]; **to ~ sth from sth** extraire qch par distillation de qch; **2** (make) distiller [*alcohol*] (**from** à partir de); **3** sout (cull) distiller [*thought, wisdom*]; **to ~ sth from** extraire qch de.
II *vi* (*p prés etc* **-ll-** GB) (all contexts) distiller.
III distilled *pp adj* [*knowledge, wisdom*] accumulé.
■ **distil off**: **~ off [sth]** éliminer [qch] par distillation.

distillation /ˌdɪstɪˈleɪʃn/ *n* **1** (of liquids) distillation *f*; **2** (of emotions, images, ideas) condensé *m*.

distilled water *n* eau *f* distillée.

distiller /dɪˈstɪlə(r)/ *n* distillateur *m*.

distillery /dɪˈstɪlərɪ/ *n* distillerie *f*.

distinct /dɪˈstɪŋkt/ *adj* **1** [*image, object*] (not blurred) net/nette; (easily visible) distinct; **2** (definite) [*resemblance, preference, progress, impression, memory*] net/nette; [*possibility, advantage, improvement*] indéniable; **3** (separable) distinct (**from** de); **4** (different) différent (**from** de); **X, as ~ from Y** X, par opposition à Y.

distinction /dɪˈstɪŋkʃn/ *n* **1** (differentiation) distinction *f*; **a fine ~** une distinction subtile; **to make** ou **draw a ~ between A and B** faire une distinction entre A et B; **the ~ of A from B** la distinction de A et de B; **class ~** distinction *f* de niveau social; **2** (difference) différence *f* (**between** entre); **to blur the ~ between** estomper la différence entre; **3** (pre-eminence) mérite *m*; **with ~** avec mérite; **of ~** réputé; **to win ~** se distinguer; **to have the ~ of doing** (have the honour) avoir le mérite de faire; (to be the only one) avoir la particularité de faire; **4** (elegance) distinction *f*; **a woman of great ~** une femme d'une grande distinction; **5** (specific honour) distinction *f*; **to win a ~ for bravery** être décoré pour acte d'héroïsme; **6** Mus, Sch, Univ mention *f* très bien; **with ~** avec mention très bien.

distinctive /dɪˈstɪŋktɪv/ *adj* **1** gen caractéristique (**of** de); **2** Ling [*feature*] pertinent.

distinctly /dɪˈstɪŋktlɪ/ *adv* **1** [*speak, hear, see*] distinctement; [*remember*] nettement; [*say, tell*] explicitement; **2** (very noticeably) [*possible, embarrassing, odd*] vraiment.

distinguish /dɪˈstɪŋgwɪʃ/ **I** *vtr* **1** (see, hear) distinguer; **2** (mark out, separate) distinguer (**from** de; **between** entre); **to be ~ed from** se distinguer de; **to be ~ed by** se caractériser par; **to ~ one from another** distinguer l'un de l'autre.
II *v refl* **to ~ oneself** aussi iron se distinguer (**as** en tant que; **in** dans; **by doing** en faisant).
III distinguishing *pres p adj* [*factor, feature, mark*] distinctif/-ive; **~ing marks** (on passport) signes *mpl* particuliers; Zool caractéristiques *fpl*.

distinguishable /dɪˈstɪŋgwɪʃəbl/ *adj* **1** (able to be told apart) que l'on peut distinguer (**from** de); **the two cars are not easily ~** il est difficile de distinguer les deux voitures; **2** (visible) visible; **3** (audible) perceptible.

distinguished /dɪˈstɪŋgwɪʃt/ *adj* **1** (elegant) distingué; **~-looking** à l'air distingué; **2** (famous) éminent.

distort /dɪˈstɔːt/ **I** *vtr* **1** (misrepresent) dénaturer [*statement, opinion, fact, understanding*]; déformer [*truth*]; fausser [*assessment*]; falsifier [*history*]; **2** (skew) fausser [*figures, competition*]; **3** (physically) déformer [*vision, features, sound, metal*].
II *vi* [*metal*] se déformer.
III distorted *pp adj* **1** (skewed) [*report, interpretation*] dénaturé; [*figures*] faussé; **2** (twisted) [*face, features*] déformé; [*structure, metal*] tordu; [*image, sound*] déformé.

distortion /dɪˈstɔːʃn/ *n* **1** (of truth, reality, opinion, facts) déformation *f*; **2** (of figures) distorsion *f*; **3** (physical) (of metal) déformation *f*; (of sound) distorsion *f*; (of features) distorsion *f*; **4** (visual) distorsion *f*.

distract /dɪˈstrækt/ *vtr* **1** (break concentration) distraire [*driver, player, worker*]; **to be (easily) ~ed by** se laisser (facilement) distraire par; **to ~ sb from sth** distraire ou détourner qn de qch; **to ~ sb from doing** empêcher qn de faire; **I was ~ed by the noise** le bruit m'a empêché de me concentrer; **2** (divert) **to ~ attention** détourner l'attention (**from** de); **to ~ sb's attention** détourner l'attention de qn (**from** de); **3** (amuse) distraire.

distracted /dɪˈstræktɪd/ *adj* **1** (anxious) affolé; **~ with** fou/folle de [*grief, worry*]; **2** (abstracted) [*look*] égaré; **3†** (mad) fou/folle.

distractedly /dɪˈstræktɪdlɪ/ *adv* **1** [*look, wander*] d'un air égaré; **2** [*run, weep*] comme un fou/une folle; **to love sb ~** aimer qn à la folie.

distracting /dɪˈstræktɪŋ/ *adj* [*sound, presence, flicker*] gênant; **I found the noise too ~** le bruit m'empêchait de me concentrer.

distraction /dɪˈstrækʃn/ *n* **1** (from concentration) distraction *f*; **I don't want any ~s** (environmental) je ne veux pas être distrait; (human) je ne veux pas qu'on me dérange; **2** (being distracted) inattention *f*; **a moment's ~** un moment d'inattention; **3** (diversion) diversion *f*; **to be a ~ from** détourner l'attention de [*problem, priority*]; **4** (entertainment) distraction *f*; **a ~ from** un dérivatif à; **to come as a welcome ~ from** être un dérivatif agréable à; **5†** (madness) folie *f*; **to drive sb to ~** rendre qn fou/folle; **to love sb to ~** aimer qn à la folie.

distrain /dɪˈstreɪn/ *vi* Jur **to ~ upon sb** saisir les biens de qn; **to ~ upon sb's goods** opérer la saisie des biens de qn.

distraint /dɪˈstreɪnt/ *n* saisie-exécution *f*.

distraught /dɪˈstrɔːt/ *adj* [*person*] éperdu (**with** de); **to be ~ at** ou **over sth** être bouleversé par qch; **they were ~ to learn that** ils ont été bouleversés d'apprendre que.

distress /dɪˈstres/ **I** *n* **1** (anguish) désarroi *m*, affliction *f*; **to be in ~** être complètement bouleversé, être désemparé; (stronger) être dans un grand désarroi; **to cause sb ~** faire de la peine à qn; **in his ~** dans son désarroi; **to my/his ~, they...** à mon/son grand chagrin, ils...; **2** (physical trouble) souffrance(s) *f(pl)*; **to be in ~** aller très mal; **foetal ~** Med souffrance *f* fœtale; **3** (poverty) détresse *f*; **in ~** [*person*] dans la détresse; **4** Naut **in ~** en détresse; **5** Jur saisie *f*.
II *vtr* faire de la peine à [*person*] (**to do** de faire) ; (stronger) bouleverser [*person*] (**to do** de faire).
III *v refl* **to ~ oneself** s'inquiéter.

distress call *n* appel *m* de détresse.

distressed /dɪˈstrest/ *adj* **1** (upset) [*person*] peiné (**at, by** par; **to do** de faire); (stronger) bouleversé (**at, by** par; **to do** de faire); **to be ~ that** être peiné que (+ *subj*); **in a ~ state** dans un état de détresse; **2** (poor) [*area*] pauvre; **in ~ circumstances** sout dans une extrême pauvreté; **~ gentlewomen†** femmes *fpl* de bonne famille dans le besoin; **3** (artificially aged) [*furniture*] vieilli artificiellement.

distressing /dɪˈstresɪŋ/ *adj* [*case, consequence, event, idea*] pénible; [*news*] navrant; [*sight*] affligeant; **it is ~ that** il est pénible que (+ *subj*); **it is/was ~ for him** il est/était pénible pour lui (**to do** de faire).

distress: **~ merchandise** *n* US marchandises *fpl* vendues à perte; **~ rocket** *n* fusée *f* de détresse; **~ sale** *n* Comm vente *f* au rabais; **~ signal** *n* signal *m* de détresse.

distributary /dɪˈstrɪbjʊtərɪ, US -terɪ/ *n* défluent *m*.

distribute /dɪˈstrɪbjuːt/ *vtr* **1** (share out) distribuer [*information, documents, supplies, money*] (**to** à; **among** entre); **2** Comm distribuer [*goods, books*]; **3** Cin distribuer [*films*]; **4** (spread out) répartir [*weight*, load, tax burden]; **5** (disperse) **to be ~d** [*flora, fauna, mineral deposits*] être réparti; **6** Journ, Print distribuer [*type*].

distribute: **~d data processing**, **DDP** *n* informatique *f* répartie; **~d system** *n* système *m* d'information réparti.

distribution /ˌdɪstrɪˈbjuːʃn/ **I** *n* **1** (sharing) (of funds, information, food, resources) distribution *f* (**to sb** à qn; **to sth** dans qch); **for ~ to schools** pour être distribué dans les écoles; **the ~ of wealth** Pol la répartition des richesses; **2** Comm, Cin distribution *f*; **3** (of flora, fauna, minerals) répartition *f*; **4** Stat répartition *f*; **5** (of weight, burden) répartition *f*.
II *modif* Comm, Econ [*channel, company, costs, network, system*] de distribution; Cin [*rights*] de distribution; Comput [*network*] de distribution.

distributor /dɪˈstrɪbjʊtə(r)/ *n* **1** Comm, Cin distributeur *m* (**for sth** de qch); **sole ~ for** concessionnaire *m* de; **2** Aut (engine part) distributeur *m*.

district /ˈdɪstrɪkt/ **I** *n* **1** (in country) région *f*; **2** (in city) quartier *m*; **3** (sector) (administrative) district *m*; US (electoral) circonscription *f* électorale; (postal) secteur *m* postal; **health ~** GB *circonscription des services de santé*.
II US Pol *vtr* découper [qch] en circonscriptions électorales.

district attorney *n* US représentant *m* du ministère public.

district council *n* GB ≈ conseil *m* général; **urban ~** conseil *m* de district urbain.

district: **~ court** *n* US cour *f* fédérale; **~ manager** *n* directeur/-trice *m/f* régional/-e; **~ nurse** *n* GB infirmière *f* visiteuse; **District of Columbia**, **DC** ▶ **1744** *pr n* District of Columbia *m*.

distrust /dɪsˈtrʌst/ **I** *n* méfiance *f* (**of** à l'égard de).
II *vtr* se méfier de [*person, motive, government*].

distrustful /dɪsˈtrʌstfl/ *adj* méfiant (**of** à l'égard de); **to be ~ of sb/sth** se méfier de qn/qch.

disturb /dɪˈstɜːb/ **I** *vtr* **1** (interrupt) déranger [*person, work, burglar*]; troubler [*silence, sleep*]; **'do not ~'** (on notice) 'ne pas déranger'; **2** (upset) troubler [*person*]; (concern) inquiéter [*person*]; **to ~ the peace** Jur troubler l'ordre public; **it ~s me that** cela m'inquiète que (+ *subj*); **they were ~ed to learn...** ils étaient troublés d'apprendre...; **3** (disarrange) déranger [*papers, bedclothes*]; troubler [*surface of water*]; remuer [*sediment*].
II *v refl* **to ~ oneself** (be inconvenienced) se déranger; **please don't ~ yourself on my account** ne vous dérangez pas pour moi.

disturbance /dɪˈstɜːbəns/ *n* **1** (interruption, inconvenience) dérangement *m*; **2** (riot) troubles *mpl*, émeute *f*; (fight) altercation *f*; **to cause a ~ of the peace** troubler l'ordre public; **3** Meteorol perturbation *f*; **4** Psych trouble *m*; (more serious) perturbation *f*.

disturbed /dɪˈstɜːbd/ *adj* **1** Psych perturbé; **emotionally ~** qui a des troubles psychologiques; **mentally ~** dérangé; **2** (concerned) (*jamais épith*) inquiété (**by** par; **to do** de faire); **3** (restless) [*sleep, night*] agité.

disturbing /dɪˈstɜːbɪŋ/ *adj* [*book, film, painting*] dérangeant, troublant; [*report, increase,* *development*] inquiétant; (stronger) alarmant; **it is ~ that** il est inquiétant que (+ *subj*); **it is ~ to see/hear...** il est inquiétant de voir/d'entendre...

disturbingly /dɪˈstɜːbɪŋlɪ/ *adv* **the quality is ~ low** ce qui est inquiétant, c'est la mauvaise qualité; **~, unemployment has risen** le chômage a augmenté de façon inquiétante; **~ for them/the team, they lost again** ce qui était inquiétant pour eux/les joueurs de l'équipe c'est qu'ils avaient encore perdu.

disunite /ˌdɪsjuːˈnaɪt/ sout **I** *vtr* désunir.
II disunited *pp adj* désuni.

disunity /dɪsˈjuːnətɪ/ *n* sout désunion *f*.

disuse /dɪsˈjuːs/ *n* (of machinery) abandon *m*; **to be in ~** [*plant, buildings*] être à l'abandon; **to fall into ~** [*plant, building*] être laissé à l'abandon; [*practice, tradition*] tomber en désuétude.

disused /dɪsˈjuːzd/ *adj* abandonné, désaffecté.

disyllabic /daɪsɪˈlæbɪk, dɪ-/ *n, adj* dissyllabe (*m*).

ditch /dɪtʃ/ **I** *n* fossé *m*.
II○ *vtr* **1** (get rid of) laisser tomber [*friend, ally*]; virer○ [*employee*]; abandonner [*system, agreement, machine*]; plaquer○ [*girlfriend, boyfriend*]; **2** US (evade) échapper à [*police*]; **to ~ school** faire l'école buissonnière; **3** (crash-land) **to ~ a plane** faire un amerrissage forcé; **4** US (crash) emboutir○ [*voiture*].
III *vi* faire un amerrissage forcé.

ditchdigger /ˈdɪtʃdɪgə(r)/ *n* US terrassier *m*.

ditcher /ˈdɪtʃə(r)/ *n* terrassier *m*.

ditching /ˈdɪtʃɪŋ/ *n* **1** Agric (digging) creusement *m* des fossés; (maintenance) curage *m* des fossés; **hedging and ~** entretien *m* des haies et fossés; **2** Aviat amerrissage *m* forcé.

ditchwater /ˈdɪtʃwɔːtə(r)/ *n*: IDIOMS **as dull as ~** ennuyeux comme la pluie.

dither /ˈdɪðə(r)/ **I**○ *n* (*sans pl*) **to be in a ~, to be all of a ~** être dans tous ses états.
II *vi* tergiverser (**about, over** sur); **stop ~ing!** arrête de tergiverser!; **she's not one to ~** elle n'est pas du genre à se poser des questions.

ditherer /ˈdɪðərə(r)/ *n* péj indécis/-e *m/f*.

ditsy○, **ditzy**○ /ˈdɪtsɪ/ *adj* US péj [*woman*] évaporé.

ditto /ˈdɪtəʊ/ **I** *n* US copie *f*.
II○ *adv* idem; **the food is awful and ~ the nightlife** la nourriture est affreuse la vie nocturne idem; **'I'm fed up○'—'~'** 'j'en ai marre○'—'moi aussi'.
III *vtr* US polycopier.

ditto marks *npl* guillemets *mpl* de répétition.

ditty† /ˈdɪtɪ/ *n* chansonnette *f*.

diuretic /ˌdaɪjʊˈretɪk/ *n, adj* diurétique (*m*).

diurnal /daɪˈɜːnl/ *adj* diurne.

diva /ˈdiːvə/ *n* (*pl* **~s** ou **~e**) diva *f*.

divan /dɪˈvæn, US ˈdaɪvæn/ *n* divan *m*.

divan bed *n* divan-lit *m*.

dive /daɪv/ **I** *n* **1** gen, Sport (plunge into water) plongeon *m*; **2** (swimming under sea) plongée *f* sous-marine; **to be on a ~** être en plongée; **3** (descent) (of plane, bird) piqué *m*; **to pull out of a ~** sortir d'un piqué; **to take a ~** fig [*prices*] chuter; **the party's fortunes have taken a ~** le destin du parti a basculé; **4** (lunge) **to make a ~ for sth** foncer vers qch; **5**○ (deliberate fall) (in fixed fight) **to take a ~** aller au tapis; (in football) **that was a ~!** c'est du chiqué○!; **6**○ péj (bar, club) tripot○ *m*.
II *vi* (*prét* **~d** GB, **dove** US) **1** gen, Sport (into water) plonger (**off, from** de; **into** dans; **down to** jusqu'à); **2** [*plane, bird*] plonger, descendre en piqué (**from** de); **3** (go diving) (as hobby) faire de la plongée; (as job) être plongeur; **4** (lunge, throw oneself) **to ~ into the bushes/under the bed** plonger dans les buissons/sous le lit; **to ~ into a bar/shop** s'engouffrer dans un bar/un magasin; **he ~d into his pocket and produced some money** il a plongé la main dans sa poche et a sorti de l'argent.
■ **dive for**: **~ for [sth] 1** [*diver*] pêcher [*pearls, coral*]; **2** [*player*] plonger sur [*ball*]; **3** [*person*] foncer vers [*exit, door*]; **to ~ for cover** foncer à l'abri.
■ **dive in 1** lit plonger; **2** fig (act impulsively) se lancer○.

dive: **~-bomb** *vtr* Mil bombarder [qch] en piqué; (in swimming pool) faire la bombe; **~-bomber** *n* bombardier *m*; **~-bombing** *n* bombardement *m* en piqué.

diver /ˈdaɪvə(r)/ ▶ **1692** *n* **1** (for sport or in flippers) plongeur/-euse *m/f*; **2** (deep-sea) scaphandrier *m*; **3** Zool (species of bird) plongeon *m*; (diving bird generally) plongeur *m*.

diverge /daɪˈvɜːdʒ/ *vi* **1** [*interests, opinions, experiences*] diverger; **2 to ~ from** s'écarter de [*truth, norm, belief, stance*]; **3** [*railway line, road*] se séparer (**from** de); **their paths ~d** fig leurs chemins ont divergé.

divergence /daɪˈvɜːdʒəns/ *n* divergence *f* (**between** entre).

divergent /daɪˈvɜːdʒənt/ *adj* divergent; **~ thinking** raisonnement *m* divergent.

divers† /ˈdaɪvəz/ *adj* littér divers.

diverse /daɪˈvɜːs/ *adj* **1** (varied) divers; **2** (different) différent.

diversification /daɪˌvɜːsɪfɪˈkeɪʃn/ *n* diversification *f*.

diversify /daɪˈvɜːsɪfaɪ/ **I** *vtr* diversifier.
II *vi* se diversifier.

diversion /daɪˈvɜːʃn, US daɪˈvɜːrʒn/ *n* **1** (redirection) (of watercourse, money) détournement *m*; (of traffic) déviation *f*; **~ of funds** Fin Jur détournement *m* de fonds; **2** (distraction, break) diversion *f* (**from** à); **to create a ~** faire diversion; Mil opérer une diversion; **3** GB (detour) déviation *f*; **4**† (entertainment) divertissement *m*.

diversionary /daɪˈvɜːʃənərɪ, US daɪˈvɜːrʒənerɪ/ *adj* [*tactic, attack, manoeuvre*] de diversion; [*argument, laughter*] destiné à faire diversion.

diversion sign *n* GB panneau *m* de déviation.

diversity /daɪˈvɜːsətɪ/ *n* diversité *f* (**of** de).

divert /daɪˈvɜːt/ **I** *vtr* **1** (redirect) détourner [*watercourse, flow*]; dévier [*traffic*] (**onto** vers; **through** par); dérouter [*flight, plane*] (**to** sur); détourner [*resources, supplies, funds, manpower*] (**from** de; **to** au profit de); **to ~ funds** Fin Jur détourner des fonds; **2** (distract) détourner [*attention, efforts, conversation*] (**from** de); détourner [*person, government, team*] (**from** de); **3**† (amuse) divertir.
II *vi* **to ~ to** se détourner sur.

diverting /daɪˈvɜːtɪŋ/ *adj* divertissant.

divest /daɪˈvest/ sout **I** *vtr* **to ~ sb of sth** (of power, rights etc) dépouiller qn de qch; (of robes, regalia) ôter qch à qn.
II *v refl* **to ~ oneself of** se débarrasser de [*robes, regalia*]; se défaire de [*ideas, beliefs*]; Comm, Fin se défaire de [*asset, subsidiary*].

divestiture /daɪˈvestʃə(r)/, **divestment** /daɪˈvestmənt/ *n* dessaisissement *m*.

divide /dɪˈvaɪd/ **I** *n* **1** (split) division *f* (**between** entre); **the North-South ~** l'opposition Nord-Sud; **2** (watershed) fig démarcation *f* (**between** entre); lit Geog ligne *f* de partage des eaux.
II *vtr* **1** (split up into parts) partager [*area, food, money, time, work*]; diviser [*class, house, room*] (**into** en); **to ~ the house into flats/the class into three groups** diviser la maison en appartements/la classe en trois groupes; **he ~d the pupils into boys and girls** il a séparé les garçons des filles; **2** (share) partager (**between** entre); **he ~s his time** ou **attention between home and office** il partage son temps entre la maison et le bureau; **they ~d the profits among themselves** ils ont partagé les bénéfices; **3** (separate) séparer (**from** de); **4** (cause disagreement) diviser [*friends, management, nation, party*]; **~ and rule** diviser pour régner; **5** GB Pol faire voter [*House*]; **6** Math diviser [*number*]; **to ~ 2 into 14** ou **to ~ 14 by 2** diviser 14 par 2; **will 14 ~ by 2?** est-ce que 14 est divisible par 2?
III *vi* **1** lit [*road, river, train*] se séparer en deux; [*group*] se répartir; [*crowd*] s'écarter; [*cell, organism*] se diviser; **2** GB Pol [*House*] voter; **3** Math être divisible.
IV divided *pp adj* [*party, government, society*] divisé; [*interests, opinions*] divergent; **~d highway** US route *f* à quatre voies; **the party is ~d on the issue** le parti est divisé sur la question.
IDIOMS **to cross the great ~** (death) faire le grand saut.
■ **divide off**: **~ [sth] off, ~ off [sth]** séparer (**from** de).
■ **divide out**: **~ [sth] out, ~ out [sth]** distribuer.
■ **divide up**: **~ [sth] up, ~ up [sth]** partager (**among** entre).

divided skirt *n* jupe-culotte *f*.

dividend /ˈdɪvɪdend/ *n* **1** Fin (share) dividende *m*; **final ~** dividende *m* annuel; **to raise/pass the ~** augmenter/ approuver le dividende; **to pay ~s** lit, fig rapporter; **2** fig (bonus) avantage *m*; **peace ~** Pol dividendes *mpl* de la paix; **3** Math dividende *m*; **4** (in football pools) gains *mpl*.

dividend: **~ cover** *n* marge *f* de dividende; **~ yield** *n* rendement *m* d'une action.

divider /dɪˈvaɪdə(r)/ *n* (in room) cloison *f*; (in file) intercalaire *m*.

dividers /dɪˈvaɪdəz/ *npl* compas *m* à pointes sèches.

dividing /dɪˈvaɪdɪŋ/ *adj* [*wall, fence*] mitoyen/-enne.

dividing: **~ line** *n* ligne *f* de démarcation (**between** entre); **~ point** *n* point *m* de divergence.

divination /ˌdɪvɪˈneɪʃn/ *n* divination *f*.

divine /dɪˈvaɪn/ **I** *n* **1** (also **Divine**) (God) **the ~** le divin *m*; **2** (priest) ecclésiastique *m*.
II *adj* **1** [*inspiration, retribution, service, intervention*] divin (*after n*); **~ providence** la divine Providence; **2**○ (wonderful) divin.
III *vtr* **1** littér (intuit) deviner; **2** (dowse) découvrir [qch] par la radiesthésie.

divinely /dɪˈvaɪnlɪ/ *adv* **1** (by God) [*revealed*] divinement; **to be ~ inspired** [*texts*] être d'inspiration divine; [*prophet*] être inspiré par Dieu; **a ~ ordained event** un événement résultant de la volonté divine; **2**○ (wonderfully) [*dance, smile*] divinement; **~ simple** d'une simplicité divine.

diviner /dɪˈvaɪnə(r)/ *n* gen radiesthésiste *mf*; (for water only) sourcier/-ière *m/f*.

divine right *n* droit *m* divin.

diving /ˈdaɪvɪŋ/ **I** *n* **1** (from a board) plongeon *m*; **2** (swimming under the sea) plongée *f* sous-marine; **to go ~** faire de la plongée sous-marine.
II *modif* [*club, equipment, gear, helmet*] de plongée.

diving: **~ bell** *n* cloche *f* à plongeur; **~ board** *n* plongeoir *m*; **~ suit** *n* scaphandre *m*.

divining rod *n* baguette *f* de sourcier.

divinity /dɪˈvɪnətɪ/ *n* **1** (of deity, person) divinité *f*; **2** (deity) divinité *f*; **the Divinity** la Divinité; **3** (theology) théologie *f*.

divisible /dɪˈvɪzəbl/ *adj* divisible (**by** par).

division /dɪˈvɪʒn/ *n* **1** (splitting) gen, Biol, Bot, Math division *f* (**into** en); **2** (sharing) (of one thing) répartition *f*; (of several things) distribution *f*; **3** Mil, Naut division *f*; Admin circonscription *f*; **4** Comm (branch, sector) division *f*; (department, team) service *m*; **chemicals ~** division chimique; **sales ~** service des ventes; **5** (in football) division *f*; **to be in ~ one** ou **in the first ~** être en première division; **a second ~ club** un club de deuxième division; **6** (dissent) désaccord *m* (**between** entre); **7** (in container) compartiment *m*; **8** GB Pol vote *m*; **to claim a ~** demander la mise aux voix; **9** US Univ faculté *f*.

divisional /dɪˈvɪʒənl/ *adj* [*commander, officer*] Mil divisionnaire; [*championship*] Sport de division.

Divisional Court *n* GB Jur tribunal *m* composé de deux juges ou plus qui se prononcent sur les appels.

division: **~ bell** *n* GB Pol sonnerie *f* qui annonce la mise aux voix; **~ of labour** *n* division *f* du travail; **~ sign** *n* signe *m* de division.

divisive /dɪˈvaɪsɪv/ *adj* [*measure, policy*] qui sème la discorde; **to be socially/racially ~** semer la discorde sociale/raciale.

divisor /dɪˈvaɪzə(r)/ *n* diviseur *m*.

divorce /dɪˈvɔːs/ **I** *n* lit, fig divorce *m* (**from** avec; **between** entre); **she's asked me for a ~** elle m'a dit qu'elle veut divorcer; **to file for ~, to sue for ~** Jur intenter une action en divorce; **to grant a ~** Jur prononcer le divorce.
II *vtr* **1** lit **to ~** divorcer de or d'avec [*husband, wife*]; **she ~d him, she was ~d from him** elle a divorcé; **they were ~d in 1987** ils ont divorcé en 1987; **2** fig dissocier (**from** de); **to ~ science from morality** dissocier la science de la morale; **~d from reality** détaché de la réalité.
III *vi* divorcer.

divorce court *n*: *tribunal chargé des affaires matrimoniales.*

divorcee /dɪˌvɔːˈsiː/ *n* divorcé/-e *m/f*.

divorce proceedings *n* procédure *f* de divorce; **to start ~** intenter une action en divorce.

divorce settlement *n* (conditions) conditions *fpl* de divorce; (sum of money) ≈ pension *f* alimentaire.

divot /ˈdɪvət/ *n* motte *f* de gazon.

divulge /daɪˈvʌldʒ/ *vtr* divulguer (**that** que; **to** à).

divvy○† /ˈdɪvɪ/ *n* GB (*abrév* = **dividend**) dividende *m*.
■ **divvy up**: **~ [sth] up, ~ up [sth]** répartir.

dixie /ˈdɪksɪ/ *n* GB Mil gamelle *f*.

Dixie /ˈdɪksɪ/ *pr n* (also **~land**) États *mpl* du sud des États-Unis.
IDIOMS **I'm not just whistling ~** US je ne plaisante pas.

Dixie: **~ cup**® *n* US gobelet *m* en carton; **~land jazz** *n* dixieland *m*.

DIY GB *n*: *abrév* ▸ **do-it-yourself**.

dizzily /ˈdɪzɪlɪ/ *adv* [*stagger, reel*] pris de vertige; [*rise, spiral*] vertigineusement.

dizziness /ˈdɪzɪnɪs/ *n* ¢ vertiges *mpl*; **to suffer from ~** souffrir de vertiges.

dizzy /ˈdɪzɪ/ **I** *adj* **1** (physically) pris de vertige; **to make sb ~** donner le vertige à qn; **to suffer from ~ spells** avoir des vertiges; **to feel ~** avoir la tête qui tourne; **2** (mentally) **to be ~ with** être ivre de [*delight, surprise*]; **3** [*height, spell*] vertigineux/-euse; **4** (scatterbrained) écervelé.
II *vtr* littér donner le vertige à [*person*].
III dizzying *pres p adj* [*height, drop*] vertigineux/-euse.

DJ *n* **1** (*abrév* = **disc jockey**) DJ; **2** GB *abrév* ▸ **dinner jacket**.

Djibouti /dʒɪˈbuːtɪ/ ▸ **1131** *pr n* Djibouti *m*.

DMA *n*: *abrév* ▸ **direct memory access**.

DMZ *n* (*abrév* = **demilitarized zone**) zone *f* démilitarisée.

DNA **I** *n* (*abrév* = **deoxyribonucleic acid**) ADN *m*.
II *modif* [*test, testing*] de l'empreinte *f* génétique; [*molecule, synthetizer*] d'ADN.

D-notice *n* GB Pol, Journ *circulaire ministérielle portant interdiction de publier pour cause de secret défense.*

do[1] /duː, də/ **I** *vtr* (*prét* **did**, *pp* **done**) **1** (perform task, be busy) faire [*washing up, ironing etc*]; **lots/nothing to ~** beaucoup/rien à faire; **it all had to be done again** il a fallu tout refaire; **what are you ~ing?** qu'est-ce que tu fais?; **are you ~ing anything tonight?** tu fais quelque chose ce soir?; **she's been ~ing too much lately** elle en fait trop ces derniers temps; **she does nothing but moan** elle ne fait que se plaindre; **what can I ~ for you?** que puis-je faire pour vous?; **will you ~ something for me?** peux-tu me rendre un service?; **2** (make smart) **to ~ sb's hair** coiffer qn; **to ~ one's teeth** se laver les dents; **to ~ the living room in pink** peindre le salon en rose; **3** (finish) faire [*military service, period of time*]; finir [*job*]; **I've already done three months** j'ai déjà fait trois mois; **the job's almost done** le travail est presque fini; **to have done**○ **doing sth** avoir fini de faire qch; **have you done**○ **complaining?** tu as fini de te plaindre?; **tell him now and have done with it** dis-lui maintenant, ce sera fait; **it's as good as done** c'est comme si c'était fait; **that's done it** (task successfully completed) ça y est; (expressing dismay) il ne manquait plus que ça; **4** (complete through study) [*student*] faire [*subject, book, author, degree, homework*]; **5** (write) faire [*translation, critique, biography*]; **6** (effect change) faire; **to ~ sb good/harm** faire du bien/mal à qn; **what have you done to the kitchen?** qu'est-ce que vous avez fait à la cuisine?; **has she done something to her hair?** est-ce qu'elle a fait quelque chose à ses cheveux?; **I haven't done anything with your pen!** je n'ai pas touché à ton stylo!; **what are we to ~ with you!** qu'allons-nous faire de toi!; **that hat/dress etc does a lot for her** ce chapeau/cette robe etc lui va bien; **7** (cause harm) faire; **to ~ something to one's foot/arm** se faire mal au pied/bras; **I won't ~ anything to you** je ne te ferai rien; **I'll ~**○ **you!** ça va être ta fête!; **8**○ (deal with) **the hairdresser says she can ~ you now** la coiffeuse dit qu'elle peut vous prendre maintenant; **they don't ~ theatre tickets** ils ne vendent pas de places de théâtre; **to ~ breakfasts** servir des petits déjeuners; **9** (cook) faire [*sausages, spaghetti etc*]; **I'll ~ you an omelette** je te ferai une omelette; **well done** [*meat*] bien cuit; **10** (prepare) préparer [*vegetables*]; **11** (produce) monter [*play*]; faire [*film, programme*] (**on** sur); **12** (imitate) imiter [*celebrity, voice, mannerism*]; **13** (travel at) faire; **to ~ 60** faire du 60 à l'heure; **14** (cover distance of) faire; **we've done 30 km since lunch** nous avons fait 30 km depuis le déjeuner; **15**○ (see as tourist) faire [*Venice, the Louvre etc*]; **16**○ (satisfy needs of) **will this ~ you?** ça vous ira?; **17**○ (cheat) **we've been done** on s'est fait avoir; **to ~ sb out of** escroquer qn de [*money*]; **he did me out of the job** il m'a pris la place; **18**○ (sterilize) **to be done** [*person, animal*] être stérilisé; **19**○ (rob) **to ~ a bank** faire un casse○ dans une banque; **20**○ (arrest, convict) **to get done for** se faire prendre pour [*illegal parking etc*]; **to ~ sb for speeding** prendre qn pour excès de vitesse.
II *vi* (*prét* **did**, *pp* **done**) **1** (behave) faire; **'~ as you're told'** (here and now) fais ce que je te dis; (when with others) fais ce qu'on te dit; **2** (serve purpose) faire l'affaire; **that box/those trousers will ~** cette boîte/ce pantalon fera l'affaire; **3** (be acceptable) **this really won't ~!** (as reprimand) ça ne peut pas continuer comme ça!; **4** (be sufficient) suffire; **will five dollars ~?** cinq dollars, ça suffira?; **that'll ~!** (as reprimand) ça suffit!; **5** (finish) finir; **have you done?** tu as fini?; **6** (get on) (in competitive situation) [*person*] s'en sortir; [*business*] marcher; (in health) [*person*] aller; **how will they ~ in the elections?** comment est-ce qu'ils s'en sortiront aux élections?; **he's ~ing as well as can be expected** (of patient) il va aussi bien que possible; **my lettuces are ~ing well** mes laitues poussent bien; **7** GB ○†(clean) faire le ménage; **the woman who does for us** la dame qui fait le ménage pour nous; **8**○ GB (be active) **you'll be up and ~ing again in no time** tu seras sur pied très vite.
III *v aux* (*prét* **did**, *pp* **done**) **1** (with questions, negatives) **did he like his present?** est-ce qu'il a aimé son cadeau?; **own up, did you or didn't you take my pen?** avoue, est-ce que c'est que tu as pris mon stylo ou pas?; **didn't he look wonderful!** est-ce qu'il n'était pas merveilleux!; **2** (for emphasis) **he did ~ it really!** il l'a vraiment fait!; **so you ~ want to go after all!** alors tu veux vraiment y aller finalement!; **I ~ wish you'd let me help you** j'aimerais tant que tu me laisses t'aider; **3** (referring back to another verb) **he said he'd tell her and he did** il a dit qu'il le lui dirait et il l'a fait; **he says he'll come along but he never does** il dit toujours qu'il viendra mais il ne le fait jamais; **you draw better than I ~** tu dessines mieux que moi; **you either did or you didn't** de deux choses l'une soit tu l'as fait, soit tu ne l'as pas fait; **4** (in requests, imperatives) **~ sit down** asseyez-vous, je vous en prie; **'may I take a leaflet?'—'~'** 'puis-je prendre un dépliant?'—'je vous en prie'; **~ shut up!** tais-toi veux-tu!; **don't you tell me what to do!** surtout ne me dis pas ce que j'ai à faire!; **5** (in tag questions and responses) **he lives in France, doesn't he?** il habite en France, n'est-ce pas?; **'who wrote it?'—'I did'** 'qui l'a écrit?'—'moi'; **'shall I tell him?'—'no don't'** 'est-ce que je le lui dis?'—'non surtout pas'; **'he knows the President'—'does he?'** 'il connaît le Président'—'vraiment?'; **so ~ they/you** eux/vous aussi; **neither does he/she etc** lui/elle etc non plus; **6** (with inversion) **only rarely does he write letters** c'est très rare qu'il écrive des lettres; **little did he suspect/think that** il était loin de se douter/de penser que.
IV○ *n* GB fête *f*; **his leaving ~** son pot○ de départ.
IDIOMS **~ as you would be done by** ne faites pas ce que vous ne voudriez pas qu'on vous fasse; **how ~ you ~** enchanté; **it doesn't ~ to be** ce n'est pas une bonne chose d'être; **it's a poor ~**○ **if** c'est vraiment grave si; **it was all I could ~ not to...** je me suis retenu pour ne pas...; **nothing ~ing !** (no way) pas question!; **there's nothing ~ing here** ici il ne se passe rien; **well done!** bravo!; **what are you ~ing with yourself these days?** qu'est-ce que tu deviens?; **what are you going to ~ for...?** comment est-ce que tu vas te débrouiller pour...? [*money, shelter etc*]; **what's done is done** ce qui est fait est fait; **what's this doing here?** qu'est-ce que ça fait ici?; **all the ~s and don'ts** tout ce qu'il faut/fallait faire et ne pas faire.
■ **do away with**: ¶ **~ away with [sth]** se débarrasser de [*procedure, custom, rule, feature*]; supprimer [*bus service etc*]; démolir [*building*]; ¶ **~ away with [sb]**○ (kill) se débarrasser de [*person*].
■ **do down**○ GB: **~ [sb] down** dire du mal de [*person*]; **don't ~ yourself down** ne te sous-estime pas.
■ **do for**○: **~ for [sb/sth]** (kill) [*illness*] achever [*person*]; fig mettre fin à [*ambition, project*]; **I'm done for** fig je suis foutu○.
■ **do in**○: **~ [sb] in 1** (kill) tuer; **2** (exhaust) épuiser; **I feel done in** je suis crevé○.
■ **do out**○: **~ [sth] out, ~ out [sth]** faire or nettoyer à fond [*spare room, garage*].
■ **do over**: ¶ **~ [sth] over** US (redo) refaire [*job, work*]; ¶ **~ [sb] over**○ passer [qn] à tabac○.
■ **do up**: ¶ **~ up** [*dress, coat*] se fermer; ¶ **~ [sth] up, ~ up [sth] 1** (fasten) refaire [*laces*]; fermer [*zip*]; **~ up your buttons** boutonne-toi; **2** (wrap) faire [*parcel*]; **to ~ one's hair up into a bun** se remonter les cheveux en chignon; **3** (renovate) restaurer [*house, furniture*]; ¶ **~ oneself up** se faire beau/belle; **I was all done up** je m'étais fait tout beau.
■ **do with**: **~ with [sth/sb] 1** (involve) **it**

do¹

The direct French equivalent of the verb *to do* in *subject + to do + object* sentences is *faire*:

she's doing her homework = elle fait ses devoirs
what are you doing? = qu'est-ce que tu fais?
what has he done with the newspaper? = qu'est-ce qu'il a fait du journal?

faire functions in very much the same way as *to do* does in English and it is safe to assume it will work in the great majority of cases. For the conjugation of the verb *faire*, see the French verb tables.

Grammatical functions

In questions

In French there is no use of an auxiliary verb in questions equivalent to the use of *do* in English.

When the subject is a pronoun, the question is formed in French either by inverting the subject and verb and putting a hyphen between the two (*veux-tu?*) or by prefacing the *subject + verb* by *est-ce que* (literally *is it that*):

do you like Mozart? = aimes-tu Mozart? *or* est-ce que tu aimes Mozart?
did you put the glasses in the cupboard? = as-tu mis les verres dans le placard? *or* est-ce que tu as mis les verres dans le placard?

When the subject is a noun there are again two possibilities:

did your sister ring? = est-ce que ta sœur a téléphoné? *or* ta sœur a-t-elle téléphoné?
did Max find his keys? = est-ce que Max a trouvé ses clés? *or* Max a-t-il trouvé ses clés?

In negatives

Equally, auxiliaries are not used in negatives in French:

I don't like Mozart = je n'aime pas Mozart
you didn't feed the cat = tu n'as pas donné à manger au chat
don't do that! = ne fais pas ça!

In emphatic uses

There is no verbal equivalent for the use of *do* in such expressions as *I DO like your dress*. A French speaker will find another way, according to the context, of expressing the force of the English *do*. Here are a few useful examples:

I DO like your dress = j'aime beaucoup ta robe
I DO hope she remembers = j'espère qu'elle n'oubliera pas
I DO think you should see a doctor = je crois vraiment que tu devrais voir un médecin

When referring back to another verb

In this case the verb *to do* is not translated at all:

I don't like him any more than you do = je ne l'aime pas plus que toi
I live in Oxford and so does Lily = j'habite à Oxford et Lily aussi
she gets paid more than I do = elle est payée plus que moi
I haven't written as much as I ought to have done = je n'ai pas écrit autant que j'aurais dû
'I love strawberries' 'so do I' = 'j'adore les fraises' 'moi aussi'

In polite requests

In polite requests the phrase *je vous en prie* can often be used to render the meaning of *do*:

do sit down = asseyez-vous, je vous en prie
do have a piece of cake = prenez un morceau de gâteau, je vous en prie
'may I take a peach?' 'yes, do' = 'puis-je prendre une pêche?' 'je vous en prie'

In imperatives

In French there is no use of an auxiliary verb in imperatives:

don't shut the door = ne ferme pas la porte
don't tell her anything = ne lui dis rien
do be quiet! = tais-toi!

In tag questions

French has no direct equivalent of tag questions like *doesn't he?* or *didn't it?* There is a general tag question *n'est-ce pas?* (literally *isn't it so?*) which will work in many cases:

you like fish, don't you? = tu aimes le poisson, n'est-ce pas?
he lives in London, doesn't he? = il habite à Londres, n'est-ce pas?

However, *n'est-ce pas* can very rarely be used for positive tag questions and some other way will be found to express the meaning contained in the tag: *par hasard* can often be useful as a translation:

Lola didn't phone, did she? = Lola n'a pas téléphoné par hasard?
Paul doesn't work here, does he? = Paul ne travaille pas ici par hasard?

In many cases the tag is not translated at all and the speaker's intonation will convey what is implied:

you didn't tidy your room, did you? (i.e. *you ought to have done*) = tu n'as pas rangé ta chambre?

In short answers

Again, there is no direct French equivalent for short answers like *yes I do*, *no he doesn't* etc. Where the answer *yes* is given to contradict a negative question or statement, the most useful translation is *si*:

'Marion didn't say that' 'yes she did' = 'Marion n'a pas dit ça' 'si'
'they don't sell vegetables at the baker's' 'yes they do' = 'ils ne vendent pas les légumes à la boulangerie' 'si'

In response to a standard enquiry the tag will not be translated:

'do you like strawberries?' 'yes I do' = 'aimez-vous les fraises?' 'oui'

For more examples and particular usages, see the entry **do¹**.

---

has something/nothing to ~ with ça a quelque chose à voir/n'a rien à voir avec; **what's that got to ~ with it?** qu'est-ce que cela a à voir là-dedans?; **what's it (got) to ~ with you?** en quoi ça te regarde?; **it's got everything to ~ with it** c'est là qu'est tout le problème; **his shyness is to ~ with his childhood** sa timidité est liée à son enfance; (talk to) **he won't have anything to ~ with me any more** il ne veut plus rien avoir à faire avec moi; (concern) **it has nothing to ~ with you** cela ne vous concerne pas; **2** (tolerate) supporter; **I can't ~ with loud music/all these changes** je ne supporte pas la musique trop forte/tous ces changements; **3** (need) **I could ~ with a drink/with a holiday** j'aurais bien besoin d'un verre/de partir en vacances; **4** (finish) **it's all over and done with** c'est bien fini; **have you done with my pen/the photocopier?** tu n'as plus besoin de mon stylo/la photocopieuse?; **I've done with all that** fig j'en ai fini avec tout ça.

■ **do without**: **~ without [sb/sth]** se passer de [*person, advice etc*]; **I can ~ without your sympathy** je me passe de ta pitié; **I can't ~ without the car** je ne peux pas me passer de la voiture; **you'll have to ~ without!** il va falloir que tu t'en passes!

do² /dəʊ/ *n* Mus = **doh**.

do. *abrév écrite* = **ditto**.

DOA *adj*: *abrév* ▶ **dead on arrival**.

dob /dɒb/: ■ **dob in**○ **~ in [sb]**, **~ [sb] in** cafarder○, dénoncer [*person*].

d.o.b. *abrév écrite* = **date of birth**.

Doberman (pinscher) /ˌdəʊbəmən'pɪnʃə/ *n* doberman *m*.

doc○ /dɒk/ *n* (doctor) toubib○ *m*, docteur *m*.

docile /'dəʊsaɪl, US 'dɒsl/ *adj* docile.

docility /dəʊ'sɪlətɪ/ *n* docilité *f*.

dock /dɒk/ **I** *n* **1** Naut, Ind dock *m*, bassin *m*; (for repairing ship) cale *f*; **to come into ~** entrer dans le dock or le bassin; **to be in ~** (for repairs) être en réparation; **2** US (wharf) appontement *m*; **3** GB Jur banc *m* des accusés or des prévenus; **the prisoner in the ~** l'accusé; **to put sb/sth in the ~** fig faire le procès de qn/qch; **4** US (also **loading ~**) zone *f* de chargement; **5** Bot patience *f*.
II docks *npl* Naut, Ind docks *mpl*; **to work in** ou **at the ~s** travailler dans les docks.
III *modif* (also **~s**) Naut, Ind [*area*] des docks; [*strike*] des dockers.
IV *vtr* **1** Naut mettre [qch] à quai [*ship*]; **2** GB (reduce) faire une retenue sur [*wages*]; enlever [*points, marks*]; **they had their pay ~ed for going on strike** on leur a fait une retenue sur leur salaire parce qu'ils avaient fait la grève; **to ~ £50 from sb's wages** faire une retenue de 50 livres sur le salaire de qn; **3** Aerosp amarrer, arrimer; **4** Vet écourter, couper [*tail*].
V *vi* **1** Naut [*ship*] (come into dock) arriver or entrer au port; (moor) accoster, se mettre à quai; **the ship ~ed at Southampton** (at end of voyage) le navire est arrivé à Southampton; (as stage on voyage) le navire a fait escale à Southampton; **they were refused permission to ~ in Britain** on leur a interdit d'entrer dans un port de Grande-Bretagne; **2** Aerosp s'arrimer.

docker /'dɒkə(r)/ ▶ **1692** *n* docker *m*.

docket /'dɒkɪt/ **I** *n* **1** Comm, Admin (label) étiquette *f* de reconnaissance or de signalisation; (customs certificate) récépissé *m* de douane; **2** US (list) gen registre *m*; Jur registre *m* des jugements rendus; (list of cases to be tried) rôle *m*; **the court has several other cases on its ~** le tribunal a plusieurs autres cas à traiter.
II *vtr* **1** Comm étiqueter [*parcel, package*]; **2** US Jur (summarize) faire un compte-rendu de [*case, proceedings*]; (prepare for trial) porter [qch] sur le rôle (des causes) [*case*].

docking /'dɒkɪŋ/ *n* Naut, Aerosp amarrage *m*.

dock labourer *n* = **dock worker**.

dockland /'dɒklənd/ *n* (also **~s**) zone *f* des docks.

Docklands /'dɒkləndz/ *pr n*: *à Londres, ancien quartier des docks, entièrement rénové.*

dock: **~ leaf** *n* feuille *f* de patience; **~side(s)** *n(pl)* zone *f* des docks; **~ walloper**○ *n* US docker *m*; **~worker** *n* docker *m*; **~yard** *n* chantier *m* naval or de constructions navales.

doctor /'dɒktə(r)/ ▶ **1692**, **1268** **I** *n* **1** Med médecin *m*, docteur *m*; **thank you, ~** merci, docteur; **to go to the ~('s)** aller chez le médecin; **she's a ~** elle est médecin; **who is your ~?** qui est votre médecin (traitant)?; **he trained as a ~** il a fait des études de médecine; **to be under a ~** GB être suivi par un médecin; **Doctor Armstrong** le docteur Armstrong; **to play ~s and nurses** jouer au docteur; **2** Univ docteur *m*.
II *vtr* **1** (tamper with) frelater [*food, wine*];

falsifier [*accounts, figures*]; altérer [*document, text*]; **2** GB Vet châtrer [*animal*].
IDIOMS **that's just what the ~ ordered!** c'est exactement ce qu'il me/te etc fallait!

doctoral /'dɒktərəl/ *adj* [*thesis*] de doctorat; [*research*] pour un doctorat; [*student*] en doctorat.

doctorate /'dɒktərət/ *n* doctorat *m*; **~ in science/theology** doctorat ès sciences/en théologie.

doctor: **Doctor of Divinity**, **DD** *n* doctorat *m* en Théologie; **Doctor of Philosophy**, **PhD**, **DPhil** *n* ≈ doctorat *m*; **~'s note** *n* certificat *m* médical.

doctrinaire /ˌdɒktrɪ'neə(r)/ *n, adj* doctrinaire (*mf*).

doctrinal /dɒk'traɪnl, US 'dɒktrɪnl/ *adj* doctrinal.

doctrine /'dɒktrɪn/ *n* doctrine *f*.

docudrama /'dɒkjʊdrɑːmə/ *n* docudrame *m*.

document /'dɒkjʊmənt/ **I** *n* gen document *m*; Jur acte *m*; **legal ~** acte judiciaire; **to study all the ~s in a case** Jur étudier le dossier d'une affaire; **travel/insurance/identity ~s** papiers *mpl* de voyage/d'assurance/d'identité; **policy ~** Pol déclaration *f* de politique générale.
II *vtr* **1** (give account of, record) décrire [*development, events*]; **this chapter in her career is not well ~ed** on sait peu de choses sur cette période de sa carrière; **the only ~ed case of this phenomenon** le seul cas connu de ce phénomène; **2** (support or prove with documents) documenter [*case, claim*]; **all applications must be properly ~ed** toutes les demandes doivent être accompagnées des pièces justificatives requises; **3** Naut munir [qch] des papiers nécessaires [*ship*].

documentary /ˌdɒkjʊ'mentrɪ, US -terɪ/ **I** *n* documentaire *m* (**about, on** sur); **television/radio ~** documentaire *m* télévisé/radiophonique.
II *adj* [*film, realism, technique, source*] documentaire; **~ evidence** Jur preuves *fpl* écrites; (in historical research) documents *mpl* de l'époque.

documentary: **~ bill** *n* Comm, Fin traite *f* documentaire; **~ credit** *n* Comm, Fin crédit *m* documentaire; **~ letter of credit** *n* Comm, Fin lettre *f* de crédit documentaire.

documentation /ˌdɒkjʊmen'teɪʃn/ *n* ȼ **1** (documents) gen documentation *f*; Comm documents *mpl*, pièces *fpl* justificatives; **2** (act of recording) **one of the historian's tasks is the ~ of social change** l'une des tâches de l'historien est de rendre compte des changements sociaux.

document: **~ case**, **~ holder** *n* porte-documents *m inv*; **~ reader** Comput lecteur *m* de documents; **~ retrieval** *n* Comput recherche *f* documentaire; **~ wallet** *n* chemise *f* (*en carton*).

DOD *n*: *abrév* US ▶ **Department of Defense**.

dodder /'dɒdə(r)/ **I** *n* Bot cuscute *f*.
II *vi* tituber, marcher d'un pas titubant.

dodderer /'dɒdərə(r)/ *n* croulant○/-e *m/f* pej.

doddering /'dɒdərɪŋ/, **doddery** /'dɒdərɪ/ *adj* **1** [*person*] (unsteady) branlant; [*movement*] titubant, vacillant; **2** (senile) gaga○, gâteux/-euse○.

doddle○ /'dɒdl/ *n* GB **it's a ~** c'est du gâteau○!, c'est simple comme bonjour!

dodecahedron /ˌdəʊdekə'hiːdrən, US -rɒn/ *n* dodécaèdre *m*.

Dodecanese /ˌdəʊdɪkə'niːz/ *pr npl* Dodécanèse *m*.

dodge /dɒdʒ/ **I** *n* **1** (movement) gen mouvement *m* de côté; Sport (in boxing, football) esquive *f*; **he made a quick ~ to the right** gen il a fait un saut vers la droite; (in boxing) il a fait une esquive vers la droite; **2**○ GB (trick) combine○ *f*, truc○ *m*; **a ~ for avoiding taxation** une combine○ pour éviter de payer les impôts; **to be up to all the ~s** connaître toutes les combines○.
II *vtr* esquiver [*bullet, blow*]; échapper à [*pursuers*]; fig esquiver [*difficulty, question, duty*]; se dérober à [*confrontation, accusation*]; éviter de payer [*tax*]; éviter [*person*]; **to ~ the issue** escamoter la question; **to ~ military service, to ~ the draft** US se faire réformer.

dodgem (**car**) /'dɒdʒəm/ *n* GB auto *f* tamponneuse; **to go on the ~s** faire un tour d'autos tamponneuses.

dodger /'dɒdʒə(r)/ *n* **1** (trickster) combinard/-e○ *m/f*; (shirker) tire-au-flanc○ *m inv*; **2** Naut taud *m*. ▶ **draft dodger**, **tax dodger etc**.

dodgy○ /'dɒdʒɪ/ *adj* GB **1** (untrustworthy) [*person, business, establishment, method*] louche○, douteux/-euse; **2** (risky, dangerous) [*decision, plan, investment*] risqué; [*situation, moment*] délicat; [*finances*] précaire; [*weather*] instable; **his health is a bit ~** sa santé est plutôt fragile.

dodo /'dəʊdəʊ/ *n* Zool dronte *m*, dodo *m*.
IDIOMS **to be as dead as a ~** être tombé aux oubliettes.

doe /dəʊ/ *n* (deer) biche *f*; (rabbit) lapine *f*; (hare) hase *f*.

DOE *n* **1** GB *abrév* ▶ **Department of the Environment**; **2** US *abrév* ▶ **Department of Energy**.

doe-eyed /'dəʊaɪd/ *adj* aux yeux de biche.

doer /'duːə(r)/ *n* (active person) homme/femme *m/f* dynamique.

does /dʌz, dəz/ (*3e pers sing prés*) ▶ **do**.

doeskin /'dəʊskɪn/ **I** *n* daim *m*.
II *modif* [*gloves, jacket*] de daim.

doesn't /'dʌznt/ (= **does not**) ▶ **do**.

doff† /dɒf, US dɔːf/ *vtr* ôter, enlever [*hat, coat*]; **to ~ one's hat to sb** se découvrir devant qn, soulever son chapeau devant qn (*en guise de salut*).

dog /dɒg, US dɔːg/ **I** *n* **1** Zool chien *m*; (female) chienne *f*; **2** (male fox, wolf, etc) mâle *m*; **3**○ (person) **you lucky ~!** sacré veinard○!; **you dirty** ou **vile ~!** sale type○!; **he's a crafty old ~!** c'est un vieux rusé!; **4**◑ (unattractive woman) mochetée○ *f*, cageot◑ *m* offensive; **5**○ US (poor quality machine, object etc) **it's a ~**○ c'est de la cochonnerie○; **6** Tech gen crampon *m*; (on roof) clameau *m*; (pawl) cliquet *m*.
II○ **dogs** *npl* GB Sport (greyhound racing) **the ~s** les courses *fpl* de lévriers.
III *vtr* (*p prés etc* **-gg-**) **1** (follow) talonner, suivre [qn] de près [*person*]; **to ~ sb's footsteps** être sur les talons de qn, être toujours derrière qn; **2** (plague) suivre; **to be ~ged by misfortune** être poursuivi par la malchance; **to be ~ged by uncertainty/controversy** être en proie à l'incertitude/la controverse; **poor health had ~ged his childhood** il avait été affligé d'une mauvaise santé pendant toute son enfance.
IDIOMS **it's ~ eat ~** c'est chacun pour soi, c'est la foire d'empoigne; **every ~ has its day** à chacun vient sa chance, à chacun son heure de gloire; **give a ~ a bad name (and hang him)** Prov celui qui veut noyer son chien l'accuse de la rage Prov; **to put on the ~**○ US frimer○; **love me, love my ~** aime-moi tel que je suis; **to go and see a man about a ~** euph hum (relieve oneself) aller se soulager; (go on unspecified business) aller voir le pape hum; **they don't have a ~'s chance** ils n'ont pas la moindre chance or l'ombre d'une chance; **it's a ~'s life** c'est une vie de chien; **to lead a ~'s life** mener une vie de chien; **to lead sb a ~'s life** mener une vie de chien à qn; **there's life in the old ~ yet** (of oneself) je ne suis pas encore grabataire; (of sb else) il/elle n'est pas encore grabataire; **to go to the ~s**○ [*company, country*] aller à vau-l'eau; [*person*] filer un mauvais coton○; **to treat sb like a ~** traiter qn comme un chien; **to be dressed** ou **got up like a ~'s dinner**○ être accoutré de façon ridicule; **it's a real ~'s breakfast**○! c'est n'importe quoi!; **you wouldn't put a ~ out on a night like this!** il fait un temps de chien ce soir! ▶ **teach**.

dog: **~ basket** *n* panier *m* pour chien; **~ biscuit** *n* biscuit *m* pour chien; **~ breeder** ▶ **1692** *n* éleveur/-euse *m/f* de chiens; **~ cart** *n* dog-cart *m*, charrette *f* anglaise.

dog collar *n* **1** lit collier *m* de chien; **2**○ hum (clergyman's collar) col *m* romain.

dog days *npl* **1** (warm weather) canicule *f*; **2** fig (slack period) période *f* creuse.

doge /dəʊdʒ/ *n* Hist doge *m*.

dog: **~-eared** *adj* écorné; **~-end**○ *n* mégot○ *m*.

dogfight /'dɒgfaɪt, US 'dɔːg-/ *n* **1** lit bagarre *f* de chiens; (between people) bagarre *f*; **2** Mil Aviat combat *m* aérien.

dog: **~fighting** *n* combat *m* de chiens; **~fish** *n* Zool chien *m* de mer; Culin roussette *f*; **~ food** *n* nourriture *f* pour chiens.

dogged /'dɒgɪd, US 'dɔːgɪd/ *adj* [*attempt*] obstiné, soutenu; [*persistence, insistence*] tenace; [*refusal*] obstiné, tenace; [*resistance*] opiniâtre; [*person*] tenace, persévérant; **a ~ campaigner for human rights** un militant acharné des droits de l'homme.

doggedly /'dɒgɪdlɪ, US 'dɔːg-/ *adv* [*persist*] obstinément; [*work*] avec ténacité; [*resist*] opiniâtrement.

doggedness /'dɒgɪdnɪs, US 'dɔːg-/ *n* obstination *f*, ténacité *f*.

Dogger Bank /ˌdɒgə'bæŋk/ *pr n* Dogger Bank *m*.

doggerel /'dɒgərəl, US 'dɔːg-/ *npl* Literat vers *mpl* de mirliton.

doggie○ *n* = **doggy I**.

doggo○ /'dɒgəʊ, US 'dɔːgəʊ/ *adv* GB **to lie ~** faire le mort.

doggone○ /'dɒgɒn, US 'dɔːgɔːn/ US **I** *adj* (also **~d**) sacré○ (*before n*), foutu◑ (*before n*).
II *adv* (also **~d**) sacrément○, vachement○.
III *excl* **~ it**○! bon sang○!, merde◑!

doggy○ /'dɒgɪ, US 'dɔːgɪ/ **I** *n* toutou○ *m*, chien *m*.
II *adj* [*odour*] de chien.

doggy: **~ bag** *n*: *petit sac pour emporter les restes*; **~ fashion**○ *adv* [*eat, swim*] comme un chien; [*make love*] en levrette; **~ paddle**○ *n, vi* = **dog paddle**.

dog handler ▶ **1692** *n* maître-chien *m*.

doghouse /'dɒghaʊs, US 'dɔːg-/ *n* US niche *f* (*à chien*).
IDIOMS **to be in the ~**○ être tombé en disgrâce; **to be in the ~ with sb**○ ne pas être dans les petits papiers de qn, ne plus avoir la cote○ avec qn.

dogie /'dəʊgɪ/ *n* US veau *m* sans mère.

dog in the manger **I** *n* empêcheur/-euse *m/f* de tourner en rond.
II **dog-in-the-manger** *modif* [*attitude, behaviour*] égoïste.

dog: **~ Latin** *n* latin *m* de cuisine; **~leg** *n* Aut virage *m* brusque, coude *m*; **~ licence** *n*: *redevance payée pour la possession d'un chien*; **~like** *adj* [*devotion, fidelity*] de chien.

dogma /'dɒgmə, US 'dɔːgmə/ *n* dogme *m*.

dogmatic /dɒg'mætɪk, US dɔːg-/ *adj* dogmatique (**about** sur).

dogmatically /dɒg'mætɪklɪ, US dɔːg-/ *adv* [*insist, maintain*] dogmatiquement; [*refuse, oppose, say*] d'une façon catégorique.

dogmatism /'dɒgmətɪzəm, US 'dɔːg-/ *n* dogmatisme *m*.

dogmatist /'dɒgmətɪst, US 'dɔːg-/ *n* dogmatique *mf*.

dogmatize /'dɒgmətaɪz, US 'dɔːg-/ *vi* dogmatiser (**about** sur).

do-gooder○ /duː'gʊdə(r)/ *n* péj bonne âme *f*, pilier *m* de bonnes œuvres pej.

dog paddle **I** *n* nage *f* à la manière d'un chien.

II *vi* nager à la manière d'un chien.

dog rose *n* **1** (flower) églantine *f*; **2** (shrub) églantier *m* (commun).

dog: **~sbody**○ *n* GB (also **general ~**) (man, woman) bonne *f* à tout faire; **~'s home**○ *n* chenil *m*; **~show** *n* exposition *f* canine; **Dog Star** *n* Sirius *m*; **~ tag**○ *n* US Mil plaque *f* d'identification (*portée par le personnel militaire américain*); **~-tired**○ *adj* claqué○, crevé○; **~tooth** *n* (*pl* **~teeth**) Archit dent-de-chien *f*; **~-tooth check** *n, adj* pied-de-poule (*m*) *inv*; **~tooth violet** *n* dent-de-chien *f*, erythronium *m*; **~track** *n* piste *f* (pour les courses de lévriers); **~trot** *n* Equit petit trot *m*; **~watch** *n* Naut petit quart *m*; **~wood** *n* cornouiller *m*.

dogy *n* US = **dogie**.

doh /dəʊ/ *n* Mus do *m*, ut *m*.

doily /ˈdɔɪlɪ/ *n* napperon *m*.

doing /ˈduːɪŋ/ **I** *p prés* ▶ **do**.

II *n* **this is her ~** c'est son ouvrage; **all of this is your ~** c'est toi qui es la cause de tout cela; **it's none of my ~** ce n'est pas moi qui l'ai fait; **it takes some ~!** ce n'est pas facile du tout!

III **doings** *npl* **1** (actions) faits et gestes *mpl*, agissements *mpl* pej; (events) événements *mpl*; **2**○ GB machin○ *m*, truc○ *m*.

do-it-yourself /ˌduːɪtjɔːˈself/, **DIY I** *n* bricolage *m*.

II *modif* [*shop, book, materials*] de bricolage; [*enthusiast*] du bricolage; **~ kit** kit *m* (à monter soi-même).

do-it-yourselfer /ˌduːɪtjɔːˈselfə(r)/ *n* bricoleur/-euse *m/f*.

dojo /ˈdəʊdʒəʊ/ *n* dojo *m*, salle *f* d'entraînement (*pour les arts martiaux*).

Dolby (stereo)® /ˈdɒlbɪ/ *n* (système) Dolby® *m*.

doldrums /ˈdɒldrəmz/ *npl* **1** Meteorol (area) zone *f* des calmes équatoriaux; (weather) calme *m* équatorial; **2** fig (stagnation) **to be in the ~** [*person*] broyer du noir, être en pleine déprime; [*economy, company*] être en plein marasme.

dole○ /dəʊl/ *n* GB Soc Admin allocation *f* de chômage; **to be/go on the ~** être/s'inscrire au chômage.

■ **dole out**: **~ out** [**sth**], **~** [**sth**] **out** distribuer.

doleful /ˈdəʊlfl/ *adj* dolent, triste.

dolefully /ˈdəʊlfəlɪ/ *adv* [*say, remark*] d'un ton dolent; [*look, gesture*] d'un air triste.

dole queue *n* GB **1** lit ≈ file *f* d'attente à l'agence pour l'emploi; **2** fig (also **~s**) nombre *m* de chômeurs.

dolichocephalic /ˌdɒlɪˌkəʊsɪˈfælɪk/ *adj* dolichocéphale.

doll /ˈdɒl, US dɔːl/ *n* **1** poupée *f*; **to play with a ~** ou **with one's ~s** jouer à la poupée; **~'s bed/clothes** lit *m*/vêtements *mpl* de poupée; **2**○ (pretty girl) jolie nana○ *f*; (attractive man) beau mec○ *m*; **hi, ~!** (to woman) salut, ma belle○! or poupée!; (to man) salut, beau mec○!; **3** (nice person) **you're a ~!** tu es un chou○!

■ **doll up**: **~ up** [**sb/sth**]○, **~** [**sb/sth**] **up**○ pomponner○ [*person*]; bichonner○ [*room, house*]; **she was all ~ed up** elle était sur son trente et un○; **to ~ oneself up, to get ~ed up** se pomponner○, se faire beau/belle.

dollar /ˈdɒlə(r)/ ▶ **1143** *n* dollar *m*.

IDIOMS **the 64 thousand ~ question** la question à mille francs.

dollar: **~ area** *n* zone *f* dollar; **~ bill** *n* billet *m* d'un dollar; **~ diplomacy** *n* diplomatie *f* qui s'appuie sur le pouvoir financier; **~ sign** *n* symbole *m* du dollar.

dollop○ /ˈdɒləp/ *n* lit cuillerée *f* (**of** de); fig bonne dose *f* (**of** de).

doll: **~'s hospital** *n* atelier *m* où on répare les poupées; **~'s house** *n* maison *f* de poupée.

dolly /ˈdɒlɪ, US ˈdɔːlɪ/ **I** *n* **1**○ (doll) poupée *f*; **2** (mobile platform) chariot *m* or plate-forme *f* (de manutention); Cin, TV dolly *m*; **3** (for washing clothes) battoir *m*, batte *f* de blanchisseuse; **4** US Rail (locomotive) diabolo *m*, locotracteur *m*; **5** Tech (for rivet) enclumette *f*; **6** Constr avant-pieu *m inv*; **7** Sport coup *m* or passe *f* facile.

II *vi* Cin, TV **to ~ in/out** faire un travelling avant/arrière.

dolly: **~ bird**○ *n* GB pej ravissante idiote○ *f*; **~ mixture** *n* petit bonbon *m*.

dolmades /dɒlˈmɑːðez/ *npl* dolmas *mpl*, feuilles *fpl* de vigne farcies.

dolman sleeve /ˌdɒlmənˈsliːv/ *n* manche *f* chauve-souris.

dolmen /ˈdɒlmən/ *n* dolmen *m*.

dolomite /ˈdɒləmaɪt/ *n* (mineral) dolomie *f*; (rock) dolomite *f*.

Dolomites /ˈdɒləmaɪts/ *pr npl* Dolomites *fpl*.

dolphin /ˈdɒlfɪn/ *n* Zool dauphin *m*.

dolphinarium /ˌdɒlfɪˈneərɪəm/ *n* delphinarium *m*.

dolphin striker *n* Naut arc-boutant *m* de martingale.

dolt /dəʊlt/ *n* péj abruti○ *m*, balourd *m*.

domain /dəʊˈmeɪn/ *n* (all contexts) domaine *m* (**of** de).

dome /dəʊm/ *n* gen dôme *m*; Archit coupole *f*, dôme *m*.

domed /dəʊmd/ *adj* [*skyline, tower, city*] à dômes, à coupoles; [*roof, ceiling*] en dôme; [*forehead, helmet*] bombé.

Domesday Book /ˈduːmzdeɪ bʊk/ *n* GB Hist Domesday Book *m* (*recueil compilé à la fin du XIe siècle pour répertorier les terres anglaises*).

domestic /dəˈmestɪk/ **I** *n* **1**† (servant) domestique† *mf*; **2**○ (argument) dispute *f* conjugale.

II *adj* **1** Pol (home) [*market, affairs, consumption, policy, flight, demand, price*] intérieur; [*consumer*] du pays; [*crisis, issue*] de politique intérieure; **2** (of house) [*activity, animal*] domestique; **~ chores** tâches *fpl* ménagères; **~ staff** domestiques *mfpl*; **3** (family) [*life, situation, harmony*] familial; [*dispute*] conjugal; **~ bliss** hum le bonheur familial.

domestically /dəˈmestɪklɪ/ *adv* Pol, gen [*produced, sold*] à l'intérieur du pays; **these are difficult times for the president ~** le président doit faire face à une situation difficile à l'intérieur du pays; **~, the decision was a disaster** au niveau de la politique intérieure, la décision a été un désastre.

domestic appliance *n* appareil *m* électroménager.

domesticate /dəˈmestɪkeɪt/ **I** *vtr* domestiquer [*animal*].

II **domesticated** *pp adj* **1** [*animal*] domestiqué; [*countryside, landscape*] léché; **2 to be ~d** [*person*] aimer s'occuper de la maison.

domestication /dəˌmestɪˈkeɪʃn/ *n* domestication *f*.

domestic help *n* aide *f* ménagère.

domesticity /ˌdɒməˈstɪsətɪ, ˌdəʊ-/ *n* **1** (home life) vie *f* de famille, vie *f* familiale; **2** (household duties) tâches *fpl* ménagères.

domestic science **I** *n* GB arts *mpl* ménagers.

II *modif* [*teacher, exam*] d'arts ménagers.

domestic servant *n* domestique *mf*.

domestic service **I** *n* **to be in ~** être domestique.

II **domestic services** *npl* services *mpl* d'entretien.

domestic violence *n* violence *f* dans la famille.

domicile /ˈdɒmɪsaɪl/ *n* Admin, Jur domicile *m*.

domiciled /ˈdɒmɪsaɪld/ *adj* domicilié.

domiciliary /ˌdɒmɪˈsɪlɪərɪ, US -erɪ/ *adj* [*visit, care, health service*] à domicile; [*rights, information*] relatif/-ive au domicile; [*premises*] du domicile.

dominance /ˈdɒmɪnəns/ *n* **1** (fact of dominating group or individual) domination *f* (**of** de); **2** (numerical strength) prépondérance *f* (**of** de); **3** Biol, Zool dominance *f*.

dominant /ˈdɒmɪnənt/ **I** *n* **1** Mus (fifth note) dominante *f*; (chord) accord *m* de dominante; (key) ton *m* de dominante; **2** Biol gène *m* dominant; **3** Ecol (animal species) espèce *f* dominante; (plant) dominante *f*.

II *adj* gen, Biol dominant; Mus [*chord, key*] de dominante.

dominate /ˈdɒmɪneɪt/ **I** *vtr* dominer [*person, region, town*]; **to ~ the market/industry** dominer le marché/dans l'industrie; **to be ~d by** [*market, industry*] être entre les mains de [*company, group*]; [*committee, university*] être dominé par [*group*]; **life in the West is ~d by the car/by television** c'est la voiture/la télévision qui prédomine dans les pays occidentaux; **an area ~d by factories/shops** une zone très industrielle/commerçante.

II *vi* **1** (control others) [*person*] dominer; **2** (predominate) [*issue, topic, question*] prédominer.

dominating /ˈdɒmɪneɪtɪŋ/ *adj* dominateur/-trice.

domination /ˌdɒmɪˈneɪʃn/ *n* domination *f* (of de; **by** par); **the ~ of the curriculum by science subjects** la prépondérance des disciplines scientifiques dans le programme.

domineer /ˌdɒmɪˈnɪə(r)/ *vi* jouer le grand chef.

domineering /ˌdɒmɪˈnɪərɪŋ/ *adj* [*person, behaviour, attitude*] despotique; [*ways*] de despote; [*tone, voice*] autoritaire.

Dominica /dəˈmɪnɪkə/ ▶ **1131** *pr n* Dominique *f*.

Dominican /dəˈmɪnɪkən/ ▶ **1486** **I** *n* **1** Geog Dominicain/-e *m/f*; **2** Relig Dominicain *m*.

II *adj* **1** Geog [*person, river, economy*] dominicain, de (la) Dominique; **2** Relig dominicain.

Dominican Republic ▶ **1131** *pr n* République *f* dominicaine.

dominion /dəˈmɪnɪən/ *n* **1** (authority) domination *f* (**over** sur); **2** (area ruled) terres *fpl*; **3** GB Hist (of empire) (also **Dominion**) dominion *m*.

domino /ˈdɒmɪnəʊ/ ▶ **1282** **I** *n* **1** Games (piece) domino *m*; **2** Hist Fashn (cloak) domino *m*; (eye-mask) loup *m*.

II **dominoes** *npl* Games dominos *mpl*.

domino: **~ effect** *n* réaction *f* en chaîne; **~ theory** *n* Pol théorie *f* des dominos.

don /dɒn/ **I** *n* **1** GB Univ professeur *m* d'université; **2** US (in mafia) don *m*.

II *vtr* (*p prés etc* **-nn-**) littér mettre [*hat, gloves*].

donate /dəʊˈneɪt, US ˈdəʊneɪt/ **I** *vtr* faire don de [*money, kidney, body*] (**to** à); **to be ~d by sb** être un don de qn.

II *vi* faire un don.

donation /dəʊˈneɪʃn/ *n* don *m* (**of** de; **à** to).

done /dʌn/ **I** *pp* ▶ **do**.

II *pp adj* (socially acceptable) **it's not the ~ thing** ça ne se fait pas; **it's not ~ to do** ça ne se fait pas de faire.

III *excl* (making deal) marché conclu!

doner kebab /ˌdəʊnə kəˈbæb/ *n* ≈ sandwich *m* grec.

dong /dɒŋ/ ▶ **1143** *n* **1** (sound of bell) dong *m*; **2** (currency) dông *m*; **3**● (penis) bite● *f*, pénis *m*.

donjon /ˈdɒndʒən/ *n* donjon *m*.

Don Juan /ˌdɒn ˈdʒuːən/ *n* lit, fig Don Juan *m*.

donkey /ˈdɒŋkɪ/ *n* Zool âne *m*.

IDIOMS **she could talk the hind leg off a ~!** c'est un vrai moulin à paroles○!; **~'s years ago**○ il y a une éternité; **I've known him for ~'s years**○ je le connais depuis des années or une éternité.

donkey engine *n* **1** Naut moteur *m* auxiliaire; **2** Mech petit cheval *m*, cheval *m* alimentaire.

donkey: **~ jacket** *n* grosse veste *f* de travail; **~ ride** *n* promenade *f* à dos d'âne; **~ work** *n* travail *m* pénible.

donnish /ˈdɒnɪʃ/ *adj* [*person*] intellectuel/-elle.

donor /ˈdəʊnə(r)/ *n* (of organ) donneur/-euse *m/f*; (of money) donateur/-trice *m/f*; **blood/kidney ~** donneur/-euse de sang/de rein.

donor: **~ card** *n* carte *f* de donneur d'organes; **~ organ** *n* transplant *m*.

Don Quixote /ˌdɒnˈkwɪksət/ *pr n* Don Quichotte.

don't /dəʊnt/ = **do not**.

donut *n* US = **doughnut**.

doodah○ GB /ˈduːdɑː/, **doodad**○ US /ˈduːdæd/ *n* machin○ *m*, truc○ *m*.

doodle /ˈduːdl/ **I** *n* gribouillage *m*.
II *vi* gribouiller (**on** sur).

doodlebug /ˈduːdlbʌɡ/ *n* GB Mil Hist missile *m* sol-sol V1.

doolally○ /ˈduːlælɪ/ *adj* hum zinzin○, dérangé; **to go ~** devenir zinzin○.

doom /duːm/ **I** *n* (death) mort *f*; (unhappy destiny) (of person) perte *f*; (of country, group) catastrophe *f*; **to have a sense of impending ~** avoir de sombres pressentiments; **to prophecy ~** prédire une catastrophe.
II *vtr* condamner [*person, project*] (**to** à); **to be ~ed to do** être condamné à faire; **to be ~ed to failure** être voué à l'échec; **to be ~ed from the start** être voué à l'échec avant même de commencer.
IDIOMS **to spread** ou **preach ~ and gloom** jouer les Cassandre; **it's not all ~ and gloom!** il reste une lueur d'espoir!

doom-laden /ˈduːmleɪdn/ *adj* [*pronouncement, forecast*] sombre, alarmiste.

doomsday /ˈduːmzdeɪ/ **I** *n* fin *f* du monde; **until ~** hum jusqu'à la saint-glinglin○.
II *modif* **a ~ scenario** un scénario catastrophe.

doomwatch /ˈduːmwɒtʃ/ *n* Ecol catastrophisme *m*.

door /dɔː(r)/ *n* **1** gen porte *f* (**to** de; **in** dans); **the ~ to the terrace/kitchen** la porte de la terrasse/de la cuisine; **their house is a few ~s down** ils habitent quelques maisons plus bas; **behind closed ~s** à huis clos **to shut/slam the ~ on sb** ou **in sb's face** lit fermer/claquer la porte au nez de qn; **to shut** ou **close the ~ on sth** fig fermer la porte à qch; **to slam the ~ in sb's face** fig envoyer promener qn; **2** Aut, Rail porte *f*, portière *f*; **a four-~ car** une voiture à quatre portes; **'mind the ~s please'** 'attention à la fermeture automatique des portes'; **3** (entrance) entrée *f*; **to be on the ~** être à l'entrée; **'pay at the ~'** 'payez à l'entrée'.
IDIOMS **to be at/look as if one is at death's ~** être/avoir l'air d'être à l'article de la mort; **to get a foot in the ~** mettre un pied dans la place; **to lay sth at sb's ~** imputer qch à qn; **to open the ~(s) to sth** ouvrir la voie à qch; **to leave the ~ open for** ou **to sth** laisser la porte ouverte à qch; **this will open ~s for him** cela va lui ouvrir des portes; **one ~ shuts, another opens** une porte se ferme, une autre s'ouvre; **to show sb the ~** mettre qn à la porte.

door: **~ bell** *n* sonnette *f*; **~ chime** *n* carillon *m* de porte; **~ frame** *n* chambranle *m* (de porte); **~ handle** *n* gen (lever type) poignée *f* de porte; (turning type) bouton *m* de porte; Aut poignée *f*; **~ jamb** *n* jambage *m*; **~keeper** *n* portier *m*; **~-knob** *n* bouton *m* de porte; **~man** *n* (at hotel) portier *m*; (at cinema) contrôleur *m*; **~mat** *n* lit, fig paillasson *m*.

doornail /ˈdɔːneɪl/: IDIOMS **to be as dead as a ~** être mort et bien mort.

door: **~ plate** *n* (of doctor, lawyer) plaque *f* (de porte); **~post** *n* montant *m*.

doorstep /ˈdɔːstep/ **I** *n* **1** (step) pas *m* de porte; **2** (threshold) seuil *m*; **on the** ou **one's ~** (nearby) tout près; (unpleasantly close) juste à côté; **3**○ (chunk of bread) grosse tartine *f*.
II *vtr* GB Pol (canvass) **to ~ sb** aller chez qn pour faire du démarchage électoral.

door: **~-stepping** *n* GB Pol démarchage *m* électoral à domicile; **~stop** *n* butoir *m* (de porte).

door-to-door /ˌdɔːtəˈdɔː/ **I** *adj* [*canvassing, car service, salesman*] à domicile; **~ selling** porte à porte *m inv*.
II door to door *adv phr* [*sell*] à domicile; **it's 90 minutes ~** le trajet prend 90 minutes de porte à porte.

doorway /ˈdɔːweɪ/ *n* **1** (frame of door) embrasure *f* (de porte); **2** (area in front of door) porche *m*; **to shelter in a shop ~** s'abriter sous le porche d'une boutique; **to block the ~** bloquer l'entrée.

dopamine /ˈdəʊpəmiːn/ *n* dopamine *f*.

dope /dəʊp/ **I** *n* **1**○ (cannabis) cannabis *m*, shit◑ *m*; **2**○ (fool) andouille○ *f*, imbécile *mf*; **3**○ (information) tuyaux○ *mpl* (**on** sur); **OK, what's the ~ on Joe?** qu'est ce qu'on a comme tuyaux sur Joe○?; **4** Aut, Tech (additive) dope *m*; **5** Ind (in dynamite manufacture) absorbant *m*; **6** (varnish) enduit *m*.
II *vtr* **1** (give drug to) Sport doper [*horse, athlete*]; gen droguer [*person*]; **2** (put drug in) mettre un somnifère dans [*food, drink*].
III doped *pp adj* (also **~d up**) [*horse, athlete*] dopé; [*person*] drogué.
■ **dope out**: **~ out [sth], ~ [sth] out** découvrir [*plan, answer*].

dope: **~ fiend**○ *n* toxicomane *mf*; **~ peddler** *n* dealer○ *m*.

dope test I *n* Sport contrôle *m* antidopage.
II dope-test *vtr* soumettre [qn/qch] à un contrôle antidopage [*horse, athlete*].

dopey○ /ˈdəʊpɪ/ *adj* **1** (silly) abruti; **2** (not fully awake) groggy○, vaseux/-euse○.

doping /ˈdəʊpɪŋ/ *n* Sport dopage *m*.

doppelganger /ˈdɒplɡeŋə(r)/ *n* double *m*.

Doppler effect /ˈdɒplə(r)/ *n* effet *m* Doppler.

Dordogne /dɔːˈdɔɪn/ ▶ **1163** *pr n* Dordogne *f*; **in/to the ~** en Dordogne.

Doric /ˈdɒrɪk/ *adj* dorique.

dork○ /dɔːk/ *n* US, Austral abruti/-e○ *m/f*.

dorm○ /dɔːm/ *n* GB Sch *abrév* ▶ **dormitory** I 1.

dormant /ˈdɔːmənt/ *adj* **1** (latent) [*emotion, sensuality, talent, potential*] latent, qui sommeille; **to lie ~** sommeiller; **2** Geol [*volcano*] au repos, en sommeil; **3** Herald couché; **4** Bot dormant.

dormer /ˈdɔːmə(r)/ *n* (also **~ window**) lucarne *f*.

dormitory /ˈdɔːmɪtrɪ, US -tɔːrɪ/ **I** *n* **1** GB dortoir *m*; **2** US Univ résidence *f*, foyer *m*.
II *modif* [*suburb, town*] dortoir *inv*.

Dormobile® /ˈdɔːməbiːl/ *n* auto-caravane *f*, camping-car *m*.

dormouse /ˈdɔːmaʊs/ *n* (*pl* **dormice**) Zool muscardin *m*.

dorsal /ˈdɔːsl/ *adj* dorsal.

Dorset /ˈdɔːsɪt/ ▶ **1624** *pr n* Dorset *m*.

dory /ˈdɔːrɪ/ *n* **1** US Naut doris *m*; **2** Zool saint-pierre *m*.

DOS /dɒs/ *n* Comput *abrév* ▶ **disk operating system**.

dosage /ˈdəʊsɪdʒ/ *n* posologie *f*.

dose /dəʊs/ **I** *n* Med, fig dose *f* (**of** de); **a ~ of originality/optimism** une dose d'originalité/d'optimisme; **to have a ~ of shingles/measles** avoir un zona/la rougeole; **a ~ of flu** une bonne grippe; **to catch a ~**○ (of VD) attraper la vérole◑.
II *vtr* **to ~ sb with medicine** bourrer○ qn de médicaments.
III *v refl* **to ~ oneself up** se bourrer○ de médicaments.
IDIOMS **like a ~ of salts** à la vitesse grand V; **he's all right in small ~s** il est supportable à doses homéopathiques.

dosh○ /dɒʃ/ *n* GB fric○ *m*, argent *m*.

doss○ /dɒs/ *n* GB **it's a ~**○! facile!
■ **doss down**○ pieuter◑, dormir.

dosser○ /ˈdɒsə(r)/ *n* **1** (tramp) clodo○ *m*, clochard/-e *m/f*; **2** (lazy person) glandeur/-euse◑ *m/f*, paresseux/-euse *m/f*.

dosshouse○ /ˈdɒshaʊs/ *n* asile *m* de nuit.

dossier /ˈdɒsɪə(r), -ɪeɪ/ *n* dossier *m* (**on** sur).

dost‡ = **do you**.

Dostoevsky /ˌdɒstɔɪˈefskɪ/ *pr n* Dostoïevski.

dot /dɒt/ **I** *n* gen point *m*; (on fabric, wallpaper) pois *m*; **'~, ~, ~'** 'points *mpl* de suspension'.
II *vtr* (*p prés etc* **-tt-**) **1** (in writing) mettre un point sur [*letter*]; **2** Culin parsemer [*chicken, joint*] (**with** de); **3** (be scattered along) **fishing villages ~ the coast, the coast is ~ted with fishing villages** il y a des ports de pêche éparpillés le long de la côte; **there were houses/people ~ted around** il y avait des maisons/des gens çà et là; **they were ~ted around the town/square** ils étaient répartis dans la ville/sur la place.
IDIOMS **since the year ~**○ depuis des siècles; **on the ~** pile; **at two o'clock on the ~** à deux heures pile.

DOT *n* US (*abrév* = **Department of Transportation**) ministère *m* des transports.

dotage /ˈdəʊtɪdʒ/ *n* **to be in one's ~** être dans ses vieux jours pej, devenir gâteux/-euse.

dote /dəʊt/ *vi* **to ~ on sb/sth** adorer qn/qch.

doth‡ /dʌθ/ = **does**.

doting /ˈdəʊtɪŋ/ *adj* **her ~ parents** ses parents qui l'adorent/l'adoraient; **he's a ~ son** il adore ses parents.

dotingly /ˈdəʊtɪŋlɪ/ *adv* [*look, gaze*] avec adoration.

dot matrix printer *n* imprimante *f* matricielle.

dotted /ˈdɒtɪd/ *adj* **1** Fashn (spotted) à pois; **2** Mus [*note*] pointé.

dotted line *n* Print pointillé *m*; **'tear along ~'** 'découpez suivant le pointillé'; **to sign on the ~** lit signer à l'endroit indiqué; fig donner son accord.

dotterel /ˈdɒtərəl/ *n* Zool pluvier *m* guignard.

dotty○ /ˈdɒtɪ/ *adj* GB [*person*] toqué○, farfelu○; [*scheme*] farfelu○.

double /ˈdʌbl/ **I** *n* **1 I'll have a ~ please** (drink) je prendrai un double, s'il vous plaît; **2** (of person) sosie *m*; Cin, Theat doublure *f*; **he's your ~!** c'est ton sosie!; **3** (in horse-racing) (bet) pari *m* sur deux chevaux (*dans deux courses consécutives*); **4** Games (in bridge) contre *m*; (in dominoes) double *m*, doublet *m*; **to throw a ~** (in darts, board game) faire un double.
II doubles *npl* (in tennis) double *m*; **ladies'/men's/mixed ~s** double dames/messieurs/mixte; **to play a game of ~s** faire un double.
III *adj* **1** (twice as much) [*portion, dose*] double (*before n*); **he was given a ~ helping of strawberries** on lui a servi une double portion de fraises or deux fois plus de fraises; **a ~ vodka** une double vodka, une vodka double; **2** (when spelling, giving number) **Anne is spelt** GB ou **spelled** US **with a ~ 'n'** Anne s'écrit avec deux 'n'; **eight ~ five four (8554)** quatre-vingt cinq, cinquante-quatre; **two ~ four (244)** deux cent quarante-quatre; **3** (dual, twofold) **~ advantage** double avantage *m*; **to serve a ~ purpose** avoir une double fonction; **a remark with a ~ meaning** une remarque à double sens; **~ murder** double meurtre *m*; **~-page advertisement** publicité *f* sur double page; **4** (intended for two people or things) [*sheet, blanket, garage etc*] double; [*ticket, invitation*] pour deux; **5** Bot double.
IV *adv* **1** (twice) deux fois; **she earns ~ what I earn** elle gagne deux fois plus que

moi; **I need ~ this amount** j'en ai besoin de deux fois plus; **it'll take ~ the time** ça va prendre le double de temps; **she's ~ his age** elle a deux fois son âge, elle a le double de son âge; **unemployment is ~ what it was last year** le chômage est deux fois plus important que l'année dernière; **~ three is six** deux fois trois égale six; **2** [*fold, bend*] en deux; **to bend ~** se plier en deux; **to be bent ~ with pain/laughter** être plié en deux de douleur/rire; **to see ~** voir double.

V *vtr* **1** (increase twofold) doubler [*amount, price, rent, dose etc*]; multiplier [qch] par deux [*number*]; **2** (also **~ over**) (fold, bend) plier [qch] en deux or en double [*blanket, dressing etc*]; doubler [*thread*]; **3** (in spelling) doubler [*letter*]; **4** (in cards) (when making call in bridge) contrer; **to ~ the stakes** doubler la mise; **5** Mus doubler; **to ~ a part** doubler une partie; **6** Naut doubler [*cape*].

VI *vi* **1** [*sales, prices, salaries etc*] doubler; **to ~ in value** doubler de valeur; **2** (in bridge) contrer; **3 to ~ for sb** Cin, Theat doubler qn; **4** (serve dual purpose) **the sofa ~s as a bed** le canapé fait aussi lit; **the study ~s as a bedroom** le bureau sert aussi de chambre; **the gardener ~s as a chauffeur** le jardinier a aussi la fonction de chauffeur; **this actor ~s as the king in Act II** cet acteur joue aussi le rôle du roi dans le deuxième acte.

IDIOMS **on** ou **at the ~** fig au plus vite; Mil au pas redoublé, au pas de gymnastique; **~ or quits!** (in gambling) quitte ou double!

■ **double back** [*person, animal*] rebrousser chemin, faire demi-tour; [*road, track etc*] former un demi-tour.

■ **double over** = **double** V 2.

■ **double up**: ¶ **~ up 1** (bend one's body) se plier en deux; **to ~ up in pain/with laughter** être plié en deux de douleur/de rire; **2** (share sleeping accommodation) partager la même chambre; **3** GB (in betting) parier sur deux chevaux (*dans deux courses consécutives*); ¶ **to be ~d up** [*person, audience*] être plié en deux (**with** de).

double: **~ act** *n* Theat, fig duo *m*; **~-acting** *adj* à double effet; **~ agent** *n* agent *m* double; **~ album** *n* album *m* double; **~ bar** *n* Mus double barre *f*.

double-barrelled GB, **double-barreled** US /ˌdʌbl'bærəld/ *adj* [*gun*] à deux coups; **~ name** GB fig nom *m* à rallonge, ≈ nom à particule.

double: **~ bass** ▶1481 *n* (instrument) contrebasse *f*; (player) contrebassiste *mf*; **~ bassoon** ▶1481 *n* contrebasson *m*; **~ bed** *n* lit *m* double or à deux places, grand lit; **~-bedded** *adj* [*room*] avec or à lit double; **~ bend** *n* Aut virage *m* en S; **~ bill** *n* Theat représentation *f* avec deux œuvres au programme; Cin séance *f* avec deux films à la suite.

double bind *n* **1** gen impasse *f*; **to be caught in a ~** être pris dans une impasse; **2** Psych double contrainte *f*, double-bind *m*; **to put sb in a ~** exercer la double contrainte sur qn.

double: **~-blind** *adj* [*test, experiment, method*] en double aveugle; **~ bluff** *n*: *fait de dire la vérité à quelqu'un en faisant croire que c'est un mensonge*; **~ boiler** *n* US ≈ bain-marie *m*.

double-book I *vtr* **to ~ a room/seat etc** réserver la même chambre/place etc pour deux personnes; **they had ~ed the whole flight** (deliberately) ils avaient surbooké le vol.

II *vi* [*hotel, airline, company*] (as practice) surbooker.

double: **~ booking** *n* surbooking *m*; **~ bounce** *n* (in tennis) double rebond *m*; **~-breasted** *adj* [*jacket*] croisé.

double check I *n* deuxième or nouveau contrôle *m*.

II **double-check** *vtr* vérifier [qch] à nouveau [*figures, arrangements, date, time etc*].

double chin *n* double menton *m*; **to have several ~s** avoir plein de plis sous le menton.

double: **~-chinned** *adj* qui a un double menton; **~-clutch** *vi* US Aut = **double-declutch**; **~ consonant** *n* consonne *f* double or géminée; **~ cream** *n* GB Culin ≈ crème *f* fraîche.

double-cross○ /ˌdʌbl'krɒs/ I *n* trahison *f*.

II *vtr* doubler, trahir [*person*].

double: **~-crosser**○ *n* traître *m*; **~ cuff** *n* poignet *m* mousquetaire; **~ daggers** *npl* Print croix *f* double.

double date US I *n* **to go on a ~** sortir à deux couples.

II **double-date** *vi* sortir à deux couples.

double-dealing I *n* fourberie *f*.

II *adj* hypocrite, fourbe.

double-decker *n* **1** GB (bus) autobus *m* à impériale or à deux étages; **2** (sandwich) sandwich *m* double.

double: **~-declutch** *vi* GB Aut faire un double débrayage; **~ density** *adj* double densité.

double-digit *adj* à deux chiffres; **~ inflation** inflation *f* à deux chiffres.

double door(s) *n(pl)* porte *f* à deux battants.

double Dutch○ *n* baragouinage○ *m*; **to talk ~** baragouiner○; **it's all ~ to me!** c'est du chinois or de l'hébreu pour moi○!

double-edged *adj* lit, fig à double tranchant.

double entendre /ˌdu:bl ɑ:n'tɑ:ndrə/ *n* **1** (word, phrase) sous-entendu *m* (grivois); **2** (act, practice) **to resort to ~** faire des sous-entendus grivois.

double entry Accts I *n* comptabilité *f* en partie double.

II **double-entry** *modif* [*bookkeeping, accounts, system*] en partie double.

double exposure *n* Phot (act, process) surimpression *f*; (photograph) photo *f* en surimpression.

double-faced *adj* **1** [*fabric, material, shelving*] à double face; **2** péj [*person*] hypocrite.

double fault I *n* double faute *f*.

II **double-fault** *vi* faire une double faute.

double: **~ feature** *n* Cin séance *f* avec deux films à la suite; **~-figure** *adj* à deux chiffres.

double figures *npl* **to go into ~** [*inflation*] passer la barre de 10%.

double flat I *n* double bémol *m*.

II **double-flat** *adj* double bémol *inv*.

double-fronted *adj* [*house*] avec une fenêtre de part et d'autre.

double game *n* **to play a ~** jouer un double jeu.

double-glaze *vtr* mettre du double vitrage à [*window*]; **all the houses are fully ~d** toutes les maisons sont équipées de double vitrage.

double glazing *n* double vitrage *m*; **to put in ~** installer du double vitrage.

double: **~ helix** *n* double hélice *f*; **~ indemnity** *n* US *clause d'une assurance-vie selon laquelle la prime est doublée en cas de mort accidentelle*; **~ jeopardy** *n* US Jur remise *f* en accusation; **~-jointed** *adj* [*person, limb, finger*] souple.

double knit I *n* double-étoffe *f*.

II **double-knit** *modif* [*garment*] en double-étoffe.

double: **~ knitting (wool)** *n* grosse laine *f*; **~ knot** *n* double nœud *m*; **~-length cassette** *n* cassette *f* double durée.

double lock I *n* serrure *f* de sécurité.

II **double-lock** *vtr* fermer [qch] à double tour [*door*].

double negative *n* Ling double négation *f*.

double-park I *vtr* garer [qch] en double file [*vehicle*].

II *vi* se garer en double file.

double: **~ parking** *n* stationnement *m* en double file; **~ pneumonia** ▶1354 *n* pneumonie *f* double.

double-quick I *adj* **in ~ time** en un rien de temps.

II *adv* en vitesse, le plus vite possible.

double: **~ room** *n* chambre *f* double, chambre *f* pour deux personnes; **~ saucepan** *n* GB ≈ bain-marie *m inv*.

double sharp I *n* double dièse *m*.

II *adj* double dièse *inv*.

double: **~-sided disk** *n* Comput disquette *f* double face; **~-sided tape** *n* scotch® *m* double-face; **~-space** *vtr* taper [qch] en double interligne [*letter, text*]; **~ spacing** *n* double interligne *m*; **~ spread** *n* Journ article *m* (or publicité *f*) sur double page.

double standard *n* **to have ~s** faire deux poids deux mesures.

double: **~ star** *n* étoile *f* double; **~-stop** *vtr, vi* jouer en double corde; **~ stopping** *n* double corde *f*.

doublet /'dʌblɪt/ *n* **1** Fashn, Hist pourpoint *m*; **2** Ling doublet *m*.

double take *n* **to do a ~** avoir une réaction (de surprise) à retardement.

double: **~ talk** *n* péj langue *f* de bois; **~ taxation agreement** *n* convention *f* de double imposition.

double think *n* **to do a ~** *tenir un raisonnement dont on sait qu'il est fondé sur une contradiction flagrante*.

double time *n* **1 to be paid ~** être payé double; **2** US Mil pas *m* redoublé, pas *m* de gymnastique; **in ~** au pas redoublé, au pas de gymnastique.

doubleton /'dʌbltən/ *n* Games bigleton *m*.

double vision *n* **to have ~** voir double.

double wedding *n* **the sisters had a ~** les deux sœurs ont été mariées en même temps.

double: **~ whammy**○ *n* double coup *m* de malchance; **~ yellow line(s)** *n(pl)* GB Aut *marquage au sol interdisant le stationnement*.

double yolk *n* **an egg with a ~** un œuf double.

doubling /'dʌblɪŋ/ *n* (of cost, salary, amount, size, strength) doublement *m*; (of number, letter) (re)doublement *m*; **the new tax will result in the ~ of prices** cette nouvelle taxe va faire doubler les prix.

doubly /'dʌblɪ/ *adv* [*punished, deprived, disappointed*] doublement; [*difficult, confident*] deux fois plus (*before n*); **I made ~ sure that** j'ai bien vérifié que; **to be ~ careful** redoubler de prudence; **she is ~ gifted—as a writer and as an artist** elle a à la fois des dons d'écrivain et d'artiste.

doubry○ /'du:brɪ/ *n* (whatsit) truc○ *m*, machin○ *m*.

Doubs ▶1163 *pr n* Doubs *m*; **in/to the ~** dans le Doubs.

doubt /daʊt/ I *n* doute *m*; **there is no ~ (that)** il ne fait aucun doute que; **there is little ~ (that)** il est presque certain que; **there is no ~ about sth** il n'y a aucun doute sur qch; **there is no ~ about her guilt** ou **that she is guilty** il n'y a aucun doute sur sa culpabilité; **(there's) no ~ about it** il n'y a aucun doute là-dessus; **there is some ~ about its authenticity** son authenticité est mise en doute; **there's (some) ~ about** ou **as to whether he will be able to come** on ne sait pas s'il pourra venir; **there is no ~ in my mind that I'm right** je suis convaincu que j'ai raison or d'avoir raison; **to have no ~ (that)** ne pas douter que (+ *subj*); **I have no ~ about her guilt** ou **that she is guilty** je n'ai aucun doute sur sa culpabilité, je ne doute pas qu'elle soit coupable; **to have one's ~s about sth** avoir des doutes sur qch, douter de qch; **I have my ~s!** j'ai des doutes!, j'en doute!; **to have one's ~s (about)**

whether douter que (+ *subj*); **I have my ~s about whether he's telling the truth** je doute qu'il dise la vérité; **to have one's ~s about doing** hésiter à faire; **no ~** sans doute; **no ~ the police will want to speak to you, the police will no ~ want to speak to you** la police voudra sans doute vous parler; **to leave sb in no ~ about sth** ne laisser à qn aucun doute quant à qch; **to be in ~** [*outcome, project, future*] être incertain; [*honesty, innocence, guilt*] gen être douteux; (on particular occasion) être mis en doute; [*person*] être dans le doute; **this report has put the whole project in ~** ce rapport a mis tout le projet en question; **the election result is not in any ~** le résultat de l'élection ne fait pas l'ombre d'un doute; **if/when in ~** dans le doute; **to be open to ~** [*evidence, testimony*] être sujet à caution; **to cast** ou **throw ~ on sth** [*person*] mettre qch en doute; [*evidence, book*] jeter le doute sur qch; **beyond (all) ~, without (a) ~** sans aucun doute; **to prove sth beyond (all) ~** prouver qch de façon indubitable; **without the slightest ~** sans l'ombre d'un doute; **there is room for ~** le doute n'est pas exclu; **there is no room for ~** il n'y a aucun doute à avoir. ▶ **benefit**.

II *vtr* douter de [*fact, evidence, value, ability, honesty, person*]; **I ~ it (very much)!** j'en doute (beaucoup)!; **to ~ (if** ou **that** ou **whether)** douter que (+ *subj*); **I don't ~ that you're telling the truth** je ne doute pas que vous disiez la vérité; **I didn't ~ that she would succeed** je ne doutais pas qu'elle réussirait.

III *vi* douter.

doubter /ˈdaʊtə(r)/ *n* sceptique *mf*, douteur/-euse *m/f* liter.

doubtful /ˈdaʊtfl/ **I** *n* Pol indécis *m*.

II *adj* **1** (unsure) [*person, expression*] incertain, sceptique; [*future, weather, argument, evidence, result*] incertain; [*benefit*] douteux/-euse, incertain; **it is ~ if** ou **that** ou **whether** il n'est pas certain que (+ *subj*); **I am ~ that** ou **whether** je doute que (+*subj*); **to be ~ about doing** hésiter à faire; **to be ~ about** ou **as to** être peu convaincu par [*idea, explanation, plan*]; avoir des doutes sur [*job, object, purchase*]; **she was ~ about this** elle était peu convaincue; **I am ~ as to his suitability for the job** je ne suis pas convaincu qu'il convienne pour ce poste; **to be ~** [*person*] avoir des doutes; **2** (questionable) [*character, past, activity, taste*] douteux/-euse.

doubtfully /ˈdaʊtfəlɪ/ *adv* **1** (hesitantly) [*speak, say*] d'un ton hésitant or incertain; [*look, listen*] d'un air hésitant or incertain; **2** (with disbelief) [*speak, say*] d'un ton sceptique; [*look, listen*] d'un air sceptique; **3** (not convincingly) [*argue*] de façon discutable.

doubtfulness /ˈdaʊtfəlnɪs/ *n* **1** (uncertainty) indécision *f*; (scepticism) scepticisme *m*; **2** (questionable nature) (of person's past, of taste) caractère *m* suspect or douteux.

doubting Thomas /ˌdaʊtɪŋ ˈtɒməs/ *n* incrédule *mf*; **to be a ~** être comme Saint Thomas.

doubtless /ˈdaʊtlɪs/ *adv* sans doute.

douche /duːʃ/ **I** *n* gen, Med douche *f*.

II *vtr* gen, Med doucher.

III *v refl* **to ~ oneself** gen, Med se doucher.

dough /dəʊ/ *n* **1** Culin pâte *f*; **bread/pizza ~** pâte à pain/à pizza; **2**○ (money) fric○ *m*, argent *m*.

doughboy† /ˈdəʊbɔɪ/ *n* US argot des militaires sammy○ *m* (*soldat américain, surtout dans la première guerre mondiale*).

doughnut, **donut** US /ˈdəʊnʌt/ *n* beignet *m*; **jam/cream ~** beignet à la confiture/à la crème.

IDIOMS **it's dollars to ~s that**○ je te parie que○.

doughty† /ˈdaʊtɪ/ *adj* [*person, courage, defence*] vaillant; [*deed*] de bravoure.

doughy /ˈdəʊɪ/ *adj* [*substance, consistency, bread, taste*] pâteux/-euse; [*skin, complexion*] terreux/-euse.

Douglas fir /ˌdʌgləsˈfɜː(r)/ *n* (sapin *m* de) Douglas *m*.

dour /dʊə(r)/ *adj* [*person, expression*] renfrogné; [*resentment, landscape*] morne; [*mood, indifference*] maussade; [*building*] austère.

dourly /ˈdʊəlɪ/ *adv* [*say, speak*] d'un ton maussade; [*smile, frown*] d'un air renfrogné.

douse, **dowse** /daʊs/ *vtr* tremper [*person, room*]; noyer, éteindre [*flame, fire*] (**with** avec); **to ~ sb/sth with water** tremper qn/qch; **to ~ sb/sth with** ou **in petrol** arroser qn/qch d'essence.

dove I /dʌv/ *n* Zool, Pol colombe *f*.

II /dəʊv/ US *prét* ▶ **dive**.

dovecot(e) /ˈdʌvkɒt, ˈdʌvkəʊt/ *n* pigeonnier *m*, colombier *m*.

dove-grey ▶**1104** *n, adj* gris (*m*) perle *inv*.

doveish, **dovish** /ˈdʌvɪʃ/ *adj* Pol [*person, policy, speech, opinion*] (à tendance) pacifiste.

Dover /ˈdəʊvə(r)/ ▶**1818** *pr n* Douvres; **the Straits of ~** le Pas *m* de Calais.

Dover sole *n* sole *f* de Douvres.

dovetail /ˈdʌvteɪl/ **I** *n* Constr (joint) assemblage *m* à queue-d'aronde; (part of joint) queue-d'aronde *f*.

II *vtr* **1** fig faire concorder [*plans, policies, research, arguments*] (**with** avec); **2** Constr assembler [qch] à queue-d'aronde [*pieces*].

III *vi* fig (also **~ together**) bien cadrer ensemble; **to ~ with sth** cadrer avec qch.

dowager /ˈdaʊədʒə(r)/ *n, adj* douairière (*f*) also hum.

dowdiness /ˈdaʊdɪnɪs/ *n* manque *m* d'élégance.

dowdy /ˈdaʊdɪ/ *adj* [*woman*] sans élégance; [*clothes*] vieux jeu *inv*; [*image*] vieillotte○; **I look so ~!** j'ai l'air d'un sac○!

dowel /ˈdaʊəl/ **I** *n* cheville *f*.

II *vtr* (*p pres etc* **-ll-** GB, **-l-** US) cheviller.

Dow-Jones (industrial average) /ˌdaʊˈdʒəʊnz/ *n* indice *m* Dow Jones.

down[1] /daʊn/

■ **Note** *down* often occurs as the second element in verb combinations in English (*go down, fall down, get down, keep down, put down etc*). For translations, consult the appropriate verb entry (***go***, ***fall***, ***get***, ***keep***, ***put*** etc).
– When used to indicate vague direction, *down* often has no explicit translation in French: *to go down to London* = aller à Londres; *down in Brighton* = à Brighton.
– For examples and further usages, see the entry below.

I *adv* **1** (from higher to lower level) **to go ~** ou **come ~** descendre; **to fall ~** tomber; **to sit ~ on the floor** s'asseoir par terre; **to pull ~ a blind** baisser un store; **I'm on my way ~** je descends; **I'll be right ~** je descends tout de suite; **~!** (to dog) couché!; **'~'** (in crossword) 'verticalement'; **read ~ to the end of the paragraph** lire jusqu'à la fin du paragraphe; **2** (indicating position at lower level) **~ below** en bas; (when looking down from height) en contrebas; **the noise was coming from ~ below** le bruit venait d'en bas; **they could see the lake ~ below** ils voyaient le lac en contrebas; **~ there** là-bas; **'where are you?'—'~ here!'** 'où es-tu?'—'ici!'; **to keep one's head ~** garder la tête baissée; **the blinds were ~** les stores étaient baissés; **a sports car with the hood ~** une voiture de sport avec la capote baissée; **several trees were blown ~** plusieurs arbres ont été abattus par le vent; **a bit further ~** un peu plus bas; **their office is two floors ~** leur bureau est deux étages plus bas; **it's on the second shelf ~** c'est au deuxième rayon en partant du haut; **the coal lies 900 metres ~** le charbon se trouve neuf cents mètres plus bas; **it's ~ at the bottom of the lake** c'est tout au fond du lac; **the telephone lines are ~** les lignes téléphoniques sont coupées; **3** (from upstairs) **is Tim ~ yet?** est-ce que Tim est déjà descendu?; **4** (indicating direction) **to go ~ to Nice/Brighton** descendre à Nice/Brighton; **to go ~ to London** aller à Londres; **~ in Brighton** à Brighton; **they've gone ~ to the country for the day** ils sont allés passer la journée à la campagne; **they moved ~ here from Scotland a year ago** ils ont quitté l'Écosse pour venir s'installer ici il y a un an; **they live ~ south**○ ils habitent dans le sud; **5** (in a range, scale, hierarchy) **children from the age of 10 ~** les enfants de moins de dix ans; **everybody from the Prime Minister ~** tout le monde depuis le Premier Ministre; **everybody from the lady of the manor ~ to the lowliest servant** tout le monde, de la châtelaine au domestique le plus humble; **from the sixteenth century ~ to the present day** du seizième siècle à nos jours; **6** (indicating loss of money, decrease in profits etc) **hotel bookings are ~ by a half this year** les réservations dans les hôtels ont baissé de moitié par rapport à l'année dernière; **this year's profits are well ~ on last year's** les bénéfices de cette année sont nettement inférieurs à ceux de l'année dernière; **I'm £10 ~** il me manque 10 livres sterling; **tourism is ~ 40% this year** le tourisme a chuté de 40% cette année; **7** (indicating decrease in extent, volume, quality, process) **to get one's weight ~** maigrir; **we managed to get the price ~ to £200** nous avons réussi à faire baisser le prix à 200 livres sterling; **in the end she managed to get the article ~ to five pages** finalement elle a réussi à réduire l'article à cinq pages; **I'm ~ to my last fiver**○ **cigarette** il ne me reste plus que cinq livres sterling/qu'une cigarette; **he described her exactly, right ~ to the colour of her eyes** il l'a décrite très précisément, jusqu'à la couleur de ses yeux; **'dollar fever ~ on Wall St'** journ 'la spéculation sur le dollar en baisse à Wall Street'; **that's seven ~, three to go!** en voilà sept de faits, il n'en reste plus que trois à faire!; **8** (in writing) **to put sth ~ (on paper** ou **in writing)** mettre qch par écrit; **it's set ~ here in black and white** c'est écrit ici noir sur blanc; **9** (on list, programme, schedule) **to put sb's name ~ for sth** inscrire qn pour qch; **you're ~ to speak next** c'est toi qui es le prochain à intervenir; **I've got you ~ for next Thursday** (in appointment book) vous avez rendez-vous jeudi prochain; **10** (incapacitated) **to be ~ with the flu/with malaria** avoir la grippe/la malaria; **11** Sport (behind) **to be two sets/six points ~** [*tennis player*] avoir deux sets/six points de retard; **the team is ~ 12–6** l'équipe est menée 12 à 6; **12** (as deposit) **to pay £40 ~** payer 40 livres sterling comptant; **13** (downwards) **he was lying face ~** il était couché, le visage face au sol; **the bread fell with the buttered side ~** la tartine est tombée avec la face beurrée sur le sol.

II *prep* **1** (from higher to lower point) **they came running ~ the hill** ils ont descendu la colline en courant; **tears ran ~ his face** les larmes coulaient le long de ses joues; **did you enjoy the journey ~?** est-ce que tu as fait bon voyage?; **she's gone ~ town** elle est allée en ville; **2** (at a lower part of) **they live ~ the road** ils habitent un peu plus loin dans la rue; **it's ~ the corridor to your right** c'est dans le couloir sur la droite; **it's a few miles ~ the river from here** c'est à quelques kilomètres en aval de la rivière; **the kitchen is ~ those stairs** la cuisine est en bas de cet escalier; **3** (along) **to go ~ the street** descendre la rue; **a dress with buttons all ~ the front** une robe boutonnée sur le devant; **he looked ~ her throat** il a regardé au fond de sa gorge; **to look ~ a tunnel/telescope** regarder dans un tunnel/télescope; **4** (throughout) **~ the ages** ou **centuries** au cours des siècles, à travers les siècles.

III *adj* **1**○ (depressed) déprimé; **to feel ~**

avoir le cafard○, être déprimé; **2** [*escalator, elevator*] qui descend; GB Rail [*train, line*] descendant; **3** Comput en panne.
IV○ *vtr* **1** abattre, terrasser [*person*]; descendre [*plane*]; **2** (drink) **he ~ed his beer** il a descendu○ son verre de bière.
IDIOMS **to have a ~ on sb, to be ~ on sb**○ avoir une dent contre qn, en vouloir à qn; **you don't hit a man when he's ~** Prov on ne frappe pas un homme à terre; **it's ~ to you to do it** c'est à toi de le faire; **it's ~ to you now** c'est à toi de jouer maintenant; **~ with tyrants/the king!** à bas les tyrans/le roi!

down² /daʊn/ *n* (all contexts) duvet *m*.

Down /daʊn/ ▶ 1624 *pr n* comté *m* de Down.

down-and-out /ˌdaʊnən'aʊt/ I *n* clochard/-e *m/f*.
II *adj* **to be ~** être à la rue.

down-at-heel /ˌdaʊnət'hiːl/ *adj* miteux/-euse.

downbeat /'daʊnbiːt/ I *n* Mus temps *m* fort.
II *adj*○ **1** (depressed) [*person*] abattu; (pessimistic) [*view, assessment*] pessimiste; **2** (laid-back) décontracté.

down-bow /'daʊnbəʊ/ *n* Mus tiré *m*.

downcast /'daʊnkɑːst, US -kæst/ *adj* **1** (directed downwards) [*eyes, look*] baissé; **2** (dejected) découragé.

downdraught /'daʊndraːft, US -dræft/ *n* US courant *m* descendant.

downer○ /'daʊnə(r)/ *n* **1 to be on a ~** (be depressed) déprimer; **2** (pill) calmant *m*.

downfall /'daʊnfɔːl/ *n* **1** (of person, government, dynasty) chute *f*; **she/drink proved to be his ~** c'est elle/la boisson qui a causé sa perte; **2** (of rain, snow) chute *f*.

downgrade /'daʊngreɪd/ I *n* US (route *f* en) pente *f*; **to be on the ~** fig baisser, être sur le déclin.
II *vtr* **1** (demote) rétrograder [*employee*]; **the hotel has been ~d to a guest house** l'hôtel a été déclassé et c'est maintenant une pension de famille; **2** (degrade) dévaloriser [*task, occupation*].

downhearted /'daʊnhaːtɪd/ *adj* abattu.

downhill /ˌdaʊn'hɪl/ I *adj* [*path, road*] en pente, qui descend.
II *adv* **to go ~** [*path, road, person, vehicle*] descendre; fig [*person*] être sur le déclin; **she has gone ~ a lot since you saw her last** sa santé s'est beaucoup détériorée depuis la dernière fois que tu l'as vue; **since he took over as manager business has gone ~** depuis qu'il est directeur les affaires vont mal; **from now on it's ~ all the way** fig (easy) à partir de maintenant il ne devrait plus y avoir de problèmes; (disastrous) à partir de maintenant c'est le déclin.

down: **~hill race** *n* (épreuve *f* de) descente *f*; **~hill ski(ing)** *n* ski *m* de descente; **~-home**○ *adj* US (from Southern states) du Sud (des États-Unis); (rustic) campagnard, rustique.

Downing Street /'daʊnɪŋˈstriːt/ *n* GB (*rue où est située*) *la résidence du premier ministre britannique*; fig *le premier ministre ou le gouvernement britannique* cf Matignon.

down: **~-in-the-mouth**○ *adj* abattu, triste; **~load** *vtr* Comput télécharger; **~loading** *n* Comput téléchargement *m*; **~market** *adj* [*products, goods, hotel, restaurant*] bas de gamme *inv*; [*area, neighbourhood*] populaire; [*newspaper, programme*] grand public *inv*.

down payment *n* acompte *m*; **to make a ~ of £50** verser un acompte de 50 livres sterling.

down: **~pipe** *n* GB gouttière *f*; **~play**○ *vtr* minimiser l'importance de [*event, incident*]; **~pour** *n* averse *f*.

downright /'daʊnraɪt/ I *adj* **1** (absolute) [*insult*] véritable (*before n*); [*refusal*] catégorique; [*liar*] fieffé (*before n*); **he's a ~ fool** c'est un imbécile fini; **that's a ~ lie!** c'est un mensonge éhonté!; **2** (forthright) [*person*] franc/franche, direct.
II *adv* [*stupid, rude*] carrément.

downriver /ˌdaʊn'rɪvə(r)/ *adj, adv* en aval.

downs /daʊnz/ *npl* GB (hills) collines *fpl*; **the Downs** les Downs *fpl* (*collines du sud de l'Angleterre*).

downshift /'daʊnʃɪft/ US Aut I *n* passage *m* à une vitesse inférieure.
II *vi* rétrograder.

downside○ /'daʊnsaɪd/ I *n* gen inconvénient *m* (**of** de).
II **downside up** *adj phr, adv phr* US sens dessus dessous.

downsize /ˌdaʊn'saɪz/ *vi* **1** (streamline) réduire les effectifs; **2** Comput micromiser.

downspout *n* US = **downpipe**.

Down's syndrome /'daʊnz sɪndrəʊm/ I *n* trisomie *f* 21.
II *modif* [*person*] trisomique.

downstage /'daʊnsteɪdʒ/ *adj, adv* vers le devant de la scène (**from** par rapport à).

downstairs /ˌdaʊn'steəz/ I *n* rez-de-chaussée *m inv*.
II *adj* [*room*] gen en bas; (on ground-floor specifically) du rez-de-chaussée; **the ~ flat** GB ou **apartment** US l'appartement du rez-de-chaussée; **'with ~ bathroom'** 'avec salle de bains au rez-de-chaussée'.
III *adv* en bas; **to go** ou **come ~** descendre (l'escalier); **a noise came from ~** il y a eu un bruit venant d'en bas.

downstate /'daʊnsteɪt/ US I *n* **to come from ~** (south) venir du sud (*d'un État*); (rural) venir du fin fond d'un État.
II *adj* du sud (*d'un État*).
III *adv* [*go*] vers le sud (*d'un État*).

downstream /'daʊnstriːm/ *adj, adv* lit, fig en aval (**of** de); **to go ~** descendre le courant.

downstream industry *n*: *secteur de l'industrie pétrolière en aval de la production*.

down: **~stroke** *n* (in writing) plein *m*; **~swept** *adj* Aviat [*wings*] surbaissé.

downswing /'daʊnswɪŋ/ *n* **1** (in golf) downswing *m*; **2** Econ = **downtrend**.

downtime /'daʊntaɪm/ *n* **1** Comput temps *m* d'indisponibilité, temps *m* mort; **2** US (in factory, workplace) *temps pendant lequel les ouvriers ne sont pas productifs*.

down-to-earth /'daʊntə'ɜːθ/ *adj* [*person, approach*] pratique; **she's very ~** (practical) elle a les pieds sur terre; (unpretentious) elle est très simple.

downtown /'daʊntaʊn/ surt US I *adj* [*store, hotel, streets etc*] du centre ville; **~ New York/Boston** le centre de New York/Boston.
II *adv* en ville.

down: **~trend** *n* Econ tendance *f* à la baisse; **~trodden** *adj* [*person, country*] opprimé; **~turn** *n* (in economy) déclin *m* (**in** de); (in demand, profits) chute *f*, baisse *f* (**in** de).

down under○ I *n* (Australia) Australie *f*; (New Zealand) Nouvelle-Zélande *f*.
II *adv* **to go ~** aller en Australie (or en Nouvelle-Zélande).

downward /'daʊnwəd/ I *adj* [*movement, glance, stroke*] vers le bas; [*path*] en pente, qui descend; **to be on the ~ path** fig être sur une pente glissante.
II *adv* = **downwards**.

downward mobility *n* régression *f* sociale.

downwards /'daʊnwədz/ *adv* [*look*] en bas, vers le bas; [*gesture*] vers le bas; **to slope ~** descendre en pente (**to** vers); **read the list from the top ~** lire la liste de haut en bas; **she laid the cards face ~ on the table** elle a mis les cartes sur la table sans les retourner; **he was floating face ~** il flottait le visage dans l'eau; **from the 15th century ~** depuis le quinzième siècle; **everybody from the boss ~** tout le monde depuis le patron.

downward trend *n* Econ tendance *f* à la baisse.

downwind /ˌdaʊn'wɪnd/ *adv* dans le sens du vent; **to be ~ of sth** Hunt avoir le vent de qch; **the ashes drifted ~ from the fire** les cendres étaient emportées par le vent.

downy /'daʊnɪ/ *adj* **1** [*skin, cheek, fruit*] duveté, duveteux/-euse; **2** [*pillow, bed*] duveteux/-euse.

dowry /'daʊərɪ/ *n* dot *f*.

dowse /daʊz/ I *vtr* = **douse**.
II *vi* (for water) faire de la rhabdomancie; Miner faire de la radiesthésie.

dowser /'daʊzə(r)/ *n* (water diviner) sourcier/-ière *m/f*; Miner radiesthésiste *mf*.

doxology /dɒk'sɒlədʒɪ/ *n* doxologie *f*.

doxy○‡ /'dɒksɪ/ *n* ribaude○† *f*.

doyen /'dɔɪən/ *n* sout doyen *m* (d'âge).

doyenne /dɔɪ'en/ *n* sout doyenne *f*.

doz *abrév écrite* = **dozen**.

doze /dəʊz/ I *n* somme *m*; **to have a ~** faire un somme; **to fall into a ~** s'assoupir.
II *vi* [*person, cat*] somnoler.
■ **doze off**: **~ off** (momentarily) s'assoupir; (to sleep) s'endormir.

dozen /'dʌzn/ *n* **1** Meas (twelve) douzaine *f*; **two ~ eggs** deux douzaines d'œufs; **a ~ people** une douzaine de personnes; **'£1 a ~'** 'une livre sterling la douzaine'; **by the ~** à la douzaine; **2** (several) **I've told you a ~ times!** je te l'ai déjà dit cent fois!; **~s of** des dizaines de [*people, things, times*]; **I can think of a ~ good reasons** (**for doing**) je peux trouver dix bonnes raisons (pour faire).

dozer○ /'dəʊzə(r)/ *n* bulldozer *m*.

dozy /'dəʊzɪ/ *adj* **1** (drowsy) somnolent; **2**○ GB (stupid) gourde○.

DPhil *n*: *abrév* ▶ **Doctor of Philosophy**.

DPP *n* GB *abrév* ▶ **Director of Public Prosecutions**.

Dr *n* **1** *abrév écrite* = **Doctor**; **2** *abrév écrite* = **Drive**.

drab /dræb/ I *n* **1** Tex (fabric) toile *f* bise.
II *adj* [*colour, decor, lifestyle*] terne; [*day*] gris; [*building, suburb*] triste.

drabness /'dræbnɪs/ *n* (of colour, decor, clothes) aspect *m* terne; (of building, place, life) grisaille *f*.

drachm /dræm/ *n* **1** Pharm drachme *f*; **2** = **drachma**.

drachma /'drækmə/ *n* (*pl* **~s**, **~e**) drachme *f*.

draconian /drə'kəʊnɪən/ *adj* draconien/-ienne.

draft /drɑːft, US dræft/ I *n* **1** (of letter, article, speech) brouillon *m*; (of novel, play) ébauche *f*; (of contract, law, plan) avant-projet *m*; **2** Fin traite *f* (**on** sur); **to make a ~ on a bank** tirer sur une banque; ▶ **bank draft**; **3** US Mil (conscription) service *m* militaire; **4** (intake) Mil contingent *m*; **5** US = **draught**.
II *modif* gen, Jur [*agreement, resolution, version*] préliminaire; **~ directive** EC directive *f* préliminaire; **~ legislation/report** avant-projet *m* de loi/de rapport; **~ ruling** décision *f* préliminaire.
III *vtr* **1** faire le brouillon de [*letter, article, speech*]; faire l'avant-projet de [*contract, law, plan*]; **2** US Mil (conscript) incorporer (**into** dans); **3** GB (transfer) détacher [*personnel*] (**to** auprès de; **from** de); **he's been ~ed to India** il a été détaché pour l'Inde; **4** Sport sélectionner; **5** US (choose) **to ~ sb to do** charger qn de faire.
■ **draft in** GB: **~ in [sb]**, **~ [sb] in** faire venir, amener [*personnel, experts, police*] (**to do** pour faire).

draft: **~ board** *n* US Mil conseil *m* de révision; **~ card** *n* US Mil ordre *m* d'incorporation; **~ dodger** *n* US Mil insoumis *m*.

draftee /drɑːf'tiː, US dræf'tiː/ *n* US Mil recrue *f*.

draftiness US = **draughtiness**.

draft: **~ing table** *n* US table *f* à dessin; **~sman** US = **draughtsman** 1, 2; **~smanship** US = **draughtsmanship**.

drafty US = **draughty**.

drag /dræg/ **I** *n* **1**○ (bore) (person) raseur/-euse *m/f*; **Peter's a ~** Peter est un raseur○; **the lecture was a ~** la conférence était rasante○; **I know it's a ~ but** je sais que c'est embêtant○ mais; **it's such a ~ having to do** quelle barbe○ d'être obligé de faire; **what a ~!** quelle barbe○!; **2** Aviat, Phys traînée *f*; **3** fig (hindrance) frein *m* (**to** à); **4** (sledge) traîneau *m*; **5** (hook) grappin *m*, araignée *f*; **6** Hunt drag *m*; **7**○ (puff) taffe◑ *f*, bouffée *f*; **to have a ~ on** tirer une taffe sur; **8** (women's clothes worn by men) vêtements *mpl* de travesti; **to dress up in ~** se travestir; **to be in ~** être en travesti; **9**○ US (influence) piston○ *m*; **10**○ (road) **the main ~** la rue *f* principale.
II *modif* **1** Theat [*act, artist, show*] de travesti; [*ball*] travesti; **2** Aut Sport [*race, racing*] de dragsters; [*racer*] de dragster.
III *vtr* (*p prés etc* **-gg-**) **1** (pull) tirer [*boat, log, sledge*] (**to, up to** jusqu'à; **towards** vers); **to ~ a chair over to the window** tirer une chaise vers la fenêtre; **to ~ sth along the ground** faire traîner qch par terre; **to ~ sb from** arracher qn de [*chair, bed*]; **to ~ sb to** traîner qn à [*match*]; traîner qn chez [*dentist*]; **to ~ sb into** traîner qn dans [*room, bushes*]; vouloir mêler qn à [*argument, dispute*]; **don't ~ me into this** je ne veux pas me mêler de ça; **don't ~ my mother into this** ne mêle pas ma mère à ça; **to ~ sb through the courts** traîner qn devant les tribunaux; **to ~ sb's name through** ou **in the mud** traîner qn dans la boue; **2** (search) draguer [*river, pond*]; **3** Comput déplacer, faire glisser [*icon*]; **4** (trail) traîner; **to ~ sth in the dirt** traîner qch dans la boue; **to ~ one's feet** ou **heels** lit traîner les pieds; fig faire preuve de mauvaise volonté (**on** quant à).
IV *vi* (*p prés etc* **-gg-**) **1** (go slowly) [*hours, days*] traîner ; [*story, plot*] traîner en longueur; **the third act ~ged** le troisième acte était interminable; **2** (trail) **to ~ in** [*hem, belt*] traîner dans [*mud*]; **3** (rub) [*brake*] frotter; **4** (inhale) **to ~ on** tirer une bouffée de [*cigarette*].
V *v refl* **to ~ oneself to** se traîner jusqu'à [*work*].
■ **drag along**: ¶ **~ [sth] along** traîner; ¶ **~ [sb] along to** traîner [qn] à [*opera, show, lecture*].
■ **drag away**: ¶ **~ [sb] away** emmener [qn] de force; **to ~ sb away from** arracher qn à [*TV, party*]; ¶ **~ [oneself] away from [sth]** partir à regret de [*party*]; **I couldn't ~ myself away** j'étais cloué sur place.
■ **drag down**: **~ [sth] down** rabaisser [*level, standard*]; **to be ~ged down to sb's level** être rabaissé au niveau de qn; **he ~ged me down with him** fig il m'a entraîné dans sa chute.
■ **drag in**: **~ [sth] in, ~ in [sth]** mentionner, placer [*name, story*].
■ **drag on** [*conflict, speech*] traîner en longueur; **to let sth ~ on** laisser qch traîner en longueur; **the war ~ged on until 1918** la guerre s'est prolongée jusqu'en 1918.
■ **drag out**: ¶ **~ [sth] out** faire traîner [*speech, meeting*]; ¶ **~ [sth] out of sb** arracher [qch] à qn [*apology, truth*].
■ **drag up**: **~ [sth] up, ~ up [sth]** déterrer [*secret, past*]; **where were you ~ged up?** hum où est-ce que tu as été élevé?

drag coefficient, **drag factor** *n* Aut, Aviat coefficient *m* de traînée.

draggy○ /ˈdrægɪ/ *adj* rasoir○.

drag: **~ harrow** *n* Agric herse *f*; **~ hunt** *n* Hunt drag *m*; **~ lift** *n* Sport tire-fesses○ *m inv*.

dragnet /ˈdrægnet/ *n* **1** Fishg drège *f*; **2** Hunt tirasse *f*; **3** (raid) rafle *f*.

dragoman‡ /ˈdrægəmən/ *n* drogman† *m*.

dragon /ˈdrægən/ *n* dragon *m* also pej or hum.
IDIOMS **to chase the ~** argot des drogués se camer (*à l'opium ou à l'héroïne*).

dragonfly /ˈdrægənflaɪ/ *n* libellule *f*.

dragoon /drəˈɡuːn/ **I** *n* Mil dragon *m*.
II *vtr* **to ~ sb into doing sth** forcer qn à faire qch.

drag queen○ *n* Theat travesti *m*.

dragster /ˈdrægstə(r)/ *n* Aut Sport dragster *m*.

dragstrip /ˈdrægstrɪp/ *n* Aut Sport piste *f* de vitesse.

drain /dreɪn/ **I** *n* **1** (in street) canalisation *f*; **to unblock the ~s** déboucher les canalisations; **open ~** canalisation à ciel ouvert; **to drop sth down a ~** faire tomber qch dans une bouche d'égout; **2** (in building) (sewer) canalisation *f* d'évacuation; (waste water pipe) descente *f* d'eau; **3** (ditch) fossé *m* d'écoulement; (on marshland) fossé *m* d'assainissement; **4** (loss) (of people, skills, money) hémorragie *f* (**of** de); **to be a ~ on** représenter une ponction sur [*profits, funds, resources*]; **5** Med drain *m*.
II *vtr* **1** drainer [*land, lake*]; purger [*radiator, boiler*]; **2** Culin égoutter [*pasta, canned food, dishes*]; **3** (sap) épuiser [*strength, energy, resources, funds*]; **to ~ sb of strength/energy** vider qn de ses forces/son énergie; **to ~ sth of resources/funds** épuiser les ressources/les fonds de qch; **4** (drink) vider [*glass*]; boire [qch] jusqu'à la dernière goutte [*contents, drink*]; **5** [*river*] collecter les eaux de [*area, basin*]; **6** Med drainer [*wound*].
III *vi* **1** (empty) [*water, liquid*] s'écouler (**out of, from** de); [*bath, radiator, sink*] se vider; **to ~ into** s'écouler dans [*sea, river, gutter, ditch*]; s'infiltrer dans [*soil, rock*]; **the blood** ou **colour ~ed from her face** le sang reflua de son visage; **I can see the life ~ing out of him** je vois la vie le quitter peu à peu; **2** (become dry) [*dishes, food*] (s')égoutter; **to leave sth to ~** laisser qch (s')égoutter.
IDIOMS **to go down the ~**○ fig tomber à l'eau○; **that's £100 down the ~**○ ça fait 100 livres sterling de fichues en l'air○; **to laugh like a ~**○ être mort de rire○.
■ **drain away**: **1** [*water, liquid*] s'écouler; **2** [*courage, hope, strength, funds*] s'épuiser.
■ **drain off**, **drain out**: ¶ **~ off** [*water, liquid*] s'écouler; ¶ **~ [sth] off, ~ off [sth]** vider [*fluid, water*].

drainage /ˈdreɪnɪdʒ/ **I** *n* **1** (of land, marsh, wound) drainage *m*; **2** (system of pipes, ditches) tout-à-l'égout *m inv*.
II *modif* [*channel, hole, pipe, technique*] de drainage.

drainage: **~ area, ~ basin** *n* bassin *m* de drainage or hydrographique spec; **~ tube** *n* Med drain *m*.

drainboard /ˈdreɪnbɔːd/ *n* US égouttoir *m*.

drained /dreɪnd/ *adj* [*person, face*] épuisé, vidé○.

drained weight *n* poids *m* net égoutté.

drainer /ˈdreɪnə(r)/ *n* égouttoir *m*.

draining /ˈdreɪnɪŋ/ **I** *n* (of marsh, land) assainissement *m*; (of rain, water in pipes) écoulement *m*.
II *adj* (emotionally, physically) épuisant, vidant○.

draining board *n* égouttoir *m*.

drainpipe /ˈdreɪnpaɪp/ **I** *n* (for rain water) descente *f* de gouttière; (for waste water, sewage) descente *f*.
II drainpipes○ *npl* GB (also **drainpipe trousers**) pantalon *m* moulant.

drake /dreɪk/ *n* canard *m* (mâle).

dram /dræm/ *n* **1** Pharm drachme *f*; **2**○ Scot (drink) petit verre *m*.

drama /ˈdrɑːmə/ **I** *n* **1** (genre) gen théâtre *m*; TV, Radio (as opposed to documentary programme) fiction *f*; **modern ~** le théâtre moderne; **2** (acting, directing) art *m* dramatique; **3** (play) drame *m*; TV, Radio dramatique *f*; **4** Journ hum (dramatic event) drame *m*; **a human ~** un drame humain; **5** (fuss) drame *m*; **to make a ~ out of sth** faire tout un drame de qch; **6** ¢ (excitement) **her life was full of ~** elle menait une vie très mouvementée.
II *modif* [*school, course, student*] d'art dramatique; **~ critic** critique *m* dramatique; **~ documentary** TV reportage *m* fiction.

dramatic /drəˈmætɪk/ *adj* **1** Literat, Theat [*literature, art, irony, effect*] dramatique; [*gesture, entrance, exit*] théâtral; **for ~ effect** pour produire un effet dramatique; **2** (tense, exciting) [*situation, event*] dramatique; **3** (sudden, radical) [*change, impact, goal, landscape*] spectaculaire.

dramatically /drəˈmætɪklɪ/ *adv* **1** (radically) radicalement; **2** (causing excitement) de façon spectaculaire; **3** Literat, Theat du point de vue théâtral; **4** (in a theatrical way) [*gesture, pause*] de façon théâtrale.

dramatics /drəˈmætɪks/ *npl* **1** art *m* dramatique; **2** péj cinéma *m* pej.

dramatic society *n* groupe *m* de théâtre amateur.

dramatis personae /ˌdræmətɪs pɜːˈsəʊnaɪ/ *npl* sout (characters) personnages *mpl* (d'une pièce); (actors) distribution *f*.

dramatist /ˈdræmətɪst/ *n* auteur *m* dramatique.

dramatization /ˌdræmətaɪˈzeɪʃn, US -tɪˈz-/ *n* **1** (dramatized version) (of novel, event) version *f* théâtrale; **TV/musical ~** version *f* pour la télévision/musicale; **2** (technique) (for stage) adaptation *f* pour la scène; (for screen) adaptation *f* pour l'écran; **3** (exaggeration) dramatisation *f*.

dramatize /ˈdræmətaɪz/ **I** *vtr* **1** (adapt) Theat adapter [qch] pour la scène; Cin, TV adapter [qch] pour l'écran; Radio adapter [qch] pour la radio; **2** (enact, depict) dépeindre; **3** (make dramatic) donner un caractère dramatique à; pej dramatiser [*event, problem*].
II *vi* dramatiser.
III dramatized *pp adj* [*account, series, version*] dramatique; **~d documentary** docudrame *m*.

drank /dræŋk/ *prét* ▶ **drink**.

drape /dreɪp/ **I** *n* **1** US (curtain) (*gén pl*) rideau *m*; **2** (of fabric) drapé *m*.
II *vtr* **to ~ sth with sth, to ~ sth over sth** draper qch de qch; **walls ~d with...** murs tendus de...; **~d in sth** [*person, statue*] enveloppé dans qch; **to ~ oneself over an armchair** s'étaler sur un fauteuil; **she was ~d around his neck**○ hum elle était pendue à son cou○.

draper† /ˈdreɪpə(r)/ GB *n* marchand/-e *m/f* de nouveautés; **~'s shop** magasin *m* de nouveautés.

drapery /ˈdreɪpərɪ/ **I** *n* (decorative) tentures *fpl*.
II draperies *npl* US rideaux *mpl*.

drastic /ˈdræstɪk/ *adj* **1** (severe) [*policy, step, measure*] draconien/-ienne; [*reduction, remedy*] drastique; [*effect*] catastrophique; **2** (dramatic) [*change*] radical.

drastically /ˈdræstɪklɪ/ *adv* **1** (profoundly) [*change, reduce*] radicalement; **2** (severely) [*reduce, limit*] sévèrement; **things went ~ wrong** les choses ont pris une très mauvaise tournure.

drat○ /dræt/ *excl* **~ (it)!** diable†!, zut○!; **~ that man!** il m'agace cet homme○!; **you're right, ~ you!** tu as raison, sale bête○!

dratted○ /ˈdrætɪd/ *adj* [*person, thing*] maudit.

draught GB, **draft** US /drɑːft/, US dræft/ **I** *n* **1** (cold air) courant *m* d'air; **2** (in fireplace) tirage *m*; **3 on ~** [*beer etc*] à la pression; **4** (of liquid, air) trait *m*; **in a single ~** d'un seul trait; **taking long ~s of cool air** aspirant l'air frais à longs traits; **5**‡ (potion) potion *f*; **6** (of ship) tirant *m* d'eau; **7** GB Games (piece) pion *m* (de jeu de dames).
II *modif* **1** [*beer, cider*] (à la) pression; **2** [*animal, horse*] de trait.
IDIOMS **to feel the ~**○ en ressentir les effets.

draught: **~board** *n* GB damier *m*;

~ excluder *n* bourrelet *m* (de porte, de fenêtre).

draughtiness GB, **draftiness** US /ˈdrɑːftɪnɪs, US ˈdræftɪnɪs/ *n* courants *mpl* d'air.

draughtproof GB, **draftproof** US /ˈdrɑːftpruːf, US ˈdræft-/ **I** *adj* calfeutré. **II** *vtr* calfeutrer.

draughtproofing GB, **draftproofing** US /ˈdrɑːftpruːfɪŋ, US ˈdræft-/ *n* **1** (insulation) calfeutrage *m*; **2** (material) matériau *m* de calfeutrage.

draughts /drɑːfts, US dræfts/ **▶ 1282** *n* GB (+ *v sg*) (set) (jeu *m* de) dames *fpl*; **to play ~** jouer aux dames.

draughtsman GB, **draftsman** US /ˈdrɑːftsmən, US ˈdræft-/ **1** Tech dessinateur/-trice *m/f* (industriel/-ielle); **2** Art dessinateur/-trice *m/f*; **3** GB Games pion *m* (de jeu de dames).

draughtsmanship GB, **draftsmanship** US /ˈdrɑːftsmənʃɪp, US ˈdræft-/ *n* **1** Tech art *m* du dessin industriel; **2** Art coup *m* de crayon.

draughty GB, **drafty** US /ˈdrɑːftɪ, US ˈdræftɪ/ *adj* [*room*] plein de courants d'air; **I was sitting in a ~ seat** j'étais assis dans un courant d'air.

draw /drɔː/ **I** *n* **1** (raffle) tirage *m* (au sort); **to win (sth in) a ~** gagner (qch) dans une loterie; **2** (tie) (in match) match *m* nul; **it was a ~** (in match) ils ont fait match nul; (in race) ils sont arrivés ex aequo; **3** (attraction) (person, film, event, place) attraction *f*; **Bob Dylan was the big ~** Bob Dylan était la grande attraction; **4** (on cigarette, pipe) bouffée *f*; **5** US (hand of cards) main *f*.
II *vtr* (*prét* **drew**, *pp* **drawn**) **1** (on paper etc) faire [*picture, plan, portrait, sketch, cartoon*]; dessiner [*person, face, object, diagram*]; tracer [*line, circle, square*]; **to ~ a picture** lit faire un dessin, dessiner; **to ~ (a picture of) a boat** dessiner un bateau; **to ~ a map** (giving directions) faire un plan; (in school) dessiner une carte; **to ~ sb sth, to ~ sth for sb** faire qch à qn [*picture, plan, cartoon, sketch*]; dessiner qch à qn [*person, face, object, diagram*]; **2** fig dépeindre [*character, picture*]; faire [*analogy, comparison, distinction, parallel*]; **3** (pull) [*animal, car, engine*] tirer [*object, cart, rope, plough*]; [*machine, suction*] aspirer [*liquid, gas*]; **to ~ a plough along** tirer une charrue; **the water is drawn along the pipe** l'eau est aspirée dans le tuyau; **I drew the book towards me** j'ai tiré le livre vers moi; **he drew the child towards him** il a attiré l'enfant vers lui; **to ~ a bolt/the curtains** tirer un verrou/les rideaux; **I drew the string as tight as I could** j'ai tiré sur la ficelle aussi fort que j'ai pu; **she drew a ten pound note from her purse** elle a tiré un billet de dix livres de son porte-monnaie; **he drew his finger along the shelf** il a passé un doigt sur l'étagère; **to ~ a handkerchief across one's forehead/a comb through ones' hair** se passer un mouchoir sur le front/un peigne dans les cheveux; **she drew his arm through hers** elle a passé son bras sous le sien; **she drew her shawl round her shoulders** elle a resserré son châle autour de ses épaules; **to ~ water from a well** tirer de l'eau d'un puits; **to ~ a pint of beer** ≈ tirer un demi-litre de bière à la pression; **to ~ blood** lit provoquer un saignement; **to ~ a bow** bander un arc; **4** (derive) tirer [*conclusion*] (**from** de); **I drew comfort from the fact that/from doing** cela m'a un peu réconforté de savoir que/de faire; **to ~ a lesson/a moral from sth** tirer une leçon/une morale de qch; **to ~ inspiration from sth** puiser de l'inspiration dans qch; **he drew hope/encouragement from this** cela lui a donné de l'espoir/du courage; **to be drawn from** [*energy, information*] provenir de; **his friends/our readers are drawn from all walks of life** ses amis/nos lecteurs viennent de tous les horizons; **5** (cause to talk) faire parler [*person*] (**about, on** de); **I'd hoped she'd tell me, but she wouldn't be drawn** ou **she refused to be drawn** j'avais espéré qu'elle me le dirait, mais elle a refusé de parler; **to ~ sth from** ou **out of sb** obtenir qch de qn [*information*]; faire dire or arracher qch à qn [*truth*]; **she drew tears of laughter from the audience** elle a fait rire son public aux larmes; **I managed to ~ a smile from him** j'ai réussi à lui arracher un sourire; **6** (attract) [*person, event, film*] attirer [*crowd, person*] (**to** vers); susciter [*reaction, criticism, praise, interest*]; **the idea drew much criticism from both sides/from the experts** l'idée a suscité de nombreuses critiques des deux côtés/chez les experts; **the course ~s students from all over the world** le cours attire des étudiants du monde entier; **his speech drew great applause** son discours a soulevé des applaudissements; **to ~ sb's attention to sth** attirer l'attention de qn sur qch; **to ~ attention to oneself** attirer l'attention sur soi; **to feel drawn to sb** se sentir attiré vers qn; **to ~ sb to** attirer qn vers [*person, religion*]; pousser qn vers [*profession*]; **the sound of the explosion drew her to the window** le bruit de l'explosion l'a attirée à la fenêtre; **to ~ sb into** mêler qn à [*conversation*]; entraîner qn dans [*argument, battle*]; **I'm not going to be drawn into an argument with you** je ne vais pas me laisser entraîner dans une dispute avec toi; **they were drawn together by their love of animals** leur amour des animaux les a rapprochés; **to ~ the enemy fire** offrir un cible au feu ennemi; **I'll ~ their fire** je ferai diversion; **7** Fin (take out) retirer [*money*] (**from** de); tirer [*cheque, bill of exchange, promissory note*] (**on** sur); (receive) toucher [*wages, pension*]; **8** Games (choose at random) tirer [qch] au sort [*name, ticket, winner*]; **they asked him to ~ the winner (out of the hat)** ils lui ont demandé de tirer au sort le gagnant; **to ~ a winning ticket** [*competitor*] tirer un billet gagnant; **Italy has been drawn against Spain** ou **to play Spain** le tirage au sort a désigné l'Italie comme adversaire de l'Espagne; **Jones drew Smith in the first round** le tirage au sort a désigné Smith comme adversaire de Jones au premier tour; **9** Sport **to ~ a match** faire match nul; **10** (remove, pull out) extraire [*tooth*]; retirer, enlever [*thorn, splinter, sting*] (**from** de); retirer [*cork*] (**from** de); dégainer, sortir [*sword, dagger*]; sortir [*knife, gun*]; tirer [*card*]; **to ~ a gun on sb** sortir un pistolet et le braquer sur qn; **to ~ a knife on sb** sortir un couteau pour en menacer qn; **with drawn sword** l'épée dégainée; **11** (disembowel) vider [*chicken, turkey, goose*]; Hist étriper [*prisoner*]; **12** Hunt suivre la voie de [*animal*]; **13** Games **to ~ trumps** tirer ses atouts; **14** Tech étirer [*wire, metal, glass*]; **15** Naut **the ship ~s six metres** le navire a un tirant d'eau de six mètres; **16†** (run) faire couler [*bath*].
III *vi* (*prét* **drew**, *pp* **drawn**) **1** (make picture) dessiner; **he ~s very well** il dessine très bien; **to ~ round** ou **around sth** dessiner en suivant les contours de [*hand, template*]; **2** (move) **to ~ ahead (of sth/sb)** lit [*vehicle, person*] gagner du terrain (sur qch/qn); fig [*person, company*] prendre de l'avance (sur qch/qn); **to ~ alongside** [*boat*] accoster; **the car drew alongside the lorry** la voiture s'est mise à côté du camion; **to ~ close** ou **near** [*time, date, ordeal*] approcher; **the time/day is ~ing close when...** l'heure/le jour approche où...; **they drew nearer to listen** ils se sont rapprochés pour écouter; **to ~ into** [*bus*] arriver à [*station*]; **the train drew into the station** le train est entré en gare; **to ~ level** se retrouver au même niveau; **to ~ level with the other athletes** (in score) se retrouver au même niveau que les autres athlètes; (in race) rattraper les autres athlètes; **to ~ over** [*vehicle*] (stop) se ranger; (still moving) se rabattre vers le bascôté; **the lorry drew over to the right-hand side of the road** le camion s'est rangé sur la voie de droite; **to ~ to one side** [*person*] s'écarter; **to ~ round** ou **around** [*people*] se rassembler; **they drew round the teacher** ils se sont rassemblés autour du professeur; **to ~ to a halt** s'arrêter; **to ~ to a close** ou **an end** [*day, event, life*] toucher à sa fin; **3** gen, Sport (in match) [*teams*] faire match nul; (finish at same time in race) [*runners, racers*] arriver ex aequo; (finish equal, with same points) se retrouver ex aequo; **they drew for second place** ils sont arrivés deuxièmes ex aequo; **X drew with Y** (in match) X a fait match nul avec Y; (in race) X est arrivé ex aequo avec Y; **4** (choose at random) **to ~ for sth** tirer qch (au sort); **they drew for partners** ils ont tiré leurs partenaires (au sort); **5** [*chimney, pipe*] tirer; [*pump, vacuum cleaner*] aspirer; **to ~ on** ou **at one's pipe/cigarette** tirer sur sa pipe/sa cigarette; **6** [*tea*] infuser.

IDIOMS **to be quick/ slow on the ~**○ (in understanding) avoir l'esprit vif/lent; (in replying) avoir/ne pas avoir la repartie facile; [*cowboy*] dégainer/ne pas dégainer vite; **to beat sb to the ~** [*rival, competitor*] devancer qn; [*cowboy*] dégainer plus vite que qn; **to ~ the line** fixer des limites; **you've got to ~ the line somewhere** il faut savoir fixer des limites; **to ~ the line at doing** se refuser à faire; **she drew the line at blackmail** elle se refusait à faire du chantage; **I ~ the line at violence** je n'irai pas jusqu'à la violence; **the union agreed to longer working hours but drew the line at wage cuts** le syndicat a accepté une augmentation des heures de travail mais a refusé une baisse des salaires.

■ **draw apart**: **~ apart** [*two people*] se séparer; **the land masses drew apart** les masses de terre se sont éloignées les unes des autres.

■ **draw aside**: ¶ **~ [sth] aside, ~ aside [sth]** écarter [*curtain, screen, object*]; ¶ **~ [sb] aside** prendre qn à part.

■ **draw away**: ¶ **~ away** [*vehicle, train, person*] (move off) s'éloigner (**from** de); (move ahead) prendre de l'avance (**from** sur); [*person*] (move away, recoil) avoir un mouvement de recul; ¶ **~ [sth] away, ~ away [sth]** retirer [*hand, foot*]; **~ the chair away from the fire** éloigne la chaise du feu; ¶ **~ [sb] away from** éloigner qn de [*fire, scene*]; distraire qn de [*book, task*].

■ **draw back**: ¶ **~ back** (move back, recoil) reculer; ¶ **~ [sth] back, ~ back [sth]** ouvrir [*curtains*]; [*person*] retirer [*hand, foot*]; ¶ **~ [sb] back, ~ back [sb]** faire revenir [*person*]; **the company will have difficulty ~ing its customers back** la société aura du mal à récupérer ses clients.

■ **draw down**: **~ [sth] down, ~ down [sth]** baisser [*blind, screen, veil*].

■ **draw in**: ¶ **~ in 1** [*days*] raccourcir; **the nights are ~ing in** les jours raccourcissent; **2** (arrive) [*bus*] arriver; [*train*] entrer en gare; ¶ **~ [sth] in, ~ in [sth] 1** gen, Art (in picture) ajouter [*background, detail*]; **2** tirer sur [*reins, rope, lead*]; rentrer [*stomach, claws*]; **3** (suck in) [*person*] aspirer [*air*]; [*pump, machine*] aspirer [*liquid, gas, air*]; **to ~ in one's breath** inspirer; **4** (attract) attirer [*people, funds*].

■ **draw off**: ¶ **~ off** [*vehicle, train*] partir; [*army*] battre en retraite; ¶ **~ [sth] off, ~ off [sth]** tirer [*beer, water*]; Med évacuer [*fluid*]; retirer, ôter [*gloves*].

■ **draw on**: ¶ **~ on** (approach) [*time, date, season*] approcher; (pass) [*time*] passer; [*evening, day, season*] (s')avancer; ¶ **~ on [sth]** puiser dans, exploiter [*skills, strength, reserves, savings*]; **in her novels she ~s on childhood memories** pour écrire ses romans elle s'inspire de ses souvenirs d'enfance; **the report ~s on information from...** le rapport tire des informations de...; **to ~ on one's experience** faire

appel à son expérience; ¶ **~ on** [**sth**], **~** [**sth**] **on** enfiler [*gloves, shoes, garment*].
■ **draw out**: ¶ **~ out 1** (leave) [*train, bus*] partir; **the train drew out of the station** le train a quitté la gare; **a car drew out in front of me** une voiture a déboîté devant moi; **2** (get longer) [*day, night*] rallonger; **the nights are ~ing out** les jours rallongent; ¶ **~** [**sth**] **out**, **~ out** [**sth**] **1** gen tirer [*handkerchief, purse, cigarette, knife*] (**from, out of** de); retirer [*splinter, nail, cork*] (**from, out of** de); extraire [*tooth*]; aspirer [*liquid, air*]; **2** Fin retirer [*cash, money, balance*]; **3** (cause to last longer) faire durer [*meeting, speech, meal*]; (unnecessarily) faire traîner [*meeting, speech, meal*]; **4** (extract) obtenir [*information, confession*]; (using force) soutirer [*information, confession*]; **they managed to ~ a confession out of him** ils ont réussi à lui soutirer des aveux; **5** Tech (stretch) étirer [*wire, thread, glass, metal*]; ¶ **~** [**sb**] **out** (make less shy) faire sortir [qn] de sa coquille; **I managed to ~ him out of his silence** j'ai réussi à le sortir de son silence; **I drew the old man out about the war** j'ai fait parler le vieil homme de la guerre.
■ **draw up**: ¶ **~ up** [*vehicle*] s'arrêter; [*boat*] accoster; ¶ **~ up** [**sth**], **~** [**sth**] **up 1** établir [*contract, criteria, budget, programme, proposals, questionnaire*]; dresser, établir [*list, inventory, plan*]; rédiger, établir [*report*]; faire [*will*]; **2** (pull upwards) hisser [*bucket*]; **3** (bring) approcher [*chair, stool*] (**to** de); **4** (gather up) tirer sur [*thread, drawstring*]; ¶ **~ oneself up** se redresser; **she drew herself up to her full height** elle s'est redressée de toute sa hauteur.

drawback /ˈdrɔːbæk/ *n* **1** gen inconvénient *m*, désavantage *m*; **it has its ~s** cela présente des inconvénients or des désavantages; **the ~ of doing that is that**... l'inconvénient de faire cela, c'est que...; **2** Comm (on exports) rembours *m*, drawback *m*.

drawbridge /ˈdrɔːbrɪdʒ/ *n* (over moat) pont-levis *m*; (over river) pont *m* basculant.

drawee /drɔːˈiː/ *n* Fin tiré *m*.

drawer /ˈdrɔː(r)/ **I** *n* **1** (in chest, cabinet, table etc) tiroir *m*; **cutlery/desk ~** tiroir à couverts/de bureau; **2** (of pictures) dessinateur/-trice *m/f*; **3** Fin tireur/-euse *m/f*.
II drawers† *npl* (for man) caleçon *m*; (for woman) culotte *f*.

drawer liner *n* garniture *f* de tiroir.

drawing /ˈdrɔːɪŋ/ **I** *n* **1** (picture) dessin *m*; **pencil/charcoal ~** dessin au crayon/au fusain; **a rough ~** une ébauche; **2** (action, occupation) le dessin *m*; **classes in ~** cours de dessin; **most of the ~ is done by Rolf** la plupart des dessins sont faits par Rolf.
II *modif* [*course, class, teacher, tools*] de dessin; [*paper, pen, book*] à dessin.

drawing account *n* (current account) compte *m* de prélèvement.

drawing board *n* **1** lit (board) planche *f* à dessin; (table) table *f* à dessin; **2** fig **we'll have to go back to the ~** il faudra tout recommencer; **the project never got off the ~** le projet n'a jamais dépassé le stade de l'étude.

drawing card *n* **1** (popular artiste, event) valeur *f* sûre; **2** US (marketable skill, asset) atout *m*.

drawing: **~ office** *n* bureau *m* de dessin industriel; **~ pin** *n* punaise *f*; **~ room** *n* salon *m*, salle *f* de réception.

drawl /drɔːl/ **I** *n* voix *f* traînante; **in a thick Texas ~** avec un fort accent traînant du Texas.
II *vtr* **'how about that!' she ~ed** 'ça alors!' dit-elle d'une voix traînante.
III *vi* parler d'une voix traînante.

drawn /drɔːn/ **I** *pp* ▶ **draw**.
II *adj* **1** [*face, look*] tiré; **he looked pale and ~** il était pâle et avait les traits tirés; **her face ~ with sorrow** les traits tirés par le chagrin; **2** Sport [*game, match*] nul/nulle.

drawn: **~ butter** *n* beurre *m* fondu (assaisonné); **~(-thread) work** *n* ouvrage *m* à jours.

draw: **~ poker** ▶ **1282** *n* US poker *m* (*joué en pariant sur les cartes retournées*); **~sheet** *n* alèse *f*.

drawstring /ˈdrɔːstrɪŋ/ **I** *n* cordon *m* de serrage.
II *modif* [*bag*] à coulisse; [*hood*] coulissé; (**with a**) **~ waist** (à) ceinture coulissante.

draw: **~ ticket** *n* billet *m* de tombola; **~-top table** *n* table *f* à rallonge.

dray /dreɪ/ *n* Hist Transp (for general use) fardier *m*; (at brewery) haquet *m*.

drayhorse /ˈdreɪhɔːs/ *n* Hist cheval *m* de trait.

dread /dred/ **I** *n* terreur *f*; **to have a ~ of sth** (real fear) être terrifié par qch; (weaker) avoir horreur de qch; **to live in ~ of sth/sb** redouter qch/qn; **to live in ~ of sth happening** redouter que qch n'arrive; **it's his constant ~** il le redoute constamment; **her ~ that her husband might return** sa crainte du retour de son mari.
II *vtr* appréhender (**doing sth** de faire qch); (stronger) redouter (**doing sth** de faire qch); **to ~ that** redouter que (+ *subj*); **she ~s him coming** elle appréhende de le voir arriver; **'what would she say?'—'I ~ to think!'** 'qu'est-ce qu'elle dirait?'—'je préfère ne pas y penser!'
III dreaded *pp adj* (*épith*) (tant) redouté.

dreadful /ˈdredfl/ *adj* **1** (unpleasant) [*weather, person*] affreux/-euse; [*day*] épouvantable; (emphatic) **what a ~ nuisance!** quelle barbe○!; **a ~ mess/waste of time** une pagaille/une perte de temps incroyable; **he made a ~ fuss** il a fait des histoires à n'en plus finir; **I had a ~ time trying to convince him** j'ai eu toutes les peines du monde à le convaincre; **2** (poor quality) [*film, book, meal*] lamentable; **3** (horrifying) [*accident, injury*] épouvantable; [*crime*] atroce; **4** (ill) **to feel/look ~** ne pas se sentir/ne pas avoir l'air bien du tout; **5** littér (inspiring fear) [*foe, weapon*] redoutable; **6** (embarrassed) **to feel ~ about sth/about doing/about having done** avoir honte de qch/de faire/d'avoir fait.

dreadfully /ˈdredfəlɪ/ *adv* **1** (emphatic) [*disappointed, cross, short of money*] terriblement; [*sorry, wrong*] vraiment; **I miss her ~** elle me manque terriblement; **2** (horribly) [*suffer*] affreusement; [*treat*] affreusement mal; [*behave*] abominablement.

dreadlocks /ˈdredlɒks/ *npl* dreadlocks *fpl* (*coiffure rasta*).

dreadnought /ˈdrednɔːt/ *n* Mil dreadnought *m*.

dream /driːm/ **I** *n* **1** (while asleep) rêve *m*; **I had a ~ about sth/about doing** j'ai rêvé de qch/que je faisais; **to have a ~ that** rêver que; **'sweet** ou **pleasant ~s!'** 'fais de beaux rêves!'; **it was like a bad ~** c'était comme un mauvais rêve; **2** (while awake) rêverie *f*, rêve *m*; **to be in a ~** être dans les nuages or dans la lune; **to be living in a ~** (because of happiness) vivre dans un rêve; (because of shock) vivre dans un autre monde; **3** (hope) rêve *m*; **I have a ~ that** mon rêve, c'est que; **to have ~s of doing** rêver de faire; **it was (like) a ~ come true** c'était comme dans un rêve; **to make sb's ~ come true** faire que le rêve de qn devienne réalité; **the car/man of your ~s** la voiture/l'homme de tes rêves; **to have success beyond one's wildest ~s** avoir un succès qui dépasse ses rêves les plus fous; **to be rich beyond one's wildest ~s** être plus riche qu'on ne l'aurait jamais espéré; **never in her wildest ~s had she thought**... jamais, même dans ses rêves les plus fous, elle n'avait imaginé...; **you couldn't imagine a more vicious person, even in your wildest ~s** sa méchanceté dépasse l'imagination; **4** (wonderful person or thing) **the car is a ~ to drive** c'est un vrai plaisir de conduire cette voiture; **he's a ~** il est adorable; **the house/dress is a ~** la maison/robe est magnifique; **this cake is a ~** ce gâteau est délicieux; **to go like a ~** [*car, engine*] marcher à merveille; **it worked like a ~** ça a marché à merveille.
II *modif* [*house, kitchen, car, vacation*] de rêve; [*job*] rêvé.
III *vtr* (*prét, pp* **dreamt** /dremt/, **~ed**) **1** (while asleep) rêver (**that** que); **2** (imagine) **I never dreamt (that)** je n'aurais jamais pensé que; (stronger) je n'aurais jamais imaginé un seul instant que.
IV *vi* (*prét, pp* **dreamt** /dremt/, **~ed**) **1** (while asleep) rêver; **he dreamt about** ou **of sth/doing** il a rêvé de qch/qu'il faisait; **2** (while awake) rêver, être dans les nuages; pej rêvasser; **to ~ about** ou **of sth** rêver à qch; **3** (hope) rêver; **to ~ of sth/of doing** rêver de qch/de faire; **you're** ou **you must be ~ing if you think**... tu te fais des illusions si tu crois que...; **~ on!** iron l'espoir fait vivre!; **4** (consider) **I/he wouldn't ~ of doing** il ne me/lui viendrait jamais à l'esprit de faire; **'don't tell them!'—'I wouldn't ~ of it!'** 'ne le leur dis pas!'—'bien sûr que non!'
■ **dream away**: **to ~ away the hours/the afternoon** passer son temps/l'après-midi à rêvasser.
■ **dream up**: **~ up** [**sth**] concevoir, inventer [*plan, excuse, idea, theory*]; imaginer [*character, plot*].

dreamboat○ /ˈdriːmbəʊt/ *n* hum apollon *m*.

dreamer /ˈdriːmə(r)/ *n* **1** (inattentive person) rêveur/-euse *m/f*, distrait/-e *m/f*; **2** (idealist) idéaliste *mf*, utopiste *mf*; **3** (person having dream) personne *f* qui rêve.

dreamily /ˈdriːmɪlɪ/ *adv* **1** (in a dream) [*look, move, wander, smile, say*] d'un air rêveur; **2** (gently) suavement.

dreamland /ˈdriːmlænd/ *n* pays *m* des rêves, monde *m* imaginaire.

dreamless /ˈdriːmlɪs/ *adj* [*sleep*] sans rêves.

dreamlessly /ˈdriːmlɪslɪ/ *adv* [*sleep*] d'un sommeil sans rêves.

dreamlike /ˈdriːmlaɪk/ *adj* irréel/irréelle.

dreamt /dremt/ *prét, pp* ▶ **dream**.

dreamtime /ˈdriːmtaɪm/ *n* Austral Anthrop ≈ âge *m* d'or.

dreamworld /ˈdriːmwɜːld/ *n* **1** (place of dreams) monde *m* de rêves; **2** (imagination) **to be (living) in a ~** être dans les nuages; **she's living in a ~ if she thinks**... elle se fait des illusions si elle croit que...

dreamy /ˈdriːmɪ/ *adj* **1** (distracted) rêveur/-euse, distrait; **2** (gentle) [*sound, music*] doux/douce; **3** (dreamlike) [*story, scene, day*] irréel/irréelle; **4**○†(attractive) [*person*] séduisant, attirant; [*house, car, dress*] ravissant.

dreariness /ˈdrɪərɪnɪs/ *n* (of life, landscape) monotonie *f*; (of weather) aspect *m* maussade; (of person) côté *m* ennuyeux.

dreary /ˈdrɪərɪ/ *adj* [*weather, landscape*] morne; [*person*] ennuyeux/-euse; [*life, routine*] monotone.

dredge /dredʒ/ **I** *n* Naut **1** (machine) drague *f*; **2** (boat) = **dredger**.
II *vtr* **1** draguer [*mud, river, channel*]; **2** Culin saupoudrer (**with** de).
III *vi* draguer.
■ **dredge up**: **~ up** [**sth**], **~** [**sth**] **up** lit remonter qch (à la drague); fig retrouver [qch] enfoui au fond de sa mémoire [*memories*]; exhumer [*unpleasant story, idea etc*].

dredger /ˈdredʒə(r)/ *n* **1** (boat) dragueur *m*; **2** Culin saupoudreuse *f*.

dregs /dregz/ *npl* **1** (of wine) lie *f* (*never pl*); (of coffee) marc *m* (*never pl*); (last drops) **she threw away the ~ of the tea** elle a jeté le thé qui restait dans la tasse; **to drink sth (down) to the ~s** boire qch jusqu'à la lie; **2** fig **the ~ of society/humanity** péj la lie de la société/l'humanité pej.

drench /drentʃ/ **I** *vtr* (in rain, sweat) tremper

[*person, clothes*] (**in** de); (in perfume) asperger (**in** de).
II **drenched** *pp adj* trempé (**in** de); **~ed to the skin** trempé jusqu'aux os; **she was ~ed in perfume** elle s'était aspergée de parfum.

drenching /'drentʃɪŋ/ I *n* **to get a ~** se faire tremper.
II *adj* **~ rain** pluie *f* battante.

Dresden /'drezdən/ *n* (also **~ china**) (porcelaine *f* de) saxe *m*; **a piece of ~** un saxe.

dress /dres/ **▶1703** I *n* **1** (item of women's clothing) robe *f*; **a silk/cotton ~** une robe de soie/de coton; **2** ¢ (clothing) vêtements *mpl*, tenue *f*; **his style of ~** son style vestimentaire; **casual/formal ~** tenue décontractée/habillée; **military ~** tenue militaire.
II *modif* [*material, pattern, design*] de robe.
III *vtr* **1** (put clothes on) habiller [*person*]; **to get ~ed** s'habiller; **2** (decorate) décorer [*Christmas tree*]; Naut pavoiser [*ship*]; **to ~ a shop window** faire une vitrine; **3** Culin assaisonner [*salad*]; préparer, parer [*chicken, crab, game*]; **4** Med panser [*wound*]; **5** (finish) dresser [*stone, timber*]; corroyer [*hide*]; **6** Agric (fertilize) fertiliser [*land*]; **7** Hort (prune) tailler [*tree, shrub*]; **8** Mil aligner [*troops*].
IV *vi* **1** (put on clothes) s'habiller; **to ~ in a suit/uniform** mettre un costume/un uniforme; **to ~ in red/black** s'habiller en rouge/noir; **to ~ for dinner/for the theatre** s'habiller pour dîner/pour aller au théâtre; **2** Mil [*troops*] s'aligner.
V *v refl* **to ~ oneself** s'habiller.
VI **dressed** *pp adj* habillé, vêtu (**in** de); **well ~ed** bien habillé.
IDIOMS **~ed to kill** habillé de façon irrésistible; ▶ **nine**.
■ **dress down**: ¶ **~ down** [*person*] s'habiller 'décontracté'; ¶ **~ [sb] down, ~ down [sb]** réprimander.
■ **dress up**: ¶ **~ up 1** (smartly) s'habiller, se mettre sur son trente et un○; **2** (in fancy dress) se déguiser (**as** en); ¶ **~ [sb] up, ~ up [sb]** (disguise) déguiser; ¶ **~ [sth] up, ~ up [sth]** (improve) agrémenter [*garment, outfit*]; fig agrémenter, enjoliver [*facts, policy*].

dressage /'dresɑːʒ/ *n* Equit dressage *m*.

dress: **~ circle** *n* Theat premier balcon *m*; **~ clothes** *npl* US habits *mpl* du dimanche; **~ coat** *n* queue-de-pie *f*; **~ code** *n* code *m* vestimentaire; **~ designer ▶1692** *n* dessinateur/-trice *m/f* de mode, modéliste *mf*.

dresser /'dresə(r)/ *n* **1** (person) **to be a sloppy/stylish ~** s'habiller mal/avec chic; **2** (piece of furniture) (for dishes) buffet *m*, vaisselier *m*; US (for clothes) commode-coiffeuse *f*; **3** Theat habilleur/-euse *m/f*; **4** (tool) (for wood) raboteuse *f*; (for stone) chemin *m* de fer, rabotin *m*.

dressing /'dresɪŋ/ I *n* **1** Med pansement *m*; **2** (sauce) assaisonnement *m*, sauce *f*; **3** US (stuffing) farce *f*; **4** Tech (of stone, wood) dressage *m*; **5** (of hide) corroyage *m*; **6** Agric (fertilizer) engrais *m*.
II **dressings** *npl* Archit parements *mpl*.

dressing case *n* vanity-case *m*.

dressing-down *n* réprimande *f*; **to give sb a ~** réprimander qn.

dressing: **~ gown** *n* robe *f* de chambre; **~ room** *n* Theat loge *f*; (in house) dressing *m*, vestiaire *m*; **~ station** *n* Mil Med poste *m* de secours; **~ table** *n* coiffeuse *f*; **~ table set** *n* accessoires *mpl* de toilette.

dress: **~maker ▶1692** *n* couturière *f*; **~making** *n* couture *f*; **~ parade** *n* Mil défilé *m* en grande tenue; **~ rehearsal** *n* Theat, fig (répétition *f*) générale *f*.

dress sense *n* **to have ~** s'habiller avec goût; **to have no ~** s'habiller sans aucun goût.

dress: **~ shield** *n* dessous-de-bras *m inv*; **~ shirt** *n* chemise *f* habillée; **~ suit** *n* queue-de-pie *f*; **~ uniform** *n* uniforme *m* de cérémonie.

dressy○ /'dresɪ/ *adj* habillé, élégant.

drew /druː/ *prét* ▶ **draw**.

dribble /'drɪbl/ I *n* **1** (of liquid) filet *m*; **2** (of saliva) bave *f*; **3** Sport dribble *m*.
II *vtr* **1** (spill) laisser dégouliner [*paint*] (**on, onto** sur); **he's dribbling soup all down his bib** la soupe lui dégouline sur le bavoir; **2** Sport dribler [*ball*]; **he ~d the ball past two defenders** il a driblé deux défenseurs.
III *vi* **1** [*liquid*] dégouliner (**on, onto** sur; **from** de); **soup ~d down his bib** la soupe dégoulinait sur son bavoir; **2** [*baby, old person*] baver; **3** Sport dribler.
■ **dribble in** [*money, contributions*] rentrer au compte-gouttes.
■ **dribble out**: **~ [sth] out, ~ out [sth]** distribuer [qch] au compte-gouttes [*cash, funds*].

dribbler /'drɪblə(r)/ *n* **1** (baby) **he's a ~** il bave beaucoup; **2** Sport dribbleur *m*.

driblet /'drɪblɪt/ *n* gouttelette *f*.

dribs and drabs /ˌdrɪbz ən 'dræbz/: **in ~** *adv phr* [*arrive, leave*] par petits groupes; [*pay, receive*] par petits bouts.

dried /draɪd/ I *pret, pp* ▶ **dry**.
II *adj* [*fruit, herb, bean, pulse*] sec/sèche; [*flower, vegetable*] séché; [*milk, egg*] en poudre.

dried-up /ˌdraɪd'ʌp/ *adj* **1** lit [*river bed, reservoir etc*] à sec; **2** péj [*person*] desséché.

drier /'draɪə(r)/ *n* **1** (for clothes, hair) séchoir *m*; (helmet type for hair) casque *m*; **2** (for paint, varnish) siccatif *m*.

drift /drɪft/ I *n* **1** (flow, movement) **the ~ of the current** le sens du courant; **to be carried downstream by the ~ of the current** être emporté en aval par le courant; **the ~ of events** fig le cours des événements; **the ~ from the land** l'exode *m* rural; **the ~ of refugees to the border** l'afflux *m* des réfugiés à la frontière; **the slow ~ of strikers back to work** le lent retour des grévistes au travail; **2** (ocean current) also Geol dérive *f*; **North Atlantic ~** dérive nord-atlantique; **3** (deviation) (of projectile) dérivation *f*; (of ship, plane) dérive *f*; **4** (mass) (of snow) congère *f*; (of leaves, sand) tas *m*, amoncellement *m*; (of smoke, mist) nuage *m*, traînée *f*; **the rain/snow was falling in ~s** il y avait des bourrasques de pluie/de neige; **5** (general meaning) sens *m* (général); **to catch the ~ of sb's argument** comprendre où quelqu'un veut en venir; **I don't catch** ou **follow your ~** je ne comprends pas où vous voulez en venir; **get the ~**○**?** tu piges○?; **6** Geol (glacial deposit) drift *m*, sédiments *mpl* glaciaires; **7** (in mining) galerie *f* en allongement; **8** Ling évolution *f*; **9** Elec, Radio dérive *f*.
II *vi* **1** (be carried by tide, current) [*boat*] dériver; (by wind) [*balloon*] voler à la dérive; [*smoke, fog*] flotter; **to ~ out to sea** dériver vers le large; **to ~ off course** [*boat*] dériver hors-cap; [*plane*] dériver hors de route; **to ~ downstream** être emporté ou entraîné en aval par le courant; **to ~ onto the rocks** s'échouer sur les rochers; **clouds ~ed across the sky** des nuages traversaient le ciel; **mist was ~ing in from the sea** il y avait de la brume qui venait de la mer; **voices ~ed into the garden** des voix parvenaient dans le jardin; **2** (pile up) [*snow*] former des congères *fpl*; [*leaves*] s'amonceler; **~ing snow** des bourrasques *fpl* de neige; **~ed snow** des congères; **3 to ~ along** [*person*] lit flâner; fig se laisser aller; **to ~ around** ou **about the house** traîner sans but dans la maison; **the strikers are ~ing back to work** les grévistes retournent progressivement au travail; **to ~ into/out of the room** entrer dans une/sortir d'une pièce d'un pas nonchalant; **to ~ from job to job** passer d'un emploi à un autre; **to ~ from town to town** errer de ville en ville; **to ~ through life** errer sans but dans la vie; **the country is ~ing towards recession/war** le pays glisse vers la récession/la guerre; **I'm content to let things ~** je me borne à laisser les événements suivre leur cours; **4** fig (stray) **to ~ into teaching/publishing** se retrouver dans l'enseignement/l'édition; **to ~ into crime/prostitution** sombrer dans la criminalité/la prostitution; **the conversation ~ed onto politics** la conversation a dérivé vers la politique.
■ **drift apart** [*friends, couple, lovers*] se détacher progressivement (**from** de); **we have ~ed apart** nous sommes moins proches qu'avant.
■ **drift away** [*crowd, spectators*] s'éloigner (**from** de); fig [*person*] (from belief etc) s'éloigner progressivement (**from** de).
■ **drift off 1** (doze off) s'assoupir; **2** (leave) s'en aller lentement.

drift anchor *n* ancre *f* flottante.

drifter /'drɪftə(r)/ *n* **1** Fishg harenguier *m*; **2** (aimless person) vagabond/-e *m/f*.

drift: **~ ice** *n* ¢ glaces *fpl* flottantes; **~-net** *n* filet *m* dérivant; **~wood** *n* bois *m* flotté.

drill /drɪl/ I *n* **1** (tool) (for wood, metal, masonry) perceuse *f*; (for oil) trépan *m*; (for mining) foreuse *f*; Dent roulette *f*, fraise *f* spec; **power/hand ~** perceuse *f* électrique/à main; **2** Mil exercice *m*; **rifle ~** maniement *m* d'armes; **3** (practice) **lifeboat/fire ~** exercice *m* de sauvetage/d'évacuation en cas d'incendie; **4** Scol (repetition) drill *m*; **5**○†GB (procedure) **the ~** la marche à suivre; **6** (furrow) sillon *m*; **7** Agric (machine) semoir *m*; **8** Tex coutil *m*.
II *vtr* **1** percer [*wood, metal, masonry*]; forer [*shaft, well, tunnel*]; Dent passer la roulette à [*tooth*]: **to ~ a hole** percer un trou (**in** dans); **2** Mil entraîner [*troops*]; **3 to ~ sb in sth** former (intensivement) qn à qch; **4** Agric semer [qch] en sillons.
III *vi* **1** (in wood, metal, masonry) percer un trou (**into** dans); Dent passer la roulette (**into** à); **to ~ for** faire des forages pour trouver [*oil, water*]; **2** Mil faire de l'exercice; **they're ~ing** ils sont à l'exercice; **3 to ~ sth into sb** faire entrer qch dans la tête de qn; **we had good manners ~ed into us** on nous a inculqué à fond les bonnes manières.

drilling /'drɪlɪŋ/ *n* (for oil, gas, water) forage *m* (**for** pour trouver); (in wood, metal, masonry) perçage *m*; Dent fraisage *m*; **oil/gas ~** forage pétrolier/de gaz; **the ~ has been going on all day!** la perceuse a marché toute la journée!

drilling: **~ derrick** *n* tour *f* de forage; **~ platform** *n* plateforme *f* de forage; **~ rig** *n* (at sea) plateforme *f* de forage; (on land) derrick *m*, tour *f* de forage.

drill sergeant *n* sergent *m* instructeur.

drily /'draɪlɪ/ *adv* **1** (with dry wit) d'un ton pince-sans-rire; **2** (coldly) sèchement.

drink /drɪŋk/ I *n* **1** (nonalcoholic) boisson *f*; **orange/pineapple ~** boisson à l'orange/à l'ananas; **to have a ~** boire quelque chose; **could I have a ~ of water?** est-ce que je pourrais boire un verre d'eau; **to give sb a ~** donner à boire à qn; **to give a plant a ~** arroser une plante; **2** (alcoholic) boisson *f* (alcoolisée), verre *m*; **to have a ~** prendre or boire un verre; **would you like a ~?** tu veux prendre un verre?; **a quick ~** un petit verre; **to go for a ~** aller boire un verre; **he likes a ~** il aime bien la bouteille; **3** (act of drinking) **to take** ou **have a ~ of sth** boire une gorgée de qch; **4** ¢ (collectively) boisson *f*; (alcoholic) alcool *m*; **food and ~** la nourriture et la boisson; **to smell of ~** sentir l'alcool; **to be under the influence of ~** être en état d'ivresse; **to take to ~** se mettre à boire; **5**○ (sea) **in the ~** à la flotte○.
II *vtr* (*prét* **drank**, *pp* **drunk**) boire [*liquid, glass*]; **he's had nothing to ~ all day** il n'a rien bu de toute la journée; **to ~ sth from a cup/glass/can** boire qch dans une tasse/un verre/une boîte; **you can ~ some**

red wines chilled certains vins rouges se boivent frais; **to ~ a toast to sb** porter un toast à qn; **'...and what would you like to ~?'** (in restaurant) '...et comme boisson?'; **what are you ~ing?** qu'est-ce que vous voulez boire?

III *vi* (*prét* **drank**, *pp* **drunk**) **1** (consume liquid) boire (**from, out of** dans); **to ~ (straight) from the bottle** boire à la bouteille; **2** (consume alcohol) boire; **his mother drank** sa mère buvait; **have you been ~ing?** tu as bu?; **don't ~ and drive** ne conduisez pas si vous avez bu; **3** (as toast) **to ~ to the bride/to the health of Mr X** boire à la mariée/à la santé de M. X.

IV *v refl* **to ~ oneself stupid** ou **silly** se soûler.

IDIOMS **to drive sb to ~** pousser qn à la boisson or à boire; **I'll ~ to that!** excellente idée!; **don't listen to him, it's the ~ talking** ne l'écoute pas, l'alcool lui fait dire n'importe quoi.

■ **drink away**: **~ away [sth]**, **~ [sth] away** noyer [qch] dans l'alcool [*troubles, sorrows*]; boire [*fortune, inheritance, wages*]; **to ~ the night away** passer la soirée à boire.

■ **drink in**: **~ in [sth]** [*person*] respirer, humer [*air*]; s'imbiber de [*atmosphere*]; boire [*words*]; [*plant, roots*] absorber [*water*].

■ **drink up**: ¶ **~ up** finir son verre; ¶ **~ up [sth]**, **~ [sth] up** finir [*milk, beer etc*].

drinkable /ˈdrɪŋkəbl/ *adj* **1** (safe to drink) potable; **2** (acceptable) buvable.

drink-driver /ˌdrɪŋkˈdraɪvə(r)/ *n* GB personne *f* qui conduit en état d'ivresse.

drink-driving /ˌdrɪŋkˈdraɪvɪŋ/ GB **I** *n* conduite *f* en état d'ivresse.

II *modif* [*offence, charge*] de conduite en état d'ivresse; [*fine*] pour conduite en état d'ivresse.

drinker /ˈdrɪŋkə(r)/ *n* **1** gen buveur/-euse *m/f*; **coffee/beer ~s** les buveurs de café/bière; **2** (habitual consumer of alcohol) **to be a ~** boire; **Bill's not much of a ~** Bill boit très peu d'alcool; **he's a heavy ~** c'est un grand buveur; **3** (person in bar) client *m*; (consumer) consommateur *m* d'alcool.

drinking /ˈdrɪŋkɪŋ/ **I** *n* (consumption of alcohol) consommation *f* d'alcool; **~ and driving** l'alcool au volant; **there was a lot of ~ at the party** on a beaucoup bu à la soirée.

II *modif* [*laws*] sur l'alcool; [*companion*] de beuverie; **a ~ session** une beuverie; **you must change your ~ habits** vous devez réduire votre consommation d'alcool.

III -drinking (*dans composés*) **beer/whisky-~** buveur/-euse de bière/de whisky.

drinking: **~ chocolate** *n* GB chocolat *m* en poudre; **~ fountain** *n* (outdoor) fontaine *f* d'eau potable; (indoor) jet *m* d'eau potable; **~ problem** *n* US = **drink problem**; **~ song** *n* chanson *f* à boire; **~-up time** *n* GB *période de quelques minutes pour finir son verre avant la fermeture du pub*; **~ water** *n* eau *f* potable.

drink problem GB *n* GB penchant *m* pour la boisson; **to have a ~** (serious) être alcoolique; (less serious) avoir un penchant pour la boisson.

drink: **~s cabinet**, **~s cupboard** *n* GB bar *m*, meuble-bar *m*; **~s dispenser** *n* GB distributeur *m* de boissons; **~s machine** *n* GB machine *f* à boissons; **~s party** *n* GB cocktail *m*.

drip /drɪp/ **I** *n* **1** (drop) goutte *f* (qui tombe); **to catch the ~s** recueillir les gouttes qui tombent; **2** (sound) ploc-ploc○ *m*; **the constant ~ of rain/a tap** le bruit continuel de la pluie/d'un robinet qui goutte; **3** GB Med (device) goutte-à-goutte *m inv*; (solution) sérum *m*; **to be on a ~** être sous perfusion; **4**○ (insipid person) péj mauviette○ *f* pej.

II *vtr* (*p prés etc* **-pp-**) **1** [*leak, roof, brush*] laisser tomber [qch] goutte à goutte [*rain, water, paint*]; [*person, fingers*] dégouliner de [*sweat, blood*]; **the engine was ~ping** le moteur avait une fuite d'huile; **to ~ sth onto** ou **down sth** faire goutter qch sur qch; **to ~ sth all over sth** cribler qch de gouttes de qch; **2** fig (ooze) **he ~ped contempt/charm** son mépris/son charme exsudait de toutes parts; **his voice ~ped smugness** la suffisance émanait de sa voix.

III *vi* (*p prés etc* **-pp-**) **1** [*water, blood, oil, rain*] tomber goutte à goutte; **to ~ from** ou **off** dégouliner de, suinter de; **to ~ down sth** dégouliner le long de qch; **to ~ into/onto** tomber goutte à goutte dans/sur; **2** [*tap, branches*] goutter; [*washing, wet cloth*] s'égoutter (**onto** sur); [*engine*] fuir; [*wound*] suinter; **to be ~ping with** lit dégouliner de [*blood, oil, grease*]; ruisseler de [*sweat*]; fig exsuder liter [*sentiment, condescension*]; **~ping with greasy sauce** dégoulinant d'une sauce grasse.

drip-dry /ˌdrɪpˈdraɪ/ **I** *adj* qui se lave et s'étend sans essorage.

II *vtr* **'wash and ~'** 'laver et étendre sans essorer'.

drip feed I /ˈdrɪpfiːd/ *n* alimentation *f* par perfusion.

II /ˌdrɪpˈfiːd/ *vtr* alimenter [qn] par perfusion.

drip: **~ mat** *n* dessous-de-verre *m inv*; **~ pan** *n* lèchefrite *f*.

dripping /ˈdrɪpɪŋ/ **I** *n* Culin graisse *f* de rôti.

II *adj* [*tap*] qui goutte; [*branches, eaves*] ruisselant; [*washing, clothes*] trempé.

dripping: **~ pan** *n* lèchefrite *f*; **~ wet** *adj* [*cloth, clothes, person*] trempé.

drive /draɪv/ **I** *n* **1** (car journey) **to go for a ~** faire un tour (en voiture); **to take sb for a ~** emmener qn faire un tour; **to take the car for a ~** faire un tour avec la voiture; **it's only five minutes' ~ from here** ce n'est qu'à cinq minutes d'ici en voiture; **it's a 40 km ~ to the hospital** il y a 40 km de route d'ici à l'hôpital; **it's an easy ~** le trajet ne pose aucun problème; **it's a magnificent ~** c'est un trajet magnifique; **2** (campaign, effort) campagne *f* (**against** contre; **for, towards** pour; **to do** pour faire); (military) offensive *f*; **sales ~** campagne *f* de vente; **3** (motivation, energy) dynamisme *m*, énergie *f*; **human ~s** instincts *mpl* humains; **the ~ to win** la volonté de vaincre; **her ~ for perfection** sa recherche acharnée de la perfection; **4** Comput entraînement *m* de disques; **5** Mech (mechanism to transmit power) transmission *f*; **6** (path) (of house) allée *f*; **the car is in** ou **on the ~** la voiture est dans l'allée; **7** Sport (in golf) drive *m*; (in tennis) drive *m*, coup *m* droit.

II *modif* Mech [*mechanism, system*] de transmission.

III *vtr* (*prét* **drove**, *pp* **driven**) **1** [*driver*] conduire [*car, bus, van, train, passenger*]; piloter [*racing car*]; transporter [*cargo, load*]; parcourir [qch] (en voiture) [*distance*]; **what (car) do you ~?** qu'est-ce que tu as comme voiture? **to ~ sb to school /to the station** conduire qn à l'école/à la gare; **to ~ tourists round town** faire visiter la ville à des touristes; **she drove me home** elle m'a reconduit chez moi; **he hates being driven** il a horreur de se faire conduire; **I ~ 15 km every day** je fais 15 km en voiture chaque jour; **to ~ sth into** rentrer qch dans [*garage, carpark, space*]; **he drove his truck into a wall** il a embouti un mur avec son camion; **he drove the car straight at me** il a dirigé la voiture droit sur moi; **she drove her car over a cliff** sa voiture s'est écrasée du haut d'une falaise; **2** (force, compel) [*poverty, greed, urge*] pousser [*person*] (**to do** à faire); **he was driven to suicide/to drink** il a été poussé au suicide/à la boisson (**by** par); **hunger drove him to it** c'est la faim qui l'a poussé; **to be driven into debt** être contraint à s'endetter; **to be driven out of business** être conduit à la faillite; **to ~ the rate up/down** faire baisser/augmenter le taux; **to ~ sb mad** ou **crazy**○ lit, fig rendre qn fou/folle or dingue○; **3** (chase or herd) conduire [*herd, cattle*]; rabattre [*game*]; flotter [*logs*]; **to ~ sheep into a field** conduire des moutons dans un champ; **to ~ sb off one's land/out of her home** chasser qn de son terrain/de chez elle; **he was driven from** ou **out of the country** il a été chassé du pays; **to ~ evil thoughts from one's mind** écarter de mauvaises pensées de son esprit; **4** (power, propel) actionner [*engine, pump, fan*]; **the generator is driven by steam** le générateur fonctionne à la vapeur; **what ~s the economy?** quel est le moteur de l'économie?; **what ~s you?** qu'est-ce qui vous fait courir?; **5** (push) [*tide, wind*] pousser [*boat, snow, rain, clouds, person*]; **the wind drove the clouds along** le vent chassait les nuages; **to ~ a nail in(to)** enfoncer un clou (dans); **to ~ a tunnel through sth** percer un tunnel dans qch; **to ~ a road through an area** faire passer une route à travers une région; **to ~ sth into sb's head** fig faire rentrer qch dans la tête de qn; **6** (force to work hard) pousser [*pupil, recruit*]; **you're driving that child too hard** tu pousses trop cet enfant; **7** Sport (in golf) envoyer [*ball*]; (in tennis) envoyer [qch] d'un coup droit [*ball*]; **to ~ the ball into the rough** (in golf) envoyer son drive dans le rough.

IV *vi* (*prét* **drove**, *pp* **driven**) **1** Aut [*driver*] conduire; **can you ~?** est-ce que tu sais conduire?; **will you ~?** est-ce que tu peux conduire?; **he ~s for Ferrari** Sport il pilote pour Ferrari; **to ~ along** rouler; **I took pictures as we drove along** j'ai pris des photos en route; **you can't ~ along the High Street** on n'a pas le droit de circuler dans la grand-rue; **to ~ on the left/at 80 km per hour/on the main road** rouler à gauche/à 80 km à l'heure/sur la grand-route; **to ~ to work/to London** aller au travail/à Londres en voiture; **to ~ into** entrer dans [*garage, carpark, space*]; rentrer dans [*tree, lamppost*]; **I drove into a ditch** je suis allé dans le fossé; **to ~ up/down a hill** monter/descendre une côte; **to ~ past** passer; **to ~ at sb** se diriger sur qn; **the taxi drove out of the station** le taxi a quitté la gare; **you use a lot of petrol driving around town** la conduite en ville consomme beaucoup d'essence; **2** Sport (in golf) driver; (in tennis) faire un drive.

V *v refl* **to ~ oneself 1** Aut conduire soi-même; **the Minister ~s himself** le Ministre conduit sa voiture lui-même; **to ~ oneself to hospital** se conduire soi-même à l'hôpital; **2** (push oneself) **to ~ oneself to do** se forcer à faire; **to ~ oneself too hard** se surmener.

■ **drive away**: ¶ **~ away** démarrer; ¶ **~ away [sth/sb]**, **~ [sth/sb] away 1** Aut [*driver*] faire démarrer [*vehicle*]; **2** (get rid of) chasser, faire partir [*wolves, insects*]; faire partir [*tourists, visitors, thieves, clients*]; écarter [*lover, friend*]; dissiper [*doubt, suspicion*]; chasser [*fear, cares*].

■ **drive at**: **what are you driving at?** où veux-tu en venir?, que veux-tu dire?

■ **drive back**: ¶ **~ back** rentrer; **to ~ there and back in one day** faire l'aller-retour dans la même journée; ¶ **~ back [sth/sb]**, **~ [sth/sb] back 1** (repel) repousser [*crowd, enemy, animals*]; **we were driven back by bad weather** le mauvais temps nous a fait rebrousser chemin; **2** Aut ramener [*car, passenger*].

■ **drive forward** (in football) attaquer.

■ **drive off 1** Aut démarrer; **2** Sport jouer le premier drive.

■ **drive on**: ¶ **~ on** (continue) poursuivre sa route; (set off again) repartir; ¶ **~ [sb] on** pousser; **to ~ sb on to do** pousser qn à faire.

■ **drive out**: **~ out [sth/sb]**, **~ [sth/sb] out** chasser [*people, invader, spirits, thought*].

drive-by (shooting) *n* US attaque *f* criminelle (*exécutée d'une voiture en marche*).

drive-in /ˈdraɪvɪn/ **I** *n* **1** (cinema) drive-in *m*, ciné-parc *m*; **2** (restaurant) restaurant *m* drive-in.
II *modif* [*restaurant, bank*] drive-in, accessible aux clients sans qu'ils sortent de leur voiture.

drivel○ /ˈdrɪvl/ **I** *n* ¢ bêtises *fpl*; **to talk ~** dire n'importe quoi.
II *vi* (*p prés etc* **-ll-** GB, **-l-** US) (also **~ on**) dire n'importe quoi (**about** sur).

driveline /ˈdraɪvlaɪn/ *n* transmission *f*.

driven /ˈdrɪvn/ **I** *pp* ▶ **drive**.
II *adj* [*person*] passionné, motivé.
III -driven (*dans composés*) **petrol-/motor-/steam-~** à essence/moteur/vapeur; **market-~** déterminé par le marché; ▶ **menu-driven**.

driver /ˈdraɪvə(r)/ *n* **1** gen conducteur/-trice *m/f*; Aut automobiliste *mf*; (for a living) chauffeur *m*; **to be a good/bad ~** être un bon/mauvais conducteur, conduire bien/mal; **a careful/reckless ~** un conducteur prudent/imprudent; **2** (mechanical component) actionneur *m*; **3** (golf club) driver *m*, bois *m* n°1. ▶ **slave driver**.

driver: **~'s education** *n* US cours *m* de conduite (*dans le cadre scolaire*); **~'s license** *n* US = **driving licence**; **~'s seat** *n* = **driving seat**.

drive: **~ shaft** *n* Tech arbre *m* de transmission; **~-through** *n* US comptoir *m* de vente à l'extérieur; **~time** *n* heure *f* de pointe; **~-time music** *n* US Radio musique *f* passée à une heure de grande écoute; **~ unit** *n* unité *f* de disques; **~-up window** *n* US *guichet bancaire où on peut retirer de l'argent sans quitter sa voiture*; **~way** *n* allée *f*.

driving /ˈdraɪvɪŋ/ **I** *n* conduite *f*; **motorway/night ~** conduite *f* sur autoroute/de nuit; **~ is difficult/fun** c'est difficile/amusant de conduire; **his ~ has improved** il conduit mieux qu'avant.
II *modif* [*skills, habits, offence, position*] de conduite.
III *adj* [*rain*] battant; [*wind, hail*] cinglant.

driving: **~ belt** *n* courroie *f* de transmission; **~ examiner** *n* inspecteur/-trice *m/f* (du permis de conduire); **~ force** *n* (person) force *f* agissante (**behind** de); (money, ambition, belief) moteur *m* (**behind** de); **~ instructor** ▶ **1692** *n* moniteur/-trice *m/f* d'auto-école; **~ lesson** *n* cours *m* de conduite; **~ licence** GB, **driver's license** US *n* permis *m* de conduire; **~ mirror** *n* rétroviseur *m*; **~ range** *n* (in golf) practice *m*; **~ school** *n* auto-école *f*.

driving seat *n* place *f* du conducteur.
IDIOMS **to be in the ~** être aux commandes, tenir les rênes.

driving test *n* examen *m* du permis de conduire; **to take/pass/fail one's ~** passer/réussir/rater son permis (de conduire).

driving wheel *n* Tech roue *f* motrice.

drizzle /ˈdrɪzl/ **I** *n* bruine *f*.
II *vtr* Culin **~ the salad with oil** verser un filet d'huile sur la salade.
III *vi* Meteorol bruiner; **it's drizzling** il bruine.

drizzly /ˈdrɪzlɪ/ *adj* [*day, weather*] de bruine.

droll /drəʊl/ *adj* **1** (amusing) drôle; **2**† (quaint, odd) bizarre.

Drôme ▶ **1163** *pr n* Drôme *f*; **in/to the ~** dans la Drôme.

dromedary /ˈdrɒmədərɪ, US -ədern/ *n* dromadaire *m*.

drone /drəʊn/ **I** *n* **1** (of engine) ronronnement *m*; (loud) vrombissement *m*; (of insects) bourdonnement *m*; **I could hear his monotonous ~** j'entendais son murmure monotone; **2** Zool faux bourdon *m*; fig (parasite) parasite *m*; **3** (pilotless aircraft) drone *m*; **4** Mus (chord, pipe) bourdon *m*.
II *vtr* **'as you like,' he ~d** 'comme vous voulez,' débita-t-il d'un ton monotone.
III *vi* [*engine*] ronronner; (loudly) vrombir; [*person*] parler d'un ton monotone; [*insect*] bourdonner; **bombers ~d overhead** des bombardiers passaient en vrombissant dans le ciel.
■ **drone on** péj faire de longs discours rasants○ (**about** sur).

drongo○ /ˈdrɒŋgəʊ/ *n* Austral péj imbécile *m*.

drool /druːl/ *vi* lit baver; ○fig baver (d'envie); **to ~ over sth/sb** s'extasier (à n'en plus finir) sur qch/qn; **to ~ at the thought of sth** baver (d'envie) en pensant à qch; **to ~ at the mouth** (in admiration) en baver d'admiration; (in envy) en baver d'envie.

droop /druːp/ **I** *n* affaissement *m*.
II *vi* **1** (sag) [*eyelids, head*] tomber; [*branch, shoulders, wings*] s'affaisser; [*moustache*] retomber; [*flower, plant*] commencer à se faner; **2** (flag) [*person*] flancher.

drooping /ˈdruːpɪŋ/ *adj* **1** lit [*eyelids, head, moustache*] tombant; [*shoulders, branch*] affaissé; [*flower, plant*] fané; **2** fig **~ spirits** abattement *m*.

droopy /ˈdruːpɪ/ *adj* [*moustache*] tombant; [*flower, leaf*] fané; [*stomach, bottom*] flasque.

drop /drɒp/ **I** *n* **1** (drip, globule) gen, Med goutte *f*; **~ by ~** goutte à goutte; **add the oil in ~s** ajouter l'huile goutte à goutte; **would you like a ~ of milk/whisky?** voulez-vous une goutte de lait/de whisky?; **just a ~** juste une goutte; **a ~ more milk** encore un peu de lait; **this isn't a bad ~ of wine/whisky** il n'est pas mauvais ce petit vin/whisky; **he's definitely had a ~ too much!** euph il a bu un verre de trop!; **2** (decrease) (in prices, inflation, numbers, birthrate, exports, demand) baisse *f* (**in** de), diminution *f* (**in** de); (in speed, pressure, noise) diminution *f* (**in** de); (in temperature) baisse *f* (**in** de); **there has been a sharp ~ in unemployment** on constate une forte baisse or diminution du nombre de chômeurs; **a 5% ~ in sth, a ~ of 5% in sth** une baisse de 5% de qch; **3** (vertical distance, slope) **there's a ~ of 100 m from the top to the water below** il y a une hauteur de 100 m du sommet jusqu'à l'eau; **don't lean out—it's a big ~** ne te penche pas—c'est haut; **it's quite a ~ from the top of the cliff/tower** la falaise/la tour est très haute; **there was a steep ~ on either side of the ridge** il y avait une pente abrupte de chaque côté de l'arête; **a sheer ~ (of 200 m) to the rocks below** une brusque dénivellation (de 200 m) jusqu'aux rochers en contrebas; **4** (delivery) (from aircraft) largage *m*, parachutage *m*; (from lorry, van) livraison *f*; (parachute jump) saut *m* en parachute; **to make a ~** [*parachutist*] faire un saut en parachute; **a ~ of food and blankets was made to the stricken area** des denrées et des couvertures ont été larguées or parachutées sur la zone sinistrée; **5** (on necklace, earring) goutte *f*; (on chandelier) pendeloque *f*; **6** (sweet) **pear/lemon ~** bonbon *m* à la poire/au citron; **chocolate ~** crotte *f* en chocolat; **7** (gallows) potence *f*; **8** Theat = **drop curtain**.
II *vtr* (*p prés etc* **-pp-**) **1** (allow to fall) (by accident) laisser tomber; (on purpose) mettre, lâcher; **mind you don't ~ it!** fais attention de ne pas le laisser tomber or le lâcher; **she ~ped a stone into the well** elle a laissé tomber or a lâché une pierre dans le puits; **~ it!** lit lâche ça!; **she ~ped a coin into the slot/a letter into the box** elle a mis une pièce dans la fente/une lettre dans la boîte; **he ~ped a 30-foot putt** ≈ il a rentré un putt de 9 mètres; **she ~ped the shuttlecock over the net** elle a fait passer le volant juste derrière le filet; **2** (deliver) [*aircraft*] lâcher, parachuter [*supplies, equipment*]; parachuter [*person*]; larguer, lâcher [*bomb, shell*]; **3** (leave) (also **~ off**) déposer [*person, object*]; **can you ~ me (off) at the post office/at Claire's, please?** est-ce que vous pouvez me déposer devant la Poste/chez Claire, s'il vous plait?; **4** (lower) baisser [*curtain, sail, hem, neckline, price*]; **to ~ one's eyes/gaze/voice** baisser les yeux/le regard/la voix; **to ~ one's trousers**○ baisser son pantalon; **to ~ one's speed** ralentir; **5** (give casually) **to ~ a hint about sth** faire allusion à qch; **to ~ sb a card/a note/a letter** envoyer une carte/un mot/une lettre à qn; **he just ~ped it into the conversation that he was leaving** il a juste fait allusion, dans la conversation, à son départ; **6** (exclude) (deliberately) supprimer [*article, episode, word*]; écarter [*team member, player*]; (by mistake) omettre [*figure, letter, digit, item on list*]; ne pas prononcer [*syllable, sound*]; **he's been ~ped from the team** il a été écarté de l'équipe; **7** (abandon) laisser tomber○ [*friend, boyfriend*]; (give up) abandonner, laisser tomber○ [*school subject, work*]; renoncer à [*habit, custom, idea, plan*]; abandonner [*conversation, matter*]; retirer [*charges, accusation, claim*]; **to ~ everything** tout laisser tomber; **can we ~ that subject, please?** on ne pourrait pas parler d'autre chose?; **just ~ it**○**, will you!** laisse tomber, tu veux bien○!; **let's ~ the formalities** ne nous embarrassons pas de formalités; **8** gen, Sport (lose) perdre [*money, point, game, serve*]; **9** Zool (give birth to) mettre bas [*calf, foal, young*]; **10** argot des drogués **to ~ acid** prendre du LSD.
III *vi* (*p prés etc* **-pp-**) **1** (fall, descend) [*object, liquid, curtain, leaf*] tomber; [*person*] (deliberately) se laisser tomber; (by accident) tomber; **we ~ped to the ground as the plane flew over** nous nous sommes jetés à terre quand l'avion est passé au-dessus de nous; **to ~ to one's knees** tomber à genoux; **to ~ into a chair** se laisser tomber dans un fauteuil; **the pen ~ped from** ou **out of his hand** le stylo lui est tombé des mains; **the key must have ~ped out of the hole in my pocket** la clé a dû passer par le trou de ma poche; **his arm ~ped to his side** il a laissé retomber le bras; **his mouth ~ped open** (from surprise) il en est resté bouche bée; (in sleep) il a ouvert la bouche; **the sun ~ped below the horizon** le soleil a disparu à l'horizon; **the plane ~ped to an altitude of 1,000 m** l'avion est descendu à une altitude de 1000 m; **2** (fall away) **the cliff ~s into the sea** la falaise tombe dans la mer; **the road ~s steeply down the mountain** la route descend abruptement le long de la montagne; ▶ **drop away**; **3** (decrease, lower) [*prices, inflation, noise, wind, temperature, level, speed*] baisser; **to ~ (from sth) to sth** [*prices, inflation, temperature, speed*] tomber (de qch) à qch; [*person*] descendre (de qch) à qch; **the temperature ~ped (from 6°C) to 0°C** la température est tombée (de 6°C) à 0°C; **she ~ped to third place** elle est descendue à la troisième place; **4**○ (collapse) **he was ready** ou **fit to ~** il tombait de fatigue; **to do sth until one ~s** ou **is ready to ~** faire qch jusqu'à l'épuisement; **5** (come to an end) **to let sth ~** laisser tomber qch [*matter, subject, conversation, course, job*]; **6** Sewing [*curtain, garment*] s'allonger; **the hem of my skirt has ~ped** l'ourlet de ma jupe s'est défait.
IDIOMS **to ~ a brick**○ ou **clanger**○ faire une gaffe○; **a ~ in the bucket** ou **ocean** une goutte d'eau dans la mer; **to ~ sb in it**○ mettre qn dans le pétrin○; **to get/have the ~ on sb** US prendre/avoir l'avantage sur qn.
■ **drop away 1** (diminish) [*attendance, numbers, support, interest*] diminuer; [*concentration*] faiblir; **2** (fall steeply) [*path, road*] descendre brusquement; (end) s'arrêter brusquement.
■ **drop back** (deliberately) rester en arrière, se laisser distancer; (because unable to keep up) prendre du retard.
■ **drop behind 1** = **drop back**; **2** fig (in school, at work) prendre du retard; **to ~ behind sb/sth** lit (deliberately) se laisser

distancer par qn/qch; fig prendre du retard sur qn/qch.

■ **drop by** passer ; **if there's anything you need just ~ by** si vous avez besoin de quoi que ce soit, passez me/nous voir; **I ~ped by to see her today** je suis passé la voir aujourd'hui.

■ **drop in**: **~ in** passer; **~ in and have a cup of tea** passez prendre une tasse de thé; **to ~ in on sb** passer voir qn; **to ~ in at the baker's** passer chez le boulanger; **I'll ~ it in (to you) later** je passerai te le donner plus tard.

■ **drop off**: ¶ **~ off 1** (fall off) [*handle, leaf, label, hat*] tomber; **2 ~ off (to sleep)** s'endormir; **3** (become weaker, fewer etc) [*attendance, numbers, business, demand, interest*] diminuer; ¶ **~ [sth/sb] off, ~ off [sth/sb]** = **drop II** 3.

■ **drop out 1** (fall out) [*object, handkerchief, contact lens, page*] tomber (**of** de); **2** (withdraw) (from contest, race) se désister; (from project) se retirer; (from school, university) abandonner ses études; (from society) se marginaliser; **to ~ out of** se retirer de [*contest, race*]; abandonner [*politics*]; **to ~ out of school/university** abandonner l'école/ses études; **that word has virtually ~ped out of the language** ce mot a pratiquement disparu de la langue; **terms that ~ped out of usage years ago** des termes qui ne sont plus utilisés depuis de nombreuses années; **the coins will gradually ~ out of circulation** les pièces seront progressivement retirées de la circulation.

■ **drop over** = **drop round**.

■ **drop round**: **~ round** passer; **I'll ~ round (to your house) later** je passerai te voir plus tard; **I'll ~ your books round after school** je passerai te donner tes livres après l'école.

drop: **~-add period** *n* US Univ *période de réflexion pendant laquelle on peut changer son choix initial de cours*; **~cloth** *n* US bâche *f*; **~ curtain** *n* Theat rideau *m*; **~-down menu** *n* Comput menu *m* déroulant; **~ forge** *n* marteau-pilon *m*.

drop goal *n* drop *m*; **to score a ~** réussir un drop.

drop: **~ hammer** *n* = **drop forge**; **~ handlebars** *npl* guidon *m* de course; **~ kick** *n* coup *m* de pied tombé; **~ leaf** *n* (of table) rallonge *f*; **~-leaf table** *n* table *f* pliante, table *f* anglaise.

droplet /ˈdrɒplɪt/ *n* gouttelette *f*.

drop-off /ˈdrɒpɒf/ *n* baisse *f*, diminution *f* (**in** de).

dropout /ˈdrɒpaʊt/ *n* **1** (from society) marginal/-e *m/f*; (from school) étudiant/-e *m/f* qui abandonne ses études; **2** Sport (in rugby) remise *f* en jeu.

dropper /ˈdrɒpə(r)/ *n* compte-gouttes *m inv*.

droppings /ˈdrɒpɪŋz/ *npl* (of mouse, rabbit, sheep) crottes *fpl*; (of horse) crottin *m*; (of bird) fiente *f*; (of insect) chiures *fpl*, crottes *fpl*.

drop: **~ping zone** *n* = **drop zone**; **~ scone** *n* crêpe *f* écossaise (*faite avec de la pâte à crêpes additionnée de levure et de sucre*); **~ shipment** *n* livraison *f* directe (*facturée au grossiste mais livrée directement au détaillant*).

drop shot *n* Sport amorti *m*; **to play a ~** faire un amorti.

dropsy /ˈdrɒpsɪ/ *n* hydropisie *f*.

drop: **~ tank** *n* Aviat réservoir *m* largable; **~ zone, ~ping zone** *n* (for supplies etc) zone *f* de largage; (for parachutist) zone *f* de saut.

drosophila /drəˈsɒfɪlə/ *n* drosophile *f*.

dross /drɒs/ *n* **1** (rubbish) rebut *m*; **it's ~** ça ne vaut rien; **2** Ind crasse *f*, laitier *m*.

drought /draʊt/ *n* sécheresse *f*.

drove /drəʊv/ **I** *pret* ▶ **drive**.

II *n* (of animals) troupeau *m* en marche; **~s of people** des foules *fpl* de gens; **in ~s** fig en masse.

drover /ˈdrəʊvə(r)/ *n* conducteur *m* de bestiaux.

drown /draʊn/ **I** *vtr* **1** (kill by immersion) noyer [*person, animal*]; **20 people were ~ed in the accident** 20 personnes sont mortes noyées dans l'accident; **the entire crew was ~ed** l'équipage entier est mort noyé; **2** (make inaudible) couvrir [*song, sound, voice*]; **3** (flood) submerger, inonder [*land, village, valley*]; fig noyer [*drink, food*] (**in** dans).

II *vi* se noyer.

III *v refl* **to ~ oneself** se noyer.

IDIOMS **to ~ one's sorrows** noyer son chagrin dans l'alcool.

■ **drown out**: ¶ **~ [sth] out, ~ out [sth]** couvrir [*noise, sound, music*]; ¶ **~ [sb] out** couvrir la voix de [*person*].

drowning /ˈdraʊnɪŋ/ **I** *n* noyade *f*.

II *adj* [*person*] qui se noie.

IDIOMS **a ~ man will clutch at a straw** Prov tout est bon à qui se noie.

drowse /draʊz/ **I** *n* **to be in a ~** être à moitié endormi.

II *vi* (be half asleep) être à moitié endormi (sleep lightly) somnoler; **to ~ the afternoon away** passer l'après-midi à somnoler.

drowsily /ˈdraʊzɪlɪ/ *adv* [*say*] d'un ton à moitié endormi; [*move*] d'un air à moitié endormi.

drowsiness /ˈdraʊzɪnɪs/ *n* somnolence *f*; **'may cause ~'** (on medication) 'risque de somnolence'.

drowsy /ˈdraʊzɪ/ *adj* **1** [*person*] à moitié endormi; [*look, smile*] somnolent; **to feel ~** avoir envie de dormir; **to grow ~** s'assoupir; **2** littér (sleep-inducing) assoupissant.

drubbing○ /ˈdrʌbɪŋ/ *n* râclée○ *f*; **to give sb a (good) ~** administrer une (belle) râclée à qn; **to get a ~** prendre une râclée.

drudge /drʌdʒ/ **I** *n* besogneux/-euse *m/f*; **to be the household ~** faire la bonne.

II *vi* (physically) trimer; (in office) besogner.

drudgery /ˈdrʌdʒərɪ/ *n* ¢ corvée *f*; **household ~** les corvées ménagères; **it's sheer ~** c'est une vraie corvée.

drug /drʌg/ **I** *n* **1** Med, Pharm médicament *m*; **a pain-relieving ~** un médicament pour calmer la douleur; **a ~ to fight infection** un médicament pour lutter contre l'infection; **to be on ~s** prendre des médicaments; **2** (narcotic) lit, fig drogue *f*; **hard/soft ~s** drogues *fpl* dures/douces; **to be on** ou **to take ~s** gen se droguer, Sport se doper; **to do ~s**○ se camer○.

II *modif* **1** (narcotic) [*problem, shipment, smuggler, trafficking*] de drogue; [*culture, use*] de la drogue; [*crime*] lié à la drogue; **2** Med, Pharm [*company, industry*] pharmaceutique.

III *vtr* (*p prés etc* **-gg-**) **1** (sedate) [*kidnapper*] administrer des somnifères à [*victim*]; [*vet*] endormir [*animal*]; **2** (dope) [*person*] mettre un somnifère dans [*drink*]; [*vet*] mettre un narcotique dans [*meal*]; [*trainer*] doper [*horse*].

IDIOMS **a ~ on the market** un produit qui se vend mal.

drug: **~ abuse** *n* consommation *f* de stupéfiants; **~ abuser** *n* drogué/-e *m/f*; **~ addict** *n* toxicomane *mf*; **~ addiction** *n* toxicomanie *f*.

drugged /drʌgd/ *adj* **1** (under the influence of medicine) [*person*] drogué; [*state, feeling*] d'abrutissement; **to be ~ up to the eyeballs**○ être bourré○ de médicaments; **to be in a ~ sleep** dormir comme sous l'effet d'un somnifère; **2** (poisoned) [*drink*] additionné d'un narcotique.

drugget /ˈdrʌgɪt/ *n* Tex thibaude *f*.

druggist /ˈdrʌgɪst/ **▶ 1692** *n* US pharmacien/-ienne *m/f*.

druggy○ /ˈdrʌgɪ/ *n* camé/-e○ *m/f*, toxicomane *mf*.

drug: **~ habit** *n* accoutumance *f* à la drogue; **~ peddler, ~ pusher** *n* revendeur/-euse *m/f* de drogue; **~-related** *adj* lié à la drogue; **~s charges** *npl* infraction *f* à la législation sur les stupéfiants; **~s offence** *n* infraction *f* à la législation sur les stupéfiants; **Drug Squad, Drugs Squad** *n* GB brigade *f* des stupéfiants; **~s raid** *n* opération *f* antidrogue; **~s ring** *n* réseau *m* de trafiquants de drogue; **~store** *n* US drugstore *m*; **~store cowboy**○ *n* US traîne-savates○ *m inv*; **~ taker** *n* toxicomane *mf*; **~-taking** *n* gen usage *m* de stupéfiants; Sport dopage *m*; **~ test** *n* Med Sport contrôle *m* antidopage; **~ user** *n* toxicomane *mf*.

druid /ˈdruːɪd/ *n* druide *m*.

druidism /ˈdruːɪdɪzəm/ *n* druidisme *m*.

drum /drʌm/ **I** *n* **▶ 1481** **1** Mus, Mil tambour *m*; **2** Ind, Comm bidon *m*; (larger) baril *m*; **a 10 litre ~** un bidon de 10 litres; **3** Tech, Aut tambour *m*; **4** (spool for rope, cable) tambour *m*.

II drums *npl* batterie *f*; **Joe Morello on ~s** Joe Morello à la batterie.

III *vtr* (*p prés etc* **-mm-**) **to ~ one's fingers/feet** tambouriner des doigts/des pieds (**on** sur); **to ~ sth into sb** fig enfoncer qch dans le crâne de qn○.

IV *vi* (*p prés etc* **-mm-**) **1** (beat drum) jouer du tambour; **2** (make drumming sound) [*rain*] tambouriner; **to ~ on the table with one's fingers** tambouriner sur la table avec les doigts.

IDIOMS **to beat the ~ for sth** fig faire du battage pour qch.

■ **drum home**: **~ [sth] home** réussir à faire comprendre [*lesson, point*]; réussir à faire passer [*message*].

■ **drum out**: **~ [sb] out** expulser [*person*].

■ **drum up**: ¶ **~ up [sth]** trouver [*business, custom, trade*]: ¶ **~ up [sb]** racoler [*clients, customers*]; **to ~ up sb's support for** obtenir le soutien de qn en faveur de [*candidate, plan*].

drum: **~beat** *n* battement *m* de tambour; **~beater**○ *n* US agent *m* publicitaire; **~ brake** *n* frein *m* à tambour; **~head** *n* peau *f* de tambour; **~head court-martial** *n*: *tribunal militaire convoqué d'urgence pendant les combats*; **~ kit** *n* batterie *f*.

drumlin /ˈdrʌmlɪn/ *n* drumlin *m*.

drum: **~ machine** *n* batterie *f* électronique; **~ major** *n* tambour-major *m*; **~ majorette** *n* majorette *f*.

drummer /ˈdrʌmə(r)/ **▶ 1692**, **1481** *n* **1** (in military band) tambour *m*; **2** (jazz or pop musician) batteur *m*; **3** (classical musician) percussionniste *mf*; **4**○ US (salesman) représentant *m* de commerce, commis *m* voyageur.

drummer boy *n* jeune tambour *m*.

drumming /ˈdrʌmɪŋ/ *n* **1** (activity) jouer de la batterie; (in orchestra) jouer des percussions; **2** (noise made on drum) bruit *m* de tambour; **the ~ faded away** le bruit du tambour s'est éteint; **3** (of fingers, feet, rain) tambourinement *m*.

drumroll /ˈdrʌmrɒl/ *n* roulement *m* de tambour.

drumstick /ˈdrʌmstɪk/ *n* **1** Mus baguette *f* de tambour; **2** Culin (of chicken) pilon *m*.

drunk /drʌŋk/ **I** *pp* ▶ **drink**.

II *n* ivrogne/-esse *m/f*.

III *adj* **1** lit ivre, soûl; **to get ~** s'enivrer (**on** de); **to get sb ~** faire boire qn; **~ driver** conducteur/-trice *m/f* en état d'ivresse; **~ driving** conduite *f* en état d'ivresse; **to be ~ and disorderly** Jur être en état d'ivresse publique; **it is illegal to be ~ in charge of a motor vehicle** Jur il est illégal de conduire en état d'ivresse; **to be arrested for being ~ in charge of a motor vehicle** Jur être arrêté pour conduite en état d'ivresse; **2** fig **~ with** ivre de [*power, passion, freedom*].

IDIOMS **as ~ as a lord** GB ou **skunk**○ US soûl comme une grive.

drunkard /ˈdrʌŋkəd/ *n* ivrogne/-esse *m/f*.

drunken /ˈdrʌŋkən/ *adj* [*person*] ivre, en état d'ivresse; [*party, evening*] bien arrosé; [*sleep, stupor*] éthylique; [*state*] d'ivresse; [*rage, fury*] causé par l'ivresse.

drunkenly /ˈdrʌnkənlı/ *adv* lit [*say, shout, laugh*] d'une voix avinée; [*walk*] en titubant; fig (as if drunk) **to lurch ~** [*person*] tituber; [*vehicle*] zigzaguer.

drunkenness /ˈdrʌŋkənnıs/ *n* **1** (state) ivresse *f*, ébriété *f* fml; **2** (habit) ivrognerie *f*.

drunkometer /ˌdrʌŋˈkɒmıtə(r)/ *n* US alcootest *m*.

druthers○ /ˈdrʌðəz/ *npl* US **if I had my ~** s'il ne tenait qu'à moi.

dry /draı/ **I** *n* GB Pol ultraconservateur/-trice *m/f*.

II *adj* **1** (not wet or moist) [*clothing, ground, hair, hand, paint, crackle, rustle*] sec/sèche; [*skin, hair, throat, mouth, cough*] sec/sèche; [*riverbed, well*] à sec; **to run ~** [*river, funds, supplies*] se tarir; **~ bread** pain sec; **to be** ou **feel ~** (thirsty) [*person*] avoir le gosier sec○; **to keep sth ~** tenir qch au sec; **to keep (oneself) ~** rester au sec; **to get ~** se sécher; **to get sth ~** (faire) sécher qch; **to wipe sth ~** essuyer qch; **the kettle has boiled ~** toute l'eau de la bouilloire s'est évaporée; **on ~ land** sur la terre ferme; **2** (not rainy) [*weather, climate, season, month, heat*] sec/sèche; [*day, spell*] sans pluie; **it will be ~ tomorrow** il ne pleuvra pas demain; **3** (not sweet) [*wine, sherry etc*] sec/sèche; **4** (ironic) [*wit, person, remark*] pince-sans-rire *inv*; (cold) [*person, remark*] sec/sèche; **5** (dull) [*book, reading, subject matter*] aride; **6** (forbidding alcohol) [*state, country*] qui interdit la vente de boissons alcoolisées; **7** GB Pol [*view, minister*] ultraconservateur/-trice; **a ~ Tory** un/-e ultraconservateur/-trice *m/f*.

III *vtr* faire sécher [*clothes, washing*]; sécher [*fruit, meat, flowers*]; **to ~ the dishes** essuyer la vaisselle; **to ~ sb's hair** sécher les cheveux de qn; **to ~ one's hair/hands** se sécher les cheveux/les mains; **to ~ one's eyes** sécher ses larmes.

IV *vi* [*sheet, clothes, hair, paint, blood, concrete*] sécher.

V *v refl* **to ~ oneself** se sécher.

IDIOMS **(as) ~ as a bone** sec/sèche comme un coup de trique; **(as) ~ as dust** ennuyeux/-euse comme la pluie.

■ **dry off**: ¶ **~ off** [*material, object*] sécher; [*person*] se sécher; ¶ **~ off [sb/sth]**, **~ [sb/sth] off** sécher [*person, object*]; **to ~ oneself off** se sécher.

■ **dry out**: ¶ **~ out 1** lit [*wood, walls, clay, soil*] sécher; **don't let the plant ~ out** ne laissez pas la plante se dessécher; **2**○ [*alcoholic*] se faire désintoxiquer; ¶ **~ out [sth/sb]**, **~ [sth/sb] out 1** lit sécher [*wood, clay*]; [*sun*] dessécher [*skin, earth*]; **2**○ désintoxiquer [*alcoholic*].

■ **dry up**: ¶ **~ up 1** lit [*river, well, spring*] s'assécher, se tarir; [*ground, jar of liquid*] sécher; **2** fig (run out) [*supply, source, funds, money*] se tarir; **3** (wipe crockery etc) [*person*] essuyer la vaisselle; **4**○ (be unable to speak) [*speaker, actor, interviewee*] sécher○; **oh, ~ up will you!** GB boucle-la, tu veux bien○!; ¶ **~ up [sth]**, **~ [sth] up 1** [*heat, drought*] assécher [*puddle, river, pond*]; **2** [*person*] essuyer [*plates, crockery*].

dryad /ˈdraıæd, ˈdraıəd/ *n* dryade *f*.

dry: **~asdust** *adj* fig aride, dépourvu d'intérêt; **~ cell** *n* pile *f* sèche.

dry-clean /ˌdraıˈkli:n/ *vtr* nettoyer [qch] à sec; **to have sth ~ed** faire nettoyer qch (chez le teinturier); **'~ only'** 'nettoyage à sec'.

dry: **~-cleaner's** ▶ **1692** *n* teinturerie *f*; **~-cleaning** *n* nettoyage *m* à sec; **~ dock** *n* cale *f* sèche.

dryer /ˈdraıə(r)/ *n* = **drier**.

dry-eyed /ˌdraıˈaıd/ *adj* [*person*] qui a les yeux secs; **to be/remain ~** avoir/garder les yeux secs.

dry: **~ farming** *n* culture *f* sèche, dry-farming *m*; **~ fly** *n* mouche *f* sèche; **~ goods**† *npl* US articles *mpl* de mercerie; **~ goods store**† *n* US magasin *m* de nouveautés† or de tissus; **~ ice** *n* neige *f* carbonique.

drying /ˈdraııŋ/ **I** *n* (of fruit, clothes) séchage *m*.

II *adj* [*wind, weather*] qui fait sécher; **a good ~ day** un beau temps pour faire sécher la lessive.

drying: **~ rack** *n* séchoir *m*; **~ room** *n* séchoir *m*.

drying-up /ˌdraııŋˈʌp/ *n* GB **to do the ~** essuyer la vaisselle.

drying-up cloth *n* GB torchon *m* à vaisselle.

dryly /ˈdraılı/ *adv* = **drily**.

dry: **~ martini** *n* martini-dry *m*; **~ measure** *n* mesure *f* de capacité pour matières sèches.

dryness /ˈdraınıs/ *n* **1** (of skin, weather, soil) sécheresse *f*; **2** (of wit, humour) causticité *f*.

dry: **~ rot** *n* pourriture *f* sèche (*du bois*); **~ run** *n* répétition *f* d'essai; **~ shampoo** *n* shampooing *m* sec; **~-shod**† *adj, adv* à pied sec; **~ ski slope** *n* piste *f* (de ski) artificielle; **~stone wall** *n* mur *m* de pierres sèches.

DSc *n* (*abrév* = **Doctor of Science**) doctorat *m* de sciences.

DSS *n* GB Soc Admin (*abrév* = **Department of Social Security**) **1** (ministry) ministère *m* des affaires sociales; **2** (local office) *service social responsable des chômeurs*.

DST *n*: *abrév* ▶ **daylight saving time**.

DT *n*: *abrév* ▶ **data transmission**.

DTI *n* GB *abrév* ▶ **Department of Trade and Industry**.

DTP *n* (*abrév* = **desktop publishing**) PAO *f*.

DT's○ *npl* (*abrév* = **delirium tremens**) **the ~** le delirium tremens.

dual /ˈdju:əl, US ˈdu:əl/ **I** *n* Ling duel *m*.

II *adj* double.

dual: **~ carriageway** *n* GB route *f* pour automobiles, route *f* à quatre voies; **~-circuit brakes** *npl* freins *mpl* à double circuit; **~-control** *adj* à double commande; **~ controls** *npl* double commande *f*.

dualism /ˈdju:əlızəm, US du:-/ *n* dualisme *m*.

duality /dju:ˈælətı, US du:-/ *n* dualité *f*.

dual: **~ nationality** *n* double nationalité *f*; **~ personality** *n* dédoublement *m* de la personnalité; **~-purpose** *adj* à double usage.

dub /dʌb/ **I** *vtr* (*p prés etc* **-bb-**) **1** (into foreign language) doubler [*film*] (**into** en); (add sound track) post-synchroniser [*film*]; mixer [*sound effect*] (**onto** à); **2** journ (nickname) surnommer [*person*]; (describe as) [*person, affair*] qualifier de; **3** (knight) **to ~ sb (a) knight** adouber qn.

II dubbed *pp adj* [*film*] doublé.

Dubai /du:ˈbaı/ *pr n* Dubaï *m*.

dubbin /ˈdʌbın/ *n* GB dégras *m*.

dubbing /ˈdʌbıŋ/ *n* **1** (into foreign language) doublage *m*; **2** (adding soundtrack) postsynchronisation *f*; (sound mixing) mixage *m*.

dubious /ˈdju:bıəs, US ˈdu:-/ *adj* **1** (showing doubt) [*response, look*] dubitatif/-ive; [*person*] **to be ~ (about sth)** avoir des doutes (en ce qui concerne qch); **I am ~ about accepting** il n'est pas sûr que j'accepte; **to be ~ whether sth is true** douter que qch soit vrai; **2** (arguable) [*translation, answer*] douteux/-euse; **that's a ~ point** c'est contestable; **3** (suspect) [*motive, claim*] suspect; [*reputation, person*] douteux/-euse; **4** (equivocal) [*distinction*] discutable; **a ~ honour/compliment** un honneur/un compliment qui n'en est pas un.

dubiously /ˈdju:bıəslı, US ˈdu:-/ *adv* **1** (expressing doubt) [*say*] dubitativement; [*look at*] d'un air incertain; **2** (arousing doubt) **he claims, ~, to be ill** il prétend être malade, ce qui semble peu probable.

dubiousness /ˈdju:bıəsnıs, US ˈdu:-/ *n* ¢ **1** (doubt) doutes *mpl*; **2** (of claim, evidence, motive) caractère *m* douteux; **3** (of distinction) caractère *m* discutable.

Dublin /ˈdʌblın/ ▶ **1818** *pr n* Dublin.

Dublin Bay prawn *n* GB langoustine *f*.

Dubliner /ˈdʌblınə(r)/ *n* (native) natif/-ive *m/f* de Dublin; (living there) habitant/-e *m/f* de Dublin.

ducal /ˈdju:kl, US ˈdu:-/ *adj* ducal.

ducat /ˈdʌkət/ *n* Hist ducat *m*.

duchess /ˈdʌtʃıs/ ▶ **1268** *n* duchesse *f*.

duchy /ˈdʌtʃı/ *n* duché *m*.

duck /dʌk/ **I** *n* **1** Zool, Culin (*pl* **~s**, *collective* **~**) canard *m*; (female of species) cane *f*; **2** (in cricket) **to be out for** ou **to make a ~** ne marquer aucun point; **to break one's ~** marquer son premier point; fig remporter sa première victoire; **3**○ GB dial (also **~s**) (form of address) (to child) mon chéri/ma chérie *m/f*; (to woman) ma petite dame; **4** Tex coutil *m*.

II ducks *npl* Fashn pantalon *m* de coutil.

III *vtr* **1** (lower) **to ~ one's head** baisser la tête; **2** (dodge) esquiver [*punch, ball*]; **3** fig (avoid) esquiver [*issue, question*]; se dérober à [*responsibility*]; **4** (push under water) faire boire la tasse à○ [*person*].

IV *vi* [*person*] baisser la tête; [*boxer*] esquiver un coup; **I ~ed into a side-street to avoid meeting her** je me suis engouffré dans une ruelle pour éviter de la rencontrer; **to ~ behind sth** se cacher derrière qch.

IDIOMS **he took to it like a ~ to water** il s'y est mis comme s'il avait fait ça toute sa vie; **(there's no point in telling him off) it's like water off a ~'s back** (c'est inutile de le réprimander) ça ne le touche absolument pas.

■ **duck out**○: ¶ **~ out of [sth]** quitter [*office, room*]; ¶ **~ out of doing** arriver à éviter de faire.

duck: **~-billed platypus** *n* ornithorynque *m*; **~board** *n* caillebotis *m*; **~-egg blue** *n, adj* turquoise (*m*) clair *inv*.

duckie○ *n* = **ducky** I.

ducking /ˈdʌkıŋ/ *n* **to get a ~** prendre un bain forcé.

ducking stool *n* Hist sellette *f* à plongeon.

duckling /ˈdʌklıŋ/ *n* caneton/canette *m/f*.

duck pond *n* mare *f* aux canards.

ducks and drakes /ˌdʌks ən ˈdreıks/ *n* Games **to play ~** s'amuser à faire des ricochets (sur l'eau); fig **to play ~ with sb** traiter qn avec désinvolture.

duck shooting *n* chasse *f* aux canards.

duck soup○ *n* US **it's ~!** (c'est) du gâteau○!

duckweed /ˈdʌkwi:d/ *n* Bot lentille *f* d'eau.

ducky○ /ˈdʌkı/ **I** *n* GB dial = **duck I 3**.

II○ *adj* US (cute) mignon/-onne.

duct /ˈdʌkt/ *n* **1** Tech (for air, water) conduit *m*; (for wiring) canalisation *f*; **2** Anat conduit *m*.

ductile /ˈdʌktaıl, US -tl/ *adj* **1** [*metal*] ductile; **2** fig sout [*person*] malléable.

ductless gland *n* glande *f* endocrine.

dud○ /dʌd/ **I** *n* **to be a ~** [*coin, banknote*] être faux/fausse; [*engine, machine*] être détraqué; [*battery*] être à plat; [*person, book, movie*] être nul/nulle○; [*firework*] être défectueux/-euse.

II†○ **duds** *npl* vêtements *mpl*.

III *adj* [*coin, banknote*] faux/fausse; [*cheque*] en bois○; [*engine, radio etc*] détraqué; [*battery*] à plat; [*book, movie*] nul/nulle○; [*firework*] défectueux/-euse.

dude○ /dju:d, US du:d/ *n* **1** (man) mec○ *m*; **a cool ~** un mec cool; **2** US (city dweller) citadin *m*; (dandy) dandy *m*.

■ **dude up**: **~ [sth] up**, **~up [sth]** habiller [*apartment, car*]; **to get ~d up** se fringuer○; **to be ~d up** être bien fringué.

dude ranch *n* US ranch *m* de vacances.

dudgeon /ˈdʌdʒən/ *n*: IDIOMS **in high ~†** (offended) profondément offensé; (angry) furieux/-ieuse.

due /djuː, US duː/ **I** *n* dû *m*; **it was his ~** gen ce n'était que son dû; (of money, inheritance etc) ça devait lui revenir; (of praise, recognition etc) il le méritait; **I must give her her ~, she...** il faut lui rendre cette justice, elle...; **the Tax Office, give them their ~, actually refunded the money** il faut bien le reconnaître que le centre des impôts a finalement remboursé l'argent.
II dues *npl* (for membership) cotisation *f*; (for import, taxes etc) droits *mpl*; **to pay one's ~s** lit payer sa cotisation; fig payer son dû.
III *adj* **1** (payable) (*jamais épith*) **to be/fall ~** [*rent, next instalment*] arriver/venir à échéance; **when ~** à l'échéance ; **the rent is ~ on/no later than the 6th** le loyer doit être payé le 6/avant le 6; **the balance ~** le solde dû; **debts ~ to the company/by the company** dettes actives/passives; **2** (entitled to) **they should pay him what is ~ to him** on devrait lui payer l'argent auquel il a droit; **the prisoner made the phone calls ~○ him** US le prisonnier a passé les coups de téléphone auxquels il avait droit; **3○** (about to be paid, given) **I'm ~ some back pay/four days' holiday** on me doit des arriérés/quatre jours de congé; **we are ~ (for) a wage increase soon** (as is normal) nos salaires doivent bientôt être augmentés; (if all goes well) nos salaires devraient bientôt être augmentés; **4** (appropriate) (*tjrs épith*) **with ~ solemnity** avec toute la solennité qui s'impose/s'imposait etc; **after ~ consideration** après mûre réflexion; **with all ~ respect to a man of his age** malgré tout le respect que l'on doit à un homme de son âge; **to show ~ respect** ou **consideration for sb/sth** témoigner le respect dû à qn/qch; **to give all ~ praise to sb** rendre un hommage bien mérité à qn; **you will receive a letter in ~ course** vous recevrez une lettre en temps utile; **in ~ course it transpired that** à la longue il est apparu que; **5** Jur (in phrases) **in ~ form** en bonne et due forme; **~ diligence** diligence normale; **to be charged with driving without ~ care and attention** être inculpé de conduite imprudente; **6** (scheduled, expected) **to be ~ to do** devoir faire; **we are ~ to leave there in the evening** nous devons partir de là-bas le soir; **the changes ~ in the year 2000** les changements qui doivent se produire en l'an 2000; **to be ~ (in)** ou **~ to arrive** [*train, bus*] être attendu; [*person*] devoir arriver; **to be ~ back soon/at 8** devoir revenir bientôt/à 8 heures; **to be ~ out** [*coach, boat etc*] devoir partir; [*book*] devoir sortir; **the book is ~ out in the shops soon** le livre doit sortir bientôt (en librairie); **to be ~ for completion/demolition** devoir être terminé/démoli.
IV *adv* (directly) **to face ~ north/east etc** [*building*] être orienté plein nord/est etc; [*hiker etc*] regarder vers le nord/l'est etc; **to go ~ south/west etc** aller droit vers le sud/l'ouest etc; **to sail ~ south** avoir le cap au sud; **to march ~ north** marcher tout droit en direction du nord; **~ east there is...** à l'est il y a...
V due to *prep phr* **1** (because of) en raison de; **~ to bad weather/a fall in demand** en raison du mauvais temps/d'une baisse de la demande; **~ to the fact that the satellite link had broken down** en raison d'une rupture de liaison avec le satellite; **he resigned ~ to the fact that** il a démissionné parce que; **to be ~ to** [*delay, cancellation etc*] être dû/due à; **~ to unforeseen circumstances** pour des raisons indépendantes de notre volonté; **'closed ~ to illness'** 'fermé pour cause de maladie'; **'cancelled ~ to high winds'** 'annulé pour cause de vent trop fort'; **2** (thanks to) grâce à; **it's all ~ to you** c'est uniquement grâce à toi.

due: **~ bill** *n* US Fin reconnaissance *f* de dette; **~ date** *n* échéance *f*, date *f* d'échéance.

duel /ˈdjuːəl, US ˈduːəl/ **I** *n* lit, fig duel *m*; **to fight a ~** se battre en duel.
II *vi* (*p prés etc* **-ll-**) lit se battre en duel; fig se livrer à un duel.

duellist /ˈdjuːəlɪst, US ˈduː-/ *n* duelliste *m*.

duenna /djuːˈenə, US ˈduː-/ *n* duègne *f*.

due process of law *n* US Jur *clauses de sauvegarde des libertés individuelles*.

duet /djuːˈet, US duː-/ *n* (composition) duo *m* also fig; **to play a duet** jouer en duo; **guitar/piano ~** duo pour guitare/piano.

duff○ /dʌf/ **I** *n* derrière *m*.
II *adj* GB **1** (defective) [*machine*] déglingué○; **2** Mus [*note*] faux/fausse; **3** Sport **a ~ shot** un loupé○; **4** (stupid) [*idea, suggestion*] débile○.
III *vtr* **1** (disguise stolen goods) maquiller; **2** GB Sport louper○ [*shot*].
■ **duff in, duff up**: **~ [sb] in, ~ [sb] up** tabasser○.

duffel, duffle /ˈdʌfl/ *n* molleton *m*.

duffel: **~ bag** *n* sac *m* (de) marin; **~ coat** *n* duffel-coat *m*.

duffer○† /ˈdʌfə(r)/ *n* (ungifted person) nullité *f*; **to be a ~ at** GB ou **in** US **French** être nul/nulle en français.

dug /dʌg/ **I** *pret, pp* ▶ **dig III, IV.**
II *n* **1** (udder) mamelle *f*; **2†** (breast) péj mamelle *f* pej.

dugout /ˈdʌgaʊt/ *n* **1** (boat) pirogue *f*; **2** Sport banc *m* des remplaçants et des officiels; **3** Mil tranchée-abri *f*.

duke /djuːk, US duːk/ **I** ▶ **1268** *n* duc *m*; **the Duke of York** le duc d'York.
II○ dukes *npl* US poings *mpl*; **to put up one's ~s** se mettre en garde.

dukedom /ˈdjuːkdəm, US ˈduːk-/ *n* (territory) duché *m*; (title) titre *m* de duc.

dulcet /ˈdʌlsɪt/ *adj* littér (*épith*) mélodieux/-ieuse; **her ~ tones** hum sa voix suave.

dulcimer /ˈdʌlsɪmə(r)/ *n* **1** (percussion instrument) tympanon *m*; **2** (in folk music) dulcimer *m*.

dulia /ˈdjuːlɪə, US ˈduː-/ *n* dulie *f*.

dull /dʌl/ **I** *adj* **1** (uninteresting) [*person, lecture, play, book*] ennuyeux/-euse; [*life, journey*] monotone; [*music*] sans intérêt; [*meal, dish*] médiocre; [*appearance, outfit, hairstyle*] triste, sans goût; **never a ~ moment!** on ne s'ennuie jamais!; **2** (not bright) [*eye, colour*] éteint; [*weather, day, sky*] maussade; [*glow, complexion*] terne; **3** (muffled) [*explosion, thud*] sourd; **4** (not sharp) [*ache, pain*] sourd; [*blade*] émoussé; **to have a ~ wit** ne pas avoir l'esprit vif; **5** Fin [*market*] terne, calme.
II *vtr* **1** (make matt) ternir [*shine, finish*]; **2** (make blunt) émousser [*blade, senses, appetite, pain*].
III *vi* [*sound*] s'amortir; [*colour*] passer.

dullard† /ˈdʌləd/ *n* péj empoté *m*.

dullness /ˈdʌlnɪs/ *n* (of life) ennui *m*; (of routine) monotonie *f*; (of company, conversation) manque *m* d'intérêt; (of weather) grisaille *f*.

dullsville○ /ˈdʌlsvɪl/ *n* (dull town) trou○ *m*; **~!** (of a situation) on s'ennuie comme des rats morts!

dully /ˈdʌllɪ/ *adv* **1** [*say, repeat*] d'un ton morne; **2** [*gleam*] faiblement; **3** [*move, trail*] lourdement.

duly /ˈdjuːlɪ, US ˈduː-/ *adv* **1** (in proper fashion) gen, Jur dûment; **2** (as expected, as arranged) comme prévu.

dumb /dʌm/ *adj* **1** (handicapped) muet/muette voir note; **a ~ person** un muet/une muette *m/f*; **~ animals** les bêtes; **2** (temporarily) muet/muette (**with** de); **to be struck ~** rester muet/muette; **3○** (stupid) [*person*] bête; [*question, action, idea*] idiot; **to act ~** jouer les imbéciles.

■ Note Ce mot peut être perçu comme injurieux dans cette acception. Lui préférer *speech impaired.*

dumb-ass◐ /ˈdʌmæs/ *n* US con/conne◐ *m/f*.

dumbbell /ˈdʌmbel/ *n* **1** Sport haltère *m*; **2○** US abruti/-e *m/f*.

dumb: **~ blonde** *n* péj blonde *f* évaporée pej; **~ cluck○** *n* nullité *f*.

dumbfound /dʌmˈfaʊnd/ *vtr* abasourdir.

dumbfounded /dʌmˈfaʊndɪd/ *adj* abasourdi.

dumbly /ˈdʌmlɪ/ *adv* sans mot dire.

dumbness /ˈdʌmnɪs/ *n* **1** (handicap) injur mutité *f*; **2○** (stupidity) bêtise *f*.

dumbo○ /ˈdʌmbəʊ/ *n* empoté/-e○ *m/f*.

dumb show *n* Theat pantomime *f*.

dumbstruck /ˈdʌmstrʌk/ *adj* interloqué, ébahi.

dumb terminal *n* Comput terminal *m* passif.

dumbwaiter /ˌdʌmˈweɪtə(r)/ *n* **1** (elevator) monte-plats *m inv*; **2** (food trolley) table *f* roulante; **3** GB (revolving tray) plateau *m* tournant.

dumdum /ˈdʌmdʌm/ *n* **1** Mil (also **~ bullet**) (balle *f*) dum-dum *f*; **2○** andouille○ *f*, abruti/-e○ *m/f*.

Dumfries and Galloway /dʌmˈfriːs/ ▶ **1624** *pr n* (also **~ Region**) Dumfries and Galloway *m*.

dummy /ˈdʌmɪ/ **I** *n* **1** (model) mannequin *m*; **tailor's ~** mannequin de couturier; **ventriloquist's ~** poupée *f* de ventriloque; **2** GB (for baby) tétine *f*, sucette *f*; **3** GB Sport feinte *f*; **to sell sb a ~** faire une feinte à qn; **4○** (stupid person) abruti/-e○ *m/f*, andouille○ *f*; **5** (imitation, object) imitation *f*; **6** Publg, Print maquette *f*; **7** Fin prête-nom *m*; **8** (in Bridge) (hand) jeu *m* du mort; (player) mort *m*; **to play from ~** jouer du mort; **9** Ling explétif *m*.
II *modif* [*fruit, furniture, drawer*] factice; [*passport, document*] faux/fausse; [*bullet*] à blanc; [*shell, bomb*] d'exercice; Fin [*company*] bidon○ *inv*.
III GB *vtr, vi* Sport feinter.
■ **dummy up○** US refuser de parler.

dummy: **~ bridge** ▶ **1282** *n* Games bridge *m* à trois; **~ element** *n* Ling élément *m* explétif; **~ load** *n* Elec charge *f* fictive; **~ pass** *n* GB Sport feinte *f* de passe; **~ run** *n* gen (trial) essai *m*; Mil attaque *f* simulée; **~ symbol** *n* Ling symbole *m* postiche; **~ variable** *n* Math variable *f* muette.

dump /dʌmp/ **I** *n* **1** (public) décharge *f* publique; **municipal ~, town ~** décharge *f* publique; **rubbish ~** GB, **garbage ~** US dépôt *m* d'ordures; **2** (rubbish heap) tas *m* d'ordures; **3** Mil **arms/munitions ~** dépôt *m* d'armes/de munitions; **4○** péj (town, village) trou○ *m*; (house) baraque○ *f* minable; (hotel) hôtel *m* minable; **5** Comput vidage *m*; **6●** US **to take a ~** chier●.
II *vtr* **1** [*person*] jeter [*refuse*]; déverser [*sewage*]; ensevelir [*nuclear waste*]; [*factory, ship*] déverser [*waste, pollutants*]; **2** (sell) **to ~ goods on the market** (on home market) écouler des produits à bas prix; (abroad) faire du dumping; **3○** (get rid of) plaquer○ [*boyfriend*]; larguer○ [*tedious person*]; se débarrasser de [*car, shopping*]; laisser tomber, abandonner [*idea, policy*]; **4○** (put down) poser [*bag, object*]; **5** Comput clicher, faire un vidage de [*data*]; **6** Mil (store) entreposer [*weapons, explosives*].
IDIOMS **to be down in the ~s○** avoir le cafard○.
■ **dump on○**: **~ on [sb]◐** US traiter [qn] comme du poisson pourri○.

dumper /ˈdʌmpə(r)/ *n* **1** (small) motobasculeur *m*; **2** (large truck) tombereau *m*, dumper *m*.

dumper truck, dump truck *n* = **dumper** 2.

dumping /ˈdʌmpɪŋ/ *n* **1** (of liquid waste, sand) déversement *m*; **'no ~', '~ prohibited'** 'interdiction de déposer des ordures'; **2** Fin, Comm dumping *m*.

dumping ground *n* lit, fig dépotoir *m* (**for** pour).

dumpling /ˈdʌmplɪŋ/ *n* **1** Culin boulette *f* de pâte; **fruit ~** fruit *m* enrobé de pâte sucrée; **2**○ (person) patapouf○ *m*.
dumpy /ˈdʌmpɪ/ *adj* **1** (plump) boulot/-otte; **2**○ US (run-down) moche○.
dun /dʌn/ **I** *n* **1** (colour) gris brun *m*; **2** (horse) isabelle *mf*.
II *adj* [*material*] bis; [*horse*] isabelle *inv*.
III *vtr* (*p prés etc* **-nn-**) harceler (**for** pour).
dunce /dʌns/ *n* cancre *m*; **to be a ~ at maths** être nul/nulle en maths.
dunce's cap *n* bonnet *m* d'âne.
dunderhead† /ˈdʌndəhed/ *n* bêta/bêtasse○ *m/f*.
dune /djuːn, US duːn/ *n* dune *f*.
dune buggy *n* buggy *m*.
dung /dʌŋ/ *n* ¢ gen excrément *m*; (for manure) fumier *m*; (of cow) bouse *f*; (of horse) crottin *m*; (of deer, gazelle) fumées *fpl*.
dungarees /ˌdʌŋɡəˈriːz/ *npl* **1** (fashionwear) salopette *f*; **2** (workwear) bleu *m* de travail.
dung beetle *n* bousier *m*.
dungeon /ˈdʌndʒən/ *n* cachot *m*, oubliettes *fpl*.
dung heap, **dunghill** /ˈdʌŋhɪl/ *n* tas *m* de fumier.
dunk /dʌŋk/ *vtr* **1** (dip) tremper [*bread, biscuit*] (**in** dans); plonger [*person, head*] (**in** dans; **under** sous); **2** (in basketball) faire un lancer coulé.
Dunkirk /dʌnˈkɜːk/ ▶ **1818** *pr n* Dunkerque.
dunk shot *n* lancer *m* coulé.
dunlin /ˈdʌnlɪn/ *n* bécasseau *m* variable.
dunno○ /dəˈnəʊ/ = **don't know**.
dunnock /ˈdʌnək/ *n* accenteur *m* mouchet.
dunny○ /ˈdʌnɪ/ *n* Aust, NZ chiottes◑ *fpl*, WC *mpl*.
duo /ˈdjuːəʊ, US ˈduːəʊ/ *n* (*pl* **~s**) **1** Theat (double act) duo *m* also fig; **musical/comedy ~** duo musical/comique; **2** Mus (duet) duo *m*.
duodecimal /ˌdjuːəʊˈdesɪml, US ˌduːəˈdesəml/ *adj* duodécimal.
duodecimo /ˌdjuːəʊˈdesɪməʊ, US ˌduːəˈdesəməʊ/ *n* (*pl* **~s**) (book, format) in-douze *m*.
duodenal /ˌdjuːəˈdiːnl, US ˌduːəˈdiːnl/ *adj* [*ulcer*] duodénal.
duodenum /ˌdjuːəʊˈdiːnəm, US ˌduːəˈdiːnəm/ *n* duodénum *m*.
duologue /ˈdjuːəlɒɡ, US ˈduː-/ *n* gen, Theat dialogue *m*.
duopoly /djuːˈɒpəlɪ, US duː-/ *n* duopole *m*.
dupe /djuːp, US duːp/ **I** *n* dupe *f*.
II *vtr* duper [*victim, investor*]; **to be ~d** être dupé; **to ~ sb into doing sth** amener qn à faire qch en le/la dupant; **we've been ~d!** on nous a eus!○
duple time /ˌduːpl ˈtaɪm/ *n* rythme *m* binaire.
duplex /ˈdjuːpleks, US ˈduː-/ **I** *n* US (apartment) duplex *m*; (house) maison *f* jumelée.
II *adj* Comput duplex *inv*.
duplicate I /ˈdjuːplɪkət, US ˈduːpləkət/ *n* **1** (copy) (of document) double *m* (**of** de); Jur duplicata *m*; (of painting, cassette, video) copie *f*; (of film) contretype *m*; **in ~** en deux exemplaires; Jur en duplicata; **2** (photocopy) photocopie *f*; **3** (repetition) (of performance, action) réplique *f*.
II /ˈdjuːplɪkət, US ˈduːpləkət/ *adj* **1** (copied) [*cheque, receipt*] en duplicata; **a ~ key/document** un double de clé/de document; **2** (in two parts) [*form, invoice*] en deux exemplaires.
III /ˈdjuːplɪkeɪt, US ˈduːpləkeɪt/ *vtr* **1** (copy) faire un double de [*document*]; copier [*painting, cassette, video*]; faire un contretype de [*film*]; **2** (photocopy) photocopier; **3** (repeat) refaire [qch] inutilement [*work*]; répéter [*action, performance*]; **to ~ resources** avoir des ressources qui font double-emploi.
IV /ˈdjuːplɪkeɪt, US ˈduːpləkeɪt/ *vi* Biol se dédoubler.
duplicating machine *n* duplicateur *m*.
duplication /ˌdjuːplɪˈkeɪʃn, US ˌduːpləˈkeɪʃn/ *n* **1** (copying) reproduction *f*; **2** (copy) (of cassette, book etc) copie *f*; **3** (repeating) (of effort, work) répétition *f* inutile; **the ~ of resources** la multiplication (inutile) des ressources.
duplicator /ˈdjuːplɪkeɪtə(r), US ˈduːpləkeɪtə(r)/ *n* duplicateur *m*.
duplicitous /djuːˈplɪsətəs, US duː-/ *adj* fourbe.
duplicity /djuːˈplɪsətɪ, US duː-/ *n* **1** (character trait) duplicité *f*; **2** (double-dealing) fourberie *f*.
durability /ˌdjʊərəˈbɪlətɪ, US ˌdʊərə-/ *n* (of material) longévité *f*, durabilité *f*; (of friendship, marriage) solidité *f*.
durable /ˈdjʊərəbl, US ˈdʊərəbl/ **I durables** *npl* biens *mpl* durables.
II *adj* [*material*] résistant; [*equipment*] solide; [*friendship, tradition*] durable.
Duralumin® /djʊəˈræljʊmɪn, US dʊə-/ *n* duralumin® *m*.
duration /djʊˈreɪʃn, US dʊˈreɪʃn/ *n* durée *f*; **of long ~** de longue durée; **of two years' ~** d'une durée de deux ans; **for the ~ of the war/meeting** pendant toute la durée de la guerre/la réunion.
IDIOMS **for the ~**○ (for ages) pour une durée indéterminée.
duress /djʊˈres, US dʊˈres/ *n* gen, Jur contrainte *f*; **to do sth under ~** faire qch sous la contrainte.
Durex® /ˈdjʊəreks, US ˈdʊəreks/ *n* préservatif *m*.
during /ˈdjʊərɪŋ/ *prep* pendant, au cours de; **~ this time** pendant ce temps.
dusk /dʌsk/ *n* (twilight) nuit *f* tombante, crépuscule *m* liter; (semidarkness) semi-obscurité *f*; **at ~** à la nuit tombante; **in the ~** dans la semi-obscurité; **~ was falling** la nuit tombait; **I don't like driving at ~** je n'aime pas conduire entre chien et loup; **~ to dawn curfew** couvre-feu du coucher au lever du soleil.
duskiness /ˈdʌskɪnɪs/ *n* (of person, limbs, cheeks) peau *f* mate; (of room) semi-obscurité *f*.
dusky /ˈdʌskɪ/ *adj* [*complexion*] mat; [*person, limbs*] à la peau mate; [*room, colour*] sombre.
dusky pink *n, adj* vieux rose (*m*) *inv*.
dust /dʌst/ **I** *n* **1** (grime, grit) poussière *f*; **chalk/coal ~** poussière de craie/charbon; **cosmic/radioactive/volcanic ~** poussières *fpl* cosmiques/radioactives/volcaniques; **thick with ~** couvert de poussière; **a speck of ~** (on a surface) un grain de poussière; (in the eye) une poussière; **to allow the ~ to settle** lit laisser retomber la poussière; fig laisser les choses se calmer; **2** (fine powder) Art, Ind poudre *f*; **gold ~** poudre d'or; **3** littér (ground) poussière *f*.
II *vtr* **1** (clean) épousseter [*furniture, house*]; **2** (coat lightly) saupoudrer [*cake*] (**with** de, avec); poudrer [*face*] (**with** de, avec).
III *vi* épousseter, faire les poussières○.
IDIOMS **to throw ~ in sb's eyes** embrouiller qn; **to shake the ~ (of sth) off one's feet** partir (de qch); **to bite the ~** [*person*] mordre la poussière; [*plan, idea*] tomber à l'eau.
■ **dust down**: ¶ **~ [sth] down, ~ down [sth]** épousseter [*chair, table*]; ¶ **to ~ oneself down** s'épousseter.
■ **dust off**: **~ [sth] off, ~ off [sth] 1** (clean) épousseter [*surface, table*]; **2** (brush off) brosser [*crumbs, powder*] (**from** de).
dust: **~ bag** *n* sac *m* d'aspirateur; **~ bath** *n* bain *m* de poussière; **~bin** *n* GB poubelle *f*; **~bin lid** *n* GB couvercle *m* de poubelle; **~bin man** *n* GB éboueur *m*.
dust bowl I *n* Geog zone *f* désertique.
II Dust Bowl *pr n* US *zone des États-Unis affectée par des tempêtes de poussière*.
dust: **~cart** *n* GB benne *f* à ordures; **~ cloth** *n* US chiffon *m* à poussière; **~ cloud** *n* nuage *m* de poussière; **~ cover** *n* (on book) jaquette *f*; (on furniture) housse *f* (de protection); **~ devil** *n* tourbillon *m* de poussière.
duster /ˈdʌstə(r)/ *n* **1** (cloth) chiffon *m* à poussière; (for blackboard) chiffon *m*; (block) brosse *f*; ▶ **feather duster**; **2** US (housecoat) blouse *f*; **3** Agric avion *m* pulvérisateur.
dust-free room *n* salle *f* blanche.
dust heap *n* **1** lit tas *m* d'ordures; **2** fig rebut *m*; **to be thrown on the ~** être jeté au rebut.
dusting /ˈdʌstɪŋ/ *n* **1** (cleaning) époussetage *m*; **to do the ~** épousseter, faire les poussières○; **2** (of snow) fine couche *f*; **3** Culin (of sugar, chocolate etc) saupoudrage *m*.
dusting powder *n* talc *m*.
dust: **~ jacket** *n* Publg jaquette *f*; **~man** *n* GB éboueur *m*; **~ mite** *n* acarien *m*; **~ mote** *n* grain *m* de poussière.
dustpan /ˈdʌstpæn/ *n* pelle *f* (à poussière); **a ~ and brush** une pelle (à poussière) et une balayette.
dust: **~ sheet** *n* drap *m* de protection (contre la poussière); **~ storm** *n* tempête *f* de poussière.
dust-up○ /ˈdʌstʌp/ *n* **1** (quarrel) prise *f* de bec○; **2** (fight) bagarre *f*; **to get into** ou **have a ~ with sb** se bagarrer avec qn.
dusty /ˈdʌstɪ/ *adj* [*house, table, road*] poussiéreux/-euse; [*climb, journey*] dans la poussière (*after n*); **to get ~** prendre la poussière.
IDIOMS **to give sb a ~ answer** envoyer qn sur les roses○.
dusty: **~ blue** *n, adj* bleu-gris (*m*) *inv*; **~ pink** *n, adj* vieux rose (*m*) *inv*.
Dutch /dʌtʃ/ ▶ **1486**, **1402** **I** *n* **1** Ling néerlandais *m*, hollandais *m*; **2 the ~** (+ *v pl*) les Néerlandais *mpl*, les Hollandais *mpl*.
II *adj* [*culture, food, football, politics*] néerlandais, hollandais; [*teacher, lesson, textbook, dictionary*] de néerlandais.
IDIOMS **to be in ~ with sb**○ être en disgrâce auprès de qn; **to go ~**○ payer chacun sa part; **to go ~ with sb**○ faire fifty-fifty avec qn○; **to talk to sb like a ~ uncle** sermonner qn.

■ Note *hollandais* is used to apply to the whole of the Netherlands as well as the Dutch language but this usage is incorrect. Strictly speaking it should be applied only to the province of the Netherlands called *Hollande* in French.

Dutch: **~ auction** *n* enchères *fpl* au rabais; **~ barn** *n* hangar *m* à récoltes; **~ cap** *n* diaphragme *m* (*contraceptif*).
Dutch courage *n* courage *m* puisé dans l'alcool; **I need (some) ~** j'ai besoin d'alcool pour me donner du courage.
Dutch: **~ door** *n* US porte *f* d'étable; **~ East Indies** *pr n* Hist Indes *fpl* orientales (néerlandaises); **~ elm disease** *n* maladie *f* parasitaire de l'orme, graphiose *f* spec; **~ Guiana** *pr n* Hist Guyane *f* hollandaise.
Dutchman /ˈdʌtʃmən/ *n* (*pl* **-men**) Néerlandais *m*, Hollandais *m* controv.
IDIOMS **'it's true, or I'm a ~,' said Bob** 'c'est vrai, ou je ne m'appelle plus Bob,' a dit Bob.
Dutch: **~ oven** *n* grosse marmite *f*, cocotte *f*; **~ School** *n* Art école *f* hollandaise; **~ treat** *n* sortie *f* où chacun paie sa part; **~ West Indies** *pr n* Antilles *fpl* néerlandaises.
Dutchwoman /ˈdʌtʃwʊmən/ *n* Néerlandaise *f*, Hollandaise *f* controv.
dutiable /ˈdjuːtɪəbl, US ˈduː-/ *adj* Tax taxable; (at customs) passible de droits de douane.
dutiful /ˈdjuːtɪfl, US ˈduː-/ *adj* **1** (obedient) [*person*] dévoué; [*act*] de dévouement; [*smile*] poli; **2** (conscientious) [*person*] consciencieux/-ieuse.
dutifully /ˈdjuːtɪfəlɪ, US ˈduː-/ *adv* **1** (obediently) scrupuleusement; **2** (conscientiously) [*work*] consciencieusement.
duty /ˈdjuːtɪ, US ˈduːtɪ/ **I** *n* **1** (obligation)

devoir *m* (**to** envers); **to have a ~ to do** avoir le devoir de faire; **to make it one's ~ to do** considérer de son devoir de faire; **it is my ~ to do** il est de mon devoir de faire; **to do one's ~** accomplir son devoir; **to do one's ~ by sb** remplir son devoir envers qn; **in the course of ~** Mil en service; gen dans l'exercice de ses fonctions; **~ calls!** le devoir m'appelle!; **to feel ~ bound to do** se sentir le devoir de faire; **to neglect one's duties** manquer à ses devoirs; **out of a sense of ~** par devoir; **moral ~** obligation *f* morale; **legal ~, statutory ~** obligation *f* légale; **2** (task) (*gén pl*) fonction *f*; **to take up one's duties** prendre ses fonctions; **to perform** ou **carry out one's duties** remplir ses fonctions (**as** de); **3 ¢** (work) service *m*; **to be on/off ~** Mil, Med être/ne pas être de service; Sch être/ne pas être de surveillance; **to go on/off ~** commencer/finir son service; **day/night ~** service *m* de jour/de nuit; **to do ~ for** ou **as sth** servir de qch; **to do ~ for sb** remplacer qn; **4** Tax taxe *f*; **customs duties** droits *mpl* de douane; **to pay ~ on sth** payer des droits de douane sur qch.
II *modif* [*nurse, security guard*] (during the day) de service; (outside hours) de permanence.

duty: **~ call** *n* visite *f* de politesse; **~ chemist** *n* pharmacien/-ienne *m/f* de garde.

duty-free /ˌdjuːtɪˈfriː, US ˌduː-/ *adj, adv* hors taxes *inv*.

duty: **~-free allowance** *n* quantité *f* autorisée de marchandises hors taxes; **~-frees** *npl* marchandises *fpl* hors taxes; **~-free shop** *n* boutique *f* hors taxes or duty-free; **~-free shopping** *n* achat *m* de marchandises hors taxes; **~ officer** *n* Mil officier *m* de service; (in police) officier *m* de permanence.

duty-paid /ˌdjuːtɪˈpeɪd, US ˌduː-/ *adj* [*sale*] à l'acquitté; [*goods*] dédouané.

duty: **~ roster, ~ rota** *n* Admin tableau *m* de service; **~ solicitor** *n* GB Jur avocat/-e *m/f* de permanence (*auprès d'un tribunal ou poste de police*).

duvet /ˈduːveɪ/ *n* GB couette *f*.

duvet cover *n* GB housse *f* de couette.

DVM *n* US Vet (*abrév* = **Doctor of Veterinary Medicine**) docteur *m* vétérinaire.

dwarf /dwɔːf/ **I** *n* nain/naine *m/f*.
II *adj* (all contexts) nain/naine.
III *vtr* (make appear small, insignificant) faire paraître [qn/qch] tout petit [*person, object etc*]; éclipser [*achievement, issue*]; **the houses were ~ed by the tower block** les maisons étaient écrasées par la tour.

dwarfish /ˈdwɔːfɪʃ/ *adj* nabot.

dwell /dwel/ *vi* (*prét, pp* **dwelt**) littér **1** (live) habiter, demeurer liter (**in** dans); **2** fig littér **~ in** demeurer dans [*mind, heart*]; habiter [*person*].
■ **dwell on**: **~ on** [sth] (talk about) s'étendre sur; (think about) [*person, mind*] s'attarder sur; **to ~ on the past** ruminer le passé; **don't ~ on it!** ne rumine pas là-dessus!

dweller /ˈdwelə(r)/ *n* habitant/-e *m/f*; **city ~, town ~** citadin/-e *m/f*; **country ~** habitant/-e *m/f* de la campagne.

dwelling /ˈdwelɪŋ/ *n* littér, Admin habitation *f*, domicile *m* Admin.

dwelling: **~ house** *n* maison *f* d'habitation; **~ place** *n* lieu *m* d'habitation.

dwelt /dwelt/ *prét, pp* ▶ **dwell**.

DWI *n* US Jur (*abrév* = **driving while intoxicated**) conduite *f* en état d'ivresse.

dwindle /ˈdwɪndl/ *vi* (also **~ away**) [*numbers, resources, strength*] diminuer; [*interest, enthusiasm*] tomber; [*health*] décliner; **to ~ to** se réduire à.

dwindling /ˈdwɪndlɪŋ/ **I** *n* (of numbers, resources, strength) diminution *f*; (of enthusiasm, interest) baisse *f*.
II *adj* [*numbers, resources, audience, interest*] en baisse; [*strength, health*] déclinant.

dye /daɪ/ **I** *n* **1** (commercial product) teinture *f*; **hair ~** teinture pour les cheveux; **2** (substance) colorant *m*; **vegetable/synthetic ~** colorant *m* végétal/artificiel.
II *vtr* teindre [*fabric*]; **to ~ sth red/black** teindre qch en rouge/noir; **to ~ one's hair** se teindre les cheveux.
III *vi* [*fabric*] se teindre.
IV dyed *pp adj* [*hair, fabric*] teint.

dyed-in-the-wool /ˌdaɪdɪnðəˈwʊl/ *adj* invétéré.

dyeing /ˈdaɪɪŋ/ *n* teinture *f*.

dyer /ˈdaɪə(r)/ *n* teinturier/-ière *m/f*.

dye: **~stuff** *n* colorant *m*; **~works** *n* usine *f* de colorants.

Dyfed /ˈdʌvɪd/ ▶ **1624** *pr n* Dyfed *m*.

dying /ˈdaɪɪŋ/ **I** *p prés* ▶ **die**.
II *n* **1** (people) **the ~** (+ *v pl*) les mourants *mpl*, les agonisants *mpl*; **prayer for the ~** prière pour les mourants; **2** (death) mort *f*.
III *adj* **1** (about to die) [*person, animal, forest*] mourant; **the ~ man's wish** la dernière volonté du défunt; **the ~ woman** la mourante; **to his ~ day** jusqu'à sa dernière heure or son dernier jour; **with her ~ breath** dans son dernier souffle; **2** (disappearing) [*art, practice, industry, tradition*] en voie de disparition; [*town, community*] moribond; **she's one of a ~ breed** elle fait partie d'une espèce en voie de disparition; **3** (final) [*minutes, stages, moments*] dernier/-ière (*before n*); **4** (fading) [*sun, light, fire, embers*] mourant.
IDIOMS **to look like a ~ duck (in a thunderstorm)**○ hum avoir l'air piteux or pitoyable.

dyke /daɪk/ *n* **1** (US **dike**) (embankment) (to prevent flooding) digue *f*; (beside ditch) remblai *m*; **2** GB (ditch) fossé *m*; **3** (US **dike**) Geol filon *m*; **4** Scot (wall) muret *m*; **5**◑ injur (lesbian) gouine◑ *f*, lesbienne *f*.

dynamic /daɪˈnæmɪk/ **I** *n* dynamique *f*.
II dynamics *npl* (all contexts) dynamique *f*.
III *adj* (all contexts) dynamique.

dynamically /daɪˈnæmɪklɪ/ *adv* **1** gen dynamiquement; **2** Phys **~-tested** soumis à des tests dynamiques.

dynamism /ˈdaɪnəmɪzəm/ *n* (all contexts) dynamisme *m*.

dynamite /ˈdaɪnəmaɪt/ **I** *n* **1** lit dynamite *f*; **2** fig **this story is political ~** cette affaire est une bombe politique; **he's ~** (sexy) il déborde de sensualité; (dynamic) il déborde d'énergie.
II○ *adj* US extra○.

dynamo /ˈdaɪnəməʊ/ *n* **1** Elec dynamo *f*; **2**○ fig (person) **he's a real ~** il déborde d'énergie.

dynast /ˈdɪnæst, US ˈdaɪ-/ *n* souverain/-e *m/f* héréditaire.

dynastic /dɪˈnæstɪk, US daɪ-/ *adj* dynastique.

dynasty /ˈdɪnəstɪ, US ˈdaɪ-/ *n* dynastie *f*; **the Tudor ~** la dynastie des Tudor.

dyne /daɪn/ *n* dyne *f*.

dysenteric /ˌdɪsənˈterɪk/ *adj* dysentérique.

dysentery /ˈdɪsəntrɪ, US -terɪ/ ▶ **1354** *n* dysenterie *f*.

dysfunction /dɪsˈfʌŋkʃn/ *n* dysfonctionnement *m*.

dysfunctional /dɪsˈfʌŋkʃənl/ *adj* dysfonctionnel/-elle.

dyslexia /dɪsˈleksɪə, US dɪsˈlekʃə/ *n* dyslexie *f*; **to suffer from ~** être dyslexique.

dyslexic /dɪsˈleksɪk/ *n, adj* dyslexique (*mf*).

dysmenorrhea /ˌdɪsmenəˈriːə/ *n* dysménorrhée *f*.

dyspepsia /dɪsˈpepsɪə/ ▶ **1354** *n* dyspepsie *f*.

dyspeptic /dɪsˈpeptɪk/ *adj* **1** (with indigestion) dyspepsique, dyspeptique; **2**† (irritable) atrabilaire†.

dysphasia /dɪsˈfeɪzɪə/ *n* dysphasie *f*.

dystopia /dɪsˈtəʊpɪə/ *n* contre-utopie *f*.

dystrophy /ˈdɪstrəfɪ/ ▶ **1354** *n* dystrophie *f*.

Ee

e, E /iː/ *n* **1** (letter) e, E *m*; **2 E** Mus mi *m*; **3 E** Geog (*abrév* = **east**) E; **4**○ **E** (ecstasy) ecstasy *m*.

each /iːtʃ/

■ **Note** When used as a determiner *each* is translated by *chaque* when an object or person is singled out: *each document was examined* = chaque document a été examiné. *Tout/toute* and *tous les/toutes les* are also used to express *each and every*: *each passport must be checked* = chaque passeport *or* tout passeport doit être contrôlé.
– When used as a pronoun *each* (= each one) is almost always translated by *chacun/chacune*. For examples and exceptions see below.

I *det* [*person, group, object*] chaque *inv*; **~ time I/you do** chaque fois que je/tu fais; **~ morning** chaque matin, tous les matins; **~ person will receive** chaque personne or tout le monde recevra; **~ and every day** tous les jours sans exception; (exasperatedly) tous les jours que Dieu fait○; **he lifted ~ box in turn, ~ one heavier than the last** il soulevait des boîtes de plus en plus lourdes.
II *pron* chacun/-e *m/f*; **~ will receive** chacun recevra; **we ~ want something different** chacun de nous veut une chose différente; **~ of you/of them etc** chacun de vous/d'eux etc, chacun d'entre vous/d'entre eux etc; **three bundles of ten notes ~** trois liasses de dix billets chacune; **~ is equally desirable** (of two) les deux sont également souhaitables; (of several) tous sont également souhaitables; **I'll try a little of ~** je prendrais bien un peu de chaque; **oranges at 30p ~** des oranges à 30 pence pièce.

each other /ˌiːtʃˈʌðə(r)/

■ **Note** *each other* is very often translated by using a reflexive pronoun (*nous, vous, se*).
– For examples and particular usages see the entry below.

pron (also **one another**) **they know ~** ils se connaissent; **we hate ~** nous nous détestons; **they're fond of ~** ils s'aiment beaucoup; **to help ~** s'aider mutuellement, s'entraider; **they wear ~'s clothes** ils se prêtent leurs vêtements; **to worry about ~** s'inquiéter l'un pour l'autre; **kept apart from ~** séparés l'un de l'autre.

each way /ˌiːtʃˈweɪ/ *adj, adv* Turf **to place an ~ bet on a horse/dog, to bet on a horse/dog ~** parier qu'un cheval/chien va arriver dans les trois premiers d'une course.

eager /ˈiːgə(r)/ *adj* **1** (keen) désireux/-euse (**to do** de faire); **2** (impatient) pressé (**to do** de faire); **to be ~ for** être avide de [*wealth, experience, fame*]; **the people are ~ for change** les gens ont soif de changement; **to be ~ to please** chercher à faire plaisir; **3** (excited) [*supporter, crowd*] enthousiaste; [*face, look*] où se lit l'enthousiasme; [*acceptance*] enthousiaste; [*anticipation*] impatient; [*student*] plein d'enthousiasme.

eager beaver○ *n* **to be an ~** être zélé.

eagerly /ˈiːgəlɪ/ *adv* [*talk*] avec passion; [*listen*] avidement; [*seize upon*] avec enthousiasme; [*wait*] impatiemment; [*pursue*] ardemment; **~ awaited** impatiemment attendu.

eagerness /ˈiːgənɪs/ *n* **1** (keenness) empressement *m* (**to do** à faire); **2** (impatience) impatience *f* (**to do** de faire); **their ~ for sacrifice** leur empressement au sacrifice; **3** (enthusiasm) enthousiasme *m*; **the ~ of their faces** l'enthousiasme qui se lisait sur leur visage.

eagle /ˈiːgl/ *n* **1** Zool aigle *m*; **2** (emblem) aigle *f*; **3** (lectern) aigle *m*; **4** Sport eagle *m*.

eagle: **~ eye** *n* (sharp) œil *m* perçant; (watchful) œil *m* vigilant; **~-eyed** *adj* (sharp-eyed) à l'œil *m* perçant; (vigilant) vigilant; **~ owl** *n* grand duc *m*; **~ ray** *n* aigle *m* de mer; **~ scout** *n* US scout *m*.

eaglet /ˈiːglɪt/ *n* aiglon *m*.

ear /ɪə(r)/ **▶ 1037** **I** *n* **1** Anat, Zool oreille *f*; **inner/middle/outer ~** oreille *f* interne/moyenne/externe; **2** (hearing, perception) oreille *f*; **pleasant to the ~** agréable à l'oreille; **to the trained/untrained ~** pour une oreille exercée/qui n'est pas exercée; **to sound odd to the English ~** sonner bizarrement pour l'oreille d'un Anglais; **to play music by ~** jouer de la musique à l'oreille; **to have a good ~ for languages** avoir une bonne oreille pour les langues; **to have an ~ for music** avoir l'oreille musicale; **to have a good ~ for accents** reconnaître les accents; **to have good ~s** avoir une bonne ouïe; **3** Bot (of wheat, corn) épi *m*.
II *modif* [*infection, operation*] (of one ear) de l'oreille; (of both ears) des oreilles.
IDIOMS **he is wet behind the ~s** c'est un petit jeunot; **it has come to my ~s that** il m'est arrivé aux oreilles que; **about** ou **around one's ~s** tout autour de soi; **my ~s are burning** j'ai les oreilles qui sifflent; **to be all ~s**○ être tout ouïe; **to be on one's ~**○ Ir (drunk) être rond○ or ivre; **to bend sb's ~** insister auprès de qn; **to be out on one's ~**○ (from job) avoir été mis à la porte○; (from home) être or se retrouver à la rue; **to be up to one's ~s in debt/work** être endetté/avoir du travail jusqu'au cou; **to get a thick ~**○ recevoir une baffe○; **to give sb a thick ~**○ coller une baffe○ à qn; **to have a word in sb's ~** parler à qn en privé; **to close** ou **shut one's ~(s) to sth/sb** refuser d'écouter qch/qn; **to go in one ~ and out the other** entrer par une oreille et sortir par l'autre; **to have** ou **keep one's ~ to the ground** garder l'œil ouvert; **to have the ~ of sb** avoir l'oreille de qn; **I'll keep my ~s open** si j'entends parler de quelque chose, je te le dirai; **to lend** ou **give a sympathetic ~ to sb** prêter une oreille compatissante à qn; **to listen with (only) half an ~** n'écouter que d'une oreille; **to play it/sth by ~** fig improviser; **to set** ou **put sb on his/her ~**○ US provoquer la colère de qn; ▶ **deaf**, **bend**, **flap**.

earache /ˈɪəreɪk/ *n* **to have ~** GB ou **an ~** avoir une otite.

earbashing○ /ˈɪəbæʃɪŋ/ *n* **to give sb an ~** passer un savon○ à qn.

ear: **~drops** *npl* Med gouttes *fpl* pour les oreilles; **~drum** *n* tympan *m*; **~flap** *n* (on hat) oreillette *f*.

earful○ /ˈɪəfʊl/ *n* **to give sb an ~** (scold) passer un savon○ à qn; (talk excessively) assommer qn de paroles; **to get an ~** (be scolded) recevoir un savon○; **to get an ~ of sb's problems** subir les jérémiades de qn○; **get an ~ of this!** écoute un peu ça!

earl /ɜːl/ *n* comte *m*.

earldom /ˈɜːldəm/ *n* **1** (title) titre *m* de comte; **2** (land) comté *m*.

earlobe /ˈɪələʊb/ *n* lobe *m* de l'oreille.

early /ˈɜːlɪ/ **I** *adj* **1** (one of the first) [*attempt, role, years, play*] premier/-ière; **in an ~ role** dans un de ses premiers rôles; **the author's ~ novels** les premiers romans de l'auteur; **the ~ weeks of the strike** les premières semaines de la grève; **one of the earliest attempts** une des premières tentatives; **~ man** les premiers hommes; **in an earlier life** dans une vie antérieure; **2** (sooner than usual) [*death*] prématuré; [*delivery, settlement*] rapide; [*vegetable, fruit*] précoce; **to have an ~ lunch/night/lecture** déjeuner/se coucher/avoir cours tôt; **to catch the earlier train** prendre le train d'avant; **to take an ~ holiday** GB ou **vacation** US prendre des vacances tôt en saison; **to take ~ retirement** partir en préretraite; **at the earliest possible opportunity** le plus tôt possible, à la première occasion; **at your earliest convenience** sout à votre convenance fml; **3** (in period of time) **in ~ childhood** dans la petite ou première enfance; **at an ~ age** à un très jeune âge; **to be in one's ~ thirties** avoir entre 30 et 35 ans; **to make an ~ start** partir tôt; **to take the ~ train** prendre le premier train; **at the earliest** au plus tôt; **the earliest I can manage is Monday** je ne peux rien faire avant lundi; **at an ~ hour** très tôt; **in the ~ hours** au petit matin; **in the ~ Middle Ages/60's** au début du Moyen Âge/des années 60; **in the ~ spring** au début du printemps; **in the ~ afternoon** en début d'après-midi; **at an ~ date** (in future) très bientôt or prochainement; **the earliest days of the cinema** les tout débuts du cinéma; **an earlier attempt/experience** une tentative/expérience précédente; **4** Biol [*gene*] précoce.
II *adv* **1** (in period of time) [*leave, arrive, book, start*] tôt; [*get up, go to bed*] tôt, de bonne heure; **it's still ~** il est encore tôt; **it's too ~ to say** il est trop tôt pour le dire; **Easter falls** ou **is ~ this year** Pâques tombe tôt cette année; **can you let me know as ~ as possible?** pouvez-vous me le dire aussitôt que possible?; **can you make it earlier?** (arranging date) pouvez-vous○ plus tôt?; **five minutes earlier** cinq minutes plus tôt; **Fred can't get there earlier than 3 pm** Fred ne peut pas y être avant 15 h; **as ~ as 1983** dès 1983; **~ next year/in the film** au début de l'année prochaine/du film; **~ in the afternoon** en début d'après-midi; **(very) ~ on** dès le début; **~ on in her career** au début de sa carrière; **I realized ~ on that** j'ai compris rapidement que; **as I said earlier** comme je l'ai déjà dit; **'post** GB **~ for Christmas'** Post envoyez vos vœux de

Noël à l'avance; **2** (before expected, too soon) [*arrive, leave, ripen*] en avance; **I'm sorry to arrive a bit ~**, **I'm sorry I'm a bit ~** je suis désolé d'arriver un peu en avance; **the postman called** ou **was ~ today** le facteur est passé tôt aujourd'hui; **the strawberries are ~ this year** les fraises sont en avance cette année; **to do sth two days/three weeks ~** faire qch avec deux jours/trois semaines d'avance; **to retire ~** partir en préretraite.

IDIOMS **~ to bed ~ to rise** tôt couché tôt levé; **it's ~ days yet** ce n'est que le début; **it's the ~ bird that catches the worm!** Prov l'avenir appartient à ceux qui se lèvent tôt; **to be an ~ bird** être un/-e lève-tôt; **to be a bit ~ in the day to say** être un peu tôt pour le dire.

Early American *adj* [*architecture, furniture*] de style pionnier.

early closing day *n* GB **Thursday is ~** le jeudi, les magasins sont fermés l'après-midi.

early: **Early English** *n, adj* Archit gothique (*m*) anglais; **~ riser** *n* lève-tôt *mf.*

early warning I *n* **to be** ou **come as an ~ of sth** être le signe avant-coureur de qch.

II *modif* [*sign*] avant-coureur; [*symptom*] premier/-ière (*before n*).

early warning system *n* Mil système *m* d'alerte avancée.

earmark /ˈɪəmɑːk/ **I** *n* (on livestock) marque *f*; fig caractéristique *f*; **to have all the ~s of sth** avoir toutes les caractéristiques de qch.

II *vtr* marquer [*animal*]; fig désigner [*money, person, site*] (**for** pour).

earmuffs /ˈɪəmʌfs/ *npl* cache-oreilles *m inv.*

earn /ɜːn/ *vtr* **1** [*person*] lit gagner [*money, sum*] (**by doing** en faisant); toucher [*salary, wage*]; **to earn a** ou **one's living** gagner sa vie; **2** fig **it ~ed her the respect/admiration of her colleagues** cela lui a valu le respect/l'admiration de ses collègues; **to ~ sb's respect** se faire respecter de qn; **he's ~ed it!** il l'a mérité!; **well-~ed** bien mérité; **3** Fin [*investment, shares*] rapporter [*interest, profit*].

earned income *n* revenus *mpl* professionnels.

earner /ˈɜːnə(r)/ *n* **1** (person) salarié/-e *m/f*; **2**○ GB (source of money) **a nice little ~** une belle petite source de revenus.

earnest /ˈɜːnɪst/ **I** *n* **1** (seriousness) **to be in ~** être sérieux/-ieuse; **to begin** ou **start in ~** commencer vraiment (**to do** à faire); **2** (also **~ money**) Comm acompte *m*; **3** Fin, Comm (guarantee) gage *m*.

II *adj* **1** (serious) [*person*] sérieux/-ieuse; **2** (sincere) [*intention*] ferme; [*desire*] profond; [*promise, wish*] sincère; **3** (fervent) [*plea, prayer*] fervent.

earnestly /ˈɜːnɪstlɪ/ *adv* **1** (seriously) [*speak, discuss, ask*] sérieusement; **2** (sincerely) [*hope, wish*] sincèrement; **3** (fervently) [*plead, pray*] avec ardeur.

earnestness /ˈɜːnɪstnɪs/ *n* **1** (seriousness) sérieux *m*; **2** (sincerity) sincérité *f*; **3** (fervour) ardeur *f*.

earning power *n* capacité *f* de gain.

earnings /ˈɜːnɪŋz/ *npl* (of person) salaire *m*, revenu *m* (**from** de); (of company) profits *mpl*, gains *mpl* (**from** de); Fin (from shares) (taux *m* de) rendement *m*; **export ~** gains *mpl* à l'exportation.

earnings: **~ growth** *n* augmentation *f* des revenus; **~-related** *adj* fonction du salaire.

ear: **~ nose and throat department**, **ENT department** *n* service *m* d'oto-rhino-laryngologie, service *m* ORL; **~ nose and throat specialist**, **ENT specialist** **▶ 1692** *n* oto-rhino-laryngologiste *mf*; **~phones** *npl* (over ears) casque *m*; (in ears) écouteurs *mpl*.

earpiece /ˈɪəpiːs/ *n* **1** Telecom écouteur *m*; **2** (of glasses) embout *m* (*d'une branche de lunettes*); **3** Journ oreille *f*.

ear: **~plug** *n* (for noise) boule *f* Quiès®; (for water) bouchon *m* d'oreille; **~ring** *n* boucle *f* d'oreille; **~ shell** *n* ormeau *m*.

earshot /ˈɪəʃɒt/ *n* **out of/within ~** hors de/à portée de voix; **out of/within ~ of** trop loin/assez près pour entendre [*person, call, noise, conversation*].

earsplitting /ˈɪəsplɪtɪŋ/ *adj* [*scream, shout*] strident; [*noise*] fracassant.

earth /ɜːθ/ **I** *n* **1** (also **Earth**) (planet) terre *f*, Terre *f*; **life on ~** la vie sur terre; **here on ~** Relig ici-bas; **the ~'s atmosphere/surface** l'atmosphère/la surface terrestre; **to vanish off the face of the ~** disparaître de la surface de la terre; **to the ends of the ~** jusqu'au bout du monde; **the oldest city on ~** la ville la plus ancienne du monde; **to come down to ~** lit, fig revenir sur terre; **to bring sb back down to ~** ramener qn sur terre; **2**○ (as intensifier) **how/where/who on ~...?** comment/où/qui...?; **what on ~ do you mean?** qu'est-ce que tu veux dire?; **nothing on ~ would persuade me to do** pour rien au monde je ne ferais; **3** (soil) terre *f*; **4** (foxhole) terrier *m*; **to go to ~** lit, fig se terrer; **to run sb/sth to ~** fig dénicher○ qn/qch, trouver qn/qch; **5** GB Elec terre *f*; **6** Chem terre *f*; **7**○ (huge amount) **to cost the ~** coûter les yeux de la tête○; **to expect the ~** demander la lune.

II *modif* GB Elec [*electrode, cable, terminal, wire*] de terre.

III *vtr* GB Elec mettre [qch] à la terre.

IDIOMS **did the ~ move for you**○**?** hum euph tu as pris ton pied○?; **to look like nothing on ~** [*person*] ressembler à un épouvantail; [*food*] avoir l'air très louche; **I feel like nothing on ~** (ill) je me sens très mal.

■ **earth up** Hort: **~ up [sth]**, **~ [sth] up** butter [*roots*].

earthborn /ˈɜːθbɔːn/ *adj* (mortal) humain.

earthbound /ˈɜːθbaʊnd/ *adj* **1** (which cannot fly) terrestre; **2** [*meteorite, spaceship*] se dirigeant vers la Terre.

earth closet *n* GB fosse *f* d'aisances.

earthen /ˈɜːθn/ *adj* **1** (made of earth) en terre; **2** (made of clay) [*pot*] en faïence.

earthenware /ˈɜːθnweə(r)/ **I** *n* faïence *f*.

II *modif* [*crockery*] en faïence.

earthiness /ˈɜːθɪnɪs/ *n* truculence *f*.

earthing /ˈɜːθɪŋ/ *n* GB Elec mise *f* à la terre.

earthling /ˈɜːθlɪŋ/ *n* Terrien/-ienne *m/f*.

earthly /ˈɜːθlɪ/ *adj* **1** (terrestrial) terrestre; **2**○ **it's no ~ use** ça ne sert à rien du tout; **there's no ~ reason** il n'y a aucune raison; **I haven't an ~ (idea)** GB aucune idée.

earth mother *n* **1**○ (maternal woman) image *f* de la maternité; **2** Relig (goddess) déesse *f* de la fertilité; (the earth) Terre *f* mère.

earth: **~mover** *n* engin *m* de terrassement; **~-moving equipment** *n* engins *mpl* de terrassement; **~quake** *n* tremblement *m* de terre; **~quake-resistant construction** *n* construction *f* parasismique; **~ science** *n* science *f* de la Terre; **~shaking**○, **~shattering**○ *adj* bouleversant; **~ sign** *n* Astrol signe *m* de terre; **~ tone** *n* Art, Fashn couleur *f* d'automne; **~ tremor** *n* secousse *f* sismique.

earthwards /ˈɜːθwədz/ *adv* vers la Terre.

earth: **~work** *n* (*pl* **~** ou **~s**) (embankment) rempart *m*, levée *f* de terre; (excavation work) terrassement *m*; **~worm** *n* ver *m* de terre.

earthy /ˈɜːθɪ/ *adj* **1** (natural) [*person, wisdom, humour*] truculent; [*vigour*] primitif/-ive; **2** [*taste, smell, colour*] de terre; **3** (covered in soil) terreux/-euse.

ear: **~ trumpet** *n* cornet *m* acoustique; **~wax** *n* cérumen *m*; **~wig** *n* perce-oreille *m*.

ease /iːz/ **I** *n* **1** (lack of difficulty) facilité *f*; **for ~ of** pour faciliter [*use, reference*]; **with ~** avec facilité, facilement; **2** (freedom from anxiety) **at ~** gen à l'aise; **at ~!** Mil repos!; **ill at ~** mal à l'aise; **to put sb at ~/at their ~** mettre qn à l'aise/à son aise; **to take one's ~** se détendre; **to put sb's mind at ~** rassurer qn (**about** à propos de); **her mind was at ~ at last** elle avait enfin l'esprit tranquille; **3** (confidence of manner) aisance *f*; **4** (affluence) aisance *f*; **to live a life of ~** vivre dans l'aisance.

II *vtr* **1** (lessen) atténuer, soulager [*pain, tension, worry*]; atténuer [*crisis, shortage, problem*]; réduire [*congestion, restrictions*]; diminuer [*burden*]; **2** (make easier) détendre [*situation*]; faciliter [*communication, development, transition*]; **3** (move carefully) **to ~ sth into** introduire qch délicatement dans; **to ~ sth out of** sortir qch délicatement de.

III *vi* **1** (lessen) [*tension, pain, pressure*] s'atténuer; [*congestion, overcrowding, rain, snow, rate*] diminuer; [*fog*] se dissiper; **2** (become less difficult) [*situation*] se détendre; [*problem*] s'atténuer; **3** Fin [*price*] être en légère baisse.

IV *v refl* **to ~ oneself into** se laisser glisser délicatement dans [*seat, bath*]; **to ~ oneself out of** se lever délicatement de [*chair*]; **to ~ oneself through** se glisser par [*gap*].

■ **ease back**: **~ [sth] back**, **~ back [sth]** ôter délicatement [*cover, bandage*].

■ **ease off**: ¶ **~ off 1** (lessen) [*business*] se ralentir; [*demand, congestion*] se réduire; [*traffic, rain, snow*] diminuer; [*fog*] se dissiper; **2** (work less hard) [*person*] relâcher son effort; ¶ **~ [sth] off**, **~ off [sth]** (remove gently) ôter délicatement [*lid, boot*].

■ **ease up** (relax) se détendre, se reposer; **to ~ up on sb/on sth** être moins sévère envers qn/pour qch.

easel /ˈiːzl/ *n* chevalet *m*.

easement /ˈiːzmənt/ *n* Jur droit *m* de passage.

easily /ˈiːzɪlɪ/ *adv* **1** (with no difficulty) [*move, win, open*] facilement, aisément; **to be ~ forgotten/obtainable** être facile à oublier/à obtenir; **~ accessible** facilement accessible; **2** (readily) [*trust, laugh, cry*] facilement, vite; **to get bored ~** s'ennuyer facilement or vite; **3** (comfortably) [*sleep, breathe*] bien; [*talk*] à l'aise; **4** (unquestionably) de loin, sans aucun doute; **~ the funniest film** de loin or sans aucun doute le film le plus amusant; **it's ~ 80 kilometres** ça fait facilement 80 kilomètres; **5** (probably) **she could ~ die** elle pourrait bien mourir.

easiness /ˈiːzɪnɪs/ *n* **1** (lack of difficulty) (of question, problem, exam) simplicité *f*; (of task, job, walk, climb) facilité *f*; **2** (comfortableness) (of life, conditions) aisance *f*.

east /iːst/ **▶ 1568** **I** *n* gen est *m*.

II East *pr n* **1** Geog **the ~** (Orient) l'Orient *m*; (of country, continent) l'Est *m*; **2** (in cards) Est *m*.

III *adj* [*side, face, coast, door*] est *inv*; [*wind*] d'est.

IV *adv* [*live, lie*] à l'est (**of** de); [*move*] vers l'est; **to go ~ of sth** passer à l'est de qch.

IDIOMS **~ or west, home is best** Prov on n'est nulle part si bien que chez soi.

East Africa *pr n* Afrique *f* de l'Est.

East African I *n* habitant/-e *m/f* de l'Afrique de l'Est.

II *adj* [*state, town, river*] d'Afrique de l'Est.

east: **East Anglia** *pr n* East Anglia *m*; **East Berlin** *pr n* Pol Hist Berlin-Est.

eastbound /ˈiːstbaʊnd/ *adj* [*carriageway, traffic*] en direction de l'est; **the ~ platform/train** GB (in underground) le quai/la rame direction est.

East End *pr n* quartiers *mpl* est de Londres.

Easter /ˈiːstə(r)/ **I** *n* **1** Relig (festival) Pâques *m*; **at ~** à Pâques; **over ~** pendant les fêtes de Pâques; **2** (in greetings) pâques *fpl*; **Happy ~** joyeuses pâques.

II *modif* [*Sunday, bunny, egg, bonnet*] de

Pâques; [*candle*] pascal; [*parade*] de printemps.

easterly /'i:stəlɪ/ **I** *n* (wind) vent *m* d'est.
II *adj* [*wind*] d'est; [*point*] à l'est; [*area*] de l'est; [*breeze*] venant de l'est; **in an ~ direction** en direction de l'est.

eastern /'i:stən/ **▶1568** *adj* **1** [*coast, border*] est; [*town, custom, accent*] de l'est; [*Europe, United States*] de l'Est; **~ France** l'est de la France; **2** (also **Eastern**) (oriental) oriental.

Eastern bloc *n* Pol Hist **the ~** le bloc *m* des pays de l'Est.

eastern: **~ bloc country** *n* pays *m* du bloc de l'Est; **Eastern Church** *n* Église *f* de rite oriental; **Eastern Daylight Time**, **EDT** *n* US heure *f* d'été de l'Est.

easterner /'i:stənə(r)/ *n* US homme/femme *m/f* de l'Est des États-Unis.

eastern: **Eastern European Time**, **EET** *n* heure *f* de l'Europe orientale; **~most** *adj* à l'extrême est, le/la plus à l'est; **Eastern Standard Time**, **EST** *n* heure *f* normale de l'Est.

east-facing /ˌi:st'feɪsɪŋ/ *adj* exposé à l'est.

East German Pol Hist **▶1486** **I** *n* Allemand/-e *m/f* de l'Est.
II *adj* est-allemand.

east: **East Germany** **▶1131** *pr n* Pol Hist Allemagne *f* de l'Est; **East Indies** *pr npl* Indes *fpl* orientales; **East Side** *pr n* quartiers *mpl* est de New-York.

East Sussex /ˌi:st 'sʌsɪks/ **▶1624** *pr n* East Sussex *m*.

eastward /'i:stwəd/ **▶1568** **I** *adj* [*side*] est *inv*; [*wall, slope*] du côté est; [*journey, route, movement*] vers l'est; **in an ~ direction** en direction de l'est, vers l'est.
II *adv* (also **~s**) vers l'est.

East-West relations *npl* Pol relations *fpl* Est-Ouest.

easy /'i:zɪ/ **I** *adj* **1** (not difficult) [*job, question, victory, life*] facile; **that's ~ to fix** c'est facile à réparer; **it's not ~ to talk to him, he's not an ~ man to talk to** ce n'est pas facile de lui parler; **that's ~ for you to say!** c'est facile à dire pour toi!; **it's all** ou **only too ~ to** il n'est que trop facile de; **she makes it look ~** cela a l'air facile avec elle; **it's an ~ walk from here** c'est facilement accessible à pied d'ici; **to be an ~ winner** gagner très facilement; **within ~ reach** tout près (**of** de); **that's easier said than done** c'est plus facile à dire qu'à faire, c'est vite dit; **to make it** ou **things easier** faciliter les choses (**for** pour); **to make life easier** (**for sb**) faciliter la vie à qn; **to make life** ou **things too ~ for** être trop complaisant avec [*criminal, regime*]; **to have an ~ ride** fig avoir la vie facile; **we didn't have an ~ time of it** ça a été une période difficile; **to take the ~ way out** choisir la solution de facilité; **2** (untroubled, relaxed) [*smile, grace, elegance*] décontracté; [*style, manner*] plein d'aisance; **at an ~ pace** d'un pas tranquille; **to feel ~** (**in one's mind**) **about** ne pas se faire de souci à propos de; **3** (weak) [*victim, prey*] facile, tout trouvé; **he's ~ game** ou **meat** c'est une proie facile; **4**○ péj (promiscuous) [*person*] facile○; **▶lay**; **5**○ (having no preference) **I'm ~** ça m'est égal; **6** Fin [*market*] en légère baisse.
II *adv* **1** (in a relaxed way) **to take it** ou **things ~** ne pas s'en faire; **take it ~!** (stay calm) du calme!, doucement!; **stand ~!** Mil repos!; **2**○ (in a careful way) **to go ~ on** ou **with** y aller doucement or mollo○ avec [*person*]; **go ~ on the milk/gin** vas-y doucement avec le lait/gin; **~ does it!** doucement!
IDIOMS **to be ~ on the eye** être agréable à regarder; **as ~ as pie** ou **ABC** ou **anything** ou **falling off a log** facile comme tout, simple comme bonjour; **~ come, ~ go** c'est de l'argent vite gagné vite dépensé; **~ does it** doucement.

easy: **~-care** *adj* [*fabric, shirt, curtain*] d'entretien facile; **~ chair** *n* ≈ chauffeuse *f*.

easygoing /ˌi:zɪ'gəʊɪŋ/ *adj* [*person*] accommodant; [*manner, attitude*] souple.

easy: **~ listening** *n* musique *f* légère; **~ money** *n* argent *m* vite gagné; **~ over** *n* US œuf *m* au plat retourné à mi-cuisson.

Easy Street○ *n* **to be on ~** se la couler douce○.

easy terms *n* Fin, Comm facilités *fpl* de paiement.

eat /i:t/ **I** *vtr* (*prét* **ate**; *pp* **eaten**) **1** (consume) [*person, animal*] manger [*cake, food, snack*]; prendre [*meal*]; **I don't ~ meat** je ne mange pas de viande; **to ~ (one's) breakfast** prendre le petit déjeuner; **to ~ (one's) lunch** déjeuner; **to ~ one's dinner** dîner; **I ate lunch in town** j'ai déjeuné en ville; **to ~ sth for lunch/dinner** manger qch pour le déjeuner/dîner; **to ~ oneself sick**○ s'empiffrer○, se donner une indigestion (**on** de); **it's not fit to ~** (poisonous) ce n'est pas comestible; (inedible) c'est immangeable; **it looks too good to ~** c'est si beau qu'on n'ose pas en manger; **she looks good enough to ~!** elle est belle à croquer○!; **to ~ one's way through a whole cake** engloutir un gâteau entier; **to ~ sb/sth alive** [*person, piranha, mosquitoes*] dévorer qn/qch; [*seductress*] **she'll ~ you alive**○! elle te mangera tout cru○!; **don't be afraid, I won't ~ you!** n'aie pas peur, je ne vais pas te manger; **to ~ one's words** fig ravaler ses paroles; **2**○ (guzzle) [*car*] bouffer○, consommer [*petrol*]; **3**○ (worry) chiffonner○; **what's ~ing you?** qu'est-ce qui te chiffonne○?
II *vi* (*prét* **ate**; *pp* **eaten**) **1** (take food) manger; **to ~ from** ou **out of** manger dans [*plate, bowl*]; **I'll soon have him ~ing out of my hand** fig bientôt j'en ferai ce que je voudrai!; **2** (have a meal) manger; **I never ~ in the canteen** je ne mange jamais à la cantine; **we ~ at six** nous dînons à 18 heures.
IDIOMS **~ your heart out!** souffre en silence!; **to ~ sb out of house and home** manger la laine sur le dos de qn○.
■ **eat away**: ¶ **~ [sth] away**, **~ away [sth]** [*water, wind*] ronger, éroder [*cliff, stone*]; [*acid, rust, termites*] ronger; ¶ **~ away at [sth]** lit [*acid, disease, rust, woodworm*] ronger; fig [*bills, fees*] manger [*profits, savings*].
■ **eat into**: **~ into [sth]** **1** (damage) [*acid, rust*] faire un trou dans [*metal, paint*]; **2** (encroach on) [*duties, interruptions*] empiéter sur [*day, leisure*]; **3** (use up) [*bills, fees*] entamer [*profits, savings*].
■ **eat out** aller au restaurant.
■ **eat up**: ¶ **~ up** finir de manger; **~ up!** finis ce que tu as dans ton assiette!; ¶ **~ [sth] up**, **~ up [sth]** **1** (finish) finir [*meal, vegetables*]; **2** (guzzle) [*car*] dévorer [*miles*]; bouffer○, consommer [*petrol*]; **3** (use up) [*bills*] engloutir [*savings*]; **4** fig **to be ~en up with** [*person*] être dévoré de [*curiosity, desire, envy*]; être dévoré par [*guilt*]; être rongé par [*worry*].

eatable /'i:təbl/ *adj* = **edible**.

eaten /'i:tn/ *pp* **▶eat**.

eater /'i:tə(r)/ *n* **1** (consumer of food) mangeur/-euse *m/f*; **a big ~** un gros mangeur; **a big fruit ~** un gros mangeur de fruits; **she's a fussy ~** elle est difficile pour la nourriture; **he's a fast/messy ~** il mange vite/salement; **2** (apple) pomme *f* à couteau.

eatery /'i:tərɪ/ *n* surtout US petit restaurant *m*.

eating /'i:tɪŋ/ *n* **~ is a pleasure** manger est un plaisir; **healthy ~ is essential** il est essentiel de manger sainement; **to make excellent/poor ~** être excellent/mauvais.

eating: **~ apple** *n* pomme *f* à couteau; **~ disorder** *n* Med trouble *m* du comportement alimentaire; **~ habits** *npl* habitudes *fpl* alimentaires; **~ house** restaurant *m*.

eating out *n* **I love ~** j'adore manger au restaurant.

eating place *n* restaurant *m*.

eats○ /i:ts/ *npl* bouffe○ *f*, nourriture *f*.

eau de cologne /ˌəʊ də kə'ləʊn/ *n* eau *f* de Cologne.

eaves /i:vz/ *npl* avant-toit *m*.

eavesdrop /'i:vzdrɒp/ *vi* (*p prés etc* **-pp-**) écouter aux portes; **to ~ on** écouter [qch] de manière indiscrète [*person, conversation*]; **to ~ on sb** (electronically) mettre qn sur table d'écoute.

ebb /eb/ **I** *n* reflux *m*; **the tide is on the ~** la marée descend; **the ~ and flow** le flux et le reflux also fig.
II *vi* **1** [*tide*] descendre, refluer; **to ~ and flow** monter et descendre; **2** fig [*support*] décliner.
IDIOMS **to be at a low ~** être au plus bas.
■ **ebb away** [*strength, enthusiasm, support*] décliner.

ebb tide *n* marée *f* descendante.

ebonite /'ebənaɪt/ *n* ébonite *f*.

ebony /'ebənɪ/ **I** *n* **1** (wood) ébène *f*; **2** (tree) ébénier *m*; **3** **▶1104** (colour) noir *m* d'ébène.
II *modif* [*casket, veneer*] d'ébène ou en ébène; [*branch, bark*] d'ébénier; [*skin, eyes*] d'un noir d'ébène.

EBRD *n*: *abrév* **▶European Bank for Reconstruction and Development**.

ebullience /ɪ'bʌlɪəns, ɪ'bʊlɪəns/ *n* exubérance *f*.

ebullient /ɪ'bʌlɪənt, ɪ'bʊlɪənt/ *adj* exubérant.

EC *n* (*abrév* = **European Community**) CE *f*.

eccentric /ɪk'sentrɪk/ **I** *n* **1** (person) excentrique *mf*; **2** Tech excentrique *m*.
II *adj* (all contexts) excentrique.

eccentrically /ɪk'sentrɪklɪ/ *adv* de manière excentrique.

eccentricity /ˌeksen'trɪsətɪ/ *n* excentricité *f*.

Eccles cake /'ekəlz/ *n* GB pâtisserie *f* aux raisins secs.

Ecclesiastes /ɪˌkli:zɪ'æsti:z/ *pr n* Ecclésiaste *m*.

ecclesiastic /ɪˌkli:zɪ'æstɪk/ *n* ecclésiastique *m*.

ecclesiastical /ɪˌkli:zɪ'æstɪkl/ *adj* ecclésiastique.

ecclesiology /ɪˌkli:zɪ'ɒlədʒɪ/ *n* ecclésiologie *f*.

ECG *n* (*abrév* = **electrocardiogram**, **electrocardiograph**) ECG *m*.

echelon /'eʃəlɒn/ *n* gen, Mil échelon *m*.

echinoderm /ɪ'kaɪnədɜ:m, 'ekɪn-/ *n* échinoderme *m*.

echo /'ekəʊ/ **I** *n* (*pl* **~es**) **1** (of sound) écho *m*; **to cheer to the ~** applaudir à tout rompre; **2** (overtone) écho *m*; **3** (of idea, opinion etc) **to have ~es of sth** rappeler qch.
II *vtr* **1** lit répercuter, renvoyer [qch] en écho; **2** (repeat) reprendre [*idea, opinion etc*]; **3** (resemble) rappeler [*artist, style*].
III *vi* retentir, résonner (**to, with** de; **around** dans).

echo chamber *n* Radio, TV chambre *f* résonnante.

echoing /'ekəʊɪŋ/ *adj* sonore.

echo sounder *n* sondeur *m* à ultrasons.

éclair /eɪ'kleə(r), ɪ'kleə(r)/ *n* Culin éclair *m*.

eclampsia /ɪ'klæmpsɪə/ **▶1354** *n* éclampsie *f*.

éclat /'eɪklɑ:/ *n* éclat *m*.

eclectic /ɪ'klektɪk/ *n, adj* éclectique (*mf*).

eclecticism /ɪ'klektɪsɪzəm/ *n* éclectisme *m*.

eclipse /ɪ'klɪps/ **I** *n* **1** Astron éclipse *f* (**of** de); **partial/total ~** éclipse partielle/totale; **solar/lunar ~** éclipse solaire/de lune; **the moon is in ~** il y a une éclipse de lune; **2** fig éclipse *f* (**of** de); **to be in, to go into ~** [*person, movement*] connaître une éclipse.
II *vtr* (all contexts) éclipser.

eclipsing binary *n* binaire *f* à éclipse.

ecliptic /ɪ'klɪptɪk/ *adj* écliptique.

eclogue /ˈeklɒg/ *n* églogue *f*.

eclosion /ɪˈkləʊʒn/ *n* éclosion *f*.

eco /ˈiːkəʊ-/ **I** *n*: *abrév* = **ecology**.
II *modif* [*group*] écologiste.
III eco+ (*dans composés*) éco-.

eco-aware /ˌiːkəʊəˈweə(r)/ *adj* sensibilisé aux problèmes de l'environnement.

ecocatastrophe /ˌiːkəkəˈtæstrəfɪ/ *n* catastrophe *f* écologique.

ecocide /ˈiːkəsaɪd/ *n* écocide *m*.

eco: **~-freak**○ *n* péj fana○ *mf* de l'écologie; **~-friendly** *adj* qui ne nuit pas à l'environnement.

ecological /ˌiːkəˈlɒdʒɪkl/ *adj* écologique.

ecologically /ˌiːkəˈlɒdʒɪklɪ/ *adj* écologiquement.

ecologist /iːˈkɒlədʒɪst/ *n*, *adj* écologiste (*mf*).

ecology /ɪˈkɒlədʒɪ/ **I** *n* (all contexts) écologie *f*.
II *modif* Pol [*movement, issue*] écologique.

Ecology Party *n* Pol parti *m* écologique.

econometric /ɪˌkɒnəˈmetrɪk/ *adj* économétrique.

econometrician /ɪˌkɒnəməˈtrɪʃn/ ▶ **1692** *n* économétricien/-ienne *m/f*.

econometrics /ɪˌkɒnəˈmetrɪks/ *n* (+ *v sg*) économétrie *f*.

econometrist /ɪˌkɒnəˈmetrɪst/ *n* = **econometrician**.

economic /ˌiːkəˈnɒmɪk, ˌek-/ *adj* **1** [*change, crisis, forecast, performance, policy, sanction*] économique; **to make ~ sense** être intéressant d'un point de vue économique; **2** (profitable) [*proposition, business*] rentable; **to make ~ sense** être financièrement intéressant.

economical /ˌiːkəˈnɒmɪkl, ˌek-/ *adj* **1** [*car, machine, method*] économique; **to be ~ to run** être économique à utiliser; **to be ~ on petrol** consommer peu d'essence; **2** [*person*] économe; **3** fig [*style, writer*] concis; **to be ~ with words** s'exprimer avec concision; **to be ~ with the truth** iron ne pas dire toute la vérité.

economically /ˌiːkəˈnɒmɪklɪ, ek-/ *adv* **1** [*strong, weak, viable, united*] économiquement; **2** (sparingly) [*run, operate*] de façon économique; **3** [*write, convey*] avec concision.

economic: **~ analyst** ▶ **1692** *n* analyste *mf* économique; **~ and monetary union**, **EMU** *n* Union *f* économique et monétaire; **~ cost** *n* coût *m* économique; **~ development** *n* développement *m* économique; **~ geography** *n* géographie *f* économique; **~ growth** *n* croissance *f* économique; **~ history** *n* histoire *f* de l'économie; **~ indicator** *n* indicateur *m* économique or de conjoncture; **~ management** *n* gestion *f* de l'économie.

economics /ˌiːkəˈnɒmɪks, ˌek-/ **I** *n* **1** (science) (+ *v sg*) économie *f*; **an expert on ~** un/une spécialiste en économie; **2** Sch, Univ (subject of study) (+ *v sg*) sciences *fpl* économiques; **to study ~** étudier les sciences économiques; **3** (financial aspects) (+ *v pl*) aspects *mpl* économiques (**of** de).
II *modif* [*degree, textbook, faculty*] de sciences économiques; [*editor, expert, correspondent*] en économie.

economic: **~ system** *n* système *m* économique; **~ theory** *n* théorie *f* économique.

economist /ɪˈkɒnəmɪst, ˌek-/ ▶ **1692** *n* économiste *mf*; **business ~** économiste *mf* d'entreprise.

economize /ɪˈkɒnəmaɪz/ **I** *vtr* économiser.
II *vi* économiser (**on** sur).

economy /ɪˈkɒnəmɪ/ *n* (all contexts) économie *f*; **to make economies** faire des économies; **for reasons of ~** pour des raisons d'économie; **with (an) ~ of effort** à moindre effort; **economies of scale** économies d'échelle; **the ~** l'économie du pays.

economy: **~ class** *n* Aviat classe *f* économique; **~ drive** *n* campagne *f* de restriction; **~ pack**, **~ size** *n* paquet *m* économique.

ecosphere /ˈiːkəʊsfɪə(r)/ *n* écosphère *f*.

ecosystem /ˈiːkəʊsɪstəm/ *n* écosystème *m*.

eco-terrorist /ˌiːkəˈterərɪst/ *n* terroriste *mf* écologiste.

ecotone /ˈiːkətəʊn/ *n* écotone *m*.

ecotype /ˈiːkətaɪp/ *n* écotype *m*.

ecru /ˈeɪkruː/ ▶ **1104** *n*, *adj* écru (*m*).

ECSC *n* (*abrév* = **European Coal and Steel Community**) CECA *f*.

ecstasy /ˈekstəsɪ/ *n* **1** extase *f*; **religious/sexual ~** extase religieuse/sexuelle; **to be in ~** ou **ecstasies** être en extase (**over** sur); **2** (also **Ecstasy**, **E**, **XTC**) (drug) ecstasy *m*.

ecstatic /ɪkˈstætɪk/ *adj* **1** (happy) [*person*] enchanté (**about** par); **2** [*happiness, joy, trance, state, smile*] extatique; [*welcome, reception, crowd, fan*] enthousiaste.

ecstatically /ɪkˈstætɪklɪ/ *adv* [*applaud, read, welcomed*] avec un enthousiasme délirant; **~ happy** radieux/-ieuse; **to be ~ reviewed** recevoir des critiques délirantes.

ECT *n* Med *abrév* ▶ **electroconvulsive therapy**.

ectomorph /ˈektəʊmɔːf/ *n* ectomorphe *mf*.

ectopic pregnancy /ekˌtɒpɪk ˈpregnənsɪ/ *n* grossesse *f* extra-utérine.

ectoplasm /ˈektəplæzəm/ *n* ectoplasme *m*.

ecu, **ECU** /eɪˈkuː/ ▶ **1143** **I** *n* (*abrév* = **European Currency Unit**) ÉCU *m*, écu *m*; **hard ~** écu *m* dur.
II *modif* [*value*] en écus; **~ bond** euro-obligation *f* libellée en écus.

Ecuador /ˈekwədɔː(r)/ ▶ **1131** *pr n* Équateur *m*.

Ecuadorian /ˌekwəˈdɔːrɪən/ ▶ **1486** **I** *n* Équatorien/-ienne *m/f*.
II *adj* équatorien/-ienne.

ecumenical /ˌiːkjuːˈmenɪkl, ˈek-/ *adj* œcuménique.

ecumenism /iːˈkjuːmənɪzəm/ *n* œcuménisme *m*.

eczema /ˈeksɪmə, US ɪgˈziːmə/ ▶ **1354** *n* eczéma *m*; **to suffer from ~** avoir de l'eczéma.

eczema sufferer *n* eczémateux/-euse *m/f*.

Ed.B *n* US Univ (*abrév* = **Bachelor of Education**) diplôme *m* universitaire de pédagogie.

EDD *n*: *abrév* ▶ **estimated date of delivery**.

eddy /ˈedɪ/ **I** *n* tourbillon *m*.
II *vi* [*tide, liquid*] faire des tourbillons, tourbillonner; [*smoke, crowd*] tournoyer.

edelweiss /ˈeɪdlvaɪs/ *n* (*pl* **~**) edelweiss *m*.

edema *n* US = **oedema**.

Eden /ˈiːdn/ *pr n* Bible, fig Éden *m*, paradis *m* terrestre also fig; **the garden of ~** le jardin d'Éden.

edentate /ɪˈdenteɪt/ *n*, *adj* Zool édenté (*m*).

edge /edʒ/ **I** *n* **1** (outer limit) (of table, road, lake, field) bord *m*; (of coin) bordure *f*; (of wood, clearing) lisière *f*; **at the water's ~** au bord de l'eau; **on the ~ of the city** en bordure de la ville; **the film had us on the ~ of our seats** le film nous a tenus en haleine; **2** (sharp side) tranchant *m*; **a blade with a sharp ~** une lame bien aiguisée; **to put an ~ on** aiguiser, affûter [*blade*]; **3** (side) (of book, plank) tranche *f*; **4** (sharpness) **to give an ~ to** aiguiser [*appetite*]; **to take the ~ off** gâter [*pleasure*]; calmer [*anger, appetite*]; soulager [*pain*]; **there was an ~ to his voice** sa voix avait quelque chose de tendu; **to lose one's ~** [*writing, style*] perdre sa vivacité; [*person*] perdre sa vigueur; **5** (advantage) **to have the ~ over** ou **on** avoir l'avantage sur [*competitor, rival*]; **to give sb the ~ over** donner à qn l'avantage sur; **to have a slight ~** avoir une légère avance (**over** sur); **6** (touchy) **to be on ~** [*person*] être énervé; **my nerves are on ~** j'ai les nerfs fatigués; **that sound sets my teeth on ~** ce bruit me fait grincer des dents; **7** fig (extremity) **to live on the ~** vivre dangereusement; **the news pushed him over the ~** cette nouvelle l'a achevé.
II *vtr* **1** (move slowly) **to ~ sth towards** approcher qch de; **he ~d the car closer to the kerb** il a rapproché la voiture du trottoir; **to ~ one's way along** longer la bordure de [*cliff, parapet*]; **2** (trim) border [*collar, handkerchief*]; **3** Hort border [*lawn*].
III *vi* (advance) **to ~ forward** avancer doucement; **to ~ up to** s'approcher doucement de; **to ~ out of a parking space** se dégager lentement d'une place de parking; **to ~ closer to** se rapprocher de [*victory, independence*]; **to ~ towards** s'approcher à petits pas de [*door, victory*].
■ **edge out** [*car, driver*] (of space) se dégager petit à petit (**of** de); (of side street) sortir petit à petit (**of** de); **I ~d out of the room/door** je me suis glissé hors de la pièce/par la porte; **to ~ sb out of** évincer qn de [*job*]; **we've ~d our competitors out of the market** nous avons éliminé tous nos concurrents du marché.
■ **edge up**: **~ up 1** [*prices, figure*] augmenter lentement; **2 to ~ up to sb** s'approcher à petits pas de qn.

edgeways /ˈedʒweɪz/, **edgewise** /ˈedʒwaɪz/ *adv* (sideways) [*move*] latéralement; (along its side) [*lay, put*] sur le côté.
IDIOMS **I can't get a word in ~** je n'arrive pas à placer un mot.

edgily /ˈedʒɪlɪ/ *adv* nerveusement.

edginess /ˈedʒɪnɪs/ *n* nervosité *f*.

edging /ˈedʒɪŋ/ *n* **1** (border) bordure *f*; **2** (making a border) (in garden) entretien *m* des bordures; (on fabric) pose *f* d'une bordure.

edging shears *n* cisaille *f* de jardinier.

edgy /ˈedʒɪ/ *adj* énervé, anxieux/-ieuse.

edible /ˈedɪbl/ *adj* [*fruit, plant, mushroom, snail*] comestible; [*meal*] mangeable.

edict /ˈiːdɪkt/ *n* **1** Hist édit *m*; **2** Jur, Pol décret *m*; **to issue an ~** faire paraître un décret.

edification /ˌedɪfɪˈkeɪʃn/ *n* sout édification *f*.

edifice /ˈedɪfɪs/ *n* édifice *m* also fig.

edify /ˈedɪfaɪ/ *vtr* édifier, porter [qn] à la vertu.

edifying /ˈedɪfaɪɪŋ/ *adj* édifiant.

Edinburgh /ˈedɪnbərə/ ▶ **1818** *pr n* Édimbourg.

edit /ˈedɪt/ **I** *n* (of film) montage *m*; (for publication) mise *f* au point.
II *vtr* **1** (check for publishing) réviser [*text, novel*]; **2** (annotate, select) éditer [*essays, letters, anthology, author, works*]; **3** (cut down) couper [*account, version, reader's letter*]; **4** Journ être le rédacteur/la rédactrice *m/f* en chef de [*newspaper, journal*]; être le rédacteur/la rédactrice *m/f* adjoint/-e de [*section, page*]; **5** TV, Cin réaliser le montage de [*film, programme*]; **6** Comput éditer [*data*].
■ **edit out**: Cin **~ out [sth]**, **~ [sth] out** couper [qch] au montage.

editing /ˈedɪtɪŋ/ *n* **1** (tidying for publication) mise *f* au point; **2** (of essays, letters, author, collection, anthology) édition *f*; **3** (of film) montage *m*; **4** (of newspaper) rédaction *f*; **5** Comput (of data) édition *f*.

edition /ɪˈdɪʃn/ *n* **1** Publg, Journ édition *f*; **first/new ~** première/nouvelle édition; **morning/evening ~** édition du matin/du soir; **2** TV (of soap opera) feuilleton *m*; (of news) édition *f*; (generally) émission *f*; **3** (of coins, porcelain) série *f*.

editor /ˈedɪtə(r)/ ▶ **1692** *n* **1** (of newspaper) rédacteur/-trice *m/f* en chef (**of** de); **political/sports/fashion ~** rédacteur politique/sportif/de mode; **2** (of book, manuscript) correcteur/-trice *m/f*; **3** (of writer, works, anthology) éditeur/-trice *m/f*; **he's the ~ of Keats' letters** il a édité les lettres de Keats; **4** (of dictionary) rédacteur/-trice *m/f*; **5** (of film) monteur/-euse *m/f*.

editorial /ˌedɪˈtɔːrɪəl/ **I** *n* éditorial *m* (**on** sur).
II *adj* **1** Journ [*policy, office, staff, freedom,*

independence] de la rédaction; [*interference*] dans la rédaction; **to have ~ control** avoir la direction de la rédaction; **the ~ page** la page de l'éditorial; **2** Publg [*policy, decision*] éditorial; **to have ~ control** avoir le contrôle du texte; **to do ~ work** faire du travail d'édition.

editorialist /ˌedɪ'tɔːrɪəlɪst/ *n* US éditorialiste *mf*.

editorialize /ˌedɪ'tɔːrɪəlaɪz/ *vi* lit [*newspaper*] déclarer dans son éditorial; fig déclarer.

editorship /'edɪtəʃɪp/ *n* direction *f*; **under the ~ of** sous la direction de.

EDS *n*: *abrév* ▶**exchangeable disk storage**.

EDT *n* US *abrév* ▶**Eastern Daylight Time**.

educable /'edʒʊkəbl/ *adj* éducable.

educate /'edʒʊkeɪt/ **I** *vtr* **1** (teach) [*teacher*] instruire [*pupil, student*]; **2** (provide education for) [*school, parent*] assurer l'instruction de [*child, pupil*]; **to ~ one's children privately/at a state school** mettre ses enfants dans une école privée/publique; **to be ~d at Oxford/in Paris** faire ses études à Oxford/à Paris; **3** (inform) [*campaign, person, book*] informer [*public, smokers, drivers*] **(about, in** sur); **to ~ sb to do** montrer à qn comment faire; **4** (refine) éduquer [*palate, tastes, mind*].

II *v refl* **to ~ oneself** s'instruire tout seul; **to ~ oneself to do** apprendre tout seul à faire.

educated /'edʒʊkeɪtɪd/ **I** *n* **the ~** (+ *v pl*) (having an education) les gens *mpl* instruits; (cultivated) les gens *mpl* cultivés.

II *adj* [*person*] (having an education) instruit; (cultivated) cultivé; [*mind, palate, taste, judgment*] raffiné; [*language, style*] dénotant un certain niveau d'instruction; [*accent*] élégant; **to be very poorly ~** ne pas avoir fait beaucoup d'études.

IDIOMS **to make an ~ guess** avancer une hypothèse.

education /ˌedʒʊ'keɪʃn/ **I** *n* **1** (training) gen éducation *f*, instruction *f*; (in health, road safety) information *f*; **musical/political/moral ~** éducation musicale/politique/morale; **~ is the key to success** l'éducation est la clé de la réussite; **2** (formal schooling) études *fpl*; **private/state school ~** études dans une école privée/dans une école publique; **to continue one's ~** poursuivre ses études; **~ should be available to all** l'instruction devrait être accessible à tous; **to have had a university** ou **college ~** avoir fait des études supérieures; **to get a good ~** faire de solides études; **she has had little ~** elle n'a pas beaucoup d'instruction; **3** (national system) enseignement *m*; **primary /secondary ~** enseignement primaire/secondaire; **government spending on ~** le budget de l'éducation; **4** Univ (field of study) sciences *fpl* de l'éducation.

II *modif* [*budget, spending, crisis*] de l'enseignement; [*method*] Scol, Univ d'enseignement; [*Minister, Ministry*] Admin de l'éducation; [*department*] Univ des sciences de l'éducation; [*diploma*] Univ en sciences de l'éducation; [*allowance*] d'études; **~ standards** Sch niveau *m* scolaire; Univ niveau *m* universitaire; **the ~ system in France/Britain** le système éducatif français/britannique.

education: **~ act** *n* loi *f* sur l'éducation; **~ adviser** *n* ≈ conseiller/-ère *m/f* pédagogique.

educational /ˌedʒʊ'keɪʃənl/ *adj* **1** [*establishment, system*] d'enseignement; [*method*] d'enseignement, pédagogique; [*developments*] de l'enseignement; [*policy*] en matière de l'éducation; [*standards, supplies*] Sch scolaire; Univ universitaire; **what kind of ~ background does she have?** quelles études a-t-elle faites?; **2** (instructive) [*toy, game, programme, value*] éducatif/-ive; [*experience, talk*] instructif/-ive.

educationalist /ˌedʒʊ'keɪʃənəlɪst/ *n* spécialiste *mf* des sciences de l'éducation.

educationally /ˌedʒʊ'keɪʃənəlɪ/ *adv* **1** gen [*worthless, useful*] pédagogiquement; **2** Sch [*disadvantaged, privileged*] sur le plan scolaire.

educationally subnormal, **ESN** **I** *n* **the ~** (+ *v pl*) les arriérés *mpl*.

II *adj* arriéré.

educational: **~ psychologist** ▶**1692** *n* psychologue *mf* scolaire; **~ psychology** *n* psychologie *f* scolaire; **~ television**, **ETV** US télévision *f* scolaire; **Educational Welfare Officer** *n* GB ≈ assistante sociale en milieu scolaire.

education: **~ authority** *n* GB *administration locale ou régionale qui gère les affaires scolaires*; **~ committee** *n* GB *comité de membres élus et de membres choisis gérant les affaires scolaires ordinaires d'une région*.

education department *n* **1** GB **Education Department** (also **Department of Education and Science**) ministère *m* de l'éducation; **2** GB (in local government) service *m* chargé des affaires d'enseignement; **3** (in university, college) département *m* des sciences de l'éducation.

education officer *n*: *membre du comité gérant les affaires scolaires ordinaires d'une région*.

educative /'edʒʊkətɪv/ *adj* éducatif/-ive.

educator /'edʒʊkeɪtə(r)/ *n* éducateur/-trice *m/f*.

educe /ɪ'dʒuːs/ *vtr* sout mettre [qch] à jour.

Edward /'edwəd/ *pr n* Édouard.

Edwardian /ed'wɔːdɪən/ **I** *n* Hist contemporain/-e *m/f* d'Édouard VII.

II *adj* de l'époque d'Édouard VII; **in ~ times** à l'époque d'Édouard VII; **the ~ Age** ou **Era** ≈ la Belle Époque *f*.

EEC **I** *n* (*abrév* ▶**European Economic Community**) CEE *f*.

II *modif* [*policy, directive*] de la CEE, communautaire; [*country*] de la CEE.

EEG *n*: *abrév* ▶**electroencephalogram, electroencephalograph**.

eel /iːl/ *n* anguille *f*.

IDIOMS **he's as slippery as an ~** il vous glisse entre les doigts.

eelworm /'iːlwɜːm/ *n* anguillule *f*.

e'en /iːn/ *adv*‡ ou littér = **even**[1].

EEOC *n* US (*abrév* = **Equal Employment Opportunity Commission**) *commission chargée de veiller sur l'égalité des chances dans le monde du travail*.

e'er‡ /eə(r)/ *adv* = **ever**.

eerie /'ɪərɪ/ *adj* [*scream, silence*] angoissant; [*place, feeling*] étrange.

eerily /'ɪərɪlɪ/ *adv* étrangement.

eeriness /'ɪərɪnɪs/ *n* atmosphère *f* angoissante.

EET *n*: *abrév* ▶**Eastern European Time**.

eff○ /ef/ *vi* **to ~ and blind** jurer comme un charretier; **~ off**○**!** vas te faire voir○!

efface /ɪ'feɪs/ *vtr* effacer also fig.

effect /ɪ'fekt/ **I** *n* **1** (net result) effet *m* **(of** de; **on** sur); **to have the ~ of doing** avoir pour effet de faire; **the ~ of advertising is to increase demand** la publicité a pour effet d'accroître la demande; **to have an ~ on sth/sb** avoir un effet sur qch/qn; **to have a damaging ~ on sth** avoir un effet néfaste sur qch; **to have little ~ on sth/sb** avoir peu d'effet sur qch/qn; **criticism doesn't seem to have any ~ on him** la critique semble n'avoir aucun effet sur lui; **the film had quite an ~ on me** ce film m'a fait forte impression; **to use sth to good ~** employer qch avec succès; **to use sth to dramatic ~** obtenir un effet spectaculaire en utilisant qch; **to feel the ~(s) of sth** sentir les effets de qch; **2** (repercussions) répercussions *fpl* **(of** de; **on** sur); **3** (power, efficacy) efficacité *f*; **the treatment loses ~ over time** le traitement cesse de faire effet avec le temps; **my advice was of no ~** mes conseils ont été sans effet; **she warned him, but to little ~** elle l'a averti, mais sans grand résultat; **we took precautions, to no ~** nous avons pris des précautions mais en vain; **to take ~** [*price increases*] prendre effet; [*law, ruling*] entrer en vigueur; [*pills, anaesthetic*] commencer à agir; **to come into ~** Jur, Admin entrer en vigueur; **to put policies into ~** appliquer des directives; **with ~ from January 1, contributions will increase by 5%** à dater du 1er janvier, les cotisations augmenteront de 5%; **4** (theme) **the ~ of what he is saying is that** il veut dire par là que; **she left a note to the ~ that** elle a laissé un mot pour dire que; **rumours to this ~** des rumeurs en ce sens; **yes, she made a remark to that ~** oui, elle a fait une remarque en ce sens; **she said 'I do not intend to resign' or words to that ~** elle a dit 'je n'ai pas l'intention de démissionner' ou quelque chose de ce genre; **5** (impression) effet *m*; **the overall ~** l'effet d'ensemble; **the lighting gives** ou **creates the ~ of moonlight** l'éclairage crée un effet de clair de lune; **to achieve an ~** obtenir un effet; **she uses her wit to deadly ~** elle a un sens de l'humour ravageur; **he paused for ~** il a fait une pause théâtrale; **she dresses like that for ~** elle s'habille comme ça pour faire de l'effet; **a beautiful marbled ~** un bel effet de marbre; **6** Sci effet *m*; **the Doppler/placebo ~** l'effet Doppler/placebo.

II effects *npl* Jur (belongings) effets *mpl*.

III in effect *adv phr* dans le fond.

IV *vtr* effectuer [*reduction, repair, sale, transformation, reform*]; apporter [*improvement*]; parvenir à [*reconciliation, settlement*].

effective /ɪ'fektɪv/ *adj* **1** [*deterrent, drug, protest, device, treatment*] efficace **(against** contre; **in doing** pour faire); **it's more ~ to replace the whole system** il est plus efficace de remplacer tout le système; **I'm only 50% ~** je ne suis efficace qu'à 50%; **2** (operational) [*legislation, regulation*] en vigueur; **to become ~** entrer en vigueur; **the new rates will be ~ from August 27** les nouveaux taux entreront en vigueur à partir du 27 août; **3** (striking, impressive) [*speech, contrast, demonstration*] percutant; **4** (actual) [*exchange rate, value, income*] Fin réel/réelle; [*control*] effectif/-ive; **they have lost ~ power** ils ont perdu le pouvoir réel.

effectively /ɪ'fektɪvlɪ/ *adv* **1** (efficiently) [*work, solve, cure, compete, communicate*] efficacement; **2** (in effect) en réalité; **3** (impressively) **the design works very ~** la conception est très réussie; **the statistics ~ demonstrate the failure of the policy** les statistiques démontrent avec force l'échec de la politique mise en œuvre.

effectiveness /ɪ'fektɪvnɪs/ *n* **1** (efficiency) efficacité *f* **(of** de); **2** (impressiveness) **the ~ of the decor/of the lecture** l'effet *m* réussi du décor/de la conférence.

effector /ɪ'fektə(r)/ *n* effecteur *m*.

effects man *n* Cin bruiteur *m*.

effectual /ɪ'fektʃʊəl/ *adj* **1** (effective) sout [*method, cure, punishment*] efficace; **2** Jur [*agreement, document*] valide.

effectually /ɪ'fektʃʊəlɪ/ *adv* efficacement.

effectuate /ɪ'fektjʊeɪt/ *vtr* mener [qch] à bien [*change, reform*]; **to ~ the policies of the Act** Jur appliquer les mesures prévues par la loi.

effeminacy /ɪ'femɪnəsɪ/ *n* caractère *m* efféminé.

effeminate /ɪ'femɪnət/ *adj* efféminé.

efferent /'efərənt/ *adj* efférent.

effervesce /ˌefə'ves/ *vi* **1** [*liquid*] être en effervescence; [*drink*] pétiller; [*gas*] se dégager par effervescence; **2** fig [*person*] être exubérant.

effervescence /ˌefə'vesns/ *n* lit effervescence *f*.

effervescent /ˌefə'vesnt/ *adj* **1** lit effervescent; **2** fig [*person, personality*] exubérant.

effete /ɪ'fi:t/ *adj* **1** pej [*person*] mou/molle; [*civilization*] déliquescent; [*philosophy*] inefficace; **2** Zool, Bot stérile.

effeteness /ɪ'fi:tnɪs/ *n* **1** péj (of person) mollesse *f*; (of civilization) déliquescence *f*; (of philosophy) inefficacité *f*; **2** Zool, Bot stérilité *f*.

efficacious /ˌefɪ'keɪʃəs/ *adj* efficace (**to do** de faire).

efficaciously /ˌefɪ'keɪʃəslɪ/ *adv* de manière efficace.

efficacy /'efɪkəsɪ/ *n* efficacité *f* (**of** de); **the drug's ~ in curing TB** l'efficacité du médicament dans le traitement de la tuberculose.

efficiency /ɪ'fɪʃnsɪ/ *n* **1** (of person, staff, method, organization) efficacité *f* (**in doing** à faire); **to improve/impair ~** améliorer/diminuer l'efficacité; **2** (of machine, engine) rendement *m*; **the (fuel) ~ of a car** le rendement d'une voiture; **to produce electricity at 50% ~** produire de l'électricité avec un rendement de 50%.

efficiency apartment *n* US studio *m* (meublé).

efficient /ɪ'fɪʃnt/ *adj* **1** [*person, employee, management*] efficace (**at doing** pour ce qui est de faire); **to make ~ use of energy** faire une utilisation rationnelle de l'énergie; **2** [*machine, engine*] économique; **to be 40% ~** avoir un rendement de 40%.

efficiently /ɪ'fɪʃntlɪ/ *adv* [*work, deal with, carry out*] de façon efficace; **the machine operates ~** la machine a un bon rendement.

effigy /'efɪdʒɪ/ *n* (all contexts) effigie *f*; **to burn an ~ of sb** brûler l'effigie de qn.

effing○ /'efɪŋ/ *adj, adv* **the ~ computer is down again** cette saleté○ d'ordinateur est encore en panne; **what ~ business is it of yours?** qu'est-ce que ça peut bien te faire○?

efflorescence /ˌeflɔː'resns/ *n* **1** Chem, Geol, Med, fig efflorescence *f*; **2** Bot floraison *f*.

efflorescent /ˌeflɔː'resnt/ *adj* Chem, Bot efflorescent.

effluence /'efluəns/ *n* émanation *f*.

effluent /'efluənt/ **I** *n* (all contexts) effluent *m*.
II *modif* [*treatment, management*] des effluents.

effluvium /ɪ'flu:vɪəm/ *n* **1** (waste) effluent *m*; **2** (offensive gas) effluves *mpl*.

effort /'efət/ *n* **1** (energy) efforts *mpl*; **all our ~** ou **~s** tous nos efforts; **to put a lot of ~ into sth/into doing** se donner beaucoup de peine or de mal pour qch/pour faire; **to put all one's ~(s) into doing** consacrer tous ses efforts pour faire; **to redouble one's ~** redoubler d'efforts; **to spare no ~** ne ménager aucun effort; **it's a waste of ~** c'est du travail pour rien; **to be worth the ~** en valoir la peine; **2** (difficulty) effort *m*; **with ~** avec difficulté; **without ~** sans effort; **it is/was an ~ to do** il est/était pénible de faire; **3** (attempt) **to make the ~** faire l'effort; **he made no ~ to apologize** il n'a fait aucun effort pour s'excuser; **his ~s at doing** ses tentatives pour faire; **her ~s on my behalf** ses efforts pour m'aider; **to make every ~** faire tout son possible; **in an ~ to do** pour essayer de faire; **joint ~** initiative *f* commune; **this painting is my latest/first ~** cette peinture est ma toute dernière/première œuvre; **not a bad ~ for a first try** pas mal pour un début; **4** (initiative) initiative *f*; **peace ~** initiative de paix; **war ~** effort de guerre; **5** fig (exercise) effort *m*; **an ~ of will/imagination** un effort de volonté/d'imagination.

effortless /'efətlɪs/ *adj* **1** (easy) aisé; **2** (innate) [*grace, skill, superiority*] naturel/-elle.

effortlessly /'efətlɪslɪ/ *adv* sans effort, sans peine.

effortlessness /'efətlɪsnɪs/ *n* **1** (ease) facilité *f*; **2** (naturalness) aisance *f*, facilité *f*.

effrontery /ɪ'frʌntərɪ/ *n* effronterie *f*.

effulgence /ɪ'fʌldʒns/ *n* littér effulgence *f*.

effusion /ɪ'fju:ʒn/ *n* **1** (flowing) (of blood) épanchement *m*; (of liquid) écoulement *m*; (of gas) fuite *f*; **2** fig (enthusiasm) débordements *mpl*; **3** (emotional outpouring) effusion *f*; (written) épanchement *m*.

effusive /ɪ'fju:sɪv/ *adj* [*person, style*] expansif/-ive; [*thanks*] très chaleureux/-euse; **to bestow ~ praise on sb** se répandre en éloges sur qn; **to give sb an ~ welcome** accueillir qn très chaleureusement.

effusively /ɪ'fju:sɪvlɪ/ *adv* [*speak*] avec effusion; [*welcome*] très chaleureusement; **to thank sb ~** prodiguer des remerciements à qn.

effusiveness /ɪ'fju:sɪvnɪs/ *n* (of welcome) chaleur *f*; (in manner) expansivité *f*; (stylistic) débordements *mpl*.

EFL I *n* (*abrév* = **English as a Foreign Language**) anglais *m* langue étrangère.
II *modif* [*teacher, course*] d'anglais langue étrangère.

eft /eft/ *n* triton *m*.

EFT *n*: *abrév* ▶ **electronic funds transfer**.

EFTA /'eftə/ *n* (*abrév* = **European Free Trade Association**) AELE *f*.

EFTPOS /'eftpɒs/ *n* (*abrév* = **electronic funds transfer at point of sale**) transfert *m* électronique de fonds.

eg (*abrév* = **exempli gratia**) par ex.

egalitarian /ɪˌgælɪ'teərɪən/ **I** *n* égalitariste *mf*.
II *adj* [*person*] égalitariste; [*principles, tradition*] égalitaire.

egalitarianism /ɪˌgælɪ'teərɪənɪzəm/ *n* égalitarisme *m*.

egest /i:'dʒest/ *vtr* évacuer.

egg /eg/ **I** *n* **1** Culin, Biol, Zool œuf *m*; **a chocolate ~** un œuf en chocolat; **2**†○(fellow) **he's a good/bad ~** c'est un brave/sale type○.
II *modif* [*sandwich*] à l'œuf; [*collector*] d'œufs; [*farm*] producteur/-trice d'œufs; [*mayonnaise, noodles, sauce*] aux œufs.
III○ *vtr* US (throw eggs at) jeter des œufs sur [*person*].
IDIOMS **to kill sth in the ~** tuer qch dans l'œuf; **to put all one's ~s in one basket** mettre tous ses œufs dans le même panier; **to have ~ on one's face**○ avoir l'air fin○; **as sure as ~s is ~s** aussi vrai que deux et deux font quatre; **to lay an ~**○ US Theat faire un four○.
■ **egg on**: **~ [sb] on** forcer qn; **to ~ sb on to do** pousser qn à faire.

egg-and-spoon race *n*: *course dans laquelle on tient un œuf dans une cuillère*.

eggbeater /'egbi:tə(r)/ *n* **1** Culin fouet *m* à œufs; **2**○ US (helicopter) hélico○ *m*, hélicoptère *m*.

egg: **~ box** *n* (*pl* **~es**) boîte *f* à œufs; **~ cream** *n* US milk-shake *m* au chocolat; **~cup** *n* coquetier *m*; **~ custard** *n* (baked) flan *m* aux œufs; **~ flip** *n* = **eggnog**; **~ foo yong** *n* US omelette *f* foo young; **~ fried rice** *n* riz *m* cantonnais; **~head**○ *n* péj grosse tête○ *f*, intellectuel/-elle *m/f*; **~nog** *n* (with milk) lait *m* de poule; (with alcohol) flip *m*; **~plant** *n* US aubergine *f*; **~s Benedict** *n* (+ *v sg*) US *œufs pochés sur un toast avec du jambon*; **~-shaped** *adj* ovoïde.

eggshell /'egʃel/ *n* coquille *f* d'œuf.

egg: **~shell blue** *n* bleu *m* pâle; **~shell china** *n* porcelaine *f* coquille d'œuf; **~shell finish** *n* peinture *f* coquille d'œuf (*inv*); **~ slicer** *n* coupe-œuf *m*; **~ timer** *n* sablier *m*; **~ whisk** *n* fouet *m* à œufs; **~ white** *n* blanc *m* d'œuf.

eggy○ /'egɪ/ *adj* GB **to be ~** être de mauvais poil○; **to get ~ with sb** se mettre en rogne contre qn○.

egg yolk *n* jaune *m* d'œuf.

eglantine /'egləntaɪn/ *n* (flower) églantine *f*; (bush) églantier *m*.

ego /'egəʊ, 'i:gəʊ, US 'i:gəʊ/ *n* **1** (self-esteem) amour-propre *m*; **it was a real ~ trip for her** ça flattait terriblement sa vanité; **to be on an ~-trip** chercher à se faire voir or mousser○; **it boosted his ~** ça lui a redonné confiance en lui-même; **to have an inflated ~** avoir une très haute opinion de soi-même; **2** Psych moi *m*, ego *m*.

egocentric /ˌegəʊ'sentrɪk, ˌi:gəʊ-, US ˌi:g-/ *adj* égocentrique.

egocentricity /ˌegəʊsən'trɪsətɪ, ˌi:gəʊ-, US ˌi:g-/ *n* égocentrisme *m*.

egoism /'egəʊɪzəm, 'i:g-, US 'i:g-/ *n* égoïsme *m*.

egoist /'egəʊɪst, 'i:g-, US 'i:g-/ *n* égoïste *mf*.

egoistic(al) /ˌegəʊ'ɪstɪk(l), ˌi:g-, US ˌi:g-/ *adj* égoïste.

egomania /ˌegəʊ'meɪnɪə, ˌi:g-, US ˌi:g-/ *n* manie *f* égocentrique.

egomaniac /ˌegəʊ'meɪnɪæk, ˌi:g-, US ˌi:g-/ **I** *n* égocentrique *mf*.
II *adj* égocentrique.

egotism /'egəʊtɪzəm, 'i:g-, US 'i:g-/ *n* égotisme *m*.

egotist /'egəʊtɪst, 'i:g-, US 'i:g-/ *n* égotiste *mf*.

egotistic(al) /ˌegəʊ'tɪstɪk, ˌi:g-, US ˌi:g-/ *adj* égotiste.

egregious /ɪ'gri:dʒɪəs/ *adj* [*error, exception*] flagrant.

egress /'i:gres/ *n* sout (action) sortie *f*; (exit point) issue *f*; **right of ~** Jur droit *m* de sortie.

egret /'i:grɪt/ *n* aigrette *f*.

Egypt /'i:dʒɪpt/ ▶ 1131 *pr n* Égypte *f*.

Egyptian /ɪ'dʒɪpʃn/ ▶ 1486, 1402 **I** *n* Égyptien/-ienne *m/f*.
II *adj* égyptien/-ienne.

Egyptologist /ˌi:dʒɪp'tɒlədʒɪst/ ▶ 1692 *n* égyptologue *mf*.

Egyptology /ˌi:dʒɪp'tɒlədʒɪ/ *n* égyptologie *f*.

eh○ /eɪ/ *excl* hein○.

EIB *n*: *abrév* ▶ **European Investment Bank**.

eider /'aɪdə(r)/ *n* eider *m*.

eiderdown /'aɪdədaʊn/ *n* **1** (quilt) édredon *m*; **2** (down) duvet *m* (de canard).

eidetic /aɪ'detɪk/ *adj* eidétique.

Eiffel Tower /'aɪfl/ *pr n* tour *f* Eiffel.

eight /eɪt/ ▶ 1505, ▶ 971, ▶ 1096 **I** *n* (number, rowing team) huit *m inv*.
II *adj* huit *inv*; **~-hour day** journée *f* de huit heures; **to work ~-hour shifts** faire les trois-huit.
IDIOMS **to have had** ou **to be one over the ~**○ avoir un verre dans le nez○.

eighteen /eɪ'ti:n/ ▶ 1505, ▶ 971 **I** *n* dix-huit *m*.
II *adj* dix-huit *inv*; **~-hole golf course** golf à dix-huit trous.

eighteenth /eɪ'ti:nθ/ ▶ 1505, 1150 **I** *n* **1** (in order) dix-huitième *mf*; **2** (of month) dix-huit *m*; **3** (fraction) dix-huitième *m*.
II *adj* dix-huitième.
III *adv* [*come, finish*] dix-huitième, en dix-huitième position.

eighth /eɪtθ/ ▶ 1505, 1150 **I** *n* **1** (in order) huitième *mf*; **2** (of month) huit *m inv*; **3** (fraction) huitième *m*; **4** Mus octave *f*.
II *adj* huitième.
III *adv* [*come, finish*] huitième, en huitième position.

eighth note *n* US Mus croche *f*.

eightieth /'eɪtɪəθ/ ▶ 1505 **I** *n* **1** (in order) quatre-vingtième *mf*; **2** (fraction) quatre-vingtième *m*.
II *adj, adv* quatre-vingtième.

eighty /'eɪtɪ/ ▶ 1505, 971 **I** *n* quatre-vingts *m*.
II *adj* quatre-vingts.

eighty-one ▶ 1505 *n, adj* quatre-vingt-un (*m*).

eighty-six ▶ 1505 **I** *n, adj* quatre-vingt-six (*m inv*).
II○ *vtr* US expédier○ [*person*].

einsteinium /aɪn'staɪnɪəm/ *n* einsteinium *m*.

Éire /ˈeərə/ ▶1131 *pr n* République *f* d'Irlande.

Eisteddfod /ˌaɪˈstedfəd, ˌaɪˈsteðvɒd/ *n*: *concours littéraire et musical gallois.*

either /ˈaɪðər, US ˈiːðər/ **I** *pron* **1** (one or other) l'un/l'une ou l'autre; **you can take ~ (of them)** tu peux prendre l'un ou l'autre; **I don't like ~ (of them)** je n'aime ni l'un ni l'autre; **I don't believe ~ of you** je ne vous crois ni l'un ni l'autre; **without ~ (of them)** sans l'un ni l'autre; **there was no sound from ~ of the rooms** aucun bruit ne provenait ni d'une chambre ni de l'autre; **~ or both of you can do it** l'un de vous peut le faire or vous pouvez le faire tous les deux; **2** (both) **~ of the two is possible** les deux sont possibles; **~ would be difficult to repair** les deux seraient aussi difficiles à réparer l'un que l'autre; **~ of us could win** nous avons tous les deux les mêmes chances de gagner; **'which book do you want?'—'~'** 'quel livre veux- tu?'—'l'un ou l'autre'.
II *det* **1** (one or the other) n'importe lequel/laquelle; **you can take ~ road** tu peux prendre n'importe laquelle des deux routes; **~ one will do** n'importe lequel fera l'affaire; (in the negative) **I can't see ~ child** je ne vois aucun des deux enfants; **2** (both) **~ one of the solutions is acceptable** les deux solutions sont acceptables; **in ~ case** dans les deux cas; **at ~ side of the street** des deux côtés de la rue; **at ~ side of the fire** de part et d'autre de la cheminée; **in ~ hand** dans chaque main; **~ way, you win** vous gagnez dans les deux cas; **~ way, it will be difficult** de toute manière, ce sera difficile; **I don't care ~ way** ça m'est égal; **I don't have strong views ~ way** je ne suis ni pour ni contre; **~ way, you can't confirm it** de toute manière, vous ne pouvez pas le confirmer.
III *adv* non plus; **I can't do it ~** je ne peux pas le faire non plus; **there's no answer to that question ~** il n'y a pas de réponse à cette question non plus; **not only was it expensive, but it didn't work ~** non seulement c'était cher, mais en plus ça ne marchait pas.
IV *conj* **1** (as alternatives) **I was expecting him ~ Tuesday or Wednesday** je l'attendais soit mardi, soit mercredi, je l'attendais (ou) mardi ou mercredi; **you ~ love him or hate him** soit on l'adore, soit on le déteste, on l'adore ou on le déteste; **~ by cheating or by lying** soit en trichant soit en mentant, (ou) en trichant ou en mentant; **it's ~ him or me** c'est lui ou moi; **available in ~ pink or blue** disponible en rose ou en bleu; **I confessed, it was ~ that or be tortured** j'ai avoué, c'était ça ou la torture; **2** (in the negative) **I wouldn't reward ~ Patrick or Emily** je ne donnerais de récompense ni à Patrick ni à Emily; **you're not being ~ truthful or fair** tu n'es ni honnête ni juste; **3** (as an ultimatum) **~ you finish your work or you will be punished!** ou tu finis ton travail ou je te punis!; **put the gun down, ~ that or I call the police** pose ton arme sinon j'appelle la police.

either-or *adj* **it's an ~ situation, you have to decide** c'est l'un ou l'autre, il faut que tu te décides.

ejaculate /ɪˈdʒækjʊleɪt/ **I** *vtr* **1** (exclaim) s'exclamer; **2** Physiol éjaculer.
II *vi* éjaculer.

ejaculation /ɪˌdʒækjʊˈleɪʃn/ *n* **1** (verbal) exclamation *f*; **2** Physiol éjaculation *f*.

ejaculatory /ɪˈdʒækjʊleɪtərɪ, US -təːrɪ/ *adj* [*function*] éjaculatoire; [*vessel, muscle*] éjaculateur/-trice.

eject /ɪˈdʒekt/ **I** *vtr* **1** (give out) [*machine, system*] rejeter [*gases, waste*] (**from** de); [*volcano*] cracher [*lava, rocks*]; **2** Audio faire sortir [*cassette*]; **3** (throw out) expulser, éjecter○ [*troublemaker, intruder, enemy*] (**from** de).
II *vi* [*pilot*] s'éjecter.

eject button *n* Audio touche *f* d'éjection.

ejection /ɪˈdʒekʃn/ *n* **1** (of gases, waste) rejet *m*; (of lava) éruption *f*; **2** (of troublemaker, enemy) expulsion *f*, éjection○ *f* (**from** de); **3** Aviat (of pilot) éjection *f*.

ejection seat *n* US Aviat siège *m* éjectable.

ejector /ɪˈdʒektə(r)/ *n* Tech éjecteur *m*.

ejector seat *n* siège *m* éjectable.

eke /iːk/ *vtr*: ■ **eke out**: **~ out sth, ~ sth out** (by saving) faire durer [*income, supplies*] (**by** à force de; **by doing** en faisant); (by supplementing) accroître un peu [*income, supplies*] (**with** par; **by doing** en faisant); **to ~ out a living** ou **an existence** essayer de joindre les deux bouts.

el /el/ *n* US (*abrév* = **elevated railroad**) métro *m* aérien.

elaborate **I** /ɪˈlæbərət/ *adj* **1** [*system, network, apparatus, plan*] complexe; [*solution, compromise, attempt, meal, ritual, game*] compliqué; **2** [*architecture, design, carving*] travaillé; [*painting, sculpture*] ouvragé; [*costume, clothes*] recherché; **3** [*joke, excuse, explanation, anecdote, question*] compliqué; [*precaution, preparation*] minutieux/-ieuse.
II /ɪˈlæbəreɪt/ *vtr* élaborer [*theory, hypothesis, scheme*]; développer [*point, statement, idea*].
III /ɪˈlæbəreɪt/ *vi* entrer dans les détails; **to ~ on** s'étendre sur [*plan, proposal*]; développer [*remark, offer, statement*].
IV elaborated *pp adj* [*theory, hypothesis, idea, view, plan, proposal*] développé.

elaborately /ɪˈlæbərətlɪ/ *adv* **1** [*carved, decorated, dressed*] de manière recherchée; **2** [*defined, described, arranged, constructed*] minutieusement.

elaborateness /ɪˈlæbərətnɪs/ *n* (complexity) complexité *f*.

elaboration /ɪˌlæbəˈreɪʃn/ *n* (of plan, theory, point etc) élaboration *f* (**of** de).

elapse /ɪˈlæps/ *vi* s'écouler; **~d time** le temps écoulé.

elastic /ɪˈlæstɪk/ *n, adj* élastique (*m*).

elasticated /ɪˈlæstɪkeɪtɪd/ *adj* [*waistband, bandage*] élastique, élastiqué.

elastic band *n* élastique *m*.

elasticity /ˌelæsˈtɪsətɪ, US ɪˌlæ-/ *n* élasticité *f*.

elate /ɪˈleɪt/ *vtr* transporter [qn] de joie.

elated /ɪˈleɪtɪd/ *adj* au comble de l'allégresse litter, transporté de joie; **I was ~ at having won** j'exultais d'avoir gagné; **she was ~ by this success** ce succès la transportait de joie.

elation /ɪˈleɪʃn/ *n* joie *f*, allégresse *f*; **to be filled with ~** être au comble de l'allégresse.

Elba /ˈelbə/ ▶1381 *pr n* île *f* d'Elbe.

elbow /ˈelbəʊ/ **I** *n* (all contexts) coude *m*; **to lean on one's ~s** être accoudé; **at sb's ~** à portée de main; **to wear sth through at the ~s** percer or trouer qch aux coudes; **there is an ~ in the pipe** le tuyau est coudé.
II *vtr* **to ~ sb in the stomach** donner un coup de coude dans l'estomac de qn; **to ~ sb aside** ou **out of the way** écarter qn du coude or d'un coup de coude.
III *vi* **to ~ through sth** jouer des coudes à travers qch; **to ~ (one's way) forward** avancer en jouant des coudes.
IDIOMS **more power to your/his etc ~** GB je te/lui souhaite bien du courage○; **to be out at (the) ~(s)** [*person*] être loqueteux; [*garment*] être miteux; **to be up to the ~s in sth** être dans qch jusqu'au cou; **to bend the** ou **an ~**○ lever le coude○; **to give sb the ~**○ se débarrasser de qn; **to rub ~s with sb**○ US fréquenter qn.

elbow: **~ grease** *n* huile *f* de coude○; **~ joint** *n* articulation *f* du coude.

elbowroom /ˈelbəʊruːm/ *n* **1** (room to move, work) espace *m* vital; **there isn't much ~ in this kitchen/office** on est un peu à l'étroit dans cette cuisine/ce bureau; **2** fig (room for manœuvre) marge *f* de manœuvre.

elder /ˈeldə(r)/ **I** *n* **1** (older person) aîné/-e *m/f*; **respect your ~s and betters** respecte tes aînés; **2** (in tribe etc) ancien *m*; **village ~** aîné or ancien du village; **party ~** Pol ancien du parti; **3** Relig (in early church) ancien *m*; **4** Relig (in Presbyterian church) ancien *m* (*qui assiste le pasteur dans l'administration d'une église*); **5** Bot sureau *m*.
II *adj* aîné; **the ~ girl** l'aînée *f*, la fille aînée *f*.

elder: **~berry** *n* baie *f* de sureau; **~berry wine** *n* vin *m* de sureau; **~flower** *n* fleur *f* de sureau.

elderly /ˈeldəlɪ/ **I** *n* **the ~** (+ *v pl*) les personnes *fpl* âgées; **care of the ~** soins *mpl* aux personnes âgées.
II *adj* **1** [*person, population*] âgé; **her ~ father** son vieux père; **an ~ couple** un couple de personnes âgées; **2** [*vehicle, machinery, aircraft*] vieux/vieille (*before n*).

elder statesman *n* (*pl* **-men**) (all contexts) doyen *m*.

eldest /ˈeldɪst/ **I** *n* aîné/-e *m/f*; **my ~** mon aîné/-e.
II *adj* aîné; **the ~ child** l'aîné/-e; **I'm the ~ girl** je suis l'aînée des filles.

elect /ɪˈlekt/ **I** *n* **the ~** (+ *v pl*) les élus.
II *vtr* **1** (by vote) élire [*representative, president etc*] (**from, from among** au sein de); **to be ~ed to a post/an assembly** être élu à un poste/à une assemblée; **to ~ sb (as) president** élire qn président; **2** (choose) choisir [*method, system etc*]; **to ~ to do** choisir de faire; **to be ~ed a member/as leader** être élu membre/chef.
III elected *pp adj* [*authority, government, officer, representative*] élu; **~ office** fonction *f* élective.
IV *adj* (*after n*) futur (*before n*) **the president ~** le président élu n'ayant pas encore pris ses fonctions.

electable /ɪˈlektəbl/ *adj* [*party*] en position de gagner les élections; **to make sb more ~** améliorer la popularité de qn.

election /ɪˈlekʃn/ **I** *n* **1** (ballot) élection *f*, scrutin *m*; **in** ou **at the ~** aux élections; **to win/lose an ~** gagner/perdre aux élections; **2** (appointment) élection *f* (**to** à); **to stand for ~** se porter candidat aux élections.
II *modif* [*agent, campaign, manifesto, fever*] électoral; [*day, results*] du scrutin.

electioneering /ɪˌlekʃəˈnɪərɪŋ/ *n* (campaigning) campagne *f* électorale; pej électoralisme *m*.

elective /ɪˈlektɪv/ **I** *n* US Sch, Univ cours *m* facultatif.
II *adj* **1** (elected) [*office, official, committee*] électif/-ive, élu; (empowered to elect) [*assembly, body*] électoral; **2** Sch, Univ [*course, subject*] facultatif/-ive.

elector /ɪˈlektə(r)/ *n* **1** (voter) électeur/-trice *m/f*; **2** US Pol membre *m* du collège électoral.

electoral /ɪˈlektərəl/ *adj* électoral.

electoral: **~ boundary** *n* limite *f* de circonscription électorale; **~ college** *n* collège *m* électoral; **~ district** *n* circonscription *f* électorale.

electorally /ɪˈlektərəlɪ/ *adv* [*necessary, damaging*] sur le plan électoral.

electoral: **~ register**, **~ roll** *n* listes *fpl* électorales; **~ vote** *n* US vote *m* des grands électeurs.

electorate /ɪˈlektərət/ *n* électorat *m*, électeurs *mpl*.

Electra /ɪˈlektrə/ *pr n* Électre.

Electra complex *n* complexe *m* d'Électre.

electric /ɪˈlektrɪk/ **I**○ **electrics** *npl* GB Aut circuits *mpl* électriques (d'une voiture).
II *adj* électrique also fig.

electrical /ɪˈlektrɪkl/ *adj* électrique.

electrical: **~ engineer** ▶1692 *n* ingénieur *m* électricien, électrotechnicien *m*; **~ engineering** *n* électrotechnique *f*.

electrically /ɪˈlektrɪklɪ/ *adv* électriquement.

electric blanket *n* couverture *f* chauffante.
electric blue ▶1104 *n, adj* bleu (*m*) électrique *inv*.
electric: **~ chair** *n* chaise *f* électrique; **~ eel** *n* anguille *f* électrique; **~ field** *n* champ *m* électrique.
electrician /ˌɪlekˈtrɪʃn/ ▶1692 *n* électricien/-ienne *m/f*.
electricity /ˌɪlekˈtrɪsətɪ/ **I** *n* lit, fig électricité *f*; **to turn off/on the ~** couper/rétablir le courant (électrique).
II *modif* [*generator, cable*] électrique; [*bill, charges*] d'électricité.
electricity: **~ board** *n* GB compagnie *f* d'électricité; **~ supply** *n* alimentation *f* en électricité.
electric shock *n* décharge *f* électrique; **to get an ~** prendre le courant.
electric storm *n* orage *m*.
electrification /ɪˌlektrɪfɪˈkeɪʃn/ *n* **1** (of railway, region etc) électrification *f*; **2** Phys électrisation *f*.
electrify /ɪˈlektrɪfaɪ/ *vtr* **1** gen électrifier [*railway, region*]; **2** Phys électriser; **3** fig électriser, galvaniser [*audience*].
electrifying /ɪˈlektrɪfaɪɪŋ/ *adj* [*speech*] électrisant.
electroanalysis /ɪˈlektrəʊəˈnæləsɪs/ *n* électroanalyse *f*.
electrocardiogram, **ECG** /ɪˌlektrəʊˈkɑːdɪəgræm/ *n* électrocardiogramme *m*.
electrocardiograph, **ECG** /ɪˌlektrəʊˈkɑːdɪəgrɑːf, US -græf/ *n* électrocardiographe *m*.
electrochemical /ɪˌlektrəʊˈkemɪkl/ *adj* électrochimique.
electrochromatography /ɪˌlektrəʊˌkrəʊməˈtɒgrəfɪ/ *n* électrochromatographie *f*.
electroconvulsive therapy, **ECT** /ɪˌlektrəʊkənˌvʌlsɪv ˈθerəpɪ/ *n* électroconvulsivothérapie *f*, électrochocs *mpl*; **he had ~** on lui a fait des électrochocs.
electrocute /ɪˈlektrəkjuːt/ **I** *vtr* électrocuter; **to be ~d** (accidentally) s'électrocuter; (in electric chair) être électrocuté, passer sur la chaise électrique.
II *v refl* **to ~ oneself** s'électrocuter.
electrocution /ɪˌlektrəˈkjuːʃn/ *n* électrocution *f*.
electrode /ɪˈlektrəʊd/ *n* électrode *f*.
electrodialysis /ɪˌlektrəʊdaɪˈæləsɪs/ *n* électrodialyse *f*.
electrodynamics /ɪˌlektrəʊdaɪˈnæmɪks/ *n* (+ *v sg*) électrodynamique *f*.
electroencephalogram /ɪˌlektrəʊɪnˈsefələgræm/ *n* électroencéphalogramme *m*.
electroencephalograph /ɪˌlektrəʊɪnˈsefələgrɑːf, US -græf/ *n* électroencéphalographie *f*.
electrolyse /ɪˈlektrəlaɪz/ *vtr* électrolyser.
electrolysis /ˌɪlekˈtrɒləsɪs/ *n* **1** Chem électrolyse *f*; **2** (hair removal) épilation *f* électrique.
electrolyte /ɪˈlektrəlaɪt/ *n* électrolyte *m*.
electrolyze *vtr* US = **electrolyse**.
electromagnet /ɪˌlektrəʊˈmægnɪt/ *n* électroaimant *m*.
electromagnetic /ɪˌlektrəʊmægˈnetɪk/ *adj* électromagnétique.
electromagnetism /ɪˌlektrəʊˈmægnɪtɪzəm/ *n* électromagnétisme *m*.
electromechanical /ɪˌlektrəʊmɪˈkænɪkl/ *adj* électromécanique.
electrometer /ˌɪlekˈtrɒmɪtə(r)/ *n* électromètre *m*.
electromotive force /ɪˌlektrəʊˌməʊtɪv ˈfɔːs/ *adj* force *f* électromotrice.
electron /ɪˈlektrɒn/ *n* électron *m*.
electronegative /ɪˌlektrəʊˈnegətɪv/ *adj* électronégatif/-ive.
electron gun *n* canon *m* à électrons.
electronic /ˌɪlekˈtrɒnɪk/ *adj* (all contexts) électronique.
electronically /ˌɪlekˈtrɒnɪklɪ/ *adv* électroniquement.
electronic: **~ directory** *n* annuaire *m* électronique; **~ engineer** ▶1692 *n* électronicien/-ienne *m/f*; **~ engineering** *n* électronique *f*; **~ eye** *n* cellule *f* photoélectrique; **~ funds transfer**, **EFT** *n* transfert *m* électronique de fonds; **~ funds transfer system** *n* système *m* de transfert électronique de fonds; **~ mail**, **E-mail** *n* messagerie *f* électronique; **~ mail system** *n* télématique *f*; **~ media** *npl* moyens *mpl* électroniques de diffusion de l'information; **~ news gathering** *n* journalisme *m* électronique; **~ office** *n* bureau *m* équipé de moyens informatiques; **~ pointer** *n* = **electronic stylus**; **~ publishing** *n* éditique *f*.
electronics /ˌɪlekˈtrɒnɪks/ *n* (+ *v sg*) électronique *f*.
electronic: **~ stylus** *n* photostyle *m*; **~ surveillance** *n* surveillance *f* électronique.
electron: **~ microscope** *n* microscope *m* électronique; **~ volt** *n* électronvolt *m*.
electrophysiology /ɪˌlektrəʊˌfɪsɪˈɒlədʒɪ/ *n* électrophysiologie *f*.
electroplate /ɪˈlektrəpleɪt/ *vtr* recouvrir [qch] d'une couche de métal par galvanoplastie.
electroplating /ɪˌlektrəˈpleɪtɪŋ/ *n* **1** (technique, process) galvanoplastie *f*; **2** (coating) couche *f* galvanoplastique.
electropositive /ɪˌlektrəʊˈpɒsɪtɪv/ *adj* électropositif/-ive.
electroshock therapy, **electroshock treatment**, **EST** /ɪˌlektrəʊˈʃɒk/ *n* électroconvulsivothérapie *f*, électrochocs *mpl*; **he had ~** on lui a fait des électrochocs.
electrostatics /ɪˌlektrəʊˈstætɪks/ *n* (+ *v sg*) électrostatique *f*.
electrosurgery /ɪˌlektrəʊˈsɜːdʒərɪ/ *n* électrochirurgie *f*.
electrotechnology /ɪˌlektrəʊtekˈnɒlədʒɪ/ *n* électrotechnique *f*.
electrotherapist /ɪˌlektrəʊˈθerəpɪst/ ▶1692 *n* électrothérapeute *mf*.
electrotherapy /ɪˌlektrəʊˈθerəpɪ/ *n* électrothérapie *f*.
electrotype /ɪˈlektrəʊtaɪp/ **I** *n* galvanotype *m*.
II *vtr* clicher [qch] par galvanotypie.
electrovalency /ɪˌlektrəʊˈveɪlənsɪ/ *n* électrovalence *f*.
electrovalent /ɪˌlektrəʊˈveɪlənt/ *adj* [*bond*] électrovalent.
electrum /ɪˈlektrəm/ *n* électrum *m*.
elegance /ˈelɪgəns/ *n* élégance *f*.
elegant /ˈelɪgənt/ *adj* **1** (refined, graceful) [*person, gesture*] élégant; [*manners*] distingué; [*clothes*] élégant, chic (*inv*); [*restaurant*] chic (*inv*); **2** (neat) [*solution, proof*] élégant; [*novel, essay*] plein d'élégance.
elegantly /ˈelɪgəntlɪ/ *adv* [*dress, write*] avec élégance; [*dressed, furnished*] élégamment.
elegiac /ˌelɪˈdʒaɪək/ *adj* [*lament, couplet*] élégiaque.
elegy /ˈelədʒɪ/ *n* élégie *f* (**for** à).
element /ˈelɪmənt/ *n* **1** (constituent) élément *m*; **a key/important ~ in her philosophy** un élément essentiel/important de sa philosophie; **the key ~ in his success** l'élément clé de son succès; **the poor salary was just one ~ in my dissatisfaction** le salaire médiocre n'expliquait que partiellement mon mécontentement; **2** (factor) facteur *m*; **the time ~** le facteur temps; **the ~ of luck** le facteur chance; **3** (small part) part *f*; **an ~ of risk/danger** une part de risque/danger; **4** (rudiment) (of courtesy, diplomacy) élément *m*, rudiment *m*; (of grammar, mathematics etc) base *f*; **5** (constituent group) élément *m*; **the violent ~ in the audience** l'élément violent du public; **6** (air, water etc) élément *m*; **the four ~s** les quatre éléments; **the ~s** (weather) les éléments; **to brave the ~s** hum affronter les éléments; **exposed to the ~s** exposé aux intempéries; **7** Chem, Math, Radio élément *m*; **8** Elec résistance *f*.
IDIOMS **to be in/out of one's ~** être/ne pas être dans son élément.
elemental /ˌelɪˈmentl/ *adj* (all contexts) élémentaire.
elementary /ˌelɪˈmentrɪ/ *adj* **1** gen, Sci (basic, simple, fundamental) élémentaire; **2** GB Hist, US Sch [*school*] primaire; [*teacher*] de primaire.
elephant /ˈelɪfənt/ *n* éléphant *m*; **baby ~** éléphanteau *m*.
IDIOMS **to have a memory like an ~** avoir une mémoire d'éléphant; **to see pink ~s** voir des éléphants roses, avoir des hallucinations.
elephantiasis /ˌelɪfənˈtaɪəsɪs/ ▶1354 *n* éléphantiasis *m*.
elephantine /ˌelɪˈfæntaɪn/ *adj* **1** fig [*joke, humour*] lourd; [*person*] éléphantesque; **2** Zool éléphantin.
elephant seal *n* éléphant *m* de mer.
elevate /ˈelɪveɪt/ *vtr* **1** (in rank, status) élever [*person, principle, quality*] (**to** au rang de); **to ~ sth to (the status of) a religion** élever qch au rang d'une religion; **to ~ sb to the status of a star** élever qn au rang de vedette; **to ~ sb to the peerage** élever qn à la pairie; **2** (uplift) élever [*mind, soul*].
elevated /ˈelɪveɪtɪd/ *adj* **1** [*tone, language, rank*] élevé; **2** [*site*] élevé; [*railway, canal*] surélevé.
elevated: **~ highway** *n* US autoroute *f* surélevée; **~ railroad** *n* US métro *m* aérien.
elevation /ˌelɪˈveɪʃn/ *n* **1** (in rank, status) élévation *f* (**to** au rang de); **2** Archit élévation *f*; **side/front ~** élévation latérale/de la façade; **3** (height) altitude *f*; **at an ~ of 200 metres** à 200 mètres d'altitude; **angle of ~** angle *m* d'élévation; **4** (of gun) élévation *f*; **5** (also **Elevation**) Relig Élévation *f*; **6** (hill) hauteur *f*, éminence *f*.
elevator /ˈelɪveɪtə(r)/ *n* **1** US (in building) ascenseur *m*; **2** (hoist) élévateur *m*; **3** US (for grain) silo *m* à grain; **4** (of aircraft) gouvernail *m* de profondeur.
elevator operator *n* US liftier/-ière *m/f*.
eleven /ɪˈlevn/ ▶1505, ▶1037, ▶1096 **I** *n* **1** onze *m*; **2** Sport **the football ~** le onze; **a football ~** une équipe de football; **the first/second ~** la première /seconde équipe; **to play for the first ~** jouer en première équipe; **a cricket ~** une équipe de cricket; GB Sch **~ plus** ≈ examen *m* à la fin du primaire.
II *adj* onze *inv*.
elevenses○ /ɪˈlevnzɪz/ *n* GB pause-café *f* (*dans la matinée*).
eleventh /ɪˈlevnθ/ ▶1505, 1150 **I** *n* **1** (in order) onzième *mf*; **2** (of month) onze *m inv*; **3** (fraction) onzième *m*; **4** Mus onzième *f*.
II *adj* onzième.
III *adv* [*come, finish*] onzième, en onzième position.
eleventh hour **I** *n* **at the ~** à la toute dernière minute.
II **eleventh-hour** *modif* [*intervention, decision*] de dernière minute.
elf /elf/ *n* (*pl* **elves**) lit, fig lutin *m*.
elfin /ˈelfɪn/ *adj* [*charm, magic, features*] de lutin.
elicit /ɪˈlɪsɪt/ *vtr* obtenir [*judgment, opinion*] (**from** de); provoquer [*reaction, response*] (**from** de); tirer [*explanation*] (**from** de).
elide /ɪˈlaɪd/ *vtr* Ling élider.
eligibility /ˌelɪdʒəˈbɪlətɪ/ *n* (to sit exam, for pension, benefit, award) droit *m* (**for** à; **to do** de faire); **this may affect your ~** ceci pourrait modifier vos droits; **to determine sb's ~ for** décider si qn a droit à.
eligible /ˈelɪdʒəbl/ *adj* **1** (qualifying) **to be ~ for** avoir droit à [*allowance, benefit, membership*]; **to be ~ for appointment** remplir les conditions pour être nommé; **to be ~**

to do être en droit de faire; **the ~ candidates/students** les candidats/étudiants qui remplissent les conditions requises; **the 4 million ~ voters** les 4 millions de personnes en droit de voter; **2**†(marriageable) **an ~ bachelor** un beau or bon parti.

Elijah /ɪˈlaɪdʒə/ *pr n* Élie.

eliminate /ɪˈlɪmɪneɪt/ *vtr* **1** (omit from consideration) éliminer [*candidate, team*]; éliminer, exclure [*hypothesis, possibility*]; écarter [*suspect*]; **2** (eradicate) éliminer [*costs, fat, disease*]; **3** (kill) éliminer, supprimer [*person*]; **4** Math, Physiol éliminer.

elimination /ɪˌlɪmɪˈneɪʃn/ *n* élimination *f*; **by a process of ~** en procédant par élimination.

Elisha /ɪˈlaɪʃə/ *pr n* Élisée.

elision /ɪˈlɪʒn/ *n* Ling élision *f*.

élite /eɪˈliːt/ **I** *n* **1** (group) (+ *v sg ou pl*) élite *f*; **2** Print caractère *m* élite.

II *adj* [*group, minority*] élitaire; [*restaurant, club*] réservé à l'élite; [*troop, team, squad*] d'élite.

élitism /eɪˈliːtɪzəm/ *n* élitisme *m*.

élitist /eɪˈliːtɪst/ *n, adj* élitiste (*mf*).

elixir /ɪˈlɪksɪə(r)/ *n* élixir *m*; **the ~ of life** l'élixir de longue vie.

elk /elk/ *n* **1** (European, Asian) élan *m*; **2** US (wapiti) wapiti *m*.

ellipse /ɪˈlɪps/ *n* Math, Ling ellipse *f*.

ellipsis /ɪˈlɪpsɪs/ *n* (*pl* **-ses**) **1** Ling ellipse *f*; **2** Print points *mpl* de suspension.

ellipsoid /ɪˈlɪpsɔɪd/ *n, adj* ellipsoïde (*m*).

elliptic(al) /ɪˈlɪptɪk(l)/ *adj* (all contexts) elliptique.

elm /elm/ *n* (tree, wood) orme *m*.

elocution /ˌeləˈkjuːʃn/ *n* élocution *f*, diction *f*.

elongate /ˈiːlɒŋgeɪt, US ɪˈlɔːŋ-/ **I** *vtr* (lengthen) allonger; (stretch) étirer.

II *vi* s'allonger.

elongated /ˈiːlɒŋgeɪtɪd, US ɪˈlɔːŋ-/ *adj* allongé; **to become ~** s'allonger.

elongation /ˌiːlɒŋˈgeɪʃən/ *n* gen, Astron élongation *f*.

elope /ɪˈləʊp/ *vi* [*couple*] s'enfuir ensemble; [*man, woman*] s'enfuir (**with** avec).

elopement /ɪˈləʊpmənt/ *n* fugue *f* amoureuse.

eloquence /ˈeləkwəns/ *n* éloquence *f*.

eloquent /ˈeləkwənt/ *adj* [*orator, speech, praise, gesture*] éloquent; **her silence was ~** son silence en disait long.

eloquently /ˈeləkwəntlɪ/ *adv* [*speak, argue, express*] éloquemment, avec éloquence.

El Salvador /ˌel ˈsælvədɔː(r)/ **▶ 1131** *pr n* Salvador *m*; **in ~** au Salvador.

else /els/ **I** *adv* d'autre; **somebody ~** quelqu'un d'autre; **nobody/nothing ~** personne/rien d'autre; **something ~** autre chose; **somewhere** ou **someplace** US **~** ailleurs, autre part; **where ~ can it be?** où est-ce que ça peut être d'autre?; **who ~ is coming?** qui d'autre vient?; **who ~'s can we borrow?** celui de qui d'autre pouvons-nous emprunter?; **how ~ can we do it/explain it?** comment le faire/l'expliquer autrement?; **what ~ would you like?** qu'est-ce que tu voudrais d'autre?; **there's little** ou **not much ~ to do/say** il n'y a pas grand-chose d'autre à faire/dire; **he talks of little ~** il ne parle presque que de ça; **everyone ~ but me went to the football match** tout le monde est allé voir le match de football sauf moi; **was anyone ~ there?** y avait-il quelqu'un d'autre?; **anyone ~ would go to bed early, but you**... à ta place n'importe qui irait se coucher tôt, mais toi, tu...; **if it were** ou **was anybody ~ but him I'd help** si c'était n'importe qui d'autre je l'aiderais; **anywhere ~ it wouldn't matter** en tout autre lieu ça n'aurait aucune importance; **he didn't see anybody ~** il n'a vu personne d'autre; **she didn't say anything ~** elle n'a rien dit d'autre; **nothing ~ but a change of government can save the economy** seul un changement de gouvernement peut sauver l'économie; **if nothing ~ he's polite** à défaut d'autre chose il est poli; **whatever ~ he might be he's not a liar** il a peut-être d'autres défauts, mais en tout cas il n'est pas menteur; **she's something ~**○! (very nice) elle est géniale!; (unusual) elle est spéciale!; **'is that you, David?'—'who ~?'** 'c'est toi, David?'—'à ton avis!'; **'so what ~ is new?'** iron 'comme si on ne le savait pas!'

II or else *conj phr* sinon, ou; **eat this or ~ you'll be hungry later** mange ça ou or sinon tu vas avoir faim plus tard; **either he's already left or ~ he can't hear the phone** soit il est déjà sorti, soit il n'entend pas le téléphone, ou bien il est déjà sorti, ou bien il n'entend pas le téléphone; **stop that now, or ~**...○! arrête tout de suite, sinon...

elsewhere /ˌelsˈweə(r), US ˌelsˈhweər/ *adv* ailleurs, autre part; **from ~** venu/-e d'ailleurs.

ELT *n*: *abrév* **▶ English Language Teaching**.

elucidate /ɪˈluːsɪdeɪt/ **I** *vtr* élucider [*mystery, problem*]; expliquer [*text, concept*].

II *vi* expliquer.

elucidation /ɪˌluːsɪˈdeɪʃn/ *n* explication *f*.

elude /ɪˈluːd/ *vtr* **1** (escape) échapper à [*pursuer, observer, attention*]; se dérober à [*police*]; esquiver [*blow*]; **2** (be beyond the reach of) échapper à [*person, understanding, definition*]; **her name ~s me** son nom m'échappe.

elusive /ɪˈluːsɪv/ *adj* [*person, animal, happiness, concept*] insaisissable; [*prize, victory*] hors d'atteinte; [*scent, memory, dream*] évanescent liter, fugace.

elusively /ɪˈluːsɪvlɪ/ *adv* de façon élusive.

elusiveness /ɪˈluːsɪvnɪs/ *n* (of person, victory, concept) nature *f* insaisissable; (of dream, scent, memory) fugacité *f*, nature *f* fugace.

elver /ˈelvə(r)/ *n* civelle *f*.

elves /elvz/ *pl* **▶ elf.**

Elysian /ɪˈlɪzɪən/ *adj* Mythol élyséen/-éenne; **the ~ fields** les champs *mpl* Élysées.

Elysium /ɪˈlɪzɪəm/ *pr n* Mythol Élysée *m*.

elytron /ˈelɪtrɒn/ *n* (*pl* **-tra**) élytre *m*.

em /em/ *n* Print **1** (piece of type) cadratin *m*; **2** (pica) cicéro *m*.

'em○ /əm/ = **them**.

emaciated /ɪˈmeɪʃɪeɪtɪd/ *adj* [*person, face, feature*] émacié; [*limb, body*] décharné; [*animal*] étique; **to become ~** [*person, face*] s'émacier; [*limbs, body*] se décharner.

emaciation /ɪˌmeɪsɪˈeɪʃn/ *n* émaciation *f*, amaigrissement *m*.

email *n* = **E-mail**.

E-mail /ˈiːmeɪl/ *n* (*abrév* = **electronic mail**) courrier *m* or messagerie *f* électronique.

emanate /ˈeməneɪt/ **I** *vtr* émettre, dégager [*radiation*]; rayonner de [*serenity*].

II *vi* [*light, gas, heat*] émaner (**from** de); [*order, report, rumour, tradition*] émaner, provenir (**from** de).

emanation /ˌeməˈneɪʃn/ *n* (all contexts) émanation *f*.

emancipate /ɪˈmænsɪpeɪt/ *vtr* émanciper, affranchir [*slave, serf*]; émanciper [*women*]; **to become ~d** [*woman*] s'émanciper.

emancipated /ɪˈmænsɪpeɪtɪd/ *adj* [*woman*] émancipé.

emancipation /ɪˌmænsɪˈpeɪʃn/ *n* (of slaves, serfs) émancipation *f*, affranchissement *m*; (of women) émancipation *f*.

emasculate /ɪˈmæskjʊleɪt/ *vtr* lit, fig émasculer.

emasculation /ɪˌmæskjʊˈleɪʃn/ *n* lit, fig émasculation *f*.

embalm /ɪmˈbɑːm, US -bɑːlm/ *vtr* lit, fig embaumer.

embalmer /ɪmˈbɑːmə(r)/ **▶ 1692** *n* embaumeur/-euse *m/f*.

embalming /ɪmˈbɑːmɪŋ/ *n* embaumement *m*.

embankment /ɪmˈbæŋkmənt/ *n* **1** (to carry railway, road) talus *m*, remblai *m*; **2** (to hold back water) quai *m*, digue *f*.

embargo /ɪmˈbɑːgəʊ/ **I** *n* Pol, Econ embargo *m* (**on** sur; **against** contre); **trade/oil ~** embargo *m* commercial/pétrolier; **arms ~** embargo *m* sur les livraisons d'armes; **to impose an ~ on sb/on sth** instaurer un embargo contre qn/sur qch; **to lift an ~** lever un embargo.

II *vtr* instaurer un embargo sur [*trade*].

embark /ɪmˈbɑːk/ **I** *vtr* Naut embarquer.

II *vi* **1** Naut (board) s'embarquer (**for** pour); **2 to ~ on** entreprendre [*journey, tour, visit*]; se lancer dans [*campaign, career, reform, relationship, process, project*]; pej s'embarquer sur [*dubious path*]; s'embarquer dans [*dubious process*].

embarkation /ˌembɑːˈkeɪʃn/ *n* (of passengers, goods, vehicles) embarquement *m*.

embarrass /ɪmˈbærəs/ *vtr* gêner, embarrasser, plonger [qn] dans l'embarras [*person, government, celebrity*]; **to be/feel ~ed** être/se sentir gêné; **to be ~ed by** ou **about** être embarrassé or gêné par [*situation, remark, joke, compliment*]; avoir honte de [*person, spouse, ignorance*]; **to be ~ed about doing** trouver gênant de faire; **I feel ~ed about doing** ça me gêne de faire; **to be financially ~ed** avoir des embarras d'argent, être gêné euph.

embarrassing /ɪmˈbærəsɪŋ/ *adj* [*situation, experience, question*] embarrassant; [*person*] gênant; [*performance, attempt*] gênant, embarrassant; **to put sb in an ~ position** mettre qn dans l'embarras; **how ~!** comme c'est gênant!

embarrassingly /ɪmˈbærəsɪŋlɪ/ *adv* [*behave*] de façon gênante; **~ frank** d'une franchise embarrassante; **it was ~ obvious** c'était tellement évident que cela en était gênant; **most ~**... chose on ne peut plus embarrassante...

embarrassment /ɪmˈbærəsmənt/ *n* **1** (feeling) embarras *m*, confusion *f*, gêne *f* (**about, at** devant); **to cause sb ~** mettre qn dans l'embarras; **to my ~** à ma grande confusion or mon grand embarras; **she left the room in ~** confuse, elle a quitté la pièce; **2** (person, action, event etc) **to be an ~ to sb** [*person*] faire honte à qn; **his past is an ~ to him** il a honte de son passé; **3** (superfluity) sout embarras *m*; **an ~ of riches** l'embarras du choix.

embassy /ˈembəsɪ/ *n* ambassade *f*; **the Italian ~** l'ambassade d'Italie.

embattled /ɪmˈbætld/ *adj* **1** fig [*person*] harcelé; [*government, organization*] assailli; **2** Mil [*city, country*] assiégé; [*army, forces*] encerclé.

embed /ɪmˈbed/ *vtr* (*p prés etc* **-dd-**) **1** lit (fix) **to be ~ded in** [*thorn, splinter, nail, screw*] être enfoncé dans [*paw, flesh, wood, wall*]; [*plant*] être ancré dans [*soil*]; [*plaque*] être encastré dans [*floor, paving*]; [*rock*] être enfoncé dans [*mud, lawn*]; **to be ~ded in sb's eye** s'être logé dans l'œil de qn; **2** fig [*notion, belief, value*] **to be ~ded in** être ancré dans [*language, thinking, memory*]; **3** Ling enchâsser [*clause*] (**in** dans); **4** Comput incorporer (**in** dans).

embedding /ɪmˈbedɪŋ/ *n* Ling enchâssement *m*.

embellish /ɪmˈbelɪʃ/ *vtr* **1** (exaggerate) enjoliver, embellir [*account, description, story*]; embellir [*truth*]; **2** (decorate) enjoliver [*garment, manuscript*]; orner, embellir [*building, architecture*].

embellishment /ɪmˈbelɪʃmənt/ *n* **1** (of story) enjolivement *m*; **2** (ornament) ornement *m*.

ember /ˈembə(r)/ *n* morceau *m* de braise; **the ~s** les braises *fpl*.

embezzle /ɪmˈbezl/ *vtr* détourner [*funds*] (**from** de).

embezzlement /ɪm'bezlmənt/ *n* détournement *m* de fonds.

embezzler /ɪm'bezlə(r)/ *n* escroc *m*.

embitter /ɪm'bɪtə(r)/ *vtr* aigrir, remplir [qn] d'amertume [*person*].

embittered /ɪm'bɪtəd/ *adj* [*person*] aigri; **to become ~** s'aigrir.

emblazon /ɪm'bleɪzn/ *vtr* **1** (decorate) décorer [*shirt, flag*] (**with** de); **to be ~ed with a crest** porter un blason; **to be ~ed across** [*logo, name*] s'étaler sur [*garment, newspapers*]; **2** Herald blasonner.

emblem /'embləm/ *n* emblème *m*.

emblematic /ˌemblə'mætɪk/ *adj* emblématique (**of** de).

embodiment /ɪm'bɒdɪmənt/ *n* (incarnation of quality, idea) incarnation *f*.

embody /ɪm'bɒdɪ/ *vtr* **1** (incarnate) [*person, institution*] incarner, être l'incarnation de [*virtue, evil, ideal*]; **to be embodied in** s'incarner dans; **2** [*work, chapter*] donner corps à [*theory, philosophy*]; **3** (legally incorporate) incorporer [*rights, proposals, statutes*] (**in** dans).

embolden /ɪm'bəʊldən/ **I** *vtr* enhardir; **to ~ sb to do** donner à qn le courage de faire.
II emboldened *pp adj* enhardi.

embolism /'embəlɪzəm/ *n* Med embolie *f*.

emboss /ɪm'bɒs/ *vtr* gaufrer [*fabric, paper*]; estamper [*leather*]; repousser, travailler [qch] en relief [*metal*].

embossed /ɪm'bɒst/ *adj* [*fabric, paper*] gaufré; [*leather*] estampé; [*metal*] repoussé; **~ lettering** caractères *mpl* en relief.

embouchure /'ɒmbʊʃʊə(r)/ *n* Mus embouchure *f*.

embrace /ɪm'breɪs/ **I** *n* **1** lit (affectionate) étreinte *f*; **to hold sb in a warm/fond ~** étreindre qn chaleureusement/affectueusement; **2** fig (of ideology etc) soutien *m*.
II *vtr* **1** lit (hug) embrasser, étreindre; **2** fig (espouse, adopt) embrasser [*religion, ideology*]; épouser [*cause*]; s'engager dans [*policy*]; adopter [*principle, technology, method*]; **to ~ the challenge of Europe** relever le défi de l'Europe; **3** fig (include) comprendre [*subject areas*]; englober [*cultures, opinions, beliefs*].
III *vi* s'embrasser, s'étreindre.

embrasure /ɪm'breɪʒə(r)/ *n* embrasure *f*.

embrocation /ˌembrəʊ'keɪʃn/ *n* embrocation *f*.

embroider /ɪm'brɔɪdə(r)/ **I** *vtr* **1** lit broder (**with** de); **2** fig enjoliver, embellir [*story*]; broder sur [*fact*]; embellir [*truth*].
II *vi* broder, faire de la broderie.

embroidered /ɪm'brɔɪdəd/ *adj* brodé.

embroidery /ɪm'brɔɪdərɪ/ **I** *n* broderie *f*.
II *modif* [*frame, silk, thread*] à broder.

embroil /ɪm'brɔɪl/ *vtr* entraîner (**in** dans); **to become ~ed in** se laisser entraîner dans [*dispute, controversy*].

embryo /'embrɪəʊ/ **I** *n* Biol, fig embryon *m*; **in ~** à l'état embryonnaire.
II *adj* = **embryonic**.

embryological /ˌembrɪə'lɒdʒɪkl/ *adj* embryologique.

embryologist /ˌembrɪ'ɒlədʒɪst/ **▶ 1692** *n* embryologiste *mf*.

embryology /ˌembrɪ'ɒlədʒɪ/ *n* embryologie *f*.

embryonic /ˌembrɪ'ɒnɪk/ *adj* **1** Biol embryonnaire; **2** fig embryonnaire, en germe.

emcee /ˌem'siː/ US **I** *n* animateur/-trice *m/f*.
II *vtr* animer.

emend /ɪ'mend/ *vtr* corriger.

emendation /ˌiːmen'deɪʃn/ *n* correction *f*.

emerald /'emərəld/ **I** *n* **1** (stone) émeraude *f*; **2 ▶ 1104** (colour) émeraude *m*.
II *adj* **1** [*ring, necklace*] d'émeraudes; **2** (colour) émeraude *inv*.

emerald: **~ green ▶ 1104** *n, adj* vert (*m*) émeraude *inv*; **Emerald Isle** *n* île *f* d'Émeraude, Irlande *f*.

emerge /ɪ'mɜːdʒ/ **I** *vi* **1** lit [*person, animal*] sortir (**from** de); **2** fig [*issue, news, problem, result*] se faire jour; [*trend, pattern*] se dégager; [*design, model, truth, doubt, surprise*] apparaître; [*talent*] voir le jour; [*evidence, message*] ressortir; [*new nation, ideology, religion*] naître; **a picture is beginning to ~** (of situation) on commence à avoir une vision plus claire de la situation; **to ~ as an influence/priority** ressortir comme une influence/une priorité; **to ~ from the education system** sortir du système d'éducation; **to ~ victorious** ressortir vainqueur; **it ~ed that** il est apparu que.
II emerging *pres p adj* [*market*] naissant; [*democracy*] qui émerge; [*opportunity*] qui apparaît ; [*writer, actor etc*] qui devient connu.

emergence /ɪ'mɜːdʒəns/ *n* (of truth, ideas, problem) apparition *f*; (of religion, movement, literary genre) apparition *f*, naissance *f*.

emergency /ɪ'mɜːdʒənsɪ/ **I** *n* **1** (crisis) cas *m* d'urgence; **in an ~, in case of ~** en cas d'urgence; **in times of ~** en temps de crise; **state of ~** Pol état *m* d'urgence; **to declare a state of ~** déclarer l'état d'urgence; **2** Med (hospital case) urgence *f*.
II *modif* [*plan, measures, operation, repairs, situation, accommodation*] d'urgence; [*stores*] pour dépanner; Pol [*meeting, session*] extraordinaire; Aut [*brakes, vehicle*] de secours.

emergency: **~ aid** *n* secours *m* d'urgence; **~ ambulance service** *n* service *m* ambulancier de secours d'urgence; cf SAMU; **~ blanket** *n* couverture *f* de survie; **~ call** *n* appel *m* d'urgence; **~ case** *n* Med urgence *f*.

emergency centre GB, **emergency center** US *n* (for refugees etc) centre *m* d'accueil (*pour sinistrés*); Med poste *m* de secours; Aut poste *m* de dépannage.

emergency: **~ exit** *n* issue *f* de secours, sortie *f* de secours; **~ landing** *n* Aviat atterrissage *m* forcé; **~ laws** *npl* Pol lois *fpl* d'exception; **~ medical service, EMS** *n* US service *m* ambulancier de secours d'urgence; cf SAMU; **~ number** *n* numéro *m* des urgences; **~ powers** *npl* Pol ≈ pleins pouvoirs *mpl*; **~ rations** *npl* vivres *mpl* de secours; **~ room** *n* US = **emergency ward**.

emergency service *n* Med service *m* de garde; Aut service *m* de dépannage.

emergency services *npl* (police) police *f* secours; (ambulance) service *m* d'aide médicale d'urgence; (fire brigade) (sapeurs-) pompiers *mpl*.

emergency stop *n* arrêt *m* d'urgence.

emergency surgery *n* **to undergo ~** être opéré d'urgence.

emergency: **~ ward** *n* salle *f* des urgences; **~ worker** *n* secouriste *mf*.

emergent /ɪ'mɜːdʒənt/ *adj* **1** [*industry, nation*] jeune; [*superpower, artist, literary genre*] naissant; **2** Philos émergent.

emerging /ɪ'mɜːdʒɪŋ/ *adj* = **emergent 1**.

emeritus /ɪ'merɪtəs/ *adj* honoraire.

emery /'emərɪ/ *n* émeri *m*.

emery: **~ board** *n* lime *f* à ongles; **~ cloth** *n* toile *f* émeri; **~ paper** *n* papier-émeri *m*.

emetic /ɪ'metɪk/ *n, adj* émétique (*m*).

emigrant /'emɪgrənt/ **I** *n* (about to leave) émigrant/-e *m/f*; (settled elsewhere) émigré/-e *m/f*.
II *modif* [*worker*] émigré; [*family*] d'émigrés.

emigrate /'emɪgreɪt/ *vi* émigrer.

emigration /ˌemɪ'greɪʃn/ *n* émigration *f*.

émigré /'emɪgreɪ, US ˌemɪ'greɪ/ *n* émigré/-e *m/f*.

eminence /'emɪnəns/ *n* **1** (distinction, fame) renommée; **2** (honour) distinction *f*; **3** liter (hill, height) éminence *f*.

eminency /'emɪnənsɪ/ *n* = **eminence**.

eminent /'emɪnənt/ *adj* [*person, scholar, career*] éminent; **to be ~ in one's field** être une personnalité éminente.

eminently /'emɪnəntlɪ/ *adv* [*respectable*] éminemment; [*capable, fair, sensible, suitable*] parfaitement; [*desirable, plausible*] hautement.

emir /e'mɪə(r)/ *n* émir *m*.

emirate /'emɪəreɪt/ *n* émirat *m*.

emissary /'emɪsərɪ/ *n* émissaire *m* (**to** auprès de).

emission /ɪ'mɪʃn/ *n* (all contexts) émission *f* (**from** provenant de).

emission spectrum *n* spectre *m* d'émission.

emit /ɪ'mɪt/ *vtr* **1** (discharge) émettre [*gas, heat, radiation, lava, signal*]; dégager [*smell, vapour*]; lancer [*spark*]; **2** (utter) émettre, rendre [*sound*]; laisser échapper [*cry*]; **3** (issue) émettre [*banknote*].

emitter /ɪ'mɪtə(r)/ *n* Electron émetteur *m*.

Emmy /'emɪ/ *n* US TV *récompense décernée par la télévision américaine*.

emollient /ɪ'mɒlɪənt/ *n, adj* émollient (*m*).

emoluments /ɪ'mɒljʊmənts/ *npl* sout (salary) émoluments *mpl*, rémunération *f*; (fee) honoraires *mpl*.

emote /ɪ'məʊt/ *vi* donner dans le sentiment○.

emotion /ɪ'məʊʃn/ *n* **1** (reaction such as anger, joy, fear) émotion *f*; (feeling such as love, hate, jealousy) sentiment *m*; **he won't talk about his ~s** il ne veut pas parler de ses sentiments; **2** (strong feeling) émotion *f*; **to show no ~** ne manifester aucune émotion or aucun émoi.

emotional /ɪ'məʊʃənl/ *adj* [*development, impact, need, problem*] émotif/-ive; [*distress, charge, content, power, reaction, state*] émotionnel/-elle; [*tie, response*] affectif/-ive; [*film*] émouvant; [*campaign, speech*] passionné; [*atmosphere, farewell, occasion, scene*] chargé d'émotion; **to feel ~** se sentir ému (**about** par); **she's rather ~** elle est facilement émue; **he gets rather ~** (cries easily) il a la larme facile; (gets irrational) il a tendance à s'énerver; **~ health** santé *f* mentale; **~ abuse** Psych sévices *mpl* psychologiques.

emotionalism /ɪ'məʊʃənəlɪzəm/ *n* émotivité *f*.

emotionally /ɪ'məʊʃənəlɪ/ *adv* **1** (with emotion) [*speak, react*] avec émotion; **~ charged** [*relationship*] intense; [*atmosphere*] chargée d'émotion; [*language*] vibrant d'émotion; **an ~ worded tribute** un hommage vibrant; **2** (from an emotional standpoint) [*drained, involved*] émotionnellement; [*immature*] sur le plan affectif; **~ deprived** privé d'affection; **~ disturbed** caractériel/-ielle.

emotionless /ɪ'məʊʃnlɪs/ *adj* impassible.

emotionlessly /ɪ'məʊʃnlɪslɪ/ *adv* impassiblement.

emotionlessness /ɪ'məʊʃnlɪsnɪs/ *n* impassibilité *f*.

emotive /ɪ'məʊtɪv/ *adj* [*issue*] brûlant, qui soulève les passions; [*word*] chargé de connotations.

empanel /ɪm'pænl/ *vtr* (*p prés etc* **-ll-**, **-l-** US) (place on list) inscrire sur une liste [*juror*]; (select) constituer [*jury*].

empathetic /ˌempæ'θetɪk/ *adj* = **empathic**.

empathic /em'pæθɪk/ *adj* [*person*] empathique, qui sait s'identifier aux autres.

empathize /'empəθaɪz/ *vi* **to ~ with** s'identifier à [*person*].

empathy /'empəθɪ/ *n* empathie *f*.

emperor /'empərə(r)/ *n* empereur *m*.

emphasis /'emfəsɪs/ *n* (*pl* **-ses**) **1** (importance) accent *m*; **to lay** ou **place** ou **put the ~ on sth** mettre l'accent sur qch; **to shift the ~ from sth to sth** mettre l'accent sur qch plutôt que sur qch; **the ~ is on sth** on met l'accent sur qch; **the government is**

placing more ~ on training le gouvernement accorde plus d'importance à la formation; **the new ~ on training** l'importance récemment accordée à la formation; **to put special ~ on sth** insister sur l'importance de qch; **2** (vocal stress) accentuation *f*.

emphasize /ˈemfəsaɪz/ *vtr* **1** (give importance to) mettre l'accent sur [*policy, need, support, etc*]; **to ~ that** insister sur le fait que; **to ~ the importance of sth** insister sur l'importance de qch; **2** (stress vocally) accentuer; **3** (highlight) mettre [qch] en valeur [*eyes etc*].

emphatic /ɪmˈfætɪk/ *adj* **1** (insistent, firm) [*statement, refusal, denial*] catégorique; [*voice, manner*] énergique; [*tone, style*] vigoureux/-euse; **to be ~ about** insister sur, être formel/-elle sur; **to be ~ that** insister pour que (+ *subj*); **he was most ~ that I should go** il a insisté pour que j'y aille; **2** (clear) [*victory*] écrasant; **3** Ling (with emphasis) emphatique.

emphatically /ɪmˈfætɪklɪ/ *adv* **1** (vehemently) [*speak*] énergiquement; [*insist*] lourdement; [*condemn, refuse, deny*] catégoriquement, énergiquement; **and I say this most ~** et je ne saurais trop insister là-dessus; **2** (undeniably) [*win*] haut la main; [*be defeated*] de manière spectaculaire; **he is most ~ not a genius** il n'a vraiment rien d'un génie.

emphysema /ˌemfɪˈsiːmə/ **▶ 1354** *n* emphysème *m*.

empire /ˈempaɪə(r)/ *n* lit, fig empire *m*.

Empire /ˈempaɪə(r)/ *adj* [*furniture, fashions*] style Empire *inv*.

Empire: **~ line** *adj* [*dress*] à taille haute; **~ State** *pr n* État *m* de New York.

empirical /ɪmˈpɪrɪkl/ *adj* empirique.

empirically /ɪmˈpɪrɪklɪ/ *adv* empiriquement.

empiricism /ɪmˈpɪrɪsɪzəm/ *n* empirisme *m*.

empiricist /ɪmˈpɪrɪsɪst/ *n, adj* empiriste (*mf*).

emplacement /ɪmˈpleɪsmənt/ *n* Mil emplacement *m* (d'une arme lourde).

employ /ɪmˈplɔɪ/ **I** *n* sout **the firm has 40 workers in its ~** l'entreprise emploie 40 personnes, l'entreprise compte 40 employés; **in his ~** à son service.
II *vtr* **1** employer [*person, company*]; **to ~ sb as** employer qn en qualité de [*driver, accountant etc*]; **she is ~ed as a secretary** elle est employée comme secrétaire; **2** (use) utiliser [*machine, tool*]; employer [*method, practice, strategy, tactics, technique*]; recourir à [*measures*]; utiliser, employer [*expression, term, metaphor*]; **to be ~ed in doing** (busy) être en train de faire; **her talents/skills would be better ~ed in advertising** son talent/savoir faire serait mieux utilisé dans la publicité.

employable /ɪmˈplɔɪəbl/ *adj* [*person*] capable de travailler.

employed /ɪmˈplɔɪd/ **I** *n* **the ~** (+ *v pl*) les actifs *mpl*.
II *adj* (in work) qui a un emploi; (an employee) salarié.

employee /ˌemplɔɪˈiː, ɪmˈplɔɪiː/ *n* salarié/-e *m/f*.

employer /ɪmˈplɔɪə(r)/ *n* employeur/-euse *m/f*; **~s' organizations** associations *fpl* patronales.

employment /ɪmˈplɔɪmənt/ *n* (paid activity) travail *m*, emploi *m*; (action) emploi *m*; **to take up ~** commencer un travail; **to seek ~** chercher du travail, rechercher un emploi; **to find ~** trouver du travail or un emploi; **to be in ~** avoir un emploi, travailler; **without ~** sans emploi; **people in ~** les actifs *mpl*; **conditions of ~** conditions *fpl* d'emploi; **place of ~** lieu de travail; **the ~ of sb as sth/to do** l'emploi de qn comme qch/pour faire; **the service industries give ~ to several million people** le secteur tertiaire fournit un emploi à or emploie plusieurs millions de personnes.

employment: **~ agency** *n* bureau *m* de recrutement; **~ contract** *n* contrat *m* de travail; **~ exchange** *n* agence *f* pour l'emploi; **Employment Minister**, **Employment Secretary** *n* ministre *m* du Travail.

emporium /ɪmˈpɔːrɪəm/ *n* (*pl* **~s** ou **-ria**) sout ou hum grand magasin *m*.

empower /ɪmˈpaʊə(r)/ *vtr* **1** (legally) **to ~ sb to do** donner le droit à qn de faire; **the police are ~ed to do** la police a pleins pouvoirs pour faire; **2** (politically) donner du pouvoir à [*women, young, consumer*]; **to feel ~ed** se sentir moins impuissant (**by** grâce à).

empress /ˈemprɪs/ *n* impératrice *f*.

emptiness /ˈemptɪnɪs/ *n* (of ideas, hopes) inanité *f*; (of space, house, life) vide *m*; (of promise, threat) vacuité *f*; (in stomach) creux *m*; **I was surprised by the ~ of the cinema/train** j'étais surpris de voir le cinéma/train aussi désert.

empty /ˈemptɪ/ **I empties**○ *npl* GB (bottles) bouteilles *fpl* vides; (glasses) verres *mpl* vides.
II *adj* **1** (lacking people) [*room, building, theatre, beach, street*] désert; [*desk*] libre; **to stand ~** [*house, office*] être inoccupé; **2** (lacking contents) [*container, pocket*] vide; [*desktop*] débarrassé; [*diary, page*] vierge; [*stomach*] vide; **3** (unfulfilled) [*promise, threat*] en l'air; [*argument, dream, rhetoric*] creux/creuse; [*gesture*] vide de sens, dénué de sens; **~ of meaning** vide de sens, dénué de sens; **4** (purposeless) [*life, days, person*] vide (**of** de).
III *vtr* = **empty out**.
IV *vi* = **empty out**.
■ **empty out** ¶ [*building, container, public place, vehicle*] se vider; [*river*] se jeter; [*contents*] se répandre; ¶ **~ [sth] out, ~ out [sth]** **1** (clear) vider [*building, theatre, container, mind*]; **2** (pour) verser [*liquid*]; vider [*substance, contents*].

empty-handed /ˌemptɪˈhændɪd/ *adj* [*arrive, leave*] les mains vides; [*return*] bredouille *inv*; **to be ~** avoir les mains vides.

empty-headed /ˌemptɪˈhedɪd/ *adj* écervelé.

empyema /ˌempaɪˈiːmə, ˌempɪ-/ *n* empyème *m*.

EMS *n* **1** (*abrév* = **European Monetary System**) SME *m*; **2** *abrév* **▶ emergency medical service**.

emu /ˈiːmjuː/ *n* émeu *m*.

emulate /ˈemjʊleɪt/ *vtr* fml **1** (imitate) imiter; (rival) rivaliser avec; **2** Comput émuler.

emulation /ˌemjʊˈleɪʃn/ *n* gen Comput émulation *f*; **in ~ of sb/sth** à l'imitation de qn/qch.

emulator /ˈemjʊleɪtə(r)/ *n* Comput émulateur *m*.

emulsifier /ɪˈmʌlsɪfaɪə(r)/ *n* émulsifiant *m*.

emulsify /ɪˈmʌlsɪfaɪ/ **I** *vtr* émulsionner, émulsifier.
II *vi* être émulsionné or émulsifié.

emulsion /ɪˈmʌlʃn/ *n* **1** Chem, Phot émulsion *f*; **2 ~ (paint)** émulsion *f*, peinture *f* acrylique.

en /en/ *n* Print demi-cadratin *m*.

enable /ɪˈneɪbl/ *vtr* **1 to ~ sb to do** (allow) permettre à qn de faire; (give opportunity) donner à qn la possibilité de faire; (give right) donner à qn le droit de faire; **2** (facilitate) faciliter [*development, growth*]; favoriser [*learning*]; **3** (encourage) **to ~ sb** donner à qn les moyens de se réaliser.

enabler /ɪˈneɪblə(r)/ *n* **to be an ~** [*teacher, trainer*] favoriser l'apprentissage.

enabling /ɪˈneɪblɪŋ/ *adj* **1** Jur **~ act** ou **legislation** loi *f* d'habilitation; **2** [*teaching method etc*] favorisant l'épanouissement.

enact /ɪˈnækt/ *vtr* **1** (perform) jouer [*scene, play, part*]; **the scene that was being ~ed before us** la scène qui se déroulait devant nous; **2** Jur Pol (pass) voter; (bring into effect) promulguer; **to ~ that** statuer que; **as by law ~ed** aux termes de la loi.

enactment /ɪˈnæktmənt/ *n* **1** (of play, scene) interprétation *f*; **2** Jur Pol promulgation *f*.

enamel /ɪˈnæml/ **I** *n* **1** ¢ gen, Dent (substance, coating) émail *m*; **2** (object) émail *m*; **3**† (also **~ paint**) peinture *f* laquée.
II *modif* [*bowl, pan*] en émail; [*ring, box*] en émaux.
III *vtr* émailler.
IV enamelled, **enameled** US *pp adj* [*glass, pottery*] émaillé; [*saucepan*] en émail; [*ornament*] en émaux; **enamelled cast iron** fonte *f* émaillée.

enamelling, **enameling** US /ɪˈnæmlɪŋ/ *n* (process) émaillage *m*; (art) émaillerie *f*.

enamel: **~ware** *n* vaisselle *f* en métal émaillé; **~work** *n* Art émaillerie *f*.

enamoured GB, **enamored** US /ɪˈnæməd/ *adj* **to be ~ of** être épris/-e or amoureux/-euse de [*person*]; avoir une passion pour [*activity*]; **his boss is not too ~ with him at the moment** ce n'est pas le grand amour entre lui et son patron en ce moment!; **I'm not too ~ of the idea of spending a whole day with him** l'idée de passer toute une journée avec lui ne m'emballe○ pas.

en bloc /ˌɒn ˈblɒk/ *adv* en bloc.

enc. *abrév* = **encl.**

encamp /ɪnˈkæmp/ *vi* établir son camp.

encampment /ɪnˈkæmpmənt/ *n* gen campement *m*; Mil cantonnement *m*.

encapsulate /ɪnˈkæpsjʊleɪt/ *vtr* **1** (summarize) résumer, renfermer; **2** (include, incorporate) contenir, inclure; **more information than can be ~d in one article** plus de détails que n'en peut contenir un seul article.

encase /ɪnˈkeɪs/ *vtr* revêtir, recouvrir (**in** de); **to be ~d in** être pris dans [*concrete*]; être serré dans [*plaster*].

encash /ɪnˈkæʃ/ *n* GB encaisser [*money order*].

encashment /ɪnˈkæʃmənt/ *n* GB encaissement *m*.

encaustic /ɪnˈkɔːstɪk/ **I** *n* Art encaustique *f*.
II *adj* [*tile*] émaillé.

encephalic /ˌenkɪˈfælɪk/ *adj* encéphalique.

encephalitis /ˌenkefəˈlaɪtɪs/ *n* encéphalite *f*.

encephalogram /enˈkefələgræm/ *n* encéphalogramme *m*.

encephalon /enˈkefəlɒn/ *n* encéphale *m*.

enchain /ɪnˈtʃeɪn/ *vtr* lit, fig enchaîner.

enchant /ɪnˈtʃɑːnt, US -tʃænt/ **I** *vtr* **1** (delight) enchanter, ravir; **2** (cast spell on) enchanter.
II enchanted *pp adj* [*garden, wood*] enchanté; [*ring*] magique; [*place*] merveilleux/-euse.

enchanter /ɪnˈtʃɑːntə(r), US -tʃæntər/ *n* enchanteur *m*.

enchanting /ɪnˈtʃɑːntɪŋ, US -tʃænt-/ *adj* [*vision, place*] merveilleux/-euse, enchanteur/-eresse; [*person, smile, village*] ravissant, enchanteur/-eresse.

enchantingly /ɪnˈtsɑːntɪŋlɪ, US -tʃænt-/ *adj* [*sing, dance*] à ravir; [*smile*] d'une façon charmante or ravissante; **she is ~ beautiful** elle est belle à ravir.

enchantment /ɪnˈtʃɑːntmənt, US -tʃænt-/ *n* **1** (delight) enchantement *m*, ravissement *m*; **2** (spell) charme *m*, enchantement *m*.

enchantress /ɪnˈtʃɑːntrɪs, US -tʃænt-/ *n* lit, fig enchanteresse *f*.

enchilada /ˌentʃɪˈlɑːdə/ *n* **1** Culin enchilada *f*; **2**○ US (big shot) **big ~** huile◑ *f*, grosse légume○ *f*.

encircle /ɪnˈsɜːkl/ *vtr* [*troops, police*] encercler [*building*]; [*fence, wall*] entourer; [*belt, bracelet*] enserrer, ceindre littér.

encirclement /ɪnˈsɜːklmənt/ *n* encerclement *m*.

encl. **I** *n* (*abrév* = **enclosure**) PJ *f*.
II *adj* (*abrév* = **enclosed**) ci-joint.

enclave /ˈenkleɪv/ *n* enclave *f*.

enclitic /enˈklɪtɪk/ *n, adj* enclitique (*m*).

enclose /ɪnˈkləʊz/ *vtr* **1** (surround) gen entourer (**with, by** de); (with fence, wall) clôturer (**with, by** avec); (in outer casing) enfermer (**in** dans); (within brackets) insérer (**in** dans); **2** (insert in letter) joindre (**with, in** à); **a cheque for £10 is ~d** veuillez trouver ci-joint un chèque de dix livres; **I'll ~ your letter with mine** je mettrai votre lettre dans la même enveloppe que la mienne; **a letter enclosing a cheque** une lettre accompagnée d'un chèque; **please find ~d** veuillez trouver ci-joint.

enclosed /ɪn'kləʊzd/ *adj* [*shelter, cabin, sea*] fermé; [*passage, precinct*] couvert; [*bath, appliance*] encastré; [*life*] cloîtré; [*garden*] clos; **~ space** espace clos; **~ order** Relig ordre cloîtré.

enclosure /ɪn'kləʊʒə(r)/ *n* **1** (space) (for animals) enclos *m*; (for racehorses) paddock *m*; (for officials) enceinte *f*; **2** (fence) clôture *f*; **3** GB Hist Agric enclosure *f*; **4** (with letter) pièce *f* jointe.

encode /ɪn'kəʊd/ *vtr, vi* gen coder, chiffrer; Comput, Ling encoder.

encoder /ɪn'kəʊdə(r)/ *n* Comput, Ling encodeur *m*.

encoding /ɪn'kəʊdɪŋ/ *n* Comput, Ling encodage *m*.

encomium /en'kəʊmɪəm/ *n* (*pl* **~s** or **-mia**) sout panégyrique *m*.

encompass /ɪn'kʌmpəs/ *vtr* **1** (include) couvrir, comprendre; [*activities, aspects, range of subjects*]; couvrir, contenir [*themes*]; regrouper [*people, ideas, theories*]; **2** (cover) [*empire, state*] englober, regrouper [*districts, territories, empire, estate*]; couvrir [*acres, hectares*].

encore /'ɒŋkɔː(r)/ Theat **I** *n* bis *m*; **to give** ou **play an ~** jouer un bis; **to get** ou **receive an ~** être bissé.
II *excl* **~!** bis!

encounter /ɪn'kaʊntə(r)/ **I** *n* **1** gen rencontre *f* (**with** avec); **brief ~** brève rencontre; **chance ~** rencontre inattendue; **through a chance ~** au hasard d'une rencontre; **his frequent ~s with the law** ses démêlés fréquents avec la police; **I had a close ~ with a lamppost** hum je suis rentré dans un réverbère; **2** Mil affrontement *m*.
II *vtr* rencontrer; se heurter à [*resistance*]; essuyer [*setback*]; rencontrer [*problem, difficulties*]; croiser [*person*]; Sport rencontrer.

encounter group *n* Psych atelier *m* relationnel.

encourage /ɪn'kʌrɪdʒ/ *vtr* **1** (boost, support) encourager; (raise morale of) encourager, réconforter; (reassure) rassurer; **to ~ sb to do** gen encourager qn à faire; [*parent, government, policy*] inciter qn à faire; **this only ~d him in his desire to do** cela n'a fait qu'accroître son désir de faire; **these observations ~d him in his belief that** ces observations l'ont conforté dans l'idée que; **don't laugh at his jokes, it'll only ~ him!** ne ris pas de ses blagues, on ne l'arrêtera plus!; **to ~ sb to do** encourager or inciter qn à faire; **2** (foster) stimuler [*investment*]; favoriser [*rise, growth*].

encouragement /ɪn'kʌrɪdʒmənt/ *n* (support) encouragement *m* (**to** pour); (inducement) incitation *f* (**to** à); **she needs no ~ to do** elle ne se fait pas prier pour faire; **to give ~ to sb, to be an ~ to sb** encourager qn; **without ~ from me** sans mon soutien.

encouraging /ɪn'kʌrɪdʒɪŋ/ *adj* encourageant.

encouragingly /ɪn'kʌrɪdʒɪŋlɪ/ *adv* [*say, smile*] d'un air encourageant; **complaints are ~ few** heureusement, il y a peu de réclamations; **an ~ high percentage** un pourcentage encourageant.

encroach /ɪn'krəʊtʃ/ *vi* **to ~ on** [*vegetation*] gagner du terrain sur, envahir; [*sea*] gagner (du terrain) sur, avancer sur; [*enemy*] empiéter or déborder sur [*territory*]; empiéter sur [*rights*]; **to ~ on sb's privacy** violer l'intimité de qn; **to ~ on sb's territory** ou **turf** fig empiéter sur le territoire de qn, marcher sur les plates-bandes de qn○.

encroachment /ɪn'krəʊtʃmənt/ *n* (of sea, enemy) empiètement *m* (**on** sur); fig (on sb's rights) empiètement *m* (**on** sur); (on sb's privacy) intrusion *f* (**on** dans).

encrust /ɪn'krʌst/ *vtr* **to be ~ed with** être recouvert de [*moss, ice, dried blood*]; être incrusté de [*jewels*].

encrustation /ˌɪnkrʌs'teɪʃn/ *n* **1** (of blood, earth) croûte *f*; **2** (of jewels) incrustation *f*.

encryption /en'krɪpʃən/ *n* Telecom cryptage *m*.

encumber /ɪn'kʌmbə(r)/ *vtr* encombrer [*person, traffic, room, street*] (**with** de); **to be ~ed with debts** [*estate*] être grevé de dettes.

encumbrance /ɪn'kʌmbrəns/ *n* **1** (to movement) gêne *f*, entrave *f* (**to** à); (to one's freedom) entrave *f*, handicap *m* (**to** pour); **2** (burden) (person) charge *f* (**to** pour); (possession) embarras *m* (**to** pour); **3** Jur **an estate free from ~(s)** un bien sans servitudes ni hypothèques.

encyclical /en'sɪklɪkl/ *n, adj* encyclique (*f*).

encyclop(a)edia /ɪnˌsaɪklə'piːdɪə/ *n* encyclopédie *f*; **she's a walking ~** hum c'est une encyclopédie vivante.

encyclop(a)edic /ɪnˌsaɪklə'piːdɪk/ *adj* encyclopédique.

encyclop(a)edist /ɪnˌsaɪklə'piːdɪst/ *n* encyclopédiste *mf*.

end /end/ **I** *n* **1** (finish, final part) (of week, holiday, journey, game, story, sentence) fin *f*; **'The End'** (of film, book etc) 'Fin'; **at the ~ of** à la fin de [*year, story*]; **at the ~ of May** fin mai; **by the ~ of** à la fin de [*year, journey, game*]; **to put an ~ to sth, to bring sth to an ~** mettre fin à qch, mettre un terme à qch; **to get to the ~ of** arriver à la fin de [*holiday*]; arriver au bout de [*story, work*]; **to come to an ~** se terminer; **to be at an ~** être terminé; **in the ~ I went home** finalement je suis rentré chez moi; **in the ~, at the ~ of the day** (all things considered) en fin de compte; **it's the ~ of the line** ou **road for the project** le projet arrive en fin de course; **for days/months on ~** pendant des jours et des jours/des mois et des mois; **there is no ~ to his talent** son talent n'a pas de limites; **no ~ of○ letters/trouble** énormément de lettres/problèmes; **that really is the ~○!** c'est vraiment le comble○!; **you really are the ~○!** tu exagères!; **I'm not going and that's the ~ of that!** je n'y vais pas, un point c'est tout!; **2** (extremity) (of nose, tail, branch, string, queue, bed, table, road) bout *m*, extrémité *f*; **at the ~ of, on the ~ of** au bout de [*bed, road, nose*]; **at the ~ of the garden** au fond du jardin; **from one ~ to another** d'un bout à l'autre; **from ~ to ~** de bout en bout, d'un bout à l'autre; **to lay sth ~ to ~** poser qch bout à bout; **the lower ~ of the street** le bas de la rue; **the northern ~ of the town** la partie nord de la ville; **the front/back ~ of the car** l'avant/l'arrière de la voiture; **the third from the ~** le/la troisième avant la fin; **to look at sth ~ on** regarder qch de front; **to stand sth on its ~** ou **on end** mettre qch debout; **it will come out the other ~** hum (of swallowed object) ça va sortir à l'autre bout; **3** (side of conversation, transaction) côté *m*; **things are fine at my** ou **this ~** de mon côté tout va bien; **how does it look from your ~?** qu'en est-il de ton côté?; **she takes care of the business ~** c'est elle qui s'occupe du côté commercial; **to keep one's ~ of the bargain** remplir sa moitié du contrat; **there was silence at the other ~** c'était le silence au bout du fil; **4** (of scale, spectrum) extrémité *f*; **at the lower ~ of the scale** au plus bas de l'échelle; **this suit is from the cheaper** ou **bottom ~ of the range** ce costume est un des moins chers de la gamme; **5** (aim) but *m*; **to this** ou **that ~** dans ce but, à cette fin; **an ~ in itself** une fin en soi; **a means to an ~** un moyen d'arriver à ses fins; **6** Sport côté *m*, camp *m*; **to change ~s** changer de camp; **7** (scrap) (of rope, string) bout *m*; (of loaf, joint of meat) reste *m*; **candle ~** bout de chandelle; **8** (death) mort *f*; **to meet one's ~** trouver la mort; **to be nearing one's ~** sentir sa fin proche; **to come to a bad** ou **sticky ~** mal finir; **and that was the ~ of the witch!** et ce fut la fin de la sorcière!
II *modif* [*house, seat*] du bout; [*carriage*] de queue.
III *vtr* mettre fin à [*strike, war, friendship, rumour, search*]; mettre fin à, conclure [*meeting, debate, programme*]; rompre [*marriage*]; achever [*match*]; **to ~ sth with** conclure or terminer qch par; **to ~ sth by doing** terminer qch en faisant; **he ~ed his days in hospital** il a fini ses jours à l'hôpital; **they ~ed the day in a restaurant** ils ont fini la journée au restaurant; **we ~ed the first half ahead** on avait l'avantage à la fin de la première mi-temps; **to ~ one's life** mettre fin à ses jours; **to ~ it all** en finir avec la vie; **the sale to ~ all sales** ce qu'il y a de mieux comme soldes.
IV *vi* **1** (finish in time) [*day, meeting, career, relationship, book, war*] finir, se terminer; [*contract, agreement*] expirer; **to ~ in** se terminer par [*failure, tragedy, divorce*]; **it ~ed in a fight/in victory** cela s'est terminé par une bagarre/une victoire; **to ~ with** se terminer par; **it ~s with him being murdered** cela se termine par son assassinat; **the word ~s in** ou **with an 'e'** le mot finit par 'e'; **where will it all ~?** comment tout cela finira-t-il?; **2** (finish in space) [*path, line, queue, river*] se terminer, s'arrêter.
IDIOMS **all's well that ~s well** tout est bien qui finit bien; **to get one's ~ away**◑ s'envoyer en l'air○; **to keep one's ~ up**○ ne pas se laisser impressionner; ▶ **justify, stick**.
■ **end up**: **~ up [sth]** finir par devenir [*president, alcoholic*]; finir par être [*rich, bored*]; **to ~ up as** finir par devenir; **I don't know how he'll ~ up** je ne sais pas comment il va finir; **to ~ up (by) doing** finir par faire; **to ~ up in** se retrouver à [*London, hospital*]; **to ~ up at home** se retrouver chez soi; **to ~ up with** se retrouver avec [*person, prize*].

endanger /ɪn'deɪndʒə(r)/ *vtr* mettre [qch] en danger [*health, life*]; constituer une menace pour [*environment, species*]; compromettre [*reputation, career, prospects*]; **~ed species** espèce menacée; fig, hum race qui se perd.

endear /ɪn'dɪə(r)/ **I** *vtr* **to ~ sb to** faire aimer qn de [*person*]; **his humanity ~ed him to the nation** son humanité l'a fait aimer de tout le pays; **what ~s her to me is her simplicity** ce qui me touche chez elle or ce qui me la rend chère c'est sa simplicité.
II *v refl* **to ~ oneself to sb** se faire aimer or apprécier de qn.

endearing /ɪn'dɪərɪŋ/ *adj* [*child, personality, habit*] attachant; [*quality*] attachant, touchant; [*remark*] touchant; [*smile*] séduisant; **there's nothing very ~ about him** il n'a rien de bien attachant.

endearingly /ɪn'dɪərɪŋlɪ/ *adv* [*smile, remark*] de manière touchante; **~ honest** d'une honnêteté touchante.

endearment /ɪn'dɪəmənt/ *n* terme *m* d'affection; **terms of ~** termes *mpl* d'affection; **words of ~** paroles *fpl* affectueuses, mots *mpl* doux.

endeavour, endeavor US /ɪn'devə(r)/ **I** *n* **1** (attempt) tentative *f* (**to do** de faire); **to make every ~ to do** faire tout son possible pour faire; **2** (industriousness) effort *m*; **3** (project) projet *m*.
II *vtr* **to ~ to do** (do one's best) faire tout son possible pour faire; (find a means) trouver un moyen de faire; (succeed) réussir à faire.

endemic /en'demɪk/ **I** *n* endémie *f*.

II *adj* endémique (**in, to** dans).

endgame /ˈendgeɪm/ *n* Games fin *f* de partie.

ending /ˈendɪŋ/ *n* **1** (of book, play, film) fin *f*, dénouement *m*; **2** Ling terminaison *f*, désinence *f* spec.

endive /ˈendɪv, US -daɪv/ *n* **1** (curly lettuce) frisée *f*, chicorée *f* frisée; **2** (blanched chicory) endive *f*.

endless /ˈendlɪs/ *adj* **1** (unlimited) [*patience, energy, choice, possibility*] infini; [*supply, stock*] inépuisable; **to go to ~ trouble to do** se donner une peine infinie pour faire; **2** (interminable) [*line, path, drop, list, meeting, search, journey*] interminable; **~ letters** une lettre après l'autre.

endlessly /ˈendlɪslɪ/ *adv* **1** (unlimitedly) infiniment; **~ patient/tolerant** infiniment patient/tolérant; **2** (without stopping) [*talk, cry, argue*] sans s'arrêter; [*search, play, try*] inlassablement; **3** (to infinity) [*stretch, extend*] à perte de vue, à l'infini.

end: **~line** *n* US Sport ligne *f* de fond; **~ matter** *n* Publg appendices *mpl*.

endocarditis /ˌendəʊkɑːˈdaɪtɪs/ **▶ 1354** *n* endocardite *f*.

endocardium /ˌendəʊˈkɑːdɪəm/ *n* (*pl* **-cardia**) endocarde *m*.

endocarp /ˈendəʊkɑːp/ *n* endocarpe *m*.

endocrine /ˈendəʊkraɪn, -ˌkrɪn/ *adj* [*glands, secretions*] endocrine; [*system, disorder*] endocrinien/-ienne.

endocrinologist /ˌendəʊkrɪˈnɒlədʒɪst/ **▶ 1692** *n* endocrinologue *mf*.

endocrinology /ˌendəʊkrɪˈnɒlədʒɪ/ *n* endocrinologie *f*.

end of term **I** *n* GB Sch, Univ fin *m* de trimestre.
II end-of-term *modif* GB Sch, Univ [*party, ball, exam, report*] de fin de trimestre.

endogamous /enˈdɒgəməs/ *adj* endogame.

endogamy /enˈdɒgəmɪ/ *n* endogamie *f*.

endogenous /enˈdɒdʒɪnəs/ *adj* endogène.

endolymph /ˈendəʊlɪmf/ *n* endolymphe *f*.

endometriosis /ˌendəʊmiːtrɪˈəʊsɪs/ **▶ 1354** *n* endométriose *f*.

endometrium /ˌendəʊˈmiːtrɪəm/ *n* (*pl* **-metria**) endomètre *m*.

endomorph /ˈendəʊmɔːf/ *n* endomorphe *mf*.

endorphin /enˈdɔːfɪn/ *n* endorphine *f*.

endorse /ɪnˈdɔːs/ *vtr* **1** donner son aval à [*view, policy, principle*]; appuyer [*candidate, decision*]; Comm approuver [*product*]; endosser [*cheque, bill*]; approuver [*claim*]; **2** GB Aut **to have one's licence ~d** ≈ perdre des points sur son permis de conduire.

endorsement /ɪnˈdɔːsmənt/ *n* **1** (of opinion) approbation *f* (**of** de); (of candidate) appui *m* (**of** à); (of decision) sanction *f* (**of** à propos de); (of claim) approbation *f* (**of** de); (of cheque) endossement *m*; **expenses claims should be submitted to your superior for ~** les notes de frais doivent être portées à votre supérieur pour être approuvées; **2** Aut **he has had two ~s for speeding** ≈ il a perdu des points pour excès de vitesse.

endoskeleton /ˈendəʊskelɪtn/ *n* endosquelette *m*.

endothermic /ˌendəʊˈθɜːmɪk/ *adj* endothermique.

endow /ɪnˈdaʊ/ *vtr* **1** (with money) doter [*hospital, charity*]; subventionner [*hospital bed, ward*]; fonder [*academic post*]; **2** (bestow) doter [*person*] (**with** de); **she is well-~ed**○ il y a du monde au balcon○, elle a une poitrine opulente; **he's well-~ed**○ il est bien monté●.

endowment /ɪnˈdaʊmənt/ *n* **1** (action) (of hospital, school) dotation *f*; (of prize, academic post) fondation *f*; **2** (money given) dotation *f*; **capital ~** dotation *f* en capital; **3** (talent, ability) don *m*, talent *m* (naturel).

endowment: **~ insurance** *n* assurance *f* à capital différé or en cas de vie; **~ mortgage** *n* hypothèque *f* liée à une assurance en cas de vie; **~ policy** *n* = **endowment insurance**.

end: **~paper** *n* Publg page *f* de garde, garde *f*; **~ product** *n* Comm produit *m* fini; **~ result** *n* résultat *m* final; **~ table** *n* US table *f* basse.

endurable /ɪnˈdjʊərəbl, US -ˈdʊə-/ *adj* supportable, endurable.

endurance /ɪnˈdjʊərəns, US -dʊə-/ *n* (physical) endurance *f*; (moral) courage *m* (**of** face à); (of cold) résistance *f* (**of** à); **to test your powers of ~ to the full** pour mettre votre endurance à l'épreuve; **to show great powers of ~** faire preuve d'une grande endurance; **past** ou **beyond** (**all**) **~** intolérable; **to provoke sb beyond ~** pousser qn à bout.

endurance test *n* Sport, Mil épreuve *f* d'endurance; péj hum vrai supplice *m*.

endure /ɪnˈdjʊə(r), US -ˈdʊər/ **I** *vtr* endurer [*personal experience, humiliation, hardship*]; supporter [*behaviour, sight, lifestyle, person*]; subir [*attack, defeat, imprisonment*].
II *vi* (last) durer.

enduring /ɪnˈdjʊərɪŋ, US -ˈdʊə-/ *adj* [*influence, fame*] durable; [*ability, grudge*] constant; [*government*] stable; [*charm*] immuable.

enduringly /ɪnˈdjʊərɪŋlɪ, US -ˈdʊə-/ *adv* **to be ~ popular** rester populaire.

end user *n* Comm, Comput utilisateur *m* final.

enema /ˈenɪmə/ *n* Med lavement *m*; **to give sb an ~** faire un lavement à qn.

enemy /ˈenəmɪ/ **I** *n* (*pl* **-mies**) **1** gen, fig ennemi/-e *m/f*; **to make enemies** se faire des ennemis; **to make an ~ of sb** se faire un ennemi de qn; **his arrogance made him many enemies** son arrogance lui a valu beaucoup d'ennemis; **public ~ number one** l'ennemi public numéro un; **to be one's own worst ~** être son pire ennemi; **the ~ within** l'ennemi intérieur; **2** Mil **the ~** (+ *v sg ou pl*) l'ennemi; **to go over to the ~** passer à l'ennemi.
II *modif* [*forces, aircraft, propaganda, territory*] ennemi; [*agent*] de l'ennemi; **~ alien** ressortissant/-e *m/f* d'un pays ennemi; **killed by ~ action** tombé sous le feu de l'ennemi; **under ~ occupation** occupé par l'ennemi.

energetic /ˌenəˈdʒetɪk/ *adj* **1** (full of life) [*person*] énergique, dynamique; [*exercise*] vigoureux/-euse; [*child*] débordant d'énergie; **I'm not feeling very ~ today** je ne me sens pas d'attaque aujourd'hui; **2** (vigorous) [*reforms, programme, administration, campaign*] énergique; [*debate*] animé.

energetically /ˌenəˈdʒetɪklɪ/ *adv* [*work, exercise*] avec vigueur; [*argue, speak*] énergiquement, avec force; [*deny*] énergiquement, vigoureusement; [*promote, publicize*] avec force; **to stride ~** marcher d'un pas énergique.

energetics /ˌenəˈdʒetɪks/ *n* Phys (+ *v sg*) énergétique *f*.

energize /ˈenədʒaɪz/ *vtr* **1** (invigorate) stimuler; **2** Elec alimenter [qch] en courant.

energizing /ˈenədʒaɪzɪŋ/ *adj* [*influence, work*] stimulant.

energy /ˈenədʒɪ/ *n* **1** (strength, vitality) énergie *f*; **to have the ~ to do** avoir l'énergie or le courage de faire; **to devote all one's ~ to sth/to doing** consacrer toute son énergie à qch/à faire; **it would be a waste of ~** ce serait se donner du mal pour rien; **2** (power, fuel) énergie *f*; **nuclear ~** énergie *f* nucléaire; **to save/waste ~** conserver/gaspiller l'énergie; **3 Department of Energy** ministère *m* de l'Énergie; **Energy Secretary**, **Energy Minister** ministre *m* de l'Énergie; **4** Phys énergie *f*.

energy: **~ consumption** *n* consommation *f* d'énergie; **~ efficiency** *n* économies *fpl* d'énergie; **~ level** *n* Phys niveau *m* énergétique; **~ resources** *npl* ressources *fpl* énergétiques.

energy saving **I** *n* économies *fpl* d'énergie.
II energy-saving *adj* [*device, measure*] anti-gaspillage d'énergie.

enervate /ˈenəveɪt/ *vtr* débiliter.

enervating /ˈenəveɪtɪŋ/ *adj* (all contexts) débilitant.

enfant terrible /ˌɒnfɒn teˈriːbl/ *n* enfant *mf* terrible.

enfeeble /ɪnˈfiːbl/ *vtr* affaiblir.

enfeeblement /ɪnˈfiːblmənt/ *n* affaiblissement *m*.

enfilade /ˌenfɪˈleɪd/ Mil **I** *n* tir *m* d'enfilade.
II *vtr* soumettre [qch] à un tir d'enfilade.

enfold /ɪnˈfəʊld/ *vtr* envelopper; **to ~ sb in one's arms** étreindre qn.

enforce /ɪnˈfɔːs/ *vtr* **1** (impose) appliquer [*rule, policy, decision*]; faire respecter [*law, court order*]; faire valoir [*legal rights*]; imposer [*silence, discipline*]; exiger [*payment*]; faire exécuter [*contract*]; **2** (strengthen) renforcer [*opinion, hypothesis*]; appuyer [*argument, theory*].

enforceable /ɪnˈfɔːsəbl/ *adj* gen qui peut être imposé; Jur [*law, ruling, verdict*] exécutoire, [*rule*] applicable; **to be ~** Jur avoir force exécutoire.

enforced /ɪnˈfɔːst/ *adj* [*acceptance, abstinence, redundancy*] forcé; [*discipline*] imposé par la force.

enforcement /ɪnˈfɔːsmənt/ *n* (of law, regulation) application *f*, exécution *f*; (of policy, decision) application *f*; (of discipline) imposition *f*; **~ action**, **~ measures** Jur mesures *fpl* d'exécution.

enfranchise /ɪnˈfræntʃaɪz/ *vtr* **1** (give right to vote to) admettre [qn] au suffrage; (give political rights to) donner or octroyer des droits politiques à; **2** (emancipate) affranchir.

enfranchisement /ɪnˈfræntʃɪzmənt/ *n* **1** Pol admission *f* au suffrage; **2** (emancipation) affranchissement *m*.

engage /ɪnˈgeɪdʒ/ **I** *vtr* **1** sout (interest, attract) retenir [*person, attention*]; éveiller [*interest, sympathy*]; séduire [*imagination*]; **to ~ sb in conversation** engager la conversation avec qn; **to be otherwise ~d** être pris ailleurs; **2** (involve) **to be ~d in** se livrer à [*activity, practice, search*]; prendre part à [*conspiracy*]; **to be ~d in discussions/negotiations** être en discussion/négociations; **to be ~d in doing** être en train de faire; **3** (employ) prendre [*lawyer*]; engager [*cleaner, secretary, interpreter*]; embaucher [*worker*]; **4** Mech passer, enclencher [*gear*]; **to ~ the clutch** embrayer; **5** Mil engager le combat avec [*enemy*].
II *vi* sout (be, become involved) **to ~ in** se livrer à [*activity, practice*]; se lancer dans [*argument, research*]; engager, entamer [*discussion, dialogue, negotiations*]; Mil engager [*combat, hostilities*].

engaged /ɪnˈgeɪdʒd/ *adj* **1** (before marriage) **to be ~** être fiancé (**to** à); **to get ~d** se fiancer (**to** à); **we were ~ for three years before getting married** nous sommes restés fiancés pendant trois ans avant de nous marier; **2** [*toilet*] occupé; [*phone, line*] occupé; [*taxi*] pris.

engaged tone *n* GB tonalité *f* 'occupé'; **I keep getting an ~** ça sonne toujours occupé.

engagement /ɪnˈgeɪdʒmənt/ *n* **1** sout (appointment) rendez-vous *m*; (for performer, artist) engagement *m*; **official** ou **public ~** obligation *f* officielle; **social ~** obligation *f* sociale; **prior ~** obligation *f*; **I have a dinner ~ tomorrow evening** j'ai un dîner demain soir; **2** (before marriage) fiançailles *fpl*; **to break off one's ~** rompre ses fiançailles; **3** Mil (initial skirmish) engagement *m* (**with** avec); (battle) combat *m* (**with** avec).

engagement: **~ book** *n* agenda *m*; **~ ring** *n* bague *f* de fiançailles.

engaging /ɪnˈgeɪdʒɪŋ/ *adj* [*shyness, character*] attachant; [*person, laugh, tale*] charmant; [*smile*] engageant; [*performance*] intéressant.

engagingly /ɪn'geɪdʒɪŋlɪ/ *adv* [*behave, smile, write*] de façon charmante; **he is ~ frank** sa franchise est charmante.

engender /ɪn'dʒendə(r)/ *vtr* engendrer, causer.

engine /'endʒɪn/ *n* **1** (motor) (in car, train, aeroplane, boat) moteur *m*; (in jet aircraft) réacteur *m*; (in ship) machines *fpl*; **steam ~** machine *f* à vapeur; **jet ~** moteur à réaction; **2** Rail (locomotive) locomotive *f*; **diesel/steam ~** locomotive diesel/à vapeur; **to sit facing/with one's back to the ~** être assis dans le sens de la marche/dans le sens contraire à la marche.

engine driver *n* mécanicien *m*.

engineer /ˌendʒɪ'nɪə(r)/ **▶1692** **I** *n* (graduate) ingénieur *m*; (in factory) mécanicien *m* monteur; (repairer) dépanneur *m*, réparateur *m*, technicien *m*; (on ship) mécanicien *m*; US Rail mécanicien *m*; **the (Royal) Engineers** Mil le génie; **chief ~** Naut mécanicien *m* chef; **heating ~** chauffagiste *m*; **telephone ~** technicien *m* des télécommunications; **▶ civil engineer etc.**

II *vtr* **1** (plot) manigancer [*revolt, fall, success, conspiracy*]; ourdir [*plot*]; **2** (build) construire.

engineering /ˌendʒɪ'nɪərɪŋ/ *n* **1** (subject, science) gen ingénierie *f*; **civil/chemical ~** génie *m* civil/chimique; **to study ~** faire des études d'ingénieur; **an extraordinary feat of ~** une belle réalisation technologique; **2** (industry) industrie *f* mécanique; **light/heavy ~** génie *m* léger/lourd; **3** (structure) construction *f* mécanique.

engineering: **~ and design department** *n* Ind bureau *m* d'études techniques; **~ company** *n* société *f* de constructions mécaniques; **~ course** *n* Univ école *f* d'ingénieurs; **~ degree** *n* Univ diplôme *m* d'ingénieur; **~ department** *n* Univ département *m* d'ingénierie; **~ drawing** *n* dessin *m* industriel; **~ factory**, **~ works** *n* usine *f* de constructions mécaniques; **~ industry** *n* industrie *f* mécanique; **~ science** *n* Univ ingénierie *f*; **~ student** *n* Univ élève *mf* ingénieur; **~ worker** *n* métallurgiste *m*.

engine: **~ failure** *n* gen, Aut, Aviat panne *f* de moteur; (in jet aircraft) panne *f* de réacteur; **~ oil** *n* huile *f*; **~ room** *n* salle *f* des machines; **~ shed** *n* Rail dépôt *m*.

England /'ɪŋglənd/ **▶1131** *pr n* Angleterre *f*.

english /'ɪŋglɪʃ/ *n* US (in billiards) effet *m*.

English /'ɪŋglɪʃ/ **▶1486**, **1402** **I** *n* **1** Ling anglais *m*; **the King's** ou **Queen's ~** l'anglais correct; **2 the ~** (+ *v pl*) les Anglais *mpl*.

II *adj* anglais.

English: **~ as a Foreign Language**, **EFL** *n* anglais *m* langue étrangère; **~ as a Second Language**, **ESL** *n* anglais *m* deuxième langue; **~ breakfast** *n* petit déjeuner *m* anglais.

English Channel *n* **the ~** la Manche.

English: **~ for Special Purposes**, **ESP** *n* anglais *m* de spécialités; **~ Language Teaching**, **ELT** *n* enseignement *m* de l'anglais.

Englishman /'ɪŋglɪʃmən/ *n* (*pl* **-men**) Anglais *m*.

IDIOMS **an ~'s home is his castle** Prov ≈ charbonnier est maître dans sa maison Prov.

Englishness /'ɪŋglɪʃnɪs/ *n* (of custom, behaviour etc) caractère *m* typiquement anglais; (of person) côté *m* typiquement anglais.

English: **~ rose** *n* jeune fille *f* au teint frais; **~ speaker** *n* anglophone *mf*; **~-speaking** *adj* [*country, community, world*] anglophone; [*person*] qui parle anglais, anglophone; **~ walnut** *n* US noix *f*; **~woman** *n* Anglaise *f*.

Eng Lit /'ɪŋ lɪt/ *n* (*abrév* = **English Literature**) littérature *f* anglaise.

engraft /ɪn'grɑːft/ *vtr* greffer (**on** sur).

engram /'engræm/ *n* engramme *m*.

engrave /ɪn'greɪv/ *vtr* gen, Print graver; **~d on the heart/mind** gravé dans le cœur/la mémoire.

engraver /ɪn'greɪvə(r)/ **▶1692** *n* graveur/-euse *m/f*.

engraving /ɪn'greɪvɪŋ/ *n* gravure *f*.

engraving plate *n* planche *f* à graver or d'imprimerie.

engross /ɪn'grəʊs/ *vtr* **1** captiver [*audience*]; **to be ~ed in** être absorbé or plongé dans [*book, spectacle, work*]; être absorbé dans [*problems*]; **2** Jur rédiger; **3** US (dominate) accaparer [*market*].

engrossing /ɪn'grəʊsɪŋ/ *adj* [*book, programme*] absorbant, captivant; [*activity, problem*] absorbant.

engrossment /ɪn'grəʊsmənt/ *n* rédaction *f* définitive.

engulf /ɪn'gʌlf/ *vtr* [*sea, waves, fire*] engloutir; [*silence*] envelopper; [*panic*] s'emparer de; **to be ~ed by hatred/grief** être déchiré par la haine/accablé de chagrin.

enhance /ɪn'hɑːns, US -hæns/ *vtr* **1** (improve) améliorer [*prospects, status, reputation*]; accroître [*rights, privileges, authority, power*]; retoucher [*image, photo*]; rehausser, mettre [qch] en valeur [*appearance, beauty*]; mettre en valeur, faire valoir [*qualities*]; **2** (increase) augmenter [*value*]; majorer [*pension, salary*].

enhancement /ɪn'hɑːnsmənt, US -hæns-/ *n* (of reputation, prospects, status) amélioration *f*; (of rights, privileges, power) accroissement *m*; (of beauty, quality) mise *f* en valeur; (of pension, salary) majoration *f*.

enharmonic /ˌenhɑː'mɒnɪk/ *adj* enharmonique.

enigma /ɪ'nɪgmə/ *n* énigme *f*.

enigmatic /ˌenɪg'mætɪk/ *adj* énigmatique.

enigmatically /ˌenɪg'mætɪklɪ/ *adv* de façon énigmatique.

enjambement /ɪn'dʒæmmənt/ *n* Literat enjambement *m*.

enjoin /ɪn'dʒɔɪn/ *vtr* **1** (impose, urge) imposer [*silence, obedience, discipline*] (**on** à); prescrire [*discretion, caution*] (**on** à); **to ~ sb to do** ordonner or enjoindre liter à qn de faire; **2** US (prohibit) **to ~ sb from doing** interdire à qn de faire.

enjoy /ɪn'dʒɔɪ/ **I** *vtr* **1** (get pleasure from) aimer [*reading, swimming, sport, hobby etc*]; aimer, apprécier [*art, music, wine*]; aimer, s'amuser à [*party*]; **I ~ gardening/cooking** j'aime jardiner/faire la cuisine; **don't worry, I'll ~ looking after Paul** ne vous inquiétez pas, ça me fait plaisir de m'occuper de Paul; **she ~s life** elle aime la vie; **he knows how to ~ life** il sait vivre; **I ~ed the match/film** le match/le film m'a plu, j'ai bien aimé le match/film; **I ~ed my day/stay in London** j'ai passé une bonne journée/un bon séjour à Londres; **I didn't ~ the party** je ne me suis pas bien amusé à la soirée; **we ~ed it immensely** cela nous a beaucoup plu, nous avons beaucoup aimé; **the tourists are ~ing the good weather** les touristes profitent du beau temps; **~ your meal!** bon appétit!; **~ our hotel's excellent restaurant** appréciez l'excellent restaurant de notre hôtel; **he ~ed a meal/coffee in the restaurant** il a pris un repas/café au restaurant; **2** (benefit from) jouir de [*privilege, right, advantage, good health, popularity, success*].

II *vi* **~!** US amusez-vous (or amuse-toi) bien!

III *v refl* **to ~ oneself** s'amuser; **to ~ oneself doing** s'amuser à faire; **~ yourselves!** amusez-vous bien!

enjoyable /ɪn'dʒɔɪəbl/ *adj* agréable.

enjoyably /ɪn'dʒɔɪəblɪ/ *adv* [*chat, dine*] d'une manière agréable; **we spent the morning ~ in the museum** nous avons passé une matinée agréable au musée.

enjoyment /ɪn'dʒɔɪmənt/ *n* **1** ¢ (pleasure) plaisir *m*; **much to the ~ of** au grand plaisir de; **my ~ of sport/reading** le plaisir que je prends au sport/à la lecture; **to get ~ from chess/television** prendre plaisir à jouer aux échecs/regarder la télévision; **he never reads for ~** il ne lit jamais pour le plaisir; **2** sout (of privileges, rights) jouissance *f* (**of** de).

enlarge /ɪn'lɑːdʒ/ **I** *vtr* agrandir [*space, opening, document, photograph*]; élargir [*empire*]; développer [*business*]; augmenter [*capacity*]; **to have a photograph ~d** faire agrandir une photo.

II *vi* **1** (get bigger) [*space, opening*] s'agrandir; [*influence, majority, population*] s'accroître; **2** Med [*pupil*] se dilater; [*tonsils, joint*] enfler; **3 to ~ on** (explain) s'étendre sur [*subject*]; développer [*theory, idea*]; **can you ~ on what has just been said?** pouvez-vous développer un peu ce qui vient d'être dit?

III enlarged *pp adj* Med [*pupil, pore*] dilaté; [*tonsils, joint*] enflé; [*heart, liver*] hypertrophié.

enlargement /ɪn'lɑːdʒmənt/ *n* **1** (of space, opening) agrandissement *m*; (of territory) élargissement *m*; (of business) accroissement *m*; (of index) augmentation *f*; (of photograph, document) agrandissement *m*; **2** Med (of pupil) dilatation *f*; (of heart, liver) hypertrophie *f*.

enlarger /ɪn'lɑːdʒə(r)/ *n* Phot agrandisseur *m*.

enlighten /ɪn'laɪtn/ *vtr* éclairer (**on** sur); **I'm waiting to be ~ed** iron j'attends qu'on éclaire ma lanterne iron; **I'm no more ~ed now than I was at the beginning** je n'en sais pas plus long or je ne suis pas plus avancé qu'au début.

enlightened /ɪn'laɪtnd/ *adj* [*person, mind, opinions*] éclairé; **in these ~ days** iron dans ce siècle de lumières, dans ce siècle éclairé.

enlightening /ɪn'laɪtnɪŋ/ *adj* [*book*] instructif/-ive; **that conversation was most ~** iron cette conversation était très instructive or édifiante.

enlightenment /ɪn'laɪtnmənt/ **I** *n* **1** (edification) instruction *f*, édification *f*; **2** (clarification) éclaircissement *m* (**on** sur); **for your ~** pour votre instruction.

II Enlightenment *pr n* (also **Age of the Enlightenment**) Hist Siècle *m* des lumières.

enlist /ɪn'lɪst/ **I** *vtr* Mil enrôler, recruter [*soldier*]; fig recruter [*volunteer, helper*]; **to ~ sb's help/co-operation** s'assurer l'aide/le concours de qn.

II *vi* Mil s'enrôler, s'engager.

enlisted man *n* US Mil simple soldat *m*.

enlistment /ɪn'lɪstmənt/ *n* Mil enrôlement *m*, recrutement *m*.

enliven /ɪn'laɪvn/ *vtr* animer [*conversation, meal*]; colorer [*speech*].

enmesh /ɪn'meʃ/ *vtr* **to become ~ed in** [*person*] s'empêtrer dans [*net, rope*]; [*fish*] se prendre dans les mailles de [*net*]; **to be ~ed in a family feud** se trouver mêlé à une querelle de famille.

enmity /'enmətɪ/ *n* inimitié *f*, hostilité *f* (**towards** envers; **for** pour).

ennoble /ɪ'nəʊbl/ *vtr* lit anoblir [*person*]; fig ennoblir [*person, mind, spirit*].

enologist *n* US = **oenologist**.

enology *n* US = **oenology**.

enormity /ɪ'nɔːmətɪ/ *n* **1** (of crime, problem, task) énormité *f*; **2** sout (crime) atrocité *f*; **3** (mistake) énormité *f*.

enormous /ɪ'nɔːməs/ *adj* [*house, animal, difference, problem*] énorme; [*effort*] prodigieux/-ieuse; **an ~ amount of** énormément de; **an ~ number of people** un monde fou; **to his ~ delight** à sa très grande joie.

enormously /ɪ'nɔːməslɪ/ *adv* [*change, enjoy, vary*] énormément; [*big, long, complex, impressed*] extrêmement; **we enjoyed ourselves ~** on s'est beaucoup or follement amusé○.

enough /ɪˈnʌf/

■ **Note** When *enough* is used as an adverb or a pronoun, it is most frequently translated by *assez*: *is the house big enough?* = est-ce que la maison est assez grande? (Note that *assez* comes before the adjective); *will there be enough?* = est-ce qu'il y en aura assez? Note that if the sentence does not specify what it is enough of, the pronoun *en*, meaning *of it/of them*, must be added before the verb in French.
– When used as a determiner, *enough* is generally translated by *assez de*: *we haven't bought enough meat* = nous n'avons pas acheté assez de viande; *there's enough meat for two meals/six people* = il y a assez de viande pour deux repas/six personnes; *have you got enough chairs?* = avez-vous assez de chaises?
– For more examples and particular usages, see the entry below.

adv, det, pron **tall/sweet ~** assez grand/sucré; **big ~ for us** assez grand pour nous; **big ~ to hold 50 people** assez grand pour contenir 50 personnes; **quite big ~** bien assez grand (**for** pour; **to do** pour faire); **just wide ~** juste assez large (**for** pour; **to do** pour faire); **to eat/have ~** manger/en avoir assez; **have you had ~ to eat?** avez-vous assez mangé?; **~ money/seats** assez d'argent/de sièges; **he has ~ money to buy a car** il a assez d'argent pour acheter une voiture; **there's more than ~ for everybody** il y en a plus qu'assez or largement assez pour tout le monde; **she seems happy ~** elle a l'air assez heureuse; **it's a common ~ complaint** c'est un sujet de plainte assez courant; **there was hardly ~** il y en avait à peine assez; **is there ~?** y en a-t-il assez?; **is he old ~ to vote?** a-t-il l'âge de voter?; **you're not trying hard ~** tu ne fais pas assez d'efforts; **curiously ~, I like her** aussi bizarre que cela puisse paraître, je l'aime bien; **will that be ~ (money)?** est-ce que ça suffira?; **I've had ~ of him/of his rudeness** j'en ai assez de lui/de sa grossièreté; **I've had ~ of working for one day** j'ai assez travaillé pour aujourd'hui; **I've got ~ to worry about** j'ai assez de soucis (comme ça); **I think you have said ~** je crois que vous en avez dit assez; **once was ~ for me!** une fois m'a suffi!; **that's ~ (from you)!** assez!; **~ said!** j'ai compris!; **it's ~ to put you off** ça suffirait à vous dégoûter; **he's ~ of a fool** ou **he's fool ~ to believe it** il est suffisamment or assez bête pour le croire; **she's a nice ~ woman** elle n'est pas désagréable; **~'s ~** ça suffit (comme ça); **and sure ~...!** et ça n'a pas manqué...!
IDIOMS **~ is as good as a feast** Prov ≈ il ne faut pas abuser des bonnes choses.

enquire *vtr, vi* = **inquire**.

enquiry *n* = **inquiry**.

enrage /ɪnˈreɪdʒ/ *vtr* mettre [qn] en rage, rendre [qn] furieux/-ieuse; **to be ~d at sb** être furieux/-ieuse contre qn.

enraged /ɪnˈreɪdʒd/ *adj* [*person*] enragé, furieux/-ieuse; [*bull, dog*] furieux/-ieuse.

enrapture /ɪnˈræptʃə(r)/ *vtr* enchanter, ravir.

enrich /ɪnˈrɪtʃ/ *vtr* (all contexts) enrichir; **this experience has ~ed her** cette expérience a été très enrichissante pour elle.

enriched nuclear fuel *n* combustible *m* nucléaire enrichi.

enrichment /ɪnˈrɪtʃmənt/ *n* enrichissement *m*.

enrol, enroll US /ɪnˈrəʊl/ (*p prés etc* **-ll-**) **I** *vtr* inscrire [*member, student, child*]; Mil enrôler [*recruit*].
II *vi* gen s'inscrire; Mil s'engager (**in** dans); **to ~ on a course/at a university** s'inscrire à un cours/à une université; **to ~ in history** s'inscrire en histoire.

enrolment, enrollment US /ɪnˈrəʊlmənt/ *n* gen inscription *f* (**in, on** à); Mil enrôlement *m*; **school ~s** les inscriptions à l'école; **the total ~ in each class** le total des inscriptions dans chaque classe; **the drop in ~s** la baisse des inscriptions.

en route /ˌɒn ˈruːt/ *adv* en route.

ensconce /ɪnˈskɒns/ **I** *vtr* **to be ~d** (in a room) être bien installé; (in an armchair) être bien installé; (in a job, situation) être casé.
II *v refl* **to ~ oneself** bien s'installer.

ensemble /ɒnˈsɒmbl/ *n* (all contexts) ensemble *m*.

enshrine /ɪnˈʃraɪn/ *vtr* Relig enchâsser [*relic*]; fig conserver [qch] pieusement [*memory*]; renfermer [*principle, tradition*]; **~d in law** consacré par la loi.

ensign /ˈensən/ *n* **1** (flag) pavillon *m*; **to fly the ~** battre pavillon; **red ~** pavillon de la marine marchande; **white ~** pavillon de la marine de guerre; **blue ~** pavillon des bâtiments de soutien; **2** US Naut, GB Mil Hist (officer) enseigne *m*.

enslave /ɪnˈsleɪv/ *vtr* lit asservir, réduire [qn] à l'esclavage; fig asservir; **to be ~d by passion** être l'esclave de la passion.

enslavement /ɪnˈsleɪvmənt/ *n* asservissement *m*.

ensnare /ɪnˈsneə(r)/ *vtr* lit prendre [qn/qch] au piège, attraper; **he was ~d by her charms** fig il s'est laissé prendre par ses charmes.

ensue /ɪnˈsjuː, US -ˈsuː/ *vi* s'ensuivre; **to ~ from** résulter de.

ensuing /ɪnˈsjuːɪŋ, US -ˈsuː-/ *adj* qui s'ensuivit.

en suite /ˌɒn ˈswiːt/ **I** *n* Tourism salle *f* de bains attenante.
II *adj* attenant, contigu/-uë; **with an ~ bathroom, with bathroom ~** avec salle de bains (attenante).

ensure /ɪnˈʃɔː(r), US ɪnˈʃʊər/ *vtr* garantir; **to ~ that** s'assurer que, faire en sorte que (+ *subj*); **to ~ sb** garantir or assurer [qch] à qn [*place, ticket*].

ENT *n* (*abrév* = **Ear, Nose and Throat**) ORL *f*.

entail /ɪnˈteɪl/ **I** *n* Jur substitution *f* (d'un héritage).
II *vtr* **1** impliquer [*travel, action, work*]; exiger [*patience, sacrifice, discretion*]; entraîner [*change, development, expense, responsibility, study*]; nécessiter [*effort, time, journey, modification*]; **to ~ sb doing** impliquer que qn fasse; **to ~ that** impliquer que (+ *subj*); **2** Jur substituer; **3** Philos, Math impliquer.

entailment /ɪnˈteɪlmənt/ *n* Philos, Math, Ling implication *f*.

entangle /ɪnˈtæŋgl/ *vtr* **1** lit **to become ~d** s'enchevêtrer (**in** dans); **to be ~d in sth** être pris dans qch; **2** fig (involve) **to be ~d with** [*person*] être étroitement lié à [*ideology*]; (sexually) se compromettre avec [*person*]; **to be ~d in** [*person*] être mêlé de près à [*conspiracy*].

entanglement /ɪnˈtæŋglmənt/ *n* **1** (complicated situation) imbroglio *m*; **the legal ~s** l'imbroglio juridique; **2** (involvement) liaison *f* (**with** avec); **his sexual ~s** ses aventures sexuelles; **3** Mil **barbed wire ~s** réseaux *mpl* de barbelés.

enter /ˈentə(r)/ **I** *vtr* **1** (go into) entrer dans, pénétrer dans [*room, building*]; **to ~ the house by the back door** entrer dans la maison par la porte de derrière; **here the river ~s the sea** ici le fleuve se jette dans la mer; **2** (commence) entrer dans [*phase, period*]; entamer [*new term, final year*]; **she is ~ing her third year as president** elle entame sa troisième année comme présidente; **he is ~ing his fiftieth year** il entre dans sa cinquantième année; **the country is ~ing a recession** le pays s'engage dans la récession; **3** (join, sign up for) entrer dans [*profession, firm*]; participer à, prendre part à [*race, competition*]; entrer à [*school, university, convent, army, party, EC*]; **to ~ parliament** entrer au parlement; **to ~ the war** entrer en guerre; **to ~ the Church** entrer en religion or dans les ordres; **4** (put forward) inscrire [*competitor, candidate, pupil*] (**for** à); engager [*horse*] (**for** dans); présenter [*poem, picture*] (**for** à); **5** (register, record) (on form, list, ledger) inscrire [*detail, figure, fact*] (**in** dans); (in diary, notebook) noter [*fact, appointment*] (**in** dans); **to ~ an item in the books** Accts porter un article or passer une écriture (sur le livre de comptes); **to ~ an objection** élever une objection; **to ~ a plea of guilty** plaider coupable; **6** (penetrate) pénétrer dans, entrer dans; **the bullet ~ed the lung** la balle a pénétré dans le poumon; **7** fig (come into) **to ~ sb's mind** ou **head** venir à l'idée or à l'esprit de qn; **it never ~ed my mind that** il ne m'était jamais venu à l'idée que; **a note of anger ~ed her voice** il y avait une pointe de colère dans sa voix; **8** Comput entrer [*data*].
II *vi* **1** [*person, animal*] entrer; **the bullet ~ed above the ear** la balle est entrée or a pénétré au-dessus de l'oreille; **'~ Ophelia'** Theat 'entre Ophélie'; **2** (enrol) **to ~ for** s'inscrire à [*exam*]; s'inscrire pour [*race*]; **I hope they don't ~** j'espère qu'ils ne participeront pas à l'épreuve.
■ **enter into**: **~ into [sth] 1** (embark on) entrer en [*correspondence, conversation*]; entamer [*negotiations, debate, argument*]; se lancer dans [*explanations, apologies*]; conclure [*deal, alliance*]; passer [*agreement, contract*]; **to ~ into detail** entrer dans les détails; **2** (become involved in) entrer dans, se laisser gagner par [*spirit*]; partager [*problem*]; **to ~ into the spirit of the game** entrer dans le jeu; **3** (be part of) faire partie de [*plans, calculations*]; **that doesn't ~ into it** c'est sans rapport.
■ **enter on** = **enter upon**.
■ **enter up**: **~ up [sth], ~ [sth] up** inscrire [*figure, total, detail*].
■ **enter upon**: **~ upon [sth] 1** (undertake) s'engager dans [*war, marriage*]; **2** Jur prendre possession de [*inheritance*].

enteric /enˈterɪk/ *adj* entérique.

enteric fever ▶ **1354** *n* fièvre *f* typhoïde.

enteritis /ˌentəˈraɪtɪs/ ▶ **1354** *n* entérite *f*.

enterostomy /ˌentəˈrɒstəmɪ/ *n* entérostomie *f*.

enterotomy /ˌentəˈrɒtəmɪ/ *n* entérotomie *f*.

enterovirus /ˌentərəʊˈvaɪərəs/ *n* entérovirus *m*.

enterprise /ˈentəpraɪz/ *n* **1** (undertaking) entreprise *f*; (venture) aventure *f*; **business ~** affaire *f* commerciale; **2** (initiative) esprit *m* d'initiative or d'entreprise; **3** (company, firm) entreprise *f*, affaire *f*; **4** Econ entreprise *f*; **private ~** l'entreprise privée.

enterprise: **~ allowance** *n* GB Admin *allocation pour la création d'une entreprise*; **~ zone** *n* zone *f* de développement économique.

enterprising /ˈentəpraɪzɪŋ/ *adj* [*person*] entreprenant; [*plan*] audacieux/-ieuse; **it was very ~ of you to organize a concert** vous avez fait preuve de beaucoup d'initiative en organisant ce concert.

enterprisingly /ˈentəpraɪzɪŋlɪ/ *adv* [*act, say*] de sa propre initiative, de son propre chef.

entertain /ˌentəˈteɪn/ **I** *vtr* **1** (keep amused) divertir; (make laugh) amuser; (keep occupied) distraire, occuper; (keep company with) tenir compagnie à; **2** (play host to) recevoir; **to ~ sb to dinner** recevoir qn à dîner; **she's being ~ed to dinner by some friends** elle est invitée à dîner chez des amis; **3** (nurture) entretenir [*idea*]; retenir [*suggestion*]; nourrir [*doubt, hope, ambition, passion, illusion*]; **I couldn't ~ the thought that** je n'arrivais pas à me faire à l'idée que.
II *vi* recevoir; **we don't ~ much** nous ne recevons pas souvent.

entertainer /ˌentəˈteɪnə(r)/ ▶ **1692** *n* (comic) comique *mf*; (performer, raconteur) amuseur/-euse *m/f*; **an all-round ~** une bête de spectacle.

entertaining /ˌentəˈteɪnɪŋ/ **I** *adj* divertissant.
II *n* (art) art *m* de recevoir; **they do a lot of ~** ils reçoivent beaucoup; **I love ~** j'adore recevoir; **ideal for ~!** parfait pour recevoir vos amis!

entertainingly /ˌentəˈteɪnɪŋlɪ/ *adv* de façon divertissante.

entertainment /ˌentəˈteɪnmənt/ *n* **1** ¢ divertissement *m*, distractions *fpl*; **what do you do for ~ here?** qu'est-ce qu'il y a comme distractions ici?; **television is her only ~** la télévision est sa seule distraction; **for sb's ~** pour l'amusement or le divertissement de qn; **for her own ~** pour le plaisir; **(much) to the ~ of sb** à la grande joie de qn; **the world of ~, the ~ world** le monde du spectacle; **2** (performance, event) spectacle *m*.

entertainment: **~ allowance** *n* indemnité *f* or prime *f* de représentation; **~ expenses** *n* frais *mpl* de représentation; **~ industry** *n* industrie *f* du spectacle.

enthral(l) /ɪnˈθrɔːl/ *vtr* (*p prés etc* **-ll-**) **1** (captivate) [*performance, novel, scenery*] captiver, passionner; [*beauty, charm*] séduire, charmer; **to be ~ed by sb's beauty** être captivé or saisi par la beauté de qn; **2†** (enslave) asservir.

enthralling /ɪnˈθrɔːlɪŋ/ *adj* [*novel, performance*] captivant, passionnant; [*beauty*] saisissant.

enthrone /ɪnˈθrəʊn/ *vtr* introniser, placer [qn] sur le trône [*monarch*]; introniser [*bishop*]; **to sit ~d** littér trôner; **~d in the hearts of millions** vénéré par des millions d'admirateurs.

enthronement /ɪnˈθrəʊnmənt/ *n* lit, fig intronisation *f*.

enthuse /ɪnˈθjuːz, US -θuːz/ **I** *vtr* enthousiasmer; **'superb!' he ~d** 'magnifique!' dit-il enthousiaste or en s'extasiant.
II *vi* s'extasier (**about, over** devant); iron s'enflammer.

enthusiasm /ɪnˈθjuːzɪæzəm, US -ˈθuːz-/ *n* **1** ¢ enthousiasme *m* (**for** pour); **to show ~ for** ou **about doing** faire preuve d'enthousiasme pour faire; **to arouse ~ in sb** susciter l'enthousiasme de qn; **to arouse sb to ~** enthousiasmer qn; **to feel ~ for sth** être tout enthousiasmé par qch; **to fill sb with ~** remplir qn d'enthousiasme; **I haven't much ~ for going** je n'ai guère envie d'y aller; **2** (hobby) passion *f*.

enthusiast /ɪnˈθjuːzɪæst, US -ˈθuːz-/ *n* (for sport, gardening, DIY) passionné/-e *m/f*; (for music, composer) fervent/-e *m/f*; **a rugby ~** un passionné de rugby; **to be an ~ for sth** se passionner pour qch or être passionné de qch.

enthusiastic /ɪnˌθjuːzɪˈæstɪk, US -ˌθuːz-/ *adj* [*crowd, response, welcome*] enthousiaste; [*singing, discussion*] exalté; [*worker, gardener*] passionné; [*member*] fervent; **to be ~ about sth** (present or future activity) être enthousiasmé par qch; (past event) parler de qch avec enthousiasme; **they were not very ~ about going to the museum** ils n'étaient pas très enthousiasmés à l'idée d'aller au musée; **he's not very ~ about his work** il ne montre pas beaucoup d'enthousiasme pour son travail.

enthusiastically /ɪnˌθjuːzɪˈæstɪklɪ, US -ˌθuːz-/ *adv* avec enthousiasme.

entice /ɪnˈtaɪs/ *vtr* (with offer, charms, prospects) attirer, tenter; (with food, money) appâter, allécher; **to ~ sb to do** persuader qn de faire; **the sunshine ~d them into the water** le soleil les incitait à la baignade.
■ **entice away**: **~ [sb] away** détourner; **to ~ sb away from** détourner qn de [*activity, work*].

enticement /ɪnˈtaɪsmənt/ *n* **1** (offer, prospect) attrait *m*; **2** (act) **the ~ of new recruits into the army is no easy matter** il n'est pas facile d'attirer de nouvelles recrues dans l'armée.

enticing /ɪnˈtaɪsɪŋ/ *adj* [*prospect, offer*] attrayant, tentant; [*person, look*] séduisant; [*food, smell*] alléchant, appétissant.

enticingly /ɪnˈtaɪsɪŋlɪ/ *adv* de manière séduisante; **~ picturesque** d'un pittoresque séduisant; **~ cool** d'une fraîcheur tentante.

entire /ɪnˈtaɪə(r)/ *adj* **1 the ~ family** toute la famille, la famille (tout) entière; **our ~ support** notre soutien absolu; **2** (of time) tout, entier/-ière; **an ~ day** toute une journée, une journée entière; **throughout her ~ career** pendant toute sa carrière; **3 the ~ world** le monde entier; **throughout the ~ house** dans toute la maison; **the ~ length of the street** toute la longueur de la rue; **4** [*number, sum*] **the ~ 50,000 dollars** les 50 000 dollars dans leur totalité; **the ~ three million population** toute la population de trois millions d'habitants; **5** (emphasizing) **the ~ atmosphere changed** l'atmosphère a complètement changé; **the ~ purpose of his visit** le seul objet de sa visite; **we are in ~ agreement with you** nous sommes entièrement d'accord avec vous.

entirely /ɪnˈtaɪəlɪ/ *adv* [*destroy, escape, cancel*] entièrement; [*reject*] totalement; [*innocent, different, unnecessary*] complètement; **that changes things ~** ça change tout; **I ~ agree** je suis entièrement d'accord; **I was ~ to blame** c'était entièrement ma faute; **that's ~ up to you** cela dépend entièrement de vous; **~ free of additives** sans additifs; **~ at your own risk** entièrement à vos risques et périls; **not ~** pas tout à fait.

entirety /ɪnˈtaɪərətɪ/ *n sans pl* ensemble *m*, totalité *f*; **in its ~** dans son ensemble; **the film will be shown in its ~** le film sera présenté en version intégrale; **they have not rejected the report in its ~** ils n'ont pas rejeté la totalité du rapport.

entitle /ɪnˈtaɪtl/ *vtr* **1** (authorize) **to ~ sb to sth** donner droit à qch à qn; **to ~ sb to do** autoriser qn à faire; **to be ~d to sth** avoir droit à qch; **to be ~d to do** avoir le droit de faire; **I'm only claiming what I'm ~d to** je ne réclame que mon dû or ce à quoi j'ai droit; **after three hours she's ~d to a rest** après trois heures elle a bien le droit de se reposer; **everyone's ~d to their own opinion** à chacun ses opinions; **2** (call) intituler [*text, music*]; donner un titre à [*work of art*]; **the sculpture is ~d 'The Apple Tree'** la sculpture s'intitule 'le Pommier'; **the poem is ~d 'Love'** le poème s'intitule 'L'amour'.

entitlement /ɪnˈtaɪtlmənt/ *n* droit *m* (**to sth** à qch; **to do** de faire); **~ to vote** droit de vote.

entity /ˈentətɪ/ *n* entité *f*.

entomb /ɪnˈtuːm/ *vtr* littér enterrer, mettre au tombeau; fig ensevelir, enfouir.

entombment /ɪnˈtuːmənt/ *n* littér ensevelissement *m*, mise *f* au tombeau; fig ensevelissement *m*.

entomological /ˌentəməˈlɒdʒɪkl/ *adj* entomologique.

entomologist /ˌentəˈmɒlədʒɪst/ ▶ **1692** *n* entomologiste *mf*.

entomology /ˌentəˈmɒlədʒɪ/ *n* entomologie *f*.

entourage /ˌɒntʊˈrɑːʒ/ *n* entourage *m*.

entr'acte /ˈɒntrækt/ *n* entracte *m*.

entrails /ˈentreɪlz/ *npl* lit, fig entrailles *fpl*.

entrain /ɪnˈtreɪn/ US **I** *vtr* faire monter [qn] dans un train.
II *vi* monter dans un train.

entrance I /ˈentrəns/ *n* **1** (door, gate, passage) entrée *f*; (hallway) entrée *f*, vestibule *m*; **main ~** entrée principale; **2** (act of entering) entrée *f*; **to make an ~** Theat, fig faire son entrée; **to give ~ to** donner accès à; **3** (right of way) admission *f*; **to gain ~ to** être admis à or dans [*club, university*]; **to deny** ou **refuse sb ~** refuser de laisser entrer qn.
II /ɪnˈtrɑːns, US -ˈtræns/ *vtr* transporter, ravir.

entrance examination *n* GB **1** Sch, Univ examen *m* d'entrée; **2** (for civil service) concours *m* d'entrée.

entrance /ˈentrəns/: **~ fee** *n* droit *m* d'entrée; **~ hall** *n* (in house) vestibule *m*; (in public building, mansion) hall *m*; **~ requirements** *npl* diplômes *mpl* requis.

entrance ticket /ɪnˈtrɑːns/ *n* billet *m* d'entrée.

entrancing /ɪnˈtrɑːnsɪŋ, US -træns-/ *adj* enchanteur/-eresse, ravissant.

entrancingly /ɪnˈtrɑːnsɪŋlɪ, US -træns-/ *adv* [*smile*] de façon séduisante; [*dance, sing*] à ravir; **she is ~ beautiful** elle est belle à ravir.

entrant /ˈentrənt/ *n* (in race, competition) participant/-e *m/f*; (in exam) candidat/-e *m/f*; (to profession) nouveau venu/nouvelle venue *m/f*; (to police force) nouvelle recrue *f*.

entrap /ɪnˈtræp/ *vtr* (*p prés etc* **-pp-**) prendre [qn] au piège; **to ~ sb into doing** pousser qn à faire par la ruse.

entrapment /ɪnˈtræpmənt/ *n* US Jur *incitation par la police à faire commettre un délit par une personne dans le seul but de la faire arrêter.*

entreat /ɪnˈtriːt/ *vtr* implorer, supplier (**to do** de faire); **to ~ sth of sb** implorer qch de qn; **spare his life, I ~ you!** épargnez-le, je vous en supplie!

entreating /ɪnˈtriːtɪŋ/ *adj* suppliant, implorant.

entreatingly /ɪnˈtriːtɪŋlɪ/ *adv* [*beg, ask*] d'une voix suppliante or implorante; [*gaze*] d'un air suppliant or implorant.

entreaty /ɪnˈtriːtɪ/ *n* prière *f*, supplication *f*; **at sb's ~** aux instances *fpl* de qn, à la requête de qn; **a look/gesture of ~** un regard/geste suppliant; **he was deaf to all ~** il était sourd à toutes les supplications.

entrée /ˈɒntreɪ/ *n* **1** GB Culin entrée *f*; **2** US (main course) plat *m* principal; **3** (into society) **her wealth gave her an ~ into high society** sa fortune lui a ouvert les portes de la haute société.

entrench /ɪnˈtrentʃ/ *vtr* Mil retrancher.

entrenched /ɪnˈtrentʃt/ *adj* **1** Mil retranché; **2** fig [*opinion*] inébranlable, ferme; [*idea*] bien arrêté; [*tradition*] bien établi, vivace; [*rights, powers*] bien établi; **he is ~ in his views** il a des opinions bien arrêtées; **a society ~ in superstition** une société figée dans la superstition.

entrenchment /ɪnˈtrentʃmənt/ *n* Mil, fig retranchement *m*.

entrepôt /ˈɒntrəpəʊ/ *n* entrepôt *m*.

entrepreneur /ˌɒntrəprəˈnɜː(r)/ *n* Comm entrepreneur/-euse *m/f*.

entrepreneurial /ˌɒntrəprəˈnɜːrɪəl/ *adj* **to have ~ spirit/skills** avoir le sens/le don des affaires.

entropy /ˈentrəpɪ/ *n* entropie *f*.

entropy diagram *n* diagramme *m* entropique.

entrust /ɪnˈtrʌst/ *vtr* confier; **to ~ sb with sth, to ~ sth to sb** confier qch à qn; **to ~ sb with the task of doing sth** confier à qn le soin de faire qch; **I ~ed the child to her (care)** je lui ai confié la garde de l'enfant.

entry /ˈentrɪ/ *n* **1** (act of entering) entrée *f*; **sb's ~ into** l'entrée de qn dans [*room, politics, profession, EC*]; **to gain ~ to** ou **into** s'introduire dans [*building*]; accéder à [*computer file*]; **he failed to gain ~** (to building) il n'a pas réussi à entrer; **to force ~ to** ou **into** s'introduire de force dans; **2** (admission) (to club, institution, university) admission *f*; (to country) entrée *f*; **he was refused ~** on a refusé de le laisser entrer (**to** dans); **free ~** entrée gratuite; **'no ~'** (on door) 'défense d'entrer'; (in one way street) 'sens interdit'; **3** (door, gate, passage) entrée *f*; **4** (recorded item) (in dictionary, ship's log) entrée *f*; (in encyclopedia) article *m*; (in diary) note *f*; (in register) inscription *f*; (in ledger, accounts book) écriture *f*; **to make an ~ in one's diary** écrire or noter quelque chose dans son journal; **there is no ~ in his diary for July 13** il n'a rien noté dans son journal à la date du 13 juillet; **to make an ~ in a ledger** passer une écriture; **5** (for poetry, painting, writing competition) œuvre *f* présentée à un concours; (for song contest) titre *m*; **the winning ~** le titre gagnant, l'œuvre gagnante; **this is my ~ for the fancy dress contest** c'est le déguisement que je présente au concours; **we received 1,000 entries for the crossword competition** il y a eu 1 000 réponses au concours de mots croisés; **send your ~ to...** envoyez votre réponse à...; **there was a large ~ for the contest** la participation au concours a été élevée.

entry: **~ fee** *n* droit *m* d'entrée; **~ form** *n* fiche *f* d'inscription; **~ permit** *n* visa *m* d'entrée; **~ phone** *n* interphone *m*; **~ requirements** *npl* diplômes *mpl* requis; **~ word** *n* US entrée *f*, adresse *f*.

ents○ /ents/ *npl* GB Univ (*abrév* = **entertainments**) animation *f* culturelle (*dans une université*).

entwine /ɪn'twaɪn/ **I** *vtr* entrelacer [*ribbon, stems, initials*]; mêler [*fate, lives*] (**with** à).
II *vi* [*ribbons, stems, initials*] s'entrelacer; [*bodies, arms*] s'enlacer; [*memories, lives*] s'entremêler; **to ~ around** enlacer [*pole, tree, body*].

E number *n* GB (number) *numéro d'additif alimentaire (approuvé par la CEE)*; (additive) additif *m* alimentaire.

enumerate /ɪ'nju:məreɪt, US -'nu:-/ *vtr* sout énumérer.

enumeration /ɪˌnju:mə'reɪʃn, US -ˌnu:-/ *n* sout (list) énumération *f*; (counting) dénombrement *m*.

enunciate /ɪ'nʌnsɪeɪt/ *vtr* articuler [*words, lines*]; énoncer [*truth, clause*]; exposer [*principle, policy*].

enunciation /ɪˌnʌnsɪ'eɪʃn/ *n* (of sound, word) articulation *f*; (of facts, clause) énonciation *f*; (of law, problem) énoncé *m*; (of principle, policy) exposé *m*.

enuresis /ˌenjʊə'ri:sɪs, US ˌenʊə-/ *n* énurésie *f*.

enuretic /ˌenjʊə'retɪk, US ˌenʊə-/ *adj* énurétique.

envelop /ɪn'veləp/ *vtr* envelopper; **~ed in** enveloppé dans [*cape, blanket*]; enveloppé par [*flames, smoke*].

envelope /'envələʊp, 'ɒn-/ *n* **1** Post enveloppe *f*; **to put sth in an ~** mettre qch sous enveloppe; **in the same ~** dans la même enveloppe, sous le même pli; **in a sealed ~** sous enveloppe cachetée, sous pli cacheté; **2** (membrane) Aviat enveloppe *f*; Anat tunique *f*; Biol, Bot enveloppe *f*, membrane *f*; **3** Math enveloppe *f*.

envelopment /ɪn'veləpmənt/ *n* Mil enveloppement *m*.

envenom /ɪn'venəm/ *vtr* envenimer.

enviable /'envɪəbl/ *adj* enviable.

enviably /'envɪəblɪ/ *adv* **he was ~ slim/rich** sa minceur/sa richesse faisait envie.

envious /'envɪəs/ *adj* [*person*] envieux/-ieuse; [*look*] d'envie, envieux/-ieuse; **to be ~ of sb/sth** envier qn/qch; **to make sb ~** rendre qn jaloux/-ouse; **some people were ~ of her good fortune** son bonheur faisait des envieux.

enviously /'envɪəslɪ/ *adv* avec envie.

environment /ɪn'vaɪərənmənt/ *n* **1** gen, Biol, Zool (physical) environnement *m*; **2** (cultural, moral) climat *m*, environnement *m*; (social) milieu *m*; **friendly ~** ambiance *f* amicale; **working ~** conditions *fpl* de travail; **3** GB Ecol **the ~** l'environnement *m*; **Department of the Environment** ministère *m* de l'Environnement; **Secretary of State** ou **Minister for the Environment** ministre *m* de l'Environnement; **4** Psych environnement *m*.

environmental /ɪnˌvaɪərən'mentl/ *adj* **1** gen, Biol, Zool [*conditions, changes*] du milieu; **2** Ecol [*concern, issue*] lié à l'environnement, écologique; [*damage, protection, pollution*] de l'environnement; **~ effect** conséquences *fpl* sur l'environnement; **~ group** groupe *m* écologiste; **~ disaster** catastrophe *f* écologique; **3** Psych lié à l'environnement.

environmental: **~ health** *n* hygiène *f* publique; **Environmental Health Officer** *n* ≈ inspecteur *m* de l'Hygiène publique.

environmentalist /ɪnˌvaɪərən'mentəlɪst/ *n* Pol, Ecol écologiste *mf*.

environmentally /ɪnˌvaɪərən'mentəlɪ/ *adv* **~ safe**, **~ sound** qui ne nuit pas à l'environnement; **~ speaking** en ce qui concerne l'environnement; **~ friendly product** produit qui respecte l'environnement; **~ aware** sensibilisé au problème de l'environnement.

environmental: **Environmental Protection Agency**, **EPA** *n* commission *f* pour la protection de l'Environnement; **~ scientist** *n* écologiste *mf*; **Environmental Studies** *npl* GB Sch études *fpl* géographiques et biologiques de l'environnement.

environs /ɪn'vaɪərənz/ *npl* environs *mpl*; **in the ~ of** dans les environs de.

envisage /ɪn'vɪzɪdʒ/ *vtr* (anticipate) prévoir (**doing** de faire); (visualize) envisager (**doing** de faire); **it is ~d that** (anticipated) il est prévu que, on envisage que.

envoy /'envɔɪ/ *n* **1** gen envoyé/-e *m/f*, émissaire *m*; **2** (also **~ extraordinary**) ministre *m* plénipotentiaire; **3** (also **envoi**) Literat envoi *m*.

envy /'envɪ/ **I** *n* (brief) envie *f*; (long-term) jalousie *f*; **out of ~** par jalousie; **in ~** par envie; **to be the ~ of sb** faire envie à qn; **her success caused considerable ~** sa réussite a fait beaucoup de jaloux.
II *vtr* envier; **to ~ sb sth** envier qch à qn.
IDIOMS **to be green with ~** être vert de jalousie.

enzyme /'enzaɪm/ *n* enzyme *f*.

EOC *n* GB *abrév* ▸ **Equal Opportunities Commission**.

eon *n* = **aeon**.

eosin(e) /'i:əsɪn/ *n* éosine *f*.

EPA *n*: *abrév* ▸ **Environmental Protection Agency**.

epaulet(te) /'epəlet/ *n* gen, Mil épaulette *f*.

ephedrine /'efədrɪn/ *n* éphédrine *f*.

ephemeral /ɪ'femərəl/ *adj* (all contexts) éphémère.

ephemerid /ɪ'femərɪd/ *n* éphémère *m*.

ephemeris /ɪ'femərɪs/ *n* (*pl* **-ides**) Astron éphémérides *fpl*.

Ephesian /ɪ'fi:ʒən/ **I** *n* Éphésien/-ienne *m/f*.
II Ephesians *npl* Bible l'Épître *f* aux Éphésiens.
III *adj* éphésien/-ienne.

epic /'epɪk/ **I** *n* Literat gen épopée *f*; (poem) épopée *f*, poème *m* épique; (prose) récit *m* épique; (film) film *m* à grand spectacle; (novel) roman-fleuve *m*.
II *adj* Literat épique; fig [*task*] herculéen/-éenne; [*struggle, undertaking, voyage*] épique.

epicarp /'epɪkɑ:p/ *n* épicarpe *m*.

epicene /'epɪsi:n/ *adj* **1** sout (effeminate) [*person, tastes*] efféminé; **2** Ling épicène.

epicentre GB, **epicenter** US /'epɪsentə(r)/ *n* épicentre *m*.

epicure /'epɪkjʊə(r)/ *n* gourmet *m*.

epicurean /ˌepɪkjʊ'ri:ən/ *n, adj* épicurien/-ienne (*m/f*).

epicureanism /ˌepɪkjʊ'ri:ənɪzəm/ *n* épicurisme *m*.

Epicurus /epɪ'kjʊərəs/ *pr n* Épicure.

epidemic /ˌepɪ'demɪk/ **I** *n* lit, fig épidémie *f*.
II *adj* épidémique.

epidermis /ˌepɪ'dɜ:mɪs/ *n* épiderme *m*.

epidiascope /ˌepɪ'daɪəskəʊp/ *n* épidiascope *m*.

epidural /ˌepɪ'djʊərəl/ **I** *n* Med (anaesthetic) péridurale *f*.
II *adj* épidural; Med [*anaesthetic*] péridural.

epiglottis /ˌepɪ'glɒtɪs/ *n* épiglotte *f*.

epigram /'epɪgræm/ *n* gen, Literat épigramme *f*.

epigrammatic(al) /ˌepɪgrə'mætɪk(l)/ *adj* épigrammatique.

epigraph /'epɪgrɑ:f, US -græf/ *n* épigraphe *f*.

epilepsy /'epɪlepsɪ/ ▸ **1354** *n* épilepsie *f*.

epileptic /ˌepɪ'leptɪk/ **I** *n* épileptique *mf*.
II *adj* [*person*] épileptique; **~ fit** crise *f* d'épilepsie.

epilogue /'epɪlɒg/ *n* épilogue *m* also fig.

epinephrine /ˌepɪ'nefrɪn/ *n* US Med adrénaline *f*.

Epiphany /ɪ'pɪfənɪ/ *n* Épiphanie *f*, jour *m* des Rois.

epiphenomenon /ˌepɪfɪ'nɒmɪnən/ *n* (*pl* **-na**) épiphénomène *m*.

epiphytic /ˌepɪ'fɪtɪk/ *adj* épiphyte.

episcopacy /ɪ'pɪskəpəsɪ/ *n* épiscopat *m*.

episcopal /ɪ'pɪskəpl/ *adj* épiscopal; **~ ring** anneau *m* pastoral or épiscopal.

Episcopal Church *pr n* Église *f* épiscopalienne.

Episcopalian /ɪˌpɪskə'peɪlɪən/ *n, adj* épiscopalien/-ienne (*m/f*).

episcopate /ɪ'pɪskəpət/ *n* épiscopat *m*.

episcope /'epɪskəʊp/ *n* GB épiscope *m*.

episiotomy /əˌpi:zɪ'ɒtəmɪ/ *n* épisiotomie *f*.

episode /'epɪsəʊd/ *n* (all contexts) épisode *m*.

episodic /ˌepɪ'sɒdɪk/ *adj* épisodique.

epistemological /ɪˌpɪstɪmə'lɒdʒɪkl/ *adj* épistémologique.

epistemology /ɪˌpɪstɪ'mɒlədʒɪ/ *n* épistémologie *f*.

epistle /ɪ'pɪsl/ *n* Literat épître *f* also hum; **Epistle to the Corinthians** Bible Épître aux Corinthiens.

epistolary /ɪ'pɪstələrɪ, US -lerɪ/ *adj* épistolaire.

epitaph /'epɪtɑ:f, US -tæf/ *n* épitaphe *f* also fig.

epithelium /ˌepɪ'θi:lɪəm/ *n* (*pl* **-liums** ou **-lia**) épithélium *m*.

epithet /'epɪθet/ *n* épithète *f*.

epitome /ɪ'pɪtəmɪ/ *n* (abstract) épitomé *m*; fig **the ~ of kindness** la bonté incarnée; **the ~ of a philosopher** le philosophe par excellence.

epitomize /ɪ'pɪtəmaɪz/ *vtr* (embody) personnifier, incarner.

EPNS *n* (*abrév* = **electroplated nickel silver**) ruolz *m*.

epoch /'i:pɒk, US 'epək/ *n* gen, Geol époque *f*; **to mark an ~** marquer une époque.

epoch-making *adj* [*invention, event*] marquant.

eponym /'epənɪm/ *n* éponyme *m*.

eponymous /ɪ'pɒnɪməs/ *adj* Literat éponyme.

EPOS /'i:pɒs/ *n* (*abrév* = **electronic point of sale**) TPV *m*; **~ terminal** terminal *m* point de vente, TPV *m*.

epoxy /ɪ'pɒksɪ/ *adj* époxy *inv*.

epoxy resin *n* résine *f* époxy.

EPROM /'i:prɒm/ *n* (*abrév* = **erasable programmable read-only memory**) EPROM *f*.

Epsom salts /'epsəm/ *npl* (+ *v sg* ou *pl*) sel *m* d'Epsom, epsomite *f*.

equable /'ekwəbl/ *adj* [*climate*] tempéré; [*temperament*] égal.

equably /'ekwəblɪ/ *adv* calmement.

equal /'i:kwəl/ **I** *n* égal/-e *m/f*; **to be the ~ of** être l'égal de; **to treat sb as an ~** traiter qn en égal.

II *adj* **1** (numerically the same) [*number, quantity*] égal (**to** à); **a sum ~ to one month's salary** une somme égale à un mois de salaire; **'~ work ~ pay'** 'à travail égal salaire égal'; **to fight for ~ pay** lutter pour l'égalité des salaires; **to demand ~ time on television** demander le même temps d'antenne; **2** (equivalent, similar) [*skill, ease, delight*] même, égal; **with ~ pleasure/violence** avec le même plaisir/la même violence; **to have ~ difficulty** avoir autant de difficulté; **they're about ~** [*candidates*] ils se valent à peu près; **3** (not inferior or superior) [*partner*] égal; **on ~ terms** [*fight, compete*] à armes égales; [*judge, place*] sur un pied d'égalité; **to have an ~ relationship** avoir des rapports d'égal à égal; **4** (up to) **to be/feel ~ to** être/se sentir à la hauteur de [*task, job*]; **to feel ~ to doing** se sentir à même de faire.

III *adv* Sport [*finish*] à égalité; **to come ~ third** arriver troisième ex aequo (**with** avec).

IV *vtr* **1** (add up to) égaler; **health plus money ~s happiness** la santé plus la richesse, c'est le bonheur; **2** (match) égaler [*record, time*].

IDIOMS **all things being ~** sauf imprévu.

equality /ɪˈkwɒlətɪ/ *n* égalité *f*; **sexual ~** égalité des sexes; **~ of opportunity** égalité des chances.

equalize /ˈiːkwəlaɪz/ *vtr, vi* égaliser.

equalizer /ˈiːkwəlaɪzə(r)/ *n* **1** Sport but *m* égalisateur; **2** Audio correcteur *m* de fréquence; **3**○ US (gun) pétard○ *m*, flingue◑ *m*.

equally /ˈiːkwəlɪ/ *adv* **1** [*divide, share*] en parts égales; **~ difficult/pretty** tout aussi difficile/joli; **2** (in the same way) de même; **~, we might say that...** de même, on pourrait dire que...

Equal Opportunities Commission, **EOC** *n* GB Commission *f* de l'égalité de traitement.

equal opportunity **I** **equal opportunities** *npl* égalité *f* des chances.

II *modif* [*employer*] appliquant la non-discrimination; [*legislation*] qui assure l'égalité d'accès.

equal: **~ rights** *npl* égalité *f* des droits; **Equal Rights Amendment**, **ERA** *n* US Amendement *m* sur l'égalité des droits; **~s sign** GB, **~ sign** US *n* signe *m* égal.

equanimity /ˌekwəˈnɪmətɪ/ *n* sérénité *f*, équanimité *f* liter.

equate /ɪˈkweɪt/ *vtr* **1** (identify) assimiler (**with** à); **2** (compare) comparer (**with** à); **3** Math mettre en équation (**with** avec).

equation /ɪˈkweɪʒn/ *n* **1** Math équation *f*; **2** fig **the ~ of wealth with happiness is misguided** on aurait tort d'assimiler la richesse au bonheur; **the other side of the ~ is...** l'autre aspect du problème, c'est...; **there is an ~ between...** il y a un rapport direct entre...

equator /ɪˈkweɪtə(r)/ *n* équateur *m*.

equatorial /ˌekwəˈtɔːrɪəl/ *adj* équatorial.

Equatorial Guinea *pr n* Guinée *f* équatoriale.

equerry /ˈekwərɪ, ɪˈkwerɪ/ *n* écuyer *m* (*à la cour d'Angleterre*).

equestrian /ɪˈkwestrɪən/ **I** *n* gen cavalier/-ière *m/f*; (acrobat) écuyer/-ère *m/f*.

II *adj* [*statue, portrait*] équestre; [*dress, gloves, studies*] d'équitation; [*event, competition*] hippique.

equidistant /ˌiːkwɪˈdɪstənt/ *adj* **1** gen à égale distance (**from** de); **2** Math équidistant (**from** de).

equilateral /ˌiːkwɪˈlætərəl/ *adj* équilatéral.

equilibrist /ɪˈkwɪlɪbrɪst/ *n* équilibriste *mf*.

equilibrium /ˌiːkwɪˈlɪbrɪəm/ *n* (*pl* **-riums** ou **-ria**) (all contexts) équilibre *m*; **in ~** en équilibre.

equine /ˈekwaɪn/ *adj* [*disease*] équin; [*species, face, features*] chevalin.

equinoctial /ˌiːkwɪˈnɒkʃl, ˌek-/ *adj* [*year, line*] équinoxial; [*gales, tides*] d'équinoxe.

equinox /ˈiːkwɪnɒks, ˈek-/ *n* équinoxe *m*; **spring/autumnal ~** équinoxe de printemps/d'automne.

equip /ɪˈkwɪp/ *vtr* (*p prés etc* **-pp-**) **1** lit équiper [*person, building, factory, room*] (**for** pour); **to ~ sth with sth** équiper qch de qch; **to ~ sb with sth** munir qn de qch; **to ~ a room/building as sth** aménager une pièce/un bâtiment en qch; **well ~ped** bien équipé; **well ~ped with sth** bien pourvu en qch; **fully ~ped kitchen** cuisine équipée; **2** fig (psychologically) préparer [*person*]; **~ped for life** préparé à la vie; **she wasn't ~ped to cope with the problem** elle n'avait pas les ressources nécessaires pour faire face au problème; **we were well ~ped to answer their questions** nous étions à même de répondre à leurs questions.

equipment /ɪˈkwɪpmənt/ *n* **1** Mil, Sport, Ind équipement *m*; **2** (office, electrical, photographic) matériel *m*; **a piece** ou **item of ~** un article.

equisetum /ˌekwɪˈsiːtəm/ *n* (*pl* **-tums** ou **-ta**) prêle *f*.

equitable /ˈekwɪtəbl/ *adj* équitable.

equitably /ˈekwɪtəblɪ/ *adv* de manière équitable, équitablement.

equitation /ˌekwɪˈteɪʃn/ *n* sout équitation *f*.

equity /ˈekwətɪ/ **I** *n* **1** (fairness) équité *f*; **2** Fin (investment) participation *f*; **shareholders' ~** participation des actionnaires.

II **equities** *npl* Fin actions *fpl* ordinaires.

III **Equity** *pr n* Theat syndicat *m* des acteurs.

equity: **~ capital** *n* Fin capital *m* en actions; **Equity card** *n* carte *f* d'adhérent au syndicat des acteurs; **~ financing** *n* Fin financement *m* par émission d'actions; **~ market** *n* Fin marché *m* des actions; **~ of redemption** *n* Jur droit *m* de grâce.

equivalence /ɪˈkwɪvələns/ *n* équivalence *f*.

equivalent /ɪˈkwɪvələnt/ **I** *n* équivalent *m*.

II *adj* équivalent; **to be ~ to sth** être équivalent à qch, équivaloir à qch.

equivocal /ɪˈkwɪvəkl/ *adj* **1** (ambiguous) [*words, reply, attitude*] équivoque; [*result, conclusion*] incertain, ambigu/-uë; **2** (dubious) [*behaviour, circumstances*] suspect; [*reputation*] équivoque.

equivocally /ɪˈkwɪvəklɪ/ *adv* d'une manière équivoque.

equivocate /ɪˈkwɪvəkeɪt/ *vi* user de faux-fuyants.

equivocation /ɪˌkwɪvəˈkeɪʃn/ *n* faux-fuyants *mpl*; **without ~** sans équivoque.

er /ə, ɜː/ *excl* euh.

ER (*abrév* = **Elizabeth Regina**) la Reine Élisabeth.

era /ˈɪərə/ *n* Geol, Hist ère *f*; (in politics, fashion etc) époque *f*; **the ~ of the mini-skirt** l'époque de la mini-jupe; **the Christian ~** l'ère chrétienne; **to mark the end of an ~** marquer la fin d'une époque; **the Hollywood ~** l'époque hollywoodienne.

ERA *n*: *abrév* ▶ **Equal Rights Amendment**.

eradicate /ɪˈrædɪkeɪt/ *vtr* éradiquer [*disease*]; éliminer, faire disparaître [*poverty, weeds, crime, superstition*].

eradication /ɪˌrædɪˈkeɪʃn/ *n* (of disease) éradication *f*; (of weeds, superstition, crime) élimination *f*.

erase /ɪˈreɪz, US ɪˈreɪs/ *vtr* **1** gen, Comput, Audio effacer; (with rubber) gommer, effacer; **2** fig éliminer [*hunger, poverty*]; effacer [*memory*]; **3**○ US (kill) liquider○.

erase head *n* Audio, Comput tête *f* d'effacement.

eraser /ɪˈreɪzə(r), US -sər/ *n* (for paper) gomme *f*; (for blackboard) brosse *f* feutrée.

eraser head *n* = **erase head**.

Erasmus /ɪˈræzməs/ *pr n* Érasme.

Erasmus scheme *n* Univ programme *m* Erasmus.

erasure /ɪˈreɪʒə(r)/ *n* (act) effacement *m*; (result) rature *f*.

ere /eə(r)/‡ ou littér **I** *prep* avant; **~ long** (future) sous peu; (past) peu après; **~ now** jusque-là.

II *conj* avant que (+ *subj*).

erect /ɪˈrekt/ **I** *adj* [*posture*] droit; [*tail*] dressé; [*ears*] droit, dressé; [*construction*] debout; [*penis*] en érection; **with head ~** la tête haute; **to hold oneself ~** se tenir droit; **to stand ~** se tenir debout.

II *vtr* **1** ériger [*monument, building*]; monter [*scaffolding*]; dresser, monter [*tent*]; placer, monter [*sign, screen*]; **2** fig ériger [*system*].

erectile /ɪˈrektaɪl, US -tl/ *adj* érectile.

erection /ɪˈrekʃn/ **1** (putting up) (of monument) érection *f*; (of building, bridge) construction *f*; (of tent) installation *f*, montage *m*; (of sign) mise *f* en place; **2** (edifice) édifice *m*; **3** (of penis) érection *f*.

erector /ɪˈrektə(r)/ *n* **1** (muscle) érecteur *m*; **2** (person) monteur *m*.

erector set *n* US meccano® *m*.

erg /ɜːg/ *n* erg *m*.

ergative /ˈɜːgətɪv/ **I** *n* ergatif *m*.

II *adj* Ling ergatif/-ive.

ergo /ˈɜːgəʊ/ *adv* sout par conséquent.

ergonomics /ˌɜːgəˈnɒmɪks/ *n* (+ *v sg*) ergonomie *f*.

ergonomist /ɜːˈgɒnəmɪst/ ▶ **1692** *n* ergonome *mf*.

ergot /ˈɜːgət/ *n* **1** Agric ergot *m*; **2** Pharm ergot *m* de seigle, ergotine *f*.

ergotism /ˈɜːgətɪzəm/ *n* ergotisme *m*.

Erie /ˈɪərɪ/ *pr n* **Lake ~** le lac Érié.

Erin /ˈerɪn, ˈɪərɪn/ *pr n* ‡ ou littér Erin *f* liter, l'Irlande *f*.

Eritrea /erɪˈtreɪə/ ▶ **1131** *pr n* Érythrée *f*.

Eritrean /erɪˈtreɪən/ **I** *n* Érythréen/-éenne *m/f*.

II *adj* érythréen/-éenne.

erk○ /ɜːk/ *n* GB Aviat soldat *m* de l'armée de l'air; GB Naut mataf○ *m*.

ERM *n* EC *abrév* ▶ **Exchange Rate Mechanism**.

ermine /ˈɜːmɪn/ *n* (animal, fur) hermine *f*.

Ernie /ˈɜːnɪ/ *n* GB (*abrév* = **Electronic random number indicator equipment**) *ordinateur qui sert au tirage au sort des numéros gagnants des bons à lots*.

erode /ɪˈrəʊd/ *vtr* éroder [*coastline, rock*]; éroder, ronger [*metal*]; fig saper [*confidence, authority*].

erogenous /ɪˈrɒdʒənəs/ *adj* érogène.

Eros /ˈɪərɒs/ *pr n* **1** Mythol Éros; **2** Psych éros *m*.

erosion /ɪˈrəʊʒn/ *n* **1** (of coastline) érosion *f*; **2** (of metal) corrosion *f*; **soil ~** érosion des sols; **3** fig érosion *f*.

erotic /ɪˈrɒtɪk/ *adj* érotique.

erotica /ɪˈrɒtɪkə/ *npl* Literat littérature *f* érotique; Cin films *mpl* érotiques; Art art *m* érotique.

eroticism /ɪˈrɒtɪsɪzəm/ *n* érotisme *m*.

err /ɜː(r)/ *vi* **1** (make mistake) faire erreur; **to ~ in one's judgment** faire une erreur de jugement; **2** (stray) pécher; **to ~ on the side of caution/generosity** pécher par excès de prudence/générosité.

IDIOMS **to ~ is human** Prov l'erreur est humaine.

errand /ˈerənd/ *n* commission *f*, course *f*; **to go on** ou **to run an ~ for sb** aller faire une commission pour qn; **to send sb on an ~** envoyer qn faire une commission; **~ of mercy** mission *f* de charité.

IDIOMS **to go** ou **be sent on a fool's ~** se dépenser pour rien.

errand boy *n* garçon *m* de courses.

errant /ˈerənt/ *adj* sout (misbehaving) dévoyé.

errata /eˈrɑːtə/ *pl* ▶ **erratum**.

erratic /ɪˈrætɪk/ **I** *n* Geol bloc *m* erratique.

II *adj* [*behaviour*] imprévisible; [*performance*] inégal; [*person, driver*] lunatique, imprévisible; [*moods*] changeant; [*movements, attempts*] désordonné; [*timetable*] fantaisiste; [*deliveries*] irrégulier/-ière; **the clock is rather ~** l'horloge n'est pas très fiable; **he's a very ~ player** son jeu est très inégal.

erratically /ɪ'rætɪklɪ/ *adv* [*play, perform*] de façon inégale; [*work, drive*] de manière fantaisiste or imprévisible.

erratum /e'rɑ:təm/ *n* (*pl* **-ta**) erratum *m*.

erroneous /ɪ'rəʊnɪəs/ *adj* erroné, faux/fausse.

erroneously /ɪ'rəʊnɪəslɪ/ *adv* à tort.

error /'erə(r)/ *n* **1** (in spelling, grammar, typing) faute *f*; (in arithmetic) erreur *f*; **to make a serious ~** (in arithmetic) faire une erreur grave; (of judgment) commettre une grave erreur; **an ~ of/in sth** une erreur de/dans qch; **by ~, in ~** par erreur; **~ of judgment** erreur *f* de jugement; **~ of 10%, 10% ~** erreur de 10%; **margin of ~** marge *f* d'erreur; **human ~** erreur *f* humaine; **~s and omissions excepted** Comm sauf erreur ou omission; **2** Comput erreur *f*; **~ message** message *f* d'erreur; **~ correction** correction *f* d'erreur.
IDIOMS **to see the ~ of one's ways** revenir de ses erreurs.

ersatz /'eəzæts, 'ɜ:sɑ:ts/ **I** *n* ersatz *m*, succédané *m*.
II *adj* **it's ~ tobacco/culture** c'est de l'ersatz de tabac/de culture.

erstwhile /'ɜ:stwaɪl/ littér **I** *adj* ancien/-ienne (*avant n*), d'autrefois.
II *adv* jadis, autrefois.

eruct *vi* US = **eructate**.

eructate /e'rʊkteɪt/ *vi* sout éructer.

erudite /'eru:daɪt/ *adj* [*person*] érudit; [*book, discussion*] savant.

eruditely /'eru:daɪtlɪ/ *adv* avec érudition.

erudition /ˌeru:'dɪʃn/ *n* érudition *f*.

erupt /ɪ'rʌpt/ *vi* **1** [*volcano*] entrer en éruption; **2** fig [*war, violence, gunfire*] éclater; [*laughter, cry*] jaillir, éclater; [*person*] (with anger) éclater (**with** de); **3** Med [*rash*] apparaître; Dent [*tooth*] percer.

eruption /ɪ'rʌpʃn/ *n* **1** (of volcano) éruption *f*; **2** fig (of violence, laughter) accès *m*, explosion *f*; (of hostilities) déclenchement *m*; (of political movement) apparition *f*; **3** Med, Dent éruption *f*.

erysipelas /ˌerɪ'sɪpɪləs/ **▶1354** *n* érysipèle *m*.

erythrocyte /ɪ'rɪθrəʊsaɪt/ *n* érythrocyte *m*.

ESA *n* (*abrév* = **European Space Agency**) ASE *f*.

Esau /'i:sɔ:/ *pr n* Ésaü.

escalate /'eskəleɪt/ **I** *vtr* intensifier [*war, problem, efforts*]; aggraver [*inflation*].
II *vi* [*conflict, violence*] s'intensifier; [*prices, inflation*] monter en flèche, s'envoler; [*unemployment*] augmenter rapidement; **to ~ into a major crisis** se transformer en crise grave.

escalation /ˌeskə'leɪʃn/ *n* (of violence, war) intensification *f*, escalade *f* (**in, of** de); (of prices, inflation) montée *f* en flèche (**in, of** de).

escalation clause *n* = **escalator clause**.

escalator /'eskəleɪtə(r)/ *n* escalier *m* mécanique, escalator® *m*.

escalator clause *n* clause *f* d'indexation.

escalope /'eskələʊp/ *n* escalope *f*.

escapade /'eskəpeɪd, ˌeskə'peɪd/ *n* (adventure) équipée *f*; (prank) frasque *f*.

escape /ɪ'skeɪp/ **I** *n* **1** (of person) lit évasion *f*, fuite *f* (**from** de; **to** vers); fig fuite *f*; **to make good one's ~** lit réussir son évasion; fig réussir à se sauver; **to make an** ou **one's ~** s'évader; **to have a narrow** ou **lucky ~** l'échapper belle; **2** (leak) (of water, gas) fuite *f* (**from** de).
II *vtr* **1** (avoid) **to ~ death/danger/persecution** échapper à la mort/au danger/aux persécutions; **to ~ responsibility/defeat** éviter une responsabilité/la défaite; **to ~ detection** [*person*] échapper aux recherches (de la police); [*fault*] ne pas être détecté; **we cannot ~ the fact that** on ne peut pas ignorer le fait que; **he cannot ~ the accusation** ou **charge** il ne peut pas échapper à l'accusation; **to ~ reality** fuir la réalité; **2** (elude) [*name, fact*] échapper à [*person*]; **to ~ sb's attention** ou **notice** échapper à (l'attention de) qn.
III *vi* **1** (get away) lit [*person*] s'enfuir, s'évader; [*animal*] s'échapper (**from** de); fig s'évader; **to ~ into** ou **to somewhere** se réfugier quelque part; **to ~ unharmed** ou **without a scratch** s'en sortir indemne; **to ~ by the skin of one's teeth** l'échapper belle; **to (manage to) ~ with one's life** s'en sortir vivant; **2** (leak) [*water*] fuir; [*gas*] fuir, s'échapper.
IV escaped *pp adj* [*prisoner, convict*] évadé; [*animal*] qui s'est enfui.

escape: **~ artist** *n* spécialiste *mf* de l'évasion; **~ character** *n* Comput caractère *m* d'échappement; **~ chute** *n* Aviat toboggan *m*; **~ clause** *n* Jur Comm clause *f* dérogatoire; **~ cock** *n* Tech soupape *f* d'échappement.

escapee /ɪˌskeɪ'pi:/ *n* évadé/-e *m/f*.

escape: **~ hatch** *n* Naut sas *m* de secours; **~ key** *n* touche *f* d'échappement.

escapement /ɪ'skeɪpmənt/ *n* Mech échappement *m*.

escape: **~ plan** *n* projet *m* d'évasion; **~ road** *n* voie *f* de ralentissement d'urgence; **~ route** *n* (in case of fire etc) plan *m* d'évacuation; (for fugitives) itinéraire *m* d'évasion; **~ sequence** *n* Comput séquence *f* d'échappement; **~ shaft** *n* Mining galerie *f* de secours; **~ valve** *n* Tech soupape *f* d'échappement; **~ velocity** *n* Aerosp vitesse *f* de libération; **~ wheel** *n* Tech roue *f* d'échappement.

escapism /ɪ'skeɪpɪzəm/ *n* péj (in literature, cinema, etc) évasion *f* (du réel); (of person) refus *m* d'affronter la réalité; **it's pure ~** c'est du pur divertissement.

escapist /ɪ'skeɪpɪst/ **I** *n* **she's an ~** elle fuit la réalité.
II *adj* [*literature, film*] d'évasion (*after n*), détaché du réel.

escapologist /ˌeskə'pɒlədʒɪst/ **▶1692** *n*: *artiste dont la spécialité est de se libérer de liens.*

escapology /ˌeskə'pɒlədʒɪ/ *n*: *l'art de se libérer de liens.*

escarpment /ɪ'skɑ:pmənt/ *n* escarpement *m*.

eschatological /ˌeskətə'lɒdʒɪkl/ *adj* eschatologique.

eschatology /ˌeskə'tɒlədʒɪ/ *n* eschatologie *f*.

eschew /ɪs'tʃu:/ *vtr* sout éviter [*discussion, temptation*]; rejeter [*violence*].

escort **I** /'eskɔ:t/ *n* **1** Mil, Naut (in police) escorte *f*; **military ~** escorte militaire; **police ~** escorte de police; **armed ~** escorte de soldats; **to put under ~** placer sous escorte; **2** (companion) compagnon/compagne *m/f*; (to a dance) cavalier/-ière *m/f*; (in agency) hôtesse *f*.
II /'eskɔ:t/ *modif* **~ agency** agence or bureau d'hôtesses; Naut, Mil **~ duty** service *m* d'escorte; **~ vessel** bâtiment *m* d'escorte.
III /ɪ'skɔ:t/ *vtr* **1** Mil escorter, faire escorte à; **to ~ sb in/out** faire entrer/sortir qn sous escorte; **2** (to a function) accompagner; (home, to the door) raccompagner.

escrow /e'skrəʊ/ *n* Jur séquestre *m*; **in ~** en séquestre.

escrow account *n* US Jur compte *m* séquestre.

escutcheon /ɪ'skʌtʃən/ *n* **1** Herald écu *m*, écusson *m*; **2** (on lock) cache-entrée *m inv*.
IDIOMS **to be a blot on the ~** être la honte de la famille.

esker /'eskə(r)/ *n* Geol os *m*.

Eskimo /'eskɪməʊ/ **▶1486**, **1402** **I** *n* **1** (person) Esquimau/-aude *m/f*; **2** Ling esquimau *m*.
II *adj* esquimau/-aude; **~ dog** chien *m* esquimau.

ESL *n*: *abrév* **▶English as a Second Language**.

ESN *adj*: *abrév* **▶educationally subnormal**.

esophagus *n* US = **oesophagus**.

esoteric /ˌi:səʊ'terɪk, ˌe-/ *adj* [*language, knowledge, practices*] ésotérique; [*argument*] obscur.

esoterica /ˌi:səʊ'terɪkə, ˌe-/ *npl* US objets *mpl* ésotériques.

esp *abrév écrite* = **especially**.

ESP *n* **1** *abrév* **▶extrasensory perception**; **2** *abrév* **▶English for Special Purposes**.

espalier /ɪ'spælɪeɪ, US ɪ'spæljər/ **I** *n* (tree) arbre *m* en espalier *m*; (trellis) treillis *m* d'espalier.
II *vtr* cultiver [qch] en espalier.

esparto /e'spɑ:təʊ/ *n* (also **esparto grass**) alfa *m*.

especial /ɪ'speʃl/ *adj* sout exceptionnel/-elle; [*benefit*] particulier/-ière.

especially /ɪ'speʃəlɪ/ *adv* **1** (above all) surtout, en particulier; **~ as it's so hot** d'autant plus qu'il fait si chaud; **he ~ ought to be told** lui surtout devrait être informé; **why her ~?** pourquoi elle en particulier?; **2** (on purpose) exprès, spécialement; **he came ~ to see me** il est venu exprès pour me voir; **3** (unusually) particulièrement.

Esperantist /ˌespə'ræntɪst/ *n* espérantiste *mf*.

Esperanto /ˌespə'ræntəʊ/ **▶1402** *n* espéranto *m*.

espionage /'espɪənɑ:ʒ/ *n* espionnage *m*.

esplanade /ˌesplə'neɪd/ *n* esplanade *f*.

espouse /ɪ'spaʊz/ *vtr* **1** sout épouser, embrasser [*cause*]; **2**‡ (marry) épouser.

espresso /e'spresəʊ/ *n* (*pl* **~s**) express *m inv*, café *m* express.

espy /ɪ'spaɪ/ *vtr* ‡ ou littér apercevoir, aviser liter.

Esq GB (*abrév écrite* = **esquire**) (on letter) **John Roberts Esq** M. John Roberts.

essay /'eseɪ/ **I** *n* **1** Sch rédaction *f*, composition *f* (**on, about** sur); (extended) dissertation *f* (**on** sur); US Univ mémoire *m* de maîtrise (**on** sur); Literat essai *m* (**on** sur); **2** littér (endeavour) tentative *f*.
II *modif* **~ question** sujet *m* de dissertation; **~ test** US Univ épreuve *f* écrite.
III *vtr* littér **1** (attempt) tenter, essayer (**to do** de faire); **2** (test) essayer, mettre à l'essai.

essayist /'eseɪɪst/ **▶1692** *n* essayiste *mf*.

essence /'esns/ **I** *n* **1** (soul, kernel) Phil, Theol essence *f*; **the ~ of the problem/of the argument** l'essentiel du problème/de l'argumentation; **this is the very ~ of jazz** c'est l'essence même du jazz; **it's the ~ of stupidity/greed** c'est la stupidité/la gourmandise même; **time is of the ~** la vitesse s'impose; **2** Cosmet, Culin essence *f*.
II in ~ *adv phr* essentiellement.

essential /ɪ'senʃl/ **I** *n* (object) objet *m* indispensable; (quality, element) qualité *f* essentielle; **I packed a few ~s** j'ai emballé quelques objets indispensables; **food and other ~s** de la nourriture et d'autres articles indispensables; **a car is not an ~** une auto n'est pas indispensable; **there are two ~s in comedy** il y a deux éléments essentiels dans la comédie; **money is an ~** l'argent est un élément essentiel.
II essentials *npl* **the ~s** l'essentiel *m*; **to get down to ~s** en venir à l'essentiel.
III *adj* **1** (vital) [*services*] de base; [*role*] essentiel/-ielle; [*ingredient*] indispensable; **~ goods** produits de première nécessité; **~ maintenance work** les travaux d'entretien indispensables; **it is ~ to do** il est indispensable de faire; **it is ~ that** il est

indispensable que (+ *subj*); **to be ~ for sth** être indispensable à qch; **it is ~ for us to agree** il est indispensable que nous soyons d'accord; **2** (basic) [*feature, element*] essentiel/-ielle; [*difference*] fondamental; [*reading*] indispensable; **humanity's ~ goodness** la bonté intrinsèque de l'humanité; **his ~ humility** son humilité intrinsèque.

essentially /ɪ'senʃəlɪ/ *adv* **1** (basically) essentiellement; **~, it's an old argument** en fait, c'est une vieille discussion; **2** (emphatic) (above all) avant tout; **our role is ~ supervisory** nous jouons avant tout un rôle de surveillance; **3** (more or less) [*correct, true*] en gros.

essential oil *n* huile *f* essentielle.

Essonne ▶ **1163** *pr n* Essonne *f*; **in/to ~** dans l'Essonne.

est *abrév écrite* = **established**.

EST *n* **1** US *abrév* ▶ **Eastern Standard Time**; **2** Med *abrév* ▶ **electroshock therapy**.

establish /ɪ'stæblɪʃ/ **I** *vtr* **1** (set up) établir [*firm, tribunal, state, guidelines, basis, relations*]; **2** (gain acceptance for) établir [*principle, theory, authority, supremacy*]; **to ~ a reputation for oneself as** se faire connaître en tant que [*singer, actor, expert*]; se faire une réputation de [*cheat, liar*]; **3** (determine, prove) établir [*guilt, innocence, ownership, paternity, facts*]; déterminer [*cause*]; **to ~ that** montrer que; **to ~ what/why/whether** montrer ce que/pourquoi/si; **to ~ the cause of death** déterminer les causes du décès.

II *v refl* **to ~ oneself** s'installer; **to ~ oneself as a butcher** s'installer boucher.

established /ɪ'stæblɪʃt/ *adj* [*institution, artist, procedure, view*] établi; **it's a well ~ fact that** c'est un fait bien établi que; **~ in 1920** fondé en 1920; **the ~ church** l'église d'État or officielle.

establishment /ɪ'stæblɪʃmənt/ **I** *n* **1** (setting up) (of business) création *f*, établissement *m* (**of** de); (of law, rule) institution *f*, instauration *f*; **2** (institution, organization) établissement *m*; **research ~** établissement *m* de recherche; **3** (shop, business) établissement *m*, maison *f* de commerce; **4** (staff) personnel *m* (**of** de); (of household) train *m* de maison.

II Establishment *pr n* GB (ruling group) classe *f* dominante, establishment *m*; (social order) ordre *m* établi; **the literary/art ~** l'establishment littéraire/du monde de l'art; **the medical/legal ~** les institutions *fpl* médicales/judiciaires; **to join** ou **become part of the Establishment** s'embourgeoiser.

III *modif* [*values, artist, figure, views*] de l'ordre établi.

estate /ɪ'steɪt/ *n* **1** (stately home and park) domaine *m*, propriété *f*; **2** = **housing estate**; **3** (assets) biens *mpl*; **to divide one's ~** partager ses biens; **a large ~** une grande fortune; **4** (condition) état *m*; **the (holy) ~ of matrimony** le saint état de mariage; **to reach man's ~**† atteindre l'âge adulte; **5**‡ ou Hist (class) état *m*; **the three ~s of the realm** les trois états; **of high/low ~** de haute/basse condition; **6** GB = **estate car**.

estate: **~ agency** *n* GB agence *f* immobilière; **~ agent** *n* GB agent *m* immobilier; **~ car** *n* GB break *m*; **~ duty** *n* GB droits *mpl* de succession; **Estates General** *npl* États *mpl* Généraux; **~ tax** *n* US droits *mpl* de succession.

esteem /ɪ'sti:m/ **I** *n* estime *f*; **to hold sb in high ~** tenir qn en haute estime; **a book held in high ~** un livre très prisé; **to go up/down in sb's ~** remonter/baisser dans l'estime de qn.

II *vtr* sout **1** (admire) avoir de l'estime pour, estimer [*person*]; apprécier [*quality*]; priser [*work*]; **our highly ~ed colleague** notre très estimé/-e collègue fml; **2** (think) considérer; **I ~ it an honour to be here** je considère comme un honneur d'être ici fml.

esthete *n* US = **aesthete**.

estimable /'estɪməbl/ *adj* sout estimable; **my ~ colleague** mon honorable collègue.

estimate I /'estɪmət/ *n* **1** (assessment of size, quantity etc) estimation *f*, évaluation *f*; **to make an ~** faire une estimation; **by the government's ~** selon une estimation du gouvernement; **by his own ~** à l'en croire; **at a rough ~** très approximativement, à vue de nez○; **at a conservative ~** sans exagération; **2** Comm (quote) devis *m*; **to put in an ~ for sth** établir un devis pour qch; **a higher/lower ~** un devis plus/moins élevé; **3** Admin (budget) (*souvent pl*) prévisions *fpl* budgétaires; **defence ~s** prévisions *fpl* budgétaires pour la défense; **4** (estimation) jugement *m* (**of sb** quant à qn).

II /'estɪmeɪt/ *vtr* **1** (guess) évaluer [*price, value*]; évaluer [*size, speed, distance*]; **to ~ that** estimer que; **to ~ sth to be** estimer que qch est; **the cost was ~d at 1,000 francs** le coût a été évalué à 1 000 francs; **2** (submit) [*builder, tenderer*] évaluer [*price, cost*]; **to ~ (a price) for sth** évaluer le prix de qch.

III estimated *pp adj* [*cost, figure*] approximatif/-ive; **an ~ 300 people** environ 300 personnes; **the ~ 1,000 victims** les victimes, qu'on estime à 1 000.

estimate: **~d time of arrival**, **ETA** *n* heure *f* d'arrivée prévue; **~d time of departure**, **ETD** *n* heure *f* de départ prévue; **estimated date of delivery**, **EDD** *n* Med date *f* présumée de l'accouchement.

estimation /ˌestɪ'meɪʃn/ *n* **1** (esteem) estime *f*; **to go up/down in sb's ~** monter/descendre dans l'estime de qn; **2** (judgment) opinion *f*; **in her ~** à son avis, d'après elle; **3** ₵ (evaluating) évaluation *f*.

Estonia /ɪ'stəʊnɪə/ ▶ **1131** *pr n* Estonie *f*.

Estonian /ɪ'stəʊnɪən/ ▶ **1486**, **1402** **I** *n* **1** (person) Estonien/-ienne *m/f*; **2** Ling estonien *m*.

II *adj* estonien/-ienne.

estrange /ɪ'streɪndʒ/ **I** *vtr* éloigner (**from** de), brouiller (**from** avec).

II estranged *pp adj* **to be ~d from sb** être séparé de qn; **her ~d husband** son mari dont elle est/était séparée.

estrangement /ɪ'streɪndʒmənt/ *n* séparation *f*.

estrogen *n* US = **oestrogen**.

estrone *n* US = **oestrone**.

estrus *n* US = **oestrus**.

estuary /'estʃʊərɪ, US -uerɪ/ *n* estuaire *m*.

E Sussex *n* GB Post *abrév écrite* ▶ **East Sussex**.

ETA *abrév* ▶ **estimated time of arrival**.

et al (*abrév* = **et alii**) et autres; hum et tutti quanti.

etc *adv* (*abrév* = **et cetera**) etc.

et cetera, etcetera /ɪt 'setərə, et-/ *adv* et cætera, et cetera.

etceteras /ɪt'setərəz, et-/ *npl* extras *mpl*.

etch /etʃ/ **I** *vtr* Art, Print graver [qch] à l'eau-forte; **~ed on her memory** fig gravé dans sa mémoire.

II *vi* Art, Print graver à l'eau-forte.

etching /'etʃɪŋ/ *n* **1** (technique) gravure *f* à l'eau-forte; **2** (picture) eau-forte *f*.

IDIOMS **come up and see my ~s** hum viens voir mes estampes japonaises.

ETD *n*: *abrév* ▶ **estimated time of departure**.

eternal /ɪ'tɜ:nl/ **I** *adj* gen, Philos, Relig éternel/-elle; [*chatter*] éternel/-elle (*before n*); [*complaints*] sempiternel/-elle pej (*before n*); **he's an ~ optimist** c'est un éternel optimiste; **the ~ feminine** l'éternel féminin; **it is to his eternal credit that** il faut reconnaître en son honneur que.

II Eternal *n* Relig **the Eternal** l'Éternel *m*.

Eternal City *pr n* Ville *f* éternelle.

eternally /ɪ'tɜ:nəlɪ/ *adv* éternellement; **~ grateful** éternellement reconnaissant.

eternal triangle *n* ≈ ménage *m* à trois.

eternity /ɪ'tɜ:nətɪ/ *n* gen, Relig éternité *f*; **for ~** [*remain, survive*] pour toujours; **to wait for an ~** attendre une éternité; **it seemed an ~ before he answered** il a mis une éternité à répondre.

eternity ring *n*: *bague donnée en gage de fidélité.*

ethane /'eθeɪn, 'i:θ-/ *n* éthane *m*.

ethanol /'eθənɒl/ *n* alcool *m* éthylique, éthanol *m*.

ether /'i:θə(r)/ *n* (all contexts) éther *m*.

ethereal /ɪ'θɪərɪəl/ *adj* éthéré, aérien/-ienne.

ethic /'eθɪk/ *n* Philos éthique *f*, morale *f*; **the success ~** le culte du succès.

ethical /'eθɪkl/ *adj* [*problem, objection, principle*] moral; [*theory*] éthique; **~ code** code *m* déontologique; **not to be ~** être contraire à la morale.

ethically /'eθɪklɪ/ *adv* moralement.

ethics /'eθɪks/ *n* **1** (+ *v sg*) Philos éthique *f*, morale *f*; **2** (+ *v pl*) (moral code) morale *f*; (of group, profession) sens *m* moral; **professional ~** déontologie *f*; **medical ~** déontologie *f* médicale.

Ethiopia /ˌi:θɪ'əʊpɪə/ ▶ **1131** *pr n* Éthiopie *f*.

Ethiopian /ˌi:θɪ'əʊpɪən/ ▶ **1486**, **1402** **I** *n* Éthiopien/-ienne *m/f*.

II *adj* éthiopien/-ienne.

ethnic /'eθnɪk/ **I** *n* injur membre *m* d'une minorité ethnique.

II *adj* [*group, minority, unrest*] ethnique; [*food, music*] exotique; [*clothes*] inspiré du folklore (*indien, africain etc*).

ethnically /'eθnɪklɪ/ *adv* sur le plan ethnique.

ethnic: **~ cleansing** *n* purification *f* ethnique; **~ minority** *n* minorité *f* ethnique.

ethnocentric /ˌeθnəʊ'sentrɪk/ *adj* ethnocentrique.

ethnography /eθ'nɒgrəfɪ/ *n* ethnographie *f*.

ethnolinguistics /ˌeθnəʊlɪŋ'gwɪstɪks/ *n* ethnolinguistique *f*.

ethnologist /eθ'nɒlədʒɪst/ ▶ **1692** *n* ethnologue *mf*.

ethnology /eθ'nɒlədʒɪ/ *n* ethnologie *f*.

ethology /i:'θɒlədʒɪ/ *n* éthologie *f*.

ethos /'i:θɒs/ *n* (spirit) esprit *m*; (approach) philosophie *f*; **company ~** philosophie de l'entreprise.

ethyl /'i:θaɪl, 'eθɪl/ *n* éthyle *m*.

ethyl: **~ acetate** *n* acétate *m* d'éthyle; **~ alcohol** *n* alcool *m* éthylique.

ethylene /'eθɪli:n/ *n* éthylène *m*.

etiquette /'etɪket, -kət/ *n* **1** (social) bienséance *f*, étiquette *f*; **2** (professional, diplomatic) protocole *m*; **professional ~** déontologie *f*; **3** (ceremonial) étiquette *f*.

Etna /'etnə/ *pr n* (also **Mount ~**) l'Etna *m*, le mont Etna.

Etruria /ɪ'trʊərɪə/ ▶ **1131** *pr n* Hist Étrurie *f*.

Etruscan /ɪ'trʌskən/ ▶ **1486**, **1402** **I** *n* **1** (person) Étrusque *mf*; **2** Ling étrusque *m*.

II *adj* étrusque.

ETV *n* US *abrév* ▶ **educational television**.

etymological /ˌetɪmə'lɒdʒɪkl/ *adj* étymologique.

etymologically /ˌetɪmə'lɒdʒɪklɪ/ *adv* étymologiquement.

etymology /ˌetɪ'mɒlədʒɪ/ *n* étymologie *f*.

eucalyptus /ju:kə'lɪptəs/ **I** *n* Bot, Pharm eucalyptus *m*.

II *modif* [*oil, leaf*] d'eucalyptus.

Eucharist /'ju:kərɪst/ *n* Eucharistie *f*.

euchre /'ju:kə(r)/ ▶ **1282** **I** *n* US Games euchre *m*.

II○ *vtr* US (trick) **to ~ sb out of sth** carotter○ qch à qn.

Euclid /'ju:klɪd/ *pr n* Euclide.

Euclidean /ju:'klɪdɪən/ *adj* euclidien/-ienne.

eugenic /ju:'dʒenɪk/ *adj* eugénique.

eugenics /ju:ˈdʒenɪks/ *n* (+ *v sg*) eugénisme *m*.

eulogize /ˈju:lədʒaɪz/ **I** *vtr* faire l'éloge or le panégyrique de.
II *vi* **to ~ over sth** faire l'éloge or le panégyrique de qch.

eulogy /ˈju:lədʒɪ/ *n* gen panégyrique *m*; Relig éloge *m* funèbre; **to deliver** ou **say the ~ for sb** US faire l'éloge funèbre de qn.

eunuch /ˈju:nək/ *n* eunuque *m*.

euphemism /ˈju:fəmɪzəm/ *n* euphémisme *m*.

euphemistic /ˌju:fəˈmɪstɪk/ *adj* euphémique.

euphemistically /ˌju:fəˈmɪstɪklɪ/ *adv* par euphémisme.

euphonium /ju:ˈfəʊnɪəm/ *n* euphonium *m*.

euphony /ˈju:fənɪ/ *n* euphonie *f*.

euphorbia /ju:ˈfɔ:bɪə/ *n* euphorbe *f*.

euphoria /ju:ˈfɔ:rɪə/ *n* euphorie *f*.

euphoric /ju:ˈfɒrɪk, US -ˈfɔ:r-/ *adj* euphorique.

Euphrates /ju:ˈfreɪti:z/ ▶ **1644** *pr n* Euphrate *m*.

euphuism /ˈju:fju:ɪzəm/ *n* euphuisme *m*.

Eurasia /jʊəˈreɪʒə/ *pr n* Eurasie *f*.

Eurasian /jʊəˈreɪʒn/ **I** *n* Eurasien/-ienne *m/f*.
II *adj* [*people, region*] eurasien/-ienne; [*continent*] eurasiatique.

EURATOM /ˈjʊərətɒm/ *n* (*abrév* = **European Atomic Energy Community**) CEEA *f*.

Eure ▶ **1163** *pr n* Eure *m*; **in/to ~** dans l'Eure.

Eure-et-Loir ▶ **1163** *pr n* Eure-et-Loir *m*; **in/to ~** dans l'Eure-et-Loir.

eureka /jʊəˈri:kə/ *excl* eurêka!

eurhythmics GB, **eurythmics** US /ju:ˈrɪðmɪks/ *n* (+ *v sg*) gymnastique *f* rythmique.

Euripides /ju:ˈrɪpɪdi:z/ *pr n* Euripide.

Euro+ /ˈjʊərəʊ-/ *dans composés* euro-.

Eurobeach /ˈjʊərəʊbi:tʃ/ *n* plage *f* portant le label CEE.

Eurobond /ˈjʊərəʊbɒnd/ *n* euro-obligation *f*.

eurocentric /ˌjʊərəʊˈsentrɪk/ *adj* eurocentrique.

eurocentrism /ˌjʊərəʊˈsentrɪzəm/ *n* eurocentrisme *m*.

eurocheque /ˈjʊərəʊtʃek/ *n* Eurochèque *m*; **~ card** carte *f* Eurochèque.

Eurocrat /ˈjʊərəʊkræt/ *n* eurocrate *mf*.

Eurocurrency /ˈjʊərəʊkʌrənsɪ/ *n* eurodevise *f*, euromonnaie *f*; **~ market** marché *m* des eurodevises.

Eurodollar /ˈjʊərəʊdɒlə(r)/ *n* eurodollar *m*.

Euromarket /ˈjʊərəʊmɑ:kɪt/ *n* marché *m* européen; **in the ~** au sein du marché européen.

Euro-MP /ˌjʊərəʊemˈpi:/ *n* député *m* européen.

Europe /ˈjʊərəp/ ▶ **1131** *pr n* Europe *f*; **to go into ~** entrer dans le Marché commun.

European /ˌjʊərəˈpɪən/ **I** *n* Européen/-éenne *m/f*.
II *adj* européen/-éenne.

European: **~ Atomic Energy Community** *n* Communauté *f* Européenne de l'Énergie Atomique; **~ Bank for Reconstruction and Development**, **EBRD** *n* Banque *f* européenne pour la reconstruction et le développement, BERD *f*; **~ Commission** *n* Commission *f* européenne; **~ Court of Human Rights** *n* Cour *f* européenne des droits de l'homme; **~ Court of Justice** *n* Cour *f* européenne de justice, Cour *f* de justice des communautés européennes; **~ Economic Community**, **EEC**, **EC** *n* Communauté *f* économique européenne *f*, CEE; **~ Free Trade Association**, **EFTA** *n* Association *f* européenne de libre-échange, AELE; **~ Investment Bank**, **EIB** *n* Banque *f* européenne d'investissement, BEI *f*.

Europeanize /ˌjʊərəˈpɪənaɪz/ *vtr* européaniser; **to become ~d** s'européaniser.

European: **~ Monetary System**, **EMS** système *m* monétaire européen, SME *m*; **~ Monetary Union** *n* Union *f* monétaire européenne; **~ Parliament** *n* Parlement *m* européen; **~ standard** *n* EC Ind, Comm normes *fpl* européennes; **~ Union** *n* Union *f* européenne.

eurosceptic /ˈjʊərəʊskeptɪk/ *n* GB eurosceptique *mf*.

Eurotunnel /ˈjʊərəʊˌtʌnl/ *n* Eurotunnel *m*.

Eurovision /ˈjʊərəʊvɪʒn/ *n* Eurovision *f*.

eurythmics *n* US = **eurhythmics**.

Eustachian tube /ju:ˌsteɪʃn ˈtju:b, US ˈtu:b/ *n* trompe *f* d'Eustache.

eustatic /ju:ˈstætɪk/ *adj* eustatique.

euthanasia /ˌju:θəˈneɪzɪə, US -ˈneɪʒə/ *n* euthanasie *f*.

eutrophication /ˌju:trəfɪˈkeɪʃn/ *n* Ecol eutrophisation *f*.

evacuate /ɪˈvækjʊeɪt/ *vtr* gen, Physiol évacuer.

evacuation /ɪˌvækjʊˈeɪʃn/ *n* évacuation *f*.

evacuee /ɪˌvækju:ˈi:/ *n* évacué/-e *m/f*.

evade /ɪˈveɪd/ *vtr* esquiver [*look, blow*]; éluder [*question, problem*]; se dérober à, fuir [*responsibility*]; échapper à [*pursuer*]; **to ~ taxes** se rendre coupable d'évasion fiscale; **so far he has ~d capture** il est toujours en fuite.

evaluate /ɪˈvæljʊeɪt/ *vtr* évaluer [*situation, performance, method, results, ability*]; mesurer [*progress*]; déterminer [*responsibilities*]; juger, évaluer [*person, application*].

evaluation /ɪˌvæljʊˈeɪʃn/ *n* (all contexts) évaluation *f*.

evanescent /ˌi:vəˈnesnt, US ˌe-/ *adj* littér évanescent.

evangelical /ˌi:vænˈdʒelɪkl/ *adj* évangélique.

evangelicalism /ˌi:vænˈdʒelɪkəlɪzəm/, **evangelism** /ɪˈvændʒəlɪzəm/ *n* évangélisme *m*.

evangelist /ɪˈvændʒəlɪst/ **I** *n* (preacher, missionary) évangélisateur/-trice *m/f*.
II Evangelist *n* Bible évangéliste *m*; **St John the Evangelist** St Jean l'Évangéliste.

evangelize /ɪˈvændʒəlaɪz/ **I** *vtr* évangéliser.
II *vi* prêcher l'Évangile.

evaporate /ɪˈvæpəreɪt/ **I** *vtr* faire évaporer [*liquid*].
II *vi* **1** [*liquid*] s'évaporer; **2** fig [*hopes, enthusiasm, confidence*] s'évaporer; [*anger, fears*] se dissiper.

evaporated milk *n* lait *m* condensé non sucré.

evaporation /ɪˌvæpəˈreɪʃn/ *n* évaporation *f*.

evasion /ɪˈveɪʒn/ *n* **1** (of responsibility) dérobade *f* (**of** à); **tax ~** évasion *f* fiscale; **2** (excuse) faux-fuyant *m*; **3** (making excuses) **he resorted to ~** il eut recours à des faux-fuyants.

evasive /ɪˈveɪsɪv/ *adj* évasif/-ive; [*look*] fuyant; **an ~ answer** une réponse évasive; **to take ~ action** Naut, Aviat changer de cap pour éviter un accident; GB Aut donner un coup de volant pour éviter un accident; fig esquiver la difficulté.

evasively /ɪˈveɪsɪvlɪ/ *adv* d'une manière évasive, évasivement.

evasiveness /ɪˈveɪsɪvnɪs/ *n* (manner) manière *f* évasive; (remarks) faux-fuyants *mpl*.

eve /i:v/ *n* **1** veille *f*; **on the ~ of** à la veille de; **2**‡ (evening) soir *m*. ▶ **Christmas eve, etc.**

Eve /i:v/ *pr n* Bible Ève.

even[1] /ˈi:vn/

■ **Note** *even* can always be translated by *même* when it is used to express surprise or for emphasis. For examples and other uses, see below.

I *adv* **1** (showing surprise) même; **he didn't ~ try** il n'a même pas essayé; **don't you ~ remember?** tu ne t'en souviens même pas?; **~ when I explained it to him** même quand je le lui ai expliqué; **without ~ apologizing** sans même s'excuser; **2** (emphasizing point) même; **disease or ~ death** la maladie ou même la mort; **I can't ~ swim, never mind dive** je ne sais même pas nager, encore moins plonger; **don't tell anyone, not ~ Bob** ne dis rien à personne, pas même à Bob; **not ~ you could believe that!** même toi, tu ne pourrais pas croire ça!; **~ scrubbing won't shift that stain** même si on frotte, la tache ne partira pas; **~ if** même si; **~ now** même maintenant; **~ today** même aujourd'hui; **3** (with comparative) encore; **it's ~ colder today** il fait encore plus froid aujourd'hui; **~ more carefully** avec encore plus de prudence, encore plus prudemment; **4** sout (just) **~ as I watched** alors même que je regardais; **she died ~ as she had lived** elle est morte comme elle a vécu.
II even so *adv phr* quand même; **it was interesting ~ so** c'était quand même intéressant.
III even then *adv phr* (at that time) même à ce moment-là; (all the same) de toute façon.
IV even though *conj phr* bien que (+ *subj*) ; **he rents his house ~ though he's so rich** riche comme il est, il loue quand même sa maison or il loue sa maison bien qu'il soit si riche.

even[2] /ˈi:vn/ **I** *n* ‡ou littér soir *m*.
II *adj* **1** (level) [*ground, surface*] égal; **to be ~ with** être au même niveau que [*wall, floor*]; **2** (regular) [*teeth, hemline*] régulier/-ière; [*temperature*] constant; **3** (calm) [*voice, tone, disposition, temper*] égal; **4** (equal) [*contest*] égal; **to be ~** [*competitors*] être à égalité (**with** avec); **5** (fair) [*exchange, distribution*] équitable; **6** (quits, owing nothing) **we're ~** nous sommes quittes; **to get ~ with sb** rendre à qn la monnaie de sa pièce; **7** Math [*number*] pair.
■ **even out**: ¶ **~ out** [*differences, imbalance, inequalities*] s'atténuer; ¶ **~ [sth] out, ~ out [sth]** répartir [*distribution, burden*]; réduire [*disadvantage, inequalities*].
■ **even up**: **~ [sth] up, ~ up [sth]** équilibrer [*contest*]; **it will ~ things up** ce sera plus équilibré.

even-handed /ˌi:vnˈhændɪd/ *adj* impartial.

evening /ˈi:vnɪŋ/ ▶ **1096** **I** *n* **1** soir *m*; (with emphasis on duration) soirée *f*; **in the ~** le soir; **during the ~** pendant la soirée; **at 6 o'clock in the ~** à six heures du soir; **this ~** ce soir; **later this ~** plus tard dans la soirée; **tomorrow/yesterday ~** demain/hier soir; **on the ~ of the 14th** le 14 au soir; **on Friday ~** vendredi soir; **on Friday ~s** le vendredi soir; **on the following** ou **next ~** le lendemain soir; **the previous ~**, **the ~ before** la veille au soir; **on the ~ of their arrival** le soir de leur arrivée; **every ~** tous les soirs; **every Thursday ~** tous les jeudis soir; **on a fine summer ~** par une belle soirée d'été; **the long winter ~s** les longues soirées d'hiver; **I'll be in all ~** je serai à la maison toute la soirée; **what do you do in the ~s?** qu'est-ce-que tu fais le soir?; **she came in the ~** elle est arrivée dans la soirée; **let's have an ~ in for a change** passons la soirée à la maison pour une fois; **to work ~s** travailler le soir; **to be on ~s** être du soir; **2 musical/theatrical ~** soirée musicale/théâtrale; **3** fig littér **in the ~ of one's life** au soir de sa vie.
II *modif* [*bag, shoe*] habillé; [*meal, newspaper, walk*] du soir.
III○ *excl* (also **good ~**) bonsoir!

evening class *n* cours *m* du soir.

evening dress *n* **1** (formal clothes) tenue *f*

de soirée; **in ~** en tenue de soirée; **2** (gown) robe *f* de soirée.

evening: **~ fixture** *n* GB Sport nocturne *f*; **~ game**, **~ match** *n* = **evening fixture**; **~ meal** *n* repas *m* du soir; **~ paper** *n* journal *m* du soir; **~ performance** *n* représentation *f* en soirée; **~ prayers** *npl* vêpres *fpl*; **~ primrose** *n* onagre *f*; **~ service** office *m* du soir; **~ shift** *n* équipe *f* du soir; **~ showing** *n* Cin séance *f* du soir; **~ star** *n* étoile *f* du berger.

evenly /ˈiːvnlɪ/ *adv* **1** [*spread, apply*] uniformément; [*breathe*] régulièrement; [*share, divide*] en parts égales; **~ distributed** [*money*] équitablement distribué; [*paint, colour*] uniformément étalé; [*disease, phenomenon*] également répandu; **to be ~ matched** être de force égale; **2** (placidly) [*say*] posément.

evenness /ˈiːvnnɪs/ *n* (of ground, surface) uniformité *f*, égalité *f*; (of distribution) équité *f*; (of breathing, movement) régularité *f*; (of temperament) égalité *f*; (of quality) constance *f*.

evens /ˈiːvnz/ **I** *npl* **I'll give you ~ that** pour moi il y a une chance sur deux que (+ *subj*).
II *modif* **to be ~ favourite** être favori et coté à un contre un.

evensong /ˈiːvnsɒŋ/ *n* office *m* du soir.

event /ɪˈvent/ *n* **1** (incident) événement *m*; **a chain of ~s** une suite d'événements; **~s are moving so fast** les événements se succèdent tellement vite; **the police were unable to control ~s** la police a été incapable de contrôler la situation; **the course of ~s** les circonstances; **2** (eventuality) cas *m*; **in the ~ of** en cas de [*fire, accident etc*]; **in the unlikely ~ that he (should) fail the exam** au cas improbable où il raterait son examen; **in that ~** dans ce cas; **in either ~** en tout cas; **in the ~** GB (as things turned out) en l'occurrence; **in any ~**, **at all ~s** de toute façon; **3** (occasion) **social ~** événement *m* mondain; **it was quite an ~** c'était un événement; **4** (in athletics) épreuve *f*; **field/track ~** épreuve *f* d'athlétisme/de vitesse; **men's/women's ~** épreuve *f* pour hommes/pour femmes; **5** Equit **three-day ~** concours *m* complet d'équitation (*se déroulant sur trois jours*).
IDIOMS **after the ~** après la bataille.

even-tempered /ˈiːvnˈtempəd/ *adj* d'une humeur égale.

eventer /ˌiːvnˈtempəd/ *n* Equit (person) participant/-e *m/f* à un concours complet; **he's a good ~** (horse) c'est un bon cheval de concours complet.

eventful /ɪˈventfl/ *adj* mouvementé, riche en événements.

eventide /ˈiːvntaɪd/ *n* littér crépuscule *m*.

eventide home *n* GB maison *f* de retraite.

eventing /ɪˈventɪŋ/ *n* GB Equit concours *m* complet.

eventual /ɪˈventʃʊəl/ *adj* [*aim, hope*] à long terme; **it led to the ~ collapse of the talks** cela a finalement entraîné l'échec des négociations; **his ~ success** le succès qu'il finit par remporter.

eventuality /ɪˌventʃʊˈælətɪ/ *n* éventualité *f*.

eventually /ɪˈventʃʊəlɪ/ *adv* (at last) finalement; (after series of events) finalement; **to do sth ~** finir par faire qch.

eventuate /ɪˈventʃʊeɪt/ *vi* sout finir par se produire; **to ~ in** mener à.

ever /ˈevə(r)/ **I** *adv* **1** (at any time) **nothing was ~ said** rien n'a jamais été dit; **no-one will ~ forget** personne n'oubliera jamais; **I don't think I'll ~ come back/she'll ~ come back** je ne pense pas revenir un jour/qu'elle revienne un jour; **I doubt if I'll ~ come back/he'll ~ come back** je ne suis pas sûr de revenir un jour/qu'il revienne un jour; **the money is unlikely ~ to be paid back** il est peu probable que l'argent soit remboursé un jour; **I don't remember ~ seeing them** je ne me souviens pas de les avoir (jamais) vus; **I don't remember her ~ saying that** je ne me souviens pas de l'avoir entendue dire ça; **I can't say I ~ noticed it** je ne l'ai jamais remarqué; **seldom** ou **rarely, if ~** rarement sinon jamais; **hardly ~** rarement; **we hardly ~ meet** nous nous rencontrons rarement, nous ne nous rencontrons presque jamais; **she never ~ comes** elle ne vient jamais; **something I would never ~ do** quelque chose que je ne ferais jamais de ma vie; **has he ~ lived abroad?** est-ce qu'il a déjà vécu à l'étranger?, a-t-il jamais vécu à l'étranger?; **haven't you ~ been to Greece?** est-ce que tu n'es jamais allé en Grèce?; **will she ~ forget?** est-ce qu'elle oubliera un jour?; **do you ~ make mistakes?** est-ce qu'il t'arrive de te tromper?; **if you ~ see, if ~ you see** si jamais tu vois; **he said if ~ I was passing through Oxford**... il m'a dit que si jamais je passais par Oxford...; **if ~ someone deserved a rise, she did** si jamais quelqu'un méritait une augmentation, c'était bien elle; **this was proof if ~ proof was needed** c'était la preuve, s'il fallait une preuve; **she's a genius if ~ I saw one** ou **if ~ there was one!** c'est un génie ou je ne m'y connais pas!; **2** (when making comparisons) **more beautiful/difficult than ~** encore plus beau/difficile que jamais; **it's windier than ~ today** il y a encore plus de vent aujourd'hui; **more than ~ before** plus que jamais; **competition is tougher than ~ before** la concurrence n'a jamais été aussi acharnée; **more women than ~ before are working** les femmes n'ont jamais été aussi nombreuses à travailler; **we have more friends than ~ before** nous n'avons jamais eu autant d'amis; **he's happier than he's ~ been** il n'a jamais été aussi heureux; **she's more gifted than he'll ~ be!** elle est plus douée qu'il ne le sera jamais!; **you work harder than I ~ did** tu travailles plus que je n'ai jamais travaillé; **the worst mistake I ~ made** la pire erreur que j'aie jamais faite ; **the best film ~ made** le meilleur film jamais fait or tourné; **she's the funniest actress ~!** c'est l'actrice la plus drôle que j'aie jamais vue!; **the first/last time anyone ~ saw him** la première/dernière fois qu'on l'a vu; **the first ~** le tout premier; **my first ~ car** ma toute première voiture; **3** (at all times, always) toujours; **~ loyal/hopeful** toujours loyal/plein d'espérance; **to be as cheerful as ~** être toujours aussi gai; **peace seems as far away as ~** la paix paraît toujours aussi improbable; **the same as ~** toujours le même; **they're the same as ~** ils sont toujours les mêmes; **they lived happily ~ after** ils vécurent toujours heureux; **~ the optimist/diplomat** l'éternel optimiste/diplomate; **your ~ loving father**† ton père qui t'aime; **~ yours, yours ~** bien à toi or à vous; **4** (expressing anger, irritation) **you never ~ write to me!** tu ne m'écris jamais!; **don't (you) ~ do that again!** ne refais jamais ça!; **if you ~ speak to me like that again** si jamais tu me reparles sur ce ton; **do you ~ think about anyone else?** ça ne t'arrive jamais de penser à quelqu'un d'autre?; **that's the last time he ~ comes here!** c'est la dernière fois qu'il vient ici!; **have you ~ heard such rubbish!** as-tu jamais entendu de telles âneries?; **did you ~ see such a mess?** as-tu jamais vu une telle pagaille?; **why did I ~ leave?** pourquoi est-ce que je suis parti?; **you were a fool ~ to believe it!** tu étais idiot de le croire (ne serait-ce qu'une minute)!; **that's all he ~ does!** c'est tout ce qu'il sait faire!; **all you ~ do is moan!** tout ce que tu sais faire c'est râler !; **5** (expressing surprise) **why ~ not?** GB pourquoi pas?; **who ~ would have guessed?** qui donc aurait deviné?; **what ~ do you mean?** que voulez-vous dire par là?; **6** GB (very) **~ so** si; **I'm ~ so glad you came!** je suis si heureux que tu sois venu!; **it's ~ so slightly damp** c'est très légèrement humide; **thanks ~ so much!** merci mille fois!; **he's ~ so much better** il va beaucoup mieux; **I've received ~ so many letters** j'ai reçu beaucoup de lettres; **be it ~ so humble** sout aussi humble soit-il fml; **she's ~ such a bright child** c'est une enfant si intelligente; **it's ~ such a shame!** c'est vraiment dommage!; **7**○ (in exclamations) **is he ~ dumb!** ce qu'il peut être bête!; **am I ~ glad to see you!** qu'est-ce que je suis content de te voir!; **do I ~!** (emphatic yes) et comment!
II ever- (*dans composés*) toujours; **~-growing** ou **-increasing** toujours croissant; **~-present** toujours présent; **~-changing** qui évolue sans cesse.
III as ever *adv phr* comme toujours; **they were, as ~, ready to**... comme toujours ils étaient prêts à...
IV ever more *adv phr* de plus en plus.
V ever since *adv phr*, *conj phr* depuis; **~ since we arrived** depuis que nous sommes arrivés, depuis notre arrivée.
VI before ever *conj phr* avant même (**doing** de faire); **she was unhappy before ~ we left** elle était malheureuse avant même que nous soyons partis.

Everest /ˈevərɪst/ *pr n* (**Mount**) **~** l'Everest *m*.

evergreen /ˈevəgriːn/ **I** *n* Bot (tree) arbre *m* à feuillage persistant or à feuilles persistantes; (plant) plante *f* à feuillage persistant or à feuilles persistantes.
II *adj* (*épith*) **1** Bot [*plant, tree*] à feuillage persistant, à feuilles persistantes; **2** fig (popular) [*song, programme*] toujours populaire, toujours en vogue.

everlasting /ˌevəˈlɑːstɪŋ, US -ˈlæst-/ *adj* éternel/-elle.

every /ˈevrɪ/

■ **Note** *every* is most frequently translated by *tous les*/*toutes les* + plural noun: *every day* = tous les jours. When *every* is emphasized to mean *every single*, it can also be translated by *chaque*. For examples and exceptions, see the entry below.

I *det* **1** (each) **~ house in the street** toutes les maisons de la rue; **she answered ~ (single) question** elle a répondu à chaque question or à toutes les questions; **~ time I go there** chaque fois que j'y vais; **I've read ~ one of her books** j'ai lu tous ses livres; **he ate ~ one of them** il les a tous mangés; **~ one of us is implicated** chacun de nous est impliqué, nous sommes tous impliqués; **that goes for ~ one of you!** c'est valable pour tout le monde!; **I enjoyed ~ minute of it** chaque minute a été un plaisir; **she ate ~ last crumb of the cake** elle a mangé le gâteau jusqu'à la dernière miette; **he spent ~ last penny of the money** il a dépensé jusqu'au dernier sou; **~ second/third day** tous les deux/trois jours; **he had none but ~ other child had one** il n'en avait pas mais tous les autres enfants en avaient un; **five out of ~ ten** cinq sur dix; **there are three women for ~ ten men** il y a trois femmes seulement pour dix hommes; **from ~ side** de toutes parts; **in ~ way** (from every point of view) à tous les égards; (using every method) par tous les moyens; **2** (emphatic) **her ~ word/action** ses moindres paroles/gestes; **your ~ wish** tout ce que vous désirez, votre moindre désir; **I have ~ confidence in you** j'ai toute confiance en vous; **there is ~ chance of a good harvest** il y a toutes les chances que la récolte soit bonne; **we have ~ expectation that** nous avons tous les espoirs que; **you have ~ reason to be pleased** tu as toutes les raisons d'être content; **they have ~ right to complain** ils ont tous les droits de se plaindre; **I wish you ~ success** je vous souhaite beaucoup de succès; **not ~ family is so lucky** toutes les familles n'ont pas autant de chance; **he is ~ bit as handsome as his father** il est tout aussi beau que son père; **it was ~ bit as good as her last film** c'était tout aussi bien que son dernier film; **~ bit as much as** tout autant que; **3** (indicating frequency) **~ day/Thursday** tous les jours/jeudis; **~ month/year** tous les mois/ans; **~ week** toutes les semaines; **once ~ few minutes** toutes les cinq minutes; **once ~ few days** plusieurs fois par semaine; **it' s not ~ day that** ce n'est pas tous les jours que; **~ 20 kilometres** tous les 20 kilomètres.

II **every other** *adj phr* (alternate) **~ other day** tous les deux jours; **~ other Sunday** un dimanche sur deux; **~ other page** toutes les deux pages.

IDIOMS **~ now and then, ~ now and again, ~ so often, ~ once in a while** de temps en temps; **~ little (bit) helps** (when collecting money) tous les dons sont bienvenus; (when saving money) les petits ruisseaux font les grandes rivières; **it's ~ man for himself** c'est chacun pour soi; **~ man for himself!** sauve qui peut!; **~ man Jack of them** tous sans exception; **~ which way** dans tous les sens.

everybody /ˈevrɪbɒdɪ/ *pron* tout le monde; **~ else** tous les autres; **~ knows ~ else around here** ici tout le monde se connaît; **you can't please ~** on ne peut pas faire plaisir à tout le monde; **he's mad, ~ knows that** il est fou, tout le monde le sait; **~ who is anybody** tous les gens importants.

everyday /ˈevrɪdeɪ/ *adj* [*activity, routine*] quotidien/-ienne; [*clothes*] de tous les jours; **~ life** la vie de tous les jours, la vie quotidienne; **this is not an ~ occurrence** cela n'arrive pas tous les jours; **~ English** l'anglais de tous les jours; **in ~ use** [*object, device, word*] d'usage courant.

everyone /ˈevrɪwʌn/ *pron* = **everybody**.

everyplace○ /ˈevrɪpleɪs/ *adv* US = **everywhere**.

everything /ˈevrɪθɪŋ/

■ **Note** *everything* is almost always translated by *tout*. For examples and particular usages, see below.

pron tout; **is ~ all right?** est-ce que tout va bien?; **you mustn't believe ~ you hear** il ne faut pas croire tout ce que tu entends; **they've eaten ~ else** ils ont mangé tout le reste; **money isn't ~** l'argent n'est pas tout; **he's got ~ going for him** il a tout pour lui; **she meant ~ to him** elle était tout pour lui; **have you got your papers and ~?** est-ce que vous avez vos papiers et tout le reste?; **I like him and ~**○**, but I wouldn't choose to go on holiday with him** je l'aime bien, c'est vrai, mais je ne choisirais pas de partir en vacances avec lui.

everywhere /ˈevrɪweə(r), US -hweər/ *adv* partout; **~ else** partout ailleurs; **~ I go it's the same** partout où je vais, c'est la même chose; **she's been ~** elle a voyagé partout; **~ people are becoming concerned** partout les gens commencent à se sentir concernés; **~ looks different at night** n'importe quel endroit change d'aspect la nuit.

evict /ɪˈvɪkt/ *vtr* expulser **(from** de).

eviction /ɪˈvɪkʃn/ *n* expulsion *f* **(from** de).

eviction notice, **eviction order** *n* mandat *m* d'expulsion.

evidence /ˈevɪdəns/ I *n* **1** gen, Jur (proof) ¢ preuves *fpl* **(that** que; **of, for** de; **against** contre); **a piece of ~** une preuve; **insufficient ~** preuves insuffisantes; **video ~** preuves fournies par une bande-vidéo; **~ to support/show sth** preuves qui appuient/démontrent qch; **there is ~ to suggest that** il y a de bonnes raisons de penser que; **there is no ~ that** rien ne prouve que; **all the ~ is** ou **suggests that** tout indique que; **to show ~ of genius** faire preuve de génie; **to believe the ~ of one's own eyes** croire ce qu'on a vu de ses propres yeux; **on the ~ of his last performance he...** si on en juge par sa dernière performance, il...; **2** Jur (testimony) témoignage *m* **(from** de) ; **to take** ou **hear sb's ~** entendre le témoignage de qn; **on the ~ of sb** d'après qn; **to be convicted on the ~ of sb** être condamné sur le témoignage de qn; **to be used in ~ against sb** servir de témoignage contre qn; **to give ~** témoigner, déposer **(for sb** en faveur de qn; **against sb** contre qn); **to give ~ for the prosecution/the defence** être témoin à charge/à décharge; **3** (trace) trace *f* **(of** de); **to be (much) in ~** être (bien) visible; **she's not very much in ~ these days** on ne la voit pas beaucoup en ce moment; **he was nowhere in ~** il était invisible.

II *vtr* sout attester; **(as) ~d by sth** comme l'atteste qch.

evident /ˈevɪdənt/ *adj* [*anger, concern, relief*] manifeste; **to be ~ from sth that** être clair d'après qch que; **it is ~ to me that** pour moi il est évident que; **his fear is ~ in his behaviour/expression** son comportement/expression trahit sa peur; **this reaction is most ~ in men** cette réaction s'observe plus particulièrement chez les hommes.

evidently /ˈevɪdəntlɪ/ *adv* **1** (obviously) [*afraid, happy*] manifestement; **2** (apparently) apparemment; **'isn't it illegal?'—'~ not!'** 'n'est-ce pas illégal?'—'il semblerait que non!' or 'apparemment, non'.

evil /ˈiːvl/ I *n* **1** (wickedness) mal *m*; **to speak ~ of sb** dire du mal de qn; **the forces of ~** les forces du Mal; **2** (bad thing) (of war, disease, social problem) fléau *m*; (of doctrine, regime) mal *m*; **the ~s of drink/drugs** le fléau de l'alcool/la drogue; **the ~s of racism** les maux du racisme.

II *adj* [*person*] méchant; [*act, destiny, intent, genius, smell, tongue, temper*] mauvais; [*plan, spirit*] maléfique; **The Evil One** le Malin.

IDIOMS **to give sb the ~ eye** jeter le mauvais œil à qn; **the lesser of two ~s** le moindre mal; **hear no ~, see no ~, speak no ~** Prov il vaudrait mieux ne pas s'en mêler; **money is the root of all ~** l'argent est la source de tous les maux ; **to put off the ~ hour** ou **day** repousser le moment fatidique; **to return good for ~** rendre le bien pour le mal.

evil: **~doer** *n* littér malfaiteur *m*; **~-minded** *adj* porté au mal; **~-smelling** *adj* nauséabond.

evince /ɪˈvɪns/ *vtr* sout faire preuve de, manifester [*intelligence, talent*].

eviscerate /ɪˈvɪsəreɪt/ *vtr* sout éviscérer.

evocation /ˌevəˈkeɪʃn/ *n* évocation *f*.

evocative /ɪˈvɒkətɪv/ *adj* évocateur/-trice.

evocatively /ɪˈvɒkətɪvlɪ/ *adv* [*described*] de façon évocatrice.

evoke /ɪˈvəʊk/ *vtr* **1** évoquer [*memory, feeling*]; **2** susciter [*response, interest, admiration*].

evolution /ˌiːvəˈluːʃn/ *n* évolution *f* **(from** à partir de).

evolutionary /ˌiːvəˈluːʃənərɪ, US -nerɪ/ *adj* évolutionniste.

evolve /ɪˈvɒlv/ I *vtr* élaborer, mettre au point [*theory, system, policy*].

II *vi* **1** [*theory, situation*] évoluer; **to ~ from sth** se développer à partir de qch; **2** [*animal, organism*] évoluer; **to ~ from sth** descendre de qch.

ewe /juː/ *n* brebis *f*; **~ lamb** agnelle *f*.

ewer /ˈjuːə(r)/ *n* aiguière *f*.

ex /eks/ I○ *n* (former partner) ex○ *mf*.

II *prep* Comm **~ works, ~ factory** [*price*] départ usine; **~ wharf, ~ dock** à quai dédouané; **~ coupon** Fin ex coupon.

III **ex+** (*dans composés*) ex-, ancien/-ienne (*before n*).

exacerbate /ɪgˈzæsəbeɪt/ *vtr* exacerber [*pain, disease*]; aggraver [*situation*].

exact /ɪgˈzækt/ I *adj* [*amount, calculation, copy, description, detail, number, replica, time*] exact; [*moment, instant*] précis; **it's not an ~ science** ce n'est pas une science exacte; **it's the ~ opposite** c'est exactement le contraire; **tell me your ~ whereabouts** dis-moi où tu te trouves exactement; **those were her ~ words** voilà exactement ce qu'elle a dit; **to be (more) ~** plus précisément; **it was in summer, July to be ~** c'était en été, plus précisément en juillet; **can you be more ~?** pourriez-vous être plus précis?; **the ~ same**○ **hat** exactement le même chapeau; **he did the ~ same**○ **thing** il a fait exactement la même chose.

II *vtr* exiger [*price, payment, ransom, obedience*] **(from** de); **to ~ revenge** prendre sa revanche.

exacting /ɪgˈzæktɪŋ/ *adj* astreignant.

exaction /ɪgˈzækʃn/ *n* exaction *f*.

exactitude /ɪgˈzæktɪtjuːd, US -tuːd/ *n* exactitude *f*.

exactly /ɪgˈzæktlɪ/ *adv* **1** (just, precisely) exactement; **~ as promised** exactement comme promis; **no-one knew ~ why/who** personne ne savait exactement pourquoi/qui; **not ~** pas exactement; **it would have been ~ the same** (of situation) ça aurait été exactement la même chose; **my feelings** ou **opinion ~!** exactement!; **what ~** ou **~ what were you doing?** que faisais-tu au juste?; **she wasn't ~ overjoyed/surprised** iron elle n'était pas précisément ravie/surprise; **2** (with exactitude) [*calculate, know, describe*] avec exactitude, exactement.

exactness /ɪgˈzæktnɪs/ *n* exactitude *f*.

exaggerate /ɪgˈzædʒəreɪt/ I *vtr* exagérer; (in one's own mind) s'exagérer [*problem, importance, risk*]; (highlight) exagérer [*effect, size, movement, expression*].

II *vi* exagérer.

exaggerated /ɪgˈzædʒəreɪtɪd/ *adj* exagéré; **he has an ~ sense of his own importance** il se fait une idée exagérée de son importance.

exaggeration /ɪgˌzædʒəˈreɪʃn/ *n* exagération *f*; **it's no ~ to say that** on peut dire sans exagération que; **...and that's no ~** sans exagérer.

exalt /ɪgˈzɔːlt/ *vtr* sout **1** (glorify) exalter, glorifier; **2** (raise in rank, power) élever [qn] à un rang important.

exaltation /ˌegzɔːlˈteɪʃn/ *n* exaltation *f*.

exalted /ɪgˈzɔːltɪd/ *adj* sout **1** (elevated) [*rank, position*] élevé, haut; [*person*] haut placé; **2** (jubilant) [*person, mood*] exalté; **3** (exaggerated) **to have an ~ opinion of oneself** se faire des illusions sur soi-même.

exam○ /ɪgˈzæm/ *n* examen *m*. ▶ **examination**.

examination /ɪgˌzæmɪˈneɪʃn/ I *n* **1** Sch, Univ examen *m* **(in** de); **French/Biology ~** examen *m* de français/de biologie; **to take an ~** passer un examen; **to pass an ~** réussir un examen; **2** (inspection) gen, Med examen *m*; Accts vérification *f*; **medical ~** examen *m* médical; **on ~** après examen; **under ~** à l'examen; **after close/further ~** après un examen attentif/approfondi; **to have an ~** Med passer un examen médical; **to give sb an ~** Med faire passer un examen médical à qn; **3** Jur (of accused, witness) interrogatoire *m*.

II *modif* Sch, Univ [*certificate, question, results*] d'examen; [*candidate*] à un examen.

examination: **~ board** *n* comité *m* responsable de l'organisation des examens nationaux; **~ paper** *n* sujets *mpl* d'examen; **~ script** *n* copie *f*.

examine /ɪgˈzæmɪn/ *vtr* **1** (intellectually) considérer [*facts*]; examiner [*evidence*]; étudier [*problem, question, theory*]; **2** (visually) examiner [*object, document, evidence*]; fouiller [*luggage*]; vérifier [*accounts*]; Med examiner [*person, part of body*]; **to have sth ~ed** Med faire examiner qch; **3** Sch, Univ faire

passer un examen à [*candidate, pupil*] (**in** en; **on** sur); **they are ~ed in maths every year** ils passent un examen en math chaque année; **4** Jur interroger [*person*].
IDIOMS **you need your head ~d**○**!** tu devrais te faire soigner○!

examinee /ɪg,zæmɪ'ni:/ *n* candidat/-e *m/f* (à un examen).

examiner /ɪg'zæmɪnə(r)/ *n* examinateur/-trice *m/f*.

examining board, **examining body** *n* Sch comité *m* responsable de l'organisation des examens nationaux.

examining justice, **examining magistrate** *n* juge *m* d'instruction.

exam nerves *npl* stress *m* des examens.

example /ɪg'zɑ:mpl, US -'zæmpl/ *n* exemple *m*; **for ~** par exemple; **to follow sb's ~** suivre l'exemple de qn; **following the ~ of Gandhi** à l'exemple de Gandhi; **to set a good ~** donner l'exemple; **he's an ~ to us all** c'est notre modèle à tous; **you're setting a bad ~ for the others** tu ne donnes pas le bon exemple aux autres; **to offer sth as an ~** proposer qch en exemple; **he was punished as an ~ to others** il a été puni pour que cela serve d'exemple aux autres; **to make an ~ of sb** punir qn pour l'exemple; **children learn by ~** les enfants apprennent par imitation.

exasperate /ɪg'zæspəreɪt/ *vtr* exaspérer.

exasperated /ɪg'zæspəreɪtɪd/ *adj* exaspéré (**by, at** par); **she was ~ with him** il l'avait portée à bout; **to get ~** s'énerver.

exasperating /ɪg'zæspəreɪtɪŋ/ *adj* exaspérant.

exasperatingly /ɪg'zæspəreɪtɪŋlɪ/ *adv* **~ clumsy/stupid** d'une maladresse/stupidité exaspérante.

exasperation /ɪg,zæspə'reɪʃn/ *n* exaspération *f*; **he stamped his foot in ~** exaspéré, il a tapé du pied.

ex cathedra /,eks kə'θi:drə/ *adj, adv* ex cathedra.

excavate /'ekskəveɪt/ **I** *vtr* **1** Archeol fouiller [*site*]; exhumer [*object*]; **2** Constr creuser [*ground, trench, tunnel*].
II *vi* Archeol faire des fouilles.

excavation /,ekskə'veɪʃn/ **I** *n* **1** (of land) excavation *f*, creusement *m*; **2** (tunnel) excavation *f*; **~ work** travaux *mpl* d'excavation.
II excavations *npl* Archeol fouilles *fpl*.

excavator /'ekskəveɪtə(r)/ *n* **1** (machine) excavateur *m*; **2** Archeol (person) fouilleur/-euse *m/f*.

exceed /ɪk'si:d/ *vtr* outrepasser [*functions, authority*]; dépasser [*speed limit, sum of money*] (**by** de); **when expenses ~ income** quand les dépenses sont supérieures aux revenus; **to ~ all expectations** dépasser toute attente; **arrested for ~ing the speed limit** arrêté pour excès de vitesse.

exceedingly /ɪk'si:dɪŋlɪ/ *adv* sout extrêmement.

excel /ɪk'sel/ **I** *vtr* surpasser (**in** en).
II *vi* exceller (**at, in** en; **at** ou **in doing** à faire).
III *v refl* **to ~ oneself** se surpasser also iron.

excellence /'eksələns/ **I** *n* excellence *f*.
II Excellence *n* = **Excellency**.

Excellency /'eksələnsɪ/ *n* Excellence *f*; **Your ~** Votre Excellence.

excellent /'eksələnt/ **I** *adj* excellent.
II *excl* parfait!

excellently /'eksələntlɪ/ *adv* admirablement, merveilleusement bien.

excelsior /ɪk'selsɪɔ:(r)/ *n* US copeaux *mpl* d'emballage.

except /ɪk'sept/

■ **Note** There are four frequently used translations for *except* when used as a preposition. By far the most frequent of these is *sauf*; the others are *excepté*, *à l'exception de* and *hormis*. Note, however, that in *what*/*where*/*who* questions, *except* is translated by *sinon*. For examples and the phrase *except for* see below.

I *prep* **everybody ~ Lisa** tout le monde sauf Lisa, tout le monde à l'exception de or excepté or hormis Lisa, tout le monde Lisa exceptée; **nothing ~** rien d'autre que; **nobody ~** personne d'autre que; **~ if/when** sauf si/quand; **~ that** sauf que, si ce n'est que; **who could have done it ~ him?** qui aurait pu le faire sinon lui?; **where could she be ~ at home?** où est-ce qu'elle pourrait être sinon chez elle?
II except for *prep phr* à part, à l'exception de.
III‡ *conj* **~ he be dead** à moins qu'il ne soit mort.
IV *vtr* excepter, exclure (**from** de); **not ~ing** sans oublier, y compris; **present company ~ed** exception faite des personnes présentes.

excepting /ɪk'septɪŋ/ *prep* à l'exception de; **always ~** à l'exception bien sûr de.

exception /ɪk'sepʃn/ *n* **1** (special case) exception *f* (**for** pour); **with the (possible) ~ of** à l'exception (peut-être) de; **the only ~ being** à la seule exception de; **without ~** sans exception; **with some ~s** à quelques exceptions près; **with certain ~s** à quelques exceptions près; **to make an ~** faire exception; **there can be no ~s** il n'y aura pas d'exception; **an ~ to the rule** une exception à la règle; **a notable ~** une exception remarquable; **the ~ proves the rule** c'est l'exception qui confirme la règle; **2 to take ~ to** (dislike) prendre [qch] comme une insulte [*remark, suggestion*].

exceptional /ɪk'sepʃənl/ *adj* **1** gen exceptionnel/-elle; **2** US Sch (handicapped) désavantagé; (gifted) particulièrement doué.

exceptionally /ɪk'sepʃənəlɪ/ *adv* exceptionnellement.

excerpt /'eksɜ:pt/ *n* extrait *m*.

excess /ɪk'ses/ **I** *n* **1** gen excès *m* (**of** de); **to eat/drink to ~** faire des excès de table/de boisson, trop manger/boire; **carried to ~** poussé à l'excès; **a life of ~** une vie d'excès; **any ~ can be frozen** tout ce qui est en trop peut être congelé; **to be in ~ of** excéder, dépasser; **it is far in ~ of what is reasonable** cela dépasse largement les limites du raisonnable; **the ~ of supply over demand** Econ l'excès *m* or l'excédent *m* de l'offre sur la demande; **2** GB Insur (insurance) franchise *f*.
II excesses *npl* excès *mpl*, abus *mpl*.
III *adj* **~ alcohol/speed/weight** excès *m* d'alcool/de vitesse/de poids; **to drive with ~ alcohol** GB conduire en état d'ivresse; **drain off the ~ water** égoutter l'excédent d'eau; **remove ~ fat** (on meat) dégraisser.

excess: **~ baggage**, **excess luggage** *n* excédent *m* de bagages; **~ fare** *n* supplément *m*.

excessive /ɪk'sesɪv/ *adj* gen excessif/-ive; **~ drinking** abus *m* d'alcool.

excessively /ɪk'sesɪvlɪ/ *adv* **1** (inordinately) [*harsh, long, expensive*] excessivement; [*drink, spend*] avec excès; **2**○ (very) [*dull, embarrassing*] excessivement controv, extrêmement.

excess: **~ postage** *n* surtaxe *f* postale; **~ profits** *npl* superbénéfices *mpl*; **~ profits tax** *n* impôt *m* sur les superbénéfices; (in wartime) contribution *f* extraordinaire sur les bénéfices de guerre.

exchange /ɪks'tʃeɪndʒ/ **I** *n* **1** (swap) échange *m*; **in ~** en échange (**for** de); **~ of ideas/information** échange d'idées/d'informations; **~ of contracts** Comm Jur ≈ signature *f* de l'acte de vente; **~ of vows** échange *m* des serments; **2** Comm, Fin change *m*; **the rate of ~** le taux de change; **bill of ~** lettre *f* de change; **first/second/third of ~** première/deuxième/troisième de change; **3** (discussion) discussion *f*; (in parliament) débat *m*; **a heated** ou **an angry ~** une discussion houleuse; **4** (visit) échange *m*; **to go on an ~** partir dans le cadre d'un échange; **~ student** étudiant/-e *m/f* participant à un échange; **~ visit** voyage *m* d'échange; **5** Comm, Fin (place of business) Bourse *f*; **6** Telecom (also **telephone ~**) central *m* (téléphonique).
II *vtr* échanger; **to ~ sth for sth** échanger qch contre qch; **to ~ sth with sb** échanger qch avec qn; **to ~ contracts** Comm Jur ≈ signer le contrat de vente; **to ~ looks/blows** échanger un regard/des coups (**with** avec); **they ~d hostages** ils ont échangé leurs otages.

exchangeable /ɪks'tʃeɪndʒəbl/ *adj* échangeable (**for, against** contre).

exchangeable: **~ disk** *n* Comput disque *m* amovible; **~ disk storage**, **EDS** *n* Comput unité *f* de disques à chargeur.

exchange: **~ bureau** *n* bureau *m* de change; **~ control** *n* contrôle *m* des changes; **~ controls** *npl* mesures *fpl* de contrôle des changes; **~ rate** *n* taux *m* de change; **Exchange Rate Mechanism**, **ERM** *n* (Mécanisme *m* de change du) système *m* monétaire européen.

exchequer /ɪks'tʃekə(r)/ **I** *n* **1** Admin ministère *m* des finances; **2** hum (funds) fonds *mpl*.
II Exchequer *pr n* ministère *m* britannique des finances.

excisable /ɪk'saɪzəbl/ *adj* sujet/-ette aux droits de régie.

excise I /'eksaɪz/ *n* (also **excise duty**) excise *f*, taxe *f*.
II /ɪk'saɪz/ *vtr* **1** Med exciser; **2** (from text) supprimer.

excision /ɪk'sɪʒn/ *n* **1** Med excision *f*; **2** (from text) suppression *f*.

excitable /ɪk'saɪtəbl/ *adj* [*person, animal, disposition*] nerveux/-euse; Med [*nerve*] excitable; **an ~ child** un enfant qui s'excite facilement.

excitant /'eksɪtənt/ *n* excitant *m*.

excite /ɪk'saɪt/ *vtr* **1** (make excited) exciter; (fire with enthusiasm) enthousiasmer; (sexually) exciter; **2** (stimulate) exciter [*imagination*]; susciter [*interest, controversy, admiration, anger*]; **3** (give rise to) éveiller [*curiosity, suspicion, passion*]; faire naître [*envy*]; **4** (incite) provoquer [*rebellion, riot*]; **5** Med, Physiol exciter.

excited /ɪk'saɪtɪd/ *adj* [*person, crowd, animal*] excité; (sexually) excité; [*voice, conversation, look*] animé; [*imagination*] exalté; Physiol excité; **to be ~ about sth** (enthusiastic) s'enthousiasmer pour qch; (in anticipation) être emballé○ à l'idée de qch; **she's ~ about going to Greece** elle est emballée○ à l'idée de partir en Grèce; **to get ~** [*person, crowd*] s'exciter; **it's nothing to get ~ about!** il n'y a pas de quoi s'exciter; **don't get ~!** (cross) ne t'énerve pas!

excitedly /ɪk'saɪtɪdlɪ/ *adv* avec animation; **they were whispering ~** ils chuchotaient tout excités; **'listen!' she said ~** 'écoute!' dit-elle tout excitée.

excitement /ɪk'saɪtmənt/ *n* **1** (emotion) excitation *f*; **what an ~!** quelle émotion!; **in the ~ we forgot to lock the car** dans l'agitation générale nous avons oublié de fermer la voiture; **the news caused great ~** la nouvelle a fait sensation; **I want some ~ out of life** je veux une vie plus excitante; **he was in a state of great ~** il était tout excité; **2** (exciting experience) événement *m* excitant.

exciting /ɪk'saɪtɪŋ/ *adj* [*idea, event, experience, film*] passionnant; **an ~ new acting talent** un acteur qui promet; **that's not a very ~ prospect** ça promet de ne pas être bien excitant.

excl. *abrév* = **excluding**.

exclaim /ɪk'skleɪm/ **I** *vtr* s'écrier (**that** que); **'what?' he ~ed** 'quoi?' s'exclama-t-il.
II *vi* gen s'exclamer (**at** devant); (in protest) se récrier (**at** devant); **to ~ in anger** s'exclamer avec colère.

exclamation /ˌekskləˈmeɪʃn/ *n* exclamation *f*.

exclamation mark, **exclamation point** US point *m* d'exclamation.

exclamatory /ɪkˈsklæmətrɪ, US -tɔːrɪ/ *adj* exclamatif/-ive.

exclude /ɪkˈskluːd/ *vtr* (keep out) exclure [*person, group*] (**from** de); (leave out) ne pas retenir, ne pas inclure [*name*]; exclure [*issue, possibility*]; **~d from membership of the party** exclu du parti; **they are ~d from (applying for) these jobs** ils n'ont pas le droit de postuler ces emplois; **they have been ~d from the inquiry** ils ont été éliminés de l'enquête; **to ~ from the jurisdiction of a court** Jur soustraire à la compétence d'un tribunal.

excluding /ɪkˈskluːdɪŋ/ *prep* mis/-e à part; **£38 ~ breakfast** 38 livres petit déjeuner non compris.

exclusion /ɪkˈskluːʒn/ *n* (expulsion) exclusion *f* (**from** de); (refusal of entry, participation) fait *m* d'être exclu (**from** de); **the ~ of women from...** le fait que les femmes soient exclues de...; **to the ~ of** à l'exclusion de.

exclusion: **~ order** *n* Jur *disposition interdisant à un conjoint violent l'accès du domicile conjugal*; **~ zone** *n* (all contexts) zone *f* interdite.

exclusive /ɪkˈskluːsɪv/ **I** *n* Journ, TV, Radio exclusivité *f*; **a BBC ~** une exclusivité de la BBC.
II *adj* **1** [*occasion*] choisi; [*club, social circle*] fermé; [*hotel, goods*] de luxe; [*school, district*] huppé; [*friendship*] exclusif/-ive; **2** Comm, Journ, TV [*story, report*] exclusif/-ive; **an ~ interview with sb** un entretien en exclusivité avec qn; **~ to Harrods** une exclusivité de Harrods; **to have ~ (marketing) rights for sth** avoir l'exclusivité (de vente) de qch; **to have ~ coverage of sth** avoir l'exclusivité de la couverture de qch; **to have ~ use of sth** être le seul à utiliser qch, avoir l'usage exclusif de; **to be mutually ~** s'exclure mutuellement; **~ of meals** les repas non compris.

exclusively /ɪkˈskluːsɪvlɪ/ *adv* exclusivement.

excommunicate /ˌekskəˈmjuːnɪkeɪt/ *vtr* excommunier.

excommunication /ˌekskəˌmjuːnɪˈkeɪʃn/ *n* excommunication *f*.

ex-con○ /ˌeksˈkɒn/ *n* ex-taulard○ *m*, ex-prisonnier *m*.

excrement /ˈekskrɪmənt/ *n* excrément *m*.

excrescence /ɪkˈskresns/ *n* lit excroissance *f*; fig verrue *f*.

excreta /ɪkˈskriːtə/ *n* sout (faeces) excréments *mpl*; (waste matter) excrétions *fpl*.

excrete /ɪkˈskriːt/ *vtr* Physiol excréter; Bot exsuder.

excretion /ɪkˈskriːʃn/ *n* Physiol excrétion *f*; Bot exsudation *f*.

excretory /ɪkˈskriːtərɪ, US -tɔːrɪ/ *adj* excréteur/-trice.

excruciating /ɪkˈskruːʃɪeɪtɪŋ/ *adj* **1** [*situation, pain, unhappiness*] atroce, insoutenable; [*noise*] infernal; **2**○ (awful) [*performance*] exécrable.

excruciatingly /ɪkˈskruːʃɪeɪtɪŋlɪ/ *adv* [*painful, embarrassing*] atrocement; [*boring*] mortellement; **~ funny** à mourir de rire.

exculpate /ˈekskʌlpeɪt/ *vtr* disculper.

excursion /ɪkˈskɜːʃn/ *n* **1** (organized) excursion *f*; (casual) promenade *f*; **2** (into subject, field) incursion *f* (**into** dans); **3** (digression) digression *f*.

excursion: **~ ticket** *n* billet *m* d'excursion; **~ train** *n* train *m* spécial.

excusable /ɪkˈskjuːzəbl/ *adj* excusable.

excuse **I** /ɪkˈskjuːs/ *n* **1** (reason) excuse *f*; (pretext) prétexte *m* (**for** à; **for doing** pour faire; **to do** pour faire); **to make** ou **find an ~** trouver une excuse; **you're always making ~s!** tu cherches toujours des prétextes!; **to be an ~ to do** ou **for doing** être ou servir de prétexte pour faire; **I have a good ~ for not doing it** j'ai une bonne excuse pour ne pas le faire; **this gave me an ~ to leave early** ceci m'a fourni un bon prétexte pour partir tôt; **so what's his ~ this time?** alors c'est quoi son excuse, cette fois?; **is that the best ~ you can come up with?** c'est tout ce que tu as trouvé comme excuse?; **any ~ for a day off work!** toutes les excuses sont bonnes or tous les prétextes sont bons pour ne pas aller au travail! ; **this is a poor ~ for a meal!** c'est un piètre repas!; **he's a poor ~ for a man!** c'est un homme minable!; **2** (justification) excuse *f*; **there's no ~ for cheating** rien n'excuse or ne justifie la tricherie; **there's no ~ for such behaviour** ce genre de conduite est inexcusable; **that's no ~** ce n'est pas une excuse or une raison; **without ~** sans excuse, sans motif valable.
II excuses *npl* **to make one's ~s** présenter ses excuses (**to** à); **to make ~s to sb** s'excuser auprès de qn.
III /ɪkˈskjuːz/ *vtr* **1** (forgive) excuser [*person, error, rudeness*]; **to ~ sb for doing** excuser qn d'avoir fait; **you could be ~d for misinterpreting him** vous êtes excusable de l'avoir mal compris; **if you'll ~ the expression** pardonnez-moi l'expression; **~ me!** excusez-moi!, pardon!; **~ me, is this the London train?** excusez-moi, est-ce que c'est le train de Londres?; **~ me for asking, but do you live here?** excusez-moi, mais est-ce que vous habitez ici?; **you'll have to ~ me for not inviting you in** vous voudrez bien m'excuser de ne pas vous inviter à entrer; **~ me, but I think you're mistaken** excusez-moi, mais je crois que vous faites erreur; **~ me, but I did not get the sack**○ je regrette, mais je n'ai pas été viré○; **if you'll ~ me, I have work to do** si vous voulez bien m'excuser, j'ai du travail à faire; **'would you like a drink?'—'~ me?'** US 'vous voulez un verre?'—'pardon?'; **may I be ~d?** GB euph (requesting permission from teacher) est-ce que je peux sortir?, est-ce que je peux aller aux toilettes?; **2** (justify) justifier [*action, measure*]; excuser, trouver des excuses à [*person*]; **3** (exempt) dispenser (**from** de; **from doing** de faire); **to be ~d from games** être dispensé des cours d'éducation physique.
IV /ɪkˈskjuːz/ *v refl* **to ~ oneself** (from table, gathering) s'excuser; **to ~ oneself for sth/for doing** s'excuser de qch/d'avoir fait.

ex-directory /ˌeksdaɪˈrektərɪ, -dɪ-/ *adj* GB **an ~ number** un numéro sur la liste rouge; **he's ~, his number is ~** il est sur la liste rouge; **to go ~** se faire mettre sur la liste rouge.

ex dividend /ˌeks ˈdɪvɪdend/ *adj* ex dividende.

exec○ /ɪkˈzek/ *n* US (*abrév* = **executive**) cadre *m*.

execrable /ˈeksɪkrəbl/ *adj* sout exécrable.

execrably /ˈeksɪkrəblɪ/ *adv* sout exécrablement.

execrate /ˈeksɪkreɪt/ *vtr* sout **1** (abhor) exécrer; **2** (curse) maudire.

execration /ˌeksɪˈkreɪʃn/ *n* sout **1** (abhorrence) exécration *f*; **2** (curse) malédiction *f*.

executant /ɪgˈzekjʊtnt/ *n* Mus interprète *mf*.

execute /ˈeksɪkjuːt/ *vtr* **1** (kill) exécuter; **to be ~d for sth** être exécuté pour qch; **2** (carry out) exécuter [*order, plan, task, wish, idea, artistic concept*]; **3** Comput exécuter.

execution /ˌeksɪˈkjuːʃn/ *n* **1** (killing) exécution *f* (**by** par); **2** (of plan, task, artistic concept) exécution *f*; (by musician) interprétation *f*; **to put sth into ~** mettre qch à exécution; **in the ~ of his duty** dans l'exercice de ses fonctions; **3** Comput exécution *f*; **4** Jur exécution *f*.

executioner /ˌeksɪˈkjuːʃənə(r)/ *n* bourreau *m*, exécuteur *m* (des hautes œuvres).

executive /ɪgˈzekjʊtɪv/ **I** *n* **1** (administrator) Comm cadre *m*; (in Civil Service) cadre *m* administratif; **finance ~** cadre *m* financier; **sales ~** cadre *m* commercial; **top ~** cadre *m* supérieur; **he's an ~ with Cayard** il est cadre chez Cayard; **2** (committee) Admin, comité *m* directeur; instances *fpl* dirigeantes; Pol exécutif *m*, comité *m* exécutif; **party ~** bureau *m* du parti; **trade union ~** bureau *m* du syndicat; **3** US **the ~** le pouvoir executif.
II *adj* **1** (administrative) [*power, section*] exécutif/-ive; [*status, post*] de cadre; **to have ~ ability/potential** avoir des aptitudes/des dispositions pour occuper un poste à responsabilité; **2** (luxury) [*chair, desk*] directorial, de luxe.

executive: **~ agreement** *n* Pol accord *m* en forme simplifiée; **~ arm** *n* organe *m* exécutif; **~ board** *n* conseil *m* de direction; **~ branch** *n* = **executive arm**; **~ briefcase** *n* attaché-case *m*; **~ committee** *n* Pol comité *m* exécutif; **~ council** *n* (of company) conseil *m* de direction; (of trade union, political party) commission *f* exécutive; **~ director** *n* directeur/-trice *m/f* exécutif/-ive ; **~ jet** *n* jet *m* privé, avion *m* privé.

Executive Mansion *pr n* US (White House) **the ~** la Maison Blanche.

executive: **~ member** *n* membre *m* du comité exécutif; **~ officer** *n* cadre *m* dirigeant; **~ order** *n* US décret *m* présidentiel; **~ privilege** *n* US *droit du président à ne pas divulguer certaines informations*; **~ producer** *n* Cin producteur *m* en chef or exécutif; **~ program** *n* Comput superviseur *m*; **~ secretary** *n* Admin secrétaire *m* exécutif; (manager's secretary) secrétaire *mf* de direction; **~ session** *n* séance *f* parlementaire à huis clos; **~ suite** *n* bureaux *mpl* de la direction; **~ toy** *n* gadget *m* (*pour se calmer les nerfs*).

executor /ɪgˈzekjʊtə(r)/ *n* Jur exécuteur *m* testamentaire.

executrix /ɪgˈzekjʊtrɪks/ *n* exécutrice *f* testamentaire.

exegesis /ˌeksɪˈdʒiːsɪs/ *n* exégèse *f*.

exemplar /ɪgˈzemplə(r), -plɑː(r)/ *n* sout modèle *m*.

exemplary /ɪgˈzemplərɪ, US -lerɪ/ *adj* **1** [*behaviour, virtue, life*] exemplaire; [*student*] modèle; **2** [*punishment*] exemplaire; **~ damages** Jur dommages et intérêts exemplaires.

exemplify /ɪgˈzemplɪfaɪ/ *vtr* (all contexts) exemplifier, illustrer.

exempt /ɪgˈzempt/ **I** *adj* exempt (**from** de).
II *vtr* exempter [*person*] (**from sth** de qch); **to ~ sb from doing** dispenser qn de faire.

exemption /ɪgˈzempʃn/ *n* exemption *f* (**from** de); (from exam) dispense *f* (**from** de); **tax ~** dégrèvement *m* d'impôts.

exercise /ˈeksəsaɪz/ **I** *n* **1** (operation) gen, Admin, Comm, Pol opération *f*; (long-term or large-scale) stratégie *f*; **academic ~** (pointless) exercice *m* d'école; **marketing ~** opération *f* de marketing; **public relations ~** campagne *f* de relations publiques; **an ~ in democracy/diplomacy** un exercice de démocratie/de diplomatie; **2** ¢ (exertion) exercice *m*; **physical ~** exercice *m* physique; **3** (training task) gen, Mus, Sch, Sport exercice *m*; **intellectual ~** exercice intellectuel; **maths ~** exercice de maths; **4** (application) (of duties, intellect, imagination, power, rights) exercice *m* (**of** de); **5** Mil manœuvres *fpl*; **to go on (an) ~** partir en manœuvres; **6** Fin levée *f*.
II exercises *npl* US cérémonie *f*.
III *vtr* **1** (apply) faire preuve de [*authority, care, caution, control, patience, restraint, tolerance*]; exercer [*power, right*]; faire valoir, exercer [*rights*]; **2** (exert physically) exercer [*body, mind*]; faire travailler [*limb, muscles*]; promener [*dog*]; sortir [*horse*]; **3** (worry) préoccuper; **a problem which has ~d many great minds** un problème qui a

préoccupé de nombreux savants; **4** Fin lever [*option*].
IV *vi* faire de l'exercice.

exercise: **~ area** *n* terrain *m* d'exercice; **~ bicycle** *n* (in gym) vélo *m* d'entraînement; (at home) vélo *m* d'appartement; **~ book** *n* cahier *m*; **~ programme** *n* Med, Sport programme *m* d'exercices.

exerciser /ˈeksəsaɪzə(r)/ *n* US **1** = **exercise bicycle**; **2** (person) personne *f* qui fait de l'exercice.

exert /ɪɡˈzɜːt/ **I** *vtr* exercer [*pressure, influence*] (**on** sur); employer [*force*]; **to ~ every effort** faire tout son possible (**to do** pour faire).
II *v refl* **to ~ oneself** se fatiguer; **you shouldn't ~ yourself** tu ne devrais pas faire trop d'efforts; **don't ~ yourself!** iron ne te fatigue pas!

exertion /ɪɡˈzɜːʃn/ *n* **1** (physical effort) effort *m*; **the ~s of the climb** les fatigues *fpl* de l'escalade; **2** (exercising) (of pressure) exercice *m*; (of force) emploi *m*; **the ~ of influence on sb** le fait d'exercer une influence sur qn.

exeunt /ˈeksɪənt/ *vi* (*tjrs pl*) Theat ils sortent; **~ soldiers** les soldats sortent.

exfoliate /ˌeksˈfəʊlɪeɪt/ **I** *vtr* exfolier [*bark, rock*]; gommer, exfolier [*skin*].
II *vi* [*bark, rock*] s'exfolier; [*skin*] se desquamer.

exfoliating scrub *n* Cosmet exfoliant *m*.

exfoliation /eksˌfəʊlɪˈeɪʃn/ *n* Geol exfoliation *f*; Med desquamation *f*; Cosmet gommage *m*.

ex gratia /ˌeks ˈɡreɪʃə/ *adj* [*award, payment*] à titre gracieux.

exhalation /ˌekshəˈleɪʃn/ *n* (of breath) expiration *f*; (of fumes, smoke) émission *f*; (from soil) émanation *f*.

exhale /eksˈheɪl/ **I** *vtr* [*person*] expirer [*air, smoke*]; [*chimney*] dégager [*smoke*].
II *vi* [*person*] expirer.

exhaust /ɪɡˈzɔːst/ **I** *n* Aut **1** (pipe) pot *m* d'échappement; **2** (fumes) gaz *mpl* d'échappement.
II *vtr* épuiser [*option, person, supply, topic*].
III *v refl* **to ~ oneself** s'épuiser.
IV exhausted *pp adj* épuisé.

exhaust: **~ centre** GB, **~ center** US *n* centre *m* de réparation de pots d'échappement; **~ emissions** *npl* gaz *mpl* d'échappement; **~ fumes** *npl* gaz *mpl* d'échappement.

exhausting /ɪɡˈzɔːstɪŋ/ *adj* épuisant.

exhaustion /ɪɡˈzɔːstʃn/ *n* **1** (tiredness) épuisement *m*, extrême fatigue *f*; **2** (of supply) épuisement *m*.

exhaustive /ɪɡˈzɔːstɪv/ *adj* [*inquiry, study, report*] exhaustif/-ive; [*coverage, list*] complet/-ète; [*analysis, description, notes, survey*] très détaillé, exhaustif/-ive; [*inspection, investigation, research*] approfondi.

exhaustively /ɪɡˈzɔːstɪvlɪ/ *adv* exhaustivement.

exhaust: **~ pipe** *n* tuyau *m* d'échappement; **~ system** *n* système *m* d'échappement; **~ valve** *n* soupape *f* d'échappement.

exhibit /ɪɡˈzɪbɪt/ **I** *n* **1** (work of art) œuvre *f* exposée; (item on display) objet *m* exposé; **2** US (exhibition) exposition *f*; **to be on ~** être exposé; **a Gauguin ~** une exposition Gauguin; **3** Jur pièce *f* à conviction; **~ A** pièce à conviction numéro un.
II *vtr* (display) exposer [*artefact, goods*]; manifester [*curiosity, preference, sign*] faire preuve de [*heroism, devotion*].
III *vi* exposer.

exhibition /ˌeksɪˈbɪʃn/ **I** *n* **1** (of art, goods) exposition *f*; **art ~** exposition; **the Picasso ~** l'exposition Picasso; **to be on ~** être exposé; **to make an ~ of oneself** péj se faire remarquer; **2** (of skill, technique) démonstration *f*; **3** fig (of arrogance, rudeness) étalage *m*; **4** (of film) présentation *f*; **5** GB Univ bourse *f* d'études.
II *modif* [*catalogue, gallery, hall, stand*] d'exposition.

exhibition centre GB, **exhibition center** US *n* palais *m* des expositions.

exhibitioner /ˌeksɪˈbɪʃənə(r)/ *n* GB Univ boursier/-ière *m*/*f*.

exhibitionism /ˌeksɪˈbɪʃənɪzəm/ *n* gen, Psych exhibitionnisme *m*.

exhibitionist /ˌeksɪˈbɪʃənɪst/ *n, adj* gen, Psych exhibitionniste (*mf*).

exhibitor /ɪɡˈzɪbɪtə(r)/ *n* **1** (of art, goods) exposant/-e *m*/*f*; **2** US (of cinema) exploitant *m* d'une salle de cinéma.

exhilarate /ɪɡˈzɪləreɪt/ *vtr* [*breeze*] vivifier; [*atmosphere, music, speed*] griser; [*action, scene, thought*] exciter; **to be ~d at** ou **by the thought of** être transporté à la pensée de.

exhilarating /ɪɡˈzɪləreɪtɪŋ/ *adj* [*breeze*] vivifiant; [*contest, game*] acharné; [*experience, ride, run*] exaltant; [*music, dance*] grisant; [*speed*] enivrant.

exhilaration /ɪɡˌzɪləˈreɪʃn/ *n* joie *f* intense.

exhort /ɪɡˈzɔːt/ *vtr* exhorter (**to do** à faire); **to ~ sb to action** exhorter qn à l'action.

exhortation /ˌeɡzɔːˈteɪʃn/ *n* exhortation *f* (**to** à; **to do** à faire).

exhumation /eksˌhjuːˈmeɪʃn, US ɪɡˌzuːm-/ *n* exhumation *f*.

exhumation order *n* Jur permis *m* d'exhumer.

exhume /eksˈhjuːm, US ɪɡˈzuːm/ *vtr* exhumer.

ex-husband /ˌeksˈhʌsbənd/ *n* ex-mari *m*.

exigencies /ˈeksɪdʒənsɪz/ *npl* sout exigences *fpl*.

exigent /ˈeksɪdʒənt/ *adj* sout exigeant.

exiguity /ˌeɡzɪˈɡjuːətɪ/ *n* (of income, means) modicité *f*; (of room) exiguïté *f*.

exiguous /eɡˈzɪɡjʊəs/ *adj* [*income, means*] modique; [*room*] exigu/-uë.

exile /ˈeksaɪl/ **I** *n* **1** (person) exilé/-e *m*/*f*; **2** (expulsion) exil *m* (**from** de); **in ~** en exil; **political ~** exil politique; **to live in/go into ~** vivre/partir en exil; **a place of ~** un lieu d'exil.
II Exile *pr n* Relig **the Exile** l'Exil *m*.
III *vtr* exiler; **to ~ for life** exiler à vie; **to ~ sb from a country** bannir qn d'un pays.
IV exiled *pp adj* en exil; **the ~d Mr X today said...** M. X, qui est en exil, a dit aujourd'hui que...

exist /ɪɡˈzɪst/ *vi* **1** (be) exister; **it really does ~** ça existe vraiment; **2** (survive) survivre; **they can do no more than ~ on that wage** ce salaire leur permet tout juste de survivre; **3** (live) vivre; **to ~ on a diet of potatoes** ne vivre que de pommes de terre; **how can he ~ without friends?** comment peut-il vivre sans amis?

existence /ɪɡˈzɪstəns/ *n* **1** (being) existence *f* (**of** de); **the largest plane in ~** le plus grand avion qui existe (*subj*); **I wasn't aware of its ~** je ne connaissais pas son existence; **to come into/go out of ~** naître/mourir; **2** (life) existence *f*; **to struggle for one's very ~** lutter pour survivre.

existent /ɪɡˈzɪstənt/ *adj* sout existant.

existential /ˌeɡzɪˈstenʃl/ *adj* existentiel/-ielle.

existentialism /ˌeɡzɪˈstenʃəlɪzəm/ *n* existentialisme *m*.

existentialist /ˌeɡzɪˈstenʃəlɪst/ *n, adj* existentialiste (*mf*).

existing /ɪɡˈzɪstɪŋ/ *adj* [*product, laws, order, institution*] existant; [*policy, management, leadership*] actuel/-elle.

exit /ˈeksɪt/ **I** *n* gen, Theat, Transp sortie *f*; **'no ~'** 'interdit'; **to make an ~** gen faire une sortie; Theat quitter la scène; Sport être éliminé; **to make a quick** ou **hasty ~** s'éclipser; **to make one's final ~** euph mourir.
II Exit *pr n* GB *association en faveur de l'euthanasie*.
III *vi* gen, Comput, Theat sortir; **to ~ stage left/right** sortir côté cour/jardin; **'~ Hamlet'** 'Hamlet sort'.

exit: **~ point** *n* Comput point *m* de sortie; **~ poll** *n* Pol sondage *m* fait à la sortie du scrutin; **~ ramp** *n* US Transp bretelle *f* de sortie; **~ sign** *n* panneau *m* (de) sortie; **~ visa** *n* visa *m* de sortie.

Exocet /ˈeksəset/ *pr n* (also **~ missile**) Mil (missile *m*) Exocet *m*.

exocrine /ˈeksəʊkraɪn/ *adj* exocrine.

exodus /ˈeksədəs/ **I** *n* exode *m*.
II Exodus *pr n* **the book of Exodus** le livre de l'Exode; **the Exodus** Bible l'Exode *m*.

ex officio /ˌeks əˈfɪʃɪəʊ/ **I** *adj* [*member*] de droit.
II *adv* [*attend, speak*] ès qualités.

exogenous /ekˈsɒdʒɪnəs/ *adj* exogène.

exonerate /ɪɡˈzɒnəreɪt/ *vtr* disculper (**from** de); **to ~ sb from blame** disculper qn.

exoneration /ɪɡˌzɒnəˈreɪʃn/ *n* disculpation *f*.

exorbitance /ɪɡˈzɔːbɪtəns/ *n* extravagance *f*.

exorbitant /ɪɡˈzɔːbɪtənt/ *adj* [*price, rent, increase*] exorbitant; [*demand*] excessif/-ive; **to go to ~ lengths to do** faire n'importe quoi pour faire; **to an ~ degree** à l'excès.

exorbitantly /ɪɡˈzɔːbɪtəntlɪ/ *adv* [*charge, pay, reward, spend*] de façon excessive; [*paid*] de façon démesurée; [*expensive*] excessivement; **~ priced** excessivement cher, à un prix exorbitant.

exorcism /ˈeksɔːsɪzəm/ *n* exorcisme *m*; **to carry out an ~ of sth/on sb** exorciser qch/qn.

exorcist /ˈeksɔːsɪst/ *n* exorciste *mf*.

exorcize /ˈeksɔːsaɪz/ *vtr* exorciser [*demon, memory, past*].

exoskeleton /ˌeksəʊˈskelɪtn/ *n* exosquelette *m*.

exosphere /ˈeksəʊsfɪə(r)/ *n* exosphère *f*.

exoteric /ˌeksəʊˈterɪk/ *adj* exotérique.

exothermic /ˌeksəʊˈθɜːmɪk/ *adj* exothermique.

exotic /ɪɡˈzɒtɪk/ **I** *n* **1** (person) personnage *m* original; **2** (animal, plant) espèce *f* exotique.
II *adj* **1** (foreign) exotique; **2** euph (erotic) [*appeal, pleasure*] sensuel/-elle; [*dancer, literature*] érotique.

exotica /ɪɡˈzɒtɪkə/ *n* objets *mpl* exotiques.

exoticism /ɪɡˈzɒtɪsɪzəm/ *n* exotisme *m*.

expand /ɪkˈspænd/ **I** *vtr* **1** Comm, Fin, gen développer [*activity, business, network, provision, range, scope*]; élargir [*concept, horizon, knowledge*]; accroître [*influence, production, sales, workforce*]; étendre [*empire*]; gonfler [*lungs, muscles*]; **2** Math, Comput développer.
II *vi* **1** [*activity, business, provision, sector, skill, town*] se développer; [*capacity, population, production, sales*] s'accroître; [*market, economy*] être en expansion; [*gas, metal*] se dilater; [*accommodation, building, institution*] s'agrandir; [*chest*] se gonfler; [*universe*] être en expansion; **heat makes it ~** la chaleur le dilate; **the company is ~ing into overseas markets** Comm la société commence à s'implanter sur les marchés étrangers; **2** (relax) [*person*] se détendre.
III expanded *pp adj* **1** gen [*programme*] élargi; [*article*] développé; [*version*] long/longue; **2** Tech [*metal*] déployé; [*plastic, polystyrene*] expansé.
■ **expand (up)on**: **~ (up)on [sth]** s'étendre sur [*argument, aspect, theory*].

expandable /ɪkˈspændəbl/ *adj* extensible.

expanding /ɪkˈspændɪŋ/ *adj* **1** fig (growing) [*business, economy, population, service, sector*] en expansion; [*area, town, project*] en développement; [*possibilities*] élargi; [*role*] de plus en plus grand; **2** lit [*file, bracelet, suitcase*] extensible.

expanse /ɪkˈspæns/ *n* (of land, water) étendue *f*; (of flesh) étalage *m*; (of fabric) surface *f*.

expansion /ɪkˈspænʃn/ *n* **1** gen, Fin, Comm (of business, production, range, trade) développement *m* (**in** de; **into** dans); (of economy) expansion *f*; (of population, membership, borrowing) accroissement *m*; (of buildings, site) agrandissement *m*; (of sales, sales figures) progression *f*; **rate of ~** taux d'accroissement; **2** Phys (of metal, gas) dilatation *f*; **3** Math (of expression) développement *m*; **4** Tech (in engine) détente *f*.

expansionary /ɪk'spænʃənərɪ/ *adj* expansionniste.

expansion: **~ board**, **~ card** *n* Comput carte *f* d'extension; **~ bolt** *n* vis *f* à cheville expansible.

expansionism /ɪk'spænʃənɪzəm/ *n* Econ, Pol expansionnisme *m*.

expansionist /ɪk'spænʃənɪst/ *n, adj* Econ, Pol expansionniste (*mf*).

expansion: **~ joint** *n* joint *m* de dilatation; **~ programme**, **~ scheme** *n* Comm programme *m* de développement; **~ slot** *n* Comput emplacement *m* libre (pour extension); **~ tank** *n* Aut réservoir *m* à expansion.

expansive /ɪk'spænsɪv/ *adj* **1** (effusive) [*person, mood*] expansif/-ive; [*gesture*] large; (grand) [*theme, vision*] grandiose; **2** (extensive) [*brow, chest*] large; [*desert, square*] vaste; **3** (extendable) [*gas*] expansible; [*material*] extensible; **4** (exerting force) [*force*] expansif/-ive.

expansively /ɪk'spænsɪvlɪ/ *adv* **1** (effusively) [*greet, smile, speak*] avec effusion; [*gesture, wave*] avec élan; **2** (in detail) [*describe*] avec profusion.

expansiveness /ɪk'spænsɪvnɪs/ *n* (of person) expansivité *f*; (of gesture) largeur *f*; (of landscape) immensité *f*.

expat○ /eks'pæt/ *n, adj*: *abrév* ▶ **expatriate**.

expatiate /ɪk'speɪʃɪeɪt/ *vi* disserter (**upon, on** sur).

expatriate I /ˌeks'pætrɪət/ *n* expatrié/-e *m/f*.
II /ˌeks'pætrɪət/ *adj* expatrié.
III /ˌeks'pætrɪeɪt/ *vtr* expatrier.

expect /ɪk'spekt/ I *vtr* **1** (anticipate) s'attendre à [*event, victory, defeat, trouble*]; **to ~ the worst** s'attendre au pire; **we ~ fine weather** il devrait faire beau; **what did you ~?** qu'est-ce que tu croyais?; **I ~ed as much** je m'y attendais; **you knew what to ~** tu savais à quoi t'attendre; **to ~ sb to do** s'attendre à ce que qn fasse; **she is ~ed to win** on s'attend à ce qu'elle gagne, elle devrait gagner; **he is ~ed to arrive at six** son arrivée est prévue pour six heures, on l'attend pour six heures; **to ~ that** s'attendre à ce que (+ *subj*); **I ~ (that) I'll lose** je m'attends à perdre, je pense que je vais perdre; **it is only to be ~ed that he should go** il est bien naturel qu'il y aille; **it was hardly to be ~ed that she should agree** il n'était guère probable qu'elle accepterait; **more/worse than ~ed** plus/pire que prévu; **not as awful as I had ~ed** pas aussi terrible que je le craignais; **2** (rely on) s'attendre à [*sympathy, help*] (**from** de la part de); **don't ~ any sympathy from me!** ne t'attends à aucune compassion de ma part!; **I ~ you to be punctual** je vous demande d'être ponctuel; **3** (await) attendre [*baby, guest, company*]; **I'm ~ing someone** j'attends quelqu'un; **what time shall we ~ you?** à quelle heure penses-tu venir?; **~ me when you see me** GB je ne sais pas à quelle heure j'arriverai; **4** (require) demander, attendre [*commitment, hard work*] (**from** de); **to ~ sb to do** demander à qn de faire, attendre de qn qu'il/elle fasse; **you will be ~ed to work at weekends** vous devrez travailler le week-end, on attendra de vous que vous travailliez le week-end; **I can't be ~ed to know everything** je ne peux pas tout savoir; **it's too much to ~** c'est trop demander; **5** GB (suppose) **I ~ so** je pense que oui; **I don't ~ so** je ne pense pas; **I ~ you're tired** vous devez être fatigué; **I ~ you'd like a bath** voulez-vous prendre un bain?
II *vi* **1** (anticipate) **to ~ to do** s'attendre à faire; **I ~ to lose/to be working late** je m'attends à perdre/à devoir travailler tard; **I was ~ing to do better** je comptais faire mieux; **2** (require) **to ~ to do** bien compter faire; **I ~ to see you there** je compte bien vous y voir; **3** (be pregnant) **to be ~ing** attendre un enfant, être enceinte.
III **expected** *pp adj* [*guest, letter*] attendu; [*attack, reaction*] prévu, escompté; [*income, price rise, sales*] prévu; **the ~ed $9 million loss** la perte prévue de neuf millions de dollars.

expectancy /ɪk'spektənsɪ/ *n* **to have an air of ~** avoir l'air d'attendre quelque chose; **a feeling of ~** un sentiment d'attente.

expectant /ɪk'spektənt/ *adj* **1** [*look, expression*] plein d'attente; **to look ~** avoir l'air d'attendre quelque chose; **2** [*mother, father*] futur (*before n*).

expectantly /ɪk'spektəntlɪ/ *adv* [*wait, look, listen*] avec l'air d'attendre quelque chose.

expectation /ˌekspek'teɪʃn/ *n* **1** (assumption, prediction) prévision *f*; **it is my ~ that** je m'attends à ce que (+ *subj*); **to have ~s of success** avoir des espoirs de succès; **against all ~(s)** à l'encontre des prévisions générales; **beyond all ~(s)** au-delà de toute attente; **it is in line with ~(s)** c'est conforme à nos prévisions; **you have been chosen in the ~ that** on vous a choisi dans l'espoir que; **in the ~ of a shortage** en prévision d'une pénurie; **2** (aspiration, hope) aspiration *f*, attente *f*; **to live up to/fail to live up to sb's ~s** répondre à/ne pas répondre à l'attente de qn; **I don't want to raise their ~s** je ne veux pas trop leur promettre; **to have great ~s of** attendre beaucoup de; **an atmosphere of ~** une atmosphère d'attente; **3** (requirement, demand) exigence *f*; **to have certain ~s of** attendre or demander certaines choses de [*police, employee*].

expectorant /ɪk'spektərənt/ *n, adj* expectorant (*m*).

expectorate /ɪk'spektəreɪt/ *vtr, vi* expectorer.

expediency /ɪk'spiːdɪənsɪ/ *n* **1** (appropriateness) opportunité *f*; **2** (self-interest) opportunisme *m*.

expedient /ɪk'spiːdɪənt/ I *n* expédient *m*.
II *adj* **1** (appropriate) opportun; **2** (advantageous) politique.

expediently /ɪk'spiːdɪəntlɪ/ *adv* opportunément.

expedite /'ekspɪdaɪt/ *vtr* sout **1** (speed up) accélérer [*operation, process*]; faciliter [*task, work*]; **2** (finish) expédier [*business*]; **3** (send) expédier [*data, document*].

expedition /ˌekspɪ'dɪʃn/ *n* **1** (to explore) expédition *f*; **to go on an ~** partir en expédition; **2** (for leisure) **climbing ~** expédition *f* en montagne; **hunting/fishing ~** partie *f* de chasse/pêche; **sightseeing ~** visite *f* touristique; **to go on a shopping ~** aller faire des courses; **3** sout (speed) **with ~** avec rapidité.

expeditionary force *n* corps *m* expéditionnaire.

expeditious /ˌekspɪ'dɪʃəs/ *adj* sout [*action, decision, response*] rapide; [*method, procedure*] expéditif/-ive.

expeditiously /ˌekspɪ'dɪʃəslɪ/ *adv* sout [*act, respond*] promptement.

expel /ɪk'spel/ *vtr* (*p prés etc* **-ll-**) **1** expulser [*alien, diplomat, dissident, tenant*]; chasser [*invader*]; exclure [*member, player, pupil*]; **2** expulser [*air, gas, water*].

expend /ɪk'spend/ *vtr* **1** (devote) consacrer [*effort, time*]; (spend) dépenser [*energy, money*]; prodiguer [*sympathy*]; **2** (exhaust) épuiser [*resources, supply*].

expendability /ɪkˌspendə'bɪlətɪ/ *n* **to make decisions about the ~ of troops and tanks** prendre des décisions quant aux taux de pertes acceptables en hommes et en chars; **the ~ of staff** le fait que le personnel ne soit pas indispensable.

expendable /ɪk'spendəbl/ *adj* **1** Mil [*troops, equipment*] sacrifiable; **2** (disposable) [*booster, fuel tank, launcher*] largable; [*materials, stationery, stores*] consommable; **~ goods** biens non durables; **to be ~** [*worker*] ne pas être indispensable.

expenditure /ɪk'spendɪtʃə(r)/ *n* **1** (amount spent) dépenses *fpl*; **~ on education/defence** dépenses *fpl* d'éducation/militaires or de défense; **income and ~** revenus *mpl* et dépenses *fpl*; **capital/consumer ~** dépenses *fpl* d'investissement/de consommation; **public ~** dépense *f* publique; **2** (in bookkeeping) sortie *f*; **3** (spending) (of energy, time, money) dépense *f*; (of resources) consommation *f*, utilisation *f*; **a useful ~ of time** du temps bien employé.

expense /ɪk'spens/ I *n* **1** (cost) frais *mpl*; **at vast/at one's own ~** à grands/à ses propres frais; **at public ~** aux frais de l'État; **to go to some ~** faire des frais; **to go to great ~, to go to a great deal of ~** dépenser beaucoup d'argent (**to do** pour faire); **to put sb to ~** faire faire des frais à qn; **to spare no ~** ne pas regarder à la dépense; **no ~ has been spared** on n'a pas regardé à la dépense; **to go to the ~ of renting a villa** faire la dépense de la location d'une villa; **to save oneself the ~ of a hotel** éviter la dépense d'une nuit à l'hôtel; **2** (cause for expenditure) dépense *f*; **a wedding is a big ~** un mariage revient cher; **petrol is a big ~ for me** l'essence représente une grosse dépense pour moi; **3** (loss) **at the ~ of** au détriment de [*health, public, safety*]; **at the ~ of jobs** au risque de perdre des emplois; **at sb's ~** [*laugh, joke*] aux dépens de qn.
II **expenses** *npl* Comm frais *mpl*; **tax-deductible ~s** frais déductibles; **to cover sb's ~s** [*person*] prendre à sa charge les frais de qn; [*sum*] couvrir les frais de qn; **to get one's ~s paid** se faire rembourser ses frais; **all ~s paid** tous frais payés; **to claim ~s** présenter sa note de frais; **to fiddle○ ~s** trafiquer○ sa note de frais.

expense account *n* frais *mpl* de représentation.

expensive /ɪk'spensɪv/ *adj* [*area, car, coat, house*] cher/chère; [*holiday, procedure, mistake, repair*] coûteux/-euse; [*taste*] de luxe; **~ to maintain** cher à entretenir; **it's getting ~ to eat out** ça revient de plus en plus cher d'aller au restaurant.

expensively /ɪk'spensɪvlɪ/ *adv* [*live, eat*] luxueusement; **~ furnished** luxueusement meublé; **to be ~ dressed** porter des toilettes chères.

expensiveness /ɪk'spensɪvnɪs/ *n* prix *m* élevé, cherté *f*.

experience /ɪk'spɪərɪəns/ I *n* **1** (expertise) expérience *f*; **driving/management/teaching ~** expérience *f* de la conduite automobile/de la gestion/de l'enseignement; **from my/his etc own ~** d'après mon/son etc expérience; **in my ~** à ma connaissance; **in all my 20 years' ~ as headmistress, I have never**... depuis 20 ans que je suis directrice, je n'ai jamais...; **to have ~ of sth** avoir l'expérience de qch; **to have ~ with children/animals** avoir de l'expérience avec les enfants/les animaux; **to have ~ (in working) with computers/cars** avoir de l'expérience en informatique/dans le domaine des voitures; **to acquire** ou **gain ~** acquérir de l'expérience; **to know from/learn by ~** savoir/apprendre d'expérience; **to judge from ~** juger d'expérience; **2** (incident) expérience *f*; **to have** ou **go through a new experience** faire une nouvelle expérience; **a world tour: the ~ of a lifetime!** le tour du monde: l'aventure de toute une vie!; **that was quite an ~!** ça a été une expérience mémorable!
II *vtr* connaître [*change, difficulty, defeat, ill-treatment, loss, problem, misfortune*]; éprou-

ver [*emotion, sensation*]; ressentir [*physical pleasure*]; **to ~ sth personally** ou **at first hand** faire l'expérience de qch soi-même.

experienced /ɪkˈspɪərɪənst/ *adj* [*worker, professional*] expérimenté; [*eye*] entraîné; **to be ~ in working with computers** avoir de l'expérience en informatique; **an ~ traveller** un grand voyageur.

experiment /ɪkˈsperɪmənt/ **I** *n* gen, Sci expérience *f* (**in** en; **on** sur); **to conduct** ou **carry out an ~** faire or effectuer une expérience; **as** ou **by way of an ~** à titre d'expérience.
II *vi* expérimenter, faire des expériences (**on** sur); **to ~ with sth** expérimenter qch, essayer qch.

experimental /ɪkˌsperɪˈmentl/ *adj* [*design, method, music, scheme, theatre*] expérimental; [*season, week*] d'essai; [*laboratory*] d'essais; [*novelist, writing*] d'avant-garde; **~ model**, **~ machine** prototype *m*; **on an ~ basis** à titre d'expérience.

experimentally /ɪkˌsperɪˈmentəlɪ/ *adv* [*establish, test*] expérimentalement; [*lick, nibble*] pour goûter; [*touch, try*] à titre d'expérience.

experimentation /ɪkˌsperɪmenˈteɪʃn/ *n* **1** (use of experiments) expérimentation *f*; **2** (experiment) expériences *fpl*; **recent ~** des expériences *fpl* récentes; **animal ~** expériences *fpl* sur les animaux.

expert /ˈekspɜːt/ **I** *n* spécialiste *mf* (**in** en, de), expert *m* (**in** en); **to be an ~ in law** être spécialiste en droit; **to be an ~ at doing** être un expert dans l'art de faire; **forensic ~** expert *m* médico-légal; **computer ~** spécialiste *mf* en informatique; **to ask the ~s** s'adresser aux spécialistes; **you're the ~!** c'est toi qui t'y connais!
II *adj* [*knowledge*] spécialisé; [*opinion, advice*] autorisé; **an ~ cook** un cordon bleu; **to be ~ at doing** être expert dans l'art de faire; **an ~ eye** un œil exercé; **to require ~ handling** [*situation*] exiger beaucoup de doigté.

expertise /ˌekspɜːˈtiːz/ *n* compétences *fpl*; (very specialized) expertise *f* (**in** dans le domaine de); **~ in** compétence *f* dans le domaine de [*subject*]; **French ~ in telecommunications** l'expertise française dans le domaine des télécommunications; **his ~ as a builder** sa compétence dans le domaine du bâtiment; **to have/lack the ~ to do** avoir/ne pas avoir les compétences requises pour faire.

expertly /ˈekspɜːtlɪ/ *adv* [*constructed, cooked, presented*] de manière experte; **~ he knotted his tie** il a noué sa cravate d'une main experte.

expert: **~ system** *n* système *m* expert; **~ witness** *n* témoin *m* expert.

expiate /ˈekspɪeɪt/ *vtr* expier [*crime, sin*]; réparer, racheter [*fault*]; effacer [*guilt*].

expiation /ˌekspɪˈeɪʃn/ *n* (of crime, guilt, sin) expiation *f*; (of fault) réparation *f*, rachat *m*.

expiatory /ˈekspɪətərɪ, US -tɔːrɪ/ *adj* expiatoire.

expiration /ˌekspɪˈreɪʃn/ *n* **1** (termination) expiration *f*; **2** (exhalation) (of breath) expiration *f*; (of gas, vapour) rejet *m*.

expiration date *n* US = **expiry date**.

expire /ɪkˈspaɪə(r)/ *vi* Admin, Comm **1** (end) [*document, contract, deadline, offer*] expirer; [*period*] arriver à terme; **my passport has ~d** mon passeport est périmé; **2** (exhale) expirer; **3** (die) (souvent hum) [*person, machine*] rendre l'âme, expirer; [*show*] s'essouffler.

expiry /ɪkˈspaɪərɪ/ *n* (of contract, document, time period) expiration *f*; (of deadline, mandate) terme *m*.

expiry date GB *n* (of perishable item) date *f* de péremption; (on label) 'à utiliser avant…'; (of credit card, permit) date *f* d'expiration; (of contract) terme *m*; (of loan) date *f* d'échéance.

explain /ɪkˈspleɪn/ **I** *vtr* (all contexts) expliquer (**that** que; **to** à); **'it's like this,' he ~ed** 'c'est ainsi,' a-t-il expliqué; **can you ~?** peux-tu m'/lui etc expliquer?; **I can't ~** je ne peux pas l'expliquer; **that ~s it!** ça explique tout!
II *v refl* **to ~ oneself** s'expliquer.
■ **explain away**: **~ away [sth]**, **~ [sth] away** trouver des justifications à [*problem, change*].

explainable /ɪkˈspleɪnəbl/ *adj* explicable.

explanation /ˌekspləˈneɪʃn/ *n* explication *f* (**of** de; **for** à); **to accept sb's ~ that** accepter l'explication de qn selon laquelle; **by way of ~, in ~** en guise d'explication; **there is no ~** il n'y a pas d'explication; **we want a full ~** nous voulons toutes les explications; **it needs no ~** c'est clair.

explanatory /ɪkˈsplænətrɪ, US -tɔːrɪ/ *adj* [*notes, leaflet, film, diagram*] explicatif/-ive; [*letter, statement*] d'explication.

expletive /ɪkˈspliːtɪv, US ˈeksplətɪv/ sout **I** *n* (exclamation) exclamation *f*; euph (swearword) juron *m*; Ling explétif *m*.
II *adj* explétif/-ive.

explicable /ɪkˈsplɪkəbl, ˈek-/ *adj* explicable; **to be ~ in terms of/in the light of** s'expliquer par/à la lumière de.

explicit /ɪkˈsplɪsɪt/ *adj* **1** (precise) [*instructions, directions, reasons*] explicite; **2** (open) [*denial, declaration, command*] formel/-elle; [*aim*] avoué; [*permission*] explicite; [*opposition, support*] déclaré; **to be ~** être explicite (**about** sur); **sexually ~** sexuellement explicite; **3** Math explicite.

explicitly /ɪkˈsplɪsɪtlɪ/ *adv* [*mention, forbid, show*] explicitement; [*deny, order*] formellement; [*admit*] ouvertement.

explode /ɪkˈspləʊd/ **I** *vtr* faire exploser [*bomb*]; fig pulvériser [*theory, argument, rumour, myth*].
II *vi* **1** lit [*bomb, gas, firework, gunpowder*] exploser; [*boiler, building, ship*] sauter; [*thunder*] gronder; **2** fig [*person*] (with anger) exploser; [*issue, controversy*] éclater; [*population*] exploser; **to ~ with rage** exploser; **to ~ with laughter** éclater de rire; **the streets ~d into life** les rues s'animèrent subitement; **the country ~d into civil war** la guerre civile a éclaté dans le pays; **they ~d**° **onto the rock music scene in 1977** ils ont fait irruption dans le monde du rock en 1977.

exploded /ɪkˈspləʊdɪd/ *adj* Tech **~ drawing** ou **diagram** éclaté *m*.

exploding star *n* étoile *f* variable.

exploit **I** /ˈeksplɔɪt/ *n* exploit *m*; **amorous ~s** hum exploits amoureux.
II /ɪkˈsplɔɪt/ *vtr* (all contexts) exploiter.

exploitable /ɪkˈsplɔɪtəbl/ *adj* exploitable.

exploitation /ˌeksplɔɪˈteɪʃn/ *n* (all contexts) exploitation *f*.

exploitative /ɪkˈsplɔɪtətɪv/ *adj* [*system*] fondé sur l'exploitation des individus; [*organization, firm*] qui exploite ses employés.

exploration /ˌekspləˈreɪʃn/ *n* gen, Aerosp, Med exploration *f*; **oil ~** prospection *f* pétrolière.

exploratory /ɪkˈsplɒrətrɪ, US -tɔːrɪ/ *adj* **1** (investigative) [*expedition*] d'exploration; **2** (preliminary) gen, Pol [*talks, calculations*] exploratoire; **3** Med [*surgery*] explorateur/-trice.

explore /ɪkˈsplɔː(r)/ *vtr* **1** gen, Aerosp, Med explorer; **to go exploring** partir en exploration; **a few hours to ~ the city** quelques heures pour explorer or découvrir la ville; **2** fig étudier [*idea, issue, opportunity*]; **to ~ ways and means of doing** explorer tous les moyens de faire; **to ~ every avenue** examiner toutes les possibilités; **to ~ for oil** chercher du pétrole.

explorer /ɪkˈsplɔːrə(r)/ *n* explorateur/-trice *m/f*.

explosion /ɪkˈspləʊʒn/ *n* **1** (of bomb, boiler, gas, building, ship, dynamite) explosion *f*; **to hear an ~** entendre une détonation; **2** fig (of mirth, rage, activity) explosion *f*; (of group, movement) essor *m*; (of prices) flambée *f*; **population ~** explosion *f* démographique.

explosive /ɪkˈspləʊsɪv/ **I** *n* **1** explosif *m*; **to be charged with possessing ~s** être inculpé de possession d'explosifs; **2** Ling = **plosive**.
II *adj* **1** [*bomb, device, force*] explosif/-ive; [*substance, mixture*] explosible; **2** fig [*situation, violence, temperament, issue*] explosif/-ive; **3** Ling = **plosive**.

exponent /ɪkˈspəʊnənt/ *n* **1** (of policy, theory, method) avocat/-e *m/f*, défenseur *m*; **2** (of instrument, artform) interprète *mf*; (of sport) adepte *mf*; **3** Math (symbol) exposant *m*.

exponential /ˌekspəʊˈnenʃl/ *adj* exponentiel/-ielle.

exponentially /ˌekspəʊˈnenʃəlɪ/ *adv* gen [*expand, rise*] exponentiellement; Math exponentiellement.

export **I** /ˈekspɔːt/ *n* exportation *f* (**of** de); **'for ~ only'** (on product) 'exportation'; **visible and invisible ~s** exportations visibles et invisibles; **a ban on ~s** un embargo sur les exportations; **it's our best-known ~** c'est notre meilleur produit d'exportation also fig.
II /ɪkˈspɔːt/ *vtr* (all contexts) exporter (**from** de); **to ~ sth to France/to several countries** exporter qch en France/dans plusieurs pays.
III /ɪkˈspɔːt/ *vi* exporter; **to ~ to France/to many countries** exporter vers la France/dans plusieurs pays.

exportable /ɪkˈspɔːtəbl/ *adj* exportable.

export agent *n* agent *m* exportateur.

exportation /ˌekspɔːˈteɪʃn/ *n* exportation *f*; **for ~ only** pour l'exportation seulement.

export: **~ control** *n* contrôle *m* des exportations; **~ credit** *n* crédit *m* à l'exportation; **~ drive** *n* campagne *f* d'exportation; **~ duty** *n* droit *m* à l'exportation; **~ earnings** *npl* gains *mpl* à l'exportation.

exporter /ɪkˈspɔːtə(r)/ *n* exportateur/-trice *m/f* (**of** de).

export: **~ finance** *n* financement *m* des exportations; **~-import company** *n* société *f* d'import-export; **~ licence** GB, **~ license** US *n* licence *f* d'exportation; **~ manager** *n* responsable *m* du service export; **~-orientated** GB, **~-oriented** US *adj* à vocation exportatrice; **~ trade** *n* exportations *fpl*.

expose /ɪkˈspəʊz/ **I** *vtr* **1** (display) gen exposer [*body, skin*]; montrer [*teeth*]; (provocatively) exhiber [*chest, thighs*]; **to ~ one's ignorance** étaler son ignorance; **2** (make public) révéler [*fact, identity, secret*]; dénoncer [*injustice, person, scandal*]; **to ~ sb as a spy** démasquer qn comme espion; **to ~ sb for what they are** dévoiler la vraie nature de qn; **3** (uncover) exposer [*contents, inside, dirt*]; dénuder [*wire*]; exposer [*nerve*]; [*low tide*] découvrir [*rocks*]; [*excavations*] mettre à jour [*fossil, remains*]; **4** (introduce) **to ~ sb to** initier qn à [*opera, politics*]; exposer qn à [*effect, influence, reality*]; **5** (make vulnerable) **to ~ sb/sth to** exposer qn/qch à [*danger, infection, light*]; livrer qn/qch à [*ridicule, temptation*]; **6** Phot exposer [*film*]; **7** Antiq (abandon) exposer [*baby*].
II *v refl* **1 to ~ oneself** (exhibit one's body) s'exhiber (**to** à); Jur commettre un outrage à la pudeur; **2 to ~ oneself to** (make oneself vulnerable) s'exposer à [*risk, danger*].
III exposed *pp adj* [*area, chest, film*] exposé; [*wire*] à nu; Constr [*beam, stonework*] apparent.

exposé /ekˈspəʊzeɪ, US ˌekspəˈzeɪ/ *n* **1** (exposure) révélations *fpl* (**of sth** sur qch); **2** (study) exposé *m*.

exposition /ˌekspəˈzɪʃn/ *n* **1** (presentation) (of facts, theory) présentation *f*; Literat, Mus, Relig exposition *f*; **2** (exhibition) exposition *f*.

expostulate /ɪkˈspɒstjʊleɪt/ sout **I** *vtr* **'no,' he ~d** 'non,' s'exclama-t-il, indigné.
II *vi* (remonstrate) faire des remontrances (**with** à).

expostulation /ɪkˌspɒstjʊˈleɪʃn/ *n* sout remontrances *fpl*.

exposure /ɪk'spəʊʒə(r)/ *n* **1** (disclosure) (of secret, crime) révélation *f*; **to fear ~** craindre d'être démasqué; **to threaten sb with ~** menacer qn de dénonciation; **2** (to light, sun, radiation) gen, Phot exposition *f* (**to** à); fig (to art, ideas, politics) contact *m* (**to** avec); **too much ~ to the sun is bad for you** il est dangereux de s'exposer trop longtemps au soleil; **3** (to cold, weather) **to die of ~** Med mourir de froid; **to suffer from ~** souffrir du froid; **4** Journ, TV, Radio couverture *f* médiatique; **film stars get a lot of press ~** la presse consacre beaucoup d'articles aux vedettes; **5** (orientation) exposition *f*; **to have a northern ~** être exposé or orienté au nord; **6** (display of body) exhibition *f* (**of** de); **7** Phot (aperture and shutter speed) temps *m* de pose; (picture) pose *f*; **a 24 ~ film** une pellicule de 24 poses; **8** Fin, Insur risque *m*.

exposure: **~ meter** *n* Phot posemètre *m*; **~ time** *n* Phot temps *m* de pose.

expound /ɪk'spaʊnd/ **I** *vtr* exposer [*theory, opinion*].
II *vi* **~ on** disserter sur.

ex-president /ˌeks'prezɪdənt/ *n* gen, Pol ex-président/-e *m/f*.

express /ɪk'spres/ **I** *n* (train *m*) express *m*, (train *m*) rapide *m*.
II *adj* **1** (rapid) [*letter, parcel*] exprès; [*delivery, coach, train*] rapide; [*goods*] envoyé en exprès; **2** sout (explicit) [*instruction, order, promise, undertaking*] formel/-elle; **on the ~ condition that** à la condition expresse que (+ *subj*); **I left ~ instructions not to admit visitors** j'ai expressément demandé qu'on ne laisse entrer personne; **with the ~ aim** ou **purpose of doing** dans le but précis de faire.
III *adv* **to send sth ~** Post envoyer qch en exprès.
IV *vtr* **1** (show) exprimer [*desire, doubt, hatred, fear, wish, thanks*]; exprimer, manifester [*interest, support*]; énoncer [*truth*]; **he ~ed anxiety about** il a exprimé son anxiété à propos de; **I can hardly ~ my gratitude** je ne sais comment exprimer ma reconnaissance; **words can't ~ how I feel** il n'y a pas de mots assez forts pour exprimer ce que je ressens; **2** Math exprimer [*number, quantity*]; **to ~ sth as a percentage** exprimer qch en pourcentage; **to ~ sth in its simplest form** réduire qch à sa plus simple expression; **3** (squeeze out) extraire, exprimer [*fluid*]; **4** US Comm expédier [qch] rapidement.
V *v refl* **to ~ oneself** s'exprimer (**in** en; **through** à travers).

expressage /ɪk'spresɪdʒ/ *n* US Comm **1** (conveyance) transport *m* rapide; **2** (fee) frais *mpl* de transport rapide.

expression /ɪk'spreʃn/ *n* **1** (phrase) expression *f*; **if you'll pardon the ~** si vous me passez l'expression; **2** (look) expression *f*; **from her ~ I knew she was sad** j'ai compris à son expression qu'elle était triste; **there was a puzzled ~ on her face** elle avait l'air perplexe; **not a flicker of ~ crossed his face** il est demeuré impassible; **3** (utterance) expression *f*; **freedom of ~** liberté *f* d'expression; **to give ~ to one's fears/feelings** exprimer ses craintes/sentiments; **beautiful beyond ~** d'une beauté indescriptible; **4** (manifestation) gen expression *f*; (of friendship, gratitude) témoignage *m*; **the riots are an ~ of social unrest** les émeutes sont l'expression du malaise social; **my feelings find their ~ in music** mes sentiments s'expriment dans la musique; **as an ~ of my gratitude** en témoignage de ma reconnaissance; **5** (feeling) expression *f*; **put some ~ into your playing!** sois un peu plus expressif!; **to read with ~** lire avec le ton; **6** Math expression *f*.

expressionism /ɪk'spreʃənɪzəm/ *n* expressionnisme *m*.

expressionist /ɪk'spreʃənɪst/ *n, adj* expressionniste (*mf*).

expressionless /ɪk'spreʃnlɪs/ *adj* [*eyes, face*] inexpressif/-ive; [*tone, voice*] monocorde; [*playing*] plat; **he remained ~ throughout the interview** il est resté impassible tout au long de l'entretien.

expression mark *n* Mus consigne *f* pour l'exécution.

expressive /ɪk'spresɪv/ *adj* [*eyes, face, features, function, language*] expressif/-ive; [*look*] éloquent; [*potential, power*] d'expression; **to be ~ of sth** exprimer qch.

expressively /ɪk'spresɪvlɪ/ *adv* de façon expressive.

expressiveness /ɪk'spresɪvnɪs/ *n* (of face) expressivité *f*; (of words) force *f* expressive; (of work of art, performance) (force *f* d')expression *f*.

expressivity /ɪkˌspre'sɪvətɪ/ *n* **1** (of style, picture) force *f* d'expression; **2** Biol expressivité *f*.

expressly /ɪk'spreslɪ/ *adv* **1** (explicitly) [*ask, authorize, promise, tell*] expressément; [*forbid*] formellement; **smoking is ~ forbidden** il est formellement interdit de fumer; **2** (specifically) [*designed, intended*] expressément, spécialement.

express: **~ rifle** *n* Hunt fusil *m* de chasse express, express *m*; **~way** *n* US Transp autoroute *f*.

expropriate /ˌeks'prəʊprɪeɪt/ *vtr* Jur exproprier; hum s'approprier.

expropriation /ˌeksˌprəʊprɪ'eɪʃn/ *n* expropriation *f* (**of** de).

expulsion /ɪk'spʌlʃn/ *n* (of pupil) exclusion *f*, renvoi *m*; (of diplomat, alien, dissident) expulsion *f*; (of member, player) exclusion *f*.

expunge /ɪk'spʌndʒ/ *vtr* **1** sout lit rayer (**from** de); **2** fig anéantir.

expurgate /'ekspəgeɪt/ *vtr* expurger.

exquisite /'ekskwɪzɪt, ɪk'skwɪzɪt/ *adj* **1** (lovely, perfect) [*face, features, manners, object*] exquis; [*setting*] charmant; [*tact, precision*] parfait; **she has ~ taste** elle a un goût exquis; **of ~ craftsmanship** finement ouvragé; **2** (intense) [*pleasure, pain, relief*] vif/vive.

exquisitely /ek'skwɪzɪtlɪ/ *adv* **1** (perfectly) [*dressed, made, written*] d'une façon exquise; [*timed, judged*] parfaitement; **~ beautiful/polite** d'une beauté/politesse exquise; **2** (intensely) extrêmement.

ex-serviceman /ˌeks'sɜːvɪsmən/ *n* ancien militaire *m*.

ex-servicewoman /ˌeks'sɜːvɪswʊmən/ *n* ancienne combattante *f*.

extant /ek'stænt, US 'ekstənt/ *adj* (surviving) encore existant; (currently existing) existant.

extemporaneous /ɪkˌstempə'reɪnɪəs/, **extemporary** /ɪk'stempərərɪ, US -rerɪ/ *adj* improvisé.

extempore /ek'stempərɪ/ *adj, adv* impromptu.

extemporize /ɪk'stempəraɪz/ *vi* improviser.

extend /ɪk'stend/ **I** *vtr* **1** (enlarge) agrandir [*house, factory*]; prolonger [*road, runway*]; élargir [*knowledge, vocabulary*]; étendre [*circle of friends, influence, powers*]; élargir, étendre [*range, scope*]; accroître, élargir [*clientele*]; approfondir [*research, study*]; **2** (prolong) prolonger [*visit, visa*]; proroger [*loan, contract*]; prolonger [*show*]; **the deadline was ~ed by six months** un délai supplémentaire de six mois a été accordé; **3** (stretch) étendre [*arm, leg, wing*]; tendre [*neck*]; **to ~ one's hand** (in greeting) tendre la main; **4** (offer) sout présenter [*congratulations*]; accorder [*credit, loan*]; apporter [*help*]; faire [*invitation*]; **to ~ a welcome to sb** souhaiter la bienvenue à qn; **5** Accts reporter [*balance, total*].
II *vi* **1** (stretch) [*beach, carpet, damage, forest, lake, weather*] s'étendre (**as far as, up to** jusqu'à; **beyond** au-delà de; **from** de); **the railway ~s from Moscow to Vladivostok** la voie ferrée va de Moscou à Vladivostok; **the rail network ~s over the whole of England** le réseau ferroviaire couvre toute l'Angleterre; **2** (last) **to ~ into September/next week** se prolonger jusqu'en septembre/jusqu'à la semaine prochaine; **to ~ over a month/two weeks** [*course, strike*] s'étendre sur un mois/deux semaines; **3** (reach) **to ~ beyond** [*enthusiasm, interest*] aller au-delà de, dépasser [*politeness*]; [*experience, knowledge*] s'étendre au-delà de, dépasser; **4** fig (go as far as) **to ~ to doing** aller jusqu'à faire; **my charity doesn't ~ to writing cheques** ma générosité ne va pas jusqu'à signer des chèques.
III extended *pp adj* [*stay, visit, guarantee*] prolongé; [*contract, leave, programme, sentence*] de longue durée; [*area*] étendu; [*bulletin*] détaillé; [*family*] étendu; [*premises*] agrandi; [*credit*] à long terme.

extendable /ɪk'stendəbl/ *adj* **1** (of adjustable length) [*handle, cable, lead*] extensible; [*ladder*] coulissant; **2** (renewable) [*contract, lease, visa*] renouvelable (**by** de).

extender /ɪk'stendə(r)/ *n* **1** (in paint) (to add body) matière *f* de charge; (to dilute) diluant *m*; **2** (in plastics) diluant *m*.

extensible /ɪk'stensəbl/ *adj* gen, Comput extensible.

extension /ɪk'stenʃn/ *n* **1** (extra section) (of cable, table) rallonge *f*; (of road, track) prolongement *m*; **the new ~ to the hospital** le nouveau bâtiment de l'hôpital; **I had a kitchen ~ built** j'ai fait agrandir ma cuisine; **a good tool functions as an ~ of the hand** un bon outil fonctionne comme un prolongement de la main; **2** Telecom (appliance) poste *m* supplémentaire; (number) (numéro *m* de) poste *m*; **he's on ~ 243** il est au poste 243; **3** (prolongation) (of contract, visa, loan) prorogation *f*; (for piece of work, essay) délai *m* supplémentaire; **4** (widening) (of powers, rights, scheme, services) extension *f*; (of knowledge) élargissement *m*; (of meaning) extension *f*; (of idea, theory) développement *m*; (of demand) augmentation *f*; (of business) développement *m*; **by ~** (logically) par extension; **5** Anat extension *f*; **6** (in hairdressing) tresse *f* artificielle.

extension: **~ cable** *n* Electron rallonge *f*; **~ ladder** *n* échelle *f* coulissante; **~ lead** *n* Elec rallonge *f*; **~ ring** *n* Phot bague-allonge *f*; **~ tube** *n* Phot tube-allonge *m*.

extensive /ɪk'stensɪv/ *adj* **1** (wide-ranging) [*network, range, programme*] vaste (*before n*); [*list*] long/longue (*before n*); [*investigation, study, knowledge, tests*] approfondi; [*operations, changes, developments*] de grande envergure; [*consultation, training*] complet/-ète; [*tour*] grand; [*powers*] étendu; **2** (substantial) [*garden, forest*] vaste (*before n*); [*investment*] considérable; **we make ~ use of computers** nous utilisons beaucoup les ordinateurs; [*damage, loss*] grave, considérable; [*flooding*] important; [*burns*] grave; **3** Agric, Phys extensif/-ive.

extensively /ɪk'stensɪvlɪ/ *adv* [*correct*] considérablement; [*discuss, quote, write*] abondamment; [*read, travel, advertise, publish*] énormément; [*damaged*] considérablement; [*used*] couramment.

extensor /ɪk'stensə(r)/ *n* (muscle *m*) extenseur *m*.

extent /ɪk'stent/ *n* **1** (size) (of park, garden, universe, empire, problem) étendue *f*; **to open to its full ~** s'ouvrir complètement; **2** (amount) (of damage) ampleur *f*; (of knowledge, power, influence) étendue *f*; (of commitment, involvement) importance *f*; **3** (degree) mesure *f*; **to what ~...?** dans quelle mesure...?; **to a certain** ou **to some ~** dans une certaine mesure; **to a great** ou **large ~** dans une large mesure; **to the ~ that we have any control over our lives** dans la mesure où nous contrôlons notre vie; **he did not participate to any great ~** il a très peu participé; **to do sth to such an ~ that** faire qch à tel point que.

extenuate /ɪk'stenjʊeɪt/ *vtr* atténuer.

extenuating /ɪkˈstenjʊeɪtɪŋ/ *adj* atténuant; **~ circumstances** circonstances atténuantes.

extenuation /ɪkˌstenjʊˈeɪʃn/ *n* atténuation *f*.

exterior /ɪkˈstɪərɪə(r)/ **I** *n* **1** (of building, vehicle) extérieur *m* (**of** de); **on the ~** à l'extérieur; **beneath his tough ~ he's very sensitive** sous un extérieur rude c'est une âme sensible; **her liberal ~** péj son vernis libéral; **2** Art, Cin extérieur *m*.
II *adj* **1** gen extérieur (**to** à); **~ decorating** peintures *fpl* extérieures; **for ~ use** (paint) pour extérieurs; **2** Cin, Phot **~ shots** prises *fpl* de vue en extérieur.

exterior angle *n* angle *m* externe.

exteriorize /ɪkˈstɪərɪəraɪz/ *vtr* Med, Psych extérioriser.

exterminate /ɪkˈstɜːmɪneɪt/ *vtr* éliminer [*vermin*]; exterminer [*people, race*].

extermination /ɪkˌstɜːmɪˈneɪʃn/ *n* (of vermin) élimination *f*; (of people, race) extermination *f*.

exterminator /ɪkˈstɜːmɪneɪtə(r)/ *n* US (for insects) employé/-e *m/f* des services de désinsectisation; (for rats) employé/-e *m/f* des services de dératisation.

extern /ˈekstɜːn/ *n* US externe *mf*.

external /ɪkˈstɜːnl/ *adj* **1** (outer) [*appearance, world, object, reality*] extérieur (**to** à); [*surface, injury*] externe; **'for ~ use only'** 'usage externe'; **2** (from outside) [*auditor, examiner*] externe; [*student*] inscrit dans un autre établissement; [*examination*] *ouvert à des étudiants inscrits dans d'autres établissements*; [*source, force, influence, mail, call*] extérieur; **3** (foreign) [*affairs, trade, debt*] extérieur; **4** Comput externe.

external: **~ angle** *n* angle *m* extérieur; **~ degree** *n*: *diplôme accordé sans assiduité aux cours;* **~ diameter** *n* diamètre *m* externe.

externalize /ɪkˈstɜːnəlaɪz/ *vtr* extérioriser.

externally /ɪkˈstɜːnəlɪ/ *adv* **1** (on the outside) [*calm, healthy*] en apparence; **in good condition ~** en bon état extérieurement; **to resemble sth ~** avoir l'apparence de qch; **2** [*examined, investigated*] par quelqu'un d'indépendant.

externals /ɪkˈstɜːnlz/ *npl* apparences *fpl*.

extinct /ɪkˈstɪŋkt/ *adj* [*species, animal, plant*] disparu; [*custom*] d'autrefois; [*value*] mort; [*fire, volcano, emotion, passion*] éteint; **to become ~** [*species, animal, plant, way of life*] disparaître; [*fire, volcano*] s'éteindre.

extinction /ɪkˈstɪŋkʃn/ *n* **1** (of species, plant, animal) extinction *f*, disparition *f*; (of fire, light) extinction *f*; (of hopes) anéantissement *m*; **to be threatened with ~** être en voie de or menacé d'extinction; **2** Comm, Fin (of debt) amortissement *m*.

extinguish /ɪkˈstɪŋgwɪʃ/ *vtr* **1** éteindre [*fire, light, cigarette*]; éteindre [*passion, enthusiasm*]; effacer [*memory*]; anéantir [*hope*]; **2** Comm, Fin éteindre [*debt*].

extinguisher /ɪkˈstɪŋgwɪʃə(r)/ *n* extincteur *m*.

extirpate /ˈekstəpeɪt/ *vtr* extirper.

extirpation /ˌekstəˈpeɪʃn/ *n* extirpation *f*.

extirpator /ˈekstəpeɪtə(r)/ *n* Agric extirpateur *m*.

extn *abrév écrite* = **extension**.

extol GB, **extoll** US /ɪkˈstəʊl/ *vtr* louer [*person, deity, deeds, merits, performance*]; prôner [*idea, system*]; **to ~ the virtues of** chanter les louanges de.

extort /ɪkˈstɔːt/ *vtr* extorquer [*money, promise, signature*] (**from** à); arracher [*confession*] (**from** à); exiger [*price*] (**from** de).

extortion /ɪkˈstɔːʃn/ *n* gen, Jur extorsion *f*.

extortionate /ɪkˈstɔːʃənət/ *adj* exorbitant.

extortionist /ɪkˈstɔːʃənɪst/ *n* extorqueur/-euse *m/f* (de fonds).

extra /ˈekstrə/ **I** *n* **1** (additional charge) supplément *m*; **there are no hidden ~s** il n'y a pas de faux frais; **2** (additional feature) option *f*; **the sunroof is an ~** le toit ouvrant est en option; **the little ~s in life** (luxuries) les petits agréments *mpl* de l'existence; **3** Cin, Theat figurant/-e *m/f*; **4** Journ édition *f* spéciale.
II *adj* [*bus, expense, fabric, hour, staff*] supplémentaire; **it will cost an ~ £1,000** cela coûtera 1000 livres de plus; **delivery/postage is ~** la livraison/l'expédition est en supplément or en sus; **to take ~ trouble** ou **pains to do** se donner beaucoup de mal pour faire; **you need to take ~ care when washing wool** il faut prendre des précautions particulières quand vous lavez de la laine.
III *adv* **to be ~ careful/kind** être encore plus prudent/aimable (que d'habitude); **he tried ~ hard to be patient** il s'est efforcé d'être le plus patient possible; **she worked ~ hard today** elle a travaillé encore plus aujourd'hui; **we charge ~ for postage** nous demandons un supplément pour les frais d'expédition; **the deluxe model costs ~** le modèle de luxe coûte plus cher; **you have to pay ~ for a sunroof** il faut payer un supplément pour le toit ouvrant.

extra charge *n* supplément *m*; **at no ~** sans supplément.

extract **I** /ˈekstrækt/ *n* (all contexts) extrait *m* (**from** de); **meat/vanilla ~** extrait de viande/de vanille.
II /ɪkˈstrækt/ *vtr* **1** (pull out) extraire [*tooth, bullet, splinter*] (**from** de); (from pile, drawer, pocket) sortir, extraire [*wallet, paper, object*] (**from** de); **2** fig (obtain) arracher [*confession, promise, secret*] (**from** à); tirer [*money, energy, heat, pleasure*] (**from sth** de qch); **to ~ money from sb** soutirer de l'argent à qn; **3** Chem extraire [*mineral, oil, essence*] (**from** de); **4** fig (derive) dégager [*sense, nuance*].

extraction /ɪkˈstrækʃn/ *n* **1** (of mineral, peat) extraction *f* (**of** de); (of fumes, air, smell) extraction *f*, évacuation *f* (**of** de); **2** Med, Dent (of tooth, bullet, etc) extraction *f*; **to have an ~** Dent se faire arracher une dent; **3** (origin) origine *f*; **of French ~** d'origine française.

extractive /ɪkˈstræktɪv/ *adj* [*industry, process*] extractif/-ive; **~ crop** culture *f* qui appauvrit les sols.

extractor /ɪkˈstræktə(r)/ *n* **1** gen extracteur *m*; **2** = **extractor fan**.

extractor fan *n* ventilateur *m* d'extraction.

extra-curricular /ˌekstrəkəˈrɪkjʊlə(r)/ *adj* Sch, Univ [*activity*] parascolaire.

extraditable /ˈekstrədaɪtəbl/ *adj* [*person*] passible d'extradition; [*offence, crime*] pouvant donner lieu à l'extradition.

extradite /ˈekstrədaɪt/ *vtr* extrader (**from** de; **to** vers).

extradition /ˌekstrəˈdɪʃn/ **I** *n* extradition *f* (**from** de; **to** vers).
II *modif* [*proceedings, treaty*] d'extradition.

extra: **~-dry** *adj* [*sherry, wine*] extra-sec; [*champagne*] brut; **~-fast** *adj* ultrarapide; **~-fine** *adj* extra-fin.

extragalactic /ˌekstrəgəˈlæktɪk/ *adj* extragalactique.

extra-large /ˌekstrəˈlɑːdʒ/ *adj* [*pullover, shirt*] extra-large, grand patron; [*coat*] grand patron, de grande taille; **an ~ bottle/tin** une maxi-bouteille/boîte.

extralinguistic /ˌekstrəlɪŋˈgwɪstɪk/ *adj* extralinguistique.

extramarital /ˌekstrəˈmærɪtl/ *adj* extraconjugal.

extra-mural /ˌekstrəˈmjʊərəl/ *adj* **1** GB Univ [*course, lecture*] ouvert à tous et assuré par un universitaire; **2** US Sch **~ sports** matchs *mpl* inter-établissements.

extraneous /ɪkˈstreɪnɪəs/ *adj* **1** (outside) [*element, event*] extérieur; [*noise, people*] de l'extérieur; **2** (not essential) [*issue, detail, information*] superflu; [*considerations*] sans rapport avec la question; **to be ~ to sth** être étranger à or sans rapport avec qch.

extraordinarily /ɪkˈstrɔːdnrəlɪ, US -dənerəlɪ/ *adv* [*able, gifted, kind*] extraordinairement; [*large, difficult, complex*] extraordinairement, particulièrement.

extraordinary /ɪkˈstrɔːdnrɪ, US -dənerɪ/ *adj* **1** (exceptional) [*person, ability, career*] extraordinaire; **to go to ~ lengths to do sth** se donner un mal extraordinaire pour faire qch; **there's nothing ~ about her playing** son jeu n'a rien d'extraordinaire; **2** (peculiar) extraordinaire, incroyable; **the most ~ thing has happened** il s'est passé quelque chose d'absolument extraordinaire; **to find it ~ that** trouver extraordinaire que (+ *subj*); **it seems ~ that he should resign** ça paraît incroyable qu'il démissionne; **isn't it ~ how people react** c'est incroyable de voir comment les gens réagissent; **3** (special) [*meeting, session*] extraordinaire; **4** Pol **ambassador ~** ambassadeur extraordinaire.

extraordinary general meeting *n* assemblée *f* générale extraordinaire.

extra pay *n* supplément *m* de salaire.

extrapolate /ɪkˈstræpəleɪt/ *vtr* extrapoler (**from** de).

extrapolation /ɪkˌstræpəˈleɪʃn/ *n* extrapolation *f* (**from** de).

extrasensory /ˌekstrəˈsensərɪ, US -sɔːrɪ/ *adj* extrasensoriel/-ielle.

extrasensory perception, ESP *n* perception *f* extrasensorielle.

extra: **~-special** *adj* exceptionnel/-elle; **~-strong** *adj* [*coffee*] très serré; [*paper*] extra-strong; [*thread*] extra-solide; [*disinfectant, weed killer*] super-puissant.

extraterrestrial /ˌekstrətəˈrestrɪəl/ *n, adj* extraterrestre (*mf*).

extraterritorial /ˌekstrəˌterɪˈtɔːrɪəl/ *adj* [*rights, privileges*] d'exterritorialité; [*water*] international.

extraterritorial possessions *n* possessions *fpl* outre-mer.

extra time *n* Sport prolongation *f*; **to go into** ou **play ~** jouer les prolongations.

extravagance /ɪkˈstrævəgəns/ *n* **1** (prodigality) péj prodigalité *f*; **2** (luxury) luxe *m*; **3** (exaggeratedness) (of behaviour, claim) extravagance *f*.

extravagant /ɪkˈstrævəgənt/ *adj* **1** [*person*] prodigue, dépensier/-ière; [*needs, tastes, way of life*] dispendieux/-ieuse; **to be ~ with sth** gaspiller qch; **2** (luxurious) [*meal, dish*] luxueux/-euse; [*plan*] coûteux/-euse; **3** [*praise, claim, demand, idea, behaviour*] extravagant.

extravagantly /ɪkˈstrævəgəntlɪ/ *adv* **1** [*furnished, decorated*] luxueusement; **to spend ~** dépenser sans compter; **to use sth ~** faire un usage immodéré de qch; **2** [*praise, claim*] à outrance; [*behave*] de façon extravagante.

extravaganza /ɪkˌstrævəˈgænzə/ *n* spectacle *m* somptueux; **football ~** grande messe *f* du football.

extravehicular /ˌekstrəviːˈhɪkjʊlə(r)/ *adj* [*activity*] extravéhiculaire.

extra virgin olive oil *n* Culin huile *f* d'olive extra vierge.

extreme /ɪkˈstriːm/ **I** *n* (all contexts) extrême *m*; **to go from one ~ to the other** passer d'un extrême à l'autre; **to take** ou **carry sth to its logical ~** pousser qch à l'extrême; **at one ~ of sth** à une extrémité de qch; **the ~s of love and hate** les extrêmes de l'amour et de la haine; **to withstand ~s of temperature** résister à des écarts extrêmes de température; **to take/carry sth to ~s** pousser/porter qch à l'extrême; **to go to ~s** pousser les choses à l'extrême; **to be driven to ~s** être poussé à bout; **~s of passion/cruelty** sommets *mpl* de la passion/la cruauté; **to go to any ~** ne s'arrêter devant rien; **cautious/naïve in the ~** prudent/naïf à l'extrême.
II *adj* **1** (as intensifier) extrême; **to live in ~ poverty** vivre dans une extrême pauvreté;

to have ~ difficulty doing avoir énormément de difficulté à faire; **2** (outside normal range) [*example, case, weather conditions, situation*] extrême; [*view, idea, step, measure, reaction, nationalist*] extrémiste; **this is Cubism at its most ~** c'est du cubisme poussé à l'extrême; **to believe sth to an ~ degree** être profondément convaincu de qch; **to be on the ~ right/left** être à l'extrême droite/gauche; **to go to ~ lengths to do** ne reculer devant rien pour faire; **to be ~ in one's views** avoir des opinions extrémistes; **I find him rather ~** je le trouve un peu trop extrémiste; **3** (furthest, highest, lowest etc) [*heat, cold, temperature, fringe, edge, limit*] extrême; **in the ~ north/south** à l'extrême nord/sud, tout au nord/sud.

extremely /ɪk'stri:mlɪ/ *adv* extrêmement, très; **to do ~ well** réussir extrêmement or très bien.

extreme unction *n* extrême-onction *f*.

extremism /ɪk'stri:mɪzəm/ *n* extrémisme *m*.

extremist /ɪk'stri:mɪst/ *n, adj* extrémiste (*mf*).

extremity /ɪk'streməti/ *n* **1** (furthest point) lit, fig extrémité *f* (**of** de); **they stand at opposite extremities** ils sont le contraire l'un de l'autre; **2** (of body) extrémité *f*; **3** (extremeness) degré *m* extrême (**of** de); **4** (dire situation) situation *f* désespérée; **to do sth in ~** faire qch en dernier recours; **to be reduced to extremities** être à bout.

extricate /'ekstrɪkeɪt/ **I** *vtr* (from trap, net) dégager (**from** de); (from situation) sortir (**from** de).
II *v refl* **to ~ oneself from** s'extirper de [*place*]; se dégager de [*embrace*]; se sortir de [*situation*].

extrinsic /ek'strɪnsɪk/ *adj* [*factor, advantage*] extrinsèque; [*stimulus, influence*] extérieur.

extroversion /ˌekstrə'vɜ:ʃn, US -vɜ:rʒn/ *n* extraversion *f*.

extrovert /'ekstrəvɜ:t/ *n, adj* extraverti/-e (*m/f*).

extrude /ɪk'stru:d/ *vtr* **1** (force out) faire sortir [*glue, toothpaste*] (**from** de); **2** Ind extruder [*metal, plastic*]; **~d plastic** plastique extrudé.

extrusion /ɪk'stru:ʒn/ *n* extrusion *f*.

exuberance /ɪg'zju:bərəns, US -'zu:-/ *n* exubérance *f*.

exuberant /ɪg'zju:bərənt, US -'zu:-/ *adj* (all contexts) exubérant.

exuberantly /ɪg'zju:bərəntlɪ, US -'zu:-/ *adv* [*play, sing*] avec exubérance; [*shout, wave*] joyeusement.

exude /ɪg'zju:d, US -'zu:d/ **I** *vtr* **1** (radiate) respirer [*charm, authority, affluence*]; **2** (give off) exsuder [*sap*]; exhaler [*smell*].
II *vi* **1** [*confidence, conviction*] se dégager (**from** de); **2** [*sap, gum*] exsuder (**from** de); [*smell*] se dégager (**from** de).

exult /ɪg'zʌlt/ *vi* exulter (**in doing** de faire); **to ~ at** ou **in sth** se réjouir de qch; **to ~ over one's enemy** chanter victoire sur son ennemi.

exultant /ɪg'zʌltənt/ *adj* [*tone, mood, look*] triomphant; [*cry*] de triomphe; **to be ~** exulter.

exultantly /ɪg'zʌltəntlɪ/ *adv* triomphalement.

exultation /ˌegzʌl'teɪʃn/ *n* exultation *f*; **with** ou **in ~** avec exultation.

exurbia /ˌeks'ɜ:bɪə/ *n* US banlieue *f* résidentielle.

ex-wife /ˌeks'waɪf/ *n* (*pl* **ex-wives**) exfemme *f*.

ex-works /ˌeks'wɜ:ks/ *adj* [*price, value*] départ-usine.

eye /aɪ/ ▶ 1037 **I** *n* **1** Anat œil *m*; **with blue/green ~s** aux yeux bleus/verts; **to raise/lower one's ~s** lever/baisser les yeux; **in front of** ou **before your (very) ~s** sous vos yeux; **to the expert/untrained ~** pour un œil exercé/non exercé; **there was sorrow/fear in his ~s** son regard exprimait le chagrin/la crainte; **with sorrow/fear in his ~s** les yeux remplis de chagrin/crainte; **I wouldn't have believed it, if I hadn't seen it with my own ~s** je ne l'aurais pas cru, si je ne l'avais vu de mes propres yeux; **I could do it with my ~s closed** je pourrais le faire les yeux fermés; **keep your ~s on the road!** c'est la route qu'il faut regarder!, regarde la route!; **keep your ~ on the ball!** ne quitte pas la balle des yeux!; **to keep an ~ on sth** surveiller qch; **to keep an ~ on sb** surveiller qn; (suspiciously) avoir or tenir qn à l'œil; **under the watchful/critical ~ of sb** sous le regard vigilant/critique de qn; **to have one's ~ on sb/sth** (watch) surveiller qn/qch; (desire) avoir envie de [*dress, car, house*]; (lust after) loucher○ sur [*food, dress, car, person*]; (aim for) viser [*job*]; **with an ~ to doing** en vue de faire; **they have their ~ on you for the director's job** ils vous ont en vue pour le poste de directeur; **she had one ~ on her work and the other on the clock** elle travaillait en gardant un œil sur l'horloge; **to keep one** ou **half an ~ on sth/sb** garder un œil sur qch/qn; **I've never clapped**○ ou **laid** ou **set ~s on him before in my life** je ne l'ai jamais vu de ma vie; **the first time I clapped** ou **laid** ou **set ~s on it, I knew**... au premier coup d'œil, j'ai compris...; **all ~s were on him** tous les yeux or tous les regards étaient fixés sur lui; **to cast** ou **run one's ~ over sth** parcourir qch du regard; **to catch sb's ~** attirer l'attention de qn; **to close** ou **shut one's ~s** lit fermer les yeux; **to close** ou **shut one's ~s to sth** fig se refuser à reconnaître qch; **to open one's ~s** lit ouvrir les yeux; **to open sb's ~s to sth** fig ouvrir les yeux à qn sur qch; **to do sth with one's ~s open** fig faire qch en toute connaissance de cause; **to go around with one's ~s shut** vivre sans rien voir; **to keep an ~ out** ou **one's ~s open for sb/sth** essayer de repérer qn/qch; **to keep one's ~s peeled** ou **skinned** rester attentif or vigilant; **to keep one's ~ peeled** ou **skinned for sb/sth** ouvrir l'œil pour essayer de repérer qn/qch; **London, seen through the ~s of a child, a child's ~ view of London** Londres, vu par un enfant; **as far as the ~ can see** à perte de vue; **I've got ~s in my head!** j'ai des yeux pour voir!; **use your ~s! it's on the table in front of you!** tu es aveugle? c'est sur la table devant toi!; **to take one's ~ off sth/sb** quitter qch/qn des yeux; **she couldn't take her ~s off him** elle le dévorait des yeux, elle ne le quittait pas des yeux; **to get one's ~ in** GB Sport s'habituer aux conditions de jeu; **'my ~○!'** 'mon œil○!'; **'~s right/left!'** Mil 'tête à droite/à gauche!'; **2** (opinion) **in the ~s of the church/law/world** aux yeux de l'église/de la loi/du monde; **in my father' s/teacher's ~s**... aux yeux de mon père/mon professeur...; **in your/his ~s**... à tes/ses yeux...; **3** (flair) **to have a good ~** avoir un bon coup d'œil; **to have an ~ for** avoir le sens de [*detail, colour*]; s'y connaître en [*antiques, livestock*]; **to have an ~ for a bargain** savoir flairer une bonne affaire; **4** Sewing (hole in needle) chas *m*; (to attach hook to) œillet *m*; **5** (on potato) œil *m*; **6** (on peacock's tail) œil *m*, ocelle *m*; **7** Meteorol (of hurricane, tornado, storm) œil *m*; **the ~ of the storm** fig (place of calm) l'œil de la tempête; (place of intense activity) le cœur de la tempête; **the ~ of the wind** le lit du vent.
II *modif* [*operation*] de l'œil; [*muscle, tissue*] de l'œil, oculaire; [*movement*] des yeux, oculaire; [*ointment, lotion*] pour les yeux; **~ disease** maladie *f* des yeux; **to have ~ trouble** avoir des troubles oculaires.
III -eyed (*dans composés*) **blue-/brown-~d** aux yeux bleus/marron.
IV *vtr* **1** (look at) regarder [*person, object*]; **to ~ sth/sb with suspicion/caution** regarder qch/qn d'un air soupçonneux /méfiant; **to ~ sth with envy** regarder qch avec envie; **2**○ (ogle at) ▶ **eye up**.
IDIOMS **to be all ~s** être tout yeux; **to be in it up to one's ~s** être compromis jusqu'au cou; **to be up to one's ~s in** être submergé de [*mail, complaints, work*]; **to be up to one's ~s in debt** être endetté jusqu'au cou; **an ~ for an ~ (a tooth for a tooth)** œil pour œil, (dent pour dent); **it was one in the ~ for him** c'était bien fait pour lui iron; **to have ~s in the back of one's head** avoir des yeux derrière la tête or dans le dos; **to make ~s at sb** faire les yeux doux à qn; **to give sb the glad ~** faire de l'œil à qn; **to see ~ to ~ with sb (about sth)** partager le point de vue de qn (au sujet de qch); **what the ~ doesn't see (the heart doesn't grieve over)** Prov bienheureux celui qui ne connaît pas la vérité.
■ **eye up**○: **~ [sb] up, ~ up [sb]** lorgner○, reluquer○.
■ **eye up and down**: **~ [sb] up and down** (suspiciously) toiser [qn] de haut en bas; (appreciatively) dévorer [qn] des yeux.

eyeball /'aɪbɔ:l/ **I** *n* Anat globe *m* oculaire; **to be ~ to ~ with sb** faire face à qn.
II *vtr* lancer des regards agressifs à [*person*].

eye: **~ bank** *n* banque *f* des yeux; **~bath** *n* œillère *f*; **~bolt** *n* Tech boulon *m* à œil.

eyebrow /'aɪbraʊ/ *n* sourcil *m*; **to raise one's** ou **an ~** (in surprise) hausser les sourcils; (in disapproval) froncer les sourcils; **to raise a few ~s** provoquer quelques froncements de sourcils.

eye: **~brow pencil** *n* Cosmet crayon *m* à sourcils; **~-catching** *adj* [*colour, design, poster*] attrayant; [*dress, hat*] original; [*advertisement, headline*] accrocheur/-euse.

eye contact *n* échange *m* de regards; **to make ~ with sb** croiser le regard de qn.

eyecup /'aɪkʌp/ *n* **1** Phot œilleton *m*; **2** US (for bathing eyes) œillère *f*.

eyedrops /'aɪdrɒps/ *npl* gouttes *fpl* pour les yeux.

eyeful /'aɪfʊl/ *n* **1** (amount) **to get an ~ of** avoir [qch] plein les yeux [*dust, sand*]; **2**○ (good look) **to get an ~ (of sth)** se rincer l'œil○ (au spectacle de qch); **get an ~ of that!** vise○ un peu ça!; **she's an ~!** US elle est mignonne!

eyeglass /'aɪglɑ:s, US -glæs/ *n* **1** (monocle) monocle *m*; **2** = **eyepiece**.

eye: **~glasses** *npl* US lunettes *fpl* (de vue); **~lash** *n* cil *m*.

eyelet /'aɪlɪt/ *n* œillet *m*.

eye level /'aɪlevl/ **I** *n* niveau *m* de l'œil; **at ~** au niveau de l'œil, à hauteur des yeux.
II eye-level *adj* [*grill, display, shelf*] à hauteur des yeux.

eye: **~lid** *n* paupière *f*; **~liner** *n* Cosmet eye-liner *m*; **~ make-up** *n* Cosmet maquillage *m* pour les yeux; **~ make-up remover** *n* Cosmet démaquillant *m* pour les yeux.

eye-opener○ /'aɪəʊpnə(r)/ *n* **1** (revelation) révélation *f*; **the trip was a real ~ for him** le voyage a été une véritable révélation pour lui, le voyage lui a ouvert les yeux; **2** US (drink) petit verre *m* du matin.

eye: **~-patch** *n* bandeau *m*, coque *f* oculaire spec; **~piece** *n* oculaire *m*; **~ rhyme** *n* Literat rime *f* pour l'œil; **~shade** *n* visière *f*; **~ shadow** *n* Cosmet fard *m* à paupières.

eyesight /'aɪsaɪt/ *n* vue *f*; **to have good/poor ~** avoir une bonne/mauvaise vue.

eye: **~ socket** *n* Anat orbite *f*; **~s-only** *adj* US confidentiel/-ielle.

eyesore /ˈaɪsɔː(r)/ *n* **to be an ~** choquer la vue.

eye: **~ specialist** ▶ **1692** *n* ophtalmologue *mf*, oculiste *mf*; **~ splice** *n* œil *m*, épissure *f* à œillet; **~ strain** *n* fatigue *f* oculaire; **~ surgeon** ▶ **1692** *n* chirurgien *m* oculiste; **~ test** *n* examen *m* de la vue.

eyetooth /ˈaɪtuːθ/ *n* (*pl* **-teeth**) Dent canine *f* supérieure.

IDIOMS **I'd give my eyeteeth for that job/car** je donnerais n'importe quoi pour obtenir ce poste/avoir cette voiture.

eyewash /ˈaɪwɒʃ/ *n* **1** Med collyre *m*; **2** fig (nonsense) poudre *f* aux yeux, fadaises *fpl*.

eyewitness /ˈaɪwɪtnɪs/ **I** *n* témoin *m* oculaire.

II *modif* [*account*, *report*] d'un témoin oculaire.

eyrie /ˈeərɪ, ˈaɪərɪ/ *n* aire *f*, nid *m* d'aigle.

Ezekiel /ɪˈziːkjəl/ *pr n* Ézéchiel.

Ff

f, F /ef/ *n* **1** (letter) f, F *m*; **2 F** Mus (note, key) fa *m*; **3 F** (*abrév* = **Fahrenheit**) F.

fa /fɑː/ *n* Mus fa *m*.

FA *n* GB **1** (*abrév* = **Football Association**) fédération *f* britannique de football; cf FFF; **2**◑ (*abrév* = **Fanny Adams**) **sweet ~** que dalle◑; **3**◑ (*abrév* = **fuck all**●) **sweet ~** que dalle◑.

FAA *n* US (*abrév* = **Federal Aviation Association**) direction *f* générale de l'aviation civile américaine.

fab○ /fæb/ *adj* GB (*abrév* = **fabulous**) sensas(s)○.

Fabian Society /ˈfeɪbɪən/ *n* Fabian Society *f* (*association socialiste anglaise à l'origine du Labour Party*).

fable /ˈfeɪbl/ *n* **1** Literat (moral tale) fable *f*; (legend) légende *f*; **2** (play, film) apologue *m* liter, histoire *f* moraliste; **3** (lie) histoire *f*.

fabled /ˈfeɪbld/ *adj* **1** (of legend) légendaire; **2** (acclaimed) fameux/-euse.

Fablon® GB /ˈfæblɒn/ *n* ≈ Vénilia® *m* adhésif.

fabric /ˈfæbrɪk/ *n* **1** (cloth) tissu *m*, étoffe *f*; **2** fig (basis) **the ~ of society** le tissu social; **3** (of building) structure *f*.

fabricate /ˈfæbrɪkeɪt/ *vtr* **1** inventer [qch] de toutes pièces [*story, excuse, evidence*]; **2** fabriquer [*object, document*].

fabrication /ˌfæbrɪˈkeɪʃn/ *n* **1** (lie) fabrication *f*; **2** (invention) invention *f*; **that's pure** ou **complete ~** c'est de l'invention pure et simple; **3** (of object, document) fabrication *f*.

fabric softener *n* (produit *m*) assouplissant *m*.

fabulous /ˈfæbjʊləs/ **I** *adj* **1**○ (wonderful) sensationnel/-elle○; **2**○ [*price, income*] fabuleux/-euse; **3** [*beast, realm*] fabuleux/-euse.
II○ *excl* génial!

fabulously /ˈfæbjʊləslɪ/ *adv* [*beautiful*] merveilleusement; [*rich*] fabuleusement; **~ expensive** hors de prix; **to be ~ successful** avoir un succès fou.

façade, facade /fəˈsɑːd/ *n* lit, fig façade *f* (**of** de).

face /feɪs/ **I** *n* **1** Anat, gen (of person) visage *m*, figure *f*; (of animal) face *f*; **to have an honest ~** avoir un visage franc; **to have ink on one's ~** avoir de l'encre sur le visage; **he punched me in the ~** il m'a donné un coup de poing au visage; **to spit in sb's ~** cracher à la figure de qn; **to slam the door in sb's ~** claquer la porte au nez de qn; **to laugh in sb's ~** rire au nez de qn; **I know that ~!** je connais cette tête-là!; **to look sb in the ~** lit, fig regarder qn en face; **I told him to his ~ that he was lazy** je lui ai dit en face qu'il était paresseux; **I dare not show my ~** fig j'ai peur de me montrer; **don't you dare show your ~ in here again!** et que je ne vous revoie plus!; **to be ~ up/down** [*person*] être sur le dos/ventre; **to put one's ~ on**○ hum se maquiller; **2** (expression) air *m*; **the smug ~ of the interviewer** l'air suffisant de l'interviewer; **she looked at me with a puzzled ~** elle m'a regardé d'un air perplexe; **a long ~** un air triste; **to pull** ou **make a ~** faire la grimace; **I can't wait to see his ~ when you tell him!** j'ai hâte de voir la tête qu'il va faire quand tu lui diras○!; **you should have seen their ~s!** tu aurais vu la tête qu'ils ont fait○!; **3** fig (outward appearance) **to change the ~ of** changer le visage de [*industry, countryside*]; **the changing ~ of education/Europe** la face changeante de l'éducation/l'Europe; **the ugly ~ of the regime** l'aspect monstrueux du régime ; **the acceptable ~ of capitalism** le bon côté du capitalisme; **on the ~ of it, it sounds easy** à première vue ou au premier abord, ça paraît facile; **4** (dignity) **to lose ~** perdre la face; **to save ~** sauver la face; **to avoid a loss of ~ he lied** pour ne pas perdre la face il a menti; **5**○ GB (nerve) culot○ *m*, audace *f*; **they had the ~ to ask for more money!** ils ont eu le culot○ de redemander de l'argent!; **6** (dial) (of clock, watch) cadran *m*; **7** (surface) (of gem, dice) face *f*; (of coin) côté *m*; (of planet) surface *f*; **the largest island on the ~ of the earth** ou **globe** la plus grande île du monde; **to disappear** ou **vanish off the ~ of the earth**○ [*person, keys*] disparaître de la circulation; **the hidden ~ of the moon** la face cachée de la lune; **8** Geol (of cliff, mountain) face *f*; (of rock) paroi *f*; (of mineral seam) face *f*; **9** (printed surface) (of playing card) face *f*; (of document) recto *m*; **~ up/down** à l'endroit/l'envers; **10** Print œil *m*.
II in the face of *prep phr* **1** (despite) en dépit de [*overwhelming odds*]; **2** (in confrontation with) face à, devant [*opposition, enemy, danger*].
III *vtr* **1** (look towards) [*person*] faire face à [*person, audience*]; [*building, room*] donner sur [*park, beach*]; **to ~ north/south** [*person*] regarder au nord/sud; [*building*] être orienté au nord/sud; **he turned to ~ the door/class** il se retourna vers la porte/la classe; **she stood facing the class** elle était debout face à la classe; **facing me/our house, there is...** en face de moi/de notre maison, il y a...; **a seat facing the engine** un siège dans le sens de la marche; **~ the front!** regarde devant toi!; **2** (confront) se trouver face à [*challenge, crisis*]; se voir contraint de payer [*fine*]; se trouver menacé de [*defeat, redundancy, ruin*]; être contraint de faire [*choice*]; être contraint de prendre [*decision*]; affronter [*attacker*]; se retrouver face à [*rival, team*]; **to be ~d with** se trouver confronté à [*problem, decision*]; **~d with such a hard decision, I panicked** face à une décision aussi difficile, j'ai paniqué; **to be ~d with the task of doing** devoir faire qch; **~d with the prospect of having to resign/move house** devant la perspective d'avoir à démissionner/déménager; **to ~ sb with** confronter qn à [*truth, evidence*]; **he ~s 18 months in prison** il va devoir faire 18 mois de prison; **I'm facing the prospect of being unemployed** je vais me retrouver au chômage; **the president has agreed to ~ the press/cameras** le président a accepté de faire face à la Presse/aux caméras; **3** (acknowledge) **~ the facts, you're finished!** regarde la réalité en face, tu es fini!; **let's ~ it, nobody's perfect** admettons-le, personne n'est parfait; **4** (tolerate prospect) **I can't ~ doing** je n'ai pas le courage de faire; **I can't ~ him** je n'ai pas le courage de le voir; **he couldn't ~ the thought of walking/eating** l'idée de marcher/manger lui était insupportable; **I don't think I can ~ another curry tonight** l'idée de remanger du curry ce soir me rend malade; **5** (run the risk of) risquer [*fine, suspension*]; **you ~ spending 20 years in jail** vous risquez vingt ans de prison; **6** Sewing (reinforce) mettre des parements à [*armhole*]; (trim) mettre des revers à [*cuff, jacket*]; **7** Constr revêtir [*façade, wall*] (**with** de); **8** Print, Publ [*photo etc*] être face à [*page*].
IV *vi* **1 to ~ towards** [*person*] regarder [*camera, audience*]; [*chair*] être tourné vers [*fire*]; [*window, house*] donner sur [*street, garden*]; **to ~ forward** regarder devant soi; **to ~ backwards** [*person*] tourner le dos; **to be facing forward/backwards** [*person*] être de face/de dos; **to be facing up/down** [*card, exam, paper*] être à l'envers/à l'endroit; **2** Mil **about ~!** demi-tour!; **left ~!** à gauche!
IDIOMS in your ~○! US bien fait pour toi!; **to feed** ou **fill** ou **stuff one's ~**○ s'empiffrer○ (**with** de); **to set one's ~ against sth** s'élever contre qch.
■ **face down** US: **~ [sb] down** intimider.
■ **face out**: ¶ **~ [sb] out** tenir tête à [*opponent, critic*]; ¶ **~ [sth] out** faire front à [*criticism*].
■ **face up**: ¶ **~ up to [sth]** faire face à [*problem, responsibilities, fears*]; ¶ **~ up to [sb]** affronter.

faceache○ /ˈfeɪseɪk/ *n* **1** Med (neuralgia) névralgie *f* faciale; **2**◑ GB (miserable person) face *f* de rat○.

face: **~ card** *n* US Games figure *f*; **~cloth** *n* GB gant *m* de toilette; **~ cream** *n* crème *f* pour le visage; **~guard** *n* Ind, Tech visière *f* de protection; Sport masque *m* protecteur.

faceless /ˈfeɪslɪs/ *adj* fig anonyme.

face-lift /ˈfeɪslɪft/ *n* **1** Cosmet lifting *m*; **to have a ~** se faire faire un lifting; **2** fig rénovation *f*; **to give sth a ~** rénover qch [*building*]; réaménager qch [*town-centre*]; changer la formule de qch [*magazine*]; rénover qch [*political party*].

face-off /ˈfeɪsɒf/ *n* **1** US (confrontation) confrontation *f*; **2** Sport (in ice hockey) remise *f* en jeu.

face: **~-pack** *n* masque *m* de beauté; **~ powder** *n* poudre *f* (de riz).

facer○ /ˈfeɪsə(r)/ *n* GB **1** (blow) coup *m* au visage; **2** fig tuile○ *f*; **what a ~!** quelle tuile!; **that's the ~** voilà le hic○.

face-saver /ˈfeɪsseɪvə(r)/ *n* moyen *m* de sauver la face; **his resignation was nothing more than a ~** sa démission n'était qu'un moyen de sauver la face.

face-saving /ˈfeɪsseɪvɪŋ/ *adj* [*plan, solution*] qui permet de sauver la face (*after n*); **he offered me a ~ solution** il m'a proposé une solution qui me permettait de sauver la face.

facet /ˈfæsɪt/ *n* **1** (of gemstone) facette *f*; **2** (of question, problem) aspect *m*; **3** (of personality) facette *f*.

facetious /fəˈsiːʃəs/ *adj* [*remark*] facétieux/-ieuse; **she's being ~** elle dit ça pour plaisanter.

facetiously /fəˈsiːʃəslɪ/ *adv* [*laugh*] facétieusement; [*say, remark*] d'un ton facétieux.

facetiousness /fəˈsiːʃəsnɪs/ *n* gouaillerie *f*.

face-to-face /ˌfeɪstəˈfeɪs/ **I** *adj* **a ~ discussion** ou **interview** ou **meeting** un face-à-face *inv*.

II face to face *adv* [*be seated*] face à face; **to come ~ with sb/sth** se retrouver face à [*person, death*]; **to meet sb ~** rencontrer qn en face-à-face; **to tell sb sth ~** dire qch à qn en face; **to talk to sb ~** parler à qn en personne.

face value *n* **1** Fin valeur *f* nominale; **2** fig **to take sth at ~** prendre qch au pied de la lettre [*claim, figures*]; prendre qch pour argent comptant [*remark, compliment*]; **to take sb at ~** juger qn sur les apparences; **at ~ it looks like a good idea** au premier abord, ça paraît être une bonne idée.

facial /ˈfeɪʃl/ **I** *n* soin *m* (complet) du visage; **to have a ~** se faire faire un soin du visage.

II *adj* [*muscle, hair*] du visage; [*injury*] au visage; [*angle, massage, nerve*] facial; **~ expression** expression *f*.

facial palsy /ˌfeɪʃl ˈpɔːlzɪ/ **▶1354** *n* Med paralysie *f* faciale.

facies /ˈfeɪʃiːz/ *npl* faciès *m*.

facile /ˈfæsaɪl, US ˈfæsl/ *adj* **1** (specious, glib) [*assumption, comparison, suggestion*] spécieux/-ieuse, facile; **2** (easy) [*success, victory*] facile.

facilitate /fəˈsɪlɪteɪt/ *vtr* faciliter [*change, choice, progress, talks, sale*]; favoriser [*development, growth*]; **his rudeness didn't exactly ~ matters** son impolitesse n'a guère arrangé les choses.

facilities management *n* gestion *f* des installations.

facility /fəˈsɪlətɪ/ **I** *n* **1** (building) complexe *m*, installation *f*; **manufacturing ~** complexe industriel; **computer ~** installation informatique; **warehouse ~** entrepôt *m*; **cold-storage ~** entrepôt *m* frigorifique; **2** (ease) facilité *f*; **with ~** avec facilité; **3** (ability) talent *m*; **to have a ~ for** être doué pour [*languages, painting*]; **4** (feature) fonction *f*; **a pause/spell-check ~** une fonction pause/de dictionnaire orthographique; **5** Admin, Comm facilités *fpl*; **credit/overdraft ~** facilités de crédit/de découvert; **we have facilities to send books** nous avons les possibilités d'envoyer des livres; **I have no facilities for photocopying** je n'ai pas de possibilités de faire des photocopies; **'fax facilities available'** 'télécopieur disponible'; **6** (department) service *m*.

II facilities *npl* **1** (equipment) équipement *m*, installation *f*; **medical/leisure facilities** équipement médical/de loisir; **computing facilities** installation *f* informatique; **facilities for the disabled** installations *fpl* pour les handicapés; **toilet facilities** toilettes; **to have cooking and washing facilities** être équipé d'une cuisine et d'une laverie; **2** (infrastructure) infrastructure *f*; **harbour facilities** installations *fpl* portuaires; **shopping facilities** magasins *mpl*, infrastructure commerciale; **tourist facilities** infrastructure touristique; **sporting facilities** infrastructure sportive; **postal facilities** service *m* postal; **3** (area) **changing facilities** vestiaire *m*; **parking facilities** (aire *f* de) parking *m*.

facing /ˈfeɪsɪŋ/ *n* **1** Archit, Constr revêtement *m*; **stone/stucco ~** revêtement en pierres/stuc; **2** Sewing entoilage *m*; **3** Fashn (*gén pl*) revers *m*; **a jacket with contrasting ~s** une veste avec des revers d'une couleur différente.

facsimile /fækˈsɪməlɪ/ **I** *n* **1** gen fac-similé *m*; **in ~** en fac-similé; **2** (sculpture) reproduction *f*; **3** (fax) sout télécopie *f*.

II *modif* [*manuscript, edition*] en fac-similé; **~ machine** télécopieur *m*.

fact /fækt/ **I** *n* **1** (accepted thing) fait *m*; **the ~ that** (beginning sentence) le fait que (+ *subj*); **it is a ~ that** il est vrai que; **to know for a ~ that** savoir de source sûre que; **owing** ou **due to the ~ that** étant donné que; **the ~ (of the matter) is (that)** le fait est que; **the ~ remains (that)** toujours est-il que; **~s and figures** les faits et les chiffres; **2** ¢ (truth) réalité *f*, vrai *m*; **~ and fiction** la fiction et la réalité; **to mix (up) ~ and fiction** mélanger la fiction et la réalité; **it is not speculation it is ~** ce n'est pas une supposition c'est un fait; **to accept sth as ~** admettre que qch est vrai; **the story was presented as ~** l'histoire a été présentée comme véridique; **to be based on ~** être fondé sur des faits réels; **3** (thing which really exists) réalité *f*; **the ~ of recession means that** la réalité de la récession implique que; **space travel is now a ~** les voyages dans l'espace sont désormais une réalité; **4** Jur (deed) fait *m*.

II in fact, as a matter of fact *adv phr* en fait; (when reinforcing point) en fait, effectivement; **they promised to pay and in ~ that's what they did** ils ont promis de payer et en fait or effectivement c'est ce qu'ils ont fait; (when contrasting, contradicting) en fait, au contraire; **I don't mind at all, in ~ I'm delighted** ça ne me fait rien, en fait or au contraire je suis ravi.

IDIOMS **I'm bored and that's a ~** je suis ennuyé vraiment; **is that a ~?** aussi iron vraiment?; **to know/learn the ~s of life** (sex) savoir/apprendre comment les enfants viennent au monde; **the ~s of life** (unpalatable truths) les réalités de la vie; **the economic/political ~s of life** les réalités économiques/politiques.

fact-finding /ˈfæktfaɪndɪŋ/ *adj* [*mission, trip, tour*] d'information; **~ committee** commission *f* d'enquête.

faction /ˈfækʃn/ *n* **1** (group) faction *f*; **2** (discord) dissension *f*; **3** Theat, TV docudrame *m*.

factional /ˈfækʃənl/ *adj* **1** [*leader, activity*] de faction; **2** [*fighting, arguments*] entre factions.

factious /ˈfækʃəs/ *adj* factieux/-ieuse.

factitious /fækˈtɪʃəs/ *adj* factice.

factitive /ˈfæktɪtɪv/ *adj* factitif/-ive.

factor /ˈfæktə(r)/ **I** *n* **1** gen, Math facteur *m*; **to rise by a ~ of** gen, Math être multiplié par; **common ~** gen point *m* commun; Math facteur commun; **human ~** élément *m* humain; **unknown ~** inconnue *f*; **plus ~** atout *m*; **~ of safety** Tech coefficient *m* de sécurité; **protection ~** (of suntan lotion) indice *m* de protection; **2** Comm (agent) courtier *m*; (of debts) facteur *m*; **3** (of commodities) commissionnaire *m*; **4** Scot (estate manager) régisseur *m*.

II *vtr* US Math = **factorize**.

III *vi* Comm agir en tant qu'agent à la commission.

■ **factor in**: **~ [sb] in, ~ in [sb]** prendre [qn] en compte.

factor: **~ 8** *n* Med facteur *m* 8; **~ analysis** *n* analyse *f* factorielle.

factorial /fækˈtɔːrɪəl/ **I** *n* factorielle *f*.

II *adj* factoriel/-ielle.

factoring /ˈfæktərɪŋ/ *n* **1** (of debts) affacturage *m*; **2** (by agent) courtage *m*.

factorize /ˈfæktəraɪz/ *vtr* Math mettre [qch] en facteurs.

factory /ˈfæktərɪ/ **I** *n* **1** gen usine *f*; **car/shoe ~** usine d'automobiles/de chaussures; **tobacco ~** manufacture *f* de tabac; **2** (illegal) **bomb ~** atelier *m* clandestin (de fabrication de bombes); **drugs ~** laboratoire *m* clandestin (de fabrication de drogue).

II *modif* [*owner, chimney, price*] d'usine.

Factory Acts *npl* GB Hist législation *f* industrielle (*du XIXe siècle*).

factory: **~ farm** *n* ferme *f* d'élevage industriel; **~ farming** *n* élevage *m* industriel; **~ floor** *n* (place) ateliers *mpl*; (workers) ouvriers/-ières *mpl/fpl*; **~ inspector ▶1692** *n* inspecteur/-trice *m/f* du travail; **~-made** *adj* fabriqué en usine; **~ ship** *n* navire-usine *m*; **~ shop** *n* magasin *m* d'usine; **~ system** *n* production *f* en usine; **~ unit** *n* unité *f* de production; **~ worker ▶1692** *n* ouvrier/-ière *m/f* (d'usine).

factotum /fækˈtəʊtəm/ *n* factotum *m*; **general ~** hum homme/femme *m/f* à tout faire.

fact sheet *n* fiche *f* d'informations.

factual /ˈfæktʃʊəl/ *adj* [*information, evidence*] factuel/-elle; [*account, description*] basé sur les faits; **~ error** erreur de fait; **~ programme** GB TV, Radio reportage *m*.

factually /ˈfæktʃʊəlɪ/ *adv* [*incorrect, complete*] dans les faits.

faculty /ˈfæklɪ/ *n* (*pl* **-ties**) **1** (power, ability) faculté *f* (**of** de; **for** de; **for doing** de faire); **to be in possession** ou **command of all one's faculties** jouir de toutes ses facultés; **critical faculties** esprit *m* critique; **2** GB Univ faculté *f*; **~ of Arts/Science** faculté des Lettres/des Sciences; **3** US Univ, Sch (staff) corps *m* enseignant.

faculty advisor *n* **1** US Univ directeur/-trice *m/f* d'études; **2** Sch animateur/-trice *m/f*.

Faculty Board *n* GB Univ conseil *m* de faculté.

faculty: **~ lounge** *n* US Sch salle *f* des professeurs; **~ meeting** *n* US Sch, Univ réunion *f* des enseignants.

fad /fæd/ *n* **1** (craze) engouement *m* (**for** pour); **2** (whim) lubie *f* (**about** de); **3** (person) **she's a food ~** elle fait très attention à ce qu'elle mange.

faddish /ˈfædɪʃ/, **faddy** /ˈfædɪ/ *adj* GB difficile (**about** pour).

fade /feɪd/ **I** *vtr* [*light, age*] faner [*curtains, clothes, colour*].

II *vi* **1** (get lighter) [*fabric*] se décolorer, se faner; [*colour*] passer; [*lettering, typescript*] s'effacer; **to ~ in the wash** [*garment, fabric*] se décolorer au lavage; [*colour*] passer au lavage; **the cloth ~d to a dull blue** le bleu du tissu s'est fané; **jeans guaranteed to ~** jeans à délavage garanti; **guaranteed not to ~** garanti grand teint; **2** (wither) [*flowers*] se faner; **3** (disappear) [*image, drawing*] s'estomper; [*sound*] s'affaiblir; [*smile, memory*] s'effacer; [*interest, excitement, hope*] s'évanouir; [*credits*] disparaître en fondu; **to ~ into the crowd/background** se fondre dans la foule/dans l'arrière-plan; **her looks are beginning to ~** elle n'est plus aussi belle qu'autrefois; **4** (deteriorate) [*hearing, light, sight*] baisser.

■ **fade away** [*sound*] s'éteindre; [*sick person*] dépérir; [*actor, star*] disparaître de la circulation; [*distinction, division*] s'estomper.

■ **fade in**: **~ [sth] in** monter [*sound, voice*]; faire apparaître [qch] en fondu [*image*]; ouvrir [qch] en fondu [*scene*].

■ **fade out**: ¶ **~ out** [*speaker, scene*] disparaître en fondu: ¶ **~ [sth] out** Cin faire disparaître [qch] en fondu [*picture, scene*].

faded /ˈfeɪdɪd/ *adj* [*clothing, carpet, decor*] décoloré; [*colour, glory*] passé; [*jeans*] délavé; [*drawing, picture*] estompé; [*photo, wallpaper*] jauni; [*flower, beauty*] fané; [*writing, lettering*] à demi effacé; [*aristocrat*] sur le déclin.

fade: **~-in** *n* Cin, Radio, TV fondu *m*; **~-out** *n* Cin, Radio, TV fondu *m*.

faecal, fecal US /ˈfiːkəl/ *adj* fécal.

faeces, feces US /ˈfiːsiːz/ *npl* matières *fpl* fécales, fèces *fpl* spec.

faerie‡ /ˈfeərɪ/ *n* **1** (being) = **fairy 1**; **2** (land) royaume *m* des fées.

faff /fæf/: ■ **faff about**○, **faff around**○ GB tournicoter○.

fag /fæg/ **I** *n* **1**○ (cigarette) clope○ *f*; **2** GB ○(nuisance) corvée *f*; **3**○ US injur pédé○ *m* offensive; **4**† GB argot des écoliers jeune élève *m* au service d'un grand (*dans les écoles privées anglaises*).

II† *vi* (*p prés etc* **-gg-**) GB argot des écoliers être au service d'un grand élève.

IDIOMS **I can't be ~ged**○ **to do it** je n'ai aucune envie de le faire.

■ **fag out**○: **~** [sb] **out** éreinter; **I'm completely ~ged out** je suis complètement claqué○.

fag end /'fægend/ *n* **1**○ (cigarette) mégot○ *m*; **2** fig bout *m*.

faggot /'fægət/ *n* **1** (meatball) boulette *f* de viande; **2** (firewood) fagot *m*; **3**◑ US injur (homosexual) pédale◑ *f* offensive.

faggoting /'fægətɪŋ/ *n* Sewing broderie *f* en faisceau.

fah /fɑː/ *n* Mus fa *m*.

Fahrenheit /'færənhaɪt/ *adj* Fahrenheit *inv*.

faience /ˌfaɪ'ɑːns/ *n* faïence *f*.

fail /feɪl/ **I** *n* Sch, Univ échec *m*; **to get a ~** GB échouer, être collé (**in** en).

II without fail *adv phr* [*arrive, do*] sans faute; [*happen*] à coup sûr, immanquablement; **I'll be there at six o'clock without ~** je serai là à six heures sans faute.

III *vtr* **1** Sch, Univ échouer à, rater○ [*exam, driving test*]; échouer or être collé○ en [*subject*]; coller○, refuser [*candidate, pupil*]; **to ~ sb** coller○ qn (**in** en); **2** (omit) **to ~ to do** manquer de faire; **to ~ to keep one's word** manquer à ses promesses; **it never ~s to annoy her** ça ne manque jamais de l'agacer; **it never ~s to work** ça marche à tous les coups; **to ~ to mention that...** omettre de signaler que...; **to ~ to appear (in court)** Jur ne pas comparaître (devant le juge); **if you ~ to complete/return the form** si vous ne remplissez/retournez pas ce formulaire; **3** (be unable) **to ~ to do** ne pas réussir à faire; **I ~ed to recognize her** je ne l'ai pas reconnue; **one could hardly ~ to notice that** il était évident que; **I ~ to see/understand why** je ne vois pas/je n'arrive pas à comprendre pourquoi; **the machine ~ed to meet our standards** la machine ne correspondait pas à nos critères; **to ~ to respond to treatment** ne pas réagir à un traitement; **4** (let down) laisser tomber [*friend*]; manquer à ses engagements envers [*dependant, supporter*]; [*courage*] manquer à [*person*]; [*memory*] faire défaut à [*person*]; **I've never ~ed you yet!** tu as toujours pu compter sur moi!; **the government has ~ed the nation** le gouvernement n'a pas tenu ses engagements envers la nation; **words ~ me!** les mots me manquent!

IV *vi* **1** (be unsuccessful) [*exam candidate*] échouer, être collé○; [*attempt, technique, plan, negotiations*] échouer; **he ~ed in the exams/in history** il a échoué or il a été collé○ aux examens/en histoire; **to ~ in one's attempt to do** échouer dans sa tentative de faire; **to ~ miserably** échouer lamentablement; **to ~ in one's duty** manquer or faillir à son devoir; **if all else ~s** en dernier recours; **2** (weaken) [*eyesight, hearing*] baisser; [*health, person*] décliner; [*voice*] s'affaiblir; [*light*] baisser, décliner; **to be ~ing fast** [*person , health*] décliner à vue d'œil; **3** (not function) [*brakes*] lâcher; [*engine*] tomber en panne; [*power, electricity, water supply*] être coupé; [*food supply*] manquer; **4** Agric [*crop*] être mauvais; **5** (go bankrupt) faire faillite; **6** Med [*heart*] lâcher; **his liver/kidneys ~ed** il a eu une défaillance du foie/des reins.

V failed *pp adj* [*actor, writer, coup d'état, project*] raté○.

failing /'feɪlɪŋ/ **I** *n* défaut *m*.

II *pres p adj* **to have ~ eyesight** avoir la vue qui baisse; **to be in ~ health** être en mauvaise santé.

III *prep* **~ that**, **~ this** autrement.

failing grade *n* US Sch échec *m*.

fail: **~-safe** *adj* [*device, machine, system*] à sûreté or sécurité intégrée; **~ soft** *adj* [*system*] à dégradation progressive.

failure /'feɪljə(r)/ *n* **1** (lack of success) gen échec *m* (**in** à); Fin faillite *f*; **his ~ to understand the problem** son incapacité à comprendre le problème; **to end in ~** se solder par un échec; **2** (unsuccessful person) raté/-e○ *m/f*; (unsuccessful venture or event) échec *m*; **he was a ~ as a teacher** comme professeur il ne valait rien; **to be a ~ at sports** ne pas être doué en sport; **to feel a ~** penser avoir raté sa vie; **the operation was a ~** l'opération a été un échec or a échoué; **3** (breakdown) (of engine, machine, power) panne *f*; Med (of organ) défaillance *f*; **crop ~** perte *f* de récolte; **power ~** panne de courant; **due to a mechanical ~** dû à une défaillance mécanique; **4** (omission) **~ to keep a promise** manquement *m* à une promesse; **~ to appear (in court)** Jur défaut *m* de comparution (en justice); **~ to comply with the rules** non-respect *m* de la réglementation; **~ to pay** non-paiement *m*; **they were surprised at his ~ to attend the meeting** ils étaient surpris qu'il n'assiste (*subj*) pas à la réunion.

fain‡ /feɪn/ *adv* de bonne grâce‡, volontiers.

faint /feɪnt/ **I** *n* évanouissement *m*; **to fall into a ~** s'évanouir; **to fall to the floor in a ~** tomber par terre évanoui; **a dead ~** une syncope.

II *adj* **1** (slight) [*smell, trace, breeze*] léger/-ère; [*glow, sound*] faible; [*accent*] léger/-ère; [*markings, streak*] à peine visible; [*signature*] à peine lisible; **2** [*recollection, suspicion*] vague; [*chance*] minime; **there is only a ~ possibility that he'll come** il y a très peu d'espoir qu'il vienne; **I haven't the ~est idea** je n'en ai pas la moindre idée; **he hadn't the ~est idea who she was** il ne savait pas du tout qui elle était; **to give a ~ smile** esquisser un sourire; **3** (weak) [*voice, breathing*] faible; **4** (dizzy) **to feel ~** se sentir mal, défaillir; **I'm ~ with hunger** je vais défaillir de faim; **5** (ineffectual) [*attempt*] timide; [*protest*] faible.

III *vi* s'évanouir; (more seriously) tomber en syncope; **to ~ from** s'évanouir de [*heat, exhaustion, hunger*]; **she ~ed from loss of blood** elle avait perdu tellement de sang qu'elle s'est évanouie.

IDIOMS **~ heart never won fair lady** Prov qui n'ose rien n'a rien Prov; **to damn sb with ~ praise** éreinter qn sous couleur d'éloge.

fainthearted /ˌfeɪnt'hɑːtɪd/ **I** *n* **the ~** (+ *v pl*) (cowardly) les timorés *mpl*; (oversensitive) les natures *fpl* sensibles.

II *adj* [*attempt, reform*] timide.

fainting /'feɪntɪŋ/ *n* évanouissements *mpl*.

fainting fit *n* évanouissement *m*.

faintly /'feɪntlɪ/ *adv* **1** (slightly) [*glisten, shine*] faiblement; [*coloured, tinged*] légèrement; [*disappointed, disgusted, silly*] légèrement; **not even ~ amusing** pas amusant du tout; **to be ~ reminiscent of sth** rappeler vaguement qch; **2** (weakly) [*breathe, smile*] faiblement; (gently) [*snore*] légèrement; [*murmur*] doucement.

faintness /'feɪntnɪs/ *n* **1** (of sound, cry, breathing) faiblesse *f*; **2** (dizziness) vertiges *mpl*.

fair /feə(r)/ **I** *n* **1** (funfair, market) foire *f*; (for charity) kermesse *f*; **2** Comm (exhibition) salon *m*; **book/food ~** salon du livre/de l'alimentation.

II *adj* **1** (just, reasonable) [*arrangement, person, punishment, ruling, share, trial, wage*] équitable (**to** envers); [*comment, decision, point*] juste; **it's only ~ that he should go/that she should be first** ce n'est que justice qu'il parte/qu'elle soit la première; **to give sb a ~ deal** ou **shake** US être tout à fait honnête envers qn; **I give you ~ warning** je te le dis tout net; **it's ~ to say that...** il est juste de dire que...; **that's a ~ question** c'est une question raisonnable; **a ~ sample** un échantillon représentatif ; **to be ~ he did try to pay** il faut dire à sa décharge qu'il a essayé de payer; **it is** ou **seems only ~ to do** ce serait la moindre des choses de faire; **~'s ~** il faut être juste; **it (just) isn't ~!** ce n'est pas juste!; **~ enough!** très bien, d'accord!; **a plea of ~ comment** Jur une invocation en défense (*du droit de commenter un fait d'intérêt général*); **that's a ~ comment** c'est vrai; **2** (moderately good) [*chance, condition, performance, skill*] assez bon/bonne; **it's a ~ bet**○ **that...** il est assez probable que...; **3** (quite large) [*amount, number, size*] important; **we were going at a ~ old**○ **pace** ou **speed** nous allions bon train; **he's had a ~ bit**○ **of luck/trouble** il a eu pas mal○ de chance/d'ennuis; **I've travelled around a ~ amount** j'ai pas mal○ voyagé; **the car was still a ~ way off** la voiture était encore à bonne distance; **4** Meteorol (fine) [*weather*] beau/belle; [*forecast*] bon/bonne; [*wind*] favorable; **to be set ~** [*weather, barometer*] être au beau fixe; fig [*arrangements*] être en ordre; **5** (light-coloured) [*hair*] blond; [*complexion, skin*] clair; **6** littér (beautiful) [*lady, maid, city, promises, words*] beau/belle; **with her own ~ hands** hum de ses belles mains; **the ~ sex** hum le beau sexe.

III *adv* [*play*] franc jeu.

IDIOMS **to be ~ game for sb** être une proie rêvée pour qn; **to be in a ~ way to do sth** avoir de bonnes chances de faire qch; **~ dos**○ à chacun son dû; **you can't say ~er than that**○ on ne saurait mieux dire; **~ and square** indiscutablement; **to win ~ and square** remporter une victoire indiscutable.

fair copy *n* version *f* au propre; **to make a ~ of sth** recopier qch au propre.

fair: **~ground** *n* champ *m* de foire; **~-haired** *adj* blond; **~-haired boy**○ *n* US fig (of public, media, teacher) chouchou○ *m*, chéri *m*; (of influential person) protégé *m*.

fairing /'feərɪŋ/ *n* Aut, Aviat carénage *m*.

fairly /'feəlɪ/ *adv* **1** (quite, rather) assez; [*sure*] pratiquement; **the hours ~ flew past** les heures semblaient vraiment passer à toute allure; **the house ~ shook to the loud music** le volume de la musique faisait pratiquement trembler la maison; **2** (justly) [*describe, obtain, win*] honnêtement; [*say*] à juste titre.

fair-minded /ˌfeə'maɪndɪd/ *adj* impartial.

fairness /'feənɪs/ *n* **1** (justness) (of person) équité *f*; (of judgment) impartialité *f*; **in all ~** en toute justice; **in ~ to him, he did phone** il faut dire à sa décharge qu'il a téléphoné; **2** (lightness) (of complexion) blancheur *f*; (of hair) blondeur *f*.

fair play *n* **to have a sense of ~** jouer franc jeu, être fair-play; **to ensure ~** faire respecter les règles du jeu.

fair: **~-sized** *adj* assez grand; **~-skinned** *adj* à la peau claire.

fair trade *n* **1** *accords de réciprocité dans les transactions commerciales internationales*; **2** US régime *m* des prix imposés.

fairway /'feəweɪ/ *n* **1** (in golf) parcours *m* normal; **2** Naut chenal *m*.

fair-weather friend *n* péj **he's a ~** dès que j'ai des ennuis, il n'est plus mon ami.

fairy /'feərɪ/ *n* **1** (magical being) fée *f*; **the bad ~** la fée Carabosse; **2**◑ injur (homosexual) tapette offensive *f*.

IDIOMS **to be away with the fairies**○ être à côté de ses pompes○.

fairy godmother *n* bonne fée *f*; **to play ~** jouer les bonnes fées.

fairy: **~land** *n* royaume *m* des fées; **~ lights** GB guirlande *f* électrique; **~-like** *adj* féerique; **~ queen** *n* reine *f* des fées; **~ story** *n* conte *m* de fées.

fairy tale I *n* **1** lit conte *m* de fées; **2** euph (lie) histoire *f* à dormir debout.

II *modif* [*romance, princess*] de conte de fées.

faith /feɪθ/ *n* **1** (confidence) confiance *f*; **to**

have ~ in sb avoir confiance en qn; **to have ~ in sb's ability** avoir confiance dans les compétences de qn; **to have ~ in a party** avoir confiance dans un parti; **to have ~ in a method** avoir foi dans une méthode; **to put one's ~ in sth** mettre sa confiance dans qch; **he has no ~ in socialism** il ne croit pas au socialisme; **I have no ~ in her** elle ne m'inspire pas confiance; **in good ~** en toute bonne foi; **to act in bad ~** agir avec mauvaise foi; **2** (belief) foi *f* (**in** en); **3** (system of beliefs) foi *f*; **the Christian/Muslim ~** la foi chrétienne/musulmane; **4** (denomination) religion *f*; **people of all ~s** les gens de toutes confessions.

faithful /ˈfeɪθfl/ **I** *n* **the ~** (+ *v pl*) lit, fig les fidèles *mpl*.
II *adj* **1** (loyal) fidèle (**to** à); **the ~ few** les vrais fidèles; **2** (accurate) [*representation, adaptation*] fidèle (**of** de; **to** à); [*quotation*] exact.

faithfully /ˈfeɪθfəlɪ/ *adv* **1** [*follow, serve*] fidèlement; **2** (accurately) [*reproduced, adapted*] fidèlement; [*recreated*] avec exactitude; **3** (in letter writing) **yours ~** veuillez agréer, Monsieur/Madame, mes/nos sincères salutations.

faithfulness /ˈfeɪθflnɪs/ *n* **1** (loyalty) fidélité *f* (**to sb** envers qn; **to sth** à qch); **2** (accuracy) (of reproduction, adaptation) fidélité *f*; (of reconstruction) exactitude *f*.

faith: **~ healer** *n* guérisseur *m*; **~ healing** *n* guérison *f* par la foi.

faithless /ˈfeɪθlɪs/ *adj* littér [*friend, husband*] infidèle; [*servant*] déloyal.

fake /feɪk/ **I** *n* **1** (jewel, work of art etc) faux *m*; **to be a ~** être un faux; **the bomb was a ~** c'était une fausse bombe; **2** (person) imposteur *m*; **3** US Sport feinte *f*.
II *adj* **1** [*fur, gem*] faux/fausse; [*flower*] artificiel/-ielle; **it's ~ wood/granite** c'est de l'imitation bois/granit; **~ Louis XV furniture** du faux Louis XV; **2** [*interview, trial*] truqué; [*emotion, smile*] feint; **3** (counterfeit) [*passport*] faux/fausse.
III *vtr* **1** (forge) contrefaire [*signature, document*]; **2**○ (falsify) truquer○ [*election*]; falsifier [*results*]; **3** (pretend) feindre [*emotion, illness*]; **to ~ one's way through a speech** US réussir à faire illusion dans un discours; **to ~ it** (pretend illness etc) jouer la comédie; (pretend knowledge) US bluffer○; (ad-lib) US improviser; **4** US Sport **to ~ a pass** feindre une passe.
■ **fake out**○ US: **~ [sb] out, ~ out [sb]** **1** Sport feinter; **2** fig feinter, bluffer○; **he really ~d me out** il m'a bien eu○.

fakeout /ˈfeɪkaʊt/ *n* US Sport, fig feinte *f*.

fakir /ˈfeɪkɪə(r), US fəˈkɪə(r)/ *n* fakir *m*.

falcon /ˈfɔːlkən, US ˈfælkən/ *n* faucon *m*.

falconer /ˈfɔːlkənə(r), US ˈfæl-/ *n* fauconnier *m*.

falconry /ˈfɔːlkənrɪ, US ˈfæl-/ *n* fauconnerie *f*.

Falkland Islander /ˌfɔːklənd'aɪləndə(r)/ *n* habitant/-e *m/f* des îles Malouines.

Falklands /ˈfɔːkləndz/ ▶ 1381 (also **Falkland Islands**) *pr npl* **the ~** les îles *fpl* Malouines.

fall /fɔːl/ ▶ 1671 **I** *n* **1** lit (of person, horse, rocks, curtain) chute *f* (**from** de); (of snow, hail) chutes *fpl*; (of earth, soot) éboulement *m*; (of axe, hammer, dice) coup *m*; **a ~ of 20 metres, a 20-metre ~** une chute de 20 mètres; **a heavy ~ of rain** une grosse averse; **to have a ~** faire une chute, tomber; **2** (in temperature, shares, production, demand, quality, popularity) baisse *f* (**in** de); (more drastic) chute *f* (**in** de); **the pound has suffered a sharp ~/a slight ~** la livre a subi une forte chute/une légère baisse; **a ~ in value** une dépréciation; **a ~ of 10% to 125** une baisse de 10% pour arriver à 125; **3** (of leader, regime, empire, fortress, town) chute *f*; (of monarchy) renversement *m*; (of seat) perte *f*; **the government's ~ from power** la chute du gouvernement; **4 ~ from grace** ou **favour** disgrâce *f*; **the Fall** Relig la chute; **5** US (autumn) automne *m*; **in the ~ of 1992** à l'automne 1992; **6** (in pitch, intonation) descente *f*; **7** (in wrestling) tombé *m*; (in judo) chute *f*.
II falls *npl* chutes *fpl*.
III *vi* (*prét* **fell**, *pp* **fallen**) **1** (come down) tomber; **~ing rain** la pluie qui tombe; **he was hurt by ~ing masonry** il a été blessé par une pierre qui tombait de la façade; **to ~ 10 metres** tomber de 10 mètres; **five centimetres of snow fell** il est tombé cinq centimètres de neige; **to ~ from** ou **out of** tomber de [*boat, nest, bag, hands*]; **to ~ off** ou **from** tomber de [*chair, table, roof, bike, wall*]; **the skirt ~s in pleats from a waistband** la jupe tombe en plis à partir de la ceinture; **to ~ on** tomber sur [*person, town*]; **it fell on my head** cela m'est tombé sur la tête; **to ~ on the floor** tomber par terre; **to ~ on one's back** tomber sur le dos; **to ~ in** ou **into** tomber dans [*bath, river, sink*]; **to ~ down** tomber dans [*hole, shaft, stairs*]; **to ~ under** tomber sous [*table*]; passer sous [*bus, train*]; **to ~ through** passer à travers [*ceiling, hole*]; tomber dans [*sky, air*]; **to ~ to earth** tomber sur terre; **to ~ to the floor** ou **to the ground** tomber par terre; **2** (drop) [*speed, volume, quality, standard, level*] diminuer; [*temperature, price, inflation, wages, production, number, attendance, morale*] baisser; (more dramatically) chuter○, tomber; **to ~ in the charts** perdre des places dans le hit-parade; **to ~ (by)** baisser de [*amount, percentage*]; **to ~ to** descendre à [*amount, place*]; **to ~ from** descendre de; **to ~ below zero/5%** descendre au-dessous de zéro/5%; **3** (yield position) tomber; **to ~ from power** tomber; **to ~ to** tomber aux mains de [*enemy, allies*]; **the seat fell to Labour** le siège a été perdu au profit des travaillistes; **to ~ from grace in sb's eyes** perdre la cote auprès de qn; **4** euph (die) tomber; **to ~ on the battlefield** tomber au champ d'honneur; **5** fig (descend) [*darkness, night, beam, silence, gaze*] tomber (**on** sur); [*blame*] retomber (**on** sur); [*shadow*] se projeter (**over** sur); **suspicion fell on her husband** les soupçons se sont portés sur son mari; **6** (occur) [*stress*] tomber (**on** sur); **Christmas ~s on a Monday** Noël tombe un lundi; **to ~ into/outside a category** rentrer/ne pas rentrer dans une catégorie; **to ~ under the heading of...** se trouver sous la rubrique de...; **7** (be incumbent on) **it ~s to sb to do** c'est à qn de faire, c'est à qn qu'il incombe de faire fml; **8** (throw oneself) **to ~ into bed/into a chair** se laisser tomber sur son lit/dans un fauteuil; **to ~ to** ou **on one's knees** tomber à genoux; **to ~ at sb's feet** se jeter aux pieds de qn; **to ~ into sb's/each other's arms** tomber dans les bras de qn/l'un de l'autre; **to ~ on each other** s'embrasser, tomber dans les bras l'un de l'autre; **to ~ on sb's neck** se jeter au cou de qn; **9** [*ground*] = **fall away 2**; **10** Relig succomber; **11** GB dial (get pregnant) tomber enceinte.
IDIOMS **did he ~ or was he pushed?** hum est-ce qu'il est parti de lui-même ou est-ce qu'on l'a forcé?; **the bigger you are** ou **the higher you climb, the harder you ~** plus dure sera la chute; **to stand or ~ on sth** reposer sur qch, dépendre de qch.
■ **fall about**○ GB **to ~ about (laughing** ou **with laughter)** se tordre○ de rire.
■ **fall apart** **1** [*bike, table*] être délabré; [*shoes*] être usé; [*car, house, hotel*] tomber en ruine; **2** [*marriage, country*] se désagréger; **3**○ [*person*] craquer○, perdre ses moyens.
■ **fall away** **1** [*paint, plaster*] se détacher (**from** de); **2** [*ground*] descendre en pente (**to** vers); **3** [*demand, support, numbers*] diminuer.
■ **fall back** gen reculer; Mil se replier (**to** sur).
■ **fall back on**: **~ back on [sth]** avoir recours à [*savings, parents, old method*]; **to have something to ~ back on** avoir quelque chose sur quoi se rabattre.
■ **fall behind**: ¶ **~ behind** [*runner, country, student*] se laisser distancer; [*work, studies*] prendre du retard; **to ~ behind with** GB ou **in** US prendre du retard dans [*work, project*]; être en retard pour [*payments, rent, correspondence*]; ¶ **~ behind [sth/sb]** se laisser devancer par [*horses, classmates, competitors*].
■ **fall down**: **~ down** **1** lit [*person, child, tree, poster*] tomber; [*tent, wall, house, scaffolding*] s'effondrer; **this whole place is ~ing down** tout tombe en ruine ici; **2** GB fig [*argument, comparison, plan*] faiblir; **where he ~s down is...** là où il faiblit, c'est...; **to ~ down on** échouer à cause de [*detail, question, obstacle*]; **to ~ down on a promise/on the job** être incapable de tenir sa promesse/de faire le travail.
■ **fall for**: ¶ **~ for [sth]** se laisser prendre à, se faire avoir○ par [*trick, story*]; ¶ **~ for [sb]** tomber amoureux/-euse de [*person*].
■ **fall in** **1** [*sides, walls, roof*] s'écrouler, s'effondrer; **2** Mil [*soldier*] rentrer dans les rangs; [*soldiers*] former les rangs; **~ in!** à vos rangs!
■ **fall in with**: **~ in with [sth/sb]** **1** (get involved with) faire la connaissance de [*group*]; **to ~ in with a bad crowd** avoir de mauvaises fréquentations; **2** (go along with) se conformer à [*timetable, plans, action*]; **3** (be consistent with) être conforme à [*expectations, concerns*].
■ **fall off** **1** lit [*person, leaf, hat, label*] tomber; **2** fig [*attendance, takings, sales, output*] diminuer; [*enthusiasm, standard, quality*] baisser; [*support, interest*] retomber; [*curve on graph*] décroître.
■ **fall on**: ¶ **~ on [sth]** se jeter sur [*food, treasure*]; ¶ **~ on [sb]** attaquer, tomber sur [*person*].
■ **fall open** [*book*] tomber ouvert; [*robe*] s'entrebâiller.
■ **fall out**: **~ out** **1** [*page, person*] tomber; **his hair/tooth fell out** il a perdu ses cheveux/une dent; **2** [*soldiers*] rompre les rangs; **~ out!** rompez!; **3**○ (quarrel) se brouiller, se fâcher (**over** à propos de); **to ~ out with sb** GB (quarrel) se brouiller or se fâcher avec qn; US (have fight) se disputer avec qn; **I've ~en out with him** GB je suis brouillé or fâché avec lui; **4** GB (turn out) se passer; **it fell out that...** il s'avéra que...
■ **fall over**: ¶ **~ over** [*person*] tomber (par terre); [*object*] se renverser; ¶ **~ over [sth]** trébucher sur [*object*]; **to ~ over oneself to do**○ se décarcasser○ pour faire; **people were ~ ing over themselves to buy shares** c'était à qui achèterait les actions.
■ **fall through** [*plans, deal*] échouer, tomber à l'eau○.
■ **fall to**: ¶ **~ to** attaquer; ¶ **~ to doing** se mettre à faire.
■ **fall upon** = **fall on**.

fallacious /fəˈleɪʃəs/ *adj* erroné.

fallaciously /fəˈleɪʃəslɪ/ *adv* à tort.

fallaciousness /fəˈleɪʃəsnɪs/ *n* caractère *m* erroné.

fallacy /ˈfæləsɪ/ *n* (belief) erreur *f*; (argument) faux raisonnement *m*.

fallback position *n* lit, fig position *f* de repli.

fallen /ˈfɔːlən/ **I** *pp* ▶ **fall**.
II *n* **the ~** (+ *v pl*) les morts *mpl* au champ d'honneur.
III *pp adj* [*leaf, soldier*] mort; [*tree*] abattu; **~ woman**† fille perdue†.

fall guy○ *n* (scapegoat) bouc *m* émissaire; (dupe) pigeon○ *m*.

fallibility /ˌfæləˈbɪlətɪ/ *n* faillibilité *f*.

fallible /ˈfæləbl/ *adj* faillible.

falling-off /ˌfɔːlɪŋˈɒf/ *n* (also **falloff**) diminution *f* (**in** de).

falling star /ˌfɔːlɪŋ ˈstɑː(r)/ *n* étoile *f* filante.

fall line *n* **1** (in skiing) ligne *f* de plus grande pente; **2** Geog ressaut *m*.

Fallopian tube /fə'ləʊpɪən/ *n* trompe *f* de Fallope.

fall: **~out** *n* ¢ (all contexts) retombées *fpl*; **~out shelter** *n* abri *m* antiatomique.

fallow /'fæləʊ/ *adj* [*land*] en jachère; **to lie ~** [*land*] être en jachère; [*idea*] rester inexploité; **a ~ period** Comm un passage à vide.

fallow deer *n* daim *m*.

false /fɔ:ls/ *adj* **1** (mistaken) [*impression, idea, information*] faux/fausse (*after n*); [*belief*] erroné; (proved wrong) [*allegations, rumour, statement*] faux/fausse (*before n*); **their fears/expectations may well prove ~** il se peut fort bien que leurs craintes/espoirs s'avèrent sans fondement; **a ~ sense of security** une fausse impression de sécurité; **2** (fraudulent) [*banknotes, passport*] faux/fausse; [*tax returns, name, address*] faux/fausse; **to give ~ information** Jur donner de faux renseignements; **to give ~ evidence** Jur faire un faux témoignage; **to bear ~ witness** Jur porter un faux témoignage; **charged with ~ accounting** Accts, Jur inculpé de faux en écritures; **3** (artificial) [*eyelashes, nose, hem*] faux/fausse (*before n*); [*floor, ceiling*] faux/fausse (*before n*); **4** [*person*] (affected, disloyal) faux/fausse.

false: **~ alarm** *n* lit, fig fausse alerte *f*; **~ bottom** *n* (in bag, box) double fond *m*; **~ economy** *n* fausse économie *f*.

falsehood /'fɔ:lshʊd/ *n* **1** (dishonesty) **to tell truth from ~** faire la différence entre le vrai et le faux; **2** (lie) mensonge *m*; **to tell a ~** mentir.

false imprisonment *n* sequestration *f*.

falsely /'fɔ:lslɪ/ *adv* **1** (wrongly) [*represent, state*] faussement; **~ accused** (accidentally) accusé à tort; (deliberately) faussement accusé; **to ~ imprison sb** Jur séquestrer qn; **2** (mistakenly) [*confident*] à tort; [*assume, believe*] à tort; **3** [*smile, laugh*] avec affectation.

false move *n* fausse manœuvre *f*.

falseness /'fɔ:lsnɪs/ *n* fausseté *f*.

false note *n* gen couac○ *m*; (in film, novel) son *m* discordant; **to strike a ~** [*person*] faire une gaffe.

false pretences *npl* **on** ou **under ~** gen en utilisant un subterfuge; Jur (by an action) par des moyens frauduleux; (in speech, writing) grâce à de fausses allégations.

false: **~ rib** *n* fausse côte *f*; **~ start** *n* lit, fig faux départ *m*; **~ step** *n* faux pas *m*.

false teeth *npl* dentier *m*; **to put in/take out one's ~** mettre/enlever son dentier.

falsetto /fɔ:l'setəʊ/ **I** *n* (voice) voix *f* de fausset; (singer) fausset *m*.
II *adj* [*voice, whine*] de fausset.

falsies○† /'fɔ:lsɪz/ *npl* faux seins *mpl*.

falsification /ˌfɔ:lsɪfɪ'keɪʃn/ *n* **1** (alteration) (of document, of figures) falsification *f*; **~ of accounts** Jur faux en écritures; **2** (distortion) (of the truth, of facts) déformation *f*.

falsify /'fɔ:lsɪfaɪ/ *vtr* **1** (alter) falsifier [*documents, results, accounts*]; **2** (distort) déformer [*facts, story*]; fausser [*sb's judgment*].

falsity /'fɔ:lsətɪ/ *n* (of accusation, statement) faux *m*; (of beliefs) caractère *m* erroné.

falter /'fɔ:ltə(r)/ **I** *vtr* (also **~ out**) balbutier [*word, phrase*].
II *vi* **1** [*demand, economy*] fléchir; **2** [*person, team, courage*] faiblir; **3** (when speaking) [*person*] bafouiller; [*voice*] trembloter; **to speak without ~ing** parler avec assurance; **4** (when walking) [*person*] chanceler; [*footstep*] hésiter; **to walk without ~ing** marcher d'un pas assuré.

faltering /'fɔ:ltərɪŋ/ *adj* [*economy, demand*] en déclin; [*footsteps, voice*] hésitant; **to make a ~ start** mal commencer.

falteringly /'fɔ:ltərɪŋlɪ/ *adv* [*speak*] avec hésitation; [*walk*] d'un pas hésitant; **to start ~** mal commencer.

fame /feɪm/ *n* renommée *f* (**as** en tant que); **to rise to ~** atteindre la renommée; **the film brought him ~** le film lui a valu la renommée; **to acquire ~** se faire une renommée; **this was her (chief) claim to ~** c'était son titre de gloire; **~ and fortune** la gloire et la fortune; **the road to ~** le chemin de la gloire.

famed /feɪmd/ *adj* célèbre (**for** pour; **as** en tant que).

familiar /fə'mɪlɪə(r)/ **I** *n* **1** (animal spirit) démon *m* familier; **2** (friend) intime *mf*.
II *adj* **1** (well-known) [*landmark, phrase, sight, shape, sound*] familier/-ière (**to** à); [*face, figure, name, story, voice*] bien connu (**to** de); **her face looked ~ to me** il me semblait que je l'avais déjà vue quelque part; **that name has a ~ ring to it, that name sounds ~** ce nom me dit quelque chose; **I thought her voice sounded ~** il me semblait que j'avais déjà entendu sa voix quelque part, il me semblait reconnaître sa voix; **to be on ~ ground** fig être en terrain connu; **2** (customary) [*argument, complaint, excuse, feeling*] habituel/-elle; **3** (acquainted) **to be ~ with sb/sth** bien connaître qn/qch; **to make oneself ~ with sth** se familiariser avec qch; **4** (intimate) [*language, manner, tone*] familier/-ière; **to be on ~ terms with sb** être assez intime avec qn; **to be too ~ with sb** se montrer trop familier/-ière avec qn.

familiarity /fəˌmɪlɪ'ærətɪ/ *n* **1** (acquaintance) (with author, art, subject, politics etc) connaissance *f* (**with** de), familiarité *f* (**with** avec); **2** (of surroundings, place) caractère *m* familier; **3** (informality) familiarité *f*; **the ~ of his tone/style** son ton/style familier.
IDIOMS **~ breeds contempt** Prov plus on est habitué à quelqu'un (ou à quelque chose) moins on l'apprécie.

familiarize /fə'mɪlɪəraɪz/ **I** *vtr* **to ~ sb with** familiariser qn avec [*area, fact, job, procedure*]; habituer qn à [*environment, person*].
II *v refl* **to ~ oneself with** se familiariser avec [*facts, system, work*]; s'habituer à [*person, place*].

familiarly /fə'mɪlɪəlɪ/ *adv* [*address, speak*] avec familiarité; [*behave*] de façon familière (**towards** envers).

family /'fæməlɪ/ **I** *n* gen, Ling, Zool (group) famille *f*; (children) enfants *mpl*; **to run in the ~** tenir de famille; **to be one of the ~** faire partie de la famille; **to start a ~** essayer d'avoir un enfant; **do you have any ~?** avez-vous des enfants?; **a ~ of four** une famille de quatre personnes.
II *modif* [*affair, feud, home*] de famille; [*member, friend*] de la famille; [*responsibilities, accommodation*] familial; **for ~ reasons** pour raisons familiales.
IDIOMS **to be in the ~ way**○ hum être enceinte.

family: **Family Allowance** *n* GB Soc Admin ≈ allocations *fpl* familiales; **~ business** *n* entreprise *f* familiale; **~ butcher** *n* boucher *m* de quartier.

family circle *n* **1** (group) cercle *m* familial; **2** US Theat deuxième balcon *m*.

family: **~ court** *n* US Jur tribunal *m* des affaires familiales; **Family Credit** *n* GB Soc Admin cf Complément *m* Familial; **Family Crisis Intervention Unit** *n* police *f* secours (*cellule spécialisée agissant en cas de drames familiaux*).

family doctor *n* (profession) médecin *m* généraliste; (of a particular family) médecin *m* de famille.

family: **~ entertainment** *n* spectacle *m* pour les petits et les grands; **~ grouping** *n* GB Sch *système de classes à double niveau dans les écoles maternelles*; **Family Health Service Authority, FHSA** *n* GB Soc Admin cf service des relations avec les professions de santé; **Family Income Supplement** *n* Soc Admin ≈ allocation *f* de soutien familial; **~ man** *n* bon père *m* de famille; **~ name** *n* nom *m* de famille; **~-owned** *adj* [*business*] familial; **~ planning** *n* planning *m* familial; **Family Planning Association, FPA** *n* ≈ Planning *m* Familial; **~ planning clinic** *n* centre *m* de planning familial.

family practice *n* US **to have a ~** être médecin *m* généraliste.

family: **~ practitioner** ▶ 1692 *n* Med médecin *m* généraliste; **Family Practitioner Committee** *n* Soc Admin (formerly) cf service des relations avec les professions de santé; **~ romance** *n* US Psych roman *m* familial; **~ room** *n* US salle *f* de jeu; **~-size(d)** *adj* [*packet*] familial; **~ style** *adj*, *adv* US ≈ table d'hôte; **~ tree** *n* arbre *m* généalogique; **~ unit** *n* Sociol cellule *f* familiale; **~ viewing** *n* émission *f* pour les petits et les grands.

famine /'fæmɪn/ *n* famine *f*.

famished○ /'fæmɪʃt/ *adj* **I'm ~** je meurs de faim, j'ai la fringale○.

famous /'feɪməs/ *adj* gen célèbre (**for** pour); [*school, university*] réputé (**for** pour); **a ~ victory** une grande victoire; **~ last words!** iron c'est ce que tu crois○!

famously /'feɪməslɪ/ *adv* **1** (wonderfully) à merveille; **to get on** ou **along ~** s'entendre à merveille; **2 Churchill is ~ quoted as saying...** tout le monde connaît les célèbres mots de Churchill...

fan /fæn/ **I** *n* **1** (enthusiast) gen fan○ *mf*; (of team) supporter *m*; **football/jazz ~** fan○ de football/de jazz; **2** (of star, actor etc) fan○ *mf*; (admirer) admirateur/-trice *m/f*; **he's a Presley ~** c'est un fan○ de Presley; **I'm not one of her ~s** je ne fais pas partie de ses admirateurs; **I'm a ~ of American TV** j'adore la télé américaine; **3** (for cooling) (electric) ventilateur *m*; (hand-held) éventail *m*; **4** Aut ventilateur *m*; **5** Agric (manual) van *m*; (mechanical) tarare *m*.
II *vtr* (*p prés etc* **-nn-**) **1** (stimulate) attiser [*fire, hatred, passion, hostility, hysteria*]; aviver [*spark, flame, hopes, anxiety*]; **2** (cool) [*breeze*] rafraîchir; **to ~ one's face** s'éventer le visage; **3**○ US (spank) fesser○.
III *v refl* (*p prés etc* **-nn-**) **to ~ oneself** s'éventer (**with** avec).
IDIOMS **to ~ the air** US battre l'air sans frapper.
■ **fan out** ¶ [*lines, railway lines*] se diviser et partir dans toutes les directions; [*police*] se déployer (en éventail) **they ~ned out across the plain** ils se déployèrent dans la plaine; ¶ **~ [sth] out, ~ out [sth]** ouvrir [qch] en éventail [*cards, papers*]; **the bird ~ned out its feathers** l'oiseau déploya ses plumes.

fanatic /fə'nætɪk/ *n* (all contexts) fanatique *mf*.

fanatical /fə'nætɪkl/ *adj* (all contexts) fanatique; **to be ~ about sth** être un/une fanatique de qch.

fanatically /fə'nætɪklɪ/ *adv* fanatiquement.

fanaticism /fə'nætɪsɪzəm/ *n* fanatisme *m*.

fan belt *n* Aut courroie *f* de ventilateur.

fanciable○ /'fænsɪəbl/ *adj* GB [*person*] pas mal du tout○.

fancier /'fænsɪə(r)/ *n* (of animals etc) (breeder) éleveur/-euse *m/f*; (lover) amateur/-trice *m/f*.

fanciful /'fænsɪfl/ *adj* [*person*] fantasque; [*idea, name*] extravagant; [*explanation*] fantaisiste; [*building*] orné; **to be ~** [*person*] se faire des idées.

fancifully /'fænsɪfəlɪ/ *adv* [*decorated*] d'une manière très ornée; [*named*] d'une manière fantaisiste; **to think** ou **imagine ~ that** s'imaginer que.

fancily /'fænsɪlɪ/ *adv* [*dressed, displayed*] en grande pompe.

fan club *n* lit, fig club *m* de fans○, fan-club *m*.

fancy /'fænsɪ/ **I** *n* **1** (liking) **to catch** ou **take sb's ~** [*object*] faire envie à qn; **he had taken her ~** (sexually) il lui avait tapé dans l'œil○; (not sexually) il lui plaisait bien; **have**

whatever takes your ~ prenez tout ce qui vous chante; **to take a ~ to sb** (sexually) GB s'enticher de qn; (non-sexually) s'attacher à qn; **I've taken a ~ to that dress/car** cette robe/voiture m'a tapé dans l'œil○; **2** (whim) caprice *m*; **a passing ~** un caprice passager; **as/when the ~ takes me** comme/quand ça me prend; **3** (fantasy) imagination *f*; **is it fact or ~?** c'est vrai ou c'est une invention?; **a flight of ~** une lubie; **4** GB sout (vague idea) **to have a ~ (that)** avoir (dans l')idée que; **5** GB (cake) petit gâteau *m* (glacé).

II *adj* **1** (elaborate) [*lighting, equipment*] sophistiqué; **nothing ~** (meal) rien de spécial; **2**○ péj (pretentious) [*place*] snobinard○; [*price*] exorbitant; [*idea, project*] fantaisiste; [*name*] tordu; [*food, gadget, equipment*] compliqué; [*clothes*] chic; **3** (decorative) [*paper, box*] fantaisie *inv*; **4** Comm [*food*] de luxe; **5** Zool [*breed*] d'agrément.

III *vtr* **1**○ (want) avoir (bien) envie de [*food, drink, object, plan, entertainment*]; **~ a coffee?** tu veux un café?; **what do you ~ for lunch?** qu'est-ce qui te plairait pour le déjeuner?; **to ~ doing** avoir envie de faire; **do you ~ going to the cinema/coming out with me?** ça te dirait○ d'aller au cinéma/de sortir avec moi?; **I don't ~ the idea of sharing a flat** l'idée de partager un appartement ne me dit rien; **2**○ GB (feel attracted to) **I ~ her** elle me plaît, elle m'a tapé dans l'œil○; **3** (expressing surprise) **~ her remembering my name!** figure-toi qu'elle se souvenait de mon nom!; **~ anyone buying that old car!** tu imagines quelqu'un acheter cette vieille bagnole○!; **~ seeing you here**○**!** tiens donc, toi ici?; **~ that**○**!** pas possible○!; **4**† (believe) croire, avoir l'impression; (imagine) s'imaginer; **5** Sport, Turf voir [qn/qch] gagnant [*athlete, horse*].

IV *v refl* **1**○ péj (be conceited) **he fancies himself** il ne se prend pas pour rien; **she fancies herself in that hat** elle n'arrête pas de frimer○ avec ce chapeau; **she fancies herself with a tennis racquet** elle se croit très bonne au tennis; **2**○ (wrongly imagine) **to ~ oneself as** se prendre pour; **he fancies himself as James Bond** il se prend pour James Bond.

V fancied *pp adj* Sport, Turf [*contender*] favori; **to be fancied for** [*competitor, horse*] être donné favori dans [*competition*]; [*candidate, party*] être donné gagnant de [*election*].

IDIOMS **a little of what you ~ does you good** ça ne peut pas te faire de mal; **to ~ one's chances**○ GB être très sûr de soi; **I don't ~ his chances**○ à mon avis il n'a aucune chance.

fancy dress I *n* ¢ GB déguisement *m*; **to wear ~** porter un déguisement; **in ~** déguisé.

II *modif* [*ball, party*] costumé; [*prize, competition*] de déguisement.

fancy: **~ goods** *npl* GB articles *mpl* de fantaisie; **~ man**○† *n* péj jules○ *m*; **~ woman**○† *n* pej poule○ *f* péj; **~work** *n* Sewing ouvrages *mpl* d'agrément.

fandango /fæn'dæŋgəʊ/ *n* (*pl* **~s**) fandango *m*.

fanfare /'fænfeə(r)/ *n* lit fanfare *f*; **in** ou **with a ~ of publicity** fig en fanfare.

fang /fæŋ/ *n* (of dog, wolf) croc *m*; (of snake) crochet *m* (à venin).

fan: **~ heater** *n* radiateur *m* soufflant; **~jet** *n* (engine) turbo *m*; (plane) turbojet *m*; **~ letter** *n* lettre *f* de fan; **~light** *n* fenêtre *f* en demi-lune; **~ magazine** *n* = **fanzine**; **~ mail** *n* lettres *fpl* envoyées par des admirateurs.

fanny /'fænɪ/ *n* **1**● GB (vagina) chatte● *f*, vagin *m*; **2**○ US (buttocks) fesses *fpl*.

fanny pack *n* US (sacoche *f*) banane *f*.

fan: **~(-assisted) oven** *n* four *m* à chaleur tournante; **~-shaped** *adj* [*leaf, stain*] en forme d'éventail; [*window*] en demi-lune; **~tail (pigeon)** *n* pigeon paon *m*.

fantasia /fæn'teɪzɪə, US -'teɪʒə/ *n* Mus fantaisie *f*.

fantasize /'fæntəsaɪz/ **I** *vtr* rêver (**that** que).

II *vi* fantasmer (**about** sur); **to ~ about doing** rêver de faire.

fantastic /fæn'tæstɪk/ *adj* **1**○ (wonderful) [*holiday, news*] formidable; [*view, weather*] magnifique; **you look ~!** tu es superbe!; **2** (unrealistic) invraisemblable; **3**○ (huge) [*profit*] fabuleux/-euse; [*speed, increase*] vertigineux/-euse; **4** (magical) fabuleux/-euse.

IDIOMS **to trip the light ~** hum danser.

fantastically /fæn'tæstɪklɪ/ *adv* **1**○ [*wealthy*] immensément; [*expensive*] terriblement; **2**○ [*increase*] de façon vertigineuse; [*perform*] incroyablement; **3** [*coloured, portrayed*] fabuleusement.

fantasy /'fæntəsɪ/ **I** *n* **1** (desired situation) rêve *m*; Psych fantasme *m*; **2** (imagination) imagination *f*; **3** (untruth) idée *f* fantaisiste; **4** (genre) fantastique *m*; **5** (story, film etc) histoire *f* fantastique; **6** Mus fantaisie *f*.

II *modif* **a ~ world** un monde imaginaire.

fan: **~ vault** *n* voûte *f* en éventail; **~ vaulting** *n* ¢ voûtes *fpl* en éventail.

fanzine /'fænziːn/ *n* magazine *m* des fans, fanzine *m*.

FAO *n* (*abrév* = **Food and Agriculture Organization**) FAO *f*.

far /fɑː(r)/ **I** *adv* **1** (to, at, from a long distance) loin; **is it ~?** c'est loin?; **it's not very ~** ce n'est pas loin; **have you come ~?** est-ce que vous venez de loin?; **is it ~ to York?** est-ce que York est loin d'ici?; **~ off, ~ away** au loin; **he doesn't live ~ away** il n'habite pas loin; **to be ~ from home/the city** être loin de chez soi/la ville; **~ beyond the city** bien au-delà de la ville; **~ above the trees** bien au-dessus des arbres; **~ out at sea** en pleine mer; **~ into the jungle** au fin fond de la jungle; **2** (expressing specific distance) **how ~ is it to Leeds?** combien y a-t-il (de kilomètres) jusqu'à Leeds?; **how ~ is Glasgow from London?** combien y a-t-il de kilomètres entre Glasgow et Londres?; **I don't know how ~ it is to Chicago from here** je ne sais pas combien il y a de kilomètres d'ici à Chicago; **he didn't go as ~ as the church** il n'est pas allé jusqu'à l'église; **he walked as ~ as her** ou **as she did** il a marché aussi loin qu'elle; **3** (to, at a long time away) **~ back in the past** loin dans le passé; **I can't remember that ~ back** je ne peux pas me rappeler quelque chose qui s'est passé il y a si longtemps; **as ~ back as 1965** déjà en 1965; **as ~ back as he can remember** d'aussi loin qu'il s'en souvienne; **the holidays are not ~ off** c'est bientôt les vacances; **he's not ~ off 70** il n'a pas loin de 70 ans; **peace seems very ~ away** ou **off** on est bien loin d'arriver à un accord de paix; **a change in government cannot be ~ away** un changement de gouvernement ne va pas tarder; **he worked ~ into the night** il a travaillé tard dans la nuit; **4** (to a great degree, very much) bien; **~ better/shorter/more expensive** bien mieux/plus court/plus cher; **~ too fast/cold** bien trop vite/froid; **~ too much money** bien trop d'argent; **~ too many people** bien trop de gens; **~ more** bien plus; **~ above/below the average** bien au-dessus/au-dessous de la moyenne; **the results fell ~ short of expectations** les résultats étaient bien loin de ce qu'on espérait; **interest rates haven't come down very ~** les taux d'intérêt n'ont pas beaucoup baissé; **they are ~ ahead of their competitors** ils sont largement en tête de leurs concurrents; **5** (to what extent, to the extent that) **how ~ is it possible to...?** dans quelle mesure est-il possible de...?; **how ~ have they got with the work?** où en sont-ils dans leur travail?; **we must wait and see how ~ the policy is successful** nous devons attendre pour voir dans quelle mesure cette politique réussit; **I wouldn't trust him very ~** je ne lui ferais pas confiance; **as** ou **so ~ as we can, as** ou **so ~ as possible** autant que possible, dans la mesure du possible; **as** ou **so ~ as we know/can see** pour autant que nous le sachions/nous puissions le constater; **as** ou **so ~ as I can remember** pour autant que je me souvienne; **as** ou **so ~ as I am/they are concerned** quant à moi/eux; **as** ou **so ~ as the money is concerned** pour ce qui est de l'argent; **as** ou **so ~ as that goes** pour ce qui est de cela; **it's OK as ~ as it goes, but**... c'est bien dans une certaine limite, mais...; **6** (to extreme degree) loin; **to go too ~** aller trop loin; **this has gone ~ enough!** ça ne peut pas continuer comme ça !; **she took** ou **carried the joke too ~** elle a poussé la plaisanterie un peu loin; **to push sb too ~** pousser qn à bout; **to go so ~ as to do** aller jusqu'à faire; **I wouldn't go so ~ as to say that** je n'irais pas jusqu'à dire que.

II *adj* **1** (remote) **the ~ north/south (of)** l'extrême nord/sud (de); **the ~ east/west (of)** tout à fait à l'est/l'ouest (de); **a ~ country** un pays lointain; **2** (further away, other) autre; **at the ~ end of the room** à l'autre bout de la pièce; **on the ~ side of the wall** de l'autre côté du mur; **3** Pol (*épith*) **the ~ right/left** l'extrême droite/gauche.

III by far *adv phr* de loin; **it's by ~ the nicest/the most expensive, it's the nicest/the most expensive by ~** c'est de loin le plus beau/le plus cher.

IV far and away *adv phr* de loin; **he's ~ and away the best/the most intelligent** il est de loin le meilleur/le plus intelligent.

V far from *prep phr* loin de; **~ from satisfied/certain** loin d'être satisfait/certain; **~ from complaining, I am very pleased** loin de me plaindre, je suis ravi; **I'm not tired, ~ from it!** je ne suis pas fatigué, loin de là!; **'are you angry?'—'~ from it!'** 'es-tu fâché?'—'pas du tout!'

VI so far *adv phr* **1** (up till now) jusqu'ici, pour l'instant; **she's only written one book so ~** jusqu'ici elle n'a écrit qu'un livre; **we've managed so ~** nous nous sommes débrouillés jusqu'ici; **we have £3,000 so ~** pour l'instant or jusqu'ici nous avons 3 000 livres sterling; **so ~, so good** pour l'instant tout va bien; **2** (up to a point) **the money will only go so ~** l'argent ne va pas durer éternellement; **they will only compromise so ~** ils ne sont prêts à accepter qu'un certain nombre de compromis; **you can only trust him so ~** tu ne peux pas lui faire entièrement confiance.

VII thus far *adv phr* jusqu'ici, jusqu'à présent; **thus ~ we don't have any information** jusqu'ici or jusqu'à présent nous n'avons pas d'informations.

IDIOMS **not to be ~ off** ou **out** ou **wrong** ne pas être loin du compte; **~ and wide, ~ and near** partout; **~ be it from me to do** loin de moi l'idée de faire; **to be a ~ cry from** être bien loin de; **he is pretty ~ gone** (ill) il est vraiment dans un état grave; (drunk) il est complètement bourré○; **how ~ gone** ou US **along is she (in her pregnancy)?** à quel stade de sa grossesse est-ce qu'elle en est?; **she will go ~** elle ira loin; **this wine/food won't go very ~** on ne va pas aller loin avec ce vin/ce qu'on a à manger.

farad /'færəd/ *n* farad *m*.

faraway /'fɑːrəweɪ/ *adj* (*épith*) lit, fig lointain.

farce /fɑːs/ *n* Theat, fig farce *f*; **the trial was a ~** fig le procès était une farce.

farcical /'fɑːsɪkl/ *adj* ridicule.

far-distant /ˌfɑː'dɪstənt/ *adj* [*land, mountains, region*] lointain; **in the ~ future** dans un lointain futur.

fare /feə(r)/ **I** *n* **1** (cost of travelling) (on bus, underground) prix *m* du ticket or du billet; (on

train, plane) prix du billet; **air/train/bus ~** prix d'un billet d'avion/de train/d'autobus; **taxi ~** prix *m* de la course; **child/adult ~** tarif *m* enfants/adultes; **half/full ~** demi-/plein tarif *m*; **return ~** prix *m* d'un aller-retour; **~s are going up** les tarifs augmentent; **the ~ to Piccadilly (on the underground) is 80p** le prix du ticket (de métro) pour Piccadilly est 80 pence; **he paid my (air) ~ to Tokyo** il a payé mon billet (d'avion) pour Tokyo; **how much is the ~ to London by train?** quel est le prix du billet de train pour Londres?; **I haven't got the ~ for the bus** je n'ai pas assez pour (acheter) un ticket d'autobus; **'please have the correct ~ ready'** 'les passagers sont priés d'avoir la monnaie exacte'; **2** (taxi passenger) client/-e *m/f* (d'un taxi); **3†** (food) nourriture *f*; **plain ~** nourriture simple; **hospital/prison ~** régime *m* d'hôpital/de prison; **bill of ~** menu *m*.
II *vi* **1** (get on) **how did you ~?** comment ça s'est passé?; **we ~d badly/well** les choses se sont mal/bien passées pour nous; **the team ~d well in the final** l'équipe s'est bien comportée dans la finale; **2** (progress) [*economy, industry, political party*] se porter; **the company is faring well despite the recession** la société se porte bien malgré la récession.

far: **Far East** *pr n* Extrême-Orient *m*; **Far Eastern** *adj* [*affairs, influence, markets*] de l'Extrême-Orient.

fare: **~ dodger** *n* voyageur/-euse *m/f* sans billet; **~-paying passenger** *n* passager/-ère *m/f* muni/-e d'un billet; **~ stage** *n* Transp section *f*.

fare-thee-well /ˌfeəðiːˈwel/: **to a fare-thee-well** *adv phr* US **1** (perfectly) à la perfection; **2** (very hard) [*thrash*] très sévèrement.

farewell /ˌfeəˈwel/ **I** *n, excl* adieu *m*; **to say one's ~s** faire ses adieux.
II *modif* [*party, gift, speech*] d'adieu.

far-fetched /ˌfɑːˈfetʃt/ *adj* tiré par les cheveux○.

far-flung /ˌfɑːˈflʌŋ/ *adj* **1** (remote) [*area, country, outpost*] lointain; **2** (widely distributed) [*countries, towns, regions etc*] éloignés les uns des autres; [*network*] étendu.

farinaceous /ˌfærɪˈneɪʃəs/ *adj* féculent.

farm /fɑːm/ **I** *n* ferme *f*; **chicken/pig/sheep ~** élevage *m* de poulets/de porcs/de moutons; **to work on a ~** travailler sur une ferme.
II *modif* [*building, animal*] de ferme.
III *vtr* cultiver, exploiter [*land*].
IV *vi* être fermier.
V **farmed** *pp adj* [*fish*] élevé dans une pisciculture.
■ **farm out**: ¶ **~ out [sth]** sous-traiter [*work*] (**to** à); ¶ **~ [sb] out 1** confier [*child, pupil, guest*] (**to** à); **2** US Sport *envoyer un joueur de baseball à une équipe locale*.

farm club *n* US Sport équipe *f* locale de baseball.

farmer /ˈfɑːmə(r)/ **▶1692|** *n* (in general) fermier *m*; (in official terminology) agriculteur *m*; (arable) cultivateur *m*; **chicken/pig/sheep ~** éleveur *m* de poulets/de porcs/de moutons; **~'s wife** fermière *f*.

farm: **~ gate price** *n* prix *m* reçu par les producteurs; **~ hand ▶1692|** *n* = **farm worker**.

farmhouse /ˈfɑːmhaʊs/ *n* (where farmer lives) habitation *f* du fermier; (house in country) ferme *f*.

farmhouse loaf *n* GB ≈ pain *m* de campagne.

farming /ˈfɑːmɪŋ/ **I** *n* **1** (profession) agriculture *f*; **2** (of area, land) exploitation *f*; **chicken/pig/sheep ~** élevage *m* de poulets/de porcs/de moutons.
II *modif* [*community*] rural; [*method*] de culture; [*subsidy*] à l'agriculture.

farm: **~ labourer** *n* = **farm worker**; **~land** *n* (for cultivation) terres *fpl* arables; (under cultivation) cultures *fpl*; **~ produce** *n* produits *mpl* de la ferme; **~ shop** *n* magasin *m* attaché à une ferme (*qui distribue directement les produits de celle-ci*); **~stead†** *n* ferme *f*; **~ worker ▶1692|** *n* ouvrier/-ière *m/f* agricole.

farmyard /ˈfɑːmjɑːd/ *n* cour *f* de ferme.

farmyard chicken *n* poulet *m* de basse-cour.

Faroes /ˈfeərəʊz/ **▶1381|** (also **Faroe Islands**) *pr npl* **the ~** les îles *fpl* Féroé.

far-off /ˈfɑːrɒf/ *adj* lointain.

far out○ **I** *adj* (modern) d'avant-garde.
II *excl* (great) super○!

farrago /fəˈrɑːgəʊ/ *n* ramassis *m*.

far-reaching /ˌfɑːˈriːtʃɪŋ/ *adj* [*effect, implication*] considérable; [*change, reform*] radical; [*investigation*] approfondi; [*programme, plan, proposal*] d'une portée considérable.

farrier /ˈfærɪə(r)/ *n* GB maréchal-ferrant *m*.

farrow /ˈfærəʊ/ **I** *n* portée *f*.
II *vi* mettre bas.

far-seeing /ˌfɑːˈsiːɪŋ/ *adj* ▶ **far-sighted**.

far-sighted /ˌfɑːˈsaɪtɪd/ *adj* **1** (prudent) [*person, policy, view, idea*] avisé; **2** US Med [*person*] presbyte.

fart◑ /fɑːt/ **I** *n* **1** (wind) pet◑ *m*; **2** (stupid person) **you silly old ~!** espèce de vieux schnoque○!
II *vi* péter◑.
■ **fart about**◑, **fart around**◑ **1** (fool about) faire l'andouille○; **2** (do nothing) traînasser○.

farther /ˈfɑːðə(r)/ (*comparative of* **far**) **I** *adv* ▶ **further I** 1, 2.
II *adj* ▶ **further II** 2.

■ Note Au sens littéral on préférera *farther* et au sens figuré *further*.

farthest /ˈfɑːðɪst/ *adj, adv* (*superl of* **far**) ▶ **furthest**.

■ Note Au sens littéral on préférera *farthest* et au sens figuré *furthest*.

farthing /ˈfɑːðɪŋ/ *n* GB Hist *ancienne pièce de très petite valeur*; **I haven't got a ~**○ je n'ai pas le sou.

FAS *n*: *abrév* ▶ **foetal alcohol syndrome**.

fascia /ˈfeɪʃə/ *n* **1** GB Aut (dashboard) tableau *m* de bord; **2** GB (over shop) panneau *m*; **3** Zool, Bot bande *f*; **4** Anat fascia *m*.

fascicle /ˈfæsɪkl/ *n* **1** Anat, Bot faisceau *m*; **2** (also **fascicule**) Print fascicule *m*.

fascinate /ˈfæsɪneɪt/ *vtr* **1** (interest) passionner; (stronger) fasciner; **2** (petrify) [*snake etc*] hypnotiser.

fascinated /ˈfæsɪneɪtɪd/ *adj* (by spectacle) captivé (**by** par); (by person) fasciné (**by** par); (by subject) passionné (**by** par).

fascinating /ˈfæsɪneɪtɪŋ/ *adj* [*book, discussion*] passionnant; [*person*] fascinant.

fascination /ˌfæsɪˈneɪʃn/ *n* **1** (interest) passion *f* (**with, for** pour); **in ~** captivé; (stronger) fasciné; **2** (power) (pouvoir *m* de) fascination *f*; **this subject has** ou **holds a great ~ for me** ce sujet me passionne.

fascism /ˈfæʃɪzəm/ *n* fascisme *m*.

fascist /ˈfæʃɪst/ *n, adj* fasciste (*mf*) also pej.

fashion /ˈfæʃn/ **I** *n* **1** (manner) façon *f*, manière *f*; **in my own ~** à ma manière; **in the Chinese/French ~** à la chinoise/française; **I can swim/cook after a ~** je nage/cuisine plus ou moins bien; **2** (vogue, trend) mode *f*; **in ~** à la mode; **out of ~** démodé; **to come into ~** devenir à la mode; **to go out of ~** se démoder, passer de mode; **the ~ for mini-skirts** la mode or la vogue des mini-jupes; **the latest ~** la dernière mode; **the ~ is for long coats this winter** les manteaux longs sont à la mode or sont en vogue cet hiver; **to be a slave to ~** être l'esclave de la mode; **to start a ~** lancer une mode; **to be all the ~** faire fureur; **to set the ~** donner le ton.
II *modif* [*accessory*] de mode; [*jewellery, tights*] fantaisie *inv*; **to make a ~ statement** essayer de lancer une mode.
III **fashions** *npl* **ladies' ~s** vêtements *mpl* pour femmes; **Paris/1930s ~s** la mode parisienne/des années 30.
IV *vtr* **1** (mould) façonner [*clay, wood*] (**into** en); **2** (make) fabriquer [*artefact*] (**out of, from** de).

fashionable /ˈfæʃnəbl/ *adj* [*colour, garment, name, style*] à la mode (**among, with** parmi); [*area, resort, restaurant*] chic *inv* (**among, with** parmi); [*opinion, pastime, topic*] en vogue (**among, with** parmi); **it's ~ to be cynical about these theories** il est de bon ton de se montrer cynique à propos de ces théories; **it's no longer ~ to do** cela ne se fait plus de faire.

fashionably /ˈfæʃnəblɪ/ *adv* à la mode.

fashion: **~ business** *n* industrie *f* de la mode; **~ buyer ▶1692|** *n* acheteur/-euse *m/f* (*d'un magasin de mode*); **~-conscious** *adj* [*person*] qui suit la mode.

fashion designer ▶1692| *n* modéliste *mf*; **the great ~s** les grands couturiers.

fashion: **~ editor ▶1692|** *n* Journ rédacteur/-trice *m/f* de mode; **~ house** *n* maison *f* de couture; **~-magazine** *n* journal *m* ou revue *f* de mode; **~ model ▶1692|** *n* mannequin *m*; **~ parade** *n* défilé *m* de mannequins; **~-plate** *n* lit, fig gravure *f* de mode; **~ show** *n* présentation *f* de collection; **~ victim** *n* victime *f* de la mode.

fast /fɑːst, US fæst/ **I** *n* (abstinence) jeûne *m*; **to break one's ~** rompre le jeûne.
II *adj* **1** (speedy) rapide; **a ~ train** un express; **a ~ time** Sport un bon temps; **to be a ~ walker/reader/writer** marcher/lire/écrire vite; **he's a ~ worker**○ gen ça ne traîne pas avec lui○; (in seduction) il ne perd pas son temps; **2** Sport [*court, pitch, track*] rapide; **3** (ahead of time) **my watch is ~** ma montre avance; **you're five minutes ~** ta montre avance de cinq minutes; **4** (immoral) péj [*person*] léger/-ère; **to lead a ~ life** faire les quatre cents coups○; **5** Phot [*film, exposure*] rapide; **6** (firm) (*jamais épith*) [*door, lid*] bien fermé; [*rope*] bien attaché; **to make sth ~** amarrer qch [*boat*]; attacher [*rope*]; **7** (loyal) [*friend*] fidèle; [*friendship*] solide; **8** (permanent) **~ dye** grand teint *m*; **is this dye ~?** est-ce que c'est du grand teint?
III *adv* **1** (rapidly) [*move, speak, write*] vite, rapidement; **how ~ can you knit/read?** est-ce que tu tricotes/lis vite?; **I need help ~** j'ai besoin d'aide tout de suite; **I ran as ~ as my legs would carry me** je me suis sauvé à toutes jambes; **these customs are ~ disappearing** ces coutumes se perdent; **education is ~ becoming a luxury** l'éducation va bientôt devenir un luxe; **the time is ~ approaching when I will do** dans peu de temps je ferai; **not so ~!** minute!○; **as ~ as I make the toast, he eats it** il mange les toasts à mesure que je les fais; **I couldn't get out of there ~ enough**○! je n'avais qu'une hâte, c'était de partir!; **2** (firmly) [*hold*] ferme; [*stuck*] bel et bien (*before pp*); [*shut*] bien; **to stand ~** tenir ferme; **to be ~ asleep** dormir d'un profond sommeil.
IV **fast by** *adv phr* littér tout à côté de.
V *vi* (abstain from food) jeûner.
IDIOMS **to pull a ~ one on sb** rouler qn○; **he pulled a ~ one on me** je me suis fait rouler○ or avoir; **to play ~ and loose** faire les quatre cents coups○; **to play ~ and loose with sb** traiter qn à la légère.

fast: **~back** *n* GB Aut voiture *f* à l'arrière profilé; **~ breeder reactor** *n* Nucl surgénérateur *m*; **~ day** *n* Relig jour *m* maigre or de jeûne.

fasten /ˈfɑːsn, US ˈfæsn/ **I** *vtr* **1** (close) fermer [*bolt, lid, case*]; attacher [*belt, sandals, necklace*]; boutonner [*coat*]; boucler [*buckle*]; **2** (attach) fixer [*notice, shelf*] (**to** à; **onto** sur); attacher [*lead, rope*] (**to** à); **to ~**

the ends together attacher les bouts ensemble; **to ~ onto sb** s'attacher or s'accrocher○ à qn; **3** fig (fix) **his eyes ~ed on me** son regard s'est fixé sur moi; **to ~ the blame/responsibility on** rejeter la faute/responsabilité sur.
II *vi* [*box*] se fermer; [*necklace, belt, skirt*] s'attacher; **to ~ at the back/side** s'attacher dans le dos/sur le côté.
■ **fasten down**: **~ down [sth]**, **~ [sth] down** fermer [*hatch*, *lid*].
■ **fasten on**: ¶ **~ on** [*lid, handle*] s'attacher; ¶ **~ [sth] on** attacher [*lid, handle*]; ¶ **~ on [sth]** fig se mettre [qch] dans la tête [*idea*]; **he ~ed on the idea of escaping** il s'est mis dans la tête de s'évader.
■ **fasten up**: **~ up [sth]**, **~ [sth] up** fermer [*case*]; attacher [*shoe*]; boutonner [*coat*].

fastener /ˈfɑːsnə(r)/, US ˈfæsnə(r)/ *n* **1** Sewing, Tech (hook) agrafe *f*; **2** (tie) attache *f*; (clasp) fermoir *m*; **snap ~** (fermoir *m* à) pression *f*.

fastening /ˈfɑːsnɪŋ, US ˈfæsnɪŋ/ **I** *n* (hook) agrafe *f*; (tie) attache *f*; (clasp) fermoir *m*.
II -fastening (*dans composés*) **front-/back-~** qui s'attache par devant/derrière (*after n*).

fast-flowing /ˌfɑːstˈfləʊɪŋ, US ˌfæst-/ *adj* au cours *m* rapide (*after n*).

fast food /ˌfɑːstˈfuːd, US ˌfæst-/ **I** *n* prêt-à-manger *m*, nourriture *f* de fast-food.
II *modif* [*chain*] de restauration rapide ou de fast-food; [*outlet, counter*] de fast-food; [*industry*] de la restauration rapide or du fast-food; **a ~ restaurant** un fast-food.

fast-forward /ˌfɑːstˈfɔːwəd, US ˌfæst-/ **I** *n* Audio avance *f* rapide.
II *modif* [*key, button*] d'avance rapide (*after n*).
III *vtr* faire avancer rapidement.

fast-growing /ˌfɑːstˈgrəʊɪŋ, US ˌfæst-/ *adj* en pleine expansion.

fastidious /fæˈstɪdɪəs/ *adj* **1** (extremely careful) [*person*] méticuleux/-euse (**about** sur); **2** (easily disgusted) [*person*] délicat, vite dégoûté.

fastidiously /fæˈstɪdɪəslɪ/ *adv* [*work*] méticuleusement; [*tidy*] extrêmement; [*dressed*] avec beaucoup de soin.

fastidiousness /fæˈstɪdɪəsnɪs/ *n* méticulosité *f*.

fastigiate /fæˈstɪdʒət/ *adj* fastigié.

fasting /ˈfɑːstɪŋ, US ˈfæstɪŋ/ *n* jeûne *m*.

fast lane /ˈfɑːstleɪn, US ˈfæst-/ *n* Aut voie *f* de dépassement; **to live in the ~** fig vivre à cent à l'heure○; **to enjoy life in the ~** fig aimer la vie à cent à l'heure○.

fast: **~ living** *n* débauche *f*; **~-moving** *adj* rapide.

fastness /ˈfɑːstnɪs, US ˈfæst-/ *n* **1** (speed) rapidité *f*; **2** (of dye) solidité *f*; **3** (*pl* **-es**) (stronghold) litér forteresse *f*.

fast rewind *n* Audio rembobinage *m* rapide.

fast-talk○ /ˌfɑːstˈtɔːk, US ˌfæst-/ *vtr* baratiner○ [*person*]; **to ~ sb into doing** baratiner○ qn pour qu'il fasse.

fast-talking○ /ˌfɑːstˈtɔːkɪŋ, US ˌfæst-/ *adj* [*salesperson*] baratineur/-euse○.

fast-track /ˈfɑːsttræk, US ˈfæst-/ **I** *n* promotion *f* accélérée; **to apply for the ~** vouloir entrer dans la promotion accélérée.
II *modif* [*scheme, plan*] accéléré; [*place*] à promotion accélérée.
III /ˌfɑːstˈtræk, US ˌfæst-/ *vtr* former [qn] de façon accélérée [*employee*].

fat /fæt/ **I** *n* **1** (in diet) matières *fpl* grasses; **~ intake** consommation *f* de matières grasses; **animal/vegetable ~s** graisses *fpl* animales/végétales; **2** (on meat) gras *m*; **you can leave the ~** tu peux laisser le gras; **3** (for cooking) gen matière *f* grasse; (from meat) graisse *f*; **beef/mutton/goose ~** graisse de bœuf/de mouton/d'oie; **fried in ~** frit dans de la matière grasse; **4** (in body) graisse *f*; **body ~** tissu adipeux; **to lay down reserves of ~** accumuler des réserves de graisse; **to run to ~** prendre du poids; **5** Chem corps *m* gras.
II *adj* **1** (overweight) [*person, animal, body*] gros/grosse; [*cheek, tummy, bottom*] rebondi; [*thigh, arm, finger*] dodu; **to get ~** grossir; **to get ~ on chocolates** grossir à force de manger des chocolats; **to get** ou **grow ~ on sth** fig s'engraisser sur qch; **2** (full, swollen) [*wallet, envelope*] rebondi; [*file, novel, magazine*] épais/épaisse; [*cushion*] moelleux/-euse; [*fruit, peapod*] gros/grosse; **3** (remunerative) [*profit, cheque, fee*] gros/grosse; **a nice ~ job** un travail grassement payé; **4** (fertile) [*land, valley, year*] fertile; **5** (worthwhile) [*rôle*] beau/belle; **6** (fatty) [*meat, bacon*] gras/grasse; **7**○ iron (not much) **that's a ~ lot of good!** ça me/nous etc rend drôlement service!○ iron; **you're a ~ lot of use!** tu es vraiment d'un grand secours! iron; **a ~ lot you know!/you care!** pour ce que tu en sais!/que ça t'intéresse○!; **'will she go?'—'~ chance!'** 'elle ira?'—'tu crois au père Noël○!'
IDIOMS **the ~'s in the fire**○ ça va faire des étincelles○; **to be in ~ city**○ US être plein aux as○; **to live off the ~ of the land** vivre grassement.

fatal /ˈfeɪtl/ *adj* **1** (lethal) [*accident, injury, blow, shot, toxin*] mortel/-elle (**to** pour); [*delay*] fatal (**to** pour); **2** (disastrous) [*weakness, flaw, mistake*] fatal; [*decision*] funeste; [*day, hour*] fatidique; **to be ~ to sb/sth** porter un coup fatal à qn/qch; **it would be ~ to do** ce serait une grave erreur de faire.

fatalism /ˈfeɪtəlɪzəm/ *n* fatalisme *m*.

fatalist /ˈfeɪtəlɪst/ *n* fataliste *mf*.

fatalistic /ˌfeɪtəˈlɪstɪk/ *adj* fataliste.

fatalistically /ˌfeɪtəˈlɪstɪklɪ/ *adv* [*react, accept*] avec fatalisme.

fatality /fəˈtælətɪ/ *n* **1** (person killed) mort *m*; **there have been no fatalities** il n'y a pas eu de morts; **road fatalities** accidents *mpl* mortels de la route; **2** (deadliness) caractère *m* mortel; **3** (fate) fatalité *f*.

fatally /ˈfeɪtəlɪ/ *adv* **1** [*injured, wounded*] mortellement; **to be ~ ill** être condamné; **2** fig [*flawed, compromised*] irrémédiablement.

fat: **~-ass**● *n* US péj gros lard○ *m*, grosse truie○ *f*; **~back** *n* US lard *m* maigre; **~ cat**○ *n* huile○ *f*.

fate /feɪt/ *n* **1** (controlling power) (also **the ~s**) sort *m*; **~ was on my side/against me** le sort était avec moi/contre moi; **a (cruel) twist of ~** un (cruel) caprice du sort; **to tempt ~** tenter le sort; **2** (death) mort *f*; **to meet a sad ~** finir tristement; **3** (destiny) sort *m*; **to be resigned/left to one's ~** être résigné/abandonné à son sort; **his ~ is sealed** son sort est scellé; **a ~ worse than death** hum un sort pire que la mort; **4** Mythol **the Fates** les Parques *fpl*.

fated /ˈfeɪtɪd/ *adj* **1** (destined) **to be ~ to do** être destiné à faire; **2** (doomed) voué (**to do** à faire); **3** (decreed by fate) prédestiné.

fateful /ˈfeɪtfl/ *adj* [*decision, event, words*] fatal; [*day*] fatidique.

fat: **~ farm**○ *n* clinique *f* d'amaigrissement; **~-free** *adj* sans matières grasses; **~head**○ *n* péj débile○ *mf*; **~-headed**○ *adj* péj débile○.

father /ˈfɑːðə(r)/ **I** *n* **1** (parent) père *m*; **to be like a ~ to sb** être un vrai père pour qn; **from ~ to son** de père en fils; **2** (ancestor) père *m*, ancêtre *m*; **land of our ~s** patrie de nos pères or aïeux; **3** (originator) père *m*; **the ~ of the motor car/of English theatre** le père de l'automobile/du théâtre anglais.
II *vtr* engendrer [*child*].
IDIOMS **like ~ like son** tel père tel fils; **the ~ and mother of a row**○ une prise de bec maison○.

Father /ˈfɑːðə(r)/ ▶ **1268** *n* **1** Relig (God) Père *m*; **the Our ~** (prayer) le Notre Père; **God the ~** Dieu le Père; **2** (title for priest) père *m*; **~ Smith** le père Smith; **thank you, ~** merci, mon père.

Father Christmas GB *n* père *m* Noël.

father confessor *n* Relig confesseur *m*; fig (confidant) directeur *m* de conscience.

father figure *n* figure *f* du père; **he's a ~ figure to her** il est la figure du père pour elle.

fatherhood /ˈfɑːðəhʊd/ *n* paternité *f*.

father: **~-in-law** *n* (*pl* **~s-in-law**) beau-père *m*; **~land** *n* patrie *f*.

fatherless /ˈfɑːðəlɪs/ *adj* sans père.

fatherly /ˈfɑːðəlɪ/ *adj* paternel/-elle.

father: **Father's Day** *n* fête *f* des pères; **Father Time** *n* le Temps *m*.

fathom /ˈfæðəm/ **I** *n* Meas Naut brasse *f* anglaise (= *1,83 m*).
II *vtr* **1** Meas Naut sonder; **2** (also GB **~ out**) (understand) comprendre.

fathomless /ˈfæðəmlɪs/ *adj* [*ocean, eyes*] insondable.

fatigue /fəˈtiːg/ **I** *n* **1** (of person) épuisement *m*; **muscle/mental ~** épuisement *m* musculaire/intellectuel; **battle ~** commotion *f*, état *m* de choc dû aux combats; **2** Tech **metal ~** fatigue *f* du métal; **3** US Mil corvée *f*.
II fatigues *npl* Mil **1** (uniform) treillis *m*; **camouflage ~s** tenue *f* de camouflage; **2** (duties) corvée *f*; **to be on ~s** être de corvée.
III *modif* Mil [*duty, detail, party*] de corvée.
IV *vtr* gen, Tech fatiguer [*person, metal*].
V fatigued *pp adj* épuisé.

fatiguing /fəˈtiːgɪŋ/ *adj* fatigant.

fatless /ˈfætlɪs/ *adj* sans matières grasses.

fatness /ˈfætnɪs/ *n* corpulence *f*.

fatso○ /ˈfætsəʊ/ *n* péj (man) gros lard○ *m*; (woman) grosse truie○ *f* pej.

fat: **~-soluble** *adj* soluble dans la graisse; **~stock** *n* GB animaux *mpl* de boucherie.

fatten /ˈfætn/ **I** *vtr* = **fatten up**.
II *vi* [*animal*] engraisser.
■ **fatten up**: **~ [sb/sth] up**, **~ up [sb/sth]** **1** engraisser [*animal*]; faire grossir [*person*]; **2** fig investir gros dans [*industry*].

fattening /ˈfætnɪŋ/ **I** *n* engraissement *m*.
II *adj* [*food, drink*] qui fait grossir (*after n*); **beer is very ~** la bière fait beaucoup grossir.

fatty /ˈfætɪ/ **I**○ *n* péj (man) gros lard○ *m*; (woman) grosse truie○ *f*.
II *adj* **1** [*tissue, deposit*] graisseux/-euse; **2** [*food, meat*] gras/grasse.

fatty: **~ acid** *n* acide *m* gras; **~ degeneration** *n* dégénérescence *f* graisseuse.

fatuity /fəˈtjuːətɪ, US -ˈtuːətɪ/ *n* (of person) fatuité *f*; (of remark) inanité *f*.

fatuous /ˈfætʃʊəs/ *adj* [*attempt, comment, decision, smile*] stupide; [*exercise, activity*] futile.

fatuousness /ˈfætʃʊəsnɪs/ *n* = **fatuity**.

faucet /ˈfɔːsɪt/ *n* US robinet *m*.

fault /fɔːlt/ **I** *n* **1** (flaw in system, wiring, machine, person) défaut *m* (**in** dans); (electrical failure, breakdown) panne *f*; **structural/design/software ~** défaut structurel/de conception/de logiciel; **my greatest ~** mon défaut principal; **for all his ~s** malgré tous ses défauts; **to be generous/scrupulous to a ~** être généreux/scrupuleux à l'excès; **2** (responsibility, guilt) faute *f*; **to be sb's ~**, **to be the ~ of sb** être (de) la faute de qn; **to be sb's ~ that** être à cause de qn que; **it's all your ~** c'est (de) ta faute; **it's my own ~** c'est de ma faute; **it's your own silly ~**○ c'est ta faute, idiot○; **it's not my ~** ce n'est pas (de) ma faute ; **it's hardly their ~** ce n'est vraiment pas (de) leur faute; **whose ~ was it?** à qui la faute?; **whose ~ will it be if we're late?** iron à qui devra-t-on d'être en retard?; **my ~ entirely** c'est ma faute, je l'avoue; **the ~ lies with him/the company** c'est lui/la compagnie qui est entièrement responsable; **through no ~ of**

his/her own indépendamment de lui/d'elle; **to be at ~** être en tort, être à blamer; **he's always finding ~** il trouve toujours quelque chose à redire; **3** Sport (call) faute!; **to serve a ~** faire une faute au service; **4** Geol faille *f*; **5** Jur faute *f*; **no-~ compensation** indemnisation *f* sans égard à la responsabilité; **no-~ divorce** divorce *m* à l'amiable; **no-~ insurance** US Aut assurance *f* avec indemnisation automatique de l'assuré.

II *vtr* prendre [qch/qn] en défaut; **you can't ~ her** on ne peut pas la prendre en défaut; **it cannot be ~ed** c'est irréprochable; **to ~ sb for sth** reprocher qch à qn; **to ~ sb for doing** reprocher à qn d'avoir fait.

fault-finding /ˈfɔːltfaɪndɪŋ/ **I** *n* **1** Tech (locating built-in flaw) localisation *f* du défaut; (locating breakdown) localisation *f* de la panne; **2** (of person) habitude *f* de tout critiquer.

II *adj* [*person*] qui critique tout; [*attitude*] négatif/-ive.

faultless /ˈfɔːltlɪs/ *adj* **1** [*performance, German, manners*] impeccable; [*taste*] irréprochable; **2** Equit [*round*] sans faute.

faultlessly /ˈfɔːltlɪslɪ/ *adv* de façon impeccable.

fault: **~ line** *n* (ligne *f* de) faille *f*; **~ plane** *n* plan *m* de faille.

faulty /ˈfɔːltɪ/ *adj* **1** [*wiring, car part, machine, product*] défectueux/-euse; **2** [*logic, policy, philosophy, argument*] erroné.

faun /fɔːn/ *n* faune *m*.

fauna /ˈfɔːnə/ *n* (*pl* **~s** ou **-ae**) faune *f*.

Faust /faʊst/ *pr n* Faust *m*.

Faustian /ˈfaʊstɪən/ *adj* faustien/-ienne.

faux pas /ˌfəʊ ˈpɑː/ *n* (*pl* **~**) sout impair *m*.

favour GB, **favor** US /ˈfeɪvə(r)/ **I** *n* **1** (approval) **to look with ~ on sb/sth**, **look on sb/sth with ~** approuver qn/qch; **to regard sb/sth with ~** considérer qn/qch avec bienveillance; **to win/lose ~ with sb ~** s'attirer/perdre les bonnes grâces de qn; **to find ~ with sb** trouver grâce aux yeux de qn; **to gain ~ with sb** remporter la faveur de qn; **to be out of ~ with sb** [*person*] ne plus être dans les bonnes grâces de qn; [*idea, fashion, method*] ne plus être en vogue auprès de qn; **to fall out of** ou **from ~ with sb** [*person*] tomber en disgrâce auprès de qn; **to fall** ou **go out of ~** [*idea, fashion, method*] passer de mode; **2** (kindness) service *m*; **to do sb a ~** rendre service à qn; **in return for all your ~s** en remerciement de tous les services que vous m'avez rendus; **they're not doing themselves any ~s** ils desservent leur (propre) cause (**by doing** en faisant); **do me a ~!** lit fais-moi plaisir!; (as prelude to rebuff) tu veux me faire plaisir?; (ironic) qu'est-ce que tu crois!; (in exasperation) et quoi encore!; **as a (special) ~** à titre de service exceptionnel; **she did it as a ~ to her boss** elle l'a fait pour rendre service à son chef; **to ask a ~ of sb**, **to ask sb a ~** demander un service à qn; **to owe sb a ~** avoir une dette envers qn; **you owe me a ~** tu me dois bien ça; **to return a ~** lit, **to return the ~** iron rendre la pareille (**by doing** en faisant); **3** (favouritism) **to show ~ to sb**, **to show sb ~** accorder un traitement de faveur à qn; **4** (advantage) **to be in sb's ~** [*situation*] être avantageux pour qn; [*financial rates, wind*] être favorable à qn; **to have sth in one's ~** avoir qch pour soi; **everything was in her ~** elle avait tout pour elle; **the plan has a lot in its ~** le projet présente beaucoup d'avantages; **if the case doesn't go in our ~** si nous n'obtenons pas gain de cause; **in your ~** [*money, balance*] à votre crédit; **5†** (small gift) petit cadeau *m*; **6** Hist (token) faveur *f*.

II favours *npl* euph (sexual) faveurs *fpl*.

III in favour of *prep phr* **1** (on the side of) en faveur de; **to be in ~ of sb/sth** être pour qn/qch; **to vote in ~ of sth** voter pour qch; **I'm in ~ of that** je suis pour; **to be in ~ of changing the law** être pour un changement de la loi; **to speak in ~ of** soutenir [*motion, idea, plan*]; **to speak in sb's ~** se prononcer en faveur de qn; **to come out in ~ of** exprimer son soutien à [*plan, person*]; **2** (to the advantage of) **to work** ou **be weighted in ~ of sb** avantager qn; **to decide in sb's ~** gen donner raison à qn; Jur donner gain de cause à qn; **3** (out of preference for) [*reject etc*] au profit de.

IV *vtr* **1** (prefer) être pour [*choice, method, solution, horse, team*]; préférer [*clothing, colour, date*]; être partisan de [*political party*]; **to ~ sb** gen montrer une préférence pour qn; (unfairly) accorder un traitement de faveur à qn; **I ~ closing the business** je suis pour la fermeture de l'entreprise; **2** (benefit) [*plans, circumstances*] favoriser; [*law, balance of power*] privilégier; **3** (approve of) être partisan de [*course of action*]; approuver [*proposal*]; **4** sout ou iron (honour) **to ~ sb with sth** faire à qn la faveur or l'honneur de qch.

V favoured *pp adj* **1** (most likely) [*course of action, date, plan, view*] privilégié; [*candidate*] favori/-ite; **2** (favourite) favori/-ite.

favourable GB, **favorable** US /ˈfeɪvərəbl/ *adj* **1** (good) [*conditions, impression, reaction, reply, time, position, weather*] favorable (**to** à); [*report, result, sign*] bon/bonne (*before n*); **to have a ~ reception** être bien reçu; **in a ~ light** sous un jour favorable; **conditions are ~ to setting up a business** les conditions financières sont favorables à la création d'une entreprise; **2** (in agreement) **to be ~** être d'accord (**to sth** avec qch); **my father is not ~ to my going alone** mon père n'est pas d'accord pour que j'y aille toute seule.

favourably GB, **favorably** US /ˈfeɪvərəblɪ/ *adv* [*speak, write*] en termes favorables; [*look on, consider*] d'un œil favorable; [*impress, review*] favorablement; **to be ~ situated** être bien situé; **to be ~ disposed to sb/to sth** être bien disposé à l'égard de qn/en ce qui concerne qch; **to be ~ received** être accueilli favorablement; **to compare ~ with sth** soutenir la comparaison avec qch.

favourite GB, **favorite** US /ˈfeɪvərɪt/ **I** *n* **1** [*person, activity, thing*] préféré/-e *m/f*; **a ~ of his** un de ses préférés; **to be a great ~ with sb** avoir beaucoup de succès auprès de qn; **my ~!** c'est ce que je préfère!; **2** Sport, Turf favori/-ite *m/f*.

II *adj* préféré, favori/-ite; **his ~ way of relaxing** ce qu'il préfère faire pour se détendre.

favouritism GB, **favoritism** US /ˈfeɪvərɪtɪzəm/ *n* favoritisme *m*.

fawn /fɔːn/ **▶1104** **I** *n* **1** Zool faon *m*; **2** (colour) beige *m* foncé.

II *adj* beige foncé.

III *vi* **to ~ on sb** [*dog*] faire la fête à qn; [*person*] péj flagorner qn.

fawning /ˈfɔːnɪŋ/ *adj* servile.

fax /fæks/ **I** *n* (*pl* **~es**) télécopie *f*, fax *m*.

II *vtr* télécopier, faxer [*document*]; envoyer une télécopie or un fax à [*person*].

fax: **~ directory** *n* annuaire *m* de la télécopie; **~ machine** *n* télécopieur *m*, fax *m*; **~ message** *n* télécopie *f*, fax *m*; **~ number** *n* numéro *m* de télécopie or de fax.

faze○ /feɪz/ *vtr* dérouter.

FBI *n* US (*abrév* = **Federal Bureau of Investigation**) Police *f* judiciaire fédérale.

FCA *n* US (*abrév* = **Farm Credit Administration**) *organisme d'État chargé de la gestion du crédit des agriculteurs.*

FCC *n* US (*abrév* = **Federal Communications Commission**) *organisme gouvernemental chargé des télécommunications.*

FCO *n* GB (*abrév* = **Foreign and Commonwealth Office**) ministère *m* des Affaires étrangères et du Commonwealth.

FDA *n* US (*abrév* = **Food and Drug Administration**) *organisme gouvernemental de contrôle pharmaceutique et alimentaire.*

fealty‡ /ˈfiːəltɪ/ *n* fidélité *f*; **to take an oath of ~** faire serment de fidélité.

fear /fɪə(r)/ **I** *n* **1** (dread, fright) peur *f*; **~ of death** peur de la mort; **I couldn't move for** ou **from ~** j'étais paralysé par la peur; **he accepted out of ~** c'est la peur qui l'a fait accepter; **have no ~!** littér ou hum n'ayez pas peur!; **to live in ~** vivre dans la peur; **to live** ou **go in ~ of one's life** craindre pour sa vie; **he lives in ~ of being found out** ou **that he will be found out** il vit dans la crainte perpétuelle d'être découvert; **for ~ of doing** de peur de faire; **for ~ that** de peur que (+ *subj*); **I kept quiet for ~ of waking them/that they would wake up** j'ai fait le moins de bruit possible de peur de les réveiller/de peur qu'ils (ne) se réveillent; **for ~ of death/punishment** de peur de mourir/d'être puni; **to have no ~ of sth** ne pas avoir peur de qch; **to have no ~ that** ne pas avoir peur que (+ *subj*); **~ of God** crainte *f* de Dieu; **the news struck ~ into his heart** littér la nouvelle l'a rempli d'effroi; **2** (worry, apprehension) crainte *f* (**for** pour); **their ~s for their son/the future** leurs craintes pour leur fils/pour l'avenir; **my ~s proved groundless** mes craintes se sont révélées injustifiées; **my worst ~s were confirmed (when...)** mes pires craintes se sont trouvées confirmées (quand...); **my ~s about the company collapsing** ou **that the company would collapse** mes craintes que la société (ne) fasse faillite; **~s are growing for sb** on craint de plus en plus pour qn; **~s are growing that his life may be in danger** on craint de plus en plus que sa vie (ne) soit en danger; **(grave) ~s have arisen that** on craint (fort) que; **I told him my ~s that** je lui ai dit que je craignais que (+ *subj*); **the future/the operation holds no ~s for her** elle n'a pas peur de l'avenir/de l'opération; **3** (possibility) **there's not much ~ of sb('s) doing** il n'y a guère de danger que qn fasse; **there's no ~ of him** ou **his being late** il n'y a pas de danger qu'il soit en retard; **there's no ~ of that happening** il n'y a pas de danger que cela arrive; **no ~!** sûrement pas!

II *vtr* **1** (be afraid of) craindre; **to ~ to do** craindre de faire; **experts ~ a crisis if the situation continues to worsen** les experts craignent une crise si la situation continue à empirer; **to ~ that** craindre que (+ *subj*); **she ~ed that her proposals might not be accepted** elle craignait que ses propositions ne soient pas acceptées; **I ~ (that) she may be dead** j'ai (bien) peur or je crains qu'elle (ne) soit morte; **it is ~ed (that)** on craint que (+ *subj*); **it is ~ed (that) the recession may get worse** on craint que la récession empire or n'empire; **the substance is ~ed to cause cancer** on craint que la substance ne provoque le cancer; **20 people are ~ed to have died** ou **are ~ed dead in the accident** on craint que 20 personnes ne soient mortes dans l'accident; **a ruler who was greatly ~ed** un chef qui inspirait la crainte; **she's a woman to be ~ed** c'est une femme redoutable; **to ~ the worst** craindre le pire, s'attendre au pire; **2** (think) **I ~ not** je crains (bien) que non; **I ~ so** (to positive question) je crains bien que oui; (to negative question) j'ai bien peur que si; **I ~ I'm late/it's raining** j'ai bien peur d'être en retard/qu'il (ne) pleuve.

III *vi* **to ~ for sth/sb** craindre pour qch/qn; **I ~ for her safety/life** je crains pour sa sécurité/vie; **never ~!** ne craignez rien, n'ayez crainte!

IDIOMS **without ~ or favour** de façon impartiale; **in ~ and trembling** tremblant de peur.

fearful /ˈfɪəfl/ *adj* **1** (afraid) craintif/-ive; **to be ~** avoir peur; **to be ~ of sth/of doing** avoir peur de qch/de faire; **to be ~ for sb** craindre pour qn; **2** (dreadful) [*noise, sight*] affreux/-euse; [*rage, argument,* *anxiety, heat*] terrible; **it's a ~ nuisance** c'est terriblement or affreusement gênant; **he's a ~ bore** il est terriblement ennuyeux.

fearfully /ˈfɪəfəlɪ/ *adv* **1** (timidly) craintivement; **2** (dreadfully) [*cold, hot, complicated, old-fashioned*] terriblement; [*nice, discreet*] extrêmement; [*expensive*] horriblement.

fearless /ˈfɪəlɪs/ *adj* sans peur, intrépide.

fearlessly /ˈfɪəlɪslɪ/ *adv* sans peur, sans la moindre frayeur.

fearlessness /ˈfɪəlɪsnɪs/ *n* intrépidité *f*.

fearsome /ˈfɪəsəm/ *adj* **1** (frightening) effrayant; **2** (frightful) effroyable; **3** (formidable) redoutable.

feasibility /ˌfiːzəˈbɪlətɪ/ *n* **1** (of idea, plan, proposal) faisabilité *f* (**of** de); **the ~ of doing** la possibilité de faire; **2** (of claim, story) vraisemblance *f* (**of** de).

feasibility study *n* étude *f* de faisabilité.

feasible /ˈfiːzəbl/ *adj* **1** (possible) [*project*] réalisable; **it is/was ~ that** il est/était possible que (+ *subj*); **to be ~ to do sth** être possible de faire qch; **2** [*excuse, explanation*] plausible.

feast /fiːst/ **I** *n* **1** (sumptuous meal) festin *m*; (formal, celebratory) banquet *m*; **wedding ~** banquet de mariage; **midnight ~** festin nocturne (*organisé en cachette*); **2** fig (for eyes, senses) régal *m* (**to, for** pour); **there will be a ~ of music** il y aura de la musique à profusion; **3** Relig fête *f*; **~ day** jour *m* de fête.

II *vtr* **1** fig **to ~ one's eyes on sth** se délecter à regarder qch; **2** lit régaler [*person*] (**on, with** de).

III *vi* se régaler (**on** de).

IDIOMS **enough is as good as a ~** il ne faut pas abuser des bonnes choses.

feasting /ˈfiːstɪŋ/ *n* festoiement *m*.

feat /fiːt/ *n* **1** (achievement) exploit *m*; **it was no mean ~ to do** cela n'a pas été une mince affaire de faire; **2 a ~ of** une prouesse de [*technology, surgery etc*].

feather /ˈfeðə(r)/ **I** *n* plume *f*.

II *modif* [*boa, cushion, mattress*] de plumes.

III *vtr* **1** (in rowing) plumer [*blade*]; **2** Aviat mettre [qch] en drapeau.

IV feathered *pp adj* [*garment*] à plumes; **our ~ed friends** nos amis les oiseaux.

IDIOMS **as light as a ~** léger comme une plume; **birds of a ~** (**flock together**) Prov qui se ressemble s'assemble Prov; **in full ~** en excellente forme; **that'll make the ~s fly** ils vont se voler dans les plumes; **that's a ~ in his cap** c'est un bon point pour lui; **you could have knocked me down with a ~** j'en avais le souffle coupé.

feather bed I *n* lit *m* de plumes.

II feather-bed *vi* Ind réduire la productivité pour éviter le chômage.

feather: **~-bedding** *n* Ind réduction *f* de la productivité (*d'une industrie*) pour éviter le chômage; **~brain** *n* écervelé/-e *m/f*; **~-brained** *adj* écervelé; **~ cut** *n* coupe *f* courte féminine; **~ duster** *n* plumeau *m*.

featherstitch /ˈfeðəstɪtʃ/ **I** *n* point *m* d'épine.

II *vtr* coudre [qch] au point d'épine.

featherweight /ˈfeðəweɪt/ **I** *n* poids *m* plume.

II *modif* [*champion, title*] (des) poids plume.

feathery /ˈfeðərɪ/ *adj* [*touch*] doux/douce comme de la plume; [*snowflake*] duveteux/-euse; [*leaf, shape*] plumeux/-euse.

feature /ˈfiːtʃə(r)/ **I** *n* **1** (distinctive characteristic) trait *m*, caractéristique *f*; **a ~ of those times** une caractéristique de cette époque; **a stylistic/unique ~ of sth** un trait stylistique/exceptionnel de qch; **to become a permanent ~** devenir un trait permanent; **to make a ~ of sth** mettre qch en valeur; **2** (aspect) aspect *m*, côté *m*; **the plan has some good ~s** le plan a de bons côtés; **a worrying ~ of the incident** un aspect inquiétant de l'incident; **to have no redeeming ~s** n'avoir rien pour soi; **3** (of car, computer, product) accessoire *m*; **optional ~s** accessoires en option; **built-in safety ~s** équipement *m* de sécurité intégré; **4** (of face) trait *m*; **with sharp/coarse ~s** aux traits anguleux/grossiers; **his eyes are his best ~** ce qu'il a de mieux, ce sont ses yeux; **5** (film) long métrage *m*, film *m*; **a double ~** une double séance; **6** Journ article *m* de fond (**on** sur); **to have** ou **do a ~ on** publier un article de fond sur; **she does a ~ in the Times** elle est chroniqueuse au 'Times'; **7** TV, Radio reportage *m* (**on** sur); **8** Ling trait *m*.

II -featured (*dans composés*) **coarse-/sharp-/fine-~d** aux traits grossiers/anguleux/fins.

III *vtr* **1** (present) [*film, magazine, concert, event*] présenter [*story, photo, place, star, work*]; [*advert, poster*] représenter, montrer [*person, scene*]; **to be ~d in sth/on the cover of sth** figurer dans qch/sur la couverture de qch; **2** (highlight) [*car, computer, new model*] être équipé de [*facility, accessory*]; **3**○ US (imagine) se figurer.

IV *vi* **1** (figure) figurer; **Shakespeare ~s prominently** Shakespeare figure à la place d'honneur; **2** TV, Cin [*performer*] jouer (**in, on** dans).

feature: **~ article** *n* article *m* de fond; **~ film** *n* long métrage *m*; **~-length** *adj* long métrage *inv*.

featureless /ˈfiːtʃəlɪs/ *adj* sans caractère.

feature writer ▶ **1692** *n* chroniqueur/-euse *m/f*.

Feb /feb/ *n*: *abrév écrite* = **February**.

febrifuge /ˈfebrɪfjuːdʒ/ *n, adj* fébrifuge (*m*).

febrile /ˈfiːbraɪl/ *adj* **1** gen [*condition, activity*] fébrile; **2** Med [*patient*] fiévreux/-euse; [*convulsion*] hyperpyrétique.

February /ˈfebrʊərɪ, US -ʊrɪ/ ▶ **1472** *n* février *m*.

fecal *adj* US = **faecal**.

feces *npl* US = **faeces**.

feckless /ˈfeklɪs/ *adj* **1** (improvident) irresponsable; **2** (helpless) incapable; **3** (inept) maladroit.

fecund /ˈfiːkənd, ˈfekənd/ *adj* littér (all contexts) fécond.

fecundity /fɪˈkʌndətɪ/ *n* littér fécondité *f*.

fed /fed/ *prét, pp* ▶ **feed**.

Fed /fed/ **1**○ US agent *m* fédéral, fédé○ *m*; **2** *abrév* ▶ **federal, federation**; **3** *abrév* ▶ **Federal Reserve Board**.

federal /ˈfedərəl/ **I Federal** *pr n* US **1** Hist (party supporter) Fédéraliste *mf*; (soldier) nordiste *m*; **2** = **Fed**○**1**.

II *adj* Admin, Pol [*court, judge, police*] fédéral; [*architecture*] US nordiste; **the ~ government** US le gouvernement fédéral.

IDIOMS **to make a ~ case out of sth** US faire toute une histoire de qch○.

federal: **Federal Communications Commission** *n* US organisme *m* exerçant un contrôle sur l'audiovisuel; **Federal Energy Regulating** *n* US Commission *f* nationale de contrôle de l'énergie; **~ holiday** *n* US jour *m* férié; **Federal Housing Administration, FHA** *n* mission *f* de contrôle des prêts au logement.

federalism /ˈfedərəlɪzəm/ *n* fédéralisme *m*.

federalist /ˈfedərəlɪst/ *n, adj* fédéraliste (*mf*).

Federal Land Bank *n* US *banque fédérale accordant des prêts aux agriculteurs*.

federally /ˈfedərəlɪ/ *adv* **1** [*elect, govern*] à un niveau fédéral; **2** US [*funded, built*] par le gouvernement fédéral.

federal: **Federal Republic of Germany** *n* République *f* fédérale d'Allemagne; **Federal Reserve Bank** *n* US banque *f* régionale des États-Unis; **Federal Reserve Board** *n* US (anciennement) = **Federal Reserve System**; **Federal Reserve System** *n* US *système bancaire aux États-Unis contrôlant les 12 banques régionales*; **Federal Trade Commission, FTC** *n* US cf Direction *f* générale de la concurrence, de la consommation et de la répression des fraudes.

federate /ˈfedəreɪt/ **I** *adj* fédéré.

II *vtr* fédérer.

III *vi* se fédérer.

federation /ˌfedəˈreɪʃn/ *n* fédération *f*.

fedora /fɪˈdɔːrə/ *n* feutre *m* (*à larges bords*), chapeau *m*.

fed up○ /ˌfed ˈʌp/ *adj* **to be ~** en avoir marre○ (**about, with, of** de; **with** ou **of doing** de faire); **he's ~ about her leaving** il ne digère pas○ qu'elle soit partie.

fee /fiː/ *n* **1** (for professional, artistic service) honoraires *mpl*; **the ~ for the X-ray is £20** le coût de la radiographie est de 20 livres sterling; **school ~s** frais *mpl* de scolarité; **service ~** commission *f*; **to pay a ~** payer; **he charged us a ~ of $200** il nous a fait payer 200 dollars; **to be paid on a ~ basis** recevoir des honoraires; **he will do it for a ~** il le fera s'il est payé; **2** (for admission) droit *m* d'entrée; (for membership) cotisation *f*; **to pay/receive a ~** payer/recevoir une somme d'argent; **admission ~, entry ~** droit *m* d'entrée; **registration ~** frais *mpl* d'inscription; **what is the membership ~?** quel est le montant de la cotisation?

feeble /ˈfiːbl/ *adj* **1** [*person, animal, intellect, institution*] faible; **2** [*light, sound, increase, movement*] faible; **3** [*argument, excuse*] peu convaincant; [*joke, attempt, performance*] médiocre.

feeble-minded /ˌfiːblˈmaɪndɪd/ *adj* **1** (stupid) imbécile; **2** euph (handicapped) faible d'esprit; **3** (indecisive) irrésolu.

feeble-mindedness /ˌfiːblˈmaɪndɪdnɪs/ *n* **1** (stupidity) imbécilité *f*; **2** euph (handicap) faiblesse *f* d'esprit; **3** (indecision) irrésolution *f*.

feebleness /ˈfiːblnɪs/ *n* faiblesse *f*; **the ~ of the light** le peu de lumière.

feebly /ˈfiːblɪ/ *adv* **1** [*burn, cry, fight, smile, wave*] faiblement; **2** [*protest, explain, joke*] mollement.

feed /fiːd/ **I** *n* GB **1** (meal) (for animal) ration *f* de nourriture; (for baby) (breast) tétée *f*; (bottle) biberon *m*; **2**○ (hearty meal) bouffe○ *f*; **to have a ~** se faire une bouffe○; **to have a good ~** bien bouffer○; **3** Agric (also **~ stuffs**) aliments *mpl* pour animaux; **4** Ind, Tech (material) alimentation *f*; (mechanism) mécanisme *m* d'alimentation; **sheet paper ~** Comput chargeur *m* feuille à feuille; **paper ~** (for photocopier) chargeur *m* de papier; **5** (in comedy) (actor) faire-valoir *m inv*; (also **~-line**) réplique *f*.

II *vtr* (*prét, pp* **fed**) **1** (supply with food) nourrir [*animal, plant, family, starving people*] (**on** de); donner à manger à [*pet*]; ravitailler [*army*]; faire la cuisine pour [*guests*]; donner la becquée à [*fledgling*]; **to ~ a baby** (on breast) donner le sein à un bébé; (on bottle) donner le biberon à un bébé; **I shall have ten to ~** je ferai la cuisine pour dix; **2** (give food to) **to ~ sth to sb, ~ sb sth** donner qch à manger à qn; **she was ~ing bread to the ducks** ou **~ing the ducks bread** elle donnait du pain aux canards; **3** (supply) alimenter [*lake, fire, machine*]; mettre des pièces dans [*meter*]; fournir [*information, secrets*] (**to** à); **to ~ sth into** mettre qch dans [*meter, slot machine*]; introduire qch dans [*slot, hole, pipe, machine*]; rentrer qch dans [*computer*]; **to ~ a machine with** alimenter une machine en [*paper, materials*]; **4** fig (fuel) alimenter [*ambition, prejudice, desire*]; **to ~ a drug habit** se procurer de la drogue; **5** Sport faire passer [*ball*] (**to** à); **6** Theat donner la réplique à [*comedian*].

III *vi* (*prét, pp* **fed**) **1** (eat) manger; **the baby's ~ing** (on milk) le bébé prend son lait; (on solids) le bébé mange; **2** (survive) **to ~ on** se nourrir de [*substance, prey*]; **3** fig (thrive) **to ~ on** être alimenté par [*emotion, conditions*]; **4** (enter) **to ~ into** [*paper, tape*] s'introduire dans [*machine*].

IV *v refl* **to ~ oneself** [*child, invalid*] manger tout seul.

■ **feed back**: **~ [sth] back**, **~ back [sth]** retransmettre [*information, results*] (**to** à).
■ **feed up** GB: **~ [sth/sb] up** bien nourrir [*child, invalid*]; engraisser [*animal*].

feedback /ˈfi:dbæk/ *n* **1** gen (from people) impressions *fpl*, remarques *fpl* (**on** sur; **from** de la part de); (from test, experiment) répercussion *f* (**from** de; **on** sur); **2** Comput feed-back *m inv*; **3** Audio (on hifi) réaction *f* parasite.

feedbag /ˈfi:dbæg/ *n* musette *f* mangeoire.

feeder /ˈfi:də(r)/ *n* **1** (person, animal) **he's a good/poor ~** il a/n'a pas beaucoup d'appétit; **to be a noisy/slow ~** manger bruyamment/lentement; **2** (also **~ bib**) GB bavette *f*; **3** Transp (also **~ road** GB) bretelle *f* de raccordement; (also **~ canal**) canal *m* d'amenée; **4** (also **~ line**) Rail embranchement *m*; **5** (for printer, photocopier) chargeur *m*; **6** Agric mangeoire *f* automatique; **7** Elec (conductor) ligne *f* d'alimentation; **8** (also **~ stream**) Geog affluent *m*.

feeder primary (school) *n* école *f* primaire (*associée avec une école secondaire*).

feed grains *npl* céréales *fpl* fourragères.

feeding /ˈfi:dɪŋ/ *n* alimentation *f*.

feeding: **~ bottle** *n* GB biberon *m*; **~ stuffs** *npl* aliments *mpl* pour animaux; **~ time** *n* heure *f* de nourrir les animaux.

feed pipe *n* tuyau *m* d'alimentation.

fee income *n* revenus *mpl* d'un membre d'une profession libérale.

feel /fi:l/ **I** *n* **1** (atmosphere, impression created) atmosphère *f*; **I like the ~ of the place** j'aime l'atmosphère de cet endroit; **there was a relaxed/conspiratorial ~ about it** il régnait une atmosphère détendue/de conspiration; **it has the ~ of a country cottage** cela a l'allure d'une maison de campagne; **the town has a friendly ~** il y a une atmosphère accueillante dans cette ville; **2** (sensation to the touch) toucher *m*, sensation *f*; **the ~ of sand between one's toes** la sensation du sable entre les orteils; **you can tell by the ~ (that)** on voit bien au toucher que; **to have an oily/slimy ~** être huileux/gluant au toucher; **I like the ~ of leather** j'aime le contact du cuir; **3** (act of touching, feeling) **to have a ~ of sth**, **to give sth a ~** tâter qch; **let me have a ~**, **give me a ~** (touch) laisse-moi toucher; (hold, weigh) laisse-moi soupeser; **4** (familiarity, understanding) **to get the ~ of** se faire à [*controls, system*]; **to get the ~ of doing** s'habituer à faire; **it gives you a ~ of** ou **for the controls/the job market** cela vous donne une idée des commandes/du marché du travail; **5** (flair) don *m* (**for** pour); **to have a ~ for languages** avoir le don des langues; **to have a ~ for language** bien savoir manier la langue.
II *vtr* (*prét, pp* **felt**) **1** (experience) éprouver, ressentir [*affection, desire, envy, pride, unease*]; ressentir [*bond, hostility, obligation, effects, consequences, strain*]; **to ~ a sense of isolation** éprouver un sentiment de solitude; **I no longer ~ anything for her** je n'éprouve plus rien pour elle; **the impact of the legislation is still being felt** les effets de la loi se font encore sentir; **the effects will be felt throughout the country** les effets se feront sentir dans tout le pays; **to make one's displeasure felt** manifester son mécontentement; **to ~ sb's loss very deeply** être très affecté par la perte de qn; **I felt my spirits rise** j'ai senti que mon moral remontait; **2** (believe, think) **to ~ (that)** estimer que; **she ~s she has no option** elle estime qu'elle n'a pas le choix; **I ~ I should warn you** je me sens dans l'obligation de vous prévenir; **I ~ he's hiding something** j'ai l'impression qu'il cache quelque chose; **I ~ deeply** ou **strongly that they are wrong** j'ai la profonde conviction qu'ils ont tort; **to ~ sth to be** estimer que qch est; **I felt it best to refuse** j'ai estimé qu'il valait mieux refuser; **we ~ it necessary to complain** nous pensons que nous devons nous plaindre; **3** (physically) sentir [*blow, pressure, motion, draught, heat, object*]; ressentir [*twinge, ache, stiffness, effects*]; **I felt something soft** j'ai senti quelque chose de mou; **you can ~ the vibrations** on sent les vibrations; **I can't ~ anything in my leg** je ne sens plus rien dans la jambe; **she ~s/doesn't ~ the cold** elle est/n'est pas frileuse; **you'll ~ the cold when you go back to England** tu sentiras le froid quand tu rentreras en Angleterre; **I felt the house shake** j'ai senti la maison qui tremblait; **I felt something crawl(ing) up my arm** j'ai senti quelque chose qui grimpait le long de mon bras; **I can ~ it getting warmer** je sens que ça se réchauffe; **I felt the tablets doing me good** j'ai senti que les cachets me faisaient du bien; **4** (touch deliberately) tâter, toucher [*carving, texture, washing, leaf, cloth*]; palper [*patient, body part, parcel*]; **to ~ the weight of sth** soupeser qch; **to tell what it is by ~ing it** dire ce que c'est au toucher; **to ~ how cold/soft sth is** sentir comme qch est froid/mou; **to ~ one's breasts for lumps** se palper les seins pour voir si on a des grosseurs; **to ~ sb for weapons** fouiller qn pour trouver des armes; **to ~ one's way** lit avancer à tâtons; fig tâter le terrain; **to ~ one's way out of the room** se diriger à tâtons vers la sortie; **to ~ one's way towards a solution** avancer à tâtons vers une solution; **5** (sense, be aware of) sentir, avoir conscience de [*presence, tension, resentment*]; avoir conscience de [*importance, seriousness, justice, irony*]; **I could ~ her frustration** je ressentais sa frustration; **can't you ~ which notes come next?** ne peux-tu pas deviner quelles notes viennent ensuite?
III *vi* (*prét, pp* **felt**) **1** (emotionally) se sentir [*sad, happy, stupid, nervous, safe*]; être [*sure, angry, surprised*]; avoir l'impression d'être [*trapped, betrayed, cheated*]; **to ~ afraid/ashamed** avoir peur/honte; **to ~ like a star** avoir l'impression d'être une vedette; **to ~ as if** ou **as though** avoir l'impression que; **I felt as if nobody cared** j'avais l'impression que tout le monde s'en moquait; **how do you ~?** que ressens-tu?; **how do you feel about being in charge?** qu'est-ce que ça te fait d'être responsable?; **how do you ~ about marriage?** qu'est-ce que tu penses du mariage?; **how do you ~ about Tim?** (for a job, role) que penses-tu de Tim?; (emotionally) que ressens-tu pour Tim?; **how does it ~** ou **what does it ~ like to be a dad?** qu'est-ce que ça fait d'être papa?; **now you know how it ~s!** maintenant tu sais ce que ça fait!; **how would you ~?** qu'est-ce que ça te ferait, à toi?; **what made her ~ that way?** qu'est-ce qui lui a fait cet effet?; **if that's the way you ~...** si c'est comme ça que tu le prends...; ▶ **feel for**; **2** (physically) se sentir [*ill, better, tired, young, fat*]; **to ~ hot/cold/hungry/thirsty** avoir chaud/froid/faim/soif; **how do you ~?**, **how are you ~ing?** comment te sens-tu?; **I'll see how I ~** ou **what I ~ like tomorrow** je verrai comment je me sens demain; **it ~s like being hit with a hammer** c'est comme si on te frappait avec un marteau; **I ~ as if** ou **as though I haven't slept a wink** j'ai l'impression de ne pas avoir fermé l'œil; **it felt as if I was floating** j'avais l'impression de flotter; **you're as young as you ~** l'important c'est de se sentir jeune; **she isn't ~ing herself today** elle n'est pas dans son assiette aujourd'hui○; **3** (create certain sensation) être [*cold, soft, slimy, smooth*]; avoir l'air [*eerie*]; **the house ~s empty** la maison fait vide; **that ~s nice!** ça fait du bien!; **your arm will ~ sore at first** votre bras vous fera mal au début; **something doesn't ~ right** il y a quelque chose qui ne va pas; **it ~s strange living alone** ça me fait tout drôle de vivre seul; **it ~s like leather** on dirait du cuir; **it ~s like (a) Sunday** on se croirait un dimanche; **the bone ~s as if it's broken** on dirait que l'os est cassé; **it ~s as if it's going to rain**, **it ~s like rain** on dirait qu'il va pleuvoir; **it ~s to me as if there's a lump** j'ai l'impression qu'il y a une bosse; **4** (want) **to ~ like sth/like doing** avoir envie de qch/de faire; **I ~ like crying** j'ai envie de pleurer; **I ~ like a drink** je prendrais bien un verre; **what do you ~ like for lunch?** qu'est-ce qui te ferait envie pour le déjeuner?; **I don't ~ like it** je n'en ai pas envie; **stop whenever you ~ like it** arrête quand ça te chante○; **'why did you do that?'—'I just felt like it'** 'pourquoi as-tu fait ça?'—'ça m'a pris comme ça'; **5** (touch, grope) **to ~ in** fouiller dans [*bag, pocket, drawer*]; **to ~ along** tâtonner le long de [*edge, wall*]; **to ~ down the back of the sofa** chercher (à tâtons) derrière le canapé; ▶ **feel around**, **feel for**.
IV *v refl* **to ~ oneself doing** se sentir faire; **she felt herself losing her temper** elle sentait la colère la gagner; **he felt himself falling in love** il sentait qu'il tombait amoureux.
IDIOMS **to ~ a fool** (ridiculous) se trouver ridicule; (stupid) se sentir bête○.
■ **feel around**, **feel about**: **~ around** tâtonner; **to ~ around in** fouiller dans [*bag, drawer*]; **to ~ around for** chercher [qch] à tâtons.
■ **feel for**: ¶ **~ for [sth]** chercher; **to ~ for a ledge with one's foot** chercher un appui du pied; **to ~ for broken bones** examiner qn pour savoir s'il s'est cassé quelque chose; ¶ **~ for [sb]** plaindre, compatir à la douleur de liter [*person*].
■ **feel out** US: **~ out [sb]**, **~ [sb] out** tester [*person*].
■ **feel up**○: **~ up [sb/sth]**, **~ [sb/sth] up** tripoter○, peloter○ [*person, body part*]; **to be felt up** se faire peloter○; **to ~ each other up** se peloter○.
■ **feel up to**: **~ up to [sth]** se sentir d'attaque○ or assez bien pour; **to ~ up to doing** se sentir d'attaque○ or assez bien pour faire; **do you ~ up to it?** est-ce que tu te sens d'attaque○?

feeler /ˈfi:lə(r)/ *n* gen antenne *f*; (of snail) corne *f*.
IDIOMS **to put out ~s** tâter le terrain, lancer un ballon d'essai.

feeler gauge *n* calibre *m* (d'épaisseur).

feelgood /fi:lgʊd/ *n* pej [*speech, rhetoric, imagery, atmosphere*] faussement rassurant; **the government is playing on the ~ factor** le gouvernement essaie de créer un sentiment de bien-être illusoire.

feeling /ˈfi:lɪŋ/ **I** *n* **1** (emotion) sentiment *m*; **~ and reason** le cœur et la raison; **a guilty ~** un sentiment de culpabilité; **it is a strange ~ to be** c'est une sensation étrange que d'être; **to hide/show one's ~s** cacher/montrer ses sentiments; **to put one's ~s into words** trouver des mots pour dire ce que l'on ressent; **to spare sb's ~s** ménager qn; **to hurt sb's ~s** blesser qn; **what are your ~s for her?** quels sont tes sentiments pour elle?; **to have tender ~s for** ou **towards sb** éprouver de la tendresse pour qn; **I know the ~!** je connais ça!; **'never!' she said with ~** 'jamais!' dit-elle avec emportement; **2** (opinion, belief) sentiment *m*; **there is a growing ~ that** on a de plus en plus le sentiment que; **the ~ among Russians is that** le sentiment des Russes est que; **my own ~ is that**, **my own ~s are that** mon sentiment est que; **to have strong ~s about sth** avoir des opinions tranchées sur qch; **popular/religious ~** le sentiment populaire/religieux; **~s are running high** les esprits s'échauffent; **3** (sensitivity) sensibilité *f*; **a person of ~** une personne sensible; **have you no ~?** n'as-tu pas de cœur?; **he played with ~** son interprétation était pleine de sensibilité; **to speak with great ~** parler avec beaucoup de passion; **to have no ~ for nature** être insensible à la

nature; **4** (impression) impression *f*; **it's just a ~** ce n'est qu'une impression; **a ~ of being trapped** l'impression d'être coincé; **I've got a horrible ~ (that) I've forgotten my passport** j'ai l'horrible impression d'avoir oublié mon passeport; **I had a ~ you'd say that** je sentais que tu allais dire ça; **I had a ~ (that) I might see you** je me disais bien que j'aurais des chances de te voir; **I get the ~ he doesn't like me** iron j'ai comme l'impression qu'il ne m'aime pas iron; **I've got a bad ~ about this** j'ai le pressentiment que cela va mal se passer; **I've got a bad ~ about her** je me méfie d'elle; **5** (physical sensation) sensation *f*; **a dizzy ~** une sensation de vertige; **a loss of ~ in sth** une perte de sensation dans qch; **6** (atmosphere) ambiance *f*; **an eerie ~** une ambiance sinistre; **there was a general ~ of tension** l'ambiance était tendue; **the general ~ was that you were right** la majorité des gens te donnent raison; **7** (instinct) don *m* (**for** pour).
II *adj* [*person*] sensible; [*gesture, remark*] sympathique.

feelingly /ˈfiːlɪŋlɪ/ *adv* [*describe, play, write, speak*] avec passion; [*say, comfort*] avec compassion.

fee-paying /ˈfiːpeɪɪŋ/ **I** *n* paiement *m* des frais de scolarité.
II *adj* [*school*] payant; [*parent, pupil*] qui paie les frais de scolarité.

fee: **~ simple** *n* (*pl* **fees simple**) propriété *f* inconditionnelle; **~-splitting** *n* US Med partage *m* des honoraires (*contraire à l'éthique médicale*).

feet /fiːt/ *pl* ▶ **foot**.

feign /feɪn/ *vtr* sout feindre [*innocence, surprise*]; simuler [*illness, sleep*]; **with ~ed surprise** avec une surprise feinte.

feint /feɪnt/ **I** *n* **1** Sport, Mil feinte *f*; **2** Print réglure *f* fine; **narrow ~ paper** papier à réglure fine.
II *vi* Sport, Mil feinter.

feisty○ /ˈfiːstɪ/ *adj* **1** (lively) fougueux/-euse; **2** US (quarrelsome) bagarreur/-euse○.

feldspar /ˈfeldspɑː(r)/ *n* feldspath *m*.

felicitate /fəˈlɪsɪteɪt/ *vtr* sout féliciter (**on** pour).

felicitation /fəˌlɪsɪˈteɪʃn/ *n* sout félicitation *f* (**on** à l'occasion de).

felicitous /fəˈlɪsɪtəs/ *adj* sout (all contexts) heureux/-euse.

felicity /fəˈlɪsətɪ/ sout **I** *n* **1** (appropriateness) justesse *f*; **2** (happiness) félicité *f*.
II **felicities** *npl* (remarks, effects) bonheurs *mpl* liter.

feline /ˈfiːlaɪn/ **I** *n* félin *m*.
II *adj* lit, fig félin.

fell /fel/ **I** *prét* ▶ **fall**.
II *n* montagne *f* (*dans le nord de l'Angleterre*).
III *vtr* abattre [*tree*]; assommer [*person*].
IDIOMS **in one ~ swoop** d'un seul coup; **with one ~ blow** d'un seul coup.

fella○ /ˈfelə/ *n* mec○ *m*.

fellatio /fəˈleɪʃiːəʊ/ *n* fellation *f*.

feller○ /ˈfelə(r)/ *n* mec○ *m*.

felling /ˈfelɪŋ/ *n* coupe *f*.

fellow /ˈfeləʊ/ **I** *n* **1**○ (man) type○ *m*, homme *m*; **a nice ~** un type sympa○; **an old ~** un vieux; **poor old ~** pauvre vieux; **poor little ~** brave petit bonhomme; **my dear ~** mon cher; **look here old ~** écoute, mon vieux; **a strange ~** un drôle de type; **what do you ~s think?** qu'est-ce que vous en pensez, vous autres?; **some poor ~ will have to do it** il y aura un pauvre malheureux qui devra le faire; **give a ~ a bit of room!** laissez-moi un peu de place!; **2** (of society, association) (also in titles) membre *m* (**of** de); **3** GB Univ (lecturer) *membre du corps enseignant d'un collège universitaire*; (governor) *membre du comité de direction d'un collège universitaire*; **4** US (researcher) universitaire *mf* titulaire d'une bourse de recherche; **5**○ †(boyfriend) petit ami *m*, jules○ *m*.
II *modif* **her ~ lawyers/teachers** ses collègues avocats/professeurs; **he and his ~ students/sufferers** lui et les autres étudiants/malades; **a ~ Englishman** un compatriote anglais.

fellow: **~ being** *n* semblable *mf*; **~ citizen** *n* concitoyen/-enne *m/f*; **~ countryman** *n* compatriote *m*; **~ countrywoman** *n* compatriote *f*; **~ creature** *n* semblable *mf*; **~ drinker** *n* compagnon *m* de boisson; **~ feeling** *n* (understanding) compréhension *f*; (solidarity) solidarité *f*; **~ human being** *n* semblable *mf*; **~ man** *n* semblable *mf*, frère *m*; **~ member** *n* (of club) autre adhérent/-e *m/f*; (of learned society) confrère *m*, consœur *f*; **~ passenger** *n* compagnon/compagne *m/f* de voyage.

fellowship /ˈfeləʊʃɪp/ *n* **1** (companionship) (social) camaraderie *f*; (religious) fraternité *f*; **2** (association) (social) association *f*; (religious) confrérie *f*; **3** Univ (post) poste *m* de recherche et d'enseignement universitaire; funding) bourse *f* de recherche.

fellow ~ traveller GB, **~ traveler** US *n* lit compagnon/compagne *m/f* de voyage; fig Pol compagnon *m* de route, communisant/-e *m/f*; **~ worker** *n* collègue *mf*.

fell-walking /ˈfelwɔːkɪŋ/ *n* GB randonnée *f* en montagne.

felon /ˈfelən/ *n* Hist, Jur criminel *m*.

felony /ˈfelənɪ/ *n* Hist, Jur crime *m*.

felt /felt/ **I** *prét, pp* ▶ **feel**.
II *n* (cloth) (thick) feutre *m*; (thinner) feutrine *f*.
III *modif* [*cloth, cover*] (thick) en feutre; (thinner) en feutrine; **~ hat** feutre *m*, chapeau *m* en feutre.

felt-tip (pen) *n* feutre *m*.

fem○ /fem/ *n* (lesbian) lesbienne *f* (*qui a le rôle passif*).

female /ˈfiːmeɪl/ **I** *n* **1** Biol, Zool femelle *f*; **in the ~** chez la femelle; **the ~s** (of species) la femelle; **2**○ pej (woman) bonne femme○ *f*; (younger) greluche○ *f*.
II *adj* **1** Bot, Zool femelle; **~ cat** chatte *f*; **~ rabbit** lapine *f*; **2** (relating to women) [*condition, population, role, sex, trait*] féminin; [*company, emancipation*] des femmes; **a ~ voice** une voix de femme; **the ~ body/voice** le corps/la voix de la femme; **~ singer** chanteuse *f*; **~ student** étudiante *f*; **~ employee** employée *f* (femme); **3** Elec femelle.

female circumcision *n* excision *f*.

feminine /ˈfemənɪn/ **I** *n* Ling féminin *m*; **in the ~** au féminin.
II *adj* **1** [*clothes, colour, style, features*] féminin; [*occupation*] de femme; [*issue*] concernant les femmes; **the ~ side of his nature** son côté féminin; **2** Ling féminin.

femininity /ˌfeməˈnɪnətɪ/ *n* féminité *f*.

feminism /ˈfemɪnɪzəm/ *n* féminisme *m*.

feminist /ˈfemɪnɪst/ **I** *n* féministe *mf*.
II *modif* [*lobby, response*] féministe.

femme *n* US = **fem**.

femoral /ˈfemərəl/ *adj* fémoral.

femur /ˈfiːmə(r)/ *n* fémur *m*.

fen /fen/ **I** *n* marais *m*.
II **the Fens** *pr npl*: *région de basses terres dans l'est de l'Angleterre*.

fence /fens/ **I** *n* **1** (barrier) clôture *f*; **steel/wooden ~** clôture métallique/en bois; **security ~** enceinte *f* de sécurité; **2** (in showjumping) obstacle *m*; (in horseracing) haie *f*; **3**○ (receiver of stolen goods) receleur/-euse *m/f*; **4** Tech (on saw) protection *f*.
II *vtr* **1** clôturer [*area, garden*]; **2**○ fourguer○ [*stolen goods*].
III *vi* **1** Sport faire de l'escrime; **2** (be evasive) se dérober; **3**○ (receive stolen goods) receler des marchandises.
IDIOMS **to mend ~s** se raccommoder (**with** avec); **to sit on the ~** ne pas prendre position.
■ **fence in**: ¶ **~ [sth] in, ~ in [sth]** entourer [qch] d'une clôture [*area, garden*]; parquer [*animals*]; ¶ **~ [sb] in** fig étouffer; **to feel ~d in** se sentir enfermé.
■ **fence off**: **~ [sth] off, ~ off [sth]** clôturer [qch].

fencer /ˈfensə(r)/ *n* Sport escrimeur/-euse *m/f*.

fencing /ˈfensɪŋ/ ▶ **1282** **I** *n* **1** Sport escrime *f*; **2** (fences) gen clôtures *fpl*; (wire) grillage *m*.
II *modif* [*mask, lesson*] d'escrime; **~ teacher** maître *m* d'armes.

fend /fend/ *v*
■ **fend for**: **to ~ for oneself** se débrouiller (tout seul).
■ **fend off**: **~ off [sb/sth], ~ [sb/sth] off** repousser [*attacker*]; parer [*blow*]; écarter [*question*].

fender /ˈfendə(r)/ *n* **1** (for fire) garde-cendre *m*; **2** US Aut aile *f*; **3** US Rail chasse-pierres *m inv*; **4** Naut défense *f*.

fender-bender○ *n* US Aut (accident) accrochage *m*.

fenestration /ˌfenɪˈstreɪʃn/ *n* **1** Archit fenêtrage *m*; **2** Med fenestration *f*.

fennel /ˈfenl/ *n* fenouil *m*.

fenugreek /ˈfenuːgriːk/ *n* fenugrec *m*.

feral /ˈfɪərəl, US ˈferəl/ *adj* sauvage.

Fermanagh /ˌfəˈmænə/ ▶ **1624** *pr n* comté *m* de Fermanagh.

ferment **I** /ˈfɜːment/ *n* (unrest) effervescence *f*; **in (a state of) ~** en effervescence; (political, racial) agitation *f*.
II /fəˈment/ *vtr* faire fermenter [*beer, wine*]; fig fomenter [*trouble*].
III /fəˈment/ *vi* [*wine, beer, yeast, fruit etc*] fermenter.

fermentation /ˌfɜːmenˈteɪʃn/ *n* fermentation *f*.

fern /fɜːn/ *n* fougère *f*.

ferocious /fəˈrəʊʃəs/ *adj* [*animal*] féroce; [*attack, violence*] sauvage; [*dagger, spike*] redoutable; [*vent*] violent; [*heat*] accablant; [*climate*] rude.

ferociously /fəˈrəʊʃəslɪ/ *adv* [*attack*] (verbally) violemment; (physically) férocement; [*bark*] avec férocité; **a ~ fought campaign** une campagne impitoyable.

ferocity /fəˈrɒsətɪ/ *n* férocité *f*.

ferret /ˈferɪt/ **I** *n* lit, fig furet *m*.
II *vi* (*p prés etc* **-tt-**) **1** Hunt chasser au furet; **2** (search) **to ~ for** chercher [qch] partout [*keys*].
■ **ferret about** fureter, fouiller (**in** dans).
■ **ferret out**○: ¶ **~ [sth] out, ~ out [sth]** dégoter○ [*bargain*]; découvrir [*truth, information*]; ¶ **~ [sb] out** dénicher [*agent, thief*].

ferrety /ˈferətɪ/ *adj* [*features*] de fouine.

ferrite /ˈferaɪt/ *n* ferrite *f*.

ferroconcrete /ˌferəʊˈkɒŋkriːt/ *n* béton *m* armé.

ferrous /ˈferəs/ *adj* ferreux/-euse.

ferrule /ˈferuːl, US ˈferəl/ *n* virole *f*.

ferry /ˈferɪ/ **I** *n* (over short distances) bac *m*; (long-distance) ferry *m*; **car ~** car-ferry *m*, transbordeur *m*.
II *modif* [*crossing*] en ferry; [*disaster*] maritime; **~ sailing times** les horaires *mpl* des ferries; **~ services** les services *mpl* de ferry.
III *vtr* transporter [*passenger, person, goods*]; **to ~ sb to** emmener qn à [*school, station*]; **to ~ sb away** emmener qn; **he's always ~ing them to and from school** il passe son temps à faire le trajet entre l'école et la maison.

ferryman /ˈferɪmæn/ *n* passeur *m*.

fertile /ˈfɜːtaɪl, US ˈfɜːrtl/ *adj* lit [*land, valley, soil*] fertile; [*human, animal, egg*] fécond; fig [*imagination, mind, environment*] fertile.

fertility /fəˈtɪlətɪ/ **I** *n* **1** lit (of land) fertilité *f*, fécondité *f*; (of human, animal, egg) fécondité *f*; **2** fig (of mind, imagination) fertilité *f*.
II *modif* [*symbol, rite*] de fertilité.

fertility drug *n* médicament *m* contre la stérilité.

fertilization /ˌfɜːtɪlaɪˈzeɪʃn, US -lɪˈz-/ *n* (of

land) fertilisation *f*; (of human, animal, plant, egg) fécondation *f*.

fertilize /ˈfɜːtɪlaɪz/ *vtr* fertiliser, mettre de l'engrais sur [*land*]; féconder [*human, animal, plant, egg*].

fertilizer /ˈfɜːtɪlaɪzə(r)/ *n* engrais *m*; **organic/chemical ~** engrais organique/chimique.

fervent /ˈfɜːvənt/ *adj* [*admirer*] fervent; [*support*] inconditionnel; **to be a ~ believer in sth** croire passionnément en qch.

fervently /ˈfɜːvəntlɪ/ *adv* [*declare*] avec ferveur; [*hope*] vivement; **to believe ~ in sth** croire passionnément en qch.

fervid /ˈfɜːvɪd/ *adj* sout passionné.

fervour GB, **fervor** US /ˈfɜːvə(r)/ *n* ferveur *f*.

fester /ˈfestə(r)/ *vi* [*wound, sore*] suppurer; [*situation*] pourrir; [*feeling*] s'envenimer.

festival /ˈfestɪvl/ *n* gen fête *f*; (arts event) festival *m*.

festive /ˈfestɪv/ *adj* [*occasion, person*] joyeux/-euse; **a festive air** un air de fête; **the ~ season** la saison des fêtes, les fêtes; **to be in (a) ~ mood** être plein d'entrain.

festivity /feˈstɪvətɪ/ **I** *n* ¢ (merriment) réjouissance *f*; **the wedding was an occasion of great ~** le mariage donna lieu à toutes sortes de réjouissances.
II festivities *npl* réjouissances *fpl*.

festoon /feˈstuːn/ **I** *n* guirlande *f*.
II *vtr* orner (**with** de).
III *modif* [*curtains*] en festons.

fetal *adj* US = **foetal**.

fetch /fetʃ/ *vtr* **1** (bring) gen aller chercher; **(go and) ~ a ladder/the foreman** va chercher une échelle/le contremaître; **to ~ sth for sb** aller chercher qch pour qn; (carry back) (r)apporter qch à qn; **~ him a chair please** apporte-lui une chaise s'il te plaît; **she'll come and ~ you** elle viendra vous chercher; **~!** (to dog) rapporte!; **to ~ sb back** ramener qn; **2** (bring financially) [*goods*] rapporter; **to ~ a good price** rapporter un bon prix; **it won't ~ much** ça ne rapportera pas grand-chose; **these vases can ~ up to £600** le prix de ces vases peut atteindre 600 livres; **3**○ (hit) **to ~ sb a blow** flanquer○ un coup à qn.
IDIOMS **to ~ and carry for sb** faire les quatre volontés de qn.
■ **fetch in**○: ¶ **~ [sth] in, ~ in [sth]** rentrer [*chairs, washing etc*]; ¶ **~ [sb] in** faire rentrer.
■ **fetch out**○: ¶ **~ [sth] out, ~ out [sth]** sortir [*object*]; ¶ **~ [sb] out, ~ out [sb]** faire sortir [*person*].
■ **fetch up**○: **to ~ up in Rome** finir par débarquer○ à Rome.

fetching /ˈfetʃɪŋ/ *adj* [*child, habit, photo*] charmant; [*outfit, hat*] ravissant.

fetchingly /ˈfetʃɪŋlɪ/ *adv* [*smile, say*] avec charme; **she was dressed very ~** elle était délicieusement vêtue.

fete /feɪt/ **I** *n* (church, village) kermesse *f* (paroissiale); **charity ~** fête *f* de bienfaisance.
II *vtr* fêter [*celebrity, hero*].

fetid, **foetid** /ˈfetɪd, US ˈfiːtɪd/ *adj* fétide, nauséabond.

fetish /ˈfetɪʃ/ *n* **1** (object) fétiche *m* (also sexual); **2** (obsessive interest) manie *f*; **3** (excessive devotion) culte *m*; **to make a ~ of sth** vouer un culte à qch; **4** Anthrop fétiche *m*, objet *m* de culte.

fetishism /ˈfetɪʃɪzəm/ *n* fétichisme *m*.

fetlock /ˈfetlɒk/ *n* **1** (joint) boulet *m*; **2** (tuft of hair) fanon *m*.

fetter /ˈfetə(r)/ **I fetters** *npl* **1** (of prisoner, slave) fers *m*; **in ~s** aux fers; **2** fig **the ~s of authority/totalitarianism** les entraves de l'autorité/du totalitarisme.
II *vtr* **1** mettre [qn] aux fers; **2** fig entraver l'influence de [*union, party*].

fettle /ˈfetl/ *n* IDIOMS **in fine** ou **good ~** en excellente forme.

fetus *n* US = **foetus**.

feu /fjuː/ *n* Scot Jur bail *m* perpétuel.

feud /fjuːd/ **I** *n* querelle *f* (**with** avec; **between** entre); **to carry on a ~ with sb** avoir une querelle avec qn; **family ~** querelle de famille; **blood ~** brouille *f* ancestrale.
II *vi* se quereller (**with** avec; **about** au sujet de).

feudal /ˈfjuːdl/ *adj* féodal.

feudalism /ˈfjuːdəlɪzəm/ *n* féodalisme *m*.

feuding /ˈfjuːdɪŋ/ **I** *n* querelle *f*.
II *adj* [*factions, families*] en conflit.

feu duty *n* Scot Jur redevance *f* fixe annuelle.

fever /ˈfiːvə(r)/ *n* **1** (temperature) fièvre *f*; **to have a ~** avoir de la fièvre; **her ~ has broken** ou **subsided** sa fièvre a baissé; **2** (excited state) fièvre *f*; **in a ~ of excitement** dans un état d'excitation fébrile; **3** (craze) fièvre *f*; **gold/rock-and-roll ~** la fièvre de l'or/du rock; **he's got gambling ~** le démon du jeu le poursuit.

fevered /ˈfiːvəd/ *adj* [*brow*] fiévreux/-euse; [*imagination*] fébrile.

feverish /ˈfiːvərɪʃ/ *adj* **1** [*person, eyes*] fiévreux/-euse; [*dreams*] délirant; **2** [*excitement*] fébrile; **in a burst of ~ activity** dans un élan d'activité fébrile.

feverishly /ˈfiːvərɪʃlɪ/ *adv* **1** Med fiévreusement; **2** (frenetically) fébrilement.

fever pitch *n* **to bring sb to ~** [*music, orator*] déchaîner [*crowd*]; **our excitement had reached ~** notre excitation était à son comble.

few /fjuː/ (*comp* **fewer**, *superl* **fewest**)

■ **Note** When *few* is used as a quantifier to indicate the smallness or insufficiency of a given number or quantity (*few horses, few shops, few people*) it is translated by *peu de*: *peu de maisons, peu de gens, peu de magasins*. Equally *the few* is translated by *le peu de*: *the few people who knew her* le peu de gens qui la connaissaient. For examples and particular usages see I 1 in entry.
– When *few* is used as a quantifier in certain expressions to mean *several*, translations vary according to the expression: see I 2 in entry.
– When *a few* is used as a quantifier (*a few books*), it can often be translated by *quelques*: quelques livres; however, for expressions such as *quite a few books, a good few books*, see II in the entry.
– For translations of *few* used as a pronoun (*few of us succeeded, I only need a few*) see III in the entry.
– For translations of *the few* used as a noun (*the few who voted for him*) see IV in the entry.

I *quantif* **1** (not many) peu de; **~ visitors/letters** peu de visiteurs/lettres; **~ people came to the meeting** peu de gens sont venus à la réunion; **very ~ houses/families** très peu de maisons/familles; **there are very ~ opportunities for graduates** il y a très peu de débouchés pour les diplômés; **one of my ~ pleasures** un de mes rares plaisirs; **on the ~ occasions that she has visited this country** les rares fois qu'elle a visité ce pays; **their needs are ~** ils ont peu de besoins; **their demands are ~** ils sont peu exigeants, ils revendiquent peu de chose; **to be ~ in number** être peu nombreux; **there are too ~ women in this profession** il y a trop peu de femmes dans ce métier; **with ~ exceptions** à quelques exceptions près; **a man of ~ words** gen un homme peu loquace; (approvingly) un homme qui ne se perd pas en paroles inutiles; **2** (some, several) **every ~ days** tous les deux ou trois jours; **over the next ~ days/weeks** (in past) dans les jours/semaines qui ont suivi; (in future) dans les jours/semaines à venir; **these past ~ days** ces derniers jours; **the first ~ weeks** les premières semaines; **the ~ books she possessed** le peu de livres qu'elle possédait.
II a few *quantif* quelques; **a ~ people/houses** quelques personnes/maisons; **I would like a ~ more** j'aimerais en avoir quelques-uns (ou quelques-unes) de plus; **quite a ~ people/houses** pas mal○ de gens/maisons, un certain nombre de gens/maisons; **we've lived here for a good ~ years** nous vivons ici depuis un bon nombre d'années; **a ~ weeks earlier** quelques semaines plus tôt; **in a ~ minutes** dans quelques minutes; **in a ~ more months** dans quelques mois; **a ~ more times** quelques fois de plus.
III *pron* **1** (not many) peu; **~ of us succeeded** peu d'entre nous ont réussi; **~ of them could swim** ils n'étaient pas nombreux à savoir nager; **~ of them survived** peu d'entre eux ont survécu, il y a eu peu de survivants; **there are so ~ of them that** (objects) il y en a tellement peu que; (people) ils sont tellement peu nombreux que; **there are four too ~** il en manque quatre; **as ~ as four people turned up** quatre personnes seulement sont venues; **~ can deny that** il y a peu de gens qui nieraient que; **2** (some) **a ~ of the soldiers/countries** un certain nombre des soldats/pays; **I only need a ~** il ne m'en faut que quelques-uns/quelques-unes; **a ~ of us** un certain nombre d'entre nous; **there were only a ~ of them** (objects) il n'y en avait que quelques-uns/quelques-unes; (people) ils étaient peu nombreux; **quite a ~ of the tourists come from Germany** un bon nombre des touristes viennent d'Allemagne; **a good ~ of the houses were damaged** un bon nombre des maisons ont été endommagées; **there are only a very ~ left** (objects) il n'en reste que très peu; (people) il ne reste que quelques personnes; **a ~ wanted to go on strike** quelques-uns voulaient faire la grève.
IV *n* **the ~ who voted for him** les rares personnes qui ont voté pour lui; **great wealth in the hands of the ~** une grande richesse entre les mains d'une minorité; **music that appeals only to the ~** une musique qui ne s'adresse qu'à l'élite.
IDIOMS **to be ~ and far between** être rarissimes; **such people/opportunities are ~ and far between** de telles personnes/occasions sont rarissimes; **villages in this area are ~ and far between** il y a très peu de villages dans cette région; **to have had a ~ (too many)**○ avoir bu quelques verres de trop, être bien parti○.

fewer /ˈfjuːə(r)/ *comp of* **few I** *adj* moins de; **there are ~ trains on Sundays** il y a moins de trains le dimanche; **there were ~ people/cases than last time** il y avait moins de monde/cas que la dernière fois; **~ and ~ people** de moins en moins de gens; **there are ~ and ~ opportunities for doing this kind of thing** les occasions de faire ce genre de chose se font de plus en plus rares.
II *pron* moins; **~ than 50 people** moins de 50 personnes; **no ~ than** pas moins de; **I have seen ~ recently** j'en ai moins vu récemment; **they were ~ than before** ils étaient moins nombreux qu'avant.

fewest /ˈfjuːɪst/ *superl of* **few I** *adj* le moins de; **they have the ~ clothes** ce sont eux qui ont le moins de vêtements; **the ~ accidents happened in this area** c'est dans cette région qu'il y a eu le moins d'accidents.
II *pron* **he sold the ~** c'est lui qui en a vendu le moins; **the country where the ~ survived** le pays où il y a eu le moins de survivants.

fey /feɪ/ *adj* **1** (clairvoyant) extralucide; **2** (whimsical) loufoque○.

fez /fez/ *n* (*pl* **~zes**) fez *m*.

ff (*abrév écrite* = **following**) et les lignes (ou pages) qui suivent.

FHA *n* US (*abrév* = **Federal Housing Administration**) *organisme gouvernemental de prêts immobiliers*.

FHSA *n* GB Soc Admin *abrév* ▶ **Family Health Service Authority**.

fiancé /fɪˈɒnseɪ, US ˌfiːɑːnˈseɪ/ *n* fiancé *m*.

fiancée /fɪˈɒnseɪ, US ˌfiːɑːnˈseɪ/ *n* fiancée *f*.

fiasco /fɪˈæskəʊ/ *n* fiasco *m*; **to turn into a ~** tourner au fiasco; **to end in ~** se terminer en fiasco; **a complete/an utter ~** un fiasco complet/total.

fiat /ˈfaɪæt, US ˈfiːət/ *n* sout **1** (decree) décret *m*, ordre *m*; **2** (permission) autorisation *f*.

fiat money *n* Fin monnaie *f* fiduciaire.

fib○ /fɪb/ **I** *n* bobard○ *m*, mensonge *m*; **to tell ~s**○ raconter des bobards○, mentir.
II *vi* (*p prés etc* **-bb-**) raconter des bobards○, mentir.

fibber○ /ˈfɪbə(r)/ *n* menteur/-euse *m/f*; **you ~!** espèce de menteur!

fibre GB, **fiber** US /ˈfaɪbə(r)/ *n* **1** (filament, strand) (of thread, wood) fibre *f*; **2** Tex fibre *f*; **a synthetic/artificial ~** une fibre synthétique/artificielle; **3** (in diet) fibres *fpl*; **a high ~ diet** une alimentation riche en fibres; **4** Bot (cell) fibre *f*; Physiol (of muscle, nerve) fibre *f*; **root ~s** radicelles *fpl*; **5** fig (strength) courage *m*.

fibreboard GB, **fiberboard** US /ˈfaɪbəbɔːd/ *n* aggloméré *m*; **a piece of ~** un panneau en fibres de verre.

fibrefill GB, **fiberfill** US /ˈfaɪbəfɪl/ *n* rembourrage *m* synthétique.

fibreglass GB, **fiberglass** US /ˈfaɪbəglɑːs/ *n* ¢ fibres *fpl* de verre; **a ~ panel** un panneau en fibres de verre.

fibre: **~ optic** GB, **fiber optic** US *adj* [*cable*] à fibres optiques; [*link*] par fibres optiques; **~optics** GB, **fiberoptics** US *n* (*v sg* ou *pl*) fibres *fpl* optiques.

fibril /ˈfaɪbrɪl/ *n* fibrille *f*.

fibrillation /ˌfaɪbrɪˈleɪʃn/ *n* fibrillation *f*.

fibrin /ˈfaɪbrɪn/ *n* fibrine *f*.

fibrinogen /faɪˈbrɪnədʒən/ *n* fibrinogène *m*.

fibroid /ˈfaɪbrɔɪd/ **I** *n* fibrome *m*.
II *adj* fibreux/-euse.

fibroma /faɪˈbrəʊmə/ *n* (*pl* **-mas** ou **-mata**) fibrome *m*.

fibrositis /ˌfaɪbrəˈsaɪtɪs/ ▶ **1354** *n* rhumatismes *mpl* musculaires.

fibrous /ˈfaɪbrəs/ *adj* fibreux/-euse.

fibula /ˈfɪbjʊlə/ *n* (*pl* **~s** ou **-ae**) **1** Anat péroné *m*; **2** (brooch) fibule *f*.

fiche /fiːʃ/ *n* microfiche *f*.

fickle /ˈfɪkl/ *adj* [*lover*] inconstant; [*fate, follower, public opinion*] changeant; [*weather*] capricieux/-ieuse; [*friend*] imprévisible; [*stock market*] fluctuant; [*wine*] irrégulier/-ière.

fickleness /ˈfɪklnɪs/ *n* (of lover, friend) inconstance *f*; (of behaviour) instabilité *f*; (of weather) caprices *mpl*; (of fortune, of stock market) fluctuations *fpl*; **the ~ of his moods** ses sautes d'humeur.

fiction /ˈfɪkʃn/ *n* **1** (literary genre) romanesque *m*, roman *m*; **2** (books) romans *mpl*; **to write ~** écrire des romans; **light ~** romans *mpl* de lecture facile; **American ~** le roman américain; **in ~** dans les romans; **children's ~** littérature *f* pour enfants; **3** (delusion) illusion *f*; **liberty is a ~** la liberté est une illusion; **4** (untruth) histoire *f*; **his address is a ~** son adresse est fictive; **do you really believe that ~ that she was sick?** est-ce que tu crois vraiment à cette histoire de maladie?; **5** (creation of the imagination) fiction *f*; **6** (pretence) **they keep up the ~ that** ils font croire à tout le monde que.

fictional /ˈfɪkʃənl/ *adj* **1** [*character, event*] imaginaire; **2** [*device*] romanesque; **3** (false) [*address, identity*] fictif/-ive.

fictionalize /ˈfɪkʃənəlaɪz/ *vtr* romancer; **a ~d account** une histoire romancée.

fiction: **~ list** *n* liste *f* des romans; **~ writer** ▶ **1692** *n* romancier/-ière *m/f*.

fictitious /fɪkˈtɪʃəs/ *adj* **1** (false) [*name, address*] fictif/-ive; [*justification, report*] fallacieux/-ieuse; **2** (imaginary) imaginaire; **all the characters in this film are ~** tous les personnages dans ce film sont imaginaires.

fiddle /ˈfɪdl/ ▶ **1481** **I** *n* **1**○ (dishonest scheme) magouille○ *f* ¢; **to work a ~** magouiller○ qch; **it's a complete ~!** c'est de la grosse magouille○!; **tax ~** fraude *f* fiscale; **to be on the ~** traficoter○; **2** (violin) violon *m*.
II *vtr*○ (illegally) truquer○, maquiller○ [*tax return*]; traficoter○ [*figures*].
III *vi* **1** (fidget) **to ~ with sth** tripoter qch; **2** (adjust) **to ~ with** tourner [*knobs, controls*]; **3** (interfere) **to ~ with sth** tripoter, jouer avec [*possessions*].
IDIOMS **to be as fit as a ~** être en pleine santé; **to ~ while Rome burns** se ficher de tout comme de l'an 40○; **to have a face as long as a ~** faire une tête d'enterrement or de six pieds de long○; **to play second ~ to sb** être le sous-fifre○ de qn.
■ **fiddle around** **1** (be idle) traîner sa flemme○; **2 to ~ around with sth** (readjust) bricoler [*typewriter, engine*]; (fidget) jouer avec [*corkscrew, elastic band*].

fiddle-faddle○ /ˈfɪdlfædl/ *n* (**what**) **~!** (c'est de la) foutaise○!

fiddler /ˈfɪdlə(r)/ ▶ **1692**, **1481** *n* violoniste *mf*.

fiddler crab *n* crabe *m* appelant.

fiddlesticks○† /ˈfɪdlstɪks/ *excl* flûte alors○!

fiddling○ /ˈfɪdlɪŋ/ *n* embrouille○ *f*; **tax ~** embrouille *f* fiscale○.

fiddly /ˈfɪdlɪ/ *adj* [*job, task*] délicat; [*clasp, fastening*] pas pratique; **~ to open/attach** difficile à ouvrir/attacher.

fidelity /fɪˈdelətɪ/ *n* gen, Electron, Telecom fidélité *f* (**of** de; **to** à).

fidget /ˈfɪdʒɪt/ **I** *n* **they're real ~s** ils n'arrêtent pas de gigoter○.
II fidgets *npl* **to have the ~s** ne pas tenir en place.
III *vi* (move about) ne pas tenir en place; (get impatient) s'impatienter; **he's always ~ing** il ne tient jamais en place; **stop ~ing!** tiens-toi tranquille!
■ **fidget about**,
■ **fidget around** gigoter○.

fidgety /ˈfɪdʒɪtɪ/ *adj* (physically) (child) remuant; (adult) agité; (psychologically) nerveux/-euse; **meetings/concerts make me ~** je ne tiens pas en place aux réunions/concerts.

fiduciary /fɪˈdjuːʃərɪ/ *adj* Jur fiduciaire.

fief /fiːf/ *n* fief *m*.

fiefdom /ˈfiːfdəm/ *n* fief *m*.

field /fiːld/ **I** *n* **1** Agric, Geog, gen champ *m* (**of** de); **ice/lava/snow ~** champ de glace/de lave/de neige; **wheat ~** champ de blé; **2** Sport (ground) terrain *m*; **football/sports ~** terrain de football/de sport; **to take to the ~** [*team*] arriver sur le terrain; **3** Sport (competitors) (athletes) concurrents *mpl*; (horses) partants *mpl*, champ *m*; Hunt chasseurs *mpl* (à courre); **to lead** ou **be ahead of the ~** Sport mener le peloton; fig être en tête; **4** (area of knowledge) domaine *m* (**of** de); **it's outside his ~** ça ne relève pas de sa compétence; **5** Ling champ *m* sémantique; **6** (real environment) **to test sth in the ~** faire des essais de qch sur le terrain; **to work in the ~** travailler sur le terrain; **7** Mil **the ~ of battle** le champ de bataille; **to die in the ~** tomber or mourir au champ d'honneur; **to take the ~** se mettre en campagne; **to hold the ~** se maintenir sur ses positions; fig [*theory*] dominer; **8** (range) champ *m*; **~ of force** Elec champ de force; **~ of vision** ou **view** champ de vision; **~ of fire** Mil secteur *m* de tir; **9** Comput, Math, Phys champ *m*; **10** Art, Herald champ *m*; **11** (airfield) terrain *m* d'aviation.
II *vtr* **1** Sport attraper , réceptionner [*ball*]; **2** Sport, gen (select) faire jouer [*team, player*]; présenter [*candidate*]; **3** (put at disposal) mettre [qn/qch] en action [*equipment, nurses, soldiers*]; **4** (respond to) répondre à [*questions*].
III *vi* Sport jouer dans l'équipe de défense.
IDIOMS **to play the ~** sortir avec tout le monde.

field ambulance *n* Mil Med ambulance *f* de campagne.

field day *n* **1** Sch, Univ sortie *f* (éducative); **a geography ~** une sortie pour le cours de géographie; **2** Mil journée *f* de manœuvres; **3** US (sports day) journée *f* sportive.
IDIOMS **to have a ~** (have fun) s'amuser comme un fou/une folle; (maliciously) [*press, critics*] jubiler; (make money) [*bookmakers, ice-cream vendors*] faire d'excellentes affaires; **the press had a ~ with the story/scandal** la presse a fait ses choux gras○ de l'affaire/du scandale.

field drain *n* drain *m*.

fielder /ˈfiːldə(r)/ *n* Sport homme *m* de champ, défenseur *m*.

field: **~ event** *n* Sport épreuve *f* sportive (*de saut et de lancer*); **~fare** *n* Zool (grive *f*) litorne *f*; **~ glasses** *npl* jumelles *fpl*; **~ goal** *n* US (in football, rugby) ≈ drop *m*; (in basket ball) panier *m*; **~ gun** *n* Mil canon *m* (de campagne); **~ hand** *n* US ouvrier/-ière *m/f* agricole; **~ hockey** ▶ **1282** *n* US Sport hockey *m* sur gazon; **~ hospital** *n* Mil, Med hôpital *m* de campagne.

field house *n* US Sport **1** (changing room) vestiaire *m*; **2** (sports centre) complexe *m* sportif.

field: **~ kitchen** *n* cuisine *f* roulante; **~ label** *n* Ling marqueur *m* de champ sémantique; **~ marshal, FM** ▶ **1612** *n* Mil maréchal *m*; **~mouse** *n* Zool mulot *m*; **~ officer** *n* Mil officier *m* supérieur; **~sman** *n* US Sport = **fielder**; **~ sports** *npl* Sport sports *mpl* de plein air; **~ strength** *n* Radio, TV intensité *f* du champ; **~strip** *vtr* Mil démonter [*firearm*]; **~ study** *n* études *fpl* sur le terrain.

field test **I** *n* essai *m* sur le terrain.
II *vtr* soumettre [qch] à des essais sur le terrain [*weapon*].

field: **~ trials** *npl* essais *mpl* sur le terrain; **~ trip** *n* Sch, Univ (one day) sortie *f* éducative; (longer) voyage *m* d'études; **~work** *n* travail *m* de terrain; **~worker** ▶ **1692** *n* Sci scientifique *mf* qui travaille sur le terrain; (for social organization) homme/femme *m/f* qui travaille sur le terrain.

fiend /fiːnd/ *n* **1** (evil spirit) démon *m*; **2** (cruel person) monstre *m*; **a cruel/selfish ~** un monstre de cruauté/d'égoïsme; **3**○ (mischievous person) petit monstre *m*; **4**○ (fanatic) **he's a racing/football ~** c'est un fana○ des courses/du football; **dope ~** amateur/-trice *m/f* de dope○; **fresh-air ~** maniaque *mf* de l'air frais.

fiendish /ˈfiːndɪʃ/ *adj* **1** (cruel) [*tyrant, cruelty*] monstrueux/-euse; [*expression, glee*] diabolique; **to take a ~ delight in sth/in doing** prendre un plaisir malin à qch/à faire; **2** (ingenious) [*plan, gadget*] diabolique; **3**○ (difficult) [*problem, job*] épouvantable; **4**○ (awful) [*traffic*] infernal.

fiendishly /ˈfiːndɪʃlɪ/ *adv* **1** [*smile, scheme, plot*] diaboliquement; **2** [*difficult, ambitious*] extrêmement.

fierce /fɪəs/ *adj* [*animal, expression, person*] féroce; [*battle, storm, hatred, anger*] violent; [*determination, loyalty*] farouche; [*advocate, supporter*] fervent; [*criticism, speech*] virulent; [*competition*] acharné; [*flames, heat*] intense; **he has a ~ temper** c'est un caractère explosif.

fiercely /ˈfɪəslɪ/ *adv* **1** [*compete, defend, hit, oppose*] avec acharnement; [*fight*] sauvagement; [*stare*] férocement; [*shout, speak*] violemment; [*burn, blaze*] avec intensité; **2** [*competitive, critical, hot, jealous*] extrêmement; [*determined, loyal*] farouchement.

fierceness /ˈfɪəsnɪs/ *n* **1** (ferocity) (of animal) férocité *f*; (of person, expression, storm, battle) violence *f*; **2** (intensity) (of heat, flames) intensité *f*; (of anger, criticism) violence *f*; (of competition) acharnement *m*; (of loyalty, determination) ardeur *f*.

fiery /ˈfaɪərɪ/ *adj* [*person, orator, wound, gas*] enflammé; [*speech, performance*] passionné; [*sunset, sky*] embrasé; [*eyes*] ardent; [*heat*] brûlant; [*food, drink*] qui emporte la bouche; [*volcano, furnace*] rougeoyant; **~ red/orange** rouge/orange feu; **he has a ~ temper** il a un caractère explosif.

fiesta /fɪˈestə/ *n* fête *f*.

FIFA /ˈfiːfə/ *n* (*abrév* = **Fédération internationale de football association**) FIFA *f*.

fife /faɪf/ ▶1481 *n* fifre *m*.

Fife /faɪf/ ▶1624 *pr n* (also **~ Region**) Fife *m*.

fifteen /ˌfɪfˈtiːn/ ▶1505, 971, 1096 **I** *n* **1** (number) quinze *m inv*; **2** (rugby) quinze *m*.
II *adj* quinze *inv*.

fifteenth /ˌfɪfˈtiːnθ/ ▶1505, 1150 **I** *n* **1** (in order) quinzième *mf*; **2** (of month) quinze *m inv*; **3** (fraction) quinzième *m*.
II *adj* quinzième.
III *adv* [*come, finish*] quinzième, en quinzième position.

fifth /fɪfθ/ ▶1505, 1150 **I** *n* **1** (in order) cinquième *mf*; **2** (of month) cinq *m*; **3** (fraction) cinquième *m*; **4** Mus quinte *f*; **5** (also **~ gear**) Aut cinquième *f*; **6** US Meas ≈ 75 cl.
II *adj* cinquième.
III *adv* [*come, finish*] cinquième, en cinquième position.

Fifth Amendment *n* US Jur cinquième amendement *m*; **to take** ou **invoke the ~** invoquer le cinquième amendement pour ne pas répondre à une question.

fifth: **~ column** *n* Hist cinquième colonne *f*; **~ columnist** *n* élément *m* subversif; **~ generation** *adj* Comput [*computer*] de cinquième génération.

fifthly /ˈfɪfθlɪ/ *adv* cinquièmement, en cinquième lieu.

fifth wheel *n* IDIOMS **to be the ~** être la cinquième roue de la charrette.

fiftieth /ˈfɪftɪəθ/ ▶1505 **I** *n* **1** (in sequence) cinquantième *mf*; **2** (fraction) cinquantième *m*.
II *adj* [*person, birthday*] cinquantième.
III *adv* [*come, finish*] cinquantième, en cinquantième position.

fifty /ˈfɪftɪ/ ▶1505, 971, 1096 *n, adj* cinquante (*m inv*).

fifty-fifty /ˌfɪftɪˈfɪftɪ/ **I** *adj* **her chances of success are only ~** elle n'a qu'une chance sur deux de réussir; **to have a ~ chance** avoir une chance sur deux (**of doing** de faire).
II *adv* **to split** ou **share sth ~** partager qch moitié-moitié; **to go ~** faire moitié-moitié; **to go ~ on sth** partager qch moitié-moitié or fifty-fifty○.

fig /fɪg/ **I** *n* (fruit) figue *f*; **dried/fresh ~s** figues sèches/fraîches.
II *adj* (*abrév* = **figurative**) figuré.

fig. *n* (*abrév écrite* = **figure**) fig.; **see ~ 3** voir fig. 3.

fight /faɪt/ **I** *n* **1** fig (struggle) lutte *f* (**against** contre; **for** pour; **to do** pour faire); **the ~ for survival** la lutte pour la survie; **the ~ for life** le combat contre la mort; **to keep up the ~** continuer le combat; **to put up a ~** se défendre (**against** contre); **a ~ to the death** lit, fig une lutte à mort; **2** (outbreak of fighting) (between civilians) bagarre *f* (**between** entre; **over** pour); Mil bataille *f* (**between** entre; **for** pour); (between animals) combat *m* (**between** entre); **to get into** ou **have a ~ with sb** se bagarrer contre or avec qn; **to start a ~** provoquer une bagarre (**with** contre or avec); **3** (in boxing) combat *m* (**between** entre); **to win/lose a ~** gagner/perdre un combat; **a straight ~** (**between**) un combat loyal (entre) also fig; **4** (argument) dispute *f* (**over** au sujet de; **with** avec); **to have a ~ with sb** se disputer avec qn; **5** (combative spirit) (physical) envie *f* de se battre; (psychological) envie *f* de lutter; **there was no ~ left in her** elle n'avait plus envie de lutter.
II *vtr* (*prét, pp* **fought**) **1** gen, fig lutter contre [*disease, evil, opponent, emotion, problem, proposal, tendency*]; combattre [*fire*]; mener [*campaign, war*] (**against** contre); **to ~ one's way through** se frayer un passage dans [*crowd*]; négocier [*difficulties, obstacles*]; **to ~ sb** lit, Sport se battre contre qn; fig lutter contre qn; **to ~ each other** se battre; **2** Pol [*candidate*] disputer [*seat, election*]; [*candidates*] se disputer [*seat, election*]; **3** Jur défendre [*case, cause*].
III *vi* (*prét, pp* **fought**) **1** fig (campaign) lutter (**for** pour; **against** contre; **to do** pour faire); **to ~ hard** lutter ferme; **2** lit, Mil se battre (**against** contre; **with** avec); **to ~ for one's country** se battre pour sa patrie; **to ~ in a battle** combattre dans une bataille; **to ~ for one's life** lutter pour la vie; **to ~ for breath** suffoquer; **to stand and ~** résister; **to go down ~ing** lit mourir au combat; fig lutter jusqu'à la mort; **to ~ over** se disputer [*land, possessions*]; **3** (squabble) se quereller (**over** à propos de).
IDIOMS **to ~ the good ~** se battre pour la bonne cause.
■ **fight back**: ¶ **~ back** (physically, tactically) se défendre (**against** contre); (emotionally) ne pas se laisser faire; ¶ **~ back [sth]** ravaler [*tears*]; refréner [*fear, anger*].
■ **fight down**: **~ down [sth]** refréner [*emotion*].
■ **fight off**: ¶ **~ off [sth], ~ [sth] off** lit se libérer de [*attacker*]; vaincre [*troops*]; repousser [*attack*]; ¶ **~ off [sth]** fig lutter contre [*illness, despair*]; rejeter [*challenge, criticism, proposal, takeover bid*].
■ **fight on** poursuivre la lutte.
■ **fight out**: **~ out [sth], ~ [sth] out** se battre pour régler [*differences etc*]; **leave them to ~ it out** laissez-les régler cela entre eux.

fighter /ˈfaɪtə(r)/ *n* **1** (determined person) lutteur/-euse *m/f*; **to be a ~** avoir du ressort; **2** (also **~ plane**) avion *m* de chasse; **3** (boxer) boxeur *m*.

fighter: **~ bomber** *n* Aviat chasseur-bombardier *m*; **~ pilot** ▶1692 *n* pilote *m* de chasse.

fighting /ˈfaɪtɪŋ/ **I** *n* **1** Mil combat *m* (**between** entre); **heavy ~** combat intense; **~ has broken out** la bataille a éclaté; **2** gen bagarre *f*; **no ~ in the playground** il est interdit de se battre dans la cour.
II *pres p adj* **1** Mil [*unit, force*] de combat; **~ man** soldat *m*; **~ strength** effectifs *mpl* (militaires); **2** (aggressive) [*talk, words*] agressif/-ive; **to have a ~ spirit** être combatif.

fighting chance *n* **to have a ~** avoir de bonnes chances (**of doing** de faire).

fighting cock *n* coq *m* de combat.
IDIOMS **to live like ~s** vivre comme des coqs en pâte.

fighting fit *adj* **to be ~** être en pleine forme○.

fig leaf *n* Bot feuille *f* de figuier; (in painting) feuille *f* de vigne; fig **it's just a ~!** c'est juste pour la forme.

figment /ˈfɪgmənt/ *n* **a ~ of the/of your imagination** un produit de l'imagination/de ton imagination.

fig tree *n* figuier *m*.

figurative /ˈfɪgərətɪv/ *adj* **1** Ling figuré; **in the ~ sense** au sens figuré; **2** Art figuratif/-ive.

figuratively /ˈfɪgərətɪvlɪ/ *adv* [*speak, mean*] au (sens) figuré; **~ speaking,...** métaphoriquement parlant,...; **literally and ~** au sens propre comme au figuré.

figure /ˈfɪgə(r), US ˈfɪgjər/ **I** *n* **1** (number, amount) chiffre *m*; **a provisional/disappointing ~** un chiffre provisoire/décevant; **a ~ of 15 million** un chiffre de 15 millions; **a ~ of £150** la somme de 150 livres; **government/official ~s** les chiffres gouvernementaux/officiels; **a four-/six-~ sum** un montant de quatre/six chiffres; **her salary runs into six ~s** elle gagne plus de 100 000 livres GB or dollars US; **inflation is in single/double ~s** le taux d'inflation est à un chiffre/à deux chiffres; **to have a head for ~s, to be good with ~s** être doué pour le calcul; **2** (known or important person) personnalité *f*, personnage *m*; **controversial/well-known/political ~** personnalité controversée/célèbre /politique; **a minor** ou **marginal ~** une personnalité peu importante; **a legendary ~ in rugby/rock music** un personnage légendaire du rugby/du rock; **3** (person, human form) personnage *m*; (in painting, sculpture) figure *f*; **a familiar/imposing/diminutive ~** un personnage familier/imposant/minuscule; **human/reclining ~** Art figure humaine/allongée; **a ~ appeared through the mist** une silhouette est apparue dans le brouillard; **to cut a sorry/fine ~** faire piètre/bonne figure; **to cut a dashing ~** avoir l'air fringant; **4** (representative or symbol) **mother/father ~** image *f* de la mère/du père; **authority ~** symbole *m* de l'autorité; **hate ~** bête *f* noire; **she is something of a Cassandra/Lady Macbeth ~** c'est une sorte de Cassandre/Lady Macbeth; **5** (body shape) ligne *f*; **to keep one's ~** garder la ligne; **to lose one's ~** prendre de l'embonpoint; **to watch one's ~** surveiller sa ligne; **to have a great ~**○ avoir une silhouette sensationnelle○; **made for a man's/woman's ~** fait pour une silhouette masculine/féminine; **6** (geometric or other shape) figure *f*; **plane/solid ~** figure plane/à trois dimensions; **7** (diagram) figure *f*; **see ~ 4** voir figure 4; **8** (in dance, skating) figure *f* de style.
II *vtr* **1**○ (suppose) **to ~ (that)** penser or se dire que; **2** Literat (express) symboliser.
III *vi* **1** (feature, appear) figurer; **to ~ in** ou **on a list** figurer sur une liste; **to ~ in a novel/report** figurer dans un roman/rapport; **2**○ (make sense) se comprendre; **that ~s** ça se comprend; **it doesn't ~** ça n'a pas de sens.
■ **figure in** US: **~ in [sth], ~ [sth] in** inclure, compter.
■ **figure on**○: **~ on [sth]** s'attendre à; **I hadn't ~d on that!** je ne m'attendais pas à ça!; **to ~ on doing** compter faire; **to ~ on sb doing** s'attendre à ce que qn fasse.
■ **figure out**: **~ out [sth], ~ [sth] out** trouver [*answer, reason, best way*]; **to ~ out who/why/how etc** arriver à comprendre qui/pourquoi/comment etc; **I can't ~ him out** je ne comprends rien à cet homme-là; **she's got her future ~d out** elle a son avenir tout tracé.

figured bass /ˌfɪgəd ˈbeɪs, US ˈfɪgjəd/ *n* Mus basse *f* chiffrée.

figurehead /ˈfɪgəhed, US ˈfɪgjər-/ *n* **1** (symbolic leader) personnalité *f* de prestige; **2** (of ship) figure *f* de proue.

figure of eight /ˌfɪgərəvˈeɪt, US ˌfɪgjər-/ *n* huit *m*; **to do a ~** [*skater, plane*] faire un huit.

figure of speech /ˌfɪgə əv ˈspiːtʃ, US ˌfɪgjər-/ *n* Literat, Ling figure *f* de rhétorique; **it's just a ~** c'est juste une façon de parler.

figure: **~ skater** *n* patineur/-euse *m/f* artistique; **~ skating** ▶1282 *n* patinage *m* artistique.

figurine /ˌfɪgəriːn, US ˌfɪgjəˈriːn/ *n* figurine *f*.

figwort /ˈfɪgwɒːt/ *n* scrofulaire *f*.

Fiji /ˌfiːˈdʒiː/ ▶1131, 1381 *pr n* Fidji *fpl*; **the ~ Islands** les îles Fidji; **in/to ~** aux Fidji.

Fijian /fɪˈdʒiːən/ ▶1486, 1402 **I** *n* **1** (person) Fidjien/-ienne *m/f*; **2** Ling fidgien *m*.
II *adj* fidgien/-ienne.

filament /ˈfɪləmənt/ *n* **1** Elec, Electron filament *m*; **2** (of fibre) fil *m*.

filbert /ˈfɪlbət/ *n* **1** (nut) aveline *f*; **2** (shrub) avelinier *m*.

filch○ /fɪltʃ/ *vtr* chiper○, voler (**from** à).

file /faɪl/ **I** *n* **1** (for papers etc) gen dossier *m*;

(cardboard) chemise *f*; (ring binder) classeur *m*; (card tray) fichier *m*; **2** (record) dossier *m* (**on** sur); **to have** ou **keep a ~ on sb** avoir/conserver un dossier sur qn; **his fingerprints/details are on ~** ses empreintes digitales/coordonnées sont classées; **she's on ~** elle est fichée; **to open a ~ on sb/sth** établir un dossier sur qn/qch; **it's time to close the ~** fig il est temps de classer l'affaire; **3** Comput fichier *m*; **computer ~** fichier; **4** (tool) lime *f*; **5** (line) file *f*; **to walk in single ~** marcher en file indienne.

II *modif* Comput [*editing, management, name, organization, protection*] de fichiers.

III *vtr* **1** Admin classer [*invoice, letter, record*]; **to ~ sth under (the heading) 'clients'** classer qch sous (la rubrique) 'clients'; **2** Jur déposer [*application, complaint, request*] (**with** auprès de); **to ~ a petition in bankruptcy** déposer son bilan; **to ~ a lawsuit (against sb)** intenter or faire un procès (à qn); **to ~ papers for adoption** faire une demande d'adoption; **to ~ a claim for damages against sb** intenter un procès pour dommages et intérêts à or contre qn; **3** Journ envoyer [*report*]; **4** limer [*wood, metal*]; **to ~ one's nails** se limer les ongles; **to ~ through a bar** couper un barreau à la lime.

IV *vi* **1** Jur **to ~ for (a) divorce** demander le divorce; **2** (walk) marcher en file; **they ~d into/out of the classroom** ils sont entrés dans/sortis de la salle l'un après l'autre; **we ~d past the coffin** nous avons défilé devant le cercueil.

■ **file down**: **~ [sth] down, ~ down [sth]** niveler [qch] à la lime [*surface*]; égaliser [qch] à la lime [*tooth*]; limer [*claw*].

file: **~ cabinet** *n* US = **filing cabinet**; **~ card** *n* US fiche *f*; **~ clerk** *n* US = **filing clerk**; **~-closer** *n* Mil serre-file *m*; **~ copy** *n* copie *f* de classement; **~ manager** *n* Comput gestionnaire *m* de fichier; **~ server** *n* Comput serveur *m* de fichiers.

filial /ˈfɪlɪəl/ *adj* filial.

filibuster /ˈfɪlɪbʌstə(r)/ **I** *n* obstruction *f* parlementaire.

II *vi* faire de l'obstruction parlementaire.

filigree /ˈfɪlɪgriː/ **I** *n* filigrane *m*.

II *modif* [*work, brooch*] en filigrane; **~ silver** argent *m* filigrané.

filing /ˈfaɪlɪŋ/ *n* classement *m*.

filing: **~ box** *n* boîte *f* à fiches; **~ cabinet** *n* classeur *m* à tiroirs; **~ card** *n* fiche *f*; **~ clerk** ▶ 1692 *n* employé/-e *m/f* de bureau chargé/-e du classement.

filings /ˈfaɪlɪŋz/ *npl* limaille *f* ¢.

filing: **~ system** *n* système *m* de classement; **~ tray** *n* corbeille *f* de classement.

Filipino /ˌfɪlɪˈpiːnəʊ/ ▶ 1486 **I** *n* Philippin/-e *m/f*.

II *adj* [*art, culture, food*] philippin; [*capital, embassy, industry, population*] des Philippines.

fill /fɪl/ **I** *n* **to eat/drink one's ~** manger/boire tout son content; **to have had one's ~** en avoir assez (**of** de; **of doing** de faire).

II *vtr* **1** [*person, water, rain, fruit, soil*] remplir [*container*] (**with** de); **fruit ~ed the baskets, the baskets were ~ed with fruit** les paniers étaient remplis de fruits; **tears ~ed his eyes** ses yeux se remplirent de larmes; **to ~ the kettle** mettre de l'eau dans la bouilloire; **2** [*crowd, audience, sound, laughter*] remplir [*building, room, street, train*]; [*smoke, gas, sunlight, protesters*] envahir [*building, room*]; **the speaker had ~ed the hall** l'orateur avait rempli la salle; **to ~ one's house with flowers/antiques** remplir sa maison de fleurs/d'antiquités; **the smell of flowers ~ed the house** l'odeur des fleurs s'est répandue dans toute la maison; **3** (plug) boucher [*crack, hole, hollow*] (**with** avec); boucher les trous de [*wall, doorframe*]; fig boucher [*vacuum, gap, void*] (**with** de); **4** (fulfil) répondre à [*need*]; **5** (occupy, take up) remplir [*page, chapter, volumes, tape*] (**with** de); occuper [*time, day, hours*]; **to ~ one's days with work** occuper ses journées en travaillant; **~ (one's) time doing** occuper son temps à faire; **6** [*company, university*] pourvoir [*post, vacancy, place, chair*]; [*applicant*] occuper [*post, vacancy*]; **there are still 10 places to ~** il reste encore 10 places à pourvoir; **7** [*emotion, thought*] remplir [*heart, mind, person*]; **to ~ sb's mind/heart with** remplir l'esprit/le cœur de qn de; **to ~ sb's head with nonsense** mettre des absurdités dans la tête de qn; **8** (stuff, put filling in) garnir [*cushion, quilt, pie, sandwich*] (**with** de); **9** [*dentist*] plomber, obturer spec [*tooth, cavity*]; **10** [*wind*] gonfler [*sail*]; **11** (carry out) exécuter [*order*]; **12** (with food) ▶ **fill up**.

III *vi* **1** [*bath, bucket, theatre, hall, streets, eyes*] se remplir (**with** de); **to ~ with light/smoke** être envahi de lumière/de fumée; **2** [*sail*] se gonfler.

IV -filled (*dans composés*) rempli de; **smoke-/book-~ed room** pièce remplie de fumée/de livres.

■ **fill in**: ¶ **~ in** [*person*] faire un remplacement; **to ~ in for sb** remplacer qn; ¶ **~ in [sth]** passer [*time, hour, day*]; ¶ **~ in [sth], ~ [sth] in 1** (complete) remplir [*form, box, section*]; **2** (plug) boucher [*hole, crack, gap*] (**with** avec); **3** (supply) donner [*detail, information, name, date*]; **4** (colour in) remplir [*shape, panel*]; **to ~ sth in with pencil/in red** remplir qch au crayon/en rouge; ¶ **~ in [sb], ~ [sb] in 1** (inform) mettre [qn] au courant (**on** de); **2**○ GB (beat up) tabasser○ [*person*].

■ **fill out**: ¶ **~ out** [*person*] prendre du poids; [*face, cheeks*] s'arrondir; ¶ **~ out [sth], ~ [sth] out** remplir [*form, application*]; faire [*certificate, prescription*].

■ **fill up**: ¶ **~ up** [*bath, theatre, bus*] se remplir (**with** de); [*person*] **to ~ up on** se bourrer○ de [*bread, sweets*]; ¶ **~ up [sth], ~ [sth] up** remplir [*kettle, box, room*] (**with** de); **to ~ up the whole room** occuper toute la pièce; **~ it** ou **her up!** (with petrol) faites le plein!; **to ~ up the time** tuer le temps; ¶ **~ up [sb], ~ [sb] up** bourrer○ qn (**with** de); **it ~s you up** c'est bourratif○; **to ~ oneself up** se bourrer○ (**with** de).

filler /ˈfɪlə(r)/ **I** *n* **1** (for wood) bouche-pores *m inv*; (for car body) mastic *m*; (for wall) enduit *m* de rebouchage, reboucheur *m*; **2** Journ, TV (article, photo, music) bouche-trou *m*; **to use sth as a ~** se servir de qch comme bouche-trou or pour faire du remplissage.

II *modif* [*article, photo, material*] de remplissage.

filler cap *n* GB Aut bouchon *m* de réservoir.

fillet /ˈfɪlɪt/ **I** *n* filet *m*; **400 g of beef ~** 400 g de filet de bœuf; **a pork ~** un filet de porc; **three sole ~s** ou **three ~s of sole** trois filets de sole.

II *vtr* enlever les arêtes de, fileter [*fish*]; **~ed cod** filets *mpl* de cabillaud.

fillet steak *n* filet *m* de bœuf.

fill-in○ /ˈfɪlɪn/ *n* remplaçant/-e *m/f*.

filling /ˈfɪlɪŋ/ **I** *n* **1** Culin (of sandwich, baked potato) garniture *f*; (stuffing for vegetable, meat, pancake) farce *f*; **pie with blackberry/meat ~** tourte *f* fourrée aux mûres/à la viande; **use jam as a ~ for the cake** fourrez le gâteau à la confiture; **2** (for tooth) plombage *m*, obturation *f* spec; **to have a ~ (done)** se faire faire un plombage; **3** (of quilt, pillow, cushion) garnissage *m*; (of bed, mattress) garniture *f*.

II *adj* [*food, dish*] bourratif/-ive○.

filling station *n* station-service *f*.

fillip /ˈfɪlɪp/ *n* coup *m* de fouet fig; **to give a ~ to** donner un coup de fouet à.

filly /ˈfɪlɪ/ *n* pouliche *f*.

film /fɪlm/ **I** *n* **1** Cin (movie) film *m*; **there's a new ~ on** un nouveau film passe; **to be** ou **work in ~s** travailler dans le cinéma; **short ~** court métrage; **2** Phot (for snapshots) pellicule *f*; (for movies) film *m*; **a colour ~** une pellicule couleur; **to capture sth on ~** enregistrer qch sur film; **3** (layer) pellicule *f*; **a ~ of oil/of dust** une pellicule d'huile/de poussière; **to look at sb through a ~ of tears** regarder qn à travers un voile de larmes; **4** Culin scellofrais® *m*.

II *vtr* [*person*] filmer [*event, programme*]; [*person*] adapter [qch] pour le cinéma [*novel, play*]; [*camera*] enregistrer [*action, scene*].

III *vi* [*camera man, crew*] tourner; **the cast are ~ing in Egypt** l'équipe tourne en Égypte.

■ **film over** [*glass, windscreen*] s'embuer.

film: **~ archive** *n* archives *fpl* cinématographiques; **~ award** *n* prix *m* de cinéma; **~ badge** *n* Tech dosimètre *m* photographique personnel; **~ buff**○ *n* mordu/-e○ *m/f* de cinéma; **~ camera** *n* caméra *f*; **~ club** *n* ciné-club *m*; **~ contract** *n* contrat *m* de tournage; **~ coverage** *n* couverture *f* cinématographique; **~ critic** ▶ 1692 *n* critique *m* de films; **~ director** ▶ 1692 *n* réalisateur/-trice *m/f*, metteur *m* en scène; **~ festival** *n* festival *m* de cinéma; **~goer** *n* cinéphile *mf*; **~ industry** *n* industrie *f* cinématographique.

filming /ˈfɪlmɪŋ/ *n* Cin tournage *m*.

film: **~ laboratory** *n* laboratoire *m* cinématographique; **~ library** *n* cinémathèque *f*; **~ magazine** *n* revue *f* de cinéma; **~-maker** ▶ 1692 *n* cinéaste *m*; **~-making** *n* cinéma *m*.

filmography /fɪlˈmɒgrəfɪ/ *n* filmographie *f*.

film: **~ premiere** *n* première *f*; **~ producer** ▶ 1692 *n* producteur/-trice *m/f* de cinéma; **~ production** *n* production *f* de films; **~ rights** *n* droits *mpl* cinématographiques; **~ script** *n* scénario *m*; **~ sequence** *n* séquence *f* (filmée).

filmset /ˈfɪlmset/ **I** *n* Cin plateau *m* de tournage.

II *vtr* (*p prés* **-tt-**, *prét, pp* **~**) Print photocomposer.

film: **~setter** *n* Print photocomposeuse *f*; **~setting** *n* Print photocomposition *f*; **~ show** *n* présentation *f* de films; **~ star** ▶ 1692 *n* vedette *f* de cinéma; **~ strip** *n* film *m* pour projection fixe; **~ studio** *n* studio *m* cinématographique; **~ test** *n* bout *m* d'essai; **~ version** *n* version *f* filmée.

filmy /ˈfɪlmɪ/ *adj* **1** (thin) [*dress*] très léger/-ère; [*fabric, screen*] transparent; [*cloud, layer*] léger/-ère; **2** (cloudy) [*glass, lens*] sale.

filter /ˈfɪltə(r)/ **I** *n* **1** Sci, Tech filtre *m*; **air/oil/water ~** filtre à air/huile/eau; **2** Audio, Phot, Telecom filtre *m*; **3** Cosmet filtre *m*; **sun ~** filtre solaire; **4** (also **~ lane**) GB Transp voie *f* réservée aux véhicules qui tournent, voie *f* de stockage spéc; **5** GB Transp (arrow) flèche *f* (directionnelle).

II *vtr* filtrer [*liquid, gas*]; faire passer [*coffee*].

III *vi* **1** (also **~ off**) GB Transp **to ~ off to the left** passer sur la voie de gauche pour tourner; **2** (trickle) **to ~ into** [*light, sound, water*] pénétrer dans [*area*]; **to ~ back/out** [*crowd, people*] revenir/sortir par petits groupes.

■ **filter in** [*light, sound, details*] filtrer.

■ **filter out**: ¶ **~ out** [*details, news*] filtrer; [*light, noise*] filtrer à l'extérieur; ¶ **~ out [sth], ~ [sth] out** éliminer [*applicants, impurities, light, noise*].

■ **filter through**: ¶ **~ through** [*details, light, sound*] filtrer; **to ~ through to sb** [*news*] filtrer jusqu'à qn; ¶ **~ through [sth]** [*sound, light*] filtrer à travers [*screen, curtain*].

filter: **~ bed** *n* bassin *m* de filtration; **~ cigarette** *n* cigarette *f* (à bout) filtre; **~ coffee** *n* (cup of coffee) café *m* (filtre); (ground coffee) café *m* moulu pour filtres; **~ coffee maker, ~ coffee machine** *n* cafetière *f* électrique; **~ funnel** *n* entonnoir *m* (à filtre); **~ paper** *n* Culin, Sci papier-filtre *m*; **~ pump** *n* Tech pompe *f* à filtrer; **~ tip** *n* (cigarette) filtre *m*; **~-tipped** *adj* [*cigarette*] (à bout) filtre *inv*.

filth /fɪlθ/ *n* **1** (dirt) crasse *f*; **2** (vulgarity) obscénités *fpl*; (swearing) grossièretés *fpl*; **3**○ GB injur (police) **the ~** les flics○ *mpl*.

filthy /ˈfɪlθɪ/ *adj* **1** (dirty) crasseux/-euse; (revolting) répugnant; **that's a ~ habit** c'est dégoûtant; **2** (vulgar) [*language*] ordurier/-ière; [*mind*] mal tourné; **3** GB (unpleasant) [*weather*] épouvantable; [*look*] noir; **he's in a ~ temper** il est d'une humeur massacrante.

filthy rich○ *adj* plein aux as○.

filtrate /ˈfɪltreɪt/ *n* filtrat *m*.

filtration /fɪlˈtreɪʃn/ *n* filtration *f*.

fin /fɪn/ *n* **1** Zool (of fish, seal) nageoire *f*; (of shark) aileron *m*; **2** Aerosp empennage *m*; **3** Tech, Aut ailette *f*; **4** Naut dérive *f*.

finagle○ /fɪˈneɪgl/ *vtr* US **1** (wangle) se débrouiller pour avoir [*grade, ticket etc*]; **2** (trick) **to ~ sb into doing** se débrouiller pour que qn fasse.

finagler○ /fɪˈneɪglə(r)/ *n* US péj magouilleur/-euse○ *m/f*.

finagling○ /fɪˈneɪglɪŋ/ *n* US ¢ magouille○ *f*.

final /ˈfaɪnl/ **I** *n* **1** Sport finale *f*; **2** Journ (edition) dernière édition *f*; **the late ~** la dernière édition du soir.
II *adj* **1** (last) (*épith*) dernier/-ière [*day, question, book, meeting*]; **~ examinations** GB Univ examens *mpl* de fin d'études; US Univ examens *mpl* de fin de semestre; **~ instalment** Comm dernier versement *m*; **2** (definitive) [*decision, answer*] définitif/-ive; [*result*] final; [*judgment*] irrévocable; **that's ~!** un point, c'est tout○!; **to have the ~ word** avoir le dernier mot; **she has the ~ say** c'est à elle de décider; **the referee's decision is ~** la décision de l'arbitre est sans appel.

final: **~ approach** *n* Aviat approche *f*; **~ cause** *n* Philos cause *f* finale; **~ demand** *n* Comm dernier rappel *m*; **~ dividend** *n* Fin superdividende *m*.

finale /fɪˈnɑːlɪ, US -nælɪ/ *n* Mus, Theat, gen finale *f*; **grand ~** apothéose *f*.

final invoice *n* Comm facture *f* définitive.

finalist /ˈfaɪnəlɪst/ *n* finaliste *mf*.

finality /faɪˈnælətɪ/ *n* irrévocabilité *f*; **with ~** avec détermination.

finalization /ˌfaɪnəlaɪˈzeɪʃn, US -lɪˈz-/ *n* finalisation *f*, dernière mise *f* au point.

finalize /ˈfaɪnəlaɪz/ *vtr* conclure [*letter, purchase, contract, deal*]; arrêter [*plan, decision, details*]; finaliser [*report*]; boucler [*team*]; fixer [*timetable, route*]; prononcer [*divorce*].

finally /ˈfaɪnəlɪ/ *adv* **1** (eventually) [*decide, accept, arrive, happen*] finalement, enfin; **they ~ arrived** ils sont finalement arrivés, ils ont fini par arriver; **2** (lastly) finalement; **~ I would like to thank...** pour finir je voudrais remercier...; **3** (definitively) [*settle, resolve, decide*] définitivement.

final notice *n* Comm dernier appel *m*.

finals /ˈfaɪnlz/ *npl* **1** Univ GB examens *mpl* de fin d'études; US examens *mpl* de fin de semestre; **2** Sport (last few games) phase *f* finale; (last game) finale *f*.

Final Solution *n* Solution *f* finale.

finance /ˈfaɪnæns, fɪˈnæns/ **I** *n* **1** (banking, money systems) finance *f*; **high ~** la haute finance; **2** (funds) fonds *mpl*; **to get** ou **obtain ~** trouver les fonds (**for** pour; **from** auprès de); **3** (credit) crédit *m*; **free ~!, 0% ~!** crédit gratuit!
II finances *npl* (financial situation) (of person) finances *fpl*; (of company, country) situation *f* financière.
III *modif* [*minister, ministry*] des Finances; [*committee, director, page, correspondent*] financier/-ière.
IV *vtr* financer [*project*].

finance: **~ bill** *n* projet *m* de loi de finances; **~ company**, **~ house** *n* société *f* de financement.

financial /faɪˈnænʃl, fɪ-/ *adj* [*adviser, backing, institution, problem, service*] financier/-ière.

financial: **~ backer** *n* commanditaire *m*; **~ futures market** *n* marché *m* à terme d'instruments financiers, MATIF.

financially /faɪˈnænʃəlɪ, fɪ-/ *adv* financièrement.

financial: **Financial Times (Industrial Ordinary Share) Index**, **FT Index** *n*: *indice du cours des actions de 30 sociétés britanniques sélectionnées par le Financial Times*; **Financial Times-Stock Exchange Index**, **FTSE 100** *n* indice *m* de la Bourse de Londres; **~ year** *n* GB exercice *m*, année *f* budgétaire.

financier /faɪˈnænsɪə(r), US ˌfɪnənˈsɪər/ *n* financier *m*.

financing /ˈfaɪnænsɪŋ, fɪˈnænsɪŋ/ *n* financement *m*.

finch /fɪntʃ/ *n* fringillidé *m*.

find /faɪnd/ **I** *n* (discovery) gen découverte *f*; (lucky purchase) trouvaille *f*; **an arms ~** la découverte d'une cache d'armes; **she's a real ~**○ c'est une vraie perle.
II *vtr* (*prét, pp* **found**) **1** (discover by chance) trouver [*thing, person*]; **'found: black kitten'** 'trouvé: chaton noir'; **I found a letter lying on the table** j'ai trouvé une lettre sur la table; **to leave sth as one found it** laisser qch dans l'état où on l'a trouvé; **to ~ sb doing** trouver qn en train de faire; **to ~ sth locked/sb dead** trouver qch fermé/qn mort; **to ~ sth to be locked/sb to be dead** constater que qch est fermé/que qn est mort; **to ~ that** constater que; **she arrived (only) to ~ that the train had left** elle est arrivée pour constater que le train était parti; **2** (discover by looking) trouver, retrouver [*thing, person*]; **I can't ~ my keys** je ne trouve pas mes clés; **to ~ sth on a map** trouver qch sur un plan; **to ~ one's place in a book** retrouver sa page; **I found her glasses for her** je lui ai trouvé ses lunettes; **to ~ one's** ou **the way** trouver or retrouver son chemin; **to ~ one's way out of** trouver la sortie de [*building, forest, city*]; **to ~ one's own way home** se débrouiller tout seul pour rentrer chez soi; **3** (discover desired thing) trouver [*job, vocation, flat, car, seat, solution*]; **you'll ~ lingerie downstairs** (in shop) vous trouverez la lingerie à l'étage inférieur; **to ~ room for** trouver de la place pour [*object, food*]; **to ~ (the) time/the energy/ the money for** trouver le temps/l'énergie/ l'argent pour; **to ~ sth for sb**, **to ~ sb sth** trouver qch pour qn; **to ~ something for sb to do**, **to ~ sb something to do** trouver quelque chose à faire pour qn; **to ~ oneself sth** se trouver qch; **4** (encounter) trouver [*word, term, species*]; **it is not found in Europe** on ne le trouve pas en Europe; **it is to be found in the Louvre** on peut le voir au Louvre; **5** (judge, consider) trouver (**that** que); **how did you ~ her?** comment l'as-tu trouvée?; **to ~ sb polite/a bore** trouver qn poli/ennuyeux; **to ~ sb/sth to be** trouver que qn/qch est; **to ~ sth easy/hard etc to do** trouver qch facile/difficile etc à faire; **to ~ it easy/painful/difficult to do** trouver que c'est facile/douloureux/difficile de faire; **to ~ it incredible/encouraging that** trouver cela incroyable/encourageant que (+ *subj*); **6** (experience) éprouver [*pleasure, satisfaction*] (**in** dans; **in doing** à faire); trouver [*comfort*] (**in** dans; **in doing** à faire); **7** (reach) **to ~ its mark/its target** toucher son but/sa cible; **to ~ its/one's (own) level** trouver son propre niveau; **to ~ its way to/into** arriver dans [*bin, pocket, area*]; **how did it ~ its way into your bag?** comment est-ce que c'est arrivé dans ton sac?; **8** Jur **to ~ that** conclure que; **to ~ sb guilty/not guilty** déclarer qn coupable/non coupable; **to be found guilty** être déclaré coupable; **how do you ~ the accused?** quel est votre verdict?; **9** (arrive to find) [*letter, card, day*] trouver [*person*]; **I hope this card ~s you well** j'espère que cette carte vous trouvera en bonne santé; **the next day found him feeling ill** le lendemain il se sentait malade; **10** Comput rechercher.
III *vi* Jur **to ~ for/against sb** se prononcer en faveur de/contre qn.
IV *v refl* **to ~ oneself 1** (discover suddenly) se retrouver; **to ~ oneself in Crewe/ trapped** se retrouver à Crewe/ coincé; **to ~ oneself unable to do** se sentir incapable de faire; **to ~ oneself agreeing/wishing that** se surprendre à être d'accord/à souhaiter que; **to ~ oneself being swept along by the crowd** se retrouver entraîné par la foule; **2** (discover one's vocation) se découvrir.
IDIOMS **all found** logé et nourri; **to ~ one's feet** prendre pied; **to take sb as one ~s him/her** prendre qn comme il/elle est.
■ **find out**: ¶ **~ out** apprendre; **I hope no-one ~s out** j'espère que personne ne l'apprendra; ¶ **~ out [sth]**, **~ [sth] out** découvrir [*fact, answer, name, cause, truth*]; ¶ **~ out who/why/where etc** trouver qui/pourquoi/où etc; ¶ **~ out that** découvrir or apprendre que; ¶ **~ [sb] out** découvrir [*person*]; **to be found out** être découvert; ¶ **~ out about 1** (discover, learn by chance) découvrir [*plan, affair, breakage*]; **2** (research, investigate) faire des recherches sur [*subject, topic*].

finder /ˈfaɪndə(r)/ **I** *n* **1** (of treasure, lost thing) celui/celle *m/f* qui trouve; **the ~ will receive a reward** la personne qui trouvera recevra une récompense; **2** (telescope) chercheur *m* de télescope.
II -finder (*dans composés*) **job-~** prospecteur-placier *m*; **house-~** agent *m* immobilier; **fact-~** ouvrage *m* de référence.
IDIOMS **~s keepers (losers weepers)** celui qui le trouve le garde.

finding /ˈfaɪndɪŋ/ *n* (of court, committee, research) conclusion *f*; **they made the following ~s** ils ont tiré les conclusions suivantes.

fine /faɪn/ **I** *n* gen amende *f*; (for traffic offence) contravention *f* (**for** pour); **to get/be given a ~** recevoir/attraper une amende; **to impose a ~ of £50/the maximum ~ on sb** condamner qn à 50 livres sterling d'amende/à l'amende la plus lourde; **'no smoking—maximum ~ £50'** 'défense de fumer sous peine d'amende pouvant s'élever à 50 livres sterling'.
II *adj* **1** (very good) [*performance, writer, example, specimen, quality, standard*] excellent; **to be in ~ form** être en pleine forme; **a ~ figure of a woman** † ou hum une superbe créature†; **2** (satisfactory) [*holiday, meal, arrangement*] bien; **that's ~** très bien; **to be/feel ~** aller/se sentir très bien; **'~, thanks'** 'très bien, merci'; **'we'll go now, OK?'—'~'** 'on y va maintenant?'—'d'accord'; **that's ~ by** ou **with me** je n'y vois pas d'inconvénient; **3**○ iron **a ~ friend you are!** en voilà un ami!; **you picked a ~ time to tell me!** tu as bien choisi le moment pour me le dire!; **you're/she's etc a ~ one to talk!** c'est bien à toi/elle etc de dire ça!; **that's all very ~, but...** c'est bien beau tout ça, mais...; **4** Meteorol [*weather, morning, day*] beau/belle; **it's** ou **the weather's ~** il fait beau; **to keep** ou **stay ~** continuer à faire beau; **one ~ day, one of these ~ days** fig un beau jour; **5** (very thin, delicate) [*hair, thread, line, feature, comb, fabric, spray, mist, layer*] fin; [*sieve, net, mesh*] à mailles fines; **6** (small-grained) [*powder, soil, particles*] fin; **7** (subtle) [*adjustment, detail, distinction, judgment*] subtil; **8** (delicate and high quality) [*china, crystal, lace, linen, wine*] fin; **9** (refined, grand) [*lady, gentleman, clothes, manners*] beau/belle; **sb's finer feelings** la délicatesse

de qn; **10** (commendable) [*person*] merveilleux/-euse; **he's a ~ man** c'est quelqu'un; **11** (pure) [*gold, silver*] pur.
III *adv* **1** [*get along, come along, do*] très bien; **you're doing ~** tu te débrouilles○ très bien; **that suits me ~** ça me va très bien; **2** [*cut, chop, slice*] controv fin.
IV *vtr* gen condamner [qn] à une amende [*offender*] (**for** pour; **for doing** pour avoir fait); (for traffic offence) donner une contravention à [*offender*]; **to ~ sb £50** condamner qn à 50 livres sterling d'amende.
IDIOMS **not to put too ~ a point on it** bref, à franchement parler; **a chance would be a ~ thing**○! ça serait trop beau○!; **to cut it a bit ~** faire trop juste, être un peu juste; **there is a ~ line between X and Y** il y a une distinction subtile entre X et Y; **to tread a ~ line** jouer serré.

fine art *n* beaux-arts *mpl*; **to study ~** étudier les beaux-arts; **the ~s** les beaux-arts.
IDIOMS **to have sth down to a ~** avoir élevé qch au rang d'un art.

fine: **~-drawn** *adj* [*distinction*] subtil; **~ grain** *adj* Phot à grain fin.

fine-grained /ˌfaɪnˈɡreɪnd/ *adj* **1** [*wood, leather*] au grain fin; **2** [*salt, sugar*] fin.

finely /ˈfaɪnlɪ/ *adv* **1** [*chopped, grated, ground, minced*] finement; **2** [*balanced, controlled, judged, poised*] soigneusement; **3** [*carved, wrought*] délicatement; **4** [*written, painted, executed*] splendidement; **5** (sumptuously) [*dressed, furnished*] splendidement.

fineness /ˈfaɪnnɪs/ *n* (of metal) titre *m*.

fineness ratio *n* rapport *m* de finesse.

fine print *n* petits caractères *mpl*.

finery /ˈfaɪnərɪ/ *n* parure *f*; **in all her ~** dans ses plus beaux atours liter.

finespun /ˈfaɪnspʌn/ *adj* [*notion, argument*] très subtil.

finesse /fɪˈnes/ ▶ 1282 **I** *n* **1** gen finesse *f*; **2** (in cards) impasse *f*.
II *vtr* **1** (handle adroitly) manipuler adroitement [*situation, person*]; contourner [*objections*]; **2** (in cards) faire l'impasse en jouant [*card, king, queen*].
III *vi* (in cards) faire une impasse.

fine-tooth(ed) comb /ˌfaɪnˈtuːθkəʊm/ *n* peigne *m* fin.
IDIOMS **to go over** ou **through sth with a ~** passer qch au peigne fin.

fine: **~-tune** *vtr* ajuster; **~ tuning** *n* ajustement *m*.

finger /ˈfɪŋɡə(r)/ **I** *n* ▶ 1037 **1** Anat doigt *m*; **first** ou **index ~** index *m*; **second ~** majeur *m*, médius *m*; **third** ou **ring ~** annulaire *m*; **fourth** ou **little ~** auriculaire *m*; **to wear a ring on one's index ~** porter une bague à l'index; **he put a ring on her ~** il lui a passé une bague au doigt; **to point one's ~ at sb/sth** montrer qn/qch du doigt; **she ran her ~s through his hair** elle lui a passé la main dans les cheveux; **to run one's ~s over sth** passer les doigts sur qch; **something is wrong, but I can't quite put my ~ on it** fig quelque chose ne va pas mais je n'arrive pas à mettre le doigt dessus; **he didn't lift** ou **raise a ~ to help** il n'a pas levé le petit doigt pour aider; **I didn't lay a ~ on her** je ne l'ai pas touchée; **if you so much as lay a ~ on my hi-fi I'll...** si jamais tu touches à ma chaîne hi-fi, je...; **I didn't lay a ~ on it** je n'y ai pas touché; **to put two ~s up at sb**○ GB, **to give sb the ~**○ US envoyer qn se faire foutre◑ (avec un geste obscène); **I can count the number of beers he has bought me on the ~s of one hand** iron je peux compter les bières qu'il m'a payées sur les doigts de la main; **2** (of glove) doigt *m*; **3** (narrow strip) (of land) bande *f*; (of mist, smoke) volute *f*; **4** (small amount) doigt *m*; **two ~s of whisky** deux doigts de whisky.
II *vtr* toucher, tripoter○ [*fruit, goods*]; toucher [*fabric, silk*]; tripoter○ [*tie, necklace*]; **to ~ one' s beard** se tripoter la barbe○.
IDIOMS **to get one's ~s burnt** se brûler les doigts; **to twist** ou **wrap sb around one's little ~** mener qn par le bout du nez; **to keep one's ~s crossed** croiser les doigts (**for sb** pour qn); **to point the ~ at sb** accuser qn; **to point the ~ of suspicion at sb** jeter des soupçons sur qn; **to put the ~ on sb**○ moucharder qn○; **to pull one's ~ out**◑ se grouiller○; **to slip through sb's ~s** [*opportunity*] passer sous le nez de qn; [*wanted man*] filer entre les doigts de qn.

finger: **~ biscuit** *n* Culin ≈ boudoir *m*; **~board** *n* Mus touche *f*; **~ bowl** *n* rince-doigts *m inv*; **~ buffet** *n* Culin buffet *m* sans couverts; **~ cymbal** *n* Mus cymbale *f* de danseur égyptien.

finger-dry /ˌfɪŋɡəˈdraɪ/ *vtr* **to ~ one's hair** passer les doigts dans ses cheveux pour les aider à sécher.

finger: **~ exercises** *n* Mus exercices *mpl* de doigté; **~ food** *n* Culin buffet *m* froid à consommer sans couverts; **~ hole** *n* Mus trou *m* (*sur flûte, clarinette etc*).

fingering /ˈfɪŋɡərɪŋ/ *n* Mus doigté *m*.

finger: **~less glove** *n* mitaine *f*; **~ mark** *n* trace *f* de doigt; **~-nail** *n* ongle *m*; **~-paint** *vi* peindre avec les doigts.

finger painting *n* **1** (technique) peinture *f* avec les doigts; **2** (picture) peinture *f* faite avec les doigts.

finger: **~ plate** *n* plaque *f* de propreté; **~ post** *n* panneau *m* indicateur (*en forme de doigt*).

fingerprint /ˈfɪŋɡəprɪnt/ **I** *n* empreinte *f* digitale; **to take sb's ~s** prendre les empreintes digitales de qn; **a set of ~s** une série d'empreintes digitales; **genetic ~, DNA ~** empreinte *f* génétique.
II *modif* [*expert*] en empreintes digitales.
III *vtr* prendre les empreintes digitales de [*person*]; relever les empreintes digitales sur [*glass, surface, weapon*].

finger: **~printing** *n* prise *f* d'empreintes digitales; **~printing kit** *n* nécessaire *m* utilisé pour relever des empreintes digitales; **~-stall** *n* doigtier *m*; **~ tight** *adj* vissé (à fond) à la main.

fingertip /ˈfɪŋɡətɪp/ *n* bout *m* du doigt; **to touch sth with one's ~s** toucher qch du bout des doigts.
IDIOMS **to have sth at one's ~s** connaître qch sur le bout des doigts; **she's an aristocrat to her ~s** elle est aristocrate jusqu'au bout des ongles.

fingertip control *n* contrôle *m* digital.

finger trouble○ *n* Comput erreur *f* de manipulation des touches.

fingerwagging /ˈfɪŋɡəwæɡɪŋ/ **I** *n* fig accusation *f*.
II *modif* [*memo, minister*] accusateur/-trice.

finial /ˈfɪnɪəl/ *n* Archit fleuron *m*.

finicky /ˈfɪnɪkɪ/ *adj* [*person*] difficile (**about** pour); [*job, task*] minutieux/-ieuse.

finish /ˈfɪnɪʃ/ **I** *n* (*pl* **~es**) **1** (end) fin *f*; **from start to ~** du début (jusqu')à la fin; **it will be a fight to the ~** lit ce sera un combat à mort; fig la partie va être serrée; **to be in at the ~** assister au dénouement; **2** Sport arrivée *f*; **it was a close ~** l'arrivée a été serrée; **an athlete with a good ~** un athlète bon au sprint final; **3** (surface, aspect) (of clothing, wood, car) finition *f*; (of fabric, leather) apprêt *m*; **a car with a metallic ~** une voiture métallisée; **paint with a matt/silk ~** peinture mate/satinée; **a wine with a smooth ~** un vin épanoui.
II *vtr* **1** (complete) finir, terminer [*chapter, sentence, task*]; terminer, achever [*building, novel, sculpture, opera*]; **to ~ doing** finir de faire; **I must get this report ~ed** il faut que je finisse or que je termine ce rapport; **2** (leave) finir [*work, studies*]; **I ~ work at 5.30 pm** je finis (le travail) à 17 h 30; **she ~es school/university next year** elle finira l'école/l'université l'année prochaine; **3** (consume) finir [*cigarette, drink, meal*]; **who ~ed all the biscuits?** qui a fini les biscuits?; **4** (put an end to) briser [*career*]; **5**○ (exhaust, demoralize) achever○ [*person*]; **that long walk ~ed me!** cette longue promenade m'a achevé○!; **this news nearly ~ed him** cette nouvelle a failli l'achever○.
III *vi* **1** (end) [*conference, programme, term*] finir, se terminer; [*holidays*] prendre fin; **the meeting ~es at 3 pm** la réunion se termine à 15 h; **the film ~es on Thursday** le film ne passe plus à partir de jeudi; **I'll see you when the concert ~es** je te verrai à la fin du concert; **wait until the music ~es** attends la fin du morceau (de musique); **as the concert was ~ing** alors que le concert touchait à sa fin; **after the lecture ~es we'll have lunch** nous déjeunerons quand la conférence sera terminée; **I'm waiting for the washing machine to ~** j'attends que ma lessive soit finie; **2** (reach end of race) arriver; **my horse ~ed first** mon cheval est arrivé premier; **the horse/the athlete failed to ~** le cheval/l'athlète n'a pas fini la course; **3** (conclude) [*speaker*] finir, conclure; **he won't let me ~** il ne me laisse pas finir (de parler); **let me ~** laissez- moi finir (de parler); **she ~ed with a quotation** elle a conclu par une citation; **4** (leave employment) **I ~ed at the bank yesterday** j'ai quitté mon travail à la banque hier.
IV finished *pp adj* **1 beautifully ~ed** [*furniture, interior etc*] avec des finitions soignées; **interior ~ed in marble/grey** intérieur avec des finitions en marbre/finitions grises; **walls ~ed in blue gloss** murs laqués bleu; **the ~ed product** le produit fini; **2** (accomplished) [*performance*] accompli; **3** (ruined) fini, fichu○; **as a boxer he's ~ed** en tant que boxeur il est fini or fichu○; **after the scandal her career was ~ed** après le scandale, sa carrière était finie.
■ **finish off**: ¶ **~ [sth] off, ~ off [sth] 1** (complete) finir, terminer [*letter, task*]; **I'll just ~ off the ironing** je vais juste finir le repassage; **2** (round off) **to ~ off the meal with a glass of brandy** terminer le repas avec un verre de cognac; ¶ **~ [sb] off 1** (exhaust, demoralize) achever○ [*person*]; **2** (kill) achever [*person, animal*].
■ **finish up**: ¶ **~ up** [*person*] (at end of journey) se retrouver; (in situation) finir; **they ~ed up in London** il se sont retrouvés à Londres; **he ~ed up in prison** il a fini en prison; **to ~ up as a teacher** finir par devenir professeur; **to ~ up (by) doing** finir par faire; ¶ **~ [sth] up, ~ up [sth]** finir [*milk, paint, cake*].
■ **finish with**: ¶ **~ with [sth]** finir avec; **have you ~ed with the newspaper?** tu as fini avec le journal?; **hurry up and ~ with the scissors, I need them** dépêche-toi avec les ciseaux, j'en ai besoin; **pass the pen to me when you've ~ed with it** passe-moi le stylo quand tu auras fini; **I'm ~ed with school/politics!** j'en ai assez de l'école!/de la politique!; ¶ **~ with [sb] 1** (split up) rompre avec [*girlfriend, boyfriend*]; **2** (stop punishing) **I haven't ~ed with you yet!** je n'en ai pas encore fini avec toi!; **you'll be sorry when I've ~ed with you!** tu vas voir ce que tu vas voir○!

finisher /ˈfɪnɪʃə(r)/ ▶ 1692 *n* finisseur/-euse *m/f*, apprêteur/-euse *m/f*.

finish: **~ing line** GB, **~ line** US *n* Sport, fig ligne *f* d'arrivée; **~ing post** *n* Sport poteau *m* d'arrivée; **~ing school** *n* Sch *pension pour jeunes filles de bonne famille.*

finishing touch *n* touche *f* finale; **to put the ~es to** mettre la touche finale à [*painting, speech, room*].

Finistère ▶ 1163 *pr n* Finistère *m*; **in/to ~** dans le Finistère.

finite /ˈfaɪnaɪt/ *adj* **1** gen [*resources*] limité; **2** Math, Philos, Ling fini.

fink◑ /fɪŋk/ US péj **I** *n* **1** (informer) mouchard/-e *m/f* pej; **2** (contemptible person) sale type○ *m*.
II *vi* (inform) **to ~ on sb** dénoncer qn.

■ **fink out**◐ se défiler○; **to ~ out on sb** laisser qn en plan○.

Finland /ˈfɪnlənd/ ▶ 1131 pr n Finlande *f*.

Finn /fɪn/ ▶ 1486 *n* **1** (citizen) Finlandais/-e *m/f*; **2** (speaker) Finnois/-e *m/f*.

Finnish /ˈfɪnɪʃ/ ▶ 1486, 1402 **I** *n* Ling finnois *m*.
II *adj* finlandais.

Finno-Ugric /ˌfɪnəʊˈuːgrɪk/ ▶ 1402 **I** *n* finno-ougrien *m*.
II *adj* finno-ougrien/-ienne.

fiord *n* = **fjord**.

fir /fɜː(r)/ *n* (also **~ tree**) sapin *m*.

fir cone *n* pomme *f* de pin.

fire /ˈfaɪə(r)/ **I** *n* **1** (element) feu *m*; **to set ~ to sth, to set sth on ~** mettre le feu à qch; **to be on ~** être en feu; **to be destroyed by ~** être détruit par le feu; **to catch ~** prendre feu; **to be on ~ with love/desire** brûler d'amour/de désir; **2** (blaze) incendie *m*; **to start a ~** provoquer un incendie; **a ~ broke out** un incendie s'est déclaré; **the ~ is out** l'incendie est éteint; **3** (for warmth) feu *m*; **to make** ou **build a ~** faire un feu; **to sit by the ~** s'asseoir au coin du feu; **a lovely** ou **roaring ~** une belle flambée; **electric ~** GB radiateur *m* électrique; **4** (shots) coups *mpl* de feu; **to open ~ on sb** ouvrir le feu sur qn, faire feu sur qn; **to exchange ~** échanger des coups de feu; **to be** ou **come under enemy ~** essuyer le feu de l'ennemi; **the police/passers-by came under ~** on a tiré sur la police/les passants; **to be under ~** fig être vivement critiqué (**from** par); **to draw sb's ~** offrir une cible au tir ennemi; **to hold one's ~** (refrain) ne pas tirer; (stop) arrêter de tirer; **to return sb's ~** riposter; **a burst of machine-gun ~** une rafale de mitraillette; **5** (verve) fougue *f*.
II *excl* **1** (raising alarm) au feu!; **2** (order to shoot) feu!
III *vtr* **1** Mil, gen décharger [*gun, weapon*]; tirer [*shot*]; lancer [*arrow, rock, missile*]; **to ~ a shot at sb/sth** tirer sur qn/qch; **2** (ceremonially) **to ~ a (21 gun) salute** tirer une salve (de 21 coups de canon); **3** fig (shoot) **to ~ questions at sb** bombarder qn de questions; **4** (inspire) **to be ~d with enthusiasm** s'enthousiasmer (**for** pour); **to ~ sb's imagination** enflammer l'imagination de qn; **5** (dismiss) renvoyer, licencier, virer○ [*person*]; **you're ~d!** vous êtes renvoyé ou viré○; **6** Tech cuire [*ceramics*].
IV *vi* **1** Mil, gen tirer (**at, on** sur); **2** Mech [*engine*] démarrer.
IDIOMS **~ away!** allez-y!; **to hang ~** Mil faire long feu; fig [*plans, project, person*] traîner; **to hold ~** attendre; **to play with ~** jouer avec le feu; **he'll never set the world on ~**○ il ne fera jamais de miracles; **to go through ~ and water for sb** faire n'importe quoi pour qn; ▶ **house**.
■ **fire off**: **~ off [sth]** **1** lit décharger [*gun*]; tirer [*round, bullets*]; **2** fig hum (send) expédier [*letter, memo*].
■ **fire up**: **~ [sb] up, ~ up [sb]** gonfler [qn] à bloc; **to be all ~d up** être gonflé à bloc.

fire: **~ alarm** *n* alarme *f* incendie; **~-and-brimstone** *adj* [*sermon, preacher*] *qui menace l'auditoire des flammes de l'Enfer*; **~ appliance** *n* voiture *f* de pompiers; **~arm** *n* arme *f* à feu; **~back** *n* plaque *f* de cheminée, contrecœur *m*.

fireball /ˈfaɪəbɔːl/ *n* **1** Nucl boule *f* de feu; **2** Astron bolide *m*; **3** Meteorol éclair *m* en boule; **4** fig (person) personne *f* dynamique.

fire: **~base** *n* Mil base *f* de feux; **~ bell** *n* sonnerie *f* d'alarme; **~boat** *n* bateau-pompe *m*.

firebomb /ˈfaɪəbɒmb/ **I** *n* bombe *f* incendiaire.
II *vtr* incendier [*building*].

fire: **~box** *n* Hist Rail foyer *m*; **~brand** *n* fig semeur *m* de discordes; **~break** *n* pare-feu *m inv*; **~brick** *n* brique *f* réfractaire; **~ brigade** *n* pompiers *mpl*; **~bug** *n* incendiaire *mf*; **~ chief** *n* US chef *m* des pompiers; **~clay** *n* argile *f* réfractaire; **~ cover** *n* assurance-incendie *f*; **~cracker** *n* pétard *m*; **~-damaged** *adj* endommagé par le feu; **~damp** *n* grisou *m*; **~ department** *n* US pompiers *mpl*; **~dog** *n* chenet *m*; **~ door** *n* porte *f* coupe-feu; **~ drill** *n* exercice *m* d'évacuation en cas d'incendie; **~-eater** *n* cracheur/-euse *m/f* de feu; **~ engine** *n* voiture *f* de pompiers; **~ escape** *n* escalier *m* de secours; **~ exit** *n* sortie *f* de secours; **~ extinguisher** *n* extincteur *m*; **~fighter** ▶ 1692 *n* pompier *m*.

firefighting /ˈfaɪəfaɪtɪŋ/ **I** *n* lutte *f* contre l'incendie.
II *modif* [*operation, plane*] de lutte contre l'incendie.

fire: **~fly** *n* luciole *f*; **~guard** *n* pare-étincelles *m inv*.

fire hazard *n* risque *m* d'incendie; **to be a ~ hazard** constituer un risque d'incendie.

fire: **~house** *n* US caserne *f* de pompiers; **~ hydrant** *n* bouche *f* d'incendie; **~ insurance** *n* assurance-incendie *f*; **~ irons** *npl* accessoires *mpl* pour faire du feu.

firelight /ˈfaɪəlaɪt/ *n* lueur *f* du feu; **in the ~, by ~** à la lueur du feu.

fire: **~lighter** *n* allume-feu *m inv*; **~ loss adjuster** *n* Insur expert *m* en sinistre incendie; **~man** ▶ 1692 *n* pompier *m*; **~ marshall** *n* US pompier *m* responsable de la prévention; **~place** *n* cheminée *f*; **~ plug** *n* US bouche *f* d'incendie ; **~ power** *n* puissance *f* de feu; **~ practice** *n* = **fire drill**.

fireproof /ˈfaɪəpruːf/ **I** *adj* [*door, clothing*] ignifugé.
II *vtr* ignifuger.

fire: **~ raiser** *n* GB pyromane *mf*; **~-raising** *n* GB pyromanie *f*; **~ regulations** *npl* (laws) normes *fpl* de protection contre les incendies; (instructions) consignes *fpl* en cas d'incendie; **~ risk** *n* risque *m* d'incendie.

fire sale *n*: *vente de marchandises légèrement endommagées dans un incendie*; **to have a ~ of assets** Fin se débarrasser au plus vite de ses actifs.

fire: **~ screen** *n* écran *m* de cheminée; **~ service** *n* (sapeurs-)pompiers *mpl*; **~side** *n* coin *m* du feu; **~ station** *n* caserne *f* de pompiers; **~ tower** *n* poste *m* de vigie; **~trap** *n* souricière *f* (*en cas d'incendie*); **~truck** *n* US voiture *f* de pompiers; **~ wall** *n* mur *m* coupe-feu; **~warden** ▶ 1692 *n* responsable *mf* de la lutte contre l'incendie; **~water**○ *n* gnôle○ *f*; **~wood** *n* bois *m* à brûler.

firework /ˈfaɪəwɜːk/ **I** *n* feu *m* d'artifice.
II fireworks *npl* **1** lit feu *m* d'artifice; **2** fig (trouble) **there'll be ~s!** ça va péter○!; **to wait for the ~s to die down** attendre que ça se calme○.

firework: **~s display** *n* feu *m* d'artifice; **~s factory** *n* usine *f* pyrotechnique.

firing /ˈfaɪərɪŋ/ *n* **1** (of guns) tir *m*; **there was continuous ~** il y avait un tir continu; **2** (of ceramics) cuisson *f*.

firing line *n* **to be in the ~** lit être dans la ligne de tir; **to be first in the ~** fig (under attack) faire l'objet de violentes critiques.

firing pin *n* percuteur *m*.

firing squad *n* peloton *m* d'exécution; **to face the ~** être fusillé.

firm /fɜːm/ **I** *n* (business) entreprise *f*; **electronics/haulage ~** entreprise d'électronique/de transports; **small ~** petite entreprise *f*; **taxi ~** compagnie *f* de taxi; **security ~** société *f* de surveillance; **~ of architects** cabinet *m* d'architecte; **law ~** cabinet *m* juridique.
II *adj* **1** (hard) [*mattress, fruit, handshake*] ferme; **to get a ~ grip on sth** tenir fermement qch; **to give sth a ~ tap/tug** taper/tirer qch d'un coup sec; **2** (steady) [*table, ladder*] solide; **3** fig (strong) [*foundation, base, basis, grasp, friend*] solide; **one must keep a ~ grip on the facts** il faut bien saisir les faits; **it's my ~ belief that** je crois fermement que; **the ~ favourite** le grand favori; **4** (definite) [*offer, commitment, intention, assurance, refusal*] ferme; [*date*] définitif/-ive; [*evidence*] concret/-ète; **5** (resolute) [*person, voice, stand, leadership, purpose, response*] ferme (**with sb** avec qn); **he needs a ~ hand** il a besoin qu'on soit ferme avec lui; **6** Fin [*pound, dollar, yen, market*] ferme.
III *adv* **to stand ~** tenir bon (**against** contre); **to remain** ou **hold ~** [*person, currency*] rester ferme (**against** par rapport à).
IV *vi* Fin [*share, price*] (stabilize) se stabiliser (**at** à); (rise) se raffermir (**to** à).
■ **firm up**: ¶ **~ up** [*arrangement, deal*] se confirmer; [*muscle, flesh*] se raffermir; ¶ **~ up [sth], ~ [sth] up** confirmer [*arrangement, deal*]; raffermir [*muscle, flesh*].

firmament /ˈfɜːməmənt/ *n* littér firmament *m* liter.

firmly /ˈfɜːmlɪ/ *adv* **1** [*say, answer, state*] d'une voix ferme, d'un ton ferme; **tell him ~ but politely...** dis-lui fermement mais poliment...; **to deal ~ with sb/sth** traiter qn/qch avec fermeté; **2** [*believe, deny, be committed, be convinced, reject, resist*] fermement; **~ held beliefs** de fermes convictions; **3** [*clasp, grip, hold, push, press*] fermement; [*attach, fasten, tie*] solidement; **to be ~ rooted/embedded in sth** fig être solidement enraciné/ancré dans qch; **we have it ~ under control** nous l'avons bien en main; **she keeps her feet ~ on the ground** elle a les pieds sur terre.

firmness /ˈfɜːmnɪs/ *n* **1** gen fermeté *f*; **2** Fin (of price, pound, share) stabilité *f*, bonne tenue *f*.

firmware /ˈfɜːmweə(r)/ *n* Comput microprogramme *m*, micrologiciel *m*.

first /fɜːst/ ▶ 1505, 1150 **I** *pron* **1** (of series, group) premier/première *m/f* (**to do** à faire); **Beethoven's ~** Mus la première de Beethoven; **she'd be the ~ to complain/to admit it** elle serait la première à se plaindre/à l'admettre; **she was one of** ou **among the ~ to arrive** elle est arrivée parmi les premiers/-ières; **2** (of month) **the ~ (of May)** le premier (mai); **3 First** (in titles) **Charles the First** Charles Ier; **Elizabeth the First** Elisabeth Première; **4** (initial moment) **the ~ I knew about his death was a letter from his wife** c'est par une lettre de sa femme que j'ai appris qu'il était mort; **that's the ~ I've heard of it!** première nouvelle!; **5** (beginning) début *m*; **at ~** au début; **from the (very) ~** dès le début; **from ~ to last** du début jusqu'à la fin; **6** (new experience) **a ~ for sb/sth** une première pour qn/qch; **another ~ for Germany!** une autre première pour l'Allemagne!; **7** Aut (gear) **to be in ~** [*driver, car*] être en première; ▶ **gear**; **8** GB Univ (degree) ≈ mention *f* très bien; **to get a ~ in history** ou **a history ~** avoir sa licence d'histoire avec mention très bien.
II *adj* **1** (of series, group) premier/-ière (*before n*); **the ~ three pages/people** or **the three ~ pages/people** les trois premières pages/personnes; **the ~ few minutes** les toutes premières minutes; **the ~ person to do** la première personne à faire; **the ~ person that did** (first of several) la première personne qui a fait; (first ever) la première personne qui ait fait; **2** (in phrases) **at ~ glance** ou **sight** à première vue; **for the ~ time** pour la première fois; **I warned him not for the ~ time that** ce n'était pas la première fois que je le prévenais que; **for the ~ and last time** une fois pour toutes; **I'll ring ~ thing tomorrow/in the morning** je vous appellerai demain au plus tôt/en tout début de matinée; **I'll do it ~ thing** je le ferai dès que possible; **3** (slightest) **he doesn't know the ~ thing about politics** il ne connaît absolument rien à la politique; **I don't know the ~ thing about him** je

ne sais absolument rien à son sujet or de lui; **she didn't have the ~ idea what to do/where to go** elle ne savait absolument pas quoi faire/où aller.

III *adv* **1** (before others) [*arrive, leave*] le premier/la première; **Louise left ~** Louise est partie la première; **to get there ~** lit, fig arriver le premier/la première; **you go ~!** après vous!, passez devant!; **ladies ~!** les dames d'abord!; **women and children ~** les femmes et les enfants d'abord; **2** (at top of ranking) **to come ~** Games, Sport terminer premier/première (**in** à); fig passer avant tout; **his career comes ~ with him** sa carrière passe avant tout pour lui; **to put sb/sth ~** fig faire passer qn/qch avant tout; **put your family ~** faites passer votre famille avant tout; **3** (to begin with) d'abord; **~ of all** tout d'abord; **~ we must decide** nous devons d'abord décider; **~ mix the eggs and sugar** mélanger d'abord les œufs et le sucre; **~ she tells me one thing, then something else** elle commence par me dire une chose puis elle me dit le contraire; **there are two reasons**: **~**... il y a deux raisons: d'abord...; **at ~** au début; **when we were ~ married** tout au début de notre mariage; **when he ~ arrived** quand il est arrivé; **he was a gentleman ~ and last** c'était avant tout un gentleman; **4** (for the first time) pour la première fois; **I ~ met him in Paris** je l'ai rencontré pour la première fois à Paris; **5** (rather) plutôt; **move to the country? I'd die ~!** déménager à la campagne? plutôt mourir!

IDIOMS **~ come ~ served** les premiers arrivés sont les premiers servis; **there are only a few tickets**: **it's ~ come ~ served** il n'y a que quelques billets: les premiers arrivés seront les premiers servis; **seats are allocated on a ~ come ~ served basis** les places sont allouées sur la base des premiers arrivés, premiers servis; **~ things ~** chaque chose en son temps; **to put ~ things ~** penser aux choses importantes d'abord.

first aid I *n* **1** gen premiers soins *mpl*; **to give sb ~** donner les premiers soins à qn; **2** (as skill) secourisme *m*; **lessons in ~** des leçons de secourisme.

II first-aid *modif* [*equipment, room, station*] de secours; [*training*] de secourisme.

first aider○ *n* secouriste *mf*.

first aid: **~ kit** *n* trousse *f* de secours; **~ officer** *n* secouriste *mf*.

first base *n* Sport première base *f*; **to get to ~** Sport atteindre la première base; **not to get to ~** fig ne pas franchir le premier stade.

first-born /ˈfɜːstbɔːn/ **I** *n* premier-né/première-née *m/f*.

II *adj* **their ~ child/son** leur premier-né; **their ~ daughter** leur première-née.

first class I *n* **1** Transp première *f* (classe *f*); **2** Post tarif *m* normal or rapide.

II first-class *adj* **1** Tourism, Transp [*accommodation, compartment, hotel, seat, ticket*] de première (classe); **2** Post [*stamp*] (au) tarif normal or rapide; [*send*] en tarif normal or rapide; **a ~ letter** une lettre en tarif normal or rapide; **~ mail** courrier (au tarif) rapide; **3** GB Univ [*degree*] avec mention très bien; **4** (excellent) excellent, de premier ordre.

III *adv* **1** Transp [*travel*] en première (classe); **2** Post en tarif normal or rapide.

first: **~ course** *n* (of meal) entrée *f*; **~ cousin** *n* (male) cousin *m* germain; (female) cousine *f* germaine; **~ day cover** *n* Post émission *f* du premier jour; **~ degree burn** *n* brûlure *f* au premier degré; **~ degree murder** *n* US Jur meurtre *m* avec préméditation; **~ edition** *n* première édition *f*, édition *f* originale; **~ estate** *n* Pol Hist premier état *m*; **~-ever** *adj* tout premier/toute première; **First Family** *n* US Pol famille *f* présidentielle.

first floor I *n* GB premier étage *m*; US rez-de-chaussée *m*.

II first-floor *modif* [*room, apartment etc*] GB au premier étage; US au rez-de-chaussée.

first-footing /ˌfɜːstˈfʊtɪŋ/ *n* Scot **to go ~** *aller rendre visite à quelqu'un après minuit la nuit de Saint-Sylvestre*.

first: **~ form** *n* GB Sch (classe *f* de) sixième *f*; **~-former** *n* GB Sch élève *mf* de sixième; **~ fruits** *npl* fig littér premiers fruits *mpl*; **~-generation** *adj* (all contexts) de la première génération; **~ grade** *n* US Sch cours *m* préparatoire.

firsthand /ˌfɜːstˈhænd/ *adj, adv* de première main; **at first hand** de première main.

first: **First Lady** *n* US Pol première dame *f*; fig grande dame *f*; **~ language** *n* langue *f* maternelle.

first light *n* premières lueurs *fpl*; **at ~** aux premières lueurs.

firstly /ˈfɜːstlɪ/ *adv* premièrement.

first mate *n* Naut second *m*.

first name *n* prénom *m*; **to be on ~ terms with sb** appeler qn par son prénom.

first night I *n* Theat première *f*.

II first-night *modif* [*nerves, audience*] de la première; [*ticket, party*] pour la première.

first: **~-nighter** *n* Theat habitué/-e *m/f* des premières; **~ offender** *n* Jur délinquant/-e *m/f* primaire; **~ officer** ▶1612 *n* Aviat, Naut second *m*; **~ performance** *n* Mus, Theat première *f* mondiale.

first person *n* Ling première personne *f*; **in the ~** à la première personne; **~ singular/plural** première personne du singulier/du pluriel.

first principle *n* principe *m* premier; **to go back to ~s** retourner aux principes premiers.

first: **~-rate** *adj* excellent; **~ school** *n* GB Sch école *f* préparatoire; **~-strike** *adj* Mil [*missile, capability*] de première frappe; **~-time buyer** *n* personne *f* qui achète sa première maison.

first-timer○ /ˌfɜːstˈtaɪmə(r)/ *n* (in sport, activity) débutant/-e *m/f*; (in new experience) quelqu'un qui n'a pas l'habitude; **he's a ~** il n'a pas l'habitude.

first violin *n* premier violon *m*.

first water *n* **of the ~** lit [*diamond*] d'une belle eau; fig de l'espèce la plus pure.

First World *n* (also **First World countries**) pays *mpl* industrialisés.

first year I *n* Sch, Univ (group) première année *f*; (pupil) élève *mf* en première année; (student) étudiant/-e *m/f* en première année.

II first-year *modif* [*student*] en première année; [*course, teacher, class*] de première année.

firth /fɜːθ/ *n* estuaire *m*.

fiscal /ˈfɪskl/ *adj* fiscal.

fiscal year *n* exercice *m* budgétaire or fiscal.

fish /fɪʃ/ **I** *n* (*pl* **~**, **~es**) **1** Zool poisson *m*; **to catch a ~** attraper or prendre un poisson; **freshwater/saltwater** ou **sea ~** poisson *m* d'eau douce/de mer; **2** Culin ¢ poisson *m*; **to eat/cook ~** manger/préparer du poisson; **wet ~** poisson *m* frais.

II *modif* [*course, bone, glue*] de poisson; [*knife, fork*] à poisson.

III *vtr* pêcher [*waters, river*].

IV *vi* **1** lit pêcher; **to ~ for trout/cod** pêcher la truite/la morue; **2** fig (test for response) **'why did he ask me that?'—'he was just ~ing!'** 'pourquoi m'a-t-il demandé ça?'—'il voulait te faire parler'; **to ~ for information** chercher à dénicher des renseignements; **to ~ for compliments** quêter des compliments.

IDIOMS **to be neither ~ nor fowl (nor good red herring)** n'être ni chair ni poisson; **to be like a ~ out of water** ne pas se sentir dans son élément; **to drink like a ~**○ boire comme un trou; **to have other ~ to fry** avoir d'autres chats à fouetter; **he's a queer ~**○ c'est un drôle d'oiseau; **he's a cold ~**○ il est très froid; **there are plenty more ~ in the sea** un de perdu, dix de retrouvés.

■ **fish around**: farfouiller (**in** dans; **for** pour trouver).

■ **fish out**: **~ out [sth] 1** (from bag, pocket, box) sortir [*money, handkerchief, pen*] (**of** de); **2** (from water) repêcher [*body, object*] (**of** de).

fish: **~ and chips** *n* poisson *m* frit avec des frites; **~ and chip shop** ▶1692 *n* GB friterie *f*; **~bowl** *n* bocal *m* (à poissons); **~ cake** *n* croquette *f* de poisson.

fisher /ˈfɪʃə(r)/ *n* pêcheur/-euse *m/f*.

fisherman /ˈfɪʃəmən/ ▶1692 *n* pêcheur *m*.

fishery /ˈfɪʃərɪ/ *n* **1** (processing plant) pêcherie *f*; **2** (activity) pêche *f*.

fishery protection vessel *n* navire *m* de surveillance des zones de pêche.

fish: **~-eye lens** *n* Phot objectif *m* à très grand angle; **~ farm** *n* centre *m* de pisciculture; **~ farming** *n* pisciculture *f*; **~ finger** *n* GB bâtonnet *m* de poisson; **~ food** *n* aliments *mpl* pour poissons; **~ fry** *n* US *pique-nique où l'on sert de la friture*; **~ hook** *n* hameçon *m*.

fishing /ˈfɪʃɪŋ/ **I** *n* pêche *f*; **deep-sea/offshore ~** pêche hauturière/côtière; **mackerel/salmon ~** pêche au maquereau/au saumon; **to go ~** aller à la pêche.

II *modif* [*boat, fleet, port, line, net*] de pêche.

fishing: **~ ground** *n* pêche *f*, lieu *m* de pêche; **~ net** *n* filet *m* de pêche; **~ rod** *n* canne *f* à pêche; **~ tackle** *n* gen attirail *m* de pêche; (in shop) articles *mpl* de pêche; **~ village** *n* port *m* de pêche.

fish: **~ kettle** *n* poissonnière *f*; **~ ladder** *n* barrages *mpl* à saumons; **~ market** *n* halle *f* aux poissons; **~ meal** *n* farine *f* de poisson.

fishmonger /ˈfɪʃmʌŋɡə(r)/ ▶1692 *n* GB poissonnier/-ière *m/f*; **~'s (shop)** poissonnerie *f*.

fish: **~net** *adj* [*tights, stockings*] à résille; **~ paste** *n* GB ≈ beurre *m* de poisson; **~plate** *n* Tech, Rail éclisse *f*.

fishpond /ˈfɪʃpɒnd/ *n* **1** gen étang *m* à poissons; (ornamental) bassin *m*; **2** (at fish farm) vivier *m*.

fish: **~ restaurant** *n* restaurant *m* de poisson; **~ shop** GB, **~ store** US ▶1692 *n* poissonnerie *f*; **~ slice** *n* (for frying) spatule *f*; (for serving at table) pelle *f* à poisson; **~tail** *vi* Aut, Aviat chasser (de gauche à droite); **~ tank** *n* aquarium *m*.

fishwife /ˈfɪʃwaɪf/ *n* marchande *f* de poisson; **to shout like a ~** crier comme une poissonnière.

fishy /ˈfɪʃɪ/ *adj* **1** lit [*smell, taste*] de poisson; **2**○ fig (suspect) louche○, douteux/-euse; **it sounds a bit ~ to me** ça m'a l'air plutôt louche○, ça ne me paraît pas très catholique.

fissile /ˈfɪsaɪl, US ˈfɪsl/ *adj* fissile.

fission /ˈfɪʃn/ *n* **1** (also **nuclear ~**) Phys fission *f*; **2** Biol fissiparité *f*.

fissionable /ˈfɪʃənəbl/ *adj* Phys fissible.

fissure /ˈfɪʃə(r)/ *n* **1** (in ground) crevasse *f*; (in wood, wall) fissure *f*; **2** Anat scissure *f*.

fissured /ˈfɪʃəd/ *adj* fissuré.

fist /fɪst/ *n* poing *m*; **to shake one's ~ at sb** menacer qn du poing.

IDIOMS **to make money hand over ~** gagner des mille et des cents; **to make a good/poor ~ of doing sth** bien/mal faire qch.

fist fight *n* pugilat *m*.

fistful /ˈfɪstfʊl/ *n* poignée *f* (**of** de).

fisticuffs○ /ˈfɪstɪkʌfs/ *n* bagarre *f*.

fistula /ˈfɪstjʊlə/ *n* (*pl* **~s** ou **-ae**) fistule *f*.

fit /fɪt/ **I** *n* **1** Med crise *f*, attaque *f*; **to have a ~** (unspecified) avoir une attaque or une crise; (epileptic) avoir une crise d'épilepsie; **2** gen (of rage, passion, jealousy, panic) accès *m*; **in a ~ of anger** dans un accès de colère; **~ of coughing** quinte *f* de toux; **~ of crying** crise de larmes; **to have a ~ of the**

giggles avoir le fou rire; **to have sb in ~s**○ donner le fou rire à qn; **to have** ou **throw a ~**○ (be mad) piquer○ une crise; **3** (of garment) **to be a good/poor ~** être/ne pas être à la bonne taille; **to be a tight ~** être juste.

II *adj* **1** [*person*] (in trim) en forme; (not ill) en bonne santé; **you're looking ~ and well!** tu as l'air en pleine forme!; **to keep/feel ~** se maintenir/se sentir en forme; **to get ~** se mettre en bonne condition; **2** (suitable, appropriate) **to be ~ company for** être une bonne compagnie pour; **it's not a ~ time to do** ce n'est pas le moment de faire; **to be ~ for** (worthy of) être digne de, convenir à [*person, hero, king*]; (capable of) être capable de faire [*job*]; être capable de remplir [*role*]; **a land ~ for heroes** une terre digne des héros or qui convient aux héros; **to be only ~ for the bin** être juste bon/bonne à mettre à la poubelle; **to be ~ for nothing** n'être plus bon/bonne à rien; **~ for human consumption** propre à la consommation; **not ~ for swimming** impropre à la baignade; **to be ~ to do** (worthy of) être digne de faire; (in a condition to) être en état de faire; (qualified to) être apte à faire; **he's not ~ to live** il n'est pas digne de rester en vie; **to be ~ to drive** être en état de conduire; **to be ~ to govern** être apte à gouverner; **~ to drink** potable; **~ to eat** mangeable; **~ to live in** habitable; **I'm not ~ to be seen!** je ne suis pas présentable!; **to see** ou **think ~ to do** juger or trouver bon de faire; **do as you see** ou **think ~** faites comme bon vous semble; **when one sees** ou **thinks ~** quand on le juge bon; **to be in no ~ state to do** ne pas être en état de faire; **it is ~ that** fml il est convenable que (+ *subj*); **3**○ (in emphatic phrases) **to laugh ~ to burst** se tordre de rire; **to cry ~ to burst/to break your heart** pleurer comme une Madeleine/à vous fendre le cœur; **to be ~ to drop** tomber de fatigue.

III *vtr* (*prét* **fitted**, **fit** US; *pp* **fitted**) **1** (be the right size) [*garment*] être à la taille de; [*shoe*] être à la pointure de; [*object*] aller sur [*top, surface*]; aller dans [*envelope, space*]; **that dress doesn't ~ me** cette robe n'est pas à ma taille; **the key ~s this lock/this box** la clé va dans cette serrure/ouvre cette boîte; **to ~ size X to Y** correspondre aux tailles X à Y; **to ~ ages 3 to 5** convenir aux enfants de 3 à 5 ans; **the jacket doesn't ~ me across the shoulders** la veste ne me va pas aux épaules; **'one size ~s all'** 'taille unique'; **2** (make or find room for) **to ~ sth in** ou **into** loger qch dans, trouver de la place pour qch dans [*room, house, car*]; **can you ~ this on your desk?** peux-tu trouver de la place pour ça sur ton bureau?; **3** (install) mettre [qch] en place [*lock, door, window, kitchen, shower*]; **to have sth ~ted** faire mettre qch en place; **to ~ A to B, to ~ A and B together** assembler A avec B; **to ~ sth into place** mettre qch en place; **to ~ sth with** équiper qch de [*attachment, lock*]; **to be ~ted with a radio** être équipé d'une radio; **4 to ~ sb for** prendre les mesures de qn pour [*garment, uniform*]; **he's being ~ted for a suit** on est en train de lui prendre ses mesures pour un costume; **to ~ sb with** pourvoir qn de [*hearing aid, prosthesis, pacemaker*]; **5** (be compatible with) correspondre à [*description, requirements*]; aller avec [*decor, colour scheme*]; **we have no-one ~ting that description** nous n'avons personne qui corresponde à cette description; **the punishment should ~ the crime** la punition devrait être proportionnée à la faute; ▶**bill**; **6** (qualify, make suitable) **to ~ sb for/to do** [*experience, qualifications*] rendre qn apte à/à faire; **to be ~ted for a role** être apte à remplir un rôle.

IV *vi* (*prét* **fitted**, **fit** US; *pp* **fitted**) **1** (be the right size) [*garment*] être à ma/ta/sa taille, aller; [*shoes*] être à ma/ta/sa pointure, aller; [*object, lid, sheet*] aller; **these jeans ~, I'll take them** ce jean est à ma taille, je le prends; **your jeans ~ really well** ton jean te va très bien; **this key doesn' t ~** cette clé ne va pas; **2** (have enough room) tenir (**into** dans); **the toys should ~ into that box** les jouets devraient tous tenir dans cette boîte; **will the table ~ in that corner?** y a-t-il de la place pour la table dans ce coin?; **3** (go into designated place) **to ~ inside one another** aller or se mettre les uns dans les autres; **to ~ into a slot** s'adapter or aller dans une fente; **to ~ into place** [*part, handle*] bien aller; [*cupboard, brick*] bien rentrer; **4** fig (tally, correspond) **his story doesn't ~** son histoire ne tient pas debout; **something doesn't quite ~ here** il y a quelque chose qui ne va pas ici; **to ~ with** correspondre à [*statement, story, facts*]; **to ~ into** aller avec [*ideology, colour scheme*]; **it all ~s into place!** tout concorde!

IDIOMS **by** ou **in ~s and starts** par à-coups.

■ **fit in**: ¶ **~ in 1** lit [*key, object*] aller; **will you all ~ in?** (to car, room) est-ce qu'il y a de la place pour vous tous?; **these books won't ~ in** je n'arrive pas à caser ces livres; **2** fig (be in harmony) s'intégrer (**with** à); **he doesn't ~ in** il ne s'intègre pas; **I'll ~ in with your plans** j'accorderai mes projets avec les vôtres; ¶ **~ [sth] in, ~ in [sth] 1** (find room for) caser [*books, objects*]; faire entrer [*key*]; **2** (find time for) caser [*game, meeting, break*]; ¶ **~ [sb] in, ~ in [sb]** trouver le temps pour voir [*patient, colleague*].

■ **fit on**: ¶ **~ on** aller; **where does it ~ on?** où est-ce que ça va?; ¶ **~ on(to) [sth]** aller sur; **this part ~s on(to) this section** ce morceau va sur cette partie; ¶ **~ [sth] on** mettre [*top, piece*].

■ **fit out, fit up**: **~ [sth] out** ou **up, ~ out** ou **up [sth]** équiper (**with** de); **to ~ sth out as an office** équiper qch pour en faire un bureau; **to ~ sb out** ou **up with** mettre [qch] à qn [*costume, garment, hearing aid*].

fitful /ˈfɪtfl/ *adj* [*sleep*] troublé, agité; [*night*] agité; [*wind, mood*] capricieux/-ieuse, changeant; [*showers, light*] intermittent.

fitfully /ˈfɪtfəlɪ/ *adv* [*sleep, rain, shine*] par intermittence.

fitment /ˈfɪtmənt/ *n* (in bathroom) appareil *m* sanitaire; **the ~s** les installations *fpl* sanitaires, le sanitaire *m*.

fitness /ˈfɪtnɪs/ I *n* **1** (physical condition) forme *f*; **2** (aptness) (of person) aptitude *f* (**for, to do** à faire); **to doubt sth's ~ for a task** douter que qch soit approprié à une tâche; **to doubt sb's ~ for a job** douter de la compétence de qn.

II *modif* [*club, centre, room*] de culture physique; [*gym, plan*] de mise en condition physique; **~ level** condition *f* physique.

fitness: **~ consultant** *n* conseiller/-ère *m/f* en culture physique; **~ fanatic** *n* fou/folle *m/f* de culture physique; **~ test** *n* test *m* de condition physique; **~ training** *n* exercices *mpl* physiques.

fitted /ˈfɪtɪd/ *adj* **1** [*clothes*] ajusté; **2** [*wardrobe, furniture, unit*] encastré; [*bedroom, kitchen*] intégré.

fitted: **~ carpet** *n* moquette *f*; **~ sheet** *n* drap-housse *m*.

fitter /ˈfɪtə(r)/ **▶1692** *n* **1** (of machines, electrical equipment) monteur/-euse *m/f*; **2** (also **carpet ~**) poseur *m* de moquette; **3** (of garment) essayeur/-euse *m/f*.

fitting /ˈfɪtɪŋ/ I *n* **1** (standardized part) (bathroom, electrical, gas) installation *f*; **furniture and ~s** mobilier et installations; **kitchen ~s** éléments *mpl* de cuisine; ▶**light fitting, shop fitting**; **2** (for clothes, hearing aid) essayage *m*; **to go for a ~** aller faire un essayage; **3** (width of shoe) largeur *f*.

II *adj* **1** (apt) [*description, language, site*] adéquat; [*memorial, testament*] qui convient; **it was a ~ end for such a man** c'était la fin qui convenait à un tel homme; **a ~ tribute to her work** un hommage mérité à son œuvre; **it is ~ that** il est convenable que (+ *subj*); **2** (seemly) [*behaviour*] bienséant.

III **-fitting** (*dans composés*) **well-~** à la bonne taille; **badly-~** [*garment*] qui ne va pas; [*dentures*] mal ajusté; **loose-/tight-~** ample/étroit.

fittingly /ˈfɪtɪŋlɪ/ *adv* (appropriately) [*situated, named*] de façon appropriée.

fitting room *n* salon *m* d'essayage.

five /faɪv/ **▶1505**, **971**, **1096** I *n* **1** (numeral) cinq *m inv*; **2**○ US (five dollar note) billet *m* de cinq dollars.

II **fives** *npl* GB Sport *variante du squash pratiquée avec une batte ou un gant*.

III *adj* cinq *inv*.

IDIOMS **to take ~**○ US faire une pause.

five-and-dime /ˌfaɪvənˈdaɪm/ *n* US bazar *m*.

five-a-side /ˌfaɪvəˈsaɪd/ GB I *n* (also **~ football**) football *m* à cinq (joueurs).

II *modif* [*tournament, match*] de football à cinq (joueurs).

five: **Five Nations Championship** *n* (in rugby) tournoi *m* des cinq nations; **~ o'clock shadow** *n* barbe *f* de fin de journée.

fiver○ /ˈfaɪvə(r)/ *n* GB billet *m* de cinq livres.

five: **~ spot**○ *n* US billet *m* de cinq dollars; **~-star hotel** *n* hôtel *m* cinq étoiles; **~-year man** *n* US péj éternel redoublant *m*; **~-year plan** *n* plan *m* quinquennal.

fix /fɪks/ I *n* **1**○ (quandary) pétrin○ *m*; **to be in a ~** être dans le pétrin○; **2**○ (dose) (of drugs) argot des drogués shoot○ *m*; (of entertainment) séance *f*; **to get a ~** se piquer○; **3** (means of identification) **to take a ~ on sth** Aviat, Naut déterminer la position de qch; **to get a ~ on sth** fig cerner qch; **let's get a ~ on the problem** cernons le problème; **4**○ (rigged arrangement) **it was a ~** c'était truqué.

II *vtr* **1** (establish, set) fixer [*date, time, venue, amount, price, limit*]; déterminer [*chronology, position on map*]; **to ~ tax at 20%** établir un impôt de 20%; **on the date ~ed** à la date convenue; **nothing is ~ed yet** il n'y a encore rien d'arrêté; **2** (organize) arranger [*meeting, trip, visit*]; préparer [*drink, meal, snack*]; **to ~ one's hair** se donner un coup de peigne; **to ~ one's face** se faire une beauté; **how are we ~ed for time/money?** qu'est-ce qu'on a comme temps/argent?○; **how are you ~ed for tonight/next week?** quels sont tes projets pour ce soir/la semaine prochaine?; **3** (mend) réparer [*article, equipment*]; (sort out) régler [*problem*]; **4** (attach, insert) fixer [*curtain, handle, shelf, notice*] (**on** sur; **to** à); planter [*post, stake*] (**into** dans); enfoncer [*hook, nail*] (**into** dans); attacher [*rope, string*] (**to** à); fig faire peser [*suspicion*] (**on** sur) ; rejeter [*blame*] (**on** sur); **to ~ sth into place** mettre qch en place; **her name was firmly ~ed in my mind** son nom était profondément gravé dans mon esprit; **5** (concentrate) fixer [*attention*] (**on** sur); placer [*hopes*] (**on** dans); tourner [*thoughts*] (**on** vers); **to ~ one's gaze on sb** regarder qn fixément; **she ~ed him with an angry stare** elle l'a fixé d'un regard furieux; **his hopes were ~ed on going to university** son plus cher espoir était d'aller à l'université; **6**○ (rig, corrupt) truquer [*contest, election, match*]; soudoyer [*judge, jury, witness*]; **7**○ (get even with) régler son compte à [*bully, criminal*]; **I'll soon ~ him (for you)!** je vais lui régler son compte!; **8** Art, Biol, Chem, Phot, Tex fixer.

III○ *vi* (inject oneself) argot des drogués se piquer○.

IV **fixed** *pp adj* [*address, gaze, vacation, idea, income, focus, order, price, rate*] fixe; [*intervals*] régulier/-ière; [*behaviour, method*] immuable; [*aim*] arrêté; [*determination*] inébranlable; [*desire*] tenace; [*intention*] ferme;

[*proportion*] constant; [*smile, expression*] figé; [*menu*] à prix fixe; **of no ~ed address** sans domicile fixe.

■ **fix on, fix upon**: ¶ **~ on** [**sth**] choisir [*person, place, food, object*]; fixer [*date, time, venue, amount*]; ¶ **~ on** [**sth**], **~** [**sth**] **on** (attach) fixer [*object*].

■ **fix up**: ¶ **~ up** [**sth**], **~** [**sth**] **up 1** (organize) arranger, organiser [*holiday, meeting*]; décider de [*date*]; **to ~ up to do** convenir de faire; **it's all ~ed up** tout est arrangé; **2** (decorate) refaire [*room, house*]; **he ~ed up the bedroom as a study** il a transformé la chambre en bureau; **3** (construct, put up) fixer [*shelf, notice*]; (amateurishly) bricoler [*shelter, storage*]; ¶ **~ sb up with sth** trouver qch à qn [*accommodation, drink, equipment, vehicle*]; faire avoir qch à qn [*ticket, pass, meal, document*]; ¶ **~ sb up with sb**○ monter une baraque à qn avec qn○.

fixated /fɪk'seɪtɪd/ *adj* **to be ~ on sb/sth** faire une fixation sur qn/qch.

fixation /fɪk'seɪʃn/ *n* **1** gen, Psych fixation *f*; **to have a ~ on** ou **about** faire une fixation sur; **mother ~** fixation à la mère; **2** Phot fixage *m*; **3** Chem fixation *f*.

fixative /'fɪksətɪv/ *n* gen, Dent, Tex produit *m* fixateur; (for hair, perfume) fixateur *m*; Art fixatif *m*; Phot fixateur *m*.

fix: **~ed assets** *npl* immobilisations *fpl*, actif *m* immobilisé; **~ed charge** *n* frais *mpl* fixes; **~ed costs** *npl* frais *mpl* fixes.

fixedly /'fɪksɪdlɪ/ *adv* [*look, gaze*] fixement; **to smile ~** garder un sourire figé.

fix: **~ed point** *n* Comput, Math virgule *f* fixe; **~ed rate financing** *n* financement *m* à taux fixe; **~ed star** *n* étoile *f* fixe; **~ed term contract** *n* contrat *m* (de travail) à durée déterminée.

fixer /'fɪksə(r)/ *n* **1**○ (schemer) magouilleur/-euse○ *m/f*; **2** Phot fixateur *m*.

fixings /'fɪksɪŋz/ *npl* Culin garniture *f*.

fixity /'fɪksətɪ/ *n* fixité *f*; **~ of purpose** détermination *f*.

fixture /'fɪkstʃə(r)/ *n* **1** Constr, Tech installation *f*; **~s and fittings** équipements *mpl*; **2** Sport rencontre *f*; **3**○ (person) personne *f* qui fait partie du décor○; **4** Jur immeuble *m* par destination.

fixture list *n* Sport agenda *m* des rencontres.

fizz /fɪz/ **I** *n* **1** (of drink) pétillement *m*; **2** (of match, firework) crépitement *m*; **3**○ GB (drink) (champagne) champagne *m*, champ○ *m*; (sparkling wine) mousseux *m*.

II *vi* **1** [*drink*] pétiller; **2** [*match, firework*] crépiter.

■ **fizz up** mousser.

fizzle /'fɪzl/ ■ **fizzle out** [*interest, enthusiasm, romance*] s'éteindre; [*strike, campaign, project*] faire fiasco; [*story*] se terminer en queue de poisson; [*firework*] faire long feu.

fizzy /'fɪzɪ/ *adj* gazeux/-euse.

fjord /fɪ'ɔ:d/ *n* fjord *m*.

FL US Post *abrév écrite* = **Florida**.

flab○ /flæb/ *n* chair *f* flasque.

flabbergast /'flæbəgɑ:st, US -gæst/ *vtr* sidérer; **to be ~ed** être sidéré (**at** à).

flabby /'flæbɪ/ *adj* **1** [*skin, muscle*] flasque; [*person*] aux chairs flasques; [*handshake*] mou/molle; **2** fig [*person, temperament*] mou/molle; [*excuse, argument*] inconsistant.

flaccid /'flæsɪd/ *adj* flasque, mou/molle.

flaccidity /,flæ'sɪdətɪ/ *n* mollesse *f*, flaccidité *f* spec.

flack /flæk/ US **I** *n* attaché/-e *m/f* de presse.

II *vi* **to ~ for sb** faire l'attaché/-e *m/f* de presse de qn.

flag /flæg/ **I** *n* **1** (national symbol) drapeau *m*; **to hoist** ou **run up a ~** hisser un drapeau; **to wave a ~** brandir un drapeau; **a ~ flew from every building** sur chaque bâtiment un drapeau flottait au vent; **to sail under the Panamanian ~** Naut battre pavillon panaméen; **2** (as signal) Naut pavillon *m*; Rail drapeau *m*; **to show the white ~** lit hisser le drapeau blanc; fig baisser pavillon; **with ~s flying** Naut pavillon haut; **3** (on map) drapeau *m*; **4** Bot iris *m* des marais; **5** (stone) dalle *f*; **6** Comput drapeau *m*.

II *vtr* (*p prés etc* **-gg-**) **1** (mark with tab) baliser [*text*]; **2** (signal) signaler [*problem*]; **3** Comput signaler [qch] au moyen d'un drapeau.

III *vi* (*p prés etc* **-gg-**) [*interest*] faiblir; [*morale, strength*] baisser; [*conversation*] languir; [*athlete, campaigner*] flancher○.

IDIOMS **to fly the ~** représenter son pays (à l'étranger); **we must keep the ~ flying** nous devons le faire pour l'honneur de notre pays; **to wave the ~** faire des déclarations patriotiques.

■ **flag down**: **~** [**sth**] **down**, **~ down** [**sth**] faire signe de s'arrêter à [*train*]; héler [*taxi*].

flag: **~ carrier** *n* compagnie *f* nationale (de transport aérien); **~ day** *n* GB jour *m* de collecte (*au profit d'une œuvre caritative*); **Flag Day** *n* US le 14 juin (*jour où le drapeau américain fut adopté*).

flagellant /'flædʒələnt/ *n* **1** Hist Relig flagellant *m*; **2** (sexual) (sadist) flagellateur/-trice *m/f*; (masochist) adepte *mf* de la flagellation.

flagellate /'flædʒəleɪt/ **I** *n* Biol flagellé *m*.

II *adj* Biol (also **~d**) flagellé.

III *vtr* flageller.

IV *v refl* **to ~ oneself** se flageller.

flagellation /,flædʒə'leɪʃn/ *n* flagellation *f*.

flagelliform /flə'dʒelɪfɔ:m/ *adj* Biol flagelliforme.

flagellum /flə'dʒeləm/ *n* (*pl* **-la** ou **~s**) Biol flagelle *m*.

flageolet /,flædʒə'let, 'flædʒ-/ *n* (all contexts) flageolet *m*.

flagged /flægd/ *adj* [*floor, room*] dallé.

flagging /'flægɪŋ/ *n* (stones) dalles *fpl*.

flag: **~ of convenience** *n* pavillon *m* de complaisance; **~ officer** ▶ **1612** *n* Naut ≈ officier *m* général.

▶ 1612

flagon /'flægən/ *n* (bottle) grosse bouteille *f*; (jug) pichet *m*.

flagpole /'flægpəʊl/ *n* mât *m* (*de drapeau*); **we'll run it** ou **the idea up the ~** fig on va lancer un ballon d'essai fig.

flagrant /'fleɪgrənt/ *adj* flagrant.

flagrantly /'fleɪgrəntlɪ/ *adv* [*behave, do*] de façon flagrante; [*artificial, dishonest etc*] manifestement.

flagship /'flægʃɪp/ **I** *n* Naut vaisseau *m* amiral.

II *modif* [*company, product*] vedette.

flag: **~stone** *n* dalle *f*; **~ stop** *n* US arrêt *m* facultatif.

flag-waving /'flægweɪvɪŋ/ *n* péj (patriotism) comportement *m* chauvin; (patriotic statements) déclarations *fpl* cocardières.

flail /fleɪl/ **I** *n* fléau *m*.

II *vtr* **1** Agric battre [qch] au fléau [*corn*]; **2** gen ▶ **flail about**.

III *vi* ▶ **flail about**.

■ **flail about, flail around**: ¶ **~ about, ~ around** [*person*] se débattre; [*arms, legs*] s'agiter; ¶ **~** [**sth**] **about, ~** [**sth**] **around** agiter [*arms, legs*].

flair /'fleə(r)/ *n* **1** (talent) don *m* (**for** pour; **for doing** pour faire); **2** (style) classe *f*.

flak /flæk/ *n* ¢ **1** Mil tirs *mpl* des batteries antiaériennes; **2**○ fig (criticism) critiques *fpl*; **to get** ou **take a lot of ~** se faire mitrailler○.

flake /fleɪk/ **I** *n* **1** (of snow, cereal) flocon *m*; (of soap) paillette *f*; (of chocolate, cheese) copeau *m*; **2** (of paint, metal, rust) écaille *f*; (of rock, flint) éclat *m*; **3**○ US (eccentric) toqué/-e○ *m/f*.

II *vtr* émietter [*fish*]; **~d almonds** amandes effilées.

III *vi* **1** (also **~ off**) [*paint, varnish*] s'écailler; [*plaster, stone*] s'effriter; [*skin*] peler; **2** [*fish*] s'émietter.

■ **flake off**◑ US se barrer○.

■ **flake out**○ (fall asleep) s'endormir comme une masse; (flop) tomber comme une masse.

flake white *n* blanc *m* de plomb or de céruse.

flakey○ = **flaky** 3.

flak jacket GB, **flack vest** US *n* gilet *m* pare-balles.

flaky /'fleɪkɪ/ *adj* **1** [*paint*] qui s'écaille; [*skin*] qui pèle; [*plaster, rock, statue*] qui s'effrite; **2** [*snow*] floconneux/-euse; **3**○ US (eccentric) [*person*] toqué○; [*idea, movie*] farfelu○.

flaky pastry *n* pâte *f* feuilletée.

flamboyant /flæm'bɔɪənt/ *adj* **1** [*person*] haut en couleur; [*lifestyle, image, behaviour*] exubérant; [*colour, clothes, style*] voyant; [*gesture*] expansif/-ive; **2** Archit de style flamboyant.

flame /fleɪm/ **I** *n* **1** lit flamme *f*; **a naked ~** une flamme nue; **to be in ~s** être en flammes; **to go up in ~s** s'enflammer; **to burst into ~s** s'embraser; **over a low/high ~** Culin à feu doux/vif; **to be shot down in ~s** être descendu en flammes also fig; **2** fig feu *m* (**of** de); **to burn with a brighter ~** brûler d'un feu plus vif; **to fan** ou **fuel the ~s of love** attiser le feu de l'amour; **to fan the ~s of violence** attiser les flambées de violence; **an old ~**○ (person) un ancien flirt○; **3** (colour) rouge *m* feu.

II *adj* [*hair, leaf, flower*] rouge feu *inv*.

III *vtr* Culin flamber.

IV *vi* **1** [*fire , torch*] flamber; **2** [*sunset, tree*] flamboyer; [*face*] s'enflammer (**with** de); **3** [*emotion*] brûler.

■ **flame up** [*fire*] flamber.

flame-coloured GB, **flame-colored** US /'fleɪmkʌləd/ *adj* [*tree, hair*] rouge feu *inv*; [*sky, fabric*] couleur de feu.

flamenco /flə'meŋkəʊ/ **I** *n* flamenco *m*.

II *modif* [*dancer, music*] de flamenco; **~ dancing** flamenco *m*.

flameproof /'fleɪmpru:f/ *adj* qui va au feu.

flame retardant I *n* ignifugeant *m*.

II *adj* [*substance, chemical*] ignifuge; [*furniture, fabric*] ignifugé.

flamethrower /'fleɪmθrəʊə(r)/ *n* lance-flammes *m inv*.

flaming /'fleɪmɪŋ/ *adj* **1** [*garment, vehicle, building*] en flammes; [*torch*] allumé; **2** [*face*] cramoisi; [*sky, colour*] flamboyant; **3** [*row*] violent; **4**○ (emphatic) fichu○; **~ idiot!** fichu imbécile○!

flamingo /flə'mɪŋgəʊ/ *n* (*pl* **~s** ou **-oes**) flamant *m* (rose).

flammable /'flæməbl/ *adj* inflammable; **highly ~** hautement inflammable.

flan /flæn/ *n* (savoury) quiche *f*, tarte *f*; (sweet) tarte *f*; **apricot ~** tarte aux abricots; **cheese ~** quiche au fromage.

Flanders /'flɑ:ndəz/ *pr n* les Flandres *fpl*.

flange /flændʒ/ *n* (on wheel) boudin *m*; (on pipe) bride *f*; (on tool) collet *m*; (on beam) aile *f*.

flanged /flændʒd/ *adj* [*wheel*] à boudin; [*pipe*] à bride; [*tool*] à collet; [*beam*] à ailes.

flank /flæŋk/ **I** *n* **1** (of animal, mountain) flanc *m*; **2** Mil flanc *m*; **3** Pol, Sport aile *f*; **4** Culin flanchet *m*.

II *vtr* flanquer [*person, door*]; border [*path, area*]; **~ed by** [*person, door*] flanqué de; [*path, area*] bordé de.

flanker /'flæŋkə(r)/ *n* (in rugby) ailier *m*.

flannel /'flænl/ **I** *n* **1** Tex (wool) flanelle *f*; (cotton) pilou *m*; **2** GB (also **face ~**) gant *m* de toilette; **3**○ GB (talk) baratin○ *m*.

II○ *vi* GB (*prés part etc* **-ll-**, US **-l-**) baratiner○.

flannelette /,flænə'let/ *n* pilou *m*.

flannels /'flænəlz/ *npl* **1** pantalon *m* de flanelle; **2** US pyjama *m* de flanelle.

flap /flæp/ **I** *n* **1** (on pocket, envelope, hat, tent) rabat *m*; **2** (made of wood) (on table, bar) abattant *m*; (of trapdoor) trappe *f*; (for cat) chatière *f*; **3** (movement) (of wings) battement *m* (**of** de); (of sail) claquement *m* (**of** de); **4** Aviat volet *m*; **5**○ (panic) **to be in a ~** être affolé; **to get into a ~** s'affoler; **6** Ling battement *m*.

II *vtr* (*p prés etc* **-pp-**) [*wind*] claquer [*sail, cloth*]; faire voleter [*paper, clothes*]; [*person*] secouer [*sheet, cloth etc*]; agiter [*paper, letter*]; **to ~ sth at sb/sth** agiter qch en direction de qn/qch; **the bird was ~ping its wings** l'oiseau battait des ailes; **he ~ped his arms around** il battait l'air de ses bras.

III *vi* (*p prés etc* **-pp-**) **1** (move) [*wing*] battre; [*sail, flag, material, door*] claquer; [*paper, clothes*] voleter; **the birds ~ped away** les oiseaux se sont éloignés en battant des ailes; **2**○ (panic) s'affoler; **stop ~ping!** calme-toi!

flapjack /ˈflæpdʒæk/ *n* Culin **1** GB biscuit *m* au müesli; **2** US crêpe *f*.

flapper○ /ˈflæpə(r)/ *n* (also **~ girl**) jeune femme *f* délurée (*des années vingt*).

flare /fleə(r)/ **I** *n* **1** (light signal) Aviat (on runway) balise *f* lumineuse; Mil (on target) fusée *f* éclairante; Naut (distress signal) fusée *f* (de détresse); **2** (burst of light) (of match, lighter) lueur *f*; (of fireworks) flamboiement *m*; **3** Ind (in petroleum processing) torche *f*; **4** Fashn évasement *m*; **5** Astron (also **solar ~**) éruption *f* solaire; **6** Phot lumière *f* parasite.

II flares *npl* (trousers) pantalon *m* à pattes d'éléphant; **a pair of ~s** un pantalon à pattes d'éléphant.

III *vtr* **1** (widen) évaser [*skirt, trouser leg*]; **a ~d skirt** une jupe évasée; **a pair of ~d trousers** un pantalon à pattes d'éléphant; **2** Ind brûler [qch] en torche [*gases*].

IV *vi* **1** (burn briefly) [*firework, match, torch*] jeter une brève lueur; **2** (erupt) [*violence*] éclater, se déchaîner; **tempers started to ~** les esprits ont commencé à s'échauffer; **3** (also **~ out**) (widen) [*skirt*] s'évaser; **4** [*nostrils*] se dilater.

■ **flare up** **1** (burn brightly) [*fire*] s'embraser; **2** fig (erupt) [*trouble, violence*] éclater, se déchaîner; [*anger, revolution*] éclater; [*person*] s'emporter; [*epidemic*] se déclarer; **3** (recur) [*illness, symptoms*] réapparaître; [*pain*] se réveiller , revenir.

flare path *n* Aviat piste *f* balisée.

flare-up /ˈfleərʌp/ *n* **1** (of fire, light) flamboiement *m*; **2** (outburst) (of fighting, trouble) recrudescence *f*; (of dispute) reprise *f*; (of war) intensification *f*; (of anger) crise *f*; **a violent ~** une flambée de violence; **3** (argument) altercation *f*; **4** (recurrence) (of feeling) regain *m*; (of disease) recrudescence *f*.

flash /flæʃ/ **I** *n* **1** (sudden light) (of torch, headlights) lueur *f* soudaine; (of jewels, metal, knife) éclat *m*; **a ~ of lightning** un éclair; **a ~ of light** une lueur soudaine; **2** fig **a ~ of colour** un éclair de couleur; **a ~ of inspiration/genius** un éclair d'inspiration/de génie; **a ~ of intuition** une intuition soudaine; **a ~ of wit** une boutade; **it came to him in a ~ that** l'idée lui est soudain venue que; **it was all over in** ou **like a ~** tout était fini en un clin d'œil; **3** Phot flash *m*; **4** (bulletin) flash *m* (d'information); **5** (stripe) (on clothing) parement *m*; (on car) bande *f*; **6** (on horse) (on head) étoile *f*; (elsewhere) tache *f* blanche; **7**○ GB (display) **give us a quick ~!** hum fais-nous voir!

II○ *adj* (posh) péj [*hotel*] luxueux/-ueuse; [*car, suit*] tape-à-l'œil *inv*; [*friend*] frimeur/-euse.

III *vtr* **1**○ (display) [*person*] montrer [qch] rapidement [*ID card, credit card, money*]; **to ~ sth at sb** [*person*] montrer qch rapidement à qn; (flaunt) exhiber qch devant qn; **2** (shine) **to ~ a signal/message to sb** envoyer un signal/message à qn avec une lampe; **to ~ a torch on** ou **at sth** diriger le faisceau d'une lampe de poche sur qch; **~ your torch three times** allume ta lampe de poche trois fois de suite; **to ~ one's headlights (at)** faire un appel de phares (à); **3** (send) fig lancer [*look, smile*] (**at** à); **4** (transmit) [*TV station*] transmettre [*pictures, news*] (**to** à); (briefly) faire apparaître [*message*].

IV *vi* **1** (shine) [*lighthouse, warning light*] clignoter; [*jewels*] étinceler; [*eyes*] lancer des éclairs; **to ~ on and off** clignoter; **his right indicator was ~ing** il avait mis son clignotant droit; **2** (appear suddenly) **a thought ~ed through my mind** une pensée m'a traversé l'esprit; **3**○ (expose oneself) [*man*] faire l'exhibitionnisme (**at** devant).

IDIOMS **to be a ~ in the pan** être un feu de paille; **quick as a ~** vif/vive comme l'éclair.

■ **flash about, flash around**: **~ [sth] about** exhiber [*credit card, banknote*]; étaler [*money*].

■ **flash back** [*film*] faire un retour en arrière (**to** sur).

■ **flash by, flash past** [*person, bird*] passer comme un éclair; [*time*] passer à la vitesse de l'éclair; [*landscape*] défiler.

■ **flash up**: ¶ **~ up** [*message, result*] s'afficher; ¶ **~ [sth] up, ~ up [sth]** afficher [*message, results*] (**on** sur).

flashback /ˈflæʃbæk/ *n* **1** Cin flash-back *m* (**to** à), retour *m* en arrière (**to** sur); **2** (memory) flash-back *m*, souvenir *m*.

flash: **~bulb** *n* ampoule *f* de flash; **~ burn** *n* Med brûlure *f* causée par une explosion atomique; **~ card** *n* (for teaching) carte *f* (de support visuel); (for awarding points) carte *f* de pointage; **~ cube** *n* cube-flash *m*.

flasher○ /ˈflæʃə(r)/ *n* **1** (exhibitionist) exhibitionniste *m*; **2** Aut clignotant *m*.

flash: **~ flood** *n* crue *f* éclair; **~-forward** *n* Cin flash-forward *m*; **~-fry steak** *n* Culin ≈ steak *m* minute; **~ gun** *n* Phot flash *m*; **~ Harry**○ *n* GB péj frimeur○ *m*.

flashily /ˈflæʃɪlɪ/ *adv* [*dress*] de façon voyante.

flashing /ˈflæʃɪŋ/ **I** *n* **1** Constr solin *m*; **2**○ (exhibitionism) exhibitionnisme *m*.

II *adj* [*light, sign*] clignotant.

flash: **~ light** *n* lampe *f* de poche; **~ photography** *n* photographie *f* au flash.

flashpoint /ˈflæʃpɔɪnt/ *n* **1** Chem point *m* d'éclair; **2** fig (trouble spot) point *m* chaud; **3** fig (explosive situation) point *m* critique.

flashy○ /ˈflæʃɪ/ *adj* péj [*driver, player*] frimeur/-euse; [*move, stroke*] pour la frime (*after n*); [*car, dress, tie*] tape-à-l'œil *inv*; [*colour*] criard; [*jewellery*] clinquant; [*campaign, image, presentation*] tape-à-l'œil *inv*; **he's a ~ dresser** il porte toujours des vêtements tape-à-l'œil.

flask /flɑːsk, US flæsk/ *n* **1** Chem (large) flacon *m*; (small) (round-bottomed) ballon *m*; (flat-bottomed) fiole *f*; **2** gen (large) bonbonne *f*; (small) bouteille *f*; (vacuum) thermos® *f* or *m inv*; (**hip**) **~** flasque *f*.

flat /flæt/ **I** *n* **1** GB (apartment) appartement *m*; **one-bedroom** deux-pièces *m inv* **~**; **2 the ~ of** le plat de [*hand, oar, sword*]; **on the ~** GB [*walk, park*] sur le plat; **3**○ (on car, bike) pneu *m* à plat; **4** Mus (note, sign) bémol *m*; **5** Theat châssis *m*; ▶ **salt flat**.

II flats *npl* **1**○ US (shoes) chaussures *fpl* plates; **2** Geog (marshland) marécage *m*.

III *adj* **1** (level) [*surface, landscape, road, roof*] plat; (not rounded) [*stone*] plat; [*stomach, chest*] plat; [*nose, face*] aplati; (shallow) [*dish, basket, box*] plat; **to be ~ on one's back/face** être sur ledeux pièces *m inv* dos/à plat ventre; **to hammer sth ~** aplatir qch au marteau; **to be squashed ~** être écrasé; **2** (deflated) [*tyre, ball*] dégonflé; **to have a ~ tyre** avoir un pneu à plat; **to go ~** se dégonfler; **3** (pressed close) **her feet ~ on the floor** les pieds bien à plat sur le sol; **4** Fashn [*shoes, heels*] plat; **5** (absolute) [*refusal, rejection, denial*] catégorique; **you're not going and that's ~**○**!** tu n'iras pas, un point c'est tout!; **6** (standard) [*fare, fee*] forfaitaire; [*charge*] fixe; **7** (monotonous) [*voice, tone*] plat, monocorde; (unexciting) [*performance, story, style*] plat; [*colour*] terne; [*taste*] plat; **8** (not fizzy) [*beer, lemonade*] éventé; **to go ~** [*beer*] s'éventer; **9** (depressed) **to feel ~** [*person*] se sentir déprimé; **he sounded a bit ~** il n'avait pas l'air en forme; **10** GB [*battery*] Elec usé; Aut à plat; **to go ~** Elec être usé; Aut être à plat; **11** Comm, Fin (slow) [*market, trade*] languissant; [*spending, profits*] stagnant; **12** Mus [*note*] bémol *inv*; (off key) [*voice, instrument*] faux; **in the key of B ~ minor** en si bémol mineur; **13** (matt) [*paint, surface*] mat.

IV *adv* **1** (horizontally) [*lay, lie*] à plat; [*fall*] de tout son long; **to knock sb ~** terrasser qn; **to lay sb ~** étendre raide qn○; **they laid the village ~** ils ont rasé le village; **to lie ~** [*person*] s'étendre; [*hair*] s'aplatir; [*pleat*] être aplati; **to lie/land ~ on one's back** s'allonger/atterrir sur le dos; **I was lying ~ on my back** j'étais allongé sur le dos; **to fall ~ on one's face** lit tomber à plat ventre; fig se casser la figure○; **2** (in close contact) **we pressed ~ against the wall** nous nous sommes aplatis contre le mur; **she pressed her nose ~ against the window** elle a collé son nez à la vitre; **3** (exactly) **in 10 minutes ~** en 10 minutes pile; **4**○ (absolutely) carrément; **she told me ~ that...** elle m'a carrément dit que...; **to turn [sth] down ~** refuser tout net [*offer, proposal*]; **they went ~ against their orders** ils ont carrément enfreint les ordres; **5** Mus [*sing, play*] faux.

IDIOMS **to fall ~** [*play*] faire un bide○; [*joke*] tomber à plat; [*party, evening*] tourner court; [*plan*] tomber à l'eau.

flat: **~-bed lorry** *n* camion *m* à plateau; **~-bottomed** *adj* [*boat*] à fond plat; **~ broke**○ *adj* fauché○, à sec○; **~ cap** *n* GB casquette *f* plate; **~car** *n* US wagon *m* plat.

flat-chested /ˌflætˈtʃestɪd/ *adj* [*woman*] à la poitrine plate.

flat course *n* US plat *m*.

flat feet *npl* pieds *mpl* plats; **to have ~** avoir les pieds plats.

flat: **~fish** *n* poisson *m* plat; **~ foot**○† *n* GB péj poulet○† *m*, policier *m*.

flat-footed /ˌflætˈfʊtɪd/ *adj* **1** Med [*person*] aux pieds plats; **to be ~** avoir les pieds plats; **2**○ (clumsy) [*person*] lourdaud péj; **3**○ péj (tactless) [*attempt, manner, remark*] maladroit.

IDIOMS **to catch sb ~**○ prendre qn au dépourvu.

flat-hunting /ˈflæthʌntɪŋ/ *n* GB **to go ~** chercher un appartement.

flat: **~iron** *n* Hist fer *m* à repasser (*qu'on chauffe sur le poêle*); **~ jockey** ▶ **1692** *n* jockey *m* spécialisé dans les courses de plat; **~lands** *npl* plaine *f*.

flatlet /ˈflætlɪt/ *n* GB ≈ studio *m*.

flatly /ˈflætlɪ/ *adv* **1** (absolutely) [*refuse, contradict, reject*] catégoriquement; [*deny*] formellement; **to be ~ opposed to sth** s'opposer catégoriquement à qch; **2** (unemotionally) [*say etc*] d'une voix monocorde.

flatmate /ˈflætmeɪt/ *n* GB colocataire *mf* (*personne avec qui on partage un appartement*).

flatness /ˈflætnɪs/ *n* **1** (of terrain, landscape) manque *m* de relief; (of roof, stone, surface) aspect *m* plat; **2** (dullness) (of voice) caractère *m* monocorde; (of colours) fadeur *f*; (of style, description, story) platitude *f*.

flat out /ˌflætˈaʊt/ **I** *adj* GB (also **~ tired** US) KO○, épuisé.

II *adv* [*drive, go, ride*] à fond de train; [*work*] d'arrache-pied; **it only does 120 km per hour ~** elle ne monte qu'à 120 km à l'heure, pied au plancher; **to tell sb ~ that** US dire carrément à qn que.

IDIOMS **to go ~ for sth** se mettre en quatre○ pour faire qch.

flat: **~ race** *n* course *f* de plat; **~ racing** *n* courses *fpl* de plat.

flat rate /ˌflætˈreɪt/ **I** *n* taux *m* fixe.

II flat-rate *modif* [*contribution, fee, tax*] forfaitaire.

flat: **~ season** *n* saison *f* des courses de plat; **~ silver** *n* US couverts *mpl* en argent.

flat spin /ˌflætˈspɪn/ *n* Aviat vrille *f* à plat.
IDIOMS **to be in a ~**○ être affolé.

flatten /ˈflætn/ **I** *vtr* **1** (level) [*rain, storm*] coucher [*crops, grass*]; abattre [*tree, fence*]; [*bombing, earthquake*] raser [*building, town*]; **he ~ed him with a single punch** il l'a étendu raide○ d'un seul coup de poing; **he'll ~ you**○! il va te casser la figure○!; **2** (smooth out) aplanir [*surface, ground, road*]; aplatir [*metal*]; **3** (crush) écraser [*animal, fruit, hat, box etc*]; **4**○ fig (beat) écraser [*person, team*]; **5** Mus baisser (le ton de) [*note*]; **6** GB Aut, Elec user [*radio battery*]; décharger [*car battery*].
II *vi* = **flatten out**.
III *v refl* **to ~ oneself** s'aplatir (**against** contre) [*wall, door etc*].
IV flattened *pp adj* [*shape, nose, head*] aplati; [*box, can*] écrasé; (by rain, storm) [*grass, weeds*] couché; (by earthquake, bombs) [*building, district*] rasé.
■ **flatten out**: ¶ **~ out** [*slope, road, ground*] s'aplanir; [*graph, curve, flight path*] se redresser; [*growth, exports, decline*] se stabiliser; ¶ **~ out [sth], ~ [sth] out** aplanir [*ground, road*]; **he ~ed the map out on the table** il a étalé la carte bien à plat sur la table.

flattening /ˈflætnɪŋ/ *n* **1** (of metal) aplatissement *m*; (of ground) aplanissement *m*; **2**○ GB (humiliation) humiliation *f*.

flatter /ˈflætə(r)/ **I** *vtr* **1** (compliment) flatter (**on** sur); **to be ~ed that** être flatté que; **2** (enhance) [*light, dress, portrait*] flatter.
II *v refl* **to ~ oneself** se flatter (**on being** d'être); **I ~ myself that I know a bit about computers** je me flatte de m'y connaître un peu en informatique.

flatterer /ˈflætərə(r)/ *n* flatteur/-euse *m/f*.

flattering /ˈflætərɪŋ/ *adj* [*remark, portrait etc*] gen flatteur/-euse; **she was wearing a ~ hat/dress** elle portait un chapeau/une robe qui la flattait.

flatteringly /ˈflætərɪŋlɪ/ *adv* flatteusement; **~ attentive** d'une prévenance flatteuse.

flattery /ˈflætərɪ/ *n* flatterie *f*.
IDIOMS **~ will get you nowhere** la flatterie ne mène à rien.

flatties○ /ˈflætiːz/ *npl* GB chaussures *fpl* plates.

flat-topped /ˈflættɒpt/ *adj* [*hill, mountain*] à sommet plat.

flatulence /ˈflætjʊləns/ *n* flatulence *f*.

flatulent /ˈflætjʊlənt/ *adj* **1** Med [*person*] ballonné; [*indigestion*] flatulent; [*food*] qui provoque des flatulences; **2** fig [*style*] enflé.

flatware /ˈflætweə(r)/ *n* US **1** (cutlery) couverts *mpl*; **2** (crockery) assiettes *fpl*.

flatworm /ˈflætwɜːm/ *n* ver *m* plat, plathelminthe *m* spec.

flaunt /flɔːnt/ **I** *vtr* péj étaler [*wealth*]; faire étalage de [*knowledge, superiority, charms*]; afficher [*opinion, ability, quality, lover*]; exhiber [*possession*].
II *v refl* **to ~ oneself** s'exhiber.

flautist /ˈflɔːtɪst/ **▶ 1692**, **1481** *n* flûtiste *mf*.

flavour GB, **flavor** US /ˈfleɪvə(r)/ **I** *n* **1** Culin goût *m*; (subtler) saveur *f*; **with a coffee ~** au café; **to bring out the ~** relever le goût; **banana ~ yoghurt** yaourt à la banane; **full of ~** plein de saveurs; **2** (atmosphere) (of period, place) atmosphère *f*; (hint) idée *f*; **the ~ of life in 1900** la saveur de la vie de 1900.
II *vtr* **1** Culin (improve taste) donner du goût à; (add specific taste) parfumer (**with** à); **2** fig assaisonner (**with** de).
III flavoured GB, **flavored** US *pp adj* **1** Culin parfumé; **coffee-~ed** parfumé au café; **fully-~ed** plein de saveurs; **2** fig assaisonné.
IDIOMS **to be ~ of the month**○ [*thing*] être en vogue; [*person*] être la coqueluche du moment.

flavour-enhancer GB, **flavor-enhancer** US *n* exhausteur *m* de goût.

flavouring GB, **flavoring** US /ˈfleɪvərɪŋ/ *n* (for sweet taste) parfum *m*; (for meat, fish) assaisonnement *m*; **natural/artificial ~** arôme *m* naturel/artificiel.

flavourless GB, **flavorless** US /ˈfleɪvəlɪs/ *adj* insipide.

flaw /flɔː/ *n* (in object, suggestion, character) défaut *m* (**in** dans); (in reasoning, theory) faille *f* (**in** dans); (in contract) Jur vice *m* de forme.

flawed /ˈflɔːd/ *adj* gen défectueux/-euse; [*character, person*] vicié.

flawless /ˈflɔːlɪs/ *adj* [*complexion*] sans défaut; [*argument*] sans faille; [*performance, technique*] irréprochable.

flax /flæks/ *n* Bot, Tex lin *m*.

flaxen /ˈflæksn/ *adj* de lin; **a ~-haired child** un enfant aux cheveux de lin.

flay /fleɪ/ *vtr* **1** (remove skin) écorcher; **2** (beat) fouetter; **3** (criticize) éreinter.

flea /fliː/ *n* puce *f*.
IDIOMS **to send sb away with a ~ in their ear**○ envoyer promener○ qn.

fleabag○ /ˈfliːbæg/ *n* péj **1** GB (person) pouilleux/-euse○ *m/f*; (animal) sac *m* à puces; **2** US (hotel) hôtel *m* miteux.

fleabite /ˈfliːbaɪt/ *n* **1** lit piqûre *f* de puce; **2** fig (trifle) vétille *f*.

flea-bitten /ˈfliːbɪtn/ *adj* **1** lit [*animal*] infesté de puces; [*part of body*] dévoré par les puces; **2**○ (shabby) miteux/-euse.

flea: **~ collar** *n* collier *m* antipuce; **~ market** *n* marché *m* aux puces; **~pit**○ *n* GB péj cinéma *m* miteux; **~ powder** *n* poudre *f* antiparasitaire.

fleck /flek/ **I** *n* (of colour) moucheture *f*; (of light) tache *f*; (of foam) flocon *m*; (of blood, paint) petite tache *f*; (of dust, powder) particule *f*.
II *vtr* **to be ~ed with** être moucheté de [*colour*]; être tacheté de [*blood, paint, light*]; **hair ~ed with grey** des cheveux grisonnants; **eyes ~ed with green** des yeux piquetés de vert.

fled /fled/ *prét, pp* ▶ **flee**.

fledged /fledʒd/ *adj* ▶ **fully-fledged**.

fledg(e)ling /ˈfledʒlɪŋ/ **I** *n* Zool oisillon *m*.
II *modif* fig [*artist, barrister etc*] frais émoulu/fraîche émoulue; [*party, group*] naissant; [*democracy, enterprise*] jeune.

flee /fliː/ (*prét, pp* **fled**) **I** *vtr* fuir.
II *vi* **1** [*person, animal*] fuir (**before, in the face of** devant); **to ~ from sth** fuir qch; **2** fig littér [*hope, happiness etc*] s'envoler.

fleece /fliːs/ **I** *n* **1** (on animal) toison *f*; **2** Tex molleton *m*; (for sportswear) laine *f* pôlaire; **3** (garment) fourrure *f* pôlaire; **~-lined** fourré.
II○ *vtr* (overcharge) estamper○; (swindle) plumer○.

fleecy /ˈfliːsɪ/ *adj* [*fabric*] laineux/-euse; [*clouds*] floconneux/-euse.

fleet /fliːt/ *n* **1** (of ships, planes) flotte *f*; (of small vessels) flottille *f*; **fishing ~** flottille de pêche; **2** (of vehicles) (in reserve) parc *m*; (on road) convoi *m*; **car ~** parc automobile.

fleet: **~ admiral ▶ 1612** *n* US amiral *m* de la flotte; **Fleet Air Arm** *n* GB aéronavale *f*; **~ chief petty officer ▶ 1612** *n* GB major *m*; **~-footed**, **~ of foot** *adj* agile.

fleeting /ˈfliːtɪŋ/ *adj* [*memory, pleasure*] fugace; [*visit, moment*] bref/brève; [*glance*] rapide.

fleetingly /ˈfliːtɪŋlɪ/ *adv* [*appear, glimpse*] fugitivement; [*glance*] rapidement.

Fleet Street *n* la presse *f* (londonienne).

Fleming /ˈflemɪŋ/ *n* Flamand/-e *m/f*.

Flemish /ˈflemɪʃ/ **▶ 1486** **I** *n* **1** (language) flamand *m*; **2 the ~** les Flamands *mpl*.
II *adj* flamand.

flesh /fleʃ/ *n* **1** (of human, animal) chair *f*; **2** (of fruit) chair *f*, pulpe *f*; **3** fig **I'm only ~ and blood** je ne suis qu'un être humain; **it's more than ~ and blood can bear** c'est plus qu'un être humain ne peut supporter; **one's own ~ and blood** la chair de sa chair; **in the ~** en chair et en os; **the pleasures/sins of the ~** les plaisirs/péchés de la chair; **it makes my ~ creep** ça me donne la chair de poule.
IDIOMS **to demand one's pound of ~** exiger son dû impitoyablement; **to go the way of all ~** littér euph aller où va toute chose; **to press the ~**○ prendre un bain de foule.
■ **flesh out**: **~ [sth] out, ~ out [sth]** étayer [*speech, article, report*] (**with** de).

flesh: **~ colour** GB, **~-color** US *n* couleur *f* chair; **~-coloured** GB, **~-colored** US *adj* (couleur) chair *inv*; **~-eating** *adj* carnivore.

fleshings /ˈfleʃɪŋz/ *npl* collant *m* (de danseuse).

fleshly /ˈfleʃlɪ/ *adj* charnel/-elle.

flesh: **~pots** *npl* mauvais lieux *mpl*; **~ wound** *n* blessure *f* superficielle.

fleshy /ˈfleʃɪ/ *adj* [*arm, leg, lip, fruit, leaf*] charnu; [*breasts, buttocks*] rebondi; [*person*] bien en chair.

flew /fluː/ *prét* ▶ **fly**.

flex /fleks/ **I** *n* GB (for electrical appliance) fil *m*.
II *vtr* **1** (contract) faire jouer [*muscle*]; **to ~ one's muscles** fig chercher à en imposer; **2** (bend and stretch) fléchir [*limb*]; plier [*finger, toe*].

flexibility /ˌfleksəˈbɪlətɪ/ *n* souplesse *f*, flexibilité *f*; **to allow ~ in doing sth** permettre une certaine souplesse pour faire qch.

flexible /ˈfleksəbl/ *adj* **1** [*working hours, arrangement*] flexible, souple; [*plan, agenda*] souple; [*repayment plan*] à échéances variables; **2** [*person*] souple (**over, about** en ce qui concerne); **3** [*tube, wire, stem*] flexible, souple; [*plastic, glass, road surface*] souple.

flexible response *n* Mil riposte *f* graduée.

flexibly /ˈfleksəblɪ/ *adv* de façon souple.

flexi disc /ˈfleksɪdɪsk/ *n* Audio disque *m* souple.

flexion /ˈflekʃn/ *n* flexion *f*.

flexitime /ˈfleksɪtaɪm/ *n* horaire *m* flexible or souple; **to work ~** avoir un horaire flexible or souple.

flexor /ˈfleksə(r)/ *n* Anat (muscle *m*) fléchisseur *m*.

flibbertigibbet○ /ˌflɪbətɪˈdʒɪbɪt/ *n* écervelé/-e *m/f*.

flick /flɪk/ **I** *n* **1** (blow) (with finger) chiquenaude *f*; (with whip, cloth, tongue) petit coup *m*; **to give sb a ~ with sth** donner un petit coup de qch à qn; **2** (movement) gen, Sport petit coup *m*; **with a ~ of the wrist/its tail** d'un petit coup de poignet/de queue; **at the ~ of a switch** rien qu'en appuyant sur un bouton; **to have a ~ through a book** feuilleter un livre; **3**○ (film) film *m*.
II flicks○ *npl* cinéma *m*.
III *vtr* **1** (strike) (with finger) donner une chiquenaude à; (with tail, cloth) donner un petit coup à; **to ~ a crumb off sth** enlever une miette de qch d'un petit geste; **to ~ sth at sb** (with finger) envoyer or lancer qch à qn d'une chiquenaude; **to ~ sth open** ouvrir d'un coup sec; **he ~ed his ash onto the floor** il a fait tomber sa cendre par terre; **to ~ a duster over the chairs** donner un coup de chiffon aux chaises; **2** (press) appuyer sur [*switch*]; **to ~ the television on/off** allumer/éteindre la télévision; **3** Sport donner un petit coup à [*ball*].
■ **flick away**: **~ [sth] away, ~ away [sth]** (with finger) enlever [qch] d'une chiquenaude; (with tail, object) éloigner.
■ **flick back**: **~ [sth] back, ~ back [sth]** rejeter [qch] en arrière [*hair*].
■ **flick off**: **~ [sth] off, ~ off [sth]** (with finger) enlever [qch] d'une chiquenaude; (with tail, cloth) enlever [qch] d'un petit geste.
■ **flick out**: ¶ **~ out** [*tongue*] sortir rapi-

dement; ¶ **~** [sth] **out**, **~ out** [sth] sortir rapidement [*tongue, blade*].

■ **flick over**: **~** [sth] **over**, **~ over** [sth] feuilleter [*pages*].

■ **flick through**: **~ through** [sth] feuilleter [*book, report*]; **to ~ through the channels** TV zapper.

flicker /ˈflɪkə(r)/ **I** *n* **1** (unsteady light) (of light, flame, candle) vacillation *f*, tremblotement *m*; (of image) scintillement *m*; (of lightning) vacillement *m*; **2** (slight sign) (of interest, surprise, anger, guilt) lueur *f* (**of** de); **the ~ of a smile** l'ombre d'un sourire; **3** (movement) (of eye, eyelid) clignement *m*; (of indicator) oscillation *f*; **4** US Zool pic *m* d'Amérique.

II *vi* **1** (shine unsteadily) [*fire, light, flame*] vaciller, trembloter; [*image*] clignoter; [*lightning*] jeter une lueur vacillante; **2** (pass quickly) **a suspicion ~ed across** ou **through his mind** un doute lui a traversé l'esprit; **3** (move) [*eye, eyelid*] cligner.

flickering /ˈflɪkərɪŋ/ *adj* [*light, flame, candle*] vacillant, tremblotant; [*image*] tremblotant.

flick knife *n* GB couteau *m* à cran d'arrêt.

flier /ˈflaɪə(r)/ *n* **1** (person or thing which flies) (pilot) aviateur/-trice *m/f*; **a swift/powerful ~** (bird) un oiseau au vol rapide/puissant; **to be a graceful ~** avoir un vol gracieux; **2** (handbill) prospectus *m*.

flight /flaɪt/ **I** *n* **1** Aerosp, Aviat, Transp (journey) vol *m* (**to** vers; **from** de); **a scheduled/charter ~** un vol régulier/charter; **the ~ to/from Paris** (in airport, announcement) le vol à destination de/en provenance de Paris; **the ~ from Dublin to London** le vol Dublin-Londres; **the ~ over the Alps was superb** le survol des Alpes était magnifique; **we hope you enjoyed your ~** nous espérons que vous avez fait un bon voyage; **we took the next ~ (out) to New York** nous avons pris l'avion suivant pour New York; **2** (course) (of bird, insect) vol *m*; (of missile, bullet) trajectoire *f*; **3** (power of locomotion) vol *m*; **to have the power of ~** avoir la capacité de voler; **in ~** [*bird, plane*] en vol; **in full ~** lit en plein vol; fig en plein élan; **4** (group) **a ~ of** un vol de, une volée de [*birds*]; une troupe de [*angels*]; une volée de [*arrows*]; une escadrille de [*aircraft*]; **5** (escape) fuite *f*; **~ from** fuite devant [*enemy, poverty, war, starvation*]; **to take ~** prendre la fuite; **to put sb to ~** mettre qn en fuite; **a ~ of capital** Econ une fuite des capitaux; **6** (set) **a ~ of steps** ou **stairs** une volée de marches; **six ~s (of stairs)** six étages; **we live four ~s up** nous habitons au quatrième; **a ~ of hurdles** Sport une série de haies; **a ~ of locks** une série d'écluses; **a ~ of terraces** un étagement de terrasses; **7** (display) (*gén pl*) **~s of imagination** élans *mpl* d'imagination; **~s of rhetoric** envolées *fpl* oratoires; **a ~ of fancy** une invention.

II *modif* [*delay, information, schedule, time*] de vol.

IDIOMS **to be in the top ~** être parmi les meilleurs; **he's in the top ~ of goalkeepers** il est parmi les meilleurs gardiens de but.

flight: **~ attendant** ▶1692 *n* Aviat (male) steward *m*; (female) hôtesse *f* de l'air; **~ bag** *n* bagage *m* à main.

flight control *n* **1** (by radio) contrôle *m* de vol; **2** (control system) commande *f* de vol.

flight deck *n* **1** Aviat (compartment) poste *m* de pilotage; (personnel) navigants *mpl* techniques; **2** Naut pont *m* d'envol.

flight engineer ▶1692 *n* mécanicien *m* navigant.

flightless /ˈflaɪtlɪs/ *adj* [*bird, insect*] incapable de voler; **the order of ~ birds** l'ordre des oiseaux coureurs.

flight: **~ lieutenant** ▶1612 *n* Mil capitaine *m* (de l'armée de l'air); **~ log** *n* journal *m* de bord; **~ path** *n* route *f* de vol; **~ plan** *n* plan *m* de vol; **~ recorder** *n* enregistreur *m* de vol; **~ sergeant** ▶1612 *n* Mil sergent *m* (de l'armée de l'air); **~ simulator** *n* Aviat simulateur *m* de vol; **~-test** *vtr* essayer [qch] en vol.

flighty /ˈflaɪtɪ/ *adj* [*person, imagination, account, mind*] écervelé; [*partner*] volage.

flimflam○ /ˈflɪmflæm/ US **I** *n* **1** (nonsense) balivernes *fpl*; **2** (trick) coup *m* fourré○.

II *vtr* rouler○.

flimsily /ˈflɪmzɪlɪ/ *adv* [*dressed*] légèrement; **~ built** peu solide.

flimsiness /ˈflɪmzɪnɪs/ *n* (of clothes) légèreté *f*; (of paper, fabric) minceur *f*; (of construction) manque *m* de solidité; (of evidence) minceur *f*; (of excuse) futilité *f*.

flimsy /ˈflɪmzɪ/ **I**† *n* GB papier *m* pelure.

II *adj* [*clothes, fabric*] léger/-ère; [*structure, appliance*] peu solide; [*argument, excuse*] futile; [*evidence*] mince, piètre (*before n*).

flinch /flɪntʃ/ *vi* (psychologically) hésiter; (physically) tressaillir; **without ~ing** sans broncher; **to ~ from doing sth** hésiter à faire qch; **to ~ at** tiquer sur [*criticism, insult etc*].

fling /flɪŋ/ **I** *n* **1**○ (spree) bon temps *m*; **to have a ~** se payer du bon temps; **to have a last** ou **final ~** faire la fête avant de se ranger; **2**○ (affair) (sexual) aventure *f*; (intellectual) flirt○ *m*; **to have a brief ~ with Marxism** flirter brièvement avec le marxisme.

II *vtr* (*prét, pp* **flung**) (throw) lancer [*ball, grenade, stone*] (**onto** sur; **into** dans); lancer [*insult, accusation*] (**at** à); **to ~ a scarf around one's shoulders** se jeter une écharpe sur les épaules; **to ~ a few things into a suitcase** jeter quelques affaires dans une valise; **to ~ sb to the ground** [*person*] jeter qn à terre; [*blast*] projeter qn à terre; **to ~ sb against sth** [*blast, person*] projeter qn contre qch; **I flung my arms around her neck** je me suis jeté à son cou; **to ~ sb into prison** jeter qn en prison.

III *v refl* **to ~ oneself** se jeter (**across** en travers de; **into** dans; **onto** sur; **over** par dessus; **under** sous); **to ~ oneself off sth** sauter de [*bridge, cliff*]; **he flung himself at her feet** il s'est jeté à ses pieds.

IDIOMS **to ~ oneself at sb's head** se jeter à la tête de qn; **youth must have its ~** il faut que jeunesse se passe.

■ **fling about**, **~ around**: **~** [sth] **around** gaspiller [*money*].

■ **fling away**: **~** [sth] **away** jeter qch.

■ **fling back**: **~** [sth] **back**, **~ back** [sth] renvoyer [*ball, keys*]; rejeter [qch] en arrière [*hair, head*]; ouvrir [qch] brusquement [*door*].

■ **fling down**: **~** [sth] **down**, **~ down** [sth] jeter [qch] par terre [*coat, newspaper*].

■ **fling on**: **~ on** [sth] enfiler [qch] rapidement [*dress, coat*].

■ **fling open**: **~** [sth] **open**, **~ open** [sth] ouvrir [qch] brusquement [*door*]; ouvrir [qch] tout grand [*window*].

■ **fling out**: **~** [sb] **out** mettre [qn] à la porte [*lover, troublemaker*].

flint /flɪnt/ **I** *n* **1** Geol silex *m*; **2** Anthrop éclat *m* de silex; **3**† (for kindling) pierre *f* à feu; **4** (in lighter) pierre *f* à briquet.

II *modif* [*church, arrowhead*] en silex; [*axe*] de silex; [*nodule, pebble*] siliceux/-euse.

flint: **~ glass** *n* flint-glass *m*; **~lock** *n* pistolet *m* à pierre.

flinty /ˈflɪntɪ/ *adj* **1** Geol [*soil, cliff*] siliceux/-euse; **2** (hard) lit, fig [*surface, face, expression*] dur.

flip /flɪp/ **I** *n* **1** (of finger) chiquenaude *f*; **to give sth a ~** donner une chiquenaude à qch; **with a ~ (of the fingers)** d'une pichenette; **to decide sth by the ~ of a coin** décider qch à pile ou face; **2** Aviat, Sport (somersault) tour *m*; **3** (glance) **to have a ~ through** feuilleter rapidement [*magazine, guide*].

II *adj* [*person, attitude, remark, reply*] désinvolte.

III○ *excl* GB **~!** zut○!, flûte○!

IV *vtr* (*p prés etc* **-pp-**) **1** (toss) lancer [*coin*]; faire sauter [*pancake*]; **let's ~ a coin to decide** décidons à pile ou face; **2** (flick) basculer [*switch*]; **to ~ sth on/off** allumer/éteindre qch d'un mouvement rapide; **to ~ sth open/shut** ouvrir/fermer qch rapidement.

V○ *vi* (*p prés etc* **-pp-**) **1** (get angry) se mettre en rogne○; **2** (go mad) perdre la boule○; **3** (get excited) devenir dingue○ (**over** de).

IDIOMS **to ~ one's lid** ou **top** US ou **wig** sortir de ses gonds○.

■ **flip out**○ **1** (get angry) se mettre en rogne○; **2** (go mad) perdre la boule○.

■ **flip over**: ¶ **~ over** [*vehicle, plane*] se retourner (complètement); ¶ **~** [sth] **over**, **~ over** [sth] **1** (toss) retourner [*omelette, pancake, coin*]; **2** (turn) feuilleter [*pages*].

■ **flip through**: **~ through** [sth] feuilleter [*book, magazine, index*].

flipboard GB, **flipchart** *n* tableau *m* de conférence, paperboard *m*.

flip-flop /ˈflɪpflɒp/ *n* **1** (sandal) tong *f*; **2** Comput (device) bascule *f*; **3** US (about-face) volte-face *f inv*.

flippancy /ˈflɪpənsɪ/ *n* désinvolture *f*; **the ~ of his tone** son ton cavalier.

flippant /ˈflɪpənt/ *adj* (not serious) [*remark, person*] désinvolte; (lacking respect) [*tone, attitude, behaviour*] cavalier/-ière; **don't be ~!** un peu de sérieux!; **I'm not being ~** je parle sérieusement.

flippantly /ˈflɪpəntlɪ/ *adv* [*ask, observe*] avec désinvolture.

flipper /ˈflɪpə(r)/ *n* **1** Zool nageoire *f*; **2** (for swimmer) palme *f*.

flipping○ /ˈflɪpɪŋ/ GB **I** *adj* fichu○; **~ heck**○**!** mince alors○!

II *adv* [*stupid, rude, painful, cold*] drôlement○; **that tastes ~ horrible!** ça a un goût vraiment horrible!

flip: **~ side** *n* Mus (on record) face *f* B; fig (other side) envers *m* (**of, to** de); **~-top** *n* capsule *f* à charnière.

flirt /flɜːt/ **I** *n* **1** (person) flirteur/-euse *m/f*; péj dragueur/-euse○ *m/f* pej; **2** (act) **to have a ~ with sb**○ flirter avec qn.

II *vi* flirter; **to ~ with** flirter avec [*person*]; jouer avec [*danger, image*]; caresser [*idea*]; friser [*sentimentality*].

flirtation /ˌflɜːˈteɪʃn/ *n* **1** (relationship) flirt *m*; **to have a ~ with sb** flirter avec qn; (longer-lived) avoir une aventure avec qn; **2** (interest) engouement *m* (**with** pour).

flirtatious /ˌflɜːˈteɪʃəs/ *adj* [*person, glance, wink*] charmeur/-euse, dragueur/-euse○ pej; [*laugh*] qui cherche à séduire.

flirting /ˈflɜːtɪŋ/ *n* flirt *m*.

flit /flɪt/ **I** *n* **1** (move) **to do a ~**○ (move house) déménager à la cloche de bois○; (leave) filer à l'anglaise; **2**◐ US (homosexual) injur tapette◐ *f* offensive.

II *vi* (*p prés etc* **-tt-**) **1** (fly) (also **~ about**) [*bird, bat, moth*] voleter; **to ~ from tree to tree** voleter d'arbre en arbre; **2** (move quickly and lightly) [*person*] aller d'un pas léger; **she was ~ting about the house** elle allait et venait dans la maison d'un pas précipité; **3** (flash) **a look of panic ~ted across his face** une expression de panique lui traversa le visage; **an idea ~ted through my mind** une idée me traversa l'esprit; **4** (move restlessly) **to ~ from one thing to another** passer rapidement d'une chose à l'autre; **to ~ from one country to another** aller et venir d'un pays à l'autre.

flitch /flɪtʃ/ *n* flèche *f* (de lard).

flitty /flɪtɪ/, **flitting**○ /ˈflɪtɪŋ/ *adj* US injur efféminé.

flivver○† /ˈflɪvə(r)/ *n* US guimbarde○ *f*, vieille voiture *f*.

float /fləʊt/ **I** *n* **1** Fishg (on net) flotteur *m*; (on line) bouchon *m*; **2** Aviat flotteur *m*; **3** (in plumbing) flotteur *m*; **4** GB (swimmer's aid) planche *f*; US (life jacket) gilet *m* de sauvetage; **5** (vehicle) char *m*; **carnival ~** char de carnaval; **milk ~** GB voiture *f* de laitier;

6 Comm (also **cash ~**) (in till) fonds *m* de caisse; **7** US (drink) *soda avec une boule de glace*; **8** GB Constr taloche *f*, bouclier *m*; **9** US Fin (time period) délai *m* avant l'encaissement d'un chèque; (value) masse *f* des effets en circulation (*qui n'ont pas été encaissés*).

II *vtr* **1** [*person*] faire flotter [*boat*]; [*tide*] mettre à flot [*ship*]; **to ~ logs down a waterway** faire flotter du bois sur un cours d'eau; **2** Fin introduire [qch] en Bourse, émettre [*shares, securities*]; lancer [qch] en Bourse [*company*]; lancer, émettre [*loan*]; laisser flotter [*currency*]; **3** (propose) lancer [*idea, suggestion*].

III *vi* **1** (on liquid, in air) flotter; **there were leaves ~ing on the water** des feuilles flottaient à la surface de l'eau; **to ~ on one's back** [*swimmer*] faire la planche; **to ~ back up to the surface** remonter à la surface; **the logs ~ed down the river** les troncs d'arbre descendaient la rivière; **the boat was ~ing out to sea** le bateau voguait vers le large; **the balloon ~ed up into the air** le ballon s'est envolé; **2** fig (waft) [*smoke, mist*] flotter; **clouds ~ed across the sky** des nuages traversaient lentement le ciel; **music from the ballroom ~ed out into the garden** on entendait la musique qui venait de la salle de bal jusque dans le jardin; **she ~ed into the room** elle est entrée dans la pièce d'un pas léger; **the thought ~ed through his mind** l'idée lui a traversé l'esprit; **3** Fin [*currency*] flotter.

■ **float about, float around 1** (circulate) [*idea, rumour*] circuler; **2**○ (be nearby) **are my keys ~ing around?** mes clés sont-elles par ici?; **your glasses are ~ing around somewhere** tes lunettes sont quelque part par là; **3**○ (aimlessly) [*person*] traîner; **he just ~s about the house all day** il passe ses journées à traîner dans la maison.

■ **float away** = **float off**.

■ **float off** [*boat*] dériver; [*balloon, feather*] s'envoler; [*person*] partir d'un pas léger.

floater /ˈfləʊtə(r)/ *n* US **1** (employee) employé/-e *m/f* polyvalent/-e; **2** (at party, reception) *personne dont le rôle est de circuler dans une soirée*; **3**○ Pol (voter) électeur/-trice *m/f* qui vote plus d'une fois; **4** Insur = **floating policy**.

float glass *n* verre *m* flotté.

floating /ˈfləʊtɪŋ/ **I** *n* **1** (of ship, logs) mise *f* à flot; **2** Fin (of company, loan) lancement *m* (en Bourse); (of shares) émission *f*; (of currency) flottement *m*.

II *adj* **1** (on water) [*bridge, debris*] flottant; **2** (unstable) [*population*] instable.

floating: **~ assets** *npl* Fin actif *m* circulant; **~ capital** *n* Fin capital *m* disponible, fonds *mpl* de roulement; **~ cheque** *n*: *chèque qui n'a pas encore été encaissé*; **~ currency** *n* Fin devise *f* flottante; **~ debt** *n* Fin dette *f* flottante or à court terme; **~ decimal (point)** *n* Math virgule *f* flottante; **~ dock** *n* Naut dock *m* flottant; **~ exchange rate** *n* Fin taux *m* de change flottant; **~ islands** *npl* Culin œufs *mpl* à la neige; **~ kidney** *n* Anat rein *m* flottant; **~ point representation** *n* notation *f* en virgule flottante; **~ policy** *n* Insur police *f* flottante; **~ rate** *n* Fin taux *m* flottant; **~ rate interest** *n* Fin intérêt *m* à taux flottant ou variable; **~ rate note** *n* Fin bon *m* à taux flottant ou révisable; **~ restaurant** *n* bateau-restaurant *m*; **~ rib** *n* Anat côte *f* flottante; **~ vote** *n* Pol vote *m* flottant; **~ voter** *n* Pol électeur *m* indécis.

flocculent /ˈflɒkjʊlənt/ *adj* (*tjrs épith*) floconneux/-euse.

flock /flɒk/ **I** *n* **1** (of sheep, goats) troupeau *m*; (of birds) volée *f*; **2** (of people) foule *f*; **in ~s** en masse; **3** ₵ Relig ouailles *fpl*; **4** Tex bourre *f*; **wool ~** bourre de laine; **5** (fleecy tuft) flocon *m*.

II *vi* [*animals, people*] affluer (**around** autour de; **into** dans); **to ~ to do** affluer pour faire; **to ~ together** [*people*] s'assembler; [*animals*] se rassembler. ▶ **feather**.

flock wallpaper *n* papier peint *m* floqué.

floe /fləʊ/ *n* banquise *f*.

flog /flɒg/ *vtr* (*p prés etc* **-gg-**) **1** (beat) flageller; **2**○ GB (sell) fourguer○, vendre; **to ~ sb sth, to ~ sth to sb** fourguer○ qch à qn.

IDIOMS **to ~ sth into the ground**○ ou **to death**○ GB bousiller○ qch; **to ~ oneself into the ground**○ ou **to death**○ GB se crever○ au travail; **to ~ a joke/story to death**○ rabâcher une plaisanterie/une histoire.

flogging /ˈflɒgɪŋ/ *n* (beating) flagellation *f*; **to give sb a ~** fouetter qn.

flood /flʌd/ **I** *n* **1** lit inondation *f*; **destroyed by ~** détruit par une inondation; **insured against ~** assuré contre l'inondation; **'~!'** (on roadsign) 'attention, route inondée!'; **the river is in ~** la rivière est en crue; **the Flood** Bible le Déluge; **2** fig **a ~ of** un flot de [*people, visitors, light, memories*]; un déluge de [*letters, complaints*]; **to be in ~s of tears** verser des torrents de larmes; **3**○ Phot, Theat = **floodlight**.

II *vtr* **1** lit inonder [*area, house*]; faire déborder [*river*]; **2** fig [*light, tears, mail*] inonder; **memories ~ed her mind** les souvenirs affluaient; **relief ~ed his face** le soulagement illumina son visage; **3** Comm (over-supply) inonder [*shops, market*] (**with** de); **4** Aut noyer [*engine, carburettor*].

III *vi* **1** [*meadow, street, cellar*] être inondé; [*river*] déborder; **2** fig **to ~ into sth** [*light*] inonder qch; [*people*] envahir qch; **tears ~ed down his cheeks** les larmes lui inondaient les joues; **a blush ~ed over his face** la rougeur lui envahit le visage; **to ~ over** ou **through sb** [*emotion*] envahir qn.

IV flooded *pp adj* [*area, house*] inondé; **to be ~ with** être inondé de [*light, calls, complaints, tears, refugees*].

■ **flood back** [*memories*] remonter à la surface.

■ **flood in** [*light, water*] entrer à flot; fig [*contributions, refugees*] affluer.

■ **flood out**: ¶ **~ out** [*water, liquid*] jaillir à flot; ¶ **~ [sth/sb] out** inonder; **to be ~ed out** [*person*] être évacué à cause des inondations.

flood: **~bank** *n* berge *f* inondable; **~ control** *n* prévention *f* des inondations; **~ damage** *n* dégât *m* des eaux.

floodgate /ˈflʌdgeɪt/ *n* lit vanne *f*; **to open the ~s** fig laisser entrer le flot (**to, for sb/sth** de qn/qch); **this decision/conference may open the ~s** fig cette décision/conférence risque de créer un précédent; **to open the ~s of revolution** fig laisser libre cours à la révolte.

flooding /ˈflʌdɪŋ/ *n* **1** (floods) inondation *f*; **'road liable to ~'** 'chaussée inondable'; **2** (overflowing) (of river) crue *f*.

flood level *n* niveau *m* des eaux.

floodlight /ˈflʌdlaɪt/ **I** *n* projecteur *m*; **to play under ~s** jouer à la lumière des projecteurs, jouer en nocturne.

II *vtr* (*prét, pp* **floodlit**) illuminer [*building*]; éclairer [*match, stage*].

III floodlit *pp adj* [*match*] joué en nocturne; [*building, pageant*] illuminé.

flood: **~mark** *n* indicateur *m* de niveau de crue; **~plain** *n* plaine *f* inondable; **~ tide** *n* marée *f* haute; **~waters** *n* eaux *fpl* d'inondation; **~way** *n* chenal *m* d'inondation.

floor /flɔː(r)/ **I** *n* **1** (of room) (wooden) plancher *m*, parquet *m*; (stone) sol *m*; (of car, lift) plancher *m*; **dance ~** piste *f* de danse; **to polish the ~** cirer le parquet; **to fall/sit/sleep on the ~** tomber/s'asseoir/coucher par terre; **to take the ~** [*dancer*] se lancer sur la piste de danse; **2** (of sea, tunnel, valley) fond *m*; **the forest ~** le tapis forestier; **3** (of Stock Exchange) parquet *m*; (of debating Chamber) auditoire *m*; (of factory) atelier *m*; **questions from the ~** des questions de l'auditoire; **to have/hold/take the ~** avoir/garder/prendre la parole; **the ~ is yours** la parole est à vous; **to be elected from the ~** être élu à vote ouvert; **4** (storey) étage *m*; **on the first ~** GB au premier étage; US au rez-de-chaussée; **the top ~** le dernier étage; **ground ~, bottom ~** GB rez-de-chaussée *m*; **we're six ~s up** (on the sixth storey) nous sommes au sixième étage; (six storeys above this storey) nous sommes six étages plus haut; **5** Fin (of prices, charges) plancher *m* (**on** sur).

II *vtr* **1** (in cement) faire le sol de; (in wood) mettre un plancher dans [*room*]; **an oak-~ed room** une pièce avec un plancher en chêne; **2** (knock over) terrasser [*attacker, boxer*]; **3** fig (silence) réduire [qn] au silence [*person, critic*]; (stump) [*question*] décontenancer [*candidate*]; **the news ~ed me** la nouvelle m'a laissé sans voix; **4**○ US Aut appuyer à fond sur [*accelerator*]; **to ~ it**○ appuyer sur le champignon○.

IDIOMS **to wipe the ~ with sb** battre [qn] à plates coutures; **to cross the ~** changer de camp.

floor: **~ area** *n* superficie *f*; **~board** *n* latte *f*, planche *f* (*de plancher*); **~ cloth** *n* serpillière *f*; **~ covering** *n* revêtement *m* de sol; **~ exercises** *npl* exercices *mpl* au sol.

flooring /ˈflɔːrɪŋ/ *n* revêtement *m* de sol.

floor: **~ lamp** *n* US lampadaire *m*; **~ leader** *n* US Pol *personne chargée d'encourager les membres d'un parti politique à voter dans la ligne*; **~-length** *adj* qui va jusqu'au sol.

floor manager ▶ **1692** *n* **1** TV régisseur *m* de plateau; **2** Comm gérant/-e *m/f* de magasin.

floor: **~ plan** *n* Archit plan *m*; **~ polish** *n* encaustique *f*, cire *f*; **~ polisher** *n* cireuse *f*; **~ rate** *n* Fin taux *m* plancher; **~ show** *n* spectacle *m* (*de cabaret*).

floor space *n* espace *m* (au sol); **we have 400 m² of ~ to let** nous avons 400 m² à louer.

floorwalker /ˈflɔːwɔːkə(r)/ *n* US chef *m* de rayon.

floosie○, **floozy**○ /ˈfluːzɪ/ *n* péj pouffiasse◐ *f*.

flop /flɒp/ **I** *n* **1** (heavy movement) **to sit down with a ~** s'affaler sur une chaise; **2**○ (failure) fiasco○ *m*; **3**○ US = **flophouse**.

II *vi* (*prés p etc* **-pp-**) **1** (move heavily) **to ~ down** s'effondrer; **to ~ down on** s'affaler sur [*bed, sofa*]; **2** (hang loosely) [*hair, ear*] retomber; [*head*] tomber; **3**○ (fail) [*play, film*] faire un four○; [*project, business venture*] être un fiasco○; **4**○ US (sleep) crécher○, dormir.

■ **flop out**○ US (rest) se reposer; (sleep) s'endormir.

■ **flop over**○ US ¶ changer d'avis; ¶ **~ over to [sth]** adopter [*idea*].

flophouse○ /ˈflɒphaʊs/ *n* US (shelter) refuge *m* de nuit; (sordid hotel) bouge○ *m*.

floppy /ˈflɒpɪ/ **I** *n* Comput disquette *f*.

II *adj* [*ears, hair*] pendant; [*hat*] à bords tombants; [*clothes*] large; [*flesh, body*] mou/molle; **to let one's arm go ~** détendre le bras.

floppy: **~ disk** *n* Comput disquette *f*; **~ drive** *n* lecteur *m* de disquettes.

flora /ˈflɔːrə/ *n* (+ *v sg*) flore *f*; **the ~ and fauna** la flore et la faune.

floral /ˈflɔːrəl/ *adj* [*design, fabric*] à fleurs; [*arrangement, art, fragrance*] floral; **~ tribute** composition *f* florale.

Florence /ˈflɒrəns/ ▶ **1818** *pr n* Florence.

Florentine /ˈflɒrəntaɪn/ *adj* florentin.

floribunda /ˌflɒrɪˈbʌndə/ *n* floribunda *m inv*.

florid /ˈflɒrɪd, US ˈflɔːr-/ *adj* **1** (ornate) [*writing, style, language*] fleuri; **2** (ruddy) [*person, face*] rougeaud.

Florida /ˈflɒrɪdə/ ▶ **1744** *pr n* Floride *f*.

florin /ˈflɒrɪn, US ˈflɔːrɪn/ ▶ **1143** *n* florin *m*.

florist /ˈflɒrɪst, US ˈflɔːrɪst/ ▶ **1692**, *n* (person) fleuriste *mf*; **~'s** (shop) fleuriste *m*.

floss /flɒs, US flɔːs/ **I** *n* **1** (fluff) bourre *f*; **2** (of silk) bourre *f* de soie; **3** (for embroidery) soie *f* floche; **4** Dent fil *m* dentaire.
II *vtr* **to ~ one's teeth** utiliser du fil dentaire.

flossy○ /ˈflɒsɪ/ *adj* US tape-à-l'œil○ *inv*.

flotation /fləʊˈteɪʃn/ **I** *n* **1** Fin (of a company, industry, loan) lancement *m*; (of shares, stock) introduction *f* en Bourse, émission *f*; (of currency) flottement *m*; **stock market ~** lancement en Bourse; **2** Chem, Ind flottation *f*.
II *modif* [*costs, plan, price, prospectus*] d'émission.

flotation: **~ bag** *n* ballon *m* de flottaison; **~ device** *n* US (life jacket) gilet *m* de sauvetage; Aviat flotteur *m*; **~ tank** *n* cellule *f* de flottation.

flotilla /fləˈtɪlə/ **I** *n* flottille *f*.
II *modif* [*yacht*] de croisière; **~ holiday** GB croisière *f* (à plusieurs bateaux).

flotsam /ˈflɒtsəm/ *n* ¢ épave *f* flottante; **~ and jetsam** (on water) épaves *fpl* flottantes; fig (odds and ends) bric-à-brac *m inv*; (people) épaves *fpl* de la société.

flounce /flaʊns/ **I** *n* **1** (movement) mouvement *m* vif (**de** of); **2** Fashn (frill) volant *m*.
II *vi* **1 to ~ in/out/off** (indignantly) entrer/sortir/partir dans un mouvement d'indignation; (angrily) entrer/sortir/partir dans un mouvement de colère; **2** (show off) (also **~ around**, **~ about**) se démener.

flounced /flaʊnst/ *adj* Fashn à volants.

flounder /ˈflaʊndə(r)/ **I** *n* **1** GB flet *m*; **2** US poisson *m* plat.
II *vi* **1** (move with difficulty) [*animal, person*] se débattre (**in** dans); **to ~ through** se débattre dans [*mud, water*]; **2** fig (falter) [*speaker*] bredouiller; [*economy*] stagner; [*career, company, leader, project*] piétiner; **to ~ through a speech** faire un discours en bredouillant.
III floundering *pres p adj* [*company, economy, industry*] stagnant.
■ **flounder about, flounder around** se débattre (**in** dans).

flour /ˈflaʊə(r)/ **I** *n* farine *f*; **~ and water paste** colle *f* à base de farine.
II *modif* [*bin, bomb, sifter*] à farine.
III *vtr* saupoudrer [qch] de farine [*cake tin, board*].

flourish /ˈflʌrɪʃ/ **I** *n* **1** (gesture) geste *m* théâtral; **to do sth with a ~** faire qch de façon théâtrale; **2** (detail, touch) **with a rhetorical** ou **an emphatic ~** avec emphase; **the show began with a ~** la représentation commença de façon grandiose; (in a piece of music) **the final ~** le bouquet final; **the opening ~** le brio des premiers accords; **3** (ornamental) (in style) fioriture *f*; **to sign sth with a ~** signer qch d'un paraphe or d'un grand trait de plume.
II *vtr* brandir [*ticket, document*]; **to ~ sth in sb's face** brandir qch devant qn.
III *vi* [*tree, plant, bacteria*] prospérer; [*child*] s'épanouir; [*firm, democracy*] prospérer; **the family is ~ing** la famille est en pleine forme.

flourishing /ˈflʌrɪʃɪŋ/ *adj* [*business, society, town*] prospère; [*plants, wildlife, garden*] florissant; [*trade, industry*] florissant.

floury /ˈflaʊərɪ/ *adj* [*hands, apron*] couvert de farine; [*potato, apple*] farineux/-euse.

flout /flaʊt/ *vtr* se moquer de [*convention, rules*].

flow /fləʊ/ **I** *n* **1** (movement) (of liquid) écoulement *m*; (of refugees, words) flot *m*; (of information) circulation *f*; (of time) cours *m*; **the ~ of refugees into a country** le flot de réfugiés vers un pays; **to go with the ~**○ suivre le mouvement; **the ~ of oil to the West** l'approvisionnement de l'Ouest en pétrole; **in full ~** fig en plein discours; **2** (circulation) (of blood, water, electricity) circulation *f*; **to impede traffic ~** entraver la circulation; **to increase the ~ of adrenalin** augmenter le taux d'adrénaline; **3** Geog (of tide) flux *m*.
II *vi* **1** (move) [*liquid, gas*] couler (**into** dans); **to ~ south** couler vers le sud; **to ~ in/back** affluer/refluer; **to ~ upwards/downwards** s'élever/tomber; **to ~ past sth** passer devant qch; **to ~ from** lit s'écouler de; fig (follow) découler de; **the river ~s into the sea** le fleuve se jette dans la mer; **2** (be continuous) [*conversation, words*] couler; [*wine, beer*] couler à flots; **the days ~ed past** les jours s'écoulaient; **money is ~ing in** l'argent afflue; **3** (move within a system) [*blood, water, electricity, adrenalin*] circuler (**through, round** dans); **pleasure ~ed through her** le plaisir l'a envahie; **4** (move gracefully) [*hair, dress*] flotter; [*pen*] courir (**across** sur); **5** Geog [*tide*] monter.

flowchart, **flow sheet** /ˈfləʊtʃɑːt, -ʃiːt/ *n* Comput, Ind organigramme *m*.

flower /ˈflaʊə(r)/ **I** *n* **1** (bloom, plant) fleur *f*; **to be in ~** être en fleur; **to come into ~** fleurir; **the roses are just coming into ~** les roses commencent à fleurir; **in full ~** en pleine floraison; **'No ~s by request'** 'Ni fleurs ni couronnes'; **2** fig (best part) **the ~ of** la fine fleur de [*age, era, group*]; **in the ~ of her youth** dans la fleur de l'âge; **in full ~** en plein épanouissement.
II *vi* lit [*flower, tree*] fleurir; [*idea, love, person, talent*] s'épanouir.

flower: **~ arrangement** *n* composition *f* florale; **~ arranging** *n* décoration *f* florale; **~bed** *n* parterre *m* de fleurs; **~ child** *n* hippie *mf*.

flowered /ˈflaʊəd/ *adj* [*fabric, plant*] à fleurs.

flower: **~ garden** *n* jardin *m* d'agrément; **~ girl** *n* (bride's attendant) demoiselle *f* d'honneur; **~ head** *n* capitule *m*.

flowering /ˈflaʊərɪŋ/ **I** *n* **1** Bot, Hort floraison *f* (**of** de); **2** fig (development) épanouissement *m* (**of** de).
II *adj* **1** (producing blooms) [*shrub, tree*] à fleurs; **2** (in bloom) [*plant, shrub*] en fleurs; **early-/late-~** à floraison précoce/tardive; **summer-~** à floraison estivale.

flower: **~pot** *n* pot *m* de fleurs; **~ power** *n*: *message d'amour et de paix des hippies*; **~ seller** ▶ **1692** *n* marchand/-e *m/f* de fleurs.

flower shop ▶ **1692** *n* boutique *f* de fleurs.

flower: **~ show** *n* (large) floralies *fpl*; (amateur) exposition *f* florale; **~ stall** *n* étal *m* de fleurs.

flowery /ˈflaʊərɪ/ *adj* [*hillside, field*] fleuri; [*design, fabric*] à fleurs; [*wine*] parfumé; [*scent*] floral; [*language, speech, style*] fleuri.

flowing /ˈfləʊɪŋ/ *adj* [*style, movement, handwriting*] coulant; [*rhythm, melody*] berceur/-euse; [*line*] doux/douce; [*hair, mane, clothes*] flottant.

flown /fləʊn/ *pp* ▶ **fly**.

fl oz *abrév écrite* = **fluid ounce**(**s**).

flu /fluː/ ▶ **1354** **I** *n* grippe *f*; **to come down with ~** attraper une grippe.
II *modif* [*victim, virus*] de la grippe; [*attack, epidemic*] de grippe; [*injection, vaccine*] contre la grippe.

flub○ /flʌb/ US **I** *n* (also **~-up**) gaffe○ *f*.
II *vtr* (*p prés etc* **-bb-**) rater.
■ **flub up**○: ¶ **~ up** se planter○; ¶ **~ up** [**sth**] se planter○ dans.

fluctuate /ˈflʌktjʊeɪt/ **I** *vi* gen, Fin [*rate, temperature, mood*] fluctuer (**between** entre).
II fluctuating *pres p adj* [*mood, mortgage rate*] fluctuant.

fluctuation /ˌflʌktjʊˈeɪʃn/ *n* gen, Fin fluctuation *f* (**in, of** de).

flue /fluː/ *n* (of chimney) conduit *m*; (of stove, boiler) tuyau *m*.

flue gas *n* gaz *m* de haut fourneau.

fluency /ˈfluːənsɪ/ *n* (all contexts) aisance *f*; **with great ~** avec une grande aisance; **you must improve your ~** tu dois acquérir une plus grande aisance; **the ~ of his writing** l'aisance de son écriture; **sb's ~ in sth** l'aisance de qn à s'exprimer en qch.

fluent /ˈfluːənt/ *adj* **1** (in language) **~ French** français *m* parlé couramment; **her French is ~** elle parle couramment le français; **I speak ~ Greek** je parle grec couramment; **a ~ Greek speaker** une personne qui parle grec couramment; **he answered in ~ English** il a répondu dans un anglais parfait; **to be ~ in sth** parler couramment qch; **2** (eloquent) [*account, speech, speaker*] éloquent; [*writer*] qui a la plume facile; **3** (graceful) [*style*] coulant; [*movement*] fluide.

fluently /ˈfluːəntlɪ/ *adv* **1** (accurately) [*speak a language*] couramment; **2** (with ease) avec facilité.

flue pipe *n* Mus tuyau *m* à bouche.

fluff /flʌf/ **I** *n* **1** (down) (on clothes) peluche *f*; (on carpet) poussière *f*; (under furniture) mouton *m*, flocon *m* de poussière; (on animal) duvet *m*; **2**○ (girl) **a bit of ~** péj une gonzesse○; **3**○ (mistake) gaffe○ *f*; **4**○ US (trivia) frivolités *fpl*.
II *vtr* **1** (also **~ up**) (puff up) [*bird, cat*] hérisser [*feathers, tail*]; faire bouffer [*cushion, hair*]; **2**○ (get wrong) rater [*cue, exam, line, note, shot*]; **I ~ed it!** j'ai raté mon coup!

fluffy /ˈflʌfɪ/ *adj* **1** [*animal, down*] duveteux/-euse; [*fur*] ébouriffé; [*rug, sweater*] moelleux/-euse; [*hair*] bouffant; [*toy*] en peluche; **2** (light) [*mixture*] léger/-ère; [*egg white, rice*] moelleux/-euse.

fluid /ˈfluːɪd/ **I** *n* **1** gen, Biol liquide *m*; **2** Chem, Tech fluide *m*; **cleaning ~** liquide *m* de nettoyage.
II *adj* **1** gen liquide; **2** Chem, Tech fluide; **3** (flexible) [*arrangement, situation*] vague; **my opinions/ideas are fairly ~** mes opinions/idées ne sont pas arrêtées; **4** (graceful) [*gesture, movement, style, lines*] fluide.

fluid: **~ assets** *npl* US Fin disponibilités *fpl*; **~ capital** *n* ¢ US Fin fonds *mpl* de roulement.

fluidity /fluːˈɪdətɪ/ *n* **1** (of substance) fluidité *f*; **2** (of plans, ideas) caractère *m* changeant; **3** (of style, movement, lines) fluidité *f*.

fluid: **~ mechanics** *n* (+ *v sg*) Phys mécanique *f* des fluides; **~ ounce** *n* Meas once *f* liquide.

fluke /fluːk/ **I** *n* **1** (lucky chance) coup *m* de veine○; **by a** (**sheer**) **~** (tout à fait) par hasard; **2** Naut (of anchor) patte *f* (*d'une ancre*); (of harpoon, arrow) barbelure *f*; **3** Zool douve *f*; **liver/blood ~** douve du foie/du sang.
II *adj* = **fluky**.
III *vtr* gagner [qch] à la chance.

fluky, **flukey** /ˈfluːkɪ/ *adj* **1** (lucky) [*coincidence*] heureux/-euse; [*circumstances, goal, shot*] dû au hasard; [*winner*] par hasard; **2** (changeable) [*wind, weather*] capricieux/-ieuse.

flume /fluːm/ *n* Geog (ravine) ravin *m*; (channel) canal *m* jaugeur.

flummery /ˈflʌmərɪ/ *n* **1** Culin *dessert à base de farine, œufs, miel et alcool*; **2**† (nonsense) balivernes *fpl*.

flummox○ /ˈflʌməks/ *vtr* sidérer○.

flummoxed○ /ˈflʌməkst/ *adj* sidéré○.

flung /flʌŋ/ *prét, pp* ▶ **fling**.

flunk○ /flʌŋk/ **I** *vtr* US Sch, Univ **1** [*student*] rater○ [*exam*]; sécher sur○ [*subject*]; **2** [*teacher*] coller○ [*class, pupil*].
II *vi* [*student*] sécher○.
■ **flunk out** [*student*] se faire virer○; **I ~ed out of high school** je me suis fait virer○ du lycée.

flunkey GB, **flunky** US /ˈflʌŋkɪ/ *n* (*pl* **-eys** GB, **-ies** US) **1** (servant) laquais *m*; **2** fig, péj larbin *m* pej.

fluorescein /flɔːˈresiːn, US ˌflʊəˈresiːn/ *n* fluorescéine *f*.

fluorescence /flɔːˈresəns, US flʊəˈr-/ *n* fluorescence *f*.

fluorescent /flɔːˈresənt, US flʊəˈr-/ *adj* (all contexts) fluorescent.

fluoridate /ˈflɔːrɪdeɪt, US ˈflʊər-/ *vtr* traiter [qch] par fluoration.

fluoridation /ˌflɔːrɪˈdeɪʃn, US ˌflʊər-/ *n* fluoration *f*.

fluoride /ˈflɔːraɪd, US ˈflʊəraɪd/ **I** *n* fluorure *m*.
II *modif* [*toothpaste, mouthwash*] au fluor.

fluorinate *vtr* = **fluoridate**.

fluorine /ˈflɔːriːn, US ˈflʊər-/ *n* fluor *m*.

fluorite /ˈflʊəraɪt/ *n* US = **fluorspar**.

fluorspar /ˈflɔːspɑː(r)/ *n* spath *m* fluor, fluorine *f*.

flurry /ˈflʌrɪ/ **I** *n* **1** (gust) (of rain, snow, wind) rafale *f*; (of dust, leaves) tourbillon *m*; **2** (bustle) agitation *f* soudaine; **a ~ of activity** un tourbillon d'activité; **a ~ of excitement** un frisson d'agitation; **a ~ of interest** un mouvement d'intérêt; **a ~ of wings** un bruissement d'ailes; **3** (burst) (of complaints, enquiries) vague *f*; **4** Fin (on shares) accès *m* de fièvre (**on** sur); **a ~ of buying** une vague d'achats.
II *vtr* affoler [*person*].

flush /flʌʃ/ **I** *n* **1** (blush) (on cheeks, skin) rougeur *f*; (in sky) lueur *f*; **there was a ~ in her cheeks** elle avait les joues rouges; **2** (surge) **a ~ of** un élan de [*pleasure, excitement, desire, pride*]; un accès de [*anger, shame*]; **in the first ~ of success/victory** dans l'ivresse du succès/de la victoire; **they were no longer in the first ~ of youth** ils n'étaient plus de la première jeunesse; **3** Constr (toilet device) chasse *f* d'eau; **to give the toilet a ~** tirer la chasse d'eau; **4** Games (set) floche *f*.
II *adj* **1** Constr (level) **to be ~ with** être dans l'alignement de [*wall, work surface*]; **2**○ (rich) **to be/feel ~** être/se sentir en fonds.
III *vtr* **1** (clean with water) **to ~ the toilet** tirer la chasse (d'eau); **to ~ sth down the toilet** faire partir qch dans les toilettes; **to ~ (out) a pipe/drain with water** nettoyer un tuyau/une canalisation à grande eau; **2** (colour) **to ~ sb's cheeks/face** empourprer les joues/le visage de qn.
IV *vi* **1** (redden) rougir (**with** de); **2** (operate) **the toilet doesn't ~** la chasse d'eau ne fonctionne pas; **we heard the toilet ~** on a entendu le bruit de la chasse d'eau.
■ **flush away**: **~ [sth] away, ~ away [sth]** faire partir [*waste, evidence*].
■ **flush out**: **~ out [sb/sth]** débusquer [*sniper, rebel, spy*]; déloger [*pest, rodent*]; **to ~ sb/sth out of** faire sortir qn/qch de [*shelter, hiding place*].

flushed /flʌʃt/ *adj* **1** (reddened) [*face, cheeks*] rouge; **~ with** rouge de [*shame, excitement*]; **to be ~** avoir les joues rouges; **2** (glowing) **~ with** [*person*] rayonnant de [*happiness, pleasure, pride*]; **~ with success/victory, they...** rayonnants après leur succès/victoire, ils...

fluster /ˈflʌstə(r)/ **I** *n* agitation *f*; **(to be) in a ~** (être) énervé.
II *vtr* énerver; **to get** ou **become ~ed** s'énerver; **to look ~ed** avoir l'air énervé.

flute /fluːt/ **▶1481** **I** *n* **1** Mus flûte *f*; **2** Archit cannelure *f*; **3** (glass) flûte *f*.
II *modif* [*part, lesson*] de flûte; [*case*] à flûte; [*composition*] pour flûte.

fluted /ˈfluːtɪd/ *adj* [*collar*] tuyauté; [*glass, flan tin*] à cannelures; [*column*] cannelé.

fluting /ˈfluːtɪŋ/ *n* (of fabric) tuyauté *m*; (on china, glass, column) cannelure *f*.

flutist /ˈfluːtɪst/ **▶1692**, **1481** *n* US flûtiste *mf*.

flutter /ˈflʌtə(r)/ **I** *n* **1** (rapid movement) (of wings, lashes) battement *m*; (of leaves, papers) voltigement *m*; (of flags, bunting) flottement *m*; **with a ~ of her eyelashes** d'un battement de cils; **heart ~** Med palpitations *fpl* cardiaques; **2** (stir) **a ~ of excitement/panic** un surcroît d'excitation/de panique; **to be all in** ou **of a ~** GB être tout en émoi; **to cause a ~** causer l'émoi; **3**○ GB (bet) **to have a ~ on the horses** faire un petit pari aux courses; **she likes the odd ~** elle aime bien parier de temps en temps; **to have a ~ on the Stock Exchange** faire une spéculation à la Bourse; **4** Electron (in sound) pleurage *m*; **5** Aviat (fault) vibration *f*.
II *vtr* **1** (beat) **the bird/moth ~ed its wings** l'oiseau/le papillon de nuit battait des ailes; **2** (move) agiter [*fan, handkerchief*]; **to ~ one's eyelashes (at sb)** battre des cils (en regardant qn).
III *vi* **1** (beat) **the bird's wings still ~ed** l'oiseau battait encore des ailes; **2** (fly rapidly) voleter; **3** (move rapidly) [*flag, bunting, ribbons*] flotter; [*clothes, curtains, fans, hand*] s'agiter; [*eyelids, lashes*] battre; **flags ~ed in the breeze/above the streets/from the mast** des drapeaux flottaient au vent/au-dessus des rues/sur le mât; **4** (spiral) (also **~ down**) [*petals, leaves*] tomber en voltigeant; **5** (beat irregularly) [*heart*] palpiter (**with** de); [*pulse*] battre faiblement.

fluttering /ˈflʌtərɪŋ/ **I** *n* **1** (flapping) (of birds, insects, wings) voletement *m*; (of flag, clothes, fan) flottement *m*; (of leaves) voltigement *m*; **2** (beating) (of heart) palpitations *fpl*; (of pulse) battement *m*.
II *adj* (*épith*) [*flag, bunting, dress*] flottant; [*birds*] voletant.

fluvial /ˈfluːvɪəl/ *adj* fluvial.

flux /flʌks/ *n* **1** (uncertainty) changement *m* continuel; **in (a state of) ~** dans un état de perpétuel changement; **2** Phys flux *m*; **3** Tech (for metals) fondant *m*; **4** Med flux *m*.

flux density *n* Phys densité *f* de flux.

fly /flaɪ/ **I** *n* **1** Zool, Fishg mouche *f*; **2** (of trousers) = **flies 1**; **3** (of tent) = **fly sheet 1**; **4** (of flag) (outer edge) bord *m* flottant; (length) battant *m*; **5** GB Hist (carriage) fiacre *m*.
II flies *npl* **1** (of trousers) braguette *f*; **your flies are undone** ta braguette est ouverte; **2** Theat cintres *mpl*.
III *adj*○ **1** US chic; **2** GB (clever) malin.
IV *vtr* (*prét* **flew**; *pp* **flown**) **1** (operate) piloter [*aircraft, spacecraft, balloon*]; faire voler [*model aircraft, kite*]; **the pilot flew the plane to...** le pilote a emmené l'avion jusqu'à...; **to ~ sth to the moon** piloter qch jusqu'à la lune; **2** (transport by air) emmener [qn] par avion [*person*]; transporter [qch/qn] par avion [*animal, wounded, supplies, food*]; **we will ~ you to New York for £150** nous vous emmènerons à New York (en avion) pour 150 livres sterling; **to ~ troops/food out to the scene** acheminer des troupes/des vivres sur les lieux par avion; **3** (cross by air) traverser [qch] en avion [*Atlantic, Channel*]; **4** (cover by air) [*bird, aircraft, spacecraft*] parcourir [*distance*]; **I ~ over 10,000 km a year** (as passenger) je vole plus de 10 000 km par an; (as pilot) je fais plus de 10 000 km par an; **5** (display) [*ship*] arborer [*flag, ensign, colours*]; [*organization, person*] agiter [*flag*]; **the embassy was ~ing the German flag** le drapeau allemand flottait sur l'ambassade; **6** sout (flee) quitter [*country*].
V *vi* (*prét* **flew**; *pp* **flown**) **1** [*bird, insect, aircraft, rocket, balloon, kite*] voler (**from** de; **to** à); **to ~ north/south** voler vers le nord/vers le sud; **to ~ over** ou **across sth** survoler qch; **to ~ past** ou **over(head)** passer dans le ciel; **a swan flew past the window** un cygne est passé devant la fenêtre (en volant); **to ~ into a cage** entrer dans une cage (en volant); **to ~ into a tree** percuter un arbre (en vol); **to ~ into Gatwick** atterrir à Gatwick; **the bird flew down and ate the bread** l'oiseau s'est abattu sur le pain et l'a mangé; **there's a mosquito ~ing around** il y a un moustique; **rumours were ~ing (around)** des bruits circulaient; **2** [*passenger*] voyager en avion, prendre l'avion; [*pilot*] piloter, voler; **to ~ from Orly** partir d'Orly; **to ~ from Rome to Athens** aller de Rome à Athènes en avion; **to ~ in Concorde** prendre le Concorde; **she flew to Madrid in a helicopter** elle est allée à Madrid en hélicoptère; **we ~ to Boston twice a day** [*airline*] nous avons deux vols par jour pour Boston; **to ~ over** ou **across sth** survoler [*Alps, Paris, Atlantic*]; **to ~ out to** s'envoler pour; **to ~ home** rentrer en avion; **to ~ around the world** faire le tour du monde en avion; **3** (be propelled) [*bullet, glass, sparks, insults, threats*] voler; **to ~ over the wall/across the room/into the room** voler par-dessus le mur/à travers la pièce/dans la pièce; **a splinter flew into his eye** une écharde s'est fichée dans son œil; **to ~ in all directions** voler dans toutes les directions; **to ~ off** s'envoler; **to ~ open** s'ouvrir brusquement; **to go ~ing**○ [*person*] faire un vol plané; [*object, objects*] valdinguer○; **to send sb ~ing**○ jeter qn sur le carreau○; **to send sth ~ing**○ envoyer valdinguer○ qch; **to ~ at sb** sauter sur qn; **to ~ into a rage** ou **temper** fig se mettre en colère; **to ~ into a panic** fig paniquer, s'affoler; **4** (rush, hurry) **I must ~!** il faut que je file○!; **to ~ past/ in/out etc** passer/entrer/sortir etc en trombe○; **5** (go quickly) (also **~ past**, **~ by**) [*time, holidays*] passer vite, filer○; **time flies when you're having fun!** le temps passe vite quand on s'amuse!; **6** (flutter, wave) [*flag, scarf, cloak, hair*] flotter; **to ~ in the wind** flotter au vent; **7** sout (flee) s'enfuir; **to ~ from sb/sth** fuir qn/qch.
IDIOMS **to drop/die like flies** tomber/mourir comme des mouches; **he wouldn't hurt** ou **harm a ~** il ne ferait pas de mal à une mouche; **there are no flies on her** elle n'est pas née de la dernière pluie; **to ~ in the face of** (defy) défier [*authority, danger, tradition*]; (contradict) être en contradiction flagrante avec [*evidence, proof*]; **to let ~ (with)** lit tirer [*arrow, hail of bullets*]; **to let ~ a stream of abuse** lancer un flot d'injures; **to let ~ at sb** s'en prendre à qn; **he really let ~** il a piqué une crise terrible.
■ **fly away** lit, fig s'envoler.
■ **fly in**: ¶ **~ in** [*person*] accourir en avion; **to ~ in from Oslo** accourir d'Oslo en avion; ¶ **~ [sth/sb] in, ~ in [sth/sb]** acheminer [qch] par avion [*food, supplies*]; **to have sb/sth flown in** faire venir qn/qch par avion.
■ **fly off** [*bird, insect*] s'envoler.

fly: **~ agaric** *n* amanite *f* tue-mouches; **~away** *adj* [*hair*] indiscipliné.

flyblown /ˈflaɪbləʊn/ *adj* **1** (not bright and new) [*furniture, object*] défraîchi; [*joke, metaphor*] éculé; **2** (infested with fly eggs) [*meat, food*] plein d'œufs de mouche.

flyby /ˈflaɪbaɪ/ *n* **1** Aerosp survol *m*; **2** Aviat (flypast) défilé *m* aérien.

fly-by-night○ /ˈflaɪbaɪnaɪt/ **I** *n* **1** (person) irresponsable *mf*; **2** (business) entreprise *f* douteuse.
II *adj* [*company, operation*] douteux/-euse; [*person*] irresponsable.

fly: **~-by-wire (control) system** *n* commandes *fpl* de vol électriques; **~catcher** *n* Zool gobe-mouches *m inv*; **~-drive** *adj* Tourism avec formule avion plus voiture.

flyer /ˈflaɪə(r)/ *n* = **flier**.

fly: **~-fishing** **▶1282** *n* pêche *f* à la mouche; **~-half** *n* Sport demi *m* d'ouverture.

flying /ˈflaɪɪŋ/ **I** *n* **1** (in plane) **to be afraid of ~** avoir peur de l'avion; **to take up ~** apprendre à piloter; **my hobby is ~** mon hobby c'est l'aviation; **2** (by bird, animal) vol *m*; **adapted for ~** adapté au vol.
II *modif* [*course, lesson, instructor, school*] de pilotage; [*goggles, helmet, jacket*] d'aviateur; [*suit*] de vol.
III *adj* **1** (able to fly) [*animal, insect, machine, trapeze*] volant; **2** (in process of flying) [*object, broken glass*] qui vole; **the dancer's ~ feet** les pieds agiles du danseur; **to take a ~ leap** ou **jump** sauter avec élan.
IDIOMS **with ~ colours** [*emerge, pass, come through*] haut la main.

flying: **~ boat** *n* hydravion *m*; **~ bomb** *n* bombe *f* volante; **~ buttress** *n* arc-boutant *m*; **~ doctor** *n* médecin *m* volant.

Flying Dutchman *n* **the ~** (in legend) le Vaisseau fantôme.

flying: **~ fish** *n* poisson *m* volant, exocet *m*; **~ fox** *n* (bat) roussette *f*; **~ officer** ▶1612 *n* GB lieutenant *m* de l'armée de l'air; **~ picket** *n* piquet *m* de grève volant; **~ saucer** *n* soucoupe *f* volante; **~ squad** *n* brigade *f* volante.

flying start *n* Sport départ *m* lancé; **to get off to a ~** fig prendre un très bon départ.

flying: **~ tackle** *n* Sport plaquage *m* en pleine course; **~ visit** *n* visite *f* éclair.

fly: **~ kick** *n* coup *m* de pied à suivre; **~leaf** *n* garde *f* volante.

fly-on-the-wall /ˌflaɪɒnðəˈwɔːl/ *adj* [*documentary, film*] pris sur le vif; **a ~ report** un reportage sur le vif.

flyover /ˈflaɪəʊvə(r)/ *n* **1** GB Transp pont *m* routier; **2** US Aviat défilé *m* aérien.

fly: **~paper** *n* papier *m* tue-mouches; **~past** *n* GB Aviat défilé *m* aérien; **~posting** *n* affichage *m* illégal.

fly sheet *n* **1** (of tent) double-toit *m*; **2** (handbill) prospectus *m*.

fly: **~ spray** *n* bombe *f* insecticide; **~ swatter** *n* tapette *f* à mouches; **~tipping** *n* GB dépôt *m* d'ordures sauvage.

flyweight /ˈflaɪweɪt/ **I** *n* poids *m* mouche.
II *modif* [*champion, boxer, title*] poids-mouche; [*match, contest*] de poids-mouche.

fly: **~wheel** *n* Mech volant *m*; **~ whisk** *n* chasse-mouches *m inv*.

FM *n* **1** Mil *abrév* ▶ **field marshal**; **2** Radio (*abrév* = **frequency modulation**) FM *f*.

FMB *n* US (*abrév* = **Federal Maritime Board**) ≈ Conseil *m* supérieur de la marine marchande.

FO *n* GB *abrév* ▶ **Foreign Office**.

foal /fəʊl/ **I** *n* poulain *m*; **to be in ~** être pleine.
II *vi* mettre bas.

foam /fəʊm/ **I** *n* **1** (on sea) écume *f*; (on drinks, bath) mousse *f*; **the ~** littér (sea) les flots; **2** (on animal) sueur *f*; **3** (from mouth) écume *f*; **4** (chemical) mousse *f*; **5** (made of rubber, plastic) mousse *f*.
II *vi* **1** (froth) [*beer, water*] mousser; [*sea*] se couvrir d'écume; **to ~ at the mouth** lit écumer; fig écumer de rage; **2** (sweat) [*horse*] suer.
■ **foam up** [*beer, lemonade*] mousser.

foam: **~-backed** *adj* avec un envers en mousse; **~ bath** *n* bain *m* moussant; **~-filled** *adj* en mousse; **~ insulation** *n* isolation *f* thermique en mousse; **~ mattress** *n* matelas *m* mousse; **~ rubber** *n* caoutchouc *m* mousse.

foamy /ˈfəʊmɪ/ *adj* [*sea*] écumeux/-euse; [*beer, lemonade*] mousseux/-euse.

fob /fɒb/ *n* **1** (pocket) gousset *m*; **2** (watch-chain) chaine *f*; **3** (ornament) breloque *f*; **key ~** porte-clés *m inv*.
■ **fob off** (*p prés etc* **-bb-**): ¶ **~ [sb] off, ~ off [sb] 1** (palm off) se débarrasser de [*enquirer, customer*]; **I ~bed him off with an excuse** j'ai inventé un prétexte pour me débarrasser de lui; **2** (get rid of) envoyer [qn] balader○ [*person*]; ¶ **~ off [sth]** rejeter [*attempt, enquiry*]; **to ~ off sth onto sb** refiler qch à qn.

FOB *adj, adv*: *abrév* ▶ **free on board**.

fob watch *n* montre *f* de gousset.

FOC *adj, adv*: *abrév* ▶ **free of charge**.

focal /ˈfəʊkl/ *adj* focal.

focal: **~ infection** *n* infection *f* focale; **~ length** *n* distance *f* focale; **~ plane** *n* plan *m* focal.

focal point *n* **1** (in optics) foyer *m*; **2** (of village, building) point *m* de convergence (**of** de; **for** pour); **the room lacks a ~** cette pièce n'a pas de coin qui attire l'œil; **3** (main concern) point *m* central; **to act as a ~ for discussion** constituer le point central de la discussion.

fo'c'sle *n* = **forecastle**.

focus /ˈfəʊkəs/ **I** *n* (*pl* **~es, foci**) **1** (focal point) foyer *m*; **to be out of ~** [*device*] ne pas être au point; [*image*] être flou; **to be in ~** être au point; **to go out of ~** [*device*] se dérégler; [*image*] devenir flou; **to bring sth into ~** mettre qch au point; **to come into ~** se rapprocher de la mise au point; **2** (device on lens) mise *f* au point; **to get the ~ right** régler la mise au point; **3** (centre of interest) centre *m*, foyer *m*; **to become the ~ of controversy** devenir le centre de la controverse; **to become a ~ for the press** devenir le centre d'intérêt de la presse; **to provide a ~ for research** fournir un centre d'intérêt à la recherche; **4** (emphasis) accent *m*; **the ~ will be on health** l'accent sera mis spécialement sur la santé.
II *vtr* (*p prés etc* **-s-** ou **-ss-**) **1** (direct) concentrer [*ray, beam*] (**on** sur); fixer [*eyes, gaze*] (**on** sur); **2** (adjust) mettre [qch] au point, régler [*lens, microscope, camera*]; **to ~ one's lens on** faire la mise au point sur [*object*]; **3** (concentrate) concentrer [*attention, mind*] (**on** sur).
III *vi* (*p prés etc* **-s-** ou **-ss-**) **1** (home in) **to ~ on** [*rays*] converger sur; [*astronomer, photographer, camera*] faire le point or la mise au point sur; [*eyes, gaze, attention*] se fixer or se concentrer sur; **2** (concentrate) **to ~ on** [*person, report, survey, study*] se concentrer sur.
IV focused, focussed *pp adj* **1** [*telescope, image*] au point; **2** [*person*] déterminé; **she's very ~** elle est très déterminée.

fodder /ˈfɒdə(r)/ *n* **1** (for animals) fourrage *m*; **2** hum (for people) écuelle *f*; **3** fig (raw material) matière *f*.

foe /fəʊ/ *n* littér ennemi/-e *m/f* also fig.

FoE *n*: *abrév* ▶ **Friends of the Earth**.

foetal, fetal US /ˈfiːtl/ *adj* fœtal; **in the ~ position** en position fœtale.

foetal alcohol syndrome, FAS *n* embryo-fœtopathie *f* alcoolique.

foetid *adj* = **fetid**.

foetus, fetus US /ˈfiːtəs/ *n* fœtus *m*.

fog /fɒg/ **I** *n* **1** Meteorol brouillard *m*; **a patch/blanket of ~** une nappe/un manteau de brouillard; **we get thick ~s here** nous avons du brouillard très épais dans la région; **a ~ of cigarette smoke** un nuage épais de fumée de cigarette; **2** fig (confusion) brouillard *m*; **a ~ of ignorance** un brouillard d'ignorance; **to be in a ~** être dans le brouillard; **3** Phot voile *m*.
II *vtr* (*p prés etc* **-gg-**) **1** lit (also **~ up**) [*steam*] embuer [*glass*]; [*light*] voiler [*film*]; **2** fig (confuse) **to ~ the issue** (unwittingly) embrouiller les choses; (deliberately) noyer le poisson.

fog: **~ bank** *n* banc *m* de brume; **~bound** *adj* [*plane, passenger*] bloqué par le brouillard; [*airport*] paralysé par le brouillard.

fogey○ /ˈfəʊgɪ/ *n* péj vieille baderne *f* pej; **he's a young ~** à son âge il est déjà vieux jeu.

foggy /ˈfɒgɪ/ *adj* **1** Meteorol [*day, landscape, weather*] brumeux/-euse; **it will be ~ tomorrow** il y a aura du brouillard demain; **2** fig [*idea, notion*] confus; **I haven't the foggiest idea**○ je n'en ai pas la moindre idée.

Foggy Bottom○ *n* US *surnom pour le ministère des affaires étrangères américain*.

foghorn /ˈfɒghɔːn/ *n* Naut corne *f* de brume; **to have a voice like a ~** avoir une voix de stentor.

fog: **~lamp, ~light** *n* Aut feu *m* de brouillard; **~ patch** *n* nappe *f* de brouillard.

foible /ˈfɔɪbl/ *n* petite manie *f*.

foil /fɔɪl/ **I** *n* **1** (for wrapping) papier *m* d'aluminium; **a sheet of ~** une feuille de papier d'aluminium; **silver/gold ~** papier argenté/doré; **~-wrapped** emballé dans du papier d'aluminium; **2** Sport fleuret *m*; **3** (deterrent) repoussoir *m*; **4** (setting) **to be** ou **act as a ~ to** ou **for** faire ressortir.
II *modif* [*container, wrapper*] en papier d'aluminium.
III *vtr* contrecarrer [*person*]; déjouer [*attempt, hope, plot*]; **to be ~ed in one's attempt to do sth** être déjoué dans sa tentative de faire qch; **~ed again!** encore raté!

foist /fɔɪst/ *vtr* **to ~ sth/sb on sb** (impose) imposer qch/qn à qn; **to ~ sth on sb** (off-load) repasser qch à qn.

fold /fəʊld/ **I** *n* **1** (crease) (in fabric, paper, skin) pli *m*; **the skirt/the curtain hung in soft ~s** la jupe/le rideau faisait des plis souples; **2** Geog repli *m*; **a ~ in the hills** un repli des collines; **3** Geol plissement *m*; **4** (group) bercail *m*; **5** Agric parc *m*; **sheep ~** parc à moutons.
II -fold (*dans composés*) **to increase twofold/threefold** doubler/tripler; **the problems are threefold** il y a trois problèmes; **interest rates have increased ninefold** les taux d'intérêt ont été multipliés par neuf.
III *vtr* **1** (crease) plier [*paper, towel, shirt, chair, table, umbrella*]; replier [*wings*]; **~ the paper in half** ou **two** plie le papier en deux; **a ~ed sheet/newspaper** un drap/journal plié; **~ some newspaper around the vases** enveloppe les vases dans du papier journal; **2** (intertwine) croiser [*arms*]; joindre [*hands*]; **he ~ed his arms across his chest** il a croisé les bras; **she sat with her legs ~ed under her** elle était assise les jambes repliées sous elle; **to ~ sb into one's arms** serrer qn dans ses bras; **3** Culin (add) incorporer (**into** à).
IV *vi* **1** [*chair, table*] se plier; **2** (fail) [*play*] quitter l'affiche; [*company*] fermer; [*project*] échouer; [*course*] cesser.
IDIOMS **to stay in/return to the ~** rester/rentrer au bercail; **to return to the family/party ~** retourner au sein de sa famille/du parti.
■ **fold away**: ¶ **~ away** [*bed, table*] se plier: ¶ **~ away [sth], ~ [sth] away** plier et ranger [*clothes, linen*]; replier [*chair*].
■ **fold back**: ¶ **~ back** [*door, shutters*] se rabattre (**against** contre): ¶ **~ back [sth], ~ [sth] back** rabattre [*shutters, sheet, sleeve, collar*].
■ **fold down**: ¶ **~ down** [*car seat, pram hood*] se rabattre; ¶ **~ [sth] down, ~ down [sth]** replier [*collar, flap, sheets*]; rabattre [*seat, pram hood*]; **to ~ down the corner of the page** corner la page.
■ **fold in**: **~ in [sth], ~ [sth] in** incorporer [*sugar, flour*].
■ **fold out**: **~ out [sth], ~ [sth] out** déplier [*map, newspaper*].
■ **fold over**: ¶ **~ over** se rabattre; ¶ **~ [sth] over** rabattre [*flap*].
■ **fold up**: ¶ **~ up** [*chair, pram, umbrella*] se plier; ¶ **~ [sth] up, ~ up [sth]** plier [*newspaper, chair, umbrella*]; **to ~ sth up again** replier qch.

foldaway /ˈfəʊldəweɪ/ *adj* [*bed*] escamotable, pliant; [*table*] pliant.

folder /ˈfəʊldə(r)/ *n* **1** (for papers) chemise *f*; **cardboard/plastic ~** chemise cartonnée/en plastique; **2** (for artwork) carton *m*; **3** (brochure) prospectus *m*; **4** Tech plieuse *f*, machine *f* à plier; **5** Comput dossier *m*.

folding /ˈfəʊldɪŋ/ *adj* [*bed, bicycle, table, umbrella*] pliant; [*camera*] à soufflet; [*door*] en accordéon.

folding: **~ money** *n* billets *mpl* de banque; **~ seat** *n* strapontin *m*; **~ stool** *n* (siège *m*) pliant *m*.

folding top *n* Aut capote *f*; **a car with a ~ top** une voiture décapotable.

fold: **~ mark** *n* repère *m* de page; **~out** *n* encart *m*.

foliage /ˈfəʊlɪɪdʒ/ *n* feuillage *m*.

foliation /ˌfəʊlɪˈeɪʃn/ *n* **1** Bot foliation *f*; **2** Print foliotage *m*; **3** Geol foliation *f*; **4** Archit rinceaux *mpl*.

folic acid /ˌfəʊlɪk ˈæsɪd/ *n* acide *m* folique.

folio /ˈfəʊlɪəʊ/ **I** *n* (paper) folio *m*; (book) in-

folio *m*; **to publish a book in ~** publier un livre in-folio.
II *modif* [*edition, volume*] in-folio.

folk /fəʊk/ I *n* **1** (people) (+ *v pl*) gens *mpl*; **country/city ~** les gens de la campagne/des villes; **old/young/poor ~** les vieux/jeunes/pauvres; **2** Mus (+ *v sg*) folk *m*.
II **folks** *npl* **1**○ (parents) parents *mpl*, vieux○ *mpl*; **2**○ (addressing people) **that's all, ~s**○! c'est tout, messieurs-dames○!
III *modif* **1** (traditional) [*dance, dancing, song, singer, music, tale*] folklorique; [*art, culture, tradition*] populaire, folklorique; **2** (modern) [*music, concert, song, singer*] folk *inv*; [*club, group*] de musique folk.

folk: **~ etymology** *n* étymologie *f* populaire; **~ hero** *n* héros *m* populaire.

folkie○ /ˈfəʊkɪ/ *n* fana○ *mf* de musique folk.

folk: **~lore** *n* folklore *m*; **~ medicine** *n* médecine *f* traditionnelle; **~ memory** *n* mémoire *f* collective; **~ rock** *n* folk-rock *m*.

folksy○ /ˈfəʊksɪ/ *adj* **1** (rustic) [*person*] amoureux/-euse de la vie de campagne; [*clothes, house*] campagnard; **2** pej (hippy) baba (cool)○ *inv*; **3** US pej **to act ~** jouer les péquenauds◑.

folk wisdom *n* (knowledge) savoir *m* populaire; (beliefs) sagesse *f* populaire.

follicle /ˈfɒlɪkl/ *n* (all contexts) follicule *m*.

follow /ˈfɒləʊ/ I *vtr* **1** (move after) suivre [*person, car*] (**into** dans); **~ that cab!** suivez ce taxi!; **to have sb ~d** faire suivre qn; **I think I'm being ~ed** je crois qu'on me suit; **~d by** suivi par; **to ~ sb in/out** entrer/sortir derrière qn; **she ~d her father into politics** elle est entrée dans la politique comme son père; **they'll ~ us on a later flight** ils nous rejoindront par un autre vol; **2** (come after in time) suivre [*event, period, incident, item on list*]; succéder à [*leader, monarch*]; **I chose the salad and ~ed it with fish** j'ai choisi la salade, et ensuite j'ai commandé du poisson; **I ~ed up my swim with a sauna** après la piscine j'ai fait un sauna; **~ed by** suivi de; **3** (go along, be guided by) suivre [*clue, path, river, arrow, map, line of inquiry, tradition, fashion, instinct, instructions*]; **if you ~ this argument to its logical conclusion...** si vous poursuivez le raisonnement jusqu'au bout...; **4** (support, be led by) suivre [*teachings, example*]; pratiquer [*religion*]; adhérer à [*faith, ideas*]; être le disciple de [*person, leader*]; **on this question I ~ Freud** sur cette question j'adhère à la théorie de Freud; **he ~s his sister in everything** il imite sa sœur en tout; **5** (watch or read closely) suivre [*sport, stock market, serial, trial, lecture, film*]; **to ~ sth with one's eyes** suivre qch des yeux; **to ~ the play in one's book** suivre la pièce dans le texte; **to ~ the fortunes of** suivre la carrière de [*person*]; suivre [*team*]; **6** (understand) suivre [*explanation, reasoning, plot*]; **do you ~ me?** tu me suis?; **if you ~ my meaning, if you ~ me** si tu vois ce que je veux dire; **7** (practise) exercer [*trade, profession*]; poursuivre [*career*]; avoir [*way of life*]; **8** (be a logical consequence) **it ~s that...** il s'ensuit que...; **it doesn't necessarily ~ that...** ça ne veut pas forcément dire que...
II *vi* **1** (move after) suivre; **she ~ed on her bike** elle a suivi en vélo; **to ~ in sb's footsteps** suivre les traces de qn; **2** (come after in time) suivre; **in the days that ~ed** dans les jours qui ont suivi; **there ~ed a lengthy debate** il s'ensuivit un débat interminable; **what ~s is just a summary** ce qui suit n'est qu'un résumé; **there's ice cream to ~** ensuite il y a de la glace; **the results were as ~s** les résultats ont été les suivants; **the sum is calculated as ~s** la somme est calculée comme suit or de la façon suivante; **3** (be logical consequence) s'ensuivre; **problems are sure to ~** il en résultera forcément des problèmes; **that doesn't ~** ce n'est pas évident; **that ~s** ça me paraît logique; **to ~ from sth that...** découler de qch que...; **4** (understand) suivre; **I don't ~** je ne suis pas.
IDIOMS **~ that**○! faut le faire○!
■ **follow about**, **follow around**: **~ [sb] around** suivre [qn] partout.
■ **follow on**: **~ on** [*person*] suivre; **to ~ on from** faire suite à; **~ing on from yesterday's lecture...** à la suite du cours d'hier...
■ **follow out** US: **~ out [sth]** suivre [*orders, instructions, advice*].
■ **follow through**: ¶ **~ through** Sport faire un swing complet; ¶ **~ through [sth]**, **~ [sth] through** mener [qch] à terme [*project, scheme, experiment*]; tenir [*promise*]; mettre [qch] à exécution [*threat*]; aller jusqu'au bout de [*idea, theory, argument*].
■ **follow up**: ¶ **~ up [sth]**, **~ [sth] up** **1** (reinforce, confirm) confirmer [*victory, success*] (**with** par); consolider [*good start, debut*] (**with** par); donner suite à [*letter, visit, threat*] (**with** par); **to ~ up a letter with sth** faire suivre une lettre de qch; **he ~ed up with a left hook** [*boxer*] il a enchaîné avec un crochet de la gauche; **2** (act upon, pursue) suivre [*story, lead*]; donner suite à [*complaint, offer, call, article*]; examiner [*suggestion*]; utiliser [*tip, hint*]; ¶ **~ up [sb]**, **~ [sb] up** (maintain contact with) suivre [*patient, person*].

follower /ˈfɒləʊwə(r)/ *n* **1** (of religious leader, thinker, artist) disciple *m*; (of political or military leader) partisan/-e *m/f*; (of religion, teachings, theory, tradition) adepte *mf*; **2** (of sport) amateur *m*; (of TV series, soap opera) fidèle *mf*; (of team) supporter *m*; **~s of politics/her career will know that...** ceux qui s'intéressent à la politique/à sa carrière sauront que...; **dedicated ~s of fashion** les inconditionnels de la mode; **3** (not a leader) suiveur *m*; **4**† (suitor) admirateur *m*.

following /ˈfɒləʊwɪŋ/ I *n* **1** (of theorist, religion, cult) adeptes *mfpl*; (of party, political figure) partisans/-anes *m/fpl*; (of soap opera, show) public *m*; (of sports team) supporters *mpl*; **the cult has a huge/small ~** la secte a énormément/peu d'adeptes; **a writer with a loyal/young ~** un écrivain qui a un public fidèle/jeune; **the party wants to build up its ~ in the south** le parti veut se faire des partisans dans le sud; **2** (before list or explanation) **you will need the ~** vous aurez besoin des choses suivantes; **the ~ have been elected** les personnes suivantes ont été élues; **the ~ is a guide to...** ce qui suit est un guide sur...
II *adj* (*tjrs épith*) **1** (next) [*day, year, article, chapter, remark*] suivant (*after n*); **they were married the ~ June** ils se sont mariés au mois de juin suivant; **the ~ women/reasons** les femmes/les raisons suivantes; **2** (from the rear) [*wind*] arrière; **my car will do 120 km/h with a ~ wind** hum ma voiture peut faire du 120 km/h avec le vent en poupe.
III *prep* suite à, à la suite de [*incident, allegation, publication*]; **~ your request for information** suite à votre demande de renseignements.

follow-my-leader ▶ 1282 *n* jeu *m* d'imitation (*en file indienne*).

follow-on /ˌfɒləʊˈɒn/ *n* suite *f*; **as a ~ from sth** dans le prolongement de qch.

follow-up /ˈfɒləʊʌp/ I *n* **1** (film, record, single, programme) suite *f* (**to** à); **as a ~ to the programme/conference** à la suite de l'émission/la conférence; **this letter is a ~ to my call** cette lettre fait suite à mon appel; **2** (of patient, socialwork case) suivi *m*; **after the operation there is no ~** il n'y a pas de suivi postopératoire.
II *modif* **1** (supplementary) [*study, survey, work*] de suivi; [*interview, inspection, check*] de contrôle; [*discussion, article, programme, meeting*] complémentaire; [*letter*] de rappel; **2** (of patient, ex-inmate) [*visit*] de contrôle; **~ care for ex-prisoners** suivi *m* social pour la réinsertion des ex-prisonniers; **~ care for patients** suivi *m* des malades.

folly /ˈfɒlɪ/ *n* **1** (madness) folie *f*; **it would be ~ to accept** accepter serait de la folie; **an act of ~** un acte de folie; **2** (foolish act) folie *f*; **the follies of youth** les folies de jeunesse; **3** Archit folie *f*.

foment /fəʊˈment/ *vtr* Med, fig fomenter.

fomentation /ˌfəʊmenˈteɪʃn/ *n* Med, fig fomentation *f*.

fond /fɒnd/ *adj* **1** (loving) [*embrace, farewell, gesture, person*] affectueux/-euse; [*eyes, heart*] tendre; **~ memories** de très bons souvenirs; **'with ~est love, Julie'** 'je t'embrasse affectueusement, Julie'; **2** (heartfelt) [*ambition, hope, wish*] cher/chère; **3** (naive) [*imagination*] naïf/naïve; **in the ~ hope that** bercé par la conviction que; **4** (partial) **to be ~ of sb** aimer beaucoup qn; **to be ~ of sth** aimer qch; **to be ~ of doing** aimer faire; **to be very ~ of sb/sth** adorer qn/qch; **5** (irritatingly prone) **to be ~ of doing** aimer bien faire.

fondle /ˈfɒndl/ *vtr* caresser.

fondly /ˈfɒndlɪ/ *adv* **1** (lovingly) affectueusement; **2** (naively) [*believe, imagine*] naïvement.

fondness /ˈfɒndnɪs/ *n* **1** (love for person) tendresse *f* (**for** pour); **2** (liking for thing, activity) passion *f* (**for** pour); **3** (irritating penchant) tendance *f*; **his ~ for criticizing** sa tendance à critiquer.

font /fɒnt/ *n* **1** Relig fonts *mpl* baptismaux; **2** Print fonte *f*; **3** Comput police *f* de caractères.

fontanelle GB, **fontanel** US /ˌfɒntəˈnel/ *n* fontanelle *f*.

food /fuːd/ I *n* **1** (sustenance) nourriture *f*, alimentation *f*; **~ and drink** la nourriture et la boisson; **~ is short** il y a une pénurie alimentaire; **2** (foodstuffs) aliments *mpl*; **cat/frozen ~** aliments pour chat/surgelés; **3** (provisions) provisions *fpl*; **to shop for ~** acheter des provisions; **we have no ~ in the house** on n'a rien à manger à la maison; **4** (cuisine, cooking) cuisine *f*; **Chinese ~** la cuisine chinoise; **is the ~ good in Japan?** on mange bien au Japon?; **to be a lover of good ~** être gourmet; **to like one's ~** bien aimer manger, avoir bon appétit; **to be off one's ~** ne pas avoir d'appétit; **5** (fuel) **~ for speculation/argument** matière *f* à spéculer/discuter; **that's ~ for thought** ça donne à réfléchir.
II *modif* [*additive, industry, product, rationing, sales*] alimentaire; [*producer, production*] d'aliments; [*shop, counter*] d'alimentation.

food: **~ aid** *n* aide *f* alimentaire; **Food and Agriculture Organization**, **FAO** *n* Organisation *f* des Nations unies pour l'Alimentation et l'Agriculture, OAA *f*; **Food and Drug Administration**, **FDA** *n* US *organisme gouvernemental de contrôle pharmaceutique et alimentaire*; **~ chain** *n* Ecol chaîne *f* alimentaire; **~ crop** *n* Agric culture *f* vivrière.

foodie○ /ˈfuːdɪ/ *n* amateur *m* de bonne bouffe○.

food: **~ parcel** *n* colis *m* de vivres; **~ poisoning** *n* intoxication *f* alimentaire; **~ processing** *n* préparation *f* industrielle des aliments; **~ processor** *n* robot *m* ménager; **~ science** *n* diététique *f*; **~stuff** *n* denrée *f* alimentaire; **~ subsidies** *npl* subventions *fpl* à l'industrie agro-alimentaire.

food supply *n* **1** (of the world, a country) ressources *fpl* alimentaires; **2** (for army, town) vivres *mpl*; **to cut off sb's ~ supplies** couper les vivres à qn.

food value *n* valeur *f* nutritive.

foofaraw○ /ˈfuːfərɔː/ *n* US **1** fig (frill) fioriture *f*; **2** (fuss) tapage *m* inutile.

fool /fuːl/ I *n* **1** (silly person) idiot/-e *m/f* (**to do** de faire); **the poor ~** le pauvre idiot; **you stupid ~**○! espèce d'idiot!; **don't be (such) a ~!** ne sois pas idiot!; **to make sb**

look a ~, to make a ~ of sb faire passer qn pour un/-e idiot/-e; **to be ~ enough to agree** être assez stupide pour accepter; **she's no ~, she's nobody's ~** elle n'est pas si bête; **any ~ could do that**○ le premier imbécile venu pourrait faire ça○; **(the) more ~ you**○**!** quelle imbécilité!; **to act** ou **play the ~** faire l'imbécile, faire le pitre; **2** Hist (jester) fou *m*; **3** GB Culin **rhubarb/fruit ~** crème *f* à la rhubarbe/aux fruits.
II○ *modif* US [*politician*] idiot; **that's a ~ thing to do/say** c'est vraiment stupide de faire/dire ça.
III *vtr* tromper, duper; **you don't ~ anybody** tu ne trompes personne; **don't let that ~ you!** ne t'y trompe pas!; **who are you trying to ~?** à qui veux-tu faire croire ça?; **you don't ~ me for a minute** je ne te crois pas un seul instant; **to ~ sb into doing** amener qn à faire; **to ~ sb into** ou **believing that** faire croire à qn que; **to ~ sb out of** escroquer qn de [*money*]; **to be ~ed** se laisser abuser (**by** par); **don't be ~ed!** ne te laisse pas abuser!; **you really had me ~ed!** tu m'as vraiment fait marcher○!
IV *vi* (joke, tease) plaisanter; **no ~ing!** iron sans blague○!
V *v refl* **to ~ oneself** se faire des illusions; **to ~ oneself into doing sth** se persuader de faire qch.
IDIOMS **a ~ and his money are soon parted** Prov aux idiots l'argent file entre les doigts; **there is no ~ like an old ~** il n'y a pire imbécile qu'un vieil imbécile; **you could have ~ed me**○**!** tu m'en diras tant○!
■ **fool about**○ GB, **fool around**○ GB ¶ **1** (waste time) perdre son temps; **2** (act stupidly) faire l'imbécile (**with** avec); **3** (have affairs) papillonner○; ¶ **~ around with [sb/sth] 1** (flirt) batifoler○ avec [*lover*]; **2** (mess around) s'amuser avec [*gadget, toy*].

foolhardiness /ˈfuːlhɑːdɪnɪs/ *n* témérité *f*.

foolhardy /ˈfuːlhɑːdɪ/ *adj* téméraire.

foolish /ˈfuːlɪʃ/ *adj* **1** (naïvely silly) [*person*] bête (**to do** de faire); **to be ~ enough to do** être assez bête pour faire; **2** (stupid) [*grin, look*] ridicule; **to look/feel ~** avoir l'air/se sentir ridicule; **to make sb look ~** rendre qn ridicule; **3** (misguided) [*decision, question, remark*] idiot; **that was a ~ thing to do** c'était idiot de faire cela.

foolishly /ˈfuːlɪʃlɪ/ *adv* **1** [*behave, believe, forget, ignore, reject*] bêtement; **~, I believed him** bêtement, je l'ai cru; **2** [*smile, grin, stare, stand there*] stupidement.

foolishness /ˈfuːlɪʃnɪs/ *n* bêtise *f*; **it is (sheer) ~ to do** c'est de la folie (pure) de faire.

foolproof /ˈfuːlpruːf/ *adj* **1** [*method, way, plan*] infaillible; **2** [*camera, machine*] d'utilisation très simple.

foolscap /ˈfuːlskæp/ **I** *n* GB (paper) papier *m* ministre.
II *adj* [*format*] ministre; [*book*] au format ministre; [*sheet*] de papier ministre.

fool's gold *n* (iron pyrites) pyrite *f* (de fer); (copper pyrites) chalcopyrite *f*.

foot /fʊt/ **▶ 1037**, **1412** **I** *n* (*pl* **feet**) **1** gen, Anat (of person, horse) pied *m*; (of rabbit, cat, dog, cow) patte *f*; (of stocking, sock, chair) pied *m*; **on ~** à pied; **to be soft under ~** être doux sous le pied; **he hasn't set ~ in this house/in England for 10 years** il n'a pas mis les pieds dans cette maison/en Angleterre depuis 10 ans; **from head to ~** de la tête aux pieds; **to rise to one's feet** se mettre debout, se lever; **to help sb to their feet** aider qn à se lever; **her speech brought the audience to its feet** toute l'audience s'est levée pour applaudir son discours; **to be on one's feet** lit être debout; **to be on one's feet again** fig être rétabli; **to get sb back on their feet** (after illness) rétablir or remettre qn d'aplomb; **to get sb/sth back on their/its feet** (after setback) remettre qn/qch sur pied; **to be quick on one's feet** être rapide; **bound** ou **tied hand and ~** pieds et poings liés; **to put one's ~ down** (accelerate) appuyer sur le champignon○; (act firmly) mettre le holà; **to sweep sb off their feet** lit faire perdre l'équilibre à qn; fig faire perdre la tête à qn; **to sit at sb's feet** lit s'asseoir aux pieds de qn; fig être aux pieds de qn; **my ~**○**!** mon œil○!; **2** (measurement) pied *m* (anglais) (= *0,3048 m*); **3** (bottom) (of mountain) pied *m* (**of** de); **at the ~ of** au pied de [*bed*]; à la fin de [*list, letter*]; en bas de [*page, stairs*]; en bout de [*table*]; **4** Sewing pied *m*; **5** Mil infanterie *f*; **6** Literat (in poetry) pied *m*.
II *vtr* **to ~ the bill** payer la facture (**for** pour).
IDIOMS **not to put a ~ wrong** ne pas commettre la moindre erreur; **to be/get under sb's feet** être/se mettre dans les jambes de qn; **to be rushed off one's feet** être débordé; **to catch sb on the wrong ~** prendre qn au dépourvu; **to cut the ground from under sb's feet** couper l'herbe sous les pieds de qn; **to dance/walk sb off their feet** faire danser/marcher qn jusqu'à l'épuisement; **to fall** ou **land on one's feet** retomber sur ses pieds; **to keep both** ou **one's feet on the ground** avoir les pieds sur terre; **to have two left feet** être maladroit; **to leave somewhere feet first** sortir de quelque part les pieds devant; **to put one's ~ down**○ (accelerate) appuyer sur le champignon○; (be firm) mettre le holà; **to put one's best ~ forward** (do one's best) faire de son mieux; (hurry) se dépêcher; **to put one's ~ in it**○ faire une gaffe; **to put one's feet up** se reposer, décompresser○; **to stand on one's own (two) feet** se débrouiller tout seul; **to start off** ou **get off on the wrong/right ~** mal/bien commencer (**with sb** avec qn); **to wait on sb hand and ~** faire tout pour qn.

footage /ˈfʊtɪdʒ/ *n* ¢ **1** Cin (piece of film) film *m*, pellicule *f*; **some ~ of** des images de; **news ~** des informations filmées; **2** Meas dimensions *fpl* en pieds (anglais), ≈ métrage *m*.

foot and mouth (disease) *n* Vet fièvre *f* aphteuse.

football /ˈfʊtbɔːl/ **▶ 1282** **I** *n* **1** (game) GB football *m*; US football *m* américain; **to play ~** jouer au football; **to be good/bad at ~** être bon/mauvais en football; **2** (ball) ballon *m* de football.
II *modif* [*boot, club, kit, match, pitch, practice, season, team*] de football; US [*helmet, uniform*] de football (américain).

football: **~ coach ▶ 1692** *n* entraîneur *m* de football; **~ coupon** *n* GB bulletin *m* de (participation au) loto sportif.

footballer /ˈfʊtbɔːlə(r)/ **▶ 1692** *n* GB joueur/-euse *m/f* de football.

football: **~ game** *n* US match *m* de football (américain); **Football League** *n* GB Sport (competition) championnat *m* de football; (association of clubs) ligue *f* de football; **~ player ▶ 1692** *n* joueur/-euse *m/f* de football; **~ pools** *npl* GB ≈ loto *m* sportif (*limité aux matchs de football*); **~ special** *n* GB train *m* des supporters (*d'une équipe de football*); **~ supporter** *n* supporter *m* (d'une équipe de football).

footbath /ˈfʊtbɑːθ/ *n* **1** (at home) bain *m* de pieds; **2** (at swimming pool) pédiluve *m*.

footboard /ˈfʊtbɔːd/ *n* **1** (on carriage, boat) (to stand on) marchepied *m*; (to rest foot on) repose-pied *m*; **2** (on bed) panneau *m* de pied.

foot: **~ brake** *n* Aut frein *m* (à pied); **~bridge** *n* passerelle *f*.

footer /ˈfʊtə(r)/ **I**○ *n* GB foot○ *m*.
II -footer (*dans composés*) **1 he's a six-~** il mesure 1,80 m; **2** (boat) **a 50-~** un 15 mètres.

foot: **~fall** *n* (bruit *m* de) pas *m*; **~ fault** *n* (in tennis) faute *f* de pied; **~hills** *npl* contreforts *mpl*.

foothold /ˈfʊthəʊld/ *n* lit prise *f* (de pied); **to gain a/lose one's ~** lit prendre/perdre pied; **to gain** ou **get a ~** fig [*company*] prendre pied; [*ideology*] s'imposer; [*plant, insect*] se propager.

footing /ˈfʊtɪŋ/ *n* **1** (basis) **on a firm ~** sur une base solide; **on a war ~** sur le pied de guerre; **to place** ou **put sth on a legal ~** légaliser qch; **to be on an equal** ou **even ~ with sb** être sur un pied d'égalité avec qn; **to be on a friendly/formal ~ with sb** avoir des rapports amicaux/formels avec qn; **2** (grip for feet) **to keep one's ~** conserver l'équilibre; **to lose one's ~** perdre pied.

footle○ /ˈfuːtl/ *v* GB ■ **~ about, ~ around** s'amuser, glander◑.

footlights /ˈfʊtlaɪts/ *npl* Theat rampe *f*; **to go behind the ~** fig monter sur les planches, devenir acteur.

footling○ /ˈfuːtlɪŋ/ *adj* futile.

footlocker /ˈfʊtlɒkə(r)/ *n* US Mil vestiaire *m* (*à la base du lit*).

footloose /ˈfʊtluːs/ *adj* libre comme l'air.
IDIOMS **~ and fancy free** sans attache.

foot: **~man‡** *n* valet *m* de pied; **~mark** *n* trace *f* (de pas); **~note** *n* lit note *f* de bas de page; fig (additional comment) post-scriptum *m*; **~ passenger** *n* passager *m* sans véhicule; **~path** *n* (in countryside) sentier *m*; (in town) trottoir *m*; **~ patrol** *n* (in police) patrouille *f* à pied; **~plate** *n* Hist Rail tablier *m* (*de locomotive à vapeur*); **~print** *n* empreinte *f* (de pied), trace *f* (de pas); **~ pump** *n* pompe *f* à pied; **~rest** *n* repose-pied *m*; **~ rot** *n* Vet piétin *m*.

footsie○ /ˈfʊtsɪ/ *n* **to play ~ with sb** faire du pied à qn.

Footsie (Index)○ /ˈfʊtsɪ/ *n* Fin (*abrév* = **Financial Times Stock Exchange Index**) indice *m* de la Bourse de Londres.

foot: **~slogging** *n* longue marche *f*; **~ soldier** *n* Mil Hist fantassin *m*; (in mafia) homme *m* de main.

footsore /ˈfʊtsɔː(r)/ *adj* [*person*] aux pieds douloureux; **to be ~** avoir mal aux pieds.

footstep /ˈfʊtstep/ *n* pas *m*.
IDIOMS **to follow in sb's ~s** suivre les traces de qn.

foot: **~stool** *n* repose-pied *m*; **~wear** *n* ¢ chaussures *fpl*; **~work** *n* jeu *m* de jambes.

fop /fɒp/ *n* péj dandy *m*, minet○ *m*.

foppish /ˈfɒpɪʃ/ *adj* péj [*person*] maniéré; [*clothes*] prétentieux/-ieuse; [*manners*] précieux/-ieuse.

for /fɔː(r), fə(r)/ **I** *prep* **1** (intended to belong to or be used by) pour; **who are the flowers ~?** pour qui sont les fleurs?; **~ her** pour elle; **to buy sth ~ sb** acheter qch pour or à qn; **she bought a book ~ me** elle a acheté un livre pour moi, elle m'a acheté un livre; **she bought presents ~ the family** elle a acheté des cadeaux pour la famille; **a club ~ young people** un club pour les jeunes; **a play area ~ children** une aire de jeux pour les enfants; **keep some pancakes ~ us!** garde-nous des crêpes!; **not ~ me thanks** pas pour moi merci; **2** (intended to help or benefit) pour; **to do sth ~ sb** faire qch pour qn; **you risked your life ~ us** tu as risqué ta vie pour nous; **let me carry it ~ you** laisse-moi le porter pour toi; **could you book a seat ~ me?** est-ce que tu pourrais réserver une place pour moi or me réserver une place?; **he cooked dinner ~ us** il nous a préparé à manger; **play a tune ~ us** joue-nous quelque chose; **3** (indicating purpose) pour; **what's it ~?** c'est pour quoi faire?, ça sert à quoi?; **it's ~ removing stains** c'est pour enlever or ça sert à enlever les taches; **what's this spring ~?** c'est pour quoi faire ce ressort?; **it's not ~ cleaning windows** ce n'est pas fait pour nettoyer les vitres; **an attic ~ storing furniture** un grenier pour entreposer les meubles; **'I need it'—'what ~?'** 'j'en ai besoin'—'pourquoi ?'; **what did you say**

for

When *for* is used as a preposition, followed by a noun or pronoun, it is translated by *pour*:

for my sister = pour ma sœur
for the garden = pour le jardin
for me = pour moi

For particular usages see the entry ***for***.

When *for* is used as a preposition indicating purpose followed by a verb it is translated by *pour* + infinitive:

for cleaning windows = pour nettoyer les vitres

When *for* is used in the construction
to be + adjective + *for* + pronoun + infinitive the translation in French is *être* + indirect pronoun + adjective + *de* + infinitive:

it's impossible for me to stay = il m'est impossible de rester
it was hard for him to understand that ... = il lui était difficile de comprendre que ...
it will be difficult for her to accept the changes = il lui sera difficile d'accepter les changements

For the construction *to be waiting for sb to do* see the entry ***wait***.
For particular usages see the entry ***for***.

In time expressions

for is used in English after a verb in the progressive present perfect tense to express the time period of something that started in the past and is still going on. To express this French uses a verb in the present tense + *depuis*:

I have been waiting for three hours
(and I am still waiting) = j'attends depuis trois heures
we've been together for two years
(and we're still together) = nous sommes ensemble depuis deux ans

When *for* is used in English after a verb in the past perfect tense, French uses the *imperfect* + *depuis*:

I had been waiting for two hours
(and was still waiting) = j'attendais depuis deux heures

for is used in English negative sentences with the present perfect tense to express the time that has elapsed since something has happened. To express this French uses the same tense as English (the perfect) + *depuis*:

I haven't seen him for ten years
(and I still haven't seen him) = je ne l'ai pas vu depuis dix ans

In spoken French, there is another way of expressing this: *ça fait* or *il y a dix ans que je ne l'ai pas vu*.

When *for* is used in English in negative sentences after a verb in the past perfect tense French uses the past perfect + *depuis*:

I hadn't seen him for ten years = je ne l'avais pas vu depuis dix ans, or (*in spoken French*) ça faisait or il y avait dix ans que je ne l'avais pas vu

for is used in English after the preterite to express the time period of something that happened in the past and is no longer going on. Here French uses the present perfect + *pendant*:

last Sunday I gardened for two hours = dimanche dernier j'ai jardiné pendant deux heures

for is used in English after the present progressive tense or the future tense to express an anticipated time period in the future. Here French uses the present or the future tense + *pour*:

I'm going to Rome for six weeks = je vais à Rome pour six semaines
or *I will go to Rome for six weeks* or j'irai à Rome pour six semaines

Note, however, that when the verb *to be* is used in the future with *for* to emphasize the period of time, French uses the future + *pendant*:

I will be in Rome for six weeks = je serai à Rome pendant six semaines
he will be away for three days = il sera absent pendant trois jours

For particular usages see **I 13, 14, 15** and **16** in the entry ***for***.

for is often used in English to form a structure with nouns, adjectives and verbs (*weakness for, eager for, apply for, fend for* etc.). For translations, consult the appropriate noun, adjective or verb entry (***weakness, eager, apply, fend*** etc.).

that ~? pourquoi as-tu dit cela?; **let's stop ~ a rest** arrêtons-nous pour nous reposer; **to do sth ~ a laugh** faire qch pour rigoler○; **to go ~ a swim/ meal** aller nager/manger; **I need something ~ my cough** j'ai besoin de quelque chose contre la toux; **she's being treated ~ depression** elle suit un traitement contre la dépression; **a cure ~ Aids** un remède contre le sida; **I sent it away ~ cleaning** je l'ai renvoyé pour qu'il soit nettoyé; **I brought her home ~ you to meet her** je l'ai amenée à la maison pour que tu puisses la rencontrer; **the bell rang ~ class to begin** la cloche a sonné pour indiquer le début du cours; **~ this to be feasible** pour que ce soit réalisable; **more investment is needed ~ economic growth to occur** il faut qu'il y ait plus d'investissements pour relancer la croissance économique ; **the idea was ~ you to work it out yourself** le but était que tu trouves (*subj*) la réponse tout seul; **4** (as representative, member, employee of) pour, de; **to work ~ a company** travailler pour une entreprise; **to play ~ France** jouer pour la France; **the MP ~ Oxford** le député d'Oxford; **Minister ~ Foreign Affairs** ministre des Affaires étrangères; **5** (indicating cause or reason) pour; **the reason ~ doing** la raison pour laquelle on fait; **~ this reason, I'd rather...** pour cette raison je préfère...; **grounds ~ divorce/~ hope** des motifs de divorce/d'espoir; **to jump ~ joy** sauter de joie; **imprisoned ~ murder** emprisonné pour meurtre; **she left him ~ another man** elle l'a quitté pour un autre homme; **famous ~ its wines** réputé pour ses vins; **to praise sb ~ his actions** féliciter qn pour ses actes; **she's been criticized ~ her views** on lui a reproché ses opinions; **I was unable to sleep ~ the pain/the noise** je ne pouvais pas dormir à cause de la douleur/du bruit; **the car is the worse ~ wear** la voiture est abîmée; **if it weren't ~ her we wouldn't be here** sans elle nous ne serions pas là; **if it hadn't been ~ the traffic jams, we'd have made it** sans les embouteillages nous serions arrivés à temps; **the plant died ~ want of water** la plante est morte parce qu'elle manquait d'eau; **she is annoyed with me ~ contradicting her** elle m'en veut parce que je l'ai contredite; **6** (indicating consequence) pour que (+ *subj*); **it's too cold ~ her to go out** il fait trop froid pour qu'elle sorte; **they spoke too quickly ~ us to understand** ils parlaient trop vite pour que nous les comprenions; **she said it loudly enough ~ all to hear** elle l'a dit suffisamment fort pour que tout le monde puisse entendre; **I haven't the patience** ou **enough patience ~ sewing** je n'ai pas la patience qu'il faut pour coudre; **there's not enough time ~ us to have a drink** nous n'avons pas le temps de prendre un verre; **7** (indicating person's attitude) pour; **to be easy ~ sb to do** être facile pour qn de faire; **~ her it's almost like a betrayal** pour elle c'est presque une trahison; **the film was too earnest ~ me** le film était trop sérieux pour moi; **it was a shock ~ him** ça a été un choc pour lui; **what counts ~ them is...** ce qui compte pour eux c'est...; **living in London is not ~ me** je ne suis pas fait pour vivre à Londres, vivre à Londres, très peu pour moi○!; **that's good enough ~ me!** ça me suffit!; **8** (stressing particular feature) pour; **~ further information write to...** pour plus de renseignements écrivez à...; **I buy it ~ flavour/freshness** je l'achète pour le goût/la fraîcheur ; **~ efficiency, there is no better system** pour ce qui est de l'efficacité il n'y a pas de meilleur système; **9** (considering) pour; **to be mature ~ one's age** être mûr pour son âge; **she's very young ~ a doctor** elle est très jeune pour un médecin; **it's warm ~ the time of year** il fait chaud pour la saison; **it's not a bad wine ~ the price** ce vin n'est pas mauvais pour le prix; **suitably dressed ~ the climate** habillé comme il faut pour le climat; **10** (towards) pour; **to have admiration/respect ~ sb** avoir de l'admiration/du respect pour qn ; **to feel sorry ~ sb** avoir de la peine pour qn; **to feel contempt ~ sb** mépriser qn; **11** (on behalf of) pour; **to be delighted/pleased ~ sb** être ravi/content pour qn; **to be anxious ~ sb** être inquiet pour qn; **say hello to him ~ me** dis-lui bonjour de ma part; **I can't do it ~ you** je ne peux pas le faire à ta place; **let her answer ~ herself** laisse-la répondre elle-même; **I speak ~ everyone here** je parle au nom de toutes les personnes ici présentes; **12** (as regards) **to be a stickler ~ punctuality** être à cheval sur la ponctualité; **she's a great one ~ jokes** on peut toujours compter sur elle pour raconter des blagues; **to be all right ~ money** avoir assez d'argent; **luckily ~ her** heureusement pour elle; **13** (indicating duration) (taking account of past events) depuis; (stressing expected duration) pour; (stressing actual duration) pendant; **this is the best show I've seen ~ years** c'est le meilleur spectacle que j'aie vu depuis des années; **we've been together ~ 2 years** nous sommes ensemble depuis 2 ans, ça fait 2 ans que nous sommes ensemble; **she hasn't slept ~ a week** elle n'a pas dormi depuis une semaine, ça fait une semaine qu'elle n'a pas dormi; **they hadn't seen each other ~ 10 years** ils ne s'étaient pas vus depuis 10 ans, ça faisait 10 ans qu'ils ne s'étaient pas vus; **she's off to Paris ~ the weekend** elle va à Paris pour le week-end; **I'm going to Spain ~ 6 months** je vais en Espagne pour 6 mois; **they are stored in the cellar ~ the winter** ils sont entreposés dans la cave pour l'hiver; **will he be away ~ long?** est-ce qu'il sera absent longtemps?; **you can stay ~ a year** vous pouvez rester un an; **to be away ~ a year** être absent pendant un an; **they were married ~ 25 years** ils ont été mariés pendant 25 ans; **he hasn't been seen ~ several days** on ne l'a pas vu depuis plusieurs jours; **she remained silent ~ a few moments** elle est restée silencieuse pendant quelques instants; **I was in Paris ~ 2 weeks** j'étais à Paris pendant 2 semaines; **to last ~ hours** durer des heures; **14** (indicating a deadline) pour; (in negative constructions) avant; **it will be ready ~ Saturday** ça sera prêt pour samedi; **when is the essay ~?** la rédaction, c'est pour quand?; **the car won't be ready ~ another 6 weeks** la voiture ne sera pas prête avant 6 semaines; **you don't have to decide ~ a week yet** tu n'as pas à prendre ta décision avant une semaine; **15** (on the occasion of) pour; **to go to China ~**

Christmas aller en Chine pour Noël; **invited ~ Easter** invité pour Pâques; **he got a bike ~ his birthday** il a eu un vélo pour son anniversaire; **16** (indicating scheduled time) pour; **the summit scheduled ~ next month** le sommet prévu pour le mois prochain; **that's all ~ now** c'est tout pour le moment; **I'd like an appointment ~ Monday** je voudrais un rendez-vous pour lundi; **I have an appointment ~ 4 pm** j'ai rendez-vous à 16h 00; **it's time ~ bed** c'est l'heure d'aller au lit; **now ~ some fun/food!** on va s'amuser/manger!; **17** (indicating distance) pendant; **to drive ~ miles** rouler pendant des kilomètres; **lined with trees ~ 3 km** bordé d'arbres pendant or sur 3 km; **the last shop ~ 30 miles** le dernier magasin avant 50 kilomètres; **there is nothing but desert ~ miles around** on ne voit que le désert à des kilomètres à la ronde; **18** (indicating destination) pour; **a ticket ~ Dublin** un billet pour Dublin; **the train leaves ~ London** le train part pour Londres; **to leave ~ work** partir travailler; **to head ~ the beach** partir à la plage; **to swim ~ the shore** nager vers la rive; **19** (indicating cost, value) pour; **it was sold ~ £100** ça s'est vendu (pour) 100 livres sterling; **they bought the car ~ £6000** ils ont acheté la voiture pour 6 000 livres sterling; **10 apples ~ £1** 10 pommes pour une livre sterling; **he'll fix it ~ £10** il le réparera pour 10 livres sterling; **I wouldn't do it ~ anything!** je ne le ferais pour rien au monde!; **you paid too much ~ that dress!** tu as payé cette robe trop cher!; **I'll let you have it ~ £20** je vous le laisse à 20 livres sterling; **a cheque ~ £20** un chèque de 20 livres sterling; **to exchange sth ~ sth else** échanger qch contre qch d'autre; ▶**nothing**; **20** (in favour of) **to be ~** être pour [*peace, divorce, reunification*]; **to be all ~ it** être tout à fait pour; **I'm ~ going to a nightclub** je suis pour qu'on aille en boîte○; **who's ~ a game of football?** qui veut jouer au football?; **21** (stressing appropriateness) **she's the person ~ the job** elle est la personne qu'il faut pour le travail; **that's ~ us to decide** c'est à nous de décider; **it's not ~ him to tell us what to do** ce n'est pas à lui de nous dire ce qu'il faut faire; **22** (in support of) en faveur de; **to vote ~ change** voter en faveur de la réforme; **the argument ~ recycling** l'argument en faveur du recyclage; **there's no evidence ~ that** ce n'est absolument pas prouvé; **23** (indicating availability) **~ sale** à vendre; **'caravans ~ hire'** 'caravanes à louer'; **24** (as part of ratio) pour; **one teacher ~ five pupils** un professeur pour cinq élèves; **~ every female judge there are ten male judges** il y a une femme juge pour dix hommes juges; **25** (equivalent to) **T ~ Tom** T comme Tom; **what's the French ~ 'boot'?** comment dit-on 'boot' en français?; **the technical term ~ it is 'chloasma'** 'chloasme' c'est le terme technique; **what is CD ~?** qu'est-ce que CD veut dire?; **green is ~ go** le vert veut dire qu'on a le droit de passer; **26** (in explanations) **~ one thing... and ~ another...** premièrement... et deuxièmement...; **~ that matter** d'ailleurs; **~ example** par exemple; **I, ~ one, agree with her** en tout cas moi, je suis d'accord avec elle; **27** (when introducing clauses) **it would be unwise ~ us to generalize** il serait imprudent pour nous de généraliser ; **it's not convenient ~ them to come today** ce n'est pas pratique pour eux de passer aujourd'hui; **the best thing would be ~ them to leave** le mieux serait qu'ils s'en aillent; **it must have been serious ~ her to cancel the class** cela a dû être grave pour qu'elle annule (*subj*) le cours; **there's nothing worse than ~ someone to spy on you** il n'y a rien de pire que quelqu'un qui t'espionne; **there's no need ~ people to get upset** il n'y a pas de quoi s'énerver; **28** (after) **to name a child ~ sb** donner à un enfant le nom de qn.

II *conj* sout car, parce que.

IDIOMS **oh ~ a nice hot bath!** je rêve d'un bon bain chaud!; **I'll be (in) ~ it if...**○ GB ça va être ma fête si...○; **right, you're ~ it**○! GB bon, ça va être ta fête○!; **to have it in ~ sb**○ avoir qn dans le collimateur○; **that's adolescents ~ you!** que voulez-vous, c'est ça les adolescents!; **there's gratitude ~ you!** c'est comme ça qu'on me (or vous etc) remercie!, quelle ingratitude!

FOR *adj, adv: abrév* ▶**free on rail**.

forage /ˈfɒrɪdʒ, US ˈfɔːr-/ **I** *n* **1** (animal feed) fourrage *m*; **2** (search) **to go on a ~ for** aller faire provision de [*food, wood*].

II *vtr* affourager [*animals*].

III *vi* **to ~ (about** ou **around) for sth** lit, fig fouiller pour trouver qch.

forage cap *n* calot *m*.

forasmuch /ˌfɔːrəzˈmʌtʃəz/ *conj* sout **~ as** pour autant que (+ *subj*) fml.

foray /ˈfɒreɪ, US ˈfɔːreɪ/ **I** *n* **1** (first venture) incursion *f* also hum (**into** dans); **to make a ~ into** s'essayer à [*politics, acting, sport*]; **2** Mil (raid) incursion *f* (**into** en).

II *vi* Mil **to ~ into** faire une incursion dans.

forbad(e) /fɔːˈbæd, US fəˈbeɪd/ *prét* ▶**forbid**.

forbear /fɔːˈbeə(r)/ *vi* (*prét* **-bore**, *pp* **-borne**) sout s'abstenir (**from sth** de qch; **from doing, to do** de faire).

forbearance /fɔːˈbeərəns/ *n* sout indulgence *f*; **to show ~ towards** être indulgent envers.

forbearing /fɔːˈbeərɪŋ/ *adj* sout indulgent.

forbears *n* = **forebears**.

forbid /fəˈbɪd/ **I** *vtr* (*p prés* **-dd-**, *prét* **forbad(e)**, *pp* **forbidden**) **1** (disallow) défendre, interdire; **~ sb to do** défendre or interdire à qn de faire; **~ sb sth** défendre or interdire qch à qn; **to ~ sth categorically** ou **expressly** interdire formellement qch; **2** (prevent, preclude) interdire; **his health ~s it** sa santé le lui interdit; **God ~!** Dieu m'en/l'en etc garde!; **God ~ she should do that!** pourvu qu'elle ne fasse pas cela!

II *v refl* **to ~ oneself sth/to do** s'interdire qch/de faire.

forbidden /fəˈbɪdn/ *adj* défendu, interdit (**to do** de faire); **he is ~ to do** on lui interdit de faire; **smoking is ~** il est interdit de fumer; **~ place** lieu *m* interdit; **~ subject/fruit** sujet/fruit défendu.

forbidding /fəˈbɪdɪŋ/ *adj* [*edifice*] intimidant; [*landscape*] inhospitalier/-ière; [*expression, look*] rébarbatif/-ive.

forbiddingly /fəˈbɪdɪŋlɪ/ *adv* [*scowl, frown*] de façon rébarbative; [*rise*] de façon imposante.

forbore /fɔːˈbɔː(r)/ *prét* ▶**forbear**.

forborne /fɔːˈbɔːn/ *pp* ▶**forbear**.

force /fɔːs/ **I** *n* **1** (physical strength, impact) (of blow, explosion, collision, earthquake) force *f*; (of sun's rays) puissance *f*; (of fall) choc *m*; **he was knocked over by the ~ of the blast/the blow** il est tombé sous la force de l'explosion/du coup; **I hit him with all the ~ I could muster** je l'ai frappé de toutes mes forces; **2** gen, Mil (physical means) force *f*; **to use ~** recourir à or employer la force; **by ~** par la force; **by ~ of arms, by military ~** à la force des armes; **3** fig (strength) (of intellect, memory, enthusiasm, logic, grief) force *f*; **by** ou **out of** ou **from ~ of habit/of circumstance/of numbers** par la force de l'habitude/des circonstances/du nombre; **'no,' she said with some ~** 'non,' a-t-elle dit avec force; **to have the ~ of law** avoir force de loi; **4** (strong influence) force *f*; **a ~ for good/change** une force agissant pour le bien/le changement; **the ~s of evil** les forces du mal; **she's a ~ in the democratic movement** c'est un personnage important du mouvement démocratique; **market ~s** forces du marché; **this country is no longer a world ~** ce pays n'est plus une puissance mondiale; **5** (organized group) forces *fpl*; **expeditionary/peacekeeping ~** forces expéditionnaires/de maintien de la paix; **naval/ground ~** forces navales/terrestres; ▶**labour force**, **workforce**, **task force etc**; **6** (police) (also **Force**) **the ~** la police; **7** Phys force *f*; **centrifugal/centripetal ~** force centrifuge/centripète; **~ of gravity** pesanteur *f*; **8** Meteorol force *f*; **a ~ 10 gale** un vent de force 10.

II forces *npl* Mil (also **armed ~s**) **the ~s** les forces *fpl* armées.

III in force *adv phr* **1** (in large numbers, strength) en force; **2** gen, Jur [*law, act, prices, ban, curfew*] en vigueur; **to come into ~** entrer en vigueur.

IV *vtr* **1** (compel, oblige) forcer; **to ~ sb/sth to do** gen forcer qn/qch à faire; **to be ~d to do** gen être forcé de faire; **he ~d his voice to remain calm** il s'est forcé à garder une voix calme; **to ~ a smile/a laugh** se forcer à sourire/ à rire; **the earthquake ~d the evacuation of hundreds of residents** le tremblement de terre a provoqué or entraîné l'évacuation de plusieurs centaines d'habitants; **protesters have ~d a public inquiry** les protestataires ont exigé et obtenu que l'on ouvre une enquête publique; **to ~ a bill through parliament** forcer or obliger le parliament à voter un projet de loi; **2** (push, thrust) **to ~ one's way through [sth]** se frayer un chemin à travers or dans [*crowd, jungle*]; **to ~ sb to the ground/up against sth** plaquer qn au sol/contre qch; **she ~d him to his knees** elle l'a forcé à se mettre à genoux; **the car ~d the motorbike off the road/into the ditch** la voiture a forcé la moto à quitter la route/à aller au fossé; **bad weather ~d him off the road for a week** le mauvais temps l'a empêché de prendre la route pendant une semaine; **she ~d her way to the top through sheer perseverance** elle est parvenue au sommet grâce à beaucoup de persévérance; **3** (apply great pressure to) forcer [*door, window, lock, safe, engine, meter*]; forcer sur [*screw*]; **to ~ an entry** Jur entrer par effraction; **to ~ the pace** forcer l'allure; **4** Agric, Hort (speed up growth) forcer [*plant*]; engraisser [*animal*].

V *v refl* **1** (push oneself) **to ~ oneself** se forcer (**to do** à faire); **2** (impose oneself) **to ~ oneself on sb** imposer sa présence à qn; **I wouldn't want to ~ myself on you** je ne cherche pas à m'imposer.

IDIOMS **to ~ sb's hand** forcer la main à qn.

■ **force back**: **~ [sth] back, ~ back [sth] 1** lit repousser, obliger [qch] à reculer [*crowd, army*]; **she ~d him back against the wall** elle l'a repoussé or plaqué contre le mur; **2** fig réprimer [*emotion, tears, anger*].

■ **force down**: **~ [sth] down, ~ down [sth] 1** (cause to land) forcer [qch] à se poser [*aircraft*]; **2** (eat reluctantly) se forcer à avaler [*food*]; **to ~ sth down sb** forcer qn à manger qch; **don't ~ your ideas down my throat**○! ne m'impose pas tes idées!; **3** (reduce) gen, Fin diminuer [qch] (de force) [*prices, wages, output*]; réduire [qch] (de force) [*currency value, demand, profits, inflation*]; **to ~ down unemployment** faire baisser le taux de chômage; **4** (squash down) tasser [*contents, objects*].

■ **force in**: **~ [sth] in, ~ in [sth]** (into larger space) faire entrer [qch] de force; (into small opening) enfoncer [qch] de force.

■ **force into**: **~ [sb/sth] into sth/doing 1** (compel) forcer [qn/qch] à faire; **to be ~d into doing** être forcé de faire; **I was ~d into it** on m'a forcé à le faire; **2** (push, thrust) **she ~d him into the car** elle l'a fait entrer de force dans la voiture; **he ~d his clothes into a suitcase** il a tassé ses vêtements dans une valise; **he ~d his way into the house** il est entré de force dans la maison.

■ **force on**: **~ [sth] on sb** imposer [qch] à

qn, forcer qn à accepter [qch]; **the decision was ~d on him** il a été forcé de prendre cette décision; **team X ~d a draw on team Y** l'équipe X a arraché un match nul à l'équipe Y.

■ **force open**: **~ [sth] open**, **~ open [sth]** forcer [*door, window, box, safe*]; **she ~d the patient's mouth open** elle a ouvert la bouche du malade de force; **he ~d his eyes open** il s'est forcé à ouvrir les yeux.

■ **force out**: **~ [sth] out**, **~ out [sth]** (by physical means) faire sortir [qch] par la force [*invader, enemy, object*]; enlever [qch] de force [*cork*]; **the government was ~d out in the elections** les élections ont forcé or obligé le gouvernement à quitter le pouvoir; **she ~d out a few words** elle s'est forcée à dire quelques mots; **to ~ one's way out (of sth)** s'échapper (de qch) par la force; **to ~ sth out of sb** arracher qch à qn [*information, apology, smile, confession*]; **the injury ~d him out of the game** cette blessure l'a forcé à abandonner le jeu.

■ **force through**: **~ [sth] through**, **~ through [sth]** faire adopter [*legislation, measures*].

■ **force up**: **~ [sth] up**, **~ up [sth]** [*inflation, crisis, situation*] faire augmenter [*prices, costs, demand, unemployment*]; [*government, company, minister*] augmenter (de force) [*prices, output, wages*]; relever [*exchange rate*].

forced /fɔːst/ *adj* **1** (false) [*laugh, smile, interpretation*] forcé; [*conversation*] peu naturel/-elle; **2** (imposed) [*labour, marriage, landing, march, saving*] forcé; **3** Hort [*plant*] forcé.

force-feed /ˈfɔːsfiːd/ *vtr* (*prét, pp* **-fed**) gaver [*animal, bird*] (**on, with** de); alimenter [qn] de force [*person*] (**on, with** de); **her parents ~ her (on** ou **with) Mozart** fig ses parents la gavent○ de Mozart.

force: **~-feeding** *n* (of animal, bird) gavage *m*; (of person) alimentation *f* de force; **~ field** *n* champ *m* de force.

forceful /ˈfɔːsfl/ *adj* [*person, character, behaviour*] énergique; [*attack, defence, speech*] vigoureux/-euse.

forcefully /ˈfɔːsfəlɪ/ *adv* [*say, argue*] avec vigueur; [*hit*] avec force.

forcemeat /ˈfɔːsmiːt/ *n* GB Culin farce *f*.

forceps /ˈfɔːseps/ **I** *n* (*pl* **~**) forceps *m*.
II *modif* [*birth, delivery*] par forceps.

forcible /ˈfɔːsəbl/ *adj* [*repatriation, eviction, removal*] forcé.

forcibly /ˈfɔːsəblɪ/ *adv* [*restrain, remove, repatriate*] de force.

forcing: **~ bid** *n* enchère *f*; **~ house** *n* Hort forcerie *f*; fig pépinière *f*.

ford /fɔːd/ **I** *n* gué *m*.
II *vtr* **to ~ a river** passer une rivière à gué.

fore /fɔː(r)/ **I** *n* **1 to the ~** en vue, en avant; fig **to be** ou **come to the ~** [*person*] se faire connaître; [*issue*] attirer l'attention; [*quality*] ressortir; [*team, party, competitor*] commencer à dominer; **to bring to the ~** faire ressortir [*talent, quality*]; mettre au premier plan [*issue, problem*]; **2** Naut avant *m*.
II *adj* gen, Naut à l'avant.
III *excl* (in golf) gare!

fore-and-aft /ˌfɔːrənˈɑːft/ *adj* Naut **~ sail** voile *f* aurique; **~ rig** gréement *m* aurique.

forearm /ˈfɔːrɑːm/ *n* avant-bras *m inv*.

forebears /ˈfɔːbeəz/ *n* sout aïeux *mpl*.

forebode /fɔːˈbəʊd/ *vtr* (*prét* **-bode**) sout présager.

foreboding /fɔːˈbəʊdɪŋ/ *n* pressentiment *m*; **to have a ~ that** avoir le pressentiment que; **to have ~s about sth** avoir de sombres pressentiments quant à qch; **a sense of ~** un sentiment d'appréhension; **full of ~** plein d'appréhension.

forecast /ˈfɔːkɑːst, US -kæst/ **I** *n* **1** (also **weather ~**) météo○ *f*, bulletin *m* météorologique; **the ~ is for rain** la météo prévoit de la pluie; **2** Comm, Econ, Fin prévisions *fpl* (**about** sur); **profits/sales ~** prévisions de bénéfices/de ventes; **3** Turf **a (racing) ~** pronostics *mpl* des courses; **4** gen (outlook) pronostics *mpl*.
II *vtr* (*prét, pp* **-cast**) (all contexts) prévoir (**that** que); **as ~** comme prévu; **sunshine is ~ for tomorrow** on prévoit du soleil pour demain; **investment is ~ to fall** on prévoit une chute de l'investissement.
III *pp adj* [*growth, demand, deficit, fall*] prévu.

forecaster /ˈfɔːkɑːstə(r), US -kæst-/ *n* **1** (of weather) spécialiste *mf* de la météorologie; **2** (economic) conjoncturiste *mf*; **3** gen, Sport pronostiqueur/-euse *m/f*.

forecasting /ˈfɔːkɑːstɪŋ, US -kæst-/ *n* **1** gen prévisions *fpl*; **2 weather ~** prévisions *fpl* météorologiques; **3** Comm, Econ, Pol **economic ~** conjoncture *f*; **electoral/market ~** prévisions *fpl* électorales/du marché.

forecastle, **fo'c'sle** /ˈfəʊksl/ *n* poste *m* d'équipage.

foreclose /fɔːˈkləʊz/ **I** *vtr* sout **1** Fin, Jur saisir [*mortgage, loan*]; **2** (remove) exclure [*possibility, chance*].
II *vi* forclore; **to ~ on** forclore [*person*]; saisir [*mortgage, loan*].

foreclosure /fɔːˈkləʊʒə(r)/ *n* sout saisie *f*.

forecourt /ˈfɔːkɔːt/ *n* **1** GB (of shop, hypermarket) parking *m*; (of garage) aire *f* de stationnement; **the price on the ~** le prix à la pompe; **2** GB Rail (of station) cour *f* de la gare; **3** (of church) ≈ parvis *m*; (of castle) avant-cour *f*; **4** (in tennis) carrés *mpl* de service.

foredoom /fɔːˈduːm/ *vtr* sout condamner [qn/qch] d'avance.

forefathers /ˈfɔːfɑːðəz/ *n* ancêtres *mpl*.

forefinger /ˈfɔːfɪŋgə(r)/ *n* index *m*.

forefoot /ˈfɔːfʊt/ *n* (*pl* **-feet**) patte *f* antérieure.

forefront /ˈfɔːfrʌnt/ *n* **at** ou **in the ~ of** [*change, research, debate*] à la pointe de; [*campaign, struggle*] au premier plan de; **it's in the ~ of my mind** c'est ma première préoccupation; **the issue should be brought to the ~** il faut mettre la question au premier plan.

forego *vtr* = **forgo**.

foregoing /ˈfɔːgəʊɪŋ/ **I** *n* **the ~** sout les faits précités.
II *adj* susdit fml.

foregone /ˈfɔːgɒn, US -ˈgɔːn/ *adj* **it is/was a ~ conclusion** c'est/c'était couru d'avance.

foreground /ˈfɔːgraʊnd/ **I** *n* premier plan *m*; **in the ~** au premier plan.
II *vtr* mettre en relief.

forehand /ˈfɔːhænd/ Sport **I** *n* coup *m* droit; **to sb's ~** sur le coup droit de qn.
II *modif* [*return, volley*] de coup droit.

forehead /ˈfɒrɪd, ˈfɔːhed, US ˈfɔːrɪd/ *n* front *m*; **high/low ~** front haut/bas; **on one's ~** au front.

foreign /ˈfɒrən, US ˈfɔːr-/ *adj* **1** [*country, imports, company, investment*] étranger/-ère; [*trade, travel*] à l'étranger; **in ~ parts** à l'étranger; **on the ~ market** sur le marché extérieur; **2** (alien, unknown) [*concept, idea*] étranger/-ère (**to** à).

foreign affairs *npl* affaires *fpl* étrangères.

foreign aid *n* (received) aide *f* étrangère; (given) aide *f* aux pays étrangers.

foreign: **~ aid budget** *n* budget *m* d'aide aux pays étrangers; **Foreign and Commonwealth Office**, **FCO** *n* GB = **foreign office**; **~ body** *n* corps *m* étranger; **~ correspondent** ▶ 1692 *n* correspondant/-e *m/f* à l'étranger.

foreigner /ˈfɒrənə(r)/ *n* étranger/-ère *m/f*.

foreign: **~ exchange** *n* devises *fpl*; **~ exchange dealer** ▶ 1692 *n* cambiste *m*, courtier/-ière *m/f* en devises; **~ exchange market** *n* marché *m* des changes; **~ legion** *n* légion *f* étrangère; **~ minister** *n* ministre *m* des affaires étrangères; **~ ministry** *n* ministère *m* des affaires étrangères; **Foreign Office**, **FO** *n* GB ministère *m* des affaires étrangères; **~-owned** *adj* [*company*] à capital étranger; **~ policy** *n* politique *f* étrangère; **~ secretary** *n* GB = **foreign minister**; **~ service** *n* service *m* diplomatique.

foreknowledge /ˌfɔːˈnɒlɪdʒ/ *n* sout **to have ~ of** avoir une connaissance préalable de [*crime*]; avoir la prescience fml de [*disaster*].

foreland /ˈfɔːlənd/ *n* promontoire *m*.

foreleg /ˈfɔːleg/ *n* gen patte *f* avant; (of horse) (membre *m*) antérieur *m*.

forelock /ˈfɔːlɒk/ *n* (of person, horse) toupet *m*; **to touch** ou **tug one's ~** montrer de la déférence (*en tirant sur la mèche de son front*).

foreman /ˈfɔːmən/ ▶ 1692 *n* **1** (supervisor) contremaître *m*; **2** Jur président *m* (d'un jury).

foremast /ˈfɔːmɑːst, -məst/ *n* mât *m* de misaine.

foremost /ˈfɔːməʊst/ **I** *adj* plus grand; **one of the city's ~ experts/jazz bands** un des plus grands experts/orchestres de jazz de la ville; **we have many problems, ~ among these are...** nous avons beaucoup de problèmes, les premiers d'entre eux sont...; **the issue is ~ in our minds** c'est la question qui nous préoccupe le plus.
II *adv* **first and ~** avant tout.

forename /ˈfɔːneɪm/ *n* prénom *m*.

forenoon /ˈfɔːnuːn/ *n* matinée *f*.

forensic /fəˈrensɪk, US -zɪk/ **I forensics** *npl* US (public speaking) art *m* oratoire.
II *adj* **1** (in crime detection) **~ tests** expertises *fpl* médico-légales; **~ evidence** résultats *mpl* des expertises médico-légales; **~ expert** expert *m* en médecine légale; **2** sout (in debate) [*skill, eloquence*] consommé; [*attack*] dévastateur/-trice.

forensic: **~ medicine**, **~ science** *n* médecine *f* légale; **~ scientist** ▶ 1692 *n* médecin *m* légiste.

forepaw /ˈfɔːpɔː/ *n* patte *f* de devant.

foreplay /ˈfɔːpleɪ/ *n* ¢ excitation *f* préliminaire.

forequarter /ˈfɔːkwɔːtə(r)/ **I** *n* (of carcass) quartier *m* de devant.
II forequarters *npl* (of horse) avant-main *f*.

forerunner /ˈfɔːrʌnə(r)/ *n* **1** (predecessor) (person) précurseur *m*; (institution, invention, model) ancêtre *m*; **2** (sign) signe *m* avant-coureur.

foresee /fɔːˈsiː/ *vtr* (*prét* **foresaw**, *pp* **foreseen**) prévoir (**that** que); **nobody foresaw her being elected** personne ne prévoyait qu'elle serait élue; **I don't ~ any problems** je ne prévois aucun problème.

foreseeable /fɔːˈsiːəbl/ *adj* prévisible (**that** que); **for the ~ future** dans l'immédiat; **in the ~ future** dans un avenir prévisible.

foreshadow /fɔːˈʃædəʊ/ *vtr* annoncer.

foreshore /ˈfɔːʃɔː(r)/ *n* laisse *f* de mer.

foreshorten /fɔːˈʃɔːtn/ **I** *vtr* Art (in drawing) [*artist*] faire un raccourci de; [*angle, distance*] raccourcir, déformer [qch] par un effet de grand angle.
II foreshortened *pp adj* raccourci.

foreshortening /fɔːˈʃɔːtnɪŋ/ *n* Art représentation *f* en raccourci.

foresight /ˈfɔːsaɪt/ *n* prévoyance *f* (**to do** de faire).

foreskin /ˈfɔːskɪn/ *n* Anat gen prépuce *m*; (of horse) fourreau *m*.

forest /ˈfɒrɪst, US ˈfɔːr-/ *n* forêt *f*; **oak/pine ~** forêt de chênes/de pins; **(tropical) rain ~** forêt tropicale; **500 hectares of ~** 500 hectares de forêt.

forestall /fɔːˈstɔːl/ *vtr* empêcher [*action, event, discussion*]; prévenir [*person*].

forest decline *n* recul *m* de la forêt.

forested /ˈfɒrɪstɪd, US ˈfɔːr-/ *adj* boisé; **densely ~** très boisé.

forester /ˈfɒrɪstə(r), US ˈfɔːr-/ *n* forestier/-ière *m/f*.

forest: **~ fire** *n* incendie *m* de forêt; **~ floor** *n* sol *m* de la forêt; **~ management** *n* exploitation *f* des forêts; **~ ranger** *n* US (garde *m*) forestier *m*.

forestry /ˈfɒrɪstrɪ, US ˈfɔːr-/ *n* (science) sylviculture *f*; (industry) exploitation *f* des forêts.

forestry: **Forestry Commission** *n* GB *l'office britannique des forêts*; **~ worker** ▶ **1692** *n* GB (maintenance) (garde *m*) forestier *m*; (lumberjack) bûcheron/-onne *m/f*.

foretaste /ˈfɔːteɪst/ *n* avant-goût *m* (**of** de).

foretell /fɔːˈtel/ *vtr* (*prét, pp* **foretold**) prédire (**that** que); **to ~ the future** prédire l'avenir.

forethought /ˈfɔːθɔːt/ *n* prévoyance *f*.

forever /fəˈrevə(r)/ *adv* **1** (also **for ever**) (eternally) [*last, live, love*] pour toujours; **captured ~ in a photo** fixé pour toujours sur la pellicule; **it can't go on** ou **last ~** [*situation, success*] ça ne peut pas durer éternellement; **I want it to be like this ~** je voudrais que ça reste toujours comme ça; **~ after(wards)** pour toujours; **the desert seemed to go on ~** le désert semblait ne pas avoir de limites; ▶ **ever**; **2** (also **for ever**) (definitively) [*leave, lose, close, change*] pour toujours, définitivement; [*stay, exile, disappear, destroy*] à jamais, pour toujours; **I can't keep doing this ~!** je ne peux pas continuer à faire ça éternellement!; **3** (persistently) **to be ~ doing sth** faire qch sans arrêt; **he's ~ moaning**○ il n'arrête pas de râler○; **4**○ (also **for ever**) (ages) **to take ~** [*task, procedure*] prendre un temps fou○; [*person*] mettre un temps fou○ (**to do** pour faire); **it seemed to go on ~** [*pain, noise*] ça m'a semblé (or lui a semblé etc) durer une éternité; **5** (always) toujours; **~ patient** toujours patient; **~ on the brink of doing** toujours sur le point de faire; **6** (in acclamations) **the Blues ~!** vive les Bleus!

forevermore /fəˌrevəˈmɔː(r)/ *adv* pour toujours.

forewarn /fɔːˈwɔːn/ *vtr* avertir (**of** de; **that** que).

IDIOMS **~ed is forearmed** Prov un homme averti en vaut deux Prov.

foreword /ˈfɔːwɜːd/ *n* avant-propos *m inv*.

forfeit /ˈfɔːfɪt/ **I** *n* **1** (action, process) confiscation *f* (**of** de); **2** (sum, token) gage *m*; **3** (in game) gage *m*; **to play ~s** jouer à un jeu de gages; **4** Jur, Comm (fine) amende *f*; (for breach of contract) dédit *m*.
II *adj* **to be ~** sout [*property*] être confiscable (**to** au profit de).
III *vtr* **1** (under duress) perdre [*right, support*]; être privé de, perdre [*liberty*]; **2** (voluntarily) renoncer à [*right, free time*]; **3** Jur, Comm verser [*sum*].

forfeiture /ˈfɔːfɪtʃə(r)/ *n* Jur (of property, money) confiscation *f* (**of** de); (of right) déchéance *f* (**of** de).

forgave /fəˈgeɪv/ *pret* ▶ **forgive**.

forge /fɔːdʒ/ **I** *n* forge *f*.
II *vtr* **1** forger [*metal*]; **2** (fake) contrefaire [*banknotes, signature, branded goods*]; **a ~d passport** un faux passeport; **to ~ a painting** faire un faux; **3** (alter) falsifier [*date, certificate, will*]; **4** (establish) forger [*alliance*]; établir [*identity, link*]; élaborer [*plan*].
III *vi* **to ~ ahead** accélérer; fig [*company, industry*] être en plein essor; **to ~ ahead** ou **forward with** aller de l'avant dans [*plan*]; **to ~ into the lead** prendre la tête.

forger /ˈfɔːdʒə(r)/ *n* **1** (of documents) faussaire *m*; **2** (of artefacts) contrefacteur/-trice *m/f*; **3** (of money) faux-monnayeur *m*.

forgery /ˈfɔːdʒərɪ/ *n* **1** (counterfeiting) (of document) faux *m*; (of work of art, banknotes) contrefaçon *f*; **2** (fake item) (signature, banknote) contrefaçon *f*; (picture, document) faux *m*.

forget /fəˈget/ (*p prés* **-tt-**; *prét* **-got**; *pp* **-gotten**) **I** *vtr* **1** (not remember) oublier [*date, face, number, appointment, poem*]; **that** oublier que; **to ~ to do** oublier de faire; **to ~ how** oublier comment; **three people, not ~ting the baby** trois personnes, sans oublier le bébé; **I'm in charge and don't you ~ it!** rappelle-toi que c'est moi le responsable; **~ it!** (no way) n'y compte pas!; (drop the subject) laisse tomber!; (think nothing of it) ce n'est rien!; **2** (put aside) oublier [*past, quarrel*]; **~ I ever mentioned him** faites comme si je n'avais pas parlé de lui; **she'll never let me ~ it** elle n'est pas près de me le faire oublier; **3** (leave behind) lit oublier [*hat, passport*]; fig oublier [*inhibitions, traditions, family*].
II *vi* oublier; **'how many?'—'I ~'** 'combien?'—'j'ai oublié'.
III *v refl* **to ~ oneself** s'oublier.

IDIOMS **once seen, never forgotten** inoubliable.

■ **forget about**: **~ about [sth/sb]** (overlook) oublier [*appointment, birthday, person*].

forgetful /fəˈgetfl/ *adj* **1** (absent-minded) [*person*] distrait; **to become** ou **grow ~** perdre un peu la mémoire; **2** (negligent) **~ of the danger, she...** oublieuse du danger, elle...; **to be ~ of one's duties** négliger ses responsabilités.

forgetfulness /fəˈgetflnɪs/ *n* **1** (absent-mindedness) distraction *f*, perte *f* de mémoire; **2** (carelessness) étourderie *f*.

forget: **~-me-not** *n* myosotis *m*; **~-me-not blue** ▶ **1104** *n* bleu *m* myosotis *inv*.

forgettable /fəˈgetəbl/ *adj* [*day, fact, film*] peu mémorable; [*actor, writer*] sans grand intérêt.

forgivable /fəˈgɪvəbl/ *adj* pardonnable.

forgive /fəˈgɪv/ (*prét* **-gave**, *pp* **-given**) **I** *vtr* pardonner à [*person*]; pardonner [*act, crime, remark*]; annuler [*debt*]; **to ~ sb sth** pardonner qch à qn; **to ~ sb for doing** pardonner à qn d'avoir fait; **he could be forgiven for believing her** on ne peut pas lui reprocher de l'avoir crue; **such a crime cannot be forgiven** un tel crime ne se pardonne pas; **~ my curiosity, but...** excusez mon indiscrétion, mais...; **~ me for interrupting** excusez-moi de vous interrompre; **to ~ and forget** pardonner et oublier.
II *v refl* **to ~ oneself** se pardonner.

forgiveness /fəˈgɪvnɪs/ *n* **1** (for action, crime) pardon *m*; **2** (of debt) annulation *f*; **3** (willingness to forgive) mansuétude *f*; **to be full of ~** être très indulgent.

forgiving /fəˈgɪvɪŋ/ *adj* [*attitude, person*] indulgent; [*climate, terrain*] clément; [*equipment*] robuste.

forgo /fɔːˈgəʊ/ *vtr* (*prét* **-went**, *pp* **-gone**) renoncer à [*opportunity, pleasure*].

forgot /fəˈgɒt/ *prét* ▶ **forget**.

forgotten /fəˈgɒtn/ *pp* ▶ **forget**.

fork /fɔːk/ **I** *n* **1** (for eating) fourchette *f*; **2** (tool) fourche *f*; **3** (division) (in tree) fourche *f*; (in river) fourche *f*; (on bicycle) fourche *f*; (in railway) embranchement *m*; (in road) bifurcation *f*; **to come to a ~ in the road** arriver à une bifurcation; **4** (in chess) fourchette *f*.
II *vtr* **1** (lift with fork) fourcher [*hay, manure, earth*]; **2** (in chess) fourcher [*opponent, chess-piece*].
III *vi* (also **~ off**) [*road, river, railway line, driver*] bifurquer; **you ~ to the left** vous bifurquez à gauche.

■ **fork out**○: ¶ **~ out** casquer○ (**for** pour); ¶ **~ out [sth]** débourser [*money*].

■ **fork over**: **~ [sth] over**, **~ over [sth]** **1** (turn over) retourner à la fourche [*hay, manure, garden*]; **2**○ US fig (hand over) **~ it over!** allez, allonge○!

■ **fork up** = **fork over**.

forked /fɔːkt/ *adj* [*twig, branch, tongue*] fourchu.

IDIOMS **to speak with ~ tongue** avoir la langue fourchue.

forked lightning *n* éclair *m* en zigzag.

forkful /ˈfɔːkfʊl/ *n* (of food) bouchée *f* sur une fourchette; (of hay) fourchée *f*.

forklift /ˈfɔːklɪft/ **I** *n* US = **forklift truck**.
II *vtr* soulever [qch] à l'aide d'un élévateur à fourche [*pallets*].

fork: **~lift truck** *n* GB chariot *m* élévateur à fourche; **~ spanner** *n* clé *f* plate; **~ supper** *n* buffet *m* (froid).

forlorn /fəˈlɔːn/ *adj* **1** (sad) [*child, appearance*] malheureux/-euse; [*place, landscape*] morne; [*sight, scene*] triste; **2** (desperate) [*attempt*] désespéré; **in the ~ hope of doing** dans le fol espoir de faire.

forlornly /fəˈlɔːnlɪ/ *adv* [*wander, search*] d'un air triste; [*echo*] tristement.

form /fɔːm/ **I** *n* **1** (kind, manifestation) (of activity, energy, exercise, transport, government, protest, work, substance) forme *f*; (of entertainment, taxation, disease) sorte *f*; **different ~s of life** ou **life ~s** différentes formes de vie; **it's a ~ of blackmail** c'est une forme de chantage; **some ~ of control is needed** un système de contrôle est nécessaire; **in the ~ of crystals/a loan** sous forme de cristaux/de prêt; **in a new/different ~** sous une nouvelle/autre forme; **to publish articles in book ~** réunir des articles dans un livre; **he won't touch alcohol in any ~** il évite l'alcool sous toutes ses formes; **to take various ~s** prendre diverses formes; **to take the ~ of a strike** prendre la forme d'une grève; **2** (document) formulaire *m*; **to fill in** ou **fill out** ou **complete a ~** remplir un formulaire; **blank ~** formulaire vierge; **3** (shape) forme *f*; **to take** ou **assume the ~ of a man/a swan** prendre la forme d'un homme/d'un cygne; **4** (of athlete, horse, performer) forme *f*; **to be in good ~** être en bonne or pleine forme; **to be on ~** être très en forme; **to return to ~** retrouver la forme; **to return to one's best ~** retrouver sa meilleure forme; **to study the ~** étudier le tableau des performances; **true to ~, she was late** fidèle à elle-même, elle était en retard; **5** Literat, Art (structure) forme *f*; (genre) genre *m*; **~ and content** la forme et le fond; **a literary ~** un genre littéraire; **theatrical ~s** formes du théâtre; **verse ~s** genres en vers; **the limitations of this ~** les limites de ce genre; **6** (etiquette) **it is bad ~** cela ne se fait pas (**to do** de faire); **purely as a matter of ~** purement par politesse or pour la forme; **I never know the ~ at these ceremonies** je ne sais jamais comment me comporter à ces cérémonies; **you know the ~** tu sais ce qu'il faut faire; **7** GB Sch classe *f*; **in the first/fourth ~** ≈ en sixième/troisième; **8** (prescribed set of words) formule *f*; **they object to the ~ of words used** ils ne sont pas d'accord avec la formulation; **9**○ GB (criminal record) **to have ~** avoir fait de la taule○ (**for** pour); **10** Ling forme *f*; **in question ~** à la forme interrogative; **11** (hare's nest) gîte *m*, forme *f*; **12** (bench) banc *m*.
II *modif* GB Sch [*captain, room*] de classe.
III *vtr* **1** (organize or create) former [*queue, circle, barrier, club, cartel, alliance, government, union, band*] (**from** avec); nouer [*friendship, relationship*]; former [*sentence, tense*]; **to ~ one's letters** former ses lettres; **please ~ a circle** s'il vous plaît, formez un cercle; **how are stalactites ~ed?** comment se forment les stalactites?; **to ~ part of sth** faire partie de qch; **to ~ a large part/the basis of sth** constituer une grande partie/la base de qch; **2** (conceive) se faire [*impression, image, picture, opinion, idea*]; concevoir [*admiration*]; **to ~ the habit of doing** prendre l'habitude de faire; **3** (mould) former [*child, pupil, personality, taste, ideas, attitudes*]; **tastes ~ed by television** des goûts formés par la télévision; **4** (constitute) former [*jury, cabinet, panel*]; **the 12 people who ~ the jury** les 12 personnes qui forment le jury.
IV *vi* (all contexts) se former.
V -formed (*dans composés*) **half-/perfectly-~ed** à moitié/parfaitement formé.

■ **form into**: **~ into [sth]** [*people*] former [*groups, classes, teams*]; **to ~ sth into**

Forms of address

Only those forms of address in frequent use are included here; titles of members of the nobility or of church dignitaries are not covered; for the use of military ranks as titles ▶ **1612**; *for letter formulae (openings and closings), and ways of addressing envelopes, see the* ***French correspondence*** *section.*

Speaking to someone

Where English puts the surname after the title, French normally uses the title alone (note that when speaking to someone French does not use a capital letter for monsieur, madame *and* mademoiselle, *unlike English* Mr *etc., nor for titles such as* docteur).

good morning, Mr Johnson	=	bonjour, monsieur
good evening, Mrs Jones	=	bonsoir, madame
goodbye, Miss Smith	=	au revoir, mademoiselle

The French monsieur *and* madame *tend to be used more often than the English* Mr X *or* Mrs Y. *Also, in English, people often say simply* Good morning *or* Excuse me; *in the equivalent situation in French, they might say* Bonjour, monsieur *or* Pardon, madame. *However, the French are slower than the British, and much slower than the Americans, to use someone's first name, so* hi there, Peter! *to a colleague may well be simply* bonjour!, *or* bonjour, monsieur; bonjour, cher ami; bonjour, mon vieux *etc., depending on the degree of familiarity that exists.*

In both languages, other titles are also used, e.g.:

hallo, Dr. Brown *or* hallo, Doctor = bonjour, docteur

In some cases where titles are not used in English, they are used in French, e.g. bonjour, Monsieur le directeur *or* bonjour, Madame la directrice *to a head teacher, or* bonjour, maître *to a lawyer of either sex. Other titles, such as* professeur *(in the sense of* professor*), are used much less than their English equivalents in direct address. Where in English one might say* Good morning, Professor, *in French one would probably say* Bonjour, monsieur *or* Bonjour, madame.

Titles of important positions are used in direct forms of address, preceded by Monsieur le *or* Madame le *or* Madame la, *as in:*

yes, Chair	=	oui, Monsieur le président
		or (*to a woman*) oui, Madame la présidente
yes, Minister	=	oui, Monsieur le ministre
		or (*to a woman*) oui, Madame le ministre

Note the use of Madame le *when the noun in question, like* ministre *here, or* professeur *and other titles, has no feminine form, or no acceptable feminine. A woman Member of Parliament is addressed as* Madame le député, *a woman Senator* Madame le sénateur, *a woman judge* Madame le juge *and a woman mayor* Madame le maire. *Women often prefer the masculine word even when a feminine form does exist, as in* Madame l'ambassadeur *to a woman ambassador,* Madame l'ambassadrice *being reserved for the wife of an ambassador.*

Speaking about someone

Mr Smith is here	=	monsieur Smith est là
Mrs Jones phoned	=	madame Jones a téléphoné
Miss Black has arrived	=	mademoiselle Black est arrivée
Ms Brown has left	=	madame Brown *or* (*as appropriate*) mademoiselle Brown est partie

(*French has no equivalent of* Ms.)

When the title accompanies someone's name, the definite article must be used in French:

Dr Blake has arrived	=	le docteur Blake est arrivé
Professor Jones spoke	=	le professeur Jones a parlé

This is true of all titles:

Prince Charles	=	le prince Charles
Princess Marie	=	la princesse Marie

Note that with royal etc. titles, only Ier *is spoken as an ordinal number* (premier) *in French; unlike English, all the others are spoken as cardinal numbers* (deux, trois, *and so on*).

King Richard I	=	le roi Richard Ier (*say Richard premier*)
Queen Elizabeth II	=	la reine Elizabeth II (*Elizabeth deux*)
Pope John XXIII	=	le pape Jean XXIII (*Jean vingt-trois*)

mettre qch en [*sentence, paragraphs, circle*]; séparer [qch] en [*groups, teams, classes*]; **to ~ objects into patterns** grouper des objets pour former des motifs.

■ **form up** [*people*] se mettre en rangs.

formal /ˈfɔːml/ *adj* **1** (official) [*agreement, announcement, application, complaint, enquiry, interview, invitation, protest, reception*] officiel/-ielle; **2** (not casual) [*language, register, style*] soutenu; [*occasion*] solennel/-elle; [*welcome, manner*] cérémonieux/-ieuse; [*clothing, outfit, jacket*] habillé; (on invitation) **'dress: ~'** 'tenue de soirée'; **'assistance' is a ~ word for 'help'** 'assistance' est plus soutenu que 'aide'; **he sounded very ~** il avait l'air très guindé pej; **~ teaching methods** méthodes traditionnelles d'enseignement; **3** (structured) [*logic, proof, grammar, linguistics, reasoning*] formel/-elle; **4** (in recognized institution) [*training*] professionnel/-elle; [*qualification*] reconnu; **he had no ~ education** il n'était jamais allé à l'école; **5** Literat, Art [*brilliance, symmetry, weakness*] formel/-elle.

formaldehyde /fɔːˈmældɪhaɪd/ *n* formaldéhyde *m*.

formal: **~ dress** *n* gen tenue *f* de soirée; Mil tenue *f* de cérémonie; **~ garden** *n* jardin *m* à la française.

formalin /ˈfɔːməlɪn/ *n* formol *m*.

formalism /ˈfɔːməlɪzəm/ *n* formalisme *m*.

formalist /ˈfɔːməlɪst/ *n, adj* formaliste (*mf*).

formality /fɔːˈmælətɪ/ *n* **1** (legal or social convention) formalité *f*; **to dispense with** ou **skip**○ **the formalities** se dispenser de formalités; **a mere ~, just a ~** une simple formalité; **customs formalities** formalités *fpl* de douane; **2** (formal nature) (of occasion, manner) solennité *f*; (of dress) caractère *m* habillé; (of room, layout, table setting) caractère *m* cérémonieux; (of language, register, style) caractère *m* soutenu; **with a minimum of ~** avec un minimum de cérémonie.

formalize /ˈfɔːməlaɪz/ *vtr* **1** (make official) officialiser [*arrangement, agreement, relations*]; **2** (in logic, computing) formaliser.

formally /ˈfɔːməlɪ/ *adv* **1** (officially) [*accuse, admit, announce, declare, end, notify, offer, recognize, withdraw*] officiellement; **2** (not casually) [*speak, write, address, greet, entertain, celebrate*] cérémonieusement; **to dress ~** s'habiller, mettre une tenue habillée; **he was not dressed ~ enough** sa tenue n'était pas suffisamment habillée.

format /ˈfɔːmæt/ **I** *n* **1** (general formulation) (of product, publication, passport, game) format *m*, présentation *f*; (of band, musical group) formation *f*; **the standard VHS ~** le format standard VHS; **available in all ~s: cassette, CD...** disponible sous toutes les présentations: cassette, compact...; **2** Publg (size, style of book or magazine) format *m*; **folio ~** format folio; **3** TV, Radio formule *f*; **a new ~ for quiz shows** une nouvelle formule pour les jeux télévisés; **4** Comput (of document, data) format *m*; **in tabular ~** sous forme de tableau; **standard display ~** mode *f* d'affichage standard.

II *vtr* (*p prés etc* **-tt-**) Comput formater.

formation /fɔːˈmeɪʃn/ **I** *n* **1** (creation) (of government, committee, alliance, company, crater, new word, character, impression, idea) formation *f*; (of friendship, relationship) établissement *m*; **2** (shape, arrangement) gen, Mil, Geol formation *f*; **to fly in ~** voler en formation; **in close/V-~** en formation serrée/triangulaire; **a cloud ~** une masse nuageuse.

II *modif* [*dancing, flying*] en formation.

formative /ˈfɔːmətɪv/ **I** *n* Ling formant *m*, élément *m* de formation.

II *adj* **1** [*period, influence, expérience*] formateur/-trice; **2** Ling [*element, affix*] de formation.

formatter /ˈfɔːmætə(r)/ *n* formateur *m*.

formatting /ˈfɔːmætɪŋ/ *n* formatage *m*.

former /ˈfɔːmə(r)/ **I** *n* **1 the ~** (the first of two) le premier/la première *m/f*, celui-là/celle-là *m/f*; **the ~ is simple, the latter is complex** celui-là est simple, celui-ci est complexe, le premier est simple, le dernier est complexe; **2** Aerosp couple *m*.

II *adj* **1** (earlier) [*era, life*] antérieur; [*size, state*] initial, original; **to restore sth to its ~ glory** rendre sa beauté première à qch; **of ~ days** ou **times** d'autrefois; **in ~ times** autrefois; **he's a shadow of his ~ self** il n'est plus que l'ombre de lui-même; **2** (no longer) [*leader, employer, husband, champion*] ancien/-ienne (*before n*); **3** (first of two) [*proposal, course, method*] premier/-ière (*before n*).

III -former (*dans composés*) GB Sch **fourth-~** ≈ élève *mf* de troisième.

formerly /ˈfɔːməlɪ/ *adv* **1** (in earlier times) autrefois; **2** (no longer) anciennement; **Mr Green, ~ with Grunard's** M. Green anciennement employé chez Grunard; **Mrs Vincent, ~ Miss Martin** Mme Vincent née Martin.

Formica® /fɔːˈmaɪkə/ **I** *n* formica® *m*.

II *modif* [*surface*] en formica®.

formic acid /ˈfɔːmɪk/ *n* acide *m* formique.

formidable /ˈfɔːmɪdəbl, fɔːˈmɪd-/ *adj* **1** (intimidating) redoutable; **2** (awe-inspiring) impressionnant.

formless /ˈfɔːmlɪs/ *adj* [*mass, object*] informe; [*novel, music, work*] mal construit.

form master, **form mistress**, **form teacher** *n* GB Sch ≈ professeur *m* principal.

form of address *n* formule *f* (de politesse); **what is the correct ~ for an archbishop?** comment doit-on s'adresser à un archevêque?

Formosa /fɔːˈməʊsə/ ▶ **1381** *pr n* Hist Formose *m*.

formula /ˈfɔːmjʊlə/ **I** *n* (*pl* **-lae** ou **~s**) **1** gen, Sci formule *f* (**for** de; **for doing** pour faire); **2** US (for babies) (powder) lait *m* en poudre; (also **~ milk**) lait *m* reconstitué.

II Formula *modif* Aut Sport **~ One/Two** de formule un/deux.

formulate /ˈfɔːmjʊleɪt/ *vtr* élaborer [*rules, plan, principles*]; formuler [*idea, design, reply, charge, bill, programme, policy*].

formulation /ˌfɔːmjʊˈleɪʃn/ *n* (of idea, reply, charge, bill) formulation *f*; (of principles, strategy) élaboration *f*.

fornicate /ˈfɔːnɪkeɪt/ *vi* forniquer.

fornication /ˌfɔːnɪˈkeɪʃn/ *n* fornication *f*.

forsake /fəˈseɪk/ *vtr* (*prét* **-sook**, *pp* **-saken**) sout abandonner [*person, home*]; renoncer à [*habit*].

forsaken /fəˈseɪkən/ *pp adj* abandonné.

forsook /fəˈsʊk/ *prét* ▶ **forsake**.

forsooth‡ /fəˈsuːθ/ *excl* foi d'animal!†.

forswear /fɔːˈsweə(r)/ *vtr* (*prét* **forswore**, *pp* **forsworn**) sout **1** (renounce) renoncer à [*claim, ambition, vice*]; **2** Jur (deny) nier [*knowledge, collusion*].

forsythia /fɔːˈsaɪθɪə, US fərˈsɪθɪə/ *n* forsythia *m*.

fort /fɔːt/ *n* fort *m*.
IDIOMS **to hold** ou US **hold down the ~** garder la maison, s'occuper de tout.

forte /ˈfɔːteɪ, US fɔːrt/ **I** *n* **1** (strong point) **to be sb's ~** être le fort de qn; **2** Mus forte *m inv*.
II *adj, adv* forte.

fortepiano /ˌfɔːteɪpɪæˈnəʊ/ ▶ 1481 *n* Mus Hist piano-forte *m inv*.

forth /fɔːθ/

■ **Note** *forth* often appears in English after a verb (*bring forth, set forth, sally forth*). For translations, consult the appropriate verb entry (***bring, sally***).
– For further uses of *forth*, see the entry below.

adv (onwards) **from this day ~** à partir d'aujourd'hui; **from that day ~** à dater de ce jour; ▶ **back, so.**

forthcoming /ˌfɔːθˈkʌmɪŋ/ *adj* **1** (happening soon) [*book, event, election, season*] prochain (*before n*); **2** (available) (*jamais épith*) disponible; **no information/money was ~ from the government** le gouvernement n'était pas disposé à fournir des informations/donner de l'argent; **the loan was not ~** le prêt n'a pas été accordé; **3** (communicative) [*person*] affable, ouvert; **to be ~ about sth** être disposé à parler de qch; **he wasn't very ~ about it** il n'était pas disposé à en parler, il était plutôt réservé à ce sujet.

forthright /ˈfɔːθraɪt/ *adj* [*person, manner*] direct; [*reply, statement*] sans détours; **in ~ terms** sans ambiguïté; **to be ~ in condemning/in pronouncing** condamner/prononcer sans ambiguïté.

forthwith /fɔːθˈwɪθ, US -ˈwɪð/ *adv* sout sur-le-champ; **to become effective ~** Jur prendre effet immédiatement.

fortieth /ˈfɔːtɪɪθ/ ▶ 1505 **I** *n* **1** (in order) quarantième *mf*; **2** Math (fraction) quarantième *m*.
II *adj* quarantième.
III *adv* [*finish*] en quarantième position.

fortification /ˌfɔːtɪfɪˈkeɪʃn/ *n* fortification *f* (**of** de).

fortify /ˈfɔːtɪfaɪ/ **I** *vtr* **1** fortifier [*person, place*] (**against** contre); **2** corser [*wine*]; **fortified wine** vin *m* doux, vin *m* de liqueur; **fortified milk/diet** lait/régime vitaminé; **fortified with vitamins** [*cereal etc*] vitaminé.
II *v refl* **to ~ oneself** se donner du courage.

fortissimo /fɔːˈtɪsɪməʊ/ *n, adj, adv* fortissimo (*m*).

fortitude /ˈfɔːtɪtjuːd, US -tuːd/ *n* détermination *f*.

Fort Knox /ˌfɔːtˈnɒks/ *pr n* Fort Knox *m*.
IDIOMS **as secure as ~** ≈ aussi sûr que les coffres de la Banque de France.

fortnight /ˈfɔːtnaɪt/ ▶ 1807 *n* GB quinze jours *mpl*, deux semaines *fpl*; **a ~'s holiday** quinze jours de vacances; **the first ~ in August** la première quinzaine d'août, les deux premières semaines d'août.

fortnightly /ˈfɔːtnaɪtlɪ/ GB **I** *adj* [*meeting, visit*] qui a lieu toutes les deux semaines; [*magazine*] publié toutes les deux semaines.
II *adv* [*publish, meet*] toutes les deux semaines.

Fortran /ˈfɔːtræn/ Comput **I** *n* fortran *m*.
II *modif* [*statement*] en fortran.

fortress /ˈfɔːtrɪs/ *n* forteresse *f*.

fortuitous /fɔːˈtjuːɪtəs, US -ˈtuː-/ *adj* sout fortuit.

fortuitously /fɔːˈtjuːɪtəslɪ/ *adv* sout fortuitement.

fortunate /ˈfɔːtʃənət/ *adj* [*person, coincidence, event*] heureux/-euse; **it was ~ for him that you arrived** heureusement pour lui que tu es arrivé; **to be ~ in sb/sth** avoir de la chance avec qn/qch; **to be ~ in doing** avoir la chance de faire; **to be ~ (enough) to do** avoir la chance or le bonheur de faire; **he is ~ in that he doesn't have to work** il a la chance or le bonheur de ne pas devoir travailler; **how ~ that...** quelle chance que... (+ *subj*); **we should remember those less ~ than ourselves** nous devrions garder à l'esprit ceux qui n'ont pas notre chance.

fortunately /ˈfɔːtʃənətlɪ/ *adv* heureusement (**for** pour).

fortune /ˈfɔːtʃuːn/ **I** *n* **1** (wealth) fortune *f*; **a small ~** une petite fortune; **to make a ~** faire fortune; **to spend/cost a ~** dépenser/coûter une fortune; **a man of ~** un homme riche; **to seek fame and ~** chercher fortune; **2** (luck) chance *f*; **to have the good ~ to do** avoir la chance or le bonheur de faire; **by good ~** par chance, par un heureux hasard; **ill ~** malchance *f*; **to tell sb's ~** dire la bonne aventure à qn.
II fortunes *npl* (of team, party, country) destin *m*; **the ~s of war** les hasards de la guerre.
IDIOMS **~ favours the brave** Prov la fortune sourit aux audacieux Prov; **~ smiled on us** la chance nous a souri.

fortune: **~ cookie** *n* US petit gâteau *m* sec (renfermant une prédiction); **~ hunter** *n* péj (man) coureur *m* de dot; (woman) croqueuse *f* de diamants○; **~-teller** *n* diseur/-euse *m/f* de bonne aventure; **~-telling** *n* divination *f*.

forty /ˈfɔːtɪ/ ▶ 1505, 971, 1096 *n, adj* quarante (*m inv*).
IDIOMS **to have ~ winks** faire un petit somme.

forty-niner *n* US Hist chercheur *m* d'or (*en Californie, pendant la ruée de 1849*).

forum /ˈfɔːrəm/ *n* (*pl* **~s** ou **fora**) gen, Antiq forum *m* (**for** de); **in an open ~** en débat ouvert.

forward /ˈfɔːwəd/ **I** *n* Sport avant *m*.
II *adj* **1** (bold) effronté; **it was ~ of me to ask** c'était assez effronté de ma part de demander; **2** (towards the front) [*roll*] avant *inv*; [*gears*] avant *inv*; **~ pass** (in rugby) en-avant *m*; **~ troops** Mil ligne *f* avant; **to be too far ~** [*seat, headrest*] être trop en avant; **3** (advanced) [*season, plant*] avancé; **how far ~ are you?** où en êtes-vous?; **I'm no further ~** je ne suis pas plus avancé; **we're not very far ~ yet** nous ne sommes pas encore très avancés; **4** Fin [*buying, delivery, market, purchase, rate*] à terme; **~ price** cours *m* à terme.
III *adv* **1** (ahead) **to step/leap ~** faire un pas/bond en avant; **to fall** ou **topple ~** tomber en avant; **to go** ou **walk ~** avancer; **to rush ~** se précipiter; **to move sth ~** lit, fig avancer qch; **'~ march!'** 'en avant, marche!'; **a seat facing ~** une place dans le sens de la marche; **a way ~** une solution; **there is no other way ~** il n'y a pas d'autre solution; **it's the only way ~** c'est la seule solution; ▶ **backward**; **2** (towards the future) **to travel** ou **go ~ in time** voyager dans le futur; **from this day ~** à partir d'aujourd'hui; **from that day** ou **time ~** à partir de ce jour-là, désormais; **3** (from beginning to end) **to wind sth ~** faire défiler qch en avance rapide [*cassette, tape*].
IV *vtr* **1** (dispatch) expédier [*goods*] (**to** à); envoyer [*catalogue, document, parcel*] (**to** à); **2** (send on) faire suivre, réexpédier [*mail*] (**to** à); **'please ~'** 'faire suivre, svp'.

forward defence *n* Mil défense *f* avancée.

forwarder /ˈfɔːwədə(r)/ *n* (of freight) transitaire *m*; (of mail) expéditeur *m*.

forwarding /ˈfɔːwədɪŋ/ *n* (of freight) transport *m*; (of mail) expédition *f*.

forwarding address *n* nouvelle adresse *f* (pour faire suivre le courrier); **to leave no ~** partir sans laisser d'adresse.

forwarding: **~ agent** *n* transitaire *m*; **~ charges** *npl* frais *mpl* d'expédition; **~ country** *n* pays *m* expéditeur; **~ instructions** *npl* indications *fpl* relatives à l'expédition; **~ station** *n* gare *f* d'expédition or de départ.

forward-looking *adj* [*company, person*] tourné vers l'avenir.

forwardness /ˈfɔːwədnɪs/ *n* (of child, behaviour) impertinence *f*.

forward planning *n* planification *f* à long terme.

forwards /ˈfɔːwədz/ *adv* = **forward** III; ▶ **backwards.**

Fosbury flop /ˌfɒzbrɪˈflɒp/ *n* Sport Fosbury *m*.

fossil /ˈfɒsl/ **I** *n* **1** Geol fossile *m*; **2** pej (person) fossile *m*.
II *modif* [*hunter, collection*] de fossiles; [*organism*] fossile.

fossil fuel *n* combustible *m* fossile.

fossilized /ˈfɒsəlaɪzd/ *adj* **1** lit [*bone, shell*] fossilisé; **2** fig [*thinking, system*] sclérosé.

foster /ˈfɒstə(r)/ **I** *adj* (*épith*) [*parent, brother, child*] adoptif/-ive (*dans une famille de placement*).
II *vtr* **1** (encourage) encourager [*attitude, spirit*]; promouvoir [*activity, image*]; **2** (cherish) entretenir [*hope, thought*]; **3** (act as parent to) prendre [qn] en placement [*child*]; **4** (place in care of) **to ~ sb with** mettre qn (en placement) dans [*family*].

foster care *n* **in ~** dans une famille de placement.

foster: **~ family** *n* famille *f* de placement; **~ home** *n* foyer *m* de placement.

fostering /ˈfɒstərɪŋ/ *n* (by family) prise *f* en charge d'un enfant placé; (by social services) placement *m* d'un enfant.

fought /fɔːt/ **I** *pret, pp* ▶ **fight.**
II -fought (*dans composés*) **close-~** serré; **hard-~** ardemment combattu.

foul /faʊl/ **I** *n* Sport faute *f* (**by** de; **on** sur); **sent off for a ~** éliminé pour faute; **cries of ~** fig des cris de protestation.
II *adj* **1** (putrid) [*place, slum, conditions*] répugnant; [*air, breath, smell*] fétide; [*water, stream*] putride; [*taste*] infect; **2** (grim) [*weather, day, atmosphere*] épouvantable; **to be in a ~ humour** ou **mood** être d'une humeur massacrante○; **to have a ~ temper** avoir un sale caractère; **it's a ~ job!** c'est une sale corvée!; **in fair weather or ~** qu'il pleuve ou qu'il vente; **3** (evil) [*person, act, crime, deed, treachery, creature*] odieux/-ieuse; **'murder most ~'** 'horrible assassinat'; **4** (offensive) [*language*] ordurier/-ière; **to have a ~ tongue** être grossier/-ière; **5** Sport (unsporting) déloyal.
III *adv* **to taste ~** avoir un goût infect.
IV *vtr* **1** (pollute) polluer [*atmosphere, environment, sea*]; souiller [*pavement, play area*]; **2** (become tangled) [*weeds, nets, ropes*] s'emmêler dans [*engine, propeller*]; **the propeller was ~ed by nets** des filets de pêche étaient emmêlés dans l'hélice; **3** (clog) bloquer [*mechanism, device*]; obstruer [*pipe, channel*]; **4** Sport (obstruct) commettre une faute contre [*player*]; **5** Naut (collide) heurter [*vessel*].
V *vi* **1** Sport commettre des fautes; **2** Naut **to ~ on** s'emmêler dans [*pulley, rocks*].
IDIOMS **to fall** ou **run ~ of sb** (fall out with) se brouiller avec qn; (lose favour) s'attirer le mécontentement de qn; **to fall ~ of the law** tomber sous le coup de la loi.
■ **foul out** (in baseball) être exclu (pour fautes personnelles).
■ **foul up**○ ¶ faire des erreurs or des bourdes○; ¶ **~ up [sth], ~ [sth] up 1** (bungle) ruiner [*plan, opportunity*]; abîmer [*system*]; **he always manages to ~ things up** il trouve toujours le moyen de tout louper○; **2** (pollute) polluer [*air, soil*].

foully /ˈfaʊlɪ/ *adv* [*treated, abused, slandered*] de façon scandaleuse; [*swear*] de façon extrêmement grossière.

foul-mouthed /ˌfaʊlˈmaʊðd/ *adj* péj grossier/-ière.

foul play /ˌfaʊlˈpleɪ/ *n* **1** (malicious act) acte *m* criminel; **2** Sport jeu *m* irrégulier; **several instances of ~** plusieurs irrégularités.

foul: **~-smelling** *adj* puant, nauséabond fml; **~-tasting** *adj* infect; **~-up**○ *n* cafouillage○ *m*.

found /faʊnd/ **I** *prét, pp* ▶ **find II, III**.
II *vtr* **1** (establish) fonder [*school, town, organization*]; **'~ed 1875'** 'fondé en 1875'; **2** (base) fonder (**on** sur); **to be ~ed on** [*society, philosophy, opinion, suspicion*] être fondé sur; **to be ~ed on fact** s'appuyer sur les faits; **3** Tech fondre [*metal, glass*].

foundation /ˌfaʊnˈdeɪʃn/ *n* **1** (base) (man-made) fondations *fpl*; (natural) base *f*; fig (of society, culture, belief) fondements *mpl* (**of, for** de); **to lay the ~s for sth** lit poser les fondations de qch; fig jeter les fondements de qch; **to rock** ou **shake sth to its ~s** lit fait trembler qch jusque dans ses fondations; fig ébranler qch jusque dans ses fondements; **2** fig (truth) **without ~** sans fondement; **there is no ~ in the report that** il n'y a aucun fondement dans le rapport selon lequel; **3** (founding) (of school, town, organization) fondation *f* (**of** de); **4** Fin (also **Foundation**) (trust) fondation *f*.

foundation: **~ course** *n* GB Univ année *f* de préparation à des études supérieures; **~ garment**† *n* (girdle) gaine *f*; (with bodice) combiné *m*; **~ stone** *n* Constr première pierre *f*.

founder /ˈfaʊndə(r)/ **I** *n* fondateur/-trice *m/f*.
II *vi* **1** (sink) [*ship*] sombrer (**on** sur); [*car, person*] s'embourber (**in** dans); **2** (fail) [*marriage*] être en difficultés; [*hopes*] s'en aller en fumée; [*career, plans, talks*] être compromis (**on** par).

founder: **~ member** *n* GB membre *m* fondateur; **Founder's Day** *n* GB Sch anniversaire *m* de la fondation; **~s' shares** *npl* GB Fin parts *fpl* de fondateur.

founding /ˈfaʊndɪŋ/ **I** *n* fondation *f*.
II *adj* fondateur/-trice.

founding father *n* fig père *m* fondateur; **the Founding Fathers** US Hist les pères *mpl* fondateurs (des États-Unis).

foundling‡ /ˈfaʊndlɪŋ/ *n* enfant trouvé/ enfant trouvée *m/f*.

foundry /ˈfaʊndrɪ/ *n* fonderie *f*.

foundry worker ▶ **1692** *n* ouvrier *m* fondeur.

fount /faʊnt/ *n* **1** littér source *f*; **2** Print fonte *f*.

fountain /ˈfaʊntɪn, US -tn/ *n* **1** (structure) fontaine *f*; **drinking ~** fontaine d'eau potable; **2** (spray) (of water) jet *m*; (of sparks, light) gerbe *f*.

fountain: **~head** *n* lit, fig source *f*; **~ pen** *n* stylo *m* (à encre).

four /fɔː(r)/ ▶ **1505**, **971**, **1096** **I** *n* quatre *m inv*; **to make up a ~** compléter un quatuor○.
II *adj* quatre *inv*.
IDIOMS **on all ~s** à quatre pattes; **to the ~ winds** aux quatre vents.

four-ball /ˈfɔːbɔːl/ *adj* (in golf) [*match*] par équipes de deux.

fourchette /ˌfʊəˈʃet/ *n* Anat fourchette *f* vulvaire.

four: **~-colour process** GB, **~-color process** US *n* Print quadrichromie *f*; **~-door** *adj* Aut [*model*] quatre portes; **~-engined** *adj* Aviat quadrimoteur; **~ eyes** *n* injur binoclard/-e○ *m/f* offensive; **~-flush** *vi* US (in cards) bluffer.

four-four time *n* Mus **in ~** à quatre-quatre.

four: **~-handed** *adj* Mus à quatre mains; (in cards) à quatre; **~-H club** *n* US club *m* d'activités rurales pour les enfants; **~-in-hand** *n* Equit attelage *m* à quatre chevaux; **~-leaf clover**, **~-leaved clover** *n* trèfle *m* à quatre feuilles; **~-legged friend** *n* ami *m* à quatre pattes; **~-letter word** *n* mot *m* grossier; **~-piece band** *n* (jazz) quartette *m*; (classical) quatuor *m*; **~-ply** *adj* [*wool*] quatre fils; **~-poster (bed)** *n* lit *m* à baldaquin; **~score** *n, adj*‡ quatre-vingts (*m*); **~-seater**○ *n* Aut voiture *f* quatre places; **~some**○ *n* quatuor○ *m*; **~some reel** *n* quadrille *m*.

foursquare /ˌfɔːˈskweə(r)/ **I** *adj* [*building, style*] cubique; [*account, attitude*] loyal; [*decision*] inébranlable.
II *adv* [*stand, place*] inébranlablement.

four-star /ˈfɔːstɑː(r)/ **I** *n* GB (also **~ petrol**) super(carburant) *m*.
II *adj* [*hotel, restaurant*] quatre étoiles.

four-stroke /ˈfɔːstrəʊk/ *adj* Aut [*engine*] à quatre temps.

fourteen /ˌfɔːˈtiːn/ ▶ **1505**, **971** **I** *n* quatorze *m inv*.
II *adj* quatorze *inv*.

fourteenth /ˌfɔːˈtiːnθ/ ▶ **1505**, **1150** **I** *n* **1** (in order) quatorzième *mf*; **2** (of month) quatorze *m inv*; **3** (fraction) quatorzième *m*.
II *adj* quatorzième.
III *adv* [*come, finish*] quatorzième, en quatorzième position.

fourth /fɔːθ/ ▶ **1505**, **1150** **I** *n* **1** (in order) quatrième *mf*; **2** (of month) quatre *m inv*; **3** (fraction) quatrième *m*; **4** Mus quarte *f*; **5** (also **~ gear**) Aut quatrième *f*.
II *adj* quatrième; **the moon is in its ~ quarter** la lune est à son dernier quartier.
III *adv* [*come, finish*] quatrième, en quatrième position.

fourth-class /ˌfɔːθˈklɑːs, US -ˈklæs/ **I** *adj* **1** US Post [*mail, matter*] non urgent; **2**○ pej [*citizen*] minable.
II *adv* US Post [*send*] en courrier non urgent.

fourth dimension *n* Phys, fig quatrième dimension *f*.

fourth estate *n* **the ~** la presse, le quatrième pouvoir.

fourthly /ˈfɔːθlɪ/ *adv* quatrièmement.

fourth-rate /ˌfɔːθˈreɪt/ *adj* péj [*job, hotel, film*] de seconde zone.

four-wheel /ˈfɔːwiːl, US -hwiːl/ *adj* Aut [*brakes*] quatre roues; [*drive*] à quatre roues motrices; **~ drive (vehicle)** quatre-quatre *m inv*, 4 x 4 *m inv*.

fowl /faʊl/ **I** *n* gen, Culin (one bird) poulet *m*; (group) volaille *f*; **the ~ of the air** Bible les oiseaux *mpl* du ciel.
II *vi* **to go ~ing** aller à la chasse au gibier à plumes.
IDIOMS **neither fish nor ~** ni chair ni poisson.

fowl: **~ing piece**† *n* fusil *m* (de chasse); **~ pest** *n* peste *f* aviaire.

fox /fɒks/ **I** *n* **1** (animal) renard *m* also fig; **2**○ US (attractive man or woman) canon○ *m*.
II *modif* (also **~ fur**) [*coat, hat*] en renard.
III○ *vtr* dérouter; **that's got me ~ed** GB ça m'a désarçonné.

fox: **~ cub** *n* renardeau *m*; **~ fur** *n* (skin) (peau *f* de) renard *m*; (coat) (manteau *m* en) renard *m*; **~glove** *n* digitale *f*; **~hole** *n* gen terrier *m* de renard; Mil trou *m* (creusé); **~hound** *n* fox-hound *m*; **~ hunt** *n* chasse *f* au renard; **~ hunting** *n* chasse *f* au renard; **~ terrier** *n* fox-terrier *m*.

foxtrot /ˈfɒkstrɒt/ **I** *n* fox-trot *m*.
II *vi* danser le fox-trot.

foxy /ˈfɒksɪ/ *adj* **1** (crafty) rusé; **2**○ (sexy) sexy.

foyer /ˈfɔɪeɪ, US ˈfɔɪər/ *n* Archit foyer *m*.

FPA *n*: *abrév* ▶ **Family Planning Association**.

fr Fin *abrév écrite* = **franc**.

Fr Relig *abrév écrite* = **Father**.

fracas /ˈfrækɑː, US ˈfreɪkəs/ *n* altercation *f*, accrochage *m*.

fraction /ˈfrækʃn/ *n* **1** gen, Math (portion) fraction *f* (**of** de); **2** (tiny amount) part *f* infime; **a ~ of what I need** une part infime de ce dont j'ai besoin; **to miss by a ~** manquer d'un cheveu; **to move a ~** bouger d'un rien; **a ~ higher/lower** un tout petit peu plus haut/plus bas.

fractional /ˈfrækʃənl/ *adj* **1** [*rise, decline, difference*] infime; **2** Math [*equation*] fractionnaire; **~ part** fraction *f*.

fractional: **~ currency** *n* Fin monnaie *f* divisionnaire; **~ distillation** *n* Chem distillation *f* fractionnée.

fractionally /ˈfrækʃənəlɪ/ *adv* légèrement.

fractionation /ˌfrækʃəˈneɪʃn/ *n* Biol fractionnement *m*.

fractious /ˈfrækʃəs/ *adj* [*person, personality*] grognon; [*situation, confrontation*] tendu.

fracture /ˈfræktʃə(r)/ **I** *n* gen, Med fracture *f*.
II *vtr* fracturer [*bone, rock*]; fig fissurer [*economy, unity*].
III *vi* [*bone*] se fracturer; [*pipe, masonry*] se fissurer.

fragile /ˈfrædʒaɪl, US -dʒl/ *adj* **1** (delicate) [*glass, structure, system, state*] fragile; **to feel ~** (physically) se sentir patraque○; (emotionally) être fragile; **2** (tenuous) [*link, hold*] ténu.

fragility /frəˈdʒɪlətɪ/ *n* fragilité *f*.

fragment **I** /ˈfrægmənt/ *n* (of rock, shell, music, manuscript) fragment *m*; (of china, glass) morceau *m*; (of food) miette *f*; **~s of conversation** bribes *fpl* de conversation; **to break into ~s** se briser en mille morceaux.
II /frægˈment/ *vtr* morceler [*organization, task*].
III /frægˈment/ *vi* [*party, system*] se fractionner (**into** en).

fragmental /ˌfrægˈmentl/ *adj* Geol détritique.

fragmentary /ˈfrægməntrɪ, US -terɪ/ *adj* **1** gen [*evidence, recollection, nature*] fragmentaire; **2** Geol [*material*] détritique.

fragmentation /ˌfrægmənˈteɪʃn/ *n* morcellement *m*.

fragmentation bomb *n* Mil bombe *f* à fragmentation.

fragmented /ˈfrægmentɪd/ *adj* [*account, argument, play*] décousu; [*group, civilization*] dispersé; [*job*] morcelé; [*system, world, rhythm*] fragmenté; **to become ~** se disperser.

fragrance /ˈfreɪgrəns/ *n* parfum *m*.

fragrance-free /ˈfreɪgrənsfriː/ *adj* non parfumé.

fragrant /ˈfreɪgrənt/ *adj* odorant; **~ memories** littér souvenirs enchanteurs.

fraidy-cat○ /ˈfreɪdɪkæt/ *n* US lang enfantin poule *f* mouillée○.

frail /freɪl/ *adj* **1** (delicate) [*health*] précaire; [*person*] frêle; **2** (fragile) [*hope, state*] précaire; **human nature is ~** la nature humaine est faible.

frailty /ˈfreɪltɪ/ *n* (of person, human nature) fragilité *f*; (of structure, health, state) précarité *f*.

frame /freɪm/ **I** *n* **1** (structure) (of building, boat, roof) charpente *f*; (of car) châssis *m*; (of bicycle, racquet) cadre *m*; (of bed) sommier *m*; (of tent) armature *f*; **2** (border) (of picture, window) cadre *m*; (of door) encadrement *m*; **3** fig (context) cadre *m*; **4** Anat (skeleton) ossature *f*; (body) corps *m*; **his huge/athletic ~** son corps énorme/athlétique; **5** (picture) Cin photogramme *m*; TV, Phot image *f*; **6** (for weaving) métier *m*; **7** (in snooker) (triangle) triangle *m*; (single game) manche *f*; **8** Comput (of transmitted data) bloc *m*; **9**○ (set-up) coup *m* monté; **to put sb in the ~** monter un coup contre qn.
II frames *npl* monture *f*.
III *vtr* **1** (enclose) lit, fig encadrer [*picture, photograph, face, view*]; [*hair*] encadrer [*face*]; **2** (formulate in words) formuler [*question, reply etc*]; **3** (devise) élaborer [*plan, policy*]; rédiger [*legislation*]; **4** (mouth) articuler [*words*]; **5**○ (set up) [*police*] monter une machination contre [*suspect*]; [*criminal*] faire porter les soupçons sur [*associate*]; **I've been ~d!** c'est un coup monté!
IV -framed (*dans composés*) **steel/timber-~d** [*house*] à charpente d'acier/de bois.

frame: **~ frequency** *n* Cin, TV fréquence *f* de trame or d'image; **~ house** *n* maison *f* à charpente en bois.

frameless /ˈfreɪmlɪs/ *adj* [*spectacles*] avec

monture à griffes; [*mirror, picture*] sans cadre.

frame line *n* Cin séparation *f* d'image.

frame of mind *n* état *m* d'esprit; **to be in the right ~ for sth/to do** être d'humeur pour qch/à faire; **to be in the wrong ~ for sth/to do** ne pas être d'humeur pour qch/à faire.

frame of reference *n* Math, Sociol, gen système *m* or cadre *m* de référence.

framer /ˈfreɪmə(r)/ ▶ 1692 *n* encadreur *m*.

frame: **~ rucksack** *n* sac *m* à dos à armature; **~ tent** *n* tente *f* à armature; **~-up**○ coup *m* monté.

framework /ˈfreɪmwɜːk/ *n* **1** lit structure *f*; **2** fig (basis) (of society, system) cadre *m*; (of agreement, theory) base *f*; (of novel, play) structure *f*; **legal/political/moral ~** cadre juridique/politique/moral; **a ~ for sth/for doing** un cadre pour qch/pour faire; **within the ~ of the UN/the constitution** dans le cadre de l'ONU/de la Constitution.

framing /ˈfreɪmɪŋ/ *n* **1** (of picture, photograph) encadrement *m*; **2** Cin cadrage *m*.

franc /fræŋk/ ▶ 1143 *n* franc *m*.

France /frɑːns/ ▶ 1131 *pr n* France *f*.

Franche-Comté ▶ 1273 *pr n* Franche-Comté *f*; **in/to the ~** en Franche-Comté.

franchise /ˈfræntʃaɪz/ **I** *n* **1** Pol droit *m* de vote; **universal ~** suffrage *m* universel; **2** Comm franchise *f*.
II *modif* Comm [*auction*] de franchises; [*business, chain*] franchisé; [*holder*] de franchise.
III *vtr* US (subcontract) franchiser [*product, service*].

Francis /ˈfrɑːnsɪs/ *pr n* Francis, François; **St ~ of Assisi** Saint François d'Assise.

Franciscan /frænˈsɪskən/ *n, adj* franciscain/-e (*m/f*).

franco /ˈfræŋkəʊ/ *adv* Comm franco; **~ domicile/frontier** franco domicile/frontière.

Franco+ /ˈfræŋkəʊ/ (*dans composés*) franco-.

francophile /ˈfræŋkəʊfaɪl/ *n, adj* francophile (*mf*).

francophobe /ˈfræŋkəʊfəʊb/ *n, adj* francophobe (*mf*).

francophone /ˈfræŋkəfəʊn/ *n, adj* francophone (*mf*).

frangipane /ˈfrændʒɪpeɪn/ *n* **1** Culin frangipane *f*; **2** = **frangipani**.

frangipani /ˌfrændʒɪˈpɑːnɪ/ *n* (*pl* **~** ou **~s**) (shrub, perfume) frangipanier *m*.

Franglais /ˈfrɑːŋgleɪ/ *n* franglais *m*.

frank /fræŋk/ **I** *adj* franc/franche (**about** en ce qui concerne); **to be perfectly ~,...** pour être tout à fait franc,...
II *vtr* Post affranchir [*letter, parcel*]; oblitérer [*stamp*].

Frank /fræŋk/ *n* Hist Franc/Franque *m/f*.

Frankfurt /ˈfræŋkfət/ ▶ 1818 *pr n* Francfort.

frankfurter /ˈfræŋkfɜːtə(r)/ *n* saucisse *f* de Francfort.

frankincense /ˈfræŋkɪnsens/ *n* encens *m*.

franking machine *n* machine *f* à affranchir.

Frankish /ˈfræŋkɪʃ/ **I** *n* Ling francique *m*.
II *adj* franc/franque.

frankly /ˈfræŋklɪ/ *adv* franchement.

frankness /ˈfræŋknɪs/ *n* franchise *f*.

frantic /ˈfræntɪk/ *adj* **1** (wild) [*activity, excitement, applause, rate*] frénétique; **2** (desperate) [*effort, struggle, search*] désespéré; [*shout, tone*] éperdu; [*person*] surexcité; **to be ~ with** être fou/folle de; **in a ~ state** dans un état de surexcitation; **to drive sb ~** rendre qn fou/folle.

frantically /ˈfræntɪklɪ/ *adv* **1** (wildly) [*wave, cheer*] frénétiquement; **2** (desperately) [*struggle, search*] désespérément.

frappé /ˈfræpeɪ/ **I** *n* US (frozen drink) boisson *f* glacée; (milkshake) milk-shake *m*.
II *adj* GB (*après n*) [*drink*] frappé.

fraternal /frəˈtɜːnl/ *adj* fraternel/-elle.

fraternity /frəˈtɜːnətɪ/ *n* **1** (brotherhood) fraternité *f*; **2** parfois péj (sharing profession) confrérie *f* also pej; **medical/banking ~** confrérie des médecins/des banquiers; **3** US Univ fraternité *f*.

fraternity pin *n* US Univ insigne *m* de fraternité.

fraternization /ˌfrætənaɪˈzeɪʃn, US -nɪˈz-/ *n* fraternisation *f* (**with** avec).

fraternize /ˈfrætənaɪz/ *vi* fraterniser; pej frayer (**with** avec).

fratricide /ˈfrætrɪsaɪd/ *n* fratricide *m*.

fraud /frɔːd/ **I** *n* fraude *f*; **computer/credit card ~** fraude informatique/sur carte de crédit.
II *modif* [*allegations, charge, claim*] de fraude; [*investigation, investigator*] sur une fraude; [*trial*] pour fraude.

Fraud Squad *n* GB Service *m* de répression des fraudes.

fraudulence /ˈfrɔːdjʊləns, US -dʒʊ-/ *n* **1** = **fraud**; **2** (of signature, figures) caractère *m* frauduleux.

fraudulent /ˈfrɔːdjʊlənt, US -dʒʊ-/ *adj* [*system, practice, dealing, use*] frauduleux/-euse; [*signature, cheque*] falsifié; [*statement*] faux/fausse; [*application, claim*] indu; [*gain, earnings*] illicite.

fraudulent conversion *n* Jur détournement *m*.

fraudulently /ˈfrɔːdjʊləntlɪ, US -dʒʊ-/ *adv* [*borrow, act*] frauduleusement.

fraught /frɔːt/ *adj* [*meeting, situation, atmosphere, relationship*] tendu; [*person*] accablé (**with** de); **to be ~ with** [*situation*] être lourd de [*danger, difficulty, etc*].

fray /freɪ/ **I** *n* sout **the ~** la bataille; **to enter** ou **join the ~** entrer dans la bataille.
II *vtr* **1** [*friction*] râper [*material*]; rogner [*rope*]; [*person*] effilocher [*material, rope*]; **2** fig (irritate) mettre [qch] à vif [*nerves*].
III *vi* [*material, rope*] s'effilocher; [*temper, nerves*] craquer○.
IV frayed *pp adj* [*material*] effiloché; [*nerves*] à bout; **tempers were ~ed** les gens s'énervaient.

frazzle○ /ˈfræzl/ **I** *n* **to burn sth to a ~** calciner qch; **to be worn to a ~** [*person*] être lessivé○.
II *vtr* **1** (burn) calciner; **2** mettre [qch] totalement à vif [*nerves*]; **to feel ~d** être lessivé○.

freak /friːk/ **I** *n* **1** (deformed person) lit, fig injur monstre *m*; **2** (strange person) original/-e *m/f*; **3** (unusual occurrence) aberration *f*; **a ~ of nature** une bizarrerie de la nature; **4**○ (enthusiast) mordu/-e○ *m/f*, fana○ *mf*; **he's a jazz/fitness ~** c'est un mordu○ du jazz/de la forme; **he's a religious ~** c'est un fanatique religieux; **5**† ○(hippy) hippie *mf*.
II *modif* [*accident, occurrence, weather, storm*] exceptionnel/-elle; [*variable*] aléatoire.
III○ *vi* (also **~ out**) (get upset) piquer une crise○.
■ **freak out**○: ¶ **~ out 1** (get angry) piquer une crise○; **2** (get excited) se défouler; **to ~ out on LSD** se défoncer au LSD; ¶ **~ [sb] out, ~ out [sb]** (upset) faire paniquer [qn].

freakish /ˈfriːkɪʃ/ *adj* **1** (monstrous) [*appearance, person, creature*] grotesque; **2** (surprising) [*event, success, weather*] exceptionnel/-elle; **3** (unusual) [*person, behaviour, clothes*] bizarre.

freak show *n* exhibition *f* de monstres.

freaky○ /ˈfriːkɪ/ *adj* bizarre.

freckle /ˈfrekl/ **I** *n* tache *f* de rousseur.
II *vi* [*person*] attraper des taches de rousseur; [*skin*] se couvrir de taches de rousseur.

freckled /ˈfrekld/ *adj* couvert de taches de rousseur.

Frederick /ˈfredrɪk/ *pr n* Frédéric.

free /friː/ **I** *n* (also **~ period**) Sch ≈ heure *f* de libre.
II *adj* **1** (unhindered, unrestricted) [*person, country, election, press, translation*] libre (*after n*); [*access, choice*] libre (*before n*); **to be ~ to do** être libre de faire; **to leave sb ~ to do** laisser qn libre de faire; **to feel ~ to do** ne pas hésiter à faire; **feel ~ to ask questions** n'hésitez pas à poser des questions; **'may I use your phone?'—'feel ~'** 'puis-je me servir de votre téléphone?'—'je vous en prie'; **feel ~ to make yourself a coffee** si tu veux un café, fais comme chez toi; **to break ~ of** ou **from** se libérer de [*influence, restriction*]; **to set sb ~ from** libérer qn de [*situation, task*]; **to set sb ~ to do** donner toute liberté à qn pour faire; **a school where children are allowed ~ expression** une école où les enfants peuvent s'exprimer librement; **there will be ~ movement of workers within the country** les ouvriers auront le droit de circuler librement dans les limites du pays; **I oiled the hinges to allow ~ movement** j'ai graissé les gonds pour faciliter le mouvement; **roadworks have restricted the ~ movement of traffic** des travaux ont réduit la fluidité de la circulation; **2** (not captive or tied) [*person, limb*] libre; [*animal, bird*] en liberté; **she grabbed it with her ~ hand** elle l'a saisi de sa main libre; **one more tug and the rope/my shoe was ~** un coup de plus et la corde/ma chaussure était dégagée; **to set [sb/sth] ~** libérer [*prisoner, hostage*]; rendre la liberté à [*animal, bird*]; **to pull a person/an animal ~** extirper une personne/un animal (**from, of** de); **to pull sth ~** dégager qch [*object, shoe*]; **to break ~** [*person, animal*] se libérer (de ses liens); **the boat broke ~ from** ou **of its moorings** le bateau a rompu ses amarres; **how did the parrot get ~?** comment le perroquet s'est-il évadé?; **they had to cut the driver ~ from his car** on a dû couper la tôle de la voiture pour dégager le chauffeur; **we managed to cut the rabbit ~** (from trap) nous avons réussi à libérer or dégager le lapin; **3** (devoid) **to be ~ from** ou **of sb** [*person*] être libéré de qn; **~ from** ou **of litter/weeds/pollution** dépourvu de déchets/mauvaises herbes/pollution; **he's not entirely ~ from** ou **of blame** il n'est pas tout à fait irréprochable; **a day ~ from** ou **of interruptions** une journée sans interruptions; **she was ~ from** ou **of any bitterness/hatred** elle n'éprouvait aucune amertume/haine; **I'm finally ~ from** ou **of debt** je suis enfin débarrassé de mes dettes; **to be ~ from** ou **of pain** ne pas souffrir; **this soup is ~ from** ou **of artificial colourings** cette soupe ne contient pas de colorants artificiels; **~ of** ou **from tax** Fin exonéré d'impôts; **~ of** ou **from interest** Fin sans intérêts; **4** (costing nothing) [*ticket, meal, delivery, sample*] gratuit; **'admission ~'** 'entrée gratuite'; **~ gift** Comm cadeau *m*; **she only came with us in the hope of a ~ meal/ride** elle nous a accompagnés dans le seul espoir de gagner or d'économiser un repas/trajet; **you can't expect a ~ ride** fig on n'a rien pour rien; **he's had a ~ ride** fig il n'a pas trop sué○ pour en arriver là; **5** (not occupied) [*person, time, morning, chair, room*] libre; **are you ~ for lunch on Monday?** es-tu libre lundi pour déjeuner?; **is this seat ~?** cette place est-elle libre?; **I'm trying to keep Tuesday ~ to go and see her** j'essaie de garder mon mardi libre pour pouvoir aller la voir; **'please leave** ou **keep this parking space ~ for disabled drivers'** 'stationnement réservé aux conducteurs handicapés'; **6** (generous, lavish) **to be ~ with** être généreux/-euse avec [*food, drink*]; être prodigue de [*compliments, advice*]; **they've always been very ~ with money** ils ont toujours dépensé sans compter; **to make ~ with sth** se servir généreusement de qch; **7** (familiar) familier/-ière; **he's too ~ in his manner** il a des manières trop familières; **to make ~ with sb** se permettre des familiarités avec qn; **8** Chem [*atom, nitrogen*] libre; **9** Ling [*form, morpheme*] non lié; [*vowel, stress*] libre.

III *adv* **1** (at liberty) [*run, roam*] librement, en toute liberté; **to go ~** [*hostage*] être libéré; [*murderer, criminal*] circuler en toute liberté; **the rapist walked ~ from the court** le violeur a pu sortir libre du tribunal; **2** (without payment) [*give, mend, repair, travel*] gratuitement; **buy two, get one ~** un produit de gratuit pour l'achat de deux; **children are admitted ~** l'entrée est gratuite pour les enfants.

IV for free *adv phr* [*give, mend, repair, work*] gratuitement; **I'll tell you this for ~**○ ça, je peux te le dire.

V *vtr* **1** (set at liberty) (from prison, captivity, slavery, chains, trap) libérer [*person, animal*]; (from wreckage) dégager; **to ~ sth from sth** dégager or libérer qch de qch; **to ~ sb from** libérer qn de [*prison*]; débarrasser qn de [*burden, prejudice*]; décharger qn de [*blame, responsibility*]; délivrer qn de [*oppression, anxiety, guilt*]; soulager qn de [*suffering, disease*]; **to ~ sth from state control** libérer qch du contrôle de l'État; **2** (make available) débloquer [*money, capital, resources*]; libérer [*person, hands*]; **early retirement ~d him to pursue his hobby** la retraite anticipée lui a donné toute liberté pour se consacrer à son passe-temps favori; **she wants to ~ ou ~ up some time for interviewing** elle veut se réserver un peu de temps pour des entretiens.

VI *v refl* **to ~ oneself** (from chains, wreckage) se dégager; **to ~ oneself from** se dégager de [*chains, wreckage*]; se libérer de [*control, restriction, influence*]; se débarrasser de [*burden*]; se décharger de [*blame, responsibility*]; se délivrer de [*anxiety, guilt*].

VII -free (*dans composés*) **smoke/oil/sugar/additive-~** sans fumée/matières grasses/sucre/additifs; **interest-~** Fin sans intérêt; **dust-~** exempt de poussière; ▶ **tax-free**, **lead-free**, **troublefree etc**.

IDIOMS **to give sb a ~ hand** donner carte blanche à qn (**in** pour); **to have a ~ hand** avoir carte blanche (**in** pour; **in doing** pour faire); **~ as a bird** ou **the air** libre comme l'air; **the best things in life are ~** dans la vie les meilleures choses sont gratuites; ▶ **country**, **lunch**.

free agent *n* **to be a ~** pouvoir agir à sa guise.

free: **~ alongside ship** *adj* franco long du bord; **~ and easy** *adj* gen décontracté; pej désinvolte; **~ association** *n* Psych association *f* libre.

freebie○, **freebee**○ /ˈfriːbiː/ **I** *n* (free gift) cadeau *m*; (newspaper) journal *m* gratuit; (trip) voyage *m* gratuit.

II *modif* [*object, meal, trip*] gratuit.

free: **~board** *n* franc-bord *m*; **~booter** *n* lit pilleur *m*; fig jouisseur/-euse *m/f*; **Free Church** *n* Église *f* nonconformiste; **~ city** *n* ville *f* libre; **~ climbing** *n* (in mountaineering) escalade *f* libre; **~ collective bargaining** *n* négociations *fpl* libres syndicats-employeurs.

freedom /ˈfriːdəm/ *n* **1** (liberty) liberté *f* (**to do** de faire); **~ of choice/of the press** liberté de choix/de la presse; **~ of action/of speech** liberté d'agir/d'expression; **~ of information** libre accès *m* à l'information; **~ of movement** gen liberté de mouvement; Tech (of part, screw etc) jeu *m*; **to give sb his/her ~** rendre sa liberté à qn; **2** (entitlement to use) **they gave us the ~ of their house while they were away** ils nous ont laissé le plein usage de leur maison pendant leur absence; **to give sb/receive the ~ of a city** nommer qn/devenir citoyen d'honneur d'une ville; **~ of the seas** liberté des mers; **3 ~ from** (lack of) absence *f* de [*fear, control, hunger, influence*]; (immunity from) immunité *f* contre [*fear, hunger, influence, disease*]; **to have** ou **enjoy ~ from** gen être à l'abri de [*war, famine, fear, hunger*]; **the new government promised ~ from hunger/from want to all its people** le nouveau gouvernement a promis d'affranchir toute la population de la faim/du besoin; **4** (ease of manner) aisance *f*.

freedom fighter *n* combattant *m* de la liberté.

free enterprise I *n* libre entreprise *f*.

II *modif* [*economy*] de marché; [*system*] basé sur la libre entreprise.

freefall /ˈfriːfɔːl/ **I** *n* chute *f* libre.

II free-fall *modif* [*bomb, racket*] nonguidé.

free: **~ flight** *n* vol *m* libre; **~-floating** *adj* [*object*] qui flotte librement; [*idea*] en l'air; [*emotion*] qui ne repose sur rien; **~-flowing** *adj* [*liquid*] coulant, qui coule librement; [*music, conversation*] coulant; [*idea*] qui vient librement.

Freefone®, **Freephone**® /ˈfriːfəʊn/ **I** *n* ≈ numéro *m* vert®.

II *modif* **~ service** ≈ numéro *m* vert®; **dial ~ 123** ≈ appelez le numéro vert 123; **dial ~ recovery service** appelez le numéro vert du service de dépannage.

free: **~-for-all** *n* mêlée *f* générale; **~hand** *adj, adv* à main levée; **~ hit** *n* coup *m* franc.

freehold /ˈfriːhəʊld/ **I** *n* pleine propriété *f*, propriété *f* foncière perpétuelle et libre; **to have the ~ of sth** avoir la pleine propriété de qch.

II *modif* [*property, tenancy, tenant, land*] en pleine propriété.

free: **~holder** *n* propriétaire *mf* foncier/-ière à perpétuité; **~ house** *n* GB pub *m* indépendant; **~ kick** *n* coup *m* franc; **~ labour** GB, **~ labor** US *n* main-d'œuvre *f* non syndiquée.

freelance /ˈfriːlɑːns, US -læns/ **I** *n* free-lance *mf*, travailleur/-euse *m/f* indépendant/-e.

II *adj* [*journalist*] free-lance; [*work*] en free-lance; **on a ~ basis** en free-lance.

III *adv* [*work*] en free-lance.

IV *vi* travailler en free-lance.

freelancer *n* = **freelance I**.

free: **~load**○ *vi* vivre en parasite; **~loader**○ *n* parasite *m*; **~ love** *n* amour *m* libre.

freely /ˈfriːlɪ/ *adv* **1** (without restriction) [*act, travel, sell*] librement; [*speak*] librement, franchement; [*breathe*] lit aisément; fig librement; (abundantly) [*spend, give*] sans compter; [*perspire*] abondamment; **to move ~** [*part of body*] bouger aisément; [*machinery*] jouer librement; [*person*] (around building, country) se déplacer librement; **to be ~ available** (easy to find) [*commodity, drug, help, information*] se trouver facilement; (accessible) [*information, education*] être ouvert à tous; **wine flowed ~** le vin coulait à profusion; **2** (willingly) [*admit, confess*] volontiers; **3** (not strictly) [*translate, adapt*] librement.

freeman /ˈfriːmən/ *n* (also **~ of the city**) citoyen *m* d'honneur d'une ville.

free market I *n* (also **~ economy**) économie *f* de marché; **in a ~** dans une économie de marché.

II *modif* [*forces, policy*] du marché; [*system*] de l'économie de marché.

free: **~ marketeer** *n* libéral/-e *m/f*, partisan *m* de l'économie de marché; **Freemason** *n* franc-maçon/-onne *m/f*; **Freemasonry** *n* franc-maçonnerie *f*.

free of charge, **FOC I** *adj* [*delivery, service, admission*] gratuit.

II *adv* [*mend, repair, replace*] gratuitement.

free: **~ on board**, **FOB** *adj, adv* GB franco à bord, FAB; US franco à destination; **~ on rail**, **FOR** *adj* franco wagon; **~ period** *n* ≈ heure *f* de libre; **Freephone**® *n, adj* = **Freefone**; **~ port** *n* port *m* franc.

freepost /ˈfriːpəʊst/ GB **I** *n* (also on envelope) port *m* payé.

II *modif* [*system, service, address*] dispensé d'affranchissement.

free: **~-range** *adj* [*hen, chicken, pig*] élevé en plein air; **~-range eggs** *npl* œufs *mpl* de poules élevées en plein air; **~ school** *n* école *f* privée spécialisée; **~ sheet** *n* journal *m* gratuit.

freesia /ˈfriːzɪə, US ˈfriːʒər/ *n* freesia *m*.

free speech *n* liberté *f* d'expression.

free spirit *n* **to be a ~** être très libre d'esprit.

free: **~-spirited** *adj* [*person*] libre d'esprit; [*character, outlook*] libre; **~-standing** *adj* lit [*lamp, statue, furniture, heater*] sur pied; [*cooker, bath*] nonencastré; fig [*organization, company*] indépendant; **Free State** *n* US Hist État *m* antiesclavagiste; **~stone** *n* pierre *f* de taille.

freestyle /ˈfriːstaɪl/ **I** *n* (in swimming) nage *f* libre; (in skiing) figures *fpl* libres; (in wrestling) lutte *f* libre.

II *modif* [*swimming, skiing, wrestling*] libre; [*race, event*] (in swimming) de nage libre; (in skiing) de figures libres; (in wrestling) de lutte libre.

freethinker /ˌfriːˈθɪŋkə(r)/ *n* libre penseur/-euse *m/f*.

freethinking /ˌfriːˈθɪŋkɪŋ/ **I** *n* (also **free thought**) libre pensée *f*.

II *adj* [*person*] libre penseur/-euse.

free: **~ throw** *n* (in basketball) lancer *m* franc; **~-throw line** *n* (in basketball) ligne *f* de lancer franc.

free trade I *n* libre-échange *m*.

II *modif* [*agreement, economist, movement*] de libre-échange; **~ zone** zone *f* franche.

free: **~ trader** *n* partisan *m* du libre-échange; **~ university** *n* US Univ *système d'enseignement universitaire par correspondance ouvert à tous*; **~ verse** *n* vers *m* libre; **~ vote** *n* ≈ vote *m* de conscience; **~ware** *n* Comput logiciel *m* gratuit; **~way** *n* US autoroute *f*.

freewheel /ˌfriːˈwiːl, US -ˈhwiːl/ **I** *n* Mech (of bicycle, vehicle) roue *f* libre.

II *vi* lit (on bike, in car) être or rouler en roue libre; fig [*person*] être insouciant.

freewheeler /ˌfriːˈwiːlə(r), US -ˈhwiːlə(r)/ *n* **to be a ~** être insouciant.

freewheeling /ˌfriːˈwiːlɪŋ, US -ˈhwiːlɪŋ/ *adj* [*person*] insouciant; [*style, imagination*] débridé; [*attitude, approach*] libre.

free will *n* **1** Philos libre arbitre *m*; **2** gen **to do sth of one's (own) ~** faire qch de son plein gré or de son propre chef.

freeze /friːz/ **I** *n* **1** Meteorol gelées *fpl*; **the big ~** les fortes gelées; **2** Econ, Fin (of credits, assets) gel *m* (**on** de); (of prices, wages) gel *m*, blocage *m*; **benefit/price/rent/wage ~** gel des allocations sociales/des prix/des loyers/des salaires.

II *vtr* (*prét* **froze**; *pp* **frozen**) **1** congeler [*food*]; [*cold weather*] geler [*liquid, pipes*]; **the lock was frozen** la serrure était gelée; **2** Econ, Fin bloquer, geler [*price, loan, wages, assets*]; **3** Cin arrêter [*frame, picture*]; **4** (anaesthetize) insensibiliser [*gum, wart, skin*]; **5** Comput figer [*window*].

III *vi* (*prét* **froze**; *pp* **frozen**) **1** (become solid) [*water, river, pipes*] geler; [*food*] se congeler; **to ~ to sth** être collé à qch par le gel; **2** (feel cold) [*person, room*] geler; **to be freezing to death** mourir de froid; **3** fig (become motionless) [*person, animal, blood*] se figer; **the smile froze on his face** son sourire s'est figé sur ses lèvres; **~!** pas un geste!; **to ~ with horror/surprise** se figer d'horreur/de surprise; **4** fig (become haughty) [*person*] devenir glacial.

IV *v impers* Meteorol geler; **it's freezing hard** il gèle dur.

IDIOMS **I can wait until hell ~s over** je peux attendre aussi longtemps qu'il faudra; **when hell ~s over!** jamais!

■ **freeze out**: **~ [sb/sth] out**, **~ out [sb/sth]** gen [*person*] tourner le dos à [*colleague, friend*]; Comm supplanter [*competitor, company*]; éliminer [qch] du marché [*goods*].

■ **freeze over** [*lake, river*] geler; [*window, windscreen*] se couvrir de givre; **the windscreen is frozen over** le pare-brise est couvert de givre.

French provinces and regions

Both traditional pre-Revolution regions and modern administrative regions usually take the definite article as in l'Alsace, la Champagne *etc.:*

I like Alsace	= j'aime l'Alsace
Champagne is beautiful	= la Champagne est belle

For names which have a compound form, such as Midi-Pyrénées *or* Rhône-Alpes, *it is safer to include the words* la région*:*

do you know Midi-Pyrénées?	= connaissez-vous la région Midi-Pyrénées?

In, to and from somewhere

There are certain general principles regarding names of French provinces and regions. However, usage is sometimes uncertain; doubtful items should be checked in the dictionary.

For in *and* to, *with feminine names and with masculine ones beginning with a vowel, use* en *without the definite article:*

to live in Burgundy	= vivre en Bourgogne
to go to Burgundy	= aller en Bourgogne
to live in Anjou	= vivre en Anjou
to go to Anjou	= aller en Anjou

For in *and* to *with masculine names beginning with a consonant, use* dans le*:*

to live in the Berry	= vivre dans le Berry
to go to the Berry	= aller dans le Berry

For from *with feminine names and with masculine ones beginning with a vowel, use* de *without the definite article:*

to come from Burgundy	= venir de Bourgogne
to come from Anjou	= venir d'Anjou

For from *with masculine names beginning with a consonant, use* du*:*

to come from the Berry	= venir du Berry

Regional adjectives

Related adjectives and nouns exist for most of the names of provinces and regions. Here is a list of the commonest:

Alsace	alsacien(ne)	Flandre	flamand(e)
Anjou	angevin(e)	Franche-Comté	franc-comtois(e)
Aquitaine	aquitain(e)	Jura	jurassien(ne)
Auvergne	auvergnat(e)	Languedoc	languedocien(ne)
Béarn	béarnais(e)	Limousin	limousin(e)
Berry	berrichon(ne)	Lorraine	lorrain(e)
Bourbonnais	bourbonnais(e)	Normandie	normand(e)
Bourgogne	bourguignon(ne)	Périgord	périgourdin(e)
Bresse	bressan(e)	Picardie	picard(e)
Bretagne	breton(ne)	Poitou	poitevin(e)
Cévennes	cévenol(e)	Provence	provençal(e)
Champagne	champenois(e)	Savoie	savoyard(e)
Charente	charentais(e)	Touraine	tourangeau(-elle)
Corse	corse	Vendée	vendéen(ne)
Dauphiné	dauphinois(e)	Vosges	vosgien(ne)

These adjectives mean of X, *as in the following (where* alsacien *stands for any of them):*

an Alsace accent	= un accent alsacien
Alsace costume	= le costume alsacien
the Alsace countryside	= les paysages alsaciens
Alsace traditions	= les traditions alsaciennes
Alsace villages	= les villages alsaciens

These words can also be used as nouns, meaning a person from X*; in this case they are written with a capital letter:*

a person from Alsace	= un Alsacien
an Alsace woman	= une Alsacienne
the people of Alsace	= les Alsaciens *mpl*

■ **freeze up** [*pipe, lock*] geler; [*window*] se couvrir de givre.

freeze: **~-dried** *adj* lyophilisé; **~-dry** *vtr* lyophiliser; **~ frame** *n* Cin, TV, Video arrêt *m* sur image.

freezer /ˈfriːzə(r)/ *n* **1** (for food storage) congélateur *m*; **2** US (ice-cream maker) sorbetière *f*.

freezer: **~ bag** *n* sac *m* pour congélateur; **~ compartment** *n* freezer *m*; **~ trawler** *n* chalutier *m* frigorifique.

freezing /ˈfriːzɪŋ/ **I** *n* **1** Meteorol zéro *m* (degré *m*); **below ~** en-dessous de zéro; **2** Fin, gen gel *m*; (of prices) gel *m*, blocage *m*.
II *adj* [*person*] (*jamais épith*) gelé; [*room, conditions, weather*] glacial; **I'm ~** je suis gelé; **it's ~ in here** on gèle ici; **~ fog** brouillard *m* givrant.

freezing cold I *n* froid *m* glacial.
II *adj* [*room, wind*] glacial; [*shower, water*] glacé.

freezing point *n* point *m* de congélation.

freight /freɪt/ **I** *n* **1** (goods) fret *m*, marchandises *fpl*; **2** (transport system) transport *m*; **air/rail/sea ~** transport aérien/ferroviaire/maritime; **3** (cost) (frais *mpl* de) port *m*.
II *modif* Comm [*company, route, service*] de transport; [*transport, wagon, train*] de marchandises; **~ traffic** circulation *f* des marchandises.
III *vtr* Comm [*person, company*] acheminer [*goods*].

freightage /ˈfreɪtɪdʒ/ *n* **1** (charge) frais *mpl* de transport; **2** (goods) fret *m*.

freight: **~ car** *n* Rail wagon *m* de marchandises; **~ charges** *npl* Comm frais *mpl* de transport; **~ collect** *adv* US Comm contre paiement à la livraison, port dû; **~ costs** *npl* frais *mpl* de transport.

freighter /ˈfreɪtə(r)/ *n* **1** Naut cargo *m*; **2** Aviat avion-cargo *m*.

freight: **~ forward** *adv* GB Comm contre paiement à la livraison, port dû; **~ forwarder**, **~ forwarding agent** ▶ 1692 *n* Comm transitaire *m*, transporteur *m*; **~ insurance** *n* assurance *f* du fret; **~liner** *n* Rail train *m* de transport de marchandises en container; **~ note** *n* lettre *f* de voiture; **~ operator** ▶ 1692 *n* Comm transporteur *m*; **~ terminal** *n* aérogare *f* de fret; **~ ton** *n* Meas tonneau *m* d'affrètement; **~ yard** *n* gare *f* de marchandises.

French /frentʃ/ ▶ 1486, 1402 **I** *n* **1** Ling français *m*; **2 the ~** (+ *v pl*) les Français.
II *adj* français.
IDIOMS **to take ~ leave** filer à l'anglaise; **pardon my ~** hum si vous me passez l'expression.

French: **~ Academy** *n* Académie *f* française; **~ bean** *n* haricot *m* vert.

French Canadian ▶ 1486, 1402 **I** *n* **1** (person) Canadien/-ienne *m/f* francophone; **2** Ling français *m* du Canada.
II *adj* [*person*] canadien/-ienne *m/f* francophone; [*accent*] franco-canadien/-ienne; [*town, custom*] du Canada francophone.

French: **~ chalk** *n* craie *f* de tailleur; **~ doors** *npl* US porte-fenêtre *f*; **~ dressing** *n* GB vinaigrette *f*; US sauce *f* mayonnaise; **~ fried potatoes** *npl* pommes *fpl* frites; **~ fries** *npl* frites *fpl*; **~ Guiana** ▶ 1163 *pr n* Guyane *f* française; **~ horn** ▶ 1481 *n* cor *m* (d'harmonie); **~ horn player** ▶ 1692 *n* corniste *mf*.

Frenchified○ /ˈfrentʃɪfaɪd/ *adj* francisé.

Frenchify /ˈfrentʃɪfaɪ/ *vtr* péj ou hum franciser.

French kiss○ *n* patin◑ *m*; **to give sb a ~** rouler un patin◑ à qn.

French: **~ knickers** *npl* culotte *f* flottante; **~ letter**○† *n* (contraceptive) capote *f* anglaise○; **~ loaf** *n* baguette *f*; **~man** *n* Français *m*; **~ marigold** *n* œillet *m* d'Inde; **~ mustard** *n* moutarde *f* douce.

French pleat *n* **1** Sewing pli *m* plat; **2** (hairstyle) (roll) chignon *m* banane; (pleat) natte *f* africaine.

French polish I *n* vernis *m* à l'alcool.
II *vtr* passer au vernis à l'alcool.

French: **~ poodle** *n* caniche *m*; **~ Revolution** *n* Révolution *f* française; **~ Riviera** *n* Côte *f* d'Azur; **~ seam** *n* couture *f* anglaise; **~-speaking** *adj* francophone; **~ stick** *n* baguette *f*; **~ toast** *n* pain *m* perdu; **~ West Africa** *pr n* Afrique *f* occidentale française; **~ window** *n* porte-fenêtre *f*; **~woman** *n* Française *f*.

frenetic /frəˈnetɪk/ *adj* [*activity*] fébrile, frénétique; [*life, lifestyle*] trépidant.

frenetically /frəˈnetɪklɪ/ *adv* frénétiquement.

frenzied /ˈfrenzɪd/ *adj* [*activity*] frénétique; [*passion, lust*] déchaîné; [*mob*] (happy) en délire; (angry) déchaîné; [*attempt, effort*] désespéré; **to make a ~ attack on sb** attaquer violemment qn; **to be the victim of a ~ attack** être attaqué par un forcené; **we had to make a ~ dash to the airport** hum on a dû rouler comme des fous○ pour arriver à l'aéroport.

frenzy /ˈfrenzɪ/ *n* frénésie *f*, délire *m*; **media ~** délire des médias; **to be in a state of ~** être exalté; **to drive** ou **rouse sb/sth to a ~** exciter qn/qch [*crowd*]; rendre qn fou/folle [*person*]; hum **cooking for ten reduces me to a state of ~** faire la cuisine pour dix me met dans tous mes états; **there is/was a ~ of activity** ça grouille/grouillait d'activité; **to be in a ~ of anticipation/joy/anxiety** être au paroxysme de l'impatience/la joie/l'angoisse.

frequency /ˈfriːkwənsɪ/ *n* (all contexts) fréquence *f* (**of** de); **in order of ~** par ordre de fréquence; **these incidents have been occurring with increasing ~** ces incidents sont de plus en plus fréquents.

frequency: **~ band** *n* bande *f* de fréquence; **~ distribution** *n* distribution *f* des fréquences; **~ hopping** *n* Telecom saut *m* de fréquence; **~ modulation** *n* modulation *f* de fréquence.

frequent I /ˈfriːkwənt/ *adj* **1** (common, usual) [*expression, use*] courant; **it's quite ~, it's quite a ~ occurrence** c'est très courant, cela arrive très souvent; **2** (happening often) [*attempt, change, departure, discussion, visit*] fréquent; **to make ~ use of sth** se servir souvent or fréquemment de qch; **to be in ~ contact with sb** être en contact régulier avec qn; **she's a ~ visitor to our house** elle vient souvent chez nous; **to be sb's ~ companion** accompagner souvent qn.
II /frɪˈkwent/ *vtr* fréquenter [*place, circle*].

frequentative /frɪˈkwentətɪv/ **I** *n* fréquentatif *m*.
II *adj* fréquentatif/-ive.

frequently /ˈfriːkwəntlɪ/ *adv* souvent, fréquemment.

fresco /ˈfreskəʊ/ *n* (*pl* **-oes**) fresque *f*.

fresh /freʃ/ *adj* **1** (not old) [*foodstuff*] frais/fraîche; **to look ~** avoir l'air frais; **to feel ~** être frais au toucher; **to taste ~** avoir un goût frais; **to smell ~** avoir une odeur fraîche; **eggs ~ from the farm** des œufs frais de la ferme; **flowers ~ from the garden** des fleurs fraîchement cueillies dans le jardin; **bread ~ from the oven** du pain frais sorti du four; **2** Culin (not processed) [*herbs, pasta, coffee*] frais/fraîche; **~ orange juice** jus d'orange pressée; **3** (renewed, other) [*clothes, linen*] propre; [*cigarette*] nouveau/-elle (*before n*); [*ammunition*] supplémentaire; [*information, evidence, supplies*] nouveau/-elle (*before n*); [*attempt, assignment, inquiry*] nouveau/-elle (*before n*); **a ~ coat of paint** une nouvelle couche de peinture; **a ~ glass of wine** un nouveau verre de vin; **to take a ~ look at sth** regarder qch d'un œil neuf; **to make a ~ start** prendre un nouveau départ; **4** (recent) [*cut, fingerprint, blood*] frais/fraîche; [*memory, news*] récent; **write it down while it is still ~ in your mind** écris-le tant que tu l'as tout frais à l'esprit; **the accident is still ~ in her memory** l'accident est encore tout frais dans sa mémoire; **5** (recently returned) **young people ~ from** ou **out of school** des jeunes à peine sortis de l'école; **to be ~ from a trip abroad** être tout frais débarqué d'un voyage à l'étranger; **6** (refreshing, original) [*approach, outlook, way*] (tout) nouveau/(toute) nouvelle (*before n*); **a ~ approach to the problem** une toute nouvelle approche du problème; **7** (energetic, alert) **to feel** ou **be ~** être plein d'entrain; **you will feel ~er in the morning** tu auras plus d'entrain demain matin; **8** (cool, refreshing) [*air, day, water*] frais/fraîche; **9** US○ (over-familiar) impertinent; **to be ~ with sb** être un peu familier/-ière avec qn; **to get ~ with sb** (sexually) prendre des libertés avec qn; **10** Meteorol **a ~ breeze** une bonne brise.

IDIOMS **to be ~ out of**○ être en panne de○ [*supplies etc*].

fresh air *n* air *m* frais; **to let in some ~** laisser entrer de l'air frais; **to get some ~** prendre l'air, s'oxygéner; **~ and exercise** le grand air et l'exercice; **they don't get enough ~** ils ne prennent pas assez l'air.

fresh-air fiend○ /ˌfreʃˈeə fiːnd/ *n* **1** (outdoor type) fana○ *mf* du grand air; **2** (liking ventilation) maniaque○ *mf* de l'air frais.

freshen /ˈfreʃn/ *vi* Meteorol **winds ~ing from the east** des vents d'est fraîchissants.
■ **freshen up** faire un brin de toilette.

fresher○ /ˈfreʃə(r)/ *n* GB Univ étudiant/-e *m/f* de première année; **~'s week** semaine *f* d'accueil des étudiants.

freshet /ˈfreʃɪt/ *n* **1** (stream) cours *m* d'eau; **2** (flood) crue *f* soudaine.

fresh-faced /ˌfreʃˈfeɪst/ *adj* au teint frais.

freshly /ˈfreʃlɪ/ *adv* [*cut, cooked, ground, picked*] fraîchement; [*painted*] fraîchement; **~ baked bread** du pain qui sort du four; **~ ironed sheets** des draps qui viennent d'être repassés; **~ washed, ~ laundered** qui vient d'être lavé, tout propre; **~ brewed coffee** du café qui vient d'être fait.

freshman /ˈfreʃmən/ *n* **1** Univ étudiant/-e *m/f* de première année; **2** US fig (in Congress, in firm) nouveau venu/nouvelle venue *m/f*.

fresh money *n* Fin argent *m* frais.

freshness /ˈfreʃnɪs/ *n* **1** (of produce, linen, paintwork) fraîcheur *f*; **2** (coolness) fraîcheur *f*; **3** (of skin, complexion) fraîcheur *f*; **4** (originality) originalité *f*, fraîcheur *f*; **the ~ of her approach** l'originalité de son approche.

fresh water I *n* eau *f* douce.
II **freshwater** *modif* [*fish, plant, lake*] d'eau douce.

freshwoman /ˈfreʃwʊmən/ *n* Univ étudiante *f* de première année.

fret /fret/ I *n* Mus frette *f*, touche *f*.
II *vtr* (*p prés etc* **-tt-**) chantourner [*wood, screen*].
III *vi* (*p prés etc* **-tt-**) **1** (be anxious) s'inquiéter (**over**, **about** pour, au sujet de); **don't ~** ne t'inquiète pas, calme-toi; **she has been ~ting all week** elle est dans tous ses états depuis une semaine; **2** (cry) [*baby*] pleurer, pleurnicher; **3** (pine) **he's ~ting for his mother** sa mère lui manque.
IV **fretted** *pp adj* [*screen*] chantourné; [*instrument*] avec frettes.

fretful /ˈfretfl/ *adj* [*child*] grognon; [*adult*] énervé, agité.

fretfully /ˈfretfəlɪ/ *adv* [*ask, speak*] avec énervement; **to pace ~ to and fro** faire nerveusement les cent pas; **to cry ~** pleurnicher.

fret: **~saw** *n* scie *f* à découper; **~work** *n* découpure *f*.

Freudian /ˈfrɔɪdɪən/ *n, adj* freudien/-ienne *m/f*; **my analyst is a ~** mon analyste est freudien.

Freudian slip *n* lapsus *m*; **to make a ~** faire un lapsus.

Fri *abrév écrite* = **Friday**.

friable /ˈfraɪəbl/ *adj* friable.

friar /ˈfraɪə(r)/ *n* frère *m*, moine *m*.

Fribourg ▶ **1818**, **1776** *pr n* Fribourg; **the canton of ~** le canton de Fribourg.

fricassee /ˈfrɪkəsiː/ *n* fricassée *f*.

fricative /ˈfrɪkətɪv/ I *n* fricative *f*, spirante *f*.
II *adj* [*consonant*] fricatif/-ive, spirant.

friction /ˈfrɪkʃn/ *n* **1** Phys friction *f*; **2** gen (rubbing) frottement *m*; **3** Ling friction *f*; **4** fig (conflict) conflits *mpl* (**between** entre); **there is growing ~ between management and workforce** il y a de plus en plus de conflits entre la direction et les employés; **there is a certain amount of ~ in any family** il y a toujours des conflits dans les familles; **this decision is bound to cause ~** cette décision va être cause de friction.

friction: **~-driven** *adj* [*toy*] à friction; **~ tape** *n* US ruban *m* isolant.

Friday /ˈfraɪdeɪ, -dɪ/ ▶ **1883** *n* vendredi *m*.

fridge /frɪdʒ/ *n* GB frigo○ *m*.

fridge-freezer /ˌfrɪdʒˈfriːzə(r)/ *n* réfrigérateur *m* avec congélateur.

fried /fraɪd/ I *pp* ▶ **fry II**, **III**.
II *pp adj* frit; **~ fish** poisson *m* frit; **~ food** friture *f*; **~ egg** œuf *m* au plat; **~ potatoes** pommes *fpl* de terre sautées.

friend /frend/ I *n* **1** (person one likes) ami/-e *m/f* (**of** de); **he's a ~ of my father's** c'est un ami de mon père; **to make ~s** se faire des amis; **to make ~s with sb** devenir ami/-e *m/f* avec qn; **to be ~s with sb** être ami/-e *m/f* avec qn; **they've been ~s for 15 years** ils sont amis depuis 15 ans; **to be the best of ~s** être les meilleurs amis du monde; **to be a good ~ to sb** gen être un véritable ami; (in crisis) être un soutien pour qn; **he's no ~ of mine!** ce n'est pas un ami!; **Rosie is a ~ of mine** Rosie est une amie; **the house belongs to a photographer ~ of his** la maison appartient à un photographe de ses amis; **we're just good ~s** nous sommes amis, c'est tout; **that's what ~s are for** c'est à ça que servent les amis; **let's be ~s!** (after quarrel) on fait la paix?; **who goes there? ~ or foe?** qui va là, ami ou ennemi?; **not forgetting our old ~ the taxman** iron sans oublier notre cher ami le fisc; **2** fig (supporter, fellow-member, ally) ami/-e *m/f*; **the party has many ~s in industry** le parti a des amis influents ou de nombreux alliés dans l'industrie; **the Friends of Covent Garden** les Amis de Covent Garden; **~s in high places** des amis influents; **3** fig (familiar object) ami *m*; **this book is an old ~** ce livre est un vieil ami.
II **Friend** *pr n* Relig Quaker *mf*, Ami/-e *m/f*.
IDIOMS **with ~s like him/her, who needs enemies?** avec des amis de ce genre, on n'a pas besoin d'ennemis; **a ~ in need is a ~ indeed** Prov c'est dans le besoin que l'on connaît ses vrais amis Prov.

friendless /ˈfrendlɪs/ *adj* sans amis.

friendliness /ˈfrendlɪnɪs/ *n* gentillesse *f* (**of** de).

friendly /ˈfrendlɪ/ I *n* Sport match *m* amical.
II *adj* [*person*] amical, sympathique; [*animal*] affectueux/-euse; [*behaviour, attitude, argument*] amical; [*smile*] (polite) aimable; (warm) amical; [*government, nation*] ami *inv* (*after n*); [*hotel, shop*] accueillant; [*match*] amical; [*agreement*] à l'amiable; **a ~ gathering** une réunion d'amis; **to be ~ with sb** être ami/-e *m/f* avec qn; **to get** ou **become ~ with sb** se lier d'amitié avec qn; **to be on ~ terms with sb** être en bons termes avec qn; **to be ~ to** être réceptif/-ive à [*new ideas*]; être bien disposé envers [*small firms, local groups*]; **to have a ~ relationship with sb** avoir de bonnes relations avec qn; **the people round here are very ~** les gens par ici sont très gentils; **he's very ~ with the boss all of a sudden** il est très copain○ avec le patron tout d'un coup; **we're ~ enough, but...** on s'entend assez bien, mais...; **let me give you some ~ advice** laisse moi te donner un conseil d'ami; **that's not very ~!** ce n'est pas très gentil!
III **-friendly** (*dans composés*) **environment-~/dolphin-~** qui ne nuit pas à l'environnement/aux dauphins; **user-~** d'utilisation facile, convivial; **child-/customer-~** adapté aux besoins des enfants/clients.

friendly fire *n* Mil euph feu *m* allié; **to be killed by ~** tomber sous le feu allié.

friendly: **Friendly Islands** ▶ **1381** *pr n* Tonga *m*, îles *fpl* des Amis; **~ society** *n* GB Insur mutuelle *f*.

friendship /ˈfrendʃɪp/ *n* (all contexts) amitié *f*; **to form ~s** se faire des amis.

Friends of the Earth, **FoE** *n* Amis *mpl* de la Terre.

fries○ /fraɪz/ *npl* US frites *fpl*.

Friesian /ˈfriːzjən, ˈfriːʒən/ *n* **1** (cow) frisonne *f*; **2** Ling = **Frisian**.

frieze /friːz/ *n* frise *f*.

frig /frɪg/ *v*: ■ **frig about**● faire l'imbécile.

frigate /ˈfrɪgɪt/ *n* frégate *f*.

frigging● /ˈfrɪgɪŋ/ *adj* foutu●.

fright /fraɪt/ *n* **1** (feeling of terror) peur *f*; (more sudden) frayeur *f*, effroi *m*; **to be paralyzed with ~** être paralysé par la peur; **she gave a cry of ~** elle a poussé un cri de frayeur or d'effroi; **to take ~** prendre peur, s'effrayer; **the horse took ~ at the noise** le cheval a été effrayé par le bruit; **the government took ~ at the increase in crime** le gouvernement a pris peur or s'est effrayé devant l'augmentation de la criminalité; **2** (shock) frayeur *f*, peur *f*; **to have** ou **get a ~** avoir peur; **to give sb a ~** faire peur à qn, effrayer qn; **it gave me such a ~** ça m'a fait une de ces peurs; **the accident gave him such a ~ that he'll be more careful in future** l'accident lui a causé une telle frayeur qu 'il n'est pas près de recommencer; **I had the ~ of my life!** j'ai cru mourir de peur!; **3**○ (person) épouvantail *m*, horreur *f*; **I look a ~!** quel épouvantail!, quelle horreur!; **doesn't he look a ~?** quel épouvantail!, quelle horreur!

frighten /ˈfraɪtn/ *vtr* [*person, situation*] faire peur à, effrayer; **~ sb into doing** faire tellement peur à qn qu'il finit par faire; **to ~ sb into submission** faire tellement peur à qn qu'il finit par se soumettre.
■ **frighten away**: **~ away [sb/sth]**, **~ [sb/sth] away** effaroucher.
■ **frighten off**: **~ off [sb]**, **~ [sb] off** chasser [*intruder*]; effaroucher [*rival, buyer, bidder*].

frightened /ˈfraɪtnd/ *adj* apeuré; **to be ~** avoir peur (**of** de; **to do** de faire); **to be ~ that** craindre que (+ *subj*), avoir peur que (+ *subj*); **to be too ~ even to look** avoir tellement peur qu'on n'ose même pas regarder; **to be ~ about what might happen/about losing one's job** redouter ce qui pourrait se passer/d'être au chômage; **to be ~ at the thought of doing** avoir peur à l'idée de faire; **I've never been so ~ in my life** je n'ai jamais eu aussi peur de ma vie; **he's a very ~ man** il a très peur. ▶ **death**, **wit**.

frightening /ˈfraɪtnɪŋ/ *adj* **1** lit (scary) [*monster, story, experience, accident*] terrifiant;

[*statistics*] effarant; **that story is ~** cette histoire me fait peur; **2** fig (alarming, disturbing) [*prospect, rate, speed*] effrayant, terrifiant; [*statistics, results*] effrayant.

frighteningly /ˈfraɪtnɪŋlɪ/ *adv* [*close, expensive, simple*] terriblement.

frightful /ˈfraɪtfl/ *adj* **1** (inducing horror) [*scene, sight*] abominable, épouvantable; **2**○ (terrible, bad) [*prospect*] terrible; [*possibility*] horrible; [*mistake*] épouvantable, terrible; [*headache*] affreux/-euse; **he had a ~ time of it** ça a été épouvantable pour lui; **he's a ~ bore** il est terriblement ennuyeux; **3**○ (expressing disgust) [*person, child*] épouvantable; [*decor*] affreux/-euse; **that wallpaper looks ~** ce papier peint est affreux or moche○; **that ~ woman!** cette femme détestable!; **4** GB (great) **this strike is a ~ nuisance** cette grève est vraiment dérangeante; **would it be a ~ nuisance for you to bring it round?** cela vous dérangerait-il beaucoup de l'apporter?; **it's a ~ shame** c'est vraiment dommage.

frightfully /ˈfraɪtfəlɪ/ *adv* GB terriblement; **we're going to be ~ late** nous allons être terriblement en retard; **he was ~ tired** il était terriblement fatigué; **I'm ~ sorry** je suis vraiment désolé; **it's ~ kind of you** vous êtes trop aimable; **I'm not ~ keen** ça ne m'emballe pas○.

frigid /ˈfrɪdʒɪd/ *adj* **1** Med [*woman*] frigide; **2** Geog [*zone*] glacial.

frigidity /frɪˈdʒɪdətɪ/ *n* **1** Med frigidité *f*; **2** fig froideur *f*.

frigidly /ˈfrɪdʒɪdlɪ/ *adv* [*reply, respond*] froidement.

frill /frɪl/ **I** *n* **1** Fashn (on dress) volant *m*; (on shirt front) jabot *m*; **2** Culin (on chop) papillotte *f*.
II frills *npl* **1** (on clothes, furniture) fanfreluches *fpl*; **2** (on car, appliance) options *fpl*; **this is the basic model, with no ~s** c'est le modèle standard, sans options; **give us a reliable system, with no ~s** donnez-nous un système fiable, nous nous passons du superflu; ▶**no-frills**; **3** (in writing, drawing) fioritures *fpl*.

frilled /frɪld/ *adj* [*garment, collar*] à volants.

frilly /ˈfrɪlɪ/ *adj* [*garment*] à froufrous; [*underwear*] avec des dentelles.

fringe /frɪndʒ/ **I** *n* **1** GB (of hair) frange *f*; **2** (decorative trim) frange *f*; **3** (edge) (of forest) lisière *f*, orée *f* (**of** de); (of town) abords *mpl*, périphérie *f* (**of** de); **to be on the ~ of the crowd** être au bord de la foule; **4** Pol, Sociol (group) frange *f*, élément *m*; **the extremist ~ of the movement** la frange extrémiste du mouvement; **5** Theat **the ~** théâtre *m* alternatif.
II fringes *npl* **on the (outer) ~s of the town** à la périphérie or aux abords de la ville; **on the ~s of society** en marge de la société; **he drifted around the ~s of showbusiness/ the art world** il traînait à la périphérie du monde du spectacle/ du monde artistique.
III *modif* **1** Theat [*theatre, performance*] alternatif/-ive; **2** Pol, Sociol [*group, activity*] marginal; **~ elements** marginaux *mpl*.
IV *vtr* **1** (put trim on) orner [qch] d'une frange [*curtains, cloth*]; **2** (form border) [*trees*] border [*field*].
V fringed *pp adj* **1** Fashn, Sewing [*garment*] à franges; **2** (edged) bordé (**with, by** de); **a lagoon ~d with palms** une lagune bordée de palmiers.

fringe benefits *npl* **1** (pensions, life or medical cover) avantages *mpl* sociaux; **2** (of job) avantages *mpl* en nature.

fringing reef *n* récif *m* frangeant.

frippery /ˈfrɪpərɪ/ *n* **1** ¢ (trivia) frivolités *fpl*; **2** (impractical item) frivolité *f*.

frisbee® /ˈfrɪzbiː/ *n* frisbee® *m*.

Frisian /ˈfrɪzɪən/ ▶**1486**, **1402** **I** *n* **1** (person) Frison/-onne *m/f*; **2** Ling frison *m*.
II *adj* frison/-onne *m/f*; **the ~ Islands** l'archipel *m* Frison.

frisk /frɪsk/ **I** *vtr* fouiller [*person*].
II *vi* [*lamb, puppy*] gambader.

frisky /ˈfrɪskɪ/ *adj* **1** (playful, high-spirited) [*puppy*] joueur/-euse; **2** (skittish) [*horse*] nerveux/-euse, chaud; **3**○ (sexy) **to be feeling ~** hum avoir envie de faire l'amour.

fritillary /frɪˈtɪlərɪ/ *n* **1** Bot fritillaire *f*; **2** Zool nymphalidé *m*.

fritter /ˈfrɪtə(r)/ *n* beignet *m*.
■ **fritter away**: **~ away [sth]**, **~ [sth] away** gaspiller [*money, resources, opportunities, time*]; **he ~s away his money on silly things** il gaspille tout son argent en bêtises.

fritz /frɪts/: **on the fritz** *adj phr* US en panne.

frivolity /frɪˈvɒlətɪ/ *n* (all contexts) frivolité *f*.

frivolous /ˈfrɪvələs/ *adj* **1** (not serious) [*person, attitude, comment, activity*] frivole; **2** péj (time-wasting) [*allegation, enquiry*] pas sérieux/-ieuse.

frivolously /ˈfrɪvələslɪ/ *adv* [*behave, spend money*] avec insouciance.

frivolousness /ˈfrɪvələsnɪs/ *n* frivolité *f*.

frizz /frɪz/ *vtr* friser [*hair*]; **to have one's hair ~ed** se faire friser les cheveux.

frizzle /ˈfrɪzl/ *vtr, vi* grésiller.

frizzy /ˈfrɪzɪ/ *adj* [*hair*] crépu; **~-haired** aux cheveux crépus.

frock /frɒk/ ▶**1703** *n* **1** Fashn robe *f*; **2** (of monk) bure *f*.

frock coat *n* redingote *f*.

frog /frɒg, US frɔːg/ **I** *n* **1** Zool grenouille *f*; **2** (on violin bow) hausse *f*.
II Frog○ *n* injur Français/-e *m/f*.
IDIOMS **to have a ~ in one's throat** avoir un chat dans la gorge.

frogman /ˈfrɒgmən, US ˈfrɔːg-/ *n* homme-grenouille *m*.

frog-march /ˈfrɒgmɑːtʃ, US ˈfrɔːg-/ *vtr* GB conduire [qn] de force.

frog: **~s' legs** *npl* cuisses *fpl* de grenouille; **~-spawn** *n* ¢ œufs *mpl* de grenouille.

frolic /ˈfrɒlɪk/ **I** *n* **1** (bit of fun) ébats *mpl*; **2** Theat, Cin (lively film) comédie *f*; (play) farce *f*.
II *vi* lit s'ébattre, gambader; fig faire la fête; **to ~ in the waves** batifoler dans les vagues.

from /frɒm, frəm/

■ **Note** When *from* is used as a straightforward preposition in English it is translated by *de* in French: *from Rome* = de Rome; *from the sea* = de la mer; *from Lisa* = de Lisa. Remember that *de* + *le* always becomes *du*: *from the office* = du bureau, and *de* + *les* always becomes *des*: *from the United States* = des États-Unis.
– *from* is often used after verbs in English (*suffer from, benefit from, protect from etc*). For translations, consult the appropriate verb entry (***suffer***, ***benefit***, ***protect*** etc).
– *from* is used after certain nouns and adjectives in English (*shelter from, exemption from, free from, safe from etc*). For translations, consult the appropriate noun or adjective entry (***shelter***, ***exemption***, ***free***, ***safe*** etc).
– This dictionary contains Usage Notes on such topics as nationalities, countries and continents, provinces and regions. Many of these use the preposition *from*. For the index to these Notes ▶**1919**.
– For examples of the above and particular usages of *from*, see the entry below.

prep **1** (indicating place of origin) **goods/paper ~ Denmark** de la marchandise/du papier provenant du Danemark; **a flight/train ~ Nice** un vol/train en provenance de Nice; **a friend ~ Chicago** un ami (qui vient) de Chicago; **a colleague ~ Japan** un collègue japonais; **people ~ Spain** les Espagnols; **where is he ~?** d'où est-il?, d'où vient-il?; **she comes ~ Oxford** elle vient d'Oxford; **a tunnel ~ X to Y** un tunnel qui relie X à Y; **the road ~ A to B** la route qui va de A à B; **noises ~ upstairs** du bruit venant d'en-haut; **to take sth ~ one's bag/one's pocket** sortir qch de son sac/sa poche; **to take sth ~ the table/the shelf** prendre qch sur la table/l'étagère; **~ under the table** de dessous la table; **2** (expressing distance) **10 km ~ the sea** à 10 km de la mer; **it's not far ~ here** ce n'est pas loin d'ici; **the journey ~ A to B** le voyage de A à B; **3** (expressing time span) **open ~ 2 pm until 5 pm** ouvert de 14 à 17 heures; **~ June to August** du mois de juin au mois d'août; **15 years ~ now** dans 15 ans; **one month ~ now** dans un mois, d'ici un mois; **~ today/July** à partir d'aujourd'hui/du mois de juillet; **deaf ~ birth** sourd de naissance; **~ the age of 8 he wanted to act** depuis l'âge de 8 ans il a toujours voulu être acteur; **~ day to day** de jour en jour; **~ that day on** à partir de ce jour-là; **4** (using as a basis) **~ a short story by Maupassant** d'après un conte de Maupassant; **~ life** d'après nature; **to grow geraniums ~ seed** planter des graines de géranium; **to speak ~ notes** parler en consultant ses notes; **to speak ~ experience** parler d'expérience; **5** (representing, working for) **a man ~ the council** un homme qui travaille pour le conseil municipal; **a representative ~ Grunard and Co** un représentant de chez Grunard et Cie; **6** (among) **to select** ou **choose** ou **pick ~** choisir parmi; **7** (indicating a source) **a card ~ Pauline** une carte de Pauline; **a letter ~ them** une lettre de leur part; **where did it come ~?** d'où est-ce que ça vient?; **where does he come ~?** d'où vient-il?; **an extract/a quote ~ sb** un extrait/une citation de qn; **to read ~ the Bible** lire un extrait de la Bible; **I got no sympathy ~ him** il n'a fait preuve d'aucune compassion à mon égard; **you can tell him ~ me that** tu peux lui dire de ma part que; **8** (expressing extent, range) **wine ~ £5 a bottle** du vin à partir de 5 livres la bouteille; **children ~ the ages of 12 to 15** les enfants de 12 à 15 ans; **to rise ~ 10 to 17%** passer de 10 à 17%; **it costs anything ~ 50 to 100 dollars** cela coûte entre 50 et 100 dollars; **everything ~ paperclips to wigs** tout, des trombones aux perruques; **~ start to finish**, **~ beginning to end** du début à la fin; **9** (in subtraction) **10 ~ 27 leaves 17** 27 moins 10 égale 17; **10** (because of, due to) **I know ~ speaking to her that** j'ai appris en lui parlant que; **he knows her ~ work** il la connaît du travail; **11** (judging by) d'après; **~ what she said** d'après ce qu'elle a dit; **~ what I saw** d'après ce que j'ai vu; **~ his expression, I'd say he was furious** étant donné la tête qu'il faisait, je pense qu'il était furieux; **~ the way he talks you'd think he was an expert** à l'entendre, on dirait un spécialiste.

frond /frɒnd/ *n* (of fern, seaweed) fronde *f*; (of palm) feuille *f*.

front /frʌnt/ **I** *n* **1** (forward facing area) (of house) façade *f*; (of shop) devanture *f*; (of cupboard, box) devant *m*; (of sweater) devant *m*; (of book, folder) couverture *f*; (of card, coin, banknote) recto *m*; (of car, boat) avant *m*; (of fabric) endroit *m*; **the dress buttons at the ~** la robe se boutonne sur le devant; **write the address on the ~ of the envelope** écrivez l'adresse au recto de l'enveloppe; **2** (furthest forward part) (of train, queue) tête *f*; (of building) devant *m*; (of auditorium) premier rang *m*; **at the ~ of the line/procession** en tête de la file/procession; **at the ~ of the house** sur le devant de la maison; **to sit at the ~ of the class** s'asseoir au premier rang de la classe; **he pushed to the ~ of the crowd** il s'est faufilé au premier rang de la foule; **face the ~!** regardez devant!; **I'll sit in the ~ with the driver** je vais m'asseoir devant, à côté du chauffeur; **there's room at the ~ of the coach** il y a de la place à l'avant du car; **from ~ to back of the house** du devant à l'arrière de la maison; **how long is the car from ~ to back?** la voiture fait combien de long?; **3**

Mil, Pol front *m*; **at the ~** au front; **4** (stomach) ventre *m*; **to sleep/lie on one's ~** dormir/se coucher sur le ventre; **to spill sth down one's ~** se renverser qch sur le devant; **5** GB (promenade) front *m* de mer, bord *m* de mer; **on the sea/river ~** au bord de la mer/de la rivière; **a hotel on the ~** un hotel en bord de mer or sur le bord de mer; **6** Meteorol front *m*; **7** (area of activity) côté *m*; **changes on the domestic** ou **home ~** Pol des changements côté politique intérieure; **there's nothing new on the wages ~** il n'y a rien de neuf côté salaires; **there are problems on the financial ~** il y a des problèmes sur le plan financier; **8** fig (outer appearance) façade *f*; **his cynicism is just a ~** son cynisme n'est qu'une façade; **to put on a brave ~** faire bonne figure; **to present a united ~** présenter un front uni; **9**○ (cover) couverture *f*; **to be a ~ for sth** servir de couverture à qch.

II *adj* **1** (facing street) [*entrance*] côté rue; [*garden, window, wall*] de devant; [*bedroom*] sur la rue; **2** (furthest from rear) [*tyre, wheel*] avant (*after n*); [*seat*] (in cinema) au premier rang; (in vehicle) de devant; [*leg, paw, tooth*] de devant; [*edge, panel*] avant (*after n*); [*carriage, coach*] de tête (*after n*); **in the ~ row** au premier rang; **go and sit in the ~ seat** va t'asseoir devant; **3** (first) [*page*] premier/-ière (*before n*); [*racing car, horse*] de tête; **4** (head-on) [*view*] de face (*after n*).

III **in front** *adv phr* (ahead) **who's in ~?** qui gagne?; **I'm 30 points in ~** j'ai 30 points d'avance; **the Italian car is in ~ on the tenth lap** c'est la voiture italienne qui mène au dixième tour.

IV **in front of** *prep phr* **1** (before) devant; **sit/walk in ~ of me** asseyez-vous/marchez devant moi; **in ~ of the mirror/TV/house** devant la glace/télé/maison; **2** (in the presence of) devant; **not in ~ of the children!** pas devant les enfants!

V *vtr* **1** (face) [*house*] donner sur [*river, sea*]; **2**○ (lead) être à la tête de [*band, company, party*]; **3** TV présenter [*TV show*].

VI *vi* **1** (face) **to ~ onto** GB ou **on** US [*house, shop*] donner sur [*sea, main road*]; **2** (serve as a cover) **to ~ for** [*person, organization*] servir de couverture à [*group*].

frontage /ˈfrʌntɪdʒ/ *n* **1** Archit (of house) façade *f*; (of shop) devanture *f*; **2** (access) **with ocean/river ~** avec accès direct sur la mer/rivière.

frontal /ˈfrʌntl/ **I** *n* Relig parement *m* d'autel; ▶ **full-frontal**.

II *adj* **1** (head-on) [*assault, attack*] de front (*after n*); **2** Anat [*lobe*] frontal; **3** Meteorol [*system*] frontal; **4** Cin, Phot [*lighting*] de face.

front bench /ˌfrʌntˈbentʃ/ **I** *n* GB Pol **1** (seats) rangs *mpl* du gouvernement; **the opposition ~** les rangs de l'opposition; **2** (members) députés *mpl* membres du gouvernement; **the opposition ~** les députés de l'opposition, porte-parole dans un domaine spécifique.

II **front-bench** *modif* [*spokesperson, politician, revolt*] du gouvernement.

front: **~bencher**○ *n* GB Pol (government) député *m* membre du gouvernement; (opposition) député *m* porte-parole dans un domaine spécifique; **~ cover** *n* couverture *f*; **~ door** *n* porte *f* d'entrée.

front-end /ˌfrʌntˈend/ Comput **I** *n* (also **~ processor**) ordinateur *m* frontal.

II *modif* [*processor, system*] frontal.

front: **~-end fee** *n* Fin frais *mpl* initiaux or de démarrage; **~-end load** *n* Fin, Insur frais *mpl* prélevés sur les premiers versements.

frontier /ˈfrʌntɪə(r), US frʌnˈtɪər/ **I** *n* lit, fig frontière *f*; **the ~s of science** les frontières de la science; **the ~ between France and Spain** la frontière franco-espagnole; **the wild ~** la frontière sauvage.

II *modif* [*town, zone*] frontière *inv* (*after n*), frontalier/-ière; [*controls*] de frontière, frontalier/-ière.

frontier: **~ post** *n* poste *m* frontière; **~sman** *n* homme *m* de la frontière.

frontispiece /ˈfrʌntɪspiːs/ *n* Print, Publg frontispice *m*.

front line /ˈfrʌntlaɪn/ **I** *n* **1** Mil front *m*; **troops in** GB ou **on** US **the ~** les troupes du front; **2** fig (exposed position) première ligne *f*; **to be in** GB ou **on** US **the ~** être en première ligne; **I don't want to be in the ~ when the complaints start** je ne veux pas que ce soit à moi que l'on vienne se plaindre; **3** Sport (in rugby) **the ~** les avants *mpl* première ligne.

II **front-line** *modif* **1** Mil [*troops, units*] de front; [*aircraft, positions*] de première ligne; **2** Pol [*area*] proche des combats; [*country, state*] frontalier/-ière avec un État en guerre.

Front line States *npl* Pol États *mpl* frontaliers avec l'Afrique du Sud.

front-loader○ /ˌfrʌntˈləʊdə(r)/ *n* machine *f* à laver à chargement frontal.

frontman /ˈfrʌntmən/ *n* **1** (figurehead) homme *m* de paille (**for** de); **2** (TV presenter) présentateur *m*; **3** (lead musician) leader *m*.

front: **~ matter** *n* Publg pages *fpl* liminaires; **~ money** *n* US acompte *m*; **~ office** *n* US (management) administration *f*, direction *f*.

front of house GB **I** *n* Theat foyer *m*.

II **front-of-house** *modif* [*staff, manager, duties*] du foyer.

front page **I** *n* (of newspaper, book) première page *f*; **the merger made the ~** Journ la fusion a fait les gros titres.

II **front-page** *modif* [*picture, story*] à la une○; **the ~ headlines** les gros titres, la manchette; **to be ~ news** faire les gros titres.

front-runner /ˌfrʌntˈrʌnə(r)/ *n* **1** Pol, gen (favourite) favori/-ite *m/f* (**in** de); **2** Sport *coureur qui aime se positionner en tête de course*.

front vowel *n* Ling voyelle *f* antérieure.

front-wheel drive, **FWD** **I** *n* traction *f* avant.

II *modif* **a ~ car** une traction avant.

frost /frɒst/ **I** *n* **1** (weather condition) gel *m*; **10° of ~** moins 10°, 10° au-dessous de zéro; **there may be a touch of ~ tonight** il pourrait geler cette nuit; **there's a touch of ~ in the air** l'air est glacial; **2** C (one instance) gelée *f*; **there was a hard ~** il a gelé dur; **3** (icy coating) givre *m* (**on** sur).

II *vtr* Culin glacer [*cake*].

III **frosted** *pp adj* **1** Cosmet [*nail varnish, eye shadow*] nacré; **2** (iced) [*cake*] recouvert de glaçage; **3** (opaque) [*glass*] dépoli, opaque; **4** (chilled) [*drinking glass*] givré.

■ **frost over**, **frost up** [*window, windscreen*] se couvrir de givre; **the windshield has ~ed over** le pare-brise est couvert de givre.

frostbite /ˈfrɒstbaɪt/ *n* gelures *fpl*; **to have** ou **get ~** avoir des gelures.

frostbitten /ˈfrɒstbɪtn/ *adj* gelé.

frosting /ˈfrɒstɪŋ/ *n* glaçage *m*.

frost-resistant /ˈfrɒstrɪzɪstənt/ *adj* [*variety, vegetable*] résistant au gel.

frosty /ˈfrɒstɪ/ *adj* **1** [*air, weather, morning*] glacial; [*windscreen, windowpane*] couvert de givre; **it was a ~ night/day** il gelait cette nuit-là/ce jour-là; **it has been a ~ night** il a gelé cette nuit; **tomorrow will start ~** demain il y aura des gelées matinales; **we're in for a spell of ~ weather** nous entrons dans une période de grand froid; **2** fig [*smile, atmosphere, reception*] glacial.

froth /frɒθ, US frɔːθ/ **I** *n* **1** (foam) (on beer, champagne) mousse *f*; (on water) écume *f*; (around the mouth) écume *f*; **2** ₵ fig (trivia) futilités *fpl*.

II *vi* [*water, liquid*] écumer; **the beer ~ed over the edge of the glass** la mousse de la bière a débordé du verre; **to ~ at the mouth** lit écumer; fig écumer or baver de rage.

frothy /ˈfrɒθɪ, US ˈfrɔːθɪ/ *adj* **1** (foamy) [*beer*] mousseux/-euse; [*coffee, liquid*] mousseux/-euse, écumeux/-euse; [*surface of sea, weir*] écumeux/-euse; **2** (lacy) [*lingerie*] léger/-ère, vaporeux/-euse.

frown /fraʊn/ **I** *n* froncement *m* de sourcils; **a worried ~** un froncement de sourcils inquiet; **to reply/say with a ~** répondre/dire en fronçant les sourcils.

II *vi* froncer les sourcils; **to ~ at sb** regarder qn en fronçant les sourcils; **he ~ed at the bad news/interruption** la mauvaise nouvelle/l'interruption lui a fait froncer les sourcils.

■ **frown on**, **frown upon**: **~ on** ou **upon [sth]** désapprouver, critiquer [*behaviour, activity, attitude*]; **to be ~ed upon** [*behaviour, dress*] être mal vu.

frowning /ˈfraʊnɪŋ/ *adj* **1** [*face*] renfrogné, sombre; **2** littér [*cliff, crag*] menaçant.

frowsy /ˈfraʊzɪ/ *adj* [*person*] sale, peu soigné; [*room, atmosphere*] qui sent or sentait le renfermé.

froze /frəʊz/ *prét* ▶ **freeze** II, III.

frozen /ˈfrəʊzn/ **I** *pp* ▶ **freeze II, III**.

II *adj* **1** [*lake, ground, person, fingers, pipe*] gelé; **I'm ~** je suis gelé; **to be ~ stiff** ou **to the bone** être transi de froid; **the ~ North** le Grand Nord; **2** fig **to be ~ with fear** être paralysé par la peur; **to be ~ to the spot** être cloué sur place; **3** Culin [*vegetables, meat etc*] (bought) surgelé; (home-prepared) congelé; **4** Fin, Econ [*prices, assets, capital*] bloqué, gelé.

FRS *n* (*abrév* = **Fellow of the Royal Society**) membre *m* de la Royal Society.

fructification /ˌfrʌktɪfɪˈkeɪʃn/ *n* Bot, littér fructification *f*.

fructify /ˈfrʌktɪfaɪ/ *vi* Bot, littér fructifier.

frugal /ˈfruːgl/ *adj* [*person*] économe (**with** de); [*life, lifestyle*] frugal; [*meal*] simple, frugal.

frugality /fruːˈgæləti/ *n* frugalité *f*.

frugally /ˈfruːgəlɪ/ *adv* [*live*] frugalement, simplement; [*manage, stock*] avec parcimonie.

fruit /fruːt/ **I** *n* (*pl* (for collective) **~**) **1** Bot (edible, inedible) fruit *m*; **a piece of ~** un fruit; **have some ~** prenez un fruit or des fruits; **to be in ~** [*tree, plant*] porter des fruits; **to bear ~** [*tree, plant*] donner des fruits; **the ~s of the earth** littér les fruits de la terre; **2** fig fruit *m*; **to enjoy the ~(s) of one's labours/of victory** jouir des fruits de son travail/de la victoire; **her efforts finally bore ~** ses efforts ont finalement porté leurs fruits; **the ~ of their union** littér le fruit de leur union; **3**◑ US injur pédé◑ *m*.

II *vi* [*tree, plant*] donner des fruits.

fruit bowl *n* (large) coupe *f* à fruits; (individual) coupelle *f* à fruits.

fruit cake *n* **1** Culin cake *m*; **2**○ hum **he's a ~** il est cinglé○.

IDIOMS **to be as nutty as a ~** être complètement cinglé○.

fruit: **~ cocktail** *n* Culin macédoine *f* de fruits; **~ cup** *n* cocktail *m* de fruits; **~ dish** *n* compotier *m*, coupe *f* à fruits; **~ drop** *n* bonbon *m* (aromatisé) aux fruits.

fruiterer† /ˈfruːtərə(r)/ *n* **▶ 1692** marchand/-e *m/f* de fruits.

fruit farm *n* (place) exploitation *f* (*spécialisée dans la production de fruits*); **he runs a ~** il est producteur de fruits.

fruit: **~ farmer** **▶ 1692** *n* producteur/-trice *m/f* de fruits; **~ farming** *n* culture *f* fruitière; **~ fly** *n* drosophile *f*, mouche *f* du vinaigre.

fruitful /ˈfruːtfl/ *adj* **1** fig [*partnership, relationship, discussion, years*] fructueux/-euse; [*source*] fertile; **this is not a ~ line of enquiry** cette piste ne nous mènera nulle part; **2** littér [*earth*] fertile, fécond.

fruitfully /ˈfruːtfəlɪ/ *adv* **1** (with positive results) [*teach*] avec succès; **2** (usefully) [*spend time*] de façon fructueuse.

fruitfulness /ˈfruːtflnɪs/ *n* **1** littér (of earth) fécondité *f*; **2** fig (of approach, line of questioning) utilité *f*.

fruit gum *n* ≈ pastille *f*, bonbon *m* aux fruits.

fruition /fruːˈɪʃn/ *n* **to come to ~** se réaliser; **to be close to ~** être sur le point de se réaliser; **to bring sth to ~** (effect) réaliser qch; (conclude) concrétiser qch.

fruit knife *n* couteau *m* à fruits.

fruitless /ˈfruːtlɪs/ *adj* [*attempt, search, trip*] vain; [*discussion*] stérile.

fruit: **~ machine** *n* machine *f* à sous; **~ salad** *n* salade *f* de fruits; **~s of the forest** *npl* fruits *mpl* de la forêt; **~ tree** *n* arbre *m* fruitier.

fruity /ˈfruːtɪ/ *adj* **1** (flavoured) [*wine, fragrance, olive oil*] fruité; **2** (mellow) [*voice, tone*] timbré; **3** (salacious) [*joke*] salé; **4**○ US (crazy) dingue○.

frump /frʌmp/ *n* péj femme *f* mal fagotée.

frumpish /ˈfrʌmpɪʃ/ *adj* péj [*woman*] mal fagoté.

frustrate /frʌˈstreɪt, US ˈfrʌstreɪt/ *vtr* **1** (irk, annoy) énerver [*person*]; **it really ~s me having to wait so long!** c'est vraiment énervant de devoir attendre si longtemps!; **2** (thwart) réduire [qch] à néant [*effort*]; contrarier [*plan, project*]; entraver [*attempt, move*].

frustrated /frʌˈstreɪtɪd, US ˈfrʌst-/ *adj* **1** (irritated) énervé; **a ~ President told reporters...** journ c'est un Président énervé qui a dit aux journalistes...; **to become ~ at sth** s'énerver de qch; **I'm so ~, my work is going really badly** le travail va mal, ça m'énerve; **2** (unfulfilled in aspirations) [*person*] frustré; [*desire, urge*] inassouvi; **why stay in a job where you feel so ~?** pourquoi restes-tu à un poste qui est si frustrant pour toi?; **3** (thwarted) [*plan*] contrarié; [*effort*] réduit à néant; [*attempt*] vain; **4** (would-be) **a ~ diplomat** un diplomate manqué; **5** (sexually) frustré.

frustrating /frʌˈstreɪtɪŋ, US ˈfrʌst-/ *adj* **1** (irritating) énervant; **you locked yourself out? how ~!** vous vous êtes fermé dehors? comme c'est énervant!; **there's nothing more ~!** il n'y a rien de plus énervant!; **2** (unsatisfactory, thwarting) [*morning, situation*] frustrant; **it was a ~ experience** c'était frustrant; **it is ~ to be unable** ou **not being able to do** c'est frustrant de ne pas pouvoir faire.

frustratingly /frʌˈstreɪtɪŋlɪ, US ˈfrʌst-/ *adv* [*difficult, elusive*] désespérément; **I find my spare time is ~ short** je trouve que j'ai désespérément peu de temps libre; **~, my team lost** à ma grande déception, mon équipe a perdu.

frustration /frʌˈstreɪʃn/ *n* **1** (thwarted feeling) frustration *f* (**at, with** quant à); **to feel anger and ~** se sentir en colère et frustré; **in ~, he...** frustré, il...; **to seethe with ~** être très contrarié; **the delay has caused ~** le retard a mis tout le monde sur les nerfs; **2** (annoying aspect) **one ~ of watching sport on television is that** ce qui est frustrant dans le sport à la télévision, c'est que; **the ~s of house-buying are endless** acheter une maison est une entreprise longue et frustrante; **3** (ruination) anéantissement *m*; **the ~ of all my hopes** l'anéantissement de tous mes espoirs; **4** (sexual) frustration *f*.

fry /fraɪ/ **I** *n* **1** Zool (+ *v pl*) fretin *m*; **2** fig **small ~** (+ *v pl*) (children) loupiots○ *mpl*, mioches○ *mpl*; (unimportant people) menu fretin *m*.

II *vtr* (*prét, pp* **fried**) Culin faire frire.

III *vi* (*prét, pp* **fried**) Culin frire; **there's a smell of ~ing** ça sent la friture.

IV fried *pp adj* frit; **fried fish** poisson *m* frit; **fried eggs** œufs *mpl* au plat; **fried food** friture *f*; **fried potatoes** pommes *fpl* de terre sautées.

frying pan GB *n* poêle *f* (à frire).

IDIOMS **to jump out of the ~ into the fire** tomber de Charybde en Scylla.

fry-up /ˈfraɪʌp/ *n* GB *repas constitué d'aliments cuits à la poêle.*

ft *abrév écrite* = **foot, feet**.

FTSE 100 *n* (*abrév* = **Financial Times Stock Exchange Index**) indice *m* de la Bourse de Londres.

fuchsia /ˈfjuːʃə/ *n* fuchsia *m*.

fuck● /fʌk/ **I** *n* **1** (act) baise● *f*; **to have a ~** baiser●; **2** (person) **to be a good ~** bien baiser●, être un bon coup●.

II *excl* merde●!, putain de merde●!; **~ you!** va te faire foutre●; **what the ~ is he doing here?** qu'est-ce qu'il fout◑ ici?

III *vtr* baiser●, coucher avec○ [*person*].

IV *vi* baiser●.

IDIOMS **I'm ~ed● if I know, ~ knows●!** je n'en sais foutre◑ rien!; **it's ~ed●** (broken) c'est foutu○; **we're ~ed●** on est dans la merde●.

■ **fuck about**●, **fuck around**●: ¶ **~ about** ou **around** déconner◑; ¶ **~ [sb] about** ou **around** se foutre◑ de la gueule◑ de qn; **they really ~ you around in this place** on se fout◑ vraiment de ta gueule◑ ici.

■ **fuck off**●: **~ off** foutre le camp◑; **~ off!** fous(-moi) le camp◑!

■ **fuck up**●: ¶ **~ up** foutre la merde●; ¶ **~ [sb] up, ~ up [sb]** foutre◑ [qn] dans un sale état; **he's a ~ed up kid** c'est un gosse foutu○; ¶ **~ [sth] up** foutre la merde● dans.

fuck-all● /ˌfʌkˈɔːl/ *adv* GB rien; **he knows ~ about it** il (n')en sait foutre◑ rien; **he does ~ in this office** il ne fout◑ rien dans ce bureau.

fucking● /ˈfʌkɪŋ/ **I** *adj* **this ~ machine!** cette putain● de machine!; **what a ~ shambles!** quel bordel◑!; **you ~ idiot!** espèce de con●!

II *adv* vachement○.

fuddle○ /ˈfʌdl/ **I** *vtr* [*drugs, drink*] embrouiller [*brain*].

II fuddled *pp adj* **1** (confused) [*idea, brain*] confus, embrouillé; [*state*] de confusion; [*person*] désorienté; **2** (the worse for drink) éméché.

fuddy-duddy○ /ˈfʌdɪdʌdɪ/ **I** *n* schnock○ *mf*.

II *adj* [*style, institution*] vieux jeu *inv*, ringard○; **to have ~ ways** être vieux jeu.

fudge /fʌdʒ/ **I** *n* **1** Culin (soft sweet) caramels *mpl* mous, fudge *m*; **have a piece of ~** prends un caramel; **2** US Culin (hot sauce) sauce *f* au chocolat; **3** Journ, Print (stop press news) dernières nouvelles *fpl*; (box or column for stop press) emplacement *m* de la dernière heure; **4**○ (compromise) **it's a ~** c'est flou; **the wording is a classic ~** l'énoncé est flou à merveille.

II○ *vtr* **1** (evade) esquiver, éluder [*issue, problem*]; **2** (falsify) truquer [*figures, accounts*].

III○ *vi* (dodge issue) se dérober.

fudge sauce *n* Culin sauce *f* au chocolat.

fuel /ˈfjuːəl/ **I** *n* **1** gen, Nucl combustible *m*; (for car, plane, machinery) carburant *m*; **several types of ~** plusieurs types de combustible; **2** fig **to provide ~ for** rajouter du poids à [*claims*]; attiser [*hatred, discord*].

II *modif* [*costs, prices, crisis*] du combustible, du carburant; [*shortage, bill*] de combustible, de carburant.

III *vtr* (*p prés etc* **-ll-**, **-l-** US) **1** (make run) [*gas, oil*] alimenter [*furnace, engine*]; **to be ~led by oil/gas** marcher au pétrole/gaz; **2** (put fuel into) [*person*] ravitailler [*plane, vehicle*]; **3** fig (spur) aggraver [*tension, fears*]; attiser [*hatred, discord*]; susciter [*speculation*].

IDIOMS **to add ~ to the flames** ou **fire** jeter de l'huile sur le feu.

fuel: **~ consumption** *n* (of plane, car) consommation *f* de carburant; (in industry) consommation *f* de combustible; **~-efficient** *adj* [*system, engine*] économique; **~ injection** *n* injection *f* (de carburant); **~ injection engine** *n* moteur *m* à injection; **~ injector** *n* injecteur *m*; **~ oil** *n* mazout *m*, fioul *m*; **~ pump** *n* pompe *f* d'alimentation; **~ rod** *n* barreau *m* de combustible.

fuel saving I *n* économie *f* d'énergie.

II *adj* [*measure, policy*] favorisant les économies d'énergie.

fuel tank *n* (of car) réservoir *m*; (of plane, ship) réservoir *m* de carburant.

fug○ /fʌg/ *n* GB atmosphère *f* enfumée; **there was a terrible ~ in the bar** l'atmosphère du bar était horriblement enfumée; **the ~ of exhaust fumes** les fumées des pots d'échappement.

fuggy /ˈfʌgɪ/ *adj* GB [*atmosphere*] (smoky) enfumé; (airless) confiné.

fugitive /ˈfjuːdʒətɪv/ **I** *n* fugitif/-ive *m/f*; fuyard/-e *m/f*; **to be a ~ from justice** fuir la justice.

II *adj* **1** littér (fleeting) [*happiness*] éphémère, fugace; [*impression, sensation*] fugitif/-ive; **2** (in flight) [*leader, criminal*] fugitif/-ive, en fuite.

fugue /fjuːg/ *n* **1** Mus fugue *f*; **a Bach ~** une fugue de Bach; **2** Psych amnésie *f* d'identité.

fulcrum /ˈfʊlkrəm/ *n* (*pl* **~s** ou **-cra**) lit point *m* d'appui; fig pivot *m*.

fulfil GB, **fulfill** US /fʊlˈfɪl/ (*p prés etc* **-ll-**) **I** *vtr* **1** (realize, carry out) réaliser [*ambition, prophecy, dream*]; tenir [*promise*]; répondre à [*desire, hope, need*]; **to ~ one's potential** se réaliser; **2** (satisfy) [*job, life, role*] combler [*person*]; **to be/feel ~led** être/se sentir comblé; **3** (satisfy requirements of) remplir [*role, duty, conditions, contract*]; **unless these conditions are ~led** à moins que ces conditions ne soient remplies.

II *v refl* **to ~ oneself** s'épanouir.

fulfilling /fʊlˈfɪlɪŋ/ *adj* [*job, career, marriage*] épanouissant; [*experience*] enrichissant.

fulfilment GB, **fulfillment** US /fʊlˈfɪlmənt/ *n* **1** (satisfaction) épanouissement *m*; **sexual ~** épanouissement sexuel; **personal ~** accomplissement *m* de soi; **~ still eluded her** elle n'était toujours pas satisfaite; **to seek/find ~** rechercher/trouver la plénitude; **to find ~ in acting/nursing** trouver son équilibre dans le théâtre/son métier d'infirmière; **2** (realization) **the ~ of** la réalisation de [*ambition, desire, need*]; l'accomplissement de [*prophecy, promise*]; **3** (carrying-out) (of role, duty, obligation) accomplissement *m*; **4** (meeting requirements) **the ~ of the contract/the requirements will entail...** pour remplir le contrat/répondre aux conditions requises, il faudra...

full /fʊl/ **I** *adj* **1** (completely filled) [*box, glass, room, cupboard*] plein; [*hotel, flight, car park*] complet/-ète; [*theatre*] comble; **a ~ tank of petrol** un plein réservoir d'essence; **a ~ bottle of whisky** une pleine bouteille de whisky; **~ to the brim** plein à ras bord; **~ to overflowing** [*bucket*] plein à déborder; [*room, suitcase*] plein à craquer○; **I've got my hands ~** lit j'ai les mains pleines; fig je suis débordé; **don't speak with your mouth ~** ne parle pas la bouche pleine; **~ of** plein de [*ideas, life, energy, surprises*]; **the hotel/the train is ~ of tourists** l'hôtel/le train est plein de touristes; **the papers are ~ of the accident** les journaux ne parlent que de l'accident; **he's ~ of his holiday plans** il ne parle que de ses projets de vacances; **to be ~ of oneself** péj être imbu de soi-même; **to be ~ of one's own importance** être plein de suffisance; **2** (sated) (also **~ up**) [*stomach*] plein; **to drink/swim on a ~ stomach** boire/se baigner le ventre plein; **I'm ~**○ je n'en peux plus; **3** (busy) [*day, week*] chargé, bien rempli; **my diary is ~ for this week** mon agenda est complet pour cette semaine; **she leads a very ~ life** elle mène une vie très remplie; **4** (complete) [*pack of cards, set of teeth*] complet/-ète; [*name, breakfast, story, details*] complet/-ète;

[*price, control*] total; [*responsibility*] entier/-ière; [*support*] inconditionnel/-elle; [*understanding, awareness*] total; [*inquiry, investigation*] approfondi; **the ~ extent of the damage/of the disaster** l'ampleur des dégâts/du désastre; **the ~ implications of** toutes les implications de, toute la portée de; **he has a ~ head of hair** il a tous ses cheveux; **to be in ~ view** être parfaitement visible; **in ~ view of sb** sous les yeux de qn; **5** (officially recognized) [*member, partner*] à part entière; [*right*] plein (*before n*); **6** (maximum) [*employment, bloom, power*] plein (*before n*); **he has the radio at ~ volume** il a mis la radio à plein volume; **at ~ speed** à toute vitesse; **in ~ sunlight** en plein soleil; **to make ~ use of sth, to use sth to ~ advantage** profiter pleinement de qch [*opportunity, situation*]; **to get ~ marks** GB obtenir la note maximale; **she deserves ~ marks for courage** GB elle mérite des félicitations pour son courage; **7** (for emphasis) [*hour, kilo, month*] bon/bonne (*before n*); **it took them three ~ weeks to reply** ils ont mis trois bonnes semaines pour répondre; **turn the knob a ~ 180 degrees** tourne complètement le bouton à 180 degrés; **8** (rounded) [*cheeks, face*] rond; [*lips*] charnu; [*figure*] fort; [*skirt, sleeve*] ample; **clothes for the ~er figure** vêtements pour personnes fortes; **9** Astron [*moon*] plein; **there's a ~ moon** c'est la pleine lune; **when the moon is ~** à la pleine lune; **10** (rich) [*flavour, tone*] riche.

II *adv* **1** (directly) **to hit sb ~ in the face/stomach** frapper qn en plein visage/ventre; **to look sb ~ in the face** regarder qn droit dans les yeux; **2** (very) **to know ~ well that** savoir fort bien que; **as you know ~ well** comme tu le sais fort bien; **3** (to the maximum) **is the volume turned up ~?** est-ce que le volume est à fond?; **with the heating up ~** avec le chauffage à fond.

III **in full** *adv phr* **to write sth in ~** écrire qch en toutes lettres; **to pay sb in ~** payer qn intégralement; **to publish/describe sth in ~** publier/décrire qch intégralement.

IDIOMS **to enjoy** ou **live life to the ~** profiter pleinement de l'existence.

full: **~-back** /ˈfʊlbæk/ *n* Sport arrière *m*; **~ beam** *n* Aut pleins phares.

full blast○ /ˌfʊlˈblɑːst/ *adv* **the TV/radio was on** ou **going at ~** la télé/radio marchait à pleins tubes○ or à pleine gomme○; **we had the heater on at ~** nous avions mis le chauffage au maximum.

full-blooded /ˌfʊlˈblʌdɪd/ *adj* **1** (vigorous) [*argument, condemnation*] vigoureux/-euse; **2** (committed) [*socialism, monetarism*] pur et dur *inv*; **3** (pure bred) [*person*] de race pure; [*horse*] pur sang.

full-blown /ˌfʊlˈbləʊn/ *adj* **1** Med [*disease*] déclaré; [*epidemic*] qui fait rage; **to have ~ Aids** être atteint d'un sida avéré; **2** (qualified) [*doctor, lawyer*] diplômé; **3** (large-scale) [*recession, crisis, war*] à grande échelle; **4** [*rose*] épanoui.

full: **~ board** *n* Tourism pension *f* complète; **~-bodied** *adj* [*wine*] corsé.

full colour I *n* Print **with 20 illustrations in ~** avec 20 illustrations en couleur.

II **full-colour** *modif* [*illustration, plate*] en couleur.

full-cream milk *n* GB lait *m* entier.

full dress I *n* gen tenue *f* de cérémonie; Mil grande tenue *f*; **officers in ~** des officiers en grande tenue.

II **full-dress** *modif* **1** Mil [*uniform*] de cérémonie; [*officer, parade*] en grande tenue; **2** Pol [*debate*] officiel/-ielle.

fuller /ˈfʊlə(r)/ ▶ 1692 *n* Tex fouleur/-euse *m/f*.

fuller's earth *n* terre *f* à foulon.

full: **~-face** *adj, adv* de face; **~-frontal** *adj* [*photograph*] nu de face; [*nudity*] intégral; **~-grown** *adj* adulte.

full house *n* **1** Theat **to have a ~** faire salle comble; **to play to a ~** jouer à guichets fermés; **2** Games (in poker) full *m*.

full-length /ˌfʊlˈleŋθ/ I *adj* **1** Cin **a ~ film** un long métrage; **2** (head to toe) [*portrait, photo*] en pied; [*mirror*] qui permet de se voir en pied; **~ window** baie *f* vitrée; **3** (long) [*coat, curtain, sleeve*] long/longue; [*novel, opera*] grand (*before n*).

II *adv* [*lie*] de tout son long.

full name *n* nom *m* et prénom *m*.

fullness /ˈfʊlnɪs/ *n* **1** (width) (of sleeve, dress) ampleur *f*; **2** (roundness) (of breasts) rondeur *f*; (of lips) épaisseur *f*; **3** (of flavour) richesse *f*.

IDIOMS **in the ~ of time** (with the passage of time) avec le temps; (eventually) en temps et lieu.

full: **~-page** *adj* Advertg, Print pleine page; **~ pay** *n* traitement *m* intégral; **~ price** *adj, adv* au prix fort.

full-scale /ˌfʊlˈskeɪl/ *adj* **1** (in proportion) [*drawing, plan*] grandeur *f* nature; **2** (extensive) [*operation, search*] de grande envergure; [*investigation*] approfondi; [*study*] exhaustif/-ive; **3** (total) [*alert, panic*] général; [*war, crisis*] généralisé; **4** (complete) [*performance*] grand (*before n*).

full-size(d) /ˌfʊlˈsaɪz(d)/ *adj* **1** (large) grand format *inv*; **2** (not for children) [*violin, bike*] pour adulte.

full stop *n* GB **1** (in punctuation) point *m*; **I'm not leaving, ~!** je ne pars pas, point final!; **2** (impasse) **negotiations have come to a ~** les négociations ont abouti à une impasse; **3** (halt) **work has come to a ~** les travaux ont été entièrement interrompus.

full-throated /ˌfʊlˈθrəʊtɪd/ *adj* **to give a ~ laugh** rire à gorge déployée; **to give a ~ cry** crier à pleine gorge.

full time I *n* Sport fin *m* du match; **he blew the whistle for ~** il a sifflé la fin du match.

II **full-time** *modif* **1** Sport [*score, whistle*] final; **2** (permanent) [*job, worker, student, secretary*] à plein temps; **to be in full-time education** [*schoolchild*] être élève à plein temps; [*student*] être étudiant à plein temps.

III *adv* [*study, teach, work*] à plein temps.

full: **~-timer** *n* employé/-e *m/f* à plein temps; **~ word** *n* Ling mot *m* plein.

fully /ˈfʊlɪ/ *adv* **1** (completely) [*understand*] très bien; [*succeed, recover*] tout à fait; [*equipped, furnished, dressed, illustrated*] entièrement; [*awake, developed*] complètement; [*aware, informed*] parfaitement; **to be ~ qualified** avoir obtenu tous ses diplômes; **I ~ intend to do it** j'ai bien l'intention de le faire; **he doesn't ~ realize what he's doing** il n'est pas pleinement conscient de ce qu'il fait; **2** (to the maximum) [*open, closed*] à fond; [*stretched, unwound*] complètement; **~ booked** complet/-ète; **a ~ loaded truck** un camion à pleine charge; **my time is ~ occupied** je suis entièrement pris; **3** (comprehensively) [*examine, study*] à fond; [*explain, describe*] de façon détaillée; **I'll write more ~ later** j'écrirai plus longuement plus tard; **4** (at least) **it's ~ ten years since I last saw you** je ne t'ai pas vu depuis dix ans au moins; **the hotel is ~ 20 km from the station** l'hôtel est au moins à 20 km de la gare; **it took me ~ two hours** j'ai mis deux bonnes heures.

fully-fashioned /ˌfʊlɪˈfæʃnd/ *adj* Fashn ajusté.

fully-fledged /ˌfʊlɪˈfledʒd/ *adj* **1** Zool [*bird*] qui a toutes ses plumes; **2** (established) [*member, officer*] à part entière; [*accountant, lawyer*] diplômé.

fulmar /ˈfʊlmə(r)/ *n* fulmar *m*.

fulminate /ˈfʌlmɪneɪt, US ˈfʊl-/ I *n* Chem fulminate *m*.

II *vi* fulminer, pester (**against** contre).

fulsome /ˈfʊlsəm/ *adj* sout [*praise, compliments*] excessif/-ive, exagéré; [*manner*] obséquieux/-ieuse; **to be ~ in one's praise of sth** vanter qch avec excès.

fulsomely /ˈfʊlsəmlɪ/ *adv* avec effusion.

fulsomeness /ˈfʊlsəmnɪs/ *n* outrance *f*.

fumarole /ˈfjuːmərəʊl/ *n* fumerolle *f*.

fumble /ˈfʌmbl/ I *n* US Sport échappé *m*.

II *vtr* **1** Sport mal attraper [*ball*]; **2** (fluff, bungle) rater [*entrance, attempt*].

III *vi* **1** (fiddle clumsily) **to ~ in one's bag for a cigarette/a tissue** fouiller dans son sac pour trouver une cigarette/un mouchoir en papier; **to ~ with** manier maladroitement [*zipper, buttons*]; **2** (search clumsily) = **fumble about**; **3** fig **to ~ for words** chercher ses mots.

■ **fumble about**: **~ about** (in dark) tâtonner (**to do** pour faire); **to ~ about in** fouiller dans [*bag, drawer*].

fume /fjuːm/ *vi* **1**○ [*person*] fulminer, être furibond○; **he was fuming at the delay** il était furibond○ à cause du retard; **to ~ with anger/with impatience** bouillonner de colère/d'impatience; **2** [*mixture, chemical*] fumer.

fumes /fjuːmz/ *npl* émanations *fpl*; **petrol ~** GB, **gas ~** US vapeurs *fpl* d'essence; **factory ~** fumées *fpl* d'usine; **traffic** ou **exhaust ~** fumée *f* des pots d'échappement.

fumigate /ˈfjuːmɪgeɪt/ *vtr* fumiger, désinfecter [qch] par fumigation.

fun /fʌn/ I *n* plaisir *m*, amusement *m*; **to have ~** s'amuser (**doing** en faisant; **with** avec); **have ~!** amusez-vous!; **we had great/good ~** nous nous sommes beaucoup/bien amusés; **it is ~ to do sth, doing sth is ~** c'est amusant de faire qch; **card games are great ~** jouer aux cartes est très amusant; **to do sth for ~, to do sth for the ~ of it** faire qch pour s'amuser; **it's just for ~** c'est seulement pour rire; **to do sth in ~** faire qch pour rire or pour plaisanter; **half the ~ of sth/of doing is...** le plus beau de qch/de faire est...; **it's all good clean ~** il n'y a rien de mal; **it's not much ~** ce n'est pas très amusant (**for** pour); **it's no ~ doing sth** ce n'est pas très amusant de faire qch; **it's not my idea of ~** je ne trouve pas ça drôle; **to spoil sb's ~** gâcher le plaisir de qn; **it takes the ~ out of it** cela en gâche le plaisir; **to be full of ~** être très drôle; **to have a sense of ~** avoir de l'humour; **he's (such) ~** il est (tellement) drôle; **she is great ~ to be with** on s'amuse beaucoup avec elle; **we had ~ cleaning up** iron on s'est bien amusé à tout nettoyer; **that looks like ~!** iron on doit s'amuser!

II *adj* [*person*] marrant○, rigolo○; **it's a ~ thing to do** c'est amusant.

III○ *vi* plaisanter.

IDIOMS **to become a figure of ~** devenir un objet de risée; **to have ~ and games** s'amuser comme des petits fous also iron; **like ~**○**!** tu parles○!; **to make ~ of** ou **poke ~ at sb/sth** se moquer de qn/qch.

function /ˈfʌŋkʃn/ I *n* **1** (role) (of body, organ, tool) fonction *f*; (of person) fonction *f*, charge *f*; **to fulfil a ~** [*person*] remplir une fonction; **to perform a ~ as** [*person, object*] faire fonction de; **in her ~ as...** en sa qualité de...; **that is not part of my ~** cela n'entre pas dans mes fonctions; **the ~ of the heart is to do** le cœur a pour fonction de faire; **bodily ~s** fonctions physiologiques; **2** (occasion) (reception) réception *f*; (ceremony) cérémonie *f* (officielle); **3** Comput, Math fonction *f*; **to be a ~ of** être fonction de also fig.

II *vi* **1** (work properly) fonctionner; **2** (operate as) **to ~ as** [*object*] faire fonction de, servir de; [*person*] jouer le rôle de.

functional /ˈfʌŋkʃənl/ *adj* [*design, furniture*] fonctionnel/-elle; (in working order) opérationnel/-elle; **~ disorder** Med trouble *m* fonctionnel; **he's barely ~ before 10 o'clock** hum il a du mal à émerger avant 10 heures.

functionalism /ˈfʌŋkʃənəlɪzəm/ *n* fonctionnalisme *m*.

functionalist /ˈfʌŋkʃənəlɪst/ *n, adj* fonctionnaliste (*mf*).

functionary /ˈfʌŋkʃənərɪ, US -nerɪ/ *n* gen fonctionnaire *mf*; péj bureaucrate *mf*, rond-de-cuir *m* pej.

function: **~ key** *n* touche *f* de fonction; **~ room** *n* salle *f* de réception; **~ word** *n* mot *m* grammatical, mot-outil *m*.

fund /fʌnd/ **I** *n* **1** (cash reserve) fonds *m*; **emergency/relief/unemployment ~** caisse *f* de prévoyance/secours/chômage; **strike/disaster ~** collecte *f* en faveur des grévistes/des sinistrés; **2** fig (store) **she's a ~ of wisdom** c'est un puits de sagesse; **he has a ~ of wit/experience** il a énormément d'humour/d'expérience.
II funds *npl* **1** (capital) fonds *mpl*, capitaux *mpl*; **to be in ~s** avoir de l'argent; **government ~, public ~** fonds publics; **2** (credit balance) (of individual) argent *m*; (of company) capitaux *mpl*; **3** (on cheque) **'No ~s', 'insufficient ~s'** 'défaut de provision'.
III Funds *pr npl* GB **the Funds** les fonds *mpl* d'État.
IV *vtr* **1** (finance) financer [*company, project*]; **2** (convert) consolider [*debt*].
V funded *pp adj* **government-~ed** financé par l'État; **a publicly ~ed project** un projet à fonds publics; **under-~ed** insuffisamment financé.

fundamental /ˌfʌndəˈmentl/ **I fundamentals** *npl* **the ~s** (of abstract ideas) les fondements *mpl* (**of** de); (of technique, skill) les règles *fpl* de base; **let's get down to ~s** venons-en à l'essentiel.
II *adj* [*question, issue, meaning*] fondamental (**to** pour); [*error*] capital; [*concern*] principal; **to be ~ to** être essentiel à; **of ~ importance** d'une importance capitale.

fundamentalism /ˌfʌndəˈmentəlɪzəm/ *n* gen fondamentalisme *m*; (Islam) intégrisme *m*.

fundamentalist /ˌfʌndəˈmentəlɪst/ *n, adj* gen fondamentaliste (*mf*); (Islam) intégriste (*mf*).

fundamentally /ˌfʌndəˈmentəlɪ/ *adv* [*opposed, flawed*] fondamentalement; [*incompatible*] foncièrement; [*change*] radicalement; **what concerns me ~ is...** ma préoccupation essentielle est...; **~, I think that...** au fond, je pense que...; **he's ~ a socialist** au fond, il est socialiste; **you are ~ mistaken** tu te trompes complètement.

funding /ˈfʌndɪŋ/ *n* Econ, Fin **1** (financial aid) financement *m*; **~ from the private sector** financement provenant du secteur privé; **to receive ~ from sb** être financé par qn; **self-~** autofinancé; **under-~** manque *m* de financement; **2** (of debt) consolidation *f*.

funding body, funding agency *n* organisme *m* de subvention.

fund: **~ manager** *n* Fin gestionnaire *mf* de fonds; **~-raiser** *n* (person) collecteur/-trice *m/f* de fonds; (event) collecte *f*.

fund-raising /ˈfʌndreɪzɪŋ/ **I** *n* collecte *f* de fonds.
II *adj* [*event*] pour collecter des fonds.

funeral /ˈfjuːnərəl/ **I** *n* gen enterrement *m*; (ceremonious) obsèques *fpl*, funérailles *fpl* liter; (in announcement) obsèques *fpl*.
II *modif* [*march, oration, service*] funèbre.
IDIOMS **that's your/her ~**○! c'est ton/son problème○!

funeral: **~ director ▶1692⌋** *n* entrepreneur *m* de pompes funèbres; **~ parlour** *n*, **~ home** US, **~ parlor** US *n* chambre *f* mortuaire (*chez un entrepreneur de pompes funèbres*); **~ procession** *n* (on foot) cortège *m* funèbre; (by car) convoi *m* funèbre; **~ pyre** bûcher *m* funéraire; **~ service** *n* service *m* funèbre.

funereal /ˈfjuːnɪərɪəl/ *adj* [*atmosphere*] lugubre, funèbre; [*voice*] lugubre.

fun: **~ fair** *n* fête *f* foraine; **~ fur** *n* fausse fourrure *f*.

fungal /ˈfʌŋgl/ *adj* [*spore, growth*] fongique; **~ infection** mycose *f* fongique.

fungi /fʌŋgaɪ, -dʒaɪ/ *pl* ▶ **fungus**.

fungible /ˈfʌndʒɪbl/ *adj* fongible.

fungoid /ˈfʌŋgɔɪd/ *adj* fongoïde.

fungous /ˈfʌŋgəs/ *adj* fongueux/-euse.

fungus /ˈfʌŋgəs/ *n* (*pl* **-gi**) **1** (plant) champignon *m*; **2** (mould) moisissure *f*; **3** Med champignon *m*, mycose *f* spec.

fun house *n* US ≈ palais *m* des miroirs.

funicular /fjuːˈnɪkjʊlə(r)/ *n, adj* funiculaire (*m*).

funk /fʌŋk/ **I** *n* **1** Mus funk *m*; **2**○ †(fear) trouille○ *f*; (coward) froussard/-e○ *m/f*; **to be in a (blue) ~** avoir une trouille bleue○.
II○ †*vtr* **to ~ it** se dégonfler.

funky○ /ˈfʌŋkɪ/ *adj* funky○.

fun-loving /ˈfʌnlʌvɪŋ/ *adj* [*person*] qui aime s'amuser; **he's very ~** il aime beaucoup s'amuser.

funnel /ˈfʌnl/ **I** *n* **1** (for liquids etc) entonnoir *m*; **2** (on ship, engine) cheminée *f*.
II *vtr* **1** lit **to ~ sth into/through** faire passer qch dans/par; **to ~ sth out** évacuer qch; **2** fig (channel) acheminer [*funds, aid*] (**to** vers); **to ~ funds into doing** débloquer des crédits pour faire.
III *vi* **to ~ into/through** [*crowd, wind*] s'engouffrer dans/à travers; [*liquid*] passer dans/par.

funnies○ /ˈfʌnɪz/ *npl* US bandes *fpl* dessinées.

funnily /ˈfʌnɪlɪ/ *adv* (oddly) [*walk, talk*] curieusement; **~ enough,...** chose curieuse,...

funny /ˈfʌnɪ/ **I** *adj* **1** (amusing) [*person, incident, film, joke*] drôle, amusant; **are you trying to be ~**○**?** tu essaies d'être drôle par hasard○?; **very ~!** iron très drôle!; **2** (odd) [*hat, smell, noise, man*] bizarre; **a ~ voice** une drôle de voix, une voix bizarre; **it's ~ that she hasn't phoned** c'est drôle or bizarre qu'elle n'ait pas appelé; **it's ~ how people change** c'est drôle or bizarre comme les gens changent; **there's something ~ about him** il a quelque chose de bizarre, c'est un drôle d'homme; **something ~'s going on** il se passe des choses bizarres; **it's a ~ feeling but...** c'est une drôle d'impression mais...; **it's ~ you should mention it** c'est drôle que tu en parles; **3**○ (unwell) **to feel ~** se sentir tout/-e chose○.
II *adv*○ [*walk, talk, act*] de façon bizarre.
IDIOMS **~ peculiar or ~ ha-ha?** drôle-bizarre ou drôle-amusant?

funny: **~ bone**○ *n* petit juif○ *m*; **~ business**○ *n* ¢ magouilles○ *fpl*; **~ farm**○ *n* cabanon○ *m*; **~ money**○ *n* fausse monnaie *f*.

fun run /ˈfʌnrʌn/ *n*: *course à pied pour amateurs, souvent organisée pour collecter des fonds*.

fur /fɜː(r)/ **I** *n* ¢ **1** (on animal) poils *mpl*, pelage *m*; (for garment) fourrure *f*; **she was dressed in ~s** elle portait de la fourrure or des fourrures; **2** GB (in kettle, pipes) tartre *m*.
II *modif* [*collar, lining, jacket*] de fourrure; **~ coat** manteau *m* de fourrure.
IDIOMS **that'll make the ~ fly!** ça va chauffer○! or barder○!
■ **fur up** GB [*kettle, pipes*] s'entartrer.

furbelow‡ /ˈfɜːbɪləʊ/ *n* falbala *m*.

furbish /ˈfɜːbɪʃ/ *vtr* (renovate) refaire [*room*]; rénover [*building*].

furious /ˈfjʊərɪəs/ *adj* **1** (angry) furieux/-ieuse (**with, at** contre); **I was ~ with myself** j'étais furieux contre moi-même; **he's ~ about it** cela l'a rendu furieux; **I was ~ with her for coming** ou **that she had come** j'étais furieux qu'elle soit venue; **he was ~ at being cheated** ou **that he'd been cheated** il était furieux d'avoir été trompé; **I was ~ to learn that...** j'étais furieux d'apprendre que...; **he was absolutely ~** il était fou furieux; **2** fig (violent) [*debate, energy, struggle*] acharné; [*storm*] déchaîné; **at a ~ rate** à un rythme effréné.
IDIOMS **the pace was fast and ~** le rythme était endiablé; **the questions came fast and ~** les questions fusaient.

furiously /ˈfjʊərɪəslɪ/ *adv* furieusement; [*struggle*] avec acharnement; **he was ~ angry** il était hors de lui; **he was waving his hands ~** il gesticulait frénétiquement.

furl /fɜːl/ **I** *vtr* ferler [*sail*]; rouler [*umbrella, flag*].
II *vi* [*smoke*] **to ~ out/upwards** sortir/monter en volutes.

furlong /ˈfɜːlɒŋ, US -lɔːŋ/ **▶1412⌋** *n* furlong *m* (= *201 m*).

furlough /ˈfɜːləʊ/ *n* Mil permission *f*; gen congé *m*.

furnace /ˈfɜːnɪs/ *n* **1** lit gen chaudière *f*; (in foundry) fourneau *m*; (for forging) four *m*; **2** fig fournaise *f*.

furnish /ˈfɜːnɪʃ/ **I** *vtr* **1** (put furniture in) meubler [*room, apartment*] (**with** avec); **2** (provide) fournir [*document, facts, excuse*]; **to ~ sb with sth** fournir qch à qn [*document, facts, clothing, equipment*].
II furnished *pp adj* [*apartment*] meublé.

furnishing /ˈfɜːnɪʃɪŋ/ **I** *n* (action) ameublement *m* (**of** de).
II furnishings *npl* (complete décor) ameublement *m*; (furniture) mobilier *m*.
III *modif* [*fabric*] d'ameublement; **~ department** rayon *m* ameublement.

furniture /ˈfɜːnɪtʃə(r)/ **I** *n* ¢ mobilier *m*, meubles *mpl*; **bedroom ~** meubles *fpl* de chambre à coucher; **door ~** plaques *fpl* et poignées *fpl*, ferrures *fpl*; **garden** ou **lawn ~** mobilier *m* de jardin; **mental ~** univers *m* intellectuel; **office ~** mobilier *m* de bureau; **street ~** mobilier *m* urbain; **a piece of ~** un meuble.
II *modif* [*shop, business, factory, maker, restorer*] de meubles; [*industry*] du meuble.
IDIOMS **to be part of the ~**○ hum faire partie des meubles○.

furniture: **~ depot** *n* garde-meubles *m inv*; **~ polish** *n* encaustique *f*; **~ remover ▶1692⌋** *n* GB déménageur *m*; **~ store** *n* magasin *m* de meubles; **~ van** *n* camion *m* de déménagement.

furore /fjʊˈrɔːrɪ/, **furor** US /ˈfjuːrɔːr/ *n* (acclaim) enthousiasme *m*; (criticism) scandale *m*; **to cause a ~** (reaction, excitement) soulever les passions; (outrage) faire scandale; (acclaim) provoquer l'enthousiasme; **there was a ~ over** ou **about** il y a eu beaucoup de bruit autour de.

furred /fɜːd/ *adj* **1** GB [*kettle, pipes*] entartré; **2** [*tongue*] chargé.

furrier /ˈfʌrɪə(r)/ **▶1692⌋** *n* fourreur *m*.

furrow /ˈfʌrəʊ/ **I** *n* **1** (in earth, snow) sillon *m*; **2** (on brow) pli *m*.
II *vtr* plisser [*brow*]; **her ~ed brow** son front plissé; **his brow was ~ed in concentration** la concentration lui faisait plisser le front.
IDIOMS **to plough a lonely ~** faire son chemin en solitaire.

furry /ˈfɜːrɪ/ *adj* **1** [*toy*] en peluche; [*kitten*] au poil touffu; **2** GB [*tongue*] chargé.

further /ˈfɜːðə(r)/ **I** *adv* (*comparative of* **far**) **1** (to or at a greater physical distance) (also **farther**) plus loin; **I can't go any ~** je ne peux pas aller plus loin; **John walked ~ than me** John a marché plus loin que moi; **how much ~ is it?** c'est encore loin?; **how much ~ have they got to go?** est-ce qu'ils vont encore loin?; **to get ~ and ~ away** s'éloigner de plus en plus; **~ north** plus (loin) au nord; **~ back/forward** plus en arrière/en avant; **~ away** ou **off** plus loin, plus éloigné; **~ on** encore plus loin; **to move ~ back** reculer encore; **2** fig (at or to a more advanced point) (also **farther**) **I'll go so far but no ~** j'irai jusque là mais pas plus loin; **the government went even ~** le gouvernement est allé encore plus loin; **she didn't get any ~ with him than I did**

elle n'est arrivée à rien de plus avec lui que moi; **we're ~ forward than we thought** on est plus avancé qu'on ne le pensait; **all that work and we're no ~ forward** tout ce travail ne nous a pas avancés du tout; **nothing could be ~ from the truth/from my mind** rien n'est plus loin or éloigné de la vérité/de mes pensées; **3** (to or at a greater distance in time) (also **farther**) **~ back than 1964** avant 1964; **a year ~ on** un an plus tard; **we must look ~ ahead** nous devons regarder plus vers l'avenir; **I haven't read ~ than page twenty** je n'ai pas lu au-delà de la page vingt; **4** (to a greater extent, even more) **prices fell/increased (even) ~** les prix ont baissé/ont augmenté encore plus; **his refusal to co-operate angered them ~** son refus de coopérer les a agacés encore plus; **we will enquire ~ into the matter** nous nous renseignerons davantage sur la question; **I won't delay you any ~** je ne vous retarderai pas davantage; **they didn't question him any ~** ils ne lui ont plus posé de questions; **5** (in addition, furthermore) de plus, en outre; **the company ~ agrees to...** en outre, l'entreprise accepte de...; **she ~ argued that** de plus, elle a affirmé que; **~, I must say that** de plus or en outre, je dois dire que.

II *adj* (*comparative of* **far**) **1** (additional) **a ~ 10%/500 people** encore 10%/500 personnes, 10%/500 personnes de plus; **~ reforms/changes/increases/questions** d'autres réformes/changements/augmentations/questions; **there have been ~ allegations that** on a affirmé de nouveau que; **~ research** des recherches plus approfondies; **~ details can be obtained by writing to the manager** pour plus de renseignements, adressez-vous à la direction; **to have no ~ use for sth** ne plus avoir besoin de qch; **without ~ delay** sans plus attendre; **there's nothing ~ to discuss** il n'y a rien d'autre à discuter; **is there anything ~?** c'est tout?; **2** (more distant) (also **farther**) autre; **the ~ end/bank/side** l'autre bout/rive/côté.

III further to sout suite à; **~ to your letter of 2nd May** suite à votre lettre du 2 mai.

IV *vtr* augmenter [*chances*]; faire avancer [*career, plan*]; servir [*cause*].

furtherance /'fɜ:ðərəns/ *n* (of aim) poursuite *f*; **in (the) ~ of** pour servir [*ambition, cause*].

further education *n* GB ≈ enseignement *m* professionnel.

furthermore /ˌfɜ:ðə'mɔ:(r)/ *adv* de plus, en outre.

furthermost /'fɜ:ðəməʊst/ *adj* le plus éloigné (**from** de); **the ~ point** le point le plus éloigné; **the ~ chair** la chaise la plus éloignée.

furthest /'fɜ:ðɪst/ **I** *adj* (*superlative of* **far**) (the most distant) [*point, place, part, side, bank*] le plus éloigné; **the tree ~ (away) from the window** l'arbre le plus éloigné de la fenêtre; **the houses ~ (away) from the river** les maisons les plus éloignées de la rivière; **which of the three is (the) ~?** lequel des trois est le plus éloigné or loin?

II *adv* **1** (to, at the greatest distance in space) (also **the ~**) le plus loin; **Tim can swim/run (the) ~** c'est Tim qui nage/court le plus loin; **the ~ north/west** le plus au nord/à l'ouest; **this plan goes ~ towards solving the problem** fig c'est ce projet qui s'approche le plus de la solution du problème; **2** (at, to greatest distance in time) **the ~ back I can remember is 1970** je ne me rappelle rien avant 1970; **the ~ ahead we can look is next week** nous ne pouvons rien prévoir au-delà de la semaine prochaine.

furtive /'fɜ:tɪv/ *adj* [*glance, movement*] furtif/-ive; [*person*] agissant subrepticement; [*behaviour*] suspect; [*deal, meeting*] subreptice; **~ drink/photograph** boisson/photo prise en cachette.

furtively /'fɜ:tɪvlɪ/ *adv* [*glance*] furtivement; [*act*] subrepticement; [*eat, smoke*] en cachette.

fury /'fjʊərɪ/ **I** *n* **1** fureur *f*; fig (of storm, sea) violence *f*; **to be in a ~** être en fureur; **to clench one's fists in ~** serrer les poings de rage; **he flew at her in a ~** il se rua sur elle dans un accès de rage; **2** fig (woman) furie *f*.

II Furies *pr npl* **the Furies** Mythol les Furies *fpl*.

IDIOMS **to do sth like ~**○ faire qch comme un fou○/une folle○.

furze /fɜ:z/ *n* ¢ ajoncs *mpl*.

fuse /fju:z/ **I** *n* **1** Elec fusible *m*, plomb *m*; **a ~ has blown** un fusible a sauté; **to blow a ~** lit faire sauter un fusible; fig○ piquer une crise○; **2** (cord) (for explosive device) mèche *f*; **3** (detonator) détonateur *m*.

II *vtr* **1** GB Elec **to ~ the lights** faire sauter○ les plombs; **2** munir [qch] d'un fusible [*plug*]; amorcer [*bomb*]; **3** Tech (unite) souder [*wires*]; fondre [qch] ensemble [*metals*]; **4** fig faire fusionner [*ideas, images*].

III *vi* **1** GB Elec **the lights have ~d** les plombs ont sauté; **2** Tech [*metals, chemicals*] amalgamer; **3** fig (also **~ together**) [*images, ideas*] fusionner.

IV fused *pp adj* Elec [*plug*] avec fusible incorporé.

IDIOMS **to be on a short ~** être soupe au lait.

fuse box *n* Elec boîte *f* à fusibles.

fusel /'fju:zl/ *n* (also **~ oil**) huile *f* de fusel.

fuselage /'fju:zəlɑ:ʒ, -lɪdʒ/ *n* fuselage *m*.

fuse wire *n* Elec fusible *m*.

fusible /'fju:zəbl/ *adj* [*metal, alloy*] fusible; **~ interfacing** (for sewing) entoilage *m* thermocollant.

fusilier /ˌfju:zə'lɪə(r)/ *n* fusilier *m*.

fusillade /ˌfju:zə'leɪd, US -sə-/ *n* **1** Mil fusillade *f*; **2** fig (of criticism, questions) avalanche *f*.

fusion /'fju:ʒn/ *n* **1** Phys fusion *f*; **2** fig (of styles) mélange *m*; (of ideas, images, parties) fusion *f*.

fuss /fʌs/ **I** *n* **1** (agitation) remue-ménage *m inv*; (verbal) histoires *fpl*; **to make a ~** faire des histoires; **to make a ~ about sth** faire toute une histoire à propos de qch; **to make a lot of ~ over accepting** faire un tas d'histoires pour accepter; **what's all the ~ about?** pourquoi tout ce remue-ménage?; **there's no need to make such a ~** il n'y a pas de quoi en faire une histoire; **with a minimum of ~** avec le moins d'histoires possible; **to make a big ~ about nothing** faire un tas d'histoires pour rien; **I don't see what all the ~ is about** je ne vois pas où est le problème; **2** (angry scene) tapage *m*; **to kick up a ~ about sth** piquer une crise○ à propos de qch; **there was a big ~ when she found out** elle a piqué une crise○ quand elle l'a appris; **3** (attention) **to make a ~ of** être aux petits soins avec or pour [*person*]; caresser [*animal*]; **there's no need to make a ~ of him** il ne faut pas s'occuper de lui; **he likes to be made a ~ of** (of person) il aime qu'on fasse grand cas de lui; (animal) il aime qu'on le caresse; **she doesn't want any ~** (of dignitary, visitor) elle veut qu'on la reçoive simplement.

II *vtr* US (bother) asticoter○.

III *vi* **1** (worry) se faire du souci (**about** pour); **he's always ~ing over** ou **about his appearance** il est obsédé par son apparence; **don't ~, I've got a key** ne t'affole pas, j'ai une clé; **2** (be agitated) s'agiter; **stop ~ing!** arrête de t'agiter pour rien!; **3** (show attention) **to ~ over sb**○ être aux petits soins avec or pour qn.

fussbudget○ /'fʌsbʌdʒɪt/ *n* US = **fusspot**.

fussily /'fʌsɪlɪ/ *adv* **1** (anxiously) avec maniaquerie; **2** (ornately) de manière tarabiscotée.

fussiness /'fʌsɪnɪs/ *n* **1** (of decoration) tarabiscotage *m*; (of prose style) emphase *f*; **2** (choosiness) maniaquerie *f*.

fussing /'fʌsɪŋ/ *n* maniaquerie *f*; **endless ~ about** ou **over details** de la maniaquerie à n'en plus finir sur les détails; **endless ~ about nothing** des histoires à n'en plus finir pour rien.

fusspot○ /'fʌspɒt/ *n* GB **1** (finicky person) maniaque *mf*; **2** (worrier) éternel inquiet/éternelle inquiète *m/f*.

fussy /'fʌsɪ/ *adj* **1** (difficult to please) **to be ~ about one's food/about details** être difficile sur la nourriture/maniaque sur les détails; **'when do you want to leave?'—'I'm not ~'** 'quand est-ce que tu veux partir?'—'ça m'est égal'; **2** (over-elaborate) [*furniture, decoration*] tarabiscoté; [*pattern*] trop chargé; [*curtains*] surchargé; [*prose style*] emphatique, tarabiscoté; **this dress is too ~** cette robe n'est pas assez simple.

fustian /'fʌstɪən, US -tʃən/ *n* futaine *f*.

fusty /'fʌstɪ/ *adj* **1** [*smell*] de moisi; **to smell ~** sentir le moisi; **2** (old-fashioned) [*person, idea, attitude*] vieux jeu *inv*.

futile /'fju:taɪl, US -tl/ *adj* **1** (vain) vain; **it is ~ to do** il est vain de faire; **2** (inane) futile.

futility /fju:'tɪlətɪ/ *n* inutilité *f*.

futon /'fu:tɒn/ *n* futon *m*.

future /'fju:tʃə(r)/ **I** *n* **1** (on time scale) avenir *m*; **in the ~** dans l'avenir; **in the near** ou **not too distant ~** dans un proche avenir; **in ~** à l'avenir; **the train/shopping centre of the ~** le train/le centre commercial du futur or de demain; **who knows what the ~ holds** ou **might bring?** qui sait ce que l'avenir nous réserve?; **to see into the ~** lire l'avenir; **2** (prospects) (of person, industry, company, sport) avenir *m*; **she/the company has a ~** elle/la compagnie a de l'avenir; **to have a (bright) ~** avoir un (bel) avenir; **there's no ~ in this kind of work** ce genre de travail n'a aucun avenir; **3** Ling (also **~ tense**) futur *m*; **in the ~** au futur.

II futures *npl* Fin (in Stock Exchange) contrats *mpl* à terme; **currency ~s** devises achetées à terme; **to deal in ~s** faire des opérations à terme.

III *adj* (*épith*) [*generation, developments, investment, earnings*] futur; [*prospects*] d'avenir; [*queen, prince etc*] futur (*before n*); **at some ~ date** à une date ultérieure; **I'll keep it for ~ reference** je vais le garder au cas où on en aurait besoin fml or au cas où○; **that would be useful for ~ reference** cela pourrait être utile dans l'avenir.

future: **~ perfect** *n* futur *m* antérieur; **~s contract** *n* contrat *m* à terme; **~s exchange** *n* marché *m* à terme; **~s market** *n* marché *m* de contrats à terme; **~s options** *npl* options *fpl* sur contrats à terme; **~s trader** ▶ 1692 *n* opérateur *m* sur les contrats à terme.

futurism /'fju:tʃərɪzəm/ (also **Futurism**) *n* futurisme *m*.

futurist /'fju:tʃərɪst/ (also **Futurist**) *n, adj* futuriste (*mf*).

futuristic /ˌfju:tʃə'rɪstɪk/ *adj* futuriste.

futurity /fju:'tjʊərətɪ, US -tʊər-/ *n* sout futur *m*.

futurologist /ˌfju:tʃə'rɒlədʒɪst/ *n* futurologue *mf*.

futurology /ˌfju:tʃə'rɒlədʒɪ/ *n* futurologie *f*.

fuze *n* US = **fuse**.

fuzz /fʌz/ **I** *n* **1** (mop of hair) tignasse *f* bouclée; (beard) barbiche *f*; (downy hair) duvet *m*; **2**○ (police) **the ~** (+ *v pl*) les flics○ *mpl*.

II *vtr* brouiller [*image, vision*].

III *vi* (also **~ over**) [*image, vision*] se brouiller.

fuzziness /'fʌzɪnɪs/ *n* **1** (of image, photograph) flou *m*; **2** (of idea, understanding) caractère *m* confus.

fuzzy /'fʌzɪ/ *adj* **1** [*hair, beard*] (curly) crépu; (downy) duveteux/-euse; **2** (blurry) [*image, vision, photo*] flou; **3** (vague) [*idea, mind, understanding, logic*] confus; [*distinction*] flou.

fwd *abrév écrite* = **forward**.

FWD *n*: *abrév* ▶ **front-wheel drive**.

g, G /dʒiː/ *n* **1** (letter) g, G *m*; **2 G** Mus sol *m*; **3 g** (*abrév écrite* = **gram(s)**) g; **4 g** Phys g *m*.

G7 *n* G7 *m*.

GA US Post *abrév écrite* = **Georgia**.

gab○ /gæb/ *vi* (*p prés etc* **-bb-**) jacasser; **to ~ on about sth** ne pas arrêter de parler de qch; **what's he ~bing on about?** qu'est-ce qu'il raconte?

IDIOMS **to have the gift of the ~**○ avoir du bagou(t)○.

gabardine /ˈgæbədiːn, -ˈdiːn/ *n* (fabric, raincoat) gabardine *f*.

gabbing○ /ˈgæbɪŋ/ *n* jacassement *m*; **stop your ~!** arrête de jacasser!

gabble /ˈgæbl/ I *n* charabia○ *m*; **~ of conversation** brouhaha *m* des conversations.

II *vtr* **1** avaler [*words*]; **2** = **gabble out**.

III *vi* bredouiller.

■ **gabble away**, **gabble on** baragouiner○.

■ **gabble out**: **~ out [sth]** bafouiller [*excuse, apology*].

gabbro /ˈgæbrəʊ/ *n* gabbro *m*.

gable /ˈgeɪbl/ I *n* pignon *m*.

II **gabled** *pp adj* à pignons (*after n*).

gable: **~ end** *n* mur-pignon *m*; **~ roof** *n* toit *m* à double pente.

Gabon /gəˈbɒn/ ▶ **1131** *pr n* Gabon *m*.

Gabonese /ˌgæbəˈniːz/ I *n* Gabonais/-e *m/f*.

II *adj* gabonais.

gad /gæd/ *excl*† (also **by ~**) sapristi†.

■ **gad about**, **gad around**○ (*p prés etc* **-dd-**) vadrouiller○.

gad: **~about**○ *n* vadrouilleur/-euse○ *m/f*; **~fly** *n* taon *m*; fig mouche *f* du coche.

gadget /ˈgædʒɪt/ *n* gadget *m* (**for doing, to do** pour faire).

gadgetry /ˈgædʒɪtrɪ/ *n* ¢ gadgets *mpl*.

Gaelic /ˈgeɪlɪk, ˈgæ-/ ▶ **1402** *n, adj* gaélique (*m*).

gaff /gæf/ I *n* **1** Fishg gaffe *f*; **2** Naut corne *f*; **3**○ GB (home) piaule○ *f*.

II *vtr* Fishg gaffer.

IDIOMS **to blow the ~**○ GB vendre la mèche○; **to blow the ~ on sth**○ GB révéler la vérité sur [*conspiracy*]; **to stand the ~**○ US encaisser○.

gaffe /gæf/ *n* bévue *f*; **to make a ~** commettre une bévue.

gaffer /ˈgæfə(r)/ *n* **1** GB (foreman) contremaître *m*; **2** GB (boss) patron *m*; **3** Cin, TV (electrician) éclairagiste *mf*; **4**† (old man) vieux bonhomme *m*.

gag /gæg/ I *n* **1** (piece of cloth) bâillon *m*; **to put a ~ over sb's mouth** bâillonner qn; **2**○ (censorship) journ bâillon *m*; **to put a ~ on democracy/free speech** bâillonner ceux qui parlent de démocratie/de liberté de la presse; **to put a ~ on the press** bâillonner la presse; **3**○ (joke) blague○ *f*.

II *vtr* (*p prés etc* **-gg-**) bâillonner [*hostage*]; journ bâillonner [*media*]; museler [*journalist, informant*]; **to ~ sb with a handkerchief** bâillonner qn avec un mouchoir.

III *vi* (*p prés etc* **-gg-**) (choke) avoir un haut-le-cœur; **he ~ged on his soup** il s'est étouffé en mangeant sa soupe.

gaga○ /ˈgɑːgɑː/ *adj* gaga○ *inv*, gâteux/-euse; **to go ~** devenir gaga○.

gage /geɪdʒ/ *n, vtr* US = **gauge** I, II.

gaggle /ˈgægl/ *n* troupeau *m*.

gag law, **gag rule** *n* US *règle permettant d'éviter ou de limiter les débats*.

gaiety /ˈgeɪətɪ/ *n* gaieté *f*.

gaiety girl *n* danseuse *f* de music-hall.

gaily /ˈgeɪlɪ/ *adv* **1** (brightly) [*laugh*] de bon cœur; [*say*] joyeusement; **~ coloured** GB, **~ colored** US aux couleurs gaies; **~ decorated** gaiement décoré; **~ dressed** habillé de couleurs gaies; **2** (casually) [*announce, reveal*] avec désinvolture.

gain /geɪn/ I *n* **1** (increase) augmentation *f*; **~ in weight/value** augmentation de poids/de valeur; **~ in time** gain *m* de temps; **~s in productivity** gains *mpl* de productivité; **2** (profit) profit *m*, gain *m*; **material/financial ~** gain *m* matériel/financier; **to do sth for material ~** faire qch pour l'argent; **3** (advantage, improvement) gen gain *m*; (in status, knowledge) acquis *m*; **electoral/diplomatic ~s** gains électoraux/diplomatiques; **the ~s of women's liberation** les acquis de la libération féminine; **to make ~s** [*political party*] se renforcer; **it's her loss but our ~** elle y perd mais nous y gagnons.

II **gains** *npl* Comm, Fin (profits) gains *mpl*, profits *mpl*; (winnings) gains *mpl*; (on stock market) gains *mpl*, hausses *fpl*; **losses and ~s** pertes *fpl* et profits; **to make ~s** [*currency, shares*] être en hausse.

III *vtr* **1** (acquire) acquérir [*experience*] (**from** de); obtenir [*information*] (**from** grâce à); gagner [*respect, support, approval*]; conquérir [*freedom*]; **to ~ popularity** gagner en popularité; **to ~ time** gagner du temps; **to ~ sth by doing** gagner qch en faisant; **to ~ credibility by doing** gagner en crédibilité en faisant; **the advantages to be ~ed from adopting this strategy** les avantages qu'on peut obtenir en adoptant cette stratégie; **we have nothing to ~ from this investment** nous n'avons rien à gagner dans cet investissement; **to ~ the impression that** avoir l'impression que; **to ~ control of sth** prendre le contrôle de qch; **to ~ possession of sth** s'assurer la possession de qch; **to ~ ground** gagner du terrain (**on** sur); **2** (increase) (in speed, height, etc) **to ~ speed/momentum** [*driver, vehicle, plane*] prendre de la vitesse/de l'élan; **to ~ weight** prendre du poids; **to ~ 4 kilos** prendre 4 kilos; **to ~ 3 minutes** (watch, clock, competitor) prendre 3 minutes d'avance; **my watch has started to ~ time** ma montre s'est mise à avancer; **3** (win) **to ~ points** gagner des points; **the Republicans ~ed four seats** les Républicains ont gagné quatre sièges; **they ~ed four seats from the Democrats** ils ont pris quatre sièges aux Démocrates; **to ~ a comfortable victory** remporter une victoire confortable; **to ~ the upper hand** prendre le dessus; **we have everything to ~ and nothing to lose** nous avons tout à gagner et rien à perdre; **4** (reach) gagner, atteindre [*place*].

IV *vi* **1** (improve) **to ~ in prestige/popularity** gagner en prestige/en popularité; **to ~ in confidence** prendre de l'assurance; **2** (profit) **she's not ~ed by it** cela ne lui a rien rapporté; **do you think we'll ~ by adopting this strategy?** pensez-vous que nous y gagnerons en adoptant cette stratégie?

■ **gain on**: **~ on [sb/sth]** rattraper [*person, vehicle*]; **the opposition are ~ing on the government** l'opposition l'emporte sur le gouvernement; **the sea is ~ing on the land** la mer gagne sur la terre.

gainer /ˈgeɪnə(r)/ *n* **1** (person, group) gagnant/-e *m/f*; **2** Fin (share) valeur *f* en hausse.

gainful /ˈgeɪnfl/ *adj* [*occupation, employment*] rémunéré.

gainfully /ˈgeɪnfəlɪ/ *adv* **to be ~ employed** avoir un emploi rémunéré.

gainsay /ˌgeɪnˈseɪ/ *vtr* (*prét, pp* **gainsaid**) sout réfuter [*argument*]; contredire [*person*]; **there's no ~ing it** c'est indéniable.

gait /geɪt/ *n* littér (of person) démarche *f*; (of animal) allure *f*.

gaiter /ˈgeɪtə(r)/ *n* guêtre *f*.

gaitered /ˈgeɪtəd/ *adj* chaussé de guêtres.

gal /gæl/ *n* **1**† = **girl** I 1; **2** *abrév écrite* = **gallon**.

gala /ˈgɑːlə/ I *n* gala *m*; **swimming ~** gala *m* de natation.

II *modif* de gala.

galactic /gəˈlæktɪk/ *adj* galactique.

galantine /ˈgælәntiːn/ *n* galantine *f*.

Galapagos /gəˈlæpəgəs/ ▶ **1381** *pr npl* (also **~ Islands**) **the ~** les (îles *fpl*) Galapagos *fpl*.

Galapagos tortoise *n* tortue *f* des (îles) Galapagos.

Galatians /gəˈleɪʃnz/ *n* (+ *v sg*) Galates *mpl*.

galaxy /ˈgæləksɪ/ *n* Astron galaxie *f*; fig pléiade *f*.

gale /geɪl/ *n* vent *m* violent, coup *m* de vent; **a force 9 ~** un vent force 9; **~force winds** vents violents; **a ~ was blowing, it was blowing a ~** le vent soufflait en tempête; **~s of laughter** fig éclats *mpl* de rire.

galena /gəˈliːnə/ *n* galène *f*.

gale warning *n* avis *m* de coup de vent.

Galicia /gəˈlɪsjə/ *pr n* (in Central Europe) Galicie *f*; (in Spain) Galice *f*.

Galilean /ˌgælɪˈliːən/ Astron, Bible, Geog I *n* Galiléen/-éenne *m/f*.

II *adj* galiléen/-éenne.

Galilee /ˈgælɪliː/ ▶ **1511** *pr n* Galilée *f*; **the Sea of ~** le lac de Tibériade, la mer de Galilée.

Galileo /ˌgælɪˈleɪəʊ/ *pr n* Galilée.

gall /gɔːl/ I *n* **1** Med bile *f*; **2** (of edible animal) fiel *m*; **3** (resentment) amertume *f*; **4** (cheek) impudence *f*; **to have the ~ to do** avoir l'impudence de faire; **5** Bot galle *f*; **6** Vet écorchure *f* (*causée par le frottement*).

II *vtr* exaspérer; **it ~s me to see/hear that** ça m'exaspère de voir/d'apprendre que; **that's what ~s me** c'est ça qui m'exaspère; **it ~s me to say so** il m'en coûte de dire ça.

gallant /ˈgælənt/ I‡ or hum *n* galant *m*.

Games and sports

With or without the definite article?

French normally uses the definite article with names of games and sports:

football	= le football
bridge	= le bridge
chess	= les échecs *mpl*
marbles	= les billes *fpl*
cops and robbers	= les gendarmes et les voleurs
to play football	= jouer au football
to play bridge	= jouer au bridge
to play chess	= jouer aux échecs
to play marbles *or* at marbles	= jouer aux billes
to play cops and robbers *or* at cops and robbers	= jouer aux gendarmes et aux voleurs
to like football	= aimer le football
to like chess	= aimer les échecs

But most compound nouns (e.g. saute-mouton, colin-maillard, pigeon vole*) work like this:*

hide-and-seek	= cache-cache *m*
to play at hide-and-seek	= jouer à cache-cache
to like hide-and-seek	= aimer jouer à cache-cache

Names of other 'official' games and sports follow the same pattern as bridge *in the following phrases:*

to play bridge with X against Y	= jouer au bridge avec X contre Y
to beat sb at bridge	= battre qn au bridge
to win at bridge	= gagner au bridge
to lose at bridge	= perdre au bridge
she's good at bridge	= elle joue bien au bridge
a bridge club	= un club de bridge

Players and events

a bridge player	= un joueur de bridge

but

I'm not a bridge player	= je ne joue pas au bridge
he's a good bridge player	= il joue bien au bridge
a game of bridge	= une partie de bridge
a bridge champion	= un champion de bridge
the French bridge champion	= le champion de France de bridge
a bridge championship	= un championnat de bridge
to win the French championship	= gagner le championnat de France
the rules of bridge	= les règles du bridge

Playing cards

The names of the four suits work like club *here:*

clubs	= les trèfles *mpl*
to play a club	= jouer un trèfle
a high/low club	= un gros/petit trèfle
the eight of clubs	= le huit de trèfle
the ace of clubs	= l'as de trèfle
I've no clubs left	= je n'ai plus de trèfle
have you any clubs?	= as-tu du trèfle?
clubs are trumps	= l'atout est trèfle
to call two clubs	= demander deux trèfles

Other games vocabulary can be found in the dictionary at match, game, set, trick *etc.*

II *adj* **1** (courageous) [*soldier*] vaillant, brave; [*struggle, attempt*] héroïque; **~ deeds** actes *mpl* de bravoure; **2†** (courteous) [*man, manners*] galant; **3‡** [*ship, steed*] noble.

gallantly /ˈgæləntlɪ/ *adv* **1** (bravely) vaillamment; **2†** (courteously) galamment.

gallantry /ˈgæləntrɪ/ *n* **1** (courage) bravoure *f*; **2†** (courtesy) galanterie *f*.

gall bladder ▶ 1037 *n* vésicule *f* biliaire.

galleon /ˈgælɪən/ *n* galion *m*.

gallery /ˈgælərɪ/ *n* **1** (also **art ~**) (public) musée *m*; (private) galerie *f*; (part of museum) galerie *f*; **2** Archit gen galerie *f*; (in parliament: for press, public) tribune *f*; **3** Theat dernier balcon *m*, poulailler○ *m*; **4** (in cave) galerie *f*; **5** US (auction room) salle *f* des ventes.

IDIOMS **to play to the ~** chercher à épater la galerie.

galley /ˈgælɪ/ *n* **1** (ship) galère *f*; **2** (ship's kitchen) cuisine *f*; **3** Aviat office *m*; **4** Print (also **~ proof**) galée *f*.

galley slave *n* lit, fig galérien *m*.

gallic /ˈgælɪk/ *adj* Chem gallique.

Gallic /ˈgælɪk/ *adj* gen français; Hist gaulois; **the ~ wars** la guerre des Gaules; **the ~ nation** la France.

gallicism /ˈgælɪsɪzəm/ *n* gallicisme *m*.

gallimaufry‡ /ˌgælɪˈmɔːfrɪ/ *n* fatras *m*.

galling /ˈgɔːlɪŋ/ *adj* [*remark, criticism*] vexant; **it was ~ to hear that** c'était vexant d'apprendre que; **I find it ~ that** je trouve vexant que (+ *subj*).

gallium /ˈgælɪəm/ *n* gallium *m*.

gallivant /ˈgælɪvænt/: ■ **gallivant around, gallivant about**: ¶ **~ around** se balader; **he's off ~ing around somewhere** il est parti se balader quelque part; ¶ **~ around [sth]** se balader en [*Europe*]; se balader dans [*region*]; se balader à travers [*countryside*].

gallon /ˈgælən/ ▶ 1068 *n* gallon *m* (GB = *4.546 litres*; US = *3.785 litres*); **a 5 ~ drum** un bidon de 5 gallons.

gallop /ˈgæləp/ I *n* Equit, fig galop *m*; **to go for a ~** aller faire un galop; **to break into a ~** prendre le galop; **at a ~** au galop also fig; **at full ~** au grand galop; **a ~ through European history** fig un aperçu rapide de l'histoire européenne.

II *vtr* galoper [*horse*].

III *vi* **1** Equit galoper; **to ~ away/back** partir/revenir au galop; **2** fig **he came ~ing down the stairs/street** il a descendu l'escalier/la rue à toute allure; **Japan is ~ing ahead in this field** le Japon dépasse tout le monde dans ce domaine; **to ~ through one's work** expédier son travail à toute vitesse.

galloping /ˈgæləpɪŋ/ *adj* **1** [*horse*] au galop; **2** fig [*inflation, consumption*] galopant.

gallows /ˈgæləʊz/ *n* gibet *m*, potence *f*; **to die on the ~** mourir au gibet; **to end up on the ~** finir à la potence.

gallows: **~ bird†** *n* gibier *m* de potence; **~ humour** GB, **~ humor** US *n* humour *m* macabre.

gallstone /ˈgɔːlstəʊn/ *n* calcul *m* biliaire.

Gallup poll /ˈgæləp pəʊl/ *n* sondage *m* Gallup.

galoot○ /gəˈluːt/ *n* lourdaud *m*.

galop /ˈgæləp/ *n* galop *m*.

galore /gəˈlɔː(r)/ *adv* [*prizes, bargains, goals, nightclubs*] à profusion; [*cocktails, whisky, sandwiches*] à volonté.

galosh /gəˈlɒʃ/ *n* caoutchouc *m*.

galumph /gəˈlʌmf/ hum *vi* (also **~ about**) se déplacer maladroitement.

galvanic /gælˈvænɪk/ *adj* **1** Elec galvanique; **2** fig **to have a ~ effect on sb** faire l'effet d'une décharge électrique sur qn.

galvanism /ˈgælvənɪzəm/ *n* Med galvanisation *f*.

galvanization /ˌgælvənaɪˈzeɪʃn, US -nɪˈz-/ *n* Ind galvanisation *f*.

galvanize /ˈgælvənaɪz/ *vtr* **1** Ind galvaniser; **2** fig galvaniser [*group, community*]; rallier [*support*]; relancer [*campaign*]; **to ~ sb into doing** pousser qn à faire; **to ~ sb into action** pousser qn à agir.

galvanometer /ˌgælvəˈnɒmɪtə(r)/ *n* galvanomètre *m*.

galvanoscope /ˈgælvənəskəʊp/ *n* galvanoscope *m*.

Gambia /ˈgæmbɪə/ ▶ 1131 *pr n* **the ~** la Gambie.

Gambian /ˈgæmbɪən/ ▶ 1486 I *n* Gambien/-ienne *m/f*.

II *adj* gambien/-ienne.

gambit /ˈgæmbɪt/ *n* **1** tactique *f*; **opening ~** tactique pour entrer en matière; **2** (in chess) gambit *m*.

gamble /ˈgæmbl/ I *n* **1** (bet) pari *m*; **to have a ~ on sth** faire un pari sur qch; **2** fig (risk) pari *m*; **to take a ~** faire un pari; **that's a bit of a ~** c'est un peu risqué; **a safe ~** un pari sûr; **his ~ paid off** son pari or son coup de poker a réussi.

II *vtr* jouer [*money*]; fig miser (**on** sur); **to ~ everything on sth** tout miser sur qch.

III *vi* (at cards) jouer; Turf parier; fig miser (**on** sur); **to ~ on the horses** parier aux courses; **to ~ at cards** jouer de l'argent aux cartes; **to ~ for high stakes** lit, fig jouer gros; **to ~ on the Stock Exchange** jouer à la Bourse; **to ~ with sb's life** jouer avec la vie de qn; **he ~d that the shares would rise** il a misé sur l'augmentation des actions; **she hadn't ~d on his being there** elle n'avait pas prévu qu'il serait là.

■ **gamble away**: **~ away [sth]**, **~ [sth] away** perdre [qch] au jeu [*money, fortune*]; **he had ~d all his money away** il avait perdu tout son argent au jeu.

gambler /ˈgæmblə(r)/ *n* joueur/-euse *m/f*; **heavy ~** flambeur *m*.

Gamblers Anonymous *n*: *association qui aide les joueurs invétérés à arrêter de parier.*

gambling /ˈgæmblɪŋ/ I *n* jeu *m* (d'argent); **his compulsive ~** sa passion du jeu.

II *modif* [*syndicate, hall, table, house, debt*] de jeu.

gambling: **~ casino** *n* casino *m*; **~ den** *n* tripot *m*; **~ joint**○ *n* tripot○ *m*; **~ losses** *n* pertes *fpl* au jeu; **~ man** *n* parieur *m*.

gamboge /gæmˈbəʊʒ, -ˈbuːʒ/ *n* gomme-gutte *f*.

gambol /ˈgæmbl/ *vi* (*p prés etc* **-ll-**, US **-l-**) littér [*child*] gambader; [*animal*] cabrioler.

game /geɪm/ I *n* **1** (activity) jeu *m*; **to play a ~** jouer à un jeu; **a ~ for three players** un jeu à trois (joueurs); **~ of chance/of skill** jeu de hasard/d'adresse; **it's only a ~!** ce n'est qu'un jeu! **this isn't a ~, you know!** ce n'est pas un jeu, tu sais!; **to play the ~** fig jouer franc jeu; **don't play ~s with me!** (tell me the truth) ne me fais pas marcher! (don't try to be smart) n'essaie pas de jouer au plus fin avec moi!; **2** (session, match) (of chess, cards, poker, darts, hide-and-seek) partie *f*; (of football, hockey, cricket) match *m*; **to have** ou **play a ~ of cards/of chess** faire or disputer une partie de cartes/d'échecs; **let's have a ~ of football** on fait une partie de foot○? **let's have a ~ of cowboys** on joue aux cowboys?; **3** US (professional sporting event) match *m*; **4** (section of tournament) (in tennis) jeu *m*; (in bridge) manche *f*; **four ~s to one** quatre jeux à un; **we're two ~s all** nous sommes à deux jeux partout; **~ to Hadman** jeu Hadman; **~, set and match** jeu, set et match; **5** (skill at playing) jeu *m*; **how to improve your ~** comment améliorer votre jeu; **grass suits my ~** j'aime bien jouer sur gazon; **she plays a great ~ of chess** c'est une excellente joueuse d'échecs; **to put sb off his/her**

~ distraire qn; 6○ (trick, scheme) jeu *m*, manège *m*; **what's your ~?** à quoi joues-tu? **so that' s his ~!** c'est donc ça sa combine○! **I have no choice but to play his ~** je n'ai pas d'autre choix que d'entrer dans son jeu; **I decided to play the same ~** j'ai décidé de rendre la pareille; **he's up to his old ~s again** il refait des siennes; 7○ (activity, occupation) péj ou hum **the insurance/marketing ~** le domaine de l'assurance/du marketing; **the politics ~** le jeu de la politique; **I've been in this ~ 10 years** je suis dans la partie depuis 10 ans; **he's new to this ~** il est nouveau dans la partie; 8 Hunt, Culin gibier *m*.
II **games** *npl* 1 GB Sch sport *m*; **good at ~s** bon/bonne en sport; 2 (also **Games**) (sporting event) Jeux *mpl*.
III *modif* 1 [*pâté, dish, stew*] de gibier; [*soup*] à base de gibier; 2 **games** GB [*teacher, lesson, master, mistress*] d'éducation physique.
IV *adj* 1 (willing to try) partant○; **he's ~ for anything** il est toujours partant○; **she's always ~ for an adventure/a laugh** elle est toujours prête à tenter l'aventure/à rire; **OK, I'm ~** d'accord, j'en suis; 2 (plucky) courageux/-euse; 3 [*leg*] estropié; **to have a ~ leg** boiter.
IDIOMS **that's the name of the ~** c'est ce qui compte; **the ~'s up** tout est fichu○; **to beat sb at his/their own ~** battre qn à son/leur propre jeu; **to be/go on the ~**○ GB faire/se mettre à faire le trottoir○; **to give the ~ away** vendre la mèche; **two can play at that ~** à bon chat, bon rat Prov.

game: **~ bag** *n* gibecière *f*; **~ bird** *n* gibier *m* à plumes; **~ chips** *npl* pommes *fpl* sautées (en tranches); **~ cock** *n* coq *m* de combat; **~ fish** *n* salmonidé *m*; **~keeper** ▶1692 *n* garde-chasse *m*; **~ laws** *npl* réglementation *f* de la chasse.

gamely /ˈgeɪmlɪ/ *adv* courageusement.

game: **~ park** *n* = **game reserve**; **~ pie** *n* pâté *m* de gibier en croûte; **~ plan** *n* Sport, gen stratégie *f*; **~ point** *n* (tennis) balle *f* de jeu; **~ reserve** *n* (for hunting) réserve *f* de chasse; (for preservation) réserve *f* naturelle (*de grands fauves*); **~ show** *n* jeu *m* télévisé.

gamesmanship /ˈgeɪmzmənʃɪp/ *n* ¢ péj stratagèmes *mpl*; **that's just ~** ce n'est qu'une astuce pour gagner.

gamester /ˈgeɪmstə(r)/ *n* joueur/-euse *m/f*.

gamete /ˈgæmiːt/ *n* gamète *m*.

game: **~(s) theory** *n* théorie *f* des jeux; **~ warden** *n* garde-chasse *m*.

gamin /ˈgæmɪn/ *n* littér gosse *mf* des rues.

gamine /gæˈmiːn/ I *n* gamine *f*.
II *modif* [*hairstyle*] à la garçonne.

gaming /ˈgeɪmɪŋ/ *n* 1 (gambling) jeu *m* (d'argent); 2 (role-play games) jeu *m* de rôles.

gaming: **~ debt** *n* dette *f* de jeu; **~ house**† *n* maison *f* de jeu; **~ laws** *npl* réglementation *f* des jeux; **~ machine** *n* machine *f* à sous.

gamma /ˈgæmə/ *n* gamma *m*.

gamma radiation *n* rayons *mpl* gamma.

gamma ray I *n* rayon *m* gamma.
II *modif* [*emissions*] des rayons gamma.

gammon /ˈgæmən/ I *n* jambon *m*.
II *modif* [*steak*] de jambon; **a ~ joint** un jambon.

gammy○ /ˈgæmɪ/ *adj* [*leg, shoulder etc*] estropié; **to have a ~ leg** avoir une mauvaise jambe○.

gamp○ /gæmp/ *n* pépin○ *m*, parapluie *m*.

gamut /ˈgæmət/ *n* Mus, fig gamme *f*; **the whole ~ of sth** toute la gamme de qch; **to run the ~ of sth** passer par tout l'éventail de qch.

gamy○ /ˈgeɪmɪ/ *adj* faisandé; **the meat smells a bit ~** la viande a une légère odeur de faisandé.

gander /ˈgændə(r)/ *n* 1 Zool jars *m*; 2○ GB **to take** ou **have a ~ at sth** jeter un coup d'œil à qch.

ganef○ /ˈgænef/ *n* US filou *m*.

gang /gæŋ/ *n* 1 (group) (of criminals) gang *m*; (of youths) pej bande *f*; **in ~s** en bande; **to join a ~** entrer dans une bande; **the Gang of Four** Hist la Bande des Quatre; 2 (of friends etc) bande *f*; **to be one of the ~** faire partie de la bande; 3 (team of workmen, prisoners) équipe *f*; 4 Tech (of tools) jeu *m*.
■ **gang together** se grouper (**to do** pour faire).
■ **gang up** se coaliser (**on, against** contre; **to do** pour faire).

gangbang● /ˈgæŋbæŋ/ *n* viol *m* collectif.

ganger /ˈgæŋə(r)/ *n* GB chef *m* d'équipe (*dans les ponts et chaussées*).

Ganges /ˈgændʒiːz/ ▶1644 *pr n* Gange *m*.

gang fight *n* bagarre *f* entre bandes.

gangland /ˈgæŋlænd/ I *n* ≈ le Milieu.
II *modif* [*killing, crime*] du Milieu.

gang leader *n* chef *m* de bande.

ganglia /ˈgæŋglɪə/ *pl* ▶ **ganglion**.

gangling /ˈgæŋglɪŋ/ *adj* dégingandé; **a ~ boy** ou **youth** un échalas.

ganglion /ˈgæŋglɪən/ *n* (*pl* **-lia**) ganglion *m*.

gang: **~plank** *n* Naut passerelle *f*; **~-rape** *n* viol *m* collectif.

gangrene /ˈgæŋgriːn/ ▶1354 *n* gangrène *f* also fig.

gangrenous /ˈgæŋgrɪnəs/ *adj* gangreneux/-euse; **to go ~** se gangrener.

gangster /ˈgæŋstə(r)/ I *n* gangster *m*, bandit *m*, truand *m*.
II *modif* [*film, story, tactics*] de gangsters; [*boss*] des gangsters.

gangway /ˈgæŋweɪ/ *n* 1 (passage) allée *f*; **'~!'** dégagez!; 2 Naut passerelle *f*.

ganja /ˈgændʒə/ *n* ganja *f*.

gannet /ˈgænɪt/ *n* 1 Zool fou *m* de Bassan; 2 fig, hum **he/she's a real ~** il/elle n'arrête pas de manger.

gantry /ˈgæntrɪ/ *n* Constr portique *m*; Aerosp tour *f* de lancement.

gaol *n*, *vtr* GB = **jail**.

gaoler *n* GB = **jailer**.

gap /gæp/ *n* 1 (empty space) (between planks, curtains) interstice *m* (**in** entre); (in fence, wall) trou *m*, ouverture *f* (**in** dans); (between buildings, cars, furniture) espace *m* (**in** entre); (in text, diagram) blanc *m*, trou *m* (**in** dans); (in hills, cloud) trouée *f* (**in** dans); **to have ~s between one's teeth** avoir les dents écartées; **his death left a ~ in my life** sa mort a laissé un vide dans ma vie; **to fill a ~** lit, fig combler un vide; 2 (break in continuity) (in timetable) trou *m*, créneau *m*; (in conversation) silence *m*; (in accounts, records, report) lacune *f*, trou *m*; (of time) intervalle *m*; (in event, performance) interruption *f*; **after a ~ of six years** après un intervalle de six ans; 3 (discrepancy) (in age) différence *f*; (between opinions) divergence *f*; (between scores) différence *f* (**in** entre); (of status) écart *m*; **a 15-year age ~** une différence d'âge de 15 ans; **the ~ between the rich and the poor** l'écart entre les riches et les pauvres; **the ~ between myth and reality** l'écart ou le décalage entre le mythe et la réalité; **to close the ~** supprimer l'écart; 4 (deficiency) (in knowledge, education) lacune *f* (**in** dans); **there's a ~ in my memory** j'ai un trou de mémoire; **technology/training ~** insuffisance *f* en matière de technologie/formation; 5 Advertg, Comm créneau *m*; **to look for a ~ in the market** chercher un créneau sur le marché; **to fill a ~ in the market** répondre à un besoin réel du marché; 6 Fin déficit *m*; **trade ~** déficit commercial; **dollar ~** pénurie *f* de dollars.

gape /geɪp/ *vi* 1 (stare) rester bouche bée; **to ~ at sth/sb** regarder qn/qch bouche bée; 2 (open wide) [*chasm, hole*] s'ouvrir tout grand; [*wound*] être béant; [*garment*] être grand ouvert; **his shirt ~d open** sa chemise était grande ouverte.

gap financing *n* crédit *m* relais.

gaping /ˈgeɪpɪŋ/ *adj* 1 (staring) [*person*] bouche bée; **he was greeted by a ~ crowd** il a été accueilli par une foule qui le regardait bouche bée; **~ onlookers** badauds *mpl*; 2 (open) [*shirt, beak*] grand ouvert; [*wound, hole*] béant; **their ~ mouths** leurs bouches grandes ouvertes.

gappy○ /ˈgæpɪ/ *adj* **~ teeth** dents écartées.

gap-toothed /ˈgæptuːθt/ *n* [*person*] qui a les dents écartées; [*smile*] édenté; **to be ~** avoir les dents écartées.

garage /ˈgærɑːʒ, ˈgærɪdʒ, US gəˈrɑːʒ/ I *n* garage *m*.
II *modif* [*wall, door*] de garage.
III *vtr* mettre [qch] au garage [*vehicle*].

garage: **~ mechanic** ▶1692 *n* mécanicien *m*; **~ owner** *n* garagiste *m*; **~ sale** *n* brocante *f* à domicile.

garaging /ˈgærədʒɪŋ/ *n* **with/without ~** avec/sans garage *m*.

garb /gɑːb/ *n* costume *m*; **in peasant/clerical ~** en costume de paysan/d'ecclésiastique.

garbage /ˈgɑːbɪdʒ/ *n* ¢ 1 US ordures *fpl*; **to dispose of ~** [*person*] jeter les ordures; [*local authority*] traiter les ordures; **to put the ~ out** sortir les poubelles; 2 fig (nonsense) âneries *fpl*; **to talk ~** débiter des âneries; 3 Comput données *fpl* incorrectes.
IDIOMS **~ in ~ out** Comput à instructions incorrectes, résultats incorrects; fig on ne fait pas de bon pain avec du mauvais levain.

garbage: **~ can** *n* US poubelle *f*; **~ chute** *n* US vide-ordures *m* *inv*; **~ collector**, **~ man** ▶1692 *n* US éboueur *m*; **~ disposal** *n* traitement *m* des ordures; **~ disposal unit** *n* US broyeur *m* d'ordures; **~ truck** *n* US camion *m* des éboueurs.

garble /ˈgɑːbl/ *vtr* raconter [qch] de façon confuse [*story, facts*]; donner [qch] de façon confuse [*instructions*]; transmettre [qch] de façon confuse [*message*].

garbled /ˈgɑːbld/ *adj* [*account, instructions*] confus.

Gard ▶1163 *pr n* Gard *m*; **in/to the ~** dans le Gard.

Garda /ˈgɑːdə/ ▶1400 *pr n* 1 Geog **Lake ~** le lac de Garde; 2 (*pl* **-dai**) (in Ireland) *membre de la police d'Irlande du Sud*.

garden /ˈgɑːdn/ I *n* 1 GB (area surrounding house) jardin *m* also fig; **front/back ~** jardin situé devant/derrière la maison; **we don't have much ~** nous n'avons pas un grand jardin. 2 US (flower) platebande *f*; (vegetable) potager *m*.
II **gardens** *npl* (municipal) jardin *m* public; ▶ **botanic**.
III *modif* [*plant, furniture*] de jardin; [*wall, fence, shed*] du jardin.
IV *vi* jardiner, faire du jardinage.
IDIOMS **to lead sb up** ou US **down the ~ path**○ mener qn en bateau○; **everything in the ~'s rosy**○ iron tout va pour le mieux iron.

garden apartment *n* 1 = **garden flat**; 2 *immeubles bas entourant un jardin*.

garden: **~ centre** GB, **~ center** US *n* jardinerie *f*; **~ city** *n* GB cité-jardin *f*.

gardener /ˈgɑːdnə(r)/ ▶1692 *n* jardinier/-ière *m/f*; **to be a keen ~** (amateur) être un passionné de jardinage.

garden: **~ flat** *n* GB appartement *m* en rez-de-jardin; **~-fresh** *adj* du jardin.

gardenia /gɑːˈdiːnɪə/ *n* gardénia *m*.

gardening /ˈgɑːdnɪŋ/ I *n* jardinage *m*.
II *modif* [*tools, equipment*] de jardinage.

garden: **Garden of Eden** *n* jardin *m* d'Éden; **~ of remembrance** *n* (in cemetery) jardin *m* des souvenirs; **~ party** *n* garden-party *f*; **~ produce** *n* ¢ produits *mpl* maraîchers; **~ shears** *npl* cisailles *fpl* (de jardinier); **~ snail** *n* escargot *m*; **~ suburb** *n* banlieue *f* verte; **~-variety** *adj* US [*writer, book*] insignifiant.

garfish /ˈɡɑːfɪʃ/ *n* aiguille *f*, orphie *f* spec.

gargantuan /ɡɑːˈɡæntjʊən/ *adj* littér gargantuesque liter.

gargle /ˈɡɑːɡl/ **I** *n* (act, liquid) gargarisme *m*; **to have a ~** se gargariser.
II *vi* se gargariser (**with** avec).

gargoyle /ˈɡɑːɡɔɪl/ *n* gargouille *f*.

garish /ˈɡeərɪʃ/ *adj* [*colour, garment*] tape-à-l'œil *inv*; [*light*] cru.

garishly /ˈɡeərɪʃlɪ/ *adj* [*dressed, decorated*] de façon voyante; **~ lit** à la lumière crue.

garishness /ˈɡeərɪʃnɪs/ *n* (of decor) clinquant *m*; (of colour, clothes) aspect *m* tape-à-l'œil; (of light) crudité *f*.

garland /ˈɡɑːlənd/ **I** *n* guirlande *f*.
II *vtr* enguirlander (**with** de).

garlic /ˈɡɑːlɪk/ **I** *n* ail *m*.
II *modif* [*sausage, mushrooms*] à l'ail; [*crouton, sauce*] aillé; [*salt*] d'ail; **~ butter** beurre *m* d'ail; **~ bread**: *pain chaud tartiné de beurre et d'ail*.

garlicky○ /ˈɡɑːlɪkɪ/ *adj* [*food*] aillé; [*breath*] qui sent l'ail.

garlic press *n* presse-ail *m inv*.

garment /ˈɡɑːmənt/ *n* vêtement *m*.

garner /ˈɡɑːnə(r)/ *vtr* sout (gather) recueillir [*information, fact*] (**from sth** dans qch); (store) emmagasiner [*memories, knowledge*].

garnet /ˈɡɑːnɪt/ **I** *n* (all contexts) grenat *m*.
II *modif* [*ring, brooch*] serti d'un grenat or de grenats.
III *adj* grenat *inv*.

garnish /ˈɡɑːnɪʃ/ **I** *n* Culin garniture *f* (**of** de).
II *vtr* **1** Culin garnir (**with** de); **2** (in jewellery) orner (**with** de).

garnishee /ˌɡɑːnɪˈʃiː/ *n* Jur tiers-saisi/-e *m/f*.

garnishing /ˈɡɑːnɪʃɪŋ/ *n* garniture *f*.

garnishment /ˈɡɑːnɪʃmənt/ *n* Jur saisie-arrêt *f*.

garnishor /ˈɡɑːnɪʃə(r)/ *n* Jur saisissant *m*.

garret† /ˈɡærət/ *n* mansarde *f*.

garrison /ˈɡærɪsn/ **I** *n* garnison *f*.
II *modif* [*town, troops, life*] de garnison.
III *vtr* [*officer*] placer une garnison dans [*town, zone*]; [*troops*] tenir garnison dans [*town, zone*]; **to ~ troops in the area** mettre des troupes en garnison dans la région; **to be ~ed in** être en garnison à.

garrotte GB, **garrote** US /ɡəˈrɒt/ **I** *n* garrot *m*.
II *vtr* (officially) exécuter [qn] au garrot; (strangle) étrangler (*avec une corde ou un fil de fer*).

garrulity /ɡəˈruːlətɪ/ = **garrulousness**.

garrulous /ˈɡærʊləs/ *adj* loquace.

garrulously /ˈɡærʊləslɪ/ *adv* de façon loquace.

garrulousness /ˈɡærʊləsnɪs/ *n* loquacité *f*.

garter /ˈɡɑːtə(r)/ *n* **1** (for stocking) jarretière *f*; (for sock) fixe-chaussette *m*; **2** US (suspender) jarretelle *f*; **3** GB (title) **Knight/Order of the Garter** Chevalier *m*/Ordre *m* de la Jarretière.
IDIOMS **I'll have your guts for ~s**○**!** j'aurai ta peau○!

garter: **~ belt** *n* US porte-jarretelles *m inv*; **~ snake** *n* couleuvre *f*; **~ stitch** *n* point *m* mousse.

gas /ɡæs/ **I** *n* **1** (fuel) gaz *m*; **to cook/heat a house with ~** cuisiner/chauffer une maison au gaz; **to turn up/turn down the ~** augmenter/baisser le gaz; **on a low/medium ~** (in cooking) à feu doux/moyen; **on a high ~** à grand feu; **to use bottled ~** utiliser du gaz en bouteille; **2** Chem gaz *m*; **3** Dent (anaesthetic) anesthésie *f*; **to have ~** être anesthésié; **4** Mil gaz *m* de combat; **5** US (petrol) essence *f*; **6**○ also **~ pedal**) US (accelerator) accélérateur *m*; **7**○ †GB (chat, talk) **to have a ~** papoter○; **8**○ (funny experience, person) **it was a ~!** on s'est bien marrés○!; **what a ~!** quelle (partie de) rigolade○!; **he's a ~** c'est un marrant○.
II *modif* [*board, industry, company*] du gaz; [*explosion, pipe*] de gaz.
III *vtr* (*p prés etc* **-ss-**) gen, Mil gazer [*person, animal*].
IV *vi* (*p prés etc* **-ss-**) **1** (give off gas) dégager des gaz; **2**○ †GB (chatter) papoter○; (go on at length) parler sans arrêt.
V *v refl* (*p prés etc* **-ss-**) **to ~ oneself** se suicider au gaz.
IDIOMS **to step on the ~** appuyer sur le champignon○.
■ **gas up** US prendre de l'essence.

gas: **~bag**○ *n* moulin *m* à paroles○; **~ board** *n* compagnie *f* du gaz; **~ bracket** *n* applique *f* à gaz; **~ burner** *n* brûleur *m* à gaz; **~ carrier** *n* transporteur *m* de gaz, méthanier *m*; **~ chamber** *n* chambre *f* à gaz.

Gascon /ˈɡæskən/ **▶ 1402** **I** *n* **1** (native) Gascon/-onne *m/f*; **2** (dialect) gascon *m*.
II *adj* gen, Ling gascon/-onne.

Gascony /ˈɡæskənɪ/ **▶ 1273** *pr n* Gascogne *f*.

gas: **~ cooker** *n* cuisinière *f* à gaz; **~-cooled** *adj* à refroidissement par gaz.

gaseous /ˈɡæsɪəs, ˈɡeɪsɪəs/ *adj* gazeux/-euse.

gas: **~ fire** *n* GB (appareil *m* de) chauffage *m* à gaz; **~-fired** *adj* [*boiler, water heater*] à gaz; [*central heating*] au gaz; **~ fitter ▶ 1692** *n* chauffagiste *m*; **~ fittings** *npl* installation *f* de gaz; **~ guzzler**○ *n* US voiture *f* qui consomme beaucoup d'essence.

gash /ɡæʃ/ **I** *n* gen entaille *f* (**in, on** à); (in boiler, ship's hull) déchirure *f* (**in** à).
II○ *adj* (not needed) superflu.
III *vtr* entailler; **to ~ one's leg/hand** s'entailler la jambe/la main (**on** avec).

gas: **~ heater** *n* (for room) (appareil *m* de) chauffage *m* à gaz; (for water) chauffe-eau *m inv*; **~holder** *n* gazomètre *m*.

gas jet *n* **1** (burner) brûleur *m*; **2** (stream of gas) jet *m* de gaz.

gasket /ˈɡæskɪt/ *n* **1** Tech (in pump) garniture *f*; (in joint) joint *m* (d'étanchéité); **to blow a ~** Aut faire sauter un joint de culasse; fig hum piquer une crise○; **2** Naut (for sail) raban *m* de ferlage.

gas lamp *n* (domestic) lampe *f* à gaz; (in street) bec *m* de gaz.

gaslight /ˈɡæslaɪt/ *n* **1** C (lamp) lampe *f* à gaz; (streetlamp) bec *m* de gaz, réverbère *m*; **2** ¢ (illumination) lueur *f* d'une lampe à gaz; (of street lamp) lueur *f* d'un réverbère.

gas: **~ lighter** *n* (for cooker) allume-gaz *m inv*; **~ lighting** *n* éclairage *m* au gaz; **~ line** *n* US queue *f* à la station d'essence; **~lit** *adj* éclairé au gaz; **~ main** *n* canalisation *f* de gaz; **~ man ▶ 1692** *n* employé *m* du gaz; **~ mantle** *n* manchon *m* à incandescence; **~ mask** *n* masque *m* à gaz; **~ meter** *n* compteur *m* à gaz; **~ mileage** *n* US consommation *f* d'essence.

gasohol /ˈɡæsəhɒl/ *n* carburol *m*.

gas oil *n* gazole *m*.

gasoline /ˈɡæsəliːn/ *n* US essence *f*; **~-powered** Aut à essence.

gasometer /ɡæˈsɒmɪtə(r)/ *n* gazomètre *m*.

gas oven *n* four *m* à gaz; **she put her head in the ~** elle s'est suicidée en mettant la tête dans le four.

gasp /ɡɑːsp/ **I** *n* (breathing) halètement *m*; **to give** ou **let out a ~** avoir le souffle coupé; **to give a ~ of horror** avoir le souffle coupé par l'épouvante; **there were ~s of amazement from the crowd** la foule en avait le souffle coupé; **at the last ~** fig au dernier moment; **to be at one's last ~** lit être sur le point de mourir; fig être exténué.
II *vtr* **'Help!' he ~ed** 'Au secours!' dit-il en haletant; **she ~ed (out) a few words** elle balbutia quelques mots en haletant.
III *vi* **1** (for breath, air) haleter; **to ~ for breath** haleter; **2** (show surprise) perdre le souffle; **to ~ in** ou **with amazement** avoir le souffle coupé par la surprise; **3**○ **to be ~ing for a drink/cigarette** mourir d'envie de boire un verre/fumer une cigarette.

gas pedal *n* US accélérateur *m*.

gasper†○ /ˈɡɑːspə(r)/ *n* GB sèche†○ *f*, cigarette *f*.

gas: **~ pipeline** *n* gazoduc *m*; **~ poker** *n*: *allumeur au gaz pour feu dans la cheminée*; **~-powered** *adj* fonctionnant au gaz; **~ range** *n* fourneau *m* à gaz; **~ ring** *n* GB (fixed) brûleur *m* à gaz; (portable) réchaud *m* à gaz; **~ station** *n* US station-service *f*; **~ stove** *n* cuisinière *f* à gaz.

gassy /ˈɡæsɪ/ *adj* [*drink*] gazeux/-euse.

gas: **~ tank** *n* US Aut réservoir *m*; **~ tap** *n* robinet *m* du gaz.

gastric /ˈɡæstrɪk/ *adj* [*juices, ulcer, pain*] gastrique; **~ flu** grippe *f* intestinale.

gastritis /ɡæˈstraɪtɪs/ **▶ 1354** *n* gastrite *f*.

gastro-enteritis /ˌɡæstrəʊˌentəˈraɪtɪs/ **▶ 1354** *n* gastro-entérite *f*.

gastroenterologist /ˌɡæstrəʊˌentəˈrɒlədʒɪst/ **▶ 1692** *n* gastro-entérologue *mf*.

gastroenterology /ˌɡæstrəʊˌentəˈrɒlədʒɪ/ *n* gastro-entérologie *f*.

gastronome /ˈɡæstrənəʊm/ *n* sout gastronome *mf*.

gastronomic /ˌɡæstrəˈnɒmɪk/ *adj* sout gastronomique.

gastronomist /ɡæˈstrɒnəmɪst/ *n* sout gastronome *mf*.

gastronomy /ɡæˈstrɒnəmɪ/ *n* sout gastronomie *f*.

gastropod /ˈɡæstrəpɒd/ *n* gastéropode *m*.

gas: **~ turbine** *n* turbine *f* à gaz; **~ worker ▶ 1692** *n* employé *m* du gaz; **~works** *n* usine *f* à gaz.

gat†◑ /ɡæt/ *n* US (gun) flingue◑ *m*.

gate /ɡeɪt/ **I** *n* **1** (of field, level crossing) barrière *f*; (in underground railway) portillon *m* automatique; (of town, prison, garden) porte *f*; (of courtyard, palace) portail *m*; (at airport) porte *f*; **please proceed to ~ 12** veuillez vous rendre à la porte 12; **at the ~** à l'entrée; **2** Sport **there was a good ~ at the match** (money) le match a fait une grosse recette; **there was a ~ of 29,000** il y a eu 29 000 spectateurs; **3** (in skiing) porte *f*; **4** Comput porte *f*.
II○ *vtr* GB coller○.
IDIOMS **to give sb/get the ~**○ US mettre qn/être mis à la porte.

gâteau /ˈɡætəʊ, US ɡæˈtəʊ/ *n* (*pl* **~x, ~s**) gâteau *m* (à la crème).

gatecrash○ /ˈɡeɪtkræʃ/ **I** *vtr* (without paying) resquiller○ à [*concert*]; (without invitation) se pointer○ sans invitation à [*party*].
II *vi* (at concert) resquiller○; (at party) se pointer○ sans invitation.

gatecrasher○ /ˈɡeɪtkræʃə(r)/ *n* (at concert) resquilleur/-euse *m/f*; (at party) intrus/-e *m/f*.

gate: **~fold** *n* Publg dépliant *m* intérieur; **~house** *n* (at park, estate) maison *f* de gardien; (at lock) cabine *f* des commandes; **~keeper** *n* gardien/-ienne *m/f*; **~leg table** *n* table *f* anglaise; **~ lodge** *n* loge *f* de gardien; **~ money** *n* Sport recette *f*.

gatepost /ˈɡeɪtpəʊst/ *n* poteau *m* d'angle.
IDIOMS **between you, me and the ~**○ entre nous soit dit.

gateway /ˈɡeɪtweɪ/ *n* entrée *f*; fig voie *f* ouverte; **the ~ to success/to fame** la voie ouverte au succès/à la célébrité; **Dover is England's ~ to Europe** Douvres est la porte de l'Europe pour les Anglais.

gather /ˈɡæðə(r)/ **I** *n* Sewing fronce *f*.
II *vtr* **1** (collect) cueillir [*fruit, nuts, mushrooms, flowers*]; ramasser [*wood, fallen fruit*]; recueillir [*data, information, evidence*]; percevoir [*taxes*]; rassembler [*followers, strength, courage*]; **to ~ one's strength** rassembler ses forces; **the movement is ~ing strength** le mouvement devient plus puissant; **to ~ dust** lit prendre la poussière; fig tomber dans l'oubli; **to ~ momentum** lit prendre de la vitesse; fig gagner du terrain; **to ~ speed** prendre de la vitesse; **to ~ way** Naut prendre de la

vitesse; **we are ~ed here today to do** nous sommes réunis aujourd'hui pour faire; **2** (embrace) **to ~ sb to** serrer qn contre [*oneself, one's bosom*]; **3** (deduce, conclude) **to ~ that** déduire que; **I ~ (that) he was there** d'après ce que j'ai compris il était là; **I ~ from her (that) he was there** d'après ce qu'elle m'a dit il était là; **I ~ed from this (that) he was angry** j'en ai déduit qu'il était en colère; **as you will have ~ed** comme vous avez pu le constater; **as far as I can ~** autant que je sache; **4** Sewing faire des fronces à; **~ed at the waist** froncé à la taille; **5** Print assembler [*sections of book*].
III *vi* **1** [*people, crowd*] se rassembler; [*family*] se réunir; [*clouds*] s'amonceler; [*darkness*] s'épaissir; **the clouds were ~ing all over Europe** fig une ombre menaçante recouvrait l'Europe; **2** Med [*boil, abscess*] mûrir.
IV gather oneself *v refl* (after shock, illness) s'en remettre; (in preparation) rassembler toute son énergie.
■ **gather around:** = **gather round**.
■ **gather in:**: **~ [sth] in, ~ in [sth]** ramasser [*essays, papers, harvest, crop*]; recueillir [*money, contributions*].
■ **gather round:** ¶ se regrouper; **~ round!** approchez-vous!; ¶ **~ round [sth/sb]** se rassembler autour de [*teacher, object*]; ¶ **~ [sth] round oneself** s'envelopper dans [*shawl*].
■ **gather together:** ¶ [*family, people*] se réunir; ¶ **~ [sth] together, ~ together [sth]** rassembler [*belongings, notes, followers*]; recueillir [*data, facts, information, evidence*].
■ **gather up**: **~ [sth] up, ~ up [sth]** ramasser [*objects, belongings, skirts*]; rassembler [*strength, energy*]; **to ~ one's hair up into a bun** rassembler or ramasser ses cheveux en un chignon.

gathering /ˈgæðərɪŋ/ **I** *n* **1** (meeting) réunion *f*; **social/family ~** réunion entre amis/de famille; **2** (action of collecting) (of fruit, mushrooms, flowers) cueillette *f*; (of wood, fallen fruit) ramassage *m*; (of information, data, evidence) réunion *f*; **3** Sewing fronces *fpl*; **4** Print assemblage *m*.
II *adj* (growing) [*dusk, gloom, speed*] croissant; **the ~ clouds of war** l'ombre menaçante de la guerre.

gator○ /ˈgeɪtər/ *n* US alligator *m*.

GATT /gæt/ *n* (*abrév* = **General Agreement on Tariffs and Trade**) GATT *m*.

gauche /gəʊʃ/ *adj* [*person, attitude*] gauche; [*remark*] maladroit; [*style, writing*] maladroit.

gaucheness /ˈgəʊʃnɪs/ *n* (of person) gaucherie *f*; (of remark) maladresse *f*.

gaucho /ˈgaʊtʃəʊ/ *n* (*pl* **-chos**) gaucho *m*.

gaucho pants *npl* jupe-culotte *f*.

gaudily /ˈgɔːdɪlɪ/ *adv* **~ painted** [*banner, wagon*] bariolé; **~ dressed** vêtu de manière criarde.

gaudy /ˈgɔːdɪ/ *adj* tape-à-l'œil *inv*.

gauge /geɪdʒ/ **I** *n* **1** (standard measure) (for gun, screw) calibre *m*; (of metal, plastic sheet) épaisseur *f*; (of needle) diamètre *m*; Tex finesse *f*; **a thin-~ steel lid** un mince couvercle d'acier; **2** Rail écartement *m* (des voies); **standard/narrow ~** voie *f* normale/étroite; **3** (measuring instrument) jauge *f*; **fuel ~** Aut, Aviat jauge d'essence; **oil ~** jauge d'huile; **4** (way of judging) moyen *m* de jauger; **the best ~ of his experience** le meilleur moyen de jauger son expérience; **it's a good ~ of character** c'est un bon test de caractère; **5** Cin format *m*.
II *vtr* **1** (measure accurately) mesurer [*diameter*]; jauger [*distance, quantity*]; calibrer [*screw, shotgun*]; jauger [*oil level*]; **2** (estimate) évaluer [*mood, reaction*]; **to ~ whether their prices are too high** évaluer si leurs prix sont trop élevés; **to ~ what is happening** évaluer ce qui se passe.

Gaul /gɔːl/ *n* (country) Gaule *f*; (inhabitant) Gaulois/-e *m/f*.

Gaullist /ˈgɔːlɪst/ *n, adj* gaulliste (*mf*).

gaunt /gɔːnt/ *adj* **1** [*person, face, figure*] décharné; **2** [*landscape, building*] lugubre.

gauntlet /ˈgɔːntlɪt/ *n* **1** (protective glove) gant *m* à crispin; **2** (in armour) gantelet *m*; **3** (on shirt sleeve) ouverture *f*.
IDIOMS **to throw down the ~** fig lancer un défi; lit jeter le gant; **to pick up** ou **take up the ~** fig relever le défi; **to run the ~ of criticism/danger** s'exposer au feu de la critique/au danger.

gauss /gaʊs/ *n* (*pl* **~**) gauss *m*.

gauze /gɔːz/ **I** *n* **1** (fabric) gaze *f*; **cotton ~** gaze *f* de coton; **2** (wire mesh) grillage *m*.
II *modif* [*curtain, bandage*] de gaze.

gauzy /ˈgɔːzɪ/ *adj* transparent.

gave /geɪv/ *prét* ▶ **give**.

gavel /ˈgævl/ *n* marteau *m* (*de commissaire-priseur* ou US *de juge*).

gavotte /gəˈvɒt/ *n* gavotte *f*.

Gawd○† /gɔːd/ *excl* mince.

gawk○ /gɔːk/ *vi* regarder bêtement.

gawker○ /ˈgɔːkə(r)/ *n* US badaud/-e *m/f*.

gawky /ˈgɔːkɪ/ *adj* dégingandé.

gawp○ /gɔːp/ = **gawk**.

gay○ /geɪ/ **I** *n* homosexuel/-elle *m/f*, gay *mf*.
II *adj* **1** [*person, centre, culture*] homosexuel/-elle; [*couple, community*] gay, homosexuel/-elle; [*club, magazine, area*] gay; **~ rights** les droits des homosexuels; **2** (lively, bright) [*person, atmosphere, colour, music*] gai; [*laughter*] joyeux/-euse; [*street, café*] animé; **3** (carefree) joyeux/-euse; **she likes the ~ life** elle aime mener joyeuse vie; **to do sth with ~ abandon** faire qch le cœur léger.

gay lib○, **gay liberation** *n*: *mouvement pour la reconnaissance des droits des homosexuels.*

gayness /ˈgeɪnɪs/ *n* homosexualité *f*.

Gaza strip /ˌgɑːzə ˈstrɪp/ *pr n* bande *f* de Gaza.

gaze /geɪz/ **I** *n* regard *m*; **to hold sb's ~** soutenir le regard de qn.
II *vi* **to ~ at sb/sth** regarder qn/qch; (in wonder) contempler qn/qch; **to ~ out of the window/into the distance** regarder (vaguement) par la fenêtre/au loin.
■ **gaze about, gaze around** regarder autour de soi; **stop gazing about!** arrête de regarder ce qui se passe!

gazebo /gəˈziːbəʊ/ *n* belvédère *m*.

gazelle /gəˈzel/ *n* (*pl* **~s** ou **~**) gazelle *f*.

gazette /gəˈzet/ **I** *n* **1** Journ (newspaper title) **Gazette** Gazette *f*; **2** GB (official journal) journal *m* officiel.
II *vtr* publier [qch] officiellement.

gazetteer /ˌgæzəˈtɪə(r)/ *n* index *m* géographique.

gazpacho /gəzˈpætʃəʊ/ *n* gaspacho *m*.

gazump○ /gəˈzʌmp/ *vtr* péj GB *en immobilier, revenir sur un accord pour vendre à plus offrant.*

gazumping○ /gəˈzʌmpɪŋ/ *n* GB péj *en immobilier, action de revenir sur un accord pour vendre à plus offrant.*

GB *n* (*abrév* = **Great Britain**) G.-B.

GBH *n abrév* ▶ **grievous bodily harm**.

GC *n* GB *abrév* ▶ **George Cross**.

GCE *n* (*pl* **~s**) GB (*abrév* = **General Certificate of Education**) diplôme *m* de fin d'études secondaires.

GCHQ *n* GB (*abrév* = **General Communications Headquarters**) *centre d'interception des télécommunications étrangères.*

GCSE *n* (*pl* **~s**) GB (*abrév* = **General Certificate of Secondary Education**) certificat *m* d'études secondaires (*passé à 16 ans*).

gdn *abrév écrite* = **garden**.

Gdns *abrév écrite* = **Gardens**.

GDP *n* (*abrév* = **gross domestic product**) PIB *m*.

GDR *n* Hist (*abrév* = **German Democratic Republic**) RDA *f*.

gear /gɪə(r)/ **I** *n* **1** (equipment) matériel *m*; **climbing/fishing/gardening ~** matériel d'alpinisme/de pêche/de jardinage; **2**○ (personal possessions, stuff) affaires *fpl*; **don't leave your ~ all over the place** ne laisse pas tes affaires partout; **3** (clothes) fringues○ *fpl*; **tennis/football ~** tenue *f* de tennis/football; **4** Aut vitesse *f*; **bottom** ou **first ~** première vitesse; **to be in second/third ~** être en seconde/troisième; **to change ~** changer de vitesse; **to put a car in ~** passer la vitesse; **you're not in ~** tu es au point mort; **you're in the wrong ~** tu n'as pas passé la bonne vitesse; **'keep in low ~'** (on sign) 'utilisez votre frein moteur'; **to get (oneself) into ~ for sth** fig se préparer pour qch; **5** Tech (toothed wheel) roue *f* dentée; **6**○ (drugs) drogués *fpl*.
II gears *npl* **1** Aut changement *m* de vitesse; **2** Tech engrenage *m*.
III *vtr* **1** (tailor) **to be ~ed to** ou **towards sb/sth** [*course, policy, system, tax*] s'adresser à qn/qch; **to be ~ed to** ou **towards doing** être destiné à faire; **2** Aut, Tech (provide with gearing) équiper [qch] d'un embrayage [*car*]; équiper [qch] d'un engrenage [*other machinery*].
■ **gear up**: ¶ **~ up** se préparer; ¶ **~ [sb] up** préparer; **to be ~ed up to do** être prêt pour faire; **to be ~ed up for** être prêt pour [*party, interview, trip*].

gear: **~box** *n* boîte *f* de vitesses; **~ change** *n* changement *m* de vitesses.

gearing /ˈgɪərɪŋ/ *n* **1** Fin coefficient *m* or ratio *m* d'endettement; **2** Tech embrayage *m*.

gear: **~ lever** *n* levier *m* de vitesses; **~ ratio** *n* rapport *m* d'engrenage.

gearshift /ˈgɪəʃɪft/ *n* US **1** (lever) levier *m* de vitesses; **2** (process) changement *m* de vitesse.

gear: **~ stick** *n* GB Aut levier *m* de vitesses; **~ wheel** *n* (on bicycle) pignon *m*.

gecko /ˈgekəʊ/ *n* (*pl* **~s** ou **~es**) gecko *m*.

gee /dʒiː/ US **I**○ *excl* (in surprise) ça alors!; (in disappointment, commiseration) mince alors!; **~ it's nice to see you** tiens, ça fait plaisir de te voir.
II○ *n* (thousand) mille *m*.
■ **gee up**○: **~ [sb/sth] up, ~ up [sb/sth]** fig réveiller [*person*]; activer [*animal*]; **~ up!** (to horse) hue!

gee-gee /ˈdʒiːdʒiː/ *n* lang enfantin dada *m* baby talk.

geek◑ /giːk/ *n* US taré/-e◑ *m/f*.

geese /giːs/ *pl* ▶ **goose**.

gee-whiz○ /ˌdʒiːˈwɪz/ *adj* tout feu tout flamme○.

geezer○ /ˈgiːzə(r)/ *n* GB (man) mec○ *m*.

gefilte fish /ˌgəfɪltə ˈfɪʃ/ *n* carpe *f* à la juive.

Geiger counter /ˌgaɪgə ˈkaʊntə(r)/ *n* compteur *m* Geiger.

geisha /ˈgeɪʃə/ *n* (also **~ girl**) geisha *f*.

gel /dʒel/ **I** *n* **1** (for bath, hair) gel *m*; **2** Chem colloïde *m*.
II *vi* (*p prés etc* **-ll-**) **1** Culin prendre; **2** (take shape) [*idea, plan*] prendre forme.

gelatin(e) /ˈdʒelətiːn, -tɪn/ *n* (all contexts) gélatine *f*.

gelatinous /dʒəˈlætɪnəs/ *adj* gélatineux/-euse.

geld /geld/ *vtr* (*prét, pp* **~ed** ou **gelt**) castrer.

gelding /ˈgeldɪŋ/ *n* **1** (horse) hongre *m*; **2** (castration) castration *f*.

gelignite /ˈdʒelɪgnaɪt/ *n* plastic *m*.

gelt○ /gelt/ *n* US fric○ *m*, argent *m*.

gem /dʒem/ *n* **1** (stone) pierre *f* précieuse, gemme *f* spec; **2** (appreciative term) **the ~ of** le joyau de [*collection*]; **a ~ of a village** un village merveilleux; **this book is a real ~** ce livre est une vraie merveille; **she's a ~**○ (very capable) c'est une perle; (very pleasant) c'est un amour○; **3** (amusing feature in newspaper) perle *f*.

Gemini /ˈdʒemɪnaɪ, -niː/ **▶1916** *n* Gémeaux *mpl*.

gemology /ˌdʒemˈɒlədʒɪ/ *n* gemmologie *f*.

gemstone /ˈdʒemstəʊn/ *n* pierre *f* brute.

gen○ /dʒen/ GB **I** *n* tuyaux○ *mpl*; **to get the ~ on sb/sth** obtenir tous les tuyaux sur qn/qch; **what's the ~ on this?** qu'est-ce qu'il faut savoir là-dessus?
II *adj, adv*: *abrév* = **general**, **generally**.
■ **gen up**○ GB: ¶ **~ up** se renseigner (**on** sur); ¶ **~ [sb] up** donner tous les tuyaux à (**on** sur); **to be ~ned up on** ou **about sth** être au parfum○ de qch.

Gen. *abrév écrite* = **General**.

gender /ˈdʒendə(r)/ **I** *n* **1** Ling genre *m*; **of common ~** épicène; **to be feminine in ~** être du genre féminin; **2** (of person, animal) sexe *m*; **female ~** sexe féminin.

gender: **~-bender**○ *n* hum travesti *m*; **~ bias** *n* préjugé *m* en faveur des hommes (or des femmes); **~ dysphoria** *n* problèmes *mpl* d'identité sexuelle; **~ gap** *n* fossé *m* entre les sexes; **~ reassignment** *n* changement *m* de sexe.

gene /dʒiːn/ *n* Biol gène *m*; **it's in his ~s** gen, hum c'est héréditaire.

genealogical /ˌdʒiːnɪəˈlɒdʒɪkl/ *adj* généalogique.

genealogist /ˌdʒiːnɪˈælədʒɪst/ **▶1692** *n* généalogiste *mf*.

genealogy /ˌdʒiːnɪˈælədʒɪ/ *n* généalogie *f*.

gene: **~ cluster** *n* batterie *f* de gènes; **~ library** *n* génothèque *f*; **~ mapping** *n* = **genetic mapping**; **~ pool** *n* patrimoine *m* héréditaire.

genera /ˈdʒenərə/ *npl* ▶ **genus**.

general /ˈdʒenrəl/ **▶1612** **I** *n* **1** Mil général *m*; **~ of the army/air force** US général d'armée/d'armée aérienne; **to make sb a ~** nommer qn général; **General Franco** le général Franco; **yes, ~** à vos ordres, mon général; **2 the ~ and the particular** le général et le particulier.
II *adj* **1** (widespread) [*interest, concern, approval, effort, feeling, opinion, chaos, ban, paralysis*] général; [*reaction, response*] répandu; **to be a ~ favourite** être apprécié de tous; **in ~ use** [*word, term*] d'usage courant; [*equipment*] d'utilisation courante; **2** (overall) [*condition, appearance, standard, rise, fall, decline, impression*] général; [*attitude, behaviour*] dans l'ensemble; **to improve one's ~ fitness** améliorer sa forme; **do you get the ~ idea?** tu vois? **that's the ~ idea** en gros, c'est ça l'idée; **the ~ plan is to do** en gros, le plan c'est de faire; **3** (rough, usually applying) [*rule, principle, axiom, conclusion*] général; **as a ~ rule** en règle générale; **4** (not detailed or specific) [*description, statement, information*] général; [*promise, assurance*] vague; **to talk in ~ terms** parler en termes généraux; **a ~ discussion about** une discussion d'ensemble sur; **to keep the conversation ~** maintenir la conversation sur des sujets d'intérêt général; **to give sb a ~ idea of** donner à qn une idée d'ensemble de; **to head in the ~ direction of** aller en direction de; **5** (not specialized) [*medicine, linguistics*] général; [*programme, magazine*] d'intérêt général; [*user, reader*] moyen/-enne; [*store, shop, dealer*] qui vend de tout; **~ office duties** travail *m* de bureau; **~ assistant** employé/-e *m/f* de bureau; **6** (miscellaneous) [*category, index, enquiry, expenses*] général; **we sell ~ antiques** nous vendons toutes sortes d'antiquités; **7** (usual, normal) [*practice, method, routine*] général; **in the ~ way of things** en règle générale; **the ~ run of people** le grand public.
III in general *adv phr* **1** (usually or non-specifically) en général; **in ~ I like the theatre, but**... en général j'aime le théâtre, mais...; **adults in ~ and parents in particular** les adultes en général et les parents en particulier; **he is fed up with life in ~** il en a assez de la vie en général; **2** (overall, mostly) dans l'ensemble; **in ~ it seems quite simple** dans l'ensemble cela paraît assez simple.

general: **~ anaesthetic** GB, **~ anesthetic** US *n* anesthésie *f* générale; **~ assembly**, **General Assembly** *n* assemblée *f* générale; **~ confession** *n* confession *f* collective; **~ degree** *n* GB *diplôme sanctionnant des études universitaires*; **~ delivery** *n* US poste *f* restante; **~ election** *n* élections *fpl* législatives; **~ headquarters** *n* (+ *v sg ou pl*) quartier *m* général; **~ hospital** *n* hôpital *m*.

generalissimo /ˌdʒenrəˈlɪsɪməʊ/ *n* (*pl* **~s**) généralissime *m*.

generalist /ˈdʒenrəlɪst/ *n* généraliste *m*, non spécialiste *mf*.

generality /ˌdʒenəˈrælətɪ/ *n* **1** (general remark) généralité *f*; **to talk in/confine oneself to generalities** parler de/s'en tenir à des généralités; **2** (overall nature) caractère *m* général (**of** de); **3** (majority) (+ *v sg ou pl*) **the ~ of people/shareholders** la plupart des gens/actionnaires; **the ~** (people at large) les gens en général.

generalization /ˌdʒenrəlaɪˈzeɪʃn, US -lɪˈz-/ *n* généralisation *f* (**about** sur); **to make a ~** faire une généralisation; **he's always making ~s** péj il est toujours en train de généraliser.

generalize /ˈdʒenrəlaɪz/ **I** *vtr* **1** (make more general) généraliser [*education, curriculum, syllabus*]; **2** (draw) **to ~ a conclusion/a principle** établir une généralisation/un principe général.
II *vi* généraliser (**about** à propos de).

generalized /ˈdʒenrəlaɪzd/ *adj* **1** (widespread) [*discontent, hostility*] général; [*anxiety, sickness*] généralisé; [*use*] répandu; **2** (vague or unspecific) [*accusation, conclusion, information, promise, statement*] général.

general knowledge *n* culture *f* générale.

generally /ˈdʒenrəlɪ/ *adv* **1** (widely) [*accepted, agreed, believed, denounced, recognized, regarded, welcomed*] dans l'ensemble, en général; **a ~ accepted definition** une définition couramment acceptée; **~ available** disponible pour le grand public; **2** (usually) généralement, en général; **it's ~ best to wait** en général, il vaut mieux attendre; **~ (speaking)**... en règle générale...; **3** (overall) **the industry ~ will be affected** l'ensemble de l'industrie sera touché; **he's ~ unwell at the moment** en ce moment il n'est vraiment pas en forme; **the quality is ~ good** dans l'ensemble la qualité est bonne; **she was dancing, drinking and ~ enjoying herself** elle dansait, elle buvait, en un mot elle s'amusait bien; **4** (vaguely) [*talk, discuss, refer*] d'une manière générale.

general: **~ manager** **▶1692** *n* directeur/-trice *m/f* général/-e; **~ meeting** *n* assemblée *f* générale; **~ officer** *n* officier *m* général; **~ partner** *n* associé-gérant *m*, commandité *m*.

general practice *n* **1** (field of doctor's work) médecine *f* générale; **to go into ~** devenir (médecin) généraliste; **2** (health centre) cabinet *m* de médecine générale.

general: **~ practitioner**, **GP** **▶1692** *n* (médecin *m*) généraliste *m*; **~ public** *n* (grand) public *m*.

general-purpose *adj* [*tool, knife, detergent*] à usages multiples.

general: **~ science** *n* Sch *la physique, la chimie et les sciences naturelles*; **~ secretary** *n* secrétaire *m* général.

generalship /ˈdʒenrəlʃɪp/ *n* (duties, office, rank) généralat *m*; **his skilful ~** son habileté *f* de général.

general: **~ staff** *n* état-major *m*; **~ store** *n* bazar *m* (*qui fait aussi épicerie*); **~ strike** *n* grève *f* générale; **~ studies** *n* GB *cours d'éducation secondaire comprenant divers sujets d'intérêt général.*

generate /ˈdʒenəreɪt/ *vtr* **1** produire [*income, sales, data, documents, graphics, noise, waste*]; créer [*employment*]; susciter [*interest, debate, tension, feeling, ideas*]; entraîner [*traffic, loss, profit, publicity*]; **2** Elec produire [*electricity, power, heat*]; **3** Ling, Math générer.

generating: **~ set** *n* groupe *m* électrogène; **~ station** *n* centrale *f* électrique.

generation /ˌdʒenəˈreɪʃn/ *n* **1** (in family, society) génération *f*; **from ~ to ~** de génération en génération; **the younger/older ~** la jeune/l'ancienne génération; **people of my ~** les gens de ma génération; **a new ~ of** une nouvelle génération de; **first ~ Australian** Australien/-ienne *m/f* de première génération; **2** (period of time) génération *f*; **it's been like this for ~s** cela fait des générations qu'il en est ainsi; **3** (in product development) génération *f*; **second ~ robots** des robots de la deuxième génération; **4** (of electricity, income, traffic, data) production *f*; (of employment) création *f*.

generation gap *n* fossé *m* des générations.

generative /ˈdʒenərətɪv/ *adj* **1** gen générateur/-trice; **2** Ling génératif/-ive; **~ grammar** grammaire *f* générative; **3** Bot **~ cell** cellule *f* génératrice.

generator /ˈdʒenəreɪtə(r)/ *n* **1** Elec générateur *m*; (in hospital, on farm etc) groupe *m* électrogène; **electric ~** générateur électrique; (machine producing gas) gazogène *m*; **2** (person) (of ideas) créateur *m*.

generatrix /ˈdʒenəreɪtrɪks/ *n* (*pl* **-trices**) Math génératrice *f*.

generic /dʒɪˈnerɪk/ *adj* générique.

generically /dʒɪˈnerɪklɪ/ *adv* génériquement; **~ similar** apparenté; **~ distinct** d'espèce(s) différente(s).

generic drugs *npl* médicaments *mpl* génériques.

generosity /ˌdʒenəˈrɒsətɪ/ *n* générosité *f* (**to, towards** envers); **her ~ with her time/money** la générosité avec laquelle elle prodigue son temps/argent; **~ of mind** ou **spirit** esprit *m* généreux; **such ~!** iron quelle générosité!

generous /ˈdʒenərəs/ *adj* **1** (beneficent, lavish) [*person*] généreux/-euse; **to be ~ with** ne pas être avare de [*praise, time*]; **2** (magnanimous) [*person*] magnanime; **the most ~ interpretation is that** l'interprétation la plus charitable est que; **3** (large) [*quantity, supply, funding*] libéral, généreux/-euse; [*size*] grand; [*hem*] bon/bonne.

generously /ˈdʒenərəslɪ/ *adv* gen généreusement; Culin [*sprinkle, grease*] abondamment; **~ cut** ample; **give ~!** soyez généreux!

genesis /ˈdʒenəsɪs/ **I** *n* (*pl* **-ses**) fig genèse *f*.
II Genesis *pr n* Bible la Genèse.

gene: **~ tagging** *n* étiquetage *m* génétique; **~ therapy** *n* thérapie *f* génique.

genetic /dʒɪˈnetɪk/ *adj* génétique.

genetically /dʒɪˈnetɪklɪ/ *adv* génétiquement; **~ engineered**, **~ manipulated** obtenu par manipulation génétique.

genetic: **~ code** *n* code *m* génétique; **~ counselling** *n* conseil *m* génétique; **~ engineering** *n* génie *m* génétique; **~ fingerprinting** *n* empreintes *fpl* génétiques; **~ ID card** *n* carte *f* (d'identité) génétique.

geneticist /dʒɪˈnetɪsɪst/ **▶1692** *n* généticien/-ienne *m/f*.

genetic: **~ manipulation** *n* ¢ manipulations *fpl* génétiques; **~ map** *n* carte *f* génétique, carte *f* chromosomique; **~ mapping** *n* cartographie *f* de gènes.

genetics /dʒɪˈnetɪks/ *n* (+ *v sg*) génétique *f*.

genetic testing *n* ¢ tests *mpl* de dépistage génétique.

Geneva /dʒɪˈniːvə/ **▶1818**, **1400**, **1776** *pr n* Genève; **Lake ~** le lac Léman or de Genève; **the canton of ~** le canton de Genève.

Geneva Convention *n* Convention *f* de Genève.
genial /ˈdʒiːnɪəl/ *adj* **1** (cheerful) cordial; **2** littér [*climate*] doux/douce.
geniality /dʒiːnɪˈælətɪ/ *n* cordialité *f*.
genially /ˈdʒiːnɪəlɪ/ *adv* cordialement.
genie /ˈdʒiːnɪ/ *n* (*pl* **-nii** ou **-nies**) djinn *m*, génie *m*.
genital /ˈdʒenɪtl/ *adj* génital; **in the ~ area** au bas-ventre.
genital herpes ▶ **1354** *n* herpès *m* génital.
genitalia /ˌdʒenɪˈteɪlɪə/ *npl* = **genitals**.
genitals /ˈdʒenɪtlz/ ▶ **1037** *npl* organes *mpl* génitaux.
genitive /ˈdʒenətɪv/ **I** *n* génitif *m*; **in the ~ (case)** au génitif.
II *adj* génitif/-ive.
genius /ˈdʒiːnɪəs/ *n* **1** (*pl* **~es**) (prodigy) génie *m*; **a mathematical/musical ~** un mathématicien/musicien de génie; **you're a ~**○! tu es un génie○!; **2** (*pl* **~es**) (with special skills) **a mechanical ~** un génie de la mécanique; **3** (skill) **to have a ~ for doing** être très doué pour faire; **to have a ~ for saying the wrong thing** iron avoir le génie de la gaffe; **4** (*pl* **-ii**) littér (spirit) génie *m*.
Genoa /ˈdʒenəʊə/ ▶ **1818** *pr n* Gênes.
Genoa cake *n* Culin pain *m* de Gênes.
genocidal /ˈdʒenəsaɪdl/ *adj* génocide.
genocide /ˈdʒenəsaɪd/ *n* génocide *m*.
Genoese /ˈdʒenəʊiːz/ **I** *n* (*pl* **~**) Génois/-e *m/f*.
II *adj* génois.
genotype /ˈdʒeːnəʊtaɪp/ *n* génotype *m*.
genre /ˈʒɑːnrə/ *n* **1** gen genre *m*; **2** Art peinture *f* de genre.
gent○ /dʒent/ **I** *n* (gentleman) **he's a (real) ~** c'est un gentleman; **'this way, ~s!'** par ici, messieurs!; **~s' hairdresser's/clothing** coiffure/vêtements pour hommes.
II gents *npl* (toilets) toilettes *fpl* (*pour hommes*); (on sign) 'messieurs'.
genteel /dʒenˈtiːl/ *adj* **1**† (refined) [*person, manners*] distingué; **to live in ~ poverty** vivre dans une manière digne; **2** péj, iron (affected) [*person*] maniéré; [*behaviour*] affecté.
gentian /ˈdʒenʃn/ *n* gentiane *f*.
gentian violet *n* bleu *m* de méthylène.
Gentile /ˈdʒentaɪl/ **I** *n* gentil *m*.
II *adj* des gentils.
gentility /dʒenˈtɪlətɪ/ *n* **1**† (refinement) distinction *f*; **2** iron ou péj (affectation) affectation *f*.
gentle /ˈdʒentl/ **I** *adj* **1** (not harsh) [*person, animal, expression, reprimand*] doux/douce; [*dentist, nurse*] qui a la main douce; [*shampoo, cleanser, heat*] doux/douce; [*hint, reminder*] discret/-ète; [*teasing, parody*] anodin; **my dentist is very ~** mon dentiste a la main douce; **be ~ with her, she's tired** ne la brusque pas, elle est fatiguée; **if we use a little ~ persuasion** gen, iron si on essaie la manière douce; **the ~ sex** littér ou iron le sexe faible; **2** (quiet) [*voice, music*] doux/douce; [*noises*] léger/-ère; **3** (gradual) [*slope, curve*] doux/douce; [*stop*] en douceur; [*transition*] sans heurts; **to come to a ~ stop** s'arrêter en douceur; **4** (light) [*pressure, touch, push, breeze*] léger/-ère; [*exercise*] modéré; [*massage*] en douceur; [*stroll*] petit; **5**† (high-born) noble; **of ~ birth** bien né; **'~ reader'**†ou hum 'aimable lecteur'.
II *vtr* US **1** (mollify) nuancer [*judgment*]; **2** (placate) apaiser.
gentlefolk† /ˈdʒentlfəʊlk/ *npl* GB gens *mpl* bien nés.
gentleman /ˈdʒentlmən/ **I** *n* (*pl* **-men**) **1** (man) monsieur *m*; **this ~ wants...** ce monsieur voudrait...; **'gentlemen of the jury'** 'messieurs les jurés'; **a ~ of leisure** un rentier; **2** (well-bred) gentleman *m*; **he's a perfect ~** c'est un parfait gentleman; **he's no ~** GB ce n'est pas un gentleman; **one of nature's gentlemen** un gentleman-né; **3** (at court) gentilhomme *m* aussi Hist; **4** US Pol (congressman) député *m*; **the ~ from Ohio** le député de l'Ohio.
II Gentlemen *npl* (on sign) Messieurs.
IDIOMS **to give sb a ~'s C** US ne pas avoir une très haute opinion de qn.
gentleman: **~-at-arms** *n* gentilhomme *m* de la garde; **~-farmer** *n* gentleman-farmer *m*.
gentlemanly /ˈdʒentlmənlɪ/ *adj* [*behaviour, person, manner*] courtois; [*appearance*] distingué.
gentleman: **~'s agreement** *n* gentleman's agreement *m*; **~'s gentleman**† *n* valet *m* de chambre.
gentlemen /ˈdʒentlmən/ *npl* ▶ **gentleman**.
gentleness /ˈdʒentlnɪs/ *n* douceur *f*.
gentlewoman‡ /ˈdʒentlwʊmən/ *n* (*pl* **-men**) **1** Hist (lady-in-waiting) dame *f* d'honneur; **2** (well-born) dame *f* bien née.
gently /ˈdʒentlɪ/ *adv* **1** (not harshly) [*rock, blow, stir*] doucement; [*comb, treat, cleanse*] avec douceur; [*cook*] à feu doux; **2** (kindly) [*speak, look, tease, admonish*] gentiment; **treat her ~** soyez gentil avec elle; **to break the news ~** annoncer la nouvelle avec ménagement; **3** (lightly) [*exercise*] sans forcer; **he kissed her ~ on the cheek** il lui posa un léger baiser sur la joue; **'squeeze ~'** (washing instructions) 'presser sans tordre'; **4** (gradually) **to slope ~ up/down** monter/descendre en pente douce; **~ does it!** doucement!
gentrification /ˌdʒentrɪfɪˈkeɪʃn/ *n* péj embourgeoisement *m*, transformation *f* en quartier bourgeois.
gentrify /ˈdʒentrɪfaɪ/ *vtr* péj transformer en quartier bourgeois; **to become gentrified** s'embourgeoiser.
gentry /ˈdʒentrɪ/ *n* †ou hum haute bourgeoisie *f*.
genuflect /ˈdʒenjuːflekt/ *vi* sout faire une génuflexion.
genuflexion GB, **genuflection** US /ˌdʒenjuːˈflekʃn/ *n* sout génuflexion *f*.
genuine /ˈdʒenjʊɪn/ *adj* **1** (real) [*bargain, reason, motive*] vrai; **many poor families are in ~ difficulty** beaucoup de familles pauvres sont vraiment dans le besoin; **in case of ~ emergency** s'il y a vraiment urgence; **2** (authentic) [*work of art*] authentique; [*jewel, substance*] véritable; **it's the ~ article**○ c'est du vrai○; **he's the ~ article**○ c'est un vrai de vrai○; **3** (sincere) [*person, emotion, effort, interest*] sincère; [*simplicity*] vrai; [*inability*] non feint (*after n*); [*buyer*] sérieux/-ieuse; **it was a ~ mistake** c'était vraiment une erreur.
genuinely /ˈdʒenjʊɪnlɪ/ *adv* **1** (really and truly) [*feel, want*] vraiment; [*worried, upset*] vraiment; **2** (in reality) [*independent*] réellement.
genuineness /ˈdʒenjʊɪnnɪs/ *n* (of person) sincérité *f*; (of artwork) authenticité *f*.
genus /ˈdʒiːnəs/ *n* (*pl* **-nera** ou **~es**) (all contexts) genre *m*.
geocentric /ˌdʒiːəʊˈsentrɪk/ *adj* géocentrique.
geochemical /ˌdʒiːəʊˈkemɪkl/ *adj* géochimique.
geochemist /ˌdʒiːəʊˈkemɪst/ ▶ **1692** *n* géochimiste *mf*.
geochemistry /ˌdʒiːəʊˈkemɪstrɪ/ *n* géochimie *f*.
geode /ˈdʒiːəʊd/ *n* géode *f*.
geodesic /ˌdʒiːəʊˈdesɪk/ *n, adj* géodésique (*f*); **~ dome** dôme *m* géodésique.
geographer /dʒɪˈɒɡrəfə(r)/ ▶ **1692** *n* géographe *mf*.
geographic(al) /ˌdʒɪəˈɡræfɪkl/ *adj* géographique.
geographically /ˌdʒɪəˈɡræfɪklɪ/ *adv* géographiquement; **~ speaking** du point de vue géographique.
geographical mile *n* Naut mille *m* marin.
geography /dʒɪˈɒɡrəfɪ/ **I** *n* (study) géographie *f*; (lay-out) topographie *f*; **to have a sense of ~** avoir le sens de l'orientation.
II *modif* [*student, teacher, lesson, book*] de géographie.
geological /dʒɪəˈlɒdʒɪkl/ *adj* géologique.
geologist /dʒɪˈɒlədʒɪst/ ▶ **1692** *n* géologue *mf*.
geology /dʒɪˈɒlədʒɪ/ **I** *n* géologie *f*.
II *modif* [*course, department, degree*] de géologie.
geomagnetic /ˌdʒiːəʊmæɡˈnetɪk/ *adj* géomagnétique.
geomagnetism /ˌdʒiːəʊˈmæɡnɪtɪzəm/ *n* géomagnétisme *m*.
geometric(al) /ˌdʒɪəʊˈmetrɪk(l)/ *adj* géométrique.
geometrically /ˌdʒɪəʊˈmetrɪklɪ/ *adv* géométriquement.
geometrician /ˌdʒɪəʊməˈtrɪʃn/ ▶ **1692** *n* géomètre *mf*.
geometry /dʒɪˈɒmətrɪ/ **I** *n* géométrie *f*.
II *modif* [*lesson, book*] de géométrie; **~ set** nécessaire *m* de géométrie.
geomorphology /ˌdʒiːəʊmɔːˈfɒlədʒɪ/ *n* géomorphologie *f*.
geonomics /ˈdʒiːəʊˈnɒmɪks/ *n* (+ *v sg*) géographie *f* économique.
geophysical /ˌdʒiːəʊˈfɪzɪkl/ *adj* géophysique.
geophysicist /ˌdʒiːəʊˈfɪzɪsɪst/ ▶ **1692** *n* géophysicien/-ienne *m/f*.
geophysics /ˌdʒiːəʊˈfɪzɪks/ *n* (+ *v sg*) géophysique *f*.
geopolitical /ˌdʒiːəʊpəˈlɪtɪkl/ *adj* géopolitique.
geopolitics /ˌdʒiːəʊˈpɒlətɪks/ *n* (+ *v sg*) géopolitique *f*.
Geordie○ /ˈdʒɔːdɪ/ GB **I** *n* natif/-ive *m/f* du Tyneside.
II *adj* du Tyneside.
George /dʒɔːdʒ/ *pr n* Georges; **by ~**○†! sacrebleu○†!; **by ~ he's done it!** hum bon sang il a réussi!
George Cross, **GC** *n* GB *médaille pour actes de courage et de dévouement*.
georgette /dʒɔːˈdʒet/ *n* crêpe *m* georgette.
Georgia /ˈdʒɔːdʒjə/ ▶ **1744**, **1131** *pr n* (all contexts) Géorgie *f*.
Georgian /ˈdʒɔːdʒjən/ ▶ **1486**, **1402** **I** *n* **1** (inhabitant) Géorgien/-ienne *m/f*; **2** (language) géorgien *m*; **3** Literat Georgien/-ienne.
II *adj* **1** Geog (all contexts) géorgien/-ienne; **2** GB Literat [*poet, poetry*] georgien/-ienne; **3** GB Hist, Archit [*style, architecture*] georgien/-ienne; **the ~ period** la période allant de 1714 à 1830.
geoscience /ˌdʒiːəʊˈsaɪəns/ *n* ¢ sciences *fpl* de la Terre; **a ~** une des sciences de la Terre.
geoscientist /ˌdʒiːəʊˈsaɪəntɪst/ ▶ **1692** *n* spécialiste *mf* des sciences de la Terre.
geostationary /ˌdʒiːəʊˈsteɪʃənrɪ, US -nerɪ/ *adj* géostationnaire.
geothermal /ˌdʒiːəʊˈθɜːml/ *adj* géothermique.
geranium /dʒəˈreɪnɪəm/ *n* géranium *m*.
gerbil /ˈdʒɜːbɪl/ *n* gerbille *f*.
geriatric /ˌdʒerɪˈætrɪk/ **I** *n* **1** Med vieillard/-e *mf*; **2**○ péj hum gâteux/-euse○ *m/f*.
II *adj* **1** Med [*hospital, ward*] gériatrique; **~ care** soins aux vieillards; **~ medicine** gériatrie *f*; **2**○ péj hum gâteux/-euse○.
geriatrician /ˌdʒerɪəˈtrɪʃn/ ▶ **1692** *n* gériatre *mf*.
geriatrics /ˌdʒerɪˈætrɪks/ *n* (+ *v sg*) gériatrie *f*.
germ /dʒɜːm/ *n* **1** (microbe) microbe *m*, germe *m*; **to carry ~s** être porteur de microbes or de germes; **2** (seed) lit, fig germe *m*; **the ~ of an idea** le germe d'une idée.
German /ˈdʒɜːmən/ ▶ **1486**, **1402** **I** *n* **1** (person) Allemand/-e *m/f*; **2** Ling allemand *m*; **Low/Middle/High ~** bas/moyen/haut allemand.

II *adj* [*town, custom, food, economy etc*] allemand; [*ambassador, embassy, emperor*] d'Allemagne; [*teacher, exam, course*] d'allemand; **East/West ~** Hist est/ouest-allemand.

German Democratic Republic, **GDR** *n* Hist République *f* démocratique allemande, RDA *f*.

germane /dʒɜːˈmeɪn/ *adj* [*point, remark*] approprié; **~ to** se rapportant à [*inquiry, topic*].

Germanic /dʒɜːˈmænɪk/ *adj* gen, Ling germanique.

German measles ▶ 1354 *n* (+ *v sg*) rubéole *f*.

Germanophile /dʒɜːˈmænəfaɪl/ *n, adj* germanophile (*mf*).

Germanophobe /dʒɜːˈmænəfəʊb/ *n, adj* germanophobe (*mf*).

German: **~ sheepdog**, **~ shepherd** *n* berger *m* allemand; **~-speaking** *adj* germanophone.

Germany /ˈdʒɜːmənɪ/ ▶ 1131 *pr n* Allemagne *f*; **East/West ~** Hist Allemagne de l'Est/de l'Ouest.

germ: **~ carrier** *n* porteur/-euse *m/f* de germes or de microbes; **~ cell** *n* gamète *m*; **~-free** *adj* désinfecté.

germicidal /ˌdʒɜːmɪˈsaɪdl/ *adj* germicide.

germicide /ˈdʒɜːmɪsaɪd/ *n* germicide *m*.

germinal /ˈdʒɜːmɪnəl/ *adj* Biol germinal.

germinate /ˈdʒɜːmɪneɪt/ **I** *vtr* lit, fig faire germer.
II *vi* lit, fig germer.

germination /ˌdʒɜːmɪˈneɪʃn/ *n* germination *f*.

germ: **~-killer** *n* antiseptique *m*; **~proof** *adj* résistant aux microbes; **~ warfare** *n* guerre *f* bactériologique.

gerontocracy /ˌdʒerɒnˈtɒkrəsɪ/ *n* gérontocratie *f*.

gerontologist /ˌdʒerɒnˈtɒlədʒɪst/ ▶ 1692 *n* gérontologue *mf*.

gerontology /ˌdʒerɒnˈtɒlədʒɪ/ *n* gérontologie *f*.

gerrymander /ˌdʒerɪˈmændə(r)/ péj **I** *n* charcutage *m* électoral.
II *vtr* truquer [*boundaries, constituency*].
III *vi* pratiquer le charcutage électoral.

gerrymandering /ˌdʒerɪˈmændərɪŋ/ *n* charcutage *m* électoral.

Gers ▶ 1163 *pr n* Gers *m*; **in/to the ~** dans le Gers.

gerund /ˈdʒerənd/ *n* nom *m* verbal.

gerundive /dʒeˈrʌndɪv/ **I** *n* adjectif *m* verbal.
II *adj* du gérondif.

gesso /ˈdʒesəʊ/ *n* **1** (for bas-relief, painting) plâtre *m* de Paris; **2** (on wood) enduit *m* au plâtre.

gestalt /gəˈstɑːlt/ *n* gestalt *f*.

gestalt psychology *n* gestaltisme *m*, théorie *f* de la forme.

Gestapo /geˈstɑːpəʊ/ **I** *n* Gestapo *f*.
II *modif* [*agent, headquarters, prison*] de la Gestapo.

gestate /dʒeˈsteɪt/ **I** *vtr* **1** Biol porter [*young*]; **2** fig mûrir [*plan*].
II *vi* **1** Biol être en gestation; **2** fig mûrir.

gestation /dʒeˈsteɪʃn/ *n* **1** lit gestation *f*; **2** fig mûrissement *m*.

gesticulate /dʒeˈstɪkjʊleɪt/ *vi* gesticuler.

gesticulation /dʒeˌstɪkjʊˈleɪʃn/ *n* gesticulation *f*.

gestural /ˈdʒestʃərəl/ *adj* gestuel/-elle.

gesture /ˈdʒestʃə(r)/ **I** *n* lit, fig geste *m* (**of** de); **a nice ~** un beau geste; **a political/humanitarian ~** un geste politique/humanitaire; **a ~ of goodwill/solidarity** un geste de bonne volonté/de solidarité; **an empty ~** un geste qui ne signifie rien.
II *vtr* **to ~ one's assent** faire un geste d'assentiment.
III *vi* faire un geste; **to ~ at** ou **towards sth** désigner qch d'un geste; **to ~ to sb** faire signe à qn (**to do** de faire).

get /get/

■ **Note** This much-used verb has no multi-purpose equivalent in French and therefore is very often translated by choosing a synonym: *to get lunch* = *to prepare lunch* = préparer le déjeuner.
– *get* is used in many idiomatic expressions (*to get something off one's chest etc*) and translations will be found in the appropriate entry (***chest*** etc). This is also true of offensive comments (*get stuffed etc*) where the appropriate entry would be ***stuff***.
– Remember that when *get* is used to express the idea that a job is done not by you but by somebody else (*to get a room painted etc*) *faire* is used in French followed by an infinitive (*faire repeindre une pièce etc*).
– When *get* has the meaning of *become* and is followed by an adjective (*to get rich/drunk etc*) *devenir* is sometimes useful but check the appropriate entry (***rich***, ***drunk*** etc) as a single verb often suffices (*s'enrichir, s'enivrer etc*).
– For examples and further uses of *get* see the entry below.

I *vtr* (*p prés* **-tt-**; *prét* **got**; *pp* **got**, **gotten** US) **1** (receive) recevoir [*letter, school report, grant*]; recevoir, percevoir [*salary, pension*]; TV, Radio capter [*channel, programme*]; **did you ~ much for it?** est-ce que tu en as tiré beaucoup d'argent?; **what did you ~ for your car?** combien as-tu revendu ta voiture?; **we ~ a lot of rain** il pleut beaucoup ici; **our garden ~s a lot of sun** notre jardin est bien ensoleillé; **we ~ a lot of tourists** nous avons beaucoup de touristes; **you ~ lots of attachments with this cleaner** il y a beaucoup d'accessoires fournis avec cet aspirateur; **you ~ what you pay for** il faut y mettre le prix; **he's ~ting help with his science** il se fait aider en sciences; **2** (inherit) **to ~ sth from sb** lit hériter qch de qn [*article, money*]; fig tenir qch de qn [*trait, feature*]; **3** (obtain) (by applying) obtenir [*permission, divorce, custody, licence*]; trouver [*job*]; (by contacting) trouver [*plumber, accountant*]; appeler [*taxi*]; (by buying) acheter [*food item, clothing*] (**from** chez); avoir [*theatre seat, ticket*]; **to ~ something for nothing/at a discount** avoir qch gratuitement/avec une réduction; **to ~ sb sth, to ~ sth for sb** (by buying) acheter qch à qn; **I'll ~ sth to eat at the airport** je mangerai qch à l'aéroport; **4** (subscribe to) acheter [*newspaper*]; **5** (acquire) se faire [*reputation*]; **he got his money in oil** il s'est fait de l'argent dans le pétrole; **6** (achieve) obtenir [*grade, mark, answer*]; **he got it right** (of calculation) il a obtenu le bon résultat; (of answer) il a répondu juste; **how many do I need to ~?** (when scoring) il me faut combien?; **he's got four more points to ~** il faut encore qu'il obtienne quatre points; **7** (fetch) chercher [*object, person, help*]; **go and ~ a chair/Mr Matthews** va chercher une chaise/M. Matthews; **to ~ sb sth, to ~ sth for sb** aller chercher qch pour qn; **~ her a chair** va lui chercher une chaise; **can I ~ you your coat?** est-ce que je peux vous apporter votre manteau?; **8** (manoeuvre, move) **to ~ sb/sth upstairs/downstairs** faire monter/descendre qn/qch; **a car to me is just something to ~ me from A to B** pour moi une voiture ne sert qu'à aller de A à B; **I'll ~ them there somehow** je les ferai parvenir d'une façon ou d'une autre; **can you ~ between the truck and the wall?** est-ce que tu peux te glisser entre le camion et le mur?; **9** (help progress) **is this discussion ~ting us anywhere?** est-ce que cette discussion est bien utile?; **I listened to him and where has it got me?** je l'ai écouté mais à quoi ça m'a avancé?; **this is ~ting us nowhere** ça ne nous avance à rien; **where will that ~ you?** à quoi ça t'avancera?; **10** (contact) **did you manage to ~ Harry on the phone?** tu as réussi à avoir Harry au téléphone?; **11** (deal with) **I'll ~ it** (of phone) je réponds; (of doorbell) j'y vais; **12** (prepare) préparer [*breakfast, lunch etc*]; **13** (take hold of) attraper [*person*] (**by** à); **I've got you, don't worry** je te tiens, ne t'inquiète pas; **to ~ sth from** ou **off** prendre qch sur [*shelf, table*]; **to ~ sth from** ou **out of** prendre qch dans [*drawer, cupboard*]; **14**○ (oblige to give) **to ~ sth from** ou **out of sb** faire sortir qch à qn [*money*]; fig obtenir qch de qn [*truth*]; **15**○ (catch) gen arrêter [*escapee*]; **got you!** gen je t'ai eu!; (caught in act) vu!; **a shark got him** un requin l'a eu; **when I ~ you, you won't find it so funny** quand tu auras affaire○ à moi, tu trouveras ça moins drôle; **16** Med attraper [*disease*]; **he got the measles from his sister** sa sœur lui a passé la rougeole; **17** (use as transport) prendre [*bus, train*]; **18** (have) **to have got** avoir [*object, money, friend etc*]; **I've got a headache/bad back** j'ai mal à la tête/au dos; **19** (start to have) **to ~ (hold of) the idea** ou **impression that** se mettre dans la tête que; **20** (suffer) **to ~ a surprise** être surpris; **to ~ a shock** avoir un choc; **to ~ a bang on the head** recevoir un coup sur la tête; **21** (be given as punishment) prendre [*five years etc*]; avoir [*fine*]; **to ~ (a) detention** être collé○; **22** (hit) **to ~ sb/sth with** toucher qn/qch avec [*stone, arrow, ball*]; **got it!** (of target) touché!; **the arrow got him in the heel** la flèche l'a touché au talon; **23** (understand, hear) comprendre; **I didn't ~ what you said/his last name** je n'ai pas compris ce que tu as dit/son nom de famille; **did you ~ it?** tu as compris?; **now let me ~ this right...** alors si je comprends bien...; **'where did you hear that?'—'I got it from Paul'** 'où est-ce que tu as entendu ça?'—'c'est Paul qui me l'a dit'; **~ this! he was arrested this morning** tiens-toi bien! il a été arrêté ce matin; **24**○ (annoy, affect) **what ~s me is...** ce qui m'agace c'est que...; **what really got me was...** ce que je n'aimais pas c'était...; **25** (learn, learn of) **to ~ to do**○ finir par faire; **to ~ to like sb** finir par apprécier qn; **how did you ~ to know** ou **hear of our organization?** comment avez-vous entendu parler de notre organisation?; **we got to know them last year** on a fait leur connaissance l'année dernière; **26** (have opportunity) **to ~ to do** avoir l'occasion de faire; **do you ~ to use the computer?** est-ce que tu as l'occasion d'utiliser l'ordinateur?; **it's not fair, I never ~ to drive the tractor** ce n'est pas juste, on ne me laisse jamais conduire le tracteur; **when do we ~ to eat the cake?** quand est-ce qu'on va pouvoir manger le gâteau?; **27** (start) **to ~ (to be)** commencer à devenir; **he's ~ting to be proficient** ou **an expert** il commence à devenir expert; **it got to be quite unpleasant** ça a commencé à devenir plutôt désagréable; **he's ~ting to be a big boy now** c'est un grand garçon maintenant; **to ~ to doing**○ commencer à faire; **we got to talking/dreaming about the holidays** on a commencé à parler/rêver des vacances; **then I got to thinking that** puis je me suis dit que; **we'll have to ~ going** il va falloir y aller; **28** (must) **to have got to do** devoir faire [*homework, chore*]; **it's got to be done** il faut le faire; **you've got to realize that** il faut que tu te rendes compte que; **if I've got to go, I will** s'il faut que j'y aille, j'irai; **there's got to be a reason** il doit y avoir une raison; **29** (persuade) **to ~ sb to do** demander à qn de faire; **I got her to talk about her problems** j'ai réussi à la faire parler de ses problèmes; **did you ~ anything out of her?** est-ce que tu as réussi à la faire parler?; **30** (have somebody do) **to ~ sth done** faire faire qch; **to ~ the car repaired/valeted** faire réparer/nettoyer la voiture; **to ~ one's hair cut** se faire couper les cheveux; **how do you ever ~ anything done?** comment est-ce que tu arrives à travailler?; **31** (cause) **to ~ the car going** faire démarrer la voiture; **to ~ the dishes washed** faire la vaisselle; **this won't ~ the dishes washed!** la vaisselle ne se fera pas toute seule!; **to ~ sb pregnant**○ mettre qn enceinte○; **as hot/cold as you can ~ it** aussi chaud/froid que possible; **to ~ one's socks wet** mouiller ses chaussettes; **to ~ one's finger trapped** se coincer le doigt.

II *vi* (*p prés* **-tt-**; *prét* **got**; *pp* **got**, **gotten** US) **1** (become) devenir [*suspicious, rich, old*]; **how lucky/stupid can you ~!** il y en a qui ont de la chance/qui sont vraiment stupides!; **it's ~ting late** il se fait tard; **how did he ~ like that?** comment est-ce qu'il en est arrivé là?; **2** (forming passive) **to ~ (oneself) killed/trapped** se faire tuer/coincer; **to ~ hurt** être blessé; **3** (become involved in) **to ~ into**○ (as hobby) se mettre à [*astrology etc*]; (as job) commencer dans [*teaching, publishing*]; fig **to ~ into a fight** se battre; **4** (arrive) **to ~ there** arriver; **to ~ to the airport/Switzerland** arriver à l'aéroport/en Suisse; **to ~ (up) to the top** (of hill etc) arriver au sommet; **how did your coat ~ here?** comment est-ce que ton manteau est arrivé là?; **how did you ~ here?** (by what miracle) comment est-ce que tu es arrivé là?; (by what means) comment est-ce que tu es venu?; **where did you ~ to?** où est-ce que tu étais passé?; **we've got to page 5** nous en sommes à la page 5; **5** (progress) **it got to 7 o'clock** il était plus de 7 heures; **I'd got as far as underlining the title** j'en étais à souligner le titre; **I'm ~ting nowhere with this essay** je n'avance pas dans ma dissertation; **are you ~ting anywhere with your investigation?** est-ce que votre enquête avance?; **now we're ~ting somewhere** (making progress) on avance vraiment; (receiving fresh lead) voilà quelque chose d'intéressant; **it's a slow process but we're ~ting there** c'est un processus lent, mais on avance; **it's not perfect yet but we're ~ting there** ce n'est pas encore parfait mais on avance; **6**○ (put on) **to ~ into** mettre [*pyjamas, overalls*].

IDIOMS **~**○**!** fiche-moi le camp○!; **~ along with you**○**!** ne sois pas ridicule! ; **~ away with you**○**!** arrête de raconter n'importe quoi○!; **~ her**○**!** regarde-moi ça!; **~ him**○ **in that hat!** regarde-le avec ce chapeau!; **he got his**○ (was killed) il a cassé sa pipe○; **I'll ~ you**○ **for that** je vais te le faire payer○; **I'm ~ting there** je progresse; **it ~s me right here!** tu vas me faire pleurer!; **I've/he's got it bad**○ je suis/il est vraiment mordu; **I've got it** je sais; **to ~ above oneself** commencer à avoir la grosse tête○; **to ~ it together**○ se ressaisir; **to ~ it up**● bander●, avoir une érection ; **to ~ one's in**○ US prendre sa revanche; **to tell sb where to ~ off** envoyer qn promener; **to ~ with it**○ se mettre dans le coup○; **what's got into her/them?** qu'est-ce qui lui/leur a pris?; **where does he ~ off**○**?** pour qui se prend-il?; **you've got me there!** alors là tu me poses une colle○!

■ **get about 1** (manage to move) se déplacer (**by doing** en faisant); **she doesn't ~ about very well now** elle a du mal à se déplacer maintenant; **2** (travel) voyager, se déplacer; **do you ~ about much in your job?** vous voyagez beaucoup pour votre travail?; **he ~s about a bit** (travels) il voyage pas mal; (knows people) il connaît du monde; **3** (be spread) [*news*] se répandre; [*rumour*] courir, se répandre; **it got about that** la nouvelle s'est répandue que, le bruit a couru que.

■ **get across**: ¶ **~ across 1** (pass to other side) traverser; **2** (be communicated) [*message*] passer; ¶ **~ across [sth]** (cross) traverser [*river, road etc*]; ¶ **~ [sth] across 1** (transport) **how will we ~ it across?** (over stream, gap etc) comment est-ce qu'on le/la fera passer de l'autre côté?; **I'll ~ a copy across to you** (in separate office, building etc) je vous en ferai parvenir un exemplaire; **2** (communicate) faire passer [*message, meaning*] (**to** à); ¶ **~ across [sb]**○ US (annoy) se mettre [qn] à dos○ [*person*].

■ **get ahead 1** (make progress) [*person*] progresser; **to ~ ahead of** prendre de l'avance sur [*competitor*]; **2** (go too fast) **let's not ~ ahead of ourselves** n'anticipons pas.

■ **get along 1** (progress) **how's the project ~ting along?** comment est-ce que le projet se présente?; **how are you ~ting along?** (in job) comment ça se passe?; (to sick or old person) comment ça va?; (in school subject) comment est-ce que ça se passe?; **2** (cope) s'en sortir; **we can't ~ along without a computer/him** on ne s'en sortira pas sans ordinateur/lui; **3** (be suited as friends) bien s'entendre (**with** avec); **4** (go) **I must be ~ting along** il faut que j'y aille.

■ **get around**: ¶ **~ around 1** (move, spread) = **get about**; **2 to ~ around to doing**: **she'll ~ around to visiting us eventually** elle va bien finir par venir nous voir; **I must ~ around to reading his article** il faut vraiment que je lise son article; **I haven't got around to it yet** je n'ai pas encore eu le temps de m'en occuper; ¶ **~ around [sth]** (circumvent) contourner [*problem, law*]; **there's no ~ting around it** il n'y a rien à faire.

■ **get at**○: **~ at [sb /sth] 1** (reach) atteindre [*object*]; arriver jusqu'à [*person*]; fig découvrir [*truth*]; **let me ~ at her** (in anger) laissez-moi lui régler son compte○; **2** (spoil) **the ants have got at the sugar** les fourmis ont attaqué le sucre; **3** (criticize) être après [*person*]; **4** (intimidate) intimider [*witness*]; **5** (insinuate) **what are you ~ting at?** où est-ce que tu veux en venir?

■ **get away**: ¶ **~ away 1** (leave) partir; **2** (escape) [*person*] s'échapper; **the fish got away** le poisson s'est échappé; **3** fig (escape unpunished) **to ~ away with a crime** échapper à la justice; **you'll never ~ away with it!** tu ne vas pas t'en tirer comme ça!; **he mustn't be allowed to ~ away with it** il ne faut pas qu'il s'en tire à si bon compte; **she can ~ away with bright colours** elle peut se permettre de porter des couleurs vives; ¶ **~ [sb/sth] away** (for break) emmener [qn] se changer les idées; **to ~ sb away from a bad influence** tenir qn à l'écart d'une mauvaise influence; **to ~ sth away from sb** retirer qch à qn [*weapon, dangerous object*].

■ **get away from**: ¶ **~ away from [sth] 1** (leave) quitter [*town*]; **I must ~ away from here** ou **this place!** il faut que je parte d'ici!; **'~ away from it all'** (in advert) 'évadez-vous de votre quotidien'; **2** fig (deny) nier [*fact*]; **there's no ~ting away from it** on ne peut pas le nier; **3** fig (leave behind) abandonner [*practice, method*]; ¶ **~ away from [sb]** lit, fig échapper à.

■ **get back**: ¶ **~ back 1** (return) gen rentrer; (after short time) revenir; **when we ~ back** à notre retour; **2** (move backwards) reculer; **~ back!** reculez!; **3** (take revenge) **to ~ back at** se venger de [*aggressor*]; ¶ **~ back to [sth] 1** (return to) rentrer à [*house, city*]; revenir à [*office, centre, point*]; **we got back to Belgium** nous sommes rentrés en Belgique; **when we ~ back to London** à notre retour à Londres; **2** (return to former condition) revenir à [*teaching, publishing*]; **to ~ back to sleep** se rendormir; **to ~ back to normal** redevenir normal; **3** (return to earlier stage) revenir à [*main topic, former point*]; **to ~ back to your problem,...** pour en revenir à votre problème,...; ¶ **~ back to [sb] 1** (return to) revenir à [*group, person*]; **2** (on telephone) **I'll ~ right back to you** je vous rappelle tout de suite; ¶ **~ [sb/sth] back 1** (return) (personally) ramener [*object, person*]; (by post etc) renvoyer; Sport (in tennis etc) renvoyer [*ball*]; **when they got him back to his cell** quand ils l'ont ramené dans sa cellule; **2** (regain) récupérer [*lost object, loaned item*]; fig reprendre [*strength*]; **she got her money back** elle a été remboursée; **she got her old job back** on lui a redonné son travail; **he got his girlfriend back** il s'est remis avec sa petite amie○.

■ **get behind**: ¶ **~ behind** (delayed) prendre du retard; ¶ **~ behind [sth]** se mettre derrière [*hedge, sofa etc*].

■ **get by 1** (pass) passer; **2** (survive) se débrouiller (**on, with** avec); **we'll never ~ by without him/them** nous ne nous en sortirons jamais sans lui/eux.

■ **get down**: ¶ **~ down 1** (descend) descendre (**from, out of** de); **2** (leave table) quitter la table; **3** (lower oneself) (to floor) se coucher; (to crouching position) se baisser; **to ~ down on one's knees** s'agenouiller; **to ~ down to** (descend to reach) arriver à [*lower level etc*]; atteindre [*trapped person etc*]; (apply oneself to) se mettre à [*work*]; **to ~ down to the pupils' level** fig se mettre à la portée des élèves; **let's ~ down to business** parlons affaires; **when you ~ right down to it** quand on regarde d'un peu plus près; **to ~ down to doing** se mettre à faire; ¶ **~ down [sth]** descendre [*slope*]; **if we ~ down the mountain alive** si nous arrivons vivants en bas de la montagne; **when we got down the hill** quand nous nous sommes retrouvés en bas de la colline; ¶ **~ [sth] down, ~ down [sth] 1** (from height) descendre [*book, jar etc*]; **2** (swallow) avaler [*medicine, pill*]; **3** (record) noter [*speech, dictation*]; ¶ **~ [sb] down 1** (from height) faire descendre [*person*]; **2**○ (depress) déprimer [*person*].

■ **get in**: ¶ **~ in 1** lit (to building) entrer; (to vehicle) monter; **2** fig (participate) **to ~ in on** réussir à s'introduire dans [*project, scheme*]; **to ~ in on the deal**○ faire partie du coup; **3** (return home) rentrer; **4** (arrive at destination) [*train, coach*] arriver; **5** (penetrate) [*water, sunlight*] pénétrer; **6** Pol [*Labour, Tories etc*] passer; [*candidate*] être élu; **7** Sch, Univ [*applicant*] être admis; **8** (associate) **to ~ in with** se mettre bien avec [*person*]; **he's got in with a bad crowd** il traîne avec des gens peu recommandables; ¶ **~ [sth] in, ~ in [sth] 1** (buy in) acheter [*supplies*]; **2** (fit into space) **I can't ~ the drawer in** je n'arrive pas à faire rentrer le tiroir; **3** Agric (harvest) rentrer [*crop*]; **4** Hort (plant) planter [*bulbs etc*]; **5** (deliver, hand in) rendre [*essay, competition entry*]; **6** (include) (in article, book) placer [*section, remark, anecdote*]; **he got in a few punches** il a distribué quelques coups; **7** (fit into schedule) faire [*tennis, golf*]; **I'll try to ~ in a bit of tennis**○ j'essayerai de faire un peu de tennis; ¶ **~ [sb] in** faire entrer [*person*].

■ **get into**: ¶ **~ into [sth] 1** (enter) entrer dans [*building*]; monter dans [*vehicle*]; **2** (be admitted) (as member) devenir membre de [*club*]; (as student) être admis à [*school, university*]; **I didn't know what I was ~ting into** fig je ne savais pas dans quoi je m'embarquais; **3** (squeeze into) rentrer dans [*garment, size*]; ▶ **debt, habit, trouble**; ¶ **~ [sb/sth] into** faire entrer [qn/qch] dans [*good school, building, room, space*].

■ **get off**: ¶ **~ off 1** (from bus etc) descendre (**at** à); **2** (start on journey) partir; **3** (leave work) finir; **4**○ (escape punishment) s'en tirer (**with** avec); **5 to ~ off to** partir pour [*destination*]; **did they ~ off to school OK?** est-ce qu'ils sont partis sans problèmes pour l'école?; (make headway) **to ~ off to a good/poor start** prendre un bon/mauvais départ; **to ~ off to sleep** s'endormir; **to ~ off on doing**○ péj (get buzz from) prendre plaisir à faire; **to ~ off with**, GB rencontrer, ramasser○ pej [*person*]; ¶ **~ off [sth] 1** (climb down from) descendre de [*wall, ledge*]; **2** (alight from) descendre de [*bus etc*]; **3** (remove oneself from) **~ off my nice clean floor/the grass** ne marche pas sur mon sol tout propre/la pelouse; **4** fig (depart from) s'écarter de [*subject*]; ¶ **~ off**○ **[sb]** (leave hold) **~ off me!** lâche-moi!; ¶ **~ [sb/sth] off 1** (lift down) descendre [*object*]; faire descendre [*person*]; **2** (dispatch) envoyer [*parcel, letter, person*]; **I've got the children off to school** j'ai envoyé les enfants à l'école; **3** (remove) enlever [*stain*]; **4**○ (send to sleep) endormir [*baby*].

■ **get on**: ¶ **~ on 1** (climb aboard) monter (**at** à); **2** (work) **~ on a bit faster/more sensibly** travaille un peu plus vite/plus sérieusement; **3** (continue with work) **let's ~ on!** continuons!; **4** GB (like each other) bien s'entendre; **5** (fare) **how did you ~ on?** comment est-ce que ça s'est passé?; **6** (cope) **how are you ~ting on?** comment est-ce que tu t'en sors?; **7** GB (approach) **he's ~ting on for 40** il approche des quarante ans; **it's ~ting on for midnight** il est presque minuit; **there are ~ting on for 80 people**○ il y a presque 80 personnes; **8** (grow late) **time's ~ting on** le temps passe; **9** (grow old) **to be ~ting on a bit** commencer à vieillir; ¶ **~ on [sth]** (board) monter dans [*vehicle*]; ¶ **~ [sth] on, ~ on [sth]** (put on) mettre [*boots, clothing*]; monter [*tyre*]; mettre [*lid, tap washer etc*].

■ **get onto**: **~ onto [sth] 1** (board) monter dans [*vehicle*]; **2** (be appointed) être nommé à [*Board*]; **3** (start to discuss) arriver à parler de [*topic, subject*]; **4** GB (contact) contacter; **I'll ~ on to the authorities** je contacterai les autorités.

■ **get on with**: ¶ **~ on with [sth]** (continue to do) **to ~ on with one's work/with preparing the meal** continuer à travailler/à préparer le repas; **let's ~ on with the job!** au travail!; ¶ **~ on with [sb]** GB s'entendre avec [*person*].

■ **get out**: ¶ **~ out 1** (exit) sortir (**through, by** par); **~ out and don't come back!** va-t'en et ne reviens pas!; **they'll never ~ out alive** ils ne s'en sortiront jamais vivants; **2** (make social outing) sortir; **you should ~ out more** tu devrais sortir plus; **3** (resign, leave) partir; **4** (alight) descendre; **5** (be let out) [*prisoner*] être libéré; **he ~s out on the 8th** il sera libéré le 8; **6** (leak) [*news*] être révélé; ¶ **~ [sth] out, ~ out [sth] 1** (bring out) sortir [*handkerchief, ID card*]; **2** (extract) retirer [*cork, stuck object*]; extraire [*tooth*]; **3** (erase) enlever [*stain*]; **4** (take on loan) emprunter [*library book*]; **5** (produce) sortir [*plans, product*]; **6** (utter) **I couldn't ~ the words out** les mots ne voulaient pas sortir; **7** (solve) faire [*puzzle*]; ¶ **~ [sb] out** (release) faire libérer [*prisoner*]; **to ~ sb out of sth** (free from detention) (personally) libérer qn de qch; (by persuasion) faire libérer qn de qch [*prisoner*]; **to ~ sth out of sth** (bring out) sortir qch de qch [*handkerchief etc*]; (find and remove) récupérer qch dans qch [*required object, stuck object*]; **I can't ~ it out of my mind** je ne peux pas l'effacer de mon esprit.

■ **get out of**: **~ out of [sth] 1** (exit from) sortir de [*building, bed*]; **2** (alight from) descendre de [*vehicle*]; **3** (leave at end of) sortir de [*meeting*]; **4** (be freed from) être libéré de [*prison*]; **5** (withdraw from) quitter [*organization*]; échapper à [*responsibilities*]; **he's got out of oil**○ (as investment) il a vendu toutes ses actions dans le pétrole; **6** (avoid doing) s'arranger pour ne pas aller à [*appointment, meeting*]; **I'll try to ~ out of it** j'essaierai de me libérer; **I accepted the invitation and now I can't ~ out of it** j'ai accepté l'invitation et maintenant je ne peux pas me défiler○; **to ~ out of doing** s'arranger pour ne pas faire; **7** (no longer do) perdre [*habit*]; **8** (gain from) **what do you ~ out of your job?** qu'est-ce que ton travail t'apporte?; **what will you ~ out of it?** qu'est-ce que vous en retirerez?

■ **get over**: ¶ **~ over** (cross) passer; ¶ **~ over [sth] 1** (cross) traverser [*bridge, stream*]; **2** (recover from) se remettre de [*illness, shock*]; **to ~ over the fact that** se remettre du fait que; **I can't ~ over it** (in amazement) je n'en reviens pas; **I couldn't ~ over how she looked** ça m'a fait un choc de la voir comme ça; **I can't ~ over how you've grown** je n'en reviens pas de ce que tu as grandi; **3** (surmount) surmonter [*problem*]; **to ~ sth over with** en finir avec qch; **let's ~ it over with** finissons-en; **4** (stop loving) oublier; **she never got over him** elle ne l'a jamais oublié; ¶ **~ [sb/sth] over 1** (cause to cross) faire passer [*injured person, object*]; faire passer [qn/qch] au-dessus de [*bridge, wall etc*]; **2** (cause to arrive) **~ the plumber over here at once** faites venir tout de suite le plombier; **3** (communicate) faire passer [*message*].

■ **get round** GB: ¶ **~ round** = **get around**; ¶ **~ round [sth]** = **get around [sth]**; ¶ **~ round**○ **[sb]** persuader [qn], avoir [qn] au sentiment○; **can't you ~ round him?** est-ce que tu ne peux pas le persuader?; **she easily ~s round her father** elle fait tout ce qu'elle veut de son père.

■ **get through**: ¶ **~ through 1** (squeeze through) passer; **2** Telecom **to ~ through to sb** avoir qn au téléphone; **I couldn't ~ through** je n'ai pas réussi à l'avoir; **3 to ~ through to** (communicate with) convaincre [*person*]; **4** (arrive) [*news, supplies*] arriver; **5** (survive) s'en sortir (**by doing** en faisant); **6** Sch, Univ [*examinee*] réussir; ¶ **~ through [sth] 1** (make way through) traverser [*checkpoint, mud*]; **2** (reach end of) terminer [*book, revision*]; finir [*meal, task*]; [*actor*] finir [*performance*]; **3** (survive mentally) **I thought I'd never ~ through the week** j'ai cru que je ne tiendrais pas la semaine; **4** (complete successfully) [*candidate, competitor*] réussir à [*exam, qualifying round*]; **I got through the interview** l'entretien s'est bien passé; **5** (consume, use) manger [*supply of food*]; boire [*supply of drink*]; dépenser [*money*]; **I ~ through two notebooks a week** il me faut or j'use deux carnets par semaine; ¶ **~ [sb/sth] through 1** (squeeze through) faire passer [*car, object, person*]; **2** (help to endure) [*pills, encouragement, strength of character*] aider [qn] à continuer; **her advice/these pills got me through the day** ses conseils/ces comprimés m'ont aidé à tenir le coup○; **3** (help through frontier etc) faire passer [*person, imported goods*]; **4** Sch, Univ (help to pass) permettre à [qn] de réussir [*candidate*]; **5** Pol faire passer [*bill*].

■ **get together**: ¶ **~ together** (assemble) se réunir (**about , over** pour discuter de); ¶ **~ [sb/sth] together, ~ together [sb/sth] 1** (assemble) réunir [*different people, groups*]; **2** (accumulate) réunir [*money*]; rassembler [*food parcels, truckload*]; **3** (form) former [*company, action group*].

■ **get under**: ¶ **~ under** passer en-dessous; ¶ **~ under [sth]** passer sous [*barrier, floorboards etc*].

■ **get up**: ¶ **~ up 1** (from bed, chair etc) se lever (**from** de); **~ up off the grass!** ne reste pas sur l'herbe!; **2** (on horse, ledge etc) monter; **how did you ~ up there?** comment est-ce que tu es monté là-haut?; **3** Meteorol [*storm*] se préparer; [*wind*] se lever; **4 to ~ up to** (reach) arriver à [*page, upper floor*]; **what did you ~ up to?** fig (sth enjoyable) qu'est-ce que tu as fait de beau?; (sth mischievous) qu'est-ce que tu as fabriqué○?; ¶ **~ up [sth] 1** arriver en haut de [*hill, ladder*]; **2** (increase) augmenter [*speed*]; **3** (start, muster) former [*group*]; faire [*petition*]; obtenir [*support, sympathy*]; ¶ **~ [sth] up** organiser; ¶ **~ [oneself] up**○ **in** mettre [*outfit*].

getatable○ /ˌgetˈætəbl/ *adj* **to be/not to be ~** [*object*] être facile/difficile à atteindre.

getaway /ˈgetəweɪ/ **I** *n* **to make a quick ~** décamper vite fait○.
II *modif* **the robbers had a ~ car outside the bank** une voiture attendait les voleurs à la sortie de la banque.

get-rich-quick scheme○ *n* combine○ *f* pour s'enrichir rapidement.

get-together /ˈgettəgeðə(r)/ *n* **we ought to have a ~** il faudrait qu'on organise quelque chose pour se voir; **we had a bit of a ~** nous avons fait une petite fête.

get: **~up**○ *n* péj accoutrement *m*; **~-up-and-go** *n* dynamisme *m*; **~ well** *adj* [*card, wishes*] de prompt rétablissement.

geum /ˈdʒiːəm/ *n* benoîte *f*.

gewgaw /ˈgjuːgɔː/ *n* colifichet *m*.

geyser /ˈgiːzə(r)/ *n* **1** Geol geyser *m*; **2** GB (water heater) chauffe-eau *m* (à gaz).

G-force *n* force *f* de gravité.

Ghana /ˈgɑːnə/ **▶ 1131** *pr n* Ghana *m*.

Ghanaian /gɑːˈneɪən/ **▶ 1486** **I** *n* Ghanéen/-éenne *m/f*.
II *adj* ghanéen/-éenne.

ghastly /ˈgɑːstlɪ, US ˈgæstlɪ/ *adj* **1** (dreadful) [*accident, scene, sight*] horrible; **2** (sickly) [*person, family, decor, colour, taste*] horrible; [*light*] blafard; **to be ~ pale, to have a ~ pallor** être blême or livide.

ghee /giː/ *n* beurre *m* clarifié.

Ghent /gent/ **▶ 1818** *pr n* Gand.

gherkin /ˈgɜːkɪn/ *n* cornichon *m*.

ghetto /ˈgetəʊ/ **I** *n* (*pl* **~** ou **~es**) ghetto *m*.
II *modif* [*child, poverty*] des ghettos; [*life, upbringing*] dans les ghettos.

ghetto blaster○ *n* (gros) radiocassette *m* or *f* portable.

ghettoization /ˌgetəʊaɪˈzeɪʃn, US -əʊɪˈz-/ *n* (of people) relégation *f* dans des ghettos; **the ~ of an issue** fig la relégation d'un problème au second plan.

ghettoize /ˈgətəʊaɪz/ *vtr* lit reléguer [qn] dans des ghettos [*immigrants*]; fig reléguer [qch] au second plan [*subject, issue*].

ghost /gəʊst/ **I** *n* **1** (spectre) fantôme *m*; **to believe in ~s** croire aux fantômes; **you look as if you've seen a ~!** tu as l'air terrorisé!; **2** fig **the ~ of a smile** l'ombre *f* d'un sourire; **they haven't the ~ of a chance of winning!** ils n'ont pas la moindre chance de réussir!; **to lay the ~s of one's past** exorciser ses démons; **3** (writer) nègre *m*; **4** TV image *f* secondaire, écho *m*.
II *vtr* **to ~ sb's books** servir de nègre à qn pour ses livres.
III *vi* **to ~ for sb** servir de nègre à qn.
IDIOMS **to give up the ~** rendre l'âme.

ghost image *n* image *f* secondaire, écho *m*.

ghostly /ˈgəʊstlɪ/ *adj* spectral.

ghost: **~ ship** *n* vaisseau *m* fantôme; **~ story** *n* histoire *f* de fantômes; **~ town** *n* ville *f* morte; **~ train** *n* train *m* fantôme; **~write** *vi, vtr* (*prét* **-wrote**; *pp* **-written**) = **ghost** II, III; **~writer** *n* nègre *m*.

ghoul /guːl/ *n* **1** (spirit) goule *f*; **2** péj (person) **to be a ~** être macabre.

ghoulish /ˈguːlɪʃ/ *adj* (all contexts) macabre.

GHQ *n* (*abrév* = **General Headquarters**) GQG *m*.

GI *n* (*pl* **GIs**) GI *m inv*, soldat *m* américain.

giant /ˈdʒaɪənt/ **I** *n* (all contexts) géant *m*; **industrial ~** géant *m* de l'industrie; **intellectual ~** géant *m* sur le plan intellectuel.
II *adj* [*size, company*] géant.

giant anteater *n* grand fourmilier *m*.

giantess /ˈdʒaɪəntes/ *n* géante *f*.

giant: **~-killer** *n* vainqueur *m* surprise; **~ panda** *n* grand panda *m*; **~-size(d)** *adj* géant; **~ slalom** *n* slalom *m* géant; **~ star** *n* étoile *f* géante.

gibber /ˈdʒɪbə(r)/ *vi* **1** (with fear, rage) bafouiller; **what's he ~ing on about?**○ péj qu'est-ce qu'il bafouille?; **~ing idiot**○ péj crétin○; **2** [*monkey*] baragouiner.

gibberish /ˈdʒɪbərɪʃ/ *n* charabia *m*.

gibbet /ˈdʒɪbɪt/ *n* potence *f*, gibet *m*.

gibbon /ˈgɪbən/ *n* gibbon *m*.

gibbous moon /ˌgɪbəsˈmuːn/ *n* lune *f* gibbeuse.

gibe = **jibe**.

GI Bill *n* US *loi votée en 1944 et permettant aux GI démobilisés de poursuivre gratuitement leurs études.*

giblets /ˈdʒɪblɪts/ *npl* abats *mpl*.

Gibraltar /dʒɪ'brɔ:ltə(r)/ ▶ 1818 *pr n* Gibraltar.

GI bride *n: épouse étrangère d'un GI.*

giddily /'gɪdɪlɪ/ *adv* **1** (dizzily) vertigineusement; **2** (frivolously) étourdiment.

giddiness /'gɪdɪnɪs/ *n* **1** (dizziness) vertige *m*; **2** (frivolity) légèreté *f*, insouciance *f*.

giddy /'gɪdɪ/ *adj* **1** (dizzy) **to feel ~** avoir la tête qui tourne; **2** (exhilarating) [*height, speed*] vertigineux/-euse; [*success, social whirl*] enivrant; **3** (frivolous) [*person*] écervelé; [*behaviour*] irréfléchi.

giddy: **~ spell** *n* vertige *m*, étourdissement *m*; **~ up** *excl* hue!.

Gideon Bible /,gɪdɪən'baɪbl/ *n* Bible *f* (*placée dans les hôtels par une organisation chrétienne*).

gift /gɪft/ *n* **1** (present) cadeau *m* (**from** de; **to** à); **a farewell/wedding ~** un cadeau d'adieu/de mariage; **to give a ~ to sb, to give sb a ~** faire or offrir un cadeau à qn; **to give sb a ~ of crystal/money** offrir du cristal/de l'argent à qn; **they gave it to us as a ~** ils nous en ont fait cadeau; **it's for a ~** c'est pour offrir; **'how to claim your free ~'** Advertg 'comment recevoir votre cadeau'; **a ~ from the gods** un don du ciel; **the ~ of life/sight** le don de la vie/la vue; fig **it was a ~ of a goal**○ le but était un vrai cadeau; **at that price, it's a ~!** à ce prix-là, c'est donné or c'est un cadeau!; **2** (donation) don *m* (**from** de; **to** à); **a ~ of £10,000/of an incubator** un don de 10 000 livres sterling/d'une couveuse; **to make a ~ of sth to sb** faire don de qch à qn; **3** (talent) don *m* (**for sth** pour qch); **to have a ~ for** ou **of doing** avoir le don de faire; **4** Jur (of property) donation *f*; **to make sb a ~ of sth** faire une donation à qn de qch; **by way of a ~** en donation; **to be in sb's ~** sont être à la discrétion de qn.
IDIOMS **don't look a ~ horse in the mouth** Prov à cheval donné, on ne regarde pas les dents Prov.

GIFT /gɪft/ *n* Med (*abrév* = **gamete intrafallopian transfer**) transfert *m* tubaire des gamètes.

gift certificate *n* US chèque-cadeau *m*.

gifted /'gɪftɪd/ *adj* (talented) [*actor, athlete, musician, artist*] doué; (intellectually) [*child*] surdoué; **a linguistically/musically ~ student** un étudiant très doué pour les langues/la musique; **a ~ amateur** un amateur très doué.

gift: **~ shop** *n* magasin *m* de cadeaux; **~ token**, **~ voucher** *n* GB chèque-cadeau *m*.

gift wrap /'gɪftræp/ **I** *n* (also **~ping**) papier *m* cadeau.
II gift-wrap /,gɪft'ræp/ *vtr* (*p prés etc* **-pp-**) **would you like it ~ped?** est-ce que je vous fais un paquet-cadeau?

gig /gɪg/ *n* **1**○ Mus concert *m* de rock; **to do** ou **play a ~** donner un concert; **2** (carriage) cabriolet *m*; **3** Naut petit canot *m*, youyou *m*.

gigabyte /'gaɪgəbaɪt/ *n* gigaoctet *m*.

gigantic /dʒaɪ'gæntɪk/ *adj* gigantesque.

gigantically /dʒaɪ'gæntɪkəlɪ/ *adv* **~ tall** gigantesque; **to be ~ successful**○ avoir un succès énorme.

gigantism /'dʒaɪgəntɪzəm/ *n* gigantisme *m*.

gigawatt /'gaɪgəwɒt/ *n* gigawatt *m*.

giggle /'gɪgl/ **I** *n* **1** (silly) petit rire *m* bête; (nervous) petit rire nerveux; **to have a fit of the ~s** avoir le fou rire; **to get the ~s** attraper un fou rire; **2**○ GB (joke) **to do sth for a ~**○ faire qch pour rigoler○; **we had a good ~**○! on a bien rigolé○!
II *vtr* **'I don't know!' she ~d** 'je ne sais pas!' dit-elle en riant bêtement or nerveusement.
III *vi* (stupidly) rire bêtement; (nervously) rire nerveusement; **he was giggling helplessly** il avait le fou rire.

giggly /'gɪglɪ/ *adj* péj [*person*] qui n'arrête pas de glousser; [*laughter*] (nervous) nerveux/-euse; (silly) bête; **to be in a ~ mood** se mettre à rire pour un rien.

GIGO (*abrév* = **garbage in garbage out**); ▶ **garbage**.

gigolo /'ʒɪgələʊ/ *n* (*pl* **-los**) gigolo *m*.

Gila monster /'hi:lə 'mɒnstə/ *n* monstre *m* de Gila.

gild /gɪld/ *vtr* (*prét, pp* **gilded** ou **gilt**) **1** dorer [*frame, ornament*]; **2** (light up) [*sun, light*] illuminer.
IDIOMS **~ed youth** jeunesse *f* dorée; **to be a bird in a ~ cage** vivre dans une prison dorée.

gilding /'gɪldɪŋ/ *n* dorure *f*.

gill[1] /gɪl/ *n* **1** (of fish) branchie *f*; **2** (of mushroom) lamelle *f*.
IDIOMS **green about the ~s**○ blanc/blanche comme un linge.

gill[2] /dʒɪl/ *n* ▶ 1068 Meas quart *m* de pinte.

gillie, **gilly** /'gɪlɪ/ *n* Scot accompagnateur *m* (*d'un chasseur, d'un pêcheur*).

gillyflower /'dʒɪlɪflaʊə(r)/ *n* giroflée *f*.

gilt /gɪlt/ **I** *pp* ▶ **gild**.
II *n* dorure *f*.
III *adj* [*frame, paint*] doré.

gilt-edged /,gɪlt'edʒd/ *adj* **1** [*page*] doré sur tranche; **2** [*investment, opportunity*] en or.

gilt-edged securities, **gilt-edged stock(s)** *n* obligations et titres *mpl* d'État or de père de famille○ pej.

gilts /'gɪlts/ Fin **I** *npl* obligations et titres *mpl* d'État or de père de famille○ pej.
II *modif* [*market, profit, yield*] des obligations et titres d'État.

gimbals /'dʒɪmblz/ *npl* cardan *m*.

gimcrack /'dʒɪmkræk/ **I** *n* babiole *f*.
II *adj* en toc, de pacotille.

gimlet /'gɪmlɪt/ *n* vrille *f*.
IDIOMS **to have eyes like ~s, to be ~-eyed** avoir un regard perçant.

gimmick /'gɪmɪk/ *n* péj **1** (stunt to attract attention) truc○ *m*; (gadget) gadget *m*; **sales/publicity ~** truc○ promotionnel/publicitaire; **cheap ~s to attract customers** des combines○ *fpl* pour attirer le client; **2** US **what's his ~?** qu'est-ce qu'il veut vraiment?

gimmickry /'gɪmɪkrɪ/ *n* ¢ péj trucs○ *mpl*.

gimmicky /'gɪmɪkɪ/ *adj* péj [*theatrical production*] plein d'effets gratuits; [*clothes, jewellery*] fantaisiste; [*idea, theory*] à la mode.

gimp /gɪmp/ **I** *n* **1** Tex renfort *m*; **2**○ US **to have a ~** boiter.
II○ *vi* US boiter.

gin /dʒɪn/ *n* **1** (drink) gin *m*; **2** (engine) égreneuse *f*; **3** (also **~ trap**) Hunt piège *m*.

gin: **~ and it** *n* GB gin-vermouth *m*; **~ and tonic** *n* gin tonic *m*; **~ and tonic belt** *n* GB banlieue *f* résidentielle aisée (*des grandes villes du sud de l'Angleterre*).

ginger /'dʒɪndʒə(r)/ ▶ 1104 **I** *n* **1** Bot, Culin gingembre *m*; **root** ou **fresh ~** gingembre *m* frais; **2** (colour) (of hair) roux *m*; **3** (nickname) injur Poil *m* de carotte offensive.
II *modif* **1** Culin [*cake, biscuit*] au gingembre; **2** (reddish) [*hair, beard*] roux/rousse; [*cat*] au poil roux.
■ **ginger up**: **~ up [sth]** égayer [*evening*]; stimuler [*metabolism*].

ginger: **~ ale** *n*: *boisson gazeuse au gingembre*; **~ beer** *n*: *boisson légèrement alcoolisée à base de gingembre*.

gingerbread /'dʒɪndʒəbred/ *n* **1** Culin ≈ pain *m* d'épice; **2** (ornamentation) surtout US tarabiscotage *m*.
IDIOMS **that takes the gilt off the ~** ça change tout.

ginger: **~bread man** *n* bonhomme *m* en pain d'épice; **~ group** *n* GB groupe *m* de pression (*à l'intérieur d'un parti, d'un organisme*); **~-haired** *adj* roux/rousse.

gingerly /'dʒɪndʒəlɪ/ *adv* avec précaution.

gingernut, **ginger snap** *n* Culin biscuit *m* au gingembre.

gingery /'dʒɪndʒərɪ/ *adj* **1** (reddish) [*hair, beard, colour*] roux/rousse; **2** Culin [*flavour*] de gingembre.

gingham /'gɪŋəm/ **I** *n* vichy *m*.
II *modif* [*garment*] en vichy.

gingivitis /,dʒɪndʒɪ'vaɪtɪs/ ▶ 1354 *n* gingivite *f*.

gink○ /gɪŋk/ *n* péj type○ *m*.

gin: **~ mill**○ US *n* péj saloon *m*; **~ rummy** ▶ 1282 *n* gin-rami *m*.

ginseng /'dʒɪnseŋ/ *n* ginseng *m*.

gin sling *n* gin-fizz *m*.

Gioconda /'dʒɒkəndə/ *pr n* **La ~** la Joconde *f*.

gippo○† /'dʒɪpəʊ/ *n* GB injur (*abrév* = **gipsy**) romanichel/-elle *m/f*.

gippy○† /'dʒɪpɪ/ *adj* GB **to have a ~ tummy** avoir la colique.

gipsy *n* = **gypsy**.

giraffe /dʒɪ'rɑ:f, US dʒə'ræf/ *n* girafe *f*; **baby ~** girafeau *m*.

gird /gɜ:d/ littér **I** *vtr* ceindre liter.
II *v refl* **to ~ oneself** se préparer (**for** à).
IDIOMS **to ~ (up) one's loins** fig, hum revêtir son armure.

girder /'gɜ:də(r)/ *n* poutre *f*; **box ~** poutre-caisson *f*.

girdle /'gɜ:dl/ **I** *n* **1** (corset) gaine *f*; **2** (belt) ceinture *f*; **3** Culin = **griddle**.
II *vtr* encercler.

girl /gɜ:l/ **I** *n* **1** (child) fille *f*; (teenager) jeune fille *f*; (woman) femme *f*; **~'s bicycle/coat** bicyclette/manteau de fille; **~s' school** école de filles; **the ~s' changing room/toilets** le vestiaire/les toilettes des filles; **baby ~** petite fille *f*, bébé *m*; **little ~** petite fille *f*, fillette *f*; **teenage ~** adolescente *f*; **young ~** jeune fille; **when I was a ~** (referring to childhood) quand j'étais petite; (referring to adolescence) quand j'étais jeune; **good morning, ~s and boys** bonjour, les enfants; **come on, ~s!** (to children) allez, les filles!; (to women) hum allez, mesdames!; **be a good ~** (to child) sois sage; (to adult) hum sois gentille; **good ~!** c'est bien!; **the new ~** gen, Sch la nouvelle *f*; **2** (daughter) fille *f*; **the Smith ~** la fille Smith; **3** (employee) (servant) bonne *f*; **factory ~** ouvrière *f*; **office ~** employée *f* de bureau; **sales** ou **shop ~** vendeuse *f*; **4** (man's sweetheart) (petite) amie *f*.
II *modif* **a ~ singer** une (jeune) chanteuse; **~ talk**○ conversation entre femmes; **he's having ~ trouble** il a des problèmes avec sa petite amie.
IDIOMS **~ next door** jeune fille rangée.

girl: **~ Friday** *n* aide *f* de bureau; **~friend** *n* (sweetheart) (petite) amie *f*; gen amie *f*; **~ guide** GB, **~ scout** US *n* éclaireuse *f*.

girlhood /'gɜ:lhʊd/ *n* (childhood) enfance *f*; (adolescence) jeunesse *f*.

girlie○ /'gɜ:lɪ/ *n* fillette *f*.

girlie: **~ mag(azine)**○ *n* magazine *m* pour hommes; **~ show**○ *n* spectacle *m* de cabaret pour hommes.

girlish /'gɜ:lɪʃ/ *adj* de jeune fille.

girlishly /'gɜ:lɪʃlɪ/ *adv* comme une jeune fille.

girls' wear department *n* rayon *m* fillette.

giro /'dʒaɪrəʊ/ **I** *n* GB Fin **1** (system) système *m* de virement bancaire; **to pay by ~** payer par virement bancaire; **2** (cheque) mandat *m* (*en paiement d'allocations de chômage, de retraite etc*).
II *modif* **~ payment**, **~ transfer** (through bank) virement *m* bancaire; (through post office) virement *m* postal.

Gironde ▶ 1163 *pr n* Gironde *f*; **in/to the ~** en Gironde.

girth /gɜ:θ/ *n* **1** (of person) tour *m* de taille; (of tree, pillar) circonférence *f*; **2** Equit sangle *f*.

gismo○ *n* = **gizmo**.

gist /dʒɪst/ *n* essentiel *m* (**of** de).

git◑ /gɪt/ *n* GB pej conard◑/conasse● *m/f*.

give /gɪv/ **I** *n* élasticité *f*; **this surface has more ~** cette surface amortit mieux les chocs.

II *vtr* (*prét* **gave**; *pp* **given**) **1** (hand over) [*person*] donner [*object, money, medal, prize, punishment, hand, arm*] (**to** à); offrir [*present, drink, sandwich*] (**to** à); **to ~ sb sth** gen donner qch à qn; (politely, as gift) offrir qch à qn; **~ it me!**, **~ me it!** donne-moi ça!; **~ him a drink** donne-lui à boire; **to ~ sb sth for** offrir qch à qn pour [*birthday, Christmas*]; **how much** ou **what will you ~ me for it?** combien m'en donnes-tu?; **I'll ~ you 50 cents for it** je t'en donne 50 cents; **I'd ~ anything for/to do** je donnerais n'importe quoi pour/pour faire; **what wouldn't I ~ for...!** je donnerais cher pour...!; **to ~ sb sth as** offrir qch à qn comme [*present, token, symbol*]; **to ~ sb sth to carry/look after** donner qch à qn à porter/surveiller; **2** (cause to have) **to ~ sb sth, to ~ sth to sb** donner [*headache, indigestion, vertigo, nightmares, satisfaction*]; transmettre, passer [*disease, infection, virus*]; **he's given me his cough** il m'a passé sa toux; **to ~ sb pleasure** faire plaisir à qn; **3** (provide, produce) donner [*milk, flavour, result, answer, sum*]; apporter [*heat, light, vitamin, nutrient*]; faire [*total*]; **blue and yellow ~ (you) green** le bleu et le jaune donnent le vert; **the number was given to three decimal places/in metric units** le nombre était donné jusqu'à la troisième décimale/en unités du système métrique; **4** (allow, accord) [*authority*] accorder [*custody, grant, bursary*]; laisser qch à qn [*seat*]; [*hotelier*] donner [*room*]; **to ~ sb sth** donner or accorder qch à qn [*time, time period*] (**to do** pour faire); **~ me a minute** donne-moi une minute; **to ~ sb enough room** laisser suffisamment de place à qn; **I'll ~ him another hour, then I'm calling the police** je lui donne or accorde encore une heure, et j'appelle la police; **she gave him a week to decide** elle lui a donné or accordé une semaine pour décider; **he was given six months to live** on lui a donné six mois à vivre; **how long do you ~ the new boss/their marriage?** combien de temps donnes-tu au nouveau patron/à leur mariage?; **it is not given to all of us to do** sout il n'est pas donné à tout le monde de faire; **she can sing, I'll ~ her that** elle sait chanter, je lui reconnais au moins ça; **it's original, I'll ~ you that** c'est original, je te l'accorde; **she could ~ her opponent five years** elle a au moins cinq ans de plus que son adversaire; **the polls ~ Labour a lead** les Travaillistes sont en tête dans les sondages; **5** Med **to ~ sb sth, to ~ sth to sb** donner qch à qn [*treatment, medicine*]; greffer qch à qn [*organ*]; poser qch à qn [*artificial limb, pacemaker*]; faire qch à qn [*facelift, injection, massage*]; **can you ~ me something for the pain?** pouvez-vous me donner quelque chose contre la douleur?; **6** (communicate) gen, Telecom donner [*advice, information, appointment*]; **to ~ sb sth** passer qch à qn [*extension, number, department*]; **~ me the sales manager, please** passez-moi le directeur commercial, s'il vous plaît; **I was given to understand** ou **believe that** on m'a laissé entendre que; **7** (give birth to) **she gave him two sons** elle lui donna deux fils.

III *vi* (*prét* **gave**; *pp* **given**) **1** (contribute) donner, faire un don; **to ~ to sth** (habitually) faire des dons à qch; **she never ~s to charity** elle ne donne jamais rien aux organisations caritatives; **'please ~ generously'** 'merci (de vos dons)'; **2** (bend, flex) [*mattress, sofa*] s'affaisser (**under** sous); [*shelf, bridge, floorboard*] fléchir (**under** sous); [*branch*] ployer (**under** sous); [*leather, fabric*] s'assouplir; **3** (yield, break) = **give way**; **4** (concede, yield) [*person, side*] céder; **something has to ~** ça va finir par craquer.

IV *v refl* (*prét* **gave**; *pp* **given**) **to ~ oneself to** (devote oneself) se consacrer à [*cause, good works*]; euph (sexually) se donner à [*person*].

IDIOMS **don't ~ me that**○**!** ne (me) raconte pas d'histoires!; **~ or take an inch (or two)** à quelques centimètres près; **~ me a nice cup of tea any day** ou **every time**○**!** rien ne vaut une bonne tasse de thé!; **if this is the big city, ~ me a village every time**○ si c'est ça la ville, alors vive les petits villages; **'I ~ you the bride and groom!'** 'je bois à la santé du marié et de la mariée!'; **I'll ~ you something to cry about**○**!** tu vas savoir pourquoi tu pleures!; **I'll ~ you something to complain about**○**!** je vais t'apprendre à te plaindre!; **more money? I'll ~ you more money!**○ je vais t'en donner, moi, de l'argent!; **to ~ and take** faire des concessions; **to ~ as good as one gets** rendre coup pour coup; **to ~ it all one's got**○ (y) mettre le paquet; **to ~ sb what for**○ passer un savon à qn○; **what ~s?**○ qu'est-ce qui se passe?

■ **give away**: ¶ **~ away [sth], ~ [sth] away 1** (as gift, offer, charity) donner [*item, sample, ticket*] (**to** à); distribuer [*samples, tickets*]; **we're practically giving them away!** à ce prix-là, c'est donné!; **they're not exactly giving it away** iron on ne peut pas dire que c'est donné; **we've got 100 copies to ~ away!** il y a 100 exemplaires à gagner!; **2** (reveal) révéler [*secret, answer, story, ending*] (**to** à); **the flavour ~s it away** on le sent au goût; **3** (waste, lose carelessly) laisser échapper [*match, goal, advantage*] (**to** au bénéfice de); ¶ **~ [sb] away, ~ away [sb] 1** (betray) [*expression, fingerprints*] trahir; [*person*] dénoncer [*person*] (**to** à); **to ~ oneself away** se trahir (**by doing** en faisant); **2** (in marriage) conduire [qn] à l'autel.

■ **give back**: **~ [sth] back, ~ back [sth] 1** (restore, return) rendre [*possession, appetite, sight, freedom*] (**to** à); **~ it back!** rends (-moi) ça!; **...or we'll ~ you your money back** ...ou vous serez remboursé; **2** (reflect) renvoyer [*echo, sound, light*].

■ **give forth** littér ou hum: **~ forth [sth]** dégager [*smell*]; émettre [*sound*].

■ **give in**: ¶ **~ in 1** (to temptation, threat, person) céder (**to** à); **2** (stop trying) abandonner; **I ~ in—tell me!** je donne ma langue au chat○—dis-le moi!; ¶ **~ in [sth], ~ [sth] in** rendre [*homework, essay*]; remettre [*ticket, key, petition*].

■ **give off**: **~ off [sth]** émettre [*signal, scent, radiation, light*]; dégager [*heat, fumes, oxygen*]; **he was giving off hostile signals** il montrait des signes d'hostilité.

■ **give onto**: **~ onto [sth]** donner sur [*street, yard etc*].

■ **give out**: ¶ **~ out** [*strength, battery, ink, fuel, supplies*] s'épuiser; [*engine, machine*] tomber en panne; ¶ **~ out [sth], ~ [sth] out 1** (distribute) distribuer [*books, leaflets, gifts*] (**to** à); **2** (emit) = **give off**; **3** (announce) donner [*information, details*].

■ **give over**: ¶ **~ over**○ arrêter; **~ over!** arrête!; **to ~ over doing**○ arrêter de faire; ¶ **~ over [sth], ~ [sth] over 1** affecter or réserver [*place, room*] (**to** à); **2** consacrer [*time, life*] (**to** à); **the rest of the day was given over to** le reste de la journée était consacré à; **3** (hand over) remettre [qch] à [*person*]; ¶ **~ oneself over to 1** (devote oneself) se consacrer à [*good works, writing*]; **2** (let oneself go) s'abandonner à [*despair, joy*]; **3** (hand oneself to) se rendre à [*police*].

■ **give up**: ¶ **~ up** abandonner; **do you ~ up?** tu abandonnes?; **I ~ up!** (exasperated) j'abandonne!; **don't ~ up!** tiens bon!; **to ~ up on** laisser tomber [*diet, crossword, pupil, patient*]; ne plus compter sur [*friend, partner, associate*]; **I've given up on him** je ne compte plus sur lui!; ¶ **~ up [sth], ~ [sth] up 1** (renounce or sacrifice) renoncer à [*vice, habit, social life, throne, title, claim*]; sacrifier [*free time, Saturdays etc*]; quitter [*job, work*]; **to ~ up smoking/drinking** cesser de fumer/de boire; **to ~ everything up for sb** renoncer à tout pour qn; **to ~ up one's free time for sth** consacrer son temps libre à qch; **2** (abandon, drop) abandonner [*search, hope, struggle, school subject*]; renoncer à [*idea, thought*]; **to ~ up trying/writing** cesser d'essayer/d'écrire; **3** (surrender) céder [*seat, place, territory*]; remettre [*passport, key*]; livrer [*secret, treasure*]; ¶ **~ up [sb], ~ [sb] up 1** (hand over) livrer (**to** à); **to ~ oneself up** se livrer, se rendre (**to** à); **2** GB (stop expecting to arrive) ne plus attendre; **I'd given you up!** je ne t'attendais plus!; **3** (stop expecting to recover) considérer [qn] comme perdu; **4** (discontinue relations with) laisser tomber [*lover*]; délaisser [*friend*].

■ **give way**: **~ way 1** (collapse) [*bridge, table, chair, wall, ceiling*] s'effondrer (**under** sous); [*fence, cable, rope*] céder (**under** sous); **his legs gave way under the weight/when he heard the news** ses jambes se sont dérobées sous le poids/sous lui quand il a appris la nouvelle; **2** GB (when driving) céder le passage (**to** à); **3** (concede, yield) céder; **to ~ way to** (yield to) céder à [*pressure, demands, person, fear, temptation, urge*]; s'abandonner à [*despair, base instincts*]; (be replaced by) faire place à [*sunshine, relief, new methods*].

give-and-take *n* ¢ concessions *fpl* mutuelles.

giveaway /ˈgɪvəweɪ/ *n* **1** (revealing thing) **to be a ~** être révélateur/-trice; **her expression was a ~** son expression était révélatrice or la trahissait; **it was a dead ~**○ c'était une preuve accablante; **oops! what a ~**○**!** zut! je me suis coupé○!; **2** (free gift, sample) cadeau *m*; **at £20 it's a ~**○ vingt livres pour ça, c'est donné.

given /ˈgɪvn/ **I** *pp* ▶ **give**.

II *adj* **1** (certain, specified) [*point, level, number*] donné; [*volume, length*] déterminé; **the ~ date** la date convenue; **at any ~ moment** à un moment précis; **2** (prone) **to be ~ to sth/to doing** avoir tendance à qch/à faire; **I am not ~ to losing my temper** je n'ai pas l'habitude de me mettre en colère.

III *prep* **1** (in view of) étant donné [*fact*]; **~ that** (seeing as) étant donné que; (assuming that) à supposer que; **2** Math **~ a triangle ABC** soit un triangle ABC; **~ that x = 2** étant donné que x = 2; **3** (with) avec [*training, proper care*]; **~ the right training** avec une bonne formation; **she could have been a writer, ~ the chance** elle aurait pu être écrivain, si on lui en avait donné la chance; **~ an opportunity I'll tell her this evening** si j'en ai l'occasion je le lui dirai ce soir; **~ the right conditions the plant will grow** dans de bonnes conditions la plante poussera.

given name *n* prénom *m*.

giver /ˈgɪvə(r)/ *n* (donor to charity etc) donateur/-trice *m/f*; **the ~ of life** celui/celle qui donne la vie.

give way sign *n* GB panneau *m* 'cédez le passage'.

gizmo○ /ˈgɪzməʊ/ *n* truc○ *m*, machin○ *m*.

gizzard /ˈgɪzəd/ *n* gésier *m*.

glacé /ˈglæseɪ, US glæˈseɪ/ *adj* [*fruit, leather*] glacé; **~ icing** glaçage *m*.

glacial /ˈgleɪsɪəl, US ˈgleɪʃl/ *adj* **1** Geol glaciaire; **~ period** ère *f* glaciaire; **2** fig [*atmosphere, stare*] glacial; **3** Chem cristallisé.

glaciated /ˈgleɪsɪeɪtɪd/ *adj* Geol glaciaire.

glaciation /ˌgleɪsɪˈeɪʃn/ *n* glaciation *f*.

glacier /ˈglæsɪə(r)/ *n* glacier *m*.

glaciological /ˌgleɪsɪəˈlɒdʒɪkl/ *adj* glaciologique.

glaciologist /ˌgleɪsɪˈɒlədʒɪst/ ▶ 1692 *n* glaciologue *mf*.

glaciology /ˌgleɪsɪˈɒlədʒɪ/ *n* glaciologie *f*.

glad /glæd/ *adj* **1** (pleased) content, heureux/-euse (**about** de; **that** que; **to do** de faire); **I am ~ (that) you are able to come** je suis content que vous puissiez venir; **I'd be ~ to help you** je serais heureux de t'aider; **oh, I am ~!** que je suis heureux!; **he was only too ~ to help me** il ne demandait qu'à m'aider; **2** (cheering) [*news*] heureux/-euse.

IDIOMS **to give sb the ~ eye** faire de l'œil à qn; **to give sb the ~ hand** faire un accueil chaleureux à qn; **in one's ~ rags**○ sur son trente et un○; **I'll be ~ to see the back** ou **last of them**○ je serai content de les voir partir.

gladden /ˈglædn/ *vtr* réjouir.

glade /gleɪd/ *n* clairière *f*.

gladiator /ˈglædieɪtə(r)/ *n* gladiateur *m*.

gladiatorial /ˌglædɪəˈtɔːrɪəl/ *adj* [*combat*] de gladiateurs; fig [*politics*] agressif/-ive.

gladiolus /ˌglædɪˈəʊləs/, **gladiola** /ˌglædɪˈəʊlə/ *n* (*pl* **-li**) glaïeul *m*.

gladly /ˈglædlɪ/ *adv* (willingly) volontiers; (with pleasure) avec plaisir.

IDIOMS **she doesn't suffer fools ~** elle a du mal à supporter les gens moins brillants qu'elle.

gladness /ˈglædnɪs/ *n* joie *f*.

glam○ /glæm/ *n, adj* = **glamorous**.

glamorize /ˈglæməraɪz/ *vtr* embellir [*person*]; valoriser [*place, attitude, idea*]; peindre [qch] sous de belles couleurs [*event*].

glamorous /ˈglæmərəs/ *adj* [*person, image, look*] séduisant; [*older person*] élégant; [*dress*] splendide; [*occasion*] brillant; [*job*] prestigieux/-ieuse.

glamour, **glamor** US /ˈglæmə(r)/ *n* (of person) séduction *f*; (of job) prestige *m*; (of travel, fast cars) fascination *f*; **to lend ~ to sth** donner de l'éclat à qch.

glamour: **~ boy**○† *n* péj éphèbe *m* pej; **~ girl**○† *n* belle fille *f bien pomponnée*; **~ model** *n* pin-up *f*; **~ photography** *n* photographie *f* de pin-up; **~ puss**○ *n* = **glamour boy**, **glamour girl**; **~ stock** *n* ¢ Fin valeur *f* vedette.

glance /glɑːns, US glæns/ **I** *n* coup *m* d'œil; **to have a ~ at** jeter un œil○ or un coup d'œil sur; **to exchange ~s** échanger un coup d'œil or un regard; **to be able to tell sth at a ~** pouvoir dire qch d'un coup d'œil; **you can tell at a ~ that** un coup d'œil suffit pour comprendre que; **at first ~** au premier coup d'œil; **without a backward ~** sans se retourner.

II *vi* **to ~ at** jeter un coup d'œil à; **to ~ out of the window** jeter un coup d'œil par la fenêtre; **to ~ down** jeter un coup d'œil vers le bas; **to ~ around the room** parcourir la pièce du regard.

■ **glance off**: **~ off [sth]** [*bullet, stone*] ricocher sur or contre; [*ball*] rebondir sur or contre; [*ray, beam*] se réfléchir sur.

glancing /ˈglɑːnsɪŋ, US ˈglænsɪŋ/ *adj* [*blow, kick*] oblique; **a ~ reference** une allusion.

gland /glænd/ *n* **1** Anat glande *f*; **to have swollen ~s** avoir des ganglions; **2** Mech presse-étoupe *m inv*.

glanders /ˈglændəz/ *n* (+ *v sg*) Vet morve *f*.

glandular /ˈglændjʊlə(r), US -dʒʊ-/ *adj* Med glandulaire.

glandular fever ▶ 1354 *n* mononucléose *f* infectieuse.

glans /glænz/ *n* (*pl* **glandes**) gland *m*.

glare /gleə(r)/ **I** *n* **1** (angry look) regard *m* furieux; **2** (from light, headlights, etc) lumière *f* éblouissante; (of sun) lumière *f* éblouissante; **in the ~ of publicity** fig sous le feu des médias.

II *vi* **1** [*person*] lancer un regard furieux (**at** à); **2** [*light, sun*] éblouir.

glaring /ˈgleərɪŋ/ *adj* **1** (obvious) [*contradiction, example, error, injustice, omission*] flagrant; **2** (blinding) [*light*] éblouissant; **3** (angry) [*look*] furieux/-ieuse.

glaringly /ˈgleərɪŋlɪ/ *adv* **it's ~ obvious** c'est l'évidence même.

Glarus ▶ 1818, 1776 *pr n* Glaris; **the canton of ~** le canton de Glaris.

glasnost /ˈglæznɒst/ *n* glasnost *f*, transparence *f*.

glass /glɑːs, US glæs/ **I** *n* **1** (substance) verre *m*; **a piece of ~** un morceau de verre; (tiny) un éclat de verre; **to cultivate sth under ~** cultiver qch sous verre; **behind ~** [*books, ornaments etc*] dans des vitrines; **2** (drinking vessel) verre *m*; **wine ~** verre *m* à vin; **a ~ of wine** un verre de vin; **3** ¢ (also **~ware**) verrerie *f*; (glasses only) services *mpl* de verres; **4**† (mirror) miroir *m*; **5** (telescope) longue-vue *f*; **6** (barometer) baromètre *m*; **the ~ is rising/falling** le baromètre monte/baisse.

II *modif* [*bottle, shelf, vase*] en verre.

III glasses *npl* **1** (spectacles) lunettes *fpl*; **a pair of ~es** une paire de lunettes; **he wears reading ~es** il doit porter des lunettes quand il lit; **2** (binoculars) jumelles *fpl*.

■ **glass in**: **~ [sth] in**, **~ in [sth]** vitrer [*shelves, courtyard*].

■ **glass over** = **glass in**.

glass: **~ blower** ▶ 1692 *n* souffleur *m* de verre; **~ blowing** *n* soufflage *m* de verre; **~ case** *n* (box) vitrine *f* en verre; (dome) globe *m*; **~ ceiling** *n*: *niveau professionnel que la discrimiation empêche certains groupes sociaux de dépasser*; **~ cloth** *n* essuie-verres *m inv*; **~ cutter** ▶ 1692 *n* (worker) vitrier *m*; (tool) diamant *m*; **~ door** *n* porte *f* vitrée; **~ eye** *n* œil *m* de verre; **~ factory** *n* verrerie *f*; **~ fibre** GB, **~ fiber** US *n* fibre *f* de verre.

glassful /ˈglɑːsfʊl, US ˈglæs-/ *n* verre *m*; **three ~s of milk** trois verres de lait; **half a ~** un demi-verre.

glasshouse /ˈglɑːshaʊs, US ˈglæs-/ *n* **1** GB (greenhouse) serre *f*; **2**○ GB argot des militaires (prison) trou○ *m*; **3** US (glassworks) verrerie *f*.

IDIOMS **people in glass houses shouldn't throw stones** mieux vaut balayer devant sa porte avant de critiquer.

glass: **~making** *n* fabrication *f* du verre; **~ paper** *n* papier *m* de verre; **~ wool** *n* laine *f* de verre; **~works** *n* verrerie *f* (usine).

glassy /ˈglɑːsɪ, US ˈglæsɪ/ *adj* **1** (resembling glass) [*substance*] vitreux/-euse; [*bead, object*] qui ressemble au verre; **2** (slippery) [*surface, rock*] lisse; [*road*] (from ice) verglacé; (from rain) glissant; **3** [*waters*] (calm) lisse (comme un miroir); (clear) transparent; **4** (cold) [*air, chill*] glacé, glacial; **5** [*eyes*] (from drink, illness) vitreux/-euse; (with hostility) glacé.

glassy-eyed /ˌglɑːsɪˈaɪd, US ˌglæs-/ *adj* [*person*] (from drink, illness) aux yeux vitreux; (with hostility) au regard glacial.

Glaswegian /glæzˈwiːdʒən/ **I** *n* (inhabitant) habitant/-e *m/f* de Glasgow; (native) originaire *mf* de Glasgow.

II *adj* [*accent, humour*] de Glasgow.

glaucoma /glɔːˈkəʊmə/ ▶ 1354 *n* glaucome *m*; **to have ~** avoir un glaucome.

glaucous /ˈglɔːkəs/ *adj* glauque.

glaze /gleɪz/ **I** *n* **1** (on pottery, bricks, tiles, leather) vernis *m*; (on fabric) lustre *m*; **2** (substance) (for ceramics) glaçure *f*; (in oil painting) glacis *m*; Culin (of icing) glaçage *m*; (of jam, jelly) nappage *m*; **3** US (ice) verglas *m*.

II *vtr* **1** GB vitrer [*door, window*]; mettre [qch] sous verre [*picture*]; **2** (apply glaze to) vernisser [*ceramics*]; vernir [*leather*]; lustrer [*fabric*]; Culin, Phot glacer; **3** US [*ice*] rendre [qch] lisse.

III *vi* (also **~ over**) [*eyes*] devenir vitreux.

glazed /gleɪzd/ *adj* **1** (fitted with glass) [*door, window*] vitré; **2** [*ceramics*] vernissé; **3** (shiny) [*leather*] verni; [*fabric*] lustré; [*paper*] glacé; **4** Culin glacé; **5** fig **to have a ~ look in one's eyes** avoir les yeux vitreux; **6** US (ice-covered) verglacé; **7**○ US (drunk) bourré○.

glazier /ˈgleɪzɪə(r), US -ʒər/ ▶ 1692 *n* vitrier *m*; **the ~'s** la vitrerie *f*.

glazing /ˈgleɪzɪŋ/ *n* **1** (act, process) pose *f* de vitres; **2** (panes of glass) vitrage *m*; **3** = **glaze I 1**.

glazing bar *n* croisillon *m*.

GLC *n* (*abrév* = **Greater London Council**) *administration de Londres jusqu'en 1986*.

gleam /gliːm/ **I** *n* (of candle, lamp, moonlight) lueur *f*; (of sunshine) rayon *m*; (of gold, polished surface) reflet *m*; (of water) miroitement *m*; fig (of hope, intelligence) lueur *f*; **there was a malicious ~ in his eye** il y avait une lueur de malveillance dans ses yeux.

II *vi* [*candle, lamp, moon*] luire; [*gold, knife, leather, polished surface*] reluire; [*jewel*] rutiler; [*water*] miroiter; [*eyes, teeth*] briller; **her eyes ~ed with mischief** ses yeux pétillaient de malice.

gleaming /ˈgliːmɪŋ/ *adj* [*candle, lamp, star, moonlight*] brillant; [*brass, leather, polished surface*] reluisant; [*eyes, teeth*] brillant; [*water*] miroitant; [*jewel*] rutilant; [*bathroom, kitchen etc*] étincelant (de propreté).

glean /gliːn/ *vtr, vi* lit, fig glaner.

gleaner /ˈgliːnə(r)/ *n* glaneur/-euse *m/f*.

gleanings /ˈgliːnɪŋz/ *npl* lit glanure† *f*; fig bribes *fpl*.

glebe /gliːb/ *n* **1** GB Relig terrain *m* rattaché au presbytère; **2** liter glèbe *f*.

glee /gliː/ *n* **1** (joy) allégresse *f*; (spiteful pleasure) jubilation *f*; **to shout with** ou **in ~** crier de joie; **2** Mus chant *m* choral.

glee club *n* US chorale *f*.

gleeful /ˈgliːfl/ *adj* [*laughter, smile*] joyeux/-euse; **to be ~** (spitefully) jubiler.

gleefully /ˈgliːfəlɪ/ *adv* (happily) joyeusement; (spitefully) avec jubilation.

glen /glen/ *n* Geog gorge *f* (*en Écosse*).

glib /glɪb/ *adj* péj désinvolte.

glibly /ˈglɪblɪ/ *adv* péj avec désinvolture.

glibness /ˈglɪbnɪs/ *n* péj désinvolture *f*.

glide /glaɪd/ **I** *n* **1** (in skating, dancing) pas *m* glissé; **2** (in air) vol *m* plané; **3** Mus port *m* de voix; **4** Phon glissement *m*; **5** (castor) patin *m* glisseur.

II *vi* **1** (move smoothly) [*skater, car, boat*] glisser (**on, over** sur); **2** (in air)[*bird, plane*] planer (**for** sur).

glide path *n* trajectoire *f* d'approche.

glider /ˈglaɪdə(r)/ *n* **1** Aviat planeur *m*; **2** US (swing) balancelle *f* double.

glider pilot *n* pilote *m* de planeur.

gliding /ˈglaɪdɪŋ/ ▶ 1282 *n* Sport vol *m* à voile.

glimmer /ˈglɪmə(r)/ **I** *n* **1** (faint light) faible lueur *f* (**of** de); **2** (trace) lueur *f*; **a ~ of hope** fig une lueur d'espoir; **without a ~ of interest** sans le moindre intérêt.

II *vi* jeter une faible lueur.

glimmering /ˈglɪmərɪŋ/ **I** *n* (of lights, stars) scintillement *m*; **a ~ of hope** une lueur d'espoir; **the ~ of an idea** l'ébauche *f* d'une idée; **the first ~s of a problem** les premières manifestations d'un problème.

II *adj* [*sea, star*] scintillant.

glimpse /glɪmps/ **I** *n* **1** (sighting) vision *f* fugitive (**of** de); **to catch a ~ of sth** entrevoir qch; **2** fig (insight) aperçu *m* (**of, at** de).

II *vtr* lit, fig entrevoir.

glint /glɪnt/ **I** *n* gen reflet *m* (**of** de); (in eye) lueur *f* (**of** de); fig **to have a ~ in one's eye** fig avoir une lueur dans le regard.

II *vi* étinceler.

glissade /glɪˈseɪd, US -ˈsɑːd/ **I** *n* Sport, Dance glissade *f*, glissé *m*.

II *vi* Sport faire une glissade.

glissando /glɪˈsændəʊ/ *n* (*pl* **-di**) Mus glissando *m*.

glisten /ˈglɪsn/ *vi* [*eyes, hair, fur, surface*] luire; [*tears*] briller; [*water*] scintiller; [*silk*] chatoyer.

glistening /ˈglɪsnɪŋ/ *pres p adj* luisant (**with** de).

glister‡ /ˈglɪstə(r)/ *vi* littér = **glitter**.

glitch○ /glɪtʃ/ *n* **1** (minor problem) pépin○ *m*; **2** Comput problème *m* technique.

glitter /ˈglɪtə(r)/ **I** *n* **1** ¢ (substance) paillettes

fpl; **2** (of diamonds, performance, occasion) éclat *m*; (of frost) scintillement *m*.
II *vi* [*star, frost, diamond*] scintiller.
IDIOMS **all that ~s is not gold** Prov tout ce qui brille n'est pas or Prov.

glitterati /ˌglɪtəˈrɑːtɪ/ *npl* célébrités *fpl*.

glittering /ˈglɪtərɪŋ/ *adj* [*stars, jewels*] scintillant; fig [*career, future, social life*] brillant.

glitz○ /glɪts/ *n* clinquant *m*.

glitzy○ /ˈglɪtsɪ/ *adj* clinquant.

gloaming /ˈgləʊmɪŋ/ *n* **in the ~** au crépuscule.

gloat /gləʊt/ *vi* jubiler (**at, over** à l'idée de); **there's no need to ~** il n'y a pas de quoi triompher.

gloating /ˈgləʊtɪŋ/ *adj* triomphant.

glob○ /glɒb/ *n* (of liquid, grease) grosse goutte *f* (**of** de); (of chewing gum) boulette *f*.

global /ˈgləʊbl/ *adj* **1** (world wide) [*environment, market, problem*] mondial; **2** (comprehensive) [*analysis, discussion, view*] global; **3** (spherical) sphérique.

globalization /ˌgləʊbəlaɪˈzeɪʃən/ *n* globalisation *f*.

globally /ˈgləʊbəlɪ/ *adv* [*compete, produce*] à l'échelle mondiale; [*famous, influential*] dans le monde entier; [*sold, produced*] dans le monde.

global: **~ village** *n* village *m* planétaire; **~ warming** *n* réchauffement *m* de l'atmosphère.

globe /gləʊb/ *n* **1** (world) **the ~** le globe; **all around** ou **across the ~** sur tout le globe; **from all corners of the ~** des quatre coins du monde; **2** (model) globe *m* terrestre; **3** (lamp etc) globe *m*.

globe: **~ artichoke** *n* artichaut *m*; **~fish** *n* poisson *m* globe; **~ lightning** *n* éclair *m* en boule; **~trotter** *n* globe-trotter *m*.

globetrotting /ˈgləʊbtrɒtɪŋ/ I *n* voyages *mpl* à travers le monde.
II *adj* voyageur/-euse.

globular /ˈglɒbjʊlə(r)/ *adj* **1** (globule shaped) globuleux/-euse; **2** (globe shaped) globulaire.

globule /ˈglɒbjuːl/ *n* gouttelette *f* (**of** de).

glockenspiel /ˈglɒkənʃpiːl/ *n* glockenspiel *m*.

gloom /gluːm/ *n* **1** (darkness) obscurité *f*; **2** (dejection) morosité *f* (**about, over** à propos de); **economic ~** morosité économique; **to cast a ~ over sb** attrister qn; **to cast a ~ over sth** assombrir qch; **doom and ~** désespoir et morosité, sinistrose○ *f*; **to spread ~ and despondency** plonger tout le monde dans le découragement.

gloomily /ˈgluːmɪlɪ/ *adv* [*say, do*] d'un air lugubre.

gloomy /ˈgluːmɪ/ *adj* **1** (dark) sombre; **2** (sad) [*expression, person, voice*] lugubre; [*weather*] morose; [*news, outlook*] déprimant; **to be ~ about sth** être morose à propos de qch; **to paint a ~ picture of the economy** faire un tableau pessimiste de l'économie.

glorification /ˌglɔːrɪfɪˈkeɪʃn/ *n* gen, Relig glorification *f*.

glorify /ˈglɔːrɪfaɪ/ I *vtr* glorifier [*God*]; glorifier, chanter les louanges de [*person, event, tradition*]; (wrongly) glorifier, faire l'éloge de [*regime, terrorism, violence, war*].
II **glorified** *pp adj* **the 'villa' was a glorified bungalow** la 'villa' n'était rien de plus qu'un simple pavillon.

gloriole /ˈglɔːrɪəʊl/ *n* Meteorol halo *m*.

glorious /ˈglɔːrɪəs/ *adj* **1** (marvellous) [*sight, view, weather, colour*] magnifique; [*holiday, outing*] merveilleux/-euse; **we had a ~ day!** nous avons passé une journée formidable!; **2** (illustrious) [*exploit, reign, revolution, victory*] glorieux/-ieuse; **3** iron (dreadful) [*mess, muddle*] beau/belle; **what a ~ mess!** quel beau gâchis!

gloriously /ˈglɔːrɪəslɪ/ *adv* merveilleusement; **a ~ sunny day** une journée magnifique.

glory /ˈglɔːrɪ/ I *n* **1** (honour, distinction) also Relig gloire *f*; **to cover oneself in ~** se couvrir de gloire; **to the greater ~ of God** à la plus grande gloire de Dieu; **my hour of ~** mon heure de gloire; **2** (splendour) splendeur *f*; **in all her ~** dans toute sa splendeur; **3** (source of pride) fierté *f*; **the cathedral is the ~ of the city** la cathédrale fait la fierté or la gloire de la ville.
II **glories** *npl* splendeurs *fpl*; **the glories of nature/Venice** les splendeurs de la nature/de Venise; **past glories** passé *m* glorieux (+ *v sg*).
III *vi* **to ~ in** être très fier/fière de [*status, strength, tradition*]; **to ~ in the name Caesar** hum porter le nom ronflant de César.
IDIOMS **~ be!** Dieu merci!; **to go to ~** euph aller ad patres euph, mourir.

glory days *npl* jours *mpl* de gloire.

glory hole *n* **1** (room) capharnaüm *m*, débarras *m*; **2** Naut cambuse *f*.

Glos *n* GB Post *abrév écrite* ▶ **Gloucestershire**.

gloss /glɒs/ I *n* **1** (lustre) (of wood, metal, paintwork, leather etc) lustre *m*; (of paper) brillant *m*; (of hair) éclat *m*; fig péj (superficial glamour) clinquant *m*; **to lose its ~** lit, fig perdre (de) son éclat; **to take the ~ off** dépolir [*wood, metal*]; fig gâcher [*proceedings, ceremony*]; **2** fig (outer appearance, veneer) vernis *m*; **a ~ of respectability** un vernis de respectabilité; **to put a favourable/different ~ on sth** fig présenter qch sous un jour favorable/différent; **3** (in text) glose *f*; **4** US pej fausse interprétation *f*; **5** (paint) laque *f* (brillante); **walls painted in blue ~** murs laqués bleu.
II *vtr* **1** (polish) faire briller; **2** (explain, clarify) gloser [*word, text*]; résumer [*report*].
■ **gloss over**: **~ over [sth]** (pass rapidly over) glisser sur; (hide) dissimuler.

glossary /ˈglɒsərɪ/ *n* glossaire *m*.

gloss coat *n* couche *f* de peinture brillante.

glosseme /ˈglɒsiːm/ *n* glossème *m*.

gloss finish *n* brillant *m*.

glossolalia /ˌglɒsəˈleɪlɪə/ *n* Relig, Psych glossolalie *f*.

gloss paint *n* laque *f* (brillante).

glossy /ˈglɒsɪ/ I○ *n* (*pl* **glossies**) = **glossy magazine**.
II *adj* [*hair, fur, material*] luisant; [*wood, metal*] brillant; [*leaves*] vernissé; [*photograph*] brillant; [*brochure, catalogue*] luxueux/-euse; fig péj [*production, film, interior*] qui a un éclat plutôt superficiel.

glossy magazine *n* magazine *m* illustré (de luxe).

glottal /ˈglɒtl/ *adj* Anat glottique; Ling glottal.

glottal stop *n* Ling coup *m* de glotte.

glottis /ˈglɒtɪs/ *n* (*pl* **-tises**) glotte *f*.

Gloucestershire /ˈglɒstəʃə(r)/ ▶ **1624** *pr n* Gloucestershire *m*.

glove /glʌv/ I *n* gant *m*; **to put on/take off one's ~s** mettre/enlever ses gants; **with the ~s off** fig [*argue, quarrel*] sans prendre de gants.
II *vtr* ganter; **her ~d hands** ses mains gantées.
IDIOMS **it fits like a ~** cela me/lui etc va comme un gant; **to be hand in ~** être comme les deux doigts de la main; **to be hand in ~ with sb** être de mèche avec qn○; **an iron fist in a velvet ~** une main de fer dans un gant de velours.

glove: **~ box**, **~ compartment** *n* boîte *f* à gants; **~ factory** *n* ganterie *f* (*usine*); **~ maker** *n* gantier/-ière *m/f*; **~ puppet** *n* marionnette *f* à gaine.

glover /ˈglʌvə(r)/ ▶ **1692** *n* gantier/-ière *m/f*.

glove shop ▶ **1692** *n* ganterie *f* (*magasin*).

glow /gləʊ/ I *n* **1** (of coal, furnace) rougeoiement *m*; (of room, candle) lueur *f*; **2** (colour) éclat *m*; **there was a ~ in her cheeks** (from happiness) elle avait le visage radieux; **after the exercise there was a ~ in her cheeks** l'exercice lui avait donné des couleurs; **3** (feeling) douce sensation *f*; **a contented ~** une douce (sensation de) satisfaction; **to take on a ~ of nostalgia** se colorer de nostalgie; **it gives you a warm ~** ça fait chaud au cœur.
II *vi* **1** (give off light) [*coal, metal, furnace*] rougeoyer; [*lamp, cigarette*] luire; **the furnace ~ed a deep red** le foyer luisait d'un rouge ardent; **paint that ~s in the dark** peinture qui luit dans le noir; **the room ~ed in the firelight** la pièce baignait dans la douce clarté du feu; **2** (look vibrant) [*colour*] être éclatant; **her skin ~ed** elle avait un teint éblouissant; **to ~ with health** [*person*] être resplendissant/-e (de santé); **her cheeks ~ed with health** son visage resplendissait de santé; **to ~ with pride/delight** rayonner de fierté/joie; **his eyes ~ed with anger** son regard luisait de colère; **3** (feel warm) **she was beginning to ~** une douce chaleur l'envahissait.

glower /ˈglaʊə(r)/ I *n* regard *m* noir.
II *vi* lancer des regards noirs (**at** à).

glowering /ˈglaʊərɪŋ/ *adj* [*person, eyes, face*] courroucé; [*clouds, sky*] menaçant.

glowing /ˈgləʊɪŋ/ *adj* **1** (bright) [*ember*] rougeoyant; [*lava*] incandescent; [*face, cheeks*] (from exercise) rouge; (from pleasure) radieux/-ieuse; [*colour*] chaud; **2** (complimentary) [*account, description*] élogieux/-ieuse; **to paint a ~ picture of sth** décrire qch en termes élogieux.

glowworm /ˈgləʊwɜːm/ *n* ver *m* luisant.

gloxinia /glɒkˈsɪnɪə/ *n* gloxinia *m*.

glucose /ˈgluːkəʊs/ I *n* glucose *m*.
II *modif* [*powder, syrup, tablets*] de glucose; [*drink*] au glucose.

glue /gluː/ I *n* **1** lit colle *f*; **to sniff ~** inhaler or sniffer○ de la colle; **2** fig ciment *m*.
II *vtr* coller; **to ~ sth on** ou **down** coller qch; **to ~ sth back on** recoller qch; **to ~ two things together** coller deux choses ensemble; **to ~ two things back together** recoller deux choses; **to ~ sth (on) to sth** coller qch sur qch.
III **glued**○ *pp adj* **to have one's eyes ~d to sb/sth** avoir les yeux fixés sur qn/qch; **to be ~d to the TV** être collé○ devant la télé; **to have one's face** ou **nose ~d to sth** avoir le nez collé à qch; **to be ~d to the spot** être cloué sur place; **to stay ~d to sb's side** coller qn○, ne pas quitter qn.
IDIOMS **to stick like ~ to sb** coller qn○, ne pas quitter qn.

glue: **~ pen** *n* stylo *m* colle transparente; **~-sniffer** *n* sniffeur/-euse○ *m/f* (de colle); **~-sniffing** *n* inhalation *f* de colle; **~ stick** *n* bâton *m* de colle.

gluey /ˈgluːɪ/ *adj* (viscous) gluant; (sticky) collant.

glum /glʌm/ *adj* morose.

glumly /ˈglʌmlɪ/ *adv* d'un air morose.

glumness /ˈglʌmnɪs/ *n* morosité *f*.

glut /glʌt/ I *n* gen surabondance *f* (**of** de); excès *m* (**of** de).
II *vtr* (*p prés etc* **-tt-**) **1** inonder [*economy, market*];
III *v refl* **to ~ oneself** se gorger (**with, on** de).
IV **glutted** *pp adj* lit, fig rassasié (**with** de); **~ted with food** rassasié.

glutamic acid /gluːˈtæmɪk/ *n* acide *m* glutamique.

gluteal /ˈgluːtɪəl/ *adj* fessier/-ière.

gluten /ˈgluːtn/ *n* gluten *m*.

gluten: **~ bread** *n* pain *m* au gluten; **~ flour** *n* farine *f* de gluten; **~-free** *adj* sans gluten.

glutenous /ˈgluːtənəs/ *adj* glutineux/-euse.

gluteus /ˈgluːtɪəs/ *n* (*pl* **-ei**) muscle *m* fessier; **~ maximus/minimus** grand/petit fessier.

glutinous /ˈgluːtənəs/ *adj* gluant.

glutton /ˈglʌtn/ *n* **1** (greedy person) glouton/

-onne *m/f*; **2** fig **a ~ for punishment** un masochiste; **a ~ for hard work** un bourreau de travail.

gluttonous /ˈglʌtənəs/ *adj* glouton/-onne.

gluttony /ˈglʌtənɪ/ *n* gloutonnerie *f*.

glycerin(e) /ˈglɪsəri:n, US -rɪn/ *n* glycérine *f*.

glycerol /ˈglɪsərɒl/ *n* glycérol *m*.

glycin(e) /ˈglaɪsi:n/ *n* Chem glycine *f*.

glycogen /ˈglaɪkədʒn/ *n* glycogène *m*.

glycol /ˈglaɪkɒl/ *n* glycol *m*; **ethylene ~** glycol éthylène *m*.

gm *n* (*abrév écrite* = **gram**) g.

G-man◑ *n* US agent *m* du FBI.

GMT *n* (*abrév* = **Greenwich Mean Time**) TU.

gnarled /nɑ:ld/ *adj* noueux/-euse.

gnash /næʃ/ *vtr* **to ~ one's teeth** lit, fig grincer des dents.

gnashing /ˈnæʃɪŋ/ *n* lit, fig **~ of teeth** grincement *m* de dents.

gnat /næt/ *n* moucheron *m*.

gnat: **~ bite** *n* piqûre *f* de moucheron; **~catcher** *n* gobe-mouches *m*.

gnat's piss◑ /ˈnætspɪs/ *n* **this coffee is ~** c'est de la flotte○ ce café.

gnaw /nɔ:/ **I** *vtr* **1** (chew) ronger [*bone, wood*]; **the mice have ~ed a hole in the sack** les souris ont fait un trou dans le sac en le rongeant; **2** fig (torment) [*hunger, remorse*] tenailler; [*pain*] lanciner.
II *vi* **to ~ at** ou **on sth** ronger qch.

gnawing /ˈnɔ:ɪŋ/ **I** *n* **1** (chewing) rongement *m*; **2** (pain) douleur *f* lancinante.
II *adj* [*hunger, guilt*] tenaillant; [*pain*] lancinant.

gneiss /naɪs/ *n* gneiss *m*.

gnome /nəʊm/ *n* **1** (goblin) gnome *m*; **garden ~** petit nain *m* (en plâtre); **2**○ (financier) péj banquier *m*; **3**○ (anonymous expert) péj expert *m*.

gnomic /ˈnəʊmɪk/ *adj* gnomique.

gnostic /ˈnɒstɪk/ *n, adj* gnostique (*mf*).

gnosticism /ˈnɒstɪsɪzəm/ *n* gnosticisme *m*.

GNP *n* (*abrév* = **gross national product**) PNB *m*.

gnu /nu:/ *n* (*pl* **~** ou **~s**) gnou *m*.

GNVQ *n* GB (*abrév* = **General National Vocational Qualification**) ≈ baccalauréat *m* professionnel.

> **go**
>
> **As an intransitive verb**
>
> *go* as a simple intransitive verb is translated by *aller*:
>
> *we're going to Paris* = nous allons à Paris;
> *where are you going?* = où vas-tu?
> *Sasha went to London last week* = Sasha est allée à Londres la semaine dernière
>
> Note that *aller* conjugates with *être* in compound tenses. For the conjugation of *aller* see the French verb tables. For more examples and particular usages see the entry ***go***.
>
> The verb *go* produces a great many phrasal verbs in English (*go up, go down, go out, go back* etc.). Many of these are translated by a single verb in French (*monter, descendre, sortir, retourner* etc.). The phrasal verbs are listed separately at the end of the entry ***go***.
>
> **As an auxiliary verb**
>
> When *go* is used as an auxiliary to show intention, it is also translated by *aller*:
>
> *I'm going to buy a car tomorrow* = je vais acheter une voiture demain
> *I was going to talk to you about it* = j'allais t'en parler
> *he's not going to ask for a rise* = il ne va pas demander d'augmentation
>
> For more examples and particular usages see **I 23** in the entry ***go***.
> For all other uses see the entry ***go***.

go /gəʊ/ **I** *vi* (*3e pers prés sg* **goes**; *prét* **went**; *pp* **gone**) **1** (move, travel) aller (**from** de; **to** à, en); **to ~ to London/Paris** aller à Londres/Paris; **to ~ to Wales/to Ireland/to California** aller au Pays de Galles/en Irlande/en Californie; **to ~ to town/to the country** aller en ville/à la campagne; **they went home** ils sont rentrés chez eux; **she's gone to Paris** elle est allée à Paris; **to ~ up/down/across** monter/descendre/traverser; **I went into the room** je suis entré dans la pièce; **to ~ by bus/train/plane** voyager en bus/train/avion; **we went there by bus** nous y sommes allés en bus; **to ~ by** ou **past** [*person, vehicle*] passer; **that car's going very fast!** cette voiture roule très vite!; **there he goes again!** (that's him again) le revoilà!; fig (he's starting again) le voilà qui recommence!, c'est reparti!; **who goes there?** Mil qui va là?; **where do we ~ from here?** fig et maintenant qu'est-ce qu'on fait?; **2** (on specific errand, activity) aller; **to ~ shopping** aller faire des courses; **to ~ swimming** (in sea, river) aller se baigner; (in pool) aller à la piscine; **to ~ for a walk** aller se promener; **to ~ on a journey/on holiday** partir en voyage/en vacances; **to ~ for a drink** aller prendre un verre; **he's gone to get some wine** il est allé chercher du vin; **~ and answer the phone** va répondre au téléphone; **~ and tell them that...** va leur dire que...; **~ after him!** poursuivez-le!; **3** (attend) aller; **to ~ to school/church** aller à l'école/l'église; **to ~ to work** aller or se rendre au travail; **to ~ to the doctor's/dentist's** aller chez le médecin/dentiste; **4** (used as auxiliary with present participle) **she went running up the stairs** elle a monté l'escalier en courant; **she went complaining to the principal** elle est allée se plaindre au directeur; **5** (depart) partir; **I must ~, I must be going** il faut que je parte or que je m'en aille; **the train goes at six o'clock** le train part à six heures; **a train goes every hour** il y a un train toutes les heures; **to ~ on holiday** partir en vacances; **be gone!** va-t'en!, allez-vous en!; **6** euph (die) mourir, disparaître; **when I am gone** quand je ne serai plus là; **the doctors say she could ~ at any time** d'après les médecins elle risque de mourir d'un instant à l'autre; **7** (disappear) partir; **half the money goes on school fees** la moitié de l'argent part en frais de scolarité; **the money/cake has all gone** il ne reste plus d'argent/de gâteau; **I left my bike outside and now it's gone** j'ai laissé mon vélo dehors et il n'est plus là or il a disparu; **there goes my chance of winning!** c'en est fait de mes chances de gagner!; **8** (be sent, transmitted) **it can't ~ by post** on ne peut pas l'envoyer par la poste; **these proposals will ~ before parliament** ces propositions seront soumises au parlement; **9** (become) **to ~ red** rougir; **to ~ white** blanchir; **his hair** ou **he is going grey** il commençe à avoir les cheveux blancs; **to ~ mad** devenir fou; **to ~ bankrupt** faire faillite; **10** (change over to new system) **to ~ Labour/Conservative** Pol [*country, constituency*] voter travailliste/conservateur; **to ~ metric** adopter le système métrique; ▶ **private, public**; **11** (be, remain) **the people went hungry** les gens n'avaient rien à manger; **we went for two days without food** nous avons passé deux jours sans rien manger; **to ~ unnoticed** passer inaperçu; **to ~ unpunished** rester impuni; **the question went unanswered** la question est restée sans réponse; **to ~ naked** se promener tout nu; **he was allowed to ~ free** il a été libéré or remis en liberté; **12** (weaken, become impaired) **his memory/mind is going** il perd la mémoire/l'esprit; **his hearing is going** il devient sourd; **my voice is going** je n'ai plus de voix; **the battery is going** la batterie est presque à plat; **the engine is going** le moteur a des ratés; **13** (of time) (elapse) s'écouler; **three hours went by before...** trois heures se sont écoulées avant que... (+ *subj*); **there are only three days to ~ before Christmas** il ne reste plus que trois jours avant Noël; **how's the time going?** quelle heure est-il?; **it's just gone seven o'clock** il est un peu plus de sept heures; **14** (be got rid of) **he's totally inefficient, he'll have to ~!** il est complètement incapable, il va falloir qu'on se débarrasse de lui!; **that new lampshade is hideous, it'll have to ~!** ce nouvel abat-jour est affreux, il va falloir qu'on s'en débarrasse!; **the car will have to ~** il va falloir vendre la voiture; **either she goes or I do!** c'est elle ou moi!; **six down and four to ~!** six de faits, et encore quatre à faire!; **15** (operate, function) [*vehicle, machine, clock*] marcher, fonctionner; **to set [sth] going** mettre [qch] en marche; **to get going** [*engine, machine*] se mettre en marche; fig [*business*] démarrer; **to get the fire going** allumer le feu; **to keep going** [*person, business, machine*] tenir le coup○, se maintenir; **we have several projects going at the moment** nous avons plusieurs projets en route en ce moment; ▶ **keep**; **16** (start) **let's get going!** allons-y!, allez, on commençe!; **we'll have to get going on that translation** il va falloir qu'on se mette à faire cette traduction; **to get things going** mettre les choses en train; **ready, steady, ~!** à vos marques, prêts, partez!; **here goes!, here we ~!** c'est parti!; **once he gets going, he never stops** une fois lancé, il n'arrête pas; **17** (lead) aller, conduire, mener (**to** à); **that corridor goes to the kitchen** le couloir va or conduit à la cuisine; **the road goes down to the sea/goes up the mountain** la route descend vers la mer/monte au sommet de la montagne; **this road goes past the cemetery** ce chemin passe à côté du cimetière; **18** (extend in depth or scope) **the roots of the plant ~ very deep** les racines de la plante s'enfoncent très profondément; **the historical reasons for this conflict ~ very deep** les raisons historiques de ce conflit remontent très loin; **these habits ~ very deep** ces habitudes sont profondément ancrées or enracinées ; **as far as that goes** pour ce qui est de cela; **it's true as far as it goes** c'est vrai dans un sens or dans une certaine mesure; **she'll ~ far!** elle ira loin!; **this time he's gone too far!** cette fois il est allé trop loin!; **a hundred pounds doesn't ~ far these days** on ne va pas loin avec cent livres sterling de nos jours; **one leg of lamb doesn't ~ very far among twelve people** un gigot d'agneau n'est pas suffisant pour douze personnes; **this goes a long way towards explaining his attitude** ceci explique en grande partie son attitude; **you can make £5 ~ a long way** on peut faire beaucoup de choses avec 5 livres sterling; **19** (belong, be placed) aller; **where do these plates ~?** où vont ces assiettes?; **that table goes beside the bed** cette table va à côté du lit; **the suitcases will have to ~ in the back** il va falloir mettre les valises derrière; **20** (fit) gen rentrer; **it won't ~ into the box** ça ne rentre pas dans la boîte ; **five into four won't ~** quatre n'est pas divisible par cinq; **three into six goes twice** six divisé par trois, ça fait deux; **21** (be expressed, sung etc in particular way) **I can't remember how the poem goes** je n'arrive pas à me rappeler le poème; **how does the song ~?** quel est l'air de la chanson?; **the song goes something like this** la chanson ressemble à peu près à ça; **as the saying goes** comme dit le proverbe; **the story goes that** le bruit court que, on dit que; **her**

theory goes something like this... sa théorie consiste à peu près à dire que...; **22** (be accepted) **what he says goes** c'est lui qui fait la loi; **it goes without saying that** il va sans dire que; **that goes without saying** cela va sans dire; **anything goes** tout est permis; **23** (be about to) **to be going to do** aller faire; **it's going to snow** il va neiger; **I was just going to phone you** j'étais justement sur le point de t'appeler, j'allais justement t'appeler; **I'm going to phone him right now** je vais l'appeler tout de suite; **I'm not going to be treated like that!** je ne vais pas me laisser faire comme ça!; **we were going to ~ to Italy, but we changed our plans** nous devions aller en Italie, mais nous avons changé d'idée; **24** (happen) **the party went very well** la soirée s'est très bien passée; **so far the campaign is going well** jusqu'à maintenant la campagne a bien marché; **how did the evening ~?** comment s'est passée la soirée?; **the way things are going, I don't think we'll ever get finished** vu la façon dont les choses se passent or si ça continue comme ça, je pense qu'on n'aura jamais fini; **how's it going**○**?, how are things going?** comment ça va○?; **how goes it?** hum comment ça va○?, comment va●?; **25** (be on average) **it's old, as Australian towns ~** c'est une ville assez vieille pour une ville australienne; **it wasn't a bad party, as parties ~** c'était une soirée plutôt réussie par rapport à la moyenne; **26** (be sold) **the house went for over £100,000** la maison a été vendue à plus de 100000 livres; **we won't let the house ~ for less than £100,000** nous ne voulons pas vendre la maison à moins de 100000 livres; **those rugs are going cheap** ces tapis ne sont pas chers; **the house will ~ to the highest bidder** la maison sera vendue au plus offrant; **'going, going, gone!'** (at auction) 'une fois, deux fois, trois fois, adjugé!'; **27** (be on offer) **I'll have some coffee, if there's any going** je prendrai bien un café, s'il y en a; **are there any drinks going?** est-ce qu'il y a quelque chose à boire?; **I'll have whatever's going** je prendrai ce qu'il y a; **it's the best machine going** c'est la meilleure machine sur le marché; **there's a job going at their London office** il y a un poste libre dans leur bureau de Londres; **28** (contribute) **the money will ~ towards a new roof** l'argent servira à payer un nouveau toit; **the elements that ~ to make a great film** les éléments qui font un bon film; **everything that goes to make a good teacher** toutes les qualités d'un bon enseignant; **29** (be given) [*award, prize*] aller (**to** à); [*estate, inheritance, title*] passer (**to** à); **the money will ~ to charity** les bénéfices iront aux bonnes œuvres; **most of the credit should ~ to the author** la plus grande partie du mérite revient à l'auteur; **the job went to a local man** le poste a été donné à un homme de la région; **30** (emphatic use) **she's gone and told everybody!** elle est allée le dire à tout le monde!; **why did he ~ and spoil it?** pourquoi est-il allé tout gâcher ?; **you've gone and ruined everything!** tu t'es débrouillé pour tout gâcher!; **he went and won the competition!** il s'est débrouillé pour gagner le concours!; **you've really gone and done it now!** tu peux être fier de toi! iron; **then he had to ~ and lose his wallet** comme s'il ne manquait plus que ça, il a perdu son portefeuille; **31** (of money) (be spent, used up) **all his money goes on drink** tout son argent passe dans l'alcool; **most of his salary goes on rent** la plus grande partie de son salaire passe dans le loyer; **I don't know where all my money goes (to)!** je ne sais pas ce que je fais de mon argent!; **32** (make sound, perform action or movement) gen faire; [*bell, alarm*] sonner; **the cat went 'miaow'** le chat a fait 'miaou'; **wait until the bell goes** attends que la cloche sonne (*subj*); **she went like this with her fingers** elle a fait comme ça avec ses doigts; **so he goes 'what about my money**○**?'** et puis il dit or il fait, 'et mon argent?'; **33** (resort to, have recourse to) **to ~ to war** [*country*] entrer en guerre; [*soldier*] partir à la guerre; **to ~ to law** GB ou **to the law** US aller en justice; **34** (break, collapse etc) [*roof*] s'effondrer; [*cable, rope*] se rompre, céder ; (fuse) [*light bulb*] griller; **35** (bid, bet) aller; **I'll ~ as high as £100** j'irai jusqu'à 100 livres sterling; **I went up to £100** je suis allé jusqu'à 100 livres sterling; **36** (take one's turn) **you ~ next** c'est ton tour après, c'est à toi après; **you ~ first** après vous; **37** (be in harmony) **those two colours don't ~ together** ces deux couleurs ne vont pas ensemble; **the curtains don't ~ with the carpet** les rideaux ne vont pas avec le tapis; **white wine ~es better with fish than red wine** le vin blanc va mieux avec le poisson que le rouge; **38**○ euph (relieve oneself) aller aux toilettes; **39** US (in takeaway) **to ~** à emporter; **two hamburgers to ~!** deux hamburgers à emporter!

II *vtr* (*3e pers prés sg* **goes**; *prét* **went**; *pp* **gone**) (see usage note) **1** (travel) **we had gone ten miles before we realized that**... nous avions déjà fait dix kilomètres quand nous nous sommes rendu compte que...; **are you going my way?** tu vas dans la même direction que moi?; **to ~ one's own way** fig suivre son chemin; **2**○ (bet, bid) **I ~ two diamonds** (in cards) j'annonce deux carreaux; **he went £20** il a mis or parié 20 livres sterling.

III *n* (*pl* **goes**) **1** GB (person's turn) tour *m*; (try) essai *m*; **it's your ~** (in game) c'est ton tour, c'est à toi; **whose ~ is it?** gen à qui le tour?; (in game) à qui de jouer?; **you've had two goes** (in game) tu as eu deux tours; (two attempts at mending sth) tu as déjà essayé deux fois; **to have a ~ at sth** essayer de faire qch; **have another ~!** essaie encore une fois or un coup!; **she had several goes at the exam** elle a repassé l'examen plusieurs fois; **I had to have several goes before passing** j'ai dû m'y reprendre à plusieurs fois avant de réussir; **2**○ (energy) dynamisme *m*; **to be full of ~, to be all ~** être très dynamique, avoir beaucoup d'allant; **he has no ~ in him** il manque de dynamisme; **3**○ GB (bout) (of illness) attaque *f*; **4** ▶ 1282 (board game) go *m*.

IV *adj* **all systems are ~!** Aerosp tout est paré pour le lancement!

IDIOMS **to have a ~ at sb** s'en prendre à qn; **to make a ~ of sth** réussir qch; **she's always on the ~** elle n'arrête jamais; **he's all ~**○**!** il n'arrête pas!; **it's all the ~**○**!** ça fait fureur!; **we have several different projects on the ~ at the moment** nous avons plusieurs projets différents en chantier or en cours en ce moment; **(it's) no ~!** pas question!; **from the word ~** dès le départ; **that was a near ~**○**!** on l'a échappé belle!; **in one ~** d'un seul coup; **to ~ one better than sb** renchérir sur qn; **that's how it goes !, that's the way it goes!** ainsi va le monde!, c'est la vie!; **there you ~**○**!** voilà!

■ **go about**: ¶ **~ about 1** = **go around**; **2** Naut virer de bord; **prepare to ~ about!** parer à virer!; ¶ **~ about [sth] 1** (undertake) s'attaquer à [*task*]; **how do you ~ about writing a novel?** comment est-ce que vous vous y prenez pour écrire un roman?; **he knows how to ~ about it** il sait s'y prendre; **2** (be busy with) **to ~ about one's business** vaquer à ses occupations; **she went about her work mechanically** elle faisait son travail machinalement.

■ **go across**: ¶ **~ across** traverser; **he's gone across to the shop/neighbour's** il est allé au magasin en face/chez les voisins en face; ¶ **~ across [sth]** traverser [*street, river, bridge etc*].

■ **go after**: **~ after [sth/sb] 1** (chase) poursuivre [*person*]; **2** fig (try hard to get) **he really went after that job** il a fait tout son possible pour avoir ce travail.

■ **go against**: **~ against [sb/sth] 1** (prove unfavourable to) **the vote/verdict/decision went against them** le vote/le verdict/la décision leur a été défavorable or n'a pas été en leur faveur; **the war is going against them** la guerre tourne à leur désavantage; **2** (conflict with) être contraire à [*rules, principles*]; **to ~ against the trend** aller à l'encontre de or être contraire à la tendance; **to ~ against the party line** Pol ne pas être dans la ligne du parti; **3** (resist, oppose) s'opposer à, aller à l'inverse de [*person, sb's wishes*].

■ **go ahead 1** (go in front) **~ ahead, I'll follow you on** partez devant, je vous suis; **2** fig (proceed) **~!** (in conversation) continue!; **~ ahead and shoot!** vas-y, tire! ; **they are going ahead with the project** ils ont décidé de mettre le projet en route; **we can ~ ahead without them** nous pouvons continuer sans eux; **next week's strike is to ~ ahead** la grève de la semaine prochaine va avoir lieu.

■ **go along 1** (move along) [*person, vehicle*] aller, avancer; **to make sth up as one goes along** fig inventer qch au fur et à mesure; **2** (attend) aller; **she went along as a witch** elle y est allée déguisée en sorcière; **I went along as a witness** j'y suis allé or je me suis présenté comme témoin.

■ **go along with**: **~ along with [sb/sth]** être d'accord avec, accepter [*plans, wishes*]; **I can't ~ along with that** je ne peux pas accepter ça; **I'll ~ along with you there** je suis d'accord avec vous sur ce point.

■ **go around**: ¶ **~ around 1** (move, travel about) se promener, circuler; **to ~ around naked/barefoot** se promener tout nu/pieds nus; **she goes around on a bicycle** elle circule à bicyclette; **they ~ around everywhere together** ils vont partout ensemble; **2** (circulate) [*rumour*] courir; **there's a rumour going around that** le bruit court que; **there's a virus going around** il y a un virus qui traîne; **there isn't enough money to ~ around** il n'y a pas assez d'argent pour tout le monde; ¶ **~ around [sth]** faire le tour de [*house, shops, area*]; **to ~ around the world** faire le tour du monde; **they went around the country looking for him** ils l'ont cherché dans tout le pays.

■ **go at**: ¶ **~ at [sb]** (attack) attaquer, tomber sur; ¶ **~ at [sth]** s'attaquer à, s'atteler à [*task, activity*].

■ **go away** [*person*] partir; **to ~ away on holiday** GB ou **vacation** US partir en vacances; **~ away and leave me alone!** va-t-en et laisse-moi tranquille!; **~ away and think about it** réfléchissez-y; **don't ~ away thinking that** ne va pas croire que; **this cold/headache just won't ~ away!** je n'arrive pas à me débarrasser de ce rhume/mal de tête!; **the problems aren't just going to ~ away!** les problèmes ne vont pas disparaître tout seuls!

■ **go back 1** (return) retourner; (turn back) rebrousser chemin, faire demi-tour ; (resume work) reprendre le travail; (resume classes, studies) reprendre les cours; **as it was raining, they decided to ~ back** comme il pleuvait, ils ont décidé de faire demi-tour or de rebrousser chemin; **they went back home** ils sont rentrés chez eux; **let's ~ back to France** rentrons en France; **to ~ back to the beginning** recommencer; **to ~ back to sleep** se rendormir; **to ~ back to work/writing** se remettre au travail/à écrire; **~ back! the path isn't safe** reculez! le chemin est dangereux; **once you've committed yourself, there's no going back** une fois que vous vous êtes engagé, vous ne pouvez plus reculer; **2** (in time) remonter; **to ~ back in time** remonter dans le temps; **to understand the problem we need to ~ back 20 years** pour comprendre le problème il faut remonter 20 ans en arrière; **this tradition goes back a century** cette tradition est vieille d'un siècle; **we ~ back a long way** ça fait longtemps qu'on se connaît; **3** (revert) revenir (**to** à); **to ~ back to teaching** revenir à l'enseignement; **to ~ back to being a student** reprendre des études; **let's ~ back to what we were discussing yesterday** revenons à ce que dont nous parlions hier.

■ **go back on**: **~ back on** [sth] revenir sur [*promise, decision*].

■ **go before**: ¶ **~ before** (go in front) aller au devant; fig (in time) se passer avant; **all that had gone before** tout ce qui s'était passé avant; ¶ **~ before [sb/sth]** [*person*] comparaître devant [*court, judge*]; **the bill went before parliament** le projet de loi a été soumis au parlement.

■ **go below** gen, Naut descendre.

■ **go by**: ¶ **~ by** [*person*] passer; [*time*] passer, s'écouler; **as time goes by** avec le temps; **don't let such opportunities ~ by** il ne faut pas laisser passer de telles occasions; ¶ **~ by [sth] 1** (judge by) juger d'après; **to ~ by appearances** juger d'après or sur les apparences; **going by her looks, I'd say she was about 30** à la voir, je lui donne 30 ans; **you mustn't ~ by what you read in the papers** il ne faut pas croire tout ce que disent les journaux; **if the trailer is anything to ~ by, it should be a good film** à en juger par la bande-annonce, ça doit être un bon film; **if the father is anything to ~ by, I wouldn't like to meet the son!** quand on voit le père, on n'a pas envie de rencontrer le fils!; **2** (proceed by) **to ~ by the rules** suivre or observer le règlement; **promotion goes by seniority** la promotion se fait à l'ancienneté or en fonction de l'ancienneté.

■ **go down**: ¶ **~ down 1** (descend) gen descendre; [*diver*] effectuer une plongée; **to ~ down to the cellar** descendre à la cave; **to ~ down to the beach** aller à la plage; **to ~ down to the pub** aller au pub; **they've gone down to Brighton for a few days** ils sont allés passer quelques jours à Brighton; **'going down!'** (in elevator) 'on descend!'; **to ~ down on one's knees** se mettre à genoux; **2** (fall) [*person, aircraft*] tomber; (sink) [*ship*] couler, sombrer; [*person*] couler, disparaître sous les flots; **most of the passengers went down with the ship** la plupart des passagers ont coulé avec le navire; **the plane went down in flames** l'avion s'est écrasé en flammes; **the plane went down over Normandy/the Channel** l'avion s'est écrasé en Normandie/est tombé dans la Manche; **to ~ down for the third time** [*drowning person*] disparaître sous les flots et se noyer; **3** [*sun*] se coucher; **4** (be received) **to ~ down well/badly** être bien/mal reçu; **this remark didn't ~ down at all well** cette remarque n'a pas été appréciée du tout; **his jokes went down well/didn't ~ down well with the audience** le public a apprécié/n'a pas beaucoup apprécié ses plaisanteries; **another cup of coffee would ~ down nicely!** une autre tasse de café serait la bienvenue!; **5** (be swallowed) **it went down the wrong way** c'est passé de travers; **6** (become lower) [*water level, temperature*] baisser; [*tide*] descendre; [*price, standard*] baisser; (abate) [*storm, wind*] se calmer; [*fire*] s'éteindre; **the river has/the floods have gone down** le niveau de la rivière/des inondations a baissé; **foodstuffs are going down (in price)** les produits alimentaires deviennent moins chers; **7** (become deflated) [*swelling*] désenfler; [*tyre, balloon*] se dégonfler; **8** GB Univ (break up for holiday) terminer les cours; (leave university permanently) quitter l'université; **when do you ~ down?** quand est-ce que vous êtes en vacances?; **9** gen, Sport (fail, be defeated) perdre; (be downgraded) redescendre; **Corby went down 6-1 to Oxford** Corby a perdu 6-1 contre Oxford; **the team has gone down to the second division** l'équipe est redescendue en deuxième division; **10** (be remembered) **he will ~ down as a great statesman** on se souviendra de lui comme d'un grand homme d'État; **11** (be recorded) être noté; **it all goes down in her diary** elle note tout dans son journal; **12** (continue) **the book goes down to 1939** le livre va jusqu'en 1939; **if you ~ down to the second last line you will see that** si vous regardez à l'avant-dernière ligne, vous verrez que; **13** (be stricken) **to ~ down with flu/malaria** attraper la grippe/la malaria; **14**○ GB (be sent to prison) être envoyé en prison; **15** Comput [*computer, system*] tomber en panne; ¶ **~ down [sth] 1** lit descendre [*hill*]; descendre dans [*mine*]; **2** (be downgraded) **to ~ down a class** Sch redescendre d'une classe.

■ **go down on**: ¶ **~ down on [sth]** (set) [*sun*] se coucher sur; **when the sun went down on the Roman Empire** fig quand l'empire romain commençait à décliner; ¶ **~ down on [sb]**● (have oral sex with) tailler une pipe à● [*man*]; faire minette à● [*woman*].

■ **go for**: ¶ **~ for [sb/sth] 1**○ (favour, have liking for) craquer○ pour [*person, physical type*]; aimer [*style of music, literature etc*]; **he really goes for blondes** il craque○ pour or il adore les blondes; **I don't ~ much for modern art** je ne suis pas emballé○ par l'art moderne, je n'aime pas tellement l'art moderne; **2** (apply to) être valable pour, s'appliquer à; **that goes for all of you!** c'est valable pour tout le monde!; **the same goes for him** c'est valable pour lui aussi!, ça s'applique à lui aussi!; ¶ **~ for [sb] 1** (attack) (physically) attaquer, tomber sur; (verbally) attaquer, s'en prendre à [*person*]; **the two youths went for him** les deux jeunes l'ont attaqué or lui ont sauté dessus; **to ~ for sb's throat** [*animal*] attaquer qn à la gorge; **she really went for him!** (in argument, row) elle l'a vraiment incendié!, elle s'en est prise violemment à lui!; **2 he has a lot going for him** il a beaucoup de choses pour lui; ¶ **~ for [sth] 1** (attempt to achieve) essayer d'obtenir [*honour, victory*]; **she's going for the gold medal/world record** elle vise la médaille d'or/le record mondial; **~ for it**○! vas-y, fonce○!; **the company is going for a new image** l'entreprise cherche à se donner une nouvelle image; **the team is going for a win against Italy** l'équipe compte bien gagner contre l'Italie; **2** (choose) choisir, prendre; **I'll ~ for the blue one** je prendrai le bleu.

■ **go forth** sout [*person*] (go out) sortir; (go forward) aller, avancer; **~ forth and multiply** allez et multipliez-vous.

■ **go forward(s)** avancer.

■ **go in 1** (enter) entrer; (go back in) rentrer; **2** Mil [*army, troops*] attaquer ; **the troops went in at dawn** les troupes ont attaqué à l'aube; **3** (disappear) [*sun, moon*] se cacher.

■ **go in for**: **~ in for [sth] 1** (be keen on) aimer [*sport, hobby etc*]; **I don't ~ in for sports much** je n'aime pas tellement le sport; **he goes in for opera in a big way** il adore l'opéra, c'est un fou d'opéra○; **we don't ~ in for that sort of thing** nous n'aimons pas ce genre de chose; **they don't ~ in much for foreign languages at Ben's school** ils ne s'intéressent pas beaucoup aux langues étrangères dans l'école de Ben; **2** (take up) **to ~ in for teaching** entrer dans l'enseignement; **to ~ in for politics** se lancer dans la politique; **3** (take part in) s'inscrire à [*exam, competition*].

■ **go into**: **~ into [sth] 1** (enter) entrer dans; fig (take up) se lancer dans; **to ~ into hospital** entrer à l'hôpital; **to ~ into parliament** entrer au parlement; **to ~ into politics/business** se lancer dans la politique/les affaires; **2** (examine, investigate) étudier; **we need to ~ into the question of funding** il faut que nous étudiions la question du financement; **3** (explain, describe) **I won't ~ into why I did it** je n'expliquerai pas pourquoi je l'ai fait; **let's not ~ into that now** laissons cela de côté pour l'instant; **4** (launch into) se lancer dans; **she went into a long explanation of what had happened** elle s'est lancée dans une longue explication de ce qui s'était passé; **5** (be expended) **a lot of work/money went into this project** beaucoup de travail/d'argent a été investi dans ce projet; **a lot of effort went into organizing the party** l'organisation de la soirée a demandé beaucoup de travail; **6** (hit) [*car, driver*] rentrer dans, heurter; **the car went into a lamp post** la voiture est rentrée dans or a heurté un réverbère.

■ **go in with**: **~ in with [sb]** se joindre à [*person, ally, organization*]; **he went in with us to buy the present** il s'est mis avec nous pour acheter le cadeau.

■ **go off**: ¶ **~ off 1** (explode, fire) [*bomb*] exploser; **the gun didn't ~ off** le coup n'est pas parti; **2** [*alarm clock*] sonner; [*fire alarm*] se déclencher; **3** (depart) partir, s'en aller; **he went off to work** il est parti au travail; **she went off to find a spade** elle est allée chercher une pelle; **they went off together** ils sont partis ensemble; **4** GB (go bad) [*milk, cream*] tourner; [*meat*] s'avarier; [*butter*] rancir; (deteriorate) [*performer, athlete etc*] perdre sa forme; [*work*] se dégrader; (lose one's attractiveness) [*person*] être moins beau/belle qu'avant; **he used to be very handsome, but he's gone off a bit** il était très beau, mais il est moins bien maintenant; **the first part of the film was good, but after that it went off** la première partie du film était bien, mais après ça s'est dégradé; **5**○ (fall asleep) s'endormir; **6** (cease to operate) [*lights, heating*] s'éteindre; **7** (happen, take place) [*evening, organized event*] se passer; **the concert went off very well** le concert s'est très bien passé; **8** Theat quitter la scène; ¶ **~ off [sb/sth]** GB **I used to like him but I've gone off him** je l'aimais bien avant, mais je ne l'aime plus tellement; **I've gone off opera/whisky** je n'aime plus tellement l'opéra/le whisky; **I think she's gone off the idea** je crois qu'elle a renoncé à l'idée.

■ **go off with**: **~ off with [sb/sth]** partir avec [*person, money*]; **she went off with all his money** elle est partie avec tout son argent; **who's gone off with my pen?** qui a pris mon stylo?

■ **go on**: ¶ **~ on 1** (happen, take place) se passer; **what's going on ?** qu'est-ce qui se passe?; **there's a party going on upstairs** il y a une fête en haut; **how long has this been going on?** depuis combien de temps est-ce que ça dure?; **a lot of stealing goes on** il y a beaucoup de vols; **a lot of drinking goes on at Christmas time** les gens boivent beaucoup à Noël; **2** (continue on one's way) poursuivre son chemin; **3** (continue) continuer; **~ on with your work** continuez votre travail, continuez de travailler; **~ on looking** continuez à or de chercher; **she went on speaking** elle a continué de parler; **~ on, we're all listening!** continue, nous t'écoutons tous!; **'and another thing,' she went on, 'you're always late'** 'et autre chose', a-t-elle ajouté, 'vous êtes toujours en retard'; **if he goes on like this, he'll get into trouble !** s'il continue comme ça, il va s'attirer des ennuis; **we can't ~ on like this!** nous ne pouvons pas continuer comme ça!; **life must ~ on** la vie continue; **the meeting went on into the afternoon** la réunion s'est prolongée jusque dans l'après-midi; **you can't ~ on being a pen pusher all your life!** tu ne peux pas rester gratte-papier toute ta vie!; **the list goes on and on** la liste est infinie or interminable; **that's enough to be going on with** ça suffit pour le moment; **have you got enough work to be going on with?** est-ce que tu as assez de travail pour le moment?; **here's £20 to be going on with** voici 20 livres pour te dépanner; **~ on (with you)**○! allons donc!; **4** (of time) (elapse) **as time went on, they...** avec le temps, ils...; **as the evening went on, he became more animated** au fur et à mesure que la soirée avançait, il devenait plus animé; **5** (keep talking) **to ~ on about sth** ne pas arrêter de parler de qch, parler de qch à n'en plus finir; **he was going on about the war** il parlait de la guerre à n'en plus finir; **don't ~ on about it!** arrête de parler de ça!, change de disque!; **she went on and on about it** elle en a fait toute une histoire; **he does tend to ~ on a bit!** il a tendance à radoter○!; **the way she goes on, you'd think she was an expert on the subject!** à l'entendre, on croirait qu'elle est experte en la matière!; **6** (proceed) passer; **let's ~ on to the next item** passons au point suivant; **he went on to say that/describe how** puis il a dit que/décrit comment; **7** (go into operation) [*heating, lights*] s'allumer; **8** Theat entrer en scène; **what time do you ~ on?** à quelle heure est-ce que vous entrez en scène?; **9** (approach) **it's going on three o'clock** il est presque trois heures; **she's four going on five** elle va sur ses cinq ans; **he's thirty going on three** hum il a trente ans mais il pourrait bien en avoir trois; **10** (fit) **these gloves won't ~ on** ces gants ne m'iront pas; **the lid won't ~ on properly** le couvercle ne ferme pas bien; **¶ ~ on [sth]** se fonder sur [*piece of evidence, information*]; **that's all we've got to ~ on** tout ce que nous savons avec certitude; **we've got nothing else to ~ on** nous n'avons pas d'autre point de départ; **the police haven't got much evidence to ~ on** la police n'a pas beaucoup de preuves à l'appui.

■ **go on at**: **~ on at [sb]** s'en prendre à [*person*]; **he's always going on at me for writing badly** il s'en prend toujours à moi à cause de ma mauvaise écriture; **they're always going on at us about deadlines** ils sont toujours sur notre dos pour des histoires de délais.

■ **go out 1** (leave, depart) sortir; **she went out of the room** elle a quitté la pièce, elle est sortie de la pièce; **to ~ out walking** aller se promener; **to ~ out for a drink** aller prendre un verre; **they ~ out a lot** ils sortent beaucoup; **she likes going out** elle aime sortir; **she had to ~ out to work at 14** il a fallu qu'elle aille travailler à 14 ans; **2** (travel long distance) partir (**to** à, pour); **she's gone out to Australia/Africa** elle est partie pour l'Australie/l'Afrique; **3** (have relationship) **to ~ out with sb** sortir avec qn; **they've been going out together for six weeks** ils sortent ensemble depuis six semaines; **4** [*tide*] descendre; **the tide is going out** la marée descend, la mer se retire; **5** Ind (go on strike) se mettre en grève; **6** (become unfashionable) passer de mode; (no longer be used) ne plus être utilisé; **miniskirts went out in the 1970s** les mini-jupes ont passé de mode dans les années 70; **gas went out and electricity came in** l'électricité a remplacé le gaz; **7** (be extinguished) [*fire, light*] s'éteindre; **8** (be sent) [*invitation, summons*] être envoyé; (be published) [*journal, magazine*] être publié; Radio, TV (be broadcast) être diffusé; **9** (be announced) **word went out that he was coming back** le bruit a couru qu'il revenait; **the news went out from Washington that** Washington a annoncé que; **10** (be eliminated) gen, Sport être éliminé; **she went out in the early stages of the competition** elle a été éliminée au début de la compétition; **11** (expressing compassion, sympathy) **my heart goes out to them** je les plains de tout mon cœur, je suis de tout cœur avec eux; **our thoughts ~ out to absent friends** nos pensées vont vers nos amis absents; **12** (disappear) **all the spirit seemed to have gone out of her** elle semblait avoir perdu tout son entrain; **the romance seemed to have gone out of their relationship** leur relation semblait avoir perdu tout son charme; **13** (end) [*year, month*] se terminer; **14** (in cards) terminer.

■ **go over**: **¶ ~ over 1** (cross over) aller; **she went over to him/to the window** elle est allée vers lui/vers la fenêtre, elle s'est approchée de lui/de la fenêtre; **to ~ over to Ireland/to America** aller en Irlande/aux États-Unis; **we are now going over to Washington for more news** Radio, TV nous passons maintenant l'antenne à Washington pour plus d'informations; **2** (be received) **how did his speech ~ over?** comment est-ce que son discours a été reçu ?; **his speech went over well** son discours a été bien reçu; **to ~ over big**○ avoir un grand succès; **3** (switch over) **he went over to Labour from the Conservatives** il est passé du parti des conservateurs au parti des travaillistes; **to ~ over to the other side** fig passer dans l'autre camp; **we've gone over to gas (central heating)** nous sommes passés au chauffage central au gaz; **to ~ over to Islam** se convertir à l'Islam; **¶ ~ over [sth] 1** (review) passer [qch] en revue [*details*]; **she went over the events of the day in her mind** elle a passé en revue les événements de la journée; **we've gone over the details again and again** nous avons déjà passé les détails en revue mille fois; **to ~ over one's lines** (actor) répéter son texte; **there's no point in going over old ground** il n'y a aucune raison de revenir là-dessus; **2** (check, inspect) vérifier [*accounts, figures*]; revoir [*facts, piece of work*]; **I want to ~ over this article once more before I hand it in** je veux relire cet article une dernière fois avant de le remettre; **to ~ over a house** faire le tour d'une maison; **3** (clean) **he went over the room with a duster** il a donné un coup de chiffon dans la pièce; **after cleaning, ~ over the surface with a dry cloth** après l'avoir nettoyée, essuyez la surface avec un chiffon sec or passez un chiffon sec sur la surface; **4 to ~ over a sketch in ink** repasser un dessin à l'encre; **5** (exceed) dépasser; **don't ~ over £100** ne dépassez pas 100 livres sterling.

■ **go round** GB: **¶ ~ round 1** (turn) [*wheel, propeller etc*] tourner; **the wheels went round and round** les roues n'ont pas arrêté de tourner; **my head's going round** j'ai la tête qui tourne; **2** (call round) **to ~ round to see sb** aller voir qn; **he's gone round to Anna's** il est allé chez Anna; **3** (suffice) **there isn't enough food/money to ~ round** il n'y a pas assez de nourriture/d'argent pour tout le monde; **there was barely enough to ~ round** il y en avait à peine assez pour tout le monde; **4** (circulate) **there's a rumour going round that** le bruit court que; **5** (make detour) faire un détour; **we had to ~ round the long way** ou **the long way round** il a fallu qu'on prenne un chemin plus long; **I had to ~ round by the bridge** il a fallu que je passe par or que je fasse un détour par le pont; **¶ ~ round [sth]** (visit) faire le tour de [*shops, house, museum*].

■ **go through**: **¶ ~ through 1** (come in) entrer; **if you'll just ~ (on) through, I'll tell them you're here** si vous voulez bien entrer, je vais leur dire que vous êtes arrivé; **2** (be approved) [*law, agreement*] passer; **the law failed to ~ through** la loi n'est pas passée; **the divorce hasn't gone through yet** le divorce n'a pas encore été prononcé; **3** (be successfully completed) [*business deal*] être conclu; **¶ ~ through [sth] 1** (undergo) endurer, subir [*experience, ordeal*]; (pass through) passer par [*stage, phase*]; **in spite of all he's gone through** malgré tout ce qu'il a enduré; **we've all gone through it** nous sommes tous passés par là; **she's gone through a lot** elle a beaucoup souffert; **he went through the day in a kind of daze** toute la journée il a été dans un état second; **the country has gone through two civil wars** le pays a connu deux guerres civiles; **to ~ through a crisis** traverser une crise; **as you ~ through life** au fur et à mesure que tu vieillis, en vieillissant; **you have to ~ through the switchboard/right authorities** il faut passer par le standard/les autorités compétentes; **it went through my mind that** l'idée m'a traversé l'esprit que; **2** (check, inspect) examiner, étudier; (rapidly) parcourir [*documents, files, list*]; **to ~ through one's mail** parcourir son courrier; **let's ~ through the points one by one** étudions or examinons les problèmes un par un; **3** (search) fouiller [*person's belongings, baggage*]; **to ~ through sb's pockets/drawers** fouiller dans les poches/tiroirs de qn; **at customs they went through all my things** à la douane ils ont fouillé toutes mes affaires; **4** (perform, rehearse) répéter [*scene*]; expliquer [*procedure*]; **let's ~ through the whole scene once more** répétons or reprenons toute la scène une dernière fois; **there are still a certain number of formalities to be gone through** il y a encore un certain nombre de formalités à remplir; **I went through the whole procedure with him** je lui ai expliqué comment il fallait procéder en détail; **5** (consume, use up) dépenser [*money*]; **we went through three bottles of wine** nous avons bu or descendu○ trois bouteilles de vin; **I've gone through the elbows of my jacket** j'ai usé ma veste aux coudes.

■ **go through with**: **~ through with [sth]** réaliser, mettre [qch] à exécution [*plan*]; **in the end they decided to ~ through with the wedding** finalement ils ont décidé de se marier; **I can't ~ through with it** je ne peux pas le faire; **you'll have to ~ through with it now** il va falloir que tu le fasses maintenant.

■ **go together 1** (harmonize) [*colours, pieces of furniture etc*] aller ensemble; **these colours don't ~ together** ces couleurs ne vont pas ensemble; **2** (entail each other) aller de pair; **poverty and crime often ~ together** la pauvreté et le crime vont souvent de pair; **3**○† (have relationship) [*couple*] sortir ensemble.

■ **go under 1** [*boat, ship*] couler, sombrer; [*drowning person*] couler, disparaître sous les flots; **2** fig (succumb) [*person*] succomber; (go bankrupt) [*business, company*] faire faillite.

■ **go up**: **¶ ~ up 1** (ascend) monter; **to ~ up to bed** monter se coucher; **they've gone up to London** ils sont allés or montés à Londres; **they've gone up to Scotland** ils sont allés en Écosse; **'going up!'** (in elevator) 'on monte!'; **2** (rise) [*price, temperature*] monter; Theat [*curtain*] se lever (**on** sur); **petrol has gone up (in price)** (le prix de) l'essence a augmenté; **unemployment is ~ing up** le chômage augmente or est en hausse; **our membership has gone up** le nombre de nos adhérents a augmenté; **a cry went up from the crowd** un cri est monté or s'est élevé de la foule; **3** (be erected) [*building*] être construit; [*poster*] être affiché; **new office blocks are going up all over the place** on construit de nouveaux immeubles un peu partout; **4** (be destroyed, blown up) [*building*] sauter, exploser; **5** GB Univ (start university) entrer à l'université; (start term) reprendre les cours; **6** (be upgraded) **the team has gone up to the first division** l'équipe est passée en première division; **7** (continue) **the book/series goes up to 1990** le livre/la série va jusqu'en 1990; **¶ ~ up [sth] 1** (mount) monter, gravir [*hill, mountain*]; **2 to ~ up a class** Sch passer dans une classe supérieure.

■ **go with**: **¶ ~ with [sth] 1** (match, suit) aller avec; **your shirt goes with your blue eyes** ta chemise va bien avec tes yeux bleus; **white wine goes better with fish than red wine** le vin blanc va mieux avec le poisson que le rouge; **2** (accompany) aller de pair avec; **the car goes with the job** la voiture va de pair avec la situation; **the responsibilities that ~ with parenthood** les responsabilités qui vont de pair avec le fait d'être parent; **¶ ~ with [sb]** (date) sortir avec; (have sex with) coucher avec [*person*].

■ **go without**: **¶ ~ without** s'en passer;

you'll just have to ~ without! il va falloir que tu t'en passes!, il va falloir que tu fasses sans!; ¶ **~ without [sth]** se passer de [*food, luxuries*].

goad /ɡəʊd/ **I** *n* lit, fig aiguillon *m*.
II *vtr* **1** (prod) aiguillonner [*animal*]; **2** fig (provoke) provoquer [*person*]; **to ~ sb into doing sth** pousser qn à faire qch; **to ~ sb to violence** pousser qn à la violence.
■ **goad on: ~ [sb] on, ~ on [sb]** aiguillonner.

go-ahead○ /ˈɡəʊəhed/ **I** *n* **to give sb the ~** donner le feu vert à qn (**to do** pour faire; **for sth** pour qch); **to get the ~ from sb** recevoir le feu vert de qn.
II *adj* [*person*] dynamique, plein d'allant.

goal /ɡəʊl/ *n* **1** Sport but *m*; **to keep ~** ou **to play in ~** être gardien de but; **to score** ou **kick a ~** marquer un but; **to miss the ~** manquer le but; **to score an own ~** lit, fig marquer un but pour le compte de l'adversaire; **2** (objective) but *m*; **her ~ was to run the company** son but était de gérer l'entreprise.

goal area *n* surface *f* de but.

goalie○ /ˈɡəʊlɪ/ *n* gardien *m* de but.

goal: **~keeper** ▶ 1692 *n* gardien *m* de but; **~ kick** *n* dégagement *m* aux six.

goalless /ˈɡəʊllɪs/ *adj* **~ match** ou **draw** match *m* nul.

goal: **~ line** *n* ligne *f* de but; **~ mouth** *n* but *m* (*espace entre les poteaux*).

goalpost /ˈɡəʊlpəʊst/ *n* poteau *m* de but.
IDIOMS **to move** ou **shift the ~s** changer les règles du jeu.

goalscorer /ˈɡəʊlskɔːrə(r)/ *n* buteur *m*.

goat /ɡəʊt/ **I** *n* **1** Zool, Culin chèvre *f*; **2**○ GB (fool) andouille○ *f*; **to act the ~** faire l'andouille○; **3**○ (lecher) vieux cochon *m*○.
II *modif* [*cheese, meat, milk, stew*] de chèvre.
IDIOMS **he really gets my ~**○ il me tape sur les nerfs○; **that will separate the sheep from the ~s** cela permettra de voir ce que vaut chacun.

goatee /ɡəʊˈtiː/ *n* barbiche *f*.

goat: **~herd** *n* chevrier/-ière *m/f*; **~sbeard** *n* Bot salsifis *m* des prés.

goatskin /ˈɡəʊtskɪn/ **I** *n* **1** (leather) cuir *m* de chèvre; (pelt) peau *f* de chèvre; **2** (leather bottle) outre *f*.
II *modif* [*rug*] en peau de chèvre.

goatsucker /ˈɡəʊtsʌkə(r)/ *n* US engoulevent *m*.

gob◑ /ɡɒb/ **I** *n* **1** GB (mouth) gueule○ *f*; **2** (spittle) mollard○ *m*; **3** (soft mass) boule *f*; **4** US (sailor) mataf○ *m*; **5** US (large quantity) **~s of charm** beaucoup de charme; **~s of kids** des quantités de mômes○.
II *vi* GB (*p prés etc* **-bb-**) mollarder○.

gobbet /ˈɡɒbɪt/ *n* morceau *m*.

gobble /ˈɡɒbl/ **I** *n* (cry of turkey) glouglou *m*.
II *vtr* (also **~ down**) engloutir [*food*].
III *vi* **1** [*turkey*] (cry) glouglouter; **2** [*person*] (eat) se goinfrer○.
■ **gobble up:** lit, fig **~ [sth] up, ~ up [sth]** engloutir.

gobbledygook○ /ˈɡɒbldɪɡuːk/ *n* charabia○ *m*.

gobbler○ /ˈɡɒblə(r)/ *n* dindon *m*.

go-between /ˈɡəʊbɪtwiːn/ *n* intermédiaire *mf*.

Gobi /ˈɡəʊbɪ/ *pr n* **the ~ desert** le désert *m* de Gobi.

goblet /ˈɡɒblɪt/ *n* verre *m* à pied; **silver ~** gobelet *m* d'argent (à pied).

goblin /ˈɡɒblɪn/ *n* lutin *m*.

gobsmacked○ /ˈɡɒbsmækt/ *adj* GB estomaqué○.

goby /ˈɡəʊbɪ/ *n* (*pl* **~** ou **-bies**) Zool gobie *m*.

go-by○ /ˈɡəʊbaɪ/ *n* **to give sb the ~**○ GB snober qn.

go-cart /ˈɡəʊkɑːt/ *n* **1** US (toy cart) chariot *m*; **2** GB (child's pushchair) poussette *f*; (baby walker) trotteur *m*; **3** (handcart) charrette *f*; **4** = **go-kart**.

god /ɡɒd/ **I** *n* **1** Relig dieu *m*; **ye ~s†!** grands dieux!; **2** (person, thing) dieu *m*, idole *f*.
II God *pr n* **1** Relig Dieu *m*; **so help me God** je le jure devant Dieu; **would to God that** plût à Dieu que (+ *subj*); **a man of God** un prêtre; **2**○ in exclamations) (exasperated) zut○!, merde◑!; (surprised) ça alors○!; **my God!** mon Dieu!; **by God, I'll...!** je le jure, je vais...!; **God forbid**○**!** grands dieux, non!; **~ forbid he should find out!** pourvu qu'il ne l'apprenne pas!; **God knows**○**!** Dieu sait!; **she lives God knows where** elle habite Dieu sait où; **God knows I've tried!** Dieu sait si j'ai essayé.
III Gods○ *npl* Theat paradis *m*, poulailler○ *m*.
IDIOMS **God helps those who help themselves** aide-toi, le ciel t'aidera; **to put the fear of God into sb** faire une peur bleue à qn; **to think one is God's gift (to women)**○ se croire irrésistible avec les femmes; **she thinks she's God's gift to acting**○ elle se croit la meilleure actrice qui ait jamais existé.

God Almighty *n* **1** Relig Dieu *m* Tout-Puissant; **2** *excl* mon Dieu!
IDIOMS **he thinks he's ~** il se prend pour Dieu le père.

god: **~-awful**○ *adj* exécrable; **~child** *n* filleul/-e *m/f*.

goddammit◑ /ˈɡɒddæmɪt/ *excl* US bon sang○!

goddamn○ /ˈɡɒddæm/ **I** *n* **not to give a ~ about** se foutre◑ royalement de.
II *adj* sacré○, fichu○.
III *adv* sacrément○.
IV *excl* **~ (it)!** bon sang○!

goddaughter /ˈɡɒddɔːtə(r)/ *n* filleule *f*.

goddess /ˈɡɒdɪs/ *n* (divinity, woman) déesse *f*.

god: **~father** *n* parrain *m*; **God-fearing** *adj* pieux/pieuse; **~forsaken** *adj* [*country, place*] perdu; **~head** *n* divinité *f*.

godless /ˈɡɒdlɪs/ *adj* impie.

godlike /ˈɡɒdlaɪk/ *adj* divin.

godly /ˈɡɒdlɪ/ *adj* pieux/pieuse.

godmother /ˈɡɒdmʌðə(r)/ *n* marraine *f*.

godparent /ˈɡɒdpeərənt/ *n* parrain/marraine *m/f*; **the ~s** le parrain et la marraine.

god: **~send** *n* aubaine *f*; **~-slot**○ *n* péj Radio, TV émission *f* religieuse; **~son** *n* filleul *m*; **Godspeed** *excl* Dieu vous garde; **~squad**○ *n* péj bigots *mpl* pej.

goer /ˈɡəʊə(r)/ **I** *n*○ GB **1** (energetic person) **to be a ~** être plein d'allant; **2** péj (woman) **she's a real ~!** elle couche à droite et à gauche!
II -goer *dans composés* **theatre-~** personne *f* qui va au théâtre; (regular) amateur/-trice *m/f* de théâtre; **cinema-~** personne qui va au cinéma; (regular) cinéphile *mf*; ▶ **churchgoer, partygoer etc.**

goes /ɡəʊz/ ▶ **go**.

gofer○ /ˈɡəʊfə(r)/ *n* US factotum *m*.

go: **~-getter**○ *n* fonceur/-euse○ *m/f*, ambitieux/-ieuse *m/f*; **~-getting**○ *adj* fonceur/-euse○.

goggle○ /ˈɡɒɡl/ *vi* [*person*] ouvrir des yeux ronds○; [*eyes*] s'écarquiller; **to ~ at sb/sth** regarder qn/qch avec des yeux ronds○.

goggle: **~-box**○ *n* GB télé○ *f*; **~-eyed**○ *adj* avec des yeux ronds○.

goggles /ˈɡɒɡlz/ *npl* **1** (cyclist's, worker's) lunettes *fpl* protectrices; (skier's) lunettes *fpl* de ski; (for swimming) lunettes *fpl* de plongée; **2**○ hum (glasses) binocles○ *mpl*.

go-go /ˈɡəʊɡəʊ/ *adj* **1** US Econ, Fin [*economics, funds, market*] spéculatif/-ive; **2**○ (dynamic) [*person, culture*] dynamique; **3**○ (disco) [*dancer, dancing*] de boîte de nuit○.

go-go dancer *n* danseuse *f* de boîte de nuit.

going /ˈɡəʊɪŋ/ **I** *n* **1** (departure) départ *m*; ▶ **coming**; **2** (progress) **that's not bad ~!, that's good ~!** c'est rapide!; **it was slow ~, the ~ was slow** (on journey) ça a été long; (at work) ça n'avançait pas vite; **the conversation was heavy ~** la conversation était laborieuse; **this book is heavy ~** ce livre est difficile à lire or est d'une lecture laborieuse; **3** (condition of ground) (for riding, walking) état *m* du sol; **the ~ was hard** ou **rough, it was hard** ou **rough ~** Turf le terrain était lourd; **4** fig (conditions, circumstances) **when the ~ gets tough** quand les choses vont mal; **she finds her new job hard ~** elle trouve que son nouveau travail est difficile; **they got out while the ~ was good** ils s'en sont tirés avant qu'il ne soit trop tard or pendant que les circonstances le permettaient.
II *adj* **1** (current) [*price*] actuel, en cours; **the ~ rate for babysitters/freelancers** le tarif en vigueur pour les babysitters/les travailleurs indépendants; **they pay me twice the ~ rate** ils me paient deux fois plus que le tarif en vigueur; **the ~ rate of interest** le taux d'intérêt actuel; **2** (operating) **~ concern** Comm affaire *f* qui marche, affaire saine; **they bought the business as a ~ concern** quand ils ont acheté l'entreprise elle était déjà montée; **3** (existing) **it's the best model ~** c'est le meilleur modèle sur le marché; **he's the best film-maker ~** c'est le meilleur cinéaste en vie.
III -going (*dans composés*) **theatre-/cinema-~** la fréquentation des théâtres/des salles de cinéma; **the theatre-~ public** les amateurs *mpl* de théâtre.

going-over○ /ˌɡəʊɪŋˈəʊvə(r)/ *n* (*pl* **goings-over**) **1** (examination) (of vehicle, machine) révision *f*; (of document) vérification *f*; (cleaning) (of room, house) nettoyage *m*; **the doctor gave me a thorough ~** le médecin m'a soigneusement examiné; **this room needs a good ~** cette pièce a besoin d'un grand nettoyage; **2 to give sb a ~** (scold) passer un savon○ à qn; (beat up) rouer qn de coups, battre qn.

goings-on○ /ˌɡəʊɪŋzˈɒn/ *npl* (events) événements *mpl*; péj (activities) activités *fpl*; (behaviour) conduite *f sg*; **there are some strange ~ in that house** il se passe de drôles de choses dans cette maison; **shady ~ in the business world** des activités louches dans le monde des affaires.

goitre, goiter US /ˈɡɔɪtə(r)/ *n* goitre *m*.

go-kart /ˈɡəʊkɑːt/ *n* kart *m*.

go-karting /ˈɡəʊkɑːtɪŋ/ ▶ 1282 *n* karting *m*; **to go ~** faire du karting.

Golan /ˈɡəʊlæn/ *pr n* **the ~ Heights** le (plateau *m* du) Golan.

gold /ɡəʊld/ **I** *n* **1** Miner, Fin or *m*; **£1,000 in ~** 1000 livres sterling en or; **to strike ~** Miner découvrir un filon; (become rich) trouver le filon○; [*athlete*] obtenir la médaille d'or; **2** (colour) (couleur *f*) or *m*; **3** = **gold medal**.
II *modif* [*jewellery, cutlery, tooth*] en or; [*coin, medal, ingot, wire*] d'or; [*ore, deposit, alloy*] d'or.
III *adv* **to go ~** Mus être disque d'or.
IDIOMS **to be as good as ~** être sage comme une image; **to have a heart of ~** avoir un cœur d'or; **to be worth one's weight in ~** valoir son pesant d'or.

gold: **~ basis** *n* étalon-or *m*; **~ beetle** *n* scarabée *m* doré.

goldbrick /ˌɡəʊldˈbrɪk/ **I** *n* **1** péj (worthless item) babiole *f*; **2**○ US (shirker) tire-au-flanc○ *m inv*.
II *vi* US (shirk) tirer au flanc○.

gold: **~bug** *n* = **gold beetle**; **~ certificate** *n* US billet *m* garanti or.

Gold Coast *n* **1** Hist (Ghana) Côte-de-l'Or *f*; **2** (in Australia) *série de stations balnéaires dans l'est de l'Australie*; **3** US banlieue *f* huppée.

gold: **~-coloured** GB, **~-colored** US *adj* couleur or *inv*, doré; **~crest** *n* roitelet *m* huppé.

gold digger *n* **1** Miner chercheur *m* d'or; **2** fig péj (woman) croqueuse *f* de diamants.

gold disc *n* disque *m* d'or.

gold dust *n* lit poudre *f* d'or; **to be like ~** fig être une denrée rare.

golden /ˈɡəʊldən/ *adj* **1** (made of gold) en or, d'or; **2** (gold coloured) doré, d'or; **~ hair** cheveux *mpl* dorés; **~ beaches** plages *fpl* de sable blond; **~ sunset** coucher *m* de soleil flamboyant; **3** fig [*dream*] doré; [*summer*] idyllique; [*voice*] d'or; **a ~ opportunity** une occasion en or; **the ~ days of Hollywood** l'âge d'or de Hollywood; **the ~ world of advertising** iron le monde merveilleux de la publicité.
IDIOMS **silence is ~** le silence est d'or.

golden: **~ age** *n* âge *m* d'or; **~ anniversary** *n* = **golden jubilee**; **~ boy** *n* enfant *m* chéri.

golden-brown /ˌɡəʊldənˈbraʊn/ ▶ 1104 *n, adj* mordoré (*m*).

golden: **~ calf** *n* Bible, fig veau *m* d'or; **~ cocker (spaniel)** *n* cocker *m* roux-doré; **Golden Delicious** *n* golden *f inv* (*pomme*); **~ eagle** *n* aigle *m* royal; **~eye** *n* garrot *m* à œil d'or; **Golden Fleece** *n* Toison *f* d'Or; **Golden Gate** *pr n* Golden Gate *m*; **~ girl** *n* enfant *f* chérie.

golden goose *n*: IDIOMS **to kill the ~** tuer la poule aux œufs d'or.

golden: **~ handshake** *n* GB prime *f* de départ; **~ hello** *n* prime *f* d'embauche; **Golden Horde** *n* Horde *f* d'Or; **Golden Horn** *n* Corne *f* d'Or; **~ jubilee** *n* (wedding anniversary) noces *fpl* d'or; (other) jubilé *m*.

golden mean *n* **1** (happy medium) **the ~** le juste milieu; **2** Art = **golden section**.

golden number *n* nombre *m* d'or.

golden oldie /ˌɡəʊldən ˈəʊldɪ/ *n* (song) vieux succès *m* (de la chanson); (film) vieux succès *m* (du cinéma).

golden: **~ oriole** *n* Zool loriot *m* jaune; **~ parachute** *n* US = **golden handshake**; **~ pheasant** *n* faisan *m* doré; **~ plover** *n* pluvier *m* doré; **~ remedy** *n* remède *m* souverain; **~ retriever** *n* golden retriever *m*; **~rod** *n* verge *f* d'or; **~ rule** *n* règle *f* d'or; **~ section** *n* section *f* dorée; **~ syrup** *n* GB ≈ sirop *m* de sucre roux; **Golden Triangle** *n* Geog Triangle *m* d'Or; **~ wedding** *n* noces *fpl* d'or; **~ yellow** *n, adj* jaune *m inv* d'or.

gold: **~ exchange standard** *n* étalon *m* de change or; **~ fever** *n* fièvre *f* de l'or; **~field** *n* terrain *m* aurifère; **~-filled** *adj* Dent aurifié; **~ filling** *n* Dent obturation *f* en or; **~finch** *n* chardonneret *m*; **~fish** *n* (*pl* **-fish** ou **-fishes**) poisson *m* rouge.

goldfish bowl *n* bocal *m* à poissons rouges; **it's like living in a ~!** fig on ne peut pas faire un mouvement sans que tout le monde soit au courant!

gold foil *n* feuille *f* d'or.

Goldilocks /ˈɡəʊldɪlɒks/ *pr n* Boucles d'Or.

gold: **~ leaf** *n* feuille *f* d'or; **~ medal** *n* médaille *f* d'or.

gold mine *n* lit, fig mine *f* d'or; **to be sitting on a ~** fig être assis sur une mine d'or.

gold: **~ mining** *n* extraction *f* de l'or; **~ note** *n* US = **gold certificate**; **~ paint** *n* peinture *f* dorée.

gold plate *n* (coating) fine couche *f* d'or; (dishes) vaisselle *f* d'or.

gold: **~-plated** *adj* plaqué or *inv*; **~ point** *n* point *m* d'or, gold-point *m*; **~ pool** *n* pool *m* de l'or; **~ record** *n* disque *m* d'or; **~ reserve** réserves *fpl* d'or; **~ rush** *n* ruée *f* vers l'or; **~smith** ▶ 1692 *n* orfèvre *m*; **~ standard** *n* étalon *m* or; **~ star** *n* badge *m* en forme d'étoile *porté à la mémoire d'un soldat mort au combat*; **~stone** *n* aventurine *f*.

golf /ɡɒlf/ ▶ 1282 **I** *n* golf *m*.
II *modif* [*tournament, umbrella, equipment*] de golf.

golf ball *n* **1** Sport balle *f* de golf; **2** (on typewriter) boule *f*.

golf ball typewriter *n* machine *f* à écrire à boule.

golf club *n* **1** (place) club *m* de golf; **2** (stick) crosse *f* de golf.

golf course *n* (terrain *m* de) golf *m*.

golfer /ˈɡɒlfə(r)/ *n* joueur/-euse *m/f* de golf, golfeur/-euse *m/f*.

golfing /ˈɡɒlfɪŋ/ *n* **to go ~** faire du golf.

golf links *n* = **golf course**.

Goliath /ɡəˈlaɪəθ/ *pr n* Bible Goliath; fig colosse *m*.

golliwog /ˈɡɒlɪwɒɡ/ *n* (poupée *f* de) nègre *m* en étoffe.

golly○ /ˈɡɒlɪ/ **I** *n* GB = **golliwog**.
II *excl* ça alors!

Gomorrah /ɡəˈmɒrə/ *pr n* Gomorrhe.

gonad /ˈɡəʊnæd/ *n* gonade *f*.

gonadotrophin /ˌɡəʊnədəʊˈtrəʊfɪn/, **gonadotropin** /ˌɡəʊnədəʊˈtrəʊpɪn/ *n* gonadotrophine *f*, gonadostimuline *f*.

gonadotropic /ˌɡəʊnədəʊˈtrɒpɪk/ *adj* gonadotrope.

gondola /ˈɡɒndələ/ *n* **1** (boat) gondole *f*; **2** (under airship, balloon) nacelle *f*; (cable car) cabine *f* (de téléphérique); **3** (in shop) (shelf unit) gondole *f*; **4** (also **~ car**) US Rail wagon *m* plat; **5** US (barge) barge *f*.

gondolier /ˌɡɒndəˈlɪə(r)/ ▶ 1692 *n* gondolier *m*.

gone /ɡɒn/ **I** *pp* ▶ **go**.
II *adj* **1** [*person*] (departed) parti; euph (dead) disparu; **be ~!**† ou hum allez-vous-en!; **to be far ~** (ill) être très malade; (with drink) être complètement bourré○; (with drugs) planer○ complètement; **to be long ~** [*person*] (dead) être mort depuis longtemps; [*machine, device*] (worn) être complètement usé; (past) [*era*] être révolu; **the theatre/school is long ~** le théâtre/l'école n'existe plus depuis longtemps; **~ are the days when** ou **the days are ~ when people had servants** l'époque où les gens avaient des domestiques est révolue; **~ with the wind** autant en emporte le vent; **2** GB (pregnant) **she is seven months ~** elle est enceinte de sept mois; **how far ~ is she?** elle est enceinte depuis combien de temps?; **3**○ **to be ~ on sb** (infatuated) s'être amouraché or entiché○ de qn; **she's really ~ on him** elle s'est vraiment entichée de lui; **4** GB (past) **it's ~ six o'clock** il est six heures passées, il est plus de six heures; **it's just ~ six o'clock** il est un peu plus de six heures; **she's ~ eighty** elle a plus de quatre-vingts ans.

goner○ /ˈɡɒnə(r)/ *n* **to be a ~**○ être fichu○.

gong /ɡɒŋ/ *n* **1** gong *m*; **dinner ~** cloche *f* du dîner; **2**○ GB (medal) médaille *f*; **3**○ US (opium pipe) pipe *f* à opium.

gonna○ /ˈɡɒnə/ = **going to**.

gonorrh(o)ea /ˌɡɒnəˈrɪə/ ▶ 1354 *n* blennorragie *f*.

gonzo○ /ˈɡɒnzəʊ/ *adj* US [*style*] flamboyant; [*person*] bizarre, dingue○.

goo○ /ɡuː/ *n* **1** (gunge) matière *f* poisseuse; **2** fig péj (sentimentality) sentimentalité *f* à l'eau de rose.

good /ɡʊd/ **I** *n* **1** (virtue) bien *m*; **~ and evil** le bien et le mal; **to do ~** faire le bien; **to be up to no ~**○ mijoter qch○; **to come to no ~** [*person*] mal tourner; **2** (benefit) bien *m*; **for the ~ of the company** pour le bien de la société; **it's for your own ~** c'est pour ton bien; **for all the ~ it did me** pour le peu de bien que ça m'a fait; **much ~ may it do him!** grand bien lui fasse!; **she's too generous for her own ~** elle est trop généreuse et ça lui jouera des tours; **for the ~ of his health** lit pour sa santé; **do you think I'm doing this for the ~ of my health?** iron tu crois que ça m'amuse de faire ça?; **it didn't do my migraine any ~** ça n'a pas arrangé ma migraine; **a strike won't do the company any ~** une grève n'arrangera pas les affaires de l'entreprise; **the rain did the plants ~** la pluie a fait du bien aux plantes; **it will do you ~ to sleep** ça te fera du bien de dormir; **no ~ can** ou **will come of it** rien de bon n'en sortira; **no ~ will come of waiting** attendre ne changera rien; **to be all to the ~** être pour le mieux; **3** (use) **it's no ~ crying** ça ne sert à rien de pleurer; **it's no ~ I can't do it** ça ne sert à rien je n'y arrive pas; **would an oil change do any ~?** est-ce qu'une vidange servirait à quelque chose?; **what ~ would it do me?** à quoi cela me servirait-il?; **these books are no ~ to me now** ces livres ne me servent plus à rien; **4** GB (profit) **to be £20 to the ~** avoir 20 livres sterling à son crédit; **5** (virtuous people) **the ~** (+ *v pl*) les bons *mpl*.
II goods *npl* **1** (for sale) gen articles *mpl*, marchandise *f*; **leather ~s** articles de cuir; **stolen ~** marchandise volée; **electrical ~s** appareils *mpl* électroménagers; **~s and services** biens *mpl* de consommation et services; **2** GB Rail marchandises *fpl*; **3** (property) affaires *fpl*, biens *mpl*; **~ and chattels** biens et effets personnels; **4**○ (what is wanted) **to deliver** ou **come up with the ~s** répondre à l'attente; **that's the ~s!** c'est parfait!
III goods *modif* GB Rail [*depot, station, train, wagon*] de marchandises.
IV *adj* (*comp* **better**; *superl* **best**) **1** (enjoyable) [*book, holiday, joke, news*] bon/bonne; [*party*] réussi; **the ~ weather** le beau temps; **the ~ times** les bons moments; **to have a ~ time** bien s'amuser; **a ~ time was had by all** tout le monde s'est amusé; **have a ~ time!** amusez-vous bien!; **have a ~ day!** bonne journée!; **the ~ things in life** les petits plaisirs de l'existence; **the ~ life** la dolce vita; **it's ~ to see you again** je suis content de vous revoir; **in the ~ old days** au bon vieux temps; **2** (happy) **to feel ~ about/doing** être content de/de faire; **helping others makes me feel ~** je suis content quand j'aide les autres; **I didn't feel very ~ about lying to him** je n'ai pas été très fier de lui avoir menti; **3** (healthy) [*ear , eye, leg*] bon/bonne; [*eyesight, hearing, memory*] bon/bonne; **you don't look too ~** tu as mauvaise mine; **I don't feel too ~** je ne me sens pas très bien; **4** (high quality) [*book, condition, make, hotel, photo, soil, score*] bon/bonne; [*coat, suit, china*] beau/belle; [*degree*] avec mention (*after n*); **I'm not ~ enough for her** je ne suis pas assez bien pour elle; **nothing is too ~ for her son** rien n'est trop beau pour son fils; **5** (prestigious) (*épith*) [*address, family, marriage*] bon/bonne; **6** (obedient) [*child, dog*] sage; [*behaviour, manners*] bon/bonne; **there's a ~ boy** ou **girl!** c'est bien!; **7** (favourable) [*review, impression, opportunity, sign*] bon/bonne; **the ~ thing is that** ce qui est bien c'est que; **New York is ~ for shopping** New York est un bon endroit pour faire les magasins; **8** (attractive) [*legs, teeth*] beau/belle; [*handwriting*] beau/belle; **to look ~ with** [*garment, accessories*] aller bien avec [*garment*]; **she looks ~ in blue/that dress** le bleu/cette robe lui va bien; **a ~ figure** une belle silhouette; **9** (tasty) [*meal*] bon/bonne; **to taste ~** avoir bon goût; **to smell ~** sentir bon *inv*; **to look ~** avoir l'air bon; **that pie looks ~** cette tourte a l'air bonne; **10** (virtuous) (*épith*) [*man, life*] vertueux/-euse; [*Christian*] bon/bonne; **the ~ guys** (in films) les bons *mpl*; **11** (kind) [*person*] gentil/-ille; **a ~ deed** une bonne action; **to do sb a ~ turn** rendre service à qn; **would you be ~ enough to do, would you be so ~ as to do** auriez-vous la gentillesse de faire; **close the door, there's a ~ chap** fermez la porte, vous serez gentil; **my ~ man**† mon brave†; **how is your ~ lady†?** comment va madame votre épouse?; **12** (pleasant) [*humour, mood*] bon/bonne; **to be in a ~ mood** être de bonne humeur; **to**

be very ~ about se montrer très compréhensif au sujet de [*mistake, misunderstanding*]; **13** (reliable) **~ old Richard!** ce bon vieux Richard!; **there's nothing like ~ old beeswax** il n'y a rien de tel que la bonne vieille cire d'abeille; **14** (competent) [*accountant, hairdresser, teacher*] bon/bonne; **she's a ~ swimmer** elle nage bien; **to be ~ at** être bon en [*Latin, physics*]; être bon à [*badminton, chess*]; **she's ~ at dancing/drawing** elle danse/dessine bien; **to be no ~ at** être nul/nulle en [*tennis, chemistry*]; être nul/nulle à [*chess, cards*]; **I'm no ~ at knitting/singing/apologizing** je ne sais pas tricoter/chanter/m'excuser; **to be ~ with** savoir comment s'y prendre avec [*old people, children, animals*]; aimer [*numbers*]; **to be ~ with one's hands** être habile de ses mains; **to be ~ with words** savoir écrire; **you're really ~ at irritating people!** iron tu es doué pour énerver les gens!; **he was ~ as Hamlet** il était bien dans le rôle d'Hamlet; **15** (beneficial) **to be ~ for** faire du bien à [*person, plant*]; être bon pour [*skin, health*]; être bon pour [*business, morale*]; **exercise is ~ for you** l'exercice fait du bien; **he eats more than is ~ for him** il mange plus qu'il ne devrait; **say nothing if you know what's ~ for you** si je peux te donner un conseil, ne dis rien; **16** (effective) [*example, knife, shampoo, method*] bon/bonne (**for doing** pour faire); **to look ~** [*design, wallpaper*] faire de l'effet; **this will look ~ on your CV** GB ou **résumé** US cela fera bien sur votre CV; **17** (suitable) [*book, day, moment, name*] bon/bonne (**for** pour); **18** (fluent) **he speaks ~ Spanish** il parle bien espagnol; **her English is ~** son anglais est bon; **19** (fortunate) **this new law is a ~ thing** cette nouvelle loi est une bonne chose; **it's a ~ job** ou **thing (that)** heureusement que; **it's a ~ job** ou **thing too!** tant mieux!; **we've never had it so ~**○ les affaires n'ont jamais été aussi prospères; **industry has never had it so ~** l'industrie n'a jamais été aussi prospère; **it's too ~ to be true** c'est trop beau pour être vrai; **20** (sensible) [*choice, idea, investment*] bon/bonne; **that's a ~ question** bonne question; **that's a ~ point** tout à fait; **21** (close) (*épith*) [*friend, relationship*] bon/bonne; **22** (serviceable) **this season ticket is ~ for two more months** cette carte d'abonnement est valable encore deux mois; **he's ~ for another 20 years** il sera encore là dans 20 ans; **the car is ~ for another 10,000 km** la voiture fera encore 10 000 km; **it's as ~ a reason as any** c'est une raison comme une autre; **to be ~ for a loan** être d'accord pour prêter de l'argent; **23** (accurate) [*description, spelling*] bon/bonne; **to keep ~ time** [*clock, watch*] être très précis; **24** (fit to eat) [*meat, cheese*] bon/bonne; **25** (substantial) (*épith*) [*salary, size, kilo, length, hour, mile*] bon/bonne; **it must be worth a ~ 2,000 dollars** ça doit valoir au moins 2 000 dollars; **a ~ 20 years ago** il y a au moins 20 ans; **a ~ thick mattress** un matelas bien épais; **a ~ long walk/talk** une bonne balade/discussion; **~ and early** de très bonne heure; **26** (hard) (*épith*) [*kick, punch*] bon/bonne; **give it a ~ clean** nettoie-le bien; **we had a ~ laugh/look** on a bien ri/regardé; **27**‡ Naut **the ~ ship Neptune** le Neptune. ▶**better**[1], **best**.

V as good as *adv phr* **1** (virtually) quasiment; **the match is as ~ as lost** le match est quasiment perdu; **to be as ~ as new** être comme neuf/neuve; **2** (tantamount to) **it's as ~ as saying yes/giving him a blank cheque** c'est comme si tu disais oui/lui donnais carte blanche; **3** (by implication) **he as ~ as called me a liar** il m'a plus ou moins traité de menteur.

VI for good *adv phr* pour toujours.

VII *excl* (expressing pleasure, satisfaction) c'est bien!; (with relief) tant mieux!; (to encourage, approve) très bien!; (in assent) très bien!

IDIOMS **~ for you!** (approvingly) bravo!; (sarcastically) tant mieux pour toi!; **that's a ~ one!** [*joke, excuse*] elle est bonne celle-là!; **~ on you**○! GB bravo!; **~ thinking** bien vu!; **everything came ~ in the end** tout s'est bien terminé; **to be caught with the ~s**○ être pris en flagrant délit; **to be onto a ~ thing**○, **to have a ~ thing going**○ être sur un bon filon; **you can have too much of a ~ thing** il ne faut pas abuser des bonnes choses.

good: **~ afternoon** *excl* (in greeting) bonjour; (in farewell) au revoir; **Good Book** *n* Relig sainte Bible *f*.

goodbye /ˌɡʊdˈbaɪ/ *n, excl* au revoir; **to say ~ to sb** dire au revoir à qn; **to say** ou **kiss ~ to sth** dire adieu à qch.

good: **~ day**† *excl* (in greeting) bonjour; (in farewell) au revoir; **~ evening** *excl* bonsoir.

good-for-nothing /ˈɡʊdfənʌθɪŋ/ **I** *n* bon/bonne *m/f* à rien.

II *modif* [*layabout, idler*] bon/bonne à rien (*after n*); **her ~ husband** son bon à rien de mari.

Good Friday *pr n* Relig Vendredi *m* saint; **on ~** le Vendredi saint.

good-hearted /ˌɡʊdˈhɑːtɪd/ *adj* généreux/-euse.

good-humoured GB, **good-humored** US /ˌɡʊdˈhjuːməd/ *adj* [*audience, crowd, meeting, discussion*] détendu; [*rivalry, competitor*] amical; [*banter, joke, criticism*] innocent; [*remark, smile, wink*] plaisant; **to be ~** (of mood) être de bonne humeur; (of character) avoir bon caractère.

good-humouredly GB, **good-humoredly** US /ˌɡʊdˈhjuːmədlɪ/ *adv* [*smile*] plaisamment; [*say*] avec bonne humeur; [*tease*] gentiment.

goodies○ /ˈɡʊdɪz/ *npl* **1** (treats) (edible) friandises *fpl*; (gifts) cadeaux *mpl*; **2** (heroes) **the ~** les bons *mpl*.

goodish○ /ˈɡʊdɪʃ/ *adj* [*actor, swimmer*] assez bon/bonne; [*appetite, relationship*] assez bon/bonne; [*party, film*] pas mal *inv*; **to be in a ~ mood** être de plutôt bonne humeur; **'were the children good?'—'~'** 'les enfants ont-ils été sages?'—'ça a été'.

good: **~-looker**○ *n* bel homme/belle femme *m/f*; **~-looking** *adj* beau/belle (*before n*); **~ looks** *npl* beauté *f* ¢, physique *m* ¢.

goodly /ˈɡʊdlɪ/ *adj* (*épith*) [*sum*] beau/belle; [*amount, number, quantity*] honorable; [*part, proportion*] bon/bonne.

good morning /ˌɡʊd ˈmɔːnɪŋ/ *excl* (in greeting) bonjour; (in farewell) au revoir.

good-natured /ˌɡʊdˈneɪtʃəd/ *adj* [*person*] agréable, facile; [*animal*] qui a bon caractère (*after n*); [*discussion, meeting*] détendu; [*banter, remark*] amical; [*criticism*] bien intentionné.

good-naturedly /ˌɡʊdˈneɪtʃədlɪ/ *adv* plaisamment.

goodness /ˈɡʊdnɪs/ **I** *n* **1** (virtue) bonté *f*; **2** (kindness) bonté *f*; **would you have the ~ to close the door?** sout auriez-vous la bonté de fermer la porte? fml; **to do sth out of the ~ of one's heart** faire qch par pure gentillesse; **3** (nutritive value) **to be full of ~** être plein de bonnes choses; **don't overcook the carrots, they lose all their ~** ne faites pas trop cuire les carottes ou elles perdront toutes leurs vertus; **the soil has lost its ~** le sol s'est appauvri.

II *excl* (also **~ gracious**) mon Dieu.

IDIOMS **I hope to ~ that** je prie le ciel que (+ *subj*); **I wish to ~ that he would write** si seulement il pouvait écrire; **~ only knows!** Dieu seul le sait!; **~ only knows how/when/why** Dieu (seul) sait comment/quand/pourquoi; **for ~' sake!** pour l'amour de Dieu!

goodnight /ˌɡʊdˈnaɪt/ **I** *n, excl* bonne nuit; **to say ~ to sb** dire bonne nuit à qn.

II *modif* **I gave him a ~ kiss** je l'ai embrassé pour lui souhaiter bonne nuit.

good: **Good Samaritan** *n* Bible, fig Bon Samaritain *m*; **Good Shepherd** *n* Relig Bon Pasteur *m*; **~-sized** *adj* [*kitchen, room*] spacieux/-ieuse; [*box, garden, pocket*] de bonne taille *inv*; **~-tempered** *adj* [*person*] facile; [*animal*] qui a bon caractère (*after n*); [*debate, remark, smile*] amical; **~-time girl** *n* péj (fun-loving) fêtarde○ *f*; euph (prostitute) fille *f* de joie.

goodwill /ˌɡʊdˈwɪl/ **I** *n* **1** (helpful attitude) bonne volonté *f*; **with ~ we'll succeed** avec de la bonne volonté nous réussirons; **a man of ~** un homme de bonne volonté; **2** (kindness) **to show ~ to** ou **towards sb** faire preuve de bienveillance à l'égard de qn; **he spoke with ~** il s'est exprimé avec bienveillance; **in a spirit of ~** en toute amitié; **to do sth with ~** faire qch de bon cœur; **the season of ~** le temps de Noël; **3** Comm (non-paper value) fonds *m* commercial; (reputation) actif *m* incorporel (*constitué par sa réputation*); (customers) clientèle *f*.

II *modif* [*gesture*] de bonne volonté; [*visite*] d'amitié.

goody○ /ˈɡʊdɪ/ **I** *n* (hero) bon *m*.

II *excl* lang enfantin chouette!

goody-goody /ˈɡʊdɪɡʊdɪ/ péj **I** *n* (both sexes) sainte nitouche *f*.

II *adj* [*child*] modèle.

goody two shoes○ /ˌɡʊdɪˈtuːʃuːz/ *n* péj modèle *m* de vertu iron.

gooey○ /ˈɡuːɪ/ *adj* **1** (sticky) gluant; **2** fig (sentimental) sentimental.

goof○ /ɡuːf/ **I** *n* **1** (idiot) dingue○ *mf*; **2** (blunder) gaffe○ *f*.

II *vtr* = **goof up**.

III *vi* faire une gaffe○ or une bévue○.

■ **goof around**○ (fool around) faire l'imbécile○ *mf*; (laze about) glander◑.

■ **goof off**○ US = **goof around**.

■ **goof on** US: **~ on [sb]** taquiner.

■ **goof up**○: ¶ **~ up** faire une gaffe○; ¶ **~ [sth] up, ~ up [sth]** massacrer○.

goofball○ /ˈɡuːfbɔːl/ *n* US **1** (fool) imbécile *mf*; **2** (drug) barbiturique *m*.

goof: **~-off**○ *n* US glandeur/-euse◑ *m/f*; **~-up**○ *n* US gaffe○ *f*, bévue○ *f*.

goofy○ /ˈɡuːfɪ/ *adj* dingue○.

goo-goo eyes○ /ˈɡuːɡuː aɪz/ *n* US yeux *mpl* de merlan frit○; **to make ~ at sb** faire des yeux de merlan frit○ à qn.

gook◑ /ɡuːk, ɡʊk/ *n* substance *f* visqueuse.

goolies◑ /ˈɡuːliːz/ *n* roupettes◑ *fpl*, testicules *mpl*.

goon○ /ɡuːn/ *n* **1** (clown) cinglé/-e○ *mf*; **he's a bit of a ~** il est un peu cinglé; **he's a real ~** péj il est complètement cinglé; **2** péj (thug) homme *m* de main; **~ squad** équipe *f* d'hommes de main.

gooney bird /ˈɡuːnɪbɜːd/ *n* US albatros *m*.

goop◑ /ɡuːp/ *n* **1** (substance) substance *f* visqueuse; **2** fig sentimentalité *f* à l'eau de rose.

goosander /ɡuːˈsændə(r)/ *n* harle *m* bièvre.

goose /ɡuːs/ **I** *n* (*pl* **geese**) Zool, Culin oie *f*; **you silly ~**○! idiot/-e!

II○ *vtr* pincer les fesses de.

IDIOMS **all his geese are swans** il prend ses vessies pour des lanternes; **to cook sb's ~**○ couler○ qn; **to kill the ~ that lays the golden eggs** tuer la poule aux œufs d'or.

gooseberry /ˈɡʊzbərɪ, US ˈɡuːsberɪ/ *n* (fruit) groseille *f* à maquereau.

IDIOMS **to be a** ou **play ~** tenir la chandelle; **to feel a ~** se sentir de trop.

gooseberry bush *n* groseillier *m*; **found under a ~** hum (of boy) né dans les choux; (of girl) née dans les roses.

gooseberry fool *n*: *purée de groseilles à maquereau à la crème.*

goose: **~bumps** *npl* = **goose pimples**; **~flesh** *n* = **goose pimples**.

goosegog○ /ˈɡʊzɡɒɡ/ *n* GB = **gooseberry**.

goosegrass /ˈguːsgrɑːs/ *n* grat(t)eron *m*.

goose pimples /ˈguːspɪmplz/ *npl* chair *f* de poule; **to come out in ~** avoir la chair de poule.

goose-step /ˈguːstep/ **I** *n* pas *m* de l'oie.
II *vi* défiler au pas de l'oie.

GOP *n* US Pol (*abrév* = **Grand Old Party**) parti *m* républicain.

gopher /ˈgəʊfə(r)/ *n* Zool gaufre *m*.

gorblimey○ /ˌgɔːˈblaɪmɪ/ GB **I** *adj* **~ accent** accent *m* des faubourgs.
II *excl* nom d'un chien○!

Gordian knot /ˌgɔːdɪənˈnɒt/ *n* Mythol nœud *m* gordien; fig **to cut the ~** trancher le nœud gordien.

gore /gɔː(r)/ **I** *n* **1** (blood) sang *m*; **2** (in fabric) panneau *m*.
II *vtr* [*bull, rhino*] encorner; **to ~ sb to death** tuer qn d'un coup de corne.

gored /gɔːd/ *adj* [*skirt*] à godets.

gorge /gɔːdʒ/ **I** *n* **1** Geog gorge *f*; **Cheddar/the Rhine ~** les gorges de Cheddar/du Rhin; **2** Anat gorge *f*, gosier *m*.
II *vi* = **gorge oneself**.
III *v refl* **to ~ oneself** se gaver (**on** de).
IDIOMS **to make sb's ~ rise** dégoûter or écœurer qn.

gorgeous /ˈgɔːdʒəs/ *adj* **1**○ (lovely) [*food, cake, scenery*] formidable○; [*kitten, baby*] adorable; [*weather, day, person*] splendide; **you look ~** tu as l'air splendide; **hello ~!** salut mignon/-onne○!; **2** (sumptuous) [*colour, velvet*] somptueux/-euse.

gorgeously /ˈgɔːdʒəslɪ/ *adv* [*furnished, coloured*] somptueusement.

gorgon /ˈgɔːgən/ **I** *n* fig (fearsome woman) gorgone *f*.
II Gorgon *pr n* Gorgone *f*.

gorilla /gəˈrɪlə/ *n* Zool, fig gorille *m*.

gormandize /ˈgɔːməndaɪz/ *vi* sout faire bonne chère.

gormless○ /ˈgɔːmlɪs/ *adj* GB empoté○.

gorp /gɔːp/ *n* US cocktail *m* de fruits secs (*consommé par les randonneurs*).

gorse /gɔːs/ *n* ¢ ajoncs *mpl*.

gorse bush *n* ajonc *m*.

gory /ˈgɔːrɪ/ *adj* [*film, battle*] sanglant; **the ~ details** fig hum les détails sanglants.

gosh○ /gɒʃ/ *excl* ça alors○!

goshawk /ˈgɒshɔːk/ *n* Zool autour *m*.

gosling /ˈgɒzlɪŋ/ *n* oison *m*.

go-slow /ˌgəʊˈsləʊ/ GB **I** *n* grève *f* perlée.
II *modif* [*tactics*] de la grève perlée.

gospel /ˈgɒspl/ **I** *n* Évangile *m*; **the ~ according to** l'Évangile selon; **to spread the ~** lit, fig répandre l'Évangile; **to take sth as ~** ou **~ truth** prendre qch pour parole d'évangile.
II *modif* **1** Mus **~ music** gospel *m*; **~ singer** chanteur/-euse *m/f* de gospel; **~ song** gospel *m*; **2** Relig [*oath*] prêté sur l'Évangile.

gossamer /ˈgɒsəmə(r)/ **I** *n* **1** ¢ littér (cobweb) fils *mpl* de la Vierge; **2** (fabric) étoffe *f* très légère.
II *adj* littér [*wings*] arachnéen/-éenne liter.

gossip /ˈgɒsɪp/ **I** *n* **1** (news) (malicious) commérages *mpl*, potins○ *mpl* (**about** sur); (not malicious) nouvelles *fpl* (**about** sur); **a piece of ~** un racontar○; **2** (chat) **do come for coffee and a ~** viens chez moi prendre un café et papoter; **to have a (good) ~** tailler une (bonne) bavette○; **3** (person) bavard/-e *m/f*.
II *vi* bavarder, papoter; péj faire des commérages (**about** sur).

gossip: **~ column** *n* échos *mpl*; **~ columnist** *n* échotier/-ière *m/f*.

gossiping /ˈgɒsɪpɪŋ/ **I** *n* bavardage *m*, commérage *m* pej.
II *adj* bavard.

gossipmonger /ˈgɒsɪpmʌŋgə(r)/ *n* bavard/-e *m/f*.

gossipy○ /ˈgɒsɪpɪ/ *adj* [*person*] péj cancanier/-ière pej; [*letter, book, style*] plein de potins○.

got /gɒt/ **1** *prét, pp* ▶ **get**; **2 to have ~** avoir; **we've ~ three children** nous avons trois enfants; **I've ~ a cold** j'ai un rhume; **what have you ~ in your pocket?** qu'est-ce que tu as dans ta poche?; **their house has ~ a big garden** leur maison a un grand jardin.
IDIOMS **to feel ~ at**○ se sentir persécuté.

gotcha○ /ˈgɒtʃə/ *excl* (catching hold of sb) je t'ai eu; (catching sb in the act) vu.

goth, **Goth** /gɒθ/ *n* **1** Hist Goth *m*; **2** GB (cult member) *type de punk qui s'habille en noir*.

gothic, **Gothic** /ˈgɒθɪk/ ▶ **1402** **I** *n* **1** Archit, Print gothique *m*; **2** (language) gotique *m*.
II *adj* Archit, Print gothique; Literat, fig [*gloom, horror*] noir.

gotta○ /ˈgɒtə/ **1** = **got to**; **2** = **got a**.

gotten /ˈgɒtn/ *pp* US ▶ **get**.

gouache /ˈgʊɑːʃ/ *n* gouache *f*.

gouge /gaʊdʒ/ **I** *n* **1** (tool) gouge *f*; **2** (scratch) rainure *f*.
II *vtr* **1** (dig) creuser [*hole*] (**in** dans); **2**○ US (overcharge) estamper○.
■ **gouge out**: **~ out [sth]**, **~ [sth] out** creuser [*pattern*]; enlever [*bad bit*]; **to ~ sb's eyes out** arracher les yeux à qn.

goulash /ˈguːlæʃ/ *n* goulasch *m* ou *f*.

gourd /gʊəd/ *n* **1** (container) gourde *f*; **2** (fruit) calebasse *f*; **3**○ US (head) calebasse○ *f*.
IDIOMS **to be out of one's ~**○ US être toqué○.

gourmand /ˈgʊəmənd/ *n* gourmand/-e *m/f*.

gourmet /ˈgʊəmeɪ/ **I** *n* gourmet *m*.
II *modif* [*restaurant, food, meal*] gastronomique.

gout /gaʊt/ ▶ **1354** *n* Med goutte *f*.

gouty /ˈgaʊtɪ/ *adj* goutteux/-euse.

gov *n*: *abrév* = **guv**.

Gov *n*: *abrév écrite* = **Governor**.

govern /ˈgʌvn/ **I** *vtr* **1** Admin, Pol gouverner [*country, state, city*]; administrer [*colony, province*]; **2** (control) [*law, principle*] régir [*conduct, manufacture, sale, treatment, use*]; dominer [*relationship, person*]; **3** (determine) déterminer [*actions, character, development, decision*]; **the basic salary is ~ed by three factors** le salaire de base est déterminé par trois facteurs; **4** sout (restrain) maîtriser, gouverner fml [*feelings, temper*]; **5** Ling régir; **6** Elec, Tech régler [*flow, input, speed*].
II *vi* [*parliament, president*] gouverner; [*administrator, governor*] administrer.

governance /ˈgʌvənəns/ *n* sout gouvernement *m*.

governess /ˈgʌvənɪs/ *n* (*pl* **~es**) gouvernante *f*.

governing /ˈgʌvənɪŋ/ *adj* [*party*] au pouvoir; [*factor*] décisif/-ive; [*class*] dirigeant; **the ~ principle** ou **concept behind socialism** l'idée directrice qui sous-tend le socialisme.

governing body *n* **1** GB (of school) conseil *m* d'établissement; (of university) conseil *m* d'Université; (of hospital, prison) conseil *m* d'administration; **2** (of sport) organisation *f* dirigeante; **3** (of trade, professional organization) comité *m* directeur.

government /ˈgʌvənmənt/ **I** *n* **1** ¢ (exercise of authority) (political) gouvernement *m*; (administrative) administration *f*; **he has no experience of ~** il n'a aucune expérience du gouvernement; **democratic ~** gouvernement démocratique; **parliamentary ~** régime *m* parlementaire; **2 C** (ruling body) (+ *v sg* ou + *v pl*) gouvernement *m*; (the State) l'État *m*; **to form a ~** former un gouvernement; **the ~ of Brazil** le gouvernement du Brésil; **the Churchill ~** le gouvernement Churchill; **our party is in ~** notre parti est au pouvoir; **3** Ling rection *f*.
II *modif* [*minister, official, plan, intervention, investigator*] du gouvernement; [*agency, decree, department, grant, majority, policy, publication*] gouvernemental; [*expenditure, borrowing*] de l'État; [*loan, funds*] public/-ique.

Government Accounting Office *pr n* US service *m* de comptabilité du gouvernement américain, cf Cour *f* des Comptes.

governmental /ˌgʌvənˈmentl/ *adj* gouvernemental.

government: **~ bond** *n* Fin obligation *f* d'État; **~ contractor** *n*: *entreprise privée travaillant sous contrat pour l'État*; **~ corporation** *n* US régie *f* d'État; **~ employee** ▶ **1692** *n* agent *m* du secteur public; **~-funded** *adj* financé par l'État; **Government House** *n* GB Pol résidence *f* du gouverneur; **~ issue** *adj* [*equipment etc*] fourni par l'État; [*bonds*] émis par l'État; **~ office** *n* administration *f*; **~ official** ▶ **1692** *n* fonctionnaire *mf*; **Government Printing Office** *pr n* US *service gouvernemental chargé de l'impression des documents et formulaires officiels*; **~ securities** *npl*, **~ stock** *n* ¢ titres *mpl* d'État.

governor /ˈgʌvənə(r)/ *n* **1** (of state, province, colony) gouverneur *m*; GB (of bank) gouverneur *m*; (of prison) directeur *m*; (of school) membre *m* du conseil d'établissement; (of university) membre *m* du conseil de l'Université; (of hospital) membre *m* du conseil d'administration; **2**○ GB (boss) patron *m*; **3** Ling régissant *m*; **4** Elec, Tech régulateur *m*.

Governor-General *n* GB Pol Gouverneur *m* général.

governorship /ˈgʌvənəʃɪp/ *n* (office of governor) fonctions *fpl* de gouverneur; (act of governing) direction *f*; **during the ~ of Mr Eavis** pendant que M. Eavis était gouverneur, sous la direction de M. Eavis.

govt *n*: *abrév écrite* = **government**.

gown /gaʊn/ *n* (for evening wear) robe *f*; (of judge, academic) toge *f*; (of surgeon) blouse *f*; (of patient) chemise *f* (d'hôpital).

gowned /gaʊnd/ *adj* [*scholar, lawyer*] en toge; [*woman*] US en robe du soir.

goy /gɔɪ/ *n* (*pl* **~im** or **~s**) goy *mf*.

GP ▶ **1692** *n* (*abrév* = **General Practitioner**) médecin *m* généraliste.

GPO *n* **1** GB (*abrév* = **General Post Office**) service *m* postal; **2** US (*abrév* = **Government Printing Office**) Imprimerie *f* nationale.

gr **1** *abrév écrite* = **gram**; **2** *abrév écrite* = **gross**.

grab /græb/ **I** *n* **1** (snatch) geste *m* vif; **to make a ~ at** ou **for sth** essayer d'attraper qch; **to be up for ~s**○ être bon à prendre; **2** (on excavator) pelle *f* automatique.
II *vtr* (*p prés etc* **-bb-**) **1** (take hold of) (also **~ hold of**) empoigner [*money, toy*]; saisir, attraper [*arm, person*]; fig saisir [*opportunity, chance*]; **to ~ sth from sb** arracher qch à qn; **to ~ hold of sb/sth** se saisir de qn/qch; **to ~ sb by the arm** saisir qn par le bras; **to ~ all the attention** accaparer toute l'attention; **2** (illegally) accaparer [*land, resources*]; **3** (snatch) **to ~ some sleep** dormir un peu, piquer un roupillon○; **to ~ a snack** manger en vitesse or vite fait; **I ~bed two hours' sleep** j'ai réussi à dormir deux heures; **4**○ (impress) **how does he/the idea ~ you?** qu'est-ce que tu penses de lui/dis de cette idée?
III *vi* (*p prés etc* **-bb-**) **to ~ at** se jeter sur [*money, sweets*].

grab bag *n* US **1** (lucky-dip) sac *m* à surprises (*pour la pêche miraculeuse*); **2** (miscellany) fourre-tout *m inv*.

grace /greɪs/ **I** *n* **1** (physical charm) (of movement, body, person, architecture) grâce *f*; **to do sth with ~** faire qch avec grâce; **to have ~/no ~** avoir de la/ne pas avoir de grâce; **2** (dignity, graciousness) grâce *f*; **to do sth with (a) good/bad ~** faire qch de bonne/mauvaise grâce; **to accept sth with (good) ~** accepter qch avec bonne grâce; **to have the ~ to do** avoir la bonne grâce

de faire; **3** (spiritual) grâce *f*; **in a state of ~** en état de grâce; **to fall from ~** Relig perdre la grâce; fig tomber en disgrâce; **by the ~ of God** par la grâce de Dieu; **4** (time allowance) **to give sb two days' ~** accorder un délai de deux jours à qn; (to debtor) accorder un délai de grâce de deux jours à qn; **you have one week's ~ to do** je vous accorde un délai d'une semaine pour faire; **a period of ~** un délai; **5** (prayer) (before meal) bénédicité *m*; (after meal) grâces *fpl*; **to say ~** dire le bénédicité or les grâces; **6** (quality) **sb's saving ~** ce qui sauve qn; **the film's saving ~ is** ce qui sauve le film c'est; **7** (mannerism) **to have all the social ~s** avoir beaucoup de savoir-vivre.
II *vtr* **1** (decorate) [*statue, flowers, picture*] orner, embellir; **to be ~d with** être orné de [*façade, square*]; **2** (honour) honorer; **to ~ sb with one's presence** aussi iron honorer qn de sa présence also iron; **3** (bless) **to be ~d with** être doué de [*beauty, intelligence*].
IDIOMS **there but for the ~ of God go I** ça aurait aussi bien pu m'arriver; **to be in sb's good ~s** être dans les bonnes grâces de qn; **to put on airs and ~s** péj prendre des airs.

Grace /greɪs/ **I** ▶ 1268 *n* **1** (title of archbishop) **His/Your ~** Monseigneur; **2** (title of duke) **His/Your ~** Monsieur le duc; (of duchess) **Her/Your ~** Madame la duchesse.
II Graces *npl* Mythol **the ~s** les trois Grâces *fpl*.

grace-and-favour /ˌgreɪsən'feɪvə(r)/ *adj* GB **~ residence** *résidence prêtée par le souverain en reconnaissance de services rendus.*

graceful /'greɪsfl/ *adj* **1** [*dancer, movement, style*] gracieux/-ieuse; **2** [*person, building, city, curve*] élégant; **3** [*apology, excuse*] élégant; **to make a ~ exit** lit, fig quitter dignement la scène.

gracefully /'greɪsfəlɪ/ *adv* **1** [*move, slide, dive*] avec grâce; **2** [*admit, accept, concede*] gracieusement.
IDIOMS **to grow old ~** vieillir avec grâce.

gracefulness /greɪsflnɪs/ *n* grâce *f*.

graceless /'greɪslɪs/ *adj* [*refusal, manner*] inélégant; [*city, individual*] dépourvu de charme, sans charme.

grace: **~ note** *n* ornement *m*; **~ period** *n* délai *m* de grâce.

gracious /'greɪʃəs/ **I** *adj* **1** (generous, dignified) [*person*] affable; [*acceptance, admission*] fait de bon gré; **to be ~ (to sb) about** ne pas en vouloir à qn pour [*mistake, failure*]; **to be ~ in defeat** accepter la défaite avec bonne grâce; **it is ~ of you to say so** c'est aimable à vous de dire cela; **2** (aristocratic) [*lady, smile, wave*] (pleasant) affable; (condescending) condescendant; **~ living** vie *f* de luxe; **3** (in royal title) gracieux/-ieuse; **by ~ permission of** par la grâce de; **4** Relig [*God*] miséricordieux.
II † *excl* mon dieu!; **~ me!, good(ness) ~!** mon dieu!; **~ no!** jamais de la vie!

graciously /'greɪʃəslɪ/ *adv* [*accept, concede, wave*] gracieusement; **he ~ agreed to come** iron il a daigné venir iron; **His Majesty is ~ pleased to accept** Sa Majesté a la bonté d'accepter.

graciousness /'greɪʃəsnɪs/ *n* courtoisie *f*; **sb's ~ in defeat** la bonne grâce avec laquelle qn accepte la défaite.

gradable /'greɪdəbl/ *adj* Ling [*adjective*] non absolu.

gradate /grə'deɪt/ **I** *vtr* trier.
II *vi* se dégrader (**from** de, **to** à).

gradation /grə'deɪʃn/ *n* **1** (on a continuum) gradation *f*; **colour ~s** Art gradations *fpl* de couleurs; **~ in, ~ of** gradation de [*colour, size, tone*]; **~s of feeling** des degrés d'émotion; **2** (in power structure) échelon *m*; **3** Meas (on scale) graduation *f*.

grade /greɪd/ **I** *n* **1** Comm (of produce, article, goods) qualité *f*; (of egg) calibre *m*; **high-/low-~** de qualité supérieure/inférieure; **low-~ imitation/literature** imitation/littérature médiocre; **small-/large-~ eggs** œufs de petit/gros calibre; **2** Sch, Univ (mark) note *f* (**in** en); **to get good ~s** avoir de bonnes notes; **to get ~ A** ou **an A ~** ≈ avoir plus de 16 sur 20; **what are the ~s required to study medicine?** quel est le niveau requis pour faire des études en médecine?; **3** (in power structure) Admin échelon *m*; Mil rang *m*; **senior-/low-~ employee** employé/-e *m/f* d'un échelon supérieur/inférieur; **a top-~ civil servant** un fonctionnaire de haut rang; **salary ~** échelon *m* de salaire; **4** US Sch (class) classe *f*; **she's in the eighth ~** ≈ elle est en (classe de) quatrième; **5** (also **Grade**) (level of difficulty) niveau *m*; **~ IV piano** Mus niveau 4 de piano; **6** US (gradient) pente *f*; **on a steep ~** dans une côte raide; **7** Agric (in breeding) (horse) demi-sang *m*; (cow) vache *f* de croisement; (sheep) mouton *m* de croisement.
II *vtr* **1** (categorize) (by quality) classer [*produce, accommodation, amenities, results*] (**according to** selon); (by size) calibrer [*eggs, fruit, potatoes*] (**according to** selon); **2** Sch (in level of difficulty) graduer [*exercises, tasks, questions*] (**according to** selon); **3** US (mark) noter [*work, assignment*] (**from** de; **to** à); **4** Art (blend) dégrader [*colours, tones*]; **5** Agric (in breeding) améliorer [qch] par sélection [*animal, stock*]; **6** Civ Eng niveler [*ground*].
III graded *pp adj* (categorized) [*tests, exercises*] classé par ordre de difficulté; [*hotel*] classé NN.
IDIOMS **to make the ~** se montrer à la hauteur.
■ **grade down** GB Sch: **~ [sth] down** abaisser [*marks*].
■ **grade up** GB Sch: **~ [sth] up** relever [*marks*].

grade: **~ book** *n* US carnet *m* de notes; **~ crossing** *n* US Rail passage *m* à niveau; **~ inflation** *n* US surnotation *f*; **~ point average** *n* US Sch, Univ moyenne *f*.

grader /'greɪdə(r)/ **I** *n* **1** (of produce) (machine) calibreur *m*; (person) classeur/-euse *m/f*; **2** Civ Eng niveleuse *f*.
II -grader (*dans composés*) US **eighth/ninth-~** ≈ élève de quatrième/de troisième.

grade: **~ school** *n* US école *f* primaire; **~ school teacher** ▶ 1692 *n* US Sch instituteur/-trice *m/f*.

gradient /'greɪdɪənt/ *n* **1** (slope) pente *f*; **to be on a ~** être en pente; **2** Meas (degree of slope) rampe *f*; **a ~ of 8%** une rampe de 8%; **3** Math, Phys gradient *m*; **temperature ~** gradient *m* de température.

grading /'greɪdɪŋ/ *n* **1** (classification) gen classification *f*; (of personnel) échelonnement *m*; **2** Sch (marking) notation *f*.

grading system *n* système *m* de notation.

gradual /'grædʒʊəl/ **I** *n* Mus, Relig graduel *m*.
II *adj* **1** (slow) [*change, increase, decline, progress*] progressif/-ive; **2** (gentle) [*slope, incline*] doux/douce.

gradualism /'grædʒʊəlɪzəm/ *n* Econ, Philos gradualisme *m*.

gradualist /'grædʒʊəlɪst/ *n, adj* Econ, Philos gradualiste (*mf*).

gradually /'grædʒʊlɪ/ *adv* progressivement; **~, he...** peu à peu, il...

graduate I /'grædʒʊət/ *n* **1** Univ diplômé/-e *m/f*; (**in** en; **of, from** de); **arts/science ~** diplômé/-e *m/f* en lettres/sciences; **Oxford ~** diplômé/-e *m/f* de l'Université d'Oxford; **2** US Sch (from high school) bachelier/-ière *m/f*; **he is a high school ~** ≈ il a le baccalauréat.
II /'grædʒʊət/ *modif* [*course, student, studies*] ≈ de troisième cycle; [*accommodation, centre*] pour étudiants de troisième cycle.
III /'grædjʊeɪt/ *vtr* **1** Tech graduer [*container, scale*]; **2** US (give degree to) conférer un diplôme à [*student*]; **3**○ US (get degree from) sortir de [*institution*].
IV /'grædjʊeɪt/ *vi* **1** terminer mes/ses etc études (**at** ou **from** à); US Sch ≈ finir le lycée; **2** (progress) **to ~ (from sth) to sth** passer (de qch) à qch.
V graduated /'grædjʊeɪtɪd/ *pp adj* Soc Admin [*contribution, scale, system, tax*] proportionnel/-elle; **~ed pension scheme** régime *m* de retraite complémentaire.

graduate: **~ assistant** *n* US assistant/-e *m/f* (*chargé de TD*); **~ profession** *n* profession *f* où l'on exige un diplôme universitaire; **~ recruit** *n* recrue *f* diplômée; **~ school** *n* US ≈ troisième cycle *m*; **~ teacher** *n* professeur *m* licencié; **~ training scheme** *n* GB programme *m* de formation professionnelle pour étudiants diplômés.

graduation /ˌgrædʒʊ'eɪʃn/ *n* **1** Univ (ceremony) remise *f* des diplômes; (end of course) obtention *f* d'un diplôme; **2** (calibration) graduation *f*; **3** US = **graduation ceremony**.

graduation ceremony *n* cérémonie *f* de la remise des diplômes.

Graeco+, Greco+ US /graɪkəʊ-/ (*dans composés*) gréco-.

graffiti /grə'fi:tɪ/ *n* (+ *v sg ou pl*) graffiti *mpl*.

graffiti artist *n* tagger *m*.

graft /grɑ:ft, US græft/ **I** *n* **1** Hort, Med greffe *f*; **skin/vein ~** greffe *f* de la peau/de veine; **2**○ GB (work) boulot○ *m*; **hard ~** boulot○ *m* acharné; **3**○ (corruption) corruption *f*; (bribe) pot-de-vin *m*.
II *vtr* Hort, Med, fig greffer (**onto** sur).
III○ *vi* GB (work hard) bosser○.

grafter○ /'grɑ:ftə(r), US 'græftə(r)/ *n* **1** GB (hard worker) bourreau *m* de travail; **2** (corrupt person) individu *m* corrompu.

graft hybrid *n* hybride *m* issu de greffe.

graham: **~ cracker** *n* US *biscuit peu sucré à la farine complète*; **~ flour** *n* US farine *f* complète.

Grail /greɪl/ *n* ▶ **Holy Grail**.

grain /greɪn/ **I** *n* **1** (commodity) céréales *fpl*; **~ prices** le prix des céréales; **2** (seed) (of rice, wheat) grain *m*; **long/short ~ rice** riz *m* long/rond; **3** (small piece) (of sand, salt) grain *m*; **4** fig (of truth, hope, comfort) brin *m*; **5** (pattern) (in wood) grain *m*, veines *fpl*; (in stone) veines *fpl*; (in leather, paper, fabric) grain *m*; **to cut along/across the ~** couper dans le fil/contre le fil; **6** Phot grain *m*; **7** Meas (weight) grain *m* (= 0.0648g).
II *vtr* (stain) veiner [*wood*]; grainer [*leather, paper*].
III grained *pp adj* [*worktop, table*] veiné; [*leather, paper*] grainé.
IDIOMS **it goes against the ~** c'est contre nature.

grain: **~ alcohol** *n* alcool *m* de grain; **~ elevator** *n* Agric silo *m* à grains.

graininess /'greɪnɪnɪs/ *n* Phot grain *m* grossier.

grainy /'greɪnɪ/ *adj* **1** Phot [*photograph, picture*] qui a du grain; **2** (resembling wood) veiné; (resembling leather) grainé; **3** (granular) [*substance*] granuleux/-euse.

gram(me) /græm/ ▶ 1883 *n* gramme *m*.

grammar /'græmə(r)/ **I** *n* **1** grammaire *f*; **to use bad ~** faire des fautes de grammaire; **that's bad ~** c'est grammaticalement incorrect; **2** (also **~ book**) grammaire *f*; **a French ~** une grammaire française.
II *modif* [*book, lesson, exercise*] de grammaire.

grammarian /grə'meərɪən/ *n* grammairien/-ienne *m/f*.

grammar school *n* **1** GB ≈ lycée (*à recrutement sélectif*); **2**† US école *f* primaire.

grammatical /grə'mætɪkl/ *adj* **1** Ling [*error*] de grammaire; [*meaning, gender, analysis*] grammatical; **2** (correct) grammaticalement correct.

grammaticality /grəˌmætɪ'kælətɪ/ *n* grammaticalité *f*.

grammatically /grəˈmætɪklɪ/ *adv* grammaticalement; **to speak/write ~** avoir une bonne grammaire.

grammaticalness /grəˈmætɪklnɪs/ *n* grammaticalité *f*.

grammatology /ˌgræməˈtɒlədʒɪ/ *n* grammatologie *f*.

grammen = **gram**.

Grammy /ˈgræmɪ/ *n* (*pl* **~s** ou **-mmies**) US Mus **to win a ~** ≈ être primé aux Victoires de la musique.

gramophone† /ˈgræməfəʊn/ **I** *n* phonographe *m*, gramophone® *m*.
II *modif* [*needle, record*] de phonographe.

Grampian: **the ~s, the ~ Mountains** *pr npl* les (monts *mpl*) Grampians *mpl*.

gramps○ /græmps/ *n* lang enfantin pépé○ *m*.

grampus /ˈgræmpəs/ *n* (*pl* **-puses**) (dolphin) dauphin *m* de Risso; (orca) orque *f* or *m*.

gran○ /græn/ *n* mémé○ *f*.

Granada /grəˈnɑːdə/ **▶ 1818** *pr n* Grenade.

granary /ˈgrænərɪ/ **I** *n* (grain store) grenier *m*; **Europe's ~** fig le grenier de l'Europe.
II *modif* GB [*bread, loaf*] complet/-ète (*avec des grains broyés*).

grand /grænd/ **I** *n* **1**○ (sum of money) GB mille livres *fpl* sterling, ≈ bâton *m*; US mille dollars *mpl*; **2**○ Mus (piano) piano *m* à queue.
II *adj* **1** (impressive) [*building, ceremony*] grandiose; [*park*] magnifique; **in ~ style** en grande pompe; **on a ~ scale** sur une très grande échelle; **in the ~ manner** dans un style de grand seigneur; **to make a ~ entry** faire une entrée spectaculaire; **the ~ old man of theatre/of letters** le grand monsieur du théâtre/de la littérature; **2** (self-important) **she's very ~** elle joue à la grande dame pej; **to put on a ~ air** prendre de grands airs; **3**○ (fine, excellent) **to have a ~ time** passer un moment formidable; **'is everything all right?' — 'it's ~ thanks'** 'tout va bien?' — 'très bien merci'; **he did a ~ job** il a fait un travail splendide; **that's ~!** c'est formidable!; **4** (in titles, names) grand, Grand.

Grand Canyon *pr n* Grand Cañon *m*.

grandchild /ˈgræntʃaɪld/ *n* (girl) petite-fille *f*; (boy) petit-fils *m*; **his ~ren** ses petits-enfants *mpl*.

granddad○ /ˈgrændæd/ *n* pépé○ *m*, papy○ *m*, papi *m*.

granddaddy○ /ˈgrændædɪ/ *n* **1** (grandfather) pépé○ *m*, papy○ *m*, papi *m*; **2** fig (precursor) ancêtre *mf*; **it's the ~ of them all** hum c'est l'ancêtre.

grand: **~daughter** *n* petite-fille *f*; **~ duchess** *n* grande-duchesse *f*; **~ duchy** *n* grand-duché *m*; **~ duke** *n* grand-duc *m*.

grandee /grænˈdiː/ *n* **1** (Spanish, Portuguese) grand *m* d'Espagne; **2** (eminent person) grand personnage *m*.

grandeur /ˈgrændʒə(r)/ *n* **1** (of scenery) majesté *f*; (of building) caractère *m* grandiose; **2** (of character) noblesse *f*; (power, status) éminence *f*.

grand: **~father** /ˈgrænfɑːðə(r)/ *n* grand-père *m*; **~father clause** *n* Jur clause *f* de non-rétroactivité; **~father clock** *n* horloge *f* comtoise; **~ finale** *n* finale *m*.

grandiloquence /ˌgrænˈdɪləkwəns/ *n* sout grandiloquence *f*.

grandiloquent /ˌgrænˈdɪləkwənt/ *adj* sout grandiloquent.

grandiose /ˈgrændɪəʊs/ *adj* grandiose.

grand: **~ jury** *n* US *jury qui décide s'il y a motif à inculpation*; **~ larceny** *n* US vol *m* qualifié.

grandma, **grandmamma**† /ˈgrænmɑː/ *n* mémé *f*, mamy *f*, mamie *f*.

grand mal /grɑː ˈmæl/ **▶ 1354** *n* grand mal *m*.

grand: **~ master** *n* (in chess) grand maître *m*; **Grand Master** *n* (of Masonic lodge) Vénérable *m*; (of Templars) Grand Maître *m*.

grandmother /ˈgrænmʌðə(r)/ *n* grand-mère *f*.
IDIOMS **to teach one's ~ to suck eggs** apprendre à un vieux singe à faire la grimace.

grand: **~mother clock** *n* horloge *f* comtoise (*de petit modèle*); **Grand National** *n* GB Turf Grand National *m*; **Grand Old Party**, **GOP** *n* US Pol parti *m* républicain; **~ opera** *n* grand opéra *m*; **~pa**○ *n* pépé○ *m*, papy○ *m*, papi *m*.

grandparent /ˈgrænpeərənt/ *n* (male) grand-père *m*; (female) grand-mère *f*; **my ~s** mes grands-parents *mpl*.

grand: **~ piano** **▶ 1481** *n* piano *m* à queue; **~ prix** *n* (*pl* **~**) grand prix *m*.

grand slam /ˌgrændˈslæm/ *n* Games, Sport grand chelem *m*; **a ~ in spades** un grand chelem à pique; **a ~ tournament** un tournoi comptant pour le grand chelem.

grand: **~son** /ˈgrænsən/ *n* petit-fils *m*; **~ staircase** *n* escalier *m* d'honneur.

grandstand /ˈgrænstænd/ *n* **1** (at stadium) tribune *f*; **to have a ~ view** ou **seat** lit, fig être aux premières loges; **2** (audience) public *m*.
IDIOMS **to play to the ~** US jouer pour la galerie.

grand total *n* total *m*; **the ~ for the repairs came to £3000** en tout, les travaux sont revenus à 3 000 livres sterling.

grand tour *n* **1 he took me on a ~ of the house** il m'a fait visiter toute la maison; **2** (also **Grand Tour**) Hist tour *m* d'Europe; **to do the ~** visiter l'Europe.

grange /greɪndʒ/ *n* **1** GB (house) manoir *m*; **2** US (farm) ferme *f*.

granite /ˈgrænɪt/ **I** *n* granit(e) *m*; **heart of ~** fig cœur de granit.
II *modif* [*hill, rock*] de granite; [*building, sculpture*] de granit.

granitic /grəˈnɪtɪk/ *adj* granitique.

granny○ /ˈgrænɪ/ *n* **1** (grandmother) bonne-maman *f*, mamie○ *f*; **2** pej (fusspot, gossip) vieille mémère○.

granny: **~ bond**○ *n* GB bon *m* du Trésor indexé; **~ flat** *n* GB petit appartement *m* indépendant (*pour parent âgé*); **~ knot** *n* nœud *m* de vache; **Granny Smith** *n* Granny Smith *f inv*; **~ specs**○ *n* petites lunettes *fpl* rondes.

granola /grəˈnəʊlə/ *n* US müesli *m*.

grant /grɑːnt, US grænt/ **I** *n* **1** (from government, local authority) subvention *f* (**for** pour); (for study) Sch, Univ bourse *f*; **~s to the voluntary sector/to the poorest applicants** subventions au bénévolat/pour les candidats les plus pauvres; **a ~ to set up a new company/to improve a property** une subvention destinée à fonder une nouvelle société/à mettre en valeur une propriété; **to apply for a ~** gen faire une demande de subvention; (for study) faire une demande de bourse; **research ~** subvention *f* de recherche; **2** Jur (of property) cession *f*.
II *vtr* **1** sout (allow) accorder [*permission*]; accéder à [*request*]; **he was ~ed permission to leave early** l'autorisation de partir tôt lui a été accordée; **to refuse to ~ access to one's home** refuser l'accès à son domicile; **permission ~ed!** permission accordée!; **God ~ that** plaise à Dieu que (+ *subj*); **2** (give) **to ~ sb sth, to ~ sth to sb** accorder qch à qn [*interview, audience, leave, visa, licence, loan*]; concéder qch à qn [*citizenship, asylum, privilege*]; **3** (concede) reconnaître [*truth, validity etc*]; **to ~ that** reconnaître que; **I ~ you that he's gifted** je vous accorde qu'il est doué; **~ed that, ~ing that** en admettant que... (+ *subj*).
IDIOMS **to take sth for ~ed** considérer qch comme allant de soi; **he takes his mother for ~ed** il croit que sa mère est à son service; **he takes too much for ~ed** il croit que tout lui est dû.

grant aid /ˈgrɑːnteɪd, US ˈgrænt-/ *n* ¢ (within a country) subventions *fpl* (**for** pour); (abroad, to Third World) aide *f* au développement (**for** pour).

grant-aided /ˌgrɑːntˈeɪdɪd, US ˌgrænt-/ *adj* subventionné.

granted /ˈgrɑːntɪd, US ˈgrænt-/ *adv* **~, it's magnificent, but very expensive** c'est magnifique, soit, mais cela coûte très cher.

grantee /ˌgrɑːnˈtiː/ *n* Jur cessionnaire *mf*.

granting /ˈgrɑːntɪŋ, US ˈgrænt-/ *n* (of asylum, citizenship, bail) octroi *m*; (of licence, visa) concession *f*, octroi *m*; (of sum of money) allocation *f*; **the ~ of access** l'autorisation *f* d'accès.

grant: **~-maintained** *adj* [*school*] subventionné par l'État; **~ of probate** *n* homologation *f* (d'une succession).

grantor /grɑːnˈtɔː(r)/ *n* Jur cédant/-e *m/f*.

granular /ˈgrænjʊlə(r)/ *adj* [*surface, texture etc*] granuleux/-euse; [*fertilizer*] granulé.

granulate /ˈgrænjʊleɪt/ **I** *vtr* granuler [*metal*]; grener [*salt, sugar*]; rendre [qch] grenu [*texture*].
II granulated *pp adj* [*paper*] grenelé; [*sugar*] cristallisé.

granulation /ˌgrænjʊˈleɪʃn/ *n* (of metal) granulation *f*; (of salt, sugar) grenage *m*.

granule /ˈgrænjuːl/ *n* (of sugar, salt) grain *m*; (of instant coffee) granulé *m*; **polystyrene ~s** billes *fpl* de polystyrène.

grape /greɪp/ **I** *n* grain *m* de raisin; **a bunch of ~s** une grappe de raisin; **to eat/buy (some) ~s** manger/acheter du raisin; **I love ~s** j'adore le raisin; **to harvest** ou **bring in the ~s** vendanger.
II *modif* [*juice, jelly*] de raisin.
IDIOMS **sour ~s!** les raisins sont trop verts!

grapefruit /ˈgreɪpfruːt/ **I** *n* pamplemousse *m*.
II *modif* [*juice, marmalade*] de pamplemousse.

grape: **~ harvest** *n* vendange *f*; **~ hyacinth** *n* Bot muscari *m*; **~ ivy** *n* Bot cissus *m* rhombifolia; **~seed oil** *n* Culin huile *f* de pépins de raisin; **~shot** *n* Mil mitraille *f*.

grapevine /ˈgreɪpvaɪn/ *n* (in vineyard) pied *m* de vigne; (in greenhouse, garden) vigne *f*.
IDIOMS **to hear sth on the ~** apprendre qch par le téléphone arabe.

graph /grɑːf, US græf/ **I** *n* **1** Comput, Math graphique *m*; **a rising/falling ~** une courbe ascendante/descendante; **2** Ling unité *f* graphique.
II *vtr* tracer le graphique or la courbe de.

grapheme /ˈgræfiːm/ *n* graphème *m*.

graphic /ˈgræfɪk/ **I graphics** *npl* **1** Comput visualisation *f* graphique; **computer ~s** infographie *f*; **2** (in film, TV) images *fpl*; (in book) illustrations *fpl*; **'~s by...'** 'mise en images de...'; **3** Art arts *mpl* graphiques.
II *adj* **1** Art, Comput graphique; **2** [*account, description*] (of sth pleasant) vivant; (of sth unpleasant) cru.

graphically /ˈgræfɪklɪ/ *adv* **1** [*describe*] (sth pleasant) d'une manière vivante; (sth unpleasant) crûment; **2** (diagrammatically) graphiquement.

graphic: **~ art** *n* art *m* graphique; **~ artist** **▶ 1692** *n* graphiste *mf*; **~ arts** *npl* arts *mpl* graphiques; **~ data processing** *n* Comput infographie *f*; **~ design** *n* Art graphisme *m*; **~ designer** **▶ 1692** *n* graphiste *mf*, concepteur/-trice *m/f* graphique; **~ display**, **graphical display** *n* Comput visualisation *f* graphique; **~ equalizer** *n* Audio correcteur *m* de fréquences, égaliseur *m* graphique.

graphite /ˈgræfaɪt/ **I** *n* graphite *m*.
II *modif* [*tennis racquet, fishing rod*] en fibre de carbone.

graphologist /grəˈfɒlədʒɪst/ **▶ 1692** *n* graphologue *mf*.

graphology /grəˈfɒlədʒɪ/ *n* graphologie *f*.

graph: **~ paper** *n* papier *m* millimétré; **~ plotter** *n* Comput table *f* traçante.

grapnel /ˈgræpnəl/ *n* grappin *m*.

grapple /ˈgræpl/ **I** *vtr* Naut saisir avec un grappin.
II *vi* **to ~ with** lit lutter avec [*person*]; fig se colleter avec [*problem, difficulty*].

grappling iron *n* grappin *m*.

grasp /grɑːsp, US græsp/ **I** *n* **1** (hold, grip) prise *f*; (stronger) poigne *f*; **to hold sth in one's ~** lit tenir qch fermement; fig tenir qch bien en main; **to hold sb in one's ~** fig tenir qn sous son emprise; **to take a firm ~ of sth** empoigner fermement qch; **she managed to slip from his ~** elle a réussi à lui faire lâcher prise; **the pen slipped from his ~** le stylo lui a glissé des doigts; **success is within their ~** le succès est à leur portée; **2** (understanding) maîtrise *f*; **to have a good ~ of a subject** avoir une bonne maîtrise d'un sujet, bien maîtriser un sujet; **he has a poor ~ of maths** il ne comprend pas grand-chose aux maths; **to have a sound ~ of economics** avoir de solides notions d'économie; **it is beyond the ~ of the imagination** cela dépasse l'imagination.
II *vtr* **1** lit empoigner [*rope, hand*]; fig saisir [*opportunity*]; **to ~ hold of sb/sth** saisir qn/qch; **2** (comprehend) saisir, comprendre [*concept, subject*]; suivre [*argument*]; se rendre compte de [*situation, significance*]; **to ~ that** comprendre que; **I don't quite ~ your meaning** je ne comprends pas tout à fait ce que vous voulez dire.
III *vi* **to ~ at** tenter de saisir [*rope, hand*]; fig s'efforcer de comprendre [*idea, meaning*]; **he'll ~ at any excuse** pour lui toutes les excuses sont bonnes.

grasping /ˈgrɑːspɪŋ, US ˈgræspɪŋ/ *adj* **1** péj (greedy) cupide; **2** [*fingers, paws*] crochu.

grass /grɑːs, US græs/ **I** *n* **1** ¢ (wild) herbe *f* also Agric; **in the ~** dans l'herbe; **a blade/a tuft of ~** un brin/une touffe d'herbe; **to put out to ~** lit, fig hum mettre au vert; **2** ¢ (lawn) pelouse *f*; **on the ~** sur la pelouse; **keep off the ~!** défense de marcher sur les pelouses!; **to mow** ou **cut the ~** tondre la pelouse; **3** ¢ (in tennis) gazon *m*; **to play/to beat sb on ~** jouer/battre qn sur gazon; **4** Bot **C** graminée *f*; **5**○ ¢ (marijuana) herbe○ *f*; **6**○ GB (informer) mouchard○ *m*.
II *modif* [*field, slope, verge*] gazonné.
III *vtr* **1** recouvrir [qch] d'herbe [*field*]; gazonner [*part of garden*]; **2** US Agric donner du fourrage vert à [*cattle*].
IV○ *vi* GB (inform) moucharder○; **to ~ on sb** balancer○ qn.
IDIOMS **the ~ is greener (on the other side of the fence)** on croit toujours que c'est mieux ailleurs; **he doesn't let the ~ grow under his feet** il ne laisse pas traîner les choses; **it was so quiet you could hear the ~ growing** on aurait pu entendre une mouche voler.
■ **grass over**: **~ over [sth], ~ [sth] over** recouvrir [qch] d'herbe [*field, road*]; gazonner [*area*].

grass: **~ box** GB, **~ catcher** US *n* bac *m* de ramassage; **~ court** *n* court *m* en gazon; **~ cuttings** *npl* herbe *f* coupée ¢; **~ green** ▶ 1104 *n, adj* vert (*m*) gazon (*inv*).

grasshopper /ˈgrɑːshɒpə(r), US ˈgræs-/ *n* **1** Zool sauterelle *f*; **2**○ US Mil avion *m* d'observation.
IDIOMS **kneehigh to a ~** haut comme trois pommes.

grassland /ˈgrɑslənd, US ˈgræs-/ *n* prairie *f*.

grassroots /ˌgrɑːsˈruːts, US ˌgræs-/ **I** *npl* **the ~** le peuple.
II *modif* [*candidate*] issu du peuple; [*movement*] populaire; [*opinion, support*] de base; **at ~ level** à un niveau de base.

grass: **~-seed** *n* (*pl inv*) graine *f* de gazon; **~ skirt** *n* pagne *m* d'herbes; **~ snake** *n* couleuvre *f*.

grass widow† /ˌgrɑːsˈwɪdəʊ, US ˌgræs-/ *n* hum **to be a ~** être temporairement célibataire.

grass widower /ˌgrɑːsˈwɪdəʊə(r), US ˌgræs-/ *n* hum célibataire *m*.

grassy /ˈgrɑːsɪ, US ˈgræsɪ/ *adj* herbeux/-euse.

grate /greɪt/ **I** *n* (fire-basket) grille *f* de foyer; (hearth) âtre *m*.
II *vtr* Culin râper [*cheese, nutmeg, carrot*]; **to ~ cheese over sth** parsemer qch de fromage râpé.
III *vi* **1** [*metal object*] grincer (**on** sur); **2** (annoy) agacer; **her voice ~s** sa voix m'agace; **to ~ on sb** ou **on sb's nerves** taper sur les nerfs de qn○; **her voice ~s on my ears** sa voix m'écorche les oreilles.
IV grated *pp adj* [*cheese, nutmeg, carrot*] râpé.

grateful /ˈgreɪtfl/ *adj* **1** (thankful) [*person*] reconnaissant (**to** à; **for** de); [*letter, kiss*] de reconnaissance; **to be ~ that** être heureux/-euse que (+ *subj*); **let's be ~ that it is only two hours late** estimons-nous heureux qu'il n'ait que deux heures de retard; **I would be ~ if you could reply** je vous serais reconnaissant de bien vouloir répondre; **with ~ thanks** avec mes or nos plus sincères remerciements; **2**† littér (welcome) agréable.

gratefully /ˈgreɪtfəlɪ/ *adv* [*smile, kiss, speak*] avec reconnaissance; **all donations ~ received** tous les dons seront les bienvenus.

grater /ˈgreɪtə(r)/ *n* râpe *f*.

gratification /ˌgrætɪfɪˈkeɪʃn/ *n* satisfaction *f*; **much to my ~** à ma grande satisfaction.

gratify /ˈgrætɪfaɪ/ **I** *vtr* faire plaisir à [*person*]; satisfaire [*desire, whim*].
II gratified *pp adj* [*person*] satisfait; [*sigh, murmur*] de satisfaction; **to be gratified that** être très heureux que (+ *subj*).
III gratifying *pres p adj* [*outcome*] satisfaisant; [*change*] agréable; **it is gratifying to know that** il est agréable d'apprendre que.

grating /ˈgreɪtɪŋ/ **I** *n* **1** (bars) grille *f*; **2** (noise) grincement *m*.
II *adj* [*noise*] grinçant; [*voice*] discordant.

gratis /ˈgreɪtɪs/ *adv* gratis.

gratitude /ˈgrætɪtjuːd, US -tuːd/ *n* reconnaissance *f* (**to, towards** envers; **for** de); **to owe sb a debt of ~** avoir une dette de reconnaissance envers qn.

gratuitous /grəˈtjuːɪtəs, US -ˈtuː-/ *adj* (all contexts) gratuit.

gratuitously /grəˈtjuːɪtəslɪ, US -ˈtuː-/ *adv* gratuitement.

gratuity /grəˈtjuːətɪ, US -ˈtuː-/ *n* **1** (tip) pourboire *m*; **2** GB (bonus) prime *f*.

Graubünden ▶ 1776 *pr n* **the canton of ~** le canton des Grisons, les Grisons.

grave[1] /greɪv/ **I** *n* (burial place) tombe *f*; **beyond the ~** après la mort; **from beyond the ~** d'outre-tombe; **to go to one's ~ believing that** rester convaincu jusque dans la tombe que; **to go to an early ~** avoir une fin prématurée.
II *adj* **1** (dangerous) [*illness, injury*] grave; [*risk*] sérieux/-ieuse; [*danger*] grand (*before n*); **2** (solemn) sérieux/-ieuse; **to look ~** avoir un air grave.
IDIOMS **to dance on sb's ~** danser sur la tombe de qn; **to dig one's own ~** creuser sa propre tombe; **to have one foot in the ~** avoir un pied dans la tombe; **somebody is walking over my ~** j'ai une angoisse; **to turn in one's ~** se retourner dans sa tombe.

grave[2] /grɑːv/ *n* (also **~ accent**) accent *m* grave; **e ~** e accent grave.

gravedigger /ˈgreɪvdɪgə(r)/ ▶ 1692 *n* fossoyeur *m*.

gravel /ˈgrævl/ **I** *n* **1** ¢ Constr (coarse) graviers *mpl*; (fine) gravillons *mpl*; **2** Med calculs *mpl*.
II *adj* (also **gravelled**, **graveled** US) [*path, road*] gravillonné.
III *vtr* gravillonner.

gravelly /ˈgrævəlɪ/ *adj* [*path*] caillouteux/-euse; [*voice*] râpeux/-euse.

gravel pit *n* gravière *f*.

gravely /ˈgreɪvlɪ/ *adv* **1** (extremely) [*concerned, disruptive*] sérieusement; [*displeased*] extrêmement; [*ill*] gravement; **to be ~ mistaken** se tromper lourdement; **2** (solemnly) [*say, nod*] gravement.

graven /ˈgreɪvn/ *adj* †ou littér gravé also fig; **~ image** Bible idole *f*.

graveness /ˈgreɪvnɪs/ *n* **1** (of demeanour) sérieux *m*; **2** (of situation, illness) gravité *f*.

graverobber /ˈgreɪvrɒbə(r)/ *n* déterreur *m* de cadavres.

graveside /ˈgreɪvsaɪd/ *n* **at the ~** (beside the grave) à côté de la tombe; (at the cemetery) au cimetière; **the mourners were gathered at the ~** tout le monde était rassemblé autour de la tombe.

gravestone /ˈgreɪvstəʊn/ *n* pierre *f* tombale.

graveyard /ˈgreɪvjɑːd/ *n* cimetière *m*; **the ~ of one's hopes** littér la fin de ses espoirs.

graveyard: **~ cough** *n* toux *f* caverneuse; **~ shift** *n* équipe *f* de nuit.

gravid /ˈgrævɪd/ *adj* gravide.

gravitas /ˈgrævɪtæs, -tɑːs/ *n* envergure *f*; **he lacks ~** il manque d'envergure, il ne fait pas le poids.

gravitate /ˈgrævɪteɪt/ *vi* **to ~ to(wards) sth/sb** graviter vers qch/qn.

gravitation /ˌgrævɪˈteɪʃn/ *n* gravitation *f*.

gravitational /ˌgrævɪˈteɪʃənl/ *adj* gravitationnel/-elle; **~ field** champ *m* de gravitation; **~ force**, **~ pull** gravitation *f*.

gravity /ˈgrævətɪ/ **I** *n* **1** Phys pesanteur *f*; **law of ~** loi *f* de la pesanteur; **centre of ~** centre *m* de gravité; **the pull of the earth's ~** l'attraction terrestre; **2** (of offence, situation) gravité *f*; **3** (of demeanour) sérieux *m*.
II *modif* [*feed, lubrication*] par gravité.

gravity brake *n* frein *m* parachute.

gravy /ˈgreɪvɪ/ *n* **1** Culin sauce *f* (au jus de rôti); **2**○ surtout US (money) bénef○ *m*.
IDIOMS **he is on the ~ train**○ il a trouvé le filon○.

gravy: **~ boat** *n* saucière *f*; **~ browning** *n*: *granulés ajoutés au jus de la viande pour l'épaissir*.

gray US = **grey**.

grayling /ˈgreɪlɪŋ/ *n* (*pl* **~**) (fish) ombre *m* de rivière.

Gray's Inn /ˌgreɪz ˈɪn/ *pr n* GB Jur *une des quatre écoles de Droit de Londres*.

graze /greɪz/ **I** *n* écorchure *f*; **it's just a ~** c'est une simple égratignure.
II *vtr* **1** (scratch, scrape) **to ~ one's knee/shin** s'écorcher le genou/tibia (**on, against** sur); **2** (skim, touch lightly) [*lips, fingers, bullet*] frôler [*surface, skin*]; **3** Agric faire paître [*animal*]; utiliser [qch] comme pacage [*land*].
III *vi* **1** Agric [*sheep*] brouter; [*cow*] paître; **to put sth out to ~** mettre qch au pâturage; **2**○ [*person*] grignoter.

grazing /ˈgreɪzɪŋ/ *n* Agric pacage *m*.

grazing: **~ land** *n* pâturage *m*; **~ rights** *npl* droit *m* de pacage.

grease /griːs/ **I** *n* **1** (lubricant) graisse *f*; (black) cambouis *m*; **2** Culin (animal) graisse *f*; (vegetable) huile *f*; **3** (dirt) graisse *f*; **covered in ~** couvert de graisse; **4** (from hair, skin) sébum *m*.
II *vtr* (all contexts) graisser.

grease: **~ gun** *n* pompe *f* à graisse; **~ monkey**○ *n* mécano *m*○; **~ nipple** *n* graisseur *m*; **~paint** *n* maquillage *m* de théâtre; **~proof paper** *n* papier *m* sulfurisé.

greaser○ /ˈgriːsə(r)/ *n* **1** GB (mechanic) mécano○ *m*; **2** (motorcyclist) motard○ *m*.

grease stain *n* (oil) tache *f* d'huile; (from hair, skin, lubricant) tache *f* de graisse.

greasiness /ˈgriːsɪnɪs/ *n* (of clothes, hair, surface) aspect *m* graisseux; (of food) aspect *m* huileux.

greasing /ˈgrisɪŋ/ *n* Mech graissage *m*.

greasy /ˈgriːsɪ/ *adj* [*hair, skin*] gras/grasse; [*overalls*] graisseux/-euse; [*food*] gras/grasse. IDIOMS **to climb the ~ pole** tenter de s'élever dans une hiérarchie où la compétition est féroce.

greasy spoon○ *n* (cafe) gargote○ *f*.

great /greɪt/ **I** *n* **1** (in title) **Peter the Great** Pierre le Grand; **2** (powerful people) **the ~** (+ *v pl*) les grands *mpl*.
II greats *npl* (remarkable people or things) grands *mpl*.
III Greats *pr npl* GB Univ études *fpl* de lettres classiques.
IV *adj* **1** (large) [*height, width, distance, speed, majority, object, danger*] grand (*before n*); [*number, amount, percentage*] grand (*before n*), important; [*increase*] fort (*before n*), important; [*improvement, difference*] grand (*before n*), considérable; **at ~ speed** très vite, à grande vitesse; **a pay rise of 10% or £1200, whichever is the ~er** une augmentation de 10% ou de 1 200 livres sterling, le chiffre le plus élevé étant pris en compte; **2** (as intensifier) [*excitement, surprise, relief, success, tragedy, force, advantage*] grand (*before n*); [*heat, pain*] fort (*before n*); **a ~ deal (of)** beaucoup (de); **a ~ many people/houses** beaucoup de personnes/maisons, un grand nombre de personnes/maisons; **to have ~ difficulty doing** avoir beaucoup de mal à faire; **in ~ detail** dans les moindres détails; **the map was a ~ help** la carte a été très utile; **you're a ~ help!** iron tu m'aides vraiment beaucoup!; **3** (remarkable) [*person, writer, name, achievement, painting, discovery*] grand (*before n*); **4**○ (excellent) [*book, film, party, vacation, weather*] génial○, formidable○; [*opportunity*] formidable○; **it's ~ to be back/to see you** c'est formidable○ d'être de retour/de te revoir; **to feel ~** se sentir en pleine forme; **you look ~!** (healthy) tu as l'air en pleine forme!; (attractive) tu es superbe!; **that dress looks ~ on you** cette robe est géniale○ sur toi; **to have a ~ time** bien s'amuser; **X is the ~est!** X est génial○!; **5**○ (talented) [*teacher, singer, team*] génial○, formidable○; **to be ~ at** être un as○ à [*tennis, football*]; **to be ~ at fixing cars** être génial○ quand il s'agit de réparer des voitures; **to be ~ with** être génial○ avec [*children, animals*]; **to be ~ on** être imbattable○ sur [*history, architecture*]; **6**○ (enthusiastic) [*worrier, flirt, organizer*] de première○; [*admirer, friend, fan*] grand (*before n*); **he's a ~ theatregoer/walker** il adore aller au théâtre/marcher; **I've never been a ~ reader** la lecture n'a jamais été mon truc○.
V○ *adv* **everything's going ~** tout marche comme sur des roulettes○; **I'm doing ~** ça marche très bien pour moi○; **the car/machine is working ~** la voiture/machine marche très bien.
IDIOMS **to cross the ~ divide** faire le grand saut.

great: **~ ape** *n* grand singe *m*, anthropoïde *m*; **~ aunt** *n* grand-tante *f*; **Great Australian Bight** *n* Grande Baie *f* Australienne; **Great Barrier Reef** *n* Grande Barrière *f* de Corail; **Great Bear** *n* Grande Ourse *f*; **~ big** *adj* (très) grand (*before n*), énorme; **Great Britain** ▶ **1131** *pr n* Grande-Bretagne *f*; **~coat** *n* manteau *m*; **Great Dane** *n* danois *m*; **Great Dividing Range** *n* Cordillière *f* australienne; **Greater London** *pr n* l'agglomération *f* londonienne; **Greater Manchester** *pr n* l'agglomération *f* de Manchester; **~est common divisor**, **~est common factor** *n* Math plus grand commun diviseur *m*; **~ grandchild** *n* arrière-petit/-e enfant *mf*; **~ granddaughter** *n* arrière-petite-fille *f*; **~ grandfather** *n* arrière-grand-père *m*; **~ grandmother** *n* arrière-grand-mère *f*; **~ grandson** *n* arrière-petit-fils *m*; **~-great grandchild** *n* arrière-arrière-petit/-e enfant *mf*; **~-great grandfather** *n* arrière-arrière-grand-père *m*; **~-great grandmother** *n* arrière-arrière-grand-mère *f*; **Great Lakes** ▶ **1400** *npl* Grands Lacs *mpl*.

greatly /ˈgreɪtlɪ/ *adv* [*admire, regret, influence, impress*] beaucoup, énormément; [*exceed*] de beaucoup; [*impressed, admired, surprised, distressed, respected*] très, extrêmement; [*improved, changed, increased, reduced*] considérablement; [*superior, inferior*] bien; **it is ~ to be regretted that** il est très regrettable que.

great nephew *n* petit-neveu *m*.

greatness /ˈgreɪtnɪs/ *n* (of achievement, novel, painting) importance *f*; (of person, country, mind) grandeur *f*.

great: **~ niece** *n* petite-nièce *f*; **Great Plains** *pr n* Grandes Plaines *fpl*; **Great Power** *n* Pol grande puissance *f*; **Great Schism** *n* Hist, Relig grand schisme *m* d'Occident; **~ tit** *n* Zool mésange *f* charbonnière; **~ uncle** *n* grand-oncle *m*; **Great Vowel Shift** *n* Ling grand changement *m* vocalique; **Great Wall of China** *pr n* Grande Muraille *f* de Chine; **Great War** *pr n* Hist Grande Guerre *f*.

greave /griːv/ *n* jambière *f*.

grebe /griːb/ *n* grèbe *m*; **great crested ~** grèbe huppé.

Grecian /ˈgriːʃn/ *adj* grec/grecque.

Greece /griːs/ ▶ **1131** *pr n* Grèce *f*.

greed /griːd/ *n* **1** (for money, power) avidité *f* (**for** de); **2** (also **greediness**) (for food) gourmandise *f*.

greedily /ˈgriːdɪlɪ/ *adv* [*eat*] goulûment.

greediness /ˈgriːdɪnɪs/ *n* = **greed 2**.

greedy /ˈgriːdɪ/ *adj* **1** [*person*] (for food) gourmand; (stronger) goulu; [*look*] avide; **he's a ~ guts**○ ou **pig**○ c'est un goinfre○; **2** (for money, power, information) avide (**for** de).

Greek /griːk/ ▶ **1486**, **1402** **I** *n* **1** (person) Grec/Grecque *m/f*; **2** (language) grec *m*.
II *adj* **1** [*food, government, island*] grec/grecque; **2** [*teacher, lesson, dictionary*] de grec.
IDIOMS **beware of ~s bearing gifts** ne faites jamais confiance à un ennemi; **it's all ~ to me** c'est du chinois pour moi.

Greek: **~ alphabet** *n* alphabet *m* grec; **~ cross** *n* croix *f* grecque; **~ key** *n* Art grecque *f*; **~ Orthodox Church** *n* Église *f* orthodoxe grecque.

green /griːn/ ▶ **1104** **I** *n* **1** (colour) vert *m*; **I've seen that dress in ~** j'ai vu la même robe en vert; **dressed in ~** vêtu de vert or habillé en vert; **a shade of ~** une nuance de vert; **several different ~s** plusieurs verts différents; **a cool/pretty ~** un vert frais/délicat; **2** (in snooker) **the ~** la bille verte; **3** (grassy area) espace *m* vert; (vegetation) verdure *f*; **a strip of ~** une bande de gazon; **4** (in bowling) boulingrin *m* (*terrain gazonné pour le jeu de boules*); (in golf) green *m*; **5** Ecol, Pol écologiste *mf*; **the Greens** les Verts; **6**○ US (money) fric○ *m*, argent *m*.
II greens *npl* **1** GB (vegetables) légumes *mpl* verts; **eat up your ~s!** mange tes légumes!; **2** US (greenery) verdure *f*; **Christmas ~s** verdure *f* (décorative) de Noël.
III *adj* **1** (in colour) vert; **to go** ou **turn ~** [*traffic lights*] passer au vert; [*walls*] verdir; fig [*person*] verdir, devenir vert; **to paint/colour/dye sth ~** peindre/colorier/teindre qch en vert; **2** (with vegetation) [*countryside, valley*] verdoyant; **3** (not ready) [*fruit, wood, tobacco*] vert; **4** Culin [*bacon*] non fumé; **5** (naïve) naïf/naïve; **I'm not as ~ as you think I am** je ne suis pas aussi naïf que tu (le) crois; **6** (inexperienced) novice; **7** Ecol, Pol [*policies, candidate, issues*] écologiste; (ecologically sound) [*marketing, washing-powder*] écologique; **8** EC Econ [*currency, pound, franc*] vert; **9**○ (off-colour) patraque○.
IDIOMS **to have ~ fingers** GB, **to have a ~ thumb** US avoir la main verte; **to give sb/sth the ~ light** donner le feu vert à qn/qch.

green: **~back**○ *n* US billet *m* vert or d'un dollar; **~ bean** *n* haricot *m* vert; **~ belt** *n* Sport ceinture *f* verte; **Green Beret** *n* US Mil béret *m* vert.

green card *n* **1** (driving insurance) carte *f* verte (internationale); **2** US carte *f* de séjour (*permettant de travailler aux États-Unis*).

Green Cross Code *n* GB code *m* de prévention routière (*destiné aux enfants*).

greenery /ˈgriːnərɪ/ *n* verdure *f*.

green-eyed monster *n* **the ~** la jalousie.

green: **~field site** *n* terrain *m* vierge; **~finch** *n* verdier *m*; **~fly** *n* puceron *m* (du rosier); **~gage** *n* reine-claude *f*.

greengrocer /ˈgriːngrəʊsə(r)/ ▶ **1692** *n* (person) marchand *m* de fruits et légumes; **~'s (shop)** magasin *m* de fruits et légumes.

greenhorn○ /ˈgriːnhɔːn/ *n* péj **1** (gullible person) benêt○ *m*; **2** (newcomer) débutant/-e *m/f*; **he's a ~** il débarque○.

green: **~house** *n* serre *f*; **~house effect** *n* Ecol effet *m* de serre; **~house gases** *npl* Ecol gaz *mpl* qui provoquent l'effet de serre.

greening /ˈgriːnɪŋ/ *n* **the ~ of the Socialist Party** la prise de conscience écologique au sein du Parti Socialiste.

greenish /ˈgriːnɪʃ/ ▶ **1104** *adj* tirant sur le vert; **~-brown eyes** des yeux marrons tirant sur le vert; **~-grey stones** des pierres d'un gris verdâtre.

Greenland /ˈgriːnlənd/ ▶ **1131** *pr n* Groenland *m*; **the ~ Sea** la Mer du Groenland.

Greenlander /ˈgriːnləndə(r)/ ▶ **1486** *n* Groenlandais/-e *m/f*.

Greenlandic /ˌgriːnˈlændɪk/ **I** *n* ▶ **1402** Ling groenlandais *m*.
II *adj* groenlandais.

green monkey disease ▶ **1354** *n* virus *m* de Marburg.

greenness /ˈgriːnnɪs/ *n* **1** (of dye, pigment) verdeur *f*; (of countryside, woods) verdure *f*; **2** (unripeness) (of fruit, wood) verdeur *f*; **3** Ecol (trend, process) prise *f* de conscience écologique; (awareness) conscience *f* écologique; **4** (inexperience) inexpérience *f*.

green: **~ onion** *n* US ciboule *f*; **~ paper** *n* GB livre *m* blanc.

Greenpeace /ˈgriːnpiːs/ *pr n* Greenpeace.

green: **~ pepper** *n* poivron *m* vert; **~room** *n* Theat foyer *m* des artistes; **~ salad** *n* salade *f* verte; **~shank** *n* Zool chevalier *m* à pieds verts; **~stick fracture** *n* fracture *f* incomplète or de bois vert; **~stuff** *n* ¢ légumes *mpl* verts; **~sward** *n* ‡ou littér tapis *m* de verdure; **~ tea** *n* thé *m* vert.

Greenwich Mean Time, GMT /ˌgrenɪtʃ ˈmiːntaɪm/ *n* temps *m* universel, TU.

green: **~wood**† *n* forêt *f* verdoyante; **~ woodpecker** *n* pic *m* vert, pivert *m*.

greet /griːt/ *vtr* **1** (welcome) accueillir [*person*]; saluer [*decision, appointment*]; **to ~ sb with a smile** accueillir qn avec le sourire; **2** (salute, acknowledge) saluer [*person*]; **to ~ sb with a wave** saluer qn d'un geste de la main; **to ~ sb in the street** dire bonjour à qn dans la rue; **3** (receive, react to) **to be ~ed with** ou **by** provoquer [*dismay, outrage, amusement*]; être salué par [*jeers, applause*]; **4** (hit, confront) **an amazing sight ~ed me** une scène extraordinaire s'offrait à moi; **a lovely smell ~ed me** une bonne odeur est parvenue à mes narines.

greeter /ˈgriːtə(r)/ *n* personne *f* qui accueille les clients (*dans un restaurant*).

greeting /ˈgriːtɪŋ/ **I** *n* (salutation) salutation *f*; **~s!** salutations!; **give him my ~s** transmets-lui mes meilleures salutations; **to exchange ~s** (as preliminary) se saluer; (in passing) se dire bonjour; **he waved at me in ~** il m'a salué d'un geste de la main.
II greetings *npl* (on cards) **Christmas ~s**

vœux *mpl* de Noël; **Seasons ~s** meilleurs vœux.

greetings card GB, **greeting card** US *n* carte *f* de vœux.

gregarious /grɪˈgeərɪəs/ *adj* [*person*] sociable; [*animal, instinct*] grégaire.

gregariousness /grɪˈgeərɪəsnɪs/ *n* (of person) sociabilité *f*; (of species) instinct *m* grégaire.

Gregorian /grɪˈgɔːrɪən/ *adj* grégorien/-ienne.

Gregory /ˈgregərɪ/ *pr n* Grégoire.

gremlin /ˈgremlɪn/ *n* hum diablotin *m*.

Grenada /grəˈneɪdə/ ▶ **1131**, **1818** *pr n* (city, country) Grenade *f*.

grenade /grəˈneɪd/ *n* grenade *f*.

Grenadian /grəˈneɪdɪən/ **I** *n* ▶ **1486** Grenadien/-ienne *m/f*.
II *adj* grenadien/-ienne.

grenadier /ˌgrenəˈdɪə/ *n* Mil grenadier *m*.

grenadine /ˈgrenədiːn/ *n* (all contexts) grenadine *f*.

grew /gruː/ *prét* ▶ **grow**.

grey GB, **gray** US /greɪ/ ▶ **1104** **I** *n* **1** (colour) gris *m*; **a shade of ~** un ton gris; **2** (horse) (cheval *m*) gris *m*.
II *adj* **1** (colour) gris; **light/dark ~** gris clair/foncé *inv*; **to go** ou **turn ~** devenir gris; **2** (with grey hair) [*person*] aux cheveux gris, grisonnant; **to go** ou **turn ~** grisonner; **3** [*existence, life, day*] morne; **4** péj [*character, town*] terne.
III *vtr* [*age, worry*] grisonner [*hair, person*].
IV *vi* grisonner; **to be ~ing at the temples** avoir les tempes grisonnantes; **the population is ~ing** la population vieillit.
IDIOMS **all cats are ~ in the dark** la nuit tous les chats sont gris.

grey: **~ area** *n* zone *f* floue; **~beard** *n* vieillard *m* (à barbe grise); **~ economy** *n* économie *f* parallèle; **~ed command** *n* Comput commande *f* estompée; **~ eminence** *n* éminence *f* grise; **Grey Friar** *n* franciscain *m*; **~-haired**, **~-headed** *adj* aux cheveux gris; **~hound** *n* lévrier *m*; **~hound bitch** *n* levrette *f*; **Greyhound bus** *n car de la compagnie Greyhound aux États-Unis*; **~hound racing** ▶ **1282** *n* course *f* de lévriers; **~hound track** *n* piste *f* de course de lévriers.

greyish GB, **grayish** US /ˈgreɪɪʃ/ ▶ **1104** *adj* grisâtre.

grey: **~lag goose** *n* oie *f* cendrée; **~ market** *n* marché *m* gris; **~ matter** *n* (brain) matière *f* grise; **~ mullet** *n* mulet *m*; **~ seal** *n* phoque *m* gris; **~ squirrel** *n* écureuil *m* gris; **~ wagtail** *n* bergeronnette *f* des ruisseaux; **~ wolf** *n* loup *m* (gris).

grid /grɪd/ *n* **1** (grating) grille *f*; **2** gen, Geog (pattern) quadrillage *m*; **the city is laid out on a ~ (pattern)** les rues de la ville forment un quadrillage; **3** GB (network) réseau *m*; **the national ~** le réseau électrique national; **4** (in motor racing) grille *f* de départ; **5** Electron grille *f*; **6**○ US (gridiron) terrain *m* de football américain.

griddle /ˈgrɪdl/ **I** *n* (for meat) gril *m* en fonte; (for pancakes, buns) plaque *f* en fonte.
II *vtr* griller (sur une plaque en fonte) [*meat*]; faire cuire sur une plaque en fonte [*cake*].

griddle cake *n*: *crêpe cuite sur une plaque en fonte*.

gridiron /ˈgrɪdaɪən/ *n* **1** Culin gril *m*; **2** US terrain *m* de football américain.

gridlock /ˈgrɪdlɒk/ *n* **1** lit embouteillage *m*, bouchon *m*; **traffic is in complete ~** ça bouchonne○; **2** fig (deadlock) impasse *f*.

grid: **~ map** *n* carte *f* quadrillée; **~ reference** *n* coordonnées *fpl*.

grief /griːf/ **I** *n* **1** (sorrow) chagrin *m*; **his ~ at** ou **over her death** le chagrin qu'il a ressenti à sa mort; **2**○ (trouble, hassle) embêtements *mpl*; **to give sb ~** ennuyer qn.
II *excl* **good ~!** mon Dieu!
IDIOMS **to come to ~** (in sports, competition) (have an accident) avoir un accident; (lose) perdre; [*firm, business*] péricliter; **he nearly came to ~ in the final exam** à la dernière épreuve il a failli tout rater○.

grief-stricken /ˈgriːfstrɪkn/ *adj* accablé de douleur (*after n*).

grievance /ˈgriːvns/ *n* (all contexts) griefs *mpl* (**against** contre); **he has a genuine ~** ses griefs sont justifiés; **to air one's ~s** exposer ses griefs.

grievance: **~ committee** *n* commission *f* d'arbitrage; **~ procedure** *n* Mgmt instance *f* prud'hommale.

grieve /griːv/ **I** *vi* **to ~ for**, **to ~ over** pleurer [*person, death*]; **to ~ deeply** être affligé.
II *v impers* littér **it ~s me to hear** cela me fait de la peine d'apprendre; **it ~s me that** cela me fait de la peine que (+ *subj*).

grievous /ˈgriːvəs/ *adj* sout [*loss, disappointment*] cruel/-elle; [*mistake, damage, wound*] grave; **to do sb a ~ wrong** faire cruellement tort à qn.

grievous bodily harm, **GBH** *n* Jur coups *mpl* et blessures *fpl*.

grievously /ˈgriːvəslɪ/ *adv* [*hurt*] grièvement; [*offended, disappointed*] cruellement.

griffin, **griffon** /ˈgrɪfɪn/ *n* griffon *m*.

grifter○ /ˈgrɪftə(r)/ *n* US escroc *m*.

grill /grɪl/ **I** *n* **1** GB (on cooker) gril *m*; **cook it in** ou **under the ~** faites-le griller; **2** US (barbecue) gril *m*; **3** (dish) grillade *f*; **4** (restaurant) grill *m*, restaurant *m* servant des grillades.
II *vtr* **1** Culin faire griller [*meat, fish*]; **2**○ (interrogate) mettre [qn] sur la sellette○ (**about** à propos de).
III *vi* [*steak, fish*] griller.

grille /grɪl/ *n* gen grille *f*; (on car) calandre *f*.

grilled /grɪld/ *adj* Culin grillé; **charcoal-~ prawns** crevettes grillées au feu de bois.

grilling○ /ˈgrɪlɪŋ/ *n* interrogatoire *m* serré; **to give sb a ~** questionner qn, mettre qn sur la sellette○ (**about** à propos de).

grill pan *n* GB plateau *m* à poignée (*allant sous le gril*).

grilse /grɪls/ *n* saumon *m* d'hiver.

grim /grɪm/ *adj* **1** (depressing) [*news, town, prison*] sinistre; [*sight, conditions*] effroyable; [*reality*] dur; **her future looks ~** son avenir a l'air sombre; **it's a ~ reminder of war** cela nous remet en mémoire la guerre dans toute son horreur; **2** (unrelenting) [*struggle*] acharné; [*resolve*] terrible; **to hold onto sb like ~ death** s'agripper à qn de toutes ses forces; **3** (unsmiling) [*expression*] grave; **to be ~-faced** avoir l'air grave; **4**○ (poor) [*accommodation, food*] très mauvais; **you look ~** tu n'as pas l'air bien du tout○; **I'm feeling pretty ~** (ill) je ne me sens pas bien; (depressed) je n'ai pas le moral○; **5** (black) [*joke, humour*] macabre.

grimace /grɪˈmeɪs, US ˈgrɪməs/ **I** *n* grimace *f* (**of** de).
II *vi* (involuntary) faire une grimace (**with**, **in** de); (pull a face) faire la grimace; **she ~d at the thought** elle fit la grimace en y pensant.

grime /graɪm/ *n* (of city) saleté *f*; (on object, person) crasse *f*.

grimly /ˈgrɪmlɪ/ *adv* **1** (sadly) [*speak*] sur un ton grave; **'if I ever get a job,' he laughed ~** 'si je finis par trouver un travail,' a-t-il dit avec un rire amer; **2** (relentlessly) [*pursue, continue, cling*] avec acharnement; **a ~ determined expression** un air sombre et résolu.

grimness /ˈgrɪmnɪs/ *n* (of story, news) caractère *m* sinistre; (of landscape, town) aspect *m* sinistre; **the ~ of his future** son avenir sombre.

Grim Reaper /ˌgrɪm ˈriːpə(r)/ *n* **the ~** la Faucheuse *f*.

grimy /ˈgraɪmɪ/ *adj* [*city, façade*] noir; [*hands, window, sheet*] crasseux/-euse.

grin /grɪn/ **I** *n* sourire *m*; **her face broke into a ~** elle a souri.
II *vi* (*p prés etc* **-nn-**) sourire (**at** à; **with** de); **to ~ broadly** faire un large sourire.
IDIOMS **to ~ and bear it** souffrir en silence; **to ~ from ear to ear** sourire jusqu'aux oreilles.

grind /graɪnd/ **I** *n* **1**○ (hard work) boulot○ *m* or travail *m* monotone; **the daily ~**○ le boulot○ or le train-train○ quotidien; **back to the ~**○**!** au boulot○**!**; **marking exam papers is an awful ~**○ corriger des copies d'examen est une vraie corvée; **it was a long hard ~**○ **cycling up the hill** c'était long et pénible de monter la côte en vélo; **it'll be a long hard ~**○ ça va être très dur; **2** (harsh sound) grincement *m*; **3**○ US péj (hard-working student) bûcheur/-euse○ *m/f*.
II *vtr* (*prét, pp* **ground**) **1** (crush) moudre [*corn, coffee beans, pepper*]; écraser, broyer [*seeds, grain*]; concasser [*pebbles, stone*]; hacher [*meat*]; **to ~ sth to dust/to a powder** réduire qch en poussière/en poudre; **to ~ corn into flour** moudre du grain pour en faire de la farine; **to ~ one's teeth** grincer des dents; **to ~ sth into the ground** écraser qch par terre; **2** (sharpen) affûter or aiguiser [qch] (à la meule) [*knife, blade*]; (polish) polir [*lenses*]; égriser [*gems*]; **3** (turn) tourner [*handle*]; Mus jouer de [*barrel organ*].
III *vi* (*prét, pp* **ground**) **1** (make harsh sound) [*machine, engine*] grincer; **to ~ to a halt** [*vehicle, train*] s'arrêter avec un grincement de freins; [*machine*] s'arrêter; fig [*factory, economy, industry, production*] s'immobiliser; **2** (be crushed) [*corn, coffee beans*] se moudre; **3**○ US (swot) bûcher○, potasser○; **4**○ US [*dancer*] *danser en se déhanchant de manière provocante*.
■ **grind away** bosser○, bûcher○; **she is ~ing away at her maths** elle bûche ses maths.
■ **grind down**: ¶ **~ down [sth]**, **~ [sth] down** (crush) écraser, broyer; (pulverize) pulvériser [*substance*]: ¶ **~ [sb] down** avoir [qn] à l'usure; **to be ground down by poverty** être accablé par la misère.
■ **grind on** [*negotiations, project*] se poursuivre inexorablement.
■ **grind out**: **~ out [sth]**, **~ [sth] out** **1** (extinguish) écraser [*cigarette*]; **2** (play) **to ~ out a tune on a barrel organ** jouer un air sur un orgue de Barbarie; **she ~s out**○ **novels at the rate of one a month** elle pond○ des romans au rythme d'un par mois; **'mind your own business,' he ground out** 'occupez-vous de vos affaires,' a-t-il grommelé entre ses dents.
■ **grind up** pulvériser.

grinder /ˈgraɪndə(r)/ *n* **1** (crushing device) (industrial) broyeur *m*; (domestic) moulin *m*; (for meat) hachoir *m*; **2** Tech (for sharpening) meule *f* (à aiguiser); **3** (person) rémouleur/-euse *m/f*; **4** (tooth) molaire *f*; **5** US (sandwich) gros sandwich *m* mixte.

grinding /ˈgraɪndɪŋ/ **I** *n* (sound) grincement *m*.
II *adj* [*noise*] grinçant; **~ poverty** misère *f* noire.

grinding wheel *n* meule *f* (de rectification).

grindstone /ˈgraɪndstəʊn/ *n* meule *f* or pierre *f* à aiguiser.
IDIOMS **to keep** ou **have one's nose to the ~** travailler sans relâche; **to keep sb's nose to the ~** faire trimer○ qn, faire travailler qn sans relâche.

gringo /ˈgrɪŋgəʊ/ *n* (*pl* **-gos**) US injur gringo *m* offensive.

grip /grɪp/ **I** *n* **1** (hold) prise *f* (**on** sur); **to tighten one's ~ on sth** lit resserrer sa prise sur qch; **to relax one's ~ on sth** relâcher sa prise sur qch; **she's lost her ~ on the rope** elle a perdu prise et lâché la corde; **to have a firm ~ (on sth)** avoir une prise solide sur qch; **2** (control) **to take a firm ~ on the company/party** prendre la société/le parti bien en main; **to lose one's**

~ on reality perdre contact avec la réalité; **to come to ~s with sth** en venir aux prises avec qch; **to get to ~s with sth** attaquer qch de front; **get** ou **take a ~ on yourself!** ressaisis-toi!; **I think he's beginning to lose his ~** je crois qu'il commence à perdre confiance; **3** (ability to hold) adhérence *f*; **these shoes have no ~/have lost their ~** ces chaussures n'accrochent pas/plus au sol; **do the tyres have a good ~?** les pneus ont-ils une bonne adhérence?; **4** (clutches) **to be in the ~ of an obsession/a bad dream** être en proie à une obsession/à un cauchemar; **in the ~ of winter** paralysé par l'hiver; **5** (bag) sac *m* de voyage; **6** Cin accessoiriste *mf*.

II *vtr* (*p prés etc* **-pp-**) **1** (grab) agripper [*arm, wrist bannister*]; (hold) serrer [*handle, arm*]; **to ~ sth between one's teeth** serrer qch entre ses dents; **to ~ a rail firmly/with both hands** agripper une rampe/saisir une rampe des deux mains; **2** (adhere to) [*tyres*] adhérer à [*road*]; [*shoes*] accrocher à [*ground*]; **3** (captivate) captiver.

III *vi* (*p prés etc* **-pp-**) (hold) **the tyres failed to ~ on the ice** les pneus n'ont pas adhéré à la glace; **my shoes didn't ~ on the rock** mes chaussures n'accrochèrent pas sur la roche.

gripe /graɪp/ I *n* **1** (complaint) sujet *m* de plainte; **her biggest ~ is that** ce qui la fait le plus râler○ c'est que; **2** Med **to have the ~s** avoir des coliques *fpl*.

II *vtr*○ US (annoy) casser les pieds○ à; **it ~s his ass◑** ça lui casse le cul◑.

III *vi* (complain) râler○ (**about** à propos de; **that** que).

gripe water *n* GB calmant *m* (*pour coliques des nourrissons*); ≈ infusion *f* de fenouil.

griping /ˈgraɪpɪŋ/ I *n*○ ¢ (complaining) ronchonnements *mpl*.

II *adj* Med **to have ~ pains** avoir des coliques *fpl*.

gripper rail /grɪpə(r)/ *n* barre *f* de seuil.

gripping /ˈgrɪpɪŋ/ *adj* captivant.

grip tape /grɪp/ *n* bande *f* adhésive.

grisly /ˈgrɪzlɪ/ *adj* [*story, sight*] horrible; [*remains*] macabre.

grist /grɪst/ *n*: IDIOMS **it's all ~ to his mill** il fait flèche de tout bois; **scandals are ~ to the mill of the press** les scandales sont la pâture de la presse.

gristle /ˈgrɪsl/ *n* (in meat) cartilage *m*; **piece of ~** du cartilage.

gristly /ˈgrɪslɪ/ *adj* [*meat*] cartilagineux/-euse.

grit /grɪt/ I *n* ¢ **1** (in carpet, on lens) grains *mpl* de poussière; (sandy dirt) grains *mpl* de sable; (in wound) saletés *fpl*; **2** GB (for roads) sable *m*; **3** (courage) cran○ *m*; **she has ~ and determination** elle est courageuse et résolue; **4** (sandstone) grès *m*.

II *vtr* (*p prés etc* **-tt-**) GB sabler [*road*]; **'~ting in progress'** 'sablage'.

IDIOMS **to ~ one's teeth** serrer les dents.

grits /grɪts/ *npl* (oats) GB gruau *m* d'avoine; (corn) US gruau *m* de maïs.

gritter /ˈgrɪtə(r)/ *n* GB Aut sableuse *f*.

gritty /ˈgrɪtɪ/ *adj* **1** (sandy) plein de sable; (gravelly) graveleux/-euse; **~ particles** (in engine, carpet) grains *mpl* de poussière; **2** (realistic, tough) [*personality*] solide et terre à terre; [*novel*] réaliste; **3** (courageous) **the team gave a ~ performance** l'équipe s'est montrée courageuse et résolue.

grizzle /ˈgrɪzl/ *vi* GB (cry) pleurnicher; (complain) grogner.

grizzled /ˈgrɪzld/ *adj* [*hair, beard, person*] grisonnant.

grizzly /ˈgrɪzlɪ/ I *n* (also **~ bear**) grizzli *m*.

II *adj* [*hair, beard*] grisonnant.

groan /grəʊn/ I *n*(of pain, despair) gémissement *m*; (of disgust, protest) grognement *m*; **to give a ~** (in pain) pousser un gémissement.

II *vtr* **'I've been hit,' he ~ed** 'je suis touché,' gémit-il; **'no!,' he ~ed** 'oh non!' soupira-t-il.

III *vi* **1** (in pain) gémir; (in disgust, protest) grogner; **to ~ in** ou **with pain** pousser un gémissement de douleur; **he always ~s at my jokes** il pousse toujours des soupirs pour montrer qu'il n'apprécie pas mes blagues; **I ~ed inwardly when I heard that...** j'étais loin d'être ravi quand j'ai appris que...; **2** (creak) [*timbers*] gémir; **to ~ under the weight of sth** gémir sous le poids de qch liter; **3** (suffer) littér gémir.

groats /grəʊts/ *npl* Culin gruau *m* d'avoine or de froment.

grocer /ˈgrəʊsə(r)/ ▶ 1692, 1692 *n* (person) épicier *m*; **~'s (shop)** épicerie *f*.

groceries /ˈgrəʊsərɪz/ *npl* **1** (shopping) courses *fpl*; **2** (type of merchandise) épicerie *f* ¢.

grocery /ˈgrəʊsərɪ/ ▶ 1692 I *n* (also **~ shop** GB, **~ store**) épicerie *f*.

II *modif* [*bill, products, sales*] d'épicerie; [*chain*] d'épiceries.

grog /grɒg/ *n* grog *m*.

groggy /ˈgrɒgɪ/ *adj* sonné○, groggy; **to feel ~** avoir les jambes en coton○.

groin /grɔɪn/ ▶ 1037 I *n* **1** Anat aine *f*; **in the ~** lit à l'aine; euph dans les testicules; **2** Archit arête *f*; **3** US = **groyne**.

II *modif* [*injury, strain*] à l'aine.

grommet /ˈgrɒmɪt/ *n* **1** (eyelet) œillet *m*; **2** Med diabolo *m*, drain *m* transtympanique spec.

groom /gru:m/ I *n* **1** (bridegroom) **the ~** le jeune marié; **2** Equit palefrenier/-ière *m/f*; (for racehorse) lad *m*.

II *vtr* **1** (clean) faire la toilette de [*dog, cat*]; (professionally) toiletter [*dog, cat*]; panser [*horse*]; **to ~ oneself carefully** s'habiller et se coiffer avec soin; **2** (prepare) **to ~ sb for an examination/for the post** préparer qn à un examen/au poste; (train) **to ~ sb for a diplomatic career** former qn pour qu'il puisse devenir diplomate.

III **groomed** *pp adj* **a well ~ed young man** un jeune homme très soigné (de sa personne); **she was immaculately ~ed** elle était parfaitement coiffée et habillée; **a carefully ~ed horse** un cheval pansé avec soin.

grooming /ˈgru:mɪŋ/ *n* (of horse) pansage *m*; (of dog) toilettage *m*; **personal ~** US présentation *f*, tenue *f*.

groove /gru:v/ I *n* **1** lit (on record) sillon *m*; (for sliding door) coulisse *f*; (in joinery) rainure *f*; (on head of screw) fente *f*, creux *m*; **2** (routine) **to be stuck in a ~** s'encroûter; **I've been stuck in a ~ for too long** je commence à m'encroûter; **3** Mus rythme *m*.

II *vi* US **~ it, baby**○! amuse-toi!

groovy○† /ˈgru:vɪ/ *adj* [*party, clothes*] sensass○†; **I'm feeling ~** je me sens super bien○; **to be ~** être dans le vent○†.

grope /grəʊp/ I○ *n* **to give sb a ~**○ essayer de tripoter○ qn.

II *vtr* **1** (feel) **he ~d his way down the dark staircase/past the furniture** il descendit l'escalier à tâtons dans le noir/il contourna les meubles à tâtons; **2**○ (sexually) tripoter○.

III *vi* **to ~ for sth** chercher qch à tâtons; fig **to ~ in the dark** tâtonner.

groping /ˈgrəʊpɪŋ/ *n* **1** fig **~(s)** tâtonnements *mpl*; **2** (sexual) pelotage○ *m*.

grosgrain /ˈgrəʊsgreɪn/ *n* Tex gros-grain *m*; **~ ribbon** gros-grain *m*.

gross /grəʊs/ I *n* (*pl* **~**) (twelve dozen) grosse *f*, douze douzaines *fpl*; **by the ~** à la grosse; **per ~** la grosse.

II *adj* **1** Comm, Fin (before deductions) [*cost, income, margin, profit, salary, sum, weight, yield*] brut; **2** (serious) gen, Jur [*error, exaggeration*] grossier/-ière; [*ignorance*] crasse; [*abuse, inequality*] choquant; [*injustice*] flagrant; **~ negligence** Jur faute *f* lourde; **~ dereliction of duty** manquement *m* grave au devoir; **3** (coarse) [*behaviour, manner*] vulgaire; [*language*] cru; **4**○ (revolting) dégueulasse◑; **5**○ (obese) obèse.

III *adv* **how much are you paid ~?** quel est votre salaire brut?

IV *vtr* **to ~ two million dollars** faire un bénéfice brut de deux millions de dollars.

■ **gross out**○: **~ [sb] out** US dégoûter [qn]; **~ me out!** c'est dégoûtant!

■ **gross up**: **~ up [sth]** Fin calculer le montant brut de [*interest, profits*].

gross: **~ domestic product, GDP** *n* Econ produit *m* intérieur brut, PIB *m*; **~ indecency** *n* Jur outrage *m* à la pudeur.

grossly /ˈgrəʊslɪ/ *adv* **1** [*abuse, betray*] de façon éhontée; [*exaggerate*] grossièrement; [*irresponsible, misleading, overcrowded, overrated*] extrêmement; [*underpaid*] scandaleusement; **~ unfair** d'une injustice flagrante; **~ overweight** obèse; **2** (crudely) [*speak, behave*] de façon grossière.

gross national product, GNP *n* Econ produit *m* national brut, PNB *m*.

grossness /ˈgrəʊsnɪs/ *n* **1** (obesity) obésité *f*; **2** (vulgarity) (of conduct, manners, language) grossièreté *f*; **3** (seriousness) énormité *f*.

gross: **~ ton** *n* tonne *f* britannique (*1016 kilogrammes*); **~ tonnage** *n* Naut jauge *f* brute.

grot○ /ˈgrɒt/ *n* crasse *f*.

grotesque /grəʊˈtesk/ *n, adj* grotesque (*m*).

grotesquely /grəʊˈtesklɪ/ *adv* [*dressed*] de façon grotesque; **~ ugly** grotesque.

grotto /ˈgrɒtəʊ/ *n* (*pl* **~s** ou **~es**) grotte *f*.

grotty○ /ˈgrɒtɪ/ *adj* GB **1** (squalid) minable○; **2** (ill) **to feel ~** se sentir tout chose○.

grouch○ /graʊtʃ/ I *n* **1** (person) rouspéteur/-euse○ *m/f*; **2** (complaint) **to have a ~ against** être en rogne contre.

II *vi* rouspéter○ (**about sb** après qn; **about sth** contre qch).

grouchy○ /ˈgraʊtʃɪ/ *adj* grognon/-onne.

ground /graʊnd/ I *pret, pp* ▶ **grind** II, III.

II *n* **1** (surface underfoot) sol *m*, terre *f*; **to put/throw sth on the ~** poser/jeter qch par terre; **to sit/lie (down) on the ground** s'asseoir/s'allonger par terre; **to fall to the ~** tomber (par terre); **to pick sth up off the ~** ramasser qch (par terre); **get up off the ~** lève-toi; **to get off the ~** [*plane*] décoller; fig [*idea*] prendre fig; **to get sth off the ~** faire démarrer [*plan, undertaking, campaign*]; **to burn to the ~** brûler complètement; **above (the) ~** en surface; **below (the) ~** sous terre; **to prepare the ~** lit préparer la terre or le sol; fig ouvrir la voie (**for** à) ; **to clear the ~** lit, fig déblayer le terrain; **on the ~** lit, fig sur le terrain; **2** (area, territory) lit, fig terrain *m*; **a piece of ~** un terrain; **built on high/rocky ~** construit sur un terrain surélevé/accidenté; **holy/neutral ~** terrain consacré/neutre; **to cover a lot of ~** lit faire beaucoup de chemin; fig avancer beaucoup; **to cover the same ~** [*teachers, speakers*] traiter le même sujet; [*articles, lectures*] traiter du même sujet; **to go over the same ~** se répéter; **to break fresh** ou **new ~** innover (**by** ou **in doing** en faisant); **to break new political/legal ~** innover dans le domaine politique/légal; **it breaks no new ~** cela n'apporte rien de nouveau; **on neutral ~** en terrain neutre ; **on my/her own ~** sur mon/son propre terrain; **to be on sure** ou **firm ~** être sûr de ce qu'on avance; **to be on shaky ~** être dans une position délicate; **to be sure of one's ~** être sûr de son fait or de ce qu'on avance; **(to be) on dangerous ~** (in discussion) (être) sur un terrain miné; (in dealings) (être) dans une position délicate; **on safe ~** sur un terrain familier; **the ~ is shifting** le climat est en train de changer fig; **familiar/new ~** domaine *m* familier/nouveau; **3** gen, Sport (for specific activity) terrain *m*; **4** (reason) gen, Jur motifs *mpl*, raisons *fpl*; **5** fig (in contest, discussion) **to gain ~** gagner du terrain (**on, over** sur); **to lose ~** perdre du terrain (**to** au profit de); **to give** ou **yield ~** céder du terrain (**to** devant; **on, over** au niveau de); **to make up** ou **regain lost ~** regagner

du terrain perdu; **to hold** ou **stand (one's) ~** tenir bon; **to change** ou **shift one's ~** fig changer son fusil d'épaule (**on** au sujet de); **6** US Elec terre *f*; **7** Art fond *m*; **8** Naut **to touch ~** racler le fond; **9** (also **~ coat**) Constr sous-couche *f*.
III grounds *npl* **1** (of house, institution) parc *m* (**of** de); **private ~s** propriété *f* privée; **2 on ethical ~s** pour des raisons d'éthique; (reasons) **on compassionate ~s** pour raisons personnelles; **~s for** motifs de [*divorce, appeal, extradition, arrest, opposition, criticism, hope*]; **to have ~s for complaint/for suspicion** avoir des motifs de se plaindre/de douter; **to give sb ~s for anxiety** être un motif or une source d'angoisse pour qn; **~s for doing** motifs pour faire; **there are reasonable ~s/there are no ~s for supposing that** il y a des motifs suffisants/il n'y a aucun motif pour supposer que; **to give sb good ~s for doing** donner à qn de bonnes raisons de faire; **to have ~s to do** avoir des raisons de faire; **on (the) ~s of** en raison de [*cost, public interest*]; pour raison de [*adultery, negligence, insufficient evidence*]; **on (the) ~s of ill-health** pour raisons de santé; **to lodge an appeal on the ~s of insanity** faire appel en arguant la folie; **on the ~s that** en raison du fait que.
IV ground *pp adj* [*coffee, pepper*] moulu.
V *vtr* **1** Aviat immobiliser [*aircraft*]; déclarer [qn] inapte [*crew, pilot*]; **2** Naut faire échouer [*vessel*] (**on** sur); **to be ~ed** s'échouer; **3** (base) **to ~ sth on** ou **in** fonder qch sur; **to be ~ed on** être fondé sur [*principle, fact, experience*]; **to be ~ed in** être fondé sur [*right, truth, understanding*]; **well-~ed suspicions** des soupçons fondés; **a well-~ed theory** une théorie bien fondée; **4**○ (punish) priver [qn] de sortie [*teenager*]; **5** US Elec mettre [qch] à la terre; **6** Mil **to ~ arms** poser l'arme à la terre; **~ arms!** reposez armes!
IDIOMS **to be thick/thin on the ~** être/ne pas être légion *inv*; **to go to ~** se terrer; **to run sb/sth to ~** dénicher○ qn/qch; **to run** ou **drive oneself into the ~** s'user or se crever○ au travail; **to run sth into the ~** laisser péricliter [*business*]; **to run a car into the ~** garder une voiture jusqu'à ce qu'elle soit bonne pour la casse; **that suits me down to the ~** ça me va parfaitement.

ground: **~ almonds** *npl* poudre *f* d'amandes; **~ attack** *n* attaque *f* au sol; **~bait** *n* appât *m*; **~-based** *adj* Mil basé au sol; **~ bass** *n* basse *f* obstinée; **~ beef** *n* US bœuf *m* haché; **~ clearance** *n* Aut garde *f* au sol; **~ cloth** *n* US tapis *m* de sol; **~ control** *n* contrôle *m* au sol; **~ cover** *n* couverture *f*; **~ cover plant** *n* plante *f* tapissante or couvrante; **~ crew** *n* personnel *m* au sol; **~ effect** *n* effet *m* de sol.

ground floor surtout GB **I** *n* rez-de-chaussée *m*; **on the ~** au rez-de-chaussée.
II ground-floor *modif* [*apartment, room, window*] au rez-de-chaussée; **at ground-floor level** au rez-de-chaussée; **to come in on the ~**○ fig commencer en bas de l'échelle.

ground: **~ forces** *npl* forces *fpl* terrestres; **~ frost** *n* givre *m*; **~ glass** *n* (opaque) verre *m* dépoli; (crushed) poudre *f* de verre; **~hog** *n* US marmotte *f* d'Amérique; **Groundhog Day** *n* US le 2 février (*dans la croyance populaire, jour décisif quant à la durée de l'hiver*); **~ hostess ▶1692** *n* hôtesse *f* au sol.

grounding /ˈgraʊndɪŋ/ *n* **1** ȼ (preparation) bases *fpl* (**in** en, de); **to have a good** ou **thorough ~ in sth** avoir de bonnes or de très solides bases en qch; **2** Aviat (of plane) immobilisation *f*; (of crew) inaptitude *f* au vol; **3** Naut échouage *m* (**on** sur); **4** US Elec mise *f* à la terre (**of** de).

ground: **~ ivy** *n* lierre *m* terrestre, gléchome *m* spec; **~keeper** *n* US préposé *m* à l'entretien d'un terrain de sports.

groundless /ˈgraʊndlɪs/ *adj* [*fear, rumour, allegation, objection*] sans fondement; [*hope*] non fondé; **to prove (to be) ~** s'avérer sans fondement.

ground: **~ level** *n* Constr rez-de-chaussée *m*; (of land) niveau *m* du sol; **~nut** *n* GB arachide *f*; **~nut oil** *n* GB huile *f* d'arachide.

ground plan *n* **1** Archit plan *m* au sol; **2** gen plan *m* préliminaire.

ground: **~ rent** *n* rente *f* foncière; **~ rice** *n* semoule *f* de riz.

ground rules *npl* grands principes *mpl*; **to change the ~** modifier les règles du jeu.

groundsel /ˈgraʊnsl/ *n* séneçon *m*.

ground: **~sheet** *n* tapis *m* de sol; **~sman** *n* GB préposé *m* à l'entretien d'un terrain de sports; **~ speed** *n* vitesse *f* au sol.

groundstaff /ˈgraʊndstɑːf, US -stæf/ *n* **1** (for maintenance) personnel *m* d'entretien d'un terrain de sports; **2** Aviat personnel *m* au sol.

groundswell /ˈgraʊndswel/ *n* **1** fig (upsurge) **a ~ of** une vague de [*support, discontent*]; **a ~ of opinion for/against** une vague de soutien pour/d'hostilité contre; **2** lit, Naut raz-de-marée *m*.

ground: **~-to-air missile** *n* missile *m* sol-air; **~ troops** *npl* troupes *fpl* terrestres; **~water** *n* nappe *f* phréatique; **~ wire** *n* US fil *m* de terre.

groundwork /ˈgraʊndwɜːk/ *n* travail *m* préparatoire (**for** à); **to do the ~** faire le travail préparatoire.

ground zero *n* point *m* zéro.

group /gruːp/ **I** *n* (all contexts) groupe *m*; **in ~s** en groupes.
II *modif* [*behaviour, dynamics, mentality*] de groupe.
III *vtr* (also **~ together**) grouper [*people, objects*] (**round** autour de); **to ~ sth according to price** grouper qch en fonction du prix.
IV *vi* (also **~ together**) se grouper (**round** autour de).
V *v refl* **to ~ oneself** [*people*] (get into groups) se répartir en groupes; **to ~ oneself according to age** se répartir par groupes d'âge; (get into a group) **to ~ oneself around** se grouper autour de.

group: **~ booking** *n* réservation *f* de groupe; **~ captain ▶1612** *n* GB Mil Aviat colonel *m* (*de l'armée de l'air*).

grouper /ˈgruːpə(r)/ *n* Zool mérou *m*.

groupie○ /ˈgruːpɪ/ *n* groupie○ *f*.

grouping /ˈgruːpɪŋ/ *n* (group, alliance) groupe *m*.

group: **~ insurance** *n* Insur assurance *f* collective; **Group of Seven** *n* groupe *m* des Sept; **~ practice** *n* Med cabinet *m* médical collectif; **~ sex** *n* amour *m* en groupe, partouze◑ *f*; **~ therapy** *n* thérapie *f* de groupe; **~ work** *n* travail *m* en groupes.

grouse /graʊs/ **I** *n* (*pl* **~**) **1** (bird, meat) tétras *m*; **2**○ (complaint) sujet *m* de mécontentement.
II○ *vi* (complain) râler○ (**about** après).

grouse: **~ beating** *n* rabattage *m* de tétras; **~ moor** *n* chasse *f* gardée de tétras; **~ shooting** *n* chasse *f* au tétras.

grout /graʊt/ **I** *n* mastic *m* (*pour carreaux*).
II *vtr* mastiquer [*tile*].

grouting /ˈgraʊtɪŋ/ *n* masticage *m*.

grove /grəʊv/ *n* bosquet *m*; **lemon ~** verger *m* de citronniers.

grovel /ˈgrɒvl/ *vi* (*p prés etc* **-ll-**, US **-l-**) **1** fig (humbly) ramper (**to sb, before sb** devant qn); **to ~ at sb's feet** ramper aux pieds de qn; **2** (also **~ about**, **~ around**) marcher à quatre pattes.

grovelling, **groveling** US /ˈgrɒvlɪŋ/ *adj* [*person, apology*] obséquieux/-ieuse.

grow /grəʊ/ (*prét* **grew**, *pp* **grown**) **I** *vtr* **1** (cultivate) cultiver [*plant, crop, cells*]; **2** (increase, allow to increase) [*person*] laisser pousser [*hair, beard, nails*]; **to ~ 5 cm** [*person*] grandir de 5 cm; [*plant*] pousser de 5 cm; **the economy has grown 2%** la croissance de l'économie est de 2%.
II *vi* **1** (increase physically) [*plant, hair, nails*] pousser (**by** de); [*person*] grandir (**by** de); [*queue*] s'allonger; [*tumour, cancer*] se développer; **haven't you grown!** qu'est-ce que tu as grandi!; **to let one's hair/nails ~** laisser pousser ses cheveux/ongles; **to ~ from** pousser à partir de [*bulb, seed*]; **to ~ to a height of 4 metres** atteindre 4 mètres de hauteur; **2** (of something abstract) [*deficit, spending, crime, population, tension, anger, chances*] augmenter (**by** de); [*company*] prospérer; [*economy*] être en expansion; [*movement, opposition, support, problem*] devenir plus important; [*poverty, crisis*] s'aggraver; [*pressure, influence*] devenir plus fort; [*list*] s'allonger; [*mystery*] s'épaissir; **fears are ~ing that** on craint de plus en plus que (+ *subj*); **to ~ from x to y** [*profit, movement*] passer de x à y; **to ~ to** atteindre [*figure, level*]; **to ~ to civil war proportions** prendre les proportions d'une guerre civile; **to ~ in** acquérir plus de [*authority, strength, confidence*]; **to ~ in popularity** devenir plus populaire; **3** (become) devenir [*hotter, colder, stronger*]; **to ~ more sophisticated** devenir plus sophistiqué; **to ~ old** vieillir; **to ~ weak** s'affaiblir; **to ~ more and more impatient** s'impatienter de plus en plus; **4 to ~ to do** finir par faire; **I soon grew to like him** j'ai vite fini par l'aimer; **I was ~ing to like him** je commençais à l'aimer.

■ **grow apart**: **~ apart** [*people*] s'éloigner l'un de l'autre; **to ~ apart from** s'éloigner de [*person*].

■ **grow in**: **~ in** [*nail*] devenir incarné.

■ **grow into**: **~ into [sth] 1** (become) devenir [*frog, adult*]; **2** (fit into) s'accoutumer à [*role, position*]; **he'll ~ into it** (of garment) quand il aura un peu grandi il pourra le mettre; **3** [*skin, bone*] se fondre dans [*tissue*].

■ **grow on: to ~ on sb** [*habit*] s'imposer; **the music was starting to ~ on me** je commençais à apprécier la musique.

■ **grow out**: **~ [sth] out, ~ out [sth]** laisser pousser ses cheveux jusqu'à ce qu'il n'y ait plus de [*perm, dye*].

■ **grow out of**: **~ out of [sth] 1** (get too old for) **he's grown out of his suit** son costume est devenu trop petit pour lui; **she's grown out of discos/going to discos** elle a passé l'âge des discothèques/d'aller en discothèque; **children's games I've grown out of** des jeux d'enfants qui ne sont plus de mon âge; **2** (come from) naître de [*interest, idea, institution*].

■ **grow together 1** lit (join together) [*bones, plants, eyebrows*] se rejoindre; **2** fig (become close) [*people*] se rapprocher.

■ **grow up 1** (grow, get bigger) [*child*] grandir; [*movement, idea*] se développer; **to ~ up in London/believing that** grandir à Londres/dans l'idée que; **2** (become adult, mature) [*person, movement*] devenir adulte; **when I ~ up** quand je serai grand; **to ~ up into** devenir [*scientist, beauty*]; **~ up!** arrête tes enfantillages!

grow bag *n* sac *m* de culture.

grower /ˈgrəʊə(r)/ *n* **1** (person) (of fruit) producteur/-trice *m/f*; (of cereal crops) cultivateur/-trice *m/f*; (of flowers) horticulteur/-trice *m/f*; **2** (plant) **to be a fast/slow ~** pousser vite/lentement.

growing /ˈgrəʊɪŋ/ **I** *n* Agric, Hort culture *f*; **rose ~** culture des roses; **a fruit-~ area** une région de culture fruitière.
II *adj* **1** (physically) [*child*] en pleine croissance; [*business*] en expansion; **it could harm the ~ baby** ça pourrait nuire à l'enfant pendant son développement; **2** (increasing) [*number, amount, authority, demand*] croissant; [*alarm, pressure, optimism, criticism, opposition*] grandissant; **to have a ~ need to do** avoir de plus en plus

besoin de faire; **there is ~ concern about** on s'inquiète de plus en plus au sujet de; **she has a ~ following** elle a de plus en plus de partisans.

growing pains *npl* **1** lit douleurs *fpl* de croissance; **2** fig (of firm, project) difficultés *fpl* dans le développement.

growing season *n* période *f* de croissance.

growl /graʊl/ **I** *n* (of dog, thunder) grondement *m*; (of person) grognement *m*; **to give a ~** grogner.
II *vtr* grommeler [*insult, curse*]; **'no,' he ~ed** 'non,' grommela-t-il; **he ~ed his reply** il répondit en grommelant.
III *vi* [*dog, thunder*] gronder; [*person*] grogner (**at** après).

grown /grəʊn/ **I** *pp* ▸ **grow**.
II *adj* **a ~ man/woman** un/-e adulte; **~ men were reduced to tears** même les hommes ont pleuré.
III -grown (*dans composés*) **moss-/weed-~** envahi par la mousse/par les mauvaises herbes; ▸ **full-grown**, **home-grown**.

grown over *adj* = **overgrown** 1.

grown-up **I** /ˈgrəʊnʌp/ *n* adulte *mf*; grande personne *f*.
II /ˌgrəʊnˈʌp/ *adj* adulte; **~ son** fils *m* adulte; **what do you want to do when you're ~?** qu'est-ce que tu veux faire quand tu seras grand?; **to behave in a ~ manner** se comporter en adulte; **to be ~ for one's age** être mûr pour son âge; **to look ~** avoir l'air d'un/-e adulte; **to sound ~** parler comme un/-e adulte.

growth /grəʊθ/ *n* **1** (physical) (of person, plant) croissance *f*; (of hair, nails) pousse *f*; **2** (increase) (of population, movement, idea, feeling) croissance *f* (**in, of** de); (of economy) expansion *f* (**in, of** de); (of numbers, amount, productivity, earnings) augmentation *f* (**in** de); (of expenditure) hausse *f* (**in** de); **a ~ in crime** une augmentation du nombre de crimes; **3** Med grosseur *f*, tumeur *f*; **4** (thing growing) Bot pousse *f*; **the new ~ on a plant** la nouvelle pousse sur une plante; **a thick ~ of weeds** des mauvaises herbes qui poussent dru; **a week's ~ of beard** une barbe d'une semaine.

growth: **~ area** *n* secteur *m* en expansion; **~ factor** *n* facteur *m* de croissance; **~ hormone** *n* hormone *f* de croissance; **~ industry** *n* industrie *f* en expansion.

growth rate *n* **1** Econ taux *m* de croissance; **2** (of person, animal, plant) rythme *m* de croissance; **the population ~** le taux de croissance démographique.

growth: **~ ring** *n* Bot (on tree) anneau *m*; **~ share** *n* valeur *f* de croissance.

groyne GB, **groin** US /grɔɪn/ *n* épi *m* (*pour retenir le sable*).

grub /grʌb/ **I** *n* **1** Zool larve *f*; (in fruit) ver *m*; **2**○ (food) bouffe○ *f*; **~'s up!** à la bouffe!
II○ *vtr* (*p prés etc* **-bb-**) US **to ~ sth from sb** soutirer qch à qn.
■ **grub about**, **grub around**: **~ about** ou **~ around for sth** fouiner pour trouver qch.
■ **grub up**: **~ [sth] up**, **~ up [sth]** [*person, machine*] déraciner; [*animal, bird*] déterrer.

grubbiness /ˈgrʌbɪnɪs/ *n* lit saleté *f*; fig infamie *f*.

grubby /ˈgrʌbɪ/ *adj* lit malpropre; fig infâme.

grub screw *n* vis *f* sans tête.

grubstake○ US /ˈgrʌbsteɪk/ **I** *n* avance *f* (*pour un projet*).
II *vtr* avancer du fric○ à [*person*]; avancer du fric○ pour [*projet*].

Grub Street *n*: *le monde des plumitifs nécessiteux*.

grudge /grʌdʒ/ **I** *n* **to bear** GB ou **hold** US **a ~** avoir de la rancune (**against** contre); **to bear sb a ~** en vouloir à qn, avoir de la rancune contre qn; **to harbour** ou **nurse a ~ against sb** garder de la rancune contre qn.
II *vtr* **to ~ sb sth** en vouloir à qn de qch; **to ~ sb their success/good looks** en vouloir à qn de sa réussite/de sa beauté; **to ~ doing sth** rechigner à faire qch.

grudging /ˈgrʌdʒɪŋ/ *adj* [*acceptance, admiration*] réticent; **to give sb ~ support** donner un soutien peu enthousiaste à qn; **to treat sb with ~ respect** respecter qn malgré soi; **to be ~ in one's praise/thanks** être avare de compliments/de remerciements.

grudgingly /ˈgrʌdʒɪŋlɪ/ *adv* [*admit, tolerate*] avec réticence; **the man whom they ~ respected** l'homme qu'ils respectaient malgré eux.

gruel /ˈgru:əl/ *n* gruau *m*.

gruelling, **grueling** US /ˈgru:əlɪŋ/ *adj* exténuant.

gruesome /ˈgru:səm/ *adj* (gory) horrible (also hum); (horrifying) épouvantable.

gruff /grʌf/ *adj* bourru.

gruffly /ˈgrʌflɪ/ *adv* d'un ton bourru.

gruffness /ˈgrʌfnɪs/ *n* rudesse *f*; **the ~ of his voice** sa voix bourrue.

grumble /ˈgrʌmbl/ **I** *n* **1** (complaint) ronchonnement *m*; **to have a ~ about sb/sth** ronchonner après qn/qch; **my only ~ is...** la seule chose dont j'ai à me plaindre est...; **2** (of thunder) grondement *m*; (of stomach) gargouillement *m*.
II *vtr* **'if you insist,' he ~d** 'si vous y tenez,' ronchonna-t-il.
III *vi* **1** [*person*] ronchonner (**at sb** après qn; **to** auprès de); **to ~ about sb/sth** se plaindre de qn/qch; **'How are you?'—'Oh, mustn't ~'** 'Ça va?'—'Oh, il n'y a pas à se plaindre'; **2** [*thunder*] gronder; [*stomach*] gargouiller.

grumbler○ /ˈgrʌmblə(r)/ *n* ronchonneur/-euse○ *m/f*.

grumbling /ˈgrʌmblɪŋ/ **I** *n* **1** ₵ (complaining) plaintes *fpl*; **2** (of thunder) grondement *m*; (of stomach) gargouillement *m*.
II *adj* **1** (complaining) ronchon/-onne○; **~ appendix** appendicite *f* chronique.

grump○ /grʌmp/ *n* (person) ronchon○ *mf*; **to have the ~s**○ être de mauvais poil○.

grumpily /ˈgrʌmpɪlɪ/ *adv* [*speak*] en bougonnant; [*act*] d'un air maussade.

grumpiness /ˈgrʌmpɪnɪs/ *n* caractère *m* bourru.

grumpy /ˈgrʌmpɪ/ *adj* grincheux/-euse, grognon/-onne.

grunge○ /ˈgrʌndʒ/ *n* **1** (dirt) crasse *f*; **2** Fashn grunge *m*.

grungy○ /ˈgrʌndʒɪ/ *adj* crasseux/-euse.

grunt /grʌnt/ **I** *n* **1** (of person, animal) grognement *m*; **to give a ~ of disapproval** émettre un grognement de désapprobation; **2**○ US (soldier) troufion○ *m*.
II *vtr* **to ~ a reply** répondre en grognant; **'go away!' he ~ed** 'va-t-en!' grogna-t-il.
III *vi* **1** [*pig*] grogner; **2** [*person*] grogner, émettre un grognement; **to ~ with** ou **in pain/pleasure** grogner de douleur/plaisir.

gryphon = **griffin**.

GSM *n* (*abrév* = **Global Systems for Mobile Communications**) GSM *m*.

G: **G spot** *n* point *m* G; **G-string** *n* Mus corde *f* de sol; Fashn string *m*, cache-sexe *m inv*; **G-suit** *n* combinaison *f* spatiale or anti-g.

Gt *abrév écrite* = **Great**.

Guadeloupe /ˌgwɑ:dəˈlu:p/ ▸ **1163** *pr n* Guadeloupe; **in/to ~** à la or en Guadeloupe.

guano /ˈgwɑ:nəʊ/ *n* guano *m*.

guarantee /ˌgærənˈti:/ **I** *n* **1** Comm (warranty, document) garantie *f* (**against** contre); **to be under ~** GB être sous garantie; **there is a ~ on the vehicle** le véhicule est sous garantie; **this television comes with** ou **carries a one-year ~** cette télévision a une garantie d'un an or est garantie un an; **2** (assurance) garantie *f* (**against** contre); **to give ~s to sb** donner des garanties à qn; **you have my ~!** je vous en donne ma parole!; **beauty is not a ~ of happiness** la beauté n'est pas une garantie de bonheur; **there is no ~ that she will come** il n'est pas certain qu'elle viendra; **3** Jur (of financial liability, sb's debts) garantie *f*; **to give a ~ of sb's good behaviour** se porter garant de la bonne conduite de qn; **4** (security) (cash) caution *f*; (object) gage *m*, garantie *f*; **to give sth as a ~** [*money*] donner qch en caution; [*object*] donner qch en gage; **5** (person) = **guarantor**.
II *vtr* **1** Comm garantir [*product, goods*] (**against** contre); **it's ~d for five years** il est garanti cinq ans; **~d waterproof** garanti étanche; **to be ~d against defective workmanship** être garanti contre les vices de fabrication; **2** (assure) garantir, assurer; **to ~ to do** s'engager à faire; **to ~ sb's safety** garantir la sécurité de qn; **I can ~ that they will come** je peux vous garantir qu'ils viendront; **I can't ~ that it's true** je ne peux pas garantir que ce soit vrai; **you won't regret it, I can ~ you that!** tu ne le regretteras pas, je te le garantis!; **her new novel is a ~d bestseller** son nouveau roman sera un bestseller à coup sûr; **the plan is ~d to succeed** le succès du plan est certain; **if we go for a walk, it's ~d to rain!** si nous allons faire une promenade, c'est sûr qu'il pleuvra!; **3** Jur **to ~ a loan** se porter garant or caution d'un emprunt; **to ~ sb for a loan** servir de garant or de caution à qn pour un emprunt; **to ~ sb's debts** servir de garant or de caution pour les dettes de qn; **to ~ a cheque** garantir un chèque; **to ~ a bill** avaliser une traite; **to ~ sb's good conduct** se porter garant de la bonne conduite de qn.

guaranteed: **~ interest** *n* taux *m* d'intérêt fixe garanti; **~ loan** *n* prêt *m* garanti; **~ price** *n* prix *m* garanti.

guarantor /ˌgærənˈtɔ:(r)/ *n* caution *f*, garant/-e *m/f*; **to stand ~ for sb** se porter garant de qn.

guaranty /ˈgærəntɪ/ *n* (all contexts) garantie *f*.

guard /gɑ:d/ **I** *n* **1** (minder) (for person) surveillant/-e *m/f*; (for place, object) gardien/-ienne *m/f*; **2** (at prison) gardien/-ienne *m/f*; (soldier) garde *m*; **3** Mil (duty) garde *f*, surveillance *f*; **to be on ~** être de garde; **to go on ~** prendre son tour de garde; **to come off ~** finir son tour de garde; **to keep** ou **stand ~** monter la garde (**over** auprès de); **to mount (a) ~ over sb/sth** monter la garde auprès de qn/qch; **the changing of the ~** GB la relève de la garde; **4** (watchfulness) **to drop** ou **relax** ou **lower one's ~** baisser la garde; **to catch sb off ~** prendre qn au dépourvu; **to be on one's ~** être sur ses gardes; **to be on one's ~ against sth** se méfier de qch; **to be on one's ~ against sth happening** veiller à ce que qch n'arrive pas; **5** (group of soldiers, police etc) **to transport sth under an armed ~** transporter qch sous escorte armée; **6** GB Rail chef *m* de train; **7** (for safety) (on printer) couvercle *m*; (on industrial machinery) carter *m* de protection; **8** GB (in names of regiments) garde *m*; **the Scots Guards** la garde écossaise; **the Coldstream Guard** le régiment de Coldstream; **9** (in Ireland) (policeman) policier *m* (irlandais).
II *vtr* **1** (protect) assurer la garde de [*place, object*]; protéger [*person, reputation*]; **a dog ~s the house** un chien garde la maison; **the house/border is heavily ~ed** la maison/la frontière est sous haute surveillance; **to ~ sth with one's life** protéger qch au péril de sa vie; **to ~ one's tongue** fig surveiller sa langue; **2** (prevent from escaping) garder [*prisoner*]; **to be closely ~ed** être surveillé de près; **3** (from discovery) garder [*secret*]; **a closely ~ed secret** un secret bien gardé.
IDIOMS **the old ~** la vieille garde.
■ **guard against**: **~ against [sth]** se pré-

munir contre [*abuses, cheating, failure*]; **to ~ against doing sth** prendre garde à ne pas faire qch; **to ~ against sth happening** veiller à ce que qch n'arrive pas.

guard dog *n* chien *m* de garde.

guard duty *n* **to be on ~** être de garde.

guarded /ˈɡɑːdɪd/ *adj* circonspect (**about** à propos de).

guardedly /ˈɡɑːdɪdlɪ/ *adv* avec circonspection.

guardedness /ˈɡɑːdɪdnɪs/ *n* réserve *f*.

guardhouse *n* poste *m* de garde.

guardian /ˈɡɑːdɪən/ *n* **1** Jur tuteur/-trice *m/f*; **legal ~** tuteur/-trice *m/f* légal/-e; **2** (defender) gardien/-ienne *m/f* (**of** de).

guardian angel *n* lit, fig ange *m* gardien.

guard: **~ of honour** *n* garde *f* d'honneur; **~ rail** *n* Aut glissière *f* de sécurité; (on bridge, window) garde-fou *m*; **~room** *n* salle *f* d'arrêt(s); **~sman** *n* GB Mil garde *m* (*membre de la garde royale*); US Mil soldat *m* de la garde nationale; **~'s van** *n* GB Rail fourgon *m* à bagages.

Guatemala /ˌɡwɑːtəˈmɑːlə/ **▶1131** *pr n* Guatemala *m*.

Guatemalan /ˌɡwɑːtəˈmɑːlən/ **▶1486** **I** *n* Guatémaltèque *mf*.
II *adj* guatémaltèque.

guava /ˈɡwɑːvə, US ˈɡwɔːvə/ *n* (tree) goyavier *m*; (fruit) goyave *f*.

gubbins○ /ˈɡʌbɪnz/ *n* GB **1** (gadget) truc○ *m*; **2** (idiot) andouille○ *mf*.

gubernatorial /ˌɡuːbənəˈtɔːrɪəl/ *adj* sout du or de gouverneur.

gudgeon /ˈɡʌdʒən/ *n* Zool goujon *m*.

gudgeon pin *n* goupille *f*.

guelder rose /ˌɡeldə ˈrəʊz/ *n* boule-de-neige *f*.

Guelf, **Guelph** /ɡwelf/ *pr n* Pol Hist guelfe *m*.

guernsey /ˈɡɜːnzɪ/ *n* Fashn pull *m* marin.

Guernsey /ˈɡɜːnzɪ/ *pr n* **1** **▶1381** Geog Guernesey *f*; **2** (also **~ cow**) Guernesey *f*.

guerrilla /ɡəˈrɪlə/ **I** *n* guérillero *m*; **urban ~s** guérilla *f* urbaine.
II *modif* [*attack, organization*] de guérilleros.

guerrilla: **~ war** *n* guérilla *f*; **~ warfare** *n* guérilla *f*.

guess /ɡes/ **I** *n* supposition *f*, conjecture *f*; **to have** ou **make** ou **take a ~** essayer de deviner; **to have** ou **make** ou **take a ~ at sth** essayer de deviner qch; **my ~ is that they will lose** à mon avis ils vont perdre; **at a (rough) ~ I would say that he is about 30** au hasard je dirais qu'il a 30 ans environ; **there are, at a ~, ten families living in that building** il doit y avoir approximativement une dizaine de familles habitant cet immeuble; **I'll give you three ~es!** devine un peu!; **that was a good ~!** tu as deviné juste!; **'how did you know?' — 'just a lucky ~!'** 'comment est-ce que tu l'as su?' — 'c'est le hasard'; **to make a wild ~** deviner au hasard; **your ~ is as good as mine** je n'en sais pas plus que toi; **it's anybody's ~!** les paris sont ouverts!; **what will happen now is anybody's ~** Dieu seul sait ce qui va arriver maintenant.
II *vtr* **1** (intuit) deviner [*answer, reason, name, identity*]; deviner, estimer [*length, width*]; **to ~ that** conjecturer que, supposer que; **to ~ sb's age** (correctly) deviner l'âge de qn; (make estimate) donner un âge à qn; **I should ~ him to be about 30** je lui donnerais 30 ans environ; **I ~ed the time to be about one o'clock** il me semblait qu'il devait être environ une heure; **she had ~ed what I was thinking** elle avait deviné mes pensées; **you'll never ~ what has happened!** tu ne devineras jamais ce qui vient d'arriver!; **I ~ed as much!** je m'en doutais!; **~ what! I've won a prize!** tu sais quoi○! j'ai gagné un prix!; **~ who!** devine qui c'est!; **2** US (suppose) supposer; (believe, think) penser, croire; **I ~ (that) what he says is true** je suppose que ce qu'il dit est vrai; **I ~ (that) I must be going now** il faut que je m'en aille maintenant; **'he's right, you know' — 'I ~ so'** 'il a raison, tu sais' — 'oui, je suppose'; **'you can't be sure' — 'I ~ not'** 'tu ne peux pas être sûr' — 'non, effectivement'.
III *vi* **1** deviner; **to ~ at** faire des suppositions or des conjectures quant à [*plans, outcome*]; **to ~ right** deviner juste; **to ~ wrong** se tromper; **you're just ~ing!** tu ne fais que deviner!; **you'll never ~!** tu ne devineras jamais!; **I couldn't begin to ~** je n'en ai pas la moindre idée; **to keep sb ~ing** laisser qn dans le doute.

guesstimate○ /ˈɡestɪmət/ **I** *n* calcul *m* approximatif.
II *vtr* calculer [qch] approximativement.

guesswork /ˈɡeswɜːk/ *n* conjecture *f*; **it's pure ~** c'est de la conjecture, ce ne sont que des hypothèses.

guest /ɡest/ **I** *n* **1** (in home, at table, at reception) invité/-e *m/f*; (of hotel) client/-e *m/f*; (of boarding house) pensionnaire *mf*; (at conference, on chat show) invité/-e *m/f*; **~ of honour** invité/-e *m/f* d'honneur; **paying ~** hôte *m* payant; **house ~** invité/-e *m/f*; **three uninvited ~s** trois personnes qui n'avaient pas été invitées; **be my ~!** je vous en prie!; **2** Biol hôte *m*.
II *modif* [*singer, speaker, conductor etc*] invité; **~ book** livre *m* d'or; **~ list** liste *f* des invités; **~ night** (at club) *soirée non réservée aux membres d'un club*; **~ star** gen invité(e) d'honneur ; (in film credits) avec la participation de; **making a ~ appearance on tonight's show is X** pour notre spectacle de ce soir nous avons invité X; **our ~ speaker tonight is...** notre invité(e) ce soir est...
III *vi* **to ~ on a programme** être invité à une émission.

guest: **~house** *n* pension *f* de famille; **~ room** *n* chambre *f* d'amis; **~worker** *n* travailleur *m* immigré, travailleuse *f* immigrée.

guff○ /ɡʌf/ *n* ¢ sottises *fpl*.

guffaw /ɡəˈfɔː/ **I** *n* gros éclat *m* de rire.
II *vi* partir d'un gros éclat de rire.

Guiana /ɡaɪˈænə/ **▶1131** *pr n* Guyane *f*; **the ~s** les Guyannes.

guidance /ˈɡaɪdns/ *n* **1** (advice) conseils *mpl* (**from** de); **clear ~** conseils clairs; **~ on legal procedures** conseils en matière de procédures légales; **~ on how to do** conseils sur la façon de faire; **~ as to the resolution of conflict** conseils en vue de la résolution d'un conflit; **basic ~ in areas such as finance** des informations de base dans des domaines tels que la finance; **to give sb ~** donner des conseils à qn; **to seek ~ on a matter** demander conseil sur une (certaine) question; **to seek the ~ of one's superiors** solliciter l'avis de ses supérieurs; **this leaflet is for your ~** ce prospectus est pour vous, à titre d'information; **under the ~ of sb** sous la direction de qn; **2** Aerosp (télé) guidage *m*.

guide /ɡaɪd/ **I** *n* **1** (person) guide *m*; **tour ~** guide (touristique); **spiritual/moral ~** guide spirituel/moral; **to engage a ~** prendre un guide; **to act as a ~** servir de guide; **let reason be your ~** fig laissez-vous guider par la raison; **2** (estimate, idea) indication *f*; **a ~ as to the cost/as to his whereabouts** une indication quant aux frais/quant à l'endroit où il se trouve; **the figure is meant to be a ~** le chiffre est donné à titre d'indication; **these answers are a good ~** ces réponses sont une bonne indication; **a rough ~** une indication approximative; **as a rough ~** à titre d'indication; **3** (book) guide *m* (**to** de); **a ~ to Greece** Tourism un guide de la Grèce ; **TV ~** programme *m* de télé(vision); **user's ~** manuel *m* d'utilisation; **good food ~** guide gastronomique; **4** (also **Girl Guide**) guide *f*; **5** Tech (directing device) guide *m*.
II *vtr* **1** (steer) guider, conduire [*person*] (**to** vers; **through** à travers); **2** (influence) [*person*] guider; [*reason*] dicter; **he allowed himself to be ~d by his elders** il a consenti à se laisser guider par ses aînés; **my actions were ~d by reason** mes actions étaient dictées par la raison; **to be ~d by sb's advice** suivre les conseils de qn; **3** Aerosp, Mil (télé)guider [*rocket, missile*].

guide: **~ book** *n* guide *m*; **~d missile** *n* missile *m* (télé)guidé; **~ dog** *n* chien *m* d'aveugle; **~d tour** *n* visite *f* guidée.

guideline /ˈɡaɪdlaɪn/ *n* **1** (rough guide) indication *f* (**for** pour; **on** sur); **can you give me some ~s on how to look after it?** pouvez-vous m'indiquer en gros comment l'entretenir?; **2** Admin, Pol directive *f* (**for** pour; **on** sur); **pay ~s** base *f* des négociations salariales; **3** (advice) conseil *m* (**for** pour; **on** sur); **to follow the ~s** suivre les conseils; **health/safety ~s** conseils *mpl* de santé/sécurité.

guide: **~ post** *n* poteau *m* indicateur; **~ rail** *n* Tech rail *m*; **~ rope** *n* main *f* courante.

guiding /ˈɡaɪdɪŋ/ **I** *n* GB **the history of ~** l'histoire des Guides.
II *adj* **~ force** fig moteur *m*; **~ principle** principe *m* directeur; **~ light** (person) flambeau *m*.

guild /ɡɪld/ *n* (medieval) guilde *f*; (modern) association *f*.

guilder /ˈɡɪldə(r)/ **▶1143** *n* florin *m*.

guildhall /ˈɡɪldhɔːl/ *n* (medieval) *salle de réunion d'une guilde*; (modern) hôtel *m* de ville; **the Guildhall** la salle des banquets de la Cité de Londres.

guile /ɡaɪl/ *n* ruse *f*; **full of ~** prêt à toutes les ruses; **without ~** candide.

guileful /ˈɡaɪlfl/ *adj* rusé.

guileless /ˈɡaɪllɪs/ *adj* candide.

guillemot /ˈɡɪlɪmɒt/ *n* guillemot *m*.

guillotine /ˈɡɪlətiːn/ **I** *n* **1** (for execution) guillotine *f*; **2** (for paper) massicot *m*; **3** GB Pol *système qui limite la durée des débats parlementaires*.
II *vtr* guillotiner [*person*].

guilt /ɡɪlt/ *n* **1** (blame) gen, Jur culpabilité *f*; **to admit ~** admettre sa culpabilité; **to establish/prove sb's ~** établir/prouver la culpabilité de qn; **where does the ~ lie?** qui est le coupable?; **2** (feeling) sentiment *m* de culpabilité (**about sb** envers qn; **about** ou **over sth** pour qch); **to feel no ~** n'éprouver aucun sentiment de culpabilité; **sense of ~** sentiment de culpabilité.

guiltily /ˈɡɪltɪlɪ/ *adv* [*say, look*] d'un air coupable; [*react, do*] se sentant coupable.

guiltless /ˈɡɪltlɪs/ *adj* sout innocent.

guilty /ˈɡɪltɪ/ *adj* **1** Jur coupable; **to be ~ of/of doing** être coupable de/de faire; **to be found ~/not ~ of sth** être reconnu coupable/déclaré non coupable de qch; **the ~ party** le/la coupable *m/f*; **2** (remorseful) [*expression, feeling*] de culpabilité; [*appearance, look*] coupable; **to feel ~ about sb/sth** se sentir coupable vis-à-vis de qn/qch; **to have a ~ conscience** avoir la conscience lourde.

guinea /ˈɡɪnɪ/ *n* GB Hist guinée *f*.

Guinea /ˈɡɪnɪ/ **▶1131** *pr n* Guinée *f*.

Guinea-Bissau **▶1131** *pr n* Guinée-Bissao *f*.

guinea-fowl /ˈɡɪnɪfaʊl/, **guinea-hen** /ˈɡɪnɪhen/ pintade *f*.

guinea-pig /ˈɡɪnɪpɪɡ/ *n* **1** Zool cochon *m* d'Inde; **2** fig (in experiment) cobaye *m*; **to be a ~** servir de cobaye.

Guinness® /ˈɡɪnɪs/ *pr n* Guinness® *f* (*bière brune*).

guise /ɡaɪz/ *n* littér **in** ou **under the ~ of a joke** sous (le) couvert de la plaisanterie; **in the ~ of a champion** sous l'aspect d'un champion; **in the ~ of doing sth** sous prétexte de faire qch; **in various** ou **different ~s** sous différentes formes.

guitar /gɪ'tɑː(r)/ ▶1481 I *n* guitare *f*; **on the ~** à la guitare.
II *modif* [*lesson, player, string, teacher*] de guitare; [*concerto*] pour guitare; **~ case** étui *m* à guitare.
guitarfish /gɪ'tɑːfɪʃ/ *n* (*pl* **~** or **~es**) rhinobatos *m*.
guitarist /gɪ'tɑːrɪst/ ▶1692, 1481 *n* guitariste *mf*.
Gujarat /,guːdʒə'rɑːt/ *pr n* Gujerat *m*.
Gujarati /,guːdʒə'rɑːtɪ/ ▶1402 I *pr n* **1** (person) Goujarati *mf*; **2** Ling goujarati *m*.
II *adj* goujarati.
Gulag /'guːlæg/ *n* Goulag *m*.
gulch /gʌltʃ/ *n* US ravin *m*.
gulf /gʌlf/ *n* **1** fig fossé *m*; **the ~ between X and Y/between the two groups** le fossé qui sépare X et Y/qui sépare les deux groupes; **2** Geog golfe *m*.
Gulf /gʌlf/ *pr n* **the ~** la région *f* du Golfe.
Gulf States *pr npl* **the ~** GB les États *mpl* du Golfe; US *les États bordant le golfe du Mexique*.
Gulf Stream *pr n* **the ~** le Gulf Stream.
Gulf War *pr n* guerre *f* du Golfe.
gull /gʌl/ I *n* **1** Zool mouette *f*; (larger) goéland *m*; **2†** (dupe) dupe *f*.
II† *vtr* duper.
gullet /'gʌlɪt/ *n* (throat) gosier *m*; (oesophagus) œsophage *m*; **to have sth stuck in one's ~** lit avoir qch coincé dans la gorge; **the words stuck in my ~** fig les mots ne sont pas sortis.
gullibility /,gʌlə'bɪlətɪ/ *n* crédulité *f*.
gullible /'gʌləbl/ *adj* crédule.
gull: **~-wing** *n* Aviat aile *f* en M; **~-wing door** *n* portière *f* papillon.
gully /'gʌlɪ/ *n* **1** Geog ravin *m*; **2** (drain) caniveau *m*; **3** (in cricket) (player) gully *m*; (area) zone *f* de jeu du gully.
gulp /gʌlp/ I *n* **1** (mouthful) (of liquid) gorgée *f*, lampée○ *f*; (of air) bouffée *f*, goulée *f*; (of food) bouchée *f*; **to breathe in ~s of air** avaler l'air par bouffées; **she drained her glass with** ou **in one ~** elle a vidé son verre d'un trait; **2** (noise) (nervous) serrement *m* de gorge; (tearful) hoquet *m*; **he swallowed it with a loud ~** il l'a avalé en déglutissant bruyamment; **'it's my fault,' she said with a ~** 'c'est de ma faute,' dit-elle en hoquetant.
II *vtr* **1** (swallow) engloutir [*food, drink*]; aspirer [*air*]; **there they were, ~ing brandy** ils étaient là en train de boire du cognac à grands traits; **2** (in emotion) **'you're not angry, are you?,' he ~ed** 'tu n'es pas fâchée, j'espère,' dit-il la gorge serrée.
III *vi* avoir la gorge serrée.
■ **gulp back**: **~ back [sth]**, **~ [sth] back** ravaler [*tears*].
■ **gulp down**: **~ down [sth]**, **~ [sth] down** engloutir [*food, drink*]; **he ~ed down his drink and left** il a vidé son verre d'un trait et il est parti.
gum /gʌm/ I *n* **1** Anat gencive *f*; **2** (also **chewing ~**) chewing-gum *m*; **a piece** ou **stick of ~** un chewing-gum; **3** (for glueing) colle *f*; **4** (from tree) gomme *f*.
II *vtr* (*p prés etc* **-mm-**) (spread with glue) gommer; (join with glue) coller (**to** à; **on to** sur; **together** ensemble); **~med label** étiquette gommée.
III○ *excl* **by ~!** nom d'un chien○!
IDIOMS **to ~ up the works**○ chambouler○ tout.
■ **gum down**: **~ [sth] down**, **~ down [sth]** coller.
■ **gum up**: **~ up [sth]** coller.
gum arabic *n* gomme *f* arabique.
gumbo /'gʌmbəʊ/ *n* (*pl* **~s**) Bot, Culin gombo *m*.
gum: **~boil** *n* fluxion *f* dentaire; **~boot** *n* GB botte *f* en caoutchouc; **~ disease** ▶1354 *n* gingivite *f*; **~drop** *n* boule *f* de gomme.
gummy /'gʌmɪ/ *adj* **1** [*smile*] édenté; **2** [*liquid*] gluant.
gumption○ /'gʌmpʃn/ *n* (common sense) jugeote○ *f*; (courage) cran○ *m*.
gumshield /'gʌmʃiːld/ *n* protège-dents *m inv*.
gumshoe○ /'gʌmʃuː/ I *n* (private investigator) détective *m* privé; (police detective) agent *m* de police en civil.
II *vi* US agir furtivement.
gum tree *n* gommier *m*.
IDIOMS **to be up a ~** être en position délicate.
gun /gʌn/ I *n* **1** (weapon) gen arme *f* à feu; (revolver) revolver *m*; (rifle) fusil *m*; (cannon) canon *m*; **to carry a ~** porter une arme à feu; **to fire a ~** tirer; **to draw a ~ on sb** braquer une arme sur qn; **watch out! he's got a ~!** attention! il est armé!; **2** (tool) pistolet *m*; **glue/paint ~** pistolet à colle/à peinture; ▶**grease gun**; **3**○ US (gunman) gangster *m*; **a hired ~** un tueur à gages; **the fastest ~ in the West** le tireur le plus rapide de l'Ouest.
II *vtr* (*p prés etc* **-nn-**) **to ~ an engine** mettre les gaz○.
IDIOMS **to go great ~s**○ [*business*] marcher très fort○; [*person*] péter le feu●; **to hold a ~ to sb's head** mettre le couteau sous la gorge de qn; **to jump the ~** agir prématurément; **to stick to one's ~s**○ (in one's actions) s'accrocher○; **she's sticking to her ~s**○ (in opinions) elle s'accroche○ à ses idées; ▶**big gun**.
■ **gun down**: **~ [sb] down**, **~ down [sb]** abattre, descendre [*person*].
■ **gun for**: **~ for [sb]** chercher des crosses à○.
gun: **~ barrel** *n* canon *m* de fusil; **~boat** *n* canonnière *f*; **~boat diplomacy** *n* politique *f* de la canonnière; **~ carriage** *n* affût *m* de canon; (at funeral) prolonge *f* d'artillerie; **~dog** *n* chien *m* de chasse; **~fight** *n* échange *m* de coups de feu.
gunfire /'gʌnfaɪə(r)/ *n* ¢ (from hand-held gun) coups *mpl* de feu; (from artillery) fusillade *f*; **the sound of ~** le bruit d'une fusillade; **under ~** sous le feu.
gunge○ /gʌndʒ/ GB I *n* magma *m* répugnant.
II *vtr* **to be all ~d up**○ être tout encrassé, être crado○.
gung ho○ /,gʌŋ'həʊ/ *adj* hum ou péj (eager for war) va-t-en guerre *inv*; (overzealous) (trop) enthousiaste.
gunk○ /gʌŋk/ *n* magma○ *m* répugnant.
gun: **~ laws** *npl* législation *f* sur les armes à feu; **~ licence** *n* permis *m* de port d'armes; **~man** *n* bandit *m* armé; **~metal** *n* bronze *m* à canon; **~metal grey** *n, adj* gris (*m*) foncé.
gunner /'gʌnə(r)/ *n* GB (in navy) canonnier *m*; (in army) artilleur *m*.
gunnery /'gʌnərɪ/ *n* artillerie *f*.
gunnery sergeant *n* US *artilleur sous-officier*.
gunny /'gʌnɪ/ *n* US (fabric) toile *f* de jute.
gunnysack /'gʌnɪsæk/ *n* US sac *m* de jute.
gunplay /'gʌnpleɪ/ *n* US échange *m* de coups de feu.
gunpoint /'gʌnpɔɪnt/ *n* **to hold sb up at ~** tenir qn sous la menace d'une arme.
gun: **~powder** /'gʌnpaʊdə(r)/ *n* poudre *f*; **Gunpowder Plot** *pr n* Hist Conspiration *f* des Poudres; **~room** *n* armurerie *f*; **~runner** *n* trafiquant/-e *m/f* d'armes; **~running** *n* trafic *m* d'armes.
gunsel○ /'gʌnsl/ *n* US **1** (boy) *jeune homosexuel entretenu*; **2** (gunman) bandit *m* armé.
gunship /'gʌnʃɪp/ *n* Mil Aviat hélicoptère *m* de combat.
gunshot /'gʌnʃɒt/ *n* **1** (report) coup *m* de feu; **2** (range) **to be within ~** être à portée de tir; **to be out of ~** être hors de portée de tir.
gunshot wound *n* blessure *f* par balle.
gun-shy *adj* **~ dog** chien *m* que les coups de fusil effraient.
gun: **~slinger**○ *n* US bandit *m* armé; **~smith** ▶1692 *n* armurier *m*; **~turret** *n* Mil tourelle *f*.
gunwale /'gʌnl/ *n* plat-bord *m*; **full to the ~s** plein à ras bords.
guppy /'gʌpɪ/ *n* guppy *m*.
gurgle /'gɜːgl/ I *n* (of water) gargouillement *m*; (of baby) gazouillis *m*; **to give ~s of pleasure** gazouiller de contentement.
II *vi* [*water*] gargouiller; [*baby*] gazouiller.
Gurkha /'gɜːkə/ *n* Gurkha *m*.
gurnard /'gɜːnəd/, **gurnet** /'gɜːnɪt/ *n* grondin *m*.
guru /'gʊruː/, US gə'ruː/ *n* gourou *m*.
gush /gʌʃ/ I *n* **1** (of water, oil, blood) jaillissement *m*; **2** (of enthusiasm, pleasure) élan *m*.
II *vtr* **'darling,' he ~ed** 'ma chérie,' s'extasia-t-il.
III *vi* **1** [*water, oil, blood*] jaillir; **tears ~ed down her cheeks** ses joues ruisselaient de larmes; **2** fig **to ~ over sb/sth** s'extasier devant qn/qch.
■ **gush in** [*water, oil etc*] s'engouffrer.
■ **gush out** [*water, oil etc*] jaillir.
gusher○ /'gʌʃə(r)/ *n* (oil well) puits *m* jaillissant.
gushing /'gʌʃɪŋ/, **gushy** /'gʌʃɪ/ *adj* [*person*] hyperexpansif/-ive○; [*letter, style*] dithyrambique○.
gusset /'gʌsɪt/ *n* soufflet *m*.
gussy○ /'gʌsɪ/ US *vtr* (also **~ up**) habiller [*person*]; **to be all gussied up**○ être sur son trente et un○.
gust /gʌst/ I *n* **1** (of wind, rain, snow) rafale *f*; **a ~ of hot air** une bouffée d'air chaud; **2** (of anger) bouffée *f*; **a ~ of laughter** un éclat de rire.
II *vi* [*wind*] souffler en rafales; [*rain, snow*] tomber en rafales; **winds ~ing up to 60 mph** des vents qui atteignent 100 km/h.
gusto /'gʌstəʊ/ *n* **with ~** avec enthousiasme; **to eat with ~** manger goulûment; **to sing with ~** chanter à pleins poumons.
gusty /'gʌstɪ/ *adj* [*day, weather*] de grand vent.
gut /gʌt/ I *n* **1**○ (abdomen, belly) bide○ *m*; **he was shot in the ~** on lui a tiré dans le bide○; **beer ~** brioche○ *f* (*de buveur de bière*); **2** Anat (intestine) intestin *m*; **3** (for racket, bow) boyau *m*.
II **guts**○ *npl* **1** (insides) (of human) tripes○ *fpl*; (of animal) entrailles *fpl*; (of building) entrailles *fpl*; (of machine) rouages *mpl*; **to have a pain in one's ~s** avoir mal au bide○; **2** (courage) cran○ *m*; **to have the ~s to do sth** avoir le cran○ de faire qch; **he's a president with ~s** c'est un président qui a du cran○.
III *modif* **1** (instinctive, basic) [*feeling, nationalism, reaction*] viscéral, instinctif/-ive; [*instinct*] premier/-ière (*before n*); **it's a ~ issue** c'est une question de tripes○; **my ~ feeling is that** je pense instinctivement que; **2**○ US Sch, Univ facile, fastoche○.
IV *vtr* (*p prés etc* **-tt-**) **1** Culin vider [*fish, animal*]; **2** (destroy) [*fire*] ravager [*building*]; [*looters*] saccager [*shop*]; **3** (strip) **we ~ted the house** nous avons tout refait dans la maison.
V **gutted**○ *pp adj* GB abattu, découragé; **he was ~ted** ça lui a fichu un coup○.
IDIOMS **to hate sb's ~s**● ne pas pouvoir blairer● qn; **to work one's ~s**● **out** se crever le cul au boulot●; **to scream one's ~s**● **out** crier à s'en faire claquer le larynx○.
gutless /'gʌtlɪs/ *adj* mou/molle.
gutsy○ /'gʌtsɪ/ *adj* **1** (spirited) fougueux/-euse, plein de punch○; **2** (brave) courageux/-euse.
gutta-percha /,gʌtə 'pɜːtʃə/ *n* gutta-percha *f*.
gutter /'gʌtə(r)/ I *n* **1** (on roof) gouttière *f*; (in street) caniveau *m*; **2** fig **the language of the ~** la langue des bas-fonds; **to come up**

from the ~ venir des bas-fonds; **to drag sb (down) into the ~** traîner qn dans le ruisseau○.
II *vi* [*flame*] crépiter et vaciller; **the candle ~ed out** la bougie vacilla et s'éteignit.
guttering /ˈɡʌtərɪŋ/ *n* ¢ gouttières *fpl*.
gutter: **~ press** *n* presse *f* à sensation; **~snipe** *n* péj gosse *mf* des rues.
guttural /ˈɡʌtərəl/ **I** *n* Ling gutturale *f*.
II *adj* guttural.
guv○ /ɡʌv/ *n* GB (*abrév* = **governor**) chef○ *m*.
guvnor○ /ɡʌvnər/ *n* GB = **guv**○.
guy○ /ɡaɪ/ **I** *n* **1** (man) type○ *m*; **a good/bad ~** (in films etc) un bon/méchant; **her ~** (boyfriend) son homme○; **hey, you ~s!** (to men, mixed group) eh! vous, les mecs○!; (to women) eh! les filles○!; **2** GB *effigie de Guy Fawkes qu'on brûle le 5 novembre*; **3** (rope) = **guyrope**.
II *vtr* tourner [qn/qch] en ridicule.
Guyana /ɡaɪˈænə/ **▶ 1131** *pr n* Guyana *f*.
Guyanese /ˌɡaɪəˈniːz/ **▶ 1486** **I** *n* Guyanien/-ienne *m/f*.
II *adj* guyanien/-ienne.
Guy Fawkes Day /ˈɡaɪ fɔːks deɪ/ *n* GB le 5 novembre (*anniversaire de la Conspiration des Poudres*).
guyrope /ˈɡaɪrəʊp/ *n* (on tent) corde *f* d'attache.
guzzle○ /ˈɡʌzl/ **I** *vtr* engloutir.
II *vi* s'empiffrer○.
guzzler○ /ˈɡʌzlə(r)/ *n* goinfre○ *mf*.
Gwent /ɡwent/ **▶ 1624** *pr n* Gwent *m*.
Gwynedd /ˈɡwɪnəð/ **▶ 1624** *pr n* Gwynedd *m*.
gybe /dʒaɪb/ *vi* Naut empanner.
gym /dʒɪm/ **▶ 1282** **I** *n* **1** (*abrév* = **gymnasium**) salle *f* de gym○, gymnase *m*; **2** (*abrév* = **gymnastics**) gym○ *f*.
II *modif* [*equipment, lesson*] de gym○.
gymkhana /dʒɪmˈkɑːnə/ *n* concours *m* hippique.
gymnasium /dʒɪmˈneɪzɪəm/ *n* (*pl* **~s** ou **-ia**) gymnase *m*.
gymnast /ˈdʒɪmnæst/ *n* gymnaste *mf*.
gymnastic /dʒɪmˈnæstɪk/ *adj* de gymnastique.
gymnastics /dʒɪmˈnæstɪks/ **▶ 1282** *npl* **1** (+ *v sg*) (subject) gymnastique *f* ¢; **2** (+ *v pl*) **mental ~** gymnastique *f* mentale.
gym: **~ shoe** *n* (chaussure *f* de) tennis *f*; **~slip** *n* GB robe *f* chasuble (*faisant partie d'un uniforme scolaire*).
gynae○ /ɡaɪnɪ/ *n* gynéco○ *mf*.
gynaecological GB, **gynecological** US /ˌɡaɪnəkəˈlɒdʒɪkl/ *adj* gynécologique.
gynaecologist GB, **gynecologist** US /ˌɡaɪnəˈkɒlədʒɪst/ **▶ 1692** *n* gynécologue *mf*.
gynaecology GB, **gynecology** US /ˌɡaɪnəˈkɒlədʒɪ/ *n* gynécologie *f*.
gyp○ /dʒɪp/ **I** *n* **1** GB (pain) **my back is giving me ~** j'ai mal au dos en ce moment; **2** US (swindle) arnaque○ *f*; **3** US (swindler) arnaqueur/-euse○ *m/f*; **4** GB Univ domestique *mf*.
II *vtr* (*p prés etc* **-pp-**) **to ~ sb out of sth** arnaquer○ qn de qch; **to get ~ped** se faire arnaquer○.
gyp joint○ *n* US boîte *f* où l'on se fait plumer○.
gyppo● /ˈdʒɪpəʊ/ *n* (*pl* **-os**) GB injur (gypsy) gitan/-e *m/f*; (Egyptian) Égyptien/-ienne *m/f*.
gypsophila /dʒɪpˈsɒfɪlə/ *n* gypsophile *f*.
gypster○ /ˈdʒɪpstə(r)/ *n* US (swindler) arnaqueur/-euse *m/f*.
gypsum /ˈdʒɪpsəm/ **I** *n* Miner, Geol gypse *m*.
II *modif* [*deposit, quarry*] de gypse.
gypsy /ˈdʒɪpsɪ/ **I** *n* gen bohémien/-ienne *m/f*; (Central European) tzigane *mf*; (Spanish) gitan/-e *m/f*.
II *modif* [*camp, site*] de bohémiens; [*music*] tzigane; [*life*] de bohémien.
gypsy: **~ cab**○ *n* US taxi *m* clandestin; **~ moth** *n* zigzag *m*.
gyrate /ˌdʒaɪˈreɪt, US ˈdʒaɪreɪt/ *vi* [*dancer*] se trémousser; [*kite*] décrire des cercles.
gyration /ˌdʒaɪˈreɪʃn/ *n* (of dancer) trémoussement *m*; (of kite, fish etc) mouvement *m* giratoire.
gyratory /ˈdʒaɪrətrɪ, ˌdʒaɪˈreɪtrɪ/ *adj* giratoire.
gyrfalcon /ˈdʒɜːfɔːlkən/ *n* gerfaut *m*.
gyro○ /ˈdʒaɪərəʊ/ *n* **1** *abrév* = **gyroscope**; **2** *abrév* = **gyrocompass**.
gyrocompass /ˈdʒaɪrəʊkʌmpəs/ *n* gyrocompas *m*.
gyromagnetic /ˌdʒaɪrəʊmæɡˈnetɪk/ *adj* gyromagnétique.
gyroscope /ˈdʒaɪrəskəʊp/ *n* gyroscope *m*.
gyroscopic /ˌdʒaɪrəˈskɒpɪk/ *adj* gyroscopique.
gyrostabilizer /ˌdʒaɪrəʊˈsteɪbəlaɪzə(r)/ *n* stabilisateur *m* gyroscopique.
gyrostat /ˌdʒaɪrəˈ/ *n* gyrostat *m*.

h, **H** /eɪtʃ/ *n* h, H *m*; **aspirate/mute ~** h aspiré/muet; **to drop one's ~'s** GB ne pas aspirer les 'h', avoir un accent populaire.

ha /hɑː/ **I** *n*: *abrév écrite* = **hectare**.
II *excl* **1** (to express triumph, scorn etc) ah; **2** **'~! ~!'** (laughter) 'ah, ah, ah!'; très drôle! iron.

habeas corpus /ˌheɪbɪəs ˈkɔːpəs/ *n* Jur (right) habeas corpus *m* (*droit de qn de demander la raison de sa détention*).

haberdasher /ˈhæbədæʃə(r)/ **▶1692** *n* **1** GB mercier/-ière *m/f*; **2** US marchand/-e *m/f* de vêtements pour hommes.

haberdashery /ˈhæbədæʃərɪ/ **▶1692** *n* **1** GB (in department store) rayon *m* mercerie; **2** (goods) GB mercerie *f*; **3** US magasin *m* de vêtements pour hommes.

habit /ˈhæbɪt/ *n* **1** (custom) gen habitude *f*; Sociol coutume *f*; **a nervous ~** un tic nerveux; **a ~ of mind** une tournure d'esprit; **to get into bad ~s** prendre de mauvaises habitudes; **to have a ~ of doing** [*person*] avoir l'habitude de faire; **history has a ~ of repeating itself** l'histoire a tendance à se répéter; **to be in the ~ of doing** avoir l'habitude de faire; **I'm not in the ~ of borrowing money** ce n'est pas dans mes habitudes d'emprunter de l'argent; **don't make a ~ of it!** que ça ne devienne pas une habitude!; **to get into/out of the ~ of doing sth** prendre/perdre l'habitude de faire qch; **to do sth out of** ou **from ~** faire qch par habitude; **to be a creature of ~** avoir ses petites habitudes; **2** (addiction) accoutumance *f*; **drug/smoking ~** accoutumance à la drogue/au tabac; **to kick the ~**○ (of addiction) décrocher○; (of smoking) arrêter de fumer; **3** Relig habit *m*; **4** Equit tenue *f* d'équitation.

habitable /ˈhæbɪtəbl/ *adj* habitable.

habitat /ˈhæbɪtæt/ *n* habitat *m*.

habitation /ˌhæbɪˈteɪʃn/ *n* sout **1** (house) habitation *f*; **2** (being inhabited) **to show signs of ~** paraître habité; **unfit for human ~** Soc Admin insalubre.

habit-forming /ˈhæbɪtfɔːmɪŋ/ *adj* [*drug, activity*] qui crée une accoutumance; **to be ~** créer une accoutumance.

habitual /həˈbɪtʃʊəl/ *adj* **1** [*behaviour, reaction*] habituel/-elle; **2** [*drinker, smoker, liar*] invétéré; **~ criminal**, **~ offender** récidiviste *mf*.

habitually /həˈbɪtʃʊəlɪ/ *adv* habituellement.

habituate /həˈbɪtʃʊeɪt/ *vtr* sout **to be** ou **become ~d to sth/to doing** s'accoutumer à qch/à faire.

hack /hæk/ **I** *n* **1** (blow) coup *m* (*de hache*); **2**○ péj (writer) écrivaillon *m* pej, plumitif○ *m*; **3** Equit (horse used for riding) cheval *m* de selle; (old horse) rosse○ *f*; **4** GB (ride) promenade *f* à cheval; **5** Sport (kick) coup *m* de pied; **6** (cough) toux *f* sèche; **7**○ US (taxi) bahut○ *m*, taxi *m*; **8**○ US (taxi driver) taxi○ *m*; **9** (notch) entaille *f*; **10** Comput = **hacker**; **11**○ Pol (also **party ~**) militant/-e *m/f*.
II *vtr* **1** (strike, chop) taillader [*branch, object*] (**with** avec, à coups de); **to ~ sb (to death) with sth** frapper qn (à mort) à coups de qch; **to ~ sth/sb to pieces** tailler ou mettre qch/qn en pièces; **2** (clear, cut) tailler dans [*undergrowth, bushes*] (**with** à coups de); **to ~ a path through sth** tailler un chemin à travers qch; **to ~ one's way through/out of sth** tailler un chemin à travers/hors de qch; **3** Sport (kick) **to ~ sb/sb's shins** flanquer○ un coup de pied à qn/dans les tibias de qn; **to ~ sb's arm** (in basketball) donner un coup au bras de qn; **4** Comput pirater○, s'introduire dans [*system, database*]; **5**○ (cope with) **I can't ~ it** je ne le supporte pas; **how long do you think he will ~ it?** combien de temps tu penses qu'il va tenir?
III *vi* **1** (chop) taillader (**with** à coups de); **to ~ at sth/sb** taillader qch/qn; **to ~ through** tailler dans [*branch, object*]; **2**○ Comput (break into systems) pirater○; **to ~ into** s'introduire dans [*system*]; **3** GB Equit faire une promenade à cheval; **4** (cough) tousser (d'une toux sèche); **5**○ US (drive taxi) conduire un taxi.
■ **hack across**: **we had to ~ across the fields** nous avons dû traverser les champs.
■ **hack around**○ US glander●.
■ **hack away**: ¶ **~ away** donner des grands coups (**with** avec); **to ~ away at sth** frapper qch à grands coups; ¶ **~ away [sth]**, **~ [sth] away** tailler [*branch, undergrowth*].
■ **hack down**: **~ down [sth]**, **~ [sth] down** abattre [*grass, bush, enemy*].
■ **hack off**: **~ off [sth]**, **~ [sth] off** tailler [*piece, branch*]; trancher [*hand, head*].
■ **hack out**: **~ out [sth]**, **~ [sth] out** tailler [*foothold, clearing*].
■ **hack up**: **~ up [sth]**, **~ [sth] up** tailler [qch] en pièces [*carcass, tree*].

hack-and-slash /ˌhækənˈslæʃ/ *adj* [*video game etc*] violent.

hacker /ˈhækə(r)/ *n* Comput **1** (illegal) pirate○ *m* informatique; **2** (legal) passionné/-e *m/f* d'informatique.

hacker-proof /ˈhækəpruːf/ *adj* [*system*] protégé contre le piratage○ informatique.

hackette○ /ˌhækˈet/ *n* péj journaliste *f* qui fait la rubrique des chiens écrasés.

hacking /ˈhækɪŋ/ *n* **1** Comput piratage○ *m* informatique; **2** (riding) promenade *f* à cheval.

hacking: **~ cough** *n* toux *f* sèche et spasmodique; **~ jacket** *n* veste *f* d'équitation.

hackle /ˈhækl/ **I** *n* Zool, Fishg hackle *m*.
II hackles *npl* (on animal) poils *mpl* du cou; **the dog's ~s began to rise** le chien se hérissait; **to make sb's ~s rise** fig hérisser qn; **to get one's ~s up** fig se hérisser.

hackman○ /ˈhækmæn/ *n* US chauffeur *m* de taxi.

hackney cab /ˌhæknɪˈkæb/ *n* fiacre *m*.

hackneyed /ˈhæknɪd/ *adj* [*joke*] éculé; [*subject*] rebattu; **~ phrase**, **~ expression** cliché *m*.

hack: **~ reporter** *n* journaliste *mf* qui fait la rubrique des chiens écrasés; **~saw** *n* scie *f* à métaux; **~work** *n* écriture *f* alimentaire; **~ writer** *n* péj écrivaillon *m* pej; **~ writing** *n* péj littérature *f* alimentaire.

had /hæd, həd/ *prét, pp* ▶ **have**.

haddock /ˈhædək/ *n* (*pl* **~s** ou **~**) églefin *m*.

Hades /ˈheɪdiːz/ *pr n* les Enfers *mpl*; **in ~** aux Enfers.

hadj = **hajj**.

hadji = **hajji**.

hadn't /ˈhædnt/ = **had not**.

Hadrian /ˈheɪdrɪən/ *pr n* Hadrien.

Hadrian's Wall *n* mur *m* d'Hadrien.

haematite GB, **hematite** US /ˈhiːmətaɪt/ *n* hématite *f*.

haematological /ˌhiːmətəˈlɒdʒɪkl/ GB, **hematological** US *adj* hématologique.

haematologist GB, **hematologist** US /ˌhiːməˈtɒlədʒɪst/ **▶1692** *n* hématologue *mf*.

haematology GB, **hematology** US /ˌhiːməˈtɒlədʒɪ/ *n* hématologie *f*.

haematoma GB, **hematoma** US /ˌhiːməˈtəʊmə/ *n* (*pl* **~s** ou **-mata**) hématome *m*.

haemodialyser GB, **hemodialyser** US /ˌhiːməˈdaɪəlaɪzə(r)/ *n* hémodialyseur *m*.

haemodialysis GB, **hemodialysis** US /ˌhiːmədaɪˈæləsɪs/ *n* hémodialyse *f*.

haemoglobin GB, **hemoglobin** US /ˌhiːməˈgləʊbɪn/ *n* hémoglobine *f*.

haemolysis GB, **hemolysis** US /hiːˈmɒləsɪs/ *n* hémolyse *f*.

haemophilia GB, **hemophilia** US /ˌhiːməˈfɪlɪə/ **▶1354** *n* hémophilie *f*.

haemophiliac GB, **hemophiliac** US /ˌhiːməˈfɪlɪæk/ *n, adj* hémophile (*mf*).

haemorrhage GB, **hemorrhage** US /ˈhemərɪdʒ/ **I** *n* lit, fig hémorragie *f*; **brain/internal ~** hémorragie cérébrale/interne; **to have a ~** faire une hémorragie.
II *vi* faire une hémorragie; **to ~ badly** saigner beaucoup.

haemorrhoids GB, **hemorrhoids** US /ˈhemərɔɪdz/ *npl* hémorroïdes *fpl*; **to suffer from ~** avoir des hémorroïdes.

haft /hɑːft/ *n* gen manche *m*; (of dagger) poignée *f*.

hag /hæg/ *n* (witch) (vieille) sorcière *f*; péj (ugly woman) **old ~** vieille peau○ *f*.

haggard /ˈhægəd/ *adj* [*appearance, person*] exténué; [*face, expression*] défait; **to look ~ (and drawn)** avoir l'air exténué.

haggis /ˈhægɪs/ *n* (*pl* **~** ou **~es**) haggis *m* (*panse de brebis ou de mouton farcie*).

haggle /ˈhægl/ *vi* marchander; **to ~ about** ou **over sth** discuter du prix de qch; **after a lot of haggling** après un long marchandage.

hagiographer /ˌhægɪˈɒgrəfə(r)/ **▶1692** *n* hagiographe *mf*.

hagiography /ˌhægɪˈɒgrəfɪ/ *n* hagiographie *f*.

hagridden /ˈhægrɪdn/ *adj* littér tourmenté.

Hague /heɪg/ **▶1818** *pr n* **The ~** La Haye.

ha-ha /ˈhɑːhɑː/ *n* (ditch) saut-de-loup *m*.

hail /heɪl/ **I** *n* lit grêle *f*; fig (of bullets, insults) grêle *f* (**of** de).
II *vtr* **1** (call, signal to) héler [*person, taxi, ship*]; **within ~ing distance** à portée de voix; **2** (praise) **to ~ sb as** acclamer qn

comme; **to ~ sth as sth/as being** saluer qch comme qch/comme étant.
III *v impers* grêler.
IV *excl* **Hail!** Salut!; **~ the conquering hero!** hum salut, héros victorieux!
■ **hail down** tomber dru.
■ **hail from** sout être de, venir de.

hail-fellow-well-met /ˌheɪlfeləʊwelˈmet/ *adj* **to be ~** être très liant; **he's a bit too ~** il est un peu trop familier avec tout le monde.

hail: **Hail Mary** *n* 'Je vous salue Marie' *m inv*; **~stone** *n* grêlon *m*; **~storm** *n* averse *f* de grêle.

hair /heə(r)/ **I** *n* **1** ¢ (collectively) (human) (on head) cheveux *mpl*; (on body) poils *mpl*; (of animal) poil *m*, pelage *m*; **to have long/short ~** [*person*] avoir les cheveux longs/courts; [*cat, dog*] avoir le poil long/court; **blond/black ~** cheveux blonds/noirs; **a fine head of ~** une belle chevelure; **to brush/wash one's ~** se brosser/se laver les cheveux; **to get one's ~ cut** se faire couper les cheveux; **to have one's ~ done** se faire coiffer; **2** (individually) (human) (on head) cheveu *m*; (on body) poil *m*; (animal) poil *m*; **two blond ~s** deux cheveux blonds.
II -haired (*dans composés*) **long/short-~ed** [*person*] aux cheveux longs/courts; [*animal*] à poil long/court; **dark/curly-~ed** aux cheveux foncés/bouclés.
IDIOMS **by a ~, by a ~'s breadth** d'un poil○; **he didn't turn a ~** il n'a pas bronché; **he was perfect, not a ~ out of place** il était impeccable, tiré à quatre épingles; **it made my ~ stand on end** cela m'a fait dresser les cheveux sur la tête; **I won't let them touch** ou **harm a ~ of your head** je ne les laisserai pas toucher à un seul cheveu de ta tête; **keep your ~ on**○! GB ne t'excite pas○!; **the thought made her ~ curl** à cette pensée ses cheveux se sont dressés sur sa tête; **to get in sb's ~**○ taper sur les nerfs de qn○; **to have sb by the short ~s**◑ US tenir le couteau sous la gorge de qn; **to let one's ~ down**○ se défouler○; **to split ~s** couper les cheveux en quatre; **to tear one's ~ out** s'arracher les cheveux; **you need a ~ of the dog (that bit you)** il te faut un petit verre pour faire passer la gueule de bois○.

hair: **~ ball** *n* (in cats) boule *f* de poils; (in calves, horses) égagropile *m*; **~band** *n* bandeau *m*, serre-tête *m inv*; **~brush** *n* brosse *f* à cheveux; **~clip** *n* GB barrette *f*; **~cloth** *n* étoffe *f* de crin; **~ conditioner** *n* après-shampooing *m*, démêlant *m*; **~ curler** *n* bigoudi *m*.

haircut /ˈheəkʌt/ *n* coupe *f* (de cheveux); **to get a ~** se faire couper les cheveux.

hairdo○ /ˈheədu:/ *n* coiffure *f*.

hairdresser /ˈheədresə(r)/ ▶ **1692** *n* coiffeur/-euse *m/f*; **a ~'s salon** un salon de coiffure; **to go to the ~'s** aller chez le coiffeur.

hair: **~dressing** *n* coiffure *f*; **~drier** *n* (hand-held) sèche-cheveux *m inv*; (hood) casque *m*; **~ follicle** *n* follicule *m* pileux; **~ gel** *n* gel *m* coiffant; **~grip** *n* GB pince *f* à cheveux.

hairless /ˈheəlɪs/ *adj* [*chest, body, chin*] glabre; [*animal*] sans poils.

hairline /ˈheəlaɪn/ *n* naissance *f* des cheveux; **his ~ is receding** son front se dégarnit.

hair: **~line crack** *n* fêlure *f*; **~line fracture** *n* Med fêlure *f*; **~net** *n* filet *m* à cheveux; **~ oil** *n* huile *f* capillaire; **~piece** *n* postiche *m*; **~pin** *n* épingle *f* à cheveux; **~pin bend** *n* virage *m* en épingle à cheveux; **~-raising** *adj* [*story, adventure, escape*] à vous faire dresser les cheveux sur la tête; **~ remover** *n* Cosmet crème *f* dépilatoire; **~ restorer** *n* régénérateur *m* du cheveu; **~ shirt** *n* haire *f*; **~-slide** *n* GB barrette *f*; **~ splitting** *n* ergotage *m*; **~spray** *n* laque *f*; **~spring** *n* spiral *m* (*dans une montre*); **~style** *n* (arrangement) coiffure *f*; (cut) coupe *f* de cheveux; **~ stylist** ▶ **1692** *n* coiffeur/-euse *m/f*; **~ transplant** *n* greffe *f* de cheveux.

hair trigger **I** *n* détente *f* ultrasensible.
II *modif* [*reaction*] très rapide.

hairy /ˈheərɪ/ *adj* **1** [*coat, blanket, dog*] poilu; [*arms, legs, chest*] velu, poilu; Bot [*stem, roots*] villeux/-euse; **2**○ [*adventure, moment*] atroce○; **things got really ~** c'était l'horreur○.

Haiti /ˈheɪtɪ/ ▶ **1131**, **1381** *pr n* Haïti *m*.

Haitian /ˈheɪʃn/ ▶ **1486**, **1402** **I** *pr n* **1** (person) Haïtien/-ienne *m/f*; **2** (language) haïtien *m*.
II *adj* haïtien/-ienne.

hajj /hædʒ/ *n* hadj or hajj *m*; **to perform the ~, to make a ~** aller en pèlerinage à la Mecque.

hajji /ˈhædʒɪ/ *n* (pilgrim) hadj *m*, hadji *m*.

hake /heɪk/ *n* (*pl* **~** ou **~s**) **1** Zool merlu *m*; **2** ¢ Culin colin *m*.

halal /hɑ:ˈlɑ:l/ *adj* [*meat*] hallal *inv*; **~ butcher** boucher *m* vendant de la viande hallal.

halation /hæˈleɪʃn/ *n* Phot halo *m*.

halcyon /ˈhælsɪən/ **I** *n* Mythol alcyon *m*.
II *adj* [*time, period*] paradisiaque; **~ days** jours heureux.

hale /heɪl/ *adj* [*old person*] vigoureux/-euse; **to be ~ and hearty** gen être en pleine forme; [*old person, convalescent*] avoir bon pied bon œil.

half /hɑ:f, US hæf/ ▶ **1096** **I** *n* (*pl* **halves**) **1** (one of two parts) moitié *f*; **~ (of) the page/the people/the wine** la moitié de la page/des gens/du vin; **~ (of) 38 is 19** la moitié de 38 est 19; **he arrives late ~ (of) the time** la moitié du temps il est en retard; **to cut/tear/break sth in ~** couper/déchirer/casser qch en deux; **2** Math (fraction) demi *m*; **four and a ~** quatre et demi; **3** Sport (time period) mi-temps *f*; (pitch area) moitié *f* de terrain; **the first/second ~** la première/seconde mi-temps; **4** Sport = **halfback**; **5**○ GB (half pint) demi-pinte *f*, ≈ bock *m*; **6** GB (half fare) demi-tarif *m*.
II *adj* **a ~ apple** une moitié de pomme; **a ~ circle** un demi-cercle; **a ~-cup, a ~ cup** une demi-tasse; **a ~-litre, a ~ litre** un demi-litre; **a ~-litre pot** un pot d'un demi-litre; **a ~-page advertisement** une publicité d'une demi-page; **twelve and a ~ per cent** douze et demi pour cent; **two and a ~ cups** deux tasses et demie.
III *pron* **1** (50%) moitié *f*; **only ~ passed** seule la moitié a réussi; **you can have ~ now, the rest later** tu peux en avoir la moitié maintenant et le reste plus tard; **to cut/increase sth by ~** réduire/augmenter qch de moitié; **that was a meal and a ~**○! ça a été un sacré repas○!; **2** (in time) **an hour and a ~** une heure et demie; **~ past two/six** GB, **~ two/six**○ deux/six heures et demie; **it starts at ~ past** ça commence à la demie; **the buses run at ~ past the hour** les bus passent à la demie de chaque heure; **3** (in age) **she is ten and a ~** elle a dix ans et demi.
IV *adv* [*full, over, asleep, drunk, cooked, dressed, eaten, hidden, understood, remembered*] à moitié; **to ~ close one's eyes/the window** fermer les yeux/la fenêtre à moitié; **it's ~ the price/the size** c'est moitié moins cher/moins grand; **~ as much money/as many people** moitié moins d'argent/de personnes; **~ as big/as heavy** moitié moins grand/lourd; **~ as much/as many again** moitié plus; **~ as tall again** moitié plus grand; **he's ~ my age** il est moitié moins âgé que moi; **she's ~ Italian** elle est à moitié italienne; **he's ~ Spanish ~ Irish** il est mi-espagnol mi-irlandais; **the word is ~ Latin ~ Greek** le mot est moitié latin moitié grec; **~ woman ~ fish** mi-femme mi-poisson, moitié femme moitié poisson; **he was only ~ serious** il n'était qu'à moitié sérieux; **~ disappointed ~ relieved** mi-déçu mi-soulagé; **to be only ~ right** n'avoir qu'à moitié raison; **to be only ~ listening** n'écouter qu'à moitié; **if it was ~ as easy as they say** si c'était vraiment aussi facile qu'on le dit; **I was ~ hoping that** j'espérais presque que; **I ~ expected it** je m'y attendais plus ou moins; **not ~ old/~ big** pas jeune/petit iron; **he wasn't ~ angry/surprised**○ il était drôlement○ en colère/surpris; **it doesn't ~ stink**○! ça pue drôlement○!; **not ~**○! et comment!; **not ~ bad**○ pas mauvais or mal du tout.
IDIOMS **~ a minute** ou **second** ou **tick**○ GB ou **mo**○ une petite minute, un instant; **how the other ~ lives** comment vivent les riches; **if given ~ a chance** à la première occasion; **to have ~ a mind to do** avoir bien envie de faire; **one's better** ou **other ~** sa (douce) moitié; **that's not the ~ of it!** ce n'est pas le meilleur!; **she doesn't know the ~ of it!** elle ne sait pas le meilleur!; **to go halves with sb** se mettre de moitié avec qn; **let's go halves** faisons moitié-moitié; **never to do things by halves** ne pas faire les choses à moitié; **too clever by ~**○ un peu trop malin/-igne.

half: **~-and-half** *adj, adv* moitié-moitié; **~-assed**◑ *adj* US foireux/-euse○; **~back** *n* Sport demi *m*; **~-baked**○ *adj* bancal○; **~-binding** *n* demi-reliure *f* à coins.

half-blood /ˈhɑ:fblʌd, US ˈhæf-/ *n* **1** (sibling) consanguin/-e *m/f*; **2** US = **half-breed**; **3** US (animal) demi-sang *m*.

half: **~-board** *n* demi-pension *f*; **~ boot** *n* demi-botte *f*; **~-bound** *adj* en demi-reliure à coins; **~-breed** *n, adj* injur métis/-isse (*m/f*); **~ brother** *n* demi-frère *m*; **~-caste** *n, adj* injur métis/-isse (*m/f*); **~ century** *n* demi-siècle *m*.

half cock *n* cran *m* de sûreté; **at ~** lit au cran de sûreté.
IDIOMS **to go off at ~, to go off half-cocked** (flop) partir en eau de boudin; (be hasty) être impulsif/-ive.

half: **~ conscious** *adj* à demi conscient; **~ crown, ~-a-crown** *n* GB Hist demi-couronne *f*; **~-cup** *modif* [*bra*] à balconnet; **~-cut**○ *adj* éméché○, ivre.

half day *n* demi-journée *f*; **it's my ~** c'est ma demi-journée de congé.

half: **~-dead** *adj* lit, fig à moitié mort; **~-dollar** *n* demi-dollar *m*.

half-dozen /ˌhɑ:fˈdʌzn, US ˌhæf-/ *n, pron, adj* demi-douzaine *f*; **to be sold by the ~** se vendre à la demi-douzaine; **a ~ eggs** une demi-douzaine d'œufs.

half fare *n* demi-tarif *m*; **to travel (at** ou **for) ~** voyager à demi-tarif.

half: **~-hearted** *adj* [*attempt, smile, participation*] un peu mou/molle; **~-heartedly** *adv* sans conviction; **~-hitch** *n* demi-clé *f*; **~ holiday** *n* GB demi-journée *f* de congé.

half hour /ˌhɑ:fˈaʊə(r), US ˌhæf-/ ▶ **1807** **I** *n* demi-heure *f*; **every ~** toutes les demi-heures; **on the ~** à la demie.
II *modif* [*delay, journey, lesson, session*] d'une demi-heure.

half: **~-hourly** /ˌhɑ:fˈaʊəlɪ, US ˌhæf-/ *adj, adv* toutes les demi-heures; **~-jokingly** *adv* en plaisantant à moitié.

half-length /ˌhɑ:fˈleŋθ, US ˌhæf-/ **I** *n* **1** Art buste *m*; **2** Turf demi-longueur *f*.
II *adj* [*portrait, picture*] en buste.

half: **~-life** *n* demi-vie *f*; **~-light** *n* littér demi-jour *m*; **~ marathon** *n* demi-marathon *m*.

half-mast /ˌhɑ:fˈmɑ:st, US ˌhæf-/ *n* **at ~** (of flag) en berne; (of trousers) à mi-mollets.

half-moon /ˌhɑ:fˈmu:n, US ˌhæf-/ **I** *n* **1** Astron demi-lune *f*; **2** (of fingernail) lunule *f*.
II *modif* [*spectacles, shape*] en demi-lune.

half: **~-naked** *adj* à moitié nu; **~ nelson** *n* (in wrestling) clé *f* au cou; **~note** *n* blanche *f*; **~-open** *adj* entrouvert.

half pay *n* demi-salaire *m*; **to be on ~** avoir un demi-salaire.

halfpenny /ˈheɪpnɪ/ **I** *n* **1** lit, GB Hist demi-penny *m*; **2** fig (small amount) sou *m*.
II *modif* [*coin, piece*] d'un demi-penny; [*sweet*] à un demi-penny.
halfpennyworth /ˈheɪpnɪwɜːθ/ *n* **a ~ of** lit un demi-penny de; fig une once de.
half-pint /ˌhɑːfˈpaɪnt, US ˌhæf-/ ▶ 1068 **I** *n* **1** Meas demi-pinte *f* (GB = *0.28 l*, US = *0.24 l*); **a ~ of milk** ≈ un quart de litre de lait; **2** GB (of beer) ≈ bock *m*.
II *modif* [*glass, bottle*] d'une demi-pinte.
half: **~ price** *adv, adj* à moitié prix; **~ rest** *n* US demi-pause *f*; **~ seas over**○† *adj* GB dans les vignes du Seigneur○†; **~ sister** *n* demi-sœur *f*.
half size I *n* (of shoe) demi-pointure *f*.
II *adj* [*replica, model*] à l'échelle 1:2; [*copy*] réduit de moitié.
half: **~ size violin** *n* demi-violon *m*; **~ slip** *n* jupon *m*; **~ smile** *n* demi-sourire *m*; **~-staff** *n* US = **half-mast**; **~-starved** *adj* à demi mort de faim; **~ step** *n* US Mus demi-ton *m*.
half term GB Sch **I** *n* **1** (holiday) vacances *fpl* de demi-trimestre, petites vacances *fpl*; **2** (period) demi-trimestre *m*.
II *modif* [*holiday, trip*] de demi-trimestre.
half-timbered /ˌhɑːfˈtɪmbəd, US ˌhæf-/ *adj* à colombages.
half-time /ˌhɑːfˈtaɪm, US ˌhæf-/ **I** *n* Sport mi-temps *f*; **at ~** à la mi-temps.
II *modif* **1** Sport [*whistle*] de la mi-temps; [*score*] à la mi-temps; **~ break** mi-temps *f*; **2** Fin, Comm [*figures, profits*] semestriel/-ielle; **3** (part time) [*post, worker*] à mi-temps.
halftone /ˈhɑːftəʊn, US ˈhæf-/ *n* **1** Phot (technique) similigravure *f*; (photograph) demi-teinte *f*; **2** Art demi-teinte *f*; **3** Mus demi-ton *m*.
half-track /ˈhɑːftræk, US ˈhæf-/ *n* **1** (drive system) chenille *f*; **2** (vehicle) half-track *m*.
half: **~-truth** *n* demi-vérité *f*; **~-volley** *n* demi-volée *f*.
halfway /ˌhɑːfˈweɪ, US ˌhæf-/ **I** *adj* **the ~ stage** la mi-étape; **to reach the ~ mark** ou **point** être à la moitié (**of** de).
II *adv* **1** (at the mid-point) à mi-chemin (**between** entre; **to** de); **to be ~ there** lit être à mi-chemin; **to stop ~** s'arrêter à mi-chemin; **I went ~** j'ai fait la moitié du chemin; **~ up** ou **down** à mi-hauteur de [*stairs, tree*]; **~ down the page** à mi-page; **~ across** au milieu de [*room, ocean*]; **you could hear it ~ across town** on l'a entendu dans la moitié de la ville; **to travel ~ across** ou **round the world for sth** faire des kilomètres et des kilomètres pour qch; **~ through** au milieu; **I left ~ through** je suis parti au milieu; **~ through the film** au milieu du film; **~ through the week/morning** en milieu de semaine/de matinée; **to be ~ through doing sth** avoir à moitié fini de faire qch; **2** fig **to go ~ to** ou **towards** GB **sth/doing sth** être à mi-chemin de qch/de faire qch; **the statement only goes ~** la déclaration ne répond qu'à moitié à la question; **we're ~ there** nous avons fait la moitié du chemin; **I met him ~** j'ai fait un compromis avec lui, nous avons coupé la poire○ en deux; **to meet trouble ~** devancer les ennuis; **3**○ (in the least) [*decent, convincing, competent*] raisonnablement.
halfway house *n* **1** (compromise) compromis *m*; **2** (rehabilitation centre) centre *m* de réadaptation; **3** Hist relais *m* d'étape.
half: **~way line** *n* Sport ligne *f* médiane; **~wit**○ *n* péj abruti/-e○ *m/f*; **~witted**○ *adj* péj abruti○.
half-year /ˌhɑːfˈjɪə(r), US ˌhæf-/ Fin, Comm **I** *n* semestre *m*.
II *modif* [*profit, results, figures*] semestriel/-ielle.
half-yearly /ˌhɑːfˈjɪəlɪ, US ˌhæf-/ **I** *adj* [*meeting, statement, payment*] semestriel/-ielle.
II *adv* [*meet, pay*] tous les six mois.

halibut /ˈhælɪbət/ *n* (*pl* **~** ou **~s**) flétan *m*.
halitosis /ˌhælɪˈtəʊsɪs/ *n* mauvaise haleine *f*; **to have** ou **suffer from ~** avoir mauvaise haleine.
hall /hɔːl/ *n* **1** (in house) entrée *f*; (corridor) couloir *m*; (in hotel, airport, station) hall *m*; **arrivals/departures ~** Aviat hall d'arrivée/de départ; **2** (for public events) (grande) salle *f*; (of church) salle *f* paroissiale; (of school) (**assembly**) **~** salle *f* de réunions; **the local ~** la salle polyvalente or des fêtes; ▶ **concert hall etc**; **3** Admin (offices) ▶ **city hall**, **town hall**; **4** Univ (residence) résidence *f* universitaire; **to live in ~** loger en résidence universitaire; **5** Univ (refectory) réfectoire *m*; **to dine in ~** GB dîner au réfectoire; **6** (country house) manoir *m*.
hallal = **halal**.
hallelujah /ˌhælɪˈluːjə/ *excl* alléluia.
hallmark /ˈhɔːlmɑːk/ **I** *n* **1** (typical feature) caractéristique *f*; **to bear the ~** ou **~s of sb/sth** présenter les caractéristiques de qn/qch; **2** GB (on metal) poinçon *m*.
II *vtr* poinçonner; **to be ~ed** porter un poinçon.
hallo /həˈləʊ/ *excl* **1** GB = **hello**; **2** Hunt = **halloo**.
hall: **Hall of Fame** *n* (all contexts) panthéon *m*; **~ of residence** *n* résidence *f* universitaire.
halloo /həˈluː/ **I** *excl* Hunt taïaut.
II *vi* (*3e pers sg prés* **~s**; *prét, pp* **~ed**) Hunt crier taïaut.
hallow /ˈhæləʊ/ **I** *vtr* littér sanctifier; **~ed be Thy name** Bible que ton nom soit sanctifié.
II hallowed *pp adj* **1** (venerated) [*tradition*] vénéré; **a ~ memory** un souvenir qui est devenu sacré; **2** (sanctified) [*ground*] saint; **in these ~ed precincts** lit, fig dans ce lieu sacré.
Halloween /ˌhæləʊˈiːn/ *n* Halloween (*31 octobre, soir des fantômes et sorcières*); **on** ou **at ~** le soir de Halloween.
hallstand /ˈhɔːlstænd/ *n* portemanteau *m*.
hallucinate /həˈluːsɪneɪt/ *vi* avoir des hallucinations; **I must have been hallucinating** fig ce devait être une hallucination.
hallucination /həˌluːsɪˈneɪʃn/ *n* hallucination *f*; **to suffer from ~s** être sujet/-ette à des hallucinations.
hallucinatory /həˈluːsɪnətrɪ, US -tɔːrɪ/ *adj* **1** [*drug, substance*] hallucinogène; **2** [*film, painting, image*] onirique; [*figure*] spectral; [*effect*] hallucinatoire; **it was a ~ experience** c'était onirique.
hallucinogen /həˈluːsɪnədʒn/ *n* hallucinogène *m*.
hallucinogenic /həˌluːsɪnəˈdʒenɪk/ *adj* hallucinogène.
hallway /ˈhɔːlweɪ/ *n* entrée *f*.
halo /ˈheɪləʊ/ *n* (*pl* **~s** ou **~es**) **1** (around head) auréole *f*; **2** fig hum odeur *f* de sainteté; **can't you see my ~?** tu ne sens pas mon odeur de sainteté○? hum; **his ~ has become a bit tarnished** son image s'est un peu ternie; **3** Astron halo *m*.
halogen /ˈhælədʒn/ *n* halogène *m*.
halogen lamp *n* **1** Aut phare *m* halogène; **2** (desk lamp etc) lampe *f* halogène.
halon /ˈheɪlɒn/ *n* halon *m*; **~ gas** gaz *m* halon.
halt /hɔːlt/ **I** *n* **1** (stop) arrêt *m*; **to come to a ~** [*group, vehicle*] s'arrêter; [*fighting*] cesser; [*negotiations*] être interrompu; **to call a ~ to** mettre fin à [*fighting, dispute*]; **shall we call a ~?** (in work) on s'arrête?; **2** (temporary) (in activity) suspension *f* (**in** dans); (in proceedings) pause *f* (**in** au cours de); **a ~ in the trial** une pause au cours du procès; **a ~ in arms sales** une suspension dans les ventes d'armes; **3** Mil (rest) halte *f*; **4** GB Rail halte *f*.
II *excl* **1** halte!; **2** (on roadsigns) **'Halt Customs!'** 'Stop Douane!'
III *vtr* **1** (stop temporarily) bloquer [*car, train*]; interrompre [*proceedings, game*]; **2** (block) mettre fin à [*arms sales, experiments*]; arrêter [*inflation, offensive*].
IV *vi* [*vehicle*] s'arrêter; [*army*] faire halte.
IDIOMS **the ~ and the lame** les éclopés *mpl*.
halter /ˈhɔːltə(r)/ *n* **1** (for horse) licol *m*; **2** (for hanging) corde *f* (*de pendaison*); **3** Fashn (also **~neck**) dos *m* nu.
halterneck /ˈhɔːltənek/ *n, adj* [*dress, swimsuit*] dos (*m*) nu.
halting /ˈhɔːltɪŋ/ *adj* [*steps, attempts*] hésitant; [*verse*] boiteux/-euse; [*style*] heurté; **to speak in ~ Polish** parler un polonais hésitant.
haltingly /ˈhɔːltɪŋlɪ/ *adv* [*progress*] par à-coups; [*speak*] de façon hésitante.
halve /hɑːv, US hæv/ **I** *vtr* **1** (reduce by half) réduire [qch] de moitié [*number, production, rate*]; **2** (divide in two) couper [qch] en deux [*carrot, cake*]; **3** (in golf) faire square sur [*hole, round*].
II *vi* [*number, rate, time*] diminuer de moitié.
IDIOMS **a trouble shared is a trouble ~d** parler d'un problème c'est déjà le résoudre à moitié.
halves /hɑːvz, US hævz/ *npl* ▶ **half**.
halyard /ˈhæljəd/ *n* drisse *f*.
ham /hæm/ **I** *n* **1** Culin jambon *m*; **smoked/unsmoked ~** jambon fumé/cuit; **boiled ~** jambon blanc; **2** Anat (of animal) cuisse *f*; **3**○ (of person) hum cuisse *f*, jambon○ *m*; **4**○ (poor actor) cabotin/-e *m/f*; **she's a terrible ~** elle joue de façon très exagérée; **5** (also **radio ~**) radioamateur/-trice *m/f*.
II *modif* Culin [*omelette, sandwich*] au jambon.
III○ *adj* [*acting*] exagéré.
IV *vi* (*p prés etc* **-mm-**) forcer son rôle.
■ **ham up**: **~ [sth] up, ~ up [sth]** forcer [*role, speech*]; **to ~ it up**○ jouer de façon exagérée.
ham and eggs *npl* US Culin œufs *mpl* au jambon.
Hamburg /ˈhæmbɜːg/ ▶ 1818 *prn* Hambourg.
hamburger /ˈhæmbɜːgə(r)/ *n* **1** (shaped minced beef) hamburger *m*; **2** US (ground beef) pâté *m* de viande.
IDIOMS **to make a ~ out of sb/sth** US faire de qn/qch de la chair à pâté.
ham-fisted○ GB, **ham-handed**○ US /ˌhæmˈfɪstɪd, ˌhæmˈhændɪd/ *adj* péj maladroit.
Hamitic /həˈmɪtɪk/ *adj* Ling chamitique.
hamlet /ˈhæmlɪt/ *n* hameau *m*.
hammer /ˈhæmə(r)/ **I** *n* **1** (tool) marteau *m*; **2** (of piano) marteau *m*; **3** (gavel) marteau *m*; **to come** ou **go under the ~** être vendu aux enchères; **4** Sport (ball) marteau *m*; (discipline) lancer *m* de marteau; **to throw the ~** lancer le marteau; **5** Anat (in ear) marteau *m*; **6** (on firearm) chien *m*. ▶ **tongs**.
II *vtr* **1** lit (beat) marteler [*metal sheet, door, table, piano keys*]; **to ~ sth into** enfoncer qch dans [*wall, fence, rock*]; **to ~ sth into shape** façonner qch au marteau; **they ~ the copper into pots** ils façonnent le cuivre pour en faire des pots; **to ~ sth flat** aplatir qch à coups de marteau; **she ~ed her fists against the door** elle tapait des poings contre la porte; **2** fig (insist forcefully) **to ~ sth into** faire entrer qch dans la tête de [*pupils, recruits*]; **they had grammar/Latin ~ed into them** on leur a bien inculqué la grammaire/le latin; **to ~ home a message/warning** bien faire comprendre un message/avertissement; **3** (attack) critiquer [*government, policy, proposal*]; descendre [qch] en flammes○ [*book, film*]; **4**○ Sport (defeat) battre [qn] à plates coutures; **5** (attack) [*artillery*] pilonner [*enemy positions, target*]; [*recession, unemployment*] accabler [*district, region*].
III *vi* **1** (use hammer) frapper à coups de marteau; **2** (pound) **to ~ on** ou **at** [*person , rain, hailstones*] tambouriner contre [*door,*

window]; **hailstones ~ed against the window/on the roof** la grêle tambourinait contre la fenêtre/sur le toit; **3** (thump) [*heart*] battre fort.

■ **hammer away** lit taper à coups de marteau; fig **to ~ away at** [*lobbyist, campaigners*] s'attaquer à [*proposal, issue*]; [*artillery*] pilonner [*enemy position*]; [*caller*] tambouriner contre [*door*]; [*pupil*] taper sur [*piano*]; **he's ~ing away at his essay** il travaille sur son devoir avec acharnement.

■ **hammer in**: **~ in [sth]**, **~ [sth] in** enfoncer [qch] à coups de marteau.

■ **hammer out**: **~ out [sth]**, **~ [sth] out** (negotiate) parvenir à [qch] après maintes discussions [*agreement, policy, formula*].

hammer and sickle *n* **the ~** la faucille et le marteau.

hammer beam *n* blochet *m*.

hammer blow *n* **1** lit coup *m* de marteau; **2** fig rude coup *m* (**to** à).

hammer drill *n* **1** (with hammer action) marteau *m* perforateur; **2** (rock drill) marteau-piqueur *m*.

hammerhead, **hammer-headed shark** *n* (requin *m*) marteau *m*.

hammering /'hæmərɪŋ/ *n* **1** (noise) (bruit *m* de) martèlement *m* (**at** sur); **sounds of ~** des martèlements; **2**○ (defeat) **to take** ou **get a ~** prendre une dérouillée○; **3**○ (tough treatment) **to give sth a ~** descendre [qch] en flammes○ [*play, film*]; critiquer sévèrement [*proposal, measure*].

hammer toe *n* orteil *m* en marteau.

hammock /'hæmək/ *n* hamac *m*.

hamper /'hæmpə(r)/ **I** *n* **1** (for picnic) panier *m* à pique-nique (*rectangulaire et muni d'un couvercle*); **2** GB (from shop etc) *panier vendu avec une sélection de produits alimentaires de luxe*; **3** (for laundry) panière *f* à linge.

II *vtr* entraver [*movement, career, progress*]; handicaper [*person*]; **~ed by injury** handicapé par une blessure; **~ed by lack of funds** handicapé par le manque de fonds.

Hampshire /'hæmpʃɪə(r)/ ▶**1624** *pr n* Hampshire *m*.

hamster /'hæmstə(r)/ *n* hamster *m*.

hamstring /'hæmstrɪŋ/ **I** *n* Anat (of human) tendon *m* du jarret; (of horse) corde *f* du jarret.

II *vtr* (*prét, pp* **-strung**) paralyser [*initiative, activity, economy*]; coincer○ [*person*].

hand /hænd/ ▶**1037** **I** *n* **1** Anat main *f*; **he had a pencil/book in his ~** il avait un crayon/un livre dans la main; **she had a pistol/umbrella in her ~** elle avait un pistolet/un parapluie à la main; **he stood there, gun/suitcase in ~** il était là, un pistolet/une valise à la main; **to get** ou **lay one's ~s on** mettre la main sur [*money, information, key, person*]; **he eats/steals everything he can get** ou **lay his ~s on** il mange/vole tout ce qui lui passe sous le nez; **to keep one's ~s off sth** ne pas toucher à [*computer, money*]; **to keep one's ~s off sb** laisser qn tranquille; **they could hardly keep their ~s off each other** ils avaient du mal à se retenir pour ne pas se toucher; **to take sb's ~** prendre la main de qn; **to take sb by the ~** prendre qn par la main; **they were holding ~s** ils se donnaient la main; **to hold sb's ~** lit tenir qn par la main; fig (give support) [*person*] tenir la main à qn; [*government*] soutenir qn; **to do** ou **make sth by ~** faire qch à la main; **the letter was delivered by ~** la lettre a été remise en mains propres; **'by ~'** (on envelope) 'par porteur'; **they gave me 50 dollars in my ~** il m'ont donné 50 dollars de la main à la main; **from ~ to ~** de main en main; **look! no ~s!** regarde! sans les mains!; **to have one's ~s full** lit avoir les mains pleines; fig avoir assez à faire; **to seize an opportunity with both ~s** saisir l'occasion à deux mains; **~s up, or I shoot!** les mains en l'air, ou je tire!; **to be on one's ~s and knees** être à quatre pattes; **we can always use another pair of ~s** une autre paire de bras ne serait pas de trop; **~s off**○! pas touche○!, bas les pattes○!; **'~s off our schools'** (slogan at rally) 'ne touchez pas à nos écoles'; **please put your ~s together for Max!** s'il vous plaît applaudissez Max!; **2** (handwriting) écriture *f*; **in a neat ~** rédigé d'une belle écriture; **in her own ~** rédigé de sa propre main; **3** (influence, involvement) influence *f*; **to have a ~ in sth** prendre part à [*decision, project*]; avoir quelque chose à voir avec [*demonstration, robbery*]; **to have a ~ in planning** ou **organizing sth** prendre part à l'organisation de qch; **to stay** ou **hold one's ~** patienter; **I thought I recognized your ~** j'ai cru avoir reconnu ton style; **4** (assistance) coup *m* de main; **to give** ou **lend sb a (helping) ~** donner un coup de main à qn; **I need a ~ with my suitcases** j'ai besoin d'un coup de main pour porter mes valises; **5** (round of applause) **to give sb a big ~** applaudir qn très fort; **let's have a big ~ for the winner!** applaudissons bien fort le gagnant!; **6** (consent to marriage) **to ask for/win sb's ~ (in marriage)** demander/obtenir la main de qn (en mariage); **7** (possession) **to be in sb's ~s** [*money, painting, document, power, affair*] être entre les mains de qn; **the painting is in private ~s** le tableau est entre les mains d'un particulier; **to change ~s** changer de mains; **to fall** ou **get into sb's ~s** [*information, equipment*] tomber entre les mains de qn; **to fall** ou **get into the wrong ~s** [*documents, weapons*] tomber en mauvaises mains; **in the right ~s this information could be useful** en bonnes mains, cette information pourrait être utile; **to be in good** ou **safe ~s** [*child, money*] être en bonnes mains; **to put one's life in sb's ~s** remettre sa vie entre les mains de qn; **to place** ou **put sth in sb's ~s** confier qch à qn [*department, office*]; remettre qch entre les mains de qn [*matter, affair*]; **to play into sb's ~s** jouer le jeu de qn; **the matter is out of my ~s** cette affaire n'est plus de mon ressort; **8** (control) **to get out of ~** [*expenditure, inflation*] déraper; [*children, fans*] devenir incontrôlable; [*demonstration, party*] dégénérer; **things are getting out of ~** on est en train de perdre le contrôle de la situation; **to take sth in ~** prendre [qch] en main [*situation*]; s'occuper de [*problem*]; **to take sb in ~** prendre qn en main [*child, troublemaker*]; **9** Games (cards dealt) jeu *m*; (game) partie *f*; **to show one's ~** lit, fig montrer son jeu; **to throw in one's ~** lit, fig abandonner la partie; **10** (worker) Agric ouvrier/-ière *m/f* agricole; Ind ouvrier/-ière *m/f*; Naut membre *m* de l'équipage; **the ship went down with all ~s** le bateau a coulé corps et biens; **11** (responsibility) **to have sth/sb on one's ~s** avoir qch/qn sur les bras [*unsold stock, surplus*]; **to take sb/sth off sb's ~s** débarrasser qn de qn/qch; **to have sth off one's ~s** ne plus avoir qch sur les bras; **they'll have a strike on their ~s if they're not careful** ils vont se retrouver avec une grève sur les bras s'ils ne font pas attention; **12** (available) **to keep/have sth to ~** garder/avoir qch sous la main [*passport, pen, telephone number*]; **to be on ~** [*person*] être disponible; **the fire extinguisher was close to ~** ou **near at ~** l'extincteur n'était pas loin; **help was close at ~** les secours étaient à proximité; **to grab the first coat that comes to ~** attraper n'importe quel manteau; **13** (skill) **to try one's ~ at sth** s'essayer à [*photography, marketing*]; **to try one's ~ at driving/painting** s'essayer à la conduite/la peinture; **to set** ou **turn one's ~ to sth/doing** entreprendre qch/de faire; **she can turn her ~ to almost anything** elle sait pratiquement tout faire; **to keep/get one's ~ in** garder/se faire la main; **14** (pointer) (on clock, dial) aiguille *f*; **the hour/minute ~** l'aiguille des heures/minutes; **15** Equit, Meas = 10,16 cm; **16** Culin (of bananas) régime *m*; **a ~ of pork** un jambonneau; **17**† (signature) **to set one's ~ to** apposer sa signature à [*document*]; **18** (source) **I got the information first/second ~** j'ai eu l'information de première main/par l'intermédiaire de quelqu'un; **19** (aspect, side) **on the one ~..., on the other ~...** d'une part... d'autre part...; **on the other ~** (conversely) par contre; **on every ~** partout.

II in hand *adj phr* **1** (current) en cours (*never after v*); **the job/matter in ~** le travail/l'affaire en cours; **2** (underway) en cours; **work on the road is already in ~** les travaux sur la route sont déjà en cours; **the preparations are well in ~** les préparatifs sont bien avancés; **3** (to spare) **I've got 50 dollars in ~** il me reste 50 dollars; **she finished the exam with 20 minutes in ~** elle a terminé l'examen avec 20 minutes d'avance; **I'll do it when I have some time in ~** je le ferai quand j'aurai du temps devant moi; **stock in ~** Comm marchandises en stock.

III out of hand *adv phr* [*reject, condemn, dismiss*] d'emblée.

IV at the ~s of *prep phr* **his treatment at the ~s of his captors** la façon dont il a été traité par ses ravisseurs; **our defeat at the ~s of the French team** notre défaite contre l'équipe française.

V *vtr* (give) **to ~ sb sth** ou **to ~ sth to sb** donner qch à qn [*form, letter, ticket*]; passer qch à qn [*knife, screwdriver*]; remettre qch à qn [*trophy*]; **to ~ sb out of a car** aider qn à sortir d'une voiture.

IDIOMS **the left ~ doesn't know what the right ~ is doing** la main gauche ignore ce que fait la droite; **to know sth like the back of one's ~** connaître qch comme le dos de la main; **many ~s make light work** Prov plus on est nombreux plus ça va vite; **I could do that with one ~ tied behind my back!** je pourrais le faire les doigts dans le nez○!; **you've got to ~ it to her/them...** il faut lui/leur faire cette justice...; **he never does a ~'s turn** il ne remue pas le petit doigt; **to win ~s down** gagner haut la main.

■ **hand back**: **~ [sth] back**, **~ back [sth]** rendre [*object, essay, colony*] (**to** à).

■ **hand down**: ¶ **~ [sth] down**, **~ down [sth]** (transmit) transmettre [*heirloom, property, tradition, skill, story*] (**from** de; **to** à); ¶ **~ [sth] down to sb**, **~ down [sth] to sb 1** (pass) faire passer [qch] à qn [*boxes, books*]; **2** (pass on after use) passer [qch] à qn [*old clothes*].

■ **hand in**: **~ [sth] in**, **~ in [sth] 1** (submit) remettre [*form, petition, ticket*] (**to** à); rendre [*homework*]; **to ~ in one's notice** ou **resignation** donner sa démission; **2** (return) rendre [*equipment, keys*].

■ **hand on**: **~ [sth] on**, **~ on [sth]** passer [*collection plate, baton*].

■ **hand out**: **~ [sth] out**, **~ out [sth]** distribuer [*food, leaflets*] distribuer [*punishments, fines*]; péj prodiguer pej [*advice*].

■ **hand over**: ¶ **~ over to sb 1** TV, Radio [*presenter*] passer l'antenne à [*reporter, presenter*]; **2** (transfer power) passer la main à [*deputy, successor*]; **3** (on telephone) **I'll just ~ you over to Rosie** je te passe Rosie; ¶ **~ over [sth]**, **~ [sth] over** rendre [*weapon*]; céder [*collection, savings, territory, title, business, company*]; livrer [*secret*]; transmettre [*power, problem*]; remettre [*keys*]; céder [*microphone, controls*]; **the mugger forced him to ~ over his money** le voleur l'a obligé à lui remettre son argent; **that pen's mine, ~ it over!** ce stylo est à moi, rends-le moi!; ¶ **~ [sb] over**, **~ over [sb]** livrer [*prisoner, terrorist*] (**to** à); **to ~ a baby/patient over to sb** remettre un enfant/un malade entre les mains de qn.

■ **hand round**: **~ [sth] round**, **~ round [sth]** faire circuler [*collection plate, leaflets, drinks, sandwiches*].

■ **hand up**: **~ [sth] up to sb** passer [qch] à qn [*hammer, box*].

hand: **~bag** *n* sac *m* à main; **~ baggage** *n* bagage *m* à main.

handball /'hændbɔːl/ *n* Sport **1** ▶1282 (ballgame) handball *m*; **2** (fault in football) faute *f* de main.

hand: **~basin** *n* lavabo *m*; **~bell** *n* clochette *f*; **~bill** *n* prospectus *m*.

handbook /'hændbʊk/ *n* (textbook, guide) manuel *m*; (technical manual) livret *m* technique; **members' ~** guide *m* de l'adhérent; **staff ~** guide *m* de (présentation de) l'entreprise; **teacher's ~** livret *m* du professeur; **training/user's ~** manuel *m* de formation/d'utilisation.

hand: **~brake** *n* Aut frein *m* à main; **~cart** *n* (two-wheeled) charrette *f* à bras; (four-wheeled) chariot *m*; **~clap** *n* claquement *m* de mains; **~clasp** *n* US poignée *f* de main; **~ cream** *n* crème *f* pour les mains.

handcuff /'hændkʌf/ **I handcuffs** *npl* menottes *fpl*; **to put the ~s on sb** passer les menottes à qn.
II *vtr* passer les menottes à [*person*]; **to ~ sb to sth** attacher qn à qch avec des menottes; **the prisoners were ~ed** les prisonniers avaient des menottes aux poignets.

hand-dryer, **hand-drier** /'hændraɪə(r)/ *n* sèche-mains *m inv*.

Handel /'hændl/ *pr n* Haendel.

handful /'hændfʊl/ *n* **1** (fistful) poignée *f*; **by the ~** ou **in ~s** par poignées; **2** (small number) (of people) poignée *f*; (of buildings, events, objects, works) petit nombre *m*; **3**○ (troublesome person, animal) **to be a ~** [*child*] ne pas être de tout repos; [*horse*] être difficile à monter; [*dog*] être épuisant.

hand: **~ grenade** *n* grenade *f* (à main); **~grip** *n* manche *m* (*de raquette*); **~gun** *n* arme *f* de poing.

hand-held /ˌhænd'held/ *adj* [*camera*] de reportage; [*tool*] à main; [*device*] portatif/-ive; [*computer*] de poche; **a ~ shower** une douchette.

handhold /'hændhəʊld/ *n* prise *f* de main.

handicap /'hændɪkæp/ **I** *n* **1** (disability) handicap *m*; **a child with severe** ou **profound physical and mental ~s** un enfant très handicapé mentalement et physiquement; **2** (disadvantage) handicap *m*; **it is a ~ to have** ou **having** c'est gênant d'avoir; **3** Sport (points) handicap *m*; (race) handicap *m*; **to have a ~ of three** (in golf) avoir trois de handicap.
II *vtr* (*p prés etc* **-pp-**) **1** fig handicaper [*person, development*]; **he was ~ped by not being able to read** c'était un handicap pour lui de ne pas savoir lire; **2** Sport handicaper [*race*].

handicapped /'hændɪkæpt/ **I** *n* **the ~** (+ *v pl*) les handicapés *mpl*; **mentally/physically ~** handicapés mentaux/physiques; **the visually ~** les mal-voyants *mpl*.
II *adj* **1** [*person*] handicapé; **2** Sport [*horse, runner*] handicapé.

handicraft /'hændɪkrɑːft, US 'hændkræft/ **I** *n* **1** (object) objet *m* artisanal; **'~s'** (sign on shop) 'artisanat' *m*; **2** (skill) travail *m* artisanal.
II handicrafts *npl* Sch travaux *mpl* manuels.
III *modif* [*exhibition, shop*] d'artisanat; [*class*] de travaux manuels.

handily /'hændɪlɪ/ *adv* [*located, positioned*] bien (*before adj*).

hand in hand *adv* lit [*run, walk*] la main dans la main; **to go ~** fig aller de pair.

handiwork /'hændɪwɜːk/ *n* gen ouvrage *m*; **is this graffiti your ~?** iron ce graffiti, c'est ton œuvre?

handjob◐ /'hænddʒɒb/ *n* **to give oneself a ~**◐ se branler●.

handkerchief /'hæŋkətʃɪf, -tʃiːf/ *n* mouchoir *m*; **paper/cotton ~** mouchoir en papier/en coton; **pocket ~** gen mouchoir de poche; (for jacket) pochette *f*.

hand-knitted /ˌhænd'nɪtɪd/ *adj* tricoté à la main.

handle /'hændl/ **I** *n* **1** (on door, drawer) poignée *f*; (on bucket, cup, basket) anse *f*; (on bag, suitcase) poignée *f*; (on piece of cutlery) manche *m*; (on frying pan, saucepan) queue *f*; (on hammer, screwdriver) manche *m*; (on broom, spade) manche *m*; (on wheelbarrow, pump) bras *m*; **a knife with a wooden ~** un couteau à manche de bois; **to pick sth up by the ~** prendre qch par la poignée or par le manche; **to hold sth by the ~** tenir qch par la poignée or par le manche; **2** fig (hold) **to get a ~ on sb** comprendre qn fig; **to use sth as a ~ against sb** se servir de qch comme d'une arme contre qn; **3**○ (title) titre *m*; **to have a ~ to one's name** avoir un titre; **4**○ (on CB radio) indicatif *m*.
II *vtr* **1** (touch) manipuler [*explosives, samples, food*]; **to ~ sb gently/roughly** traiter qn gentiment/rudement; **to ~ sth gently/roughly** manier qch délicatement/brutalement; **to ~ stolen goods** faire du trafic de marchandises volées; **to ~ drugs** faire du trafic de drogue; **to ~ a gun** manier un pistolet; **'~ with care'** 'fragile'; **'please do not ~ (the goods)'** 'prière de ne pas toucher (à la marchandise)'; **to ~ the ball** (in football) faire une faute de main; **2** (manage) manier [*horse*]; manœuvrer [*car*]; **to know how to ~ children/clients** savoir s'y prendre avec les enfants/les clients; **he's hard to ~** il n'a pas un caractère facile; **this car ~s bends well** cette voiture tient bien la route dans les virages; **3** (deal with) traiter [*grievances, case, negotiations*]; affronter, faire face à [*emergency, crisis*]; supporter [*stress*]; **he couldn't ~ the pace/pressure** il n'a pas supporté le rythme/la pression; **she ~d the situation very well** elle a très bien fait face à la situation; **I can't ~ any more problems at the moment!** j'ai assez de problèmes comme ça en ce moment!; **can you ~ another sausage/drink**○**?** hum estce que tu peux encore avaler une saucisse/un verre?; **leave it to me, I can ~ it** laisse-moi faire, je peux m'en occuper; **4** (process) [*organization*] traiter [*money, clients, order*]; [*airport, port*] accueillir [*traffic, passengers, cargo*]; [*factory*] traiter [*waste, pesticides*]; [*person*] manier [*information, money, accounts*]; [*person*] examiner [*job application*]; [*computer*] manipuler [*graphics, information*]; [*department, official*] s'occuper de [*complaints, immigration, enquiries*]; [*agent*] s'occuper de [*sale*]; [*lawyer*] s'occuper de [*case*]; **5** (artistically) traiter [*theme, narrative, rhythms*].
III *vi* Aut **the car ~s well/badly** la voiture manœuvre bien/mal; **it ~s well on bends/on wet surfaces** elle prend bien les virages/elle tient bien la route sur chaussée humide.
IDIOMS **to fly off the ~**○ piquer une crise○; **to be too hot to ~** (of situation) être trop risqué.

handle: **~bar moustache** *n* moustache *f* en crocs; **~bars** *npl* guidon *m*.

handler /'hændlə(r)/ *n* **1** (of dog) maître-chien *m*; (of other animals) dresseur/-euse *m/f*; **2** (advisor) (of star) agent *m*; (of politician) conseiller *m*; **3** (worker) **food ~** employé/-e *m/f* dans la restauration; **cargo ~** transporteur *m*; **4** (dealer) **~ of stolen goods** trafiquant/-e *m/f* de marchandises volées.

handling /'hændlɪŋ/ *n* **1** (holding, touching) (of substance) manipulation *f*; (of tool, weapon) maniement *m*; **the ~ of foodstuffs/of radioactive materials** la manipulation de denrées alimentaires/de matériaux radioactifs; **old books require careful ~** les livres anciens doivent être manipulés avec soin; **the package had been subjected to rough ~** le paquet avait été maltraité; **2** (way of dealing) **her ~ of the theme/the story** sa façon de traiter le thème/l'histoire; **the bank's ~ of the affair** la façon dont la banque a traité l'affaire; **their ~ of the negotiations** leur conduite des négociations; **the president's ~ of the crisis** la façon dont le président a fait face à la crise; **the ~ of the case** Jur le traitement de l'affaire; **their ~ of the economy** leur gestion de l'économie; **sheep ~** traitement *m* des ovins; **3** Comm (storage, shipping) manutention *f*; **~ facilities** service *m* de manutention; **a grain ~ firm** une entreprise de transport de céréales; **4** (processing) (of data, documents) traitement *m*; (of process, business) gestion *f*; **speedier ~ of air traffic** une gestion plus rapide du trafic aérien; **cash ~** maniement *m* de grosses sommes; **5** (training) **dog ~** entraînement *m* des chiens.

handling charge *n* **1** Comm frais *mpl* de manutention; **2** Admin, Fin frais *mpl* administratifs.

hand: **~ lotion** *n* lotion *f* pour les mains; **~ luggage** *n* bagage *m* à main; **~made** *adj* fait à la main; **~maid**, **~maiden**‡ *n* servante *f*.

hand-me-down○ /'hændmiːdaʊn/ *n* vieux vêtement *m*; **my sister's ~s** les vieux vêtements de ma sœur.

handout /'hændaʊt/ *n* **1** (payment) péj (welfare payment) allocation *f*; (to industry) subvention *f*; (charitable) aumône *f*, don *m*; **to live off/rely on ~s** vivre de/dépendre de la charité des autres; **2** (document) (single sheet) feuille *f*; (several sheets) document *m*; **3** (leaflet) prospectus *m*.

handover /'hændəʊvə(r)/ *n* (of property, power, territory) transfert *m*; (of prisoner, ransom) remise *f*; (of product) remise *f* (**to** à).

hand: **~-painted** *adj* peint à la main; **~pick** *vtr* choisir [qch] soi-même [*vegetables, fruit*]; trier [qn] sur le volet [*staff, deputy*].

handportable /ˌhænd'pɔːtəbəl/ **I** *n* Comput portatif *m*; Telecom portable *m*.
II *adj* Comput portatif/-ive; Telecom portable.

hand: **~rail** *n* (on stairs) rampe *f*, main *f* courante; (on balcony, pier) garde-fou *m*; **~-reared** *adj* [*animal*] élevé au biberon; **~saw** *n* scie *f* manuelle; **~set** *n* Telecom combiné *m*; **~shake** *n* (friendly gesture) poignée *f* de main; Comput établissement *m* d'une liaison; **~ signal** *n* gen, Aut signe *m* de la main; **~s-off** *adj* [*manager*] qui pratique la délégation du pouvoir; [*policy*] de non-intervention; [*style, approach*] basé sur la non-intervention.

handsome /'hænsəm/ *adj* **1** (fine) [*man*] beau; [*town, bag*] beau/belle; [*building*] beau et imposant; **a ~ woman** une belle femme; **2** (appreciable) [*dividend*] bon/bonne; [*sum*] beau/belle; [*reward*] généreux/-euse; **to receive ~ remuneration** être largement payé.
IDIOMS **~ is as ~ does** Prov il faut juger quelqu'un à ses actes plutôt que se fier aux apparences.

handsomely /'hænsəmlɪ/ *adv* **1** (elegantly) **a ~ proportioned building** un bâtiment aux proportions élégantes; **a ~ written book** un livre très bien écrit; **2** (decisively) **to win ~** gagner haut la main; **3** (amply) **to pay off ~** [*investment*] être d'un bon rapport; **to be ~ rewarded** recevoir une généreuse récompense.

hand: **~s-on** *adj* [*experience, training, manager, management*] de terrain; [*control*] direct; [*museum*] interactif/-ive; [*approach*] pragmatique; **~spring** *n* saut *m* de mains, salto *m*.

handstand /'hændstænd/ *n* Sport équilibre *m*; **to do a ~** faire l'équilibre.

hand-to-hand /ˌhændtə'hænd/ **I** *adj* [*combat, fighting*] (au) corps à corps; **a ~ fight** un corps à corps.
II *adv* [*fight*] corps à corps.

hand-to-mouth /'hændtəmaʊθ/ **I** *adj* [*existence, life*] au jour le jour *inv*.
II hand to mouth *adv* [*live*] au jour le jour.

hand: **~ towel** *n* essuie-mains *m inv*; **~-woven** *adj* tissé à la main.

handwriting /ˈhændraɪtɪŋ/ *n* écriture *f*; **the message was in Brigitte's ~** le message était écrit de la main de Brigitte.

handwritten /ˈhændrɪtn/ *adj* manuscrit.

handy /ˈhændɪ/ *adj* **1** (useful) [*book, index, skill*] utile; [*bag, tool, pocket*] pratique; **to be ~ for doing** être pratique pour faire; **a ~ hint** ou **tip** un conseil utile; **to come in ~ for sb/sth** servir à qn/qch; **to come in ~ for doing** servir à faire; **don't throw the box away, it might come in ~** ne jette pas la boîte, elle peut toujours servir; **an ability to speak Spanish could come in ~** savoir parler espagnol pourrait être utile; **that's ~ to know** c'est bon à savoir; **2** (convenient) [*format, shape, size*] pratique; [*location*] bon/bonne; [*shop*] bien situé; **the hotel is ~ for the shops** l'hôtel est bien situé pour les magasins; **to keep sth ~** garder qch sous la main [*keys, passport*]; **have you got a pencil ~?** as-tu un crayon sous la main?; **3**○ (skilful) [*player, footballer*] doué (**at doing** pour faire); **to be ~ with a paintbrush/ one's fists** savoir se servir d'un pinceau/de ses poings; **to be ~ about the house** être bricoleur/-euse *m/f*.

handyman /ˈhændɪmæn/ *n* (amateur) bricoleur *m*; (professional) homme *m* à tout faire.

hang /hæŋ/ **I** *n* **1** Sewing (of curtain, garment) **the ~** le tombant; **2**○ (knack) **to get the ~ of sth○/of doing○** piger○ qch/comment faire; **you'll soon get the ~ of the computer/of using the new system** tu ne vas pas tarder à piger○ l'ordinateur/comment utiliser le nouveau système; **you're getting the ~ of it** tu as pigé○.

II *vtr* (*prét, pp* **hung**) **1** (suspend) (from projection, hook, coat-hanger) accrocher (**from** à; **by** par; **on** à); (from string, rope) suspendre (**from** à); (drape over) étendre, mettre (**over** sur); (peg up) étendre [*washing*] (**on** sur); **the cat had a bell hung round its neck** le chat avait une clochette (accrochée) au cou; **I'll ~ the washing on the line** je vais étendre le linge; **she hung the towel over the radiator** elle a mis la serviette sur le radiateur; **2** (also **~ down**) (let dangle) suspendre [*rope, line etc*] (**out of** par); laisser pendre [*arm, leg*]; baisser [*head*]; **she hung her arm over the side of the boat** elle a laissé pendre son bras hors de la barque; **we hung our heads in shame** nous avons baissé la tête de honte; **3** Art accrocher [*exhibition, picture*]; **4** (decorate with) **to be hung with** être orné de [*flags, tapestries*]; être décoré de [*garlands*]; **the walls were hung with portraits** des portraits étaient accrochés aux murs; **5** (interior decorating) poser [*wallpaper*]; **6** Constr, Tech poser [*door, gate*]; **7** Culin faisander [*game*]; **8** (*prét, pp* **hanged**) pendre [*criminal, victim*] (**for** pour; **for doing** pour avoir fait); **he was ~ed for treason** il a été pendu pour trahison; **to be ~ed drawn and quartered** être pendu, éviscéré et écartelé.

III *vi* (*prét, pp* **hung**) **1** (be suspended) (on hook) être accroché; (from height) être suspendu; (on washing line) être étendu; **a chandelier hung from the ceiling** un chandelier était suspendu au plafond; **her photo ~s over the piano** sa photo est accrochée au-dessus du piano; **she hung from the branch, then dropped** elle est restée accrochée or suspendue à la branche, puis elle s'est laissée tomber; **her arm hung limply over the arm of the chair** son bras pendait mollement de l'accoudoir; **the bed is too short: my feet ~ over the end** le lit est trop petit: mes pieds dépassent; **the children were ~ing out of the window** les enfants se penchaient à la fenêtre; **2** Sewing (drape) [*curtain, garment*] tomber; **the dress doesn't ~ properly** la robe ne tombe pas bien; **3** (float) [*fog, cloud, smoke, smell*] flotter; **4** Art être accroché; **his paintings ~ in the Louvre** ses tableaux sont accrochés au Louvre; **5** Culin [*game*] faisander; **6** (die) être pendu (**for** pour).

IV *v refl* (*prét, pp* **hanged**) **to ~ oneself** se pendre (**from** à).

IDIOMS **~ it all○!** zut○!; **~ John○!** tant pis pour John!; **~ the expense○!** au diable l'avarice!; **I'll be ~ed if...○** je veux bien être pendu si...; **~ed if I know○!** je n'en sais fichtre rien○!; **sb/sth can go ~○** GB, **let sb/sth go ~○** GB qn/qch peut aller au diable; **to let it all ~ out○** être relax○; **well I'll be ~ed○†!** ça alors! ▶ **sheep**.

■ **hang about○**, **hang around○** (waiting for sth) poireauter○; (aimlessly) traîner; **to keep sb ~ing around for three hours** faire poireauter○ qn pendant trois heures.

■ **hang around○**: ¶ **~ around** = **hang about**; **to ~ around with sb** (associate with) fréquenter qn; ¶ **~ around [sb]** (inflict oneself on) être toujours à tourner autour○ de qn; **she's always ~ing around me** elle est toujours à me tourner autour.

■ **hang back** (in fear) rester derrière; (waiting) rester; (reluctant) lit rester à la traîne; fig être réticent; **she hung back from offering help** elle était réticente à proposer son aide.

■ **hang down** gen pendre; [*hem*] être défait.

■ **hang off** pendre.

■ **hang on** ¶ **1**○ (wait) attendre; **~ on, I've a better idea** attends, j'ai une meilleure idée; (on phone) **can you ~ on a minute?** voulez-vous attendre une minute?; **2**○ (survive) tenir○; **he hung on for another five years** il a tenu cinq ans de plus; **~ on in there○!** tiens bon, accroche-toi○!; ¶ **~ on [sth] 1** (depend on) dépendre de; **we must win—everything ~s on it** il faut que nous gagnions—tout en dépend; **2** (listen attentively) **to ~ on sb's words** ou **every word** être pendu aux lèvres de qn.

■ **hang on to**: **~ on to [sth/sb] 1** (hold tight) s'agripper à [*object, rail*]; agripper [*person*]; **~ on to the branch** agrippe-toi à la branche; **~ on to that child** agrippe l'enfant; **~ on to your hat!** lit tiens bien ton chapeau!; fig accroche-toi!; **2**○ fig (retain) s'accrocher à○ [*possession, power, title, tradition, values*].

■ **hang out** ¶ **1** (protrude) [*shirt, handkerchief etc*] dépasser; **2**○ (live) crécher○; **3**○ (frequent) traîner○; ¶ **~ out [sth]**, **~ [sth] out** étendre [*washing*]; accrocher [*sign*]; sortir [*flag*].

■ **hang over**: **~ over [sb/sth]** [*threat, danger, unpleasant prospect, suspicion*] planer sur [*person, project*].

■ **hang together 1** (be consistent) se tenir; **2** (cooperate) se serrer les coudes.

■ **hang up** ¶ (on phone) raccrocher; Comput tomber en panne; **to ~ up on sb** raccrocher au nez de qn; ¶ **~ up [sth]**, **~ [sth] up 1** (on hook) accrocher; (on hanger, string) suspendre; (on washing line) étendre; **she hung it up to dry** elle l'a étendu pour le faire sécher; **2** Telecom raccrocher [*phone*]; **3** fig, hum **to ~ up one's skis/one's gloves/ one's spade** mettre ses skis/ses gants/sa bêche au rancart.

hangar /ˈhæŋə(r)/ *n* hangar *m*.

hangdog /ˈhæŋdɒg/ *adj* [*expression, look*] de chien battu.

hanger /ˈhæŋə(r)/ *n* **1** (coat hanger) cintre *m*; **2** (loop) boucle *f*.

hanger-on○ /ˌhæŋərˈɒn/ *n* parasite *m*, pique-assiette○ *mf*.

hang-glider /ˈhæŋglaɪdə(r)/ *n* (craft) deltaplane *m*; (pilot) deltaplaniste *mf*.

hang-gliding /ˈhæŋglaɪdɪŋ/ ▶ **1282** *n* deltaplane *m*; **to go ~** faire du deltaplane.

hanging /ˈhæŋɪŋ/ **I** *n* **1** (strangulation) pendaison *f*; **death by ~** mort par pendaison; **~ is too good for him** la pendaison est une mort trop douce pour lui; **2** (curtain) rideau *m*; (on wall, for decoration) tenture *f*; **3** (act of suspending) (of picture, decoration) accrochage *m*; (of door, wallpaper) posage *m*; (of game) Culin faisandage *m*.

II *adj* Jur [*offence*] passible de pendaison; [*judge*] lit partisan de la pendaison; fig à la main lourde.

hanging: **~ basket** *n* Hort suspension *f* florale, panier *m* suspendu; **~ committee** *n* Art jury *m* d'admission des tableaux; **Hanging Gardens of Babylon** *npl* jardins *mpl* suspendus de Babylone; **~ staircase** *n* escalier *m* en encorbellement; **~ valley** *n* vallée *f* suspendue.

hangman /ˈhæŋmən/ *n* **1** (at gallows) bourreau *m*; **2** ▶ **1282** (game) potence *f*.

hangnail /ˈhæŋneɪl/ *n* petite peau *f*.

hang-out○ /ˈhæŋaʊt/ *n* **his favourite ~** son endroit favori.

hangover /ˈhæŋəʊvə(r)/ **I** *n* **1** (from drink) gueule *f* de bois○; **to have a ~** avoir la gueule de bois○; **2** fig (legacy) héritage *m* (**from** de).

II *modif* [*remedy*] contre la gueule de bois.

hang-up○ /ˈhæŋʌp/ *n* (deep-rooted) complexe *m*; (specific worry) problème *m*; **to have a ~ about** avoir un complexe à cause de [*appearance, experience*]; avoir la phobie de [*spiders etc*]; **to have a ~ about doing** avoir un problème pour faire.

hank /hæŋk/ *n* (of wool etc) écheveau *m*.

hanker /ˈhæŋkə(r)/ *vi* **to ~ after** ou **for sth** (with desire) rêver de qch; (with nostalgia) regretter qch.

hankering /ˈhæŋkərɪŋ/ *n* **a ~ for sth/to do sth** une grande envie de qch/de faire qch.

hanky, **hankie**○ /ˈhæŋkɪ/ *n* mouchoir *m*.

hanky-panky○ /ˌhæŋkɪˈpæŋkɪ/ *n* hum (sexual) polissonneries *fpl*; (dishonest) friponneries *fpl*.

Hannibal /ˈhænɪbl/ *pr n* Hannibal.

Hanoi /ˌhæˈnɔɪ/ ▶ **1818** *pr n* Hanoi.

Hanover /ˈhænəʊvə(r)/ ▶ **1818** *pr n* Hanovre.

Hanoverian /ˌhænəˈvɪərɪən/ *adj* **1** Hist hanovrien/-ienne; **2** Geog de Hanovre.

Hansard /ˈhænsɑːd/ *n*: *compte-rendu officiel des débats de la Chambre des communes*.

Hanseatic League /ˌhænsɪˈætɪk/ *pr n* Hanse *f* teutonique.

hansom /ˈhænsəm/ *n* (also **~ cab**) cab *m*, cabriolet *m*.

Hants GB Post *abrév écrite* = **Hampshire**.

ha'penny /ˈheɪpnɪ/ *n* GB *abrév* ▶ **halfpenny**.

haphazard /hæpˈhæzəd/ *adj* (unorganized) peu méthodique; (random) **a ~ world** un monde incohérent; **in a ~ way** [*arranged*] de façon peu méthodique; [*guess*] au hasard; [*pick up skills, information*] par-ci par-là.

haphazardly /hæpˈhæzədlɪ/ *adv* n'importe comment.

hapless /ˈhæplɪs/ *adj* littér ou hum pauvre, infortuné liter.

happen /ˈhæpən/ *vi* **1** (occur) arriver, se passer, se produire; **when/where/how did it ~?** quand/où/comment est-ce arrivé?, quand/où/comment cela s'est-il passé or produit?; **what's happening?** qu'est-ce qui se passe?; **the accident ~ed yesterday** l'accident est arrivé or s'est produit hier; **I wonder what will ~ next** je me demande ce qui va arriver or se passer maintenant; **we must make sure this never ~s again** nous devons faire en sorte que cela ne se reproduise jamais; **you cannot expect the change to ~ overnight** ne t'attends pas à ce que le changement se produise du jour au lendemain; **so much has ~ed since our last meeting** il s'est passé tant de choses depuis notre dernière rencontre; **he reacted as if nothing had ~ed** il a réagi comme si de rien n'était; **whatever ~s, don't get out of the car** quoi qu'il arrive, ne sors pas de la voiture; **it had to ~, it was bound to ~** GB ça devait arriver; **miracles do ~!** les miracles, ça arrive!; **it may ~ that, it can ~ that** il arrive parfois que; **how does it ~** ou **how can it ~ that**

such problems are ignored? comment se fait-il qu'on ne prête pas attention à de tels problèmes?; **success doesn't just ~!** le succès n'arrive pas comme ça!; **anything might ~!** on peut s'attendre à tout!; **she's the sort of person who makes things ~** elle fait bouger les choses; **2** (befall) **to ~ to sb** arriver à qn; **the worst thing that can ~ to a man like him is** la pire chose qui puisse arriver à un homme comme lui, c'est; **old age/death is something that ~s to us all** la vieillesse/la mort nous attend tous; **3** (occur by chance) **there ~s/~ed to be a free parking space** il se trouve qu'il y a/qu'il y avait une place libre; **we ~ed to be there when she appeared** nous nous trouvions là par hasard quand elle est arrivée; **it so ~s that I have an example right here** il se trouve que j'ai un exemple juste ici; **as it ~ed, the weather that day was bad** il s'est trouvé qu'il faisait mauvais ce jour-là; **if you ~ to see her say hello** si par hasard tu la vois, salue-la de ma part; **do you ~ to have his phone number?** aurais-tu par hasard son numéro de téléphone?; **4** (materialize) arriver; **the promised reforms never ~ed** les réformes promises ne sont jamais arrivées; **5** (go wrong, cause harm) arriver; **if anything ~s to Dinah, I shall never forgive myself** s'il arrive quoi que ce soit à Dinah, je ne me le pardonnerai jamais; **do you think anything will ~?** penses-tu qu'il va arriver quelque chose?; **6** (become of) devenir; **what will ~ to the children?** que deviendront les enfants?; **what ~ed to all those fine promises?** que sont devenues toutes ces belles promesses?; **7** (used indignantly, assertively) **he just ~s to be the best actor in Britain!** il se trouve que c'est le meilleur acteur de Grande-Bretagne!; **sorry, but I ~ to disagree** désolé, mais je ne suis pas d'accord.

■ **happen on**: **~ on** [sth] trouver [qch] par hasard, tomber sur [qch] [*object*].

happening /ˈhæpənɪŋ/ **I** *n* **1** (occurrence) incident *m*; **there have been some strange ~s recently** il s'est passé des choses étranges dernièrement; **2** Art, Theat happening *m*.
II○ *adj* branché○.

happenstance /ˈhæpənstəns/ *n* US hasard *m*; **by ~** par hasard; **it was just ~** c'était le hasard.

happily /ˈhæpɪlɪ/ *adv* **1** (cheerfully) [*laugh, chat, play, say*] joyeusement; **to be ~ married** être heureux en ménage; **a ~ married man** un mari heureux; **a ~ married woman** une femme heureuse; **they all lived ~ ever after** ils vécurent heureux jusqu'à la fin de leurs jours; **2** (luckily) heureusement; **3** (willingly) [*accept, admit, agree, give up, leave, submit*] volontiers; **4** (successfully) [*blend, chosen*] avec bonheur; **a ~ worded letter** une lettre aux termes bien choisis.

happiness /ˈhæpɪnɪs/ *n* bonheur *m*.

happy /ˈhæpɪ/ *adj* **1** (cheerful) [*home, life, memory, atmosphere*] heureux/-euse; [*person*] heureux/-euse (**about** de; **with sb** avec qn; **for sb** pour qn; **that** que + *subj*); **the ~ couple** les mariés *mpl*; **the ~ event** (birth) l'heureux événement; **to be ~ doing** bien aimer faire; **I'm ~ (that) I've won/(that) they're back** je suis heureux d'avoir gagné/qu'ils soient revenus; **2** (pleased, satisfied) content; **to be ~ with sth** être satisfait de qch; **he's not ~ about it** il n'est pas d'accord; **to keep sb ~** faire plaisir à qn; **to give sb sth to keep them ~** donner qch à qn pour qu'il reste tranquille; **3** (willing) **to be ~ to do** être heureux/-euse de faire; **he's quite ~ to leave on Monday** cela ne le dérange pas de partir lundi; **are you ~ to go tomorrow?** cela ne te dérange pas d'y aller demain?; **we are ~ for them to do it** cela ne nous dérange pas qu'ils le fassent; **4** (in greetings) **Happy birthday!** Bon anniversaire!; **Happy Christmas!** Joyeux Noël!; **Happy New Year!** Bonne année!; **Happy anniversary!** Bon anniversaire!; **5** (lucky) heureux/-euse; **by a ~ coincidence** par une heureuse coïncidence; **he's in the ~ position of having no debts** il a la chance de ne pas avoir de dettes; **the ~ few** les quelques rares privilégiés; **6** (successful) [*blend, balance, choice, phrase*] heureux/-euse; **7**○ (slightly drunk) pompette○.

IDIOMS **to be as ~ as Larry** ou **as a sandboy** GB être heureux comme un poisson dans l'eau.

happy couple *n* **the ~** les mariés *mpl*.

happy ending *n* heureux dénouement *m*.

happy event *n* **the ~** l'heureux événement *m*.

happy: **Happy Families** ▶ 1282 *n* (+ *v sg*) les sept Familles *fpl*; **~-go-lucky** *adj* [*person, attitude*] insouciant; **~ hour** *n*: *dans un bar, période durant laquelle les boissons sont vendues à prix réduit*.

happy hunting ground *n* **1** (Amerindian) paradis *m* (*des Indiens d'Amérique*); **2** fig paradis *m*; **to be a ~ for sb** être le paradis pour qn.

happy medium *n* juste milieu *m*.

Hapsburg /ˈhæpsbɜːg/ *pr n* Habsbourg; **the ~s** les Habsbourg *mpl*.

hara-kiri /ˌhærəˈkɪrɪ/ *n* hara-kiri *m*; **to commit ~** faire hara-kiri.

harangue /həˈræŋ/ **I** *n* (political) harangue *f*; (moral) sermon *m*.
II *vtr* (*p prés* **haranguing**) (politically) haranguer; (morally) sermonner.

harass /ˈhærəs, US həˈræs/ **I** *vtr* [*photographer, police etc*] harceler; [*problem, event*] contrarier.
II harassed *pp adj* excédé.

harassment /ˈhærəsmənt, US həˈræsmənt/ *n* harcèlement *m*; **police ~** harcèlement par la police; **sexual ~** harcèlement sexuel; **racial ~** persécution *f* raciste.

harbinger /ˈhɑːbɪndʒə(r)/ *n* littér signe *m* annonciateur; **~ of doom** (thing) funeste présage *m*; (person) porteur/-euse *m/f* de mauvaises nouvelles.

harbour GB, **harbor** US /ˈhɑːbə(r)/ **I** *n* **1** lit port *m*; **deep-water ~** port de toute marée; **natural ~** port naturel; **2** fig (haven) refuge *m*.
II *vtr* **1** (nurse) nourrir [*emotion, suspicion, illusion*]; **to ~ a grudge** être plein de ressentiment; **2** (shelter illegally) receler [*criminal*]; **3** (contain) receler [*parasite, insect*]; retenir [*dirt, germs*].

harbour dues, **harbour fees** *npl* frais *mpl* or droits *mpl* portuaires.

harbour master ▶ 1692 *n* capitaine *m* de port.

harbourside /ˈhɑːbəsaɪd/ **I** *n* port *m*.
II *modif* [*bar, café etc*] du port.

harbour station *n* gare *f* maritime.

hard /hɑːd/ **I** *adj* **1** [*consistency, object, surface, skin, muscle, snow, butter, bread, ground, bed, pencil lead*] dur; [*paint, wax, mud, glue*] dur, durci; **to go** ou **grow** ou **become ~** durcir; **to set ~** [*concrete, plaster etc*] durcir complètement; **a ~ frost** une forte gelée; **frozen ~** complètement gelé; ▶ **hard lens**; **2** (difficult, complex) [*problem, question, puzzle*] dur, difficile; [*choice*] difficile, dur à faire; [*decision*] difficile, dur à prendre; (arduous, demanding) [*task, study, training, climb*] dur, difficile; [*bargaining, negotiations, fight*] dur, serré; **I've had a ~ day** j'ai eu une dure journée; **a ~ day's work/filming** une dure journée de travail/de tournage; **to be ~ to open/cut/find/read** être dur or difficile à ouvrir/couper/trouver/lire; **it's a ~ poem to translate** c'est un poème difficile à traduire; **to be ~ to please** être exigeant; **it's ~ to do** c'est dur or difficile à faire; **it was ~ not to laugh** il était dur or difficile de ne pas rire; **his decision was ~ for us to understand** il était dur or difficile de comprendre sa décision, nous avions du mal à comprendre sa décision; **it is ~ for sb to do sth** il est difficile à or pour qn de faire qch; **it was ~ for us to understand his decision** il nous était difficile de comprendre sa décision, nous avions du mal à comprendre sa décision; **it's ~ for old people to change their ways** il est difficile pour les personnes âgées de changer leurs habitudes; **to find it ~ to do sth** avoir du mal à faire qch, trouver dur or difficile de faire qch; **to find sth ~ to do** trouver qch dur or difficile à faire; **it's ~ to accept/believe** on a du mal à accepter/croire (**that** que); **I'm not afraid of ~ work** le travail ne me fait pas peur; **it was ~ work** ou **going** ça a été dur or difficile; **it's ~ work doing sth** c'est difficile or dur de faire qch; **it was ~ work persuading her to sell** c'était difficile or dur de la persuader de vendre; **I found the article rather ~ going** j'ai trouvé l'article plutôt ardu or difficile; **he made ~ work of moving the table** il a fait tout un plat○ pour déplacer la table; **~ work never hurt** ou **killed anybody!** le travail n'a jamais fait de mal à personne!; **it's too much like ~ work** c'est trop fatigant; **to be a ~ worker** [*student, pupil, employee*] être travailleur/-euse; [*manual worker*] être dur à la tâche; **to do things the ~ way** se compliquer la tâche; **he got the job the ~ way** il a beaucoup travaillé pour en arriver là; **to find sth out** ou **learn sth the ~ way** apprendre qch à ses dépens; **3** (harsh, unpleasant) [*life, childhood, year*] difficile; [*blow, knock*] fig dur, terrible; [*climate, winter*] rude; **he has to learn to take the ~ knocks** il faut qu'il apprenne à encaisser○; **this is a ~ world** nous vivons dans un monde cruel or sans pitié; **to be ~ on sb** [*person, court*] être dur envers qn; **don't be so ~ on yourself!** ne sois pas si dur avec toi-même!; **this tax is very ~ on the unemployed** cet impôt frappe durement les chômeurs; **this print is ~ on the eyes** ces caractères ne ménagent pas la vue; **~ luck** ou **lines**○ GB! (sympathetic) pas de chance!; **~ luck** ou **lines**○ GB ou **cheese**○ GB! (unsympathetic) tant pis pour toi!, manque de pot○!; **to take a ~ line** adopter une attitude ferme (**on sth** à propos de qch; **with sb** envers qn); **it's a ~ life** gen, hum, iron la vie est dure; **it's a ~ life being a millionaire** iron c'est dur d'être (un) millionnaire; **no ~ feelings!** sans rancune!; **I bear her no ~ feelings** je ne lui en veux pas, je ne lui en tiens pas rancune; **these are ~ times** les temps sont durs; **to fall on ~ times** connaître des revers de fortune; **he's having a ~ time (of it)** il traverse une période difficile; **to have a ~ time (of it) doing sth** avoir du mal à faire qch; **to give sb a ~ time**○ (make things difficult) rendre la vie impossible à qn; (tell off) passer un savon○ à qn; **4** (stern, cold) [*person, voice, look, words*] dur, sévère; **their hearts are ~** ils ont le cœur dur; **5** (forceful) [*shove, push, knock*] bon/bonne (*before n*); **I gave the door a ~ push** j'ai poussé fortement la porte; **6** (concrete) [*evidence, proof*] solide; [*facts*] concret/-ète, solide; [*news*] sérieux/-ieuse; **the paper that brings you the ~ news** le journal qui vous donne des nouvelles sérieuses; **the ~ facts about sth** la vérité sur qch; **7** (stark) [*outline, colour, light*] dur; [*sound*] violent; **8** (strong) [*drink, liquor*] fort; [*drug*] dur; [*pornography*] hard; **to be a ~ drinker** boire des alcools forts; **a drop of the ~ stuff**○ une goutte d'alcool (fort); **9** Pol **the ~ left/right** la gauche/droite (pure et) dure; **10** Chem [*water*] dur, calcaire; **11** Ling [*consonant*] dur; **12**○ (tough) [*person*] dur; **so you think you're ~, do you?** tu te prends pour un dur, hein○?
II *adv* **1** (strongly, energetically) [*push, pull, punch, laugh, cry*] fort; [*work*] dur; [*study, think*] sérieusement; [*rain*] fort, à verse; [*snow*] abondamment; [*look, listen*] attentivement; **to hit sb/sth ~** lit frapper qn/qch

fort; fig frapper qn/qch durement; **to be ~ hit** fig être durement frappé (**by** par); **think ~!** réfléchissez bien or sérieusement!; **to try ~** (intellectually) faire beaucoup d'efforts; (physically) essayer de toutes ses forces; **as ~ as one can** [*run, try, push, pull, work*] de toutes ses forces; **no matter how ~ I try/work, I...** j'ai beau essayer/travailler, je...; **to be ~ at it**○ ou **at work** être en plein boulot○ or travail; **she works** ou **drives her students very ~** elle fait travailler très dur ses étudiants; **to take sth (very) ~** prendre (très) mal qch; **2** (with directions) **turn ~ left at the traffic lights** aux feux tournez tout de suite à gauche; **go ~ astern** Naut machine arrière toute; **~ a-port/a-starboard** Naut à babord/à tribord toute; **3** (indicating proximity) **~ behind** juste derrière; **~ by† sth** tout près de qch; **~ (up)on sth** juste sur qch; ▶ **heel**.

IDIOMS **to play ~ to get** se faire désirer; **to be ~ put to do** avoir du mal à faire; **to be/feel ~ done by** être/se sentir brimé.

hard: **~ and fast** *adj* [*rule, distinction, category*] absolu; **~-ass**● *n* US dur/-e *m/f* à cuire○.

hardback /ˈhɑːdbæk/, **hardcover** /ˌhɑːdˈkʌvə(r)/ US **I** *n* livre *m* cartonné or relié; **in ~** en édition reliée.

II *modif* [*book*] cartonné, relié; [*sales, figures*] des livres reliés; [*publisher*] de livres reliés.

hardbacked /ˈhɑːdbækt/ *adj* [*chair*] à dossier dur.

hardball /ˈhɑːdbɔːl/ ▶ **1282** *n* US Sport base-ball *m*; **to play ~** lit jouer au baseball; fig utiliser tous les moyens possibles.

hardbitten /ˌhɑːdˈbɪtn/ *adj* [*person*] endurci.

hardboard /ˈhɑːdbɔːd/ **I** *n* aggloméré *m*.

II *modif* [*box, wall*] en aggloméré; [*sheet*] d'aggloméré.

hard-boiled /ˌhɑːdˈbɔɪld/ *adj* **1** lit [*egg*] dur; **2** fig [*person*] endurci.

hardcase○ /ˈhɑːdkeɪs/ *n* dur/-e *m/f* à cuire○.

hard cash *n* espèces *fpl*, (argent *m*) liquide *m*; **in ~** en espèces, en liquide.

hard copy *n* Comput tirage *m*.

hard core I *n* **1** (of group, demonstrators, strikers, resistance) noyau *m* dur; **2** Constr remblai *m*; **3 hardcore** Mus hardcore *m*.

II hard-core *adj* **1** (established) [*Marxist, supporter, opponent, protest*] irréductible; **2** (extreme) [*pornography, video*] hard (*inv*); **3 hardcore** Mus [*music, band, record*] hardcore *inv*.

hard court *n* Sport court *m* en dur.

hard currency I *n* monnaie *f* forte.

II *modif* [*earnings, exports, investments, reserves*] de monnaie forte.

hard: **~ disk** *n* Comput disque *m* dur; **~-drinking** *adj* qui boit beaucoup; **~-earned** *adj* [*cash, money*] durement gagné; [*position*] durement obtenu.

harden /ˈhɑːdn/ **I** *vtr* **1** lit gen (faire) durcir [*paint, glue, butter, wax, skin*]; Ind tremper [*steel*]; **2** fig [*time, experience*] endurcir [*person*] (**to** à); raffermir, renforcer [*resolve, opposition*]; durcir [*attitude, stance*]; **to ~ one's heart** s'endurcir (**to** à).

II *vi* **1** lit [*paint, glue, butter, wax, muscle, skin*] durcir; **2** fig [*face, voice*] se faire dur, se durcir; [*opposition, resolve, attitude, stance*] se durcir; **his eyes ~ed** son regard se durcit; **to ~ into** [*suspicions, dislike, guidelines*] se cristalliser en [*certainty, hatred, strict rules*]; **3** Fin [*shares, market, economy*] se raffermir; [*prices*] être en hausse.

III *v refl* **to ~ oneself to** s'endurcir à [*pain, criticism*].

■ **harden off** Hort: ¶ **~ off** [*plant*] s'endurcir; ¶ **~ [sth] off, ~ off [sth]** endurcir [*plant*].

hardened /ˈhɑːdnd/ *adj* **1** lit [*paint, wax, glue, clay, skin*] durci; Ind [*steel*] trempé; **2** fig [*criminal, terrorist, miser*] endurci; [*drinker, addict*] invétéré; **to become ~ to** s'accoutumer à [*pain, climate*]; devenir indifférent à [*insults*].

hardening /ˈhɑːdnɪŋ/ **I** *n* **1** gen lit, fig durcissement *m*; **2** Ind (of steel) trempage *m*; **3** Med **~ of the arteries** durcissement des artères.

II *adj* [*resolve, conviction*] grandissant; [*attitude*] de plus en plus dur.

hard: **~ error** *n* Comput erreur *f* permanente; **~-faced** *adj* lit [*person*] aux traits durs; fig froid; **~-fought** *adj* [*battle*] âprement mené; [*election, competition*] âprement disputé.

hard hat *n* **1** (helmet) gen casque *m*; Equit bombe *f*; **2** US (construction worker) ouvrier/-ière *m/f* du bâtiment.

hard: **~head** *n* US réaliste *mf*; **~-headed** *adj* [*person, approach*] réaliste.

hard-hearted /ˌhɑːdˈhɑːtɪd/ *adj* insensible; **to be ~ towards sb** être dur envers qn.

hard-hitting /ˌhɑːdˈhɪtɪŋ/ *adj* [*report, speech, criticism, film*] sans concession.

hardiness /ˈhɑːdɪnɪs/ *n* **1** (strength, toughness) gen robustesse *f*; Hort (of plant) résistance *f*; **2** (boldness) hardiesse *f*.

hard: **~ labour** GB, **~ labor** US travaux *mpl* forcés; **~ lens** *n* lentille *f* de contact rigide.

hardline /ˌhɑːdˈlaɪn/ *adj* [*measure, tactic, policy*] (très) ferme; [*communist, conservative, political system*] intransigeant, pur et dur; **~ approach** jusqu'au-boutisme *m*.

hardliner /ˌhɑːdˈlaɪnə(r)/ *n* gen pur et dur *m*, jusqu'au-boutiste *mf*; Pol partisan/-e *m/f* de la ligne dure.

hard-luck story *n* **to tell** ou **give sb a ~** raconter ses malheurs à qn.

hardly /ˈhɑːdlɪ/ *adv* **1** (only just, barely) [*begin, know, hear, see, be able*] à peine; **I ~ know him** je le connais à peine; **they had ~ gone out when** ils étaient à peine sortis que; **~ had they set off than** ou **when** à peine étaient-ils partis que; **2** (not really) [*expect, hope*] difficilement; **you can ~ expect me to believe that!** tu peux difficilement t'attendre à ce que je croie cela!; **it's ~ a secret!** c'est loin d'être un secret!; **it's ~ likely** c'est peu probable; **it's ~ surprising** ce n'est guère étonnant; **it's ~ worth it** cela n'en vaut pas la peine; **~!** certainement pas!; **I need ~ tell you that** il va sans dire que; **I need ~ remind you that** inutile de vous rappeler que; **I can ~ wait!** gen il me tarde d'y être; iron je meurs d'envie d'y être; **I can ~ believe it!** je n'arrive pas à y croire!; **3** (almost not) **~ any/ever/anybody** presque pas/jamais/personne; **he ~ ever writes** il n'écrit presque jamais; **~ a day goes by without sb doing sth** ou **that sb doesn't do sth** il se passe à peine un jour sans que qn fasse qch; **4** (harshly) durement.

hardness /ˈhɑːdnɪs/ *n* **1** (firmness) (of substance, object, voice) dureté *f*; **2** (difficulty) (of work, problem, life) difficulté *f*, dureté *f*; (of climate) rudesse *f*.

hard-nosed /ˌhɑːdˈnəʊzd/ *adj* (unsentimental) [*person*] résolu, qui ne fait pas de sentiment; pej [*attitude, businessman, government*] impitoyable; [*person*] sans cœur.

hard of hearing I *n* **the ~** (+ *v pl*) les malentendants *mpl*.

II *adj* **to be ~** entendre mal.

hard-on● /ˈhɑːdɒn/ *n* **to have** ou **get a ~** bander●.

hard: **~ palate** *n* voûte *f* du palais; **~ porn**○ *n* le hard○ *m*.

hard-pressed /ˌhɑːdˈprest/, **hard-pushed** /ˌhɑːdˈpʊʃt/ *adj* gen en difficulté; (for time) pressé; (under pressure) sous pression; **to be ~ for time** être pressé; **to be ~ to do** avoir du mal à faire.

hard: **~ rock** *n* Mus hard rock *m*, hard *m*; **~ sauce** *n* US Culin crème *f* au beurre parfumée; **~scrabble** *adj* US [*farm*] à très bas rendement; [*farmer*] pauvre.

hard sell I *n* vente *f* selon des méthodes agressives; **to give sb the ~, to do a ~ on sb** essayer de forcer qn à acheter.

II hard-sell *modif* [*tactic, technique, approach*] de vente agressive.

hardshell /ˈhɑːdʃel/ *adj* US [*conservative, socialist*] pur et dur.

hardship /ˈhɑːdʃɪp/ *n* **1** ¢ (difficulty) détresse *f*; (poverty) privations *fpl*; **2 C** (ordeal) épreuve *f*; **they suffered many ~s** ils ont connu beaucoup d'épreuves; **it's no great ~ for you to get up half an hour earlier** ça ne te tuera pas○ de te lever une demi-heure plus tôt.

hardship fund *n* fonds *m* d'aide.

hard: **~ shoulder** *n* GB bande *f* d'arrêt d'urgence; **~ standing** *n* place *f* de stationnement; **~tack** *n* Naut biscuit *m* (de ration).

hardtop /ˈhɑːdtɒp/ *n* **1** (car) voiture *f* avec hard-top; **2** (roof) hard-top *m*.

hard up○ /ˌhɑːdˈʌp/ *adj* fauché○, désargenté; **to be ~ for sth** être à court de qch.

hardware /ˈhɑːdweə(r)/ **I** *n* **1** Comput matériel *m* (informatique), hardware *m*; **2** Mil équipement *m*; **3** Comm (household goods) articles *mpl* de quincaillerie.

II *modif* Comput [*company, efficiency, requirements, design*] de matériel (informatique), de hardware.

hard: **~ware dealer** ▶ **1692** *n* quincaillier/-ière *m/f*; **~ware shop, ~ware store** ▶ **1692** *n* quincaillerie *f*; **~-wearing** *adj* résistant; **~-won** *adj* durement acquis.

hardwood /ˈhɑːdwʊd/ **I** *n* bois *m* dur, bois *m* de feuillu.

II *modif* [*object, furniture*] de feuillus, de bois durs.

hard-working /ˌhɑːdˈwɜːkɪŋ/ *adj* [*person*] travailleur/-euse; [*animal*] industrieux/-ieuse.

hardy /ˈhɑːdɪ/ *adj* **1** (strong) [*person, animal, constitution*] robuste; Hort [*plant*] résistant; **2** (bold) [*explorer, adventurer*] hardi.

hardy: **~ annual** *n* plante *f* annuelle résistante au gel; **~ perennial** *n* vivace *f*, plante *f* vivace.

hare /heə(r)/ *n* Zool, Culin lièvre *m*.

IDIOMS **to be as mad as a March ~** être complètement toqué○; **to run with the ~ and hunt with the hounds** miser sur les deux tableaux; **to start a ~** lit, fig lever un lièvre.

■ **hare off** GB partir en trombe○.

hare: **~ and hounds** *n* jeu *m* de piste; **~bell** *n* Bot campanule *f*.

harebrained /ˈheəbreɪnd/ *adj* [*person*] écervelé; [*scheme*] farfelu○.

hare: **~ coursing** *n* chasse *f* au lièvre (*menée par des chiens*); **~lip** *n* bec-de-lièvre *m*.

harem /ˈhɑːriːm/ *n* harem *m*.

harem pants *npl* pantalon *m* bouffant, saroual *m*.

haricot /ˈhærɪkəʊ/ *n* GB (also **~ bean**) (dried) haricot *m* blanc; (fresh) haricot *m* vert.

hark /hɑːk/ *excl*‡ écoutez!; **~ at him/her**○**!** hum écoutez-le/-la donc!

■ **hark back to**: **~ back to [sth]** (recall) rappeler; (evoke) [*style, song*] évoquer.

harken *vi* = **hearken**.

harlequin /ˈhɑːlɪkwɪn/ **I** *n* (also **Harlequin**) Arlequin *m*.

II *adj* (coloured) bigarré.

Harley Street /ˈhɑːlɪ/ *pr n* GB *bonne adresse à Londres pour les médecins spécialistes privés*.

harlot /ˈhɑːlət/ *n* littér, péj catin† *f*.

harm /hɑːm/ **I** *n* mal *m*; **to do ~ to sb, to do sb ~** faire du mal à qn; **to do ~ to sth** endommager qch; **I didn't mean him any ~** je ne voulais pas lui faire de mal; **I**

meant no ~ by ou **in doing** je ne pensais pas à mal en faisant; **it would do no ~ to do** (you have nothing to lose) tu ne risques rien à faire; (you ought to) tu ferais mieux de faire; **some hard work wouldn't do him any ~** iron ça ne lui ferait pas de mal de travailler un peu plus; **to do more ~ than good** faire plus de mal que de bien; **you'll come to no ~** il ne t'arrivera rien; **no ~ done!** il n'y a pas de mal!; **where's the ~ in it?** quel mal y a-t-il à ça?; **out of ~'s way** (in a safe place) en sûreté; (unable to harm) hors d'état de nuire.

II *vtr* **1** (damage) faire du mal à [*person, baby*]; endommager [*crops, lungs*]; **a little sugar won't ~ you** un peu de sucre ne va pas te faire de mal; **he hasn't ~ed anybody** il n'a fait de mal à personne; **he wouldn't ~ a fly!** il ne ferait pas de mal à une mouche!; **2** (affect adversely) nuire à [*population, economy*]; déparer [*landscape, village*].

harmful /ˈhɑːmfl/ *adj* **1** (physically) [*bacteria, chemical, ray*] nocif/-ive; **2** (damaging) [*behaviour, gossip, allegation*] nuisible (**to** pour).

harmless /ˈhɑːmlɪs/ *adj* **1** (not dangerous) [*chemical, virus*] inoffensif/-ive (**to** pour); [*growth, cyst*] bénin/bénigne; [*rash, bite*] sans danger; **2** (inoffensive) [*person*] inoffensif/-ive; [*fun, joke, eccentricity*] innocent; **he's ~!** hum il n'est pas dangereux!

harmonic /hɑːˈmɒnɪk/ **I** *n* Phys, Mus harmonique *m*; **second/third ~** deuxième/troisième harmonique.

II *adj* Math, Mus harmonique.

harmonica /hɑːˈmɒnɪkə/ ▶ **1481** *n* harmonica *m*.

harmonics /hɑːˈmɒnɪks/ *n* (+ *v sg*) harmonie *f*.

harmonious /hɑːˈməʊnɪəs/ *adj* harmonieux/-ieuse.

harmoniously /hɑːˈməʊnɪəslɪ/ *adv* harmonieusement.

harmonium /hɑːˈməʊnɪəm/ ▶ **1481** *n* harmonium *m*.

harmonize /ˈhɑːmənaɪz/ **I** *vtr* (all contexts) harmoniser.

II *vi* **1** [*law, practice, people*] s'accorder (**with** avec); **2** [*colour, feature*] se marier (**with** avec); **3** Mus [*player, instrument*] jouer en harmonie (**with** avec); [*singer*] chanter en harmonie (**with** avec); [*note, sound*] être en harmonie (**with** avec).

harmony /ˈhɑːmənɪ/ *n* (all contexts) harmonie *f*; **in ~ (with)** en harmonie (avec); **perfect ~** parfaite harmonie, accord *m* parfait; **domestic ~** harmonie familiale; **three-part ~** accord *m* de trois sons.

harness /ˈhɑːnɪs/ **I** *n* **1** (for horse, dog, person) harnais *m*; **safety ~** harnais de sécurité; **2** fig **to work in ~** travailler en équipe (**with** avec); **to die in ~** mourir à la tâche; **I'm back in ~** j'ai repris le collier.

II *vtr* **1** (channel, use) exploiter [*power, potential*]; **2** (put harness on) harnacher [*horse, dog*]; **3** (attach) atteler [*animal*] (**to** à).

harness race *n* course *f* attelée.

harp /hɑːp/ ▶ **1481** *n* harpe *f*.

■ **harp on**○: **~ on [sth], ~ on about [sth]** rabâcher○ la même chose à propos de.

harpist /ˈhɑːpɪst/ ▶ **1692** *n* harpiste *mf*.

harpoon /hɑːˈpuːn/ **I** *n* harpon *m*.

II *vtr* harponner.

harp seal *n* phoque *m* du Groenland.

harpsichord /ˈhɑːpsɪkɔːd/ ▶ **1481** *n* clavecin *m*.

harpsichordist /ˈhɑːpsɪkɔːdɪst/ ▶ **1692**, **1481** *n* claveciniste *mf*.

harpy /ˈhɑːpɪ/ *n* **1** Mythol harpie *f*; **2** (woman) péj mégère *f* péj.

harpy eagle *n* Zool harpie *f*.

harridan /ˈhærɪdən/ *n* péj mégère *f* péj.

harrier /ˈhærɪə(r)/ *n* **1** (bird) busard *m*; **2** (dog) harrier *m*; **3** Sport (runner) coureur *m* de cross.

Harrier /ˈhærɪə(r)/ *n* (also **~ jump jet**) Mil Harrier *m* (*avion de chasse à décollage vertical*).

Harris tweed® /ˈhærɪs/ *n*: *tweed fabriqué dans l'île de Harris*.

harrow /ˈhærəʊ/ **I** *n* Agric herse *f*.

II *vtr* Agric herser.

III **harrowed** *pp adj* tourmenté.

harrowing /ˈhærəʊɪŋ/ *adj* [*experience, ordeal*] atroce; [*film, story, image*] déchirant.

harry /ˈhærɪ/ *vtr* **1** (pursue, harass) harceler; **2** Mil (destroy) ravager.

harsh /hɑːʃ/ *adj* **1** (severe, cruel) [*punishment, measures*] sévère; [*regime, person*] dur; [*fate*] cruel/-elle; **perhaps I was too ~ in my criticism** j'ai peut-être été un peu dur; **to have ~ words for sb/sth** critiquer qn/qch; **2** [*climate, winter*] rigoureux/-euse; [*conditions*] difficile; **3** [*light, colour*] cru; **4** [*voice, sound*] rude; **5** [*chemical, cleaner*] corrosif/-ive; [*shampoo*] détergent; **6** [*cloth, fabric*] rêche.

harshly /ˈhɑːʃlɪ/ *adv* [*treat, judge, speak*] durement; [*punish, condemn*] sévèrement.

harshness /ˈhɑːʃnɪs/ *n* (of punishment, law, regime) sévérité *f*; (of criticism) dureté *f*; (of climate, winter) rigueur *f*; (of conditions) difficulté *f*; (of light, colour) dureté *f*; (of sound, voice) rudesse *f*.

hart /hɑːt/ *n* (*pl* **~s** ou *collect* **~**) cerf *m*.

harum-scarum○ /ˌheərəmˈskeərəm/ **I** *adj* [*person, behaviour*] écervelé.

II *adv* [*run*] comme un fou.

harvest /ˈhɑːvɪst/ **I** *n* **1** lit (of wheat) moisson *f*, récolte *f*; (of fruits) récolte *f*; (of grapes) vendange *f*; **to get in the ~** faire la récolte; **a good/poor ~** une bonne/mauvaise récolte; **2** fig (of investment, policy) résultat *m*; **to reap the ~ of 20 years of tyranny/work** récolter les fruits de 20 ans de tyrannie/de travail; **to reap a rich ~** récolter les fruits de ses efforts; **to reap a bitter ~** payer les pots cassés.

II *vtr* **1** lit moissonner [*corn*]; récolter [*vegetables*]; cueillir [*fruit*]; **2** fig (collect) récolter [*information*].

III *vi* (of corn) faire la moisson or la récolte; (of fruit) faire la récolte; (of grapes) faire la vendange.

harvester /ˈhɑːvɪstə(r)/ *n* **1** (machine) moissonneuse *f*; **2** (person) moissonneur/-euse *m/f*.

harvest: **~ festival** *n* fête *f* de la moisson; **~ home** *n*: *repas célébrant la fin des moissons*; **~man** *n* US Zool cousin *m*; **~ mite** *n* aoûtat *m*; **~ moon** *n* pleine lune *f* (*de l'équinoxe d'automne*); **~ mouse** *n* souris *f* des moissons.

has ▶ **have**.

has-been○ /ˈhæzbiːn/ *n* péj homme fini/femme finie *m/f*, has been○ *mf*; **a political ~** un politicien fini/une politicienne finie *m/f*.

hash /hæʃ/ **I** *n* **1** Culin hachis *m*; **2**○ (*abrév* = **hashish**) hasch○ *m*; **3**○ (mess) gâchis *m*: **he made a ~ of the interview** il s'est très mal débrouillé pendant l'entretien; **he'll make a ~ of things** il va tout gâcher.

II *vtr* Culin hacher.

IDIOMS **to settle sb's ~**○ régler son compte à qn; **to sling ~**○ US faire le serveur/la serveuse *m/f*.

■ **hash out**○: **~ out [sth], ~ [sth] out** discuter qch et arriver à une solution.

hash: **~ browns** *npl* US pommes *fpl* de terre sautées; **~ house**○ *n* US péj gargote *f* péj.

hashish /ˈhæʃiːʃ/ *n* haschisch *m*.

hasn't = **has not**.

hasp /hɑːsp/ *n* moraillon *m*.

hassle○ /ˈhæsl/ **I** *n* ¢ **1** (inconvenience, effort) complications *fpl*; **to cause (sb) ~** créer des complications (à qn); **it's too much ~** ça crée trop de complications; **it was a real ~** c'était vraiment embêtant; **the ~ of (doing) sth** les embêtements de (faire) qch; **2** (harassment, pestering) **to give sb ~** embêter qn○ (**about** à propos de); **to get a lot of ~ from sb** être embêté○ par qn; **3** US (tussle) chamaillerie *f*.

II *vtr* **1** (harass, pester) talonner (**about** à propos de); **to ~ sb to do sth** talonner qn pour qu'il/elle fasse qch; **2** (worry) [*job, etc*] stresser.

III **hassled** *pp adj* stressé.

hassock /ˈhæsək/ *n* **1** (cushion) coussin *m* (d'agenouilloir); **2** US (seat) pouf *m*.

haste /heɪst/ *n* hâte *f*; **to act in ~** agir à la hâte; **in her ~** dans sa hâte (**to do** de faire); **to make ~** se dépêcher (**to do** de faire); **with undue** ou **unseemly ~** avec un empressement mal à propos; **why the ~?** pourquoi tant de précipitation?

IDIOMS **more ~ less speed** hâte-toi lentement; ▶ **repent**.

hasten /ˈheɪsn/ **I** *vtr* accélérer [*ageing, destruction*]; précipiter [*departure, death, decline*].

II *vi* se hâter; **to ~ to do** s'empresser de faire; **they ~ed away** ils partirent en toute hâte.

hastily /ˈhæstɪlɪ/ *adv* [*do*] à la hâte; [*say*] précipitamment; **too ~** avec trop de précipitation.

hasty /ˈheɪstɪ/ *adj* **1** (hurried) [*talks, marriage, consultation, departure*] précipité; [*meal*] rapide; [*note, sketch*] fait à la hâte; **to beat a ~ retreat** hum rapidement battre en retraite; **2** (rash) [*decision*] inconsidéré; [*judgment, conclusion*] hâtif/-ive; **to be too ~ in doing** aller trop vite en besogne en faisant; **perhaps I was a little ~** j'y suis allé peut-être un peu vite.

hat /hæt/ *n* chapeau *m*; **to put on/take off one's ~** mettre/enlever son chapeau; **we'll draw the winners out of a ~** on déterminera les gagnants par un tirage au sort; **to pass the ~ around** faire la quête.

IDIOMS **at the drop of a ~** pour un oui, pour un non; **~s off!** chapeau (bas)!; **old ~** dépassé; **I'll eat my ~ (if he wins)!** je vous parie tout ce que vous voulez (qu'il ne gagnera pas)!; **to keep sth under one's ~** garder qch pour soi; **keep it under your ~!** surtout pas un mot!; **to put** ou **throw one's ~ into the ring** se porter candidat; **to take one's ~ off to sb** fig tirer son chapeau à qn; **to talk through one's ~** parler à tort et à travers; **to wear two ~s** avoir deux fonctions; **I'm wearing my legal ~ now** je vous parle maintenant en tant que juriste.

hat: **~band** *n* ruban *m* de chapeau; **~box** *n* carton *m* à chapeau.

hatch /hætʃ/ **I** *n* **1** Aviat, Aerosp panneau *m* mobile; Naut écoutille *f*; Aut portière *f*; **cargo/safety ~** panneau *m* de chargement/de secours; **under ~es** Naut dans la cale; **2** (in dining room) passe-plats *m inv*; **3** (floodgate) vanne *f* d'écluse; **4** (brood of chicks) couvée *f*.

II *vtr* **1** (incubate) faire éclore [*eggs*]; **2** (plan secretly) tramer [*plot, scheme*]; élaborer [*surprise*]; **3** Art hachurer.

III *vi* [*chicks, fish eggs*] éclore.

IDIOMS **down the ~!** cul sec! ▶ **chicken**.

hatchback /ˈhætʃbæk/ *n* (car) voiture *f* avec hayon; (car door) hayon *m*.

hat: **~check girl** *n* US préposée *f* au vestiaire; **~check man** *n* US préposé *m* au vestiaire.

hatchery /ˈhætʃərɪ/ *n* (for chicks) couvoir *m*; (for fish) incubateur *m*.

hatchet /ˈhætʃɪt/ *n* hachette *f*.

IDIOMS **to bury the ~** faire la paix.

hatchet face○ *n* visage *m* en lame de couteau.

hatchet job○ *n* critique *f* virulente; **to do a ~ job on sb/sth** démolir○ qn/qch.

hatchet man○ *n* homme *m* de main.

hatching /ˈhætʃɪŋ/ *n* **1** (incubation) incubation *f*; (emergence) éclosion *f*; **2** Art hachures *fpl*.

hatchway /ˈhætʃweɪ/ *n* Naut écoutille *f*.

hate /heɪt/ **I** *n* haine *f*; ▶ **pet hate**.

II *vtr* **1** (feel antagonism towards) détester; (violently) haïr; **they ~ each other** ils se détestent; **to ~ sb for sth/for doing** en vouloir à qn de qch/d'avoir fait; **he's someone you love to ~** c'est quelqu'un sur qui on aime bien taper○; **2** (not enjoy) avoir horreur de [*sport, food, activity*]; **to ~ doing** ou **to do** avoir horreur de faire; **he ~s to see me cry** il a horreur de me voir pleurer; **he ~s being corrected** il a horreur qu'on le corrige (*subj*); **I ~ it when** je ne supporte pas quand; **I'd ~ it if he felt excluded, I'd ~ (for) him to feel excluded** je n'aimerais pas du tout qu'il se sente exclu; **3** (regret) (in apology) **to ~ to do, to ~ doing** être désolé de faire; **I ~ to interrupt you but...** je suis désolé de vous interrompre mais...; **I ~ (having) to say it but...** (in criticism) je regrette d'avoir à le dire, mais...

III *v refl* **to ~ oneself** se détester.

hate campaign *n* campagne *f* d'incitation à la haine.

hated /'heɪtɪd/ *adj* détesté.

hateful /'heɪtfl/ *adj* **1** [*person, action, regime*] odieux/-ieuse (**to** avec); **2** littér [*glance, tone*] plein de haine, haineux/-euse.

hate: **~ mail** *n* lettres *fpl* d'injures; **~monger** *n* US personne *f* qui incite à la haine.

hatless /'hætlɪs/ *adj* sans chapeau.

hatpin /'hætpɪn/ *n* épingle *f* à chapeau.

hatrack /'hætræk/ *n* (shelf) porte-chapeaux *m inv*; (pegs) portemanteau *m*.

hatred /'heɪtrɪd/ *n* (of person, group, system, war) (violent) haine *f* (**of** de; **for** pour); (less violent) aversion *f* (**of** pour); **racial ~** haine raciale; **out of ~** [*act*] par haine; **ancient ~s** de vieilles haines.

hatshop /'hætʃɒp/ ▶ **1692** *n* gen boutique *f* de chapeaux; (women's) boutique *f* de modiste.

hat stand GB, **hat tree** US *n* portemanteau *m* (*sur pied*).

hatter /'hætə(r)/ ▶ **1692** *n* (for ladies) modiste *f*; (for men) chapelier *m*.

IDIOMS **to be as mad as a ~** être fou/folle à lier.

hat trick *n* Sport coup *m* du chapeau, triplé *m*.

haughtily /'hɔːtɪlɪ/ *adv* [*look, speak*] avec hauteur; [*ignore*] superbement.

haughtiness /'hɔːtɪnɪs/ *n* hauteur *f*.

haughty /'hɔːtɪ/ *adj* [*person, contempt*] hautain; [*manner*] altier/-ière.

haul /hɔːl/ **I** *n* **1** (taken by criminals) butin *m*; **a £2m ~** un butin d'une valeur de 2 millions de livres; **art/jewellery ~** butin d'objets d'art/de bijoux; **2** (found by police, customs) saisie *f*; **arms/heroin ~** saisie d'armes/d'héroïne; **3** Sport (of medals etc) moisson *f*; **4** (journey) **it will be a long ~** lit, fig l'étape sera longue; **it's a long ~ to Christmas** d'ici Noël, il y a du chemin; **the long ~ from Dublin to London** le long voyage de Dublin à Londres; **the long ~ to recovery** Med le long chemin de la guérison; Econ la longue remontée; **5** Transp **long/medium/short ~ flight** vol *m* long/moyen/court courrier; **long ~ transport** transport *m* long courrier; **6** (of fish) prise *f*, pêche *f*.

II *vtr* **1** (drag) tirer [*load, wagon*]; tirer, traîner [*person*]; **he ~ed himself up on the roof** il s'est hissé sur le toit; **2** Transp transporter, camionner; **3** Naut **to ~ a boat** (alter course of) lofer; (hoist out of water) haler.

III *vi* Naut [*wind*] refuser; [*ship*] naviguer vent debout.

IDIOMS **to ~ ass●** US (hurry up) se magner le cul●, se dépêcher; (move fast) foncer○; **to ~ sb over the coals** passer un savon à qn○.

■ **haul down**: **~ down [sth], ~ [sth] down** amener [*flag*]; affaler [*rope, sail*].

■ **haul in**: **~ in [sth], ~ [sth] in** amener [*net, catch, fish*]; affaler [*rope*]; tirer [qn] hors de l'eau [*person*].

■ **haul off 1** Naut passer au vent; **2 to ~ off and do sth**○ US faire qch tout d'un coup.

■ **haul out**: **~ out [sth/sb], ~ [sth/sb] out** tirer [qch/qn] hors de l'eau [*net, body*]; **to ~ sb out of bed** tirer qn du lit.

■ **haul up**: **~ up [sth], ~ [sth] up** hisser [*flag, person*]; **they ~ed the boat up onto the beach** ils ont tiré le bateau sur la plage; **to be ~ed up before sb**○ être convoqué chez qn.

haulage /'hɔːlɪdʒ/ **I** *n* ₵ **1** (transport) transport *m* routier, roulage *m*; **2** (cost) frais *mpl* de roulage or de transport.

II *modif* [*company, contractor*] de transport routier.

haulier /'hɔːlɪə(r)/ GB, **hauler** /'hɔːlə(r)/ US ▶ **1692** *n* (owner of firm) transporteur *m*; (firm) société *f* de transports routiers; (truck driver) routier *m*.

haunch /hɔːntʃ/ *n* (of human, horse) hanche *f*; (of animal) derrière *m*; **a ~ of venison** un cuisseau de chevreuil; **to squat on one's ~es** s'accroupir.

haunt /hɔːnt/ **I** *n* (of people, animals, birds) lieu *m* de prédilection; **a favourite/regular ~ of artists** un lieu de prédilection/de fréquentation des artistes.

II *vtr* **1** lit, fig hanter; **her crimes have returned to ~ her** ses crimes sont revenus la hanter; **he is ~ed by the fear of dying** il a la hantise de la mort; **2** (frequent) être un/-e habitué/-e *m/f* de [*place*]; (obsessively) hanter [*place*].

haunted /'hɔːntɪd/ *adj* [*house, castle, etc*] hanté; [*face, expression*] tourmenté.

haunting /'hɔːntɪŋ/ **I** *n* **to investigate a ~** enquêter sur des phénomènes paranormaux; **the stories of the ~** les histoires de fantôme.

II *adj* [*film, book, image, music, beauty, doubt*] lancinant; [*memory*] obsédant.

hauntingly /'hɔːntɪŋlɪ/ *adv* [*beautiful, similar*] jusqu'à la hantise.

Haute-Corse ▶ **1163** *pr n* Haute-Corse *f*; **in/to ~** en Haute-Corse.

Haute-Garonne ▶ **1163** *pr n* Haute-Garonne *f*; **in/to the ~** en Haute-Garonne.

Haute-Loire ▶ **1163** *pr n* Haute-Loire *f*; **in/to the ~** en Haute-Loire.

Haute-Marne ▶ **1163** *pr n* Haute-Marne *f*; **in/to the ~** en Haute-Marne.

Haute-Normandie ▶ **1273** *pr n* Haute-Normandie *f*; **in/to ~** en Haute-Normandie.

Hautes-Alpes ▶ **1163** *pr n* Hautes-Alpes *fpl*; **in/to the ~** dans les Hautes-Alpes.

Haute-Saône ▶ **1163** *pr n* Haute-Saône *f*; **in/to the ~** dans la Haute-Saône.

Haute-Savoie ▶ **1163** *pr n* Haute-Savoie *f*; **in/to ~** en Haute-Savoie.

Hautes-Pyrénées ▶ **1163** *pr n* Hautes-Pyrénées *fpl*; **in/to the ~** dans les Hautes-Pyrénées.

Haute-Vienne ▶ **1163** *pr n* Haute-Vienne *f*; **in/to ~** dans la Haute-Vienne.

Haut-Rhin ▶ **1163** *pr n* Haut-Rhin *m*; **in/to the ~** dans le Haut-Rhin.

Hauts-de-Seine ▶ **1163** *pr n* Hauts-de-Seine *mpl*; **in/to ~** dans les Hauts-de-Seine.

Havana /hə'vænə/ ▶ **1818** **I** *pr n* La Havane *f*; **in ~** à La Havane.

II *n* (cigar) havane *m*.

have /hæv, həv/ **I** *vtr* (uses not covered in NOTE) **1** (possess) avoir; **she has a dog** elle a un chien; **2** (consume) prendre; **to ~ a sandwich** manger un sandwich; **to ~ a whisky** boire un whisky; **to ~ a cigarette** fumer une cigarette; **to ~ breakfast** prendre le petit déjeuner; **to ~ dinner** dîner; **to ~ lunch** déjeuner; **he had a sandwich for lunch** il a mangé un sandwich au déjeuner; **I had some more cake** j'ai repris du gâteau; **3** (want) vouloir, prendre; **I'll ~ tea please** je voudrais du thé s'il vous plaît; **what will you ~?** qu'est-ce que vous prendrez or voulez?; **she won't ~ him back** elle ne veut plus de lui; **I offered her £5, but she wouldn't ~ it** je lui ai offert cinq livres sterling, mais elle les a refusées; **I wouldn't ~ it any other way** ça me convient comme ça; **I wouldn't ~ him/her any other way** c'est comme ça que je l'aime; **4** (receive, get) recevoir [*letter, parcel, information*]; **I've had no news from him** je n'ai pas eu de nouvelles de lui; **I must ~ the information/some money soon** il me faut l'information/de l'argent bientôt; **I must ~ the document by 4 o'clock** il faut que j'aie le document avant 4 heures; **to let sb ~ sth** donner qch à qn; **5** (hold) faire [*party, celebration*]; tenir [*meeting*]; organiser [*competition, ballot, exhibition*]; avoir [*conversation*]; célébrer [*church service*]; mener [*enquiry*]; passer [*interview*]; **6** (exert, exhibit) avoir [*effect, influence*]; avoir [*courage, nerve, impudence, courtesy*] (**to do** de faire); **7** (spend) passer; **to ~ a nice day/evening** passer une journée/soirée agréable; **to ~ a good time** bien s'amuser; **to ~ a hard** ou **bad time** avoir des moments difficiles; **to ~ a good vacation/a day at the beach** passer de bonnes vacances/une journée à la plage; **8** (be provided with) (also **~ got**) **to ~ sth to do** avoir qch à faire; **I ~** ou **I've got some clothes to wash** j'ai des vêtements à laver; **I ~** ou **I've got letters to write** j'au du courrier à faire; **I ~** ou **I've got a lot of work to do** j'ai beaucoup de travail; **9** (undergo, suffer) avoir; **to ~ (the) flu/measles** avoir la grippe/la rougeole; **to ~ (a) toothache/a headache** avoir mal aux dents/mal à la tête; **to ~ an accident/a heart attack** avoir un accident/une crise cardiaque; **to ~ a shock** subir un choc; **he had his car/watch stolen** il s'est fait voler sa voiture/montre, on lui a volé sa voiture/montre; **she has had her windows broken** on lui a cassé ses fenêtres; **they like having stories read to them** ils aiment qu'on leur lise des histoires; **I ~** ou **I've got a student coming in five minutes** j'ai un élève qui arrive dans cinq minutes; **10** (cause to be done) **to ~ sth done** faire faire qch; **to ~ the house painted/the washing-machine installed** faire peindre la maison/installer la machine à laver; **to ~ one's hair cut** se faire couper les cheveux; **to ~ an injection/a dental check-up/a manicure** se faire faire une piqûre/un contrôle des dents/une manucure; **to ~ sb do sth** faire faire qch à qn; **she had him close the door/wait in the corridor** elle lui a fait fermer la porte/attendre dans le couloir; **they would ~ us believe that** ils voudraient nous faire croire que; **I would ~ you know/say that** je voudrais que vous sachiez/disiez que; **to ~ sb doing** faire faire qn; **he had them laughing/crying** il les a fait rire/pleurer; **she had them digging the garden/writing poetry** elle leur a fait bêcher le jardin/écrire des poèmes; **11** (cause to become) **he had his revolver/camera ready** il avait son revolver/appareil photo prêt; **we'll soon ~ everything ready/clean** nous aurons bientôt fini de tout préparer/nettoyer; **she had the car in pieces in the garage** elle avait démonté la voiture dans le garage; **if you're not careful you'll ~ that table/that glass over** si tu ne fais pas attention tu vas renverser la table/le verre; **she had them completely baffled** elle les a complètement déroutés; **I had it finished by 5 o'clock** je l'avais fini avant 5 heures; **12** (allow) (*gén au négatif*) tolérer; **I won't ~ this kind of behaviour!** je ne tolérerai pas ce comportement!; **I won't ~ it!** ça ne va pas se passer comme ça!; **I won't ~ this any more!** je n'en supporterai pas davantage!; **I won't ~ them exploit him** je ne tolérerai pas qu'ils l'exploitent; **I won't ~ him hurt** je ne laisserai personne le blesser; **we can't ~ them staying in a hotel** on ne peut pas les

have

When used as an auxiliary in present perfect, future perfect and past perfect tenses *have* is normally translated by *avoir*:

I have seen = j'ai vu
I had seen = j'avais vu

However, some verbs in French, especially verbs of movement and change of state (e.g. *aller, venir, descendre, mourir*), take *être* rather than *avoir* in these tenses:

he has left = il est parti

In this case, remember the past participle agrees with the subject of the verb:

she has gone = elle est allée

If you are in doubt as to whether a verb conjugates with *être* or *avoir*, consult the French verb tables. Reflexive verbs (e.g. *se lever, se coucher*) always conjugate with *être*:

she has fainted = elle s'est évanouie

For translations of time expressions using *for* or *since* (*he has been in London for six months, he has been in London since June*), see the entries ***for*** and ***since***.

For translations of time expressions using *just* (*I have just finished my essay, he has just gone*), see the entry ***just¹***.

to have to meaning *must* is translated by either *devoir* or the impersonal construction *il faut que* + subjunctive:

I have to leave now = il faut que je parte maintenant *or* je dois partir maintenant

In negative sentences, *not to have to* is generally translated by *ne pas être obligé de* e.g.

you don't have to go = tu n'es pas obligé d'y aller

For examples and particular usages see entry.

When *have* is used as a straightforward transitive verb meaning *possess*, *have* (or *have got*) can generally be translated by *avoir*, e.g.

I have (got) a car = j'ai une voiture
she has a good memory = elle a une bonne mémoire
they have (got) problems = ils ont des problèmes

For examples and particular usages see entry; see also ***got***.

have is also used with certain noun objects where the whole expression is equivalent to a verb:

to have dinner = to dine
to have a try = to try
to have a walk = to walk

In such cases the phrase is very often translated by the equivalent verb in French (*dîner, essayer, se promener*). For translations consult the appropriate noun entry (***dinner***, ***try***, ***walk***).

had is used in English at the beginning of a clause to replace an expression with *if*. Such expressions are generally translated by *si* + past perfect tense, e.g.

had I taken the train, this would never have happened = si j'avais pris le train, ce ne serait jamais arrivé
had there been a fire, we would all have been killed = s'il y avait eu un incendie, nous serions tous morts

For examples of the above and all other uses of *have* see the entry.

laisser aller à l'hôtel; **13** (physically hold) tenir; **she had the glass in her hand** elle tenait le verre dans la main; **she had him by the throat/by the arm** elle le tenait à la gorge/par le bras; **he had his hands over his eyes** il avait les mains sur les yeux; **to ~ one's back to sb** tourner le dos à qn; **14** (give birth to) [*woman*] avoir [*child*]; [*animal*] mettre bas, avoir [*young*]; **has she had it yet?** est-ce qu'elle a accouché?; **she's having a baby (in May)** elle va avoir un enfant (en mai); **15** (as impersonal verb) **over here, we ~ a painting by Picasso** ici vous avez un tableau de Picasso; **what we ~ here is a small group of extremists** ce à quoi nous avons affaire ici, est un petit groupe d'extrémistes; **on the one hand you ~ the victims of crime and on the other...** d'un côté il y a les victimes des crimes, et de l'autre...; **16** (puzzle) (also **~ got**) **you ~** ou **you've got me there!** là tu me poses une colle!; **17** (have at one's mercy) (also **~ got**) **I've got you/him now!** maintenant je te/le tiens!; **I'll ~ you!** je vais te montrer!; **18**○ (have sex with) se faire◑ [*person*].

II *modal aux* **1** (must) **I ~ to leave now** je dois partir maintenant, il faut que je parte maintenant; **2** (need to) **you don't ~ to** ou **you haven't got to leave so early** tu n'as pas besoin de or tu n'es pas obligé de partir si tôt; **why did this ~ to happen?** pourquoi fallait-il que ça arrive?; **did you ~ to spend so much money?** tu avais vraiment besoin de dépenser autant d'argent?, est-ce qu'il fallait vraiment que tu dépenses autant d'argent?; **something had to be done** il fallait faire quelque chose; **3** (for emphasis) **this has to be the most difficult decision I've ever made** c'est sans doute la décision la plus difficile que j'aie jamais eu à prendre.

III *aux* **1** gen avoir; (with movement and reflexive verbs) être; **she has lost her bag** elle a perdu son sac; **she has already left/arrived** elle est déjà partie/arrivée; **she has hurt herself** elle s'est blessée; **she has washed her hands** elle s'est lavé les mains; **~ you seen her?** l'as-tu vue?, est-ce que tu l'as vue?; **we haven't lost them** nous ne les avons pas perdus; **2** (in tag questions etc) **you've seen the film, haven't you?** tu as vu le film, n'est-ce pas?; **you haven't seen the film, ~ you?** tu n'as pas vu le film?; **you haven't seen my bag, ~ you?** tu n'as pas vu mon sac, par hasard?; **'he's already left'—'has he indeed!'** 'il est déjà parti'—'vraiment!'; **'you've never met him'—'yes I ~!'** 'tu ne l'as jamais rencontré'—'mais si!'

IV having *aux* **1** (in time clauses) **having finished his breakfast, he went out** après avoir fini son petit déjeuner, il est sorti; **having said he'd be there early, he arrived late** après avoir dit or alors qu'il avait dit qu'il viendrait tôt, il est arrivé en retard; **2** (because, since) **having already won twice, he's a great favourite** comme il a déjà gagné deux fois, c'est un grand favori; **having lost money before, he was reluctant to invest in a new project** ayant déjà perdu de l'argent or comme il avait déjà perdu de l'argent, il hésitait à investir dans un nouveau projet.

IDIOMS **to ~ done with sth** en finir avec qch; **this car/TV has had it**○ cette voiture/télé est foutue○; **when your father finds out, you've had it**○**!** (in trouble) quand ton père saura, ça va être ta fête○!; **I can't do any more, I've had it**○**!** (tired) je n'en peux plus, je suis crevé○!; **I've had it (up to here)**○ j'en ai marre○; **I've had it (up to here) with him/my job**○ j'en ai marre de ce type/mon travail○; **to ~ it in for sb**○ avoir qn dans le collimateur○; **she has/doesn't ~ it in her to do** elle est capable/incapable de faire; **he will ~ it that** il soutient que; **he won't ~ it that** il n'admet pas que; **I've got it!** je sais!; **let's be having you!** hum à nous deux!; **and the ayes/noes ~ it** les oui/non l'emportent, les voix pour/contre l'emportent; **to ~ it off** ou **away with sb**◑ GB s'envoyer en l'air avec qn◑; **the ~s and the ~-nots** les riches et les pauvres; **...and what ~ you** ...etc; **there is no milk/there are no houses to be had** on ne trouve pas de lait/de maisons; **are there any more to be had?** est- ce qu'on en trouve encore? ; **these are the best spectacles to be had** ce sont les meilleures lunettes qu'on puisse trouver.

■ **have around** US = **have over, have round**.

■ **have back**: **~ [sth] back, ~ back [sth]** (have returned) **you can ~ it back tomorrow** je te le rendrai demain; **when can I ~ my car/my money back?** quand est-ce que tu me rends ma voiture/mon argent?

■ **have down**: **~ [sb] down** inviter [*person*]; **to ~ sb down for the weekend** inviter qn à passer le weekend à la maison.

■ **have in**: **~ [sb] in** (also **~ got**) faire venir [*doctor, priest*]; faire entrer [*employee, neighbour*]; **we've got decorators in at the moment** en ce moment nous avons des décorateurs à la maison.

■ **have on**: ¶ **~ [sth] on, ~ on [sth]** (also **~ got**) (be wearing) porter [*coat, skirt etc*]; **to ~ nothing on** ne rien avoir sur soi; ¶ **~ [sth] on** (be busy doing) avoir [qch] de prévu; **~ you got anything on this evening?** avez-vous quelque chose de prévu ce soir?; **I've got a lot on next week** j'ai beaucoup de choses prévues la semaine prochaine; ¶ **~ [sb] on**○ (tease) faire marcher○ [*person*]; ¶ **~ sth on sb** (have evidence about) avoir des preuves contre qn; **the police ~ got nothing on me** la police n'a aucune preuve contre moi.

■ **have out**: **~ [sth] out** se faire enlever or arracher [*tooth*]; **to ~ one's appendix out** se faire opérer de l'appendicite; **to ~ it out with sb** s'expliquer avec qn.

■ **have over, have round**: **~ [sb] over** inviter [*person*]; **to ~ sb over for the evening** inviter qn à passer la soirée chez soi.

■ **have up**○: **to be had up** être jugé (for pour).

have-a-go○ *adj* GB [*person, pensioner*] téméraire.

haven /ˈheɪvn/ *n* **1** (safe place) refuge *m* (**for** pour); **2** fig havre *m*; **a ~ of peace** un havre de paix; **3** (harbour) port *m*.

haven't /ˈhævnt/ = **have not**.

haver /ˈheɪvə(r)/ *vi* **1** (dither) vaciller; **2** Scot (talk nonsense) dire des bêtises.

haversack /ˈhævəsæk/ *n* gen sac *m* à dos; Mil musette *f*.

havoc /ˈhævək/ *n* dévastation *f*; **to wreak ~ on** dévaster [*building, landscape*]; **to play ~ with** chambouler [*plans, etc*]; **to cause ~** lit provoquer des dégâts; fig tout mettre sens dessus dessous.

haw /hɔː/ **I** *n* **1** Bot cenelle *f*; **2** Zool paupière *f* nictitante.

II† *excl* **~! ~!** ha! ha!

IDIOMS **to hum** GB ou **hem** US **and ~** balbutier.

Hawaii /həˈwaɪi/ **▶ 1381** *pr n* Hawaï *m*; **in Hawaii** à Hawaï.

Hawaiian /həˈwaɪən/ **▶ 1486**, **1402** **I** *n* **1** (person) Hawaïen/-ïenne *m/f*; **2** (language) hawaïen *m*.

II *adj* [*culture, landscape*] hawaïen/-ïenne; **the ~ Islands** les îles Hawaï.

hawfinch /ˈhɔːfɪntʃ/ *n* gros-bec *m*.

hawk /hɔːk/ **I** *n* faucon *m* also Pol.

II *vtr* péj (sell) (door-to-door) colporter; (in street) vendre.

III *vi* **1** (hunt) chasser [qch] au faucon; **2**○ (clear throat) se racler la gorge; (spit) cracher.
IDIOMS **to have eyes like a ~** avoir des yeux de lynx.

hawker /ˈhɔːkə(r)/ *n* colporteur *m*.

Hawkeye○ /ˈhɔːkaɪ/ *n* US habitant/-e *m/f* de l'Iowa.

hawk-eyed /ˈhɔːkaɪd/ *adj* aux yeux de lynx.

hawkish /ˈhɔːkɪʃ/ *adj* Pol belliciste.

hawk moth *n* sphingidé *m*.

hawser /ˈhɔːzə(r)/ *n* aussière *f*.

hawthorn /ˈhɔːθɔːn/ **I** *n* (tree, flower) aubépine *f*.
II *modif* [*blossom, hedge*] d'aubépine.

hay /heɪ/ *n* foin *m*; **to make ~** faire les foins.
IDIOMS **to make ~ while the sun shines** saisir l'occasion au vol; **to hit the ~**○ aller se coucher; **to have a roll in the ~**○† faire une partie de jambes en l'air◐.

hay: **~cock** *n* meulon *m*; **~ fever** ▶**1354** *n* rhume *m* des foins; **~ fork** *n* fourche *f* à foin; **~ loft** *n* grenier *m* à foin; **~maker** *n* faneur/-euse *m/f*; **~making** *n* fenaison *f*; **~ride** *n* promenade *f* dans une charrette de foin; **~seed**○ *n* US péj péquenaud/-e○ *m/f* pej.

haystack /ˈheɪstæk/ *n* meule *f* de foin.
IDIOMS **it is/was like looking for a needle in a ~** autant chercher une aiguille dans une botte de foin.

haywire○ /ˈheɪwaɪə(r)/ *adj* **1** (faulty) (*jamais épith*) [*plan*] fou/folle; [*machine*] détraqué; **to go ~** [*plan*] dérailler; [*machinery, system*] se détraquer; **2** US (crazy) détraqué○.

hazard /ˈhæzəd/ **I** *n* **1** (risk) risque *m* (**to** pour); **the ~s of sth** les risques que constitue qch; **the ~s of doing** les risques qu'il y a à faire; **to be a health/an environmental ~** constituer un risque pour la santé/l'environnement; **traffic ~** danger *m* pour la circulation; **fire/occupational ~** risque d'incendie/du métier; **2** (chance) hasard *m*; **3** (in golf) obstacle *m*.
II *vtr* **1** (venture) hasarder [*opinion, explanation, reply*]; **to ~ a guess** hasarder une idée; **to ~ a guess that** se hasarder à dire que; **2** (risk) risquer [*life, health, reputation etc*].

hazardous /ˈhæzədəs/ *adj* [*job, weather conditions, substance*] dangereux/-euse; [*journey*] périlleux/-euse; [*enterprise, venture*] risqué, aléatoire; **it is ~ to...** il est dangereux de...

haze /heɪz/ **I** *n* (mist) brume *f*; (of smoke, dust, blossom) nuage *m* (**of** de); **to be in an alcoholic ~** être dans les brumes de l'alcool.
II *vtr* US argot des étudiants bizuter.
■ **haze over** Meteorol se couvrir légèrement.

hazel /ˈheɪzl/ **I** *n* (tree) noisetier *m*; (wood) bois *m* de noisetier.
II *modif* [*twig, catkin*] de noisetier; **~ grove** coudraie *f*.
III ▶**1104** *adj* [*eyes*] (couleur *f* de) noisette (*inv*).

hazelnut /ˈheɪzlnʌt/ **I** *n* noisette *f*.
II *modif* [*yoghurt, meringue*] aux noisettes.

haziness /ˈheɪzɪnɪs/ *n* (of atmosphere) état *m* brumeux; fig (of memory, ideas) flou *m*.

hazing /ˈheɪzɪŋ/ *n* US argot des étudiants bizutage *m*.

hazy /ˈheɪzɪ/ *adj* [*weather, morning*] brumeux/-euse; [*sunshine*] voilé; [*image, outline*] flou; [*recollection, idea*] vague; **to be ~ about sth** être dans le vague en ce qui concerne qch.

h: **H-beam** *n* poutrelle *f* en H; **H-block** *n* GB *dans une prison, bâtiment en forme de H*; **H bomb** *n* bombe *f* H.

HC *n*: *abrév* = **hot and cold water**.

HDTV *n* (*abrév* = **high-definition television**) TVHD *f*.

he /hiː, hɪ/

■ **Note** *he* is almost always translated by *il*: *he closed the door* = il a fermé la porte. The emphatic form is *lui*.
– For exceptions and particular usages, see the entry below.

pron il; **~'s seen us** il nous a vus; **here ~ is** le voici; **there ~ is** le voilà; **~ didn't take it** ce n'est pas lui qui l'a pris; **she lives in Oxford but ~ doesn't** elle habite Oxford mais lui pas; **~'s a genius** c'est un génie; **it's a ~**○ (of baby) c'est un garçon; (of animal) c'est un mâle; **~ who...**, **~ that...** celui qui...; **~ who sees** celui qui voit; **~ and I went to the cinema** lui et moi sommes allés au cinéma.

HE 1 *abrév* ▶**high explosive**; **2** (*abrév* = **His/Her Excellency**) SE.

head /hed/ ▶**1037** **I** *n* **1** Anat (of person, animal) tête *f*; **the top of one's ~** le sommet de la tête or du crâne; **he had a beret on his ~** il avait un béret sur la tête; **she put her ~ round the door** elle a passé la tête par la porte; **my ~ aches** j'ai mal à la tête; **to nod one's ~** hocher la tête; **to have a fine ~ of hair** avoir une belle chevelure; **to get** ou **keep** ou **have one's ~ down** lit avoir or garder la tête baissée; fig (be inconspicuous) ne pas se faire remarquer; (work hard) avoir le nez sur son travail; **with one's ~ in one's hands** la tête dans les mains; **from ~ to foot** ou **toe** de la tête aux pieds, des pieds à la tête; **he pulled his sweater over his ~** il a retiré son pull; **the decision was made over the ~s of the members** la décision a été prise sans consulter les membres; **she was promoted over the ~s of her colleagues** elle a obtenu une promotion qui revenait de droit à ses collègues; **to stand on one's ~** faire le poirier; **to stand an argument/theory on its ~** fig [*person*] prendre le contre-pied d'un argument/d'une théorie; [*evidence, fact*] contredire un argument/une théorie; **~s turned at the sight of...** tout le monde s'est retourné en voyant...; **to hold a gun** ou **pistol to sb's ~** lit braquer un pistolet contre la tête de qn; fig tenir le couteau sous la gorge de qn; **2** (mind) tête *f*, crâne○ *m* pej; **her ~ was full of grand ideas** elle avait la tête pleine de grandes idées; **I can't get it into her ~ that** je n'arrive pas à lui enfoncer dans la tête or le crâne que; **he has got it into his ~ that I love him** il s'est mis dans la tête que je l'aime; **he has taken it into his ~ to resign** il s'est mis en tête de démissionner; **what(ever) put that idea into her ~?** qu'est-ce qui lui a mis cette idée dans la tête?; **I can't get the faces of those starving children out of my ~** je n'arrive pas à oublier les visages affamés de ces enfants; **I can't get that tune out of my ~** je n'arrive pas à m'ôter cet air de la tête; **you can put that idea out of your ~!** tu peux oublier cette idée!; **he put the idea of danger out of his ~** il a chassé l'idée du danger de sa tête; **all these interruptions have put it out of my ~** toutes ces interruptions me l'ont fait sortir de la tête; **the name has gone right out of my ~** le nom m'est complètement sorti de la tête; **I can't add them up in my ~** je ne peux pas les additionner de tête; **I wonder what's going on in her ~?** je me demande ce qui lui passe par la tête; **to be** ou **go above** ou **over sb's ~** (too difficult) passer par-dessus la tête de qn, dépasser qn; **don't worry** ou **bother your (pretty little) ~ about that**○! ne te casse pas la tête pour ça○!; **use your ~**○! sers-toi de tes méninges○!; **to turn sb's ~** tourner la tête à qn; **her success has turned her ~** son succès lui a tourné la tête; **to have a (good) ~ for figures/business** être doué pour le calcul/les affaires; **I have a good ~ for heights** je n'ai pas le vertige; **to have no ~ for heights** avoir le vertige; **3** Meas, Turf tête *f*; **to be a ~/half a ~ taller than sb, to be taller than sb by a ~/half a ~** dépasser qn d'une tête/d'une demi-tête; **to win by a (short) ~** Turf, fig gagner d'une (courte) tête; **4**○ (headache) mal *m* de tête; **to have a bad ~**○ gen avoir mal à la tête; (hangover) avoir mal aux cheveux○; **5** (leader, director) (of family, church, agency, section) chef *m*; (of social service, organization) responsable *mf*, directeur/-trice *m/f*; **at the ~ of** à la tête de; **a team of experts with Dubois at its ~** une équipe d'experts avec Dubois à sa tête; **~ of government/State** chef de gouvernement/d'État; **~ of department** Admin chef de service; Sch professeur principal; **~ of Maths/German** Sch responsable de la section de Maths/d'allemand; **~ of personnel/marketing** Comm chef du personnel/du marketing; **6** Admin, Comm (individual person or animal) **we paid £10 a ~** ou **per ~** nous avons payé 10 livres sterling par personne; **to count ~s** compter les gens; **50 ~ of cattle** Agric 50 têtes de bétail; **30 ~ of sheep** 30 moutons; **7** Sport, Tech (of pin, nail etc, hammer, golf club) tête *f*; (of axe, spear, arrow) fer *m*; (of tennis racquet) tamis *m*; (of stick) pommeau *m*; **8** (front or top end) (of bed) chevet *m*; (of table) (haut) bout *m*; (of procession) tête *f*; (of pier, river, valley, glacier, lake) extrémité *f*; **at the ~ of the stairs/page/list** en haut de l'escalier/de la page/de la liste; **a letter with his address at the ~** une lettre avec son adresse en en-tête; **at the ~ of the queue** en tête de la file d'attente; **9** Bot, Hort (of cabbage, lettuce) pomme *f*; (of celery) pied *m*; (of garlic) tête *f*; **to cut the dead ~s off the roses** couper les fleurs fanées des rosiers; **10** Comput, Elec (of computer, video, tape recorder) tête *f*; **reading ~, playback ~** tête *f* de lecture; **writing ~, recording ~** tête *f* d'écriture; **11** (on beer) mousse *f*; **12** Med (on boil, spot) tête *f*; **to come to a ~** lit, Med mûrir; fig [*crisis, trouble, unrest*] arriver au point critique; **to bring sth to a ~** Med faire mûrir; fig précipiter [*crisis, trouble, unrest*]; amener [qch] au point critique [*situation*]; **13** (in plumbing) (height of water) hauteur *f* de chute d'eau; (water pressure) pression *f*; **~ of water** colonne *f* d'eau; **14** Phys (of steam) pression *f*, volant *m* de vapeur spec; **to have a good ~ of steam** fig (be progressing well) avoir le vent en poupe; **15** Geog cap *m*; **16** Tech (on lathe) poupée *f*.
II heads *npl* **1** (tossing coin) face *f*; **'~s or tails?'** 'pile ou face?'; **'~s!'** 'face!'; **'~s it is!'** 'c'est face!'; **~s I win/we go** face je gagne/on y va; **2** Naut (lavatory) toilettes *fpl*.
III *modif* **1** Anat [*movement*] de tête; [*injury*] à la tête; [*covering, bandage*] sur la tête; Zool [*markings, feathers*] de la tête; **2** (chief) [*cashier, cook, gardener*] en chef.
IV *vtr* **1** lit (be at the top of) être en tête de [*column, list, procession, queue*]; **2** (be in charge of) être à la tête de [*business, firm, delegation, committee, team*]; mener [*expedition, inquiry, revolt*]; **the inquiry ~ed by Inspector Lacôte** l'enquête menée par l'inspecteur Lacôte; **3** (entitle) intituler [*article, chapter, essay*]; **this paragraph is ~ed by a quotation** ce paragraphe est précédé d'une citation; **to ~ a letter with one's address** mettre son adresse en tête d'une lettre ; **~ed writing paper, ~ed stationery** papier *m* à lettres à en-tête; **4** (steer) diriger [*vehicle*] (**towards** vers); naviguer [*boat*] (**towards** vers); **I ~ed the car for the sea** j'ai pris le volant en direction de la mer; **he ~ed the sheep away from the cliff** il a éloigné les moutons de la falaise; **5** Sport **to ~ the ball** faire une tête; **he ~ed the ball into the net** il a marqué un but de la tête.
V *vi* **where was the train ~ed** ou **~ing?** dans quelle direction est-ce que le train allait?; **to ~ south/north** Naut mettre le cap au sud/au nord; **he ~ed straight back into the room** il est retourné tout droit dans la pièce; **it's time to ~ home** ou **for home** il est temps de rentrer; **she ~ed across the dunes** elle s'est engagée à travers les dunes; **look out! he's ~ing this way** attention! il se dirige par ici!;

there's good luck ~ing your way (in horoscope) la chance va vous sourire; ▶ **head for**.

VI **-headed** (*dans composés*) **black-~ed bird** oiseau à tête noire; **red-~ed boy** garçon (aux cheveux) roux; **two-~ed monster** monstre à deux têtes.

IDIOMS **on your own ~ be it!** à tes risques et périls!; **to go to sb's ~** [*alcohol, success, praise*] monter à la tête de qn; **you've won, but don't let it go to your ~** tu as gagné, mais ne te monte pas la tête; **to go off one's ~**○ perdre la boule○; **are you off your ~?** tu as perdu la boule○?; **to keep/lose one's ~** garder/perdre son sang-froid; **to be soft** ou **weak in the ~**○ être faible d'esprit; **he's not right in the ~**○ il a un grain○; **to laugh one's ~ off**○ éclater de rire; **to shout one's ~ off**○ crier à tue-tête; **to talk one's ~ off**○ ne pas arrêter de parler; **she talked my ~ off**○ **all the way** elle m'a cassé les oreilles○ tout le long du trajet; **off the top of one's ~** [*say, answer*] sans réfléchir; **I can't think of anything off the top of my ~** rien ne me vient à l'esprit pour l'instant; **to give a horse its ~** lâcher la bride à un cheval; **to give sb their ~** lâcher la bride à qn; **to give sb ~**● US tailler une pipe● à qn; **to be able to do sth standing on one's ~** faire qch les doigts dans le nez○; **I can't make ~ (n)or tail of it** je n'y comprends rien, ça n'a ni queue ni tête; **I couldn't make ~ (n)or tail of what she was saying** je ne comprenais rien à ce qu'elle disait; **if we all put our ~s together** si nous nous y mettons tous; **so Louise and I put our ~s together and...** donc Louise et moi nous y sommes mis à deux et...; **the leaders put their ~s together** les dirigeants se sont consultés; **two ~s are better than one** Prov deux avis valent mieux qu'un.

■ **head for**: **~ for [sth] 1** lit, gen se diriger vers; Naut (set sail) mettre le cap sur; **the car was ~ing** ou **~ed for Paris** la voiture se dirigeait vers Paris; **the ship was ~ing** ou **~ed for New York** le navire faisait route vers New York; **where were they ~ing** ou **~ed for?** dans quelle direction est-ce qu'ils allaient?; **we were ~ing** ou **~ed for the coast when we broke down** nous roulions en direction de la côte quand nous sommes tombés en panne; **to ~ for home** prendre le chemin du retour; **to ~ for the whisky bottle** foncer sur la bouteille de whisky; **2** fig courir à [*defeat, victory*]; courir vers [*trouble*]; **to be ~ing for a fall** courir à l'échec.

■ **head off** ¶ partir (**for, in the direction of, towards** vers); **he ~ed off across the fields** il est parti à travers les champs; ¶ **~ off [sb/sth], ~ [sb/sth] off 1** lit (intercept) bloquer, barrer la route à [*person*]; **2** fig (forestall) éluder [*question*]; éviter [*complaint, quarrel, rebellion*]; **he ~ed her off onto a more interesting topic of conversation** il a fait dévier sa conversation vers un sujet plus intéressant.

■ **head up**: **~ up [sth]** diriger [*department, team*].

headache /ˈhedeɪk/ ▶ 1354 *n* **1** mal *m* de tête; **to have a ~** avoir mal à la tête; **to give sb a ~** donner mal à la tête à qn; **to suffer from sick ~** avoir des maux de tête et des nausées; **2** fig **to be a ~ (to sb)** causer des ennuis (à qn); **that's your ~**○! c'est ton problème○!

headachy /ˈhedeɪkɪ/ *adj* **to feel ~** avoir mal à la tête.

head: **~band** *n* bandeau *m*; **~banger**○ *n* Pol extrémiste *mf*; Mus fana○ *mf* de heavy metal; **~board** *n* tête *f* de lit; **~ boy** *n* GB Sch *élève qui représente l'école et qui a des responsabilités*; **~butt** *vtr* donner un coup de tête or de boule○ à.

head case○ *n* **to be a ~** avoir un grain○.

head: **~ cheese** *n* US fromage *m* de tête; **~ cold** ▶ 1354 *n* rhume *m* de cerveau.

headcount /ˈhedkaʊnt/ *n* **1** (counting) comptage *m*; **to do a ~** compter (les personnes présentes); **2** (total staff) effectif *m*.

headdress /ˈheddres/ *n* (of feathers) coiffure *f*; (of lace) coiffe *f*.

header /ˈhedə(r)/ *n* **1**○ (dive) **to take a ~** piquer une tête○; **I took a ~ into the lake/bushes** j'ai piqué une tête○ dans le lac/les buissons; **he took a ~ downstairs** il a dégringolé○ dans l'escalier; **2** Sport tête *f*; **3** Comput en-tête *m*; **4** Constr (brick) boutisse *f*; **5** (also **~ tank**) Tech réservoir *m* de compensation.

header: **~ block** *n* Comput bloc *m* début; **~ label** *n* Comput label *m* début.

headfirst /ˌhedˈfɜːst/ *adv* lit [*fall, plunge*] la tête la première; fig [*rush into*] tête baissée.

head gear *n* ¢ couvre-chef *m*.

head girl *n* **1** GB Sch *élève qui représente l'école et qui a des responsabilités*; **2** ▶ 1692 Equit (in riding stables) palefrenière-soigneuse *f* en chef.

head height *adv phr* **at ~** à hauteur d'homme.

head-hunt /ˈhedhʌnt/ I *vtr* (seek to recruit) chercher à recruter; (recruit successfully) recruter; **she has been ~ed several times** elle a été contactée plusieurs fois par des chasseurs de tête; **she was ~ed** elle a été recrutée par un chasseur de têtes.

II *vi* (chercher à) recruter des cadres expérimentés dans d'autres entreprises.

head-hunter /ˈhedhʌntə(r)/ *n* **1** Comm chasseur *m* de têtes; **2**○ US Pol *personne ou agence cherchant à miner l'influence d'un adversaire politique*.

head-hunting /ˈhedhʌntɪŋ/ *n* **1** Comm chasse *f* aux têtes; **2**○ US Pol déboulonnage○ *m* d'un adversaire politique.

headiness /ˈhedɪnɪs/ *n* (of wine, perfume) bouquet *m* capiteux; (of experience, success) griserie *f*.

heading /ˈhedɪŋ/ *n* **1** (of article, essay, column) titre *m*; (of subject area, topic) rubrique *f*; (inscription on notepaper, letter) en-tête *m*; **chapter ~** (quotation, résumé) tête *f* de chapitre; (title) titre *m* (de chapitre); **philosophy comes under the ~ of Humanities** la philosophie est classée sous la rubrique Sciences Humaines; **2** Aviat, Naut cap *m*.

head lad ▶ 1692 *n* (in racing stables) premier garçon *m*; (in riding stables) palefrenier-soigneur *m* en chef.

headlamp /ˈhedlæmp/ *n* **1** (of car) phare *m*; (of train) fanal *m*; **2** (for miners, climbers) lampe-chapeau *f*.

headland /ˈhedlənd/ *n* (high) promontoire *m*; (flat) pointe *f*.

headless /ˈhedlɪs/ *adj* gen sans tête; Zool acéphale spec.

IDIOMS **to run around like ~ chickens** ne plus savoir où donner de la tête.

headlight /ˈhedlaɪt/ *n* (of car) phare *m*; (of train) fanal *m*.

headline /ˈhedlaɪn/ I *n* **1** Journ gros titre *m*; **to hit the ~s** faire la une○; **the ~s were full of the crash, the crash was in all the ~s** l'accident faisait la une○ de tous les journaux; **the front-page ~** la manchette; **he'll never make the ~s** il n'aura jamais les honneurs de la presse; **2** Radio, TV titre *m*; **here are the (news) ~s again** et maintenant le rappel des (grands) titres (de l'actualité).

II *vtr* intituler [*feature*]; titrer [*newspaper article*].

III *vi* Mus [*band, singer*] (at festival) être en tête d'affiche; (on tour) jouer en vedette.

headline: **~-grabber**○ *n* nouvelle *f* qui fait la une○; **~-grabbing**○ *adj* qui fait la une○.

headlong /ˈhedlɒŋ/ I *adj* [*fall*] tête la première; **a ~ dash** ou **rush** une ruée; **a ~ drive** ou **ride** une course effrénée; **a ~ flight** un sauve-qui-peut *inv*.

II *adv* [*fall*] la tête la première; [*run, rush*] à toute vitesse; **to rush ~ into sth** fig se jeter tête baissée dans qch.

head: **~louse** *n* (*pl* **~lice**) pou *m*; **~man** *n* chef *m*; **~master** ▶ 1692, 1268 *n* directeur *m*; **~mistress** ▶ 1692, 1268 *n* directrice *f*; **~ nurse** *n* US infirmier/-ière *m/f* en chef; **~ office** *n* siège *m* social.

head-on /ˌhedˈɒn/ I *adj* lit [*crash, collision*] de front; fig [*confrontation, approach*] direct.

II *adv* [*collide, crash, hit, attack*] de front; **we collided ~ in the corridor** on s'est rentré dedans dans le couloir; **to tackle a problem ~** fig attaquer un problème de front.

headphones /ˈhedfəʊnz/ *npl* casque *m*; **a pair of ~** un casque.

headquarters /ˌhedˈkwɑːtəz/ *npl* (+ *v sg* ou *pl*) **1** gen, Comm, Admin siège *m* social; **he works at ~** il travaille au siège; **2** Mil quartier *m* général; **to set up one's ~** installer son quartier général.

head: **~ rest** *n* gen appui-tête *m*; Aut repose-tête *m inv*; **~ restraint** *n* Aut repose-tête *m inv*.

headroom /ˈhedrʊm/ *n* **I haven't got enough ~** le plafond est trop bas pour moi; **we haven't got enough ~** (in boat, vehicle) nous sommes trop hauts pour passer; **'max ~ 4 metres'** Transp 'hauteur limitée à 4 mètres'.

head: **~sail** *n* foc *m*; **~scarf** *n* (*pl* **-scarves**) foulard *m*; **~set** *n* casque *m*; (with microphone) micro-casque *m*.

headship /ˈhedʃɪp/ *n* Sch (post) poste *m* de directeur/-trice; **under her ~** sous sa direction.

head: **~shrinker**○ *n* péj psy○ *mf*, psychiatre *mf*; **~space** *n* (in container) espace *m* libre; **~square** *n* foulard *m*.

headstand /ˈhedstænd/ *n* poirier *m*; **to do a ~** faire le poirier.

head start *n* longueur *f* d'avance; **to give sb a ~ on** ou **over sb** donner à qn une longueur d'avance sur qn; **to have a ~** avoir une longueur d'avance.

headstone /ˈhedstəʊn/ *n* (grave) pierre *f* tombale.

headstrong /ˈhedstrɒŋ/ *adj* [*person*] têtu; [*attitude, behaviour*] obstiné; [*decision*] impétueux/-euse.

head: **~ tax** *n* taxe *f* individuelle; **~ teacher** ▶ 1692 *n* directeur/-trice *m/f*.

head to head I *n, modif* **to come together in a ~** ou **in a head-to-head battle** s'affronter.

II *adv* **to come ~** s'affronter.

head: **~-up display** *n* Aut, Aviat collimateur *m* de pilotage; **~ waiter** ▶ 1692 *n* maître *m* d'hôtel; **~waters** *npl* sources *fpl*.

headway /ˈhedweɪ/ *n* progrès *m*; **to make ~** lit progresser; fig faire des progrès.

head: **~wind** *n* gen vent *m* contraire; Naut vent *m* debout; **~word** *n* entrée *f*.

heady /ˈhedɪ/ *adj* [*wine, mixture*] capiteux/-euse, qui monte à la tête; [*perfume*] entêtant; fig [*experience, success*] grisant.

heal /hiːl/ I *vtr* guérir [*person, wound, injury*]; fig guérir, apaiser [*pain, suffering*]; apaiser [*quarrel*]; **I hope we can ~ the breach** ou **rift (between them)** j'espère que nous arriverons à les réconcilier.

II *vi* [*wound, cut*] se cicatriser; [*fracture, scar, ulcer*] guérir.

IDIOMS **time ~s all wounds** Prov le temps guérit les chagrins.

■ **heal over, heal up** [*wound, cut*] se cicatriser.

healer /ˈhiːlə(r)/ *n* guérisseur/-euse *m/f*; **time is a great ~** le temps apporte l'oubli.

healing /ˈhiːlɪŋ/ I *n* (of person) guérison *f*; (of cut, wound) cicatrisation *f*, guérison *f*.

II *adj* [*power, property*] curatif/-ive; [*lotion, ointment*] (for wounds) cicatrisant; **to have a**

~ effect lit, fig avoir un effet salutaire; **the ~ process** lit, fig le rétablissement.

health /helθ/ **I** *n* **1** Med santé *f*; fig (of economy) santé *f*; (of environment) qualité *f*; **mental ~** santé mentale; **in good/bad ~** en bonne/mauvaise santé; **to enjoy good ~** jouir d'une bonne santé; **2** (in toasts) **to drink (to) sb's ~** boire à la santé de qn; **here's (to your) ~!, good ~!** à votre santé!; **3** US = **health education**.
II *modif* [*problems, issues, needs*] de santé; [*reforms*] des services de santé.

health: **Health and Safety Executive** *n* GB Inspection *f* du travail; **Health and Safety Inspector** ▶ 1692 *n* GB inspecteur/-trice *m/f* du travail; **Health Authority** *n* GB administration *f* régionale de la santé publique; **~ benefits** *npl* prestations *fpl* de santé.

health care *n* **1** gen (prevention of illness) soins *mpl* médicaux, protection *f* contre les maladies; **2** Admin services *mpl* médicaux.

health: **~ centre** *n* GB centre *m* médico-social; **~ check** *n* visite *f* médicale.

health clinic *n* **1** = **health centre**; **2** (in Third World) centre *m* médical.

health: **~ club** *n* club *m* de (remise en) forme; **~ education** *n* ≈ hygiène *f* publique; **~ farm** *n*: *établissement pour cures d'amaigrissement, de rajeunissement etc*; **~ food** *n* ¢ aliments *mpl* naturels; **~ food shop** ▶ 1692 *n* magasin *m* de produits diététiques.

healthful /ˈhelθfl/, **health-giving** /ˈhelθɡɪvɪŋ/ *adj* [*exercise, food, drink*] bon/bonne pour la santé, salutaire; [*effect*] salutaire.

health hazard *n* risque *m* pour la santé.

healthily /ˈhelθɪlɪ/ *adv* [*eat, live etc*] sainement; **to be ~ sceptical of sth/sb** exprimer un scepticisme sain à l'égard de qch/qn.

health: **~ inspector** ▶ 1692 *n* inspecteur/-trice *m/f* de l'hygiène; **~ insurance** *n* assurance *f* maladie; **~ maintenance organization, HMO** *n* US ≈ mutuelle *f*; **~ officer** ▶ 1692 *n* inspecteur/-trice *m/f* de la santé.

health resort *n* (by sea) station *f* balnéaire; (in mountains) station *f* climatique; (spa town) station *f* thermale, ville *f* d'eau.

Health Secretary *n* GB ministre *m* de la Santé.

Health Service *n* **1** GB services *mpl* de santé; **2** US Univ infirmerie *f*.

health: **~ spa** *n* ville *f* d'eau; **~ visitor** ▶ 1692 *n* GB infirmier/-ière *m/f* des services sociaux; **~ warning** *n* mise *f* en garde du ministère de la Santé.

healthy /ˈhelθɪ/ *adj* [*person, animal, plant, skin, hair, lifestyle, diet, menu*] sain; [*air*] salutaire; [*exercise*] bon/bonne pour la santé; [*appetite*] robuste, bon/bonne; [*crop*] abondant; [*economy, finances, position, competition*] sain; [*profit*] excellent; [*machinery*] en bon état de marche; **it's not a very ~ occupation** (morally) ce n'est pas une occupation très saine; **she is much healthier than she was** elle se porte bien mieux qu'avant; **to have a ~ respect for sb** apprécier [qn/qch] à sa juste valeur [*opponent, sb's talents*]; craindre beaucoup [*teacher, authority figure*]; **I would have a ~ respect for those waves if I were you!** à ta place je me méfierais de ces vagues!; **(a) ~ scepticism** circonspection *f*; **his finances are none too ~** ses finances sont mal en point; **your car doesn't sound very ~** hum ta voiture fait un drôle de bruit; **to have a ~ lead** Sport avoir une avance confortable.
IDIOMS **a ~ mind in a ~ body** un esprit sain dans un corps sain.

heap /hiːp/ **I** *n* **1** (of rubble, leaves, objects) tas *m*; **to pile sth up in a ~** ou **in ~s** mettre qch en tas; **to lie in a ~** [*person*] être affalé; [*objects, bodies*] être entassés; **to fall** ou **collapse in a ~** [*person*] s'affaler; **to collapse in an exhausted ~** s'affaler épuisé; **2**○ (lot) **~s of** (plenty of) plein de [*money, food, atmosphere*]; (too much) un tas○ de [*work, problems*]; **we've got ~s of things to do** on a un tas de choses à faire; **we've got ~s of time** on a tout notre temps; **to be in a ~ of trouble** avoir plein de○ or des tas ○ de problèmes; **3**○ péj (car) guimbarde○ *f*, tacot○ *m*.
II heaps○ *adv* cent fois; **to feel ~s better** se sentir cent fois mieux; **~s more room** cent fois plus de place.
III *vtr* **1** (pile) = **heap up**; **2** fig (shower) **to ~ sth on sb** couvrir qn de qch [*praise*]; accabler qn de qch [*work*]; abreuver qn de qch [*insults*]; **to ~ scorn on sb** accabler qn de mépris.
■ **heap up**: **~ [sth] up, ~ up [sth]** entasser [*leaves, bodies*]; empiler [*food*]; submerger [*table*] (**with** de).

heaped /hiːpt/ *adj* **a ~ spoonful** Culin une bonne cuillerée; **a dish ~ with cakes** un plat avec une montagne de gâteaux.

hear /hɪə(r)/ (*prét, pp* **heard**) **I** *vtr* **1** (perceive with ears) entendre [*sound, thud, voice, car, radio*]; **she heard her brother coming up the stairs** elle a entendu son frère qui montait l'escalier; **I can ~ the train whistling** j'entends siffler le train; **an explosion was heard** on a entendu une explosion; **I can ~ you!** je t'entends!; **I heard you coming in** je t'ai entendu quand tu es rentré; **to ~ sb being beaten/thanked** entendre que l'on est en train de battre/de remercier qn; **to ~ her talk, you'd think (that)** à l'entendre, on croirait que; **we haven't heard the end** ou **last of it** on n'a pas fini d'en entendre parler; **to make oneself** ou **one's voice heard** lit se faire entendre; fig faire entendre sa voix; **I can't ~ myself think!** il y a tellement de bruit que je n'arrive pas à me concentrer; **2** (learn, find out about) apprendre [*news, story, joke, rumour*]; **to ~ (tell) of sth** entendre parler de qch; **to ~ (it said) that** apprendre que, entendre dire que; **I've heard good things about...** j'ai entendu dire du bien de...; **I've heard so much about you** on m'a tant parlé de vous; **I've heard it all before!** je connais la chanson○!; **have you heard the one about...** (joke) tu connais celle de...; **have you heard?** tu es au courant?; **what have you heard?** tu es au courant de quelque chose?; **I'm sorry to ~ (that) you can't come** je suis désolé d'apprendre que vous ne pouvez pas venir; **I ~ you want to be a doctor** il paraît que tu veux devenir médecin; **so I ~, so I've heard** c'est ce que j'ai entendu dire; **she won, I ~** elle a gagné, paraît-il; **to ~ whether/why/how** savoir si/pourquoi/comment; **3** (listen to) écouter [*lecture, speech, broadcast, concert, record*]; [*judge, court, jury*] entendre [*case, evidence, testimony, witness*]; écouter [*prayer*]; **to ~ sb do sth** écouter qn faire qch; **to ~ a child read** faire lire un enfant à voix haute; **to ~ what sb has to say** entendre ce que qn a à dire; **do you ~ (me)?** tu m'entends?; **to ~ Mass** sout assister à la messe, entendre la messe sout; **the court heard that...** Jur il a été déclaré à la cour que...
II *vi* entendre; **to ~ about** entendre parler de; **have you heard about Matt and Sarah?** tu es au courant pour Matt et Sarah?
IDIOMS **~! ~!** bravo!; **let's ~ it for Jo** on applaudit Jo bien fort.
■ **hear from**: **~ from [sb]** **1** (get news from) recevoir des nouvelles de [*friend, relative*]; **it's nice to ~ from you** je suis content d'avoir de tes nouvelles; **I'm waiting to ~ from head office/the hospital** j'attends une réponse du siège social/de l'hôpital; **don't do anything until you ~ from me** ne fais rien tant que je ne t'aurai pas fait pas signe; **you'll be ~ing from me!** (threat) tu auras de mes nouvelles!; **you'll be ~ing from my solicitor** vous en parlerez à mon avocat; **2** (hear interviewed on TV etc) entendre le point de vue de [*representative, politician*]; écouter le récit de [*survivor, eyewitness*].
■ **hear of**: **~ of [sb/sth]** **1** (be or become aware of) entendre parler de; **I've never even heard of her** je ne sais même pas qui c'est; **the first I heard of the accident was on the radio** j'ai appris l'accident par la radio; **that's the first I've heard of it!** première nouvelle!; **he hasn't been heard of since** on n'a plus jamais entendu parler de lui; **2** (countenance, consider) **I won't ~ of it!** il n'en est pas question!
■ **hear out**: **~ out [sb], ~ [sb] out** écouter [qn] jusqu'au bout.

heard /hɜːd/ *prét, pp* ▶ **hear**.

hearer /ˈhɪərə(r)/ *n* (listener) auditeur/-trice *m/f*; **his ~s were enthralled** son auditoire a été fasciné.

hearing /ˈhɪərɪŋ/ **I** *n* **1** (sense, faculty) ouïe *f*, audition *f*; **his ~ is not very good** il n'a pas l'oreille très fine; **to damage sb's ~** causer des troubles de l'ouïe à qn; **2** (earshot) **there was no-one within ~** il n'y avait personne à portée de voix; **in** ou **within my ~** en ma présence; **to be out of sb's ~** être trop loin de qn pour qu'il puisse entendre; **3** (before court, magistrate, committee etc) audience *f*; **~ of an appeal/an application** audition *f* d'un appel/d'une demande; **closed** ou **private ~** audience *f* à huis clos or privée; **4** (chance to be heard) **to get a ~** se faire entendre; **to give sb/sth a ~** écouter qn/qch; **I want a fair ~** je veux qu'on m'écoute impartialement.
II *modif* [*damage, loss, test*] d'audition.
III *adj* qui entend (bien); **deaf and ~ children** les enfants sourds et ceux doués d'une bonne ouïe.

hearing: **~ aid** *n* prothèse *f* auditive, sonotone® *m*, appareil *m*; **~-impaired** *adj* malentendant.

hearken‡ /ˈhɑːkən/ *vi* prêter l'oreille (**to** à).

hearsay /ˈhɪəseɪ/ *n* ¢ ouï-dire *m inv*, on-dit *m inv*; **based on ~** fondé sur des 'ouï-dire' or 'on-dit'.

hearsay evidence *n* Jur déposition *f* sur la foi d'autrui.

hearse /hɜːs/ *n* corbillard *m*.

heart /hɑːt/ ▶ 1282 **I** *n* **1** Anat (of human, animal) cœur *m*; **his ~ stopped beating** lit, fig son cœur s'est arrêté (de battre); **my ~ missed** ou **skipped a beat** mon cœur a fait un bond; **to clasp sb/sth to one's ~** serrer qn/qch sur son cœur; **who can say, hand on ~** ou **with their hand on their ~...?** qui peut dire, la main sur le cœur...?; **in the shape of a ~** en forme de cœur; **2** (site of emotion, love, sorrow etc) cœur *m*; **to win/capture/steal sb's ~** gagner/conquérir/prendre le cœur de qn; **to give sb one's ~** donner son cœur à qn; **to break sb's ~** briser le cœur de qn; **to break one's ~** se briser le cœur (**over sb** pour qn); **to cry fit to break one's ~** pleurer à en rendre l'âme; **it does my ~ good to see...** cela me réchauffe le cœur de voir...; **with a heavy/light ~** le cœur lourd/léger; **the way to sb's ~** le chemin du cœur de qn; **to lose one's ~ to sb** tomber amoureux/-euse de qn; **to take sb to one's ~** prendre qn en affection; **to sob one's ~ out** pleurer toutes les larmes de son corps; **to sing one's ~ out** chanter à pleins poumons; **to act one's ~ out** jouer avec tout son cœur; **my ~ goes out to you/him** je suis avec vous/lui de tout cœur; **from the bottom of one's ~** du fond du cœur; **3** (innermost feelings, nature) cœur *m*; **to open one's ~ to sb** ouvrir son cœur à qn; **to take sth to ~** prendre qch à cœur; **to follow one's ~** suivre son cœur; **from the ~** du fond du cœur; **to love sb with all one's ~** aimer qn de tout son cœur; **to wish with all one's ~ that** souhaiter de tout cœur que (+ *subj*); **in my ~ (of ~s)** au fond de moi-même; **my ~ is not in sth/doing sth** je n'ai pas le cœur à qch/à faire qch; **it is close** ou **dear** ou **near to my ~** cela me tient à cœur; **I have your interests at ~** tes intérêts me tiennent à cœur; **he's a child at ~** dans le fond, c'est toujours un enfant; **4** (capacity for pity, love etc) cœur *m*; **to have no ~** ne pas avoir de cœur; **to be all ~** avoir très bon cœur; **to have a cold/soft ~** avoir le cœur dur/tendre; **I didn't have the ~ to refuse** je n'ai pas eu le cœur de refuser; **I couldn't find it in my ~ to forgive them** je n'ai pas pu leur pardonner; **have a ~!** pitié!; **to have a change of ~** changer de sentiment; **5** (courage) courage *m*; **to take/lose ~** prendre/perdre courage; **she took ~ from the fact that** elle puisait son courage dans le fait que; **to be in good ~** avoir le moral; **6** (middle, centre) (of district) cœur *m*; **right in the ~ of London** en plein cœur de Londres; **in the ~ of the jungle/country** en pleine jungle/campagne; **the ~ of the matter** le fond du problème; **to get to the ~ of the matter** entrer dans le vif du sujet; **issues which lie at the ~ of a dispute** les questions qui se trouvent au cœur d'un conflit; **7** (in cards) cœur *m*; **two of ~s** deux de cœur; **to play a ~** jouer à cœur; **have you got any ~s?** as-tu du cœur?; **8** (of artichoke, lettuce, cabbage, celery) cœur *m*.

II *modif* [*patient, specialist, operation*] du cœur; [*muscle, valve, wall*] cardiaque; [*surgery*] du cœur, cardiaque; **to have a ~ condition** ou **a ~ complaint** être cardiaque.

III by heart *adv phr* par cœur; **to know/learn sth off by ~** savoir/apprendre qch par cœur.

IV -hearted (*dans composés*) **hard-/pure-~ed** au cœur dur/pur.

IDIOMS **a man/woman after my own ~** un homme/une femme comme je les aime; **cross my ~ (and hope to die)** croix de bois, croix de fer (si je mens je vais en enfer); **his/her ~ is in the right place** il/elle a bon cœur; **home is where the ~ is** Prov où le cœur aime, là est le foyer; **to have set one's ~ on sth/doing** ou **to have one's ~ set on sth/doing** vouloir à tout prix qch/faire; **don't set your ~ on it** n'y compte pas trop; **the way to a man's ~ is through his stomach** Prov pour conquérir un homme, préparez-lui des petits plats.

heartache /ˈhɑːteɪk/ *n* gen chagrin *m*; (romantic) peine *f* de cœur.

heart attack *n* crise *f* cardiaque, infarctus *m*; **to have a ~** lit, fig avoir une crise cardiaque.

heartbeat /ˈhɑːtbiːt/ *n* **1** (single pulse) battement *m* de cœur, pulsation *f* cardiaque spec; **2** (rhythm of heart) battements *mpl* de cœur, pulsations *fpl* cardiaques spec; **to increase sb's ~** élever le rythme cardiaque de qn.

heart: **~break** *n* déchirement *m*, douleur *f*; **~breaker** *n* (man) bourreau *m* des cœurs; (woman) femme *f* fatale.

heartbreaking /ˈhɑːtbreɪkɪŋ/ *adj* [*sight, story, news*] navrant; [*cry, appeal*] déchirant; **it is ~ to see** il est navrant de voir; **it would be ~ to fail** cela nous/me etc fendrait le cœur de ne pas réussir.

heartbroken /ˈhɑːtbrəʊkn/ *adj* **to be ~** avoir le cœur brisé.

heart: **~burn** *n* brûlures *fpl* d'estomac; **~ disease** *n* ¢ maladies *fpl* cardiaques.

hearten /ˈhɑːtn/ *vtr* encourager; **we were ~ed by the news** la nouvelle nous a encouragés.

heartening /ˈhɑːtnɪŋ/ *adj* encourageant, réconfortant.

heart failure *n* arrêt *m* du cœur.

heartfelt /ˈhɑːtfelt/ *adj* [*condolence, gratitude, passion, wish*] sincère; [*word, appeal, plea, prayer*] qui vient du cœur.

hearth /hɑːθ/ *n* foyer *m*.

IDIOMS **far from ~ and home** loin de son foyer.

hearth rug *n* petit tapis *m*.

heartily /ˈhɑːtɪlɪ/ *adv* **1** (enthusiastically) [*welcome, greet*] chaleureusement; [*support, approve, disapprove*] vigoureusement; [*sing, say, laugh, eat*] de bon cœur; **he ~ agreed with her** il était tout à fait d'accord avec elle; **2** (thoroughly) [*glad, relieved*] vraiment; **I'm ~ sick of it**° j'en ai ras le bol°.

heartiness /ˈhɑːtɪnɪs/ *n* (of laugh, slap) vigueur *f*; (of person, voice, manner) jovialité *f*; **the ~ of his appetite** son grand appétit.

heartland /ˈhɑːtlənd/ *n* (also **~s** *pl*) **1** (industrial, rural centre) cœur *m*; **2** Pol fief *m*; **3** (centre of a region, country) centre *m*.

heartless /ˈhɑːtlɪs/ *adj* [*person*] sans cœur (*predic*); [*attitude, behaviour*] sans pitié; **~ wretch!** sans-cœur!; **her ~ father** son sans-cœur de père; **how could you be so ~!** quel/quelle sans-cœur!; **~ treatment** traitement *m* cruel, cruauté *f* (**of** envers).

heartlessly /ˈhɑːtlɪslɪ/ *adv* [*treat, say, act*] sans pitié.

heartlessness /ˈhɑːtlɪsnɪs/ *n* (of person) insensibilité *f*, manque *m* de cœur; (of attitude, remark) cruauté *f*.

heart: **~-lung machine** *n* cœur-poumon *m* (artificiel); **~ monitor** *n* moniteur *m* cardiaque; **~ murmur** *n* souffle *m* au cœur; **~ rate** *n* rythme *m* or fréquence *f* spec cardiaque; **~ rate monitor** *n* = **heart monitor**.

heartrending /ˈhɑːtrendɪŋ/ *adj* [*cry, sob, appeal, plea*] déchirant; [*sight, story*] navrant.

heart-searching /ˈhɑːtsɜːtʃɪŋ/ *n* ¢ examen *m* de conscience; **after much ~** après un examen de conscience approfondi.

heart: **~sease** *n* Bot pensée *f* sauvage; **~-shaped** *adj* en forme de cœur (*after n*); **~sick** *adj* abattu, déprimé.

heartstrings /ˈhɑːtstrɪŋz/ *npl* corde *f* sensible; **to pluck** ou **tug (at) sb's ~** faire vibrer la corde sensible de qn; **to touch sb's ~** toucher la corde sensible de qn.

heart: **~ surgeon** ▶ **1692** *n* chirurgien *m* cardiaque, cardiochirurgien *m*; **~throb**° *n* idole *f*.

heart-to-heart /ˌhɑːttəˈhɑːt/ **I** *n* conversation *f* à cœur ouvert; **to have a ~** parler à cœur ouvert (**with** avec).

II *adj, adv* [*talk, chat*] à cœur ouvert.

heart: **~ transplant** *n* greffe *f* du cœur, transplantation *f* cardiaque spec; **~ transplant patient** *n* greffé/-e *m/f* du cœur.

heart trouble *n* problèmes *mpl* cardiaques; **to have ~** souffrir de problèmes cardiaques.

heart: **~-warming** *adj* réconfortant, qui réchauffe le cœur; **~wood** *n* cœur *m* du bois.

hearty /ˈhɑːtɪ/ **I**° *n* GB péj joyeux drille *m*.

II *adj* **1** (jolly and vigorous) [*person, voice, manner*] jovial; [*laugh*] franc/franche; [*slap, pat*] vigoureux/-euse; **2** [*appetite, meal, breakfast*] solide; **he's a ~ eater** c'est un gros mangeur; **3** (whole-hearted) [*approval, congratulations, admiration*] chaleureux/-euse; [*resentment, loathing*] total; **to have a ~ dislike of sth** détester cordialement qch; **4** (warm) [*welcome, greeting*] cordial.

IDIOMS **heave-ho, my hearties!** oh-hisse, les gars!

heat /hiːt/ **I** *n* **1** gen, Phys, Meteorol chaleur *f*; **the plants wilted in the ~** les plantes se sont fanées à la chaleur; **he was sweating in** ou **with the ~** il transpirait à cause de la chaleur; **she was exhausted by the ~** elle se sentait exténuée à cause de la chaleur; **the summer/afternoon ~** la chaleur de l'été/de l'après-midi; **in the ~ of the summer** au plus chaud de l'été; **in the ~ of the day** au moment le plus chaud de la journée; **we were stifling in the 30° ~** il faisait 30° et on étouffait; **in this ~ nobody feels hungry** par cette chaleur personne n'a faim; **a cream to take the ~ out of sunburnt skin** un lait apaisant pour les coups de soleil; **2** Culin (of hotplate, gas ring) feu *m*; (of oven) température *f*; **cook at a low/moderate ~** faire cuire à feu doux/moyen; (in oven) faire cuire à basse température /à température moyenne; **turn up/turn down the ~** augmenter/diminuer le feu or la température; **3** (heating) chauffage *m*; **to turn the ~ on/off** mettre/arrêter le chauffage; **to turn the ~ up/down** monter/baisser le chauffage; **4** Sport épreuve *f* éliminatoire; (in athletics) série *f*; **she won her ~** elle a remporté sa série; **5** Zool **to be on** ou **in ~** être en chaleur; **6** fig (of argument, discussion) véhémence *f*; **in the ~ of sth** dans le feu de qch; **carried away by the ~ of the discussion she...** emportée dans le feu de la discussion elle...; **in the ~ of the moment** dans le feu de l'action; **to take the ~ off sb** soulager qn; **that's taken the ~ off us** cela nous a soulagés; **to put** ou **turn the ~ on sb to do** faire pression sur qn pour qu'il fasse; **the ~ is on** il va falloir mettre le paquet (**to do** pour faire); ▶ **kitchen**.

II *vtr* gen chauffer [*room, house, pool*]; Culin faire chauffer [*food, oven*]; Med échauffer [*blood*]; **~ the oven to 180°** faire chauffer le four à 180°.

III *vi* chauffer.

■ **heat through** ¶ [*food, drink, house*] chauffer; **has the soup ~ed through?** la soupe est-elle chaude?; ¶ **~ [sth] through** faire chauffer [*food*].

■ **heat up** ¶ [*food, drink*] chauffer; [*air*] se réchauffer; **wait until the engine/radiator ~s up** attends que le moteur/radiateur soit chaud; **has the iron ~ed up yet?** est-ce que le fer est chaud?; ¶ **~ [sth] up, ~ up [sth]** (for first time) faire chauffer [*food, oven*]; (reheat) faire réchauffer [*food*].

heat: **~ barrier** *n* mur *m* thermique, mur *m* de chaleur; **~ capacity** *n* capacité *f* calorifique; **~ constant** *n* constante *f* calorifique.

heated /ˈhiːtɪd/ *adj* **1** lit [*water, pool*] chauffé; [*brush, windscreen, rollers*] chauffant; **2** fig [*debate, argument*] animé; [*denial, defence*] véhément; **to grow** or **get ~** [*debate, argument, person*] s'animer.

heatedly /ˈhiːtɪdlɪ/ *adv* avec véhémence.

heat efficiency *n* rendement *m* calorifique.

heater /ˈhiːtə(r)/ *n* gen radiateur *m*; (portable) chauffage *m* d'appoint.

heat: **~ exchanger** *n* échangeur *m* de chaleur; **~ exhaustion** *n* coup *m* de chaleur simple.

heath /hiːθ/ *n* (moor) lande *f*; (heather) bruyère *f*; **on the ~** dans la lande.

heat haze *n* brume *f* de chaleur.

heathen /ˈhiːðn/ **I** *adj* (irreligious) païen/-ïenne; (uncivilized) barbare.

II *n* (unbeliever) païen/-ïenne *m/f*; (uncivilized) barbare *mf*.

heathenism /ˈhɪðənɪzəm/ *n* paganisme *m*.

heather /ˈheðə(r)/ *n* bruyère *f*.

Heath Robinson /ˌhiːθ ˈrɒbɪnsən/ *adj* GB [*contraption, repairs*] bricolé ingénieusement.

heating /ˈhiːtɪŋ/ **I** *n* chauffage *m*; **to turn the ~ on/off** mettre/arrêter le chauffage; **to turn the ~ up/down** monter/baisser le chauffage; **the ~ is on/off** le chauffage est en marche/est arrêté.

II *modif* [*bill, costs, apparatus*] de chauffage.

heating: **~ engineer** ▶ **1692** *n* chauffagiste *m*; **~ plant** *n* chaufferie *f*; **~ system** *n* système *m* de chauffage.

heat: **~ lightning** *n* ¢ éclairs *mpl* de chaleur; **~ loss** *n* (all contexts) déperdition *f* de chaleur; **~-proof** *adj* [*mat, dish, tile*] résistant à la chaleur; [*clothing*] isolant; **~ pump** *n* thermopompe *f*; pompe *f* à chaleur; **~ rash** *n* éruption *f* cutanée due à la chaleur, miliaire *f* spec; **~-resistant** *adj* [*mat, tile, dish*] résistant à la chaleur; [*clothing*] isolant.

heat seal I *n* joint *m* d'étanchéité.
II **heat-seal** *vtr* étanchéiser, sceller [qch] à chaud.

heat: **~-seeking missile** *n* missile *m* à tête chercheuse thermique; **~-sensitive** *adj* thermosensible, sensible à la chaleur; **~ setting** *n* (of thermostat, heater, washing machine) programme *m*; (of iron, hairdrier) position *f*; **~ shield** *n* Aerosp bouclier *m* thermique; **~ stroke** *n* coup *m* de chaleur (*avec collapsus*); **~-treated** *adj* Ind traité thermiquement; **~ treatment** *n* Med thermothérapie *f*; Ind traitement *m* thermique; Agric thermisation *f*; **~wave** *n* vague *f* de chaleur.

heave /hi:v/ I *n* **1** (effort to move) effort *m*; **to give a ~** (pull) tirer de toutes ses forces; (push) pousser de toutes ses forces; **2** (swell) (of sea) houle *f*; **his stomach gave a ~** il a eu un haut-le-cœur; **3** Geol déplacement *m* latéral.
II *vtr* (*prét, pp* **heaved**, Naut **hove**) **1** (lift) hisser; (pull) traîner péniblement; **2 to ~ a sigh** pousser un soupir; **3** (throw) lancer (**at** sur); **4** Naut **to ~ a boat ahead/astern** déhaler un bateau par l'avant/l'arrière.
III *vi* (*prét, pp* **heaved**, Naut **hove**) **1** [*sea, ground*] se soulever et s'abaisser; **2** (pull) tirer de toutes ses forces; **3** (retch) avoir un haut-le-cœur; (vomit) vomir; **it made my stomach ~** ça m'a donné un haut-le-cœur; **4** Naut, fig **to ~ into sight** apparaître.
IV **heaving** *pres p adj* [*bosom, breast*] haletant.
■ **heave to** (*prét, pp* **hove**) Naut: ¶ **~ to** se mettre en panne; **to be hove to** rester en panne; ¶ **~ [sth] to** mettre en panne [*ship*].
■ **heave up**: ¶ **~ up**○ dégueuler●, vomir; ¶ **~ oneself up** se hisser (**onto** sur).

heave-ho /ˌhi:vˈhəʊ/ *excl* Naut oh-hisse!; **to give sb the (old) ~**○ hum (break off with) plaquer qn○; (dismiss) mettre qn à la porte.

heaven /ˈhevn/ *n* **1** Relig (also **Heaven**) ciel *m*, paradis *m*; **to go to/be in ~** aller/être au paradis or au ciel; **~ and earth** ciel et terre; **~ and hell** l'enfer et le paradis; **the kingdom of ~** le royaume des cieux; **our Father which art in ~** notre père qui es aux cieux; **the will of ~** la volonté céleste; **2** (in exclamations) **~s (above)!** grands dieux!; **~ forbid**, **~ forfend!** sout grands dieux, non!; **~ forbid she should realize!** pourvu qu'elle ne s'en rende pas compte!; **~ only knows!** Dieu seul sait!; **~ help us!** que Dieu nous vienne en aide!; **~ help him when I catch him**○! qu'est-ce qu'il va prendre quand je vais l'attraper○!; **good ~s!** ou **great ~s†!** grands dieux!; **God in ~!** mon Dieu!; **thank ~(s)!** Dieu soit loué!; **in ~'s name stop†!** arrêtez au nom du ciel†!; **what in ~'s name are you up to?** mais bon Dieu qu'est-ce que tu fais○?; **3** (bliss) (state, place) paradis *m*; **this beach is ~ on earth** cette plage c'est le paradis terrestre; **the dinner/the hotel was ~** le dîner/l'hôtel était divin; **4** (sky) ciel *m*; **5** Astrol, littér, hum **the ~s** le ciel; **the ~s opened** des trombes d'eau se sont abattues.
IDIOMS **to be in seventh ~** être au septième ciel; **to move ~ and earth** remuer ciel et terre (**to do** pour faire); **to stink** ou **smell to high ~** puer.

heavenly /ˈhevənlɪ/ *adj* **1** (of heaven) [*choir, vision*] céleste; (of God) [*peace, justice*] divin; **2**○ (wonderful) divin.

heavenly: **~ body** *n* corps *m* céleste; **Heavenly Father** *n* père *m* céleste.

heaven-sent /ˈhevnsent/ *adj* [*opportunity, rescue*] providentiel/-ielle.

heavenward(s) /ˈhəvnwəd(z)/ *adv* littér [*gaze*] au ciel.

heavily /ˈhevɪlɪ/ *adv* **1** (with weight) [*lean, press, fall, move, load, weigh*] lourdement; [*walk, tread*] à pas pesants; [*sleep, sigh*] profondément; [*breathe*] (noisily) bruyamment; (with difficulty) péniblement; **~ built** solidement bâti; **~ underlined** souligné d'un gros trait; **to come down ~ on sth** ne pas tolérer qch; **to come down ~ on sb** punir qn de manière exemplaire; **2** (considerably, abundantly) [*rain*] très fort; [*snow, spend, invest, smoke, drink, criticize, rely*] beaucoup; [*bleed*] abondamment; [*involved*] grandement; [*taxed, armed, in debt*] fortement; **to be too ~ dependent on** compter beaucoup trop sur; **to be ~ subsidized** bénéficier de beaucoup de subventions; **~ sedated** sous forte sédation; **~ made-up** très maquillé; **to be ~ fined** avoir une forte amende; **to lose ~** (financially) perdre beaucoup; (in game) se faire écraser; **to be ~ into**○ s'adonner à [*drug, music, sport*].

heaviness /ˈhevɪnɪs/ *n* **1** (weight, thickness) (of object, person, fabric, garment) lourdeur *f*; (of features) manque *m* de finesse; (of limbs) engourdissement *m*, lourdeur *f*; **2** (considerable nature) (of losses, casualties) importance *f*; (of gunfire, traffic) densité *f*; (of rain, snow) abondance *f*.

heavy /ˈhevɪ/ ▶ **1883** I○ *n* **1** (person) gen grosse brute *f*; (bodyguard, escort) gorille○ *m*; **2** GB (newspaper) grand journal *m*, journal *m* sérieux.
II *adj* **1** gen, Phys (having weight) [*weight, person, load, bag, parcel*] lourd; **to be too ~ to lift** être trop lourd à soulever or pour qu'on puisse le soulever; **to make sth heavier** alourdir qch; **he's 5 kg heavier than me** il pèse 5 kilos de plus que moi; **how ~ are you?** combien pèses-tu?; **to be ~ with young** [*animal*] être pleine; **2** (thick) [*fabric, coat*] lourd; [*shoes, frame*] gros/grosse (*before n*); [*line, feature, face*] épais/épaisse; **in ~ type** en caractères gras; **of ~ build** solidement bâti, de forte carrure; **to wear ~ make-up** se maquiller beaucoup, être très maquillé; **3** Mil, Ind [*machinery*] gros/grosse (*before n*), lourd; [*artillery*] lourd; **'~ plant crossing'** 'traversée d'engins'; **4** fig (weighty, ponderous) [*movement, step*] pesant, lourd; [*irony, humour, responsibility, sigh*] lourd; **my legs feel ~** j'ai les jambes lourdes; **his eyelids began to get ~** ses paupières devenaient lourdes; **with a ~ heart** le cœur gros; **to be a ~ sleeper** avoir le sommeil lourd; **a ~ thud** un bruit sourd; **a ~ blow** un coup violent; **'you told me,' he said with ~ emphasis** 'c'est toi qui me l'a dit,' dit-il en insistant lourdement; **the going is ~** le terrain est lourd; **the interview was ~ going** (slow, hard work) l'interview était laborieuse; **5** (abundant) [*traffic*] dense; [*gunfire*] nourri; [*bleeding, period*] abondant; [*charge, investment*] important ; **to be a ~ drinker/smoker** boire/fumer beaucoup; **security was ~** d'importantes mesures de sécurité avaient été prises; **~ trading on the stock market** beaucoup de transactions à la Bourse; **to have a ~ workload** avoir beaucoup de travail; **to be ~ on** (use a lot of) [*person*] avoir la main lourde sur [*ingredient, perfume*]; [*machine*] consommer beaucoup de [*fuel*]; (contain a lot of) comporter beaucoup de [*humour, ingredient*]; **6** (severe) [*defeat, loss, debt*] lourd; [*attack, bombing*] intense; [*prison sentence, penalty, fine*] sévère; [*cuts, criticism*] fort (*before n*); [*cold*] gros/grosse (*before n*); **~ casualties** un nombre élevé de victimes; **~ fighting** de violents combats; **7** (strong) [*perfume, scent, concentration*] fort; [*accent*] prononcé; **8** Meteorol [*rain, frost*] fort; [*fog, mist*] épais/épaisse; [*snow, dew*] abondant; [*cloud*] lourd; [*sky*] chargé, lourd; **it's very ~ today** il fait très lourd aujourd'hui; **to capsize in ~ seas** chavirer par grosse mer; **9** Culin [*meal, food, pastry*] lourd; [*wine*] corsé; **10** (busy, packed) [*day, month, timetable, programme*] chargé; **11** (difficult, serious) [*book, paper, film, lecture*] ardu; **this article is ~** ou **makes ~ reading** cet article n'est pas d'une lecture facile; **12** (loaded) **to be ~ with** [*air, branch, atmosphere*] être chargé de [*perfume, flowers, resentment*]; **a remark ~ with meaning** une remarque lourde de sens.
III *adv* [*weigh*] lourdement; **time hung ~ on her hands** le temps lui pesait.
IDIOMS **things started to get ~**○ (threatening) ça a commencé à mal tourner; (serious, intellectual) ça a commencé à devenir un peu ardu; (sexual) ça a commencé à devenir lourd○.

heavy breathing *n* **1** gen respiration *f* bruyante; **2** (on phone) respiration *f* bruyante obscène.

heavy crude (oil) *n* pétrole *m* brut lourd.

heavy-duty /ˌhevɪˈdju:tɪ, US -ˈdu:-/ *adj* (very strong) [*plastic, rubber, lock, battery*] à haute résistance; (for industrial use) [*machine, equipment*] à usage industriel.

heavy goods vehicle, **HGV** *n* poids *m* lourd.

heavy-handed /ˌhevɪˈhændɪd/ *adj* **1** (clumsy) [*person, remark, compliment, approach*] maladroit; **2** (authoritarian) [*person, policy, treatment*] autoritaire.

heavy-hearted /ˌhevɪˈhɑ:tɪd/ *adj* **to be ~** avoir le cœur gros.

heavy: **~ industry** *n* industrie *f* lourde; **~ metal** *n* Mus hard rock *m*; **~ petting**○ *n* pelotage○ *m*, attouchements *mpl*; **~ water** *n* eau *f* lourde.

heavyweight /ˈhevɪweɪt/ I *n* **1** Sport (boxer) poids *m* lourd; (wrestler) lutteur *m* catégorie libre; **2**○ fig (in industry, commerce) grosse légume○ *f*; (intellectual) grosse tête○ *f*.
II *modif* **1** Sport [*boxer, competition, title*] poids lourd; **2** (serious) [*paper, politician*] sérieux/-ieuse; **3** [*fabric*] lourd.

hebe /ˈhi:bɪ/ *n* **1** US injur youpin/-e *m/f* offensive; **2** (shrub) véronique *f*.

Hebraic /hi:ˈbreɪɪk/ *adj* hébraïque.

Hebrew /ˈhi:bru:/ I *n* **1** (person) Hébreu *m*, Israélite *mf*; **2** ▶ **1402** Ling hébreu *m*.
II *adj* [*person*] hébreu; [*calendar, alphabet, civilization*] hébraïque; **the ~ people** les Hébreux, les Israélites.

Hebrides /ˈhebrɪdi:z/ ▶ **1381** *pr npl* **the ~** les Hébrides *fpl*.

heck○ /hek/ I *n* **what the ~ is going on?** que diable se passe-t-il?; **what the ~ are you doing?** mais qu'est-ce que tu fiches là○?; **what the ~!** je m'en fiche○!; **so it costs $25! what the ~!** ça coûte $25! et alors?; **he earns a ~ of a lot** c'est fou ce qu'il gagne comme fric○; **it's a ~ of a long way** c'est rudement○ loin; **he's one ~ of a nice guy** il est vachement○ sympa○.
II *excl* zut!

heckle /ˈhekl/ I *vtr* (barrack) interpeller; (interrupt) interrompre grossièrement.
II *vi* chahuter.

heckler /ˈheklə(r)/ *n* chahuteur/-euse *m/f* (*qui interrompt un orateur*).

heckling /ˈheklɪŋ/ *n* ¢ interpellations *fpl*, chahut *m* (*pour interrompre un orateur*).

hectare /ˈhekteə(r)/ ▶ **1771** *n* hectare *m*.

hectic /ˈhektɪk/ *adj* **1** (busy) [*activity*] intense, fiévreux/-euse; [*period*] mouvementé, agité; [*day, week, schedule*] chargé, mouvementé; **the ~ pace of change** l'extrême rapidité avec laquelle les changements se sont faits; **at a ~ pace** très rapidement; **to have a ~ life(style)** avoir une vie trépidante; **life in the city is very ~** la vie en ville est très animée; **2** Med [*fever*] hectique; [*flush*] fiévreux/-euse.

hectogram(me) /ˈhektəgræm/ ▶ **1883** *n* hectogramme *m*.

hectolitre GB, **hectoliter** US /ˈhektəli:tə(r)/ ▶ **1869**, **1068** *n* hectolitre *m*.

hector /ˈhektə(r)/ I *vi* prendre un ton dictatorial.
II *vtr* haranguer.
III **hectoring** *pres p adj* dictatorial.

he'd /hi:d/ = **he had, he would**.

hedge /hedʒ/ I *n* **1** Bot haie *f*; **2** Fin protection *f* (**against** contre).

II *vtr* **1** lit planter une haie autour de [*area*]; **2** fig (evade) esquiver [*question*]; **3** Fin se protéger contre [*loss, risk*].
III *vi* (equivocate) se dérober.
IV **hedged** *pp adj* **1** [*field, paddock*] fermé; **~d with** bordé de; **2** fig **~d about with** truffé de [*problems, restrictions*].
IDIOMS **to ~ one's bets** se couvrir; **to look as if one has been dragged through a ~ backwards** avoir l'air tout ébouriffé.
■ **hedge against** Fin **~ against [sth]** se protéger contre [*inflation , loss*].

hedge: **~-clippers** *npl* cisailles *fpl* à haies; **~hog** *n* hérisson *m*.

hedgehop /ˈhedʒhɒp/ *vi* (*p prés etc* **-pp-**) faire du rase-mottes.

hedge: **~row** *n* haie *f*; **~ sparrow** *n* accenteur *m* mouchet; **~ trimmer** *n* taille-haies *m inv*.

hedonism /ˈhiːdənɪzəm/ *n* hédonisme *m*.

hedonist /ˈhiːdənɪst/ *n* hédoniste *mf*.

hedonistic /ˌhiːdəˈnɪstɪk/ *adj* hédoniste, hédonistique; **a ~ existence** une vie de sybarite.

heebie-jeebies○ /ˌhiːbɪˈdʒiːbɪz/ *npl* **the ~** la frousse○, le trac○.

heed /hiːd/ I *n* attention *f*, considération *f*; **to pay ~ to sb, to take ~ of sb** tenir compte de ce que dit qn; **to pay ~ to sth, to take ~ of sth** tenir compte de qch.
II *vtr* tenir compte de [*advice, warning*]; **without ~ing sth/sb** sans tenir compte de qch/des conseils de qn.

heedless /ˈhiːdlɪs/ *adj* (thoughtless) irréfléchi; (carefree) insouciant (**of** de).

heedlessly /ˈhiːdlɪslɪ/ *adv* à la légère, imprudemment.

heehaw /ˈhiːhɔː/ I *n* hi-han *m*.
II *excl* hi-han!
III *vi* faire hi-han.

heel /hiːl/ I *n* **1** Anat (of foot) talon *m*; **to turn on one's ~** tourner les talons; **a puppy at his ~(s)** un chiot sur ses talons; **to bring a dog to ~** rappeler un chien; **'~ boy!'** 'au pied!'; **to bring [sb] to ~** fig mater [*rebel*]; mettre [qn] au pas [*dissident, child, employee*]; **to come to ~** [*dog*] venir au pied; [*person*] fig se soumettre; **2** (of shoe, sock) talon *m*; **to click one's ~s** claquer des talons; **3** (of hand) talon *m*; **4** (of loaf, plant cutting) talon *m*; **5** Tech (of saw, golfclub, ski) talon *m*; **6** fig (power) botte *f*; **under the ~ of the enemy** sous la botte de l'ennemi; **7**○† GB (person) chameau○ *m*.
II **heels** *npl* (also **high ~s**) chaussures à (hauts) talons.
III *vtr* **1** (repair) refaire un talon à [*shoe*]; **2** Sport talonner [*ball*].
IDIOMS **to cool** ou **kick one's ~s** attendre, faire le pied de grue○; **we left him to cool his ~s for an hour** nous l'avons laissé poireauter○ pendant une heure; **to dig in one's ~s, to dig one's ~ in** (mulishly) se braquer; **I'm prepared to dig my ~s in on** ou **over this** je ne suis pas prêt à faire des compromis là-dessus; **to fall** ou **go head over ~s** (tumble) culbuter; **to fall/be head over ~s in love with sb** tomber/être éperdument amoureux de qn; **to be hard** ou **close on sb's ~s** être aux talons de qn; **to be hot on sb's ~s** talonner qn; **to come** ou **follow hard on the ~s of sth** suivre de près qch; **to kick up one's ~s** se défouler○; **to show a clean pair of ~s, to take to one's ~s** hum prendre ses jambes à son cou, s'enfuir.
■ **heel in**: **~ [sth] in, ~ in [sth]** Hort mettre [qch] en jauge [*plant, cutting*].
■ **heel over** [*boat*] gîter; [*object*] pencher.

heel bar ▶ 1692 *n* talon-minute *m*.

heeling /ˈhiːlɪŋ/ *n* talonnage *m*.

heelpiece /ˈhiːlpiːs/ *n* **1** (of stocking) talon *m*; **2** (of ski) talonnière *f*.

heft○ /heft/ *vtr* US (lift up) soulever; (feel weight) soupeser.

hefty /ˈheftɪ/ *adj* [*person*] costaud○; [*object*] pesant; [*blow*] puissant; [*portion*] imposant; [*bill, profit, sum*] considérable; **she earns a ~ salary** elle gagne gros; **they're paying a ~ price for it** c'est cher payé.

Hegelian /heɪˈgiːlɪən/ *n, adj* hégélien/-ienne (*m/f*).

hegemony /hɪˈdʒemənɪ, US ˈhedʒeməʊnɪ/ *n* hégémonie *f*.

Hegira /ˈhedʒɪrə, hɪˈdʒaɪərə/ *n* **the ~** l'hégire *f*; **the ~ calendar** le calendrier musulman.

heifer /ˈhefə(r)/ *n* génisse *f*.

heigh-ho /ˌheɪˈhəʊ/ *excl* allons-y gaiement○!

height /haɪt/ ▶ 1412 I *n* **1** (tallness) (of person) taille *f*; (of table, tower, tree) hauteur *f*; **a woman of average** ou **medium ~** une femme de taille moyenne; **what is your ~?** combien mesures-tu?; **to be 1 metre 60 cm in ~** [*person*] mesurer 1 mètre 60; [*pile, object*] faire 1 mètre 60 de haut; **to draw oneself up to one's full ~** se redresser; **2** (distance from the ground) (of shelf, person) hauteur *f*; (of mountain, plane) altitude *f*; **to gain/lose ~** prendre/perdre de l'altitude; **at a ~ of 200 metres** à 200 mètres d'altitude; **to fall from a ~ of 20 metres** tomber d'une hauteur de 20 mètres; **to dive from a great ~** plonger de très haut; **at shoulder ~** à hauteur d'épaule; **3** fig (peak) **at the ~ of the season** en pleine saison; **at the ~ of the rush-hour** en plein dans les heures de pointe; **at the ~ of the storm/crisis** au plus fort de l'orage/la crise; **to be at the ~ of one's success/popularity** être au faîte de son succès/sa popularité; **to be at the ~ of one's career** être au sommet de sa carrière; **a writer at the ~ of her powers** un écrivain à l'apogée de son talent; **the violence was at its ~** la violence était à son comble; **at its ~ the club had 200 members** le club au plus haut de sa fréquentation comptait 200 membres; **4** (utmost) **the ~ of** le comble de [*luxury, stupidity, cheek*]; **to be the ~ of fashion** être ce que l'on fait de plus à la mode.
II **heights** *npl* (high place) hauteurs *fpl*; **the snowy/wooded ~s** les monts enneigés/boisés; **to be scared of ~s** avoir le vertige; **to rise to** ou **reach great ~s** fig aller loin; **to reach new ~s of** aller encore plus loin dans [*perfection, skill*].

heighten /ˈhaɪtn/ I *vtr* intensifier [*emotion*]; renforcer [*desire*]; accroître [*curiosity*]; augmenter [*malaise, anxiety, tension, suspense*]; rendre [qch] plus vif/vive [*sensation*]; accentuer [*effect*]; **to ~ sb's awareness of** rendre qn plus conscient de.
II *vi* [*fear*] augmenter; [*tension*] monter; **his colour ~ed** il a rougi.
III **heightened** *pp adj* [*sensitivity*] très grand (*before n*); **a ~ed awareness of** une conscience plus grande de; **to have a ~ed sensitivity to** être plus sensible à.

heinie◑ /ˈhaɪnɪ/ *n* US fesses *fpl*.

heinous /ˈheɪnəs/ *adj* sout abominable; **a ~ crime** un crime odieux.

heir /eə(r)/ *n* **1** lit héritier/-ière *m/f* (**to** de); **his son and ~** son héritier; **~ apparent, ~ presumptive** héritier/-ière *m/f* présomptif/-ive (*sauf changement dans l'ordre de succession*); **rightful ~, ~-at-law** héritier/-ière *m/f* légitime; **to make sb one's ~** laisser ses biens à qn; **2** fig **to be ~ to** hériter de [*problems, projects*].

heiress /ˈeərɪs/ *n* héritière *f*.

heirloom /ˈeəluːm/ *n* **1** Jur héritage *m*; **2** gen **a family ~** un objet de famille.

heist○ /haɪst/ US I *n* (robbery) vol *m*; (armed) hold-up *m inv*.
II *vtr* cambrioler [*place*]; voler [*money, goods*].

held /held/ *prét, pp* ▶ **hold**.

Helen /ˈhelən/ *pr n* Hélène; **~ of Troy** Hélène de Troie.

helical /ˈhelɪkl, hiːlɪkl/ *adj* **1** Tech hélicoïdal; **2** Math hélicoïde.

helices /ˈhelɪsiːz, ˈhiː-/ *pl* ▶ **helix**.

helicopter /ˈhelɪkɒptə(r)/ I *n* hélicoptère *m*; **~ transfer/transport** transfert/transport héliporté; **by ~** en hélicoptère.
II *vtr* héliporter.
■ **helicopter in**: **~ [sth/sb] in, ~ in [sth/sb]** amener [qch/qn] en hélicoptère.
■ **helicopter out**: **~ [sth/sb] out, ~ out [sth/sb]** évacuer [qch/qn] par hélicoptère.

helicopter: **~ base** *n* hélistation *f*; **~ patrol** *n* patrouille *f* en hélicoptère; **~ pilot** ▶ 1692 *n* pilote *m* d'hélicoptère; **~ rescue** *n* opération *f* de sauvetage par hélicoptère; **~ station** *n* hélistation *f*.

helideck /ˈhelɪdek/ *n* Naut plate-forme *f* pour hélicoptères.

heliograph /ˈhiːlɪəgrɑːf, US -græf/ *n* héliographe *m*.

heliostat /ˈhiːlɪəstæt/ *n* héliostat *m*.

heliotrope /ˈhiːlɪətrəʊp/ *n, adj* héliotrope (*m*).

helipad /ˈhelɪpæd/ *n* (on ground) aire *f* d'atterrissage pour hélicoptères; (on building) plate-forme *f* pour hélicoptères.

heliport /ˈhelɪpɔːt/ *n* héliport *m*.

helium /ˈhiːlɪəm/ *n* hélium *m*.

helix /ˈhiːlɪks/ *n* (*pl* **-lices** ou **-lixes**) hélice *f*; **double ~** double hélice.

hell /hel/ I *n* **1** (also **Hell**) Relig enfer *m*; **to go to/be in ~** aller en/être en enfer; **may you rot in ~**†! que le diable t'emporte!; **I'll see him in ~ first**†! plutôt mourir!; **2**○ (unpleasant experience) enfer *m*; **life was ~ (on earth)** la vie était un enfer; **Mondays are sheer ~** le lundi, c'est l'enfer; **Oxford is ~ on a Saturday** Oxford est infernal le samedi; **to make sb's life ~ (for him/her)** rendre la vie infernale à qn; **it was ~ getting the work finished** on a eu toutes les peines du monde à terminer le travail; **to go through ~** connaître un calvaire (**doing** à faire); **3**○ (as intensifier) **a ~ of a waste/shock** un gâchis/un choc terrible; **it' s a ~ of a lot worse/easier** c'est nettement pire/plus facile; **he's one ~ of a smart guy** US c'est fou ce qu'il est intelligent○; **we had a ~ of a time** (bad) on en a bavé○; (good) on s'est payé du bon temps○; **you've got a ~ of a nerve!** tu ne manques pas de culot○!; **a ~ of a way to do sth** une drôle de façon de faire qch; **as jealous/guilty as ~** terriblement jaloux/coupable; **it sure as ~ wasn't me** une chose est sûre, ce n'était pas moi; **to run/fight like ~** courir/se battre de toutes ses forces; **let's get the ~ out of here!** barrons-nous◑!; **get the ~ out of here!** dégage!; **like ~ I will/you are!** pas question!; **'it's a good film'—'like ~ it is!'** 'c'est un bon film'—'tu rigoles○!'; **why/who the ~?** pourquoi/qui bon Dieu○?; **what the ~ are you doing?** qu'est-ce que tu fais, bon Dieu○?; **how the ~ should I know?** comment je pourrais le savoir, bon Dieu○?; **oh, what the ~!** (too bad) tant pis!; **oh, to** ou **the ~ with it!** je laisse tomber○!
II◑ *excl* bon Dieu○!; **~'s bells!, ~'s teeth!** nom de Dieu!; **go to ~**○! va te faire voir○!; **to ~ with all of you!**○ allez vous faire voir○!
IDIOMS **all ~**○ **broke** ou **was let loose** le raffut a éclaté; **come ~ or high water**○ coûte que coûte; **he/she has been to ~ and back** il/elle revient de loin; **there was/will be ~ to pay** il/elle l'a payé/le paiera cher; **to be ~**○ **on sth** US être un enfer○ pour qch; **to beat** ou **knock ~ out of sb/sth** cogner qn/qch comme un sourd○; **to catch ~**○ US prendre un savon○; **to do sth for the ~ of it**○ faire qch pour le plaisir; **to give sb ~**◑ (cause to suffer) rendre la vie dure à qn; (scold) engueuler○ qn; **go on, give 'em ~**◑ vas-y, montre-leur○; **not to have a cat in ~'s chance** ou **a snowball's chance in ~**◑ ne pas avoir une foutue◑ chance; **not to have a hope in ~**◑ **of doing** ne pas avoir une foutue◑ chance de faire; **to play (merry) ~ with sth**○

chambouler qch○; **to raise (merry) ~**○ faire une scène (**with sb** à qn).
■ **hell around**○ US mener une vie de patachon○.

he'll /'hi:əl/ = **he will**.

hellacious○ /hə'leɪʃəs/ *adj* US atroce.

hell-bent /ˌhel'bent/ *adj* **~ on doing** décidé à faire.

hellcat /'helkæt/ *n* harpie *f*.

hellebore /'helɪbɔ:(r)/ *n* ellébore *m*.

Hellene /'heli:n/ *n* Hellène *mf*.

Hellenic /he'li:nɪk, US he'lenɪk/ *adj* [*civilization, language*] hellénique; [*people*] hellène; **a ~ cruise** une croisière en Grèce.

heller◑ /'helə(r)/, **hellion**◑ /'helɪən/ *n* US fripouille *f*, casse-cou *m inv*.

hellfire /ˌhel'faɪə(r)/ **I** *n* tourments *mpl* de l'enfer.
II *modif* [*preacher, sermon*] apocalyptique.

hell: **~-for-leather**○ *adj, adv* [*run, ride*] à toute allure; [*drive*] à tombeau ouvert; **~hole** *n* (prison, trenches, war zone) enfer *m*; (hovel) bouge *m*.

hellish /'helɪʃ/ **I** *adj* **1** (hell-like) [*sight, vision*] d'enfer (*after n*); [*war, experience*] infernal; **2**○ (awful) [*motorway, traffic, racket*] infernal○.
II◑† *adv* [*dark, difficult*] drôlement.

hellishly○ /'helɪʃlɪ/ *adv* [*cold, lonely, painful*] terriblement.

hello /hə'ləʊ/ *excl* **1** (greeting) bonjour!; (on phone) (receiving a call) allô!; (making a call) allô bonjour!; **2** (in surprise) tiens!

Hell's angel *n* ≈ blouson *m* noir.

helluva◑ /'heləvə/ = **hell of a**; ▶ **hell**.

hell week *n* US Univ semaine *f* du bizutage.

helm /helm/ *n* lit, fig barre *f*; **to take the ~** prendre la barre; **to be at the ~** être à la barre.

helmet /'helmɪt/ *n* gen casque *m*; Hist heaume *m*.

helmeted /'helmɪtɪd/ *adj* casqué.

helmsman /'helmzmən/ *n* timonier *m*.

help /help/ **I** *n* **1** (assistance) aide *f*; (in an emergency) secours *m*; **to need some ~ with the cooking/gardening** avoir besoin d'aide pour faire la cuisine/le jardin; **with the ~ of** à l'aide de [*stick, knife*]; avec l'aide de [*person*]; **can I be of ~ (to you)?** puis-je faire quelque chose pour vous?; **to be of ~ to sb** [*person*] rendre service à qn; [*information, map*] être utile à qn; **the information was of little ~ to us** l'information ne nous a pas été d'un grand secours or ne nous a pas été très utile; **she was a great ~ to us** elle nous a beaucoup aidés, elle nous a été d'un grand secours; **you're a great ~!** iron tu es vraiment d'un grand secours!; **to come to sb's ~** venir au secours de qn, venir en aide à qn; **to go to sb's ~** aller au secours de qn, prêter secours or assistance à qn; **to cry** ou **shout for ~** appeler à l'aide or au secours; **he is beyond ~, he is past (all) ~** on ne peut plus rien pour lui; **it's a ~ if you can speak the language** ça aide de parler la langue; **a degree would be a ~** un diplôme aiderait bien; **the tablets were no ~** les comprimés n'ont pas servi à grand-chose; **there's no ~ for it** il n'y a rien à faire; **she needs (professional) ~** gen elle devrait consulter un professionnel; (from psychiatrist) elle devrait voir un psychiatre; **2** (also **daily ~**) (cleaning woman) femme *f* de ménage; **3** ¢ (staff) domestiques *mpl*; (on farm) ouvriers *mpl* agricoles; **they need extra ~ in the bar** ils ont besoin d'aide supplémentaire au bar.
II *excl* au secours!; **~! I've got nothing to wear for tonight!** hum mince alors○! je n'ai rien à mettre pour ce soir!
III *vtr* **1** (assist) aider (**to do** à faire); (more urgently) secourir; **we got the children to ~ us** nous nous sommes fait aider par les enfants; **we must all ~ each other** nous devons tous nous entraider or nous aider les uns les autres; **she ~ed them with the decorations** elle les a aidés pour les décorations; **can you ~ me with this sack please?** est-ce que tu peux m'aider à porter ce sac s'il te plaît?; **can I ~ you?** (in shop) vous désirez?; (on phone) j'écoute; (at reception desk) je peux vous aider?; **to ~ sb across/down/out** aider qn à traverser/descendre/sortir; **I ~ed him to his feet** je l'ai aidé à se lever; **to ~ sb on/off with** aider qn à mettre/enlever [*garment, boot*]; **she ~ed him through some difficult times** elle l'a aidé à traverser des moments difficiles; **2** (improve) améliorer [*situation, problem*]; **he didn't ~ matters by writing that letter** il n'a rien arrangé en écrivant cette lettre; **getting drenched didn't ~ my cold** le fait de me faire tremper jusqu'aux os n'a pas arrangé mon rhume; **3** (contribute) **to ~ to do** contribuer à faire; **her article ~ed (to) increase public awareness of the problem** son article a contribué à sensibiliser le public à ce problème; **the injection should ~ (to) ease the pain** la piqûre devrait soulager la douleur; **these flowers will ~ (to) brighten the room** ces fleurs devraient égayer la pièce; **this policy ~s (to) keep prices down** cette politique favorise la baisse des prix; **4** (serve) **to ~ sb to** offrir [qch] à qn [*food, wine*]; **5** (prevent) **it can't be ~ed!** on n'y peut rien!, tant pis!; **she can't ~ the way she was brought up** elle ne peut rien changer à la façon dont elle a été élevée; **I can't ~ the way I feel** je n'y peux rien; **he can't ~ being awkward/stupid!** ce n'est pas de sa faute s'il est maladroit/stupide!; **I can't ~ it if the car breaks down!** je n'y peux rien or ce n'est pas de ma faute si la voiture tombe en panne!; **I'm sorry I slammed the door—I couldn't ~ it** excusez-moi d'avoir claqué la porte—je ne l'ai pas fait exprès; **not if I can ~ it!** sûrement pas!; **he won't win if I can ~ it** je vais faire tout mon possible pour l'empêcher de gagner; **don't tell her any more than you can ~** ne lui dis pas plus qu'il n'en faut; **try not to change gear more often than you can ~** essayez de changer de vitesse le moins (souvent) possible; **she never works harder than she can ~** elle travaille toujours le strict minimum; **I can't ~ that** je n'y peux rien; **you can't ~ but pity him** on ne peut pas s'empêcher d'avoir pitié de lui.
IV *vi* **1** (assist) aider; **I was only trying to ~!** je voulais seulement aider!; **he never ~s with the cooking/housework** il n'aide jamais à faire la cuisine/le ménage; **they offered to ~ with the expenses** ils ont offert d'aider à payer les frais or de participer aux frais; **this map doesn't ~ much** cette carte n'est pas d'un grand secours or ne sert pas à grand-chose; **will it ~ if I give you a clue?** est-ce que ça t'aiderait si je te donnerait un indice?; **every little ~s** (when donating money) tous les dons sont les bienvenus; (when saving) les petits ruisseaux forment les grandes rivières; **2** (be an improvement) **would it ~ if I turned the light off?** est-ce que ce serait mieux si j'éteignais?; **it might ~ if we knew where they lived** ça nous arrangerait de savoir où ils habitent, ça serait déjà quelque chose si on savait où ils habitent; **she tried going to bed earlier, but it didn't ~ much** elle a commencé à se coucher plus tôt, mais ça n'a pas servi à grand-chose.
V *v refl* **1** (serve) **to ~ oneself** se servir; **I ~ed myself from the fruit bowl** je me suis servi dans la coupe de fruits; **~ yourselves!** servez- vous!; **~ yourselves to coffee/cigarettes** prenez du café/des cigarettes; **~ yourselves to some more cake** reprenez un peu de gâteau; **2 to ~ oneself to** (pinch) piquer○; **he has been ~ing himself to the till** il a piqué○ (de l'argent) dans la caisse; **3** (prevent) **to ~ oneself** s'en empêcher; **I tried not to laugh, but I couldn't ~ myself** j'ai essayé de ne pas rire, mais je n'ai pas pu m'en empêcher or c'était plus fort que moi.
■ **help along**: ¶ **~ [sb] along** aider [qn] à marcher [*infirm person*]; ¶ **~ [sth] along** faire avancer [*process, negotiations, project*].
■ **help out**: ¶ **~ out** aider, donner un coup de main○; ¶ **~ [sb] out** gen aider, donner un coup de main○ à; (financially) dépanner○; (in crisis) tirer [qn] d'embarras [*person*]; **his parents ~ him out with the rent** ses parents l'aident à payer le loyer.

helper /'helpə(r)/ *n* gen aide *mf*, assistant/-e *m/f*; (for handicapped person) aide *f* sociale.

helpful /'helpfl/ *adj* [*tool, machine, gadget*] utile; [*person*] serviable, obligeant; [*remedy*] efficace, utile; [*advice, suggestion, information, book, guide*] utile; **I was only trying to be ~!** j'essayais seulement de me rendre utile!; **the staff were very ~** le personnel a été serviable; **thank you, you've been most ~** merci beaucoup de votre aide; **it would be ~ if we knew how much it was going to cost** ça nous arrangerait de savoir le prix.

helpfully /'helpfəlɪ/ *adv* [*explain, suggest, indicate*] obligeamment, gentiment; **this road is not very ~ signposted** sur cette route, la signalisation n'est pas d'un grand secours.

helpfulness /'helpflnɪs/ *n* (of person) obligeance *f*; (of advice, information, guide, tool etc) utilité *f*.

helping /'helpɪŋ/ *n* gen portion *f*; **I took a small ~ of cream** j'ai pris un (tout) petit peu de crème; **would you like another ~ of meat?** voulez-vous encore de la viande?; **he took a second ~ of potatoes** il a repris des pommes de terre; **there'll be no second ~s** il n'y aura pas de rab○ or de deuxième tournée; **this is my third ~** j'en reprends pour la deuxième fois.

helping hand *n* secours *m*; **to give** ou **lend a ~ to sb** donner un coup de main à qn.

help key *n* Comput touche *f* d'aide.

helpless /'helplɪs/ *adj* **1** (powerless) [*person*] impuissant; (because of infirmity, disability) impotent; [*expression*] d'impuissance; **to feel ~** se sentir impuissant; **the government is quite ~ in this matter** le gouvernement est tout à fait impuissant or n'y peut rien dans cette affaire; **she was ~ to do anything about it** elle ne pouvait rien y faire; **I was ~ to prevent his leaving** je ne pouvais pas l'empêcher de partir; **I'm not totally ~!** je ne suis pas complètement impotent!; **they were ~ with laughter** ils étaient morts de rire○; **2** (defenceless) [*person*] sans défense; [*victim*] malheureux/-euse (*before n*); **3** (destitute) [*orphan, family*] démuni.

helplessly /'helplɪslɪ/ *adv* [*watch, observe*] sans pouvoir rien faire; [*struggle, try*] en vain, désespérément; **he looked at me ~** il m'a jeté un regard où se lisait l'impuissance; **'I don't know,' he said ~** 'je ne sais pas,' dit-il d'un air découragé or (stronger) d'un air désemparé; **to look on ~** assister en spectateur impuissant (**as** alors que); **they were laughing ~** ils étaient morts de rire○.

helplessness /'helplɪsnɪs/ *n* **1** (powerlessness) impuissance *f*; (because of infirmity, disability) impotence *f*; **2** (defencelessness) vulnérabilité *f*.

help: **~line** *n* service *m* d'assistance (téléphonique); **~mate**†, **~meet**† *n* (spouse) époux *m*, épouse *f*; (companion) compagnon *m*, compagne *f*.

Helsinki /hel'sɪŋkɪ/ ▶ **1818** *pr n* Helsinki.

helter-skelter /ˌheltə'skeltə(r)/ **I** *n* GB toboggan *m* (en spirale).
II *adj* [*rush, account*] désordonné.
III *adv* **to run ~** courir comme un dératé○ (or des dératés○).

hem /hem/ **I** *n* ourlet *m*; **to take up/let down the ~ on** raccourcir/rallonger [*garment*].

> **her**
>
> When used as a direct object pronoun, *her* is translated by *la* (*l'* before a vowel). Note that the object pronoun normally comes before the verb in French and that in compound tenses like perfect and past perfect the past participle agrees with the pronoun:
>
> *I know her* = je la connais
> *I've already seen her* = je l'ai déjà vue
>
> In imperatives, the direct object pronoun is translated by *la* and comes after the verb:
>
> *catch her!* = attrape-la!
> (*note the hyphen*)
>
> When used as an indirect object pronoun, *her* is translated by *lui*:
>
> *I've given her the book* = je lui ai donné le livre
> *I've given it to her* = je le lui ai donné
>
> In imperatives, the indirect object pronoun is translated by *lui* and comes after the verb:
>
> *phone her* = téléphone-lui
> *give them to her* = donne-les-lui
> (*note the hyphens*)
>
> After prepositions and after the verb *to be* the translation is *elle*:
>
> *he did it for her* = il l'a fait pour elle
> *it's her* = c'est elle
>
> When translating *her* as a determiner (*her house* etc.) remember that in French possessive adjectives, like most other adjectives, agree in gender and number with the noun they qualify; *her* is translated by *son* + masculine singular noun (*son chien*), *sa* + feminine singular noun (*sa maison*) BUT *son* + feminine noun beginning with a vowel or mute 'h' (*son assiette*), and *ses* + plural noun (*ses enfants*).
>
> For *her* used with parts of the body **▶ 1037**.

II *vtr* (*p prés etc* **-mm-**) faire un ourlet à [*garment*]; ourler [*linen*].
■ **hem in**: **~ [sb/sth] in, ~ in [sb/sth]** cerner [*person, troops*]; **to be ~med in** être cerné; **to feel ~med in** fig se sentir coincé (**by** par).

hemiplegia /ˌhemɪˈpliːdʒɪə/ *n* hémiplégie *f*.

hemiplegic /ˌhemɪˈpliːdʒɪk/ *n, adj* hémiplégique (*mf*).

hemisphere /ˈhemɪsfɪə(r)/ *n* Med, Geog hémisphère *m*; **the western ~** journ le monde occidental.

hemistich /ˈhemɪstɪk/ *n* hémistiche *m*.

hemline /ˈhemlaɪn/ *n* ourlet *m*; **~s are going up/coming down** les robes raccourcissent/rallongent.

hemlock /ˈhemlɒk/ *n* ciguë *f*.

hemp /hemp/ **I** *n* **1** (plant, fibre) chanvre *m*; **2** (drug) cannabis *m*; **Indian ~** chanvre indien.
II *modif* [*rope, cloth*] de chanvre.

hemstitch /ˈhemstɪtʃ/ **I** *n* point *m* d'ourlet à jours.
II *vtr* ourler [qch] à jours.

hen /hen/ **I** *n* poule *f*.
II *adj* femelle.

hence /hens/ *adv* sout **1** (from now) d'ici; **three days ~** d'ici or dans trois jours; **2** (for this reason) (*before n*) d'où; (*before adj*) donc; **there is a strike, ~ the delay** il y a une grève, d'où le retard; **she was slimmer and ~ more active** elle était plus mince et donc plus active; **3‡** (from this place) d'ici.

henceforth /ˌhensˈfɔːθ/, **henceforward** /hensˈfɔːwəd/ *adv* littér (from now on) dorénavant, désormais; (from then on) dès lors.

henchman /ˈhentʃmən/ *n* **1** (supporter) homme *m* de confiance; (accomplice) homme *m* de main; péj acolyte *m*; **2‡** (squire) écuyer *m*.

hen: **~ coop** *n* cage *f* à poules; **~ harrier** *n* busard *m* Saint-Martin; **~house** *n* poulailler *m*.

henna /ˈhenə/ **I** *n* henné *m*.
II *modif* [*rinse, treatment*] de henné; [*shampoo*] au henné.
III *vtr* (*3e pers sg prés* **~s**; *prét, pp* **~ed**) passer [qch] au henné.

hen party *n* soirée *f* passée entre femmes (*avant le mariage de l'une d'elles*).

hen-pecked /ˈhenpekt/ *adj* **he is ~, he is a ~ husband** sa femme le mène par le bout du nez.

hen run *n* enclos *m* à poules.

Henry /ˈhenrɪ/ *pr n* Henri.

hep○ /hep/ *adj* US branché○; **to be ~ to sth** être au parfum de qch.

heparin /ˈhepərɪn/ *n* héparine *f*.

hepatitis /ˌhepəˈtaɪtɪs/ **▶ 1354** *n* hépatite *f*.

heptagon /ˈheptəgən, US -gɒn/ *n* heptagone *m*.

heptathlon /hepˈtæθlən, -lɒn/ **▶ 1282** *n* heptathlon *m*.

her /hɜː(r), hə(r)/ **I** *pron* (direct object) la, l'; (indirect object) lui; **it's ~** c'est elle; **I did it for ~** je l'ai fait pour elle.
II *det* son/sa/ses.

Heraclitus /ˌherəˈklaɪtəs/ *pr n* Héraclite.

herald /ˈherəld/ **I** *n* **1** lit héraut *m*; **~-at-arms** héraut d'armes; **2** fig signe *m* avant-coureur; **the Sixties, ~ of a new era** les années soixante, qui marquent le début d'une époque.
II *vtr* (also **~ in**) annoncer, proclamer; **much ~ed** tant annoncé.

heraldic /heˈrældɪk/ *adj* héraldique; **~ device** emblème *m*.

heraldry /ˈherəldrɪ/ *n* (study, history) héraldique *f*; (pomp) cérémonial *m* somptueux; **book of ~** armorial *m*.

Hérault **▶ 1163** *pr n* Hérault *m*; **in/to the ~** dans l'Hérault.

herb /hɜːb/ *n* (plant) herbe *f*; (for cooking) herbe *f* aromatique; (with medicinal properties) plante *f* or herbe *f* médicinale; Pharm plante *f* or herbe *f* officinale; **mixed ~s** ≈ herbes de Provence; **fresh ~s** fines herbes.

herbaceous /hɜːˈbeɪʃəs/ *adj* herbacé; **~ border** massif *m*.

herbage /ˈhɜːbɪdʒ/ *n* Agric herbage *m*.

herbal /ˈhɜːbl/ **I** *n* herbier *m*.
II *adj* [*remedy*] à base de plantes; [*pillow*] parfumé.

herbalist /ˈhɜːbəlɪst/ **▶ 1692** *n* herboriste *mf*; **~'s shop** herboristerie *f*.

herb garden *n* jardin *m* d'herbes aromatiques.

herbivore /ˈhɜːbɪvɔː(r)/ *n* herbivore *m*.

herbivorous /hɜːˈbɪvərəs/ *adj* herbivore.

herb tea, herbal tea *n* tisane *f*, infusion *f*.

Herculean /ˌhɜːkjʊˈliːən/ *adj* herculéen/éenne.

Hercules /ˈhɜːkjʊliːz/ *pr n* Hercule.

herd /hɜːd/ **I** *n* (of sheep, cattle) troupeau *m*; (of horses) troupe *f*, bande *f*; (of reindeer) harde *f*; fig, pej (of people) troupeau *m*.
II *vtr* (drive) rassembler [*animals*]; rassembler [qn] en troupeau [*people*]; **the prisoners were all ~ed into one room** les prisonniers ont été entassés dans une pièce.
III *vi* **to ~ into sth** s'assembler dans qch.
IDIOMS **to follow the ~** fig être un mouton de Panurge.
■ **herd together** se rassembler; (closely) se masser.

herd instinct *n* instinct *m* grégaire.

herdsman /ˈhɜːdzmən/ **▶ 1692** *n* gardien *m* de troupeau.

here /hɪə(r)/

> ■ **Note** When *here* is used to indicate the location of an object/point etc close to the speaker, it is generally translated by *ici*: *come and sit here* = viens t'asseoir ici.
> – When the location is not so clearly defined, *là* is the usual translation: *he's not here at the moment* = il n'est pas là pour l'instant.
> – Remember that *voici* is used to translate *here is* when the speaker is drawing attention to an object/a place/a person etc physically close to him or her.
> – For examples and particular usages, see entry below.

I *adv* **1** (indicating place) ici; **let's stop ~** arrêtons-nous ici; **sign ~ please** veuillez signer ici s'il vous plaît; **stand ~** mettez-vous ici; **far from/near ~** loin/près d'ici; **two kilometres from ~** à deux kilomètres d'ici; **come over ~** venez par ici; **up to ~, down to ~** jusqu'ici; **put it in ~** mettez-le ici; **I'm up ~** je suis là-haut; **~ below** (in text) ci-dessous; **those persons ~ present** Jur les personnes ici présentes; **~ lies** (on tombstone) ci-gît; **since you were last ~** depuis ta dernière visite ici; **following a visit ~ by members** suite à la venue des membres; **~ and there** (in places) par endroits; **2** (to draw attention) **I have ~**... j'ai ici...; **~ they are/she comes!** les/la voici!; **~ comes the bus** voilà le bus; **~ you are** (offering sth) tiens, tenez; **~'s a screwdriver** tiens voilà un tournevis; **this thing ~ is** ceci est; **this paragraph/sales assistant ~** ce paragraphe/vendeur; **my colleague ~ will show you** mon collègue va vous montrer; **which one? this one ~ or that one?** lequel? celui-ci ou celui-là?; **it says ~ that** c'est marqué ici que; **~'s what you do** voilà ce qu'il faut faire; **~'s why** je vais vous expliquer pourquoi; **3** (indicating presence, arrival) **she's not ~ right now** elle n'est pas là pour le moment; **'Matthew?'—'~ sir'** (revealing whereabouts) 'Matthew?'—'ici Monsieur'; (during roll call) 'Matthew?'—'présent Monsieur'; **~ we are at last** nous voilà enfin, nous voici arrivés; **when will he be getting ~?** quand est-ce qu'il arrivera? ; **the train will be ~ any minute** le train va arriver d'un moment à l'autre; **we get off ~** c'est là qu'on descend; **4** (indicating juncture) **now that summer's ~** maintenant que c'est l'été; **~' s our chance** voilà notre chance; **I may be wrong ~** je me trompe peut-être; **so ~ you are, a bachelor of 25** te voilà donc, célibataire à vingt-cinq ans; **▶ here and now**; **5**○ (emphatic) **this ~ contraption** ce truc; **look** ou **see ~ you!** écoute-moi bien toi!
II○ *excl* **~ stop that!** hé là arrêtez ça!; **~ hang on a minute!** hé attends une minute!
IDIOMS **~ goes!** c'est parti!; **~'s hoping** j'espère; **~'s to our success/to you!** à notre succès/la tienne!; **~ there and everywhere** partout, par-ci par-là; **to be ~ there and everywhere** fig [*person*] être au four et au moulin; **it's neither ~ nor there** ce n'est pas le problème; **~ we go**○! (sneeringly) c'est parti!, nous y voilà!

hereabout US, **hereabouts** GB /ˈhɪərəbaʊt(s)/ *adv* par ici.

hereafter /hɪərˈɑːftə(r)/ **I** *n* **the ~** l'au-delà *m*.
II *adv* Jur ci-après.

here and now **I** *n* **the ~** (present) le présent; (life before death) la vie ici-bas; **a poet of the ~** un poète des temps modernes.
II *adv* immédiatement; **tell me ~ where you've been!** dis-moi immédiatement où tu as été!

hereby /hɪəˈbaɪ/ *adv* Admin, Jur **I ~ promise that** (in document) je, soussigné, promets que; **I ~ declare that** (in document) je déclare par la présente que; **I ~ declare him elected** je le déclare solennellement élu; **he is ~ licensed to sell** le présent document l'autorise à vendre.

hereditary /hɪˈredɪtrɪ, US -terɪ/ *adj* héréditaire.

heredity /hɪˈredətɪ/ *n* hérédité *f*.

Hereford and Worcester /ˈherɪfəd ənd ˈwʊstə(r)/ **▶ 1624** *pr n* Hereford and Worcester *m*.

herein /ˈhɪərɪn/ *adv* Jur (at beginning of document) ci-après; (at end) ci-dessus.

hereinafter /ˌhɪərɪnˈɑːftə(r)/ *adv* Jur = **hereafter** II.

heresy /ˈherəsɪ/ *n* (all contexts) hérésie *f*.

heretic /ˈherətɪk/ *n* hérétique *m*.

heretical /hɪˈretɪkl/ *adj* hérétique.

hereto /hɪəˈtuː/ *adv* **1** (of this fact) **as witness ~** comme témoin des faits; **2** (to this) **attached ~** ci-joint; (to this agreement) **the parties ~** les parties concernées.

heretofore /ˌhɪətuːˈfɔː(r)/ *adv* Jur jusqu'ici.

hereupon /ˌhɪərəˈpɒn/ *adv* sout **~, they began shouting** c'est à ce moment-là qu'ils ont commencé à crier.

herewith /ˌhɪəˈwɪð/ *adv* sout ci-joint.

heritable /ˈherɪtəbl/ *adj* Scot Jur transmissible.

heritage /ˈherɪtɪdʒ/ *n* **1†** sout (inheritance) héritage *m*; **2** (cultural) patrimoine *m*.

herky-jerky○ /ˌhɜːkɪˈdʒɜːkɪ/ *adj* US saccadé.

hermaphrodite /hɜːˈmæfrədaɪt/ *n, adj* hermaphrodite (*m*).

hermaphroditic /hɜːˌmæfrəˈdɪtɪk/ *adj* hermaphrodite.

hermeneutic /ˌhɜːmɪˈnjuːtɪk/ **I hermeneutics** *n* (+ *v sg*) herméneutique *f*.
II *adj* herméneutique.

Hermes /ˈhɜːmiːz/ *pr n* Hermès.

hermetic /hɜːˈmetɪk/ *adj* hermétique.

hermetically /ˈhɜːˈmetɪklɪ/ *adv* hermétiquement; **~ sealed** hermétiquement fermé.

hermit /ˈhɜːmɪt/ *n* ermite *m*.

hermitage /ˈhɜːmɪtɪdʒ/ *n* ermitage *m*.

hermit crab *n* bernard-l'ermite *m inv*.

hernia /ˈhɜːnɪə/ *n* (*pl* **~s** ou **~e**) hernie *f*.

hero /ˈhɪərəʊ/ *n* (*pl* **~es**) héros *m*; **a ~'s welcome** un accueil triomphal; **the ~ of the hour** le héros du jour.

Herod /ˈherəd/ *pr n* Hérode.

heroic /hɪˈrəʊɪk/ *adj* [*person, deed*] héroïque; **~ attempts** des efforts épiques.

heroically /hɪˈrəʊɪklɪ/ *adv* héroïquement.

heroic couplet *n* Literat distique *m* héroïque.

heroics /hɪˈrəʊɪks/ *npl* mélodrame *m*; **no ~ please** inutile de jouer les héros.

heroic treatment *n* acharnement *m* thérapeutique.

heroin /ˈherəʊɪn/ *n* héroïne *f*; **to come off ~** arrêter de prendre de l'héroïne; **to be on ~** prendre de l'héroïne.

heroin: **~ addict** *n* héroïnomane *mf*; **~ addiction** *n* héroïnomanie *f*.

heroine /ˈherəʊɪn/ *n* héroïne *f*.

heroism /ˈherəʊɪzəm/ *n* héroïsme *m*.

heron /ˈherən/ *n* héron *m*.

hero sandwich US sandwich *m* géant.

hero-worship /ˈhɪərəʊwɜːʃɪp/ **I** *n* culte *m* du héros, adulation *f*.
II *vtr* (*p prés etc* **-pp-**, US **-p-**) aduler.

herpes /ˈhɜːpiːz/ **▶ 1354** *n* herpès *m*.

herring /ˈherɪŋ/ *n* hareng *m*.

herring boat *n* harenguier *m*.

herringbone /ˈherɪŋbəʊn/ **I** *n* **1** (fabric) tissu *m* à chevrons; **2** (design) motif *m* à chevrons; **3** (ski climb) montée *f* en ciseaux.
II *modif* **in a ~ pattern** en chevron.

herringbone stitch *n* point *m* de chausson.

herring gull *n* goéland *m* argenté.

hers /hɜːz/

■ **Note** In French, possessive pronouns reflect the gender and number of the noun they are standing for; *hers* is translated by *le sien, la sienne, les siens, les siennes*, according to what is being referred to.
– For examples and particular usages, see the entry below.

pron **my car is red but ~ is blue** ma voiture est rouge mais la sienne est bleue; **the green pen is ~** le stylo vert est à elle; **which house is ~?** sa maison c'est laquelle?; **I'm a friend of ~** c'est une amie à moi; **it's not ~** ce n'est pas à elle, ce n'est pas le sien or la sienne; **the money wasn't ~ to give away** elle n'avait pas à donner cet argent; **~ was not an easy task** sa tâche n'était pas facile; **I saw her with that dog of ~!** péj je l'ai vue avec son sale chien○!

herself /həˈself/

■ **Note** When used as a reflexive pronoun, direct and indirect, *herself* is translated by *se* (*s'* before a vowel): *she's enjoying herself* = elle s'amuse bien; *she's cut herself* = elle s'est coupée.
– When used in emphasis, the translation is *elle-même*: *she herself didn't know* = elle ne le savait pas elle-même.
– After a preposition the translation is *elle* or *elle-même*: *she can be proud of herself* = elle peut être fière d'elle *or* d'elle-même.

pron **1** (refl) se, s'; **she's hurt ~** elle s'est blessée; **2** (emphatic) elle-même; **she ~ said that...** elle a dit elle-même que...; **3** (after prep) elle, elle-même; **for ~** pour elle, pour elle-même; **4** (expressions) **(all) by ~** toute seule; **she's not ~ today** elle n'est pas dans son assiette aujourd'hui.

Hertfordshire /ˈhɑːtfədʃɪə(r)/ **▶ 1624** *pr n* Hertfordshire *m*.

Herts *n* GB Post *abrév écrite* **▶ Hertfordshire**.

hertz /hɜːts/ *n* hertz *m*.

Hertzian wave /ˈhɜːtsɪən/ *n* onde *f* hertzienne.

he's /hiːz/ = **he is, he has**.

hesitancy /ˈhezɪtənsɪ/ *n* hésitation *f*; (reluctance) réticence *f*; **~ about doing** réticence à faire.

hesitant /ˈhezɪtənt/ *adj* **1** (nervous) [*person, expression, reply*] hésitant, peu assuré; [*step, policy*] incertain; **to be ~ about doing** hésiter à faire; **to be/look ~** ne pas être/ne pas avoir l'air sûr de soi; **his reading/singing was ~** il lisait/chantait d'un ton mal assuré; **2** (reticent) **to be ~ about** être réticent quant à [*plan, scheme, system*].

hesitantly /ˈhezɪtəntlɪ/ *adv* **1** (nervously) [*act, do*] avec hésitation; [*speak*] d'un ton hésitant; [*walk*] d'un pas hésitant; **2** (reticently) avec réticence.

hesitate /ˈhezɪteɪt/ *vi* hésiter (**over** sur); **to ~ to do** hésiter à faire; **I ~ to recommend this product/make a judgment** je me garderai de recommander ce produit/de faire un jugement; **she was hesitating over a new hat** elle ne pouvait décider quel chapeau acheter; **to ~ at nothing** ne reculer devant rien.
IDIOMS **he who ~s is lost** Prov à hésiter on n'obtient rien.

hesitation /ˌhezɪˈteɪʃn/ *n* hésitation *f*; **to have no ~ in doing** n'avoir aucune hésitation à faire; **there is no room for ~** il n'est plus temps de balancer; **without the slightest** ou **a moment's ~** sans la moindre hésitation.

Hesperides /heˈsperɪdiːz/ **▶ 1381** *pr npl* **the ~** (nymphs) les Hespérides *fpl*; (garden) (+ *v sg*) jardin *m* des Hespérides; (islands) les Hespérides *fpl*.

hessian /ˈhesɪən, US ˈheʃn/ *n* toile *f* de jute.

hetero○ /ˈhetərəʊ/ *adj, n* hétéro○ (*mf*), hétérosexuel/-elle (*m/f*).

heterodox /ˈhetərədɒks/ *adj* hétérodoxe.

heterodoxy /ˈhetərədɒksɪ/ *n* hétérodoxie *f*.

heterogeneous /ˌhetərəˈdʒiːnɪəs/ *adj* hétérogène.

heterosexual /ˌhetərəˈsekʃʊəl/ *n, adj* hétérosexuel/-elle (*m/f*).

heterosexuality /ˌhetərəˌsekʃʊˈælətɪ/ *n* hétérosexualité *f*.

het up○ /ˌhetˈʌp/ *adj* énervé; **to get ~ about** ou **over sth** se mettre dans tous ses états à cause de qch; **why are you so ~?** qu'est-ce que tu as à t'exciter comme ça○?

heuristic /hjʊəˈrɪstɪk/ **I heuristics** *n* (+ *v sg*) heuristique *f*.
II *adj* heuristique.

hew /hjuː/ (*pp* **hewn**) **I** *vtr* abattre [*wood, coal*]; tailler [*stone, branch*] (**out of** dans); **to be ~n in sth** [*letters, pattern*] être gravé dans qch; **to ~ a path through sth** se tailler un chemin à travers qch.
II *vi* US **to ~ to sth** se conformer à qch.

hex○ /heks/ US **I** *n* sort *m*; **to put a ~ on sth/sb** jeter un sort à qn/qch.
II *vtr* jeter un sort à.

hexadecimal /ˌheksəˈdesɪml/ *n, adj* hexadécimal (*m*).

hexadecimal notation *n* Comput numération *f* hexadécimale.

hexagon /ˈheksəgən, US -gɒn/ *n* hexagone *m*.

hexagonal /hekˈsægənl/ *adj* hexagonal.

hexagonal key *n* clé *f* à six pans.

hexagram /ˈheksəgræm/ *n* hexagramme *m*.

hexameter /hekˈsæmɪtə(r)/ *n* hexamètre *m*; **in ~s** en hexamètres.

hey○ /heɪ/ *excl* (call for attention) hé!, eh!; (in protest) dis donc!; **~ Mum, what's for lunch?** dis, maman, qu'est-ce qu'on mange?

heyday /ˈheɪdeɪ/ *n* (of movement etc) âge *m* d'or; (of person) beaux jours *mpl*; **in my ~** (at my best) quand j'étais dans la fleur de l'âge; (at peak of my fame) quand j'étais au sommet de ma gloire.

hey presto /ˌheɪ ˈprestəʊ/ *excl* ô miracle!, et passez muscade!; (in narrative) comme par miracle.

hg *n* (*abrév écrite* = **hectogram**) hg *m*.

H-girder *n* = **H-beam**.

HGV GB (*abrév* = **heavy goods vehicle**) **I** *n* PL *m*, poids *m* lourd.
II *modif* **~ licence** permis *m* poids lourd.

HHS *n* US (*abrév* = **Health and Human Services**) services *mpl* de santé américains.

hi○ /haɪ/ *excl* salut○!

HI US Post *abrév écrite* = **Hawaii**.

hiatus /haɪˈeɪtəs/ *n* (*pl* **~es** ou **~**) **1** (pause) temps *m* d'arrêt; **2** (gap in manuscript) lacune *f*; **3** Ling, Literat hiatus *m*.

hibernate /ˈhaɪbəneɪt/ *vi* hiberner.

hibernation /ˌhaɪbəˈneɪʃn/ *n* hibernation *f*; **to go into ~** entrer en hibernation; **to emerge from** ou **come out of ~** sortir d'hibernation.

hibiscus /hɪˈbɪskəs, US haɪ-/ *n* (*pl* **~es**) hibiscus *m*.

hiccup, hiccough /ˈhɪkʌp/ **I** *n* **1** lit hoquet *m*; **to have (the) ~s** avoir le hoquet; **2** fig (setback) anicroche *f*.
II *vi* (*p prés etc* **-p-** ou **-pp-**) hoqueter.

hick○ /hɪk/ US pej **I** *n* plouc◐ *mf*.
II *adj* plouc◐; **~ town** trou○ *m*.

hickey /ˈhɪkɪ/ *n* US **1**○ (spot) petit bouton *m*; **2**◐ (love-bite) suçon *m*; **3**○ (gadget) machin○ *m*.

hickory /ˈhɪkərɪ/ *n* hickory *m*, noyer *m* blanc d'Amérique.

hid /hɪd/ *prét* **▶ hide**.

hidden /ˈhɪdn/ **I** *pp* **▶ hide**.
II *adj* [*cause, danger, talent, treasure*] caché; **to be ~ from view** être caché, être invisible; **to lie ~** rester caché; **to keep sth ~ (away)** cacher [qch]; **what have you got ~ away in that drawer?** qu'est-ce que tu caches dans ce tiroir?

hide /haɪd/ **I** *n* **1** (skin) peau *f*; **2** (leather) cuir *m*; **3** (for hunter, photographer) cachette *f*.
II *vtr* (*prét* **hid**; *pp* **hidden**) cacher [*object, person*] (**from** à); ne pas montrer [*emotion, feeling*] (**from** à); **to ~ from sb the fact that** cacher à qn le fait que; **to have nothing to ~** n'avoir rien à cacher; **to ~ one's blushes** cacher sa honte.
III *vi* (*prét* **hid**; *pp* **hidden**) se cacher; **a place to ~** un endroit où se cacher; **to ~**

behind sb/sth lit, fig se cacher derrière qn/qch.
IV *v refl* (*prét* **hid**; *pp* **hidden**) **to ~ oneself** se cacher.
IDIOMS **I haven't seen ~ nor hair of him** il a complètement disparu de la circulation.
■ **hide away**: **~ [sth] away**, **~ away [sth]** cacher.
■ **hide out** GB, **hide up** US se cacher, se planquer○.

hide: **~ and seek** GB, **~-and-go-seek** US ▶ 1282 *n* cache-cache *m inv*; **~away** *n* retraite *f*.

hidebound /ˈhaɪdbaʊnd/ *adj* conventionnel/-elle, rigide.

hideous /ˈhɪdɪəs/ *adj* **1** (ugly) [*clothing*] affreux/-euse, horrible; [*object, creature, monster*] hideux/-euse; [*colour*] horrible; [*noise*] affreux/-euse; **2** (terrible) [*mistake*] terrible; [*conditions*] atroce, abominable; [*violence*] horrible; [*murder*] odieux/-ieuse, atroce.

hideously /ˈhɪdɪəslɪ/ *adv* **1** (repulsively) [*ugly, deformed*] atrocement, affreusement; **2** (terribly) [*behave, act*] d'une façon horrible.

hideout /haɪd/ *n* cachette *f*.

hiding /ˈhaɪdɪŋ/ *n* **1** (concealment) **to go into ~** se terrer, se cacher; **to be in ~** rester terré, se tenir caché; **to emerge from** ou **come out of ~** sortir de sa cachette; **2** (beating) correction *f*, raclée○ *f*; **to give sb a (good) ~** administrer une (bonne) raclée○ à qn.
IDIOMS **to be on a ~ to nothing** ne pas avoir la moindre chance de réussir or de gagner.

hiding place *n* cachette *f*.

hie‡ /haɪ/ *vi* se hâter, courir; **~ thee hence!** hors d'ici!

hierarchic(al) /ˌhaɪəˈrɑːkɪk(l)/ *adj* **1** (of a hierarchy) hiérarchique; **2** (arranged in a hierarchy) hiérarchisé.

hierarchy /ˈhaɪərɑːkɪ/ *n* hiérarchie *f*.

hieroglyph /ˈhaɪərəglɪf/ *n* lit, fig hiéroglyphe *m*.

hieroglyphic /ˌhaɪərəˈglɪfɪk/ I *n* lit, fig hiéroglyphe *m*.
II **hieroglyphics** *npl* écriture *f* hiéroglyphique, hiéroglyphes *mpl*.
III *adj* hiéroglyphique.

hifalutin○ /ˌhaɪfəˈluːtɪn/ *adj* = **highfalutin(g)**.

hi-fi /ˈhaɪfaɪ/ I *n* **1** (set of equipment) chaîne *f* hi-fi *inv*, hi-fi *f inv*; **2** (*abrév* = **high fidelity**) hi-fi *f inv*, haute-fidélité *f inv*.
II *modif* [*record, tape, sound*] hi-fi *inv*, haute-fidélité *inv*.

higgledy-piggledy /ˌhɪgldɪˈpɪgldɪ/ I *adj* pêle-mêle *inv*.
II *adv* pêle-mêle, n'importe comment.

high /haɪ/ ▶ 1412 I *n* **1** (high level) niveau *m* élevé; **an all-time** ou **a record ~** un niveau record; **to rise to** ou **hit** ou **reach a new ~** atteindre son niveau le plus élevé; **a ~ of 35°** une pointe de 35°; **a ten-year ~ of three million** un niveau record de trois millions en dix ans; **2**○ (euphoric feeling) **to give sb a ~** [*drug*] défoncer○ qn; [*success, compliment*] monter à la tête de qn; **to be on a ~** être en pleine euphorie; **3** Meteorol zone *f* de haute pression; **4**○ US Sch = **high school**.
II *adj* **1** (tall) [*building, wall, cliff, hill, pile*] haut; [*table, chair, forehead, collar, heel*] haut (*after n*); **~ cheekbones** pommettes *fpl* saillantes; **how ~ is the cliff?** quelle est la hauteur de la falaise?; **it is 50 cm ~** ça fait 50 cm de haut; **a five-metre ~ wall** un mur de cinq mètres de haut; **chest-/waist-~** à la hauteur de la poitrine/la ceinture; **I've known him since he was so ~** il n'était pas plus grand que ça quand je l'ai connu; **2** (far from the ground) [*shelf, window, ceiling, plateau*] haut; [*tier, level, floor*] supérieur; [*cloud*] d'altitude; **at ~ altitude** à haute altitude; **at ~ tide** à marée haute; **with a ~ ceiling** haut de plafond; **a dress with a ~ neck(line)** une robe montante; **how ~ (up) are we?** (on top of building) on est à combien de mètres au-dessus du sol?; (on plane, mountain) quelle est notre altitude?; **how ~ do you want the shelf?** à quelle hauteur voulez-vous l'étagère?; **3** (numerically large) [*number, ratio, price, frequency, volume*] élevé; [*wind*] violent; [*playing card*] grosse; **this will lead to ~er taxes** cela conduira à une augmentation des impôts; **at ~ speed** à grande vitesse; **to have a ~ temperature** avoir de la fièvre; **~ in** riche en [*fat, iron*]; **4** (great, intense) [*degree, intensity, risk*] élevé; [*fever, heat*] fort (*before n*); [*anxiety, tension, excitement*] extrême; [*hope, expectation*] grand (*before n*); **cook on a ~ heat** faire cuire à feu vif; **turn the grill to ~** mettre le gril sur la position maximum; **to have a ~ colour** avoir le teint rougeaud; **that is ~ praise!** c'est très flatteur!; **a moment of ~ drama** un moment de grande émotion; **the ~ seriousness of sth** le grand sérieux de qch; **the building is ~ Victorian/Gothic** le bâtiment est de la grande époque victorienne/du Gothique; **in ~ summer** au cœur de l'été; **feelings are running ~** les esprits s'échauffent; **5** (important) [*quality, status, standard, rank, class, authority*] supérieur; [*priority, place on list*] élevé; **a ~er court** une cour supérieure; **I have it on the ~est authority** je tiens cela des autorités les plus haut placées; **to have friends in ~ places** avoir des amis haut placés; **corruption in ~ places** la corruption en haut lieu; **to be ~ up** être haut placé; **to go on to ~er things** faire son chemin dans le monde; **6** (noble) [*ideal, principle, character*] noble; **those are ~ words (indeed)!** iron ce sont de (bien) grands mots!; **7** (acute) [*pitch, sound, voice*] aigu/-guë; [*note*] haut; **to reach the ~ notes** atteindre les notes les plus hautes; **8** (mature) [*game*] faisandé; [*fish, cheese*] avancé; [*butter*] rance; **I like my cheese really ~** j'aime mon fromage bien fait; **9**○ (euphoric) (on drug) défoncé○, dans un état euphorique; (happy) ivre de joie; **to be ~ on** être défoncé à [*drug*]; **she was ~ on success** son succès l'avait rendue ivre de joie; **to get ~** (deliberately) se défoncer○; (accidentally) s'intoxiquer; **10** Ling [*vowel*] fermé.
III *adv* **1** (to a great height) [*build, pile, climb, jump, throw, fly, rise, raise*] haut; **the plane flew too ~** l'avion a volé trop haut or à une altitude trop élevée; **the desk was piled ~ with papers** les papiers s'entassaient en hautes piles sur le bureau; **write it ~er up** écris-le plus haut; **to live ~ up on the 16th floor** habiter tout en haut au 16ème étage; **to climb ~er and ~er** lit [*person, animal*] grimper de plus en plus haut; fig [*figures, rate, unemployment*] augmenter de plus en plus; **interest rates may go as ~ as 15%** le taux d'intérêt peut monter jusqu'à 15%; **don't go any ~er than £5,000** ne dépasse pas 5 000 livres sterling; **2** (at a high level) [*set, turn on*] fort; **to turn sth up ~** monter qch; **don't turn it up too ~** ne le mets pas trop fort; **3** [*sing, play*] haut; **play an octave ~er** jouez à l'octave supérieure.
IV **on ~** *adv phr* gen en haut; Relig au Ciel; **from on ~** gen d'en haut; Relig du Ciel.
IDIOMS **it's ~ time that sb did** il est grand temps que qn fasse; **to have a ~ (old) time** s'amuser comme des fous; **to hold one's head (up) ~** marcher la tête haute; **to search** ou **hunt ~ and low for sth** remuer ciel et terre pour trouver qch.

high altar *n* maître-autel *m*.

high and dry *adj* lit échoué; **to leave sb ~** fig laisser qn en plan.

high: **~-angle shot** *n* plongée *f*; **~ball** *n* cocktail *m*; (with whisky) whisky-soda *m*; **~ball glass** *n* verre *m* à cocktail; **~ beam** *n* US pleins phares *mpl*; **~born** *adj* de haute naissance; **~boy** *n* US commode *f* (haute); **~brow** *n, adj* intellectuel/-elle (*m/f*); **~ chair** *n* chaise *f* haute.

High Church I *n* Haute Église *f*.
II *adj* [*service, ceremony, person*] de la Haute Église.

high-class *adj* [*hotel, shop, car*] de luxe; [*performance*] de premier ordre; [*goods, product*] de première qualité; [*area, neighbourhood*] de grand standing; [*prostitute, gigolo*] de luxe.

high comedy *n* Theat comédie *f* raffinée; **there are moments of ~ in the film** il y a des moments très comiques dans le film.

high: **~ command** *n* haut commandement *m*; **~ commission** *n* haut-commissariat *m*; **~ commissioner** ▶ 1692 *n* haut-commissaire *m*; **~ court** *n* cour *f* suprême; **High Court (of Justice)** *n*: *tribunal suprême en matière civile en Angleterre et au Pays de Galles*; **~ court judge** ▶ 1692 *n* juge *m* de la cour suprême; **High Court of Justiciary** *n*: *tribunal suprême en matière criminelle en Écosse*; **~-definition** *adj* (à) haute définition *inv*; **~ density** *adj* [*disk, tape, plastic, metal*] haute densité *inv*; **~ density housing** *n* grands ensembles *mpl*; **~ diver** *n* plongeur/-euse *m/f* de haut vol; **~ diving** ▶ 1282 *n* plongeon *m* de haut vol; **~-energy physics** *n* physique *f* des hautes énergies.

Higher /ˈhaɪə(r)/ *n* Scot Sch certificat *m* de fin d'études en Écosse (*à 17 ans*).

high: **~er education** *n* enseignement *m* supérieur; **~er mathematics** *n* (+ *v sg*) mathématiques *fpl* abstraites; **Higher National Certificate** *n* GB brevet *m* technique (*obtenu vers l'âge de 18 ans*); **Higher National Diploma** *n* GB brevet *m* technique (*intermédiaire entre le baccalauréat et un diplôme universitaire*); **~est common factor** *n* plus grand commun diviseur *m*; **~ explosive**, **HE** *n* explosif *m* brisant.

highfalutin(g)○ /ˌhaɪfəˈluːtɪŋ/ *adj* [*language, speech*] ampoulé; [*ways, ideas*] prétentieux/-ieuse.

high: **~ fashion** *n* haute couture *f*; **~-fibre** *adj* [*foodstuff*] riche en fibres; **~-fidelity** *n, adj* haute-fidélité (*f*) (*inv*); **~ finance** *n* haute finance *f*; **~ five** *n* geste *m* de victoire (*tape dans la main d'une autre personne, le bras levé*); **~-flier** *n* jeune loup *m*, ambitieux/-ieuse *m/f*; **~-flown** *adj* ampoulé; **~-flyer** *n* = **high-flier**.

high-flying /ˌhaɪˈflaɪɪŋ/ *adj* **1** lit [*aircraft*] capable de voler à haute altitude; [*bird*] de haut vol; **2** fig [*person*] ambitieux/-ieuse; [*ambition, ideal*] extravagant; [*career*] de haut vol.

high: **~-frequency** *adj* (à) haute fréquence; **High German** ▶ 1402 *n* haut allemand *m*.

high-grade /ˌhaɪˈgreɪd/ *adj* **1** Miner [*mineral, ore*] à haute teneur; **2** gen [*merchandise, substance, paper*] de haute qualité.

high ground *n* lit altitude *f*; **there will be snow on ~** il neigera en altitude; **to seize** ou **claim** ou **take the (moral) ~** fig invoquer l'impératif moral, prendre une position moraliste.

high: **~-handed** *adj* despotique; **~-handedly** *adv* despotiquement.

high hat *n* **1** (top hat) haut-de-forme *m*; **2** Mus (cymbal) cymbale *f* double à coulisse; **3**†○ snob *m*.

high: **~-heeled** *adj* [*shoe*] à talon haut; **~ heels** *npl* (shoes, heels) hauts talons *mpl*; **~-income** *adj* à revenus élevés; **~-intensity** *adj* [*lights*] à haute intensité lumineuse; **~-interest** *adj* à intérêt élevé.

high jinks○ /ˌhaɪ ˈdʒɪŋks/ *npl* du bon temps *m*; **to get up to ~** se payer du bon temps○.

high jump ▶ 1282 *n* Sport saut *m* en hauteur.
IDIOMS **to be for the ~**○ GB se retrouver dans de beaux draps○.

high kick *n* battement *m*.

highland /ˈhaɪlənd/ **I** *n* (also **~s**) région *f* montagneuse.
II *adj* [*animal*] des montagnes; [*vegetation*] de montagne.

Highland /ˈhaɪlənd/ **▶1624** **I Highlands** *pr npl* (also **Highland Region**) Highlands *mpl*, Hautes-Terres *fpl* (d'Écosse).
II *modif* [*customs, dress, cattle*] des Highlands; [*holiday*] dans les Highlands.

highlander /ˈhaɪləndə(r)/ *n* montagnard/-e *m/f*.

Highlander /ˈhaɪləndə(r)/ *n* (inhabitant) habitant/-e *m/f* de la Haute Écosse or des Highlands; (native) natif/-ive *m/f* des Highlands.

Highland: **~ fling** *n* danse *f* écossaise; **~ games** *npl* jeux *mpl* écossais.

high-level /ˌhaɪˈlevl/ *adj* **1** gen [*contracts, meeting, talks*] à haut niveau; [*diplomat, executive, official*] de haut niveau; **2** Comput [*programming language*] de haut niveau; **3** Nucl [*nuclear waste*] à forte radioactivité.

high life *n* grande vie *f*.

highlight /ˈhaɪlaɪt/ **I** *n* **1** Art rehaut *m*; **2** (in hair) (natural) reflet *m*; (artificial) mèche *f*; **3** (best part) (of exhibition) clou *m*; (of match, show, event) point *m* culminant; (of week, evening, year) point *m* fort.
II highlights *npl* Sport, Radio, TV résumé *m*.
III *vtr* (*prét, pp* **-lighted**) **1** (accentuate) [*artist*] rehausser; [*photographer*] mettre [qch] en valeur; [*sun, light*] éclairer; **2** (emphasize) mettre l'accent sur, souligner; **3** (with fluorescent pen) surligner; **4** Comput sélectionner, marquer; **5** (bleach) éclaircir; **to have one's hair ~ed** se faire faire des mèches.

highlighter /ˈhaɪlaɪtə(r)/ *n* **1** (pen) surligneur *m*; **2** (make-up) fard *m* clair.

high living *n* grande vie *f*.

highly /ˈhaɪlɪ/ *adv* **1** (very, to a large extent) [*complex, dangerous, developed, educated, intelligent, motivated, promising, respected, sensitive, unusual*] extrêmement; [*toxic, unlikely*] hautement; [*seasoned*] très, fortement; **~ important** de la plus haute importance; **to be ~ critical of sth/sb** critiquer sévèrement qch/qn; **2** (enthusiastically) **to speak/think ~ of sb** dire/penser beaucoup de bien de qn; **she is very ~ thought of** on pense le plus grand bien d'elle; **to praise sb ~** chanter les louanges de qn; **to be ~ regarded** être hautement apprécié; **to be ~ acclaimed** recevoir un excellent accueil; **3** (with a large amount) [*remunerated, rewarded*] largement; **~ priced** de grand prix; **~ populated** extrêmement peuplé.

highly-charged /ˌhaɪlɪˈtʃɑːdʒd/ *adj* [*atmosphere, meeting*] très tendu; [*narrative*] mouvementé.

highly-coloured GB, **highly-colored** US /ˌhaɪlɪˈkʌləd/ *adj* **1** lit aux couleurs vives; **2** (embellished) [*version, description, story*] enjolivé.

highly: **~-paid** *adj* très bien payé; **~ placed** *adj* haut placé; **~-polished** *adj* d'un beau poli; **~-sexed** *adj* doué d'une forte libido; **~-strung** *adj* très tendu; **~-trained** *adj* parfaitement entraîné.

high: **High Mass** *n* grand-messe *f*; **~-minded** /ˌhaɪˈmaɪndɪd/ *adj* [*person*] à l'âme noble; [*act, attitude, principle, wish*] noble; **~-necked** *adj* [*dress, blouse*] montant; [*sweater*] à col montant.

highness /ˈhaɪnɪs/ *n* (of building, voice, sound) hauteur *f*; (of wind) violence *f*, force *f*.

Highness /ˈhaɪnɪs/ **▶1268** *n* **His** ou **Her (Royal) ~** Son Altesse *f*.

high noon *n* plein midi *m*; **at ~** en plein midi.

high: **~-octane** *adj* à indice d'octane élevé; **~-performance** *adj* performant.

high-pitched /ˌhaɪˈpɪtʃt/ *adj* **1** [*voice, sound*] aigu/-uë; **2** [*roof*] à forte pente.

high point *n* fig point *m* culminant.

high-powered /ˌhaɪˈpaʊəd/ *adj* **1** (powerful) [*rifle, transmitter*] à grande portée; [*car, engine*] de grande puissance; [*telescope, microscope, lens*] à fort grossissement; **2** (dynamic) [*person, executive, solicitor*] de haut vol; [*sector, field, business*] dynamique; [*job*] de haute responsabilité.

high pressure **I** *n* Meteorol hautes pressions *f*.
II *modif* **1** (aggressive) [*selling, technique, tactic, salesperson*] agressif/-ive; **2** (stressful) [*job*] à haute responsabilité; **3** Tech [*gas, steam, pump, cylinder*] à haute pression.

high: **~ priest** *n* Relig grand prêtre *m*; fig pape *m* (**of** de); **~ priestess** *n* Relig, fig grande prêtresse *f* (**of** de); **~-principled** *adj* [*person*] de grands principes; [*stance, motivation*] dicté par de grands principes.

high-profile /ˌhaɪˈprəʊfaɪl/ *adj* [*entrepreneur, firm, politician, pressure group*] bien en vue; [*campaign, lobbying*] intensif/-ive; [*meeting, visit*] largement couvert.

high: **~-ranking** *adj* de haut rang; **~-resolution** *adj* à haute résolution.

high rise **I** *n* tour *f* (d'habitation).
II *adj* [*flat, apartment, office*] dans une tour; **~ building**, **~ block** tour *f*.

high-risk /ˌhaɪˈrɪsk/ *adj* **1** (dangerous) [*occupation, sport*] à haut risque; [*prisoner*] dangereux/-euse; **2** (in danger) [*group, person*] à haut risque.

high: **~ road** *n* grand-route *f*; **~ roller**[○] *n* US casse-cou[○] *mf inv*; **~ school** *n* US Sch ≈ lycée *m*; GB Sch établissement *m* secondaire; **~-scoring** *adj* [*player*] au score élevé.

high sea *n* haute mer *f*; **on the ~s** en haute mer.

high season *n* haute saison *f*; **in (the) ~** en haute saison.

high: **~-sided vehicle** *n* véhicule *m* qui offre prise au vent; **~ society** *n* haute société *f*; **~-sounding** *adj* ronflant; **~-speed** *adj* [*train, rail link, line, car chase, crash*] à grande vitesse; [*coach, jet, boat*] rapide; [*fax, printer, sorting machine*] rapide; [*film*] ultrarapide; [*camera, lens*] à obturation ultrarapide; **~-spending** *adj* dépensier/-ière; **~-spirited** *adj* plein d'entrain.

high spirits *npl* entrain *m*; **to be in ~** être plein d'entrain.

high spot *n* point *m* culminant.

high street GB (also **High Street**) **I** *n* (in town) rue *f* principale; (in village) grand-rue *f*; **you won't find these clothes in the ~** vous ne trouverez pas ces vêtements dans une boutique appartenant à une chaîne.
II *modif* [*retailer*] appartenant à une chaîne.

high: **~-street bank** *n* grande banque *f* (*qui a des succursales et des agences partout*); **~-street shop** **▶1692** *n* boutique *f* appartenant à une chaîne; **~-street spending** *n* dépenses *fpl* de consommation courante; **~-strung** *adj* = **highly-strung**; **~ table** *n* (at function) table *f* d'honneur; GB Univ table *f* des professeurs.

hightail[○] /ˈhaɪteɪl/ *vi* US **to ~ (it) home/to sb's house** se grouiller[○] de rentrer chez soi/d'aller chez qn.

high tea *n* GB goûter *m* dînatoire.

high tech /ˌhaɪ ˈtek/ **I** *n* (interior design) high-tech *m*.
II[○] **high-tech** *adj* [*industry, company*] de pointe; [*hospital, office, equipment, weapon, car*] ultramoderne; [*method, system*] à la pointe de la technologie; [*style, decor, furniture, room*] high-tech *inv*.

high technology **I** *n* technologie *f* de pointe.
II *modif* [*company, industry, sector*] à la pointe de la technologie; [*development, research*] technologie de pointe; [*import, export, product, equipment*] de pointe.

high: **~-tension** *adj* à haute tension; **~ tide** *n* marée *f* haute; **~ treason** *n* haute trahison *f*; **~-up**[○] *n* grosse légume[○] *f*; **~-velocity** *adj* [*bullet, missile, rifle*] à grande vitesse; [*wind, gust*] de force élevée.

high voltage **I** *n* haute tension *f*.
II high-voltage *adj* de haute tension.

high: **~-waisted** *adj* à taille haute; **~ water** *n* (high tide) marée *f* haute; (of tidal river, in harbour) hautes eaux *fpl*; **~-water mark** *n* lit niveau *m* des hautes eaux; fig apogée *m*.

highway /ˈhaɪweɪ/ *n* GB (main road) route *f* nationale; US (motorway) autoroute *f*; **public** ou **king's** ou **queen's ~** GB voie *f* publique; **~s and byways** chemins et sentiers.

highway: **Highway Code** *n* GB Code *m* de la Route; **~(s) engineer** **▶1692** *n* ingénieur *m* des ponts et chaussées; **~ maintenance** *n* entretien *m* des chaussées; **~man** *n* bandit *m* de grand chemin; **~ patrol** *n* US police *f* de la route; **~ robbery** *n* lit banditisme *m*; fig vol *m* manifeste; **Highways Department** *n* ≈ Ponts et Chaussées *mpl*.

high: **~ wire** *n* corde *f* raide; **~ yellow**[●] *n* US injur mulâtre/mulâtresse *m/f* au teint très clair.

hijack /ˈhaɪdʒæk/ **I** *n* détournement *m* d'avion.
II *vtr* **1** lit détourner [*plane*]; s'emparer de force de [*lorry, car*]; **2** fig (take over) s'approprier [*theory, subject*]; récupérer [*event, demonstration*].

hijacker /ˈhaɪdʒækə(r)/ *n* (of plane) pirate *m* (de l'air); (of bus, truck) pirate *m* (de la route).

hijacking /ˈhaɪdʒækɪŋ/ *n* détournement *m*.

hike /haɪk/ **I** *n* **1** (walk) randonnée *f*; hum longue marche *f*; **to go on** ou **for a ~** faire une randonnée; **2** Fin (rise) hausse *f* (**in** de); **wage/price ~** hausse des salaires/prix.
II *vi* faire de la randonnée; **they ~d all round Italy** ils ont fait le tour de l'Italie en randonnée.
III *vtr* (also **~ up**) remonter [*garment*]; Fin augmenter [*rate, price*].
IDIOMS **take a ~**[○]**!** va te faire voir[○]!

hiker /ˈhaɪkə(r)/ *n* randonneur/-euse *m/f*.

hiking /ˈhaɪkɪŋ/ **▶1282** *n* randonnée *f*; **a week's ~ holiday** une semaine de randonnée.

hiking boot *n* chaussure *f* de marche.

hilarious /hɪˈleərɪəs/ *adj* désopilant, hilarant; **we had a ~ time** on s'est amusé comme des fous.

hilariously /hɪˈleərɪəslɪ/ *adv* **~ funny** hilarant, vraiment marrant.

hilarity /hɪˈlærətɪ/ *n* hilarité *f*; **her hat caused much ~** son chapeau déclencha l'hilarité générale.

hill /hɪl/ *n* colline *f*; (hillside) coteau *m*; (incline) pente *f*, côte *f*; **the Hill** US le Congrès; **over ~ and dale** liter par monts et par vaux.
IDIOMS **as old as the ~s** vieux comme Hérode; **to be over the ~** ne plus être de première jeunesse.

hillbilly /ˈhɪlbɪlɪ/ *n* US péj péquenaud/-e[○] *m/f* pej; plouc[○] *mf* pej.

hill: **~ climb** *n* (motor sport) course *f* de côte; **~ farming** *n* GB élevage *m* en montagne.

hilliness /ˈhɪlɪnɪs/ *n* nature *f* accidentée.

hillock /ˈhɪlək/ *n* petite colline *f*.

hillside /ˈhɪlsaɪd/ *n* flanc *m* de coteau; **on the ~** à flanc de coteau.

hill station *n* station *f* de montagne.

hilltop /ˈhɪltɒp/ **I** *n* sommet *m* de colline.
II *modif* [*farm, settlement*] au sommet de la colline.

hill walking *n* randonnées *fpl* pédestres (en basse montagne).

hilly /ˈhɪlɪ/ *adj* [*landscape, region*] vallonné.

hilt /hɪlt/ *n* (handle) (of sword) poignée *f*; (of knife) manche *m*; **(up) to the ~** lit jusqu'à la garde; fig (in debt) jusqu'au cou; **to be taxed to the ~** être grevé d'impôts; **to back sb (up) to the ~** donner son appui inconditionnel à qn.

him /hɪm/

■ **Note** When used as a direct object pronoun, *him* is translated by *le* (*l'* before a vowel). Note that the object pronoun normally comes before the verb in French: *I know him* = je le connais; *I've already seen him* = je l'ai déjà vu.
– In imperatives, the direct object pronoun is translated by *le* and comes after the verb: *catch him!* = attrape-le (note the hyphen).
– When used as an indirect object pronoun, *him* is translated by *lui*: *I've given him the book* = je lui ai donné le livre; *I've given it to him* = je le lui ai donné.
– In imperatives, the indirect object pronoun is translated by *lui* and comes after the verb: *phone him!* = téléphone-lui; *give it to him* = donne-le-lui (note the hyphens).
– After prepositions and after the verb *to be* the translation is *lui*: *she did it for him* = elle l'a fait pour lui; *it's him* = c'est lui.

pron **1** (direct obj) le, l'; **I like ~** je l'aime bien; **catch ~!** attrape-le!; **2** (indirect obj, after prep) lui.

Himalayas /ˌhɪmə'leɪəz/ *pr npl* (montagnes *fpl* de) l'Himalaya *m*.

himbo○ /'hɪmbəʊ/ *n* journ, péj minet○ *m* pej.

himself /hɪm'self/

■ **Note** When used as a reflexive pronoun, direct and indirect, *himself* is translated by *se* (*s'* before a vowel): *he's enjoying himself* = il s'amuse bien; *he's cut himself* = il s'est coupé.
– When used in emphasis the translation is *lui-même*: *he himself didn't know* = il ne le savait pas lui-même.
– After a preposition, the translation is *lui* or *lui-même*: *he can be proud of himself* = il peut être fier de lui *or* de lui-même.
– For particular usages see below.

pron **1** (refl) se, s'; **he's hurt ~** il s'est blessé; **2** (emphatic) lui-même; **he ~ said that...** il a dit lui-même que...; **3** (after prep) lui, lui-même; **for ~** pour lui, pour lui-même; **4** (expressions) (**all**) **by ~** tout seul; **he's not ~ today** il n'est pas dans son assiette aujourd'hui.

hind /haɪnd/ **I** *n* (*pl* **~s** ou **~**) Zool biche *f*.
II *adj* de derrière, postérieur; **~ legs** pattes *fpl* de derrière; **Charles got up on his ~ legs and said...** il a fallu que Charles se lève et dise...

hinder /'hɪndə(r)/ *vtr* **1** (hamper) entraver [*development, process, career*]; faire obstacle à [*proposals, reform*]; (delay) freiner [*progress, efforts*]; retarder [*plan*]; **2** (prevent) empêcher [*action*]; retenir, arrêter [*person*]; **to ~ sb in their efforts to do** gêner les efforts de qn pour faire.

Hindi /'hɪndɪ/ ▶ **1402** *n* hindi *m*.

hindmost /'haɪndməʊst/ *adj* tout dernier, toute dernière, ultime.
IDIOMS **run, boys, and the devil take the ~!** sauve qui peut!

hindquarters /ˌhaɪnd'kwɔːtəz/ *npl* **1** gen arrière-train *m*; **2** Equit (of horse) arrière-main *f*; **a half-turn on the ~** un demi-tour sur les hanches.

hindrance /'hɪndrəns/ *n* entrave *f*; **to be a ~ to sb** [*person*] gêner qn; [*social class, lack of ability, poverty*] être un handicap pour qn; **to be a ~ to sth** être une entrave à qch; **he's more of a ~ than a help** il gêne plutôt qu'il n'aide.
IDIOMS **without let or ~** sans que personne ne s'y oppose.

hindsight /'haɪndsaɪt/ *n* **with (the benefit of) ~** avec du recul, rétrospectivement.

Hindu /ˌhɪn'duː, US 'hɪnduː/ ▶ **1486** **I** *n* Hindou/-e *m/f*.
II *adj* hindou.

Hinduism /'hɪnduːɪzəm/ *n* hindouisme *m*.

Hindustan /ˌhɪndʊ'stɑːn/ *n* Hindoustan *m*.

Hindustani /ˌhɪndʊ'stɑːnɪ/ ▶ **1402** *n, adj* hindoustani (*m*), hindi (*m*).

hinge /hɪndʒ/ **I** *n* gen charnière *f*; (lift-off) gond *m*; **to come off its ~s** [*door*] sortir de ses gonds.
II *vtr* (*p prés* **hingeing**) mettre des charnières à.
III *vi* (*p prés* **hingeing**) **to ~ on sth** Tech s'articuler sur qch; **to ~ on sth/sb** fig dépendre de qch/qn.
IV hinged *pp adj* [*lid*] à charnières; [*seat*] rabattable; [*girder*] articulé.

hinge joint *n* Anat charnière *f*.

hint /hɪnt/ **I** *n* **1** (insinuation) allusion *f* (**about** à); **broad ~** allusion transparente; **gentle** ou **subtle ~** allusion discrète; **to give a ~** faire allusion (**about** à); **he gave no ~ of knowing** rien dans son attitude (or dans ses paroles) n'indiquait qu'il savait; **to drop ~s** faire des allusions; **to drop ~s that** laisser entendre que; **to take a ~** ou **the ~** saisir l'allusion; **he took the ~ and left** il a saisi l'allusion et est parti; **all right, I can take a ~, here's £10** c'est bon, j'ai compris or j'ai saisi l'allusion, voici 10 livres; **2** (little bit) lit (of spice, flavouring) pointe *f*; (of colour) touche *f*; fig (of smile) ébauche *f*, (of disgust, irony, humour, embarrassment) soupçon *m*; (of emotion, fear) trace *f*; (of accent) pointe *f*; **a ~ of autumn** un air d'automne; **there was no ~ of impatience in her face** il n'y avait aucune trace d'impatience sur son visage; **3** (clue) indication *f*, idée *f*; **I've no idea, give me a ~** je ne vois pas, donne-moi une indication; **acting on a ~** agissant sur une indication; **4** (helpful tip) renseignement *m*, tuyau○ *m* (**for, on** pour; **for doing** pour faire).
II *vtr* **to ~ that** laisser entendre que (**to** à); **'it's someone you know,' he ~ed** 'c'est quelqu'un que vous connaissez,' a-t-il laissé entendre.
III *vi* faire des sous-entendus.
■ **hint at**: **~ at** [**sth**] faire allusion à; **the possibility has been ~ed at** on a fait allusion à la possibilité.

hinterland /'hɪntəlænd/ *n* gen arrière-pays *m inv*; (of port) arrière-pays *m inv*, hinterland *m*.

hip /hɪp/ **I** *n* **1** ▶ **1037** Anat hanche *f*; **to break one's ~** se casser le col du fémur; **2** Archit croupe *f*; **~(ped) roof** toit *m* en croupe; **3** Bot gratte-cul *m*, cynorhodon *m*.
II *adj* [*person*] branché; [*habit, style*] dans le vent○, à la page○.
III *excl* **~ ~ hurrah!** hip hip hip hourra!
IV -hipped (*dans composés*) **broad-/narrow-hipped** aux hanches fortes/étroites.
IDIOMS **to shoot from the ~** parler sans réfléchir.

hip: **~ bath** *n* bain *m* de siège; **~bone** *n* os *m* iliaque; **~ flask** *n* flasque *f*.

hip hop /ˌhɪp 'hɒp/ *n* hip hop *m*.

hip: **~-huggers** *npl* = **hipsters**; **~ measurement**, **~ size** *n* tour *m* de hanches.

hippie, **hippy** /'hɪpɪ/ *n, adj* hippie (*mf*), hippy (*mf*).

hippo /'hɪpəʊ/ *n* hippopotame *m*.

hip pocket /hɪp/ *n* poche *f* revolver.

Hippocrates /hɪ'pɒkrətiːz/ *pr n* Hippocrate.

Hippocratic /ˌhɪpə'krætɪk/ *adj* hippocratique (*inv*); **~ oath** serment *m* d'Hippocrate.

hippodrome /'hɪpədrəʊm/ *n* hippodrome *m*.

Hippolytus /hɪ'pɒlɪtəs/ *pr n* Hippolyte.

hippopotamus /ˌhɪpə'pɒtəməs/ *n* (*pl* **-muses** ou **-mi**) hippopotame *m*.

hip replacement *n* prothèse *f* de hanche; **to have a ~** se faire mettre une prothèse à la hanche.

hipsters /'hɪpstəz/ *npl* pantalon *m* taille-basse.

hire /'haɪə(r)/ **I** *n* location *f*; **car/boat/video ~** location de voitures/de bateaux/de vidéos; **on ~** en location; **to let sth out on ~** mettre qch en location; **for ~** [*boat, skis*] à louer; [*taxi*] libre.
II *vtr* louer [*equipment, services, vehicle*] (**from** de; **to** à); engager [*person*]; **~d killer** tueur *m* à gages; **to take on ~d help** engager des employés en extra.
■ **hire out**: ¶ **~ out** [**sth**], **~** [**sth**] **out** louer; ¶ **~ oneself out** offrir ses services (**as** comme).

hire: **~ car** *n* voiture *f* de location; **~ charge** *n* coût *m* de location; **~ company**, **~ firm** *n* agence *f* de location; **~d man** *n* US Agric garçon *m* de ferme.

hireling /'haɪəlɪŋ/ *n* laquais *m*.

hire purchase, **HP** *n* achat *m* à crédit; **on ~** à crédit.

hire purchase agreement, **hire purchase arrangement** *n* GB accord *m* concernant les facilités de crédit.

hirsute /'hɜːsjuːt, US -suːt/ *adj* **1** [*person*] (hairy) poilu, velu; (unkempt) hirsute; **2** Bot hirsute, velu.

his /hɪz/

■ **Note** In French determiners agree in gender and number with the noun they qualify. So *his* when used as a determiner is translated by *son* + masculine singular noun (son chien), by *sa* + feminine singular noun (sa maison) BUT by *son* + feminine noun beginning with a vowel or mute h (son assiette) and by *ses* + plural noun (ses enfants).
– When *his* is stressed, *à lui* is added after the noun: HIS *house* = sa maison à lui.
– For *his* used with parts of the body ▶ **1037**.
– In French possessive pronouns reflect the gender and number of the noun they are standing for. When used as a possessive pronoun *his* is translated by le sien, la sienne, les siens or les siennes according to what is being referred to.
– For examples and particular usages see the entry below.

I *det* son/sa/ses.
II *pron* **all the drawings were good but ~ was the best** tous les dessins étaient bons mais le sien était le meilleur; **the blue car is ~** la voiture bleue est la sienne, la voiture bleue est à lui; **it's not ~** ce n'est pas à lui; **which house is ~?** sa maison c'est laquelle?; **I'm a colleague of ~** je suis un/-e de ses collègues; **I saw him with that dog of ~** péj je l'ai vu avec son sale chien○; **~ was not an easy task** fml sa tâche n'était pas facile; **the money was not ~ to give away** il n'avait pas à donner cet argent.

Hispanic /hɪ'spænɪk/ **I** *n* Hispano-Américain/-e *m/f*, Latino-Américain/-e *m/f*.
II *adj* **1** (Spanish) [*art, culture, architecture*] hispanique; **2** (Latin American) [*person, area, custom*] latino-américain.

hiss /hɪs/ **I** *n* (of gas, steam) sifflement *m*, chuintement *m*; (of snake, person) sifflement *m*; (of tape) grésillement *m*.
II *vtr* gen siffler [*person, performance, speech*]; **'I hate you,' she ~ed** 'je te déteste,' siffla-t-elle; **he was ~ed off the stage** il a quitté la scène sous les sifflets.
III *vi* **1** [*person, wind, snake, locomotive*] siffler; [*cat*] cracher; [*steam*] chuinter; [*gas*] siffler, chuinter; [*hot fat, cassette*] grésiller; **to ~ at sb** [*person*] siffler qn; [*kettle*] siffler.

histologist /hɪ'stɒlədʒɪst/ ▶ **1692** *n* histologiste *mf*.

histology /hɪ'stɒlədʒɪ/ *n* histologie *f*.

historian /hɪ'stɔːrɪən/ ▶ **1692** *n* historien/-ienne *m/f*; **ancient ~** spécialiste *mf* d'histoire de l'Antiquité; **art ~** historien/-ienne *m/f* de l'art; **military/social ~** spécialiste *mf* d'histoire militaire/sociale.

historic /hɪ'stɒrɪk, US -'stɔːr-/ *adj* **1** gen [*event, site, moment*] historique; **of ~ importance** d'une grande importance historique; **on this ~ occasion** en ce moment historique; **2** Ling **past ~** passé simple; **~**

present présent de narration; **in the ~ present** au présent de narration.

historical /hɪˈstɒrɪkl, US -ˈstɔːr-/ *adj* historique.

historically /hɪˈstɒrɪklɪ, US -ˈstɔːr-/ *adv* (where history is concerned) historiquement; (from an historical point of view) d'un point de vue historique; **~ based** fondé sur l'histoire; **~ speaking** d'un point de vue historique.

historiography /hɪˌstɔːrɪˈɒgrəfɪ/ *n* historiographie *f*.

history /ˈhɪstrɪ/ **I** *n* **1** (past) histoire *f*; **ancient/modern ~** histoire *f* ancienne/moderne; **French ~** histoire *f* de France; **18th century French ~** histoire *f* de la France au XVIIIe siècle; **military/social ~** histoire *f* militaire/sociale; **~ of art** histoire *f* de l'art; **in all the firm's 50-year ~** dans les 50 années d'histoire de la compagnie; **a place in ~** une place dans l'histoire; **~ proved him wrong** l'histoire lui donna tort; **to make ~** entrer dans l'histoire; **to go down in ~ as** entrer dans l'histoire comme; **~ repeats itself** l'histoire se répète; **to rewrite ~** récrire l'histoire; **that's ancient** ou **past ~** c'est de l'histoire ancienne; **2** Jur, Med antécédents *mpl*; **family ~** antécédents *mpl* familiaux; **medical ~** antécédents *mpl* médicaux; **to have a ~ of heart trouble** avoir des antécédents cardiaques; **to have a ~ of violence** avoir un passé violent; **3** (account) histoire *f*; **4** (tradition) tradition *f*; **the company has a ~ of success/strikes** la compagnie connaît de nombreux succès/de nombreuses grèves.
II *modif* [*book, course, degree, lesson, student, teacher*] d'histoire.
IDIOMS **the rest is ~** tout le monde connaît la suite.

histrionic /ˌhɪstrɪˈɒnɪk/ **I histrionics** *npl* comportement *m* outrancier, cinéma° *m*; **cut out the ~s!** arrête de faire du cinéma°!, arrête de te donner en spectacle!
II *adj* péj mélodramatique, théâtral.

hit /hɪt/ **I** *n* **1** (blow, stroke in sport) coup *m*; (in fencing) touche *f*; **to give the ball a tremendous ~** frapper la balle très fort; **to score a ~** Sport, fig marquer un point; ▶ **direct hit**; **2** (success) (play, film etc) succès *m*; (record) tube° *m*; **to be a big** ou **smash ~** (show, film) avoir or remporter un succès fou; **to be a ~ with the public** avoir beaucoup de succès auprès du public; **to make a ~ with sb** [*person*] faire grosse impression sur qn; **she's a big ~ with my son** mon fils l'adore; **3**° (dose) argot des drogués injection *f*; **4**° (murder) argot des gangsters meurtre *m*, assassinat *m*.
II *modif* [*song, play, musical, record*] à succès.
III *vtr* (*p prés* **-tt-**; *prét, pp* **hit**) **1** (strike) frapper [*person, ball*]; [*head, arm*] cogner contre [*windscreen, wall*]; **to ~ one's head/knee on sth** se cogner la tête/le genou contre qch; **his father used to ~ him** son père le battait; **to ~ a good shot** (in tennis, cricket) jouer une bonne balle; **to ~ a nail with a hammer** enfoncer un clou à coups de marteau; **to ~ the brakes** écraser le frein; **2** (strike as target) [*bullet, assassin, torpedo*] atteindre [*victim, target, ship, enemy*]; **3** (collide violently) heurter [*vehicle, wall*]; (more violently) percuter; [*vehicle*] renverser [*person*]; **the plane hit the runway with a bump** l'avion s'est posé lourdement sur la piste; **4** (affect adversely) affecter, toucher [*group, incomes, industry*]; **to be hit by strikes/bad weather** être affecté par les grèves/le mauvais temps; **hardest** ou **worst hit will be small businesses** ce sont les petits commerces qui seront les plus touchés; **his father's death hit him badly** la mort de son père l'a beaucoup affecté; **5** (become apparent to) **it suddenly hit me that** je me suis soudain rendu compte que; **then it hit me!** tout d'un coup j'ai réalisé°!; **6** (reach) arriver à [qch] [*motorway, main road*]; fig [*figures, weight*] atteindre [*level*]; **7** (come upon) rencontrer [*traffic, problem, bad weather*]; **you'll ~ the worst of the rush hour** tu vas tomber en pleine heure d'affluence; **8**° (go to) **to ~ the town** sortir s'amuser; **let's ~ the pub/club** allons au pub/en boîte; **9**° (attack) [*robbers*] attaquer [*bank etc*]; **10**° (kill) refroidir°, assassiner [*person*]; **11**° (scrounge) **to ~ sb for sth** taper° qch à qn; **12**° (in cards) **'~ me!'** 'donne-moi une carte!'
IDIOMS **to ~ sb in the eye** sauter aux yeux; **a colour which ~s you between the eyes** une couleur criarde; **to ~ the big time**° réussir; **to ~ the ceiling** ou **roof**° sauter au plafond°; **to ~ the jackpot** remporter le gros lot; **to ~ it off with sb** bien s'entendre avec qn; **not to know what has hit one**° être sidéré; **a beer would just ~ the spot**°! une bière ferait (bien) l'affaire!
■ **hit back**: ¶ **~ back** riposter; ¶ **~ [sb] back** rendre un coup à [qn]; **well, if he ~s you, ~ him back!** eh bien, s'il te frappe, rends-le lui (coup pour coup)!; ¶ **~ [sth] back** renvoyer [*ball*].
■ **hit out**: **~ out** lit distribuer des coups à droite et à gauche; fig **to ~ out at** attaquer [*neglect, complacency*].
■ **hit upon, hit on**: ¶ **~ (up)on [sth]** avoir [*idea*]; découvrir [*evidence, solution*]; trouver [*present*]; tomber sur [*problem*]; **you've hit on a bad time** tu tombes mal; ¶ **~ on [sb]**° US draguer° [*person*].

hit-and-miss *adj* [*method*] approximatif/-ive; [*affair, undertaking*] hasardeux/-euse; **the way they run things is pretty ~** ils gèrent leurs affaires n'importe comment.

hit-and-run *adj* [*raid, attack*] éclair *inv*; [*accident*] où le chauffeur a pris la fuite; [*gang*] qui attaque et prend la fuite; **~ driver** chauffeur *m* en délit de fuite.

hitch /hɪtʃ/ **I** *n* **1** (problem) problème *m*, pépin° *m*; **there has been a slight ~** il y a eu un petit pépin°; **to pass off without a ~** se dérouler sans problème; **2** (knot) nœud *m*; **3** US (in prison) séjour *m*; **to do a ~ in the army** rester quelque temps dans l'armée.
II *vtr* **1** (fasten) attacher [*rope, reins, trailer*] (**to** à); atteler [*horse, team*] (**to** à); accrocher [*wagon, rail carriage*] (**to** à); **2**° (thumb) **to ~ a ride** ou **lift** faire du stop°; **I ~ed a lift to York** je suis allé à York en stop°; **can I ~ a ride to school?** tu m'emmènes à l'école?
III° *vi* **1** (hitchhike) faire du stop°; **to ~ to Paris in two days** mettre deux jours pour aller à Paris en stop; **2** US (limp) boitiller.
IDIOMS **to get ~ed**° convoler en justes noces°.
■ **hitch up**: **~ up [sth]**, **~ [sth] up 1** (pull up) retrousser [*skirt*]; remonter [*trousers, covers*]; **to ~ a bag up onto one's back** hisser un sac sur son dos; **2** (attach) accrocher [*wagon, trailer*]; atteler [*horse*].

hitchhike /ˈhɪtʃhaɪk/ *vi* faire de l'auto-stop *m*, faire du stop° *m*; **to ~ to Paris** aller à Paris en stop°; **to ~ round the world** faire le tour du monde en stop°.

hitch: **~hiker** *n* auto-stoppeur/-euse *m/f*; **~hiking** *n* auto-stop *m*.

hi-tech = **high tech**.

hither‡ /ˈhɪðə(r)/ *adv* ici; **come ~** venez là; **~ and thither** de ci, de là.

hitherto /ˌhɪðəˈtuː/ *adv* (up till now) jusqu'ici, jusqu'à présent; (up till then) jusqu'alors.

Hitler /ˈhɪtlə(r)/ *pr n* Hitler; **a little ~** fig un petit despote or dictateur.

Hitlerian /hɪtˈlɪərɪən/ *adj* hitlérien/-ienne.

Hitlerism /ˈhɪtlərɪzəm/ *n* hitlérisme *m*.

Hitler Youth Movement *n* Hist Jeunesses *fpl* hitlériennes.

hit: **~ list** *n* liste *f* noire; **~ man** *n* (gangster) tueur *m* (à gages); **~ parade** *m* palmarès *m*, hit-parade *m*; **~ single** *n* tube° *m*; **~ squad** *n* commando *m* (de tueurs).

Hittite /ˈhɪtaɪt/ ▶ **1486**, **1402** **I** *n* **1** (person) Hittite *mf*; **2** (language) hittite *m*.
II *adj* hittite.

HIV *n* (*abrév* = **human immunodeficiency virus**) (virus *m*) VIH *m*.

hive /haɪv/ **I** *n* **1** (beehive) ruche *f*; **2** (swarm) essaim *m*; **a ~ of activity** ou **industry** une vraie ruche.
II hives *npl* ▶ **1354** urticaire *f*.
III *vtr* mettre [qch] dans une ruche [*bees*].
IV *vi* [*bees*] entrer dans la ruche.
■ **hive off**: ¶ **~ off**° filer°; ¶ **~ [sth] off**, **~ off [sth]** Comm, Admin **1** (subcontract) sous-traiter; **2** (separate off) séparer [*part of company*]; **3** (sell off) céder.

HIV positive *adj* séropositif/-ive (*au virus VIH*).

hiya° /ˈhaɪjə/ *excl* salut!

hl (*abrév écrite* = **hectolitre**) hl.

HM *n* (*abrév* = **His Majesty**, **Her Majesty**) SM.

HMG *n* GB (*abrév* = **His/Her Majesty's Government**) le gouvernement de Sa Majesté.

HMI *n* (*abrév* = **His/Her Majesty's Inspector**) inspecteur *m* (*qui se rend dans les écoles*).

HMS *n* (*abrév* = **His/Her Majesty's Ship**) ≈ bâtiment *m* de Sa Majesté; **~ Victory** le (HMS) Victoire.

HMSO *n* (*abrév* = **His/Her Majesty's Stationery Office**) *service gouvernemental de publication*.

HNC *n* GB (*abrév* = **Higher National Certificate**) ≈ BTS *m*.

HND *n* GB (*abrév* = **Higher National Diploma**) *diplôme supérieur d'aptitudes techniques*.

hoard /hɔːd/ **I** *n* (of treasure) trésor *m*; (of provisions) provisions *fpl*; **a miser's ~** le magot° d'un avare.
II *vtr* **1** (build up reserves of) stocker [*supplies*] also pej; [*animal*] amasser [*food*]; **to ~ money** péj amasser de l'argent, thésauriser liter; **2** (refuse to throw away) amasser [*objects*].

hoarder /ˈhɔːdə(r)/ *n* **to be a ~ of sth** entasser qch; **I'm a terrible ~** je ne jette jamais rien.

hoarding /ˈhɔːdɪŋ/ *n* GB **1** (for advertisements) panneau *m* publicitaire; **2** (fence) palissade *f*; **3** (saving) accumulation *f*.

hoarfrost /ˈhɔːfrɒst, US -frɔːst/ *n* gelée *f* blanche, givre *m*.

hoarse /hɔːs/ *adj* [*voice*] enroué, rauque; [*cry*] rauque; **to be ~** être enroué, avoir la voix enrouée; **to shout/laugh oneself ~** s'enrouer à force de crier/rire.

hoarsely /ˈhɔːslɪ/ *adv* d'une voix rauque or enrouée.

hoarseness /ˈhɔːsnɪs/ *n* (of voice) enrouement *m*.

hoary /ˈhɔːrɪ/ *adj* **1** [*hair*] blanchi; [*person*] chenu, aux cheveux blancs; [*plant*] couvert de poils blancs ou d'un duvet blanc; **~-headed**, **~-haired** chenu, aux cheveux blancs; **2** fig (ancient) [*problem*] éternel/-elle; **a ~ old joke** une plaisanterie éculée.

hoax /həʊks/ **I** *n* (practical joke) canular *m*.
II *modif* [*call, claim, warning*] bidon°; [*bomb*] factice.
III *vtr* monter un canular° à; **we've been ~ed!** on nous a eus°!

hob /hɒb/ *n* **1** (on cooker, stove) table *f* de cuisson; **2** (on open fire) plaque *f* (*sur laquelle on tient la bouilloire au chaud*).

hobble /ˈhɒbl/ **I** *n* **1** (limp) boitillement *m*; **2** (strap for horse) entrave *f*, abot *m*.
II *vtr* (fetter) entraver [*animal*].
III *vi* (limp) boitiller, clopiner; **to ~ in/out/along** entrer/sortir/avancer clopin-clopant°.

hobbledehoy‡ /ˌhɒbəldɪˈhɔɪ/ *n* grand dadais *m*, godichon†° *m*.

hobble skirt *n* jupe *f* entravée, jupe *f* fourreau.

hobby /ˈhɒbɪ/ *n* passe-temps *m inv*, violon *m* d'Ingres; **hobbies and interests** (on cv) centres *mpl* d'intérêt.

hobby horse *n* **1** (toy) *bâton emmanché d'une tête de cheval en bois*; **2** (obsession) dada *m* pej; cheval *m* de bataille.

hobbyist /ˈhɒbɪɪst/ *n* gen amateur *m*; (collector) collectionneur/-euse *m/f*.

hobgoblin /ˈhɒbgɒblɪn/ *n* **1** (in folklore) gnome *m*, lutin *m*; **2** fig (obsession) hantise *f*.

hobnail /ˈhɒbneɪl/ *n* caboche *f*; **~(ed) boots** souliers *mpl* ferrés or à clous.

hobnob○ /ˈhɒbnɒb/ *vi* (*p prés etc* **-bb-**) **to ~ with sb** frayer○ avec qn.

hobo /ˈhəʊbəʊ/ *n* (*pl* **~s** ou **~es**) **1** (urban vagrant) clochard/-e *m/f*, vagabond/-e *m/f*; **2** US (migratory worker) (travailleur) saisonnier *m*.

Hobson /ˈhɒbsn/ *pr n*: IDIOMS **it's ~'s choice** c'est un choix qui n'en est pas un.

hock /hɒk/ **I** *n* **1** (of horse etc) jarret *m*; Culin jarret *m* (de porc); **2** Wine vin *m* du Rhin; **3**○ (pawn) **to be in ~** (pawned) être au clou○, être engagé au mont-de-piété; (in debt) être endetté; **to be in ~ to sb** devoir de l'argent à qn; **to get sth out of ~** retirer qch du clou○.
II *vtr* (pawn) mettre [qch] au clou○.

hockey /ˈhɒkɪ/ ▶ 1282 *n* **1** GB (also **field ~**) hockey *m*; **2** US (also **ice ~**) hockey *m* sur glace.

hockey player *n* hockeyeur/-euse *m/f*, joueur/-euse *m/f* de hockey.

hockey stick *n* crosse *f* de hockey; **she's rather jolly ~s** fig elle a un côté scout.

hocus-pocus /ˌhəʊkəsˈpəʊkəs/ **I** *n* **1** (conjuror's skill) tour *m* de passe-passe; **2** péj (trickery) supercherie *f*, tour *m* de passe-passe; **3** (jargon) charabia *m*; **a lot of political ~** (activities) des tours de passe-passe de politiciens; (verbal) du blabla○ de politiciens.
II *excl* abracadabra!

hod /hɒd/ *n* (for coal) seau *m* à charbon; (for bricks) oiseau *m*, auge *f*, hotte *f*.

hod carrier ▶ 1692 *n* porteur *m* de briques (*sur un chantier*).

hodgepodge *n* US = **hotchpotch**.

hoe /həʊ/ **I** *n* houe *f*, binette *f*.
II *vtr* biner [*ground*]; sarcler [*plants, flower-beds, weeds*].
IDIOMS **to have a hard row to ~** avoir une lourde tâche à accomplir.

hoedown /ˈhəʊdaʊn/ *n* US **1** (folk dance) danse *f* (de village); **2** (social evening) sauterie *f* (de village).

hog /hɒg/ **I** *n* **1** GB (castrated pig) porc *m* châtré; **2** US (pig) porc *m*, verrat *m*; **3**○ (person) pourceau *m*; **4**○ US (car) grosse américaine *f*.
II○ *vtr* (*prét, pp* **-gg-**) (monopolize) monopoliser.
IDIOMS **to go the whole ~**○ (be extravagant) voir les choses en grand; (go to extremes) aller jusqu'au bout.

Hogarthian /həˈgɑːθɪən/ *adj* à la (manière de) Hogarth; fig grotesque, caricatural.

Hogmanay /ˈhɒgmənеɪ/ *n* GB dial Saint-Sylvestre *f*, réveillon *m*.

hogshead /ˈhɒgzhed/ *n* barrique *f*.

hogtie /ˈhɒgtaɪ/ *vtr* lier les pattes de [*pig, cow*]; fig réduire [qn] à l'impuissance [*person*].

hogwash /ˈhɒgwɒʃ/ *n* (pigswill) pâtée *f* des cochons; fig foutaise○ *f*.

hoick○ /hɔɪk/ *vtr* GB (also **~ up**) hisser, soulever; **she ~ed her bag onto the table** elle a posé son sac sur la table.

hoi polloi /ˌhɔɪ pəˈlɔɪ/ *npl* péj plèbe *f* pej, populace *f*.

hoist /hɔɪst/ **I** *n* palan *m*; **to give sb a ~ (up)** faire la courte échelle à qn.
II *vtr* hisser [*flag, sail, heavy object*].
IDIOMS **to be ~ with one's own petard** être pris à son propre piège.

hoity-toity○ /ˌhɔɪtɪˈtɔɪtɪ/ *adj* péj prétentieux/-ieuse.

hoke○ /həʊk/ *vtr* US **she ~s (up) her performance too much** elle en fait trop.

hokey-cokey /ˌhəʊkɪˈkəʊkɪ/ *n* hokey-cokey *m* (*genre de farandole accompagnée de chant*).

hokum○ /ˈhəʊkəm/ *n* ¢ US (nonsense) absurdités *fpl*, niaiseries *fpl*; (sentimentality) mièvrerie *f*.

hold /həʊld/ ▶ 1068 **I** *n* **1** (grasp, grip) prise *f*; **to get ~ of** attraper [*rope, handle*]; **to keep (a) ~ of** ou **on** tenir [*ball, rail, hand*]; ▶ **catch, grab, grasp, seize, take**; **2** (possession) **to get ~ of** se procurer [*book, ticket, document*]; [*press*] avoir vent de [*story*]; découvrir [*details, information*]; **3** (contact) **to get ~ of** (by phone) joindre [*person*]; (by other means) trouver [*person*]; **4** (control) emprise *f* (**on, over** sur); **to have a ~ on** ou **over sb** avoir de l'emprise sur qn; **to get a ~ of oneself** se reprendre; **5** (storage, area) Aviat soute *f*; Naut cale *f*; **6** Sport (in wrestling) prise *f*; **to have sb in a ~** faire une prise à qn; **7** (of hairspray, gel) fixation *f*; **normal/extra ~** fixation normale/extra-forte.
II *vtr* (*prét, pp* **held**) **1** (clasp) tenir [*object, hand, person*] (**above, over** au-dessus de; **against** contre); **to ~ sth in one's hand** tenir qch à la main [*brush, pencil, stick*]; (enclosed) tenir qch dans la main [*button, coin, sweet*]; **to ~ sth/sb by** tenir qch/qn par [*handle, stem, sleeve, leg*]; **to ~ one's stomach/head (in pain)** se tenir l'estomac/la tête (à cause de la douleur); **to ~ sb (in one's arms)** serrer qn dans ses bras; **to ~ each other** se serrer l'un contre l'autre; **can you ~ my bag for me?** tu peux me tenir mon sac?; **2** (maintain) **to ~ one's head upright/still** tenir sa tête droite/immobile; **to ~ one's hands apart/still** tenir ses mains écartées/immobiles; **to ~ a pose/smile** garder une pose/un sourire; **to ~ sth in place** ou **position** maintenir qch en place; **to ~ one's speed** maintenir sa vitesse; **3** (arrange) organiser, tenir [*meeting, talks*]; organiser [*competition, ballot, demonstration, course, election*]; organiser, donner [*party, reception*]; organiser, monter [*exhibition, show*]; avoir [*conversation*]; célébrer [*church service*]; mener [*enquiry*]; faire passer [*interview*]; **to be held** avoir lieu; **4** (have capacity for) [*box, case, tank*] (pouvoir) contenir [*objects, amount*]; [*theatre, room*] avoir une capacité de [*350 people*]; **the bus ~s ten (people)** le bus a dix places; **to (be able to) ~ one's drink** ou **liquor** tenir l'alcool; **5** (contain) [*drawer, cupboard, box, case*] contenir [*objects, possessions*]; **6** (support) [*shelf, fridge, branch, roof*] supporter [*weight, load, crate*]; **the branch won't ~ you** la branche ne supportera pas ton poids; **7** (restrain) [*dam, wall*] retenir, contenir [*water, flood waters*]; [*person*] tenir [*dog*]; maîtriser [*thief*]; **there is/there'll be no ~ing him** fig on ne peut/pourra plus l'arrêter; **8** (keep against will) [*police, kidnappers*] détenir [*person*]; **to ~ sb prisoner/hostage** garder qn prisonnier/en otage; **9** (possess) détenir, avoir [*shares, power, record, playing card*]; être titulaire de [*degree, sporting title, cup*]; occuper [*job, position*]; avoir, être en possession de [*ticket, passport, licence*]; porter [*title*]; Jur, gen [*bank, computer, police, solicitor*] conserver [*document, information, money*]; avoir [*mortgage*]; **10** (keep back) garder [*place, seat, ticket*]; faire attendre [*train, flight*]; mettre [qch] en attente [*letter, order*]; **~ it**○! minute○!; **~ everything!** arrêtez tout!; **two burgers, but ~ the mustard!** deux hamburgers, sans moutarde!; **11** (believe) avoir [*opinion, belief*]; **to ~ sb/sth to be** tenir qn/qch pour, considérer qn/qch comme; **to ~ that** [*person*] soutenir que; [*law, theory*] dire que; **to ~ sb liable** ou **responsible** tenir qn pour responsable; **12** (defend successfully) Mil tenir [*territory, city, bridge*]; Pol, Sport conserver [*title, seat, lead, position*]; (in tennis) **to ~ one's serve** ou **service** gagner or remporter son service; **to ~ one's own** [*person*] se défendre tout seul (**against** contre); [*army*] tenir bon (**against** devant); **13** (captivate) captiver [*person, audience, class*]; capter, retenir [*attention, interest*]; **14** Telecom **to ~ the line** patienter, rester en ligne; **can you ~ the line please** ne quittez pas s'il vous plaît; **15** Mus tenir [*note*] (**for** pendant); **16** Aut **to ~ the road** tenir la route.
III *vi* (*prét, pp* **held**) **1** (remain intact) [*rope, shelf, bridge, dam, glue*] tenir; fig (also **~ good**) [*theory, offer, objection, law*] tenir; **2** (continue) [*weather*] rester beau/belle, se maintenir; [*luck*] continuer, durer; **3** Telecom patienter; **4** (remain steady) **~ still!** tiens-toi tranquille!
IV *v refl* (*prét, pp* **held**) **to ~ oneself upright/well** se tenir droit/bien.
V on ~ *adv phr* **1** Telecom en attente; **to put sb on ~** Telecom faire patienter qn; **to put a call on ~** Telecom mettre un appel en attente; **2 to put one's plan/a project on ~** gen laisser ses projets/un projet en suspens.

■ **hold against**: **to ~ sth against sb** reprocher qch à qn; **to ~ it against sb that** en vouloir à qn parce que; **I don't ~ it against him/them** je ne lui/leur en veux pas; **your age could be held against you** ton âge pourrait jouer en ta défaveur.

■ **hold back**: ¶ **~ back** se retenir; **to ~ back from doing** se retenir de faire, préférer ne pas faire; ¶ **~ [sb/sth] back, ~ back [sb/sth] 1** (restrain) contenir [*water, tide, crowd, animals*]; retenir [*hair, tears*]; retenir [*person*]; refouler [*feelings*]; contenir [*anger*]; **to ~ back one's laughter** se retenir or s'empêcher de rire; **2** (prevent progress of) (involuntarily) [*person*] retarder [*person, group*]; (deliberately) [*person*] retenir [*person*]; [*background, poor education*] gêner [*person*]; entraver [*production, progress, development*]; **3** (withhold) [*person, government, organization*] cacher [*information, result*]; (to protect privacy) tenir [qch] secret, ne pas divulguer [*name, information, identity*]; [*person, company*] différer [*payment*].

■ **hold down**: **~ [sb/sth] down, ~ down [sb/sth] 1** (prevent from moving) maintenir [qch] en place [*tent, carpet, piece of paper*]; tenir, maîtriser [*person*]; **2** (press down) appuyer sur [*pedal, key*]; **3** (keep at certain level) limiter [*number, rate, expenditure, costs, inflation*]; limiter l'augmentation de [*wages, taxes, prices*]; **4** (keep) (not lose) garder [*job*]; (have) avoir [*job*].

■ **hold forth** péj disserter, pérorer pej (**about, on** sur).

■ **hold in**: **~ [sth] in, ~ in [sth] 1** (restrain) réprimer, contenir [*feeling, anger, disappointment*]; **2** (pull in) rentrer [*stomach, buttocks*].

■ **hold off**: ¶ **~ off** [*enemy*] accorder un répit; [*creditors*] accorder un délai; **I hope the rain ~s off** j'espère qu'il ne pleuvra pas; **the rain held off until after the match** il s'est mis à pleuvoir après le match; **to ~ off buying/making a decision** reporter l'achat/la décision à plus tard; **he held off leaving until the weekend** il a reporté son départ au week-end; ¶ **~ [sb] off, ~ off [sb]** tenir [qn] à distance [*enemy, creditor, journalists*]; faire patienter [*client*]; ¶ **~ [sth] off** repousser [*attack*].

■ **hold on**: ¶ **~ on 1** (wait) gen attendre; Telecom patienter; **'~ on, I'll just get him'** (on telephone) 'ne quittez pas, je vais le chercher'; **2** (grip) tenir (**with** de, avec); **'~ on (tight)!'** 'tiens-toi (bien)!'; **3** (endure) [*person, company*] tenir; ¶ **~ [sth] on** [*screw, glue*] maintenir [qch] en place; **to be held on with sth** [*door, handle, wheel*] être maintenu par qch.

■ **hold on to**: **~ on to [sb/sth] 1** (grip) s'agripper à [*branch, railing, rope*]; s'agripper à, se tenir à [*person*]; (to prevent from falling) agripper, retenir [*person*]; serrer [*object, purse*]; (bien) tenir [*dog*]; **2** (retain) conserver [*power, title, lead*]; garder [*shares,* car]; **to ~ on to one's dreams** fig s'accrocher à ses rêves; **to ~ on to one's** ou **the belief that** persister à croire que; **3** (look after) garder [*object*] (**for** pour).

■ **hold out**: ¶ **~ out 1** (endure) tenir le coup, tenir bon; **to ~ out against** tenir bon devant [*enemy, changes, threat*]; **2** (remain available) [*supplies, food, stocks*] durer; ¶ **~ [sth] out, ~out [sth]** tendre [*glass, money, ticket*] (to à); **to ~ out one's hand/leg** tendre la main/la jambe; ¶ **~ out [sth]** garder, conserver [*hope*]; **I don't ~ out much hope** je ne me fais guère d'illusions, je n'ai plus beaucoup d'espoir; **they don't ~ out much hope of finding him** ils ont perdu presque tout espoir de le retrouver; **to ~ out for** insister pour obtenir [*pay rise, increase*]; **to ~ out on sb**○ cacher des choses à qn; **they know something, but they're ~ing out on us** ils sont au courant mais ils nous cachent quelque chose.

■ **hold over**: **~ [sth] over, ~ over [sth] 1** (postpone) ajourner [*question, programme*]; **2** (continue to show) maintenir [qch] à l'affiche [*film*]; prolonger [*show, exhibition*].

■ **hold to**: ¶ **~ to [sth]** s'en tenir à [*belief, opinion, decision*]; ¶ **~ sb to [sth]** faire tenir [qch] à qn [*promise*]; faire honorer [qch] à qn [*contract, offer*]; **I'll ~ you to that!** je note!, je m'en souviendrai!

■ **hold together**: ¶ **~ together 1** (not break) [*car, shoes, chair*] tenir; **2** (remain united) [*family, party*] rester uni; [*alliance*] rester intact; ¶ **~ [sth] together 1** (keep intact) faire tenir [*car, machine, chair*]; maintenir ensemble [*papers, pieces*]; **to be held together with sth** tenir avec qch; **2** (unite) assurer la cohésion de [*company, party, government*]; **my mother held the family together** la famille est restée unie grâce à ma mère.

■ **hold up**: ¶ **~ up 1** (remain intact) tenir, résister; **to ~ up well** [*currency*] résister; **2** (remain valid) [*theory, argument*] tenir; ¶ **~ [sb/sth] up, ~ up [sb/sth] 1** (support) soutenir [*shelf, picture*]; tenir [*trousers, stockings*]; **to be held up by** ou **with sth** tenir avec qch; **2** (raise) lever [*object*]; **to ~ one's hand up** lever la main; **3** (display) **to ~ sb/sth up as an example** ou **model of** présenter qn/ qch comme un exemple de; **to ~ sb up to ridicule** tourner qn en ridicule, ridiculiser qn; **4** (delay) retarder [*person, flight*]; ralentir [*production, traffic*]; arrêter, interrompre [*procession*]; **5** (rob) attaquer [*train, bank, person*].

■ **hold with**: **not to ~ with** ne pas être d'accord avec [*idea, system*]; être contre [*television, imitations etc*]; **he doesn't ~ with teaching children French** il est contre le fait qu'on enseigne le français aux enfants.

holdall /ˈhəʊldɔːl/ *n* sac *m*.

holder /ˈhəʊldə(r)/ *n* **1** (person who possesses something) (of passport, degree, post) titulaire *mf*; (of ticket, record) détenteur/-trice *m/f*; (of cup, title) tenant/-e *m/f*; (of key) détenteur/-trice *m/f*; (of shares) porteur/-euse *m/f*; **account ~** titulaire d'un compte; **credit card/passport ~** titulaire d'une carte de crédit/d'un passeport; **record/ticket ~** détenteur/-trice d'un record/billet; **cup/title ~** tenant/-e d'une coupe/d'un titre; **2** (container, stand) support *m*.

holding /ˈhəʊldɪŋ/ *n* **1** Fin avoir *m*; **2** Agric exploitation *f*.

holding: **~ company** *n* Fin holding *m*, société *f* de portefeuille or de holding; **~ paddock** *n* enclos *m* provisoire; **~ pattern** *n* Aviat circuit *m* d'attente.

hold-up /ˈhəʊldʌp/ *n* **1** (delay) gen retard *m*; (on road) embouteillage *m*, bouchon *m*; **2** (robbery) hold-up *m*, attaque *f* à main armée.

hole /həʊl/ **I** *n* **1** (in clothing, ground, hedge, pocket) trou *m* (**in** dans); **to dig a ~** creuser un trou; **the explosion blew a ~ in the plane** l'explosion a fait un trou dans l'avion; **this sweater is full of ~s** ce pull est tout troué; **2** (in wall) brèche *f*; **3** GB (in tooth) cavité *f*; **4** Aut (in road) (pothole) nid *m* de poule; (man-made) trou *m*; **5** fig (flaw) faille *f*; **to pick ~s in an argument** repérer les failles d'un raisonnement; **6** (of mouse) trou *m*; (of fox, rabbit) terrier *m*; **7** Ecol trou *m*; **a ~ in the ozone layer** un trou dans la couche d'ozone; **8** (financial) trou *m*; **a big ~ in profits** un grand trou dans les bénéfices; **that holiday made a ~ in my pocket** ces vacances ont fait un trou dans mon budget; **9**○ (place) péj trou○ *m* pej; **10** Sport (golf) (all contexts) trou *m*; **to get a ~ in one** faire un trou en un; **a nine-~ golf course** un parcours de neuf trous; **11** US (solitary confinement) trou○ *m*.

II *vtr* **1** [*shell*] crever [*building*]; **2** Naut [*iceberg, reef*] faire une brèche dans [*ship*]; **3** Sport (golf) **to ~ the ball** ou **shot** ou **putt** rentrer la balle, faire le trou (**in** en).

III *vi* Sport (in golf) faire or terminer le trou.

IDIOMS **to be 10 dollars in the ~** US en être de 10 dollars○; **to get oneself into a ~**○ se fourrer dans le pétrin○; **to get sb out of a ~** tirer qn du pétrin○; **I needed that like I need a ~ in the head**○! il ne me manquait plus que ça! ▶ **money**.

■ **hole up** se terrer.

■ **hole out** (in golf) finir le parcours (**in** en).

hole-and-corner *adj* clandestin.

hole-in-the-heart *n* (ventricular) communication *f* interventriculaire; (auricular) communication *f* interauriculaire.

holey○ /ˈhəʊlɪ/ *adj* [*garment*] troué.

holiday /ˈhɒlədeɪ/ **I** *n* **1** GB (vacation) vacances *fpl*; **the school ~s** les vacances scolaires; **the summer ~s** les vacances d'été, les grandes vacances; **half-term ~** petites vacances; **family ~** vacances en famille; **to go/be on ~** partir/être en vacances; **2** GB (time off work) congé *m*; **to take ten days' ~** prendre dix jours de congé; **four weeks' ~ with pay** quatre semaines de congés payés; **3** (public, bank) jour *m* férié; **4** US **the ~s** les fêtes (de fin d'année); **happy ~s!** bonnes fêtes!

II *modif* [*region, brochure*] touristique.

III *vi* passer les vacances.

holiday: **~ atmosphere** *n* air *m* de fête; **~ camp** *n* GB camp *m* de vacances; **~ home** *n* résidence *f* secondaire; **~ job** *n* GB (in summer) job○ *m* d'été; **~maker** *n* GB gen vacancier/-ière *m/f*; (summer visitor) estivant/-e *m/f*; **~ resort** *n* lieu *m* de villégiature; **~ season** *n* GB saison *f* des vacances; **~ traffic** *n* GB circulation *f* de la route des vacances.

holier-than-thou /ˌhəʊlɪəðənˈðaʊ/ *adj* **to be ~** se prendre pour un petit saint; **this ~ attitude** cette attitude de petit saint.

holiness /ˈhəʊlɪnɪs/ *n* sainteté *f*.

Holiness /ˈhəʊlɪnɪs/ ▶ **1268** *n* **His/Your ~** Sa/Votre Sainteté.

holism /ˈhɒlɪzəm, ˈhəʊ-/ *n* holisme *m*.

holistic /hɒˈlɪstɪk, ˈhəʊ-/ *adj* holistique.

holland† /ˈhɒlənd/ **I** *n* (cloth) toile *f* de Hollande.

II *modif* [*blind, cover*] en toile de Hollande.

Holland /ˈhɒlənd/ ▶ **1131** *pr n* Hollande *f*, Pays-Bas *mpl*; **in ~** en Hollande, aux Pays-Bas.

holler○ /ˈhɒlə(r)/ **I** *n* hurlement *m*.

II *vtr* brailler [*warning, command*].

III *vi* brailler, gueuler (**at sb** après qn).

hollow /ˈhɒləʊ/ **I** *n* **1** (depression) (in tree) creux *m*; (of hand, back) creux *m*; (in hillside) dépression *f*; **2** Geog (small valley) cuvette *f*.

II *adj* **1** (not solid) [*space, object*] creux/creuse; **the wall sounds ~** le mur sonne creux; **2** (sunken) [*cheeks, eyes*] creux/creuse; **3** (booming) [*voice, cough, clang*] caverneux/-euse; **4** (insincere) [*words*] faux/fausse; [*promise*] vain; **to give a ~ laugh** avoir un rire forcé; **to sound ~** [*excuse, explanation, advice*] sonner faux; **5** (empty) [*victory, triumph, joy*] vain.

IDIOMS **to beat sb ~**○ battre qn à plates coutures; **to hold sb in the ~ of one' s hand** tenir qn en son pouvoir.

■ **hollow out**: **~ [sth] out, ~ out [sth]** creuser [*hole, pond*]; **the centre of the log had been ~ed out** on avait évidé le centre de la bûche.

hollow: **~-cheeked** *adj* aux joues creuses; **~-eyed** *adj* aux yeux caves; **~ fibre, ~ fill** *adj* [*pillow, duvet*] garni en fibre synthétique.

hollowly /ˈhɒləʊlɪ/ *adv* [*echo, sound*] d'une manière caverneuse.

holly /ˈhɒlɪ/ **I** *n* (tree, wood) houx *m*.

II *modif* [*berry, branch*] de houx.

hollyhock /ˈhɒlɪhɒk/ *n* rose *f* trémière.

holm oak /ˌhəʊmˈəʊk/ *n* (tree, wood) chêne *m* vert.

holocaust /ˈhɒləkɔːst/ *n* **1** holocauste *m*; **2** Hist **the Holocaust** l'Holocauste *m*.

Holocene /ˈhɒləsiːn/ **I** *n* **the ~** l'holocène *m*.

II *adj* holocène.

hologram /ˈhɒləgræm/ *n* hologramme *m*.

holograph /ˈhɒləgrɑːf, US -græf/ *n* (also **~ document**) document *m* olographe.

holography /həˈlɒgrəfɪ/ *n* holographie *f*.

holophrastic /ˌhɒləˈfræstɪk/ *adj* holophrastique.

hols○ /hɒlz/ *n* GB (*abrév* = **holidays**) vacances *fpl*.

holster /ˈhəʊlstə(r)/ *n* étui *m* de revolver; (on saddle) fonte *f*.

holy /ˈhəʊlɪ/ *adj* [*writings, place, community, person*] saint; [*well, water*] bénit; **~ picture** image *f* pieuse; **to lead a ~ life** mener une vie sainte; **on ~ ground** en lieu saint; **~ cow**○!, **~ smoke**○!, **~ mackerel**○!, **~ shit**◐! zut alors○!

holy: **Holy Bible** *n* Sainte Bible *f*; **~ city** *n* ville *f* sainte; **Holy Communion** *n* sainte communion *f*; **~ day** *n* jour *m* saint; **Holy Father** *n* Saint-Père *m*; **Holy Ghost** *n* = **Holy Spirit**; **Holy Grail** *n* Saint-Graal *m*; **Holy Innocents' Day** *n* jour *m* des saints Innocents; **Holy Joe**○ *n* grenouille *f* de bénitier○; **Holy Land** *n* Terre *f* Sainte; **~ of holies** *n* Relig, fig le Saint des Saints; **Holy Roman Empire** *n* Saint Empire *m* romain germanique; **Holy Sacrament** *n* saint sacrement *m*; **Holy Saturday** *n* Samedi *m* saint; **Holy See** *n* Saint-Siège *m*; **Holy Sepulchre** *n* Saint-Sépulcre *m*; **Holy Spirit** *n* Saint-Esprit *m*; **Holy Trinity** *n* sainte Trinité *f*; **~ war** *n* guerre *f* sainte; **Holy Week** *n* semaine *f* sainte; **Holy Writ** *n* Saintes Écritures *fpl*.

homage /ˈhɒmɪdʒ/ *n* hommage *m*; **to pay ~ to sb** rendre hommage à qn; **in ~ to** en hommage à.

homburg /ˈhɒmbɜːg/ *n* chapeau *m* mou.

home /həʊm/ **I** *n* **1** (dwelling) gen logement *m*; (house) maison *f*; **new ~s for sale** journ logements neufs à vendre; **he doesn't have a ~** il n'a pas de logement; **you have a beautiful ~** vous avez une belle maison/un bel appartement; **to be far from/near ~** être loin de/près de chez soi; **a ~ of one's own** un chez-soi; **to work from ~** travailler à domicile; **to set up ~ in France/in Madrid** s'installer en France/à Madrid; **I've made my ~ in France now** je suis installé or je vis en France maintenant; **birds make their ~ in...** les oiseaux font leur nid dans...; **his ~ has been a tent for the last two weeks** il habite dans une tente depuis deux semaines; **the island is ~ to 3,000 people** l'île abrite 3 000 personnes; **2** (for residential care) maison *f*; **retirement/nursing ~** maison de retraite/de santé; **to put sb in a ~** mettre qn dans un établissement spécialisé; **3** (family base) foyer *m*; **broken ~** foyer désuni; **to make a ~ for** créer un foyer pour; **'good ~ wanted'** 'cherche foyer accueillant'; **to leave ~** quitter la maison; **4** (country) pays *m*; **to consider France (as) ~** considérer la France comme son pays; **5** (source) **~ of** [*country*] pays *m* de [*speciality*]; [*place*] lieu *m* privilégié pour [*tennis, golf*]; [*jungle, region*] habitat *m* de

[*species*]; **6**○ fig (place) place *f*; **to find a ~ for** trouver une place pour [*book, object*].
II *modif* **1** (family) [*life*] de famille; [*surroundings, background*] familial; [*comforts*] du foyer; **2** (national) [*market, affairs*] intérieur; [*news*] national; **3** Sport (local) [*match, win*] à domicile; [*team*] qui reçoit.
III *adv* **1** [*come, go, arrive*] (to house) à la maison, chez soi; (to country) dans son pays; **on the journey ~** (to house) en rentrant à la maison; (to apartment, room) en rentrant chez moi/nous etc; (by boat, plane) pendant le voyage de retour; **to see sb ~** raccompagner qn à la maison; **to take sb ~** (accompany) raccompagner qn à la maison; (to meet family) emmener qn à la maison; **is she ~?** est-ce qu'elle est à la maison?; **is she ~ yet?** elle est déjà rentrée?; **2** (to required position, effect) **to hammer** ou **drive sth ~** lit enfoncer complètement [*nail*]; fig bien faire passer [*message*]; **to press** ou **push one's point ~** enfoncer le clou fig; **to bring sth ~ to** fig faire voir qch à; **to strike ~** fig toucher juste.
IV at home *adv phr* **1** (in house) [*be, work, stay*] à la maison; **to live at ~** habiter chez ses parents; **at ~ and abroad** dans notre pays et à l'étranger; **Madam is not at ~**† Madame ne reçoit personne; **2** Sport (on own ground) [*play*] à domicile; **they're at ~ on Saturday** ils jouent à domicile samedi; **X are playing Y at ~** X reçoit Y; **3** fig (comfortable) [*be, feel*] à l'aise (**with** avec); **make yourself at ~** mets-toi à l'aise, fais comme chez toi.
V *vi* [*animal*] savoir retourner chez soi.
IDIOMS **it's/he's nothing to write ~ about** ça/il n'a rien d'extraordinaire; **it's ~ from ~** GB, **it's ~ away from ~** US c'est un second chez-soi; **~ sweet ~, there's no place like ~** Prov on n'est nulle part si bien que chez soi; **to be a bit too close to ~** être blessant; **he found it a bit close to ~** ça l'a touché au vif; **let's talk about something nearer ~** parlons de ce qui nous concerne plus particulièrement; **to be ~ and dry** être sauvé.
■ **home in** [*missile*] se diriger vers sa cible; **to ~ in on** se diriger sur [*target*].

home: **~ address** *n* (on form) domicile *m*; (personal not business) adresse *f* personnelle; **~ baked** *adj* (fait) maison; **~ banking** *n* banque *f* à domicile; **~ birth** *n* accouchement *m* à domicile; **~body**○ *n* casanier/-ière *m/f*.

homebound /ˈhəʊmbaʊnd/ *adj* surtout US **1** (housebound) confiné chez soi; **2** (heading home) [*traffic, car, traveller*] rentrant chez soi; [*train*] du retour.

home: **~ brew** *n* bière *f* (brassée) maison; **~ buying** *n* accession *f* à la propriété; **~ centre** GB, **home center** US *n* maisonnerie *f*; **~ comforts** *npl* confort *m* du foyer ¢.

homecoming /ˈhəʊmkʌmɪŋ/ **I** *n* **1** (return home) retour *m* à la maison; **2** US Sport *match de football annuel du lycée suivi d'un bal*.
II *modif* US Sport **~ king/queen** roi/reine *m/f* de la fête.

home: **~ computer** *n* ordinateur *m*, PC *m*; **~ cooking** *n* bonne cuisine *f* familiale; **Home Counties** *npl* GB comtés *mpl* limitrophes de Londres; **~ country** *n* pays *m* d'origine, patrie *f*; **~ economics** *n* (+ *v sg*) Sch cours *m* d'économie domestique.

home front *n* (during war) **the ~** l'arrière *m*; **on the ~** (in politics) pour les affaires intérieures.

home ground *n* fig terrain *m* familier; **on ~** en terrain familier; **to win on one's ~** Sport gagner à domicile.

homegrown /ˌhəʊmˈgrəʊn/ *adj* **1** [*vegetables*] du jardin; **2** fig [*idea*] bien de chez soi (*after n*).

home: **Home Guard** *n* GB Hist *groupe de volontaires recrutés pour défendre le pays en cas d'invasion*; **~ heating** *n* chauffage *m* domestique; **~ help** *n* GB aide familiale *f*; **~land** *n* pays *m* d'origine, patrie *f*; (in S. Africa) bantoustan *m*; **~ leave** *n* Mil permission *f*.

homeless /ˈhəʊmlɪs/ **I** *n* **the ~** (+ *v pl*) les sans-abri *mpl*.
II *adj* [*person, family*] gen sans abri, sans logement; (after earthquake, flood etc) sinistré.

homelessness /ˈhəʊmlɪsnɪs/ *n* **the problem of ~** le problème des sans-abri; **~ is on the increase** le nombre des sans-abri est en augmentation.

home life *n* vie *f* de famille.

homeliness /ˈhəʊmlɪnɪs/ *n* **1** (unpretentious nature) (of room, hotel, atmosphere, furniture) simplicité *f* accueillante; (of cooking) simplicité *f*; (of person) GB simplicité *f*; **2** US péj (plainness) manque *m* d'attraits.

home: **~ loan** *n* prêt *m* immobilier; **~loving** *adj* casanier/-ière.

homely /ˈhəʊmlɪ/ *adj* **1** GB (cosy) [*hotel, atmosphere*] accueillant; **2** GB (unpretentious) [*room, hotel*] sans prétention; [*person*] simple; **3** US (plain) [*person*] sans attraits.

home: **~made** *adj* (fait) maison; **~maker** *n* (woman) femme *f* d'intérieur; (woman or man) personne *f* qui tient la maison; **~ movie** *n* film *m* d'amateur; **Home Office** *n* Pol ministère *m* de l'Intérieur.

homeopath /ˌhəʊmɪəˈpæθ/ *n* homéopathe *mf*.

homeopathic /ˌhəʊmɪəˈpæθɪk/ *adj* [*medicine, clinic*] homéopathique; [*doctor*] homéopathe.

homeopathy /ˌhəʊmɪˈɒpəθɪ/ *n* homéopathie *f*.

home owner *n* propriétaire *mf*.

home ownership *n* fait *m* d'être propriétaire de son logement; **~ is on the increase** de plus en plus de gens sont propriétaires de leur logement.

home: **~ page**, *n* Comput page *f* d'accueil; **~ plate** *n* Sport marbre *m*; **~ port** *n* port *m* d'attache; **~ posting** *n* Mil affectation *f* au pays.

Homer /ˈhəʊmə(r)/ *pr n* Homère.

Homeric /həʊˈmerɪk/ *adj* homérique.

home: **~ room** *n* US Sch salle *f* de classe (*où l'appel est fait*); **~ rule** *n* Pol gouvernement *m* autonome; **~ run** *n* Sport point *m* marqué par le batteur (*s'il réussit à toucher toutes les bases*); **~ sales** *npl* Econ ventes *fpl* sur le marché intérieur; **Home Secretary** *n* Pol Ministre *m* de l'Intérieur; **~ shopping** *n* téléachat *m*.

homesick /ˈhəʊmsɪk/ *adj* **to be ~** [*child*] s'ennuyer de ses parents; [*adult*] (for country) avoir le mal du pays; **I'm ~ for my dog** mon chien me manque.

home: **~sickness** /ˈhəʊmsɪknɪs/ *n* mal *m* du pays; **~ side** *n* = **home team**.

homespun /ˈhəʊmspʌn/ *adj* **1** [*cloth*] filé à la maison; **2** fig [*wisdom, virtue*] naturel/-elle; [*person*] simple.

homestead /ˈhəʊmsted/ *n* **1** (house and land) domaine *m*; **2** (farm) ferme *f*; **3** US Admin terres *fpl* (*acquises pour leur occupation et leur exploitation*).

Homestead Act *n* US loi *f* des terres fédérales de 1862 (*accordant aux pionniers la propriété de terres qu'ils occupaient et exploitaient*).

homesteader /ˈhəʊmstedə(r)/ *n* **1** (farmer) ≈ fermier/-ière *m/f*; **2** Hist colon *m*, pionnier *m*.

home: **~ teacher** ▶ **1692** *n* US maître/maîtresse *m/f*; **~ team** *n* équipe *f* qui reçoit; **~time** *n* Sch heure *f* de rentrer à la maison; **~ town** *n* ville *f* natale; **~ video** *n* vidéo *f* d'amateur; **~ visit** *n* Med visite *f* à domicile.

homeward /ˈhəʊmwəd/ **I** *adj* [*journey*] de retour.
II *adv* **to go** ou **head** ou **travel ~(s)** rentrer; **to be ~ bound** être sur le chemin de retour; **~-bound commuters** banlieusards rentrant chez eux.

home waters *npl* Naut, Pol eaux *fpl* territoriales.

homework /ˈhəʊmwɜːk/ **I** *n* **1** Sch devoirs *mpl*; **2** (research) **to do some ~ on** faire quelques recherches au sujet de; **you haven't done your ~!** tu ne t'es pas documenté!
II *modif* [*book*] de devoirs; **~ diary** cahier de textes.

home: **~worker** *n* travailleur/-euse *m/f* à domicile; **~working** *n* travail *m* à domicile.

homey /ˈhəʊmɪ/ *adj* **1** (cosy) [*room, hotel, atmosphere*] accueillant; **2** (unpretentious) [*room, hotel, cooking*] sans prétention.

homicidal /ˌhɒmɪˈsaɪdl/ *adj* homicide.

homicide /ˈhɒmɪsaɪd/ *n* **1** (murder) homicide *m*; **culpable/justifiable ~** Jur homicide volontaire/justifiable; **2** (person) meurtrier/-ière *m/f*; **3** US = **homicide bureau**.

homicide bureau *n* US brigade *f* criminelle.

homily /ˈhɒmɪlɪ/ *n* homélie *f*.

homing /ˈhəʊmɪŋ/ *adj* Tech, Mil [*missile, weapon, rocket*] autoguidé; [*system, device*] d'autoguidage.

homing: **~ instinct** *n* Zool faculté *f* d'orientation; **~ pigeon** *n* pigeon *m* voyageur.

hominy grits /ˈhɒmɪnɪ grɪts/ *n* US (maize) maïs *m* concassé; (dish) bouillie *f* de maïs.

homo● /həʊməʊ/ *n* US injur pédé● *m* offensive, homosexuel *m*.

homogeneity /ˌhɒmədʒɪˈniːɪtɪ/ *n* homogénéité *f*.

homogeneous /ˌhɒməˈdʒiːnɪəs, ˌhɒməʊ-/ *adj* homogène.

homogenize /həˈmɒdʒɪnaɪz/ *vtr* Culin homogénéiser.

homogenous /həˈmɒdʒɪnəs/ *adj* homogène.

homograph /ˈhɒməgrɑːf, US -græf/ *n* homographe *m*.

homographic /ˌhɒməˈgræfɪk/ *adj* homographe.

homography /hɒˈmɒgrəfɪ/ *n* homographie *f*.

homologous /həˈmɒləgəs/ *adj* homologue.

homologue GB, **homolog** US /ˈhɒməlɒg/ *n* Chem homologue *m*.

homonym /ˈhɒmənɪm/ *n* homonyme *m*.

homonymic /ˌhɒməˈnɪmɪk/ *adj* homonymique.

homophobe /ˈhɒməfəʊb/ *n* personne *f* intolérante envers les homosexuels.

homophobia /ˌhɒməˈfəʊbɪə/ *n* intolérance *f* envers les homosexuels.

homophobic /ˌhɒməˈfəʊbɪk/ *adj* qui fait preuve d'intolérance envers les homosexuels.

homophone /ˈhɒməfəʊn/ *n* homophone *m*.

homophonic /ˌhɒməˈfɒnɪk/ *adj* homophone.

homophony /həˈmɒfənɪ/ *n* homophonie *f*.

Homo sapiens /ˌhəʊməʊ ˈsæpɪenz/ *n* Homo sapiens *m*.

homosexual /ˌhɒməˈsekʃʊəl/ **I** *n* homosexuel/-elle *m/f*; **practising** ou **active ~s** les homosexuels actifs.
II *adj* homosexuel/-elle.

homosexuality /ˌhɒməˌsekʃʊˈælətɪ/ *n* homosexualité *f*.

homy○ /ˈhəʊmɪ/ *adj* = **homely** 1.

Hon 1 (*abrév écrite* = **Honourable**) **the ~ Anne Grey** l'honorable Anne Grey; **2** (*abrév écrite* = **Honorary**) honoraire.

honcho○ /ˈhɒntʃəʊ/ *n* (*pl* **~s**) US (important person) gros bonnet○ *m*; (hotshot) crack○ *m*; **he's the head ~** c'est le grand chef○.

Honduran /hɒnˈdjʊərən/ ▶ **1486** **I** *n* Hondurien/-ienne *m/f*.
II *adj* du Honduras, hondurien/-ienne.

Honduras /hɒn'djʊərəs/ ▶ **1131** pr n Honduras m; **in/to ~** au Honduras.

hone /həʊn/ I n pierre f à aiguiser.
II vtr **1** (perfect) aiguiser [*technique, skill, strategy*]; affûter [*argument, wit, style*]; **2** (sharpen) aiguiser [*axe, blade, knife*].

honest /'ɒnɪst/ I adj **1** (truthful) [*person*] intègre; [*account, answer*] sincère; **to be ~ about sth** être honnête au sujet de qch; **the ~ truth** la pure vérité; **2** (trustworthy) honnête; **3** (sincere) [*face*] franc/franche; [*attempt*] fait de bon cœur; **to be ~ with sb** être franc avec qn; **to be ~ with oneself** être honnête avec soi-même; **to be less than ~ with sb** ne pas être tout à fait franc avec qn; **be ~!** sois franc!; **to be ~,...** à dire vrai...; **4** (legal) [*profit, money*] honnêtement acquis; [*price*] juste; **by ~ means** par des moyens légitimes; **to make an ~ living** gagner honnêtement sa vie; **he's never done an ~ day's work** il n'a jamais fait une vraie journée de travail de sa vie!
II excl **it wasn't me, ~**○ ou **~ to God!** ce n'était pas moi, parole d'honneur!; **~ to goodness** ou **~ to God, have you any sense!** mais, ma parole, n'as-tu aucun bon sens!
IDIOMS **to make an ~ woman of sb** hum épouser qn.

honest broker n Pol honnête courtier m.

honestly /'ɒnɪstlɪ/ adv **1** (truthfully) [*answer*] honnêtement; **2** (legally) [*earn*] honnêtement; **3** (sincerely) [*believe*] franchement; [*say*] sincèrement; **I ~ don't know** franchement, je ne sais pas; **do you ~ think you're going to win?** est-ce que tu crois sincèrement que tu vas gagner?; **quite ~,...** franchement...; **4** (as sentence adv) vraiment; **~, I mean it!** je le pense vraiment; **~? surely not!** vraiment? non, sûrement pas!; **~, there's no problem** je vous assure, il n'y a aucun problème; **5**○ (in exasperation) franchement!

honest-to-goodness adj **1** (simple) [*holiday, meal*] simple; **2** US (authentic) véritable.

honesty /'ɒnɪstɪ/ n **1** (truthfulness, integrity) honnêteté f; **to have the ~ to admit sth** avoir l'honnêteté d'admettre qch; **2** (sincerity) (of person, statement) sincérité f; **3** Bot ¢ monnaie f du pape.
IDIOMS **~ is the best policy, ~ pays** l'honnêteté est toujours récompensée.

honey /'hʌnɪ/ n **1** (food) miel m; **acacia/clover ~** miel m d'acacia/de trèfle; **clear ~** miel m liquide; **2**○ surtout US (endearment) chéri/-e m/f; (addressing woman) chérie f; **she's a ~**† c'est un amour.

honey: **~bee** n abeille f; **~bunch**○, **~bun** n US chéri/-e m/f; **~-coloured** GB, **~-colored** US ▶ **1104** adj (couleur de) miel inv.

honeycomb /'hʌnɪkəʊm/ I n **1** (in hive) rayon m de miel; **2** (for sale) gâteau m de miel.
II modif **1** [*pattern, design*] en nid-d'abeilles; **2** Aviat **~ structure** métal m alvéolé.

honeycombed /'hʌnɪkəʊmd/ adj **~ with** percé de [*holes*]; creusé de [*passages, tunnels*]; truffé de [*spies*].

honey: **~dew** n miellat m; **~dew melon** n melon m d'Espagne.

honeyed /'hʌnɪd/ adj mielleux/-euse.

honeymoon /'hʌnɪmu:n/ I n **1** (wedding trip) voyage m de noces; **they spent their ~ in Paris** ils sont allés à Paris en voyage de noces; **to be on one's ~** être en voyage de noces; **2** fig (also **~ period**) (calm spell) lune f de miel.
II vi **we ~ed in Paris** nous sommes allés à Paris en voyage de noces.

honeymoon couple n couple m en voyage de noces.

honeymooner /'hʌnɪmu:nə(r)/ n nouveau/-elle marié/-e m/f (en voyage de noces).

honeymoon suite n suite f nuptiale.

honeypot /'hʌnɪpɒt/ n **1** pot m à miel; **2**◑ US (vagina) vagin m.
IDIOMS **like bees around a ~** comme des mouches sur un pot de miel.

honeysuckle /'hʌnɪsʌkl/ n chèvrefeuille m.

Hong Kong /ˌhɒŋ 'kɒŋ/ ▶ **1818** I n Hongkong m.
II adj [*people, cuisine*] de Hongkong; **the ~ Chinese** les Chinois de Hongkong.

honk /hɒŋk/ I n (of car horn) coup m de klaxon®; (of geese) cri m (de l'oie).
II vtr **to ~ one's horn** klaxonner.
III vi [*geese*] cacarder; [*car horn*] faire tut-tut; [*driver*] klaxonner; **drivers were ~ing at them** les conducteurs les klaxonnaient.

honkie◑, **honky**◑ /'hɒŋkɪ/ n US injur sale○ Blanc/Blanche m/f offensive.

honky-tonk /'hɒŋkɪtɒŋk/ I n **1** (music) musique f de bastringue; **2**○ US (club) bastringue○ m, boîte f de nuit○.
II adj [*music*] de bastringue○; [*piano*] bastringue○.

honor n, vtr US = **honour**.

honorable adj US = **honourable**.

honorably adv US = **honourably**.

honorarium /ˌɒnə'reərɪəm/ n (pl **-ria**) honoraires mpl.

honorary /'ɒnərərɪ, US 'ɒnərerɪ/ adj **1** [*doctorate, degree*] honorifique, honoris causa inv; [*member, fellowship, membership*] honoraire; [*man, woman, Northerner*] hum pour la forme; **2** (voluntary) [*post, position*] bénévole.

honor guard n US membre m de la garde d'honneur.

honorific /ˌɒnə'rɪfɪk/ adj honorifique.

honor roll n US **1** Sch, Sport tableau m d'honneur; **2** Mil liste f des soldats tombés au champ d'honneur.

honor: **~ society** n US Sch club m des meilleurs élèves; **~ system** n US Sch système m de l'autodiscipline.

honour GB, **honor** US /'ɒnə(r)/ I n **1** (privilege) honneur m; **to consider sth a great ~** considérer qch comme un grand honneur; **place of ~** place d'honneur; **it is an ~ (for sb) to do** c'est un honneur (pour qn) de faire; **to have the ~ to do** ou **of doing** avoir l'honneur de faire; **to give sb** ou **do sb the ~ of doing** faire à qn l'honneur de faire; **to be an ~ to sb/sth** faire honneur à qn/qch; **in ~ of sb/sth** en l'honneur de qn/qch; **to what do I owe this ~?** sout ou iron que me vaut cet honneur? sout ou iron; **buried with full ~s** enterré avec les honneurs suprêmes; **2** (high principles) honneur m; **a man of ~** un homme d'honneur; **to impugn sb's ~** sout mettre en doute l'honneur de qn; **a point/an affair of ~** un point/une affaire d'honneur; **~ is satisfied** l'honneur est satisfait; **to give one's word of ~** donner sa parole d'honneur; **in ~** en tout honneur; **to be on one's ~ to do** être engagé sur l'honneur à faire; **I swear it (up)on my ~**† ou **~ bright**†! je le jure sur mon honneur†!; **3** (in titles) **Your Honour** Votre Honneur.
II **honours** npl **1** Univ **to graduate with ~s** ≈ réussir sa licence avec mention; **first/second class ~s** ≈ licence avec mention très bien/bien; **2** (in cards) honneurs mpl.
III vtr **1** (show respect for) honorer [*parents, spouse, dead, hero, artist, guest, leader, flag*]; **to feel/be ~ed** se sentir/être honoré (**by** par); **we would be ~ed** nous serions honorés; **I feel** ou **am ~ed that she trusts me** sa confiance m'honore; **to ~ sb by doing** sout faire l'honneur à qn de faire; **welcome to our ~ed guests** bienvenue à nos honorables invités; **2** (fulfil, be bound by) honorer [*cheque, contract, debt, obligation, signature, terms*]; tenir [*promise, commitment*]; remplir [*agreement, arrangement*].
IDIOMS **there is ~ among thieves** les loups ne se mangent pas entre eux; **to do the ~s** (serve food, drinks) faire les honneurs; (introduce guests) faire les présentations.

honourable GB, **honorable** US /'ɒnərəbl/ adj **1** (principled) [*man, woman, intention*] honnête; **to do the ~ thing** faire la seule chose convenable; **it is/it is not ~ to do** c'est/ce n'est pas honnête de faire; **2** (worthy) [*calling, profession, tradition*] honorable; **3** (consistent with self-respect) [*defeat, victory, war, peace, settlement, performance*] honorable; **4** ▶ **1268** (in titles) **the Honourable Mr Justice Jones** le Juge Jones; **the Honourable Gentleman/Lady** Pol Monsieur/Madame le député; **my Honourable friend** GB Pol mon honorable collègue.

honourable: **~ discharge** n libération f honorable; **~ mention** n mention f honorable.

honourably GB, **honorably** US /'ɒnərəblɪ/ adv [*acquit oneself, fight, withdraw*] honorablement; [*behave, marry*] honnêtement; **to be ~ defeated** subir une défaite honorable.

honour: **~-bound** adj tenu par l'honneur (**to do** de faire); **~s course** n GB *cours universitaire ordinaire*; US *cours universitaire réservé aux meilleurs étudiants*; **~s degree** n GB *licence ordinaire*; US *licence réservée aux meilleurs étudiants*; **Honours List** n GB *liste de distinctions honorifiques conférées par le monarque à l'occasion de son anniversaire ou du 1er janvier*.

hooch○ /hu:tʃ/ n US **1** (alcohol) boisson f alcoolisée; **2** argot des soldats (thatched hut) hutte f; (shack) cabane f.

hood /hʊd/ n **1** (head gear) (attached) capuchon m; (detached) capuche f; (balaclava) cagoule f; **2** (for falcon) chaperon m; **3** (cover) (on stove, cooker) hotte f; (on printer) capot m (antibruit); **4** GB (on car, pram) capote f; **to put the ~ up/down** relever/abaisser la capote; **5** Aviat (cockpit) verrière f; **6** US Aut (bonnet) capot m; **7** (on cobra) capuchon m; **8** Univ (ceremonial) épitoge f; **9**○ US (gangster) truand m; (juvenile delinquent) loubard○ m.

hooded /'hʊdɪd/ adj **1** [*sweatshirt, jacket*] à capuchon; **2** [*attacker, rioter, hostage*] le visage caché par une cagoule; [*figure, falcon*] encapuchonné; **3 to have ~ eyes** ou **eyelids** avoir les paupières tombantes.

hooded: **~ crow** n corneille f mantelée; **~ seal** n phoque m à capuchon.

hoodlum○ /'hu:dləm/ n **1** (hooligan) vandale m; (juvenile delinquent) loubard○ m; **2** US (crook) truand m, escroc m.

hoodoo○ /'hu:du:/ n (pl **~s**) poisse○ f.

hoodwink /'hʊdwɪŋk/ vtr tromper; **to ~ sb into doing sth** tromper qn pour qu'il fasse qch.

hooey◑ /'hu:ɪ/ n ¢ US bobards○ mpl, idioties fpl; **oh ~!** quelles salades○!

hoof /hu:f/ n (pl **~s** ou **hooves**) (of horse, cow) sabot m (d'animal); **cattle bought on the ~** du bétail acheté sur pied.
IDIOMS **to ~ it**○ aller à pinces○ or à pied; **to think up a policy on the ~** improviser une politique.

hoof-and-mouth disease n US fièvre f aphteuse.

hoofed /hu:ft/ adj [*animal*] à sabots.

hoofer○ /'hu:fə(r)/ n US danseur/-euse m/f professionnel/-elle.

hoof pick n Equit cure-pied m.

hoo-ha○ /'hu:hɑ:/ n pagaille f; **they made a real ~ about it** ils en ont fait tout un foin○.

hook /hʊk/ I n **1** (for clothing, picture) crochet m; **2** Fishg hameçon m; **3** Sewing agrafe f; **~s and eyes** agrafes fpl; **4** Agric, Hort faucille f; **5** (on stick) crosse f; **6** Telecom **to take the phone off the ~** décrocher le téléphone; **to leave the phone off the ~** laisser le téléphone décroché; **7** (boxing) crochet m; **left/right ~** crochet du gauche/du droit; **8** (golf) coup m hooké; **9** US (bend) coude m, courbe f; **10** Comm accroche f.

II *vtr* **1** (hang) accrocher (**on, onto** à; **round** autour de); **2** (pull through) faire passer [*string, loop*] (**through** dans); passer [*limb, finger, stick*] (**through** dans); **3** Fishg prendre [*fish*]; fig, hum○ mettre le grappin sur○ [*spouse*]; **4** (golf) hooker; (rugby) talonner.
IDIOMS **to be off the ~** être tiré d'affaire; **to get sb off the ~** tirer qn d'affaire; **to let sb off the ~** laisser filer○ qn; **to get one's ~s into sb** mettre le grappin sur qn○.
■ **hook on**: ¶ **~ on** s'accrocher (**to** à); ¶ **~ [sth] on, ~ on [sth]** accrocher (**to** à).
■ **hook together**: ¶ **~ together** s'accrocher ensemble; ¶ **~ [sth] together** accrocher [qch] ensemble.
■ **hook up**: ¶ **~ up** [*garment*] s'agrafer; ¶ **~ up [sth], ~ [sth] up** **1** (attach) agrafer [*garment*]; accrocher [*trailer, picture*]; **2** Radio, TV faire un duplex entre [*stations*]; **3** Elec, Tech connecter [*appliance*].

hookah /'hʊkə/ *n* narguilé *m*.

hooked /hʊkt/ *adj* **1** [*nose, claw, beak*] crochu; [*stick*] avec une crosse; **2** (addicted) accro○; **to be ~ on** se camer○ à [*crack, heroin*]; être mordu○ de [*computer games, game shows*]; **3**○ US (married) casé○, marié.

hooker /'hʊkə(r)/ *n* **1** (in rugby) talonneur *m*; **2**● (prostitute) putain● *f*, prostituée *f*.

hook: **~ nose** *n* nez *m* crochu; **~-nosed** *adj* au nez crochu.

hook-up /'hʊkʌp/ *n* **1** Radio, TV relais *m*; **2** US (in trailer park) borne *f* de raccordement.

hookworm /'hʊkwɜːm/ *n* ankylostome *m*.

hooky○, **hookey** /'hʊkɪ/ *n* US **to play ~** faire l'école buissonnière†.

hooligan /'huːlɪgən/ *n* vandale *m*, voyou *m*; **soccer ~** hooligan *m*.

hooliganism /'huːlɪgənɪzəm/ *n* vandalisme *m*.

hoop /huːp/ *n* **1** (of metal, wood, bone) cerceau *m*; **2** (in croquet) arceau *m*.
IDIOMS **to go through the ~s, to jump through ~s** se démener; **to put sb through the ~s** obliger qn à faire ses preuves.

hoopla /'huːplɑː/ ▶ **1282** *n* **1** GB (at fair) jeu *m* d'anneaux; **2**○ US (showy publicity) battage *m*; **3**○ US (fuss) pagaille *f*; (bustle) remue-ménage *m*; (noise) brouhaha *m*.

hoopoe /'huːpuː/ *n* huppe *f*.

hooray /hʊ'reɪ/ *excl* hourra.

Hooray Henry *n* GB péj fils *m* à papa pej.

hoosier○ /'huːʒə(r)/ *n* péj péquenaud/-e○ *m/f* pej.

hoot /huːt/ **I** *n* **1** (noise) (of owl) (h)ululement *m*; (of train) sifflement *m*; (of ship or factory siren) mugissement *m*; (of car) coup *m* de klaxon®; (derisive shout) huée *f*; **this was greeted with ~s of laughter** ceci a déclenché l'hilarité générale; **2**○ (person) **she's a ~** elle est impayable; **it was a ~** c'était très marrant○.
II *vi* [*owl*] (h)ululer; [*train*] siffler; [*siren*] mugir; [*car*] klaxonner; [*person, crowd*] (derisively) huer; **to ~ with laughter** éclater de rire.
III *vtr* huer [*speaker, actor*]; **to be ~ed off the stage** quitter la scène sous les huées; **to ~ one's horn** donner un coup de klaxon® (**at sb** pour avertir qn).
IDIOMS **I don't give a ~** ou **two ~s**○! je m'en fiche○ comme de l'an quarante!
■ **hoot down**: ¶ **~ down [sb], ~ [sb] down** huer; ¶ **~ down [sth], ~ [sth] down** rejeter [qch] avec dérision [*plan, proposal*].

hootenanny /,huːtə'nænɪ/ *n* réunion *f* de chanteurs folk.

hooter /'huːtə(r)/ **I** *n* **1** (siren) sirène *f*; GB Aut† (horn) cornet† *f*, klaxon® *m*; **2**○ GB (nose) pif○ *m*.
II **hooters**○ *npl* US (breasts) nichons○ *mpl*.

hoover /'huːvə(r)/ *vtr* GB **to ~ a carpet/a room** passer l'aspirateur sur un tapis/dans une pièce.

Hoover® /'huːvə(r)/ *n* GB aspirateur *m*.

hooves /huːvz/ *pl* ▶ **hoof**.

hop /hɒp/ **I** *n* **1** (movement) (of frog, rabbit, child) bond *m*; (of bird) sautillement *m*; **with a ~** d'un bond; **in a series of little ~s** en sautillant; **2**○ (short journey) **a short ~** un saut *m* (de puce); **3**○ (dance) bal *m* (populaire); **the village ~** le bal du village.
II **hops** *npl* Agric, Bot (crop) houblon *m* ¢; **to grow ~s** cultiver le houblon.
III *vtr* (*p prés etc* **-pp-**) **1** (jump over) franchir [qch] d'un bond [*fence*]; **2**○ US (board) sauter dans [*flight, train, bus*].
IV *vi* (*p prés etc* **-pp-**) **1** (jump) [*person*] sauter; **to ~ off a wall** sauter d'un mur; **to ~ over a puddle/ditch** sauter par-dessus une flaque/un fossé; **to ~ up and down with rage/delight** trépigner de rage/de joie; **2** (on one leg) sauter à cloche-pied; **to ~ (over) to the door** sauter à cloche-pied jusqu'à la porte; **to ~ up/down the path** monter/descendre le sentier à cloche-pied; **3** [*animal*] sauter; [*bird*] sautiller; **a rabbit ~ped across the road** un lapin traversa la route en quelques bonds; **4** (move speedily) **to ~ into bed/on a plane/off a bus** sauter dans son lit/dans un avion/d'un bus; **I'll give you a lift, ~ in!** je t'emmène, vas-y, monte!; **5**○ (travel) **to ~ over** ou **across to** faire un saut○ à [*city, country*].
IDIOMS **to be ~ping mad**○ être fou furieux/folle furieuse; **to catch sb on the ~**○ GB prendre qn au dépourvu; **to ~ into bed with sb** se fourrer○ au lit avec qn; **to ~ it**○ GB déguerpir○; **go on, ~ it!** allez, du balai○!; **to keep sb on the ~**○ GB maintenir qn sous pression; **to be (kept) on the ~**○ être sous pression.
■ **hop about**, **hop around** [*child, bird*] sautiller.
■ **hop off**○ partir.

hope /həʊp/ **I** *n* **1** (desire, expectation) espoir *m*, espérance *f* (**of** de); (cause for optimism) espoir *m*; **in the ~ of sth/of doing** dans l'espoir de qch/de faire; **she cherishes the ~ that he is still alive** elle nourrit l'espoir qu'il soit encore vivant; **my (only) ~ is that he will be happy** mon (seul) espoir est qu'il soit heureux; **to have high ~s of sb/sth** fonder de grands espoirs sur qn/qch; **to have ~s of doing** avoir l'espoir de faire; **to have great** ou **high ~s of doing** avoir bon espoir de faire; **there is little/no ~ left for them** il y a peu/il n'y a plus d'espoir pour eux; **to pin** ou **set one's ~s on sth** mettre tout son espoir dans qch; **to set one's ~s on doing** espérer de tout cœur faire; **to be beyond (all) ~, to be without ~** être sans espoir; **to live in ~** vivre dans l'espoir; **to live in (the) ~ of sth** vivre dans l'espoir de qch; **to keep one's ~s high** garder espoir; **there are grounds for ~** il y a des raisons d'espérer; **to give sb new ~** ranimer l'espoir de qn; **all ~ is lost** c'est sans espoir; **to raise sb's ~s** faire naître l'espoir chez qn; **don't raise their ~s too much** ne leur donne pas trop d'espoir; **to dash sb's ~s** anéantir l'espoir de qn; **to lose/give up ~** perdre/abandonner espoir; **a glimmer** ou **ray of ~** une lueur d'espoir; **'~s rise for a peace settlement in the Middle East'** journ 'espoir de paix au Moyen-Orient'; **2** (chance) chance *f*, espoir *m*; **to have no ~ of sth/of doing sth** n'avoir aucune chance de qch/de faire qch; **there is little/no ~ that he will come** il y a peu de chances/il n'y a aucune chance qu'il vienne; **there is no ~ of an improvement** on ne peut pas s'attendre à une amélioration; **if the champion loses, what ~ is there for me?** si le champion perd, quelles sont mes chances à moi?; **our only ~ is to fight on** notre seule chance or seul espoir est de poursuivre la lutte; **his best ~ is that the champion may be tired** tout ce qu'il peut espérer est que le champion soit fatigué; **what a ~**○!, **some ~**○! il ne faut pas rêver!; **he hasn't got a ~ in hell**○ il n'a pas la moindre chance; **it's/she's my last ~** c'est/elle est mon dernier espoir; **3** (promising person) espoir *m*.
II *vtr* espérer (**that** que); **to ~ to do** espérer faire; **it is to be ~d that** il faut espérer que (+ *indic*); **I ~ (that) he'll come** j'espère qu'il viendra; **we cannot ~ to compete with big firms** nous n'avons aucune chance de rivaliser avec de grosses entreprises; **I only** ou **just ~ he remembers** j'espère seulement qu'il s'en souviendra; **we had hoped to make a profit this year, but...** nous espérions faire un bénéfice cette année, mais...; **I (do) ~ so/not** j'espère (bien) que oui/que non; **I won't forget'—'I should ~ not!'** 'je n'oublierai pas'—'j'espère bien que non!'; **'I'm sure he'll recover'—'I ~ so'** 'je suis sûr qu'il va se remettre'—'je l'espère'; **hoping to hear from you** (in letter) dans l'espoir d'avoir de vos nouvelles.
III *vi* espérer; **to ~ for sth** attendre or espérer avoir qch; **I ~d for a letter/success** j'attendais or j'espérais avoir une lettre/du succès; **don't ~ for too much** n'en attendez pas trop; **all we can do is ~** il ne nous reste qu'à espérer; **to ~ for the best** être optimiste.
IDIOMS **abandon ~, all ye who enter here** abandonnez toute espérance, vous qui entrez; **to ~ against ~** espérer en dépit de tout; **~ springs eternal (in the human breast)** l'espérance est inépuisable.

hope chest *n* US (chest) coffre *m* à trousseau; (trousseau) trousseau *m*.

hopeful /'həʊpfl/ **I** *n* (person) (showing promise) espoir *m*; (ambitious) ambitieux/-ieuse *m/f*; **young ~** jeune espoir *m*.
II *adj* **1** (filled with hope) [*person, expression*] plein d'espoir; [*attitude, mood, period*] optimiste; **to be ~ about sth** être optimiste quant à qch; **to be ~ of doing** avoir bon espoir de faire; **he is ~ that he will win** il a bon espoir de gagner; **we remain ~ that...** nous conservons l'espoir que...; **I am not ~ of success** je n'ai pas d'espoir de succès; **2** (encouraging) [*letter, news, result, sign, situation*] encourageant; [*development, period*] prometteur/-euse.

hopefully /'həʊpfəlɪ/ *adv* **1** (with luck) avec un peu de chance; **~, he'll pay** avec un peu de chance, il paiera; **'will he pay?'—'~'** 'c'est lui qui paiera?'—'je l'espère'; **2** (with hope) [*say*] avec optimisme; **she smiled at him ~** elle lui a addressé un sourire plein d'espoir.

hopeless /'həʊplɪs/ *adj* **1** (desperate) [*attempt, case, expression, grief, situation, struggle*] désespéré; [*mess, muddle*] inextricable; [*extravagance*] incurable; **it was ~ trying to convince her** il était impossible de la convaincre; **it's ~! I give up!** inutile! j'abandonne!; **2**○ (incompetent) [*person, work*] nul/nulle○ (**as** comme; **with** avec); **to be ~ at sth** être nul/nulle○ en qch; **to be ~ at doing** être incapable de faire; **he's a ~ case!** c'est un cas désespéré! also hum; **you're ~!** (affectionately) tu es incorrigible!

hopelessly /'həʊplɪslɪ/ *adv* **1** (irretrievably) [*drunk, inadequate, lost, out of date*] complètement; [*in debt*] jusqu'au cou○; [*in love*] éperdument; [*confused*] inextricablement; **to be ~ extravagant** jeter l'argent par les fenêtres; **2** (despairingly) [*speak, weep*] avec désespoir; [*look at*] désespérément.

hopelessness /'həʊplɪsnɪs/ *n* **1** (despair) désespoir *m*; **2** (futility) futilité *f* (**of doing** de faire).

hop: **~ field** *n* houblonnière *f*; **~-flavoured** *adj* GB [*beer*] au houblon.

hopper /'hɒpə(r)/ *n* **1** (for grain, sand, coal) trémie *f*; **2** (also **~ car**) wagon-trémie *m*; **3** Comput (device) magasin *m* d'alimentation (de cartes perforées).

hop: **~-picker** ▶ **1692** *n* (person) cueilleur/-euse *m/f* de houblon; (machine) récolteuse *f* de houblon; **~-picking** *n* cueillette *f* du houblon; **~sack** *n* US sac *m* en jute; **~sacking** *n* US toile *f* de jute; **~scotch** ▶ 1282 *n* marelle *f*.

Horae /ˈhɔːriː/ *pr npl* **the ~** les Heures *fpl*.

horde /hɔːd/ *n* (mass) (of people) foule *f* (**of** de); (of insects) nuée *f* (**of** de); (of animals) horde *f* (**of** de); **the ~(s)** la horde.

horehound /ˈhɔːhaʊnd/ *n* Bot marrube *m*.

horizon /həˈraɪzn/ *n* **1** (skyline) horizon *m*; **on the ~** lit (visible) à l'horizon; fig (imminent) en vue; **2** (of ideas, interests) horizon *m*; **to open up new ~s** ouvrir de nouveaux horizons; **to widen** ou **broaden one's ~s** élargir ses horizons; **a person of narrow ~s** une personne aux vues étroites; **3** (period) **within a 10 year ~** ou **a ~ of 10 years** en l'espace de 10 ans.
IDIOMS **the only cloud on the ~** la seule ombre au tableau.

horizontal /ˌhɒrɪˈzɒntl, US ˌhɔːr-/ **I** *n* horizontale *f*.
II *adj* horizontal.

horizontal: **~ bar** *n* barre *f* fixe; **~ integration** *n* concentration *f* horizontale.

horizontally /ˌhɒrɪˈzɒntəlɪ, US ˌhɔːr-/ *adv* horizontalement.

hormonal /hɔːˈməʊnl/ *adj* hormonal.

hormone: **~ replacement therapy, HRT** *n* hormonothérapie *f* substitutive; **~ treatment** *n* traitement *m* hormonal.

horn /hɔːn/ **I** *n* **1** Zool (of animal, snail) corne *f*; (of owl) aigrette *f*; fig (on moon, anvil) corne *f*; (of devil) corne *f*; **2** Mus ▶ 1481 cor *m*; **to play the ~** jouer du cor; **for ~** pour cor; **the ~s** les cors; **3** (of car) klaxon® *m*, avertisseur *m* (sonore); (of ship) sirène *f*; **to sound one's ~** [*car*] klaxonner; [*ship*] donner un coup de sirène; **4** ¢ (substance) corne *f*; **made of ~** en corne; **5** (for drinking) corne *f*.
II *modif* Mus [*player, teacher, solo*] de cor; [*concerto, part*] pour cor.
IDIOMS **to blow one's own ~** US chanter ses propres louanges; **to draw** ou **pull in one's ~s** (feeling hurt) rentrer dans sa coquille; (financially) réduire son train de vie; **to lock ~s with sb** croiser le fer avec qn; **to take the bull by the ~s** prendre or saisir le taureau par les cornes.
■ **horn in**○ US **to ~ in (on a conversation)** mettre son grain de sel○; **stop ~ing in** ne te mêle pas de ça.

horn: **~beam** *n* Bot charme *m*; **~bill** *n* Zool calao *m*.

horned /hɔːnd/ *adj* [*animals*] à cornes; [*devil*] cornu; **long-/short-~ sheep** moutons à longues cornes/à cornes courtes.

horned owl *n* Zool hibou *m* grand duc.

horned toad *n* crapaud *m* cornu.

hornet /ˈhɔːnɪt/ *n* frelon *m*.
IDIOMS **to stir up a ~'s nest** soulever un tollé; **it's a real ~'s nest** c'est un problème épineux.

hornless /ˈhɔːnlɪs/ *adj* [*cattle, species*] sans cornes.

horn: **~ of plenty** *n* corne *f* d'abondance; **~pipe** *n* matelote *f*; **~-rimmed** *adj* [*spectacles*] à monture d'écaille; [*frames*] d'écaille; **~ rims** *npl* lunettes *fpl* à monture d'écaille.

horny /ˈhɔːnɪ/ *adj* **1** (hornlike) [*claws, carapace, growth*] corné; [*protuberance*] cornu; **2** (calloused) calleux/-euse; **3**◑ (aroused) excité○; **to feel ~** se sentir tout excité○.

horology /həˈrɒlədʒɪ/ *n* **1** (science) chronométrie *f*; **2** (skill) horlogerie *f*.

horoscope /ˈhɒrəskəʊp, US ˈhɔːr-/ *n* horoscope *m*.

horrendous /hɒˈrendəs/ *adj* [*crime, conditions, accident*] épouvantable; [*problem, mistake, cost, noise*] effroyable.

horrendously /hɒˈrendəslɪ/ *adv* effroyablement.

horrible /ˈhɒrɪbl, US ˈhɔːr-/ *adj* **1** (unpleasant) [*place, clothes, smell, thought*] affreux/-euse; [*weather, holiday, food, person*] épouvantable; **to be ~ to sb** être méchant avec qn; **2** (shocking) [*crime, death, scene*] horrible.

horribly /ˈhɒrɪblɪ, US ˈhɔːr-/ *adv* **1** [*embarrassed, rude, apt*] terriblement; **the plan went ~ wrong** le projet a très mal tourné; **2** [*burned, disfigured, tortured*] horriblement; [*die, scream*] d'une manière atroce.

horrid /ˈhɒrɪd, US ˈhɔːrɪd/ *adj* **1** [*place, smell, thought, experience*] affreux/-euse; **2**† [*person*] méchant (**to sb** avec qn); **3**† [*crime, sight*] épouvantable.

horrific /həˈrɪfɪk/ *adj* atroce.

horrified /ˈhɒrɪfaɪd, US ˈhɔːr-/ *adj* horrifié (**at, by** par; **to do** de faire; **that** que + *subj*); **a ~ silence** un silence horrifié.

horrify /ˈhɒrɪfaɪ, US ˈhɔːr-/ *vtr* [*tragedy, crime*] remplir [qn] d'horreur; [*behaviour, ignorance, suggestion*] scandaliser.

horrifying /ˈhɒrɪfaɪɪŋ, US ˈhɔːr-/ *adj* [*event, experience, idea, report, sight*] horrifiant; [*behaviour, ignorance*] effroyable.

horror /ˈhɒrə(r), US ˈhɔːr-/ **I** *n* **1** (feeling) (all contexts) horreur *f* (**at** devant); **to his ~** à sa grande horreur; **to have a ~ of sth/of doing** avoir horreur de qch/de faire; **to recoil in ~** reculer d'horreur; **the full ~** toute l'horreur; **~ of ~s!** pour comble d'horreur!; **2**○ (person) **he's a little ~**○ c'est un petit monstre○; **3**○ (ugly thing) horreur *f*.
II *modif* [*film, story*] d'épouvante.
IDIOMS **to give sb the ~s** donner le frisson à qn.

horror-stricken, horror-struck *adj* frappé d'horreur.

horse /hɔːs/ *n* **1** cheval *m*; **the ~s**○ fig (horseracing) les courses *fpl* (de chevaux); **2** (in gym) cheval *m* de saut; (pommel) cheval *m* d'arçons; **3** Mil ¢ cavalerie *f*, troupes *fpl* à cheval; **4**○ (heroin) argot des drogués cheval○ *m*, héroïne *f*; **5**○ US (condom) préservatif *m*.
IDIOMS **I could eat a ~** j'ai une faim de loup; **to back the wrong ~** miser sur le mauvais cheval; **to eat like a ~** manger comme quatre; **to flog** GB ou **beat** US **a dead ~**○ s'acharner en pure perte; **(straight) from the ~'s mouth** de source sûre; **to get on one's high ~** monter sur ses grands chevaux; **hold your ~s!**○ arrêtez!, une minute! ; **it's ~s for courses** c'est la solution idoine; **you can take** ou **lead a ~ to water but you can't make it drink** Prov on ne saurait faire boire un âne qui n'a pas soif Prov; **that's a ~ of a different colour** ça c'est une autre paire de manches; **to work like a ~** travailler comme un forcené or une bête de somme; **wild ~s wouldn't drag it out of me** pour rien au monde je ne le révélerais; **wild ~s wouldn't drag me there** je n'irais pas pour tout l'or du monde!
■ **horse about, horse around** chahuter.

horse: **~-and-buggy**○ *adj* US péj antédiluvien/-ienne; **~ artillery** *n* artillerie *f* montée.

horseback /ˈhɔːsbæk/ **I** *n* **on ~** à cheval.
II *adv* US **to ride ~** faire du cheval.

horseback riding ▶ 1282 *n* US équitation *f*.

horse: **~box** *n* van *m*; **~ brass** *n* médaillon *m* de cuivre (*utilisé à l'origine comme décoration sur les harnais de chevaux de gros trait*); **~breaker** *n* dresseur/-euse *m/f* de chevaux; **~breeder** ▶ 1692 *n* éleveur/-euse *m/f* de chevaux; **~ chestnut** *n* (tree) marronnier *m* (d'Inde); (fruit) marron *m* (d'Inde); **~ collar** *n* collier *m* (de harnais); **~ dealer** *n* maquignon/-onne *m/f*; **~ doctor**○ *n* péj (vet) vétérinaire *mf*; (doctor) charlatan *m*; **~-drawn** *adj* [*carriage, vehicle*] tiré par des chevaux; **~flesh** *n* (horses collectively) chevaux *mpl*; (meat) viande *f* de cheval; **~fly** *n* taon *m*; **Horse Guards** *npl* GB Mil régiment *m* de la Garde à cheval.

horsehair /ˈhɔːsheə(r)/ **I** *n* crin *m* (de cheval).
II *modif* [*sofa, mattress*] de crin (de cheval).

horse: **~hide** *n* cuir *m* de cheval; **~ latitudes** *npl* zone *f* des calmes tropicaux; **~laugh** *n* gros rire *m*; **~man** *n* cavalier *m*; **~manship** *n* (activity) équitation *f*; (art, skill) aptitude *f* à l'équitation; **~ manure** *n* crottin *m* de cheval; **~meat** *n* viande *f* de cheval; **~ opera**○ *n* US western *m*; **~play** *n* chahut *m*.

horsepower /ˈhɔːspaʊə(r)/ *n* puissance *f* (en chevaux); (unit of power) cheval-vapeur *m*, cheval *m*; **a 90 ~ engine** un moteur de 90 chevaux.

horse: **~ race** *n* course *f* de chevaux; **~racing** *n* courses *fpl* de chevaux, courses *fpl* hippiques; **~radish** *n* raifort *m*; **~radish sauce** *n* sauce *f* au raifort; **~riding** ▶ 1282 *n* équitation *f*; **~ sense**○ *n* (gros) bon sens *m*; **~shoe** *n* fer *m* à cheval; **~shoe crab** *n* crabe *m* des Moluques, limule *f*; **~show** *n* concours *m* hippique; **~tail** *n* Bot prêle *f*; **~ trader** ▶ 1692 *n* lit, fig maquignon/-onne *m/f*; **~-trading** *n* lit, fig maquignonnage *m*; **~ trials** *npl* concours *m* complet d'équitation; **~ vaulting** *n* voltige *f*.

horsewhip /ˈhɔːswɪp/ **I** *n* cravache *f*.
II *vtr* (*p prés etc* **-pp-**) cravacher.

horsewoman /ˈhɔːswʊmən/ *n* cavalière *f*, écuyère *f*.

hors(e)y /ˈhɔːsɪ/ *adj* **1** (like a horse) péj [*face, appearance*] chevalin; **2** (interested in horses) passionné de chevaux; **the ~ set** le milieu de l'équitation.

horticultural /ˌhɔːtɪˈkʌltʃərəl/ *adj* horticole.

horticulture /ˈhɔːtɪkʌltʃə(r)/ *n* horticulture *f*.

horticulturist /ˌhɔːtɪˈkʌltʃərɪst/ ▶ 1692 *n* horticulteur/-trice *m/f*.

hose /həʊz/ **I** *n* **1** (also **~pipe** GB) (for garden) tuyau *m* d'arrosage; (for cleaning) jet *m* d'eau; **2** (also **fire ~**) lance *f* à incendie; **3** Aut (in engine) tuyau *m*; **4** (tubing) tuyau *m*; **a length of ~** un bout de tuyau; **5** GB (hosiery) bonneterie *f*; **6** Hist (garment) haut-de-chausses *m*; **7** GB†, US (stockings) bas *mpl*.
II *vtr* arroser [*garden*].
■ **hose down**: **~ [sth] down, ~ down [sth]** laver [qch] au jet.
■ **hose out**: **~ out [sth], ~ [sth] out** laver [qch] à grande eau.

hosepipe /ˈhəʊzpaɪp/ GB *n* **1** (garden) tuyau *m* d'arrosage; **2** (fire) lance *f* à incendie.

hosepipe ban *n* GB interdiction *f* d'utiliser les tuyaux d'arrosage.

hosier† /ˈhəʊzɪə(r), US ˈhəʊʒə(r)/ ▶ 1692 *n* bonnetier/-ière *m/f*.

hosiery‡ /ˈhəʊzɪərɪ, US ˈhəʊʒərɪ/ *n* bonneterie *f*.

hospice /ˈhɒspɪs/ *n* **1** (for the terminally ill) établissement *m* de soins palliatifs; **2** (for travellers) hospice *m*.

hospitable /hɒˈspɪtəbl/ *adj* [*person, family, country*] hospitalier/-ière (**to** envers); [*gesture, invitation*] accueillant; [*climate, conditions, terrain*] favorable.

hospitably /ˈhɒspɪtəblɪ, ˌhɒˈspɪt-/ *adv* avec hospitalité.

hospital /ˈhɒspɪtl/ **I** *n* hôpital *m*; **to/from ~** GB ou **the ~** US à/de l'hôpital; **to be taken to** ou **admitted to ~ with...** être hospitalisé pour...; **I've never been in ~** je n'ai jamais été hospitalisé; **he died in ~** il est mort à l'hôpital.
II *modif* [*facilities, staff, treatment, ward*] hospitalier/-ière; [*administration, food, waiting list*] des hôpitaux; **~ beds** lits *mpl* d'hôpital; **~ patient** patient/-e *m/f*.

hospital: **~ administrator** ▶ 1692 *n* directeur/-trice *m/f* d'hôpital; **~ authorities** *npl* comité *m* de gestion (d'un hôpital).

hospital corner *n* **to do ~s** ≈ faire un lit au carré.

hospital doctor ▶ 1692 *n* médecin *m* d'hôpital.

hospitality /ˌhɒspɪˈtælətɪ/ *n* hospitalité *f*.

hospitality suite *n* TV salon *m* d'accueil.

hospitalize /ˈhɒspɪtəlaɪz/ *vtr* hospitaliser.

hospital: **~ nurse** ▶1692 *n* infirmier/-ière *m/f* d'hôpital; **~ porter** ▶1692 *n* GB brancardier *m*; **~ ship** *n* navire-hôpital *m*.

host /həʊst/ **I** *n* **1** (to guests, visitors) hôte *m*; **to play ~ to sb** recevoir or accueillir qn; **2** Bot, Zool hôte *m*; **3** Rad, TV animateur/-trice *m/f*; **4**† ou hum (innkeeper) aubergiste *mf*; **mine ~** hum notre hôte hum; **5** (multitude) foule *f* (**of** de); **6**‡ (army) armée *f*; **7** Relig hostie *f*.
II *modif* [*animal, plant, cell*] hôte; **~ country** pays *m* hôte or d'accueil.
III *vtr* **1** [*city, country, institution etc*] être l'hôte de, accueillir; **2** Rad, TV animer.

hostage /ˈhɒstɪdʒ/ *n* otage *m*; **to take/hold sb ~** prendre/garder qn en otage.
IDIOMS **to give a ~ to fortune** prendre un gros risque.

hostage-taker /ˈhɒstɪdʒteɪkə(r)/ *n* preneur/-euse *m/f* d'otages.

hostel /ˈhɒstl/ **I** *n* **1** (residence) (for students, workers, refugees etc) foyer *m*; **(youth) ~** auberge *f* de jeunesse; **2**‡ = **hostelry**.
II *vi* passer ses vacances en auberge de jeunesse.

hosteller /ˈhɒstələ(r)/ *n* habitué/-e *m/f* des auberges de jeunesse.

hostelry‡ /ˈhɒstəlrɪ/ *n* auberge *f*.

hostess /ˈhəʊstɪs/ *n* **1** (to guests, visitors) hôtesse *f*, maîtresse *f* de maison; **2** (on plane, train, coach, in administration) hôtesse *f*; **3** Radio, TV animatrice *f*; **4** euph (in night-club etc) entraîneuse *f*.

hostile /ˈhɒstaɪl, US -tl/ *adj* hostile (**to** à); **~ takeover (bid)** Comm OPA *f* inamicale.

hostility /hɒˈstɪlətɪ/ **I** *n* hostilité *f*; **to show ~ to** ou **towards sb/sth** manifester de l'hostilité à l'égard de qn/à qch.
II hostilities *npl* Mil hostilités *fpl*.

hostler‡ /ˈɒslə(r)/ *n* palefrenier *m*.

hot /hɒt/ *adj* **1** (very warm) [*season, country, bath, plate, hands, feet*] chaud; [*sun*] chaud; [*food, drink*] (bien) chaud; **it's ~ here** il fait chaud ici; **the weather is ~ in July** il fait un temps chaud au mois de juillet; **it was a ~ day** il faisait chaud ce jour-là; **to be** ou **feel ~** [*person*] avoir chaud; **to get ~** [*person*] commencer à avoir trop chaud; [*parked car*] devenir chaud; [*engine, iron, oven, radiator*] chauffer; [*weather*] se réchauffer; **it gets ~ in this office** il fait parfois chaud dans ce bureau; **the room feels ~** il fait chaud dans cette pièce; **the sun felt ~ on his back** il sentait la chaleur du soleil sur son dos; **your forehead feels ~** tu as le front chaud; **digging is ~ work** ça donne chaud de bêcher le jardin; **she's had a ~ walk from the station** elle a eu chaud en venant à pied de la gare; **the sun is at its ~test at this time of day** c'est l'heure où le soleil est le plus chaud; **how ~ should I have the oven/iron?** à quelle température dois-je régler le four/le fer?; **to be ~ from the oven** [*bread, cake*] sortir du four; **to go ~ and cold** (with fever) être fiévreux/-euse; (with fear) avoir des sueurs froides; **it's terribly ~!** on étouffe!; **2** Culin [*mustard, spice, chili powder*] fort; [*curry, sauce, dish*] épicé; **3** (new, fresh) [*trail*] tout chaud; [*news*] tout chaud; **~ gossip** les derniers potins○; **4** (newly arrived) **Dr Mayer, ~ from the New York conference** le docteur Mayer, tout frais arrivé de la conférence de New York; **~ from** ou **off the press** tout chaud sorti de la presse; **5** (fierce, keen) [*competition*] acharné; [*pace*] rapide; **the pace got too ~ for him** le rythme est devenu trop rapide pour lui; **6** (short) **to have a ~ temper** s'emporter facilement; **7** (in demand)○ **to be ~** US [*entertainer, show, film*] faire un tabac○; **to be a ~ property** être demandé; **8**○ (good) **a ~ tip** un bon tuyau○; **the team is ~** US l'équipe marche fort; **a ~ streak** US une bonne passe; **to be the ~ favourite** être le grand favori; **if you think you are so ~, try it yourself!** puisque tu es si doué, fais-le toi-même!; **to be ~ on sth** (knowledgeable) être calé○ en qch; (keen, insistent) être très à cheval sur qch; **not so ~** pas terrible; **9**○ (difficult, unpleasant) **to make it** ou **things ~ for sb** mener la vie dure à qn; **10**○ (stolen) volé; **11** (bright) [*colour*] chaud; **~ pink** rose bonbon; **12** Mus [*jazz*] hot; **13** Nucl (radioactive) radioactif/-ive; **14** (close) **to be ~ on sb's trail** être sur les talons de qn; **to be ~ on the trail of sth** être sur la piste de qch; **to set off in ~ pursuit of sb** se lancer à la poursuite de qn; **a truck with two police cars in ~ pursuit** un camion avec deux voitures de police à ses trousses; (in guessing games) **you're getting ~** tu chauffes; **15**○ US (erotic) [*movie, scene*] érotique.
IDIOMS **to be in/get into ~ water** être/se mettre dans le pétrin○; **to blow ~ and cold** être d'humeur changeante; **to be/get all ~ and bothered** être/se mettre dans tous ses états; **to have the ~s for sb**○ en pincer pour qn○; **when you're ~ you're ~, and when you're not you're not** US il y a des jours avec et des jours sans.
■ **hot up**: ¶ **~ up 1** (become exciting) [*match*] s'animer; [*election campaign*] s'intensifier; **things are ~ting up** ça commence à chauffer○; **2** (get faster) **the pace is ~ting up** l'allure s'accélère; **3** (intensify) [*raids, war*] s'intensifier; ¶ **~ [sth] up** forcer [*pace*]; donner du punch○ à [*broadcast, campaign, speech, music*].

hot air○ *n* paroles *fpl* en l'air; **it's just so much ~!** ce ne sont que des paroles en l'air!

hot: **~ air balloon** *n* montgolfière *f*; **~bed** *n* foyer *m* (**of** de); **~-blooded** *adj* [*response, reaction*] passionné; [*race*] au tempérament fougueux or passionné.

hot cake *n* US ≈ crêpe *f*.
IDIOMS **to sell like ~s** GB, US se vendre comme des petits pains.

hotchpotch /ˈhɒtʃpɒtʃ/ *n* GB mélange *m*, mixture *f*.

hot cross bun *n* ≈ brioche *f* du vendredi saint.

hot dog I *n* hot-dog *m*.
II† *excl* US (expressing approval, pleasure) ça, alors!
III *vtr* (*p prés etc* **-gg-**) **1**○ (show off) faire de l'épate○; **2** (in skiing) faire du ski acrobatique.

hot dogging ▶1282 *n* ski *m* acrobatique.

hotel /həʊˈtel/ **I** *n* hôtel *m*.
II *modif* [*room, lobby, manager, restaurant, receptionist*] d'hôtel; [*price, industry, service*] hôtelier/-ière.

hotelier /həʊˈtelɪə(r)/ ▶1692 *n* hôtelier/-ière *m/f*.

hotelkeeper /ˌhəʊˈtelkiːpə(r)/ ▶1692 *n* GB hôtelier/-ière *m/f*.

hotel work *n* travail *m* dans l'hôtellerie.

hot flush GB, **hot flash** US *n* bouffée *f* de chaleur.

hotfoot /ˈhɒtfʊt/ **I** *adv* hum, iron [*go*] à toute vitesse or allure.
II○ *vtr* **to ~ it down to the pub/over to a friend's house** courir au pub/chez un ami.

hot: **~ gospeller** *n* GB péj, hum *prédicateur évangélique qui prêche avec enthousiasme*; **~ hatch(back)**○ *n* GB Aut petite voiture *f* puissante (*à trois ou cinq portes*); **~head** *n* péj tête *f* brûlée, exalté/-e *m/f*.

hot-headed /ˌhɒtˈhedɪd/ *adj* [*person*] impétueux/-euse, exalté; [*decision*] précipité.

hot-headedly /ˌhɒtˈhedɪdlɪ/ *adv* [*react*] sans réfléchir; **to rush ~ into things** foncer○ tête baissée.

hotheadedness /ˌhɒtˈhedɪdnɪs/ *n* impétuosité *f*.

hothouse /ˈhɒthaʊs/ **I** *n* **1** Hort serre *f* (chaude); **2** fig milieu *m* protégé.
II *modif* [*atmosphere*] de serre chaude; **~ child** enfant *mf* surdoué/-e; **~ school** école *f* pour enfants surdoués.
III *vtr* stimuler [*child*].

hothouse plant *n* lit, fig plante *f* de serre.

hothousing /ˈhɒthaʊzɪŋ/ *n* Sch *enseignement intensif destiné aux enfants surdoués*.

hotline /ˈhɒtlaɪn/ *n* **1** ligne *f* ouverte, permanence *f* téléphonique; **Aids/drugs ~** numéro *m* spécial SOS sida/drogue; **2** (between heads of state) téléphone *m* rouge.

hotly /ˈhɒtlɪ/ *adv* [*say, retort, exclaim*] passionnément; [*disputed, denied*] violemment; **the race/match was ~ contested** la lutte a été chaude.

hot: **~ money** *n* capitaux *mpl* spéculatifs or fébriles; **~ pants** *npl* short *m* moulant; **~ pepper** *n* piment *m* rouge; **~plate** *n* plaque *f* de cuisson; **~pot** *n* GB ragoût *m*.

hot potato○ *n* sujet *m* brûlant.
IDIOMS **to drop sb like a ~** laisser tomber qn du jour au lendemain.

hot rod *n* voiture *f* au moteur gonflé.

hot seat○ *n* US (electric chair) chaise *f* électrique.
IDIOMS **to be in the ~** être sur la sellette.

hot shit○ US **I** *n* **he thinks he's ~** il ne se prend pas pour rien.
II *excl* ça alors!

hot shoe *n* griffe *f* porte-flash.

hotshot○ /ˈhɒtʃɒt/ **I** *n* gen crack○ *m*; pej gros bonnet○ *m*.
II *adj* souvent péj [*executive*] de classe.

hot spot○ *n* **1** Journ, Pol point *m* chaud or névralgique; **2** Tourism pays *m* du soleil, destination *f* au soleil; **3** (nightclub) boîte *f* de nuit.

hot spring *n* source *f* chaude.

hot stuff○ *n* **to be ~** (talented) [*person*] être un crack; [*pop group*] être super○; (attractive) être sexy; (titillating) [*book, film*] être osé; **he thinks he's ~** il ne se prend pas pour rien.

hot-tempered /ˌhɒtˈtempəd/ *adj* colérique.

Hottentot /ˈhɒtntɒt/ ▶1402 **I** *n* **1** (person) Hottentot *mf*; **2** Ling hottentot *m*.
II *adj* hottentot.

hotter○ /ˈhɒtə(r)/ *n* GB jeune chauffard *m* en voiture volée.

hotting○ /ˈhɒtɪŋ/ *n* GB rodéo *m* (à la voiture volée).

hot: **~ tub** *n* US ≈ jacuzzi *m* de jardin; **~ war** *n* guerre *f* ouverte; **~ water bottle** *n* bouillotte *f*.

hot-wire○ /ˈhɒtwaɪə(r)/ *vtr* **to ~ a car** faire démarrer une voiture en trafiquant les fils.

houm(o)us *n* = **hummus**.

hound /haʊnd/ **I** *n* **1** Hunt chien *m* de chasse, chien *m* courant, chien *m* de meute; **a pack of ~s** une meute de chiens; **to ride to** ou **follow the ~s** chasser à courre; **2** hum (dog) clébard○ *m*; **3**○ (enthusiast) **autograph ~** chasseur/-euse *m/f* d'autographes; **publicity ~** personne *f* qui recherche la publicité.
II *vtr* (harass) harceler, traquer [*person*].
IDIOMS **to be like a ~ out of hell** être fou de rage.
■ **hound down**: **~ down [sb]**, **~ [sb] down** débusquer qn.
■ **hound out**: **~ [sb] out** chasser; **to be ~ed out of town** être chassé de la ville; **he was ~ed out of politics** il a été chassé de la vie politique.

hound-dog○ /ˈhaʊnddɒg/ *n* US **1** (dog) chien *m* (de meute); **2** (scoundrel) vaurien *m*.

houndstooth (check) /ˈhaʊndztuːθ/ **I** *n* Fashn, Tex pied-de-poule *m*.
II *modif* [*fabric, jacket, pattern*] pied-de-poule *inv*.

hour /aʊə(r)/ ▶1807, 1096 **I** *n* **1** (60 minutes) heure *f*; **an ~ ago** il y a une heure; **after an ~** au bout d'une heure; **a solid** ou **full ~** une heure entière; **for ~s** pendant des heures; **he'll be here within** ou **inside an ~** il sera là d'ici une heure; **it's an ~ (away) from London** c'est à une heure de Londres; **at 14.00 ~s** à 14 heures; **twice an ~** deux fois par heure; **£10 per ~** 10 livres sterling (de) l'heure; **to be paid by the ~** être payé à l'heure; **2** (time of day) heure *f*; **the clock strikes the ~** l'horloge sonne les heures; **the bus leaves on the ~** le bus part à l'heure juste; **she got home in the early ~s** elle est rentrée au petit matin; **at an early ~** de bonne heure; **to stay out until all ~s** rentrer très tard dans la nuit; **at this ~?** à l'heure qu'il est?; **at this late ~** fig au point où nous en sommes; **3** (point in time) heure *f*; **the ~ of his execution has come** l'heure de son exécution est arrivée; **your ~ has come** ton heure a sonné; **her finest/darkest ~** son heure de gloire/la plus sombre; **in my ~ of need** au temps de ma détresse.

II hours *npl* **1** (times) heures *fpl*; **business** ou **opening ~s** heures *fpl* d'ouverture; **office/visiting/working ~s** heures *fpl* de permanence/de visite/de travail; **our business ~s are 9 am to 2 pm** nous sommes ouverts de 9 h à 14 h; **I can't serve drinks after ~s** je ne peux pas vous servir à boire après l'heure de fermeture; **out of ~s** en dehors des heures d'ouverture; **to keep early/late ~s** se coucher tôt/tard; **to keep regular ~s** se coucher et se lever à des heures régulières; **2** Relig heures *fpl*; **book of ~s** livre *m* d'heures.

hour: **~glass** *n* sablier *m*; **~glass figure** *n* taille *f* mannequin; **~ hand** *n* aiguille *f* des heures.

hourly /ˈaʊəlɪ/ **I** *adj* **1** (every hour) [*bulletin*] horaire; **the buses are ~** les bus partent toutes les heures; **2** (per hour) [*pay, rate*] horaire; **on an ~ basis** à l'heure; **3** (continual) [*expectation, fear*] perpétuel/-elle.

II *adv* **1** (every hour) [*arrive, chime, depart, phone*] toutes les heures; **2** (per hour) **to pay sb ~** payer qn à l'heure; **3** (at any time) [*expect*] d'une heure à l'autre.

house I /haʊs *pl* haʊzɪz/ *n* **1** (home) maison *f*; **at my/his ~** chez moi/lui; **to go/come to sb's ~** aller/venir chez qn; **to be good around the ~** aider à la maison; **to keep ~** tenir la maison (**for** de); **you'll wake the whole ~** tu vas réveiller toute la maison; **the children were playing ~** les enfants jouaient au papa et à la maman; **2** (also **House**) Pol Chambre *f*; **the bill before the ~** le projet de loi soumis à la Chambre; **this ~ deplores** les députés ici présents déplorent; **3** Comm maison *f*; **on the ~** aux frais de la maison; **the drinks are on the ~!** c'est la maison qui offre!; **4** Theat (audience) assistance *f*; (auditorium) salle *f*; (performance) séance *f*; **'~ full'** (on notice) 'complet'; **is there a doctor in the ~?** y a-t-il un médecin dans la salle?; **there wasn't a dry eye in the ~** la salle entière était en émoi; **to bring the ~ down** faire crouler la salle de rire; **5** (also **House**) (family line) maison *f*; **the ~ of Windsor** la Maison des Windsor; **6** Relig maison *f*; **7** GB Sch (team) groupe *m* (*formé à l'entrée de l'école pour les activités extra-scolaires*); **8** Astrol maison *f*; **9** (also **House**) house music *f* (*musique de discothèque*).

II /haʊz/ *vtr* **1** (give lodging to) (permanently) loger [*person*]; (temporarily) héberger [*homeless, refugees*]; **to be badly** ou **poorly ~d** être mal logé; **2** (contain) [*building, room, library*] abriter [*books, collection, exhibition*].

IDIOMS **to put** ou **set one's ~ in order** mettre de l'ordre dans ses affaires; **first set your own ~ in order** vous devriez d'abord mettre de l'ordre dans vos propres affaires; **to get on like a ~ on fire**° s'entendre à merveille.

house: **~ agent** ▶1692 *n* GB agent *m* immobilier; **House Appropriations Committee** *n* US comité *m* qui détermine le budget.

house arrest *n* résidence *f* surveillée; **to be under ~** être en résidence surveillée.

houseboat /ˈhaʊsbəʊt/ *n* **1** (house shaped) habitation *f* flottante; **2** (barge) péniche *f* aménagée.

housebound /ˈhaʊsbaʊnd/ **I** *n* **the ~** (+*v pl*) les personnes *fpl* confinées chez elles.

II *adj* confiné chez soi; **she is ~** elle est confinée chez elle.

housebreak /ˈhaʊsbreɪk/ *vtr* US **to ~ a dog** apprendre à un chien à être propre.

housebreaker /ˈhaʊsbreɪkə(r)/ *n* cambrioleur/-euse *m/f*.

housebreaking /ˈhaʊsbreɪkɪŋ/ *n* **1** Jur cambriolage *m* par effraction; **2** US (of pet) éducation *f* à la propreté.

house: **~broken** *adj* US [*pet*] propre; **~ call** *n* visite *f* à domicile; **~clean** *vi* US faire le ménage; **~cleaning** *n* US ménage *m*; **~ clearance sale** *n* vente *f* de mobilier à la suite d'un décès; **~coat** *n* déshabillé *m*, peignoir *m*; **~father** ▶1692 *n* responsable *m* des enfants (*dans une institution*); **~fly** *n* mouche *f* domestique.

houseful /ˈhaʊsfʊl/ *n* maisonnée *f*, pleine maison *f*; **a ~ of** une maison pleine de.

houseguest /ˈhaʊsgest/ *n* invité/-e *m/f* (*pour quelques jours*).

household /ˈhaʊshəʊld/ **I** *n* gen maison *f*; Admin (in census, survey) ménage *m*; **the whole ~** toute la maison; **a large ~** une grande maisonnée; **the head of the ~** le chef de famille.

II *modif* [*accounts, expenses, bill*] du ménage; [*chore, dust, item, waste*] ménager/-ère.

household: **~ ammonia** *n* ammoniaque *f* domestique; **~ appliance** *n* appareil *m* électroménager; **Household Cavalry** *n* GB cavalerie *f* de la Garde royale.

householder /ˈhaʊshəʊldə(r)/ *n* gen habitant/-e *m/f*; (owner) propriétaire *mf*; (tenant) locataire *mf*; (head of household) chef *m* de famille.

household: **~ gods** *npl* pénates *mpl*, dieux *mpl* du foyer; **~ insurance** *n* assurance *f* de l'habitation; **~ linen** *n* linge *m* de maison.

household name *n* **he's a ~** tout le monde connaît son nom.

household: **~ policy** *n* Insur assurance *f* multirisque habitation; **~ soap** *n* savon *m* de Marseille; **~ troops** *npl* Garde *f* royale.

house-hunt /ˈhaʊshʌnt/ *vi* chercher une maison.

house-hunting /ˈhaʊshʌntɪŋ/ *n* **to go ~** se lancer à la recherche d'une maison (à acheter).

house: **~ husband** *n* homme *m* au foyer; **~ journal** *n* = **house magazine**.

housekeeper /ˈhaʊskiːpə(r)/ ▶1692 *n* (in house) gouvernante *f*; (in institution) responsable *mf* du personnel d'entretien.

housekeeping /ˈhaʊskiːpɪŋ/ **I** *n* **1** (domestic) (money) argent *m* du ménage; (managing of money) gestion *f* de l'argent du ménage; **2** Pol, Fin, Comm gestion *f*.

II *modif* [*money, allowance*] du ménage; Biol [*gene*] domestique.

house: **~ lights** *npl* Theat éclairage *m*; **~ magazine** *n* bulletin *m* interne; **~maid** ▶1692 *n* femme *f* de chambre; **~maid's knee** *n* inflammation *f* du genou; **~man** ▶1692 *n* GB Med interne *mf*; **~martin** *n* hirondelle *f* de fenêtre; **~master** *n* GB Sch enseignant *m* responsable d'un groupe d'enfants (*dans un internat britannique*); **~mistress** *n* GB Sch enseignante *f* responsable d'un groupe d'enfants (*dans un internat britannique*); **~mother** ▶1692 *n* responsable *f* des enfants (*dans une institution*); **~ mouse** *n* souris *f* grise; **~ music** *n* = **house** I 9; **~ of cards** *n* lit, fig château *m* de cartes; **House of Commons** *n* Chambre *f* des communes; **~ officer** ▶1692 *n* GB Med interne *mf*; **House of God** *n* maison *f* de Dieu; **House of Keys** *n*: *Chambre basse du Parlement de l'Île de Man*; **House of Lords** *n* GB Chambre *f* des lords, Chambre *f* haute; **House of Representatives** *n* Chambre *f* des représentants; **~ organ** *n* = **house magazine**; **~owner** *n* propriétaire *mf* de maison; **~ painter** ▶1692 *n* peintre *m* en bâtiment; **~parent** *n* responsable *mf* des enfants (*dans une institution*); **~ party** *n* réception *f*; **~ physician** ▶1692 *n* GB Med interne *mf*; **~plant** *n* plante *f* d'intérieur; **~ prices** *npl* prix *mpl* du marché immobilier; **~-proud** *adj* fier/fière de son intérieur; **~ red** *n* vin *m* rouge cuvée du patron.

houseroom /ˈhaʊsruːm/ *n* **I wouldn't give it ~** (of object) je n'en voudrais pour rien au monde; (of idea) je ne perdrais pas mon temps sur ça.

house: **~ sales** *npl* ventes *fpl* immobilières; **~-sit** *vi* garder une maison (**for** pour); **~-sitter** *n* personne *f* qui garde une maison; **Houses of Congress** *npl* US *le Sénat et la Chambre des représentants*; **Houses of Parliament** *n* GB Parlement *m* Britannique; **~ sparrow** *n* moineau *m* domestique; **~ style** *n* Publg, Journ style *m* maison; **~ surgeon** ▶1692 *n* GB interne *mf* en chirurgie.

house-to-house *adj* [*search, enquiries, canvass*] de maison en maison; **to carry out a ~ collection** faire une quête à domicile.

house: **~top** *n* = **rooftop**; **~-trained** *adj* GB [*pet*] propre; **~wares** *npl* Comm articles *mpl* de ménage.

house-warming (party) *n* pendaison *f* de crémaillère; **to have** ou **give a ~** pendre la crémaillère.

house white *n* vin *m* blanc cuvée du patron.

housewife /ˈhaʊswaɪf/ *n* (*pl* **-wives** /waɪvz/) (not employed outside home) femme *f* au foyer; (with emphasis on domestic labour) ménagère *f*.

housewifely /ˈhaʊswaɪflɪ/ *adj* de ménagère.

housewifery /ˈhaʊswɪfərɪ/ *n* tenue *f* d'un ménage.

house wine *n* cuvée *f* maison or du patron.

housewives /ˈhaʊswaɪvz/ *npl* ▶ **housewife**.

housework /ˈhaʊswɜːk/ *n* (cleaning only) ménage *m*; (including ironing, washing) travaux *mpl* ménagers; **to do the ~** gen s'occuper de la maison; (clean) faire le ménage.

housey-housey /ˌhaʊsɪˈhaʊsɪ/ ▶1282 *n* GB ≈ jeu *m* de loto.

housing /ˈhaʊzɪŋ/ **I** *n* **1** (houses, flats) logements *mpl*; **the problem of ~** le problème du logement; **2** Tech (casing) boîtier *m*; **engine/axle ~** carter *m* moteur/d'essieu; **3** Archit, Constr (in timber) encastrement *m*, logement *m*.

II *modif* [*crisis, problem, department*] du logement; [*conditions*] de logement; [*shortage*] de logements; [*density*] de l'habitat.

housing: **~ association** *n* GB *organisation à but nonlucratif qui s'occupe de rénover les habitations et d'aider les locataires et les propriétaires*; **~ benefit** *n* GB ≈ allocation *f* logement; **~ development** *n* (large) cité *f*; (small) lotissement *m*.

housing estate *n* GB (large) cité *f*; (small) lotissement *m*; (council-run) ≈ cité *f* or lotissement *m* HLM.

housing: **~ project** US *n* (large) ≈ cité *f* HLM; (small) ≈ lotissement *m* HLM; **~ stock** *n* parc *m* de logements.

hove /həʊv/ *pp, prét* Naut ▶ **heave**.

hovel /ˈhɒvl/ *n* taudis *m*.

hover /ˈhɒvə(r)/ *vi* **1** lit [*small bird, insect*] voleter (**over, above** au-dessus de); [*bird of prey*] planer (**over, above** au-dessus de); [*helicopter*] faire du surplace (**over, above** au-dessus de); fig [*smile*] errer (**on** sur); [*danger, suspicion etc*] planer (**over, above** au-dessus de); [*price, costs etc*] tourner (**around** autour de); **to ~ around sb/sth** tourner autour de qn/qch; **a question ~ed on her lips** elle avait une question au bord des lèvres; **2** (vacillate) vaciller (**between** entre); **country**

~ing on the brink of war pays au bord de la guerre; **to be ~ing between life and death** rester suspendu entre la vie et la mort.

hover: **~craft** *n* (*pl* **~**) aéroglisseur *m*; **~fly** *n* syrphe *m*; **~port** *n* hoverport *m*; **~train** *n* aérotrain® *m*.

how /haʊ/

■ **Note** When *how* is used as a question word meaning *in what way?* or *by what means?* (*how did you get here?*, *how will you do it?*) it is almost always translated by *comment*: comment es-tu arrivé ici?; comment le feras-tu?
– When *how* is used as a conjunction meaning *the way in which* it is often translated by *comment*: *I don't know how they did it* = je ne sais pas comment ils l'ont fait; *tell me how you make a curry* = dis-moi comment on fait un curry.
– When *how* is used as a conjunction meaning *that* it is almost always translated by *que*: *he told me how he had stolen the money* = il m'a dit qu'il avait volé l'argent; *it's amazing how they survived* = c'est étonnant qu'ils aient survécu.
– For more examples and particular usages see below.

I *adv*, *conj* **1** (in what way, by what means) comment; **how did you make it?** comment l'as-tu fait?; **I wonder ~ it works** je me demande comment ça marche; **I don't know ~ he does it!** je ne sais pas comment il le fait!; **to know ~ to do** savoir faire; **I learned ~ to do it** j'ai appris à le faire or comment on le fait; **~ do you feel about it?** qu'en penses-tu?; **~ does the tune go?** c'est quoi l'air?; **2** (enquiring about success, health etc) **~ are you?** comment allez-vous?; **~'s your foot/head?** comment va ton pied/ta tête?; **~'s your brother?** comment va ton frère?; **tell me ~ she/your family is?** dis-moi comment elle/ta famille va, dis-moi si elle/ta famille va bien; **~ did the exam/interview go?** comment s'est passé l'examen/l'entretien?; **~ was the film/book?** comment était le film/livre?; **~ did you like the party/house?** la fête/maison t'a plu?; **~'s everything?**, **~ are things?** comment ça va?; **~ do you do!** (greeting) enchanté!; **3** (in number, quantity etc questions) **~ much does this cost?**, **~ much is this?** combien ça coûte?; **~ much do you/does it weigh?** combien pèses-tu/pèse-t-il?; **~ many times have you been to France?** combien de fois es-tu allé en France?; **~ many years have you lived here?** depuis combien d'années habitez-vous ici?; **I don't know ~ many people will come** je ne sais pas combien de personnes vont venir; **~ much time/money is there left?** combien de temps/d'argent reste-t-il?; **~ long is the rope?** de quelle longueur est cette corde?; **~ long do you want it?** de quelle longueur le veux-tu?; **~ long will it take?** combien de temps cela va-t-il prendre?; **~ old is she ?** quel âge a-t-elle? ; **~ tall is the tree/your father?** combien mesure l'arbre/ton père?; **~ big is the garden?** de quelle taille est le jardin?; **~ far is it?** c'est à quelle distance?; **tell me ~ old she is** dis-moi son âge or quel âge elle a; **~ often do you go there?** tu y vas tous les combien?; **~ soon can he get here?** dans combien de temps peut-il venir?; **4** (in exclamations) **~ wonderful/horrible!** c'est fantastique/horrible!; **~ nice you look!** qu'est-ce que tu es beau!, comme tu es beau!; **~ clever of you/him!** comme c'est intelligent de ta/sa part!; **~ wrong I was!** qu'est-ce que j'ai eu tort!, comme j'ai eu tort!; **~ it rained!** qu'est-ce qu'il a plu!, comme il a plu!; **~ you've grown!** qu'est-ce que tu as grandi!, comme tu as grandi!; **~ they shouted!** qu'est-ce qu'ils ont crié!; **5**○ (in whichever way) comme; **you can decorate it ~ you like** tu peux le décorer comme tu veux; **6** (why) **~ could you?** comment as-tu pu faire ça?; **~ can he say that?** comment peut-il dire une chose pareille?; **7** (that) que; **he told me ~ he had found it on the bus** il m'a dit qu'il l'avait trouvé dans l'autobus; **you know ~ he always arrives late** tu sais qu'il arrive toujours en retard.

II○ **how come** *adv phr* pourquoi; **'I don't like him'—'~ come?'** 'je ne l'aime pas'—'pourquoi?'; **~ come you always get the best place/arrive first?** comment se fait-il que tu aies toujours la meilleure place/tu arrives toujours le premier?

III how so *adv phr* comment ça.

IV how's that *adv phr* **1** (what do you think?) **I'll take you home, ~'s that?** je te ramènerai chez toi, ça te va?; **~'s that for an honest answer/an interesting job** ça c'est une réponse honnête/un emploi intéressant!; **2** (pardon?) **'he's called Nicholas'—'~'s that?'** 'il s'appelle Nicholas'—'répète'.

IDIOMS **the ~ and the why of sth** le pourquoi et le comment de qch; **and ~!** et comment!; **'did your mother tell you off?'—'and ~!'** 'est-ce que ta mère t'a passé un savon○?'—'et comment!'

howdy○ /ˈhaʊdɪ/ *excl* US salut○!

how-d'ye-do○ /ˌhaʊdjəˈdu:/ *n* **this is a fine** ou **real ~!** en voilà une histoire!

however /haʊˈevə(r)/ **I** *adv* **1** (nevertheless) toutefois, cependant, pourtant; **~, he did say that he would look into the matter** il a toutefois dit qu'il examinerait la question; **~, the recession is not over yet** toutefois, la récession n'est pas encore terminée; **they can, ~, explain why** ils peuvent, cependant, expliquer pourquoi; **if, ~, you prefer not to accept the offer, we...** si, toutefois, vous préférez refuser cette offre, nous...; **today, ~, it looks as though the sun might come out** aujourd'hui, pourtant, on a l'impression que le soleil va briller; **2** (no matter how) **~ hard I try, I can't** j'ai beau essayer de toutes mes forces, je ne peux pas; **~ difficult the task is** ou **may be, we can't give up** si difficile que soit la tâche, nous ne pouvons pas abandonner; **~ profitable the company is** ou **may be...** la compagnie a beau faire des bénéfices,...; **~ rich/small she is** ou **may be** si riche/petite soit-elle; **everyone, ~ poor/inexperienced** chacun, si pauvre/inexpérimenté soit-il; **~ often you tell me, I still won't believe you** tu peux me le répéter aussi souvent que tu veux, je ne te croirai pas davantage; **~ much it costs** quel que soit le prix; **~ many people go** quel que soit le nombre de personnes qui y vont; **~ long it takes, I'm not leaving** quel que soit le temps que ça prendra, je ne partirai pas; **3** (how on earth) comment; **~ did you guess?** comment as-tu deviné?

II *conj* **~ you like** comme tu veux; **~ he does it, she won't like it** quelle que soit la façon dont il s'y prend, ça ne lui plaira pas; **~ they travel, they will find it difficult** quelle que soit la façon dont ils voyagent, ça va leur paraître difficile.

howitzer /ˈhaʊɪtsə(r)/ *n* obusier *m*.

howl /haʊl/ **I** *n* **1** (wail) hurlement *m*; **a ~ of pain/rage** un hurlement de douleur/rage; **to give a ~** pousser un hurlement; **2** (shout) **a ~ of laughter** un éclat de rires; **~s of protest** des huées *fpl*; **3**○ **to be a ~** (funny) être hilarant.

II *vtr* hurler [*insult, slogan*] (**at** à); **'come back!' she ~ed** 'reviens!' hurla-t-elle.

III *vi* [*child*] hurler, pousser des hurlements; [*dog, wind*] hurler; **to ~ with rage/terror** hurler de rage/terreur; **to ~ with laughter** éclater de rire.

■ **howl down**: **~ [sb] down** conspuer [*speaker*].

howler○ /ˈhaʊlə(r)/ *n* bourde○ *f*, gaffe *f*, perle *f*.

howling /ˈhaʊlɪŋ/ **I** *n* **1** ¢ (of animal, wind) hurlement *m*; **2** (of baby, crowd) hurlements *mpl*.

II *adj* **1** [*child, animal*] qui hurle, hurlant; **the ~ wind** les hurlements du vent; **2**○ fig [*mistake*] criant; [*success*] retentissant.

hoy /hɔɪ/ *excl* ohé!

hoyden /ˈhɔɪdn/ *n* péj garçon *m* manqué.

hoydenish /ˈhɔɪdənɪʃ/ *adj* péj [*girl*] aux allures de garçon manqué; [*behaviour*] de garçon manqué; [*shout*] tapageur/-euse.

hp *n* (*abrév* = **horse power**) CV *m*.

HP *n* GB *abrév* ▶ **hire purchase**.

HQ *n* Mil (*abrév* = **headquarters**) QG *m*.

hr *n* (*abrév écrite* = **hour**) h.

HRH *n* (*abrév* = **Her** ou **His Royal Highness**) Son Altesse Royale.

HRT *n*: *abrév* ▶ **hormone replacement therapy**.

HS *n*: *abrév écrite* = **high school**.

HT *n*, *adj* (*abrév* = **high tension**) HT.

HUAC *n* (*abrév* = **House Un-American Activities Committee**) Commission *f* des activités anti-américaines.

hub /hʌb/ *n* Tech moyeu *m*; fig centre *m*.

hubbub /ˈhʌbʌb/ *n* (noise) brouhaha *m*; (turmoil) tohu-bohu *m*.

hubby○ /ˈhʌbɪ/ *n* hum mari *m*.

hubcap /ˈhʌbkæp/ *n* Aut enjoliveur *m*.

hubris /ˈhju:brɪs/ *n* sout prétention *f* démesurée.

huckleberry /ˈhʌklbərɪ, US -berɪ/ *n* US myrtille *f*.

huckster /ˈhʌkstə(r)/ *n* US **1** (pedlar) camelot *m*; **2** péj (salesman) bonimenteur *m*; **3** péj (swindler) escroc *m*.

HUD *n* US (*abrév* = **Department of Housing and Urban Development**) *Département du logement et de l'urbanisme*.

huddle /ˈhʌdl/ **I** *n* **1** (cluster) (of people) petit groupe *m*; (of buildings) entassement *m*; (of objects) amas *m*; **they were in a ~ around the radio** ils s'étaient regroupés autour du poste de radio; **to go into a ~** se réunir en petit comité; **2** US Sport (of footballers) regroupement *m* (*pour mettre au point la stratégie à adopter*).

II *vi* **they ~d at the bus stop** ils se pressaient à l'arrêt de bus; **he was huddling over a fire/in a corner** il était blotti près du feu/dans un coin; **she ~d under the bushes** elle se recroquevillait sous les buissons; **the village ~s between the mountains and the sea** le village est blotti entre les montagnes et la mer; **to ~ around** se presser autour de [*fire, radio, speaker*].

III huddled *pp adj* [*figure, group*] blotti; **~d in** recroquevillé dans [*chair, bed, car*]; **they lay ~d together in the tent** ils étaient blottis ensemble dans la tente; **houses ~d around the square** des maisons serrées autour de la place.

■ **huddle together** se serrer les uns contre les autres.

Hudson Bay /ˌhʌdsən ˈbeɪ/ *pr n* Baie *f* d'Hudson.

hue /hju:/ **I** *n* **1** littér (shade) nuance *f*; (colour) couleur *f*, teinte *f*; **2** fig (political) tendance *f*; (physical, moral) caractère *m*.

II -hued (*dans composés*) littér **violet/rose-~** teinté de violet/de rose.

hue and cry *n* tollé *m*; **to raise a ~ and cry against** ou **about sth** crier haro sur qch.

huff○ /hʌf/ **I** *n* **to be in a ~** être vexé; **to go** ou **get into a ~** prendre la mouche.

II *vi* souffler; **to ~ and puff** lit souffler et haleter; fig faire toute une histoire (**about** à propos de).

huffily○ /ˈhʌfɪlɪ/ *adv* d'un air vexé.

huffiness /ˈhʌfɪnɪs/ *n* mauvaise humeur *f*.

huffish○ /ˈhʌfɪʃ/, **huffy**○ /ˈhʌfɪ/ *adj* (annoyed) vexé; (irritable) susceptible; (sulky) boudeur/-euse.

hug /hʌg/ **I** *n* étreinte *f*; **to give sb a ~** serrer qn dans ses bras.

II *vtr* (*p prés etc* **-gg-**) **1** (embrace) [*person*] serrer [qn] dans ses bras; [*bear, gorilla*] écraser [qn/qch] entre ses bras; **to ~ one's knees** serrer ses genoux dans ses bras; **2** (keep close to) [*boat, vehicle*] raser; [*road, path*] longer; **to ~ the coast** Naut serrer la côte; **to ~ the walls** [*person*] raser les murs; **3** (fit tightly) mouler; **figure-~ging** moulant.

huge /hju:dʒ/ *adj* [*country, city, garden, room*] immense; [*building, person, animal*] gigantesque; [*portion, appetite*] énorme; [*debts, profits, sum of money*] gros/grosse (*before n*); [*success*] énorme.

hugely /ˈhju:dʒlɪ/ *adv* **1** (emphatic) [*successful, enjoyable, expensive etc*] extrêmement; **2** [*increase, vary etc*] considérablement; [*enjoy*] énormément.

hugeness /ˈhju:dʒnɪs/ *n* immensité *f*.

hugger-mugger /ˈhʌgəmʌgə(r)/ **I** *n* **1** (confusion) pagaille *f*; **2** (secrecy) secret *m*.
II *adj* **1** (confused) désordonné; **2** (secret) secret/-ète.

Huguenot /ˈhju:gənəʊ/ **I** *n* Huguenot/-e *m/f*.
II *adj* huguenot.

huh○ /hə/ *excl* (in surprise, inquiry) hein!; (in derision, disgust) pff!

hulk /hʌlk/ *n* **1** (of abandoned ship) épave *f*, carcasse *f*; (of machine, tank) carcasse *f*; **2** pej (ship) rafiot *m*; Hist (prison ship) navire *m* pénitencier; **3** fig (of building, mountain) masse *f* gigantesque; **a great ~ of a man** un mastodonte.

hulking /ˈhʌlkɪŋ/ *adj* énorme; **a great ~ brute** (man) une énorme brute; (dog) un molosse.

hull /hʌl/ **I** *n* **1** (of ship, plane) coque *f*; (of tank) carcasse *f*; **2** (of peas, beans) cosse *f*; (of nut) coquille *f*; (of barley) balle *f*; (of rice) glume *f*; (of strawberry) queue *f*.
II *vtr* **1** écosser [*peas, beans*]; écaler [*nuts*]; décortiquer [*rice, grain*]; monder [*barley*]; équeuter [*strawberries*]; **2** Naut, Aviat percer la coque de.

hullabaloo○ /ˌhʌləbəˈlu:/ *n* **1** (fuss, outcry) esclandre *m*; **2** (noise) raffut○ *m*.

hullo /hʌˈləʊ/ *excl* = **hallo**.

hum /hʌm/ **I** *n* **1** (sound) (of insect, aircraft, engine, traffic, voices) bourdonnement *m*; (of machinery) ronronnement *m*; **2**○ GB (bad smell) puanteur *f*.
II *excl* (in hesitation) heu.
III *vtr* (*p prés etc* **-mm-**) [*person*] fredonner [*tune*] (**to, for** à).
IV *vi* (*p prés etc* **-mm-**) **1** (make a low sound) [*person*] fredonner; [*insect, aircraft*] bourdonner; [*machine*] ronronner; **to ~ along to a tune** fredonner sur un air; **to ~ to oneself** fredonner tout bas; ▶ **haw**; **2** (bustle) [*factory floor, office*] bourdonner; **to ~ with activity/life** bourdonner d'activité/de vie; **3**○ GB (smell) sentir mauvais.

human /ˈhju:mən/ **I** *n* humain *m*; **fellow ~** semblable *mf*.
II *adj* **1** (not animal) [*behaviour, affairs, body, population, reproduction, weakness*] humain; [*characteristic, rights*] de l'homme; **he's only ~** il a ses faiblesses comme tout le monde; **2** (sympathetic) humain; **to lack the ~ touch** manquer de chaleur humaine.

human being *n* être *m* humain.

humane /hju:ˈmeɪn/ *adj* **1** [*person, régime*] humain; [*act*] d'humanité; **2** [*slaughter, culling*] sans cruauté; **3**† [*studies, education*] classique.

human ecology *n* écologie *f* humaine.

humane killer *n* instrument *m* d'abattage sans cruauté.

humanely /hju:ˈmeɪnlɪ/ *adv* sans cruauté.

humaneness /hju:ˈmeɪnɪs/ *n* humanité *f*.

human engineering *n* **1** (ergonomics) ergonomie *f*; **2** (in industry) gestion *f* des ressources humaines.

humane: **~ society** *n* US société *f* américaine pour la protection des animaux, cf SPA *f*; **~ trap** *n* (for mouse) boîte-piège *f*; (for animal trapped for fur) piège *m* à masse.

human interest **I** *n* Journ aspect *m* humain.
II *modif* **a ~ story** un récit de vie quotidienne.

humanism /ˈhju:mənɪzəm/ *n* humanisme *m*; **liberal/secular ~** humanisme libéral/séculaire.

humanist /ˈhju:mənɪst/ *n, adj* humaniste (*mf*).

humanistic /ˌhju:məˈnɪstɪk/ *adj* humaniste.

humanitarian /hju:ˌmænɪˈteərɪən/ **I** *n* humaniste *mf*.
II *adj* humanitaire.

humanity /hju:ˈmænətɪ/ **I** *n* **1** (the human race) humanité *f*; **2** (kindness) humanité *f*; **3** (human condition) condition *f* d'être humain.
II humanities *npl* Univ humanités *fpl*.

humanize /ˈhju:mənaɪz/ **I** *vtr* **1** gen humaniser; **2** Art, Cin donner un visage humain à; **a ~d mouse** une souris à visage humain.
II humanizing *pres p adj* [*influence*] humanisant.

humankind /ˌhju:mənˈkaɪnd/ *n* humanité *f*.

humanly /ˈhju:mənlɪ/ *adv* humainement; **~ possible** humainement possible.

human nature *n* nature *f* humaine; **it's only ~ to...** c'est tout à fait humain de...

humanoid /ˈhju:mənɔɪd/ *n, adj* humanoïde (*mf*).

human: **~ race** *n* race *f* humaine; **~ resources manager** ▶ 1692 *n* directeur/-trice *m/f* des ressources humaines; **~ resources** *npl* ressources *fpl* humaines; **~ rights** *npl* droits *mpl* de l'homme; **~ rights activist** *n* militant/-e *m/f* pour les droits de l'homme; **~ rights campaign** *n* mouvement *m* pour les droits de l'homme; **~ rights campaigner** *n* = **human rights activist**; **~ rights group** *n* groupe *m* de défense des droits de l'homme; **~ rights movement** *n* mouvement *m* pour les droits de l'homme; **~ rights record** *n* réputation *f* dans le domaine des droits de l'homme; **~ shield** *n* bouclier *m* humain.

Humberside /ˈhʌmbəˌsaɪd/ ▶ 1624 *pr n* Humberside *m*.

humble /ˈhʌmbl/ **I** *adj* **1** (lowly) [*origin, position*] modeste; **2** (unpretentious) [*dwelling, gift*] modeste; **3** (deferential) humble; **please accept my ~ apologies** sout je vous prie d'accepter mes humbles excuses fml; **in my ~ opinion** iron à mon humble avis; **your ~ servant** hum votre humble serviteur; **4** (showing humility) [*person, gratitude*] humble; [*reply, remark*] empreint d'humilité.
II *vtr* humilier [*person, opponent*].
III humbled *pp adj* humilié, modeste.
IV *v refl* **to ~ oneself** s'humilier (**before** devant).
IDIOMS **to eat ~ pie** aller à Canossa.

humble-bee† /ˈhʌmblbi:/ *n* bourdon *m*.

humbleness /ˈhʌmblnɪs/ *n* (of apology, rank) humilité *f*; **despite the ~ of his birth** ou **origins** malgré ses humbles origines.

humbling /ˈhʌmblɪŋ/ *adj* humiliant, salutaire.

humbly /ˈhʌmblɪ/ *adv* **1** (meekly) [*reply, ask, pray*] humblement; **2** (modestly) [*live*] humblement; **~ born** d'origine modeste.

humbug /ˈhʌmbʌg/ *n* **1**○ (dishonesty) tromperie *f*; **2**○ (nonsense) fumisterie○ *f*; **to talk ~** raconter des sornettes *fpl*; **3** (person) charlatan *m*; **4** GB (sweet) bonbon *m* à la menthe.

humdinger○ /ˌhʌmˈdɪŋə(r)/ *n* **it's a real ~!** c'est génial!; **a ~ of a match/an argument** un match/une dispute du tonnerre.

humdrum /ˈhʌmdrʌm/ *adj* monotone.

humerus /ˈhju:mərəs/ *n* (*pl* **-ri**) humérus *m*.

humid /ˈhju:mɪd/ *adj* [*climate, conditions*] humide; [*weather*] lourd.

humidifier /hju:ˈmɪdɪfaɪə(r)/ *n* humidificateur *m*.

humidity /hju:ˈmɪdətɪ/ *n* humidité *f*; **relative ~** humidité relative.

humidor /ˈhju:mɪdɔ:(r)/ *n* cave *f* à cigares.

humiliate /hju:ˈmɪlɪeɪt/ *vtr* humilier.

humiliated /hju:ˈmɪlɪeɪtɪd/ *adj* humilié.

humiliating /hju:ˈmɪlɪeɪtɪŋ/ *adj* humiliant.

humiliatingly /hju:ˈmɪlɪeɪtɪŋlɪ/ *adv* [*fail, be defeated*] de façon humiliante.

humiliation /hju:ˌmɪlɪˈeɪʃn/ *n* (feeling, act) humiliation *f*.

humility /hju:ˈmɪlətɪ/ *n* humilité *f*.

humming /ˈhʌmɪŋ/ *n* (of insect, aircraft) bourdonnement *m*; (of machine) ronronnement *m*; (of person) fredonnement *m*.

humming: **~ bird** *n* oiseau-mouche *m*, colibri *m*; **~ top** *n* toupie *f* sifflante.

hummock /ˈhʌmək/ *n* **1** (of earth) monticule *m*; **2** (of ice) hummock *m*.

hummus /ˈhʊməs/ *n* hoummos *m*.

humor *n* US = **humour**.

humorist /ˈhju:mərɪst/ *n* humoriste *mf*.

humorless *adj* US = **humourless**.

humorlessly *adv* US = **humourlessly**.

humorous /ˈhju:mərəs/ *adj* **1** (amusing) [*anecdote, book, incident, remark*] humoristique; **2** (amused) [*look, person, smile, tone*] plein d'humour.

humorously /ˈhju:mərəslɪ/ *adv* avec humour.

humour GB, **humor** US /ˈhju:mə(r)/ **I** *n* **1** (wit) humour *m*; **to have a/no sense of ~** avoir/ne pas avoir le sens de l'humour; **a good sense of ~** le sens de l'humour; **the ~ of the situation** le côté humoristique de la situation; **2** (mood) humeur *f*; **to be in good ~** être de bonne humeur; **to be in no ~ for jokes/arguing** ne pas être d'humeur à plaisanter/discuter; **to be out of ~** être de mauvaise humeur; **to be out of ~ with sb** sout être en froid avec qn; **when the ~ takes me** quand l'envie m'en prend; **3**‡ Med humeur *f*.
II *vtr* amadouer [*person*]; se plier à [*request, whim, wish*].
III -humoured (*dans composés*) **good-humoured** [*person, smile*] aimable; **bad-humoured** désagréable.

humourless GB, **humorless** US /ˈhju:məlɪs/ *adj* [*person*] qui manque d'humour; [*description, laugh, voice*] dépourvu d'humour.

humourlessly GB, **humorlessly** US /ˈhju:məlɪslɪ/ *adv* sans humour.

hump /hʌmp/ **I** *n* lit (all contexts) bosse *f*; **road ~**, **speed ~** ralentisseur *m*, dos-d'âne *m*.
II *vtr* **1**○ GB (lift, carry) porter, trainer; **2** (bend) courber [*back*]; **3**● (have sex with) baiser●, coucher avec○.
III *vi* **1**● (have sex) faire l'amour; **2**◐ US (exert oneself) se défoncer○; **3**◐ US (hurry) se grouiller○.
IDIOMS **to have (got) the ~**○ GB faire la tête○; **to get/be over the ~** passer/avoir passé le cap difficile.

humpback /ˈhʌmpbæk/ *n* **1** (also **~ whale**) baleine *f* à bosse, mégaptère *f* spec; **2** = **hunchback**.

humpback(ed) bridge *n* pont *m* en dos d'âne.

humpy /ˈhʌmpɪ/ *adj* **1** [*land, field*] bosselé; **2**○ GB (grumpy) bougon/-onne.

humus /ˈhju:məs/ *n* humus *m*.

Hun /hʌn/ *n* **1** (of Asiatic people) Hun *m*; **2**† injur Boche *m* offensive.

hunch /hʌntʃ/ **I** *n* intuition *f*; **to work on a ~** travailler sur une intuition; **to have a ~ that** avoir l'intuition que; **to play a ~** agir sur une intuition; **it's just a ~** ce n'est qu'une idée.
II *vtr* **to ~ one's shoulders** rentrer les épaules.
III *vi* **to ~ over one's desk/work** se tenir penché à son bureau/sur son travail.
■ **hunch down** se recroqueviller.

hunch: **~back** /ˈhʌntʃbæk/ *n* injur bossu/-e *m/f*; **~backed** *adj* bossu.

hunched /hʌntʃt/ *adj* [*figure, person*] voûté;

[*back*] voûté; [*shoulders*] rentré; **he was ~ up in the corner** il était tassé dans le coin.

hundred /'hʌndrəd/ **▶1505** I *n* cent *m*; **two ~** deux cents; **two ~ and one** deux cent un; **a ~ to one** cent contre un; **it was a ~ to one chance** il y avait une chance sur cent; **sold in ~s** ou **by the ~** vendu par centaines; **in the ~s** dans les cents; **in nineteen ~** en mille neuf cents; **in nineteen ~ and three** en mil neuf cent trois; **~s of times/of girlfriends** des centaines de fois/de petites amies.
II *adj* cent; **two ~ francs** deux cents francs; **two ~ and five francs** deux cent cinq francs; **about a ~ people/metres** une centaine de personnes/de mètres; **to be a ~ (years old)** être centenaire; **to be a ~ percent correct** [*person*] avoir raison à cent pour cent; **the Hundred Days** Hist les Cent Jours.
IDIOMS **not if I live to be a ~** jamais au grand jamais.

hundred-and-one **▶1505** I *n* cent un.
II *adj* lit, fig hum mille.

hundredfold /'hʌndrədfəʊld/ I *adj* multiplié par cent.
II *adv* **a ~** par cent; **to increase ~** centupler.

hundreds and thousands *npl* Culin nonpareilles *fpl*.

hundredth /'hʌndrətθ/ **▶1505** I *n* (all contexts) centième *m*.
II *adj* centième.

hundredweight /'hʌndrədweɪt/ **▶1883** *n* GB = *50,80 kg*; US = *45,36 kg*.

hundred-year-old **▶971** I *n* (person) centenaire *mf*.
II *adj* [*object, building etc*] vieux/vieille de cent ans; [*person*] centenaire.

Hundred Years' War *pr n* guerre *f* de Cent Ans.

hung /hʌŋ/ I *pret, pp* ▶ **hang**.
II *adj* Pol [*jury, parliament*] en suspens.

Hungarian /hʌŋ'geərɪən/ **▶1486**, **1402** I *n* **1** (person) Hongrois/-e *m/f*; **2** (language) hongrois *m*.
II *adj* hongrois.

Hungary /'hʌŋgərɪ/ **▶1131** *pr n* Hongrie *f*.

hunger /'hʌŋgə(r)/ I *n* faim *f*; fig désir *m* ardent (**for** de).
II *vi* **to ~ for, to ~ after** fig avoir faim de.

hunger march *n* GB Hist **the ~es** les Marches *fpl* de la faim (sur Londres).

hunger strike *n* grève *f* de la faim; **to go on/be on ~** entamer/faire une grève de la faim.

hunger striker *n* gréviste *mf* de la faim.

hung-over○ /ˌhʌŋ'əʊvə(r)/ *adj* **to be** ou **feel ~** avoir la gueule de bois○.

hungrily /'hʌŋgrɪlɪ/ *adv* lit avec voracité; fig avec avidité.

hungry /'hʌŋgrɪ/ I *adj* **1** lit **to be** ou **feel ~** avoir faim; (stronger) être affamé; **to make sb ~** donner faim à qn; **to be ~ for dinner** être en appétit pour le dîner; **to go ~** (from necessity) souffrir de la faim; (by choice) se priver de manger; **I'd rather go ~ than eat that!** je préfère me passer de manger plutôt que de manger ça!; **this is ~ work!** c'est un travail qui donne faim!; **2** fig [*look, eye*] avide; **to be ~ for** être affamé de.
II **-hungry** (*dans composés*) **power-/sex-~** assoiffé de pouvoir/de sexe.

hung-up○ /hʌŋ'ʌp/ *adj* **1** (tense) complexé; **2** (obsessed with) **to be ~ on sb/sth** être dingue○ de qn/qch.

hunk /hʌŋk/ *n* **1** (of bread, cheese) gros morceau *m*; **2**○ (man) beau mec○ *m*.

hunker○ /'hʌŋkə(r)/ I **hunkers** *npl* **to sit on one's ~s** s'accroupir; **to be on one's ~s** être accroupi.
II *vi* (also **~ down**) s'accroupir.

hunky○ /'hʌŋkɪ/ *adj* **a ~ man** un beau mec.

hunky-dory○ /ˌhʌŋkɪ'dɔ:rɪ/ *adj* super○, au poil○.

hunt /hʌnt/ I *n* **1** (search) recherche *f* (**for** de); **to join the ~ for sb/sth** participer à la recherche de qn/qch; **the ~ is on for the terrorists** on recherche les terroristes; **the ~ is on for the best cook in Britain** la course est engagée pour trouver le meilleur cuisinier de Grande-Bretagne; **2** Hunt (activity) chasse *f*; **lion ~** chasse au lion; **3** Hunt (fox-hunting group, area) chasse *f* à courre; **to be a member of the ~** être membre de l'équipage de chasse.
II *vtr* **1** (seek, pursue) rechercher [*murderer, prisoner, suspect, witness*]; **to ~ sb out of** ou **off sth** faire sortir qn de qch; **2** Hunt (pursue) chasser [*game, fox, bear*]; (pursue over) battre [*area, estate*]; **3** Hunt (use for hunting) monter [qch] à la chasse [*horse*]; **to ~ (a pack of) hounds** diriger une meute.
III *vi* **1** (for prey) [*animal*] chasser; **2** (search) **to ~ for** chercher [qch] partout [*object, person, address*]; être à la recherche de [*truth, cure*]; **to ~ for sth in/among sth** fouiller dans/parmi qch pour trouver qch; **to ~ around** ou **about for sth** chercher qch partout; **to ~ high and low for sth** remuer ciel et terre pour trouver qch; **3** (oscillate) [*gauge, indicator*] s'affoler (**around** au tour de); [*device, aircraft*] osciller.
■ **hunt down**: **~ down [sth/sb]**, **~ [sth/sb] down** **1** Hunt forcer [*animal*]; **2** (find) retrouver, dénicher○ [*lost object, address*]; traquer [*war criminal, terrorist*]; persécuter [*victim, minority*].
■ **hunt out**: **~ out [sth]**, **~ [sth] out** découvrir, dénicher○.
■ **hunt up**: **~ up [sb/sth]**, **~ [sb/sth] up** s'enquérir de [*old friend, person*]; finir par retrouver [*lost object*].

hunted /'hʌntɪd/ *adj* **1** (sought) [*animal, killer*] traqué; **2** (harassed) [*look, expression, feeling*] accablé.

hunter /'hʌntə(r)/ *n* **1** (person who hunts) chasseur/-euse *m/f*; (in fox-hunting) chasseur/-euse *m/f* à courre; (animal that hunts) prédateur *m* (**of** de); **2** (horse) cheval *m* de chasse; **3** (dog) chien *m* de chasse; **4** (watch) montre *f* à double boîtier; **5** (collector) **fossil/souvenir ~** collectionneur/-euse *m/f* de fossiles/de souvenirs.

hunter: **~-killer** *n* navire *m* d'un groupe de recherche et d'attaque; **~'s moon** *n*: *pleine lune qui suit l'équinoxe d'automne*.

hunting /'hʌntɪŋ/ *n* chasse *f* (**of** à), vénerie *f* spec; **to go ~** aller à la chasse; **to live by ~** vivre de la chasse.
IDIOMS **happy ~!** bonne chasse!

hunting: **~ boot** *n* botte *f* de chasse; **~ crop** *n* cravache *f*; **~ ground** *n* terrain *m* de chasse; ▶ **happy hunting ground**; **~ horn** *n* cor *m* de chasse; **~ knife** *n* couteau *m* de chasse; **~ lodge** *n* pavillon *m* de chasse; **~ pink** *n* veste *f* de veneur; **~ season** *n* saison *f* de chasse.

huntress /'hʌntrɪs/ *n* littér chasseuse *f*, chasseresse *f* liter.

hunt saboteur, **hunt sab**○ *n* GB opposant/-e *m/f* à la chasse au renard.

huntsman /'hʌntsmən/ *n* **1** (hunter) gen chasseur *m*; (fox-hunter) chasseur *m* à courre; **2** (trainer of hounds) veneur *m*.

hunt the thimble **▶1282** *n* cache-tampon *m inv*.

hurdle /'hɜ:dl/ I *n* **1** **▶1282** Sport, Turf haie *f*; **the 100m ~s** le 100m haies; fig obstacle *m*; **to clear a ~** lit franchir une haie; fig surmonter un obstacle; **2** Agric claie *f*.
II *vi* Sport, Turf faire de la course de haies.

hurdler /'hɜ:dlə(r)/ *n* coureur *m* de haies.

hurdle race *n* course *f* de haies.

hurdling /'hɜ:dlɪŋ/ **▶1282** *n* course *f* de haies.

hurdy-gurdy /ˌhɜ:dɪ'gɜ:dɪ/ **▶1481** *n* orgue *m* de Barbarie.

hurl /hɜ:l/ I *vtr* **1** lancer [*projectile*] (**at** sur); **to be ~ed to the ground** être projeté au sol; **2** fig **to ~ insults/accusations at sb** accabler qn d'injures/d'accusations.
II *v refl* **to ~ oneself** lit se précipiter; fig se jeter (**into** dans).

hurler /'hɜ:lə(r)/ *n* joueur *m* de hockey irlandais.

hurley /'hɜ:lɪ/, **hurling** /'hɜ:lɪŋ/ **▶1282** *n* hockey *m* irlandais.

hurly-burly /ˌhɜ:lɪ'bɜ:lɪ/ *n* tohu-bohu *m*.

hurrah, **hurray** /hʊ'rɑ:/ *n, excl* hourra (*m*); **~ for Paul!** vive Paul!; **last ~** US dernière envolée *f*.

hurricane /'hʌrɪkən, US -keɪn/ *n* ouragan *m*; **~ force wind** vent soufflant en ouragan.

hurricane lamp *n* lampe-tempête *f*.

hurried /'hʌrɪd/ *adj* [*note, call, visit*] rapide; [*meal*] pris à la hâte; [*job, work*] fait à la va-vite; [*departure*] précipité.

hurriedly /'hʌrɪdlɪ/ *adv* [*dress, pack, wash, finish, write*] en toute hâte; [*leave*] précipitamment; **'I don't mean you,' he added ~** 'ce n'est pas de toi que je parle,' a-t-il ajouté vivement.

hurry /'hʌrɪ/ I *n* hâte *f*, empressement *m*; **to be in a ~** être pressé (**to do** de faire); **in my ~, I forgot...** dans ma hâte, j'ai oublié...; **there's no ~** il n'y a rien d'urgent, il n'y a pas le feu○; **what's (all) the ~?** qu'est-ce qui presse?; **to do sth in a ~** faire qch à la hâte; **I'm not in any ~ to have children** je ne suis pas pressée d'avoir des enfants; **I won't forget that in a ~!** je ne suis pas près d'oublier ça!; **she won't do that again in a ~!** elle ne recommencera pas de sitôt!
II *vtr* **1** (do hastily) brusquer [*meal, task, performance, speech*]; **2** (rush, bustle) bousculer [*person*]; **to ~ sb in/out** faire entrer/sortir qn en toute hâte; **to ~ sb to his seat** faire asseoir qn rapidement; **to ~ sb away from the scene** faire quitter précipitamment les lieux à qn.
III *vi* [*person*] se dépêcher, se presser; **to ~ over doing** se dépêcher de faire; **to ~ over one's homework/a meal** se dépêcher de faire ses devoirs/de manger; **to ~ in/out** entrer/sortir précipitamment; **to ~ home** se dépêcher de rentrer chez soi.
■ **hurry along**: ¶ **~ along** se presser, se dépêcher; **~ along there please!** allons, pressons s'il vous plait!; ¶ **~ along [sth]**, **~ [sth] along** faire accélérer, faire activer [*process*].
■ **hurry away** se sauver.
■ **hurry back** (to any place) se dépêcher or s'empresser de retourner (**to** à); (to one's home) se dépêcher de rentrer (chez soi) ; **~ back!** dépêche-toi de rentrer!
■ **hurry off** se sauver.
■ **hurry up**: ¶ **~ up** se dépêcher; **~ up!** dépêche-toi! magne-toi○!; ¶ **~ [sb] up**, **~ up [sb]** bousculer [*person*]; ¶ **~ [sth] up** faire accélérer, faire activer [*process*].

hurt /hɜ:t/ I *n* blessure *f*; **his sense of ~ and betrayal** son sentiment d'avoir été blessé et trahi; **there is a lot of ~ on both sides** ils en ont souffert tous les deux; **emotional ~** blessure affective.
II *adj* [*feelings, look*] blessé; **I was more angry than ~** j'étais plus fâché que blessé; **she was ~ not to have been invited** elle était blessée de ne pas avoir été invitée; **he felt ~ about the way he had been treated** il était blessé par la façon dont il avait été traité; **to sound** ou **look ~** avoir l'air peiné; **to feel ~** être peiné.
III *vtr* (*prét, pp* **hurt**) **1** (injure) **to ~ one's hand/back** se blesser or se faire mal à la main/au dos; **the dog ~ its paw** le chien s'est blessé à la patte; **she ~ her shoulder when she fell** elle s'est blessée à l'épaule en tombant; **he ~ his back moving the piano** il s'est fait mal au dos en déplaçant le piano; **was anybody ~?** y a-t-il eu des blessés?; **they were seriously/slightly ~** ils ont été grièvement or gravement/légèrement blessés; **somebody's going to get ~**

quelqu'un va se faire mal; **hard work never ~ anybody** travailler dur n'a jamais fait de mal à personne; **it wouldn't ~ her to apologize** ça ne lui ferait pas de mal de s'excuser; **2** (cause pain to) faire mal à [*person*]; **you're ~ing my arm** vous me faites mal au bras; **these shoes ~ my feet** ces chaussures me font mal aux pieds; **it ~s him to bend his knee** il a mal quand il plie le genou; **3** (emotionally) gen blesser; (offend) froisser, offusquer; **he ~ them by leaving early** il les a froissés en partant tôt; **to ~ sb's feelings** blesser quelqu'un; **to ~ sb's pride** blesser quelqu'un dans son amour-propre; **she's afraid of getting ~** elle a peur d'être blessée; **it's often the children who get ~** ce sont souvent les enfants qui en pâtissent; **4** (affect adversely) [*prices, inflation*] nuire à.

IV *vi* (*prét, pp* **hurt**) **1** (be painful, cause pain) faire mal; **my foot/my throat ~s** j'ai mal au pied/à la gorge; **this small print makes my eyes ~** ces petits caractères me donnent mal aux yeux; **where does it ~?** où est-ce que vous avez mal?; **my shoes ~** mes chaussures me font mal; **it ~s when I turn my head** j'ai mal quand je tourne la tête; **2** (take effect) [*sanctions, taxes*] se faire sentir; **3** (emotionally) **what really ~ was knowing that she had lied** ce qui m'avait vraiment blessé c'était de savoir qu'elle m'avait menti; **her indifference really ~s** son indifférence me blesse; **the truth often ~s** le vérité est souvent cruelle.

V *v refl* **to ~ oneself** se blesser, se faire mal.

hurtful /ˈhɜːtfl/ *adj* [*accusation, rumour, remark, words*] blessant; **the truth is often ~** la vérité est souvent cruelle.

hurtfully /ˈhɜːtfəlɪ/ *adv* de façon blessante.

hurtfulness /ˈhɜːtfəlnɪs/ *n* méchanceté *f*.

hurtle /ˈhɜːtl/ *vi* **to ~ down sth** dévaler qch; **to ~ along a road** foncer sur une route; **to ~ through the air** fendre l'air; **a stone ~d through the window/past me** une pierre vola à travers la fenêtre/devant moi.

husband /ˈhʌzbənd/ **I** *n* gen mari *m*; Admin époux *m*; **ex-~** ex-mari *m*; **to live as ~ and wife** vivre maritalement; **to work as a ~ and wife team** travailler en couple; **to take a ~**† prendre mari†.

II *vtr* **1** (manage prudently) bien gérer; **2** (economize) économiser.

husbandry /ˈhʌzbəndrɪ/ *n* **1** Agric agriculture *f*; **animal ~** élevage *m*; **2** (of resources) gestion *f*.

hush /hʌʃ/ **I** *n* silence *m*; **a ~ fell over the crowd** un silence envahit la foule.

II *excl* (all contexts) chut.

III *vtr* **1** (silence) faire taire [*person*]; faire cesser [*bruit*]; **2** (pacify) calmer [*baby*].

IV *vi* [*person*] se taire.

■ **hush up**: ¶ **~ up** se taire; ¶ **~ up [sth]** étouffer [*scandal, affair*]; ¶ **~ up [sb]**, **~ [sb] up** faire taire [*person*].

hushed /hʌʃt/ *adj* **1** [*room, conversation, whisper*] feutré; **to speak in ~ tones** ou **a ~ voice** parler à voix feutrée; **2** [*person, audience*] muet; **they watched in ~ admiration** ils regardaient muets d'admiration.

hush-hush○ /ˌhʌʃˈhʌʃ/ *adj* très confidentiel/-ielle; **to keep sth ~** garder qch pour soi.

hush money○ *n* prix *m* du silence; **to pay sb ~** acheter le silence de qn.

hush puppy *n* US beignet *m* soufflé.

husk /hʌsk/ **I** *n* (of grains) enveloppe *f* also fig.

II *vtr* décortiquer.

huskily /ˈhʌskɪlɪ/ *adv* d'une voix enrouée.

huskiness /ˈhʌskɪnɪs/ *n* enrouement *m*.

husky /ˈhʌskɪ/ **I** *n* (dog) husky *m*.

II *adj* **1** (hoarse) [*voice*] enroué; [*cough*] rauque; **2** (burly) costaud.

hussar /hʊˈzɑː(r)/ *n* hussard *m*; **the 2nd ~s** le 2e de hussards.

hussy○† /ˈhʌsɪ/ *n* pej dévergondée *f*.

hustings /ˈhʌstɪŋz/ *n* (+ *v sg* ou *pl*) tribune *f* (*pour élections*); fig **at/on the ~** pendant la campagne électorale.

hustle /ˈhʌsl/ **I** *n* **1** (lively activity) tourbillon *m* d'activité; ▶ **bustle**; **2**○ US (illegal activity) escroquerie *f*.

II *vtr* **1** (push) pousser, bousculer [*person*]; **to ~ sb into a building** faire entrer qn précipitamment dans un bâtiment; **he ~d her through the crowd** il lui a frayé un chemin à travers la foule; **2** (urge) pousser [*person*]; **to ~ sb into doing** pousser qn à faire; **3**○ US (sell illegally) vendre [qch] illégalement; **4**○ US (obtain by dubious means) soutirer [*money*]; dégoter○ [*job, contact*]; **5** (hurry) précipiter [*negotiations*]; bousculer [*person*].

III *vi* **1** (hurry) [*person*] se dépêcher; **2**○ US (make an effort) se démener; (work hard) trimer○; **3**○ US (be a prostitute) faire le trottoir○, racoler○.

hustler○ /ˈhʌslə(r)/ *n* US **1** (swindler) arnaqueur/-euse◑ *m/f*; **2** (prostitute) prostitué/-e *m/f*.

hut /hʌt/ *n* (in garden) cabane *f*; (in shanty town) bicoque○ *f*; (on building site) baraque *f* (de chantier); (temporary classroom) baraque *f* préfabriquée; (for climbers, shepherds) refuge *m*; (native type) hutte *f*; (larger) case *f*; (grass) paillote *f*; (on beach) cabine *f* (de plage).

hutch /hʌtʃ/ *n* **1** (for animals) gen cage *f*; (for rabbits) clapier *m*; **2** fig pej (house) clapier *m*; **3** US (furniture) dressoir *m*.

hyacinth /ˈhaɪəsɪnθ/ *n* **1** Bot jacinthe *f*; **wild/wood ~** jacinthe sauvage/des bois; **2** (gemstone) hyacinthe *f*.

hyaena = **hyena**.

hybrid /ˈhaɪbrɪd/ **I** *n* (all contexts) hybride *m*.

II *adj* **1** gen, Hort hybride; **2** Biol hybride; [*DNA*] hybride; [*gene*] chimère.

hybrid bill *n* GB Pol projet *m* de loi mixte.

hybridism /ˈhaɪbrɪdɪzəm/ *n* hybridation *f*.

hybridization /ˌhaɪbrɪdaɪˈzeɪʃn, US -dɪˈz-/ *n* **1** lit hybridation *f*; **2** fig métissage *m*.

hybridize /ˈhaɪbrɪdaɪz/ *vtr* hybrider.

hybrid system *n* Comput système *m* mixte.

hydra /ˈhaɪdrə/ **I** *n* (*pl* **~e** ou **~s**) hydre *f* also fig.

II *pr n* **the Hydra** l'Hydre *f*.

hydrangea /haɪˈdreɪndʒə/ *n* hortensia *m*.

hydrant /ˈhaɪdrənt/ *n* **1** gen prise *f* d'eau; **2** (also **fire ~**) bouche *f* d'incendie.

hydrate /ˈhaɪdreɪt/ **I** *n* hydrate *m*.

II *vtr* hydrater.

hydraulic /haɪˈdrɔːlɪk/ *adj* (all contexts) hydraulique.

hydraulic ramp *n* Aut pont-élévateur *m*.

hydraulics /haɪˈdrɔːlɪks/ *n* (+ *v sg*) hydraulique *f*.

hydraulics engineer ▶ **1692** *n* hydraulicien/-ienne *m/f*.

hydro /ˈhaɪdrəʊ/ *n* GB établissement *m* thermal.

hydrocarbon /ˌhaɪdrəˈkɑːbən/ **I** *n* hydrocarbure *m*.

II *modif* [*compound, gas*] d'hydrocarbures.

hydrocephalus /ˌhaɪdrəʊˈsefələs/ ▶ **1354** *n* hydrocéphalie *f*.

hydrochloric acid /ˌhaɪdrəˈklɒrɪk, US -ˈklɔːrɪk/ *n* acide *m* chlorhydrique.

hydrocyanic /ˌhaɪdrəsaɪˈænɪk/ *adj* cyanhydrique.

hydrodynamics /ˌhaɪdrədaɪˈnæmɪks/ *n* (+ *v sg*) hydrodynamique *f*.

hydroelectric /ˌhaɪdrəʊɪˈlektrɪk/ *adj* hydroélectrique.

hydroelectricity /ˌhaɪdrəʊɪlekˈtrɪsətɪ/ *n* hydroélectricité *f*.

hydrofoil /ˈhaɪdrəfɔɪl/ *n* **1** (craft) hydroptère *m*; **2** (foil) aile *f* portante.

hydrogen /ˈhaɪdrədʒən/ *n* hydrogène *m*.

hydrogen: **~ bomb** *n* bombe *f* à hydrogène; **~ peroxide** *n* eau *f* oxygénée.

hydrography /haɪˈdrɒgrəfɪ/ *n* hydrographie *f*.

hydrolysis /haɪˈdrɒləsɪs/ *n* hydrolyse *f*.

hydrometer /haɪˈdrɒmɪtə(r)/ *n* aréomètre *m*.

hydropathic /ˌhaɪdrəˈpæθɪk/ *adj* hydrothérapique.

hydrophilic /ˌhaɪdrəˈfɪlɪk/ *adj* hydrophile.

hydrophobia /ˌhaɪdrəˈfəʊbɪə/ *n* **1** Psych (fear of water) hydrophobie *f*; **2**† Med (rabies) rage *f*.

hydrophobic /ˌhaɪdrəˈfəʊbɪk/ *adj* gen, Chem hydrophobe.

hydroplane /ˈhaɪdrəpleɪn/ *n* **1** (boat) hydroglisseur *m*; **2** (submarine rudder) barre *f* de plongée; **3** US (seaplane) hydravion *m*.

hydroplaning /ˌhaɪdrəˈpleɪnɪŋ/ *n* aquaplanage *m*.

hydroponics /ˌhaɪdrəˈpɒnɪks/ *n* (+ *v sg*) culture *f* hydroponique.

hydrotherapy /ˌhaɪdrəʊˈθerəpɪ/ *n* hydrothérapie *f*.

hydroxide /haɪˈdrɒksaɪd/ *n* hydroxyde *m*.

hyena /haɪˈiːnə/ *n* Zool hyène *f*; fig requin *m*.

hygiene /ˈhaɪdʒiːn/ **I** *n* hygiène *f*; **in the interests of ~** pour des raisons d'hygiène; **food ~** hygiène alimentaire.

II *modif* [*standards*] d'hygiène.

hygienic /haɪˈdʒiːnɪk/ *adj* hygiénique.

hygienist /ˈhaɪdʒiːnɪst/ ▶ **1692** *n* hygiéniste *mf*.

hymen /ˈhaɪmen/ *n* hymen *m*.

hymn /hɪm/ *n* (song) cantique *m*; fig (expression of praise) hymne *m* (**to** à).

hymnal /ˈhɪmnəl/ *n* recueil *m* de cantiques.

hymnbook /ˈhɪmbʊk/ *n* livre *m* de cantiques.

hype○ /haɪp/ **I** *n* **1** (publicity) battage *m* publicitaire; **media ~** battage *m* médiatique, médiatisation *f* à outrance; **2** US (*abrév* = **hypodermic**) seringue *f*; **3** US toxico○ *mf*.

II *vtr* **1** (promote) faire du battage pour [*film, book, star*]; **2** (blow up) gonfler [*issue, news story, case*]; **3** (force up price of) faire grimper [qch] par des achats massifs [*record, share*]; **4** (stimulate) doper○ [*sales, demand, economy, market*].

■ **hype up**: **~ up [sth]**, **~ [sth] up** (stimulate) doper [*sales, economy*]; (promote) faire du battage pour [*film, star, book*]; (blow up) gonfler [*issue, story*].

hyped up○ /ˌhaɪptˈʌp/ *adj* **1** [*product, performance, film, star*] qu'on a fait mousser○; **2** (overstimulated) [*person, behaviour*] surexcité; [*economy*] dopé.

hyper○ /ˈhaɪpə(r)/ *adj* surexcité.

hyper+ /ˈhaɪpə(r)/ (*dans composés*) hyper-.

hyperacidity /ˌhaɪpərəˈsɪdətɪ/ *n* hyperacidité *f*.

hyperactive /ˌhaɪpərˈæktɪv/ *adj* gen, Med, Psych hyperactif/-ive.

hyperactivity /ˌhaɪpərækˈtɪvətɪ/ *n* hyperactivité *f*.

hyperbola /haɪˈpɜːbələ/ *n* (*pl* **-las** ou **-le**) Math hyperbole *f*.

hyperbole /haɪˈpɜːbəlɪ/ *n* hyperbole *f*.

hyperbolic /ˌhaɪpəˈbɒlɪk/ *adj* hyperbolique.

hypercorrection /ˌhaɪpəkəˈrekʃn/ *n* hypercorrection *f*.

hypercritical /ˌhaɪpəˈkrɪtɪkl/ *adj* excessivement critique.

hyperglycaemia /ˌhaɪpəglaɪˈsiːmɪə/ *n* hyperglycémie *f*.

hyperinflation /ˌhaɪpərɪnˈfleɪʃn/ *n* hyperinflation *f*.

hyperkinesis /ˌhaɪpəkɪˈniːsɪs/ *n* hyperkinésie *f*.

hyperkinetic /ˌhaɪpəkɪˈnetɪk/ *adj* hyperkinétique.

hypermarket /ˈhaɪpəmɑːkɪt/ *n* GB hypermarché *m*.

hypermetropia /ˌhaɪpəmɪˈtrəʊpɪə/ *n* hypermétropie *f*.

hypernym /ˈhaɪpənɪm/ *n* hyperonyme *m*.

hyperrealism /ˌhaɪpəˈriːəlɪzəm/ *n* hyperréalisme *m*.

hypersensitive /ˌhaɪpəˈsensətɪv/ *adj* hypersensible (**to** à).

hypersonic /ˌhaɪpəˈsɒnɪk/ *adj* Aviat, Tech hypersonique.

hypertension /ˌhaɪpəˈtenʃn/ *n* hypertension *f*.

hypertext /ˈhaɪpətekst/ *n*, *modif* Comput hypertext (*m*).

hypertrophy /haɪˈpɜːtrəfɪ/ *n* hypertrophie *f*.

hyperventilate /ˌhaɪpəˈventɪleɪt/ *vi* être en hyperventilation.

hyperventilation /ˌhaɪpəventɪˈleɪʃn/ *n* hyperventilation *f*.

hyphen /ˈhaɪfn/ *n* trait *m* d'union.

hyphenate /ˈhaɪfəneɪt/ *vtr* mettre un trait d'union à [*word*]; **to be ~d** s'écrire avec un trait d'union.

hyphenation /haɪfəˈneɪʃn/ *n* **1** (use of hyphen) emploi *m* du trait d'union; **2** Comput césure *f*, coupure *f* en fin de ligne.

hypnagogic /ˌhɪpnəˈgɒdʒɪk/ *adj* hypnagogique.

hypnosis /hɪpˈnəʊsɪs/ *n* hypnose *f*; **under ~** sous hypnose.

hypnotherapy /ˌhɪpnəˈθerəpɪ/ *n* hypnothérapie *f*.

hypnotic /hɪpˈnɒtɪk/ *n*, *adj* (all contexts) hypnotique (*m*).

hypnotism /ˈhɪpnətɪzəm/ *n* hypnotisme *m*.

hypnotist /ˈhɪpnətɪst/ *n* hypnotiseur *m*.

hypnotize /ˈhɪpnətaɪz/ *vtr* hypnotiser.

hypo /ˈhaɪpəʊ/ *n* **1** Chem, Phot hyposulfite *m* (de soude); **2**○ (*abrév* = **hypodermic syringe**) seringue *f* hypodermique.

hypoallergenic /ˌhaɪpəʊæləˈdʒenɪk/ *adj* hypoallergique.

hypocentre GB, **hypocenter** US /ˈhaɪpəsentə(r)/ *n* **1** Geol hypocentre *m*; **2** Nucl (ground zero) point *m* zéro.

hypochondria /ˌhaɪpəˈkɒndrɪə/ *n* hypocondrie *f*.

hypochondriac /ˌhaɪpəˈkɒndrɪæk/ *n*, *adj* hypocondriaque (*mf*).

hypocrisy /hɪˈpɒkrəsɪ/ *n* hypocrisie *f*.

hypocrite /ˈhɪpəkrɪt/ *n* hypocrite *mf*.

hypocritical /ˌhɪpəˈkrɪtɪkl/ *adj* hypocrite.

hypocritically /ˌhɪpəˈkrɪtɪklɪ/ *adv* hypocritement.

hypodermic /ˌhaɪpəˈdɜːmɪk/ **I** *n* **1** (syringe) hypodermique *f*; **2** (injection) piqûre *f* hypodermique.

II *adj* **1** [*injection, needle, syringe*] hypodermique; **2** [*infection*] sous-cutané.

hypoglycaemia /ˌhaɪpəʊglaɪˈsiːmɪə/ *n* hypoglycémie *f*.

hyponym /ˈhaɪpənɪm/ *n* hyponyme *m*.

hyponymy /haɪˈpɒnəmɪ/ *n* hyponymie *f*.

hypostasis /haɪˈpɒstəsɪs/ *n* (*pl* **-tases**) (all contexts) hypostase *f*.

hypostatic(al) /ˌhaɪpəˈstætɪk(l)/ *adj* hypostatique.

hypostatize /haɪˈpɒstətaɪz/ *vtr* hypostasier.

hypotaxis /ˌhaɪpəˈtæksɪs/ *n* Ling hypotaxe *f*.

hypotension /ˌhaɪpəʊˈtenʃən/ *n* hypotension *f*.

hypotenuse /haɪˈpɒtənjuːz, US -tnuːs/ *n* hypoténuse *f*.

hypothalamus /ˌhaɪpəˈθæləməs/ *n* (*pl* **-mi**) hypothalamus *m*.

hypothermia /ˌhaɪpəʊˈθɜːmɪə/ *n* hypothermie *f*.

hypothesis /haɪˈpɒθəsɪs/ *n* (*pl* **-theses**) hypothèse *f*; **working ~** hypothèse de travail.

hypothesize /haɪˈpɒθəsaɪz/ *vi* émettre une hypothèse; **to ~ that** émettre l'hypothèse que.

hypothetic(al) /ˌhaɪpəˈθetɪk(l)/ *adj* [*question, argument*] hypothétique.

hypothetically /ˌhaɪpəˈθetɪklɪ/ *adv* hypothétiquement.

hyssop /ˈhɪsəp/ *n* hysope *f*.

hysterectomy /ˌhɪstəˈrektəmɪ/ *n* hystérectomie *f*.

hysteria /hɪˈstɪərɪə/ *n* (all contexts) hystérie *f*; **mass ~** hystérie collective.

hysterical /hɪˈsterɪkl/ *adj* **1** gen [*person, behaviour*] hystérique; [*sob*] convulsif/-ive; [*demand, speech*] délirant; **~ laughter** fou rire *m*; **2**○ (funny) délirant.

hysterically /hɪˈsterɪklɪ/ *adv* **1** [*funny*] follement; **2 to sob ~** avoir une violente crise de larmes; **to laugh ~** avoir le fou rire; **to shout ~** hurler comme un/-e hystérique.

hysterics /hɪˈsterɪks/ *n* **1** gen, Psych (fit) crise *f* de nerfs; **to have** ou **go into ~** avoir une crise de nerfs; **2** (laughter) **to be in ~** rire aux larmes; **he had us in ~** il nous a fait mourir de rire.

i, I /aɪ/ *n* **1** (letter) i, I *m*; **2 I** (*abrév écrite* = **Island**) île *f*.
IDIOMS **to dot the i's and cross the t's** mettre les points sur les i.

I /aɪ/

■ **Note** *I* is almost always translated by *je* which becomes *j'* before a vowel or mute h: *I closed the door* = j'ai fermé la porte. The emphatic form is *moi*.
– For exceptions and particular uses see below.

pron je, j'; **I live in London** j'habite à Londres; **here I am** me voici; **there I am** me voilà; **I didn't take it** ce n'est pas moi qui l'ai pris; **he's a student but I'm not** il est étudiant mais moi pas; **I who**... moi qui...; **I who have seen** moi qui ai vu; **he and I went to the cinema** lui et moi sommes allés au cinéma.

IA US Post *abrév écrite* = **Iowa**.

IAAF *n* (*abrév* = **International Amateur Athletic Federation**) FIAA *f*.

IAEA *n* (*abrév* = **International Atomic Energy Agency**) AIEA *f*.

iambic /aɪˈæmbɪk/ **I** *n* (also **iamb**) iambe *m*.
II *adj* iambique; **~ metre** mètre *m* iambique.

ib /ɪb/ (*abrév* = **ibidem**) ib.

IBA *n* GB *abrév* ▶ **Independent Broadcasting Authority**.

Iberia /aɪˈbɪərɪə/ *pr n* Ibérie *f*.

Iberian /aɪˈbɪərɪən/ **I** *n* (person) Ibère *mf*.
II *adj* ibérique.

Iberian Peninsula *pr n* péninsule *f* ibérique.

ibex /ˈaɪbeks/ *n* bouquetin *m*.

ibid /ˈɪbɪd/ (*abrév* = **ibidem**) ibid.

ibis /ˈaɪbɪs/ *n* ibis *m*.

IBRD *n* (*abrév* = **International Bank for Reconstruction and Development**) BIRD *f*.

Icarus /ˈɪkərəs/ *pr n* Icare.

ice /aɪs/ **I** *n* **1** gen glace *f*; (on roads) verglas *m*; (in drinks) glaçons *mpl*; **the car skidded on the ~** la voiture a dérapé sur le verglas; **there's ~ on the roads** il y a du verglas sur les routes; **a show on ~** un spectacle sur glace; **a whisky with ~** un whisky avec des glaçons; **to put sth on ~** lit mettre [qch] à rafraîchir [*champagne*]; fig mettre [qch] en attente [*plans, project*]; **'danger! thin ~'** (on sign) 'il est dangereux de s'aventurer sur la glace'; **your feet are like ~**! tu as les pieds glacés!; **2** GB (ice cream) glace *f*; **vanilla ~** glace à la vanille; **water ~** sorbet *m*; **3**○ **₵** (diamonds) diams○ *mpl*, diamants *mpl*; **4**○ argot des drogués (amphetamine) ice○ *m*.
II *vtr* **1** Culin glacer [*cake*]; **2**○ US (kill) refroidir○, tuer [*person*]; (defeat) battre [qn] à plates coutures○ [*team*].
III iced *pp adj* [*water*] avec des glaçons; [*tea*] glacé; [*coffee*] frappé; [*cake*] glacé.
IDIOMS **to break the ~** rompre la glace; **to cut no ~** ne faire aucun effet; **this argument cut no ~ with them** cet argument ne leur a fait aucun effet; **his excuses cut no ~ with me** ses excuses ne m'impressionnent guère; **to be treading** ou **skating on thin ~** s'aventurer sur un terrain glissant.
■ **ice over** [*roads, runway*] se couvrir de verglas; [*windscreen*] se couvrir de glace; [*river, pond*] geler.
■ **ice up** [*lock, windscreen wipers, airplane*] givrer; [*windows*] se couvrir de givre.

ice age I *n* période *f* glaciaire.
II ice-age *modif* [*phenomenon*] de la période glaciaire.

ice axe *n* piolet *m*.

iceberg /ˈaɪsbɜːɡ/ *n* **1** lit iceberg *m*; **2**○ péj (cold person) glaçon *m*.
IDIOMS **the tip of the ~** la partie visible de l'iceberg.

iceberg lettuce *n* laitue *f* croquante.

ice: **~ blue** *adj* bleu glacier *inv*; **~boat** *n* Sport char *m* à voile sur glace; **~bound** *adj* [*ship*] pris dans les glaces; [*port, road*] bloqué par les glaces.

icebox /ˈaɪsbɒks/ *n* **1** GB (freezer compartment) compartiment *m* à glace, freezer *m*; **2** US (fridge) réfrigérateur *m*; **3** (cool box) glacière *f*.

ice: **~breaker** *n* Naut brise-glace *m inv*; **~ bucket** *n* seau *m* à glace; **~cap** *n* calotte *f* glaciaire; **~-cold** *adj* [*hand, water*] glacé; [*room, wind*] glacial; [*beer*] bien frais/fraîche; fig [*person, reception*] glacial.

ice cream *n* Culin glace *f*; **I like ~** j'aime la glace; **two vanilla ~s** deux glaces à la vanille.

ice: **~-cream bar** *n* US ≈ esquimau *m*, glace *f*; **~-cream cone**, **~-cream cornet** *n* (cornet *m* de) glace *f*; **~-cream maker** *n* sorbetière *f*; **~-cream parlour** GB, **~-cream parlor** US *n* Comm glacier *m*; **~-cream seller** ▶ 1692 *n* marchand/-e *m/f* de glaces; **~-cream soda** *n* US *boule de glace servie dans un soda*; **~-cream sundae** *n* coupe *f* glacée; **~-cream van** GB, **~-cream truck** US *n* camionnette *f* de marchand de glaces; **~-cube** *n* glaçon *m*; **~ dancer** ▶ 1282 *n* danseur/-euse *m/f* sur glace; **~ dancing** ▶ 1282 *n* danse *f* sur glace; **~ field** *n* champ *m* de glace; **~ floe** *n* banquise *f*, glace *f* flottante; **~-hammer** *n* marteau-piolet *m*; **~ hockey** ▶ 1282 *n* hockey *m* sur glace; **~house** *n* glacière *f*.

Iceland /ˈaɪslənd/ ▶ 1131 *pr n* Islande *f*.

Icelander /ˈaɪsləndə(r)/ ▶ 1486 *n* Islandais/-e *m/f*.

Icelandic /aɪsˈlændɪk/ ▶ 1486, 1402 **I** *n* Ling islandais *m*.
II *adj* islandais.

ice: **~ lolly** *n* GB ≈ sucette *f* (glacée); **~ machine** *n* machine *f* à glaçons; **~man** *n* US livreur *m* de glace; **~ pack** *n* poche *f* de glace; **~ pick** *n* Sport poinçon *m* à glace; Culin pic *m* à glace; **~ piton** *n* broche *f* à glace; **~ rink** *n* patinoire *f*; **~ show** *n* spectacle *m* sur glace.

iceskate /ˈaɪsskeɪt/ ▶ 1282 **I** *n* patin *m* à glace.
II *vi* gen patiner; (as a hobby) faire du patinage or patin (sur glace).

ice: **~ skater** ▶ 1282 *n* patineur/-euse *m/f* (sur glace); **~-skating** ▶ 1282 *n* patinage *m* sur glace; **~ storm** *n* US tempête *f* de pluie verglaçante; **~-tray** *n* bac *m* à glaçons; **~ water** *n* US eau *f* glacée; **~ yacht** *n* char *m* à voile sur glace.

ichthyologist /ˌɪkθɪˈɒlədʒɪst/ ▶ 1692 *n* ichtyologiste *mf*.

ichthyology /ˌɪkθɪˈɒlədʒɪ/ *n* ichtyologie *f*.

ichthyosaurus /ˌɪkθɪəˈsɔːrəs/ *n* ichtyosaure *m*.

icicle /ˈaɪsɪkl/ *n* stalactite *f* (de glace).

icily /ˈaɪsɪlɪ/ *adv* [*stare*] de façon glaciale; [*reply, say*] d'un ton glacial.

icing /ˈaɪsɪŋ/ *n* **1** Culin glaçage *m*; **chocolate ~** glaçage au chocolat; **2** (on aeroplane) givrage *m*.
IDIOMS **to be the ~ on the cake** être la cerise sur le gâteau.

icing sugar *n* GB sucre *m* glace.

icky○ /ˈɪkɪ/ *adj* **1** (dirty, unpleasant) dégoûtant; **to feel ~** se sentir patraque○; **2** (sentimental) écœurant.

icon /ˈaɪkɒn/ *n* **1** Art, Relig icône *f*; **2** fig (idol, symbol) (person) idole *f*; (object) symbole *m*; **she is a feminist ~** elle est une idole pour les féministes; **3** Comput icône *f*.

iconoclast /aɪˈkɒnəklæst/ *n* iconoclaste *mf*.

iconoclastic /aɪˌkɒnəˈklæstɪk/ *adj* iconoclaste.

iconographer /ˌaɪkəˈnɒɡrəfə(r)/ *n* iconographe *mf*.

iconography /ˌaɪkəˈnɒɡrəfɪ/ *n* (*pl* **-phies**) lit iconographie *f*; fig image *f*.

ICPO *n* (*abrév* = **International Criminal Police Organization**) OIPC *f*.

icy /ˈaɪsɪ/ *adj* **1** [*pavement, road*] verglacé; **there are ~ patches on the roads** il y a des plaques de verglas sur les routes; **2** (cold) [*draught, water, wind*] glacial; [*hands*] glacé; **3** fig [*look, reception*] glacial.

icy-cold *n* [*hand, water*] glacé; [*room, wind*] glacial.

id /ɪd/ *n* **the ~** le ça.

I'd /aɪd/ = **I had**, **I should**, **I would**.

ID I *n* **1** (*abrév* = **identification**, **identity**) pièce *f* d'identité; **2** US Post *abrév écrite* = **Idaho**.
II *modif* (*abrév* = **identity**) [*card, papers, disc*] d'identité; **~ code** Comput code *m* d'identification.

Idaho /ˈaɪdəhəʊ/ ▶ 1744 *n* Idaho *m*; **in/to ~** dans l'Idaho.

IDD *n* GB (*abrév* = **International Direct Dialling**) (service *m* d'appel) international *m*.

idea /aɪˈdɪə/ *n* **1** (suggestion) idée *f*; **a good ~** une bonne idée; **it was Sophie's ~ to sell the car** c'est Sophie qui a eu l'idée de vendre la voiture; **he came up with** ou **hit on the ~ of buying a farm** l'idée lui est venue d'acheter une ferme; **to be full of ~s** avoir plein d'idées; **2** (plan) idée *f*; **to have some vague ~ of doing** avoir dans l'idée de faire; **it's a good ~ to take a raincoat** c'est une bonne idée d'emporter un imperméable; **to put an ~ into sb's head** mettre une idée dans la tête de qn; **don't start getting ~s!** ne commence pas à te faire des idées!; **you can get** ou **put that ~ out of your head!** il n'en est pas question!; **3** (thought) idée *f* (**about, on** sur); **what are your ~s on this portrayal?** qu'est-ce que vous pensez de cette interprétation?; **4** (concept, notion) conception *f*; **he's got strange ~s about women/education** il a une drôle de conception des femmes/de l'enseignement; **you've got a funny ~ of loyalty** tu as une drôle de conception de la loyauté; **if that's your ~ of good work/of a joke...** si c'est ça que tu appelles du bon travail/une plaisanterie...; **a hamburger isn't my ~ of a good meal** un hamburger n'est pas vraiment ce que j'appelle un bon repas; **5** (impression) impression *f*; **to give sb the ~ that** donner à qn l'impression que (+ *indic*); **he's got the ~ that everybody is lying to him** il a l'impression que tout le monde lui ment; **whatever gave you that~!** qu'est-ce qui t'a fait croire une chose pareille!; **6** (knowledge) idée *f*; **do you have any ~ how/where etc...?** as-tu une idée sur la manière dont/où etc...?; **I have no ~** je n'en ai pas la moindre idée; **to have no ~ why/how etc** ne pas savoir pourquoi/comment etc; **to have an ~ of how long it takes to do** avoir une idée du temps qu'il faut pour faire; **he hadn't the slightest ~ who I was** il ne savait absolument pas qui j'étais; **he's 55? I had no ~!** il a 55 ans? je ne savais pas!; **to have no ~ of** ou **about** n'avoir aucune idée de [*price, time*]; **I have no ~ whether he's arrived or not** je ne sais pas du tout s'il est arrivé ou non; **you've no ~ how pleased I was!** tu ne peux pas savoir combien j'étais content!; **I have a vague ~ what you mean** j'ai une idée de ce que tu veux dire; **what a funny ~!** quelle drôle d'idée!; **7** (theory) idée *f*; **I've an ~ that he might be lying** j'ai dans l'idée qu'il ment; **he's got funny ~s on management** il a de drôles d'idées sur la gestion; **I've got a pretty good ~ who stole the money** je crois bien savoir qui a volé l'argent; **8** (aim) but *m*; **the ~ of a diet is to lose weight** le but d'un régime est de perdre du poids; **that's the whole ~!** c'est bien là tout le but; **what's the ~ behind the offer?** quel est le but de cette proposition?; **9** (gist) **now I get the ~** ah, maintenant je vois; **do you get the ~?** tu vois?; **now you're getting the ~** voilà, tu commences à comprendre; **that's the ~!** c'est ça!; **10** (estimate) **to give sb an ~ of** donner une idée à qn de [*cost, price*].

IDIOMS **the very ~!** quelle idée!; **what's the big ~○?** qu'est-ce qui te prend○?

ideal /aɪˈdiːəl/ **I** *n* **1** (principle) idéal *m*; **2** (model) idéal *m* (**of** de); **the feminine/Christian ~** l'idéal féminin/chrétien; **3** Philos idéal *m*.

II *adj* (all contexts) idéal (**for** pour; **to do** pour faire).

Ideal Home Exhibition *n* salon *m* britannique des arts ménagers.

idealism /aɪˈdɪəlɪzəm/ *n* gen, Philos idéalisme *m*; **out of ~** [*act*] par idéalisme.

idealist /aɪˈdɪəlɪst/ *n* gen, Philos idéaliste *mf*.

idealistic /ˌaɪdɪəˈlɪstɪk/ *adj* idéaliste.

idealize /aɪˈdɪəlaɪz/ *vtr* idéaliser.

ideally /aɪˈdɪəlɪ/ *adv* **1** (preferably) **~, the tests should be free, the tests should ~ be free** l'idéal serait que les examens soient gratuits **~, we'd like a house/to stay** l'idéal pour nous, ce serait une maison/ce serait de rester; **what would you like, ~?** qu'est-ce que tu aimerais, de préférence?; **2** (perfectly) **~ located, ~ situated** idéalement situé; **to be ~ suited** [*couple, colours*] être parfaitement assortis; **to be ~ suited for** être parfait pour [*job, role*].

ideas man○ *n* concepteur *m*.

identical /aɪˈdentɪkl/ *adj* identique (**to, with** à); **they look ~** ils ont l'air identiques.

identically /aɪˈdentɪklɪ/ *adv* [*dressed, constructed*] de façon identique; [*operate, function*] de façon identique; **to be ~ alike** [*people*] se ressembler tout à fait; [*objects*] être absolument identiques.

identical: **~ proposition** *n* principe *m* d'identité; **~ twin** *n* vrai jumeau/vraie jumelle *m/f*.

identifiable /aɪˌdentɪˈfaɪəbl/ *adj* **1** (recognizable) identifiable (**as** comme étant); **~ by sth** reconnaissable à qch; **2** (visible) visible.

identifiably /aɪˌdentɪˈfaɪəblɪ/ *adv* manifestement.

identification /aɪˌdentɪfɪˈkeɪʃn/ *n* **1** (of body, species, person) identification *f* (**from** à partir de); **to make an ~ of a criminal** procéder à l'identification d'un criminel; **2** (empathy) identification *f* (**with** à); **3** (proof of identity) pièce *f* d'identité; **have you got any ~?** est-ce que vous avez une pièce d'identité?

identification: **~ parade** *n* GB séance *f* d'identification; **~ tag** *n* badge *m* (d'identification).

identifier /aɪˈdentɪfaɪə(r)/ *n* Comput identificateur *m*.

identify /aɪˈdentɪfaɪ/ **I** *vtr* **1** (establish identity of) identifier [*person, body, culprit*] (**as** comme étant; **to** à); **2** (pick out) distinguer; **3** (consider as equivalent) **to ~ sb/sth with sb/sth** identifier qn/qch à qn/qch.

II *vi* (empathize) **to ~ with** s'identifier à.

III *v refl* **to ~ oneself** (establish identity) donner son identité; **to ~ oneself with sb/sth** s'identifier à or avec qn/qch.

identikit /aɪˈdentɪkɪt/ **I** *n* (also **Identikit**®, **identikit picture**) portrait-robot *m*.

II *adj* péj [*novel, house*] fait en série.

identity /aɪˈdentətɪ/ *n* (all contexts) identité *f*; **to change one's ~** changer d'identité; **to protect/reveal sb's ~** protéger/révéler l'identité de qn; **have you any proof of ~?** avez-vous une pièce d'identité?; **sense of ~** sens *m* de son identité; **national/religious ~** identité nationale/religieuse; **mistaken ~** erreur *f* d'identité.

identity: **~ bracelet** *n* gourmette *f*; **~ card** *n* carte *f* d'identité; **~ crisis** *n* crise *f* d'identité; **~ number** *n* numéro *m* d'identification; **~ papers** *npl* papiers *mpl* d'identité; **~ parade** *n* GB séance *f* d'identification.

ideogram /ˈɪdɪəgræm/, **ideograph** /ˈɪdɪəgrɑːf, US -græf/ *n* idéogramme *m*.

ideographic /ˌɪdɪəʊˈgræfɪk/ *adj* idéographique.

ideological /ˌaɪdɪəˈlɒdʒɪkl/ *adj* idéologique.

ideologically /ˌaɪdɪəˈlɒdʒɪklɪ/ *adv* d'un point de vue idéologique.

ideologist /ˌaɪdɪˈɒlədʒɪst/, **ideologue** /ˈaɪdɪəlɒg/ *n* idéologue *mf*.

ideology /ˌaɪdɪˈɒlədʒɪ/ *n* idéologie *f*.

ides /aɪdz/ *npl* **the ~ of March** les ides *fpl* de mars.

idiocy /ˈɪdɪəsɪ/ *n* **1** (stupidity) idiotie *f*; **2** (stupid remark) bêtise *f*.

idiolect /ˈɪdɪəlekt/ *n* idiolecte *m*.

idiom /ˈɪdɪəm/ *n* **1** Ling (phrase) idiome *m*, idiotisme *m* spec; **2** (language) (of speakers) parler *m*; (of theatre, sport) langue *f*; **3** (of music, art, architecture) style *m*; **in the jazz ~** dans le style jazz.

idiomatic /ˌɪdɪəˈmætɪk/ *adj* idiomatique; **~ expression** tournure *f* idiomatique.

idiomatically /ˌɪdɪəˈmætɪklɪ/ *adv* [*speak, write*] de façon idiomatique.

idiosyncrasy /ˌɪdɪəˈsɪŋkrəsɪ/ *n* **1** (of machine, system, person) particularité *f*; **2** hum (foible) manie *f*.

idiosyncratic /ˌɪdɪəsɪŋˈkrætɪk/ *adj* [*account, need, character*] particulier/-ière; [*reaction, attitude*] caractéristique.

idiot /ˈɪdɪət/ *n* **1** (fool) idiot/-e *m/f*; **to act/talk like an ~** faire/dire des idioties; **to feel like an ~** se sentir idiot; **that ~ Martin** cet imbécile de Martin; **you bloody◐ ~!** espèce de crétin◐!; **2**† Med injur idiot/-e *m/f* offensive.

idiot: **~ board○** *n* télésouffleur *m*; **~ box○**† US télé○ *f*.

idiotic /ˌɪdɪˈɒtɪk/ *adj* [*question, reply, grin*] idiot; [*remark, idea*] stupide.

idiotically /ˌɪdɪˈɒtɪklɪ/ *adv* [*talk, smile*] bêtement.

idiot tape *n* Comput frappe *f* au kilomètre.

idle /ˈaɪdl/ **I** *adj* **1** (lazy) péj [*person, worker*] paresseux/-euse, fainéant; **2** (vain, pointless) [*boast, threat*] vain; [*speculation, question, curiosity*] oiseux/-euse; [*conversation, chatter, remark*] inutile; **it would be ~ to attempt to do** ce serait vain de tenter de faire; **3** (without occupation) [*person*] oisif/-ive; [*day, hour, moment*] de loisir; **the ~ rich** les riches oisifs; **100 men made ~** 100 hommes mis au chômage; **4** (not functioning) [*port, dock, mine*] à l'arrêt; [*machine*] arrêté; **to lie** ou **stand ~** [*machine, factory*] être à l'arrêt; [*land*] rester inexploité; **5** Fin [*capital*] dormant.

II *vi* **1** [*engine*] tourner au ralenti; **2** [*person*] paresser, flemmarder○.

IDIOMS **the devil makes work for ~ hands** Prov oisiveté est mère de tous les vices Prov.

■ **idle away**: **~ away [sth], ~ [sth] away** passer [qch] à ne rien faire [*time, day, hours*].

idle character *n* Comput caractère *m* blanc.

idleness /ˈaɪdlnɪs/ *n* **1** (inaction) inactivité *f*; **enforced ~** oisiveté *f* forcée; **2** (laziness) paresse *f*.

idler /ˈaɪdlə(r)/ *n* **1** (person) (slacker) paresseux/-euse *m/f*; (loiterer) badaud/-e *m/f*; **2** Tech (wheel, gear, roller) roue *f* folle; (pulley) poulie *f* folle.

idly /ˈaɪdlɪ/ *adv* **1** (not doing anything) [*gaze, sit*] paresseusement; **to sit** ou **stand ~ by** [*person*] rester les bras croisés; [*country*] ne pas agir; **2** (vainly, aimlessly) [*wonder*] vaguement; [*chat, talk*] pour passer le temps.

idol /ˈaɪdl/ *n* **1** (pagan) idole *f*; **2** (hero) idole *f*; **cinema/teen ~** idole du cinéma/des jeunes; **fallen ~** idole déchue.

idolater /aɪˈdɒlətə(r)/ *n* idolâtre *m*.

idolatress /aɪˈdɒlətrɪs/ *n* idolâtre *f*.

idolatrous /aɪˈdɒlətrəs/ *adj* idolâtre.

idolatry /aɪˈdɒlətrɪ/ *n* idolâtrie *f* also fig.

idolize /ˈaɪdəlaɪz/ *vtr* adorer [*parent, friend*]; idolâtrer [*star, personality*]; **he was ~d by his fans** ses fans○ l'idolâtraient.

idyll /ˈɪdɪl, US ˈaɪdl/ *n* idylle *f* also Literat.

idyllic /ɪˈdɪlɪk, US aɪˈd-/ *adj* idyllique.

ie (*abrév* = **that is**) c-à-d.

if /ɪf/

■ **Note** *if* is almost always translated by *si*, except in the case of a very few usages which are shown below.

I *conj* **1** (in the event that, supposing that) si; **I'll help you ~ you pay me** je t'aiderai si tu me paies; **I'm not coming ~ you invite her** je ne viens pas si tu l'invites; **~ he dies** ou **~ he should die, it will have been your fault** s'il meurt, ça sera de ta faute; **~ she is to be believed** si on l'en croit; **~ possible** si possible; **tomorrow, ~ convenient** demain, si possible; **~ asked, I would say that** si on me posait la question, je dirais que; **I'll come with you ~ you like** je t'accompagnerai si tu veux; **he answers in monosyllables, ~ he answers at all** quand il daigne répondre, il répond par monosyllabes; **it was a milestone in our history, ~ you like** ça a été une étape importante dans notre histoire, en quelque sorte or si vous voulez; **~ I were you, I...** (moi) à ta place, je...; **~ it were to snow** s'il neigeait; **~ it were not for the baby, we could go camping** s'il n'y avait pas le bébé, on pourrait faire du camping; **~ so** si c'est le cas; **~ not** sinon; **tomorrow, ~ not sooner** demain au plus tard, demain ou même avant; **~ I'm not mistaken** si je ne me trompe; **2** (whenever) si; **~ in doubt, consult the manual** pour plus de précisions, consultez le manuel; **~ you mention his name, she cries** il suffit de prononcer son nom pour qu'elle pleure; **~ they need any advice they always come to me** quand ils ont besoin d'un conseil, c'est toujours moi qu'ils viennent voir; **3** (whether) si; **I wonder ~ they will come** je me demande s'ils vont venir; **do you know ~ they survived or not?** est-ce que tu sais s'ils ont survécu?; **can you remember ~ he told you?** est-ce que tu te souviens s'il te l'avait dit?; **4** (functioning as *that*) **I'm sorry ~ she doesn't like it but...** je suis désolé que cela ne lui plaise pas mais...; **do you mind ~ I smoke?** cela vous dérange si je fume?; **I don't care ~ he is married!** cela m'est égal qu'il soit marié!; **5** (although, accepting that) si; **we'll go even ~ it's dangerous** nous irons même si c'est dangereux; **(even) ~ they are old, at least they are not alone** même s'ils sont vieux, au moins ils ne sont pas seuls; **it's a good shop, ~ a little expensive** c'est un bon magasin, bien qu'un peu cher; **a pleasant, ~ rather small, apartment** un appartement agréable, bien qu'un peu petit; **it was interesting, ~ nothing else** au moins c'était intéressant; **6** (as polite formula) **~ you would sign here please/follow me please** si vous voulez bien signer ici/me suivre; **7** (expressing surprise, dismay etc) **~ it isn't our old friend Mr Pivachon!** tiens, mais voilà notre vieil ami M. Pivachon!; **well, ~ she didn't try and hit him!** je vous jure, elle a essayé de le battre!; **8** (used with *what*) **what ~ he died?** et s'il mourait?; **what ~ I say no?** et si je dis non?; **(so) what ~ he** (ou **I** etc) **did?** et alors?

II if only *conj phr* **~ only because (of)** ne serait-ce qu'à cause de; **~ only for a moment** ne serait-ce que pour un instant; **~ only for one reason** ne serait-ce que pour la bonne raison que...; **~ only I had known!** si (seulement) j'avais su!; **~ only I could get my hands on them!** si seulement je les tenais!

IDIOMS **there are lots of ~s and buts about it** beaucoup de doutes planent là-dessus; **~, and it's a very big ~, he agrees...** s'il est d'accord, ce qui est loin d'être évident...; **it's a very big ~** c'est loin d'être sûr.

iffy○ /ˈɪfɪ/ *adj* **1** (dubious) suspect; **it sounds a bit ~ to me** ça me paraît un peu suspect; **2** (undecided) [*person*] indécis; [*outcome*] incertain; **he's a bit ~ about going** il n'est pas très chaud○ pour y aller.

igloo /ˈɪgluː/ *n* igloo *m*, iglou *m*.

Ignatius /ɪgˈneɪʃəs/ *pr n* Ignace; **St ~ Loyola** Saint Ignace de Loyola.

igneous /ˈɪgnɪəs/ *adj* Geol igné; **~ rock** roche *f* ignée.

ignite /ɪgˈnaɪt/ **I** *vtr* démarrer [*motor*]; faire exploser [*fuel*]; enflammer [*material*]; **to ~ tensions** enflammer les passions.

II *vi* [*petrol, gas*] s'enflammer; [*engine*] démarrer; [*rubbish, timber*] prendre feu; [*situation*] s'enflammer.

ignition /ɪgˈnɪʃn/ *n* **1** Aut (system) allumage *m*; **electronic ~** allumage électronique; **to adjust the ~** régler l'allumage; **2** Aut (starting mechanism) contact *m*; **to switch on/off the ~** mettre/couper le contact; **3** Aut, Tech (igniting) allumage *m*.

ignition: **~ coil** *n* bobine *f* d'allumage; **~ key** *n* clé *f* de contact; **~ point** *n* point *m* d'allumage; **~ switch** *n* contact *m*.

ignoble /ɪgˈnəʊbl/ *adj* sout **1** [*thought, feeling, conduct, act*] infâme; [*nature, character*] vil; **2** littér [*origins*] humble.

ignominious /ˌɪgnəˈmɪnɪəs/ *adj* sout **1** [*defeat, retreat, failure, fate*] ignominieux/-ieuse; **2** [*act, conduct*] scandaleux/-euse.

ignominiously /ˌɪgnəˈmɪnɪəslɪ/ *adv* sout ignominieusement.

ignominy /ˈɪgnəmɪnɪ/ *n* sout ignominie *f*.

ignoramus /ˌɪgnəˈreɪməs/ *n* (*pl* **-muses**) ignare *mf*.

ignorance /ˈɪgnərəns/ *n* (of person) ignorance *f*; (of behaviour, manners) manque *m* d'éducation; **through ~** par ignorance; **to be in ~ of sth** ignorer qch; **his ~ of things scientific** son ignorance des choses de la science or de tout ce qui est scientifique; **to keep sb in ~ of sth** laisser qn dans l'ignorance de qch.

IDIOMS **~ of the law is no excuse** nul n'est censé ignorer la loi; **~ is bliss** l'ignorance est salvatrice.

ignorant /ˈɪgnərənt/ *adj* [*person*] (of a subject) ignorant; (uneducated) inculte; (boorish) grossier/-ière; [*remark, idea*] d'ignorant; **to be ~ about** tout ignorer de [*subject*]; **to be ~ of** ignorer [*options, possibilities, rights*]; **pig ~** bête comme un âne.

ignorantly /ˈɪgnərəntlɪ/ *adv* [*say, affirm*] par ignorance; [*behave*] d'une manière grossière.

ignore /ɪgˈnɔː(r)/ *vtr* ignorer [*person*]; ne pas relever [*request, remark*]; ne pas faire attention à [*criticism*]; passer sur [*behaviour, mistake*]; ne pas tenir compte de [*feeling, fact*]; ne pas respecter [*instructions, rule*]; ne pas suivre [*advice*]; se désintéresser complètement de [*issue, problem*]; brûler [*traffic lights*]; **to ~ sb's very existence** faire comme si qn n'existait pas.

iguana /ɪgˈwɑːnə/ *n* (*pl* **~** ou **~s**) iguane *m*.

IKBS *n* Comput *abrév* ▶ **intelligent knowledge-based system**.

ikon *n* = **icon**.

IL US Post *abrév écrite* = **Illinois**.

ILEA /ˈɪlɪə/ *n* (*abrév* = **Inner London Education Authority**) *organisme autrefois chargé de l'éducation pour la ville de Londres*.

Ile-de-France ▶ **1273** *pr n* Île-de-France *f*; **in/to the ~** en Île-de-France.

ileum /ˈɪlɪəm/ *n* (*pl* **ilea**) iléon *m*.

Iliad /ˈɪlɪəd/ *n* Iliade *f*.

ilium /ˈɪlɪəm/ *n* (*pl* **ilia**) ilion *m*.

ilk /ɪlk/ *n* (*sans pl*) espèce *f*; **of that ~** de cette espèce; **of his/their ~** de la même espèce.

ill /ɪl/ **I** *n* **1** (evil) **to wish sb ~** souhaiter du mal à qn; **for good or ~** pour le meilleur ou pour le pire; **2** (ailment) mal *m*; **economic ~s** les maux de l'économie.

II *adj* **1** (having particular illness) malade; **to be ~ with sth** (serious illness) être atteint de qch; (less serious) souffrir de qch; **to be taken ~, to fall ~** tomber malade; **2** (nauseous) **to feel ~** avoir mal au cœur or des nausées; **the smell made him feel ~** l'odeur lui a donné mal au cœur or des nausées.

III *adv* sout **1** (badly) **they have been ~ served by their government** leur gouvernement les a desservis; **he is ~ suited to the post** il n'est guère fait pour ce poste; **to speak ~ of sb** dire du mal de qn; **to bode** ou **augur ~ for sth** littér être de mauvais augure pour qch; **2** (scarcely) **he ~ deserves your praise** il ne mérite guère vos louanges; **it ~ becomes you to criticize** il ne vous sied guère de critiquer.

IDIOMS **it's an ~ wind (that blows nobody any good)** Prov à quelque chose malheur est bon Prov.

I'll /aɪl/ = **I shall, I will**.

ill-acquainted *adj* peu familier/-ière (**with** de).

ill-advised *adj* [*approach, decision, policy*] malavisé; [*action, remark*] inconsidéré, malavisé; **he was ~ to wait** il a été malavisé d'attendre.

ill: **~-assorted** *adj* mal assorti; **~ at ease** *adj* gêné, mal à l'aise; **~-bred** *adj* mal élevé; **~-concealed** *adj* mal dissimulé; **~-conceived** *adj* mal conçu; **~-considered** *adj* [*remark, decision*] irréfléchi; [*measure*] hâtif/-ive; **~-defined** *adj* mal défini; **~-disposed** *adj* mal disposé (**towards** envers).

Ille-et-Vilaine ▶ **1163** *pr n* Ille-et-Vilaine *f*; **in/to ~** en Ille-et-Vilaine.

ill effect *n* conséquence *f* néfaste.

illegal /ɪˈliːgl/ **I** *n* US immigrant/-e *m/f* clandestin/-e.

II *adj* **1** (unlawful) [*act, sale, profits, use*] illégal; [*parking*] illicite; [*immigrant*] clandestin; **2** Games, Sport [*pass, move, tackle*] irrégulier/-ière; **3** Comput [*character, operation*] interdit.

illegality /ˌɪlɪˈgælətɪ/ *n* **1** (unlawfulness) illégalité *f*; **2** Sport (of pass, move, tackle) irrégularité *f*; **3** (unlawful act) illégalité *f*.

illegally /ɪˈliːgəlɪ/ *adv* [*import, sell, work*] illégalement; [*park*] en infraction.

illegible /ɪˈledʒəbl/ *adj* illisible.

illegibly /ɪˈledʒəblɪ/ *adv* de façon illisible.

illegitimacy /ˌɪlɪˈdʒɪtɪməsɪ/ *n* (all contexts) illégitimité *f*; **the rate of ~** le taux de naissances illégitimes.

illegitimate /ˌɪlɪˈdʒɪtɪmət/ *adj* (all contexts) illégitime.

illegitimately /ˌɪlɪˈdʒɪtɪmətlɪ/ *adv* illégitimement.

ill: **~-equipped** *adj* mal équipé; **~-fated** *adj* [*expedition, enterprise, person*] malheureux/-euse; [*day*] fatal; **~-favoured** GB, **~-favored** US *adj* au physique ingrat; **~ feeling** *n* ressentiment *m*; **~-fitting** *adj* [*garment, shoe*] qui va mal; **~-founded** *adj* sans fondement; **~-gotten** *adj* mal acquis.

ill health *n* (chronic) mauvaise santé *f*; **~ prevented him from taking part** (temporary) un problème de santé l'a empêché de participer.

illiberal /ɪˈlɪbərəl/ *adj* [*society, state*] intolérant; [*views*] étroit; [*person*] à l'esprit étroit.

illicit /ɪˈlɪsɪt/ *adj* illicite.

illicitly /ɪˈlɪsɪtlɪ/ *adv* **1** (illegally) de manière illicite; **2** (secretly) [*meet, have sex*] clandestinement.

ill-informed *adj* mal informé.

Illinois /ˌɪlɪˈnɔɪ/ ▶ **1744** *pr n* Illinois *m*.

illiteracy /ɪˈlɪtərəsɪ/ *n* analphabétisme *m*; **60% ~** un taux d'analphabétisme de 60%.

illiterate /ɪˈlɪtərət/ **I** *n* **1** (person) analphabète *mf*; **2 the ~** (+ *v pl*) les analphabètes.

II *adj* **1** [*person*] analphabète; **2** (uncultured) [*person*] illettré; [*letter, writing*] d'illettré.

ill: **~-judged** *adj* peu judicieux/-ieuse; **~ luck** *n* malchance *f*; **~-mannered** *adj* grossier/-ière; **~-natured** *adj* désagréable.

illness /ˈɪlnɪs/ ▶ **1354** *n* maladie *f*; **minor/fatal/serious ~** maladie bénigne/mortelle/grave.

illocutionary /ˌɪləˈkjuːʃənərɪ, US -nerɪ/ *adj* Philos illocutoire.

illogical /ɪˈlɒdʒɪkl/ *adj* illogique.

illogicality /ˌɪlɒdʒɪˈkælətɪ/ *n* illogisme *m*.

illogically /ɪˈlɒdʒɪklɪ/ *adv* **1** [*feel, react*] en dépit de toute logique; **2** [*reason, argue*] illogiquement.

ill: **~-prepared** *adj* mal préparé; **~-starred** *adj* littér infortuné fml; **~ temper** *n* mauvaise humeur *f*; **~-tempered** *adj* désagréable, déplaisant; **~-timed** *adj* [*remark, arrival*] inopportun; [*takeover, campaign*] malencontreux/-euse; **~-treat** *vtr* maltraiter; **~ treatment** *n* mauvais traitements *mpl*.

illuminate /ɪˈluːmɪneɪt/ *vtr* **1** (light) éclairer; (for effect) illuminer; **2** (enlighten) éclairer; **3** Art enluminer [*manuscript*].

illuminated /ɪˈluːmɪneɪtɪd/ *adj* **1** (lit up) [*sign, panel*] lumineux/-euse; (for effect) illuminé; **2** Art [*manuscript*] enluminé.

illuminating /ɪˈluːmɪneɪtɪŋ/ *adj* fig éclairant.

Illnesses, aches and pains

Where does it hurt?

where does it hurt? = où est-ce que ça vous fait mal? *or* (*more formally*) où avez-vous mal?
his leg hurts = sa jambe lui fait mal

(*Do not confuse* faire mal à qn *with the phrase* faire du mal à qn, *which means* to harm sb.)

he has a pain in his leg = il a mal à la jambe

Note that with avoir mal à *French uses the definite article* (la) *with the part of the body, where English has a possessive* (his), *hence:*

his head was aching = il avait mal à la tête

English has other ways of expressing this idea, but avoir mal à *fits them too:*

he had toothache = il avait mal aux dents
his ears hurt = il avait mal aux oreilles

Accidents

she broke her leg = elle s'est cassé la jambe

Elle s'est cassé la jambe *means literally* she broke to herself the leg; *because the* se *is an indirect object, the past participle* cassé *does not agree. This is true of all such constructions:*

she sprained her ankle = elle s'est foulé la cheville
they burned their hands = ils se sont brûlé les mains

Chronic conditions

Note that the French often use fragile (*weak*) *to express a chronic condition:*

he has a weak heart = il a le cœur fragile
he has kidney trouble = il a les reins fragiles
he has a bad back = il a le dos fragile

Being ill

Mostly French uses the definite article with the name of an illness:

to have flu = avoir la grippe
to have measles = avoir la rougeole
to have malaria = avoir la malaria

This applies to most infectious diseases, including childhood illnesses. However, note the exceptions ending in -ite (*e.g.* une hépatite, une méningite) *below.*

When the illness affects a specific part of the body, French uses the indefinite article:

to have cancer = avoir un cancer
to have cancer of the liver = avoir un cancer du foie
to have pneumonia = avoir une pneumonie
to have cirrhosis = avoir une cirrhose
to have a stomach ulcer = avoir un ulcère à l'estomac

Most words in -ite (*English* -itis) *work like this:*

to have bronchitis = avoir une bronchite
to have hepatitis = avoir une hépatite

When the illness is a generalized condition, French tends to use du, de la *or* des:

to have rheumatism = avoir des rhumatismes
to have emphysema = avoir de l'emphysème
to have asthma = avoir de l'asthme
to have arthritis = avoir de l'arthrite

One exception here is:

to have hay fever = avoir le rhume des foins

When there is an adjective for such conditions, this is often preferred in French:

to have asthma = être asthmatique
to have epilepsy = être épileptique

Such adjectives can be used as nouns to denote the person with the illness, e.g. un/une asthmatique *and* un/une épileptique *etc.*

French has other specific words for people with certain illnesses:

someone with cancer = un cancéreux/une cancéreuse

If in doubt check in the dictionary.

English with *is translated by* qui a *or* qui ont, *and this is always safe:*

someone with malaria = quelqu'un qui a la malaria
people with Aids = les gens qui ont le Sida

Falling ill

The above guidelines about the use of the definite and indefinite articles in French hold good for talking about the onset of illnesses.

French has no general equivalent of to get. *However, where English can use* catch, *French can use* attraper:

to catch mumps = attraper les oreillons
to catch malaria = attraper la malaria
to catch bronchitis = attraper une bronchite
to catch a cold = attraper un rhume

Similarly where English uses contract, *French uses* contracter:

to contract Aids = contracter le Sida
to contract pneumonia = contracter une pneumonie
to contract hepatitis = contracter une hépatite

For attacks of chronic illnesses, French uses faire une crise de:

to have a bout of malaria = faire une crise de malaria
to have an asthma attack = faire une crise d'asthme
to have an epileptic fit = faire une crise d'épilepsie

Treatment

to be treated for polio = se faire soigner contre la polio
to take something for hay fever = prendre quelque chose contre le rhume des foins
he's taking something for his cough = il prend quelque chose contre la toux
to prescribe something for a cough = prescrire un médicament contre la toux
malaria tablets = des cachets contre la malaria
to have a cholera vaccination = se faire vacciner contre le choléra
to be vaccinated against smallpox = se faire vacciner contre la variole
to be immunized against smallpox = se faire immuniser contre la variole
to have a tetanus injection = se faire vacciner contre le tétanos
to give sb a tetanus injection = vacciner qn contre le tétanos
to be operated on for cancer = être opéré d'un cancer
to operate on sb for appendicitis = opérer qn de l'appendicite

illumination /ɪˌluːmɪˈneɪʃn/ **I** *n* **1** (lighting) (of building, panel, sign) éclairage *m*; (for effect) illumination *f*; **2** (enlightenment) illumination *f*; **3** Art (of manuscript) enluminure *f*.
II illuminations *npl* GB illuminations *fpl*.

illuminator /ɪˈluːmɪneɪtə(r)/ *n* Art enlumineur/-euse *m/f*.

illumine /ɪˈluːmɪn/ *vtr* éclairer.

ill-use /ˌɪlˈjuːz/ *vtr* sout maltraiter.

illusion /ɪˈluːʒn/ *n* illusion *f*; **to have ~s about** se faire des illusions sur; **to be** ou **to labour under the ~ that** se faire l'illusion que; **she has no ~s left about the future** elle ne se fait plus aucune illusion sur l'avenir; **it's an ~ to think that...** c'est s'illusionner que de croire que...; **an ~ of space** une illusion d'espace.

illusionist /ɪˈluːʒənɪst/ *n* illusionniste *mf*.

illusive /ɪˈluːsɪv/, **illusory** /ɪˈluːsərɪ/ *adj* (misleading) trompeur/-euse; (apparent) illusoire.

illustrate /ˈɪləstreɪt/ **I** *vtr* illustrer [*book, point, principle*]; **to ~ that...** illustrer le fait que...; **to ~ how...** illustrer la façon dont...
II illustrated *pp adj* [*book, story, poem*] illustré; **an ~d talk** une conférence avec support visuel.

illustration /ˌɪləˈstreɪʃn/ *n* (all contexts) illustration *f*.

illustrative /ˈɪləstrətɪv, US ɪˈlʌs-/ *adj* **~ material** illustrations *fpl*; **it is ~ of...** cela illustre bien...; **'may be reproduced for ~ purposes'** Publg 'peut être reproduit à titre d'illustration'.

illustrator /ˈɪləstreɪtə(r)/ **▶ 1692** *n* illustrateur/-trice *m/f*.

illustrious /ɪˈlʌstrɪəs/ *adj* **1** (famous) [*person, name*] illustre; (distinguished) [*career, past*] glorieux/-ieuse; **2** sout (glorious) [*emperor, queen*] glorieux/-ieuse.

illustriously /ɪˈlʌstrɪəslɪ/ *adv* glorieusement.

ill will *n* rancune *f*; **I bear them no ~** je ne leur garde pas rancune fml.

ILO *n* **1** (*abrév* = **International Labour Organization**) OIT *f*; **2** (*abrév* = **International Labour Office**) BIT *m*.

I'm /aɪm/ = **I am**.

image /ˈɪmɪdʒ/ *n* **1** (concept) (mental picture) image *f*; (notion) idée *f*; **the popular ~ of life in the north** l'idée que les gens se font de la vie dans le nord; **2** (epitome) image *f*; **the ~ of the successful working mother** l'image de la mère qui travaille et qui a réussi; **3** (public impression) (of company, personality) image *f* de marque; **4** TV, Phot, Cin (picture) image *f*; **visual ~** image réelle; **the moving ~** l'image en mouvement; **5** (likeness) image *f*; **God created Man in his own ~** Dieu créa l'homme à son image; **he is the (spitting) ~ of you** fig c'est toi tout craché; **6** Literat image *f*; **7** Math image *f*.

image: **~ builder**, **~ maker** *n* professionnel/-elle *m/f* de l'image de marque; **~-conscious** *adj* conscient de son image de marque.

imagery /ˈɪmɪdʒərɪ/ *n* ¢ Art, Literat images *fpl*.

imaginable /ɪˈmædʒɪnəbl/ *adj* [*situation, solution, danger, threat*] imaginable; **the funniest/most horrible thing ~** la chose la plus amusante/horrible qu'on puisse imaginer.

imaginary /ɪˈmædʒɪnərɪ, US -nerɪ/ *adj* (all contexts) imaginaire.

imaginary number *n* Math nombre *m* imaginaire.

imagination /ɪˌmædʒɪˈneɪʃn/ *n* imagination *f*; **to show ~** faire preuve d'imagination; **to have a fertile ~** avoir l'imagination fertile; **to see sth in one's ~** voir qch en imagination; **in his ~ he has a friend called Vic** il s'imagine avoir un ami qui s'appelle Vic; **I'll leave the rest to your ~** je te laisse le soin d'imaginer la suite; **it leaves nothing to the ~** cela ne laisse rien à l'imagination; **is it my ~, or...?** je rêve, ou...?; **it's all in your ~!** c'est tout dans la tête!, tu te fais des idées!; **use your**

~! réfléchis un peu!; **not by any stretch of the ~ could you say**... même en faisant un grand effort d'imagination on ne pourrait pas dire...

imaginative /ɪˈmædʒɪnətɪv, US -əneɪtɪv/ *adj* [*person, child, story, film, design, performance*] plein d'imagination; [*artist, mind*] imaginatif/-ive; [*solution, system, budget, method, device*] ingénieux/-ieuse.

imaginatively /ɪˈmædʒɪnətɪvlɪ, US -əneɪtɪvlɪ/ *adv* [*written, designed, devised, performed, solved*] avec imagination.

imaginativeness /ɪˈmædʒɪnətɪvnɪs, US -əneɪtɪvnɪs/ *n* esprit *m* d'invention.

imagine /ɪˈmædʒɪn/ *vtr* **1** (picture, visualize) (s')imaginer, se représenter [*object, scene, scenario*]; **to ~ that**... imaginer que...; **to ~ sb doing** imaginer qn en train de faire; **I can't ~ him travelling alone** je ne le vois pas en train de voyager seul; **I can't ~ her liking that, I can't ~ (that) she liked that** je ne crois pas qu'elle ait aimé ça; **to ~ (oneself) flying** s'imaginer en train de voler; **to ~ being rich/king** s'imaginer riche/roi; **I can't ~ (myself) saying that** je ne me vois pas (en train de) dire ça; **to ~ how/what/why** imaginer comment/ce que/pourquoi; **you can well/you can't ~ the trouble I've had** tu peux bien/tu ne peux pas t'imaginer les ennuis que j'ai eus; **I can ~ only too well** j'imagine trop bien; **just ~!, just ~ that!** tu t'imagines!, tu te rends compte!; **just ~ my surprise** imagine un peu ma surprise; **you can just ~ how I felt** tu imagines ma tête○; **2** (fancy, believe wrongly) (s')imaginer, se figurer (**that** que); **don't ~ you'll get away with it!** ne te figure pas que tu vas t'en tirer comme ça!; **surely you don't ~ that**...? tu ne vas pas tout de même imaginer que...?; **you must have ~d it** ce doit être un effet de ton imagination; **you're imagining it!** tu te fais des idées!; **3** (suppose, think) (s')imaginer, supposer (**that** que); **he's dead, I ~** il est mort, j'imagine or je suppose; **I ~ so** j'imagine, je suppose; **you would ~ he'd be more careful** on aurait pu croire qu'il serait plus prudent.

imaging /ˈɪmɪdʒɪŋ/ *n* Comput, Med imagerie *f*.

imaginings /ɪˈmædʒɪnɪŋz/ *npl* fantaisies *fpl*; **sb's horrible/dark ~** les horribles/sombres fantaisies de qn; **never in my worst ~** jamais dans mes rêves les plus horribles.

imam /ɪˈmɑːm/ *n* imam *m*.

imbalance /ˌɪmˈbæləns/ *n* déséquilibre *m* (**between** entre); **to correct an ~** corriger un déséquilibre; **trade ~** Econ déséquilibre des échanges commerciaux; **hormonal ~** Med déséquilibre hormonal.

imbecile /ˈɪmbəsiːl, US -sl/ **I** *n* **1** gen imbécile *mf*; **2**‡ Med débile *mf*.
II *adj* **1** gen imbécile; **2**‡ Med débile.

imbecility /ˌɪmbəˈsɪlətɪ/ *n* **1** (stupidity) stupidité *f*; (stronger) folie *f*; **2** (act, remark) imbécillité *f*; **3**‡ Med imbécillité *f*.

imbibe /ɪmˈbaɪb/ **I** *vtr* sout **1** (drink) boire; **2** (take in) absorber [*knowledge, propaganda*].
II *vi* hum (tipple) être porté sur la bouteille.

imbroglio /ɪmˈbrəʊlɪəʊ/ *n* imbroglio *m*.

imbue /ɪmˈbjuː/ **I** *vtr* imprégner (**with** de).
II imbued *pp adj* **~d with** imprégné de.

IMF *n* (*abrév* = **International Monetary Fund**) FMI *m*.

imitate /ˈɪmɪteɪt/ *vtr* **1** (behave similarly to) imiter; **2** (mimic) imiter; **to ~ sb to the life** imiter qn à merveille; **to ~ a cock crowing** imiter le chant du coq; **art ~s life** l'art imite le réel; **3** (copy) copier [*handwriting, design*].

imitation /ˌɪmɪˈteɪʃn/ **I** *n* (all contexts) imitation *f*; **in ~ of** à l'imitation de; **to learn by ~** apprendre par imitation; **to do an ~ of sb/sth** faire une imitation de qn/qch; **beware of ~s!** méfiez-vous des contrefaçons!
II *adj* [*plant, snow*] artificiel/-ielle; **~ fur** imitation *f* de fourrure; **~ fur coat** manteau en imitation de fourrure; **~ gold** similor *m*; **~ jewel** faux bijou *m*; **~ leather** similicuir *m*; **~ marble** faux marbre *m*; **~ mink** imitation *f* vison.
IDIOMS **~ is the sincerest form of flattery** l'imitation est la plus sincère des flatteries.

imitative /ˈɪmɪtətɪv, US -teɪtɪv/ *adj* [*person*] imitateur/-trice; [*sound*] imitatif/-ive; [*style*] sans originalité; **the ~ arts** les arts imitatifs.

imitator /ˈɪmɪteɪtə(r)/ *n* imitateur/-trice *m/f*.

immaculate /ɪˈmækjʊlət/ *adj* **1** [*person, dress, house, manners*] impeccable; [*performance, timing, technique*] parfait; **~ condition** (in advertisement) état impeccable; **2** Relig immaculé; **the Immaculate Conception** l'Immaculée Conception *f*.

immaculately /ɪˈmækjʊlətlɪ/ *adv* [*dressed, presented*] de façon impeccable; [*furnished*] avec beaucoup de goût.

immanent /ˈɪmənənt/ *adj* immanent.

immaterial /ˌɪməˈtɪərɪəl/ *adj* **1** (unimportant) sans importance; **it's ~ (to me) whether you like it or not** peu m'importe que vous l'aimiez ou non; **to be ~ to sth** n'avoir rien à voir avec qch; **2** (intangible) immatériel/-ielle.

immature /ˌɪməˈtjʊə(r), US -tʊər/ *adj* **1** (not fully grown) [*animal, plant*] immature; [*fruit*] vert; **2** pej (childish) immature; **don't be so ~!** ne te conduis pas comme un enfant!; **to be ~ for one's age** manquer de maturité pour son âge.

immaturity /ˌɪməˈtjʊərətɪ, US -tʊər-/ *n* **1** (of plant, animal) immaturité *f*; **2** pej (childishness) manque *m* de maturité.

immeasurable /ɪˈmeʒərəbl/ *adj* [*difference, damage, quantity*] incommensurable; [*gulf, depth*] insondable.

immeasurably /ɪˈmeʒərəblɪ/ *adv* incommensurablement.

immediacy /ɪˈmiːdɪəsɪ/ *n* immédiateté *f*; **a sense of ~** le sens de l'immédiat.

immediate /ɪˈmiːdɪət/ *adj* **1** (instant) [*effect, reaction, delivery*] immédiat; [*thought, idea*] premier/-ière; **2** (urgent, current) [*concern, responsibility, goal*] premier/-ière; [*problem, crisis*] urgent; [*information*] frais/fraiche; **~ steps must be taken** il faut prendre des mesures immédiates; **there is no ~ danger of this happening** il n'y a pas de danger que cela se produise dans l'immédiat; **the patient is not in ~ danger** les jours du patient ne sont pas en danger; **3** (near) [*prospects*] immédiat; **in the ~ vicinity** dans le voisinage immédiat; **his ~ family** ses proches; **in the ~ future** dans l'avenir proche; **4** (with no intermediary) [*cause*] immédiat; [*neighbours*] immédiat; **on my ~ left** juste à ma gauche.

immediate: **~ annuity** *n* rente *f* immédiate; **~ constituent** *n* constituant *m* immédiat.

immediately /ɪˈmiːdɪətlɪ/ **I** *adv* **1** (at once) [*notice, depart, reply, understand*] immédiatement; [*apparent, clear*] tout de suite; [*condemn, denounce*] tout de suite; **serve ~** Culin servez sur-le-champ; **~ at** ou **to hand** sous la main; **2** (directly) [*threatened, affected*] immédiatement; **he is not ~ at risk** il n'est pas directement menacé; **3** (straight) **~ after/before** juste avant/après [*event, activity*]; **4** (near) **~ next door** dans la maison juste à côté; **~ under the window** juste en dessous de la fenêtre.
II *conj* GB dès que, aussitôt que; **he left ~ he received the call** il est parti dès qu'il a reçu le coup de fil.

immemorial /ˌɪməˈmɔːrɪəl/ *adj* (timeless) immémorial; **from** ou **since time ~** de temps immémorial.

immense /ɪˈmens/ *adj* (all contexts) immense.

immensely /ɪˈmenslɪ/ *adv* [*enjoy, help*] énormément; [*complicated, popular, useful*] extrêmement, infiniment.

immensity /ɪˈmensətɪ/ *n* (all contexts) immensité *f*.

immerse /ɪˈmɜːs/ **I** *vtr* (in liquid) plonger (**in** dans).
II *v refl* **to ~ oneself** se plonger (**in** dans).

immersed /ɪˈmɜːst/ *adj* **1** (in liquid) immergé (**in** dans); **2** (in book, task, etc) absorbé (**in** dans).

immersion /ɪˈmɜːʃn, US -ʒn/ *n* (all contexts) immersion *f* (**in** dans); **baptism by total ~** baptême par immersion totale.

immersion: **~ course** *n* GB cours *m* avec immersion linguistique; **~ heater** *n* chauffe-eau *m* électrique.

immigrant /ˈɪmɪgrənt/ **I** *n* (recent) immigrant/-e *m/f*; (established) immigré/-e *m/f*.
II *adj* (recent) immigrant; (established) immigré.

immigrate /ˈɪmɪgreɪt/ *vi* immigrer (**to** à, en).

immigration /ˌɪmɪˈgreɪʃn/ **I** *n* (all contexts) immigration *f*; **to go through ~** passer l'immigration.
II *modif* [*procedures, restrictions*] d'immigration.

immigration: **~ authorities** *npl* services *mpl* de l'immigration; **~ control** *n* (system) contrôle *m* de l'immigration; (office) services *mpl* de l'immigration; **~ laws** *npl* lois *fpl* sur l'immigration; **~ officer, ~ official** *n* fonctionnaire *mf* des services de l'immigration; **Immigration Service** *n* GB services *mpl* de l'immigration.

imminence /ˈɪmɪnəns/ *n* imminence *f*.

imminent /ˈɪmɪnənt/ *adj* [*arrival, danger, release*] imminent; **rain/a storm is ~** la pluie/l'orage menace.

immobile /ɪˈməʊbaɪl, US -bl/ *adj* **1** (motionless) immobile; **2** (unable to move) [*person*] impotent; [*object*] fixe.

immobility /ˌɪməˈbɪlətɪ/ *n* **1** (of traffic, vehicle) immobilité *f*; **2** (inability to move) (of person) impotence *f*; **~ of labour** manque de mobilité de la main-d'œuvre; **3** (lack of change) inertie *f*.

immobilize /ɪˈməʊbɪlaɪz/ **I** *vtr* **1** (stop operating) paralyser [*traffic, market, organization*]; immobiliser [*car, engine*]; paralyser [*enemy installation*]; **2** (keep still) immobiliser [*patient, limb, animal*]; **3** Fin bloquer [*funds*].
II immobilized *pp adj* [*car, person*] immobilisé; [*market, traffic*] paralysé.

immoderate /ɪˈmɒdərət/ *adj* sout (all contexts) immodéré.

immoderately /ɪˈmɒdərətlɪ/ *adv* sout immodérément.

immodest /ɪˈmɒdɪst/ *adj* **1** (boastful) présomptueux/-euse; **2** (improper) indécent.

immodestly /ɪˈmɒdɪstlɪ/ *adv* **1** [*claim*] présomptueusement; **she claims, not ~, that** elle prétend, à juste titre, que; **2** [*dress, behave*] indécemment.

immodesty /ɪˈmɒdɪstɪ/ *n* **1** (of claim) présomption *f*; **without ~** sans être présomptueux/-euse; **2** (sexual) impudeur *f*.

immolate /ˈɪməleɪt/ **I** *vtr* immoler.
II *v refl* **to ~ oneself** s'immoler.

immoral /ɪˈmɒrəl, US ɪˈmɔːrəl/ *adj* (all cases) immoral; **to live off ~ earnings** Jur vivre de gains illicites (*en tant que proxénète*).

immorality /ˌɪməˈrælətɪ/ *n* (all contexts) immoralité *f*.

immortal /ɪˈmɔːtl/ **I** *n* **1** (god) (also **Immortal**) immortel/-elle *m/f*; **2** (writer) auteur *m* immortel; **3** (star) vedette *f* immortelle.
II *adj* (all contexts) immortel/-elle.

immortality /ˌɪmɔːˈtælətɪ/ *n* (all contexts) immortalité *f*; **to achieve ~** entrer dans l'immortalité.

immortalize /ɪˈmɔːtəlaɪz/ **I** *vtr* immortaliser [*person, place, event*].
II immortalized *pp adj* immortalisé; **~ in verse** immortalisé en vers; **~ in a book/film** immortalisé dans un livre/film.

immovable /ɪˈmuːvəbl/ **I immovables** *npl* biens *mpl* immeubles.

II *adj* 1 (immobile) fixe; 2 (unchanging) [*position, opinion*] inébranlable; [*government, person*] immuable; 3 (impassive) impassible; 4 Jur [*goods, property*] immeuble.

immovably /ɪ'mu:vəblɪ/ *adv* [*opposed, resolved*] irrévocablement.

immune /ɪ'mju:n/ *adj* 1 Med [*person, organism*] immunisé (**to** contre); [*reaction*] immunitaire; [*substance*] immunisant; **~ deficiency** déficience *f* immunitaire, immunodéficience *f*; **~ system** système *m* immunitaire; **to become ~ to** acquérir l'immunité contre; 2 (oblivious) **~ to** insensible à [*flattery, criticism*]; 3 (exempt) **to be ~ from** être à l'abri de [*attack, arrest*]; être exempté de [*tax*]; **to be ~ from prosecution** ne pas faire l'objet de poursuite.

immunity /ɪ'mju:nətɪ/ *n* 1 Med, Admin immunité *f* (**to, against** contre); **tax/legal ~** exemption *f* fiscale/légale; **to be granted ~** se voir accorder l'immunité; 2 (to criticism) impassibilité *f* (**to** devant).

immunization /ˌɪmjʊnaɪ'zeɪʃn, US -nɪ'z-/ *n* immunisation *f* (**against** contre); **mass ~** immunisation généralisée.

immunize /'ɪmjʊnaɪz/ *vtr* immuniser (**against** contre).

immunodeficiency /ˌɪmju:ˌnəʊdɪ'fɪʃənsɪ/ *n* déficience *f* immunitaire, immunodéficience *f*.

immunodeficient /ˌɪmjʊnəʊdə'fɪʃənt/ *adj* immunodéficitaire.

immunogenic /ˌɪmju:nəʊ'dʒenɪk/ *adj* immunogène.

immunoglobulin /ˌɪmju:nəʊ'glɒbjʊlɪn/ *n* immunoglobuline *mf*.

immunological /ˌɪmju:nə'lɒdʒɪkl/ *adj* immunologique.

immunologist /ˌɪmjʊ'nɒlədʒɪst/ *n* immunologiste *mf*.

immunology /ˌɪmjʊ'nɒlədʒɪ/ *n* immunologie *f*.

immunosuppressive /ˌɪmju:nəsə'presɪv/ I *n* immunodépresseur *m*.
II *adj* immunodépressif/-ive.

immure /ɪ'mjʊə(r)/ littér I *vtr* 1 (imprison) enfermer; 2 (wall in) emmurer.
II *v refl* **to ~ oneself** fig se cloîtrer.

immutability /ɪˌmju:tə'bɪlətɪ/ *n* immuabilité *f*, immutabilité *f*.

immutable /ɪ'mju:təbl/ *adj* immuable.

immutably /ɪ'mju:təblɪ/ *adv* définitivement.

imp /ɪmp/ *n* 1 (elf) lutin *m*; 2 fig (child) **she's a little ~**○ c'est un petit diable○ fig.

impact I /'ɪmpækt/ *n* 1 (effect) impact *m* (**on** sur); **to have** ou **make an ~ on sb/sth** avoir un impact sur qn/qch; 2 (violent contact) (of explosion, hammer, vehicle) choc *m*; (of bomb, bullet) impact *m* (**against** contre; **on** sur); **on ~** au moment de l'impact; 3 (impetus of collision) choc *m*.
II /ɪm'pækt/ *vtr* 1 (affect) avoir un impact sur; 2 (hit) percuter.
III /ɪm'pækt/ *vi* avoir un impact (**on** sur).

impacted /ɪm'pæktɪd/ *adj* 1 Med [*tooth*] inclus; [*fracture*] engrené; 2 Aut **two ~ cars** deux voitures encastrées; 3 US Econ [*area*] dont les ressources sont utilisées au maximum; 4 US (entrenched) [*attitude*] arrêté.

impair /ɪm'peə(r)/ *vtr* affecter [*performance, walk*]; diminuer [*ability, concentration*]; affaiblir [*memory, hearing, vision*]; détériorer [*health, relationship*]; compromettre [*attempt, investigation, reputation*]; diminuer, affecter [*efficiency, productivity, progress*].

impaired /ɪm'peəd/ *adj* [*hearing, vision*] affaibli; [*memory*] défaillant; [*mobility*] réduit; [*relationship*] compromis; **his speech is ~** il a des problèmes d'élocution. ▸**visually impaired**, **hearing-impaired**.

impairment /ɪm'peəmənt/ *n* **mental/physical/visual ~** troubles *mpl* mentaux/moteurs/visuels; **~ of vision/hearing** troubles *mpl* de la vue/de l'ouïe.

impala /ɪm'pɑ:lə/ *n* (*pl* **-as** ou **-a**) impala *m*.

impale /ɪm'peɪl/ I *vtr* empaler (**on** sur).
II *v refl* **to ~ oneself** s'empaler (**on** sur).

impalpable /ɪm'pælpəbl/ *adj* 1 (intangible) impalpable; 2 (hard to describe) indéfinissable.

impanel *vtr* Jur = **empanel**.

imparity /ɪm'pærətɪ/ *n* inégalité *f*.

impart /ɪm'pɑ:t/ *vtr* 1 (communicate) transmettre [*knowledge, news, skill*] (**to** à); communiquer [*information, message*] (**to** à); transmettre [*enthusiasm, optimism, wisdom*] (**to** à); 2 (add) donner [*atmosphere, flavour, texture*].

impartial /ɪm'pɑ:ʃl/ *adj* [*advice, decision, inquiry, judge, witness*] impartial; [*account, journalist, programme*] objectif/-ive.

impartiality /ˌɪmˌpɑ:ʃɪ'ælətɪ/ *n* (of judge, inquiry, verdict) impartialité *f*; (of broadcast, journalist) objectivité *f*.

impartially /ɪm'pɑ:ʃəlɪ/ *adv* [*act, choose, decide, judge*] de façon impartiale; [*divide, share out*] équitablement; [*report, write*] objectivement.

impassable /ɪm'pɑ:səbl, US -'pæs-/ *adj* [*barrier, obstacle, pass, river*] infranchissable; [*road*] impraticable.

impasse /'æmpɑ:s, US 'ɪmpæs/ *n* impasse *f*; **to reach an ~** aboutir à une impasse.

impassioned /ɪm'pæʃnd/ *adj* [*debate*] passionné; [*appeal, plea, speech*] véhément.

impassive /ɪm'pæsɪv/ *adj* 1 (expressionless) [*person, expression, features*] impassible; 2 (unruffled) [*attitude, person, reply*] imperturbable.

impassively /ɪm'pæsɪvlɪ/ *adv* 1 (without visible emotion) impassiblement; 2 (calmly) imperturbablement.

impatience /ɪm'peɪʃns/ *n* 1 (irritation) agacement *m* (**with** à l'égard de; **at** devant); **my worst fault is ~** mon plus grand défaut est mon manque de patience; 2 (eagerness) impatience *f* (**to do** de faire); **~ for sth** désir *m* impatient de qch.

impatiens /ɪm'peɪʃɪenz/ *n* impatiente *f*, balsamine *f*.

impatient /ɪm'peɪʃnt/ *adj* 1 (irritable) agacé (**at** par); **to be/get ~ with sb** s'impatienter contre qn; 2 (eager) [*person*] impatient; **to be ~ to do** être impatient or avoir hâte de faire; [*gesture, tone*] d'impatience; **to be ~ for sth** attendre qch avec impatience.

impatiently /ɪm'peɪʃntlɪ/ *adv* [*wait*] impatiemment; [*fidget, pace*] avec impatience; [*speak, say*] d'un ton agacé.

impeach /ɪm'pi:tʃ/ *vtr* 1 gen mettre en doute [*honesty, motive*]; 2 Jur, Pol mettre [qn] en accusation.

impeachment /ɪm'pi:tʃmənt/ *n* 1 (of honour) attaque *f* (**of** contre); 2 Jur, Pol mise *f* en accusation.

impeccable /ɪm'pekəbl/ *adj* [*manners, behaviour, language*] irréprochable; [*house, clothes, appearance*] impeccable; [*credentials, record*] impeccable.

impeccably /ɪm'pekəblɪ/ *adv* [*dressed*] impeccablement; [*speak, behave*] de façon irréprochable; **~ clean** impeccable.

impecunious /ˌɪmpɪ'kju:nɪəs/ *adj* sout impécunieux/-ieuse.

impedance /ɪm'pi:dəns/ *n* Elec impédance *f*.

impede /ɪm'pi:d/ *vtr* entraver [*progress, career*]; [*obstacle*] gêner [*movement, traffic*].

impediment /ɪm'pedɪmənt/ *n* 1 (hindrance) entrave *f* (**to** à); 2 (to marriage) empêchement *m* (à mariage); 3 (also **speech ~**) défaut *m* d'élocution.

impedimenta /ɪmˌpedɪ'mentə/ *n* (+ *v pl*) gen, hum impedimenta *mpl*.

impel /ɪm'pel/ *vtr* (*p prés etc* **-ll-**) 1 (drive) [*emotion, idea*] pousser [*person*] (**to do** à faire); **~led by fear** poussé par la peur; 2 (urge) [*person, speech*] inciter [*person*] (**to** à; **to do** à faire); **to feel ~led to do** se sentir obligé de faire.

impending /ɪm'pendɪŋ/ *adj* (*avant n*) imminent.

impenetrability /ɪmˌpenɪtrə'bɪlətɪ/ *n* lit, fig impénétrabilité *f*.

impenetrable /ɪm'penɪtrəbl/ *adj* [*barrier, undergrowth, layer*] impénétrable; [*jargon*] hermétique; [*mystery*] insondable; [*fog*] dense.

impenitence /ɪm'penɪtəns/ *n* impénitence *f*.

impenitent /ɪm'penɪtənt/ *adj* impénitent.

impenitently /ɪm'penɪtəntlɪ/ *adv* sans repentir.

imperative /ɪm'perətɪv/ I *n* 1 (priority) impératif *m*; **the first ~ is to do** l'impératif numéro un est de faire; 2 Ling impératif *m*; **in the ~ (mood)** à l'impératif.
II *adj* [*need*] urgent; [*tone*] impérieux/-ieuse; **it is ~ that she write** il est impératif qu'elle écrive; **it is ~ to act** il est impératif que nous agissions.

imperatively /ɪm'perətɪvlɪ/ *adv* 1 (urgently) impérativement; 2 (imperiously) impérieusement .

imperceptible /ˌɪmpə'septəbl/ *adj* imperceptible; **almost ~** à peine perceptible.

imperceptibly /ˌɪmpə'septəblɪ/ *adv* imperceptiblement.

imperceptive /ˌɪmpə'septɪv/ *adj* [*person*] peu perspicace.

imperfect /ɪm'pɜ:fɪkt/ I *n* Ling imparfait *m*; **in the ~** à l'imparfait.
II *adj* 1 (incomplete) incomplet/-ète; 2 (defective) [*goods*] défectueux/-euse; [*logic*] imparfait; [*reasoning*] faux/fausse; 3 Ling **the ~ tense** l'imparfait *m*; 4 Comm [*competition*] imparfait.

imperfection /ˌɪmpə'fekʃn/ *n* 1 (defect) (in object) défectuosité *f*; (in person) défaut *m*; 2 (state) imperfection *f*; **human ~** l'imperfection humaine.

imperfectly /ɪm'pɜ:fɪktlɪ/ *adv* imparfaitement.

imperial /ɪm'pɪərɪəl/ I *n* (beard) barbe *f* à l'impériale.
II *adj* 1 (of empire, emperor) impérial; 2 fig [*disdain, unconcern*] majestueux/-euse; 3 GB Hist de l'Empire; 4 GB Meas [*measure*] conforme aux normes britanniques.

imperialism /ɪm'pɪərɪəlɪzəm/ *n* impérialisme *m*.

imperialist /ɪm'pɪərɪəlɪst/ *n, adj* impérialiste (*mf*).

imperil /ɪm'perəl/ *vtr* (*p prés etc* **-ll-** GB, **-l-** US) menacer [*existence*]; compromettre [*security, plan, scheme*].

imperious /ɪm'pɪərɪəs/ *adj* impérieux/-ieuse.

imperiously /ɪm'pɪərɪəslɪ/ *adv* [*say*] impérieusement; **the request was ~ declined** on repoussa la demande de manière impérieuse.

imperishable /ɪm'perɪʃəbl/ *adj* 1 [*material*] qui ne périt pas; [*food*] non périssable; 2 [*memory*] impérissable.

impermanent /ɪm'pɜ:mənənt/ *adj* [*arrangement, situation, change*] provisoire.

impermeable /ɪm'pɜ:mɪəbl/ *adj* [*membrane, rock*] imperméable.

impermissible /ˌɪmpə'mɪsəbl/ *adj* sout inadmissible (**for sb to do** que qn fasse).

impersonal /ɪm'pɜ:sənl/ *adj* 1 (objective, cold) impersonnel/-elle; **coldly ~** froid et impersonnel; 2 Ling [*verb*] impersonnel/-elle.

impersonality /ɪmˌpɜ:sə'nælətɪ/ *n* (of person) froideur *f*; (of style, organization) impersonnalité *f*.

impersonally /ɪm'pɜ:sənəlɪ/ *adv* 1 (impartially) [*assess, judge*] impersonnellement; 2 (coldly) froidement; 3 Ling à la forme impersonnelle.

impersonate /ɪm'pɜ:səneɪt/ *vtr* 1 (imitate) imiter; 2 (pretend to be) se faire passer pour [*police officer etc*].

impersonation /ɪmˌpɜːsəˈneɪʃn/ *n* **1** (act) imitation *f*; **to do ~s** faire des imitations; **2** Jur usurpation *f* d'identité (**of** de).

impersonator /ɪmˈpɜːsəneɪtə(r)/ *n* (actor) imitateur/-trice *m/f*; **animal ~** imitateur/-trice *m/f* (*des cris d'animaux*); **female ~** artiste *m* travesti.

impertinence /ɪmˈpɜːtɪnəns/ *n* impertinence *f*; **to have the ~ to do** avoir l'impertinence de faire.

impertinent /ɪmˈpɜːtɪnənt/ *adj* [*person, remark*] impertinent; **to be ~** se montrer impertinent (**to** envers).

impertinently /ɪmˈpɜːtɪnəntlɪ/ *adv* [*act, say, reply*] avec impertinence.

imperturbable /ˌɪmpəˈtɜːbəbl/ *adj* [*person, manner*] imperturbable.

imperturbably /ˌɪmpəˈtɜːbəblɪ/ *adv* [*continue, speak*] imperturbablement; **'of course,' she said ~** 'bien sûr,' dit-elle, imperturbable; **~ polite/calm** poli/calme et imperturbable.

impervious /ɪmˈpɜːvɪəs/ *adj* **1** (to water, gas) imperméable (**to** à); **2** fig (to charm, sarcasm, events, suffering) indifférent (**to** à); (to argument, idea, demands, economic conditions) imperméable (**to** à).

impetigo /ˌɪmpɪˈtaɪgəʊ/ ▶ 1354 *n* impétigo *m*.

impetuosity /ɪmˌpetʃʊˈɒsətɪ/ *n* (of person) impétuosité *f*; (of action) impulsivité *f*.

impetuous /ɪmˈpetʃʊəs/ *adj* [*person*] impétueux/-euse; [*action*] impulsif/-ive.

impetuously /ɪmˈpetʃʊəslɪ/ *adv* impétueusement; **~ generous** d'une générosité impulsive.

impetuousness = **impetuosity**.

impetus /ˈɪmpɪtəs/ *n* **1** (trigger) impulsion *f*; **the ~ for the project came from X** le projet a commencé sous l'impulsion de X; **2** (momentum) élan *m*; **to gain/lose ~** prendre/perdre de l'élan; **to give ~ to sth** donner de l'élan à qch; **3** Phys impulsion *f*.

impiety /ɪmˈpaɪətɪ/ *n* **1** Relig impiété *f*; **2** (disrespect) manque *m* de respect.

impinge /ɪmˈpɪndʒ/ *vi* **to ~ on** (restrict) empiéter sur; (affect) affecter; **to ~ on sb's consciousness** parvenir jusqu'à la conscience de qn.

impious /ˈɪmpɪəs/ *adj* **1** Relig impie; **2** (disrespectful) irrespectueux/-euse.

impiously /ˈɪmpɪəslɪ/ *adv* **1** Relig avec impiété; **2** (disrespectfully) irrespectueusement.

impish /ˈɪmpɪʃ/ *adj* espiègle.

implacable /ɪmˈplækəbl/ *adj* implacable.

implacably /ɪmˈplækəblɪ/ *adv* implacablement.

implant **I** /ˈɪmplɑːnt, US -plænt/ *n* Med implant *m*; **oestrogen ~** implant d'œstrogène.

II /ɪmˈplɑːnt, US -ˈplænt/ *vtr* Med, fig implanter (**in** dans).

implantation /ˌɪmplɑːnˈteɪʃn, US -plænt-/ *n* (of fertilized egg) (naturally) nidation *f*; (artificially) implantation *f*.

implausible /ɪmˈplɔːzəbl/ *adj* peu plausible.

implausibly /ɪmˈplɔːzəblɪ/ *adv* [*claim, explain*] d'une manière peu plausible; **~, he denied everything** il nia tout, ce qui semble peu plausible.

implement **I** /ˈɪmplɪmənt/ *n* gen instrument *m*; (tool) outil *m*; **farm ~s** outillage *m* agricole; **garden ~s** outils *mpl* de jardinage; **set of ~s** Culin série *f* d'ustensiles; **an ~ for sth/for doing** un instrument destiné à qch/à faire.

II /ˈɪmplɪment/ *vtr* **1** gen, Jur exécuter [*contract, idea, decision*]; mettre [qch] en application [*law*]; **2** Comput implanter [*software*]; implémenter [*system*].

implementation /ˌɪmplɪmenˈteɪʃn/ *n* (of contract, idea, decision) exécution *f*; (of law, policy) mise *f* en application; Comput implémentation *f*.

implicate /ˈɪmplɪkeɪt/ *vtr* impliquer (**in** dans); **he is in no way ~d** il n'est en aucune façon impliqué.

implication /ˌɪmplɪˈkeɪʃn/ *n* **1** (possible consequence) implication *f*; **what are the ~s for the future/for the disabled?** quelles sont les implications pour l'avenir/pour les handicapés?; **2** (suggestion) insinuation *f*; **the ~ is that** cela signifie que; **they said there were younger applicants, the ~ being that he was too old** ils ont dit qu'il y avait de plus jeunes candidats, insinuant qu'il était trop vieux; **by ~, the government is also responsible** cela signifie que le gouvernement est aussi responsable.

implicit /ɪmˈplɪsɪt/ *adj* **1** (implied) implicite (**in** dans); **2** (absolute) [*faith, confidence, trust*] absolu.

implicitly /ɪmˈplɪsɪtlɪ/ *adv* **1** (tacitly) [*assume, admit, recognize*] implicitement; **2** (absolutely) [*trust, believe*] sans réserve.

implied /ɪmˈplaɪd/ *adj* implicite.

impliedly /ɪmˈplaɪdlɪ/ *adv* Jur implicitement; **expressly or ~** explicitement ou implicitement.

implode /ɪmˈpləʊd/ **I** *vtr* **1** Phon **to ~ a consonant** prononcer une consonne implosive; **2** faire imploser [*vessel, flask*].

II *vi* imploser.

implore /ɪmˈplɔː(r)/ *vtr* conjurer [*person*] (**to do** de faire); **to ~ sb's forgiveness** littér implorer le pardon de qn liter.

imploring /ɪmˈplɔːrɪŋ/ *adj* implorant.

imploringly /ɪmˈplɔːrɪŋlɪ/ *adv* [*say*] d'un ton implorant; **to look at sb ~** implorer qn du regard.

implosion /ɪmˈpləʊʒn/ *n* implosion *f*.

implosive /ɪmˈpləʊsɪv/ *adj* Phon implosif/-ive.

imply /ɪmˈplaɪ/ *vtr* **1** [*person*] (insinuate) insinuer (**that** que); (make known) laisser entendre (**that** que); **he didn't mean to ~ anything** il ne voulait rien insinuer; **what are you ~ing?** qu'est-ce que vous insinuez (par là)?; **he implied that they were guilty** il a laissé entendre qu'ils étaient coupables; **2** [*argument*] (mean) impliquer; **silence does not necessarily ~ approval** le silence n'implique pas nécessairement l'approbation; **to ~ that** (corroboratively) impliquer que (+ *indic*); (erroneously) impliquer que (+ *subj*); **3** [*term, word*] (mean) laisser supposer (**that** que); **as their name implies...** comme leur nom le laisse supposer...

impolite /ˌɪmpəˈlaɪt/ *adj* impoli (**to** envers).

impolitely /ˌɪmpəˈlaɪtlɪ/ *adv* [*act, behave*] de manière impolie; [*say*] avec impolitesse.

impoliteness /ˌɪmpəˈlaɪtnɪs/ *n* impolitesse *f*.

impolitic /ɪmˈpɒlɪtɪk/ *adj* impolitique.

imponderable /ɪmˈpɒndərəbl/ *n, adj* impondérable (*m*).

import **I** /ˈɪmpɔːt/ *n* **1** Comm, Econ (item of merchandise) importation *f*, produit *m* importé; (act of importing) importation *f* (**of, from** de); **foreign ~s** importations *fpl* étrangères; **2** (cultural borrowing) apport *m* (**from** à); **3** sout (meaning) signification *f* (**in** à); **4** (importance) importance *f*; **of no (great) ~** de peu d'importance; **of political ~** qui a une importance politique.

II /ˈɪmpɔːt/ *modif* [*ban, cost, price, quota, surcharge, surplus*] d'importation; [*bill, increase, rise*] des importations.

III /ɪmˈpɔːt/ *vtr* Comm, Econ, gen importer (**from** de; **to** en).

IV imported *pp adj* [*goods*] importé.

importance /ɪmˈpɔːtns/ *n* importance *f* (**of doing** de faire); **her career is of great ~ to her** sa carrière est très importante or compte beaucoup pour elle; **a healthy diet is of great ~ to children** un régime sain est essentiel pour les enfants; **it is of great ~ that** il est essentiel que (+ *subj*); **it is of great ~ that the pound should remain stable** il est essentiel que la livre sterling reste stable; **to be of national ~** être d'importance nationale; **an event of great political ~** un événement d'une grande portée politique; **it is a matter of the utmost ~** c'est une question de la plus haute importance; **great ~ is attached to success** on attache une grande importance au succès; **the ~ of France as a world power** l'importance de la France en tant que puissance mondiale; **list the priorities in order of ~** classez les priorités par ordre d'importance; **a person of no ~** une personne sans importance; **it's of no ~** ça n'a pas d'importance.

important /ɪmˈpɔːtnt/ *adj* [*statement, factor, role, figure, writer*] important; **it is ~ that** il est important que (+ *subj*); **it is ~ to remember that...** il est important de se rappeler que..., il faut se rappeler que...; **this is ~ for our success/health** c'est important pour notre succès/santé; **it is ~ for us to succeed** il est important pour nous de réussir; **his children are very ~ to him** ses enfants comptent beaucoup or sont très importants pour lui; **it is ~ to me that you attend the meeting** il est important pour moi que vous assistiez à la réunion, votre présence à la réunion compte beaucoup pour moi; **is anybody ~ coming?** est-ce qu'il y a des gens importants qui viennent?; **he's an ~ social figure** c'est une personne en vue.

importantly /ɪmˈpɔːtntlɪ/ *adv* **1** (significantly) d'une manière importante; **more ~, he succeeded where she had failed** plus important encore, il a réussi là où elle avait échoué; **and, more ~,...** et, plus important encore,...; **most ~, it means** mais surtout, cela signifie; **these changes have taken place most ~ in the agricultural sector** ces changements se sont manifestés essentiellement dans le secteur agricole; **2** (pompously) [*announce, strut*] d'un air important.

importation /ˌɪmpɔːˈteɪʃn/ *n* Comm (act, object) importation *f*.

import duty *n* taxe *f* à l'importation.

importer /ɪmˈpɔːtə(r)/ *n* importateur/-trice *m/f*; **car/oil ~** importateur/-trice *m/f* de voitures/de pétrole.

import-export /ˌɪmpɔːtˈekspɔːt/ **I** *n* import-export *m*.

II *modif* [*growth, merchant*] de l'import-export; **~ trade** import-export *m*.

importing /ɪmˈpɔːtɪŋ/ **I** *n* importation *f* (**of** de).

II *adj* [*country, business*] importateur/-trice; **oil-~ country** pays *m* importateur de pétrole.

import licence GB, **import license** US *n* licence *f* d'importation.

importunate /ɪmˈpɔːtʃʊnət/ *adj* importun.

importune /ˌɪmpɔːˈtjuːn/ *vtr* **1** (pester) importuner [*person*] (**for** pour; **with** avec); **2** Jur [*prostitute*] racoler.

importuning /ˌɪmpɔːˈtjuːnɪŋ/ *n* Jur racolage *m*.

importunity /ˌɪmpɔːˈtjuːnətɪ/ *n* sout **1** (request) importunité *f*; **2** (instance) sollicitation *f*.

impose /ɪmˈpəʊz/ **I** *vtr* **1** imposer [*embargo, condition, opinion, constraint, rule, obedience*] (**on sb** à qn; **on sth** sur qch); infliger [*sanction, punishment*] (**on** à); **to ~ a fine on sb** frapper qn d'une amende; **to ~ a tax on tobacco** imposer le tabac; **2 to ~ one's presence on sb** s'imposer à qn; **3** Print imposer.

II *vi* s'imposer; **to ~ on sb** déranger qn; **to ~ on sb's kindness/hospitality** abuser de la bienveillance/de l'hospitalité de qn.

III *v refl* **to ~ oneself on sb** s'imposer à qn.

imposing /ɪmˈpəʊzɪŋ/ *adj* [*person, appearance*] imposant; [*sight, array, collection*] impressionnant.

imposition /ˌɪmpəˈzɪʃn/ *n* **1** (exploitation) **|**

hope it's not too much of an ~ j'espère que je n'abuse pas de votre bienveillance; **I think it's rather an ~** je trouve qu'il/qu'elle abuse un peu; **2** (of tax) imposition *f*; **3** Print imposition *f*.

impossibility /ɪmˌpɒsəˈbɪlətɪ/ *n* impossibilité *f* (**of** de; **of doing** de faire); **a physical ~** une impossibilité matérielle; **it's a near ~!** c'est pratiquement impossible!; **that's a logical ~** c'est logiquement impossible.

impossible /ɪmˈpɒsəbl/ **I** *n* **the ~** l'impossible *m*.
II *adj* [*person, situation, idea, suggestion*] impossible; **it is ~ to do** il est impossible de faire; **it's almost ~ for me to come** il m'est pratiquement impossible de venir; **to make it ~ for sb to do sth** mettre qn dans l'impossibilité de faire qch; **it is ~ that he should have missed the train** il est impossible qu'il ait raté le train; **difficult, if not ~** difficile, pour ne pas dire impossible; **it's ~, I won't stand for it!** c'est intolérable, je ne le supporterai pas!

impossibly /ɪmˈpɒsəblɪ/ *adv* (appallingly) affreusement; (amazingly) incroyablement; **it's ~ early/expensive** c'est vraiment trop tôt/cher.

impost /ˈɪmpəʊst/ *n* US taxe *f* à l'importation.

impostor /ɪmˈpɒstə(r)/ *n* imposteur *m*.

imposture /ɪmˈpɒstʃə(r)/ *n* imposture *f*.

impotence /ˈɪmpətəns/ *n* lit, fig impuissance *f*.

impotent /ˈɪmpətənt/ *adj* lit, fig impuissant; **to render sb/sth ~** réduire qn/qch à l'impuissance.

impound /ɪmˈpaʊnd/ *vtr* emmener [qch] à la fourrière [*vehicle*]; confisquer [*goods*]; saisir, déposer [qch] au greffe [*passport, papers*].

impoverish /ɪmˈpɒvərɪʃ/ *vtr* (all contexts) appauvrir.

impoverished /ɪmˈpɒvərɪʃt/ *adj* (all contexts) appauvri.

impoverishment /ɪmˈpɒvərɪʃmənt/ *n* (all contexts) appauvrissement *m*.

impracticability /ɪmˌpræktɪkəˈbɪlətɪ/ *n* impraticabilité *f*.

impracticable /ɪmˈpræktɪkəbl/ *adj* [*idea, plan*] impraticable.

impractical /ɪmˈpræktɪkl/ *adj* **1** (unworkable) [*plan, solution*] impraticable, peu réalisable; **2** (unrealistic) [*suggestion, idea*] peu réaliste; **3** [*person*] **to be ~** manquer d'esprit pratique.

impracticality /ɪmˌpræktɪˈkælətɪ/ *n* **1** (unworkable nature) impraticabilité *f*; **2** (of person) manque *m* d'esprit pratique.

imprecation /ˌɪmprɪˈkeɪʃn/ *n* sout imprécation *f* fml.

imprecise /ˌɪmprɪˈsaɪs/ *adj* (all contexts) imprécis.

imprecision /ˌɪmprɪˈsɪʒn/ *n* (of language, expression) imprécision *f*.

impregnable /ɪmˈpregnəbl/ *adj* [*castle, defences*] imprenable; [*leader, party*] invincible.

impregnate /ˈɪmpregneɪt, US ɪmˈpreg-/ *vtr* **1** (soak, pervade) imprégner (**with** de); **2** (fertilize) féconder [*woman, animal, egg*].

impregnation /ˌɪmpregˈneɪʃn/ *n* (of female, egg) fécondation *f*.

impresario /ˌɪmprɪˈsɑːrɪəʊ/ *n* impresario *m*.

impress **I** /ˈɪmpres/ *n* sout empreinte *f*.
II /ɪmˈpres/ *vtr* **1** (arouse respect) impressionner [*person, public, audience, panel*] (**with** par; **by doing** en faisant); **to be ~ed by** ou **with sb/sth** être impressionné par qn/qch; **to be easily ~ed** se laisser facilement impressionner; **they were (favourably) ~ed** ça leur a fait bonne impression; **they weren't too ~ed by his attitude/with the results** ils n'ont guère apprécié son attitude/les résultats; **she/the company is not ~ed** elle/la société n'apprécie pas beaucoup; **she does it just to ~ people** elle ne fait ça que pour la galerie○; **2** (emphasize) **to ~ sth (up)on sb** faire bien comprendre qch à qn; **to ~ upon sb that** faire (bien) comprendre à qn que; **3** (imprint) **to ~ sth on** marquer qch sur [*surface, material*]; **to ~ sth in** faire une empreinte de qch dans [*wax, plaster*].
III /ɪmˈpres/ *vi* [*person, quality, feature*] faire bonne impression.

impression /ɪmˈpreʃn/ *n* **1** (idea) impression *f*; **to give the ~ of doing** donner l'impression de faire; **she had the ~ that she knew him/he knew her** elle avait l'impression de le connaître/qu'il la connaissait; **to get the (distinct) ~ that** avoir (bien) l'impression que; **to be under the ~ that** avoir l'impression que; **2** (impact) impression *f*; **to make a good/bad ~** faire bonne/mauvaise impression (**on** sur); **to make (quite) an ~** faire impression or de l'effet; **it left a deep ~ on him** cela l'a profondément marqué; **what kind of ~ did they make?** quelle impression ont-ils faite?; **3** (perception) impression *f*; **to have the ~ of doing** avoir l'impression de faire; **to give** ou **create an ~ of sth** faire l'effet de qch; **an artist's ~ of the building** le bâtiment vu par un artiste; **what's your ~ of the new boss?** quelle est ton impression sur le nouveau patron?; **first ~s count** les premières impressions sont souvent les meilleures; **4** (imitation) imitation *f*; **to do ~s (of famous people)** faire des imitations (de personnes célèbres); **she does a good ~ of Valerie** elle imite bien Valérie; **5** (imprint) (of weight, foot, hand) impression *f*; (from teeth) marque *f*; (of hoof) empreinte *f*; **to leave an ~ on** laisser une trace sur [*surface, sand, wax*]; **to take an ~ of** faire une empreinte de [*key, fossil*]; **6** Print, Publg (reprint) réimpression *f*; **7** Print (process) impression *f*.

impressionable /ɪmˈpreʃənəbl/ *adj* [*child, mind, youth*] influençable; **at an ~ age** à l'âge où l'on est influençable.

Impressionism /ɪmˈpreʃənɪzəm/ *n* (also **impressionism**) impressionnisme *m*.

impressionist /ɪmˈpreʃənɪst/ *n* **1** Art, Mus impressionniste *mf*; **2** (mimic) imitateur/-trice *m/f*.

Impressionist /ɪmˈpreʃənɪst/ *n, adj* Art, Mus impressionniste (*mf*).

impressionistic /ɪmˌpreʃəˈnɪstɪk/ *adj* impressionniste.

impressive /ɪmˈpresɪv/ *adj* [*achievement, cast, collection, display, result, total*] impressionnant; [*building, monument, sight*] imposant; **she is very ~** elle en impose.

impressively /ɪmˈpresɪvlɪ/ *adv* [*behave, perform, argue, demonstrate*] de manière impressionnante; [*assured, cohesive, competent, large*] remarquablement.

impressment /ɪmˈpresmənt/ *n* Hist (requisition) réquisition *f*.

imprimatur /ˌɪmprɪˈmeɪtə(r), -ˈmɑːtə(r)/ *n* Relig, fig imprimatur *m*.

imprint **I** /ˈɪmprɪnt/ *n* **1** (impression) lit, fig empreinte *f*; **to leave an ~** laisser une empreinte; **2** Publg (on title page) marque *f* d'éditeur; (publishing house) maison *f* d'édition; **published under the Grunard ~** édité chez Grunard.
II /ɪmˈprɪnt/ *vtr* **1** (fix) graver [*idea, image, belief*] (**on** dans); **2** (print) imprimer [*mark, design*] (**on** sur); **3** Psych, Zool (affect by imprinting) imprégner.

imprinter /ɪmˈprɪntə(r)/ *n* (for credit card) imprimante *f* à carte.

imprinting /ɪmˈprɪntɪŋ/ *n* Psych, Zool empreinte *f*.

imprison /ɪmˈprɪzn/ *vtr* **1** (put in prison) emprisonner, mettre [qn] en prison; **to be ~ed for/for doing** être emprisonné pour/pour avoir fait; **to be ~ed for ten years** (sentenced) être condamné à dix ans de prison; **2** fig (trap) emprisonner [*finger, limb*] (**in** dans).

imprisonment /ɪmˈprɪznmənt/ *n* emprisonnement *m*; **to be sentenced to ten years' ~/to ~ for life** être condamné à dix ans de prison/à la prison à vie; **to threaten sb with ~** menacer qn de le/la mettre en prison.

improbability /ɪmˌprɒbəˈbɪlətɪ/ *n* **1** (of something happening) improbabilité *f*; (of something being true) invraisemblance *f*; **2** (unlikely story, event) improbabilité *f*.

improbable /ɪmˈprɒbəbl/ *adj* **1** (unlikely to happen) improbable; **it is ~ that** il est improbable or peu probable que (+ *subj*); **2** (unlikely to be true) invraisemblable; **it is ~ that** il est peu vraisemblable que (+ *subj*).

improbably /ɪmˈprɒbəblɪ/ *adv* [*claim, state*] invraisemblablement; **her hair was ~ red** ses cheveux étaient d'un roux invraisemblable.

impromptu /ɪmˈprɒmptjuː, US -tuː/ **I** *n* Mus impromptu *m*.
II *adj* [*call, party, speech*] impromptu.

improper /ɪmˈprɒpə(r)/ *adj* **1** (unseemly, not fitting) [*behaviour, pride*] malséant, peu convenable; **2** (irregular) [*conduct, dealing, use*] irrégulier/-ière; **3** (indecent) [*suggestion, remark*] indécent; **4** (incorrect) [*use*] impropre, abusif/-ive; **it is ~ to do** il est incorrect de faire.

improper: **~ fraction** *n* expression *f* fractionnaire; **~ integral** *n* intégrale *f* impropre.

improperly /ɪmˈprɒpəlɪ/ *adv* **1** (irregularly, dishonestly) [*act, obtain, deal*] de manière irrégulière; **2** (unsuitably) [*behave*] de manière malséante; **to be ~ dressed** ne pas être habillé comme il convient; **3** (indecently) [*suggest, behave*] indécemment; **4** (incorrectly) [*use*] improprement, abusivement.

impropriety /ˌɪmprəˈpraɪətɪ/ *n* **1** (irregularity) irrégularité *f*; **to accuse sb of financial ~** accuser qn d'avoir commis des irrégularités financières; **2** (unseemliness) inconvenance *f*; **to commit an ~** commettre une inconvenance; **3** (indecency) indécence *f*.

improve /ɪmˈpruːv/ **I** *vtr* **1** (qualitatively) améliorer [*conditions, hygiene, efficiency, appearance, diet, quality, relations*]; **to ~ one's German** se perfectionner en allemand; **~ your memory** améliorez votre mémoire; **the new arrangements did not ~ matters** les nouveaux accords n'ont pas arrangé les choses; **to ~ one's mind** se cultiver (l'esprit); **to ~ one's lot** améliorer son sort; **to ~ the lot of the disabled/of pensioners** améliorer les conditions de vie des handicapés/des retraités; **2** (quantitatively) (increase) augmenter [*wages*]; accroître [*productivity, output, profits*]; **to ~ one's chances of winning/of getting of a job** augmenter ses chances de gagner/d'obtenir un travail; **3** Archit, Constr aménager [*building, site*]; **4** Agric amender [*soil*]; accroître [*yield*].
II improved *pp adj* **1** (better) [*diet, efficiency, conditions*] amélioré; **~d access** accès facilité; **new ~d formula** Comm nouvelle formule améliorée; **2** (increased) [*offer*] meilleur.
III *vi* **1** [*relations, health, handwriting, weather*] s'améliorer; **to ~ with age** [*cake, wine*] s'améliorer avec le temps; **the cake/wine will ~ in flavour** le gâteau/le vin s'améliorera; **living conditions have ~d greatly over the past twenty years** les conditions de vie se sont beaucoup améliorées ces vingt dernières années; **your Spanish is improving** ton espagnol s'améliore; **things are improving** la situation s'améliore; **he's improving** Med son état s'améliore, il va mieux; **2 to ~ on** (better) améliorer [*score*]; renchérir sur [*offer*]; **she has ~d on last year's result** elle a obtenu de meilleurs résultats que l'année dernière; **3** (increase) [*productivity, profits*] augmenter; **4** Agric [*yield*] augmenter.

improvement /ɪmˈpruːvmənt/ *n* **1** (change for the better) amélioration *f* (**in, of, to** de); **an ~ on last year's performance** une amélioration par rapport aux résultats de l'an dernier; **an ~ on his previous offer** Fin une offre plus intéressante que son offre précédente; **the new edition is an ~ on the old one** la nouvelle édition est bien meilleure que l'ancienne; **there have been a lot of safety ~s** ou **~s in safety** il y a eu beaucoup d'amélioration en matière de sécurité; **a 2% ~** ou **an ~ of 2% on last year's profits** une amélioration de 2% par rapport aux bénéfices de l'an dernier; **2** (progress) progrès *mpl*; **he has made a big ~** (in schoolwork, behaviour) il a fait de gros progrès; Med son état s'est beaucoup amélioré; **she has made some ~ in maths** elle a fait des progrès en maths; **he has come on a lot but there is still room for ~** il a fait des progrès mais il peut encore faire mieux; **there is room for ~ in the industry** on pourrait encore faire mieux dans l'industrie; **3** (alteration) aménagement *m*; **an ~ to the road network** un aménagement du réseau routier; **to make ~s to** apporter des aménagements à [*house*]; **home ~s** aménagements *mpl* du domicile; **a road ~ scheme** un projet d'aménagement des routes.

improvement grant *n* GB subvention *f* pour l'amélioration d'un logement.

improver /ɪm'pruːvə(r)/ *n* GB **1** (student) perfectionnant/-e *m/f*; **2** Ind (in flour) additif *m*.

improvidence /ɪm'prɒvɪdəns/ *n* imprévoyance *f*, manque *m* de prévoyance.

improvident /ɪm'prɒvɪdənt/ *adj* **1** (heedless of the future) imprévoyant; **2** (extravagant) prodigue, dépensier/-ière.

improving /ɪm'pruːvɪŋ/ *adj* **1** (enhanced) [*position, performance, situation*] qui s'améliore; [*trade deficit*] qui diminue; [*inflation rate*] qui baisse; **2†** (edifying) [*literature*] édifiant.

improvisation /ˌɪmprəvaɪ'zeɪʃn, US *also* ɪmˌprɒvə'zeɪʃn/ *n* (all contexts) improvisation *f*.

improvise /'ɪmprəvaɪz/ **I** *vtr* improviser; **an ~d table/screen** une table/un écran de fortune.
II *vi* (all contexts) improviser.

imprudence /ɪm'pruːdns/ *n* imprudence *f*.

imprudent /ɪm'pruːdnt/ *adj* imprudent.

imprudently /ɪm'pruːdntlɪ/ *adv* [*act*] imprudemment; **she ~ suggested that...** elle a commis l'imprudence de suggérer que...

impudence /'ɪmpjʊdəns/ *n* effronterie *f*, impudence *f*.

impudent /'ɪmpjʊdənt/ *adj* insolent, impudent.

impudently /'ɪmpjʊdəntlɪ/ *adv* [*say, answer*] avec insolence, impudemment.

impugn /ɪm'pjuːn/ *vtr* contester [*sincerity, judgment*]; attaquer [*reputation*].

impulse /'ɪmpʌls/ *n* **1** (urge) impulsion *f*; **to have a sudden ~ to do** avoir une envie soudaine de faire; **her immediate ~ was to say no** sur le coup elle a eu envie de refuser; **to act on (an) ~** (rashly) agir sur un coup de tête; (spontaneously) obéir or céder à une impulsion; **on a sudden ~ she turned back** cédant à une impulsion elle a fait demi-tour; **the ~ to communicate** l'envie de communiquer; **a generous ~** un élan de générosité; **a person of ~** un/-e impulsif/-ive *m/f*; **2** (stimulus) impulsion *f*; **to give an ~ to economic recovery** donner une impulsion au redressement économique; **3** Physiol influx *m* nerveux; **4** Elec, Phys impulsion *f*.

impulse: **~ buy**, **~ purchase** *n* achat *m* d'impulsion; **~ buying** *n* ¢ achat *m* d'impulsion.

impulsion /ɪm'pʌlʃn/ *n* sout envie *f* irrésistible (**to do** de faire).

impulsive /ɪm'pʌlsɪv/ *adj* **1** (spontaneous) [*gesture, reaction*] spontané; **2** (rash) [*person, gesture*] impulsif/-ive; [*remark, reaction*] irréfléchi; **3** Phys bref/brève.

impulsively /ɪm'pʌlsɪvlɪ/ *adv* **1** (on impulse) [*speak, behave, act*] impulsivement; **2** (rashly) [*decide, act*] sur un coup de tête.

impulsiveness /ɪm'pʌlsɪvnɪs/ *n* impulsivité *f*.

impunity /ɪm'pjuːnətɪ/ *n* impunité *f*; **with ~** en toute impunité.

impure /ɪm'pjʊə(r)/ *adj* **1** (polluted) [*water, thoughts*] impur; [*drug*] frelaté; **2** Archit, Art [*style*] bâtard.

impurity /ɪm'pjʊərətɪ/ *n* lit, fig impureté *f*; **tested for impurities** pureté testée.

imputation /ˌɪmpjuː'teɪʃn/ *n* **1** (attribution) attribution *f*, imputation *f* (**of** de; **to** à); **2** (accusation) imputation *f*.

impute /ɪm'pjuːt/ *vtr* imputer, attribuer (**to** à).

in /ɪn/

■ **Note** *in* is often used after verbs in English (*join in, tuck in, result in, write in etc*). For translations, consult the appropriate verb entry (***join***, ***tuck***, ***result***, ***write*** etc).
– If you have doubts about how to translate a phrase or expression beginning with *in* (*in a huff, in business, in trouble etc*) you should consult the appropriate noun entry (***huff***, ***business***, ***trouble*** etc).
– This dictionary contains Usage Notes on such topics as age, countries, dates, islands, months, towns and cities etc. Many of these use the preposition *in*. For the index to these Notes ▶ **1919**.
– For examples of the above and particular functions and uses of *in*, see the entry below.

I *prep* **1** (expressing location or position) **~ Paris** à Paris; **~ Spain** en Espagne; **~ hospital/school** à l'hôpital/l'école; **~ prison/class/town** en prison/classe/ville; **~ the film/dictionary/newspaper** dans le film/dictionnaire/journal; **~ the garden** dans le jardin, au jardin; **I'm ~ here!** je suis là!; ▶ **bath**, **bed**; **2** (inside, within) dans; **~ the box** dans la boîte; **there's something ~ it** il y a quelque chose dedans or à l'intérieur; **3** (expressing a subject or field) dans; **~ insurance/marketing** dans les assurances/le marketing; ▶ **course**, **degree**, **expert**; **4** (included, involved) **to be ~ the army** être dans l'armée; **to be ~ politics** faire de la politique; **to be ~ the team/group/collection** faire partie de l'équipe/du groupe/de la collection; **to be ~ on**○ être dans [*secret*]; **to be ~ on the plan**○ être dans le coup○; **I wasn't ~ on it**○ je n'étais pas dans le coup○; **to be ~ at the finish** être là à la fin; **5** (in expressions of time) **~ May** en mai; **~ 1987** en 1987; **~ the night** pendant la nuit; **~ the twenties** dans les années 20; **at four ~ the morning** à quatre heures du matin; **at two ~ the afternoon** à deux heures de l'après-midi; **day ~ day out** tous les jours (sans exception); **6** (within the space of) en; **to do sth ~ 10 minutes** faire qch en 10 minutes; **~ a matter of seconds** en quelques secondes; **7** (expressing the future) dans; **I'll be back ~ half an hour** je serai de retour dans une demi-heure; **8** (for) depuis; **it hasn't rained ~ weeks** il n'a pas plu depuis des semaines, ça fait des semaines qu'il n'a pas plu; **9** (during, because of) dans; **~ the confusion, he escaped** dans la confusion, il s'est échappé; **~ his hurry he forgot his keys** dans sa précipitation il a oublié ses clés; **10** (with reflexive pronouns) **it's no bad thing ~ itself** ce n'est pas une mauvaise chose en soi; **how do you feel ~ yourself?** est-ce que tu as le moral?; ▶ **itself**; **11** (present in, inherent in) **you see it ~ children** on le rencontre chez les enfants; **it's rare ~ cats** c'est rare chez les chats; **we lost a talented surgeon ~ Jim** nous avons perdu un chirurgien brillant en la personne de Jim; **he hasn't got it ~ him to succeed** il n'est pas fait pour réussir; **there's something ~ what he says** il y a du vrai dans ce qu'il dit; **12** (expressing colour, composition) en; **it comes ~ green** il existe en vert; **available ~ several colours** disponible en plusieurs couleurs; **bags ~ leather and canvas** des sacs en cuir et en toile; **13** (dressed in) en; **~ jeans/a skirt** en jean/jupe; **~ sandals** en sandales; **dressed ~ black** habillé en noir; **14** (expressing manner or medium) **~ German** en allemand; **~ one dollar bills** en billets d'un dollar; **~ B flat** en si bémol; **'no,' he said ~ a whisper** 'non,' a-t-il chuchoté; **chicken ~ a white wine sauce** du poulet à la sauce au vin blanc; **peaches ~ brandy** des pêches à l'eau de vie; **~ pencil/~ ink** au crayon/à l'encre; **15** (as regards) **rich/poor ~ minerals** riche/pauvre en minéraux; **deaf ~ one ear** sourd d'une oreille; **10 cm ~ length** 10 cm de long; **equal ~ weight** du même poids; **16** (by) **~ accepting** en acceptant; **~ doing so** en faisant cela; **17** (in superlatives) de; **the tallest tower ~ the world** la plus grande tour du monde; **18** (in measurements) **there are 100 centimetres ~ a metre** il y a 100 centimètres dans un mètre; **what's that ~ centimetres?** combien ça fait en centimètres?; **have you got it ~ a 16?** est-ce que vous l'avez en 42?; **~ a smaller size** dans une plus petite taille; **there's only 1 cm ~ it** il n'y a qu'un cm de différence; **there's nothing ~ it** ils se valent; **the temperature was ~ the thirties** il faisait dans les trente degrés; **19** (in ratios) **a gradient of 1 ~ 4** une pente de 25%; **a tax of 20 pence ~ the pound** une taxe de 20 pence par livre sterling; **to have a one ~ five chance** avoir une chance sur cinq; **20** (in approximate amounts) **~ their hundreds** ou **thousands** par centaines; **to cut/break sth ~ three** couper/casser qch en trois; **21** (expressing arrangement) **~ a circle** en cercle; **~ rows of 12** par rangées de douze; **~ pairs** deux par deux; **~ bundles** en liasses; **22** (expressing age) **she's ~ her twenties** elle a une vingtaine d'années; **people ~ their forties** les gens qui ont la quarantaine; **~ old age** avec l'âge, en vieillissant.
II in and out *prep phr* **to come ~ and out** entrer et sortir; **he's always ~ and out of the house** ou **room** il n'arrête pas d'entrer et de sortir; **to weave ~ and out of** se faufiler entre [*traffic, tables*]; **to be ~ and out of prison all one's life** passer la plus grande partie de sa vie en prison; **to be ~ and out of hospital a lot** passer beaucoup de temps à l'hôpital.
III in that *conj phr* dans la mesure où.
IV *adv* **1** (indoors) **to come ~** entrer; **to run ~** entrer en courant; **to ask** ou **invite sb ~** faire entrer qn; **~ with you!** allez, rentrez!; **2** (at home, at work) **to be ~** être là; **you're never ~** tu n'es jamais là; **I'm usually ~ by 9 am** j'arrive généralement à 9 heures; **to come ~ two days a week** venir au bureau deux jours par semaine; **to be ~ by midnight** être rentré avant minuit; **to spend the evening ~, to have an evening ~** passer la soirée à la maison; ▶ **keep**, **stay**; **3** (in prison, in hospital) **he's ~ for murder** il a été emprisonné pour meurtre; **she's ~ for a biopsy** elle est entrée à l'hôpital pour une biopsie; **4** (arrived) **the train is ~** le train est en gare; **the ferry is ~** le ferry est à quai; **the sea** ou **tide is ~** c'est marée haute; ▶ **come**, **get**; **5** Sport (within the boundary) **the ball** ou **shot is ~** la balle est bonne; (batting) **England is ~** l'équipe anglaise est à la batte; **6** (gathered) **the harvest is ~** la moisson est rentrée; **7** (in supply) **we don't have any ~** nous n'en avons pas en stock; **I should get some ~ tomorrow** je devrais en recevoir demain; **we've got some new titles ~** on a reçu quelques nouveaux titres; **to get some beer/a video ~** aller chercher de la bière/une vidéocassette; **8** (submitted) **applications must be ~ by the 23rd** les candidatures doivent être déposées avant le 23; **the homework has to be ~ tomorrow** le

devoir doit être rendu demain; ▶ **get, power, vote**.

V○ *adj* (fashionable) **to be the ~, to be the ~ thing** être à la mode; **it's the ~ place to eat** c'est le restaurant à la mode.

IDIOMS **to know the ~s and outs of an affair** connaître une affaire dans les moindres détails; **to have an ~ with sb** US avoir ses entrées chez qn; **to have it ~ for sb**○ avoir qn dans le collimateur○; **you're ~ for it**○ tu vas avoir des ennuis; **he's ~ for a shock/surprise** il va avoir un choc/être surpris.

in. *abrév écrite* = **inch**.

IN US Post *abrév écrite* = **Indiana**.

inability /ˌɪnəˈbɪlətɪ/ *n* (to drive, pay, concentrate) incapacité *f* (**to do** de faire); (to help) impuissance *f* (**to do** à faire).

in absentia /ˌɪn æbˈsentɪə/ *adv* en son/leur etc absence.

inaccessibility /ˌɪnæksesəˈbɪlətɪ/ *n* inaccessibilité *f*.

inaccessible /ˌɪnækˈsesəbl/ *adj* **1** (out of reach) [*place, person*] inaccessible; **2** (hard to grasp) [*play, art form*] peu accessible (**to** à).

inaccuracy /ɪnˈækjərəsɪ/ *n* **1** ¢ (of report, account, estimate, term) inexactitude *f*; (of person) manque *m* d'exactitude or de précision; **2** (in account, estimate) inexactitude *f*; **the report is full of inaccuracies** le rapport contient de nombreuses inexactitudes.

inaccurate /ɪnˈækjʊrət/ *adj* [*data, calculation, information, translation*] inexact; [*account, statement*] contenant des inexactitudes; [*instrument*] pas juste; [*word, term*] impropre; **her description was ~** sa description contenait des inexactitudes; **it would be ~ to say so** cela serait inexact; **he tends to be ~** il a tendance à faire des erreurs.

inaccurately /ɪnˈækjʊərətlɪ/ *adv* [*report, quote, state*] inexactement; **a condition known ~ as** une maladie connue sous le nom inexact de; **~ described as** qualifié à tort de.

inaction /ɪnˈækʃn/ *n* (failure to act) inaction *f*; (not being active) inactivité *f*.

inactive /ɪnˈæktɪv/ *adj* **1** (not active) [*person, life, mind*] inactif/-ive; **2** (not working) [*machine*] inactif/-ive, qui n'est pas en service; **3** (dormant) [*volcano*] inactif/-ive, éteint.

inactivity /ˌɪnækˈtɪvətɪ/ *n* inactivité *f*, manque *m* d'activité.

inadequacy /ɪnˈædɪkwəsɪ/ *n* **1** (insufficiency) insuffisance *f*; **2** (defect) défaut *m*; **to have** ou **suffer from feelings of ~** être complexé, avoir le sentiment de ne pas être à la hauteur.

inadequate /ɪnˈædɪkwət/ *adj* [*funding, heating, resources, measures, preparation, knowledge*] insuffisant (**for** pour; **to do** pour faire); [*budget, control*] déficient, insuffisant; [*system, means, legislation, response, planning, facilities, services*] inadéquat; [*word, expression*] faible; **the law is hopelessly ~ on this subject** cette situation est très mal couverte par la loi; **to feel ~** [*person*] être complexé, avoir le sentiment de ne pas être à la hauteur.

inadequately /ɪnˈædɪkwətlɪ/ *adv* [*heated, lit, paid, prepared*] insuffisamment; **it is ~ staffed** il n'y a pas assez de personnel; **they are ~ trained** leur formation est insuffisante.

inadmissible /ˌɪnədˈmɪsəbl/ *adj* **1** Jur [*evidence*] irrecevable; **2** (unacceptable) [*behaviour, act*] inadmissible; [*proposal*] inacceptable.

inadvertence /ˌɪnədˈvɜːtəns/ *n* manque *m* d'attention, étourderie *f*.

inadvertent /ˌɪnədˈvɜːtənt/ *adj* **1** (accidental) [*omission, error, action*] involontaire; **2** (inattentive) inattentif/-ive.

inadvertently /ˌɪnədˈvɜːtəntlɪ/ *adv* **1** (unintentionally) involontairement; **2** (unthinkingly) par mégarde.

inadvisable /ˌɪnədˈvaɪzəbl/ *adj* [*plan, action*] inopportun, à déconseiller; **it is ~ for sb to do** il est déconseillé à qn de faire.

inalienable /ɪnˈeɪlɪənəbl/ *adj* Jur inaliénable.

inamorata /ˌɪnæməˈrɑːtə/ *n* littér ou hum amoureuse *f*.

inane /ɪˈneɪn/ *adj* [*person, conversation*] idiot; [*programme, question*] débile○.

inanely /ɪˈneɪnlɪ/ *adv* [*grin, laugh*] de façon idiote.

inanimate /ɪnˈænɪmət/ *adj* inanimé.

inanition /ˌɪnəˈnɪʃn/ *n* sout inanition *f*.

inanity /ɪˈnænətɪ/ *n* ineptie *f*.

inapplicable /ɪnˈæplɪkəbl, ˌɪnəˈplɪk-/ *adj* inapplicable (**to** à).

inappropriate /ˌɪnəˈprəʊprɪət/ *adj* **1** (improper, unsuitable) [*behaviour, action, reaction*] inconvenant, peu convenable; [*remark, reference*] inopportun; **shorts are ~ for work** le short n'est pas une tenue convenable pour aller travailler; **this is quite ~ for children** ce n'est vraiment pas pour les enfants; **2** (not what is needed, incorrect) [*advice, treatment, site, building, name, word*] qui n'est pas approprié; **he was an ~ choice for leader** il a été mal choisi pour tenir le poste de dirigeant.

inappropriately /ˌɪnəˈprəʊprɪətlɪ/ *adv* [*behave, laugh*] inopportunément, mal à propos; **to be ~ dressed** (unsuitably) être habillé de façon inconvenante; (impractically) ne pas être habillé de manière adéquate.

inappropriateness /ˌɪnəˈprəʊprɪətnɪs/ *n* (of remark) inopportunité *f*, manque *m* d'à-propos; (of behaviour, dress) inconvenance *f*; (of choice, site) inadéquation *f*.

inapt /ɪnˈæpt/ *adj* (inappropriate) [*expression, term*] impropre, inconvenant; [*behaviour, remark*] déplacé, inconvenant.

inarticulate /ˌɪnɑːˈtɪkjʊlət/ *adj* **1** (unable to express oneself) **to be ~** ne pas savoir s'exprimer; **she was ~ with rage** elle était tellement en colère qu'elle n'arrivait plus à s'exprimer; **2** (indistinct) [*mumble, cry, grunt*] inarticulé; [*speech*] inintelligible; **3** (defying expression) [*rage, despair, grief, longing*] inexprimable; **4** Zool inarticulé.

inartistic /ˌɪnɑːˈtɪstɪk/ *adj* [*person*] peu artiste; [*work*] sans valeur artistique.

inasmuch /ˌɪnəzˈmʌtʃ/: **inasmuch as** /ˌɪnəzˈmʌtʃəz/ *conj phr* (insofar as) dans la mesure où; (seeing as, since) vu que.

inattention /ˌɪnəˈtenʃn/ *n* inattention *f*, manque *m* d'attention.

inattentive /ˌɪnəˈtentɪv/ *adj* [*pupil*] inattentif/-ive; [*audience, lover*] peu attentif/-ive; **to be ~ to** être peu attentif/-ive à [*person, needs*]; ne pas être attentif/-ive à [*speech*].

inattentively /ˌɪnəˈtentɪvlɪ/ *adv* [*listen*] distraitement, sans prêter attention.

inaudible /ɪnˈɔːdəbl/ *adj* [*sound*] inaudible; **he was almost ~** on l'entendait à peine; **her reply was mostly ~** la plus grande partie de sa réponse était inaudible.

inaudibly /ˌɪnˈɔːdəblɪ/ *adv* [*reply, mumble*] de façon inaudible.

inaugural /ɪˈnɔːgjʊrəl/ *adj* **1** (first in series) [*meeting, session*] inaugural; **~ lecture** GB cours *m* d'ouverture; **2** (of an inauguration) [*ceremony, address*] d'inauguration, inaugural.

inaugurate /ɪˈnɔːgjʊreɪt/ *vtr* **1** (begin, open) inaugurer [*exhibition, era, tradition*]; **2** (induct) investir [qn] de ses fonctions [*president, official*]; introniser [*bishop*].

inauguration /ɪˌnɔːgjʊˈreɪʃn/ *n* **1** (into office) (of president) investiture *f*; (of bishop) intronisation *f*; **2** (beginning) (of exhibition, era, tradition) inauguration *f*.

Inauguration Day *n* US Pol jour *m* de l'investiture présidentielle.

inauspicious /ˌɪnɔːˈspɪʃəs/ *adj* **1** (unpromising) [*beginning, circumstances*] peu propice, de mauvais augure; **2** (unfortunate) [*meeting, occasion*] malencontreux/-euse.

inauspiciously /ˌɪnɔːˈspɪʃəslɪ/ *adv* [*begin, start*] mal.

in-between *adj* intermédiaire.

inboard /ˈɪnbɔːd/ *adj* Naut in-bord, intérieur; Aviat intérieur.

inborn /ˈɪnbɔːn/ *adj* **1** (innate) [*talent, tendency*] inné, naturel/-elle; **2** (inherited) [*deficiency*] congénital.

inbred /ˌɪnˈbred/ *adj* **1** (innate) [*tendency, confidence*] naturel/-elle, inné; **2** (produced by inbreeding) [*animal*] résultant de croisements entre animaux de même souche; [*family, tribe*] qui est caractérisé par un haut degré de consanguinité; [*characteristic*] résultant de croisement consanguin.

inbreeding /ɪnˈbriːdɪŋ/ *n* (in animals) croisement *m* d'animaux de même souche; (in humans) croisement *m* consanguin, consanguinité *f*.

inbuilt /ˌɪnˈbɪlt/ *adj* **1** (ingrained) [*trait, belief*] profondément ancré; **2** (built in) [*bias, limitation*] intrinsèque.

Inc US (*abrév* = **incorporated**) SA; **Macron ~** Macron SA.

incalculable /ɪnˈkælkjʊləbl/ *adj* **1** [*harm, loss, effect*] incalculable; **2** (unpredictable) [*person, mood*] changeant.

incandescence /ˌɪnkænˈdesns/ *n* incandescence *f*.

incandescent /ˌɪnkænˈdesnt/ *adj* **1** (with heat) incandescent; **2** fig (radiant) rayonnant.

incandescent lamp *n* lampe *f* à incandescence.

incantation /ˌɪnkænˈteɪʃn/ *n* incantation *f*.

incapability /ɪnˌkeɪpəˈbɪlɪtɪ/ *n* gen, Jur incapacité *f* (**to do** de faire).

incapable /ɪnˈkeɪpəbl/ *adj* [*person, organization*] incapable (**of doing** de faire); **he's ~ of action/of any emotion** il est incapable d'agir/d'éprouver une émotion; **to be ~ of killing/of dishonesty** être incapable de tuer/d'être malhonnête; **actions ~ of justification** sout des actions impossibles à justifier; **drunk and ~** Jur en état d'ivresse publique.

incapacitate /ˌɪnkəˈpæsɪteɪt/ *vtr* **1** (immobilize) [*accident, disability, illness*] immobiliser; **severely ~d** infirme, invalide; **2** (temporarily) [*pain, headache*] rendre [qn] incapable de faire quoi que ce soit; **3** (disarm) mettre [qn] hors d'état de nuire.

incapacity /ˌɪnkəˈpæsətɪ/ *n* **1** gen incapacité *f* (**to do** de faire), impuissance *f* (**to do** à faire); **2** Jur incapacité *f* (**to do** de faire).

in-car /ɪnˈkɑː(r)/ *adj* **~ stereo** ou **entertainment system** autoradio *m*.

incarcerate /ɪnˈkɑːsəreɪt/ *vtr* incarcérer.

incarceration /ɪnˌkɑːsəˈreɪʃn/ *n* incarcération *f*.

incarnate I /ɪnˈkɑːnet/ *adj* incarné; **the devil ~** le diable incarné.

II /ˈɪnkɑːneɪt/ *vtr* incarner; **to be ~d in** ou **as** s'incarner en.

incarnation /ˌɪnkɑːˈneɪʃn/ *n* Relig, fig incarnation *f*.

incautious /ɪnˈkɔːʃəs/ *adj* imprudent, irréfléchi.

incautiously /ɪnˈkɔːʃəslɪ/ *adv* imprudemment.

incendiary /ɪnˈsendɪərɪ, US -dɪerɪ/ I *n* **1** (bomb) engin *m* incendiaire; **2** (arsonist) incendiaire *mf*; **3** (agitator) agitateur/-trice *m/f*.

II *adj* lit, fig incendiaire.

incendiary: **~ attack** *n* attaque *f* à la bombe incendiaire; **~ device** *n* engin *m* incendiaire.

incense I /ˈɪnsens/ *n* encens *m*.

II /ɪnˈsens/ *vtr* (enrage) faire enrager, mettre [qn] en fureur.

incense: **~ bearer** *n* thuriféraire *m*; **~ burner** *n* encensoir *m*.

incensed /ɪnˈsenst/ *adj* outré (**at** de; **by** par), révolté (**at, by** par).

incentive /ɪnˈsentɪv/ *n* **1** (motivation) **to give**

sb the ~ to do donner envie à qn de faire; **there is no ~ for people to save** rien n'incite les gens à faire des économies; **they've no ~ to work** ils ne sont pas motivés dans leur travail; **there are strong ~s to join a union** on a tout intérêt à adhérer à un syndicat; **2** Fin, Comm prime *f*; **export ~** prime à l'exportation.

incentive: **~ bonus**, **~ payment** *n* prime *f* d'encouragement; **~ scheme** *n* système *m* de primes d'encouragement.

inception /ɪn'sepʃn/ *n* commencement *m*, début *m*; **from** ou **since its ~ in 1962** depuis ses débuts en 1962.

incessant /ɪn'sesnt/ *adj* incessant.

incessantly /ɪn'sesntlɪ/ *adv* sans cesse.

incest /'ɪnsest/ *n* inceste *m*; **to commit ~** commettre un inceste.

incestuous /ɪn'sestjʊəs, US -tʃʊəs/ *adj* lit incestueux/-euse; **it's a very ~ world** fig c'est une mafia.

inch /ɪntʃ/ ▶**1412** **I** *n* (*pl* **~es**) **1** Meas pouce *m* (= *2,54 cm*); **2** fig (small amount) **~ by ~** petit à petit; **I couldn't see an ~ in front of me in the fog** je ne voyais rien à deux pas dans le brouillard; **to miss being run over by ~es** être à deux doigts de se faire écraser; **to come within an ~ of winning/succeeding** passer à deux doigts de la victoire/du succès; **to be within an ~ of death/victory** être à deux doigts de la mort/victoire; **she won't give** ou **budge an ~** elle ne veut pas bouger d'un pouce.

II *vtr* **to ~ sth forward** faire avancer [qch] petit à petit [*car*]; **to ~ the car into the garage** rentrer la voiture au garage avec précaution; **to ~ one's way across sth** traverser [qch] petit à petit.

III *vi* **to ~ across sth** traverser [qch] petit à petit [*floor*]; **to ~ along sth** franchir [qch] petit à petit [*ledge, plank*]; **to ~ towards sth** lit se diriger petit à petit vers [*door*]; fig parvenir petit à petit à [*solution, completion*].

IDIOMS **give her an ~ and she'll take a mile** ou **yard** plus on lui en donne, plus elle en veut; **I don't trust him an ~** je n'ai pas la moindre confiance en lui; **to fight every ~ of the way** lutter pied à pied; **to know every ~ of sth** connaître qch comme sa poche; **to search every ~ of the car/carpet** passer la voiture/le tapis au peigne fin; **to be every ~ an aristocrat/soldier** être aristocrate/soldat jusqu'à la moelle.

■ **inch up** [*inflation, interest rate, price*] monter graduellement.

inchoate /ɪn'kəʊeɪt, 'ɪn-/ *adj* [*idea, plan*] à peine ébauché; [*desire, longing*] vague.

inchoative /ɪn'kəʊətɪv/ *adj* Ling inchoatif/-ive.

inch worm *n* Zool géomètre *m*, arpenteuse *f*.

incidence /'ɪnsɪdəns/ *n* **1** (occurrence) **the ~ of** la fréquence de [*thefts, attacks, deaths*]; **a high ~ of sth** un taux élevé de qch; **the low ~ of sth** le faible taux de qch; **2** Phys (of ray) incidence *f*; **angle of ~** angle *m* d'incidence.

incident /'ɪnsɪdənt/ **I** *n* **1** (event) (in life) incident *m*; (in narrative) épisode *m*; **2** (disturbance) incident *m*; **border/diplomatic ~** incident frontalier/diplomatique; **stabbing ~** agression *f* à coups de couteau; **without ~** sans incident.

II *adj* **1** sout (related) **~ to** propre à [*membership, ownership, role*]; **2** Phys [*ray*] incident.

incidental /ˌɪnsɪ'dentl/ **I** *n* détail *m*.

II incidentals *npl* Comm faux-frais *mpl*.

III *adj* **1** (minor) [*detail, by-product, fact, remark*] secondaire; [*flaw, error*] mineur; **2** (occurring as minor consequence) **to be ~ to** accompagner [*activity, job, undertaking*]; **3** (accidental) usage critiqué fortuit.

incidental: **~ damages** *npl* Jur dommages-intérêts *mpl* indirects; **~ expenses** *npl* faux-frais *mpl*.

incidentally /ˌɪnsɪ'dentlɪ/ *adv* **1** (by the way) à propos; **~, did you see...?** à propos, as-tu vu...?; **...who, ~, owes me £10** ...qui, soit dit en passant, me doit dix livres; **2** (as a by-product) par la même occasion.

incidental music *n* Cin musique *f* de film; Theat musique *f* de scène.

incident: **~ room** *n* GB bureau *m* des enquêteurs; **~ tape** *n* Transp ruban *m* de signalisation.

incinerate /ɪn'sɪnəreɪt/ *vtr* incinérer.

incineration /ɪnˌsɪnə'reɪʃn/ *n* incinération *f*.

incinerator /ɪn'sɪnəreɪtə(r)/ *n* (industrial, domestic) incinérateur *m*; (in crematorium) four *m* crématoire.

incipient /ɪn'sɪpɪənt/ *adj* [*disease, crisis*] à ses débuts; [*baldness*] naissant; **a sign of ~ madness** le signe du début de la folie.

incise /ɪn'saɪz/ *vtr* **1** (cut) inciser; **2** (engrave) graver.

incised /ɪn'saɪzd/ *adj* **1** [*surface, design*] gravé; **2** Bot [*leaf*] incisé.

incision /ɪn'sɪʒn/ *n* **1** Med incision *f*; **2** Bot incisure *f*.

incisive /ɪn'saɪsɪv/ *adj* (keen, decisive) [*remark*] perspicace; [*criticism, mind*] pénétrant; [*manner, presentation*] précis; [*style*] incisif/-ive.

incisively /ɪn'saɪsɪvlɪ/ *adv* [*argue, present*] d'une manière précise.

incisiveness /ɪn'saɪsɪvnɪs/ *n* (of remark) perspicacité *f*; (of criticism, mind) caractère *m* pénétrant.

incisor /ɪn'saɪzə(r)/ *n* incisive *f*.

incite /ɪn'saɪt/ *vtr* **to ~ violence/a riot** inciter à la violence/à l'émeute; **to ~ sb to do** pousser ou inciter qn à faire.

incitement /ɪn'saɪtmənt/ *n* incitation *f* (**to** à).

incivility /ˌɪnsɪ'vɪlətɪ/ *n* incivilité *f*.

incl **1** (*abrév écrite* = **including**) compris; **£20,000 ~ bonuses** 20 000 livres, primes comprises; **2** (*abrév* = **inclusive**) TTC; **£110 ~** 110 livres sterling TTC.

inclemency /ɪn'klemənsɪ/ *n* (of weather, winter) inclémence *f*; (of climate) rigueur *f*.

inclement /ɪn'klemənt/ *adj* **1** [*weather, winter*] inclément; [*climate*] rigoureux/-euse; **2** [*judge*] inclément, dur.

inclination /ˌɪŋklɪ'neɪʃn/ *n* **1** (tendency) tendance *f*, inclination *f*; (**to, towards** à); **I have an ~ to forget** j'ai tendance à oublier; **to be lazy by ~** être paresseux par nature; **to follow one's own ~s** suivre ses penchants naturels; **2** (desire) envie *f*, désir *m* (**for** de); (liking) goût *m* (**for** pour); **to have an ~ to do/to be** avoir envie de faire/d'être; **to have no ~ to do** n'avoir aucune envie de faire; **to have no ~ for sth** n'avoir aucun goût pour qch; **3** (degree of slope) inclinaison *f*.

incline I /'ɪŋklaɪn/ *n* (slope) pente *f*.

II /ɪn'klaɪn/ *vtr* **1** (bend) incliner [*head*]; **2 to be ~d to do** (have tendency) avoir tendance à faire; (have desire) avoir envie de faire; **if you feel so ~d** si l'envie vous en prend; **he was not ~d to help/listen** il n'était pas disposé à aider/écouter; **to be artistically ~d** avoir un goût pour l'art; **I didn't know he was that way ~d** euph péj je ne savais pas qu'il en était○ euph pej, je ne savais pas qu'il était homosexuel; **3** sout (persuade) **to ~ sb to do** porter qn à faire; **4** (tilt) incliner [*mirror, seat*].

III /ɪn'klaɪn/ *vi* **1** (tend) **to ~ to** ou **towards** [*ideas, politics*] tendre vers [*extremism, socialism*]; **to ~ to** ou **towards greed/severity** [*person*] avoir tendance à être gourmand/sévère; **to ~ towards the opinion that** avoir tendance à penser que; **2** (lean) [*person, road, tower, tree*] s'incliner.

inclined plane *n* plan *m* incliné.

inclose *vtr* ▶ **enclose**.

inclosure *n* ▶ **enclosure**.

include /ɪn'klu:d/ *vtr* gen inclure; (followed by list of names, items etc) comprendre; **most people, children ~d** la plupart des gens, enfants inclus; **all the ministers, Blanc ~d** tous les ministres, Blanc inclu; **the guests ~d Karl Marx** parmi les invités il y avait Karl Marx; **breakfast is ~d in the price** le petit déjeuner est compris; **£50 to ~ taxes** 50 livres sterling y compris les taxes; **your duties ~ answering the phone** répondre au téléphone fait partie de vos fonctions; **does that ~ me?** est-ce que cela s'adresse aussi à moi?

including /ɪn'klu:dɪŋ/ *prep* (y) compris; **~ July** y compris juillet; **not ~ July** sans compter juillet; **£10, ~ coffee** 10 livres sterling, café compris; **up to and ~ Monday** jusqu'à lundi inclus; **~ service** service compris; **~ Mary/not ~ Mary we'll be six** avec Mary/sans Mary nous serons six.

inclusion /ɪn'klu:ʒn/ *n* gen, Math inclusion *f* (**of** de; **in** dans); **advertisements for ~ in next week's issue** petites annonces à paraître dans le numéro de la semaine prochaine.

inclusive /ɪn'klu:sɪv/ *adj* [*charge*] inclus; [*price*] forfaitaire; [*terms*] tout compris; **from the 15th to the 21st ~** du 15 au 21 inclus; **those aged 17–24 ~** les personnes âgées de 17 à 24 ans inclus; **prices are all-~** tout est compris dans le prix indiqué; **book an ~ holiday with us** GB réservez des vacances tout compris chez nous; **the price ~ of delivery** le prix, livraison comprise; **the price is not ~ of delivery** le prix ne comprend pas la livraison.

inclusively /ɪn'klu:sɪvlɪ/ *adv* inclusivement.

incognito /ˌɪnkɒg'ni:təʊ, US ɪŋ'kɒgnətəʊ/ **I** *n* incognito *m*.

II *adj* **to be ~** rester dans l'incognito; **to remain ~** garder l'incognito.

III *adv* [*travel, go*] incognito.

incoherence /ˌɪŋkəʊ'hɪərəns/ *n* incohérence *f*.

incoherent /ˌɪŋkəʊ'hɪərənt/ *adj* incohérent.

incoherently /ˌɪŋkəʊ'hɪərəntlɪ/ *adv* de façon incohérente.

incombustible /ˌɪŋkəm'bʌstəbl/ *adj* incombustible.

income /'ɪŋkʌm/ *n* revenu *m*, revenus *mpl*; **an ~ of £1,000 per month** un revenu de 1 000 livres sterling par mois; **to be on an ~ of £20,000 per year** gagner 20 000 livres par an; **to live within/beyond one's ~** vivre dans la limite de/au-delà de ses moyens; **low-~ households** ménages *mpl* à bas revenus; **loss of ~** perte *f* de revenus; **disposable/taxable ~** revenu disponible/imposable; **gross ~** revenu brut; **sources of ~** sources *fpl* de revenus; **earned ~** revenus professionnels; **unearned ~** ≈ rentes *fpl*.

income bracket, **income group** *n* tranche *f* de revenu; **low-/high-~** tranche des petits/des gros revenus.

incomer /'ɪnkʌmə(r)/ *n* GB (immigrant) immigrant/-e *m/f*.

income: **~s policy** *n* politique *f* des revenus; **~ support** *n* GB Soc Admin *allocation chômage minimum*; **~ tax** *n* impôt *m* sur le revenu; **~ tax form** *n* feuille *f* d'impôts; **~ tax inspector** *n* inspecteur/-trice *m/f* des impôts; **~ tax return** *n* déclaration *f* des revenus, feuille *f* d'impôts.

incoming /'ɪnkʌmɪŋ/ **I incomings** *npl* Accts rentrées *fpl*, recettes *fpl*.

II *adj* **1** (received) [*call, mail*] qui vient de l'extérieur; [*order, missile*] qui arrive; **this phone only takes ~ calls** ce téléphone ne peut que recevoir des appels; **2** (arriving) [*aircraft, passenger*] qui arrive; **~ flights have been diverted** les avions qui devaient atterrir ont été détournés; **3** (new) [*president, government*] nouveau/-elle; **4** [*tide*] montant.

incommensurable /ˌɪŋkə'menʃərəbl/ *adj* incommensurable (**with** avec).

incommensurate /ˌɪŋkəˈmenʃərət/ *adj* **1 to be ~ with** (out of proportion) être disproportionné à; (inadequate) être insuffisant pour; **2** = **incommensurable**.

incommode /ˌɪŋkəˈməʊd/ *vtr* sout incommoder, gêner.

incommunicable /ˌɪŋkəˈmjuːnɪkəbl/ *adj* incommunicable.

incommunicado /ˌɪŋkəˌmjuːnɪˈkɑːdəʊ/ **I** *adj* (by choice) injoignable; (involuntarily) sans contact avec l'extérieur.

II *adv* [*held, detained*] sans contact avec l'extérieur.

in-company *adj* [*training*] interne.

incomparable /ɪnˈkɒmprəbl/ *adj* [*beauty, splendour*] sans pareil/-eille; **the ~ Greta Garbo** Greta Garbo, qui n'a pas sa pareille.

incomparably /ɪnˈkɒmprəblɪ/ *adv* [*better*] infiniment; **~ the best** sans comparaison le/la meilleur/-e; **~ beautiful** d'une beauté sans pareille.

incompatibility /ˌɪŋkəmˌpætəˈbɪlətɪ/ *n* (all contexts) incompatibilité *f*.

incompatible /ˌɪŋkəmˈpætɪbl/ *adj* [*person, computer, drug*] incompatible (**with** avec); [*idea, activity*] inconciliable (**with** avec).

incompetence /ɪnˈkɒmpɪtəns/, **incompetency** /ɪnˈkɒmpɪtənsɪ/ *n* **1** (of professional) incompétence *f*; (of person, child) inaptitude *f*; **2** Jur (of person, court) incompétence *f*.

incompetent /ɪnˈkɒmpɪtənt/ **I** *n* incapable *mf*.

II *adj* **1** [*doctor, management, government*] incompétent; [*work, performance*] mauvais; **to be ~ to do** ne pas avoir les compétences nécessaires pour faire; **2** Jur (in law) [*person, child*] incompétent; [*witness*] récusé; [*evidence*] irrecevable.

incompetently /ɪnˈkɒmpɪtəntlɪ/ *adv* de façon incompétente.

incomplete /ˌɪŋkəmˈpliːt/ *adj* **1** (unfinished) [*work, building*] inachevé; **2** (lacking parts) [*set, collection, machine*] incomplet/-ète; **3** (imperfect) [*success, victory*] incomplet/-ète, partiel/-ielle.

incompletely /ˌɪŋkɒmˈpliːtlɪ/ *adv* incomplètement.

incompleteness /ˌɪŋkəmˈpliːtnɪs/ *n* (of work) état *m* inachevé; (of set) caractère *m* incomplet.

incomprehensible /ɪnˌkɒmprɪˈhensəbl/ *adj* [*reason, attitude*] incompréhensible; [*speech, style*] inintelligible.

incomprehensibly /ɪnˌkɒmprɪˈhensəblɪ/ *adv* [*act, react*] de façon incompréhensible; [*worded, written*] de façon inintelligible; **~, she didn't react** inexplicablement, elle n'a pas réagi.

incomprehension /ɪnˌkɒmprɪˈhenʃn/ *n* incompréhension *f*; **to look at sb in ~** regarder qn avec stupeur.

inconceivable /ˌɪŋkənˈsiːvəbl/ *adj* inconcevable; **it is ~ that** il est inconcevable que (+ *subj*).

inconceivably /ˌɪŋkənˈsiːvəblɪ/ *adv* [*tall, difficult*] incroyablement; **~ lazy** d'une paresse inconcevable.

inconclusive /ˌɪŋkənˈkluːsɪv/ *adj* [*discussion, meeting*] sans conclusion véritable; [*debate, election*] sans résultat clair; [*argument, evidence*] peu concluant.

inconclusively /ˌɪŋkənˈkluːsɪvlɪ/ *adv* [*end*] sans conclusion véritable; [*argue*] de manière peu concluante.

incongruity /ˌɪŋkɒŋˈgruːətɪ/ *n* **1** (of appearance, behaviour) incongruité *f*, bizarrerie *f*; (of situation) absurdité *f*; **2** (act, event) incongruité *f*.

incongruous /ɪnˈkɒŋgrʊəs/ *adj* [*sight, building*] déconcertant, inattendu; [*appearance, clothing*] surprenant; [*behaviour*] déplacé, inconvenant; **it seems ~ that** ça paraît bizarre que (+ *subj*).

incongruously /ɪnˈkɒŋgrʊəslɪ/ *adv* [*dress*] bizarrement; **~ modern** d'une modernité déconcertante.

inconsequential /ɪnˌkɒnsɪˈkwenʃl/ *adj* **1** (unimportant) sans importance; **2** (illogical) illogique, inconséquent.

inconsiderable /ˌɪŋkənˈsɪdrəbl/ *adj* insignifiant; **not ~** non négligeable.

inconsiderate /ˌɪŋkənˈsɪdərət/ *adj* [*person*] peu attentif/-ive à autrui; [*remark, behaviour*] maladroit; **to be ~ towards sb** manquer d'égards envers qn; **it was most ~ of her to leave like that** c'était très impoli de sa part de partir comme ça; **that was a very ~ thing to say** c'était manquer de tact que de dire cela.

inconsiderately /ˌɪŋkənˈsɪdərətlɪ/ *adv* sans aucune considération.

inconsistency /ˌɪŋkənˈsɪstənsɪ/ *n* (of argument, statement) incohérence *f*; **the ~ of his work** son travail inégal; **the ~ of her behaviour** sa conduite changeante.

inconsistent /ˌɪŋkənˈsɪstənt/ *adj* **1** (erratic) [*work, performance*] inégal; [*behaviour*] changeant; [*argument, beliefs*] incohérent; [*attitude*] inconsistant; **2** (incompatible) **to be ~ with** être en contradiction avec.

inconsolable /ˌɪŋkənˈsəʊləbl/ *adj* inconsolable.

inconsolably /ˌɪŋkənˈsəʊləblɪ/ *adv* inconsolablement.

inconspicuous /ˌɪŋkənˈspɪkjʊəs/ *adj* [*person*] qui passe inaperçu, qui ne se fait pas remarquer; [*place, clothing*] discret/-ète; **try to be ~** essaie d'être discret/-ète.

inconspicuously /ˌɪŋkənˈspɪkjʊəslɪ/ *adv* discrètement.

inconstancy /ɪnˈkɒnstənsɪ/ *n* **1** (unfaithfulness) inconstance *f*; **2** (discontinuity) irrégularité *f*.

inconstant /ɪnˈkɒnstənt/ *adj* [*friend, lover*] inconstant; [*conditions, feelings, temperature*] instable.

incontestable /ˌɪŋkənˈtestəbl/ *adj* incontestable.

incontinence /ɪnˈkɒntɪnəns/ *n* Med, fig incontinence *f*.

incontinence pad *n* Med couche *f* (pour incontinents).

incontinent /ɪnˈkɒntɪnənt/ *adj* Med, fig incontinent.

incontrovertible /ˌɪŋkɒntrəˈvɜːtəbl/ *adj* [*evidence, proof, sign*] indéniable; [*argument, statement*] irréfutable.

incontrovertibly /ˌɪŋkɒntrəˈvɜːtəblɪ/ *adv* incontestablement [*true, wrong*]; [*demonstrate, prove*] de façon incontestable.

inconvenience /ˌɪŋkənˈviːnɪəns/ **I** *n* **1** (trouble) dérangement *m*; **to put sb to great ~** causer beaucoup de dérangement à qn; **I don't want to cause you any ~** je ne veux pas vous causer le moindre dérangement; **'the management apologizes for any ~ caused to customers during renovations'** 'la direction s'excuse auprès de ses clients pour les désagréments occasionnés pendant la période de rénovation'; **2** (disadvantage) inconvénient *m*; **the ~s of having no car** l'inconvénient de ne pas avoir de voiture; **there are ~s in working part-time** le travail à temps partiel présente des inconvénients.

II *vtr* déranger.

inconvenient /ˌɪŋkənˈviːnɪənt/ *adj* **1** [*location, arrangement, device*] incommode; [*time*] inopportun; **if it's not ~** si cela ne vous/les/etc dérange pas; **it's rather an ~ time to call** ce n'est pas une heure pour une visite; **living so far from the station is very ~** ce n'est vraiment pas pratique d'habiter si loin de la gare; **2** euph (embarrassing) [*fact, incident*] gênant.

inconveniently /ˌɪŋkənˈviːnɪəntlɪ/ *adv* [*arranged, located*] de façon peu pratique.

inconvertibility /ˌɪŋkənˌvɜːtəˈbɪlətɪ/ *n* Fin inconvertibilité *f*, non-convertibilité *f*.

inconvertible /ˌɪŋkənˈvɜːtəbl/ *adj* Fin inconvertible, non convertible.

incorporate /ɪnˈkɔːpəreɪt/ **I** *vtr* **1** (make part of sth) **~ sth into sth** incorporer qch dans qch; **he has ~d our employees/your ideas into his new plan** il a incorporé nos employés/vos idées dans son nouveau projet; **2** (have as part of itself) comporter; **the society ~s many new features** la société comporte beaucoup de nouveaux éléments; **the new society ~s the two old ones** la nouvelle société regroupe les deux anciennes; **3** Comm, Jur constituer en société (commerciale).

II *vi* Comm, Jur se constituer en société commerciale.

III incorporated *pp adj* constitué en société commerciale; **Smith and Brown Incorporated** Smith et Brown SA.

incorporation /ɪnˌkɔːpəˈreɪʃn/ *n* **1** gen incorporation *f* (**into** dans); **to collect information for ~ into sth** rassembler des informations pour les incorporer à qch; **2** Jur constitution *f* (d'une société).

incorporator /ɪnˈkɔːpəreɪtə(r)/ *n* Fin, Jur membre *m* fondateur d'une société (commerciale).

incorporeal /ˌɪŋkɔːˈpɔːrɪəl/ *adj* gen, Jur incorporel/-elle; **~ chattels, ~ property** Jur biens *mpl* incorporels.

incorrect /ˌɪŋkəˈrekt/ *adj* **1** (false, inaccurate) incorrect (**to do** de faire); **to be ~ in doing** faire erreur en faisant; **2** (improper, unsuitable) incorrect.

incorrectly /ˌɪŋkəˈrektlɪ/ *adv* incorrectement; **we assumed ~ that** nous nous sommes trompés en pensant que.

incorrigible /ɪnˈkɒrɪdʒəbl, US -ˈkɔːr-/ *adj* incorrigible.

incorrigibly /ɪnˈkɒrɪdʒəblɪ, US -ˈkɔːr-/ *adv* incorrigiblement.

incorruptibility /ˌɪŋkəˌrʌptəˈbɪlətɪ/ *n* incorruptibilité *f*.

incorruptible /ˌɪŋkəˈrʌptəbl/ *adj* incorruptible.

increase **I** /ˈɪŋkriːs/ *n* **1** (in amount) augmentation *f* (**in** de); **price/pay ~** augmentation de prix/de salaire; **a sudden ~ in unemployment** une soudaine augmentation du taux de chômage; **an ~ of 5%, a 5% ~** une augmentation de 5%; **an ~ of 20% in the cost of sth** une augmentation de 20% du prix de qch; **2** (in degree) accroissement *m*; **an ~ in support for the policy** un nombre croissant de personnes favorables à la politique; **there has been an ~ in public interest** le public s'y intéresse de plus en plus; **to be on the ~** être en progression.

II /ɪnˈkriːs/ *vtr* **1** gen augmenter [*sales, grant, offer, temperature, anxiety*]; **to ~ one's chances of doing** augmenter ses chances de faire; **to ~ the risk of** augmenter les risques de [*failure, disease etc*]; **to ~ sth by** augmenter qch de [*amount, percentage*]; **to ~ life expectancy by five years** prolonger l'espérance de vie de cinq ans; **to ~ sth to** augmenter qch jusqu'à; **I ~d my offer to $100** je suis monté à 100 dollars; **2** (in knitting) augmenter de [*stitch*].

III /ɪnˈkriːs/ *vi* **1** gen [*output, sales, volume, strength, intensity*] augmenter; [*appetite*] grandir; [*workload*] s'accroître; **to ~ by** augmenter de [*amount, percentage*]; **to ~ in number/value** augmenter en nombre/valeur; **to ~ in volume** augmenter de volume; **to ~ in size** s'agrandir; **to ~ from... to** passer de... à; **2** Meteorol [*wind*] se lever; (at sea) forcir; **3** (in knitting) augmenter.

IV increasing *pres p adj* [*prices, number*] croissant; **with increasing frequency** de plus en plus fréquemment.

V increased *pp adj* [*choice, demand, probability*] plus grand; [*attacks*] plus fréquent; [*inequality*] plus marqué; **an ~d risk of cancer** un risque accru de cancer.

increasingly /ˈɪŋkriːsɪŋlɪ/ *adv* [*popular, difficult*] de plus en plus; **~, he came to**

accept this petit à petit, il a fini par accepter cela.

incredible /ɪnˈkredəbl/ *adj* **1** (unbelievable) incroyable; **2**○ (wonderful) fantastique.

incredibly /ɪnˈkredəblɪ/ *adv* **1** (astonishingly) incroyablement; **~, she didn't hear a thing** chose incroyable, elle n'a rien entendu; **2**○ (extremely) extrêmement.

incredulity /ˌɪŋkrɪˈdju:lətɪ, US -du:-/ *n* incrédulité *f*; **a look** ou **expression of ~** un air incrédule.

incredulous /ɪnˈkredjʊləs, US -dʒə-/ *adj* incrédule; **he was ~ at the news/your success** il n'arrivait pas à croire la nouvelle/à ta réussite; **I was ~ that** je n'arrivais pas à croire que (+ *subj*).

incredulously /ɪnˈkredjʊləslɪ, US -dʒə-/ *adv* [*ask, exclaim, repeat*] d'un ton incrédule; [*look, stare*] d'un air incrédule; [*listen*] d'une oreille incrédule.

increment /ˈɪŋkrəmənt/ **I** *n* **1** Fin (on salary) augmentation *f* (automatique); **2** (addition) Comput, Math incrément *m*; **3** (number added) Comput pas *m* de progression; Math valeur *f* de progression.
II *vtr* **1** Fin augmenter (automatiquement) [*salary*]; **2** Comput, Math incrémenter; **to ~ a value by one** incrémenter une valeur d'une unité.

incremental /ˌɪŋkrəˈmentl/ *adj* **1** Comput, Math [*backup, computer, display*] incrémentiel/-ielle; **2** (increasing) [*benefit, effect*] cumulatif/-ive; [*measures, steps*] progressif/-ive.

incremental: **~ cost** *n* coût *m* marginal or différentiel; **~ scale** *n* échelle *f* mobile des salaires.

incriminate /ɪnˈkrɪmɪneɪt/ **I** *vtr* [*evidence, documents*] incriminer; **to ~ sb in** impliquer qn dans [*crime, activity*].
II *v refl* **to ~ oneself** s'incriminer.

incriminating /ɪnˈkrɪmɪneɪtɪŋ/ *adj* [*statement, document, testimony, weapon*] compromettant; **~ evidence** preuves *fpl* incriminantes.

incrimination /ɪnˌkrɪmɪˈneɪʃn/ *n* incrimination *f*.

incriminatory /ɪnˈkrɪmɪneɪtərɪ, -nətrɪ, US -tɔ:rɪ/ *adj* Jur [*testimony, document*] compromettant; **~ evidence** preuves incriminantes.

in-crowd○ /ˈɪnkraʊd/ *n* **to be in with the ~** fréquenter les gens à la mode.

incrust *vtr* = **encrust**.

incrustation /ˌɪŋkrʌˈsteɪʃn/ *n* **1** (layer) (of shells, gems) incrustation *f*; (of salt, lime) dépôt *m*; **2** (process) lit incrustation *f*; fig (of habits, customs) encroûtement *m*.

incubate /ˈɪŋkjʊbeɪt/ **I** *vtr* **1** Agric [*breeder*] incuber; [*hen*] couver; **2** (grow) faire incuber [*bacteria, culture, embryo*]; **3** fig mûrir [*scheme, idea*].
II *vi* **1** [*eggs*] être en incubation; **2** [*bacteria, embryo*] être en incubation; **the disease takes four weeks to ~** la durée d'incubation de la maladie est de quatre semaines; **3** fig [*revolt*] couver.

incubation /ˌɪŋkjʊˈbeɪʃn/ *n* **1** (of eggs, bacteria) incubation *f*; **2** fig (of scheme, play) maturation *f*; **3** Med incubation *f*.

incubation period *n* période *f* d'incubation.

incubator /ˈɪŋkjʊbeɪtə(r)/ *n* **1** (for child) couveuse *f*; **2** (for eggs, embryos, bacteria) incubateur *m*.

incubus /ˈɪŋkjʊbəs/ *n* **1** (devil) incube *m*; **2** fig (fear) cauchemar *m*.

inculcate /ˈɪnkʌlkeɪt, US ɪnˈkʌl-/ *vtr* **to ~ sth in sb**, **~ sb with sth** inculquer qch à qn.

inculcation /ˌɪnkʌlˈkeɪʃn/ *n* inculcation *f*.

incumbency /ɪnˈkʌmbənsɪ/ *n* sout exercice *m* d'une charge; **during his ~ at the ministry** pendant l'exercice de sa charge au ministère.

incumbent /ɪnˈkʌmbənt/ **I** *n* sout **1** Admin, Pol, gen personne *f* exerçant une charge; (minister) ministre *m*; (delegate) représentant/-e *m/f*; **2** (in Anglican church) pasteur *m* (*chargé d'une paroisse*).
II *adj* **1** (morally) **to be ~ on** ou **upon sb to do** incomber à qn de faire; **2** (in office) [*minister, administrator*] en exercice; **the ~ president** le président actuel.

incunabulum /ˌɪnkju:ˈnæbjʊləm/ *n* (*pl* **-bula**) Hist incunable *m*.

incur /ɪnˈkɜ:(r)/ *vtr* (*p prés etc* **-rr-**) **1** Comm, Fin contracter*n* [*debts*]; subir [*loss*]; encourir [*expense, charge, penalty, risk*]; **2** (bring down) encourir [*wrath, displeasure*].

incurable /ɪnˈkjʊərəbl/ **I** *n* incurable *mf*.
II *adj* **1** [*disease, disorder*] incurable; **2** [*romanticism, optimism*] incorrigible.

incurably /ɪnˈkjʊərəblɪ/ *adv* **1** Med **to be ~ ill** souffrir d'une maladie incurable; **2** fig **to be ~ romantic/inquisitive** être d'un romantisme/d'une curiosité incorrigible.

incurious /ɪnˈkjʊərɪəs/ *adj* indifférent.

incursion /ɪnˈkɜ:ʃn, US -ʒn/ *n* **1** Mil incursion *f* (**into** dans); **2** (intrusion) intrusion *f* (**into** dans).

indebted /ɪnˈdetɪd/ *adj* **1** (grateful) **to be ~ to sb** être redevable à qn; **to be ~ to sb for sth/for doing sth** être obligé à qn de qch/de faire qch; **2** Econ, Fin (*tjrs épith*) [*company, country, economy*] endetté.

indebtedness /ɪnˈdetɪdnɪs/ *n* **1** Econ, Fin endettement *m*; **2** (gratitude) dette *f* (**to** envers; **for** pour).

indecency /ɪnˈdi:snsɪ/ *n* **1** (lack of decency) indécence *f*; **2** Jur (offence) attentat *m* à la pudeur; **gross ~** outrage *m* à la pudeur.

indecent /ɪnˈdi:snt/ *adj* **1** (sexually) indécent; **2** (unseemly) [*haste*] malséant; **an ~ amount of work/money** une somme de travail/d'argent choquante.

indecent: **~ assault** *n* attentat *m* à la pudeur (**on** contre); **~ exposure** *n* outrage *m* public à la pudeur.

indecently /ɪnˈdi:sntlɪ/ *adv* **1** (offensively) [*behave, act*] d'une manière indécente; [*dressed*] d'une manière indécente; **2** (inappropriately) **they got married ~ soon** ils se sont mariés avec une rapidité malséante; **~ early** plus tôt que nécessaire.

indecipherable /ˌɪndɪˈsaɪfrəbl/ *adj* indéchiffrable.

indecision /ˌɪndɪˈsɪʒn/ *n* indécision *f* (**about** quant à); **after months of ~** après des mois d'hésitation.

indecisive /ˌɪndɪˈsaɪsɪv/ *adj* **1** [*person*] (momentarily) indécis (**about** quant à); (by nature) **he's an ~ person** c'est un indécis; **2** [*reply, result*] indécis; [*battle, victory, election, debate*] peu concluant.

indecisively /ˌɪndɪˈsaɪsɪvlɪ/ *adv* [*speak, reply*] d'un ton indécis; [*behave*] d'une manière indécise.

indeclinable /ˌɪndɪˈklaɪnəbl/ *adj* indéclinable.

indecorous /ɪnˈdekərəs/ *adj* sout inconvenant.

indecorously /ɪnˈdekərəslɪ/ *adv* sout [*behave, guffaw*] d'une manière inconvenante; [*short, skimpy*] impudemment.

indecorum /ˌɪndɪˈkɔ:rəm/ *n* sout manque *m* de correction.

indeed /ɪnˈdi:d/ *adv* **1** (certainly) en effet, effectivement; **it is ~ likely that** il est en effet or effectivement probable que; **there had ~ been a plot** il y avait effectivement eu un complot; **'it's unfair'—'~!'** 'c'est injuste'—'en effet!'; **'are you interested?'—'~ I am!'** ou **'yes ~!'** 'ça t'intéresse?'—'bien sûr que oui!'; **'can you see it from there?'—'~ you can'** ou **'you can ~'** 'est-ce qu'on peut le voir de là?'—'bien sûr que oui'; **'he's not coming, is he?'—'~ he is!'** 'lui, il ne vient pas?'—'bien sûr que si!'; **'did she really leave him?'—'she did ~!'** 'est-ce qu'elle l'a vraiment laissé tomber?'—'oui!'; **2** (in fact) en fait; **it won't harm them—~ it might be to their advantage** cela ne leur nuira pas—en fait cela peut tourner à leur avantage; **he was a colleague, ~ a friend** c'était un collègue et en fait or et même un ami; **she is polite, ~ charming** elle est polie et même charmante; **I feel, ~ I am convinced, that** je pense, je suis même convaincu que; **if ~ that is what consumers want** si c'est vraiment ce que veulent les consommateurs; **3** (for emphasis) vraiment; **very clever/traditional ~** vraiment très intelligent/traditionnel; **it was very hot ~** il faisait vraiment très chaud; **I was very sad ~ to hear** j'ai été vraiment attristé d'apprendre; **that's very good news ~** ce sont vraiment de bonnes nouvelles; **to know very little ~ about sth** savoir vraiment très peu sur qch; **that was praise ~ coming from him!** venant de lui c'était vraiment un compliment!; **we are very grateful ~ for...** nous sommes profondément reconnaissants de...; **thank you very much ~** merci mille fois; **4** iron (expressing surprise, disbelief) **'he knows you'—'does he ~?'** 'il te connaît'—'ah bon?', 'vraiment?'; **a bargain ~! it's a rip-off**○**!** tu parles d'une affaire! c'est de l'arnaque◐!; **'why did she do it?'—'why ~?'** 'pourquoi est-ce qu'elle l'a fait?'—'ça je me le demande', 'ça c'est une bonne question'.

indefatigable /ˌɪndɪˈfætɪgəbl/ *adj* [*campaigner, worker, director*] inlassable; **she's ~!** elle est infatigable!

indefatigably /ˌɪndɪˈfætɪgəblɪ/ *adv* inlassablement.

indefensible /ˌɪndɪˈfensəbl/ *adj* **1** (morally) [*crime, cruelty, behaviour, attitude*] inexcusable; [*severity, penalty*] injustifiable; **2** (logically) [*reasoning, opinion, cause*] indéfendable; **3** Mil [*position, territory*] indéfendable.

indefensibly /ˌɪndɪˈfensəblɪ/ *adv* [*act, behave*] d'une manière inexcusable; **to be ~ cruel/rude** être d'une cruauté/d'une impolitesse inexcusable.

indefinable /ˌɪndɪˈfaɪnəbl/ *adj* indéfinissable.

indefinably /ˌɪndɪˈfaɪnəblɪ/ *adv* vaguement; **there was something ~ sad about her** elle avait quelque chose de vaguement triste.

indefinite /ɪnˈdefɪnət/ *adj* **1** (vague) [*idea, plan, intention, emotion, answer*] vague; [*duties, responsibilities*] imprécis; **2** (without limits) [*period, delay, curfew, strike*] illimité; [*amount, number*] indéterminé; **~ ban** Sport interdiction pour une durée indéterminée; **3** Ling **the ~ article** l'article *m* indéfini.

indefinitely /ɪnˈdefɪnətlɪ/ *adv* [*continue, last, stay, detain*] indéfiniment; [*adjourn, cancel, postpone, ban*] pour une durée indéterminée.

indelible /ɪnˈdeləbl/ *adj* **1** [*ink, mark*] indélébile; **2** [*memory, impression*] ineffaçable; **an ~ part of** une part indélébile de [*background, culture*].

indelibly /ɪnˈdeləblɪ/ *adv* **1** lit [*marked, printed*] de manière indélébile; **2** fig [*impressed, imprinted*] de manière ineffaçable.

indelicacy /ɪnˈdelɪkəsɪ/ *n* sout **1** (tactlessness) indélicatesse *f*; **2** euph (coarseness) grossièreté *f*; **3** euph (remark) indélicatesse *f*.

indelicate /ɪnˈdelɪkət/ *adj* sout **1** (tactless) [*action, remark*] indélicat; **it was ~ of her to mention it** c'était indélicat de sa part d'en parler; **2** euph (coarse) [*comment, act*] grossier/-ière.

indemnification /ɪnˌdemnɪfɪˈkeɪʃn/ *n* **1** (protection) assurance *f* (**against** contre); **2** (compensation) indemnisation *f* (**for** de).

indemnify /ɪnˈdemnɪfaɪ/ *vtr* **1** (protect) assurer (**against, from** contre); **2** (compensate) indemniser (**for** de).

indemnity /ɪnˈdemnətɪ/ *n* **1** (protection) assurance *f* (**against** contre); **letter of ~** lettre

f de garantie; **2** (payment) indemnité *f*; **3** Jur (exemption) décharge *f*.
indemnity fund *n* fonds *m* de garantie.
indene /ˈɪndiːn/ *n* indène *m*.
indent I /ˈɪndent/ *n* **1** GB Comm commande *f*; **to place an ~ for goods** passer une commande de marchandises; **2** Print (of first line) alinéa *m*; **3** (incision) entaille *f*.
II /ɪnˈdent/ *vtr* **1** Print renfoncer [*line, text, word*]; **new paragraphs should be ~ed** on doit faire un alinéa pour les nouveaux paragraphes; **2** denteler [*edge*].
III /ɪnˈdent/ *vi* GB Comm passer une commande; **to ~ on a supplier for goods** faire une commande de marchandises auprès d'un fournisseur.
IV indented *pp adj* **1** Print en alinéa; **2** [*coastline*] découpé; [*edge*] dentelé.
indentation /ˌɪndenˈteɪʃn/ *n* **1** (depression) gen marque *f*; (in metal) bosse *f*; **2** (in coastline) (action) découpage *m*; (inlet) échancrure *f*; **3** Print (also **indent**) alinéa *m*.
indent house *n* US Comm maison *f* d'importation (*spécialisée dans les produits manufacturés à l'étranger*).
indenture /ɪnˈdentʃə(r)/ **I** *n* Jur contrat *m* synallagmatique.
II indentures *npl* Hist (of apprentice) contrat *m* d'apprentissage; (of worker) contrat *m* sous conditions.
III *vtr* Hist [*craftsman*] prendre [qn] en apprentissage; [*landowner*] engager [qn] sous contrat [*labourer*].
independence /ˌɪndɪˈpendəns/ *n* indépendance *f* (**from** vis-à-vis de).
Independence Day *n* US fête *f* de l'Indépendance.
independent /ˌɪndɪˈpendənt/ **I** *n* **1** Pol candidat/-e *m/f* indépendant/-e; **2** (film or record company) indépendant *m*, compagnie *f* indépendante.
II *adj* **1** (self-reliant) [*person, life, attitude, style*] indépendant (**of** de); **~ means, an ~ income** des revenus personnels; **2** Pol [*country*] indépendant (**of** de); **3** (impartial) [*body, expert, observer, inquiry, investigation*] indépendant; [*witness, evidence, account*] objectif/-ive; **4** (separate, unconnected) [*complaint, source*] indépendant; **two ~ surveys give the same result** deux sondages indépendants donnent le même résultat; **5** (not part of an organization) gen, Pol [*candidate, cinema, company, newspaper*] indépendant; **6** (not state run) [*school, hospital, radio station*] privé; **7** Ling, Math indépendant.
independent: **Independent Broadcasting Authority**, **IBA** *n* GB organisme *m* de contrôle des stations privées de radio et télédiffusion; **~ clause** *n* Ling proposition *f* indépendante.
independently /ˌɪndɪˈpendəntlɪ/ *adv* **1** (without help) [*act, live*] de façon indépendante; **2** (separately) [*administer, negotiate, research*] individuellement, de façon indépendante; **~ of** indépendamment de; **~ of each other** indépendamment l'un de l'autre; **3** (impartially) [*investigated, monitored, confirmed*] par une autorité extérieure.
independent: **~ suspension** *n* Aut suspension *f* indépendante; **Independent Television Commission**, **ITC** *n* GB organisme *m* de contrôle des chaînes privées de télédiffusion; **~ variable** *n* Math variable *f* indépendante.
in-depth /ˌɪnˈdepθ/ **I** *adj* [*analysis, study, knowledge*] approfondi, détaillé; [*guide*] détaillé; [*interview*] en profondeur.
II in depth *adv phr* [*examine, study*] en détail.
indescribable /ˌɪndɪˈskraɪbəbl/ *adj* [*chaos, noise, smell*] indescriptible; [*pleasure, peace, beauty*] inexprimable, ineffable liter.
indescribably /ˌɪndɪˈskraɪbəblɪ/ *adv* **to be ~ dirty/beautiful/sad** être d'une saleté/beauté/tristesse inexprimable; **an ~ boring film** un film incroyablement ennuyeux; **she felt ~ happy** elle sentait en elle une joie inexprimable.
indestructibility /ˌɪndɪstrʌktɪˈbɪlətɪ/ *n* indestructibilité *f*.
indestructible /ˌɪndɪˈstrʌktəbl/ *adj* indestructible.
indeterminable /ˌɪndɪˈtɜːmɪnəbl/ *adj* indéterminable.
indeterminacy /ˌɪndɪˈtɜːmɪnəsɪ/ *n* sout indétermination.
indeterminate /ˌɪndɪˈtɜːmɪnət/ *adj* **1** gen (imprecise) indéterminé; **of ~ age** d'un âge indéterminé; **2** Math, Ling indéterminé.
indeterminately /ˌɪndɪˈtɜːmɪnətlɪ/ *adv* [*assessed, measured*] de façon indéterminée; [*known, ascertained*] vaguement.
index /ˈɪndeks/ **I** *n* (*pl* **~es** ou **-ices**) **1** Print index *m inv*; **thumb ~** index à onglets; **2** (card catalogue) catalogue *m*; **author/subject ~** catalogue par auteur/sujet; **card ~** fichier *m*; **3** Math (of power) exposant *m*; (of radical) indice *m*; **4** Econ, Fin indice *m*; **cost-of-living ~** GB, **consumer price ~** US indice des prix à la consommation; **share ~**, **stock ~** indice boursier; **5** Phys **~ of refraction**, **refractive ~** indice *m* de réfraction; **6** (indication) indice *m* (**of** de); **7** (list) répertoire *m*; **8** Comput index *m inv*; **9** Aut (registration number) numéro *m* d'immatriculation.
II *modif* [*file*] des index; [*register, word*] d'index.
III *vtr* **1** Print munir [qch] d'un index [*book*]; indexer [*word*]; **this book is badly ~ed** l'index de ce livre est mal fait; **2** (catalogue) classer, cataloguer [*article, book, data, information, subject*] (**under** sous, à); **3** Econ, Fin **to ~ sth to sth** indexer qch sur qch; **~ed to inflation** indexé sur l'inflation; **4** Comput indexer.
IV *vi* établir un index.
V indexed *pp adj* Comput [*address, addressing, file*] indexé.
indexation /ˌɪndekˈseɪʃn/ *n* Econ, Fin indexation *f* (**to** sur).
index: **~ card** *n* fiche *f*; **~ figure** *n* Econ, Stat (nombre *m*) indice *m*; **~ finger** *n* index *m inv*.
indexing /ˈɪndeksɪŋ/ *n* Comput indexation *f*.
index: **~-linked** *adj* Econ, Fin indexé; **~ number** *n* Math (nombre *m*) indice *m*.
India /ˈɪndɪə/ **▶ 1131** *pr n* Inde *f*.
India ink *n* US encre *f* de Chine.
Indian /ˈɪndɪən/ **▶ 1486** **I** *n* **1** (from India) Indien/-ienne *m/f*; **2** (American) Indien/-ienne *m/f* d'Amérique; **3** (language) indien *m*.
II *adj* **1** (of India) [*people, culture, politics*] indien/-ienne; [*ambassador, embassy*] de l'Inde; **the ~ Empire** Hist l'Empire des Indes; **2** (American) [*tribe, village, culture*] indien/-ienne, amérindien/-ienne spec; **an ~ reservation** une réserve indienne.
Indiana /ˌɪndɪˈænə/ **▶ 1744** *pr n* Indiana *m*.
Indian: **~ club** *n* massue *f* (de gymnastique); **~ corn** *n* US maïs *m*; **~ elephant** *n* éléphant *m* d'Asie.
Indian file *n* **in ~** en file indienne, à la queue leu leu.
Indian: **~ giver** *n* US péj *personne qui reprend son cadeau*; **~ hemp** *n* chanvre *m* indien; **~ ink** *n* GB encre *f* de Chine.
Indian Ocean **▶ 1511** *pr n* **the ~** l'océan *m* Indien.
Indian: **~ red** *n* rouge *m* indien; **~ summer** *n* été *m* de la Saint Martin also fig; **~ wrestling** *n* US bras *m* de fer.
India: **~ paper** *n* papier *m* bible; **india rubber**† *n* (material) caoutchouc *m*; (eraser) gomme *f*.
indicate /ˈɪndɪkeɪt/ **I** *vtr* **1** (designate) indiquer; **he ~d the door with a nod of his head** il a indiqué la porte de la tête; **2** (show) indiquer (**that** que); **the speedometer ~d 100** le compteur de vitesse indiquait 100; **3** (recommend) **to be ~d** être indiqué; **surgery is usually ~d in such cases** la chirurgie est généralement indiquée en pareils cas; **4** (make known) faire savoir [*intentions, feelings*] (**to** à); **he has ~d that he will retire** il a fait savoir qu'il va prendre sa retraite; **5** Aut **to ~ that one is going to do** indiquer son intention de faire.
II *vi* [*driver*] mettre son clignotant; [*cyclist*] faire signe.
indication /ˌɪndɪˈkeɪʃn/ *n* indication *f*, indice *m*; **clear ~ of economic recovery** indice certain de reprise économique; **to be an ~ of** indiquer; **it is an ~ that** c'est signe que; **to give no ~ that** [*person*] ne pas laisser entrevoir que; **the test gave no ~ that he had cancer** les analyses n'ont pas révélé de cancer chez lui; **to give no ~ of who/how etc** [*person*] ne rien dire qui permette de savoir qui/comment etc; [*letter, speech*] ne pas permettre de savoir qui/comment etc; **can you give us some ~ of the sum involved?** pouvez-vous nous donner une idée de la somme dont il est question?; **there is every ~ that, all the ~s are that** tout porte à croire que.
indicative /ɪnˈdɪkətɪv/ **I** *n* Ling indicatif *m*; **in the ~** à l'indicatif.
II *adj* **1 to be ~ of** montrer; **2** Ling indicatif/-ive.
indicator /ˈɪndɪkeɪtə(r)/ *n* **1** (pointer) aiguille *f*; (device) indicateur *m* also fig; **pressure/growth ~** indicateur de pression/de croissance; **2** Rail (also **~ board**) tableau *m*; **arrivals/departures ~** tableau des arrivées/des départs; **3** Aut clignotant *m*; **4** Ling, Chem indicateur *m*.
indices /ˈɪndɪsiːz/ *npl* **▶ index**.
indict /ɪnˈdaɪt/ *vtr* gen accuser; Jur inculper.
indictable /ɪnˈdaɪtəbl/ *adj* Jur [*act, person*] passible de poursuites; **~ offence** délit *m*.
indictment /ɪnˈdaɪtmənt/ *n* **1** Jur (written) acte *m* d'accusation; (spoken) accusation *f* (**against** contre; **for** pour); **to bring an ~** intenter une accusation; **to be under ~ for murder** être inculpé/-e de meurtre; **bill of ~** GB Hist acte d'accusation; **2** gen mise *f* en accusation.
indie○ /ˈɪndɪ/ **I** *n* US Cin indépendant *m*.
II *adj* US Cin, GB Mus indépendant; **~ music** rock *m* indépendant.
indifference /ɪnˈdɪfrəns/ *n* indifférence *f* (**to, towards** envers); **it is a matter of ~ to him** cela lui est indifférent; **seeming ~** une feinte indifférence.
indifferent /ɪnˈdɪfrənt/ *adj* **1** (uninterested) indifférent (**to, as to** à); (to charms) insensible (**to** à); **2** (mediocre) médiocre.
indifferently /ɪnˈdɪfrəntlɪ/ *adv* **1** (without caring) avec indifférence; **2** (equally) indifféremment; **3** (not well) médiocrement.
indigence /ˈɪndɪdʒəns/ *n* sout indigence *f*.
indigenous /ɪnˈdɪdʒɪnəs/ *adj* indigène (**to** à).
indigent /ˈɪndɪdʒənt/ *adj* sout indigent.
indigestible /ˌɪndɪˈdʒestəbl/ *adj* (all contexts) indigeste.
indigestion /ˌɪndɪˈdʒestʃn/ **I** *n* crise *f* de foie; **to suffer from ~** être sujet aux crises de foie.
II *modif* [*cure, remedy*] contre l'indigestion.
indignant /ɪnˈdɪgnənt/ *adj* indigné (**at** de; **about, over** par); **to become** ou **get ~** s'indigner (**at, about** de).
indignantly /ɪnˈdɪgnəntlɪ/ *adv* [*do, say, protest*] avec indignation; [*leave, look*] d'un air indigné.
indignation /ˌɪndɪgˈneɪʃn/ *n* indignation *f* (**at** devant; **over, about** au sujet de; **with** contre); **her ~ at hearing that...** son indignation d'apprendre que...; **(much) to his ~** à sa grande indignation; **righteous ~** la vertueuse indignation.
indignity /ɪnˈdɪgnətɪ/ *n* indignité *f* (**of** de; **of being** d'être).
indigo /ˈɪndɪgəʊ/ **▶ 1104** **I** *n* Art, Bot, Tex indigo *m*.
II *adj* indigo *inv*; **~ blue** bleu indigo *inv*.

indirect /ˌɪndɪˈrekt, -daɪˈr-/ *adj* indirect.

indirect: **~ advertising** *n* publicité *f* indirecte; **~ costs** *npl* frais *mpl* indirects; **~ labour costs** *npl* frais *mpl* indirects de main-d'œuvre; **~ lighting** *n* éclairage *m* indirect.

indirectly /ˌɪndɪˈrektlɪ, -daɪˈr-/ *adv* indirectement.

indirectness /ˌɪndɪˈrektnɪs, -daɪˈr-/ *n* manière *f* détournée.

indirect: **~ object** *n* Ling objet *m* indirect; **~ proof** *n* démonstration *f* par l'absurde; **~ speech** *n* discours *m* indirect; **~ tax** *n* impôt *m* indirect; **~ taxation** *n* imposition *f* indirecte.

indiscernible /ˌɪndɪˈsɜːnəbl/ *adj* [*object*] imperceptible; [*reason*] obscur.

indiscipline /ɪnˈdɪsɪplɪn/ *n* indiscipline *f*.

indiscreet /ˌɪndɪˈskriːt/ *adj* indiscret/-ète.

indiscretion /ˌɪndɪˈskreʃn/ *n* **1** (lack of discretion) manque *m* de discrétion; **2** (act) indiscrétion *f*.

indiscriminate /ˌɪndɪˈskrɪmɪnət/ *adj* **1** (generalized) sans distinction; **2** (not fussy) sans discernement; **to be ~ in** manquer de discernement dans.

indiscriminately /ˌɪndɪˈskrɪmɪnətlɪ/ *adv* **1** (without distinction) sans distinction; **2** (uncritically) sans discernement.

indispensable /ˌɪndɪˈspensəbl/ *adj* indispensable (**to** à; **for doing** pour faire).

indisposed /ˌɪndɪˈspəʊzd/ *adj* sout **1** (ill) gen, hum souffrant; **2** (unwilling) mal disposé (**to do** à faire).

indisposition /ˌɪndɪspəˈzɪʃn/ *n* sout **1** (illness) indisposition *f*; **2** (unwillingness) manque *m* d'inclination (**to do** à faire).

indisputable /ˌɪndɪˈspjuːtəbl/ *adj* [*leader, champion*] indiscuté; [*fact, reason*] indiscutable; [*logic*] irrécusable.

indisputably /ˌɪndɪˈspjuːtəblɪ/ *adv* indiscutablement.

indissoluble /ˌɪndɪˈsɒljʊbl/ *adj* [*bond, tie*] indissoluble; [*friendship*] indestructible.

indissolubly /ˌɪndɪˈsɒljʊblɪ/ *adv* indissolublement.

indistinct /ˌɪndɪˈstɪŋkt/ *adj* [*sound, voice, path, markings*] indistinct; [*memory*] confus; [*photograph*] flou.

indistinctly /ˌɪndɪˈstɪŋktlɪ/ *adv* [*see, hear, speak*] indistinctement; [*remember*] confusément.

indistinguishable /ˌɪndɪˈstɪŋgwɪʃəbl/ *adj* **1** (identical) impossible à distinguer; **2** (indiscernible) indiscernable.

indistinguishably /ˌɪndɪˈstɪŋgwɪʃəblɪ/ *adv* [*resemble*] au point qu'on ne peut les distinguer.

individual /ˌɪndɪˈvɪdʒʊəl/ **I** *n* **1** (person) individu *m* also pej; **each ~** chaque individu; **2** (eccentric) personnage *m*.

II *adj* **1** (for or from one person) [*contribution, effort, freedom, portion, pursuit, sport*] individuel/-elle; [*comfort, convenience, attitude*] personnel/-elle; [*tuition*] particulier/-ière; **2** (taken separately) **each ~ person/article** chaque personne/article individuellement; **3** (idiosyncratic) particulier/-ière.

individualism /ˌɪndɪˈvɪdʒʊəlɪzəm/ *n* individualisme *m*.

individualist /ˌɪndɪˈvɪdʒʊəlɪst/ *n* **1** (idiosyncratic) individualiste *mf*; **2** (supporter of individualism) partisan/-e *m/f* de l'individualisme.

individualistic /ˌɪndɪˌvɪdʒʊəˈlɪstɪk/ *adj* individualiste.

individuality /ˌɪndɪˌvɪdʒʊˈælətɪ/ *n* individualité *f*.

individualize /ˌɪndɪˈvɪdʒʊəlaɪz/ *vtr* donner une note personnelle à [*gift, clothing*]; adapter [qch] aux besoins personnels [*teaching, arrangements*].

individually /ˌɪndɪˈvɪdʒʊəlɪ/ *adv* (personally, in person) individuellement; (one at a time) (of things) séparément; **~ designed, ~ planned** de conception individualisée; **each item is ~ priced** le prix est indiqué sur chaque article.

individuation /ˌɪndɪˌvɪdʒʊˈeɪʃn/ *n* individuation *f*.

indivisibility /ˌɪndɪˌvɪzɪˈbɪlətɪ/ *n* Math, Phys indivisibilité *f*.

indivisible /ˌɪndɪˈvɪzəbl/ *adj* **1** gen, Math, Phys [*entity*] indivisible; **2** (inseparable) **to be ~ from** être inséparable de.

indivisibly /ˌɪndɪˈvɪzəblɪ/ *adv* [*joined, linked*] de manière indivisible.

Indochina /ˌɪndəʊˈtʃaɪnə/ *pr n* Indochine *f*.

Indochinese /ˌɪndəʊtʃaɪˈniːz/ **I** *n* Indochinois/-e *m/f*.

II *adj* indochinois.

indoctrinate /ɪnˈdɒktrɪneɪt/ *vtr* endoctriner; **to ~ sb with sth** inculquer qch à qn.

indoctrination /ɪnˌdɒktrɪˈneɪʃn/ *n* endoctrinement *m* (**of** de).

Indo-European /ˌɪndəʊjʊərəˈpɪən/ **I** *n* indo-européen *m*.

II *adj* indo-européen/-éenne.

indole /ˈɪndəʊl/ *n* indole *m*.

indolence /ˈɪndələns/ *n* indolence *f*.

indolent /ˈɪndələnt/ *adj* gen, Med indolent.

indolently /ˈɪndələntlɪ/ *adv* [*lie, stretch*] indolemment; [*stroll, move, gesture*] nonchalamment.

indomitable /ɪnˈdɒmɪtəbl/ *adj* invincible.

indomitably /ɪnˈdɒmɪtəblɪ/ *adv* sans se laisser décourager.

Indonesia /ˌɪndəʊˈniːzjə/ **▶1131** *pr n* Indonésie *f*.

Indonesian /ˌɪndəʊˈniːzjən/ **I** *n* **▶1486**, **1402** **1** (person) Indonésien/-ienne *m/f*; **2** (language) indonésien *m*.

II *adj* indonésien/-ienne.

indoor /ˈɪndɔː(r)/ *adj* [*activity, sport, competition*] en salle; [*pool, tennis court*] couvert; [*lavatory, restaurant table*] à l'intérieur; [*TV aerial*] intérieur; [*photography, plant, shoes*] d'intérieur; **~ and outdoor** [*sports facilities*] en salle et à l'extérieur.

indoors /ˌɪnˈdɔːz/ *adv* (under cover, in the main house) à l'intérieur; (at home) à la maison; **~ and outdoors** dedans et dehors; **to go ~** rentrer.

indorse *vtr* = **endorse**.

Indre **▶1163** *pr n* Indre *m*; **in/to ~** dans l'Indre.

Indre-et-Loire **▶1163** *pr n* Indre-et-Loire *m*; **in/to ~** en Indre-et-Loire.

indubitable /ɪnˈdjuːbɪtəbl, US -ˈduː-/ *adj* indubitable.

indubitably /ɪnˈdjuːbɪtəblɪ, US -duː-/ *adv* indubitablement.

induce /ɪnˈdjuːs, US -duːs/ **I** *vtr* **1** (persuade) persuader (**to do** de faire); (stronger) inciter (**to** à; **to do** à faire); **nothing would ~ me to fly again** rien ne pourrait me convaincre de reprendre l'avion; **2** (bring about) provoquer [*emotion, response*]; **this drug ~s sleep** ce médicament fait dormir; **3** Med **to ~ labour** provoquer l'accouchement; **~d labour** accouchement *m* provoqué; **she was ~d** on a provoqué son accouchement; **4** Elec, Philos induire.

II -induced *dans composés*: **drug-/stress-~d** provoqué par la drogue/le stress; **▶ self-induced**.

inducement /ɪnˈdjuːsmənt, US -duː-/ *n* **1** (promised reward) récompense *f*; euph (bribe) pot-de-vin *m*; **financial ~** avantage *m* pécuniaire; **as an ~ to first-time buyers** Comm comme cadeau de bienvenue aux nouveaux clients; **2** ¢ (incentive) motivation *f* (**to do** pour faire); **to be an ~ to sth** encourager qch.

induct /ɪnˈdʌkt/ *vtr* **1** (inaugurate) installer [*priest, president etc*]; **to be ~ed into the priesthood** être admis à la prêtrise; **to be ~ed into the mysteries of sth** hum être initié aux mystères de qch; **2** US Mil incorporer.

induction /ɪnˈdʌkʃn/ *n* **1** Elec, Math, Philos, Tech induction *f*; **2** Med (of labour) déclenchement *m*; **3** (inauguration) (of priest, president) installation *f*; **4** US Mil incorporation *f*.

induction: **~ ceremony** *n* cérémonie *f* de prise de fonctions; **~ coil** *n* bobine *f* d'induction; **~ course** *n* GB stage *m* d'introduction; **~ heating** *n* chauffage *m* par induction; **~ loop** *n* boucle *f* magnétique.

inductive /ɪnˈdʌktɪv/ *adj* **1** [*reasoning, process*] inductif/-ive; **2** Elec, Phys inducteur/-trice.

indulge /ɪnˈdʌldʒ/ **I** *vtr* **1** (satisfy) céder à [*interest, passion, whim, desire, fantasy*]; **she can ~ her love of music** elle peut donner libre cours à sa passion pour la musique; **2** (humour) gâter [*child*]; céder à [*adult*]; **don't ~ him!** ne lui cède pas!

II *vi* gen se laisser tenter; euph (drink) boire de l'alcool; **to ~ in** se livrer à [*gossip, speculation, banter*]; se complaire dans [*nostalgia, sentimentality*]; se laisser tenter par [*food, wine, cigar*].

III *v refl* **to ~ oneself** se faire plaisir; **to ~ oneself in** ou **with** s'offrir [*luxury*]; **to ~ oneself by doing** se faire une gâterie en faisant.

indulgence /ɪnˈdʌldʒəns/ *n* **1** (luxury) péché *m* mignon; **it is my one ~** c'est mon péché mignon; **2** (tolerance) indulgence *f* (**towards** envers; **for** pour); **if I may crave your ~** sout si vous m'accordez la faveur de votre attention; **3** (act of indulging) **~ in food** gourmandise *f*; **~ in nostalgia** abandon *m* à la nostalgie; **4** (enjoyment) plaisir *m*; **to live a life of ~** ne se refuser aucun plaisir; **5** Relig indulgence *f*.

indulgent /ɪnˈdʌldʒənt/ *adj* indulgent (**to, towards** pour, envers).

indulgently /ɪnˈdʌldʒəntlɪ/ *adv* [*smile, laugh, listen*] avec indulgence; [*say*] d'un ton indulgent.

industrial /ɪnˈdʌstrɪəl/ *adj* **1** (relating to industry) [*area, archeology, architecture, development, espionage, policy, sector*] industriel/-ielle; [*accident, injury, medicine, safety*] du travail; **2** (active in industry) [*analyst, chemist, city, nation, spy, worker*] industriel/-ielle; **3** (for use in industry) [*chemical, robot, tool*] à usage industriel; [*size*] industriel/-ielle.

industrial action *n* GB gen action *f* revendicative; (strike) grève *f*; **to take ~** gen entreprendre une action revendicative; (strike) faire la grève.

industrial: **~ arts** *npl* US Sch cours *mpl* de technologie; **~ base** *n* tissu *m* industriel, base *f* industrielle; **~ democracy** *n* participation *f* ouvrière; **~ design** *n* esthétique *f* industrielle, conception *f* industrielle; **~ designer** *n* concepteur/-trice *m/f* industriel/-ielle; **~ diamond** *n* diamant *m* industriel; **~ disablement benefit** *n* indemnité *f* pour accident du travail et maladies professionnelles; **~ disease** *n* maladie *f* professionnelle; **~ dispute** *n* conflit *m* social; **~ engineering** *n* génie *m* industriel; **~ estate** *n* GB zone *f* industrielle.

industrialism /ɪnˈdʌstrɪəlɪzəm/ *n* industrialisme *m*.

industrialist /ɪnˈdʌstrɪəlɪst/ *n* industriel *m*.

industrialization /ɪnˌdʌstrɪəlaɪˈzeɪʃn, US -lɪˈz-/ *n* industrialisation *f*.

industrialize /ɪnˈdʌstrɪəlaɪz/ *vtr* industrialiser.

industrial: **~ park** *n* parc *m* industriel; **~ psychologist** **▶1692** *n* psychologue *mf* d'entreprise; **~ rehabilitation** *n* rééducation *f* professionnelle; **~ relations** *npl* relations *fpl* entre les patrons et les ouvriers; **Industrial Revolution** *n* révolution *f* industrielle; **~ tribunal** *n*: *conseil qui règle les conflits entre le patronat et les employés ou les syndicats*; cf conseil *m* des prud'hommes; **~ union** *n* syndicat *m* ouvrier; **~ unrest** *n* agitation *f* ouvrière; **~ vehicle** *n* véhicule *m* utilitaire; **~ waste** *n* déchets *mpl* industriels.

industrious /ɪnˈdʌstrɪəs/ *adj* diligent.
industriously /ɪnˈdʌstrɪəslɪ/ *adv* avec diligence.
industriousness /ɪnˈdʌstrɪəsnɪs/ *n* zèle *m* au travail.
industry /ˈɪndəstrɪ/ *n* **1** industrie *f*; **heavy/light ~** industrie lourde/légère; **the catering/advertising ~** l'industrie hôtelière/de la publicité; **the coal/oil ~** l'industrie du charbon/du pétrole; **the Shakespeare/Joyce ~** fig péj le filon Shakespeare/Joyce; **2** sout (diligence) zèle *m* (au travail).
inebriate I /ɪˈniːbrɪət/ *n, adj* sout ivrogne (*mf*).
II /ɪˈniːbrɪeɪt/ *vtr* enivrer.
III **inebriated** *pp adj* enivré (**with, by** par).
inebriation /ɪˌniːbrɪˈeɪʃn/, **inebriety** /ˌɪniːˈbraɪətɪ/ *n* sout ébriété *f* fml; **in a state of ~** dans un état d'ébriété.
inedible /ɪnˈedɪbl/ *adj* [*dish, meal*] immangeable; [*plants*] non comestible; [*fungi*] incomestible.
ineducable /ɪnˈedʒʊkəbl/ *adj* inéducable.
ineffable /ɪnˈefəbl/ *adj* gen, Relig ineffable; [*sorrow*] inexprimable.
ineffaceable /ˌɪnɪˈfeɪsəbl/ *adj* ineffaçable.
ineffective /ˌɪnɪˈfektɪv/ *adj* [*method, plan, theory*] inefficace (**in doing** à faire); [*worker*] incapable; **to make an ~ attempt to do** essayer en vain de faire.
ineffectively /ˌɪnɪˈfektɪvlɪ/ *adv* [*try*] en vain; [*teach, demand*] sans succès.
ineffectiveness /ˌɪnɪˈfektɪvnɪs/ *n* inefficacité *f*.
ineffectual /ˌɪnɪˈfektʃʊəl/ *adj* [*person*] incapable; [*policy*] inefficace; [*attempt*] infructueux/-euse; [*movement, gesture*] sans effet.
ineffectually /ˌɪnɪˈfektʃʊəlɪ/ *adv* en vain.
inefficacious /ˌɪnefɪˈkeɪʃəs/ *adj* inefficace.
inefficacy /ˌɪnˈefɪkəsɪ/ *n* inefficacité *f*.
inefficiency /ˌɪnɪˈfɪʃnsɪ/ *n* **1** (of person, company) (lack of organization) manque *m* d'organisation; (incompetence) incompétence *f*; **2** (of machine, method, system) inefficacité *f*.
inefficient /ˌɪnɪˈfɪʃnt/ *adj* **1** [*person, company*] (disorganized) mal organisé; (incompetent) incompétent; **2** [*machine, method, system, use*] inefficace.
inefficiently /ˌɪnɪˈfɪʃntlɪ/ *adv* [*organize, work*] d'une manière inefficace; [*perform task*] d'une manière incompétente.
inelastic /ˌɪnɪˈlæstɪk/ *adj* **1** [*rules, system*] rigide; **2** [*material*] non élastique; **3** Econ, Phys inélastique.
inelegant /ˌɪnˈelɪgənt/ *adj* inélégant.
inelegantly /ˌɪnˈelɪgəntlɪ/ *adv* inélégamment.
ineligibility /ɪnˌelɪdʒəˈbɪlətɪ/ *n* (for job) fait *m* de ne pas remplir des conditions de candidature (**for** à); (for election) Pol inéligibilité *f*; (for grant, benefit) le fait de ne pas avoir droit (**for** à).
ineligible /ɪnˈelɪdʒəbl/ *adj* **to be ~** (for job, competition) ne pas remplir les conditions pour poser sa candidature (**for** à); (for election) être inéligible; (for grant, pension, benefit, award) ne pas avoir droit (**for** à); **to be ~ to vote** ne pas avoir le droit de vote.
ineluctable /ˌɪnɪˈlʌktəbl/ *adj* inéluctable.
inept /ɪˈnept/ *adj* **1** (incompetent) incompétent; **2** (tactless) maladroit.
ineptitude /ɪˈneptɪtjuːd, US -tuːd/, **ineptness** /ɪˈneptnɪs/ *n* **1** (inefficiency) incompétence *f*; **2** (tactlessness) maladresse *f*.
ineptly /ɪˈneptlɪ/ *adv* **1** (inefficiently) de façon incompétente; **2** (tactlessly) maladroitement.
inequality /ˌɪnɪˈkwɒlətɪ/ *n* gen, Math inégalité *f*.
inequitable /ɪnˈekwɪtəbl/ *adj* inéquitable.
inequity /ɪnˈekwətɪ/ *n* injustice *f*.
ineradicable /ˌɪnɪˈrædɪkəbl/ *adj* gen indéracinable; [*disease*] inextirpable.
inert /ɪˈnɜːt/ *adj* gen, Chem, Phys inerte; Pharm inactif/-ive; **~ gas** gaz *m* rare.
inertia /ɪˈnɜːʃə/ *n* gen, Phys inertie *f*.
inertial /ɪˈnɜːʃl/ *adj* **1** Mil, Phys [*force, mass*] d'inertie; **2** Naut [*navigation*] inertiel/-ielle.
inertia: **~ reel seatbelt** *n* ceinture *f* de sécurité à enrouleur; **~ selling** *n* GB vente *f* par envoi de marchandises non commandées.
inertly /ɪˈnɜːtlɪ/ *adv* de façon inerte.
inescapable /ˌɪnɪˈskeɪpəbl/ *adj* indéniable.
inessential /ˌɪnɪˈsenʃl/ *adj* superflu.
inestimable /ˌɪnˈestɪməbl/ *adj* inestimable.
inevitability /ɪnˌevɪtəˈbɪlətɪ/ *n* caractère *m* inévitable.
inevitable /ɪnˈevɪtəbl/ I *n* **the ~** l'inévitable *m*; **the ~ happened** l'inévitable s'est produit.
II *adj* gen, hum inévitable; **it is/was ~ that he should do** il est/était inévitable qu'il fasse; **it is ~ that she will do** il est inévitable qu'elle fera or qu'elle fasse.
inevitably /ɪnˈevɪtəblɪ/ *adv* inévitablement.
inexact /ˌɪnɪgˈzækt/ *adj* inexact.
inexactitude /ˌɪnɪgˈzæktɪtjuːd, US -tɪtuːd/ *n* inexactitude *f*.
inexactly /ˌɪnɪgˈzæktlɪ/ *adv* inexactement.
inexcusable /ˌɪnɪkˈskjuːzəbl/ *adj* inexcusable (**that** que + *subj*); **it is ~ of her/them** il est inexcusable de sa/leur part (**to do** de faire).
inexcusably /ˌɪnɪkˈsjuːzəblɪ/ *adv* [*overlook, neglect*] de façon impardonnable or inexcusable; **~ lazy/rude** d'une paresse/impolitesse inexcusable.
inexhaustible /ˌɪnɪgˈzɔːstəbl/ *adj* [*supply, reserve*] inépuisable.
inexorable /ɪnˈeksərəbl/ *adj* [*logic, advance, progress, fate*] inexorable; [*person*] implacable.
inexorably /ɪnˈeksərəblɪ/ *adv* inexorablement.
inexpedient /ˌɪnɪkˈspiːdɪənt/ *adj* inopportun.
inexpensive /ˌɪnɪkˈspensɪv/ *adj* pas cher; **a good but ~ wine** un vin qui est bon et pas cher.
inexpensively /ˌɪnɪkˈspensɪvlɪ/ *adv* à peu de frais.
inexperience /ˌɪnɪkˈspɪərɪəns/ *n* inexpérience *f* (**of** de).
inexperienced /ˌɪnɪkˈspɪərɪənst/ *adj* inexpérimenté (**in** en).
inexpert /ɪnˈekspɜːt/ *adj* [*sailor, gardener etc*] amateur *inv*; [*translation, repair*] maladroit; [*eye*] de néophyte.
inexpertly /ɪnˈekspɜːtlɪ/ *adv* de façon maladroite.
inexpiable /ɪnˈekspɪəbl/ *adj* inexpiable.
inexplicable /ˌɪnɪkˈsplɪkəbl/ *adj* inexplicable; **for some ~ reason** pour une raison inexplicable.
inexplicably /ˌɪnɪkˈsplɪkəblɪ/ *adv* inexplicablement.
inexpressible /ˌɪnɪkˈspresəbl/ *adj* inexprimable.
inexpressibly /ˌɪnɪkˈspresəblɪ/ *adv* [*dull, relieved*] au-delà de toute expression.
inexpressive /ˌɪnɪkˈspresɪv/ *adj* inexpressif/-ive.
inextinguishable /ˌɪnɪkˈstɪŋgwɪʃəbl/ *adj* inextinguible.
in extremis /ɪn ɪkˈstriːmɪs/ *adv* sout in extremis.
inextricable /ɪnˈekstrɪkəbl, ˌɪnɪkˈstrɪk-/ *adj* (all contexts) inextricable.
inextricably /ɪnˈekstrɪkəblɪ, ˌɪnɪkˈstrɪk-/ *adv* inextricablement.
infallibility /ɪnˌfæləˈbɪlətɪ/ *n* infaillibilité *f*.
infallible /ɪnˈfæləbl/ *adj* infaillible.
infallibly /ɪnˈfæləblɪ/ *adv* **1** (always) immanquablement; **2** (faultlessly) infailliblement.
infamous /ˈɪnfəməs/ *adj* [*person*] tristement célèbre; [*conduct, crime*] infâme.
infamy /ˈɪnfəmɪ/ *n* infamie *f*.
infancy /ˈɪnfənsɪ/ *n* **1** (young childhood) première enfance *f*, petite enfance *f*; **from (one's) ~** de sa petite enfance; **in early ~** dans la toute petite enfance; **in (one's) ~** en bas âge; **2** fig débuts *mpl*; **in its ~** à ses débuts; **in the ~ of** au tout début de [*career, movement*]; **to be still in its ~** fig [*company, project*] en être encore à ses débuts or à ses premiers balbutiements; **3** Jur minorité *f*.
infant /ˈɪnfənt/ I *n* **1** (baby) bébé *m*; (very young child) enfant *mf* en bas âge; (young child) petit/-e enfant *m/f*; **a newborn ~** un nouveau-né; **2** GB Sch enfant *mf* (*entre 4 et 7 ans*); **3** Jur mineur/-e *m/f*.
II **Infants** *npl* GB Sch petites classes *fpl*.
III *modif* **1** [*daughter, son*] petit; [*voice*] d'enfant; [*disease*] infantile; **2** fig [*organization*] tout jeune; [*movement*] naissant.
infanta /ɪnˈfæntə/ *n* infante *f*.
infante /ɪnˈfæntɪ/ *n* infant *m*.
infanticide /ɪnˈfæntɪsaɪd/ *n* **1** (crime) infanticide *m*; **2** (killer) infanticide *mf*.
infantile /ˈɪnfəntaɪl/ *adj* **1** péj infantile, puéril; **2** Med infantile.
infantilize /ɪnˈfæntəlaɪz/ *vtr* infantiliser.
infant: **~ mortality** *n* mortalité *f* infantile; **~ prodigy** *n* enfant *mf* prodige.
infantry /ˈɪnfəntrɪ/ *n* infanterie *f*, fantassins *mpl*.
infantryman /ˈɪnfəntrɪmən/ *n* (*pl* **-men**) fantassin *m*.
infant school *n* ≈ école *f* maternelle.
infatuate /ɪnˈfætʃʊeɪt/ *vtr* **~d with** entiché de; **to become ~d with** s'éprendre de [*person*]; s'engouer de or pour [*idea, object, music*].
infatuation /ɪnˌfætʃʊˈeɪʃn/ *n* engouement *m* (**with** pour); **to develop an ~ for sb** s'éprendre de qn; **a passing ~** une amourette.
infeasible /ɪnˈfiːzəbl/ *adj* impraticable.
infect /ɪnˈfekt/ *vtr* **1** gen, Med contaminer [*person, blood*]; infecter [*person, wound*]; contaminer [*food*]; **to ~ sb/sth with sth** transmettre qch à qn/qch; **to become ~ed** [*wound*] s'infecter; [*person, blood*] être contaminé; **2** fig (influence) (negatively) corrompre [*person, society*]; **to ~ sb with one's enthusiasm** communiquer son enthousiasme à qn.
infection /ɪnˈfekʃn/ I *n* **1** gen Med (of wound, organ) infection *f*; (of person, blood) contamination *f*; **to be exposed to ~** [*person*] être exposé à la contagion; **2** Med (specific disease) infection *f*; **urinary/viral ~** infection urinaire/virale; **3** fig péj contamination *f*.
II *modif* [*rate, level*] gen de contagion, d'infection; (by physical contact) de contamination.
infectious /ɪnˈfekʃəs/ *adj* **1** Med [*disease, agent*] infectieux/-ieuse; [*person*] contagieux/-ieuse; **2** fig [*enthusiasm, laughter*] contagieux/-ieuse, communicatif/-ive; [*accent*] qui s'attrape facilement.
infectiousness /ɪnˈfekʃəsnɪs/ *n* Med nature *f* infectieuse; fig nature *f* contagieuse.
infective /ɪnˈfektɪv/ *adj* pathogène.
infelicitous /ˌɪnfɪˈlɪsɪtəs/ *adj* sout [*expression, translation*] maladroit.
infelicity /ˌɪnfɪˈlɪsətɪ/ *n* sout (unfortunate expression, translation) maladresse *f*.
infer /ɪnˈfɜː(r)/ *vtr* (*p prés etc* **-rr-**) **1** (deduce) inférer fml, déduire (**from** de); **2** usage critiqué (imply) suggérer.
inference /ˈɪnfərəns/ *n* **1** (act, process) déduction *f*, inférence *f* fml; **by ~** par déduction, par voie de conséquence; **2** (conclusion) conclusion *f*, déduction *f*; **the ~ is that** on en conclut or déduit que; **to draw an ~ from** tirer une conclusion de; **3** usage critiqué (hint, implication) suggestion *f*.
inferior /ɪnˈfɪərɪə(r)/ I *n* inférieur/-e *m/f*; Mil subalterne *mf*, subordonné/-e *m/f*.

II *adj* **1** (poor quality) [*goods, workmanship*] de qualité inférieure; **2** [*position*] inférieur; **to make sb feel ~** donner un sentiment d'infériorité à qn; **3** Print [*symbol, letter, number*] en indice; **4** Bot infère.

inferior court *n* tribunal *m* inférieur.

inferiority /ɪnˌfɪərɪˈɒrətɪ, US -ˈɔːr-/ *n* infériorité *f* (**to** vis-à-vis de).

inferiority complex *n* complexe *m* d'infériorité.

infernal /ɪnˈfɜːnl/ *adj* **1**○ (damned) [*cat, phone, child etc*] maudit○; (appalling) [*noise, row, weather*] infernal○; **2** (of hell) infernal; **the ~ regions** les enfers *mpl*; **3** (devilish) [*cruelty, wickedness*] abominable.

infernally /ɪnˈfɜːnəlɪ/ *adv* [*difficult, noisy*] abominablement.

inferno /ɪnˈfɜːnəʊ/ *n* **1** (conflagration) brasier *m*; **2** (hell) enfer *m* also fig.

infertile /ɪnˈfɜːtaɪl, US -tl/ *adj* **1** [*land, soil*] infertile, stérile; **2** [*person, couple*] stérile.

infertility /ˌɪnfəˈtɪlətɪ/ *n* **1** (of land, soil) stérilité *f*, infertilité *f*; **2** (of person) stérilité *f*.

infertility: **~ clinic** *n* centre *m* d'examens et de soins pour les personnes stériles; **~ treatment** *n* traitement *m* contre la stérilité.

infest /ɪnˈfest/ *vtr* infester; **~ed with rats**, **rat-~ed** infesté de rats.

infestation /ˌɪnfesˈteɪʃn/ *n* infestation *f*.

infidel /ˈɪnfɪdəl/ *n, adj* Hist, Relig infidèle (*mf*).

infidelity /ˌɪnfɪˈdelətɪ/ *n* infidélité *f*.

infighting /ˈɪnfaɪtɪŋ/ *n* **1** (internal conflict) conflits *mpl* internes; **2** (in boxing) corps à corps *m*.

infill /ˈɪnfɪl/ *n* (all contexts) remplissage *m*.

infiltrate /ˈɪnfɪltreɪt/ **I** *vtr* **1** infiltrer [*liquid, gas*]; **2** Mil, Pol infiltrer [*meeting, territory*]; noyauter, infiltrer [*organization, group*].
II *vi* [*liquid, gas, light, troops*] s'infiltrer (**into** dans).

infiltration /ˌɪnfɪlˈtreɪʃn/ *n* gen infiltration *f*; Mil, Pol infiltration *f*, noyautage *m*.

infinite /ˈɪnfɪnət/ **I** *n* **the ~** l'infini *m*.
II *adj* **1** (boundless) [*patience, number, variety*] infini; [*wealth*] illimité; **in his ~ wisdom** Relig ou iron dans son immense sagesse; **to give ~ pleasure to sb** faire infiniment plaisir à qn; **with ~ care** avec infiniment de soin; **2** Math [*series, decimal*] infini.

infinitely /ˈɪnfɪnətlɪ/ *adv* infiniment.

infinitesimal /ˌɪnfɪnɪˈtesɪml/ *adj* **1** [*amount*] infinitésimal, infime; [*increase, chance*] infime; **2** Math infinitésimal.

infinitive /ɪnˈfɪnətɪv/ *n* Ling infinitif *m*; **in the ~** à l'infinitif.

infinitive marker *n* Ling marqueur *m* d'infinitif.

infinitude /ɪnˈfɪnɪtjuːd, US -tuːd/ *n* littér infinitude *f*.

infinity /ɪnˈfɪnətɪ/ *n* **1** gen, Math, Phot infini *m*; **to ~** à l'infini; **2** (incalculable number) **an ~ of**... une infinité de...

infirm /ɪnˈfɜːm/ **I** *n* **the ~** (+ *v pl*) les infirmes *mpl*, les invalides *mpl*.
II *adj* **1** (weak) infirme, invalide; **2**‡ **~ of purpose** irrésolu.

infirmary /ɪnˈfɜːmərɪ/ *n* **1** (in school, prison) infirmerie *f*; **2** (hospital) hôpital *m*.

infirmity /ɪnˈfɜːmətɪ/ *n* (illness) infirmité *f*.

infix /ɪnˈfɪks/ *n* Ling infixe *m*.

in flagrante delicto /ɪn flæɡræntɪ ˌdeɪˈlɪktəʊ/ *adv phr* en flagrant délit.

inflame /ɪnˈfleɪm/ *vtr* **1** (fire up) enflammer [*imagination*]; exacerber [*passion*]; enflammer, échauffer [*crowd, audience*]; **to be ~d with desire** brûler de désir; **2** (exacerbate) aggraver [*conflict, situation*]; **3** Med enflammer.

inflamed /ɪnˈfleɪmd/ *adj* Med enflammé.

inflammable /ɪnˈflæməbl/ *adj* inflammable.

inflammation /ˌɪnfləˈmeɪʃn/ *n* Med inflammation *f*.

inflammatory /ɪnˈflæmətrɪ, US -tɔːrɪ/ *adj* **1** [*speech, remarks, language*] incendiaire; **2** Med inflammatoire.

inflatable /ɪnˈfleɪtəbl/ **I** *n* gen objet *m* gonflable; (dinghy) canot *m* pneumatique; (toy) jouet *m* gonflable.
II *adj* [*mattress, dinghy*] pneumatique; [*tube, toy, lifejacket*] gonflable.

inflate /ɪnˈfleɪt/ **I** *vtr* **1** gonfler [*balloon, tyre, toy, lifejacket*]; dilater, gonfler [*lung*]; **2** fig gonfler [*price, bill, ego*]; **3** Econ **to ~ the economy** accroître la circulation monétaire.
II *vi* [*tyre, toy*] se gonfler.

inflated /ɪnˈfleɪtɪd/ *adj* **1** (excessive) [*price*] gonflé; [*fee, salary*] excessif/-ive; [*claim, reputation, importance*] exagéré; [*style, language*] boursouflé; **to have an ~ ego** avoir une très haute opinion de soi-même; **2** [*tyre, lifejacket*] gonflé; **3** Med [*lung*] dilaté, gonflé.

inflation /ɪnˈfleɪʃn/ *n* **1** Econ inflation *f*; **with ~ (running) at 10%** avec une inflation de 10%; **rate of ~** taux *m* d'inflation; **2** (of dinghy, tyre) gonflement *m*, gonflage *m*; **3** Med (of lung) dilatation *f*, gonflement *m*.

inflation-adjusted *adj* ajusté sur l'inflation.

inflationary /ɪnˈfleɪʃnrɪ, US -nerɪ/ *adj* Econ [*pressure, spiral, wage claim*] inflationniste.

inflation rate *n* taux *m* d'inflation.

inflect /ɪnˈflekt/ **I** *vtr* **1** Ling conjuguer [*verb*]; décliner [*noun, adjective*]; **to be ~ed with 'ed'** prendre la terminaison 'ed'; **2** (modulate) moduler [*voice*]; Mus altérer; **3** (curve) (in)fléchir [*ray*].
II *vi* Ling [*verb*] se conjuguer; [*noun, adjective*] se décliner; **this word does not ~ in the plural** ce mot reste invariable au pluriel.

inflected /ɪnˈflektɪd/ *adj* Ling [*language*] flexionnel/-elle; [*form*] fléchi.

inflection /ɪnˈflekʃn/ *n* **1** Ling (of radical) flexion *f*; (of vowel) inflexion *f*; **the ~ of nouns and verbs** la flexion nominale et verbale; **2** (modulation) (of voice, tone) inflexion *f*; Mus altération *f*; **3** Math, Phys inflexion *f*; **4** (bend) (of body) inflexion *f*.

inflectional /ɪnˈflekʃənl/ *adj* [*language*] flexionnel/-elle; **an ~ ending** une flexion suffixale.

inflexibility /ɪnˌfleksəˈbɪlətɪ/ *n* **1** (of attitude, will, rule) inflexibilité *f*; (of system, method) rigidité *f*; **2** (of material, structure) rigidité *f*.

inflexible /ɪnˈfleksəbl/ *adj* **1** fig [*person, attitude, will*] inflexible; [*system*] rigide; **2** [*material*] rigide.

inflexion *n* GB = **inflection**.

inflict /ɪnˈflɪkt/ *vtr* infliger [*pain, torture, defeat, punishment*] (**on** à); causer [*damage*]; **to ~ a wound on sb** blesser qn; **to ~ one's presence/one's diet on sb** hum infliger sa présence/son régime à qn.

in-flight /ˌɪnˈflaɪt/ *adj* (all contexts) en vol.

inflow /ˈɪnfləʊ/ *n* **1** (of cash, goods, people) afflux *m*; **capital ~** afflux de capitaux; **2** (into tank, reservoir) arrivée *f*.

inflow pipe *n* tuyau *m* d'arrivée.

influence /ˈɪnflʊəns/ **I** *n* **1** (force, factor affecting sth) influence *f* (**on** sur); **to be** ou **have an important ~** avoir une influence importante; **to have** ou **be a good/bad ~** avoir une bonne/mauvaise influence; **a moderating/evil ~** une influence modératrice/néfaste; **his ~s are Lou Reed and Bob Dylan** Lou Reed et Bob Dylan l'ont influencé; **to be under sb's ~** subir l'influence de qn; **to be under the ~ of sth** être sous l'influence de qch; **to be under the ~** euph, hum être éméché○; **to drive while under the ~ of alcohol** Jur conduire en état d'ébriété; **2** (power, capacity to affect sth) influence *f* (**with sb** auprès de qn; **over sb/sth** sur qn/qch); **to have ~** avoir de l'influence; **to use one's ~** user de son influence (**to do** pour faire); **to bring one's ~ to bear on sb** exercer son influence sur qn.
II *vtr* influencer [*child, voter, artist, jury*]; influer sur [*decision, choice, ideas, design, events, result*]; **don't let him ~ you!** ne le laisse pas t'influencer!; **I don't want to ~ you one way or the other** je ne veux pas t'influencer dans un sens ou dans l'autre; **to ~ sb in his/her choice/decision** influencer qn dans son choix/sa décision; **to ~ sb to do** inciter qn à faire; **to be ~d by sb/sth** se laisser influencer par qn/qch; **to be heavily** ou **strongly ~d by sb/sth** être fortement influencé par qn/qch.

influence peddling *n* trafic *m* d'influence.

influential /ˌɪnflʊˈenʃl/ **I** *n* **the ~** (+ *v pl*) les gens qui comptent, les gens en place.
II *adj* **1** (respected) [*theory, movement, theorist, artist, programme*] très suivi; [*newspaper, commentator*] très écouté; [*study, survey, work*] très remarqué; **2** (key) [*factor, event, fact*] déterminant; **3** (powerful) [*businessman, banker, person*] influent, qui compte; **she's very ~** c'est quelqu'un qui compte; **to have ~ friends** avoir des amis importants ou en place.

influenza /ˌɪnflʊˈenzə/ ▶ **1354** *n* grippe *f*.

influx /ˈɪnflʌks/ *n* **1** (of people, money) afflux *m*; **a sudden ~ of refugees into the area** un afflux soudain de réfugiés dans la région; **2** (of liquid) arrivée *f*.

info○ /ˈɪnfəʊ/ *n* renseignements *mpl*, tuyaux○ *mpl*.

inform /ɪnˈfɔːm/ **I** *vtr* **1** (notify, tell) informer [*person, authorities, police, public, consumer*] (**of, about** de; **that** du fait que); **I ~ed him (that) his visit was unnecessary** je lui ai fait savoir que sa visite était inutile; **I would like to be ~ed** j'aimerais être averti; **why wasn't I ~ed?** pourquoi n'ai-je pas été informé or averti?; **to keep sb ~ed** tenir qn informé or au courant (**of, as to** de); **I ~ed him of my views** je lui ai fait part de mes vues; **I am pleased/sorry to ~ you that** j'ai le plaisir/le regret de vous informer du fait que; **to ~ sb if/when** avertir qn si/quand; **2** (pervade, give essential features to) [*idea, premise, sense*] guider [*writing, work, policy, law*].
II *vi* **1** (denounce) **to ~ on** ou **against** dénoncer; **2** (give information) informer.
III *v refl* **to ~ oneself** s'informer (**about** sur).

informal /ɪnˈfɔːml/ *adj* **1** (unaffected) [*person*] sans façons; [*manner, style, tone*] simple; **to greet sb in an ~ manner** ou **way** accueillir qn en toute simplicité; **2** (casual) [*language*] familier/-ière; **~ clothes** vêtements *mpl* de tous les jours; **dress ~** (on invitation) tenue *f* de ville; **3** (relaxed) [*atmosphere, mood*] décontracté; [*club, group*] informel/-elle; [*meal*] sans cérémonies; **4** (unofficial) [*announcement, request*] officieux/-ieuse; [*visit*] privé; [*invitation*] verbal; [*discussion, interview*] informel/-elle; **on an ~ basis** de façon informelle; **we have an ~ arrangement** nous avons un arrangement entre nous.

informality /ˌɪnfɔːˈmælətɪ/ *n* **1** (of person, event) simplicité *f*; (of arrangement, meeting) caractère *m* informel; (of gathering, workplace) ambiance *f* décontractée; **I liked the ~ of the ceremony** j'ai apprécié la simplicité de la cérémonie; **2** Ling (of language) style *m* familier.

informally /ɪnˈfɔːməlɪ/ *adv* **1** (without ceremony) [*dress*] en tenue décontractée; [*speak, meet*] en toute simplicité; [*greet*] sans cérémonie; **2** (unofficially) [*act, agree, arrange, discuss, suggest*] officieusement; **to invite sb ~** [*statesman*] inviter qn à titre privé.

informant /ɪnˈfɔːmənt/ *n* **1** Journ, Ling, gen (source of information) informateur/-trice *m/f*; **2** (informer) indicateur/-trice *m/f*.

informatics /ˌɪnfəˈmætɪks/ *n* informatique *f*.

information /ˌɪnfəˈmeɪʃn/ *n* ¢ **1** (facts,

details) renseignements *mpl*, informations *fpl* (**on, about** sur); **a piece** ou **bit** ou **item of ~** un renseignement, une information; **to pass on ~** communiquer des renseignements or informations; **freedom of ~** liberté d'information; **I need more ~** j'ai besoin de plus amples renseignements; **I have no ~ about that** je ne dispose pas de renseignements or d'informations à ce sujet; **we have very little ~** nous avons très peu de renseignements or d'informations; **my ~ is that** selon mes renseignements or informations; **for further** ou **additional** ou **more ~** pour plus de renseignements or d'informations; **to enclose sth for ~** joindre qch pour information or à titre de renseignement; **'for ~'** 'pour information', 'à titre de renseignement'; **for your ~, I've never even met him!** au cas où tu ne le saurais pas, je ne l'ai jamais rencontré!; **2** US Telecom (service *m* des) renseignements *mpl*; **to call ~** appeler les renseignements; **3** Comput informations *fpl*.

information: **~ bureau** *n* bureau *m* des renseignements; **~ content** *n* contenu *m* informationnel; **~ desk** *n* réception *f*; **~ exchange** *n* échange *m* d'informations; **~ office** = **information bureau**.

information officer *n* **1** (PR person, press officer) préposé/-e *m/f* à l'information; **2** (responsible for IT) agent *m* d'information.

information: **~ pack** *n* documentation *f*; **~ processing** *n* traitement *m* de l'information; **~ retrieval** *n* recherche *f* documentaire; **~ retrieval system** *n* système *m* de recherche documentaire; **~ room** *n* (in police station) salle *f* radio; **~ science** *n* science *f* de l'information, informatique *f*; **~ scientist** *n* informaticien/-ienne *m/f*; **~ service** *n* service *m* de renseignements; **~ superhighway** *n* Comput autoroutes *fpl* de l'information, inforoutes *fpl*; **~ system** *n* système *m* informatique; **~ technology**, **IT** *n* technologie *f* de l'information, informatique *f*; **~ theory** *n* théorie *f* de l'information; **~ transfer** *n* transfert *m* d'information.

informative /ɪnˈfɔːmətɪv/ *adj* [*lecture, talk, leaflet, book*] riche en renseignements; [*trip, evening, day*] instructif/-ive; [*speaker, guide, lecturer*] savant.

informed /ɪnˈfɔːmd/ *adj* **1** [*choice, debate, decision, judgment, opinion, guess*] fondé; **ill-~** non fondé; **2** [*person, critic, public, consumer*] averti; [*source*] informé; **he is very well-/ill-~** il est très bien/mal informé or renseigné.

informer /ɪnˈfɔːmə(r)/ *n* **1** (to police, authorities) indicateur/-trice *m/f*; **to turn ~** dénoncer or vendre ses complices; **2** (adviser) informateur/-trice *m/f*.

infraction /ɪnˈfrækʃn/ *n* infraction *f* (**of** à).

infra dig /ˌɪnfrəˈdɪg/ *adj* hum indigne, déshonorant.

infrared /ˌɪnfrəˈred/ *adj* infrarouge.

infrared: **~ photograph** *n* photographie *m* infrarouge; **~ sensor** *n* détecteur *m* infrarouge.

infrasonic /ˌɪnfrəˈsɒnɪk/ *adj* infrasonore.

infrastructure /ˈɪnfrəstrʌktʃə(r)/ *n* (all contexts) infrastructure *f*.

infrequency /ɪnˈfriːkwənsɪ/ *n* rareté *f*.

infrequent /ɪnˈfriːkwənt/ *adj* rare.

infrequently /ɪnˈfriːkwəntlɪ/ *adv* rarement; **not ~** assez fréquemment.

infringe /ɪnˈfrɪndʒ/ **I** *vtr* enfreindre [*rule, law, ban*]; ne pas respecter [*civil liberties, rights, copyright*]; commettre une contrefaçon de [*patent*].
II *vi* **to ~ on** ou **upon** empiéter sur [*rights, sovereignty*].

infringement /ɪnˈfrɪndʒmənt/ *n* (of rule) infraction *f* (**of** à); (of rights, liberty) violation *f*; (of patent, trademark) contrefaçon *f*.

infuriate /ɪnˈfjʊərɪeɪt/ *vtr* faire rager, exaspérer [*person*].

infuriated /ɪnˈfjʊərɪeɪtɪd/ *adj* exaspéré.

infuriating /ɪnˈfjʊərɪeɪtɪŋ/ *adj* exaspérant.

infuriatingly /ɪnˈfjʊərɪeɪtɪŋlɪ/ *adv* [*laugh, reply*] de façon exaspérante; **~ slow** d'une lenteur exaspérante.

infuse /ɪnˈfjuːz/ **I** *vtr* **1** (inject, imbue) **to ~ sth with sth** insuffler qch à qch; **to ~ a project with enthusiasm** insuffler de l'enthousiasme à un projet; **to ~ sth into** insuffler qch à [*society, work, person*]; **the movement was ~d with new life** un nouvel élan a été insufflé au mouvement; **2** Culin faire infuser [*tea, herb*]; **vinegar ~d with tarragon** vinaigre aromatisé à l'estragon.
II *vi* infuser.

infusion /ɪnˈfjuːʒn/ *n* **1** (of cash, aid) injection *f*; **an ~ of new life** un souffle nouveau; **2** Culin infusion *f*.

ingenious /ɪnˈdʒiːnɪəs/ *adj* ingénieux/-ieuse, astucieux/-ieuse.

ingeniously /ɪnˈdʒiːnɪəslɪ/ *adv* [*solve, design*] ingénieusement, astucieusement; **~ designed** d'une conception ingénieuse.

ingénue /ˈænʒeɪnjuː, US ˈændʒənuː/ *n* ingénue *f*.

ingenuity /ˌɪndʒɪˈnjuːətɪ, US -ˈnuː-/ *n* ingéniosité *f*; **to use one's ~** déployer toute son ingéniosité.

ingenuous /ɪnˈdʒenjʊəs/ *adj* ingénu, candide.

ingenuously /ɪnˈdʒenjʊəslɪ/ *adv* [*ask, remark*] ingénument, candidement.

ingenuousness /ɪnˈdʒenjʊəsnɪs/ *n* ingénuité *f*, candeur *f*.

ingest /ɪnˈdʒest/ *vtr* **1** lit ingérer [*food, liquid*]; **2** fig absorber, assimiler [*fact*].

ingestion /ɪnˈdʒestʃn/ *n* lit (of food) ingestion *f*.

inglenook /ˈɪŋglnʊk/ *n* GB coin *m* du feu.

inglorious /ɪnˈglɔːrɪəs/ *adj* littér déshonorant, infamant.

ingot /ˈɪŋgət/ *n* lingot *m*.

ingrained /ɪnˈgreɪnd/ *adj* **1** [*dirt*] bien incrusté; **2** (deep-rooted) [*habit, tendency*] invétéré, enraciné; [*prejudice, hatred*] enraciné, tenace; **to be deeply ~ in** être profondément ancré dans [*person, heart, society*].

ingrate /ˈɪngreɪt/ *n* ingrat/-e *m/f*.

ingratiate /ɪnˈgreɪʃɪeɪt/ *v refl* péj **to ~ oneself** se faire bien voir (**with sb** de qn).

ingratiating /ɪnˈgreɪʃɪeɪtɪŋ/ *adj* péj doucereux/-euse.

ingratitude /ɪnˈgrætɪtjuːd, US -tuːd/ *n* ingratitude *f*.

ingredient /ɪnˈgriːdɪənt/ *n* **1** Culin ingrédient *m*; **2** fig élément *m* (**of** de).

ingress /ˈɪŋgres/ *n* Jur entrée *f*.

ingressive /ˌɪŋˈgresɪv/ Ling **I** *n* ingressive *f*.
II *adj* ingressif/-ive.

in-group /ˈɪngruːp/ *n* péj clique *f*, côterie *f*.

ingrowing toenail, **ingrown toenail** *n* ongle *m* de pied incarné.

inguinal /ˈɪŋgwɪnl/ *adj* inguinal.

inhabit /ɪnˈhæbɪt/ **I** *vtr* **1** lit habiter [*house, region, planet*]; **2** fig vivre dans [*fantasy world, milieu*].
II inhabited *pp adj* [*land, cave, planet*] habité.

inhabitable /ɪnˈhæbɪtəbl/ *adj* habitable.

inhabitant /ɪnˈhæbɪtənt/ *n* habitant/-e *m/f*.

inhalant /ɪnˈheɪlənt/ *n* inhalant *m*.

inhalation /ˌɪnhəˈleɪʃn/ *n* inhalation *f*, aspiration *f*.

inhalator /ɪnˈheɪlətə(r)/ *n* inhalateur *m*, respirateur *m*.

inhale /ɪnˈheɪl/ **I** *vtr* aspirer, inhaler [*vapour, fumes*]; avaler [*smoke, vomit*]; humer, respirer [*scent*].
II *vi* (breathe in) inspirer; (take in smoke) avaler la fumée; **to ~ deeply** inspirer profondément.

inhaler /ɪnˈheɪlə(r)/ *n* inhalateur *m*.

inharmonious /ˌɪnhɑːˈməʊnɪəs/ *adj* peu harmonieux/-ieuse.

inhere /ɪnˈhɪə(r)/ *vi* être inhérent (**in** à).

inherent /ɪnˈhɪərənt, ɪnˈherənt/ *adj* **to be ~ in** être inhérent or propre à; **the ~ limitations of** les limitations inhérentes à; **with its ~ risks** avec les risques qui lui sont inhérents.

inherently /ɪnˈhɪərəntlɪ, ɪnˈher-/ *adv* [*comic, complex, evil*] naturellement; [*involve, entail, encourage*] par sa nature.

inherit /ɪnˈherɪt/ *vtr* hériter de [*money, property*]; hériter de, succéder à [*title*]; fig hériter de [*problem, tradition*]; **to ~ sth from sb** hériter qch de qn; **she has ~ed her mother's intelligence** elle a hérité l'intelligence de sa mère; **I've ~ed my mother's cat** j'ai hérité le chat de ma mère.

inheritance /ɪnˈherɪtəns/ *n* **1** (thing inherited) héritage *m* also fig; **to come into an ~** faire un héritage; **2** (succession) succession *f*; **by** ou **through ~** par voie de succession; **3** Biol patrimoine *m* héréditaire.

inheritance tax *n* US droits *mpl* de succession.

inherited /ɪnˈherɪtɪd/ *adj* [*characteristic, disease*] héréditaire; [*wealth, debt, tradition*] hérité.

inheritor /ɪnˈherɪtə(r)/ *n* (all contexts) héritier/-ière *m/f*.

inhibit /ɪnˈhɪbɪt/ *vtr* **1** (restrain) inhiber [*person, reaction*]; entraver [*situation, activity, choice, progress*]; **to ~ sb from doing** (prevent) empêcher qn de faire; (discourage) dissuader qn de faire qch; **2** Psych inhiber [*person*]; **3** Sci inhiber [*function*]; **4** Jur (prohibit) interdire, défendre (**from doing** de faire).

inhibited /ɪnˈhɪbɪtɪd/ *adj* [*person, thinking*] inhibé, refoulé; [*activity, development*] entravé; **to be ~ by** [*person*] être handicapé par [*lack of confidence, inexperience*].

inhibiting /ɪnˈhɪbɪtɪŋ/ *adj* inhibiteur/-trice.

inhibition /ˌɪnhɪˈbɪʃn, ˌɪnɪˈb-/ *n* inhibition *f*; **to get rid of one's ~s** se libérer de ses inhibitions.

inhibitor /ɪnˈhɪbɪtə(r)/ *n* (all contexts) inhibiteur *m*.

inhibitory /ɪnˈhɪbɪtərɪ, US -tɔːrɪ/ *adj* (all contexts) inhibiteur/-trice.

inhospitable /ˌɪnhɒˈspɪtəbl/ *adj* [*country, climate, person*] inhospitalier/-ière; [*behaviour*] désobligeant.

inhospitably /ˌɪnhɒˈspɪtəblɪ/ *adv* [*act*] sans hospitalité.

inhospitality /ɪnˌhɒspɪˈtælətɪ/ *n* inhospitalité *f*.

in-house /ˈɪnhaʊs, -ˈhaʊs/ *adj* [*training, service, worker*] interne; **he is ~** il est de la maison.

inhuman /ɪnˈhjuːmən/ *adj* inhumain.

inhumane /ˌɪnhjuːˈmeɪn/ *adj* inhumain, cruel/-elle.

inhumanity /ˌɪnhjuːˈmænətɪ/ *n* inhumanité *f*, cruauté *f*; **man's ~ to man** la cruauté de l'homme envers son semblable.

inhumation /ˌɪnhjuːˈmeɪʃn/ *n* sout inhumation *f*.

inhume /ɪnˈhjuːm/ *vtr* sout inhumer.

inimical /ɪˈnɪmɪkl/ *adj* inamical, hostile; **to be ~ to** aller à l'encontre de [*interest, aim*]; être nuisible à [*unity, sovereignty*].

inimitable /ɪˈnɪmɪtəbl/ *adj* inimitable; **in her own ~ way** dans son style inimitable, à sa manière à elle.

iniquitous /ɪˈnɪkwɪtəs/ *adj* [*practice, system, tax*] inique, injuste.

iniquity /ɪˈnɪkwətɪ/ *n* (all contexts) iniquité *f*.

initial /ɪˈnɪʃl/ **I** *n* initiale *f*; **to sign one's ~s** signer de ses initiales.
II *adj* [*symptoms, shock, reaction*] initial, premier/-ière; [*shyness, reticence*] initial, du début; **~ letter** initiale *f*; **in the ~ stages** dans un premier temps.
III *vtr* (*p prés etc* GB **-ll-**, US **-l-**) gen parapher or parafer [*document*]; (authorize) viser et parapher.

initial expenses *npl* Comm frais *mpl* de premier établissement.

initialization /ˌɪnɪʃəlaɪˈzeɪʃn, US -lɪˈz-/ *n* Comput initialisation *f*.

initialize /ɪˈnɪʃəlaɪz/ *vtr* Comput initialiser.

initially /ɪˈnɪʃəlɪ/ *adv* au départ.

Initial Teaching Alphabet, ITA *n* Sch *alphabet phonétique à l'usage des enfants*.

initiate I /ɪˈnɪʃɪət/ *n* initié/-e *m/f*.
II /ɪˈnɪʃɪeɪt/ *vtr* **1** mettre en œuvre [*plan, project, reform*]; amorcer [*talks*]; entreprendre [*improvements, reorganization*]; **to ~ proceedings against sb** Jur entamer or engager des poursuites contre qn; **2** (admit) **to ~ sb into** (into membership) admettre qn au sein de [*secret society, club*]; (into knowledge) initier qn à [*astrology, art of love*]; **3** Comput lancer [*programme*]; amorcer, établir [*communication*].

initiation /ɪˌnɪʃɪˈeɪʃn/ I *n* **1** (of negotiations) amorce *f*; (of scheme, process) lancement *m*; **2** (admission) (into sect) admission *f* (**into** au sein de); (into knowledge) initiation *f* (**into** à); **3** (ceremony) cérémonie *f* d'initiation.
II *modif* [*ceremony, rite*] d'initiation.

initiative /ɪˈnɪʃətɪv/ *n* **1** (quality) initiative *f*; **to have** ou **show ~** faire preuve d'initiative; **use your ~!** (as advice) fais preuve d'initiative!; (as reproof) un peu d'initiative quand même!; **on one's own ~** de son propre chef; **2** (move) initiative *f*; **to take the ~** prendre l'initiative (**in doing** de faire); **peace ~(s)** initiative(s) de paix; **3** (upper hand) **to take/lose the ~** prendre/perdre l'initiative; **4** Pol Jur initiative *f*.

initiative test *n* Psych test *m* d'initiative.

initiator /ɪˈnɪʃɪeɪtə(r)/ *n* instigateur/-trice *m/f*.

inject /ɪnˈdʒekt/ I *vtr* **1** lit injecter [*liquid, vaccine, fuel*] (**into** dans); **to ~ sb with sth** Med faire une injection de qch à qn; **to ~ sb against sth** vacciner qn contre qch; **'to be ~ed intravenously'** 'par voie intraveineuse'; **2** fig apporter [*new ideas*] (**into** à); insuffler [*hope, life, enthusiasm*] (**into** à); injecter [*cash, capital*] (**into** dans).
II *v refl* **to ~ oneself with** se faire des injections de [*insulin*]; se piquer○ à [*heroin*].

injection /ɪnˈdʒekʃn/ *n* **1** Med piqûre *f*, injection *f* spec; **2** Tech injection *f*.

injection moulding GB, **injection molding** US *n* moulage *m* par injection.

injector /ɪnˈdʒektə(r)/ *n* Aut injecteur *m*.

in-joke /ˈɪndʒəʊk/ *n* **it's an ~** c'est une plaisanterie entre nous; **it's a BBC ~** c'est une plaisanterie interne à la BBC.

injudicious /ˌɪndʒuːˈdɪʃəs/ *adj* sout [*act, remark, statement*] peu judicieux/-ieuse.

injudiciously /ˌɪndʒuːˈdɪʃəslɪ/ *adv* [*remark, act*] peu judicieusement.

injunction /ɪnˈdʒʌŋkʃn/ *n* **1** Jur injonction *f* (**to do** de faire; **against** contre); **to ask for an ~** faire une requête en injonction; **2** (admonition) injonction *f*, recommandation *f* formelle.

injure /ˈɪndʒə(r)/ I *vtr* **1** Med blesser [*person*]; **seriously/fatally ~d** grièvement/mortellement blessé; **nobody was ~d** personne n'a été blessé; **to ~ one's hand/knee** se blesser la main/le genou; **2** (damage) nuire à [*health*]; compromettre, ternir [*reputation*]; compromettre, léser [*interests*]; porter un coup à, blesser [*self-esteem*]; **to ~ sb's feelings** faire de la peine à qn.
II *v refl* **to ~ oneself** se blesser; (slightly) se faire mal.

injured /ˈɪndʒəd/ I *n* **the ~** (+ *v pl*) gen les blessés *mpl*; (in accident) les accidentés *mpl*.
II *adj* **1** Med [*person*] blessé; (in accident) accidenté; [*limb, back*] blessé; **2** fig [*pride, feelings*] blessé; [*tone, look*] offensé, blessé; **3** (wronged) [*wife, husband*] trompé; **the ~ party** Jur la partie lésée.
III *modif* **~ list** liste *f* des blessés.

injurious /ɪnˈdʒʊərɪəs/ *adj* sout **1** (harmful) **~ to** nuisible or préjudiciable à [*health, economy*]; **2** (abusive) [*remark*] blessant, offensant.

injury /ˈɪndʒərɪ/ *n* **1** Med blessure *f*; **head/internal injuries** blessures à la tête/internes; **to do sb an ~** blesser qn; **to do oneself an ~** hum se faire mal; **2** fig (to reputation) atteinte *f*; **3** Jur préjudice *m*, dommage *m*.

injury: **~ benefit** *n* GB allocation *f* versée à un/-e accidenté/-e du travail; **~ time** *n* Sport arrêts *mpl* de jeu.

injustice /ɪnˈdʒʌstɪs/ *n* injustice *f*; **to do sb an ~** être or se montrer injuste envers qn.

ink /ɪŋk/ I *n* (all contexts) encre *f*; **in ~** à l'encre.
II *modif* [*bottle, stain*] d'encre; [*eraser*] à encre.
III *vtr* encrer.
IDIOMS **as black as ~** d'un noir d'encre.
■ **ink in**: **~ in [sth]**, **~ [sth] in** repasser [qch] à l'encre [*form, drawing*].

ink: **~blot** *n* tache *f* d'encre, pâté *m*; **~blot test** *n* test *m* de Rorschach; **~ drawing** *n* dessin *m* à l'encre; **~jet printer** *n* imprimante *f* à jet d'encre.

inkling /ˈɪŋklɪŋ/ *n* petite idée *f*; **to have an ~ that** avoir l'idée que; **to have no ~ that** ne pas avoir la moindre idée que; **her expression gave no ~ of how she felt** son visage ne laissait rien deviner de ses sentiments; **that was the first ~ I had that all was not well** c'est alors que j'ai commencé à me douter que tout n'allait pas bien.

ink: **~pad** *n* tampon *m* encreur; **~pot** *n* encrier *m*; **~ sac** *n* poche *f* à encre; **~stand** *n* écritoire *f*; **~well** *n* encrier *m* de pupitre.

inky /ˈɪŋkɪ/ *adj* **1** lit [*fingers, page*] taché d'encre; **2** fig [*sky*] noir comme de l'encre.

inlaid /ˌɪnˈleɪd/ I *prét, pp* ▸ **inlay**.
II *adj* [*jewellery*] incrusté; [*box, furniture*] marqueté; [*sword*] damasquiné.

inland I /ˈɪnlənd/ *adj* **1** (not coastal) [*area, town, harbour*] intérieur; **~ navigation** navigation *f* intérieure; **~ waterways** canaux *mpl* et rivières *fpl*; **2** GB (domestic) [*communications, mail, trade, transport*] intérieur; **~ postage rate** tarif postal intérieur.
II /ˌɪnˈlænd/ *adv* [*travel, be situated*] à l'intérieur des terres; **to move further ~** pénétrer plus avant dans les terres.

inland: **~ bill** *n* GB Fin lettre *f* de change sur l'intérieur; **Inland Revenue** *n* GB service *m* des impôts britannique; **Inland Revenue Stamp** *n* timbre *m* fiscal.

in-laws /ˈɪnlɔːz/ *npl* (parents) beaux-parents *mpl*; (other relatives) belle-famille *f*; parents *mpl* par alliance.

inlay I /ˈɪnleɪ/ *n* **1** (on jewellery) incrustation *f*; (on box, furniture) marqueterie *f*; (on metal) damasquinage *m*; **brooch with enamel ~(s)** broche incrustée d'émail; **2** Dent inlay *m*, incrustation *f*.
II /ˌɪnˈleɪ/ *vtr* incruster [*jewellery*] (**with** de); marqueter [*wood*]; damasquiner [*sword*].

inlet /ˈɪnlet/ *n* **1** (of sea) bras *m* de mer, crique *f*; (of river) bras *m* de rivière; **2** Tech (for fuel, air) arrivée *f*, admission *f*.

inlet: **~ pipe** *n* tuyau *m* d'arrivée; **~ valve** *n* soupape *f* d'admission.

in loco parentis /ɪn ˌləʊkəʊ pəˈrentɪs/ *adj phr, adv phr* Jur in loco parentis, en lieu et place des parents.

inmate /ˈɪnmeɪt/ *n* **1** (of institution) (of hospital) malade *mf*; (of mental hospital) interné/-e *m/f*; (of prison) détenu/-e *m/f*, pensionnaire○ *mf*; **2**† (of house) occupant/-e *m/f*, résident/-e *m/f*.

inmost *adj* = **innermost**.

inn /ɪn/ *n* **1** (hotel) (small) auberge *f*; (larger) hôtellerie *f*; **2** (pub) pub *m*.

innards /ˈɪnədz/ *npl* lit, fig entrailles *fpl*.

innate /ɪˈneɪt/ *adj* [*quality, attribute, tendency*] inné, naturel/-elle.

innately /ɪˈneɪtlɪ/ *adv* naturellement.

inner /ˈɪnə(r)/ I *n* cercle *m* intérieur (d'une cible).
II *adj* (*épith*) **1** [*room, courtyard, wall, layer*] intérieur; **2** [*voice, conflict, life*] intérieur; [*emotion, thought*] intime; **the ~ circle** le petit groupe; **the ~ man** (spirit) l'homme *m* intérieur; hum l'estomac *m*.

inner city I *n* **the ~** les quartiers *mpl* déshérités.
II **inner-city** *modif* [*problems, crime, regeneration*] des quartiers déshérités; **an ~ area** ou **district** un quartier déshérité.

inner: **~-directed** *adj* individualiste; **~ ear** *n* oreille *f* interne.

innermost /ˈɪnəməʊst/ *adj* (*épith*) **1** (most intimate) **sb's ~ feelings/thoughts** les sentiments/les pensées les plus intimes de qn; **his ~ self** ou **being** le tréfonds de son âme liter; **2** (inmost) **the ~ part of** le cœur de [*country, island, continent*].

inner: **~ sanctum** *n* souvent hum antre *m*, saint *m* des saints; **~spring** *adj* US [*mattress*] à ressorts; **Inner Temple** *n* GB *une des quatre écoles de droit à Londres*; **~ tube** *n* chambre *f* à air.

inning /ˈɪnɪŋ/ *n* US (in baseball) tour *m* de batte.

innings /ˈɪnɪŋz/ *n* GB **1** (in cricket) (+ *v sg*) tour *m* de batte; **2** fig **to have had a good ~** (when dead) avoir bien profité de l'existence; (when leaving) avoir fait son temps.

innkeeper /ˈɪnkiːpə(r)/ *n* (of small inn) aubergiste *mf*; (larger) hôtelier/-ière *m/f*.

innocence /ˈɪnəsns/ *n* **1** (guilelessness) innocence *f*; **in all ~** en toute innocence; **an air of ~** un air innocent; **2** (naïvety) innocence *f*, naïveté *f*; **in my ~, I thought that...** dans mon innocence or naïf comme je suis, j'ai pensé que...; **3** Jur (of accused) innocence *f*; **to prove one's ~** prouver son innocence.

innocent /ˈɪnəsnt/ I *n* innocent/-e *m/f*, naïf/-ïve *m/f*; **they're no ~s!** ce ne sont pas des enfants de chœur!
II *adj* **1** Jur (not guilty) innocent (**of** de); **2** (blameless) [*victim, civilian, bystander*] innocent; **3** (innocuous) [*enjoyment, fun*] innocent, inoffensif/-ive; [*question, remark*] innocent, sans malice; [*error*] bénin/-igne; [*explanation, meeting*] anodin; **4** (naïve) innocent, naïf/-ïve; **she was ~ about such things** elle ne savait rien de ces choses-là; **5** (unaware) innocent; **~ of** inconscient de [*reaction, effect*].

innocent infringement (**of patent**) *n* Jur contrefaçon *f* involontaire.

innocently /ˈɪnəsntlɪ/ *adv* [*ask, reply, say*] innocemment; [*act, become involved*] en toute innocence.

innocent misrepresentation *n* Jur déclaration *f* inexacte non frauduleuse.

innocuous /ɪˈnɒkjʊəs/ *adj* **1** (inoffensive) [*remark, statement*] inoffensif/-ive, innocent; **2** (harmless) [*substance*] inoffensif/-ive.

innovate /ˈɪnəveɪt/ *vi* innover.

innovation /ˌɪnəˈveɪʃn/ *n* innovation *f*; **~s in medicine/in animal breeding** des innovations en médecine/dans l'élevage des animaux; **to make ~s in sth** apporter des innovations à qch.

innovative /ˈɪnəvətɪv/ *adj* innovateur/-trice.

innovator /ˈɪnəveɪtə(r)/ *n* innovateur/-trice *m/f*.

innovatory /ˌɪnəˈveɪtərɪ/ *adj* = **innovative**.

Inns of Court /ˌɪnz əv ˈkɔːt/ *npl* GB Jur Institut *m* britannique d'études judiciaires.

innuendo /ˌɪnjuːˈendəʊ/ *n* (*pl* **~s** ou **~es**) **1** (veiled slights) insinuations *fpl*; **a campaign of ~** une campagne d'insinuations; **2** (sexual references) allusions *fpl* grivoises.

innumerable /ɪˈnjuːmərəbl, US ɪˈnuː-/ *adj* innombrable, sans nombre.

innumeracy /ɪˈnjuːmərəsɪ, US ɪˈnuː-/ *n* GB

(inability to count) incapacité *f* de compter; (unfamiliarity with maths) ignorance *f* en calcul.

innumerate /ɪ'nju:mərət, US ɪ'nu:-/ *adj* GB **to be ~** (unable to count) être incapable de compter; (uncomfortable with maths) ne pas être à l'aise avec les chiffres.

inoculate /ɪ'nɒkjʊleɪt/ *vtr* Med vacciner (**against** contre); **to ~ sb with sth** inoculer qch à qn.

inoculation /ɪ,nɒkjʊ'leɪʃn/ *n* Med vaccination *f*, inoculation *f*.

inoffensive /,ɪnə'fensɪv/ *adj* inoffensif/-ive.

inoperable /ɪn'ɒpərəbl/ *adj* [*tumour, condition*] inopérable.

inoperative /ɪn'ɒpərətɪv/ *adj* inopérant.

inopportune /ɪn'ɒpətju:n, US -tu:n/ *adj* inopportun.

inopportunely /ɪn'ɒpətju:nlɪ, US -tu:n-/ *adv* inopportunément.

inordinate /ɪn'ɔ:dɪnət/ *adj* [*appetite, size*] énorme, démesuré; [*quantity, cost, pride*] démesuré; [*desire, passion*] immodéré; **an ~ amount of time** un temps infini.

inordinately /ɪn'ɔ:dɪnətlɪ/ *adv* [*long, wide*] démesurément; [*pleased, proud, careful*] extrêmement.

inorganic /,ɪnɔ:'gænɪk/ *adj* inorganique.

inorganic chemistry *n* chimie *f* inorganique.

in-patient /'ɪnpeɪʃnt/ *n* malade *mf* hospitalisé/-e.

input /'ɪnpʊt/ **I** *n* **1** ¢ (of money) apport *m*; (of energy) alimentation *f* (**of** en); **electrical ~** courant *m* d'entrée; **2** ¢ (contribution) contribution *f*; **her ~ was minimal** elle a fourni un minimum d'effort; **3** C Ind (resource) facteur *m* de production; **4** ¢ Comput (action) saisie *f* des données; (data) données *fpl* d'entrée or à traiter; (part of computer) bloc *m* d'entrée.
II *modif* [*device, protection*] d'entrée.
III *vtr* (*p prés* **-tt-**; *prét, pp* **-put** ou **-putted**) Comput saisir [*data*]; **to ~ data into a computer** entrer des données dans un ordinateur.

input data *n* Comput données *fpl* d'entrée or à traiter.

input-output /,ɪnpʊt'aʊtpʊt/ **I** *n* **1** Comput entrée-sortie *f*; **2** Econ échanges *mpl* interindustriels.
II *modif* **1** Comput [*unit, device, storage*] d'entrée-sortie; **2** Econ [*analysis, table*] des échanges interindustriels.

inquest /'ɪŋkwest/ *n* gen, Jur enquête *f* (**on, into** sur); **to hold an ~** mener or conduire une enquête (**into** sur).

inquire /ɪn'kwaɪə(r)/ **I** *vtr* demander; **to ~ the way to** ou **how to get to the bank** demander le chemin pour aller à la banque; **to ~ sth of** ou **from sb** demander qch à qn; **I ~d what age he was/whether he was ill** je lui ai demandé quel âge il avait/s'il était malade.
II *vi* se renseigner (**about** sur); **to ~ after sb** demander des nouvelles de qn, s'enquérir de qn fml; **to ~ into** (ask for information about) se renseigner sur; (research) faire des recherches sur; Admin, Jur enquêter sur; **to ~ into the truth of an allegation** vérifier si une accusation est fondée; **I'll go and ~** je vais demander; **'~ within'** 's'adresser ici'; **'~ at the information desk'** 's'adresser au bureau de renseignements'.

inquiring /ɪn'kwaɪərɪŋ/ *adj* [*look, voice*] interrogateur/-trice; [*mind*] curieux/-ieuse.

inquiringly /ɪn'kwaɪərɪŋlɪ/ *adv* [*look*] d'un air interrogateur.

inquiry /ɪn'kwaɪərɪ, US 'ɪŋkwərɪ/ **I** *n* **1** (request for information) demande *f* de renseignements; **to make an ~ about** ou **into** se renseigner sur; **to make inquiries** demander des renseignements (**about** sur); **on ~, it was discovered that** renseignements pris, on a découvert que; **'all inquiries to...'** 'pour tous renseignements, s'adresser à...'; **in answer to** ou **with reference to your ~** (by letter) en réponse à votre courrier; (by phone) suite à votre appel téléphonique; **2** Admin, Jur enquête *f*, investigation *f* (**into** sur); **police/public/judicial ~** enquête policière/publique/judiciaire; **murder ~** enquête criminelle; **to hold/conduct an ~** faire/ mener une enquête (**into** sur); **to set up** ou **open** ou **launch an ~** ouvrir une enquête; **a man is helping the police with their inquiries** un homme est interrogé par les policiers dans le cadre de leur enquête; **line of ~** piste *f*.
II *modif* [*report*] d'enquête; [*findings*] de l'enquête.
III inquiries *npl* bureau *m* or service *m* de renseignements *mpl*.

inquiry: **~ agent** *n* GB détective *m* privé; **~ response system** *n* Comput système *m* d'interrogation-réponse; **~ terminal** *n* Comput poste *m* d'interrogation-réponse.

inquisition /,ɪnkwɪ'zɪʃn/ **I** *n* (enquiry) enquête *f*; **why the ~?** hum pourquoi cet interrogatoire?
II Inquisition *pr n* Hist Inquisition *f*.

inquisitive /ɪn'kwɪzətɪv/ *adj* [*person, mind*] curieux/-ieuse, inquisiteur/-trice.

inquisitively /ɪn'kwɪzətɪvlɪ/ *adv* avec curiosité.

inquisitiveness /ɪn'kwɪzətɪvnɪs/ *n* curiosité *f*.

inquisitor /ɪn'kwɪzɪtə(r)/ *n* interrogateur/-trice *m/f*.

Inquisitor General *n* Hist Relig grand Inquisiteur *m*.

inquisitorial /ɪn,kwɪzɪ'tɔ:rɪəl/ *adj* [*interrogation*] inquisitorial.

inquisitorial system *n* Jur procédure *f* inquisitoire.

inquorate /ɪn'kwɔ:reɪt/ *adj* **the meeting is ~** le quorum n'a pas été atteint pour cette réunion.

inroad /'ɪnrəʊd/ *n* **1 to make ~s into** ou **on** US (advance, encroach on) faire une avancée sur [*market*]; entamer [*savings*]; réduire [*lead*]; **2** Mil incursion *f*.

inrush /'ɪnrʌʃ/ *n* (of air, water) irruption *f*.

insalubrious /,ɪnsə'lu:brɪəs/ *adj* (insanitary) insalubre; (sleazy) sordide.

insane /ɪn'seɪn/ *adj* **1** gen [*person*] fou/folle; [*idea, desire, decision*] fou/folle, insensé; [*plan*] démentiel/-ielle; **to go** ou **become ~** perdre la raison; **to drive sb ~** rendre qn fou; **is he ~?** mais il est fou ou quoi?; **2** Jur [*person*] aliéné; **to be declared ~** être reconnu aliéné.

insanely /ɪn'seɪnlɪ/ *adv* [*act, behave*] de façon insensée; **to be ~ jealous** être fou/folle de jalousie.

insanitary /ɪn'sænɪtərɪ, US -terɪ/ *adj* insalubre, malsain.

insanity /ɪn'sænətɪ/ *n* **1** gen (of person, plan) folie *f*; **2** Jur aliénation *f* mentale; **to enter a plea of ~** Jur faire valoir une exception d'irresponsabilité pour cause d'aliénation mentale.

insatiable /ɪn'seɪʃəbl/ *adj* insatiable.

insatiably /ɪn'seɪʃəblɪ/ *adv* [*hunger for, thirst for*] insatiablement; **~ curious** d'une curiosité insatiable.

inscribe /ɪn'skraɪb/ *vtr* **1** (write) (in book) inscrire (**in** dans); (engrave) (on stone, metal etc) graver (**on** sur); **to ~ sth with a verse, to ~ a verse on sth** graver des vers sur [*monument*]; inscrire des vers sur [*book*]; **a plaque ~d with his name** une plaque gravée à son nom; **the book was ~d 'To Bruno'** le livre portait l'inscription 'À Bruno'; **2** (sign) dédicacer [*book, photograph*]; **~d copy** exemplaire avec envoi; **3** Math inscrire.

inscription /ɪn'skrɪpʃn/ *n* gen inscription *f*; (in book) envoi *m*.

inscrutability /ɪn,skru:tə'bɪlətɪ/ *n* impénétrabilité *f*.

inscrutable /ɪn'skru:təbl/ *adj* [*smile, remark, person*] énigmatique; [*expression*] énigmatique, insondable.

inseam /'ɪn'si:m/ *n* US longueur *f* d'un pantalon (à partir de l'entrejambe).

insect /'ɪnsekt/ *n* insecte *m*.

insect: **~ bite** *n* piqûre *f* d'insecte; **~ eater** *n* insectivore *m*.

insecticide /ɪn'sektɪsaɪd/ *n, adj* insecticide (*m*).

insectivore /ɪn'sektɪvɔ:(r)/ *n* insectivore *m*.

insectivorous /,ɪnsek'tɪvərəs/ *adj* insectivore.

insect: **~ powder** *n* poudre *f* insecticide; **~ repellent** *n* insectifuge *m*, produit *m* anti-insecte; **~ spray** *n* bombe *f* insecticide.

insecure /,ɪnsɪ'kjʊə(r)/ *adj* **1** [*person*] (lacking confidence) qui manque d'assurance; (anxious) anxieux/-ieuse; **to be (very) ~** manquer (complètement) d'assurance; **to feel very ~ about the future** avoir des inquiétudes pour l'avenir; **2** Psych insécurisé; **3** (not reliable) [*arrangement, plan*] fragile; [*job, situation*] précaire; [*investment*] risqué; **4** (unsafe, loose) [*screw*] mal serré; [*bolt*] qui tient mal; [*lock*] peu sûr; [*rope*] mal attaché; [*structure*] branlant; [*door, window*] qui ferme mal; [*grip, foothold*] mal assuré; **5** (inadequately protected) [*fortress, outpost*] peu sûr.

insecurity /,ɪnsɪ'kjʊərətɪ/ *n* **1** (psychological) manque *m* d'assurance; (stronger) inquiétude *f*; **to suffer from feelings of ~** éprouver un sentiment d'insécurité; **2** (of position, situation) insécurité *f*; (of income) précarité *f*; **financial ~** précarité financière.

inseminate /ɪn'semɪneɪt/ *vtr* inséminer.

insemination /ɪn,semɪ'neɪʃn/ *n* insémination *f*.

insensate /ɪn'senseɪt/ *adj* **1** (inanimate, insentient) inanimé, insensible; **2** (insensitive, inhuman) insensible; **3** (senseless) insensé.

insensibility /ɪn,sensə'bɪlətɪ/ *n* **1** (indifference) insensibilité *f* (**to** à); **2** Med (to stimuli) insensibilité *f*; (unconsciousness) inconscience *f*.

insensible /ɪn'sensəbl/ *adj* **1** (indifferent) (to emotion, criticism) insensible, indifférent (**to** à); **2** Med (to stimuli) insensible (**to** à); (unconscious) inconscient, sans connaissance; **3** (unaware) inconscient (**of, to** de); **4** (imperceptible) [*change*] insensible, imperceptible.

insensitive /ɪn'sensətɪv/ *adj* **1** [*person*] (tactless) sans tact; (unfeeling) insensible (**to** à); **2** [*remark*] indélicat; [*attitude, policy*] peu compréhensif/-ive.

insensitivity /ɪn,sensə'tɪvətɪ/ *n* (all contexts) insensibilité *f* (**to** à).

inseparable /ɪn'seprəbl/ *adj* [*people, couple, notion, part*] inséparable (**from** de).

inseparably /ɪn'seprəblɪ/ *adv* [*linked, joined*] indissociablement; [*close*] inséparablement.

insert I /ɪn'sɜ:t/ *vtr* insérer [*word, clause*] (**in** dans); introduire, insérer [*key, knife, finger*] (**in** dans); insérer [*advertisement*] (**in** dans); insérer, encarter spec [*page, leaflet*] (**in** dans); **to ~ sth between two words** intercaler qch entre deux mots.
II /'ɪnsɜ:t/ *n* **1** = **insertion 2**; **2** Fashn (in dress) incrustation *f*; (in shoe) talonnette *f*; **3** (in machine) pièce *f* ajoutée, ajout *m*.

insertion /ɪn'sɜ:ʃn/ *n* **1** (action) insertion *f*, introduction *f*; **2** Journ (enclosed page, leaflet) encart *m*; (advertisement, amendment) insertion *f*; **3** Fashn incrustation *f*; **4** Anat insertion *f*.

in-service training *n* formation *f* continue.

inset /'ɪnset/ **I** *n* **1** (boxed picture) (map) insert *m*; (photo) photographie *f* en médaillon; **'~: the writer'** 'en médaillon: l'écrivain'; **2** (in sewing) entre-deux *m inv*.
II *vtr* (*p prés* **-tt-**; *prét, pp* **inset**) insérer [*map, picture*].

inshore /,ɪn'ʃɔ:(r)/ **I** *adj* [*fishing, current, area*] côtier/-ière; [*diving*] près de la côte; **~ lifeboat** canot *m* de sauvetage côtier.

II *adv* [*swim, drift*] vers la côte; [*fish, anchor*] près de la côte.

inside I /ˈɪnsaɪd/ *n* **1** (inner area or surface) intérieur *m*; **the ~ of the box/house** l'intérieur de la boîte/maison; **on the ~** à l'intérieur; **locked from the ~** fermé de l'intérieur; **the ~ of the leg/of the arm** l'intérieur de la jambe/du bras; **2** Sport, Transp **to be on the ~** [*runner*] être dans le couloir intérieur or à la corde; [*horse*] tenir la corde; [*car*] gen être sur or dans la voie de droite; GB, Austral être sur or dans la voie de gauche; **to overtake on the ~** (in Europe, US etc) doubler à droite; (in GB, Australia etc) doubler à gauche; **the favourite is coming up on the ~** le favori reprend du terrain en tenant la corde; **3** (area furthest from the road) **to walk on the ~** marcher loin du bord du trottoir; **4** (position of trust) **our sources on the ~** nos informateurs qui sont dans la place; **sb on the ~** qn dans la place; **5**○ (prison) **life on the ~** la vie en taule○.
II insides○ /ɪnˈsaɪdz/ *npl* (intestines) (of animal) entrailles *fpl*; (of human) intestin *m*, estomac *m*, boyaux○ *mpl*; **it upset his ~s** ça lui détraque l'intestin; **my ~s hurt** j'ai mal au ventre.
III /ɪnˈsaɪd/ *prep* (also US **~ of**) **1** (in the interior of) à l'intérieur; **~ the box/house/car** à l'intérieur de or dans la boîte/maison/voiture; **to be ~ (the house)** être à l'intérieur (de la maison); **put it ~ the envelope** mets-le dans l'enveloppe; **get some food ~ you!** mange donc quelque chose!; **you'll feel better with some food/a drink ~ you** tu te sentiras mieux après avoir mangé/bu quelque chose; **anger surged up ~ me** la colère montait en moi; **the thoughts ~ my head** mes pensées; **I knew deep down ~ that she was right** au fond de moi, je savais qu'elle avait raison; **2** (within an area, organization) à l'intérieur de; **conditions ~ the refugee camp** les conditions de vie à l'intérieur du camp de réfugiés; **my contacts ~ the company** mes contacts à l'intérieur de l'entreprise; **3** (under) **~ (of) an hour/a year** en moins d'une heure/d'un an; **to be ~ the world record** battre le record mondial; **to be ~ the speed limit** être en deçà de la vitesse maximale autorisée; **to finish ~ the permitted time** finir dans les limites du temps imparti.
IV /ˈɪnsaɪd/ *adj* **1** (interior) [*angle, cover, pocket, surface, measurement*] intérieur; [*toilet*] à l'intérieur; **the ~ pages of a paper** les pages intérieures d'un journal; **2** (first-hand) [*information, news*] de première main; **the ~ story** la vérité; **I got the ~ story from Clare** Clare était présente et m'a raconté ce qui s'était passé; **3** (within an organization) **an ~ source** un informateur dans la place; **it's an ~ job** c'est un coup monté de l'intérieur or par quelqu'un de la maison; **4** Sport, Transp **the ~ lane** (of road) (in Europe, US etc) la voie de droite; (in GB, Australia etc) la voie de gauche; (of athletics track) le couloir intérieur.
V /ɪnˈsaɪd/ *adv* **1** (indoors) à l'intérieur; (in a container) à l'intérieur, dedans; **she's ~** elle est à l'intérieur; **to dash** ou **hurry ~** se précipiter à l'intérieur; **to look ~** regarder à l'intérieur or dedans; **put the books ~ it** mets les livres dedans; **to go** ou **come** ou **step ~** entrer; **to bring sth ~** rentrer [*pram, shopping, chairs*]; **the lining ~ is silk** la doublure est en soie; **2**○ GB (in prison) **to be ~** être en taule○; **he's been ~** il a fait de la taule○; **to put sb ~** mettre qn en taule○.
VI inside out /ˈɪnsaɪd,aʊt/ *adv phr* **your sweater is ~ out** ton pull est à l'envers; **to turn sth ~ out** (reverse) retourner [*bag, coat*]; (ransack) mettre qch sens dessus dessous [*room, house*]; **to blow sth ~ out** [*wind*] retourner [*umbrella*]; **to know sth ~ out** connaître qch à fond [*subject*].

inside: **~ forward** *n* Sport intérieur *m*, inter *m*; **~ left** *n* Sport intérieur *m* gauche, inter *m* gauche; **~ leg** *n* entrejambes *m*; **~ leg measurement** *n* hauteur *f* de l'entrejambes.

insider /ɪnˈsaɪdə(r)/ **I** *n* gen, Fin initié/-e *m/f*.
II *modif* [*knowledge, information*] d'initié.

insider: **~ dealer**, **~ trader** *n* Fin initié *m*; **~ dealing**, **~ trading** *n* Fin délit *m* d'initié.

inside right *n* Sport intérieur *m* droit, inter *m* droit.

inside track *n* **1** Sport couloir *m* intérieur; **2** US fig **to have an ~ into** avoir un informateur au sein de [*organization*].

insidious /ɪnˈsɪdɪəs/ *adj* insidieux/-ieuse.

insidiously /ɪnˈsɪdɪəslɪ/ *adv* insidieusement.

insight /ˈɪnsaɪt/ *n* **1** (enlightening fact, revealing glimpse) aperçu *m*, idée *f*; **a fascinating ~ into** un aperçu fascinant sur; **to give an ~ into** donner une idée de; **the book provides no new ~s** le livre n'apporte rien de nouveau (**into** sur); **to gain an ~ into sth** arriver à mieux connaître qch; **we didn't gain much ~** ou **many ~s into** on n'a pas appris grand-chose sur; **2** (perceptiveness, intuition) perspicacité *f*, intuition *f*; **to have ~** avoir de la perspicacité or de l'intuition; **her remarkable ~ into male psychology** sa compréhension remarquable de la psychologie masculine; **3** Psych (in psychoanalysis) compréhension *f* de soi, insight *m*.

insightful /ˈɪnsaɪtfʊl/ *adj* [*person*] perspicace; [*analysis*] pénétrant.

insignia /ɪnˈsɪgnɪə/ *npl* **1** (symbols) insigne *m*; **2** (medals) insigne *m*.

insignificance /,ɪnsɪgˈnɪfɪkəns/ *n* insignifiance *f*; **to pale** ou **fade into ~** devenir dérisoire.

insignificant /,ɪnsɪgˈnɪfɪkənt/ *adj* **1** (negligible) [*cost, difference*] négligeable; **2** (unimportant) [*person, detail*] insignifiant.

insincere /,ɪnsɪnˈsɪə(r)/ *adj* [*person, voice, smile, compliment*] hypocrite; **to be ~** [*person, speech, remark*] manquer de sincérité; **an ~ answer** une réponse qui n'est pas sincère.

insincerity /,ɪnsɪnˈserətɪ/ *n* (of person) manque *m* de sincérité; (of smile, remark, compliment) hypocrisie *f*.

insinuate /ɪnˈsɪnjʊeɪt/ **I** *vtr* insinuer (**that** que).
II *v refl* **to ~ oneself into sth** s'insinuer dans qch.

insinuating /ɪnˈsɪnjʊeɪtɪŋ/ *adj* [*smile*] plein de sous-entendus; **an ~ remark** une insinuation.

insinuation /ɪn,sɪnjʊˈeɪʃn/ *n* insinuation *f*; **he made all sorts of ~s about the firm/about me** il a insinué toutes sortes de choses à propos de la société/à mon propos; **to make an ~ that** insinuer que.

insipid /ɪnˈsɪpɪd/ *adj* (all contexts) fade.

insipidity /,ɪnsɪˈpɪdətɪ/ *n* fadeur *f*, insipidité *f*.

insist /ɪnˈsɪst/ **I** *vtr* **1** (demand) insister; (authoritatively) exiger; **to ~ that** insister pour que (+ *subj*); (authoritatively) exiger que (+ *subj*); **I ~ you tell me!** j'exige que tu me le dises!; **2** (maintain forcefully) affirmer, soutenir; **they ~ed that it was true** ils ont affirmé que c'était la vérité; **she ~ed that she was innocent** elle a protesté de son innocence.
II *vi* insister; **I won't ~** je n'insisterai pas; **all right, if you ~** très bien, puisque tu insistes or puisque tu y tiens; **to ~ on** exiger [*punctuality, silence*]; **to ~ on doing** tenir à faire; **he will ~ on getting up early/paying for everything** il tient absolument à se lever tôt/à tout payer; **to ~ on sb doing** tenir à ce que qn fasse, insister pour que qn fasse; **I really must ~** j'insiste, il le faut.

insistence /ɪnˈsɪstəns/ *n* insistance *f*; **with ~** avec insistance ou instance; **to do sth at** ou **on sb's ~** faire qch devant l'insistance de qn; **her ~ on doing** l'insistance qu'elle met/a mise etc à faire; (stronger) son obstination à faire; **his ~ on his innocence was not convincing** ses protestations d'innocence n'étaient pas convaincantes.

insistent /ɪnˈsɪstənt/ *adj* [*person, noise*] insistant; [*demand*] pressant; [*rhythm*] implacable; **to be ~** insister (**about** sur; **that** pour que + *subj*); **he was most ~ that we should attend** il a beaucoup insisté pour que nous venions.

insistently /ɪnˈsɪstəntlɪ/ *adv* avec insistance.

in situ /ɪn ˈsɪtjuː/ *adv* sur place, in situ fml.

insofar /,ɪnsəˈfɑː(r)/: **insofar as** *conj phr* **~ as** dans la mesure où; **~ as (it is) possible** dans la mesure du possible; **~ as I can** dans la mesure de mes moyens; **~ as X is concerned** en ce qui concerne X.

insole /ˈɪnsəʊl/ *n* semelle *f* (intérieure).

insolence /ˈɪnsələns/ *n* insolence *f*.

insolent /ˈɪnsələnt/ *adj* insolent; **an ~ remark** une remarque insolente, une insolence.

insolently /ˈɪnsələntlɪ/ *adv* avec insolence.

insolubility /ɪn,sɒljʊˈbɪlətɪ/ *n* gen, Chem insolubilité *f*.

insoluble /ɪnˈsɒljʊbl/ *adj* **1** [*problem, conflict*] insoluble; **2** Chem, Med insoluble (**in** dans).

insolvable /ɪnˈsɒlvəbl/ *adj* US [*problem*] insoluble.

insolvency /ɪnˈsɒlvənsɪ/ *n* insolvabilité *f*; **~ expert** expert *m* en faillites.

insolvent /ɪnˈsɒlvənt/ *adj* insolvable; **the firm declared that it was ~** la société a déposé son bilan.

insomnia /ɪnˈsɒmnɪə/ *n* insomnie *f*; **to suffer from ~** souffrir d'insomnie.

insomniac /ɪnˈsɒmnɪæk/ *n* insomniaque *mf*; **to be an ~** être insomniaque.

insomuch /,ɪnsəʊˈmʌtʃ/ *adv* **~ as** (to the extent that) dans la mesure où; (seeing that) vu que.

insouciance /ɪnˈsuːsɪəns/ *n* sout insouciance *f*.

insouciant /ɪnˈsuːsɪənt/ *adj* sout insouciant.

inspect /ɪnˈspekt/ *vtr* **1** examiner [qch] de près [*document, picture, product*]; contrôler, vérifier [*accounts, books*]; inspecter [*school, teacher, factory, weapons-site, machinery, pitch, wiring*]; contrôler [*passport*]; contrôler, visiter [*luggage*]; **to ~ sth for defects** examiner [qch] de près pour s'assurer qu'il n'y a pas de défauts; **right to ~** Jur droit *m* de communication or de regard; **2** GB Transp contrôler [*ticket*]; **3** Mil (routinely) inspecter; (at ceremony) passer en revue.

inspection /ɪnˈspekʃn/ *n* **1** (of document, picture) examen *m*, inspection *f*; (of school, teacher, factory, weapons-site, machinery, wiring) inspection *f*; (of passport) contrôle *m*; **to make** ou **carry out an ~** procéder à une inspection; **customs ~** passage *m* à la douane; **on closer ~** en y regardant de plus près, après un examen plus approfondi; **2** GB Transp contrôle *m*; **3** Mil (routine) inspection *f*; (at ceremony) revue *f*.

inspection: **~ certificate** *n* certificat *m* de contrôle de fabrication; **~ chamber** *n* puits *m* de visite; **~ copy** *n* Publg spécimen *m*; **~ pit** *n* fosse *f* de visite or de réparation.

inspector /ɪnˈspektə(r)/ *n* **1** gen inspecteur/-trice *m/f*; **~ general** inspecteur/-trice *m/f* général/-e; **~ of weights and measures** inspecteur/-trice *m/f* des poids et mesures; **2** GB (in police) inspecteur *m* de police; **3** GB Sch (also **~ of schools**) inspecteur/-trice *m/f*; **4** GB Transp contrôleur/-euse *m/f*.

inspectorate /ɪnˈspektərət/ *n* **1** (inspectors collectively) corps *m* des inspecteurs, inspection *f*; **2** (rank) inspectorat *m*; **3** GB Sch (district) (primary) ≈ circonscription *f*; (secondary) ≈ académie *f*.

inspiration /,ɪnspəˈreɪʃn/ *n* **1** (stimulus)

inspiration *f* (**for** pour); **to draw one's ~ from sth** s'inspirer de qch; **to search for ~** chercher l'inspiration; **2** (person, thing that inspires) source *f* d'inspiration; **she is an ~ to us all!** elle est un exemple pour nous tous!; **3** (sudden idea) inspiration *f*; **4** Physiol inspiration *f*.

inspirational /ˌɪnspəˈreɪʃənl/ *adj* **1** (inspiring) inspirateur/-trice; **2** (inspired) inspiré.

inspire /ɪnˈspaɪə(r)/ *vtr* **1** (give rise to) inspirer [*person, work of art, fashion, idea*]; motiver [*decision, gesture*]; **the revolution was ~d by these ideals** la révolution s'est inspirée de ces idéaux; **2** (arouse) **to ~ love/respect/trust in sb** inspirer de l'amour/du respect/de la confiance à qn; **to ~ sb with hope/courage** donner de l'espoir/du courage à qn; **to ~ enthusiasm in sb** enthousiasmer qn; **he doesn't ~ much confidence** il n'inspire guère confiance; **3** (incite) inciter, encourager (**to do** à faire); **what ~d you to suggest that?** qu'est-ce qui vous a donné l'idée de proposer cela?

inspired /ɪnˈspaɪəd/ **I** *adj* [*person, work of art, performance*] inspiré; [*idea*] lumineux/-euse; **to make an ~ guess** avoir une heureuse inspiration.

II -inspired (*dans composés*) **French/surrealist-~** d'inspiration française/surréaliste.

inspiring /ɪnˈspaɪərɪŋ/ *adj* [*teacher, leader, speech*] enthousiasmant; [*thought, music*] exaltant; **it's not particularly ~** cela n'a rien de très inspirant.

inst. (*abrév écrite* = **instant**) Comm **your letter of the 3rd ~** votre lettre du 3 courant.

instability /ˌɪnstəˈbɪlətɪ/ *n* instabilité *f*.

instal(l) /ɪnˈstɔːl/ **I** *vtr* **1** installer [*computer system, new equipment etc*] (**in** dans); poser [*windows*]; **we had a new kitchen ~ed** on a fait installer une nouvelle cuisine; **2** (in official post) **to ~ sb in office** installer qn.

II *v refl* **to ~ oneself** s'installer.

installation /ˌɪnstəˈleɪʃn/ *n* (all contexts) installation *f*; **computer/military ~** installation informatique/militaire; **nuclear/oil ~** installation nucléaire/pétrolière.

installment plan *n* contrat *m* de vente à crédit or tempérament; **to buy sth on the ~** acheter qch à crédit or à tempérament.

instalment, **installment** US /ɪnˈstɔːlmənt/ *n* **1** (partial payment) versement *m* partiel; **monthly ~** mensualité *f*; **annual ~** annuité *f*; **to pay an ~** faire un versement partiel; **to pay for/repay sth in ~s** payer/rembourser qch en plusieurs versements; **2** (section) (of story, serial) épisode *m*; (of novel) feuilleton *m*; **to publish sth in weekly ~s** publier qch en feuilletons hebdomadaires.

instalment credit *n* crédit *m* échelonné.

instance /ˈɪnstəns/ **I** *n* **1** (case) cas *m*; **in the first ~** en premier lieu; **in many ~s** dans bien des cas; **in this (particular) ~** dans le cas présent; **as an ~ of** comme exemple de; **2** (request) **at the ~ of sb** à or sur la demande de qn; **3** (example) exemple *m*; **for ~** par exemple.

II *vtr* **1** (cite) citer [qch] en exemple; **2** (illustrate) illustrer.

instant /ˈɪnstənt/ **I** *n* **1** (moment) instant *m*; **at that (very) ~** à l'instant même; **for an ~** pendant un instant; **in an ~** dans un instant; **an ~ later** un instant plus tard; **come here this ~!** viens ici à l'instant!; **the ~ we saw him** dès que nous l'avons vu; **2**○ (coffee) nescafé® *m*, café *m* instantané; **do you mind ~?** un nescafé®, ça te va?

II *adj* **1** (immediate) [*access, act, dismissal, effect, obedience, rapport, relief, replay, response, success*] immédiat; [*solution*] instantané; [*hot water*] courant; **~ camera** polaroïd® *m*; **2** Culin [*coffee, soup*] instantané; [*mashed potato*] déshydraté; [*milk, mix*] en poudre; [*dish, meal*] à préparation rapide; **3**† **your letter of the 3rd ~** votre courrier du 3 courant.

instantaneous /ˌɪnstənˈteɪnɪəs/ *adj* [*death, event, response*] instantané; [*dislike*] immédiat.

instantaneously /ˌɪnstənˈteɪnɪəslɪ/ *adv* instantanément.

instantly /ˈɪnstəntlɪ/ *adv* gen immédiatement; [*die*] sur le coup.

instant replay *n* US Sport répétition *f* d'une séquence; **to show an ~ of a goal** repasser un but au ralenti.

instead /ɪnˈsted/ **I** *adv* **we didn't go home—we went to the park ~** au lieu de rentrer nous sommes allés au parc; **forget the theory and concentrate ~ on the practice** laisse tomber la théorie et concentre-toi plutôt sur la pratique; **next time try camping ~** la prochaine fois essaie plutôt le camping; **I don't feel like walking—let's take a taxi ~** je n'ai pas envie de marcher—prenons plutôt un taxi; **she didn't go to London. Instead she decided to go to Oxford** au lieu d'aller à Londres elle a décidé d'aller à Oxford; **I was going to phone but wrote ~** j'allais téléphoner mais finalement j'ai écrit; **we have no tea—will you take coffee ~?** nous n'avons pas de thé—voudriez-vous du café à la place?; **she couldn't attend so her son went ~** elle ne pouvait pas y assister alors son fils est allé à sa place; **to choose ~ to do** préférer faire.

II instead of *prep phr* **~ of doing** au lieu de faire; **you should be helping us ~ of moaning!** au lieu de râler○ tu devrais nous aider!; **~ of sth** au lieu de qch; **why not visit several castles ~ of just one?** pourquoi ne pas visiter plusieurs châteaux au lieu d'un seul?; **the interest was 30% ~ of 23%** l'intérêt était de 30% au lieu de 23%; **use oil ~ of butter** utilisez de l'huile à la place du beurre; **~ of sb** à la place de qn; **you can go ~ of me** tu peux y aller à ma place.

instep /ˈɪnstep/ *n* (of foot, shoe) cou-de-pied *m*; **to have a high ~** avoir le pied cambré.

instigate /ˈɪnstɪgeɪt/ *vtr* lancer [*attack, strike*]; ouvrir [*inquiry*]; engager [*proceedings*].

instigation /ˌɪnstɪˈgeɪʃn/ *n* **at the ~ of sb** à l'instigation de qn; **he stole the car at her ~** c'est elle qui l'a incité à voler la voiture.

instigator /ˈɪnstɪgeɪtə(r)/ *n* instigateur/-trice *m/f*.

instil GB, **instill** US /ɪnˈstɪl/ *vtr* (*p prés etc* **-ll-**) inculquer [*pride, respect, attitude, belief*] (**in** à); donner [*confidence*] (**in sb** à qn); insuffler [*fear*] (**in** à).

instinct /ˈɪnstɪŋkt/ *n* instinct *m*; **the ~ for survival** l'instinct de conservation; **the ~ to do** l'instinct qui pousse à faire; **her ~ is to fight back** lit, fig elle se défend d'instinct; **follow your ~(s)** (when making decision) laisse-toi guider par ton intuition; (in sport etc) fais ce qui te semble le plus naturel; **my first ~ was to...** ma première réaction fut de...; **death/life ~** Psych pulsion *f* de mort/de vie; **the killer ~** lit l'instinct qui pousse à tuer; fig la combativité.

instinctive /ɪnˈstɪŋktɪv/ *adj* instinctif/-ive.

instinctively /ɪnˈstɪŋktɪvlɪ/ *adv* [*react, behave, realize*] d'instinct; **~, he...** instinctivement, il...

institute /ˈɪnstɪtjuːt, US -tuːt/ **I** *n* **1** (organization) institut *m*; **2** US (course) stage *m*.

II *vtr* **1** (initiate) instituer, instaurer [*custom, rule, prize*]; établir [*scheme*]; ouvrir [*inquiry*] (**into** sur); **2** (found) fonder, constituer [*society*]; Univ créer [*chair*]; **newly ~d** [*post*] nouvellement créé; [*organization*] de fondation récente; **3** Jur intenter [*action*] (**against** contre); **to ~ (legal) proceedings** entamer or engager des poursuites (**against** contre); **4** Relig investir, instituer.

institution /ˌɪnstɪˈtjuːʃn, US -tuːʃn/ *n* **1** Admin, Pol institution *f* also fig; **she has become a national ~** hum elle est devenue une institution nationale; **charitable/religious ~** institution caritative/religieuse; **financial ~** organisme *m* financier; **2** Soc Admin gen établissement *m* spécialisé; (old people's home) asile *m* de vieillards; (mental hospital) hôpital *m* psychiatrique; **she has spent most of her life in ~s** elle a passé la plus grande partie de sa vie dans toutes sortes d'établissements spécialisés; **3** (establishment) (of custom, rule, body, prize) institution *f*; **~ of legal proceedings** Jur introduction *f* d'instance; **4** Relig investiture *f*, institution *f*; **5** US = **institute I 1**.

institutional /ˌɪnstɪˈtjuːʃənl, US -tuː-/ *adj* **1** [*structure, reform*] institutionnel/-elle; [*food, meals*] de collectivité; **~ life** la vie réglementée d'un établissement spécialisé; **to be put in ~ care** [*child*] être placé dans un établissement spécialisé; [*old person*] être placé dans un asile de vieillards; **2** Comm [*buying, advertising, investor*] institutionnel/-elle; **~ economics** institutionnalisme *m*.

institutionalize /ˌɪnstɪˈtjuːʃənəlaɪz, US -tuː-/ **I** *vtr* **1** (place in special care) gen placer [qn] dans un établissement spécialisé; (in mental hospital) interner; **to become ~d** [*patient, resident*] être marqué par la vie réglementée d'un établissement spécialisé; **2** (establish officially) institutionnaliser, donner un caractère officiel à [*event, practice, system*].

II institutionalized *pp adj* [*racism, violence*] institutionnalisé; **to become ~d** [*custom, practice*] prendre un caractère officiel, s'institutionnaliser.

in-store /ˈɪnstɔː(r)/ *adj* [*adviser, beauty consultant*] sur place, dans le magasin; **~ promotion** publicité *f* sur le lieu de vente; **~ bakery** rayon *m* boulangerie.

instruct /ɪnˈstrʌkt/ *vtr* **1** (direct) **to ~ sb to do** [*superior, boss*] donner l'ordre à qn de faire; [*tribunal, commission*] enjoindre à qn de faire; **to be ~ed to do** recevoir l'ordre de faire; **to ~ sb when/how to do** indiquer à qn quand/comment faire; **2** (teach) instruire; **to ~ sb in** enseigner [qch] à qn, instruire qn en [*subject, discipline, craft*]; **to ~ sb how to do** enseigner à qn comment faire; **3** GB Jur (engage) **to ~ a solicitor** louer les services d'un avocat.

instruction /ɪnˈstrʌkʃn/ **I** *n* **1** (directive) instruction *f* (**to** à); **to issue** ou **give ~s to sb to do** donner l'ordre à qn de faire; **to receive ~s** recevoir un ordre or des instructions; **to carry out ~s** exécuter des ordres ou des instructions; **I have ~s to do/not to do** j'ai reçu l'ordre de faire/de ne pas faire; **to be under ~s to do** être chargé de faire; **according to ~s** conformément aux instructions reçues; **failing ~s to the contrary** sauf contre-ordre; **2** ¢ (teaching) instruction *f*; **the language of ~** la langue d'enseignement; **to give sb ~ in sth** instruire qn en qch, enseigner qch à qn; **to receive ~ in** recevoir une instruction en; **3** Comput instruction *f*; **print ~** instruction d'impression.

II instructions *npl* (for product use) instructions *fpl*; **to follow the ~s** suivre les instructions; **~s for use** mode *m* d'emploi.

instructional /ɪnˈstrʌkʃənl/ *adj* éducatif/-ive.

instruction: **~ book** *n* livret *m* de l'utilisateur; **~ manual** *n* manuel *m* d'utilisation; **~ sheet** *n* notice *f* explicative.

instructive /ɪnˈstrʌktɪv/ *adj* [*talk, report, incident*] instructif/-ive; [*book, film*] instructif/-ive, éducatif/-ive; **it is ~ to compare...** il est instructif de comparer...

instructor /ɪnˈstrʌktə(r)/ ▶ 1692 *n* **1** (trainer) (in sports, driving, flying) moniteur/-trice *m/f* (**in** de); (military) instructeur *m*; (in prison) éducateur/-trice *m/f*; **2** US (in university) ≈ assistant/-e *m/f*; (any teacher) professeur *m*.

instructress /ɪnˈstrʌktrɪs/ *n* monitrice *f*.

instrument /ˈɪnstrʊmənt/ ▶ 1481 **I** *n* **1** (tool, implement) instrument *m* also fig; **to be**

the ~ of fate être l'instrument du destin; **to be an ~ for good/evil** exercer une bonne/mauvaise influence; **2** Mus instrument *m*; **to play an ~** jouer d'un instrument; **3** Aviat, Aut instrument *m*; **to fly on ~s** piloter aux instruments; **4** Jur (document) instrument *m*, acte *m* juridique.
II *modif* Aviat [*landing, flying*] aux instruments.
III *vtr* **1** Mus orchestrer; **2** Ind équiper [*factory, machine*].

instrumental /ˌɪnstrʊˈmentl/ **I** *n* instrumental *m*.
II **instrumentals** *npl* partie *f* instrumentale.
III *adj* **1 to be ~ in sth** contribuer à qch; **to be ~ in doing** contribuer à faire; **he played an ~ role in creating the company** il a été pour beaucoup dans la création de l'entreprise; **she was ~ in his release** il a été libéré grâce à elle; **to be ~ in sb's downfall** être l'instrument de la chute de qn; **2** Mus instrumental.

instrumentalist /ˌɪnstrʊˈmentəlɪst/ *n* instrumentiste *mf*.

instrumentation /ˌɪnstrʊmenˈteɪʃn/ *n* Aviat, Tech, Mus instrumentation *f*.

instrument panel *n* Aviat, Aut tableau *m* de bord.

insubordinate /ˌɪnsəˈbɔːdɪnət/ *adj* [*person*] insubordonné; **~ behaviour** insubordination *f*.

insubordination /ˌɪnsəˌbɔːdɪˈneɪʃn/ *n* gen indiscipline *f*; Mil insubordination *f*.

insubstantial /ˌɪnsəbˈstænʃl/ *adj* **1** (small) [*meal*] peu nourrissant; [*helping*] mesquin; **2** (flimsy) [*building*] peu solide; [*plant*] fragile; [*evidence*] insuffisant; [*accusation*] sans substance; **3** (unreal) insaisissable.

insufferable /ɪnˈsʌfrəbl/ *adj* [*heat, conditions*] insupportable; [*rudeness*] intolérable; **he's an ~ bore** il est assommant.

insufferably /ɪnˈsʌfrəblɪ/ *adv* **to be ~ rude/arrogant** être d'une impolitesse/arrogance insupportable.

insufficiency /ˌɪnsəˈfɪʃnsɪ/ *n* insuffisance *f*.

insufficient /ˌɪnsəˈfɪʃnt/ *adj* **there are ~ copies/workers/resources** il n'y a pas assez d'exemplaires/d'ouvriers/de ressources (**to do** pour faire); **to be ~ for** être insuffisant pour; **to have ~ time/resources** ne pas avoir assez de temps/de ressources.

insufficiently /ˌɪnsəˈfɪʃntlɪ/ *adv* gen pas assez; [*protected, understood, paid*] mal.

insular /ˈɪnsjʊlə(r), US -sələr/ *adj* **1** pej [*outlook, lifestyle*] étriqué; **to be ~** [*person*] avoir des vues étroites; **2** Geog insulaire.

insularity /ˌɪnsjʊˈlærətɪ, US -səˈl-/ *n* péj (of nation, group) étroitesse *f* d'esprit.

insulate /ˈɪnsjʊleɪt, US -səˈl-/ **I** *vtr* **1** Constr (against cold, heat) isoler [*roof, room*] (**against** contre); calorifuger [*water tank*]; (against noise) insonoriser, isoler [*room*]; **2** Elec isoler; **3** fig (protect) protéger (**from** de; **against** contre); (segregate) isoler, tenir à l'écart (**from, against** de).
II **insulated** *pp adj* [*wire, cable*] isolé; [*handle, pliers*] isolant; [*water tank*] calorifugé; [*room*] (against cold, heat) isolé; (against noise) insonorisé; **a well-~d house** une maison bien isolée.

insulating /ˈɪnsjʊˌleɪtɪŋ, US -səˈl-/ *pres p adj* isolant; **~ board** panneau *m* isolant; **~ material** isolant *m*; **~ tape** ruban *m* isolant.

insulation /ˌɪnsjʊˈleɪʃn, US -səˈl-/ *n* **1** (thermal) (of house, room) isolation *f*; (of water tank) calorifugeage *m*; **loft** ou **roof ~** isolation *f* du comble or du toit; **2** (acoustic) isolation *f* (acoustique); **sound ~** insonorisation *f*; **3** (material) isolant *m*; **4** Elec isolation *f*.

insulator /ˈɪnsjʊleɪtə(r), US -səl-/ *n* **1** (substance) isolant *m*; **2** Elec isolateur *m*.

insulin /ˈɪnsjʊlɪn, US -səl-/ *n* insuline *f*.

insulin: **~ level** *n* taux *m* d'insuline; **~ treatment** *n* insulinothérapie *f*.

insult I /ˈɪnsʌlt/ *n* (remark) insulte *f*, injure *f*; (action) insulte *f*, affront *m*; **an ~ to sb's intelligence/memory** une insulte à l'intelligence/la mémoire de qn; **to take sth as an ~** percevoir qch comme une insulte or un affront; **and to add ~ to injury**... et pour comble d'insulte...
II /ɪnˈsʌlt/ *vtr* (verbally) insulter, injurier; (by one's behaviour) insulter, faire un affront à.

insulting /ɪnˈsʌltɪŋ/ *adj* [*remarks, language*] insultant, injurieux/-ieuse; [*behaviour*] insultant, offensant.

insultingly /ɪnˈsʌltɪŋlɪ/ *adv* [*act, speak, worded*] de façon injurieuse; **~ brief** d'une brièveté injurieuse.

insuperable /ɪnˈsuːpərəbl, ɪnˈsjuː-/ *adj* insurmontable.

insuperably /ɪnˈsuːpərəblɪ/ *adv* **our task was ~ difficult** notre tâche était d'une difficulté insurmontable.

insupportable /ˌɪnsəˈpɔːtəbl/ *adj* sout insupportable.

insurable /ɪnˈʃɔːrəbl, US -ˈʃʊər-/ *adj* assurable.

insurance /ɪnˈʃɔːrəns, US -ˈʃʊər-/ *n* **1** ¢ (contract) assurance *f* (**against** contre); (policy) police *f* d'assurance; **~ for the house/car** une assurance pour la maison/la voiture; **to take out ~ against sth** s'assurer contre qch; **to pay the ~ on sth** payer l'assurance de qch; **the ~ runs out soon** la police d'assurance expire bientôt; **accident/fire ~** assurance contre les accidents/contre l'incendie; **travel ~** assurance voyage; **2** (amount paid to or by company) assurance *f*; **I pay £500 in ~ on the car** je paie 500 livres sterling d'assurance pour la voiture; **the company paid out two million dollars in ~** la société a versé deux millions de dollars d'assurance; **3** (profession) **he works in ~** il travaille dans les assurances; **4** fig (precaution) protection *f*; **I see my investments as a form of ~ against inflation** je considère mes investissements comme une protection contre l'inflation.

insurance: **~ agent** ▶1692 *n* agent *m* d'assurances; **~ assessor** ▶1692 *n* expert *m* en assurances; **~ broker** ▶1692 *n* courtier *m* en assurances; **~ broking** *n* courtage *m* d'assurances; **~ certificate** *n* certificat *m* d'assurance; **~ claim** *n* demande *f* d'indemnité; **~ company** *n* compagnie *f* d'assurances; **~ plan** *n* US régime *m* d'assurances; **~ policy** *n* (police *f* d')assurance *f*; **~ premium** *n* prime *f* d'assurance; **~ scheme** *n* GB régime *m* d'assurances.

insure /ɪnˈʃɔː(r), US -ˈʃʊər/ **I** *vtr* **1** (protect) assurer [*baggage, person, property*]; **to ~ sb/sth against sth** assurer qn/qch contre qch; **to insure oneself** ou **one's life** prendre une assurance-vie, s'assurer sur la vie; **2** (take precautions) **to ~ against delay/shortages** se garantir contre les retards/les ruptures de stock; **to ~ against disappointment, please book early** pour éviter une déception, il est conseillé de réserver à l'avance; **3** US = **ensure**.
II **insured** *pp adj* assuré; **a parcel ~d for £50** un paquet assuré pour une valeur déclarée de 50 livres sterling; **~d value** montant *m* de l'assurance.

insured party *n* assuré/-e *m/f*.

insurer /ɪnˈʃɔːrə(r), US -ˈʃʊər-/ *n* assureur *m*.

insurgent /ɪnˈsɜːdʒənt/ **I** *n* (rebel) insurgé/-e *m/f*.
II *adj* [*population, troops*] insurgé.

insurmountable /ˌɪnsəˈmaʊntəbl/ *adj* insurmontable.

insurrection /ˌɪnsəˈrekʃn/ *n* insurrection *f*.

insurrectionary /ˌɪnsəˈrekʃənərɪ, US -nerɪ/ *adj* insurrectionnel/-elle.

insurrectionist /ˌɪnsəˈrekʃənɪst/ **I** *n* insurgé/-e *m/f*.
II *adj* insurgé.

int. *adj* **1** *abrév écrite* = **international**; **2** *abrév écrite* = **internal**.

intact /ɪnˈtækt/ *adj* intact; **to survive ~** rester intact.

intaglio /ɪnˈtɑːlɪəʊ/ **I** *n* (gem, seal) intaille *f*.
II *modif* [*engraving*] en creux.

intake /ˈɪnteɪk/ *n* **1** (consumption) consommation *f*; **a high sugar ~** une forte consommation de sucre; **the daily calorie ~ of a baby** les besoins quotidiens en calories d'un bébé; **2** Sch, Univ, Admin (admissions) (+ *v sg ou pl*) admissions *fpl*; **the new ~** (at school) les nouveaux élèves *mpl*; (into training, job) les nouvelles recrues *fpl*; **the 1987 ~ of students** les étudiants de l'année 1987; **3** (inhalation) **an ~ of breath** une inspiration *f*; **there was a sharp ~ of breath** tout le monde a retenu son souffle; **4** Tech (inlet) arrivée *f*; **air/fuel ~** arrivée d'air/de carburant.

intake valve *n* soupape *f* d'admission.

intangible /ɪnˈtændʒəbl/ **I** *n* impondérable *m*.
II *adj* **1** (undefinable) [*atmosphere, nuance*] insaisissable; **2** Comm Jur [*benefit, property*] incorporel/-elle; **~ asset** immobilisation *f* incorporelle.

integer /ˈɪntɪdʒə(r)/ *n* nombre *m* entier relatif.

integral /ˈɪntɪgrəl/ **I** *n* intégrale *f*.
II *adj* **1** (intrinsic) [*member, part, feature*] intégrant; **to be an ~ part of** être une or faire partie intégrante de; **to be ~ to** être intrinsèque à; **2** Tech (built-in) [*power supply, lighting, component*] incorporé; [*garage*] intégré; **3** Math [*number*] intégral; **4** (whole) intégral.

integrate /ˈɪntɪgreɪt/ **I** *vtr* **1** (incorporate) intégrer, incorporer [*region, company, system, design*] (**into** dans; **with** à); **to be well ~d with its surroundings** bien s'intégrer à son environnement; **2** (blend, combine) combiner [*systems, companies*]; **to ~ two systems** combiner deux systèmes; **3** Sociol (absorb) intégrer [*minority, immigrant*] (**into** dans); **4** Pol (desegregate as policy) rendre [qch] accessible à tous [*school, sport, beach, facility*]; **5** Math intégrer [*number, function*].
II *vi* **1** (mix) [*minority, ethnic group, person*] s'intégrer (**with** à; **into** dans); **2** (desegregate) [*school, sport, facility*] devenir accessible à tous.

integrated /ˈɪntɪgreɪtɪd/ *adj* **1** (planned as a whole) [*system, service, scheme*] intégré; **2** (ethnically or religiously) mixte.

integrated: **~ accounting package** *n* Comput logiciel *m* intégré de comptabilité; **~ circuit** *n* circuit *m* intégré; **~ course** *n* GB stage *m* d'apprentissage; **~ data network** *n* réseau *m* de données intégré; **~ day** *n* GB *à la maternelle ou à l'école primaire, journée sans emploi du temps structuré*.

integration /ˌɪntɪˈgreɪʃn/ *n* (all contexts) intégration *f* (**into** dans; **with** à; **between** entre).

integrity /ɪnˈtegrətɪ/ *n* intégrité *f* (**of** de); **a man of ~** un homme intègre.

integument /ɪnˈtegjʊmənt/ *n* tégument *m*.

intellect /ˈɪntəlekt/ *n* **1** (intelligence) intelligence *f*; **2** (person) esprit *m*, intellect *m*.

intellectual /ˌɪntəˈlektʃʊəl/ **I** *n* intellectuel/-elle *m/f*.
II *adj* intellectuel/-elle; **~ snob** intellectuel/-elle *m/f* snob.

intellectualism /ˌɪntəˈlektʃʊəlɪzəm/ *n* intellectualisme *m*.

intellectualize /ˌɪntəˈlektʃʊəlaɪz/ **I** *vtr* intellectualiser [*problem*].
II *vi* philosopher (**about** sur); péj pérorer pej (**about** sur).

intellectually /ˌɪntəˈlektʃʊəlɪ/ *adv* intellectuellement.

intellectual property rights *npl* propriété *f* intellectuelle.

intelligence /ɪnˈtelɪdʒəns/ *n* **1** intelligence *f*; **to have the ~ to do** avoir l'intelligence de faire; **to be of low ~** être peu intelligent; **use your ~!** réfléchis!; **that's an**

insult to my ~! c'est me prendre pour un/une imbécile!; **2** gen, Mil (information) renseignements *mpl*; **according to the latest ~** selon les informations de dernière minute; **3** Mil (secret service) services *mpl* de renseignements; **military/naval ~** service de renseignements de l'armée de terre/de la marine; **to be in ~** être dans les services de renseignements; **4** sout (intelligent being) intelligence *f*.

intelligence: **~ agent** *n* agent *m* de renseignements; **Intelligence Corps** *n* GB ≈ service *m* de renseignements de l'armée; **~ quotient, IQ** *n* quotient *m* intellectuel; **Intelligence Service** *n* service *m* de renseignements; **~ test** *n* test *m* d'aptitude intellectuelle.

intelligent /ɪn'telɪdʒənt/ *adj* intelligent.

intelligent: **~ card** *n* carte *f* à puce; **~ knowledge-based system, IKBS** *n* système *m* expert.

intelligently /ɪn'telɪdʒəntlɪ/ *adv* intelligemment, avec intelligence.

intelligentsia /ɪn,telɪ'dʒentsɪə/ *n* **the ~** l'intelligentsia *f*.

intelligent terminal *n* terminal *m* intelligent.

intelligibility /ɪn,telɪdʒə'bɪlətɪ/ *n* intelligibilité *f*.

intelligible /ɪn'telɪdʒəbl/ *adj* intelligible (**to** à).

intelligibly /ɪn'telɪdʒəblɪ/ *adv* intelligiblement.

Intelsat /'ɪntelsæt/ *n* Telecom (satellite *m*) Intelsat *m*.

intemperance /ɪn'tempərəns/ *n* intempérance *f*.

intemperate /ɪn'tempərət/ *adj* **1** (unrestrained) [*remark, attack, language*] incontrôlé; **2** (given to excess) [*person*] intempérant; **3** [*weather*] rigoureux/-euse.

intend /ɪn'tend/ **I** *vtr* **1** (have in mind) vouloir, avoir en tête [*outcome, meaning, result, marriage*]; **as I ~ed** comme je le voulais, comme je l'entendais fml; **just what/where I ~ed** exactement ce que/là où je voulais; **sooner/more than I had ~ed** plus tôt/plus que je ne voulais; **to ~ to do, to ~ doing** avoir l'intention de faire; **to ~ sb to do** avoir l'intention or vouloir que qn fasse; **to ~ that...** avoir l'intention que... (+ *subj*); **2** (mean) **to ~ sth as a joke/an insult** dire qch pour plaisanter/blesser; **no insult ~ed** sans vouloir offenser; **it was clearly ~ed as a reference to...** c'était manifestement une allusion à...; **to be ~ed for sb** être destiné à qn; **to be ~ed for sth** être prévu pour qch; **I never ~ed it to be a serious analysis** je n'ai jamais prétendu que c'était une analyse sérieuse; **she ~ed it to be affectionate/cruel** son intention était affectueuse/cruelle; **the law is ~ed to prevent...** la loi vise à empêcher...; **it was not ~ed to be used like that** il n'était pas prévu qu'on s'en serve de cette façon.
II intending *pres p adj* [*applicant, traveller*] potentiel/-ielle.

intendant /ɪn'tendənt/ *n* Hist intendant *m*.

intended /ɪn'tendɪd/ **I**† *n* **her/his ~** son/sa promis/-e† *m/f*, son/sa futur/-e *m/f*.
II *adj* **1** (meant, desired) [*meaning, result, effect, insult*] voulu; **2** (planned) [*visit, purchase*] projeté; [*output, conditions of use*] prévu; **~ for sb** destiné à qn; **the ~ victim** la personne visée.

intense /ɪn'tens/ *adj* **1** (great) [*activity, emotion, pain, pressure*] intense; [*interest, satisfaction*] vif/vive (*before n*); [*colour*] intense; **2** (serious) [*person*] sérieux/-ieuse.

intensely /ɪn'tenslɪ/ *adv* [*curious, problematic*] extrêmement; [*dislike, hate*] profondément.

intensification /ɪn,tensɪfɪ'keɪʃn/ *n* intensification *f* (**of** de).

intensifier /ɪn'tensɪfaɪə(r)/ *n* Ling intensif *m*.

intensify /ɪn'tensɪfaɪ/ **I** *vtr* intensifier.
II *vi* s'intensifier.

intensity /ɪn'tensətɪ/ *n* intensité *f* (**of** de); **to speak with ~** parler avec ferveur.

intensive /ɪn'tensɪv/ **I** *adj* (all contexts) intensif/-ive; **an ~ course in French** un cours intensif or accéléré de français.
II -intensive (*dans composés*) **energy-~** à forte consommation en énergie; **technology-~** à fort niveau technologique. ▶ **capital-intensive, labour-intensive**.

intensive care *n* **to be in ~** être en réanimation; **to be in need of ~** avoir besoin de soins intensifs.

intensive care unit *n* service *m* de soins intensifs.

intensively /ɪn'tensɪvlɪ/ *adv* [*farmed, cultivated*] intensivement.

intent /ɪn'tent/ **I** *n* **1** (intention) intention *f*, dessein *m* (**to do** de faire); **with ~** [*act, say*] à dessein, intentionnellement; **it is political in ~** le but en est politique; **2** Jur intention *f*; **with (criminal) ~** avec une intention criminelle or délictueuse; **with ~ to do** avec l'intention de faire.
II *adj* **1 to be ~ on doing** être résolu or décidé à faire; **~ on victory/privatization** résolu or décidé à gagner/à privatiser; **2** (absorbed) [*person, expression, silence*] absorbé (**on** par; **on doing** à faire).
IDIOMS **to all ~s and purposes** quasiment.

intention /ɪn'tenʃn/ *n* intention *f* (**to do, of doing** de faire); **to come with the ~ of doing** venir dans l'intention de faire; **it is our ~ to do, our ~ is to do** nous avons l'intention de faire; **the ~ is to do** l'objectif or le but est de faire; **she has no/she hasn't the slightest ~ of doing** elle n'a aucune intention/elle n'a nullement l'intention de faire; **with good ~s** dans une bonne intention; **with the best of ~s** avec les meilleures intentions du monde; **to be full of good ~s** être plein de bonnes intentions.

intentional /ɪn'tenʃənl/ *adj* [*action, insult*] intentionnel/-elle; [*effect*] voulu.

intentionally /ɪn'tenʃənəlɪ/ *adv* [*act, mislead, injure*] intentionnellement, exprès; [*ambiguous, vague*] délibérément; **to make oneself ~ homeless** GB Jur choisir de quitter son domicile.

intently /ɪn'tentlɪ/ *adv* attentivement.

inter /ɪn'tɜː(r)/ *vtr* (*p prés etc* **-rr-**) sout ensevelir.

interact /,ɪntər'ækt/ *vi* [*factors*] agir l'un sur l'autre; [*phenomena*] avoir une action réciproque l'un sur l'autre; [*people*] communiquer; Comput [*computers, users*] dialoguer; **to ~ with sb** communiquer avec qn.

interaction /,ɪntər'ækʃn/ *n* gen, Phys, Comput interaction *f* (**between, among** entre); **the ~ of A with B** l'interaction de A et B.

interactive /,ɪntər'æktɪv/ *adj* gen, Comput interactif/-ive.

interactive: **~ computing** *n* informatique *f* conversationnelle; **~ learning** *n* apprentissage *m* interactif.

interactively /,ɪntər'æktɪvlɪ/ *adv* Comput en mode interactif.

interactive: **~ mode** *n* mode *m* conversationnel or interactif; **~ terminal** *n* terminal *m* interactif; **~ video** *n* vidéo *f* interactive.

interbreed /,ɪntə'briːd/ **I** *vtr* (*prét, pp* **-bred**) croiser [*cattle, stock, plants*].
II *vi* (*prét, pp* **-bred**) se croiser, se métisser (**with** avec).

interbreeding /,ɪntə'briːdɪŋ/ *n* croisement *m*.

intercalate /ɪn'tɜːkəleɪt/ *vtr* intercaler.

intercalation /ɪn,tɜːkə'leɪʃn/ *n* intercalation *f*.

intercede /,ɪntə'siːd/ *vi* **1** (plead) intercéder (**with** auprès de; **on sb's behalf** en faveur de qn); **2** (mediate) intervenir comme médiateur/-trice *m/f* (**between** entre).

intercept /,ɪntə'sept/ **I** *n* **1** Telecom, US Sport interception *f*; **2** Math intersection *f*.
II *vtr* intercepter.

interception /,ɪntə'sepʃn/ *n* Telecom, Sport interception *f*.

interceptor /,ɪntə'septə(r)/ *n* Aviat intercepteur *m*.

intercession /,ɪntə'seʃn/ *n* **1** (intervention) intercession *f* (**with** auprès de); **2** (mediation) médiation *f* (**between** entre).

interchange **I** /'ɪntətʃeɪndʒ/ *n* **1** (road junction) échangeur *m*; **2** (exchange) échange *m*.
II /,ɪntə'tʃeɪndʒ/ *vtr* (exchange) échanger; (change places of) permuter.

interchangeable /,ɪntə'tʃeɪndʒəbl/ *adj* interchangeable.

interchangeably /,ɪntə'tʃeɪndʒəblɪ/ *adv* de façon interchangeable.

inter-city /,ɪntə'sɪtɪ/ **I** *n* GB Transp rapide *m*, train *m* de grandes lignes.
II *adj* interurbain.

intercollegiate /,ɪntəkə'liːdʒət/ *adj* GB Univ (between colleges) entre collèges; US (between universities) interuniversitaire.

intercom /'ɪntəkɒm/ *n* interphone® *m*; **over the ~** par l'interphone®; **the voice on the ~** la voix dans l'interphone®.

intercommunicate /,ɪntəkə'mjuːnɪkeɪt/ *vi* [*people, rooms*] communiquer.

intercommunication /,ɪntəkə,muːnɪ'keɪʃn/ *n* communication *f* (**between** entre).

intercommunion /,ɪntəkə'mjuːnɪən/ *n* Relig intercommunion *f*.

interconnect /,ɪntəkə'nekt/ **I** *vtr* raccorder [*parts*].
II *vi* [*components*] se connecter; [*rooms*] communiquer; Comput [*computers, systems, workstations*] être raccordé.
III interconnected *pp adj* raccordé.

interconnecting /,ɪntəkə'nektɪŋ/ *adj* [*rooms, apartments*] communicant; [*cable*] de connexion.

interconnection /,ɪntəkə'nekʃn/ *n* Comput raccordement *m* (en réseau).

intercontinental /,ɪntə,kɒntɪ'nentl/ *adj* intercontinental.

intercontinental ballistic missile *n* missile *m* balistique intercontinental.

intercostal /,ɪntə'kɒstl/ *adj* Anat intercostal.

intercourse /'ɪntəkɔːs/ *n* **1** (social) relations *fpl*; **2** (sexual) rapports *mpl* (sexuels).

interdenominational /,ɪntədɪ,nɒmɪ'neɪʃənl/ *adj* Relig interconfessionnel/-elle.

interdepartmental /,ɪntə,diːpɑːt'mentl/ *adj* **1** Univ entre départements; **2** Admin, Comm entre services; **3** Pol interministériel/-ielle.

interdependence /,ɪntədɪ'pendəns/ *n* interdépendance *f* (**between** entre; **of** de).

interdependent /,ɪntədɪ'pendənt/ *adj* interdépendant.

interdict **I** /'ɪntədɪkt/ *n* sout **1** Jur interdiction *f*; **2** Relig interdit *m*.
II /,ɪntə'dɪkt/ *vtr* gen, Jur, Relig interdire.

interdiction /,ɪntə'dɪkʃn/ *n* gen, Jur, Relig interdiction *f*.

interdisciplinarity /,ɪntə,dɪsɪplɪ'nærətɪ/ *n* interdisciplinarité *f*.

interdisciplinary /,ɪntə,dɪsɪ'plɪnərɪ, US -nerɪ/ *adj* interdisciplinaire.

interest /'ɪntrəst/ **I** *n* **1** ¢ (enthusiasm) intérêt *m* (**in** pour); **a lively ~ in politics** un vif intérêt pour la politique; **full of ~** plein d'intérêt; **to add to the ~ of sth** ajouter un certain intérêt à qch; **to be of great/no ~ to sb** être d'un grand/sans intérêt pour qn; **to be of little ~ to sb** être de peu d'intérêt pour qn; **we've had a lot of ~ from Europe** beaucoup de gens en Europe nous ont manifesté leur intérêt; **I collect stamps just for ~** je collectionne les

timbres pour le plaisir; **to hold sb's ~** retenir l'attention de qn; **as a matter of ~**... juste pour savoir...; **2** (hobby, passion) centre *m* d'intérêt; **what are your main ~s?** quels sont vos centres d'intérêt principaux?; **he has wide/limited ~s** il s'intéresse à énormément de/à peu de choses; **3** (benefit) intérêt *m*; **in the ~(s) of** (to promote) dans l'intérêt de [*peace, freedom*]; (out of concern for) par souci de [*hygiene, justice*]; **it is in your (own) ~(s) to do** il est dans ton intérêt de faire; **I have an ~ in doing** il est de mon intérêt de faire; **to act in sb's ~s** agir dans l'intérêt de qn; **to look after one's own ~s** veiller sur ses propres intérêts; **to have a vested ~ in sth** être directement concerné par qch; **to have sb's best ~s at heart** vouloir le bien de qn; **4** (concern) intérêt *m*; **of public ~** d'intérêt public; **majority/minority ~** Fin participation majoritaire/minoritaire; **to declare one's ~s** faire état de ses participations personnelles; **5** Fin (accrued monies) intérêts *mpl* (**on** de); **5% ~** intérêts de 5%; **simple/compound ~** intérêts *mpl* simples/composés; **overdraft ~ charges** intérêts sur un découvert; **to earn ~** [*investment*] rapporter des intérêts; **account paying/not paying ~** compte rémunéré/non rémunéré; **to return sth with ~** fig revaloir qch au centuple; **6** Fin, Comm (share) intérêts *mpl*, participation *f* (**in** dans); **~ in a grocery business** intérêts dans un commerce d'alimentation; **business ~s** intérêts *mpl* commerciaux; **cereal/tobacco ~s** intérêts dans les céréales/dans le tabac.
II *vtr* **1** (provoke curiosity, enthusiasm) intéresser [*person*] (**in** à); **it may ~ you to know** ça pourrait t'intéresser de savoir; **can I ~ you in buying some insurance/playing for us?** vous laisserez-vous convaincre de souscrire une assurance/de jouer pour notre équipe?; **can I ~ you in our new range?** Comm permettez-moi d'attirer votre attention sur notre nouvelle gamme; **2** (concern) [*problem, plight, policy*] concerner.

interest-bearing *adj* Fin [*investment, account*] porteur/-euse d'intérêts.

interested /ˈɪntrəstɪd/ *adj* [*expression, onlooker, listener*] intéressé; **to be ~ in** s'intéresser à [*subject, activity*]; **I am ~ in doing** ça m'intéresse de faire; **we're just not ~** ça ne nous intéresse pas; **to get sb ~ in** intéresser qn à [*activity, subject*]; **to become ~ in** commencer à s'intéresser à; **the ~ parties** les intéressés.

interest: **~-free loan** *n* prêt *m* sans intérêt; **~ group** *n* groupement *m* d'intérêt.

interesting /ˈɪntrəstɪŋ/ *adj* intéressant.

interestingly /ˈɪntrəstɪŋlɪ/ *adv* **1** (worthy of note) chose intéressante; iron chose curieuse; **~, there is no equivalent** chose intéressante, il n'y a pas d'équivalent; **~, his wife isn't with him** chose curieuse, sa femme n'est pas avec lui; **~ enough**... ce qui est très intéressant...; **2** (inspiring interest) [*speak, write*] d'une façon intéressante; **~ complex/constructed** d'une intéressante complexité/construction.

interest rate *n* Fin taux *m* d'intérêt.

interface /ˈɪntəfeɪs/ **I** *n* **1** Comput, fig interface *f* (**between** entre; **with** avec); **2** Tech jonction *f* (**between** entre; **with** avec).
II *vtr* **1** Tech connecter, relier (**to** à; **with** avec); **2** Sewing entoiler.
III *vi* se connecter (**to** à; **with** avec).

interface: **~ board** *n* Comput carte *f* d'interface; **~ routine** *n* Comput routine *f* d'interface; **~ software** *n* Comput logiciel *m* d'interface.

interfacing /ˈɪntəfeɪsɪŋ/ *n* Sewing entoilage *m*.

interfere /ˌɪntəˈfɪə(r)/ *vi* **1** péj (involve oneself) [*person*] **to ~ in** s'immiscer dans [*affairs*]; **don't ~!** ne te mêle pas de ça!; **she never ~s** elle ne se mêle jamais de ce qui ne la regarde pas; **2** (intervene) [*government, court, police*] intervenir; **to ~ in** s'ingérer dans [*internal affairs, private life*]; **3** (touch, mess with) **to ~ with** toucher, traficoter○ [*machine, bird's nest*]; **to ~ with a child** GB euph se livrer à des attouchements sexuels sur un enfant; **4** (hinder) [*activity*] **to ~ with** empiéter sur [*family life, freedom, right*]; déranger [*sleep, healing*]; **5** Phys interférer.

interference /ˌɪntəˈfɪərəns/ *n* **1** (by government, editor, boss) ingérence *f* (**in** dans); (by family) immixtion *f* (**in** dans); **I don't want any ~** je ne veux pas qu'on se mêle de mes affaires; **2** (of sound waves, light waves) brouillage *m*, interférence *f*; (on radio) parasites *mpl*; **3** Ling interférence *f*.

interfering /ˌɪntəˈfɪərɪŋ/ *adj* péj [*person, family*] envahissant, qui se mêle de ce qui ne le/la regarde pas.

interferon /ˌɪntəˈfɪərən/ *n* interféron *m*.

intergalactic /ˌɪntəgəˈlæktɪk/ *adj* intergalactique.

intergovernmental /ˌɪntəˌgʌvnˈmentl/ *adj* intergouvernemental.

interim /ˈɪntərɪm/ **I** *n* entre-temps *m*; **in the ~** entre-temps.
II *adj* [*arrangement, measure, government*] provisoire; [*bond, certificate*] provisoire; [*interest, payment, loan*] intermédiaire; [*post, employee*] intérimaire; **~ dividend** acompte *m* sur dividende; **~ financing** préfinancement *m*; **~ profits** résultats *mpl* semestriels; **~ report** comptes *mpl* semestriels; **the ~ period** l'intérim *m*.

interior /ɪnˈtɪərɪə(r)/ **I** *n* **1** (inside) (of house) intérieur *m*; (of fridge, bag) intérieur *m*; **a Vermeer ~** Art une scène d'intérieur de Vermeer; **2** (of country, continent) intérieur *m*; **people from the ~** personnes venues de l'intérieur (du pays); **Secretary/Department of the Interior** US Pol ministre *m*/ministère *m* de l'Intérieur.
II *adj* **1** (inside) [*wall, paintwork*] intérieur; **2** Cin, TV [*shot*] en intérieur; [*scene*] d'intérieur; **3** (inner) [*motive, impulse*] intérieur.

interior: **~ angle** *n* angle *m* intérieur; **~ decoration** *n* décoration *f*; **~ decorator** ▶ 1692 *n* décorateur/-trice *m/f*; **~ design** *n* (colours, fabrics etc) design *m*; (walls, space) architecture *f* intérieure; **~ designer** ▶ 1692 *n* (of colours, fabrics etc) designer *m*; (of walls, space) architecte *mf* d'intérieur; **~ sprung** *adj* à ressorts.

interject /ˌɪntəˈdʒekt/ *vtr* placer [*word, comment*]; introduire [*warning*]; **'I disagree,' she ~ed** 'je ne suis pas d'accord,' dit-elle.

interjection /ˌɪntəˈdʒekʃn/ *n* **1** Ling interjection *f*; **2** (interruption) interruption *f*.

interlace /ˌɪntəˈleɪs/ **I** *vtr* entrecroiser.
II *vi* s'entrelacer, s'entrecroiser.

interlard /ˌɪntəˈlɑːd/ *vtr* émailler (**with** de).

interleave /ˌɪntəˈliːv/ **I** *vtr* intercaler.
II *vi* s'intercaler.

interlibrary loan *n* prêt *m* interbibliothèques.

interline /ˌɪntəˈlaɪn/ *vtr* **1** Print interligner; **2** Sewing mettre de la triplure dans.

interlinear /ˌɪntəˈlɪnɪə(r)/ *adj* interlinéaire.

interlining /ˈɪntəlaɪnɪŋ/ *n* Sewing triplure *f*.

interlink /ˌɪntəˈlɪŋk/ **I** *vtr* **to be ~ed** être lié (**with** à).
II *vi* [*aspects, problems*] se lier.

interlock **I** /ˈɪntəlɒk/ *n* **1** Comput verrouillage *m*; **2** Tex interlock *m*.
II /ˌɪntəˈlɒk/ *vtr* emboîter [*pipes, tiles*]; enclencher [*mechanisms*]; entrelacer [*fingers, bodies*].
III /ˌɪntəˈlɒk/ *vi* [*pipes, tiles*] s'emboîter; [*mechanisms*] s'enclencher; [*fingers*] s'entrelacer; [*systems, factors, objectives*] être intimement lié.

interlocutor /ˌɪntəˈlɒkjʊtə(r)/ *n* interlocuteur/-trice *m/f*.

interloper /ˈɪntələʊpə(r)/ *n* intrus/-e *m/f*.

interlude /ˈɪntəluːd/ *n* **1** Cin, Theat, Mus (interval) entracte *m*; **2** (brief entertainment) Theat intermède *m*; Mus interlude *m*; **3** (pause in events) intervalle *m* (**between** entre); **in the ~** dans l'intervalle.

intermarriage /ˌɪntəˈmærɪdʒ/ *n* **1** (within a family) intermariage *m*; **2** (between groups) mariage *m* mixte.

intermarry /ˌɪntəˈmærɪ/ *vi* **1** (within a family) pratiquer l'intermariage; **2** (between groups) se marier (*entre membres de groupes ethniques ou raciaux différents*).

intermediary /ˌɪntəˈmiːdɪərɪ, US -dɪerɪ/ **I** *n* intermédiaire *mf* (**between** entre).
II *adj* intermédiaire.

intermediate /ˌɪntəˈmiːdɪət/ **I** *n* **1** (mediator) intermédiaire *mf*; **2** US Aut automobile *f* de taille moyenne; **3** Chem produit *m* intermédiaire.
II *adj* **1** [*point, step, stage*] intermédiaire; **2** Sch [*book, exam*] de difficulté moyenne; [*course*] de niveau moyen; [*level, student*] moyen/-enne; **3** Fin [*credit*] à moyen terme.

intermediate: **~ host** *n* hôte *m* intermédiaire; **~ range** *adj* [*missile, weapon*] à moyenne portée; **~ technology** *n* technologie *f* intermédiaire.

interment /ɪnˈtɜːmənt/ *n* inhumation *f*.

intermezzo /ˌɪntəˈmetsəʊ/ *n* intermezzo *m*.

interminable /ɪnˈtɜːmɪnəbl/ *adj* interminable.

interminably /ɪnˈtɜːmɪnəblɪ/ *adv* [*argue, talk*] pendant des heures; **~ long** interminable.

intermingle /ˌɪntəˈmɪŋgl/ **I** *vtr* mêler [*themes*]; mélanger [*colours, patterns*] (**with** à).
II *vi* [*people, themes*] se mêler (**with** à); [*colours, patterns*] se mélanger (**with** à).

intermission /ˌɪntəˈmɪʃn/ *n* **1** Cin, Theat entracte *m*; **2** (pause) gen interruption *f*; (in fighting, quarrel) trêve *f*; **3** Med intermission *f*.

intermittent /ˌɪntəˈmɪtənt/ *adj* [*noise, activity*] intermittent; [*use*] occasionnel/-elle.

intermittently /ˌɪntəˈmɪtəntlɪ/ *adv* par intermittence.

intern **I** /ˈɪntɜːn/ *n* surtout US **1** Med interne *mf*; **2** gen stagiaire *mf*.
II /ɪnˈtɜːn/ *vtr* Mil, Pol interner.
III /ɪnˈtɜːn/ *vi* surtout US faire un stage.

internal /ɪnˈtɜːnl/ *adj* **1** (inner) [*mechanism*] interne; [*pipe*] intérieur; **the theory has ~ consistency** la théorie est cohérente en soi; **2** Med [*organ*] interne; **~ bleeding** hémorragie *f* interne; **~ injuries** lésions *fpl* internes; **~ examination** toucher *m* vaginal; **3** (within organization) [*problem, dispute*] interne; [*call, phone, mail*] interne; [*candidate*] interne à l'entreprise; **~ memorandum** note *f* de service; **~ financing** autofinancement *m*; **4** (within country) [*security, flight*] intérieur; [*debt, trade*] intérieur; **~ revenue** revenus *mpl* fiscaux; **~ affairs** Pol affaires *fpl* internes; **~ fighting** luttes *fpl* intestines.

internal: **~ combustion engine** *n* moteur *m* à combustion interne; **~ examiner** *n* GB Sch, Univ examinateur/-trice *m/f* (*faisant passer un examen dans son propre établissement*).

internalize /ɪnˈtɜːnəlaɪz/ *vtr* intérioriser.

internally /ɪnˈtɜːnəlɪ/ *adv* **1** (on the inside) à l'intérieur; **'not to be taken ~'** Med 'médicament à usage externe'; **he was bleeding ~** il faisait une hémorragie interne; **2** (within organization) [*recruit*] au sein de l'entreprise; **3** [*visualize*] mentalement.

Internal Revenue Service *n* US ≈ fisc *m*.

international /ˌɪntəˈnæʃnəl/ **I** *n* Sport (fixture) match *m* international; (player) international/-e *m/f*.
II *adj* international; **~ waters** eaux *fpl* internationales.

International Court of Justice *n* cour *f* internationale de justice.

Internationale /ˌɪntənæʃəˈnɑːl/ *n* Mus, Pol Internationale *f*.

internationalism /ˌɪntəˈnæʃnəlɪzəm/ *n* internationalisme *m*.

internationalist /ˌɪntəˈnæʃnəlɪst/ *n* internationaliste *mf*.

internationalization /ˌɪntəˌnæʃnəl aɪˈzeɪʃn, US -lɪˈz-/ *n* internationalisation *f*.

internationalize /ˌɪntəˈnæʃnəlaɪz/ *vtr* internationaliser.

internationally /ˌɪntəˈnæʃnəlɪ/ *adv* [*known*] dans le monde entier, mondialement; [*famous, recognized, respected*] dans le monde entier; **~, the situation is even worse** sur le plan international, la situation est encore pire.

international: **International Monetary Fund**, **IMF** *n* Fonds *m* monétaire international, FMI *m*; **~ money order** *n* mandat-poste *m* international; **International Phonetic Alphabet**, **IPA** *n* alphabet *m* phonétique international, API *m*; **~ relations** *n* (+ *v sg*) Univ relations *fpl* internationales; **~ reply coupon** *n* coupon-réponse *m* international.

internecine /ˌɪntəˈniːsaɪn/ *adj* **1** (destructive) [*conflict, warfare*] fratricide; **2** (internal) [*feud, rivalry*] intestin.

internee /ˌɪntɜːˈniː/ *n* Mil, Pol interné/-e *m/f*.

Internet /ˈɪntənet/ *n* Comput Internet *m*; **~ service provider** fournisseur *m* d'accès à l'Internet; **~ user** internaute *mf*.

internist /ɪnˈtɜːnɪst/ *n* US, Med interniste *mf*.

internment /ɪnˈtɜːnmənt/ *n* internement *m*.

internship /ɪnˈtɜːnʃɪp/ *n* US **1** gen stage *m*; **2** Med internat *m*.

interpersonal /ˌɪntəˈpɜːsənl/ *adj* [*skills*] de communication; [*relations*] humain; **~ communications** communication *f*.

interplanetary /ˌɪntəˈplænɪtrɪ, US -terɪ/ *adj* interplanétaire.

interplay /ˈɪntəpleɪ/ *n* interaction *f* (**between** entre; **of** de).

Interpol /ˈɪntəpɒl/ *n* Interpol *m*.

interpolate /ɪnˈtɜːpəleɪt/ *vtr* placer [*remark*] (**into** dans); insérer [*anecdote, song*] (**into** dans); interpoler [*passage*] (**into** dans); Math interpoler; **'that's not true!' she ~d** 'cela est faux!' coupa-t-elle.

interpolation /ɪnˌtɜːpəˈleɪʃn/ *n* **1** (addition) interpolation *f* (**of** de); **2** (interruption) interruption *f*.

interpose /ˌɪntəˈpəʊz/ **I** *vtr* **1** (insert) interposer (**between** entre); **2** (introduce) placer [*comment, remark*].
II *vi* intervenir.
III *v refl* **to ~ oneself** s'interposer (**between** entre).

interpret /ɪnˈtɜːprɪt/ **I** *vtr* interpréter (**as** comme; **to** pour).
II *vi* faire l'interprète (**for** pour).

interpretation /ɪnˌtɜːprɪˈteɪʃn/ *n* interprétation *f* (**by** par; **of** de); **open to ~** sujet à interprétation; **to place an ~ on sth** donner une interprétation à qch.

interpretative /ɪnˈtɜːprɪtətɪv/ *adj* [*difficulties, differences, skills*] d'interprétation; [*article, guide*] donnant une interprétation.

interpreter /ɪnˈtɜːprɪtə(r)/ *n* **1** interprète *mf*; **to speak through an ~** parler par l'intermédiaire d'un/d'une interprète; **2** Comput (machine) traductrice *f*; (program) interpréteur *m*.

interpreting /ɪnˈtɜːprɪtɪŋ/ *n* (subject, profession) interprétariat *m*.

interregnum /ˌɪntəˈregnəm/ *n* (*pl* **-a** ou **~s**) interrègne *m*.

interrelate /ˌɪntərɪˈleɪt/ **I** *vtr* mettre [qch] en corrélation.
II *vi* [*events, facts, ideas*] être étroitement lié; [*people*] sympathiser.
III interrelated *pp adj* [*components, parts*] interdépendant; [*ideas*] étroitement lié.

interrelation /ˌɪntərɪˈleɪʃn/, **interrelationship** /ˌɪntərɪˈleɪʃnʃɪp/ *n* **1** (of facts, events) corrélation *f* (**between** entre; **of** de; **with** avec); **2** (of people, groups) relation *f* (**between** entre; **of** de; **with** avec).

interrogate /ɪnˈterəgeɪt/ *vtr* **1** gen interroger; (more rigorous) soumettre [qn] à un interrogatoire; **2** Comput interroger.

interrogation /ɪnˌterəˈgeɪʃn/ **I** *n* interrogatoire *m* (**by** par; **of** de); **he confessed under ~** il a avoué pendant son interrogatoire.
II *modif* [*procedure, room*] d'interrogatoire.

interrogation mark *n* Ling point *m* d'interrogation.

interrogative /ˌɪntəˈrɒgətɪv/ **I** *n* Ling interrogatif *m*; **in the ~** à la forme interrogative.
II *adj* **1** Ling interrogatif/-ive; **2** gen [*look, remark, tone*] interrogateur/-trice.

interrogatively /ˌɪntəˈrɒgətɪvlɪ/ *adv* **1** [*look*] d'un air interrogateur; [*speak*] d'un ton interrogateur; **2** Ling [*function*] à la forme interrogative.

interrogator /ɪnˈterəgeɪtə(r)/ *n* interrogateur/-trice *m/f*.

interrogatory /ˌɪntəˈrɒgətrɪ, US -tɔːrɪ/ *adj* [*tone*] interrogateur/-trice; [*manner*] interrogatif/-ive.

interrupt /ˌɪntəˈrʌpt/ **I** *n* Comput interruption *f*.
II *vtr* **1** (cut in) interrompre, couper la parole à [*person*]; **2** (disturb) déranger [*person*]; interrompre [*meeting, lecture*]; **3** (block) gêner [*view*]; **the skyline was ~ed by pylons** quelques pylônes brisaient la ligne d'horizon; **4** (stop) couper [*supply*].
III *vi* interrompre; **stop ~ing!** arrête de m'interrompre!

interruption /ˌɪntəˈrʌpʃn/ *n* interruption *f*; **there are constant ~s** on est constamment interrompu.

intersect /ˌɪntəˈsekt/ **I** *vtr* **1** gen croiser; **a field ~ed by ditches** un champ coupé par des fossés; **2** Math couper.
II *vi* **1** [*roads, wires, ideas*] se croiser; **two ~ing paths** deux chemins qui se croisent; **to ~ with** croiser; **2** Math se couper.

intersection /ˌɪntəˈsekʃn/ *n* gen, Math intersection *f* (**of** de; **with** avec).

interservice /ˌɪntəˈsɜːvɪs/ *adj* Mil interarmées (*inv*).

intersperse /ˌɪntəˈspɜːs/ *vtr* (with jokes) parsemer (**with** de); (with music, breaks) entrecouper (**with** de); (with colour, flowers, trees) parsemer (**with** de); **houses ~d among the trees** des maisons éparpillées parmi les arbres; **laughter ~d between sarcastic comments** des commentaires sarcastiques parsemés d'éclats de rire; **sunshine ~d with showers** des éclaircies en alternance avec des averses.

interstate /ˌɪntəˈsteɪt/ **I** *n* (also **~ highway**) autoroute *f* (inter-États).
II *adj* US [*commerce, communications, links*] entre États.

interstellar /ˌɪntəˈstelə(r)/ *adj* interstellaire.

interstice /ɪnˈtɜːstɪs/ *n* interstice *m*.

intertwine /ˌɪntəˈtwaɪn/ **I** *vtr* entrelacer [*fingers, threads*].
II *vi* [*bodies, fingers, threads*] s'entrelacer; [*lives, destinies, themes*] se croiser; **intertwining branches** branches entrelacées.
III intertwined *pp adj* lit entrelacé (**with** à); fig lié (**with** à).

interurban /ˌɪntərˈɜːbən/ *adj* interurbain.

interval /ˈɪntəvl/ *n* **1** (in time, space) intervalle *m*; **there was a long ~ between the two visits** il y a eu un long intervalle entre les deux visites; **he is fed at four-hourly ~s** on lui donne à manger toutes les quatre heures; **at regular ~s** à intervalles réguliers; **at weekly ~s** toutes les semaines; **they were positioned at ~s of 100 metres** ou **at 100 metre ~s** ils étaient placés à 100 mètres d'intervalle; **bright ~s** Meteorol belles éclaircies *fpl*; **to have lucid ~s** Med avoir des périodes de lucidité; **2** GB Theat entracte *m*; Sport (during match) pause *f*, mi-temps *f inv*; **3** Mus intervalle *m*; **an ~ of a third/a fifth** un intervalle d'une tierce/d'une quinte.

intervene /ˌɪntəˈviːn/ *vi* **1** (take action) intervenir; **to ~ on sb's behalf** intervenir en faveur de qn; **to ~ in a dispute** intervenir dans un conflit; **2** (happen) arriver, survenir; **if nothing ~s** si rien n'arrive entre-temps; **10 years had ~d** 10 années s'étaient écoulées; **3** (mediate) s'interposer (**between** entre).

intervening /ˌɪntəˈviːnɪŋ/ *adj* **in the ~ period** ou **hours** entre-temps; **in the ~ 10 years** dans les 10 dernières années; **I had grown taller during the ~ years** les années s'étaient écoulées et j'avais grandi; **he could see across the ~ fields to the hills** par-delà les champs il pouvait apercevoir les collines.

intervention /ˌɪntəˈvenʃn/ **I** *n* intervention *f*; **an ~ on my behalf** une intervention en ma faveur.
II *modif* EC [*beef, butter*] acheté à un prix d'intervention; [*price, stocks*] d'intervention.

interventionist /ˌɪntəˈvenʃənɪst/ *n, adj* interventionniste (*mf*).

interview /ˈɪntəvjuː/ **I** *n* **1** (for job etc) entretien *m* (**with** avec); **job ~** entretien; **to be called** ou **invited for (an) ~** être convoqué à un entretien; **who is on the ~ panel?** quelles sont les personnes qui font passer l'entretien?; **2** Journ interview *f*; **TV/radio ~** interview à la télévision/à la radio; **to conduct/give an ~** mener/accorder une interview; **in an ~ with the Gazette** dans une interview accordée au journal la Gazette; **3** (formal talks) entretien *m* (**between** entre).
II *vtr* **1** (for job, place) faire passer un entretien à [*candidate*]; **2** (call to interview) convoquer [qn] pour un entretien; **3** Journ interviewer [*celebrity*]; [*police*] interroger [*suspect*].
III *vi* [*candidate*] passer un entretien; [*manager, company*] faire passer des entretiens; **to ~ well** être bon lors de l'entretien.

interviewee /ˌɪntəvjuːˈiː/ *n* **1** (for job, place) candidat/-e *m/f*; **2** (on TV, radio) personne *f* interviewée; **3** (in survey) personne *f* interrogée.

interviewer /ˈɪntəvjuːə(r)/ *n* **1** (for job, course) personne *f* faisant passer l'entretien; **2** Journ intervieweur/-euse *m/f*; **TV ~** journaliste *mf* qui fait des interviews à la télévision; **3** (for survey) enquêteur/-trice *m/f*.

intervocalic /ˌɪntəvəˈkælɪk/ *adj* intervocalique.

interwar /ˌɪntəˈwɔː(r)/ *adj* [*history, literature, politics*] de l'entre-deux-guerres; **during the ~ period** ou **years** pendant l'entre-deux-guerres.

interweave /ˌɪntəˈwiːv/ (*prét* **-wove** /-ˈwəʊv/; *pp* **-woven** /-ˈwəʊvn/) **I** *vtr* entrelacer [*fingers, threads*]; mêler [*themes, rhythms*].
II *vi* [*fibres*] s'entrelacer; [*destinies*] être lié; [*themes, melodies, voices*] se mêler.
III interwoven *pp adj* lit entrelacé (**with** à); fig mêlé (**with** à).

intestate /ɪnˈtesteɪt/ *adj* Jur intestat (*inv*); **to die ~** décéder intestat.

intestate estate *n* succession *f* ab intestat.

intestinal /ɪnˈtestɪnl, ˌɪntesˈtaɪnl/ *adj* intestinal; **~ blockage** occlusion *f* intestinale; **to have ~ fortitude** US avoir qch dans le ventre○.

intestine /ɪnˈtestɪn/ *n* intestin *m*.

intifada /ɪntɪˈfɑːdə/ *n* intifada *f*.

intimacy /ˈɪntɪməsɪ/ **I** *n* **1** (closeness) intimité *f*; **to be on terms of ~ with sb** être intimement lié à qn; **2** euph (sexual relations) relations *fpl* (sexuelles); **there had been no ~ between them** ils n'avaient pas eu une relation très poussée; **3** (closed environment) intimité *f*.
II intimacies *npl* (gestures) gestes *mpl* familiers; (words) familiarités *fpl*.

intimate I /ˈɪntɪmət/ *n* intime *mf*.
II /ˈɪntɪmət/ *adj* **1** (personal) [*biography, detail, diary, friend, secret, style*] intime;

[*belief, friendship*] profond; [*life*] privé; **~ apparel** US lingerie *f*; **to have an ~ relationship with sb** être intime avec qn; **to be on ~ terms with sb** être intime avec qn; **2** (sexual) [*relationship*] intime; **to be ~ with sb** avoir des relations sexuelles avec qn; **3** (cosy) [*atmosphere, occasion, meal, restaurant*] intime; **4** (close) [*bond, connection*] intime; **to have an ~ acquaintance with, to have an ~ knowledge of** avoir une connaissance approfondie de.

III /ˈɪntɪmeɪt/ *vtr* **1** (hint) laisser entendre [*desires, wishes*]; **to ~ that** laisser entendre que; **2** (announce) annoncer [*content, composition, refusal*]; **to ~ that** faire savoir que.

intimately /ˈɪntɪmətlɪ/ *adv* **1** (in a personal way) [*know*] intimement; [*greet, speak, write*] de façon intime; **2** (sexually) [*caress, touch*] intimement; **to be ~ involved with sb** avoir une liaison avec qn; **3** (deeply) **to be ~ aware of sth** être profondément conscient de qch; **to be ~ acquainted** ou **familiar with sth** connaître qch intimement; **4** (closely) [*connected, related*] intimement; **to be ~ involved in** ou **with sth** être impliqué de près à qch.

intimation /ˌɪntɪˈmeɪʃn/ *n* **1** (hint) indication *f*; **she gave me no ~ that she was leaving** rien ne m'a laissé présager qu'elle allait partir; **he gave her an ~ that** il lui a laissé entendre que; **to have an ~ of danger** pressentir un danger; **2** (announcement) gen, Relig annonce *f*.

intimidate /ɪnˈtɪmɪdeɪt/ *vtr* intimider; **to ~ sb into doing** faire pression sur qn pour qu'il fasse.

intimidating /ɪnˈtɪmɪdeɪtɪŋ/ *adj* [*behaviour, experience, person*] intimidant; [*obstacle, sight, size*] impressionnant; [*prospect*] angoissant.

intimidatingly /ɪnˈtɪmɪdeɪtɪŋlɪ/ *adv* [*say, look etc*] d'une façon intimidante; [*large, long etc*] effroyablement.

intimidation /ɪnˌtɪmɪˈdeɪʃn/ *n* intimidation *f* (**by** de la part de; **of** de).

into /ˈɪntu, ˈɪntə:/

■ **Note** *into* is used after certain nouns and verbs in English (*way into, change into, stray into etc*). For translations, consult the appropriate noun or verb entry (***way***, ***change***, ***stray*** etc).
– *into* is used in the structure *verb + sb + into + doing* (*to bully sb into doing, to fool sb into doing*). For translations of these structures see the appropriate verb entry (***bully***, ***fool*** etc).
– For translations of expressions like *get into trouble, go into detail, get into debt etc* you should consult the appropriate noun entry (***trouble***, ***detail***, ***debt*** etc).

prep **1** (indicating change of position, location) dans; **to put sth ~** mettre qch dans [*container, envelope, drainer, room*]; **to come/go ~** entrer dans [*room, building, zone*]; **to disappear ~** disparaître dans [*forest, mist*]; **pour the mixture ~ it** verser le mélange dedans; **to move sth ~ the shade** mettre qch à l'ombre; **to go ~ town/~ the office** aller en ville/au bureau; **to get ~ a car/a train** monter dans une voiture/un train; **to get ~ bed** se mettre au lit; **to help sb ~ bed** aider qn à se mettre au lit; **2** (indicating change of shape, form, value) en; **to cut/fold sth ~ triangles** couper/plier qch en triangles; **to curl up ~ a ball** se rouler en boule; **to break ~ pieces** se briser; **divided ~ apartments** divisé en appartements; **to translate sth ~ Greek** traduire qch en grec; **to change dollars ~ francs** changer des dollars en francs; **to turn ~** se métamorphoser en [*butterfly, frog*]; **to turn ~ a young woman** devenir une jeune femme; **to roll sth ~ a ball** faire une boule de qch; **3** (indicating duration) **to last/continue ~ the 18th century** durer/continuer jusqu'au XVIIIᵉ siècle; **to go on ~ the afternoon** se prolonger dans l'après-midi; **long** ou **far ~ the night** jusque tard dans la nuit; **4** (indicating a point in a process) **we were well ~ 1988 when...** l'année 1988 était bien entamée quand...; **well ~ the second half** bien après le début de la deuxième mi-temps; **she was well ~ the fourth month of her pregnancy** elle en était bien à son quatrième mois de grossesse; **to be (well) ~ one's thirties** avoir une bonne trentaine d'années; **5** (indicating direction) dans; **to speak ~ the microphone** parler dans le microphone; **to stare ~ space** regarder dans le vide; **to gaze ~ the distance** regarder au loin; **to ride off ~ the sunset** partir vers le soleil couchant; **6**○ (keen on) **to be ~** être fana○ de [*jazz, athletics, architecture etc*]; **she's ~ art in a big way, she's heavily ~ art** c'est vraiment une fana d'art○; **to be ~ drugs** se droguer; **7** (indicating impact) dans; **to run ~ sth** rentrer dans qch; **he bumped ~ me** il m'est rentré dedans; **to bang ~ sb/sth** heurter qn/qch; **8** Math **8 ~ 24 goes 3 times** ou **is 3** 24 divisé par 8 égale 3. ▶ **get into, go into**.

IDIOMS **to be ~ everything** [*child*] toucher à tout.

intolerable /ɪnˈtɒlərəbl/ *adj* [*behaviour, conceit, heat, state*] intolérable (**to** à); [*position, situation*] insupportable (**to** à); **it is ~ that** il est intolérable que (+ *subj*); **it is ~ to do** il est insupportable de faire.

intolerably /ɪnˈtɒlərəblɪ/ *adv* [*act, behave*] d'une façon insupportable; [*painful, possessive, long*] horriblement.

intolerance /ɪnˈtɒlərəns/ *n* gen, Med intolérance *f* (**of, towards** vis-à-vis de; **to** à).

intolerant /ɪnˈtɒlərənt/ *adj* intolérant (**of, towards** vis-à-vis de; **with** envers).

intolerantly /ɪnˈtɒlərəntlɪ/ *adv* avec intolérance.

intonation /ˌɪntəˈneɪʃn/ *n* Ling, Mus intonation *f*.

intone /ɪnˈtəʊn/ **I** *vtr* psalmodier [*prayer, psalm*]; déclamer [*lecture, speech*].
II *vi* déclamer.

intoxicant /ɪnˈtɒksɪkənt/ *n* **1** (alcohol) boisson *f* alcoolisée; **2** (poison) substance *f* toxique; **3** fig (stimulant) drogue *f*.

intoxicate /ɪnˈtɒksɪkeɪt/ *vtr* **1** (inebriate) enivrer (**with** avec); **2** (poison) intoxiquer (**with** avec); **3** fig griser (**with** avec).

intoxicated /ɪnˈtɒksɪkeɪtɪd/ *adj* **1** lit ivre; **to drive while ~** conduire en état d'ivresse; **2** fig grisé (**by, with** par).

intoxicating /ɪnˈtɒksɪkeɪtɪŋ/ *adj* **1** lit [*drink*] alcoolisé; [*effect, substance*] toxique; **2** fig [*perfume, smell*] enivrant; [*experience, sensation*] grisant.

intoxication /ɪnˌtɒksɪˈkeɪʃn/ *n* **1** lit ivresse *f*, ébriété *f*; **in a state of ~** en état d'ivresse or d'ébriété; **2** fig ivresse *f*.

intoximeter® /ɪnˈtɒksɪmətə(r)/ *n* alcootest *m*.

intractability /ɪnˌtræktəˈbɪlətɪ/ *n* **1** (of person, opinion) inflexibilité *f*; **2** (of substance) manque *m* de malléabilité; **3** (of illness, problem) caractère *m* rebelle.

intractable /ɪnˈtræktəbl/ *adj* [*person, personality*] intraitable; [*opinion*] inflexible; [*substance*] dur à travailler; [*illness, problem*] rebelle.

intramural /ˌɪntrəˈmjʊərl/ **I intramurals** *npl* US matchs *mpl* entre équipes d'un même établissement.
II *adj* [*course, studies*] dispensé dans l'établissement; [*game, match*] US interclasse (*inv*).

intramuscular /ˌɪntrəˈmʌskjʊlə(r)/ *adj* intramusculaire.

intransigence /ɪnˈtrænsɪdʒəns/ *n* intransigeance *f* (**about, over** sur; **towards** envers).

intransigent /ɪnˈtrænsɪdʒənt/ *adj* [*attitude, behaviour, person*] intransigeant (**about, over** sur; **towards** envers).

intransitive /ɪnˈtrænsətɪv/ **I** *n* intransitif *m*.
II *adj* intransitif/-ive.

intrauterine /ˌɪntrəˈju:tərɪn/ *adj* intra-utérin.

intrauterine device, IUD *n* Med stérilet *m*.

intravenous /ˌɪntrəˈvi:nəs/ *adj* intraveineux/-euse.

intravenous: **~ drip** *n* perfusion *f* intraveineuse; **~ drug use** *n* toxicomanie *f* intraveineuse; **~ drug user** *n* usager *m* de drogues par voie intraveineuse; **~ injection** *n* (piqûre *f*) intraveineuse *f*.

intravenously /ˌɪntrəˈvi:nəslɪ/ *adv* par voie *f* intraveineuse.

in-tray /ˈɪntreɪ/ *n* corbeille *f* arrivée.

intrepid /ɪnˈtrepɪd/ *adj* intrépide.

intrepidity /ˌɪntrɪˈpɪdətɪ/ *n* intrépidité *f*.

intrepidly /ɪnˈtrepɪdlɪ/ *adv* [*attack, march*] hardiment; [*act, speak*] avec intrépidité.

intricacy **I** /ˈɪntrɪkəsɪ/ *n* complexité *f*.
II intricacies *npl* **1** (of story) subtilités *fpl*; **2** (of the law) méandres *mpl*.

intricate /ˈɪntrɪkət/ *adj* [*carving, mechanism, pattern, plot, task*] compliqué; [*problem, relationship, solution*] complexe.

intricately /ˈɪntrɪkətlɪ/ *adv* de façon complexe.

intrigue **I** /ˈɪntri:g, ɪnˈtri:g/ *n* ¢ (plotting) intrigue *f*; **political ~** les intrigues politiques; **to engage in an ~** intriguer.
II /ɪnˈtri:g/ *vtr* (fascinate) intriguer; **she was ~d by his story** son histoire l'intriguait; **I'm ~d to know how you got here** je suis curieux de savoir comment vous êtes arrivé ici.
III /ɪnˈtri:g/ *vi* (plot) comploter (**against** contre; **with** avec).

intriguing /ɪnˈtri:gɪŋ/ **I** *n* ¢ intrigues *fpl*.
II *adj* [*person, smile*] fascinant; [*person, story*] curieux/-ieuse, intéressant.

intriguingly /ɪnˈtri:gɪŋlɪ/ *adv* **the question was ~ worded** la question était formulée de façon à susciter la curiosité; **~, she said nothing** chose curieuse, elle n'a rien dit.

intrinsic /ɪnˈtrɪnzɪk, -sɪk/ *adj* intrinsèque (**to** à).

intrinsically /ɪnˈtrɪnzɪklɪ, -sɪk-/ *adv* intrinsèquement.

intro○ /ˈɪntrəʊ/ *n* Mus, gen (*abrév* = **introduction**) intro○ *f*.

introduce /ˌɪntrəˈdju:s, US -du:s/ **I** *vtr* **1** (make known) présenter [*person*] (**as** comme); **to ~ sb to** présenter qn à [*guest, friend*]; initier qn à [*painting, camping, drugs, smoking*]; **she ~d me to Mozart/French cooking** elle m'a fait connaître Mozart/la cuisine française; **this book ~s us to the subject/ideas of...** ce livre nous présente le sujet/les idées de...; **have you been ~d?** avez-vous été présentés?; **introducing Abigail Bond** Cin pour la première fois à l'écran, Abigail Bond; **2** (cause to enter) introduire [*liquid, tube, needle*] (**into** dans); introduire [*species, plant, disease*] (**into** dans); introduire [*camera, bomb*] (**into** dans); introduire [*character, theme*] (**into** dans); **she tried to ~ the subject into the conversation** elle a essayé d'aborder le sujet; **3** (establish) mettre [qch] en place [*law, system, examination, reform*] (**into** dans); introduire [*word, product, change*] (**into** dans); **4** (preface) introduire [*talk, article, chapter*] (**with** par); **5** (present for debate) présenter [*bill, proposal*]; **6** TV, Radio [*presenter*] présenter [*programme*].
II *v refl* **to ~ oneself** se présenter (**to** à).

introduction /ˌɪntrəˈdʌkʃn/ *n* **1** (making known) présentation *f*; **to make** ou **do the ~s** faire les présentations; **'our next guest needs no ~'** 'il est inutile de présenter notre prochain intervenant'; **a letter of ~** une lettre de recommandation; **2** (insertion) (of liquid, tube, needle) introduction *f* (**into** dans); (of species, plant, character, theme) introduction *f* (**into** dans); **3** (establishing) (of law, system, examination, reform) introduction *f* (**into** dans); **this system is a recent ~** ce système a été introduit récemment; **4** (initiation) (to art, music, alcohol, drugs) premier contact *m* (**to** avec); **5** (preface) (to speech, article, book) introduction *f* (**to** de); **6** Mus prologue *m*; **7** (beginner's guide) initiation *f*; **'An Introduction to French'** 'Initiation au français'; **8** Pol, Admin (presentation for debate) (of bill, proposal) présentation *f*.

introduction agency *n* club *m* de rencontres.

introductory /ˌɪntrəˈdʌktərɪ/ *adj* **1** (prefatory) [*remark, speech, paragraph, explanation*] préliminaire; **2** Comm [*offer*] de lancement.

introit /ˈɪntrɔɪt/ *n* Relig introït *m*.

introspection /ˌɪntrəˈspekʃn/ *n* introspection *f*.

introspective /ˌɪntrəˈspektɪv/ *adj* [*person*] introspectif/-ive; [*tendency*] à l'introspection.

introspectiveness /ˌɪntrəˈspektɪvnɪs/ *n* introspection *f*.

introversion /ˌɪntrəˈvɜːʃn, US -ˈvɜːrʒn/ *n* introversion *f*.

introvert /ˈɪntrəvɜːt/ **I** *n* introverti/-e *m/f*.
II *adj* = **introverted**.

introverted /ˈɪntrəvɜːtɪd/ *adj* introverti.

intrude /ɪnˈtruːd/ **I** *vtr* imposer [*opinions*].
II *vi* **1** (meddle, interfere) **I don't wish to ~** je ne veux pas me mêler de ce qui ne me regarde pas; **to ~ in(to) sb's affairs** s'immiscer dans les affaires de qn; **2** (encroach) **I don't wish to ~ (up)on her grief** je ne veux pas la déranger quand elle a du chagrin; **to ~ (up)on sb's privacy** être importun; **I don't want to ~ on a family gathering** je ne veux pas m'imposer dans une réunion de famille; **3** (disturb) **I don't wish to ~** je ne veux pas vous déranger.

intruder /ɪnˈtruːdə(r)/ *n* (all contexts) intrus/-e *m/f*; **the trawler is an ~ in our coastal waters** le chalutier pénètre illégalement dans nos eaux territoriales; **we were made to feel like ~s** on nous a fait sentir que nous étions de trop.

intruder alarm *n* sonnerie *f* d'alarme.

intrusion /ɪnˈtruːʒn/ *n* **1** (interruption, unwelcome arrival) intrusion *f* (**into** dans); **she apologized for the ~** elle s'est excusée de nous avoir dérangés; **2** (interference) ingérence *f*, immixtion *f* (**into** dans); **it's an ~ into my affairs** on se mêle de mes affaires; **3** Ling (at beginning of word) prothèse *f*; (between words) épenthèse *f*; (at end of word) paragoge *f*.

intrusive /ɪnˈtruːsɪv/ *adj* **1** (indiscreet) [*question, journalist, cameras*] indiscret/-ète; (persistent) [*neighbours*] envahissant; **2** (disturbing) [*phone call, presence*] importun; **3** Ling [*consonant, vowel*] d'appui.

intuit /ɪnˈtjuːɪt, US -tuː-/ *vtr* sentir intuitivement; **to ~ that** avoir l'intuition que.

intuition /ˌɪntjuːˈɪʃn, US -tuː-/ *n* intuition *f* (**about** concernant); **to have an ~ that** avoir l'intuition que; **to know sth by ~** savoir qch intuitivement.

intuitive /ɪnˈtjuːɪtɪv, US -tuː-/ *adj* intuitif/-ive.

intuitively /ɪnˈtjuːɪtɪvlɪ, US -tuː-/ *adv* intuitivement.

Inuit /ˈɪnjuːɪt, ˈɪnʊɪt/ (*pl* **~** ou **~s**) **I** *n* Inuit/-e *m/f*.
II *adj* inuit.

inundate /ˈɪnʌndeɪt/ *vtr* **1** lit inonder [*field, land*]; **2** fig submerger [*person, organization*] (**with** de); inonder [*market*] (**with** de).

inundation /ˌɪnʌnˈdeɪʃn/ *n* inondation *f*.

inure /ɪˈnjʊə(r)/ **I** *vtr* endurcir (**to** à).
II *v refl* **to ~ oneself to sth** s'endurcir à qch.
III inured *pp adj* endurci (**to** à).

invade /ɪnˈveɪd/ *vtr* lit, fig envahir; **to ~ sb's privacy** s'immiscer dans la vie privée de qn.

invader /ɪnˈveɪdə(r)/ *n* envahisseur/-euse *m/f*.

invading /ɪnˈveɪdɪŋ/ *adj* [*troops, army*] d'invasion; [*fans, tourists, bacteria*] envahisseur/-euse; **the ~ Germans** l'envahisseur allemand.

invalid I /ˈɪnvəliːd, ˈɪnvəlɪd/ *n* infirme *mf*; (in official terminology) invalide *mf*; **I'm not an ~!** je ne suis pas infirme!
II /ˈɪnvəliːd, ˈɪnvəlɪd/ *modif* [*parent, relative*] infirme.
III /ɪnˈvælɪd/ *adj* **1** [*argument, claim, conclusion*] sans fondement; **2** Admin, Jur [*contract, will, marriage*] nul/nulle; [*statute, judgment*] caduc/caduque; [*claim*] non valable; [*passport, ticket*] périmé.
IV /ˈɪnvəliːd, ˈɪnvəlɪd/ *vtr* **~ed out of the army** GB réformé (pour raisons de santé).

invalidate /ɪnˈvælɪdeɪt/ *vtr* **1** infirmer [*argument, criticism*]; annuler [*claim*]; **2** Admin, Jur annuler.

invalid car /ˈɪnvəliːd, ˈɪnvəlɪd/ *n* voiturette *f* pour handicapés.

invalidity /ˌɪnvəˈlɪdətɪ/ *n* **1** (of argument, claim) manque *m* de validité; **2** (of person) invalidité *f*.

invalidity: **Invalidity Addition** *n* GB Soc Admin supplément *m* d'invalidité; **Invalidity benefit** *n* GB Soc Admin pension *f* d'invalidité.

invaluable /ɪnˈvæljʊəbl/ *adj* **1** (useful) [*assistance, advice, experience*] inestimable; [*person, machine, service*] précieux/-ieuse; **2** (priceless) [*jewel, painting*] inestimable.

invariable /ɪnˈveərɪəbl/ *adj* invariable.

invariably /ɪnˈveərɪəblɪ/ *adv* invariablement.

invasion /ɪnˈveɪʒn/ *n* invasion *f*; **~ of (sb's) privacy** atteinte *f* à la vie privée (de qn).

invasive /ɪnˈveɪsɪv/ *adj* [*plant*] envahissant; [*cancer*] invasif/-ive; [*treatment*] chirurgical.

invective /ɪnˈvektɪv/ *n* ¢ invectives *fpl*.

inveigh /ɪnˈveɪ/ *vi* **to ~ against sb/sth** fulminer contre qn/qch.

inveigle /ɪnˈveɪgl/ *vtr* péj **to ~ sb into doing** convaincre qn de faire (par la ruse).

invent /ɪnˈvent/ *vtr* inventer.

invention /ɪnˈvenʃn/ *n* **1** C (something invented) invention *f*; **2** ¢ (act of inventing) invention *f*; **3** (lie) invention *f*, mensonge *m*; **that story is pure** ou **a complete ~** cette histoire est inventée de toutes pièces.

inventive /ɪnˈventɪv/ *adj* inventif/-ive.

inventiveness /ɪnˈventɪvnɪs/ *n* créativité *f*, esprit *m* d'invention.

inventor /ɪnˈventə(r)/ *n* inventeur/-trice *m/f*.

inventory /ˈɪnvəntrɪ, US -tɔːrɪ/ **I** *n* **1** (list) inventaire *m*; **2** US (stock) stock *m*; **~ of fixtures** état *m* des lieux.
II *vtr* inventorier.

inventory control *n* US Comm gestion *f* des stocks.

inverse I /ˈɪnvɜːs/ *n* Math inverse *m*.
II /ˌɪnˈvɜːs/ *adj* Math, gen inverse; **in ~ proportion to** inversement proportionnel à; **in ~ order** en sens inverse.

inversely /ˌɪnˈvɜːslɪ/ *adv* [*vary*] de façon inversement proportionnelle; [*proportionate*] inversement.

inversion /ɪnˈvɜːʃn, US ɪnˈvɜːrʒn/ *n* **1** Ling, Med inversion *f*; **2** (homosexuality) inversion *f*; **3** Mus renversement *m*.

invert I /ˈɪnvɜːt/ *n* inverti/-e *m/f*.
II /ɪnˈvɜːt/ *vtr* **1** (reverse) inverser [*word order*]; fig renverser [*values*]; **2** (upend) retourner [*object*].
III inverted *pp adj* **1** (reversed) [*word order*] inversé; Mus [*chord*] renversé; (in optics, photography) [*image*] renversé; **it's ~ snobbery** c'est du snobisme à rebours; **2** (upended) [*object*] à l'envers.

invertebrate /ɪnˈvɜːtɪbreɪt/ *n, adj* invertébré (*m*).

inverted commas /ˌɪnvɜːtɪd ˈkɒməz/ *npl* GB guillemets *mpl*; **in ~** entre guillemets.

inverter, **invertor** /ɪnˈvɜːtə(r)/ *n* Elec onduleur *m*.

invert sugar *n* sucre *m* inverti.

invest /ɪnˈvest/ **I** *vtr* **1** (commit) investir, placer [*money, capital*]; consacrer [*time, energy, resources*] (**in** à); **to ~ £50,000 in shares** ou **stock** US investir or placer 50 000 livres sterling en valeurs; **we've ~ed a lot of effort in this project** nous nous sommes beaucoup investis dans ce projet; **2** (bestow) **to ~ sb with** investir qn de [*right, authority, power*]; **to be ~ed with significance** se voir attribuer une certaine signification; **to be ~ed with mystery** être empreint de mystère; **3** (install) investir [*president*]; **to ~ sb as sth** élever qn au rang de qch; **4** Mil investir.
II *vi* **1** Fin (in Stock Exchange) investir, placer son argent; **to ~ in shares** placer son argent en valeurs; **2** (spend money on) **to ~ in** [*government, company*] investir dans [*industry, company, equipment*]; (buy) [*person*] investir dans [*car, hi-fi*].

investigate /ɪnˈvestɪgeɪt/ **I** *vtr* **1** (inquire into) enquêter sur [*crime, cause, case*]; faire une enquête sur [*person*]; vérifier [*allegation, story*]; **they are being ~d** ils font l'objet d'une enquête; **2** (study) examiner [*question, possibility, report*]; étudier [*subject, culture*]; Comm sonder [*market, sector*]; **3** (try out) essayer [*restaurant, club*]; **it's worth investigating whether** il faudrait se renseigner pour savoir si.
II *vi* [*police*] enquêter; **I went to ~** gen je suis allé voir.

investigation /ɪnˌvestɪˈgeɪʃn/ **I** *n* **1** (inquiry) (in police) enquête *f* (**of, into sth** sur qch); **the crime is still under ~** on enquête encore sur le crime; **he is under ~** il fait l'objet d'une enquête; **2** (study) Comm, Med, Sci étude *f* (**of sth** de qch); **the matter under ~** la question (actuellement) à l'étude; **on (further) ~** après enquête (plus approfondie); **3** Accts, Jur vérification *f*; (of company) vérification *f* de comptabilité (**of** de).
II *modif* (in police) [*report, committee*] d'enquête.

investigative /ɪnˈvestɪgətɪv, US -geɪtɪv/ *adj* [*committee, mission, journalism, reporting*] d'investigation; **~ journalist** ou **reporter** journaliste *mf* d'investigation.

investigator /ɪnˈvestɪgeɪtə(r)/ *n* (in police) enquêteur/-trice *m/f*; **private ~** US détective *m* privé.

investigatory /ɪnˌvestɪˈgeɪtərɪ/ *adj* [*group, methods, procedures*] d'enquête.

investiture /ɪnˈvestɪtʃə(r), US -tʃʊər/ *n* cérémonie *f* d'investiture; **the ~ of sb as** l'élévation de qn au rang de.

investment /ɪnˈvestmənt/ **I** *n* **1** Fin investissement *m*, placement *m*; **~ in shares** placement en valeurs; **he called for more government ~ in industry** il a demandé que le gouvernement investisse plus dans l'industrie; **a good/bad ~** un bon/mauvais placement or investissement; **2** (commitment) **a better ~ of one's time** une meilleure utilisation de son temps; **the ~ of time and energy in sth** le temps et l'énergie consacrés à qch; **a huge emotional ~** un énorme engagement personnel; **3** Mil investissement *m*.
II *modif* Fin [*club, company, grant, opportunity*] d'investissement.

investment: **~ analyst** ▶**1692** *n* analyste *mf* financier/-ière; **~ bank** *n* US investment bank *f*; **~ income** *n* revenu *m* de portefeuille de titres; **~ management** *n* gestion *f* de portefeuille; **~ manager** ▶**1692** *n* gérant/-e *m/f* de portefeuille; **~ trust** *n* société *f* d'investissement.

investor /ɪnˈvestə(r)/ *n* investisseur/-euse *m/f* (**in** dans); (in shares) actionnaire *mf*; **big/small ~s** gros/petits actionnaires; **private ~** petit porteur *m*.

inveterate /ɪnˈvetərət/ *adj* invétéré.

invidious /ɪnˈvɪdɪəs/ *adj* [*position, task*] délicat; [*choice, comparison*] difficile.

invigilate /ɪnˈvɪdʒɪleɪt/ **I** *vtr* surveiller [*examination*].

II *vi* être de surveillance (**at** pour).

invigilator /ɪn'vɪdʒɪleɪtə(r)/ *n* surveillant/-e *m/f*.

invigorate /ɪn'vɪgəreɪt/ *vtr* revigorer.

invigorating /ɪn'vɪgəreɪtɪŋ/ *adj* revigorant.

invincibility /ɪnˌvɪnsə'bɪlətɪ/ *n* (of person, army) invincibilité *f*; (of will, belief) irréductibilité *f*.

invincible /ɪn'vɪnsəbl/ *adj* [*person, army, power*] invincible; [*will, belief*] irréductible.

inviolability /ɪnˌvaɪələ'bɪlətɪ/ *n* inviolabilité *f*.

inviolable /ɪn'vaɪələbl/ *adj* inviolable.

inviolably /ɪn'vaɪələblɪ/ *adv* inviolablement.

inviolate /ɪn'vaɪələt/ *adj* sout [*law*] inviolable; [*treaty*] inviolé; [*group, institution*] intouchable.

invisibility /ɪnˌvɪzə'bɪlətɪ/ *n* invisibilité *f*.

invisible /ɪn'vɪzəbl/ *adj* (all contexts) invisible.

invisible: **~ exports** *npl* exportations *fpl* invisibles; **~ ink** *n* encre *f* sympathique; **~ mending** *n* stoppage *m*.

invisibly /ɪn'vɪzəblɪ/ *adv* invisiblement; **to have sth ~ mended** faire stopper [*garment*].

invitation /ˌɪnvɪ'teɪʃn/ *n* **1** (request, card) invitation *f*; **an ~ to lunch/dinner** une invitation à déjeuner/à dîner; **to send/accept/decline an ~** envoyer/accepter/décliner une invitation; **thank you for your kind ~** je vous remercie de votre aimable invitation; **we regret we are unable to accept your kind ~** nous regrettons de ne pouvoir accepter votre aimable invitation; **to receive an ~ to do** être invité à faire; **2** ¢ (act of inviting) invitation *f*; **'by ~ only'** 'entrée sur invitation uniquement'; **at sb's ~** à or sur l'invitation de qn; **3** Ind (summons, bidding) offre *f*; **the rail union issued an urgent ~ to talks** le syndicat des chemins de fer a lancé une offre pressante de négociations; **4** Fin **an ~ to bid** un appel d'offres; **an ~ to tender** une adjudication; **5** fig (encouragement) incitation *f*; **unlocked doors are an open ~ to burglars** les portes non fermées à clé sont une incitation manifeste pour les cambrioleurs; **this was an ~ to him to feel persecuted** cela l'a incité à se considérer comme persécuté.

invitation card *n* carton *m* (d'invitation).

invite I○ /'ɪnvaɪt/ *n* invitation *f*.
II /ɪn'vaɪt/ *vtr* **1** inviter [*person*]; **to ~ sb to a party/to dinner/for a drink** inviter qn à une soirée/à dîner/à prendre un verre; **why don't we ~ Tara along?** pourquoi ne pas inviter Tara à venir avec nous?; **to ~ sb to do** inviter qn à faire; **to be ~d by sb to do** être invité par qn à faire; **to be ~d back** (repaying hospitality) être invité en retour; (a second time) être invité de nouveau; **to ~ sb in** inviter qn à entrer; **he ~d her out** il l'a invitée à sortir avec lui; **to ~ sb over** ou **round** (**to one's house**) inviter qn chez soi; **to ~ sb over to one's table** inviter qn à (venir s'asseoir à) sa table; **to ~ sb for (an) interview** convoquer qn pour un entretien; **2** (ask for) solliciter [*comments, suggestions*]; **he ~d questions from the audience** il invita l'auditoire à poser des questions; **3** (court) chercher [*disaster, trouble*] **why ~ trouble?** pourquoi chercher les ennuis?; **4** Fin **to ~ a bid** faire un appel d'offres; **to ~ tenders** faire une adjudication.

inviting /ɪn'vaɪtɪŋ/ *adj* [*room, apartment*] accueillant; [*smile*] engageant; [*meal*] appétissant; [*prospect*] alléchant, tentant.

invitingly /ɪn'vaɪtɪŋlɪ/ *adv* [*smile*] d'un air engageant; **the fire flickered ~** un feu accueillant pétillait dans la cheminée.

in vitro /ˌɪn'viːtrəʊ/, **IV** *adj, adv* in vitro *inv*.

in vitro fertilization, **IVF** *n* fécondation *f* in vitro.

invocation /ˌɪnvə'keɪʃn/ *n* invocation *f*.

invoice /'ɪnvɔɪs/ **I** *n* facture *f*.
II *vtr* envoyer une facture à [*person, company*]; **to ~ sb for sth** facturer qch à qn; **to be ~d** recevoir une facture (**for** pour).

invoicing /'ɪnvɔɪsɪŋ/ *n* facturation *f*.

invoke /ɪn'vəʊk/ *vtr* invoquer [*God, law, right, help*]; évoquer [*spirit, demon*].

involuntarily /ɪn'vɒləntrəlɪ, US -terɪlɪ/ *adv* involontairement.

involuntary /ɪn'vɒləntrɪ, US -terɪ/ *adj* involontaire; **~ repatriation** rapatriement *m* forcé.

involuntary: **~ manslaughter** *n* Jur homicide *m* involontaire or non prémédité; **~ muscle** *n* muscle *m* involontaire.

involve /ɪn'vɒlv/ **I** *vtr* **1** (entail) impliquer, nécessiter [*effort, travel*]; entraîner [*danger, problems*]; **to ~ doing** [*job, sport, policy, plan*] impliquer or nécessiter de faire; **it ~s leaving early** cela implique or nécessite de partir tôt; **there is a lot of work/effort ~d** cela implique beaucoup de travail/d'efforts; **there is some travelling/lifting ~d** cela nécessite de voyager/porter des charges; **the work ~s computers** le travail concerne les ordinateurs; **2** (cause to participate) gen faire participer [*person, group*] (**in** à); (implicate) impliquer, mêler [*person, group*] (**in** dans); **to be ~d in** (positive) participer à, être engagé dans [*business, project*]; (negative) être mêlé à [*scandal, robbery, fight*]; **to be ~d in doing** s'occuper de faire; **to get ~d in** ou **with sth** gen se trouver engagé dans qch; (in sth dubious) se trouver mêlé à qch; **not to get ~d in** ou **with sth** rester à l'écart de qch; **it will ~ them in heavy expenditure** ça va les entraîner à de grosses dépenses; **to feel ~d** se sentir impliqué; **3** (affect) concerner, impliquer [*person, animal, vehicle*]; **three people were ~d in the accident** trois personnes étaient impliquées dans l'accident; **our future/their safety is ~d** notre avenir/leur sécurité est en jeu; **4** (engross) [*film, play, book*] faire participer, prendre [*person, audience*]; **to be ~d in** être pris par, être plongé dans [*film, book, work*]; **to get ~d in** se laisser prendre par, se plonger dans [*film, play, book, work*]; **5** (get emotionally attached) **to be/get ~d with** être/devenir proche de [*patient, client*]; (romantically) avoir une liaison avec [*person*]; **to be (too) ~d in** ou **with sth** prendre [qch] à cœur [*problem, situation*]; **you're too ~d to make a judgment** tu es trop concerné pour porter un jugement; **6** (make a commitment) **to get ~d** s'engager; **I don't want to get ~d** je ne veux pas m'engager.
II *v refl* **to ~ oneself in** ou **with** (participate) prendre part à [*project, task*].

involved /ɪn'vɒlvd/ *adj* **1** (complicated) [*discussion, explanation, story, problem*] compliqué; **2** (affected) (*après n*) [*person, group*] concerné; **3** (implicated) (*après n*) [*person, group*] impliqué; **4** (necessary) (*après n*) [*expense, effort, problems*] inhérent.

involvement /ɪn'vɒlvmənt/ *n* **1** (participation) (in activity, campaign, task) participation *f* (**in** à); (commitment) (in party, enterprise, politics) engagement *m* (**in** dans); **2** ¢ (connections) (with group, organization) liens *mpl* (**with** avec); (with person) relations *fpl* (**with** avec); **3** (relationship) relation *f* privée (**with** avec); (sexual or romantic) relation *f*; **4** (engrossment) (in film, book) (vif) intérêt *m* (**in** pour).

invulnerability /ɪnˌvʌlnərə'bɪlətɪ/ *n* invulnérabilité *f*.

invulnerable /ɪn'vʌlnərəbl/ *adj* invulnérable.

inward /'ɪnwəd/ **I** *adj* **1** (inner) [*satisfaction*] personnel/-elle; [*relief, calm*] intérieur; **to give an ~ sigh/shudder** soupirer/frémir intérieurement; **her ~ reaction was to do** intérieurement or en son for intérieur, elle avait envie de faire; **2** (towards the inside) [*bend, curve*] vers l'intérieur.
II *adv* = **inwards**.

inward: **~ bill of lading** *n* connaissement *m* d'entrée; **~-bound** *adj* [*journey, flight*] de retour; [*ship*] en retour; [*cargo*] de retour; **~ investment** *n* Fin investissements *mpl* étrangers; **~-looking** *adj* [*society, organization*] replié sur soi-même; [*person*] introverti, replié sur soi-même; [*policy*] nombriliste○.

inwardly /'ɪnwədlɪ/ *adv* [*relieved, happy, calm*] intérieurement; [*rage, sigh, gloom, curse*] intérieurement; [*know, feel*] en son for intérieur.

inwards /'ɪnwədz/ *adv* [*fold, open, move, bend, grow*] vers l'intérieur; [*freight, invoice*] à l'arrivée; **to face ~** [*room*] donner sur la cour; **to look ~** [*person, organization*] se replier sur soi-même.

in-your-face /'ɪnjəˌfeɪs/ *adj* agressif/-ive; [*style*] percutant.

iodine /'aɪədiːn, US -daɪn/ *n* **1** (element) iode *m*; **2** (antiseptic) teinture *f* d'iode.

iodize /'aɪədaɪz/ *vtr* ioder.

iodoform /aɪ'ɒdəfɔːm/ *n* iodoforme *m*.

ion /'aɪən/ *n* ion *m*.

Iona /aɪ'əʊnə/ ▶ **1381** *pr n* (île *f* d')Iona.

Ionian /aɪ'əʊnɪən/ ▶ **1381** *adj* ionien/-ienne; **~ islands** îles *fpl* Ioniennes; **~ sea** mer *f* Ionienne.

ionic /aɪ'ɒnɪk/ *adj* Phys ionique.

Ionic /aɪ'ɒnɪk/ *adj* Archit ionique.

ionize /'aɪənaɪz/ *vtr* ioniser.

ionosphere /aɪ'ɒnəsfɪə(r)/ *n* ionosphère *f*.

iota /aɪ'əʊtə/ *n* **1** lit iota *m*; **2** fig **not an** ou **one ~ of truth** pas une once de vérité; **it hasn't changed one ~** ça n'a pas changé d'un iota.

IOU *n* (*abrév* = **I owe you**) reconnaissance *f* de dette; **an ~ for £500** un reçu pour 500 livres sterling.

Iowa /'aɪəʊə/ ▶ **1744** *pr n* Iowa *m*.

IPA *n* (*abrév* = **International Phonetic Alphabet**) API *m*.

ipecac(uanha) /'ɪpɪkæk(ˌwɑːnə)/ *n* ipéca *m*.

IQ *n* (*abrév* = **intelligence quotient**) QI *m*.

IRA *n* **1** (*abrév* = **Irish Republican Army**) IRA *f*; **2** US (*abrév* = **Individual Retirement Account**) *plan de retraite complémentaire*.

Irak *pr n* = **Iraq**.

Iraki *adj* = **Iraqi**.

Iran /ɪ'rɑːn/ ▶ **1131** *pr n* Iran *m*.

Iranian /ɪ'reɪnɪən/ ▶ **1486**, **1402** **I** *n* **1** (person) Iranien/-ienne *m/f*; **2** (language) iranien *m*.
II *adj* iranien/-ienne.

Iraq /ɪ'rɑːk/ ▶ **1131** *pr n* Iraq *m*.

Iraqi /ɪ'rɑːkɪ/ ▶ **1486** **I** *n* (person) Iraquien/-ienne *m/f*.
II *adj* iraquien/-ienne.

irascibility /ɪˌræsə'bɪlətɪ/ *n* irascibilité *f*.

irascible /ɪ'ræsəbl/ *adj* irascible.

irascibly /ɪ'ræsəblɪ/ *adv* [*reply, say*] sur un ton irascible.

irate /aɪ'reɪt/ *adj* furieux/-ieuse, courroucé liter (**about** au sujet de).

IRBM *n* (*abrév* = **Intermediate Range Ballistic Missile**) IRBM *m*.

ire /'aɪə(r)/ *n* littér courroux *m* liter.

Ireland /'aɪələnd/ ▶ **1131** *pr n* Irlande *f*; **the Republic of ~** la République d'Irlande.

irides /'aɪərɪdiːz/ *pl* ▶ **iris** 1.

iridescence /ˌɪrɪ'desns/ *n* chatoiement *m*.

iridescent /ˌɪrɪ'desnt/ *adj* chatoyant, iridescent.

iridium /aɪ'rɪdɪəm/ *n* iridium *m*.

iridology /ˌɪrɪ'dɒlədʒɪ/ *n* iridiologie *f*.

iris /'aɪərɪs/ *n* **1** Anat (*pl* **irides**) iris *m*; **2** Bot (*pl* **~es**) iris *m*.

Irish /'aɪərɪʃ/ ▶ **1402**, **1486** **I** *n* **1** Ling irlandais *m*; **2** (people) **the ~** les Irlandais *mpl*.
II *adj* irlandais.

Irish: **~ coffee** *n* irish coffee *m*; **~ Free State** *n* État *m* libre d'Irlande; **~man** *n*

Irlandais *m*; ~ **Republic** ▶ 1131 *n* République *f* d'Irlande; ~ **sea** ▶ 1511 *n* mer *f* d'Irlande; ~ **setter** *n* setter *m* irlandais; ~ **stew** *n* irish stew *m* (*ragoût de mouton*); ~ **wolfhound** *n* irish wolfhound *m*; ~**woman** *n* Irlandaise *f*.

irk /ɜːk/ *vtr* agacer.

irksome /ˈɜːksəm/ *adj* agaçant.

iron /ˈaɪən, US ˈaɪərn/ **I** *n* **1** (metal) fer *m*; **old** ou **scrap** ~ ferraille *f*; ~ **and steel works/industry** usine/industrie *f* sidérurgique; **a man/will of** ~ fig un homme/une volonté de fer; **2** (for clothes) fer *m* (à repasser); **electric** ~ fer *m* électrique; **with a hot/cool** ~ à fer chaud/doux; **to run the** ~ **over sth, to give sth an** ~ donner un coup de fer à qch; **3** (golf) fer *m*; **a six-**~ un fer six; **4** (splint) attelle *f*; **5** Med fer *m*.
II irons *npl* fers *mpl*; **to put sb in** ~**s** mettre qn aux fers.
III *modif* lit [*bar, gate, railing*] en fer; ~ **sheet** tôle *f*.
IV *adj* fig [*constitution, grip, will*] de fer; [*rule*] draconien/-ienne.
V *vtr* repasser [*clothes*]; **do not** ~ (on label) ne pas repasser; **to** ~ **sth under a damp cloth** repasser qch à la pattemouille.
VI *vi* [*person*] repasser; [*garment, fabric*] se repasser.
IDIOMS **to have a lot of** ~**s in the fire** avoir beaucoup d'affaires en train; **the** ~ **had entered his soul** littér il avait la mort dans l'âme; **to strike while the** ~ **is hot** battre le fer pendant qu'il est chaud.
■ **iron out**: ~ **out [sth]**, ~ **[sth] out 1** lit faire partir [qch] au fer [*creases*]; **2** fig aplanir [*problem, difficulty*]; **to** ~ **the wrinkles out of sth** fig peaufiner qch.

Iron Age *n* âge *m* de fer.

ironclad /ˌaɪənˈklæd, US ˌaɪərn-/ **I** *n* Hist (ship) cuirassé *m*.
II *adj* fig [*guarantee*] à toute épreuve; [*argument, defence*] inattaquable.

Iron Cross *n* Mil Croix *f* de Fer.

Iron Curtain *n* Pol Hist rideau *m* de fer; **behind the** ~ au-delà du rideau de fer; **an** ~ **country** un pays du bloc communiste.

iron: ~ **filings** *npl* limaille *f* de fer; ~ **fist**, ~ **hand** *n* fig poigne *f* de fer; ~ **horse** *n* US Hist locomotive *f* à vapeur.

ironic(al) /aɪˈrɒnɪk(l)/ *adj* ironique.

ironically /aɪˈrɒnɪklɪ/ *adv* [*say, ask*] ironiquement; ~, **she never replied** l'ironie, c'est qu'elle n'a jamais répondu.

ironing /ˈaɪənɪŋ, US ˈaɪərn-/ *n* repassage *m*; **to do the** ~ faire le repassage.

ironing board *n* planche *f* à repasser.

iron: **Iron Lady** *n* GB Pol Dame *f* de Fer; ~ **lung** *n* poumon *m* d'acier.

ironmonger /ˈaɪənmʌŋgə(r), US ˈaɪərn-/ ▶ 1692 *n* quincaillier/-ière *m/f*; ~**'s (shop)** quincaillerie *f*.

iron: ~**mongery** *n* quincaillerie *f*; ~ **ore** *n* minerai *m* de fer; ~ **oxide** *n* oxyde *m* de fer; ~ **pyrites** *n* pyrite *f* de fer.

iron rations *npl* vivres *mpl* or rations *fpl*; **to be on** ~ vivre sur ses rations.

iron: ~**stone** *n* minerai *m* de fer; ~**stone china** *n* faïence *f* fine dure, lithocérame *f* spéc; ~ **work** *n* ferronnerie *f*; ~**works** *n* (+ *v sg* ou *pl*) usine *f* sidérurgique.

irony /ˈaɪərənɪ/ *n* ironie *f*; **the** ~ **is that** l'ironie c'est que (+ *subj*); **one of life's little ironies** une des ironies du sort.

Iroquois /ˈɪrəkwɔɪ/ ▶ 1402, 1486 **I** *n* **1** (person) Iroquois/-e *m/f*; **2** (language) iroquois *m*.
II *adj* iroquois.

irradiate /ɪˈreɪdɪeɪt/ *vtr* **1** Med, Nucl irradier; **2** Culin irradier, ioniser [*fruit, vegetable*].

irradiation /ɪˌreɪdɪˈeɪʃn/ *n* **1** Nucl, Med irradiation *f*; **2** Culin (of fruit, vegetables) irradiation *f*, ionisation *f*.

irrational /ɪˈræʃənl/ *adj* [*behaviour*] irrationnel/-elle; [*fear, hostility*] sans fondement; **he's rather** ~ il n'est pas très raisonnable; **she has become quite** ~ **about the divorce** elle a perdu le sens des proportions en ce qui concerne le divorce; **he's** ~ **about it** on ne peut pas le raisonner là-dessus.

irrationally /ɪˈræʃənəlɪ/ *adv* [*act*] d'une façon déraisonnable or irrationnelle; [*angry, happy*] sans raison.

irreconcilable /ɪˈrekənsaɪləbl, ɪˌrekənˈsaɪləbl/ *adj* [*opponents*] irréconciliable (**with** avec); [*ideas*] incompatible (**with** avec); [*conflict*] inconciliable.

irrecoverable /ˌɪrɪˈkʌvərəbl/ *adj* [*object*] irrécupérable; [*loss*] irréparable; Fin [*debt*] irrécouvrable.

irredeemable /ˌɪrɪˈdiːməbl/ *adj* **1** Relig [*sinner*] incorrigible; **2** (irrecoverable) [*loss*] irrémédiable; **3** Fin [*shares, bonds*] irremboursable; [*loan*] non amortissable; [*paper money*] non remboursable.

irredeemably /ˌɪrɪˈdiːməblɪ/ *adv* irrémédiablement.

irreducible /ˌɪrɪˈdjuːsəbl, US -ˈduːs-/ *adj* sout irréductible.

irrefutable /ɪˈrefjʊtəbl, ˌɪrɪˈfjuː-/ *adj* irréfutable, irrécusable.

irregular /ɪˈregjʊlə(r)/ **I** *n* Mil irrégulier/-ière *m/f*.
II irregulars *npl* US Comm (clothing) vêtements *mpl* dégriffés; (other merchandise) articles *mpl* de second choix.
III *modif* [*army, force*] irrégulier/-ière.
IV *adj* **1** gen, Ling irrégulier/-ière; **at** ~ **intervals** à intervalles irréguliers; **to keep** ~ **hours** avoir des horaires irréguliers; **to lead an** ~ **life** mener une vie décousue; **2** US Comm [*merchandise*] de second choix.

irregularity /ɪˌregjʊˈlærətɪ/ *n* (of pulse, shape, surface) irrégularité *f*; (in machine) anomalie *f*; (in report, election, dealings) anomalie *f*, irrégularité *f*.

irregularly /ɪˈregjʊləlɪ/ *adv* irrégulièrement; ~**-shaped** à la forme irrégulière.

irrelevance /ɪˈreləvəns/, **irrelevancy** /ɪˈreləvənsɪ/ *n* **1** (lack of importance) (of fact, remark, question) manque *m* d'à-propos; ~ **to sth** manque de rapport avec qch; **2** (unimportant thing) **to be an** ~ ne pas avoir d'importance; **a document full of** ~**s** un document truffé de remarques sans rapport avec le sujet.

irrelevant /ɪˈreləvnt/ *adj* **1** (unconnected) [*remark*] hors de propos; [*facts*] hors du sujet; [*question*] sans rapport avec le sujet; **to be** ~ **to sth** n'avoir aucun rapport avec qch; **2** (unimportant) **the money's** ~ ce n'est pas l'argent qui compte.

irrelevantly /ɪˈreləvəntlɪ/ *adv* [*say, ask*] hors de propos.

irreligious /ˌɪrɪˈlɪdʒəs/ *adj* irréligieux/-ieuse.

irremediable /ˌɪrɪˈmiːdɪəbl/ *adj* sout [*harm, loss*] irrémédiable; [*fault*] incorrigible.

irremediably /ˌɪrɪˈmiːdɪəblɪ/ *adv* sout [*damaged, lost*] irrémédiablement; [*vain, stupid*] incorrigiblement.

irreparable /ɪˈrepərəbl/ *adj* irréparable.

irreparably /ɪˈrepərəblɪ/ *adv* irréparablement.

irreplaceable /ˌɪrɪˈpleɪsəbl/ *adj* irremplaçable.

irrepressible /ˌɪrɪˈpresəbl/ *adj* [*high spirits*] débordant, irrépressible; [*desire, sense of humour, enthusiasm*] inextinguible; **he's (absolutely)** ~! il est infatigable!

irrepressibly /ˌɪrɪˈpresəblɪ/ *adv* ~ **cheerful/enthusiastic** d'une bonne humeur/d'un enthousiasme à toute épreuve.

irreproachable /ˌɪrɪˈprəʊtʃəbl/ *adj* irréprochable.

irresistible /ˌɪrɪˈzɪstəbl/ *adj* irrésistible.

irresistibly /ˌɪrɪˈzɪstəblɪ/ *adv* irrésistiblement; ~ **beautiful/charming** d'une beauté/d'un charme irrésistible.

irresolute /ɪˈrezəluːt/ *adj* irrésolu, indécis.

irresolutely /ɪˈrezəluːtlɪ/ *adv* d'un air indécis.

irrespective /ˌɪrɪˈspektɪv/: **irrespective of** *prep phr* sans tenir compte de [*age, class, ability*]; ~ **of race** sans distinction de race; **everyone,** ~ **of who they are** tous, sans exception; ~ **of whether it rains** qu'il pleuve ou non.

irresponsibility /ˌɪrɪˌspɒnsəˈbɪlətɪ/ *n* irresponsabilité *f*.

irresponsible /ˌɪrɪˈspɒnsəbl/ *adj* [*behaviour, remark, person*] irresponsable; **it was** ~ **of him to do that** c'était irresponsable de sa part de faire cela.

irresponsibly /ˌɪrɪˈspɒnsəblɪ/ *adv* de façon irresponsable.

irretrievable /ˌɪrɪˈtriːvəbl/ *adj* [*loss, harm*] irrémédiable, irréparable.

irretrievably /ˌɪrɪˈtriːvəblɪ/ *adv* irrémédiablement.

irreverence /ɪˈrevərəns/ *n* irrévérence *f*.

irreverent /ɪˈrevərənt/ *adj* irrévérencieux/-ieuse.

irreverently /ɪˈrevərəntlɪ/ *adv* irrévérencieusement.

irreversible /ˌɪrɪˈvɜːsəbl/ *adj* [*process, decision*] irréversible; [*disease*] incurable.

irreversibly /ˌɪrɪˈvɜːsəblɪ/ *adv* irréversiblement.

irrevocable /ɪˈrevəkəbl/ *adj* irrévocable.

irrevocably /ɪˈrevəkəblɪ/ *adv* irrévocablement.

irrigable /ˈɪrɪgəbl/ *adj* irrigable.

irrigate /ˈɪrɪgeɪt/ *vtr* Agric, Med irriguer.

irrigation /ˌɪrɪˈgeɪʃn/ **I** *n* Agric, Med irrigation *f*; **to be under** ~ être irrigué.
II *modif* [*canal, system*] d'irrigation.

irritability /ˌɪrɪtəˈbɪlətɪ/ *n* irritabilité *f*.

irritable /ˈɪrɪtəbl/ *adj* irritable.

irritable bowel syndrome ▶ 1354 *n* colopathie *f* fonctionnelle.

irritably /ˈɪrɪtəblɪ/ *adv* [*say*] d'un ton irrité; [*look, shrug*] d'un air irrité.

irritant /ˈɪrɪtənt/ **I** *n* **1** (noise, situation etc) source *f* d'irritation; **2** (substance) irritant *m*.
II *adj* irritant.

irritate /ˈɪrɪteɪt/ *vtr* **1** (make angry) irriter, agacer; **2** Med irriter.

irritating /ˈɪrɪteɪtɪŋ/ *adj* gen irritant, agaçant; Med irritant.

irritatingly /ˈɪrɪteɪtɪŋlɪ/ *adv* [*behave, say*] d'une façon irritante or agaçante; ~ **patient/punctual** d'une patience/ponctualité agaçante.

irritation /ˌɪrɪˈteɪʃn/ *n* gen, Med irritation *f*.

irruption /ɪˈrʌpʃn/ *n* irruption *f*.

is /ɪz/ 3e *pers. du prés de* **be**.

Isaiah /aɪˈzaɪə/ *pr n* Isaïe.

ISBN *n* (*abrév* = **International Standard Book Number**) ISBN *m*.

ISDN *n* (*abrév* = **International Services Digital Network**) RNIS *m*.

Isère ▶ 1163 *pr n* Isère *f*; **in/to** ~ en Isère.

-ish /ɪʃ/ *suffix* **1** (with adjs, advs) **greenish** tirant sur le vert, verdâtre pej; **darkish** plutôt sombre; **earlyish** assez tôt; **2** (with figures, numbers etc) **he's thirtyish** il a dans les trente ans, il a la trentaine; **they came at fourish** ils sont venus vers quatre heures.

isinglass /ˈaɪzɪŋglɑːs, US -glæs/ *n* **1** Agric, Culin (gelatin) ichtyocolle *f*; **2** (mica) mica *m*.

Isis /ˈaɪsɪs/ *pr n* Isis.

Islam /ˈɪzlɑːm, -læm, -ˈlɑːm/ *n* **1** (religion) islam *m*; **2** (Muslims collectively) Islam *m*.

Islamabad /ɪzˈlæməbæd/ ▶ 1818 *pr n* Islamabad.

Islamic /ɪzˈlæmɪk/ *adj* islamique.

Islamism /ˈɪzləmɪzəm/ *n* islamisme *m*.

island /ˈaɪlənd/ **I** *n* **1** île *f*; (small) îlot *m*; ~ **of peace/hope** fig îlot de paix/d'espoir; **2** Transp ▶ **traffic island**.
II *modif* (of particular island) de l'île; (of islands generally) des îles; **an** ~ **community** une

communauté insulaire; **the ~ community** les habitants de l'île.

IDIOMS **no man is an ~** on ne peut pas se passer des autres.

islander /ˈaɪləndə(r)/ *n* habitant/-e *m/f* d'une île (or de l'île), insulaire *mf*.

island hopping *n* **to go ~** aller d'île en île.

Islands Council *n* GB *conseil régional responsable de la gestion d'un groupe d'îles*.

isle /aɪl/ **▶1381** *n* **1** Geog île *f*; **Isle of Man** île *f* de Man; **Isle of Wight** île *f* de Wight; **2** littér île *f*.

islet /ˈaɪlɪt/ *n* littér îlot *m*.

ism /ˈɪzəm/ *n* péj idéologie *f*; **Marxism and other ~s** le marxisme et autres idéologies.

isn't /ˈɪznt/ = **is not**.

ISO *n* (*abrév* = **International Standards Organization**) ISO *f*, Organisation *f* des normes internationales.

isobar /ˈaɪsəbɑː(r)/ *n* isobare *f*.

isolate /ˈaɪsəleɪt/ *vtr* (all contexts) isoler (**from** de).

isolated /ˈaɪsəleɪtɪd/ *adj* isolé.

isolation /ˌaɪsəˈleɪʃn/ *n* (all contexts) isolement *m*; **in ~** dans l'isolement; **in splendid ~** hum superbement isolé.

isolation hospital *n* GB hôpital *m* pour maladies infectieuses.

isolationism /ˌaɪsəˈleɪʃənɪzəm/ *n* isolationnisme *m*.

isolationist /ˌaɪsəˈleɪʃənɪst/ *n, adj* isolationniste (*mf*).

isolation ward *n* GB salle *f* des contagieux.

Isolde /ɪˈzɒldə/ *pr n* Iseult, Iseut.

isometric /ˌaɪsəʊˈmetrɪk/ **I isometrics** *npl* exercices *mpl* musculaires isométriques.
II *adj* isométrique.

isomorphic /ˌaɪsəˈmɔːfɪk/ *adj* Chem, Math, Ling isomorphe; Biol homomorphique.

isomorphism /ˌaɪsəˈmɔːfɪzəm/ *n* Chem, Math, Ling isomorphisme *m*; Biol homomorphisme *m*.

isosceles /aɪˈsɒsəliːz/ *adj* isocèle.

isotherm /ˈaɪsəθɜːm/ *n* isotherme *f*.

isotope /ˈaɪsətəʊp/ *n* isotope *m*.

Israel /ˈɪzreɪl/ **▶1131** *pr n* Israël (*never with article*); **in ~** en Israël.

Israeli /ɪzˈreɪlɪ/ **▶1486** **I** *n* Israélien/-ienne *m/f*.
II *adj* israélien/-ienne.

Israelite /ˈɪzrɪəlaɪt, -rəlaɪt/ *n* Israélite *mf*.

issue /ˈɪʃuː, ˈɪsjuː/ **I** *n* **1** (topic for discussion) problème *m*, question *f* (**of** de); **a political ~** une question or un problème politique; **that's not the ~** ce n'est pas la question or le problème; **to force the ~** précipiter la solution d'une question or d'un problème; **to make an ~ (out) of** faire une histoire de; **the point at ~** ce qui est en cause; **her beliefs are not at ~** ses croyances ne sont pas en question; **our future is at ~ here** c'est notre avenir qui est en question ici; **to be at ~** (in disagreement) être en désaccord (**over, about** sur); **to take ~ with** entrer en désaccord avec; **I must take ~ with you on that** je dois vous signifier mon désaccord sur ce point; **2** (allocation) (of blankets, food, arms, uniforms) distribution *f*; (of passport, licence, summons, writ) délivrance *f*; **3** (official release) (of stamps, coins, shares) émission *f*; (of book) publication *f*; **4** Publg (copy) (of newspaper, magazine, journal) numéro *m*; **back ~** ancien numéro *m*; **5** (flowing out) (of liquid) écoulement *m*; **6** (outcome) résultat *m*; **7** (offspring) descendance *f*; **to die without ~** mourir sans laisser de descendance.
II *vtr* **1** (allocate) distribuer [*book, food, arms, uniforms*] (**to** à); **to ~ sb with sth** fournir qch à qn; **to be ~d with** recevoir; **2** (make public) délivrer [*declaration, statement, ultimatum*]; émettre [*order, warning*]; **3** (release officially) émettre [*stamps, coins, shares*]; **4** (publish) publier [*book, magazine*].

Islands

In French, some names of islands always have the definite article and some never do.

Island names with definite article

These behave like the names of countries **▶1131**, *with different constructions depending on gender and number:*

Corsica = la Corse
in Corsica = en Corse
to Corsica = en Corse
from Corsica = de Corse

Note that where the English has the definite article, French normally has as well:

the Balearics = les Baléares *fpl*
in the Balearics = aux Baléares
to the Balearics = aux Baléares
from the Balearics = des Baléares

Islands without definite article

As in English, most island names have no definite article; these work like names of towns **▶1818**:

Cyprus = Chypre
in Cyprus = à Chypre
to Cyprus = à Chypre
from Cyprus = de Chypre
Cyprus sherry = le sherry de Chypre

English uses on with the names of small islands; there is no such distinction in French:

on St. Helena = à Sainte-Hélène
on Naxos = à Naxos

As with names of cities and towns, it is safest to avoid explicit genders; use l'île de ... *instead:*

Cuba is beautiful = l'île de Cuba est belle

Names with or without île in them

English and French tend to work the same way in this respect:

Guernsey = Guernesey
the island of Guernsey = l'île de Guernesey
the Balearics = les Baléares
the Balearic Islands = les îles Baléares
the Orkney Isles = les îles Orcades

Exceptions

There are some exceptions to these rules, e.g. Fiji, Samoa, Jamaica. *If in doubt, look up island name in the dictionary.*

III *vi* **1** (flow out) **to ~ from** [*water, liquid*] s'écouler de; [*gas, smoke*] émaner de; [*shouts, laughter, insults*] provenir de; **2** (result) **to ~ from** résulter de.

issuer /ˈɪʃʊə(r)/ *n* Fin émetteur *m*.

Istanbul /ˌɪstænˈbʊl/ **▶1818** *pr n* Istanbul.

isthmus /ˈɪsməs/ *n* isthme *m*.

Istria /ˈɪstrɪə/ *n* Istrie *f*.

it /ɪt/ *pron* **1** (in questions) **who is ~?** qui est-ce?, qui c'est○?; **~'s me** c'est moi; **where is ~?** où est-il/elle?, où est-ce que c'est?, c'est où○?; **what is ~?** (of object, noise etc) qu'est-ce que c'est?, c'est quoi○?; (what's happening?) qu'est-ce qui se passe?; (what is the matter?) qu'est-ce qu'il y a?; **how was ~?** comment cela s'est-il passé?, ça s'est passé comment○?; **2** Games **you're ~!** c'est toi le chat!

IDIOMS **I didn't have ~ in me to refuse** je n'ai pas eu le cœur de refuser; **he's just not got ~ in him to do any better** il ne peut vraiment pas faire mieux; **the best/worst of ~ is that** ce qu'il y a de mieux/de pire la-dedans c'est que; **that's ~!** (in triumph) voilà!, ça y est!; (in anger) ça suffit!; **we've had ~ now**○! on est fichu○!; **the cooker's had ~**○! la cuisinière est fichue○!; **I've had ~ (with this job)** j'en ai ras le bol○ (de ce travail); **to have ~ in for sb**○ en vouloir à qn; **to be with ~**○ être branché○, être dans le vent.

IT *n*: *abrév* **▶information technology**.

ITA *n*: *abrév* **▶Initial Teaching Alphabet**.

Italian /ɪˈtæljən/ **▶1486**, **1402** **I** *n* **1** (person) Italien/-ienne *m/f*; **2** Ling italien *m*.
II *adj* italien/-ienne.

Italianate /ɪˈtæljəneɪt/ *adj* à l'italienne.

italic /ɪˈtælɪk/ **I** *adj* italique.
II italics *npl* italique *m*; **in ~s** en italique; **'my ~s'** 'les italiques sont de moi'.

italicize /ɪˈtælɪsaɪz/ *vtr* Print imprimer [qch] en italique; (by hand) mettre [qch] en italique; **this word is ~d** ce mot est en italique.

Italy /ˈɪtəlɪ/ **▶1131** *pr n* Italie *f*.

ITC *n* GB *abrév* **▶Independent Television Commission**.

itch /ɪtʃ/ **I** *n* **1** (physical) démangeaison *f*; **to relieve an ~** soulager des démangeaisons; Med **the ~** la gale; **2**○ (hankering) envie *f* (**for** de; **to do** de faire); **I had an ~ to travel** l'envie de voyager me démangeait○.
II *vtr* US (scratch) gratter.
III *vi* **1** (physically) avoir des démangeaisons; **my back is ~ing** j'ai le dos qui me démange; **these socks make me** ou **my feet ~** ces chaussettes me démangent; **2 to be ~ing for sth/to do** mourir○ d'envie de qch/de faire.

itching /ˈɪtʃɪŋ/ **I** *n* démangeaisons *fpl*.
II *adj* = **itchy**.

itching powder *n* poil *m* à gratter.

itchy○ /ˈɪtʃɪ/ *adj* **I have an ~ back** j'ai le dos qui me démange; **I feel ~ all over** ça me gratte partout.

IDIOMS **to have ~ feet**○ avoir la bougeotte○; **to have ~ fingers**○ être chapardeur/-euse○ *m/f*.

it'd /ˈɪtəd/ = **it had, it would**.

item /ˈaɪtəm/ **I** *n* **1** gen, Comput article *m*; **household ~** article *m* ménager; **luxury ~** produit *m* de luxe; **an ~ of furniture** un meuble; **~s of clothing** vêtements *mpl*; **2** Admin Pol point *m*; **an ~ on the agenda** un point à l'ordre du jour; **~ nine** le point neuf; **~s of business** questions au programme; **3** Journ, Radio, TV article *m* (**about** sur); **news ~** article *m*; **the main ~** Radio, TV le titre principal; Journ le gros titre; **4** Mus morceau *m*; (in show) numéro *m*; **5** Ling item *m*.
II *adv* Comm (when listing) sout item.

itemize /ˈaɪtəmaɪz/ *vtr* détailler; **~d bill** facture *f* détaillée.

item veto *n* US Pol veto *m* partiel.

iterative /ˈɪtərətɪv/ *adj* Ling itératif/-ive, fréquentatif/-ive.

itinerant /aɪˈtɪnərənt, ɪ-/ **I** *n* vagabond/-e *m/f*.
II *adj* [*life, preacher, worker*] itinérant; [*tribe*] nomade; **~ teacher** US professeur *m* qui exerce sur plusieurs établissements.

itinerary /aɪˈtɪnərərɪ, ɪ-, US -rerɪ/ *n* itinéraire *m*.

it'll /ˈɪtl/ = **it will**.

ITN *n* GB (*abrév* = **Independent Television News**) *chaîne indépendante d'actualités télévisées*.

its /ɪts/

■ **Note** In French determiners agree in number and gender with the noun they qualify. *its* is translated by *son + masculine noun*: *its nose* = son nez; by *sa + feminine noun*: *its tail* = sa queue; BUT by *son + feminine noun beginning with a vowel or mute h*: *its ear* = son oreille; and by *ses + plural noun*: *its ears* = ses oreilles.

det son/sa/ses.

it's /ɪts/ = **it is, it has**.

itself /ɪtˈself/

■ **Note** When used as a reflexive pronoun, direct and indirect, *itself* is translated by *se* (*s'* before a vowel or mute h): *the cat hurt itself* = le chat s'est fait mal; *a problem presented itself* = un problème s'est présenté.
– When used for emphasis *itself* is translated by *lui-même* when standing for a masculine noun and *elle-même* when standing for a femi-

it

When *it* is used as a subject pronoun to refer to a specific object (or animal) *il* or *elle* is used in French according to the gender of the object referred to:

'where is the book/chair?' 'it's in the kitchen' = 'où est le livre/la chaise?' 'il/elle est dans la cuisine'
'do you like my skirt?' 'it's lovely' = 'est-ce que tu aimes ma jupe?' 'elle est très jolie'

However, if the object referred to is named in the same sentence, *it* is translated by *ce* (*c'* before a vowel):

it's a good film = c'est un bon film

When *it* is used as an object pronoun it is translated by *le* or *la* (*l'* before a vowel) according to the gender of the object referred to:

it's my book/my chair and I want it = c'est mon livre/ma chaise et je le/la veux

Note that the object pronoun normally comes before the verb in French and that in compound tenses like the perfect and the past perfect, the past participle agrees with it:

I liked his shirt – did you notice it? = j'ai aimé sa chemise – est-ce que tu l'as remarquée? *or* l'as-tu remarquée?

In imperatives only, the pronoun comes after the verb:

it's my book – give it to me = c'est mon livre – donne-le-moi (note the hyphens)

When *it* is used vaguely or impersonally followed by an adjective the translation is *ce* (*c'* before a vowel):

it's difficult = c'est difficile
it's sad = c'est triste

But when *it* is used impersonally followed by an adjective + verb the translation is *il*:

it's difficult to understand how … = il est difficile de comprendre comment …

If in doubt consult the entry for the adjective in question.

For translations for impersonal verb uses (*it's raining, it's snowing*) consult the entry for the verb in question.

it is used in expressions of days of the week (*it's Friday*) and clock time (*it's 5 o'clock*). This dictionary contains usage notes on these and many other topics. For the index to these notes ▶ **1919**. For other impersonal and idiomatic uses see the entry ***it***.

When *it* is used after a preposition in English the two words (prep + *it*) are often translated by one word in French. If the preposition would normally be translated by *de* in French (e.g. *of, about, from* etc.) the *prep* + *it* = *en*:

I've heard about it = j'en ai entendu parler

If the preposition would normally be translated by *à* in French (e.g. *to, in, at* etc.) the prep + *it* = *y*:

they went to it = ils y sont allés

For translations of *it* following prepositions not normally translated by *de* or *à* (e.g. *above, under, over* etc.) consult the entry for the preposition.

nine noun: *the car itself was not damaged* = la voiture elle-même n'était pas endommagée.
– For examples and particular usages see the entry below.
– For uses with prepositions (*by itself etc*) see 3 below.

pron **1** (refl) se, s'; **2** (emphatic) lui-même/elle-même; **the house ~ was pretty** la maison elle-même était jolie; **the library is not in the university ~** la bibliothèque n'est pas dans l'université même or dans l'université elle-même; **he was kindness ~** c'était la bonté personnifiée; **3** (after prepositions) **the heating comes on by ~** le chauffage se met en marche tout seul; **the house stands by ~ in the middle of a field** la maison est toute seule au milieu d'un champ; **the library is a fine building in ~** la bibliothèque par elle-même est un beau bâtiment; **learning French is not difficult in ~** l'apprentissage du français n'est pas difficile en soi.

ITV *n* GB (*abrév* = **Independent Television**) *chaîne indépendante de télévision.*

IUD *n*: *abrév* ▶ **intrauterine device.**

IV *n*: *abrév* ▶ **intraveinous drip.**

I've /aɪv/ = **I have.**

ivory /ˈaɪvərɪ/ **I** *n* **1** ȼ (substance) ivoire *m*; **2** (ornament) (objet *m* en) ivoire *m*; **3** (colour) ivoire *m inv*.
II *modif* [*object*] d'ivoire, en ivoire.
III *adj* [*skin, complexion*] ivoire *inv*.
IDIOMS **to tickle the ivories**† hum pianoter○.

ivory: **Ivory Coast** ▶ **1131** *pr n* Côte *f* d'Ivoire; **~ tower** *n* fig tour *f* d'ivoire.

ivy /ˈaɪvɪ/ *n* lierre *m*.

ivy-leaf geranium *n* géranium-lierre *m*.

Ivy League *adj* US ≈ bon chic bon genre; **the ~ colleges** *les huit universités prestigieuses de la côte est américaine* (*Harvard, Yale, etc*).

Jj

j, J /dʒeɪ/ *n* j, J *m*.

jab /dʒæb/ **I** *n* **1** GB Med (vaccination) vaccin *m*; (injection) piqûre *f*; **2** (poke) petit coup *m*; **3** (in boxing) direct *m*.
II *vtr* **to ~ sth into sth** planter qch dans qch; **he ~bed his finger into my arm, he ~bed my arm (with his finger)** il a planté son doigt dans mon bras; **to ~ sth at sb** pointer qch en direction de qn.
III *vi* **1** gen **she ~bed at the page with her finger** elle tapait sur la page avec son doigt; **2** (in boxing) envoyer des directs (**at** à).

jabber /ˈdʒæbə(r)/ **I** *vtr* baragouiner.
II *vi* (chatter) jacasser; (in foreign language) baragouiner.

jabbering /ˈdʒæbərɪŋ/ *n* (chatter) jacasseries *fpl*; (incomprehensible talk) baragouin *m*.

jabot /ˈʒæbəʊ/ *n* Fashn jabot *m*.

jacaranda /ˌdʒækəˈrændə/ *n* jacaranda *m*.

jack /dʒæk/ **I** *n* **1** (crank for car etc) cric *m*; **2** (in cards) valet *m* (**of** de); **3** (in bowls) cochonnet *m*; **4** Elec, Telecom jack *m*; **5** Naut pavillon *m*.
II jacks ▶ 1282 *npl* Games osselets *mpl*.
IDIOMS **every man ~** tout un, chacun; **every man ~ of them** jusqu'au dernier; **to be (a) ~ of all trades (and master of none)** être un/-e touche-à-tout *inv*; **to have an I'm all right Jack attitude** ne s'occuper que de sa petite personne.
■ **jack around**○ US: ¶ **~ around 1** (idle around) traînasser○; **2 to ~ around with sth** traficoter○ qch; ¶ **~ around [sb]**, **~ [sb] around** agacer.
■ **jack in**○ GB: **~ in [sth]**, **~ [sth] in** plaquer○, laisser tomber [*job, task*]; **to ~ it in** tout plaquer.
■ **jack off**● US se branler●, se masturber.
■ **jack up**: **~ up [sth]**, **~ [sth] up 1** soulever [qch] avec un cric [*vehicle*]; **2**○ fig faire grimper [*price, charge*]; **3**○ US (encourage) chauffer○ [*crowd*].

jackal /ˈdʒækɔːl, US -kl/ *n* chacal *m*.

jackanapes† /ˈdʒækəneɪps/ *n* polisson/-onne *m/f*.

jack: **~ass** *n* lit, fig âne *m*; **~boot** *n* botte *f* militaire; fig botte *f* (**of** de); **~-booted** *adj* [*soldier, troops*] botté; [*regime, repression*] musclé, autoritaire; **~daw** *n* choucas *m*.

jacket /ˈdʒækɪt/ ▶ 1703 **I** *n* **1** (garment) veste *f*; (short) veston *m*; **potatoes (baked) in their ~s** Culin pommes *fpl* de terre en robe des champs (au four); **2** (of book) (also **dust ~**) jaquette *f*; US (of record) pochette *f*; **3** Tech (insulating) enveloppe *f* isolante.
II *modif* **1** [*sleeve, pocket*] de veste; **~ potato** Culin pomme *f* de terre en robe des champs (au four); **2** [*illustration, design*] de couverture.

jack: **Jack Frost** *pr n* ≈ le Bonhomme Hiver; **~hammer** *n* marteau-piqueur *m*; **~-in-the-box** *n* diable *m* à ressort.

jackknife /ˈdʒæknaɪf/ **I** *n* **1** (knife) couteau *m* pliant; **2** = **jackknife dive**.
II *vi* [*lorry*] se mettre en portefeuille.

jackknife dive *n* saut *m* carpé.

jack-o'-lantern /ˌdʒækəʊˈlæntən/ *n* **1** US citrouille *f* taillée en forme de visage; **2** GB feu-follet *m*.

jack plug *n* jack *m*.

jackpot /ˈdʒækpɒt/ *n* gros lot *m*.
IDIOMS **to hit the ~** (win prize) gagner le gros lot; (have great success) faire un tabac○.

jack: **~rabbit** *n* lièvre *m* (*du nord-ouest américain*); **~ shit**◑ *n* US que dalle◑; **~straws** *n* (+ *v sg*) (jeu *m* de) jonchets *mpl*; **~ tar, Jack Tar** *n* marin *m*, matelot *m*; **Jack-the-lad**○ *n* GB esbroufeur○ *m*.

Jacobean /ˌdʒækəˈbɪən/ *adj* jacobéen/-éenne.

Jacobite /ˈdʒækəbaɪt/ *n* Jacobite *mf*.

jacuzzi® /dʒəˈkuːzɪ/ *n* jacuzzi® *m*, bain *m* bouillonnant.

jade /dʒeɪd/ **I** *n* **1** (stone) jade *m*; **2** ▶ 1104 (colour) vert *m* jade; **3**‡ péj (woman) friponne *f*; **4**‡ péj (horse) rossinante† *f*.
II *modif* [*ring, statue*] en jade.
III *adj* vert jade *inv*.

jaded /ˈdʒeɪdɪd/ *adj* **1** (exhausted) fatigué; **2** (bored) [*person, palate*] blasé; **to have a ~ appetite** ne pas avoir d'appétit.

jade green ▶ 1104 *n, adj* vert (*m*) jade *inv*.

Jag○ /dʒæg/ *n* Jag○ *f*, Jaguar® *f*.

jagged /ˈdʒægɪd/ *adj* [*rock, cliff, wreck*] déchiqueté; [*knife, saw*] dentelé; **a ~ tear** une déchirure en zig-zag.

jaguar /ˈdʒægjʊə(r)/ *n* jaguar *m*.

jail /dʒeɪl/ **I** *n* prison *f*; **to be in/go to ~** être/aller en prison (**for sth** pour qch); **to go to ~ for 10 years** faire 10 ans de prison; **sentenced to 14 days in ~** condamné à 14 jours de réclusion criminelle ou de prison.
II *modif* **~ sentence** peine *f* de prison.
III *vtr* emprisonner; Admin, Jur incarcérer (**for sth** pour qch); **~ed for life** condamné à la réclusion criminelle à perpétuité.

jail: **~bait**◑ *n* US mineure *f*; **~bird**○ *n* taulard/-e○ *m/f*; (habitual) récidiviste *mf*; **~break** *n* évasion *f*.

jailer† /ˈdʒeɪlə(r)/ *n* geôlier/-ière† *m/f*.

jakes○† /dʒeɪks/ *npl* **the ~** les cabinets *mpl*.

jalopy○ /dʒəˈlɒpɪ/ *n* guimbarde○ *f*, vieille voiture *f*.

jalousie /ˈʒælʊziː/ *n* jalousie *f*, persienne *f*.

jam /dʒæm/ **I** *n* **1** Culin confiture *f*; **apricot ~** confiture d'abricots; **2** (congestion) (of people) foule *f*; (of traffic) embouteillage *m*; ▶ **log jam**; **3** (failure, blockage of machine, system, department) blocage *m*; **4**○ (difficult situation) pétrin○ *m*; **this is a real ~** on est vraiment dans le pétrin○; **to be in/get into a ~** être/se mettre dans le pétrin○; **to help sb out of a ~** tirer qn du pétrin○; **5** Mus (also **~ session**) bœuf○ *m*, jam-session *f*.
II *modif* Culin [*tart, doughnut etc*] à la confiture.
III *vtr* (*p prés etc* **-mm-**) **1** (stuff , pile) **to ~ things into** entasser des choses dans [*small space, suitcase, box*]; **she ~med her clothes into the drawer** elle a entassé ses vêtements dans le tiroir; **reporters were ~ming microphones into our faces** les journalistes nous fourraient○ des micros sous le nez; **to ~ one's hat on** enfoncer son chapeau sur sa tête; **to ~ one's foot on the brake, to ~ the brake on** freiner à bloc; **2** (fix firmly, wedge) coincer; **I was ~med between the wall and the door** j'étais coincé entre le mur et la porte; **I got my finger ~med in the door** je me suis coincé le doigt dans la porte; **the key's ~med in the lock** la clé s'est coincée dans la serrure; **3** (also **~ up**) (crowd, fill up) gen encombrer; **cars ~med (up) the roads** les routes étaient embouteillées; **to be ~med (solid) with, to be ~med full of** [*room, entrance, shelf*] être bourré de [*people, books, objects*]; **4** (also **~ up**) (cause to stop functioning, block) [*dirt, malfunction, person*] enrayer [*mechanism*]; coincer [*lock, door, window, system*]; **sand had ~med (up) the mechanism** le sable avait enrayé le mécanisme; **to be ~med** ou **~med up** [*mechanism*] s'enrayer (**by sth** à cause de qch); [*lock, door, window*] se coincer or se bloquer (**by sth** à cause de qch); [*system*] se bloquer; **5** Radio, Telecom brouiller [*frequency, transmission*].
IV *vi* (*p prés etc* **-mm-**) **1** (become stuck) [*mechanism, switch, lever*] s'enrayer; [*lock, door, window*] se coincer, se bloquer; **2** Mus faire un bœuf○, improviser.
IDIOMS **it's real ~**○**!** (job, task) c'est du gâteau○!; **you want ~ on it**○**!** GB et puis quoi encore!; **(it's a case of) ~ tomorrow** les beaux jours sont pour demain; ▶ **money, bread**.
■ **jam in**: ¶ **~ in** [*people*] s'entasser; ¶ **~ [sth/sb] in 1** (trap, wedge) coincer; **to be ~med in** être coincé; **2** (pack in) entasser; **there were 30 people ~med into the room** il y avait 30 personnes entassées dans la pièce.

Jamaica /dʒəˈmeɪkə/ ▶ 1131, ▶ 1381 *pr n* Jamaïque *f*; **in ~** à la Jamaïque.

Jamaican /dʒəˈmeɪkən/ ▶ 1486 **I** *n* Jamaïquain/-e *m/f*.
II *adj* jamaïquain.

jamb /dʒæm/ *n* chambranle *m*.

jamboree /ˌdʒæmbəˈriː/ *n* **1** (for scouts) jamboree *m*; **2** (party) grande fête *f*.

James /dʒeɪmz/ *pr n* Jacques.

jam: **~-full** *adj* = **jam-packed**; **~jar**, **~ pot** *n* pot *m* à confitures.

jamming /ˈdʒæmɪŋ/ *n* **1** Radio, Telecom brouillage *m*; **2** Mus improvisation *f*; **3** (in mountaineering) coincement *m*.

jammy /ˈdʒæmɪ/ *adj* **1**○ GB [*person*] veinard○; [*job*] de planqué; **2** lit [*fingers, face*] plein de confiture.

jam-packed /ˌdʒæmˈpækt/, **jam-full** /ˌdʒæmˈfʊl/ *adj* bondé; **to be jam-full of** ou **jam-packed with sth** être bourré de qch.

jam pot *n* = **jamjar**.

Jan *abrév écrite* = **January**.

jangle /ˈdʒæŋgl/ **I** *n* (of bells, pots) tintement *m*; (of keys) cliquetis *m*; (of alarm) bruit *m* strident.
II *vtr* faire tinter [*bell*]; faire cliqueter [*keys*].
III *vi* **1** (make noise) [*bells, pots*] tinter; [*keys, bangles*] cliqueter; **2** [*nerves*] **my nerves are jangling** j'ai les nerfs à vif.

jangling /ˈdʒæŋglɪŋ/ **I** *n* = **jangle I**.
II *adj* [*noise*] métallique; [*alarm*] strident.
janitor /ˈdʒænɪtə(r)/ *n* US, Scot gardien *m*.
Jansenism /ˈdʒænsənɪzəm/ *n* jansénisme *m*.
Jansenist /ˈdʒænsənɪst/ *n, adj* janséniste (*mf*).
January /ˈdʒænjʊərɪ, US -jʊerɪ/ **▶ 1472** *n* janvier *m*.
Jap○ /dʒæp/ péj **I** *n* Japonais/-e *m/f*.
II *adj* japonais.
japan /dʒəˈpæn/ **I** *n* laque *f*.
II *vtr* (*p prés etc* **-nn-**) laquer, vernir.
Japan /dʒəˈpæn/ **▶ 1131** *pr n* Japon *m*.
Japanese /ˌdʒæpəˈniːz/ **▶ 1486**, **1402** **I** *n* **1** (person) Japonais/-e *m/f*; **2** Ling japonais *m*.
II *adj* [*culture, industry*] japonais.
jape† /dʒeɪp/ *n* farce *f*, plaisanterie *f*.
japonica /dʒəˈpɒnɪkə/ *n* cognassier *m* du Japon.
jar /dʒɑː(r)/ **I** *n* **1** gen pot *m*; (large) (for sweets, pickles, preserves) bocal *m*; (earthenware) jarre *f*; **2**○ GB (drink) pot○ *m*; **to go for a ~**○ aller prendre un pot○ or un verre; **3** (jolt) lit, fig secousse *f*, choc *m*; **4** (noise) crissement *m*.
II *vtr* (*p prés etc* **-rr-**) **1** (give shock to) lit, fig ébranler, secouer [*person, structure, building*]; **to ~ one's shoulder/neck** se cogner l'épaule/le cou; **2** US (spur) **to ~ sb into action** pousser qn à agir.
III *vi* (*p prés etc* **-rr-**) **1** (make discordant noise) [*instrument, music, voice*] rendre un son discordant; **to ~ on** agacer [*person*]; **the noise ~red on her nerves** le bruit lui tapait○ sur les nerfs; **that music ~s on my ears** cette musique m'écorche○ les oreilles; **2** (rattle) [*windows*] trembler; **3** (clash) [*colours*] jurer; [*note*] sonner faux; [*ideas, opinions*] ne pas s'accorder; [*comments, criticism*] être déplacé.
jargon /ˈdʒɑːgən/ *n* jargon *m*.
jarring /ˈdʒɑːrɪŋ/ *adj* [*sound, voice, colour, effect*] discordant.
jasmine /ˈdʒæsmɪn, US ˈdʒæzmən/ *n* jasmin *m*.
jasper /ˈdʒæspə(r)/ *n* jaspe *m*.
jaundice /ˈdʒɔːndɪs/ **▶ 1354** *n* jaunisse *f*.
jaundiced /ˈdʒɔːndɪst/ *adj* **1** (bitter, cynical) [*attitude, person, account*] négatif/-ive; **to look on sth with a ~ eye** voir qch d'un mauvais œil; **2** (affected with jaundice) qui a la jaunisse; **to look ~** avoir l'air de quelqu'un qui a la jaunisse.
jaunt /dʒɔːnt/ *n* balade○ *f*; **to go for a ~** faire une balade○.
jauntily /ˈdʒɔːntɪlɪ/ *adv* de façon guillerette.
jaunty /ˈdʒɔːntɪ/ *adj* [*person, appearance*] guilleret/-ette; **to wear one's hat at a ~ angle** porter crânement son chapeau.
java○† /ˈdʒɑːvə/ *n* US café *m*.
Java /ˈdʒɑːvə/ **▶ 1381** *pr n* Java *f*.
Javanese /ˌdʒɑːvəˈniːz/ **▶ 1486** **I** *n* **1** (native) Javanais/-e *m/f*; **2** Ling javanais *m*.
II *adj* javanais.
javelin /ˈdʒævlɪn/ **▶ 1282** *n* **1** (object) javelot *m*; **2** (event) **the ~** le javelot, le lancer du javelot.
javelin: **~ thrower** *n* lanceur/-euse *m/f* de javelot; **~ throwing** **▶ 1282** *n* lancer *m* du javelot, javelot *m*.
jaw /dʒɔː/ **I** *n* **1** **▶ 1037** (bone) mâchoire *f*; **to set one's ~** prendre un air décidé; **2**○ (chat) **to have a good ~** tailler une bavette○.
II jaws *npl* (of animal, tool) mâchoires *fpl*; **the ~s of death** littér les griffes de la mort liter; **to snatch victory from the ~s of defeat** arracher la victoire à l'ennemi.
III○ *vi* (chat) papoter○.
IDIOMS **his ~ dropped** les bras lui en sont tombés.
■ **jaw on**○ (lecture) faire des sermons (**at** à).
jawbone /ˈdʒɔːbəʊn/ **I** *n* mâchoire *f*, maxillaire *m* spec.
II *vtr* US exercer des pressions sur [*person*].
jawbreaker○ /ˈdʒɔːbreɪkə(r)/ *n* **1** (word) mot *m* imprononçable; **2** (candy) bonbon *m* à sucer.
jawline /ˈdʒɔːlaɪn/ *n* menton *m*.
jay /dʒeɪ/ *n* geai *m*.
jaywalk /ˈdʒeɪwɔːk/ *vi* traverser en dehors des passages pour piétons.
jaywalker /ˈdʒeɪwɔːkə(r)/ *n* personne *f* qui traverse en dehors des passages pour piétons.
jazz /dʒæz/ **I** *n* Mus jazz *m*; **to play ~** jouer du jazz.
II *modif* [*concert, musician, singer, fan*] de jazz.
IDIOMS **and all that ~**○ et tout le bataclan○.
■ **jazz up**○: **~ up [sth], ~ [sth] up** **1** (liven up) rajeunir [*dress, outfit*]; égayer [*room, decor*]; ranimer [*party, atmosphere*]; **2** (play like jazz) faire une version jazz de [*tune*].
jazz: **~ band** *n* jazz-band *m*; **~ dance** *n* modern-jazz *m*; **~man** *n* musicien *m* de jazz.
jazzy /ˈdʒæzɪ/ *adj* **1** (bright) [*colour*] voyant; [*pattern, dress, wallpaper*] bariolé; **2** [*music*] jazzy *inv*.
JCB® *n* JCB® *m*, tracto-pelle *m*.
JCS *n* US *abrév* **▶ Joint Chiefs of Staff**.
JD *n* US (*abrév* = **Jurum Doctor**) doctorat *m* de droit.
jealous /ˈdʒeləs/ *adj* (all contexts) jaloux/-ouse (**of** de); **to feel ~** être jaloux; **to make sb ~** rendre qn jaloux; **to keep a ~ eye on sth** surveiller qch d'un œil jaloux.
jealously /ˈdʒeləslɪ/ *adv* [*watch, behave*] jalousement; **~ guarded** jalousement gardé.
jealousy /ˈdʒeləsɪ/ *n* jalousie *f*; **his petty jealousies** ses petites crises de jalousie.
jean /dʒiːn/ **I** *modif* (denim) [*jacket, skirt*] en jean.
II jeans *npl* jean *m*; **a pair of ~s** un jean.
Jean /dʒiːn/ *pr n* Jeanne.
jeep® /dʒiːp/ *n* jeep *f*.
jeer /dʒɪə(r)/ **I** *n* (from crowd) huée *f*; (from person) raillerie *f*.
II *vtr* huer.
III *vi* se moquer; **to ~ at** se moquer de [*idea, suggestion*]; [*crowd*] huer [*person*]; [*individual*] railler [*person*].
jeering /ˈdʒɪərɪŋ/ **I** *n* ¢ huées *fpl*.
II *adj* railleur/-euse.
Jehovah /dʒɪˈhəʊvə/ *pr n* Jéhovah; **~'s Witness** Témoin *m* de Jéhovah.
jejune /dʒɪˈdʒuːn/ *adj* littér **1** (naive) naïf/naïve; **2** (dull) fade.
Jekyll and Hyde /ˌdʒekɪl ən ˈhaɪd/ *n* **to lead a ~ existence** mener une double vie.
jell /dʒel/ *vi* = **gel II**.
jellied /ˈdʒelɪd/ *adj* en aspic; **~ eels** anguilles *fpl* en gelée.
Jell-o® /ˈdʒeləʊ/ *n* US gelée *f* de fruits.
jelly /ˈdʒelɪ/ *n* **1** Culin (savoury) gelée *f*; (sweet) gelée *f* de fruits; **2** (clear preserve) gelée *f*; **3** US (jam) confiture *f*; **to set into a ~** se gélifier; **4** (gelatinous substance) gelée *f*; **5**○ *abrév* = **gelignite**.
IDIOMS **to shake like a ~** trembler comme une feuille; **my legs turned to ~** j'avais les jambes en coton.
jelly: **~ baby** *n* bonbon *m*; **~ bean** *n* bonbon *m* fourré à la gelée.
jellyfish /ˈdʒelɪfɪʃ/ *n* (*pl* **~** ou **~es**) méduse *f*.
jelly: **~ mould** GB, **~ mold** US *n* moule *m* à gelée; **~ roll** *n* US biscuit *m* roulé.
jemmy /ˈdʒemɪ/ GB **I** *n* pince-monseigneur *f*.
II *vtr* **to ~ sth open** forcer qch à la pince-monseigneur.
je ne sais quoi /ˌʒə nə seɪ ˈkwɑː/ *n* je-ne-sais-quoi *m*.
jeopardize /ˈdʒepədaɪz/ *vtr* compromettre [*career, chance, plans*]; mettre [qch] en péril [*lives, troops*].
jeopardy /ˈdʒepədɪ/ *n* **to be in ~** être en péril, être menacé; **to put sb/sth in ~** mettre qn/qch en péril; **▶ double jeopardy**.
jerboa /dʒɜːˈbəʊə/ *n* gerboise *f*.
jeremiad /ˌdʒerɪˈmaɪæd/ *n* jérémiade *f* (**about** à propos de).
Jeremiah /ˌdʒerɪˈmaɪə/ *pr n* Jérémie.
Jericho /ˈdʒerɪkəʊ/ **▶ 1818** *pr n* Jéricho.
jerk /dʒɜːk/ **I** *n* **1** (jolt) gen secousse *f*, saccade *f*; (twitch) (of muscle, limb) tressaillement *m*, (petit) mouvement *m* brusque; **with a ~ of his hand/head** avec un brusque mouvement de la main/tête; **to pull the knife/drawer out with a ~** tirer le couteau/le tiroir d'un coup sec; **to start off with a ~** [*vehicle*] démarrer avec une secousse; **2**○ péj (obnoxious man) salaud● *m*; (stupid man) crétin○ *m*, abruti○ *m*.
II○ *modif* US **my ~ cousins** mes imbéciles○ de cousins.
III *vtr* tirer brusquement [*object*]; **she ~ed her head back** elle releva brusquement le menton; **he ~ed his hand away** d'un mouvement brusque il a retiré la main; **try not to ~ the camera** essaie de ne pas faire bouger l'appareil.
IV *vi* **1** (jolt) **to ~ to a halt** [*vehicle*] s'arrêter avec une secousse; **to ~ around/bolt upright** [*person*] se retourner/se redresser brusquement; **2** (twitch) [*person, limb, muscle*] tressaillir.
■ **jerk around**○ US: ¶ **~ around** (idle about) fainéanter○; ¶ **~ [sb] around** (harass) asticoter○ [*person*].
■ **jerk away** [*person*] se dégager brusquement; **to ~ away from sb/sth** reculer brusquement devant qn/qch.
■ **jerk off**● **1** (masturbate) se branler●, se masturber; **~ off●!** fous● (-moi) le camp!; **2** US (idle about) se tourner les pouces○.
■ **jerk out**: **~ out [sth]** **1** (stammer) bafouiller [*reply, excuse, apology*]; **2** (pull out) sortir brusquement [*gun, knife etc*].
jerkily /ˈdʒɜːkɪlɪ/ *adv* [*move*] par à-coups, par saccades; [*speak*] d'une voix saccadée.
jerkin /ˈdʒɜːkɪn/ *n* gilet *m*.
jerkwater town *n* US péj trou *m* or bled○ *m* perdu.
jerky /ˈdʒɜːkɪ/ **I** *n* US Culin bœuf *m* séché.
II *adj* [*movement*] saccadé; [*style, phrase*] haché.
jeroboam /ˌdʒerəˈbəʊəm/ *n* jéroboam *m*.
jerry○† /ˈdʒerɪ/ *n* GB pot *m* de chambre.
Jerry○† /ˈdʒerɪ/ GB injur **I** *n* **1** (soldier) Fritz○† *m* offensive; **2** (the Germans) les Boches○† *mpl* offensive.
II *modif* [*bomber, tank*] boche○† offensive.
jerry-building /ˈdʒerɪbɪldɪŋ/ *n* péj construction *f* de mauvaise qualité.
jerry-built /ˈdʒerɪbɪlt/ *adj* péj construit à la va-vite.
jerrycan /ˈdʒerɪkæn/ *n* jerrican *m*, nourrice *f*.
jersey /ˈdʒɜːzɪ/ **I** *n* **1** (sweater) pull-over *m*, tricot *m*; **football ~** maillot *m* de football; **2** (fabric) jersey *m*.
II *modif* [*garment*] en jersey.
Jersey /ˈdʒɜːzɪ/ **▶ 1381** *pr n* **1** GB (island) Jersey *f*; **2**○ US (= **New Jersey**) New Jersey *m*; **3** (also **~ cow**) vache *f* de race jersiaise.
Jerusalem /dʒəˈruːsələm/ **▶ 1818** *pr n* Jérusalem.
Jerusalem artichoke *n* topinambour *m*.
jest /dʒest/ **I** *n* plaisanterie *f*; **in ~** pour plaisanter.
II *vi* plaisanter.
IDIOMS **many a true word is spoken in ~** Prov plus d'une vérité est dite en plaisantant.
jester /ˈdʒestə(r)/ *n* bouffon *m*.
Jesuit /ˈdʒezjʊɪt, US ˈdʒeʒəwət/ *n, adj* jésuite (*m*).
Jesuitical /ˌdʒezjʊˈɪtɪkl, US ˌdʒeʒʊ-/ *adj* jésuitique.
Jesus /ˈdʒiːzəs/ **I** *pr n* Jésus; **~ Christ** Jésus-Christ.

II● *excl* ~ **(Christ)**●! nom de Dieu●!

Jesus: ~ **freak**○ *n* péj chrétien/-ienne *m/f* charismatique branché/-e; ~ **sandals** GB, **Jesus shoes** US *npl* nu-pieds *mpl*.

jet /dʒet/ **I** *n* **1** (plane) jet *m*, avion *m* à réaction; **2** (of water, flame) jet *m*; **3** (on gas ring) brûleur *m*; (of engine) gicleur *m*; **4** (stone) jais *m*.
II *modif* [*necklace, brooch*] en jais.
III *vi* (*p prés etc* **-tt-**) **to ~ off to the USA** s'envoler pour les USA; **to ~ around the world** passer son temps dans les avions.

jet: ~ **aircraft** *n* jet *m*, avion *m* à réaction; **~-black** *adj* [*hair, eyes*] de jais *inv*; ~ **engine** *n* moteur *m* à réaction, réacteur *m*; ~ **fighter** *n* chasseur *m* à réaction; **~foil** *n* hydroglisseur *m*; ~ **fuel** *n* kérosène *m*; **~lag** *n* décalage *m* horaire.

jetlagged /ˈdʒetlægd/ *adj* **to be ~** souffrir du décalage horaire.

jet: **~liner** *n* avion *m* à réaction; **~-powered**, **jet-propelled** *adj* à réaction; ~ **propulsion** *n* propulsion *f* par réaction.

jetsam /ˈdʒetsəm/ *n* ▶ **flotsam**.

jet set *n* jet-set *m*.

jet setter *n* **to be a ~** faire partie du jet-set.

jet-ski ▶ 1282 **I** *n* jet-ski *m*.
II *vi* faire du jet-ski.

jet-skiing ▶ 1282 *n* jet-ski *m*.

jet stream *n* jet-stream *m*, courant-jet *m*.

jettison /ˈdʒetɪsn/ *vtr* **1** (dump) (from ship) jeter [qch] par-dessus bord; (from plane, spacecraft) larguer; **2** (discard) se débarrasser de [*old clothes, jumble*]; **3** fig (reject) rejeter [*idea, theory*].

jetty /ˈdʒetɪ/ *n* (of stone) jetée *f*; (of wood) appontement *m*.

Jew /dʒuː/ *n* juif/juive *m/f*.

Jew-baiting *n* persécution *f* des juifs.

jewel /ˈdʒuːəl/ *n* **1** (gem) pierre *f* précieuse; **2** (piece of jewellery) bijou *m*; **3** Tech (in watch) rubis *m*; **4** fig (person) perle *f*; (town, building, object) joyau *m*; **to be the ~ in the crown of** être le plus beau fleuron de [*collection, company, range*].

jewel case *n* coffret *m* à bijoux.

jewelled GB, **jeweled** US /ˈdʒuːəld/ *adj* lit orné de pierres précieuses; Tech [*watch*] à rubis.

jeweller GB, **jeweler** US /ˈdʒuːələ(r)/ ▶ 1692 *n* (person) bijoutier/-ière *m/f*; **~'s (shop)** bijouterie *f*.

jewellery GB, **jewelry** US /ˈdʒuːəlrɪ/ *n* gen bijoux *mpl*; (in shop, workshop) bijouterie *f*; **a piece of ~** un bijou.

jewellery: ~ **box** GB *n* boîte *f* à bijoux; ~ **case** GB *n* coffret *m* à bijoux; ~ **store** *n* US bijouterie *f*.

Jewess /ˈdʒuːes/ *n* juive *f*.

Jewish /ˈdʒuːɪʃ/ *adj* juif/juive.

Jewish calendar *n* calendrier *m* juif.

Jewishness /ˈdʒuːɪʃnɪs/ *n* judaïté *f*.

Jewry /ˈdʒʊərɪ/ *n* communauté *f* juive.

Jew's harp *n* Mus guimbarde *f*.

Jezebel /ˈdʒezəbl, -bel/ *n* **1** (hussy) dévergondée *f*; **2** (schemer) intrigante *f*.

jib /dʒɪb/ **I** *n* **1** Naut foc *m*; **2** (of crane) flèche *f*.
II *vi* (*p prés etc* **-bb-**) [*person*] rechigner (**at** à; **at doing** à faire); [*horse*] faire un refus; **to ~ at** [*horse*] refuser [*fence*].
IDIOMS **I don't like the cut of his ~**† je n'aime pas son allure.

jib: ~ **boom** *n* Naut bout-dehors *m*; ~ **crane** *n* grue *f* à flèche.

jibe /dʒaɪb/ **I** *n* moquerie *f*.
II *vi* **1** (mock) **to ~ at sb/sth** se moquer de qn/qch; **2**○ US (match) coller○ (**with** avec); **3** Naut [*boat*] virer lof pour lof; [*sail*] passer d'un bord à l'autre du mât.

jiff(y)○ /ˈdʒɪfɪ/ *n* seconde *f*, instant *m*; **I'll be with you in a ~** une seconde et je suis à toi; **it won't take a ~** ce sera fait en moins de deux○.

Jiffy bag® *n* enveloppe *f* matelassée.

jig /dʒɪg/ **I** *n* **1** Mus gigue *f*; **to dance** ou **do a ~** danser une gigue; **2** Tech (guide) dispositif *m* de serrage; (template) gabarit *m*.
II *vtr* (*p prés etc* **-gg-**) remuer [*feet*]; **to ~ a baby (up and down) on one's knee** faire sauter un bébé sur ses genoux.
III *vi* (*p prés etc* **-gg-**) (also **~ about, ~ around**) gigoter○; (impatiently) se trémousser.
IDIOMS **the ~ is up**○ US c'est cuit○.

jigger /ˈdʒɪgə(r)/ *n* **1** (measure) petite mesure *f* (à liqueur); **2**○ US (thingummyjig) truc○ *m*, machin○ *m*; **3** Zool chique *f*.

jiggered○ /ˈdʒɪgəd/ *adj* **1** (astonished) sidéré; **I'll be ~!** nom d'une pipe○!; **2** (exhausted) crevé○.

jiggery-pokery○ /ˌdʒɪgərɪˈpəʊkərɪ/ *n* GB micmac○ *m*.

jiggle /ˈdʒɪgl/ **I** *vtr* agiter.
II *vi* (also **~ about, ~ around**) se trémousser.

jigsaw /ˈdʒɪgsɔː/ *n* **1** (also **~ puzzle**) puzzle *m*; **2** Tech scie *f* sauteuse.

jihad /dʒɪˈhɑːd/ *n* **1** Relig djihad *m*; **2** fig croisade *f*.

jilt /dʒɪlt/ *vtr* abandonner, plaquer○.

Jim Crow○ /ˌdʒɪm ˈkrəʊ/ *n* US ségrégation *f* raciale; **~ policies** politique *f* ségrégationniste.

jim dandy○† /ˌdʒɪmˈdændɪ/ *excl* US chouette○!

jimjams○ /ˈdʒɪmdʒæmz/ *npl* **1** (fear) frousse○ *f*; **2** (from alcohol) delirium tremens *m*; **3** GB (pyjamas) lang enfantin pyjama *m*.

jimmy /ˈdʒɪmɪ/ US **I** *n* (crowbar) pince-monseigneur *f*.
II jimmies *npl* nonpareilles *fpl*.
III *vtr* forcer [qch] à la pince-monseigneur.

jingle /ˈdʒɪŋgl/ **I** *n* **1** (noise) (of bells, coins) tintement *m*; (of keys, bracelet) cliquetis *m*; **2** (verse) ritournelle *f*; **3** Advertg jingle *m*, refrain *m* publicitaire, sonal *m*.
II *vtr* faire tinter [*coins, keys*].
III *vi* [*bells*] tintinnabuler; [*keys, coins*] cliqueter.

jingo† /ˈdʒɪŋgəʊ/ *excl* **by ~!** sapristi†!

jingoism /ˈdʒɪŋgəʊɪzəm/ *n* péj chauvinisme *m*.

jingoist /ˈdʒɪŋgəʊɪst/ *n, adj* péj chauvin/-e (*m/f*) Pol.

jingoistic /ˌdʒɪŋgəʊˈɪstɪk/ *adj* péj chauvin.

jink /dʒɪŋk/ Sport **I** *n* mouvement *m* d'esquive.
II *vi* courir en zigzag. ▶ **high jinks**.

jinx /dʒɪŋks/ **I** *n* **1** (curse) sort *m*; **to put a ~ on sb/sth** jeter un sort à qn/qch; **there's a ~ on this car** il y a toujours quelque chose qui ne va pas avec cette voiture; **there's a ~ on me** j'ai la poisse○; **2** (unlucky person, object) porte-malheur *m inv*.
II *vtr* porter la poisse○ à [*person*]; **I must be ~ed** j'ai la poisse○.

jitterbug /ˈdʒɪtəbʌg/ *n* **1** Dance jitterbug *m*; **2**○ (nervous person) paquet *m* de nerfs.

jitters /ˈdʒɪtəz/ *npl* Econ, Pol courant *m* de nervosité; **to have the ~** [*person, stock market*] être nerveux/-euse; [*actor*] avoir le trac; **to give sb the ~** rendre qn nerveux/-euse.

jittery /ˈdʒɪtərɪ/ *adj* nerveux/-euse.

jive /dʒaɪv/ **I** *n* **1** Mus swing *m*; **2**○ US (glib talk) salades○ *fpl*; **3** US argot *m* des musiciens de jazz.
II *vi* Dance danser le swing.
III *vtr* US○ **1** (mislead) embobiner○; **2** (tease) charrier○.

Jnr *adj*: *abrév écrite* = **junior**.

Joan of Arc *pr n* Jeanne d'Arc.

job /dʒɒb/ **I** *n* **1** (employment) emploi *m*; (post) poste *m*; **to look for/get a ~** chercher/trouver un emploi; **to give sb a ~** donner un emploi à qn; **to give up/keep one's ~** quitter/conserver son emploi; **a ~ in a bookshop/an office** un emploi dans une librairie/un bureau; **a teaching/civil service ~** un poste d'enseignant/de fonctionnaire; **to have a good ~** avoir un bon poste; **what's her ~?** qu'est-ce qu'elle fait (comme travail)?; **to have a ~ as a secretary/in local government** être employé comme secrétaire/dans l'administration locale; **to be out of a ~** être sans emploi; **we'll all be out of a ~** nous nous retrouverons tous sans emploi; **2** (role) fonction *f*; **the ~ of the curator is to...** la fonction du conservateur est de...; **the ~ of the heart/liver is to...** la fonction du cœur/du foie est de...; **to have the ~ of doing** avoir pour fonction de faire; **it's the jury's/my ~ to do** c'est au jury/à moi de faire; **3** (duty) travail *m*; **her main ~ is to...** son travail principal consiste à...; **she's only doing her ~** elle ne fait que son travail; **4** (task) travail *m*, boulot○ *m*; **to find/have a ~ for sb to do** trouver/avoir du travail or un boulot○ pour qn; **to do odd ~s around the house** faire des bricoles○ dans la maison; **5** (assignment) (of company) projet *m*; (of individual) tâche *f*; **to do a ~ for the local council** exécuter un projet pour le conseil municipal; **the next ~ is to convince him** la tâche suivante consistera à le convaincre; **to have the ~ of doing** avoir la tâche de faire; **the ~ of building the theatre went to X** la construction du théâtre a été confiée à X; **6** (result of work to do) **a good/poor/lovely ~** du bon/du mauvais/de l'excellent travail; **to make a good ~ of doing sth** faire du bon travail en faisant qch; **you've made a good ~ of the chair** tu as fait du bon travail avec la chaise; **you haven't made a very good ~ of it** tu n'as pas fait du très bon travail; **7**○ (difficult activity) **a real ~, quite a ~** toute une affaire○ **(to do, doing** de faire); **we had a real ~ on there!** on ne s'est pas amusés!; **8**○ (crime, theft) coup○ *m*; **to do** ou **pull off a ~** faire un coup○; **bank ~** attaque *f* de banque; **to do a bank ~** dévaliser une banque; **9** Comput travail *m*, job○ *m*; **10**○ (thing) truc○ *m*; **11**○ (plastic surgery) **to have a nose ~** se faire refaire le nez.
II *modif* [*advert, offer, opportunities, title*] d'emploi; [*analysis, evaluation, specification*] de poste; [*pages, supplement*] des emplois; [*creation, cuts, losses*] d'emplois.
III *vi* (*p prés etc* **-bb-**) **1** (do casual work) faire des petits travaux; **2** (do piece-work) travailler à la tâche.
IDIOMS **(and a) good ~ too!** GB et c'est une bonne chose!; **it's a good ~ that** GB heureusement que; **~s for the boys** des planques○ pour les copains; **just the ~** tout à fait ce qu'il faut; **to do a big ~**○ faire caca○; **on the ~** (working) au travail or boulot○; **to learn on the ~** apprendre sur le tas; **to lie down** ou **fall asleep on the ~** s'endormir à la tâche; **to be on the ~**○ GB hum être en train de faire l'amour; **to do the ~** fig faire l'affaire; **to give sth/sb up as a bad ~** GB laisser tomber qch/qn; **to make the best of a bad ~** GB faire contre mauvaise fortune bon cœur; ▶ **on-the-job**.

Job /dʒəʊb/ *pr n* Bible Job.
IDIOMS **to be a ~'s comforter** être totalement décourageant; **to have the patience of ~** avoir une patience d'ange.

job action /dʒɒb/ *n* US mouvement *m* de revendication.

jobber /ˈdʒɒbə(r)/ *n* travailleur/-euse *m/f* à la tâche; US grossiste *mf*.

jobbery /ˈdʒɒbərɪ/ *n* péj tripatouillage○ *m*, trafic *m* d'influence.

jobbing /ˈdʒɒbɪŋ/ *adj* [*gardener, builder, printer*] à la tâche.

job /dʒɒb/: **Job Centre** *n* GB bureau *m* des services nationaux de l'emploi; ~ **control** *n* Comput contrôle *m* des travaux; ~ **control language** *n* Comput langage *m* de contrôle des travaux; ~ **description** *n* description *f* de poste; **~holder** *n* employé/-e *m/f*; **~-hunting** *n* chasse *f* à l'emploi.

jobless /ˈdʒɒblɪs/ **I** *n* **the ~** (+ *v pl*) les sans-emploi *mpl*.
II *modif* [*total*] des sans-emploi; [*rate, figures*] du chômage.
III *adj* sans emploi.

joblessness /ˈdʒɒblɪsnɪs/ *n* chômage *m*.

job lot /ˌdʒɒbˈlɒt/ *n* **1** (at auction) lot *m*; **2** fig (collection) ramassis *m* pej.

job queue /dʒɒb/ *n* Comput file *f* d'attente de travaux.

job satisfaction /dʒɒb/ *n* satisfaction *f* dans le travail; **I get a lot of ~** mon travail me donne beaucoup de satisfaction.

job security /dʒɒb/ *n* sécurité *f* de l'emploi.

job-share /ˈdʒɒbʃeə(r)/ **I** *n* poste *m* partagé.
II *modif* [*scheme, system*] de partage de poste; [*position*] partagé.

job /dʒɒb/: **~ sharing** *n* partage *m* de poste; **-~sworth**○ *n* GB péj employé/-e *m/f* borné/-e.

jock○ /dʒɒk/ *n* **1** GB injur Écossais *m*; **2** US athlète *m*.

jockey /ˈdʒɒkɪ/ **I** *n* jockey *m*.
II *vtr* **to ~ sb into doing sth** amener qn à faire qch.
III *vi* **to ~ for position** lit [*runners, riders*] lutter pour la première place; fig jouer des coudes; **the managers were ~ing for the post** les dirigeants jouaient des coudes pour obtenir le poste; **politicians ~ing for power** des politiciens engagés dans la lutte pour le pouvoir.

jockey: **Jockey Club** *n* Jockey-club *m*; **~ shorts** *n* US slip *m* (d'homme).

jockstrap○ /ˈdʒɒkstræp/ *n* suspensoir *m*.

jocose /dʒəʊˈkəʊs/ *adj* littér facétieux/-ieuse.

jocular /ˈdʒɒkjʊlə(r)/ *adj* (all contexts) badin.

jocularity /ˌdʒɒkjʊˈlærətɪ/ *n* jovialité *f*.

jocularly /ˈdʒɒkjʊləlɪ/ *adv* [*say, announce*] d'un ton badin.

jocund /ˈdʒɒkənd/ *adj* littér jovial.

jodhpurs /ˈdʒɒdpəz/ *npl* Sport, Fashn jodhpurs *mpl*; **a pair of ~** des jodhpurs.

joe○ /dʒəʊ/ *n* US gars *m*.

Joe Bloggs GB, **Joe Blow** US *n* Monsieur Tout-le-Monde.

jog /dʒɒg/ **I** *n* **1** (knock) gen petite secousse *f*; (with elbow) coup *m* de coude; **2** (trot) petit trot○ *m*; **to set off at a ~** partir au petit trot○; **3** Sport **to go for a ~** aller faire un jogging; **4** US (in road) coude *m*.
II *vtr* (*p prés etc* **-gg-**) pousser [*elbow*]; heurter [*table*]; **to ~ sb with one's elbow** donner un coup de coude à qn; **to ~ sb's memory** rafraîchir la mémoire de qn.
III *vi* (*p prés etc* **-gg-**) **1** Sport faire du jogging; **2**○ US [*road*] faire un coude.
■ **jog along, jog on** [*vehicle*] cahoter; fig [*person, business*] suivre son petit bonhomme de chemin○, se maintenir.

jogger /ˈdʒɒgə(r)/ *n* joggeur/-euse *m/f*.

jogging /ˈdʒɒgɪŋ/ ▶ 1282 **I** *n* jogging *m*.
II *modif* [*clothes, gear*] de jogging; **~ suit** jogging *m*, survêtement *m*.

joggle○ /ˈdʒɒgl/ **I** *n* **1** (jolt) légère secousse *f*; **2** Constr goujon *m*.
II *vtr* secouer légèrement.
III *vi* brinquebaler○, ballotter.

jog trot *n* petit trot *m*.

Johannesburg /dʒəʊˈhænɪsbɜːg/ ▶ 1818 *pr n* Johannesburg.

john○ US /dʒɒn/ *n* **1** (lavatory) **the ~** les WC○ *mpl*; **2**◐ (prostitute's client, dupe) micheton◐ *m*.

John /dʒɒn/ *pr n* Jean; **(Saint) ~ the Baptist** Saint Jean-Baptiste; **(Saint) ~ of the Cross** (Saint) Jean de la Croix.

John: **~ Bull** *n* (Englishman) l'Anglais *m* moyen; (xenophobic) l'Anglais *m* xénophobe; **~ Doe** *n* US l'homme *m* de la rue; **~ Dory** *n* (fish) (European) saint-pierre *m inv*; (South Seas) dorée *f*; **~ Hancock**○ US *n* signature *f*.

johnny /ˈdʒɒnɪ/ *n* **1** US Med blouse *f* de patient; **2**○ GB (condom) capote *f* anglaise○, préservatif *m*; **3**○† (fellow) GB type○ *m*.

johnny: **~-cake** *n* US crêpe *f*; **Johnny-come-lately** *n* (*pl* **-lies**) (newcomer) nouveau venu *m*; (upstart) parvenu *m*.

John Q Public○ *n* US l'homme *m* de la rue.

join /dʒɔɪn/ **I** *n* raccord *m*.
II *vtr* **1** (meet up with) rejoindre [*colleague, family*]; **I'll ~ you in Paris** je te rejoindrai à Paris; **come and ~ us for dinner/drinks** venez dîner/prendre un verre avec nous; **may I ~ you?** (sit down) puis-je me joindre à vous?; **we're going to the opera, would you like to ~ us?** nous allons à l'opéra, voulez-vous venir avec nous?; **2** (go to the end of) se mettre dans [*line, queue*]; se mettre au bout de [*row*]; ajouter son nom à [*list*]; **3** (become a member of) devenir membre de [*EC, organization, team*]; adhérer à [*club, party*]; s'inscrire à [*class, library*]; s'engager dans [*army*]; devenir membre de [*church*]; **to ~ a union** se syndiquer; **~ the club!** tu n'es pas le seul/la seule!; **4** (become part of) se joindre à [*crowd, exodus, rush*]; **to ~ battle** entrer dans la bataille; **the province voted to ~ the federation** la province a voté l'union avec la fédération; **5** (become an employee) entrer dans [*firm, company*]; **to ~ Lloyds/Ford** entrer chez Lloyds/Ford; **6** (participate in) ▶ **join in**; **7** (associate with) gen se joindre à [*person*] **(to do, in doing** pour faire); (professionally) [*actor, businesswoman*] s'associer à [*colleague, partner*] **(to do, in doing** pour faire); **to ~ forces** s'unir, s'allier; **to ~ forces with sb/sth** (merge) s'allier à qn/qch; (co-operate) collaborer avec qn/qch; **to ~ sb in the struggle** se joindre à qn dans la lutte; **Martin ~s me in sending his congratulations** Martin se joint à moi pour vous féliciter; **8** (board) monter dans [*train*]; monter à bord de [*ship*]; **9** (attach) réunir, joindre [*ends, halves, pieces*]; assembler [*parts*]; **to ~ one end to another** ou **the other** joindre un bout à l'autre; **to ~ two pieces together** joindre deux morceaux; **10** (link) relier [*points, towns, dots*] **(to** à); **to ~ hands** lit se prendre par la main; fig collaborer; **11** (merge with) [*road*] rejoindre [*motorway*]; [*river*] se jeter dans [*sea*]; **12** Relig [*priest*] unir [*bride and groom*]; **to ~ two people in marriage** unir deux personnes par le mariage.
III *vi* **1** (become a member) (of party, club) adhérer; (of group, class) s'inscrire; **2** (connect, meet) [*edges, pieces*] se joindre; [*pipes, wires*] se raccorder; [*rivers, roads*] se rejoindre.
■ **join in**: ¶ **~ in** participer; ¶ **~ in [sth]** participer à [*talks, discussion, campaign, game, activity*]; prendre part à [*strike, demonstration*]; **to ~ in the bidding** prendre part aux enchères; **to ~ in the fun** se joindre à la fête; **to ~ in the dancing/singing** se mettre à danser/chanter avec les autres.
■ **join on**: ¶ **~ on** se fixer; ¶ **~ [sth] on, ~ on [sth]** (fasten) attacher, fixer; (add) ajouter.
■ **join up**: ¶ **~ up 1** Mil (enlist) s'engager; **2** (meet up) [*people*] se retrouver; **3** (merge) [*roads, tracks*] se rejoindre; ¶ **~ up [sth], ~ [sth] up** relier [*characters, dots*]; assembler [*pieces*]; **~ed-up writing** écriture *f* liée.

joinder /ˈdʒɔɪndə(r)/ *n* Jur jonction *f* d'instance.

joiner /ˈdʒɔɪnə(r)/ ▶ 1692 *n* Constr menuisier/-ière *m/f*.

joinery /ˈdʒɔɪnərɪ/ *n* menuiserie *f*.

joint /dʒɔɪnt/ **I** *n* **1** Anat articulation *f*; **elbow/knee/ankle ~** articulation du coude/du genou/de la cheville; **to dislocate a ~** se déboîter une articulation; **to put one's shoulder out of ~** se déboîter l'épaule; **to be out of ~** [*shoulder, knee*] être déboîté; **to have stiff** ou **aching ~s** avoir des douleurs articulaires; **2** Tech, Constr (in carpentry) assemblage *m*; (in metalwork) joint *m*; (of pipes, tubes) raccord *m*; **3** Culin rôti *m*; **4**○ pej (place) gen endroit *m*; (nightclub, office, workplace) boîte○ *f*; (café) boui-boui○ *m*; **burger ~** fast-food○ *m*; **pizza ~** pizzeria *f*; **5**○ (cannabis cigarette) joint○ *m*.
II *modif* Med [*problem, pain*] articulaire; [*replacement*] d'articulation.
III *adj* [*action*] collectif/-ive; [*programme, working party, session, company*] mixte; [*measures, procedure*] commun; [*winner, third*] ex aequo; [*negotiations, talks*] multilatéral; **he is ~ favourite** c'est l'un des deux favoris.
IV *vtr* **1** Culin découper [*poultry*]; **2** Tech raccorder [*pipes*].
IDIOMS **to have one's nose put out of ~** être dépité.

joint account *n* compte *m* joint.

joint agent *n* GB **the house is in the hands of ~s** la maison est en vente dans deux agences.

joint: **~ agreement** *n* convention *f* collective; **~ and several** *adj* Fin, Jur conjoint et solidaire; **~ author** *n* coauteur *m*; **~ beneficiary** *n* bénéficiaire *mf*; **Joint Chiefs of Staff**, **JCS** *npl* US, Mil chefs *mpl* d'états-majors interarmés; **~ committee** *n* comité *m* mixte; **~ creditor** *n* cocréancier/-ière *m/f*; **~ custody** *n* garde *f* partagée; **~ debtor** *n* codébiteur/-trice *m/f*.

jointed /ˈdʒɔɪntɪd/ *adj* **1** Culin [*chicken*] découpé; **2** (doll, puppet) articulé; **3** (rod, pole) démontable.

joint: **~ effort** *n* collaboration *f*; **~ heir** *n* cohéritier/-ière *m/f*; **~ honours** *npl* GB Univ licence *f* combinée.

jointly /ˈdʒɔɪntlɪ/ *adv* [*manage, publish, own, organize*] conjointement; **~ owned** en copropriété; **to be ~ owned by X et Y** être la copropriété de X et Y; **to be ~ liable for damages** être solidaire des dommages-intérêts; **they are ~ responsible** ils sont conjointement responsables.

jointly and severally *adv* conjointement et solidairement.

joint management *n* cogestion *f*.

joint meeting *n* réunion *f* des intéressés; **a ~ of the two committees** une réunion entre les deux comités.

joint: **~ owner** *n* copropriétaire *mf*; **~ ownership** *n* copropriété *f*; **~ partnership** *n* participation *f* mixte; **~ resolution** *n* résolution *f* commune; **~ signatory** *n* cosignataire *m*; **~-stock company** *n* société *f* par actions.

jointure /ˈdʒɔɪntʃə(r)/ *n* Jur douaire *m*.

joint venture *n* **1** Econ, Fin coentreprise *f*, joint-venture *m*; **2** gen projet *m* en commun.

joist /dʒɔɪst/ *n* Constr solive *f*.

jojoba /həʊˈhəʊbə/ *n* jojoba *m*.

joke /dʒəʊk/ **I** *n* **1** (amusing story) plaisanterie *f*, blague○ *f* **(about** sur); **to tell a ~** raconter une blague○; **to get**○ **the ~** saisir la plaisanterie; **bad ~** plaisanterie nulle; fig mauvaise plaisanterie; **it's our private ~** c'est une plaisanterie entre nous; **to have a ~ about sth** plaisanter sur qch; **can't you see the ~?** tu ne vois pas ce que ça a de drôle?; **2** (laughing matter) plaisanterie *f*; **to do sth as a ~** faire qch par plaisanterie; **to turn sth into a ~** tourner qch à la plaisanterie; **to carry** ou **take a ~ too far** pousser trop loin la plaisanterie; **the ~ is on you** la plaisanterie se retourne contre toi; **this is getting beyond a ~** la plaisanterie a assez duré; **she can't take a ~** elle prend mal la plaisanterie; **can't you take a ~?** tu ne supportes pas la plaisanterie?; **it's no ~ doing** ce n'est pas drôle de faire; **it's no ~ trying to find a job** trouver un emploi n'est pas une mince affaire; **to make a ~ of sth** prendre qch à la rigolade○; **3** (prank) tour *m*, farce *f*; **to play a ~**

on sb jouer un tour or faire une farce à qn; **4** (object of ridicule) (person) guignol *m* pej; (event, situation) farce *f*; **the exam was a ~** l'examen était une farce.

II *vi* plaisanter, blaguer○; **to ~ about sth** plaisanter sur qch; (maliciously) se moquer de qch; **you must be joking!** tu plaisantes!; tu veux rire!; **I was only joking!** ce n'était qu'une plaisanterie!, c'était pour rire!; **I'm not joking!** je ne plaisante pas!; **it's no joking matter** ça n'a rien de drôle.

joker /ˈdʒəʊkə(r)/ *n* **1** (who tells jokes) blagueur/-euse○ *m/f*; (who plays tricks) farceur/-euse *m/f*; **2**○ pej (person) type○ *m*; **3** (in cards) joker *m*; **4** Jur *clause ambiguë d'une loi*.

IDIOMS **the ~ in the pack** l'exception à la règle.

jokester† /ˈdʒəʊkstə(r)/ *n* farceur/-euse *m/f*.

jokey○ /ˈdʒəʊkɪ/ *adj* rigolo/-ote○, cocasse.

joking /ˈdʒəʊkɪŋ/ I *n* ¢ plaisanterie *f*, blague○ *f*; **~ apart** ou **aside** blague à part, toute plaisanterie mise à part.

II *adj* [*tone*] de plaisanterie; **to speak in a ~ way** parler en plaisantant.

jokingly /ˈdʒəʊkɪŋlɪ/ *adv* [*say*] en plaisantant; **he was ~ called Buster** on l'appelait Buster pour plaisanter.

jollification /ˌdʒɒlɪfɪˈkeɪʃn/ *n* (also **jollifications** *pl*) réjouissances *fpl*.

jollily /ˈdʒɒlɪlɪ/ *adv* gaiement.

jollity /ˈdʒɒlətɪ/ *n* gaieté *f*; (of person) bonne humeur *f*.

jolly /ˈdʒɒlɪ/ I *adj* **1** (cheerful) [*person*] enjoué; [*tune*] joyeux/-euse; [*bunting, party hats*] qui donne un air de fête; **2**○† (enjoyable) amusant; **what a ~ time we had!** qu'est-ce qu'on s'est bien amusé!; **3**○ (drunk) éméché○.

II○ *adv* GB (emphatic) drôlement; **she's a ~ good singer** elle chante drôlement bien; **he was ~ lucky** il a eu une sacrée veine○; **'I'm not going'—'you ~ well are!'** 'je n'y vais pas'—'c'est ce qu'on va voir!'; **~ good**○! formidable!

III *vtr* **to ~ sb along** amadouer qn; **we jollied him into staying** nous avons fini par le convaincre de rester avec nous.

IDIOMS **to get one's jollies**○ **doing sth** US prendre son pied○ à faire qch.

jolly: **~ boat** *n* canot *m*; **Jolly Roger** *n* pavillon *m* noir.

jolt /dʒəʊlt/ I *n* **1** (jerk) secousse *f*; **2** (shock) choc *m*; **to give sb a ~** secouer qn; **3**○ US (drink) coup○ *m*.

II *vtr* **1** lit secouer; **I was ~ed out of my seat** j'ai été violemment projeté hors de mon siège; **2** fig (shock) secouer [*person*].

III *vi* [*vehicle*] cahoter; **to ~ to a halt** ou **a standstill** s'arrêter avec des soubresauts.

jolting /ˈdʒəʊltɪŋ/ I *n* (of vehicle) secousses *fpl*, cahots *mpl*.

II *adj* cahotant.

Jonah /ˈdʒəʊnə/ *pr n* Bible Jonas; fig oiseau *m* de malheur.

jonquil /ˈdʒɒŋkwɪl/ *n* (white) narcisse *m*; (yellow) jonquille *f*.

Jordan /ˈdʒɔːdn/ ▶ **1131**, **1644** *pr n* **1** (country) Jordanie *f*; **2** (river) Jourdain *m*.

Jordanian /dʒɔːˈdeɪnɪən/ ▶ **1486** I *n* Jordanien/-ienne *m/f*.

II *adj* [*ambassador*] de Jordanie; [*agriculture, education*] jordanien/-ienne.

josh○ /dʒɒʃ/ US I *n* taquinerie *f*.

II *vtr* taquiner.

III *vi* blaguer.

joss stick /ˈdʒɒstɪk/ *n* bâtonnet *m* d'encens.

jostle /ˈdʒɒsl/ I *vtr* bousculer.

II *vi* **1** lit (push) [*supporters, shoppers*] se bousculer (**for** pour; **to do** pour faire); **2** fig (compete) se bousculer (**with** avec; **for** pour).

jot /dʒɒt/ I *n* **he doesn't care a ~** il s'en fiche○ complètement; **it doesn't matter a ~** cela n'a pas la moindre importance; **it makes not a ~ of difference** ça ne fait pas un poil○ de différence; ▶ **tittle**.

II *vtr* (*p prés etc* **-tt-**) = **jot down**.

■ **jot down**: **~ [sth] down**, **~ down [sth]** noter [*ideas, names*]; **he ~ted down some notes** il a griffonné quelques notes.

jotter /ˈdʒɒtə(r)/ *n* GB (pad) bloc-notes *m inv*.

jottings /ˈdʒɒtɪŋz/ *npl* notes *fpl*.

joual /ʒwɑːl/ *n* joual *m*.

joule /dʒuːl/ *n* Phys joule *m*.

journal /ˈdʒɜːnl/ *n* **1** (diary) journal *m*; (periodical) revue *f*; (newspaper) journal *m*; Accts journal *m*; **2** Tech (also **~ bearing**) palier *m*.

journalese /ˌdʒɜːnəˈliːz/ *n* péj jargon *m* journalistique.

journalism /ˈdʒɜːnəlɪzəm/ *n* journalisme *m*.

journalist /ˈdʒɜːnəlɪst/ *n* journaliste *mf*; **newspaper/television ~** journaliste *mf* de la presse écrite/à la télévision.

journalistic /ˌdʒɜːnəˈlɪstɪk/ *adj* [*career, skill*] de journaliste; [*assignment, ethics, style*] journalistique.

journey /ˈdʒɜːnɪ/ I *n* **1** (trip) (long) voyage *m*; (short or habitual) trajet *m*; **metro/bus ~** trajet en métro/bus; **to go on a ~** partir en voyage; **did you have a pleasant ~?** avez-vous fait bon voyage?; **(have a) safe ~!** bon voyage!; **she had never made the ~ to Glasgow** elle n'était jamais allée à Glasgow; **we broke our ~ in Paris** nous nous sommes arrêtés à Paris; **2** (distance covered) trajet *m*; **3** (time taken) **it's a two-hour ~ to Lille** il faut deux heures pour aller à Lille; **4** (spiritual) voyage *m*.

II *modif* **~ time** (in car, bus etc) durée *f* du trajet; (in plane) durée *f* du vol.

III *vi* voyager (**from** de; **to** à); **to ~ on** continuer son voyage.

journeyman /ˈdʒɜːnɪmən/ *n* (*pl* **-men**) Hist (qualified worker) compagnon *m*.

joust /dʒaʊst/ *vi* jouter.

jousting /ˈdʒaʊstɪŋ/ *n* joute *f* (à cheval).

Jove /dʒəʊv/ *pr n* Mythol Jupiter; **by ~**○†! parbleu○!

jovial /ˈdʒəʊvɪəl/ *adj* [*person, mood*] jovial; [*remark*] enjoué; [*company*] joyeux/-euse.

joviality /ˌdʒəʊvɪˈælətɪ/ *n* jovialité *f*.

jowl /dʒaʊl/ *n* (jaw) mâchoire *f*; (fleshy fold) bajoue *f*; **heavy/square ~ed** à la mâchoire lourde/carrée.

IDIOMS **to live/work cheek by ~ with sb** vivre/travailler coude à coude avec qn.

joy /dʒɔɪ/ *n* **1** (delight) joie *f* (**at** devant); **to my great ~, he recovered** à ma grande joie, il a guéri; **to jump/shout for ~** sauter/crier de joie; **2** (pleasure) plaisir *m*; **the ~ of doing** le plaisir de faire; **to do sth for the sheer ~ of it** faire qch uniquement pour le plaisir; **his dancing is a ~ to behold** c'est un plaisir de le regarder danser; **3**○ GB (success) **I got no ~ out of the bank manager** mon entretien avec le directeur de banque n'a rien donné; **I wish you ~ (of it)** iron je vous souhaite bien du plaisir iron.

IDIOMS **to be full of the ~s of spring** être en pleine forme.

joyful /ˈdʒɔɪfl/ *adj* joyeux/-euse; **we were ~ at** ou **about the news of her release** la nouvelle de sa libération nous a remplis de joie.

joyfully /ˈdʒɔɪfəlɪ/ *adv* joyeusement; **the news was ~ received** la nouvelle a été reçue avec joie.

joyfulness /ˈdʒɔɪflnɪs/ *n* (habitual) allégresse *f*; (on one occasion) gaieté *f*.

joyless /ˈdʒɔɪlɪs/ *adj* [*marriage*] malheureux/-euse; [*occasion*] triste; [*workers*] morose; [*production*] terne; [*existence*] morne.

joyous /ˈdʒɔɪəs/ *adj* littér [*heart, song, person, shout*] joyeux/-euse; [*occasion*] heureux/-euse.

joyously /ˈdʒɔɪəslɪ/ *adv* [*shout, welcome*] joyeusement.

joyrider /ˈdʒɔɪraɪdə(r)/ *n* jeune chauffard *m* en voiture volée.

joyriding /ˈdʒɔɪraɪdɪŋ/ *n* rodéo *m* à la voiture volée.

joystick /ˈdʒɔɪstɪk/ *n* Aviat manche *m* à balai; (in video games) manette *f*.

JP *n* GB *abrév* ▶ **Justice of the Peace**.

Jr *adj*: *abrév écrite* = **junior**.

jubilant /ˈdʒuːbɪlənt/ *adj* [*person*] exultant; [*crowd*] en liesse; [*expression, mood*] réjoui; **to be ~** exulter (**about, at, over** devant).

jubilation /ˌdʒuːbɪˈleɪʃn/ *n* (joy) jubilation *f* (**about, at, over** devant); (rejoicing) réjouissance *f*.

jubilee /ˈdʒuːbɪliː/ I *n* jubilé *m*.

II *modif* [*festivity, year*] du jubilé.

Judaea /dʒuːˈdɪə/ *pr n* Judée *f*.

Judah /ˈdʒuːdə/ *pr n* Bible Juda.

Judaic /dʒuːˈdeɪɪk/ *adj* judaïque.

Judaism /ˈdʒuːdeɪɪzəm, US -dɪɪzəm/ *n* judaïsme *m*.

judas /ˈdʒuːdəs/ *n* (peephole) judas *m*.

Judas /ˈdʒuːdəs/ *pr n* Judas also fig.

Judas tree *n* arbre *m* de Judée.

judder /ˈdʒʌdə(r)/ GB I *n* secousse *f*.

II *vi* être agité de violentes secousses; **to ~ to a halt** s'arrêter avec de violentes secousses.

judge /dʒʌdʒ/ I *n* **1** ▶ **1268** Jur juge *m*; **2** (adjudicator) (at competition) membre *m* du jury; Sport juge *m*; **the ~s' decision is final** (at show etc) la décision du jury est sans appel; **3** fig **to be a good ~ of character** être un fin psychologue, savoir juger les gens; **to be no ~ of** ne pas s'y connaître en [*art, wine*]; **I think it's lovely—not that I'm any ~** je trouve ça très beau—bien que je ne sois pas vraiment juge en la matière; **let me be the ~ of that** je suis mieux à même d'en juger.

II **Judges** *pr npl* Bible Juges *mpl*.

III *vtr* **1** gen, Jur juger [*person*]; **to ~ a prisoner guilty** juger qu'un accusé est coupable; **who are you to ~ others?** de quel droit te permets-tu de juger les autres?; **2** (adjudicate) faire partie du jury de [*show, competition*]; **3** (estimate) (currently) estimer [*distance, age*]; (in the future) prévoir [*outcome, reaction*]; **it is hard to ~ who will win the election** il est difficile de prévoir qui va gagner les élections; **4** (consider) juger, estimer; **the operation was ~d a great success** on a estimé or jugé que l'opération avait été un grand succès; **~d by their usual standards, their concert was disappointing** par rapport à ce qu'ils font d'habitude, leur concert était décevant.

IV *vi* juger; **I am in no position to ~** ce n'est pas à moi de juger; **as far as one can ~** autant qu'on puisse en juger; **judging by** ou **from...** à en juger par or d'après...

IDIOMS **to be as sober as a ~** (not drunk) ne pas être ivre du tout; (solemn) être sérieux comme un pape.

judge advocate *n* GB assesseur *m*; US commissaire *m* du gouvernement.

judgeship /ˈdʒʌdʒʃɪp/ *n* US fonctions *fpl* de juge.

judgment, **judgement** /ˈdʒʌdʒmənt/ *n* **1** gen, Jur jugement *m*; **to pass/give ~** prononcer/rendre un jugement (**on** sur); **to make ~s about sth** juger qch; **to sit in ~ on** ou **over** juger [*person, situation*]; **2** (opinion) avis *m*, opinion *f*; **in my ~** à mon avis; **to reserve ~** réserver son jugement; **to do sth against one's better ~** faire qch en sachant que l'on fait une erreur; **3** (discernment) jugement *m*; **an error of ~** une erreur de jugement; **to lack ~** manquer de jugement; **use your own ~** (in assessing) c'est à vous de juger; (in acting) faites comme bon vous semblera; **4** (punishment) punition *f*.

judgmental, **judgemental** /ˌdʒʌdʒˈmentl/ *adj* **to be (too) ~** juger les autres de façon trop catégorique; **don't be so ~!** ne juge pas tant les autres!

Judgment Day *n* le jour du Jugement dernier.

judicature /ˈdʒuːdɪkətʃə(r)/ *n* (administration of justice) justice *f*; (court system) institution *f* judiciaire.

judicial /dʒuːˈdɪʃl/ *adj* **1** [*inquiry, process*] judiciaire; [*decision*] jurisprudentiel/-ielle; **to bring/take ~ proceedings against sb** engager une procédure contre qn; **2** (wise) [*mind*] pondéré; **3** (impartial) [*silence*] réfléchi.

judicially /dʒuːˈdɪʃəlɪ/ *adv* [*observe, remark*] de manière pondérée, avec pondération.

judicial review *n* **1** GB Jur pouvoir *m* de regard de la Haute Cour sur les activités des tribunaux subalternes; **2** US Jur pouvoir *m* d'examen de la constitutionnalité d'une loi.

judicial separation *n* GB séparation *f* de corps (*ordonnée par juridiction*).

judiciary /dʒuːˈdɪʃɪərɪ, US -ʃɪerɪ/ **I** *n* Jur **1** (system of courts) système *m* judiciaire; **2** (judges) magistrature *f*; **3** (power, authority) pouvoir *m* judiciaire.
II *modif* [*system, reforms*] judiciaire.

judicious /dʒuːˈdɪʃəs/ *adj* judicieux/-ieuse (**to do** de faire).

judiciously /dʒuːˈdɪʃəslɪ/ *adv* judicieusement.

judo /ˈdʒuːdəʊ/ **▶ 1282** **I** *n* judo *m*.
II *modif* [*contest, hold, lesson, throw*] de judo; [*expert*] en judo.

judy○ /ˈdʒuːdɪ/ *n* GB nana○ *f*.

jug /dʒʌg/ **I** *n* **1** GB (glass) carafe *f*; (earthenware) pichet *m*; (pot-bellied) cruche *f*; (for cream, milk) pot *m*; **water ~** pot à eau, carafe; **2** US (earthenware) cruche *f*; **wine ~** grande cruche à vin; **3**○ (prison) taule◑ *f*; **in ~** GB, **in the ~** US en taule.
II◑ **jugs** *npl* US (breasts) nichons◑ *mpl*, seins *mpl*.
III *vtr* (*p prés etc* **-gg-**) **1** Culin cuire [qch] à l'étuvée; **~ged hare** civet *m* de lièvre; **2**○ (jail) coffrer◑.

jug band *n* US orchestre *m* improvisé.

jugful /ˈdʒʌgfʊl/ *n* **1** GB carafe *f*; **three ~s of water** trois carafes d'eau; **2** US cruche *f*.

juggernaut /ˈdʒʌgənɔːt/ *n* **1** GB (truck) poids *m* lourd; **2** (irresistible force) poids *m* écrasant.

juggle /ˈdʒʌgl/ **I** *vtr* (all contexts) jongler avec.
II *vi* (all contexts) jongler (**with** avec).

juggler /ˈdʒʌglə(r)/ *n* jongleur/-euse *m/f*.

jughead○ /ˈdʒʌghed/ *n* US andouille○ *f*, imbécile *mf*.

jugular /ˈdʒʌgjʊlə(r)/ **I** *n* jugulaire *f*.
II *adj* jugulaire.
IDIOMS **to go (straight) for the ~** frapper au point sensible.

juice /dʒuːs/ **I** *n* **1** Culin jus *m*; **2** Bot, Physiol suc *m*; **3**○ (petrol) essence *f*; **4**○ (electricity) jus○ *m*; **5**○ US (alcohol) alcool *m*.
II *vtr* US presser.
III juiced○ *pp adj* US beurré○.

juice: **~ extractor** *n* GB centrifugeuse *f* (*pour fruits*); **~head**○ *n* US poivrot/-ote○ *m/f*.

juicer /ˈdʒuːsə(r)/ *n* US centrifugeuse *f* (*pour fruits*).

juiciness /ˈdʒuːsɪnɪs/ *n* teneur *f* en jus.

juicy /ˈdʒuːsɪ/ *adj* **1** Culin juteux/-euse; **2**○ (racy) [*story*] croustillant; [*blonde*] appétissant○; **3**○ (profitable) juteux/-euse○; **4**○ (interesting) [*role*] intéressant.

jujitsu /dʒuːˈdʒɪtsuː/ **▶ 1282** *n* jiu-jitsu *m*.

juju /ˈdʒuːdʒuː/ *n* **1** (talisman) grigri *m*; **2** (power) pouvoir *m* magique.

jujube /ˈdʒuːdʒuːb/ *n* jujube *m*.

jukebox /ˈdʒuːkbɒks/ *n* juke-box *m*.

Jul *abrév écrite* = **July**.

julep /ˈdʒuːlɪp/ *n* (also **mint ~**) boisson *f* à la menthe.

Julian /ˈdʒuːlɪən/ **I** *pr n* Julien.
II *adj* julien/-ienne.

Julius /ˈdʒuːlɪəs/ *pr n* Jules; **~ Caesar** Jules César.

July /dʒuːˈlaɪ/ **▶ 1472** *n* juillet *m*.

jumble /ˈdʒʌmbl/ **I** *n* **1** (of papers, objects) tas *m*; (of ideas) fouillis *m*; (of words) fatras *m*; **her clothes were in a ~** ses habits étaient en fouillis; **there was a ~ of ideas in my head** ma tête était remplie d'idées confuses; **2** GB (items for sale) bric-à-brac *m*, vieux objets *mpl*; **have you any ~?** avez-vous de vieux objets dont vous voudriez vous débarrasser?
II *vtr* brouiller [*ideas*]; mélanger [*words, letters*]; **to be ~d together** [*objects*] être entassé en désordre.
■ **jumble up**: **~ [sth] up, ~ up [sth]** mélanger [*letters, shapes, images*].

jumble sale *n* GB vente *f* de charité.

jumbo /ˈdʒʌmbəʊ/ **I** *n* **1** lang enfantin éléphant *m*; **2** = **jumbo jet**.
II *modif* (also **~-sized**) [*packet, size*] géant.

jumbo jet *n* gros-porteur *m*.

jump /dʒʌmp/ **I** *n* **1** (leap) saut *m*, bond *m*; **in a single ~** d'un seul bond; **parachute ~** saut en parachute; **2** Equit obstacle *m*; **water ~** rivière *f*; **3** fig (step) **to be one ~ ahead** avoir une longueur d'avance (**of sb** sur qn); **4** (sudden increase) bond *m* (**in** dans); **prices start at £50 then there's a big ~ to £200** les prix commencent à 50 livres et ensuite ils passent d'un bond à 200 livres; **she's made the ~ from deputy to director** elle est passée d'un bond du poste d'adjointe à celle de directrice; **it's a big ~ from school to university** il y a un grand décalage entre l'école et l'université; **5** Comput instruction *f* de saut.
II *vtr* **1** (leap over) sauter [*obstacle, ditch*]; **he ~ed three metres** il a sauté trois mètres; **she can ~ the horse over the fence** elle peut faire sauter la barrière à son cheval; **2** (anticipate) **to ~ the gun** lit [*athlete*] partir avant le signal; fig anticiper; **to ~ the lights** [*motorist*] passer au feu rouge; **to ~ the queue** passer devant tout le monde; **3** (escape) **to ~ ship** [*crewman*] ne pas rejoindre son bâtiment; **to ~ bail** ne pas comparaître au tribunal; **4** (miss) [*stylus*] sauter [*groove*]; [*disease*] sauter [*generation*]; **to ~ the rails** [*train*] dérailler; **to ~ a stage** (in argument) omettre un point; (in promotion, hierarchy) brûler une étape; **5**○ (attack) [*mugger*] sauter sur [*victim*]; **6**○ (board) **to ~ a train** sauter dans un train en marche.
III *vi* **1** (leap) sauter; **to ~ for joy** sauter de joie; **to ~ across** ou **over** franchir [qch] d'un bond [*ditch, hole*]; **to ~ clear of sth** faire un bond pour éviter qch; **to ~ to one's feet** se lever d'un bond; **to ~ to sb's defence** se précipiter pour défendre qn; **to ~ to conclusions** tirer des conclusions hâtives; **to ~ up and down** [*gymnast*] sautiller; [*child*] sauter en l'air; fig (in anger) trépigner de colère; **2** (start) [*person*] sursauter; **you made me ~** tu m'as fait sursauter; **he ~ed out of his skin**○ il a sauté au plafond○; **3** (rise) [*prices, profits, birthrate*] monter en flèche; **4** (move) **I ~ed to the last page** je suis passé directement à la dernière page; **the film ~s from 1800 to 1920** le film passe d'un seul coup de 1800 à 1920; **5** (welcome) **to ~ at** saisir, sauter sur [*opportunity*]; accepter [qch] avec enthousiasme [*offer, suggestion*]; **6** Comput **to ~ to** sauter à [*address*].
IDIOMS **~ to it!** et que ça saute○!; **go and ~ in the lake**○! va te faire voir○!
■ **jump about, jump around** sauter.
■ **jump back** [*person*] faire un bond en arrière; [*lever, spring*] reprendre sa place initiale.
■ **jump down** [*person*] sauter (**from** de).
■ **jump in** [*person*] monter.
■ **jump on**: ¶ **~ on [sth]** (mount) sauter dans [*bus, train*]; sauter sur [*bicycle, horse*]; **~ on!** monte!; ¶ **~ on [sb]** lit, fig sauter sur qn; **she ~ed on me** lit, fig elle m'a sauté dessus.
■ **jump out** [*person*] sauter; **to ~ out of** sauter par [*window*]; sauter de [*bed, chair, train*]; **to ~ out in front of sb** surgir devant qn.
■ **jump up** [*person*] se lever d'un bond; **to ~ up on** sauter sur [*table etc*].

jumped-up /ˈdʒʌmptʌp/ *adj* péj prétentieux/-ieuse; **you're just/he's just a ~ waiter** tu n'est/ce n'est qu'un serveur qui a pris du galon.

jumper /ˈdʒʌmpə(r)/ **▶ 1703** *n* **1** GB (sweater) pull *m*, pull-over *m*; **2** US (pinafore) robe *f* chasuble; **3** Tech barre *f* à mine.

jumper cables *npl* US Aut câbles *mpl* de démarrage.

jumping /ˈdʒʌmpɪŋ/ *adj* US animé.

jumping: **~ bean** *n* pois *m* sauteur; **~ gene** *n* transposon *m*.

jumping jack *n* **1** Games pantin *m* articulé; **2** (firework) pétard *m* sauteur.

jumping-off place *n* fig point *m* de départ.

jump: **~-jet** *n* avion *m* à décollage vertical; **~ jockey ▶ 1692** *n* Equit jockey *m* de steeple-chase; **~ leads** *npl* câbles *mpl* de démarrage; **~-off** *n* Equit épreuve *f* finale contre la montre, barrage *m*; **~ rope** *n* US corde *f* à sauter; **~ seat** *n* strapontin *m*.

jump-start /ˈdʒʌmpstɑːt/ **I** *n* **to give sb a ~** aider qn à démarrer sa voiture avec des câbles.
II /ˌdʒʌmpˈstɑːt/ *vtr* démarrer [qch] avec des câbles [*car*].

jump suit *n* Fashn combinaison *f*.

jumpy○ /ˈdʒʌmpɪ/ *adj* [*person*] nerveux/-euse; [*market*] instable.

Jun *abrév écrite* = **June**.

junction /ˈdʒʌŋkʃn/ *n* **1** (of two roads) carrefour *m*; (on motorway) échangeur *m*; **2** Rail (of railway lines) nœud *m* ferroviaire; (station) gare *f* de jonction ou de raccordement; **3** Tech (point *m* de) raccordement *m*; **thermocouple ~** jonction *f* thermocouple; **4** fig sout fusion *f*.

junction box *n* boîte *f* de raccordement.

juncture /ˈdʒʌŋktʃə(r)/ *n* **1** gen point *m*; **at this ~** à ce moment; **2** Ling joncture *f*.

June /dʒuːn/ **▶ 1472** *n* juin *m*.

June bug *n* hanneton *m*.

Jungian /ˈjʊŋɪən/ *n, adj* jungien/-ienne (*m/f*).

jungle /ˈdʒʌŋgl/ **I** *n* lit, fig jungle *f*; **the law of the ~** la loi de la jungle.
II *modif* [*fauna, flora*] de la jungle; [*life, path*] dans la jungle.

jungle: **~ fowl** *n* coq/poule *m/f* bankiva; **~ gym** *n* cage *f* à poules; **~ juice**○ *n* tord-boyaux○ *m*; **~ warfare** *n* guerre *f* dans la jungle.

junior /ˈdʒuːnɪə(r)/ **I** *n* **1** (younger person) cadet/-ette *m/f*; **to be 10 years sb's ~** être le cadet/la cadette de qn de 10 ans; **2** (low-ranking worker) subalterne *mf*; **3** GB Sch élève *mf* du primaire; **to teach ~s** enseigner dans une école primaire; **4** US Univ ≈ étudiant/-e *m/f* de premier cycle; (in high school) ≈ élève *mf* de première; **5** Sport (young player) cadet/-ette *m/f*; **6** GB = **junior doctor**; **7** GB = **junior minister**.
II *adj* **1** (low-ranking, not senior) [*colleague, worker*] (inferior) subalterne; (trainee) débutant; [*post, rank, position*] subalterne; **to be ~** débuter, avoir peu d'expérience ; **more ~** moins expérimenté; **he's very ~** il a très peu d'expérience; **he is ~ to me in the firm** il a un grade inférieur au mien dans la compagnie; **2** (young) [*person*] jeune; [*fashion, activity, wing of organization*] pour les jeunes; **to be ~ to sb** être plus jeune que qn (**by** de); **3** Sport [*championship, race, league, team, 100 metres*] des cadets; [*champion*] jeune, des cadets; [*player, high-jumper*] jeune; **4** (the younger) (also **Junior**) **Bob Mortimer ~** Bob Mortimer fils or junior.

junior: **~ clerk** *n* employé/-e *m/f*; **~ college** *n* US premier cycle *m* universitaire; **Junior Common Room** *n* GB Univ (room) salle *f* des étudiants; (student body) (+ *v sg ou pl*) étudiants *mpl*; **~ doctor** *n* médecin *m* des hôpitaux; **~ executive** *n* cadre *m* débutant; **~ high school** *n* US ≈ collège *m*; **~ lightweight** *n* poids *m* super-plume; **~ middleweight** *n* poids *m* super mi-moyen.

junior minister *n* secrétaire *m* d'État; **she is the junior health minister** elle est secrétaire d'État à la Santé.

junior: **~ miss** *n* US fillettes *fpl*; **~ partner** *n* (simple) associé/-e *m/f*; **~ rating** *n* GB Naut matelot *m*; **~ school** *n* GB école *f* (primaire); **~ seaman** ▶ **1612** *n* GB matelot *m*; **~ technician** ▶ **1612** *n* GB soldat *m* de 1e classe (*dans l'Armée de l'Air*); **~ welterweight** *n* poids *m* super-léger.

juniper /ˈdʒuːnɪpə(r)/ **I** *n* genièvre *m*.
II *modif* **~ berries** baies *fpl* de genièvre.

junk /dʒʌŋk/ **I** *n* **1**○ péj (poor quality) (furniture, merchandise) camelote○ *f*; (possessions) vieilleries *fpl*; **clear your ~ off the table!** dégage ton bazar○ de la table!; **how can you read that ~?** comment peux-tu lire ces bêtises?; **2** (second-hand) bric-à-brac *m*, vieilleries *fpl*; **3** (boat) jonque *f*.
II○ *vtr* bazarder○ [*appliance*]; mettre [qch] à la ferraille [*car*]; mettre [qch] au rancart○ [*idea*].

junk bond *n* obligation *f* à haut rendement et à risque élevé.

junket /ˈdʒʌŋkɪt/ **I** *n* **1** Culin entremets *m* au lait caillé; **2**○ (spree) fête *f*; (paid trip) voyage *m* aux frais de la princesse.
II *vi* faire la fête.

junket(t)ing○ /ˈdʒʌŋkɪtɪŋ/ *n* (celebrating) fête *f*; (paid trip) voyage *m* aux frais de la princesse.

junk food *n* nourriture *f* industrielle.

junkie○ /ˈdʒʌŋkɪ/ *n* drogué/-e *m/f*.

junk: **~ jewellery** *n* bijoux *mpl* de fantaisie; **~ mail** *n* ¢ prospectus *mpl*; **~man** *n* US chiffonnier-ferrailleur *m*; **~ shop** *n* boutique *f* de bric-à-brac; **~yard** *n* (for scrap) dépotoir *m*; (for old cars) cimetière *f* de voitures.

Juno /ˈdʒuːnəʊ/ *pr n* Junon.

Junoesque /ˌdʒuːnəʊˈesk/ *adj* d'une beauté gracieuse.

junta /ˈdʒʌntə/ *n* junte *f*.

Jupiter /ˈdʒuːpɪtə(r)/ *pr n* **1** Mythol Jupiter *m*; **2** Astron Jupiter *f*.

Jura /ˈdʒʊərə/ ▶ **1163**, **1273**, **1776** *pr n* **the ~** le Jura; **in the ~** dans le Jura; **the Swiss ~** le Jura suisse.

Jurassic /dʒʊəˈræsɪk/ **I** *n* **the ~** le jurassique.
II *adj* jurassique.

juridical /dʒʊəˈrɪdɪkl/ *adj* juridique.

jurisdiction /ˌdʒʊərɪsˈdɪkʃn/ *n* **1** gen, Admin compétence *f* (**over** sur); **to come within** ou **under sb's ~** relever de la compétence de qn; **to be outside sb's ~** ne pas être de la compétence de qn; **2** Jur juridiction *f* (**over** sur); **to be within/outside sb's ~** relever/ne pas relever de la juridiction de qn; **3** US (court) juridiction *f*.

jurisdictional /ˌdʒʊərɪsˈdɪkʃənl/ *adj* juridictionnel/-elle.

jurisprudence /ˌdʒʊərɪsˈpruːdns/ *n* **1** (philosophy) philosophie *f* du droit; **2** (precedents) jurisprudence *f*.

jurist /ˈdʒʊərɪst/ ▶ **1692** *n* juriste *mf*.

juror /ˈdʒʊərə(r)/ *n* juré *m*.

jury /ˈdʒʊərɪ/ **I** *n* **1** Jur jury *m*; **to be** ou **to serve on a ~** faire partie d'un jury; **to be picked for a ~** être appelé à faire partie d'un jury; **to instruct the ~** donner des indications aux jurés; **'members of the ~'** 'mesdames et messieurs les jurés'; **the ~ is still out** Jur le jury est en train de délibérer; fig on ne peut encore rien dire; **2** (at competition) jury *m*.
II *modif* Naut [*mast*] de fortune.

jury: **~ box** *n* banc *m* des jurés; **~ duty** *n* US = **jury service**; **~man** *n* juré *m*.

jury service *n* GB **to do ~** faire partie d'un jury.

jury: **~ shopping** *n* US sélection *f* des jurés (*pour une plus grande objectivité*); **~ system** *n* système *m* de jugement par jury; **~woman** *n* femme *f* juré.

just[1] /dʒʌst/ **I** *adv* **1** (very recently) **to have ~ done** venir (juste) de faire; **she's ~ arrived** elle vient juste d'arriver; **I'm ~ back** je viens juste de rentrer; **it has ~ been varnished** ça vient juste d'être verni; **2** (immediately) juste; **~ after your birthday** juste après ton anniversaire; **~ after you left/arrived** juste après ton départ/arrivée; **~ before** juste avant; **it's ~ after 10 am/midnight** il est 10 heures passées/minuit passé de quelques minutes; **3** (slightly) (with quantities) un peu; (indicating location or position) juste; **~ over 20 kg** un peu plus de 20 kg; **~ under 15 cm** un peu moins de 15 cm; **~ beyond** ou **past** ou **after the station** juste après la gare; **~ below the knee** juste en-dessous du genou; **~ on the left** juste à gauche; **4** (only, merely) juste; **~ a cup of tea** juste une tasse de thé; **~ for fun** juste pour rire; **there will be ~ the three of us** il y aura juste nous trois; **not cross, ~ disappointed** pas fâché, juste déçu; **~ two days ago** il y a juste deux jours; **~ last week** pas plus tard que la semaine dernière; **he's ~ a child** ce n'est qu'un enfant; **not ~ men** pas seulement les hommes; **5** (purposely) exprès; **he did it ~ to annoy us** il l'a fait exprès pour nous embêter; **I came ~ to see you** je suis venu exprès pour te voir; **6** (barely) tout juste; **~ on time** tout juste à l'heure; **he's ~ 20** il a tout juste 20 ans; **I've got ~ enough money** j'ai tout juste assez d'argent; **the oven is ~ hot enough** le four est tout juste assez chaud; **I (only) ~ caught the train** j'ai eu le train de justesse; **he (only) ~ passed the exam** il a réussi à l'examen de justesse; **7** (simply) tout simplement; **~ tell the truth** dis la vérité, tout simplement; **she ~ won't listen** elle ne veut tout simplement pas écouter; **I was ~ wondering if...** je me demandais tout simplement si...; **that's ~ the way it is** c'est comme ça, c'est la vie; **~ a moment** ou **minute** ou **second** (please wait) un instant; (when interrupting, disagreeing) un instant, minute○; **8** (exactly, precisely) exactement; **that's ~ what I suggested** c'est exactement ce que j'ai suggéré; **it's ~ what she wants** c'est exactement ce qu'elle veut; **it's ~ what you were expecting** c'est bien ce à quoi tu t'attendais; **~ as I thought, we're too late** c'est bien ce que je pensais, nous arrivons trop tard; **~ how do you hope to persuade him?** comment espères-tu le persuader au juste?; **~ how many there are isn't known** on ne sait pas au juste combien il y en a; **it's ~ right** c'est parfait; **~ at that moment, Paul arrived** juste à ce moment-là Paul est arrivé; **it's ~ on 8 am** GB il est exactement 8 heures, il est 8 heures pile; **he likes everything to be ~ so** il aime que les choses soient parfaitement en ordre; **she looks ~ like her father** elle ressemble énormément à son père; **it's ~ like him to forget** c'est bien lui d'oublier; **it's ~ like you to be late** c'est bien toi d'être en retard; **~ so!** tout à fait; **that's ~ it** ou **the trouble** c'est bien ça le problème; **that's ~ the point!** justement!; **9** (possibly, conceivably) **it might** ou **could ~ be true** il se peut que ça soit vrai; **he may ~ make it in time** il se peut qu'il arrive à temps; **10** (at this or that very moment) **to be ~ doing** être en train de faire; **to be ~ about to do** être sur le point de faire; **I'm ~ finishing the letter** je suis en train de finir la lettre; **I'm ~ coming** j'arrive; **he was ~ leaving** il partait; **I'm ~ off!** j'y vais!; **11** (positively, totally) **that was ~ wonderful/delicious** c'était vraiment merveilleux/délicieux; **that's ~ ridiculous/wrong** c'est tout à fait ridicule/faux; **that's ~ typical!** iron ça ne m'étonne vraiment pas!; **that's ~ great!** (enthusiastically) c'est vraiment formidable!; (ironically) il ne manquait plus que ça!; **12** (easily) **I can ~ imagine her as president** je n'ai aucun mal à l'imaginer présidente; **can't you ~ picture the scene!** ce n'est pas difficile d'imaginer la scène!; **I can ~ smell the pineforests** je sens déjà l'odeur des pins; **13** (with imperatives) donc; **~ keep quiet!** tais-toi donc!; **~ look at the time!** regarde donc l'heure qu'il est!; **~ you dare!** essaie donc voir!; **~ imagine!** imagine donc!; **~ think, you could have been hurt!** mais tu te rends compte? tu aurais pu être blessé!; **14** (in requests) **if I could ~ interrupt you** si je peux me permettre de vous interrompre; **if you could ~ hold this box** si vous pouvez tenir cette boite; **could you ~ wait five minutes?** est-ce que vous pourriez attendre cinq minutes?; **15** (for emphasis in responses) **'he's adorable'—'isn't he ~'** 'il est adorable'—'ah, ça oui'; **'that film was dreadful'—'wasn't it ~!'** 'ce film était absolument nul!'—'ah, ça oui!; **'she's really full of herself'—'isn't she ~'** 'elle est vraiment imbue de sa personne'—'ça tu peux le dire'; **'I bet you're furious'—'aren't I ~'** 'je parie que tu es furieux'—'et comment!'; **16** (equally) **~ as big/funny/well as...** aussi grand/drôle/bien que...; **I can ~ as easily walk** je peux tout aussi bien y aller à pied.
II just about *adv phr* presque; **~ about cooked/finished** presque cuit/fini; **'are you ready?'—'~ about'** 'es-tu prêt?'—'presque'; **it's ~ about 10 o'clock** il est presque 10 heures; **~ about everything/anything** à peu près tout/n'importe quoi; **I can ~ about see it/reach it** je peux tout juste le voir/l'attraper; **~ about enough for two** juste assez pour deux; **I've had ~ about enough!** j'en ai marre○!; **~ about here** à peu près ici; **it's ~ about the most boring film I've seen** c'est sans doute le film le plus ennuyeux que j'aie vu; **it's ~ about the best holiday we've had** ce sont sans doute les meilleures vacances que nous ayons passées.
III just now *adv phr* (a short time ago) **I saw him ~ now** je viens juste de le voir; (at the moment) en ce moment.
IV just as *conj phr* juste au moment où; **he arrived ~ as I was leaving** il est arrivé juste au moment où je partais.
IDIOMS **it's ~ as well it's waterproof** heureusement que c'est imperméable; **~ as well!** tant mieux! ; **it would be ~ as well if you asked him** tu ferais bien de lui demander; **I'd ~ as soon you didn't mention it** j'aimerais autant que tu le gardes pour toi; **take your raincoat ~ in case it rains** prends ton imperméable au cas où il pleuvrait; **I always check ~ in case** je vérifie toujours, on ne sait jamais.

just[2] /dʒʌst/ **I** *n* **the ~** (+ *v pl*) les justes *mpl*.
II *adj* **1** (fair) [*person, society, decision, cause, comment, war*] juste; [*action, complaint, demand*] justifié; [*anger, claim, criticism, suspicion*] légitime; [*reward*] mérité; **as is only ~** à juste titre; **it's only ~** ce n'est que justice (**to do** de faire; **that** que + *subj*); **to be ~ in one's dealings with sb** faire preuve d'équité dans ses relations avec qn; **without ~ cause** sans raison valable; **2** (exact) [*account, balance, calculation*] juste, exact; **3** Jur [*claim*] fondé; [*title, request*] valable; [*inheritance*] légitime.
IDIOMS **to sleep the sleep of the ~** dormir du sommeil du juste.

justice /ˈdʒʌstɪs/ *n* **1** (fairness) justice *f*; **is there any ~ in her accusations?** est-ce que ses accusations sont justes?; **it can be said, with some ~, that** il faut bien reconnaître que; **to do sb ~, to do ~ to sb** rendre justice à qn; **the portrait doesn't do her ~** le portrait ne l'avantage pas;

I couldn't do ~ to it (refusing food) je ne pourrais pas y faire honneur; **2** (the law) justice *f*; **a court of ~** une cour de justice; **to bring sb to ~** traduire qn en justice; **she is a fugitive from ~** elle fuit la justice; **3** (judge) GB juge *m*; US juge *m* de la Cour Suprême; **Mr Justice Murphy** GB le juge Murphy.

justice: **Justice Department** *n* US ministère *m* de la justice; **Justice Minister**, **Minister of Justice** *n* ministre *m* de la Justice; **Justice of the Peace**, **JP** *n* juge *m* de paix.

justifiable /ˈdʒʌstɪfaɪəbl/ *adj* (that is justified) légitime; (that can be justified) justifiable.

justifiable homicide *n* homicide *m* justifié par les circonstances.

justifiably /ˈdʒʌstɪfaɪəblɪ/ *adv* à juste titre; **he's ~ angry** il est en colère, non sans raison or à juste titre; **she is ~ proud** elle a de bonnes raisons d'être fière (**of** de).

justification /ˌdʒʌstɪfɪˈkeɪʃn/ *n* **1** (reason) raison *f*; **to have some ~ for doing** avoir des raisons de faire; **you have no ~ for being so rude** rien ne vous autorise à être aussi impoli; **in ~ of sth** en justification à qch; **what can they say in ~ of his behaviour?** qu'est-ce qu'ils peuvent dire pour justifier sa conduite?; **with some ~** non sans raison; **without any ~** sans aucune raison valable; **2** Comput, Print (of margins) justification *f*; Comput (moving of data) cadrage *m*; **right/left ~** justification à droite/à gauche; **3** Relig justification *f*.

justified /ˈdʒʌstɪfaɪd/ *adj* **1** [*feeling, belief, complaint, increase, policy*] justifié; **to be ~ in doing** avoir de bonnes raisons de faire; **to feel ~ in doing** se sentir en droit de faire; **you are quite ~ in refusing** vous avez absolument raison de refuser; **2** Comput, Print [*margin*] justifié; **3** Comput [*text, data*] cadré.

justify /ˈdʒʌstɪfaɪ/ *vtr* **1** justifier [*feeling, belief, complaint, increase, policy*]; **how can you ~ such cruelty?** qu'est-ce qui justifie une telle cruauté?; **what justifies its inclusion in the collection?** qu'est-ce qui justifie qu'on le mette dans la collection?; **2** Comput, Print justifier [*margins*]; **3** Comput cadrer [*text, data*].

IDIOMS **the end justifies the means** la fin justifie les moyens.

just-in-time /dʒʌst/ *adj* [*manufacture, production*] en flux tendus; [*stock control*] à flux tendus.

justly /ˈdʒʌstlɪ/ *adv* **1** (equitably) avec justice; **2** (justifiably) à juste titre.

justness /ˈdʒʌstnɪs/ *n* **1** (aptness) justesse *f*; **2** (reasonableness) (of claim, request) caractère *m* justifié.

jut /dʒʌt/ **I** *vi* (*p prés etc* **-tt-**) (also **~ out**) **1** (horizontally) [*cape, promontory*] s'avancer en saillie (**into** dans); [*balcony*] faire saillie (**over** sur); **2** (vertically) [*mountain*] se dresser.

II jutting *p prés adj* (also **jutting out**) saillant.

jute /dʒuːt/ *n* jute *m*.

juvenile /ˈdʒuːvənaɪl/ **I** *n* **1** sout (young person) jeune *mf*; Jur mineur/-e *m/f*; **2** Bot, Zool jeune *mf*.

II *adj* **1** (young) [*person*] jeune; [*group, gang*] de jeunes; **2** pej (childish) puéril; **3** Bot, Zool juvénile.

juvenile: **~ court** *n* tribunal *m* pour enfants; **~ crime** *n* criminalité *f* juvénile; **~ delinquency** *n* délinquance *f* juvénile; **~ delinquent** *n* jeune délinquant/-e *m/f*; **~ lead** *n* Theat jeune premier/-ière *m/f*; **~ offender** *n* Jur délinquant/-e *m/f* mineur/-e.

juxtapose /ˌdʒʌkstəˈpəʊz/ *vtr* juxtaposer (**with** à).

juxtaposition /ˌdʒʌkstəpəˈzɪʃn/ *n* juxtaposition *f* (**with** à); **in ~** en juxtaposition.

k, K /keɪ/ *n* **1** (letter) k, K *m*; **2 K** *abrév* = **kilo**; **3 K** Comput (*abrév* = **kilobyte**) K *m*; **4 K** (*abrév* = **thousand**) mille; **he earns £50 K** il gagne 50 000 livres sterling.

Kabul /ˈkɑːbl/ **▶ 1818** *pr n* Kaboul.

kaffeeklatsch /ˈkæfeɪklætʃ/, **coffee klatch** *n* US réunion *f* autour d'une tasse de café.

kaffir /ˈkæfə(r)/ *n* injur nègre/négresse *m/f* offensive d'Afrique du Sud.

Kafkaesque /ˈkæfkaesk/ *adj* kafkaïen/-ïenne.

kaftan /ˈkæftæn/ *n* caftan *m*.

kagoule *n* = **cagoule**.

kail *n* = **kale**.

kainite /ˈkaɪnaɪt/ *n* kaïnite *f*.

Kaiser /ˈkaɪzə(r)/ *n* Kaiser *m*.

Kalahari /ˌkæləˈhɑːrɪ/ *pr n* **the ~** le Kalahari; **the ~ desert** le désert du Kalahari.

kale /keɪl/ *n* **1** Agric (also **curly ~**) chou *m* frisé; **2**° US (money) fric° *m*.

kaleidoscope /kəˈlaɪdəskəʊp/ *n* lit, fig kaléidoscope *m*.

kaleidoscopic /kəˌlaɪdəˈskɒpɪk/ *adj* kaléidoscopique.

kamikaze /ˌkæmɪˈkɑːzɪ/ *n, adj* kamikaze (*m*).

Kampuchea /ˌkæmpʊˈtʃɪə/ *pr n* Hist Kampuchéa *m*; **People's Republic of ~** République populaire du Kampuchéa.

Kampuchean /ˌkæmpʊˈtʃɪən/ Hist **I** *n* Kampuchéen/-éenne *m/f*.
II *adj* kampuchéen/-éenne.

kangaroo /ˌkæŋɡəˈruː/ *n* kangourou *m*.

kangaroo court *n* péj tribunal *m* irrégulier.

Kansas /ˈkænzəs/ **▶ 1744** *pr n* Kansas *m*.

Kantian /ˈkæntɪən/ *adj* kantien/-ienne.

kaolin /ˈkeɪəlɪn/ *n* kaolin *m*.

kapok /ˈkeɪpɒk/ *n* kapok *m*.

kapok tree *n* kapokier *m*.

kaput° /kæˈpʊt/ *adj* kaput° *inv*.

karabiner /ˌkærəˈbiːnə(r)/ *n* mousqueton *m*.

karaoke /ˌkerɪˈəʊkeɪ, -kɪ/ *n* karaoké *m*.

karat /ˈkærət/ *n* US **▶ carat**.

karate /kəˈrɑːtɪ/ **▶ 1282** **I** *n* karaté *m*.
II *modif* [*class*] de karaté; **~ chop** coup de karaté; **~ expert** karatéka *mf*.

karma /ˈkɑːmə/ *n* lit, fig karma *m*.

kart /kɑːt/ *n* kart *m*.

karting /ˈkɑːtɪŋ/ **▶ 1282** *n* karting *m*; **to go ~** faire du karting.

Kashmir /kæʃˈmɪə/ *pr n* Cachemire *m*.

Kashmiri /kæʃˈmɪərɪ/ **▶ 1486**, **1402** **I** *n* **1** (person) Cachemirien/-ienne *m/f*; **2** Ling cachemirien *m*.
II *adj* cachemirien/-ienne.

Kat(h)mandu /ˌkætmænˈduː/ **▶ 1818** *pr n* Katmandou.

katydid /ˈkeɪtɪdɪd/ *n* sauterelle *f* (*d'Amérique du Nord*).

katzenjammer° /ˈkætsənjæmə(r)/ *n* US **1** (uproar) brouhaha *m*; **2** (hangover) gueule *f* de bois°.

kayak /ˈkaɪæk/ *n* kayak *m*.

Kazakhstan /ˌkɑːzɑːkˈstɑːn, ˌkæz-/ **▶ 1131** *pr n* Kazakhstan *m*.

kazoo /kəˈzuː/ *n* mirliton *m*.

KB *n* Comput (*abrév* = **kilobyte**) Ko *m*.

KC *n* **1** GB Jur *abrév* **▶ King's Counsel**; **2** US Post *abrév* = **Kansas City**.

KD *adj* US *abrév* = **knocked down**.

kebab /kɪˈbæb/ *n* (also **shish ~**) chiche-kebab *m*.

kedge /kedʒ/ **I** *n* (also **~ anchor**) Naut ancre *f* à jet.
II *vtr* touer.
III *vi* se touer.

kedgeree /ˈkedʒəriː, ˌkedʒəˈriː/ *n* GB pilaf *m* de poisson.

keel /kiːl/ *n* Naut quille *f*; Aviat arête *f* ventrale spec, ventral fin *m*; **to be on an even ~** Naut être dans ses lignes; **he's on a more even ~ now** fig il est plus équilibré qu'avant; **my finances are back on an even ~** fig mes finances sont revenues à la normale.
■ **keel over** [*boat*] chavirer; [*person*] s'écrouler; [*tree*] s'abattre.

keelhaul /ˈkiːlhɔːl/ *vtr* Naut Hist *faire passer qn sous la quille en guise de châtiment*; fig (rebuke) passer un savon° à.

keen /kiːn/ **I** *n* lamento *m* funèbre.
II *adj* **1** (eager) [*admirer, attentions*] fervent; [*applicant, candidate*] motivé; **to be ~ on** tenir à [*plan, project*]; être chaud° pour [*idea*]; **I'm not too ~** ou **not over-~ on the idea** je ne suis pas très chaud°; **to be ~ on doing** ou **to do** tenir à faire; **to be ~ for sb to do** ou **on sb's doing** tenir à ce que qn fasse; **to be ~ that sb should do** tenir à ce que qn fasse; **to look ~** avoir l'air tenté or partant°; **my wife wants to go but I'm not (too) ~** ou **less than ~** ma femme veut y aller, mais je ne suis pas (trop) partant°; **2** (enthusiastic) [*amateur, artist, campaigner, sportsplayer, supporter*] enthousiaste; [*student*] assidu; **to be ~ on** être passionné de [*activity*]; avoir une passion pour [*animals*]; **he's ~ on my sister, but my father's not too ~ on him**° il en pince° pour ma sœur mais mon père ne l'encaisse° pas; **mad ~**° GB fana°; **3** (intense) [*anticipation, appetite, delight, desire, interest*] vif/vive; [*admiration, sense of loss*] intense; **4** (acute) [*eye, intelligence*] vif/vive; [*sight*] perçant; [*hearing, sense of smell*] fin; **to have a ~ eye for sth** avoir l'œil pour qch; **5** (sharp) lit [*blade*] acéré; fig [*wit*] vif/vive, mordant; [*draught, wind*] pénétrant; [*air*] vif/vive; **6** (competitive) [*price*] défiant toute concurrence; [*competition, rivalry*] intense; [*demand*] Comm fort, dynamique; [*debate*] animé.
III *vi* gémir (**over** sur).

keenly /ˈkiːnlɪ/ *adv* [*interested*] vivement; [*awaited*] ardemment; [*aware*] parfaitement; [*feel, contest, debate*] vivement.

keenness /ˈkiːnnɪs/ *n* **1** (enthusiasm) enthousiasme *m*; **2** (sharpness) (of feelings) intensité *f*; (of senses) acuité *f*; (of wind, air) mordant *m*; (of blade) tranchant *m*.

keep /kiːp/ **I** *n* **1** (maintenance) pension *f*; **to pay for one's ~** payer une pension; **to work for one's ~** travailler pour payer sa pension; **to earn one's ~** [*person*] gagner de quoi vivre; [*factory, branch*] fig être viable; **2** Archit donjon *m*.
II *vtr* (*prét, pp* **kept**) **1** (cause to remain) **to ~ sb in hospital/indoors** [*person*] garder qn à l'hôpital/à l'intérieur; [*illness*] retenir qn à l'hôpital/à l'intérieur; **to ~ sth/sb clean** garder qch/qn propre; **to ~ sth warm/cool** garder qch au chaud/au frais; **to ~ sb warm/cool** protéger qn du froid/de la chaleur; **to be kept clean/warm/locked** rester propre/au chaud/fermé (à clé); **to ~ sb talking/waiting** retenir/faire attendre qn; **I won't ~ you to your promise** tu n'es pas obligé de tenir ta promesse; **to ~ an engine/machine running** laisser un moteur/une machine en marche; **bronchitis kept him in bed** une bronchite l'a obligé à garder le lit; **2** (detain) retenir; **there's nothing to ~ me here** (plus) rien ne me retient ici; **don't let me ~ you!** je ne veux pas vous retenir!; **what kept you?** qu'est-ce qui t'a retenu?; **I won't ~ you a minute** je n'en ai pas pour longtemps; **the police are ~ing him for questioning** la police le garde à vue pour l'interroger; **3** (retain) garder, conserver [*book, letter, money, receipt*]; garder [*job*]; garder [*seat, place*] (**for** pour); garder, mettre [qch] de côté [*ticket, bread*] (**for** pour); **we ~ these glasses for special occasions** nous gardons ces verres pour les grandes occasions; **this pullover has kept its colour/shape** ce pullover a gardé sa couleur/forme; **4** (have and look after) tenir [*shop, restaurant*]; avoir [*dog, cat*]; élever [*sheep, chickens*]; **5** (sustain) **to ~ sth going** entretenir qch [*conversation, fire, tradition*]; **I'll make you a sandwich to ~ you going** je te ferai un sandwich pour que tu tiennes le coup; **it was only his work that kept him going** sans son travail il n'aurait pas tenu le coup; **have you got enough work to ~ you going?** avez-vous assez de travail pour vous occuper?; **6** (store) mettre, ranger; **I ~ my money in a safe** je mets mon argent dans un coffre-fort; **where do you ~ your cups?** où rangez-vous vos tasses?; **I ~ a spare key in the cupboard** j'ai un double de la clé dans le placard; **7** (have in stock) [*shop, shopkeeper*] vendre, avoir [*brand, product*]; **8** (support financially) faire vivre, entretenir [*husband, wife, family*]; entretenir [*lover*]; avoir [*servant*]; **to ~ sb in beer** approvisionner qn en bière; **9** (maintain by writing in) tenir [*accounts, list, diary, record*]; **10** (conceal) **to ~ sth from sb** taire or cacher qch à qn; **11** (prevent) **to ~ sb from doing** empêcher qn de faire; **12** (observe) tenir [*promise*]; garder [*secret*]; se rendre à, venir à [*appointment, date*]; célébrer [*occasion, festival*]; observer [*commandments, sabbath, Lent*]; **13** Mus **to ~ time** ou **the beat** battre la mesure; **14**† (protect) [*God*] garder†, protéger [*person*] (**from** de); [*person*] défendre [*gate, bridge*]; **15** (maintain) entretenir [*car, house*]; **well/badly kept** bien/mal entretenu.
III *vi* (*prét, pp* **kept**) **1** (continue) **to ~ doing** continuer à or de faire, ne pas arrêter

de faire; **to ~ going** lit continuer; **I don't know how she ~s going!** je ne sais pas comment elle tient le coup!; **~ at it!** persévérez!; **~ west/straight on** continuez vers l'ouest/tout droit; **'~ left/right'** 'tenez votre gauche/droite'; **2** (remain) **to ~ indoors** rester à l'intérieur; **to ~ out of the rain** se protéger de la pluie; **to ~ warm/cool** se protéger du froid/de la chaleur; **to ~ calm** rester calme; **to ~ silent** ou **quiet** garder le silence; **3** (stay in good condition) [*food*] se conserver, se garder; **4** (wait) [*news, business, work*] attendre; **I've got something to tell you, it won't ~** j'ai quelque chose à te dire, ça ne peut pas attendre; **5** (in health) **'how are you ~ing?'** 'comment allez-vous?'; **she's ~ing well** elle va bien.

IV *v refl* **to ~ oneself** subvenir à ses propres besoins; **to ~ oneself warm/cool** se protéger du froid/de la chaleur; **to ~ oneself healthy** rester en forme; **to ~ oneself to oneself** ne pas être sociable; **to ~ oneself from doing** s'empêcher de faire.

V for ~s *adv phr* pour de bon, pour toujours.

IDIOMS **to ~ in with sb** rester en bons termes avec qn; **to try to ~ up with the Joneses** rivaliser avec ses voisins; **you can't ~ a good man down** la compétence finit par être reconnue; ▶ **clear**.

■ **keep after**: **~ after** [**sb**] **1** (pursue) pourchasser; **2** (chivvy) harceler.

■ **keep at**: ¶ **~ at** [**sb**] US harceler, casser les pieds○ à [*person*]; ¶ **~ at it** persévérer.

■ **keep away**: ¶ **~ away** ne pas s'approcher (**from** de); ¶ **~** [**sth/sb**] **away** empêcher [qch/qn] de s'approcher, tenir [qch/qn] à distance; **to ~ sb away from** (prevent from getting close to) empêcher qn de s'approcher de, tenir qn à distance de [*person, fire*]; (cause to be absent from) tenir qn éloigné de [*family*]; **to ~ sb away from his work** empêcher qn de travailler.

■ **keep back**: ¶ **~ back** rester en arrière, ne pas s'approcher; **~ back!** ne vous approchez pas!, n'avancez pas!; **to ~ back from sth** ne pas s'approcher de qch; ¶ **~** [**sth/sb**] **back**, **~ back** [**sth/sb**] **1** (prevent from advancing) empêcher [qn] de s'approcher [*person, crowd*] (**from** de); faire redoubler [*pupil, student*]; [*barrier, dam*] retenir [*water*]; **he kept his hair back with an elastic band** il avait les cheveux retenus en arrière par un élastique; **2** (retain) garder [*money*]; conserver [*food, objects*]; **3** (conceal) cacher [*information, fact, detail*] (**from** à); **4** (prevent from doing) retenir [*person*].

■ **keep down**: ¶ **~ down** rester allongé; **~ down!** ne bougez pas!; ¶ **~** [**sth**] **down**, **~ down** [**sth**] **1** (cause to remain at a low level) limiter [*number, speed, costs, expenditure, inflation*]; limiter l'augmentation de [*prices, costs, wages, unemployment*]; maîtriser, juguler [*inflation*]; **to ~ one's weight down** surveiller son poids; **~ your voice down!** baisse la voix!; **~ the noise down!** faites moins de bruit!; **2** (retain in stomach) garder [*food*]; ¶ **~** [**sb**] **down 1** GB Sch (cause to repeat a year) faire redoubler [*pupil*]; **2** (repress) opprimer [*people*]; réprimer [*revolt*].

■ **keep in**: ¶ **~ in** [*car, cyclist, driver etc*] GB tenir sa gauche; (elsewhere) tenir sa droite; ¶ **~** [**sb/sth**] **in 1** (cause to remain inside) empêcher [qn/qch] de sortir [*person, animal*]; garder [*dentures, contact lenses*]; **they're ~ing her in** (in hospital) ils la gardent; **2** (restrain) rentrer [*stomach, elbows*]; réprimer [*emotions, anger, impatience*]; **3** Sch (cause to stay at school) garder [qn] en retenue, coller○ [*pupil*].

■ **keep off**: ¶ **~ off 1** (stay at a distance) **~ off!** n'avancez pas!; **2** (not start) **I hope the rain/storm ~s off** j'espère qu'il ne pleuvra pas/que l'orage n'éclatera pas; ¶ **~ off** [**sth**] **1** (stay away from) ne pas marcher sur; **'Please ~ off the grass'** 'Défense de marcher sur la pelouse'; **2** (refrain from) s'abstenir de consommer, éviter [*fatty food, alcohol*]; s'abstenir de parler de [*subject*]; **to ~ off cigarettes** ne pas fumer; ¶ **~** [**sth**] **off**, **~ off** [**sth**] **1** (prevent from touching) éloigner [*animals, insects*]; **this plastic sheet will ~ the rain/ dust off** cette housse en plastique protège contre la pluie/la poussière; **2** (continue not to wear) ne pas remettre [*shoes, hat*]; ¶ **~ sb off** [**sth**] (cause to refrain from) éviter de donner [qch] à qn [*food, alcohol*]; empêcher qn de parler de [*subject*].

■ **keep on**: ¶ **~ on doing** continuer à faire, ne pas cesser de faire; **to ~ on with sth** poursuivre qch; **to ~ on about sth** ne pas arrêter de parler de qch; **to ~ on at sb** harceler qn, casser les pieds○ à qn (**to do** pour qu'il fasse); ¶ **~** [**sb/sth**] **on** garder [*employee, flat, hat, shoes*].

■ **keep out**: ¶ **~ out of** [**sth**] **1** (not enter) ne pas entrer dans [*area, house*]; **'~ out!'** (on notice) 'défense d'entrer'; **2** (avoid being exposed to) rester à l'abri de [*sun, rain, danger*]; **3** (avoid getting involved in) ne pas se mêler de [*argument*]; **~ out of this!** ne t'en mêle pas!; **to ~ out of sb's way, to ~ out of the way of sb** (not hinder) ne pas encombrer qn; (avoid seeing) éviter qn; **try to ~ out of trouble!** essaie de bien te conduire!; ¶ **~** [**sb/sth**] **out**, **~ out** [**sb/sth**] (not allow to enter) ne pas laisser entrer [*person, animal*]; **to ~ the rain out** empêcher la pluie d'entrer; **I wore an extra pullover to ~ out the cold** j'ai mis un pullover de plus pour me protéger du froid; **to ~ sb out of sth** (not allow to get involved in) ne pas vouloir mêler qn à qch; (not allow to enter) ne pas laisser entrer qn dans qch; **to ~ sb out of trouble** empêcher qn de faire des bêtises; **to ~ sb/sth out of sb's way** faire en sorte que qn/qch ne soit pas sur le chemin de qn.

■ **keep to**: ¶ **~ to** [**sth**] (stick to) lit ne pas s'écarter de, rester sur [*road, path*]; fig respecter, s'en tenir à [*timetable, facts, plan*]; respecter [*law, rules*]; **'~ to the left/right'** 'tenez votre gauche/droite'; **to ~ to one's bed** garder le lit; **to ~ to one's home** rester chez soi; ¶ **~ sb to** [**sth**] (cause to remain on) empêcher qn de s'écarter de [*route*]; forcer qn à tenir [*promise*]; ¶ **~** [**sth**] **to** (restrict) limiter [qch] à [*weight, number*]; **to ~ sth to oneself** garder qch pour soi [*secret, information, opinion*]; **he can't ~ his hands to himself**○ il a les mains baladeuses○; **~ your hands to yourself!** bas les pattes○!

■ **keep under**: **~** [**sb**] **under 1** (dominate) assujettir, soumettre [*race, slaves, inhabitants*]; **2** (cause to remain unconscious) maintenir [qn] inconscient.

■ **keep up**: ¶ **~ up 1** (progress at same speed) (all contexts) [*car, runner, person*] suivre; [*business rivals, competitors*] rester à la hauteur; **2** (continue) [*price*] se maintenir; **if the rain ~s up I'm not going** s'il continue à pleuvoir je n'y vais pas; ¶ **~** [**sth**] **up**, **~ up** [**sth**] **1** (cause to remain in position) tenir [*trousers*]; **'~ your hands up!'** (by gunman) 'gardez les mains en l'air!'; **2** (continue) continuer [*attack, bombardment, studies*]; entretenir [*correspondence, friendship*]; maintenir [*membership, tradition*]; garder [*pace*]; **to ~ up the pressure** continuer à faire pression (**for** pour obtenir; **on** sur); **he kept up his German by going to evening classes** il a entretenu son allemand en suivant des cours du soir; **to ~ up one's strength/spirits** garder ses forces/le moral; **~ it up!, ~ up the good work!** continuez comme ça!; ¶ **~** [**sb**] **up** (maintain awake) maintenir [qn] réveillé [*child, person*]; [*noise, illness*] empêcher [qn] de dormir; **I hope I'm not ~ing you up** (politely) j'espère que je ne vous oblige pas à veiller; (ironically) j'espère que je ne vous empêche pas de dormir.

■ **keep up with**: **~ up with** [**sb/sth**] **1** (progress at same speed as) (physically) aller aussi vite que [*person, group*]; (mentally) suivre [*class, work, lecture*]; [*company, country*] se maintenir à la hauteur de [*competitors*]; Econ [*wages, pensions*] suivre [*prices, inflation, cost of living*]; faire face à [*demand*]; **2** (be informed about) suivre [*fashion, developments, news*]; **3** (remain in contact with) garder le contact avec [*schoolfriends, colleagues*]. ▶ **end**, **pecker**.

keeper /ˈkiːpə(r)/ *n* **1** (in zoo) gardien/-ienne *m/f*; **2** Sport (in football) gardien/-ienne *m/f* (de but); (in cricket) gardien/-ienne *m/f* (de guichet); **3** (curator) conservateur/-trice *m/f*; **4** (guard) gardien/-ienne *m/f*; **the ~ of the gate** le gardien de la porte; **5** (person in charge of someone else) **am I my brother's ~?** est-ce que je suis responsable de mon frère?; **I'm not his ~** je ne suis pas son ange gardien. ▶ **finder**.

keep fit /ˌkiːp ˈfɪt/ **I** *n* gymnastique *f* d'entretien.

II keep-fit *modif* [*class, teacher, fanatic*] de gymnastique.

keep fit exercises *npl* gymnastique *f* d'entretien.

keeping /ˈkiːpɪŋ/ **I** *n* (custody) **in sb's ~, in the ~ of sb** à la garde de qn; **to put sb/sth in sb's ~** confier qn/qch à qn.

II in ~ with *prep phr* conforme à [*status, law, rules, image, tradition*]; **to be in ~ with** correspondre à [*law, rules, policy, image, character*] s'harmoniser avec [*surroundings, area, village*].

III out of ~ with *prep phr* **to be out of ~ with** ne pas correspondre à [*character, image, style*]; ne pas convenir à [*occasion*].

keepsake /ˈkiːpseɪk/ *n* souvenir *m*.

keg /keg/ **I** *n* (for liquid) fût *m*; (for gunpowder) baril *m*.

II *modif* [*beer*] pression *inv*.

keister○ /ˈkiːstə(r), ˈkaɪstə(r)/ *n* US derrière *m*.

kelp /kelp/ *n* laminaire *f*.

kelvin /ˈkelvɪn/ *n* degré *m* Kelvin; **~ scale** échelle *f* Kelvin.

ken /ken/ **I** *n* **beyond my ~** au-delà de mon entendement; **to be beyond sb's ~** dépasser l'entendement de qn.

II *vtr* Scot dial = **know**.

kennel /ˈkenl/ *n* **1** GB (for dog) niche *f*; (for several dogs) chenil *m*; **2** (GB **kennels** + *v sg*) (establishment) chenil *m*; **to be in ~s** GB, **to be in a ~** US être dans un chenil.

Kent /kent/ ▶ **1624** *pr n* Kent *m*.

Kentucky /kenˈtʌkɪ/ ▶ **1744** *pr n* Kentucky *m*.

Kenya /ˈkenjə/ ▶ **1131** *pr n* Kenya *m*; **in ~** au Kenya.

Kenyan /ˈkenjən/ ▶ **1486**, **1402** **I** *n* Kényan/-e *m/f*.

II *adj* kényan/-e.

kepi /ˈkeɪpɪ/ *n* képi *m*.

kept /kept/ **I** *prét, pp* ▶ **keep**.

II *adj* [*man, woman*] entretenu.

keratin /ˈkerətɪn/ *n* kératine *f*.

kerb /kɜːb/ *n* GB (edge of pavement) bord *m* du trottoir; **stop at the ~** arrête-toi au bord du trottoir; **to draw up at the ~** se ranger le long du trottoir; **to pull away from/pull into the ~** s'éloigner/se rapprocher du trottoir.

kerb: **~ broker** *n* Fin coulissier *m*; **~ crawler** *n* GB dragueur○ *m* au volant; **~ crawling** *n* GB drague○ *f* au volant; **~ drill** *n* GB code *m* de prévention routière (*pour enfants*); **~ market** *n* Fin marché *m* en coulisse; **~stone** *n* GB pierre *f* (*de bordure d'un trottoir*).

kerchief† /ˈkɜːtʃɪf/ *n* fichu *m*.

kerfuffle○ /kəˈfʌfl/ *n* GB cirque○ *m*.

kernel /ˈkɜːnl/ *n* **1** (of nut, fruitstone) amande *f*; (whole seed) grain *m*; **walnut ~** cerneau *m* de noix; **2** fig fond *m*; **a ~ of truth** un fond de vérité; **3** Comput, Ling noyau *m*.

kernel sentence *n* Ling phrase *f* noyau, phrase *f* nucléaire.

kernite /ˈkɜːnaɪt/ *n* kernite *f*.

kerosene, **kerosine** /ˈkerəsiːn/ *n* **1** US, Austral (paraffin) pétrole *m* (lampant); **2** (aircraft fuel) kérosène *m*.

kestrel /ˈkestrəl/ *n* (faucon *m*) crécerelle *f*.

ketch /ketʃ/ *n* ketch *m*.

ketchup /ˈketʃəp/ GB *n* ketchup *m*.

kettle /ˈketl/ *n* bouilloire *f*; **did you put the ~ on?** est-ce que tu as mis l'eau à chauffer?; **the ~'s boiling** l'eau bout.
IDIOMS **a different ~ of fish** une toute autre affaire; **it's the pot calling the ~ black** c'est l'hôpital qui se moque de la charité.

kettledrum /ˈketldrʌm/ ▶ 1481 *n* timbale *f*.

key /kiː/ **I** *n* **1** (locking device) clé *f*, clef *f*; **a front-door/car ~** une clé de maison/voiture; **a set** ou **bunch of ~s** un jeu de clés; **to leave the ~ in the door** laisser la clé sur la porte; **under lock and ~** sous clé; **2** (winding device) gen remontoir *m* (**for** de); (for clock) clé *f* (de pendule), remontoir *m*; **3** Tech clé *f*; **radiator ~** clavette *f* à radiateur; **4** (control) (on typewriter, computer, piano, phone) touche *f*; (on oboe, flute) clé *f*; **5** fig (vital clue) (to happiness, success etc) clé *f*, secret *m* (**to** de); **his diary holds the ~ to the mystery** son journal renferme la clé du mystère; **exercise is the ~ to health** l'exercice est le secret de la santé; **the ~ to being a good teacher is to listen** le secret pour devenir un bon enseignant est d'écouter; **6** (explanatory list) (on map) légende *f*; (to abbreviations, symbols) liste *f*; (for code, cryptogram) clé *f*; **'pronunciation ~'** 'liste phonétique', 'tableau *m* phonétique'; **7** (answers) (to test, riddle) solutions *fpl*; Sch corrigé *m*; **8** Mus ton *m*, tonalité *f*; **what ~ is the sonata in?** dans quel ton est la sonate?; **change of ~** lit, fig changement *m* de ton; **a major ~** un ton majeur; **in a major/minor ~** en majeur/mineur; **to sing/play in ~** chanter/jouer juste; **to sing/ play off ~** chanter/jouer faux; **9** Geog caye *m*.
II *modif* [*industry, job, element, document, figure, role*] clé *inv* (*after n*); [*difference, point*] capital; [*problem*] essentiel/-ielle; **~ workers** des travailleurs occupant des postes clés.
III *vtr* **1** (type) saisir [*data, information*]; **2** (adapt) adapter [*remarks, speech*] (**to** à).
■ **key in**: **~ [sth] in, ~ in [sth]** saisir [*data*].

keyboard /ˈkiːbɔːd/ ▶ 1481 **I** *n* Comput, Print, Mus clavier *m*.
II keyboards *npl* Mus synthétiseur *m*.
III *vtr* saisir.

keyboarder /ˈkiːbɔːdə(r)/ *n* opérateur/-trice *m/f* de saisie.

keyboarding /ˈkiːbɔːdɪŋ/ **I** *n* Comput, Publg saisie *f*.
II *modif* [*error, problem*] de saisie, de frappe.

keyboard: **~ instrument** *n* instrument *m* à clavier; **~ operator** *n* = **keyboarder**; **~ skills** *npl* ≈ connaissances *fpl* en traitement de texte; **~s player** *n* joueur/-euse *m/f* de synthétiseur.

keyed-up /ˌkiːdˈʌp/ *adj* [*person, team*] (excited) excité; (tense) tendu; **to get ~** (excited) s'exciter; (nervous) devenir tendu; **she was all ~ about the exams** elle était remontée à bloc○ pour les examens.

key holder *n*: *personne responsable des clés*.

keyhole /ˈkiːhəʊl/ *n* trou *m* de serrure; **to look through the ~** regarder par le trou de la serrure.

key: **~hole journalism** *n* reportages *mpl* à sensation; **~hole saw** *n* Tech scie *f* à guichet; **~hole surgery** *n* Med chirurgie *f* endoscopique.

keying /ˈkiːɪŋ/ *n* Comput, Publg saisie *f*.

key money *n* (for business premises) pas-de-porte *m inv*; (for apartment) reprise *f*.

keynote /ˈkiːnəʊt/ *n* **1** Mus tonique *f*; **2** fig (main theme) (of speech, policy, report) thème *m* principal.

keynote: **~ lecture** *n* communication *f* inaugurale; **~ speaker** *n* intervenant/-e *m/f* principal/-e; **~ speech** *n* gen, Pol discours *m* programme.

key: **~-pad** *n* Comput pavé *m* numérique; Telecom clavier *m* numérique; **~ punch** *n* Comput perforatrice *f* à clavier; **~-ring** *n* porte-clés *m inv*; **~ signature** *n* armature *f*; **~stone** *n* Archit, fig clé *f* de voûte; **~stroke** *n* Comput frappe *f*; **~word** *n* mot *m* clé.

kg *n* (*abrév* = **kilogram**) kg *m*.

KGB *n* KGB *m*.

khaki /ˈkɑːkɪ/ **I** *n* Tex kaki *m*; **in ~** en kaki.
II *adj* kaki *inv*.

Khmer /kmeə(r)/ ▶ 1486, 1402 **I** *n* **1** (person) Khmer/Khmère *m/f*; **2** (language) khmer *m*.
II *adj* khmer/khmère.

Khmer Rouge *n* Khmers *mpl* rouges.

Khyber Pass /ˌkaɪbəˈpɑːs/ *pr n* passe *f* de Khaybar.

kHz *n* (*abrév* = **kiloherz**) kHz.

kibbutz /kɪˈbʊts/ *n* (*pl* **~es** ou **~im**) kibboutz *m*.

kibitz○ /ˈkɪbɪts/ *vtr* US **1** kibitzer (*au bridge*); **2** (interfere) fourrer○ son nez dans les affaires d'autrui.

kibitzer○ /ˈkɪbɪtsə(r), kɪˈbɪtsə(r)/ *n* US **1** spectateur/-trice *m/f* (*qui donne des conseils qu'on n'a pas demandés*); **2** (busybody) mouche *f* du coche.

kibosh○ /ˈkaɪbɒʃ/ *n*: IDIOMS **to put the ~ on sth** mettre fin à qch.

kick /kɪk/ **I** *n* **1** (of person, horse) coup *m* de pied; (of donkey, cow, goat) coup *m* de sabot; (of swimmer) battement *m* de pieds; (of footballer) tir *m*; **to give sb/the door a ~** donner un coup de pied à qn/dans la porte; **to aim** ou **take a ~ at sb/sth** [*person*] lancer un coup de pied à qn/dans qch; **she aimed a ~ at the goal** elle a tiré vers le but; **to get a ~ on the leg/in the stomach** (from person, horse) recevoir un coup de pied à la jambe/dans l'estomac; (from donkey, cow) recevoir un coup de sabot à la jambe/dans l'estomac; **to give sb a ~ up the backside**○ ou **in the pants**○ lit, fig botter le derrière○ de qn; ▶ **free kick**, **penalty kick**; **2**○ (thrill) **it gives her a ~ to do** elle prend plaisir à faire; **to get a ~ from doing** prendre plaisir à faire; **3** (of firearm) recul *m*; **4**○ (strength, zest) (of person, organization) dynamisme *m*; **this punch has quite a ~ (to it)** ce punch est assez costaud○; **5**○ (craze) marotte *f*, manie *f*; **to be on a health-food ~** manger bio○.
II *vtr* gen (once) [*person*] donner un coup de pied à [*person*]; donner un coup de pied dans [*table, door*]; [*person*] shooter dans [*ball, tin can*]; [*horse*] botter; [*donkey, cow, goat*] donner un coup de sabot à [*person*]; donner un coup de sabot dans [*gate, bucket*]; (repeatedly) donner des coups de pied à [*person*]; donner des coups de pieds dans [*object*]; **to ~ sb on the leg/in the face/in the stomach** [*person, horse*] donner à qn un coup or des coups de pied à la jambe/au visage/dans l'estomac; [*donkey, cow*] donner à qn un coup de sabot dans la jambe/au visage/dans l'estomac; **to ~ sth over a wall/under the bed/through the window** envoyer qch par-dessus un mur/sous le lit/par la fenêtre d'un coup de pied; **to ~ sth away** éloigner qch d'un coup de pied; **he ~ed dust into my face** d'un coup de pied il m'a envoyé de la poussière à la figure; **to ~ a hole** ou **dent in sth** défoncer qch d'un coup de pied; **to ~ one's legs (in the air)** [*baby*] pédaler; **to ~ a goal** marquer un but; **to ~ the ball into touch** (in rugby) envoyer le ballon en touche.
III *vi* **1** gen [*person*] (once) donner un coup de pied; (repeatedly) donner des coups de pied; [*swimmer*] faire des battements de pieds; [*dancer*] lancer la jambe; [*cow*] ruer; [*horse*] botter; **to ~ at sb/sth** [*person*] lancer un coup de pied à qn/dans qch; **the horse ~ed at me** le cheval a voulu me botter; **to ~ for touch** (in rugby) chercher la touche; **2** (recoil) [*gun*] reculer.
IDIOMS **a (real) ~ in the teeth**○ ou **ass**◑ US une gifle; **it's better than a ~ in the teeth**○ c'est mieux que rien; **to ~ sb when they're down** frapper un homme à terre; **to ~ the habit**○ gen décrocher○, arrêter; (of smoking) arrêter de fumer; **I could have ~ed myself** je me serais donné des claques○ (**for doing** d'avoir fait); **to be alive and ~ing** être bien vivant; **to ~ over the traces** ruer dans les brancards○; ▶ **heel**, **scream**, **upstairs**.
■ **kick around**, **kick about**: ¶ **~ around**○ [*objects, clothes*] traîner○; **that idea's been ~ing around for years** cette idée traîne○ dans l'air depuis des années; **he's been ~ing around Europe for a year**○ il se balade○ en Europe depuis un an; ¶ **~ [sth] around** ou **about 1** lit donner des coups de pied dans, s'amuser avec [*ball, object*]; **2**○ discuter de, explorer [*idea*]; ¶ **~ [sb/sth] around** or **about** (treat badly) maltraiter [*person*]; malmener [*toys, objects*]; **I won't be ~ed around by anyone** je ne me laisserai pas marcher dessus.
■ **kick against**: **~ against [sth]** (resist) résister à [*idea, suggestion*]; (fight against) lutter contre [*rules, system*]; **to ~ against doing** résister à l'idée de faire.
■ **kick back**: ¶ **~ back** [*firearm*] avoir du recul; ¶ **~ [sth] back, ~ back [sth] 1** renvoyer (du pied) [*ball, object*]; **2** US Fin accorder une ristourne de [*money*].
■ **kick down**: **~ [sth] down, ~ down [sth]** enfoncer [qch] d'un coup de pied or à coups de pied [*door*]; [*horse*] renverser [*fence*].
■ **kick in**: ¶ **~ in**○ US (contribute) verser sa quote part; ¶ **~ [sth] in, ~ in [sth]** enfoncer [qch] d'un coup de pied or à coups de pied [*door, window, box*]; **to ~ sb's teeth** ou **face in**◑ casser la figure○ or la gueule◑ de qn.
■ **kick off**: ¶ **~ off 1** Sport donner le coup d'envoi; **2**○ [*person, meeting, tour, concert*] commencer, démarrer; ¶ **~ off [sth], ~ [sth] off 1** enlever [*shoes*]; **2**○ commencer [*meeting, tour, concert*]; ¶ **~ [sb] off**○ exclure [qn] de, virer○ [qn] de [*committee, board of directors*].
■ **kick out**: ¶ **~ out** [*animal*] ruer; [*person*] lancer des coups de pied; **to ~ out at sb** [*person*] lit lancer des coups de pied à qn; **to ~ out against** se rebeller contre [*idea, system, injustice*]; ¶ **~ [sb] out, ~ out [sb]**○ vider○, virer○ [*troublemaker, intruder*]; éjecter○ [*team member*]; virer○ [*employee*].
■ **kick over**: **~ [sth] over, ~ over [sth]** renverser [qch] (d'un coup de pied or à coups de pied).
■ **kick up**: **~ [sth] up, ~ up [sth]** soulever [*sand, dust*]; **to ~ up a fuss**○ ou **stink**○ faire des histoires○ (**about** à propos de).

kick: **~back** *n* pot-de-vin *m*, dessous-de-table *m inv*; **~boxer** *n* kick-boxeur *m*; **~boxing** *n* kick-boxing *m*; **~ chart** *n* Med grille *f* de coups de pied d'un fœtus.

kicker /ˈkɪkə(r)/ *n* Sport (in rugby) botteur *m*; **that horse is a ~** attention, ce cheval botte.

kick-off /ˈkɪkɒf/ *n* Sport coup *m* d'envoi; fig **what time's the ~○?** à quelle heure on décolle○?

kick: **~ pleat** *n* pli *m* d'aisance; **~-stand** *n* Transp béquille *f*.

kick-start /ˈkɪkstɑːt/ **I** *n* (also **~-starter**) (on motorbike) kick *m*.
II *vtr* **1** lit démarrer [qch] au pied [*motorbike*]; **2** fig relancer [*economy*].

kick turn *n* (in skiing) conversion *f*.

kid /kɪd/ **I** *n* **1**○ (child) enfant *mf*, gosse○ *mf*; (youth, teenager) gamin/-e○ *m/f*; **their ~s are grown up** leurs gosses○ sont grands; **2** (young goat) chevreau/-ette *m/f*; **3** (of antelope) (male) faon *m*; (female) biche *f*; **4** (goatskin) chevreau *m*.

II *modif* [*bag, shoe*] en chevreau.
III○ *vtr* (*p prés etc* **-dd-**) **1** (tease) charrier○; **to ~ sb about sth** charrier○ qn à propos de qch; **I ~ you not** je ne charrie○ pas; **2** (fool, deceive) faire marcher○ [*person*]; **to ~ sb into believing that** faire croire à qn que; **you can't ~ me** je ne marche pas○.
IV○ *vi* (*p prés etc* **-dd-**) (tease) rigoler○; **you're ~ding!** tu rigoles!; **you've got to be ~ding!** tu veux rire!; **no ~ding!** sans blague○!
V○ *v refl* **to ~ oneself** se faire des illusions.
IDIOMS **it's ~'s stuff**○ c'est un jeu d'enfant.

kid brother○ *n* frérot○ *m*.

kiddy○ /'kɪdɪ/ *n* enfant *mf*, gosse○ *mf*.

kid glove *n* gant *m* en chevreau.
IDIOMS **to treat sb with ~s** prendre des gants avec qn.

kidnap /'kɪdnæp/ **I** *n* enlèvement *m*.
II *modif* [*attempt*] d'enlèvement; [*victim*] d'un enlèvement.
III *vtr* (*p prés etc* **-pp-**) enlever.

kidnapper /'kɪdnæpə(r)/ *n* ravisseur/-euse *m/f*.

kidnapping /'kɪdnæpɪŋ/ *n* enlèvement *m*.

kidney /'kɪdnɪ/ **I** *n* **1** (of person) rein *m*; **artificial ~** rein artificiel; **floating ~** rein flottant; **2** (of animal) Anat rein *m*; Culin rognon *m*; **lamb/beef ~s** rognons d'agneau/de bœuf.
II *modif* [*operation*] du rein; [*disease*] des reins; **to have ~ trouble** souffrir de troubles rénaux.
IDIOMS **a man of a different ~** littér un homme d'un autre acabit liter.

kidney: **~ bean** *n* haricot *m* rouge; **~ dialysis** *n* dialyse *f*; **~ dish** *n* Med haricot *m*; **~ donor** *n* donneur/-euse *m/f* de rein; **~ failure** *n* défaillance *f* rénale.

kidney machine *n* rein *m* artificiel; **to be on a ~** être en dialyse.

kidney: **~ shaped** *adj* [*table, swimming pool*] en forme de haricot; **~ specialist** *n* néphrologue *mf*; **~ stone** *n* calcul *m* rénal; **~ transplant** *n* transplantation *f* rénale.

kid sister○ *n* sœurette○ *f*.

kif /kɪf/ *n* kif *m*.

kike○ /kaɪk/ *n* injur youpin/-e○ *m/f* offensive.

kill /kɪl/ **I** *n* **1** (in bullfighting, hunting) mise *f* à mort; **to be in at the ~** lit assister à la mise à mort; **I wanted to be in at the ~** fig je voulais assister au dénouement; **2** (prey) proie *f*.
II *vtr* **1** (cause to die) tuer [*person, animal*]; **he ~ed her with a knife** il l'a tuée avec un couteau; **he was ~ed by the disease** la maladie l'a tué; **he was ~ed by a drunken driver** il a été tué par un conducteur ivre; **they ~ed one another** ou **each other** ils se sont entre-tués; **~ed outright** tué sur le coup; **drink is slowly ~ing him** l'alcool le détruit lentement; **~ed in action** ou **battle** tombé au champ d'honneur; **I'll do it, even if it ~s me**○! je le ferai, même si je dois y laisser ma peau○!; **I could have ~ed her!** je l'aurais tuée!; **she didn't say anything, but if looks could ~...** elle n'a rien dit mais ses yeux lançaient des éclairs; **2**○ (make effort) **it wouldn't ~ you to turn up on time** cela ne te ferait pas de mal d'arriver à l'heure; **3**○ (hurt) **my feet are ~ing me** j'ai mal aux pieds; **what ~s me is not knowing** ce qui me tue, c'est de ne pas savoir; **4** (end, stop) arrêter [*rumour*]; supprimer [*paragraph, story*] Journ; faire échouer [*idea, proposal*]; **it ~ed her chances of getting a job** cela a anéanti toutes ses chances d'obtenir un emploi; **that remark ~ed the conversation dead** cette remarque a jeté un froid dans la conversation; **5** (deaden) tuer [*smell, flavour*]; **smoking ~s the appetite** fumer ôte tout appétit; **to ~ the pain** faire disparaître la douleur; **6**○ (turn off) couper [*engine, machine*]; éteindre [*television, radio, light*]; **7** (spend) **to ~ time** tuer le temps (**by doing** en faisant); **I have two hours to ~** j'ai deux heures à attendre; **8**○ (amuse) **what ~s me is that he knew all along** le plus drôle, c'est qu'il le savait déjà.
III *vi* [*cancer, drinking*] tuer.
IV *v refl* **to ~ oneself** se suicider; **to ~ oneself doing** fig se tuer à faire; **don't ~ yourself!** iron surtout ne te fatigue pas trop!; **to ~ oneself laughing** être mort de rire; **they were all ~ing themselves laughing** ils étaient tous morts de rire.
■ **kill off**: **~ off [sth], ~ [sth] off** détruire [*weeds, crops*]; éliminer [*pests, opponents*]; **he ~s off the heroine in the third act** il fait mourir l'héroïne au troisième acte.

killer /'kɪlə(r)/ **I** *n* **1** (illness, poison) **cold/heroin/cancer is a ~** le froid/l'héroïne/le cancer tue; **cancer is a major ~** le cancer est l'une des principales causes de mortalité; **2** (person) meurtrier *m*; (animal) tueur/-euse *m/f*; **the hunt for the ~** la chasse au meurtrier.
II *modif* [*disease, virus*] mortel/-elle; [*drug*] qui tue; [*insect*] tueur/-euse.
IDIOMS **it's a ~**○! (hill) c'est crevant○!; (joke) c'est tordant○!

killer instinct *n* lit instinct *m* de tuer; **to lack the ~** fig manquer d'agressivité.

killer: **~ satellite** *n* satellite *m* tueur; **~ whale** *n* épaulard *m*.

killing /'kɪlɪŋ/ **I** *n* (of individual) (person) meurtre *m* (**of** de); (animal) mise *f* à mort (**of** de); **the ~ of civilians/elephants** le massacre de civils/d'éléphants; **the ~ must stop** il faut que la tuerie cesse.
II○ *adj* [*pace*] infernal○; [*work*] crevant○.
IDIOMS **to make a ~**○ ramasser un joli paquet○.

killingly○† /'kɪlɪŋlɪ/ *adv* **a ~ funny film** un film à mourir de rire; **it was ~ funny** c'était à mourir de rire.

kill: **~joy** *n* rabat-joie *mf inv*; **~ or cure** *adj* [*methods, approach*] radical.

kiln /kɪln/ *n* four *m*.

Kilner jar® /'kɪlnə(r)/ *n* GB bocal *m* à conserves.

kilo /'kiːləʊ/ **▶ 1883** *n* kilo *m*.

kiloampere /'kiːləʊæmpeə(r)/ *n* kiloampère *m*.

kilobyte /'kɪləbaɪt/ *n* kilo-octet *m*.

kilocycle /'kiːləʊsaɪkl/ *n* kilocycle *m*.

kilogram(me) /'kɪləgræm/ **▶ 1883** *n* kilogramme *m*.

kilohertz /'kɪləhɜːts/ *n* kilohertz *m*.

kilolitre GB, **kiloliter** US /'kiːləʊliːtə(r)/ **▶ 1883** *n* kilolitre *m*.

kilometre /kɪ'lɒmɪtə(r)/ GB, **kilometer** /'kɪləmiːtə(r)/ US **▶ 1412** *n* kilomètre *m*.

kilometric /ˌkɪlə'metrɪk/ *adj* kilométrique.

kiloton /'kɪlətən/ *n* kilotonne *f*.

kilovolt /'kɪləvɒlt/ *n* kilovolt *m*.

kilowatt /'kɪləwɒt/ *n* kilowatt *m*.

kilowatt-hour *n* kilowattheure *m*.

kilt /kɪlt/ *n* kilt *m*.

kilted /'kɪltɪd/ *adj* [*person*] en kilt.

kilter○ /'kɪltə(r)/ *n* **to be out of ~** (out of line) [*post etc*] être mal aligné; (not working properly) [*engine, machine*] avoir quelque chose qui cloche; **to be out of ~ with sth** [*policy, ideas*] être décalé par rapport à qch.

kimono /kɪ'məʊnəʊ, US -nə/ *n* kimono *m*.

kin /kɪn/ *n* ₵ parents *mpl*, famille *f*.

kind /kaɪnd/ **I** *n* **1** (sort, type) sorte *f*, genre *m*, type *m*; **this ~ of book/film** ce genre or type de livre/film; **this ~ of dog/person** ce genre de chien/personne; **all ~s of people/cars/music/activities, people/cars/music/activities of all ~s** toutes sortes de gens/de voitures/de musiques/d'activités; **various ~s of cheese/car, cheeses/cars of various ~s** diverses sortes de fromages/de voitures; **what ~ of dog/car is it?** qu'est-ce que c'est comme chien/voiture?; **what ~ of person is she?** quelle sorte de personne est-elle?; **what ~ of person does he think I am?** pour qui me prend-il?; **what ~ of (a) person would do a thing like that?** qui pourrait faire une chose pareille?; **what ~ of a question/an answer is that?** qu'est-ce que c'est que cette question/cette réponse?; **what ~ of talk is that?** en voilà des façons de parler!; **I won't do anything of the ~** je n'en ferai rien; **I don't believe anything of the ~** je n'en crois rien; **ideas of a dangerous/subversive ~** des idées dangereuses/subversives; **decisions of a difficult/momentous ~** des décisions difficiles/capitales; **a criminal/racist of the worst ~** un criminel/un raciste de la pire espèce; **they could find no information/food of any ~, they could not find any ~ of information/food** ils n'ont pas trouvé la moindre information/nourriture; **this sculpture is the oldest (example) of its ~** c'est la plus vieille sculpture du genre; **this is the only one of its ~, this is one of a ~** c'est unique en son genre; **he must be some ~ of idiot/sadist** ça doit être un imbécile/un sadique; **they found a fossil/picture of some ~** ils ont trouvé une sorte de fossile/tableau; **they needed some ~ of success/progress** ils avaient besoin d'avoir du succès/de faire des progrès; **I think it's some ~ of detective story/cleaning device** ce doit être une histoire policière/un système de nettoyage; **'what do you need?'—'books, toys, that ~ of thing'** 'de quoi avez-vous besoin?'—'de livres, de jouets, ce genre de choses'; **I like tennis, squash, that ~ of thing** j'aime le tennis, le squash, ce genre de sport; **what ~ of thing(s) does he like/do?** qu'est-ce qu'il aime/fait?; **that's my ~ of film/man!** c'est le genre de film/d'homme que j'aime!; **that's the ~ of person I am/she is** je suis/elle est comme ça; **I'm not/he's not that ~ of person** ce n'est pas mon/son genre; **she's not the ~ of person who tells lies** ou **to tell lies** ce n'est pas son genre de mentir; **they found a solution of a ~** ils ont trouvé une solution qui n'était pas merveilleuse; **it's wine/butter of a ~** c'est du vin/du beurre de mauvaise qualité; **2** (expressing vague classification) **a ~ of** une sorte de; **a ~ of handbag/toy/soup** une sorte de sac à main/de jouet/de soupe; **a ~ of anarchist/genius/servant** une sorte d'anarchiste/de génie/de serviteur; **a ~ of depression/intuition** une sorte de dépression/d'intuition; **I heard a ~ of rattling noise** j'ai entendu comme un cliquetis; **I felt a ~ of apprehension** j'ai ressenti une certaine appréhension; **3** (classified type) espèce *f*, genre *m*; **I know your/his ~** je connais les gens de votre/son espèce; **they stick with their own ~** ils ne fréquentent que les gens de leur espèce.
II **in kind** *adv phr* **1** (in goods) en nature; **to pay in ~** payer en nature; **2** (in same way) **to repay sb in ~** (good deed) rendre la pareille à qn; (bad deed) rendre la monnaie de sa pièce à qn; **3** (in essence) **they are/are not different in ~** ils sont/ils ne sont pas très différents.
III○ **kind of** *adv phr* **he's ~ of cute/forgetful/clever** il est plutôt mignon/distrait/intelligent; **they were ~ of frightened/happy** en fait, ils avaient un peu peur/ça leur faisait plutôt plaisir; **I ~ of like him** en fait, je l'aime bien; **we ~ of thought/heard that...** nous pensions/avons entendu dire que...; **'is it interesting/dangerous?'—'~ of'** 'est-ce que c'est intéressant/dangereux?'—'plutôt, oui'; **'did you have a good time?'—'~ of'** 'est-ce que vous vous êtes bien amusés?'—'oui, c'était pas mal'.
IV *adj* **1** (caring, helpful) [*person*] gentil/-ille; [*act*] bon/bonne; [*remark, gesture, words*] gentil/-ille; [*thought*] délicat; **to be ~ to sb** être gentil avec qn; **'Sudso is ~ to your hands/skin'** 'Sudso respecte vos

mains/votre peau'; **to be ~ to animals** bien traiter les animaux; **the critics were not ~ to the play** les critiques n'ont pas épargné la pièce; **life has been ~ to me** j'ai eu de la chance dans la vie; **life has not been ~ to him** la vie ne l'a pas épargné; **time has been ~ to him** il ne fait pas son âge; **that's very ~ of you** c'est très gentil/aimable de votre part; **it's very ~ of you/him to give us a lift/lend me some money** c'est très gentil de ta/sa part de nous ramener/de me prêter de l'argent; (in polite formulas) **would you be ~ enough** ou **so ~ as to pass me the salt?** auriez-vous l'amabilité de me passer le sel; **she was ~ enough to give me a lift home/offer me a drink** elle a eu la gentillesse de me ramener/de m'offrir un verre; **'you're too ~!'** 'vous êtes trop aimable!'

kinda○ /ˈkaɪndə/ = **kind of**.

kindergarten /ˈkɪndəgɑ:tn/ *n* jardin *m* d'enfants.

kind-hearted *adj* [*person*] de cœur; **she's very ~** elle a bon cœur.

kind: **~-heartedly** *adv* très gentiment; **~-heartedness** *n* bonté *f*.

kindle /ˈkɪndl/ **I** *vtr* **1** (set light to) allumer [*fire*]; mettre le feu à, enflammer [*wood*]; **2** fig attiser [*desire, passion, jealousy*]; susciter [*enthusiasm, interest*].
II *vi* [*wood*] s'enflammer, prendre feu.

kindliness /ˈkaɪndlɪnɪs/ *n* bonté *f*, bienveillance *f*.

kindling /ˈkɪndlɪŋ/ *n* petit bois *m*, bois *m* d'allumage.

kindly /ˈkaɪndlɪ/ **I** *adj* [*person, nature*] gentil/-ille; [*smile, interest*] bienveillant; [*voice*] plein de gentillesse; [*face*] sympathique; **she's a ~ soul** elle est très gentille.
II *adv* **1** (in a kind, nice way) [*speak, look, treat*] avec gentillesse; **to speak ~ of sb** avoir un mot gentil pour qn; **thank you ~**† tous mes remerciements; **2** (obligingly) gentiment; **she ~ agreed to do** elle a gentiment accepté de faire; **would you ~ do/refrain from doing** auriez-vous l'amabilité de faire/de ne pas faire; **'would visitors ~ do'**, **'visitors are ~ requested to do'** GB 'les visiteurs sont priés de faire'; **3** (favourably) **to look ~ on** approuver [*activity*]; **to think ~ of** avoir une bonne opinion de [*person*]; **to take ~ to** apprécier [*idea, suggestion, person*]; **I don't think he'll take ~ to being kept waiting** je ne crois pas qu'il va apprécier qu'on le fasse attendre.

kindness /ˈkaɪndnɪs/ *n* **1** ¢ (quality) gentillesse *f* (**to, towards** envers, à l'égard de); **to show sb ~, to show ~ to** ou **towards sb** témoigner de la gentillesse à l'égard de or envers or à qn; **I never showed you anything but ~** j'ai toujours été gentil avec toi; **an act of ~** un acte de bonté; **out of ~** par gentillesse; **2 C** (instance) gentillesse *f*; **your little ~es towards me** tes petites gentillesses envers moi; **to do sb a ~** rendre service à qn; **it's no ~ to him to do** on ne lui rend pas service en faisant.
IDIOMS **out of the ~ of one's heart** par pure gentillesse; **to kill sb with ~** trop gâter qn; **to be full of the milk of human ~** être pétri d'humanité.

kindred /ˈkɪndrɪd/ **I** *n* ¢ **1** (family) (+ *v pl ou v sg*) famille *f*, parents *mpl*; **2** (blood relationship) parenté *f*.
II *adj* **1** [*family, tribe, language*] apparenté; **2** [*activity*] semblable.

kindred spirit *n* âme *f* sœur.

kinetic /kɪˈnetɪk/ *adj* cinétique.

kinetic: **~ art** *n* art *m* cinétique; **~ energy** *n* énergie *f* cinétique.

kinetics /kɪˈnetɪks/ *n* (+ *v sg*) cinétique *f*.

king /kɪŋ/ **▶1268** *n* **1** (monarch) roi *m*; **King Charles** le roi Charles; **the ~ of Spain** le roi d'Espagne; **the ~ of ~s** le roi des rois; **the ~ of the jungle** ou **beasts** le roi des animaux; **2** fig (of comedy, cinema, wines etc) roi *m* (**of** de); **3** Games (in chess, cards) roi *m*; (in draughts, checkers) dame *f*.
IDIOMS **to live like a ~** vivre comme un roi or un coq en pâte; **to be the ~ of the castle** être seigneur du château; **a cat may look at a ~** Prov un chien regarde bien un évêque Prov; **to ~ it over sb** traiter qn de haut.

king: **~bird** *n* Zool tyran *m*; **~bolt** *n* pivot *m* central, cheville *f* ouvrière; **~ cobra** *n* cobra *m* royal; **~cup** *n* (buttercup) bouton *m* d'or; (marsh marigold) souci *m* d'eau.

kingdom /ˈkɪŋdəm/ *n* **1** (monarchy) lit, fig royaume *m*; **the ~ of God** ou **heaven/the imagination** le royaume des cieux/de l'imagination; **2** Bot, Zool règne *m*; **the plant/animal ~** le règne végétal/animal.
IDIOMS **until ~ come** jusqu'à la fin des temps; **to send** ou **knock sb to ~ come** envoyer qn ad patres○ or dans l'autre monde.

king: **~fisher** *n* martin-pêcheur *m*; **King James Version** *n* version *f* de la Bible autorisée.

kingly /ˈkɪŋlɪ/ *adj* lit, fig royal, de roi.

king: **~maker** *n* Pol personnage *m* influent; **~ penguin** *n* manchot *m* royal; **~pin** *n* Tech, fig cheville *f* ouvrière; **~ post** *n* poinçon *m*; **~ prawn** *n* grosse crevette *f*.

Kings /kɪŋz/ *npl* Bible (livre *m* des) Rois *mpl*.

king: **King's Bench** *n* ▶ **Queen's Bench**; **King's Counsel, KC** *n* ▶ **Queen's Counsel**; **King's English** *n* ▶ **Queen's English**; **King's evidence** *n* ▶ **Queen's evidence**; **King's highway** *n* ▶ **Queen's highway**.

kingship /ˈkɪŋʃɪp/ *n* royauté *f*.

king-size(d) /ˈkɪŋsaɪzd/ *adj* [*cigarette*] extra-longue; [*packet*] géant; [*portion, garden*] énorme; **~ bed** grand lit *m* (*qui fait 1,95 m de large*).

king: **King's Regulations** *n* ▶ **Queen's Regulations**; **King's shilling** *n* ▶ **Queen's shilling**; **King's speech** *n* ▶ **Queen's speech**.

kink /kɪŋk/ **I** *n* **1** (in wire, rope, tube, pipe) nœud *m*; **the hosepipe has a ~ in it** le tuyau d'arrosage est tordu; **his hair has a ~ in it** ses cheveux frisent légèrement; **2** fig (in personality) aberration *f*, perversion *f*.
II *vi* [*rope, cable*] s'entortiller.

kinky /ˈkɪŋkɪ/ *adj* **1**○ [*person, behaviour, sex, clothes*] pervers, bizarre; **2** [*hair*] ondulé.

kinsfolk /ˈkɪnsfəʊk/ *n* (+ *v pl*) parents *mpl*, famille *f*.

kinship /ˈkɪnʃɪp/ *n* **1** (blood relationship) parenté *f*; **2** fig (empathy) affinité *f* (**with** avec).

kin: **~sman**† *n* parent *m*; **~swoman**† *n* parente *f*.

kiosk /ˈki:ɒsk/ *n* **1** (stand) kiosque *m*; **2** GB Telecom cabine *f*.

kip○ /kɪp/ GB **I** *n* (sleep) roupillon○ *m*; **to have a ~, to get some ~** piquer un roupillon○.
II *vi* (*p prés etc* **-pp-**) (also **~ down**) se pieuter○, roupiller○.

kipper /ˈkɪpə(r)/ GB **I** *n* hareng *m* fumé et salé, kipper *m*.
II *vtr* fumer et saler [*herring*].

Kirbigrip® /ˈkɜ:bɪgrɪp/ *n* épingle *f* à cheveux.

Kirghiz /ˈkɜ:gɪz/ **▶1486**, **1402** **I** *n* **1** (person) Kirghiz/-e *m/f*; **2** Ling kirghize *m*.
II *adj* kirghiz.

Kirghizia /ˌkɜ:ˈgi:zɪə/ **▶1131** *pr n* ▶ **Kirghizstan**.

Kirghizstan /ˈkɜ:gɪstæn/ **▶1131** *pr n* Kirghizstan *m*, Kirghizie *f*.

kirk /kɜ:k/ *n* Scot église *f*; **the Kirk** l'Église *f* presbytérienne d'Écosse.

kiss /kɪs/ **I** *n* baiser *m*; **to give sb a ~** donner un baiser à qn, embrasser qn; **give me a ~!** gen embrasse-moi!; (to child) fais-moi une bise○!; **to have a ~ and a cuddle** se faire des mamours○; **love and ~es** (at end of letter) bons baisers, grosses bises○.
II *vtr* embrasser, donner un baiser à [*person*]; baiser [*hand, ring*]; **to ~ sb on** embrasser qn sur [*cheek, lips*]; **to ~ hands** (ceremoniously) faire le baisemain; **we ~ed each other** nous nous sommes embrassés; **she ~ed him back** elle lui a rendu son baiser; **to ~ sb goodnight/goodbye** souhaiter bonne nuit/dire au revoir à qn en l'embrassant; **let me ~ it better!** un petit bisou et ça ira mieux après!; **to ~ sb's tears away** embrasser qn pour le/la consoler; **you can ~ your money goodbye!** fig tu peux dire adieu à ton argent!
III *vi* **1** s'embrasser; **to ~ and make up** se réconcilier; **2** (in billiards) se frôler.
IDIOMS **to ~ and tell** avoir une liaison et le faire savoir publiquement; **to ~ ass◑** US faire de la lèche○; **~ my ass◑!** va te faire mettre●!

kissagram *n* ▶ **kissogram**.

kiss: **~ ass◑** *n* US lèche-cul● *mf inv*; **~ curl** *n* (adult's) accroche-cœur *m*; (baby's) bouclette *f*.

kisser○ /ˈkɪsə(r)/ *n* gueule○ *f*.

kiss of death *n* fig coup *m* fatal; **to be the ~** porter le coup fatal (**for, to** à).

kiss-off○ /ˈkɪsɒf/ *n* US **to give sb the ~** [*lover*] plaquer○ qn; [*employer*] virer○ qn.

kiss of life *n* GB bouche-à-bouche *m inv*; **to give sb the ~** faire le bouche à bouche à qn; **to give sth the ~** fig donner un nouveau souffle à qch.

kissogram /ˈkɪsəgræm/ *n*: *service de baisers livrés à domicile par porteur spécial.*

kit /kɪt/ *n* **1** (set of tools or implements) trousse *f*; **repair ~** trousse de réparation; **2** ¢ GB gen, Sport (gear, clothes) affaires *fpl*; **football/tennis ~** affaires de football/de tennis; **riding ~** tenue *f* d'équitation; **3** (set of parts for assembly) kit *m*; **to buy sth in a ~** acheter qch en kit; **to come in ~ form** être vendu en kit; **model aircraft ~** maquette *f* d'avion; **4** Mil paquetage *m*, barda◑ *m*; **in full ~** en tenue de campagne; **to pack one's ~** faire son paquetage.
■ **kit out** GB: **~ out [sb/sth], ~ [sb/sth] out** équiper [*person, interior*] (**with** de); **to be ~ted out** être accoutré de vêtements.

kitbag /ˈkɪtbæg/ *n* GB **1** gen (for sport) sac *m* de sport; (for travel) sac *m* de voyage; **2** Mil (sailor's) sac *m* de marin; (soldier's) sac *m* de soldat.

kitcar /ˈkɪtkɑ:(r)/ *n* voiture *f* en kit.

kitchen /ˈkɪtʃɪn/ **I** *n* cuisine *f*.
II *modif* [*furniture, appliance, utensil, salt, staff*] de cuisine; [*door, window*] de la cuisine.
IDIOMS **if you can't stand the heat get out of the ~** si tu trouves la situation insupportable, tu n'es pas obligé de rester.

kitchen area *n* (in room, apartment) coin *m* cuisine.

kitchen cabinet *n* **1** lit buffet *m* de cuisine; **2** fig, Pol conseillers *mpl* intimes du chef du gouvernement.

kitchenette /ˌkɪtʃɪˈnet/ *n* kitchenette *f*.

kitchen: **~ foil** *n* papier *m* d'aluminium; **~ garden** *n* jardin *m* potager; **~maid** *n* fille *f* de cuisine; **~ paper** *n* essuie-tout *m inv*, sopalin® *m*; **~ police, KP** *n* US Mil soldats *mpl* qui sont de corvée de cuisine; **~ porter** *n* garçon *m* de cuisine; **~ range** *n* fourneau *m* (de cuisine); **~ roll** *n* essuie-tout *m*; **~ scales** *npl* balance *f* de cuisine.

kitchen sink *n* évier *m*.
IDIOMS **to take everything but the ~** (on holiday) tout emporter sauf les meubles; **to steal everything but the ~** tout voler sauf les murs.

kitchen: **~ sink drama** *n* GB théâtre *m* naturaliste; **~ soap** *n* ≈ savon *m* de Marseille; **~ unit** *n* élément *m* de cuisine;

~ware *n* ¢ (implements) ustensiles *mpl* de cuisine; (crockery) vaisselle *f*; **~ waste** *n* ¢ déchets *mpl* domestiques.

kite /kaɪt/ *n* **1** (toy) cerf-volant *m*; **to fly a ~** lit faire voler un cerf-volant; fig lancer un ballon d'essai; **2** Zool milan *m*.
IDIOMS **as high as a ~**○ (drunk) complètement bourré○; (on drugs) défoncé○; **go (and) fly a ~**○! va te faire voir○!

kitemark /ˈkaɪtmɑːk/ *n* GB label *m* de qualité (*du British Standards Institution*).

kit furniture *n* ¢ meubles *mpl* en kit, prêt-à-monter *m* ¢.

kith /kɪθ/ *n* **~ and kin** amis *mpl* et parents *mpl*.

kitsch /kɪtʃ/ *n, adj* kitsch (*m*).

kitten /ˈkɪtn/ *n* chaton *m*.
IDIOMS fig **to have ~s**○ piquer une crise○.

kittenish /ˈkɪtənɪʃ/ *adj* [*person*] aguicheur/-euse.

kittiwake /ˈkɪtɪweɪk/ *n* Zool mouette *f* tridactyle.

kitty /ˈkɪtɪ/ *n* **1**○ (cat) minet *m*, minou○ *m*; **2** (of money) cagnotte *f*, caisse *f* commune.

kiwi /ˈkiːwiː/ **I** *n* Zool kiwi *m*.
II○ **Kiwi** *n* Néo-Zélandais/-e *m/f*.

kiwi fruit *n* kiwi *m*.

KKK *n*: *abrév* ▶ **Ku Klux Klan**.

Klansman /ˈklænzmən/ *n* membre *m* du Ku Klux Klan.

Klaxon® /ˈklæksn/ *n* Aut Hist klaxon® *m*.

Kleenex® /ˈkliːneks/ *n* Kleenex® *m*.

kleptomania /ˌkleptəˈmeɪnɪə/ *n* kleptomanie *f*.

kleptomaniac /ˌkleptəˈmeɪnɪæk/ *n, adj* kleptomane (*mf*).

klutz◑ /klʌts/ *n* US empoté/-e○ *m/f*.

klystron /ˈklaɪstrɒn/ *n* klystron *m*.

km (*abrév écrite* = **kilometre**) km.

kmh (*abrév écrite* = **kilometres per hour**) km/h.

knack /næk/ *n* **1** (physical dexterity) tour *m* de main (**of doing** pour faire); **to get the ~** attraper le tour de main; **to lose the ~** perdre la main; **2** (talent) don *m*; **to have the ~ of** ou **for doing** avoir le don de faire.

knacker /ˈnækə(r)/ **I** *n* **1** GB (horse butcher) équarrisseur *m*; **to send a horse to the ~'s yard** envoyer un cheval à l'équarrissage; **2** GB (salvage man) démolisseur *m*; **3**◑ (testicle) couille◑ *f*, testicule *m*.
II◑ *vtr* **1** (exhaust) [*activity, journey*] mettre [qn] à plat [*person*]; **2** (ruin, break) [*person*] bousiller○ [*car, gadget*].
III◑ **knackering** *pres p adj* [*day, journey, activity*] crevant○.
IV◑ **knackered** *pp adj* **1** (tired) [*person*] crevé○, à plat○; **2** (broken) [*car, TV etc*] foutu◑, cassé.

knapsack /ˈnæpsæk/ *n* sac *m* à dos.

knave /neɪv/ *n* **1** (in cards) valet *m*; **2**‡ (rogue) coquin‡ *m*.

knead /niːd/ *vtr* **1** [*baker, cook*] pétrir [*dough*]; **2** (massage) masser.

knee /niː/ **I** ▶ **1037** *n* Anat genou *m*; lit, fig **to be on/fall to one's ~s** être/tomber à genoux; **to be up to one's ~s in water** avoir de l'eau jusqu'aux genoux; **to sit on sb's ~** s'asseoir sur les genoux de qn; **come and sit on my ~** viens t'asseoir sur mes genoux; **to have the paper open on one's ~** avoir le journal ouvert sur les genoux; **to eat on one's ~** manger sur ses genoux; **on (one's) hands and ~s** à quatre pattes; **to go down on bended ~ (to sb)** se mettre à genoux (devant qn).
II *vtr* donner un coup de genou à [*person*].
IDIOMS **to bring** ou **force sb/sth to his/its ~s** mettre qn/qch à genoux; **to go weak at the ~s** avoir les jambes qui flageolent.

knee-breeches *n* knickers *mpl*.

kneecap /ˈniːkæp/ **I** *n* rotule *f*.
II *vtr* briser les rotules à [*person*].

kneecapping /ˈniːkæpɪŋ/ *n*: *mutilation de qn en lui brisant les rotules*.

knee-deep /ˌniːˈdiːp/ *adj* **the water was ~** l'eau arrivait aux genoux; **to be ~ in paperwork/problems** fig être dans les papiers/problèmes jusqu'au cou.

knee: **~-high** *adj* gen [*grass, corn*] à hauteur des genoux; hum [*person*] haut comme trois pommes; **~-jerk** *adj* [*reaction, response*] automatique, inconsidéré.

kneel /niːl/ **I** *vi* (also **~ down**) (*prét, pp* **kneeled**, **knelt**) gen se mettre à genoux; (in prayer) s'agenouiller.
II kneeling *pres p adj* [*person*] gen à genoux; (in prayer) agenouillé; **in a ~ position** à genoux.

knee: **~-length** *adj* [*skirt, dress*] à hauteur du genou; **~-pad** *n* genouillère *f*; **~s-up**○ *n* GB fête *f*.

knell /nel/ *n* littér lit, fig glas *m*.
IDIOMS **to sound the death ~ for sth** sonner le glas de qch.

knelt /nelt/ *prét, pp* ▶ **kneel**.

knew /njuː, US nuː/ *prét* ▶ **know**.

knickerbocker glory *n* coupe *f* glacée.

knickerbockers /ˈnɪkəbɒkəz/ *npl* knickers *mpl*.

knickers /ˈnɪkəz/ ▶ **1703** **I** *npl* **1** GB (underwear) petite culotte *f*, slip *m*; **a pair of ~** une petite culotte; **2** US (knickerbockers) knickers *mpl*.
II *excl* zut○!
IDIOMS **to get one's ~ in a twist**○ GB s'énerver.

knick-knack /ˈnɪknæk/ *n* bibelot *m*.

knife /naɪf/ **I** *n* (*pl* **knives**) **1** gen couteau *m*; **2** Ind (blade) lame *f*.
II *vtr* donner un coup de couteau à [*person*] (**in** dans); **to be ~d** recevoir un coup de couteau.
IDIOMS **an accent you could cut with a ~** un accent à couper au couteau; **before you could say ~**○ en moins de temps qu'il n'en faut pour le dire; **to be under the ~**○ être sur le billard○; **to have one's ~ into sb**○ en avoir après qn○; **to put the ~ in** descendre qn en flèche; **to twist the ~ in the wound** remuer le couteau dans la plaie; **the knives are out!** fig c'est la guerre!

knife box *n* bloc *m* porte-couteaux.

knife-edge *n* fig **to be on a ~** [*result, success, negotiations*] ne tenir qu'à un fil; **to be (living) on a ~** [*person*] être au bord de l'abîme.

knife: **~ grinder** *n* rémouleur *m*; **~ pleated** *adj* [*skirt*] plissée soleil.

knife-point *n* **at ~** sous la menace d'un couteau.

knife: **~-rest** *n* porte-couteau *m*; **~ sharpener** *n* aiguisoir *m*; **~ switch** *n* Elec interrupteur *m* à lames.

knifing /ˈnaɪfɪŋ/ *n* attaque *f* au couteau.

knight /naɪt/ **I** *n* **1** gen, Hist chevalier *m*; **to be made a ~** être fait chevalier; **2** Games (in chess) cavalier *m*.
II *vtr* GB anoblir [*person*] (**for** pour).
IDIOMS **you're my ~ in shining armour!** tu es mon sauveur!

knight errant *n* chevalier *m* errant.

knighthood /ˈnaɪthʊd/ *n* **1** (title) titre *m* de chevalier; **he received a ~** la reine or le roi lui a conféré le titre de chevalier; **2** (chivalry) chevalerie *f*.

knightly /ˈnaɪtlɪ/ *adj* chevaleresque.

Knight Templar *n* ▶ **Templar**.

knit /nɪt/ **I** *n* (garment) tricot *m*; **cotton/silk ~** tricot *m* en coton/soie.
II *vtr* (*prét, pp* **knitted**, **knit**) tricoter [*garment, blanket*] (**for** pour); **to ~ sb sth** tricoter qch pour qn; **~ one, purl one** une maille à l'endroit, une maille à l'envers.
III *vi* (*prét, pp* **knitted**, **knit**) **1** (with wool etc) [*person*] tricoter; **2** (join together) [*broken bones*] se souder.
IV knitted *pp adj* [*garment*] en tricot.
IDIOMS **to ~ one's brows** froncer les sourcils.
■ **knit together**: ¶ **~ together 1** (join) [*bones*] se souder (les uns aux autres); **2** (unite) [*community*] s'unir; ¶**~ [sth] together**, **~ together [sth] 1** lit tricoter [qch] ensemble [*colours, strands*]; **2** fig (bring together) entrelacer [*themes, ideas*]; **3** (unite) unir [*community, group*].
■ **knit up**: ¶ **~ up** [*wool*] se tricoter; ¶ **~ up [sth]** tricoter [*wool, garment*].

knitter /ˈnɪtə(r)/ *n* tricoteur/-euse *m/f*.

knitting /ˈnɪtɪŋ/ **I** *n* (all contexts) tricot *m*.
II *modif* [*bag*] à tricot; [*machine, needle, wool*] à tricoter.

knitwear /ˈnɪtweə(r)/ *n* ¢ tricots *mpl*.

knives /naɪvz/ *pl* ▶ **knife**.

knob /nɒb/ *n* **1** (handle) (of door, drawer) bouton *m*; (of cane) pommeau *m*; **2** (decorative) (on bannister, furniture) boule *f*; **3** (control button) bouton *m*; **4** (of butter etc) noix *f*; **5**◑ GB (penis) queue◑ *f*; **6**◑ (idiot) imbécile *mf*.
IDIOMS **...and the same to you with (brass) ~s on**○! ...et toi encore plus○!

knobbly /ˈnɒblɪ/ GB, **knobby** /ˈnɒbɪ/ US *adj* noueux/-euse.

knock /nɒk/ **I** *n* **1** (blow) coup *m*; **a ~ on the head** un coup sur la tête; **to take a ~** prendre un coup; **a ~ with a hammer** un coup de marteau; **a ~ at the door** un coup à la porte; **I'll give you a ~ at 7.30** je frapperai à ta porte à 7 h 30; **I thought I heard a ~** je crois qu'on a frappé; **2** onomat **~! ~!** toc! toc!; **3** fig (setback) coup *m*; **to take a ~** en prendre un coup; **it gave his confidence a ~** son assurance en a pris un coup; **I've had worse ~s** j'ai subi pire que ça; **you must learn to take the ~s** tu dois apprendre à encaisser○ (les coups).
II *vtr* **1** (strike) cogner [*object*]; **to ~ one's head/arm on sth** se cogner la tête/le bras contre qch; **to ~ sb on the head/arm with sth** donner un coup sur la tête/le bras de qn avec qch; **to ~ sb/sth into/against/across** projeter qn/qch dans/contre/à travers; **to ~ sb unconscious** ou **senseless** ou **silly**○ [*person, object, blow*] assommer qn; **to ~ a hole in sth** faire un trou dans qch; **to ~ sth straight/flat** redresser/aplatir qch; **to ~ two rooms into one** abattre la cloison entre deux pièces; **2** (cause to move) **to ~ sth off** ou **out of sth** faire tomber qch de qch; **to ~ sb/sth over sth** envoyer qn/qch par-dessus qch; **to ~ sb/sth to the ground** faire tomber qn/qch par terre; **she ~ed the ball into the pond** elle a envoyé la balle dans l'étang; **to ~ a nail/peg into sth** enfoncer un clou/une cheville dans qch; **to ~ the handle off the jug** casser l'anse du pot; **to ~ sb off his feet** [*blast, wave*] soulever qn; **to ~ sb/sth out of the way** écarter qn/qch; **to ~ sb flat** étendre qn par terre; **3** (beat) **to ~ the enthusiasm/spirit out of sb** faire perdre son enthousiasme/sa joie de vivre à qn; **I'll ~ that stupid smile off his face** je vais lui faire passer ce sourire stupide; **that will ~ a bit of sense into him** ça va peut-être lui inculquer un peu de bon sens; **4**○ (criticize) critiquer [*method, opposition, achievement*]; dénigrer [*person*]; **don't ~ it!** hum arrête de critiquer!
III *vi* **1** (make sound) (involuntarily) [*branch, object*] cogner (**on, against** contre); (deliberately) [*person*] frapper (**at, on** à); [*engine, water pipes*] cogner; **2** (collide) **to ~ into** ou **against sth** heurter qch; **to ~ into each other** se heurter.
IDIOMS **his knees were ~ing** ses genoux s'entrechoquaient de peur; **to ~ sth on the head**○ mettre fin à qch; **to be ~ing on a bit**○ commencer à se faire vieux; **it must be ~ing on**○ **30 years since...** ça ne doit pas faire loin de 30 ans que...; **I'll ~ your heads together!** je vous ferai entendre raison!
■ **knock about**○, **knock around**○: ¶ **~ about** traîner; ¶ **~ about [sth]** [*object*] traîner dans [*house, area*]; **to ~ about with sb**○ fréquenter qn; **to ~ about**

together○ [*adults*] se fréquenter; ¶ **~ [sb] about**○ malmener; ¶ **~ [sth] about 1** (buffet) [*storm*] ballotter [*boat*]; **2** Sport **let's just ~ the ball about** faisons juste des balles.

■ **knock back**: ¶ **~ back [sth], ~ [sth] back 1** (return) [*player*] renvoyer [*ball*]; **2**○ (swallow) descendre○ [*drink*]; **3**○ (reject) rejeter [*offer*]; refuser [*invitation*]; ¶ **~ [sb] back 1** (surprise) [*news*] secouer [*person*]; **2**○ (cost) **that dress must have ~ed her back a few quid**○ cette robe a dû lui coûter une fortune; **3** (refuse) jeter○ [*person*].

■ **knock down**: **~ [sb/sth] down, ~ down [sb/sth] 1** (cause to fall) (deliberately) [*aggressor*] jeter [qn] à terre [*victim, opponent*]; [*police*] défoncer [*door*]; [*builder*] abattre [*building*]; (accidentally) [*person, vehicle, animal*] renverser [*person, object*]; [*lightning, wind*] abattre [*tree, fence*]; fig [*person*] abattre [*obstacle, barrier*]; **2** (reduce) [*buyer*] faire baisser [*price*]; [*seller*] baisser [*price*]; **I managed to ~ him down by a few pounds** j'ai réussi à le faire baisser de plusieurs livres; **3** (allocate) [*auctioneer*] adjuger [*lot*].

■ **knock in**: **~ [sth] in, ~ in [sth]** (deliberately) [*person*] planter [*nail, peg*]; [*golfer*] rentrer○ [*ball*]; (accidentally) [*blow*] enfoncer [*side, top*].

■ **knock into**: **~ into [sb/sth]** heurter.

■ **knock off**: ¶ **~ off**○ [*worker*] arrêter de travailler; ¶ **~ [sb/sth] off, ~ off [sb/sth] 1** (cause to fall) [*person, blow, force*] faire tomber [*person, object*]; [*movement, blow*] désarçonner [*rider*]; [*person*] écarter [*insect*]; [*wind, person*] décapiter [*flower heads*]; [*person, blow*] desceller [*handle, end, car mirror*]; **2** (reduce) **I'll ~ £10 off for you** je vous ferai une réduction de 10 livres; **she wouldn't ~ anything off** elle ne voulait faire aucune réduction; **he ~ed 20% off the bill** il a déduit 20% de la note; **3**○ (steal) subtiliser [*car, object*]; **4**○ (stop) **~ it off!** ça suffit!; **5**◑ (have sex with) culbuter◑ [*person*].

■ **knock out**: ¶ **~ [sb/sth] out, ~ out [sb/sth] 1** (dislodge) [*person, blow*] casser [*tooth*]; [*blast*] souffler [*window*]; [*person, blow*] arracher [*peg, nail, support*]; [*person, blow*] vider [*contents*]; **2** (make unconscious) [*person, blow*] assommer [*person, animal*]; [*drug*] endormir [*person, animal*]; [*boxer*] mettre [qn] au tapis [*opponent*]; **don't drink the punch, it will ~ you out!** ne bois pas le punch, ça va t'assommer!; **all that walking has ~ed him out**○ ça l'a épuisé de marcher si longtemps; **3** (destroy) [*enemy, shell*] faire sauter [*tank*]; [*enemy, shell*] mettre [qch] hors service [*factory*]; [*strike action, breakdown*] paralyser [*production, service*]; **4** Sport (eliminate) [*competitor*] éliminer [*opponent, team*]; **5** Aut (straighten) [*mechanic*] redresser [*dent, metal*]; **6**○ (produce) [*machine*] débiter [*quantity*]; [*person*] jouer [*tune*]; **7**○ (overwhelm) [*performance, appearance, good news*] émerveiller [*person*]; [*bad news*] consterner; ¶ **~ oneself out 1** (become unconscious) s'assommer; **2**○ (become exhausted) s'éreinter○.

■ **knock over**: **~ [sb/sth] over, ~ over [sb/sth]** [*person, animal, vehicle, force*] renverser [*person, animal, object*].

■ **knock through** Constr **you could ~ through into the dining-room** vous pourriez abattre le mur de la salle à manger.

■ **knock together**: ¶ **~ together** [*knees, objects*] s'entrechoquer; ¶ **~ [sth] together, ~ together [sth]**○ **1** (create) bricoler [*furniture, shelter*]; confectionner [*meal*]; mettre [qch] sur pied [*show, reception*]; **2** (bang together) cogner l'un contre l'autre; **they need their heads ~ing together** fig ils auraient besoin d'une bonne leçon.

■ **knock up**: ¶ **~ up** (in tennis) faire des balles (**with** avec); ¶ **~ [sth] up, ~ up [sth] 1**○ (make) bricoler [*furniture, shelter*]; confectionner [*meal, outfit*]; **2**○ Sport [*competitor, player*] totaliser [*points*]; réaliser [*score*]; ¶ **~ [sb] up, ~ up [sb] 1** (awaken) réveiller [*person*]; **2**○ (exhaust) mettre [qn] à plat○; **3**◑ (make pregnant) mettre [qn] en cloque○.

knockabout /ˈnɒkəbaʊt/ **I** *n* **1** Sport échange *m* de balles; **2** US Naut dériveur *m*.
II *adj* [*comedy, comedian*] loufoque.

knockdown /ˈnɒkdaʊn/ *adj* [*price*] sacrifié.

knocker /ˈnɒkə(r)/ **I** *n* (on door) heurtoir *m*.
II knockers *npl* **1**○ (critics) détracteurs *mpl*; **2**◑ (breasts) nichons◑ *mpl*.

knock-for-knock *adj* Insur à torts partagés.

knocking /ˈnɒkɪŋ/ **I** *n* gen coups *mpl*; (in engine) cognement *m*; **to hear a ~ at the door** entendre des coups à la porte.
II *adj* **a ~ sound** gen des coups; (in engine) un cognement.

knocking copy *n* Advertg publicité *f* comparative.

knocking-off time○ /ˌnɒkɪŋˈɒftaɪm/ *n* heure *f* de la sortie.

knock: **~ing shop**◑ *n* maison *f* close; **~-kneed** *adj* cagneux/-euse; **~ knees** *npl* genoux *mpl* cagneux; **~-on** *n* (in rugby) passe *f* en avant; **~-on effect** *n* implications *fpl*.

knock-out /ˈnɒkaʊt/ **I** *n* **1** (in boxing) knock-out *m*; **to win by a ~** gagner par knock-out; **2**○ (show etc) réussite *f*; **to be a ~** [*person*] être fantastique; **he's a ~ on the drums** il est sublime à la batterie.
II *adj* **1** Sport [*competition*] avec tours éliminatoires; **2**○ (incapacitating) [*pills, injection*] sédatif/-ive; **~ drops** sédatif *m*; **3**○ (brilliant) [*idea*] sublime; **to look a ~** être superbe.

knock-up○ /ˈnɒkʌp/ *n* Sport échauffement *m*; **to have a ~** faire des balles○.

knoll /nəʊl/ *n* butte *f*.

knot /nɒt/ **I** *n* **1** (tied part) nœud *m*; **to tie sth in a ~** nouer qch; **2** (tangle in hair, rope) nœud *m*; **to comb the ~s out of one's hair** se démêler les cheveux avec un peigne; **3** (in wood) nœud *m*; **4** fig (group) petit groupe *m* (**of** de); **5** fig (tense feeling) **to have a ~ in one's stomach** avoir l'estomac noué; **6** Naut nœud *m*; **to do 15 ~s** filer 15 nœuds.
II *vtr* (*p prés etc* **-tt-**) nouer [*strings, ends, scarf, handkerchief*] (**together** ensemble); **to ~ one's tie** faire un nœud à sa cravate.
III *vi* (*p prés etc* **-tt-**) [*stomach, muscles*] se nouer.
IDIOMS **to do sth at a rate of ~s** faire qch à toute allure; **to get tied up in ~s** s'embrouiller; **to tie the ~** se marier.

knothole /ˈnɒthəʊl/ *n* trou *m* (laissé par un nœud).

knotty /ˈnɒtɪ/ *adj* **1** (gnarled) [*fingers, joints, wood*] noueux/-euse; **2** fig [*problem*] épineux/-euse.

know /nəʊ/ **I** *vtr* (*prét* **knew** /njuː/; *pp* **known** /nəʊn/) **1** (have knowledge of) connaître [*person, place, characteristics, name, taste, opinion, result, figures, value, rules, decision, situation, system, way*]; savoir, connaître [*answer, language, reason, truth, words*]; **he ~s everything/something** il sait tout/quelque chose; **to ~ sb by name/sight/reputation** connaître qn de nom/vue/réputation; **you ~ Frank, he's always late** tu connais Frank, il est toujours en retard; **to ~ sth by heart** savoir or connaître qch par cœur; **to ~ how to do** savoir faire; (stressing method) savoir comment faire; **I ~ how to swim** je sais nager; **she ~s how to improve it/use it** elle sait comment l'améliorer/l'utiliser; **he certainly ~s how to upset people/make a mess** iron pour contrarier les gens/faire du désordre, il s'y connaît○; **to ~ that...** savoir que...; **to ~ for certain** ou **for sure that...** savoir avec certitude que...; **I wasn't to ~ that** je ne pouvais pas savoir que; **to ~ who/when** savoir qui/quand; **to ~ why/whether** savoir pourquoi/si; **to ~ what love is** savoir ce que c'est que l'amour; **you ~ what children are/she is** tu sais comment sont les enfants/elle est; **to ~ sb/sth as** connaître qn/qch sous le nom de; **Edward, better known as Ted** Edward, plus connu sous le nom de Ted; **Virginia known as Ginny to her friends** Virginia ou Ginny pour ses amis; **I ~ him for** ou **to be a liar** je sais que c'est un menteur; **to let it be known** ou **to make it known that** faire savoir que; **to have known sb/sth to do** avoir déjà vu qn/ qch faire; **I've never known him to lose his temper** je ne l'ai jamais vu se mettre en colère; **it has been known to snow there** il est arrivé qu'il neige ici; **if I ~ you/him** tel que je te/le connais; **he is known to the police** il est connu de la police; **just how well did you ~ the accused?** iron dans quelle mesure connaissiez-vous ou ne connaissiez-vous pas l'inculpé?; **I ~ all about redundancy!** je sais ce que c'est que le chômage!; **as you well ~** comme tu le sais bien; **as well she ~s** elle le sait parfaitement; **(do) you ~ something?, do you ~ what?** tu sais quoi?; **there's no ~ing how/whether** on ne peut pas savoir comment/si; **to ~ one's way home** connaître le chemin pour rentrer chez soi; **to ~ one's way around** fig savoir se débrouiller; **to ~ one's way around a town** bien connaître une ville; **to ~ one's way around a computer/an engine** savoir se débrouiller avec les ordinateurs/les moteurs; **I ~ that for a fact** j'en suis absolument sûr; **I ~ what! you could...** j'ai une idée! tu pourrais...; **he ~s all/nothing about it** il est/il n'est pas au courant; **maybe you ~ something I don't** peut-être que tu sais quelque chose que je ne sais pas; **2** (feel certain) être sûr; **he's dead, I ~ it** il est mort, j'en suis sûr; **I knew it!** j'en étais sûr!; **to ~ that...** être sûr que...; **I ~ my key is here somewhere** je suis sûr que ma clé est quelque part par ici; **I don't ~ that we can** je ne suis pas sûr que nous puissions; **I don't ~ that I want to go really** je ne suis pas vraiment sûr d'avoir envie d'y aller; **I don't ~ that opening the window/taking medicine will make much difference** je ne pense pas que le fait d'ouvrir la fenêtre/de prendre des médicaments puisse changer quelque chose; **3** (realize) se rendre compte; **to ~ to do** savoir qu'il faut faire; **does he ~ to switch off the light?** sait-il qu'il faut éteindre?; **do you ~ how expensive that is?** tu te rends compte combien ça coûte?; **she doesn't ~ just how lucky she's been** elle ne se rend pas compte de la chance qu'elle a eue; **you don't ~ how pleased I am** tu ne peux pas savoir comme je suis content; **she's attractive and doesn't she ~ it!** elle est séduisante et elle le sait!; **don't I ~ it!** ne m'en parle pas!; **4** (recognize) reconnaître (**by** à; **from** de); **I hardly knew him** je l'ai à peine reconnu; **I ~ her by her walk** je la reconnais à sa démarche; **she doesn't ~ a peach from a plum!** elle ne sait pas reconnaître une pêche d'une prune!; **only their parents ~ one from the other** il n'y a que leurs parents qui sachent les distinguer; **she ~s a bargain when she sees one** elle sait repérer les bonnes affaires; **5** (acknowledge) **to be known for sth** être connu pour qch; **to be known for doing** être connu pour faire; **he's known for providing a good service** il est connu pour offrir un bon service; **6** (experience) connaître [*joy, sadness, love*]; **you have to ~ sorrow to ~ what happiness is** il faut avoir connu le chagrin pour savoir ce qu'est le bonheur; **7**‡ Bible connaître†.
II *vi* (*prét* **knew**; *pp* **known**) **1** (have knowledge) savoir; **as you ~** comme vous le savez; **you'll ~ next time** tu le sauras pour la prochaine fois; **I wouldn't ~** je ne saurais dire; **to ~ about** (have information) être au courant de [*event*]; (have skill) s'y connaître en [*computing, engines*]; **he ~s about such things** il s'y connaît; **to ~ of** (from experience) connaître; (from information) avoir entendu parler de; **do you ~ of a...**

short cut? est-ce que tu connais un raccourci?; I ~ of somebody who... j'ai entendu parler de quelqu'un qui...; not that I ~ of pas que je sache; to let sb ~ of ou about tenir qn au courant de [*plans, arrangement, job*]; we'll let you ~ nous vous tiendrons au courant; how should I ~○! comment veux-tu que je sache!; if you must ~ si tu veux tout savoir; wouldn't you like ou love to ~ t'aimerais bien le savoir○; if you drop it on your foot, you'll ~ about it○ si tu le laisses tomber sur ton pied, tu vas le sentir passer○; if the brakes fail, you'll ~ about it si les freins lâchent tu t'en rendras compte; if I were angry with you, you'd ~ about it si j'étais fâché contre toi, je te le ferais savoir; I'd ou I'll have you ~○ je te signale○; you ~ better than to argue with him tu as mieux à faire que de te disputer avec lui; you left her alone? you ought to have known better tu l'as laissée seule? tu n'aurais pas dû; he says he came home early but I ~ better il dit qu'il est rentré tôt mais je n'en crois rien; they don't ~ any better ils n'en savent pas plus; they don't ~ any better, you do! eux ils ne savent peut-être pas, mais toi tu n'as aucune excuse!; **2** (feel certain) 'he won't win'—'oh I don't ~' 'il ne va pas gagner'—'oh je n'en suis pas si sûr'; 'I'll take the morning off'—'I don't ~ about that! ' 'je vais prendre ma matinée'—'c'est ce que vous croyez?'; 'is it useful?'—'I don't ~ about useful, but it was cheap' 'c'est utile?'—'je ne sais pas si c'est utile mais ce n'était pas cher'; I don't ~ about you but... je ne sais ce que tu en penses, mais...; I don't ~! look at this mess! non mais○, regarde un peu ce fouillis!

IDIOMS it takes one to ~ one qui se ressemble s'assemble; not to ~ what to do with oneself ne pas savoir quoi faire de son temps; not to ~ where ou which way to turn fig ne pas savoir à quel saint se vouer; not to ~ where to put oneself ne pas savoir où se mettre; not to ~ whether one is coming or going ne plus savoir ce qu'on fait; it's not what you ~ but who you ~ ce qui compte ce n'est pas d'avoir des connaissances mais des relations; to be in the ~○ être bien informé, être à la coule◐; to be in the ~ about sth○ être au courant de qch; I ~ my place hum je sais que je ne compte pas; well what do you ~! iron en voilà une surprise! iron.

knowable /ˈnəʊəbl/ *adj* susceptible d'être connu.

know: ~-all○ *n* GB je-sais-tout *mf inv*; ~-how○ *n* savoir-faire *m inv*.

knowing /ˈnəʊɪŋ/ *adj* [*look, smile*] entendu; she smiled in a ~ way elle a souri d'un air entendu.

knowingly /ˈnəʊɪŋlɪ/ *adv* **1** (intentionally) [*offend, mislead*] délibérément; **2** (with understanding) [*smile, look*] d'un air entendu.

know-it-all○ *n* US = know-all.

knowledge /ˈnɒlɪdʒ/ *n* **1** (awareness) connaissance *f*; to bring sth to sb's ~ porter qch à la connaissance de qn; it has come to our ~ that il a été porté à notre connaissance que fml, nous avons appris que; to my/your ~ à ma/ta connaissance; with the full ~ of sb au vu et au su de qn; to have ~ of avoir connaissance de; he has no ~ of what happened il ne sait pas ce qui s'est passé; to my certain ~ he... je sais de façon certaine qu'il...; without sb's ~ à l'insu de qn; **2** (factual wisdom) gen connaissances *fpl*; (of specific field) connaissance *f*; ~ of the subject connaissance du sujet; human/technical ~ connaissances humaines/techniques; a thirst for ~ une soif de connaissances; ~ of computing/Monet's work connaissance de l'informatique/des œuvres de Monet; all branches of ~ toutes les branches de la connaissance.

knowledgeable /ˈnɒlɪdʒəbl/ *adj* [*person*] savant; [*article*] bien documenté (about sur); [*remark*] pertinent (about sur); to be ~ about [*person*] s'y connaître en [*subject*].

knowledgeably /ˈnɒlɪdʒəblɪ/ *adv* [*speak, write*] en connaissance de cause.

knowledge: ~-based system *n* système *m* expert; ~ engineer *n* ingénieur *m* de la connaissance, cogniticien/-ienne *m/f*; ~ engineering *n* génie *m* cognitif.

known /nəʊn/ **I** *pp* ▶ know.

II *pp adj* **1** (recognized) [*authority, danger, source*] reconnu; **2** (from acquaintance, experience) [*celebrity, cure*] connu; the most dangerous substance ~ to man la substance la plus dangereuse que l'homme connaisse; **3** (measured) [*weight, quantity*] défini.

knuckle /ˈnʌkl/ *n* **1** (of person) jointure *f* (du doigt), articulation *f* (du doigt); to crack one's ~s faire craquer ses doigts; to rap sb on ou over the ~s lit, fig taper sur les doigts de qn; to get a rap over the ~s lit, fig se faire taper sur les doigts; **2** (on animal) jarret *m*; **3** Culin (of lamb, mutton) gigot *m*; (of pork, veal) jarret *m*; pig's ~s jambonneau *m*.

IDIOMS to be near the ~○ être limite○; to give sb a ~ sandwich◐ balancer son poing dans la figure de qn○.

■ **knuckle down**○ s'y mettre (sérieusement); to ~ down to se mettre sérieusement à [*task, work*].

■ **knuckle under**○ se soumettre, céder.

knuckle: ~bone *n* articulation *f*, jointure *f*; ~bones ▶ 1282 *npl* Games osselets *mpl*; ~-duster *n* coup-de-poing *m* américain; ~head○ *n* crétin○ *m*; ~ joint *n* Anat articulation *f* du doigt, jointure *f* du doigt; Tech (articulation *f* à) genouillère *f*.

knurl /nɜːl/ **I** *n* (in wood) nœud *m*; (in metal) godron *m*.

II *vtr* gen godronner; Tech moleter.

KO○ **I** *n* (*abrév* = knock-out) KO○ *m*.

II *vtr* (*abrév* = knock out) mettre [qn] KO○.

koala (bear) /kəʊˈɑːlə/ *n* koala *m*.

kohl /kəʊl/ *n* Cosmet khôl *m*.

kohlrabi /ˌkəʊlˈrɑːbɪ/ *n* chou-rave *m*.

kook○ /kuːk/ *n* US dingue○ *mf*.

kookaburra /ˈkʊkəbʌrə/ *n* kookaburra *m*.

kookie○, **kooky**○ /ˈkuːkɪ/ *adj* US dingue○.

kopeck /ˈkəʊpek/ ▶ 1143 *n* kopeck *m*.

Koran /kəˈrɑːn/ *n* Coran *m*.

Koranic /kəˈrænɪk/ *adj* coranique.

Korea /kəˈrɪə/ ▶ 1131 *pr n* Corée *f*.

Korean /kəˈrɪən/ ▶ 1486, 1402 **I** *n* **1** (person) Coréen/-éenne *m/f*; **2** Ling coréen *m*.

II *adj* coréen/-éenne; the ~ War la guerre de Corée.

korma /ˈkɔːmə/ *n*: *sorte de curry à la crème et à la noix de coco.*

kosher /ˈkəʊʃə(r)/ *adj* **1** Relig [*meat, food, restaurant*] casher; **2**○ fig (legitimate) it's ~ c'est impeccable, c'est OK○; there's something not quite ~ about it il y a quelque chose de pas très catholique○ là-dedans.

Kosovo /ˈkɒsəvəʊ/ *pr n* Kosovo *m*.

Kowloon /ˌkaʊˈluːn/ *pr n* Kowloon; the ~ Peninsula la péninsule de Kowloon.

kowtow /ˌkaʊˈtaʊ/ *vi* pej courber l'échine; to ~ to sb faire des courbettes à qn pej; to ~ to sth s'incliner devant qch.

KP *n* US *abrév* ▶ kitchen police.

kph (*abrév écrite* = kilometres per hour) km/h.

Kraut○ /kraʊt/ *n, adj* injur boche○ (*mf*) offensive.

Kremlin /ˈkremlɪn/ *pr n* Kremlin *m*.

krill /krɪl/ *n* krill *m*.

Krishna /ˈkrɪʃnə/ *pr n* Krishna.

Krugerrand /ˈkruːgərænd/ *n* Krugerrand *m*.

krypton /ˈkrɪptɒn/ *n* krypton *m*.

KS US Post *abrév écrite* = Kansas.

Kt *n*: *abrév* = knight.

kudos○ /ˈkjuːdɒs/ *n* prestige *m*; to have ~ avoir du prestige; to gain (the) ~ for sth tirer le prestige de qch.

Ku Klux Klan /ˌkuː klʌks ˈklæn/ *n* Ku Klux Klan *m*.

kumquat /ˈkʌmkwɒt/ *n* kumquat *m*.

kung fu /ˌkʊŋ ˈfuː/ ▶ 1282 *n* kung-fu *m*.

Kurd /kɜːd/ *n* Kurde *mf*.

Kurdish /ˈkɜːdɪʃ/ ▶ 1402 **I** *n* Ling kurde *m*.

II *adj* kurde.

Kurdistan /ˌkɜːdɪˈstæn/ *pr n* Kurdistan *m*.

Kuwait /kʊˈweɪt/ ▶ 1131, 1818 *pr n* Koweït *m*.

Kuwaiti /kʊˈweɪtɪ/ ▶ 1486, 1402 **I** *n* Kuweitien/-ienne *m/f*.

II *adj* kuweitien/-ienne.

kvetch○ /kvetʃ/ *vi* US (complain) se plaindre.

kW (*abrév écrite* = kilowatt) kW.

kwashiorkor /kwæʃɪˈɔːkɔː(r)/ ▶ 1354 *n* kwashiorkor *m*.

kWh *n* (*abrév* = kilowatt-hour) kWh.

KY US Post *abrév écrite* = Kentucky.

l, L /el/ *n* **1** (letter) l, L *m*; **2 L** (*abrév écrite* = **litre(s)** GB, **liter(s)** US) l; **3 L** GB Aut (*abrév écrite* = **Learner**) élève *m* conducteur accompagné; **4 L** US Rail **the L** le métro aérien; **5 L** *abrév écrite* = **Lake**; **6 L** *abrév écrite* = **left**; **7 l** (*abrév écrite* = **line**) (in poetry) V; (in prose) l; **8 L** (*abrév écrite* = **large**) L.

la *n* = **lah**.

LA 1 US (*abrév* = **Los Angeles**) LA; **2** US Post *abrév écrite* = **Louisiana**.

lab /læb/ *n* labo○ *m*; ▶ **laboratory**.

Lab. GB Pol (*abrév écrite* = **Labour (Party)**) **H. Moore ~** H. Moore parti travailliste.

lab coat *n* blouse *f* blanche.

label /ˈleɪbl/ **I** *n* **1** lit (on clothing, jar, bottle, luggage) étiquette *f*; (on diagram) légende *f*; **address ~** étiquette d'adresse; **price ~** étiquette (indiquant le prix); **gummed/sticky ~** étiquette gommée/adhésive; **tie-on ~** étiquette à attacher; **own ~** Comm marque *f* de distributeur; **this shop sells own-~ products** ce magasin vend des produits sous sa propre marque; **2** fig étiquette *f*; **to hang** ou **stick a ~ on sb/sth** coller○ une étiquette à qn/qch; **the ~ has stuck** l'étiquette lui est restée; **3** Mus (also **record ~**) label *m*; **a jazz classic on the Bluenote ~** un classique de jazz sorti chez Bluenote or sous le label Bluenote; **4** Comput label *m*; **5** Ling (in grammar) étiquette *f*; (in dictionary) marqueur *m*.
II *vtr* (*p prés etc* **-ll-**, US **-l-**) **1** lit (stick label on) étiqueter [*clothing, jar, bottle, luggage*]; mettre des légendes sur [*diagram*]; **a jar ~led 'rice'** un pot portant l'étiquette 'riz'; **to be ~led 'confidential'/'ozone-friendly'** porter la mention 'confidentiel'/'protège la couche d'ozone'; **a requirement to ~ pasteurized/irradiated products** une obligation d'indiquer si un produit est pasteurisé/irradié; **2** fig (pigeon-hole) classer, étiqueter pej [*person, work*] (**as** comme); **he is usually ~led (as) an impressionist** on le classe or l'étiquète en général comme parmi les impressionnistes; **3** Ling étiqueter.

labelling /ˈleɪblɪŋ/ **I** *n* étiquetage *m*.
II *modif* [*device, scheme, system*] d'étiquetage; [*machine*] à étiqueter.

labia /ˈleɪbɪə/ *npl* lèvres *fpl* (*de la vulve*).

labial /ˈleɪbɪəl/ **I** *n* Ling labiale *f*.
II *adj* Anat, Ling labial.

labiodental /ˌleɪbɪəʊˈdentl/ **I** *n* labiodentale *f*.
II *adj* labiodental.

labiovelar /ˌleɪbɪəʊˈviːlə(r)/ *n, adj* labiovélaire (*f*).

labor *n* US = **labour**.

laboratory /ləˈbɒrətrɪ, US ˈlæbrətɔːrɪ/ **I** *n* laboratoire *m*; **in the ~** au laboratoire.
II *modif* [*animal, equipment, experiment, job, test, manager, staff, report*] de laboratoire; [*research*] en laboratoire.

laboratory: **~ assistant** *n* laborantin/-e *m/f*; **~ technician** *n* technicien/-ienne *m/f* de laboratoire.

labor: **Labor Day** *n* US fête *f* du travail; **Labor Department** *n* US ministère *m* du travail.

labored *adj* US = **laboured**.

laborer *n* US = **labourer**.

laborious /ləˈbɔːrɪəs/ *adj* laborieux/-ieuse.

laboriously /ləˈbɔːrɪəslɪ/ *adv* laborieusement.

labor union *n* US syndicat *m*.

labour GB, **labor** US /ˈleɪbə(r)/ **I** *n* **1** gen (work) travail *m*, labeur *m* liter; **the fruits of one's ~s** les fruits de son travail or son labeur; **to rest from one's ~s** se reposer de son travail; **the division of ~** la division du travail; **to withdraw one's ~** se mettre en grève; **a withdrawal of ~** une grève *f*; **2** Ind (workforce) gen main-d'œuvre *f*; (in contrast to management) ouvriers *mpl*; **material and ~** fournitures et main-d'œuvre; **skilled/unskilled ~** main-d'œuvre *f* qualifiée/non qualifiée; **3** Med accouchement *m*, travail *m* spec; **her ~ lasted 16 hours** son accouchement a duré 16 heures; **an easy/difficult ~** un accouchement facile/difficile; **to be in ~** être en train d'accoucher; **to go into** ou **begin ~** commencer à avoir des contractions; **~ pains** douleurs *fpl* de l'accouchement.
II *modif* [*costs*] de la main-d'œuvre; [*dispute, relations*] ouvriers-patronat *inv*; [*market*] du travail; [*shortage*] de main-d'œuvre; [*leader*] syndical.
III *vi* **1** (work, try hard) travailler (dur) (**at** à; **on** sur; **to do** pour faire); **2** (have difficulties) peiner (**to do** à faire); **he was ~ing to breathe** il peinait à respirer, il respirait péniblement; **to ~ up/down/along** monter/descendre/avancer avec peine or péniblement; **3** Aut [*engine*] peiner; **4 to ~ under** être victime de [*delusion, illusion, misapprehension*]; **he's ~ing under the illusion that he's going to be offered the post** il se fait l'illusion or il s'imagine qu'on va lui offrir la place.
IDIOMS **a ~ of love** une tâche demandant beaucoup de passion; **a ~ of Hercules** un travail de Romain or de titan; **to ~ the point** insister lourdement.

Labour /ˈleɪbə(r)/ **I** *pr n* (+ *v pl*) le parti *m* travailliste.
II *adj* [*supporter, view, manifesto*] du parti travailliste; [*opponent*] au parti travailliste; [*MP*] travailliste; **the ~ vote** le vote travailliste; **to vote ~** voter travailliste.

labour camp *n* camp *m* de travaux forcés, bagne *m*.

laboured GB, **labored** US /ˈleɪbəd/ *adj* **1** (difficult) [*movement*] pénible, laborieux/-ieuse; [*breathing*] difficile; **2** (showing effort) [*joke, humour, speech*] lourd; **it was a rather ~ start** le début était un peu laborieux.

labourer GB, **laborer** US /ˈleɪbərə(r)/ ▶ **1692** *n* ouvrier/-ière *m/f* du bâtiment; **farm ~** ouvrier/-ière *m/f* agricole.

labour: **~ exchange** *n* GB Bourse *f* du Travail; **~ force** *n* main-d'œuvre *f*.

labour-intensive *adj* Ind [*industry*] à forte valeur ajoutée; **to be ~** [*method, process, work*] nécessiter une main-d'œuvre importante.

labour: **~ law** *n* législation *f* or droit *m* du travail; **~ movement** *n* mouvement *m* travailliste; **Labour Party** *n* GB parti *m* travailliste; **~ relations** *npl* relations *fpl* du travail.

labour-saving *adj* [*equipment, feature, system*] qui allège or facilite le travail; **~ device** appareil *m* ménager.

labour ward *n* (room) salle *f* d'accouchement; (ward) salles *fpl* d'accouchement.

labrador /ˈlæbrədɔː(r)/ *n* Zool labrador *m*.

laburnum /ləˈbɜːnəm/ *n* cytise *m*, faux ébénier *m*.

labyrinth /ˈlæbərɪnθ/ *n* Mythol, fig labyrinthe *m*, dédale *m*.

labyrinthine /ˌlæbəˈrɪnθaɪn, US -θɪn/ *adj* labyrinthique.

lace /leɪs/ **I** *n* **1 ¢** (fabric) dentelle *f*; **made of ~** en dentelle; **a piece of ~** une dentelle; **2 C** (on shoe, boot, dress) lacet *m*; (on tent) cordon *m*; **shoe ~s** lacets *mpl* de chaussures; **to tie one's ~s** nouer or attacher ses lacets.
II *modif* [*curtain, dress, handkerchief*] en dentelle; [*industry*] de la dentelle.
III *vtr* **1** (fasten, tie) lacer [*shoes, corset, dress*]; attacher [*tent flap*]; **to ~ sb into** lacer qn dans [*corset*]; **2** (add substance to) **to ~ a drink with sth** mettre qch dans une boisson [*alcohol, poison*]; **his drink was ~d with whisky** on avait mis du whisky dans sa boisson; **to be ~d with** fig être mêlé de [*irony, humour, colour*].
IV *vi* = **lace up**.
■ **lace up**: ¶ **~ up** [*shoe, corset, dress*] se lacer; **the dress ~s up at the back** la robe se lace dans le dos; ¶ **~ [sth] up, ~ up [sth]** lacer [*shoes, boots, corset, dress*]; attacher [*tent flap*].

lace: **~-maker** ▶ **1692** *n* Sewing dentellière *f*; **~-making** *n* Sewing fabrication *f* de la dentelle, dentellerie *f*; **~ punching** *n* Comput perforation *f* en grille.

lacerate /ˈlæsəreɪt/ *vtr* lit lacérer; fig blesser profondément.

laceration /ˌlæsəˈreɪʃn/ *n* gen, Med lacération *f*.

lace: **~-up (shoe)** *n* chaussure *f* à lacet; **~wing** *n* chrysope *f*.

lachrymal /ˈlækrɪml/ *adj* lacrymal.

lachrymose /ˈlækrɪməʊs/ *adj* sout larmoyant.

lacing /ˈleɪsɪŋ/ *n* Comput perforation *f* en grille.

lack /læk/ **I** *n* manque *m* (**of** de); **for** ou **through ~ of** par manque de; **there is no ~ of volunteers** il ne manque pas de volontaires.
II *vtr* manquer de [*confidence, humour, funds, moisture*].
III *vi* **to be ~ing** manquer; **funding was ~ing** le financement manquait; **to be ~ing in** manquer de; **to ~ for nothing** ne manquer de rien.

lackadaisical /ˌlækəˈdeɪzɪkl/ *adj* [*person, attitude*] nonchalant (**about** à l'égard de).

lackey /ˈlækɪ/ *n* laquais *m* also fig, pej.

lacking /ˈlækɪŋ/ *adj* **to be ~** euph [*person*] être un peu simplet/-ette.

Lakes

Normally, English Lake X *becomes* le lac X *in French (note the small* l *at* lac*):*

Lake Michigan = le lac Michigan
Lake Victoria = le lac Victoria

But when a lake shares its name with a town, English Lake X *becomes* le lac de X *in French:*

Lake Annecy = le lac d'Annecy
Lake Constance = le lac de Constance
Lake Como = le lac de Côme

Sometimes English can drop the word Lake *but it is always safe to keep the word* lac *in French:*

Trasimeno = le lac Trasimène
Balaton = le lac Balaton

Loch *and* Lough *in names are normally not translated (note the use of the definite article and the small* l *in French):*

Loch Ness = le loch Ness
Lough Erne = le lough Erne

lacklustre GB, **lackluster** US /ˈlæklʌstə(r)/ *adj* [*person, performance, style*] terne.

laconic /ləˈkɒnɪk/ *adj* laconique.

laconically /ləˈkɒnɪklɪ/ *adv* laconiquement.

lacquer /ˈlækə(r)/ **I** *n* **1** (varnish) also Cosmet laque *f*; **2** Art (ware) laques *mpl*.
II *vtr* **1** laquer [*surface*]; **2** GB mettre de la laque sur [*hair*].

lacrosse /ləˈkrɒs, US -ˈkrɔːs/ ▶ 1282 *n* lacrosse *m*.

lacrosse stick *n* crosse *f*.

lactase /ˈlækteɪz, -teɪs/ *n* lactase *f*.

lactate I /ˈlækteɪt/ *n* lactate *m*.
II /lækˈteɪt/ *vi* produire du lait.

lactation /lækˈteɪʃn/ *n* lactation *f*.

lacteal /ˈlæktɪəl/ **I** *n* vaisseau *m* chylifère.
II *adj* **1** (lymphatic) [*vessel*] chylifère; **2** [*fever, secretion*] lacté.

lactic /ˈlæktɪk/ *adj* lactique.

lactic acid *n* acide *m* lactique.

lactiferous /lækˈtɪfərəs/ *adj* lactifère.

lactogenic /ˌlæktəˈdʒenɪk/ *adj* galactogène.

lactose /ˈlæktəʊs/ *n* lactose *m*.

lacuna /ləˈkjuːnə/ *n* (*pl* **~ae**) lacune *f*.

lacustrine /ləˈkʌstraɪn/ *adj* sout lacustre.

lacy /ˈleɪsɪ/ *adj* en or de dentelle.

lad○ /læd/ **I** *n* **1** (boy) gars○ *m*, garçon *m*; **2** GB (lively man) gars○ *m*; **3** Equit (in racing stables) lad *m*; (in riding stables) palefrenier *m*.
II lads *npl* **the ~s** les copains *mpl*; **to go out with the ~s** sortir avec les copains; **come on ~s!** allez les gars!

ladder /ˈlædə(r)/ **I** *n* **1** (for climbing) échelle *f* also fig; **social/career ~** échelle sociale/professionnelle; **to be at the bottom/top of the ~** lit être au pied/en haut de l'échelle; fig être au bas/au sommet de l'échelle; **to work one's way up the ~** fig gravir les échelons; **2** GB (in stockings) échelle *f*, maille *f* filée.
II *vtr* filer [*stocking*].
III *vi* [*stocking*] filer.

ladder: **~proof** *adj* GB [*stockings*] indémaillable; **~ tournament** *n* Sport ≈ tournoi *m* éliminatoire.

laddie○ /ˈlædɪ/ *n* Scot garçon *m*, petit gars○ *m*; **look here ~** écoute-moi bien petit gars.

laddish○ /ˈlædɪʃ/ *adj* péj macho○ *inv*.

lade /leɪd/ *vtr* (*prét* **laded**, *pp* **laden**) charger.

laden /ˈleɪdn/ **I** *pp* ▶ **lade**.
II *pp adj* [*lorry, cart*] en pleine charge; **~ with** chargé de [*supplies, fruit*]; fig littér accablé de [*remorse, guilt*].

la-di-da○ /ˌlɑːdɪˈdɑː/ *adj* péj [*behaviour, manners*] chochotte○, prétentieux/-ieuse.

ladies' gallery *n* GB Pol galerie *f* des femmes (*à la Chambre des Communes*).

lading /ˈleɪdɪŋ/ *n* chargement *m*.

ladle /ˈleɪdl/ **I** *n* **1** Culin louche *f*; **2** Ind cuillère *f* de coulée.
II *vtr* servir [qch] à la louche [*soup, sauce*].

■ **ladle out**: **~ [sth] out, ~ out [sth] 1** Culin servir [qch] à la louche [*soup, sauce*]; **2** fig se répandre en [*compliments*]; prodiguer [*money, information, advice*].

ladle crane *n* Tech pont *m* de coulée.

lady /ˈleɪdɪ/ (*pl* **ladies**) **I** *n* **1** (woman) dame *f*; **ladies first** les dames d'abord; **ladies and gentlemen** mesdames et messieurs; **the young ~ at the desk** la demoiselle à la réception; **behave yourself, young ~!** (to child) sois sage, ma petite!; **his young ~**† sa bonne amie†; **your good ~**† votre dame†; **my old ~**○ ma bourgeoise○; **a little old ~** une petite vieille; **my dear ~** chère madame; **look here, ~**○**!** écoutez, ma petite dame!; **she's a real ~** fig elle est très distinguée; **the ~ of the house** la maîtresse de maison; **a ~ by birth** une aristocrate de naissance; **2** ▶ 1268 GB (in titles) **Lady Churchill** Lady Churchill.
II Ladies *npl* (on toilets) 'Dames'; **where's the Ladies?** où sont les toilettes?
III *modif* **a ~ doctor/writer** une femme médecin/écrivain.

ladybird /ˈleɪdɪbɜːd/ *n* coccinelle *f*.

Lady Bountiful *n* dame *f* patronnesse; **she likes to play ~** elle joue les mécènes.

lady: **Lady Chapel** *n* chapelle *f* de la Vierge; **Lady Day** *n* Relig fête *f* de l'Annonciation; **~ fern** *n* fougère *f* femelle; **~finger** *n* Culin boudoir *m*; **~ friend** *n* amie *f*; **~-in-waiting** *n* dame *f* d'honneur; **~-killer**○ *n* tombeur○ *m*.

ladylike /ˈleɪdɪlaɪk/ *adj* [*person, behaviour*] distingué; **it is not ~ to do** il n'est pas distingué pour une femme de faire.

ladylove† /ˈleɪdɪlʌv/ *n* dulcinée *f*.

lady mayoress ▶ 1268 *n* GB **1** (mayor's wife) *titre officiel de la femme du lord-maire*; **2 Lady Mayoress** (as form of address) Madame le (lord-)maire.

Lady Muck○ *n* **she thinks she's ~** péj elle se prend pour une grande dame.

lady: **~ orchid** *n* orchis *m* pourpre; **~'s finger** *n* (okra) okra *m*.

Ladyship /ˈleɪdɪʃɪp/ ▶ 1268 *n* **her/your ~** Madame (la baronne or la comtesse etc); **her ~ wants you!** fig, péj Madame la comtesse te demande!

lady's maid *n* femme *f* de chambre.

lag /læg/ **I** *n* **1** (time period) (lapse) décalage *m*; (delay) retard *m*; **2**○ (criminal) **old ~** repris *m* de justice.
II *vtr* (*p prés etc* **-gg-**) calorifuger [*pipe, tank*]; isoler [*roof*].

■ **lag behind**: ¶ **~ behind** [*person, prices*] être à la traîne; ¶ **~ behind [sb/sth]** traîner derrière [*person*]; fig être en retard sur [*rival, comparable product*]; **wages are ~ging behind prices** les salaires sont en retard sur les prix.

lager /ˈlɑːgə(r)/ *n* bière *f* blonde.

lager lout *n* GB péj voyou○ *m* (*qui se soûle à la bière*).

laggard† /ˈlægəd/ *n* traînard/-e *m/f*.

lagging /ˈlægɪŋ/ *n* (material) isolant *m*.

lagging jacket *n* Tech garniture *f* de chaudière.

lagniappe /ˈlænjæp, lɑːnˈjæp/ *n* US (gift) cadeau-réponse *m*; (bonus) prime *f*.

lagoon /ləˈguːn/ *n* lagune *f*.

lah /lɑː/ *n* Mus la *m*.

laicize /ˈleɪɪsaɪz/ *vtr* laïciser.

laid /leɪd/ *prét, pp* ▶ **lay**.

laidback○ /ˌleɪdˈbæk/ *adj* [*approach, attitude*] décontracté.

lain /leɪn/ *pp* ▶ **lie** III 2, 3, 4, 5, 6, 7, 8.

lair /leə(r)/ *n* repaire *m* also fig.

laird /ˈleəd/ *n* Scot propriétaire *m* foncier, laird *m*.

lake /leɪk/ *n* lac *m*.
IDIOMS **go and jump in the ~**○**!** va te faire voir ailleurs○!

lake: **~ dweller** *n* Hist habitant/-e *m/f* d'une cité lacustre; **~ dwelling** *n* Hist habitation *f* lacustre; **Lake Poets** *npl* poètes *mpl* lakistes.

lakeside /ˈleɪksaɪd/ **I** *n* **by the ~** au bord du lac.
II *modif* [*café, scenery*] de bord de lac.

lam○ /læm/ *vtr* (*p prés etc* **-mm-**) **1** (hit) assommer [*person*]; propulser○ [*ball*]; **2** (criticize) = **lam into**.

■ **lam into**: **~ into [sb/sth]** éreinter [*writing, production*]; rentrer dans○ [*person*].

lama /ˈlɑːmə/ *n* lama *m*.

Lamaism /ˈlɑːmeɪzəm/ *n* Relig lamaïsme *m*.

Lamaist /ˈlɑːmeɪst/ *n* Relig lamaïste *mf*.

lamb /læm/ **I** *n* **1** (animal) agneau *m*; **2** ¢ Culin agneau *m*; **leg of ~** gigot *m* d'agneau; **spring ~** agneau de printemps; **3** (term of endearment) ange *m*.
II *modif* Culin [*chops, stew*] d'agneau.
III *vi* [*ewe*] mettre bas; [*farmer*] aider les brebis à mettre bas.

■ **lamb down** agneler.

lambast(e) /læmˈbeɪst/ *vtr* sout **1** (beat) rosser; **2** (censure) vilipender [*person, organization*].

lambent /ˈlæmbənt/ *adj* littér [*flame, sky*] chatoyant; [*humour*] brillant.

lambing /ˈlæmɪŋ/ **I** *n* agnelage *m*.
II *modif* [*season*] de l'agnelage; [*pen*] d'agnelage.

lambrequin /ˈlæmbəkɪn/ **I** *n* lambrequin *m*.
II *modif* [*pattern*] à lambrequins.

lambskin /ˈlæmskɪn/ **I** *n* peau *f* d'agneau.
II *modif* [*garment, rug*] en agneau.

lamb: **~'s lettuce** *n* mâche *f*; **~'s tails** *npl* Bot chatons *mpl*.

lamb's wool /ˈlæmzwʊl/ **I** *n* laine *f* d'agneau, lambswool *m*.
II lamb's-wool, **lambswool** *modif* [*jumper, glove*] en laine d'agneau.

lame /leɪm/ **I** *n* **the ~** (+ *v pl*) les estropiés *mpl*.
II *adj* **1** (unable to walk) [*person, animal*] boiteux/-euse; **to be ~ in the left/right leg** boiter de la jambe gauche/droite; **to go ~** se mettre à boiter; **to be slightly ~** boiter légèrement; **2** fig [*excuse, argument*] boiteux/-euse.
III *vtr* estropier [*person, animal*].

lamé /ˈlɑːmeɪ/ *n* lamé.

lamebrain○ /ˈleɪmbreɪn/ *n* idiot/-e *m/f*, débile○ *mf*.

lame duck I *n* canard *m* boiteux.
II *modif* **~ president/government** *président/gouvernement vaincu qui assure la transition entre les élections et la prise de fonctions du nouveau président*.

lamely /ˈleɪmlɪ/ *adv* [*say*] sans conviction.

lameness /ˈleɪmnɪs/ *n* (of person, animal) claudication *f*; fig (of argument, excuse) faiblesse *f*.

lament /ləˈment/ **I** *n* **1** (expression of grief) lamentation *f*, pleurs *mpl* (**for** pour); **2** Literat (song) complainte *f* (**for** pour); (poem) élégie *f* (**for** à).
II *vtr* **1** (grieve over) pleurer [*wife, loss, death*]; se lamenter sur [*fate, misfortune*]; **the late ~ed John Adams** le regretté John Adams also iron; **2** (complain about) déplorer [*lack, weakness*]; **to ~ that** déplorer que (+ *subj*); **'no-one told me,' he ~ed** 'personne ne me l'a dit,' déplora-t-il.

lamentable /ˈlæməntəbl/ *adj* [*state, situation, result, performance*] déplorable, lamentable; [*incident, affair, lack, loss*] fâcheux/-euse, regrettable.

lamentably /ˈlæməntəblɪ/ *adv* lamentablement.

lamentation /ˌlæmənˈteɪʃn/ *n* **1 C** (expression of grief) lamentation *f*; **2** ¢ (lamenting) lamentations *fpl*.

Lamentations /ˌlæmənˈteɪʃnz/ *pr npl* Bible livre *m* des Lamentations.

laminate I /ˈlæmɪnət/ *n* (plastic) stratifié *m*; (metal) laminé *m*.
II /ˈlæmɪneɪt/ *vtr* laminer [*metal*].

laminated /ˈlæmɪneɪtɪd/ *adj* [*plastic, surface, worktop*] stratifié; [*metal*] laminé;

[*wood*] contreplaqué; [*glass, windscreen*] feuilleté; [*card, cover*] plastifié.

lamp /læmp/ *n* (all contexts) lampe *f*.

lamp: **~black** *n* noir *m* de fumée; **~ bracket** *n* applique *f*.

lampern /ˈlæmpən/ *n* lamproie *f* de rivière.

lamplighter /ˈlæmplaɪtə(r)/ *n* Hist allumeur/-euse *m/f* de réverbères.

lampoon /læmˈpuːn/ **I** *n* satire *f*.
II *vtr* railler [*person, institution*].

lampoonist /læmˈpuːnɪst/ *n* auteur *m* satirique.

lamppost /ˈlæmppəʊst/ *n* réverbère *m*.
IDIOMS **between you, me and the ~** entre nous.

lamprey /ˈlæmprɪ/ *n* lamproie *f*.

lampshade /ˈlæmpʃeɪd/ *n* abat-jour *m*.

LAN *n*: *abrév* ▶ **local area network**.

Lancashire /ˈlæŋkəʃə(r)/ ▶**1624** *pr n* Lancashire *m*.

Lancaster /ˈlæŋkəstə(r)/ *pr n* Hist (house) Lancastre.

lance /lɑːns, US læns/ **I** *n* **1** (weapon) lance *f*; **2** Med lancette *f*.
II *vtr* Med percer [*boil, abscess*].

lance corporal ▶**1612** *n* GB soldat *m* de première classe.

lancer /ˈlɑːnsə(r), US ˈlænsə(r)/ *n* Mil lancier *m*.

lancers /ˈlɑːnsəz, US ˈlænsəz/ *n* (+ *v sg*) quadrille *m* des lanciers.

lancet /ˈlɑːnsɪt, US ˈlæn-/ *n* Med lancette *f*.

lancet: **~ arch** *n* Archit arc *m* en lancette, arc *m* lancéolé; **~ window** *n* Archit fenêtre *f* à lancettes.

Lancs *n* GB Post *abrév écrite* = **Lancashire**.

land /lænd/ **I** *n* **1** Constr, Jur (terrain, property) terrain *m*; (very large) terres *fpl*; **building ~** terrain à bâtir; **the lie** GB ou **lay** US **of the ~** lit le relief du terrain; fig de quoi il en retourne; **get off my ~!** dégagez° de mon terrain!; **private/public ~** propriété *f* privée/publique; **2** Agric (farmland) terre *f*; **barren/fertile ~** terre stérile/fertile; **to live off/work the ~** vivre de/travailler la terre; **a movement back to the ~** un retour à la terre; **3** (countryside) campagne *f*; **to live on/leave the ~** vivre à/quitter la campagne; **4** Pol, gen (country) pays *m*; **foreign/tropical ~** pays étranger/tropical; **from many ~s** de nombreux pays; **throughout the ~** dans tout le pays; **the ~ of** le pays de [*dreams, opportunity*]; **5** (not sea) terre *f*; **dry ~** terre ferme; **I can see ~** je vois la terre; **to reach** ou **make ~** toucher terre; **to remain on ~** rester à terre; **by ~** par voie de terre; **on ~ the bird is clumsy** sur la terre ferme l'oiseau est maladroit; **~ was sighted** la terre était en vue; **~ ahoy!** Naut terre en vue!; **the war on (the) ~** la guerre terrestre.
II *modif* **1** Agric, Constr [*clearance, drainage, development*] du terrain; [*worker*] agricole; **2** Jur [*purchase, sale*] de terrain; [*prices*] du terrain; [*deal, tax*] foncier/-ière; [*law, tribunal*] agraire; **3** gen, Mil [*battle, forces, transport, animal*] terrestre.
III *vtr* **1** Aerosp, Aviat [*pilot*] poser [*aircraft, spacecraft*]; débarquer [*passengers, astronaut*]; décharger [*cargo, luggage*]; **NASA wants to ~ a space capsule on Mars** la NASA veut faire atterrir une capsule spatiale sur Mars; **2** Naut débarquer [*person*] (**on** sur); décharger [*cargo, luggage*] (**on** sur); **3** Fishg prendre [*fish*]; **4**° fig (secure) décrocher° [*job, contract, prize*]; **I ~ed myself a job at the palace** je me suis dégoté° un boulot° au palais; **5**° (saddle with problem) **to ~ sb with** refiler à qn [*task*]; **he ~ed me with washing the car** il m'a refilé la voiture à laver; **to be ~ed with sb/sth** se retrouver avec qn/qch sur les bras; **I was ~ed with the children/with cleaning the equipment** je me suis retrouvé avec les enfants/avec le nettoyage du matériel sur les bras; **now you've really ~ed her in it** ou **in a fine mess!** tu l'as vraiment fichue° dans de beaux draps!; **he ~ed us in court** on s'est retrouvé au tribunal par sa faute; **6**° (deliver) flanquer° [*blow, punch*]; **she ~ed him one (in the eye)** elle lui en a collé une° (dans l'œil).
IV *vi* **1** Aerosp, Aviat [*aircraft, balloon, passenger*] atterrir; [*spacecraft*] (on earth) atterrir; (on moon) atterrir sur la lune, alunir controv; (on planet) se poser; [*passengers, crew*] débarquer; **as the plane came in to ~** alors que l'avion se préparait à atterrir; **2** Naut [*passenger*] débarquer; [*ship*] accoster; **3** Sport, gen [*sportsman, gymnast, animal, insect, bird*] atterrir; [*object, substance*] tomber; hum atterrir; [*ball*] toucher le sol; **he fell and ~ed at the bottom of the stairs** il est tombé et a atterri au bas de l'escalier; **did you see where it ~ed?** tu as vu où c'est tombé or où ça a atterri?; **most of the paint ~ed on me** presque toute la peinture m'est tombée dessus; **the petition ~ed on my desk** fig la pétition a atterri sur mon bureau; **the punch ~ed on his chin** le coup de poing l'a touché au menton; **only one of the darts ~ed on the board** une seule fléchette s'est retrouvée sur la cible.
V *v refl* **to ~ oneself in** se mettre dans [*difficult situation*]; **to ~ oneself with**° se retrouver avec [*task, problem*].
IDIOMS **to find out how the ~ lies** tâter le terrain.
■ **land up**°: ¶ **~ up** (end up) [*person*] se retrouver; [*lost property, object, vehicle*] finir; **the stolen watch/car ~ed up in the river** la montre/voiture volée a fini dans la rivière; **he ~ed up with the bill/in Berlin** il s'est retrouvé avec la facture/à Berlin; ¶ **~ up doing** finir par faire; **she ~ed up doing everything herself/working in a factory** elle a fini par tout faire elle-même/travailler dans une usine.

land: **~ agent** ▶**1692** *n* (on estate) régisseur *m*; (broker) expert *m* foncier; **~ army** *n* GB Hist *corps de femmes employées aux travaux agricoles pendant la guerre*.

landau /ˈlændɔː/ *n* landau *m*.

land: **~ breeze** *n* brise *f* de terre; **~ bridge** *n* pont *m* terrestre; **~ crab** *n* crabe *m* terrestre.

landed /ˈlændɪd/ *adj* [*class*] terrien/-ienne; **the ~ gentry** l'aristocratie terrienne; [*property, estates*] foncier/-ière; **~ cost** Comm prix franco dédouané.

Landes ▶**1163** *pr n* Landes *fpl*; **in/to the ~** dans les Landes.

landfall /ˈlændfɔːl/ *n* Naut (land reached or sighted) escale *f*; **to make ~** [*boat, person*] accoster; [*hurricane*] atteindre la terre.

land: **~fill** *n* enfouissement *m* des déchets; **~fill site** *n* site *m* d'enfouissement des déchets; **~form** *n* Geol relief *m* (du sol); **~ girl** *n* GB Hist *jeune femme employée aux travaux agricoles pendant la guerre*; **~ grant college** *n* US Univ *école ou université d'État où l'enseignement de l'agriculture est obligatoire*.

landing /ˈlændɪŋ/ **I** *n* **1** (at turn of stairs) palier *m*; (storey) étage *m*; **his room is on the next ~** sa chambre est à l'étage supérieur; **2** Mil (of troops) (from boat) débarquement *m*; (from plane) (by parachute) parachutage *m*; (on runway) largage *m*; **a paratroop ~** un parachutage; **3** Naut (of people) débarquement *m*; (of cargo) déchargement *m*; **4** Aerosp, Aviat atterrissage *m* (**on** sur); **night ~** atterrissage de nuit; **moon ~** atterrissage sur la lune; **5** Sport, gen (of animal, athlete, hanglider) réception *f*; (of parachutist, bird, insect) atterrissage *m*.
II *modif* **1** (on stairs) [*light, carpet*] du palier; **2** (at port) [*charges, platform*] de débarquement; **3** Aerosp, Aviat [*procedure*] d'atterrissage.

landing beacon *n* balise *f* d'atterrissage.

landing beam *n* faisceau-guide *m* d'atterrissage.

landing: **~ card** *n* Aviat, Naut carte *f* de débarquement; **~ craft** *n* péniche *f* de débarquement; **~ field** *n* terrain *m* d'aviation; **~ gear** *n* train *m* d'atterrissage; **~ lights** *npl* (on plane) phares *mpl* d'atterrissage; (on airfield) balises *fpl* d'atterrissage; **~ net** *n* Fishg épuisette *f*; **~ party** *n* Mil commando *m* de débarquement; **~ platform** *n* aire *f* d'atterrissage; **~ speed** *n* vitesse *f* d'atterrissage; **~ stage** *n* débarcadère *m*; **~ strip** *n* piste *f* d'atterrissage.

land: **~lady** *n* (owner of property) propriétaire *f*; (living-in) logeuse *f*; (of pub) patronne *f*; **~less** *adj* sans terre; **~ line** *n* Telecom ligne *f* de terre; **~locked** *adj* sans débouché sur la mer; **~lord** *n* (owner of property) propriétaire *m*; (living in) logeur *m*; (of pub) patron *m*; **~lubber** /ˈlændˌlʌbə(r)/ *n* hum ou péj marin *m* d'eau douce.

landmark /ˈlændmɑːk/ **I** *n* point *m* de repère; fig étape *f* importante (**in** dans).
II *modif* [*discovery, reform, speech, victory, event*] décisif/-ive.

land: **~mass** *n* masse *f* terrestre; **~ mine** *n* Mil mine *f* terrestre; **~ of Nod** *n* fig pays *m* des rêves; **~owner** *n* propriétaire *mf* foncier/-ière; **~ ownership** *n* propriété *f* foncière; **~ reform** *n* réforme *f* agraire; **~ registry** *n* cadastre *m*; **Land Rover®** *n* Land Rover® *f*.

landscape /ˈlænskeɪp/ **I** *n* (all contexts) paysage *m*.
II *modif* **1** Art, Phot [*painter, photographer*] spécialiste des paysages; [*art, photography*] paysagiste; [*picture, photo*] de paysage; **2** Archit, Hort [*gardening*] paysagiste; [*architecture, design*] paysager/-ère.
III *vtr* aménager [*grounds*]; **~d garden** jardin aménagé.

landscape: **~ architect** ▶**1692** *n* architecte *mf* paysagiste; **~ format** *n* gen, Comput format *m* horizontal, présentation *f* à l'italienne; **~ gardener** ▶**1692** *n* jardinier/-ière *m/f* paysagiste.

landscaper /ˈlænskeɪpə(r)/ ▶**1692** *n* paysagiste *mf*.

landscaping /ˈlænskeɪpɪŋ/ *n* (art, process) aménagement *m* paysager; (end result) aménagement *m*.

landscapist /ˈlænskeɪpɪst/ ▶**1692** *n* Art (artiste *mf*) paysagiste *mf*.

landslide /ˈlænslaɪd/ **I** *n* **1** Geol glissement *m* de terrain; **2** fig Pol victoire *f* écrasante; **to win by a ~** remporter une victoire écrasante.
II *modif* Pol [*victory, majority*] écrasant.

land: **~slip** *n* glissement *m* de terrain; **~ surveyor** ▶**1692** *n* géomètre *m*; **~ tax** *n* impôt *m* foncier; **~ use** *n* Agric répartition *f* des terres; (in town planning) aménagement *m* du territoire.

landward /ˈlændwəd/ **I** *adj* [*side, boat, island*] face à la terre; [*wind, view*] de mer; [*progress, journey, direction*] vers la terre.
II *adv* [*move, sail*] vers la terre; [*face, gaze*] en direction de la terre.

land yacht *n* char *m* à voile.

lane /leɪn/ *n* **1** (narrow road) (in country) chemin *m*, petite route *f*; (in town) ruelle *f*; **'Church ~'** 'chemin de l'Église'; **2** (of road) voie *f*, file *f*; Aviat, Naut, Sport couloir *m*; **a three-~ road** une route à trois voies; **to keep in ~** GB rester sur la même voie; **'get in ~'** GB 'mettez-vous sur la bonne file'; **to be in the wrong ~** être sur la mauvaise file; **to change ~s** changer de voie or file.

lane: **~ closure** *n* fermeture *f* de voie; **~ discipline** *n* respect *m* du marquage au sol; **~ markings** *n* lignes *fpl* blanches, marquage *m* au sol.

langlauf /ˈlæŋlaʊf/ *n* ski *m* de fond.

language /ˈlæŋgwɪdʒ/ *n* **1** ¢ (system) langage *m*; **the development of ~** le développement du langage; **2** (of a particular nation) langue *f*; **the English ~** la langue anglaise; **3** ¢ (words used by a particular group) gen, Comput langage *m*; **formal/legal ~** langage

Languages

Note that names of languages in French are always written with a small letter, not a capital as in English; also, French almost always uses the definite article with languages, while English does not. In the examples below the name of any language may be substituted for French *and* français*:*

French is easy = le français est facile
I like French = j'aime le français
to learn French = apprendre le français

However, the article is never used after en:

say it in French = dis-le en français
a book in French = un livre en français
to translate sth into French = traduire qch en français

and it may be omitted with parler:

to speak French = parler français *or* parler le français

When French *means* in French *or* of the French, *it is translated by* français:

a French expression = une expression française
the French language = la langue française
a French proverb = un proverbe français
a French word = un mot français

and when you want to make it clear you mean in French *and not* from France, *use* en français:

a French book = un livre en français
a French broadcast = une émission en français

When French *means* relating to French *or* about French *it is translated by* de français:

a French class = une classe de français
a French course = un cours de français
a French dictionary = un dictionnaire de français
a French teacher = un professeur de français

but

a French-English dictionary = un dictionnaire français-anglais

See the dictionary entry for -speaking *and* speaker *for expressions like* Japanese-speaking *or* German speaker. *French has special words for some of these expressions:*

English-speaking = anglophone
a French speaker = un/une francophone

Note also that language adjectives like French *can also refer to nationality e.g.* a French tourist, ▶ 1486, *or to the country e.g.* a French town, ▶ 1131.

formel/juridique; **spoken ~** langue *f* parlée; **bad** ou **strong** ou **foul ~** langage *m* grossier; **mind your ~!** sois poli!; **don't use that ~ with me!** ne me parle pas de cette façon!

IDIOMS **to speak the same ~** parler la même langue.

language: **~ barrier** *n* obstacle *m* or barrière *f* de la langue; **~ laboratory, ~ lab** *n* laboratoire *m* de langues.

Languedoc-Roussillon ▶ 1273 *pr n* Languedoc-Roussillon *m*; **in the ~** dans le Languedoc-Roussillon.

languid /ˈlæŋgwɪd/ *adj* languissant.

languidly /ˈlæŋgwɪdlɪ/ *adv* avec langueur.

languish /ˈlæŋgwɪʃ/ *vi* **1** (remain neglected) **to ~ in** [*person*] languir en [*prison*]; languir dans [*bed*]; [*object*] traîner dans [*garage, box*]; **2** (lose strength) dépérir; **to ~ in the heat** mourir de chaleur; **3** (pine) **to ~ for** se languir de l'absence de [*person*].

languishing /ˈlæŋgwɪʃɪŋ/ *adj* **1** (pathetic) [*look, sigh*] languissant; **2** (failing) [*project, programme, discussion*] infructueux/-euse.

languor /ˈlæŋgə(r)/ *n* langueur *f*.

languorous /ˈlæŋgərəs/ *adj* langoureux/-euse.

languorously /ˈlæŋgərəslɪ/ *adv* d'une manière langoureuse.

lank /læŋk/ *adj* [*hair*] plat.

lanky /ˈlæŋkɪ/ *adj* (grand et) maigre.

lanolin /ˈlænəlɪn/ *n* lanoline *f*.

lantern /ˈlæntən/ *n* **1** (light) lanterne *f*; **2** Archit lanterne *f*, lanterneau *m*.

lantern: **~ fish** *n* poisson-lanterne *m*; **~ fly** *n* fulgore *m* porte-lanterne; **~-jawed** *adj* aux joues creuses; **~ slide** *n* plaque *f* de lanterne magique.

lanthanum /ˈlænθənəm/ *n* lanthane *m*.

lanyard /ˈlænjəd/ *n* **1** (cord round neck) cordon *m*; **2** Naut (rope) ride *f* de hauban.

Lao /ˈlɑːɒ, laʊ/ ▶ 1486, 1402 **I** *n* **1** (person) Laotien/-ienne *m/f*; **2** (language) laotien *m*.
II *adj* laotien/-ienne.

Laos /ˈlɑːɒs, laʊs/ ▶ 1131 *pr n* Laos *m*.

Laotian /ˈlɑːɒʃn, ˈlaʊʃɪən/ *n, adj* = **Lao**.

lap /læp/ **I** *n* **1** (area of body) genoux *mpl*; **to have sth in one's ~** avoir qch sur les genoux; **to be in** ou **on sb's ~** être sur les genoux de qn; **to spill sth in sb's ~** renverser qch sur les genoux de qn; **I spilled coffee in his ~** j'ai renversé du café sur son pantalon; **2** Sport (of track) tour *m* de piste; (of racecourse) tour *m* de circuit; **to run a ~** faire un tour de piste; **a ten-~ race** une course en dix tours; **on the first ~** au premier tour; **a ~ of honour** un tour d'honneur; **to be on the last ~** lit faire le dernier tour; fig en être à la dernière étape; **3** (part of journey) étape *f*.
II *vtr* (*p prés etc* **-pp-**) **1** Sport avoir un tour d'avance sur [*person*]; **2** (drink) laper [*water, milk*]; **3** (overlap) chevaucher.
III *vi* (*p prés etc* **-pp-**) **1** (splash) [*water*] clapoter (**against, at** contre; **on** sur); **2** (overlap) **to ~ over** chevaucher.

IDIOMS **in the ~ of the gods** entre les mains des dieux; **in the ~ of luxury** dans le plus grand luxe; **to drop** ou **dump**○ **a problem in sb's ~** se décharger d'un problème sur qn; **to fall into sb's ~** tomber tout cuit dans le bec de qn○.

■ **lap up**: **~ [sth] up, ~ up [sth] 1** lit laper [*milk, water*]; **2** fig boire [qch] comme du petit lait [*compliment, flattery*]; avaler [*lies, news*].

lap and shoulder belt *n* Aut, Aviat ceinture *f* trois points.

laparoscope /ˈlæpərəskəʊp/ *n* Med laparoscope *m*.

laparoscopy /ˌlæpəˈrɒskəpɪ/ *n* Med laparoscopie *f*.

laparotomy /ˌlæpəˈrɒtəmɪ/ *n* Med laparotomie *f*.

lap belt *n* Aut, Aviat ceinture *f* ventrale.

lapdog *n* **1** lit chien *m* de salon; **2** (person) péj **he's her ~** elle le mène par le bout du nez.

lapel /ləˈpel/ *n* revers *m*; **to grab sb by his ~s** saisir qn par les revers de sa veste.

lapel microphone *n* micro *m* cravate.

lapidary /ˈlæpɪdərɪ, US -derɪ/ *n, adj* lapidaire (*m*).

lapis lazuli /ˌlæpɪs ˈlæzjʊlɪ, US ˈlæzəlɪ/ *n* lapis-lazuli *m*.

lap joint *n* Tech joint *m* à recouvrement.

Lapland /ˈlæplænd/ ▶ 1131 *pr n* Laponie *f*.

Laplander /ˈlæplændə(r)/ *n* Lapon/-onne *m/f*.

Lapp /læp/ ▶ 1486, 1402 **I** *n* **1** (person) Lapon/-onne *m/f*; **2** (language) lapon *m*.
II *adj* lapon/-onne.

lapping /ˈlæpɪŋ/ *n* (sound) clapotis *m*.

lap: **~ riveting** *n* Tech rivetage *m* par recouvrement; **~ robe** *n* US plaid *m*.

lapse /læps/ **I** *n* **1** (slip) défaillance *f*; **a ~ of memory** un trou de mémoire; **a ~ in concentration** un relâchement de l'attention; **2** (moral error) écart *m* de conduite; **a ~ from** un manquement à [*virtue*]; **3** (interval) intervalle *m*, laps *m* de temps; **4** (expiry) (of right, patent, cover, policy) déchéance *f*; **5** (departure) **his ~s into jargon** son passage involontaire au jargon.
II *vi* **1** (drift) **to ~ into** tomber dans [*jargon, slang, coma*]; **to ~ into silence** se taire; **to ~ into unconsciousness** perdre connaissance; **to ~ into bad habits** prendre de mauvaises habitudes; **to ~ into German/dialect** passer à l'allemand/au dialecte; **2** (expire) [*right, patent, act, law*] tomber en désuétude; [*contract, policy, membership*] expirer; [*subscription, insurance, cover*] prendre fin; **3** (slip, slide) [*standard*] baisser; **to ~ from** manquer à [*virtue, principle, standard*].
III lapsed *pp adj* **1** (expired) [*patent, policy*] caduc/-uque; [*contract*] périmé; **2** Relig [*Catholic*] qui n'est plus pratiquant.

lapsus linguae /ˌlæpsəs ˈlɪŋgwaɪ/ *n* Ling lapsus *m*.

laptop /ˈlæptɒp/ Comput **I** *n* portable *m*.
II *modif* [*computer, PC*] portable.

lap welding *n* Tech soudure *f* à recouvrement.

lapwing /ˈlæpwɪŋ/ *n* vanneau *m*.

larceny /ˈlɑːsənɪ/ *n* vol *m*.

larch /lɑːtʃ/ *n* mélèze *m*.

lard /lɑːd/ **I** *n* saindoux *m*.
II *vtr* **1** Culin larder [*meat*]; **2** fig (embellish) **to ~ sth with** truffer qch de [*quotations, allusions*].

larder /ˈlɑːdə(r)/ *n* garde-manger *m inv*.

large /lɑːdʒ/ ▶ 1703 **I** *adj* **1** (big) [*area, car, city, feet, house*] grand (*before n*); [*appetite, piece, fruit, hand, nose, eye*] gros/grosse; **to take a ~ size** prendre une grande taille; **to grow** ou **get ~** grandir; **2** (substantial) [*amount, fortune, sum*] important, gros/grosse (*before n*); [*part*] gros/grosse (*before n*); [*number, quantity*] grand (*before n*); [*population, percentage*] fort (*before n*), important; [*crowd, family*] nombreux/-euse (*after n*); [*proportion*] gros/grosse, fort (*before n*); **to be out in ~ numbers** [*people*] être nombreux/-euses; **3** (fat) [*person*] gros/grosse; **to grow** ou **get ~** grossir, prendre du poids; **4** (extensive) [*selection, range, choice*] grand (*before n*); **in ~ measure, to a ~ extent** en grande partie; **on a ~ scale** [*plan, demolish, reorganize*] sur une grande échelle; [*emigrate, desert*] en grand nombre.
II at large *adj phr* **1** (free) [*prisoner, killer*] en liberté; **2** (in general) [*society, population*] en général, dans son ensemble; **in the country at ~** dans l'ensemble du pays; **the public at ~** le grand public.

IDIOMS **by and ~** de façon générale, en général; **~r than life** [*character, personality*] exubérant; **he turned up two days later as ~ as life** il a réapparu deux jours plus tard bien vivant.

large: **~hearted** *adj* au grand cœur (*after n*); **~ intestine** *n* gros intestin *m*.

largely /ˈlɑːdʒlɪ/ *adv* [*ignored, obsolete, responsible*] en grande partie; **they are ~ children** pour la plupart ce sont des enfants.

largemouth bass *n* perche *f* truitée.

largeness /ˈlɑːdʒnɪs/ *n* (of body, object) grandeur *f*; (of quantity, sum) importance *f*.

large-scale *adj* (all contexts) à grande échelle.

largesse /lɑːˈdʒes/ *n* **1** (generosity) largesse *f*; **2** (gift of money) largesses *fpl*.

large white *n* **1** Agric (pig) porc *m* charcutier; **2** Zool = **cabbage white**.

largish /ˈlɑːdʒɪʃ/ *adj* [*amount, sum*] assez important; [*crowd, house, town*] assez grand (*before n*).

largo /ˈlɑːgəʊ/ *n, adv* largo (*m*).

lariat /ˈlærɪət/ *n* (for catching) lasso *m*; (for tethering) longe *f*.

lark /lɑːk/ *n* **1** Zool alouette *f*; **to be up with the ~** se lever au chant du coq; **2**○ (fun) rigolade○ *f*; **a great ~, a bit of a ~** GB une vraie rigolade○; **to do sth for a ~** faire qch pour rigoler○; **3**○ (unpleasant business) histoire *f*; **I don't think much of this dieting ~** je n'aime pas beaucoup cette histoire de régime.
IDIOMS **to sing like a ~** chanter comme un rossignol.
■ **lark about, lark around**○ GB faire l'idiot.

larkspur /ˈlɑːkspɜː(r)/ *n* pied *m* d'alouette, delphinium *m*.

larva /ˈlɑːvə/ *n* (*pl* **-vae**) larve *f*.

larval /ˈlɑːvəl/ *adj* larvaire.

laryngitis /ˌlærɪnˈdʒaɪtɪs/ ▶ **1354** *n* laryngite *f*.

larynx /ˈlærɪŋks/ *n* larynx *m*.

lasagne /ləˈzænjə/ *n* lasagnes *fpl*.

lascivious /ləˈsɪvɪəs/ *adj* lascif/-ive.

lasciviously /ləˈsɪvɪəslɪ/ *adv* lascivement.

lasciviousness /ləˈsɪvɪəsnɪs/ *n* lascivité *f*.

laser /ˈleɪzə(r)/ *n* laser *m*.

laser: **~ beam** *n* faisceau *m* laser; **~ disc** *n* disque *m* laser; **~-guided** *adj* guidé par laser; **~ printer** *n* imprimante *f* à laser; **~ show** *n* spectacle *m* laser; **~ surgery** *n* chirurgie *f* au laser; **~ treatment** *n* thérapie *f* au laser.

lash /læʃ/ **I** *n* **1** Anat (eyelash) cil *m*; **2** (whipstroke) coup *m* de fouet; **40 ~es** 40 coups de fouet; **3** (whip) lanière *f*; **4** (flogging) supplice *m* du fouet; **to be sentenced to the ~** être condamné au fouet.
II *vtr* **1** lit (whip) fouetter [*animal, person*]; **2** fig (batter) [*rain*] cingler [*windows*]; [*storm*] balayer [*region*]; [*waves*] fouetter [*shore*]; **3** (criticize) (also **~ into**) s'en prendre à [*person*]; **to ~ sb with one's tongue** faire des remarques cinglantes à qn; **4** (secure) attacher (**to** à); **to ~ two things together** attacher deux choses ensemble; **5** (swish) [*animal*] fouetter l'air de [*tail*].
■ **lash down**: ¶ **~ down** [*rain*] tomber violemment; ¶ **~ [sth] down, ~ down [sth]** (secure) arrimer [*cargo, crates*].
■ **lash out 1** (hit out) [*person*] devenir violent, se démener; [*tiger, cat*] donner un coup de patte; **to ~ out at** [*person*] frapper; [*tiger*] donner un coup de patte à; **to ~ out with one's foot** donner des coups de pied; **2** (verbally) invectiver; **to ~ out at** ou **against** invectiver [*person, institution*]; **3** (spend freely) faire une folie; **to ~ out on** faire une folie et acheter [*coat, car*].

lashing /ˈlæʃɪŋ/ **I** *n* **1** (flogging) **to get a ~** recevoir le fouet; **to give sb a ~** fouetter qn; **2** (fastening) amarre *f*.
II lashings○ *npl* GB **~s of** une montagne de [*cream, food*].
III *adj* [*wind*] violent; [*rain*] battant.

lash-up○ /ˈlæʃʌp/ *n* bricolage *m*, installation *f* provisoire.

lass /læs/ *n* GB Dial jeune fille *f*.

lassie /ˈlæsɪ/ *n* GB Dial jeune fille *f*.

lassitude /ˈlæsɪtjuːd, US -tuːd/ *n* sout lassitude *f*.

lasso /læˈsuː/ **I** *n* (*pl* **-oes**) lasso *m*.
II *vtr* attraper [qch] au lasso.

last /lɑːst, US læst/ ▶ **1807** **I** *n* **1** (for shoes) forme *f*; **2** (end of life) **to the ~** jusqu'au bout.
II *pron* **1** (final) **the ~** le dernier/la dernière *m/f* (**to do** à faire); **that was the ~ I saw of her** c'est la dernière fois que je l'ai vue; **I thought we'd seen the ~ of him!** je croyais qu'on en avait fini avec lui!; **I hope we've seen the ~ of the cold weather** j'espère qu'on en a fini avec le froid; **you haven't heard the ~ of this!** l'affaire n'en restera pas là!; **to leave sth till ~** s'occuper de qch en dernier (lieu); **2** (of series) **the ~** le dernier/la dernière *m/f*; **to be the ~ in a long line of Kings** être le dernier (en date) d'une longue lignée de rois; **his new novel is better than the ~** son nouveau roman est meilleur que le dernier or le précédent; **the ~ I heard, he was living in Spain** aux dernières nouvelles, il habitait en Espagne; **the ~ but one** l'avant-dernier/-ière; **the night before ~** (evening) avant-hier soir; (night) la nuit d'avant-hier; **the week before ~** il y a deux semaines; **lovely dresses, this ~ being the most expensive** de belles robes, cette dernière étant la plus coûteuse; **3** (all that remains) **the ~** le dernier/la dernière *m/f*; **'are there any more cakes?'—'no, this is the ~'** 'est-ce qu'il reste des gâteaux?'—'non, c'est le dernier'; **he poured out the ~ of the whisky** il a versé ce qui restait de whisky; **the ~ of the guests were just leaving** les derniers invités prenaient congé.
III *adj* **1** (final) [*hope, novel, time*] dernier/-ière (*before n*); **to the ~ detail** jusqu'au dernier détail; **the ~ car to be made in Abingdon** la dernière voiture fabriquée à Abingdon; **the ~ person to do** la dernière personne à faire; **it is the ~ time that I/you do** c'est la dernière fois que je/tu fais; **for the ~ time, will you be quiet!** c'est la dernière fois que je vous le dis, taisez-vous!; **your ~ name please?** votre nom de famille s'il vous plaît?; **in my ~ job** là où je travaillais avant; **every ~ one of them** tous jusqu'au dernier; **2** (final in series) dernier/-ière; **the ~ house before the garage** la dernière maison avant le garage; **the ~ building/horse but one** l'avant-dernier bâtiment/cheval; **his name is ~ but two on the list** son nom est le troisième à partir de la fin de la liste; **the ~ few children/buildings** les deux ou trois derniers enfants/bâtiments; **3** (describing past time) dernier/-ière; **~ week/year** la semaine/l'année dernière; **~ Tuesday** mardi dernier; **I was in Spain ~ Christmas** j'étais en Espagne à Noël l'an dernier; **in** ou **over the ~ ten years** durant ces dix dernières années; **Anne has been in Cambridge for the ~ eight months** Anne est à Cambridge depuis huit mois; **~ night** (evening) hier soir; (nighttime) cette nuit; **late ~ night** tard hier soir; **this time ~ year** l'an dernier à cette époque-ci; **~ week's figures** les chiffres de la semaine dernière; **~ night's broadcast** l'émission d'hier soir; **4** fig (most unlikely) dernier/-ière; **he's the ~ person I'd ask!** c'est la dernière personne à qui je m'adresserais!; **to be the ~ person to do** être le dernier/la dernière à faire; **I'd be the ~ person to suggest that...** je serais le dernier/la dernière à suggérer que...; **the ~ thing they want is publicity!** la publicité, c'est vraiment ce qu'ils souhaitent le moins!; **the ~ thing I need is guests for the weekend** il ne me manquait plus que des invités pour le week-end iron; **another cat is the ~ thing we need** nous n'avons certainement pas besoin d'un autre chat.
IV *adv* **1** (in final position) **to come in ~** [*runner, racing car*] arriver en dernier; **to be placed ~** être classé dernier/-ière; **the girls left ~** les filles sont parties les dernières; **~ of all** en dernier lieu; **to put sb/sth ~** faire passer qn/qch après tout le reste; **2** (most recently) **she was ~ in Canada in 1976** la dernière fois qu'elle est allée au Canada, c'était en 1976; **the play was ~ performed in 1925** la dernière représentation de la pièce a eu lieu en 1925, la pièce a été jouée pour la dernière fois en 1925.
V *vtr* **a loaf ~s me two days** un pain me fait deux jours; **a loaf of bread lasts my mother a week** ma mère, un pain lui fait la semaine; **we have enough food to ~ (us) three days** nous avons assez de provisions pour trois jours; **there's enough to ~ me a lifetime!** il y en a assez jusqu'à la fin de mes jours!
VI *vi* **1** (extend in time) [*marriage, ceasefire, performance*] durer; **the exhibition ~ed two months** l'exposition a duré deux mois; **it won't ~!** ça ne durera pas longtemps!; **it's too good to ~!** c'est trop beau pour que ça dure!; **he won't ~ long in this place** il ne tiendra pas longtemps ici; **that beer didn' t ~ long** cette bière n'a pas fait long feu○; **I'm afraid the poor dog won't ~ long** je crains que le pauvre chien n'en ait plus pour longtemps; **2** (maintain condition) [*fabric*] faire de l'usage; [*perishables*] se conserver; **these shoes will ~ and ~** ces chaussures sont inusables.
■ **last out**: ¶ **~ out 1** (not run out) [*money*] suffire; [*supplies*] durer; **2** (persist) [*person*] tenir; **she says she's given up smoking, but she'll never ~ out!** elle dit qu'elle a cessé de fumer, mais elle ne tiendra jamais!; **3** (endure siege) [*inhabitants, town*] tenir; ¶ **~ out [sth]** tenir jusqu'à la fin de [*siege*]; **she' ll never ~ out the month** elle ne finira pas le mois.

last-ditch *adj* [*attempt, stand*] désespéré, ultime.

lasting /ˈlɑːstɪŋ, US ˈlæstɪŋ/ *adj* [*effect, impression, contribution*] durable; [*relationship*] sérieux/-ieuse; [*damage*] irréparable; **she made a contribution of ~ value to the community** elle a apporté une contribution durable à la communauté.

Last Judgment *n* Jugement *m* dernier.

lastly /ˈlɑːstlɪ, US ˈlæstlɪ/ *adv* enfin, finalement.

last: **~-mentioned** *pron, adj* dernier/-ière; **~-minute** *adj* [*change, cancellation*] de dernière minute.

last post *n* **the ~** (each evening) la retraite au clairon; (at funeral) la sonnerie aux morts.

last rites *npl* Relig **the ~** les derniers sacrements.

Last Supper *n* Cène *f*.

latch /lætʃ/ **I** *n* **1** (fastening) loquet *m*; **to lift/drop the ~** soulever/abaisser le loquet; **2** (spring lock) serrure *f* (de sûreté); **to put the door on the ~** bloquer le verrou en position ouverte.
II *vtr* fermer [qch] au loquet; **it wasn't properly ~ed** le loquet n'était pas bien mis.
■ **latch on**○: ¶ **~ on** (understand) saisir○; ¶ **~ on to [sth] 1** (seize on) lit s'accrocher à [*handle, object*]; (exploit) exploiter [*idea, trend*]; reprendre [*mistake, weakness*]; **2** (gain possession of) s'emparer de [*ball*]; **3** (realize) se rendre compte de [*truth, secret, fact*]; ¶ **~ on to [sb]** s'accrocher à [*person*].

latch: **~key** *n* clé *f* plate; **~key child, ~key kid**○ *n* GB péj enfant *mf* laissé/-e à lui-/elle-même; **~lock** *n* serrure *f* avec bouton de verrouillage.

late /leɪt/ **I** *adj* **1** (after expected time) [*arrival, rains, publication, implementation*] tardif/-ive; **in case of ~ delivery** en cas de retard de livraison; **~ essays will not be marked** les dissertations rendues en retard ne seront pas corrigées; **to have a ~ lunch** déjeuner plus tard que d'habitude; **to make a ~ start** (getting up) se lever tard; (setting off) partir tard; **to get off to a ~ start** [*meeting, event*] commencer tard; **sorry I'm ~** désolé d'être en retard; **the secretary/her application form was ~** la secrétaire/sa demande est arrivée en retard; **to be ~ for** être en retard pour [*work, school, appointment*]; **to make sb ~** retarder qn; **to be ~ leaving** partir en retard; **to be ~ with the rent** payer son loyer avec du retard; **dinner will be a bit ~** le dîner sera retardé; **Easter is ~ this year** Pâques tombe tard cette année; **if the payment is more than three days ~** si le paiement a

plus de trois jours de retard; **2** (towards end of day, season, life etc) [*hour, supper, date, pregnancy*] tardif/-ive; [*plant, variety*] Bot tardif/-ive; **to have a ~ lecture on Mondays** avoir un cours tard le lundi; **to take a ~ holiday** GB ou **vacation** US prendre des vacances tard en saison; **to keep ~ hours** se coucher tard; **to have a ~ night** (aller) se coucher tard; **you've had too many ~ nights this week** tu t'es couché trop tard toute la semaine; **to watch the ~ film on television** regarder le dernier film à la télévision; **in ~r life** plus tard dans la vie; **to be in one's ~ fifties** approcher de la soixantaine; **a man in his ~ thirties** un homme proche de la quarantaine; **to be a ~ starter** commencer tard; **at this ~ stage** à ce stade avancé; **in ~ January** (à la) fin janvier; **in the ~ 50's/18th century** à la fin des années 50/du XVIIIe siècle; **~ Renaissance art** l'art de la fin de la Renaissance; **~ Victorian** [*architecture etc*] de la fin de l'époque victorienne; **in the ~ Middle Ages** au bas moyen âge; **it will be ~ afternoon when I arrive** j'arriverai en fin d'après-midi; **the ~st appointment is at 4 pm** le dernier rendez-vous est à 16 h; **the ~st date you can apply** la date limite de dépôt des candidatures; **3** (towards end of series) **in one of her ~r films** dans un de ses derniers films; **Shakespeare's ~r plays** les dernières pièces de Shakespeare; **in ~r editions of the newspaper** dans les dernières éditions du journal; **in a ~r novel** dans un roman postérieur; **~r models are fully automatic** les modèles postérieurs sont entièrement automatiques; **her ~r experiments** ses expériences ultérieures; **at a ~r meeting** à une réunion ultérieure; **have you a ~r recording?** avez-vous un enregistrement plus récent?; **the ~st fashions** la dernière mode; **4** (deceased) **the ~ President** feu le Président fml, le défunt Président; **my ~ husband** mon pauvre mari.
II *adv* **1** (after expected time) [*arrive, leave, start, finish*] en retard; **to be running ~** [*person*] être en retard; [*train, bus*] avoir du retard; **to start three months ~** commencer avec trois mois de retard; **2** (towards end of time period) [*get up, go to bed, open, close, end*] tard; **it's ~, let's go to bed** il est tard, allons nous coucher; **~ last night/in the evening** tard hier soir/dans la soirée; **~ last week** à la fin de la semaine dernière; **to work ~** travailler tard; **to work ~ into the night** travailler tard dans la nuit; **as ~ as that** aussi tard (que cela); **~r on** plus tard; **it's a bit ~ in the day to do** fig c'est un peu tard pour faire; **too ~!** trop tard!; **don't leave it too ~!** n'attendez pas trop (longtemps)!; **as ~ as possible** aussi tard que possible; **to leave no ~r than 6 am** partir au plus tard à 6 h; **to marry ~** se marier sur le tard; **to learn Italian ~ in life** apprendre l'italien sur le tard; **he left for Italy six months ~r** il est parti pour l'Italie six mois après; **see you ~r!** à tout à l'heure!; **3** Admin (formerly) **Miss Stewart, ~ of 48 Temple Rd** Mlle Stewart, autrefois domiciliée au 48 Temple Rd.
III of late *adv phr* dernièrement, ces jours-ci.

latecomer /'leɪtkʌmə(r)/ *n* (to lecture, event) retardataire *mf*; **to be a ~ to** venir tard à [*profession, activity*].

late developer *n* **to be a ~** [*child*] être lent; [*adult*] hum être un peu en retard.

lateen /lə'tiːn/ *n* (also **~ sail**) voile *f* latine.

late: **Late Greek** *n* grec *m* du Moyen Âge; **Late Latin** *n* bas latin *m*.

lately /'leɪtlɪ/ *adv* ces derniers temps; **have you seen Rosie ~?** as-tu vu Rosie ces derniers temps?; **until ~** jusqu'à ces derniers temps; **~, she's been working at home** ces derniers temps, elle travaille à la maison.

latency /'leɪtnsɪ/ *n* latence *f*.

lateness /'leɪtnɪs/ *n* **1** (of person, train etc) retard *m*; **~ will not be tolerated** les retards ne seront pas admis; **2** (of time) **because of the ~ of the hour** fml à cause de l'heure tardive.

late-night *adj* [*film*] dernier/-ière (*before n*); [*session*] en nocturne; **it's ~ shopping on Thursdays** les magasins restent ouverts tard le jeudi.

latent /'leɪtnt/ *adj* [*heat, image, talent*] latent; **~ defect** vice *m* caché; **~ period** période *f* de latence.

lateral /'lætərəl/ *adj* latéral; **~ thinking** la pensée latérale.

laterally /'lætərəlɪ/ *adv* latéralement.

late riser *n* lève-tard *mf inv*.

latest /'leɪtɪst/ **I** *superl* ▶ **late**.
II *pron* **1** (news etc) **have you heard the ~?** est-ce que tu connais la dernière○?; **what's the ~ on her condition?** quoi de neuf sur son état de santé?; **2** (most recent) **the ~ in children's fashion/modern technology** la dernière mode enfantine/technologie moderne, la mode enfantine/la technologie moderne dernier cri; **the ~ in a series of attacks/incidents** la dernière attaque/le dernier incident de la série; **3**○ hum (lover) **his/her ~** sa dernière conquête.
III *adj* (most recent) [*book, edition, fashion, model, news etc*] dernier/-ière.
IV at the latest *adv phr* au plus tard.

latex /'leɪteks/ *n* latex *m*.

lath /lɑːθ, US læθ/ *n* latte *f*; **~ and plaster wall** mur *m* fait de lattes recouvertes de plâtre.

lathe /leɪð/ *n* tour *m*.

lather /'lɑːðə(r), 'læðə(r), US 'læð-/ **I** *n* **1** (of soap) mousse *f*; **to work up a ~** faire de la mousse; **2** (frothy sweat) écume *f*; **the horse was in a ~** le cheval était couvert d'écume; **he was in a real ~**○ fig il était dans tous ses états○.
II *vtr* **1** savonner [*face, chin*]; **2**○ (thrash) flanquer une dérouillée○ à.
III *vi* mousser.

latifundia /ˌlætɪ'fʊndɪə/ *npl* latifundia *mpl*.

Latin /'lætɪn, US 'lætn/ ▶ **1402** **I** *n* **1** Ling latin *m*; **low ~** bas latin; **late/vulgar ~** latin décadent/vulgaire; **dog ~** latin de cuisine; **2** (person) Latin/-e *m/f*.
II *adj* **1** Ling [*grammar, author*] latin; [*lesson*] de latin; **2** [*person, culture, country, temperament*] latin; **~ lover** péj ou hum séducteur méditerranéen.

Latin America *pr n* Geog Amérique *f* latine.

Latin American **I** *n* Latino-Américain/-e *m/f*.
II *adj* latino-américain.

Latinist /'lætɪnɪst/ *n* latiniste *mf*.

Latinization /ˌlætɪnaɪ'zeɪʃn, US -nɪ'z-/ *n* latinisation *f*.

Latinize /'lætɪnaɪz/ *vtr* latiniser.

Latino /læ'tiːnəʊ/ *n* US Latino-Américain/-e *m/f*, Latino○ *mf*.

Latin Quarter *n* quartier *m* latin.

latish○ /'leɪtɪʃ/ **I** *adj* [*meal*] tardif/-ive.
II *adv* [*come, arrive*] assez tard.

latitude /'lætɪtjuːd, US -tuːd/ *n* **1** Geog latitude *f*; **57 degrees ~ north** 57 degrés de latitude nord; **in these ~s** sous ces latitudes; **2** (liberty) latitude *f*.

latitudinal /ˌlætɪ'tjuːdɪnl, US -tuːdənl/ *adj* [*mountain, ridge*] qui va d'est en ouest; **~ position** latitude *f*.

latrine /lə'triːn/ *n* latrines *fpl*.

latter /'lætə(r)/ **I** *n* **the ~** ce dernier/cette dernière *m/f*; **he loves dogs and cats, especially the ~** il aime les chiens et les chats, surtout ces derniers or ceux-ci.
II *adj* **1** (second) dernier/-ière; **do you prefer the former or the ~ explanation?** est-ce que vous préférez la première ou la deuxième explication?; **these ~ problems are more serious** ces problèmes-ci sont plus graves; **2** (later) [*half*] deuxième; **in the ~ part of the evening** vers la fin de la soirée; **in his/her ~ years** dans les dernières années de sa vie.

latterday /ˌlætə'deɪ/ *adj* **1** (modern equivalent of) [*crusader, pilgrim, personage*] des temps modernes; **2** (present, recent) [*invention, technique*] d'aujourd'hui.

Latterday Saints *npl* membres *mpl* de l'Église des saints des derniers jours, Mormons *mpl*.

latterly /'lætəlɪ/ *adv* **1** (recently) dernièrement; **2** (in later times) (pendant) les dernières années; **she was with the company for 30 years, ~ as managing director** elle a travaillé pour cette entreprise pendant 30 ans, les dernières années en tant que P-DG.

lattice /'lætɪs/ *n* (screen) treillis *m*; (fence, plant support) treillage *m*.

latticed /'lætɪst/ *adj* treillissé.

lattice: **~ girder** *n* poutre *f* en treillis; **~ window** *n* fenêtre *f* à croisillons de plomb; **~ work** *n* treillis *m*.

Latvia /'lætvɪə/ ▶ **1131** *pr n* Lettonie *f*.

Latvian /'lætvɪən/ ▶ **1486**, **1402** **I** *n* **1** (person) Letton/-on(n)e *m/f*; **2** (language) letton *m*.
II *adj* letton/-on(n)e.

laud /lɔːd/ *vtr* sout louer.

laudable /'lɔːdəbl/ *adj* louable.

laudably /'lɔːdəblɪ/ *adv* [*behave*] de façon louable.

laudanum /'lɔːdənəm/ *n* laudanum *m*.

laudatory /'lɔːdətərɪ, US -tɔːrɪ/ *adj* élogieux/-ieuse.

laugh /lɑːf, US læf/ **I** *n* **1** (amused noise) rire *m*; **he gave a scornful ~** il a eu un rire de dédain; **she gave a loud ~** elle a ri bruyamment; **with a ~** en riant; **to like a good ~** aimer bien rire; **to get** ou **raise a ~** faire rire; **the sketch that got the biggest ~** le sketch qui a provoqué le plus de rires; **if you want a ~ listen to him sing!** si vous voulez rire écoutez-le chanter!; **read this, it'll give you a ~** lis ceci, ça va te faire rire; **2** (source of amusement) **to do sth for a ~**○ faire qch pour rigoler○; **just for a ~** ou **for ~s, they hid her keys**○ ils lui ont caché ses clés, histoire de rigoler○ or de rire; **the film was a good ~** le film était vraiment très drôle; **their brother is a real ~** leur frère est très drôle or marrant○; **she's always good for a ~**○ on s'amuse toujours bien avec elle; **let's go to the party, it will be a ~**○ allons à la fête, on va bien s'amuser; **they had a ~ rehearsing the scene** ils se sont drôlement bien amusés quand ils ont répété la scène; **the script isn't exactly full of ~s** le scénario n'est pas ce qu'on peut appeler hilarant; **what a ~**○! iron quelle bonne blague○!
II *vtr* **he ~ed a sinister/triumphant ~** il a eu un rire sinistre/triomphant; **'of course not!' she ~ed** 'bien sûr que non!' dit-elle en riant.
III *vi* **1** (be audibly amused) rire (**about, over** de); **to make sb ~** faire rire qn; **to ~ out loud** rire aux éclats, rire tout haut; **to ~ at sb/sth** rire de qn/qch; **you shouldn't ~ at your own jokes!** il ne faut pas rire des ses propres blagues○; **she never ~s at my jokes** mes blagues○ ne la font jamais rire; **the children ~ed at the clown** le clown a fait rire les enfants; **I ~ed until the tears ran down my cheeks** j'ai ri aux larmes; **she soon had the audience ~ing** il ne lui a pas fallu longtemps pour faire rire le public; **we're ~ing with you not at you** on ne rit pas méchamment; **he ~ed nervously** il a eu un rire nerveux; **2** (feel amused) rire; **to ~ to oneself** rire en soi-même, rire tout bas; **don't make me ~!** iron laisse-moi rire!, ne me fais pas rire!; **it makes me ~ when I hear him boasting!** ça me fait doucement rire quand je l'entends se vanter!; **I don't know whether to ~ or cry!** je ne sais pas si je dois rire ou bien pleurer!; **to ~ at sb/sth** se moquer de qn/qch ; **he's afraid of being ~ed at** il a peur qu'on se moque de lui; **to be able to**

~ at oneself être capable de se moquer de soi-même; **he doesn't have much to ~ at** ou **about these days** ce n'est pas drôle pour lui en ce moment.
IDIOMS **he who ~s last ~s longest** Prov rira bien qui rira le dernier Prov; **~ and the world ~s with you** celui qui rit s'entoure d'amis; **you'll be ~ing on the other side of your face** tu riras jaune, ça va t'ôter l'envie de rire; **this news will make him ~ on the other side of his face** cette nouvelle va lui ôter l'envie de rire; **to be ~ing all the way to the bank** remplir ses poches; **to have the last ~ over sb** l'emporter finalement sur qn; **she had the last ~** finalement c'est elle qui a bien ri; **to ~ in sb's face** rire au nez de qn; **to ~ oneself sick** ou **silly** se tordre de rire.
■ **laugh off**: **~ [sth] off, ~ off [sth]** écarter [qch] par la plaisanterie [*speculation, accusation*]; dédramatiser [qch] par la plaisanterie [*mistake, defeat*]; choisir de rire de [*criticism, insult*]; **she ~ed the matter off** elle a tourné la chose en plaisanterie; **they won't be able to ~ this one off!** cette fois-ci, ils ne s'en tireront pas par une plaisanterie!

laughable /ˈlɑːfəbl, US ˈlæf-/ *adj* [*attempt, proposal*] ridicule, risible; [*offer, sum*] dérisoire.

laughably /ˈlɑːfəblɪ, US ˈlæf-/ *adv* [*small, naïve*] ridiculement.

laughing /ˈlɑːfɪŋ, US ˈlæfɪŋ/ *adj* [*person*] qui rit; [*eyes, face, expression*] rieur/rieuse; **it's no ~ matter** il n'y a pas de quoi rire; **he's in no ~ mood** (in bad temper) il n'est pas d'humeur à rire; (in low spirits) il n'a pas le cœur à rire.

laughing: **~ gas** *n* gaz *m* hilarant; **~ hyena** *n* hyène *f* (tachetée); **~ jackass** *n* martin-chasseur *m* géant.

laughingly /ˈlɑːfɪŋlɪ, US ˈlæf-/ *adv* [*say, explain*] en riant; **it is ~ called a hotel** cela porte pompeusement le nom d'hôtel.

laughing stock *n* risée *f*; **the ~ of Europe/the neighbourhood** la risée de toute l'Europe/tout le quartier; **they have made us into a ~** ils ont fait de nous un objet de risée.

laughter /ˈlɑːftə(r), US ˈlæf-/ *n* ¢ rires *mpl*; **she could hear ~** elle entendait des rires; **there was ~ at this remark** cette remarque a déclenché les rires; **he announced amid ~ that** au milieu des rires il a annoncé que; **to roar** ou **howl with ~** hurler de rire; **a fit of ~** un fou rire.

laughter line GB, **laugh line** US *n* ≈ ride *f* d'expression.

laughtrack /ˈlɑːftræk, US ˈlæf-/ *n* (bande *f* sonore de) rires *mpl* enregistrés.

launch /lɔːntʃ/ **I** *n* **1** Naut (also **motor ~**) (for patrolling) vedette *f*; (for pleasure) bateau *m* de plaisance; **customs'/police ~** vedette *f* de la douane/de la police; **2** (setting in motion) (of new boat, rocket, satellite) lancement *m*; (of dinghy, lifeboat) mise *f* à l'eau; Advertg, Comm (of campaign, product, publication) lancement *m*.
II *vtr* **1** Naut mettre [qch] à l'eau [*dinghy, lifeboat*]; lancer [*new ship*]; **2** (fire) lancer [*missile, rocket*] (**against, at** sur); **air-/sea-~ed** lancé du ciel/depuis la mer; **3** (start) lancer [*campaign, career, company, hunt, project*]; ouvrir [*investigation*]; mettre [qch] en action [*plan*]; **to ~ an attack on sb/sth** lit lancer une attaque contre qn/qch; fig attaquer qn/qch; **4** Advertg, Comm lancer [*magazine, product, range*].
III *vi* **to ~ (forth) into** se lancer dans [*description, story*]; attaquer [*chorus, song*].
IV *v refl* **to ~ oneself at sb/sth** se lancer sur qn/qch.
■ **launch out** [*company, designer*] se diversifier; **to ~ out into** [*person, company*] se lancer dans [*cosmetics, consultancy, design*].

launch complex *n* Aerosp ensemble *m* de lancement.

launcher /ˈlɔːntʃə(r)/ *n* lanceur *m*.

launching /ˈlɔːntʃɪŋ/ *n* **1** Naut (of boat) mise *f* à l'eau; (of new boat) lancement *m*; **2** Aerosp lancement *m*; **3** Advertg, Comm (starting) (of campaign, product, project) lancement *m*; (of scheme) mise *f* en route.

launch: **~ pad**, **~ing pad** *n* Aerosp aire *f* de lancement; fig tremplin *m* (**for** pour); **~ party** *n* réception *f* (*pour le lancement d'un produit*); **~ platform**, **~ing platform** *n* Aerosp rampe *f* de lancement; **~ site**, **~ing site** *n* Aerosp base *f* de lancement; **~ vehicle** *n* Aerosp fusée *f* de lancement.

launder /ˈlɔːndə(r)/ **I** *vtr* **1** laver [*clothes, linen*]; **freshly ~ed** impeccable; **2** blanchir [*money, profits*].
II *vi* se laver; **it won't ~** vous ne pouvez pas le laver.

launderette /lɔːnˈdret, ˌlɔːndəˈret/ GB, **laundromat** /ˈlɔːndrəmæt/ US *n* laverie *f* automatique.

laundering /ˈlɔːndərɪŋ/ *n* (all contexts) blanchissage *m*.

laundress /ˈlɔːndrɪs/ *n* blanchisseuse *f*.

laundrette *n* GB = **launderette**.

laundromat *n* US = **launderette**.

laundry /ˈlɔːndrɪ/ *n* **1** (place) (commercial) blanchisserie *f*; (in hotel, house) laverie *f*; **2** (linen) linge *m*; **dirty ~** linge sale; **to do the ~** faire la lessive.

laundry: **~ basket** *n* panier *m* à linge; **~ list** *n* lit liste *f* de blanchissage; fig liste *f* interminable; **~ van** *n* camionnette *f* de la blanchisserie; **~ worker** ▶ **1692** *n* employé/-e *m/f* de (la) blanchisserie.

laureate /ˈlɒrɪət, US ˈlɔː-/ *n* lauréat/-e *m/f*; **a Nobel ~** un/-e lauréat/-e du prix Nobel; **the poet ~** GB le poète lauréat.

laurel /ˈlɒrəl, US ˈlɔːrəl/ **I** *n* **1** Bot laurier *m*; **2** (honours) (also **laurels**) lauriers *mpl*; **to crown sb with ~(s)** ceindre la tête de qn de lauriers.
II *modif* [*crown, wreath*] de lauriers.
IDIOMS **to look to one's ~s** veiller à la concurrence; **to rest on one's ~s** se reposer or s'endormir sur ses lauriers.

Laurence /ˈlɒrəns/ *pr n* Laurent.

lav○ /læv/ *n* GB (*abrév* = **lavatory**) toilettes *fpl*.

lava /ˈlɑːvə/ **I** *n* lave *f*.
II *modif* [*bed, flow*] de lave.

lavalier /lɑːˈvɑːlɪə/ *n* US pendentif *m*.

lavatorial /ˌlævəˈtɔːrɪəl/ *adj* [*humour*] scatologique.

lavatory /ˈlævətrɪ, US -tɔːrɪ/ **I** *n* toilettes *fpl*; **gents'/ladies' ~** toilettes pour hommes/dames.
II *modif* [*bowl, door, seat*] des toilettes.

lavatory: **~ attendant** ▶ **1692** *n* employé/-e *m/f* à l'entretien des toilettes, (female) dame *f* pipi○; **~ humour** *n* humour *m* scatologique; **~ paper** *n* papier *m* hygiénique.

lavender /ˈlævəndə(r)/ **I** *n* (all contexts) lavande *f*; **the scent of ~** le parfum de la lavande.
II ▶ **1104** *adj* (colour) lavande *inv*.
III *modif* [*bag, flower, leaf, seed*] de lavande.

lavender blue ▶ **1104** *n, adj* bleu (*m*) lavande *inv*.

laverbread /ˈlɑːvəbred/ *n* gâteau *m* d'algues.

lavish /ˈlævɪʃ/ **I** *adj* [*party, home, lifestyle*] somptueux/-euse; [*hospitality*] généreux/-euse; **to be ~ with sth** être généreux avec qch; **to be ~ in one's praise for sth/sb** être prodigue de louanges sur qch/qn.
II *vtr* prodiguer [*money, affection*] (**on** à); **to ~ praise on sth/sb** se répandre en louanges sur qch/qn.

lavishly /ˈlævɪʃlɪ/ *adv* [*decorated, furnished*] luxueusement; [*spend*] sans compter; [*entertain, give*] généreusement.

lavishness /ˈlævɪʃnɪs/ *n* (of hospitality) générosité *f*; (of decor) luxe *m*.

law /lɔː/ *n* **1** ¢ (body of rules) loi *f*; **to obey/break the ~** respecter/enfreindre la loi; **to be against the ~** être contraire à la loi fml, être interdit; **it is against the ~ to do** il est interdit de faire; **the ~ is on our side** nous avons la loi pour nous; **to be above the ~** être au-dessus des lois; **to remain within the ~** rester dans les limites de la légalité; **the ~ of the land** la législation du pays; **the ~ as it stands** la législation en vigueur; **under Italian ~** d'après la loi italienne; **by ~** conformément à la loi; **it's required by ~** c'est obligatoire légalement; **the bill became ~ yesterday** le projet de loi a été adopté hier; **divine ~** la loi divine; **his word is ~** sa parole fait loi; **2** Jur (rule) loi *f*; **a ~ against** une loi interdisant [*gambling, vagrancy*]; **the ~s on** les lois sur [*gambling, vagrancy*]; **there has been a change in the ~** la loi a été modifiée; **there ought to be a ~ against it** ça devrait être interdit; **3** (justice) justice *f*; **court of ~** cour *f* de justice; **to go to ~** recourir à la justice (**about, over** pour); **in the eyes of the ~** aux yeux de la loi; **to take the ~ into one's own hands** faire justice soi-même; **4**○ (police) police *f*; **I'll have the ~ on you!** je vais appeler la police!; **5** (academic discipline) droit *m*; **to study ~** faire son droit; **6** (principle) loi *f*; **the ~s of nature/motion** les lois de la nature/du mouvement; **the ~s of perspective** les règles *fpl* de la perspective; **the second ~ of thermodynamics** le deuxième principe *m* de la thermodynamique.
IDIOMS **to be a ~ unto oneself** être un peu original.

law: **~-abiding** *adj* respectueux/-euse des lois; **~ and order** *n* ordre *m* public; **~breaker** *n* personne *f* qui enfreint la loi, contrevenant/-e *m/f* à la loi.

law-breaking *n* violation(s) *f(pl)* de la loi; **to encourage ~** encourager à violer la loi.

law: **~ court** *n* tribunal *m*; **~ enforcement agency** *n* US organisme *m* responsable du maintien de l'ordre; **~ enforcement officer** *n* US personne *f* responsable du maintien de l'ordre; **~ faculty** *n* faculté *f* de droit.

lawful /ˈlɔːfl/ *adj* [*custody, owner, strike, excuse*] légal; [*conduct*] licite; [*wife, husband*] légitime; **it is not ~ to do** il est illégal de faire; **to do sth without ~ authority** faire qch illégalement; **to go about one's ~ business** vaquer à ses occupations.

lawfully /ˈlɔːfəlɪ/ *adv* [*act*] légalement.

lawfulness /ˈlɔːflnɪs/ *n* légalité *f*.

lawgiver /ˈlɔːgɪvə(r)/ *n* législateur/-trice *m/f*.

lawless /ˈlɔːlɪs/ *adj* **1** (anarchic) [*period, society*] anarchique; [*area, town*] tombé dans l'anarchie; **2** (rebellious) [*person*] sans foi ni loi.

lawlessness /ˈlɔːlɪsnɪs/ *n* (of period, streets) anarchie *f*; (of person) manque *m* de respect des lois.

law: **Law Lord** *n* GB juge *m* (*siégeant à la Chambre des Lords*); **~man** *n* US policier *m*.

lawn /lɔːn/ *n* **1** (grass) pelouse *f*; **2** (fabric) linon *m*, batiste *f*.

lawnmower /ˈlɔːnməʊə(r)/ *n* tondeuse *f* (à gazon).

lawn tennis ▶ **1282** *n* **1** gen tennis *m*; **2** (on grass) tennis *m* sur gazon.

law school *n* faculté *f* de droit; **to go to ~** faire du or son droit; **to be at ~** être étudiant/-e en droit.

law student *n* étudiant/-e *m/f* en droit.

lawsuit /ˈlɔːsuːt/ *n* procès *m*; **to bring a ~ against** intenter un procès à.

lawyer /ˈlɔːjə(r)/ ▶ **1692** *n* **1** (who practises law) avocat/-e *m/f*; **to hire a ~** engager un avocat; **2** (expert in law) juriste *mf*.

lax /læks/ *adj* **1** (not strict) [*law, regulation, government*] laxiste; [*security*] relâché; **2** Phon lâche, relâché; **3** Med relâché.

laxative /ˈlæksətɪv/ **I** *n* laxatif *m*.
II *adj* laxatif/-ive.

laxity /ˈlæksətɪ/, **laxness** /ˈlæksnɪs/ *n* laxisme *m*.

lay /leɪ/ **I** *prét* ▶ **lie**.
II *n* **1**◑ injur (sexual partner) **she's an easy ~** injur c'est une fille facile offensive; **she's a good ~** injur elle baise● bien offensive; (sex act) baise● *f*; **2** Literat lai *m*.
III *adj* **1** gen [*helper, worker*] non initié; **~ person** profane *mf*; **~ opinion** l'opinion des profanes; **2** Relig [*preacher, member, reader*] laïque; [*brother, sister*] lai.
IV *vtr* (*prét, pp* **laid**) **1** lit (place) poser; (spread out) étaler [*rug, blanket, covering*]; (arrange) disposer; (ceremonially, as offering) déposer [*wreath*]; coucher [*baby, patient*]; **~ the cards face down** posez les cartes face en dessous; **~ the blanket on the ground** étalez la couverture sur le sol; **~ the slices of apple on top** disposez les pommes coupées en tranches sur le dessus; **she laid the baby in the cot** elle a couché le bébé dans le berceau; **to ~ the newspaper on the table** étaler le journal sur la table; **he laid his hand on my forehead** il a posé sa main sur mon front; **he laid his cheek against hers** il a mis sa joue contre la sienne; **to ~ hands on sth** fig (find) mettre la main sur qch; **to ~ hands on sb** Relig imposer les mains à qn; **2** (set for meal) mettre [*table, cutlery, crockery*]; **to ~ the table for lunch** mettre la table pour le déjeuner; **to ~ the table for four** mettre le couvert pour quatre; **to ~ the table with the best china** disposer la plus belle porcelaine sur la table; **to ~ an extra place** ajouter un couvert; **3** (prepare) préparer [*fire, plan, trail*]; poser [*basis, foundation*]; tendre [*trap*]; **4** Constr, Hort, Mil poser [*carpet, tiles, bricks, paving, turf, cable, mine, pipe*]; construire [*railway, road, sewer*]; **5** Zool pondre [*egg*]; **6** fig (attribute) porter [*charge, accusation*]; déposer [*complaint*]; jeter [*curse, spell*] (**on** à); **to ~ stress** ou **emphasis on sth** mettre l' accent sur qch; **to ~ the blame for sth on sb** rejeter la responsabilité de qch sur qn; **7** (bet) gen, Turf parier [*money*] (**on** sur); **8** (suppress) fig dissiper [*fears, doubts, suspicions*]; arrêter [*rumour*]; **9**◑ (have sex with) baiser● avec; **to get laid** se faire sauter●.
V *vi* (*prét, pp* **laid**) **1** Agric, Zool pondre; **2** Naut jeter l'ancre (**off** au large de; **alongside** le long de).
IDIOMS **to ~ it on the line** ne pas mâcher ses mots; **to ~ a finger** ou **hand on sb** (beat) lever la main sur qn; (touch) toucher qn.
■ **lay about**: **~ about [sb]** rouer [qn] de coups; **to ~ about sb with a stick** rouer qn de coups de bâton.
■ **lay aside**: **~ aside [sth], ~ [sth] aside 1** lit (for another activity) poser [*book, sewing, toy*]; (after one stage in process) mettre [qch] de côté [*part-finished dish, model*]; **2** fig (relinquish) abandonner [*studies, cares*]; renoncer à [*responsibility, principle, feeling, inhibition, doubt*].
■ **lay back**: **~ back [sth], ~ [sth] back** coucher [*ears, patient*]; poser [*head*].
■ **lay before**: **~ [sth] before sb** soumettre [qch] à qn [*law, bill*]; exposer [qch] à qn [*case, facts, evidence*]; **I laid the facts before them** je leur ai exposé les faits.
■ **lay by**: **~ by [sth], ~ [sth] by** mettre [qch] de côté [*money, provisions*].
■ **lay down**: **~ down [sth], ~ [sth] down 1** (put horizontal) coucher [*object, baby, patient*]; étaler [*rug, garment, cards*]; **2** (put down) poser [*book, implement, suitcase*]; déposer [*weapon, arms*]; **3** fig (relinquish) **to ~ down one's life for sb/sth** sacrifier sa vie pour qn/qch; **4** (establish) établir [*rule, procedure, plan, course of action*]; poser [*condition*]; donner [*order*]; fixer [*price, charge, wage*]; **it is laid down that...** il est stipulé que...; **5** Constr jeter, poser [*foundations*]; installer [*cable, pipe, drain*]; construire [*road, railway*]; **6** Wine mettre [qch] en cave [*bottles, wine*]; **7** (record) enregistrer [*track*].
■ **lay in**: **~ in [sth]** faire provision de; **we've laid in plenty of beer** nous avons fait une grande provision de bière; **to ~ in supplies of sth** s'approvisionner en qch.
■ **lay into**: **~ into [sb] 1** lit bourrer [qn] de coups; **she laid into me with her umbrella** elle m'a donné des coups de parapluie; **2**○ fig (abuse) **she laid into me** elle m'est tombée dessus○; **the teacher laid into them for being late** le professeur leur est tombé dessus○ à cause de leur retard.
■ **lay off** ¶ (stop)○ arrêter; **~ off! it hurts!** arrête! ça fait mal!; ¶ **~ off [sb], lay [sb] off** (sack) (temporarily) mettre [qn] en chômage technique; (permanently) licencier; ¶ **~ off [sb]** (leave alone)○ laisser [qn] tranquille.
■ **lay on**: **~ on [sth], ~ [sth] on 1** (apply) appliquer [*paint, plaster, glue*]; **2** GB (install) [*workman*] installer [*gas, electricity, water*]; [*owner*] faire installer [*gas, electricity, water*]; **3** (supply) prévoir [*meal, food, service, transport*]; **4** (organize) organiser [*entertainment, excursion*]; donner [*display*]; **5**○ fig (exaggerate) forcer un peu la dose sur○ [*praise, pathos, sarcasm, gratitude, flattery*]; **you laid it on a bit (thick)** tu as forcé un peu la dose○.
■ **lay open**: **~ [sth] open** exposer (**to** à); **to ~ oneself open to** s'exposer à [*accusations, criticism, ridicule, exploitation*].
■ **lay out**: ¶ **~ [sth] out, ~ out [sth] 1** lit (spread out, display) disposer [*goods, cards, food*]; (unfold) étaler [*map, garment, fabric*]; (put ready) préparer [*clothes*]; **2** (design) concevoir [*building, book, magazine, advertisement*]; mettre [qch] en page [*letter, illustrations*]; monter [*page*]; dessiner [*town, village, garden*]; disposer [*buildings, pattern pieces*]; **3** (explain) exposer [*reasons, demands, facts, information*]; **4**○ (spend) débourser [*sum of money*]; ¶ **~ out [sb], ~ [sb] out 1** (prepare for burial) faire la toilette mortuaire de [*dead person, corpse*]; **2**○ (knock unconscious) mettre [qn] KO○.
■ **lay up**: ¶ **~ up [sth], ~ [sth] up 1** (store away) lit faire provision de [*food, supplies*]; fig se préparer [*trouble, problems*]; **2** (take out of service) désarmer [*boat*]; ¶ **~ [sb] up** (confine to bed) forcer [qn] à s'aliter; **to be laid up** être alité; **to be laid up with** être au lit avec [*illness, injury*].

layabout○ /ˈleɪəbaʊt/ *n* péj fainéant/-e○ *m/f*.

layaway /ˈleɪəweɪ/ *n* US, Comm **to put sth on ~** garder qch moyennant caution.

lay: **~-by** *n* GB, Transp aire *f* de repos; **~ days** *npl* Naut jours *mpl* de planche.

layer /ˈleɪə(r)/ **I** *n* **1** couche *f*; **~ of clothing** épaisseur *f* de vêtements; **~ upon ~** couche sur couche; **2** (hen) pondeuse *f*.
II *vtr* **1** Hort marcotter; **2** (in hairdressing) couper [qch] en dégradé; **3** (arrange in layers) disposer [qch] en couches.

layer cake *n* gâteau *m* fourré.

layering /ˈleɪərɪŋ/ *n* Hort marcottage *m*.

layette /leɪˈet/ *n* layette *f*.

laying /ˈleɪɪŋ/ *n* **1** (of floor-covering, foundation stone, pipes, cable, mines, turf) pose *f*; **2** (of railway) construction *f*; **3** (of egg) ponte *f*; **4** Relig **the ~ on of hands** l'imposition *f* des mains.

layman /ˈleɪmən/ *n* gen profane *m*; Relig laïc *m*.

lay-off /ˈleɪɒf/ *n* (permanent) licenciement *m* (*gen pl*); (temporary) mise *f* en chômage technique.

layout /ˈleɪaʊt/ *n* (of page, book, magazine, computer screen) mise *f* en page; (of advertisement, article, report) présentation *f*; (of building, built-in units) agencement *m*; (of flat, rooms, cards) disposition *f*; (of town, village, estate, engine, machine) plan *m*; (of garden, park) dessin *m*; **page ~** mise *f* en page; **road ~** emplacement *m* de la route.

lay: **~out artist** ▶ **1692** *n* maquettiste *mf*; **~over** *n* US Transp (by road, rail) attente *f*; (by sea, air) escale *f*.

Lazarus /ˈlæzərəs/ *pr n* Lazare.

laze /leɪz/ *vi* (also **about, ~ around**) paresser, flemmarder○; **to ~ in the sun** se prélasser au soleil; **I like to ~ in bed at weekends** j'aime bien traîner○ au lit le weekend.
■ **laze away**: **to ~ the time away** passer le temps à ne rien faire.

lazily /ˈleɪzɪlɪ/ *adv* **1** (idly) [*move, wonder etc*] nonchalamment; **2** (relaxedly) [*lie, float*] mollement; **3** (gently) [*flow, bob*] doucement; **4** (out of laziness) par paresse.

laziness /ˈleɪzɪnɪs/ *n* paresse *f*.

lazy /ˈleɪzɪ/ *adj* [*person*] paresseux/-euse; [*smile*] nonchalant; [*yawn*] indolent; [*day, holiday*] paisible; [*movement, pace*] lent; [*excuse*] facile; **~ thinking** paresse *f* intellectuelle.

lazy: **~bones** *n* flemmard/-e○ *m/f*; **~ eye** *n* amblyopie *f*; **~ Susan** *n* plateau *m* tournant.

lb *abrév écrite* = **pound**.

LBO *n*: *abrév* ▶ **leveraged buyout**.

lbw (in cricket) (*abrév* = **leg before wicket**) *faute du batteur qui met la jambe devant le guichet*.

lc *abrév écrite* ▶ **lower case**.

LCD *n* (*abrév* = **liquid crystal display**) affichage *m* à cristaux liquides, LCD spec.

LCP *n*: *abrév* ▶ **link control procedure**.

L-dopa /elˈdəʊpə/ *n* L-dopa *f*.

LDS *n* (*abrév* = **Licentiate of Dental Surgery**) *diplômé en chirurgie dentiste*.

lea /liː/ *n* littér pré *m*.

LEA *n* (*abrév* = **Local Education Authority**) *administration locale qui gère les affaires scolaires*.

leach /liːtʃ/ **I** *vtr* [*rain, water*] lessiver (**from** de).
II *vi* [*substance, pollutant*] s'infiltrer.

lead[1] /liːd/ **I** *n* **1** (winning position in race, game, poll, quiz) **to be in the ~, to have the ~** être en tête; **to go into the ~, to take the ~** passer en tête; **this gave him the ~** ceci lui a permis de passer en tête; **to move into an early ~** passer rapidement en tête; **to share the ~** se partager la première place; **2** (amount by which one is winning) avance *f* (**over** sur); **to have a ~ of three points/half a lap** avoir trois points/un demi-tour de piste d'avance; **to have a six second/three-goal ~** avoir six secondes/trois buts d'avance; **to increase one's ~** creuser l'écart (**by** de); **to increase one's ~ in the polls to 20%** atteindre une avance de 20% dans les sondages; **3** (initiative) **to take the ~** prendre l'initiative; **to take the ~ in doing** être le premier/la première à faire; **to give a** ou **the ~** donner l'exemple (**in doing** en faisant); **to follow sb's ~** suivre l'exemple de qn; **4** (clue) piste *f*; **to have a number of ~s to pursue** avoir plusieurs pistes à suivre; **this was our first real ~** c'était notre première vraie piste; **to give sb a ~ as to** mettre qn sur la piste ou la voie de [*solution, perpetrator*]; **5** Theat, Cin (role) rôle *m* principal, premier rôle *m*; **to play the ~** jouer le rôle principal; **who was the male/female ~?** qui était l'acteur/l'actrice qui jouait le rôle principal?; **6** Journ (story) **to be the ~** être à la une○; **to be the ~ in all the papers** faire la une○ de tous les journaux; **7** Elec (wire) fil *m*; **8** GB (for dog) laisse *f*; **on a ~** en laisse; **to let the dog off the ~** lâcher le chien; **9** (in cards) **it's Nina's ~** c'est à Nina de jouer en premier.
II *modif* [*guitarist, guitar*] premier/-ière (*before n*); [*role, singer*] principal.
III *vtr* (*prét, pp* **led**) **1** (guide, escort) mener, conduire [*person*] (**to sth** à qch; **to sb** auprès de qn; **out of** hors de; **through** à travers); **to ~ sb into the house/into the kitchen** mener or conduire qn dans la

maison/à la cuisine; **to ~ sb up/down** mener or conduire qn en haut de/en bas de [*hill, staircase*]; **to ~ sb back** ramener or reconduire qn (**to** à); **to ~ sb away** éloigner qn (**from** de); **to ~ sb across the road** faire traverser la rue à qn; **to ~ sb to safety/into a trap** conduire qn en lieu sûr/dans un piège; **2** (pull, take by hand or bridle) mener [*child, prisoner, horse*] (**to** à; **into** dans; **by** par); **to ~ sb to his cell** conduire qn dans sa cellule; **3** (bring) [*path, route, sign, clue, sound, smell*] mener [*person*] (**to** à); **where is this discussion ~ing us?** à quoi cette conversation nous mène-t-elle?; **this ~s me to my main point** ceci m'amène à mon sujet principal; **to ~ the conversation onto** amener la conversation sur; **4** (be leader of) mener [*army, team, expedition, attack, strike, revolt, proceedings, procession, parade*]; diriger [*orchestra, research*]; **to ~ sb to victory** mener qn à la victoire; **to ~ the debate** mener les débats; **to ~ a congregation in prayer** entonner les prières; **to ~ the dancing** ouvrir le bal; **5** Sport, Comm (be ahead of) avoir une avance sur [*rival, team*]; **to be ~ing sb by 10 metres** avoir une avance de 10 mètres sur qn, devancer qn de 10 mètres; **to be ~ing Liverpool 4–2** mener par 4 buts à 2 dans le match contre Liverpool; **to ~ the world** être au premier rang mondial; **to ~ the field** (in commerce, research) être le plus avancé; (in race) mener, être en tête; **to ~ the market** être le leader du marché; **6** (cause, influence) **to ~ sb to do** amener qn à faire; **to ~ sb to believe/hope that** amener qn à croire /espérer que; **to be led to believe that** être amené à croire que; **he led me to expect that** d'après ce qu'il m'avait dit je m'attendais à ce que (+ *subj*); **what led you to this conclusion?** qu'est-ce qui vous a amené à cette conclusion?; **everything ~s me to conclude that** tout me porte à conclure que; **to be easily led** être très influençable; **7** (conduct, have) mener [*active life, lazy life*]; **to ~ a life of luxury/idleness** vivre dans le luxe/l'oisiveté; **8** Jur **to ~ a witness** interroger un témoin en lui suggérant les réponses; **9** Games (in cards) jouer [*card*].

IV *vi* (*prét, pp* **led**) **1** (go, be directed) **to ~ to** [*path, route*] mener à; [*door*] s'ouvrir sur; [*exit, trapdoor*] donner accès à; **to ~ back to** ramener à; **to ~ off the corridor** [*passage*] partir du couloir; [*door*] s'ouvrir sur le couloir; **footsteps led away from the scene** des traces de pas partaient du lieu; **2** (result in) **to ~ to** entraîner [*complication, discovery, accident, response*]; **it was bound to ~ to trouble** ça devait mal finir; **one thing led to another, and we**... de fil en aiguille, nous...; **3** (be ahead) [*runner, car, company*] être en tête; [*team, side*] mener; **to ~ by three games/15 seconds** avoir trois jeux/15 secondes d'avance; **to be ~ing in the arms race** être en tête dans la course aux armements; **4** (go first) (in walk, procession) aller devant; (in action, discussion) prendre l'initiative; **5** (in dancing) conduire; **6** Jur **to ~ for** être l'avocat principal de [*defence, prosecution*]; **7** Journ **to ~ with** mettre [qch] à la une○ [*story, headline, picture*]; **8** (in boxing) **to ~ with one's left/right** attaquer de gauche/de droite; **9** (in cards) jouer le premier/la première.

IDIOMS **to ~ the way** (go first) passer devant; (guide others) montrer le chemin; (be ahead, winning) être en tête; **to ~ the way up/down/into** passer devant pour monter/descendre/entrer dans; **to ~ the way in space research** être le numéro un dans le domaine de la recherche spatiale.

■ **lead off** (begin) commencer (**with** par).

■ **lead on**: **~ [sb] on 1** (give false hope) mener [qn] en bateau○ [*client, investor, searcher*]; **2** (sexually) provoquer; **3** (influence) influencer.

■ **lead up to**: **~ up to [sth] 1** (precede) précéder; **the years ~ing up to the war** les années qui ont précédé la guerre; **2** (culminate in) se terminer par [*argument, outburst*]; **3** (introduce) amener [*topic*]; **I had a feeling you were ~ing up to that** je sentais que tu voulais en venir là.

lead[2] /led/ **I** *n* **1** (metal) plomb *m*; **white ~** céruse *f*; **red ~** minium *m*; **2**○ fig (bullets) pruneaux○ *mpl*; **3** (also **black ~**) (graphite) mine *f* de plomb; (in pencil) mine *f*; **4** (on fishing line, in gun cartridge etc) plomb *m*; **5** Naut (for sounding) plomb *m* (de sonde); **6** Print interligne *f*; **7** Constr (of window) (baguette *f* de) plomb *m*; **~s** (of windows) plombure *f* ¢; **8** GB (for roofing) couverture *f* de plomb ¢.

II *modif* [*paint, piping, weight*] en or de plomb.

IDIOMS **to fill** ou **pump sb full of ~**○ cribler qn de balles○; **to get the ~ out**○ US (stop loafing) se bouger; (speed up) se grouiller○; **to go over** US ou **down** GB **like a ~ balloon**○ tomber à plat○; **to swing the ~**○† GB tirer au flanc○.

lead /led/: **~ acetate** *n* acétate *m* de plomb; **~ed lights** *npl* petits carreaux *mpl* (*d'une fenêtre*); **~ed petrol** GB, **~ed gasoline** US *n* essence *f* au plomb; **~ed window** *n* fenêtre *f* à petits carreaux.

leaden /'ledn/ *adj* **1** (made of lead) de plomb, en plomb; **2** (lead coloured) [*sky, clouds*] de plomb; [*complexion*] grisâtre; **3** fig [*silence*] de mort; [*atmosphere*] écrasant; [*footsteps, pace*] lourd; [*performance*] raide.

leader /'li:də(r)/ *n* **1** (chief, head) (of nation) chef *m* d'État, dirigeant/-e *m/f*; (of gang, group, team) chef *m*; (of council, club, association) président/-e *m/f*; (of party, opposition) leader *m*; (of trade union) secrétaire *mf*; (of army, troops) commandant/-e *m/f*; **2** (organizer, instigator) (of expedition) responsable *mf*; (of strike, rebellion, movement) meneur/-euse *m/f*; (of project, operation) directeur/-trice *m/f*; **3** (one in front) (in race or competition) premier/-ière *m/f*; (of procession, line of walkers) chef *m* de file; (climber) premier *m* de cordée; (horse) cheval *m* de tête; **to be among the ~s** être dans le peloton de tête; **the ~s at the end of the first round are**... à la tête du classement à la fin de la première partie nous avons...; **4** (in market, field) leader *m*; **a world ~ in car manufacturing** un leader mondial dans la fabrication des voitures; **5** Mus (in orchestra) premier violon *m*; (conductor of band) chef *m* d'orchestre; **6** Journ éditorial *m*; **7** Zool (of pack) meneur *m*; **8** Jur avocat *m* principal; **9** Hort rejet *m*; **10** Tech, Video (on tape) amorce *f*.

leader: **Leader of the House of Commons** *n* GB Pol Président/-e *m/f* de la Chambre des communes; **Leader of the House of Lords** *n* GB Pol Président/-e *m/f* de la Chambre des lords.

leadership /'li:dəʃɪp/ **I** *n* **1** (of party, state, company) **the ~** les dirigeants *mpl*, la direction *f*; **the party ~** les dirigeants or la direction du parti; **to be elected to the ~** être élu à la direction; **2** (quality) qualités *fpl* de leader; **sb's potential for ~** les capacités de qn à être un leader; **we need firm ~** nous avons besoin d'un véritable leader; **3** (fact of being leader) **during her ~** pendant son mandat; **under the ~ of** sous la direction de.

II *modif* [*struggle*] pour le pouvoir; [*qualities*] de chef, de leader.

leadership contest, **leadership election** *n* élection *f* à la direction du parti.

lead-free /'ledfri:/ *adj* sans plomb.

lead-in /'li:dɪn/ *n* préambule *m*.

leading /'li:dɪŋ/ *adj* **1** (top) [*lawyer, politician, academic etc*] éminent; [*brand*] dominant; [*position*] de premier plan; **a ~ director/actor** un des plus grands metteurs en scène/acteurs; **a ~ company/bank** une des sociétés/banques les plus importantes; **a ~ figure in theatrical circles** un personnage important du monde du théâtre; **2** (main) [*role*] principal; **to play the ~ role in** jouer le rôle principal dans; **he played a ~ role in** il a joué un rôle majeur dans; **3** Sport (in race) [*driver, car*] en tête de course; (in league) [*club, team*] en tête du classement; **4** (at the front) [*division, aircraft, car*] de tête.

leading: **~ aircraftman** ▶**1612** *n* GB Mil caporal *m* dans l'armée de l'air; **~ article** *n* éditorial *m*; **~ case** *n* Jur *affaire qui sert de précédent*; **~ counsel** *n* Jur avocat *m* principal.

leading edge I *n* **1** Aviat bord *m* d'attaque; **2** fig **at the ~ of** à la pointe de [*technology*].

II leading-edge *modif* [*organization, technology*] de pointe.

leading: **~ lady** *n* Theat, Cin vedette *f* féminine, actrice *f* principale; **~ light** *n* membre *m* très actif (**in** de); **~ man** *n* vedette *f* masculine, acteur *m* principal; **~ note** *n* septième *f*; **~ question** *n* question *f* qui suggère la réponse; **~ rein** *n* longe *f*; **~ seaman** ▶**1612** *n* GB Mil quartier-maître *m*.

lead /led/: **~ oxide** *n* oxyde *m* de plomb; **~ pencil** *n* crayon *m* à papier; **~ poisoning** *n* saturnisme *m*, intoxication *f* par le plomb; **~ shot** *n* grenaille *f* de plomb.

lead story /li:d/ *n* histoire *f* à la une○; **to be the ~** être à la une○.

lead time /li:d/ *n* (in production) délai *m* de production; (in delivery) délai *m* de livraison.

leadworks /'ledwɜ:ks/ *n* fonderie *f* de plomb.

leaf /li:f/ **I** *n* (*pl* **leaves** /li:vz/) **1** (of plant) feuille *f*; **dock/oak/lettuce ~** feuille de patience/de chêne/de salade; **autumn leaves** feuilles d'automne; **to come into ~** se couvrir de feuilles; **2** (of paper) feuille *f*; (of book) page *f*, feuillet *m* spec; **3** (of gold, silver) feuille *f*; **4** (of table) (sliding, removable) rallonge *f*; (hinged) abattant *m*.

II -leafed, -leaved (*dans composés*) **red-~** à feuilles rouges; **broad-~** à grandes feuilles.

IDIOMS **to shake like a ~** trembler comme une feuille; **to take a ~ out of sb's book** s'inspirer de qn; **to turn over a new ~** tourner la page.

■ **leaf through**: **~ through [sth]** feuilleter [*pages, papers, book, magazine*]; parcourir [*introduction*].

leaf bud *n* bourgeon *m* à feuilles.

leafless /'li:flɪs/ *adj* sans feuilles.

leaflet /'li:flɪt/ **I** *n* **1** gen dépliant *m* (**on, about** sur); (advertising) prospectus *m* (**on, about** sur); (polemic) tract *m* (**on, about** sur); **information ~** notice *f* explicative; **2** (little leaf) foliole *f*.

II *vtr* **to ~ a town/an area** [*political group*] couvrir une ville/un quartier de tracts; [*advertiser*] couvrir une ville/un quartier de prospectus; **they ~ed every home** gen ils ont distribué des dépliants chez tout le monde.

III *vi* gen distribuer des dépliants; [*advertiser*] distribuer des prospectus; [*party*] distribuer des tracts; **to advertise sth with a ~ing campaign** faire une campagne publicitaire pour qch en distribuant des prospectus.

leaf: **~ mould** GB, **~ mold** US *n* terreau *m* (de feuilles); **~ spinach** *n* épinards *mpl* en branches; **~ tobacco** *n* tabac *m* en feuilles; **~ vegetable** *n* légume *m* dont on consomme la feuille.

leafy /'li:fɪ/ *adj* **1** [*tree, wood*] luxuriant; **2** [*suburb, area*] vert.

league /li:g/ *n* **1** (alliance) gen, Pol ligue *f*; **2** (collaboration) **to be in ~ with** être allié avec; **3** Sport (GB football) (competition) championnat *m*; (association of clubs) ligue *f*; ▶**rugby league**; **4** fig (class) niveau *m*; **they're not in the same ~** ils ne sont pas comparables; **he's out of his ~** il ne fait pas le poids; **to be in the big ~** être dans le peloton de tête; **to be at the top of the exports/unemployment ~** être en tête de

liste des exportateurs/du chômage; **5**‡ Meas lieue *f*.
IDIOMS **to be ~s ahead of sth/sb** être bien meilleur que qch/qn.

league: **~ champion** *n* Sport champion *m* de ligue; **~ championship** *n* Sport championnat *m* de ligue; **~ division** *n* GB Sport division *f* (du championnat de ligue); **League of Nations** *n* Hist Société *f* des Nations; **~ standings** *npl* US = **league table**; **~ table** *n* GB Sport classement *m* du championnat; fig classement *m*.

leak /li:k/ **I** *n* **1** (crack) (in container, roof) fuite *f*; (in ship) voie *f* d'eau; **to plug/stop a ~** gen boucher/arrêter une fuite; Naut aveugler une voie d'eau; **to spring a ~** [*pipe, tank*] se mettre à fuir; **the vessel sprang a ~** une voie d'eau s'est ouverte dans le bateau; **2** (escape) (of liquid, gas) fuite *f*, échappement *m*; Elec (of charge) fuite *f* électrique or de courant; **gas/radiation ~** fuite de gaz/radioactive; **3** Journ (disclosure) fuite *f* (**about** au sujet de); **a press** ou **newspaper ~** une fuite dans la presse; **a security ~** une fuite de documents secrets.
II *vtr* **1** (disclose) divulguer [*information, report, document*]; **2** (expel) [*tank*] répandre [*oil, effluent*] (**into** dans); [*heater*] dégager [*fumes*].
III *vi* **1** (have crack) [*container, pipe, roof*] fuir; [*boat*] faire eau; **2** (seep) [*chemical, liquid, gas*] échapper (**from, out of** de); **to ~ into** se répandre dans [*sea, soil*].
IV leaked *pp adj* [*document, report, information*] divulgué.
V leaking *pres p adj* [*pipe, roof, tank, window*] qui fuit; **~ gas** une fuite de gaz.
IDIOMS **to take a ~**◐ aller se soulager○.
■ **leak away** s'écouler.
■ **leak out** [*information, news, secret*] être divulgué; [*water, chemicals, gas*] se répandre.
■ **leak in** [*water*] s'infiltrer (**through** par).

leakage /ˈli:kɪdʒ/ *n* **1** ¢ (leaking) fuite *f*; **2** (spill) fuite *f*, perte *f*; **3** ¢ (of information, secrets) fuite *f*; **4** Comm, Meas (natural loss) perte *f*.

leaker○ /ˈli:kə(r)/ *n* US taupe *f*, espion/-onne *m/f*

leaky /ˈli:kɪ/ *adj* [*container, tap, pipe, roof*] qui fuit; [*boat*] qui prend l'eau; **to be ~** [*container, tap, roof*] fuir.

lean /li:n/ **I** *n* (meat) maigre *m*.
II *adj* [*person, body, face*] mince; [*meat*] maigre; fig (difficult) [*year, times*] difficile; **to have a ~ time** ou **year** connaître les vaches maigres; **two ~ years** deux années de vaches maigres.
III *vtr* (*prét, pp* **leaned** ou **leant**) appuyer; **to ~ a bike/ladder against a wall** appuyer un vélo/une échelle contre or à un mur; **to ~ one's head on sb's shoulder** appuyer sa tête sur or contre l'épaule de qn; **to ~ one's head out of the window** se pencher par la fenêtre, mettre la tête à la fenêtre; **to ~ one's elbows on sth** s'accouder à qch; **to ~ one's back against the wall** s'adosser au mur.
IV *vi* (*prét, pp* **leaned** ou **leant**) [*wall, building*] pencher; **the bicycle/ladder was ~ing against the wall** la bicyclette/l'échelle était appuyée contre le mur or au mur; **to ~ against a wall** (for support) s'appuyer contre un mur; (with one's back) s'adosser au mur.
IDIOMS **to have a ~ time of it** manger de la vache enragée○.
■ **lean across**: ¶ **~ across** [*person*] se pencher (**to do** pour faire); ¶ **~ across [sth]** se pencher par-dessus [*desk, table*].
■ **lean back** se pencher en arrière; **to ~ back in one's chair** s'appuyer contre le dossier de sa chaise.
■ **lean down** se pencher; **to ~ down from the cab of a lorry** se pencher par la vitre d'un camion.
■ **lean forward** se pencher en avant (**to do** pour faire).
■ **lean on**: ¶ **~ on [sth]** s'appuyer sur [*stick*]; s'accouder à [*window-sill*]; **~ on my arm** appuie-toi sur mon bras; ¶ **~ on [sb] 1** lit s'appuyer sur [*person*]; **2** fig (depend on) compter sur [*person*]; **3** fig (pressurize) faire pression sur [*person*].
■ **lean out**: **~ out** se pencher au dehors; **to ~ out of [sth]** se pencher par [*window*]; se pencher par la vitre de [*vehicle*].
■ **lean over**: ¶ **~ over** [*person*] gen se pencher; (forwards) se pencher en avant; ¶ **~ over [sth]** se pencher par-dessus [*shoulder, wall*].
■ **lean towards** lit se pencher vers; fig [*person, party, object*] pencher vers.

leaning /ˈli:nɪŋ/ *adj* [*tree, post*] penché; **the ~ tower of Pisa** la tour penchée de Pise.

leanings /ˈli:nɪŋz/ *npl* (gift, predisposition) dispositions *fpl*; (tendencies) tendances *fpl*; (inclinations) inclinations *fpl*; **to have artistic ~** avoir des dispositions artistiques; **to have socialist ~** pencher vers le socialisme.

leanness /ˈli:nnɪs/ *n* **1** (of person) minceur *f*; **2** (of meat) absence *f* de gras.

leant /lent/ *prét, pp* ▶ **lean**.

lean-to /ˈli:ntu:/ **I** *n* appentis *m*.
II *modif* [*shed, garage*] en appentis.

leap /li:p/ **I** *n* **1** lit, gen saut *m*, bond *m*; Sport saut *m*; **to take a ~** sauter, faire un saut; **in** ou **at one ~** d'un bond; **2** fig (big step) bond *m* (en avant); **a great ~ forward in sth** un grand bond en avant en qch; **to make the ~ from journalist to novelist** faire le saut du journalisme au roman; **it requires a ~ of the imagination** cela réclame un grand effort d'imagination; **'a giant ~ for mankind'** 'un pas de géant pour l'humanité'; **3** (in price, demand) bond *m* (**in** dans).
II *vtr* (*prét, pp* **leapt, leaped** /li:pt, lept/) **1** (jump over) franchir [qch] d'un bond [*hedge, chasm*]; **2** [*person*] **to ~ three metres** sauter trois mètres; **3** [*rider*] faire sauter [*horse*] (**over** au dessus de).
III *vi* (*prét, pp* **leapt, leaped** /li:pt, lept/) **1** [*person, animal*] bondir, sauter; **to ~ out of the bath/to the phone/to one's feet** bondir or sauter hors de son bain/sur le téléphone/sur ses pieds; **to ~ across** ou **over sth** franchir qch d'un bond; **to ~ out of bed** sauter du lit; **to ~ to safety** sauter pour sauver sa vie; **to ~ up the stairs** monter l'escalier quatre à quatre; **to ~ to sb's defence** fig bondir au secours de qn; **2** fig [*heart*] bondir (**with** de); **her mind ~ed back to her childhood** son enfance lui est revenue brutalement à l'esprit; **the narrative ~s forward to 1950** le récit saute à 1950; **the words ~ed off the page at him** les mots lui ont sauté aux yeux; **3** [*price, profit, charge, stock market*] grimper (**by** de).
IDIOMS **look before you ~** Prov il faut réfléchir avant d'agir; **to come on in ~s and bounds** faire des progrès à pas de géant.
■ **leap around, leap about** sautiller.
■ **leap at** fig: **~ at [sth]** bondir sur [*chance, offer*].
■ **leap in** fig (with answer, retort) se lancer.
■ **leap out** ¶ lit surgir d'un bond (**from behind** de derrière); ¶ **~ out at [sb] 1** surgir en bondissant sur [*passer-by*]; **2** fig (be obvious) sauter aux yeux de [*reader, onlooker*].
■ **leap up 1** (jump to one's feet) bondir sur ses pieds; **to ~ up at sb** [*dog*] bondir sur qn; **2** (rise) [*price, rate*] grimper.

leapfrog /ˈli:pfrɒg/ ▶ 1282 **I** *n* saute-mouton *m*; **to play ~** jouer à saute-mouton.
II *vtr* (*p prés etc* **-gg-**) **1** lit sauter par dessus [*wall, obstacle*]; **2** fig devancer [*rival, opponent*].
III *vi* (*p prés etc* **-gg-**) fig **to ~ over** devancer [*rival, opponent*].

leapt /lept/ *pp, prét* ▶ **leap**.

leap year *n* année *f* bissextile.

learn /lɜ:n/ **I** *vtr* (*prét, pp* **learned** ou **learnt**) **1** (through study, practice) apprendre [*language, facts, trade*]; acquérir [*skills*] (**from** de); **to ~ to do, to ~ how to do** apprendre à faire; **I ~ed a lot from her** elle m'a beaucoup appris; **what we ~ed from the experiment was that** ce que nous pouvons tirer de l'expérience, c'est que; **what did we ~ from it?** qu'est-ce que cela nous a apporté?; **there is a lesson to be ~ed from this** on peut tirer une leçon de ceci; **we ~ed all about computers** nous avons tout appris sur les ordinateurs; **to ~ to live with sb/sth** s'adapter à qn/qch; **2** (discover) **to ~ that** apprendre que; **we'll soon ~ whether he succeeded** nous saurons bientôt s'il a réussi; **3**○ GB (teach) **I'll soon ~ you!** je t'apprendrai, va!; **that'll ~ you!** ça t'apprendra!
II *vi* (*prét, pp* **learned** ou **learnt**) **1** (acquire knowledge) apprendre; **to ~ about sth** apprendre qch; **to ~ from** ou **by experience** apprendre à force d'expérience; **to ~ from one's mistakes** tirer la leçon de ses erreurs; **it's been a ~ing experience** ça a été une expérience pleine d'enseignements; **you'll ~!** un jour tu comprendras!; **it's never too late to ~** il n'est jamais trop tard pour apprendre; **2** (hear information) apprendre (**that** que); **to ~ of** ou **about sb's death** apprendre la mort de qn.
IDIOMS **live and ~** c'est une bonne leçon.
■ **learn off**: **~ [sth] off, ~ off [sth]** apprendre [qch] par cœur.

learned /lɜ:nɪd/ *adj* **1** [*person, book, article*] érudit; [*remark, speech*] savant; [*journal*] spécialisé; [*society*] savant; **my ~ friend** Jur mon distingué confrère; **2** /lɜ:nd/ Psych [*behaviour, response*] acquis.

learnedly /ˈlɜ:nɪdlɪ/ *adv* savamment.

learner /ˈlɜ:nə(r)/ *n* apprenant/-e *m/f*; **foreign language ~s** apprenants en langue étrangère; **he's only a ~** ce n'est qu'un débutant; **to be a quick ~** apprendre vite; **slow ~** Sch élève *m/f* lent/-e; **to be a slow ~** avoir du mal à assimiler.

learner driver *n* GB élève *m/f* d'auto-école.

learning /ˈlɜ:nɪŋ/ *n* **1** (erudition) érudition *f*; **the amount of ~ in that book is phenomenal** le niveau d'érudition de ce livre est phénoménal; **to wear one's ~ lightly** ne pas faire étalage de son érudition; **2** (process) apprentissage *m*; **the ~ of social skills** l'apprentissage de la vie en société.
IDIOMS **a little ~ is a dangerous thing** Prov il est dangereux de jouer aux experts.

learning curve *n* courbe *f* d'apprentissage.

learning difficulties *npl* **children with ~** enfants *mfpl* avec des difficultés scolaires, enfants *mpl* en grande difficulté; **adults with ~** adultes *mfpl* avec des difficultés d'apprentissage.

learning: **~ disability** *n* US Sch difficultés *fpl* scolaires; **~ disabled child** *n* US Sch enfant *mf* ayant des difficultés scolaires; **~ process** *n* processus *m* d'apprentissage; **~ resources centre** *n* centre *m* de documentation et d'information.

learnt /lɜ:nt/ *prét, pp* ▶ **learn**.

lease /li:s/ **I** *n* Jur (contract, period of time) bail *m*; **to take out a ~ on an apartment** prendre un appartement à bail; **a one-year ~** un bail d'un an; **long ~** bail à long terme.
II *vtr* **1** [*tenant*] louer [qch] à bail [*house, premises*]; [*client*] louer [*car*]; **2** = **lease out**.
IDIOMS **to give sb a new ~ of** GB ou **on** US **life** [*operation, new drug*] redonner vie à qn; [*news, experience*] redonner des forces à qn; **to give a new ~ of life to** donner un second souffle à [*party, company, movement*]; **the city has been given a new ~ of** ou **on life** la ville connaît un regain de vitalité.
■ **lease out**: **~ out [sth], ~ [sth] out** louer [qch] à bail [*property*].

leaseback /ˈli:sbæk/ *n* cession-bail *f*.

leasehold /ˈliːshəʊld/ **I** *n* (property) propriété *f* louée à bail; (tenure) bail *m*.
II *adj* [*property*] loué à bail.
III *adv* à bail.

lease: **~holder** *n* locataire *mf* à bail; **~hold reform** *n* révision *f* du bail.

leash /liːʃ/ *n* **1** (for dog) laisse *f*; **to have one's dog on a ~** tenir son chien en laisse; **2** fig **to keep sb on a short** ou **tight ~** tenir la bride haute à qn; **to be straining at the ~** [*person*] brûler d'impatience.

leasing /ˈliːsɪŋ/ **I** *n* (by company) crédit-bail *m*; (by individual) location *f* avec option d'achat.
II *modif* [*company, scheme*] de leasing.

least /liːst/ (*superl of* **little**)

■ **Note** When *the least* is used as a quantifier followed by a noun to mean *the smallest quantity of* it is translated by *le moins de*: *to have the least food* = avoir le moins de nourriture.
– But when *the least* is used as a quantifier to mean *the slightest* it is translated by *le* or *la moindre*: *I haven't the least idea* = je n'en ai pas la moindre idée.
– For examples of these and particular usages see I below.
– For translations of *least* as a pronoun or adverb see II and III below.
– The phrase *at least* is usually translated by *au moins*.
– For examples and exceptions see IV below.
– For the phrase *in the least* see V below.

I *quantif* **(the) ~** (le) moins de; (in negative constructions) (le or la) moindre; **they have the ~ food** ce sont eux qui ont le moins de nourriture or le moins à manger; **they have the ~ chance of winning** ce sont eux qui ont le moins de chance de gagner; **they haven't the ~ chance of winning** ils n'ont pas la moindre chance de gagner; **I haven't the ~ idea** je n'en ai pas la moindre idée; **he didn't have the ~ difficulty in believing her** il n'a pas eu la moindre difficulté à la croire; **the ~ thing annoys him** la moindre chose l'agace; **he wasn't the ~ bit jealous/worried** il n'était pas jaloux/inquiet le moins du monde or du tout; **'were you frightened?'—'not the ~ bit!'** 'est-ce que tu avais peur?'—'pas le moins du monde!'
II *pron* le moins; **nobody has very much but we have the ~** personne n'en a beaucoup mais c'est nous qui en avons le moins; **buy the one that costs the ~** achète le moins cher (or la moins chère); **it was the ~ I could do** c'était la moindre des choses!; **the ~ he could have done was phone the police** il aurait au moins pu appeler la police; **that's the ~ of our problems!** c'est le cadet de nos soucis!; **that's the ~ of it** ce n'est pas tout; **she was surprised, to say the ~ (of it)** le moins qu'on puisse dire, c'est qu'elle était surprise.
III *adv* **1** (with adjective or noun) **the ~** le/la moins; (with plural noun) les moins; **she was the ~ satisfied of all** c'était elle la moins satisfaite de tous; **the ~ wealthy/powerful families** les familles les moins riches/puissantes; **2** (with verbs) le moins *inv*; **I like that one (the) ~** c'est celui-là que j'aime le moins; **they are the ones who need it (the) ~** ce sont eux qui en ont le moins besoin; **just when we ~ expected it** juste quand on s'y attendait le moins; **those ~ able to afford to pay** ceux qui peuvent le moins se permettre de payer; **those ~ able to cope** ceux qui ont le plus de mal à se débrouiller; **nobody was very enthusiastic about this idea, the president ~ of all** ou **~ of all the president** personne n'a accueilli cette idée avec enthousiasme, le président encore moins que les autres; **not ~ because** entre autres parce que, à commencer parce que.
IV at least *adv phr* (stating minimum quantity or advantage) au moins; (qualifying statement) du moins; **there were at ~ 50 people in the room** il y avait au moins 50 personnes dans la pièce; **it must have cost at ~ £1,000** cela a dû coûter au moins 1 000 livres sterling; **she's at ~ 40** elle a au moins 40 ans; **he's at ~ as qualified as she is** il est au moins aussi qualifié qu'elle; **they could at ~ have phoned!** ils auraient au moins pu téléphoner!; **you could at ~ have told me!** tu aurais pu au moins me le dire!; **at ~ she didn't suffer** au moins elle n'a pas souffert; **he's gone to bed—at ~ I think so** il est allé se coucher—du moins, je pense; **he has never been there—at ~, that's what he says** il n'y a jamais été—du moins, c'est ce qu'il dit; **such people are at the very ~ guilty of negligence** de telles personnes sont au moins coupables de négligence; **candidates should, at the very ~, be proficient in two foreign languages** les candidats devront maîtriser au moins deux langues étrangères.
V in the least *adv phr* **I'm not worried in the ~, I'm not in the ~ (bit) worried** je ne suis pas inquiet le moins du monde; **I'm not hungry in the ~, I'm not in the ~ (bit) hungry** je n'ai absolument pas faim; **it doesn't bother me in the ~** ça ne me dérange pas le moins du monde; **it doesn't matter in the ~** ça n'a pas la moindre importance; **not in the ~!** pas du tout!, pas le moins du monde!
IDIOMS **last but not ~, last but by no means ~** enfin et surtout.

leastways○ /ˈliːstweɪz/, **leastwise**○ /ˈliːstwaɪz/ US *adv* en tout cas.

leather /ˈleðə(r)/ **I** *n* **1** (material) cuir *m*; **2** (also **wash ~**) peau *f* de chamois; **3** = **stirrup leather**.
II leathers *npl* vêtements *mpl* en cuir.
III *modif* [*garment, object*] de cuir, en cuir.
IV○ *vtr* rosser [*person*].
IDIOMS **to go hell for ~**○ [*person, vehicle*] aller à un train d'enfer○.

leather: **~ bar**○ *n* bar-cuir *m*; **~-bound** *adj* relié en cuir.

leatherette /ˌleðəˈret/ *n* similicuir *m*.

leather goods *npl* gen articles *mpl* en cuir; (expensive) maroquinerie *f*.

leathering○ /ˈleðərɪŋ/ *n* tannée● *f*.

leather: **~jacket** *n* GB Zool larve *f* de la tipule; **~neck**○ *n* US argot des marines marine *m* (américain), fusilier-marin *m* (américain).

leathery /ˈleðərɪ/ *adj* [*skin*] tanné; [*meat*] coriace.

leave /liːv/ **I** *n* **1** (also **~ of absence**) (time off) gen congé *m*; Mil permission *f*; **to take ~** prendre des congés; **to take three days' ~** prendre trois jours de congé; **I've taken all my ~ for this year** j'ai pris tous mes congés pour cette année; **to be granted 24 hours' ~** Mil recevoir une permission de 24 heures; **to be on ~** gen être en congé; Mil être en permission; **to come home on ~** Mil rentrer en permission; **2** (permission) autorisation *f*; **to give sb ~ to do** donner à qn l'autorisation de faire; **to have sb's ~ to do** avoir l'autorisation de qn de faire; **to ask sb's ~ to do, to ask ~ of sb (to do)** sout demander à qn l'autorisation de faire; **by** ou **with your ~** avec votre permission; **without so much as a by your ~** sans autre forme de procès; **3** (departure) **to take ~ of sb** prendre congé de qn; **he took his ~** il a pris congé.
II *vtr* (*prét, pp* **left**) **1** (depart from) gen partir de [*house, station etc*]; (more permanently) quitter [*country, city etc*]; (by going out) sortir de [*room, building*]; **he left home early** il est parti tôt de chez lui; **to ~ school** (permanently) quitter l'école; **the plane/train ~s Paris for Nice at 9.00** l'avion/le train pour Nice part de Paris à 9 heures; **to ~ the road/table** quitter la route/table; **to ~ France to live in Canada** quitter la France pour aller vivre au Canada; **to ~ the track** [*train*] dérailler; **to ~ the ground** [*plane*] décoller; **to ~ one's seat** se lever; **I left him cleaning his car** quand je suis parti, il nettoyait sa voiture; **the smile left her face** fig son sourire s'est effacé; **as soon as the words left her lips...** à peine eut-elle fini de parler...; **2** (leave behind) (forgetfully) laisser [*person*]; oublier [*object*]; (deliberately) quitter [*partner*]; laisser [*key, instructions, name, tip, address*] (**for** pour; **with** chez); (permanently) abandonner [*animal, children, family*]; **he left his umbrella on the train** il a oublié son parapluie dans le train; **the kittens had been left in a sack** on avait abandonné les chatons dans un sac; **she's left her husband** elle a quitté son mari; **to ~ sb sth** laisser qch à qn; **I've left him some instructions/ the key** je lui ai laissé des instructions/la clé; **to ~ sb/sth in sb's care** confier qn/qch à qn; **3** (let remain) laisser [*food, drink, gap, choice*]; **he left his vegetables/wine** il a laissé ses légumes/son vin; **you ~ me no choice** ou **alternative but to...** vous ne me laissez pas d'autre choix que de...; **he left us in no doubt as to** ou **about his feelings** il ne nous a laissé aucun doute quant à ses sentiments; **to ~ sth lying around** laisser traîner qch; **to ~ sth tidy/open/in ruins** laisser qch en ordre/ouvert/en ruines; **to ~ sb homeless** laisser qn sans domicile; **to be left homeless** se retrouver sans domicile; **there are/we have five minutes left** il reste/il nous reste cinq minutes; **he was left short of money/time** il ne lui restait plus beaucoup d'argent/de temps; **he stared at what was left of the house** il a regardé longuement ce qui restait de la maison; **ten minus seven ~s three** Math sept ôtés de dix, il reste trois; **the accident left him an orphan/a cripple** l'accident a fait de lui un orphelin/un invalide; **the attack left her with a scar/a broken nose** elle a gardé une cicatrice/un nez cassé après l'agression; **where does that ~ me?** qu'est-ce que je vais devenir?; **4** (allow to do) **to ~ sth to sb** laisser [qch] à qn [*job, task*]; **to ~ it (up) to sb to do** laisser à qn le soin de faire; **it will be left to him to do it** on lui laissera le soin de le faire; **to ~ the decision/choice (up) to sb** laisser à qn le soin de décider/choisir; **to ~ it up to sb where/how etc to do** laisser qn décider où/comment etc faire; **to ~ sb to do** laisser qn faire; **~ him to sleep** laisse-le dormir; **to ~ sb to it** (to do something) laisser qn se débrouiller ; (to be alone) laisser qn tranquille; **to ~ sb to himself, to ~ sb be**○ laisser qn tranquille; **~ him/me alone** laisse-le/-moi tranquille; **~ it to** ou **with me** je m'en occupe, je m'en charge; **~ everything to me!** je m'en occupe, je me charge de tout!; **5** (result in) [*oil, wine, tea*] faire [*stain*]; [*cup, plate etc*] laisser [*stain, mark*]; [*cup, heel, chair*] faire [*hole, dent*]; **the operation will ~ a scar** vous garderez une cicatrice de l'opération; **6** (postpone) laisser [*task, homework, housework*]; **~ it till tomorrow/ Friday/the end** laisse ça pour demain/ vendredi/la fin; **7** (stop and agree) **to ~ it that** convenir que; **to ~ it at that** en rester là; **8** Jur (bequeath) laisser, léguer [*money, property*]; **to ~ sth to sb, to ~ sb sth** léguer qch à qn; **9** (be survived by) laisser [*widow, son, daughter*]; **10** (pass) **to ~ sth on one's left/right** passer qch à gauche/à droite.
III *vi* (*prét, pp* **left**) partir; **to ~ for** partir pour [*airport, France*]; **to ~ for work** partir travailler; **to ~ for another company** partir dans une autre société; **he left for a career in advertising** il est parti pour faire carrière dans la publicité.
IV *v refl* (*prét, pp* **left**) **to ~ oneself (with)** se réserver [*time, money*]; **to ~ oneself short of money/time** ne pas prévoir assez d'argent/de temps.

■ **leave about, leave around**: **~ [sth] around** (carelessly) laisser traîner [*books, papers, toys*]; (deliberately) disposer [*cushions, books, magazines*].

■ **leave aside**: ~ [sth] aside, ~ aside [sth] laisser [qch] de côté; **leaving aside the question of** (ignoring for now) si on laisse de côté la question de; (not mentioning) sans parler du problème de.

■ **leave behind**: ¶ ~ [sb/sth] behind 1 (go faster than) distancer [*person, competitor*]; fig (in business, intellectually) distancer [*person, competitor*]; **the teacher left the students behind** les étudiants n'arrivaient pas à suivre le professeur; 2 (move away from) [*vehicle, plane*] s'éloigner de [*coast, country, ground*]; [*traveller*] laisser [qch] derrière soi [*town, country*]; [*person*] quitter [*family, husband*]; fig en finir avec, tirer un trait sur [*past, problems, relationship*]; 3 (fail to bring) (accidentally) oublier, laisser [*object, child, animal*]; (deliberately) laisser [*object, child, animal*]; ¶ ~ [sth] behind (cause to remain) [*person*] laisser [*chaos, problems, bitterness*]; [*earthquake, storm, flood*] faire [*damage*]; **to ~ chaos behind** laisser la pagaille○; **the army/tornado left a trail of destruction behind it** l'armée/la tornade a tout détruit sur son passage; **to be** ou **get left behind** (not keep up) (physically) [*person*] se faire distancer; (intellectually) ne pas suivre, être largué○; (in business) [*country, company*] se laisser distancer; (not be taken) (accidentally) être oublié; (deliberately) **the plants were left behind** on a laissé les plantes.

■ **leave go, leave hold** (*usage critiqué*) lâcher; **to ~ go** ou **hold of sb/sth** lâcher qn/qch.

■ **leave in**: ~ [sth] in laisser [*object, paragraph, quote*].

■ **leave off**: ¶ ~ off [*rain*] cesser; [*person*] s'interrompre; **to carry on** ou **continue where one left off** reprendre là où on en était; **where did we ~ off?** où en étions-nous?; ~ **off**○! arrête○!; ¶ ~ **off doing** (stop) cesser or arrêter de faire; ¶ ~ [sth] off, ~ off [sth] 1 (not put on) ne pas mettre [*coat, tie, hat, lid, blanket*]; (not put back on) ne pas remettre [*coat, tie, hat, lid, blanket*]; 2 (not switch on) ne pas allumer [*light, TV*]; ne pas brancher [*iron, kettle*]; (leave switched off) laisser [qch] éteint [*light, central heating, TV*]; laisser [qch] débranché [*iron, kettle*]; 3 (omit) omettre [*name, item, letter*]; (by mistake) oublier [*name, item, letter*]; **to ~ sth off a list** omettre qch d'une liste.

■ **leave on**: ~ [sth] on 1 (not remove) garder [*coat, tie, hat*]; laisser [*lid, blanket, bandage, label*]; 2 (not switch off) laisser [qch] allumé [*light, TV, central heating*]; laisser [qch] branché [*iron*]; laisser [qch] ouvert [*gas, tap*]; laisser [*safety catch*].

■ **leave out**: ~ [sb/sth] out, ~ out [sb/sth] 1 (fail to include) (accidentally) omettre, oublier [*word, line, name, fact*]; oublier [*ingredient, object, person*] (deliberately) omettre [*name, fact, reference*]; ne pas mettre [*ingredient, object*]; (from social group, activity) tenir [qn] à l'écart; **to feel left out** se sentir tenu à l'écart; ~ **it out**○! arrête○!; **to ~ sth out of** omettre qch de [*text*]; **to ~ sb out of** exclure qn de [*group*]; ~ **me out of it!** ne me mêlez pas à ça!; **to ~ sth out of one's calculations** ne pas tenir compte de qch dans ses calculs; 2 (let remain outdoors) laisser [qch] dehors [*bicycle, washing, milk*]; 3 (not put away) laisser [qch] dehors [*clothes*]; 4 (not put in) ne pas mettre [*contact lenses, plug*]; (not put back) ne pas remettre [*contact lenses, plug*].

■ **leave over**: ~ [sth] over 1 (cause to remain) laisser [*food, drink*]; **there is/we have some money left over** il reste/il nous reste de l'argent; 2 (postpone) remettre [qch] à plus tard [*discussion, meeting*].

leaven /ˈlevn/ I† *n* levain *m*.

II *vtr* 1 Culin faire lever; 2 fig (enliven) relever [*speech, story*] (**with** de).

leavening /ˈlevnɪŋ/ *n* lit, fig levain *m*.

leaves /liːvz/ *npl* ▶ **leaf**.

leave-taking *n* adieux *mpl*.

leaving /ˈliːvɪŋ/ I *n* départ *m*.

II *modif* [*party, present*] d'adieu.

III **leavings** *npl* restes *mpl*.

Lebanese /ˌlebəˈniːz/ ▶ 1486 I *n* Libanais/-e *m/f*.

II *adj* libanais, du Liban.

Lebanon /ˈlebənən/ ▶ 1131 *pr n* (also **the ~**) (le) Liban *m*; **in ~** au Liban.

lech○ /letʃ/ I = **lecher**.

II *vi* **to ~ for** ou **after sb** courir après qn.

lecher /ˈletʃə(r)/ *n péj* coureur *m* de jupons.

lecherous /ˈletʃərəs/ *adj* lubrique.

lecherously /ˈletʃərəslɪ/ *adv* d'une manière lubrique.

lechery /ˈletʃərɪ/ *n* lubricité *f*.

lectern /ˈlektɜːn/ *n* (in church) lutrin *m*; (for lecture notes) pupitre *m*.

lector /ˈlektɔː(r)/ *n* lecteur/-trice *m/f*.

lecture /ˈlektʃə(r)/ I *n* 1 (public talk) conférence *f* (**on** sur); GB Univ cours *m* magistral (**on** sur); **to give a ~** (public talk) donner une conférence (**to** à); GB Univ faire un cours (**to** à); 2 (scolding) **he gave me a ~** il m'a sermonné, il m'a fait la leçon.

II *vtr* 1 GB Univ donner un cours à; **she ~s new students on computing** elle donne des cours d'informatique aux nouveaux étudiants; 2 (scold) sermonner○, faire la leçon à; **to ~ sb for having done sth** sermonner qn pour avoir fait qch.

III *vi* 1 GB Univ faire un cours (**to** à; **on** sur); **next term he'll be lecturing on Sartre** le trimestre prochain il fera un cours sur Sartre; **she ~s in mathematics** elle enseigne les mathématiques (à l'université); 2 (give public talk) donner une conférence (**on** sur).

lecture: ~ **hall** *n* US amphithéâtre *m*, amphi○ *m*; ~ **notes** *npl* GB Univ notes *fpl* de cours.

lecturer /ˈlektʃərə(r)/ ▶ 1692 *n* 1 (speaker) conférencier/-ière *m/f*; 2 GB Univ enseignant/-e *m/f* (du supérieur); **junior ~** ≈ assistant/-e *m/f*; **senior ~** ≈ maître *m* de conférences; **she's a maths ~** ou **a ~ in maths** elle enseigne les maths (à l'université); 3 US Univ ≈ chargé *m* de cours.

lecture room *n* GB Univ salle *f* de conférences.

lectureship /ˈlektʃəʃɪp/ *n* GB Univ poste *m* d'enseignant à l'université; **a ~ in linguistics** un poste en linguistique (à l'université).

lecture theatre *n* GB Univ amphithéâtre *m*, amphi○ *m*.

led /led/ *pret, pp* ▶ **lead**[1].

ledge /ledʒ/ *n* 1 (in house) (small shelf) rebord *m*; **window ~** rebord *m* de la fenêtre; 2 (natural) (on mountain, cliff) saillie *f* (rocheuse), replat *m*; (tiny) aspérité *f*; (overhang) corniche *f*; 3 (under sea) (reef) récif *m*; (projection) haut-fond *m*; 4 Sport (in climbing) vire *f*.

ledger /ˈledʒə(r)/ *n* 1 Accts registre *m* (*de comptabilité*); grand livre *m*; 2 Constr sommier *m* d'échafaudage; 3 Fishg clipot *m*, paternoster *m*.

ledger line *n* 1 Mus ligne *f* supplémentaire (de portée); 2 Fishg paternoster *m*.

lee /liː/ I *n* côté *m* sous le vent or à l'abri du vent; **in** ou **under the ~ of** à l'abri de.

II *adj* [*side, shore*] sous le vent.

leech /liːtʃ/ *n* Zool, fig, péj sangsue *f*; **to cling to sb like a ~** coller○ qn comme une sangsue.

leek /liːk/ *n* poireau *m*.

leer /lɪə(r)/ péj I *n* (cunning) regard *m* sournois; (malevolent) regard *m* malveillant; (lustful) regard *m* libidineux.

II *vi* (lustfully) jeter des regards libidineux; (slyly) jeter des regards sournois; **to ~ at sb/sth** lorgner○ qn/qch.

leery /ˈlɪərɪ/ *adj* **to be ~ of** se méfier de.

lees /liːz/ *npl* (wine sediment) lie *f*.

leeward /ˈliːwəd, ˈluːəd/ I *n* côté *m* sous le vent; **to ~** sous le vent.

II *adj, adv* sous le vent.

Leeward Islands ▶ 1381 *npl* îles *fpl* Sous-le-Vent.

leeway /ˈliːweɪ/ *n* 1 Naut, Aviat dérive *f*; 2 fig liberté *f* de manœuvre.

left /left/ ▶ 1173 I *prét, pp* ▶ **leave**.

II *n* 1 (side or direction) gauche *f*; **on the ~** sur la gauche; **on your ~** sur votre gauche; **to the ~** vers la gauche; **keep** (**to the**) **~** Aut tenez la gauche; 2 Pol **the ~** la gauche; **on the ~** à gauche; **to the ~ of sb** à gauche de qn; 3 Sport (poing *m*) gauche *m*.

III *adj* [*eye, hand, shoe*] gauche.

IV *adv* [*go, look, turn*] à gauche.

IDIOMS **~, right and centre** (everywhere) partout; (indiscriminately) [*criticize, spend money*] sans réfléchir; **to be out in ~ field**○ US être à côté de la plaque○.

left: ~ **back** *n* Sport arrière *m* gauche; **Left Bank** *n* (in Paris) Rive *f* gauche.

left-hand /ˌleftˈhænd/ *adj* [*page, side, door*] de gauche.

left-hand drive, lhd I *n* voiture *f* avec la conduite à gauche.

II *adj* [*vehicle, car*] avec la conduite à gauche.

left-handed /ˌleftˈhændɪd/ I *adj* [*person*] gaucher/-ère; [*scissors, pen*] pour gauchers.

II *adv* [*play, write*] de la main gauche.

left: ~**-handedness** *n* fait *m* d'être gaucher; ~**-hander** *n* gaucher/-ère *m/f*.

leftie○ /ˈleftɪ/ *n* aussi péj gauchiste *mf*.

leftism /ˈleftɪzəm/ *n* Pol gauchisme *m*.

leftist /ˈleftɪst/ I *n* Pol homme/femme *m/f* de gauche.

II *adj* Pol [*person, party, activity, view*] de gauche.

left: ~**-luggage** (**office**) *n* GB consigne *f*; ~ **luggage** *n* GB bagages *mpl* en consigne; ~**-of-centre** *adj* Pol centre-gauche *inv*; ~**-over** *adj* restant; ~**-overs** *npl* restes *mpl*.

left wing I *n* 1 Pol **the ~** la gauche; 2 Sport (side of field) côté *m* gauche; (player) ailier *m* gauche.

II **left-wing** *adj* Pol [*person, group, view, idea*] de gauche.

left-winger *n* Pol homme/femme *m/f* de gauche.

leg /leg/ I *n* 1 ▶ 1037 Anat (of person) jambe *f*; (of animal) gen patte *f*; (of horse) jambe *f*; **to have a bad ~**○ être infirme d'une jambe; **to stand on one ~** se tenir debout sur une jambe; **my ~s can't go any further** mes jambes ne me portent plus; 2 (of furniture) pied *m*; **table ~** pied *m* de table; 3 Culin (of lamb) gigot *m*; (of veal) cuisseau *m*; (of poultry, pork, game, frog) cuisse *f*; (of venison) cuissot *m*; 4 Sewing (of trousers) jambe *f*; **these trousers are too long in the ~** ce pantalon a les jambes trop longues; 5 (of journey, race) étape *f*; 6 Sport (in football) manche *f*.

II *modif* [*movement, muscle*] de la jambe; [*pain*] à la jambe; [*exercises*] pour les jambes.

III○ *vtr* (*p prés etc* **-gg-**) **to ~ it** (walk) arquer○; (walk fast) galoper○; (run away) cavaler○.

IV **-legged** (dans composés) **three-~ged** [*furniture*] à trois pieds; **four-/six-~ged** [*animal*] à quatre/six pattes; **long-~ged** [*person*] à jambes longues; [*animal*] à longues pattes; **bare-~ged** jambes nues.

IDIOMS **break a ~**○! Theat je te dis merde◑!; US (get lost) lâche-moi les baskets○!; **shake a ~!** remue-toi!; **she doesn't have a ~ to stand on** elle n'a rien sur quoi s'appuyer, elle n'a aucun argument valable; **show a ~**○! sors-toi○ du lit; **to be all ~s** être tout en jambe; **to be on its last ~s** [*machine, car*] avoir fait son temps; [*regime*] ne plus en avoir pour longtemps; [*company*] être au bord de la faillite; **he is on his last ~s** il n'en a plus pour longtemps; **to cost an arm and a ~** coûter les yeux de la tête; **to get one's ~ over**◑ s'envoyer en l'air◑; **to give sb a ~ up**○ faire la courte échelle à qn; fig dépanner qn○; **to pull sb's ~** faire marcher qn.

legacy /ˈlegəsɪ/ *n* **1** Jur legs *m*; **2** fig **the ~ of** l'héritage *m* de [*era, event, movement, artist etc*]; les séquelles *fpl* de [*war, suffering*]; **X's ~ to sth** la contribution de X à qch.

legal /ˈliːgl/ *adj* **1** (relating to the law) [*assistance, battle, career, department, document, matter, parlance, system, representative*] juridique; [*mistake*] judiciaire; [*medicine, process, status*] légal; [*costs, fees*] de justice; **to take** ou **get ~ advice** consulter un avocat; **2** (recognized by the law) [*abortion, act, age, heir, import, limit, obligation, right, separation*] légal; [*requirement*] requis par la loi; [*definition, guideline, precedent*] juridique; [*owner, claim*] légitime; **it is ~ to do** il est légal de faire; **it is your ~ duty to do** vous êtes dans l'obligation légale de faire.

legal action *n* poursuite *f* judiciaire; **to bring a** ou **take ~ against sb** intenter un procès à qn.

legal: **~ aid** *n* Jur aide *f* juridique; **~ capacity** *n* capacité *f*; **~ eagle**○ *n* as *m* du barreau○; **~ entity** *n* personne *f* morale.

legalese /ˌliːgəˈliːz/ *n* péj jargon *m* juridique.

legal: **~ fiction** *n* fiction *f* de droit or de la loi; **~ holiday** *n* US jour *m* férié.

legalism /ˈliːgəlɪzəm/ *n* **1** (legal term) tournure *f* juridique; **2** ¢ (rigour) légalisme *m*.

legalistic /ˌliːgəˈlɪstɪk/ *adj* péj [*approach, attitude, reasoning*] légaliste; [*terminology*] juridique.

legality /liːˈgælətɪ/ *n* légalité *f*.

legalization /ˌliːgəlaɪˈzeɪʃn, US -lɪˈz-/ *n* légalisation *f*.

legalize /ˈliːgəlaɪz/ *vtr* légaliser.

legally /ˈliːgəlɪ/ *adv* **1** (in the eyes of the law) [*liable, valid, void*] juridiquement; **to be ~ represented** être représenté par un avocat; **to be ~ qualified** être juriste; **to be ~ responsible for sth** avoir la responsabilité légale de qch; **to be ~ entitled to do** avoir le droit de faire; **~, the matter is complex** du point de vue juridique, l'affaire est compliquée; **this contract is ~ binding** ce contrat vous engage; **2** (in accordance with the law) [*act, marry*] conformément à la loi; [*buy, sell, import, work*] légalement.

legal: **~ practice** *n* (office) cabinet *m* légal; (exercise of law) pratique *f* du droit; **~ practitioner** *n* juriste *mf*; **~ proceedings** *npl* poursuites *fpl* judiciaires; **~ profession** *n* profession *f* juridique.

legal tender *n* monnaie *f* légale; **this coin is not ~** cette pièce n'a plus cours.

legate /ˈlegɪt/ *n* légat *m*.

legatee /ˌlegəˈtiː/ *n* légataire *m*.

legation /lɪˈgeɪʃn/ *n* légation *f*.

legator /lɪˈgeɪtə(r)/ *n* testateur/-trice *m/f*.

legend /ˈledʒənd/ *n* (all contexts) légende *f* (**of** de); **~ has it that** selon la légende; **a living ~** une légende vivante; **to become a ~ in one's own lifetime** passer dans la légende de son vivant.

legendary /ˈledʒəndrɪ, US -derɪ/ *adj* légendaire.

legerdemain /ˌledʒədəˈmeɪn/ *n* ¢ (of conjuror) prestidigitation *f*; fig péj manigances *fpl*.

leggings /ˈlegɪŋz/ *npl* (for walker, farmer) cuissardes *fpl*; (for baby) collant *m*; (for woman) caleçon *m* (*porté en pantalon*).

leggo○ /ˈlegəʊ/ *abrév* = **let go**.

leggy /ˈlegɪ/ *adj* **1** [*person*] aux longues jambes; **2**○ [*plant*] haut et dégarni.

Leghorn /ˌlegˈhɔːn/ **▶ 1818** *pr n* Livourne.

legibility /ˌledʒəˈbɪlətɪ/ *n* lisibilité *f*.

legible /ˈledʒəbl/ *adj* lisible.

legibly /ˈledʒəblɪ/ *adv* lisiblement.

legion /ˈliːdʒən/ **I** *n* Mil légion *f*; fig multitude *f*.
II *adj* (*jamais épith*) légion (*inv*).

legionary /ˈliːdʒənərɪ, US -nerɪ/ **I** *n* légionnaire *m*.
II *adj* de la légion.

legionnaire /ˌliːdʒəˈneə(r)/ *n* Mil légionnaire *m*.

legionnaire's disease **▶ 1354** *n* maladie *f* du légionnaire, légionellose *f*.

leg iron *n* (for convict) entrave *f*; (for disabled person) appareil *m* orthopédique.

legislate /ˈledʒɪsleɪt/ *vi* **1** (make laws) légiférer (**on** sur); **to ~ against** faire des lois contre [*discrimination, pornography*]; **2** (predict) **to ~ for** prévoir [*circumstances, event*].

legislation /ˌledʒɪsˈleɪʃn/ *n* **1** (body of laws) législation *f* (**against** contre; **on** sur; **about, relating to** concernant; **to do** pour faire); **EEC/government ~** législation *f* communautaire/gouvernementale; **industrial/financial/employment ~** législation *f* industrielle/financière/de l'emploi; **a piece of ~** une loi; **to adopt/present ~** adopter/présenter un projet de loi; **to introduce ~** faire adopter des lois; **2** (process of lawmaking) législation *f*.

legislative /ˈledʒɪslətɪv, US -leɪtɪv/ *adj* législatif/-ive; **~ drafting** US rédaction *f* d'un projet de loi.

legislator /ˈledʒɪsleɪtə(r)/ *n* Jur, Pol législateur/-trice *m/f*.

legislature /ˈledʒɪsleɪtʃə(r)/ *n* Jur, Pol législature *f*.

legist /ˈliːdʒɪst/ *n* Jur légiste *m*.

legit○ /lɪˈdʒɪt/ *adj* **1** (legal) [*job, operation, venture*] réglo○, régulier/-ière; [*goods*] de provenance honnête; **2** (genuine) [*offer, information, organization*] sérieux/-ieuse.

legitimacy /lɪˈdʒɪtɪməsɪ/ *n* **1** (legality) (of law, measure, birth) légitimité *f*; **2** (justifiability) (of comment, conclusion, objection) bien-fondé *m*; (of measure, rule) légitimité *f*; **to give ~ to sth** légitimer qch.

legitimate **I** /lɪˈdʒɪtɪmət/ *adj* **1** (justifiable) [*action, claim, question, request, target, user*] légitime; [*conclusion, excuse*] valable; **it is ~ to do** on est en droit de faire; **it is ~ for me to do** je suis en droit de faire; **2** (in accordance with the law) [*business, deal, organization*] régulier/-ière; [*act, child, claim, government, heir, owner, right, spouse*] légitime; [*killing*] justifiable; **for a ~ purpose** à des fins légitimes; **to make sth ~** rendre qch légal; **3** Theat [*theatre*] vrai (*before n*).
II /lɪˈdʒɪtɪmeɪt/ *vtr* = **legitimize**.

legitimately /lɪˈdʒɪtɪmətlɪ/ *adv* **1** (with justification) [*ask, claim, argue, refuse*] légitimement; **one might ~ wonder whether/think that...** on serait en droit de se demander si/de penser que...; **2** (legally) [*act, authorize, own*] légalement; [*operate*] en toute légalité.

legitimation /lɪˌdʒɪtɪˈmeɪʃn/ *n* Jur (of child) légitimation *f*; (of party, group) légalisation *f*.

legitimize /lɪˈdʒɪtɪmaɪz/ *vtr* **1** (legalize) légaliser [*government, bill, plan*]; rendre [qch] légal [*ruling*]; **2** (justify) justifier [*action, crime, existence, interference, plan, reputation*].

legless /ˈleglɪs/ *adj* **1** lit sans jambes; **2**○ GB (drunk) hum bituré à bloc○.

leg: **~man** *n* US reporter *m*; Pol factotum *m*; **~-of-mutton** *adj* Fashn [*sleeve*] gigot *inv*; **~-pull** *n* farce *f*; **~-pulling** *n* mise *f* en boîte○; **~room** *n* place *f* pour les jambes; **~ shield** *n* jambière *f*.

legume /ˈlegjuːm/ *n* **1** (plant) légumineuse *f*; **2** (pod) *fruit comestible d'une légumineuse*.

leguminous /lɪˈgjuːmɪnəs/ *adj* légumineux/-euse.

leg warmer *n* jambière *f*.

legwork /ˈlegwɜːk/ *n* déplacements *mpl*; **to do the ~** déblayer le terrain○ fig.

Leibnitzian /ˈlaɪbnɪtsɪən/ *adj* Leibnizien/-ienne.

Leicestershire /ˈlestəʃə(r)/ **▶ 1624** *pr n* Leicestershire *m*.

Leics GB Post *abrév écrite* = **Leicestershire**.

leisure /ˈleʒə(r), US ˈliːʒə(r)/ **I** *n* ¢ (spare time) loisir(s) *m(pl)*, temps *m* libre; (activities) loisirs *mpl*; **to do sth at (one's) ~** (unhurriedly) prendre son temps pour faire qch; (with time for thought) faire qch à tête reposée; **gentleman/lady of ~** hum rentier/-ière *m/f*.
II *modif* [*centre, company, facilities*] de loisirs; **~ industry** industrie *f* des loisirs; **~ society** civilisation *f* du loisir.

leisured /ˈleʒəd, US ˈliːʒəd/ *adj* **1** also pej privilégié; **the ~ classes** les classes *fpl* privilégiées, les nantis *mpl;* **2** (*tjrs épith*) = **leisurely I**.

leisurely /ˈleʒəlɪ, US ˈliː-/ **I** *adj* [*person*] calme; [*way of life, walk*] tranquille; [*breakfast, holiday*] détendu, tranquille; [*game*] détendu; **at a ~ pace, in a ~ way** sans se presser.
II *adv* sans se presser.

leisure: **~ suit** *n* ensemble *m* sport; **~ time** *n* loisirs *mpl*, temps *m* libre; **~ wear** *n* ¢ vêtements *mpl* de sport.

leitmotiv /ˈlaɪtməʊtiːf/ *n* leitmotiv *m*.

LEM *n* (*abrév* = **lunar excursion module**) lem *m*.

lemma /ˈlemə/ *n* Comput, Math, Ling lemme *m*.

lemmatization /ˌlemətaɪˈzeɪʃn/ *n* Comput, Math, Ling lemmatisation *f*.

lemmatize /ˈlemətaɪz/ *vtr* Comput, Math, Ling lemmatiser.

lemming /ˈlemɪŋ/ *n* lemming *m*.

lemon /ˈlemən/ **▶ 1104** **I** *n* **1** (fruit) citron *m*; **2** (colour) jaune *m* citron; **3**○ hum (idiot) **to look/feel a ~** avoir l'air/se sentir tout bête; **4**○ US (dud) (play, book, movie) navet○ *m*; **this car is a ~** cette voiture est de la camelote.
II *modif* [*peel, pip, juice, marmalade*] de citron; [*drink, sorbet*] au citron.
III *adj* (colour) jaune citron *inv*.

lemonade /ˌleməˈneɪd/ *n* (fizzy) limonade *f*; (still) citronnade *f*; (fresh) US citron *m* pressé.

lemon: **~ balm** *n* mélisse *f*; **~ cheese, ~ curd** *n* GB crème *f* de citron; **~ drop** *n* bonbon *m* au citron; **~-flavoured, ~-flavored** US *adj* parfumé au citron; **~ juice** *n* jus *m* de citron; GB (drink) citron *m* pressé; **~ sole** *n* GB limande-sole *f*; **~ squash** *n* GB ≈ sirop *m* de citron; **~ squeezer** *n* presse-citron *m inv*; **~ tea** *n* thé *m* au citron; **~ tree** *n* citronnier *m*; **~ yellow** **▶ 1104** *n, adj* jaune (*m*) citron.

lemur /ˈliːmə(r)/ *n* maki *m*.

lend /lend/ **I** *vtr* (*pp, prét* **lent**) **1** (loan) prêter [*object, money*]; **to ~ sb sth** prêter qch à qn; **I lent John my bicycle, I lent my bicycle to John** j'ai prêté ma bicyclette à John; **I've been lent a bicycle by John** John m'a prêté une bicyclette; **I've been lent a bicycle** on m'a prêté une bicyclette; **to ~ money at 10%** prêter de l'argent à 10%; **2** (add, provide) conférer [*quality, character, credibility*] (**to** à); prêter [*support*]; **to ~ support to sth** étayer qch; **to ~ an ear** prêter l'oreille; **to ~ a hand** prêter une main; **to ~ one's name to** prêter son nom à; **to ~ weight to sth** donner du poids à qch.
II *vi* (*pp, prét* **lent**) Fin prêter, accorder un prêt (**to** à); **to ~ against sth** prêter contre la garantie de qch; **to ~ at 15%** prêter à 15%.
III *v refl* (*pp, prét* **lent**) se prêter (**to** à); **her novels do not ~ themselves to being filmed** ses romans ne se prêtent pas à une adaptation pour le cinéma.
■ **lend out**: **~ out [sth], ~ [sth] out** prêter.

lender /ˈlendə(r)/ *n* prêteur/-euse *m/f*; **mortgage ~** société *f* de prêt immobilier.

lending /ˈlendɪŋ/ **I** *n* prêt *m*.
II *modif* [*agency, bank, figures, library, programme, scheme, service*] de prêt; [*agreement,*

Length measurement

Note that French has a comma where English has a decimal point.

1 in = 2,54 cm* (*centimètres*)
1 ft = 30,48 cm
1 yd = 91,44 cm
1 furlong = 201,17 m (*mètres*)
1 ml = 1,61 km (*kilomètres*)

* *There are three ways of saying* 2,54 cm, *and other measurements like it:* deux virgule cinquante-quatre centimètres, *or* (*less formally*) deux centimètres virgule cinquante-quatre, *or* deux centimètres cinquante-quatre. *For more details on how to say numbers,* ▶ **1505**).

Length

how long is the rope? = de quelle longueur est la corde?
it's ten metres long = elle fait dix mètres
a rope about six metres long = une corde d'environ six mètres de* long
A is longer than B = A est plus long que B
B is shorter than A = B est plus court que A
A is as long as B = A est aussi long que B
A is the same length as B = A a la même longueur que B
A and B are the same length = A et B ont la même longueur *or* A et B sont de* la même longueur
it's three metres too short = il est trop court de trois mètres
it's three metres too long = il est trop long de trois mètres
six metres of silk = six mètres de soie
ten metres of rope = dix mètres de corde
sold by the metre = vendu au mètre

Note the French construction with de, *coming after the noun it describes:*

a six-foot-long python = un python de six pieds de* long
an avenue four kilometres long = une avenue de quatre kilomètres de* long

* *The* de *is obligatory in these constructions.*

Height

People

how tall is he? = quelle est sa taille? *or* combien est-ce qu'il mesure?
he's six feet tall = il fait un mètre quatre-vingts *or* il mesure un mètre quatre-vingts
he's 1m 50 = il fait 1,50 m (*say* un mètre cinquante)
he's about five feet = il fait à peu près un mètre cinquante
A is taller than B = A est plus grand que B
B is smaller than A = B est plus petit que A
A is as tall as B = A est aussi grand que B
A is the same height as B = A a la même taille que B
A and B are the same height = A et B ont la même taille *or* A et B sont de* la même taille

Note the French construction with de, *coming after the noun it describes:*

a six-foot-tall athlete = un athlète d'un mètre quatre-vingts
a footballer over six feet in height = un footballeur de plus d'un mètre quatre-vingts

Things

how high is the tower? = quelle est la hauteur de la tour?
it's 50 metres = elle fait 50 mètres *or* elle mesure 50 mètres
about 25 metres high = environ 25 mètres de* haut
it's 100 metres high = elle fait cent mètres de* haut *or* elle fait cent mètres de hauteur
at a height of two metres = à une hauteur de deux mètres *or* à deux mètres de hauteur
A is higher than B = A est plus haut que B
B is lower than A = B est moins haut que A
A is as high as B = A est aussi haut que B
A is the same height as B = A a la même hauteur que B
A and B are the same height = A et B ont la même hauteur *or* A et B sont de* la même hauteur

Note the French construction with de, *coming after the noun it describes:*

a 100-metre-high tower = une tour de 100 mètres de* haut
a mountain over 4,000 metres in height = une montagne de plus de quatre mille mètres
how high is the plane = à quelle hauteur *or* à quelle altitude est l'avion?
what height is the plane flying at? = à quelle altitude l'avion vole-t-il?
the plane is flying at 5,000 metres = l'avion vole à une altitude de cinq mille mètres *or* à cinq mille mètres d'altitude*

* *The* de *is obligatory in these constructions.*

Distance

what's the distance from A to B? = quelle distance y a-t-il entre A et B?
how far is it from Paris to Nice? = combien y a-t-il de kilomètres de Paris à Nice?
how far away is the school from the church? = à quelle distance l'école est-elle de l'église?
it's two kilometres = il y a deux kilomètres
it's about two kilometres = il y a environ deux kilomètres
at a distance of five kilometres = à une distance de 5 kilomètres *or* à cinq kilomètres de distance
C is nearer B than A is = C est plus près de B que A
A is nearer to B than to C = A est plus près de B que de C
it's further than from B to C = c'est plus loin que de B à C
A is as far away as B = A est aussi loin que B
A and B are the same distance away = A et B sont à la même distance

Note the French construction with de, *coming after the noun it describes:*

a ten-kilometre walk = une promenade de dix kilomètres

Width/breadth

In the following examples, broad *may replace* wide *and* breadth *may replace* width, *but the French remains* large *and* largeur.

what width is the river? = de* quelle largeur est la rivière?
how wide is it? = combien fait-elle de* large?
about seven metres wide = environ sept mètres de* large
it's seven metres wide = elle fait sept mètres de* large *or* de* largeur
A is wider than B = A est plus large que B
B is narrower than A = B est plus étroit que A
A is as wide as B = A est aussi large que B
A is the same width as B = A a la même largeur que B
A and B are the same width = A et B ont la même largeur *or* A et B sont de* la même largeur

Note the French construction with de, *coming after the noun it describes:*

a ditch two metres wide = un fossé de deux mètres de* large
a piece of cloth two metres in width = une pièce de tissu de deux mètres de* largeur
a river 50 metres wide = une rivière de 50 mètres de* largeur

* *The* de *is obligatory in these constructions.*

Depth

what depth is the river? = de* quelle profondeur est la rivière?
how deep is it? = combien fait-elle de* profondeur?
about ten metres deep = environ dix mètres de* profondeur
it's four metres deep = elle fait quatre mètres de* profondeur
at a depth of ten metres = à dix mètres de* profondeur *or* à une profondeur de* dix mètres
A is deeper than B = A est plus profond que B
B is shallower than A = B est moins profond que A

(*note that French has no word for* shallow)

A is as deep as B = A est aussi profond que B
A is the same depth as B = A a la même profondeur que B
A and B are the same depth = A et B ont la même profondeur

Note the French construction with de, *coming after the noun it describes:*

a well 20 metres deep = un puits de vingt mètres de* profondeur

* *The* de *is obligatory in these constructions.*

rate] d'emprunt; **~ limit** plafond *m* d'endettement.

lend-lease /ˌlendˈliːs/ *n* prêt-bail *m*.

length /leŋθ/ ▶ **1412** **I** *n* **1** (linear measurement) longueur *f*; **what is the ~ of the plank?, what ~ is the plank?** quelle est la longueur de la planche?, de quelle longueur est la planche?; **cut the fabric to a ~ of two metres** couper une longueur de deux mètres dans le tissu; **to be 15 cm/50 km in ~** faire 15 cm/50 km de long; **X is twice the ~ of Y** X est deux fois plus long que Y; **the whole ~ of the street was planted with trees** la rue était plantée d'arbres sur toute sa longueur; **a river runs along the whole ~ of the valley** une rivière coule tout le long de or sur toute la longueur de la vallée; **she ran the (whole) ~ of the beach** elle a fait toute la longueur de la plage en courant; **he has cycled the (whole) ~ of Italy** il a fait l'Italie d'un bout à l'autre à bicyclette ; **there was a ladder running the (whole) ~ of her stocking** son bas était filé sur toute sa hauteur; **2** (duration) (of book, film, article, waiting list) longueur *f*; (of event, activity, situation, prison sentence) durée *f*; Ling (of vowel, syllable) longueur *f*; **for the whole ~ of the ceremony** pendant toute la durée de la cérémonie; **~ of service** Comm, Ind ancienneté *f*; **a film three hours in ~** un film de trois heures or qui dure trois heures; **a book 200 pages in ~** un livre de 200 pages or qui fait 200 pages; **the thesis wasn't of sufficient ~** la thèse n'était pas assez longue; **a significant/considerable ~ of time** un temps important/considérable; **he spends a ridiculous ~ of time in the bathroom** il passe un temps infini dans la salle de bains; **he can't concentrate for any ~ of time** il n'arrive pas à se concentrer pendant (très) longtemps; **he complained about the ~ of time he'd been in prison** il s'est plaint d'avoir passé tant de temps en prison; **the ~ of time between two events** l'intervalle (de temps) entre deux événements; **despite its three-hour ~, the play was enjoyable** bien qu'elle ait duré trois heures, la pièce était agréable; **3** (piece, section) (of string, cable, carpet, wood) morceau *m*; (of fabric) ≈ métrage *m*; (of piping, track) tronçon *m*; **to cut sth into two metre ~s** débiter qch en morceaux de deux mètres; **a six-metre ~ of rope** une corde de six mètres; **sold in ~s of five metres** [*wood, carpet*] vendu par morceaux de cinq mètres;

[*fabric*] vendu en coupons de cinq mètres; **dress/skirt ~** hauteur *f* de robe/de jupe; **4** Sport longueur *f*; **to swim 20 ~s** faire 20 longueurs (de piscine); **to win by six ~s/half a ~** gagner de six longueurs/d'une demi-longueur; **X's two-~ victory over Y** la victoire de X sur Y par deux longueurs; **to have a four-~ advantage/lead over sb** avoir une avance de quatre longueurs sur qn; **to be two ~s ahead/behind** avoir deux longueurs d'avance/de retard.
II lengths *npl* **to go to great/extraordinary ~s to do sth** se donner beaucoup/énormément de mal pour faire qch; **to be willing to go to any ~s (to do)** être prêt à faire n'importe quoi (pour faire); **I was shocked by the ~s he was prepared to go to** j'étais choqué par ce qu'il était prêt à faire; **she went to the ~s of writing to the president** elle est allée jusqu'à écrire au président.
III at length *adv phr* **1** (for a long time) longuement; **the problem has been examined at (great) ~** le problème a été examiné (très) longuement; **2** (at last) finalement; **at ~, he left** finalement il est parti.
IV -length (*dans composés*) **shoulder-~ hair** des cheveux qui arrivent aux épaules; **a knee-~ skirt** une jupe qui arrive aux genoux; **calf-~ boots** des bottes qui arrivent au mollet; **a medium-~ article** un article de longueur moyenne; **floor-~ curtains** des rideaux qui descendent jusqu'au sol. ▶ **full-length**.

lengthen /'leŋθən/ **I** *vtr* **1** rallonger [*garment*] (**by** de, par); prolonger [*wall, shelf, track*] (**by** de, par); **to ~ sth from X metres to Y metres** faire passer la longueur de qch de X mètres à Y mètres; **2** prolonger [*stay, visit*]; rallonger [*waiting period, queue, list*]; **to ~ sth from three years to four years** faire passer la durée de qch de trois à quatre ans; **3** Ling allonger [*vowel, syllable*].
II *vi* **1** [*queue, list, shadow*] s'allonger; [*skirts, trousers*] devenir plus long; Med [*bone*] s'allonger; **to ~ from X cm to Y cm** passer de X cm à Y cm; **2** [*days, nights*] s'allonger, rallonger; [*visit, silence*] se prolonger; **the intervals between her visits/migraines are ~ing** ses visites/ses migraines s'espacent.

lengthily /'leŋθılı/ *adv* longuement.

lengthwise /'leŋθwaız/, **lengthways** /'leŋθweız/ GB **I** *adj* [*cut, opening*] gen dans le sens de la longueur; (in fabric) dans (le sens de) la hauteur.
II *adv* **1** (along the length) [*cut, fold, place*] gen dans le sens de la longueur; (of fabric) dans (le sens de) la hauteur; **2** (end to end) [*place, lay*] en long.

lengthy /'leŋθı/ *adj* [*visit, illness, speech*] (assez) long/longue; **this treatment can be quite ~** ce traitement peut être assez long; **a ~ explanation** une longue explication; **we had a ~ wait** nous avons dû attendre (assez) longtemps.

lenience /'li:nıəns/, **leniency** /'li:nıənsı/ *n* (of person, institution) indulgence *f* (**with** pour; **towards** envers); (of punishment) légèreté *f*.

lenient /'li:nıənt/ *adj* [*person, institution, treatment, marking*] indulgent (**with** pour; **towards** envers); [*punishment, fine*] léger/-ère.

leniently /'li:nıəntlı/ *adv* avec indulgence.

Lenin /'lenın/ *pr n* Lénine.

Leninism /'lenınızəm/ *n* léninisme *m*.

Leninist /'lenınıst/ *n, adj* léniniste (*mf*).

lens /lenz/ *n* **1** (in optical instruments) lentille *f*; (in spectacles) verre *m*; (in camera) objectif *m*; (contact) lentille *f*; **long ~** Phot, TV téléobjectif *m*; **hard/soft ~es** lentilles *fpl* rigides/souples; **2** Anat cristallin *m*.

lens: **~ cap** *n* bouchon *m* d'objectif; **~ hood** *n* parasoleil *m*.

lent /lent/ *prét, pp* ▶ **lend**.

Lent /lent/ *n* carême *m*; **to observe ~** faire carême; **to give up sth for ~** renoncer à qch pendant le carême.

Lenten /'lentən/ *adj* littér de carême.

lentil /'lentl/ **I** *n* Bot, Culin lentille *f*; **red/green/brown ~s** lentilles rouges/vertes/blondes.
II *modif* [*soup, curry* etc] aux lentilles.

Lent term *n* GB Univ deuxième trimestre *m*.

Leo /'li:əʊ/ ▶ **1916** *pr n* **1** Astrol, Astron Lion *m*; **2** (name) Léon *m*.

Leonardo (da Vinci) /ˌli:ə'nɑ:dəʊ də 'vıntʃı/ *pr n* Léonard de Vinci.

leonine /'li:ənaın/ *adj* léonin.

leopard /'lepəd/ *n* léopard *m*.
IDIOMS **a ~ cannot change his spots** Prov chassez le naturel, il revient au galop Prov.

leopard cub *n* jeune léopard *m*.

leopardskin /'lepədskın/ **I** *n* peau *f* de léopard.
II *modif* [*garment, rug, pattern*] en peau de léopard.

leotard /'li:ətɑ:d/ *n* justaucorps *m*.

leper /'lepə(r)/ *n* Med, fig lépreux/-euse *m/f*.

leper colony *n* léproserie *f*.

lepidoptera /ˌlepı'dɒptərə/ *npl* lépidoptères *mpl*.

leprechaun /'leprəkɔ:n/ *n* lutin *m* (*en Irlande*).

leprosy /'leprəsı/ *n* lèpre *f*.

leprous /'leprəs/ *adj* [*person*] lépreux/-euse; [*body*] envahi par la lèpre.

lesbian /'lezbıən/ **I** *n* lesbienne *f*.
II *adj* lesbien/-ienne.

lesbianism /'lezbıənızəm/ *n* homosexualité *f* féminine, lesbianisme *m*.

lesion /'li:ʒn/ *n* lésion *f*.

Lesotho /lı'su:tu, lə'səʊtəʊ/ ▶ **1131** *pr n* Lésotho *m*; **in/to ~** au Lésotho.

less /les/ (*comp of* **little**) **I** *quantif* moins de; **~ beer/information/money** moins de bière/d'information/d'argent; **I have ~ money than him** j'ai moins d'argent que lui; **it took ~ time than we expected** cela a pris moins de temps que prévu; **I have ~ time for reading than I used to** j'ai moins le temps de lire qu'avant; **of ~ value/importance** de moindre valeur/importance; **to grow ~** diminuer.
II *pron* moins; **I have ~ than you** j'en ai moins que toi; **they have little money but we have even ~** ils n'ont pas beaucoup d'argent mais nous en avons encore moins; **I gave them ~ to eat** je leur ai donné moins à manger; **~ than half** moins de la moitié; **in ~ than three hours** en moins de trois heures; **in ~ than no time** en moins de deux; **13 is ~ than 18** 13 est plus petit que 18; **a sum of not ~ than £1,000** une somme qui s'élève au moins à 1 000 livres sterling; **he was ~ than honest/helpful** il était loin d'être honnête/serviable; **it's an improvement, but ~ of one than I had hoped** c'est un progrès, mais pas au point que j'aurais espéré; **she's nothing ~ than a common criminal** elle n'est rien de moins qu'une criminelle; **nothing ~ than written proof will satisfy them** ils ne seront satisfaits que quand ils auront une preuve écrite; **it's nothing ~ than a scandal!** c'est un véritable scandale!; **they want nothing ~ than the best** ils exigent le meilleur; **I offered them £800 for the car but they let me have it for ~** je leur ai proposé 800 livres sterling pour la voiture, mais ils me l'ont laissée pour moins; **he's ~ of a fool than you think** il est moins bête que tu ne le penses; **they will think all the ~ of her for it** ça va la faire descendre dans leur estime; **I think no ~ of her for that** elle n'est pas descendue dans mon estime pour autant; **the ~ she knows about it the better** moins elle en sait, mieux ça vaut; **I want £100 and not a penny ~!** je veux cent livres et pas un centime de moins!; **the ~ said about it the better** moins on en parle, mieux ça vaut; **people have been shot for ~!** il y en a qui ont été tués pour moins que ça!; **~ of your impudence!** ne sois pas insolent!; **~ of that!** (to child misbehaving) ça suffit!

> **less**
>
> When *less* is used as a quantifier (*less money*) it is translated by *moins de*: *moins d'argent*. For examples and particular usages, see **I** in the entry ***less***.
>
> When *less* is used as a pronoun (*you should have taken less*), it is translated by *moins*: *tu aurais dû en prendre moins*.
>
> *less than* is usually translated by *moins que* and *even less* by *encore moins*. For examples and particular usages of these see **II** in the entry ***less***.
>
> When *less* is used as an adverb followed by a verb, an adjective, or another adverb (*to eat less, less interesting, less often*) it is translated by *moins*: *manger moins, moins intéressant, moins souvent*. For examples and particular usages see **III** in the entry ***less***.
>
> For *less* used as a preposition (*less 10%*) see **IV** in the entry ***less***.
> For the phrase *less and less* see **V** in the entry ***less***.

III *adv* moins; **I read ~ these days** je lis moins en ce moment; **I liked it ~ than you did** je l'ai moins aimé que toi; **I dislike him no ~ than you** je ne l'aime pas plus que toi; **that's ~ urgent/serious** c'est moins urgent/grave; **much ~ important** beaucoup moins important; **it matters ~ than it did before** cela a moins d'importance qu'avant; **it's ~ complicated than you think** c'est moins compliqué que vous ne croyez; **she is no ~ qualified than you** elle n'est pas moins qualifiée que toi; **~ often** moins souvent; **it's ~ a village than a town** c'est plutôt une ville qu'un village; **the more I see him, the ~ I like him** plus je le vois, moins je l'aime; **no ~ than 30 people/85%** au moins 30 personnes/85%; **they live in Kensington, no ~!** ils habitent à Kensington, rien que ça!; **he's married to a countess, no ~!** il est marié avec une comtesse, rien que ça!; **no ~ a person than the emperor** l'empereur en personne; **one of the ~ known valleys** une des vallées les moins connues; **he was ~ offended than shocked** il était plus choqué qu'offensé; **she wasn't any the ~ happy** elle n'en était pas moins heureuse; **much** ou **still** ou **even ~** encore moins; **he can't afford to rent a house, much ~ buy one** il n'a pas les moyens de louer une maison, encore moins d'en acheter une.
IV *prep* moins; **~ 15% discount** moins 15% de remise; **a salary of £20,000, ~ tax** un salaire de 20 000 livres sterling, avant impôts.
V less and less *adv phr* de moins en moins; **we see her ~ and ~** nous la voyons de moins en moins; **~ and ~ often/busy** de moins en moins souvent/occupé.

lessee /le'si:/ *n* Jur preneur/-euse *m/f* à bail.

lessen /'lesn/ **I** *vtr* diminuer [*love, affection, influence*]; réduire [*pressure, cost, production*]; atténuer [*impact, pain, effect*]; **to ~ the need for sth** réduire or faire diminuer la demande pour qch.
II *vi* diminuer.

lessening /lesnıŋ/ *n* diminution *f*.

lesser /'lesə(r)/ **I** *adj* gen moindre; [*life form*] peu évolué; **to a ~ degree** ou **extent** à un moindre degré, dans une moindre mesure; **a ~ sum of money** une somme moins importante; **~ being** ou **mortal** être inférieur; **~ beings** ou **mortals like us** hum de simples mortels comme nous; **~ offence** ou **crime** délit *m* de moindre importance; **a ~ man would have run away** un homme plus faible se serait enfui; **the ~ works of an artist** les œuvres mineures d'un artiste.
II *adv* moins; **~ known** moins connu.

let¹

When *let* is used in English with another verb in order to make a suggestion (*let's do it at once*), the first person plural *-ons* of the appropriate verb can generally be used to express this in French: *faisons-le tout de suite*. (Note that the verb alone translates *let us do* and no pronoun appears in French.)

In the spoken language, however, which is the usual context for such suggestions, French speakers will use the much more colloquial *on* + *present tense* or *si on* + *imperfect tense*:

let's do it at once = on le fait tout de suite? *or* si on le faisait tout de suite?
let's go to the cinema tonight = si on allait au cinéma ce soir?
let's go! = allons-y *or* on y va!

These translations can also be used for negative suggestions:

let's not take or *don't let's take the bus – let's walk* = on ne prend pas le bus, on y va à pied *or* ne prenons pas le bus, allons-y à pied

For more examples and particular usages see **I 1** in the entry ***let¹***.

When *let* is used in English with another verb to express defiance or a command (*just let him try!*) the French uses the structure *que* + present subjunctive:

just let him try! = qu'il essaie!
don't let me see you here again! = que je ne te revoie plus ici!

For more examples and particular usages see **I 2** in the entry ***let¹***.

When *let* is used to mean *allow*, it is generally translated by the verb *laisser*. For examples and particular usages see **I 3** in the entry ***let¹***.

For translations of expressions such as *let fly*, *let loose*, *let slip* etc., consult the entry for the second word (***fly***, ***loose***, ***slip*** etc.).

lesson /ˈlesn/ *n* **1** gen leçon *f*; Sch cours *m*, leçon *f*; **Spanish ~** cours d'espagnol; **driving/tennis ~** leçon de conduite/de tennis; **to give ~s** donner des cours (**in** de); **to take/have ~s** prendre/suivre des cours (**in** de); **the headmaster will take today's French ~** le directeur va assurer le cours de français aujourd'hui; **we have ~s from 9 to 12** nous avons cours de 9 heures à midi; **2** Relig leçon *f*; **to read the ~** lire la leçon; **3** fig leçon *f*; **let that be a ~ to you!** que cela te serve de leçon!; **I've learned my ~!** cela m'a servi de leçon!; **I'm going to teach him a ~!** je vais lui donner une bonne leçon!; **that'll teach you a ~!** cela t'apprendra!

lesson plan *n* plan *m* de cours.

lessor /leˈsɔː(r)/ *n* Jur bailleur/-eresse *m/f*.

lest /lest/ *conj* sout **1** (for fear that) de peur de (+ *infin*), de crainte de (+ *infin*), de crainte que (+ *ne* + *subj*); (in case that) au cas où; **he wrote down the address ~ he forget it** il a noté l'adresse de peur or de crainte de l'oublier; **she burned her letters ~ he** (**should** ou **might**) **read them** elle a brûlé ses lettres de crainte qu'il ne les lise; **~ anyone should ask you** au cas où quelqu'un vous le demanderait; **'~ we forget'** ≈ 'In memoriam'; **2** (after expressions of fear) **I was afraid ~ he might** ou **should die** j'avais peur qu'il ne meure.

let¹ /let/ **I** *vtr* (*p prés* **-tt-**; *prét, pp* **let**) **1** (when making suggestion) **~'s go** allons-y; **~'s give it a try** essayons; **~'s go for a swim** allons nager; **~'s begin by doing** commençons par faire; **~'s get out of here!** sortons d'ici!; **~'s not** ou **don't ~'s** GB **talk about that!** n'en parlons pas!; **~'s see if...** voyons si...; **~ us pray** prions; **~'s pretend that this is the interview** faisons comme si c'était l'entretien; **~'s face it** soyons honnête; **~'s face it, you were wrong** il faut voir les choses en face, tu avais tort; **~ me see, ~'s see...** voyons...; **it was—~ me think—about 8 pm** il était—attends voir or voyons voir—environ 8 heures du soir; **~ me think about it** laisse-moi réfléchir; **~'s assume that...** supposons or mettons que... (+ *subj*); **~'s say (that)...** admettons que... (+ *subj*); **it's more complex than, ~'s say, a computer** c'est plus compliqué que, disons, un ordinateur; **~'s say she wasn't amused** iron disons qu'elle n'a pas vraiment apprécié; **2** (when expressing defiance or a command) **~ there be no doubt about it!** qu'il n'y ait aucun doute là-dessus!; **~ everyone make up his own mind** que chacun d'entre nous décide pour lui-même; **~ the festivities begin!** que la fête commence!; **never ~ it be said that** qu'il ne soit pas dit que; **~ there be light** que la lumière soit; **people will talk—well ~ them (talk)!** ça va faire parler les gens—eh bien laisse-les parler!; **~ that be a lesson to you!** que cela te serve de leçon!; **just ~ him try it!** qu'il essaie!; **if he wants tea, ~ him make it himself!** s'il veut du thé, qu'il le fasse lui-même!; **~ them eat cake!** qu'on leur donne de la brioche!; **~ me tell you...** crois-moi, croyez-moi...; **~ y = 25** Math soit y = 25; **~ the line AB intersect CD** Math soit la droite AB qui coupe CD; **3** (allow) **to ~ sb do sth** laisser qn faire qch; **she let us see the baby** elle nous a laissés voir le bébé; **~ me go first** laisse-moi passer devant or en premier; **~ me pay for dinner** laissez-moi vous inviter; **~ me explain** laisse-moi t'expliquer; **she let herself be intimidated** elle s'est laissée intimider; **don't ~ them see you crying** ne les laisse pas voir que tu pleures; **don't ~ them think that...** ne les laisse pas penser que...; **don't ~ it get you down** ne te laisse pas abattre; **she wanted to leave but they wouldn't ~ her** elle voulait partir mais ils ne l'ont pas laissée faire; **I won't ~ them talk to me like that!** je ne permets pas qu'on me parle sur ce ton!; **don't ~ me forget to do** rappelle-moi de faire; **~ me see, ~ me have a look** fais voir, fais-moi voir; **~ me (do that)** permettez fml, laisse-moi faire; **~ me ask you...** permettez-moi de vous demander...; **~ me introduce you to Isabelle** laissez-moi vous présenter à Isabelle; **can you ~ me have that in writing?** pourriez-vous me mettre cela par écrit?; **~ them have it!** lit donne-le-leur!; fig○ (shoot) descends-les○!; (attack verbally) rentre-leur dedans○!; **to ~ sth fall/escape** laisser tomber/échapper qch; **don't ~ the milk boil over!** ne laisse pas déborder le lait!; **to ~ one's hair/beard grow** se laisser pousser les cheveux/la barbe; **4** (allow free movement or passage to) **to ~ sb through** laisser passer qn; **to ~ sb on/off the bus** laisser qn monter dans/descendre de l'autobus; **can you ~ me off here?** pouvez-vous me déposer ici?; **~ me pass please** laissez-moi passer s'il vous plaît; **she won't ~ him out of/inside the house** elle ne le laisse pas sortir/entrer; **I let myself in** je suis entré; **to ~ air into a room** aérer une pièce; **draw the curtains and ~ some light in** ouvre les rideaux pour qu'il y ait un peu de lumière; **to ~ the air out of** dégonfler [*tyre, balloon*]; **5** (insert, inlay) **to ~ a door/window into a wall** percer une porte/fenêtre dans un mur; **a statue let into the wall** une statue encastrée dans le mur.

II let alone *conj phr* à plus forte raison; **she was too ill to stand ~ alone walk** elle était trop malade pour se tenir debout à plus forte raison pour marcher; **he couldn't look after the cat ~ alone a child** il ne serait pas capable de s'occuper du chat encore moins d'un enfant.

■ **let away**○: **~ [sb] away with doing** laisser qn faire; **don't ~ her away with that!** ne la laisse pas s'en tirer comme ça!

■ **let down**: ¶ **~ [sb] down 1** (disappoint) [*organization, person*] laisser tomber [qn]; **it has never let me down** [*technique, machine*] ça a toujours marché; **the car let us down** la voiture nous a laissé tomber; **to feel let down** être déçu; **don't ~ me down!** je compte sur toi!; ▶**side**; **2** (embarrass) faire honte à [qn]; ¶ **~ [sth] down, ~ down [sth] 1** GB (deflate) dégonfler [*tyre*]; **2** (lower) faire descendre [*bucket, basket*]; baisser [*window*]; **3** (lengthen) rallonger [*skirt, coat*]; **4** (leave loose) détacher [*hair*]; ▶**hair**.

■ **let go** ¶ lit lâcher prise; **to ~ go of sb/sth** lit lâcher qn/qch; fig se détacher de qn/qch; **he just can't ~ go** fig il ne peut pas oublier; ¶ **~ [sb] go, ~ go [sb] 1** (free) relâcher [*hostage, suspect, prisoner*]; **2** (release hold on) lâcher [*person, sleeve, arm*]; **~ me go, ~ go of me!** lâche-moi!; **3** euph (make redundant) licencier [*employee*]; **to be let go** être licencié; **4 to ~ oneself go** (all contexts) se laisser aller; ¶ **~ [sth] go, ~ go [sth] 1** (release hold on) lâcher [*rope, bar*]; **2** fig **to ~ it go** (not to react) laisser passer; (stop fretting about) ne plus y penser; **we'll ~ it go at that** restons-en là.

■ **let in**: ¶ **~ in [sth], ~ [sth] in 1** (allow to enter) [*roof, window*] laisser passer [*rain*]; [*shoes, tent*] prendre [*water*]; [*curtains, glass door*] laisser passer [*light*]; **2** Sport (concede) laisser marquer [*goal*]; **3** GB Aut **to ~ in the clutch** embrayer; ¶ **~ [sb] in, ~ in [sb] 1** (show in) faire entrer; **2** (admit) laisser entrer; **I let myself in** je suis entré avec ma clé; **3 to ~ oneself in for** (expose oneself to) aller au devant de [*trouble, problems, disappointment*]; **I had no idea what I was ~ting myself in for** je n'avais aucune idée de là où je mettais les pieds○; **4 to ~ sb in on, to ~ sb into** mettre qn au courant de [*secret, joke, news*].

■ **let off**: ¶ **~ off [sth]** tirer [*fireworks*]; faire exploser [*device, bomb*]; faire partir [*rifle, gun*]; ▶**hook, steam**; ¶ **~ [sb] off 1** GB Sch (send home) laisser sortir [*pupils*]; **2** (excuse) **to ~ sb off** dispenser qn de [*lessons, homework, chores*]; **to ~ sb off doing** dispenser qn de faire; **3** (leave unpunished) ne pas punir [*culprit*]; **to be ~ off with** s'en tirer avec [*fine, caution*]; **to ~ sb off lightly** laisser qn s'en tirer à bon compte.

■ **let on 1** (reveal) dire (**to sb** à qn); **to ~ on about sth** parler de qch; **don't ~ on!** ne dis rien!; **don 't ~ on that you speak German** ne dis pas que tu parles allemand; **she misses them more than she ~s on** ils lui manquent plus qu'elle ne veut bien l'admettre; **2** GB (pretend) **to ~ on that** faire croire que.

■ **let out**: ¶ **~ out** US [*movie, school*] finir (at à); ¶ **~ out [sth] 1** (emit) laisser échapper [*cry, scream, sigh, shriek*]; **to ~ out a roar** beugler; **2** GB (reveal) révéler (**that** que); ¶ **~ [sth] out, ~ out [sth] 1** (release) faire sortir [*animal*]; **2** donner libre cours à [*grief, anger*]; **to ~ out one's breath** expirer; ▶**cat**; **3** Aut **to ~ out the clutch** embrayer; **4** Sewing (alter) élargir [*skirt, jacket*]; rallonger [*waistband*]; ¶ **~ [sb] out 1** (release) laisser sortir [*prisoner*] (**of** de); faire sortir [*pupils, employees*] (**of** de); **2** (show out) reconduire [qn] à la porte; **I'll ~ myself out** ne vous dérangez pas, je peux sortir tout seul.

■ **let through**: ¶ **~ [sb] through, ~ through [sb] 1** (in crowd) laisser passer; **2**

Sch, Univ accorder un examen à; ¶ **~ [sth] through, ~ through [sth]** laisser passer [*error, faulty product*].

■ **let up 1** (ease off) [*rain, wind*] se calmer; [*heat*] diminuer; **the rain never once let up** il a plu sans arrêt; **2** (stop) [*conversation, pressure*] s'arrêter; **he never ~s up** (works hard) il travaille sans relâche; (exerts pressure) il ne me/lui etc laisse jamais de répit; (talks constantly) il n'arrête pas de parler; **3 to ~ up on sb**○ (be less severe) lâcher la bride à qn, être moins dur avec qn.

let[2] /let/ **I** *n* **1** GB (lease) bail *m*; **to take a three-year ~ on a house** louer une maison pour trois ans; **2** Sport let *m*, balle *f* let; **to serve a ~** jouer un let; **3** Jur ▶ **hindrance**.

II *vtr* (*p prés* **-tt-**; *prét, pp* **let**) **1** (also GB **~ out**) (lease) louer [*room, apartment, land*] (**to** à); **'room to ~'** 'chambre à louer'; **'to ~'** 'à louer'; **2**† Med **to ~ blood** faire une saignée.

■ **let off**: **~ off [sth], ~ [sth] off** louer [*part of house, property*].

letdown /'letdaʊn/ *n* **1** (disappointment) déception *f*; **it was a bit of a ~** [*film, performance, meal*] c'était décevant; **2** Aerosp descente *f*.

lethal /'li:θl/ *adj* **1** (fatal) [*poisonous substance, gas, ray, effect*] mortel/-elle; [*disease, attack, blow*] fatal; [*blow, weapon, explosion*] meurtrier/-ière; **~ dose** gen dose *f* mortelle; (of nuclear radiation) dose *f* létale; **2** (dangerous) [*toy, machine, implement, stretch of road*] très dangereux/-euse; [*attack, blow*] fig fatal; [*marksman, opponent*] redoutable; **a ~ cocktail** ou **mixture** (drink) lit un mélange meurtrier; fig, hum un mélange redoutable; (of people) hum un mélange explosif.

lethargic /lɪ'θɑ:dʒɪk/ *adj* [*person, animal*] lit léthargique; fig (lazy) apathique; [*movement*] engourdi; **to feel ~** se sentir engourdi; **to become ~** s'engourdir.

lethargically /lɪ'θɑ:dʒɪklɪ/ *adv* [*move, work*] mollement; [*sit, lie*] paresseusement; [*look, reply*] d'un air las.

lethargy /'leθədʒɪ/ *n* léthargie *f*.

let-out○ /'letaʊt/ *n* échappatoire *f*.

let-out clause *n* Jur clause *f* dérogatoire.

let's /lets/ = **let us**.

Lett /let/ *pr n* Letton/-one *m*/*f*.

letter /'letə(r)/ **I** *n* **1** (item of correspondence) lettre *f* (**to** pour; **from** de); **a ~ of apology/resignation** une lettre d'excuse/de démission; **to inform sb by ~** informer qn par lettre; **he receives a lot of ~s** il reçoit beaucoup de courrier; **~s to the editor** Journ courrier des lecteurs; **the ~s of Virginia Woolf** la correspondance de Virginia Woolf; **2** (of alphabet) lettre *f*; (character) caractère *m*; **the ~ A** la lettre A; **to write sth in big ~s** écrire qch en gros caractères; **to have a lot of ~s after one's name**○ être bardé○ de titres; **3** US Sport *récompense sportive décernée par une école sous la forme de son monogramme*.

II letters *npl* (literature) belles-lettres *fpl*; **academy of ~s** société des belles-lettres; **a man/woman of ~s** un homme/une femme de lettres.

III *vtr* marquer [qch] d'une lettre [*photograph, diagram*]; **the rows are ~ed from A to P** les rangées portent des lettres allant de A à P; **to be ~ed in gold/ink** porter des lettres en or/inscrites à l'encre.

IV *vi* US Univ **to ~ in baseball** gagner une récompense en base-ball.

IDIOMS **to respect the ~, if not the spirit, of the law** suivre la lettre, sinon l'esprit, de la loi; **to follow instructions to the ~** suivre des instructions à la lettre.

letter: **~ bomb** *n* lettre *f* piégée; **~ box** *n* boîte *f* à lettres.

lettered† /'letəd/ *adj* lettré.

letterhead /'letəhed/ *n* en-tête *m*.

lettering /'letərɪŋ/ *n* caractères *mpl*.

letter: **~man** *n* US Univ *étudiant qui a gagné une récompense sportive de son école*; **~ of credit** *n* lettre *f* de crédit; **~ opener** *n* coupe-papier *m*.

letter-perfect *adj* US [*piece of work, essay*] parfait; Theat **to be ~** connaître son texte sur le bout des doigts.

letter post *n* Post tarif *m* lettre.

letterpress /'letəpres/ *n* Print **1** (method) typographie *f*; **2** (text) texte *m* imprimé en relief.

letter: **~ rack** *n* porte-lettres *m inv*; **~s of credence** *npl* lettres *fpl* de créance; **~s page** *n* Journ courrier *m* des lecteurs; **~s patent** *npl* lettres *fpl* patentes.

letter-writer *n* **he's a keen ~** il aime beaucoup écrire (des lettres).

letting /'letɪŋ/ *n* GB **1** (property for lease) location *f*; **holiday ~s** locations *fpl* de vacances; **furnished ~s** locations *fpl* meublées; **2** ¢ (leasing) location *f* (**of** de).

lettuce /'letɪs/ **I** *n* Bot, Culin (any variety) salade *f*; (round) laitue *f*; (cos) romaine *f*; (iceberg) laitue *f* croquante; **a head of ~** une laitue, une salade.

II *modif* [*heart, leaf*] de laitue, de salade; [*soup*] de laitue.

letup /'letʌp/ *n* **1** (reduction in intensity) accalmie *f* (**in** dans); **2** (respite) pause *f*.

leucocyte /'lu:kəsaɪt/ *n* leucocyte *m*.

leucotomy /lu:'kɒtəmɪ/ *n* leucotomie *f*.

leuk(a)emia /lu:'ki:mɪə/ ▶ **1354** *n* leucémie *f*; **to have ~** être atteint de leucémie, être leucémique.

leukocyte *n* = **leucocyte**.

leukotomy *n* = **leucotomy**.

Levant /lɪ'vænt/ *pr n* **the ~** le Levant.

Levantine /lɪ'væntaɪn/ *adj* levantin.

levee /'levɪ/ *n* **1** Hist (reception) (on rising) lever *m* (*du roi*); (in afternoon) réception *f* royale; **2** US (embankment) digue *f*; (by river) levée *f* alluviale; (quay) quai *m*.

level /'levl/ **I** *n* **1** (floor) (of building, mine) niveau *m*; **2** (elevation) (of liquid, sea) niveau *m*; **3** Sch, Univ niveau *m*; **an intermediate ~ textbook** un manuel pour le niveau intermédiaire; **that course is above/below your ~** ce cours est trop difficile/facile pour toi; **4** fig (of understanding) niveau *m*; **to be on the same ~ as sb** être du même niveau que qn; **to get down/to come down to sb's ~** se mettre/s'abaisser au niveau de qn; **to talk to sb on their ~** parler à qn d'égal à égal; **5** (equal plane) **to be on a ~ with** lit [*building, window*] être à la hauteur de or au même niveau que [*building, window*]; fig [*action*] équivaloir à [*action*]; **on a ~ with the first floor** à la hauteur du premier étage; **two windows both on the same ~** deux fenêtres à la même hauteur; **at waist-/knee-~** à la hauteur de la taille/des genoux; **at street ~** au niveau de la rue; **that is on a ~ with arson** fig ça équivaut à l'incendie criminel; **6** (degree) (of pollution, noise, competence) niveau *m*; (of substance, unemployment, illiteracy) taux *m*; (of spending) montant *m*; (of satisfaction, anxiety) degré *m*; **glucose/cholesterol ~s** taux de glucose/cholestérol; **7** (position in hierarchy) échelon *m*; **at local/national/board ~** à l'échelon local/national/du conseil d'administration; **at all ~s** à tous les échelons; **at a higher/lower ~** à un échelon supérieur/inférieur; **8** fig (plane) plan *m*; **on a purely practical ~** sur un plan strictement pratique; **to be reduced to the same ~ as** être mis sur le même plan que; **on a literary/musical ~** d'un point de vue littéraire/musical; **9** fig (standard) qualité *f*; **the ~ of training/of service** la qualité de la formation/du service; **10** (tool) gen niveau *m*; (for surveying) niveau *m* à lunette.

II levels *npl* Geog **the Somerset ~s** la plaine du Somerset.

III *adj* **1** (not at an angle) [*shelf, rail, floor*] droit; [*surface*] plan; [*worktop, table*] horizontal; **to hold a compass ~** tenir une boussole horizontale; **I don't think this bed is ~** je trouve que ce lit penche; **2** (not bumpy) [*ground, surface, plain, land*] plat; [*field, garden*] nivelé; (naturally) sans dénivellation; **3** Culin (not heaped) [*teaspoonful*] ras; **4** (equally high) **to be ~** [*shoulders, windows, etc*] être à la même hauteur; [*floor, ceiling, building*] être au même niveau; **is the hem ~?** est-ce que l'ourlet est droit?; **trim the shoots so they are ~ with the ground** taillez les rejets au ras du sol; **5** fig (equal in achievement, rank) **to be ~** [*competitors*] être à égalité; **to be ~ in popularity** atteindre la même cote de popularité; **on the same ~** (of colleagues) au même échelon; **6** (stable) **to remain ~** [*growth, figures*] rester stable; **7** fig (even) [*tone*] égal.

IV *adv* (abreast) **to draw ~** [*competitors, cars*] arriver à la même hauteur (**with** que); **the pound is keeping ~ with the deutschmark** la livre se maintient par rapport au deutschmark.

V *vtr* (*p prés etc* **-ll-** GB, **-l-** US) **1** (raze to ground) raser [*village, area*]; **2** (aim) braquer [*gun, weapon*] (**at** sur); lancer [*accusation*] (**at** contre); adresser [*criticism*] (**at** à); **the criticism was ~led mainly at the board of directors** les critiques visaient essentiellement le conseil d'administration; **3**○ (knock down) mettre à terre [*opponent*].

IDIOMS **to be ~-pegging** être à égalité; **to be on the ~** (on level ground) être sur terrain plat; (trustworthy) être réglo○; **to ~ with sb** être honnête avec qn; **to keep a ~ head** garder son sang-froid; **to try one's ~ best to do sth** faire tout son possible pour faire qch.

■ **level off**: ¶ **~ off 1** [*prices, rate of growth, curve*] se stabiliser; **2** [*plane, pilot*] amorcer le vol en palier; **3** [*path*] continuer sur terrain plat; ¶ **~ [sth] off, ~ off [sth]** égaliser [*ground, floor, mortar*]; aplanir [*wooden surface*].

■ **level out**: ¶ **~ out 1** [*land, terrain*] s'aplanir; **2** [*prices, rate of growth, curve*] se stabiliser; ¶ **~ [sth] out, ~ out [sth]** niveler [*ground, floor*].

level: **~ crossing** *n* passage *m* à niveau; **~-headed** *adj* pondéré, sensé; **~-headedness** *n* gen bon sens *m*; (in crisis) sang-froid *m*.

leveller GB, **leveler** US /'levələ(r)/ *n* littér **death is the great ~** tous les hommes sont égaux devant la mort.

levelling /'levəlɪŋ/ **I** *n* **1** (making smooth) nivellement *m*; **2** (razing to ground) démolition *f*.

II *modif* [*effect*] de nivellement; **a ~ process** un nivellement.

levelling: **~-down** *n* nivellement *m* par le bas; **~-off** *n* Econ stabilisation *f*; **~ rod** *n* mire *f*; **~ screw** *n* vis *f* de réglage; **~-up** *n* réajustement *m*.

lever /'li:və(r), US 'levər/ **I** *n* **1** Aut, Tech levier *m*; (small) manette *f*; **gear ~** GB Aut levier de changement de vitesse; **to pull a ~** actionner un levier or une manette; **2** fig (also **bargaining ~**) moyen *m* de pression.

II *vtr* **1** lit **to ~ sth off sth** enlever qch de qch à l'aide d'un levier; **to ~ sth out of sth** sortir qch de qch à l'aide d'un levier; **to ~ sth into position** mettre qch en place à l'aide d'un levier; **to ~ sth open** utiliser un levier pour ouvrir qch; **2** fig **to ~ sb in/out** (of office, organization) installer/déloger qn.

■ **lever up**: **~ up [sth], ~ [sth] up** soulever (à l'aide d'un levier).

leverage /'li:vərɪdʒ, US 'lev-/ **I** *n* **1** Econ, Pol force *f* d'appui (**on, over** sur); **2** Fin effet *m* de levier; **3** Phys puissance *f* de levier.

II *vtr* exercer une influence.

III leveraged *pp adj* Econ, Fin [*company*] endetté; **highly ~d** à fort degré d'endettement.

leverage: **~d buyout, LBO** *n* rachat *m* d'entreprise par endettement;

~d management buyout, **LMBO** *n* rachat *m* d'entreprise par ses salariés.
leveret /ˈlevərɪt/ *n* levraut *m*.
leviathan /lɪˈvaɪəθn/ *n* lit, fig léviathan *m*.
Levi's® /ˈliːvaɪz/ *npl* Levi's® *m*.
levitate /ˈlevɪteɪt/ **I** *vtr* faire léviter.
II *vi* léviter.
levitation /ˌlevɪˈteɪʃn/ *n* lévitation *f*.
Levite /ˈliːvaɪt/ *pr n* Lévite *mf*.
Leviticus /lɪˈvɪtɪkəs/ *pr n* Lévitique *m*.
levity /ˈlevətɪ/ *n* désinvolture *f*; **this is no occasion for ~** ce n'est pas le moment de plaisanter.
levy /ˈlevɪ/ **I** *n* **1** (tax) taxe *f*, impôt *m* (**on** sur); (act of collecting) perception *f*; **import/production ~** taxe à l'importation/à la production; **agricultural ~** prélèvement *m* agricole; **political ~** GB cotisation *f* (*payée par les membres d'un syndicat au parti travailliste*); **2** Mil Hist levée *f*.
II *vtr* **1** (charge) percevoir, prélever [*tax, duty, amount*] (**from** de); imposer [*fine*]; **to ~ a tax on sb/sth** prélever or imposer une taxe sur qn/qch; **2** Mil Hist lever [*troops, army*].
lewd /ljuːd, US ˈluːd/ *adj* [*joke, gesture, remark*] obscène; [*person, expression*] lubrique.
lewdly /ˈljuːdlɪ, US ˈluːdlɪ/ *adv* de façon obscène.
lewdness /ˈljuːdnɪs, US ˈluːd-/ *n* (of joke, remark) obscénité *f*; (of person, behaviour) lubricité *f*.
lexeme /ˈleksiːm/ *n* lexème *m*.
lexical /ˈleksɪkl/ *adj* lexical.
lexicalize /ˈleksɪkəlaɪz/ *vtr* lexicaliser; **to become ~d** se lexicaliser.
lexicographer /ˌleksɪˈkɒɡrəfə(r)/ ▶ **1692** *n* lexicographe *mf*.
lexicographical /ˌleksɪkəˈɡræfɪkl/ *adj* lexicographique.
lexicography /ˌleksɪˈkɒɡrəfɪ/ *n* lexicographie *f*.
lexicological /ˌleksɪkəˈlɒdʒɪkl/ *adj* lexicologique.
lexicologist /ˌleksɪˈkɒlədʒɪst/ ▶ **1692** *n* lexicologue *mf*.
lexicology /ˌleksɪˈkɒlədʒɪ/ *n* lexicologie *f*.
lexicon /ˈleksɪkən, US -kɒn/ *n* gén, Ling lexique *m*.
lexis /ˈleksɪs/ *n* lexique *m*.
ley-line /leɪlaɪn/ *n*: *ligne droite imaginaire reliant des sites préhistoriques et supposée correspondre à une ligne d'énergie terrestre*.
lez◐ /lez/, **lezzie**◐ /ˈlezɪ/ *n* injur (lesbian) gouine◐ *f*, lesbienne *f* offensive.
LI US Post *abrév* = **Long Island**.
liability /ˌlaɪəˈbɪlətɪ/ **I** *n* **1** Jur (responsibility) responsabilité *f*; **to deny ~ for** décliner toute responsabilité en ce qui concerne; **~ for military service** obligations *fpl* militaires; **~ for tax/for paying tax** assujettissement *m* à l'impôt/au paiement de l'impôt; **2** (drawback) handicap *m*; **the house has become a ~ to them** la maison est devenue une trop grande charge pour eux; **the leader has become a ~ to his party** le chef est devenu un poids mort pour son parti.
II liabilities *npl* passif *m*, dettes *fpl*; **assets and liabilities** actif et passif; **to meet one's liabilities** faire face à ses engagements financiers, payer ses dettes.
liable /ˈlaɪəbl/ *adj* **1** (likely) **to be ~ to do** risquer de faire; **to be ~ to win/to get arrested** risquer de gagner/de se faire arrêter; **it's ~ to rain** il risque de pleuvoir, il se peut qu'il pleuve; **2** (prone) **to be ~ to** [*person*] être sujet/-ette à [*illness etc*]; [*thing*] être susceptible à; **she is ~ to colds/fits** elle est sujette aux rhumes/aux crises; **the contract is ~ to changes** le contrat peut faire l'objet de modifications; **to be ~ to postponement at short notice** être susceptible d'être ajourné à la dernière minute; **3** (legally subject) **to be ~ to** être passible de [*fine, prosecution*]; **to be ~ for** ou **to duty** être assujetti à des droits; **to be ~ for** ou **to tax** [*person, company*] être imposable; [*goods, property*] être soumis à l'impôt; **to be ~ for military service** être astreint au service militaire; **4** Jur (answerable) civilement responsable (**for** de); **to be ~ for sb's debts** répondre des dettes de qn; **~ for damages** tenu de payer des dommages et intérêts.
liaise /lɪˈeɪz/ *vi* travailler en liaison (**with** avec).
liaison /lɪˈeɪzn, US ˈlɪəzɒn/ *n* (all contexts) liaison *f* (**with** avec; **between** entre); **to make a** ou **the ~** Phon faire la liaison.
liaison: **~ committee** *n* comité *m* de liaison; **~ officer** *n* Mil officier *m* de liaison; Admin responsable *mf* de la communication.
liana /lɪˈɑːnə/ *n* liane *f*.
liar /ˈlaɪə(r)/ *n* menteur/-euse *m/f*.
lib○ /lɪb/ *n* (mouvement *m* de) libération *f*; **women's ~** ≈ mouvement *m* pour la libération de la femme, MLF *m*.
Lib /lɪb/ *n* GB Pol (*abrév* = **Liberal**) libéral/-e *m/f*; **~-Lab pact** coalition *f* de 1977 à 1978 entre travaillistes et libéraux (*contre les conservateurs*).
libation /laɪˈbeɪʃn/ *n* **1** Antiq libation *f* (**to** à); **2** hum libations *fpl*.
libber○ /ˈlɪbə(r)/ *n* activiste *mf*; **women's ~** féministe *f*.
Lib Dem○ *n, adj* GB Pol *abrév* = **Liberal Democrat**.
libel /ˈlaɪbl/ **I** *n* **1** (crime) diffamation *f*; **to bring an action for ~ against sb, to sue sb for ~** intenter un procès en diffamation à qn; **2** (article, statement) écrit *m* diffamatoire; **3** (slander, insult) calomnie *f*.
II *modif* [*action, case, proceedings, suit*] en diffamation; [*award, damages*] pour diffamation; [*laws*] sur la diffamation.
III *vtr* (*p prés etc* **-ll-**, US **-l-**) diffamer.
libellous GB, **libelous** US /ˈlaɪbələs/ *adj* diffamatoire.
liberal /ˈlɪbərəl/ **I** *n* gen, Pol libéral/-e *m/f*; gauchisant/-e *m/f* pej.
II *adj* **1** (open-minded, tolerant) [*person, institution*] gen libéral; Pol, Relig libéral; péj bien intentionné; [*attitude, values*] libéral; **~ intellectual** ≈ intellectuel/-elle *m/f* de gauche; **2** (generous) [*amount, offer*] généreux/-euse; [*person*] prodigue (**with** de); **the cook has been a bit ~ with the salt** la cuisinière a eu la main un peu lourde sur le sel; **to make ~ use of sth** faire amplement usage de qch; **3** [*translation, interpretation*] libre.
Liberal /ˈlɪbərəl/ *n, adj* Pol libéral/-e (*m/f*).
liberal arts *npl* **1** Univ ≈ arts *mpl* et sciences *fpl* humaines; **2** Hist arts *mpl* libéraux.
liberal democracy *n* démocratie *f* libérale.
Liberal Democrat *n* GB Pol libéral-démocrate *mf*; **the ~s** les libéraux-démocrates.
liberal education *n* ≈ éducation *f* classique.
liberalism /ˈlɪbərəlɪzəm/ *n* **1** gen, Pol, Econ libéralisme *m*; **2** = **liberality**.
liberality /ˌlɪbəˈrælətɪ/ *n* **1** (generosity) libéralité *f*; **2** (open-mindedness) libéralisme *m*.
liberalization /ˌlɪbərəlaɪˈzeɪʃn, US -lɪˈz-/ *n* libéralisation *f*.
liberalize /ˈlɪbərəlaɪz/ *vtr* libéraliser; **to become ~d** se libéraliser.
liberally /ˈlɪbərəlɪ/ *adv* **1** (generously) libéralement; **~ laced with vodka** avec une bonne dose de vodka; **2** (tolerantly) [*think, treat, govern*] de façon libérale; **3** (not literally) [*interpret, translate*] librement.
liberal: **~-minded** *adj* large d'esprit; **Liberal Party** *n* GB Pol Hist parti *m* libéral; **~ studies** *npl* GB Sch, Univ ≈ culture *f* générale.
liberate /ˈlɪbəreɪt/ **I** *vtr* **1** gen libérer [*country, group*] (**from** de); libérer, délivrer [*hostage, prisoner*]; affranchir [*slave*]; **2** Fin dégager [*funds*]; **3** Chem libérer; **4**○ hum (steal) faucher○.
II liberated *pp adj* [*attitude, lifestyle, woman*] libéré.
III liberating *pres p adj* libérateur/-trice.
liberation /ˌlɪbəˈreɪʃn/ *n* **1** gen, Pol libération *f* (**from** de); **women's/black/sexual ~** libération *f* de la femme/des noirs/sexuelle; **gay ~** mouvement *m* de libération des homosexuels; **2** Fin (of funds) dégagement *m*; **3** Hist (of France) **the Liberation** la Libération.
liberation: **~ army** *n* Pol armée *f* de libération; **~ front** *n* front *m* de libération.
liberationist /ˌlɪbəˈreɪʃənɪst/ *n* membre *m* d'un mouvement de libération.
liberation: **~ movement** *n* Pol mouvement *m* de libération; **~ theology** *n* théologie *f* de la libération; **~ war** *n* guerre *f* de libération.
liberator /ˈlɪbəreɪtə(r)/ *n* libérateur/-trice *m/f*.
Liberia /laɪˈbɪərɪə/ ▶ **1131** *pr n* Liberia *m*; **in/to ~** au Liberia.
Liberian /laɪˈbɪərɪən/ ▶ **1486** **I** *n* Libérien/-ienne *m/f*.
II *adj* libérien/-ienne.
libertarian /ˌlɪbəˈteərɪən/ *n, adj* **1** (Right wing) ultralibéral/-e (*m/f*); **2** (liberal Left) libertaire (*mf*).
libertarianism /ˌlɪbəˈteərɪənɪzəm/ *n* (Right wing) ultralibéralisme *m*.
libertinage /ˈlɪbətiːnɪdʒ/ *n* littér libertinage *m*.
libertine /ˈlɪbətiːn/ *n* littér libertin/-e *m/f*.
liberty /ˈlɪbətɪ/ *n* **1** gen, Philos, Pol (freedom) liberté *f*; **individual/political ~** liberté individuelle/politique; **civil liberties** droits *mpl* civils; **to be at/to set sb at ~** être/mettre qn en liberté; **to be at ~ to do** être libre de faire; **I am not at ~ to say** sout je n'ai pas le droit de vous le dire; **2** (presumption) **to take the ~ of doing** prendre la liberté de faire; **to take liberties with sth/sb** prendre des libertés avec qch/qn; **it is a bit of a ~** ou **rather a ~ to do** c'est plutôt effronté de faire; **what a ~**○! quel sans-gêne!; **3** US Mil Naut permission *f*.
IDIOMS **it's ~ hall here!** chacun fait comme il veut ici!
liberty: **~ bodice** *n* chemise *f* américaine; **~ cap** *n* bonnet *m* phrygien.
libidinal /lɪˈbɪdɪnl/ *adj* libidinal.
libidinous /lɪˈbɪdɪnəs/ *adj* sout hum libidineux/-euse.
libido /lɪˈbiːdəʊ, ˈlɪbɪdəʊ/ *n* (*pl* **-os**) libido *f*.
Libra /ˈliːbrə/ ▶ **1916** *n* Balance *f*.
Libran /ˈlɪːbrən/ ▶ **1916** **I** *n* Balance *f*; **he's a ~** il est Balance.
II *adj* [*characteristic*] de la Balance.
librarian /laɪˈbreərɪən/ ▶ **1692** *n* bibliothécaire *mf*.
librarianship /laɪˈbreərɪənʃɪp/ *n* (library science) bibliothéconomie *f*; **a career/studies in ~** une carrière/des études de bibliothécaire.
library /ˈlaɪbrərɪ, US -brerɪ/ **I** *n* bibliothèque *f*; **local/public ~** bibliothèque de quartier/municipale; **photo(graphic) ~** photothèque *f*; **toy ~** ludothèque *f*.
II *modif* [*book, card, service, ticket*] de bibliothèque; Comput [*program, software*] de bibliothèque.
library: **~ edition** *n* édition *f* pour bibliothèque; **~ pictures** *npl* TV images *fpl* d'archives; **~ science** *n* bibliothéconomie *f*.
librettist /lɪˈbretɪst/ *n* librettiste *mf*.
libretto /lɪˈbretəʊ/ *n* (*pl* **-tti** ou **-ttos**) livret *m*, libretto *m*.
Librium® /ˈlɪbrɪəm/ *n* Librium® *m*.
Libya /ˈlɪbɪə/ ▶ **1131** *pr n* Libye *f*; **in/to ~** en Libye.
Libyan /ˈlɪbɪən/ ▶ **1486** **I** *n* Libyen/-enne *m/f*.

II *adj* libyen/-enne.

Libyan Desert *pr n* désert *m* de Libye.

lice /laɪs/ *pl* ▶ **louse**.

licence GB, **license** US /'laɪsns/ *n* **1** (to make, sell sth) licence *f* (**to do** de faire; **for** pour); **the restaurant doesn't have a ~** le restaurant n'a pas de licence de débit de boissons; **sold/manufactured/brewed under ~ (from)** vendu/fabriqué/brassé sous licence (de); **2** (to drive, carry gun, fish) permis *m* (**to do** pour faire; **for** pour); (for TV) redevance *f*; **to lose one's (driving) ~** se faire retirer son permis (de conduire); **to be married by special ~** se marier avec dispense; **3** péj (freedom) licence *f* pej; **artistic ~** liberté *f* de l'artiste; **4** fig (permission) autorisation *f*; **this law is a ~ to harass the innocent** cette loi laisse le champ libre pour harceler les innocents.
IDIOMS **it's a ~ to print money** c'est un pactole.

licence fee *n* GB redevance *f*.

licence number *n* **1** (of car) numéro *m* minéralogique or d'immatriculation; **2** (of driver) numéro *m* de permis de conduire.

licence plate, **license tag** US *n* plaque *f* minéralogique or d'immatriculation.

license /'laɪsns/ I *n* US = **licence**.
II *vtr* **1** (authorize) autoriser (**to do** à faire); **radio stations must be ~d by the appropriate authority** les stations de radio doivent obtenir une autorisation des autorités compétentes; **2** (obtain licence for) obtenir un permis pour [*gun*]; (register) faire immatriculer [*vehicle*]; **3** (use under licence) exploiter [qch] sous licence; **the software is ~d from X** le logiciel est exploité sous licence de X.

licensed /'laɪsnst/ *adj* **1** [*restaurant, café, club*] qui a une licence de débit de boissons; **the shop is ~ for the sale of tobacco** le magasin a une licence de débit de tabac; **2** [*dealer, security firm, taxi*] agréé; [*pilot, dog-handler*] breveté; **to be ~ to carry a gun** avoir un permis de port d'armes; **to be ~ to drive a heavy goods vehicle** avoir son permis poids lourds; **3** [*firearm, TV*] déclaré; [*vehicle*] en règle.

licensed: **~ practical nurse**, **LPN** **▶ 1692** *n* US ≈ infirmier/-ière *m/f* auxiliaire; **~ premises** *npl* GB débit *m* de boissons; **~ victualler** *n* GB titulaire *mf* d'une licence de débit de boissons.

licensee /,laɪsən'si:/ *n* **1** (of pub etc) titulaire *mf* d'une licence de débit de boissons; **2** (licensed manufacturer) détenteur/-trice *m/f* d'une autorisation; **3** (holder of gun, fishing etc licence) détenteur/-trice *m/f* d'un permis.

licenser *n* = **licensor**.

licensing authority *n* **1** (for drivers, guns etc) organisme *m* délivrant les permis; **2** (for sale of alcohol) organisme *m* délivrant les licences; **3** (authorizing manufacture, use) organisme *m* délivrant les autorisations.

licensing: **~ hours** *npl* GB heures *fpl* d'ouverture des débits de boissons; **~ laws** *npl* GB lois *fpl* réglementant la vente des boissons alcoolisées; **~ magistrate** *n* GB magistrat *m* délivrant les licences de débit de boissons.

licensor /'laɪsnsə(r)/ *n* **1** (issuing licence to manufacture) organisme *m* délivrant les autorisations; **2** (issuing licence to sell) organisme *m* délivrant les licences; **3** (issuing gun, fishing licence) organisme *m* délivrant les permis.

licentiate /laɪ'senʃɪət/ *n* diplômé/-e *m/f* (**in** en).

licentious /laɪ'senʃəs/ *adj* licencieux/-ieuse.

lichen /'laɪkən/ *n* lichen *m*.

lich-gate *n* = **lychgate**.

licit /'lɪsɪt/ *adj* sout licite fml.

lick /lɪk/ I *n* **1** (with tongue) coup *m* de langue; **to give sth a ~** lécher qch; **give me a ~ of your ice cream** laisse-moi lécher ta glace un coup; **2** fig **a ~ of paint** un petit coup de peinture; **3**○ Mus (in jazz) chorus *m*; **4** (blow) coup *m*; **5**○ US (scrap) brin○ *m*.
II *vtr* **1** [*person, animal, flame, wave*] lécher; **the cat was ~ing its paws** le chat se léchait les pattes; **to ~ sth off the spoon** lécher qch sur la cuillère; **to ~ sth clean** [*animal*] nettoyer qch à coups de langue; **he ~ed his fingers clean** il s'est léché les doigts; **to ~ one's chops**○ ou **lips** lit se lécher les babines; fig (at prospect) se délecter (**at** à); **to ~ sb's boots**○**/arse**◑ lécher les bottes○/le cul◑ de or à qn; **2**○ (beat in game) écraser, battre [qn] à plate couture○ [*team, opponent*]; (beat physically) corriger, battre [*person*]; (overcome) venir à bout de [*difficulty*]; **to get ~ed** (in game) se faire battre à plate couture○, se faire écraser; **I think we've got the problem ~ed!**○ je crois que nous avons réussi à venir à bout de ce problème; **this puzzle has got me ~ed!** cette énigme me dépasse!
IDIOMS **at a fair** ou **good ~**○ à toute allure, en quatrième vitesse; **to give oneself a ~ and a promise**○† faire un brin de toilette; **to ~ one's wounds** panser ses blessures; ▶ **shape**.
■ **lick up**: **~ up [sth]**, **~ [sth] up** [*person*] lécher; [*cat, dog*] laper.

lickety-split○ /,lɪkətɪ'splɪt/ US *adv* à toute allure.

licking○ /'lɪkɪŋ/ *n* (beating) raclée○ *f*; **to take** ou **get a ~**○ prendre une raclée○.

lickspittle† /'lɪkspɪtl/ *n* flagorneur/-euse† *m/f*.

licorice *n* US = **liquorice**.

lictor /'lɪktɔ:(r)/ *n* licteur *m*.

lid /lɪd/ *n* **1** (cover) couvercle *m*; **dustbin/saucepan ~** couvercle de poubelle/de casserole; **to put on/take off the ~** mettre/enlever le couvercle; **2** (eyelid) paupière *f*.
IDIOMS **to blow the ~ off sth**○ lever le voile sur qch; **to flip one's ~**○ éclater; **to keep the ~ on sth**○ contrôler qch; **to put a ~ on sth**○ mettre un frein à qch; **to put the ~ on sth**○ (finish) mettre fin à qch; **that really puts the (tin) ~ on it!**○ ça, c'est vraiment le pompon○!

lido /'li:dəʊ/ *n* (*pl* **-os**) **1** (beach) plage *f* (aménagée); **2** GB (pool) piscine *f* (en plein air).

lie /laɪ/ I *n* **1** (falsehood) mensonge *m*; **it's all ~s** ce ne sont que des mensonges; **to tell a ~** mentir; **no I tell a ~** non je me trompe; **to give the ~ to sth/sb** démentir qch/qn; **2** (in golf) **a good/bad ~** un bon/mauvais lie.
II *vtr* (*p prés* **lying**; *prét, pp* **lied**) **'No,' I ~d** 'Non,' mentis-je; **he ~d his way into the job** il a obtenu le poste grâce à des mensonges; **she'll ~ her way out of trouble** elle s'en sortira grâce à des mensonges; **we ~d our way past the guard** nous avons amadoué le gardien grâce à des mensonges.
III *vi* **1** (*p prés* **lying**; *prét, pp* **lied**) (tell falsehood) mentir (**to sb** à qn; **about** à propos de); **he ~d about her** il a menti à son propos; **the camera never ~s** la caméra ne ment pas; **2** (*p prés* **lying**, *prét* **lay**, *pp* **lain** *also for 3, 4, 5, 6, 7, 8*) (in horizontal position) [*person, animal*] (action) s'allonger; (state) être allongé; [*bottle, packet, pile*] être couché; **don't ~ on the grass** ne t'allonge pas sur l'herbe; **he was lying on the bed** il était allongé sur le lit; **she continued to ~ there** elle est restée allongée là; **to ~ on one's back/front** être allongé or s'allonger sur le dos/ventre; **to ~ flat** être allongé or s'allonger à plat; **to ~ face down** être allongé or s'allonger sur le ventre; **the horse lay injured** le cheval blessé était couché; **to ~ awake at night** rester éveillé la nuit; **to ~ in bed all morning** rester au lit toute la matinée; **don't ~ in the sun too long** ne reste pas allongé trop longtemps au soleil; **~ still** ne bougez pas; **while her husband lay in hospital** pendant que son mari était à l'hôpital; **he lay dead** il gisait mort; **the soldier lay dying** le soldat agonisait; **the body lay...** le corps reposait...; **to ~ in state** être exposé publiquement; **here ~s John Brown** ci-gît John Brown; **3** (be situated) gen être; Math [*point*] être situé; **to ~ fifth** ou **in fifth place** occuper la cinquième place; **to ~ in pieces/open** être en morceaux/ouvert; **everything that ~s in my way** tout ce qui est sur mon chemin; **their unhappy past lay behind them** leur passé malheureux était derrière eux; **your future ~s in that direction** votre avenir est dans cette voie; **that's where our future ~s** c'est là qu'est notre avenir; **to ~ before sb** [*life, career*] s'ouvrir pour qn; [*unknown*] attendre qn; **what ~s ahead?** qu'est-ce qui nous attend?; **the toys lay all over the floor** le sol était couvert de jouets; **danger ~s all around us** nous sommes menacés de toutes parts; **4** (remain) rester; **the boat had lain there for years** le bateau était resté là pendant des années; **his clothes lay where he'd left them** ses vêtements étaient restés là où il les avait laissés; **the newspaper lay unread** le journal n'avait pas été ouvert; **his meal lay untouched** il n'avait pas touché à son assiette; **to ~ idle** [*machine*] être inutilisé; [*money*] croupir; **to ~ empty** rester vide; **5** (can be found) résider; **their interests ~ elsewhere** leurs intérêts résident ailleurs; **that's where the fault lay** c'est là que résidait la faute; **to ~ in** [*cause, secret, success, talent*] résider dans; [*popularity, strength, fault*] venir de; [*solution, cure*] consister dans; **to ~ in doing** [*solution, cure*] consister à faire; **to ~ behind** (be hidden) se cacher derrière; (instigate) être à l'origine de; **to ~ at the heart/at the root of** être au cœur/à la racine de; **my support ~s with you** mon soutien vous est acquis; **the responsibility ~s with them** c'est eux qui sont responsables; **6** lit, fig (as covering) [*snow*] tenir; **the snow lay thick** il y avait une épaisse couche de neige; **to ~ over** [*aura, atmosphere*] recouvrir [*place, gathering*]; **to ~ upon** [*burden, guilt*] reposer sur [*person*]; **7** Jur **an appeal that will not ~** un recours qui n'est pas recevable; **no appeal ~s against the action** l'action ne souffre pas d'appel; **8** Naut **to be lying at anchor** avoir jeté l'ancre.
IDIOMS **let the matter ~** laissez les choses comme elles sont; **to ~ in the hands of** dépendre de; **to ~ low** garder un profil bas; **to live a ~** vivre dans le mensonge; **to take it lying down**○ se laisser faire; **don't just ~ down and die** ne baissez pas les bras. ▶ **land**, **wait**.
■ **lie about**= **lie around**.
■ **lie around**: ¶ **~ around** [*person, object*] traîner; **to leave sth lying around** laisser traîner qch; ¶ **~ around [sth]** traîner dans [*house*].
■ **lie back** (horizontally) s'allonger (**on** sur); **she lay back on the pillow** elle s'est adossée à l'oreiller; **~ back and enjoy life** détendez-vous et profitez de la vie.
■ **lie down** (briefly) s'allonger; (for longer period) se coucher; ▶ **dead**.
■ **lie in** (in bed) faire la grasse matinée.
■ **lie off** Naut [*ship*] rester au large.
■ **lie over** [*business, matter*] être ajourné.
■ **lie to** Naut **1** (be hove to) tenir le cap; **2** (be at anchor) être à l'ancre.
■ **lie up 1** (stay in bed) garder le lit; **2** (hide) se cacher.

Liechtenstein /'lɪktənstaɪn/ **▶ 1131** *pr n* Liechtenstein *m*; **in/to ~** au Liechtenstein.

lied /li:t/ *n* (*pl* **lieder**) (song) lied *m*.

lie detector I *n* détecteur *m* de mensonge.
II *modif* [*evidence, printout*] de détecteur de mensonge; [*test*] au détecteur de mensonge.

lie-down /'laɪdaʊn/ *n* **to have a ~** aller s'allonger.

lief‡ /li:f/ *adv* **I'd as ~ go as stay** peu m'importe de partir ou de rester.

liege /li:dʒ/ *n* **1** (also **~ lord**) suzerain *m*; **my ~** mon seigneur; **2** (also **~ man**) vassal *m* lige.

lie-in /ˈlaɪɪn/ *n* **to have a ~** faire la grasse matinée.

lien /ˈlɪən/ *n* Jur droit *m* de rétention (**on** de).

lieu /ljuː/ **I in lieu** *adv phr*: **one week's holiday in ~** une semaine de vacances pour compenser.
II in lieu of *prep phr* à la place de.

Lieut *abrév écrite* = **Lieutenant**.

lieutenancy /lefˈtenənsɪ, US luːˈt-/ *n* (army) grade *m* de lieutenant; (navy) grade *m* de lieutenant de vaisseau.

lieutenant, Lt /lefˈtenənt, US luːˈt-/ ▶ **1612** *n* **1** Mil (GB army) lieutenant *m*; (GB, US navy) lieutenant *m* de vaisseau; **2** (US police) lieutenant *m*; **3** (assistant) lieutenant *m*.

lieutenant: **~ colonel** *n* lieutenant-colonel *m*; **~ commander** *n* capitaine *m* de corvette; **~ general** *n* (army) général *m* de corps d'armée; (airforce) général *m* de corps aérien; **~ Governor** *n* gouverneur *m* adjoint.

life /laɪf/ (*pl* **lives**) **I** *n* **1** (as opposed to death) vie *f*; **~ and death** la vie et la mort; **a matter of ~ and death** une question de vie ou de mort; **to cling to ~** s'accrocher à la vie; **to have a love of ~** aimer la vie; **to bring sb back to ~** gen rendre la vie à qn; Med ranimer qn; **to save sb's ~** sauver la vie de qn; **to put one's ~ at risk** risquer sa vie; **to lay down** ou **give one's ~ for sb** sacrifier sa vie pour qn; **to lose/risk one's ~ doing** perdre/risquer sa vie à faire; **to take one's own ~** se donner la mort; **to take sb's ~** sout donner la mort à qn; **to run/swim for one's ~** courir/nager aussi vite que possible; **run for your ~!** sauve qui peut!; **2** (period from birth to death) vie *f*; **short/long ~** courte/longue vie; **throughout one's ~** pendant toute sa vie; **his waking ~** sa vie éveillée; **in this ~ and the next** dans cette vie et dans l'autre; **the first time in my ~** la première fois de ma vie; **a day/year in the ~ of** une journée/année de la vie de; **romance/race of one's ~** amour/course de sa vie; **I got the fright of my ~!** j'ai eu la frayeur de ma vie!; **a job for ~** un emploi à vie; **a friend for ~** un ami pour la vie; **in later ~** plus tard dans sa vie; **to mark sb for ~** marquer qn pour la vie; **to go through** ou **spend one's ~ doing** passer sa vie à faire; **to make ~ worth living** donner un sens à la vie; **to be all for an easy ~** aimer la vie facile; **early in ~** très tôt; **in adult ~** à l'âge adulte; **in the prime of ~** dans la fleur de l'âge; **at my time of ~** à mon âge; **have you lived here all your ~?** est-ce que tu as toujours habité ici? ; **for the rest of one' s ~** pour le restant de ses jours; **in her early ~** quand elle était jeune; **to depart this ~** littér quitter ce monde; **the ~ and times of X** la vie et l'époque de X; **to write a ~ of sb** écrire une biographie de qn; **3** (animation, vigour) vie *f*, vitalité *f*; **full of ~** plein de vie or vitalité; **there was no ~ in her voice** il n'y avait aucune vitalité dans sa voix; **there's not much ~ in the town in winter** cette ville n'est pas très vivante l'hiver; **to come to ~** [*person*] reprendre conscience; fig sortir de sa réserve; [*fictional character*] prendre vie; [*party*] s'animer; **to bring a subject to ~** traiter un sujet de manière très vivante; **to bring history/a character to ~** donner de la vie à l'histoire/un personnage; **to roar/splutter into ~** se mettre en marche en vrombissant/en toussant; **put a bit of ~ into it**° mettez-y un peu de tonus°; **this drink will put new ~ into you** cette boisson te redonnera des forces; **4** (social activity, lifestyle) vie *f*; **to lead a busy/sheltered ~** mener une vie occupée/protégée; **to change one's ~** transformer sa vie; **private/family** ou **home ~** vie privée/de famille; **working/social ~** vie professionnelle/personnelle; **his way of ~** son mode de vie; **a way of ~** un style de vie; **a ~ of luxury/crime** une vie de luxe/de criminel; **to live the good** ou **high ~** mener la grande vie; **the outdoor ~** la vie au grand air; **it's no ~ for a child** ce n'est pas une vie pour un enfant; **to have a ~ of one's own** avoir sa propre vie; **to make a new ~ for oneself** se forger une nouvelle vie ; **to get on with one's ~** continuer sa vie; **what a ~!** quelle vie!; **in public ~** dans les affaires publiques; **5** (as general concept) vie *f*; **~ in general** la vie en général; **~'s been kind to me** la vie m'a été favorable; **isn't ~ wonderful?** la vie n'est-elle pas merveilleuse?; **how's ~ treating you?** comment va la vie? **to make ~ easier/difficult for sb** faciliter/compliquer la vie à qn; **don't make ~ so difficult for yourself** ne te rends pas la vie impossible; **to take ~ as it comes** prendre la vie comme elle vient; **~ has to go on** la vie continue; **that's ~** c'est la vie; **~'s a bitch**° chienne de vie°; **6** (living things) vie *f*; **origins of ~** origines de la vie; **extraterrestrial ~** la vie extraterrestre; **~ as we know it** la vie telle que nous la connaissons; **plant/marine ~** la vie végétale/marine; **~ in the hedgerows/forest** la faune des haies/forêts; **low ~** péj racaille° *f*; **7** (human being(s)) **without loss of ~** sans perte de vies humaines; **the ship sank with the loss of 500 lives** le naufrage du navire a fait 500 morts; **8** (useful duration) durée *f*; **shelf ~** durée de conservation; **the average ~ of a washing-machine** la durée moyenne d'une machine à laver; **there's plenty of ~ still left in them** ils sont encore tout à fait utilisables; **this carpet's coming to the end of its ~** ce tapis commence à avoir fait son temps; **9** Jur **to do**° ou **serve ~** être emprisonné à vie; **to sentence sb to ~** condamner qn à perpétuité; **to get ~**° se faire condamner à perpette°; **10** Games vie *f*; **to lose a ~** perdre une vie; **11** Art **from ~** [*draw, paint*] d'après nature.
II *modif* [*member, president, peer, peerage, membership*] à vie; [*ban*] définitif/-ive; Insur [*annuity*] viager/-ère.
IDIOMS **anything for a quiet ~** tout ce que tu voudras mais laisse-moi tranquille; **for dear ~** de toutes mes/ses etc forces; **not for the ~ of me** absolument pas; **he couldn't for the ~ of him see why** il n'arrivait absolument pas à comprendre pourquoi; **not on your ~!** jamais de la vie!; **this is the ~!** c'est la belle vie!, voilà la vie qu'il me/nous etc faut!; **to frighten the ~ out of sb** faire mourir qn de peur; **to have the time of one's ~** s'amuser comme un fou/une folle; **you get out of ~ what you put into it** comme on fait son lit on se couche Prov; **to take one's ~ in one's hands** risquer sa vie.

life: **~-and-death** *adj* [*decision, issue*] crucial; **~ assurance** *n* = **life insurance**; **~belt** *n* bouée *f* de sauvetage; **~ blood** *n* fig force *f* vitale; **~boat** *n* canot *m* de sauvetage; **~boatman** *n* sauveteur *m*; **~boat station** *n* poste *m* de secours (en mer); **~buoy** *n* bouée *f* de sauvetage; **~ class** *n* Art cours *m* de dessin d'après modèle; **~ cycle** *n* cycle *m* de vie; **~ drawing** *n* Art dessin *m* d'après modèle; **~ expectancy** *n* Biol espérance *f* de vie; Tech durée *f* probable; **~ force** *n* littér force *f* vitale; **~ form** *n* être *m* vivant; **~giving** *adj* vital; **~guard** ▶ **1692** *n* surveillant/-e *m/f* de baignade.

Life Guards *npl* GB *l'un des régiments de cavalerie de la garde royale britannique.*

life: **~ history** *n* Biol, Hist vie *f*; **~ imprisonment** *n* réclusion *f* à perpétuité.

life insurance I *n* assurance-vie *f*; **to take out ~** souscrire une assurance-vie.
II *modif* [*policy*] d'assurance-vie; [*salesman*] en assurance-vie.

life: **~ interest** *n* Jur usufruit *m*; **~jacket** *n* gilet *m* de sauvetage.

lifeless /ˈlaɪflɪs/ *adj* **1** (dead, appearing dead) [*body, animal*] inanimé; **2** (inanimate) [*object*] inanimé; **3** (without life) [*planet, pond*] sans vie; **4** fig [*performance*] peu vivant; [*character*] manquant de vie; [*voice*] éteint.

lifelessly /ˈlaɪflɪslɪ/ *adv* **she lay ~ on the sofa** elle était allongée sur le sofa, immobile; **his arms hung ~** il avait les bras pendants, immobiles.

lifelessness /ˈlaɪflɪsnɪs/ *n* fig (of acting, production) platitude *f*.

lifelike /ˈlaɪflaɪk/ *adj* très ressemblant.

lifeline /ˈlaɪflaɪn/ *n* **1** (rope) (on boat etc) bouée *f* de sauvetage; (safety line) corde *f* de sécurité; (in climbing) assurance *f*; **2** fig (social, financial aid) bouée *f* de sauvetage; **the telephone was her ~** pour elle le téléphone était un lien vital; **3** (in palmistry) ligne *f* de vie.

lifelong /ˈlaɪflɒŋ/ *adj* [*friendship, fear, ambition, work*] de toute une vie; **to have had a ~ fear of/ambition to do** avoir toujours eu peur de/rêvé de faire.

life: **~ mask** *n* Art masque *m*, empreinte *f* du visage; **~-or-death** *adj*= **life-and-death**; **~ preserver** *n* = **lifejacket**, **lifebuoy**.

lifer° /ˈlaɪfə(r)/ *n* condamné/-e *m/f* à perpette°.

life raft *n* radeau *m* de sauvetage.

lifesaver /ˈlaɪfseɪvə(r)/ *n* **1** (lifeguard) sauveteur *m*; **2** fig **to be a ~** [*object*] être d'une grande utilité; **you're a ~!** tu m'as sauvé la vie!

lifesaving /ˈlaɪfseɪvɪŋ/ **I** *n* **1** (swimmers' technique) sauvetage *m*; **2** Med secourisme *m*.
II *modif* [*course*] (swimming) de sauvetage; Med de secourisme; [*equipment*] de secourisme; [*technique*] (swimming) de sauvetage; (Med) du secourisme; [*drugs, treatment*] d'importance vitale.

life: **~ sciences** *npl* sciences *fpl* de la vie; **~ sentence** *n* Jur condamnation *f* à perpétuité; **~-size** *adj* grandeur nature *inv*; **~ span** *n* durée *f* de vie; **~ story** *n* vie *f*; **~style** *n* style *m* de vie; **~-support machine** *n* appareil *m* de respiration artificielle; **~-support system** *n* équipement *m* de vie; **~-threatening** *adj* [*illness*] très grave; [*situation*] critique.

lifetime /ˈlaɪftaɪm/ **I** *n* **1** (from birth to death) vie *f*; **the work of a ~** l'œuvre d'une vie; **a ~'s accumulation of junk** des vieilleries accumulées pendant toute une vie; **in her ~** de son vivant; **the chance/the holiday of a ~** la chance/les vacances de ma/ta etc vie; **2** (long period) éternité *f*; **to seem like a ~** sembler une éternité; **it felt like a ~ before...** il s'est écoulé ce qui m'a semblé une éternité avant que...; **3** (of object) durée *f*; **during its ~** pendant toute la durée de son utilisation.
II *modif* [*subscription, ban*] à vie.

life vest *n* US = **lifejacket**.

lift /lɪft/ **I** *n* **1** GB (elevator) (for people) ascenseur *m*; (for goods) monte-charge *m inv*; **to take the ~ to the fourth floor** prendre l'ascenseur pour monter au cinquième étage; **2** (ride) **she asked me for a ~** elle m'a demandé de la conduire; **I get a ~ to work from Annie** Annie me dépose à mon travail; **to give sb a ~ to the station** déposer qn à la gare; **can I give you a ~?** je peux te déposer quelque part?; **to give ~s to hitchhikers** prendre des auto-stoppeurs; **to hitch a ~** faire de l'auto-stop; **don't accept ~s from strangers** ne monte jamais dans la voiture d'un inconnu; **3**° (boost) coup *m* de fouet; **to give sb a ~** [*praise, good news*] remonter le moral à qn; **4**° (help) **can you give me a ~ with this trunk?** est-ce que tu peux m'aider à porter cette malle?; **5** Sport (in weightlifting) essai *m*; **6** Sport (height) (of gymnast, diver) détente *f*; (of ball) (in football, tennis) lift *m*; **7** (special heel) talonnette *f*; **8** Aviat sustentation *f*.
II *modif* GB [*button, door*] d'ascenseur; [*maintenance*] des ascenseurs.
III *vtr* **1** (pick up) soulever [*object, person*]; **to ~ sth off a ledge/onto the table** soulever qch d'un rebord/pour le mettre sur la

table; **to ~ sth out of the box/drawer** sortir qch de la boîte/du tiroir; **to ~ sth into the car** prendre qch pour le mettre dans la voiture; **to ~ sb into the ambulance** porter qn jusque dans l'ambulance; **to ~ sth over the wall** faire passer qch par-dessus le mur; **she ~ed the spoon/flute to her lips** elle a porté la cuillère/flûte à sa bouche; **one, two, three, ~!** oh, hisse!; **2** (raise) lever [*arm, head*]; **he ~ed his arm** il a levé le bras; **she didn't even ~ her head from her book** elle n'a même pas levé le nez de son livre; **3** Mil (transport) ▶ **lift in, lift out**; **4** (remove) lever [*siege, ban, sanctions*]; **I feel as if a great weight has been ~ed from my mind** ou **shoulders** je me sens soulagé d'un grand poids; **5** (boost) **to ~ sb's spirits** remonter le moral à qn; **6** Sport (improve) améliorer [*game, performance*]; **7**○ (steal) piquer○, voler [*file, keys, ideas*] (**from** dans); pomper○, copier [*article, passage*] (**from** sur); **he ~ed it from my briefcase** il l'a piqué dans ma serviette; **8** (dig up) arracher [*carrots, onions*]; **9**○ GB (arrest) arrêter; **10** Sport (in football, tennis) lifter [*ball*]; **to ~ weights** faire des haltères; **11** US (pay off) rembourser [*mortgage, debt*]; **12** Cosmet **to have one's face ~ed** se faire faire un lifting.

IV *vi* **1** (improve) [*bad mood, headache*] disparaître; **her spirits began to ~** elle a commencé à retrouver le moral; **2** (disappear) [*fog, mist*] se dissiper; **3** (open) se soulever; **the lid/trapdoor ~s easily** le couvercle/la trappe se soulève facilement.

IDIOMS **not to ~ a finger** ne pas lever le petit doigt.

■ **lift down**: **~ [sb/sth] down, ~ down [sb/sth]** descendre [*object*]; **to ~ a child down from a wall** soulever un enfant d'un mur et le poser par terre.

■ **lift in**: **~ [sb/sth] in, ~ in [sb/sth]** Mil transporter [qn/qch] par voie aérienne [*troops, supplies*].

■ **lift off**: ¶ **~ off** [*rocket, helicopter*] décoller; [*top, cover*] s'enlever; ¶ **~ [sth] off, ~ off [sth]** enlever [*cover, lid*].

■ **lift out**: ¶ **~ out** [*shelf, filter*] être amovible; ¶ **~ [sb/sth] out, ~ out [sb/sth]** Mil évacuer [*troops, equipment*].

■ **lift up**: ¶ **~ up** [*lid, curtain*] se soulever; ¶ **~ [sb/sth] up, ~ up [sb/sth]** soulever [*book, suitcase, lid*]; lever [*head, veil, eyes*]; relever [*jumper, coat*]; **they ~ed up their voices in prayer/song** leurs voix s'élevèrent pour prier/chanter; **to ~ a child up onto a wall** soulever un enfant et le poser sur un mur.

lift: **~boy** *n* GB liftier *m*; **~cage** *n* GB cabine *f* d'ascenseur; **~gate** *n* US Aut hayon *m*.

lifting /ˈlɪftɪŋ/ **I** *n* (ending) (of ban, siege) levée *f*.

II *modif* [*gear, tackle*] de levage.

lift-off /ˈlɪftɒf/ *n* Aerosp lancement *m*; **(we have) ~!** lancement effectué.

lift: **~-operator** ▶ **1692** *n* GB liftier *m*; **~shaft** *n* GB cage *f* d'ascenseur.

lig○ /lɪg/ *vi* GB (*p prés etc* **-gg-**) entrer sans payer.

ligament /ˈlɪgəmənt/ **I** *n* ligament *m*; **knee/ankle ~** ligament du genou/de la cheville; **torn/strained ~** ligament déchiré/froissé.

II *modif* [*tissue, fibre*] ligamenteux/-euse; [*trouble, injury*] ligamentaire.

ligature /ˈlɪgətʃə(r)/ *n* (all contexts) ligature *f*.

ligger○ /ˈlɪgə/ *n* parasite *m*.

light /laɪt/ ▶ **1883** **I** *n* **1** (brightness) lumière *f*; **a beam of ~** un faisceau de lumière; **by the ~ of** à la lumière de [*fire*]; à la clarté de [*moon*]; **in a good ~** sous une bonne lumière; **to read in a poor ~** lire avec peu de lumière; **in full ~** en pleine lumière; **in the ~ of day** lit, fig au grand jour; **I'd like to drive back in the ~** j'aimerais rentrer avant la nuit; **to cast** ou **throw** ou **shed ~ on** lit projeter or répandre de la lumière sur; fig éclaircir; **to hold sth up to the ~** tenir qch à la lumière; **against the ~** à contre-jour; **with the ~ behind her** le dos tourné à la lumière; **the ~ was failing** la nuit tombait; **2** (gleam, bright point) lumière *f*; (in eye) lueur *f*; **a ~ on the horizon** une lumière à l'horizon; **the city ~s** les lumières de la ville; **3** (electrical appliance) (in building, on machine, in oven) lumière *f*; (in street) réverbère *m*; (on ship) feu *m*; **to put** ou **switch** ou **turn a ~ on** allumer une lumière; **to put** ou **switch** ou **turn a ~ off** éteindre une lumière; **to leave a ~ on** laisser une lumière allumée; **are all the ~s off** ou **out?** est-ce que toutes les lumières sont éteintes?; **a ~ came on/went out** une lumière s'est allumée/s'est éteinte; **to turn a ~ up/down** augmenter/réduire une lumière; **the ~s went up/down** Theat les lumières se sont allumées/éteintes; **shine the ~ over here!** éclaire par ici!; **4** (part of gauge, indicator, dashboard) voyant *m* (lumineux); **a red ~ comes on/goes off** un voyant rouge s'allume/s'éteint; **5** Aut (headlight) phare *m*; (rearlight) feu *m* arrière; (inside car) veilleuse *f*; **to put one's ~s on/off** allumer/éteindre ses phares; **to have/leave one's ~s on** avoir/laisser ses phares allumés; **to check one's ~s** vérifier les phares; **to flash one's ~s at sb** faire un appel de phares à qn; **6** (flame) **to put a ~ to** allumer [*fire, gas*]; **to set ~ to** mettre le feu à; **to give sb a ~** offrir du feu à qn; **have you got a ~?** tu as du feu?; **7** fig (aspect) jour *m*; **to see sth in a good/bad/new ~** voir qch sous un bon/mauvais/nouveau jour; **I hadn't thought of it in that ~** je n'y avais pas pensé sous cet angle-là; **looking at it in that ~...** vu sous cet angle...; **to appear in a bad ~** apparaître sous un jour défavorable; **in the ~ of** compte tenu de; **to review sth in the ~ of** réexaminer qch à la lumière de [*evidence, experience*]; **to see sb/sth in a different ~** voir qn/qch sous un jour différent; **8** fig (exposure) **to bring to ~** découvrir [*fact, evidence, truth, crime*]; **to come to** ou **be brought to ~** être découvert; **9** Constr (window) vitre *f*.

II lights *npl* **1** Transp feu *m*, feux *mpl*; **the ~s are red/green** le feu est au rouge/au vert; **to stop at the ~s** s'arrêter au feu; **cross at the ~s** traversez aux feux; **the ~s aren't working** les feux ne marchent pas; **to shoot**○ ou **jump**○ **the ~s** griller○ un feu rouge; **2** (decorative display) illuminations *fpl*; **3** Culin mou *m*.

III *modif* [*switch, shade, socket*] de lampe.

IV *adj* **1** (bright) [*evening, room, house*] clair; **it is ~ enough to do** il fait assez clair pour faire; **to get** ou **grow ~er** [*sky*] s'éclaircir; **it was getting** ou **growing ~** il commençait à faire jour; **while it's still ~** pendant qu'il fait encore jour; **2** (pale) [*colour, fabric, wood, skin*] clair; [*hair*] blond; **~ blue/grey** bleu/gris clair *inv*; **~ blue socks** des chaussettes bleu clair; **3** (not heavy) [*material, substance, mist, snow, wind, clothing, plane, sleep, meal, beer, cake*] léger/-ère; [*rain*] fin; [*drinker*] modéré; [*business, trading*] peu actif/-ive; **to have a ~ touch** [*pianist*] avoir un toucher léger; [*writer, cook*] avoir une certaine légèreté; **a ~ sprinkling** ou **dusting** un saupoudrage; **a ~ soprano** une soprano légère; **to be a ~ sleeper** avoir le sommeil léger; **she is 2 kg ~er** elle pèse 2 kg de moins; **this sack of coal is 5 kg ~** il manque 5 kg à ce sac de charbon; **4** (not severe) [*damage, punishment, sentence*] léger/-ère; **5** (delicate) [*knock, tap, footsteps*] léger/-ère; [*kiss, movement*] délicat; **to be ~ on one's feet** avoir la démarche légère; **6** (not tiring) [*work*] peu fatigant; [*exercise, training*] léger/-ère; **~ duties** petits travaux *mpl*; **~ housework** petits travaux ménagers; **to make ~ work of sth** faire qch sans peine; **7** (not intellectually demanding) [*music, verse*] léger/-ère; **a bit of ~ relief** un peu de divertissement; **some ~ reading for the beach** quelque chose de facile à lire pour la plage; **8** (not important) [*affair*] pas sérieux/-ieuse; **it is no ~ matter** c'est une chose sérieuse; **to make ~ of** traiter [qch] à la légère [*rumour, problem*]; ne pas attacher d'importance à [*injury*]; **9** (cheerful) [*mood, laugh*] enjoué; **10** Culin (low-fat) [*product*] allégé, light.

V *vtr* (*prét, pp* **lit** /lɪt/ ou **lighted**) **1** (set fire to) allumer [*candle, gas, oven, cigarette*]; enflammer [*wood, paper*]; tirer [*firework*]; craquer [*match*]; **to ~ a fire** faire un or du feu; **to ~ the fire** allumer le feu; **a ~ed match** une allumette enflammée; **2** (illuminate) [*torch, lamp, sun*] éclairer.

VI *vi* (*prét, pp* **lit**) [*fire*] prendre; [*candle, cigarette, gas, wood, match*] s'allumer.

IDIOMS **the ~ of sb's life** le rayon de soleil de qn; **many hands make ~ work** Prov à plusieurs la besogne va vite; **to do sth according to one's ~s** sout faire qch comme on l'entend; **to go ~ on**○ **sth** y aller mollo◑ avec qch; **to go out like a ~** s'endormir tout de suite; **to see the ~** comprendre.

■ **light on**: **~ on [sth]** [*eyes, person*] tomber sur.

■ **light up**○: ¶ **~ up 1** (light cigarette) allumer une cigarette; (light pipe) allumer une pipe; **2** [*lamp*] s'allumer; **3** fig [*face*] s'éclairer; [*eyes*] briller de joie; ¶ **~ up [sth], ~ [sth] up 1** [*smoker*] allumer [*cigarette, cigar, pipe*]; **2** (illuminate) illuminer [*surroundings*]; allumer [*sign*].

■ **light upon** = **light on**.

light: **~ ale** *n* bière *f* blonde légère; **~ bulb** *n* ampoule *f*; **~-coloured** GB, **~-colored** US *adj* de couleur claire; **~-emitting diode**, **LED** *n* diode *f* électroluminescente, LED *f*.

lighten /ˈlaɪtn/ **I** *vtr* **1** (make brighter) éclairer [*room, surroundings*]; éclaircir [*colour, fabric, hair, wood, skin*]; **2** fig (make more cheerful) détendre [*atmosphere*]; adoucir [*mood*]; **3** (reduce weight of) alléger [*burden, load, luggage, pressure*]; atténuer [*rebuke*].

II *vi* **1** (grow brighter) [*sky, colour, hair, wood, skin*] s'éclaircir; **2** (grow less heavy) [*burden, pressure, workload*] s'alléger; **3** (become more cheerful) [*mood*] s'adoucir; [*atmosphere*] se détendre; [*expression*] s'éclairer; **his heart ~ed** il s'est senti soulagé.

■ **lighten up**○ [*person*] se détendre; **~ up!** laisse-toi vivre○!

lightener /ˈlaɪtnə(r)/ *n* (for hair) (produit *m*) décolorant *m*.

light entertainment *n* variétés *fpl*.

lighter /ˈlaɪtə(r)/ *n* **1** (for smokers) (hand-held, table) briquet *m*; (in car) allume-cigares *m*; **2** (for gas cooker) allume-gaz *m*; **3** Naut allège *f*.

lighterage /ˈlaɪtərɪdʒ/ *n* Naut, Comm (process) aconage *m*; (charge) droit *m* d'aconage.

lighter: **~ fuel** *n* (gas) gaz *m* à briquet; (liquid) essence *f* à briquet; **~ socket** *n* Aut prise *f* de l'allume-cigares.

light: **~-fingered** *adj* (thieving) chapardeur/-euse; (skilful) [*thief*] adroit; **~ fitting** *n* douille *f*; **~-footed** *adj* agile, au pied léger liter; **~-haired** *adj* [*person*] aux cheveux clairs.

light-headed /ˌlaɪtˈhedɪd/ *adj* **1** (dizzy) [*person*] étourdi; [*feeling*] d'étourdissement; **2** (frivolous) écervelé.

light-headedness /ˌlaɪtˈhedɪdnɪs/ *n* (dizziness) étourdissement *m*.

light-hearted /ˌlaɪtˈhɑːtɪd/ *adj* **1** (happy) enjoué; **2** (not serious) humoristique; **a ~ look at** un regard humoristique sur.

light-heartedly /ˌlaɪtˈhɑːtɪdlɪ/ *adv* **1** (happily) avec enjouement; **2** (jokily) de façon humoristique.

light: **~-heavyweight** *n* poids *m* mi-lourd; **~house** *n* phare *m*; **~house keeper** *n* gardien *m* de phare; **~ industry** *n* industrie *f* légère.

lighting /ˈlaɪtɪŋ/ *n* gen, Theat éclairage *m*; **indirect/frontal ~** éclairage indirect/de face.

like¹

When *like* is used as a preposition (*like a child, do it like this*) it can generally be translated by *comme*.

Note however that *be like* and *look like* meaning *resemble* are translated by *ressembler à*:

she's like her father = elle ressemble
or *she looks like her father* à son père

like is used after certain other verbs in English to express particular kinds of resemblance (*taste like, feel like, smell like* etc.). For translations, consult the appropriate verb entry.

When *like* is used as a conjunction it is translated by *comme*:

songs like my mother sings = des chansons comme celles que chante ma mère

When *like* is used to introduce an illustrative example (*big cities like London*) it can be translated by either *comme* or *tel/telle/tels/telles que*: *les grandes villes comme Londres* or *les grandes villes telles que Londres*.

For particular usages of *like* as a preposition or conjunction and for noun and adverb uses, see the entry ***like¹***.

lighting: **~ director** ▶1692 *n* Theat, Cin chef *m* éclairagiste; **~ effects** *n* effets *mpl* d'éclairage; **~ engineer** ▶1692 *n* Theat, Cin éclairagiste *m*; **~-up time** *n*: *heure où il est conseillé d'allumer ses phares*.

lightly /ˈlaɪtlɪ/ *adv* **1** (gently, delicately) [*touch, kiss, rustle, pat, toss, season*] légèrement; **~ perfumed** délicatement parfumé; **2** (frivolously) [*accuse, undertake, dismiss*] à la légère; **it is not a decision I have taken ~** ce n'est pas une décision que j'ai prise à la légère; **3** (not heavily) [*move, run, walk*] avec légèreté; [*dress*] légèrement; **to sleep ~** avoir le sommeil léger; **to wear one's learning ~** ne pas faire étalage de son savoir; **4** (with little punishment) **to get off ~** s'en tirer à bon compte; **to let sb off ~** laisser qn s'en tirer à bon compte; **5** (casually) [*say, answer*] avec désinvolture.

light meter *n* Phot photomètre *m*.

lightness /ˈlaɪtnɪs/ *n* **1** (brightness, paleness) clarté *f*; **2** (in weight, of food, of movement) légèreté *f*.

lightning /ˈlaɪtnɪŋ/ **I** *n* **1** ¢ (in sky) éclairs *mpl*; **a flash** ou **stroke of ~** un éclair; **2** (striking sth) foudre *f*; **struck by ~** frappé par la foudre; **~ struck the tree** la foudre est tombée sur l'arbre.
II *adj* [*raid, visit*] éclair (*inv*).
IDIOMS **as fast** ou **quick as ~** en un rien de temps; **~ never strikes twice (in the same place)** l'histoire ne se répète pas; **like a flash of ~** en un rien de temps; **like greased ~** ou **like a streak of ~** en quatrième vitesse.

lightning: **~ bug** *n* US luciole *f*; **~ conductor** GB, **~ rod** *n* paratonnerre *m*; **~ strike** *n* grève *f* surprise.

light opera *n* opérette *f*.

light pen *n* **1** (for computer screen) crayon *m* optique; **2** (to read barcode) lecteur *m* de code-barres.

light: **~ railway** *n* transport *m* urbain sur rail; **~-sensitive** *adj* photosensible; **~ship** *n* bateau-phare *m*; **~ show** *n* spectacle *m* avec des effets de lumière; **~-skinned** *adj* à la peau claire, clair de peau; **~ switch** *n* interrupteur *m*; **~ wave** *n* onde *f* lumineuse.

lightweight /ˈlaɪtweɪt/ **I** *n* **1** Sport poids *m* léger; **2** fig péj personne *f* médiocre; **an intellectual ~** un intellectuel médiocre.
II *adj* **1** [*garment, product*] léger/-ère; **2** Sport [*fight*] de poids légers; [*champion, title*] des poids légers; **3** fig péj [*politician, intellectual*] médiocre; [*writing, article*] léger/-ère.

light year *n* **1** Astron année-lumière *f*; **2**○ fig **to be ~s ahead of** être à des années-lumière devant; **it was ~s ago** ça fait un bail○.

ligneous /ˈlɪgnɪəs/ *adj* ligneux/-euse.

lignite /ˈlɪgnaɪt/ *n* lignite *m*.

lignum vitae /ˌlɪgnəm ˈvaɪtɪ, ˈviːtaɪ/ *n* **1** (wood) (bois *m* de) gaïac *m*; **2** (tree) gaïac *m*.

Liguria /lɪˈgjʊərɪə/ *pr n* Ligurie *f*.

like¹ /laɪk/ **I** *prep* **1** (in the same manner as) comme; **he acted ~ a professional** il a agi comme un professionnel or en professionnel; **~ the liar that she is, she...** en bonne menteuse, elle...; **eat up your dinner ~ a good boy** sois gentil et finis ton dîner; **stop behaving ~ an idiot!** arrête de faire l'idiot!; **~ me, he loves swimming** tout comme moi, il adore nager; **it's ~ this: we are asking you to take a cut in salary** voilà, nous vous demandons d'accepter une réduction de salaire; **it happened ~ this** voilà comment cela s'est passé; **look, it wasn't ~ that** écoutez, cela ne s'est pas passé comme ça; **when I see things ~ that** quand je vois des choses pareilles; **don't talk ~ that!** ne dis pas des choses pareilles!; **'how do I do it?'—'~ this'** 'comment faut-il faire?'—'comme ça'; **I'm sorry to disturb you ~ this** je suis désolé de vous déranger comme ça; **all right, be ~ that then!** et puis fais ce que tu voudras!; **they've gone to Ibiza or somewhere ~ that** ils sont allés à Ibiza ou quelque chose comme ça; **2** (similar to, resembling) comme; **to be ~ sb/sth** être comme qn/qch; **he was ~ a son to me** il était comme un fils pour moi; **you know what she's ~!** tu sais comment elle est!; **it was just ~ a fairytale!** on aurait dit un conte de fée!; **what's it ~?** c'est comment?; **it's a second-hand car but it looks ~ new** c'est une voiture d'occasion mais elle est comme neuve; **where did you get your jacket?—I want to buy one ~ it** où as-tu acheté ta veste—je veux acheter la même or une pareille; **so this is what it feels ~ to be poor, so this is what poverty feels ~!** maintenant je sais (or on sait etc) ce que c'est d'être pauvre!; **there's nothing ~ a nice warm bath!** rien ne vaut un bon bain chaud!, il n'y a rien de mieux qu'un bon bain chaud!; **I've never seen anything ~ it!** je n'ai jamais rien vu de pareil!; **that's more ~ it!** voilà ce qui est mieux!; **Paris! there's nowhere ~ it!** rien ne vaut Paris!; **I don't earn anything ~ as much as she does** je suis loin de gagner autant qu'elle; **what was the weather ~?** quel temps faisait-il?; **what's Oxford ~ as a place to live?** comment est la vie à Oxford?; **3** (typical of) **it's not ~ her to be late** ça ne lui ressemble pas or ce n'est pas son genre d'être en retard; **if that isn't just ~ him!** c'est bien (de) lui!; **it's just ~ him to be so spiteful!** c'est bien lui d'être si méchant!; **just ~ a man!** c'est typiquement masculin!; **he's not ~ himself these days** il n'est pas lui-même ces jours-ci; **4** (expressing probability) **it looks ~ rain** on dirait qu'il va pleuvoir; **it looks ~ the war will be a long one** il y a des chances pour que la guerre dure; **he was acting ~ he was crazy**○ US il se comportait comme un fou; **you seem ~ an intelligent man** tu as l'air intelligent; **5** (close to, akin to) **it cost something ~ £20** cela a coûté dans les 20 livres, cela a coûté environ 20 livres; **something ~ half the population are affected** environ la moitié de la population est touchée; **with something ~ affection/enthusiasm** avec un semblant d'affection/d'enthousiasme.
II *adj* sout pareil/-eille, semblable, du même genre; **cups, bowls and ~ receptacles** des tasses, des bols et des récipients du même genre; **cooking, ironing and ~ chores** la cuisine, le repassage et autres tâches du même genre; **to be of ~ mind** être du même avis, avoir les mêmes opinions.
III *conj* **1** (in the same way as) comme; **~ I said, I wasn't there**○ comme je vous l'ai déjà dit, je n'étais pas là; **nobody can sing that song ~ he did** personne ne peut chanter cette chanson comme lui; **it's not ~ I imagined it would be** ce n'est pas comme je l'avais imaginé; **~ they used to** comme ils le faisaient autrefois; **2**○ (as if) comme si; **she acts ~ she knows everything** elle fait comme si elle savait tout; **he acts ~ he owns the place** il se conduit comme s'il était chez lui.
IV *adv* **1** (akin to, near) **it's nothing ~ as nice as their previous house** c'est loin d'être aussi beau que leur maison précédente; **'the figures are 10% more than last year'—'20%, more ~○!'** 'les chiffres sont de 10% supérieurs à l'année dernière'—'20%, plutôt!'; **luxury hotel! boarding house, more ~○!** un hôtel de luxe! une pension, oui! iron; **2**○ (so to speak) **I felt embarrassed, ~** GB, **I felt, ~, embarrassed** US je me sentais plutôt embarrassé; **it reminds me a bit, ~, of a hospital** ça me fait penser, comment dire, à un hôpital.
V *n* **dukes, duchesses and the ~** des ducs, des duchesses et autres personnes de ce genre; **earthquakes, floods and the ~** des tremblements de terre, des inondations et autres catastrophes de ce genre; **I've never seen its ~** ou **the ~ of it** je n'ai jamais vu une chose pareille; **their ~ will never be seen again** des gens comme eux, il n'y en a plus; **scenes of unrest the ~(s) of which had never been seen before in the city** des scènes d'agitation telles qu'on n'en avait jamais vu dans la ville; **the ~(s) of Al Capone** des gens comme Al Capone; **she won't even speak to the ~s of us**○! elle refuse même de parler à des gens comme nous!; **you shouldn't associate with the ~(s) of them**○ tu ne devrais pas fréquenter des gens de leur acabit pej or des gens comme ça.
VI -like *dans composés* **bird-~** qui fait penser à un oiseau; **child-~** enfantin; **king-~** royal.
IDIOMS **~ enough, very ~**†, **(as) ~ as not** probablement; **~ father ~ son** Prov tel père tel fils Prov.

like² /laɪk/ *vtr* **1** (get on well with) aimer bien [*person*]; **I ~ Paul** j'aime bien Paul; **to ~ sb as a friend** aimer bien qn en tant qu'ami; **to ~ A better than B** préférer A à B, aimer mieux A que B; **to ~ A best** préférer A; **to be well ~d** être apprécié; **to want to be ~d** vouloir plaire; **2** (find to one's taste) aimer (bien) [*animal, artist, food, music, product, style*]; **to ~ X better than Y** préférer X à Y; **to ~ Z best** préférer Z; **to ~ one's coffee strong** aimer son café fort; **how do you ~ your tea?** comment aimes-tu boire ton thé?; **what I ~ about him/this car is...** ce que j'aime (bien) chez lui/dans cette voiture, c'est...; **we ~ the look of the house** la maison nous semble bien; **I ~ the look of the new boss** le nouveau patron me paraît sympathique or me plaît; **if the manager~s the look of you** si tu fais bonne impression sur le directeur; **she didn't ~ the look of the hotel** l'hôtel ne lui disait rien; **I don't ~ the look of that man** cet homme a une tête qui ne me revient pas; **I don't ~ the look of her, call the doctor** elle a une drôle de mine, appelle le médecin; **I don't ~ the sound of that** ça ne me dit rien qui vaille; **I don't ~ what I hear about her** ce que j'entends dire à propos d'elle ne me plaît pas beaucoup; **she hasn't phoned for weeks, I don't ~ it** ça fait des semaines qu'elle n'a pas téléphoné, je n'aime pas ça; **if you ~ that sort of thing** à condition d'aimer ce genre de choses; **you'll come with us and ~ it!** tu viendras avec nous que ça te chante○ ou pas!; **I ~ cheese but it doesn't ~ me**○ j'aime le fromage mais ça ne me réussit pas; **this plant ~s sunlight** cette plante se plaît au soleil; **3** (enjoy doing) aimer bien; (stronger) aimer; **I ~ doing, I ~ to**

do j'aime (bien) faire; **he ~s being able to do** il aime pouvoir faire; **I ~ to see people doing** j'aime (bien) que les gens fassent; **that's what I ~ to see!** je trouve ça très bien!; **I ~ it when you do** j'aime bien que tu fasses; **I don't ~ it when you do** je n'aime pas que tu fasses; **I ~ed it better when we did** j'aimais mieux quand on faisait; **how do you ~ your new job?** qu'est-ce que tu penses de ton nouveau travail?; **how do you ~ living in London?** ça te plaît de vivre à Londres?; **how would you like it if you had to do...?** ça te plairait à toi d'être obligé de faire...?; **4** (approve of) aimer; **I don't ~ your attitude** je n'aime pas ton attitude, ton attitude ne me plaît pas; **the boss won't ~ it if you're late** le patron ne sera pas content si tu arrives en retard; **she doesn't ~ to be kept waiting** elle n'aime pas qu'on la fasse attendre; **to ~ sb to do** aimer que qn fasse; **I ~ that!** iron ça, c'est la meilleure!; **I ~ his cheek** ou **nerve!** iron il ne manque pas de culot!; **I ~ it!** ça me plaît!; **~ it or not we all pay tax** que ça nous plaise ou non nous payons tous des impôts; **5** (wish) vouloir, aimer; **I would** ou **should ~ a ticket** je voudrais un billet; **I would** ou **should ~ to do** je voudrais or j'aimerais faire; **she would have ~d to do** elle aurait voulu or aimé faire; **would you ~ to come to dinner?** voudriez-vous venir dîner?, est-ce que cela vous dirait de venir dîner?; **I wouldn't ~ to think I'd upset her** j'espère bien que je ne lui ai pas fait de peine; **we'd ~ her to do** nous voudrions or aimerions qu'elle fasse; **would you ~ me to come?** voulez-vous que je vienne?; **I'd ~ to see him try**○! je voudrais bien voir ça!; **how would you ~ to come?** qu'est-ce que tu dirais de venir?; **where did they get the money from, that's what I'd ~ to know** je voudrais or j'aimerais bien savoir où ils ont trouvé l'argent; **I don't ~ to disturb her** je n'ose pas la déranger; **if you ~** (willingly agreeing) si tu veux; (reluctantly agreeing) si tu y tiens; **he's a bit of a rebel if you ~** il est un peu contestataire si tu veux; **you can do what you ~** tu peux faire ce que tu veux; **say what you ~, I think it's a good idea** tu peux dire ce que tu veux or tu diras ce que tu voudras, je pense que c'est une bonne idée; **sit (any)where you ~** asseyez-vous où vous voulez; **6** (think important) **to ~ to do** tenir à faire; **I ~ to keep fit** je tiens à me maintenir en forme.

likeable /'laɪkəbl/ *adj* [*person*] agréable, sympathique; [*animal*] attachant; [*novel, music*] agréable.

likelihood /'laɪklɪhʊd/ *n* probabilité *f*, chances *fpl*; **in all ~** selon toute probabilité; **the ~ is that she has missed the train/got lost** il est probable qu'elle ait manqué le train/se soit perdue; **there is no ~ of peace** il n'y a aucune chance de paix; **there is some/little ~ of peace** il y a quelques/peu de chances de paix; **to increase/reduce the ~ of that happening** accroître/réduire la probabilité or les chances que cela se produise.

likely /'laɪklɪ/ **I** *adj* **1** (probable) probable; [*explanation*] plausible; [*excuse, story*] iron beau/belle; **to be ~ to fail/increase/face problems** risquer d'échouer/d'augmenter/de connaître des difficultés; **to be ~ to become president/pass one's exams** avoir de fortes chances de devenir président/de réussir à ses examens; **the man most ~ to win** l'homme qui a le plus de chances de gagner; **it is** ou **seems ~ that** il est probable que; **it is not ~ that, it is hardly ~ that** il y a peu de chances que (+ *subj*); **he is not ~ to come/refuse** il y a peu de chances qu'il vienne/refuse; **he looks ~ to fail** il échouera probablement; **a ~ story!** iron à d'autres○!; **a ~ excuse!** iron belle excuse!; **2** (potentially successful) [*person, candidate*] prometteur/-euse; **3** (potential) [*customer, client, candidate*] potentiel/-ielle.

II *adv* (probably) probablement; **as ~ as not** probablement; **not ~**○! GB que tu crois○!

like-minded /laɪk'maɪndɪd/ *adj* du même avis; **an opportunity to meet ~ people** (sharing same opinions) l'occasion de rencontrer des gens qui partagent vos opinions or pensent comme vous; (sharing same tastes) l'occasion de rencontrer des gens qui ont les mêmes goûts que vous.

liken /'laɪkən/ *vtr* comparer (**to** à); **he has been ~ed to** on l'a comparé à.

likeness /'laɪknɪs/ *n* **1** (similarity) ressemblance *f* (**between** entre); **family ~** air *m* de famille; **to bear a ~ to** ressembler à; **2** (of picture) **to be a true** ou **good ~** être ressemblant; **he has caught the ~** son portrait est très ressemblant; **3** (form) **to assume** ou **take on the ~ of** se métamorphoser en.

likewise /'laɪkwaɪz/ *adv* (similarly) également, de même; (also) aussi, de même; **~, students feel that...** les étudiants également trouvent que...; **I'm leaving and I suggest you do ~** je pars, et je te conseille de faire de même; **I'm well and my parents ~** je vais bien et mes parents de même ou aussi; **'pleased to meet you!'–'~, I'm sure!'** 'enchanté!'—'et moi de même!'

liking /'laɪkɪŋ/ *n* **to have a ~ for** aimer [*activity, food*]; **to develop a ~ for swimming** prendre goût à la natation; **to take a ~ to sb** se prendre d'affection pour qn; **you should find this more to your ~** ceci devrait vous plaire davantage; **he's too smart for my ~** il est trop malin à mon goût.

lilac /'laɪlək/ **I** *n* (all contexts) lilas *m*; **a bunch of ~** un bouquet de lilas.
II ▶ **1104** *adj* (colour) lilas *inv*.

Lilliputian /ˌlɪlɪ'pjuːʃn/ **I** *n* Lilliputien/-ienne *m/f*.
II *adj* lilliputien/-ienne.

Lilo® /'laɪləʊ/ *n* matelas *m* pneumatique.

lilt /lɪlt/ *n* (of tune) cadence *f*; (of accent) intonation *f*.

lilting /'lɪltɪŋ/ *adj* mélodieux/-ieuse.

lily /'lɪlɪ/ *n* lys *m inv*.
IDIOMS **to gild the ~** en faire trop.

lily: **~-livered** *adj* poltron/-onne; **~ of the valley** *n* muguet *m*; **~ pad** *n* feuille *f* de nénuphar; **~ pond** *n* bassin *m* aux nénuphars.

lily-white *adj* littér **1** (white) **~ skin** teint *m* de lis; **her ~ hand** sa main d'une blancheur de lis; **2** (pure) [*morals*] pur; [*person*] blanc/blanche comme neige; **3**○ US [*suburb, club*] réservé aux blancs.

lima bean /'liːmə, US 'laɪmə/ *n* haricot *m* de lima.

limb /lɪm/ *n* **1** Anat membre *m*; **to stretch one's ~s** s'étirer; **2** (of tree) branche *f* (maîtresse).
IDIOMS **to be out on a ~** se retrouver isolé; **to go out on a ~** se mouiller○; **to be sound in wind and ~** avoir bon pied bon œil; **to risk life and ~** risquer sa vie; **to tear sb ~ from ~** mettre qn en pièces.

limber /'lɪmbə(r)/ *adj* littér souple.
■ **limber up** s'échauffer; **to do ~ing up exercises** faire des exercices d'assouplissement.

limbo /'lɪmbəʊ/ *n* **1** ¢ Relig, fig les limbes *mpl*; **to be in (a state of) ~** être dans les limbes; **2** (dance) limbo *m*.

lime /laɪm/ **I** *n* **1** (calcium) chaux *f*; **2** (fruit) citron *m* vert; **3** (tree) tilleul *m*.
II *vtr* chauler.

lime: **~ green** ▶ **1104** *n, adj* citron (*m*) vert *inv*; **~ juice** *n* jus *m* de citron vert; **~ kiln** *n* four *m* à chaux.

limelight /'laɪmlaɪt/ *n* vedette *f*; **to be in the ~** tenir la vedette; **to hog/share the ~** accaparer/partager la vedette; **to avoid** ou **shun the ~** ne pas se faire remarquer.

lime pit *n* plain *m*.

limerick /'lɪmərɪk/ *n* limerick *m* (*poème humoristique en cinq lignes*).

lime: **~stone** *n* calcaire *m*; **~ tree** *n* tilleul *m*.

limewash /'laɪmwɒʃ/ **I** *n* badigeon *m* (blanc).
II *vtr* blanchir [qch] à la chaux.

limey○ /'laɪmɪ/ US **I** *n* Angliche○ *mf*.
II *adj* angliche○.

limit /'lɪmɪt/ **I** *n* **1** (maximum extent) limite *f*; **there will be no ~ to the violence** la violence ne connaîtra pas de limites; **it's beyond the ~(s) of my experience** cela sort des limites de mon expérience; **to push sb to the ~** pousser qn à bout; **he has pushed my patience to the ~** ou **to its ~s** il est venu à bout de ma patience; **it's the ~**○! ça dépasse les bornes!; **you're the ~**○! tu dépasses les bornes!; **2** (legal restriction) limitation *f* (**on** sur); **public spending ~s** limitation des dépenses publiques; **speed ~** limitation de vitesse; **safety ~s** limites imposées par les normes de la sécurité; **to be over/under the ~** (of alcohol) avoir trop/ne pas avoir trop d'alcool dans le sang; **3** (boundary) (of territory, universe, power, science) limite *f* (**of** de); **within the ~s of what we can do** dans la limite de ce que l'on peut faire; **'is it possible?'—'yes, within ~s'** 'est-ce possible?'—'oui, dans une certaine limite'; **to be off ~s** Mil être interdit d'accès; **the garden is off ~s** l'accès au jardin est interdit; **my private life is off ~s** ma vie privée ne vous concerne pas.
II *vtr* (restrict) limiter [*use, imports, actions*]; **to be ~ed to doing** se limiter à faire; **spending is ~ed to two million** les dépenses sont limitées à deux millions; **places are ~ed to 60** le nombre de places est limité à 60.
III *v refl* **to ~ oneself** s'imposer des limites; **to ~ oneself to** se limiter à [*amount, quantity*]; **you're ~ing yourself by not doing** tu te limites trop en ne faisant pas.

limitation /ˌlɪmɪ'teɪʃn/ *n* **1** (restriction) restriction *f*; **to impose** ou **place ~s on** imposer des restrictions à [*right, freedom*]; **to be a ~ on sb's power** être une limitation du pouvoir de qn; **contractual/budgetary ~s** restrictions contractuelles/budgétaires; **time/space ~s** manque *m* de temps/d'espace; **2** (shortcoming) limite *f*; **his ~s as an artist** ses limites en tant qu'artiste; **to have its ~s** avoir ses limites; **to know one's (own) ~s** connaître ses propres limites.

limited /'lɪmɪtɪd/ *adj* **1** (small) [*resources, ambition, market, vocabulary, intelligence*] limité; [*imagination*] borné; **of ~ ability** aux capacités limitées; **2** (restricted) [*sample, menu, space*] limité; **3** Comm **Nolan Computers Limited** Nolan Computers SA.

limited: **~ company** *n* GB société *f* anonyme; **~ edition** *n* (book, lithograph) tirage *m* limité; (album, recording) production *f* limitée; **~ liability company** *n* société *f* à responsabilité limitée.

limitless /'lɪmɪtlɪs/ *adj* illimité.

limo○ /'lɪməʊ/ *n* limousine *f*.

Limousin ▶ **1273** *pr n* Limousin *m*; **in the ~** dans le Limousin.

limousine /'lɪməziːn, ˌlɪmə'ziːn/ *n* limousine *f*.

limp /lɪmp/ **I** *n* **to walk with** ou **have a ~** boiter; **to have a slight ~ in one's left leg** boiter légèrement du pied gauche.
II *adj* [*material, gesture, handshake, style*] mou/molle; **the lettuce is ~** la salade n'est plus croquante; **the flowers look a bit ~** les fleurs n'ont plus l'air très fraîches; **to let oneself go ~** relâcher ses muscles; **her right arm had gone ~** elle n'avait plus aucune force dans le bras droit; **I felt his**

body go ~ j'ai senti tous les muscles de son corps se relâcher.

III *vi* **to ~ along** boiter; **to ~ in/away** entrer/s'éloigner en boitant; **the trawler ~ed into port** le chalutier regagna le port tant bien que mal.

limp binding *n* Publg reliure *f* souple.

limpet /ˈlɪmpɪt/ *n* bernique *f*.

IDIOMS **to cling like a ~** être une vraie sangsue○.

limpet mine *n* mine-ventouse *f*.

limpid /ˈlɪmpɪd/ *adj* limpide.

limply /ˈlɪmplɪ/ *adv* [*dangle, hang*] mollement.

limpness /ˈlɪmpnɪs/ *n* (of body) mollesse *f*.

limp-wristed /ˌlɪmpˈrɪstɪd/ *adj* péj efféminé.

limy /ˈlaɪmɪ/ *adj* Geol, Hort calcaire.

linage /ˈlaɪnɪdʒ/ *n* (number of lines) lignage *m*, nombre *m* de lignes; **to pay by ~** payer à la ligne.

linchpin /ˈlɪntʃpɪn/ *n* **1** Tech clavette *f*, goupille *f*; **2** fig (essential element) **the ~ of** [*person*] le pilier de [*government, organization*]; [*idea, principle, institution*] la base de [*ideology, belief, theory*].

Lincolnshire /ˈlɪŋkənʃə(r)/ ▶1624 *pr n* Lincolnshire *m*.

Lincoln's Inn /ˌlɪŋkənz ˈɪn/ *n* GB Jur *l'une des quatre écoles de droit à Londres*.

Lincs GB Post *abrév écrite* = **Lincolnshire**.

linctus /ˈlɪŋktəs/ *n* sirop *m* (contre la toux).

linden (tree) /ˈlɪndən/ *n* littér tilleul *m*.

line /laɪn/ **I** *n* **1** (mark) ligne *f*; (shorter, thicker) trait *m*; Art trait *m*; Sport (on pitch, court) ligne *f*; Math ligne *f*; **~ and colour** Art le trait et la couleur; **a straight/curved ~** une ligne droite/courbe; **a solid/broken ~** une ligne continue/discontinue; **a single/double ~** une ligne simple/double; **to draw** ou **rule a ~** tracer une ligne; **to draw a ~ down the middle of the page** tracer une ligne verticale au milieu de la page; **to put a ~ through sth** barrer qch; **to cross the ~** Sport franchir la ligne; **the starting/finishing ~** Sport la ligne de départ/d'arrivée; **above/below the ~** (in bridge) (marqué) en points d'honneur/en points de marche; **the ~ AB** (in geometry) la droite AB; **the thin ~ of his mouth** ses lèvres fines; **2** (row) (of people, cars) file *f* (**of** de); (of trees) rangée *f* (**of** de); (of footprints, hills) succession *f* (**of** de); **in straight ~s** [*plant, arrange, sit*] en lignes droites; **to stand in a ~** faire la queue; **get into (a) ~!** faites la queue!; **to form a ~** [*people*] faire la queue; [*hills, houses, trees*] être aligné; **please form a ~** mettez-vous en file s'il vous plait; **she is fifth in ~** elle est la cinquième dans la file; **to be in ~** [*buildings*] être dans l'alignement; **put the desks in ~** alignez les bureaux; **to be in ~ with** [*shelving, cooker*] être dans l'alignement de [*cupboard*]; [*mark, indicator*] coïncider avec [*number*]; **to be out of ~** [*picture*] être de travers; **3** fig **to be in ~ for promotion/a pay rise** avoir des chances d'être promu/d'être augmenté; **to be in ~ for redundancy/takeover** risquer d'être mis au chômage/d'être racheté; **to be next in ~ for promotion/execution** être le prochain à être promu/exécuté; **in ~ for the post of** bien placé pour obtenir le poste de; **4** surtout US (queue) file *f*; **to stand in** ou **wait in ~** faire la queue (**for** pour); **5** (wrinkle) (on face) ride *f*; (on hand) ligne *f*; **6** Archit, Sewing (outline shape) ligne *f* (**of** de); **the classical ~s of the building** la ligne classique du bâtiment; **7** (boundary) frontière *f*; **an imaginary ~ between** une frontière imaginaire entre; **to cross the state ~** passer la frontière de l'État; **to follow the ~ of the old walls** suivre le tracé des anciens remparts; **there's a fine ~ between knowledge and pedantry** de la culture à la pédanterie il n'y a qu'un pas; **8** (rope) corde *f*; Fishg ligne *f*; **to put the washing on the ~** étendre le linge; **a ~ of washing** du linge étendu à sécher; **to throw sb a ~** lancer une corde à qn; **to cast one's ~** lancer sa ligne; **there was a fish at the end of the ~** il y avait un poisson qui mordait; **9** (cable) Elec ligne *f* (électrique); **the ~ had been cut** Elec on avait coupé la ligne; **to bring the ~s down** Telecom abattre les lignes; **the ~s are down** Telecom les lignes ont été abattues; **10** Telecom (connection) ligne *f*; **a bad ~** une mauvaise ligne; **outside ~** ligne *f* extérieure; **dial 9 to get an outside ~** faites le 9 pour appeler à l'extérieur; **to be on the ~ to sb** être en ligne avec qn; **to get off the ~**○ raccrocher; **at the other end of the ~** au bout du fil; **the ~s will be open from 8.30 onwards** vous pouvez nous appeler à partir de 8 h 30; **the ~ is dead** il n'y a pas de tonalité; **the ~ went dead** la ligne a été coupée; **11** Transp Rail (connection) ligne *f* (**between** entre); (rails) voie *f*; (shipping, air transport) (company) compagnie *f*; (route) ligne *f*; **repairs to the ~** réparations sur la voie; **at every station along the ~** à chaque gare sur la ligne; **the London-Edinburgh ~** Rail la ligne Londres-Édimbourg; **12** (in genealogy) lignée *f*; **the male/female ~** la lignée par les hommes/les femmes; **the Tudor ~** la maison des Tudor; **to found** ou **establish a ~** fonder une lignée; **the ~ died out** la lignée s'est éteinte; **to come from a long ~ of scientists** être issu d'une longue lignée de scientifiques; **to trace one's ~ back to sb** retracer son ascendance jusqu'à qn; **to trace a ~ down to sb** retracer une descendance jusqu'à qn; **to trace a ~ through sb** retracer l'ascendance du côté de qn; **the title passes to the next in ~** le titre passe au suivant dans l'ordre de succession; **she is second in ~ to the throne** elle est la deuxième dans l'ordre de succession au trône; **13** (of text) (in prose) ligne *f*; (in poetry) vers *m*; (of music) ligne *f*; **to give sb 100 ~s** donner 100 lignes à qn; **to start a new ~** aller à la ligne; **to miss a ~** sauter une ligne; **write a few ~s about your hobbies** décrivez vos passe-temps en quelques lignes; **just a ~ to say thank you** juste un petit mot pour dire merci; **a ~ from** une citation de [*poem etc*]; **a ~ of verse** ou **poetry** un vers; **the famous opening ~s** la célèbre introduction; **he has all the best ~s** il a les meilleures répliques; **to learn one's ~s** Theat apprendre son texte; **14** (conformity) **to fall into ~** être d'accord; **to make sb fall into ~** faire marcher qn au pas; **to fall into ~ with** [*person*] tomber d'accord avec [*view*]; [*group, body*] être d'accord avec [*practice, policy*]; **China fell into ~ with the other powers** la Chine s'est mise d'accord avec les autres puissances; **to bring sb into ~** ramener qn dans le rang; **to bring regional laws into ~ with federal laws** harmoniser les lois régionales et les lois fédérales; **to bring working conditions into ~ with European standards** aligner les conditions de travail sur les normes européennes; **to keep sb in ~** tenir qn en main; **his statement is out of ~ with their account** sa déclaration ne concorde pas avec leur déposition; **our prices are out of ~ with those of our competitors** nos prix ne s'accordent pas avec ceux de nos concurrents; **to be (way) out of ~** [*objection, remark*] être (tout à fait) déplacé; **you're way out of ~**○**!** franchement, tu exagères!; **15**○ (piece of information) **to have a ~ on sb/sth** avoir des informations sur qn/qch; **to give sb a ~ on sb/sth** donner un tuyau○ à qn sur qn/qch; **to give sb a ~ about sth** (story, excuse) raconter des bobards○ à qn sur qch; **don't give me that ~!** ne me raconte pas ces histoires!; **16** (stance) position *f* (**on** sur); **something along these ~s** quelque chose dans le même genre; **our rivals had been thinking along the same ~s** nos concurrents avaient pensé aux mêmes choses; **to be on the right ~s** être sur la bonne voie; **the official ~** la position officielle; (approach) ligne *f* de conduite (**with** avec); **to take a firm ~ with sb** se montrer ferme avec qn; **I don't know what ~ to take** je ne sais pas quelle ligne de conduite adopter; **17** Comm (type of product) gamme *f*; **one of our most successful ~s** une gamme qui a beaucoup de succès; **18** Mil (fortifications) ligne *f*; (position held) position *f*; **enemy ~s** lignes *fpl* ennemies; **they held their ~** ils ont conservé leurs positions; **19** Naut **~ ahead/abreast** ligne de front/de file; **20** (equator) **the ~** la ligne; **to cross the ~** traverser la ligne; **21**○ (of cocaine) ligne○ *f* (**of** de); **22** TV ligne *f*.

II in line with *prep phr* en accord avec [*approach, policy, trend, teaching, requirement*]; **to be in ~ with** [*statement, measure*] être dans la ligne de [*policy, view, recommendation*]; [*figures, increase*] être proportionnel à [*inflation, trend*]; **to increase/fall in ~ with** augmenter/baisser proportionnellement à; **to vary in ~ with** varier parallèlement à.

III *vtr* **1** (add layer) doubler [*garment*] (**with** avec); tapisser [*box, shelf, nest*] (**with** de); **to be ~d with books** être tapissé de livres; **to ~ the walls and ceilings** tapisser les murs et les plafonds d'un papier d'apprêt; **2** (stand along) [*trees, spectators*] border [*route*]; **to be ~d with trees** être bordé d'arbres; **3** (mark) **to be ~d with** être marqué par [*worry, age*].

IDIOMS **all along the ~, right down the ~** sur toute la ligne; **somewhere along the ~** (at point in time) à un certain moment; (at stage) quelque part; **something along those ~s** quelque chose dans ce goût; **to do a ~ with sb**○ sortir avec qn; **to be on the ~** [*life, job*] être en jeu.

■ **line up**: ¶ **~ up 1** (side by side) se mettre en rang (**for** pour); (one behind the other) se mettre en file (**for** pour); **to ~ up in rows** se mettre en rangs; **2** (take sides) **to ~ up with sb/sth** se ranger du côté de qn/qch; **to ~ up against sb/sth** se regrouper contre qn/qch; ¶ **~ up [sb], ~ [sb] up** (in row) faire s'aligner; **they ~d us up** (in columns) ils nous ont fait former des colonnes; **to ~ people up against a wall** aligner des gens contre un mur; ¶ **~ [sth] up, ~ up [sth] 1** (align) aligner (**with** sur); **2** (organize) sélectionner [*team*]; **to have sb/sth ~d up** [*candidate, work, project, activities*] avoir qn/qch en vue; **what have you got ~d up for us tonight?** qu'est-ce que tu nous as prévu pour ce soir○?

lineage /ˈlɪnɪɪdʒ/ *n* lignage *m*; **of noble ~** de noble lignage; **he can trace his ~ to William I** sa famille remonte à Guillaume Ier.

lineal /ˈlɪnɪəl/ *adj* **~ descent from** descendance en ligne directe de.

lineament sout /ˈlɪnɪəmənt/ *n* trait *m*.

linear /ˈlɪnɪə(r)/ *adj* linéaire.

lined /laɪnd/ *adj* **1** [*face, hands, skin*] ridé; **2** [*paper*] ligné; **3** [*garment, curtains*] doublé.

line: **~ drawing** *n* dessin *m* au trait; **~ feed** *n* changement *m* de ligne; **~ fishing** *n* pêche *f* à la ligne.

lineman /ˈlaɪnmən/ ▶1692 *n* **1** Elec technicien *m* de lignes; **2** Telecom agent *m* des lignes; **3** US Sport *au football américain, joueur qui se place sur la ligne*.

line manage *vtr* diriger [qch] au niveau opérationnel.

line management *n* **1** (system) direction *f* hiérarchique; **2** (managers) responsables *mpl* opérationnels.

line manager *n* responsable *mf* opérationnel/elle.

linen /ˈlɪnɪn/ **I** *n* **1** (fabric) lin *m*; **to wear ~** porter du lin; **2** (items) (household) linge *m* de maison; (underwear) linge *m* de corps.

II *modif* [*jacket, sheet*] en lin, de lin; [*industry*] du lin.

IDIOMS **to wash one's dirty ~ in public** laver son linge sale en public.

linen: **~ basket** *n* panier *m* à linge sale;

~ cupboard GB, **~ closet** US *n* armoire *f* à linge.

line: **~ of argument** *n* raisonnement *m*; **~ of attack** *n* lit plan *m* d'attaque; fig plan *m* d'action; **~ of communication** *n* voie *f* de communication; **~ of descent** *n* descendance *f*, lignée *f*.

line of duty *n* **killed in the ~** [*policeman*] mort en service (commandé); [*soldier*] mort au combat.

line: **~ of enquiry** *n* (in investigation) piste *f*; (in research) ligne *f* de recherche; **~ of fire** *n* ligne *f* de tir; **~ of flight** *n* trajectoire *f*; **~ of latitude** *n* ligne *f* de latitude; **~ of longitude** *n* ligne *f* de longitude; **~ of thought** *n* (way of thinking) façon *f* de penser; (association of ideas) raisonnement *m*.

line of vision *n* (when aiming) ligne *f* de mire; **to block sb's ~** boucher la vue à qn.

line of work *n* métier *m*; **to be in the same ~** faire le même genre de métier.

line: **~-out** *n* remise *f* en touche; **~-printer** *n* imprimante *f* ligne par ligne.

liner /ˈlaɪnə(r)/ *n* **1** Naut paquebot *m* de grande ligne, liner *m*; **2** Aviat liner *m*, (avion *m*) gros porteur *m*; **3** Tech (of pipe) chemise *f*.

linesman /ˈlaɪnzmən/ *n* GB **1** (in tennis) juge *m* de ligne; (in football, hockey) juge *m* de touche; **2** ▶ **1692** Telecom agent *m* des lignes; Elec technicien *m* de lignes.

line: **~-spacing** *n* interlignage *m*; **~ squall** *n* Meteorol grain *m* en ligne; **~ storm** *n* US tempête *f* d'équinoxe.

line-up /ˈlaɪnʌp/ *n* **1** Sport équipe *f*; (personnel, pop group) groupe *m*; **the management ~** la composition de la direction; **a ~ of cabaret acts** une série de numéros de cabaret; **2** (identification parade) séance *f* d'identification (*de suspects*).

ling /lɪŋ/ *n* **1** Bot bruyère *f*; **2** (fish) (saltwater) julienne *f*; (freshwater) lotte *f* de rivière.

linger /ˈlɪŋɡə(r)/ *vi* **1** [*person, eyes, gaze*] s'attarder; **he ~ed for another few weeks (before dying)** il a encore vécu quelques semaines avant de mourir; **2** [*sensation, memory, smell*] persister; **the scent ~s on the air** le parfum persiste dans l'air; **3** [*doubt, question, suspicion*] subsister.

■ **linger on** [*memory, pain*] persister.

■ **linger over**: ¶ **~ over [sth]** savourer [*meal, drink*]; ¶ **~ over doing** prendre son temps pour faire.

lingerie /ˈlænʒəriː, US ˌlɑːndʒəˈreɪ/ *n* ¢ lingerie *f*; **silk ~** une lingerie de soie.

lingering /ˈlɪŋɡərɪŋ/ *adj* **1** [*look*] prolongé; [*smell, taste, pain, pollution, mist*] persistant; **2** [*doubt, hope, regret*] qui subsiste; [*memory*] persistant; **3** [*death*] lent.

lingo° /ˈlɪŋɡəʊ/ *n* baragouin° *m*.

lingua franca /ˌlɪŋɡwə ˈfræŋkə/ *n* (*pl* **~s** ou **linguae francae**) lingua franca *f*.

linguist /ˈlɪŋɡwɪst/ *n* gen, Ling linguiste *mf*; **I'm no (great) ~** je ne suis guère doué pour les langues.

linguistic /lɪŋˈɡwɪstɪk/ *adj* gen, Ling linguistique.

linguistic atlas *n* atlas *m* linguistique.

linguistics /lɪŋˈɡwɪstɪks/ **I** *n* (+ *v sg*) linguistique *f*.

II *modif* [*course, lecturer*] de linguistique.

liniment /ˈlɪnɪmənt/ *n* (ointment) pommade *f*; (liquid) liniment *m*.

lining /ˈlaɪnɪŋ/ *n* **1** (for garment, bag) doublure *f*; **a polyester ~** une doublure en polyester; **2** Physiol paroi *f*; **the womb ~, the ~ of the womb** la paroi utérine or de l'utérus.

IDIOMS **every cloud has a silver ~** à quelque chose malheur est bon.

lining paper *n* (for decorating) papier *m* d'apprêt; (for shelves) papier *m* à tapisser.

link /lɪŋk/ **I** *n* **1** (in chain) maillon *m*; **to be the weak ~ in** constituer le point faible de [*chain, investments, argument*]; **2** Transp liaison *f* (**between** entre); **a rail ~ from A to B** une liaison ferroviaire de A à B; **3** (connection between facts, events, phenomena) rapport *m* (**between** entre); lien *m* (**with** avec); **there are possible ~s with the explosion** il est possible qu'il y ait un rapport avec l'explosion; **to have ~s with terrorist groups** avoir des liens avec des groupes terroristes; **4** (between nations, companies) (economic or trading tie) relation *f* (**with** avec; **between** entre); (historical or friendly tie) lien *m* (**with** avec; **between** entre); **to forge ~s between** forger les liens entre; **to break off/renew ~s** rompre/renouer les relations; **5** Telecom, Radio, Comput liaison *f*; **television ~** liaison par télévision.

II *vtr* **1** (connect physically) [*road, path, tunnel, staircase, cable, chain*] relier [*places, objects*]; **to ~ A to B** ou **A with B** ou **A and B** relier A à B; **to be ~ed by** être relié par [*bus, bridge, cable*]; **to ~ arms** [*people*] se donner le bras; **to ~ arms with sb** prendre qn par le bras; **to walk along arms ~ed** marcher bras dessus bras dessous; **2** (relate, establish connection between) **to ~ sth to** ou **with** lier qch à [*inflation, income*]; établir un lien entre qch et [*statistic, fact, crime, illness*]; **the gene has been ~ed to cancer** on a établi un lien entre ce gène et le cancer; **evidence ~ing sb to a crime** des preuves qui établissent un lien entre qn et un crime; **police think the crimes are ~ed** la police pense qu'il y a un lien entre les crimes; **his name has been ~ed with** son nom a été associé à [*deed, name*]; **to be ~ed by** (have in common) être lié par; **3** Comput connecter [*terminals, computers*]; **to ~ sth to** ou **with** connecter qch à [*mainframe, terminal*]; **4** TV, Radio établir une liaison entre [*places*] (**by** par); **to be ~ed to Moscow by satellite** avoir une liaison par satellite avec Moscou.

III linked *pp adj* **1** [*rings, circles, symbols*] entrelacé; **2** fig [*issues, problems, crimes, projects*] lié; **they are romantically ~ed** il y a quelque chose entre eux.

IDIOMS **a chain is as strong as its weakest ~** Prov une chaîne ne peut pas être plus solide que son maillon le plus faible.

■ **link up**: **~ up** [*firms, colleges*] s'associer; **to ~ up with** s'associer avec [*college, firm*].

linkage /ˈlɪŋkɪdʒ/ *n* **1** (connection) (in ideas) lien *m* (**between** entre); (in phenomena) rapport *m* (**between** entre); **2** (of issues in international relations) association *f* (**between** entre); **3** (in genetics) linkage *m*.

linkage: **~ editing** *n* Comput édition *f* de liens; **~ editor** *n* Comput éditeur *m* de liens.

link: **~ control procedure, LCP** *n* Comput protocole *m* de communication; **~ed subroutine** *n* Comput sous-programme *m* fermé.

linker /ˈlɪŋkə(r)/ *n* **1** Comput éditeur *m* de liens; **2** Ling mot-outil *m*.

link: **~ing loader** *n* Comput chargeur-éditeur *m* de liens; **~man** *n* présentateur *m*; **~ road** *n* GB route *f* de raccordement.

links /lɪŋks/ *n* golf *m*, terrain *m* de golf.

link-up /ˈlɪŋkʌp/ *n* **1** TV, Radio liaison *f*; **satellite ~** liaison par satellite; **2** Fin, Comm association *f* (**between** entre; **with** avec).

linkwoman /ˈlɪŋkwʊmən/ *n* présentatrice *f*.

linnet /ˈlɪnɪt/ *n* linotte *f*.

lino /ˈlaɪnəʊ/ *n* lino *m*.

lino cut, lino print *n* gravure *f* sur linoléum.

linoleum /lɪˈnəʊlɪəm/ *n* linoléum *m*.

Linotype® /ˈlaɪnəʊtaɪp/ **I** *n* linotype® *f*.

II *modif* **~ machine** linotype® *f*.

linseed /ˈlɪnsiːd/ *n* ¢ graines *fpl* de lin.

linseed oil *n* huile *f* de lin.

lint /lɪnt/ *n* **1** Med tissu *m* ouaté (*pour pansement*); **2** (fluff) peluches *fpl*.

lintel /ˈlɪntl/ *n* linteau *m*.

lion /ˈlaɪən/ *n* **1** Zool lion *m*; **the ~'s den** lit, fig l'antre *m* du lion; **2 literary ~** célébrité *f* littéraire.

IDIOMS **the ~ lies down with the lamb** c'est le lion à côté de l'agneau; **to put one's head in the ~'s jaws** ou **mouth** se jeter dans la gueule du loup; **to take the ~'s share** se tailler la part du lion; **the ~'s share of the funding has gone to the opera** l'opéra a obtenu la plus grosse partie des subventions. ▶ **beard**.

lion cub *n* lionceau *m*.

lioness /ˈlaɪənes/ *n* lionne *f*.

lion: **~-hearted** *adj* liter courageux/-euse comme un lion; **~ hunter** *n* chasseur/-euse *m/f* de lion.

lionize /ˈlaɪənaɪz/ *vtr* aduler.

lion tamer ▶ **1692** *n* dompteur/-euse *m/f* de lions.

lip /lɪp/ **I** *n* **1** Anat (of person) lèvre *f*; (of dog, ape) babine *f*; **to kiss sb on the ~s** embrasser qn sur la bouche or les lèvres; **to lick one's ~s** (to wet them) se passer la langue sur les lèvres; (in anticipation) se lécher les babines°; **to bite one's ~** se mordre les lèvres; **to read sb's ~s** lire sur les lèvres de qn; **read my ~s**°! écoutez bien!; **the name on everyone's ~s** le nom qui est sur toutes les lèvres; **my ~s are sealed!** bouche cousue°!; **2** (of cup, basin, crater) bord *m*; (of jug) bec *m*; **3**° (cheek) insolence *f*; **to give sb ~** être insolent envers qn.

II *modif* [*brush, gloss, pencil*] à lèvres; [*movements*] des lèvres.

III -lipped (*dans composés*) **thin-/thick-~ped** aux lèvres minces/charnues.

IDIOMS **to keep a stiff upper ~** rester flegmatique.

lipase /ˈlaɪpeɪs, ˈlɪpeɪs/ *n* lipase *f*.

lip balm /ˈlɪpbɑːm/ *n* baume *m* pour les lèvres.

lipid /ˈlɪpɪd/ *n* lipide *m*.

liposome /ˈlaɪpəʊsəʊm/ *n* liposome *m*.

liposuction /ˈlaɪpəʊsʌkʃn, ˈlɪpəʊ-/ *n* liposuccion *f*.

lip-read /ˈlɪpriːd/ *vi* (*prét, pp* **-read** /-red/) lire sur les lèvres de quelqu'un; **can you ~?** sais-tu lire sur les lèvres?

lip: **~reading** *n* lecture *f* sur les lèvres; **~salve** *n* baume *m* pour les lèvres.

lip service *n* péj **to pay ~ to** se dire être pour [*human rights, equality*]; **he pays ~ to feminism but…** il se dit féministe mais…

lip: **~stick** *n* rouge *m* à lèvres; **~-sync** *vi* chanter en play-back.

liquefaction /ˌlɪkwɪˈfækʃn/ *n* liquéfaction *f*.

liquefied petroleum gas, LPG *n* gaz *mpl* de pétrole liquéfiés, GPL *mpl*.

liquefy /ˈlɪkwɪfaɪ/ **I** *vtr* liquéfier.

II *vi* se liquéfier.

liqueur /lɪˈkjʊə(r), US -ˈkɜːr/ *n* liqueur *f*; **apricot ~** liqueur d'abricot.

liqueur: **~ brandy** *n* fine (champagne) *f*; **~ chocolate** *n* chocolat *m* à la liqueur; **~ glass** *n* verre *m* à liqueur.

liquid /ˈlɪkwɪd/ **I** *n* **1** (substance) liquide *m*; **drink plenty of ~s** buvez beaucoup; **2** Phon liquide *f*.

II *adj* **1** [*state, substance, air, nitrogen, consonant*] liquide; **2** (clear) [*eyes, gaze, sound*] clair.

liquid assets *npl* liquidités *fpl*.

liquidate /ˈlɪkwɪdeɪt/ *vtr* **1** Fin liquider [*assets, stock, company*]; régler [*debt*]; **2** (murder) liquider°.

liquidation /ˌlɪkwɪˈdeɪʃn/ *n* (of company, stock) liquidation *f*; (of debt) remboursement *m*; **to go into ~** entrer en liquidation.

liquidator /ˈlɪkwɪdeɪtə(r)/ *n* liquidateur/-trice *m/f*.

liquid: **~ crystal** *n* cristal *m* liquide; **~ crystal display, LCD** *n* affichage *m* à cristaux liquides.

liquid diet *n* diète *f* hydrique; **to be put on a ~** être mis à la diète hydrique.

liquidity /lɪˈkwɪdətɪ/ *n* liquidité *f*.

liquidity: **~ preference** *n* Econ préférence *f* pour la liquidité; **~ ratio** *n* Fin coefficient *m* de liquidité.

liquidize /ˈlɪkwɪdaɪz/ *vtr* GB Culin passer [qch] au mixeur.

liquidizer /ˈlɪkwɪdaɪzə(r)/ *n* GB Culin mixeur *m*.

liquid: **~ lunch** *n* hum alcool *m* en fait de déjeuner; **~ measure** *n* mesure *f* de capacité des liquides; **~ paper** *n* correcteur *m* liquide; **~ paraffin** *n* Med huile *f* de paraffine; **~ soap** *n* savon *m* liquide.

liquor /ˈlɪkə(r)/ *n* **1** (alcohol) alcool *m*; **hard** ou **strong ~** de l'alcool fort; **he can't hold his ~** il ne tient pas l'alcool; **2** Culin jus *m* (de cuisson).

■ **liquor up** US: **to be ~ed up** être soûl.

liquorice, **licorice** US /ˈlɪkərɪs/ **I** *n* **1** (plant) réglisse *f*; **2** (substance) réglisse *m*.

II *modif* [*root, stick*] de réglisse; **~ allsorts** bonbons *mpl* assortis au réglisse.

liquor store *n* US magasin *m* de vins et spiritueux.

lira /ˈlɪərə/ ▶ **1143** *n* (*pl* **lire**) lire *f*.

L-iron /ˈelaɪən/ *n* fer *m* en équerre.

Lisbon /ˈlɪzbən/ ▶ **1818** *pr n* Lisbonne.

lisle /laɪl/ **I** *n* fil *m* d'Écosse.

II *modif* **~ stockings** des bas *mpl* de fil.

lisp /lɪsp/ **I** *n* zézaiement *m*; **to have a ~** zézayer, avoir un cheveu sur la langue○.

II *vtr* dire [qch] en zézayant.

III *vi* zézayer, zozoter○.

LISP *n* Comput LISP *m*.

lissom /ˈlɪsəm/ *adj* svelte.

list /lɪst/ **I** *n* **1** (catalogue) liste *f* (**of** de); **to be on a ~** être sur une liste; **to put sb/sth on a ~** mettre qn/qch sur une liste; **to take sb/sth off a ~** rayer qn/qch d'une liste; **to be at the head** ou **top of the ~** lit arriver en tête de liste; fig être en tête des priorités; **to be high/to be low on one's ~ of priorities** figurer/ne pas figurer en tête de ses priorités; **to draw up a ~** dresser une liste; ▶ **checklist**, **price list**, **waiting list etc**; **2** Naut (leaning) bande *f*; **to have a (slight) ~** donner (légèrement) de la bande; **3** (price) = **list price**.

II lists *npl* Hist, fig lice *f*; **to enter the ~s** entrer en lice (**against** contre).

III *vtr* **1** gen faire la liste de [*objets, people*]; **to be ~ed under** être classé à; **to be ~ed among** figurer parmi; **to be ~ed in a directory/the Yellow Pages®** être repris dans un répertoire/les Pages Jaunes®; **2** Comput lister; **3** Fin **to be ~ed on the Stock Exchange** être coté en Bourse.

IV *vi* **1** Naut donner de la bande; **2** US Comm **what does it ~ for?** quel est son prix au catalogue?

V listed *pp adj* GB [*building*] classé.

listen /ˈlɪsn/ **I** *n* **to have a ~ to sth** écouter qch; **have a ~ to this!** écoute un peu ça!; **it's well worth a ~** ça vaut la peine de l'écouter.

II *vi* **1** (to words, music, sounds) écouter; **to ~ at the door** écouter aux portes; **to ~ to sb doing** écouter qn faire; **I was ~ing to her singing/playing the piano** je l'écoutais chanter/jouer du piano; **~ to this!** écoute un peu ça!; **to ~ to sb/sth** écouter qn/qch; **'you're ~ing to...'** Radio 'vous écoutez...', 'vous êtes à l'écoute de ...'; **2** (pay heed) écouter; **~ carefully!** écoutez attentivement!; **sorry, I wasn't ~ing** excusez-moi, je n'écoutais pas; **you just never ~, do you?** tu n'écoutes donc jamais (ce qu' on te dit)?; **~, can you come tomorrow?** écoute, est-ce que tu peux venir demain?; **to ~ to** écouter [*teacher, adviser*]; **to ~ to advice/reason** écouter un conseil/la voix de la raison; **don't ~ to them** ne les écoute pas; **3** (wait) **to ~ for** guetter [*voice, sound, signal*]; **I ~ed for sounds of crying** je guettais le moindre pleurnichement.

■ **listen in 1** (eavesdrop) écouter (indiscrètement); **we don't want them ~ing in** nous ne voulons pas qu'ils écoutent aux portes; **to ~ in on** ou **to** écouter [qch] indiscrètement [*conversation, phone call, meeting*]; **2** Radio **to ~ in to** écouter [*programme*].

■ **listen out**: **to ~ out for** prêter une oreille attentive à [*programme, ideas, information*].

■ **listen up**○ US **hey, ~ up a minute!** hé, écoutez un peu!

listenable○ /ˈlɪsnəbl/ *adj* US [*music*] écoutable○.

listener /ˈlɪsnə(r)/ *n* **1** (personal) **to be a good/bad ~** savoir/ne pas savoir écouter; **I found a ready ~ in my aunt** j'ai trouvé en ma tante une oreille attentive; **2** Radio (*gén pl*) auditeur/-trice *m/f* (**to** de); **the ~s were spellbound** (at lecture, reading) l'auditoire était envoûté.

listening /ˈlɪsnɪŋ/ *n* **it makes interesting/exciting ~** c'est intéressant/passionnant à écouter; **'easy ~'** Mus 'variétés' *fpl*.

listening: **~ device** *n* système *m* d'écoute; **~ post** *n* poste *m* d'écoute.

listening skills *n* **1** Sch (in language) compréhension *f* orale; **2** Psych (in counselling) écoute *f*; **trained in ~** formé à l'écoute.

listening station *n* station *f* d'écoute.

listeria /lɪˈstɪərɪə/ *n* (bacteria) listéria *f*; (illness) listériose *f*.

listeriosis /lɪˌstɪərɪˈəʊsɪs/ *n* Med listériose *f*.

listing /ˈlɪstɪŋ/ **I** *n* **1** gen, Fin inscription *f* (**in** dans); **Stock Exchange ~** liste *f* des sociétés cotées en Bourse; **2** Comput listing *m*.

II listings *npl* pages *fpl* d'informations (*comprenant les programmes de télévision, de radio, et les spectacles*).

listless /ˈlɪstlɪs/ *adj* [*person, manner*] apathique; [*gesture*] mou/molle.

listlessly /ˈlɪstlɪslɪ/ *adv* [*speak*] sans enthousiasme; [*move*] mollement.

listlessness /ˈlɪstlɪsnɪs/ *n* apathie *f*.

list price *n* prix *m* au catalogue.

lit /lɪt/ **I** *pret, pp* ▶ **light**.

II○ (*abrév* = **literature**) littérature *f*.

litany /ˈlɪtənɪ/ *n* **1** Relig litanies *fpl*; **2** fig (of complaints etc) litanie *f*.

litchi *n* = **lychee**.

liter *n* US = **litre**.

literacy /ˈlɪtərəsɪ/ **I** *n* **1** (in a population) taux *m* d'alphabétisation; **~ is good/poor** le taux d'alphabétisation est élevé/faible; **our aim is 100% adult ~** notre but est que 100% des adultes sachent lire et écrire; **2** (of individual) niveau *m* d'alphabétisation, niveau *m* scolaire; **his level of ~ is very low** il est pratiquement analphabète; **to teach ~** alphabétiser.

II *modif* [*campaign, class, level, rate, scheme, target*] d'alphabétisation.

literal /ˈlɪtərəl/ *adj* **1** [*meaning, sense, use of word, truth*] littéral; **2** [*translation, rendering*] mot à mot; **3** [*depiction, performance, adaptation*] gen fidèle; pej sans imagination péj; **4** (actual, real) véritable (*before n*); **5** pej = **literal-minded**.

literally /ˈlɪtərəlɪ/ *adv* **1** [*mean, use*] littéralement; [*translate, interpret*] mot à mot; **to take sth ~** prendre qch au pied de la lettre; **2** (without exaggeration) bel et bien; **they quite ~ danced all night** ils ont bel et bien dansé toute la nuit; **3**○ (emphatic) littéralement○; **he ~ exploded (with rage)** il a littéralement explosé (de rage).

literal-minded /ˌlɪtərəlˈmaɪndɪd/ *adj* péj qui prend tout au pied de la lettre; **to be ~** tout prendre au pied de la lettre.

literary /ˈlɪtərərɪ, US ˈlɪtərerɪ/ *adj* [*prize, criticism, talent*] littéraire; **a ~ man** un homme de lettres.

literary: **~ critic** *n* critique *m* littéraire; **~ criticism** *n* critique *f* littéraire; **~ theory** *n* théorie *f* littéraire.

literate /ˈlɪtərət/ *adj* **1** (able to read and write) **to be ~** savoir lire et écrire; **he is barely ~** il sait à peine lire et écrire; **2** (cultured) [*person*] cultivé; [*work, film*] érudit; **a visually ~ society** une société comprenant le langage de l'image.

literati /ˌlɪtəˈrɑːtɪ/ *npl* gens *mpl* de lettres.

literature /ˈlɪtrətʃə(r), US -tʃʊər/ **I** *n* **1** (literary writings) littérature *f*; **20th century French ~** la littérature française du XXe siècle; **a work of ~** une œuvre littéraire; **2** (pamphlets) documentation *f*; **sales ~** brochures *fpl* publicitaires; **campaign ~** tracts *mpl*; **described in the ~ as** décrit dans tous les ouvrages consacrés à ce sujet comme.

II *modif* [*student, course*] de littérature.

lithe /laɪð/ *adj* leste.

lithium /ˈlɪθɪəm/ *n* lithium *m*.

litho /ˈlaɪθəʊ/ *n* litho *f*.

lithograph /ˈlɪθəgrɑːf, US -græf/ **I** *n* lithographie *f*.

II *vtr* lithographier.

lithographer /lɪˈθɒgrəfə(r)/ ▶ **1692** *n* lithographe *mf*.

lithographic /ˌlɪθəˈgræfɪk/ *adj* lithographique.

lithography /lɪˈθɒgrəfɪ/ *n* lithographie *f*.

Lithuania /ˌlɪθjuːˈeɪnɪə/ ▶ **1131** *pr n* Lituanie *f*.

Lithuanian /ˌlɪθjuːˈeɪnɪən/ ▶ **1486**, **1402** **I** *n* **1** (person) Lituanien/-ienne *m/f*; **2** (language) lituanien *m*.

II *adj* lituanien/-ienne.

litigant /ˈlɪtɪgənt/ *n* Jur plaideur/-euse *m/f*.

litigate /ˈlɪtɪgeɪt/ **I** *vtr* mettre [qch] en litige.

II *vi* plaider.

litigation /ˌlɪtɪˈgeɪʃn/ *n* ¢ litiges *mpl*; **has the case come to ~?** est-ce que l'affaire a été portée au tribunal?; **to be the subject of ~** faire l'objet d'un litige.

litigious /lɪˈtɪdʒəs/ *adj* [*person*] procédurier/-ière; [*topic*] litigieux/-ieuse.

litmus /ˈlɪtməs/ *n* Chem tournesol *m*.

litmus paper *n* papier *m* de tournesol.

litmus test *n* **1** Chem réaction *f* au (papier de) tournesol; **to do a ~** étudier la réaction au tournesol; **2** fig mise *f* à l'épreuve; **a ~ of her principles** la mise à l'épreuve de ses principes.

litotes /ˈlaɪtəʊtiːz/ *npl* Literat litote *f*.

litre, **liter** US /ˈliːtə(r)/ ▶ **1068** **I** *n* litre *m*.

II *modif* [*jug, measure*] d'un litre; **a ~ bottle of wine** une bouteille d'un litre de vin.

litter /ˈlɪtə(r)/ **I** *n* **1** (rubbish) détritus *mpl*; (more substantial) ordures *fpl*; (paper) papiers *mpl*; **to drop ~** jeter des détritus; **the streets are full of ~** les rues sont pleines de détritus et d'ordures; (on sign) **'no ~, penalty £500'** 'défense de déposer des ordures sous peine d'une amende de 500 livres sterling'; **2** (random collection) fouillis *m* (**of** de); **you can hardly see the floor for the ~ of books** on aperçoit à peine le plancher à cause du fouillis de livres; **3** Zool portée *f*; **to have a ~** mettre bas; **4** (for farm stock, cat) litière *f*; **5** (stretcher) (for casualty) brancard *m*; (for dignitary) litière *f*.

II *vtr* [*leaves, books*] joncher [*ground, floor*]; **to ~ clothes around a room** laisser traîner ses vêtements partout dans une pièce; **to ~ a house with sth** semer qch dans toute la maison [*clothes, magazines*]; **to ~ the floor/ground with sth** recouvrir le plancher/sol de qch; **to ~ a surface with sth** couvrir une surface de qch; **to be ~ed with papers/corpses** [*ground, field*] être jonché de papiers/cadavres; **to be ~ed with allusions/references** fig être parsemé d'allusions/de références; **history is ~ed with crooks** l'histoire est pleine d'escrocs.

III *vi* Zool [*animal*] mettre bas.

litter: **~ basket**, **~ bin** *n* poubelle *f*; **~ box** *n* US = **litter tray**; **~bug** *n* péj *personne qui jette des détritus par terre*; **~ lout** *n* GB = **litterbug**; **~ tray** *n* bac *m* à litière.

little[1] /ˈlɪtl/ (*comp* **less**; *superl* **least**)

■ **Note** When *little* is used as a quantifier (*little hope, little damage*) it is translated by *peu de*: peu d'espoir, peu de dégâts.
– For examples and particular usages see I below.
– When *a little* is used as a pronoun (*give me a little*) it is translated by *un peu*: donne-moi un peu.
– When *little* is used alone as a pronoun (*there's little I can do*) it is very often translated by *pas grand-chose*: je ne peux pas faire grand-chose.
– For examples of these and other uses of *little* as a pronoun (*to do as little as possible etc*) see II below.
– For uses of *little* and *a little* as adverbs see the entry below.
– Note that ***less*** and ***least*** are treated as separate entries in the dictionary.

I *quantif* **~ hope/chance** peu d'espoir/de chances; **~ damage was done** il y avait peu de dégâts; **we've made ~ progress** nous avons fait peu de progrès; **there's so ~ time** il y a si peu de temps; **too ~ money** trop peu or pas assez d'argent; **there's ~ sense** ou **point** ça n'a pas beaucoup de sens; **he speaks ~ German** il ne parle presque pas allemand; **~ or no influence/training** presque pas d'influence/de formation; **~ or no time/money** presque pas de temps/d'argent; **with no ~ difficulty** non sans mal; **I have ~ time** ou **sympathy for cheats** je ne supporte pas les tricheurs; **I see ~ of Paul these days** je ne vois pas beaucoup Paul en ce moment; ▶ **chance**.
II *pron* **taste a ~** goûtez-en un peu; **save a ~ for me** gardes-en un peu pour moi; **I only ate a ~** je n'en ai mangé qu'un peu; **a ~ of the money** un peu de l'argent; **the ~ I saw wasn't very good** le peu que j'ai vu n'était pas très bien; **I did what ~ I could** j'ai fait le peu que j'ai pu; **he remembers very ~** il ne se souvient pas bien; **~ of what he says is true** il n'y a pas grand-chose de vrai dans ce qu'il dit; **there's ~ I can do** je ne peux pas faire grand-chose; **she did ~ to help** elle n'a pas fait grand-chose pour aider; **I got ~ out of the lecture** je n'ai pas compris grand-chose au cours; **age has ~ to do with it** l'âge n'a pas grand-chose à voir là-dedans; **to do as ~ as possible** faire le moins possible; **to know ~ about mechanics** ne pas s'y connaître beaucoup en mécanique; **there's ~ to worry about** il n'y a pas tellement de raisons de s'inquiéter; **~ of note** rien de bien particulier; **it says ~ for his honesty** ça en dit long sur son honnêteté; **it says very ~ for her** ce n'est pas tellement à son honneur; **~ or nothing** quasiment rien; ▶ **help**.
III *adv* **1** (rarely) [*say, speak, sleep, eat, laugh*] peu; **I go there very ~** j'y vais très peu; **she visits them as ~ as possible** elle leur rend visite le moins souvent possible; **his books are ~ read** on ne le lit plus guère; **2** (hardly, scarcely) **to be ~ changed** ne pas avoir beaucoup changé; **the next results were ~ better** les résultats suivants étaient à peine meilleurs; **~ more than an hour ago** il y a à peine une heure; **it's ~ short of madness** cela frise la folie; **a ~-known novel** un roman peu connu; **3** (not at all) **~ did she realize that the watch was stolen** elle ne s'est pas du tout rendu compte que la montre était volée ; **I ~ thought** ou **supposed that he would do it** je n'aurais jamais cru qu'il le ferait; **~ did they know that** ils étaient bien loin de douter que; **~ do you know!** si tu savais!
IV a little (bit) *adv phr* (slightly) un peu; **a ~ (bit) anxious/surprised** un peu inquiet/surpris; **a ~ less/more** un peu moins/plus; **stay a ~ longer** reste encore un peu; **I was not a ~ surprised/offended** j'étais plutôt surpris/vexé; **'I'm a genius,' he said, not a ~ proudly** 'je suis un génie,' a-t-il dit, non sans fierté.
V as little as *adv phr* **for as ~ as 10 dollars a day** pour seulement 10 dollars par jour; **it can cost as ~ as £60** cela coûte seulement 60 livres sterling; **I like Henry as ~ as you do** je n'aime Henry guère plus que toi.

little[2] /ˈlɪtl/ *adj* **1** (small) petit (*before n*); **a ~ house** une petite maison; **a ~ something** un petit quelque chose; **poor ~ thing** pauvre petit/-e *m/f*; **a ~ old lady** une petite vieille dame; **she's a nice ~ thing** elle est adorable; **2** (young) [*brother, sister, boy, girl*] petit (*before n*); **when I was ~** quand j'étais petit; **the baboon and its ~ ones** le babouin et ses petits; **Mrs Carter and all the ~ Carters** Madame Carter et tous ses enfants; **3** (feeble, weak) [*gesture, nod, smile*] petit (*before n*); **a ~ voice said**... une petite voix dit...; **4** (lacking influence) [*farmer, businessman*] petit (*before n*); **5** (expressing scorn, contempt) **he's a ~ despot** c'est un vrai petit tyran; **a poky ~ flat** un petit appartement minable; **a nasty ~ boy** un méchant petit garçon; **6** (short) [*nap, snooze*] petit (*before n*); **a ~ holiday** quelques jours de vacances; **a ~ break** une petite pause; **I'll walk with you a ~ way** je ferai un bout de chemin avec toi; **stay a ~ while** reste un moment; **a ~ while longer** encore un peu.
IDIOMS **~ by ~** petit à petit; **to make ~ of** (disparage) ne pas faire grand cas de [*achievement, victory*]; (not understand) ne pas comprendre grand-chose à [*speech, report*]; ▶ **fancy**, **learning**, **too**.

■ Note Pour le comparatif et le superlatif on préférera les formes *smaller* et *smallest* à *littler* and *littlest*.

little /ˈlɪtl/: **Little Bear** GB, **Little Dipper** US *pr n* Astron Petite Ourse *f*; **Little Dog** *pr n* GB Astron Petit Chien *m*; **~ end** *n* GB Aut pied *m* de bielle.

little finger *n* petit doigt *m*, auriculaire *m*.
IDIOMS **to wrap** ou **twist sb around one's ~** mener qn par le bout du nez.

littleness /ˈlɪtlnɪs/ *n* petitesse *f*.

little /ˈlɪtl/: **~ owl** *n* chouette *f*, chevêche *f*; **~ people** *npl* fées *fpl*.

little woman *n* péj **the ~** ma femme.

littoral /ˈlɪtərəl/ **I** *n* littoral *m*.
II *adj* littoral, du littoral.

lit up○ /ˌlɪtˈʌp/ *adj* soûl.

liturgical /lɪˈtɜːdʒɪkl/ *adj* liturgique.

liturgy /ˈlɪtədʒɪ/ *n* liturgie *f*.

livable /ˈlɪvəbl/ *adj* [*life*] vivable; [*house, flat*] habitable; **he's not ~ with**○ il est invivable○.

live[1] /lɪv/ **I** *vtr* **1** (conduct) vivre; **to ~ one's life** vivre sa vie; **to ~ a normal/peaceful/healthier life** vivre normalement/paisiblement/plus sainement; **to ~ a life of luxury/crime** vivre dans le luxe/crime; **to ~ the life of a recluse/a saint** vivre en reclus/comme un saint; **if I could ~ my life over again** si je pouvais revivre ma vie; **you can't ~ your children's lives for them** vous ne pouvez pas vivre à la place de vos enfants; **to ~ one's faith/one's politics** vivre sa foi/sa politique; **2** (undergo) vivre [*experience*].
II *vi* **1** (dwell) [*animal*] vivre; [*person*] gen vivre, habiter (**with** avec); (in permanent dwelling) habiter; **they ~ at number 7** ils habitent au numéro 7; **three sons still living at home** trois fils qui vivent encore à la maison; **animals that ~ underground** des animaux qui vivent sous terre; **to ~ together/apart/alone** vivre ou habiter ensemble/séparément/seul; **to ~ in** vivre dans, habiter [*house, apartment*]; **it isn't fit to ~ in** c'est insalubre; **he's not very easy to ~ with** il n'est pas très facile à vivre; **Devon is a nice place to ~** il fait bon vivre dans le Devon; **have you found anywhere to ~ yet?** avez-vous trouvé à vous loger?; **he ~s at the library/doctor's** iron il est toujours fourré○ à la bibliothèque/chez le médecin; **he ~s in his jeans** il est toujours en jean; **2** (lead one's life) vivre; **to ~ happily/extravagantly** vivre heureux/de manière extravagante; **to ~ in luxury/poverty** vivre dans le luxe/la pauvreté; **we ~ in the computer age** nous vivons à l'ère de l'informatique; **to ~ for** ne vivre que pour [*sport, work, family*]; **to ~ in hope/fear/etc (of sth/of doing)** vivre dans l'espoir/la peur (de qch/de faire); **to ~ through sth** vivre [*experience, period*]; **to ~ without** vivre sans [*person*]; se passer de [*drugs, TV, electricity*]; **they ~d happily ever after** (in story) ils vécurent heureux et eurent beaucoup d'enfants; **3** (remain alive) gen, fig vivre; (survive) survivre; **to ~ to be eighty/ninety** vivre jusqu'à l'âge de quatre-vingts/quatre-vingt-dix ans; **nothing can ~ in this environment** rien ne peut vivre dans ce milieu; **his grandfather is still living** son grand-père vit toujours; **as long as I ~, I'll**... tant que je vivrai, je...; **you'll regret this for as long as you ~** vous le regretterez toute votre vie; **she 's only got two months to ~** il ne lui reste que deux mois à vivre; **I don't think he'll ~** je ne pense pas qu'il survive; **the memory will ~ in my heart forever** le souvenir vivra toujours dans mon cœur; **these plants ~ through the hardest of winters** ces plantes survivent à l'hiver le plus rude; **she'll not ~ through the night** elle ne passera pas la nuit; **I'll ~!** hum je n'en mourrai pas!; **I've got nothing left to ~ for** je n'ai plus de raison de vivre; **to ~ to regret sth** en venir à regretter qch; **long ~ democracy/the King!** vive la démocratie/le roi!; **4** (subsist, maintain existence) vivre; **to ~ by hunting/begging** vivre en chassant/en mendiant; **to ~ by one's pen** vivre de sa plume; **to ~ by one's wits** vivre d'expédients; **to ~ on** ou **off** vivre de [*fruit, interest, profits, charity, promises*]; vivre sur [*wage, capital*]; **to ~ off sb** se faire entretenir par qn; **his wages aren't enough to ~ on** son salaire ne suffit pas pour le faire vivre; **her children ~ on junk food** ses enfants ne mangent que des cochonneries○; **enough food to ~ on for a week** assez de nourriture pour une semaine; **to ~ out of tins/the freezer** vivre de conserves/de surgelés; **5** (put up with) **to ~ with** accepter [*illness, situation, consequences*]; supporter [*noise, décor*]; **to learn to ~ with sth** apprendre à accepter qch; **to ~ with oneself** vivre en paix avec soi-même; **to ~ with the fact that** admettre que; **'Living with Aids'** journ 'au cœur du sida'; **6** (experience life) vivre; **this is what I call living** c'est ce que j'appelle vivre; **come on! ~ a little!** allez viens! laisse-toi vivre!; **she's really ~d** elle a beaucoup vécu; **you haven't ~d until you've been to**... tu n'as rien vu tant que tu n'es pas allé à...
IDIOMS **~ and let ~** il faut être tolérant; **to ~ it up**○ faire la fête○; **to ~ on fresh air** vivre d'amour et d'eau fraîche; **you ~ and learn** on apprend tous les jours; **I'll never ~ it down!** je ne pourrai plus marcher la tête haute!; **to ~ sth down** faire oublier qch.

■ **live in** [*teacher, caretaker*] avoir un logement de fonction; [*pupil*] être interne; [*care assistant*] résider sur place; [*nanny, maid*] être logé et nourri.

■ **live on**: **~ on** [*person*] survivre; [*reputation, tradition, work*] se perpétuer.

■ **live out**: ¶ **~ out** [*cook, nanny*] ne pas être logé; [*care assistant, teacher*] vivre en ville; [*pupil*] être externe; ¶ **~ out [sth] 1** (survive) passer [*winter, day*]; **I don't think he'll ~ out the week** je ne crois pas qu'il passera la semaine; **2** (spend) **to ~ out the rest of one's days somewhere** finir ses jours quelque part; **3** (enact) vivre [*fantasies*].

■ **live up to** [*person*] être fidèle à [*principles, standards*]; [*person*] répondre à [*expectations*]; [*person*] se montrer digne de [*name, social position*]; [*person*] être à la hauteur de [*reputation*]; [*product*] ne pas démentir [*advertising*].

live² /laɪv/ **I** *adj* **1** (not dead) [*person, animal, bait*] vivant; **~ birth** naissance *f* d'un enfant viable; **real ~** en chair et en os; **2** Radio, TV (not recorded) [*band, broadcast, orchestra*] en direct; [*concert, performance, show, recording*] sur scène; [*theatre*] vivant; [*album*] enregistré sur scène; [*communications*] public/-ique; **before a ~ audience** devant un public; **3** Elec sous tension; **4** (burning) [*coal*] ardent; [*match, cigarette end*] allumé; **5** (capable of exploding) [*ammunition, bullet*] réel/réelle; (unexploded) [*bomb*] nonexplosé; **6** (topical) [*issue*] d'actualité.
II *adv* Radio, TV [*appear, bring, broadcast, transmit*] en direct; [*play, perform*] sur scène.

lived-in○ /ˈlɪvdɪn/ *adj* **to look ~** donner l'impression d'être habité○; **to have that ~ look** donner une impression de confort.

live-in /ˈlɪvɪn/ *adj* [*cook, nanny*] à demeure; **on a ~ basis** à demeure; **to have a ~ lover** vivre en concubinage.

livelihood /ˈlaɪvlɪhʊd/ *n* gagne-pain *m*; **to lose/jeopardize one's ~** perdre/mettre en danger ses moyens d'existence; **my ~ depends on it** mon gagne-pain en dépend.

liveliness /ˈlaɪvlɪnɪs/ *n* (of place, person) gaieté *f*; (of style) vivacité *f*.

livelong /ˈlɪvlɒŋ, US ˈlaɪvlɔːŋ/ *adj* littér **all the ~ day** du matin au soir et du soir au matin.

lively /ˈlaɪvlɪ/ *adj* **1** (vivacious) [*person, community, group*] plein d'entrain; [*place, scene, atmosphere, conversation, music, evening*] animé; [*account, style*] vivant; [*intelligence, imagination, interest, mind*] vif/vive; [*campaign*] percutant; **2** (fast) [*pace, breeze*] vif/vive; [*music, dance*] entraînant.
IDIOMS **look ~**○! réveillez-vous!

liven /ˈlaɪvn/: ■ **liven up**: ¶ **~ up** s'animer; ¶ **~ up [sth], ~ [sth] up** égayer [*person, décor*]; animer [*event, evening*]; **he started singing to ~ things up (a bit)** il a commencé à chanter pour mettre un peu d'animation.

liver /ˈlɪvə(r)/ *n* **1** Culin, Med foie *m*; **grilled/lamb's ~** foie *m* grillé/d'agneau; **2** (person) **a clean ~** un/-e vertueux/-euse *m/f*; **a fast ~** un/-e débauché/-e *m/f*.

live rail /laɪv/ *n* rail *m* conducteur.

liver: **~ complaint** *n* problème *m* de foie; **~ disease** *n* maladie *f* du foie; **~ fluke** *n* douve *f* du foie.

liveried /ˈlɪvərɪd/ *adj* en livrée.

liverish /ˈlɪvərɪʃ/ *adj*: **to feel ~** avoir une crise de foie.

liver paste, ~ pâté *n* pâté *m* de foie.

Liverpudlian /ˌlɪvəˈpʌdlɪən/ **I** *n* (living there) habitant/-e *m/f* de Liverpool; (born there) natif/-ive *m/f* de Liverpool.
II *adj* de Liverpool.

liver: **~ salts** *npl* sels *mpl* pour le foie; **~ spot** *n* tache *f* brune (*de vieillesse*); **~ trouble** *n* = **liver complaint**; **~wort** *n* Bot hépatique *f*; **~wurst** *n* US ≈ pâté *m* de foie.

livery /ˈlɪvərɪ/ *n* **1** (uniform) livrée *f*; **2** Equit (care of horse) pension *f*; **at ~** en pension.

livery: **~ company** *n* corporation *f* londonienne; **~man** *n* membre *m* d'une corporation londonienne.

livery stable *n* (for care) pension *f* pour chevaux; (for hire) écurie *f* de louage.

lives /laɪvz/ *npl* ▶ **life**.

livestock /ˈlaɪvstɒk/ *n* bétail *m*.

live wire /laɪv/ *n* **1** Elec fil *m* sous tension; **2** fig **to be a ~** être très dynamique.

livid /ˈlɪvɪd/ *adj* **1**○ (furious) furieux/-ieuse (**with** contre; **at doing** de faire); **2** [*face, scar*] livide; [*sky*] plombé; **~ with rage** blême de rage.

living /ˈlɪvɪŋ/ **I** *n* **1** (livelihood) vie *f*; **to earn** ou **make a ~** gagner sa vie; **to earn** ou **make an honest/a meagre ~** gagner sa vie honnêtement/avec difficulté; **to work for a ~** travailler pour gagner sa vie; **what do you do for a ~?** qu'est-ce que vous faites dans la vie?; **it's not much of a ~** ça permet tout juste de vivre; **2** (lifestyle) vie *f*; **easy/loose ~** une vie facile/de débauche; **high ~** la grande vie; **fast ~** une vie de bâton de chaise; **3** (incumbency) cure *f*; **4 the ~** (+ *v pl*) les vivants *mpl*.
II *adj* [*person, organism, legend, symbol, language*] vivant; **to be ~ proof of** être la preuve vivante de; **the ~ word** Relig la parole vivante; **a ~ hell** un véritable enfer; **within ~ memory** de mémoire d'homme; **there wasn't a ~ soul** il n'y avait pas âme qui vive.
IDIOMS **to be still in the land of the ~** être encore de ce monde.

living: **~ conditions** *npl* conditions *fpl* de vie; **~ dead** *npl* morts-vivants *mpl*; **~ death** *n* fig enfer *m*, calvaire *m*; **~ expenses** *npl* frais *mpl* de subsistance; **~ fossil** *n* fossile *m* vivant; **~-out allowance** *n* indemnité *f* de logement; **~ quarters** *npl* quartiers *mpl*; **~ room** *n* salle *f* de séjour, salon *m*; **~ space** *n* espace *m* (pour vivre); **~ standards** *npl* niveau *m* de vie; **~ wage** *n* salaire *m* adéquat.

Livorno /lɪˈvɔːnəʊ/ ▶ **1818** *pr n* Livourne.

Livy /ˈlɪvɪ/ *pr n* Tite-Live.

lizard /ˈlɪzəd/ *n* lézard *m*.

Lizard /ˈlɪzəd/ *n* **the ~** le cap *m* Lizard.

lizardskin /ˈlɪzədskɪn/ *n* lézard *m*; **a ~ bag** un sac en lézard.

llama /ˈlɑːmə/ *n* lama *m*.

LL B *n* (*abrév écrite* = **Bachelor of Laws**) diplôme *m* universitaire de droit.

LL.B. *n* Jur licence *f* en droit.

LL D *n* (*abrév écrite* = **Doctor of Laws**) doctorat *m* de droit.

LL.D. *n* Jur doctorat *m* en droit.

LMBO *n*: *abrév* ▶ **leveraged management buyout**.

LMS *n* GB *abrév* ▶ **local management of schools**.

lo /ləʊ/ *excl* littér (also **lo and behold**) voilà.

loach /ləʊtʃ/ *n* loche *f*.

load /ləʊd/ **I** *n* **1** (sth carried) charge *f*; (on vehicle, animal) chargement *m*; (on ship, plane) cargaison *f*; fig fardeau *m*; **a lorry shed its ~ on the motorway today** aujourd'hui un camion a déversé tout son chargement sur l'autoroute; **to have a heavy ~ to bear** fig avoir un lourd fardeau à porter; **to take a ~ off sb's mind** soulager qn (d'un grand poids); **it's a ~ off my mind** je me sens soulagé; **a bus-load of children** un autobus plein d'enfants; **a whole plane-load of passengers filled the departure lounge** la salle d'embarquement de l'aéroport était remplie de passagers; **2** Tech, Mech (weight) charge *f* (**on** sur); **this beam has a ~ of 10 tons** cette poutre a une charge limite de 10 tonnes; **do not exceed maximum ~** ne pas dépasser la charge maximum; **3** (shipment, batch) (of sand, gravel etc) cargaison *f*; (of cement) fournée *f*; **I've done four ~s of washing this morning** j'ai fait quatre machines de linge ce matin; **4** Elec charge *f*; **5** fig (amount of work) travail *m*; **we must lighten the ~ of young doctors** nous devons alléger le travail des jeunes médecins; fig **let's try and spread the ~** essayons de répartir le travail à faire; **6**○ (a lot) **a ~** ou **a whole ~ of people/books** des tas○ or des quantités de gens/livres.
II○ **loads** *npl* **~s of people/photos/flowers** des tas○ de gens/photos/fleurs; **we've got ~s of time** nous avons tout notre temps or largement le temps; **there was ~s of champagne** il y avait du champagne en quantité; **we had ~s to drink** on n'a pas arrêté de boire; **I've seen/done it ~s of times before** je l'ai vu/fait je ne sais pas combien de fois; **to have ~s of energy** avoir de l'énergie à revendre; **to have ~s of work** avoir un travail fou○; **to have ~s of money** être plein aux as○, être bourré de fric○.
III *vtr* **1** gen charger [*vehicle, ship, donkey, gun, washing machine*] (**with** de); **to ~ a camera** mettre un film dans un appareil photo; **to ~ the luggage into the car** charger les bagages dans la voiture; **2** Comput charger [*program*]; **3** Elec surcharger [*system*]; **4** Insur majorer [*premium*]; **5** fig (inundate, give generously) **to ~ sb with** combler or couvrir qn de [*presents, honours*]; **6** (tamper with) piper [*dice*]; **to ~ the dice against sb** fig truquer les cartes contre qn.
IV *vi* charger.
IDIOMS **get a ~ of this!** (listen) écoute un peu ça○!; **get a ~ of that!** (look) vise un peu ça○!; **that's a ~ of old rubbish**○ ou **nonsense** ou **crap**◑ ou **cobblers**◑ c'est de la blague○ or foutaise○.
■ **load down**: **~ [sb] down** charger qn (**with** de); **to be ~ed down with sth** plier ou ployer sous le poids de qch; **to ~ sb down with work** accabler qn de travail.
■ **load up**: ¶ **~ up** [*lorry*] charger, prendre son chargement; ¶ **~ [sth] up** [*person*] charger [*van, ship*] (**with** de).

load-bearing *adj* [*wall*] porteur/-euse.

loaded /ˈləʊdɪd/ *adj* **1** (full, laden) [*tray, dress-rail, plane, lorry, gun*] chargé (**with** de); fig **~ with meaning** ou **significance** plein de sens; **2** (weighed down) [*person*] chargé (**with** de); fig **to be ~ with honours/medals** être couvert d'honneurs/de médailles; **3**○ fig (rich) plein aux as○, bourré de fric○; **4** (leading) [*question*] tendancieux/-ieuse; **5** Ind [*substance*] chargé (**with** de); **6**○ US (drunk) bourré○.

loader /ˈləʊdə(r)/ *n* (person) chargeur *m*; (machine) chargeuse *f*.

load factor *n* **1** Elec facteur *m* d'utilisation; **2** Aviat coefficient *m* de remplissage.

loading /ˈləʊdɪŋ/ *n* **1** Transp chargement *m*; **2** Insur majoration *f*.

loading bay *n* aire *f* or zone *f* de chargement.

load: **~ line** *n* ligne *f* de charge; **~ shedding** *n* délestage *m*; **~ stone** *n* magnétite *f*.

loaf /ləʊf/ **I** *n* (*pl* **loaves**) pain *m*; **a ~ of bread** un pain; **a brown/white ~** un pain complet/blanc.
II *vi* US = **loaf about**.
IDIOMS **half a ~ is better than no bread** Prov faute de grives on mange des merles; **use your ~**○! fais marcher tes méninges○!
■ **loaf about, loaf around** traînasser.

loafer /ˈləʊfə(r)/ *n* **1** (shoe) mocassin *m*; **2** (idler) flemmard/-e○ *m/f*.

loaf: **~ sugar** *n* sucre *m* en pain; **~ tin** GB, **~ pan** US *n* moule *m* à cake.

loam /ləʊm/ *n* terreau *m*.

loamy /ˈləʊmɪ/ *adj* riche en terreau.

loan /ləʊn/ **I** *n* **1** Fin (money or property) (borrowed) emprunt *m*; (lent) prêt *m*; **a £20,000 ~, a ~ of £20,000** un prêt or un emprunt de 20 000 livres sterling; **to take out a ~** faire or souscrire fml un emprunt; **to ask for/give a ~** demander/accorder un prêt; **2** (act) (of lending) prêt *m*; (of borrowing) emprunt *m*; **to have the ~ of sth** emprunter qch; **to give sb the ~ of sth** prêter qch à qn; **to be on ~** [*museum object*] être prêté (**to** à); [*person*] prêter ses services (**to** à); **this book is not for ~** consultation sur place; **the book is already on ~** le livre a déjà été emprunté.
II *vtr* prêter (also **~ out**) prêter [*object, money*] (**to** à).

loan: **~ account** *n* Fin compte *m* de prêt; **~ agreement** *n* Fin contrat *m* de prêt; **~ bank** *n* caisse *f* de prêts; **~ capital** *n* capital *m* d'emprunt; **~ certificate** *n* titre *m* de prêt; **~ facility** *n* facilité *f* de crédit; **~ portfolio** *n* portefeuille *m* de prêts; **~ shark**○ *n* péj usurier/-ière *m/f*; **~ stock** *n* emprunt *m* obligataire; **~ translation** *n* Ling calque *m*; **~ word** *n* Ling emprunt *m*.

loath /ləʊθ/ *adj* **I am ~ to do** je préférerais ne pas faire; **he was ~ to do** il aurait préféré ne pas faire; **Joseph, never ~ to do** Joseph, qui n'hésite jamais à faire; **nothing ~** sans hésitation.

loathe /ləʊð/ *vtr* détester (**doing** faire).

loathing /ˈləʊðɪŋ/ *n* répugnance *f* (**for** pour).

loathsome /ˈləʊðsəm/ *adj* répugnant.

loathsomeness /ˈləʊðsəmnɪs/ *n* caractère *m* répugnant.

loaves /ləʊvz/ *npl* ▶ **loaf**.

lob /lɒb/ **I** *n* Sport lob *m*.
II *vtr* (*p prés etc* **-bb-**) **1** gen lancer; **2** Sport lober.
III *vi* (*p prés etc* **-bb-**) lober.

lobby /ˈlɒbɪ/ **I** *n* **1** (hall) (of house) entrée *f*, vestibule *m*; (of hotel) hall *m*; (of theatre) lobby *m*; **2** Pol (to meet public) *hall de l'assemblée législative où le public rencontre les députés*; **3** GB Pol (also **division ~**) (where MPs vote) *vestibule où les députés se répartissent pour voter*; **4** (also **~ group**) lobby *m*; **the environmental/farming/pro-European ~** le lobby écologiste/des agriculteurs/pro-européen; **5** (campaign) campagne *f* de pression, lobbying *m*; **to stage a mass ~ of parliament** organiser une manifestation devant le parlement.
II *vtr* [*person, group*] faire pression sur [*person, group*] (**about** à propos de); Pol appuyer [*bill*]; **to ~ a bill through parliament** GB/**Congress** US appuyer un projet de loi pour qu'il passe au parlement/au Congrès.
III *vi* faire pression, se livrer à un travail de propagande; **to ~ for sth/to do** faire pression pour obtenir qch/pour faire.

lobby correspondent *n* journaliste *mf* parlementaire.

lobbyer /ˈlɒbɪə(r)/ *n* membre *m* d'un groupe de pression, lobbyiste *mf*.

lobby group *n* lobby *m*.

lobbying /ˈlɒbɪɪŋ/ *n* activité *f* des groupes de pression, lobbying *m*; **~ of ministers** lobbying des ministres.

lobbyist /ˈlɒbɪɪst/ *n* membre *m* d'un groupe de pression, lobbyiste *mf*; **a ~ for pensioners' rights** un lobbyiste pour les droits des retraités.

lobe /ləʊb/ *n* Anat, Bot lobe *m*; **ear ~** lobe *m* de l'oreille.

lobelia /ləˈbiːljə/ *n* lobélie *f*.

lobotomy /ləʊˈbɒtəmɪ/ *n* lobotomie *f*.

lobster /ˈlɒbstə(r)/ **I** *n* Culin, Zool homard *m*; **dressed ~** homard préparé.
II *modif* [*salad, soup*] au homard.

lobster: **~ Newburg** *n* homard *m* à la Newburg; **~ pot** *n* casier *m* à homards; **~ Thermidor** *n* homard *m* thermidor.

local /ˈləʊkl/ **I**○ *n* **1** (resident) personne *f* du pays; **the ~s** les gens *mpl* du pays; **is he a ~?** il est du coin?; **2** (pub) pub *m* du quartier; **3** (cinema) cinéma *m* du quartier; **4** Med anesthésique *m* local; **5** (newspaper) journal *m* local; **the ~s** les journaux locaux; **6** (train) omnibus *m*.
II *adj* **1** (neighbourhood) [*church, doctor, library, shop*] du quartier; **2** (of the town) [*newspaper, office, hospital, transport*] local; **3** (regional) [*newspaper, television, radio, news*] régional; [*speciality*] du pays; [*tradition*] local; [*business*] de la région; **to show ~ variations** manifester des variations d'un endroit à l 'autre; **4** (of a country) [*currency, language*] local; **~ time** heure locale; **5** Med [*pain, swelling*] localisé.

local: **~ anaesthetic** *n* anesthésique *m* local; **~ area network**, **LAN** *n* Comput réseau *m* local; **~ authority** *n* GB Admin (+ *v sg ou pl*) autorités *fpl* locales; **~ (area) call** *n* Telecom communication *f* téléphonique locale; **~ colour** GB, **~ color** US *n* couleur *f* locale; **~ council** *n* GB = **local authority**.

locale /ləʊˈkɑːl, US -ˈkæl/ *n* **1** (setting) scène *f*; **the ~ is a small village** la scène se passe dans un petit village; **2** (place) endroit *m*.

local: **~ education authority**, **LEA** *n* GB (+ *v sg ou pl*) *administration locale qui gère les affaires scolaires*; **~ election** *n* élection *f* locale; **~ government** *n* administration *f* locale; **~ government minister** *n* GB *ministre d'État chargé de déterminer les pouvoirs des autorités locales*.

locality /ləʊˈkælətɪ/ *n* **1** (local area) région *f*; **shops in the ~** les magasins de la région; **2** (place) endroit *m*; **different localities** des endroits différents.

localize /ˈləʊkəlaɪz/ **I** *vtr* **1** (pinpoint) localiser [*origin, problem*]; **2** (restrict to one area) restreindre [*damage, effect*]; **3** Admin Pol décentraliser [*control, education*].
II localized *pp adj* [*damage, pain, problem*] localisé; [*control, administration*] décentralisé.

local management of schools, **LMS** *n* GB *autonomie des écoles pour la gestion de leur budget*.

locate /ləʊˈkeɪt, US ˈləʊkeɪt/ **I** *vtr* **1** (find) retrouver [*person, object*]; localiser [*fault, problem*]; situer [*sound*]; repérer [*information*]; **2** (position) établir [*business*]; construire [*building*]; situer [*site*]; Tech positionner [*fitment, part*]; **to be ~d somewhere** être situé quelque part.
II *vi* Tech [*fitment, part*] se positionner.

location /ləʊˈkeɪʃn/ *n* **1** (place) gen endroit *m*; (exact site) emplacement *m* (**for** pour); **a central/convenient/ideal ~** un emplacement central/commode/idéal; **to know the ~ of sth** savoir où se trouve qch; **2** Cin extérieurs *mpl*; **on ~** en extérieur; **to go on ~** tourner en extérieur.

locative /ˈlɒkətɪv/ **I** *n* Ling (also **~ case**) locatif *m*; **in the ~** au locatif.
II *adj* locatif/-ive.

loch /lɒk, lɒx/ *n* Scot loch *m*, lac *m*.

loci /ˈlɒkiː/ *npl* ▶ **locus**.

lock /lɒk/ **I** *n* **1** (with key) serrure *f*; (with bolt) verrou *m*; **there's no ~ on the bathroom door** il n'y a pas de verrou à la porte de la salle de bains; **under ~ and key** sous clé; **2** (of hair) mèche *f*; **long/curly ~s** cheveux *mpl* longs/bouclés; **3** Naut écluse *f*; **4** (in wrestling) clé *f*; **arm/leg ~** clé de bras/jambe; **5** (in rugby) avant *m* de deuxième ligne; **6** Aut rayon *m* de braquage; **to have a good ~** [*car*] bien braquer; **full ~** braquage *m* à fond; **half ~** demi-braquage *m*; **7** Comput verrouillage *m*; **8** (on firearm) percuteur *m*.
II *vtr* **1** (close securely) (with key) fermer [qch] à clé; (with bolt) verrouiller; **to ~ sth into a drawer** enfermer qch dans un tiroir; **2** Comput verrouiller [*file*]; **3** fig **to be ~ed in combat** [*armies*] être aux prises; **two lovers ~ed in an embrace** deux amants enlacés; **to ~ horns** lit [*animals*] lutter cornes contre cornes; fig [*people*] se disputer violemment.
III *vi* **1** (close securely) [*door, drawer*] fermer à clé; **2** (seize up) [*wheel, steering wheel*] se bloquer.

■ **lock away**: ¶ **~ [sth] away**, **~ away [sth]** mettre [qch] sous clé; ¶ **~ [sb] away** enfermer qn.

■ **lock in**: **~ [sb] in** enfermer [*person*]; **to ~ oneself in** s'enfermer.

■ **lock on** [*capitals key, shift key*] se verrouiller; [*radar*] accrocher; **to ~ onto a target** accrocher une cible.

■ **lock out**: **~ [sb] out** enfermer [qn] dehors; **to ~ oneself out** s'enfermer dehors; **to be ~ed out** être enfermé dehors; **I've ~ed myself out of my car** j'ai fermé ma voiture avec les clés dedans; **I've ~ed myself out of my room** je me suis enfermé dehors.

■ **lock together** [*components, pieces*] s'emboîter.

■ **lock up**: ¶ **~ up** fermer; **it's time to ~ up** c'est l'heure de fermer; ¶ **~ [sth] up**, **~ up [sth]** mettre [qch] sous clé [*documents, jewellery*]; fermer [qch] à clé [*house, room*]; immobiliser [*capital*]; ¶ **~ [sb] up**, **~ up [sb]** enfermer [*captive, hostage*]; mettre [qn] sous les verrous [*killer, prisoner*]; **he should be ~ed up**○**!** il est bon à enfermer○!

locker /ˈlɒkə(r)/ *n* casier *m*, vestiaire *m*.

locker room I *n* vestiaire *m*.
II *modif* [*joke*] de corps de garde; [*humour*] paillard.

locket /ˈlɒkɪt/ *n* Fashn médaillon *m*.

lock gate *n* porte *f* d'écluse.

locking /ˈlɒkɪŋ/ **I** *n* gen, Comput verrouillage *m*; ▶ **central locking**.
II *adj* [*draw, door*] qui ferme à clé; [*petrol cap*] antivol.

lock: **~jaw** *n* tétanos *m*; **~ keeper** *n* éclusier/-ière *m/f*; **~nut** *n* (special screw) écrou *m* auto-bloquant; (additional screw) contre-écrou *m*; **~-out** *n* lock-out *m inv*, grève *f* patronale; **~smith** *n* serrurier *m*.

lock-up /ˈlɒkʌp/ *n* **1** GB (garage) garage *m* (*séparé du domicile*); (shop) boutique *f*; **2**† (cell) cellule *f*.

loco /ˈləʊkəʊ/ **I**○ *n* GB Rail loco○ *f*.
II○ *adj* (mad) timbré○, fou/folle.

locomotion /ˌləʊkəˈməʊʃn/ *n* locomotion *f*.

locomotive /ˌləʊkəˈməʊtɪv/ **I** *n* locomotive *f*; **electric/diesel/steam ~** locomotive électrique/diesel/à vapeur.
II *adj* **1** [*muscle*] locomoteur/-trice; **2** [*power*] locomotif/-ive.

locomotive shed *n* hangar *m* à locomotives.

locum /ˈləʊkəm/ *n* GB remplaçant/-e *m/f*.

locus /ˈləʊkəs/ *n* (*pl* **-ci**) Math lieu *m*.

locust /ˈləʊkəst/ *n* locuste *f*, sauterelle *f*; **swarm of ~s** nuage *m* de sauterelles.

locust: **~ bean** *n* caroube *f*; **~ tree** *n* caroubier *m*.

locution /ləˈkjuːʃn/ *n* locution *f*.

lode /ləʊd/ *n* Geol filon *m*.

loden /ˈləʊdn/ *n* (coat, fabric) loden *m*.

lodestar /ˈləʊdstɑː(r)/ *n* **1** Astron étoile *f* polaire; **2** fig guide *m*.

lodestone /ˈləʊdstəʊn/ *n* magnétite *f*.

lodge /lɒdʒ/ **I** *n* **1** (small house) pavillon *m*; (for gatekeeper) loge *f* (du gardien); (in castle) conciergerie *f*; **hunting ~** pavillon de chasse; **porter's ~** Univ loge du concierge; **2** US (hotel) hôtel *m*; **3** (Masonic) loge *f*; **4** (of beaver) abri *m*.
II *vtr* **1** (accommodate) loger [*person*]; **2** déposer [*appeal, complaint, protest*] (**with** auprès de); **3** (store) déposer [*valuables*].
III *vi* **1** (reside) se loger (**with** chez); **2** (stick) [*bullet*] loger; [*small object*] (in throat, tube) se coincer; (on surface) s'incruster; **it ~d in her memory** cela s'est incrusté dans sa mémoire.

lodger /ˈlɒdʒə(r)/ *n* (having room only) locataire *mf*; (with meals) pensionnaire *mf*; **to take in ~s** louer des chambres; (with meals) prendre des pensionnaires.

lodging /ˈlɒdʒɪŋ/ **I** *n* logement *m*; **a night's ~** hébergement *m* pour la nuit; **board and ~** (chambre *f* avec) pension *f*.
II lodgings *npl* logement *m*; **to take ~** prendre une chambre (**with** chez).

lodging house† *n* pension *f*.

loess /ˈləʊes/ *n* lœss *m*.

loft /lɒft, US lɔːft/ **I** *n* **1** (attic) grenier *m*; **hay ~** grenier à foin; **2** US (apartment) loft *m*; **3** Relig, Archit tribune *f*; **choir/organ ~** tribune de la chorale/d'orgue.
II *vtr* US lancer [qch] en chandelle [*ball*].

loft bed *n* US lit *m* en mezzanine.

loft conversion *n* **1** (process) aménagement *m* de grenier; **2** (room) grenier *m* aménagé.

loft hatch *n* trappe *f* (du grenier).
loftily /ˈlɒftɪlɪ, US ˈlɔːftɪlɪ/ *adv* avec hauteur.
loftiness /ˈlɒftɪnɪs, US ˈlɔːftɪnɪs/ *n* **1** (of building, peak, etc) hauteur *f*; **2** (of manners) hauteur *f*; (of ideas) grandeur *f*.
loft ladder *n* échelle *f* escamotable.
lofty /ˈlɒftɪ, US ˈlɔːftɪ/ *adj* **1** [*building, peak, etc*] haut; **2** [*manner*] hautain; [*ideas, words*] noble.
log /lɒg, US lɔːg/ **I** *n* **1** (of wood) rondin *m*; (for burning) bûche *f*; **2** (written record) registre *m*; **to keep a ~ of people's comings and goings** noter les allées et venues des gens; **3** Transp (of plane, ship) livre *m* de bord; **4** Comput carnet *m* d'exploitation; **5** Math logarithme *m*.
II *vtr* (*p prés etc* **-gg-**) **1** (record) noter [*reading, fact*]; **2** (clock up) (also **~ up**) avoir à son actif [*miles*]; **3** (achieve) [*car, train*] rouler à [*speed, 80 mph*]; [*plane*] voler à [*speed, 500 mph*]; [*ship*] filer [*knots*].
III *vi* (*p prés etc* **-gg-**) abattre des arbres.
IDIOMS **to sleep like a ~** dormir comme une souche.
■ **log in** = **log on**.
■ **log on** Comput ouvrir une session, se connecter.
■ **log off** Comput clore une session, se déconnecter.
■ **log out** = **log off**.
loganberry /ˈləʊgənbrɪ, US -berɪ/ *n* loganberry *m*.
logarithm /ˈlɒgərɪðəm, US ˈlɔːg-/ *n* logarithme *m*.
logarithmic spiral *n* spirale *f* logarithmique.
log book *n* **1** (of car) ≈ carte *f* grise; **2** (of plane, ship) livre *m* de bord; **3** (written record) registre *m*.
log: **~ cabin** *n* cabane *f* en rondins; **~ fire** *n* feu *m* de bois.
logger /ˈlɒgə(r)/ *n* bûcheron *m*.
loggerheads /ˈlɒgəhedz/ *npl* **to be at ~** être en désaccord (**with** avec).
loggerhead turtle *n* caret *m*.
loggia /ˈləʊdʒə, ˈlɒdʒɪə/ *n* loggia *f*.
logging /ˈlɒgɪŋ/ *n* abattage *m* des arbres.
logic /ˈlɒdʒɪk/ *n* gen, Philos, Comput logique *f*; **I can see the ~ in selling it** je vois l'intérêt que cela peut présenter de le vendre.
IDIOMS **to chop ~** discutailler.
logical /ˈlɒdʒɪkl/ *adj* logique; **~ positivism** positivisme *m* logique.
logically /ˈlɒdʒɪklɪ/ *adv* logiquement; **~ speaking** logiquement.
logic: **~ bomb** *n* bombe *f* logique; **~ chopping** *n* ergotage *m*; **~ circuit** *n* circuit *m* logique.
logician /ləˈdʒɪʃn/ *n* logicien/-ienne *m/f*.
logistic /ləˈdʒɪstɪk/ *adj* logistique.
logistically /ləˈdʒɪstɪklɪ/ *adv* d'un point de vue logistique.
logistics /ləˈdʒɪstɪks/ *n* (+ *v sg* ou *pl*) logistique *f*.
log jam *n* lit embouteillage *m* (de bois de flottage); fig blocage *m*.
logo /ˈləʊgəʊ/ *n* logo *m*.
log pile *n* tas *m* de bois.
logroll /ˈlɒgrəʊl/ **I** *vtr* voter [qch] en remerciement d'un service rendu [*bill*].
II *vi* renvoyer l'ascenseur.
logrolling /ˈlɒgrəʊlɪŋ/ *n* US Pol trafic *m* de faveurs.
log: **~ saw** *n* Agric scie *f* à bûches; **~ tables** *npl* tables *fpl* de logarithmes.
logy○ /ˈləʊgɪ/ *adj* US mou, léthargique.
loin /lɔɪn/ **I** *n* Culin **1** (of pork) GB ≈ côtes *fpl* premières, US ≈ filet *m*; **2** (of lamb) GB ≈ carré *m* de côtes premières, US ≈ filet *m*; **3** (of veal) GB ≈ longe *f*, US ≈ côtes *fpl* premières.
II † **loins** *npl* Anat reins *mpl*.
IDIOMS **to gird up one's ~s** lit, fig se ceindre les reins.
loin: **~ chop** *n* côte *f* première; **~cloth** *n* pagne *m*.

Loire /lwɑː(r)/ ▶**1644**, **1163** *pr n* Loire *f*; **in/to the ~** dans la Loire; **the ~ valley** la vallée de la Loire; **a ~ wine** un vin de la Loire.
Loire-Atlantique ▶**1163** *pr n* Loire-Atlantique *f*; **in/to the ~** en Loire-Atlantique.
Loiret ▶**1163** *pr n* Loiret *m*; **in/to the ~** dans le Loiret.
Loir-et-Cher ▶**1163** *pr n* Loir-et-Cher *m*; **in/to the ~** dans le Loir-et-Cher.
loiter /ˈlɔɪtə(r)/ *vi* (idly) traîner; (pleasurably) flâner; (suspiciously) rôder.
loiterer /ˈlɔɪtərə(r)/ *n* (idle) flâneur/-euse *m/f*; (suspicious) rôdeur/-euse *m/f*.
loitering /ˈlɔɪtərɪŋ/ *n* Jur **1 ~ (with intent)** intention *f* délictueuse; **2** (soliciting) racolage *m*.
loll /lɒl/ *vi* [*person*] se prélasser; [*part of body*] tomber; [*tongue*] pendre.
■ **loll about** traîner sans rien faire.
■ **loll back** [*person*] se prélasser; [*head*] partir en arrière.
lollipop /ˈlɒlɪpɒp/ *n* sucette *f*.
lollipop: **~ lady**○ *n* GB contractuelle *f* qui fait traverser la rue aux écoliers; **~ man**○ *n* GB contractuel *m* qui fait traverser la rue aux écoliers.
lollop /ˈlɒləp/ *vi* galoper (maladroitement).
lolly /ˈlɒlɪ/ *n* GB **1**○ (money) fric○ *m*; **2** (sweet) sucette *f*; **ice ~** glace *f* à l'eau (*sur un bâton*).
lollygag○ /ˈlɒlɪgæg/, **lallygag**○ /ˈlælɪgæg/ *vi* US **1** (loiter) traînasser; **2** (dawdle) lambiner○.
Lombard /ˈlɒmbəd/ **I** *n* Lombard/-e *m/f*.
II *adj* lombard.
Lombardy /ˈlɒmbədɪ/ *pr n* Lombardie *f*.
Lombardy poplar *n* peuplier *m* d'Italie.
London /ˈlʌndən/ ▶**1818** **I** *pr n* Londres; **in/to ~** à Londres; **Greater ~** le Grand Londres; **inner ~** Londres intra-muros; **outer ~** la banlieue de Londres.
II *modif* [*person, accent, flight, train*] de Londres.
London broil *n* US Culin steak *m* grillé.
Londoner /ˈlʌndənə(r)/ *n* Londonien/-ienne *m/f*.
London pride *n* GB Bot désespoir-des-peintres *m*, saxifrage *m*.
lone /ləʊn/ *adj* littér (lonely) solitaire; (only one) seul.
loneliness /ˈləʊnlɪnɪs/ *n* (of person) solitude *f*; (of position) isolement *m*.
lonely /ˈləʊnlɪ/ *adj* [*person, life*] solitaire; [*place, building*] isolé; [*decision*] que l'on prend seul; **I am ~ for my family** je me sens seul, loin de ma famille.
lonely: **~ hearts' club** club *m* de rencontres; **~ hearts' column** *n* annonces *fpl* matrimoniales.
lone parent *n* parent *m* isolé.
loner /ˈləʊnə(r)/ *n* solitaire *mf*.
lonesome /ˈləʊnsəm/ *adj* solitaire; **to be ~ for sb** se sentir seul loin de qn.
IDIOMS **to be all on** GB ou **by** US **one's ~** être tout seul.
lone wolf *n* solitaire *m*.
long /lɒŋ, US lɔːŋ/ ▶**1412** **I** *n* (syllable, signal) Literat, Radio longue *f*.
II *adj* **1** (lengthy, protracted) [*event, period, process, wait, conversation, book, journey, vowel*] long/longue; [*delay*] important; [*bath, sigh*] grand (*before n*); **20 minutes ~** (long) de 20 minutes; **how ~ is the interval?** combien de temps dure l'entracte?; **is an hour ~ enough?** est-ce qu'une heure suffira?; **it's been a ~ day** la journée a été longue; **to get** ou **grow** ou **become ~er** [*days*] s'allonger; **to take a ~ hard look at sth** lit, fig examiner qch attentivement; **I want to have a ~er look at the patient** je voudrais examiner le malade plus longuement; **she gave me a ~ hard stare** elle a posé sur moi un regard scrutateur; **after ~ hours of discussion** après de longues heures de discussion; **I don't like the ~ hours in this job** je n'aime pas les longues journées dans ce travail; **for five ~ years I waited** j'ai attendu pendant cinq longues années; **to be ~ in coming** tarder à venir; **a friend of ~ standing** un ami de longue date; **2** (in expressions of time) **she's been away a ~ time** elle est restée longtemps absente; **it's been a ~ time since I saw you** ça fait longtemps que je ne t'ai pas vu; **you've been a ~ time getting here** tu as mis longtemps pour arriver; **they've been a ~ time making up their minds** il leur a fallu du temps pour se décider; **six hours, that's a ~ time** six heures, c'est long; **three years seems such a ~ time** trois ans semblent si long; **I've been a teacher for a ~ time** je suis professeur depuis longtemps; **I hadn't played tennis for a ~ time** je n'avais pas joué au tennis depuis longtemps; **she hasn't been well for a ~ time** ça fait longtemps qu'elle est malade; **for a ~ time I didn't believe her** pendant longtemps je ne l'ai pas crue; **it's a ~ ~ time since I last saw her** il y a bien longtemps que je ne l'ai pas vue; **a ~ time ago** il y a longtemps; **a very ~ time ago, a ~ ~ time ago** il y a très longtemps; **to take a ~ time** [*person*] mettre longtemps; [*task etc*] prendre longtemps or du temps; **that takes a ~ time to organize** cela prend longtemps or du temps à organiser; **does it take a ~ time for the results to come through?** est-ce que les résultats mettent longtemps à arriver?; **3** (in measuring) [*arm, dress, hair, queue, rope, table*] long/longue; [*grass*] haut; [*detour*] grand; **20 m ~** (long) de 20 m, de 20 m de long; **the ~ side of the table** le grand côté de la table; **to get** ou **grow ~** [*grass, hair, nails*] devenir long, pousser; [*list, queue*] s'allonger; **she's growing her hair ~** elle se laisse pousser les cheveux; **to make sth ~er** allonger [*sleeve*]; augmenter la longueur de [*shelf*]; **to be ~ in the leg** [*person, animal*] avoir de longues jambes; [*trousers*] être trop long; **4** (in expressions of distance) **is it a ~ way to the station?** est-ce que la gare est loin (d'ici)?; **it's a ~ way** c'est loin; **he lives a ~ way away** ou **off** il habite loin; **we could hear the guns a ~ way off** dans le lointain nous entendions les canons; **January is a ~ way off** janvier est loin; **Nice is a ~ way from Paris** Nice est loin de Paris; **they're a ~ way from satisfying our requirements** ils sont loin de remplir toutes nos conditions; **don't fall, it's a ~ way down** ne tombe pas, c'est haut; **a ~ way down the road** tout au bout de la route; **a ~ way down the list** loin sur la liste; **I saw the boat a ~ way out** là-bas au loin j'ai vu le bateau; **you are a ~ way out in your calculations** vous vous trompez lourdement dans vos calculs; **it's a ~ way up to the tenth floor** c'est haut jusqu'au dixième étage; **we've come a ~ way to be here tonight/since the days of the first computers** nous avons fait beaucoup de chemin pour être ici ce soir/depuis l'époque des premiers ordinateurs; **to go a ~ way** [*person*] (be successful) aller loin; [*provision, packet, supply*] (last long) durer longtemps; **to make sth go a ~ way** faire durer qch; **a little goes a ~ way** (of paint, chemical, spice) il n'en faut pas beaucoup; **to go a ~ way towards doing** contribuer largement à faire; **to have a ~ way to go** lit [*traveller*] avoir beaucoup de chemin à faire; fig [*worker, planner*] avoir encore beaucoup d'efforts à faire (**to do** avant de faire); **it's the biggest/best by a ~ way** c'est de loin le plus grand/le meilleur; **to take the ~ way round** faire un long détour.
III *adv* **1** (a long time) longtemps; **will you be ~?** tu en as pour longtemps?; **I shan't be ~** je n'en ai pas pour longtemps; **how ~ will you be?** tu en as pour combien de temps?; **how ~ will you be in the meeting?** cette réunion va te prendre combien de temps?; **how ~ will you be in choosing?**

combien de temps te faudra-t-il pour choisir?; **not very ~** pas très longtemps; **don't be ~** dépêche-toi; **don't be ~ in getting ready** ne prends pas trop de temps pour te préparer; **how ~ will it be before I hear?** combien de temps faudra-t-il avant que j'entende?; **it won't be ~ before you're home again** tu seras rentré chez toi dans peu de temps; **I've been here ~er than anyone else** je suis ici depuis plus longtemps que tout le monde; **I can't stand it a day/moment ~er** je ne le supporterai pas un jour/une minute de plus; **the ~er we stayed the hotter it grew** plus le temps passait et plus il faisait chaud; **it's been so ~ since we last met** ça fait si longtemps que nous ne nous sommes pas vus; **it's not that ~ since the party** il ne s'est pas passé tellement de temps depuis la soirée; **it's not that ~ since I was a student** il n'y a pas si longtemps j'étais étudiant; **it wasn't ~ before people said...** il n'a pas fallu longtemps pour que les gens disent...; **has he been gone ~?** est-ce qu'il y a longtemps qu'il est parti? ; **I haven't got ~** je n'ai pas beaucoup de temps; **I've worked here ~ enough to know...** je travaille ici depuis assez longtemps pour savoir...; **if you stay ~ enough** si tu restes assez longtemps; **300 years has not been ~ enough** 300 ans n'ont pas suffi; **he paused only** ou **just ~ enough to...** il s'est interrompu juste le temps de...; **an hour? that doesn't give us ~ to have dinner** une heure? ça ne nous laisse pas beaucoup de temps pour dîner; **this won't take ~** ça ne prendra pas longtemps; **the meeting took much ~er than expected** la réunion a duré beaucoup plus longtemps que prévu; **how ~ did it take him to find out?** il lui a fallu combien de temps pour se renseigner?; **it took me ~er than I thought** il m'a fallu plus de temps que je ne pensais; **three days at the ~est** trois jours maximum; **before ~** (in past) peu après; (in future) dans peu de temps; **he'll be here before ~** il arrivera dans peu de temps; **she phoned before ~** elle a appelé peu après; **he'll be here before much ~er** il sera ici sous peu; **for ~** longtemps; **not for ~** pas longtemps; **will you be gone for ~?** seras-tu longtemps absent?; **he's happy now but not for ~** il est content à présent mais ça ne durera pas; **~ after** longtemps après; **she only knew ~ after** elle ne l'a su que longtemps après; **not ~ after** peu après; **it's ~ after** ou **past your bedtime** tu devrais être couché depuis longtemps; **~ ago** il y a longtemps; **he left not ~ ago** il n'y a pas longtemps qu'il est parti; **~ before** bien avant; **~ before we were married** bien avant notre mariage; **it wasn't ~ before he realized** il ne lui a pas fallu longtemps pour se rendre compte; **he left not ~ before lunch** il est parti peu de temps avant le déjeuner; **~ since** depuis longtemps; **they split up ~ since** ils sont séparés depuis longtemps; **they've ~ since gone home** il y a longtemps qu'ils sont partis; **he's no ~er head** il n'est plus chef; **I can't stand it any ~er** j'en ai assez; **5 minutes, no ~er!** 5 minutes, pas plus!; **I can't stay any ~er** je ne peux pas rester plus longtemps; **2** (for a long time) (*avant pp*) depuis longtemps; **I had ~ wished to meet him** j'avais envie de le rencontrer depuis longtemps; **that method has ~ been out of date** cette méthode est depuis longtemps dépassée; **those days are ~ gone** ce temps-là n'est plus; **3** (throughout) (*après n*) **all night/day ~** toute la nuit/ la journée; **her whole life ~** toute sa vie.

IV as long as, so long as *conj phr* **1** (in time) aussi longtemps que; **borrow it for as ~ as you like** tu peux le garder aussi longtemps que tu veux; **as ~ as possible/necessary** aussi longtemps que possible/qu'il le faut; **as ~ as I live** toute ma vie; **2** (provided that) du moment que (+ *indic*), pourvu que (+ *subj*); **as ~ as you're safe, that's all that matters** du moment que tu es en sécurité, c'est tout ce qui compte; **as ~ as you keep me informed** pourvu que tu me tiennes au courant.

V *vi* **to ~ for sth** avoir très envie de qch, soupirer après qch liter; **to ~ for sb to do** avoir très envie que qn fasse; **to ~ for sb** avoir très envie de voir qn, se languir de qn liter; **to ~ to do** (be impatient) être très impatient de faire; (desire sth elusive) rêver de faire, brûler de faire liter.

IDIOMS **~ time no see**○! hum ça fait une paye○ qu'on ne s'est pas vus!; **she's not ~ for this world** elle ne fera pas de vieux os; **so ~**○! salut!; **to be ~ on sth**○ avoir beaucoup de [*commonsense, experience*]; **why all the ~ faces?** vous en faites une tête○!; **to pull a ~ face** faire triste mine; **to have a ~ memory** être rancunier/-ière.

long: **~-awaited** *adj* attendu depuis longtemps, longtemps attendu; **~boat** *n* chaloupe *f*; **~bow** *n* arc *m* de guerre; **~-dated** *adj* Fin [*bills*] à longue échéance; [*investment*] à long terme; **~-delayed** *adj* longuement différé.

long-distance I *adj* [*race, runner*] de fond; [*journey*] long/longue (*before n*); [*telephone call*] (within the country) interurbain; (abroad) international; **~ flight** vol *m* long-courrier; **~ lorry driver** GB routier *m*.
II *adv* **he's phoning us ~** gen il nous appelle de loin; (from abroad) il nous appelle de l'étranger.

long: **~-drawn-out** *adj* interminable; **~ drink** *n* long drink *m*; **~-eared owl** *n* moyen duc *m*; **~ed-for** *adj* tant attendu; **~-established** *adj* fondé il y a longtemps.

longevity /lɒnˈdʒevətɪ/ *n* (of person, animal) longévité *f*; (of phenomenon, idea, tradition) persistance *f*.

long-fin tuna, **long-fin tunny** *n* thon *m* blanc.

long-haired *adj* [*person*] aux cheveux longs; [*animal*] à poil long.

longhand /ˈlɒŋhænd/ *n* **in ~** écrit à la main.

long: **~-handled** *adj* à manche long; **~-haul** *adj* Aviat long-courrier *inv*; **~horn** *n* longhorn *mf*.

longing /ˈlɒŋɪŋ, US ˈlɔːŋɪŋ/ **I** *n* grand désir *m* (**for** de; **to do** de faire); (stronger) convoitise *f* (**for** envers); (nostalgic) nostalgie *f* (**for** de); **he had a secret ~ for the gypsy life** il aspirait secrètement à une vie de bohémien.
II *adj* [*look*] (amorous) plein de désir; (greedy) plein de convoitise.

longingly /ˈlɒŋɪŋlɪ, US ˈlɔːŋ-/ *adv* (greedily) avec convoitise; (nostalgically) avec nostalgie; (amorously) amoureusement.

longish /ˈlɒŋɪʃ, US ˈlɔːŋɪʃ/ *adj* assez long/longue; **a ~ time** pas mal de temps.

longitude /ˈlɒndʒɪtjuːd, US -tuːd/ *n* longitude *f*; **at a ~ of 52°, at ~ 52°** par 52° de longitude.

longitudinal /ˌlɒndʒɪˈtjuːdɪnl, US -ˈtuːdnl/ *adj* longitudinal.

longitudinally /ˌlɒndʒɪˈtjuːdɪnəlɪ, US -ˈtuːdnəlɪ/ *adj* longitudinalement.

long: **~ johns**○ *npl* caleçon *m* long; **~ jump** ▶ 1282 *n* GB saut *m* en longueur; **~ jumper** *n* sauteur/-euse *m/f* en longueur; **~-lasting** *adj* durable, qui dure longtemps.

long-life *adj* [*milk, cream, juice*] longue conservation *inv*; [*battery*] longue durée *inv*.

long: **~-limbed** *adj* aux membres longs; **~-line** *adj* Fashn long/longue.

long-lived *adj* [*person, animal*] d'une grande longévité; [*phenomenon, tradition*] persistant.

long-lost *adj* [*relative*] perdu de vue depuis longtemps; [*object*] perdu depuis longtemps.

long: **~-overdue** *adj* attendu depuis longtemps; **~-playing record** GB, **~play record** US *n* Audio trente-trois tours *m*.

long-range *adj* [*missile, rifle*] (à) longue portée; [*forecast, plan*] à long terme; **~ aircraft** (civil) long-courrier *m*; Mil avion *m* à grand rayon d'action.

long-running *adj* [*play, serial, dispute*] qui dure depuis longtemps; **Britain's longest-running radio quiz** le plus vieux jeu radiophonique de Grande-Bretagne.

long: **~ship** *n* Hist drakkar *m*; **~shoreman** *n* US débardeur *m*, docker *m*; **~shoring** *n* débardage *m*.

long shot *n* **1** Cin plan *m* éloigné; **2** Sport, Turf outsider *m*; **3** (risky attempt) **it's a ~** c'est risqué, c'est un coup à tenter; **4** (guess) **this is a ~** je dis ça à tout hasard.

long-sighted *adj* Med presbyte; fig prévoyant.

long-sightedness *n* Med presbytie *f*; fig prévoyance *f*.

long-sleeved *adj* à manches longues.

long-standing *adj* [*arrangement, rivalry, grievance, involvement*] de longue date; [*joke*] vieux/vieille (*before n*).

long: **~-stay car park** *n* GB parc *m* de stationnement longue durée; **~-suffering** *adj* qui est d'une patience à toute épreuve.

long-tailed *adj* à longue queue; **~ tit** mésange *f* à longue queue.

long term I *n* **in the ~** à long terme.
II long-term *adj, adv* à long terme.

long-time *adj* de longue date.

long-wave I *n* grandes ondes *fpl*; **can you get ~?** peux-tu capter les grandes ondes?; **on ~** sur les grandes ondes.
II *modif* [*broadcast, signal*] en grandes ondes; [*radio, receiver*] à grandes ondes.

longways /ˈlɒŋweɪz/ *adv* dans le sens de la longueur.

long: **~ weekend** *n* long week-end *m*; **~-winded** *adj* verbeux/-euse; **~-windedness** *n* verbosité *f*.

loo○ /luː/ *n* GB toilettes *fpl*, vécés *mpl*, WC *mpl*; **he's in the ~** il est aux toilettes or vécés.

loofah /ˈluːfə/ *n* loufa *m*.

look /lʊk/ **I** *n* **1** (glance) coup *m* d'œil; **to have** ou **take a ~ at sth** (briefly) jeter un coup d'œil à or sur qch; (closely) examiner qch; **to have** ou **take a good ~ at** examiner [qch] soigneusement [*car, contract, patient*]; regarder [qch] de près [*suspect, photo*]; **I didn't get a good ~ at the thief** je n'ai pas bien vu le voleur; **to have a ~ inside/behind sth** regarder à l'intérieur de/derrière qch; **to have a ~ round** faire un tour de [*house, town*]; **I had a quick ~ round** (in town) j'ai fait un petit tour; (in shop) j'ai jeté un coup d'œil; **to have a ~ round the shops** faire le tour des magasins; **to have a ~ through** (peer) regarder dans [*telescope*]; regarder par [*crack, window*]; (scan) chercher dans [*archives, files*]; parcourir [*essay, report*]; **she took one ~ at him and screamed** elle l'a regardé et s'est mise à crier; **I took one ~ at him and knew that he was ill** j'ai tout de suite vu qu'il était malade; **let's have a ~ at that grazed knee** voyons ce genou écorché; **to take a long hard ~ at sth** fig étudier sérieusement qch; **2** (search) **to have a ~** chercher; **to have a ~ for sth** chercher qch; **I've had several ~s** j'ai regardé or cherché plusieurs fois; **I had a good ~ in the attic** j'ai bien cherché dans le grenier; **3** (expression) regard *m*; **a ~ of fear/anger** un regard rempli de terreur/de colère; **a ~ of sadness** un regard triste; **to give sb a kind/pitying ~** regarder qn avec bonté/pitié; **he gave me a ~ of sheer hatred** il m'a lancé or jeté un regard de pure haine; **did you see the ~ he gave me?** tu as vu le regard qu'il m'a jeté?; **she gave me such a ~!** elle m'a jeté un de ces regards!; **he got some odd** ou **funny ~s** on l'a regardé d'un drôle d'air; **I don't like the ~**

on his face ou **in his eye** je n'aime pas son air; **you could tell from the ~ on his face that** à sa tête○ on voyait que; **to give sb a dirty/evil ~** regarder qn d'un sale œil/d'un air méchant; **4** (appearance) (of person) air *m*; (of building, car, design, scenery) aspect *m*; **to have a ~ of weariness/sadness about one** avoir l'air abattu/triste; **the car has a dated ~** la voiture ne fait pas très moderne; **she has a ~ of her father about her** elle a quelque chose de son père; **to have the ~ of a military man/seasoned traveller** avoir l'allure d'un militaire/d'un voyageur expérimenté; **I like the ~ of it** ça a l'air bien; **I like the ~ of the new computer/car** j'aime bien la ligne du nouvel ordinateur/de la nouvelle voiture; **I like the ~ of him** il a l'air sympa○, il a une bonne tête○; **I don't like the ~ of him** il ne m'inspire pas confiance; **I don't like the ~ of the weather** le ciel n'annonce rien de bon; **I don't like the ~ of that rash** ces rougeurs m'inquiètent; **by the ~(s) of him he must be about 40** à le voir on lui donnerait la quarantaine; **by the ~(s) of the barometer** à en juger par le baromètre; **5** (style) look○ *m*, style *m*; **the ~ for the 90's** le look des années 90.

II looks *npl* **he's got the ~s, but can he act?** il a le physique, mais sait-il jouer?; **~s aren't everything** il n'y a pas que la beauté qui compte; **to keep one's ~s** rester beau/belle; **he's losing his ~s** il n'est pas aussi beau qu'autrefois; **you can't go** ou **judge by ~s alone** il ne faut pas se fier aux apparences.

III *vtr* **1** (gaze, stare) regarder; **~ what he's done!** regarde ce qu'il a fait!; **~ how/where...** regarde comment/où...; **to ~ sb in the eye/in the face** regarder qn dans les yeux/en face; **to ~ sb up and down** (appraisingly) regarder qn de haut en bas; (critically) toiser qn des pieds à la tête; **to ~ one's last on** jeter un dernier regard sur [*house, view*]; **~ what arrived this morning** regarde ce qui est arrivé ce matin; **~ who it is!** regarde qui voilà!; **~ who's just walked in!** regarde qui vient d'arriver!; **now ~ what you've done!** regarde ce que tu as fait!; **~ what time it starts!** tu as vu à quelle heure ça commence!; **2** (appear) **to ~ one's age** faire son âge; **to ~ one's best** être à son avantage; **she still ~s the same** elle n'a pas changé; **to ~ an idiot** ou **a fool** avoir l'air ridicule; **it won't ~ good if you refuse** ça sera mal vu si tu refuses; **he doesn't ~ himself today** il n'a pas l'air dans son assiette aujourd'hui.

IV *vi* **1** regarder (**into** dans; **over** par-dessus); **to ~ and see who's at the door** regarder qui est à la porte; **to ~ and see what's on TV** regarder ce qu'il y a à la télé; **to ~ at sb/sth** regarder qn/qch; **to ~ away** détourner le regard or les yeux; **to ~ in at the window** regarder (à l'intérieur) par la fenêtre ; **to ~ out of** ou **through the window** regarder par la fenêtre; **to ~ the other way** lit regarder ailleurs; fig fermer les yeux; **to ~ up and down the street** regarder partout dans la rue; **I didn't know where to ~** fig je ne savais plus où me mettre; (in shop) **I'm just ~ing** je ne fais que regarder; **2** (search) chercher, regarder; **to ~ down** parcourir [*list*]; **to ~ for sth** chercher qch; **a group of youths ~ing for trouble** une bande de jeunes qui cherchent la bagarre; **are you ~ing for a smack in the mouth○?** tu veux mon poing sur la figure○?; **3** (appear, seem) avoir l'air, paraître; **he ~s happy** il a l'air heureux, il paraît heureux; **it's nice to see you ~ing happy** ça fait plaisir de te voir heureux; **you ~ hot/cold** tu as l'air d'avoir chaud/froid; **he doesn't ~ French** il n'a pas l'air français , il ne fait pas français; **he ~s young for his age** il fait or il paraît jeune pour son âge; **she's 40 but she doesn't ~ it** elle a 40 ans mais elle ne les fait pas; **he ~s about 50** il doit avoir la cinquantaine; **that dress makes you ~ younger** cette robe te rajeunit; **how do I ~?** comment me trouves-tu?; **you ~ well** tu as bonne mine; **you don't ~ well** tu as mauvaise mine; **you ~ good in that hat** ce chapeau te va bien; **you ~ good enough to eat!** tu es mignon à croquer○!; **that cake ~s good** ce gâteau a l'air bon; **the picture will ~ good in the study** le tableau ira bien dans le bureau; **how does my tie ~?** comment est ma cravate?; **it doesn't ~ straight** il n'est pas droit, il est de travers; **it doesn't ~ right** ça ne va pas; **how does it ~ to you?** qu'est-ce que tu en penses?; **it ~s OK to me** ça m'a l'air d'aller; **does the meat ~ cooked to you?** est -ce que tu crois que la viande est cuite?; **things are ~ing good** les choses se présentent bien; **things aren't ~ing too good** ça ne va pas très bien; **it ~s to me as if** ou **though** j'ai l'impression que; **this ~s to me like the right street** j'ai l'impression que c'est la bonne rue; **it ~s as if** ou **though it will rain/snow** on dirait qu'il va pleuvoir/neiger; **it ~s likely that** il semble probable que (+ *subj*); **it ~s certain that** il semble certain que (+ *indic*); **he ~s to be the strongest** il semble être le plus fort; **it ~s to be a question of time/money** ça a l'air d'être une question de temps/d'argent; **4 to ~ like sb/sth** ressembler à qn/qch; **it doesn't ~ anything like a Picasso!** ça ne ressemble absolument pas à un Picasso!; **that photograph doesn't ~ like you** ou **~s nothing like you** on ne te reconnaît pas du tout sur cette photo; **what does she ~ like?** comment est-elle?; **what does the house ~ like?** comment est la maison?; **it ~s like being funny/interesting** cela promet d'être amusant/intéressant; **you ~ like being the only man there** il y a de fortes chances pour que tu sois le seul homme présent; **she ~s like being the first to finish** il y a de fortes chances pour qu'elle soit la première à finir; **it ~s like he's dying** tout porte à croire qu'il est mourant; **it ~s like rain/snow** on dirait qu'il va pleuvoir/neiger; **it certainly ~s like it** ça en a tout l'air; **'are you having trouble?' 'what does it ~ like?'** iron 'tu as des ennuis?' 'à ton avis?' iron; **what does it ~ like to you? murder?** qu'en pensez-vous? c'est un meurtre?; **it ~s like cancer to me** je pense que c'est un cancer; **you ~ like you could do with a drink/bath** j'ai l'impression qu'un verre d'alcool/un bain ne te ferait pas de mal; **5** (also **~ here**) écoute; **~, this is ridiculous** écoute, c'est ridicule; **~, it wasn't my fault** écoute, ce n'était pas ma faute; **~ here, I'm in no mood for jokes** écoute-moi bien, je ne suis pas d'humeur à plaisanter; **6** (be oriented) **to ~ north/south** [*house, room*] être orienté au nord/sud.

V -looking (*dans composés*) **serious/distinguished-~ing** [*person*] à l'air sérieux/distingué; **dubious/sinister-~ing** [*place, object*] à l'aspect douteux/sinistre; **he's not bad-~ing** il n'est pas mal.

IDIOMS **if ~s could kill, I'd be dead by now** il/elle/etc m'a fusillé du regard.

■ **look about** = **look around**.

■ **look after**: ¶ **~ after [sb/sth] 1** (care for) soigner [*patient, sick animal*]; garder [*child*]; s'occuper de [*customer, guest*]; s'occuper de [*animal, plant*]; entretenir [*car, equipment*]; prendre soin de [*belongings, toys*]; **he's being ~ed after by his grandparents** ce sont ses grand-parents qui le gardent; **these books have been well ~ed after** on a pris soin de ces livres; **to ~ after sb's needs** satisfaire les besoins de qn; **2** (be responsible for) s'occuper de [*administration, finances, business, shop*]; surveiller [*class, schoolchildren*]; **to ~ after sb's interests** veiller aux intérêts de qn; **~ after my luggage, I'll be back in a minute!** surveille mes bagages, je reviens tout de suite!; ¶ **~ after oneself 1** (cope) **she's too frail to ~ after herself** elle est trop fragile pour se débrouiller toute seule; **I'm old enough to ~ after myself** je suis assez grand pour me débrouiller tout seul; **2** (be careful) **safe journey, and ~ after yourself** bon voyage, sois prudent!

■ **look ahead** lit regarder devant soi; fig regarder vers l'avenir; **we must ~ ahead to the future now** nous devons penser à l'avenir maintenant; **she's ~ing ahead to the next Olympics** elle se prépare pour les prochains jeux Olympiques; **and now, ~ing ahead to tomorrow's programmes** Radio, TV et maintenant, un aperçu des émissions de demain.

■ **look around**: ¶ **~ around 1** (turn around) se retourner; **2** (glance around) regarder autour de soi; **to ~ around at one's friends/ colleagues** fig passer en revue ses amis/collègues; **3** (search) chercher; **to ~ around for sb/sth** chercher qn/qch; **4** (visit, examine) (in building, town) faire un tour; (in room) jeter un coup d'œil; ¶ **~ around [sth]** visiter [*church, town*]; faire le tour de [*room*]; **they spent the morning ~ing around London/the shops** ils ont passé la matinée à visiter Londres/à faire les magasins.

■ **look at**: **~ at [sth] 1** gen regarder; (briefly) jeter un coup d'œil sur; **~ at the state of you!** regarde un peu de quoi tu as l'air!; **just ~ at the state of this room!** regarde un peu l'état de cette pièce!; **~ at this coat/book!** regarde-moi○ ce manteau/ce livre!; **just ~ at this!** regarde-moi ça○! ; **you 'd never guess, to ~ at her** à la voir on ne devinerait jamais; **he's/it's not much to ~ at** il/ça ne paie pas de mine; **2** (examine) vérifier [*equipment*]; [*doctor*] examiner [*patient, wound*]; [*workman*] jeter un coup d'œil à [*car, plumbing*]; étudier [*problem, implications, effects, ways, offer, options*]; **you should get that wound ~ed at** tu devrais faire examiner cette blessure (par le médecin); **3** (see, view) voir [*life, events, situation*]; envisager [*problem*]; **try and ~ at it my way** essaie de voir les choses de mon point de vue; **his way of ~ing at things** sa façon de voir les choses; **~ at it this way, if he offers, I won't refuse** écoute, s'il me fait une proposition, je ne la refuserai pas; **that's how I ~ at it** c'est comme ça que je vois les choses; **the problem needs to be ~ed at from all angles** il faut envisager ce problème sous tous ses aspects; **you can't be too careful, ~ at Tom!** il faut être très prudent, regarde ce qui est arrivé à Tom!; **4** (face) **to be ~ing at** [*firm*] être au bord de [*bankruptcy, collapse*]; [*criminal*] risquer [*life sentence, fine*]; **you're ~ing at major repairs here** dites-vous bien qu'il s'agit ici de réparations importantes; **you're ~ing at a bill for about 3,000 dollars** ça va vous coûter aux alentours de 3 000 dollars.

■ **look back**: **~ back 1** (turn around) se retourner; **to ~ back at sb/sth** se retourner pour regarder qn/qch; **2** (reflect, reminisce) **let's ~ back to the year 1964** revenons à l'année 1964; **if we ~ back to the 19th century** si l'on considère le dix-neuvième siècle; **since then she's never ~ed back** depuis tout s'est très bien passé pour elle; **to ~ back on** se tourner sur [*past*]; repenser à [*experience*]; faire le bilan de [*career, marriage*]; **~ing back on it, I think I made the right decision** rétrospectivement, je pense que j'ai pris la bonne décision.

■ **look down**: ¶ **~ down** (with modesty, shame) baisser les yeux; (from a height) regarder en bas; **from the hilltop she ~ed down on the city** elle regardait la ville du haut de la colline; ¶ **~ down on [sb/sth] 1** (despise) mépriser [*person, lifestyle*]; **2** (dominate) [*fortress, tower*] dominer [*town, valley*].

■ **look for**: ¶ **~ for [sb/sth]** (search for) chercher qn/qch; ¶ **~ for [sth]** (expect) attendre [*commitment, co-operation, result, reward*] (**from** de); **what I'm ~ing for**

from you is a guarantee ce que j'attends de vous c'est une garantie; **what do you ~ for in a new recruit?** qu'est-ce que vous attendez d'une nouvelle recrue?

■ **look forward**: **to ~ forward to [sth]** attendre [qch] avec impatience; **I was so ~ing forward to it** j'attendais ça avec tant d'impatience, je m'en faisais une telle joie; **she's ~ing forward to going on holiday** elle a hâte de partir en vacances; **I'm not ~ing forward to the interview/party** la perspective de l'entretien/la fête ne me réjouit pas; **I ~ forward to hearing from you** (writing to a friend) j'espère avoir bientôt de tes nouvelles; (in formal correspondence) dans l'attente de votre réponse.

■ **look in** **1** (pay a visit) passer; **I'll ~ in again tomorrow** je repasserai demain; **to ~ in on** passer voir [*person, class, rehearsals*]; **~ in on the baby and check she's still asleep** va voir si le bébé dort; **2** (watch TV) **if there are any viewers ~ing in who want more details, please contact us** les téléspectateurs qui désirent obtenir plus de renseignements peuvent nous contacter.

■ **look into**: **~ into [sth]** examiner, étudier [*matter, possibility, problem*]; examiner [*accounts, background*]; enquêter sur [*death, disappearance, theft*].

■ **look on**: ¶ **~ on** [*crowd, spectators*] regarder; **we ~ed on admiringly as she danced** nous l'avons regardée danser avec admiration; **I was forced to ~ on as the house was ransacked** j'ai été forcé d'assister au pillage de la maison; ¶ **~ on [sb/sth]** considérer [*person, event etc*] (**as** comme; **with** avec); **we ~ on him as a son** nous le considérons comme notre fils; **I ~ on it as a privilege** je considère que c'est un privilège.

■ **look onto**: **~ onto [sth]** [*house, room*] donner sur [*sea, garden, street*].

■ **look out**: ¶ **~ out** (take care) faire attention (**for** à); (be wary) se méfier (**for** de); **you must ~ out for snakes** faites attention aux serpents; **~ out for motorists turning out of side roads** méfiez-vous des automobilistes qui débouchent des petites routes; **~ out!** attention!; ¶ **~ out for [sb/sth]** guetter [*person*]; être à l'affût de [*new recruits, talent*]; être à la recherche de [*apartment, book*]; guetter l'apparition de [*signs , symptoms*]; repérer [*cases, examples*]; être à l'affût de [*bargain, special offer*]; ¶ **~ out for [oneself]** se débrouiller tout seul, s'occuper de soi; ¶ **~ out over [sth]** [*window, balcony*] donner sur [*sea, park*].

■ **look over**: ¶ **~ [sb] over** passer [qn] en revue [*new recruits, troops*]; ¶ **~ [sth] over** examiner [*car, equipment*]; [*vet*] examiner [*animal*]; **get an expert to ~ the car over before you buy it** fais examiner la voiture par un spécialiste avant de l'acheter; ¶ **~ over [sth]** **1** (read) (in detail) examiner [*document, contract*]; (rapidly) parcourir [*essay, lines, notes*]; jeter un coup d'œil sur, parcourir [*document, report*]; **I'll get Rose to ~ it over quickly** je demanderai à Rose d'y jeter un petit coup d'œil; **2** (visit) visiter [*factory, gardens, house*].

■ **look round** ¶ **1** (look behind one) se retourner; **she ~ed round to see who it was** elle s'est retournée pour voir qui c'était; **2** (look about) regarder autour de soi; **I'm just ~ing round** (in shop) je ne fais que regarder; **we're ~ing round for a new house** nous cherchons une nouvelle maison; ¶ **~ round [sth]** visiter [*town, building*].

■ **look through**: ¶ **~ through [sth]** **1** (read) consulter [*archive, material, files*]; parcourir [*essay, list, script, report, notes*]; (scan idly) feuilleter [*book, magazine*]; **2** (search) fouiller dans [*belongings, drawers, briefcase*]; **I caught him ~ing through my diary** je l'ai trouvé en train de lire mon journal intime; **try ~ing through that pile of papers** regarde dans cette pile de papiers; ¶ **~ through [sb]** faire semblant de ne pas voir [*person*].

■ **look to**: ¶ **~ to [sb/sth]** **1** (rely on) compter sur qn/qch (**for** pour; **to do** pour faire); **they ~ to him for leadership** ils comptent sur lui pour les diriger; **2** (turn to) se tourner vers [*future*]; **he ~ed to his friends for support** il s'est tourné vers ses amis pour qu'ils le soutiennent; ¶ **~ to [sth]** (pay attention) veiller à [*defences, interests*]; ¶ **~ to do** (expect) espérer faire; **we're ~ing to break even/make a profit** nous espérons rentrer dans nos frais/faire des bénéfices.

■ **look up**: ¶ **~ up** **1** (raise one's eyes) lever les yeux (**from** de); **2** (raise one's head) lever la tête; **to ~ up at the clouds/treetops** regarder les nuages/le sommet des arbres; **3** (improve) [*business, prospects*] aller mieux; [*conditions, situation*] s'améliorer; [*property market*] reprendre; **things are ~ing up for us** les choses s'arrangent pour nous; ¶ **~ up [sth]** regarder à l'intérieur de [*chimney*]; **to ~ up sb's skirt** regarder sous la jupe de qn; ¶ **~ [sb/sth] up, ~ up [sb/sth]** **1** (check in book) chercher [*address, phone number, price, word*] (**in** dans); **~ his number up in the phone book** cherche son numéro de téléphone dans l'annuaire; **2** (visit) passer voir [*acquaintance, friend*]; **~ me up if you're ever in New York** passez me voir or faites-moi signe si jamais vous vous trouvez à New York; ¶ **~ up to [sb]** admirer [*person*].

look: **~-alike** *n* sosie *m*; **~ed-for** *adj* (*tjrs épith*) [*result, total*] attendu; [*benefit, profits*] escompté.

looker○ /ˈlʊkə(r)/ *n* (woman) belle nana○ *f*; (man) beau mec○ *m*.

looker-on *n* (*pl* **lookers-on**) gen spectateur/-trice *m/f*; (in street) badaud/-e *m/f*.

look-in /ˈlʊkɪn/ *n* GB **he monopolized the debate, nobody else got a ~** il a monopolisé la parole et n'a donné à personne d'autre la chance de s'exprimer; **we don't intend to give our competitors a ~** nous n'avons pas l'intention de laisser la moindre chance à la concurrence; **her brother was adored by her parents, but she never got a ~** son frère a été adoré par ses parents, mais ils n'ont jamais prêté attention à elle.

looking-glass *n* littér miroir *m*.

look-out /ˈlʊkaʊt/ **I** *n* **1** (surveillance) **to be on ~** [*sailor*] être de veille; [*soldier*] faire le guet; **to be on the ~ for** rechercher [*stolen vehicle, escaped prisoner*]; être à l'affût de [*bargain, rare books, new ideas*]; guetter [*visitor*]; être à l'affût de, rechercher [*new recruits, promising actors*]; **to keep a ~ for** continuer de chercher [*lost keys, first edition*]; guetter [*person*]; **2** (sentry) (on ship) vigie *f*; (in army) guetteur *m*; **3** (surveillance post) poste *m* d'observation; **4**○ GB (private concern) **that's his ~** c'est son affaire, ça le regarde.

II *modif* [*platform, post, tower*] d'observation; **to be on ~ duty** (on ship) être de veille; (in army) faire le guet.

look-over /ˈlʊkəʊvə(r)/ *n* coup *m* d'œil; **to give sth a ~** jeter un coup d'œil sur or à qch.

look-see○ /ˌlʊkˈsiː/ *n* coup *m* d'œil; **to have** ou **take a ~** jeter un coup d'œil.

look-up /ˈlʊkʌp/ *n* Comput consultation *f*.

loom /luːm/ **I** *n* métier *m* à tisser.

II *vi* **1** (also **~ up**) [*shape, figure, building*] surgir (**out of** de; **over** au-dessus de); **a figure ~ed up through the mist** une silhouette surgit dans la brume; **2** [*threat, war, strike, crisis*] menacer; [*exam, interview, deadline*] s'approcher dangereusement; **the spectre of war ~s over the country** le spectre de la guerre menace le pays; **to ~ large** [*exam, thought, horror, issue*] peser lourd; [*figure, politician*] occuper une place importante.

III looming *pres p adj* **1** fig [*crisis, threat, shortage*] qui menace; [*deadline, exam*] qui s'approche dangereusement; **2** lit [*spire, cliff, tower*] menaçant.

loon /luːn/ *n* **1** US Zool plongeon *m*; **2**† dial (idiot) imbécile *mf*.

IDIOMS **to be as crazy as a ~** US être fou à lier.

loony○ /ˈluːnɪ/ **I** *n* (*pl* **-ies**) **1** (eccentric) farfelu/-e *m/f*; **2** (crazy) dingue○ *mf*; injur (mentally ill) taré/-e○ *m/f* offensive; **you ~!** patate○!

II *adj* farfelu○.

loony: **~-bin**○ *n* asile *m* de fous; **~ left**○ GB péj activistes *mpl* du parti travailliste.

loop /luːp/ **I** *n* **1** gen boucle *f*; (for belt) boucle *f*, passant *m*; **2** Aviat looping *m*; **to ~ the ~** faire un looping; **3** Cin, Video boucle *f*; **film/video ~** film *m*/vidéo *f* en boucle; **4** Elec circuit *m* fermé; **5** Comput boucle *f*; **6** Rail (also **~-line**) voie *f* d'évitement; **7** Med stérilet *m*.

II *vtr* nouer [*string, thread etc*].

III *vi* [*road, path*] faire une boucle; **the river ~s back on itself** la rivière décrit une boucle.

IDIOMS **to throw sb for a ~** US sidérer qn.

loophole /ˈluːphəʊl/ *n* **1** fig lacune *f*; **to close** ou **plug a ~** combler une lacune; **to find/exploit a ~** trouver/exploiter une lacune; **2** Archit meurtrière *f*.

loopy○ /ˈluːpɪ/ *adj* loufoque○.

loose /luːs/ **I** *n* **1 on the ~** [*prisoner, criminal, animal*] qui s'est échappé; [*troublemakers*] déchaîné; **there's a killer/lion on the ~** il y a un tueur/lion qui s'est échappé; **there is a gang of hooligans on the ~ in the town** il y a une bande de voyous qui rôdent dans les rues de la ville; **he is still on the ~** il est toujours en liberté or en cavale○; **2** (in rugby) **the ~** la mêlée ouverte.

II *adj* **1** lit (not firm or tight) [*knot, lace, screw*] desserré; [*nail, handle*] branlant; [*joint*] lâche; [*component, section*] mal fixé; [*button*] qui se découd; [*thread*] décousu; [*tooth*] qui se déchausse; **to come** ou **work ~** [*knot, screw*] se desserrer; [*brick, handle*] être branlant; [*nail*] lâcher; [*tooth*] se déchausser; **to work [sth] ~** desserrer [*rope, knot, screw, fixture*]; dégager [*nail, post*]; desceller [*brick, bar*]; **to hang ~** [*hair*] être dénoué; [*rope, reins, thread*] pendre; **hang ~**○**!** US détends-toi!; **~ connection** Elec faux contact; **2** (free) [*animal*] échappé; **the bull's ~** le taureau s'est échappé; **to break ~** [*animal*] s'échapper (**from** de); fig rompre (**from** avec); **to cut sb ~** détacher qn; **to roam** ou **run ~** courir en liberté; **to let** ou **set** ou **turn ~** libérer [*animal, prisoner*]; **he let the dogs ~ on me** il a lâché les chiens sur moi; **I wouldn't let her ~ on a classroom** je ne la laisserais pas seule face à une classe; **I wouldn't let first year students ~ on Joyce!** je ne ferais pas lire Joyce aux étudiants de première année!; **to let ~ with criticism/insults** critiquer/insulter sans retenue; **3** Comm (not packed) [*tea, tobacco, sweets, vegetables*] en vrac; **we sell envelopes ~** nous vendons les enveloppes au détail; **just put the apples in the bag ~** mettez donc les pommes à même le sac or directement dans le sac; **~ change** petite monnaie; **4** (that has come apart) [*card, page*] volant; [*stone, fragment*] détaché; **a ~ sheet of paper** une feuille volante; **these pages have come ~** ces pages se sont détachées; **~ rust/paint** rouille/peinture friable; **'~ chippings'** GB, **'~ gravel'** US (roadsign) 'attention gravillons'; **5** (not close-fitting) [*dress, jacket, trousers*] ample; [*fold, waistband*] large; [*collar*] lâche; (flaccid) [*skin*] flasque; [*muscle*] détendu; **6** (not compacted) [*soil*] meuble; [*link, weave*] lâche; [*structure*] lâche; [*association, alliance*] vague; **to have ~ bowels** avoir la diarrhée; **~ maul** (in rugby) mêlée ouverte; **7** (not strict or exact) [*translation, version*] assez libre, approximatif/-ive; [*wording*] imprécis; [*interpretation*] assez libre, large; [*guideline*] vague; [*discipline, style*] relâché; **~ talk** propos *mpl* inconsidérés; **8** (dissolute) [*morals*] dissolu, relâché; **~ living** (vie *f* de) débauche *f*; **9** (spare) [*cash, funds*] disponible.

III *vtr* littér **1** (release) libérer; **2** (shoot) tirer [*arrow*].

IDIOMS **to be at a ~ end** GB, **to be at ~ ends** US être désœuvré, ne pas trop savoir quoi faire; **to tie up the ~ ends** régler les derniers détails; **to have a ~ tongue** ne pas savoir tenir sa langue.

■ **loose off** ¶ (shoot) tirer (**at** sur); ¶ **~ off [sth], ~ [sth] off** décharger [*gun*]; tirer [*arrow, shot*]; décocher [*abuse, insults*].

loose: **~box** *n* GB box *m*; **~ cover** *n* GB housse *f* (de fauteuil); **~-fitting** *adj* ample; **~-head prop** *n* (in rugby) ailier *m* avant droit.

loose-leaf *adj* à feuilles mobiles; **~ binder, ~ folder** classeur *m*.

loose-limbed *adj* souple.

loosely /ˈluːslɪ/ *adv* **1** lit (not tightly) [*attach, fasten, cover, hold, wrap, wind*] sans serrer; [*fit*] approximativement; (not firmly) [*fix*] pas solidement; **a jacket thrown ~ over her shoulders** une veste négligemment jetée sur ses épaules; **his clothes hung ~ on him** il flottait dans ses vêtements; **2** fig [*combined, connected, organized*] de façon souple; [*structured*] assez librement; **3** fig (imprecisely) [*describe, interpret, translate, render, associate*] assez librement, de façon approximative; [*identify, refer*] vaguement; [*supervise*] d'assez loin; **the film is ~ based on the novel** le film est une adaptation assez libre du roman; **these theories are ~ termed Marxist** ces théories sont qualifiées grossièrement de marxistes.

loosely: **~ knit** *adj* [*group, structure*] peu uni; **~ tailored** *adj* de coupe ample.

loosen /ˈluːsn/ **I** *vtr* **1** (make less tight) desserrer [*knot, belt, strap, lid, collar, screw*]; dégager [*nail, post*]; relâcher [*rope, string, link, control*]; détacher, dénouer [*hair*]; fig assouplir [*laws, restrictions*]; **~ all tight clothing** Med défaire tout vêtement qui serre; **to ~ one's grip** ou **hold on sth** lit relâcher sa prise sur qch; fig relâcher son emprise sur qch; **2** (make less compact) ameublir [*soil*]; **to ~ the bowels** Med, Pharm avoir une action laxative.

II *vi* (become less tight) [*knot, fastening, screw, point, grip, hold*] se desserrer; [*rope, string, wire*] se détendre; fig [*ties*] se relâcher.

IDIOMS **to ~ sb's tongue** délier la langue à qn.

■ **loosen up**: ¶ **~ up 1** Sport s'échauffer; **2** fig [*person*] se détendre, se dégeler○; ¶ **~ up [sth], ~ [sth] up** lit, fig assouplir [*muscle, joint, policy, system*].

looseness /ˈluːsnɪs/ *n* **1** (of knot, fastening, screw, joint) desserrement *m*; (of rope) relâchement *m*; (of clothing) ampleur *f*; **~ of the bowels** Med diarrhée *f*; **2** fig (of translation, argument, thinking) manque *m* de rigueur; (of use of term) imprécision *f*; (of structure, organization) souplesse *f*; (of morals) relâchement *m*; (of person) immoralité *f*.

loosestrife /ˈluːsstraɪf/ *n* (purple) salicaire *f*; (yellow) lysimaque *f*.

loose: **~-tongued** *adj* qui ne tient pas sa langue; **~-weave** *adj* [*fabric*] lâche.

loot /luːt/ **I** *n* **1** (stolen goods) butin *m*; **2**○ (money) fric○ *m*.

II *vtr* piller.

III *vi* se livrer au pillage.

looter /ˈluːtə(r)/ *n* pillard/-e *m/f*.

looting /ˈluːtɪŋ/ *n* pillage *m*.

lop /lɒp/ (*p prés etc* **-pp-**) *vtr* élaguer [*tree, branch*].

■ **lop off**: **~ [sth] off, ~ off [sth]** élaguer [*branch*]; trancher [*head*]; **she ~ped 10% off the price/10 seconds off the record** elle a retranché 10% du prix/10 secondes du record.

lope /ləʊp/ **I** *n* (of animal) foulée *f*; (of person) enjambée *f*.

II *vi* **to ~ off/in** partir/entrer à grandes enjambées.

lop-eared /ˈlɒpɪəd/ *adj* aux oreilles pendantes.

lopsided /ˌlɒpˈsaɪdɪd/ *adj* **1** [*clothing, object, smile*] de travers; [*drawing*] mal proportionné; **2** fig [*argument, view etc*] irrationnel/-elle.

lopsidedly /ˌlɒpˈsaɪdɪdlɪ/ *adv* de travers.

loquacious /ləˈkweɪʃəs/ *adj* sout loquace.

loquaciously /ləˈkweɪʃəslɪ/ *adv* sout de manière loquace.

loquacity /ləˈkwæsətɪ/, **loquaciousness** /ləˈkweɪʃəsnɪs/ *n* sout loquacité *f*.

lord /lɔːd/ ▶ **1268** *n* **1** (ruler) seigneur *m* (**of** de); **one's ~ and master** son seigneur et maître; **2** (peer) lord *m* (*titre des pairs britanniques*); **the (House of) Lords** la Chambre des Lords (*Chambre haute du Parlement du Royaume Uni*); **my Lord** (to noble) Monsieur le comte/duc/etc; (to bishop) Monseigneur.

IDIOMS **to ~ it over sb**○ regarder qn de haut.

Lord /lɔːd/ *n* **1** Relig Seigneur *m*; **praise the ~!** louez le Seigneur!; **in the year of our ~ 1904** en l'an de grâce 1904; **2**○ (in exclamations) Seigneur (Jésus)!; **good ~!** Grand Dieu!; **~ (only) knows!** Dieu seul le sait!; **~ knows where/why/etc** Dieu sait où/pourquoi/etc; **~ preserve us!** Dieu nous garde!

Lord: **~ Advocate** *n*: *magistrat à la tête de la justice en Écosse*; **~ Chamberlain** *n* Lord *m* Chamberlain (*officier responsable du service intérieur de la maison royale britannique*); **~ Chancellor** *n* Lord *m* Chancelier; cf ministre *m* de la Justice; **~ Chief Justice** *n*: *le plus haut magistrat de la Haute Cour de Justice en Grande-Bretagne*; **~ High Admiral** *n*: *titre donné au souverain britannique*; **~ Lieutenant** *n*: *représentant de la couronne dans un comté de Grande-Bretagne*.

lordly /ˈlɔːdlɪ/ *adj* **1** (proud) [*manner, tone, contempt*] hautain; **2** (like a lord) [*bearing, appearance*] princier/-ière.

Lord Mayor ▶ **1268** *n* lord-maire *m* (*titre des maires des grandes villes de Grande-Bretagne*).

Lord: **~ of Appeal** *n*: *membre du tribunal d'appel de la Chambre des Lords*; **~ President of the Council** *n*: *ministre qui préside au Conseil privé du souverain d'Angleterre*; **~ Privy Seal** *n* Lord *m* du Sceau privé (*ministre sans portefeuille*); **~ Provost** *n*: *maire d'une des grandes villes d'Écosse*.

lords and ladies *n* Bot arum *m* tacheté.

Lord's Day *n* jour *m* du Seigneur.

lordship /ˈlɔːdʃɪp/ ▶ **1268** *n* **1** (also **Lordship**) (title) **your/his ~** (of noble) Monsieur; (of judge) Monsieur le Juge; (of bishop) Monseigneur; **their ~s will vote tomorrow** Messieurs les représentants de la Chambre des Lords se prononceront demain; **2** souveraineté *f* (**over** sur).

Lord: **~'s Prayer** *n* Notre Père *m*; **~s Spiritual** *npl*: *évêques et archevêques siégeant à la Chambre des Lords en Grande-Bretagne*; **~'s Supper** *n* Eucharistie *f*; **~s Temporal** *npl* lords *mpl* temporels (*membres de la Chambre des Lords n'appartenant pas au clergé*).

lore /lɔː(r)/ *n* **1** (of a people) traditions *fpl*; **2** (of nature) connaissance *f* traditionnelle.

lorgnette /lɔːˈnjet/ *n* Hist (spectacles) face-à-main *m*; (for opera, races) lorgnette *f*.

Lorraine /lɒˈreɪn/ ▶ **1273** *pr n* Lorraine *f*; **in ~** en Lorraine.

Lorraine cross *n* croix *f* de Lorraine.

lorry /ˈlɒrɪ, US ˈlɔːrɪ/ *n* (*pl* **-ies**) GB camion *m*; **heavy ~** poids *m* lourd; **army ~** camion militaire.

IDIOMS **it fell off the back of a ~**○ hum c'est tombé du ciel; euph c'est de la marchandise récupérée.

lorry: **~ driver** ▶ **1692** *n* GB gen routier *m*, chauffeur *m* de poids lourd; **~ load** *n* GB camion *m* also fig.

lose /luːz/ **I** *vtr* (*prét, pp* **lost**) **1** (mislay) perdre [*object, person*]; **to ~ one's way** lit se perdre, perdre son chemin; fig s'égarer; **2** (be deprived of) perdre; **the poem has lost something in translation** le poème a perdu quelque chose à la traduction; **to ~ interest in sth** se désintéresser de qch; **to ~ touch** (with person, reality, situation) perdre contact (**with** avec); **to ~ the use of** perdre l'usage de [*limb, muscle*]; **to ~ one's life** mourir; **many lives were lost** il y a eu de nombreuses victimes; **200 jobs will be lost** 200 emplois vont être supprimés; **to ~ one's breath** s'essouffler; **to ~ one's figure** s'épaissir; **he's losing his looks** il n'est plus aussi beau qu'autrefois; **we are losing a lot of business to our competitors** nous avons perdu beaucoup d'affaires au profit de nos concurrents; **they lost both sons in the war** ils ont perdu leurs deux fils pendant la guerre; **to be lost at sea** périr en mer; **to have nothing/little to ~**○ n'avoir rien/pas grand-chose à perdre; **try it, you've nothing to ~**○! essaie, tu n'as rien à perdre!; **you've nothing to ~ by applying** tu ne risques rien en posant ta candidature; **I daren't, I've got too much to ~** je n'ose pas, c'est trop risqué; **3** (miss, waste) manquer [*chance*]; perdre [*time*]; **there's no time/not a moment to ~** il n'y a pas de temps/un instant à perdre; **stopping meant losing vital seconds** s'arrêter représentait une perte de secondes capitales; **he lost no time in replying** il n'a pas perdu de temps pour répondre; **this allusion was not lost on him** cette allusion ne lui a pas échappé; **4** (be defeated in) gen, Jur, Pol, Sport perdre [*fight, war, match, game, race, case, bet, election, vote*]; avoir le dessous dans [*argument, debate*]; perdre en [*appeal*]; **5** (not hear or understand) manquer [*remark, word*]; (not see) perdre [qch] de vue [*moving object*]; **you've lost me there**○! je ne vous suis plus!; **their cries were lost in the din** leurs cris ont été étouffés par le vacarme; **6** (shake off, get rid of) se débarrasser de [*habit, unwanted person or object*]; semer○ [*pursuer*]; supprimer [*job*]; licencier [*worker*]; **7** (go slow) [*clock, watch*] retarder de [*minutes, seconds*]; **8** (cause to forfeit) **to ~ sb sth** faire perdre qch à qn; **his speech lost the party a million votes** son discours a fait perdre au parti un million de voix.

II *vi* (*prét, pp* **lost**) **1** (be defeated) perdre (**to sb** devant qn); **they lost to the French team** ils se sont fait battre par l'équipe française; **2** (be worse off, deteriorate) perdre; **they lost on the sale of the house** ils ont vendu la maison à perte; **the novel ~s in translation** le roman y perd à la traduction; **try it, you can't ~!** essaie, tu n'as rien à perdre!; **3** [*clock, watch*] retarder.

III *v refl* (*prét, pp* **lost**) **to ~ oneself in** se plonger dans [*book*]; se perdre dans [*contemplation*].

■ **lose out** être perdant; **to ~ out on** perdre dans [*deal*]; manquer, rater○ [*chance, opportunity, bargain*]; **to ~ out to sb** se faire dépasser par qn.

loser /ˈluːzə(r)/ *n* gen, Games, Sport perdant/-e *m/f*; **to be a good/bad ~** être bon/mauvais perdant; **you won't be the ~ by it** vous n'y serez pas perdant; **a born ~** un perdant né○; **that policy's a vote-~** cette politique est destinée à faire perdre des voix.

losing /ˈluːzɪŋ/ *adj* **1** gen, Games, Sport [*team, player*] perdant; [*side*] des perdants; **2** Comm, Fin [*concern*] déficitaire.

IDIOMS **it's a ~ battle** c'est une bataille perdue d'avance; **to fight a ~ battle against** livrer une bataille perdue d'avance contre; **to be on a ~ streak** ou **wicket** ne pas être en veine○.

loss /lɒs, US lɔːs/ *n* **1** gen, Comm, Fin, Insur, Pol perte *f* (**of** de); **heat/weight ~** perte de chaleur/de poids; **~ of blood** perte de sang; **there was great ~ of life** il y a eu de nombreuses victimes; **~ of income** ou **earnings** manque *m* à gagner; **~ of sound/vision** TV interruption *f* du son/de l'image; **with the ~ of 300 jobs** avec la suppression de 300 emplois; **he is a great ~ to the arts** c'est une grande perte pour les arts; **he's no great ~** ce n'est pas une grande perte; **a sense of ~** un sentiment de vide; **to make a ~ on sth** Comm enregistrer une perte sur qch; **to trade at a ~** Comm vendre à perte; **to suffer ~es** Comm, Mil subir des pertes; **the party suffered heavy ~es in the elections** le parti a perdu beaucoup de voix aux élections; **2 to be at a ~** (puzzled) être perplexe; (helpless) être perdu; **to be at a ~ as to what to do** ne pas savoir du tout quoi faire; **I'm at a ~ to explain it** je suis dans l'impossibilité de l'expliquer; **he was at a ~ for words** les mots lui manquaient; **she's never at a ~ for words** elle a toujours quelque chose à dire.

IDIOMS **to cut one's ~es** arrêter les dégâts○; **their ~ is our gain** autant de gagné pour nous.

loss: **~ adjuster** *n* Insur expert *m* en assurances; **~ leader** *n* article *m* promotionnel (*vendu à perte*); **~-maker** *n* Comm (product) produit *m* vendu à perte; (company) entreprise *f* travaillant à perte; **~-making** *adj* [*product*] vendu à perte; [*company*] travaillant à perte; **~ ratio** *n* Insur taux *m* de perte.

lost /lɒst, US lɔːst/ **I** *prét, pp* ▶ **lose**.
II *adj* **1** [*object, child, animal*] perdu; **to get ~** se perdre; **I think we're ~** je pense que nous sommes perdus; **the ticket got ~** le billet a été perdu; **her basic point got ~** on ne savait plus où elle voulait en venir; **~ soul** Relig, fig âme en peine; **get ~○!** fiche le camp○!; **2** (wasted, vanished) [*opportunity, chance*] manqué; [*happiness, innocence, youth*] perdu; [*civilisation*] disparu; **to give sb/sth up for ~** considérer qn/qch comme perdu; **good advice is ~ on her** c'est en pure perte qu'on lui donne des conseils; **my lecture was completely ~ on them** ma conférence leur est complètement passée au-dessus de la tête; **another promising player ~ to the sport** encore un joueur prometteur perdu pour le sport; **3** (mystified) [*person, look*] perdu; **to be ~ without sb/sth** être perdu sans qn/qch; **I'd be ~ without you/a calculator** je serais perdu sans toi/une calculatrice; **to be ~ for words** être à court d'arguments; **4 to be ~ in** être plongé dans [*book, thought*]; **~ in wonder** éperdu d'émerveillement; **to be ~ to the world** être complètement ailleurs; **5** (doomed) littér ou hum perdu; **all is/is not ~** tout est/n'est pas perdu; **a ~ cause** une cause perdue.

lost and found *n* **1** (articles) objets *mpl* trouvés; **2** (also **~ office**) service *m* des objets trouvés; **3** Journ **'lost-and-found (column)'** 'objets perdus et trouvés'.

lost property GB *n* = **lost and found** 1.

lot[1] /lɒt/ **I** *pron* **1** (great deal) **a ~** beaucoup; **we buy a ~ at the market** nous achetons beaucoup de choses au marché; **he likes to spend a ~ on holidays** il aime dépenser beaucoup d'argent en vacances; **to get a ~ out of** tirer beaucoup de [*book, activity*]; **to do a ~ to help sb/improve sth** faire beaucoup pour aider qn/améliorer qch; **there's not a ~ to tell** il n'y a pas grand-chose à raconter; **they didn't have a ~ left** il ne leur restait pas grand-chose; **he knows a ~ about sport** il s'y connaît beaucoup en sport; **you've taken (rather) a ~ on** tu en fais (un peu) trop; **I'd give a ~ to be able to do** je donnerais cher pour pouvoir faire; **it says a ~ about her/the regime** ça en dit long sur elle/le régime; **it has a ~ to do with anxiety** c'est très lié à l'angoisse; **that has a ~ to do with it** c'est très lié; **an awful ~** énormément; **there's an awful ~ left to do** il reste énormément de choses à faire; **quite a ~** beaucoup, pas mal○; **to mean quite a ~ to sb** avoir beaucoup or pas mal○ d'importance pour qn; **she knows quite a ~ about cinema** elle s'y connaît très bien en cinéma; **we have such a ~ in common** nous avons tellement or tant de choses en commun; **such a ~ depends on...** tellement or tant de choses dépendent de...; **it takes such a ~ out of me** ça me fatigue tellement; **he's been through such a ~** il a tellement or tant souffert; **2**○ (entire amount or selection) **the ~** tout; **she ate the (whole) ~** elle a tout mangé, elle a mangé le tout; **they'll confiscate the ~!** ils vont tout confisquer or confisquer le tout!; **you can take the ~** tu peux tout prendre, tu peux prendre le tout; **I'll write you a cheque for the ~** je vous ferai un chèque pour le tout; **the whole ~ tied with a ribbon** le tout attaché avec un ruban; **the best speech of the ~** le meilleur de tous les discours; **the nicest dress of the ~** la plus belle de toutes les robes; **heartburn, cramps, the ~!** des brûlures d'estomac, des crampes, bref tout!; **3**○ (specific group of people) **she's the best/nicest of the ~** c'est la meilleure/la plus gentille (de tous/toutes); **that ~** péj ces gens-là pej; **I don't trust that ~** je me méfie de ces gens-là; **you ~** vous, vous autres; **listen you ~, I've had enough!** écoutez, j'en ai vraiment assez de vous!; **my ~ can't even spell properly** les miens ne savent même pas écrire correctement; **they're not a bad ~** ils ne sont pas méchants; **he's a bad ~○** c'est un sale type○; **the best of a bad ~○** le moins pire○.

II *quantif* **1** (great deal) **a ~ of** beaucoup de; **a ~ of money/energy/people** beaucoup d'argent/d'énergie/de gens; **it affects a ~ of women** cela touche beaucoup de femmes; **I don't have a ~ of time** je n'ai pas beaucoup de temps; **not a ~ of people know that** il n'y a pas beaucoup de gens qui savent ça; **I see a ~ of him** je le vois beaucoup; **you've done a ~ of teaching** tu as beaucoup enseigné; **to spend an awful○ ~ of time doing** passer énormément de temps à faire; **he has an awful○ ~ of responsibility** il a énormément de responsabilité; **there were quite a ~ of people/cars/books** il y avait beaucoup or pas mal○ de gens/voitures/livres; **quite a ~ of people disagree** il y a beaucoup de personnes qui ne sont pas d'accord; **quite a ~ of our efforts/support...** une bonne part de nos efforts/notre soutien...; **what a ~ of people/books!** que de monde/de livres!; ▶ **fat**; **2**○ (entire group) **get out, the (whole) ~ of you!** sortez tous!; **I'd sack the ~ of them!** je les mettrais tous à la porte!; **I'll outlive the ~ of you!** je vous enterrerai tous!

III lots○ *quantif, pron* **~s (and ~s) of** des tas○ de [*people, cars, shops, jobs, stories, vegetables*]; beaucoup de [*music, money, traffic, wine, blood*]; **there are ~s of things to do** il y a beaucoup de or des tas○ de choses à faire; **we have ~s in common** nous avons des or un tas○ de choses en commun; **...and ~s more** ...et beaucoup d'autres choses; **'has he got records?'—'yes, ~s!** il a des disques?—oui des tas○!'

IV lots○ *adv* **~s better/more interesting** beaucoup or vachement○ mieux/plus intéressant.

V a lot *adv phr* beaucoup; **a ~ better/easier/more useful** beaucoup mieux/plus facile/plus utile; **a ~ worse** bien pire; **they talk a ~ about justice** ils parlent beaucoup de justice; **she works at home a ~** elle travaille beaucoup à la maison; **you find this a ~ with teenagers** on rencontre beaucoup ce problème chez les adolescents; **the situation has improved a ~** la situation s'est beaucoup améliorée; **we visit them a ~** nous leur rendons

> ### lot[1]
>
> When *a lot* is used as a pronoun (*they buy a lot, he spends a lot*), it is translated by *beaucoup*: *ils achètent beaucoup, il dépense beaucoup*. For particular usages, see **I 1** in the entry ***lot***[1].
>
> When *a lot* is used to mean *much* in negative expressions (*they didn't have a lot*) it is translated by *pas grand-chose*: *ils n'avaient pas grand-chose*. For particular usages, see **I 1** in the entry ***lot***[1].
>
> When *the lot* is used as a pronoun (*they took the lot*), it is usually translated by *tout*: *ils ont tout pris*. For particular usages, see **I 2** in the entry ***lot***[1].
>
> When *a lot of* is used as a quantifier (*a lot of money*) it is translated by *beaucoup de*. For particular usages, see **II 1** in the entry ***lot***[1]. For translations of *lots of* see **III** in the entry ***lot***[1].
>
> When *a lot* is used as an adverb (*a lot stronger, he's changed a lot*) it is translated by *beaucoup*: *beaucoup plus fort, il a beaucoup changé*. For particular usages, see **V** in the entry ***lot***[1].

souvent visite; **this happens quite a ~** cela arrive très souvent; **an awful ~ cheaper** beaucoup moins cher; **you're smoking an awful ~○** tu fumes beaucoup; **it would help an awful○ ~** ça aiderait beaucoup; **he travels abroad such a ~** il voyage beaucoup à l'étranger; **thanks a ~○!** merci beaucoup!

lot[2] /lɒt/ *n* **1** (destiny) sort *m*; (quality of life) condition *f*; **to be happy with one's ~** être content de son sort; **to improve one's ~** améliorer sa condition; **to improve the ~ of the elderly** améliorer la condition des personnes âgées; **the poverty and disease which are the ~ of many** la pauvreté et la maladie qui sont le lot de beaucoup de gens; **a policeman's ~ is not a happy one** la vie d'un policier n'est pas enviable; **to throw in one's ~ with sb** allier son destin à celui de qn; **2** US (piece of land) parcelle *f* (de terrain); **vacant ~** terrain *m* vague; **used car ~** garage *m* vendant des voitures d'occasion; ▶ **parking lot**; **3** (at auction) lot *m*; **~ No. 69, an oil painting by Gauguin** lot nº 69, une huile de Gauguin; ▶ **job lot**; **4** (decision-making process) tirage *m* au sort; **to draw** ou **cast ~s** tirer au sort (**to do** pour faire); **to be chosen** ou **decided by ~** être tiré au sort; **the ~ fell to me** ou **it fell to my ~ to do** le sort a voulu que je fasse; **5** Cin (studio) studio *m*; **6** (set, batch) (of goods, articles) lot *m* (**of** de); (of produce, fish) arrivage *m* (**of** de); (of students, recruits, tourists) arrivage *m* hum.

Lot ▶ **1163** *pr n* Lot *m*; **in/to the ~** dans le Lot.

Lot-et-Garonne ▶ **1163** *pr n* Lot-et-Garonne *m*; **in/to the ~** dans le Lot-et-Garonne.

loth *adj* = **loath**.

Lothian /'ləʊðɪən/ ▶ **1624** *pr n* (also **~ Region**) Lothians *m*.

lotion /'ləʊʃn/ *n* lotion *f*.

lottery /'lɒtərɪ/ *n* lit, fig loterie *f*.

lotto /'lɒtəʊ/ ▶ **1282** *n* loto *m*.

lotus /'ləʊtəs/ *n* lotus *m*.

lotus: **~-eater** *n* lit, Mythol lotophage *m*; fig sybarite *mf*; **~ position** *n* position *f* du lotus.

loud /laʊd/ **I** *adj* **1** (noisy) [*bang, music, radio, TV, voice*] fort; [*din, crash, scream*] grand; [*comment, laugh, party*] bruyant; [*applause*] vif/vive; [*whisper*] audible; **to be ~ with sth** résonner de qch; **2** (emphatic) [*protest, objection*] vif/vive; [*agreement*] vigoureux/-euse; **to be ~ in one's praise/condemnation of sth** louer/condamner qch vivement; **3** (vulgar) péj [*colour, pattern*] criard; [*person, behaviour*] exubérant.

II *adv* fort; **out ~** à voix haute; **~ and clear** clairement; **her voice rang out ~ and clear** sa voix se fit clairement entendre; **I am receiving you ~ and clear** Radio je vous reçois cinq sur cinq○; hum je te comprends parfaitement.

IDIOMS **for crying out ~**○! mais enfin!

loudhailer /ˌlaʊdˈheɪlə(r)/ *n* GB mégaphone *m*.

loudly /ˈlaʊdlɪ/ *adv* [*bang, crash, knock, talk, laugh, sing*] bruyamment; [*play music, scream, cry*] fort; [*cheer*] chaleureusement; [*protest, praise, condemn*] vivement.

loud: **~mouth**○ *n* grande gueule◑ *f*; **~mouthed**○ *adj* fort en gueule◑.

loudness /ˈlaʊdnɪs/ *n* intensité *f*.

loud: **~speaker** *n* (for announcements) haut-parleur *m*; (for hi-fi) enceinte *f*; **~speaker system** *n* (for announcements) haut-parleurs *mpl*; (for hi-fi) enceinte *f*; **~speaker van** *n* camionnette *f* haut-parleur.

Louisiana /luːˌiːzɪˈænə/ ▶ **1744** *pr n* Louisiane *f*.

lounge /laʊndʒ/ **I** *n* **1** (in house, hotel) salon *m*; **TV ~** salle-télé *f*; **2** (in airport) hall *m*; **airport/arrivals ~** hall d'aéroport/des arrivées; **departure ~** salle *f* d'embarquement; **3** US (also **cocktail ~**) bar *m*.

II *modif* [*chairs, furniture*] de salon.

III *vi* **1** (sprawl) s'avachir (**on** sur); **to ~ against sth** s'avachir contre qch; **2** (idle) paresser.

■ **lounge about, lounge around** paresser, lambiner pej; **to ~ about the house** paresser dans la maison.

lounge: **~ bar** *n* GB grande salle *f* de pub; **~ lizard**○ *n* salonnard○ *m*.

lounge suit *n* **1** GB (man's) costume *m*, complet *m*; (on invitation) costume *m* de ville; **2** US pyjama *m* d'intérieur.

lounge: **~ suite** *n* GB sièges *mpl* de salon; **~wear** *n* US vêtements *mpl* d'intérieur.

lour /ˈlaʊə(r)/ *vi* = **lower²**.

louse /laʊs/ *n* **1** (*pl* **lice**) (insect) pou *m*; **2**◑ (*pl* **louses**) pej salaud◑ *m*.

■ **louse up**◑: **~ [sth] up, ~ up [sth]** bousiller.

lousy /ˈlaʊzɪ/ **I** *adj* **1**○ [*book, film, holiday*] mauvais; [*meal, holiday, working conditions*] infect○; [*salary*] nul/nulle○; **to be ~ at** être nul/nulle○ en [*history etc*]; **to feel ~** être mal fichu○, être patraque○; **a ~ trick** un sale tour; **2** (louse-infested) couvert de poux; **3**○ **~ with** bourré○ de [*tourists etc*].

II○ *adv* US **to do ~** foirer○ (**on** à).

lout /laʊt/ *n* (rude-mannered) malotru○ *m*; (hooligan) voyou *m*; (clumsy) rustaud *m*.

loutish /ˈlaʊtɪʃ/ *adj* (bad-mannered) grossier/-ière; (rowdy, violent) **~ youth** voyou *m*; **~ behaviour** conduite *f* de voyou.

louvre GB, **louver** US /ˈluːvə(r)/ **I** *n* (strip) lame *f* (de persienne); (door) porte *f* persiennée; (in window) vasistas *m*; (on belltower) abat-son *m*.

II *modif* [*door, shutter*] persienné.

louvred GB, **louvered** US /ˈluːvəd/ *adj* persienné.

lovable /ˈlʌvəbl/ *adj* [*person, clown, eccentric*] sympathique; [*child*] adorable.

love /lʌv/ **I** *n* **1** (affection, devotion) amour *m* (**for** pour); **to do sth for ~** faire qch par amour (**of sb** pour qn); **to do sth for the ~ of it** faire qch par goût; **for the ~ of God** ou **Mike**○†! pour l'amour de Dieu or du ciel! **to be/fall in ~** être/tomber amoureux/-euse (**with** de); **he's in ~ with the sound of his own voice** il s'écoute parler; **to fall out of ~** cesser d'être amoureux/-euse (**with** de); **to make ~** (have sex) faire l'amour (**with** avec; **to** à); **to make ~ to sb**† (court) faire la cour à qn; **2** (in polite formulas) **give my ~ to Jo** transmets mes amitiés à Jo; **~ to Don and the kids**○ baisers à Don et aux enfants; **Andy sends his ~** Andy t'embrasse; **with ~ from Bob, ~ Bob** affectueusement, Bob; **3** (object of affection) amour *m*; **he/music was my first ~** il/la musique a été mon premier amour; **my one true ~** mon seul amour; **the ~ of his life** l'amour de sa vie; **the little ~s**○! GB ce sont des amours!; **be a ~ and make some tea**○ GB sois gentil, fais-moi une tasse de thé; **4** GB (term of address) (to lover, spouse) mon amour *m*, mon chéri/ma chérie *m/f*; (to child) mon chéri/ma chérie *m/f*; **that's 25 pence please, ~** c'est 25 pence, s'il vous plaît Madame/Monsieur; **5** (in tennis) zéro *m*; **15 ~** 15 (à) zéro; **~ 15** zéro (à) 15; **two sets to ~** deux sets à zéro.

II *modif* [*letter, scene, song, story, token*] d'amour.

III *vtr* **1** (feel affection for) aimer [*lover, spouse, child, pet, friend*]; **to ~ sb very much/madly/tenderly** aimer énormément/follement/tendrement qn; **to ~ sb for sth** aimer qn pour qch; **I ~ her for saving my life/making me laugh** je l'aime parce qu'elle m'a sauvé la vie/me fait rire; **to ~ each other** s'aimer; **'he ~s me, he ~s me not'** ≈ 'il m'aime, un peu, beaucoup, passionnément, à la folie, pas du tout'; **I must ~ you and leave you** hum ce n'est pas que je m'ennuie, mais il faut que je m'en aille; **2** (be fond of, appreciate) aimer [*activity, place, thing*]; (stronger) adorer; **I ~ the scene where...** j'adore la scène où...; **I ~d the way you said that** j'ai bien aimé la façon dont tu as dit ça; **I ~ it when...** j'adore quand...; **to ~ doing, to ~ to do** aimer faire; **I would ~ to see them** j'aimerais beaucoup les voir; **I'd ~ to help him but I can't** j'aimerais bien l'aider mais je ne peux pas; **'dance?'—'I'd ~ to!'** 'tu veux danser?'—'avec plaisir!'; **'can she help?'—'she'd ~ to'** 'elle peut nous aider?'—'elle serait ravie'; **she'll ~ that!** iron elle sera vraiment ravie! iron.

IV *vi* (feel love) aimer.

IDIOMS **~ at first sight** le coup de foudre; **there's no ~ lost between them** ils/elles se détestent cordialement. ▶ **money**.

love affair *n* (with person) liaison *f* (**with** avec; **between** entre); (with place, car, era etc) histoire *f* d'amour (**with** avec).

lovebird /ˈlʌvbɜːd/ **I** *n* Zool inséparable *m*.

II lovebirds *npl* (lovers) hum tourtereaux *mpl* fig.

love: **~bite** *n* GB suçon *m*; **~ child** *n* euph enfant *mf* de l'amour; **~-hate relationship** *n* relation *f* oscillant entre l'amour et la haine; **~-in** *n* love-in *m*; **~-in-a-mist** *n* Bot nigelle *f*; **~ knot** *n* lacs *m* d'amour.

loveless /ˈlʌvlɪs/ *adj* **1** [*marriage, home, childhood, sex*] sans amour; **2** [*person*] (unloved) sans amour; (unloving) incapable d'amour.

love: **~-lies-bleeding** *n* Bot queue-de-renard *f*; **~ life** *n* vie *f* amoureuse.

loveliness /ˈlʌvlɪnɪs/ *n* beauté *f*.

lovelorn /ˈlʌvlɔːn/ *adj* qui a des peines d'amour.

lovely /ˈlʌvlɪ/ **I** *n* beauté *f*; **my ~** ma belle.

II *adj* **1** (beautiful) [*church, colour, dress, garden, hair, person, poem*] beau/belle, joli (*before n*); **you look ~ in pink/that dress** tu es ravissante en rose/dans cette robe; **the hat will look ~ with your dress** le chapeau ira très bien avec ta robe; **2** (pleasant) [*family, letter, person*] charmant; [*meal, smell, soup*] délicieux/-ieuse; [*idea, surprise*] bon/bonne (*before n*); [*evening, weekend*] excellent; [*day, present, weather*] magnifique; **it's ~ to do** c'est agréable de faire; **to smell ~** sentir bon; **to taste ~** être délicieux/-ieuse; **3** (emphatic) **~ and hot/fresh/tanned** bien chaud/frais/bronzé.

lovemaking /ˈlʌvmeɪkɪŋ/ *n* **1** (sex) **our ~** nos rapports (sexuels); **his/her ~** sa façon de faire l'amour; **2**† (flirtation) **his ~ flattered her** la cour qu'il lui faisait, l'a flattée.

love: **~ match** *n* union *f* parfaite; **~ nest** *n* journ nid *m* d'amour; **~ potion** *n* philtre *m* d'amour.

lover /ˈlʌvə(r)/ *n* **1** (sexual partner) gen partenaire *mf*; (in adultery) amant/maîtresse *m/f*; **to be/become ~s** être/devenir amants; **to take a ~** prendre un amant; **a good ~** un bon amant; **2** (person in love) amoureux/-euse *m/f*; **young ~s** jeunes amoureux; **3** (enthusiast) amateur *m* (**of** de); **jazz/opera ~** amateur de jazz/d'opéra; **I'm no great ~ of cricket** je ne suis pas très amateur de cricket.

lover boy○ *n* Don Juan *m*.

love: **~ seat** *n* confident *m*; **~sick** *adj* languissant d'amour.

lovey○ /ˈlʌvɪ/ *n* GB mon chéri/ma chérie *m/f*.

lovey-dovey○ /ˌlʌvɪˈdʌvɪ/ *adj* GB **to get all ~** se mettre à roucouler○.

loving /ˈlʌvɪŋ/ **I** *adj* [*mother, husband, look, smile*] tendre; [*couple, kiss*] amoureux/-euse; [*care, attention*] affectueux/-ueuse; **a ~ family** une famille unie; (in letter-writing) **from your ~ son, Fred** ton fils qui t'aime, Fred.

II -loving (*dans composés*) **football-/music-~** amateur de football/de musique; **peace-/freedom-/animal-~** qui aime la paix/la liberté/les animaux.

loving: **~ cup** *n* coupe *f* de l'amitié; **~-kindness**‡ *n* bonté *f*.

lovingly /ˈlʌvɪŋlɪ/ *adv* (all contexts) avec amour.

low /ləʊ/ **I** *n* **1** Meteorol dépression *f*; **2** fig **the stock market closed at a record ~** le marché boursier a été clôturé à son niveau le plus bas; **the economy has hit a ~** l'économie est dans le creux de la vague; **his popularity has hit a new ~** sa popularité a atteint son niveau le plus bas; **morale is at an all time ~** le moral est au plus bas; **the lyrics hit a new ~ in banality** les paroles (de la chanson) atteignent des sommets dans la banalité.

II *adj* **1** (close to the ground) [*branch, building, chair, wall, cloud, ground*] bas/basse; **the sun is ~ in the sky** le soleil est bas dans le ciel; **there will be flooding on ~ ground** il y aura des inondations à basse altitude; **2** (nearly depleted) [*reservoir, level*] bas/basse; [*battery*] faible; **our stocks are rather ~** nos stocks sont plutôt bas; **the fire was getting ~** le feu était bas; **we're ~ on skilled staff** nous manquons de personnel qualifié; **I'm getting ~ on petrol** je n'ai plus beaucoup d'essence; **these products are ~ in sugar/fat** ces produits contiennent peu de sucre/matière grasse; **the patient is very ~** le malade est au plus mal or bas; **3** (minimal) [*price, wage*] bas/basse; [*capacity, speed*] réduit; [*income, number, rate*] faible; [*pressure, temperature*] bas/basse; **leave the soup on a ~ heat** laissez mijoter la soupe à feu doux; **the temperature was in the ~ twenties** il faisait dans les vingt degrés; **4** (inferior) [*mark, score, quality, standard*] mauvais; [*life form*] peu évolué; **5** (depressed) déprimé; **to feel ~, to be in ~ spirits** être déprimé; **6** (deep) [*note, tone, voice*] bas/basse; **in a ~ voice** tout bas; **the sound is too ~** Radio, TV le son est trop bas; **7** (disapproved of) (vulgar) [*conversation, humour*] peu relevé; (base) [*action, behaviour*] ignoble; **that was a really ~ thing to do** c'était vraiment un sale coup○; **8** Naut **~ tide** marée *f* basse; **at ~ tide** à marée basse.

III *adv* **1** (near the ground) [*aim, fly, shoot*] bas; [*bend, crouch*] très bas; **the plane flew ~ over the desert** l'avion survolait le désert à basse altitude; **I wouldn't sink** ou **stoop so ~ as to ask him for money** fig je ne m'abaisserais pas à lui demander de l'argent; **2** (near the bottom) **it is very ~ (down) on the list** lit c'est tout à fait au bas de la liste; fig c'est tout à fait secondaire; **look ~er down the page** regarde plus bas sur la page; **3** (at a reduced level) [*buy*] à bas prix; [*speak*] bas; **to turn sth down ~**

baisser [*heating, light, radio*]; **stocks are running ~** les stocks sont en baisse; **I rate him pretty ~** je ne le tiens pas en grande estime; **4** (at a deep pitch) [*sing*] bas.
IV *vi* [*cow*] meugler.
IDIOMS **to be the ~est of the ~** être le dernier des derniers; **to be laid ~ by** être alité par [*illness*].

low: **~-alcohol** *adj* Wine peu alcoolisé; **~-angle shot** *n* Cin, Phot contre-plongée *f*; **~born**† *adj* de basse extraction†; **~boy** *n* US guéridon *m* (*avec tiroirs*).

lowbrow /ˈləʊbraʊ/ péj I *n* personne *f* peu intellectuelle.
II *adj* [*person*] peu intellectuel/-elle; [*music, literature*] de bas étage.

low: **~-budget** *adj* à petit budget; **~-calorie** *adj* [*diet*] hypocalorique; [*food*] à faible teneur en calories.

Low Church I *n* Basse Église *f* anglicane.
II *adj* de la Basse Église anglicane.

low: **~-cost** *adj* économique, bon marché; **Low Countries** *pr npl* Hist Pays-Bas *mpl*; **~-cut** *adj* décolleté.

low-down○ /ˈləʊdaʊn/ I *n* tuyau○ *m*, renseignements *mpl*; **to get the ~ on sb/sth** avoir un tuyau○ or des renseignements sur qn/qch; **to give sb the ~** tuyauter qn○, renseigner qn (**on** sur).
II *adj* [*person, trick*] sale (*before n*); **a ~ trick** un sale tour.

lower[1] /ˈlaʊə(r)/ I *vi* littér (frown) prendre un air comminatoire (**at** avec).
II **lowering** *pres p adj* [*sky, look*] menaçant.

lower[2] /ˈləʊə(r)/ I *comp adj* [*deck, jaw, level, lip, part, price*] inférieur; **a pain in the ~ back** une douleur au bas du dos.
II *vtr* **1** (bring down) baisser [*barrier, blind, curtain, flag, newspaper, rifle*]; Constr abaisser [*ceiling*]; **to ~ one's eyes/head/arms** baisser les yeux/la tête/les bras; **to ~ sb/sth into** descendre qn/qch dans [*hole*]; **to ~ sb/sth onto** descendre qn/qch sur [*roof, boat*]; **2** (reduce) baisser [*light, volume*]; réduire [*pressure, temperature*]; baisser [*prices*]; diminuer [*resistance*]; abaisser [*age limit*]; baisser [*standards*]; **to ~ one's voice** baisser la voix; **to ~ one's guard** baisser sa garde; fig relâcher sa vigilance; **to ~ sb's morale** démoraliser qn; **3** (abolish) abolir [*trade barrier*]; **4** Naut affaler [*sail*]; mettre [qch] à la mer [*lifeboat*]; amener [*mast*]; **the lifeboats were ~ed into the sea** les canots de sauvetage ont été mis à la mer.
III *v refl* **to ~ oneself 1** (demean oneself) s'abaisser; **2** (sit carefully) **to ~ oneself into** entrer lentement dans [*bath*]; s'asseoir précautionneusement dans [*chair*].
■ **lower down**: **~ [sth] down, ~ down [sth]** descendre [*parcel, stretcher*].

lower case /ˈləʊə(r)/ I *n* Print bas *m* de casse, minuscules *fpl*; **use ~ for this heading** mettez ce titre en minuscules.
II **lower-case** *modif* **~ letter** minuscule *f*.

Lower Chamber /ˈləʊə(r)/ *n* = **Lower House**.

lower class /ˈləʊə(r)/ I *n* (*pl* **~es**) **the ~, the ~es** la classe ouvrière, les classes populaires.
II *adj* gen de la classe ouvrière; [*accent, custom, district*] populaire.

lower /ˈləʊə(r)/: **~ court** *n* Jur instance *f* inférieure; **Lower House** *n* GB Pol Chambre *f* des Communes.

lowering /ˈləʊərɪŋ/ I *n* **1** (reduction) (of prices, tariffs, standards) baisse *f*; (of pressure, temperature, rate) baisse *f*; (of age limit) abaissement *m*; (of light, volume) baisse *f*; (of resistance) diminution *f*; **2** (of flag, sail) abaissement *m*; (of mast) calage *m*; **3** fig (removal) (of barriers) suppression *f*.
II *adj* (demeaning) dégradant, humiliant.

lower middle class /ˈləʊə(r)/ I *n* (*pl* **~es**) **the ~, the ~es** la petite bourgeoisie.
II *adj* petit-bourgeois/petite-bourgeoise.

lower /ˈləʊə(r)/: **~-ranking** *adj* de grade inférieur; **~ school** *n* ₵ petites classes *fpl*.

lower sixth /ˈləʊə(r)/ *n* GB Sch ≈ classe *f* de première; **to be in the ~** ≈ être en première.

lowest common denominator *n* Math, fig plus petit dénominateur *m* commun; **he reduces everything to the ~** péj il rabaisse tout à ce qu'il y a de plus trivial.

low: **~-fat** *adj* [*diet*] sans matières grasses; [*cheese, food*] allégé; [*milk*] écrémé; **~-flying** *adj* volant à faible altitude; **~-frequency** *adj* [*sound*] à basse fréquence; **Low German** *n* Ling bas allemand *m*; **~-grade** *adj* (poor quality) [*meat, steel*] de qualité inférieure; (minor) [*official*] de grade inférieur; **~-heeled** *adj* plat, à talons plats.

low-income *adj* [*family*] à faible revenu; [*bracket*] des bas salaires.

lowing /ˈləʊɪŋ/ *n* meuglement *m*.

low-key /ˌləʊˈkiː/ *adj* [*approach, lifestyle, person*] discret/-ète; [*style, mood, treatment*] sobre; [*meeting, talks*] informel/-elle; [*ceremony*] intime.

lowland /ˈləʊlənd/ I *n* (also **~s**) basses-terres *fpl*.
II *modif* [*farmer, farming*] des basses-terres; [*area*] à faible altitude; [*river*] de plaine.

Lowland /ˈləʊlənd/ I **Lowlands** *pr npl* **the Lowlands (of Scotland)** les Basses-Terres *fpl* (d'Écosse).
II *modif* des Basses-Terres (d'Écosse).

lowlander /ˈləʊləndə(r)/ *n* **1** gen homme/femme *m/f* qui vient de la plaine; **2 Lowlander** Écossais/-e *m/f* des Basses-Terres.

Lowland Scots *n* Ling dialecte *m* des Basses-Terres d'Écosse.

Low Latin *n* Ling bas latin *m*.

low-level *adj* **1** Aviat [*flight, bombing*] à basse altitude; **2** (informal) [*meeting, talks*] informel/-elle; **3** Comput [*language*] de bas niveau; **4** Nucl [*radiation*] faible.

low-life I *n* **1** ₵ (underworld) (social) bas-fonds *mpl*; (criminal) milieu *m*; **2**○ (person) (*pl* **~s**) crapule *f*.
II *modif* [*character, scene*] des bas-fonds; [*friend, contact*] du milieu; [*bar, area*] fréquenté par des voyous.

lowliness /ˈləʊlɪnɪs/ *n* modestie *f*.

low-loader *n* Transp camion *m* à plate-forme surbaissée.

lowly /ˈləʊlɪ/ *adj* modeste.

low: **~-lying** *adj* à basse altitude; **Low Mass** *n* Relig messe *f* basse; **~-necked** *adj* décolleté.

lowness /ˈləʊnɪs/ *n* **1** (lack of height) (of bridge, ceiling) faible hauteur *f*; **2** (smallness) (of offer, price) modicité *f*; **3** Meteorol, Phys **the ~ of the temperature/pressure** la basse température/pression.

low-paid I *n* **the ~** (+ *v pl*) les petits salaires *mpl*.
II *adj* [*job*] faiblement rémunéré; [*worker*] peu rémunéré.

low-pitched *adj* **1** Mus grave; **2** Archit [*roof*] en pente douce.

low: **~-priced** *adj* Comm à bas prix; **~-profile** *adj* (discreet) [*approach, job, mission*] discret/-ète; **~-quality** *adj* de qualité inférieure.

low-rise I *n* Archit barre *f* (d'immeuble).
II *adj* [*building*] bas/basse (*after n*).

low: **~-risk** *adj* Fin [*investment*] à risque limité; [*borrower*] fiable; Med, Insur [*individual, group*] ne faisant pas partie des groupes à risques; **~-scoring** *adj* Sport [*match*] avec peu de points de marqués.

low season *n* Tourism basse saison *f*; **in the ~** en basse saison.

low: **~-slung** *adj* [*chassis*] surbaissé; [*belly*] pendant; **~-start mortgage** *n* GB, Fin *emprunt-logement avec un faible taux d'intérêt de départ*; **Low Sunday** *n* Relig premier dimanche *m* après Pâques; **~-tar** *adj* à faible teneur en goudrons; **~-tech** *adj* (de type) traditionnel; **~-tension**, **LT** *adj* Elec (à) basse tension; **~ tide** *n* marée *f* basse.

low voltage I *n* basse tension *f*.
II **low-voltage** *adj* de basse tension.

low-water mark *n* niveau *m* des basses eaux.

lox /lɒks/ *n* US saumon *m* fumé.

loyal /ˈlɔɪəl/ *adj* [*friend, servant, supporter*] loyal (**to** envers); [*customer*] fidèle (**to** à).

loyalist /ˈlɔɪəlɪst/ I *n* partisan/-anne *m/f*.
II **Loyalist** *pr n* Pol *partisan du maintien de l'union entre la Grande-Bretagne et l'Irlande du Nord*.

loyally /ˈlɔɪəlɪ/ *adv* [*support, serve*] fidèlement; [*speak*] avec dévouement.

loyalty /ˈlɔɪəltɪ/ *n* loyauté *f* (**to, towards** envers); **to have divided** ou **conflicting loyalties** se sentir écartelé.

lozenge /ˈlɒzɪndʒ/ *n* **1** Pharm pastille *f*; **2** Math losange *m*.

Lozère ▶ **1163** *pr n* Lozère *f*; **in/to ~** en Lozère.

LP *n* (*abrév* = **long-playing record**) (disque *m*) 33 tours *m*.

LPG *n*: *abrév* ▶ **liquefied petroleum gas**.

L-plate /el pleɪt/ *n* GB Aut plaque *f* d'élève conducteur débutant accompagné.

LPN *n* US *abrév* ▶ **licensed practical nurse**.

LRAM *n* GB (*abrév* = **Licentiate of the Royal Academy of Music**) diplômé/-e *m/f* de musique.

LRCP *n* GB (*abrév* = **Licentiate of the Royal College of Physicians**) diplômé/-e *m/f* de médecine.

LRCS *n* GB (*abrév* = **Licentiate of the Royal College of Surgeons**) diplômé/-e *m/f* de médecine opératoire.

LSAT *n* US (*abrév* = **Law School Admission Test**) test *m* d'évaluation en vue des études de droit.

LSD *n* (*abrév* = **lysergic acid diethylamide**) LSD *m*.

L.S.D. *n* GB (*abrév* = **librae, solidi, denarii**, = **pounds, shillings, pence**) *ancien système monétaire en Grande-Bretagne*.

LSE *n* GB (*abrév* = **London School of Economics**) *faculté des Sciences économiques de l'Université de Londres*.

L-shaped *adj* en (forme de) L.

Lt *abrév écrite* ▶ **lieutenant**.

Lt. Col *abrév écrite* ▶ **Lieutenant Colonel**.

Ltd GB (*abrév écrite* = **limited (liability)**) cf SARL.

Lt. Gen *abrév écrite* = **Lieutenant General**.

lube○ /luːb/ *n* US **1** (oil) huile *f* de graissage; **2** (petroleum jelly) lubrifiant *m*; **3** (also **~ job**) graissage *m*.

lubricant /ˈluːbrɪkənt/ *n* lubrifiant *m*.

lubricate /ˈluːbrɪkeɪt/ *vtr* gen lubrifier; Aut graisser, lubrifier.

lubricating oil *n* huile *f* de graissage, lubrifiant *m*.

lubrication /ˌluːbrɪˈkeɪʃn/ *n* gen lubrification *f*; Aut, Mech graissage *m*.

lubricator /ˈluːbrɪkeɪtə(r)/ *n* (substance) lubrifiant *m*.

lubricious /luːˈbrɪʃəs/ *adj* péj lubrique, salace.

lubricity /luːˈbrɪsətɪ/ *n* péj lubricité *f*, salacité *f*.

lucerne /luːˈsɜːn/ *n* GB luzerne *f*.

Lucerne /luːˈsɜːn/ ▶ **1818**, **1776** *pr n* Lucerne; **the canton of ~** le canton de Lucerne.

lucid /ˈluːsɪd/ *adj* **1** (clear, understandable) clair; **2** (sane) [*person, mind*] lucide; [*moment*] de lucidité; **3** (luminous) littér lumineux/-euse.

lucidity /luːˈsɪdətɪ/ *n* **1** (clarity) (of account, argument etc) clarté *f*; **2** (sanity) lucidité *f*; **3** (luminosity) littér luminosité *f*.

lucidly /ˈluːsɪdlɪ/ *adv* clairement.

lucifer○‡ /ˈluːsɪfə(r)/ *n* GB allumette *f*.

luck /lʌk/ *n* **1** (fortune) **good ~** chance *f*; **bad ~** malchance *f*; **to bring sb good/bad ~** porter bonheur/malheur à qn; **to have the good ~ to do** avoir la chance de faire; **it's good ~ to do** ça porte bonheur de faire; **it is bad ~ that** ce n'est pas de chance que (+ *subj*); **I've had nothing but bad ~ with that car** je n'ai eu que de la malchance avec cette voiture; **to try one's ~** tenter sa chance; **~ was on his side** la chance était de son côté; **as ~ would have it**... le hasard a voulu que... (+ *subj*); **bad** ou **hard ~!** pas de chance!; **just my ~!** c'est bien ma chance!; **good ~!** bonne chance!; **better ~ next time!** tu auras plus de chance la prochaine fois!; **I wish you all the best of ~** je vous souhaite la meilleure chance possible; **to be down on one's ~** être dans une mauvaise passe; **2** (good fortune) chance *f*; **with ~**... avec de la chance...; **with a bit of ~**... avec un peu de chance...; **to run out of ~** ne plus avoir le vent en poupe; **our ~ ran out in the third game** notre chance a tourné dans le troisième match; **to wear sth for ~** porter qch comme porte-bonheur; **by a stroke of ~** par un coup de chance; **any ~ with the job hunting?** ça marche, les recherches pour un emploi?; **'have you found it?'—'no ~ yet'** 'tu l'as trouvé?'—'pas encore, malheureusement'; **to be in/out of ~** avoir de la/ne pas avoir de chance.
IDIOMS **it's the ~ of the draw** c'est une question de chance; **to put in two spoonfuls, and one for ~** mettre deux cuillerées plus une au cas où; **my ~' s in!** c'est mon jour de chance!; **no such ~!** hélas non!; **to ring the doorbell once more for ~** sonner encore une fois à tout hasard; **to take pot ~** (at cinema, theatre) aller au petit bonheur; **you'll have to take pot ~** (at meal) ce sera à la fortune du pot.
■ **luck out**○ US avoir de la veine○.

luckily /ˈlʌkɪlɪ/ *adv* heureusement (**for** pour).

luckless /ˈlʌklɪs/ *adj* littér [*person*] infortuné; [*occasion*] malheureux/-euse.

lucky /ˈlʌkɪ/ *adj* **1** (fortunate) **to be ~ to do/to be** avoir la chance de faire/d'être; **you're ~ to be able to do** tu as de la chance de pouvoir faire; **to be ~ to be alive** avoir eu de la chance de s'en tirer vivant; **you'll be ~ to get a taxi** tu auras bien de la chance si tu trouves un taxi; **it was ~ for me that you came** j'ai eu de la chance que tu sois venu; **it was ~ for me that I went** j'ai eu de la chance d'y être allé; **I'm ~ that I've been able to do** j'ai eu de la chance de pouvoir faire; **to be ~ enough to do** avoir la chance de faire; **those who are ~ enough to have a job** ceux qui ont la chance d'avoir un emploi; **to be ~ at the races** avoir de la chance aux courses; **I'm not a ~ person** je n'ai jamais de chance; **~ you**○! veinard/-e○ *m/f*!; **you ~ dog**○ ou **devil**○ sacré/-e veinard/-e○ *m/f*; **I/you etc should be so ~**○! GB iron ça serait trop beau!; **you should think** ou **count yourself lucky that I didn't do** tu dois te considérer heureux/-euse que je n'aie pas fait; **to have a ~ escape** l'échapper belle; **2** (bringing good luck) [*charm, colour, number*] porte-bonheur *inv*; **it's my ~ day!** c'est mon jour de chance!; **the number three is ~/is ~ for me** le numéro trois porte bonheur/me porte bonheur; **it's a ~ sign** c'est un bon signe.
IDIOMS **to strike it ~** décrocher le gros lot○; **to thank one's ~ stars** remercier le ciel.

lucrative /ˈluːkrətɪv/ *adj* lucratif/-ive.

lucre○† /ˈluːkə(r)/ *n* fric○ *m*.

Lucretia /luːˈkriːʃə/ *pr n* Lucrèce *f*.

Lucretius /luːˈkriːʃəs/ *pr n* Lucrèce *m*.

Luddite /ˈlʌdaɪt/ *n* Hist luddite *m*; fig péj réactionnaire *mf* (*qui s'oppose au progrès*).

ludic /ˈlʌdɪk/ *adj* sout ludique.

ludicrous /ˈluːdɪkrəs/ *adj* ridicule, grotesque.

ludicrously /ˈluːdɪkrəslɪ/ *adv* ridiculement.

ludo /ˈluːdəʊ/ ▶ 1282 *n* GB jeu *m* des petits chevaux.

luff /lʌf/ **I** *n* guindant *m*.
II *vi* lofer, venir au vent.

lug /lʌg/ **I** *n* **1** (on pot) oreille *f*, anse *f*; **2** Constr, Tech patte *f*; **3**◑ GB = **lughole**.
II *vtr* (*p prés etc* **-gg-**) traîner, trimbaler○ [*suitcase, heavy object*]; traîner [*person*].

luggage /ˈlʌgɪdʒ/ *n* ¢ bagages *mpl*.

luggage: **~ handler** ▶ 1692 *n* bagagiste *mf*; **~ label** *n* étiquette *f* à bagages; **~ rack** *n* compartiment *m* à bagages; **~ van** *n* GB fourgon *m* à bagages.

lugger /ˈlʌgə(r)/ *n* lougre *m*.

lughole◑ /ˈlʌgəʊl/ *n* GB esgourde◑ *f*, portugaise◑ *f*.

lugubrious /ləˈguːbrɪəs/ *adj* lugubre.

lugubriously /ləˈguːbrɪəslɪ/ *adv* lugubrement.

Luke /luːk/ *pr n* Luc.

lukewarm /ˌluːkˈwɔːm/ *adj* **1** [*food, liquid*] tiède; **2** fig [*reception, response*] tiède, peu enthousiaste; **she was a bit ~ about the idea** l'idée ne l'enthousiasmait pas.

lull /lʌl/ **I** *n* (in storm, fighting) accalmie *f*; (in conversation) pause *f*; (in trading) ralentissement *m*; **the ~ before the storm** le calme avant la tempête.
II *vtr* apaiser [*person*]; endormir [*suspicions*]; **to ~ sb to sleep** endormir qn en le berçant; **he ~ed them into thinking they were safe** il leur a fait croire qu'ils étaient en sécurité; **to be ~ed into a false sense of security** se laisser aller à un sentiment de sécurité trompeur.

lullaby /ˈlʌləbaɪ/ *n* berceuse *f*.

lulu○ /ˈluːluː/ *n* US **a ~ of a mistake/story** une sacrée○ erreur/histoire; **he's a ~** c'est un sacré○ mec○.

lumbago /lʌmˈbeɪgəʊ/ *n* lumbago *m*.

lumbar /ˈlʌmbə(r)/ *adj* lombaire; **~ puncture** ponction *f* lombaire.

lumber /ˈlʌmbə(r)/ **I** *n* **1** US (wood) bois *m* de construction; **2**† GB (junk) bric-à-brac *m*.
II *vtr* **1**○ GB **to be ~ed with sb/sth** se taper○ or se coltiner○ qn/qch; **I'm ~ed with the ironing** je me suis tapé○ or coltiné○ le repassage; **I get ~ed with the job of entertaining her parents** on m'a infligé la corvée de divertir ses parents; **I'm ~ed with the house, I can't sell it** j'ai la maison sur les bras, je n'arrive pas à la vendre; **2** US (remove timber from) exploiter [qch] (pour le bois de construction).
III *vi* **1** (also **~ along**) [*animal, person*] avancer d'un pas lourd; [*vehicle*] avancer péniblement; **to ~ away** ou **off** [*person*] s'éloigner d'un pas lourd; **to ~ in/out** entrer/sortir d'un pas lourd; **to ~ through sth** traverser qch d'un pas lourd; **2** US (cut timber) débiter le bois.

lumber company *n* US entreprise *f* de bois de construction.

lumbering /ˈlʌmbərɪŋ/ *adj* [*animal, person*] au pas lourd (*after n*); [*vehicle*] qui avance péniblement; fig [*system, bureaucracy*] pesant.

lumber: **~jack** ▶ 1692 *n* bûcheron/-onne *m/f*; **~jacket** *n* veste *f* en laine à carreaux; **~jack shirt** *n* chemise *f* épaisse à carreaux.

lumberman /ˈlʌmbəmən/ ▶ 1692 *n* US **1** (dealer) marchand *m* de bois; **2** (woodcutter) bûcheron *m*.

lumber: **~ mill** *n* scierie *f*; **~ room**† *n* GB débarras *m*; **~yard** *n* US scierie *f*.

luminary /ˈluːmɪnərɪ, US -nerɪ/ *n* **1** Astrol astre *m*; **2** fig (person) sommité *f*.

luminescence /ˌluːmɪˈnesns/ *n* **1** Phys luminescence *f*; **2** (light) littér lueur *f*.

luminosity /ˌluːmɪˈnɒsətɪ/ *n* luminosité *f*.

luminous /ˈluːmɪnəs/ *adj* lumineux/-euse.

lumme○† /ˈlʌmɪ/ *excl* GB grands Dieux!, sapristi○†!

lummox○ /ˈlʌməks/ *n* US lourdaud/-e *m/f*.

lummy○ /ˈlʌmɪ/ *excl* GB = **lumme**.

lump /lʌmp/ **I** *n* **1** (of substance) gen morceau *m*; (of soil, clay) motte *f*; (in sauce) grumeau *m*; **in one** ou **a ~** fig en bloc; **2** (on body) (from fall, knock) bosse *f* (**on** sur); (tumour) grosseur *f* (**in, on** à); **3**○ (idle person) (man) balourd○ *m*; (woman) dondon○ *f*.
II *vtr* **to ~ X with Y** regrouper X et Y; péj mettre X et Y dans le même panier○; **to ~ the science students with the arts students** regrouper les étudiants de sciences avec les étudiants d'humanités; **the two groups shouldn't be ~ed together** on ne devrait pas mettre les deux groupes dans le même panier.
III *vi* **1** US (become lumpy) [*sauce*] faire des grumeaux; **2** (also **~ along**) se traîner.
IDIOMS **to get** ou **take one's ~s** US encaisser les coups; **to have a ~ in one's throat** avoir la gorge serrée or une boule dans la gorge; **I'll/he'll have to ~ it**○ il va falloir faire avec/qu'il fasse avec○; **like it or ~ it**○ que ça te/lui etc chante ou pas○.

lumpectomy /lʌmˈpektəmɪ/ *n* ablation *f* d'une tumeur au sein.

lumpen† /ˈlʌmpn/ *adj* péj demeuré.

lumpenproletariat /ˌlʌmpənˌprəʊlɪˈteərɪət/ *n* lumpenprolétariat *m*.

lump: **~fish**, **~sucker** *n* lump *m*; **~fish roe** *n* œufs *mpl* de lump.

lumpish /ˈlʌmpɪʃ/ *adj* ahuri.

lump sugar *n* sucre *m* en morceaux.

lump sum *n* **1** Comm (complete payment) versement *m* unique; (decided in advance) somme *f* forfaitaire; **2** Insur capital *m* forfaitaire.

lump sum payment *n* Insur versement *m* d'un capital.

lumpy /ˈlʌmpɪ/ *adj* [*sauce*] grumeleux/-euse; [*mattress, pillow, soil*] défoncé; [*surface*] bosselé; **to go ~** [*sauce*] faire des grumeaux.

lunacy /ˈluːnəsɪ/ *n* **1**† Med folie *f*, démence *f*; **2**† Jur démence *f*; **3** fig folie *f*.

lunar /ˈluːnə(r)/ *adj* [*rock, sea, crater, orbit*] lunaire; [*eclipse*] de lune; [*landscape*] fig lunaire; **~ month** mois *m* lunaire, lunaison *f*; **~ landing** atterrissage *m* sur la lune, alunissage *m* controv; **~ module** module *m* lunaire.

lunatic /ˈluːnətɪk/ **I** *n* **1**† Med dément/-e *m/f*, aliéné/-e *m/f*; **2**† Jur dément/-e *m/f*; **3** fig fou/folle *m/f*; **he drives like a ~!** il conduit comme un fou or un dingue○!
II *adj* Med, Jur dément; fig [*person*] fou/folle; [*plan, idea, behaviour*] démentiel/-ielle.

lunatic: **~ asylum**† *n* asile *m* d'aliénés†; **~ fringe** *n* péj les extrémistes *mfpl*, les jusqu'au-boutistes *mfpl*.

lunch /lʌntʃ/ **I** *n* déjeuner *m*; **to have ~** déjeuner; **to eat sth for ~** manger qch au déjeuner; **I often go out for ~** je déjeune souvent dehors; **to take sb out for** ou **to ~** emmener qn déjeuner au restaurant; **come round for ~** viens déjeuner (à la maison); **she's gone to ~**, **she's at ~** elle est partie déjeuner; **I'll take my ~ early** je vais déjeuner tôt; **~!, time for ~!** à table!; **to close for ~** fermer le midi; **the bar does good ~es** le bar sert de bons repas le midi.
II *vi* déjeuner (**on, off** de).
IDIOMS **out to ~**○ dingue○; **there's no such thing as a free ~** on ne fait jamais rien pour rien.

lunch: **~ basket** *n* panier-repas *m*; **~box** *n* boîte *f* à sandwichs; **~break** *n* pause-déjeuner *f*.

luncheon /ˈlʌntʃən/ *n* sout déjeuner *m*.
luncheon: **~ meat** *n* ≈ viande *f* en conserve; **~ voucher**, **LV** *n* ticket-repas *m*, ticket-restaurant® *m*.
lunch hour *n* heure *f* du déjeuner.
lunchtime /ˈlʌntʃtaɪm/ **I** *n* heure *f* du déjeuner.
II *modif* [*news, edition*] de midi; [*speech, concert*] qui a lieu pendant l'heure du déjeuner.
lung /lʌŋ/ **I** *n* poumon *m*; **to have a good pair of ~s** hum avoir de la voix or du poumon.
II *modif* [*disease*] pulmonaire; [*transplant*] du poumon.
lung cancer *n* cancer *m* du poumon.
lunge /lʌndʒ/ **I** *n* **1** (movement) brusque mouvement *m* vers l'avant; **he made a desperate ~ for the ball** il fit un bond désespéré vers la balle; **she made a ~ for him with her fist** elle a fait un mouvement en avant pour lui donner un coup de poing; **2** (fencing) botte *f*; **3** Equit longe *f*.
II *vtr* faire tourner [qch] à la longe [*horse*].
III *vi* **1** gen bondir (**for** sur; **at, towards** GB vers; **forward** en avant); **2** (in fencing) porter or pousser une botte (**at** à).
lung: **~-power** *n* puissance *f* vocale; **~ specialist** *n* pneumologue *mf*.
lunk○ /lʌŋk/ *n* (also **lunkhead**○ /ˈlʌŋkhed/ US) balourd/-e *m*/*f*.
lunula /ˈluːnjʊlə, US ˈluːnʊlə/ *n* lunule *f*.
lupin /ˈluːpɪn/ *n* lupin *m*.
lurch /lɜːtʃ/ **I** *n* **1** lit (of vehicle) embardée *f*; **to give a ~** faire une embardée; **2** fig écart *m*.
II *vi* **1** lit [*person, vehicle*] tanguer; **to ~ forward** ou **along** s'avancer en tanguant; **to ~ to a halt** faire une embardée et s'arrêter; **2** fig **to ~ to the left/right** Pol faire un écart sur la gauche/droite; **to ~ between** balancer entre; **to ~ back to sth** retourner vers qch.
IDIOMS **to leave sb in the ~** laisser qn dans une situation difficile.
lurcher /ˈlɜːtʃə(r)/ *n* GB chien *m* de chasse (*croisé entre un collie et un lévrier*).
lure /lʊə(r)/ **I** *n* **1** (attraction) attrait *m* (**of** de); **2** Hunt, Fishg leurre *m*.
II *vtr* attirer (**with** avec); **to ~ sb into a trap/a car** attirer qn dans un piège/une voiture; **to ~ sb into doing sth** amener qn à faire qch par la ruse; **they ~d him out of his house** ils ont réussi à le faire sortir de chez lui par la ruse; **to ~ sb away from her studies** détourner qn de ses études.
lurex® /ˈlʊəreks/ **I** *n* lurex® *m*.
II *modif* [*dress, etc*] en lurex.
lurgy○ /ˈlɜːgɪ/ *n* GB **to have the dreaded ~** avoir attrapé le microbe à son tour○.
lurid /ˈlʊərɪd/ *adj* **1** [*colour*] criard; [*sky*] sanglant; **2** [*description, detail, past*] épouvantable.
lurk /lɜːk/ **I** *vi* [*person*] être tapi; [*danger, fear, suspicion*] menacer.
II lurking *pres p adj* [*doubt, fear, suspicion*] persistant.
luscious /ˈlʌʃəs/ *adj* [*food*] succulent; [*woman*]○ pulpeux/-euse.
lush /lʌʃ/ **I**● *n* poivrot/-ote○ *m*/*f*.
II *adj* [*grass*] gras/grasse; [*vegetation*] luxuriant; [*hotel, surroundings*] luxueux/-euse.
lust /lʌst/ **I** *n* gen désir *m* (**for** de); (deadly sin) luxure *f*; **the ~ for power** la soif du pouvoir.
II *vi* **to ~ for** ou **after sb/sth** convoiter qn/qch.
luster *n* US = **lustre**.
lustful /ˈlʌstfl/ *adj* concupiscent.
lustfully /ˈlʌstfəlɪ/ *adv* avec concupiscence.
lustily /ˈlʌstɪlɪ/ *adv* avec vigueur.
lustre GB, **luster** US /ˈlʌstə(r)/ *n* éclat *m*.
lustreless GB, **lusterless** US /ˈlʌstəlɪs/ *adj* sans éclat.
lustreware GB, **lusterware** US /ˈlʌstəweə(r)/ *n* poterie *f* à reflet métallique.
lustrous /ˈlʌstrəs/ *adj* littér brillant.
lusty /ˈlʌstɪ/ *adj* vigoureux/-euse.
lute /luːt/ ▶ **1481** *n* luth *m*.
lutenist /ˈluːtənɪst/ ▶ **1692**, **1481** *n* luthiste *mf*.
Lutheran /ˈluːθərən/ **I** *n* Luthérien/-ienne *m*/*f*.
II *adj* luthérien.
Lutheranism /ˈluːθərənɪzəm/ *n* luthéranisme *m*.
luv○ /lʌv, lʊv/ *n* GB mon petit monsieur○/ma petite dame○ *m*/*f*.
Luxembourg /ˈlʌksəmbɜːg/ ▶ **1131** *pr n* Luxembourg *m*; **the Grand Duchy of ~** le grand-duché de Luxembourg.
luxuriance /lʌgˈzjʊərɪəns/ *n* luxuriance *f*.
luxuriant /lʌgˈzjʊərɪənt/ *adj* luxuriant.
luxuriate /lʌgˈzjʊərɪeɪt/ *vi* **to ~ in** s'abandonner avec délices à [*warmth, bath*]; savourer [*freedom, attention*].
luxurious /lʌgˈzjʊərɪəs/ *adj* [*apartment, lifestyle*] de luxe (*never after v*); [*heat, bath*] voluptueux/-euse; **his apartment is ~** son appartement est luxueux.
luxuriously /lʌgˈzjʊərɪəslɪ/ *adv* [*furnish, decorate*] luxueusement; [*live*] dans le luxe; [*yawn, stretch*] voluptueusement.
luxuriousness /lʌgˈzjʊərɪəsnɪs/ *n* luxe *m*.
luxury /ˈlʌkʃərɪ/ **I** *n* (all contexts) luxe *m*; **to have/enjoy the ~ of doing** avoir/se payer le luxe de faire; **a life of ~** une vie de luxe; **in (the lap of) ~** dans le luxe.
II *modif* [*product, holiday, accommodation*] de luxe; **~ goods** produits de luxe.
LV *n* GB *abrév* ▶ **luncheon voucher**.
LW *n* Radio (*abrév* = **long wave**) GO *fpl*.
lycanthropy /laɪˈkænθrəpɪ/ *n* lycanthropie *f*.
lyceum /laɪˈsɪəm/ *n* **1** (building) salle *f* publique; **2** US (organization) organisme *m* culturel.
lychee /ˈlaɪtʃiː, ˌlaɪˈtʃiː/ *n* litchi *m*.
lychgate /ˈlɪtʃgeɪt/ *n* porche *m* d'entrée du cimetière.
Lycra® /ˈlaɪkrə/ *n* Lycra® *m*.
lye /laɪ/ *n* Chem lessive *f*.
lying /ˈlaɪɪŋ/ *n* ¢ mensonges *mpl*.
lying-in† *n* accouchement *m*.
lymph /lɪmf/ *n* lymphe *f*.
lymphatic /lɪmˈfætɪk/ *adj* Anat, fig lymphatique.
lymphatic drainage (**massage**) *n* drainage *m* lymphatique; **to give sb ~** faire un drainage lymphatique à qn.
lymph node *n* ganglion *m* lymphatique.
lymphocyte /ˈlɪmfəsaɪt/ *n* lymphocyte *m*.
lymphoid /ˈlɪmfɔɪd/ *adj* lymphoïde.
lymphosarcoma /ˌlɪmfəʊsɑːˈkəʊmə/ *n* (*pl* **-mata**) lymphosarcome *m*.
lynch /lɪntʃ/ *vtr* lyncher.
lynching /ˈlɪntʃɪŋ/ *n* lynchage *m*.
lynch: **~ law** *n* loi *f* de Lynch; **~ mob** *n* lyncheurs *mpl*.
lynx /lɪŋks/ *n* (*pl* **-xes**) lynx *m*.
lynx-eyed /ˈlɪŋksaɪd/ *adj* [*person*] aux yeux de lynx; **to be ~** avoir des yeux de lynx.
Lyons /ˈliːɔːŋ/ ▶ **1818** *pr n* Lyon.
lyophilize /laɪˈɒfɪlaɪz/ *vtr* lyophiliser.
lyre /ˈlaɪə(r)/ ▶ **1481** *n* lyre *f*.
lyrebird /ˈlaɪəbɜːd/ *n* oiseau-lyre *m*.
lyric /ˈlɪrɪk/ **I** *n* Literat poème *m* lyrique.
II lyrics *npl* (of song) paroles *fpl* (*d'une chanson*).
III *adj* Mus, Poetry lyrique.
lyrical /ˈlɪrɪkl/ *adj* (all contexts) lyrique; **to wax ~** (**about** ou **over sth**) disserter avec lyrisme (sur qch).
lyrically /ˈlɪrɪklɪ/ *adv* avec lyrisme.
lyricism /ˈlɪrɪsɪzəm/ *n* (all contexts) lyrisme *m*.
lyricist /ˈlɪrɪsɪst/ ▶ **1692** *n* parolier/-ière *m*/*f*.
lyric-writer ▶ **1692** *n* parolier/-ière *m*/*f*.

Mm

m, **M** /em/ *n* **1** (letter) m, M *m*; **2 m** (*abrév écrite* = **metre(s)** GB, **meter(s)** US) m; **3 M** (*abrév* = **motorway**) autoroute *f*; **on the M3** sur l'autoroute M3; **4 m** *abrév écrite* = **mile(s)**; **5 m** *abrév écrite* = **million**.

ma○ /mɑ:/ *n* maman *f*.

MA *n* **1** (*abrév* = **Master of Arts**) ≈ maîtrise *f* de lettres; **2** US Post *abrév écrite* = **Massachusetts**.

ma'am /mæm, mɑ:m/ *abrév* ▶ **madam** 1.

mac○ /mæk/ *n* GB (*abrév* = **mackintosh**) imper○ *m*.

macabre /mə'kɑ:brə/ *adj* macabre.

macadam /mə'kædəm/ *n* macadam *m*.

macaroni /ˌmækə'rəʊnɪ/ *n* ¢ macaronis *mpl*.

macaronic /ˌmækə'rɒnɪk/ *adj* macaronique.

macaroni cheese *n* gratin *m* de macaronis.

macaroon /ˌmækə'ru:n/ *n* macaron *m*.

macaw /mə'kɔ:/ *n* ara macao *m*.

mace /meɪs/ *n* **1** (spice) macis *m*; **2** (ceremonial staff) masse *f*; **3** (weapon) masse *f* d'armes.

Mace® /meɪs/ **I** *n* gaz *m* lacrymogène.
II *vtr* (also **mace**) lancer du gaz lacrymogène sur [*crowd*].

Macedonia /ˌmæsɪ'dəʊnɪə/ *pr n* Macédoine *f*.

Macedonian /ˌmæsɪ'dəʊnɪən/ **I** *n* Macédonien/-ienne *m/f*.
II *adj* macédonien/-ienne.

macerate /'mæsəreɪt/ **I** *vtr* faire macérer.
II *vi* macérer.

Mach /mɑ:k, mæk/ *pr n* Mach; **~ one/two** Mach un/deux.

macher◐ /'mɑ:xə(r)/ *n* US huile○ *f*, grosse légume◐ *f*.

machete /mə'tʃetɪ, US mə'ʃetɪ/ *n* machette *f*.

Machiavelli /ˌmækɪə'velɪ/ *pr n* Machiavel.

Machiavellian /ˌmækɪə'velɪən/ *adj* machiavélique.

machination /ˌmækɪ'neɪʃn/ *n* machination *f*.

machine /mə'ʃi:n/ **I** *n* **1** (piece of equipment) machine *f* (**for doing** à faire); **sewing/washing ~** machine à coudre/à laver; **to operate a ~** faire fonctionner une machine; **by ~** à la machine; **2** fig (apparatus) machine *f*; **publicity/electoral ~** la machine publicitaire/électorale; **the Conservative Party ~** la machine administrative du parti conservateur.
II *vtr* Ind usiner.

machine: **~ age** *n* ère *f* de la machine; **~-assisted translation**, **MAT** *n* traduction *f* assistée par ordinateur, TAO *f*; **~ code** *n* Comput code *m* machine.

machine gun I *n* mitrailleuse *f*.
II machine-gun *vtr* (*p prés etc* **-nn-**) mitrailler.

machine: **~ intelligence** *n* intelligence *f* artificielle; **~ language** *n* Comput langage *m* machine; **~-made** *adj* fait à la machine; **~ operator** *n* Ind opérateur/-trice *m/f*.

machine-readable /məˌʃi:n'ri:dəbl/ *adj* Comput [*data, text*] directement exploitable; [*passport*] vérifiable par ordinateur; **in ~ form** directement exploitable.

machinery /mə'ʃi:nərɪ/ *n* ¢ **1** (equipment) machines *fpl*; (working parts) mécanisme *m*, rouages *mpl*; (operating lift etc) machinerie *f*; **a piece of ~** une machine; **heavy ~** machines *fpl* lourdes; **the ~ of justice** fig les rouages de la justice; **2** fig (apparatus) dispositifs *mpl*; **the ~ to deal with pollution** les dispositifs de lutte contre la pollution; **the ~ to settle industrial disputes** le système mis en place pour régler les conflits sociaux.

machine shop *n* atelier *m* d'usinage.

machine stitch I *n* point *m* (de piqûre) à la machine.
II machine-stitch *vtr* piquer à la machine.

machine: **~ tool** *n* machine-outil *f*; **~ tool operator** ▶ **1692** *n* opérateur/-trice *m/f* (de machine-outil); **~ translation**, **MT** *n* traduction *f* automatique.

machinist /mə'ʃi:nɪst/ ▶ **1692** *n* opérateur/-trice *m/f*.

machismo /mə'tʃɪzməʊ, -'kɪzməʊ/ *n* machisme *m*.

Mach number *n* nombre *m* de Mach.

macho /'mætʃəʊ/ *adj* pej macho; (manly) viril; **a real ~ man** péj un vrai macho.

mackerel /'mækrəl/ *n* maquereau *m*.

mackerel sky *n* ciel *m* moutonné.

mackintosh, **macintosh** /'mækɪntɒʃ/ *n* imperméable *m*.

macramé /mə'krɑ:mɪ/ **I** *n* macramé *m*.
II *modif* [*belt, wall hanging, work*] en macramé.

macro /'mækrəʊ/ **I** *n* Comput macro *f*.
II macro+ (*dans composés*) macro-.

macrobiotic /ˌmækrəʊbaɪ'ɒtɪk/ *adj* macrobiotique.

macrobiotics /ˌmækrəʊbaɪ'ɒtɪks/ *n* (+ *v sg*) macrobiotique *f*.

macrocosm /'mækrəʊkɒzəm/ *n* macrocosme *m*.

macroeconomic /ˌmækrəʊi:kə'nɒmɪk, -ekə-/ *adj* macroéconomique.

macroeconomics /ˌmækrəʊi:kə'nɒmɪks, -ekə-/ *n* (+ *v sg*) macroéconomie *f*.

macrolinguistics /ˌmækrəʊlɪŋ'gwɪstɪks/ *n* (+ *v sg*) macrolinguistique *f*.

macron /'mækrɒn/ *n* trait *m* supérieur.

macrophage /'mækrəʊfeɪdʒ/ *n* macrophage *m*.

macrophotography /ˌmækrəʊfə'tɒgrəfɪ/ *n* macrophotographie *f*.

macroscopic /ˌmækrəʊ'skɒpɪk/ *adj* macroscopique.

mad /mæd/ *adj* **1** (insane) [*person*] fou/folle; (enraged) [*dog, bull*] enragé; **to be ~ with** être fou de [*grief, pain, joy*]; **you must be ~!** tu es (complètement) fou!; **to go ~** (insane) devenir fou/folle; **it's nationalism gone ~** fig c'est du nationalisme poussé à l'extrême; **are you/is he ~?** tu es/il est fou or malade?; **of course not, do you think I'm ~?** mais non, tu me prends pour un fou?; **2** (foolish) [*idea, hope, feeling, scheme*] insensé; **it is ~ to do** ou **doing** c'est fou or de la folie de faire; **he is/they are ~ to do** c'est de la folie de sa/leur part de faire; **you'd be ~ to give up your job** ce serait fou de démissionner; **I'm ~ even to think of it** je suis fou d'en avoir eu l'idée ; **to go ~**○ (spend money) faire des folies; **3** (angry) [*person*] (*jamais épith*) très en colère, furieux/-ieuse; **to be ~ at** ou **with sb** être très en colère contre qn; **to get ~ at** ou **with sb** se mettre en colère contre qn; **they are ~ at us for coming back late** ils sont furieux que nous soyons rentrés tard or parce que nous sommes rentrés tard; **to be ~ about sth** être en colère à cause de qch; **to be ~ (that)...** être furieux que... (+ *subj*); **she'd be ~ if she knew** elle serait furieuse si elle l'apprenait; **to go ~**○ être fou de rage; **to make sb ~** exaspérer qn; **it makes me ~ to think of it!** ça me rend furieux d'y penser!; **to drive sb ~** rendre qn fou (de rage); **4**○ (enthusiastic) **~ about** ou **on** fou de [*person, hobby, sport, music*]; **I'm not ~ about the idea** l'idée ne m'emballe○ pas tellement; **he's not ~ about the teacher/about fish** il n'aime pas beaucoup le professeur/le poisson; **to be horse-/football-/movie-~** être un passionné or un mordu○ des chevaux/de football/de cinéma; **she's money-~!** elle adore l'argent!; **5** (frantic) [*dash, panic, race, traffic*] infernal; **to be ~ for** être fou de [*film, popstar*]; réclamer [*food, blood, goods*]; **to be in a ~ rush** être très pressé; **it was a ~ scramble to finish on time** ça a été la panique○ pour finir en temps voulu; **we made a ~ dash for the bus** on a couru comme des fous pour attraper le bus.
IDIOMS **to work/laugh/run like ~** travailler/rire/courir comme un fou/une folle.

MAD *n* (*abrév* = **mutual assured destruction**) destruction *f* mutuelle assurée.

Madagascar /ˌmædə'gæskə/ ▶ **1131** *pr n* Madagascar *m*.

madam /'mædəm/ **1** (also **Madam**) (form of address) madame *f*; (in titles) Madame *f*; **Madam Chairman** Madame la Présidente; **Dear Madam** Madame; **2**○ GB (young woman) (stuck up) pimbêche○ *f*; (cheeky) insolente *f*; **3** (in brothel) mère *f* maquerelle.

madcap /'mædkæp/ **I** *n* écervelé/-e *m/f*.
II *adj* (*épith*) [*person, scheme, idea*] insensé.

mad cow disease *n* maladie *f* de la vache folle.

madden /'mædn/ *vtr* [*attitude, nuisance, situation*] exaspérer [*person*]; [*pain, heat, insects*] rendre [qn] fou [*person*]; **it ~s me to do/that** ça m'exaspère de faire/que (+ *subj*).

maddening /'mædnɪŋ/ *adj* [*person, characteristic*] énervant; [*delay, noise, situation, behaviour*] exaspérant; **it's ~ to** c'est exaspérant de.

maddeningly /'mædnɪŋlɪ/ *adv* **~ slow/inefficient/precise** d'une lenteur/inefficacité/précision exaspérante; **a ~ superior tone** un ton supérieur énervant; **he's always ~ late** c'est exaspérant, il est toujours en retard.

made /meɪd/ **I** *pret, pp* ▶ **make**.

II *adj* **to be ~** avoir réussi; **he's a ~ man** c'est un homme qui a réussi.
III **-made** (*dans composés*) **foreign-/Italian-~** fabriqué à l'étranger/en Italie.
IDIOMS **he's got it ~**○ (sure to succeed) sa réussite est assurée; (has succeeded) il n'a plus à s'en faire.

Madeira /mə'dɪərə/ ▶1381 *pr n* **1** Geog Madère; **2** (wine) madère *m*.

Madeira cake *n* GB Culin ≈ quatre-quarts *m*.

made: **~-to-measure** *adj* [*garment*] sur mesure; **~-to-order** *adj* [*garment, dish*] sur commande.

made-up /ˌmeɪd'ʌp/ *adj* **1** (wearing make-up) maquillé; **heavily ~** très maquillé; **2** (invented) [*story*] fabriqué; **3** [*road*] goudronné; **4** [*garment*] de prêt-à-porter; **5**○ GB (delighted) très content.

madhouse○ /'mædhaʊs/ *n* **1**† (asylum) asile *m* de fous†; **2** (uproar) maison *f* de fous.

Madison Avenue /ˌmædɪsn 'ævɪnjuː, US -nuː/ *pr n*: *avenue de New York célèbre pour ses agences de publicité et de relations publiques*.

madly /'mædlɪ/ *adv* **1** (frantically) [*scribble, gesticulate, rush around*] frénétiquement; **2** (extremely) [*amusing, exciting, extravagant, jealous*] follement; **~ in love (with sb)** follement or éperdument amoureux (de qn).

madman○ /'mædmən/ *n* fou○ *m*, malade○ *m*.

madness /'mædnɪs/ *n* lit, fig folie *f*; **it is/it would be ~ to do** c'est/ce serait de la folie de faire; **it is ~ for him to ignore the warning** il est fou de ne pas tenir compte de cet avertissement.
IDIOMS **there is method in his ~** il y a de la cohérence jusque dans sa folie; **that way ~ lies** littér c'est la voie ouverte à l'aberration.

Madonna /mə'dɒnə/ *n* Madone *f*.

madras /mə'dræs/ **I** *n* **1** (fabric) madras *m*; **2** GB Culin curry *m* (*très épicé*).
II *modif* [*shirt, scarf*] en madras.

Madrid /mə'drɪd/ ▶1818 *pr n* Madrid.

madrigal /'mædrɪgl/ *n* madrigal *m*.

madwoman○ /'mædwʊmən/ *n* folle○ *f*, malade○ *f*.

maelstrom /'meɪlstrəm/ *n* lit, fig maelström *m*.

maestro /'maɪstrəʊ/ *n* maestro *m*.

mae west†, **Mae West**† /ˌmeɪ 'west/ *n* gilet *m* de sauvetage (gonflable).

MAFF *n* GB (*abrév* = **Ministry of Agriculture, Fisheries and Food**) ministère *m* de l'Agriculture, de la Pêche et de l'Alimentation.

mafia, **Mafia** /'mæfɪə, US 'mɑː-/ **I** *n* **the ~** la Mafia; fig la mafia *f*.
II *modif* [*activity, gangster, killing*] de la Mafia.

mafioso /ˌmæfɪ'əʊsəʊ/ *n* (*pl* **-si** ou **-sos**) mafioso *m*.

mag○ /mæg/ *n*: *abrév* ▶ **magazine** 1.

magazine /ˌmægə'ziːn/ *n* **1** Journ revue *f*; (mainly photos) magazine *m*; **computer/glossy ~** revue d'informatique/de luxe; **monthly ~** revue mensuelle; **fashion/photography ~** magazine de mode/de photographie; **women's ~** journal *m* féminin; **2** (on radio, TV) magazine *m*; **3** (of gun, camera) magasin *m*; **4** (arms store) arsenal *m* d'artillerie.

magenta /mə'dʒentə/ ▶1104 **I** *n* magenta *m*.
II *adj* magenta *inv*.

Maggiore /ˌmædʒɪ'ɔːrɪ/ ▶1400 *pr n* **Lake ~** le Lac Majeur.

maggot /'mægət/ *n* (in fruit) ver *m*; (for fishing) asticot *m*.

maggoty /'mægətɪ/ *adj* [*cheese, meat*] plein de vers; [*fruit*] véreux/-euse.

Maghreb /'mʌgrəb/ *pr n* **the ~** le Maghreb.

Maghrebi /'mʌgrəbɪ/ **I** *n* Maghrébin/-e *m*/*f*.
II *adj* maghrébin.

Magi /'meɪdʒaɪ/ *npl* **the ~** les Rois *mpl* mages.

magic /'mædʒɪk/ **I** *n* **1** (supernatural power) magie *f*; **to believe in ~** croire à la magie; **as if by ~** comme par enchantement; **to practise ~** pratiquer la magie; **it works like ~!** c'est miraculeux!; **to work ~** faire des miracles; **black/white ~** magie *f* noire/blanche; **to do sth by ~** faire qch par magie; **2** (enchantment) magie *f* (**of** de).
II *adj* magique; **it's ~!** c'est formidable!; **the Magic Flute** la Flûte enchantée.

magical /'mædʒɪkl/ *adj* **1** (supernatural) [*properties, powers, transformation*] magique; **2** (enchanting) [*moment*] magique; [*week, stay*] merveilleux/-euse; **the landscape has a ~ quality** c'est un paysage enchanteur.

magically /'mædʒɪklɪ/ *adv* [*disappear, transform*] lit par magie; fig comme par magie or enchantement.

magic: **~ carpet** *n* tapis *m* volant; **~ circle** *n* cercle *m* magique.

magician /mə'dʒɪʃn/ *n* (wizard) magicien *m*; (entertainer) illusionniste *m*.

magic: **~ lantern** *n* lanterne *f* magique; **Magic Marker**® *n* marqueur *m*; **~ potion** *n* potion *f* magique; **~ spell** *n* formule *f* magique; **~ square** *n* carré *m* magique; **~ wand** *n* baguette *f* magique.

magisterial /ˌmædʒɪ'stɪərɪəl/ *adj* **1** (authoritative) magistral; **2** Jur [*office, duties*] de magistrat.

magistracy /'mædʒɪstrəsɪ/ *n* (all contexts) magistrature *f* (*nonprofessionnelle*).

magistrate /'mædʒɪstreɪt/ ▶1692 *n* magistrat *m* (*nonprofessionnel*); **to appear before (the) ~s** comparaître devant les magistrats.

magistrates' court, Magistrates' Court *n* ≈ tribunal *m* de police.

magma /'mægmə/ *n* magma *m*.

Magna Carta /ˌmægnə 'kɑːtə/ *n* **the ~** la Grande Charte.

magna cum laude /ˌmægnə kʊm 'laʊdeɪ/ *adv* US Univ **to graduate ~** obtenir son diplôme avec mention très bien.

magnanimity /ˌmægnə'nɪmətɪ/ *n* magnanimité *f*.

magnanimous /mæg'nænɪməs/ *adj* magnanime; **that's very ~ of you!** iron c'est trop généreux de ta part iron.

magnanimously /mæg'nænɪməslɪ/ *adv* avec magnanimité.

magnate /'mægneɪt/ *n* magnat *m*; **oil ~** magnat du pétrole; **property ~** grand propriétaire; **shipping ~** armateur *m*.

magnesia /mæg'niːʃə/ *n* magnésie *f*.

magnesium /mæg'niːzɪəm/ *n* magnésium *m*.

magnet /'mægnɪt/ *n* **1** lit aimant *m*; **2** fig pôle *m* d'attraction (**for** pour).

magnetic /mæg'netɪk/ *adj* **1** [*block, rod*] aimanté; [*force, properties*] magnétique; **2** [*appeal, smile*] irrésistible.

magnetically /mæg'netɪklɪ/ *adv* **1** lit par magnétisme; **2** fig irrésistiblement.

magnetic: **~ compass** *n* boussole *f*; **~ disk** *n* disque *m* magnétique; **~ field** *n* champ *m* magnétique; **~ north** *n* nord *m* magnétique; **~ resonance** *n* résonance *f* magnétique; **~ resonance imaging** *n* imagerie *f* par résonance magnétique; **~ storm** *n* orage *m* magnétique; **~ tape** *n* bande *f* magnétique.

magnetism /'mægnɪtɪzəm/ *n* lit, fig magnétisme *m*; **animal/personal/sexual ~** magnétisme animal/personnel/sexuel.

magnetize /'mægnɪtaɪz/ *vtr* **1** lit aimanter; **2** fig magnétiser.

magneto /mæg'niːtəʊ/ *n* magnéto *f*.

Magnificat /mæg'nɪfɪkæt/ *n* **the ~** le Magnificat.

magnification /ˌmægnɪfɪ'keɪʃn/ *n* (all contexts) grossissement *m*; **under ~** au microscope.

magnificence /mæg'nɪfɪsns/ *n* (of parade, clothes, building) magnificence *f*; (of landscape, natural feature) splendeur *f*.

magnificent /mæg'nɪfɪsnt/ *adj* magnifique.

magnificently /mæg'nɪfɪsntlɪ/ *adv* **1** [*play, perform*] magnifiquement; **2** [*dressed, decorated*] superbement.

magnify /'mægnɪfaɪ/ *vtr* **1** [*microscope, lens*] grossir; **2** (exaggerate) exagérer.

magnifying glass *n* loupe *f*.

magnitude /'mægnɪtjuːd, US -tuːd/ *n* **1** (of problem, disaster) ampleur *f*; **of the first ~** de la première importance; **an order of ~** un ordre de grandeur; **2** Astron magnitude *f*.

magnolia /mæg'nəʊlɪə/ ▶1104 **I** *n* **1** Bot (also **~ tree**) magnolia *m*; **2** (colour) crème *m*.
II *adj* (colour) crème.

magnum /'mægnəm/ *n* Wine magnum *m*.

magnum opus /ˌmægnəm 'əʊpəs/ *n* œuvre *f* maîtresse.

magpie /'mægpaɪ/ *n* **1** Zool pie *f*; **2** fig (person) collectionneur/-euse *m*/*f* d'objets hétéroclites; **3** US (chatterbox) moulin *m* à paroles.

mag tape○ *n*: *abrév* ▶ **magnetic tape**.

Magyar /'mægjɑː(r)/ ▶1486, 1402 **I** *n* **1** (person) Magyar *mf*; **2** (language) magyar *m*.
II *adj* magyar.

maharajah /ˌmɑːhə'rɑːdʒə/ *n* maharajah *m*.

maharani /ˌmɑːhə'rɑːniː/ *n* maharani *f*.

maharishi /ˌmɑːhə'rɪʃɪ/ *n* maharishi *m*.

mahatma /mə'hætmə/ *n* mahatma *m*; **Mahatma Gandhi** le mahatma Gandhi.

mah-jong(g), /ˌmɑː'dʒɒŋ/ ▶1282 *n* mahjong *m*.

mahogany /mə'hɒgənɪ/ **I** *n* (wood, tree, colour) acajou *m*.
II *modif* [*chair, table, chest*] d'acajou, en acajou.
III *adj* [*hair, colour*] acajou.

Mahomet /mə'hɒmɪt/ *pr n* = **Mohammed**.

Mahometan† /mə'hɒmɪtn/ **I** *n* mahométan/-e† *m*/*f*.
II *adj* mahométan/-e†.

mahout /mə'haʊt/ *n* cornac *m*.

maid /meɪd/ *n* **1** (in house) bonne *f*; (in hotel) femme *f* de chambre; **~ of all work** bonne à tout faire; **~ of honour** demoiselle *f* d'honneur; **2**‡ (virgin) pucelle† *f*.

maiden /'meɪdn/ **I** *n* **1** littér jeune fille *f*; **2** Turf *cheval qui n'a jamais remporté de course*; **3** (also **~ over**) (in cricket) *partie d'un match de cricket pendant laquelle aucun point n'est marqué*.
II *adj* [*flight, voyage*] inaugural.

maiden: **~ aunt**† *n* tante *f* célibataire; **~hair** *n* (also **~ fern**) capillaire *m*.

maidenhead‡ /'meɪdnhed/ *n* **1** (virginity) innocence† *f* (*d'une jeune fille*); **2** (hymen) hymen *m*.

maidenhood‡ /'meɪdnhʊd/ *n* **1** (time) adolescence *f* (*d'une jeune fille*); **2** (state) virginité *f* (*d'une jeune fille*).

maiden: **~ name** *n* nom *m* de jeune fille; **~ speech** *n* discours *m* inaugural.

maidservant /'meɪdsɜːvənt/ *n* servante *f*.

mail /meɪl/ **I** *n* **1** (postal service) poste *f*; **by ~** par la poste; **your cheque is in the ~** votre chèque a été posté; **2** (correspondence) courrier *m*; **3** Mil Hist **a coat/gloves of ~** une cotte/des gants de mailles.
II *vtr* envoyer, expédier [*letter, parcel*]; **to ~ a letter to sb, to ~ sb a letter** envoyer ou expédier une lettre à qn.

mailbag /'meɪlbæg/ *n* **1** (for transport) sac *m* postal; **2** (of postman) sacoche *f* (du facteur); **3** (correspondence) courrier *m*.

mail bomb *n* colis *m* piégé.

mailbox /'meɪlbɒks/ *n* surtout US **1** (for posting) boîte *f* aux lettres; **2** (for delivery) boîte *f* à lettres.

mail: **~ car** *n* US wagon-poste *m*; **~ carrier** *n* US préposé/-e *m/f*.

mail coach *n* **1** Rail wagon-poste *m*; **2** Hist Transp malle-poste *f*.

mail delivery *n* distribution *f* (du courrier).

mailer /ˈmeɪlə(r)/ *n* US enveloppe *f* d'expédition.

mailing /ˈmeɪlɪŋ/ *n* **1** gen (dispatch) envoi *m* (par la poste); **2** Advertg publipostage *m*, mailing *m*.

mailing: **~ address** *n* adresse *f* postale; **~ house** *n* (company) société *f* de routage; (department of company) service *m* du courrier; **~ list** *n* Comm fichier-clientèle *m*; Theat liste *f* d'abonnés.

mail: **~man** /ˈmeɪlmən/ ▶1692 *n* US (*pl* **-men**) facteur *m*; **~-merge** *n* Comput fusion *f* avec un fichier d'adresses.

mail order /ˈmeɪl ɔːdə(r)/ **I** *n* commande *f* par correspondance; **to buy/sell (by) ~** acheter/vendre par correspondance; **available by ~** disponible sur commande.

II *modif* [*business, catalogue, goods, service*] de vente *f* par correspondance.

mail room *n* (service *m* du) courrier *m*.

mail shot *n* publipostage *m*; **to do a ~** faire du publipostage.

mail: **~ slot** *n* boîte *f* à lettres; **~ train** *n* train *m* postal.

mail van *n* **1** (in train) wagon-poste *m*; **2** (delivery vehicle) camionnette *f* de la poste.

maim /meɪm/ **I** *vtr* estropier.

II maimed *pp adj* [*child, soldier*] mutilé; **~ed for life** mutilé à vie.

main /meɪn/ **I** *n* **1** (pipe, conduit) (for water, gas, electricity) canalisation *f*; (for sewage) égout *m* (collecteur); **water/gas ~** canalisation *f* d'eau/de gaz; **2** (network) (also **mains**) (of water, gas, electricity) réseau *m* de distribution; (of sewage) réseau *m* d'évacuation; **gas from the ~s** gaz de ville; **electricity from the ~s** électricité du secteur; **water from the ~s** eau courante; **to turn sth on/off at the ~(s)** mettre/couper qch (au compteur); **to work** ou **run off the ~(s)** fonctionner sur secteur; **3**† littér (sea) large *m*; **on the ~** au large; **4**‡ = **mainland**.

II mains *modif* [*gas*] de ville; [*electricity*] du secteur; [*water*] courant; [*radio, appliance*] sur secteur; [*plug, lead, voltage*] de secteur.

III *adj* [*aim, airport, character, concern, problem, building, entrance, meal, clause*] principal; **the ~ thing is to...** le principal, c'est de...; **the ~ thing to do is...** la chose principale à faire, c'est...; **that's the ~ thing!** c'est le principal!

IDIOMS **in the ~** dans l'ensemble.

main bearing *n* Aut palier *m*.

main chance *n* grande occasion *f*.

IDIOMS **to have an eye for** ou **to the ~** guetter la grande occasion.

main: **~ course** *n* plat *m* principal; **~ deck** *n* pont *m* supérieur; **~ drag**○ *n* grand-rue *f*.

Maine /meɪn/ ▶1744 *pr n* US Maine *m*; **in ~** dans le Maine.

Maine-et-Loire ▶1163 *pr n* Maine-et-Loire *m*; **in/to ~** dans le Maine-et-Loire.

mainframe /ˈmeɪnfreɪm/ **I** *n* (also **~ computer**, **~ processor**) ordinateur *m* central.

II *modif* [*system, network*] informatiquement centralisé; [*market*] d'informatique centralisée.

mainland /ˈmeɪnlənd/ **I** *n* territoire *m* continental; **from/to/on the ~** depuis/vers/sur le continent; **the Chinese ~, the ~ of China** la Chine continentale.

II *modif* [*China, Europe, town, government*] continental.

mainlander /ˈmeɪnləndə(r)/ *n* continental/-e *m/f*.

main line I /ˌmeɪnˈlaɪn/ *n* Rail grande ligne *f*; **on the ~** sur la grande ligne (**between** entre; **from** de; **to** à).

II /ˌmeɪnˈlaɪn/ *modif* Rail [*station, terminus, train*] de grande ligne.

III○ **mainline** /ˈmeɪnlaɪn/ *vtr* argot des drogués se shooter○ à [*heroin, cocaine*].

IV○ **mainline** /ˈmeɪnlaɪn/ *vi* argot des drogués se piquer.

mainliner○ /ˈmeɪnlaɪnə(r)/ *n* **1** (of drugs) argot des drogués drogué/-e *m/f* qui se pique, shooté/-e○ *m/f*; **2** (person of high status) personne *f* appartenant à la haute○.

mainly /ˈmeɪnlɪ/ *adv* surtout, essentiellement; **I read novels ~** je lis surtout des romans; **I read ~** je lis la plupart du temps.

main: **~ man**○ *n* US copain *m*, pote○ *m*; **~mast** *n* grand mât *m*; **~ memory** *n* Comput mémoire *f* centrale; **~ office** *n* (of company, organization, newspaper) siège *m* (social).

main road *n* (through country, region, estate) route *f* principale; (in town) grande rue *f* (**through** qui traverse; **out of** qui sort de; **into** qui entre dans); **off the ~** en retrait de la grand-route.

main: **~sail** *n* grand-voile *f*; **~ sheet** *n* Naut écoute *f* (*de la grand-voile*).

mainspring /ˈmeɪnsprɪŋ/ *n* **1** fig (pivotal element) (of action, plot) motif *m* essentiel (**of** de); (of life) raison *f* d'être (**of** de); **2** (of watch) ressort *m* principal.

mainstay /ˈmeɪnsteɪ/ *n* **1** fig (major element) (person) pilier *m* (**of** de); (thing) base *f* (**of** de); **2** Naut étai *m* de grand mât.

mainstream /ˈmeɪnstriːm/ **I** *n* (*tjrs sg*) courant *m* dominant (**of** de); **to be in the ~** être dans le courant dominant.

II *adj* **1** (conventional) traditionnel/-elle; **2** (main) principal; **3** Sch [*curriculum, education, school*] classique; **4** Mus **~ jazz** jazz mainstream.

III *vtr* US Sch intégrer dans le cycle scolaire normal.

mainstreaming /ˈmeɪnstriːmɪŋ/ *n* US, Sch intégration *f* dans le cycle scolaire normal.

main street *n* rue *f* principale.

maintain /meɪnˈteɪn/ *vtr* **1** (keep steady) maintenir [*temperature, confidence, control, services, prices, investment, value, speed, standards*]; **2** (support) subvenir aux besoins de [*children, spouse*]; entretenir [*army*]; garder [*lifestyle*]; **the farm can ~ a family of 6** la ferme peut faire vivre une famille de 6 personnes; **3** (look after) entretenir [*machine, road*]; **4** (assert) continuer à affirmer [*innocence*]; **to ~ that** soutenir que.

maintained school *n* GB Sch école *f* publique.

maintenance /ˈmeɪntənəns/ *n* **1** (upkeep) (of machine, road, building) entretien *m* (**of** de); **2** (of morale, standards etc) maintien *m* (**of** de); **3** Jur GB (alimony) pension *f* alimentaire; **to pay sb ~, to pay ~ to sb** verser une pension alimentaire à qn.

maintenance: **~ contract** *n* contrat *m* d'entretien; **~ crew** *n* équipe *f* d'entretien; **~ fees** *npl* frais *mpl* d'entretien; **~ grant** *n* (for student) bourse *f* (d'études); **~ man** *n* ouvrier *m* chargé de l'entretien; **~ order** *n* GB ordonnance *f* de versement de pension alimentaire.

Mainz /maɪnts/ ▶1818 *pr n* Mayence.

maisonette /ˌmeɪzəˈnet/ *n* duplex *m*.

maître d'hôtel /ˌmetrədəʊˈtel/ *n* **1** (in restaurant) maître *m* d'hôtel; **2** (in household) majordome *m*.

maize /meɪz/ *n* maïs *m*.

Maj *n*: *abrév écrite* = **Major**.

majestic /məˈdʒestɪk/ *adj* majestueux/-euse.

majestically /məˈdʒestɪklɪ/ *adv* majestueusement.

majesty /ˈmædʒəstɪ/ **I** *n* **1** (of building, ceremony) majesté *f*; (of scenery) grandeur *f*; **2** (royal authority) majesté *f*.

II *n* **Majesty** (in titles) **Her/His ~** sa Majesté; **yes, Your ~** oui, Votre Majesté; **Her/His ~'s government** le gouvernement britannique.

IDIOMS **to be detained at Her/His ~'s pleasure** sout être en or être envoyé en prison.

major /ˈmeɪdʒə(r)/ **I** *n* **1** Mil commandant *m*; **2 Major** (in titles) **Major Andrews** le commandant Andrews; **3** US Univ (subject) matière *f* principale; (student) **I'm a physics ~** ma matière principale est la physique; **4** Jur majeur/-e *m/f*; **5** Mus ton *m* majeur.

II *adj* **1** (important) [*change, championship, city, client, company, damage, decision, event, user*] important; [*crisis, contribution, difference, difficulty, effect, importance, role, work*] majeur; [*influence, significance*] capital; **a ~ operation, ~ surgery** Med une grosse opération; **2** (main) principal; **3** Mus majeur; **in a ~ key** en majeur; **4**† GB Sch **Jones ~** Jones aîné.

III *vi* US Univ **to ~ in** se spécialiser en.

Majorca /məˈjɔːkə, məˈdʒɔːkə/ ▶1381 *pr n* Majorque *f*; **in ~** à Majorque.

Majorcan /məˈjɔːkən, məˈdʒɔːkən/ **I** *n* Majorquin/-e *m/f*.

II *adj* majorquin.

majordomo /ˌmeɪdʒəˈdəʊməʊ/ *n* majordome *m* aussi hum.

majorette /ˌmeɪdʒəˈret/ *n* majorette *f*.

major-general /ˌmeɪdʒəˈdʒenrəl/ *n* Mil, Mil Naut général *m* de division.

majority /məˈdʒɒrətɪ, US -ˈdʒɔːr-/ **I** *n* **1** (greater part) (+ *v sg ou pl* GB) majorité *f* (**of** de); **the vast ~** la grande majorité; **an overwhelming ~** une majorité écrasante; **to be in a** ou **the ~** être en majorité; **the silent ~** la majorité silencieuse; **2** Pol majorité *f*; **to increase one's ~** augmenter sa majorité; **by a ~ of 50** à une majorité de 50; **a three to one/a two-thirds ~** une majorité de trois contre un/des deux-tiers; **a working ~** une majorité suffisante; **3** Jur majorité *f*.

II *modif* [*government, rule, shareholder*] majoritaire; [*support, view, opinion*] de la majorité; [*verdict*] rendu à la majorité; [*decision*] pris à la majorité.

major premise *n* Philos majeure *f*.

make /meɪk/ **I** *n* (brand) marque *f*; **what ~ is your car?** de quelle marque est ta voiture?; **what ~ of computer is it?** quelle est la marque de cet ordinateur?

II *vtr* (*prét, pp* **made**) **1** (create) faire [*dress, cake, coffee, stain, hole, will, pact, film, sketch, noise*]; **to ~ the bed** faire le lit; **to ~ a rule** établir une règle; **to ~ the law** faire or édicter fml les lois; **to ~ sth from** faire qch avec; **wine is made from grapes** le vin se fait avec du raisin; **to ~ sth for sb, to ~ sb sth** faire qch pour qn; **to be made for sb** être fait pour qn; **to be made for each other** être fait l'un pour l'autre; **to ~ room/the time for sth** trouver de la place/du temps pour qch; **to ~ sth out of** faire qch en; **what is it made (out) of?** en quoi est-ce fait?; **it's made (out) of gold** c'est en or; **to see what sb is made of** voir de quoi est fait qn; **let's see what he's made of** voyons de quoi il est fait; **show them what you're made of!** montre-leur de quel bois tu te chauffes○!; **to be as clever as they ~ them** être malin comme pas un○; **to ~ A into B** faire B à partir de A; **to ~ fruit into jam** faire de la confiture à partir des fruits; **to ~ a house into apartments** transformer une maison en appartements; **made in France/by Macron** fabriqué en France/par Macron; **God made man** Dieu a créé l'homme; **2** (cause to be or become, render) se faire [*friends, enemies*]; **to ~ sb happy/jealous/popular** rendre qn heureux/jaloux/populaire; **to ~ sb hungry/thirsty** donner faim/soif à qn; **to ~ oneself available/ill** se rendre disponible/malade; **to ~ oneself heard/understood** se faire entendre/comprendre; **to ~ sth bigger** agrandir qch; **to ~ sth better** améliorer qch; **to ~ sth worse** aggraver qch [*problem, situation*]; **to ~ sb's cold better** soulager le rhume de qn; **to ~ exams easier**, **to ~ passing exams easier**, **to ~ it easier to pass exams** faciliter les examens; **to ~ it easy/possible to do** [*person*] faire en sorte qu'il soit facile/possible de faire; **that made it easy for me to leave** cela a facilité mon départ; **3** (cause to do) **to ~ sb cry/jump/think** faire pleurer/sursauter/réfléchir qn; **I made her smile** je l'ai fait sourire; **to ~ sb do sth** faire faire qch à qn; **I made her forget her problems/lose patience** je lui ai fait oublier ses problèmes/perdre patience; **it ~s me look fat/old** ça me grossit/vieillit; **it ~s me look ill** ça me donne l'air malade; **to ~ sth do** faire que qch fasse; **to ~ sth happen** faire que qch se produise; **to ~ the story end happily** faire en sorte que l'histoire se termine bien; **to ~ sth work** [*person*] réussir à faire marcher qch [*machine etc*]; **to ~ sth grow/burn** [*person*] réussir à faire pousser/brûler qch; [*chemical, product*] faire pousser/brûler qch; **it ~s your face look rounder** ça fait paraître ton visage plus rond; **it ~s her voice sound funny** cela lui donne une drôle de voix; **4** (force, compel) **to ~ sb do** obliger qn à faire; **they made me (do it)** ils m'ont obligé, ils m'ont forcé, ils m'y ont forcé; **to be made to do** être obligé or forcé de faire; **he must be made to cooperate** il faut qu'il coopère; **to ~ sb wait/talk** faire attendre/parler qn; **5** (turn into) **to ~ sb sth**, **to ~ sth of sb** faire de qn qch; **it's been made into a film** on en a fait or tiré un film; **to ~ sb a star** faire de qn une vedette; **we made him treasurer** on l'a fait trésorier; **we made Tom treasurer** on a choisi Tom comme trésorier; **to be made president for life** être fait président à vie; **to ~ sb one's assistant** faire de qn son adjoint; **to ~ a soldier/a monster of sb** faire de qn un soldat/un monstre; **it'll ~ a man of you** hum ça fera de toi un homme; **he'll never ~ a teacher** il ne fera jamais un bon professeur; **she'll ~ a good politician** elle fera une fine politicienne; **to ~ sb a good husband** être un bon mari pour qn; **to ~ sth sth**, **to ~ sth of sth** faire de qch qch; **to ~ a habit/a success/an issue of sth** faire de qch une habitude/une réussite/une affaire; **do you want to ~ something of it?** (threatening) tu veux vraiment qu'on en discute? ; **to ~ too much of sth** faire tout un plat de qch○; **that will ~ a good shelter/a good tablecloth** cela fera un bon abri/une bonne nappe; **6** (add up to, amount to) faire; **three and three ~ six** trois et trois font six; **how much does that ~?** ça fait combien?; **that ~s ten altogether** ça fait dix en tout; **that ~s five times he's called** ça fait cinq fois qu'il appelle; **7** (earn) gagner [*salary, amount*]; **to ~ £300 a week** gagner 300 livres sterling par semaine; **he ~s more in a week than I ~ in a month** il gagne plus en une semaine que je ne gagne en un mois; **how much** ou **what do you think she ~s?** combien crois-tu qu'elle gagne?; **to ~ a living** gagner sa vie; **to ~ a profit** réaliser des bénéfices; **to ~ a loss** subir des pertes; **8** (reach, achieve) arriver jusqu'à [*place, position*]; atteindre [*ranking, level*]; faire [*speed, distance*]; **to ~ the camp before dark** arriver au or atteindre le camp avant la nuit; **to ~ the six o'clock train** attraper le train de six heures; **we'll never ~ it** nous n'y arriverons jamais; **to ~ the first team** entrer dans la première équipe; **to ~ the charts** entrer au hit-parade; **to ~ the front page of** faire la une de [*newspaper*]; **to ~ six spades** (in bridge) faire six piques; **to ~ 295** (in cricket) faire or marquer 295; **9** (estimate, say) **I ~ it about 30 kilometres** je dirais 30 kilomètres environ; **I ~ the profit £50** les bénéfices doivent s'élever à 50 livres sterling; **I ~ it five o'clock** il est cinq heures à ma montre ; **what time do you ~ it?** quelle heure as-tu?; **what do you ~ the distance (to be)?** quelle est la distance à ton avis?; **let's ~ it six o'clock/five dollars** disons six heures/cinq dollars; **can we ~ it a bit later?** peut-on dire un peu plus tard?; **what do you ~ of it?** qu'en dis-tu?; **what does she ~ of him?** qu'est-ce qu'elle pense or dit de lui?; **I don't know what to ~ of it** je ne sais quoi en penser; **I can't ~ anything of it** je n'y comprends rien; **10** (cause success of) assurer la réussite de [*holiday, day*]; **a good wine can ~ a meal** un bon vin peut assurer la réussite d'un repas; **it really ~s the room** [*feature, colour*] ça rend bien; **that interview made her career as a journalist** cette interview lui a permis de faire carrière dans le journalisme; **it really made my day** ça m'a rendu heureux pour la journée; **'go ahead, ~ my day!'** iron 'allez, vas-y!'; **to ~ or break sb/sth** décider de l'avenir de qn/qch; **11**○ (have sex with) se faire◑ [*woman*]; **12** sout (eat) prendre [*meal*]; **13** Elec fermer [*circuit*]; **14** Games (shuffle) battre [*cards*]; **15** Games (win) **to ~ a trick** faire une levée.

III *vi* (*prét, pp* **made**) **1** (act) **to ~ as if to do** faire comme si on allait faire; **she made as if to kiss him** elle a fait comme si elle allait l'embrasser; **he made like**○ **he was injured** il a fait semblant d'être blessé; **2** (move) ▶ **make after**, **make for**, **make towards**; **3** (shuffle cards) battre.

IDIOMS **to be on the ~**○ (for profit) avoir les dents longues; (for sex) être en chasse○; **to ~ it**○ (in career, life) y arriver; (to party, meeting) réussir à venir; (be on time for train etc) y être; (have sex) s'envoyer en l'air○ (**with** avec); **I'm afraid I can't ~ it** malheureusement je ne peux pas y aller; **if they don't ~ it by 10pm** s'ils n'arrivent pas avant 10h.

■ **make after**: **~ after [sb]** poursuivre.

■ **make at**: **~ at [sb]** attaquer (**with** avec).

■ **make away with** = **make off**.

■ **make do**: ¶ **~ do** faire avec; **to ~ do with** se contenter de qch; ¶ **~ [sth] do** se contenter de.

■ **make for**: ¶ **~ for [sth] 1** (head for) se diriger vers [*door, town, home*]; **2** (help create) permettre, assurer [*easy life, happy marriage*]; ¶ **~ for [sb] 1** (attack) se jeter sur; **2** (approach) se diriger vers.

■ **make good**: ¶ **~ good** réussir; **a poor boy made good** un garçon pauvre qui a réussi; ¶ **~ good [sth] 1** (make up for) réparer [*damage, omission, loss*]; rattraper [*lost time*]; combler [*deficit, shortfall*]; **2** (keep) tenir [*promise*].

■ **make off** filer○; **to ~ off across the fields/towards the town** s'enfuir à travers les champs/vers la ville; **to ~ off with sth/sb** se tirer○ avec qch/qn.

■ **make out**: ¶ **~ out 1** (manage) s'en tirer○; **how are you making out?** comment ça marche○?; **2** US (grope) se peloter○; **3** (claim) affirmer (**that** que); **he's not as stupid as he ~s out** il n'est pas aussi bête qu'il (le) prétend; ¶ **~ out [sth]**, **~ [sth] out 1** (see, distinguish) distinguer [*shape, writing*]; **2** (claim) **to ~ sth out to be** prétendre que qch est; **3** (understand, work out) comprendre [*puzzle, mystery, character*]; **to ~ out if** or **whether** comprendre si; **I can't ~ him out** je n'arrive pas à le comprendre; **4** (write out) faire, rédiger [*cheque, will, list*]; **to ~ out a cheque** GB ou **check** US **to sb** faire un chèque à qn, signer un chèque à l'ordre de qn; **it is made out to X** il est à l'ordre de X; **who shall I ~ the cheque out to?** à quel ordre dois-je faire le chèque?; **5** (expound) **to ~ out a case for sth** argumenter en faveur de qch; ¶ **~ oneself out to be** prétendre être [*rich, brilliant*]; faire semblant d'être [*stupid, incompetent*].

■ **make over**: **~ over [sth]**, **~ [sth] over 1** (transform) transformer [*building, appearance*] (**into** en); **2** (transfer) céder [*property*] (**to** à).

■ **make towards**: **~ towards [sth/sb]** se diriger vers.

■ **make up**: ¶ **~ up 1** (put make-up on) **to ~ oneself up** se maquiller; **2** (after quarrel) se réconcilier (**with** avec); **3 to ~ up for** (compensate for) rattraper [*lost time, lost sleep, missed meal, delay*]; combler [*financial loss, deficit*]; compenser [*personal loss, bereavement*]; **4 to ~ up to**○ faire de la lèche à○ [*boss, person*]; ¶ **~ up [sth]**, **~ [sth] up 1** (invent) inventer [*excuse, story*]; **you're making it up!** tu inventes!; **to ~ sth up as one goes along** inventer qch au fur et à mesure; **2** (prepare) faire [*parcel, bundle, garment, road surface, bed*]; préparer [*prescription*]; composer [*type*]; **she had the fabric made up into a jacket** elle s'est fait faire une veste avec le tissu; **3** (constitute) faire [*whole, personality, society*]; **to be made up of** être fait or composé de; **to ~ up 10% of** constituer 10% de; **4** (compensate for) rattraper [*loss, time*]; combler [*deficit, shortfall*]; **to ~ the total up to £1,000** compléter la somme pour faire 1 000 livres au total; **5** (put make-up on) maquiller [*person, face, eyes*]; **6** (stoke up) alimenter, s'occuper de [*fire*]; **7 to ~ it up** (make friends) se réconcilier (**with** avec); **I'll ~ it up to you somehow** (when at fault) j'essaierai de me faire pardonner; (when not at fault) je vais trouver quelque chose pour compenser.

■ **make with**○: ¶ **~ with [sth]** US (hurry and bring) se dépêcher d'apporter; ¶ **~ it with [sb]** se faire◑.

make-believe I /ˈmeɪkbɪliːv/ *n* fantaisie *f*; **it's pure ~** c'est de la pure fantaisie; **it's only ~** ce n'est qu'une histoire imaginaire; **the land of ~** le pays des contes de fées.
II /ˈmeɪkbɪliːv/ *modif* [*world, house, friend*] imaginaire.
III make believe /ˌmeɪkbɪˈliːv/ *vtr* **to ~ that** imaginer que; **to make believe (that) one is a pirate** imaginer que l'on est un pirate, jouer aux pirates.

make: **~-do-and-mend** *vi* faire avec, tirer le diable par la queue○; **~fast** *n* point *m* d'amarrage.

makeover /ˈmeɪkəʊvə(r)/ *n* transformation *f*; **'free ~'** 'démonstration de maquillage'.

maker /ˈmeɪkə(r)/ **I** *n* **1** (manufacturer) (of clothes, wine, food, appliance, tyres) fabricant *m*; (of cars, aircraft) constructeur *m*; **the ~'s label** la marque du fabricant; ▶ **dressmaker**, **watchmaker etc**; **2** (device) ▶ **coffee maker etc**.
II Maker *n* Relig Créateur *m*. ▶ **holidaymaker**, **troublemaker etc**.
IDIOMS **to (go to) meet one's Maker** rendre l'âme.

makeshift /ˈmeɪkʃɪft/ *adj* improvisé.

make-up /ˈmeɪkʌp/ *n* **1** (cosmetics) maquillage *m*; **to wear ~** se maquiller; **to put on one's ~** se maquiller; **2** (character) caractère *m*; **to be part of sb's ~** faire partie du caractère de qn; **to be in sb's ~** être dans le caractère de qn; **3** (composition) (of whole, committee) composition *f*; **4** TV, Theat, Cin **to work in ~** travailler dans le maquillage; **5** Print mise *f* en page.

make-up artist ▶ **1692** *n* maquilleur/-euse *m/f*.

make-up: **~ bag** *n* trousse *f* de maquillage; **~ base** *n* base *f* de maquillage.

make: **~-up girl** ▶ **1692** *n* maquilleuse *f*; **~-up man** ▶ **1692** *n* maquilleur *m*; **~-up remover** *n* démaquillant *m*.

makeweight /ˈmeɪkweɪt/ *n* **1** fig (person) solution *f* de remplacement, bouche-trou○ *m*; **2** lit poids *m* (de balance).

making /ˈmeɪkɪŋ/ *n* **1** (creation, manufacture) (of film, programme) réalisation *f*; (of industrial product) fabrication *f*; (of clothes) confection *f*; (of meal, cake) préparation *f*; **problems of sb's own ~** des problèmes du propre fait

de qn; **to see a product in the ~** voir un produit en cours de fabrication; **the film was two years in the ~** le tournage du film a duré deux ans; **a disaster is in the ~** une catastrophe est en train de se produire; **history in the ~** l'Histoire en marche; **2** (of person, personality) **to be the ~ of sb** (past events) être ce qui a fait de qn ce qu'il/elle est; **this contract will be the ~ of her** ce contrat sera le point de départ de sa carrière; **'The ~ of a president'** 'Biographie d'un président'. ▶ **matchmaking, watchmaking etc.**
IDIOMS **to have all the ~s of sth** avoir tout pour faire qch.

malachite /'mæləkaɪt/ *n* malachite *f*.
maladjusted /ˌmælə'dʒʌstɪd/ *adj* Psych inadapté.
maladjustment /ˌmælə'dʒʌstmənt/ *n* Psych inadaptation *f*.
maladministration /ˌmælədˌmɪnɪ'streɪʃn/ *n* ¢ **1** Admin, Mgmt mauvaise gestion *f*; **2** Jur malversations *fpl*.
maladroit /ˌmælə'drɔɪt/ *adj* sout maladroit.
maladroitly /ˌmælə'drɔɪtlɪ/ *adv* sout maladroitement.
maladroitness /ˌmælə'drɔɪtnɪs/ *n* sout maladresse *f*.
malady /'mælədɪ/ *n* littér **1** (illness) maladie *f*; **2** fig mal *m*.
Malagasy /ˌmælə'gæsɪ/ **▶ 1486**, **1402** **I** *n* (*pl* **-ies**) **1** (native of Madagascar) Malgache *mf*; **2** (language) malgache *m*.
II *adj* malgache.
malaise /mæ'leɪz/ *n* sout malaise *m*; **a deep-seated ~** un malaise profondément enraciné.
malapropism /'mæləprɒpɪzəm/ *n* impropriété *f* de langage.
malaria /mə'leərɪə/ **▶ 1354** *n* paludisme *m*; **a ~ attack** une crise de paludisme; **anti-~ tablet** cachet *m* antipaludique.
malarial /mə'leərɪəl/ *adj* [*fever, symptoms*] paludéen/-éenne; [*mosquito*] du paludisme.
malark(e)y○ /mə'lɑːkɪ/ *n* ¢ balivernes *fpl*.
Malawi /mə'lɑːwɪ/ **▶ 1131** *pr n* Malawi *m*.
Malawian /mə'lɑːwɪən/ **▶ 1486** **I** *n* (inhabitant) Malawien/-ienne *m/f*.
II *adj* malawien/-ienne.
Malay /mə'leɪ/, **Malayan** /mə'leɪən/ **▶ 1486**, **1402** **I** *n* **1** (inhabitant) Malais/-e *m/f*; **2** (language) malais *m*; **the ~ Peninsula** la péninsule de Malacca.
II *adj* malais.
Malaya /mə'leɪə/ *pr n* Malaisie *f* occidentale.
Malayan /mə'leɪən/ *n, adj* = **Malay**.
Malaysia /mə'leɪzɪə/ **▶ 1131** *pr n* Malaisie *f*.
Malaysian /mə'leɪzɪən/ **▶ 1486**, **1402** **I** *pr n* (inhabitant) Malaisien/-ienne *m/f*.
II *adj* malaisien/-ienne.
malcontent /'mælkəntent/ **I** *n* sout mécontent/-e *m/f*.
II *adj* sout mécontent.
Maldives /'mɔːldɪvz/ **▶ 1381**, **1131** *pr npl* (also **Maldive Islands**) **the ~** les Maldives *fpl*.
male /meɪl/ **I** *n* **1** Biol, Zool mâle *m*; **in the ~** chez le mâle; **the ~s** (of species) le mâle; **2** (man) homme *m*; hum mâle *m*.
II *adj* **1** Biol, Zool mâle; **2** (relating to men) [*condition, population, role, sex, trait*] masculin; [*company*] des hommes; **a ~ voice** une voix d'homme; **the ~ body/voice** le corps/la voix de l'homme; **~ singer** chanteur *m*; **~ student** étudiant *m*; **~ employee** employé *m* (homme); **3** Elec mâle.
male chauvinism /ˌmeɪl 'ʃəʊvɪnɪzəm/ *n* machisme *m*.
male chauvinist /ˌmeɪl 'ʃəʊvɪnɪst/ **I** *n* phallocrate *m*; **~ pig** sale phallocrate.
II *adj* [*attitude, opinion*] macho.
malediction /ˌmælɪ'dɪkʃn/ *n* sout malédiction *f*.
male-dominated /ˌmeɪl'dɒmɪneɪtɪd/ *adj* **1** (run by men) [*society, world*] dominé par les hommes; **2** (mainly masculine) [*environment, industry, profession*] où les hommes dominent.
malefactor /'mælɪfæktə(r)/ *n* sout malfaiteur *m*.
male: **~ menopause** *n* retour *m* d'âge masculin, andropause *f* spec; **~ model** *n* mannequin *m* homme or masculin; **~ voice choir** *n* chœur *m* d'hommes.
malevolence /mə'levələns/ *n* malveillance *f* (**towards** envers).
malevolent /mə'levələnt/ *adj* malveillant.
malevolently /mə'levələntlɪ/ *adv* avec malveillance.
malformation /ˌmælfɔː'meɪʃn/ *n* malformation *f*.
malformed /ˌmæl'fɔːmd/ *adj* [*limb, nose*] difforme; [*heart, kidney, leaf, shoot*] malformé.
malfunction /ˌmæl'fʌŋkʃn/ **I** *n* **1** (poor operation) mauvais fonctionnement *m*; **2** (breakdown) défaillance *f*; **an equipment/a computer ~** une défaillance technique/de l'ordinateur; **3** Med dysfonctionnement *m*.
II *vi* mal fonctionner; **the machine is ~ing** la machine fonctionne mal.
Mali /'mɑːlɪ/ **▶ 1131** *pr n* Mali *m*.
Malian /'mɑːlɪən/ **▶ 1486** **I** *n* (person) Malien/-ienne *m/f*.
II *adj* malien/-ienne.
malice /'mælɪs/ *n* **1** (spite) méchanceté *f* (**towards** à); **out of ~** par méchanceté; **there's no ~ in him** il n'est pas méchant; **I bear him no ~** je ne lui veux aucun mal; **2** Jur préméditation *f*; **with ~ aforethought** Jur avec préméditation.
malicious /mə'lɪʃəs/ *adj* **1** (spiteful) [*comment, person, smile*] malveillant; [*act*] méchant; [*allegation*] calomnieux/-ieuse; **2** Jur **with ~ intent** avec l'intention de nuire.
malicious damage *n* ¢ Jur dégâts *mpl* volontaires.
maliciously /mə'lɪʃəslɪ/ *adv* **1** (spitefully) [*speak, write*] méchamment; [*act, behave*] avec méchanceté; **2** Jur avec l'intention de nuire.
malicious: **~ prosecution** *n* poursuites *fpl* abusives Jur; **~ wounding** *n* ¢ Jur coups *mpl* et blessures *fpl* volontaires.
malign /mə'laɪn/ **I** *adj* [*effect, influence, intention*] nuisible.
II *vtr* calomnier [*person, group, organization*]; **much-~ed** tant décrié.
malignancy /mə'lɪgnənsɪ/ *n* **1** (desire to harm) malveillance *f*; **2** Med malignité *f*.
malignant /mə'lɪgnənt/ *adj* **1** (cruel) [*criticism, look, thought*] malveillant; [*person, power*] malfaisant; [*nature, personality*] cruel/-elle; **2** Med malin/-igne.
malinger /mə'lɪŋgə(r)/ *vi* péj jouer les malades.
malingerer /mə'lɪŋgərə(r)/ *n* péj tire-au-flanc○ *m inv*.
mall /mæl, mɔːl/ *n* **1** (shopping arcade) (in town) galerie *f* marchande; (in suburbs) US centre *m* commercial; **2** US (street) rue *f* piétonne.
mallard /'mælɑːd, US 'mælərd/ *n* (*pl* **~** ou **~s**) colvert *m*.
malleability /ˌmælɪə'bɪlətɪ/ *n* malléabilité *f*.
malleable /'mælɪəbl/ *adj* [*substance, person*] malléable.
mallet /'mælɪt/ *n* Sport, Tech maillet *m*.
malleus /'mælɪəs/ *n* (*pl* **-llei**) Anat marteau *m*.
mallow /'mæləʊ/ *n* Bot mauve *f*.
mall people *npl* US péj (suburbanites) banlieusards *mpl*; (unsophisticated) ploucs○ *mpl* pej.
malnutrition /ˌmælnju:'trɪʃn, US -nu:-/ *n* gen sous-alimentation *f*; Med spec malnutrition *f*.
malodorous /ˌmæl'əʊdərəs/ *adj* sout malodorant.
malpractice /ˌmæl'præktɪs/ *n* ¢ **1** Admin, Jur, Mgmt malversations *fpl*; **administrative ~** malversations *fpl*; **electoral ~** fraude *f* électorale; **professional ~** faute *f* professionnelle; **2** US Med erreur *f* médicale; **~ insurance** assurance *f* contre l'erreur médicale.
malt /mɔːlt/ **I** *n* Culin **1** (grain) malt *m*; **2** (whisky) whisky *m* pur malt; **3** US (drink) lait *m* malté, milk-shake *m*.
II *vtr* malter.
Malta /'mɔːltə/ **▶ 1131**, **1381** *pr n* Malte *f*.
maltase /'mɔːlteɪz/ *n* Biol maltase *f*.
malted○ /'mɔːltɪd/ *n* US = **malted milk 2**.
malted milk *n* **1** (hot drink) lait *m* malté (*chaud*); **2** US (milk shake) lait *m* malté, milk-shake *m*.
Maltese /ˌmɔːl'tiːz/ **▶ 1486**, **1402** **I** *n* **1** (inhabitant) Maltais/-e *m/f*; **2** (language) maltais *m*.
II *adj* maltais.
Maltese: **~ cross** *n* Croix *f* de Malte; **~ fever** *n* fièvre *f* de Malte.
malt extract *n* Culin extrait *m* de malt.
malthusianism /ˌmæl'θjuːzɪənɪzəm, US -'θuː-/ *n* malthusianisme *m*.
malt liquor /ˌmɔːlt 'lɪkə(r)/ *n* US *boisson fermentée à partir de moût de bière.*
maltreat /ˌmæl'triːt/ *vtr* maltraiter.
maltreatment /ˌmæl'triːtmənt/ *n* mauvais traitement *m*.
malt: **~ vinegar** *n* vinaigre *m* de malt; **~ whisky** *n* whisky *m* pur malt.
mam /mæm/ *n* lang enfantin maman *f*.
mama *n* **1** /'mamə/ US lang enfantin maman *f*; **2** /mə'mɑː/‡ mère *f*.
mamma /'mɑːmə/ *n* **1** (mummy) lang enfantin US maman *f*; **2**○ péj (buxom woman) grosse mémère○ *f* pej.
mammal /'mæml/ *n* mammifère *m*.
mammalian /mə'meɪlɪən/ *adj* [*animal, female*] mammifère; [*habitat, trait*] des mammifères.
mammary /'mæmərɪ/ *adj* mammaire; **~ gland** glande *f* mammaire.
mammograph /'mæməgrɑːf, US -græf/ *n* mammographie *f*.
mammography /mæ'mɒgrəfɪ/ *n* mammographie *f*.
Mammon /'mæmən/ *pr n* Relig Mammon.
IDIOMS **to worship ~** vénérer le Veau d'or.
mammoth /'mæməθ/ **I** *n* Zool mammouth *m*.
II *adj* [*project, task*] gigantesque; [*organization, structure*] géant.
mammy /'mæmɪ/ *n* **1** (mummy) lang enfantin maman *f*; **2**† US (servant) nourrice *f* (*noire*).
man /mæn/ **I** *n* (*pl* **men**) **1** (adult male) homme *m*; **middle-aged/married ~** homme d'âge mûr/marié; **as one ~ to another** entre hommes; **he's not a ~ to do** ce n'est pas le genre d'homme à faire; **a blind ~** un aveugle; **an old ~** un vieillard; **a single ~** un célibataire; **a ladies' ~** un homme à femmes; **a beer/whisky ~** un buveur de bière/de whisky; **a leg/bum ~**○ un amateur de belles jambes/de derrières; **a ~ of God/the people** un homme de Dieu/du peuple; **a ~ of iron** ou **steel** un homme de fer; **they've arrested the right ~** on a arrêté le vrai coupable; **he's your ~** c'est l'homme qu'il te faut; **he has worked for the party, ~ and boy** GB il a travaillé pour le parti toute sa vie; **~ of the match** héros *m* du match; **good ~!** (well done) bravo mon gars!; **my good ~!** mon vieux○!; **my little ~**○ mon petit; **2** (husband, partner) homme *m*; **her ~** son homme; **he is the right ~ for her** c'est l'homme qu'il lui fallait; **her young ~**† son fiancé; **~ and wife** mari et femme; **to live as ~ and wife** vivre maritalement; **3** (person) homme *m*; **no ~ could have done more** personne n'aurait pu faire davantage; **as good as the next ~** aussi bien que n'importe qui; **the common ~** l'homme

du commun; **primitive Man** l'homme primitif; **4** (person of courage) homme *m*; **be a ~** sois un homme; **to make a ~ of sb** faire un homme de qn; **5** (mankind) (also **Man**) humanité *f*; **6** Sport (team member) joueur *m*; **7** Games (piece) (in chess) pièce *f*; (in draughts) pion *m*; **8**† ou hum (servant) valet *m*.
II men *npl* Mil (subordinates) hommes *mpl*; **to address the men** s'adresser aux hommes; **'now men...'** 'soldats...'; **officers and men** Mil officiers et hommes; (in Navy) officiers et matelots.
III *excl* **1**○ (expressing surprise) mince, alors○!; **2** (addressing somebody) **hey ~!** eh mec○!
IV *vtr* (*p prés etc* **-nn-**) **1** gen tenir [*switchboard, desk*]; **will the telephone be ~ned?** est-ce qu'il y aura quelqu'un pour répondre au téléphone?; **2** Mil armer [qch] en hommes [*ship*]; assigner des hommes à [*barricade, gun*]; **who is ~ning the barricades?** qui est assigné aux barricades?; **to ~ the pumps** mettre des hommes aux pompes.
V manned *pp adj* Aerosp [*flight, spacecraft, base*] habité; **fully ~ned** (of ship) avec un équipage complet.
IDIOMS **every ~ for himself** chacun pour soi; **Man proposes, God disposes** l'homme propose et Dieu dispose; **to a ~** sans exception; **as one ~** comme un seul homme; **to sort out the men from the boys** séparer les hommes des mauviettes○; **he took it like a ~** il a pris ça en homme; **to be ~ enough to do** avoir le courage de faire; **to be a ~'s ~** aimer être entre hommes; **to be one's own ~** être son propre maître; **to be the ~ of the moment** être l'homme du jour.

manacle‡ /'mænəkl/ **I** *n* **1** (shackle) chaîne *f*; **2** (handcuff) aussi hum menotte *f*.
II *vtr* enchaîner [*convict, slave*]; mettre les menottes à [*criminal, suspect*].

manage /'mænɪdʒ/ **I** *vtr* **1** (succeed) **to ~ to do** réussir à faire, se débrouiller○ pour faire; **she ~d to find a job/finish the article** elle a réussi à trouver un emploi/finir l'article; **how does he ~ to save so much money?** comment réussit-il à faire tant d'économies?; **how did she ~ to spend so much money?** comment s'est-elle débrouillée○ pour dépenser tant d'argent?; **he ~d to offend everybody** iron il a réussi à froisser tout le monde; **I ~d not to dirty my hands** j'ai réussi à ne pas me salir les mains; **2** (find possible) **she ~d a smile** elle a réussi à sourire; **I can ~ a few words in Italian** j'arrive à dire quelques mots en italien; **can you ~ seven o'clock tomorrow?** sept heures demain soir, ça te convient?; **can you ~ lunch on Friday?** est-ce que tu seras libre pour déjeuner vendredi?; **I couldn't ~ another thing!** je n'en peux plus○!; **I'm sure you can ~ another glass of wine** tu prendras bien un autre verre de vin?; **I can't ~ more than £30** je ne peux pas dépasser 30 livres sterling; **3** (administer) diriger, administrer [*project, finances*]; diriger [*company, bank, school*]; gérer [*business, shop, hotel, estate*]; **~d economy** économie *f* dirigée; **4** (organize) gérer [*money, time*]; **5** (handle) savoir s'y prendre avec [*person, animal*]; manier [*tool, boat, oars etc*]; **they ~d the situation very badly** ils s'y sont très mal pris; **he knows how to ~ her** il sait s'y prendre avec elle.
II *vi* se débrouiller○; **they have to ~ on £50 a week** ils doivent se débrouiller○ avec 50 livres sterling par semaine; **can you ~?** tu y arrives?; **thank you, I can ~** merci, je peux me débrouiller○.

manageable /'mænɪdʒəbl/ *adj* [*size, proportions, quantity*] maniable; [*problem, issue*] maîtrisable; [*car*] maniable; [*boat*] facile à manœuvrer; [*person, animal*] docile; **~ hair** cheveux faciles à coiffer; **to keep sth at a ~ level** maintenir qch à un niveau raisonnable.

management /'mænɪdʒmənt/ **I** *n* **1** (of business, company, hotel) gestion *f*, management *m*; (of shop, bank, hospital, estate, economy, staff) gestion *f*; **the business failed due to bad ~** l'affaire a fait faillite à cause d'une mauvaise gestion; **her skilful ~ of the situation** sa façon adroite de gérer la situation; **2** (managers collectively) direction *f*; **top ~** la haute direction, les cadres dirigeants; **lower/middle ~** les cadres *mpl* subalternes/moyens; **~ and unions** la direction et les syndicats, les partenaires *mpl* sociaux; **~ and workers** (in industry) la direction et les ouvriers; (in business) la direction et les employés; **'under new ~'** 'changement de direction'; **'the ~ regrets that...'** 'la direction regrette que...'.
II *modif* [*career*] dans le management; [*job*] de cadre, de management; [*problem*] de gestion, de management; [*staff*] d'encadrement; **the ~ team** l'équipe dirigeante; **a ~ spokesman** un porte-parole de la direction.

management: **~ accounting** *n* comptabilité *f* analytique; **~ buyout**, **MBO** *n* rachat *m* d'une entreprise par ses cadres; **~ committee** *n* comité *m* de gestion; **~ company** *n* société *f* de gestion; **~ consultancy** *n* cabinet *m* de conseil; **~ consultant** ▶ **1692** *n* conseiller *m* en gestion or en management; **~ fees** *npl* frais *mpl* de gestion; **~ information system, MIS** *n* système *m* intégré de gestion, SIG *m*; **~ studies** *npl* études *fpl* de gestion.

management style *n* mode *f* de gestion du personnel; **I don't like his ~** je n'aime pas sa façon de traiter le personnel.

management trainee *n* apprenti manager *m*.

manager /'mænɪdʒə(r)/ *n* (of business, company, bank, cinema, hotel, theatre) directeur/-trice *m/f*; (of restaurant, pub, shop) gérant/-e *m/f*; (of farm) exploitant/-e *m/f*; (of project) chef *m*, directeur/-trice *m/f*; (in showbusiness) directeur/-trice *m/f* artistique; Sport manager *m*; **school ~** GB membre *m* du conseil d'établissement; **to be a good ~** gen être un/une bon/bonne gestionnaire; (of household) savoir bien gérer le budget domestique.

manageress /,mænɪdʒə'res/ *n* (of hotel, restaurant, shop) gérante *f*; (of company) directrice *f*.

managerial /,mænɪ'dʒɪərɪəl/ *adj* [*experience*] en gestion; [*decision*] de la direction; [*problem*] d'encadrement; [*training*] des cadres; **~ staff** les cadres *mpl*; **~ skills** compétences *fpl* en matière de gestion; **at ~ level** au niveau des cadres.

managing: **~ director** *n* directeur général/directrice générale *m/f*; **~ editor** *n* directeur/-trice *m/f* de la rédaction; **~ partner** *n* associé *m* gérant.

man-at-arms /,mænət'ɑ:mz/ *n* Hist homme *m* d'armes.

manatee /,mænə'ti:/ *n* lamantin *m*.

Manche ▶ **1163** *pr n* Manche *f*; **in/to the ~** dans la Manche.

man child *n* enfant *m* mâle.

Manchu /,mæn'tʃu:/ ▶ **1486**, **1402** **I** *n* (*pl* **~, ~s**) Geog, Hist **1** (person) Mandchou/-e *m/f*; **2** (language) mandchou *m*.
II *adj* mandchou.

Manchuria /,mænt'ʃʊərɪə/ *pr n* Mandchourie *f*.

Manchurian /,mæn'tʃʊərɪən/ **I** *n* (person) Mandchou/-e *m/f*.
II *adj* mandchou.

Mancunian /mæŋ'kju:nɪən/ **I** *n* (born there) natif/-ive *m/f* de Manchester; (living there) habitant/-e *m/f* de Manchester.
II *adj* de Manchester.

mandala /'mændələ/ *n* mandala *m*.

mandarin /'mændərɪn/ *n* **1** (fruit) mandarine *f*; (tree) mandarinier *m*; **2** (person) mandarin *m* also pej.

mandarin: **Mandarin Chinese** ▶ **1402** *n* Ling mandarin *m*; **~ duck** *n* canard *m* mandarin.

mandate /'mændeɪt/ **I** *n* **1** (authority) gen autorité *f*; Pol mandat *m*; **to have a ~ to do** Pol avoir reçu mandat de faire; **this gives us a clear ~ to proceed** ceci nous donne toute latitude pour poursuivre; **under British ~** sous mandat britannique; **2** Hist (territory) territoire *m* sous mandat; **3** Fin, Jur (document) procuration *f*, mandat *m*.
II *vtr* **1** (authorize) gen autoriser; Pol mandater, donner mandat à; **2** placer [qch] sous mandat [*territory*].

mandatory /'mændətərɪ, US -tɔ:rɪ/ *adj* obligatoire.

mandible /'mændɪbl/ *n* (of vertebrate) mâchoire *f* inférieure; (of bird, insect) mandibule *f*.

mandolin /,mændə'lɪn/ ▶ **1481** *n* mandoline *f*.

mandrake /'mændreɪk/ *n* mandragore *f*.

mandrill /'mændrɪl/ *n* mandrill *m*.

mane /meɪn/ *n* lit, fig crinière *f*.

man-eater /'mæni:tə(r)/ *n* **1** (animal) mangeur *m* d'hommes; **2**○ fig hum ou péj (woman) mangeuse *f* d'hommes.

man-eating /'mæni:tɪŋ/ *adj* [*animal*] mangeur/-euse d'hommes.

maneuver US *n, vtr, vi* = **manoeuvre**.

man Friday /,mæn 'fraɪdeɪ/ *n* **1** Literat Vendredi; **2** (general assistant) factotum *m*.

manful /'mænfl/ *adj* vaillant.

manfully /'mænfəlɪ/ *adv* vaillamment.

manganese /'mæŋgəni:z/ **I** *n* manganèse *m*.
II *modif* [*bronze, steel*] au manganèse.

mange /meɪndʒ/ *n* gale *f*.

mangel-wurzel /'mæŋglwɜ:zl/ *n* betterave *f* fourragère.

manger /'meɪndʒə(r)/ *n* mangeoire *f*.

mangetout /,mɑ:nʒ'tu:/ *n* pois *m* gourmand, mange-tout *m inv*.

mangle /'mæŋgl/ **I** *n* essoreuse *f* à rouleaux.
II *vtr* mutiler [*body*]; broyer [*vehicle*]; fig massacrer [*translation, piece of music*]; estropier [*message*].

mango /'mæŋgəʊ/ **I** *n* (fruit) mangue *f*; (tree) manguier *m*.
II *modif* [*juice*] de mangue; [*grove*] de manguiers; [*chutney*] à la mangue.

mangold /'mæŋgld/ *n* = **mangel-wurzel**.

mangosteen /'mæŋgəsti:n/ *n* (fruit) mangouste *f*; (tree) mangoustan *m*, mangoustanier *m*.

mangrove /'mæŋgrəʊv/ *n* palétuvier *m*, manglier *m*.

mangrove swamp *n* mangrove *f*.

mangy /'meɪndʒɪ/ *adj* [*animal*] galeux/-euse; fig [*rug, curtains, coat*] élimé; [*room, hotel*] miteux/-euse.

manhandle /'mænhændl/ *vtr* **1** (treat roughly) malmener, maltraiter; **2** (move by manpower) manutentionner.

manhattan /,mæn'hætn/ *n* (drink) manhattan *m* (*cocktail à base de whisky et vermouth*).

man: **~hole** *n* (in road) regard *m*, bouche *f* d'égout; (of boiler, tank) regard *m*; **~hole cover** *n* plaque *f* de regard.

manhood /'mænhʊd/ *n* **1** (adult state) âge *m* d'homme; **2** (masculinity) masculinité *f*; **3** littér (men collectively) hommes *mpl*.

man: **~-hour** *n* Ind heure *f* de main-d'œuvre; **~hunt** *n* chasse *f* à l'homme.

mania /'meɪnɪə/ *n* Psych manie *f*; fig (obsession) passion *f* (**for** de); **to have a ~ for doing** avoir la manie de faire; **motorcycle ~** la passion des motos.

maniac /'meɪnɪæk/ **I** *n* **1** Psych maniaque *mf*; **2**○ fig (reckless person) fou/folle *m/f*; **he's a computer ~** c'est un mordu○ d'informatique; **to drive like a ~** conduire comme un fou.

II *adj* 1 Psych maniaque; 2○ fig [*driver, behaviour, scheme*] fou/folle.

maniacal /məˈnaɪəkl/ *adj* Psych maniaque; fig fou/folle, dément.

manic /ˈmænɪk/ *adj* 1 Med, Psych (manic-depressive) maniaco-dépressif/-ive, cyclothymique; (obsessive) obsessionnel/-elle; 2 fig [*activity, behaviour*] frénétique.

manic: **~ depression** *n* psychose *f* maniaco-dépressive, cyclothymie *f*; **~ depressive** *n, adj* maniaco-dépressif/-ive (*m/f*); cyclothymique (*mf*).

Manich(a)ean /ˌmænɪˈkiːən/ *n, adj* manichéen/-éenne (*m/f*).

Manich(a)eism /ˌmænɪˈkiːɪzəm/ *n* manichéisme *m*.

manicure /ˈmænɪkjʊə(r)/ I *n* manucure *f*; **to give sb a ~** manucurer qn.
II *vtr* manucurer [*person*]; **to ~ one's nails** se faire les ongles; **her ~d nails** ses ongles manucurés; **a ~d lawn** hum une pelouse impeccable.

manicure: **~ scissors** *n* ciseaux *mpl* à ongles; **~ set** *n* trousse *f* de manucure.

manicurist /ˈmænɪkjʊərɪst/ ▶ 1692 *n* manucure *mf*.

manifest /ˈmænɪfest/ I *n* Naut, Aviat manifeste *m*.
II *adj* manifeste, évident.
III *vtr* manifester.
IV *v refl* **to ~ itself** se manifester.

manifestation /ˌmænɪfəˈsteɪʃn/ *n* manifestation *f*, signe *m* (**of** de).

Manifest Destiny *n* US Hist destinée *f* manifeste (*doctrine expansionniste des Américains*).

manifestly /ˈmænɪfestlɪ/ *adv* manifestement.

manifesto /ˌmænɪˈfestəʊ/ *n* manifeste *m*, programme *m*; **election ~** programme *m* électoral.

manifold /ˈmænɪfəʊld/ I *n* Aut collecteur *m*, tubulure *f*; **inlet** ou **induction ~** collecteur d'admission; **exhaust ~** collecteur d'échappement.
II *adj* littér multiple, nombreux/-euse; **~ wisdom** sagesse *f* infinie.

manikin *n* = **mannikin**.

Manila /məˈnɪlə/ *pr n* 1 ▶ 1818 Geog Manille; 2 (paper) papier *m* kraft.

man in the moon *n* visage *m* de la lune.

manioc /ˈmænɪɒk/ *n* manioc *m*.

manipulate /məˈnɪpjʊleɪt/ *vtr* 1 (handle, control) manipuler, manœuvrer [*gears, tool, machine*]; 2 pej manipuler [*person, situation, opinion, market*]; **she ~d him into accepting the offer** elle l'a manipulé de façon à le persuader d'accepter la proposition; **to ~ sb's emotions** jouer sur les émotions de qn; 3 (falsify) péj falsifier [*figures, facts, data*]; 4 Med (in physiotherapy) manipuler.

manipulation /məˌnɪpjʊˈleɪʃn/ *n* 1 (of gears, tool, machine) manipulation *f*, manœuvre *f*; 2 (of person, situation, public opinion) péj manipulation *f*; 3 (of figures, facts) péj falsification *f*; 4 Med manipulation *f*.

manipulative /məˈnɪpjʊlətɪv/ *adj* manipulateur/-trice.

manipulator /məˈnɪpjʊleɪtə(r)/ *n* manipulateur/-trice *m/f*.

Manitoba /ˌmænɪˈtəʊbə/ *pr n* Manitoba *m*.

mankind /ˌmænˈkaɪnd/ *n* humanité *f*.

manliness /ˈmænlɪnɪs/ *n* virilité *f*.

man lock *n* Civ Eng sas *m*.

manly /ˈmænlɪ/ *adj* viril.

man-made /ˌmænˈmeɪd/ *adj* [*fibre, dye*] chimique; [*fabric*] synthétique; [*pond, snow*] artificiel/-ielle; [*environment*] façonné par l'homme; [*object, tool*] fabriqué par l'homme; [*catastrophe*] d'origine humaine.

manna /ˈmænə/ *n* Bible, fig manne *f*.
IDIOMS **like ~ from heaven** comme une manne céleste.

mannequin /ˈmænɪkɪn/ *n* (dummy, person) mannequin *m*.

manner /ˈmænə(r)/ I *n* 1 (way, method) manière *f*, façon *f*; **in this ~** de cette manière or façon; **in like ~, in the same ~** de la même manière; **the ~ in which they were treated** la manière or la façon dont on les a traités; **to do sth in such a ~ that** faire qch de telle sorte que (+ *subj*); **the ~ of his going** littér ou **of his death** la façon dont il est mort; **in a ~ of speaking** pour ainsi dire; 2 (way of behaving) attitude *f*; **don't be put off by her ~** ne sois pas rebuté par sa façon de faire or par son attitude; **something in his ~ disturbed her** quelque chose dans son comportement la troublait; **she has a bad ~** elle a une attitude déplaisante; **to have a good telephone ~** savoir parler au téléphone; 3 littér (sort, kind) sorte *f*, genre *m*; **what ~ of man is he?** quel genre or quelle manière† d'homme est-ce?; **all ~ of delights** toutes sortes de plaisirs; **by no ~ of means** pas du tout; 4 Art, Literat (style) manière *f*; **in** ou **after the ~ of** à la manière de.
II **manners** *npl* 1 (social behaviour) manières *fpl*; **to have good/bad ~s** avoir de bonnes/mauvaises manières; **it's bad ~s to do** il est mal élevé de faire; **he has no ~s** il n'a aucun savoir-vivre; (child) il ne sait pas se tenir; **to have the ~s to do** avoir la politesse de faire; **aren't you forgetting your ~s?, where are your ~s?** en voilà une façon de se tenir!; **I'll teach him some ~s!** je vais lui apprendre les bonnes manières!; **road ~s** politesse *f* au volant; 2 (social habits, customs) mœurs *fpl*; **comedy of ~s** comédie *f* de mœurs.
III **-mannered** (*dans composés*) **ill/well-~ed** mal/bien élevé; **mild-~ed** doux/douce, aux manières douces.
IDIOMS **to do sth as if to the ~ born** faire qch comme si l'on était né pour cela.

mannered /ˈmænəd/ *adj* péj maniéré pej.

mannerism /ˈmænərɪzəm/ *n* 1 (personal habit) particularité *f*; 2 péj (quirk) manie *f* pej, tic *m* pej.

Mannerism /ˈmænərɪzəm/ *n* Art, Literat maniérisme *m*.

Mannerist /ˈmænərɪst/ *n, adj* maniériste (*mf*).

mannerliness /ˈmænəlɪnɪs/ *n* politesse *f*, savoir-vivre *m inv*.

mannerly /ˈmænəlɪ/ *adj* bien élevé.

mannikin /ˈmænɪkɪn/ *n* 1 Art, Med (also in dressmaking) mannequin *m*; 2 = **mannequin**; 3‡ (dwarf) nabot *m*.

manning /ˈmænɪŋ/ *n* 1 Mil armement *m*; 2 Ind effectifs *mpl*.

manning levels *npl* volume *m* des effectifs.

mannish /ˈmænɪʃ/ *adj* [*woman, clothing*] masculin, péj hommasse○.

manoeuvrability /məˌnuːvrəˈbɪlətɪ/ *n* maniabilité *f*.

manoeuvrable /məˈnuːvrəbl/ *adj* maniable.

manoeuvre GB, **maneuver** US /məˈnuːvə(r)/ I *n* lit, fig manœuvre *f*; **political/military ~** manœuvre politique/militaire; **to be on ~s** Mil être en manœuvres; **we have some room for ~** fig nous avons une marge de manœuvre.
II *vtr* 1 lit manœuvrer [*vehicle, object*]; **to ~ sth in/out** faire entrer/sortir qch en manœuvrant; **to ~ sth into position** manœuvrer qch pour le mettre en position; 2 fig manœuvrer [*person*]; faire dévier [*discussion*] (**to** vers); **to ~ sb into doing** manœuvrer qn pour qu'il fasse; **the Minister ~d the bill through Parliament** le Ministre a manœuvré le Parlement pour qu'il accepte le projet de loi; **he ~d the conversation round to the subject of** il a fait dévier la conversation vers le sujet de.
III *vi* manœuvrer.

manoeuvring /məˈnuːvərɪŋ/ *n* ¢ manigances *fpl*; pej magouille○ *f*.

man-of-war /ˌmænəvˈwɔː(r)/ *n* (ship) navire *m* de guerre.

manometer /mæˈnɒmɪtə(r)/ *n* manomètre *m*.

manor /ˈmænə(r)/ *n* 1 (also **~ house**) manoir *m*; Hist (estate) domaine *m* seigneurial; **Lord/Lady of the ~** châtelain/châtelaine *m/f*; 2○ GB argot des policiers secteur *m* (de police).

manorial /məˈnɔːrɪəl/ *adj* seigneurial.

manpower /ˈmænpaʊə(r)/ *n* 1 gen main-d'œuvre *f*; Mil hommes *mpl*; 2 (physical force) force *f*; **by sheer ~** à la force des poignets.

Manpower /ˈmænpaʊə(r)/ *n* GB *agence pour l'emploi*.

manse /mæns/ *n* presbytère *m* (*de pasteur*).

manservant /ˈmænsɜːvənt/ *n* valet *m*.

mansion /ˈmænʃn/ *n* (in countryside) demeure *f*; (in town) hôtel *m* particulier.

Mansion House *n* résidence *f* du Lord Mayor de Londres.

man-sized /ˈmænsaɪzd/ *adj* 1 Comm [*tissues*] grand modèle *inv*; 2 hum [*meal, portion*] sérieux/-ieuse.

manslaughter /ˈmænslɔːtə(r)/ *n* Jur homicide *m* involontaire.

mansuetude‡ /ˈmænswɪtjuːd, US -tuːd/ *n* mansuétude *f*.

mantel /ˈmæntl/ *n* = **mantelpiece**.

mantelpiece /ˈmæntlpiːs/, **mantelshelf** /ˈmæntlʃelf/ *n* (shelf) manteau *m* de cheminée; **on the ~** sur la cheminée.

mantilla /mænˈtɪlə/ *n* mantille *f*.

mantis /ˈmæntɪs/ *n* mante *f* (religieuse).

mantle /ˈmæntl/ I *n* 1‡ (cloak) cape *f*, pèlerine *f*; (woman's) mante *f*; 2 fig littér (of snow, darkness) manteau *m*; **to assume the ~ of power** assumer le pouvoir; 3 (of gas lamp) manchon *m*; 4 Geol, Biol, Zool manteau *m*.
II *vtr* littér recouvrir.

man-to-man /ˌmæntəˈmæn/ I *adj* d'homme à homme.
II **man to man** *adv* d'homme à homme.

mantrap /ˈmæntræp/ *n* piège *m* à hommes.

manual /ˈmænjʊəl/ I *n* 1 (book) manuel *m*; 2 Mus clavier *m*.
II *adj* [*labour, skills, task, work, worker*] manuel/-elle; [*gearbox, transmission, typewriter*] mécanique.

manually /ˈmænjʊəlɪ/ *adv* à la main, manuellement.

manufacture /ˌmænjʊˈfæktʃə(r)/ I *n* (of building materials, textiles, tools, electrical goods) fabrication *f*; (of food products, arms) production *f*; **car ~** construction *f* automobile.
II **manufactures** *npl* produits *mpl* manufacturés.
III *vtr* 1 lit fabriquer [*goods*]; 2 fig péj fabriquer (de toutes pièces) [*evidence, excuse*].
IV **manufactured** *pp adj* **~d goods/products** biens/produits manufacturés.

manufacturer /ˌmænjʊˈfæktʃərə(r)/ *n* gen fabricant *m* (**of** de); (of cars) constructeur *m*; **car ~** constructeur *m* automobile.

manufacturing /ˌmænjʊˈfæktʃərɪŋ/ I *n* 1 (sector of economy) industrie *f*; **the death of ~** la mort de l'industrie; **the importance of ~** l'importance de la production industrielle; 2 (making) gen fabrication *f*; (of cars, heavy machinery) construction *f*.
II *modif* [*output, sector, workforce*] industriel/-ielle; [*capacity, costs, system, technique, engineer*] de production; [*process*] de fabrication; **~ plant** usine *f*.

manufacturing base *n* tissu *m* industriel, base *f* industrielle.

manure /məˈnjʊə(r)/ I *n* 1 fumier *m*; **liquid ~** purin *m*; **horse ~** lit crottin *m* de cheval; **green ~** engrais *mpl* verts; 2○ US fig balivernes *fpl*.
II *vtr* fumer, engraisser.

manure heap *n* (tas *m* de) fumier *m*.

manuscript /ˈmænjʊskrɪpt/ I *n* manuscrit *m*; **in ~** (not yet printed) sous forme de manuscrit.
II *modif* [*letter*] manuscrit, écrit à la main.

Manx /mæŋks/ ▶ 1402 I *n* **1** Ling mannois *m*; **2 the ~** (+ *v pl*) les habitants *mpl* de l'île de Man.
II *adj* de l'île de Man.

Manx: **~ cat** *n* chat *m* (sans queue) de l'île de Man; **~man** *n* habitant *m* de l'île de Man; **~woman** *n* habitante *f* de l'île de Man.

many /'menɪ/ (*comp* **more**, *superl* **most**) I *quantif* beaucoup de, un grand nombre de; **~ people/cars** beaucoup de gens/voitures, un grand nombre de gens/voitures; **~ times** de nombreuses fois, bien des fois; **for ~ years** pendant de nombreuses années; **in ~ ways** à bien des égards; **his ~ friends** ses nombreux amis; **the ~ advantages of city life** les nombreux avantages de la vie citadine; **how ~ people/times?** combien de gens/de fois?; **too ~ people/times** trop de gens/fois; **a great ~ people** énormément de gens, un très grand nombre de gens; **for a great ~ years** pendant de nombreuses années; **a good ~ people/times** pas mal○ de gens/de fois; **like so ~ other women, she**... comme tant d'autres femmes, elle...; **I have as ~ books as you (do)** j'ai autant de livres que toi; **five exams in as ~ days** cinq examens en autant de jours; **~ a man would be glad of such an opportunity** plus d'un homme se réjouirait d'une telle occasion; **I spent ~ a night there** j'y ai passé de nombreuses nuits; **I've been there ~ a time, ~'s the time I've been there** j'y suis allé maintes fois.
II *pron* beaucoup; **not ~** pas beaucoup; **too ~** trop; **how ~?** combien?; **as ~ as you like** autant que tu veux; **I didn't know there were so ~** je ne savais pas qu'il y en avait autant; **we don't need ~ more** il ne nous en faut pas beaucoup plus; **~ of them were killed** beaucoup d'entre eux ont été tués; **there were too ~ of them** ils étaient trop nombreux; **a good ~ of the houses were damaged** un bon nombre des maisons ont été endommagées; **one/two too ~** un/deux de trop; **you've set one place too ~** tu as mis un couvert de trop.
III *n* **the ~** (the masses) la foule, les masses *fpl*; **to sacrifice the interests of the few in favour of the ~** sacrifier les intérêts d'une minorité en faveur du plus grand nombre; **the ~ who loved her** les nombreuses personnes qui l'ont aimée.
IDIOMS **to have had one too ~**○ avoir bu un coup de trop○.

many: **~-coloured**, **~-hued** littér *adj* multicolore; **~-sided** *adj* [*personality, phenomenon*] à multiples facettes.

Maoism /'maʊɪzəm/ *n* maoïsme *m*.

Maoist /'maʊɪst/ *n, adj* maoïste (*mf*).

Maori /'maʊrɪ/ ▶ 1486, 1402 I *n* **1** (person) Maori/-e *m/f*; **2** Ling maori *m*.
II *adj* maori.

map /mæp/ I *n* (of region, country) carte *f* (**of** de); (of town, underground, subway) plan *m* (**of** de); **road/tourist ~** carte routière/touristique; **weather ~** carte météo(rologique); **street ~** plan des rues; **~ of the underground** plan du métro; **I'll draw you a ~** je vais te faire un plan; **the political ~ of Europe** fig le paysage politique de l'Europe.
II *vtr* **1** Geog, Geol, Astron faire la carte de [*region, planet*]; faire le plan de [*town*]; faire un levé topographique de [*crater etc*]; **2** Comput faire une projection de.
IDIOMS **to put sb/sth on the ~** mettre qn/qch en vedette; **to be wiped off the ~** être rayé de la carte.
■ **map out**: **~ out [sth]**, **~ [sth] out** élaborer, mettre [qch] au point [*plans, strategy*]; planifier [*schedule*]; **her future is all ~ped out for her** son avenir est tout tracé.

maple /'meɪpl/ I *n* **1** (tree) érable *m*; **2** (also **~ wood**) bois *m* d'érable.
II *modif* [*leaf, syrup*] d'érable; [*floor, furniture*] en bois d'érable.

map maker ▶ 1692 *n* cartographe *mf*.

mapping /'mæpɪŋ/ *n* **1** Geog, Geol, Astron, Biol cartographie *f*; **2** Comput projection *f* topographique; ▶ **genetic mapping**.

map: **~ping pen** *n* plume *f* à dessin; **~ reader** *n* lecteur/-trice *m/f* de carte; **~ reading** *n* lecture *f* des cartes.

mar /mɑː(r)/ *vtr* (*p prés etc* **-rr-**) (*souvent au passif*) gâcher.
IDIOMS **to make or ~ sth** assurer le succès ou l'échec de qch.

Mar *abrév écrite* = **March**.

marabou /'mærəbuː/ *n* (bird) marabout *m*; (feathers) plumes *fpl*.

maraschino /ˌmærə'skiːnəʊ/ *n* marasquin *m*.

maraschino cherry *n* cerise *f* au marasquin.

marathon /'mærəθən, US -θɒn/ I *n* **1** (sport) marathon *m*; **to run (in) a ~** courir un marathon; **2** fig marathon *m*.
II *modif* **1** Sport **~ runner** marathonien/-ienne *m/f*; **2** (massive) -marathon *inv*; **a ~ session** une séance-marathon.

marauder /mə'rɔːdə(r)/ *n* maraudeur/-euse *m/f*.

marauding /mə'rɔːdɪŋ/ *adj* en maraude.

marble /'mɑːbl/ I *n* **1** (stone) marbre *m*; **made of ~** en marbre; **2** Games (glass) bille *f*; **3** Art (sculpture) marbre *m*; **4 marbles** ▶ 1282 (game) (+ *v sg*) billes *fpl*; **to play** ou **shoot ~s** US jouer aux billes.
II *modif* [*object*] de marbre.
IDIOMS **to lose one's ~s**○ perdre la boule○; **she still has all her ~s**○ elle garde toute sa tête.

marble cake *n* gâteau *m* marbré.

marbled /'mɑːbld/ *adj* **1** [*surface, appearance, paper*] marbré (**with** de); **2** Culin [*meat*] persillé.

marbling /'mɑːblɪŋ/ *n* (all contexts) marbrure *f*.

march /mɑːtʃ/ I *n* **1** Mil (foot journey) marche *f*; **a 40 km ~** une marche de 40 km; **on the ~** en marche; **it's a day's ~ from here** c'est à une journée de marche d'ici; **to be on the ~** lit [*army*] être en marche; fig [*prices*] être en hausse; **quick/slow ~** marche au pas accéléré/au pas de parade; **by forced ~** à marche forcée; **2** (demonstration) marche *f* (**against** contre; **for** pour); **peace/protest ~** marche *f* pacifiste/de protestation; **a ~ in protest at/in favour of sth** une marche de protestation contre/en faveur de qch; **a ~ on the White House** une marche sur la Maison Blanche; **3** Mus marche *f*; **4** fig (of progress) avancée *f* (**of** de); **the ~ of time** la marche du temps.
II *vtr* **she ~ed him into the office/off to the bathroom** elle l'a emmené d'autorité dans le bureau/à la salle de bains.
III *vi* **1** [*soldiers, band, prisoners*] marcher au pas; **to ~ on Rome** marcher sur Rome; **to ~ (for) 40 km** faire une marche de 40 km; **to ~ up and down the street** arpenter la rue; **forward ~!** en avant, marche!; **quick ~!** pas accéléré, marche!; **2** (in protest) manifester (**against** contre; **for** pour); **they ~ed from the hospital to the town hall** ils ont défilé de l'hôpital à la mairie; **they ~ed to Brussels in protest** ils ont organisé une marche de protestation jusqu'à Bruxelles; **they ~ed through Brussels in protest** leur marche de protestation a traversé Bruxelles; **3** (walk briskly) marcher d'un pas vif; (angrily) marcher l'air furieux; **he ~ed into/out of the room** il est entré/sorti l'air furieux; **she ~ed up to his desk** elle s'est dirigée droit sur son bureau.
IDIOMS **to give sb their ~ing orders** renvoyer qn avec perte et fracas.

March /mɑːtʃ/ ▶ 1472 *n* mars *m*.
IDIOMS **to be as mad as a ~ hare** être complètement fou.

marcher /'mɑːtʃə(r)/ *n* (in demonstration) manifestant/-e *m/f*; (in procession, band) marcheur/-euse *m/f*; **the civil rights/peace ~s** les manifestants pour les droits civiques/pour la paix.

marching /'mɑːtʃɪŋ/ I *n* marche *f*; **the ~ stopped** la marche a fait halte; **there was a sound of ~** on entendait un bruit de pas cadencés.
II *adj* [*feet, troops, demonstrators*] en marche.

marching: **~ band** *n* fanfare *f* avec majorettes; **~ song** *n* marche *f*.

marchioness /ˌmɑːʃə'nes/ *n* marquise *f*.

march-past /'mɑːtʃpɑːst/ *n* défilé *m*.

Mardi Gras /ˌmɑːdɪ 'grɑː/ *n* mardi *m* gras.

mare /meə(r)/ *n* (horse) jument *f*; (donkey) ânesse *f*.

marg○ /mɑːdʒ/ *n* GB *abrév* = **margarine**.

margarine /ˌmɑːdʒə'riːn/ *n* margarine *f*.

margarita /ˌmɑːgə'riːtə/ *n* margarita *m* (*cocktail de téquila et de jus de citron*).

marge○ /mɑːdʒ/ *n* GB *abrév* = **margarine**.

margin /'mɑːdʒɪn/ *n* **1** (on paper) marge *f*; **in the ~** dans la marge; **left/right ~** marge à gauche/droite; **2** (of wood, field) lisière *f*; (of river) bord *m*; **3** (also **winning ~**) marge *f* (**of** de); **by a wide/narrow/comfortable ~** avec une marge importante/courte/confortable; **to lose by a small ~** perdre de peu; **4** fig (fringe) (*souvent pl*) marge *f*; **at** ou **on the ~(s) of** en marge de; **5** (allowance) marge *f* (**for** pour); **~ of** ou **for error** marge d'erreur; **safety ~** marge de sécurité; **6** Comm (also **profit ~**) marge *f* bénéficiaire; **a low/high ~ sector** secteur à faible/forte marge bénéficiaire.

marginal /'mɑːdʒɪnl/ I *n* GB Pol siège *m* disputé.
II *adj* **1** (minor or peripheral) marginal; **2** GB Pol [*seat, ward*] disputé; **3** Agric [*land*] à faible rendement; **4** [*teacher's remark*] dans la marge; [*author's note*] en marge.

marginalia /ˌmɑːdʒɪ'neɪlɪə/ *npl* annotations *fpl*.

marginalize /'mɑːdʒɪnəlaɪz/ *vtr* marginaliser.

marginally /'mɑːdʒɪnəlɪ/ *adv* très légèrement.

marguerite /ˌmɑːgə'riːt/ *n* marguerite *f*.

marigold /'mærɪgəʊld/ *n* Bot souci *m*.

marijuana /ˌmærjuː'ɑːnə/ *n* marijuana *f*.

marina /mə'riːnə/ *n* marina *f*.

marinade /ˌmærɪ'neɪd/ I *n* marinade *f*.
II *vtr* faire mariner (**in** dans).
III *vi* mariner.

marinate /'mærɪneɪt/ I *vtr* faire mariner (**in** dans).
II **marinated** *pp adj* mariné.

marine /mə'riːn/ I *n* **1** (soldier) fusilier *m* marin; **the Marines** les marines *mpl*; **2** (navy) **the mercantile** ou **merchant ~** la marine marchande.
II *modif* [*mammal, ecosystem, biology*] marin; [*archeology, explorer, life*] sous-marin; [*insurance, law, equipment, transport, industry*] maritime.
IDIOMS **tell it to the ~s!** raconte ça à d'autres!

marine: **Marine Corps** *n* corps *m* des marines américains; **~ engineer** ▶ 1692 *n* ingénieur *m* du génie maritime.

mariner /'mærɪnə(r)/ *n*† marin *m*.

Mariolatry /ˌmeərɪ'ɒlətrɪ/ *n* culte *m* excessif de la Vierge.

marionette /ˌmærɪə'net/ *n* marionnette *f*.

marital /'mærɪtl/ *adj* [*relations*] conjugal; **~ status** Admin situation *f* de famille.

maritime /'mærɪtaɪm/ *adj* (all contexts) maritime.

marjoram /'mɑːdʒərəm/ *n* Bot, Culin marjolaine *f*.

mark /mɑːk/ ▶ 1143 I *n* **1** (visible patch) (stain) tache *f*; (spot on animal) tache *f*; (from injury) marque *f*; **to make one's ~** (on document) signer d'une croix; fig faire ses preuves; **2** fig (lasting impression) **to bear the ~ of** [*person*] porter l'empreinte de [*genius, greatness*]; [*face*] porter les marques de [*pain, grief*]; **to leave one's ~ on sth** [*person*] marquer qch de son influence [*company, project*]; [*recession*] marquer qch [*country*]; **3** (symbol) **as a ~ of** en signe de [*appreciation, esteem*]; **4** Sch, Univ, gen (assessment of work) note *f*; **what ~ has she given you?** quelle note t'a-t-elle mise?; **he gets no ~s for effort/ originality** fig pour l'effort/l'originalité, il mérite zéro; ▶ **full, top**; **5** (number on scale) **the 3-mile ~** la borne de trois miles; **unemployment has reached/passed the two million ~** le chômage a atteint/dépassé la barre des deux millions; **his earnings are above/below the £20,000 ~** son salaire est supérieur/inférieur à 20 000 livres; **the timer had reached the one-minute ~** cela faisait une minute au chronomètre; **the high-tide ~** le maximum de la marée haute; **at gas ~ 7** à thermostat 7; **he/his work is not up to the ~** fig il/son travail n'est pas à la hauteur; **6** Sport (starting line) (in athletics) marque *f*; **on your ~s, (get) set, go!** à vos marques! prêts! partez!; **to get off the ~** prendre le départ; **we haven't even got off the ~ yet** fig nous n'avons même pas commencé; **he's a bit slow off the ~** fig il a l'esprit un peu lent; **you were a bit slow off the ~ in not noticing the mistake sooner** tu as été un peu lent à remarquer cette erreur; **he's very quick off the ~** il a l'esprit vif; **you were a bit quick off the ~ (in) blaming her** tu l'as blâmée un peu trop vite; **he's always very quick off the ~ when it comes to money** il n'est jamais le dernier quand il s'agit d'argent; **you were quick off the ~!** (to do sth) tu n'as pas perdu de temps!; **7** (target) (in archery etc) but *m*; **to find its ~** [*arrow*] atteindre son but; fig [*criticism, remark*] mettre dans le mille; **to be (way) off the ~, to be wide of the ~** [*person , calculation*] être à côté de la plaque○; **on the ~** absolument exact; **8** Sport (in rugby) arrêt *m* de volée; **9** (also **Mark**) (model in series) Mark; **Jaguar Mark II** Jaguar Mark II; **10** (also **Deutschmark**) deutschmark *m*.

II *vtr* **1** (make visible impression on) (stain) tacher [*clothes, material, paper*]; [*bruise, scar*] marquer [*skin, face*]; (with pen etc) marquer [*map, belongings*] (**with** avec); **to ~ sb for life** (physically) défigurer qn à vie; (mentally) marquer qn à vie; **2** (indicate, label) [*person*] marquer [*name, initials, price, directions*] (**on** sur); [*cross, arrow, sign, label*] indiquer [*position, place, road*]; fig [*death, event, announcement*] marquer [*end, change, turning point*]; **to be ~ed as** être considéré comme [*future champion, criminal*]; **to ~ the occasion/sb's birthday with** marquer l'occasion/l'anniversaire de qn par [*firework display, party*]; **X ~s the spot** l'endroit est indiqué par une croix; **to ~ one's place** (in book) marquer la page; **3** (characterize) caractériser [*style, remark, behaviour, era*]; **to be ~ed by** être caractérisé par [*violence, envy, humour, generosity*]; **4** Sch, Univ (tick) corriger [*essay, homework, examination paper*]; **to ~ sb absent/present** noter qn absent/présent; **to ~ sth right/wrong** indiquer que qch est juste/faux; **5** (pay attention to) noter (bien) [*warning, comment*]; **~ him well, he will be a great man** sout souvenez-vous de lui, ce sera un grand homme; **6** Sport marquer [*player*].

III *vi* **1** Sch, Univ [*teacher*] faire des corrections; **2** (stain) [*dress, material etc*] se tacher; **3** Sport marquer.

IV mark you *conj phr* n'empêche que (+ *indic*); **~ you it won't be easy** n'empêche que ça ne va pas être facile.

IDIOMS **~ my words** crois-moi; **he'll not live long, ~ my words!** crois-moi, il ne vivra pas longtemps!; **to be an easy ~** être une poire○; **to ~ time** Mil marquer le pas; **I'm ~ing time working as a waitress until I go to France** fig je travaille comme serveuse en attendant d'aller en France; **the company is ~ing time at the moment** fig la compagnie ne fait que piétiner en ce moment.

■ **mark down**: ¶ **~ [sth] down, ~ down [sth]** (reduce price of) démarquer [*product*]; ¶ **~ [sb] down** (lower grade of) baisser les notes de [*person*]; baisser la note de [*work, essay*]; **to ~ sb down as (being) sth** (consider to be) considérer qn comme [*troublemaker, asset*].

■ **mark off**: **~ [sth] off, ~ off [sth] 1** (separate off) délimiter [*area*]; **2** (tick off) pointer [*items, names*].

■ **mark out**: ¶ **~ [sb] out, ~ out [sb] 1** (distinguish) distinguer (**from** de); **2** (select) désigner [*person*] (**for** pour); ¶ **~ [sth] out, ~ out [sth]** marquer les limites de [*court, area*].

■ **mark up**: ¶ **~ [sth] up, ~ up [sth]** (add percentage to price) [*company*] majorer le prix de [*product*] (**by** de); (increase price) [*shopkeeper*] augmenter le prix de [*product*] (**by** de); ¶ **~ [sb/sth] up** Sch, Univ (increase grade of) remonter les notes de [*person*]; remonter la note de [*work, essay*].

mark-down /'mɑːkdaʊn/ *n* Comm rabais *m*.

marked /mɑːkt/ *adj* **1** (noticeable) [*contrast, resemblance, decline, increase*] marqué, net/nette (*before n*); [*accent*] prononcé; **2** (in danger) **he's a ~ man** on en veut à sa vie; **3** Ling marqué.

markedly /'mɑːkɪdlɪ/ *adv* [*better, different, smaller*] nettement; [*increase, decline, differ, improve*] sensiblement.

marker /'mɑːkə(r)/ *n* **1** (also **~ pen**) marqueur *m*; **2** (tag) repère *m*; **3** (person who keeps score) marqueur/-euse *m/f*; **4** Sch, Univ (examiner) examinateur/-trice *m/f*; **5** (bookmark) signet *m*; **6** Sport (person) marqueur/-euse *m/f*; **7** Ling marque *f*.

market /'mɑːkɪt/ **I** *n* **1** Econ (trading structure) marché *m*; **the art/job/property ~** le marché de l'art/du travail/de l'immobilier; **the ~ in tea/sugar, the tea/sugar ~** le marché du thé/du sucre; **at ~ (price)** au prix du marché; **cars at the upper** ou **top end of the ~** les voitures haut de gamme; **to be at the upper end of the ~** [*company*] être au premier rang du marché; **to put sth on the ~** mettre qch sur le marché; **to be in the ~ for sth** chercher (à acquérir) qch; **to come onto the ~** [*goods, product*] arriver sur le marché; **2** Comm (potential customers) marché *m* (**for** pour); **domestic/foreign ~** marché intérieur/extérieur; **the Japanese/French ~** le marché japonais/français; **a good/poor/steady ~ for** une demande forte/faible/stable de; **it sells well to the teenage ~** ça se vend bien aux adolescents; **a gap in the ~** un créneau, un besoin du marché; **3** (place where goods are sold) marché *m*; **flower/fish ~** marché aux fleurs/halle *f* aux poissons; **covered/open air ~** marché couvert/en plein air; **to go to ~** aller au marché; **4** Fin (stock market) Bourse *f*; **to play the ~** spéculer.

II *modif* Comm, Econ [*share*] de marché; [*conditions, rates, trend*] du marché.

III *vtr* **1** (sell) commercialiser, vendre [*product*]; **2** (promote) lancer or mettre [qch] sur le marché.

IV *vi* US **to go ~ing** faire des courses.

V *v refl* **to ~ oneself** se vendre.

marketability /ˌmɑːkɪtə'bɪlətɪ/ *n* (of product) caractère *m* commercialisable.

marketable /'mɑːkɪtəbl/ *adj* (in demand, fit for sale) vendable; **~ value** valeur marchande or d'échange.

market: **~ analysis** *n* analyse *f* de marché; **~ analyst** ▶ **1692** *n* analyste *mf* de marché; **~-based** *adj* = **market-led**; **~capitalization** *n* capitalisation *f* boursière; **~ cross** *n*: *croix qui se trouve sur la place du marché*; **~ day** *n* jour *m* du marché; **~ economy** *n* économie *f* de marché.

marketeer /ˌmɑːkɪ'tɪə(r)/ *n* Pol (also **Marketeer, pro-~**) partisan *m* du Marché commun; **anti-~** opposant/-e *m/f* au Marché commun. ▶ **black marketeer**.

marketer /'mɑːkɪtə(r)/ *n* vendeur *m*.

market: **~ forces** *npl* forces *fpl* du marché; **~ garden** *n* jardin *m* maraîcher; **~ gardener** ▶ **1692** *n* maraîcher/-ère *m/f*; **~ gardening** *n* culture *f* maraîchère.

marketing /'mɑːkɪtɪŋ/ **I** *n* **1** (process, theory) marketing *m*, mercatique *f*; **product/service ~** marketing d'un produit/d'un service; **2** (department) service *m* de marketing.

II *modif* [*director, manager*] du marketing; [*method, department*] de marketing; [*staff*] du service de marketing.

marketing: **~ agreement** *n* accord *m* de commercialisation; **~ campaign** *n* campagne *f* de vente; **~ company** *n* Comm société *f* de marketing; **~ exercise** *n* campagne *f* de marketing; **~ man** *n* (*pl* **-men**) commercial *m*; **~ mix** *n* marchéage *m*; **~ process** *n* processus *m* de commercialisation; **~ research** *n* étude *f* de marché; **~ strategy** *n* stratégie *f* commerciale.

market: **~ leader** *n* (product) produit *m* vedette; (company) leader *m* du marché; **~-led** *adj* gen déterminé par le marché; [*economy*] de marché; **~ maker** *n* Fin opérateur *m* (en Bourse); **~ making** *n* transactions *fpl* (en Bourse); **~ opportunity** *n* créneau *m*; **~ order** *n* ordre *m* de Bourse; **~ overt** *n* GB Jur marché *m* public.

marketplace /'mɑːkɪtpleɪs/ *n* **1** (square) place *f* du marché; **2** Econ, Fin marché *m*; **in the ~** sur le marché.

market: **~ potential** *n* ressources *fpl* or possibilités *fpl* d'un marché; **~ price** *n* prix *m* du marché; **~ rent** *n* GB valeur *f* locative; **~ report** *n* résultat *m* d'étude de marché; **~ research** *n* étude *f* de marché; **~ research agency** *n* agence *f* spécialisée en études de marché; **~ researcher** ▶ **1692** *n* chargé/-e *m/f* d'études de marketing; **~ resistance** *n* réaction *f* défavorable des consommateurs; **~ square** *n* place *f* du marché; **~ stall** *n* étal *m*; **~ town** *n* bourg *m*; **~ trader** *n* vendeur/-euse *m/f* sur un marché; **~ value** *n* valeur *f* marchande or d'échange.

marking /'mɑːkɪŋ/ *n* **1** (visible impression) (spot on animal) tache *f*; (on aircraft) marque *f*; **road ~s** signalisation *f* horizontale; **2** GB Sch, Univ (process of correcting) corrections *fpl*; (marks given) notation *f*; **3** Sport marquage *m*; **man-to-man ~** marquage individuel.

marking: **~ ink** *n* encre *f* indélébile; **~ pen** *n* marqueur *m* indélébile; **~ scheme** *n* GB Sch, Univ barème *m*; **~ system** *n* GB Sch, Univ système *m* de notation.

mark: **~ reading, ~ scanning** *n* Comput lecture *f* optique de marques; **~sman** *n* Mil, Sport tireur *m* d'élite; **~smanship** *n* Mil, Sport adresse *f* au tir; **~swoman** *n* Mil, Sport tireuse *f* d'élite; **~-up** *n* (retailer's margin) marge *f*; (increase) augmentation *f*.

marl /mɑːl/ **I** *n* marne *f*.

II *vtr* marner.

marlin /'mɑːlɪn/ *n* **1** Zool marlin *m*; **2** Naut (also **marline**) lusin *m*.

marly /'mɑːlɪ/ *adj* marneux/-euse.

marmalade /'mɑːməleɪd/ *n* confiture *f* or marmelade *f* d'oranges; **grapefruit ~** confiture *f* de pamplemousse.

marmalade: **~ cat** *n* chat roux/chatte rousse *m/f*; **~ orange** *n* orange *f* amère.

Marmara /'mɑːmərə/ ▶ **1511** *pr n* **the Sea of ~** la mer de Marmara.

Marmite® /'mɑːmaɪt/ *n* GB *pâte à tartiner aux extraits de levure et de légumes*.

Marmora *pr n* = **Marmara**.

marmoreal /mɑːˈmɔːrɪəl/ *adj* littér marmoréen/-éenne liter.

marmoset /ˈmɑːməzet/ *n* ouistiti *m*.

marmot /ˈmɑːmət/ *n* marmotte *f*.

Marne ▶1163 *pr n* Marne *f*; **in/to the ~** dans la Marne.

marocain /ˈmærəkeɪn/ *n* crêpe *m* marocain.

Maronite /ˈmærənaɪt/ *n, adj* maronite (*mf*).

maroon /məˈruːn/ ▶1104 **I** *n* **1** (colour) bordeaux *m*; **2** GB (rocket) fusée *f* de détresse.
II *adj* bordeaux *inv*.
III *vtr* (strand) **to be ~ed on an island/at home** être bloqué sur une île/chez soi; **the ~ed sailors** ou **castaways** les naufragés.

marquee /mɑːˈkiː/ *n* **1** GB (tent) grande tente *f*; (of circus) chapiteau *m*; **2** US (canopy) (grand) auvent *m*.

Marquesas Islands /mɑːˈkeɪsæs aɪləndz/ *pr npl* îles *fpl* Marquises.

marquess /ˈmɑːkwɪs/ *n* marquis *m*.

marquetry /ˈmɑːkɪtrɪ/ *n* marqueterie *f*.

marquis /ˈmɑːkwɪs/ *n* marquis *m*.

Marrakech, **Marrakesh** /ˌmærəˈkeʃ/ ▶1818 *pr n* Marrakech.

marriage /ˈmærɪdʒ/ *n* **1** (ceremony, contract) mariage *m* (**to sb** avec qn); **broken ~** mariage brisé; **her first/second ~** son premier/second mariage; **proposal of ~** proposition *f* de mariage; **by ~** par alliance; **my uncle by ~** mon oncle par alliance; **we're related by ~** nous sommes parents par alliance; **2** fig (alliance) mariage *m*; **the ~ of art and science** le mariage de l'art et de la science; **3** (in cards) mariage *m*.

marriageable† /ˈmærɪdʒəbl/ *adj* [*person*] mariable; **of ~ age** en âge de se marier.

marriage: **~ bed** *n* lit *m* conjugal; **~ bonds** *npl* liens *mpl* conjugaux; **~ bureau** *n* agence *f* matrimoniale; **~ ceremony** *n* cérémonie *f* nuptiale; **~ certificate** *n* extrait *m* d'acte de mariage; **~ contract** *n* contrat *m* de mariage; **~ guidance** *n* conseil *m* conjugal; **~ guidance counsellor** *n* conseiller/-ère *m/f* conjugal/-e; **~ licence** GB, **~ license** US *n* certificat *m* de publication des bans; **~ of convenience** *n* mariage *m* de convenance; **~ proposal** *n* proposition *f* de mariage; **~ rate** *n* taux *m* de nuptialité; **~ vows** *npl* vœux *mpl* de mariage.

married /ˈmærɪd/ **I** *adj* **1** [*person*] marié (**to** à); **~ couple** couple *m*; **2** [*state, life, love*] conjugal.
II marrieds *npl* **the young ~s** les jeunes mariés *mpl*.

married: **~ name** *n* nom *m* de femme mariée; **~ quarters** *npl* quartiers *mpl* familiaux.

marrow /ˈmærəʊ/ *n* **1** Anat moelle *f*; **chilled** ou **frozen to the ~** gelé or transi jusqu'à la moelle; **2** GB Bot courge *f*; **baby ~** GB courgette *f*.

marrowbone /ˈmærəʊbəʊn/ *n* os *m* à moelle; **~ jelly** gelée *f* (d'os à moelle).

marrowfat (pea) *n* pois *m* à grain ridé.

marry /ˈmærɪ/ **I** *excl* ‡ sacrebleu!
II *vtr* **1** lit [*priest, registrar, parent*] marier; [*bride, groom*] se marier avec, épouser; **to get married** se marier (**to** avec); **they were married by his uncle** c'est son oncle qui les a mariés; **they were married in 1989** ils se sont mariés en 1989; **will you ~ me?** veux-tu m'épouser?; **2** fig marier [*ideas, styles, colours*]; **to be married to one's job** hum ne vivre que pour son travail.
III *vi* se marier; **to ~ into a family** entrer dans une famille par le mariage; **to ~ for love/money** faire un mariage d'amour/d'argent; **he's not the ~ing kind** il n'est pas du genre à se marier; **to ~ into money** épouser un homme/une femme riche; **to ~ again** se remarier; **to ~ beneath oneself** se mésallier.
■ **marry off**: **~ off [sb]**, **~ [sb] off** marier (**to** à, avec).

Mars /mɑːz/ *pr n* **1** Mythol Mars *m*; **2** Astron Mars *f*.

Marseillaise /ˌmɑːseɪˈjeɪz/ *n* **the ~** la Marseillaise.

Marseilles /mɑːˈseɪ/ ▶1818 *pr n* Marseille.

marsh /mɑːʃ/ *n* (terrain) marécage *m*; (region) marais *m*.

marshal /ˈmɑːʃl/ **I** *n* **1** Mil maréchal *m*; (as form of address) Monsieur le Maréchal; **2** GB Jur *avocat accompagnant un juge itinérant*; **3** (at rally, ceremony) membre *m* du service d'ordre; **4** US Jur ≈ huissier *m* de justice; **5** US Hist (sheriff) marshal *m*; **6** US (in fire service) capitaine *m* des pompiers.
II (*p prés* **-ll-** GB, **-l-** US) *vtr* **1** gen, Mil rassembler [*troops, vehicles, ships*]; diriger [*crowd*]; Rail trier [*wagons*]; fig rassembler [*ideas, facts, arguments*]; **2** (guide, usher) conduire [*person*]; **they were ~led out of the room** on les a conduits hors de la pièce.

marshalling yard *n* GB Rail gare *f* de triage.

marsh: **~ fever** ▶1354 *n* paludisme *m*; **~ gas** *n* gaz *m* des marais; **~ harrier** *n* busard *m* des roseaux; **~land** *n* (terrain) marécage *m*; (region) marais *m*.

marshmallow /ˌmɑːʃˈmæləʊ/ *n* **1** Bot guimauve *f*; **2** Culin pâte *f* de guimauve.

marsh: **~ marigold** *n* souci *m* d'eau; **~ tit** *n* mésange *f* nonnette.

marshy /ˈmɑːʃɪ/ *adj* marécageux/-euse.

marsupial /mɑːˈsuːpɪəl/ *n, adj* marsupial (*m*).

mart /mɑːt/ *n* **1** (shopping centre) centre *m* commercial; **2** (market) marché *m*; **auction ~** salle *f* des ventes.

marten /ˈmɑːtɪn, US -tn/ *n* martre *f*.

martial /ˈmɑːʃl/ *adj* [*music*] martial; [*spirit*] guerrier/-ière.

martial: **~ arts** *npl* arts *mpl* martiaux; **~ law** *n* loi *f* martiale.

Martian /ˈmɑːʃn/ **I** *n* Martien/-ienne *m/f*.
II *adj* martien/-ienne *m/f*.

martinet /ˌmɑːtɪˈnet, US -tnˈet/ *n* **to be a ~** être stricte en matière de discipline.

martini /mɑːˈtiːnɪ/ *n* **1** (cocktail) (martini *m*) dry *m* (*cocktail de vermouth blanc et de gin*); **2 Martini**® martini *m*.

Martinique /ˌmɑːtɪˈniːk/ ▶1163, 1381 *pr n* Martinique *f*; **in/to ~** à la or en Martinique.

Martinmas /ˈmɑːtɪnməs/ *n* la Saint-Martin.

martyr /ˈmɑːtə(r)/ **I** *n* Relig, fig martyr/-e *m/f*; **a ~ to the cause** un martyr de la cause; **she's a ~ to her rheumatism** fig ses rhumatismes lui font souffrir le martyre; **don't be such a ~!** arrête de jouer les martyrs!; **he likes playing the ~** il aime jouer les martyrs.
II *vtr* lit, fig martyriser.
III martyred *pp adj* [*sigh, look*] déchirant; [*air*] de martyr.

martyrdom /ˈmɑːtədəm/ *n* martyre *m*.

martyrize /ˈmɑːtɪraɪz/ *vtr* martyriser.

marvel /ˈmɑːvl/ **I** *n* **1** (wonderful thing) merveille *f*; **it was a ~ to behold** c'était merveilleux à voir; **it's a ~ that he can still dance** c'est merveilleux qu'il puisse encore danser; **he's a ~ with children** il est merveilleux avec les enfants; **the ~s of nature** les merveilles de la nature; **to work ~s** faire des merveilles; **2** (wonderful example) **she's a ~ of patience** elle est merveilleusement patiente; **the building is a ~ of design** ce bâtiment est merveilleusement bien conçu.
II *vtr* (*p prés etc* GB **-ll-**, US **-l-**) **to ~ that** s'étonner de ce que (+ *subj*).
III *vi* s'étonner (**at** de), être émerveillé (**at** par).

marvellous GB, **marvelous** US /ˈmɑːvələs/ *adj* [*weather, holiday etc*] merveilleux/-euse; **but that's ~!** mais c'est formidable!; **it's ~ that he was able to come** c'est formidable qu'il ait pu venir.

marvellously GB, **marvelously** US /ˈmɑːvələslɪ/ *adv* [*sing, get on*] à merveille; [*clever, painted*] merveilleusement; **~ well** merveilleusement bien.

Marxism /ˈmɑːksɪzəm/ *n* marxisme *m*.

Marxist /ˈmɑːksɪst/ *n, adj* marxiste (*mf*).

Mary /ˈmeərɪ/ *pr n* Marie; **~ Magdalene** Marie-Madeleine; **~ Queen of Scots** Marie Stuart, reine d'Écosse.

Maryland /ˈmeərɪlænd/ ▶1744 *pr n* Maryland *m*.

marzipan /ˈmɑːzɪpæn, ˌmɑːzɪˈpæn/ *n* pâte *f* d'amandes.

mascara /mæˈskɑːrə, US -ˈskærə/ *n* mascara *m*, rimmel® *m*.

mascon /ˈmæskɒn/ *n* mascon *m*.

mascot /ˈmæskət, -skɒt/ *n* mascotte *f*; **lucky ~** porte-bonheur *m*.

masculine /ˈmæskjʊlɪn/ **I** *n* masculin *m*; **in the ~** au masculin.
II *adj* **1** gen [*clothes, colour, style, features*] masculin; [*occupation*] d'homme; **the ~ side of her nature** son côté masculin; **2** Ling masculin.

masculinity /ˌmæskjʊˈlɪnətɪ/ *n* (virility) virilité *f*; (gender) masculinité *f*.

maser /ˈmeɪzə(r)/ *n* maser *m*.

mash /mæʃ/ **I** *n* **1** Agric (for dogs, poultry) pâtée *f*; (for horses) mash *m*; **bran ~** pâtée de son; **2** (in brewing) trempe *f*; **3**° GB Culin purée *f* (de pommes de terre); **bangers and ~** des saucisses avec de la purée.
II *vtr* **1** écraser [*fruit*]; **~ed potatoes/turnips** purée *f* de pommes de terre/de navets; **to ~ potatoes** faire de la purée (de pommes de terre); **2** (in brewing) brasser.
■ **mash up**: **~ up [sth]**, **~ [sth] up** écraser [*fruit, potatoes*].

MASH /mæʃ/ *n* US (*abrév* = **mobile army surgical hospital**) unité *f* médicale de campagne.

masher /ˈmæʃə(r)/ *n* (utensil) presse-purée *m inv*.

mask /mɑːsk, US mæsk/ **I** *n* **1** (for face) (for disguise, protection) masque *m*; (at masked ball) loup *m*; **a ~ of indifference** fig un masque d'indifférence; **2** (sculpture) masque *m*; **3** Cosmet **face ~** masque *m*; **4** Electron, Comput masque *m*; **5** Phot cache *m*; **6** Theat masque *m*.
II *vtr* **1** masquer [*face*]; **2** fig dissimuler [*truth, emotions*]; masquer [*taste*]; **3** Fin déguiser [*losses*]; **4** Phot masquer.

mask: **~ed ball** *n* bal *m* masqué; **~ing tape** *n* ruban *m* adhésif.

masochism /ˈmæsəkɪzəm/ *n* masochisme *m*.

masochist /ˈmæsəkɪst/ *n, adj* masochiste (*mf*).

masochistic /ˌmæsəˈkɪstɪk/ *adj* masochiste.

mason /ˈmeɪsn/ ▶1692 *n* **1** Constr maçon *m*; **2 Mason** (also **Free~**) franc-maçon *m*.

masonic /məˈsɒnɪk/ *adj* maçonnique.

Masonite, masonite® /ˈmeɪsənaɪt/ *n* US aggloméré *m*.

masonry /ˈmeɪsənrɪ/ *n* **1** Constr maçonnerie *f*; **2 Masonry** (also **Free~**) maçonnerie *f*.

masque /mɑːsk/ *n* **1** Theat mascarade *f*; **2** = **masked ball**.

masquerade /ˌmɑːskəˈreɪd, US ˌmæsk-/ **I** *n* **1** (ball) bal *m* masqué; **2** fig (pretence) mascarade *f*.
II *vi* **to ~ as sb** se faire passer pour qn; **to ~ under a false name** s'abriter sous un faux nom.

mass /mæs/ **I** *n* **1** (voluminous body) masse *f* (**of** de); (cluster) amas *m* (**of** de); **a ~ of trees** une masse d'arbres; **a ~ of particles** un amas de particules; **the tree was just a ~ of flowers** l'arbre était couvert de fleurs; **2** (large amount) (of people) foule *f* (**of** de); (of evidence, legislation, details) quantité *f* (**of** de); **3** Relig messe *f*; **to celebrate/say ~** célébrer/dire la messe; **to attend** ou **go to ~** aller à la messe; **4** Phys, Art masse *f*.
II masses *npl* **1** (the people) **the ~es** gen

la foule; (working class) les masses *fpl*; **the labouring ~es** les masses laborieuses; **2**○ GB (lots) **to have ~es of work/friends** avoir beaucoup or plein○ de travail/d'amis; **there were ~es of people** il y avait une foule de gens; **there was ~es of food** il y avait un tas○ de choses à manger; **to have ~es of time** avoir tout son temps, avoir largement le temps.
III *modif* **1** (large scale) [*audience*] de masse; [*destruction, exodus, protest, unemployment*] massif/-ive; **~ meeting** rassemblement *m* de masse; **~ shooting** massacre *m*; **2** (of the people) [*communications, consciousness, culture, demonstration, movement, tourism*] de masse; [*hysteria*] collectif/-ive; **to have ~ appeal** avoir un succès de masse; **3** (simultaneous) [*sackings, desertions*] en masse.
IV *vi* [*troops*] se regrouper; [*bees*] se masser; [*clouds*] s'amonceler.

Massachusetts /ˌmæsəˈtʃuːsɪts/ **▶ 1744** *pr n* Massachusetts *m*.

massacre /ˈmæsəkə(r)/ **I** *n* lit, fig massacre *m*.
II *vtr* **1** lit massacrer; **2** fig démolir○ [*team*]; massacrer [*language, tune*].

massage /ˈmæsɑːʒ, US məˈsɑːʒ/ **I** *n* massage *m*; **to have a ~** se faire faire un massage.
II *vtr* masser [*person*]; fig tricher sur [*figures*]; flatter [*ego*].

massage: **~ oil** *n* huile *f* de massage; **~ parlour** *n* salon *m* de massage.

mass: **~ consumption** *n* consommation *f* de masse; **~ cult**○ *n* US culture *f* de masse; **~-energy** *n* masse-énergie *f*; **~-energy equation** *n* équation *f* masse-énergie.

masseur /mæˈsɜː(r)/ **▶ 1692** *n* masseur *m*.

masseuse /mæˈsɜːz/ **▶ 1692** *n* masseuse *f*.

mass grave *n* charnier *m*, fosse *f* commune.

massicot /ˈmæsɪkət/ *n* massicot *m*.

massif /ˈmæsiːf, mæˈsiːf/ *n* massif *m*.

massive /ˈmæsɪv/ *adj* [*object, animal, amount, error, fraud, debt*] énorme; [*explosion, scandal*] retentissant; [*majority, victory*] écrasant; [*campaign, task, programme*] de grande envergure; [*increase, cut, attack*] massif/-ive; [*heart attack, haemorrhage*] grave.

massively /ˈmæsɪvlɪ/ *adv* [*reduce, increase*] énormément; [*overrated, overloaded, stretched*] considérablement; [*expensive, intensive*] extrêmement; **to be ~ successful** avoir un immense succès.

mass market /ˌmæs ˈmɑːkɪt/ **I** *n* marché *m* grand public.
II *modif* [*phone, TV set*] grand public *inv*; [*potential*] de grande diffusion.

mass-marketed /ˌmæsˈmɑːkɪtɪd/ *adj* [*goods*] destiné au grand public.

mass-marketing /ˌmæsˈmɑːkɪtɪŋ/ *n* commercialisation *f* massive.

mass: **~ media** *n* (+ *v sg* ou *pl*) (mass) médias *mpl*; **~ murder** *n* massacre *m*; **~ murderer** *n* auteur *m* d'un meurtre collectif; **~ noun** *n* nom *m* noncomptable; **~ number** *n* nombre *m* de masse; **~ observation** *n* enquête *f* sociologique (*au niveau national*).

mass-produce /ˌmæsprəˈdjuːs, US -duːs/ **I** *vtr* fabriquer [qch] en série.
II mass-produced *pp adj* fabriqué en série.

mass: **~ production** *n* fabrication *f* en série; **~ screening** *n* Med dépistage *m* systématique; **~ spectrograph** *n* spectrographe *m* de masse; **~ spectrometer** *n* spectromètre *m* de masse; **~ spectroscope** *n* spectroscope *m* de masse; **~ X-ray** *n* dépistage *m* radiographique systématique.

mast /mɑːst, US mæst/ **I** *n* **1** (on ship, for flags) mât *m*; Radio, TV pylône *m*; **the ~s of a ship** la mâture d'un navire; **2** ₵ Agric glands *mpl* et faines *fpl*.
II *vtr* mâter.
III -masted (*dans composés*) **three-~ed** à trois mâts.
IDIOMS **to nail one's colours to the ~** afficher ses opinions (une fois pour toutes); **to sail before the ~** servir comme simple matelot.

mastectomy /məsˈtektəmɪ/ *n* mastectomie *f*.

master /ˈmɑːstə(r), US ˈmæs-/ **I** *n* **1** (man in charge) maître *m*; **the ~ of the house** le maître de maison; **to be ~ in one's own house** être maître chez soi; **2** (person in control) maître/-esse *m/f*; **to be one's own ~** être son propre maître; **to be (the) ~ of one's fate/the situation** être maître/-esse de son destin/la situation; **to be ~ of oneself** être maître/-esse de soi; **3** (person who excels) maître *m*; **a ~ of** un maître de [*violin, narrative*]; un/-e expert/-e de [*tactics, public relations*]; **to be a ~ at doing** être maître dans l'art de faire; **4** Art (also **Master**) maître *m*; **the Dutch ~s** les maîtres hollandais; **5** Sch (teacher) (primary) maître *m*, instituteur *m*; (secondary) professeur *m*; (headmaster) proviseur *m*; **6** GB Univ (of college) principal *m*; **7** (also **~ copy**) original *m*; **8**† (also **Master**) (as form of address) maître *m*; **yes, Master** oui, Maître; **9** Univ (graduate) ≈ titulaire *mf* d'une maîtrise; **~'s (degree)** maîtrise *f* (**in** en, de); **to be working towards one's ~'s** préparer sa maîtrise; **10** Naut capitaine *m*; **11** (in chess, bridge etc) maître *m*; **12** (title of young man) monsieur *m*; **the young ~**† le jeune monsieur; **Master Ian Todd** (on envelope) Monsieur Ian Todd.
II Masters *npl* (+ *v sg*) Sport **the Masters** gen le championnat; (in tennis) le masters.
III *modif* [*architect, butcher, chef, craftsman*] maître (*before n*); [*smuggler, spy, terrorist, thief*] professionnel/-elle.
IV *vtr* **1** (learn, become proficient in or with) maîtriser [*subject, language, controls, computers, theory, basics, complexities*]; posséder [*art, skill*]; **2** (control) dominer [*feelings, situation, person*]; surmonter [*phobia*].

master: **~-at-arms** *n* GB **▶ 1612** capitaine *m* d'armement; **~ bedroom** *n* chambre *f* principale; **~ builder ▶ 1692** *n* maître *m* d'œuvre; **~ class** *n* master class *m*; **~ copy** *n* original *m*; **~ disk** *n* Comput disque *m* d'exploitation; **~ file** *n* Comput fichier *m* maître.

masterful /ˈmɑːstəfl, US ˈmæs-/ *adj* **1** (dominating) [*person*] dominateur/-trice; **2** (skilled, masterly) [*person*] très habile; [*technique*] magistral.

masterfully /ˈmɑːstəfəlɪ, US ˈmæs-/ *adv* **1** (dominantly) en maître; **2** (skilfully) magistralement.

masterfulness /ˈmɑːstəflnɪs, US ˈmæs-/ *n* assurance *f*.

master key *n* passe-partout *m inv*.

masterly /ˈmɑːstəlɪ, US ˈmæs-/ *adj* [*technique, writing*] magistral; **to have a ~ command of the English language** maîtriser parfaitement la langue anglaise.

master mariner *n* Naut capitaine *m* de première classe.

mastermind /ˈmɑːstəmaɪnd/ **I** *n* cerveau *m* (**of, behind** de).
II *vtr* échafauder [*crime, swindle, plot, conspiracy*]; organiser [*event, concert*].

master: **Master of Arts** *n* ≈ maîtrise *f* de lettres; **~ of ceremonies** *n* (presenting entertainment) animateur/-trice *m/f*; (at formal occasion) maître *m* des cérémonies; **~ of foxhounds**, **~ of the hounds** *n* grand veneur *m*; **Master of Science** *n* ≈ maîtrise *f* de sciences; **Master of the Rolls** *n* GB *juge de la cour d'appel et garde des archives*; **~piece** *n* chef-d'œuvre *m* also fig; **~ plan** *n* plan *m* d'ensemble; **~ print** *n* Cin copie *f* mère; **~ race** *n* race *f* supérieure; **~ sergeant ▶ 1612** *n* US Mil adjudant *m*; Aviat sergent-chef *m*; **~'s ticket** *n* Naut brevet *m* de capitaine; **~stroke** *n* (brilliant action, piece of skill) coup *m* de maître; (idea, stroke of genius) idée *f* de génie; **~ tape** *n* bande *f* mère; **~work** *n* chef-d'œuvre *m*.

mastery /ˈmɑːstərɪ, US ˈmæs-/ *n* **1** (skill, knowledge) maîtrise *f* (**of** de); **to have complete ~ of one's subject** maîtriser complètement son sujet; **2** (control, dominance) domination *f*, maîtrise *f*; **to have ~ over sb/sth** dominer qn/qch.

masthead /ˈmɑːsthed, US ˈmæst-/ **I** *n* **1** Naut tête *f* de mât; **2** (of newspaper) ≈ ours○ *m*.
II *vtr* hisser [qch] en tête de mât [*sail*].

mastic /ˈmæstɪk/ *n* mastic *m*.

masticate /ˈmæstɪkeɪt/ *vi* mastiquer, mâcher.

mastiff /ˈmæstɪf/ *n* mastiff *m*.

mastitis /mæˈstaɪtɪs/ **▶ 1354** *n* mastite *f*.

mastodon /ˈmæstədɒn/ *n* mastodonte *m*.

mastoid /ˈmæstɔɪd/ **I** *n* Anat mastoïde *f*.
II *adj* [*muscle*] mastoïdien/-ienne; **~ process** apophyse *f* mastoïde.

mastoiditis /ˌmæstɔɪˈdaɪtɪs/ *n* mastoïdite *f*.

masturbate /ˈmæstəbeɪt/ **I** *vtr* masturber.
II *vi* se masturber.

masturbation /ˌmæstəˈbeɪʃn/ *n* masturbation *f*.

masturbatory /ˌmæstəˈbeɪtərɪ, US -bəˈtɔːrɪ/ *adj* masturbatoire.

mat /mæt/ **I** *n* **1** (on floor) (petit) tapis *m*; (for wiping feet) paillasson *m*; **exercise ~** tapis; fig (of vegetation) tapis *m*; **2** (on table) (heatproof) dessous-de-plat *m inv*; (ornamental) napperon *m*; **place ~** set *m* de table.
II *adj* = **matt.**
III *vi* (*p prés etc* **-tt-**) **1** [*hair*] s'emmêler; **2** [*wool, sweater*] se feutrer.

MAT *n* (*abrév* = **machine-assisted translation**) TAO *f*.

matador /ˈmætədɔː(r)/ **▶ 1692** *n* matador *m*.

match /mætʃ/ **I** *n* **1** Sport match *m* (**against** contre; **between** entre); **2** (for lighting fire) allumette *f*; **a box/book of ~es** une boîte/pochette d'allumettes; **to put** ou **set a ~ to sth** mettre le feu à qch; **(have you) got a ~○?** tu as du feu?; **3** (equal, challenger) **to be a ~ for sb** être un adversaire à la mesure de qn; **to be no ~ for sb** être trop faible pour qn; **to meet one's ~** trouver quelqu'un à sa hauteur; **he's met his ~ in her** avec elle, il a trouvé quelqu'un à qui se mesurer; **to be more than a ~ for sb** surpasser qn; **4** (thing that harmonizes or corresponds) **to be a good ~ for sth** [*shoes, curtains, colour*] aller très bien avec qch; **those two cushions are a good ~** ces deux coussins vont bien ensemble; **I couldn't find an exact ~ for the broken cup** je n'ai pas pu trouver de tasse exactement pareille à celle qui avait été cassée; **the blood sample is a perfect ~ with that found at the scene of the crime** l'échantillon de sang correspond parfaitement au sang trouvé sur les lieux du crime; **5** (marriage) union *f*, mariage *m*; **to make a good ~** épouser un bon parti; **to be a good ~ for sb** être un bon parti pour qn; **6** (wick on explosive) mèche *f*.
II *vtr* **1** (correspond to, harmonize with) [*colour, bag, socks*] être assorti à; [*blood type, sample, bone marrow*] correspondre à; [*product, outcome, supply*] répondre à [*demand, expectations*]; [*item, word*] correspondre à [*definition, description*]; **her talent did not ~ her mother's ambitions** son talent n'était pas à la hauteur des ambitions de sa mère; **his job ideally ~es his interests** son travail correspond parfaitement à ses goûts; **2** (compete with or equal) égaler [*record, achievements*]; **we will ~ our competitors' prices** nous alignerons nos prix sur ceux de la concurrence; **the government will ~ your donation dollar for dollar** le gouvernement donnera la même somme que vous au dollar près; **his wit cannot be ~ed** il a une intelligence hors pair; **she more than ~ed him in aggression** elle le valait bien sur le plan de l'agressivité; **he is**

to be ~ed against the world champion on a organisé une rencontre entre lui et le champion du monde; **when it comes to cheating there's nobody to ~ him** pour ce qui est de tricher il n'y en a pas deux comme lui; **3** (find a match for) **to ~ sb with compatible people** trouver les personnes avec lesquelles qn peut s'entendre; **to ~ trainees with companies** mettre en rapport des stagiaires avec des sociétés; **to ~ a wire to the correct terminal** raccorder un fil à la borne qui convient; **to ~ (up) the names to the photos** trouver les noms qui correspondent aux photos.
III *vi* [*colours, clothes, curtains*] être assortis/-ies; [*components, pieces*] aller ensemble; **that button doesn't ~** ce bouton n'est pas identique aux autres; **a set of ~ing luggage** un ensemble de bagages assortis; **with gloves to ~, with ~ing gloves** avec des gants assortis.
■ **match up**: ¶ **~ up** [*pieces, bits*] aller ensemble; ¶ **~ up [sth], ~ [sth] up** ajuster [*pieces, sides, bits*]; **to ~ up to** être à la hauteur de [*expectation, hopes, reputation*].

matchbox /ˈmætʃbɒks/ *n* boîte *f* d'allumettes.

match day I *n* jour *m* de match.
II *modif* [*alcohol ban, event, parking*] pour le jour du match.

matched /mætʃt/ *adj* assorti; **they are well/badly/perfectly ~** ils sont bien/mal/parfaitement assortis.

matching /ˈmætʃɪŋ/ *adj* assorti; **they're a ~ pair** ou **set** ils sont assortis.

matchless /ˈmætʃlɪs/ *adj* [*beauty, taste*] incomparable; [*complacency, indifference*] sans pareil/-eille.

matchmaker /ˈmætʃmeɪkə(r)/ *n* **1** (for couples) marieur/-euse *m/f*, entremetteur/-euse *m/f* pej; **2** (for boxer) manager *m*; (for business etc) intermédiaire *mf*.

matchmaking /ˈmætʃmeɪkɪŋ/ *n* **to enjoy ~** aimer jouer les entremetteurs/-euses; **I'm sick of all this ~** j'en ai marre○ qu'on essaie de me marier; **a ~ service for buyers and vendors** un service qui a pour mission de mettre en contact acheteurs et vendeurs.

match play *n* match-play *m*.

match point *n* balle *f* de match; **at ~** à la balle de match.

matchstick /ˈmætʃstɪk/ **I** *n* (bois *m* d') allumette *f*.
II *modif* [*man, figure*] stylisé, filiforme.

matchwood /ˈmætʃwʊd/ *n* éclats *mpl* de bois, copeaux *mpl*; **to reduce sth to ~** réduire qch en miettes.

mate /meɪt/ **I** *n* **1**○ GB (friend) copain○ *m*; (at work, school) camarade *mf*; **hello ~!** salut mon vieux○!; **2** (sexual partner) Zool (male) mâle *m*; (female) femelle *f*; (person) hum partenaire *mf*; **3** (assistant) aide *mf*; **builder's ~** aide-maçon *m*; **4** GB Naut (in merchant navy) ≈ second *m* (capitaine); ▶ **first mate, second mate**; **5** (in chess) mat *m*.
II *vtr* **1** accoupler [*animal*] (**with** à or avec); **2** (in chess) faire mat.
III *vi* [*animal*] s'accoupler (**with** à, avec).

material /məˈtɪərɪəl/ **I** *n* **1** (information, data) documentation *f*, documents *mpl* (**about, on** sur; **for** pour); **to collect ~ on sth** se documenter sur qch; **I'm collecting ~ for a book** je recueille de la documentation pour un livre; **to draw on ~ from the archives** se baser sur des documents provenant des archives; **course** ou **teaching ~** matériel *m* pédagogique; **promotional ~, publicity ~** documentation *f* publicitaire; **reference ~** référentiel *m*; **some of the ~ in the report is inaccurate** certains passages du rapport sont inexacts; **2** (subject matter) sujet *m*; **I'll use the ~ in my next article** je traiterai ce sujet dans mon prochain article; **the ~ in the magazine is controversial** le contenu de la revue est controversé; **some of the ~ in the show is unsuitable for children** certaines parties du spectacle ne sont pas pour les enfants; **3** Theat, TV (script) texte *m*; (show) spectacle *m*; **she writes all her own ~** elle écrit ses textes elle-même; **4** Mus chansons *fpl*; **he writes all his own ~** il est auteur-compositeur; **I'm working on ~ for a new album** je suis en train de travailler à mon nouvel album; **5** (substance) gen matière *f*, substance *f*; Constr, Tech matériau *m*; **explosive ~** matière or substance explosive; **natural ~** matière or substance naturelle; **nuclear ~** matériaux *mpl* nucléaires; **packing ~** matériaux *mpl* d'emballage ; **plastic ~** matériaux *mpl* plastiques; **waste ~** déchets *mpl*; **6** (fabric) tissu *m*, étoffe *f*; **cotton ~** tissu en coton; **curtain/dress ~** tissu pour rideaux/pour robes; **furnishing ~** tissu d'ameublement; **natural/synthetic ~** étoffe naturelle/synthétique; **7** (personal potential) étoffe *f*; **she is star/executive ~** elle a l'étoffe d'une vedette/d'un cadre; **he is not really university ~** il n'est pas capable d'entreprendre des études universitaires.
II materials *npl* **1** (equipment) matériel *m*; **art ~s, artist's ~s** fournitures *fpl* de dessin; **cleaning ~s** produits *mpl* d'entretien; **2** (natural substances) matériaux *mpl*.
III *adj* **1** (significant, relevant) [*assistance, benefit, change, damage, effect*] matériel/-ielle; [*anxiety, question*] important; [*fact*] pertinent; [*witness, evidence*] matériel/-ielle; **to be ~ to sth** se rapporter à qch; **2** (physical, concrete) [*cause, comfort, consideration, gain, need, possessions, success, support*] matériel/-ielle; **in ~ terms, we are better off** nous sommes plus à l'aise sur le plan matériel; **to do sth for ~ gain** faire qch par esprit de lucre.

materialism /məˈtɪərɪəlɪzəm/ *n* matérialisme *m*.

materialist /məˈtɪərɪəlɪst/ *n, adj* matérialiste (*mf*).

materialistic /məˌtɪərɪəˈlɪstɪk/ *adj* = **materialist**.

materialize /məˈtɪərɪəlaɪz/ *vi* **1** (happen) [*hope, offer, plan, threat*] se concrétiser; [*event, situation*] se réaliser; [*idea*] prendre forme; **the threat failed to ~** la menace ne s'est pas concrétisée; **the strike failed to ~** la grève n'a pas eu lieu; **2** (appear) souvent hum [*person, object*] surgir; [*spirit*] se matérialiser; **I waited, but he failed to ~** j'ai attendu, mais il ne s'est pas montré.

materially /məˈtɪərɪəlɪ/ *adv* **1** (considerably) sensiblement; **not ~ faster/lower** pas vraiment plus rapide/bas; **2** (physically) matériellement.

maternal /məˈtɜːnl/ *adj* maternel/-elle (**towards** avec).

maternally /məˈtɜːnəlɪ/ *adv* maternellement; **she treats them very ~** elle est très maternelle avec eux.

maternity /məˈtɜːnətɪ/ **I** *n* maternité *f*.
II *modif* [*clothes*] de grossesse.

maternity: **~ benefit** *n* GB allocation *f* de maternité; **~ department** *n* (in store) rayon *m* future maman; **~ hospital** *n* maternité *f*; **~ leave** *n* congé *m* de maternité; **~ unit** *n* service *m* d'obstétrique; **~ ward** *n* maternité *f*.

matey○ /ˈmeɪtɪ/ *adj* GB copain○ (**with** avec); **they're very ~** ils sont très copains○; **just you watch it, ~ boy!** hum fais gaffe, mon vieux○!

math○ /mæθ/ *n* US = **maths**○.

mathematical /ˌmæθəˈmætɪkl/ *adj* mathématique; **to have a ~ mind** être fort en maths; **to be a ~ impossibility** être mathématiquement impossible.

mathematically /ˌmæθəˈmætɪklɪ/ *adv* mathématiquement.

mathematician /ˌmæθməˈtɪʃn/ ▶ **1692** *n* mathématicien/-ienne *m/f*.

mathematics /ˌmæθəˈmætɪks/ *n* **1** (subject) (+ *v sg*) mathématiques *fpl*; **2** (mathematical operations) (+ *v sg* ou *v pl*) calculs *mpl*.

maths○ /mæθs/ GB **I** *n* (+ *v sg*) maths○ *fpl*.
II *modif* [*class, book, teacher*] de maths.

matinée /ˈmætɪneɪ, ˈmætneɪ, US ˌmætnˈeɪ/ **I** *n* Cin, Theat matinée *f*.
II *modif* [*performance, show*] en matinée.

matinée: **~ coat, ~ jacket** *n* GB gilet *m* de bébé; **~ idol** *n* Cin acteur *m* idolâtré par les femmes (*dans les années 30 et 40*).

mating /ˈmeɪtɪŋ/ *n* accouplement *m*.

mating: **~ call** *n* chant *m* nuptial; **~ season** *n* lit, fig saison *f* des amours.

matins /ˈmætɪnz/ *npl* (in Catholic church) matines *fpl*; (in Church of England) office *m* du matin.

matriarch /ˈmeɪtrɪɑːk/ *n* (head of family) femme *f* chef de famille; (venerable woman) matrone *f*.

matriarchal /ˌmeɪtrɪˈɑːkl/ *adj* matriarcal.

matriarchy /ˈmeɪtrɪɑːkɪ/ *n* matriarcat *m*.

matrices /ˈmeɪtrɪsiːz/ *pl* ▶ **matrix**.

matricidal /ˌmeɪtrɪˈsaɪdl/ *adj* matricide.

matricide /ˈmeɪtrɪsaɪd/ *n* **1** (crime) matricide *m*; **2** (perpetrator) matricide *mf*.

matriculate /məˈtrɪkjʊleɪt/ **I** *vtr* inscrire.
II *vi* **1** (enrol) s'inscrire; **2**† GB Sch être reçu à l'examen d'entrée à l'université.

matriculation /məˌtrɪkjʊˈleɪʃn/ **I** *n* **1** Univ (enrolment) inscription *f*; **2**† GB Sch *examen donnant droit à l'inscription universitaire*.
II *modif* [*fee*] d'inscription; [*card*] d'étudiant; [*exam*] d'entrée à l'université.

matrilineal /ˌmætrɪˈlɪnɪəl/ *adj* matrilinéaire.

matrimonial /ˌmætrɪˈməʊnɪəl/ *adj* [*problems, home, state*] conjugal; [*bond*] conjugal, matrimonial; **~ causes** Jur *ensemble des affaires relatives à l'état conjugal*.

matrimony /ˈmætrɪmənɪ, US -məʊnɪ/ *n* mariage *m*; **to be united in holy ~** être uni dans le sacrement du mariage.

matrix /ˈmeɪtrɪks/ *n* (*pl* **-trices**) Anat, Comput, Ling, Math, Print, Tech matrice *f*; Miner gangue *f*.

matron /ˈmeɪtrən/ *n* **1** GB (nurse) (in hospital) infirmière *f* en chef; (in school) infirmière *f* (*chargée également de l'intendance*); **2** (person in charge) (of orphanage, nursing home) directrice *f*; **3** US (warder) gardienne *f*; **4** (woman) péj matrone *f* pej.

matronly /ˈmeɪtrənlɪ/ *adj* [*duties, manner*] de mère de famille, de matrone; [*figure*] fort, corpulent; **she already looks ~** elle fait déjà matrone pej.

matron-of-honour GB, **matron-of-honor** US *n* dame *f* d'honneur.

matt /mæt/ *adj* mat; **with a ~ finish** [*paint*] mat; [*photograph*] sur papier mat.

matte /mæt/ *adj* US = **matt**.

matted /ˈmætɪd/ *adj* [*hair*] emmêlé; [*wool, fibres*] aplati; [*cloth, woollens*] feutré; [*roots, branches*] entrelacé, enchevêtré; **to become ~** [*hair*] s'emmêler; [*fibres*] s'enchevêtrer; [*woollens*] se feutrer.

matter /ˈmætə(r)/ **I** *n* **1** gen chose *f*; (of specified nature) affaire *f*; (requiring solution) problème *m*; (on agenda) point *m*; **business ~s** affaires *fpl*; **money ~s** questions *fpl* d'argent; **the ~ in hand/under discussion** l'affaire en question/dont il est question; **it will be no easy ~** cela ne sera pas (une affaire) facile; **the ~ is closed** l'affaire est close; **I have important ~s to discuss** j'ai des choses importantes à discuter; **~s have taken an unexpected turn** les choses ont pris un tour inattendu; **report the ~ to the police** signalez la chose à la police; **the main ~ on the agenda** le point principal à l'ordre du jour; **~s arising** Admin points non inscrits à l'ordre du jour; **private ~** affaire privée; **this is a ~ for the police** c'est un problème qui relève de la police; **there's the small ~ of the £1,000 you owe me** il y a le petit problème des 1000 livres sterling que tu me dois; **Cathe-**

rine is dealing with the ~ Catherine s'occupe du problème; **that's another ~** c'est un autre problème, c'est une autre histoire; **it's no small ~** ce n'est pas une broutille; **to let the ~ drop** en rester là; **to take the ~ further/no further** aller/ne pas aller plus loin; **the fact** ou **truth of the ~ is that** la vérité est que; **I know nothing of the ~** je ne suis au courant de rien; **2** (question) question *f*; **a ~ of** une question de [*experience, importance, opinion, principle, taste*]; **it's a ~ of urgency** c'est urgent; **a ~ of life and death, a life or death ~** une question de vie ou de mort; **it will just be a ~ of months** ce ne sera qu'une question de mois; **a ~ of a few francs/days** l'affaire de quelques francs/jours; **'will he recover?'—'it's a ~ of time'** 's'en remettra-t-il?'—'c'est une question de temps'; **it's only a ~ of time before they separate** ils vont se séparer, ce n'est plus qu'une question de temps; **3 the ~** (something wrong, trouble) un problème; **is anything the ~?** y a-t-il un problème?; **there was something the ~** il y avait un problème; **there's nothing the ~** il n'y a pas de problème; **what's the ~?** qu'est-ce qu'il y a?; **there's nothing the ~ with me** je n'ai rien; **what's the ~ with Louise?** qu'est-ce qu'elle a Louise?; **there's something the ~ with her car** sa voiture a un problème; **there's something the ~ with her eye** elle a quelque chose à l'œil; **what's the ~ with doing a bit of work?** iron ça t'ennuierait de travailler un peu?; **4** Sci (substance) matière *f*; **inert ~** matière inerte; **inorganic/organic ~** matière inorganique/organique; **vegetable ~** matière végétale; **a particle of ~** une particule; **colouring ~** colorant *m*; **5** (on paper) **advertising ~** publicité *f*; **printed ~** imprimés *mpl*; **reading ~** lecture *f*; **6** (content of article, book, speech etc) contenu *m*; **subject ~** contenu *m*; **~ and style** le fond et la forme; **7** Med (pus) pus *m*.

II *vi* être important; **children/details ~** les enfants/les détails sont importants; **politeness ~s** la politesse est importante; **to ~ to sb** [*behaviour, action*] avoir de l'importance pour qn; [*person*] compter pour qn; **it ~s to me where you go and what you do** tes faits et tes gestes ont de l'importance pour moi; **it ~s to me!** c'est important pour moi!; **it ~s how you speak/where you sit** ta façon de parler/l'endroit où tu t'assieds a de l'importance; **it really doesn't ~** cela n'a absolument aucune importance; **it doesn't ~ how/when** peu importe comment/quand (+ *indic*); **it doesn't ~ whether** peu importe que (+ *subj*); **'I'm late'—'oh, it doesn't ~'** 'je suis en retard'—'oh, ça ne fait rien'; **'what about Richard?'—'oh, it doesn't ~ about him!'** 'et Richard?'—'oh, il ne faut pas s'inquiéter pour lui!'; **it ~s that she feels/is etc** c'est grave qu'elle se sente/soit etc; **does it ~ that I can' t be there?** est-ce que c'est grave si je ne peux pas venir?; **does it really ~?** (reprovingly) qu'est-ce que ça peut faire?

IDIOMS **as a ~ of course** systématiquement; **as a ~ of fact** en fait; **for that ~** d'ailleurs; **don't speak to me like that! or to anyone else, for that ~!** ne me parle pas sur ce ton! ni à qui que ce soit d'autre d'ailleurs!; **no ~!** peu importe!; **no ~ how late it is/what he did** peu importe l'heure/ce qu'il a fait; **that's the end of the ~, there's an end to the ~** c'est mon/son etc dernier mot; **to make ~s worse** pour ne rien arranger; **to take ~s into one's own hands** prendre les choses en main.

Matterhorn /ˈmætəhɔ:n/ *pr n* **the ~** le (mont) Cervin.

matter-of-fact *adj* [*voice, tone*] détaché; [*person*] terre à terre; **she told us the news in a very ~ way** elle nous a annoncé la nouvelle d'une façon très détachée.

matter-of-factly *adv* d'une façon très détachée.

Matthew /ˈmæθju:/ *pr n* Mathieu; Bible Matthieu.

matting /ˈmætɪŋ/ *n* ¢ **1** (material) revêtement *m* de sol tressé; **2** (mats) nattes *fpl*.

mattock /ˈmætək/ *n* pioche *f*.

mattress /ˈmætrɪs/ *n* matelas *m*.

mattress cover *n* gen housse *f* de matelas.

maturation /ˌmætjʊˈreɪʃn/ *n* (of tree, body) maturation *f*; (of whisky, wine) vieillissement *m*; (of cheese) affinage *m*.

mature /məˈtjʊə(r), US -ˈtʊər/ **I** *adj* **1** [*plant, animal*] adulte; **~ garden** beau jardin (*planté depuis quelques années*); **2** (psychologically) [*person*] mûr; [*attitude, reader*] adulte; **her most ~ novel** son roman le plus achevé; **after ~ consideration** après mûre réflexion; **3** Culin [*hard cheese*] fort; [*soft cheese*] affiné; [*whisky*] vieux; **~ wine** vin vieux; **4** Fin [*bill, insurance policy*] arrivé à échéance.

II *vtr* laisser vieillir [*wine, whisky*]; affiner [*cheese*].

III *vi* **1** (physically) [*person, animal*] devenir adulte; [*plant*] atteindre la taille adulte; **2** (psychologically) [*person, attitude*] mûrir; **3** fig [*idea, plan*] mûrir; **4** [*wine, whisky*] vieillir; [*cheese*] s'affiner; **5** Fin [*bill, insurance policy*] arriver à échéance.

maturely /məˈtjʊəlɪ, US -ˈtʊərlɪ/ *adv* **to behave ~** avoir un comportement adulte.

mature student *n* GB personne *f* qui reprend des études (*après un temps au foyer ou dans la vie active*).

maturity /məˈtjʊərətɪ, US -ˈtʊə-/ *n* maturité *f*; Fin échéance *f*; **to reach ~** [*person*] atteindre l'âge adulte; [*tree*] arriver à maturité; **he lacks ~** il n'est pas très mûr.

matzo /ˈmɑ:tsəʊ/ *n* pain *m* azyme.

maudlin /ˈmɔ:dlɪn/ *adj* [*song, story, tone*] larmoyant; [*person*] mélancolique; **he gets ~ when he drinks** il a le vin triste.

maul /mɔ:l/ **I** *n* **1** (hammer) masse *f*; **2** (in rugby) maul *m*.

II *vtr* **1** (attack) [*animal*] mutiler; (fatally) déchiqueter; **2** (manhandle) malmener; **3** (sexually) tripoter○ [*woman*]; **4** fig [*critics*] démolir.

mauling /ˈmɔ:lɪŋ/ *n* mutilation *f*; **to get a ~ from the critics** fig être démoli par la critique.

maulstick /ˈmɔ:lstɪk/ *n* Art appui-main *m*.

maunder /ˈmɔ:ndə(r)/ *vi* **1** (speak) divaguer; **to ~ on about sth** divaguer sur qch; **2** (wander) errer, se baguenauder○.

Maundy: **~ money** *n* GB *aumône octroyée par le souverain le jeudi saint*; **~ Thursday** *n* jeudi *m* saint.

Mauritania /ˌmɒrɪˈteɪnɪə/ ▶ **1131** *pr n* Mauritanie *f*.

Mauritanian /ˌmɒrɪˈteɪnɪən/ ▶ **1486** **I** *n* Mauritanien/-ienne *f*.

II *adj* mauritanien/-ienne.

Mauritian /məˈrɪʃn/ **I** *n* ▶ **1486** Mauricien/-ienne *m/f*.

II *adj* mauricien/-ienne.

Mauritius /məˈrɪʃəs/ ▶ **1131**, **1381** *pr n* Maurice *f*.

mausoleum /ˌmɔ:səˈli:əm/ *n* **1** (tomb) mausolée *m*; **2** (big house) péj grande baraque○ *f*.

mauve /məʊv/ ▶ **1104** *n, adj* mauve (*m inv*).

maven○ /ˈmeɪvn/ *n* US péj expert *m*; **he's an architecture ~** il se prend pour un expert en architecture.

maverick /ˈmævərɪk/ **I** *n* **1** (calf) veau *m* non marqué; **2** (person) non-conformiste *mf*.

II *adj* nonconformiste.

maw /mɔ:/ *n* **1** (of cow) caillette *f*; **2** (of bird) jabot *m*; **3** (of lion etc) gueule *f* also fig hum; **to disappear into the ~ of sth** fig être englouti par qch.

mawkish /ˈmɔ:kɪʃ/ *adj* péj **1** (sentimental) mièvre; **2** (insipid) fade.

mawkishness /ˈmɔ:kɪʃnɪs/ *n* péj **1** (sentimentality) mièvrerie *f*; **2** (insipidity) fadeur *f*.

max○ /mæks/ *abrév* = **maximum**.

maxi /ˈmæksɪ/ *n* **1** (also **~ dress**) robe *f* maxi; **2** (also **~ skirt**) jupe *f* maxi.

maxilla /mækˈsɪlə/ *n* (*pl* **-illae**) (in vertebrates) maxillaire *m* (supérieur); (in insects) maxille *f*.

maxillary /mækˈsɪlərɪ/ *adj* maxillaire.

maxim /ˈmæksɪm/ *n* maxime *f*.

maxima /ˈmæksɪmə/ *pl* ▶ **maximum**.

maximal /ˈmæksɪml/ *adj* (*tjrs épith*) maximal.

maximalist /ˈmæksɪməlɪst/ *n* maximaliste *mf*.

maximization /ˌmæksɪmaɪˈzeɪʃn/ *n* maximalisation *f*.

maximize /ˈmæksɪmaɪz/ *vtr* **1** gen maximiser [*profit, sales*]; **to ~ one's potential** utiliser à fond toutes ses capacités; **2** Comput agrandir.

maximum /ˈmæksɪməm/ **I** *n* (*pl* **-imums, -ima**) maximum *m*; **at the ~** au maximum; **the hall can hold a ~ of 300** la salle peut contenir 300 personnes au maximum; **to do sth to the ~** faire qch à fond.

II *adj* [*price*] maximum; [*temperature*] maximal; [*speed*] maximum, maximal.

III *adv* au maximum.

maximum: **~ load** *n* charge *f* limite; **~ minimum thermometer** *n* thermomètre *m* à maximum et à minimum; **~ security prison** *n* prison *f* de haute surveillance.

may[1] /meɪ/ *modal aux* **1** (possibility) **'are you going to accept?'—'I ~'** 'tu vas accepter?'—'peut-être'; **this medicine ~ cause drowsiness** ce médicament peut provoquer des réactions de somnolence; **they're afraid she ~ die** ils ont peur qu'elle (ne) meure; **even if I invite him he ~ not come** même si je l'invite il risque de ne pas venir; **that's as ~ be, but**... peut-être bien, mais...; **come what ~** advienne que pourra; **be that as it ~** quoi qu'il en soit; **2** (permission) **I'll sit down, if I ~** je vais m'asseoir si vous le permettez; **if I ~ say so** si je puis me permettre; **and who are you, ~ I ask?** iron qui êtes-vous au juste?

may[2] /meɪ/ *n* (hawthorn) aubépine *f*.

May /meɪ/ ▶ **1472** *n* (month) mai *m*.

Mayan /ˈmaɪən/ ▶ **1402**, **1486** **I** *n* **1** (person) Maya *mf*; **2** Ling maya *m*.

II *adj* maya.

maybe /ˈmeɪbi:/ **I** *adv* peut-être; **~ they'll arrive early** peut-être arriveront-ils tôt, ils arriveront peut-être tôt; **~ he's right** il a peut-être raison; **I saw him ~ three weeks ago** je l'ai vu il y a peut-être trois semaines.

II *n* **'is that a yes?'—'it's a ~'** 'c'est oui?'—'c'est peut-être'.

IDIOMS **as soon as ~** le plus rapidement possible.

May: **~ beetle, ~ bug** *n* hanneton *m*; **~day** *n* Radio mayday *m*.

May Day /ˈmeɪ deɪ/ **I** *n* premier mai *m*, fête *f* du travail.

II *modif* [*parade, celebration*] du premier mai.

Mayenne ▶ **1163** *pr n* Mayenne *f*; **in/to ~** dans la Mayenne.

Mayfair /ˈmeɪfeə(r)/ *pr n* Mayfair (*quartier chic de Londres*).

mayhem /ˈmeɪhem/ *n* **1** (chaos) désordre *m*; (violence) grabuge○ *m*; **to create ~** semer la pagaille○; **2** US Jur (crime *m* de) mutilation *f*; **to commit ~ on** ou **against sb** se rendre coupable de mutilation sur qn.

mayn't /ˈmeɪənt/ = **may not**.

mayo○ /ˈmeɪəʊ/ *n* (*abrév* = **mayonnaise**) mayonnaise *f*.

mayonnaise /ˌmeɪəˈneɪz, US ˈmeɪəneɪz/ *n* mayonnaise *f*.

mayor /meə(r), US ˈmeɪər/ ▶ **1268** *n* maire *m*;

Mr/Madam Mayor Monsieur/Madame le maire.

mayoral /ˈmeərəl, US ˈmeɪərəl/ *adj* de maire.

mayoralty /ˈmeərəltɪ, US ˈmeɪər-/ *n* (office) mairie *f*; (term of office) mairie *f*, mandat *m* de maire.

mayoress /ˈmeərɪs, US ˈmeɪə-/ ▶ **1268** *n* (wife of mayor) femme *f* du maire; (lady mayor) US mairesse *f*.

May: **maypole** *n* mât *m* (de fête) (*à l'occasion du premier mai*); **~ queen** *n* reine *f* du premier mai.

may've /ˈmeɪəv/ = **may have**.

maze /meɪz/ *n* **1** (puzzle) lit, fig labyrinthe *m*; **2** (network) (of streets) dédale *m* (**of** de); (of pipes) enchevêtrement *m* (**of** de).

mazurka /məˈzɜːkə/ *n* mazurka *f*.

mb *n* (*abrév* = **millibar**) mbar.

Mb *n* Comput (*abrév* = **megabyte**) Mo.

MB *n* **1** GB Univ (*abrev* = **Bachelor of Medicine**) diplôme *m* universitaire de médecine; **2** Comput (*abrév* = **megabyte**) Mo.

MBA *n* Univ (*abrév* = **Master of Business Administration**) ≈ maîtrise *f* de gestion.

MBE *n* GB (*abrév* = **Member of the Order of the British Empire**) *membre de l'ordre de l'empire britannique*.

MBO *n* (*abrév* = **management buyout**) rachat *m* d'entreprise par ses cadres.

MC *n* **1** (*abrév* = **Master of Ceremonies**) (in cabaret) animateur *m*; (at banquet) maître *m* de cérémonie; **2** Mus (rapper) MC *m*; **3** US Pol *abrév écrite* = **Member of Congress**; **4** Aut *abrév écrite* = **Monaco**.

MCAT *n* US Univ (*abrév* = **Medical College Admission Test**) *test d'admission aux écoles de médecine*.

MCC *n* GB (*abrév* = **Marylebone Cricket Club**) *corps arbitral du cricket britannique*.

McCarthyism /məˈkɑːθɪɪzəm/ *n* maccarthysme *m*.

McCoy /məˈkɔɪ/ *n*: IDIOMS **the real ~**○ le vrai de vrai○; **it's the real ~** c'est de l'authentique.

MCN *n*: *abrév* ▶ **Micro Cellular Network**.

MD *n* **1** Med, Univ (*abrév* = **Doctor of Medicine**) docteur *m* en médecine; **2** US Post *abrév écrite* = **Maryland**; **3** Mgmt (*abrév* = **Managing Director**) directeur *m* général.

MDT *n* US *abrév* ▶ **Mountain Daylight Time**.

me¹ /miː, mɪ/

■ **Note** When used as a direct or indirect object pronoun *me* is translated by *me* (or *m'* before a vowel): *she knows me* = elle me connaît; *he loves me* = il m'aime.
– Note that the object pronoun normally comes before the verb in French and that in compound tenses like the present perfect and past perfect, the past participle of the verb agrees with the direct object pronoun: *he's seen me* (female speaker) = il m'a vue.
– In imperatives the translation for both the direct and the indirect object pronoun is *moi* and comes after the verb: *kiss me!* = embrasse-moi!; *give it to me!* = donne-le-moi! (note the hyphens).
– After prepositions and the verb *to be* the translation is *moi*: *she did it for me* = elle l'a fait pour moi; *it's me* = c'est moi.
– For particular expressions see below.

pron me, (*before vowel*) m'; **it's for ~** c'est pour moi; **poor little ~**○ pauvre de moi; **what would you do if you were ~?** qu'est-ce que tu ferais à ma place?; **dear ~**○!, **deary ~**○! ça alors!

me² /miː/ *n* Mus mi *m*.

ME *n* **1** Med *abrév* ▶ **myalgic encephalomyelitis**; **2** US Post *abrév écrite* = **Maine**; **3** Ling *abrév* ▶ **Middle English**; **4** US Med *abrév* ▶ **medical examiner**.

mea culpa /ˌmiːə ˈkʊlpə, ˌmeɪə ˈkʊlpə/ *n*, *excl* mea culpa (*m inv*).

mead /miːd/ *n* hydromel *m*.

may¹

When *may* (or *may have*) is used with another verb in English to convey *possibility*, French will generally use the adverb *peut-être* (= perhaps) with the equivalent verb:

it may rain = il pleuvra peut-être
we may never know what happened = nous ne saurons peut-être jamais ce qui s'est passé
he may have got lost = il s'est peut-être perdu

Alternatively, and more formally, the construction *il se peut que* + subjunctive may be used: *il se peut qu'il pleuve*; *il se peut que nous ne sachions jamais*. For particular usages, see **1** in the entry ***may***.

peut-être is also used in French to convey *concession*:

he may be slow but he's not stupid = il est peut-être lent mais il n'est pas bête
you may think I'm crazy but ... = tu penses peut-être que je suis fou mais ...

When *may* is used to convey *permission*, the French equivalent is *pouvoir*:

you may close the door = vous pouvez fermer la porte

Note that the polite question *may I ...?* is translated by *puis-je ...?*:

may I make a suggestion? = puis-je faire une suggestion?

For particular usages, see **2** in the entry ***may***.

When *may* is used in rather formal English to convey purpose in the construction *in order that* + *may* the French equivalent is *pour que* + subjunctive:

in order that he may know = pour qu'il sache

When *may* is used with another verb to express a wish the French uses *que* + subjunctive:

may they be happy! = qu'ils soient heureux!
long may it last! = que ça dure!

When *may well* + *verb* is used to convey likelihood the French uses *il est fort possible que* + subjunctive:

he may well have gone elsewhere = il est fort possible qu'il soit allé ailleurs

But note:

that may well be but ... = c'est possible mais ...

In the phrase *may as well*, *may* is used interchangeably with *might*, which is more frequently used. For translations see the entry ***might¹***.

meadow /ˈmedəʊ/ *n* **1** (field) pré *m*; **2** ¢ (also **~land**) prés *mpl*, prairies *fpl*; **3** (also **water ~**) prairie *f* inondable.

meadow: **~lark** *n* sturnelle *f*; **~ rue** *n* Bot pigamon *m* jaune; **~sweet** *n* reine-des-prés *f*.

meager *adj* US = **meagre**.

meagerly *adv* US = **meagrely**.

meagre GB, **meager** US /ˈmiːgə(r)/ *adj* [*income, sum, meal, fire, crop*] maigre (*before n*); [*living, existence*] chiche; [*response, returns*] piètre (*before n*); **a ~ diet of rice** de maigres rations de riz.

meagrely GB, **meagerly** US /ˈmiːgəlɪ/ *adv* [*eat, live, spread*] chichement.

meal /miːl/ *n* **1** (food) repas *m*; **hot/cold/main ~** repas chaud/froid/principal; **they had a ~ in the canteen** ils ont mangé à la cantine; **did you enjoy your ~?** est-ce que vous avez bien mangé?; **to go out for a ~** sortir dîner; **2** (from grain) farine *f*.

IDIOMS **don't make a ~ of it**○! n'en fais pas tout un plat○!

meals on wheels *n* repas *mpl* (livrés) à domicile (*pour personnes âgées ou handicapées*).

meal ticket *n* **1** (voucher) ticket-repas *m*; **2**○ fig (quality, qualification) gagne-pain *m*; (person) **I'm just a ~ for you!** pour toi je ne suis qu'un portefeuille!

meal: **~time** *n* heure *f* de repas; **~worm** *n* ver *m* de farine.

mealy /ˈmiːlɪ/ *adj* **1** (in texture) farineux/-euse; **2** (pale) blême.

mealybug /ˈmiːlɪbʌg/ *n* pseudococcus *m* spec.

mealy-mouthed /ˌmiːlɪˈmaʊðd/ *adj* hypocrite.

mean /miːn/ **I** *n* **1** Math, gen moyenne *f*; **above/below the ~** au-dessus/en dessous de la moyenne; **2** fig (middle point) milieu *m*.

II *adj* **1** (average) [*weight, temperature*] moyen/-enne; **2** (ungenerous) [*person*] avare; [*attitude, nature*] mesquin; [*examiner*] sévère; **to be ~ with** être avare sur [*portion, quantity*]; **he's ~ with his money** il est avare; **3**○ (unkind) [*person, action*] méchant; [*trick*] sale (*before n*); **to be ~ to sb** être méchant avec qn; **to be ~ about** faire des remarques désobligeantes sur [*appearance, performance*]; **it is/was ~ of you to do** ce n'est pas chic de ta part de faire/d'avoir fait; **to feel ~ for** ou **about doing** avoir un peu honte de faire; **4** (vicious) [*animal, person, expression*] méchant; **that man/dog has got a ~ streak** cet homme/ce chien a la méchanceté en lui; **5** (tough) [*city*] implacable; [*street*] hostile; **he's a ~ character** c'est un sale type○; **6**○ (skilful) [*exponent, shot*] formidable, du tonnerre○ (*after n*); **she makes a ~ margarita** elle fait un margarita du tonnerre○; **she plays a ~ game of tennis/chess** elle touche sa bille○ au tennis/aux échecs; **you're no ~ artist/poker player!** tu es un sacré○ artiste/joueur de poker!; **7**○ (small) **to have no ~ opinion of oneself** avoir une haute opinion de soi-même; **that's no ~ feat!** ce n'est pas un mince exploit!; **8** (lowly) littér [*dwelling*] misérable ; [*birth*] bas/basse; [*origin*] modeste; **9**○ US (off colour) **to feel ~** ne pas être dans son assiette○.

III *vtr* (*prét, pp* **meant**) **1** (signify) [*word, symbol, phrase*] signifier, vouloir dire (**that** que); [*sign*] vouloir dire; **what does this word/symbol ~?** que signifie ce mot/symbole?; **the name/word ~s nothing to me** ce nom/mot ne me dit rien; **does the term ~ anything to him?** est-ce que le terme lui dit quelque chose?; **2** (intend) **to ~ to do** avoir l'intention de faire; **to ~ sb to do** GB, **to ~ for sb to do** US vouloir que qn fasse; **to be meant for sb** [*question, bomb*] être destiné à qn; **I meant it as a joke/a compliment** c'était une blague/un compliment de ma part; **he doesn't ~ you any harm** il ne te veut aucun mal; **what do you ~ by opening my letters?** qu'est-ce qui te prend d'ouvrir mon courrier?; **to ~ well** avoir de bonnes intentions (**by sb** à l'égard de qn); **he ~s trouble** ou **mischief** il a de mauvaises intentions; **she ~s business** elle est sérieuse; **he ~s what he says** (he is sincere) il est sérieux; (he is menacing) il ne plaisante pas; **she meant no offence** elle n'y entendait pas malice; **I didn't ~ to do it** je ne l'ai pas fait exprès; **I didn't ~ anything by it** je n'avais aucune arrière-pensée; **without ~ing to** par inadvertance; **my remark offended you? it was meant to!** ma remarque t'a vexé? c'était voulu!; **3** (entail) [*strike, law*] entraîner [*shortages, changes*];

[*budget*] signifier [*tax cuts*]; **his death/the accident ~s doing** à cause de sa mort/l'accident il faut faire; **4** (intend to say) vouloir dire; **do you ~ Paul Rose?** tu veux dire Paul Rose?; **what do you ~ by that remark?** qu'est-ce que tu veux dire par là?; **do you ~ me?** c'est de moi que tu parles?; **I ~ to say, who wants a car that won't start?** non mais, qui voudrait d'une voiture qui ne démarre pas?; **I know what you ~** je comprends; **5** (be of value) **a promise/designer label ~s nothing** une promesse/marque ne veut pas dire grand-chose; **she ~s everything/nothing to me** elle est tout/n'est rien pour moi; **money ~s everything/nothing to them** l'argent représente tout/ne représente rien pour eux; **your friendship ~s a lot to me** ton amitié est très importante pour moi; **what it ~s to live in a democracy!** quelle belle chose que de vivre dans une démocratie!; **6** (be destined) (*tjrs au passif*) **to be meant to do** être destiné à faire; **she was meant to be/become a doctor** elle était destinée à être/devenir médecin; **it was meant to be** ou **happen** cela devait arriver; **they were meant for each other** ils étaient faits l'un pour l'autre; **I was meant for better things** j'étais appelé à un destin meilleur; **7** (be supposed to be) (*tjrs au passif*) **he's/you're etc meant to be** il est/tu es etc censé être [*impartial, sad*]; **I'm/you're etc meant to be doing** je suis/tu es etc censé faire.

meander /mɪ'ændə(r)/ **I** *n* méandre *m*.
II *vi* **1** (wind) [*river, road*] serpenter (**through** à travers); **2** (wander) [*person*] flâner; [*thoughts*] vagabonder; **3** (lose direction) [*discussion, play*] traîner en longueur.
■ **meander on** [*speaker*] radoter.

meandering /mɪ'ændərɪŋ/ **I** *n* (*gén pl*) **1** (wandering) méandre *m*; **2** péj (conversational) radotage *m* pej.
II *adj* **1** (winding) [*river, road*] sinueux/-euse; **2** (aimless) péj [*conversation, tale etc*] décousu.

meanie○ /'mi:nɪ/ *n* **1** (miser) radin/-e *m/f*; **2** lang enfantin (spoilsport) **he's a ~** c'est un méchant○.

meaning /'mi:nɪŋ/ *n* **1** (sense) (of word, phrase, remark) sens *m*, signification *f*; (of symbol, gesture, name) signification *f*; **what is the ~ of this word?** quel est le sens de ce mot?; **a word with two ~s** un mot à double sens; **what is the ~ of this?** qu'est-ce que cela signifie?; **poverty? he doesn't know the ~ of the word!** la pauvreté? c'est un mot qui ne fait pas partie de son vocabulaire; **2** (message) (of film, dream) signification *f*; **3** (purpose) sens *m*; **my life/work no longer has any ~** ma vie/mon travail n'a plus aucun sens; **to give new ~ to** donner un sens nouveau à [*life, work*]; **4** (eloquence) **a look/gesture full of ~** un regard/geste lourd de sens; **5** (drift) **yes, I get your ~**○ oui, je vois ce que tu veux dire; **he likes a little drink, if you get my ~**○ il aime bien boire un petit verre, si tu vois ce que je veux dire; **6** Jur termes *mpl*; **within the ~ of the act** selon les termes de la loi.

meaningful /'mi:nɪŋfl/ *adj* **1** (significant) [*word, term, statement, result*] significatif/-ive; **explain it in a way that is ~ to children** explique-le de manière à ce que les enfants comprennent; **2** (profound) [*relationship, comment, lyric*] sérieux/-ieuse; [*experience*] riche; [*insight*] poussé; **my life is no longer ~** ma vie n'a plus de sens; **3** (eloquent) [*look, smile*] entendu; [*gesture*] significatif/-ive; **4** (constructive) [*discussion, talk*] constructif/-ive; [*act, work*] utile; [*process, input*] positif/-ive.

meaningfully /'mi:nɪŋfəlɪ/ *adv* [*speak*] avec sincérité; **to look ~ at sb** jeter un regard entendu à qn.

meaningless /'mi:nɪŋlɪs/ *adj* **1** (having no sense) [*claim, word, phrase*] dépourvu de sens (*after n*); [*code, figure*] incompréhensible; **the diagram/sentence is ~ to me** le diagramme/la phrase m'est incompréhensible; **2** (worthless) [*chatter, role, title*] insignifiant; [*action, contribution, remark*] sans importance; [*effort*] inutile; **a ~ exercise** une opération inutile; **3** (pointless) [*act, sacrifice, violence*] insensé; **my life is ~** ma vie n'a pas de sens.

mean-looking /'mi:nlʊkɪŋ/ *adj* **1** (vicious) [*dog, man*] méchant; **2** hum (impressive) [*drink*] géant; **3**○ (trendy) [*jacket*] d'enfer○ (*after n*).

meanly /'mi:nlɪ/ *adv* **1** (ungenerously) [*distribute*] avec mesquinerie; [*mark*] sévèrement; **2** (poorly) [*dressed, housed*] misérablement; **3** (nastily) [*behave, say*] méchamment.

mean-minded /ˌmi:n'maɪndɪd/ *adj* malintentionné.

meanness /'mi:nnɪs/ *n* **1** (stinginess) avarice *f*; **2** (nastiness) méchanceté *f* (**to** envers; **towards** à l'égard de); **to do sth out of ~** faire qch par méchanceté; **3** (smallness) (of portion) maigreur *f*; **4** (viciousness) méchanceté *f*; **5** (humbleness) littér pauvreté *f*.

means /mi:nz/ **I** *n* (*pl* **~**) (way) moyen *m*; **by illegal ~** par des moyens illégaux; **ready to use whatever ~ they can to...** prêt à utiliser tous les moyens pour...; **a ~ of** un moyen de [*communication, transport, storage*]; **a ~ of doing** un moyen de faire; **there was no ~ of knowing** il n'y avait pas moyen de savoir; **by ~ of sth** au moyen de qch; **yes, by all ~** oui, certainement; **if you wish to leave, then by all ~ do** si vous voulez partir, cela ne tient qu'à vous; **it is by no ~ certain/complete, it is not certain/complete by any ~** c'est loin d'être sûr/complet.
II *npl* (resources) moyens *mpl*, revenus *mpl*; **of moderate ~** [*person, family*] aux revenus modestes; **to live beyond/within one's ~** vivre au-dessus de/selon ses moyens; **to have the ~ to do** avoir les moyens de faire; **a man of ~** un homme riche or fortuné.
IDIOMS **by fair ~ or foul** par tous les moyens; **for him, it's just a ~ to an end** pour lui, c'est juste un moyen d'arriver à ses fins; ▶ **justify**.

mean-spirited *adj* petit, mesquin.

means test **I** *n* enquête *f* sur les ressources.
II means-test *vtr* soumettre [qn] à un examen de ressources.
III means-tested *pp adj* [*benefit, grant, fine*] dépendant des ressources.

meant /ment/ *prét, pp* ▶ **mean**.

meantime /'mi:ntaɪm/ **I** *adv* = **meanwhile I**.
II for the meantime *adv phr* pour le moment.
III in the meantime *adv phr* = **meanwhile I**.

meanwhile /'mi:nwaɪl/ **I** *adv* **1** (during this time) pendant ce temps; **~, cook the pasta** (in recipe) pendant ce temps, faire cuire les pâtes; **Gerard, ~, was cooking the dinner** Gérard, pendant ce temps, préparait le dîner; **2** (until then) en attendant; **~, if you have any questions...** en attendant, si vous avez des questions...; **3** (since or before then) entre-temps; **a lot had changed/could change ~** beaucoup de choses avaient changé/pourraient changer entre-temps; **4** (by way of contrast) au même moment; **~ in Paris...** au même moment à Paris...
II in the meanwhile *adv phr* = **meanwhile I**.

measles /'mi:zlz/ **▶ 1354** *n* (+ *v sg*) rougeole *f*.

measly○ /'mi:zlɪ/ *adj* [*amount, quality*] misérable; [*gift, result*] minable○; **I was paid a ~ £2 an hour** je gagnais deux misérables livres par heure.

measurable /'meʒərəbl/ *adj* **1** (perceptible) [*difference*] notable; **2** (quantifiable) [*change*] mesurable; [*phenomena*] quantifiable.

measurably /'meʒərəblɪ/ *adv* sensiblement.

measure /'meʒə(r)/ **▶ 1412**, **1771**, **1068**, **1869**, **1883**, **1703** **I** *n* **1** (unit) unité *f* de mesure; **weights and ~s** les poids *mpl* et mesures *fpl*; **a ~ of length** une unité de longueur; **liquid ~** mesure *f* de capacité pour les liquides; **to make sth to ~** faire qch sur mesure; **it's made to ~** (garment) c'est fait sur mesure, c'est du sur mesure; **2** (standard amount, container) mesure *f*; **a double ~ of vodka** une double mesure de vodka; **he gave me short ~, I got short ~** il a triché sur la quantité; **3** (device for measuring) instrument *m* de mesure; **4** fig (qualified amount, extent) **some** ou **a certain ~ of** un/-e certain/-e; **a ~ of respect/success/change** un certain respect/succès/changement; **to receive only a small ~ of support** ne recevoir qu'un soutien limité; **a good** ou **wide ~ of autonomy** une grande autonomie; **in large ~** dans une large mesure; **she despised them and envied them in equal ~** elle les méprisait autant qu'elle les enviait; **to distribute praise and blame in equal ~** faire autant de compliments que de critiques; **in full ~** [*feel, possess, fulfil, contribute*] pleinement; [*repay*] entièrement; [*suffer*] profondément; **5** (way of estimating, indication) (of price rises) mesure *f*; (of success, anger, frustration etc) mesure *f*, indication *f*; (of efficiency, performance) critère *m*; **to be the ~ of** donner la mesure de; **to give some ~ of** donner une idée de [*delight, failure, talent, arrogance etc*]; **to use sth as a ~ of** utiliser qch pour mesurer [*effects, impact, success*]; **this is a ~ of how dangerous it is** ceci montre à quel point c'est dangereux; **this is a ~ of how seriously they are taking the situation** ceci montre à quel point ils prennent la situation au sérieux; **that is a ~ of how well the company is run** cela mesure la qualité de la gestion de la société; **6** (assessment) **beyond ~** [*change, increase*] énormément; [*anxious, beautiful, difficult*] extrêmement; **it has improved beyond ~** il y a eu d'énormes progrès; **to take the ~ of sb** jauger qn; **I have the ~ of them** je sais ce qu'ils valent; **7** (action, step) mesure *f* (**against** contre; **to do** pour faire) ; **to take ~s** prendre des mesures; **safety** ou **security ~** mesure de sécurité; **~s aimed at doing** des mesures destinées à faire; **to do sth as a precautionary/an economy ~** faire qch par mesure de précaution/d'économie; **as a preventive ~** à titre préventif; **as a temporary ~** provisoirement; **the ~ was defeated** Pol Jur la mesure a été rejetée; **8** Dance, Mus, Literat mesure *f*.
II *vtr* **1** (by standard system) [*person, instrument*] mesurer [*length, rate, depth, person, waist*]; **to ~ sth in** mesurer qch en [*metres, inches*]; **to get oneself ~d for** faire prendre ses mesures pour; **over a ~d kilometre** Sport sur un kilomètre (*délimité par des balises*); **to ~ sth into** mesurer qch dans [*container*]; **2** (have a measurement of) mesurer; **to ~ four by five metres** mesurer quatre mètres sur cinq; **a tremor measuring 5.2 on the Richter scale** une secousse de 5,2 sur l'échelle de Richter; **3** (assess) mesurer [*performance, ability, success, popularity*]; **they ~ their progress by the number of** ils mesurent leur progrès au nombre de; **4** (compare) **to ~ sth against** comparer qch à [*achievement, standard, effort*].
III *vi* [*person, instrument*] mesurer.
IV *v refl* **to ~ oneself against sb** se mesurer à qn.
IDIOMS **for good ~** pour faire bonne mesure; **to do things by half-~s** se contenter de demi-mesures; **there can be no half-~s** il ne saurait être question de demi-mesures.
■ **measure off**: **~ off [sth]** mesurer [*fabric, ribbon etc*].
■ **measure out**: **~ out [sth]** mesurer [*land, flour, liquid*]; doser [*medicine*]; compter [*drops*].
■ **measure up**: ¶ **~ up** [*person*] avoir les qualités requises; [*product*] être de qualité; **to ~ up against sb** être l'égal de qn; **to ~ up to** être à la hauteur de [*expectations*];

soutenir la comparaison avec [*achievement*]; ¶ **~ up [sth]** mesurer [*room etc*].

measured /ˈmeʒəd/ *adj* [*tone, response, pace*] mesuré; [*analysis, comment*] circonspect.

measureless /ˈmeʒəlɪs/ *adj* littér infini.

measurement /ˈmeʒəmənt/ ▶1771, 1703 *n* **1** (of room, piece of furniture) dimension *f*; **to take the ~s of** prendre les dimensions de; **2** Sewing **to take sb's ~s** prendre les mensurations de qn; **waist/chest ~** tour *m* de taille/de poitrine; **leg/arm ~** longueur *f* de jambe/de bras.

measuring: **~ jug** *n* verre *m* gradué; **~ spoon** *n* cuillère-mesure *f*; **~ tape** *n* mètre *m* ruban, mètre *m* de couturière.

meat /miːt/ **I** *n* **1** Culin viande *f*; (flesh) chair *f*; **red/white ~** viande rouge/blanche; **chicken/crab ~** chair de poulet/de crabe; **2** fig (main part) essentiel *m* (**of** de); **3**‡ (food) nourriture *f*.

II *modif* [*dish, extract*] de viande; [*industry*] de la viande; **~ products** produits *mpl* à base de viande.

IDIOMS **~ and two veg**○ viande garnie de deux légumes; **he's a ~-and-two-veg man**○ GB, **he's a ~-and-potatoes man**○ US il est très steak-frites○; **political scandals are ~ and drink to them** ils se repaissent de scandales politiques; **to be strong ~** être choquant; **one man's ~ is another man's poison** Prov le bonheur des uns fait le malheur des autres Prov.

meatball /ˈmiːtbɔːl/ *n* **1** Culin (*gén pl*) boulette *f* de viande; **2**○ US (person) andouille○ *f*.

meat cleaver *n* couperet *m*.

meat-eater /ˈmiːtiːtə(r)/ *n* **1** (animal) carnivore *m*; **2** (person) **they're not great ~s** ils ne mangent pas beaucoup de viande.

meat: **~-eating** *adj* [*animal*] carnivore; **~-free** *adj* [*dish*] sans viande; [*diet, cookery*] végétarien/-ienne; **~ hook** *n* croc *m* de boucherie; **~ loaf** *n* pain *m* de viande.

meat market *n* **1** (butcher's) boucherie *f*; **2**○ (place to look for sex) lieu *m* de drague○.

meat: **~packer** ▶1692 *n* employé/-e *m/f* d'un abattoir; **~packing** *n* conditionnement *m* de la viande; **~ pie** *n* Culin ≈ pâté *m* en croûte; **~ processing** *n* transformation *f* de la viande; **~ safe** *n* GB garde-manger *m inv*; **~ trade** *n* boucherie *f*.

meatus /mɪˈeɪtəs/ *n* Anat (*pl* **~es** ou **~**) gen conduit *m*; (urinary) méat *m* urinaire.

meaty /ˈmiːtɪ/ *adj* **1** (with meat) [*stew, sauce*] riche en viande; [*chop*] beau/belle; [*flavour, smell*] de viande; **2** (brawny) [*person, hand*] épais/-aisse; **3** fig (interesting) [*role, story, subject*] riche.

Mecca /ˈmekə/ ▶1818 *pr n* **1** (shrine) La Mecque; **2** fig (also **mecca**) **a ~ for** la Mecque des [*tourists, scholars*].

Meccano® /mɪˈkɑːnəʊ/ *n* meccano® *m*.

mechanic /mɪˈkænɪk/ ▶1692 *n* mécanicien/-ienne *m/f*.

mechanical /mɪˈkænɪkl/ *adj* (all contexts) mécanique.

mechanical: **~ drawing** *n* US Tech dessin *m* industriel; **~ engineer** ▶1692 *n* ingénieur *m* mécanicien; **~ engineering** *n* construction *f* mécanique.

mechanically /mɪˈkænɪklɪ/ *adv* **1** Mech [*produce, perform, process, operate*] mécaniquement; **~-operated** à commande mécanique; **2** (automatically) [*behave, respond*] mécaniquement, machinalement.

mechanics /mɪˈkænɪks/ *npl* **1** (subject) (+ *v sg*) mécanique *f*; **2** (workings) (+ *v pl*) lit, fig mécanisme *m*; **the ~ of** le mécanisme de [*engine, pump*]; **the ~ of the law/of management** les mécanismes de la loi/la gestion; **the ~ of doing** la méthode pour faire.

mechanism /ˈmekənɪzəm/ *n* **1** (of machine, device) mécanisme *m*; **2** (procedure) mécanisme *m* (**of** de); **legal ~s** procédures *fpl* légales; **a ~ for regulating prices/selecting staff** une méthode pour contrôler les prix/sélectionner le personnel; **a ~ to do** un moyen de faire; **3** Biol, Psych mécanisme *m*; **4** Philos (theory) mécanisme *m*.

mechanistic /ˌmekəˈnɪstɪk/ *adj* **1** Philos mécaniste; **2** Math mécanique.

mechanization /ˌmekənaɪˈzeɪʃn, US -nɪˈz-/ *n* mécanisation *f*.

mechanize /ˈmekənaɪz/ **I** *vtr* mécaniser.

II *vi* se mécaniser.

III mechanized *pp adj* mécanisé.

med○ /med/ *adj* [*school*] de médecine; [*student*] en médecine.

med. *abrév écrite* = **medium**.

Med○ /med/ *n* GB *abrév* ▶ **Mediterranean**.

MEd /ˌemˈed/ *n* Univ (*abrév* = **Master of Education**) ≈ maîtrise *f* de pédagogie.

medal /ˈmedl/ *n* médaille *f*; **gold/silver ~** médaille d'or/d'argent.

medallion /mɪˈdælɪən/ *n* (all contexts) médaillon *m*.

medallist GB, **medalist** US /ˈmedəlɪst/ *n* médaillé/-e *m/f*; **gold/silver ~** médaillé/-e *m/f* d'or/d'argent.

medal: **Medal of Honor** *n* US Mil Médaille *f* d'honneur (*la plus haute décoration militaire des États-Unis*); **~ play** *n* (in golf) concours *m* par coups.

meddle /ˈmedl/ *vi* péj **stop meddling!** arrête de te mêler de ce qui ne te regarde pas!, mêle-toi de tes affaires!; **to ~ in** s'immiscer dans [*affairs*]; **to ~ with** toucher à [*property*].

meddler /ˈmedlə(r)/ *n* péj indiscret/-ète *m/f*.

meddlesome /ˈmedəlsəm/ *adj* péj indiscret/-ète.

meddling /ˈmedlɪŋ/ péj **I** *n* ingérence *f*.

II *adj* (*épith*) [*person*] indiscret/-ète; **his ~ ways** son habitude de mettre son nez partout.

medevac /ˈmedɪvæk/ *n* US Mil (*abrév* = **medical evacuation**) évacuation *f* sanitaire.

media /ˈmiːdɪə/ **I** *n* (+ *v pl ou sg*) **1** Journ, Radio, TV **the ~** les médias *mpl*; **mass ~** mass media *mpl*; **news ~** presse *f* d'information; **in the ~** dans les médias; **2** Art, Biol ▶ **medium I** 1, 2.

II *modif* [*advertising*] dans les médias; [*analyst, attention, industry, influence, interest, law, organization, page, power, reaction, report*] des médias; [*coverage, event, hype, image, personality*] médiatique; [*consultant, group, ownership*] de médias; [*demand, sales*] par les médias; [*man, woman*] qui travaille dans les médias; [*tycoon*] de l'industrie des médias.

media: **~ blitz** *n* prise *f* d'assaut par les médias; **~ circus** *n* défilé *m* des médias; **~-conscious** *adj* soucieux/-ieuse de son image médiatique.

mediaeval *adj* = **medieval**.

media fatigue *n* désintérêt *m* des médias.

medial /ˈmiːdɪəl/ *adj* **1** Ling [*consonant*] médial; [*position*] médian; **2** Math [*number, amount*] moyen/-enne.

median /ˈmiːdɪən/ **I** *n* **1** Math, Stat médiane *f*; **2** US Aut (also **~ strip**) terre-plein *m* central.

II *adj* **1** Stat [*price, income, sum*] moyen/-enne; **2** Math [*point, line*] médian; [*value*] moyen/-enne.

mediant /ˈmiːdɪənt/ Mus *n* médiante *f*.

media: **~-shy** *adj* qui n'aime pas les médias; **~ star** *n* personnalité *f* médiatique; **~ student** *n* étudiant/-e *m/f* en communication; **~ studies** *npl* communication *f* et journalisme *m*.

mediate /ˈmiːdɪeɪt/ **I** *vtr* **1** (as negotiator) négocier [*settlement, peace*]; **2** (affect) influencer; **3** sout (transmit) fournir [*services*]; diffuser [*idea, cult*] (**through** au moyen de, par).

II *vi* arbitrer; **to ~ in/between** servir de médiateur dans/entre.

III mediating *pres p adj* [*role, nation*] médiateur/-trice.

mediation /ˌmiːdɪˈeɪʃn/ *n* (in law, politics, industry) médiation *f*; (in marital disputes) conciliation *f*.

mediator /ˈmiːdɪeɪtə(r)/ *n* médiateur/-trice *m/f*.

medic○ /ˈmedɪk/ *n* **1** (doctor) toubib○ *m*, médecin *m*; **2** (student) étudiant/-e *m/f* en médecine; **3** Med, Mil infirmier/-ière *m/f* militaire.

Medicaid /ˈmedɪkeɪd/ *n* US Soc Admin assistance *f* médicale aux économiquement faibles.

medical /ˈmedɪkl/ **I** *n* (in school, army, for job) visite *f* médicale; (private) examen *m* médical; **army/company ~** visite médicale de l'armée/d'entreprise.

II *adj* médical; **to retire on ~ grounds** prendre sa retraite pour raisons de santé.

medical advice *n* conseils *mpl* d'un médecin; **to seek ~ advice** consulter un médecin; **against ~ advice** contre l'avis du médecin.

medical: **~ appointment** *n* rendez-vous *m* chez le médecin; **~ board** *n* Mil commission *f* médicale; **~ care** *n* ¢ gen soins *mpl* médicaux; Soc Admin assistance *f* médicale; **~ certificate** *n* certificat *m* médical; **~ check-up** *n* bilan *m* de santé; **~ doctor** ▶1692 *n* docteur *m* en médecine; **~ emergency** *n* urgence *f*; **~ ethics** *npl* éthique *f* médicale ¢; **~ examination** *n* = **medical** I; **~ examiner** *n* US Jur médecin *m* légiste; **~ expert** *n* médecin *m* expert.

medical history *n* **1** (background) antécédents *mpl* (médicaux); **2** (notes) dossier *m* médical.

medical: **~ insurance** *n* assurance-maladie *f*; **~ jurisprudence** *n* médecine *f* légale.

medically /ˈmedɪklɪ/ *adv* **to examine/test sb ~** faire passer un examen médical à qn; **~ fit** ou **sound** en bonne santé; **~ unfit** en mauvaise santé; **a ~ qualified person** une personne ayant une formation médicale; **there's nothing wrong with him ~** il n'a rien, médicalement parlant.

medical: **~ man**○ *n* toubib○ *m*, médecin *m*; **~ missionary** *n* missionnaire *mf* qui a une formation médicale; **~ officer**, **MO** *n* Mil médecin *m* militaire; Ind médecin *m* du travail.

medical opinion *n* **1** ¢ (views of the profession) **~ is divided** la profession médicale est partagée; **2 C** (view of one doctor) opinion *f* de médecin.

medical: **~ orderly** *n* (in hospital) garçon/fille *m/f* de salle; (in army) infirmier *m* militaire; **~ practitioner** ▶1692 *n* médecin *m*.

medical profession *n* **the ~** (doctors collectively) le corps médical; (occupation) la médecine.

medical: **Medical Research Council** *n* GB *institut national britannique de la recherche médicale*; **~ school** *n* faculté *f* de médecine; **~ science** *n* médecine *f*; **~ social worker** *n* assistant/-e *m/f* social/-e (*attaché/-e à un hôpital*); **~ student** *n* étudiant/-e *m/f* en médecine; **~ studies** *npl* études *fpl* de médecine; **~ unit** *n* gen centre *m* médical; (in hospital) service *m* de médecine générale; **~ ward** *n* service *m* de médecine.

medicament† /mɪˈdɪkəmənt/ *n* médicament *m*.

Medicare /ˈmedɪkeə(r)/ *n* US Soc Admin assistance *f* médicale aux personnes âgées.

medicate /ˈmedɪkeɪt/ *vtr* ajouter une substance médicamenteuse à [*gauze, soap*].

medicated /ˈmedɪkeɪtɪd/ *adj* [*bandage, powder, soap, sweet*] médical; [*shampoo*] traitant.

medication /ˌmedɪˈkeɪʃn/ *n* **1** ¢ (drug treatment) médicaments *mpl*; **to be on ~** prendre des médicaments (**for** pour); **to give sb**

~ administrer des médicaments à qn; **to put sb on/take sb off ~** prescrire/supprimer des médicaments à qn; **2 C** (medicine) médicament *m.*

medicinal /mɪˈdɪsɪnl/ *adj* [*property, quality, use*] thérapeutique; [*herb, plant*] médicinal; **~ drugs** médicaments *mpl*; **I drink brandy for ~ purposes** hum je bois du cognac à des fins thérapeutiques.

medicine /ˈmedsn, US ˈmedɪsn/ *n* **1 ¢** (discipline) médecine *f*; **to study ~** étudier la médecine; **doctor of ~** docteur *m* en médecine; **2 C** (drug) médicament *m* (**for** pour); **the best ~** lit, fig le meilleur remède.
IDIOMS **to give sb a taste of their own ~** rendre à qn la monnaie de sa pièce; **to take one's ~ like a man** avaler la pilule○; **that's pretty strong ~!** tu n'y vas pas avec le dos de la cuillère○!

medicine: **~ ball** *n* Sport médecine-ball *m*; **~ bottle** *n* fiole *f*; **~ box** *n* pharmacie *f* portative; **~ cabinet**, **~ chest**, **~ cupboard** *n* armoire *f* à pharmacie; **~ man** *n* Anthrop sorcier *m* guérisseur; **~ show** *n* US Hist boniment *m* de charlatan.

medico○ /ˈmedɪkəʊ/ **I** *n* = **medic**.
II medico+ (*dans composés*) médico-.

medieval /ˌmedɪˈiːvl, US ˌmiːd-, *also* mɪˈdiːvl/ *adj* **1** Hist [*city, period, art*] médiéval; [*merchant, knight, noble*] du Moyen Âge, médiéval; **2** fig (primitive) moyenâgeux/-euse pej.

medievalism /ˌmedɪˈiːvəlɪzəm, US ˌmiːd-, *also* mɪˈd-/ *n* civilisation *f* médiévale.

medievalist /ˌmedɪˈiːvəlɪst, US ˌmiːd-, *also* mɪˈd-/ **▶ 1692** *n* médiéviste *mf.*

Medina /meˈdiːnə/ **▶ 1818** *pr n* Médine.

mediocre /ˌmiːdɪˈəʊkə(r)/ *adj* médiocre.

mediocrity /ˌmiːdɪˈɒkrətɪ/ *n* **1** (state) médiocrité *f*; **2** (person) médiocre *mf.*

meditate /ˈmedɪteɪt/ **I** *vtr* (think about) méditer (**doing** de faire).
II *vi* méditer (**on** ou **upon** sur).

meditation /ˌmedɪˈteɪʃn/ *n* **1** Relig, gen méditation *f*; **2** Literat réflexion *f* (**on** sur).

meditative /ˈmedɪtətɪv, US -teɪt-/ *adj* [*person, expression, nature*] méditatif/-ive; [*music, experience*] contemplatif/-ive; [*silence, calm, atmosphere*] recueilli.

meditatively /ˈmedɪtətɪvlɪ/ *adv* [*gaze, wander*] d'un air méditatif.

Mediterranean /ˌmedɪtəˈreɪnɪən/ **▶ 1511** **I** *pr n* **1** (also **~ sea**) (mer *f*) Méditerranée *f*; **in the ~** dans la or en Méditerranée; **2** (region) pays *mpl* méditerranéens; **3** (native) méditerranéen/-éenne *m/f.*
II *adj* (all contexts) méditerranéen/-éenne.

medium /ˈmiːdɪəm/ **▶ 1703** **I** *n* **1** (*pl* **-iums** ou **-ia**) Cin, Radio, Theat, TV moyen *m* d'expression; **advertising ~** support *m* publicitaire; **through the ~ of** par l'intermédiaire de; **2** (*pl* **-ia**) Art (technique) technique *f*; (material) matériel *m*; **3** (midpoint) milieu *m*; **to find** ou **strike a happy ~** trouver le juste milieu; **4** (*pl* **-iums**) Biol, Bot, Hort milieu *m*; **culture ~**, **growing ~** Biol milieu de culture; **planting ~** Hort terre *f* de plantation; **5** (*pl* **-iums**) (spiritualist) médium *m.*
II *adj* **1** [*size, temperature*] moyen/-enne; **of ~ build/height** de stature/ taille moyenne; **in the ~ term** à moyen terme; **2** Radio [*wave*] moyen/-enne; **on ~ wave** sur les ondes moyennes; **~ wave radio** radio à ondes moyennes.

medium-dry /ˌmiːdɪəmˈdraɪ/ *adj* [*drink*] demi-sec.

medium-fine /ˌmiːdɪəmˈfaɪn/ *adj* [*pen*] à pointe moyenne; [*tip, point*] moyen/-enne.

medium-length /ˌmiːdɪəmˈlenθ/ *adj* [*book, film, article*] de longueur moyenne; [*hair*] milong/mi-longue.

medium: **~-level** *adj* de niveau moyen; **~-price(d)** *adj* à prix moyen; **~-range** *adj* [*missile*] à moyenne portée; **~-rare** *adj* [*meat*] à point; **~-sized** *adj* de taille moyenne.

medium-term /ˌmiːdɪəmˈtɜːm/ **I** *n* **in the ~** à moyen terme.
II *adj* à moyen terme.

medlar /ˈmedlə(r)/ *n* **1** (fruit) nèfle *f*; **2** (tree) néflier *m.*

medley /ˈmedlɪ/ *n* **1** Mus pot-pourri *m* (**of** de); **2** (in swimming) (also **individual ~**) épreuve *f* individuelle quatre nages; **~ relay** relais *m* quatre nages; **3** (mixture) (of people, groups) mélange *m.*

medulla /meˈdʌlə/ *n* (*pl* **-ae** ou **-as**) **1** (marrow) moelle *f*; **2** (also **~ oblongata**) bulbe *m* rachidien.

meek /miːk/ *adj* docile.
IDIOMS **as ~ as a lamb** doux comme un agneau; **~ and mild** humble et doux.

meekly /ˈmiːklɪ/ *adv* docilement.

meekness /ˈmiːknɪs/ *n* docilité *f.*

meerschaum /ˈmɪəʃəm/ *n* (also **~ pipe**) pipe *f* en écume (de mer).

meet /miːt/ **I** *n* **1** Sport rencontre *f* (sportive); **athletics ~** GB, **track ~** US rencontre *f* d'athlétisme; **2** GB, Hunt rendez-vous *m* de chasseurs.
II‡ *adj* séant†, convenable; **it is ~ that** il est convenable que (+ *subj*), il sied† que (+ *subj*).
III *vtr* (*prét, pp* **met**) **1** (encounter) rencontrer [*person*]; rencontrer, affronter [*team, opponent, enemy*]; **to ~ each other** se rencontrer; **to ~ one's death** fig trouver la mort; **2** (make acquaintance of) faire la connaissance de [*person*]; **'pleased to ~ you!'** 'enchanté (de faire votre connaissance)!'; **Paul, ~ my boss, Janet** (as introduction) Paul, je vous présente ma patronne, Janet; **have you met Mr Roberts?** (at gathering) est-ce que vous avez été présenté à M. Roberts?; **3** (greet) (await) attendre; (fetch) chercher [*person*]; **she went to the airport to ~ them** elle est allée à l'aéroport les attendre or chercher; **I'll be there to ~ you** je viendrai te chercher; **to ~ sb off** GB ou **at** US **the bus/plane** attendre qn à l'arrêt de bus/à l'aéroport; **4** (come into contact with) [*hand*] rencontrer, toucher [*hand*]; [*line*] rencontrer, croiser [*line*]; **his eyes met hers** son regard a rencontré or a croisé le sien; **he couldn't ~ her eye** il ne pouvait pas la regarder en face; **an incredible sight met her eye** un spectacle incroyable s'est offert à ses yeux; **5** (fulfil) satisfaire [*demand, order, needs*]; satisfaire à [*criteria*]; payer [*bills, costs*]; couvrir [*debts, overheads*]; compenser [*loss*]; faire face à [*obligations, commitments*]; remplir [*conditions*]; **6** (rise to) satisfaire à [*standards*]; se montrer à la hauteur de [*challenge*]; **7** (respond to) répondre à [*criticism, accusation, objection*].
IV *vi* (*prét, pp* **met**) **1** (come together) [*people*] se rencontrer, se voir; [*teams, armies*] se rencontrer, s'affronter; [*committee, group, parliament*] (for discussion) se réunir (**to do** pour faire); [*cars*] se croiser; **the two cars/trains met head-on** les deux véhicules/trains se sont heurtés de front or de plein fouet○; **to ~ again** [*people*] se revoir; **goodbye, till we ~ again!** au revoir! à la prochaine fois!; **2** (make acquaintance) [*people*] faire connaissance; **3** (come into contact) [*hands, lips*] se rencontrer, se toucher; [*roads, lines, eyes*] se rencontrer, se croiser.
IDIOMS **there's more to this than ~s the eye** ce n'est pas aussi clair que cela en a l'air; **there's more to him than ~s the eye** il cache bien son jeu; **to make ends ~** joindre les deux bouts.
■ **meet up**○: **~ up** se retrouver; **to ~ up with**○ retrouver [*friend*]; **they met up with each other at the theatre** ils se sont retrouvés au théâtre.
■ **meet with**: ¶ **~ with [sb]** rencontrer [*person, delegation*]; ¶ **~ with [sth]** rencontrer [*difficulties, opposition, success, criticism, suspicion*]; être accueilli avec [*approval, praise*]; subir [*failure*]; **he met with misfortune/an accident** il lui est arrivé un malheur/un accident; **his ideas/comments met with no response** ses idées/commentaires n'ont suscité aucune réaction; **to be met with** être accueilli par [*silence, shouts*]; se heurter à [*disapproval*]; être confronté par [*anger*].

meeting /ˈmiːtɪŋ/ *n* **1** (official assembly) réunion *f*; **cabinet/staff ~** réunion du conseil des ministres/des membres du personnel; **to call a ~** convoquer une réunion; **to be in a ~** être en réunion; **2** (coming together) (between individuals, groups) rencontre *f*; **a ~ of minds** fig une profonde entente; **3** GB Sport rencontre *f* (sportive); **athletics ~** rencontre d'athlétisme; **race ~** Turf réunion de courses; **4** Relig (of Quakers) service *m*, culte *m* (des quakers); **to go to ~** aller au culte.

meeting: **~ hall** *n* salle *f* de réunion; **~house** *n* Relig (of Quakers) temple *m*; **~-place** *n* (lieu *m* de) rendez-vous *m*; **~ point** *n* point *m* de rencontre.

mega /megə/ **I mega+** (*dans composés*) méga-.
II○ *excl* GB c'est géant○ or méga○!

megabucks○ /ˈmegəbʌks/ *npl* des millions de dollars; **to be making** ou **earning ~** gagner une fortune.

megabyte /ˈmegəbaɪt/ *n* Comput mégaoctet *m.*

mega-carrier /ˈmegəkærɪə(r)/ *n* géant *m* du transport aérien.

megacycle /ˈmegəsaɪkl/ *n* mégacycle *m.*

megadeath /ˈmegədeθ/ *n* mort *f* sur une vaste échelle.

megahertz /ˈmegəhɜːts/ *n* (*pl* **~**) mégahertz *m inv.*

megalith /ˈmegəlɪθ/ *n* mégalithe *m.*

megalithic /ˌmegəˈlɪθɪk/ *adj* mégalithique.

megalomania /ˌmegələˈmeɪnɪə/ *n* mégalomanie *f.*

megalomaniac /ˌmegələˈmeɪnɪæk/ *n, adj* mégalomane (*mf*).

megalopolis /ˌmegəˈlɒpəlɪs/ *n* mégalopole *f.*

megaphone /ˈmegəfəʊn/ *n* porte-voix *m inv.*

megastar /ˈmegəstɑː(r)/ *n* superstar *mf.*

megastore /ˈmegəstɔː(r)/ *n* GB mégastore *m.*

megaton /ˈmegətʌn/ *n* mégatonne *f.*

megawatt /ˈmegəwɒt/ *n* mégawatt *m.*

megillah○ /məˈgɪlə/ *n* US **the whole ~** tout le tremblement○.

meiosis /maɪˈəʊsɪs/ *n* (*pl* **-ses**) **1** Biol méiose *f*; **2** Literat litote *f.*

Mekong /ˌmiːˈkɒŋ/ **▶ 1644** *pr n* **the ~** le Mékong.

melamine /ˈmeləmiːn/ **I** *n* mélamine *f.*
II *modif* [*table, worktop, surface*] en mélamine.

melancholia /ˌmelənˈkəʊlɪə/ *n* mélancolie *f.*

melancholic /ˌmelənˈkɒlɪk/ *n, adj* mélancolique (*mf*).

melancholy /ˈmelənkəlɪ/ **I** *n* mélancolie *f.*
II *adj* [*person*] mélancolique; [*music, occasion*] triste.

Melanesia /ˌmeləˈniːzɪə/ **▶ 1131** *pr n* Mélanésie *f.*

Melanesian /ˌmeləˈniːzɪən/ **▶ 1486**, **1402** **I** *n* **1** (native) Mélanésien/-ienne *m/f*; **2** (language) mélanésien *m.* **II** *adj* mélanésien/-ienne.

mélange /ˈmeɪlɑːnʒ, US meɪˈlɑːnʒ/ *n* mélange *m.*

melanin /ˈmelənɪn/ *n* mélanine *f.*

melanoma /ˌmeləˈnəʊmə/ *n* mélanome *m.*

Melba: **~ sauce** *n* coulis *m* de framboises; **~ toast** *n* ≈ toast *m* très mince.

meld /meld/ littér **I** *vtr* mêler (**with** à).
II *vi* se mêler.

mêlée, melee /ˈmeleɪ, US meɪˈleɪ/ *n* mêlée *f.*

mellifluous /meˈlɪflʊəs/ *adj* littér mélodieux/-ieuse.

mellow /ˈmeləʊ/ **I** *adj* **1** (smooth) [*wine*] moelleux/-euse; [*flavour, taste*] suave; [*tone, voice*] mélodieux/-ieuse; **2** (soft) [*colour, light, sound*] doux/douce; **3** (juicy) [*fruit*] fondant; **4** (weathered) [*stone*] patiné par l'âge; **5** (calm) [*atmosphere, behaviour, person*] serein; **to get** ou **grow ~ with age** s'assagir avec l'âge; **6** (relaxed) [*person*] détendu; **to be in a ~ mood** être détendu.
II *vtr* **1** (calm) [*experience, time*] assagir [*person*]; **2** (relax) [*music, wine*] détendre [*person*]; **3** (ripen) faire mûrir [*fruit*]; donner du moelleux à [*wine*].
III *vi* **1** (calm down) [*person*] s'amadouer, s'assagir; [*behaviour*] s'assagir; **2** (tone down) [*attitude*] s'adoucir; **3** (ripen) [*fruit*] mûrir; [*taste, wine*] prendre du moelleux.
■ **mellow out**○ décompresser○, se détendre.

mellowing /ˈmeləʊɪŋ/ **I** *n* **1** (of fruit, wine) maturation *f*; **2** (of colour, voice) adoucissement *m*; **3** (of person, behaviour) adoucissement *m*.
II *adj* [*effect, influence*] adoucissant; **to have a ~ effect** ou **influence on sb** adoucir qn.

mellowness /ˈmeləʊnɪs/ *n* **1** (of fruit, wine) moelleux *m*; **2** (of colour, conduct, light, person, voice) douceur *f*; **3** (of stone) patine *f*.

melodeon, melodion /mɪˈləʊdɪən/ ▶ **1481** *n* (accordion) mélodion *m*.

melodic /mɪˈlɒdɪk/ *adj* **1** Mus mélodique; **2** gen mélodieux/-ieuse.

melodious /mɪˈləʊdɪəs/ *adj* mélodieux/-ieuse.

melodrama /ˈmelədrɑːmə/ *n* mélodrame *m* also fig.

melodramatic /ˌmelədrəˈmætɪk/ *adj* mélodramatique; **to sound ~** avoir l'air dramatique; **you're being ~!** tu dramatises les choses!

melodramatically /ˌmelədrəˈmætɪklɪ/ *adv* [*gesture, pause, speak*] de façon mélodramatique.

melodramatics /ˌmelədrəˈmætɪks/ *npl* péj **cut out the ~**○! arrête ton cinéma○!

melody /ˈmelədɪ/ *n* mélodie *f*.

melon /ˈmelən/ **I** *n* (fruit) melon *m*.
II *modif* [*balls, seeds*] de melon.

melt /melt/ **I** *n* **1** (thaw) dégel *m*, fonte *f* des neiges; **2** US Culin sandwich *m* recouvert de fromage fondu.
II *vtr* **1** lit [*heat, sun, person*] faire fondre [*snow, metal, plastic, butter, chocolate*]; **2** fig [*pity, plea, person*] attendrir [*heart, person*].
III *vi* **1** lit [*snow, ice, butter, metal, plastic, chocolate*] fondre (**at** à); **to ~ in the sun/in your mouth** fondre au soleil/dans la bouche; **I'm ~ing!** je suis en nage!; **2** fig (soften) [*heart, person*] fondre (**with** de); **3** (merge) **to ~ into the crowd/background/forest** se fondre dans la foule/le fond/la forêt; **to ~ into sb's arms** fondre dans les bras de qn.
■ **melt away 1** lit [*snow, ice*] fondre complètement; **2** fig (disappear) [*fear, confidence, distrust*] se dissiper; [*crowd, people*] se disperser; [*money*] fondre.
■ **melt down**: **~ down [sth], ~ [sth] down** fondre [*metal, wax, object*] (**into** en).

meltdown /ˈmeltdaʊn/ *n* **1** Nucl fusion *f* du cœur d'un réacteur; **in ~** en fusion; **2**○ Fin (crash) chute *f* des actions, krach *m* boursier.

melting /ˈmeltɪŋ/ *adj* **1** [*look, word, gaze*] attendri; **2** [*snow, ice*] fondu.

melting point *n* point *m* de fusion.

melting pot *n* (of people, nationalities) melting-pot *m*.
IDIOMS **to be in the ~** être en discussion; **to throw sth into the ~** remettre qch en question.

melt: **~-in-the-mouth** *adj* fondant; **~water** *n* eaux *fpl* de fonte.

member /ˈmembə(r)/ **I** *n* **1** (of group, committee, jury, family, organization) membre *m*; **to be a ~ of** faire partie de [*family, group*]; être membre de [*club, committee*]; **active ~** membre *m* actif; **committee ~** membre *m* du comité; **~ of staff** gen employé/-e *m/f*; (in school) professeur *m*; **~ of the audience** (listening) auditeur/-trice *m/f*; (watching) spectateur/-trice *m/f*; **~ of the armed forces** militaire *m*; **~ of the opposite sex** personne *f* de l'autre sexe; **'~s only'** 'réservé aux membres'; **~ of the public** (in the street) passant/-e *m/f*; (in theatre, cinema) spectateur/-trice *m/f*; **~s of the public were warned** la population a été avertie; **an ordinary ~ of the public** un simple citoyen; **like any other ~ of the public** comme tout le monde; **2** (also **Member**) Pol (of parliament) député *m*; (of EC etc) membre *m*; **the Member for Oxford** le député d'Oxford; **3** Constr pièce *f*; **cross ~** traverse *f*; **support ~** pièce *f* de support; **4** Math (of set) élément *m*; **5** (limb) membre *m*; **6** (penis) membre *m*; **male ~** membre viril.
II *modif* [*nation, state*] membre.

member: **Member of Congress, MC** *n* US Pol membre *m* du Congrès; **Member of Parliament, MP** ▶ **1268** *n* GB Pol député *m* (**for** de); **Member of the European Parliament, MEP** *n* membre *m* du Parlement européen; **Member of the House of Representatives, MHR** *n* US Pol membre *m* de la Chambre des représentants.

membership /ˈmembəʃɪp/ **I** *n* **1** (state of belonging) adhésion *f* (**of** à); **EC ~** adhésion à la CEE; **full ~** adhésion à part entière; **group ~** adhésion en groupe; **student ~** adhésion étudiant; **to apply for ~** faire une demande d'adhésion; **to resign/renew one's ~** rendre/renouveler sa carte de membre; **to let one's ~ lapse** ne pas payer ses cotisations; **~ of** GB ou **in** US **the club is open to all** le club est ouvert à tous; **to take out joint/family ~ of** GB ou **in** US **the club** adhérer en couple/en famille au club; **2** (fee) cotisation *f*; **3** (people belonging) (+ *v sg* ou *pl*) membres *mpl*; **it has a ~ of 200** il y a 200 membres; **~ is declining/increasing** le nombre des membres décroît/augmente; **a society with a large/small ~** une organisation qui compte beaucoup de/peu de membres.
II *modif* [*application*] d'adhésion; [*qualifications, committee*] d'admission; **~ card** carte *f* de membre; **~ fee** cotisation *f*; **~ secretary** secrétaire *mf* chargé/-e des adhésions.

Members' Lobby *n* GB Pol *local à l'entrée de la Chambre des communes où les députés rencontrent leurs électeurs.*

membrane /ˈmembreɪn/ *n* **1** Biol, Bot (tissue) membrane *f*; **2** Constr membrane *f* (d'étanchéité).

membranous /ˈmembrənəs/ *adj* membraneux/-euse.

memento /mɪˈmentəʊ/ *n* (*pl* **~s** ou **~es**) souvenir *m* (**of** de); **as a ~** en souvenir.

memento mori /mɪˌmentəʊ ˈmɔːrɪ/ *n* (*pl* **~**) memento mori *m inv*.

memo /ˈmeməʊ/ *n* (*abrév* = **memorandum**) gen note *f* (**on, about** à propos de); Admin note *f* de service.

memo board *n* tableau *m* d'affichage.

memoirs /ˈmemwɑː(r)z/ *npl* Mémoires *mpl* (**of, on** sur).

memo pad *n* bloc-notes *m*.

memorabilia /ˌmemərəˈbɪlɪə/ *n* (+ *v sg* ou *pl*) souvenirs *mpl*; **Beatles' ~** souvenirs des Beatles.

memorable /ˈmemərəbl/ *adj* [*day, event, experience, victory*] mémorable; [*person, quality, voice, book*] inoubliable.

memorably /ˈmemərəblɪ/ *adv* [*say, describe*] de façon mémorable; [*amusing, interesting*] remarquablement.

memorandum /ˌmeməˈrændəm/ *n* (*pl* **memoranda**) **1** Admin note *f* de service (**to** à l'attention de; **from** de la part de); **2** Pol mémorandum *m*.

memorandum: **~ of agreement** *n* protocole *m* d'accord; **~ of association** *n* Jur, Comm acte *m* constitutif d'une société.

memorial /məˈmɔːrɪəl/ **I** *n* **1** (monument) mémorial *m* (**to** à); **2** (reminder) **as a ~ to** à la mémoire de; **to be a ~ to sb/sth** être à la mémoire de qn/qch; **3** (document) mémoire *m*.
II *adj* commémoratif/-ive.

Memorial Day *n* US *jour de commémoration des soldats américains morts à la guerre.*

memorialize /məˈmɔːrɪəlaɪz/ *vtr* immortaliser.

memorial service *n* messe *f* commémorative.

memorize /ˈmeməraɪz/ *vtr* apprendre [qch] par cœur.

memory /ˈmemərɪ/ *n* **1** (faculty) mémoire *f*; **to have a good ~** avoir bonne mémoire; **to have a bad ~** ne pas avoir de mémoire; **to lose one's ~** perdre la mémoire; **to have an excellent ~** avoir une excellente mémoire; **to have a good ~ for names** avoir une bonne mémoire des noms; **from ~** de mémoire; **long term/short term/visual ~** Med mémoire à long terme/à court terme/visuelle; **to remain in the ~** rester gravé dans la mémoire; **to have a good ~ for faces** être physionomiste; **if my ~ serves me right** si je me souviens bien; **to have a long ~** être rancunier/-ière; **2** (recollection) (*souvent pl*) souvenir *m*; **3** (period of time) **in living** ou **recent ~** de mémoire d'homme; **4** (posthumous fame) souvenir *m*; **their ~ lives on** leur souvenir est toujours vivant; **to keep sb's ~ alive** ou **green** garder vivant le souvenir de qn; **5** (commemoration) **in (loving) ~ of** à la mémoire de; **6** Comput mémoire *f*.
IDIOMS **to take a trip down ~ lane** se pencher sur ses souvenirs.

memory: **~ bank** *n* bloc *m* mémoire; **~ card** *n* carte *f* à mémoire; **~ chip** *n* puce *f* mémoire; **~ loss** *n* perte *f* de mémoire; **~ span** *n* empan *m* mnémonique; **~ typewriter** *n* machine *f* à écrire à mémoire.

memsahib /ˈmemsɑːb/ *n* (aux Indes) Madame *f*.

men /men/ *pl* ▶ **man**.

menace /ˈmenəs/ **I** *n* **1** (threat) menace *f*; **to demand money with ~s** Jur exiger de l'argent par des menaces; **there was ~ in his eyes** il avait un regard menaçant; **2** (danger) danger *m*; **he is a ~ to other motorists** c'est un danger public; **3**○ (nuisance) **he's a real ~** c'est une vraie plaie.
II *vtr* menacer (**with** de, avec).

menacing /ˈmenəsɪŋ/ *adj* menaçant.

menacingly /ˈmenəsɪŋlɪ/ *adv* [*glare, approach*] d'une façon menaçante; [*say*] d'un ton menaçant; **~ dark** sombre et menaçant.

ménage /meɪˈnɑːʒ/ *n* ménage *m*; **~ à trois** ménage à trois.

menagerie /mɪˈnædʒərɪ/ *n* ménagerie *f* also fig.

Menai Strait /ˌmenaɪ ˈstreɪt/ *pr n* détroit *m* de Menai.

mend /mend/ **I** *n* **1** (in garment, fabric) (stitched) raccommodage *m*; (darned) reprise *f*; (patched) rapiéçage *m*; **2** fig **to be on the ~** [*person*] être en voie de guérison; [*sales, economy*] reprendre; [*company*] se porter mieux; [*weather, situation*] s'améliorer.
II *vtr* **1** lit réparer [*car, furniture, toy, road*]; (stitch) raccommoder [*garment, fabric*]; (darn) repriser [*garment, fabric*]; (add patch) rapiécer [*garment, fabric*]; **2** fig guérir [*feelings, broken heart*]; **to ~ relations with** améliorer les relations avec.
III *vi* **1** (heal) [*injury*] guérir; [*person*] se rétablir; **2** fig [*feelings, broken heart*] guérir.
IDIOMS **to ~ one's ways** s'amender. ▶ **fence**.

mendacious /menˈdeɪʃəs/ *adj* sout mensonger/-ère.

mendacity /men'dæsətɪ/ *n* sout (of person) propension *f* au mensonge; (of statement, document) caractère *m* mensonger, fausseté *f*.

mendelevium /ˌmendə'li:vɪəm/ *n* mendélévium *m*.

Mendelian /men'di:lɪən/ *adj* mendélien/-ienne.

Mendel(ian)ism /ˌmen'di:lɪənɪzəm, men'di:lɪzəm/ *n* mendélisme *m*.

mendicancy /'mendɪkənsɪ/ *n* sout mendicité *f*.

mendicant /'mendɪkənt/ *n, adj* sout mendiant/-e (*m/f*).

mendicity /men'dɪsɪtɪ/ *n* sout mendicité *f*.

mending /'mendɪŋ/ *n* (sewing together) **to do some ~** faire du raccommodage.

Menelaus /ˌmenɪ'leɪəs/ *pr n* Ménélas.

menfolk /'menfəʊk/ *npl* hommes *mpl*.

menhir /'menhɪə(r)/ *n* menhir *m*.

menial /'mi:nɪəl/ I *n* (servant) subalterne *m*; péj larbin *m*.

II *adj* [*task, job*] subalterne; [*attitude*] servile.

meningitis /ˌmenɪn'dʒaɪtɪs/ ▶ 1354 I *n* méningite *f*.

II *modif* [*epidemic, outbreak*] de méningite.

meninx /'mi:nɪŋks/ *n* (*pl* **meninges**) méninge *f*.

meniscus /mə'nɪskəs/ *n* (*pl* **-sci** ou **-scuses**) (all contexts) ménisque *m*.

menopausal /ˌmenə'pɔ:zl/ *adj* [*symptom, problem*] ménopausique; [*woman*] ménopausée.

menopause /'menəpɔ:z/ *n* ménopause *f*.

Menorca /mɪ'nɔ:kə/ ▶ 1381 *pr n* Minorque *f*.

menorrhagia /ˌmenə'reɪdʒɪə/ *n* ménorragie *f*.

mensch○ /menʃ/ *n* US (*pl* **-en**) quelqu'un de vraiment bien.

menses /'mensi:z/ *npl* Med spéc menstruation *f*.

men's room /'menzru:m, -rʊm/ *n* US toilettes *fpl* pour hommes.

menstrual /'menstrʊəl/ *adj* menstruel/-elle.

menstruate /'menstrʊeɪt/ *vi* avoir ses règles.

menstruation /ˌmenstrʊ'eɪʃn/ *n* menstruation *f*.

mensuration /ˌmensjʊə'reɪʃn/ *n* mesure *f*.

menswear /'menzweə(r)/ I *n* prêt-à-porter *m* pour hommes.

II *modif* **~ department** rayon *m* du prêt-à-porter masculin.

mental /'mentl/ *adj* **1** Med [*handicap, illness, patient*] mental; [*hospital, institution*] psychiatrique; [*ward*] de psychiatrie; **2** (of the mind) [*ability, effort, energy*] intellectuel/-elle; [*process*] mental; **~ exhaustion** surmenage *m* intellectuel; **~ state** état *m* mental; **~ strain** fatigue *f* mentale; **3** (in one's head) [*calculation, arithmetic, picture*] mental; **to make a ~ note to do** se dire qu'il faut faire; **4**○ (mad) fou/folle, malade○.

mental: **~ age** *n* Psych âge *m* mental; **~ block** *n* blocage *m* psychologique; **~ cruelty** *n* cruauté *f* mentale; **~ defective** *n* injur débile/-e *m/f* mental/-e *m/f* offensive; **~ healing** *n* thérapie *f* par suggestion mentale.

mental health I *n* **1** (of person) santé *f* mentale; **2** Admin psychiatrie *f*.

II *modif* [*programme, strategy*] de santé mentale; [*worker*] spécialisé en psychiatrie; **~ services** services *mpl* psychiatriques.

mental home *n* clinique *f* psychiatrique.

mentality /men'tælətɪ/ *n* mentalité *f*.

mentally /'mentəlɪ/ *adv* **1** Med **~ handicapped** ou **disabled** handicapé mental; **~ retarded** retardé; **the ~ ill** les malades mentaux; **she's ~ ill** c'est une malade mentale; **to be ~ deranged** avoir l'esprit dérangé; **2** (regarding the mind) **~ exhausted** surmené intellectuellement; **to be ~ alert** avoir l'esprit alerte; **~ quick/slow** rapide/lent d'esprit; **3** (inwardly) [*decide, resolve*] dans son for intérieur; [*calculate, estimate*] mentalement.

mental powers *npl* capacités *fpl* intellectuelles.

menthol /'menθɒl/ *n* menthol *m*.

mentholated /'menθəleɪtɪd/ *adj* au menthol.

mention /'menʃn/ I *n* **1** gen, Advertg (reference) mention *f* (**of** de); **to get a media** ou **a promotional ~** être mentionné dans les médias à des fins publicitaires; **the mere ~ of my name** la seule évocation de mon nom; **to make no ~ of** [*report, person*] ne pas faire mention de; **there was no ~ of the hostages** il n'a pas été fait mention des otages; **the book got a ~ on the radio** on a parlé du livre à la radio; **2** (acknowledgement) mention *f*; **honourable ~** gen mention honorable; Mil citation *f*.

II *vtr* **1** (allude to) faire mention de [*person, name, topic, event, fact*]; **he didn't ~ money** il n'a fait aucune mention d'argent; **please don't ~ my name** ne mentionnez pas mon nom; **she never ~s her work** elle ne parle jamais de son travail; **to ~ sb/sth to sb** parler de qn/qch à qn; **to ~ that** dire (en passant) que; **she ~ed (that) you were coming** elle a dit que vous veniez; **I hardly need to ~ that** inutile de signaler que; **not to ~** sans parler de; **it's difficult getting there, not to ~ finding parking space** c'est difficile d'y aller, sans parler des problèmes de stationnement; **without ~ing any names** sans nommer personne; **'as ~ed above'** 'comme il a été dit plus haut'; **the countries ~ed above** les pays déjà cités; **too numerous to ~** trop nombreux pour être cités; **to be ~ed in a will** figurer sur un testament; **just ~ my name** dis-leur que tu viens de ma part; **don't ~ it!** je vous en or je t'en prie!; **2** (acknowledge) citer [*name, person*]; mentionner [*quality, service*].

mentor /'mentɔ:(r)/ *n* mentor *m*.

menu /'menju:/ *n* (all contexts) menu *m*.

menu: **~-driven** /ˌmenju:'drɪvn/ *adj* Comput piloté par menus; **~ item** *n* Comput élément *m* de menu.

meow *n, vi* US = **miaow**.

MEP *n* (*abrév* = **Member of the European Parliament**) député *m* au Parlement européen.

Mephistopheles /ˌmefɪ'stɒfɪli:z/ *pr n* Méphistophélès.

mephistophelian /ˌmefɪstə'fi:lɪən/ *adj* méphistophélique.

mercantile /'mɜ:kəntaɪl, US -ti:l, -tɪl/ *adj* [*ship, nation*] marchand; [*law*] commercial; [*system, theory*] mercantile.

mercantile: **~ agency** *n* agence *f* de renseignements commerciaux; **~ marine** *n* marine *f* marchande.

mercantilism /'mɜ:kəntɪlɪzəm/ *n* **1** (system) mercantilisme *m*; **2** (commercialism) pratique *f* du commerce.

mercenary /'mɜ:sɪnərɪ, US -nerɪ/ I *n* mercenaire *mf*.

II *adj* [*action, person*] intéressé; [*business interest*] mercantile.

mercer‡ /'mɜ:sə(r)/ *n* GB marchand *m* de tissus.

mercerized /'mɜ:səraɪzd/ *adj* mercerisé.

merchandise /'mɜ:tʃəndaɪz/ I *n* marchandise(s) *f(pl)*.

II *vtr* (also **merchandize**) **1** (buy and sell) faire le commerce de; **2** (promote) assurer la promotion de.

merchandiser /'mɜ:tʃəndaɪzə(r)/ *n* (also **merchandizer**) marchandiseur *m*.

merchandising /'mɜ:tʃəndaɪzɪŋ/ *n* (also **merchandizing**) marchandisage *m*.

merchant /'mɜ:tʃənt/ I *n* **1** Comm (selling in bulk) négociant *m*; (selling in small quantities) marchand *m*; (retailer) détaillant *m*; **wine/silk ~** marchand de vins/de soie, négociant en vins/en soie; **2**○ (person) **speed ~** fou/folle *m/f* du volant; **rip-off ~** arnaqueur/-euse◑ *m/f*.

II *modif* [*ship, vessel, fleet, shipping*] marchand; [*sailor, seaman*] de la marine marchande.

merchantability /ˌmɜ:tʃəntə'bɪlətɪ/ *n* valeur *f* marchande.

merchantable /'mɜ:tʃəntəbl/ *adj* **1** (which is selling well) [*goods*] qui se vend bien (*after n*); **2** (which could sell well) commercialisable; **3** (saleable) [*quality*] marchand.

merchant bank *n* GB banque *f* d'affaires.

merchant banker ▶ 1692 I *n* GB **1** (executive) cadre *m* d'une banque d'affaires; **2** (owner) banquier *m* d'affaires.

II **merchant bankers** *npl* (company) banque *f* d'affaires.

merchant banking *n* GB **1** (activity) activités *fpl* des banques d'affaires; **2** (profession) banque *f* d'affaires.

merchant: **~man** *n* Naut navire *m* marchand; **~ navy** GB, **~ marine** US *n* marine *f* marchande.

merciful /'mɜ:sɪfl/ *adj* **1** (showing kindness) [*person, sentence*] clément (**to, towards** envers); [*act*] charitable; [*God*] miséricordieux/-ieuse; **2** (fortunate) [*occurrence*] heureux/-euse; **death was a ~ release** la mort fut une délivrance.

mercifully /'mɜ:sɪfəlɪ/ *adv* **1** (compassionately) avec clémence; **2** (fortunately) par bonheur, par chance; **the queue was ~ short** par bonheur la file d'attente était courte.

merciless /'mɜ:sɪlɪs/ *adj* [*ruler, behaviour, attitude, criticism*] impitoyable (**to, towards** envers); [*heat, rain, cold*] implacable.

mercilessly /'mɜ:sɪlɪslɪ/ *adv* [*act, treat, speak, tease*] de manière impitoyable; [*rain, snow*] inexorablement.

mercurial /mɜ:'kjʊərɪəl/ *adj* **1** Chem [*compound, poisoning*] au mercure; **2** (lively) [*person*] vif/vive; (changeable) [*temperament*] lunatique.

mercury /'mɜ:kjʊrɪ/ I *n* mercure *m*.

II **Mercury** *pr n* **1** Mythol Mercure *m*; **2** Astron Mercure *f*.

mercy /'mɜ:sɪ/ *n* **1** (clemency) clémence *f*; **to show ~ to** ou **towards sb** se montrer clément à l'égard de qn; **to have ~ on sb** avoir pitié de qn; **to beg for ~** demander grâce; **in his ~ he let them go** en or dans sa miséricorde il les laissa partir; **an act of ~** un acte de compassion; **a recommendation to ~** Jur un recours en grâce; **for ~'s sake**○! pitié!; **2** (power) merci *f*; **to be at the ~ of** être à la merci de; **to leave sb to the tender mercies of sb** iron abandonner qn à la merci de qn; **to throw oneself on sb's ~** s'en remettre au bon vouloir de qn; **3** (fortunate event) **it's a ~ that** c'est une chance que (+ *subj*).

IDIOMS **let's be grateful** ou **thankful for small mercies** sachons apprécier notre chance.

mercy: **~ dash** *n* action *f* (humanitaire) d'urgence; **~ flight** *n* vol *m* humanitaire.

mercy killing *n* **1** (euthanasia) ⊄ euthanasie *f*; **2** (act) C acte *m* d'euthanasie.

mercy seat *n* Bible propitiatoire *m*.

mere /mɪə(r)/ I‡ *n* lac *m*.

II *adj* **1** (common, simple) [*coincidence, propaganda, nonsense*] pur (*before n*); [*convention, fiction, formality, inconvenience*] simple (*before n*); **he's a ~ child** ce n'est qu'un enfant; **he's a ~ clerk** ce n'est qu'un (simple) employé; **a ~ nothing** trois fois rien; **he's a ~ nobody** c'est quelqu'un d'insignifiant; **2** (least, even) [*sight, thought, idea*] simple, seul; **the ~ idea of speaking in public scares me** la simple idée de parler en public m'effraie; **the ~ mention of her name** la simple évocation de son nom; **the ~ sight of her** sa seule vue; **the ~ presence of asbestos can be dangerous** le seul fait qu'il y ait de l'amiante constitue un danger; **3** (bare) seulement; **the beach is a**

~ 2 km from here la plage est seulement à 2 km d'ici or n'est qu'à 2 km d'ici; **the interview lasted a ~ 20 minutes** l'entretien a duré tout juste 20 minutes.

merely /'mɪəlɪ/ *adv* simplement, seulement; **I ~ asked him/told him** je lui ai simplement or seulement demandé/dit; **the picture is ~ a reproduction** ce tableau est simplement or seulement une reproduction, ce tableau est une simple reproduction; **his accusations ~ damaged his own reputation** ses accusations n'ont fait que nuire à sa propre réputation; **it is not enough ~ to stage a demonstration** il ne suffit pas d'organiser une manifestation; **~ thinking** ou **to think about it scares me** le seul ou simple fait d'y penser m'effraie.

meretricious /ˌmerɪ'trɪʃəs/ *adj* [*glamour, charm*] factice; [*policy*] alléchant.

merge /mɜːdʒ/ **I** *vtr* **1** (join) **to ~ sth into** ou **with sth** incorporer qch en qch [*company, group*]; **2** (blend) mélanger [*colour, design*].
II *vi* **1** (also **~ together**) (join) [*companies, departments, states*] fusionner; [*roads, rivers*] se rejoindre; **to ~ with** fusionner avec [*company, department, state*]; rejoindre [*river, road*]; **to ~ into** fusionner avec [*company*]; **2** (blend) [*colours, sounds*] se confondre; **to ~ into** se fondre avec [*colour, sky, trees*]; **to ~ into each** ou **one another** [*colours, trees*] se confondre.

merger /'mɜːdʒə(r)/ **I** *n* **1** (of companies) fusion *f*; **2** (process of merging) fusionnement *m*.
II *modif* [*plan, proposal*] de fusion; **~ talks** discussions *fpl* concernant la fusion.

meridian /mə'rɪdɪən/ **I** *n* **1** Geog, Astron, Math méridien *m*; **2** fig (peak) apogée *m*.
II *modif* [*time*] méridien/-ienne.

meridian circle *n* lunette *f* méridienne.

meridional /mə'rɪdɪənl/ **I** *n* (person) Méridional/-e *m/f*.
II *adj* **1** [*line, time*] méridien/-ienne; **2** (southern) méridional.

meringue /mə'ræŋ/ *n* meringue *f*.

meringue shell *n* fond *m* en meringue.

merino /mə'riːnəʊ/ **I** *n* (all contexts) mérinos *m*.
II *modif* [*wool, garment*] de mérinos; [*sheep, ram*] mérinos.

merit /'merɪt/ **I** *n* (of idea, philosophy, plan, behaviour) valeur *f*; (of person) mérite *m*; **to have ~** [*plan, idea*] avoir de la valeur; **to judge sb on their own ~s** juger qn selon son mérite; **to judge sth on its own ~s** juger qch selon ses qualités propres [*situation, case*]; **there's some/little ~ in his work** son œuvre a une certaine valeur/peu de valeur; **there's some/little ~ in doing** il y a du mérite/peu de mérite à faire; **certificate of ~** accessit *m*; **to give due ~ to sb for doing** reconnaître à qn le mérite d'avoir fait.
II *vtr* mériter; **her bravery ~s a reward** son courage mérite (une) récompense or d'être recompensé.

merit: **~ award** *n* récompense *f* honorifique; **~ list** *n* tableau *m* d'honneur; **~ mark**, **~ point** *n* Sch bon point *m*.

meritocracy /ˌmerɪ'tɒkrəsɪ/ *n* méritocratie *f*.

meritocratic /ˌmerɪtə'krætɪk/ *adj* méritocratique.

meritorious /ˌmerɪ'tɔːrɪəs/ *adj* méritoire.

merit system *n* US système *m* d'avancement selon le mérite.

merlin /'mɜːlɪn/ *n* émerillon *m*.

mermaid /'mɜːmeɪd/ *n* sirène *f*.

merman /'mɜːmæn/ *n* (*pl* **mermen**) triton *m*.

Merovingian /ˌmerəʊ'vɪndʒɪən/ **I** *n* Mérovingien/-ienne *m/f*.
II *adj* mérovingien/-ienne.

merrily /'merɪlɪ/ *adv* **1** (joyfully) joyeusement; **2** (unconcernedly) avec insouciance.

merriment /'merɪmənt/ *n* (fun) joie *f*; (laughter) hilarité *f*; **his impersonation provoked an outburst of ~** son imitation a suscité l'hilarité générale.

merry /'merɪ/ *adj* **1** (happy) joyeux/-euse, gai; **~ Christmas!** joyeux Noël!; **2**○ (tipsy) éméché; **3‡** (also **merrie**) (pleasant, delightful) **~ England** l'Angleterre d'autrefois; **the ~ month of May** le joli mois de mai; **Robin Hood and his ~ men** Robin des Bois et ses joyeux compagnons.
IDIOMS **the more the merrier!** Prov plus on est de fous, plus on rit Prov; **to make ~** s'amuser; **to give sb ~ hell**○ passer un bon savon à qn○.

merry-go-round /'merɪgəʊraʊnd/ *n* lit manège *m*; fig tourbillon *m*.

merry: **~maker** *n* noceur/-euse○ *m/f*; **~making** *n* réjouissances *fpl*.

Merseyside /'mɜːzɪsaɪd/ ▶**1624** *pr n* Merseyside *m*.

mesa /'meɪsə/ *n* US mesa *f*.

mescaline /'meskəliːn/ *n* mescaline *f*.

mesh /meʃ/ **I** *n* **1** (netting) (of nylon, string) filet *m*; (of metal) grillage *m*; **2** (space in net) mailles *fpl*; **5 cm ~** des mailles de 5 cm; **3** (net) mailles *fpl*; **4** Tech engrenure *f*; **in ~** engrené.
II *vtr* (also **~ together**) (co-ordinate) faire concorder [*ideas, policies*].
III *vi* **1** (also **~ together**) (become entangled) [*leaves, branches*] s'enchevêtrer; **2** fig (also **~ together**) (be compatible) [*ideas, policies, tendencies*] concorder; **to ~ with sth** être en accord avec qch; **3** Tech [*cogs, teeth*] s'engrener; **to ~ with sth** s'emboîter dans qch.

mesh: **~ bag** *n* filet *m* à provisions; **~ connection** *n* Elec couplage *m* polygonal; **~ size** *n* Fishg maillage *m*.

mesmeric /mez'merɪk/ *adj* mesmérien/-ienne.

mesmerism† /'mezmərɪzəm/ *n* mesmérisme *m*.

mesmerize /'mezməraɪz/ **I** *vtr* hypnotiser.
II mesmerized *pp adj* fig fasciné, médusé.

mesomorph /'mesəʊmɔːf/ *n* mésomorphe *mf*.

meson /'mezɒn, 'miːzɒn/ *n* Phys méson *m*.

Mesopotamia /ˌmesəpə'teɪmɪə/ *pr n* Mésopotamie *f*.

Mesozoic /ˌmesəʊ'zəʊɪk/ **I** *n* mésozoïque *m*.
II *adj* mésozoïque.

mesquite /'meskiːt/ *n* mesquite *m*.

mess /mes/ **I** *n* **1** (untidy state) désordre *m*; **what a ~** quel désordre!; **to make a ~** [*children, workmen*] mettre du désordre; **to leave sth in a ~** laisser qch en désordre; **the kitchen is (in) a ~** la cuisine est en désordre; **to tidy** ou **clear up the ~** mettre de l'ordre; **this report is a ~!** ce rapport est fait n'importe comment!; **my hair is a ~** je suis complètement décoiffée; **you look a ~!** GB, **you look like a ~!** US tu es dans un bel état!; **2** fig (muddled state) **my life is a ~** ma vie est un désastre; **the economy/country is in a terrible ~** l'économie/le pays est dans une situation catastrophique; **to make a ~ of the job** massacrer○ le travail; **to let things get into a ~** laisser aller les choses; **how did we get into this ~?** comment a-t-on fait pour en arriver là?; **you got us into this ~** c'est toi qui nous as mis dans ce pétrin○; **he'll get us out of this ~** il nous sortira de ce pétrin○; **this is a fine ~ you've got** GB ou **gotten** US **us into!** grâce à toi, nous voilà dans de beaux draps!; **3**○ (pitiful state) **his face was a ~ after the accident** il avait le visage amoché○ après l'accident; **he's a ~**○ (psychologically) il est dans un sale état; (incompetent) il est nul○; **4** (excrement) saletés *fpl*; **the dog made a ~ on the lawn** le chien a fait ses saletés sur la pelouse; **dog ~**○ crotte○ *f* de chien; **5** (stain) **to make a ~ of** ou **on the tablecloth/ carpet** salir la nappe/moquette; **to make a ~ of oneself** gen se salir; (when eating) manger salement; **6** Mil cantine *f*; **officers' ~** (in the army) mess *m*; (in the navy) carré *m* des officiers; **7**○ US portion *f*; **a ~ of greens** une portion de légumes verts.
II○ *vi* (meddle) **to ~ with** toucher à [*drugs*]; **I don't ~ with drugs** je ne touche pas à la drogue; **don't ~ with him, he's dangerous** évite-le, il est dangereux.
IDIOMS **no ~ing**○! sans blagues○!; **to sell one's birthright for a ~ of pottage** Bible vendre son droit d'aînesse pour un plat de lentilles.

■ **mess about**○, **mess around**○: ¶ **~ around 1** (act the fool) faire l'imbécile ; **to ~ around with** jouer avec [*chemicals, matches*]; **don't ~ around with drugs** ne touche pas à la drogue; **2** (potter) **to ~ around in the garden/with friends** s'amuser dans le jardin/avec des amis; **3** (sexually) **he ~es around** c'est un coureur; **to ~ around with sb** coucher avec qn; ¶ **~ [sb] around**○ faire tourner qn en bourrique○.

■ **mess up**○: ¶ **~ up** US faire l'imbécile; ¶ **~ [sth] up, ~ up [sth] 1** (muddle up) semer la pagaille dans [*papers*]; (get untidy) mettre du désordre dans [*kitchen*]; (dirty) salir [*napkin, sheets*]; **2** (do badly) bâcler [*exam, work*]; **3** (ruin) gâcher; **you've ~ed things up for everybody** tu as tout gâché pour tout le monde; **I've ~ed up my chances of promotion** j'ai gâché mes chances d'obtenir une promotion; ¶ **~ [sb] up** [*drugs, alcohol*] détruire [*person*]; [*experience*] faire perdre les pédales○ à qn.

message /'mesɪdʒ/ *n* **1** (communication) message *m* also Comput (**about** au sujet de); **a telephone/taped ~** un message téléphonique/enregistré; **to take a ~** (on telephone) prendre un message; **to give/leave sb a ~ that** transmettre/laisser un message à qn lui disant que; **2** (meaning) gen, Relig, Pol message *m*; **a film with a ~** un film contenant un message; **to get one's ~ across** (be understood) se faire comprendre; (convince people) faire passer son message; **to get the ~**○ comprendre, piger○; **his ~ isn't getting through** son message ne passe pas or passe mal; **3†** (errand) course *f*; **to go on a ~ for sb** aller faire une course pour qn; **to go for the ~s** (shopping) aller faire les courses.

message switching *n* Comput commutation *f* de messages.

messaging /'mesɪdʒɪŋ/ *n* Comput messagerie *f* électronique, télémessagerie *f*.

mess dress *n* Mil grand uniforme *m*.

messenger /'mesɪndʒə(r)/ *n* **1** gen messager/-ère *m/f*; (for hotel, company) garçon *m* de courses, coursier/-ière *m/f*; **2** Naut (light line) touline *f*; (endless belt) tournevire *m*.

messenger: **~ boy** ▶**1692** *n* garçon *m* de courses, coursier *m*; **~ RNA** *n* Biol acide *m* ribonucléique messager, ARN-m *m*.

mess hall *n* Mil réfectoire *m*.

messiah /mɪ'saɪə/ *n* messie *m* also fig; **the Messiah** le Messie.

messianic /ˌmesɪ'ænɪk/ *adj* Bible (all contexts) messianique.

mess: **~ jacket** *n* Mil vareuse *f*; **~ kit** *n* GB Mil (uniform) tenue *f* de soirée; (eating utensils) popote○ *f*; **~ room** = **mess hall**.

Messrs /'mesəz/ *n* (*abrév écrite* = **messieurs**) MM.

mess tin *n* Mil gamelle *f*.

messy /'mesɪ/ *adj* **1** (untidy) [*house, room*] en désordre; [*hair, appearance*] négligé; [*handwriting, work*] peu soigné; **2** (dirty) [*activity, work*] salissant; **he's a ~ eater** il mange salement; **3** (confused) [*divorce, lawsuit*] pénible; [*business, affair*] sale (*before n*).

mestizo /me'stiːzəʊ/ *n* (*pl* **-zoes** ou **-zos**) métis/métisse *m/f* (*issu d'un mélange de races européenne et amérindienne*).

met /met/ *pret, pp* ▶ **meet**.

Met○ /met/ *n* **1** GB (*abrév* = **Metropolitan Police**) police *f* de Londres; **2** US (*abrév* =

Metropolitan Museum) Metropolitan Museum *m*.

metabolic /ˌmetəˈbɒlɪk/ *adj* [*disease, needs, stress*] du métabolisme; **~ rate** métabolisme *m* basal.

metabolically /ˌmetəˈbɒlɪklɪ/ *adv* du point de vue métabolique.

metabolism /mɪˈtæbəlɪzəm/ *n* métabolisme *m*.

metabolize /mɪˈtæbəlaɪz/ *vtr* transformer [qch] par métabolisme.

metacarpal /ˌmetəˈkɑːpl/ **I** *n* métacarpien *m*.
II *adj* [*ligament, vein*] métacarpien/-ienne; [*bone*] du métacarpe.

metacarpus /ˌmetəˈkɑːpəs/ *n* métacarpe *m*.

metal /ˈmetl/ **I** *n* **1** Miner métal *m*; **2** (also **heavy ~**) Mus hard rock *m*; **3** (in printing) caractère *m*; **4** (in glassmaking) pâte *f* de verre.
II *modif* **1** (made of metal) [*container, tool, fitting, cable*] en métal; **2** Mus [*group, band, music, album*] de hard rock.

metalanguage /ˈmetəlæŋgwɪdʒ/ *n* métalangage *m*.

metal: **~ detector** *n* détecteur *m* de métaux; **~ fatigue** *n* fatigue *f* du métal.

metalinguistic /ˌmetəlɪŋˈgwɪstɪk/ *adj* métalinguistique.

metalinguistics /ˌmetəlɪŋˈgwɪstɪks/ *n* (+ *v sg*) métalinguistique *f*.

metallic /mɪˈtælɪk/ *adj* **1** Chem [*substance*] métallique; [*state*] de métal; **2** [*paint, finish*] métallisé; **3** (resembling metal) [*sound, appearance*] métallique; [*eyes*] d'un éclat métallique; [*taste*] de métal.

metallurgic(al) /ˌmetəˈlɜːdʒɪk(l)/ *adj* [*problem, study*] métallurgique; [*work*] de métallurgie; [*expert*] en métallurgie.

metallurgist /mɪˈtælədʒɪst, US ˈmetəlɜːrdʒɪst/ **▶ 1692** *n* métallurgiste *m*.

metallurgy /mɪˈtælədʒɪ, US ˈmetəlɜːrdʒɪ/ *n* métallurgie *f*.

metal: **~ polish** *n* produit *m* à astiquer pour métaux; **~work** *n* ferronnerie *f*; **~worker ▶ 1692** *n* ferronnier *m*.

metamorphic /ˌmetəˈmɔːfɪk/ *adj* **1** gen [*quality, technique*] de métamorphose; **2** Geol métamorphique.

metamorphism /ˌmetəˈmɔːfɪzəm/ *n* **1** Geol métamorphisme *m*; **2** gen = **metamorphosis**.

metamorphose /ˌmetəˈmɔːfəʊz/ **I** *vtr* **1** Biol, fig métamorphoser (**into** en); **2** Geol métamorphiser.
II *vi* **1** Biol, fig se métamorphoser (**into** en); **2** Geol se transformer par métamorphisme.

metamorphosis /ˌmetəˈmɔːfəsɪs/ *n* (*pl* **-phoses**) (all contexts) métamorphose *f* (**into** en).

metamorphous /ˌmetəˈmɔːfəs/ *adj* = **metamorphic**.

metaphor /ˈmetəfɔː(r)/ *n* métaphore *f*; **to mix one's ~s** faire des métaphores incohérentes.

metaphoric(al) /ˌmetəˈfɒrɪk(l)/ *adj* métaphorique; **I must put my ~ skates on** je dois, comme on dit, passer à la vitesse supérieure.

metaphorically /ˌmetəˈfɒrɪklɪ/ *adv* métaphoriquement; **~ speaking** pour employer une métaphore.

metaphysical /ˌmetəˈfɪzɪkl/ *adj* **1** Philos métaphysique; **2** (abstract) abstrait.

metaphysics /ˌmetəˈfɪzɪks/ *n* (+ *v sg*) métaphysique *f*.

metastasis /meˈtæstəsɪs/ *n* (*pl* **-tases**) métastase *f*.

metatarsal /ˌmetəˈtɑːsl/ **I** *n* métatarsien *m*.
II *adj* [*ligament, arch*] métatarsien/-ienne; [*bone, swelling*] du métatarse.

metatarsus /ˌmetəˈtɑːsəs/ *n* métatarse *m*.

metathesis /mɪˈtæθəsɪs/ *n* (all contexts) métathèse *f*.

metazoan /ˌmetəˈzəʊən/ **I** *n* métazoaire *m*.
II *adj* de la famille des métazoaires.

mete /miːt/ *v* ■ **mete out**: **~ [sth] out, ~ out [sth]** infliger [*punishment, ill treatment*]; accorder [*reward, favour*]; rendre [*justice*].

meteor /ˈmiːtɪə(r)/ **I** *n* **1** (fragment) météore *m*; **2** (streak of light) étoile *f* filante.
II *modif* [*crater, shower*] météorique.

meteoric /ˌmiːtɪˈɒrɪk, US -ˈɔːr-/ *adj* **1** [*dust, impact*] météorique; **2** fig (rapid) [*rise, progress*] fulgurant.

meteorite /ˈmiːtɪəraɪt/ **I** *n* météorite *f*.
II *modif* [*dust, impact*] météorique.

meteorological /ˌmiːtɪərəˈlɒdʒɪkl/ *adj* météorologique; **~ balloon** ballon-sonde *m* météorologique.

meteorologically /ˌmiːtɪərəˈlɒdʒɪklɪ, US ˌmiːtɪɔːr-/ *adv* sur le plan météorologique.

Meteorological Office *n*: *météorologie nationale britannique*.

meteorologist /ˌmiːtɪəˈrɒledʒɪst/ **▶ 1692** *n* météorologue *mf*.

meteorology /ˌmiːtɪəˈrɒlədʒɪ/ **I** *n* météorologie *f*.
II *modif* [*study, records*] météorologique.

meter /ˈmiːtə(r)/ **I** *n* **1** (measuring instrument) compteur *m*; **electricity/gas/water ~** compteur d'électricité/de gaz/d'eau; **to read the ~** relever le compteur; **2** (also **parking ~**) parcmètre *m*; **3** US Meas = **metre**.
II *vtr* **1** mesurer [*electricity, gas, water, pressure*]; **to have one's water supply ~ed** avoir un compteur d'eau; **2** Post affranchir [qch] à la machine.

meter: **~ maid**○ *n* contractuelle *f* (de police); **~ reader** *n* releveur *m* de compteur; **~ reading** *n* relevé *m* du compteur.

methadone /ˈmeθədəʊn/ *n* méthadone *f*.

methane /ˈmiːθeɪn/ *n* méthane *m*.

methanol /ˈmeθənɒl/ *n* méthanol *m*.

method /ˈmeθəd/ *n* **1** (system, technique, manner) (of teaching, contraception, training) méthode *f* (**for doing** pour faire); (of payment, treatment) mode *m* (**of** de); **~ of transport** moyen *m* de transport; **teaching/farming ~s** méthodes d'enseignement/agricoles; **production ~s** modes de production; **2** (orderliness) méthode *f*; **scientific/deductive ~** méthode scientifique/déductive; **a man of ~** un homme méthodique; **3** Cin, Theat méthode *f* de Stanislavski, philosophie *f* 'Actor's Studio'; **▶ madness**.

method: **~ acting** *n* méthode *f* Stanislavski, jeu *m* 'Actor's Studio'; **~ actor** *n* adepte *mf* de 'l'Actor's Studio'.

methodical /mɪˈθɒdɪkl/ *adj* méthodique.

methodically /mɪˈθɒdɪklɪ/ *adv* méthodiquement.

Methodism /ˈmeθədɪzəm/ *n* méthodisme *m*.

Methodist /ˈmeθədɪst/ *n, adj* méthodiste (*mf*).

methodological /ˌmeθədəˈlɒdʒɪkl/ *adj* méthodologique.

methodologically /ˌmeθədəˈlɒdʒɪklɪ/ *adv* [*reasonable, acceptable*] du point de vue méthodologique; [*work, think*] avec méthode.

methodology /ˌmeθəˈdɒlədʒɪ/ *n* méthodologie *f*.

meths /meθs/ *n* (+ *v sg*) GB (*abrév* = **methylated spirit**) alcool *m* à brûler.

Methuselah /mɪˈθjuːzələ/ **I** *pr n* (patriarch) Mathusalem.
II *n* (bottle) mathusalem *m*.
IDIOMS **as old as ~** vieux comme Mathusalem.

methyl /ˈmeθɪl/ **I** *n* méthyle *m*.
II *modif* [*acetate, bromide, chloride etc*] de méthyle.

methylated /ˈmeθəleɪtɪd/ *adj* méthylique.

methylated spirit(s) *n* (+ *v sg*) alcool *m* à brûler.

methylene /ˈmeθɪliːn/ **I** *n* méthylène *m*.
II *modif* [*chloride, blue*] de méthylène.

meticulous /mɪˈtɪkjʊləs/ *adj* méticuleux/-euse; **to be ~ about one's work** être méticuleux dans son travail; **she's very ~ about brushing her teeth every day** elle fait très attention à se brosser les dents tous les jours.

meticulously /mɪˈtɪkjʊləslɪ/ *adv* méticuleusement.

meticulousness /mɪˈtɪkjʊləsnɪs/ *n* méticulosité *f*.

métier /ˈmetɪeɪ/ *n* vocation *f*.

Met Office *n* GB *abrév* **▶ Meteorological Office**.

metonymy /mɪˈtɒnɪmɪ/ *n* métonymie *f*.

metre /ˈmiːtə(r)/ **▶ 1412** *n* **1** GB Meas mètre *m*; **2** Literat mètre *m*; **3** Mus mesure *f*.

metric /ˈmetrɪk/ *adj* métrique; **to go ~**○ adopter le système métrique.

metrical /ˈmetrɪkl/ *adj* **1** Meas de mesure; **2** Literat métrique; **~ psalm** psaume *m* versifié.

metricate /ˈmetrɪkeɪt/ *vtr* faire passer [qch] au système métrique.

metrication /ˌmetrɪˈkeɪʃn/ *n* (adoption) adoption *f* du système métrique; (conversion) conversion *f* au système métrique.

metrics /ˈmetrɪks/ *n* (+ *v sg*) métrique *f*.

metrological /ˌmetrəˈlɒdʒɪkl/ *adj* métrologique.

metrology /mɪˈtrɒlədʒɪ/ *n* **1** (study) métrologie *f*; **2** (system of measurement) système *m* de mesures.

metronome /ˈmetrənəʊm/ *n* métronome *m*.

metropolis /məˈtrɒpəlɪs/ *n* métropole *f*; **the ~** GB Londres.

metropolitan /ˌmetrəˈpɒlɪtən/ **I** *n* **1** gen (person) citadin/-e *m/f*; **2** Relig (also **~ bishop**) (of Catholic Church) métropolitain *m*; (of Church of England) archevêque *m*; (of Eastern churches) métropolite *m*.
II *adj* **1** (of city) [*area, park, population, organization*] urbain; [*buildings, traffic, values*] des grandes villes; **~ New York/Los Angeles** l'agglomération de New York/Los Angeles; **2** (home territory) **~ France** la France métropolitaine; **3** Relig métropolitain.

metropolitan: **~ authority** *n* GB Admin *conseil qui dirige l'une des six principales conurbations britanniques*; **~ district** *n* GB Admin circonscription *f* administrative (d'une conurbation); **Metropolitan police** *n* GB police *f* de Londres.

mettle /ˈmetl/ *n* courage *m*, ardeur *f* (**to do** pour faire); **to be on one's ~** faire de son mieux; **to put sb on his ~** amener qn à montrer de quoi il est capable.

Meurthe-et-Moselle ▶ 1163 *pr n* Meurthe-et-Moselle *f*; **in/to ~** en Meurthe-et-Moselle.

Meuse ▶ 1163 *pr n* Meuse *f*; **in/to ~** dans la Meuse.

mew /mjuː/ **I** *n* **1** (of cat) miaulement *m*; **2** (seagull) mouette *f*.
II *vi* miauler.

mews /mjuːz/ *n* GB **1** (+ *v sg*) (street) ruelle *f*; (yard) cour *f*; **2** (+ *v pl*) (stables) écuries *fpl*.

mews flat *n* GB *appartement chic aménagé dans d'anciennes écuries*.

Mexican /ˈmeksɪkən/ **▶ 1486** **I** *n* (person) Mexicain/-e *m/f*.
II *adj* mexicain.

Mexican: **~ jumping bean** *n* pois *m* sauteur; **~ stand off** *n* US impasse *f*; **~ wave** *n* ola *f* (*mouvement de vague engendré par les spectateurs qui se lèvent successivement autour du terrain*).

Mexico /ˈmeksɪkəʊ/ **▶ 1131** *pr n* Mexique *m*.

Mexico City ▶ 1818 *pr n* Mexico.

mezzanine /ˈmezəniːn/ *n* **1** (floor) mezzanine *f*, entresol *m*; (in room, apartment) mezzanine *f*; **2** Theat US corbeille *f*; GB premier dessous *m*.

mezzanine: **~ bed** *n* lit *m* en mezzanine; **~ financing** *n* financement *m* mezzanine, emprunt *m* subordonné.

mezzo-soprano /ˌmetsəʊsəˈprɑːnəʊ/ ▶ 1868 I *n* (*pl* **~s**) (voice, singer) mezzo-soprano *f*.
II *modif* [*voice, part*] de mezzo-soprano.

mezzotint /ˈmetsəʊtɪnt/ I *n* (method, print) mezzo-tinto *m*.
II *vtr* graver [qch] par mezzo-tinto.

MF /emˈef/ *n* (*abrév* = **medium frequency**) FM *f*.

MFA *n* US (*abrév* = **Master of Fine Arts**) ≈ maîtrise *f* d'arts plastiques.

mfrs *abrév écrite* = **manufacturers**.

mg *n* (*abrév* = **milligram**) mg *m*.

Mgr (*abrév écrite* = **Monseigneur**, **Monsignor**) Mgr.

MHR *n* US *abrév* ▶ **Member of the House of Representatives**.

MHz (*abrév écrite* = **Megahertz**) MHz.

mi /miː/ *n* mi *m*.

MI US *abrév écrite* = **Michigan**.

MI5 *n* (*abrév* = **Military Intelligence Section Five**) service *m* britannique de contre-espionnage.

MI6 *n* (*abrév* = **Military Intelligence Section Six**) service *m* britannique de surveillance du territoire; cf DST.

MIA *abrév* ▶ **missing in action**.

miaow /miːˈaʊ/ I *n* miaou *m*.
II *vi* miauler.

miasma /mɪˈæzmə/ *n* sout miasmes *mpl*.

mica /ˈmaɪkə/ *n* mica *m*.

mice /maɪs/ *pl* ▶ **mouse**.

Michael /ˈmaɪkl/ *pr n* Michel.

Michaelmas /ˈmɪklməs/ *pr n* la Saint-Michel.

Michaelmas: **~ daisy** *n* GB aster *m*; **~ Term** *n* GB premier trimestre *m*.

Michelangelo /ˌmaɪkəlˈændʒələʊ/ *pr n* Michel-Ange.

Michigan /ˈmɪʃɪgən/ ▶ 1744 *pr n* Michigan *m*; **Lake ~** le lac Michigan.

mick° /mɪk/ *n* injur Irlandais *m*.

mickey /ˈmɪkɪ/ *n* GB IDIOMS **to take the ~**° se payer la tête° (**out of** de); **are you taking the ~ out of me?** tu te paies ma tête?; **stop taking the ~** arrête tes persiflages!

Mickey Finn /ˌmɪkɪ ˈfɪn/ *n* boisson *f* droguée.

Mickey Mouse /ˌmɪkɪ ˈmaʊs/ I *pr n* Mickey Mouse.
II *modif* péj [*job*] idiot; [*qualifications*] sans valeur.

micro /ˈmaɪkrəʊ/ I *n* Comput micro *m*.
II **micro +** (*dans composés*) micro-.

microanalysis /ˌmaɪkrəʊəˈnæləsɪs/ *n* (*pl* **-lyses**) microanalyse *f*.

microbe /ˈmaɪkrəʊb/ *n* microbe *m*.

microbial /maɪˈkrəʊbɪəl/ *adj* microbien/-ienne.

microbiological /ˌmaɪkrəʊbaɪəˈlɒdʒɪkəl/ *adj* microbiologique.

microbiologist /ˌmaɪkrəʊbaɪˈɒlədʒɪst/ ▶ 1692 *n* microbiologiste *mf*.

microbiology /ˌmaɪkrəʊbaɪˈɒlədʒɪ/ *n* microbiologie *f*.

Micro Cellular Network, **MCN** *n* Telecom réseau *m* microcellulaire.

microcephalic /ˌmaɪkrəʊsɪˈfælɪk/ *adj* microcéphale.

microcephaly /ˌmaɪkrəʊˈsefəlɪ/ *n* microcéphalie *f*.

microchip /ˈmaɪkrəʊtʃɪp/ I *n* puce *f*, circuit *m* intégré.
II *modif* [*industry, technology*] du circuit intégré; [*factory*] de circuits intégrés.

microcircuit /ˈmaɪkrəʊsɜːkɪt/ *n* microcircuit *m*.

microcircuitry /ˌmaɪkrəʊˈsɜːkɪtrɪ/ *n* microcircuits *mpl*.

microclimate /ˈmaɪkrəʊklaɪmɪt/ *n* microclimat *m*.

micrococcus /ˌmaɪkrəʊˈkɒkəs/ *n* (*pl* **-cocci**) micrococcus *m*; (for fermentation) microcoque *m*.

microcomputer /ˌmaɪkrəʊkəmˈpjuːtə(r)/ I *n* micro-ordinateur *m*.
II *modif* [*company, network*] de micro-ordinateurs; [*software*] pour micro-ordinateur.

microcomputing /ˌmaɪkrəʊkəmˈpjuːtɪŋ/ *n* micro-informatique *f*.

microcopy /ˈmaɪkrəʊkɒpɪ/ I *n* microphotographie *f*.
II *vtr* reproduire [qch] sur microfiche or microfilm.

microcorneal lens /ˌmaɪkrəʊˌkɔːnɪəl ˈlenz/ *n* (*pl* **~es**) lentille *f* microcornéenne.

microcosm /ˈmaɪkrəkɒzəm/ *n* microcosme *m* also fig; **in ~** en réduction.

microcosmic /ˌmaɪkrəʊˈkɒzmɪk/ *adj* microcosmique.

microcrystal /ˈmaɪkrəʊkrɪstl/ *n* microcristal *m*.

microcrystalline /ˌmaɪkrəʊˈkrɪstɪlaɪn/ *adj* microcristallin.

microculture /ˈmaɪkrəʊkʌltʃə(r)/ *n* Biol, Sociol microculture *f*.

microdissection /ˌmaɪkrəʊdaɪˈsekʃn/ *n* microdissection *f*.

microdot /ˈmaɪkrəʊdɒt/ *n* **1** Phot microdot *m*; **2** (drug) comprimé *m* de LSD.

microeconomic /ˌmaɪkrəʊˌekəˈnɒmɪk, -ˌiːkəˈn-/ *adj* microéconomique.

microeconomics /ˌmaɪkrəʊˌekəˈnɒmɪks, -ˌiːkəˈn-/ *n* (+ *v sg*) microéconomie *f*.

microelectrode /ˌmaɪkrəʊɪˈlektrəʊd/ *n* microélectrode *f*.

microelectronic /ˌmaɪkrəʊɪlekˈtrɒnɪk/ *adj* microélectronique.

microelectronics /ˌmaɪkrəʊɪlekˈtrɒnɪks/ *n* (+ *v sg*) microélectronique *f*.

microenvironment /ˌmaɪkrəʊɪnˈvaɪərənment/ *n* microenvironnement *m*.

microfauna /ˈmaɪkrəʊfɔːnə/ *npl* microfaune *f*.

microfiche /ˈmaɪkrəʊfiːʃ/ *n* microfiche *f*.

microfiche reader *n* lecteur *m* de microfiches.

microfilm /ˈmaɪkrəʊfɪlm/ I *n* microfilm *m*.
II *vtr* microfilmer.

microfilm reader *n* Phot lecteur *m* de microfilms.

microflora /ˈmaɪkrəʊflɔːrə/ *npl* microflore *f*.

microform /ˈmaɪkrəʊfɔːm/ *n* **1** ¢ (process) micrographie *f*; **2** C (microcopy) microcopie *f*.

microgram US, **microgramme** GB /ˈmaɪkrəʊgræm/ ▶ 1883 *n* microgramme *m*.

micrograph /ˈmaɪkrəʊgrɑːf, US -græf/ *n* (photo, drawing) micrographie *f*.

micrographics /ˌmaɪkrəʊˈgræfɪks/ *n* (+ *v sg*) micrographie *f*.

micrography /maɪˈkrɒgrəfɪ/ *n* (all contexts) micrographie *f*.

microgravity /ˌmaɪkrəʊˈgrævətɪ/ *n* microgravité *f*.

microgroove /ˈmaɪkrəʊgruːv/ *n*, *modif* microsillon (*m*).

microhabitat /ˌmaɪkrəʊˈhæbɪtæt/ *n* microenvironnement *m*.

microimage /ˈmaɪkrəʊɪmɪdʒ/ *n* microimage *f*.

microlight /ˈmaɪkrəʊlaɪt/ *n* ULM *m*, ultra léger *m* motorisé.

microlighting /ˈmaɪkrəlaɪtɪŋ/ ▶ 1282 *n* ultra léger *m* motorisé.

microlinguistics /ˌmaɪkrəʊlɪŋˈgwɪstɪks/ *n* (+ *v sg*) microlinguistique *f*.

microlitre /ˈmaɪkrəʊliːtə(r)/ ▶ 1068 *n* microlitre *m*.

micromesh /ˈmaɪkrəʊmeʃ/ *adj* **~ tights** GB, **~ pantyhose** US collant *m* mousse.

micrometeorite /ˌmaɪkrəʊˈmiːtɪəraɪt/ *n* micrométéorite *f*.

micrometeorologist /ˌmaɪkrəʊmiːtɪəˈrɒlədʒɪst/ ▶ 1692 *n* micrométéorologue *mf*.

micrometeorology /ˌmaɪkrəʊmiːtɪəˈrɒlədʒɪ/ *n* micrométéorologie *f*.

micrometer US, **micrometre** GB /maɪˈkrɒmɪtə(r)/ *n* micromètre *m*.

micrometry /maɪˈkrɒmɪtrɪ/ *n* micrométrie *f*.

microminiature /ˌmaɪkrəʊˈmɪnətʃə(r), US -tʃʊər/ *adj* [*circuit, parts*] microminiaturisé.

microminiaturization /ˌmaɪkrəʊˌmɪnɪtʃəraɪˈzeɪʃn, US -tʃʊərɪˈz-/ *n* microminiiaturisation *f*.

microminiaturize /ˌmaɪkrəʊˈmɪnɪtʃəraɪz, US -tʃʊər-/ *vtr* microminiaturiser.

micron /ˈmaɪkrɒn/ *n*† micron† *m*.

Micronesia /ˌmaɪkrəʊˈniːzɪə/ ▶ 1131 *pr n* Micronésie *f*.

microorganism /ˌmaɪkrəʊˈɔːgənɪzəm/ *n* micro-organisme *m*.

microphone /ˈmaɪkrəfəʊn/ *n* microphone *m*.

microphotograph /ˌmaɪkrəʊˈfəʊtəgrɑːf, US -græf/ I *n* microphotographie *f*.
II *vtr* microphotographier.

microphotometer /ˌmaɪkrəʊfəʊˈtɒmɪtə(r)/ *n* microphotomètre *m*.

microphysical /ˌmaɪkrəʊˈfɪzɪkl/ *adj* microphysique.

microphysics /ˈmaɪkrəʊfɪzɪks/ *n* (+ *v sg*) microphysique *f*.

microprobe /ˈmaɪkrəʊprəʊb/ *n* microsonde *f*.

microprocessing /ˌmaɪkrəʊˈprəʊsesɪŋ/ *n* micro-informatique *f*.

microprocessor /ˈmaɪkrəʊprəʊsesə(r)/ *n* microprocesseur *m*.

microprogram /ˈmaɪkrəʊprəʊgræm/ *n* microprogramme *m*.

microprogram(m)ing /ˌmaɪkrəʊˈprəʊgræmɪŋ/ *n* microprogrammation *f*.

microreader /ˈmaɪkrəʊriːdə(r)/ *n* microlecteur *m*.

micro-reproduction /ˌmaɪkrəʊriːprəˈdʌkʃn/ *n* microreproduction *f*.

microscope /ˈmaɪkrəskəʊp/ *n* microscope *m*; **under the ~** lit, fig au microscope.

microscopic /ˌmaɪkrəˈskɒpɪk/ *adj* **1** (minute) microscopique; **2** (using a microscope) au microscope.

microscopically /ˌmaɪkrəˈskɒpɪklɪ/ *adv* [*examine, study*] au microscope; **~ small** microscopique.

microscopic section *n* coupe *f* histologique.

microscopy /maɪˈkrɒskəpɪ/ *n* microscopie *f*.

microsecond /ˈmaɪkrəʊsekənd/ *n* microseconde *f*.

microstructural /ˌmaɪkrəʊˈstrʌktʃərəl/ *adj* de microstructure.

microstructure /ˈmaɪkrəʊstrʌktʃə(r)/ *n* microstructure *f*.

microsurgery /ˈmaɪkrəʊsɜːdʒərɪ/ *n* microchirurgie *f*.

microsurgical /ˌmaɪkrəʊˈsɜːdʒɪkl/ *adj* [*technique, procedure*] de microchirurgie; [*specialist, knowledge*] en microchirurgie.

microtechnique /ˈmaɪkrəʊtekniːk/ *n* microtechnique *f*.

microvolt /ˈmaɪkrəʊvəʊlt/ *n* microvolt *m*.

microwatt /ˈmaɪkrəʊwɒt/ *n* microwatt *m*.

microwave /ˈmaɪkrəweɪv/ I *n* **1** (wave) micro-onde *f*; **2** (oven) four *m* à micro-ondes.
II *modif* [*transmitter*] à micro-ondes; [*cookery*] au four à micro-ondes.
III *vtr* passer [qch] au four à micro-ondes.
IV **microwaved** *pp adj* [*food*] fait au micro-ondes.

microwaveable /ˈmaɪkrəweɪvəbl/ *adj* [*food*] qui peut être cuit au four à micro-ondes; [*container*] pour four à micro-ondes.

micturate /ˈmɪktjʊəreɪt/ *vi* spéc uriner.
micturition /ˌmɪktjʊəˈrɪʃn/ *n* spéc miction *f*.
mid+ /mɪd/ (*dans composés*) **in the ~-1990's/20th century** au milieu des années 90/du vingtième siècle; **~-afternoon/-morning** milieu *m* de l'après-midi/de la matinée; **to stop in ~-sentence** s'arrêter au milieu de sa phrase; **(in) ~-May** (à la) mi-mai; **in ~-career, she...** à mi-chemin dans sa carrière, elle...; **he's in his ~-forties** il a environ 45 ans.
midair /ˌmɪdˈeə(r)/ **I** *adj* [*collision*] en plein vol.
II in midair *adv phr* (in mid-flight) en plein vol; (in the air) en l'air; **his fork stopped in ~** sa fourchette s'arrêta en l'air; **to leave sth in ~** fig laisser qch en suspens.
Midas /ˈmaɪdəs/ *pr n* Midas.
IDIOMS **to have the ~ touch** avoir le don de tout transformer en or.
mid-Atlantic /ˌmɪdətˈlæntɪk/ *adj* **~ accent** accent *m* à mi-chemin entre l'accent britannique et l'accent américain.
midbrain /ˈmɪdbreɪn/ *n* mésencéphale *m*.
midday /ˌmɪdˈdeɪ/ ▶ 1096 **I** *n* midi *m*.
II *modif* [*sun, meal*] de midi.
midden /ˈmɪdn/ *n* lit, fig tas *m* de fumier.
middle /ˈmɪdl/ **I** *n* **1** milieu *m*; **in the ~ of one's back/forehead** au milieu du dos/du front; **in the ~ of** au milieu de [*place, night, meal*]; **to be caught in the ~** être pris entre deux feux; **I was in the ~ of a good book when...** j'étais plongé dans un bon livre quand...; **in the ~ of May** à la mi-mai; **right in the ~ of** en plein milieu de [*meeting, crisis, debate*]; **right in the ~ of dinner** en plein dîner; **to be in the ~ of doing** être en train de faire; **to split [sth] down the ~** partager [qch] en deux [*bill, work*]; [*argument, issue*] diviser [qch] en deux [*group, opinion*]; **2**○ (waist) taille *f*; **to grab sb round the ~** attraper qn par la taille.
II *adj* gen [*door, shelf, house*] du milieu; [*price*] modéré; [*size, height, difficulty*] moyen/-enne; [*ranks*] Mil intermédiaire; **in ~ life** au milieu de ma/ta etc vie, aux alentours de la cinquantaine; **to be in one's ~ thirties** GB avoir environ 35 ans; **the ~ child** (of three children) le deuxième enfant; (of five children) le troisième enfant; **to steer** ou **take** ou **follow a ~ course** adopter une position intermédiaire; **there must be a ~ way** il doit y avoir un juste milieu.
IDIOMS **in the ~ of nowhere** dans un trou perdu.
middle age *n* l'âge *m* mûr; **the onset of ~** le début de l'âge mûr; **she took up a new career in late ~** elle avait déjà un certain âge quand elle a changé de carrière.
middle-aged /ˌmɪdlˈeɪdʒd/ *adj* [*person*] d'âge mûr; fig [*outlook, view*] vieux jeu *inv*.
Middle Ages *n* **the ~** le Moyen Âge; **the early/late ~** le bas/haut Moyen Âge.
middle: **~-age spread** *n* embonpoint *m* dû à l'âge; **Middle America** *n* (social group) *Américains aisés et aux idées conservatrices*.
middlebrow /ˈmɪdlbraʊ/ péj **I** *n* (person) personne *f* sans prétentions intellectuelles.
II *adj* [*book*] sans prétentions intellectuelles; [*writer, actor*] de deuxième zone; [*music, tastes*] sans prétentions.
middle C *n* do *m* du milieu du clavier.
middle class I *n* classe *f* moyenne.
II *adj* [*person*] de la classe moyenne (*after n*); [*attitude, view*] bourgeois.
middle distance I *n* **1** Art, Phot, Cin second plan *m*; **2** gen **in the ~** au loin; **to gaze into the ~** regarder dans le vague.
II *adj* Sport [*event, athlete*] de demi-fond.
middle ear *n* oreille *f* moyenne.
Middle East I *pr n* Moyen-Orient *m*.
II *modif* [*affairs*] du Moyen-Orient; [*talks*] sur le Moyen-Orient.
middle: **~-eastern** *adj* [*nation, politics*] du Moyen-Orient; **Middle English** *n* moyen anglais *m*; **~ finger** ▶ 1037 *n* majeur *m*; **Middle French** *n* moyen français *m*; **~ ground** *n* gen juste milieu *m*; (in argument, disagreement) terrain *m* d'entente; Pol majorité *f* silencieuse, marais *m*; **Middle High German** *n* moyen haut allemand *m*; **~-income** *adj* [*person, family, country*] aux revenus moyens; **Middle Kingdom** *n* Hist (in Egypt) Moyen Empire *m*; (in China) Empire *m* du Milieu; **~man** *n* gen, Comm intermédiaire *m*.
middle management I *n* cadres *mpl* moyens.
II *modif* [*committee, level*] des cadres moyens; **~ executive** cadre *m* moyen.
middle manager *n* cadre *m* moyen.
middle name *n* deuxième prénom *m*.
IDIOMS **patience is my ~** la patience est ma plus grande vertu.
middle-of-the-road *adj* [*clothes, music, artist*] (banal) très ordinaire; (with wide appeal) populaire; [*policy*] gen modéré; péj tiède.
middle-ranking *adj* d'un rang intermédiaire.
middle school *n* GB *école pour élèves entre 9 et 13 ans*; US *école pour élèves entre 12 et 14 ans*.
middle: **~-size(d)** *adj* [*object, person, company, town*] de taille moyenne; **Middle Temple** *pr n* GB *une des quatre écoles de droit à Londres*.
middleweight /ˈmɪdlweɪt/ **I** *n* poids *m* moyen.
II *adj* [*boxer*] poids moyen; [*competition, champion*] des poids moyens.
Middle West *n* = **Midwest**.
middling /ˈmɪdlɪŋ/ *adj* [*ability, attainment*] moyen/-enne.
IDIOMS **fair to ~** pas trop mal.
Middx *n*: *abrév écrite* = **Middlesex**.
midfield /ˌmɪdˈfiːld/ **I** *n* **1** (area) milieu *m* du terrain; **in ~** en milieu de terrain; **to play ~** jouer milieu de terrain; **2** (position) milieu *m* de terrain.
II *modif* [*player, defence*] de milieu de terrain.
midfielder /ˌmɪdˈfiːldə(r)/ *n* milieu *m* de terrain, demi *m*.
mid-flight /ˌmɪdˈflaɪt/ **I** *adj* [*crash, collision, turbulence*] en plein vol.
II in mid-flight *adv phr* en plein vol.
midge /mɪdʒ/ *n* moucheron *m*; **~ bite** piqûre *f* d'insecte.
midget /ˈmɪdʒɪt/ **I** *n* **1** (dwarf) injur nain/-e *m/f*; **2**○ (small person) nain/-e *m/f*.
II *adj* miniature; **~ submarine** Mil sous-marin *m* de poche.
Mid Glamorgan /ˌmɪd ɡləˈmɔːɡən/ ▶ 1624 *pr n* Mid Glamorgan *m*.
Midi /ˈmɪdɪ/ *adj* (*abrév* = **musical instruments digital interface**) [*guitar, instrument, hi-fi*] Midi.
Midi-Pyrénées ▶ 1273 *pr n* Midi-Pyrénées *m*; **in/to the ~** dans le Midi-Pyrénées.
Midland /ˈmɪdlənd/ **I Midlands** *pr n* (+ *v sg*) **the ~s** la région *f* des Midlands (*au centre de l'Angleterre*).
II *adj* [*region, industry, accent*] des Midlands.
midlife /ˈmɪdlaɪf/ **I** *n* âge *m* mûr.
II *modif* [*crisis, problems*] de la cinquantaine.
midnight /ˈmɪdnaɪt/ ▶ 1096 **I** *n* **1** (in time) minuit *m*; **at ~** à minuit; **it is (just) after ~** il est (un peu) plus de minuit; **she arrived just after ~** elle est arrivée juste après minuit; **it's past ~** il est minuit passé; **2** fig (despair) ténèbres *fpl*.
II *modif* [*celebration, deadline*] de minuit.
IDIOMS **to burn the ~ oil** travailler jusqu'à l'aube.
midnight: **~ blue** ▶ 1104 *n, adj* bleu (*m*) nuit (*inv*); **~ madness sale** *n* US soldes *fpl* extraordinaires en nocturne; **~ sun** *n* soleil *m* de minuit.
midpoint /ˈmɪdpɔɪnt/ *n* milieu *m*.
mid-price /ˌmɪdˈpraɪs/ **I** *n* **to sell at ~** se vendre à prix modéré.
II *modif* [*product, item*] à prix modéré.
mid-range /ˌmɪdˈreɪndʒ/ **I** *n* **to be in the ~** [*product, hotel*] être en milieu de gamme.
II *modif* [*car, hotel, product*] de milieu de gamme.
midriff /ˈmɪdrɪf/ *n* ventre *m*; **a bare ~** (of body) un ventre nu; (of dress) une ouverture sur le ventre.
mid-season /ˌmɪdˈsiːzn/ Sport, Comm **I** *n* milieu *m* de saison; **in ~** en milieu de saison.
II *modif* [*match, sale, season*] de milieu de saison.
midshipman /ˈmɪdʃɪpmən/ *n* (*pl* **-men**) **1** GB (officer) aspirant *m* (*de la Marine*); **2** US (trainee) élève *m* de l'École navale; **3** GB (rank) grade *m* d'aspirant.
midsize /ˈmɪdsaɪz/ **I** *n* US Aut voiture *f* de taille moyenne.
II *adj* de taille moyenne.
midst /mɪdst/ *n* **in the ~ of** au beau milieu de [*group, place, event*]; **in the ~ of change/war** en plein changement/pleine guerre; **in our ~** parmi nous.
midstream /ˌmɪdˈstriːm/: **in midstream** *adv phr* (in river) au milieu du courant; fig (in speech) [*stop, pause, interrupt*] en plein milieu d'une phrase; **to abandon sth in ~** abandonner qch à mi-course.
midsummer /ˌmɪdˈsʌmə(r)/ **I** *n* (high summer) milieu *m* de l'été; (solstice) solstice *m* d'été.
II *modif* [*heat, days*] de plein été.
Midsummer('s) Day *n* la Saint-Jean.
mid-term /ˌmɪdˈtɜːm/ **I** *n* **in ~** Pol (of government) au milieu *m* de son/leur etc mandat; Sch au milieu *m* du trimestre; (of pregnancy) au milieu *m* de ma/sa etc grossesse.
II *modif* Pol [*crisis, election, reshuffle*] de milieu de mandat; Sch [*results, report, test*] de milieu de trimestre.
mid-terrace /ˌmɪdˈterəs/ *modif* [*house, property*] *situé au milieu d'un alignement de maisons identiques et contiguës*.
midtown /ˈmɪdtaʊn/ *n* US centre-ville *m*.
mid-Victorian /ˌmɪdvɪkˈtɔːrɪən/ *adj* [*style, fashion*] du milieu de la période victorienne; **in the ~ period** au milieu de la période victorienne.
midway /ˌmɪdˈweɪ/ **I** *n* US attractions *fpl* foraines.
II *adj* [*post, position*] de mi-course; [*stage, point*] de mi-parcours.
III *adv* **~ between/along** à mi-chemin entre/le long de; **~ through** au milieu de [*event, process, period*].
midweek /ˌmɪdˈwiːk/ **I** *n* milieu *m* de la semaine; **in ~** en milieu de semaine.
II *modif* [*performance, edition, concession*] de milieu de semaine; **~ return** GB Rail aller-retour *m* en semaine.
III *adv* en milieu de semaine.
Midwest /ˌmɪdˈwest/ *pr n* **the ~** le Middle West, le Midwest.
Midwestern /ˌmɪdˈwestən/ *adj* [*people, accent, state*] du Middle West.
Midwesterner /ˌmɪdˈwestənə(r)/ *n* US Américain/-e *m/f* du Middle West.
midwife /ˈmɪdwaɪf/ ▶ 1692 *n* (*pl* **-wives**) Med sage-femme *f*; **male ~** homme *m* sage-femme; **to be ~ to, to act as ~ for** fig jouer l'accoucheur pour qch, aider la création de qch.
midwifery /ˈmɪdwɪfərɪ, US -waɪf-/ **I** *n* profession *f* de sage-femme; **to study ~** faire des études de sage-femme.
II *modif* [*course, service*] de sage-femme.
midwinter /ˌmɪdˈwɪntə(r)/ **I** *n* **1** (season)

might¹

Although usage shows that *may* and *might* are interchangeable in many contexts, *might* indicates a more remote possibility than *may*. French generally translates this element of possibility using *peut-être* with the appropriate verb tense:

it might snow = il va peut-être neiger

(It is also possible to translate this more formally using *il se peut* + subjunctive: *il se peut qu'il neige*). For particular examples see ***might¹* 1**.

It is possible to translate *might* differently depending on the nature of the context and the speaker's point of view:

he might not come = il risque de ne pas venir

implies that this is not a desirable outcome for the speaker;

he might not come = il pourrait ne pas venir
or il se peut qu'il ne vienne pas

however, is neutral in tone.Where there is the idea of a possibility in the past which has not in fact occurred (see ***might¹* 2**), French uses the past conditional of the verb (which is often *pouvoir*):

it might have been serious (but wasn't in fact) = ça aurait pu être grave

This is also the case where something which could have taken place did not, thus causing annoyance:

you might have said thanks! = tu aurais pu dire merci!
(see ***might¹* 7**).

Might, as the past tense of *may*, will automatically occur in instances of reported speech:

he said you might be hurt = il a dit que tu serais peut-être blessé

For more examples see the entry ***might¹*** and bear in mind the rules for the agreement of tenses.

Where there is a choice between *may* and *might* in making requests, *might* is more formal and even rather dated. French uses inversion (*je peux = puis-je?*) in this context and *puis-je me permettre de ...?* (= *might I ...?*) is extremely formal.

Might can be used to polite effect – to soften direct statements: *you might imagine that* ... or to offer advice tactfully: *it might be wise to* .... In both cases, French uses the conditional tense of the verb: *on pourrait penser que ...; ce serait peut-être une bonne idée de ...* The use of *well* in phrases such as *he might well be right* etc. implies a greater degree of likelihood.

For translations of *might well, may well*, see **II 2** in the entry ***well¹***.
For translations of the phrase *might as well* (*we might as well go home*), see ***well¹* II 2**.

milieu *m* de l'hiver; **in ~** en plein hiver; **2** (solstice) solstice *m* d'hiver.
II *modif* [*day, weather*] de plein hiver.

mien /mi:n/ *n* littér mine *f*; **of cheerful ~** à la mine joviale.

miff○ /mɪf/ *vtr* vexer.

miffed○ /mɪft/ *adj* **to be** ou **get ~** prendre la mouche○ (**about, over** à propos de).

might¹ /maɪt/ *modal aux* (*prét de* **may**; *nég* **might not, mightn't**) **1** (indicating possibility) **she ~ be right** elle a peut-être raison; **the rumour ~ not be true** cette rumeur n'est peut-être pas fondée; **they ~ not go** peut-être qu'ils n'iront pas; **'will you come?'—'I ~'** 'tu viendras?'—'peut-être'; **you ~ finish the painting before tonight** tu auras peut-être fini de peindre avant ce soir; **you ~ find that** vous trouverez peut-être que; **they ~ have to go away** il va peut-être falloir qu'ils partent; **we ~ be misjudging her** nous la jugeons peut-être mal, il se peut que nous la jugions mal fml; **you ~ have met her already** tu l'as peut-être déjà rencontrée; **they ~ have got lost** ils se sont peut-être perdus; **you ~ have guessed that** vous aurez peut-être deviné que; **the plane ~ have landed by now** l'avion a dû déjà atterrir; **it ~ be tiredness** c'est peut-être or ça pourrait être la fatigue; **I ~ (well) lose my job** je risque de perdre mon travail; **it ~ well improve the standard** ça pourrait bien améliorer le niveau; **try as I ~, I can't do it** j'ai beau essayer, je n'arrive pas à le faire; **however unlikely that ~ be** si improbable que cela puisse paraître; **whatever they ~ think** quoi qu'ils pensent (*subj*); **he wouldn't do anything which ~ damage his reputation** il ne ferait rien qui puisse nuire à sa réputation; **2** (indicating unrealized possibility) **I ~ have been killed!** j'aurais pu être tué!; **I hate to think what ~ have happened** je n'ose imaginer ce qui aurait pu arriver; **more ~ have been done to prevent it** on aurait pu faire davantage pour l'éviter; **he was thinking about what ~ have been** il pensait à ce qui se serait passé si les choses avaient été différentes; **if I had been there all this mightn't have happened** si j'avais été là tout ça ne serait peut-être pas arrivé; **if they had acted quickly he ~ well be alive today** s'ils avaient agi plus vite il serait peut-être encore en vie aujourd'hui; **3** (in sequence of tenses, in reported speech) **I said I ~ go into town** j'ai dit que j'irais peut-être en ville; **we thought you ~ be here** nous avons pensé que tu serais peut-être là; **they thought she ~ have been his lover** ils ont pensé qu'elle avait peut-être été sa maîtresse; **I thought it ~ rain** j'ai pensé qu'il risquait de pleuvoir; **she asked if she ~ leave** elle demanda si elle pouvait partir; **4** sout (when making requests) **~ I make a suggestion?** puis-je me permettre de faire une suggestion?; **~ I enquire if...** puis-je me permettre de demander si...; **I should like to invite them, if I ~** j'aimerais les inviter si vous voulez bien; **I ~ add that** j'aurais souhaité ajouter que; **~ I ask who's calling?** c'est de la part de qui s'il vous plaît?; **and who, ~ I ask, are you?, and who ~ you be?** (aggressive) on peut savoir qui vous êtes?; **5** (when making suggestions) **it ~ be a good idea to do** ce serait peut-être une bonne idée de faire; **you ~ try making some more enquiries** tu devrais essayer de te renseigner un peu plus; **they ~ do well to consult an expert** ils feraient peut-être bien de consulter un spécialiste; **we ~ go out for a meal later** nous pourrions aller manger au restaurant plus tard; **you ~ like to drop in later** tu veux peut-être passer plus tard; **you ~ take time to visit the old town** n'hésitez pas à aller visiter la vieille ville; **6** (when making statement, argument) **one ~ argue** ou **it ~ be argued that** on pourrait dire or faire valoir que; **one ~ assume that** on pourrait supposer que; **as you** ou **one ~ expect** comme de bien entendu; **what you ~ call a 'putsch'** ce qu'on pourrait appeler un 'putsch'; **as you ~ imagine, he has conservative tastes** comme vous pouvez le deviner, il a des goûts classiques; **7** (expressing reproach, irritation) **I ~ have known** ou **guessed!** j'aurais dû m'en douter!; **you ~ try helping!** tu pourrais peut-être aider!; **he ~ at least apologize!** il pourrait au moins s'excuser!; **they ~ have consulted us first** ils auraient pu nous consulter d'abord; **you ~ have warned me!** tu aurais pu me prévenir!; **8** (in concessives) **he ~ be very brilliant but he's not a politician** il est peut-être très brillant mais ce n'est pas un politique; **they ~ not be fast but they're reliable** ils ne sont peut-être pas rapides mais on peut au moins compter sur eux; ▸**well¹ II 2**.

might² /maɪt/ *n* **1** (power) puissance *f*; **2** (physical strength) force *f*; **with all his ~** de toutes ses forces.
IDIOMS **~ makes right** la raison du plus fort est toujours la meilleure; **with ~ and main†** de toutes ses forces.

mightily /ˈmaɪtɪlɪ/ *adv* **1**○ (emphatic) drôlement○; **2**‡ (powerfully) vigoureusement.

mightiness /ˈmaɪtɪnɪs/ *n* puissance *f*.

mightn't /ˈmaɪtnt/ = **might not**.

might've /ˈmaɪtəv/ = **might have**.

mighty /ˈmaɪtɪ/ **I** *n* **the ~** (+ *v pl*) les puissants.
II *adj* **1** [*nation, leader, force*] puissant; **2** littér [*river, peak, tree*] imposant; **the ~ ocean** le vaste océan; **3**○ (huge, terrific) énorme.
III○ †*adv* (emphatic) vachement○, très.
IDIOMS **how are the ~ fallen!** littér comme tombent les puissants!; **the pen is mightier than the sword** littér la plume est plus puissante que l'épée liter; **high and ~** hautain.

mignonette /ˌmɪnjəˈnet/ *n* Bot réséda *m*.

migraine /ˈmi:greɪn, US ˈmaɪ-/ **▸1354** *n* migraine *f*; **it gives her a ~** cela lui donne la migraine; **an attack of ~** une crise de migraine; **to suffer from ~** souffrir de migraines.

migrant /ˈmaɪgrənt/ **I** *n* **1** Sociol gen (person) migrant/-e *m/f*; **2** Zool (bird) oiseau *m* migrateur; (animal) animal *m* migrateur.
II *adj* **1** Sociol [*labour, labourer*] saisonnier/-ière; **~ worker** (seasonal) travailleur/-euse *m/f* saisonnier/-ière; (foreign) travailleur/-euse *m/f* immigré/-e; **2** Zool migrateur/-trice.

migrate /maɪˈgreɪt, US ˈmaɪgreɪt/ *vi* **1** [*person*] émigrer; **2** [*bird, animal, parasite, chemical*] migrer.

migration /maɪˈgreɪʃn/ *n* (all contexts) migration *f*.

migratory /ˈmaɪgrətrɪ, maɪˈgreɪtərɪ, US ˈmaɪgrətɔ:rɪ/ *adj* [*animal, bird, fish*] migrateur/-trice; [*journey, instinct, behaviour*] migratoire.

mike○ /maɪk/ *n* Audio, Radio, TV micro○ *m*.

Mike /maɪk/ *pr n*: IDIOMS **for the love of ~**○†! pour l'amour du ciel!

Milan /mɪˈlæn/ **▸1818** *pr n* Milan.

Milanese /ˌmɪləˈni:z/ *adj* milanais.

milch cow† /ˈmɪltʃ kaʊ/ *n* Agric vache *f* laitière; fig péj vache *f* à lait.

mild /maɪld/ **I** *n* GB (also **~ ale**) bière *f* anglaise brune (légère).
II *adj* **1** (moderate) [*amusement, disappointment, protest, punishment, surprise*] léger/-ère; [*interest, irritation*] modéré; **2** (not cold) [*weather, winter*] doux/douce; [*climate*] tempéré; **it was a ~ day** il faisait doux; **a ~ spell** une période de beau temps; **3** (in flavour) [*beer, taste, tobacco*] léger/-ère; [*cheese*] doux/douce; [*curry*] peu épicé; **4** Cosmet [*soap, detergent, cream*] doux/douce; **5** Med [*case, symptom, infection*] bénin/-igne; [*attack, sedative*] léger/-ère; **a ~ heart attack** une petite crise cardiaque; **6** (gentle) [*person, character, voice*] doux/douce.

mildew /ˈmɪldju:, US -du:/ **I** *n* **1** Hort (disease) mildiou *m*; **2** (mould) moisissure *f*; **the smell of ~** l'odeur de moisi.
II *vi* moisir.

mildewed /ˈmɪldju:d, US -du:d/ *adj* [*plant, produce*] mildiousé; [*material*] moisi.

mildly /ˈmaɪldlɪ/ *adv* **1** (moderately) légèrement; **to put it ~** pour dire les choses avec modération; **that's putting it ~** c'est un euphémisme; **2** (gently) [*speak*] avec douceur; [*rebuke*] légèrement.

mild-mannered /ˌmaɪldˈmænəd/ *adj* modéré.

mildness /ˈmaɪldnɪs/ *n* (of character, weather,

product, punishment, voice) douceur *f*; (of taste) légèreté *f*; (of protest) modération *f*.

mile /maɪl/ ▶ 1412, 1604 I *n* **1** Meas mile *m* (= *1609 mètres*); **it's 50 ~s away** ≈ c'est à 80 kilomètres d'ici; **a 10 ~ journey** ≈ un trajet de 15 kilomètres; **she lives 10 ~s from me** ≈ elle habite à 15 kilomètres de chez moi; **half a ~** ≈ 800 mètres; **60 ~s per hour** ≈ 100 kilomètres à l'heure; **to do over 50 ~s to the gallon** ≈ consommer moins de six litres aux cent; **2** fig **to walk for ~s** marcher pendant des kilomètres; **to stretch for ~s** s'étendre sur des kilomètres; **it's ~s away!** c'est au bout du monde; **~s from anywhere** loin de tout; **not a million ~s from here/from the truth** pas très loin d'ici /de la vérité; **to see/recognize sth a ~ off** voir/reconnaître qch de loin; **you could smell it a ~ off** on pouvait le sentir à cent lieues à la ronde; **to stand out a ~, stick out a ~** sauter aux yeux; **I'd run a ~** je prendrais mes jambes à mon cou; **to be ~s away** (daydreaming) être complètement ailleurs; **3** (race) **the ~** le mile; **the 4 minute ~** le mile en 4 minutes.

II **miles** *npl* (as intensifier) [*bigger, more important etc*] beaucoup; **~s better** bien meilleur; **to be ~s out** (wrong) [*estimate, figure*] être complètement faux; [*person*] être très loin du compte.

IDIOMS **a miss is as good as a ~** Prov rater, même de peu, c'est rater; **to go the extra ~** en faire plus; **to talk a ~ a minute** US parler à toute vitesse.

mileage /ˈmaɪlɪdʒ/ *n* **1** nombre *m* de miles; **what's the ~ for the trip?** ≈ combien de kilomètres fait l'ensemble du voyage?; **2** (done by car) kilométrage *m*; **to have a low ~/a high ~** avoir un faible kilométrage/un kilométrage élevé; **unlimited ~** kilométrage illimité; **3** (miles per gallon) consommation *f*; **4** fig (use) **he's had plenty of ~ out of that coat** ce manteau lui a beaucoup servi; **there's still some ~ left in it** cela peut encore servir; **to get political ~ out of sth** tirer un bénéfice politique de qch; **the press got maximum ~ out of the story** la presse a exploité l'histoire au maximum; **5** = **mileage allowance**.

mileage: **~ allowance** *n* ≈ indemnité *f* kilométrique; **~ indicator** *n* ≈ compteur *m* kilométrique.

milepost /ˈmaɪlpəʊst/ *n* **1** borne *f* (milliaire); **2** GB Turf dernier poteau *m*.

milestone /ˈmaɪlstəʊn/ *n* **1** lit borne *f* (milliaire); **2** fig étape *f* importante; **to be a ~ in sb's life** marquer une étape dans la vie de qn.

milieu /ˈmiːljɜː, US ˌmiːˈljɜː/ *n* sout (*pl* **-lieux** ou **-lieus**) milieu *m*.

militant /ˈmɪlɪtənt/ souvent péj I *n* (activist) agitateur/-trice *m/f*, trublion *m*; (armed) partisan/-e *m/f* de la lutte armée.

II *adj* militant.

Militant Tendency *n* Pol (*parti britannique d'extrême gauche*).

militarism /ˈmɪlɪtərɪzəm/ *n* péj militarisme *m*.

militarist /ˈmɪlɪtərɪst/ *n, adj* militariste (*mf*).

militaristic /ˌmɪlɪtəˈrɪstɪk/ *adj* péj militariste.

militarize /ˈmɪlɪtəraɪz/ *vtr* militariser; **~d zone** zone *f* militarisée.

military /ˈmɪlɪtrɪ, US -terɪ/ I *n* **the ~** (army) (+ *v sg*) l'armée *f*; (soldiers) (+ *v pl*) les militaires *mpl*.

II *adj* militaire.

military: **~ academy** *n* école *f* militaire; **~ attaché** *n* attaché *m* militaire; **~ band** *n* fanfare *f* militaire; **~-industrial complex** *n* US complexe *m* militaro-industriel; **~ junta** *n* junte *f* militaire; **~ police** *n* police *f* militaire; **~ policeman, MP** *n* membre *m* de la police militaire.

military service *n* service *m* militaire; **to be called up for ~** être appelé sous les drapeaux.

militate /ˈmɪlɪteɪt/ *vi* **to ~ against sth** compromettre qch; **to ~ for** militer en faveur de [*reform, improvement*].

militia /mɪˈlɪʃə/ *n* **1** (citizen army) milice *f*; **2** US (liable for draft) **the ~** la réserve.

militiaman /mɪˈlɪʃəmən/ *n* (*pl* **-men**) milicien *m*.

milk /mɪlk/ I *n* **1** Culin lait *m*; **baby ~** lait *m* pour bébé; **condensed ~** lait concentré sucré; **powdered/evaporated ~** lait en poudre/concentré; **full cream ~** lait entier; **long-life ~** lait longue conservation; **skimmed/semi-skimmed ~** lait écrémé/demi-écrémé; **soya ~** lait de soja; **UHT ~** lait UHT; **2** Physiol, Vet lait *m*; **breast ~** lait maternel; **to be in ~** Vet donner du lait; **to produce ~** avoir du lait; **to express ~** Med tirer le lait; **when the ~ comes in** Med quand la montée du lait se fait; **3** Cosmet, Pharm lait *m*; **cleansing ~** lait démaquillant; **4** Bot lait *m*.

II *vtr* **1** Agric, Vet traire; **2** fig (exploit) (for money) pomper [*company, state*] **(for** de); **to ~ sb dry** saigner qn à blanc; **he ~ed the audience for applause** il a extorqué des applaudissements aux spectateurs; **3** extraire [*sap, juice*].

III *vi* [*cow, goat etc*] donner du lait; [*dairyman, farmer*] faire la traite; **this cow ~s well** cette vache donne beaucoup de lait.

IDIOMS **to come home with the ~** rentrer au petit matin; **it's no good crying over spilt ~** Prov il ne sert à rien de pleurer sur le lait répandu; ▶ **kindness**.

milk: **~-and-water** *adj* insipide; **~ bar** *n* milk-bar *m*; **~ bottle** *n* bouteille *f* de lait; **~ can, ~ churn** *n* bidon *m* à lait; **~ chocolate** *n* chocolat *m* au lait; **~ diet** *n* régime *m* lacté; **~ duct** *n* canal *m* galactophore.

milker /ˈmɪlkə(r)/ *n* **1** (person) personne *f* chargée de la traite; **2** (cow) laitière *f*.

milk: **~ fever** ▶ 1354 *n* Med, Vet fièvre *f* de lait; **~ float** *n* GB camionnette *f* de laitier; **~ gland** *n* glande *f* mammaire.

milking /mɪlkɪŋ/ *n* traite *f*; **to do the ~** faire la traite.

milking: **~ herd** *n* troupeau *m* de laitières; **~ machine** *n* trayeuse *f*; **~ pail** *n* seau *m* (pour la traite); **~ parlour** GB, **~ parlor** US *n* salle *f* de traite; **~ stool** *n* tabouret *m* (de traite); **~ time** *n* heure *f* de la traite.

milk: **~ jug** *n* pot *m* à lait; **~ loaf** *n* pain *m* au lait; **~maid** *n* fille *f* de ferme (*qui s'occupe de la traite*).

milkman /ˈmɪlkmən/ ▶ 1692 *n* (delivering) laitier *m*.

milk: **~ of magnesia** *n* lait *m* de magnésie; **~ powder** *n* lait *m* en poudre; **~ products** *npl* produits *mpl* laitiers; **~ pudding** *n* dessert *m* à base de lait.

milk round *n* **1** lit tournée *f* de livraison du lait; **2**○ GB fig rencontres *fpl* étudiants-entreprises.

milk run○ *n* Aviat vol *m* de routine.

milk: **~ shake** *n* milk-shake *m*; **~sop**○† *n* chiffe *f* molle○; **~ tooth** *n* dent *f* de lait; **~ train** *n* premier train *m* du matin; **~ truck** *n* US camionnette *f* de laitier.

milkweed /ˈmɪlkwiːd/ *n* **1** Bot asclépiade *f*; **2** Zool (butterfly) danaïde *f*.

milk-white /ˌmɪlkˈwaɪt, US -hwaɪt/ I *n* blanc *m* laiteux.

II *adj* [*skin*] laiteux/-euse; [*steed*] blanc/blanche comme la neige.

milkwort /ˈmɪlkwɜːt/ *n* herbe *f* au lait.

milky /ˈmɪlkɪ/ *adj* **1** (containing milk) [*drink*] au lait; [*diet*] lacté; **she likes her tea very ~** elle aime son thé avec beaucoup de lait; **to taste ~** avoir un goût de lait; **2** [*skin, liquid, colour*] laiteux/-euse.

milky: **Milky Way** *pr n* Voie *f* lactée; **~ white** *adj* laiteux/-euse.

mill /mɪl/ I *n* **1** (building) (for flour etc) moulin *m*; (factory) fabrique *f*; **paper ~** fabrique de papier; **2** Ind (machine) (for processing) machine-outil *f*; (for tooling metal) fraiseuse *f*; (for polishing) polissoir *m*; (roller) presse *f*; **3** Culin moulin *m*; **4** fig (routine) routine *f* ardue; **5** US fig usine *f*; **diploma ~** usine à diplômes; **6**○ (fight) castagne○ *f*.

II *vtr* moudre [*flour, pepper*]; fabriquer [*steel*]; broyer [*paper*]; filer [*cotton*]; tisser [*textiles*]; moleter [*screw*]; fraiser [*nut, bolt*]; denteler [*coin*]; **~ed edge** (of coin) bord dentelé.

IDIOMS **there'll be trouble at t'mill**○ hum on va avoir des ennuis; **to go through the ~** en voir de toutes les couleurs○; **to put sb through the ~** mettre qn à rude épreuve.

■ **mill around, mill about** grouiller.

mill board *n* carton-bois *m*.

millenarian /ˌmɪlɪˈneərɪən/ *n* millénariste *mf*.

millenarianism /ˌmɪlɪˈneərɪənɪzəm/ *n* millénarisme *m*.

millennial /mɪˈlenɪəl/ *n, adj* millénaire (*m*).

millennium /mɪˈlenɪəm/ *n* (*pl* **-niums** ou **-nia**) **1** (cycle) millénaire *m*; **2** (anniversary) millième anniversaire *m*, millénaire *m*; **3** Relig, fig millénium *m*.

miller /ˈmɪlə(r)/ *n* ▶ 1692 **1** (person) Agric meunier/-ière *m/f*; Ind fraiseur/-euse *m/f*; **2** (machine) fraiseuse *f*.

millet /ˈmɪlɪt/ *n* **1** (grass) (European) millet *m* des roseaux; (Indian) millet *m* commun; **2** (seed) millet *m*.

mill: **~ girl** ▶ 1692 *n* ouvrière *f* (*des filatures*); **~ hand** ▶ 1692 *n* ouvrier/-ière *m/f* (*du textile*).

millibar /ˈmɪlɪbɑː(r)/ *n* millibar *m*.

milligram(me) /ˈmɪlɪgræm/ ▶ 1883 *n* milligramme *m*.

millilitre GB, **milliliter** US /ˈmɪlɪliːtə(r)/ ▶ 1068 *n* millilitre *m*.

millimetre GB, **millimeter** US /ˈmɪlɪmiːtə(r)/ ▶ 1412 *n* millimètre *m*.

milliner /ˈmɪlɪnə(r)/ ▶ 1692 *n* modiste *f*.

millinery /ˈmɪlɪnərɪ, US -nerɪ/ *n* **1** ¢ (hats) chapeaux *mpl* et accessoires *mpl* pour la coiffure féminine; **2** (business) industrie *f* chapelière.

milling /ˈmɪlɪŋ/ I *n* (of corn) mouture *f*; (of paper) broyage *m*; (of cloth) tissage *m*; (of metal) fraisage *m*; (on coin) dentelage *m*.

II *adj* littér [*crowd*] grouillant.

milling: **~ cutter** *n* fraise *f* Tech; **~ machine** *n* fraiseuse *f*.

million /ˈmɪljən/ ▶ 1505 I *n* **1** (figure) million *m*; **six ~** six millions; **in ~s** par millions; **the odds are a ~ to one** il y a une chance sur un million; **thanks a ~**○**!** merci mille fois!; iron merci quand même○!; **2** (money) **her first ~** son premier million; **the family ~s** la fortune de la famille; **to have ~s** être riche à millions.

II **millions** *npl* (large numbers) des millions **(of** de); **the starving ~s** les masses *fpl* affamées.

III *adj* **a ~ people/pounds** un million de personnes/de livres; **to be a ~ years old** avoir un million d'années; **a ~ dollar bid** une offre d'un million de dollars; **I've told you a ~ times**○! je te l'ai dit cent or mille fois!

IDIOMS **to feel like a ~ (dollars)**○ US se sentir des ailes; **to look like a ~ (dollars)**○ être superbe; **to be one in a ~**○ être un oiseau rare○; **a chance in a ~**○ (slim) une chance sur un million; (exceptional) une chance unique.

millionaire /ˌmɪljəˈneə(r)/ *n* millionnaire *mf*.

millionth /ˈmɪljənθ/ ▶ 1505 I *n* millionième *m* **(of** de).

II *adj* millionième.

millipede /ˈmɪlɪpiːd/ *n* mille-pattes *m inv*.

mill owner *n* propriétaire *mf* d'usine.

mill pond *n* bassin *m* de retenue (d'un moulin).
IDIOMS **to be like a** ou **as smooth as a ~** [*sea*] être d'huile.

mill race *n* (stream) bief *m*; (channel) chenal *m*.

millstone /'mɪlstəʊn/ *n* meule *f*.
IDIOMS **to be/to have a ~ round one's neck** être/avoir un boulet au pied.

mill: **~stream** *n* bief *m* de moulin; **~wheel** *n* roue *f* de moulin; **~ worker** *n* = **mill hand**.

milo /'maɪləʊ/ *n* sorgho *m*.

milometer /maɪ'lɒmɪtə(r)/ *n* GB ≈ compteur *m* kilométrique; **to turn back the ~** trafiquer le compteur.

milquetoast /'mɪlktəʊst/ *n* péj chiffe *f* molle○.

milt /mɪlt/ *n* laitance *f*.

mime /maɪm/ **I** *n* **1** (art) (modern, classical) mime *m*; **2** (performance) pantomime *f*; **3** (performer) mime *mf*.
II *vtr* mimer [*person, words, scene*]; **to ~ doing** mimer quelqu'un en train de faire.
III *vi* mimer; **to ~ to** mimer [*music, text*].

mime artist ▶ **1692** *n* mime *mf*.

mimeograph /'mɪmɪəgrɑ:f, US -græf/ **I** *n* **1** (machine) ronéo® *f*; **2** (copy) polycopié *m*.
II *vtr* polycopier.

mimesis /mɪ'mi:sɪs, maɪ-/ *n* Art mimêsis *f*; Literat, Biol mimétisme *m*.

mimetic /mɪ'metɪk/ *adj* Biol mimétique.

mimic /'mɪmɪk/ **I** *n* (person, bird) imitateur/-trice *m/f*; (professional) imitateur/-trice *m/f*.
II *vtr* (*p prés etc* **-ck-**) **1** (to amuse) imiter; (to ridicule) parodier; **2** (simulate) simuler [*ability, condition, surroundings*]; Zool imiter [*colouring*]; **3** péj (copy) singer pej.

mimicry /'mɪmɪkrɪ/ *n* **1** (mimicking) imitation *f*; **to have a talent for ~** être doué pour les imitations; **2** Zool mimétisme *m*.

mimosa /mɪ'məʊzə, US -məʊsə/ *n* mimosa *m*.

min 1 *abrév écrite* = **minute**[1]; **2** *abrév écrite* = **minimum**.

Min. GB *abrév écrite* = **Ministry**.

minaret /ˌmɪnə'ret/ *n* minaret *m*.

minatory /'mɪnətərɪ, US -tɔ:rɪ/ *adj* sout menaçant.

mince /mɪns/ **I** *n* GB Culin viande *f* hachée; **beef/pork ~** bœuf/porc haché.
II *vtr* hacher [*meat, vegetable*].
III *vi* péj (walk) marcher en se dandinant (**across** à travers; **along** le long de).
IV minced *pp adj* [*meat, vegetable*] haché.
IDIOMS **not to ~ matters** ou **one's words** ne pas mâcher ses mots.
■ **mince up**: **~ up [sth]**, **~ [sth] up** hacher.

mincemeat /'mɪnsmi:t/ *n* GB Culin *garniture composée de fruits secs et d'épices*.
IDIOMS **to make ~ of sb** ne faire qu'une bouchée de qn.

mince pie *n*: *tartelette garnie d'une pâte de fruits secs*.

mincer /'mɪnsə(r)/ *n* hachoir *m*; **to put sth through the ~** passer qch au hachoir; **to put sb through the ~**○ fig faire passer un mauvais quart d'heure à qn○.

mincing /'mɪnsɪŋ/ *adj* affecté.

mincingly /'mɪnsɪŋlɪ/ *adv* de façon affectée.

mincing machine *n* hachoir *m*.

mind /maɪnd/ **I** *n* **1** (centre of thought, feelings) esprit *m*, tête *f*; **a healthy ~** un esprit sain; **peace of ~** tranquillité d'esprit; **it's all in the ~** c'est tout dans la tête○; **to cross sb's ~** venir à l'esprit de qn; **it never crossed my ~ that...** ça ne m'est jamais venu à l'esprit que..., ça ne m'a jamais effleuré l'esprit que...; **what was in the judge's ~?** qu'est-ce que le juge avait en tête?; **at the back of my ~ I had my doubts** au fond de moi j'avais des doutes; **my ~ was full of suspicion** j'avais des soupçons sur tout; **that's a load** ou **weight off my ~** ça me soulage beaucoup; **to be clear in one's ~ about/that...** être sûr de/que...; **to build up an image in one's ~ of sb/sth** se faire une image de qn/qch; **to feel easy in one's ~ about sth** se sentir rassuré quant à qch; **to have something on one's ~** être préoccupé; **to set one's ~ on doing sth** décider de faire qch; **to set sb's ~ at rest** rassurer qn; **nothing could be further from my ~** loin de moi cette pensée; **2** (brain) esprit *m*, intelligence *f*; **with the ~ of a two-year-old** avec l'intelligence d'un enfant de deux ans; **to have a very good ~** être très intelligent; **he has a fine legal ~** c'est un brillant juriste; **the right calibre of ~ for the job** les qualités intellectuelles pour cet emploi; **it's a case of ~ over matter** c'est la victoire de l'esprit sur la matière; **3** (way of thinking) esprit *m*; **to have a logical/analytic ~** avoir l'esprit logique/d'analyse; **the criminal ~** l'esprit criminel; **to read sb's ~** lire dans les pensées de qn; **4** (opinion) avis *m*; **to be of one ~** être du même avis; **to my ~**○ à mon avis; **to make up one's ~ about/to do** se décider à propos de/à faire; **my ~'s made up** je suis décidé; **to change one's ~ about sth** changer d'avis sur qch; **I've changed my ~ about him—he's really quite nice** j'ai changé d'avis à son sujet—en fait il est assez gentil; **to keep an open ~ about sth** ne pas avoir de préjugés sur qch; **to know one's own ~** avoir des idées bien à soi; **to speak one's ~** dire ce qu'on a à dire; **5** (attention) esprit *m*; **sorry, my ~ is elsewhere** pardon, j'ai l'esprit ailleurs; **to let one's ~ wander** laisser son esprit s'égarer; **to concentrate** ou **keep one's ~ on sth** se concentrer sur; **to give** ou **put one's ~ to sth** accorder son attention à qch; **she can work very fast when she puts her ~ to it** elle peut travailler très vite quand elle se concentre; **to take sb's ~ off sth** distraire qn de qch; **to turn one's ~ to sth** se mettre à penser à qch; **6** (memory) esprit *m*; **to come to ~** venir à l'esprit; **I can't get him out of my ~** je n'arrive pas à l'oublier; **try to put it out of your ~** essaie de ne plus y penser; **my ~'s a blank** j'ai un trou de mémoire; **it went right** ou **clean** ou **completely out of my ~** cela m'est complètement sorti de la tête; **to bring sth to ~** rappeler qch à qn; **to call sth to ~** se remémorer qch; **7** (sanity) raison *f*; **her ~ is going** elle n'a plus toute sa raison; **are you out of your ~**○**?** tu es fou/folle○? ; **I was going out of my ~ with worry** j'étais fou/folle d'inquiétude; **nobody in their right ~ would do such a thing** quelqu'un de normal ne ferait jamais cela; **to be of sound ~**† Jur jouir de toutes ses facultés mentales; **8** (person as intellectual) esprit *m*; **all the great ~s of the 17th century** tous les grands esprits du dix-septième siècle.
II in mind *adv phr* **I bought it with you in ~** je l'ai acheté en pensant à toi; **I have something in ~ for this evening** j'ai une idée pour ce soir; **with holidays/the future in ~** en prévision des vacances/de l'avenir; **with this in ~,...** avec cette idée en tête,...; **what kind of present did you have in ~?** est-ce que vous avez une idée du genre de cadeau que vous voulez offrir?; **to have it in ~ to do sth** avoir l'intention de faire qch; **to put sb in ~ of sb/sth** rappeler qn/qch à qn.
III *vtr* **1** (pay attention to) faire attention à [*hazard*]; surveiller [*manners, language*]; **~ what the teacher tells you** fais attention à ce que le professeur te dit; **~ your head/the step** attention à la tête/à la marche; **~ you don't drink/he doesn't drink** fais attention à ne pas boire/à ce qu'il ne boive pas; **don't ~ them!** ne fais pas attention à eux!; **carry on, don't ~ me** gen continuez, ne faites pas attention à moi; iron allez-y, ne vous gênez pas!; **~ how you go** GB faites bien attention à vous; **it's a secret, ~**○ c'est un secret, n'oublie pas; **~ you**○**, it won't be easy** remarque, ce ne sera pas facile; **2** (object to) **I don't ~ the cold/her husband** le froid/son mari ne me dérange pas; **I don't ~ cats, but I prefer dogs** je n'ai rien contre les chats, mais je préfère les chiens; **I don't ~ having a try** ça ne me dérangerait pas d'essayer; **'do you ~ if I bring him?'—'no, I don't ~'** 'est-ce que ça te dérange si je viens avec lui?'—'bien sûr que non'; **'do you want to go today or tomorrow?'—'I don't ~'** 'tu veux y aller aujourd'hui ou demain?'—'ça m'est égal'; **they were late, not that I ~ed, but still...** ils étaient en retard, non que cela m'ait dérangé, mais tout de même...; **I don't ~ who comes** peut venir qui veut; **she doesn't ~ where he sleeps/when he turns up** hum pour elle, il peut dormir où il veut/arriver quand il veut; **will they ~ us being late?** est-ce qu'ils seront fâchés si nous sommes en retard?; **would you ~ keeping my seat for me/opening the window?** est-ce que ça vous ennuierait de garder ma place/d'ouvrir la fenêtre?; **would you ~ accompanying me to the station?** (said by policeman) je vous demanderai de bien vouloir me suivre au commissariat; **I don't ~ telling you, I was frightened** je peux te dire que j'ai eu peur; **I think you were a bit rude, if you don't ~ my saying so** pour être franc, je trouve que tu as été un peu impoli; **if you don't ~ my asking...** si ce n'est pas une question indiscrète...; **'like a cigarette?'—'don't ~ if I do'**○ 'une cigarette?'—'c'est pas de refus'○; **I wouldn't ~ a glass of wine** je prendrais volontiers un verre de vin; **if you don't ~** si cela ne vous fait rien also iron; **3** (care) se soucier de; **he ~s what you think of him** il se soucie de ce que tu penses de lui; **do you ~!** iron non mais!; **never ~** (don't worry) ne t'en fais pas; (it doesn't matter) peu importe; **never you ~**○**!** (don't worry) ne t'en fais pas; (to nosy person) cela ne te regarde pas○!; **never ~ all that now** laissons tomber tout cela pour l'instant; **never ~ who/what/when etc...** peu importe qui/ce que/quand etc...; **never ~ complaining...** GB ce n'est pas la peine de te plaindre...; **he can't afford an apartment, never ~ a big house** il ne peut pas se permettre un appartement encore moins une grande maison; **4** (look after) s'occuper de [*animal, children*]; tenir [*shop*].
IDIOMS **great ~s think alike** les grands esprits se rencontrent; **if you've a ~ to** si le cœur vous en dit; **to see sth in one's ~'s eye** imaginer qch; **~ your own business**○**!** occupe-toi de tes affaires○!; **I gave him a piece of my ~**○**!** je lui ai dit ma façon de penser!; **to have a good ~** ou **half a ~ to do** GB avoir bien envie de faire; **to have a ~ of one's own** savoir ce qu'on veut; **to have no ~ to do** ne pas avoir le cœur de faire; **to be bored out of one's ~** s'ennuyer à mourir; **travel broadens the ~** les voyages enrichissent l'esprit; ▶ **two**.
■ **mind out** faire attention; **~ out or you'll fall** fais attention à ne pas tomber; **~ out of the way**○**!** dégage○!

mind: **~bending** *adj* [*drug*] psychotrope; [*problem*] très complexe; **~-blowing**○ *adj* époustouflant○; **~-boggling**○ *adj* stupéfiant.

minded /'maɪndɪd/ **I** *adj* sout **to be ~ to do** avoir envie de faire; **you can join us if you're so ~** tu peux te joindre à nous, si ça te dit.
II -minded (*dans composés*) **1** (with certain talent) **to be mechanically-/business-~** avoir le sens de la mécanique/des affaires; **2** (with certain attitude) **to be small-/open-~** avoir l'esprit étroit/ouvert; **3** (with certain trait) **to be feeble-~** être simplet/-ette.

minder /'maɪndə(r)/ *n* GB **1**○ (bodyguard) garde *m* du corps; **2** (also **child ~**) nourrice *f*.

mind-expanding /ˌmaɪndɪks'pændɪŋ/ *adj* [*drug*] hallucinogène.

mindful /'maɪndfl/ *adj* **~ of** soucieux/-ieuse de.

mindless /'maɪndlɪs/ *adj* **1** péj (stupid) [*person, programme*] bête, débile○; [*work*] abrutissant; [*vandalism*] gratuit; **2** (requiring little thought) [*task*] machinal.

mindlessly /'maɪndlɪslɪ/ *adv* **1** péj (stupidly) stupidement; **2** (automatically) [*perform task*] machinalement.

mind-numbing *adj* abrutissant.

mindreader /'maɪndri:də(r)/ *n* télépathe *mf*; **you must be a ~** hum mais tu lis dans mes pensées; **I'm not a ~!** je ne suis pas médium!

mind: **~reading** *n* télépathie *f*; **~-set** *n* façon *f* de penser.

mine[1] /maɪn/

■ **Note** In French, pronouns reflect the gender and number of the noun they are standing for. So *mine* is translated by *le mien, la mienne, les miens, les miennes*, according to what is being referred to: *the blue car is mine* = la voiture bleue est la mienne; *his children are older than mine* = ses enfants sont plus âgés que les miens.
– For examples and particular usages, see the entry below.

pron **his car is red but ~ is blue** sa voiture est rouge mais la mienne est bleue; **the green pen is ~** le stylo vert est le mien; **which glass is ~?** lequel (de ces verres) est le mien?, mon verre c'est lequel○?; **~'s a whisky**○ un whisky pour moi; **she's a friend of ~** c'est une amie à moi; **he's no friend of ~!** ce n'est pas un ami à moi!; **it's not ~** ce n'est pas à moi; **the book isn't ~ to lend you** je ne peux pas te prêter ce livre, il n'est pas à moi; **~ is not an easy task** fml ma tâche n'est pas facile; **that brother of ~** péj mon imbécile de frère○.

mine[2] /maɪn/ **I** *n* **1** Mining mine *f*; **to work in** ou **down the ~s** travailler dans les mines; **to go down the ~** (become a miner) descendre à la mine; **2** fig mine *f*; **to be a ~ of information** être une mine de renseignements; **to have a ~ of experience to draw on** pouvoir s'appuyer sur son expérience; **3** Mil (explosive) mine *f*; **to lay a ~** (on land) poser une mine; (in sea) mouiller une mine; **to hit** ou **strike a ~** heurter une mine.
II *vtr* **1** Mining extraire [*gems, mineral*]; exploiter [*area*]; **2** Mil (lay mines in) miner [*area*]; (blow up) faire sauter [*ship, tank*].
III *vi* exploiter un gisement; **to ~ for** extraire [*gems, mineral*].
■ **mine out**: **~ out [sth]**, **~ [sth] out** extraire [*mineral*]; exploiter [*area, pit*]; **the pit is completely ~d out** la mine est épuisée.

mine /maɪn/: **~ clearing** *n* déminage *m*; **~ detector** *n* détecteur *m* de mines.

minefield /'maɪnfi:ld/ *n* **1** lit champ *m* de mines; **2** fig terrain *m* miné; **a political ~** une poudrière politique.

mine /maɪn/: **~hunter** *n* détecteur *m* de mines; **~layer** *n* Mil Naut mouilleur *m* de mines; **~laying** *n* (at sea) mouillage *m* de mines; (on land) pose *f* de mines.

miner /'maɪnə(r)/ **▸ 1692** *n* mineur *m*.

mineral /'mɪnərəl/ **I** *n* **1** Miner (substance, class) minéral *m*; **2** Mining (for extraction) minerai *m*; **3** GB (drink) boisson *f* gazeuse.
II *adj* gen minéral; **~ ore** minerai *m*.

mineral kingdom *n* règne *m* minéral.

mineralogical /ˌmɪnərə'lɒdʒɪkl/ *adj* minéralogique.

mineralogist /ˌmɪnə'rælədʒɪst/ **▸ 1692** *n* minéralogiste *mf*.

mineralogy /ˌmɪnə'rælədʒɪ/ *n* minéralogie *f*.

mineral oil *n* **1** Miner pétrole *m*; **2** US (paraffin) huile *f* minérale.

mineral: **~ rights** *npl* concession *f* d'exploitation minière; **~ spring** *n* source *f* d'eau minérale; **~ water** *n* eau *f* minérale.

miner: **~'s lamp** *n* lampe *f* de mineur; **~s' strike** *n* grève *f* des mineurs.

mineshaft /'maɪnʃɑ:ft, US -'ʃæft/ *n* puits *m* de mine.

minestrone /ˌmɪnɪ'strəʊnɪ/ *n* minestrone *m*.

mine /maɪn/: **~sweeper** *n* dragueur *m* de mines; **~sweeping** *n* dragage *m* de mines; **~worker ▸ 1692** *n* mineur *m*; **~ workings** *npl* chantier *m* de mine.

mingle /'mɪŋgl/ **I** *vtr* mêler [*quality, feeling*] (**with** à); mélanger [*sand, colour, taste*] (**with** avec).
II *vi* **1 to ~ with** (chat to) se mêler à [*crowd, guests*]; (socialize with) fréquenter [*social group*]; **he doesn't ~** il ne se mêle pas aux gens; **let's ~!** mêlons-nous aux invités; **2** (combine) [*sounds*] se confondre (**with** à); [*smells, colours, tastes, feelings*] se mêler (**with** à).
III mingled *pp adj* **~d with** mêlé de.

mingy○ /'mɪndʒɪ/ *adj* [*person*] radin○, pingre; [*amount*] maigre.

mini /'mɪnɪ/ **I** *n* mini-jupe *f*.
II mini+ (*dans composés*) mini-.

miniature /'mɪnətʃə(r), US 'mɪnɪətʃʊər/ **I** *n* (all contexts) miniature *f*; **in ~** en miniature.
II *adj* **1** [*bottle, camera, TV, world, version*] miniature; **2** [*breed, dog, horse*] nain.

miniature: **~ golf ▸ 1282** *n* mini-golf *m*; **~ railway** *n* petit train *m*; **~ village** *n* village *m* miniature.

miniaturist /'mɪnɪtʃərɪst/ **▸ 1692** *n* miniaturiste *mf*.

miniaturization /ˌmɪnɪtʃəraɪ'zeɪʃn, US -rɪ'z-/ *n* miniaturisation *f*.

miniaturize /'mɪnɪtʃəraɪz/ *vtr* miniaturiser.

miniboom /'mɪnɪbu:m/ *n* croissance *f* éclair.

minibudget /ˌmɪnɪ'bʌdʒɪt/ *n* GB Pol budget *m* provisoire.

minibus /'mɪnɪbʌs/ *n* GB minibus *m*.

minicab /'mɪnɪkæb/ *n* GB taxi *m* (non agréé).

minicomputer /ˌmɪnɪkəm'pju:tə(r)/ *n* mini-ordinateur *m*.

minicourse /'mɪnɪkɔ:s/ *n* US Univ stage *m*.

minidress *n* mini-robe *f*.

minim /'mɪnɪm/ *n* **1** Mus GB blanche *f*; **2** Meas goutte *f*.

minima /'mɪnɪmə/ *pl* **▸ minimum**.

minimal /'mɪnɪml/ *adj* **1** (very small) minime; **2** (minimum) minimal.

minimal: **~ art** *n* art *m* minimal; **~ free form** *n* Ling forme *f* libre minimale.

minimalism /'mɪnɪməlɪzəm/ *n* Art minimalisme *m*.

minimalist /'mɪnɪməlɪst/ **I** *n, adj* minimaliste (*mf*).
II *adj* minimaliste.

minimally /'mɪnɪməlɪ/ *adv* très légèrement.

minimal pair *n* paire *f* minimale.

minimarket /'mɪnɪmɑ:kɪt/, **minimart** /'mɪnɪmɑ:t/ *n* supérette *f*.

minimize /'mɪnɪmaɪz/ *vtr* **1** (reduce) réduire [qch] au maximum [*cost, damage, impact, risk*]; **2** (play down) minimiser [*incident, significance*]; **3** Comput réduire.

minim rest *n* GB demi-pause *f*.

minimum /'mɪnɪməm/ **I** *n* minimum *m* (**of** de); **to keep to a/to the ~** maintenir à un/au minimum; **to reduce to a** ou **to the ~** réduire au maximum; **the bare** ou **absolute ~** le strict minimum; **the legal/necessary ~** le minimum légal/nécessaire; **to do the ~** faire le minimum; **at the ~** au minimum.
II *adj* minimum, minimal.

minimum: **~ iron** *adj* [*fabric, garment*] qui demande peu de repassage; **~ lending rate, MLR** *n* taux *m* d'escompte minimum; **~ wage** *n* salaire *m* minimum.

mining /'maɪnɪŋ/ **I** *n* **1** Mining exploitation *f* minière; **2** Mil (minelaying) (on land) pose *f* de mines; (at sea) mouillage *m* de mines.
II *modif* [*area, company, industry, rights, town*] minier/-ière; [*family, union*] de mineurs; [*accident*] de mine.

mining: **~ engineer ▸ 1692** *n* ingénieur *m* des mines; **~ engineering** *n* génie *m* minier; **~ rights** *npl* droits *mpl* d'exploitation minière.

minion /'mɪnɪən/ *n* péj ou hum (subordinate) sous-fifre○ *mf*, subalterne *mf*.

mini-pill /'mɪnɪpɪl/ *n* micropilule *f*.

miniscule *adj* = **minuscule**.

mini-skirt /'mɪnɪskɜ:t/ *n* mini-jupe *f*.

minister /'mɪnɪstə(r)/ **▸ 1268** **I** *n* **1** GB Pol ministre *m*; **~ of** ou **for Defence/the Environment, Defence/Environment ~** ministre de la Défense/de l'Environnement; **▸ cabinet minister, junior minister, minister of state**; **2** Relig ministre *m*; **~ of religion** ministre du culte.
II *vi* **1** (care for) sout **to ~ to** donner des soins à [*person*]; **to ~ to sb's needs** pourvoir aux besoins de qn; **2** Relig **to ~ to** desservir [*parish, village*].

ministerial /ˌmɪnɪ'stɪərɪəl/ *adj* GB Pol ministériel/-ielle.

ministering angel *n* ange *m* de dévouement.

minister of state *n* GB Pol ministre *m* délégué; **Minister of State for Education** ministre délégué auprès du ministre de l'Éducation.

minister: **~ plenipotentiary** *n* (*pl* **ministers plenipotentiary**) ministre *m* plénipotentiaire; **~ resident** *n* GB Pol (*pl* **ministers resident**) ministre *m* résident; **~ without portfolio** *n* GB Pol ministre *m* sans portefeuille.

ministrations /ˌmɪnɪ'streɪʃnz/ *npl* soins *mpl*.

ministry /'mɪnɪstrɪ/ *n* **1** GB Pol (department, building) ministère *m*; **Ministry of Defence/of Education/of Health/of Transport** ministère de la Défense/de l'Éducation/de la Santé/des Transports; **2** Relig (profession, duties) ministère *m*; **to perform** ou **carry out one's ~** exercer son ministère; **to join the ~** (Protestant) devenir pasteur; **3** Pol (tenure) mandat *m* ministériel; **4** Pol (group of ministers) gouvernement *m*.

minium /'mɪnɪəm/ *n* minium *m*.

miniver /'mɪnɪvə(r)/ *n* menu-vair *m*.

mink /mɪŋk/ **I** *n* (animal, fur, coat) vison *m*.
II *modif* [*garment*] de vison.

Minnesota /ˌmɪnɪ'səʊtə/ **▸ 1744** *pr n* Minnesota *m*.

minnow /'mɪnəʊ/ *n* **1** (fish) vairon *m*; **2** fig menu fretin *m*.

Minoan /mɪ'nəʊən/ **I** *n* Minoen/-enne *m/f*.
II *adj* minoen/-enne.

minor /'maɪnə(r)/ **I** *n* **1** Jur mineur/-e *m/f*; **2** US Univ matière *f* secondaire.
II *adj* **1** [*change, consideration, repair, defect, artist, role*] mineur; **~ road** route secondaire; **~ aristocracy** petite noblesse; **they're ~ royalty** ce sont des membres peu importants de la famille royale; **2** (not serious) [*injury, burn, fracture*] léger/-ère; [*operation, surgery*] mineur; **3** Mus [*scale, chord, interval, seventh*] mineur; **C ~** Do mineur; **in a ~ key** en mineur; **4** US Univ [*subject*] secondaire; **5**† GB Sch **Smith ~** Smith junior.
III *vi* US Univ **to ~ in sth** prendre qch en matière secondaire.

Minorca /mɪ'nɔ:kə/ **▸ 1381** *pr n* Minorque *f*.

minority /maɪ'nɒrətɪ, US -'nɔ:r-/ **I** *n* **1** gen minorité *f* (**of** de); **to be in the ~** être en minorité; **vocal ~** minorité agissante; **ethnic/religious ~** minorité ethnique/religieuse; **to be in a ~ of one** être le seul/la seule à penser cela; **2** US Pol opposition *f*.
II *modif* [*government, group, interest, party, shareholder*] minoritaire; [*activity*] qui ne touche qu'une minorité de personnes.

minority: **~ leader** *n* US Pol chef *m* de l'opposition; **~ president** *n* US Pol *président dont le parti n'a pas la majorité au Congrès*; **~ programme** *n* Radio, TV *émission destinée à un groupe minoritaire*; **~ report** *n* rapport *m* d'un groupe minoritaire; **~ rule** *n* gouvernement *m* par la minorité.

minor league US Sport **I** *n* division *f* secondaire.
II *modif* [*team, player*] de division secondaire; fig [*artist, university, company*] de second ordre; **he plays ~ baseball** il joue au baseball en division secondaire.

minor: **~ offence** GB, **~ offense** US *n* délit *m* mineur; **~ planet** *n* petite planète *f*; **~ premise** *n* mineure *f*; **~ prophet** *n* petit prophète *m*; **~ suit** *n* couleur *f* mineure (*au bridge*); **~ term** *n* terme *m* mineur.

Minotaur /'maɪnətɔ:(r)/ *n* **the ~** le Minotaure.

minster /'mɪnstə(r)/ *n* (with cathedral status) cathédrale *f*; (without) église *f* abbatiale.

minstrel /'mɪnstrəl/ *n* ménestrel *m*; **wandering ~** ménestrel (itinérant).

minstrel gallery *n* tribune *f* des musiciens.

mint /mɪnt/ **I** *n* **1** Bot, Culin menthe *f*; **2** (sweet) bonbon *m* à la menthe; **after-dinner ~** chocolat *m* à la menthe; **3** (for coins) hôtel *m* des Monnaies; **the Royal Mint** GB l'hôtel de la Monnaie (*à Londres*); **4**○ (vast sum) fortune *f*; **to make a ~** gagner une fortune; **to cost a ~** coûter une fortune.
II *modif* [*jelly, sauce, tea, toothpaste*] à la menthe; [*essence, flower, leaf*] de menthe.
III *adj* (new) à l'état neuf; **in ~ condition** à l'état neuf.
IV *vtr* **1** lit frapper [*coin*]; **2** fig forger [*word, expression*].

mint: **~-flavoured** *adj* parfumé à la menthe; **~ green** *n, adj* couleur (*f*) menthe à l'eau (*inv*); **~ julep** *n* US mint julep (*cocktail de bourbon à la menthe*).

minty /'mɪntɪ/ *adj* [*flavour, taste*] de menthe.

minuet /ˌmɪnjʊ'et/ *n* menuet *m*.

minus /'maɪnəs/ **I** *n* **1** Math moins *m*; **two ~es make a plus** moins par moins égale plus; **2** (drawback) inconvénient *m*; **it has its pluses and ~es** cela a ses avantages et ses inconvénients.
II *adj* **1** Math [*sign, symbol, button*] moins; [*number, quantity, value*] négatif/-ive; **2** [*factor, point*] négatif/-ive; **on the ~ side...** pour ce qui est des inconvénients...; **3** Sch, Univ **B ~** B moins; **4** Bot [*fungus, specimen, type*] négatif/-ive.
III *prep* **1** Math moins; **what is 20 ~ 8?** combien font 20 moins 8?; **it is ~ 15 (degrees)** il fait moins 15 (degrés); **2** hum (without) sans; **he woke up ~ his passport** quand il s'est réveillé il n'avait plus son passeport; **he's ~ a tooth/a finger** il a une dent/un doigt en moins.

minuscule /'mɪnəskju:l/ **I** *n* (letter) minuscule *f*.
II *adj* (all contexts) minuscule.

minus sign *n* signe *m* moins.

minute[1] /'mɪnɪt/ ▶ **1807**, **1096** **I** *n* **1** (unit of time) minute *f*; **a few ~s earlier/later** quelques minutes avant/après; **five ~s past ten** dix heures cinq; **it's five ~s' walk away** c'est à cinq minutes à pied; **we arrived at eight o'clock to the ~** nous sommes arrivés à huit heures pile; **we arrived without a ~ to spare** nous sommes arrivés au tout dernier moment; **2** (short moment) minute *f*; **just a ~ please** une minute, s'il vous plaît; **I'll be ready in a ~** je serai prêt dans une minute; **she won't be a ~** elle sera là dans un instant; **it won't take a ~** il y en aura pour un instant; **within ~s the police were there** en l'espace de quelques minutes la police était sur les lieux; **3** (exact instant) **the ~ I heard the news I telephoned** dès que j'ai entendu la nouvelle j'ai téléphoné; **at that very ~** à cet instant précis; **they're due to arrive any ~ now** ils devraient arriver d'une minute à l'autre; **stop talking this ~!** arrêtez immédiatement de parler!; **I was just this ~ going to phone you** j'allais t'appeler à l'instant; **he's at this ~ starting his speech** il est tout juste en train de commencer son discours; **to arrive at the last ~** arriver à la dernière minute; **to leave things to the last ~** laisser les choses à la dernière minute; **to put sth off to the last ~** repousser qch au dernier moment; **not for one ~ did I think she was lying** je n'ai pas pensé un seul instant qu'elle mentait; **he's always up to the ~ with the news** il est toujours au courant des dernières nouvelles; **she's always up to the ~ in her clothes** elle est toujours à la dernière mode; **4** Geog, Math minute *f*.
II minutes *npl* **1** Jur minutes *fpl*, procès-verbal *m*; **2** Admin compte-rendu *m*; **to take the ~s** rédiger le compte-rendu; **he read the ~s of the last meeting** il a lu le compte-rendu de la dernière réunion.
III *vtr* inscrire [qch] au procès-verbal [*decision, objection, apology*].
IDIOMS **there's one** ou **a sucker born every ~**○ ce ne sont pas les gogos○ qui manquent.

minute[2] /maɪ'nju:t, US -'nu:t/ *adj* [*particle, lettering*] minuscule; [*quantity*] infime; [*risk, rise, variation*] minime; **to describe sth in ~ detail** décrire qch dans les moindres détails.

minute /'mɪnɪt/: **~ book** *n* registre *m* des procès-verbaux; **~ hand** *n* grande aiguille *f*, aiguille *f* des minutes.

minutely /maɪ'nju:tlɪ, US -'nu:tlɪ/ *adv* [*describe, examine*] minutieusement; [*vary, differ*] de manière infime; **to question sb ~** interroger qn à fond.

minute /'mɪnɪt/: **Minuteman** *n* US Hist membre *m* de l'armée indépendantiste pendant la Guerre d'indépendance; **~ steak** *n* entrecôte *f* minute.

minutiae /maɪ'nju:ʃɪi:, US mɪ'nu:ʃɪi:/ *npl* menus détails *mpl*, minuties† *fpl*.

minx† /mɪŋks/ *n* coquine *f*.

Miocene /'mɪəsi:n/ **I** *n* **the ~** le Miocène.
II *adj* miocène.

MIPS, mips /mɪps/ *n* (*abrév* = **millions of instructions per second**) millions d'instructions par seconde.

miracle /'mɪrəkl/ **I** *n* miracle *m*; **to perform/accomplish a ~** faire/accomplir un miracle; **it's a ~ that** c'est un miracle que (+ *subj*); **a minor ~** un petit miracle; **by some ~** par on ne sait quel miracle; **economic ~** miracle économique; **a ~ of** un prodige de [*efficiency etc*]; **to work** ou **perform ~s** faire des miracles (**with** avec).
II *modif* [*cure, drug, recovery*] miracle.

miracle: **~ play** *n* miracle *m*; **~ worker** *n* fig faiseur/-euse *m/f* de miracles; lit personne *f* qui fait des miracles.

miraculous /mɪ'rækjʊləs/ *adj* **1** (as by miracle) [*cure, escape, recovery, survival*] miraculeux/-euse; **2** (great, amazing) [*speed, efficiency etc*] prodigieux/-ieuse.

miraculously /mɪ'rækjʊləslɪ/ *adv* miraculeusement.

mirage /'mɪrɑ:ʒ, mɪ'rɑ:ʒ/ *n* mirage *m*.

mire /'maɪə(r)/ *n* littér **1** (area) bourbier *m*; **2** (mud) boue *f*; **3** fig (bad situation) pétrin○ *m*.
IDIOMS **to drag sb** ou **sb's name through the ~** traîner qn dans la boue.

mired /'maɪəd/ *adj* fig littér **to be ~ in** baigner dans [*blood*]; nager dans [*corruption*]; se perdre dans [*detail, trivia*].

mirror /'mɪrə(r)/ **I** *n* **1** (looking glass) miroir *m*, glace *f*; **hall of ~s** palais des glaces or des miroirs; **2** (reflecting surface) miroir *m*; **3** Aut rétroviseur *m*; **4** fig reflet *m*.
II *vtr* lit, fig refléter; **to be ~ed in** se refléter dans.
III mirrored *pp adj* [*ceiling, wall*] recouvert de miroirs.

mirror: **~ image** *n* fig image *f* inversée; **~ writing** *n* écriture *f* spéculaire, écriture en miroir.

mirth /mɜ:θ/ *n* **1** (laughter) hilarité *f*; **to provoke/cause ~** provoquer/déclencher l'hilarité; **2** (joy) joie *f*.

mirthful /'mɜ:θfl/ *adj* sout (laughing) joyeux/-euse; (happy) gai.

mirthless /'mɜ:θlɪs/ *adj* sout [*laugh*] forcé; [*account etc*] dépourvu d'humour; [*occasion*] triste.

MIRV *n* US Mil (*abrév* = **multiple independently targeted reentry vehicle**) missile *m* à ogives à charges multiples et indépendantes.

miry /'maɪərɪ/ *adj* littér bourbeux/-euse.

MIS /ˌemaɪ'es/ *n* (*abrév* = **management information system**) SIG *m*.

misadventure /ˌmɪsəd'ventʃə(r)/ *n* sout ou Jur mésaventure *f*; **verdict of death by ~** GB verdict de mort accidentelle (*n'entraînant pas la responsabilité pénale*).

misadvise /ˌmɪsəd'vaɪz/ *vtr* mal conseiller.

misalliance /ˌmɪsə'laɪəns/ *n* mésalliance *f*.

misanthrope /'mɪsənθrəʊp/ *n* sout misanthrope *mf*.

misanthropic /ˌmɪsən'θrɒpɪk/ *adj* sout [*person*] misanthrope; [*attitude, writing*] misanthropique.

misanthropist /mɪ'sænθrəpɪst/ *n* = **misanthrope**.

misanthropy /mɪ'sænθrəpɪ/ *n* sout misanthropie *f*.

misapplication /ˌmɪsæplɪ'keɪʃn/ *n* (of knowledge, skill) mauvais usage *m*.

misapply /ˌmɪsə'plaɪ/ *vtr* (misuse) mal utiliser; **the rule has been misapplied** la règle n'a pas été appliquée correctement.

misapprehend /ˌmɪsæprɪ'hend/ *vtr* sout mal comprendre.

misapprehension /ˌmɪsæprɪ'henʃn/ *n* sout malentendu *m*, erreur *f*; **to be (labouring) under a ~** se tromper.

misappropriate /ˌmɪsə'prəʊprɪeɪt/ *vtr* sout détourner [*funds*].

misappropriation /ˌmɪsəˌprəʊprɪ'eɪʃn/ *n* sout détournement *m*; **~ of funds** détournement de fonds.

misbegotten /ˌmɪsbɪ'gɒtn/ *adj* **1** [*plan*] mal conçu; [*person*] qui ne vaut rien; **2**‡ (illegitimate) bâtard; **~ child** bâtard/-e *m/f*.

misbehave /ˌmɪsbɪ'heɪv/ **I** *vi* [*child*] se tenir mal; [*adult*] se conduire mal; **stop misbehaving!** tiens-toi tranquille!
II *v refl* **to ~ oneself** = **misbehave**.

misbehaviour, **misbehavior** US /ˌmɪsbɪ'heɪvɪə(r)/ *n* gen mauvais comportement *m*; Sch mauvaise conduite *f*.

misbelief /ˌmɪsbɪ'li:f/ *n* croyance *f* fausse.

miscalculate /ˌmɪs'kælkjʊleɪt/ **I** *vtr* mal évaluer [*response, risk*]; mal calculer [*amount, distance*].
II *vi* lit faire une erreur de calcul; fig faire un mauvais calcul.

miscalculation /ˌmɪskælkjʊ'leɪʃn/ *n* lit erreur *f* de calcul; fig mauvais calcul *m*.

miscall /mɪs'kɔ:l/ **I** *vtr* **1** (in tennis) **to ~ a fault** annoncer faute par erreur; **2** (misname) appeler à tort [*place*].
II *vi* annoncer faute par erreur.

miscarriage /'mɪskærɪdʒ, ˌmɪs'kærɪdʒ/ *n* **1** Med fausse couche *f*; **to have a ~** faire une fausse couche; **2** Jur **a ~ of justice** une grave erreur judiciaire.

miscarry /ˌmɪs'kærɪ/ *vi* **1** Med [*woman*] faire une fausse couche; Vet [*cow, ewe*] avorter; **2** [*plan, attack, strategy*] échouer.

miscast /ˌmɪs'kɑ:st, US -'kæst/ *vtr* (*prét, pp* **~**) **he was badly ~ as Hamlet** il n'était pas fait pour le rôle d'Hamlet; **the film was ~** les rôles du film étaient mal distribués.

miscegenation /ˌmɪsɪdʒɪ'neɪʃn/ *n* sout métissage *m*.

miscellaneous /ˌmɪsə'leɪnɪəs/ *adj* divers; **~ expenses** frais *mpl* divers; **the letter**

was classified under '~' la lettre a été classée sous la rubrique 'divers'.

miscellany /mɪˈselənɪ, US ˈmɪsəleɪnɪ/ *n* **1** (variety) (of people, things) collection *f* disparate (**of** de); (of questions) choix *m* (**of** de); **2** Literat (anthology) morceaux *mpl* choisis; **3** TV, Radio choix *m*.

mischance /ˌmɪsˈtʃɑːns, US -tʃæns/ *n* sout **1** (bad luck) malheur *m*; **by ~** par malheur; **2** (misadventure) mésaventure *f*.

mischief /ˈmɪstʃɪf/ *n* **1** (playfulness) espièglerie *f*; (witty) malice *f*; (done by children) bêtises *fpl*; **they are full of ~** ils sont pleins d'espièglerie; **to get into ~** faire des bêtises; **it keeps them out of ~** ça les occupe; **children are always up to ~** les enfants sont toujours prêts à faire des bêtises; **her eyes twinkled with ~** ses yeux brillaient de malice; **2** littér (harm) troubles *mpl* liter; **to make** ou **create ~** susciter des troubles; **3**○ (rascal) polisson/-onne *m/f*.
IDIOMS **to do oneself a ~** GB se faire mal.

mischief-maker *n* semeur/-euse *m/f* de troubles.

mischief-making **I** *n* zizanie *f*.
II *adj* [*remarks*] malveillant.

mischievous /ˈmɪstʃɪvəs/ *adj* **1** (playful) [*child, comedy, humour*] espiègle; [*smile, eyes*] malicieux/-ieuse; **2** littér (harmful) malveillant.

mischievously /ˈmɪstʃɪvəslɪ/ *adv* **1** [*smile, laugh, tease*] malicieusement; **2** littér [*insinuate, misrepresent*] avec malveillance.

mischievousness /ˈmɪstʃɪvəsnɪs/ *n* espièglerie *f*.

misconceive /ˌmɪskənˈsiːv/ **I** *vtr* mal interpréter [*remark, meaning*]; se méprendre sur [*role, duty*].
II misconceived *pp adj* **1** (badly thought out) [*idea, argument*] mal fondé; **2** (badly planned) [*agreement, project*] mal conçu.

misconception /ˌmɪskənˈsepʃn/ *n* idée *f* fausse; **Western ~s about the East** les idées fausses que l'Occident se fait sur l'Orient; **it is a popular ~ that** on croit souvent à tort que.

misconduct **I** /ˌmɪsˈkɒndʌkt/ *n* (moral) inconduite *f*; **he is guilty of professional ~** il a commis une faute professionnelle; **it's gross ~** c'est une faute professionnelle très grave.
II /ˌmɪskənˈdʌkt/ *vtr* (mismanage) mal gérer [*business affairs*]; mal mener [*enquiry*].
III /ˌmɪskənˈdʌkt/ *v refl* **to ~ oneself** mal se conduire.

misconstruction /ˌmɪskənˈstrʌkʃn/ *n* mauvaise interprétation *f*; **open to ~** pouvant faire l'objet d'une mauvaise interprétation; **to put a ~ on sb's words** mal interpréter les paroles de qn.

misconstrue /ˌmɪskənˈstruː/ *vtr* sout mal interpréter.

miscount /ˌmɪsˈkaʊnt/ **I** *n* Pol **to make a ~** faire une erreur dans le compte des suffrages exprimés.
II *vtr, vi* gen, Pol mal compter.

miscreant /ˈmɪskrɪənt/ *n* littér scélérat/-e *m/f*.

miscue /ˌmɪsˈkjuː/ *vtr* (in football, cricket) mal frapper [*ball*]; (in billiards) toucher à faux.

misdeal /ˌmɪsˈdiːl/ **I** *n* maldonne *f*.
II (*pp, prét* **misdealt**) *vtr* mal distribuer [*cards*].
III (*pp, prét* **misdealt**) *vi* faire (une) maldonne.

misdeed /ˌmɪsˈdiːd/ *n* méfait *m*; **to rectify a ~** réparer un méfait.

misdemeanour, **misdemeanor** US /ˌmɪsdɪˈmiːnə(r)/ *n* **1** sout (minor fault) incartade *f*; **2** Jur délit *m*.

misdirect /ˌmɪsdaɪˈrekt, -dɪˈrekt/ *vtr* **1** (send in wrong direction) mal orienter [*person*]; **to ~ sb to** diriger qn par erreur vers; **2** (misuse) mal orienter [*talents, efforts*]; **his anger is ~ed against his father** il dirige sa colère à tort contre son père; **3** Post (address wrongly) mal libeller l'adresse de [*letter, parcel*]; **the letter was ~ed to our old address** la lettre a été envoyée par erreur à notre ancienne adresse; **4** Jur mal instruire [*jury*].

misdirection /ˌmɪsdaɪˈrekʃn, -dɪˈrek-/ *n* (of talents, efforts) mauvaise orientation *f*.

miser /ˈmaɪzə(r)/ *n* avare *mf*.

miserable /ˈmɪzrəbl/ *adj* **1** (gloomy, unhappy) [*person, expression*] malheureux/-euse; [*thoughts*] noir; [*event*] malheureux/-euse; [*weather*] sale (*before n*); **what a ~ afternoon!** quel après-midi maussade!; **to look ~** avoir l'air malheureux/-euse; **to feel ~** avoir le cafard; **2**○ (small, pathetic) [*helping, quantity*] misérable; [*salary, wage*] de misère; [*attempt, failure, performance, result*] lamentable; **a ~ 50 dollars** 50 misérables dollars; **3** (poverty-stricken) [*life*] de misère; [*dwelling*] misérable; **4** (abject) **a ~ sinner** un pécheur éhonté.
IDIOMS **~ as sin** malheureux comme les pierres.

miserably /ˈmɪzrəblɪ/ *adv* **1** (unhappily) [*speak*] d'un ton malheureux; [*stare*] d'un air malheureux; **he was ~ cold** il avait horriblement froid; **2** (poorly) [*fail, perform*] lamentablement; **a ~ low wage** un salaire de misère; **~ fed** mal nourri.

miserliness /ˈmaɪzəlɪnɪs/ *n* (of person) avarice *f*.

miserly /ˈmaɪzəlɪ/ *adj* **1** (avaricious) [*person*] avare; [*habits*] mesquin; **2** (meagre) [*allowance, amount*] maigre.

misery /ˈmɪzərɪ/ *n* **1** (unhappiness) souffrance *f*; (gloom) abattement *m*; **to lead** ou **live a life of ~** avoir une vie de souffrance; **human ~** la misère humaine; **to make sb's life a ~** faire de la vie de qn un enfer; **to put sb out of their ~** euph (kill) abréger les souffrances de qn euph; **to put an animal out of its ~** euph achever un animal; **tell her the answer, put her out of her ~!** ne la laisse pas languir plus longtemps, donne-lui la réponse!; **the look of ~ on his face** son air malheureux; **2** (poverty) misère *f*; **3** (difficult or painful situation) calvaire *m* (**of** de); **the ~ of depression** le calvaire de la dépression; **4**○ GB (gloomy person) gen grincheux/-euse *m/f*; (child) pleurnicheur/-euse *m/f*.

misery guts○ /ˌmɪzərɪ ˈgʌts/ *n* GB (*pl* **~**) grincheux/-euse *m/f*.

misfire /ˌmɪsˈfaɪə(r)/ *vi* **1** lit [*gun, rocket*] faire long feu; [*engine*] avoir des ratés; **2** fig [*plan, joke*] tomber à plat.

misfit /ˈmɪsfɪt/ *n* (at work, in a group) marginal/-e *m/f*; **social ~** inadapté/-e *m/f* social/-e.

misfortune /ˌmɪsˈfɔːtʃuːn/ *n* **1** (unfortunate event) malheur *m*; **2** (bad luck) malchance *f*; **to have the ~ to do** avoir la malchance de faire.

misgiving /ˌmɪsˈgɪvɪŋ/ *n* crainte *f*; **to have ~s about sth** avoir des craintes quant à qch; **to have ~s about sb** avoir des doutes au sujet de qn; **not without ~(s)** non sans appréhension.

misgovern /ˌmɪsˈgʌvn/ *vtr* mal gouverner [*country*]; mal administrer [*city, colony*].

misgovernment /ˌmɪsˈgʌvnmənt/ *n* (of country) mauvais gouvernement *m*; (of city, colony) mauvaise administration *f*.

misguided /ˌmɪsˈgaɪdɪd/ *adj* [*strategy, attempt*] peu judicieux/-ieuse; [*politicians, teacher*] malavisé.

mishandle /ˌmɪsˈhændl/ *vtr* **1** (inefficiently) mal conduire [*operation, meeting*]; ne pas savoir comment s'y prendre avec [*person*]; **the case had been badly ~d** le cas avait été très mal traité; **2** (roughly) manier [qch] sans précaution [*object*]; malmener [*animal*].

mishap /ˈmɪshæp/ *n* incident *m*; **a slight ~** un incident sans importance; **we had a slight ~ with the car** nous avons eu un petit problème avec la voiture; **without ~** sans incident.

mishear /ˌmɪsˈhɪə(r)/ *vtr* (*prét, pp* **misheard**) mal entendre; **I misheard 'sea' as 'tea'** j'ai entendu 'tea' au lieu de 'sea'.

mishmash○ /ˈmɪʃmæʃ/ *n* méli-mélo○ *m*; **this law is a ~** cette loi est un méli-mélo; **a ~ of** un ramassis de.

misinform /ˌmɪsɪnˈfɔːm/ **I** *vtr* mal renseigner.
II misinformed *pp adj* mal renseigné (**about** sur); **they were badly ~ed** ils ont été très mal renseignés.

misinformation /ˌmɪsɪnfəˈmeɪʃn/ *n* (intentional) désinformation *f*; (unintentional) renseignements *mpl* inexacts (**about** sur).

misinterpret /ˌmɪsɪnˈtɜːprɪt/ *vtr* mal interpréter.

misinterpretation /ˌmɪsɪntɜːprɪˈteɪʃn/ *n* interprétation *f* erronée; **open to ~** qui prête à une interprétation erronée.

misjudge /ˌmɪsˈdʒʌdʒ/ *vtr* mal évaluer [*speed, distance*]; mal calculer [*shot*]; mal évaluer [*popular feeling*]; mal juger [*person, character*]; **I ~d him completely** je l'ai totalement mal jugé.

misjudgment, **misjudgement** /ˌmɪsˈdʒʌdʒmənt/ *n* **1** (wrong judgment) (of speed, distance) erreur *f* d'évaluation; (of shot) mauvais calcul *m*; **2** (wrong opinion) erreur *f* de jugement; **a serious ~ of his character/motives** une grave erreur de jugement à propos de son caractère/ses motifs.

miskick GB /ˌmɪsˈkɪk/ **I** *vtr* mal envoyer [*ball*]; rater [*penalty*].
II *vi* rater son tir.

mislay /ˌmɪsˈleɪ/ *vtr* (*prét, pp* **mislaid**) égarer.

mislead /ˌmɪsˈliːd/ *vtr* (*prét, pp* **misled**) (deliberately) tromper; (unintentionally) induire [qn] en erreur; **to ~ sb about sth** tromper qn sur qch; **to ~ sb into thinking that...** faire croire à tort à qn que...

misleading /ˌmɪsˈliːdɪŋ/ *adj* [*impression, title*] trompeur/-euse; [*information*] trompeur/-euse, mensonger/-ère; [*claim, statement, advertising*] mensonger/-ère; **it would be ~ to say that...** il serait trompeur de dire que...

misleadingly /ˌmɪsˈliːdɪŋlɪ/ *adv* de manière trompeuse.

mismanage /ˌmɪsˈmænɪdʒ/ *vtr* (administratively) mal diriger; (financially) mal gérer.

mismanagement /ˌmɪsˈmænɪdʒmənt/ *n* (of economy, funds) mauvaise gestion *f*; (of company, project) mauvaise direction *f*.

mismatch /ˈmɪsmætʃ/ *n* **1** (of styles, colours) discordance *f* (**between** de); (of concepts, perceptions) disparité *f* (**between** de); **2** (in marriage) **the marriage is a ~** c'est un couple mal assorti.

mismatched /ˌmɪsˈmætʃt/ *adj* [*people, furniture*] mal assorti; [*knives, forks, socks*] dépareillé.

misname /ˌmɪsˈneɪm/ *vtr* (name incorrectly) appeler à tort; (give unsuitable name to) mal nommer; **the ~d 'Happy Valley'** 'la vallée du bonheur' la mal nommée.

misnomer /ˌmɪsˈnəʊmə(r)/ *n* appellation *f* impropre; **it's a bit of a ~** GB c'est une appellation quelque peu impropre.

misogamy /mɪˈsɒgəmɪ/ *n* misogamie *f*.

misogynist /mɪˈsɒdʒɪnɪst/ *n* misogyne *mf*.

misogyny /mɪˈsɒdʒɪnɪ/ *n* misogynie *f*.

misplace /ˌmɪsˈpleɪs/ **I** *vtr* **1** (mislay) égarer [*keys, money*]; **2** (put in wrong place) mal ranger [*book, object*].
II misplaced *pp adj* **1** [*fears, criticisms*] déplacé; **2** [*money, passport*] égaré.

misprint **I** /ˈmɪsprɪnt/ *n* coquille *f*, faute *f* typographique.
II /ˌmɪsˈprɪnt/ *vtr* faire une coquille or une faute typographique sur [*word*].

mispronounce /ˌmɪsprəˈnaʊns/ *vtr* mal prononcer.

mispronunciation /ˌmɪsprəˌnʌnsɪˈeɪʃn/ *n* **1** (act) prononciation *f* incorrecte (**of** de); **2** (instance) erreur *f* de prononciation.

misquotation /ˌmɪskwəʊˈteɪʃn/ *n* citation *f* fautive.

misquote /ˌmɪsˈkwəʊt/ *vtr* déformer les propos de [*person*]; déformer [*text*]; citer fautivement [*price, figure*]; **she was ~d as demanding his resignation** on a déformé ses propos en disant qu'elle exigeait sa démission.

misread /ˌmɪsˈriːd/ *vtr* (*prét, pp* **misread** /ˌmɪsˈred/) **1** (read wrongly) mal lire [*sentence, map, thermometer*]; mal relever [*meter*]; **2** (misinterpret) mal interpréter [*actions, conduct*]; **I ~ the signs completely** fig je n'avais pas du tout compris la situation.

misreading /ˌmɪsˈriːdɪŋ/ *n* **1** (false reading) **the ~ of a word/map** la lecture inexacte d'un mot/d'une carte; **2** (false interpretation) (of scripture, text) interprétation *f* erronée.

misrepresent /ˌmɪsˌreprɪˈzent/ *vtr* présenter [qn] sous un faux jour [*person*]; déformer [*views, intentions*]; dénaturer, déformer [*facts*]; **to ~ sb as sth** présenter qn à tort comme qch.

misrepresentation /ˌmɪsˌreprɪzenˈteɪʃn/ *n* **1** gen (of facts, opinions) déformation *f*; (of person) représentation *f* erronée; **2** Jur déclaration *f* inexacte; **fraudulent ~** déclaration frauduleuse.

misrule /ˌmɪsˈruːl/ **I** *n* **1** (bad government) mauvaise administration *f*; **2** littér (disorder) désordre *m*.
II *vtr* mal gouverner.

miss /mɪs/ **I** *n* **1** (failure to score) (in game) coup *m* manqué or raté; **the first shot was a ~** le premier coup a manqué; ▶**near miss**; **2 to give [sth] a ~**○ ne pas aller à [*activity, entertainment, lecture, meeting, work*]; se passer de [*dish, drink, meal*]; **'you still haven't done your homework'—'oh, give it a ~ Dad'** 'tu n'as toujours pas fait tes devoirs'—'oh, lâche-moi les baskets○, papa'; **3** (failure) (film, record etc) échec *m*; **4**† (little girl) petite fille *f*; (young woman) jeune fille *f*; **a pert little ~** péj une petite pimbêche.
II Miss ▶**1268** **1** (woman' s title) Mademoiselle *f*; (written abbr) Mlle; **the Misses Brown**† les demoiselles Brown†; **Miss World/Oxford** Miss Monde/Oxford; **2** gen, Sch (mode of address) mademoiselle *f*; **yes, Miss** oui, mademoiselle; **can I help you, Miss?** est-ce que je peux vous aider, mademoiselle?
III *vtr* **1** gen, Games, Sport (fail to hit) manquer [*target*]; passer à côté de [*record*]; **the stone/bullet just ~ed my head** la pierre/balle m'a frôlé la tête; **he just ~ed the other car/a pedestrian** il a failli emboutir l'autre voiture/renverser un piéton; **2** (fail to take or catch) rater [*bus, train, connection, plane, meeting, event, cue, entertainment, bargain*]; laisser passer [*chance, opportunity*]; **I ~ed her/the train by five minutes** je l'ai ratée/j'ai raté le train de cinq minutes; **the chance was too good to ~** l'occasion était trop bonne pour la laisser passer; **to ~ doing** ne pas pouvoir faire; **I ~ed going to the museum** je n'ai pas pu aller au musée; **it's wonderful, don't ~ it!** c'est génial, à ne pas rater!; **you don't know what you're ~ing!** tu ne sais pas ce que tu rates!; **you didn't ~ much, it was terrible!** tu n'as pas raté or perdu grand-chose, c'était nul!; **3** (fail to see) rater; **you can't ~ it, it's the only one** tu ne peux pas le rater, c'est le seul; **the shop's easy/hard to ~** la boutique peut facilement/difficilement se rater; **4** (fail to hear or understand) ne pas saisir [*joke, remark*]; **I ~ed that—what did she say?** je n'ai pas saisi—qu'est-ce qu'elle a dit?; **she doesn't ~ much** peu de choses lui échappent; **he doesn't ~ a thing does he?** rien ne lui échappe n'est-ce pas?; **he ~ed the point of the remark** le sens de la remarque lui a échappé; **you've ~ed the whole point!** tu n'as rien compris!; **5** (omit) sauter [*line, page, section, meal, class, lecture*]; **6** (fail to attend) manquer [*school*]; **7** (escape, avoid) échapper à [*death, injury*]; éviter [*traffic, bad weather, rush hour*]; **I/he just ~ed doing sth** j'ai/il a failli faire qch; **I just** ou **narrowly ~ed being captured/injured** j'ai failli être pris/blessé; **how she ~ed being run over I'll never know!** comment elle n'a pas été renversée je ne le saurai jamais!; **8** (notice absence of) remarquer la disparition de [*object*]; **she didn't ~ her purse till she got back** elle n'a remarqué la disparition de son portemonnaie qu'à son retour; **oh, is it mine? I hadn't ~ed it** c'est le mien? je n'avais pas remarqué qu'il avait disparu; **I didn't ~ you** je n'avais pas remarqué que tu étais sorti; **keep it, I won't ~ it** garde-le, je n'en aurai pas besoin; **9** (regret absence of) **I ~ Richard** Richard me manque; **the boys ~ them** ils manquent aux garçons; **he ~ed the office/Paris** le bureau/Paris lui manquait; **what I ~ most is...** ce qui me manque le plus, c'est...; **to ~ doing sth** regretter de ne plus faire qch; **I won't ~ having to get up at 5 am** je ne regretterai pas de ne plus avoir à me lever à 5 heures du matin; **I shall ~ having you as a neighbour** je vous regretterai comme voisine; **she'll be greatly** ou **sadly ~ed** son absence sera très regrettée; **he won't be ~ed**○! bon débarras!
IV *vi* **1** Games, Mil, Sport rater son coup; **you can't ~!** tu ne peux pas rater ton coup!; **~ed!** raté; **2** Aut [*engine*] avoir des ratés.
IDIOMS **to ~ the boat** ou **bus**○ rater le coche; ▶**mile**.
■ **miss out**○: ¶ **~ out** être lésé; **I feel I've ~ed out somewhere along the line** j'ai l'impression d'avoir été lésé quelque part; ¶ **~ out on [sth]** laisser passer [*pleasure, benefit, chance, opportunity, bargain*]; **he ~ed out on all the fun** il a laissé passer l'occasion de s'amuser; ¶ **~ out [sb/sth], ~ [sb/ sth] out** sauter [*line, section, topic, verse*]; omettre [*fact, point, person*].

missal /ˈmɪsl/ *n* missel *m*.

misshapen /ˌmɪsˈʃeɪpən/ *adj* [*body part*] difforme; [*object*] déformé.

missile /ˈmɪsaɪl, US ˈmɪsl/ **I** *n* **1** Mil missile *m*, engin *m*; **2** gen (rock, bottle etc) projectile *m*.
II *modif* [*attack, base, site*] de missiles; **~ launcher** lance-missiles *m inv*.

missing /ˈmɪsɪŋ/ *adj* [*thing*] qui manque; [*person*] disparu; **~ person** personne disparue; **the ~ link** gen, Anthrop, hum le chaînon manquant; **to be ~** manquer; **there's nothing ~** il n'y a rien qui manque, tout est là; **how many pieces are ~?** il manque combien de pièces?; **a man with a finger ~** ou **a ~ finger** un homme auquel il manque un doigt; **the book was ~ from its usual place** le livre n'était pas à sa place habituelle; **to go ~** [*person, object*] disparaître; **to report sb ~** signaler la disparition de qn; **~ presumed dead** porté disparu, présumé mort.

missing in action, **MIA** *adj* Mil porté disparu.

mission /ˈmɪʃn/ **I** *n* **1** (group of people) mission *f*; **diplomatic/trade ~** mission diplomatique/commerciale; **2** (task) mission *f*; **our ~ was to do** nous avions pour mission de faire; **to be on a ~** être en mission; **to undertake/carry out a ~** se charger/s'acquitter d'une mission; **~ accomplished!** mission accomplie! also hum; **to be sent on a ~** être envoyé en mission; **3** Relig mission *f*; **4** Mil Aviat mission *f*; **to fly 30 ~s** faire 30 missions aériennes.
II *modif* [*hospital, school*] géré par une mission.

missionary /ˈmɪʃənrɪ, US -nerɪ/ ▶**1692** **I** *n* Relig missionnaire *mf*.
II *modif* Relig [*role, vocation*] missionnaire; [*sect, settlement*] de missionnaires.
IDIOMS **to be filled with ~ zeal** avoir l'esprit missionnaire.

missionary position *n* position *f* du missionnaire.

Mission Control *n*: *partie de la NASA responsable du suivi des vols spatiaux.*

missis *n* = **missus**.

Mississippi /ˌmɪsɪˈsɪpɪ/ ▶**1744**, **1644** *pr n* Mississippi *m*.

missive /ˈmɪsɪv/ *n* sout missive *f*.

Missouri /mɪˈzʊərɪ/ ▶**1744**, **1644** *pr n* Missouri *m*.
IDIOMS **to be** ou **come from ~** US être un sceptique.

misspell /ˌmɪsˈspel/ *vtr* (*prét, pp* **-spelled** ou **-spelt** GB) mal orthographier; **to ~ sb's name** faire une faute au nom de qn.

misspelling /ˌmɪsˈspelɪŋ/ *n* faute *f* d'orthographe.

misspend /ˌmɪsˈspend/ *vtr* (*prét, pp* **misspent**) gaspiller (**on** en); **a misspent youth** une folle jeunesse.

misstate /ˌmɪsˈsteɪt/ *vtr* présenter [qch] de façon erronée.

misstatement /ˌmɪsˈsteɪtmənt/ *n* **1** (of situation, facts) présentation *f* erronée (**of** de); **2** (untruth) déclaration *f* inexacte.

missus○ /ˈmɪsɪz/ *n* **1** (wife) **his ~** sa dame○; **the ~** la bourgeoise○; **2** (as address) **yes, ~** oui, m'dame○.

missy○† /ˈmɪsɪ/ *n* mam'selle○† *f*, mademoiselle *f*.

mist /mɪst/ **I** *n* **1** (thin fog) brume *f*; **~ and fog patches** nappes *fpl* de brume et de brouillard; **2** (of perfume, spray) brume *f*; (from breath, on window) buée *f*; **3** fig (of tears) voile *m*.
II *vtr* vaporiser [*plant*].
IDIOMS **lost in the ~s of time** perdu dans la nuit des temps.
■ **mist over** [*lens, mirror*] s'embuer; [*landscape*] s'embrumer; **his eyes ~ed over with tears** les larmes embuaient ses yeux.
■ **mist up** [*lens, window*] s'embuer.

mistakable /mɪˈsteɪkəbl/ *adj* facile à confondre (**for** avec).

mistake /mɪˈsteɪk/ **I** *n* (error) (in text, spelling, typing) faute *f*; (in sum, calculation, judgment, procedure) erreur *f*; **to make a ~** gen faire une erreur, se tromper; (in spelling, typing) faire une faute; **to make a stupid ~** faire une bêtise; **to make a ~ in** se tromper dans [*calculations*]; faire une faute dans [*letter, essay*]; **to make a ~ about sb/sth** se tromper sur le compte de qn/sur qch; **to make the ~ of doing** faire ou commettre l'erreur de faire, faire la bêtise de faire; **to make the same ~ again** ou **twice** faire la même erreur; **it would be a ~ to do** ce serait une erreur de faire; **it was a ~ to leave my umbrella at home** j'ai eu tort de laisser mon parapluie à la maison; **to do sth by ~** faire qch par erreur; **she took my keys in ~ for hers** elle a pris mes clés au lieu des siennes; **to make a fatal ~** commettre une erreur fatale; **to realize/admit one's ~** se rendre compte de/reconnaître son erreur; **~s were made** il y eu des erreurs; **we all make ~s** des erreurs, on en fait tous; **there is no ~** il n'y a pas d'erreur possible; **the terrorists said the killing of X was a ~** les terroristes ont déclaré avoir tué X par erreur; **you're making a big ~**○ tu fais une grave erreur; **you'll be punished, make no ~ about it** ou **that!** tu seras puni, fais-moi confiance!; **there must be some ~** il doit y avoir erreur; **my ~!** mea culpa!; **...and no ~** il n'y a pas de doute; **to learn by one's ~s** tirer la leçon de ses erreurs.
II *vtr* (*prét* **-took**, *pp* **-taken**) **1** (confuse) **to ~ sth for sth else** prendre qch pour qch d'autre; **to ~ sb for sb else** confondre qn avec qn d'autre; **there's no mistaking him!** on ne peut pas le prendre pour qn d'autre; **there's no mistaking that voice** il est impossible de ne pas reconnaître cette voix; **there's no mistaking his intentions** on ne

peut pas se tromper sur ses intentions; **2** (misinterpret) mal interpréter [*meaning*].

mistaken /mɪ'steɪkən/ **I** *pp* ▶ **mistake**.
II *adj* **1 to be ~** avoir tort; **I'm afraid you are ~** je crois que vous avez tort; **he was ~ in thinking it was over** il avait tort de croire que c'était fini; **unless I'm very much ~** si je ne me trompe; **to do sth in the ~ belief that**... faire qch croyant à tort que...; **it's a case of ~ identity** Jur il y a erreur sur la personne; **2** [*enthusiasm, generosity*] mal placé.

mistakenly /mɪ'steɪkənlɪ/ *adv* [*think, fear, believe*] à tort; **whether ~ or not, they remain optimistic** à tort ou à raison, ils restent optimistes.

mister /'mɪstə(r)/ *n* **1** *forme complète de* **Mr**, *assez rare*; **2**○ (used by children) **please, ~, have you got the time?** s'il vous plaît, m'sieur, vous avez l'heure?; (used by adults) **now listen here, ~!** toi là, écoute-moi bien!

mistime /ˌmɪs'taɪm/ *vtr* mal calculer [*length of journey, attack, shot*]; **to ~ one's resignation** mal choisir son moment pour donner sa démission; **I ~d the announcement** j'ai mal choisi mon moment pour annoncer la nouvelle.

mistiming /ˌmɪs'taɪmɪŋ/ *n* (of remark) inopportunité *f*; **the ~ of his departure/resignation** le fait qu'il avait mal calculé l'heure de son départ/qu'il avait mal choisi son moment pour donner sa démission.

mistletoe /'mɪsltəʊ/ *n* gui *m*; **to kiss sb under the ~** embrasser qn pour lui souhaiter la bonne année.

mistook /mɪ'stʊk/ *prét* ▶ **mistake**.

mistranslate /ˌmɪstræns'leɪt/ *vtr* mal traduire.

mistranslation /ˌmɪstræns'leɪʃn/ *n* (mistake) erreur *f* de traduction.

mistreat /ˌmɪs'triːt/ *vtr* maltraiter [*person, animal*]; **don't ~ your books** prends soin de tes livres.

mistreatment /ˌmɪs'triːtmənt/ *n* mauvais traitement *m*.

mistress /'mɪstrɪs/ *n* **1** (sexual partner) maîtresse *f*; **to keep/have a ~** entretenir/avoir une maîtresse; **2** (woman in charge) (of servant, animal) maîtresse *f*; **~ of the situation** maîtresse de la situation; **the ~ of the house** la maîtresse de maison; **3**† GB (teacher) professeur *m*; **maths ~** professeur de maths.
IDIOMS **to be one's own ~** être sa propre maîtresse; **to be ~ of the situation** être maîtresse de la situation.

mistrial /ˌmɪs'traɪəl/ *n* Jur **1** (invalid trial) procès *m* entaché d'un vice de procédure de forme ou de fond; **2** US (where jury cannot agree) procès *m* ne pouvant aboutir (*le jury n'étant pas unanime*).

mistrust /ˌmɪs'trʌst/ **I** *n* méfiance *f* (**of, towards** à l'égard de).
II *vtr* se méfier de.

mistrustful /ˌmɪs'trʌstfl/ *adj* méfiant (**of** à l'égard de).

mistrustfully /ˌmɪs'trʌstfəlɪ/ *adv* (in attitude) avec méfiance; (visibly) d'un air méfiant.

misty /'mɪstɪ/ *adj* [*conditions, morning*] brumeux/-euse; [*hills, view*] embrumé; [*lens, window*] embué; [*photo*] flou; **~ rain** bruine *f*; **her eyes went all ~** les larmes embuaient ses yeux; **~ blue/grey** fig bleu/gris pâle.

misty-eyed /ˌmɪstɪ'aɪd/ *adj* [*look*] tendre; **he goes all ~ about it** il est tout ému quand il en parle.

misunderstand /ˌmɪsˌʌndə'stænd/ **I** *vtr* (*prét, pp* **-stood**) mal comprendre; (completely) ne pas comprendre; **don't ~ me** (to clarify oneself) comprends-moi bien.
II misunderstood *pp adj* **to feel misunderstood** se sentir incompris; **much misunderstood** [*concept, person, book*] souvent mal compris.

misunderstanding /ˌmɪsˌʌndə'stændɪŋ/ *n* malentendu *m*; **so as to avoid any ~** pour qu'il n'y ait pas de malentendus.

misuse I /ˌmɪs'juːs/ *n* (of equipment) mauvais usage *m*; (of word, expression) usage *m* impropre; (of talents) mauvais emploi *m*; **~ of funds** détournement *m* de fonds.
II /ˌmɪs'juːz/ *vtr* faire mauvais usage de [*equipment*]; mal employer [*word, expression, talents, resources*]; abuser de [*authority*].

mite /maɪt/ *n* **1** (child) **poor little ~!** pauvre petit!; **2**○ (small amount) **she seemed a ~ confused** elle semblait un tantinet perplexe; **he was a ~ ridiculous** il était un tantinet ridicule; **3** (animal) acarien *m*; **cheese ~** mite *f* du fromage; **harvest ~** aoûtat *m*.

miter *n* US = **mitre**.

mitigate /'mɪtɪgeɪt/ **I** *vtr* atténuer [*effects, distress*]; réduire [*risks*]; minimiser [*loss*]; Jur atténuer [*sentence*].
II mitigating *pres p adj* Jur **mitigating circumstances** ou **factors** circonstances *fpl* atténuantes.

mitigation /ˌmɪtɪ'geɪʃn/ *n* **1** (minimising) (of effects, distress) atténuation *f*; (of loss) minimisation *f*; **2** Jur (of sentence, damages) réduction *f*; **to say sth in ~ of sb's actions** dire qch à la décharge de qn; **to make a plea in ~** plaider les circonstances atténuantes.

mitosis /mɪ'təʊsɪs, maɪ-/ *n* mitose *f*.

mitral /'maɪtrəl/ *adj* mitral.

mitral valve *n* valvule *f* mitrale.

mitre GB, **miter** US /'maɪtə(r)/ **I** *n* **1** (of bishop) mitre *f*; **2** Constr = **mitre joint**.
II *vtr* Constr **1** (join) assembler [qch] à onglet; **2** (shape) tailler [qch] d'onglet.

mitre: **~ box** *n* boite *f* à onglets; **~ joint** *n* assemblage *m* à onglet.

mitt /mɪt/ *n* **1** (mitten) moufle *f*; **2**○ (hand) main *f*; **get your ~s off that!** bas les pattes○!; **3** Sport gant *m* de baseball.

mitten /'mɪtn/ *n* moufle *f*.

mix /mɪks/ **I** *n* **1** (combination) (of people, colours, objects, styles) mélange *m*; **2** Culin, Constr (for cement, paste, cake) mélange *m*; **a cake ~** (in packet) une préparation pour gâteau; **3** Mus mixage *m*, mix *m*; **in the ~** dans le mixage.
II *vtr* **1** (combine) mélanger [*ingredients, colours*] (**with** avec; **and** à); mélanger, mêler [*objects*]; combiner [*styles, types, methods, systems*] (**with** avec; **and** à); **to ~ sth into** (add to) incorporer qch à; **to ~ one's drinks** faire des mélanges; **to ~ and match** assortir [*colours, styles*]; **2** (make) préparer [*drink, cocktail*]; malaxer [*concrete, cement, paste*]; **to ~ the flour and the water into a paste** malaxer la farine et l'eau pour obtenir une pâte; **3** Mus mixer [*record, track*].
III *vi* **1** (also **~ together**) (be combined) [*ingredients, liquids, colours*] se mélanger (**with** avec, à); **2** (socialize) être sociable; **to ~ with** fréquenter.
IDIOMS **to ~ it**○ GB (stir up trouble) semer la zizanie; US (start a fight) se bagarrer.
■ **mix around**: **~ [sth] around, ~ around [sth] 1** (blend) mélanger, remuer [*mixture, ingredients, paste*]; **2** (jumble up) intervertir [*names, objects*]; permuter [*letters of word*].
■ **mix in**: **~ [sth] in, ~ in [sth]** incorporer [*ingredient, substance*] (**with** à).
■ **mix up**: **~ [sth] up, ~up [sth] 1** (get confused over) confondre [*dates, names, tickets*]; **to ~ up A and B/A with B** confondre A et B/A avec B; **to get two things ~ed up** confondre deux choses; **2** (confuse) embrouiller, désorienter [*person*] (**about, over** à propos de); **to get ~ed up about** s'embrouiller à propos de; **3** (jumble up) mélanger, mêler [*papers, photos, clothes*]; **4** (involve) **to ~ sb up in** impliquer qn dans, mêler qn à; **to get ~ed up in** se trouver mêlé à; **to be ~ed up with sb** gen fréquenter qn; (having affair with) avoir une liaison avec qn; **to get ~ed up with sb** se mettre à fréquenter qn.

mixed /mɪkst/ *adj* **1** (varied) [*collection, programme, diet*] varié; [*nuts, sweets*] assorti; [*salad*] composé; [*group, community*] (socially, in age) mélangé, hétérogène; (racially) d'origines diverses; **of ~ blood** de sang mêlé; **2** (for both sexes) [*school, team, sauna*] mixte; **in ~ company** en présence d'hommes et de femmes; **3** (contrasting) [*reaction, reception*] mitigé; **to have ~ feelings about** éprouver des sentiments mitigés or contradictoires à propos de; **with ~ feelings** avec un enthousiasme modéré.

mixed: **~ ability** *adj* Scol [*class, teaching*] sans groupes de niveau; **~ bag** *n* fig mélange *m*.

mixed blessing *n* **to be a ~** avoir ses avantages et ses inconvénients.

mixed: **~ doubles** *n* double *m* mixte; **~ economy** *n* économie *f* mixte; **~ farming** *n* agriculture *f* mixte, culture *f* et élevage *m*; **~ fruit** *n* assortiment *m* de fruits secs; **~ grill** *n* assortiment *m* de grillades; **~ marriage** *n* mariage *m* mixte; **~ media** *adj* multimédia; **~ metaphor** *n* métaphore *f* incohérente.

mixed race I *n* race *f* mêlée; **of ~** métis/-isse.
II *modif* [*person*] métis/-isse.

mixed-up○ /ˌmɪkst'ʌp/ *adj* **1** (emotionally confused) [*person*] perturbé; **2** (jumbled up) [*thoughts, memories, emotions*] confus.

mixed vegetables *npl* macédoine *f* de légumes.

mixer /'mɪksə(r)/ *n* **1** Culin (electric) batteur *m* électrique; (manual) fouet *m* mécanique; **2** (drink) boisson *f* nonalcoolisée (*à ajouter à une boisson alcoolisée*); **3** (for cement) bétonnière *f*; **4** Mus (engineer) ingénieur *m* du son; (device) mélangeur *m* de son; **5** (sociable person) **to be a good/bad ~** être très/peu sociable; **6** US (social gathering) soirée-rencontre *f*.

mixer tap, **mixer faucet** US *n* robinet *m* mélangeur.

mixing /'mɪksɪŋ/ *n* **1** (combining) (of people, objects, ingredients) mélange *m*; (of cement) malaxage *m*; **2** Mus mixage *m*.

mixing: **~ bowl** *n* bol *m* à mixer, saladier *m*; **~ desk** *n* Mus console *f* de mixage.

mixture /'mɪkstʃə(r)/ *n* **1** (combination) (of people, flavours, reasons) mélange *m* (**of** de); **2** Culin, Chem mélange *m*; Pharm mixture *f*.

mix-up /'mɪksʌp/ *n* confusion *f* (**over** sur).

miz(z)en /'mɪzn/ *n* **1** (sail) artimon *m*; **2** (mast) mât *m* d'artimon.

Mk (*abrév écrite* = **mark**) **~ II Jaguar** Jaguar Mk2.

MLitt /ˌem'lɪt/ *n* GB (*abrév* = **Master of Letters**) diplôme *m* supérieur de lettres et sciences humaines.

MLR *n*: *abrév* ▶ **minimum lending rate**.

MLS US (*abrév* = **Master of Library Science**) diplôme *m* supérieur de bibliothécaire.

mm (*abrév écrite* = **millimetre(s)**) mm.

MMC *n*: *abrév* = **Monopolies (and Mergers) Commission**.

MN US Post *abrév écrite* = **Minnesota**.

mnemonic /nɪ'mɒnɪk/ **I** *n* **1** gen moyen *m* mnémotechnique; **2** Comput mnémonique *m*.
II *adj* **1** (aiding memory) mnémotechnique; **2** (relating to memory) mnémonique.

mnemonics /nɪ'mɒnɪks/ *n* (+ *v sg*) mnémotechnique *f*.

mo○ /məʊ/ *n* GB (moment) moment *m*, instant *m*; **just a ~!** un instant!

MO 1 Mil *abrév* ▶ **Medical Officer**; **2** US Post *abrév écrite* = **Missouri**; **3** *abrév* ▶ **money order**.

moan /məʊn/ **I** *n* **1** (of person, wind) gémissement *m*; **2**○ (grouse) plainte *f* (**about** au sujet de); **to have a good ~**○ **about sth/sb** bien râler au sujet de qch/qn.
II *vtr* **1** (complain) **to ~ that** se plaindre

que; **2** (wail) **'no!' he ~ed** 'non!' dit-il en gémissant.
III *vi* **1** [*person*] (make sound) gémir, pousser des gémissements (**with** de); **2**○ (grouse) râler○ (**about** contre); **to ~ and groan** râler○; **3** [*wind*] gémir.
IV moaning *pres p adj* [*child, customer*] râleur/-euse○, rouspéteur/-euse○; **~ing minnie**○ GB péj râleur/-euse *m/f* de service○ pej.

moaner○ /'məʊnə(r)/ *n* ronchon/-onne○ *m/f*.

moaning /'məʊnɪŋ/ *n* ¢ **1** (whimpering) gémissements *mpl*; **2**○ (grumbling) jérémiades○ *fpl*; **3** (of wind) gémissement *m*.

moat /məʊt/ *n* douve *f*; **the ~ of a castle** les douves d'un château.

moated /'məʊtɪd/ *adj* entouré de douves.

mob /mɒb/ **I** *n* (+ *v sg ou pl*) **1** (crowd) foule *f* (**of** de); **an angry ~** une foule en colère; **2** (gang) gang *m*; **the Mob** la Mafia; **3**○ (group) clique○ *f* also pej; **Byron, Keats and all that ~** Byron, Keats et toute la clique; **4** (masses) souvent péj **the ~** la populace *f* pej, le peuple *m*.
II *modif* **1** (Mafia) [*boss, connection, leader*] de la Mafia; **2** (crowd) [*violence*] de la foule.
III *vtr* (*p prés etc* **-bb-**) assaillir [*person*]; envahir [*place*].

mobcap /'mɒbkæp/ *n* charlotte *f*, coiffure *f* à bord froncé.

mobile /'məʊbaɪl, US -bl, *also* -biːl/ **I** *n* **1** gen, Art mobile *m*; **2** (also **~ phone**) téléphone *m* portatif.
II *adj* **1** (moveable) [*centre, unit, missile*] mobile; [*canteen, classroom*] ambulant; [*population, workforce*] mobile; [*communications*] sans fil; **2** fig [*features*] mobile; **3** (able to get around) **to be ~** (able to walk) pouvoir marcher; (able to travel) pouvoir se déplacer; **he's not as ~ as he was** (at home) il a plus de difficultés pour marcher qu'autrefois; (on journeys) il ne se déplace pas aussi facilement qu'avant; **I'm still ~** j'arrive encore à marcher or à me déplacer.

mobile: **~ home** *n* mobile home *m*, résidence *f* mobile, **~ library** *n* GB bibliobus *m*; **~ phone** *n* téléphone *m* portatif; **~ shop** *n* commerce *m* ambulant.

mobility /məʊ'bɪlətɪ/ *n* **1** (ability to move) mobilité *f*; (of features) mobilité *f*; (agility) agilité *f*; **those with restricted ~** les personnes à mobilité réduite; **it allows unrestricted ~** cela permet de se déplacer sans mal; **2** Sociol **social ~** mobilité *f*.

mobility allowance *n* GB *allocation de transport pour personnes à mobilité réduite*.

mobilization /ˌməʊbɪlaɪ'zeɪʃn, US -lɪ'z-/ *n* gen, Mil mobilisation *f*; **to order (a) ~** donner l'ordre de mobiliser.

mobilize /'məʊbɪlaɪz/ **I** *vtr* gen, Mil mobiliser (**against** contre); **to ~ the support of sb** fig essayer de trouver du soutien auprès de qn.
II *vi* Mil mobiliser (**against** contre).

mob: **~ oratory** *n* péj éloquence *f* démagogique; **~ rule** *n* péj règne *m* de la populace; **~ scene** *n* scène *f* de foule.

mobster /'mɒbstə(r)/ *n* membre *m* de la pègre.

moccasin /'mɒkəsɪn/ *n* mocassin *m*.

mocha /'mɒkə, US 'məʊkə/ *n* **1** (coffee) moka *m*; **2** (flavouring) arôme *m* de café et de chocolat.

mock /mɒk/ **I** *n* GB Sch examen *m* blanc.
II *adj* (*before n*) **1** (imitation) [*suede, ivory*] faux/fausse (*before n*); **~ leather** similicuir *m*; **~-Gothic/-Tudor architecture** faux-gothique *m*/faux-Tudor *m*; **2** (feigned) [*innocence, horror, humility*] feint, simulé; [*accident, battle, trial*] simulé; **in ~ terror/innocence** en feignant la terreur/l'innocence; **3** (practice) [*interview, raid, rescue*] simulé; [*exam*] blanc/blanche.
III *vtr* **1** (laugh at) se moquer de [*person, action, attempt*]; **2** littér (frustrate) narguer [*attempt, effort, hopes*].
IV *vi* se moquer.
■ **mock up**: **~ [sth] up, ~ up [sth]** réaliser une maquette de.

mocker /'mɒkə(r)/ *n* moqueur/-euse *m/f*.
IDIOMS **to put the ~s on sth** GB gâcher qch.

mockery /'mɒkərɪ/ *n* **1** (ridicule) moquerie *f*; **to make a ~ of** tourner [qn/qch] en dérision [*person, group, process, report, work*]; bafouer [*law, principle, rule*]; **self-~** autodérision *f*; **2** (travesty) (of art, activity, justice) parodie *f*; **3** (object of ridicule) objet *m* de risée.

mock-heroic /ˌmɒkhɪ'rəʊɪk/ *adj* Literat héroï-comique.

mocking /'mɒkɪŋ/ **I** *n* ¢ moqueries *fpl*.
II *adj* [*manner, remark, smile, tone*] moqueur/-euse; **self-~** d'autodérision.

mockingbird /'mɒkɪŋbɜːd/ *n* oiseau *m* moqueur.

mockingly /'mɒkɪŋlɪ/ *adv* [*applaud, grin, laugh, mimic*] de façon moqueuse; [*speak*] d'un ton moqueur.

mock: **~ orange** *n* Bot seringa *m*; **~ turtle soup** *n* consommé *m* à la tête de veau; **~-up** *n* Print, Tech maquette *f*.

mod /mɒd/ **I** *n* GB (also **Mod**) mod *mf* (*jeune des années 60, adepte de la musique soul ou ska*).
II *adj*○ US (up-to-date) branché○.

MoD *n* GB (*abrév* = **Ministry of Defence**) ministère *m* de la Défense.

modal /'məʊdl/ **I** *n* (also **~ auxiliary**, **~ verb**) (auxiliaire *m*) modal *m*.
II *adj* (all contexts) modal.

modality /mə'dælətɪ/ *n* modalité *f*.

mod con /ˌmɒd'kɒn/ *n* GB (*abrév* = **modern convenience**) confort *m* (moderne); **'all ~s'** (in advert) 'tout confort'.

mode /məʊd/ *n* **1** (way, style) mode *m*; **~ of life** mode *m* de vie; **~ of behaviour** type *m* de comportement; **~ of dress** tenue *f*, façon *f* de s'habiller; **~ of speech** ou **expression** façon *f* de s'exprimer; **~ of leadership** style *m* de direction; **2** (method) **~ of funding** type *m* de financement; **~ of production** méthode *f* de production; **~ of transport** moyen *m* de transport; **3** (state) (of equipment) mode *m*; (of person) humeur *f*; **in printing/play-back/operational ~** en mode impression/lecture/opérationnel; **to switch** ou **change ~** [*machine*] changer de mode; [*person*] changer de rôle; **I'm in work ~** je pense à mon travail; **I'm in party ~** je suis d'humeur à faire la fête; **4** Mus mode *m*; **5** Stat mode *m*.

model /'mɒdl/ **I** *n* **1** (scale representation) (for planning, engineering) maquette *f* (**of** de); (made as hobby) maquette *f* (**of** de); **2** (version of car, appliance, garment) modèle *m*; **the new/latest ~** le nouveau/dernier modèle; **a 1956 ~ (car)** une voiture modèle 1956; **3** (person) (for artist, photographer) modèle *m*; (showing clothes) mannequin *m*; **top/fashion ~** mannequin de luxe/de mode; **4** (example, thing to be copied) modèle *m*; **to be a** ou **serve as a ~ for sth** servir de modèle à qch; **a ~ of** un modèle de [*tact, fairness, good government*]; **a legal system on the British ~** un système judiciaire sur le modèle britannique; **to hold sth up** ou **out as a ~** prendre qch pour modèle; **5** Math, Comput modèle *m*; **computer/climate ~** modèle informatique/climatique.
II *adj* **1** [*railway, train, soldier, village*] miniature; [*aeroplane, boat, car*] modèle réduit; **2** (new and exemplary) [*farm, hospital, prison*] modèle, pilote; **3** (perfect) [*spouse, student, conduct*] modèle.
III *vtr* (*p prés etc* **-ll-**, **-l-** US) **1 to ~ sth on sth** modeler qch sur qch; **2** [*fashion model*] présenter [*garment, design*]; **3** (shape) modeler [*clay, wax, figure, head*] (**in** en); **4** Comput, Math modéliser [*process, economy*].
IV *vi* (*p prés etc* **-ll-**, **-l-** US) **1** [*artist's model*] poser (**for** pour); **2** [*fashion model*] travailler comme mannequin (**for** pour); **3** [*sculptor, artist*] **to ~ in** modeler en [*clay, wax*].
V modelled, modeled US *pp adj* **1** [*clothes*] présenté (**by** par); **2 ~led on sth** modelé sur qch.
VI *v refl* **to ~ oneself on sb** se modeler sur qn.

model answer *n* exemple *m* de réponse.

modeler *n* US = **modeller**.

modeling *n* US = **modelling**.

modeller /'mɒdələ(r)/ *n* modéliste *mf*.

modelling /'mɒdəlɪŋ/ *n* **1** (of clothes) **to take up ~** devenir mannequin; **have you done any ~?** as-tu déjà travaillé comme mannequin?; **~ is a tough career** la carrière de mannequin est dure; **2** (for photographer, artist) **to do some ~** poser comme modèle (**for** pour); **3** (with clay etc) modelage *m*; **4** Comput modélisation *f*.

modelling clay *n* pâte *f* à modeler.

model theory *n* théorie *f* des modèles.

modem /'məʊdem/ *n* modem *m*.

moderate I /'mɒdərət/ *n* modéré/-e *m/f*.
II /'mɒdərət/ *adj* **1** (not extreme) also Pol [*person, opinion, demand, party, tone*] modéré (**in** dans); **2** (of average extent) [*gain, income, performance, success*] moyen/-enne, limité; Culin **at** ou **over a ~ heat** à feu moyen; **in a ~ oven** à four moyen; **3** Meteorol [*conditions*] tempéré; [*wind, rain*] modéré.
III /'mɒdəreɪt/ *vtr* **1** gen, Pol modérer [*person, opinion*]; **2** GB Sch, Univ harmoniser les résultats de [*examinations*].
IV /'mɒdəreɪt/ *vi* **1** (become less extreme) se modérer; **2** (chair) présider; **to ~ over sth** animer [*debate*]; **3** Meteorol [*wind, storm*] s'apaiser; [*rain*] se calmer.

moderate: **~ breeze** *n* Meteorol jolie brise *f*; **~ gale** *n* Meteorol grand frais *m*.

moderately /'mɒdərətlɪ/ *adv* **1** (averagely) [*confident, fit, interesting, successful*] moyennement; **~ priced** de milieu de gamme; **this car is ~ priced** c'est une voiture de milieu de gamme; **~ sized** de taille moyenne; **~ good** assez bon/bonne; **~ well** assez bien; **2** (restrainedly) also Pol [*criticize, speak, react*] avec modération.

moderating /'mɒdəreɪtɪŋ/ *adj* [*influence, role*] modérateur/-trice.

moderation /ˌmɒdə'reɪʃn/ *n* modération *f* (**in** dans); **in ~** avec modération; **to be taken in ~** à consommer avec modération.

moderator /'mɒdəreɪtə(r)/ *n* **1** (chairman) animateur/-trice *m/f*; **2** Scot Relig **Moderator of the Church of Scotland** président *m* de l'Assemblée générale de l'Église presbytérienne (*en Écosse*); **3** GB Sch, Univ membre *m* du jury (*chargé d'harmoniser les notes*); **4** Nucl modérateur *m*.

modern /'mɒdn/ **I** *n* moderne *mf*.
II *adj* **1** (up-to-date) [*car, factory, device, company, system, person*] moderne; **all ~ conveniences** tout confort (moderne); **2** (contemporary) [*era, literature*] moderne; [*world*] contemporain; **~ China/Berlin** la Chine/le Berlin d'aujourd'hui; **in ~ times** à l'époque moderne; **he's a sort of ~ Napoleon** c'est une sorte de Napoléon des temps modernes.

modern: **~ art** *n* l'art *m* moderne; **~-day** *adj* des temps modernes; **~ dress** *n* Theat costumes *mpl* modernes; **~ English** *n* l'anglais *m* moderne; **~ Greek** *n* le grec moderne; **~ history** *n* l'histoire *f* moderne.

modernism /'mɒdənɪzəm/ *n* (also **Modernism**) modernisme *m*.

modernist /'mɒdənɪst/ *n, adj* (also **Modernist**) moderniste (*mf*).

modernistic /ˌmɒdə'nɪstɪk/ *adj* moderniste.

modernity /mɒ'dɜːnətɪ/ *n* modernité *f*.

modernization /ˌmɒdɜːnaɪ'zeɪʃn, US -nɪ'z-/ *n* modernisation *f*; **the office is in need of ~** le bureau a besoin d'être modernisé.

modernize /'mɒdənaɪz/ **I** *vtr* moderniser.
II *vi* se moderniser.

modern language I modern languages *npl* langues *fpl* vivantes.

II *modif* (also **~s**) [*student*] en langues vivantes; [*lecturer, teacher*] de langues vivantes.

modest /ˈmɒdɪst/ *adj* **1** (unassuming) [*person*] modeste (**about** au sujet de); **he's just being ~!** il fait le modeste!; **2** (not large or showy) [*gift, aim*] modeste; [*sum, salary*] modique; **3** (demure) [*dress*] décent; [*person*] pudique.

modestly /ˈmɒdɪstlɪ/ *adv* **1** (unassumingly) [*talk, explain*] avec modestie, modestement; **2** (demurely) [*dress*] décemment; **3** (moderately) **he has been ~ successful** il a remporté un succès modeste.

modesty /ˈmɒdɪstɪ/ *n* **1** (humility) modestie *f*; **false ~** fausse modestie; **in all ~** en toute modestie; **2** (demureness) (of person) pudeur *f*; (of dress) décence *f*; **3** (smallness) (of sum) modicité *f*; (of aspirations) modestie *f*.

modicum /ˈmɒdɪkəm/ *n* minimum *m* (**of** de).

modifiable /ˈmɒdɪfaɪəbl/ *adj* modifiable.

modification /ˌmɒdɪfɪˈkeɪʃn/ *n* modification *f*; **to make ~s to** ou **in sth** apporter des modifications à qch; **the project will need ~** le projet devra être modifié; **we accept it without further ~s** nous l'acceptons tel quel.

modifier /ˈmɒdɪfaɪə(r)/ *n* Ling modificateur *m*.

modify /ˈmɒdɪfaɪ/ **I** *vtr* **1** (alter) modifier [*engine, drug, weapon*]; **in a modified form** sous une forme modifiée; **2** (moderate) modérer [*demand, statement, policy*]; atténuer [*punishment*] (**to** en); **3** Ling modifier.
II modifying *pres p adj* Ling modificatif/-ive *m/f*.

modish /ˈməʊdɪʃ/ *adj* à la mode.

modular /ˈmɒdjʊlə(r), US -dʒʊ-/ *adj* (all contexts) modulaire.

modulate /ˈmɒdjʊleɪt, US -dʒʊ-/ **I** *vtr* gen, Radio, Electron moduler.
II *vi* Mus moduler (**from** de; **to** en).

modulation /ˌmɒdjʊˈleɪʃn, US -dʒʊ-/ *n* (all contexts) modulation *f*.

module /ˈmɒdjuːl, US -dʒʊ-/ *n* **1** Aerosp, Comput, Constr, Electron module *m*; **2** Sch module *m*; Univ module *m*, unité *f* de valeur.

modulus /ˈmɒdjʊləs, US -dʒʊ-/ *n* (*pl* **-li**) Math, Phys module *m*.

modus operandi /ˌməʊdəs ˌɒpəˈrændɪ/ *n* manière *f* de procéder.

modus vivendi /ˌməʊdəs vɪˈvendɪ/ *n* (*pl* **modi vivendi**) modus vivendi *m*.

moggy○, **moggie**○ /ˈmɒgɪ/ *n* GB minou○ *m*, chat *m*.

mogul /ˈməʊgl/ *n* **1** (magnate) magnat *m*; **2** (in skiing) bosse *f*.

Mogul /ˈməʊgl/ **I** *pr n* Moghol *m*.
II *adj* [*emperor, rule*] des Moghols.

mohair /ˈməʊheə(r)/ **I** *n* mohair *m*.
II *modif* [*garment*] en mohair.

Mohammed, Mahomet /məʊˈhæmed/ *pr n* Relig Mahomet.
IDIOMS **if the mountain will not come to ~, then ~ must go to the mountain** Prov si la montagne ne va pas à Mahomet, Mahomet va à la montagne Prov.

Mohammedan /məʊˈhæmɪdən/ **I** *n* Mahométan/-e *m/f*.
II *adj* mahométan.

Mohammedanism /məʊˈhæmɪdənɪzəm/ *n* mahométisme *m*.

mohican /məʊˈhiːkən/ *n* **1** (hairstyle) iroquois *m*, crête *f*; **2 Mohican** US Hist Mohican *m*.

Mohs scale /ˈməʊz skeɪl, ˈmɔːs-/ *n* échelle *f* de Mohs.

moiré /ˈmwɑːreɪ/ *n, adj* moiré (*m*).

moist /mɔɪst/ *adj* [*climate, wind, soil, compost, stone*] humide; [*towel, cloth*] humide; [*cake, meat*] moelleux/-euse; [*hands*] (with sweat) moite; Cosmet [*skin*] bien hydraté; **his eyes ~ with tears** ses yeux mouillés de larmes; **keep the soil ~** veillez à ce que la terre soit toujours humide.

moisten /ˈmɔɪsn/ **I** *vtr* **1** gen humecter [*stamp, envelope, cloth*]; **to ~ one's fingers/lips** s'humecter les doigts/lèvres; **2** Culin mouiller légèrement.
II *vi* [*eyes*] se mouiller.

moistness /ˈmɔɪstnɪs/ *n* (of air, soil) humidité *f*; (of hand) moiteur *f*; Cosmet (of skin) hydratation *f*.

moisture /ˈmɔɪstʃə(r)/ *n* (of soil, in walls) humidité *f*; (on glass) buée *f*; (in skin) hydratation *f*; (sweat) moiteur *f*.

moisturize /ˈmɔɪstʃəraɪz/ **I** *vtr* hydrater [*skin*].
II moisturizing *pres p adj* hydratant.

moisturizer /ˈmɔɪstʃəraɪzə(r)/ *n* (lotion) lait *m* hydratant; (cream) crème *f* hydratante.

molar /ˈməʊlə(r)/ **I** *n* Dent molaire *f*.
II *adj* Dent, Phys molaire.

molasses /məˈlæsɪz/ *n* (+ *v sg*) mélasse *f*.

mold *n, vtr* US ▶ **mould**.

Moldavia /mɒlˈdeɪvɪə/ ▶ **1131** *pr n* Hist Moldavie *f*.

Moldavian /mɒlˈdeɪvɪən/ ▶ **1486**, **1402** **I** *n* **1** Hist (person) Moldave *mf*; **2** Ling moldave *m*.
II *adj* moldave.

Moldova /mɒlˈdəʊvə/ ▶ **1131** *pr n* Moldavie *f*.

Moldovan /mɒlˈdəʊvən/ ▶ **1486** *n* (person) Moldave *mf*.

mole /məʊl/ *n* **1** Zool taupe *f*; **2** fig (spy) taupe *f*; **3** (on skin) grain *m* de beauté; **4** (breakwater) môle *m*; **5** Phys, Chem mole *f*.

mole-catcher ▶ **1692** *n* taupier *m*.

molecular /məˈlekjʊlə(r)/ *adj* moléculaire.

molecule /ˈmɒlɪkjuːl/ *n* molécule *f*.

molehill /ˈməʊlhɪl/ *n* taupinière *f*.
IDIOMS **to make a mountain out of a ~** faire une montagne d'une taupinière.

moleskin /ˈməʊlskɪn/ **I** *n* **1** (fur) (peau *f* de) taupe *f*; **2** (cotton) moleskine *f*.
II *modif* **1** (fur) [*garment*] en peau de taupe; **2** (cotton) [*trousers, jacket*] en moleskine.

molest /məˈlest/ *vtr* **1** (sexually assault) agresser [qn] sexuellement [*child*]; **2** sout (annoy) importuner [*person*].

molestation /ˌməʊleˈsteɪʃn/ *n* **1** ¢ (sexual assault) agressions *fpl* sexuelles; **2** sout (annoyance) **without ~** sans être importuné.

molester *n* ▶ **child molester**.

moll○ /mɒl/ *n* compagne *f*; **a gangster's ~** la compagne d'un gangster.

mollify /ˈmɒlɪfaɪ/ *vtr* apaiser, calmer [*person*].

mollusc, **mollusk** US /ˈmɒləsk/ *n* mollusque *m*.

mollycoddle /ˈmɒlɪkɒdl/ *vtr* dorloter.

Molotov cocktail /ˈmɒlətɒf/ *n* cocktail *m* Molotov.

molt *n, vi* US = **moult**.

molten /ˈməʊltən/ *adj* (*épith*) en fusion.

Moluccan /məˈlʌkən/ **I** *n* Moluquois/-e *m/f*.
II *adj* moluquois.

Moluccas /məˈlʌkəs/ ▶ **1381** *pr npl* (also **Molucca Islands**) **the ~** les Moluques *fpl*.

molybdenum /məˈlɪbdɪnəm/ *n* molybdène *m*.

mom○ /mɒm/ *n* US maman *f*.

mom and pop store○ *n* US petit commerce *m* familial.

moment /ˈməʊmənt/ *n* **1** (instant) instant *m*; **in a ~** dans un instant; **for the ~** pour l'instant; **it will only take you a ~** tu en as pour un instant; **just for a ~ I thought you were Paul** l'espace d'un instant j'ai cru que tu étais Paul; **at any ~** à tout instant; **I didn't think for a** ou **one ~ that you were guilty** je n'ai pas pensé un (seul) instant que tu étais coupable; **I don't believe that for one ~** je ne le crois pas du tout; **I recognized him the ~ I saw him** je l'ai reconnu à l'instant où je l'ai vu; **just a ~, that's not what you said yesterday!** attends or pas si vite, ce n'est pas ce que tu m'as dit hier!; **and not a ~ too soon!** il était temps!; **the car hasn't given me a ~'s trouble** la voiture ne m'a pas créé le moindre ennui; **in a ~ of panic/weakness, I agreed** dans un moment de panique/faiblesse, j'ai accepté; **in his lucid ~s he appears quite normal** dans ses moments de lucidité il a l'air tout à fait normal; **2** (point in time) moment *m*; **a great ~ in French history** un grand moment de l'histoire de France; **at the right ~** au bon moment; **to choose one's ~** choisir le bon moment; **phone me the ~ (that) he arrives** appelle-moi dès qu'il arrivera; **I've only this ~ arrived** je viens tout juste d'arriver; **her bad luck began the ~ she was born** sa déveine a commencé le jour de sa naissance; **at this ~ in time** à l'heure actuelle; **he's the man of the ~** gen c'est l'homme du moment; **this is the ~ of truth** c'est le moment de vérité; **3** (good patch) **the film/novel had its ~s** le film/roman avait ses bons moments; **he has his ~s** il a ses bons côtés; **4** (importance) Littér importance *f*; **to be of great ~ to sb** être d'une grande importance pour qn; **5** Phys moment *m*.

momentarily /ˈməʊməntrəlɪ, US ˌməʊmənˈterəlɪ/ *adv* **1** (for an instant) [*glance, hesitate, forget, stop*] momentanément; **2** US (very soon) dans un instant; (at any moment) d'un moment à l'autre.

momentary /ˈməʊməntrɪ, US -terɪ/ *adj* **1** (temporary) [*aberration, delay, lapse*] momentané; **a ~ silence** un moment de silence; **a ~ panic** un instant de panique; **2** (fleeting) [*impulse, indecision, whim*] passager/-ère; [*glimpse*] rapide.

momentous /məˈmentəs, məʊˈm-/ *adj* capital.

momentousness /məˈmentəsnɪs, məʊˈm-/ *n* importance *f* capitale.

momentum /məˈmentəm, məʊˈm-/ *n* **1** (pace) lit, fig élan *m*; **to gain/lose ~** prendre/perdre de l'élan; **2** Phys vitesse *f*; **to gain** ou **gather/lose ~** prendre/perdre de la vitesse.

Mon *abrév écrite* = **Monday**.

Monaco /ˈmɒnəkəʊ/ ▶ **1131** *pr n* Monaco *m*.

monad /ˈmɒnæd, ˈməʊ-/ *n* Biol, Philos monade *f*.

Mona Lisa /ˌməʊnə ˈliːzə/ *pr n* **the ~** la Joconde.

monarch /ˈmɒnək/ *n* monarque *m*.

monarchic /məˈnɑːkɪk/ *adj* (also **monarchical**) monarchique.

monarchism /ˈmɒnəkɪzəm/ *n* monarchisme *m*.

monarchist /ˈmɒnəkɪst/ *n, adj* monarchiste (*mf*).

monarchy /ˈmɒnəkɪ/ *n* monarchie *f*.

monastery /ˈmɒnəstrɪ, US -terɪ/ *n* monastère *m*.

monastic /məˈnæstɪk/ *adj* **1** Relig monastique; **2** (ascetic) monacal.

monasticism /məˈnæstɪsɪzəm/ *n* monachisme *m*.

Monday /ˈmʌndeɪ, -dɪ/ ▶ **1883** *n* lundi *m*; **that ~ morning feeling** la déprime du lundi matin.

Monegasque /ˌmɒnɪˈgæsk/ ▶ **1486** **I** *n* Monégasque *mf*.
II *adj* monégasque.

monetarism /ˈmʌnɪtərɪzəm/ *n* monétarisme *m*.

monetarist /ˈmʌnɪtərɪst/ **I** *n* monétariste *mf*.
II *adj* [*policy, reform*] monétariste.

monetary /ˈmʌnɪtrɪ, US -terɪ/ *adj* [*base, reserves, standard, unit*] monétaire.

money /ˈmʌnɪ/ **I** *n* **1** (coins, notes) argent *m*; **2** (funds) argent *m*; **to make ~** (person) gagner de l'argent; (business, project) rapporter de l'argent; **to run out of ~** ne plus avoir d'argent; **to get one's ~ back**

(in shop) être remboursé; (after loan, resale) rentrer dans ses fonds; (after risky venture, with difficulty) récupérer son argent; **to find the ~ to do** trouver l'argent pour faire; **there's no ~ in it** ça ne rapporte pas; **where is the ~ going to come from?** et d'où viendra l'argent?; **there's big ~ involved**○ il y a de grosses sommes en jeu; **they made a lot of ~ when they sold the house** ils ont fait un beau bénéfice quand ils ont vendu la maison; **3** (in banking, on stock exchange) argent *m*, monnaie *f*, capitaux *mpl*; **to raise ~** trouver des capitaux; **to pay good ~** payer en bel et bon argent, payer un bon prix; **to put up ~ for a project** investir de l'argent dans un projet; **4** (salary) salaire *m*; **the job is boring but the ~ is good** le travail est ennuyeux, mais c'est bien payé; **to earn good ~** bien gagner sa vie; **5** (price) prix *m*; **it's not the best car in the world, but it's good for the ~** ce n'est pas la meilleure voiture du monde, mais elle est bien pour le prix; **6** (wealth) argent *m*, fortune *f*; **to make one's ~ in business** faire (sa) fortune dans les affaires; **to inherit one's ~** acquérir sa fortune par héritage; **there's a lot of ~ in that area** il y a beaucoup de gens riches dans la région; **there's a lot of ~ (to be made) in computing** l'informatique, ça peut rapporter.

II monies, moneys *npl* (funds) fonds *mpl*, capitaux *mpl*; (sums) sommes *fpl*.

III *modif* [*matters, problems, worries*] d'argent.

IDIOMS **not for love nor ~** pour rien au monde; **for my ~...** à mon avis...; **it's ~ well spent** c'est de l'argent bien dépensé; **~ burns a hole in her pocket, she spends ~ like water** l'argent lui file entre les doigts; **it's ~ for jam, it's ~ for old rope** c'est de l'argent facile; **~ talks** avec l'argent on obtient ce qu'on veut; **time is ~** le temps c'est de l'argent; **the smart ~ is on X** les gens bien informés misent sur X; **to be in the ~** être en fonds; **to be made of ~** être cousu d'or, rouler sur l'or; **to get one's ~'s worth, to get a good run for one's ~** en avoir pour son argent; **to give sb a good run for his/her ~** en donner à qn pour son argent; **to have ~ to burn** avoir de l'argent à ne savoir qu'en faire or à jeter par les fenêtres; **to put one's ~ where one's mouth is** sortir son portefeuille; **to throw good ~ after bad** investir en pure perte; **your ~ or your life!** la bourse ou la vie!

money: **~ belt** *n* ceinture *f* porte-monnaie; **~box** *n* tirelire *f*; **~-changer** *n* changeur *m*.

moneyed /ˈmʌnɪd/ *adj* riche.

money-grubbing /ˈmʌnɪɡrʌbɪŋ/ *adj* péj rapace fig.

moneylender /ˈmʌnɪlendə(r)/ ▶ 1692 *n* **1** Fin, Comm prêteur/-euse *m/f*; **2**† (usurer) usurier/-ière *m/f*.

money: **~-loser** *n* affaire *f* déficitaire; **~maker** *n* (product) article *m* qui rapporte beaucoup; (activity) activité *f* lucrative; **~making** *adj* [*scheme*] pour faire fortune; **~man** *n* financier *m*; **~ market** *n* marché *m* monétaire; **~ market fund** *n* fonds *m* commun de placement; **~ order, MO** *n* mandat *m* postal; **~ rate** *n* taux *m* du loyer de l'argent; **~ spider** *n* petite araignée *f* (*censée porter bonheur*); **~ spinner** *n* GB mine *f* d'or fig; **~ supply** *n* masse *f* monétaire.

moneywort /ˈmʌnɪwɜːt/ *n* sibthorpie *f* d'Europe.

mongol† /ˈmɒŋɡl/ *n, adj* Med injur mongolien/-ienne (*m/f*).

Mongol /ˈmɒŋɡl/ ▶ 1486 **I** *n* **1** (person) Mongol/-e *m/f*; **2** (language) mongol *m*.
II *adj* mongol.

Mongolia /mɒŋˈɡəʊlɪə/ ▶ 1131 *pr n* Mongolie *f*; **Outer ~** lit Mongolie-Extérieure; hum le bout du monde.

Mongolian /mɒŋˈɡəʊlɪən/ ▶ 1486 **I** *n* Mongol/-e *m/f*.
II *adj* mongol.

mongolism† /ˈmɒŋɡəlɪzəm/ *n* Med injur mongolisme *m*.

mongoloid† /ˈmɒŋɡəlɔɪd/ *n, adj* Med injur mongolien/-ienne (*m/f*).

mongoose /ˈmɒŋɡuːs/ *n* mangouste *f*.

mongrel /ˈmʌŋɡrl/ **I** *n* (chien *m*) bâtard *m*.
II *adj* bâtard.

monied /ˈmʌnɪd/ *adj* = **moneyed**.

monies /ˈmʌnɪz/ *npl* = **money** II.

moniker○† /ˈmɒnɪkə(r)/ *n* nom *m*.

monitor /ˈmɒnɪtə(r)/ **I** *n* **1** gen, Tech dispositif *m* de surveillance; (security TV) écran *m* de contrôle; **2** Med moniteur *m*; **heart ~** moniteur cardiaque; **3** Audio, Comput moniteur *m*; **~ program** moniteur *m*; **4** GB Sch *élève responsable d'une tâche* (*cahiers de texte, nettoyage du tableau etc*); **5** US Sch surveillant/-e *m/f*; **6** Journ, Radio permanencier *m*.
II *vtr* **1** gen, Tech contrôler, surveiller [*rate, result*]; **to ~ the weather** exercer une surveillance constante des phénomènes météorologiques; **2** Med surveiller [*breathing, patient*]; **to ~ sb for** suivre qn pour [*heart problems etc*]; **3** Sch suivre [*student, progress*]; **4** Radio, Journ être à l'écoute de [*broadcast*].

monitoring /ˈmɒnɪtərɪŋ/ **I** *n* **1** Tech, Med (by person) surveillance *f*; (by device) monitoring *m*; **careful ~ for problems** contrôle *m* systématique des problèmes éventuels; **2** Sch GB suivi *m*; **~ of students/progress** le suivi des étudiants/des progrès; **3** Radio, Journ (of broadcasts) service *m* d'écoute.
II *modif* [*device, equipment*] de surveillance.

monitor lizard *n* varan *m*.

monk /mʌŋk/ *n* moine *m*.

monkey /ˈmʌŋkɪ/ *n* **1** Zool singe *m*; **female ~** guenon *f*; **2**○ (rascal) galopin○ *m*; **3**○ GB cinq cents livres *fpl* sterling; **4** Tech (of piledriver) mouton *m*.

IDIOMS **I don't give a ~'s about it**○ je m'en fous complètement○; **to have a ~ on one's back**○ (be addicted) être toxicomane; (have a problem) avoir un problème; **to make a ~ out of sb**○ se payer la tête de qn○.

■ **monkey around**○ faire l'idiot (**with** avec).

monkey: **~ business**○ *n* (fooling) (-*c*) bêtises *fpl*; (cheating) grenouillage○ *m*; **~ house** *n* pavillon *m* des singes; **~ jacket** *n* veste *f* ajustée; **~ nut**○ *n* GB cacahuète *f*; **~ puzzle (tree)** *n* araucaria *m*; **~ shines** *npl* US = **monkey business**; **~ suit**○ *n* US smoking *m*; **~ tricks**○ *npl* = **monkey business**.

monkey wrench *n* clé *f* à molette.

monkfish /ˈmʌŋkfɪʃ/ *n* (*pl* **~**) (angler fish) lotte *f*; (angel shark) ange *m* de mer.

monkish /ˈmʌŋkɪʃ/ *adj* monacal.

monkshood /ˈmʌŋkshʊd/ *n* Bot aconit *m*.

mono /ˈmɒnəʊ/ **I** *n* Audio monophonie *f*; **in ~** en mono.
II *adj* Audio mono *inv*.
III mono- (*dans composés*) mono-.

monobasic /ˌmɒnəʊˈbeɪsɪk/ *adj* Chem monobasique.

monochromatic /ˌmɒnəkrəˈmætɪk/ *adj* monochromatique.

monochrome /ˈmɒnəkrəʊm/ **I** *n* **1** (technique) **in ~** Art, Phot en monochrome; Cin, TV en noir et blanc; **2** (print) monochrome *m*.
II *adj* **1** lit Cin, TV [*film*] en noir et blanc; Art, Comput, Phot monochrome; **2** fig (dull) monotone.

monocle /ˈmɒnəkl/ *n* monocle *m*.

monocoque /ˈmɒnəkɒk/ *n* **1** Aut voiture *f* monocoque; **2** Naut monocoque *m*.

monocular /məˈnɒkjʊlə(r)/ *adj* monoculaire.

monoculture /ˈmɒnəʊkʌltʃə(r)/ *n* monoculture *f*.

monocycle /ˈmɒnəsaɪkl/ *n* monocycle *m*.

monogamist /məˈnɒɡəmɪst/ *n* monogame *mf*.

monogamous /məˈnɒɡəməs/ *adj* monogame.

monogamy /məˈnɒɡəmɪ/ *n* monogamie *f*.

monogram /ˈmɒnəɡræm/ *n* monogramme *m*.

monogrammed /ˈmɒnəɡræmd/ *adj* **his ~ ties** ses cravates marquées de son monogramme.

monograph /ˈmɒnəɡrɑːf, US -ɡræf/ *n* monographie *f*.

monohull /ˈmɒnəʊhʌl/ *n* Naut monocoque *m*.

monokini /ˌmɒnəʊˈkiːnɪ/ *n* monokini *m*.

monolingual /ˌmɒnəʊˈlɪŋɡwəl/ *n, adj* monolingue (*m*).

monolith /ˈmɒnəlɪθ/ *n* (all contexts) monolithe *m*.

monolithic /ˌmɒnəˈlɪθɪk/ *adj* (all contexts) monolithique.

monologue, monolog US /ˈmɒnəlɒɡ/ *n* (all contexts) monologue *m*.

monomania /ˌmɒnəˈmeɪnɪə/ *n* monomanie *f*.

monomaniac /ˌmɒnəˈmeɪnɪæk/ **I** *n* monomane *mf*.
II *adj* monomaniaque.

monomial /məˈnəʊmɪəl/ *n* Math monôme *m*.

monomorphic /ˌmɒnəˈmɔːfɪk/ *adj* Biol monomorphe.

mononucleosis /ˌmɒnəʊˌnjuːklɪˈəʊsɪs, US -ˌnuː-/ ▶ 1354 *n* Med mononucléose *f*.

monophonic /ˌmɒnəˈfɒnɪk/ *adj* monophonique.

monophthong /ˈmɒnəfθɒŋ/ *n* monophtongue *m*.

monoplane /ˈmɒnəpleɪn/ *n* monoplan *m*.

Monopolies (and Mergers) Commission, MMC *n* GB ≈ Commission *f* de la concurrence.

monopolist /məˈnɒpəlɪst/ *n* monopoliste *mf*.

monopolistic /məˌnɒpəˈlɪstɪk/ *adj* [*advantage, position, practices, system*] monopolistique; [*authority, company*] monopoliste.

monopolization /məˌnɒpəlaɪˈzeɪʃn, US -lɪˈz-/ *n* monopolisation *f*.

monopolize /məˈnɒpəlaɪz/ *vtr* **1** Econ détenir or avoir le monopole de [*raw materials, market*]; **the media have been ~d by a small group** c'est un petit groupe qui détient le monopole des médias; **2** fig monopoliser [*bathroom*].

monopoly /məˈnɒpəlɪ/ **I** *n* Econ, fig monopole *m*; **to have a ~ on** ou **of** avoir or détenir le monopole de; **to break sb's ~ on sth** remettre en question le monopole de qch détenu par qn.
II Monopoly® *pr n* Monopoly® *m*.
III *modif* [*industry*] monopoliste; [*control, position, restrictions*] monopolistique.

monopoly: **~ capitalism** *n* capitalisme *m* monopolistique; **Monopoly money** *n* fig, hum monnaie *f* de singe.

monorail /ˈmɒnəʊreɪl/ *n* monorail *m*.

monoski /ˈmɒnəskiː/ **I** *n* monoski *m*.
II *vi* faire du monoski.

monoskiing /ˈmɒnəskiːɪŋ/ ▶ 1282 *n* monoski *m*.

monosodium glutamate /ˌmɒnəʊˌsəʊdɪəm ˈɡluːtəmeɪt/ *n* glutamate *m* (de sodium).

monosyllabic /ˌmɒnəsɪˈlæbɪk/ *adj* monosyllabique.

monosyllable /ˈmɒnəsɪləbl/ *n* monosyllabe *m*; **in ~s** par monosyllabes.

monotheism /ˈmɒnəθiːɪzəm/ *n* monothéisme *m*.

monotheist /ˈmɒnəθiːɪst/ *n* monothéiste *mf*.

monotheistic /ˌmɒnəθiːˈɪstɪk/ *adj* monothéiste.

monotone /ˈmɒnətəʊn/ *n* voix *f* or ton *m* monotone; **to speak in a ~** parler sur un ton monotone.

The months of the year

Don't use capitals for the names of the months in French, and note that there are no common abbreviations in French as there are in English (Jan, Feb *and so on*). *The French only abbreviate in printed calendars etc.*

January	= janvier	July	= juillet
February	= février	August	= août
March	= mars	September	= septembre
April	= avril	October	= octobre
May	= mai	November	= novembre
June	= juin	December	= décembre

Which month?

(May *in this note stands for any month; they all work the same way; for more information on dates in French* ▶ **1150**.)

what month is it?	= quel mois sommes-nous? *or* (*very informally*) on est quel mois?
it was May	= nous étions en mai
what month was he born?	= de quel mois est-il?

When?

in May	= en mai *or* au mois de mai
they're getting married this May	= ils se marient en mai
that May	= cette année-là en mai
next May	= en mai prochain
in May next year	= l'an prochain en mai
last May	= l'année dernière en mai
the May after next	= dans deux ans en mai
the May before last	= il y deux ans en mai

which part of the month?

at the beginning of May	= au début de mai
in early May	= début mai
at the end of May	= à la fin de mai
in late May	= fin mai
in mid-May	= à la mi-mai
for the whole of May	= pendant tout le mois de mai
throughout May	= tout au long du mois de mai

Regular events

every May	= tous les ans en mai
every other May	= tous les deux ans en mai
most Mays	= presque tous les ans en mai

Uses with other nouns

one May morning	= par un matin de mai
one May night	= par une nuit de mai *or (if evening)* par un soir de mai

For other uses, it is always safe to use du mois de:

May classes	= les cours du mois de mai
May flights	= les vols du mois de mai
the May sales	= les soldes du mois de mai

Uses with adjectives

the warmest May	= le mois de mai le plus chaud
a rainy May	= un mois de mai pluvieux
a lovely May	= un beau mois de mai

monotonous /mə'nɒtənəs/ *adj* (all contexts) monotone.

monotonously /mə'nɒtənəslɪ/ *adv* [*speak, sound*] d'un ton monotone; [*move, act*] de manière monotone.

monotony /mə'nɒtənɪ/ *n* monotonie *f*.

monotype /'mɒnətaɪp/ *n* Art monotype *m*.

Monotype® /'mɒnətaɪp/ *n* Print Monotype® *m*.

monoxide /mə'nɒksaɪd/ *n* monoxyde *m*.

Monroe doctrine /mʌn'rəʊ dɒktrɪn/ *n* Pol, Hist doctrine *f* de Monroe.

monseigneur /ˌmɒnsen'jɜː(r)/ *n* monseigneur *m*.

monsignor /mɒn'siːnjə(r)/ *n* monsignor(e) *m*.

monsoon /mɒn'suːn/ *n* mousson *f*; **during the ~ (season)** pendant la mousson.

monsoon rain(s) *n(pl)* pluies *fpl* de la mousson.

monster /'mɒnstə(r)/ **I** *n* lit, fig monstre *m*; **sea ~** monstre marin.
II *modif* géant.

monstrance /'mɒnstrəns/ *n* ostensoir *m*.

monstrosity /mɒn'strɒsɪtɪ/ *n* **1** (eyesore) horreur *f*; **2** (of act, behaviour, crime) monstruosité *f*.

monstrous /'mɒnstrəs/ *adj* **1** (odious) [*creature, crime, accusation*] monstrueux/-euse; [*building*] hideux/-euse; **it is ~ that** il est scandaleux que (+ *subj*); **that's ~!** c'est scandaleux!; **2** (huge) énorme, gigantesque.

monstrously /'mɒnstrəslɪ/ *adv* monstrueusement.

montage /mɒn'tɑːʒ/ *n* Art, Cin montage *m*; Phot photomontage *m*.

Montana /mɒn'tænə/ ▶ **1744** *pr n* Montana *m*.

monte /'mɒntɪ/ *n* US *jeu de cartes où l'on mise de l'argent*.

Montenegro /ˌmɒntɪ'niːgrəʊ/ *pr n* Monténégro *m*.

Montezuma's revenge /ˌmɒntɪˌzuːməz rɪ'vendʒ/ *n* hum turista° *f*.

month /mʌnθ/ ▶ **1807** *n* mois *m*; **in two ~s, in two ~s' time** dans deux mois; **every ~** chaque mois or tous les mois; **for ~s** pendant des mois; **~ by ~** mois après mois; **next/last ~** le mois prochain/dernier; **the ~ before last** pas le mois dernier, celui d'avant; **the ~ after next** pas le mois prochain, celui d'après; **~s later** des mois plus tard; **once a ~** une fois par mois; **every other ~** tous les deux mois; **~ in ~ out** pendant des mois et des mois; **in the ~ of June** au mois de juin; **at the end of the ~** en fin de mois; Admin, Comm fin courant; **what day of the ~ is today?** nous sommes le combien aujourd'hui?; **six ~s' pay** six mois de salaire; **a ~'s rent** un mois de loyer; **a seven-month-old baby** un bébé de sept mois; **~ after ~ he forgets to pay** (regular payment) tous les mois il oublie de payer; (single payment) ça fait des mois qu'il oublie de payer; **your salary for the ~ beginning May 15** votre salaire du 15 mai au 15 juin.
IDIOMS **it's her time of the ~** euph elle est indisposée.

monthly /'mʌnθlɪ/ **I** *n* (journal) mensuel *m*.
II *adj* mensuel/-elle; **~ instalment** mensualité *f*.
III *adv* [*pay, earn*] au mois, mensuellement; [*happen, visit, publish*] tous les mois, une fois par mois; **it is £200 ~** c'est 200 livres sterling par mois.

Montreal /ˌmɒntrɪ'ɔːl/ ▶ **1818** *pr n* Montréal *m*.

monument /'mɒnjʊmənt/ *n* lit, fig monument *m*; **~ to a war hero** monument à la gloire d'un héros de guerre; **the building is a ~ to his art/ambition** le bâtiment témoigne de son art/ambition.

monumental /ˌmɒnjʊ'mentl/ *adj* (all contexts) monumental; **~ work** Art, Literat œuvre *f* monumentale.

monumentally /ˌmɒnjʊ'mentəlɪ/ *adv* [*dull, boring*] mortellement; **~ ignorant** d'une ignorance monumentale.

monumental mason ▶ **1692** *n* marbrier *m*.

moo /muː/ **I** *n* meuglement *m*.
II *excl* meuh!
III *vi* meugler.

mooch /muːtʃ/ **I** *n* US tapeur/-euse° *m/f*.
II *vtr* US (cadge) **to ~ sth from** ou **off sb** taper° qch à qn.
III *vi* GB **to ~ along** ou **about** traîner; **to ~ around the house** traîner à la maison.

mood /muːd/ *n* **1** (frame of mind) humeur *f*; **to be in the ~ for jokes/work** être d'humeur à plaisanter/travailler; **to be in the ~ for doing** ou **to do** avoir envie de faire; **to be in no ~ for doing** ou **to do** ne pas être d'humeur à faire; **to be in a good/bad ~** être de bonne/mauvaise humeur; **to be in a stubborn/relaxed ~** se montrer entêté/détendu; **when he's in the ~** quand l'envie l'en prend; **when** ou **as the ~ takes him** selon son humeur; **I'm not in the ~** je ne suis pas d'humeur; **2** (bad temper) saute *f* d'humeur; **to be in a ~** être de mauvaise humeur; **he's in one of his ~s today** il est de mauvaise humeur aujourd'hui; **3** (atmosphere) (in room, meeting) ambiance *f*; (of place, era, artwork) atmosphère *f*; (of group, party) état *m* d'esprit; **the general ~ was one of despair** le sentiment général était au désespoir; **the ~ of the moment** l'humeur du moment; **4** Ling mode *m*; **in the subjunctive ~** au subjonctif.

moodily /'muːdɪlɪ/ *adv* [*say, speak*] d'un ton maussade; [*look, sit, stare*] d'un air morose.

moodiness /'muːdɪnɪs/ *n* humeur *f* changeante, inégalités *fpl* d'humeur.

mood: **~ music** *n* musique *f* d'ambiance; **~ swing** *n* saute *f* d'humeur.

moody /'muːdɪ/ *adj* **1** (unpredictable) lunatique; **a ~ person** un/-e lunatique *m/f*; **2** (atmospheric) [*novel, film*] sombre; **3** (sultry) [*actor, appearance*] ténébreux/-euse.

mooing /'muːɪŋ/ *n* ¢ meuglements *mpl*.

moola(h)° /'muːlə/ *n* US fric° *m*.

moon /muːn/ **I** *n* Astron (satellite) lune *f*; **the ~** (of the earth) la Lune; **the ~s of Saturn** les lunes de Saturne; **there will be a ~ tonight** il y aura clair de lune cette nuit; **there will be no ~ tonight** ce soir, ce sera une nuit sans lune; **by the light of the ~** au clair de lune; **to put a man on the ~** envoyer un homme sur la Lune.
II *vi* **1** (daydream) rêvasser (**over sth/sb** à qch/qn); **2**° (display buttocks) montrer ses fesses.
IDIOMS **to be over the ~ about sth** être aux nues à propos de qch; **many ~s ago** littér il y a des lustres; **once in a blue ~** tous les trente-six du mois°; **the man in the ~** le visage de la Lune; **to shoot the ~** US déménager à la cloche de bois°.
■ **moon about**°, **moon around**° musarder.

moon: **~beam** *n* rayon *m* de lune; **~ boots** *npl* après-ski *mpl*; **~ buggy** *n* jeep *f* lunaire; **~-faced** *adj* aux joues rondes.

Moonie° /'muːnɪ/ *n* mooniste *mf*.

moon landing *n* atterrissage *m* sur la lune.

moonless /'muːnlɪs/ *adj* sans lune.

moonlight /'muːnlaɪt/ **I** *n* clair *m* de lune; **in the** ou **by ~** au clair de lune.
II *vi* travailler au noir.
IDIOMS **to do a ~ flit**° GB filer de nuit sans payer.

moonlighter /'muːnlaɪtə(r)/ *n* travailleur *m* au noir.

moonlighting /'muːnlaɪtɪŋ/ *n* travail *m* au noir.

moonlit /'muːnlɪt/ *adj* [*sky, evening*] éclairé par la lune; **a ~ night** une nuit de lune.

moon rock *n* roche *f* lunaire.

moonshine /'muːnʃaɪn/ *n* **1** ¢ (nonsense)

fadaises○ *fpl*; **2** US (liquor) alcool *m* de contrebande.

moonshiner○ /ˈmuːnʃaɪnə(r)/ *n* US (maker) distilleur/-euse *m/f* clandestin/-e; (seller) trafiquant/-e *m/f* d'alcool.

moon: **~stone** *n* pierre *f* de lune; **~struck** *adj* lunatique.

moonwalk /ˈmuːnwɔːk/ *n* marche *f* lunaire.

moor /mɔː(r), US mʊər/ **I** *n* lande *f*; **on the ~s** sur la lande.
II *vtr* Naut amarrer.
III *vi* Naut mouiller.

Moor /mʊə(r)/ *n* Hist Maure *mf*.

moorhen /ˈmɔːhen, US ˈmʊər-/ *n* GB poule *f* d'eau.

mooring /ˈmɔːrɪŋ, US ˈmʊər-/ **I** *n* (place) mouillage *m*; **a boat at its ~s** un bateau amarré.
II moorings *npl* (ropes) amarres *fpl*; fig (ideological, emotional) attaches *fpl*.

mooring buoy *n* bouée *f* de corps-mort.

Moorish /ˈmʊərɪʃ/ *adj* mauresque.

moorland /ˈmɔːlənd, US ˈmʊər-/ **I** *n* lande *f*.
II *modif* [*air, hills, sheep*] de la lande.

moose (*pl* **moose**) /muːs/ *n* Zool (Canadian) orignal *m*; (European elk) élan *m*.

moot /muːt/ **I** *n* (also **~ court**) *pseudo-tribunal où les étudiants de droit s'entraînent.*
II *vtr* sout soulever [*possibility*]; **it has been mooted that** d'aucuns ont suggéré que.

moot point *n* **that is a ~** c'est difficile à dire.

mop /mɒp/ **I** *n* **1** (for floors) (of cotton) balai *m* à franges; (of sponge) balai *m* éponge; **2** (for dishes) lavette *f*; **3** (hair) crinière○ *f*; tignasse○ *f* pej; **a ~ of red/curly hair** une crinière rousse/bouclée.
II *vtr* (*p prés etc* **-pp-**) **1** (wash) laver [qch] à grande eau [*floor, deck*]; **2** (wipe) **to ~ one's face/brow (with sth)** s'éponger le visage/le front (avec qch); **to ~ sb's brow** éponger le front de qn.
III *vi* (*p prés etc* **-pp-**) essuyer.
■ **mop down**: **~ [sth] down, ~ down [sth]** laver [qch] à grande eau [*floor, deck*].
■ **mop up**: ¶ **~ up** éponger; ¶ **~ up [sth], ~ [sth] up 1** lit éponger [*mess, liquid*]; **he ~ped up his gravy with some bread** il a saucé son assiette avec du pain; **2** Mil, gen (get rid of) balayer [*resistance, rebels*]; **3** (absorb) engloutir [*savings, profits, surplus*]; **4** US (polish off) engloutir [*food*].

mopboard /ˈmɒpbɔːd/ *n* US plinthe *f*.

mope /məʊp/ *vi* **1** (brood) se morfondre; **to ~ about sth** broyer du noir en pensant à qch; **2** = **~ about**.
■ **mope about, mope around** traîner (comme une âme en peine).

moped /ˈməʊped/ *n* vélomoteur *m*.

mop-head○ /ˈmɒphed/ *n* ébouriffé/-e *m/f*.

moppet○† /ˈmɒpɪt/ *n* petit chou *m*, trésor *m*.

mopping-up operation *n* Mil, gen opération *f* de nettoyage.

moquette /mɒˈket, US məʊ-/ *n* ¢ moquette *f*.

moraine /məˈreɪn, mɒˈreɪn/ *n* moraine *f*.

moral /ˈmɒrəl, US ˈmɔːrəl/ **I** *n* morale *f*; **the ~ is that** la morale c'est que; **to draw a ~ from sth** tirer la leçon de qch.
II morals *npl* **1** (habits) mœurs *fpl*; **public ~s** mœurs publiques; **a person of loose ~s** une personne de mœurs faciles or légères; **2** (morality) moralité *f*; **to have no ~s** être sans moralité.
III *adj* (all contexts) moral; **on ~ grounds** pour des raisons morales; **~ certainty** certitude *f* morale; **~ support** soutien *m* moral; **to take the ~ high ground** prendre une position moraliste.

morale /məˈrɑːl, US -ˈræl/ *n* moral *m*; **to raise ~** remonter le moral à qn; **to lower sb's ~** saper le moral de qn; **~ is low at present** le moral est bas en ce moment.

morale-booster *n* **his comment was a ~** sa remarque m'a remonté le moral.

moral fibre GB, **moral fiber** /ˌmɒrəlˈfaɪbə(r), US ˌmɔːr-/ US *n* force *f* morale.

moralist /ˈmɒrəlɪst, US ˈmɔːrəlɪst/ *n* Literat, Philos, gen also pej moraliste *mf*.

moralistic /ˌmɒrəˈlɪstɪk, US ˌmɔːr-/ *adj* moralisateur/-trice.

morality /məˈrælətɪ/ *n* moralité *f*.

morality: **~ play** *n* Theat moralité *f*; **~ tale** *n* conte *m* moral.

moralize /ˈmɒrəlaɪz, US ˈmɔːr-/ *vi* moraliser (**about** sur).

moralizing /ˈmɒrəlaɪzɪŋ, US ˈmɔːr-/ **I** *n* ¢ leçons *fpl* de morale.
II *adj* moralisateur/-trice.

morally /ˈmɒrəlɪ, US ˈmɔːr-/ *adv* moralement; **~ wrong** contraire à la morale; **~ speaking** du point de vue de la morale.

moral: **~ majority** *n* majorité *f* bien-pensante; **Moral Majority** *n* Pol US *mouvement politique américain regroupant en majorité les chrétiens fondamentalistes, prônant les valeurs morales de la droite*; **~ philosopher** *n* Philos moraliste *mf*; **~ philosophy** *n* Philos morale *f*; **Moral Rearmament** *n* Réarmement *m* moral; **~ theology** *n* théologie *f* morale.

morass /məˈræs/ *n* lit, fig bourbier *m*.

moratorium (*pl* **-toria**) /ˌmɒrəˈtɔːrɪəm/ *n* moratoire *m* (**on** sur).

Moravia /məˈreɪvɪə/ **▶ 1131** *pr n* Moravie *f*.

Moravian /məˈreɪvɪən/ **▶ 1486**, **1402** **I** *n* Morave *mf*.
II *adj* morave.

moray eel /ˈmɒrɪ iːl/ *n* murène *f*.

morbid /ˈmɔːbɪd/ *adj* (all contexts) morbide.

morbid anatomy *n* anatomie *f* pathologique.

morbidity /ˌmɔːˈbɪdətɪ/ *n* **1** (of imagination, preoccupation, subject) caractère *m* morbide; **2** Med morbidité *f*.

morbidly /ˈmɔːbɪdlɪ/ *adv* **1** de façon malsaine; **2** Med morbidement.

Morbihan /ˈmɔːbɪhæn/ **▶ 1163** *pr n* Morbihan *m*; **in/to the ~** dans le Morbihan.

mordacity /mɔːˈdæsətɪ/ *n* sout causticité *f*.

mordant /ˈmɔːdnt/ *adj* sout [*wit*] mordant, caustique.

mordent /ˈmɔːdnt/ *n* pincé *m*.

more /mɔː(r)/

■ **Note** When used to modify an adjective or an adverb to form the comparative *more* is very often translated by *plus*: *more expensive* = plus cher/chère; *more beautiful* = plus beau/belle; *more easily* = plus facilement; *more regularly* = plus régulièrement. For examples and further uses see I 1 below.
– When used as a quantifier to indicate a greater amount or quantity of something *more* is very often translated by *plus de*: *more money/cars/people* = plus d'argent/de voitures/de gens. For examples and further uses see II 1 below.

I *adv* **1** (comparative) **it's ~ serious than we thought/you think** c'est plus grave que nous ne pensions/vous ne pensez; **the ~ intelligent (child) of the two** (l'enfant) le plus intelligent des deux ; **he's no ~ honest than his sister** il n'est pas plus honnête que sa sœur; **the ~ developed countries** les pays plus développés; **2** (to a greater extent) plus, davantage; **you must work/sleep/rest ~** il faut que tu travailles/dormes/te reposes davantage; **he sleeps/talks ~ than I do** il dort/parle plus que moi; **you can't paint any ~ than I can, you can no ~ paint than I can** tu ne sais pas plus peindre que moi; **the ~ you think of it, the harder it will seem** plus tu y penseras, plus ça te paraîtra dur; **he is (all) the ~ determined/angry because** il est d'autant plus déterminé/en colère que; **3** (longer) **I don't work there any ~** je n'y travaille plus; **I couldn't continue any ~** je ne pouvais pas continuer plus longtemps; **she is no ~** littér elle n'est plus; **4** (again) **once/twice ~** une fois/deux fois de plus, encore une fois/deux fois; **he's back once ~** il est de nouveau de retour; **5** (rather) **~ surprised than angry** plus étonné que fâché; **he's ~ a mechanic than an engineer** il est plus mécanicien qu'ingénieur; **it's ~ a question of organization than of money** c'est plus une question d'organisation que d'argent.
II *quantif* **~ cars than people** plus de voitures que de gens; **~ eggs than milk** plus d'œufs que de lait; **~ cars than expected/before** plus de voitures que prévu/qu'avant; **some ~ books** encore quelques livres; **a little/lot ~ wine** un peu/beaucoup plus de vin; **~ bread** encore un peu de pain; **there's no ~ bread** il n'y a plus de pain; **have some ~ beer!** reprenez de la bière; **have you any ~ questions/problems?** avez-vous d'autres questions/problèmes?; **we've no ~ time** nous n'avons plus le temps; **nothing ~** rien de plus; **something ~** autre chose, quelque chose d'autre.
III *pron* **1** (larger amount or number) plus; **it costs ~ than the other one** il/elle coûte plus cher que l'autre; **he eats ~ than you** il mange plus que toi; **the children take up ~ of my time** les enfants prennent une plus grande partie de mon temps; **many were disappointed, ~ were angry** beaucoup de gens ont été déçus, un plus grand nombre étaient fâchés; **we'd like to see ~ of you** nous voudrions te voir plus souvent; **2** (additional amount) davantage; (additional number) plus; **tell me ~ (about it)** dis-m'en davantage; **I need ~ of them** il m'en faut plus; **I need ~ of it** il m'en faut davantage; **we found several/a few ~ (of them) in the house** nous en avons trouvé plusieurs/quelques autres dans la maison; **I can't tell you any ~** je ne peux pas t'en dire plus; **have you heard any ~ from your sister?** as-tu d'autres nouvelles de ta sœur?; **I have nothing ~ to say** je n'ai rien à ajouter; **in Mexico, of which ~ later...** au Mexique, dont nous reparlerons plus tard...; **let's** ou **we'll say no ~ about it** n'en parlons plus.
IV more and more *det phr, adv phr* de plus en plus; **~ and ~ work/time** de plus en plus de travail/de temps; **to work/sleep ~ and ~** travailler/dormir de plus en plus; **~ and ~ regularly** de plus en plus régulièrement.
V more or less *adv phr* plus ou moins.
VI more so *adv phr* encore plus; **in York, and even ~ so in Oxford** à York et encore plus à Oxford; **it is very interesting, made (even) ~ so because** c'est très intéressant, d'autant plus que; **he is just as active as her, if not ~ so** ou **or even ~ so** il est aussi actif qu'elle, si ce n'est plus; **(all) the ~ so because...** d'autant plus que...; **they are all disappointed, none ~ so than Mr Lowe** ils sont tous déçus, en particulier M. Lowe; **no ~ so than usual/the others** pas plus que d'habitude/les autres.
VII more than *adv phr, prep phr* **1** (greater amount or number) plus de; **~ than 20 people/£50** plus de 20 personnes/50 livres sterling; **~ than half** plus de la moitié; **~ than enough** plus qu'assez; **2** (extremely) **~ than generous/happy** plus que généreux/ravi; **the cheque ~ than covered the cost** le chèque a amplement couvert les frais; **you ~ than fulfilled your obligations** tu as fait plus que remplir tes obligations.
IDIOMS **she's nothing ~ (nor less) than a thief, she's a thief, neither ~ nor less** c'est une voleuse, ni plus ni moins; **he's nothing** ou **no** ou **not much ~ than a servant** ce n'est qu'un serviteur; **and what is ~...** et qui plus est...; **there's ~ where that came from** ce n'est qu'un début.

moreish○ /ˈmɔːrɪʃ/ *adj* **to be ~** avoir un petit goût de revenez-y○.

morello (cherry) *n* griotte *f*.

moreover /mɔːˈrəʊvə(r)/ *adv* de plus, qui plus est.

mores /ˈmɔːreɪz, -riːz/ *npl* mœurs *fpl*.

morganatic /ˌmɔːgəˈnætɪk/ *adj* morganatique.

morgue /mɔːg/ *n* morgue *f*; **this place is like a ~**○ fig cet endroit est complètement mort.

MORI /ˈmɒrɪ/ *n* (*abrév* = **Market and Opinion Research Institute**) *institut de sondage britannique*; **a ~ poll** un sondage d'opinion réalisé par l'institut MORI.

moribund /ˈmɒrɪbʌnd/ *adj* moribond.

Mormon /ˈmɔːmən/ **I** *n* (follower) Mormon/-e *m/f*.
II *pr n* (prophet) Mormon.
III *adj* mormon.

Mormonism /ˈmɔːmənɪzəm/ *n* mormonisme *m*.

morn /mɔːn/ *n*† ou littér potron-minet† *m*.

morning /ˈmɔːnɪŋ/ ▶1096 **I** *n* matin *m*; (with emphasis on duration) matinée *f*; **during the ~** pendant la matinée; **at 3 o'clock in the ~** à 3 heures du matin; (**on**) **Monday ~** lundi matin; **on Monday ~s** le lundi matin; **this ~** ce matin; **later this ~** plus tard dans la matinée; **tomorrow/yesterday ~** demain/hier matin; **the previous ~** la veille au matin; **the following ~, the ~ after, the next ~** le lendemain matin; **on the ~ of 2 May** le matin du 2 mai; **on a cold winter's ~** par un matin froid ou une matinée froide d'hiver; **early** ou **first thing in the ~** (dawn) tôt le matin; **all right, I'll do it first thing in the ~** c'est bon, je le ferai dès demain matin; **from ~ till night** du matin au soir; **to work ~s** travailler le matin; **to be on ~s** être du matin; **we've done a good ~'s work** on a eu une bonne matinée de travail.
II *modif* [*air, flight, train, news, paper, prayers, star*] du matin; **that early ~ feeling** la torpeur matinale.
III *excl* (also **good ~**) bonjour!
IDIOMS **the ~ after the night before** un lendemain de cuite○.

morning: **~-after pill** *n* pilule *f* du lendemain; **~ coat** *n* jaquette *f*; **~ coffee** *n* pause-café *f*; **~ dress** *n* habit *m*; **~ glory** *n* volubilis *m*; **~ room**† *n* salon *m* (*utilisé le matin*); **~ service** *n* Relig office *m* du matin; **~ sickness** *n* vomissements *mpl* du matin; **~ watch** *n* Naut premier quart *m* du jour.

Moroccan /məˈrɒkən/ ▶1486 **I** *n* Marocain/-e *m/f*.
II *adj* marocain.

morocco (leather) /məˈrɒkəʊ/ **I** *n* maroquin *m*.
II *modif* [*binding, shoes*] en maroquin.

Morocco /məˈrɒkəʊ/ ▶1131 *pr n* Maroc *m*.

moron○ /ˈmɔːrɒn/ *n* crétin/-e *m/f*.

moronic /məˈrɒnɪk/ *adj* débile.

moronically /məˈrɒnɪklɪ/ *adv* de façon crétine.

morose /məˈrəʊs/ *adj* morose.

morosely /məˈrəʊslɪ/ *adv* [*sit, stare*] d'un air morose.

morph /mɔːf/ *n* morphe *m*.

morpheme /ˈmɔːfiːm/ *n* morphème *m*.

Morpheus /ˈmɔːfɪəs/ *pr n* Morphée.
IDIOMS **in the arms of ~** littér dans les bras de Morphée.

morphia† /ˈmɔːfɪə/ *n* morphine *f*.

morphine /ˈmɔːfiːn/ *n* morphine *f*.

morphine: **~ addict** *n* morphinomane *mf*; **~ addiction** *n* morphinomanie *f*.

morphological /ˌmɔːfəˈlɒdʒɪkl/ *adj* (all contexts) morphologique.

morphologically /ˌmɔːfəˈlɒdʒɪklɪ/ *adv* (all contexts) morphologiquement.

morphologist /mɔːˈfɒlədʒɪst/ ▶1692 *n* Biol, Ling morphologiste *mf*.

morphology /mɔːˈfɒlədʒɪ/ *n* (all contexts) morphologie *f*.

morris: **~ dance** *n*: *danse folklorique anglaise*; **~ dancer** *n*: *danseur folklorique anglais*; **~ dancing** *n* ¢ *danse folklorique anglaise*; **~ man** *n*: *danseur folklorique anglais*.

morrow‡ /ˈmɒrəʊ, US ˈmɔːr-/ *n* lendemain *m*; **on the ~** demain; **good ~!** bonjour!

Morse (code) /mɔːs/ **I** *n* morse *m*; **in ~** en morse.
II *modif* [*signal*] en morse; [*alphabet*] morse *inv*.

morsel /ˈmɔːsl/ *n* **1** lit (of food) morceau *m*; **a tasty ~** un morceau de choix; **2** fig (of sense, self-respect) once *f* (**of** de).

Morse set *n* morse *m*.

mortadella /ˌmɔːtəˈdelə/ *n* mortadelle *f*.

mortal /ˈmɔːtl/ **I** *n* littér mortel/-elle *m/f*.
II *adj* **1** gen [*man, life, enemy, danger*] mortel/-elle; [*injury, blow*] fatal; **2** Relig [*sin*] mortel/-elle.

mortal combat *n* lutte *f* à mort.

mortality /mɔːˈtælətɪ/ *n* mortalité *f*; ▶**infant mortality**.

mortality rate *n* taux *m* de mortalité.

mortally /ˈmɔːtəlɪ/ *adv* (all contexts) mortellement.

mortal remains *npl* dépouille *f* mortelle.

mortar /ˈmɔːtə(r)/ *n* Constr, Mil, Pharm mortier *m*.

mortarboard /ˈmɔːtəbɔːd/ *n* GB Univ toque *f* (*d'étudiant ou de professeur d'université*).

mortgage /ˈmɔːgɪdʒ/ **I** *n* emprunt-logement *m* (**on** pour); **to apply for a ~** faire une demande d'emprunt-logement; **to raise a ~** obtenir un emprunt-logement; **to take out a ~** contracter fml ou faire un emprunt-logement; **pay off** ou **clear a ~** rembourser un emprunt-logement.
II *modif* [*agreement, deed*] hypothécaire.
III *vtr* hypothéquer [*property*] (**for** pour) ; **the house is ~d to the bank** la maison est en hypothèque à la banque; fig **to ~ one's future** hypothéquer son avenir.

mortgage broker ▶1692 *n* courtier *m* en prêts hypothécaires.

mortgagee /ˌmɔːgɪˈdʒiː/ *n* créancier/-ière *m/f* hypothécaire.

mortgager, **mortgagor** /ˈmɔːgɪdʒə(r)/ *n* débiteur/-trice *m/f* hypothécaire.

mortgage: **~ rate** *n* taux *m* de l'emprunt-logement; **~ relief** *n*: *réduction d'impôt pour emprunt-logement*; **~ repayment** *n* mensualité *f* de remboursement.

mortice *n* ▶**mortise**.

mortician /mɔːˈtɪʃn/ ▶1692 *n* US entrepreneur *m* de pompes funèbres.

mortification /ˌmɔːtɪfɪˈkeɪʃn/ *n* (all contexts) mortification *f*.

mortify /ˈmɔːtɪfaɪ/ **I** *vtr* **1** (embarrass) mortifier [*person*]; **2** Relig mortifier; **to ~ the flesh** mortifier sa chair.
II mortifying *pres p adj* mortifiant.
III mortified *pp adj* mortifié.

mortise /ˈmɔːtɪs/ **I** *n* mortaise *f*.
II *vtr* mortaiser.

mortise: **~ and tenon joint** *n* Constr assemblage *m* à tenon et mortaise; **~ lock** *n* serrure *f* encastrée.

mortuary /ˈmɔːtʃərɪ, US ˈmɔːtʃʊerɪ/ **I** *n* morgue *f*.
II *adj* mortuaire.

mosaic /məʊˈzeɪɪk/ **I** *n* lit, fig mosaïque *f*.
II *modif* [*floor, pattern*] en mosaïque.

Mosaic /məʊˈzeɪɪk/ *adj* Bible mosaïque.

Moscow /ˈmɒskəʊ/ ▶1818 *pr n* Moscou.

Moselle, **Mosel** /məʊˈzel/ ▶1644, 1163 *pr n* **1** (river) Moselle *f*; **2** (department) Moselle *f*; **in/to ~** dans la Moselle; **3** Wine vin *m* de Moselle.

Moses /ˈməʊzɪz/ *pr n* Moïse; **Holy ~**○! grand Dieu!

Moses basket *n* couffin *m*.

mosey○ /ˈməʊzɪ/ **I** *n* petit tour *m*; **to have a ~ round the garden** faire un petit tour dans le jardin.
II *vi* se baguenauder; **to ~ down the street** descendre la rue en flânant; **I'd better be ~ing along** il faut que je m'en aille; **let's ~ on down to the pub** allons tranquillement au pub.

Moslem /ˈmɒzləm/ **I** *n* Musulman/-e *m/f*.
II *adj* musulman.

mosque /mɒsk/ *n* mosquée *f*.

mosquito /məsˈkiːtəʊ, mɒs-/ *n* moustique *m*.

mosquito: **~ bite** *n* piqûre *f* de moustique; **~ net** *n* moustiquaire *f*; **~ repellent** *n* antimoustique *m*.

moss /mɒs, US mɔːs/ *n* Bot mousse *f*.
IDIOMS **a rolling stone gathers no ~** Prov pierre qui roule n'amasse pas mousse Prov.

moss: **~back**○ *n* US réactionnaire *mf*; **~-covered** *adj* moussu; **~ green** *n, adj* vert (*m*) mousse (*inv*).

moss-grown /ˈmɒsgrəʊn, US ˈmɔːs-/ *adj* **1** lit moussu; **2** (antiquated) vieillot/-otte.

moss: **~ rose** *n* rose *f* moussue; **~ stitch** *n* point *m* de riz.

mossy /ˈmɒsɪ, US ˈmɔːsɪ/ *adj* moussu.

most /məʊst/

■ **Note** When used to form the superlative of adjectives *most* is translated by *le plus* or *la plus* depending on the gender of the noun and by *les plus* with plural noun: *the most beautiful woman in the room* = la plus belle femme de la pièce; *the most expensive hotel in Paris* = l'hôtel le plus cher de Paris; *the most difficult problems* = les problèmes les plus difficiles. For examples and further uses see the entry below.

I *det* **1** (the majority of, nearly all) la plupart de; **~ people/computers** la plupart des gens/des ordinateurs; **2** (superlative: more than all the others) le plus de; **she got the ~ votes/money** c'est elle qui a obtenu le plus de voix/d'argent; **we had (the) ~ success/problems in China** c'est en Chine qu'on a eu le plus de succès/de problèmes; **those with (the) ~ intelligence** ceux qui sont les plus intelligents.
II *pron* **1** (the majority) la plupart (**of** de); **~ of the people/of the computers** la plupart des gens/des ordinateurs; **~ of you/us** la plupart d'entre vous/nous; **~ of the bread/wine** presque tout le pain/vin; **~ of the money** la plus grosse part de l'argent; **for ~ of the day/evening** pendant la plus grande partie de la journée/soirée; **~ agreed** la plupart étaient d'accord; **~ were blue** la plupart étaient bleus; **2** (the maximum) **the ~ you can expect is**... tout ce que tu peux espérer c'est...; **the ~ I can do is**... tout ce que je peux faire, c'est..., le mieux que je puisse faire, c'est...; **what's the ~ we'll have to pay?** au maximum, combien aurons-nous à payer?; **3** (more than all the others) le plus; **John has got the ~** c'est John qui en a le plus.
III *adv* **1** (used to form superlative) **the ~ beautiful château in France** le plus beau château de France; **~ easily** le plus facilement; **the ~ beautifully written poetry** de très beaux poèmes; **~ interestingly (of all), he**... le plus intéressant c'est qu'il...; **2** (very) très, extrêmement; **~ encouraging/amusing/odd** très ou extrêmement encourageant/amusant/bizarre; **~ probably** très vraisemblablement; **3** (more than all the rest) le plus; **what ~ annoyed him** ou **what annoyed him ~ (of all) was** ce qui l'ennuyait le plus c'était que; **those who will benefit/suffer ~ from**... ceux qui profiteront/souffriront le plus de...; **4**○ US (almost) presque; **~ everyone** presque tout le monde.
IV at (the) most *adv phr* au maximum, au plus.
V for the most part *adv phr* (most of them) pour la plupart; (most of the time) la

plupart du temps; (basically) essentiellement, surtout; **for the ~ part, they...** pour la plupart, ils...; **for the ~ part he works in his office** la plupart du temps, il travaille dans son bureau; **the book is, for the ~ part, about sex** le livre parle essentiellement or surtout de sexe; **his experience is, for the ~ part, in publishing** son expérience est surtout or essentiellement dans l'édition.
VI **most of all** *adv phr* par-dessus tout.
IDIOMS **to make the ~ of** tirer le meilleur parti de [*situation, resources, looks, rest, abilities, space*]; profiter de [*holiday, opportunity, good weather*].

mostly /ˈməʊstlɪ/ *adv* **1** (chiefly) surtout, essentiellement; (most of them) pour la plupart; **he composes, ~ for the piano** il compose surtout pour le piano; **200 people, ~ Belgians** 200 personnes, des Belges pour la plupart; **2** (most of the time) la plupart du temps, en général; **~ we travelled by train** la plupart du temps or en général, nous avons pris le train; **~ he stays in his room** la plupart du temps or en général, il reste dans sa chambre.

MOT /ˌeməʊˈtiː/ GB Aut (*abrév* = **Ministry of Transport**) **I** *n* (also **~ test**, **~ inspection**) contrôle *m* technique des véhicules; **to take one's car in for its ~** amener sa voiture au contrôle technique; **to pass/fail the ~** obtenir/ne pas obtenir le certificat de contrôle; **'~ until June'** 'certificat de contrôle valable jusqu'à juin'.
II *modif* [*certificate, centre*] de contrôle technique.
III *vtr* effectuer le contrôle technique de [*car*].

mote /məʊt/ *n* grain *m*.
IDIOMS **to see the ~ in one's neighbour's eye but not the beam in one's own** voir la paille dans l'œil du voisin et ne pas voir la poutre dans le sien.

motel /məʊˈtel/ *n* motel *m*.

motet /məʊˈtet/ *n* motet *m*.

moth /mɒθ, US mɔːθ/ *n* **1** gen papillon *m* de nuit; **2** (in clothes) mite *f*.

mothball /ˈmɒθbɔːl, US ˈmɔːθ-/ **I** *n* boule *f* de naphtaline; **to put sth in/take sth out of ~s** fig mettre qch au/sortir qch du placard fig.
II *vtr* mettre [qch] en sommeil [*pit, shipyard*].

moth-eaten /ˈmɒθiːtn, US ˈmɔːθ-/ *adj* **1** (shabby) miteux/-euse; **2** (damaged by moths) mité.

mother /ˈmʌðə(r)/ **I** *n* **1** (parent) mère *f*; **a ~ of two** une mère de deux enfants; **she's like a ~ to me** c'est une mère pour moi; **2** (form of address) (to mother) mère *f* fml, maman *f*; **3**◐ US **a ~ of** un bon dieu de○.
II **Mother** *pr n* Relig Mère *f*; **Reverend Mother** révérende Mère.
III *vtr* **1** lit materner [*young*]; **2** (fuss over) dorloter also pej.
IDIOMS **every ~'s son (of them)** tous sans exception; **to learn sth at one's ~'s knee, to take sth in with one's ~'s milk** apprendre qch dans sa plus tendre enfance.

motherboard *n* carte *f* mère.

mother church, **Mother Church** *n* (Catholic church) notre sainte mère *f* l'Église.

mother: **~ country** *n* mère patrie *f*; **~ earth** *n* notre bonne vieille terre *f*; **~ figure** *n* image *f* de la mère; **~fucker●** *n* fils *m* de pute●; **~fucking●** *adj* putain● de *inv* (*before n*); **Mother Goose** *n* ma Mère *f* l'Oye; **~ hen** *n* fig mère *f* poule.

motherhood /ˈmʌðəhʊd/ *n* fait *m* d'être mère; **the responsibilities of ~** les responsabilités incombant à une mère de famille; **to combine ~ with a career** combiner les enfants et le travail.

mothering /ˈmʌðərɪŋ/ *n* **1** ¢ (motherly care) soins *mpl* maternels; **2** (being a mother) fait *m* d'être mère.

Mothering Sunday *n* GB fête *f* des Mères.

mother: **~-in-law** *n* (*pl* **mothers-in-law**) belle-mère *f*; **~-in-law's tongue** *n* Bot sansevière *f*; **~land** *n* (all contexts) patrie *f*.

motherless /ˈmʌðəlɪs/ *adj* [*child*] orphelin de mère; [*animal*] sans mère.

mother love *n* amour *m* maternel.

motherly /ˈmʌðəlɪ/ *adj* maternel/-elle.

mother: **~-naked** *adj* tout nu, nu comme un ver; **Mother Nature** *n* Dame *f* Nature; **Mother of God** *n* mère *f* de Dieu.

mother-of-pearl /ˌmʌðərəvˈpɜːl/ **I** *n* nacre *f*.
II *modif* [*necklace, brooch, box*] de or en nacre.

mother: **~-of-thousands** *n* ruine-de-Rome *f*, cymbalaire *f* spec; **~'s boy** *n* petit garçon *m* à sa maman○; **Mother's Day** *n* fête *f* des Mères; **~'s help** GB, **~'s helper** US *n* aide *f* maternelle; **~ ship** *n* ravitailleur *m*; **Mother Superior** *n* Mère *f* supérieure; **~-to-be** *n* future mère *f*, future maman *f*.

mother tongue *n* **1** (native tongue) langue *f* maternelle; **2** (from which another evolves) langue *f* mère.

mother wit *n* bon sens *m*.

mothproof /ˈmɒθpruːf, US ˈmɔːθ-/ *vtr* traiter [qch] à l'antimite.

motif /məʊˈtiːf/ *n* (in art, music) motif *m*; (in literature) thème *m*.

motion /ˈməʊʃn/ **I** *n* **1** (movement) mouvement *m*; **to be in ~** être en mouvement; **to set sth in ~** lit mettre qch en marche [*pendulum*]; fig mettre qch en route [*plan*]; déclencher [*chain of events*]; **to set the wheels in ~** fig mettre les choses en route; **perpetual ~** mouvement *m* perpétuel; **2** (gesture) (of hands) geste *m*; (of head, body) mouvement *m*; **3** Admin, Pol motion *f*; **to table/second the ~** déposer/appuyer la motion; **to carry/defeat the ~ by 10 votes to 8** adopter/rejeter la motion par 10 voix contre 8; **a ~ of censure** une motion de censure; **4** Med selles *fpl*; **to have a ~** aller à la selle.
II *vtr* **to ~ sb away/back** faire signe à qn de s'éloigner/reculer; **to ~ sb to approach** faire signe à qn de s'approcher.
III *vi* faire signe (**to** à).
IDIOMS **to go through the ~s** faire qch machinalement; **to go through the ~s of doing** faire mine de faire.

motionless /ˈməʊʃnlɪs/ *adj* [*sit, stand*] sans bouger; [*hawk, cloud*] immobile; **they sat ~** ils restèrent assis sans bouger.

motion picture **I** *n* film *m*.
II *modif* [*industry*] du cinéma; [*director*] de cinéma.

motion sickness *n* mal *m* des transports.

motivate /ˈməʊtɪveɪt/ **I** *vtr* (all contexts) motiver (**to do** à faire).
II **motivating** *pres p adj* [*force, factor*] motivant.
III *v refl* **to ~ oneself** se motiver.

motivated /ˈməʊtɪveɪtɪd/ *adj* **1** [*person, pupil*] motivé; **highly** ou **well ~** très motivé; **2 politically/racially ~** [*act*] politique/raciste.

motivation /ˌməʊtɪˈveɪʃn/ *n* (all contexts) motivation *f* (**for** de; **for doing, to do** pour faire).

motivation(al) research *n* étude *f* de motivation.

motivator /ˈməʊtɪveɪtə(r)/ *n* (person, thing) élément *m* moteur; **the team ~** le moteur de l'équipe; **to be a** ou **act as a ~** jouer un rôle moteur.

motive /ˈməʊtɪv/ **I** *n* **1** gen motif *m* (**for, behind** de); **sb's ~ in doing** le motif qui pousse qn à faire; **a political ~** un motif politique; **base/noble ~s** des motifs ignobles/nobles; **2** Jur mobile *m* (**for** de).
II *adj* lit [*force, power*] moteur/-trice; **she was the ~ force behind the decision** fig elle était à l'origine de la décision.

motiveless /ˈməʊtɪvlɪs/ *adj* [*crime, act*] gratuit.

motivelessly /ˈməʊtɪvlɪslɪ/ *adv* gratuitement.

motley /ˈmɒtlɪ/ **I** *n* (jester's costume) habit *m* bariolé du bouffon.
II *adj* **1** [*crowd, gathering*] bigarré; [*collection*] hétéroclite; **a ~ crew** hum un groupe curieusement assorti; **2** [*coat*] bariolé.

motocross /ˈməʊtəkrɒs/ ▶ **1282** *n* motocross *m*.

motor /ˈməʊtə(r)/ **I** *n* **1** Elec, Mech (engine) moteur *m*; **2** fig **to be the ~ for sth** être le moteur de qch; **3**○ †(car) bagnole○ *f*.
II *modif* **1** Aut [*industry, insurance, manufacturer, mechanic, racing, trade, vehicle*] automobile; [*exhibition, show*] de l'automobile; **2** Med [*activity, area of brain, disorder, function, nerve*] moteur/-trice.
III *vi* **1**† (travel by car) voyager en voiture, rouler; **to ~ along/away** passer/s'éloigner en roulant ou en voiture; **to ~ down to the coast** rouler vers la côte; **2**○ (go fast) tracer○; **she's really ~ing through the work** elle abat vraiment de la besogne.

motorail /ˈməʊtəreɪl/ *n* GB train *m* autocouchettes.

motor: **~bike** *n* moto *f*; **~boat** *n* canot *m* automobile; **~cade** *n* cortège *m* (de véhicules); **~ car**† *n* automobile† *f*; **~ court**, **~ inn** *n* US = **motor lodge**; **~cycle** *n* motocyclette *f*; **~cycle escort** *n* escorte *f* de motards; **~cycle messenger** *n* coursier/-ière *m/f* à moto; **~cycling** ▶ **1282** *n* motocyclisme *m*; **~cyclist** *n* motocycliste *mf*; **~ home** *n* auto-caravane *f*, camping-car *m*.

motoring /ˈməʊtərɪŋ/ **I**† *n* promenade *f* en voiture; **to go ~** aller se promener en voiture.
II *modif* [*organization, correspondent, magazine*] automobile; [*accident*] de voiture; [*holiday*] en voiture; [*offence*] de conduite.

motorist /ˈməʊtərɪst/ *n* automobiliste *mf*.

motorization /ˌməʊtəraɪˈzeɪʃn, US -rɪˈz-/ *n* motorisation *f*.

motorize /ˈməʊtəraɪz/ **I** *vtr* **1** motoriser [*vehicle, troops, police*]; **2** équiper [qch] d'un moteur [*system, camera, device*].
II **motorized** *pp adj* [*transport, vehicle, regiment*] motorisé; [*camera, device*] équipé d'un moteur.

motor: **~ launch** *n* vedette *f*; **~ lodge** *n* US motel *m*; **~man** ▶ **1692** *n* US machiniste *m*; **~ mechanic** ▶ **1692** *n* mécanicien/-ienne *m/f* auto(mobile); **~mouth**○ *n* moulin *m* à paroles○; **~ mower** *n* tondeuse *f* à moteur; **~ neurone disease** ▶ **1354** *n* maladie *f* de Charcot, sclérose *f* latérale amyotrophique spéc; **~ oil** *n* huile *f* de graissage; **~ scooter** *n* scooter *m*.

motorway /ˈməʊtəweɪ/ GB **I** *n* autoroute *f*.
II *modif* [*markings, police, service station, telephone*] de l'autoroute; [*traffic, network, system, junction, building programme*] autoroutier/-ière; [*crash, pile-up*] sur l'autoroute; [*driving*] sur autoroute.

Motown® /ˈməʊtaʊn/ *pr n*, *modif* Motown® (*m*).

mottled /ˈmɒtld/ *adj* [*skin, paper, file, binding*] marbré; [*hands*] tacheté; [*markings, design*] flou.

motto /ˈmɒtəʊ/ *n* **1** (of person, institution) devise *f*; **that's my ~** c'est ce que je me dis; **2** GB (in cracker) (joke) blague *f*; (riddle) devinette *f*.

mould GB, **mold** US /məʊld/ **I** *n* **1** (shape) moule *m*; **ring ~** ≈ moule à savarin; **candle ~** moule à chandelles; **2** fig moule *m*; **in the ~ of** dans le moule de; **in the same ~** dans le même moule; **to be cast in/to fit into a ~** être coulé dans/entrer dans un moule; **to break the ~** innover; **3** (pudding, jelly) entremets *m* froid; **rice ~** gâteau *m* de riz; **4** (fungi) moisissure *f*; **5** (soil) terreau *m*.

II *vtr* **1** lit modeler [*plastic, clay*] (**into sth** pour en faire qch); modeler [*sculpture, shape*] (**out of, from, in** en); **to ~ sth around sth** mouler qch sur qch; **2** fig façonner [*opinion, character, society*] (**into** pour en faire).
III *vi* **to ~ to sth**, **to ~ round sth** mouler qch; **to be ~ed to sb's body** [*dress etc*] mouler (le corps de) qn.
IV moulded *pp adj* [*plastic, chair, frame*] moulé.

mould-breaker *n* novateur/-trice *m/f*; **to be a ~** [*person, design, book, film*] être novateur/-trice; [*machine etc*] être une innovation.

mould-breaking *adj* innovateur/-trice.

moulder GB, **molder** US /'məʊldə(r)/ *vi* (also **~ away**) **1** lit [*building, ruins*] tomber en poussière; [*corpse, refuse*] se décomposer; **2** fig [*person*] pourrir.

moulding GB, **molding** US /'məʊldɪŋ/ *n* **1** (of clay, model) moulage *m*; **2** (of opinion, character) modelage *m*; **3** (trim on wall, frame, car) moulure *f*.

mouldy GB, **moldy** US /'məʊldɪ/ *adj* [*bread, food*] moisi; **a ~ smell** une odeur de moisi; **to go ~** moisir.

moult GB, **molt** US /məʊlt/ **I** *n* mue *f*.
II *vtr* perdre [*fur, feathers*].
III *vi* [*cat, dog*] perdre ses poils; [*bird*] muer.

mound /maʊnd/ *n* **1** (hillock) monticule *m*, tertre *m*; **2** (heap) monceau *m* (**of** de); **3** US Sport monticule *m* du lanceur.

mount /maʊnt/ **I** *n* **1** (mountain) mont *m*; **Mount Etna/Everest** le mont Etna/Everest; **2** (horse) monture *f*; **3** (support, surround) (of jewel, lens) monture *f*; (for picture) carton *m* de montage; (for microscope, slide) lame *f*; (for film slide) cadre *m*.
II *vtr* **1** (ascend) gravir, monter [*stairs*]; monter sur [*platform, scaffold*]; monter sur, enfourcher [*horse, bicycle*]; **to ~ the throne** fig monter sur le trône; **to ~ the pavement** Aut monter sur le trottoir; **2** (fix into place) monter [*jewel, picture, photo*] (**on** sur); coller [*stamp*]; monter [*exhibit, specimen*]; mettre [qch] en position [*gun*]; Aut, Tech installer [*engine, device*]; **3** (set up, hold) monter [*exhibition, campaign*]; monter [*production*]; organiser [*demonstration*]; Mil monter [*attack*]; Fin lancer [*raid*]; **to ~ guard** monter la garde (**at, over** sur); **4** Zool (in copulation) monter; **5** Equit monter.
III *vi* **1** [*climber, staircase*] monter (**to** jusqu'à); **the blood ~ed to his cheeks** le sang lui est monté au visage; **2** (increase) [*temperature, debts, prices*] monter; [*number, toll*] augmenter; [*concern*] grandir; **3** Equit se mettre en selle.
IV mounting *pres p adj* [*pressure, problems, tension etc*] croissant, de plus en plus important; [*bills*] de plus en plus élevé.

mountain /'maʊntɪn, US -ntn/ **I** *n* lit montagne *f*; fig montagne *f*, monceau *m* (**of** de); **in the ~s** à la montagne; **a ~ of debts** une montagne de dettes; **I've got ~s of work to do** j'ai énormément de travail à faire; **meat/butter ~** Econ excédents *mpl* de viande/de beurre.
II *modif* [*road, stream, scenery*] de montagne; [*air*] de la montagne; [*tribe*] des montagnes.
IDIOMS **to make a ~ out of a molehill** faire une montagne d'une taupinière.

mountain: **~ ash** *n* sorbier *m* des oiseleurs; **~ bike** *n* vélo *m* tout-terrain, VTT *m*; **~ cat** *n* (puma) puma *m*; (lynx) lynx *m inv*; **~ climbing** ▶ 1282 *n* alpinisme *m*; **Mountain Daylight Time**, **MDT** *n* US heure *f* d'été des Montagnes Rocheuses; **~ dew**○ *n* whisky *m* de contrebande.

mountaineer /ˌmaʊntɪ'nɪə(r), US -ntn'ɪər/ ▶ 1692 *n* **1** (climber) alpiniste *mf*; **2** US (mountain-dweller) montagnard/-e *m/f*.

mountaineering /ˌmaʊntɪ'nɪərɪŋ, US -ntn'ɪərɪŋ/ ▶ 1282 *n* alpinisme *m*.

mountain: **~ goat** *n* chèvre *f* chamoisée; **~ lion** *n* puma *m*, couguar *m*.

mountainous /'maʊntɪnəs, US -ntənəs/ *adj* [*region, landscape, country*] montagneux/-euse; fig (huge) [*wave, heap*] gigantesque.

mountain: **~ range** *n* chaîne *f* de montagnes; **~ sickness** *n* mal *m* des montagnes; **~side** *n* flanc *m* or versant *m* d'une montagne; **Mountain Standard Time**, **MST** *n* US heure *f* des Montagnes Rocheuses; **Mountain (Standard) Time**, **M(S)T** *n* US heure *f* normale des Rocheuses; **~ top** *n* cime *f*.

mountebank /'maʊntɪbæŋk/ *n* littér charlatan *m*.

mount: **~ed police** *n* (+ *v pl*) police *f* montée; **~ed policeman** *n* (*pl* **~ed policemen**) membre *m* de la police montée.

Mountie /'maʊntɪ/ *n* membre *m* de la police montée canadienne; **the ~s** la police montée canadienne.

mounting block *n* montoir *m*.

mourn /mɔːn/ **I** *vtr* pleurer [*person, death*].
II *vi* (observe ritual) porter le deuil; **to ~ for sth/sb** pleurer qch/qn.

mourner /'mɔːnə(r)/ *n* (relation) parent *m* du défunt; (other) personne *f* assistant aux obsèques; **to be the chief ~** mener le deuil.

mournful /'mɔːnfl/ *adj* [*person, expression, look, sound*] mélancolique, triste.

mournfully /'mɔːnfəlɪ/ *adv* mélancoliquement.

mourning /'mɔːnɪŋ/ *n* **1** (state, clothes) deuil *m*; **to be in ~** être en deuil (**for** de); **to be in deep ~** être en grand deuil; **to wear ~** porter le deuil; **to go into/come out of ~** prendre/quitter le deuil; **2** ¢ (wailing) lamentations *fpl*.

mourning: **~ band** *n* crêpe *m*; **~ clothes** *npl* vêtements *mpl* de deuil.

mouse /maʊs/ **I** *n* (*pl* **mice**) lit, fig, Comput souris *f*.
II *vi* [*cat*] chasser les souris.
IDIOMS **as quiet as a ~** aussi discret qu'une souris; **to play cat and ~ (with sb)** jouer au chat et à la souris (avec qn).

mousehole /'maʊshəʊl/ *n* trou *m* de souris.

mousemat, **mousepad** /'maʊsmæt, 'maʊspæd/ *n* Comput tapis *m* de souris.

mouser /'maʊsə(r)/ *n* souricier *m*.

mousetrap /'maʊstræp/ *n* souricière *f*.

mousey /'maʊsɪ/ *adj* **1** (colour) [*hair, colour*] châtain terne *inv*; **2** (timid) péj effacé; **3** [*odour*] de souris.

moussaka /muː'sɑːkə/ *n* moussaka *f*.

mousse /muːs/ *n* (all contexts) mousse *f*.

moustache /mə'stɑːʃ/ **mustache** US /'mʌstæʃ/ *n* moustache *f*; **a man with a ~** un homme moustachu.

moustachio, **mustachio** US /mə'stɑːʃɪəʊ, US -stæʃ-/ *n* grosse moustache *f*.

moustachioed, **mustachioed** US /mə'stɑːʃɪəʊd, US -stæʃ-/ *adj* à grosse moustache.

mousy *adj* = **mousey**.

mouth /maʊθ/ **I** *n* **1** (of human, horse) bouche *f*; (of other animal) gueule *f*; **in one's ~** dans la bouche; **to have five ~s to feed** avoir cinq bouches à nourrir; **to open/shut one's ~** ouvrir/fermer la bouche; **with my/his etc ~ open** bouche bée *inv*; **why did you have to open your (big) ~**○**?** qu'est-ce qui t'a pris d'ouvrir ta grande gueule◑?; **he's got a big ~**○ il a une grande gueule◑; **me and my big ~**○**!** moi et ma grande gueule◑!; **2** (of cave, tunnel) entrée *f*; (of river) embouchure *f*; (of geyser, volcano) bouche *f*; (of valley) débouché *m*; (of jar, bottle, decanter) goulot *m*; (of bag, sack) ouverture *f*; **3**○ (talk) **he's all ~ (and no action)** il cause, c'est tout ce qu'il sait faire○; **that's enough ~ from you!** je t'ai assez entendu!; **to watch one's ~** surveiller son langage.
II *vtr* **1** (move lips silently) articuler silencieusement [*word, lyrics, answer*]; **2** péj (say insincerely) débiter [*platitudes, rhetoric*].
III *vi* **1** (mime) mimer; **2** US (speak affectedly) déclamer.
IDIOMS **by word of ~** de bouche à oreille; **don't put words in my ~** ne me fais pas dire ce que je n'ai pas dit; **his heart was in his ~** son cœur battait la chamade; **to be down in the ~** être tout triste; **to leave a bad** ou **nasty taste in one's** ou **the ~** fig laisser un arrière-goût amer; **to put one's foot in one's ~** faire une gaffe○; **to shoot one's ~ off** parler sans réfléchir; **to take the words right out of sb's ~** ôter les mots de la bouche de qn; **wash your ~ out!** ne dis pas de gros mots!; **I'll wash your ~ out with soap!** je vais te faire passer l'envie de dire des gros mots!
■ **mouth off**○ péj: ¶ **~ off 1** (shout) tempêter (**about** à propos de; **at sb** contre qn); **2** US (be impudent) répondre insolemment; **3** US (speak indiscreetly) dégoiser○; ¶ **~ off [sth]** déballer○ [*opinions, prejudices*].

mouthful /'maʊθfʊl/ *n* **1** (of food) bouchée *f*; (of liquid) gorgée *f*; **to swallow a meal in one ~** ne faire qu'une bouchée d'un repas; **2**○ (long hard word) mot *m* long d'un kilomètre○; (long hard name) nom *m* à coucher dehors○; **3**○ (abuse) engueulade○ *f*; **to give sb a ~** passer une engueulade○ à qn; **to get a ~** recevoir une engueulade○; **a ~ of obscenities/of curses** un chapelet d'obscénités/de jurons; **4**○ US (pertinent remark) remarque *f* importante.

mouth organ ▶ 1481 *n* harmonica *m*.

mouthpiece /'maʊθpiːs/ *n* **1** (of musical instrument) embouchure *f*; (of telephone) microphone *m*; (of pipe, snorkel) embout *m*; **2** (person) souvent péj porte-parole *m* (**of, for** de); fig (newspaper) souvent péj organe *m* (**of** de).

mouth: **~-to-mouth** *adj* [*technique, method*] du bouche-à-bouche *inv*; **~-to-mouth resuscitation** *n* bouche-à-bouche *m inv*; **~ ulcer** *n* aphte *m*; **~wash** *n* eau *f* dentifrice.

mouth-watering /'maʊθwɔːtərɪŋ/ *adj* appétissant; **to look ~** faire venir l'eau à la bouche.

mouthy○ /'maʊðɪ/ *adj* grande gueule○ *inv*.

movable /'muːvəbl/ *adj* **1** gen mobile; **2** Jur [*goods, property*] mobilier/-ière.
IDIOMS **a ~ feast** une fête mobile; **it's a ~ feast** fig hum c'est une réjouissance dont la date n'est pas connue.

movables /'muːvəblz/ *npl* biens *mpl* mobiliers.

move /muːv/ **I** *n* **1** (movement) gen mouvement *m*; (gesture) geste *m*; **one ~ and you're dead!** un geste et vous êtes mort!; **to watch sb's every ~** surveiller chacun des gestes de qn; **don't make any sudden ~s** ne fais pas de mouvement brusque; **there was a ~ towards the door** il y a eu un mouvement vers la porte; **let's make a ~**○ si on bougeait○?; **it's time I made a ~**○ il est temps de partir; **2** (transfer) (of residence) déménagement *m*; (of company) transfert *m*; **the ~ took a day** le déménagement a pris une journée; **the firm's ~ out of town** le transfert de la société à l'extérieur de la ville; **our friends helped with the ~** nos amis nous ont aidés à déménager; **our ~ to Brighton** notre installation à Brighton; **to make the ~ to London** [*family*] s'installer à Londres; [*firm*] être transféré à Londres; [*employee*] être muté à Londres; **she made the ~ from sales to management** elle est passée des ventes à la direction; **she's due for a ~** il est temps de la muter; **3** Games coup *m*; **his last/next ~** son dernier/prochain coup; **white has the first ~** les blancs jouent en premier; **it's your ~** c'est ton tour, c'est à toi de jouer; **4** (step, act) manœuvre *f*; **a good/bad ~** une bonne/mauvaise idée; **what's our next ~?** que faisons-nous ensuite?; **to make the first ~** faire le premier pas; **they have made no ~(s) to allay public anxiety** ils n'ont rien fait pour rassurer l'opinion publique; **there has been a ~ towards liberalization** il y a eu une évolution dans le sens de la libéralisation; **in a ~ to counter opposition attacks**... pour tenter de parer les attaques de l'opposition...

II on the move *adj phr* **to be on the ~** [*army*] être en mouvement; [*train*] être en marche; **to be always on the ~** [*diplomat, family*] être tout le temps en train de déménager; [*nomad, traveller*] être toujours sur les routes or par monts et par vaux; **the circus is on the ~ again** le cirque repart à nouveau; **a society on the ~** fig une société en pleine évolution.

III *vtr* **1** (change position of) déplacer [*game piece, cursor, bus stop, car, furniture*]; transporter [*injured person, patient, army*]; (to clear a space) enlever [*object*]; **~ your things!** enlève tes affaires!; **to ~ sb to another hospital** transporter qn dans un autre hôpital; **he's too ill to be ~d** il est trop malade pour être transporté; **to ~ sth off** enlever qch de [*table, chair*]; **to ~ sth out of** enlever qch de [*room, house*]; **~ the chair out of the way** enlève la chaise de là; **~ your head, I can't see!** pousse ta tête, je ne vois rien!; **to ~ sth into** transporter qch dans [*room, garden*]; **to ~ sth upstairs/downstairs** monter/descendre qch; **to ~ sth further away/closer** éloigner/rapprocher qch; **to ~ troops to the front** envoyer des troupes au front; **2** (set in motion) [*person*] bouger, remuer [*limb, finger, head*]; [*wind, water, mechanism*] faire bouger [*leaf, branch, wheel, cog*]; **3** (to new location or job) muter [*employee, staff*]; transférer [*office, headquarters*]; **I've asked to be ~d** j'ai demandé à être muté; **4** (to new house, site) déménager [*furniture, belongings, equipment*]; **to ~ house** déménager; **a local firm ~d us** une entreprise locale a fait notre déménagement; **5** (affect) émouvoir [*person*]; **to be ~d by sth** être ému par qch; **~d to tears** ému aux larmes; **6** (prompt, motivate) **to ~ sb to/to do** [*circumstance*] amener qn à/à faire; **he was ~d to act by the letter** la lettre l'a incité à agir; **I felt ~d to protest** j'ai senti que je devais protester; **7** (propose) proposer [*amendment, adjournment*]; **to ~ that the matter (should) be put to the vote** proposer que la question soit soumise au vote; **8** (sell, shift) vendre [*goods, stock*].

IV *vi* **1** (stir, not stay still) [*person, branch, earth*] bouger; [*lips*] remuer; **don't ~!** ne bouge pas!; **it won't ~** cela ne bouge pas; **will you please ~!** veux-tu te pousser?; **I can't ~ for plants in here** GB je ne peux pas bouger ici, tellement il y a de plantes; **you can't ~ for tourists in town** GB on ne peut rien faire en ville, tellement il y a de touristes; **2** (proceed, travel) [*vehicle*] rouler; [*person*] avancer; [*procession, army*] être en marche; **we were moving at about 65 kilometres an hour** nous roulions à environ 65 kilomètres à l'heure; **we'd better keep moving** nous ferions mieux de continuer; **we must get things moving** fig nous devons faire avancer les choses; **things are starting to ~ on the job front** les choses commencent à avancer côté travail; **go on, get moving!** allez, avance!; **to ~ into** entrer dans; **to ~ out of** sortir de; **we are moving into a new era in science** nous entrons dans une nouvelle ère de la science; **to ~ along/across** avancer le long de/à travers; **his fingers ~d rapidly over the keys** ses doigts couraient sur les touches; **to ~ back** reculer; **to ~ forward** s'avancer; **to ~ away** s'éloigner; **she has ~d away from this view** elle a changé d'avis; **to ~ away from the window** s'écarter de la fenêtre; **to ~ up** monter; **to ~ down** descendre; **public opinion has ~d to the right** l'opinion publique a glissé vers la droite; **3**○ (proceed quickly) **that cat can really ~!** ce chat est très vif!; **that traffic cop's**○ **really moving!** t'as vu comme il bombe ce motard○!; **4** (change home, location) [*person, family, firm, shop*] déménager; **to ~ to** s'installer à [*countryside, Paris*]; s'installer en [*Scotland, France*]; **to ~ to a bigger/smaller house** s'installer dans une maison plus grande/plus petite; **to ~ to Avenue Gambetta/Oxford Street** s'installer avenue Gambetta/dans Oxford Street; **to ~ back to England** se réinstaller en Angleterre; **5** (change job) être muté; **to ~ to** être muté à [*accounts, different department*]; **6** (act) agir; **to ~ on** intervenir sur [*problem, question*]; **to ~ to do** intervenir pour faire; **he ~d swiftly to deny the allegations** il s'est empressé de démentir les allégations; **7** Games [*player*] jouer; [*piece*] se déplacer; **8** Comm (sell, be sold) se vendre; **this line is moving fast** ces articles se vendent bien.

V○ *v refl* **to ~ oneself** se pousser; **~ yourself!** (get out of way) pousse-toi!; (hurry up) avance!

IDIOMS **to get a ~ on**○ se magner○, se dépêcher; **to make a ~ on sb**○ draguer○ qn; **to ~ with the times** vivre avec son temps; **to put the ~s on sb**○ US faire des avances à qn.

■ **move about, move around**: ¶ **~ about 1** (to different position) [*person*] remuer; [*object*] bouger; **2** (to different home) déménager; ¶ **~ [sb/sth] about** déplacer [*object, furniture*]; **they ~ him around a lot between branches/departments** on le fait souvent changer de succursale/service.

■ **move along**: ¶ **~ along 1** (stop loitering) circuler; (proceed) avancer; (squeeze up) se pousser; **~ along please!** (on bus) avancez un peu dans le fond s'il vous plaît!; **2** fig (progress) **things are moving along nicely** les choses se mettent en place; ¶ **~ [sb/sth] along** faire circuler [*loiterers, crowd*]; faire avancer [*herd, group*].

■ **move away**: ¶ **~ away** (by moving house) déménager; (by leaving scene of activity) partir; **to ~ away from** quitter [*area, accident scene*]; ¶ **~ [sb/sth] away, ~ away [sb/sth]** faire reculer [*crowd*]; déplacer [*obstruction*].

■ **move down**: ¶ **~ down** (in list, hierarchy) descendre; ¶ **~ [sb] down, ~ down [sb] 1** GB Sch faire repasser [qn] au niveau inférieur [*pupil*]; **2** gen (in division, ranking) faire redescendre [*team, player*]; ¶ **~ [sth] down, ~ down [sth]** (to lower shelf etc) mettre [qch] plus bas.

■ **move in**: ¶ **~ in 1** (to house) emménager; **to ~ in with** s'installer avec [*friend, relative*]; aller vivre avec [*lover*]; **2** (advance, attack) [*troops, police, bulldozer*] s'avancer; **to ~ in on** [*police, attackers, demolition men*] s'avancer sur [*person, site*]; [*corporate raider, racketeer*] lancer une opération sur [*market, company*]; **3** (intervene) [*company, government*] intervenir; ¶ **~ [sb] in, ~ in [sb] 1** (place in housing) [*authorities, council*] installer [*family etc*]; **2** (change residence) **a friend helped to ~ me in** un ami m'a aidé à emménager.

■ **move off** [*procession, parade*] partir; [*vehicle*] se mettre en route; [*troops*] se mettre en marche.

■ **move on**: ¶ **~ on 1** [*person, traveller*] se mettre en route; [*vehicle*] repartir; [*time*] passer; **to ~ on to** aller à [*Manchester, Lille etc*]; **to ~ on to a new town** aller dans une autre ville; passer à [*next item*]; **to ~ on to consider sth** passer à qch; **to ~ on to sth better** faire quelque chose de mieux; **let's ~ on** (in discussion) passons au point suivant; **2** (keep moving) [*crowd, traffic*] circuler; **3** (develop) **things have ~d on since** depuis, les choses ont changé; **I'm OK now, I've ~d on** ça va maintenant, c'est du passé; ¶ **~ [sth] on, ~ on [sth]** GB faire avancer [*discussion*]; avancer [*clock hands*]; ¶ **~ [sb] on, ~ on [sb]** GB faire circuler [*busker, street trader*].

■ **move out**: ¶ **~ out** (of house) déménager; (of camp) [*soldiers, tanks*] quitter les lieux; **to ~ out of** quitter [*house, office, area*]; ¶ **~ [sb/sth] out, ~ out [sb/sth]** évacuer [*residents*]; enlever [*object*].

■ **move over**: ¶ **~ over 1** se pousser; **~ over!** pousse-toi; **2** fig (for younger generation etc) céder la place (**for sb** à qn); ¶ **~ [sb/sth] over** déplacer [*person, object*]; **~ it over to the left** déplace-le vers la gauche.

■ **move up**: ¶ **~ up 1** (make room) se pousser; **2** (be promoted) [*employee*] recevoir une promotion; **to ~ up to second place** (in list, chart) passer à la seconde place; **to ~ up to the first division** passer en première division; ¶ **~ [sb] up, ~ up [sb] 1** GB Sch faire passer [qn] au niveau supérieur [*pupil*]; **2** Sport (into higher league, division) faire monter [*team, player*]; ¶ **~ [sth] up** (to higher shelf etc) mettre [qch] plus haut.

moveable *adj* = **movable**.

movement /ˈmuːvmənt/ *n* **1** (of person, dancer, head, wave, vehicle, machine part) mouvement *m*; (of hand, arm) geste *m*; **an upward/downward ~** un mouvement ascendant/descendant; **a graceful/sudden ~** (of arm) un geste gracieux/brusque; **to watch sb's ~s** surveiller les faits et gestes de qn; **2** fig (in prices, market, situation) mouvement *m*; **very little ~ on the stock exchange/the political front** très peu de mouvement à la Bourse/sur le front politique; **an upward/downward ~ in prices** une augmentation/diminution des prix; **a ~ towards liberalization** une évolution vers la libéralisation; **a ~ away from marriage** une tendance à rejeter le mariage; **3** (organization, group) mouvement *m* (**for** en faveur de); **mass ~** mouvement de masse; **the trade union ~** le mouvement syndicaliste; **4** Mus mouvement *m*; **in three ~s** en trois mouvements; **5** (transporting) acheminement *m* (**of** de; **by** par); **6** (circulation) circulation *f*; **the free ~ of goods** la libre circulation des marchandises; **7** Tech (of clock, watch) mouvement *m*; **8** Med (of bowels) selles *fpl*; **to have a ~** aller à la selle.

mover /ˈmuːvə(r)/ ▶ 1692 *n* **1** (who proposes motion) personne *f* qui dépose une motion; **2** US (removal person) déménageur *m*; **3**○ (dancer) **to be a lovely** ou **great (little) ~**○ bien danser.

mover and shaker○ *n* US homme/femme *m/f* d'action.

movie /ˈmuːvɪ/ **I** *n* surtout US film *m*; **to go to a ~** aller voir un film.

II movies *npl* **the ~s** le cinéma; **to go to the ~s** aller au cinéma; **to be in ~s** travailler dans le cinéma.

movie: **~ camera** *n* caméra *f*; **~ director** ▶ 1692 *n* réalisateur/-trice *m/f* de cinéma.

movie film *n* **1** (for camera) pellicule *f* cinématographique; **2**† (movie) film *m*.

movie: **~goer** *n* spectateur/-trice *m/f* de cinéma; **~-maker** ▶ 1692 *n* cinéaste *mf*; **~ mogul** *n* grand/-e producteur/-trice *m/f* de cinéma; **~ producer** *n* producteur/-trice *m/f* de cinéma; **~ star** *n* vedette *f* de cinéma; **~ theater** *n* US cinéma *m*.

moving /ˈmuːvɪŋ/ *adj* **1** [*vehicle, train*] en marche; [*parts, target*] mobile; [*staircase*] roulant; **2** fig (emotional) [*story, scene, speech*] émouvant; **3** fig (motivating) **to be the ~ force** ou **spirit behind sth** être l'âme de qch.

movingly /ˈmuːvɪŋlɪ/ *adv* [*talk, describe, convey*] de façon émouvante.

moving walkway /ˈmuːvɪŋ ˈwɔːkweɪ/ *n* tapis *m* roulant.

mow /məʊ/ **I** *n* **to give the lawn a ~** tondre la pelouse.

II *vtr* (*pp* **~ed, mown**) tondre [*grass, lawn*]; couper [*hay*]; **new-mown** [*grass*] fraîchement tondu; [*hay*] fraîchement coupé.

■ **mow down**: **~ down [sb], ~ [sb] down** faucher [*person*].

mower /ˈməʊə(r)/ *n* **1** (machine) tondeuse *f* à gazon; **2** (person) faucheur/-euse *m/f*.

mowing /ˈməʊɪŋ/ *n* (of lawn) tonte *f*; (of hay) fauchage *m*.

mown /məʊn/ *pp* ▶ **mow**.

Mozambican /ˌməʊzæmˈbiːkən/ ▶ 1486 **I** *n* Mozambicain/-e *m/f*.

II *adj* mozambicain.

Mozambique /ˌməʊzæm'bi:k/ ▶**1131** *pr n* Mozambique *m.*

Mozart /'məʊtsɑ:t/ *pr n* Mozart.

MP *n* **1** GB (*abrév* = **Member of Parliament**) député *m*; **2** *abrév* ▶**military policeman**.

mpg *n* (*abrév* = **miles per gallon**) miles *mpl* au gallon; GB **35 ~** 8 litres aux cent; US **30 ~** 8 litres aux cent.

mph *n* (*abrév* = **miles per hour**) miles *mpl* à l'heure; **to travel at 50 ~** rouler à 80 km/h.

MPhil *n* Univ (*abrév* = **Master of Philosophy**) diplôme *m* supérieur de lettres et sciences humaines.

MPS *n* GB (*abrév* = **Member of the Pharmaceutical Society**) *titre de pharmacien.*

Mr /'mɪstə(r)/ ▶**1268** *n* (*pl* **Messrs**) **1** (title for man) M., Monsieur; **~ Gwyn Jones** M. Gwyn Jones; **I saw ~ Taylor** j'ai vu M. Taylor; **good morning, ~ Miller** bonjour, Monsieur Miller; **~ Right** le Prince Charmant; **2** (title for position) **~ President** Monsieur le Président; **~ Big**○ le grand chef.

MRC *n* GB *abrév* ▶**Medical Research Council**.

MRCP *n* GB (*abrév* = **Member of the Royal College of Physicians**) *titre de médecin.*

MRCS *n* GB (*abrév* = **Member of the Royal College of Surgeons**) *titre de chirurgien.*

MRCVS *n* GB (*abrév* = **Member of the Royal College of Veterinary Surgeons**) *titre de médecin vétérinaire.*

Mrs /'mɪsɪz/ ▶**1268** *n* Mme, Madame; **~ Sue Clark** Mme Sue Clark; **~ John Clark** sout Mme John Clark; **I saw ~ Evans** j'ai vu Madame Evans; **good morning, ~ Martin** bonjour, Madame Martin.

Ms /mɪz, məz/ ▶**1268** *n* ≈ Mme.

■ Note *Ms* est l'équivalent féminin de *Mr* (M.) et permet de s'adresser à une femme dont on connaît le nom sans préciser sa situation de famille: Ms Brown.

MS *n* **1** *abrév écrite* = **manuscript**; **2** *abrév* ▶**multiple sclerosis**; **3** US Post *abrév écrite* = **Mississippi**; **4** US Univ *abrév* ▶**Master of Science**.

MSc *n* Univ *abrév* ▶**Master of Science**.

MST *n* US *abrév* ▶**Mountain Standard Time**.

Mt (*abrév écrite* = **Mount**) Mt.

MT *n* **1** *abrév* ▶**machine translation**; **2** US Post *abrév écrite* = **Montana**.

mth *abrév écrite* = **month**.

much /mʌtʃ/

■ **Note** When *much* is used as an adverb, it is translated by *beaucoup*: *it's much longer* = c'est beaucoup plus long; *she doesn't talk much* = elle ne parle pas beaucoup.
– For particular usages, see I below.
– When *much* is used as a pronoun, it is usually translated by *beaucoup*: *there is much to learn* = il y a beaucoup à apprendre. However, in negative sentences *grand-chose* is also used: *I didn't learn much* = je n'ai pas beaucoup appris *or* je n'ai pas appris grand-chose.
– When *much* is used as a quantifier, it is translated by *beaucoup de*: *they don't have much money* = ils n'ont pas beaucoup d'argent.
– For particular usages see III below.

I *adv* **1** (to a considerable degree) beaucoup; **~ smaller/happier** beaucoup plus petit/content (**than** que); **they're not ~ cheaper than the originals** ils ne sont pas beaucoup moins chers que les originaux; **~ more interesting** beaucoup or bien plus intéressant; **the film was ~ better than expected** le film était bien meilleur que prévu; **it's ~ better organized** c'est beaucoup mieux organisé; **they're getting ~ less demanding** ils deviennent beaucoup moins exigeants; **the shoes are ~ too expensive** les chaussures sont beaucoup trop chères; **it's ~ too dangerous** c'est beaucoup trop dangereux; **he doesn't ~ care for them** il ne les aime pas beaucoup; **I didn't ~ like what I saw** je n'ai pas beaucoup aimé ce que j'ai vu; **she doesn't worry ~ about it** ça ne l'inquiète pas beaucoup; **we'd ~ rather stay here** nous préférerions de beaucoup rester ici; **the meeting has been ~ criticized** on a beaucoup critiqué la réunion; **they are ~ to be pitied** ils méritent qu'on ait pitié d'eux; **~ loved by her friends** très aimée de ses amis; **your comments would be ~ appreciated** tous vos commentaires seront les bienvenus; **he's not ~ good at Latin/at tennis** il n'est pas très bon en latin/au tennis; **he's not ~ good at doing** il n'est pas très doué pour faire; **does it hurt ~?** est-ce que ça fait très mal?; **it's ~ the more interesting of the two studies** c'est de loin la plus intéressante des deux études; **she's ~ the best teacher here** elle est de loin le meilleur professeur ici; **~ to our annoyance, they didn't phone back** ils n'ont pas rappelé, ce qui nous a beaucoup vexés ; **~ to my surprise** à ma grande surprise; **2** (often) beaucoup, souvent; **we don't go out ~** nous ne sortons pas beaucoup; **they didn't see each other ~** ils ne se voyaient pas beaucoup; **she doesn't talk ~ about the past** elle ne parle pas beaucoup du passé; **do you go to concerts ~?** est-ce que tu vas souvent au concert?; **a ~ married film star** une vedette de cinéma qui s'est remariée plusieurs fois; **3** (approximately, nearly) plus ou moins, à peu près; **to be ~ the same** être à peu près pareil (**as** que); **his condition is ~ the same as yesterday** son état est plus ou moins or à peu près le même qu'hier; **it's pretty ~ like driving a car** c'est plus ou moins la même chose que de conduire une voiture; **he behaved ~ the way the others did** il s'est comporté plus ou moins comme les autres; **in ~ the same way** à peu près de la même façon (**as** que); **~ the same is true of China** la situation est à peu près la même en Chine; **4** (specifying degree to which something is true) **too ~** trop; **you worry/talk too ~** tu t'inquiètes/parles trop; **very ~** (a lot) beaucoup; (absolutely) tout à fait; **he misses you very ~** tu lui manques beaucoup; **I'd appreciate it very ~ if** j'apprécierais beaucoup que (+ *subj*); **thanks very ~** merci beaucoup; **we enjoyed ourselves very ~** nous nous sommes beaucoup amusés; **she's very ~ like her mother** elle ressemble beaucoup à sa mère; **it's very ~ the norm** c'est tout à fait la norme; **I felt very ~ the foreigner** je me sentais tout à fait étranger; **so ~** tellement; **I wanted so ~ to meet you** j'avais tellement envie de vous rencontrer; **it hurts so ~** ça fait tellement mal; **it's so ~ better** c'est tellement mieux; **he hates flying so ~ that he prefers to take the boat** il déteste tellement l'avion qu'il préfère prendre le bateau; **thanks so ~ for** merci beaucoup pour; **as ~** autant (**as** que); **I like them as ~ as you (do)** je les aime autant que toi; **she doesn't worry as ~ as before** elle ne s'inquiète pas autant qu'avant; **they hated each other as ~ as ever** ils se détestaient toujours autant; **she is as ~ entitled to a visa as you** elle a autant droit à un visa que toi; **they were as ~ a part of village life as the farmers** ils faisaient autant partie de la vie du village que les fermiers; **he wasn't sure and said as ~** il n'était pas sûr et il l'a dit; **I thought as ~** c'est bien ce qui me semblait; **however ~** même si; **you'll have to accept the decision however ~ you disagree** il va falloir que tu acceptes la décision même si tu n'es pas d'accord ; **I couldn't cry out however ~ it hurt** je ne pouvais pas crier même si ça me faisait très mal; **5** (emphatic: setting up a contrast) **not so ~ X as Y** moins X que Y, plus Y que X; **it wasn't so ~ a warning as a threat** c'était moins un avertissement qu'une menace, c'était plus une menace qu'un avertissement; **the discovery wasn't so ~ shocking as depressing** la découverte était moins choquante que déprimante; **it doesn't annoy me so ~ as make me wonder** ça m'agace moins que ça ne me surprend.

II *pron* **1** (a great deal) beaucoup; (in negative sentences) grand-chose; **do you have ~ left?** est-ce qu'il vous en reste beaucoup?; **did he earn ~?** est-ce qu'il a gagné beaucoup?; **we have ~ to learn** nous avons beaucoup à apprendre (**from** de); **we didn't eat ~** nous n'avons pas mangé grand-chose; **there isn't ~ to do** il n'y a pas grand-chose à faire; **he doesn't have ~ to say** il n'a pas grand-chose à dire; **there isn't ~ one can do to prevent it** il n'y a pas grand-chose à faire pour empêcher ça; **he doesn't have ~ to complain about** il n'a pas à se plaindre; **it leaves ~ to be desired** ça laisse (vraiment) à désirer; **there's ~ to be said for** beaucoup de choses plaident en faveur de [*plan, country life, job-sharing*]; **~ of** une grande partie de; **~ of the difficulty lies in...** une grande partie de la difficulté réside dans...; **~ of the meeting was spent discussing...** une grande partie de la réunion a été consacrée à discuter...; **~ of their work involves...** une grande partie de leur travail consiste à...; **~ of what remains is useless** une grande partie de ce qui reste est inutile; **~ of the resentment is due to** le ressentiment vient en grande partie de; **I don't see ~ of them now** je ne les vois plus beaucoup maintenant; **to make ~ of sth** (focus on) insister sur qch; (understand) comprendre qch; **the report made ~ of the scandal** le rapport insistait sur le scandale or faisait grand cas du scandale; **I couldn't make ~ of her last book** je n'ai pas compris grand-chose à son dernier livre; **2** (expressing a relative amount, degree) **so ~** tant; **they are willing to pay so ~ per vehicle** ils sont prêts à payer tant par véhicule; **we'd eaten so ~ that** nous avions tant mangé que; **she spends so ~ of her life abroad** elle passe une très grande partie de sa vie à l'étranger; **she spends so ~ of her life abroad that** elle passe une si grande partie de sa vie à l'étranger que; **so ~ of her work is gloomy** il y a une grande partie de son œuvre qui est sombre; **so ~ of the earth is polluted** la terre est tellement polluée; **so ~ of the time, it's a question of patience** la plupart du temps c'est une question de patience; **too ~** trop; **it costs too ~** c'est trop cher; **you eat too ~** tu manges trop; **it's too ~!** lit c'est trop!; (in protest) c'en est trop!; **it's too ~ of a strain** c'est trop éprouvant; **she was too ~ of an egotist to do** elle était trop égoïste pour faire; **I couldn't eat all that, it's too ~ for me!** je ne pourrais jamais manger tout ça, c'est trop pour moi!; **the heat/the work was too ~ for them** ils n'ont pas pu supporter la chaleur/le travail; **the measures proved too ~ for them** ils n'ont pas pu tolérer les mesures; **he was too ~ for his opponent** il était trop fort pour son adversaire; **I bought about this ~** j'en ai acheté à peu près ça; **he's read this ~ already** il a déjà lu tout ça; **I'll say this ~ for him, he's honest** il a au moins ça pour lui, il est honnête; **this ~ is certain, we'll have no choice** une chose est certaine, nous n'aurons pas le choix; **twice as ~** deux fois autant or plus; **if we had half as ~ as you** si nous avions la moitié de ce que tu as; **I'll need half as ~ again** il me faudra encore la moitié de ça; **as ~ as possible** autant que possible; **they paid as ~ as we did** ils ont payé autant que nous; **is it as ~ as that?** est-ce que ça fait autant que ça?; **I enjoy nature as ~ as the next person** j'apprécie la nature autant que n'importe qui; **it can cost as ~ as £50** ça peut coûter jusqu'à 50 livres sterling ; **it was as**

~ as I could do not to laugh il a fallu que je me retienne pour ne pas rire; **as ~ as to say**... d'un air de dire...; **how ~?** combien?; **how ~ did you pay for it?** combien est-ce que tu l'as payé?; **tell them how ~ you won** dis-leur combien tu as gagné; **how ~ do they know?** qu'est-ce qu'ils savent au juste?; **he never knew how ~ we missed him** il n'a jamais su à quel point or combien il nous a manqué; **do you know how ~ this means to me?** est-ce que tu sais à quel point or combien c'est important pour moi?; **3** (focusing on limitations, inadequacy) **it's not** ou **nothing ~** ce n'est pas grand-chose; **it's not up to ~** GB ça ne vaut pas grand-chose; **he 's not ~ to look at** il n'est pas très beau; **she doesn't think ~ of him** elle n'a pas très bonne opinion de lui; **she doesn't think ~ of it** elle n'en pense pas beaucoup de bien; **I'm not ~ of a letter-writer/reader** je n'aime pas beaucoup écrire des lettres/lire; **it's not ~ of a film** ce n'est pas un bon film; **it wasn't ~ of a life** ce n'était pas une vie; **it wasn't ~ of a holiday for us** ce n'était vraiment pas des vacances pour nous; **that's not ~ of a consolation!** ça ne me console pas tellement!; **I'm not ~ of a one for cooking**○ la cuisine ce n'est pas mon fort○.
III *quantif* beaucoup de; **have you got ~ money/work?** est-ce que tu as beaucoup d'argent/de travail?; **I haven't got (very) ~ time** je n'ai pas beaucoup de temps; **we didn't get ~ support** nous n'avons pas eu beaucoup de soutien; **it doesn't make ~ sense** ça n'a pas beaucoup de sens; **there isn't ~ wine left** il ne reste pas beaucoup de vin; **does he watch ~ TV?** est-ce qu'il regarde beaucoup la télé○?; **she didn't speak ~ English** elle parlait peu anglais; **too ~ energy** trop d'énergie; **to spend too ~ money** dépenser trop d'argent; **we don't have too ~ time** nous n'avons pas beaucoup de temps; **don't use so ~ salt** ne mets pas tant de sel; **why does he make so ~ noise?** pourquoi fait-il tant de bruit?; **I spent so ~ time doing** j'ai passé tant de temps à faire; **she gets so ~ enjoyment out of the radio** elle a tant de plaisir à écouter la radio; **we paid twice as ~ money** nous avons payé deux fois plus d'argent; **how ~ time have we got left?** combien de temps nous reste-t-il?; **how ~ liquid does it contain?** combien de liquide est-ce que ça contient?
IV **much+** (*dans composés*) **~-loved/-respected** très apprécié/respecté; **~-maligned** tant décrié; **~-needed** indispensable.
V **much as** *conj phr* bien que (+ *subj*); **~ as he needed the money, he wouldn't beg for it** il avait vraiment besoin de cet argent et pourtant il ne pouvait se résoudre à mendier; **~ as we regret our decision we have no choice** bien que nous regrettions or nous avons beau regretter notre décision, nous n'avons pas le choix.
VI **much less** *conj phr* encore moins; **I've never seen him ~ less spoken to him** je n'ai jamais eu l'occasion de le voir encore moins de lui parler.
VII **so much as** *adv phr* **without so ~ as saying goodbye/as an apology** sans même dire au revoir/s'excuser; **if you so ~ as move/sigh** si tu fais le moindre mouvement/pousses le moindre soupir; **they can be imprisoned for so ~ as criticizing the regime** ils peuvent être emprisonnés ne serait-ce que pour avoir critiqué le régime.
IDIOMS **~ wants more** plus on en a plus on en veut; **there isn't ~ in** GB ou **to** US **it** (in contest, competition) ils se suivent de près; **there isn't ~ in it for us** (to our advantage) ça ne va pas nous apporter grand-chose; **she's late again? that's a bit ~!** elle est encore en retard? elle exagère!; ▶ **so**.

muchness /ˈmʌtʃnɪs/ *n*: IDIOMS **they're much of a ~** il n'y a pas beaucoup de différence entre eux.

mucilage /ˈmjuːsɪlɪdʒ/ *n* mucilage *m*.

mucilaginous /ˌmjuːsɪˈlædʒɪnəs/ *adj* (all contexts) mucilagineux/-euse.

muck /mʌk/ *n* **1** lit (filth, rubbish) saletés *fpl*; (mud) boue *f*; (manure) fumier *m*; **cat/dog ~** crotte *f* de chat/de chien; **bird ~** fiente *f* d'oiseau; **2**○ fig (book, film etc) bêtises *fpl*; (food) saletés *fpl*.
■ **muck about**○, **muck around**○: ¶ **~ about** (fool about) faire l'imbécile; (potter about) traîner; **to ~ about with** traficoter○ [*appliance*]; toucher à [*object*]; ¶ **~ [sb] about** se ficher de.
■ **muck in** (share task) mettre la main à la pâte○; (share accommodation) partager le gîte et le couvert (**with** avec).
■ **muck out**: **~ out [sth]** nettoyer [*cowshed, stable*].
■ **muck up**: **~ up [sth] 1** (spoil) chambouler○ [*plans*]; cochonner○, bâcler [*task*]; louper○ [*exam, interview, opportunity*]; **2** salir [*clothes, carpet*].

muckraker /ˈmʌkreɪkə(r)/ *n* péj dénicheur/-euse *m/f* de scandales.

muckraking /ˈmʌkreɪkɪŋ/ I *n* course *f* au scandale.
II *adj* [*story*] infâme; [*campaign*] de diffamation.

muck-up○ /ˈmʌkup/ *n* gâchis *m*.

mucky○ /ˈmʌkɪ/ *adj* (muddy) boueux/-euse; (dirty) sale; **what ~ weather!** quel sale temps!; **you ~ pup**○! petit cochon○!

mucous /ˈmjuːkəs/ *adj* muqueux/-euse.

mucous membrane *n* (membrane *f*) muqueuse *f*.

mucus /ˈmjuːkəs/ *n* mucus *m*, mucosités *fpl*.

mud /mʌd/ *n* boue *f*; **to sink in the ~** s'enfoncer dans la boue.
IDIOMS **here's ~ in your eye**○! à la tienne, Étienne○!; **his name is ~** ç'en est fait de sa réputation; **it's as clear as ~**○! c'est d'un clair○!; **to drag sb's name in** ou **through the ~** traîner qn dans la boue; **to sling ~ at sb** couvrir qn de boue.

mud: **~bank** *n* banc *m* de vase; **~ bath** *n* (for person, animal) bain *m* de boue; fig bourbier *m*.

muddle /ˈmʌdl/ I *n* **1** (mess) ¢ (of papers) pagaille○ *f*; (of string) embrouillamini *m*; fig (in administration) confusion *f*; **my documents are in a ~** mes documents sont en pagaille○; **the clients' records have got into a terrible ~** les dossiers des clients sont dans une pagaille○ épouvantable; **what a ~!** quelle pagaille○!; **your financial affairs are in a ~** vos affaires financières sont désordonnées; **2** (mix-up) malentendu *m*; **there was a ~ over my hotel reservation** il y a eu un malentendu à propos de ma réservation d'hôtel; **3** (mental confusion) **to be in a ~** avoir les idées embrouillées; **to be in a ~ over** ou **about** avoir les idées embrouillées à propos de; **to get into a ~** s'embrouiller.
II *vtr* = **muddle up**.
■ **muddle along** vivoter○.
■ **muddle through** se débrouiller.
■ **muddle up**: ¶ **~ [sth] up, ~ up [sth]** (disorder) semer la pagaille○ dans [*papers*]; emmêler [*string*]; ¶ **~ [sb] up** (confuse) embrouiller les idées de [*person*]; **to get sth ~d up** s'embrouiller dans qch [*dates, names*]; **I got you ~d up with Martin** je t'ai confondu avec Martin.

muddled /ˈmʌdld/ *adj* **1** (confused) **to be ~** [*person*] avoir l'esprit confus; **2** (unclear) [*account, story, thinking*] confus.

muddle-headed /ˌmʌdlˈhedɪd/ *adj* [*person*] aux idées confuses (*after n*); [*attempt, idea, plan*] confus; **he's rather ~** il est assez confus.

muddler /ˈmʌdlə(r)/ *n* esprit *m* brouillon.

muddy /ˈmʌdɪ/ I *adj* [*hand*] couvert de boue; [*shoe, garment*] crotté; [*road, water, coffee*] boueux/-euse; [*pink*] sale; [*green, yellow*] terne; [*complexion*] terreux/-euse.
II *vtr* couvrir [qch] de boue [*hands*]; crotter [*shoes, clothes*]; troubler [*water*].
IDIOMS **to ~ the waters** brouiller les pistes.

mud: **~ flap** *n* pare-boue *m inv*; **~ flat** *n* Geog laisse *f*; **~guard** *n* garde-boue *m inv*; **~ hut** *n* hutte *f* de terre; **~pack** *n* Cosmet masque *m* de beauté à l'argile; **~ pie** *n* pâté *m* de terre; **~slide** *n* éboulement *m* de terrain; **~-slinging** *n* dénigrement *m*.

muesli /ˈmjuːzlɪ/ *n* GB müesli *m*.

muezzin /muːˈezɪn, US mjuː-/ *n* muezzin *m*.

muff /mʌf/ I *n* **1** (mitten) manchon *m*; **2**● US (vulva) chatte● *f*.
II○ *vtr* louper○ [*shot, catch*]; rater○ [*chance*]; se tromper dans [*lines*].

muffin /ˈmʌfɪn/ *n* **1** GB muffin *m* (*petit pain plat et rond*); **2** US (cupcake) petite génoise *f* individuelle.

muffle /ˈmʌfl/ I *vtr* **1** (wrap up) emmitoufler [*person*] (**in** dans); **~d in furs** emmitouflé dans des fourrures; **2** (mute) assourdir [*bell, drum*]; étouffer [*voice, laughter*]; fig **to ~ the voice of protest** étouffer les protestations.
II **muffled** *pp adj* [*cough, giggle*] étouffé; [*bell, drum*] assourdi; **a ~d thump** ou **thud** un bruit sourd.

muffler /ˈmʌflə(r)/ *n* **1** Fashn cache-nez *m inv*; **2** US Aut silencieux *m*.

mufti /ˈmʌftɪ/ *n* **1** Relig mufti *m*; **2** Mil tenue *f* civile; **to wear ~** s'habiller en civil; **in ~** en pékin○.

mug /mʌg/ I *n* **1** (for tea, coffee) grande tasse *f*; (for beer) chope *f*; **2** (contents) (also **~ful**) grande tasse *f* (**of** de); **3**○ (face) gueule◑ *f*; **what an ugly ~!** quelle sale gueule◑!; **4** GB (fool) poire○ *f*; **it's a ~'s game** c'est un attrape-nigaud; **5** US (photo) = **mug shot**; **6**○ (thug) gangster *m*.
II *vtr* (*p prés etc* **-gg-**) agresser; **to be mugged** se faire agresser.
III *vi* US (*p prés etc* **-gg-**) faire des grimaces.
■ **mug up**○ GB: **~ up [sth]** potasser○ [*subject*].

mugger /ˈmʌgə(r)/ *n* agresseur *m*.

mugging /ˈmʌgɪŋ/ *n* **1 C** (attack) agression *f*; **2 ¢** (crime) agressions *fpl*; **~ is on the increase** les agressions deviennent plus fréquentes.

muggins○ /ˈmʌgɪnz/ *n* hum GB **~ here will pay the bill** c'est ma pomme○ qui paiera l'addition.

muggy /ˈmʌgɪ/ *adj* [*weather*] lourd; [*room, day*] étouffant; **it's ~ in here** on étouffe ici.

mugho pine /ˌmjuːgəʊˈpaɪn/ *n* pin *m* mugho.

mug shot *n* **1** (of criminal) photo *f* de criminel; **2** hum photo *f*.

mugwump /ˈmʌgwʌmp/ *n* US Pol indépendant/-e *m/f*.

Muhammad /məˈhæmɪd/ *pr n* Mahomet.

mujaheddin, mujahedeen /ˌmuːdʒəˈdiːn/ *npl* **the ~** les Moudjahidin *mpl*.

mulatto /mjuːˈlætəʊ, US məˈl-/ I *n* mulâtre/-esse *m/f*.
II *adj* mulâtre.

mulberry /ˈmʌlbrɪ, US -berɪ/ ▶ **1104** I *n* **1** (tree) mûrier *m*; **2** (fruit) mûre *f*; **3** (colour) lie-de-vin *f inv*.
II *modif* [*juice, wine*] de mûres; [*leaf*] de mûrier.

mulch /mʌltʃ/ I *n* paillis *m*.
II *vtr* pailler.

mule /mjuːl/ *n* **1** (animal) mulet *m*, mule *f*; **2**○ (stubborn person) tête *f* de mule; **3** (slipper) mule *f*; **4** Tex mule-jenny *f*; **5**○ (also **drug ~**) (person) mule *f*.
IDIOMS **as stubborn as a ~** têtu comme une mule or une bourrique.

mule: **~ driver** ▶ **1692** *n* muletier/-ière *m/f*; **~ path** *n* chemin *m* muletier.

muleteer† /ˌmjuːlɪ'tɪə(r)/ ▶1692 *n* muletier/-ière *m/f*.
mulish /'mjuːlɪʃ/ *adj* entêté.
mulishness /'mjuːlɪʃnɪs/ *n* entêtement *m*.
mull /mʌl/ **I** *vtr* Culin chauffer et épicer [*wine*].
II mulled *pp adj* Culin [*cider, wine*] chaud.
■ **mull over**: **~ over [sth], ~ [sth] over** retourner [qch] dans sa tête.
mullah /'mʌlə/ *n* mollah *m*.
mullet /'mʌlɪt/ *n* (*pl* **~**) (red) rouget *m*; (grey) mulet *m*.
mulligan○ /'mʌlɪgən/ *n* (also **~ stew**) US Culin ragoût *m* fourre-tout○.
mulligatawny /ˌmʌlɪgə'tɔːnɪ/ *n* (also **~ soup**) soupe *f* au curry.
mullion /'mʌlɪən/ *n* meneau *m*.
mullioned /'mʌlɪənd/ *adj* à meneaux.
multi+ /'mʌltɪ/ (*dans composés*) multi-.
multi-access /ˌmʌltɪ'ækses/ *n* Comput accès *m* multiple.
multicellular /ˌmʌltɪ'seljʊlə(r)/ *adj* pluricellulaire.
multichannel /ˌmʌltɪ'tʃænl/ *adj* [*television*] à canaux multiples; [*reception*] de plusieurs chaînes.
multicoloured GB, **multicolored** US /ˌmʌltɪ'kʌləd/ *adj* multicolore.
multicultural /ˌmʌltɪ'kʌltʃərəl/ *adj* multiculturel/-elle.
multiculturalism /ˌmʌltɪ'kʌltʃərɪzəm/ *n* multiculturalisme *m*.
multidimensional /ˌmʌltɪdaɪ'menʃənl/ *adj* multidimensionnel/-elle.
multidirectional /ˌmʌltɪdaɪ'rekʃənl, -dɪ'rek-/ *adj* multidirectionnel/-elle.
multidisciplinary /ˌmʌltɪdɪsɪ'plɪnərɪ, US -nerɪ/ *adj* Sch, Univ pluridisciplinaire.
multidisciplinary system *n* Sch, Univ pluridisciplinarité *f*.
multi-ethnic /ˌmʌltɪ'eθnɪk/ *adj* multiethnique.
multi-faceted /ˌmʌltɪ'fæsɪtɪd/ *adj* **1** (varied) [*career, character, personality*] à multiples facettes; **2** lit (gemstone) facetté.
multifarious /ˌmʌltɪ'feərɪəs/ *adj* d'une grande variété, divers.
multiflora /ˌmʌltɪ'flɔːrə/ *n, adj* multiflore *f*.
multiform /'mʌltɪfɔːm/ *adj* multiforme.
multi-function /ˌmʌltɪ'fʌŋkʃn/ *adj* [*watch, calculator, computer*] multifonctions *inv*.
multigym /'mʌltɪdʒɪm/ *n* appareil *m* de musculation (*constitué d'un jeu d'haltères*).
multihull /'mʌltɪhʌl/ *n* multicoque *m*.
multilateral /ˌmʌltɪ'lætərəl/ *adj* **1** Pol [*talks, agreement*] multilatéral; **2** Math [*shape*] à plusieurs côtés.
multilateralist /ˌmʌltɪ'lætərəlɪst/ *n, adj* Pol multilatéraliste (*mf*).
multilevel /ˌmʌltɪ'levl/ *adj* **1** [*parking, access, analysis*] à plusieurs niveaux; [*building, complex*] de plusieurs étages; **2** Comput multiniveaux *inv*.
multilingual /ˌmʌltɪ'lɪŋgwəl/ *adj* plurilingue.
multilingualism /ˌmʌltɪ'lɪŋgwəlɪzəm/ *n* plurilinguisme *m*.
multimedia /ˌmʌltɪ'miːdɪə/ *adj* (all contexts) multimédia *inv*.
multi-million /ˌmʌltɪ'mɪljən/ *adj* de plusieurs millions; **~ pound/dollar** de plusieurs millions de livres/de dollars.
multimillionaire /ˌmʌltɪˌmɪljə'neə(r)/ *n* multimillionnaire *mf*.
multi-million-pound /ˌmʌltɪˌmɪljən'paʊnd/ *adj* [*project, deal*] de plusieurs millions de livres.
multi-nation /ˌmʌltɪ'neɪʃn/ *adj* multinational.
multinational /ˌmʌltɪ'næʃənl/ **I** *n* (also **~ company**) multinationale *f*.
II *adj* [*company, corporation, force, agreement*] multinational.
multiparous /mʌl'tɪpərəs/ *adj* multipare.
multipartite /ˌmʌltɪ'pɑːtaɪt/ *adj* **1** Pol [*treaty*] multipartite; **2** [*document*] divisé en plusieurs parties.
multi-party /ˌmʌltɪ'pɑːtɪ/ *adj* Pol [*government, system*] pluripartite.
multiple /'mʌltɪpl/ **I** *n* **1** Math multiple *m* (**of** de); **sold in ~s of six** vendus par six; **2** GB (chain of shops) magasin *m* à succursales multiples; **3** Fin (share) action *f* multiple.
II *adj* (all contexts) multiple.
multiple: **~ birth** *n* naissance *f* multiple; **~ choice** *adj* [*test, question*] à choix multiple; **~ entry visa** *n* visa *m* valable pour plusieurs entrées; **~ fractures** *npl* fractures *fpl* multiples; **~ fruit** *n* infrutescence *f*; **~ injuries** *npl* blessures *fpl* multiples; **~ occupancy** *n*: *occupation d'une maison par plusieurs personnes*; **~ ownership** *n* multipropriété *f*; **~ personality** *n* Psych dissociation *f*; **~ pile-up** *n* carambolage *m*; **~ risk** *adj* [*insurance, policy*] multirisque; **~ sclerosis, MS** ▶1354 *n* sclérose *f* en plaques; **~ stab wounds** *npl* plusieurs coups *mpl* de couteau; **~ store** *n* GB magasin *m* à succursales multiples.
multiplex /'mʌltɪpleks/ **I** *n* **1** Telecom multiplex *m*; **2** US Cin complexe *m* multi-salles.
II *adj* Telecom multiplex *inv*.
III *vtr* Telecom multiplexer.
multiplexer /'mʌltɪpleksə(r)/ *n* Telecom multiplexeur *m*.
multiplexing /'mʌltɪpleksɪŋ/ *n* Telecom multiplexage *m*.
multipliable /'mʌltɪplaɪəbl/, **multiplicable** /'mʌltɪplɪkəbl/ *adj* multipliable (**by** par).
multiplicand /ˌmʌltɪplɪ'kænd/ *n* multiplicande *m*.
multiplication /ˌmʌltɪplɪ'keɪʃn/ *n* gen, Math multiplication *f*; **to do ~** faire des multiplications.
multiplication: **~ sign** *n* signe *m* de multiplication; **~ table** *n* table *f* de multiplication.
multiplicative /ˌmʌltɪ'plɪkətɪv/ *adj* multiplicatif/-ive.
multiplicity /ˌmʌltɪ'plɪsətɪ/ *n* **1** (wide variety) multiplicité *f* (**of** de); **2** (numerousness) multitude *f*.
multiplier /'mʌltɪplaɪə(r)/ *n* (all contexts) multiplicateur *m*.
multiplier effect *n* effet *m* multiplicateur.
multiply /'mʌltɪplaɪ/ **I** *vtr* (all contexts) multiplier (**by** par).
II *vi* **1** Math multiplier; **2** gen, Biol (increase) se multiplier.
multiply handicapped /ˌmʌltɪplɪ'hændɪkæpt/ **I** *n* (+ *v pl*) **the ~** les polyhandicapés *mpl*.
II *adj* polyhandicapé.
multipolar /ˌmʌltɪ'pəʊlə(r)/ *adj* multipolaire.
multiprocessing /ˌmʌltɪ'prəʊsesɪŋ/ *n* Comput multitraitement *m*.
multiprocessor /ˌmʌltɪ'prəʊsesə(r)/ *n* Comput multiprocesseur *m*.
multiprogramming /ˌmʌltɪ'prəʊgræmɪŋ/ *n* Comput multiprogrammation *f*.
multipurpose /ˌmʌltɪ'pɜːpəs/ *adj* [*tool, gadget*] à usages multiples; [*area, organization*] polyvalent.
multiracial /ˌmʌltɪ'reɪʃl/ *adj* multiracial.
multirisk /'mʌltɪrɪsk/ *adj* Insur multirisque.
multisensory /ˌmʌltɪ'sensərɪ/ *adj* multisensoriel/-ielle.
multistage /'mʌltɪsteɪdʒ/ *adj* **1** Aerosp [*rocket*] à plusieurs étages; **2** Tech [*turbine*] à étages multiples; [*compressor*] à plusieurs étages; **3** gen [*process, investigation*] à plusieurs échelons.
multistandard /ˌmʌltɪ'stændəd/ *adj* TV multistandard *inv*.
multistorey /ˌmʌltɪ'stɔːrɪ/ *adj* GB [*building*] à étages; **~ carpark** *n* parking *m* à étages.
multi-talented /ˌmʌltɪ'tæləntɪd/ *adj* [*performer*] aux talents multiples.
multitasking /ˌmʌltɪ'tɑːskɪŋ/ *n* traitement *m* multitâches.
multitrack /'mʌltɪtræk/ *adj* Audio multipiste *inv*.
multitude /'mʌltɪtjuːd, US -tuːd/ *n* multitude *f*.
IDIOMS **to hide** ou **cover a ~ of sins** hum dissimuler la dure réalité.
multitudinous /ˌmʌltɪ'tjuːdɪnəs, US -'tuːdɪnəs/ *adj* innombrable.
multiuser /ˌmʌltɪ'juːzə(r)/ *adj* Comput [*computer*] à utilisateurs multiples; [*system, installation*] multiposte *inv*.
multivalence /ˌmʌltɪ'veɪləns/, **multivalency** /ˌmʌltɪ'veɪlənsɪ/ *n* polyvalence *f*.
multivalent /ˌmʌltɪ'veɪlənt/ *adj* polyvalent.
multivitamin /ˌmʌltɪ'vɪtəmɪn US, mʌltɪ'vaɪtəmɪn/ *n* multivitamine *f*.
mum○ /mʌm/ *n* **1** GB (mother) maman *f*; **2** *abrév* ▶ **chrysanthemum**.
IDIOMS **~'s the word** motus et bouche cousue; **to keep ~** ne pas piper mot.
mumble /'mʌmbl/ **I** *n* marmonnement *m*.
II *vtr* marmonner [*apology, reply*]; **'sorry,' he ~d** 'pardon,' a-t-il marmonné.
III *vi* **to ~ to oneself** marmonner.
mumbo jumbo○ /ˌmʌmbəʊ'dʒʌmbəʊ/ *n* péj **1** (speech, writing) charabia○ *m* pej; **2** (ritual) cérémonial *m*.
mummer /'mʌmə(r)/ *n* Theat mime *mf*.
mummery /'mʌmərɪ/ *n* **1** Theat mimodrame *m*; **2** péj (ceremony) momerie *f*.
mummification /ˌmʌmɪfɪ'keɪʃn/ *n* momification *f*.
mummify /'mʌmɪfaɪ/ **I** *vtr* momifier.
II *vi* se momifier.
mummy /'mʌmɪ/ *n* **1**○ GB (mother) maman *f*; **2** (embalmed body) momie *f*.
mummy's boy *n* GB péj fils *m* à maman.
mumps /mʌmps/ ▶1354 *n* (+ *v sg*) oreillons *mpl*; **to have (the) ~** avoir les oreillons.
munch /mʌntʃ/ *vtr* **1** (eat) [*person*] mâcher [*food*]; [*animal*] mâchonner [*food*]; **to ~ one's way through** [*person, animal*] avaler, dévorer [*food*]; **2** hum [*machine*] avaler [*card, money*].
■ **munch away** mâcher; **to ~ away at sth** croquer (voracement) qch.
■ **munch on**: **~ on [sth]** croquer.
Munchhausen's syndrome /'mʊŋkhaʊzns sɪndrəʊm/ *n* syndrome *m* de Munchhausen.
munchies○ /'mʌntʃiːz/ *npl* amuse-gueule *mpl inv*; **to have the ~** avoir la dalle○.
mundane /mʌn'deɪn/ *adj* terre-à-terre, quelconque.
mung bean /'mʌŋ biːn/ *n* haricot *m* mung.
municipal /mjuː'nɪsɪpl/ *adj* municipal.
municipal court *n* US Jur tribunal *m* d'instance.
municipality /mjuːˌnɪsɪ'pælətɪ/ *n* municipalité *f*.
munificence /mjuː'nɪfɪsns/ *n* sout munificence *f*.
munificent /mjuː'nɪfɪsnt/ *adj* sout [*person*] munificent; [*gift, donation*] généreux/-euse.
muniments /'mjuːnɪmənts/ *npl* Jur titres *mpl* (*de propriété etc*).
munitions /mjuː'nɪʃnz/ **I** *npl* Mil munitions *fpl*.
II *modif* [*factory, industry*] de munitions.
Munro /mən'rəʊ/ *n* (in mountaineering) *sommet au-dessus de 1 000 mètres*.
mural /'mjʊərəl/ **I** *n* gen peinture *f* murale; (in cave) peinture *f* rupestre.
II *adj* [*art, decoration*] mural.
murder /'mɜːdə(r)/ **I** *n* **1** Jur (crime) meurtre *m*; **attempted ~** tentative *f* de meurtre or d'assassinat; **2**○ (hell) **it's ~ in town today!** c'est infernal en ville aujourd'hui○!; **finding a parking space here is sheer ~!** trouver à se garer ici, c'est infernal○!; **to be ~ on the feet/nerves** être un cauchemar pour les pieds/nerfs.

Musical instruments

Playing an instrument

Note the use of de *with* jouer:

to play the piano	= jouer du piano
to play the clarinet	= jouer de la clarinette
but	
to learn the piano	= apprendre le piano

Players

English -ist *is often French* -iste; *the gender reflects the sex of the player.*

a violinist	= un *or* une violoniste
a pianist	= un *or* une pianiste

A phrase with joueur/joueuse de X *is usually safe.*

a piccolo player	= un joueur *or* une joueuse de piccolo
a horn player	= un joueur *or* une joueuse de cor

But note the French when these words are used with good *and* bad *like this:*

he's a good pianist	= il joue bien du piano
he's not a good pianist	= il ne joue pas bien du piano
he's a bad pianist	= il joue mal du piano

As in English, the name of the instrument is often used to refer to its player:

she's a first violin	= elle est premier violon

Music

a piano piece	= un morceau pour piano
a piano arrangement	= un arrangement pour piano
a piano sonata	= une sonate pour piano
a concerto for piano and orchestra	= un concerto pour piano et orchestre
the piano part	= la partie pour piano

Use with another noun

De *is usually correct:*

to take piano lessons	= prendre des leçons de piano
a violin maker	= un fabricant de violons
a violin solo	= un solo de violon
a piano teacher	= un professeur de piano
but note the à *here:*	
a violin case	= un étui à violon

II *modif* [*inquiry, investigation*] sur un meurtre; [*scene, weapon*] du crime; [*squad, trial*] criminel/-elle; **~ hunt** chasse *f* à l'assassin; **~ suspect** meurtrier présumé/meurtrière présumée *m/f*; **~ victim** victime *f* (d'un meurtre); gen [*story, mystery*] policier/-ière.
III *vtr* **1** Jur (kill) lit assassiner (**with** avec); **2**○ fig tuer○; **I could ~ that woman**○! elle est à tuer○, cette femme!; **3**○ (ruin) massacrer○ [*language, piece of music*]; **4**○ (defeat) écraser○, battre [qn] à plates coutures [*team, opponents*]; **5**○ GB (devour) **I could ~ a pint/a sandwich!** je me taperais bien◑ une bière/un sandwich!
IV **murdered** *pp adj* **the ~ed man/woman** la victime.
IDIOMS **to get away with ~** [*dishonest people*] s'en tirer impunément; **that child gets away with ~!** on lui passe tout à cet enfant!; **to scream** ou **yell blue** GB ou **bloody** US **~**○ [*child*] crier comme un putois; [*public figure, press*] s'indigner.

murder case *n* (for police) affaire *f* d'homicide; (for court) procès *m* en homicide.

murder charge *n* inculpation *f* de meurtre; **to face ~s** être inculpé de meurtre.

murderer /'mɜːdərə(r)/ *n* assassin *m*, meurtrier *m*.

murderess /'mɜːdərɪs/ *n* meurtrière *f*.

murder one○ *n* US Jur homicide *m* volontaire (*avec circonstances aggravantes*).

murderous /'mɜːdərəs/ *adj* **1** (deadly) [*regime, expression, look*] assassin; [*attack, deeds, tendencies, thoughts*] meurtrier/-ière; [*intent*] de meurtre; **2**○ (emphatic) [*heat, conditions, pressure*] infernal; **3** (dangerous) [*route, conditions*] meurtrier/-ière.

murderous-looking /ˌmɜːdərəs'lʊkɪŋ/ *adj* [*weapon*] meurtrier/-ière; **he's a ~ individual** il a une tête d'assassin.

murderously /'mɜːdərəslɪ/ *adv* [*jealous, suspicious*] farouchement; [*difficult*] épouvantablement; **~ long** qui n'en finit plus.

murk /mɜːk/ *n* littér (of water, light, sounds) opacité *f*; (of past, feelings) impénétrabilité *f*.

murkiness /'mɜːkɪnɪs/ *n* = **murk**.

murky /'mɜːkɪ/ *adj* **1** (gloomy) [*light, water, colour, hour*] glauque; [*weather*] maussade; [*distance*] opaque; **2** (suspect) [*past, secret*] trouble.

murmur /'mɜːmə(r)/ I *n* **1** (of traffic) bourdonnement *m* (**of** de); (of voices, stream) murmure *m* (**of** de); **2** (expressing reaction) murmure *m*; **a ~ of disapproval/agreement** un murmure de désapprobation/d'approbation; **to obey without a ~** obéir sans murmurer.
II *vtr* (all contexts) murmurer.
III *vi* murmurer.

murmuring /'mɜːmərɪŋ/ I *n* (of voices, stream, sea) murmure *m*.
II **murmurings** *npl* (complaints) murmures *mpl* (**about** contre); (rumours) rumeurs *fpl*.
III *adj* [*stream*] murmurant.

Murphy's Law /'mɜːfɪz lɔː/ *n* loi *f* de l'emmerdement maximum○.

muscat /'mʌskət/ *n* (also **~ grape**) (raisin *m*) muscat *m*.

muscatel /ˌmʌskə'tel/ *n* **1** (wine) (vin *m*) muscat *m*; **2** (grape) (raisin *m*) muscat *m*.

muscle /'mʌsl/ I *n* **1** (in arm, leg etc) muscle *m*; **calf/stomach ~s** muscles du mollet/de l'estomac; **without moving a ~** sans broncher; **don't move a ~!** ne bouge pas!; **2** Anat (tissue) ¢ muscles *mpl*, tissu *m* musculaire; **3** (clout) puissance *f*; **financial/military ~** poids or puissance financière/militaire; **they have no ~** ils ne font pas le poids; **we have the ~ to compete with these firms** nous avons assez de ressources pour être en compétition avec ces entreprises; **to give ~ to** donner du poids à [*argument, threat*].
II *modif* [*exercise, relaxant*] pour les muscles; [*fatigue, injury, tissue*] musculaire.
III *vtr* **to ~ one's way into sth** essayer de s'imposer dans [*discussion*]; se frayer un chemin jusqu'à [*room*].
■ **muscle in**○ s'immiscer (**on** dans); **to ~ in on sb's territory** piétiner les plates-bandes de qn○.

muscle: **~-bound** *adj* [*person*] aux muscles hypertrophiés; **~ car**○ *n* US voiture *f* à moteur gonflé.

muscleman○ /'mʌslmæn/ *n* **1** (strong man) parfois péj monsieur *m* muscle pej; **2** (thug) péj homme *m* de main.

muscle: **~ shirt** *n* US débardeur *m*; **~ strain** *n* élongation *f*.

Muscovite /'mʌskəvaɪt/ I *n* Moscovite *mf*.
II *adj* moscovite.

muscular /'mʌskjʊlə(r)/ *adj* **1** Anat [*disease, tissue*] musculaire; **2** (strong) [*person, body, limbs*] musclé; **to have a ~ build** être tout en muscles; **3** fig (vigorous) [*attitude, pose*] musclé; **~ Christians** GB chrétiens *mpl* zélés.

muscular dystrophy ▶ **1354** *n* dystrophie *f* musculaire.

musculature /'mʌskjʊlətʃə(r)/ *n* musculature *f*.

muse /mjuːz/ I *n* muse *f*.
II *vi* (in silence) songer (**on, over, about** à); (aloud) commenter, l'air songeur.

museum /mjuː'zɪəm/ I *n* musée *m*; **science/natural history/military ~** musée des sciences/d'histoire naturelle/militaire.
II *modif* [*curator, display, collection*] de musée.

museum piece *n* péj ou hum pièce *f* de musée.

mush /mʌʃ/ *n* **1** (of vegetables) bouillie *f*; **boiled to a ~** cuit en bouillie; **2** US (corn porridge) bouillie *f* de farine de maïs; **3**○ (soppiness) mièvrerie *f*.

mushroom /'mʌʃrʊm, -ruːm/ ▶ **1104** I *n* **1** Bot, Culin champignon *m*; **to spring** ou **pop up like ~s** fig pousser comme des champignons; **2** (colour) beige *m* rosé.
II *modif* Culin [*soup, omelette*] aux champignons.
III *adj* (also **~-coloured**) (de couleur) beige rosé *inv*.
IV *vi* [*buildings, towns*] pousser comme des champignons, proliférer; [*group, organization*] se multiplier, proliférer; [*business*] se développer; [*demand, profits*] s'accroître rapidement.

mushroom: **~ cloud** *n* champignon *m* atomique; **~ growth** *n* croissance *f* rapide.

mushrooming /'mʌʃruːmɪŋ, -rʊmɪŋ/ I *n* **1** (activity) **to go ~** aller aux champignons; **2** (spread) prolifération *f*.
II *adj* [*demand*] croissant; [*trade*] florissant; [*payments, deficit*] grandissant.

mushy○ /'mʌʃɪ/ *adj* **1** (pulpy) [*mixture, texture*] pâteux/-euse; [*vegetables*] en bouillie; [*ground*] spongieux/-ieuse; **2** (sentimental) [*film, story*] à l'eau de rose; [*person*] mièvre; **to go (all) ~** faire le sentimental (**over, about** à propos de).

mushy peas *npl* purée *f* de pois.

music /'mjuːzɪk/ I *n* **1** (art, composition) musique *f*; **guitar/piano ~** musique *f* pour guitare/piano; **to write ~** écrire de la musique; **to set sth to ~** mettre qch en musique; **2** (printed) partition *f*; **to read ~** lire la musique.
II *modif* [*exam, lesson, teacher, festival*] de musique; [*appreciation, critic, practice*] musical.
IDIOMS **to face the ~** affronter l'orage; **to be ~ to sb's ears** être doux à l'oreille de qn.

musical /'mjuːzɪkl/ I *n* (also **~ comedy**) comédie *f* musicale.
II *adj* **1** [*person*] (gifted) musicien/-ienne; (interested) mélomane; **they are a very ~ family** ils sont très musiciens dans la famille; **2** [*voice, laughter*] mélodieux/-ieuse; **3** [*accompaniment, director, score*] musical.

musical box *n* GB boîte *f* à musique.

musical chairs ▶ **1282** *npl* chaises *fpl* musicales.

musical: **~ evening** *n* soirée *f* musicale; **~ instrument** ▶ **1481** *n* instrument *m* de musique.

musically /'mjuːzɪklɪ/ *adv* **1** (in a musical way) musicalement; **2** (making a pleasant sound) mélodieusement.

musicassette /ˌmjuːzɪkə'set/ *n* Audio cassette *f* de musique.

music: **~ box** *n* US boîte *f* à musique; **~ case** *n* porte-musique *m inv*; **~ centre** *n* GB chaîne *f* compacte stéréo; **~ college** *n* conservatoire *m* de musique.

music hall GB I *n* music-hall *m*.
II *modif* [*artist*] de music-hall.

musician /mjuːˈzɪʃn/ ▶1692 *n* musicien/-ienne *m/f*.
musicianship /mjuːˈzɪʃnʃɪp/ *n* talent *m* musical, maîtrise *f*.
music lover *n* mélomane *mf*.
musicologist /ˌmjuːzɪˈkɒlədʒɪst/ ▶1692 *n* musicologue *mf*.
musicology /ˌmjuːzɪˈkɒlədʒɪ/ *n* musicologie *f*.
music: **~ stand** *n* pupitre *m* à musique; **~ stool** *n* tabouret *m* de piano; **~ video** *n* clip *m* vidéo.
musing /ˈmjuːzɪŋ/ **I** *n* ¢ songeries *fpl*.
II musings *npl* songeries *fpl*.
III *adj* [*stare, way*] songeur/-euse.
musk /mʌsk/ *n* musc *m*.
musk deer *n* (chevrotain *m*) porte-musc *m inv*.
musket /ˈmʌskɪt/ **I** *n* mousquet *m*.
II *modif* [*fire, drill*] de mousquet.
musketeer /ˌmʌskɪˈtɪə(r)/ *n* Mil, Hist mousquetaire *m*.
musketry /ˈmʌskɪtrɪ/ *n* Mil, Hist tirs *mpl* (de mousquets).
musk: **~melon** *n* cantaloup *m*; **~ ox** *n* bœuf *m* musqué; **~-rat** *n* rat *m* musqué; **~ rose** *n* rose *f* muscade.
musky /ˈmʌskɪ/ *adj* musqué.
Muslim /ˈmʊzlɪm, US ˈmʌzləm/ = **Moslem**.
muslin /ˈmʌzlɪn/ **I** *n* **1** (cloth) mousseline *f*; **2** Culin (for straining) étamine *f*.
II *modif* [*apron, curtain*] en mousseline.
muslin bag *n* Culin nouet *m*.
muso○ /ˈmjuːzəʊ/ *n* musicien/-ienne *m/f*.
musquash /ˈmʌskwɒʃ/ **I** *n* (animal, fur) rat *m* musqué.
II *modif* [*jacket, stole*] en rat musqué.
muss○ /mʌs/ US **I** *n* pagaille○ *f*.
II *vtr* = **muss up**.
■ **muss up**○: **~ [sth] up, ~ up [sth]** décoiffer [*hair*]; chiffonner [*clothing*]; mettre la pagaille○ dans [*papers, belongings*].
mussel /ˈmʌsl/ *n* moule *f*.
mussel bed *n* parc *m* à moules.
must[1] /mʌst, məst/

■ **Note** When *must* indicates obligation or necessity, French tends to use either the verb *devoir* or the impersonal construction *il faut que + subjunctive*: *I must go* = je dois partir, il faut que je parte. For examples and particular usages see I 1 and I 3 below. See also ***have*** II 1 and the related usage note.
– When *must* expresses assumptions or probability, the verb *devoir* is always used: *it must strike you as odd that* = ça doit te sembler bizarre que (+ *subj*). See I 7 below for further examples.
– For the conjugation of *devoir*, see the French verb tables.

I *modal aux* (*nég* **must not, mustn't**) **1** (indicating obligation, prohibition) **you ~ check your rearview mirror before indicating** il faut regarder dans le rétroviseur avant de mettre son clignotant; **the feeding bottles ~ be sterilized** les biberons doivent être stérilisés; **they said she ~ be consulted first** ils ont dit qu'il fallait d'abord la consulter; **~ we really be up by 7 am?** est-ce qu'il faut vraiment qu'on soit levé pour 7 heures?; **you mustn't mention this to anyone** il ne faut en parler à personne, tu ne dois en parler à personne; **all visitors ~ leave the premises** tous les visiteurs doivent quitter les lieux; **the loan ~ be repaid in one year** le prêt est remboursable en un an; **withdrawals ~ not exceed £200** les retraits ne doivent pas dépasser 200 livres sterling; **they begin, as all parents ~, to adapt** comme tous les parents, ils commencent à s'habituer; **it ~ eventually have an effect** ça doit finir par avoir des conséquences; **2** (indicating requirement, condition) **candidates ~ be EC nationals** les candidats doivent être ressortissants d'un des pays de la CEE; **applicants ~ have spent at least one year abroad** les candidats doivent avoir passé au moins un an à l'étranger; **to gain a licence you ~ spend 40 hours in the air** pour obtenir son brevet il faut avoir 40 heures de vol; **3** (stressing importance, necessity) **children ~ be alerted to the dangers** les enfants doivent être avertis des dangers, il faut que les enfants soient avertis des dangers; **we ~ do more to improve standards** il faut faire plus or nous devons faire plus pour améliorer le niveau; **immigrants ~ not become scapegoats** il ne faut pas que les immigrés deviennent des boucs émissaires, les immigrés ne doivent pas devenir des boucs émissaires; **you ~ be patient** il faut que tu sois patient, tu dois être patient; **tell her she mustn't worry** dis-lui de ne pas s'inquiéter; **we ~ never forget** il ne faut jamais oublier; **I ~ ask you not to smoke** je dois vous demander de ne pas fumer; **it's very odd I ~ admit** c'est très étrange je dois l'avouer; **I feel I ~ tell you that** je pense devoir te dire que; **it ~ be said that** il faut dire que; **I ~ apologize for being late** je vous demande d'excuser mon retard; **I ~ say I was impressed** je dois dire que j'étais impressionné; **that was pretty rude I ~ say!** je dois dire que c'était assez impoli!; **very nice, I ~ say!** iron très gentil vraiment! iron; **4** (expressing intention) **we ~ ask them about it soon** il faut que nous leur demandions bientôt; **I ~ check the reference** je dois vérifier la référence , il faut que je vérifie la référence; **we mustn't forget to let the cat out** il ne faut pas or nous ne devons pas oublier de laisser sortir le chat; **5** (indicating irritation) **well, come in if you ~** bon, entre si tu insistes; **why ~ she always be so cynical?** pourquoi faut-il toujours qu'elle soit si cynique?; **he's ill, if you ~ know** il est malade si tu veux vraiment le savoir; **~ you make such a mess?** est-ce que tu as vraiment besoin de mettre le désordre?; **6** (in invitations, suggestions) **you ~ come and visit us!** il faut vraiment que vous veniez nous voir!; **we really ~ get together soon** il faudrait vraiment qu'on se voie bientôt; **you ~ meet Flora Brown** il faut absolument que tu fasses la connaissance de Flora Brown; **7** (expressing assumption, probability) **it ~ be difficult living there** ça doit être difficile de vivre là-bas; **it ~ have been very interesting for you to do** ça a dû être très intéressant pour toi de faire; **there ~ be some mistake!** il doit y avoir une erreur!; **they ~ be wondering what happened to us** ils doivent se demander ce qui nous est arrivé; **what ~ people think?** qu'est-ce que les gens doivent penser?; **viewers ~ have been surprised** les téléspectateurs ont dû être surpris; **that ~ mean we're at the terminus** ça doit vouloir dire que nous sommes au terminus; **that ~ be Marie-Hélène's tea** ça doit être le thé de Marie-Hélène; **because he said nothing people thought he ~ be shy** comme il ne disait rien les gens pensaient qu'il devait être timide; **they ~ really detest each other** ils doivent vraiment se détester; **they ~ be even richer than we thought** ils doivent être encore plus riches qu'on ne le pensait; **'he said so'—'oh well it MUST be right, mustn't it?'** iron 'c'est ce qu'il a dit'—'ça doit être vrai alors!'; **anyone who believes her ~ be naïve** il faut vraiment être naïf pour la croire; **you ~ be out of your mind!** tu es fou!; **8** (expressing strong interest, desire) **this I ~ see!** il faut que je voie ça!; **we simply ~ get away from here!** il faut à tout prix que nous sortions d'ici!
II *n* **it's a ~** c'est indispensable (**for** pour); **the book is a ~ for all gardeners** ce livre est indispensable or est un must○ pour tous les amateurs de jardinage; **Latin is no longer a ~ for access to university** le latin n'est plus indispensable pour entrer à l'université; **this film is a ~** ce film est à voir or à ne pas rater; **if you're going to Paris, a visit to the Louvre is a ~** si vous allez à Paris une visite au Louvre s'impose.
must[2] /mʌst/ *n* Wine moût *m*.
mustache *n* US = **moustache**.
mustachio /məˈstɑːʃɪəʊ, US -stæʃ-/ *n* (*pl* **~s**) grosse moustache *f*.
mustang /ˈmʌstæŋ/ *n* mustang *m*.
mustard /ˈmʌstəd/ ▶1104 **I** *n* **1** (plant, condiment) moutarde *f*; **~ and cress** moutarde blanche et cresson alénois; **2** (colour) jaune *m* moutarde *m inv*.
II *modif* [*powder, seed*] de moutarde; [*pot, spoon*] à moutarde.
III *adj* moutarde *inv*.
IDIOMS **to be as keen as ~** déborder d'enthousiasme; **he doesn't cut the ~** US il ne fait pas le poids.
mustard: **~ bath** *n* bain *m* sinapisé; **~ gas** *n* Mil gaz *m* moutarde; **~ plaster** *n* sinapisme *m*.
muster /ˈmʌstə(r)/ **I** *n* Mil rassemblement *m*.
II *vtr* **1** (also **~ up**) (summon) rassembler [*energy, enthusiasm*]; rallier [*support, majority*]; préparer [*argument*]; **with all the dignity she could ~** avec toute la dignité dont elle était capable; **2** gen, Mil (gather) rassembler [*team, volunteers, troops*].
III *vi* gen, Mil se rassembler.
IDIOMS **to pass ~** être acceptable.
■ **muster in** US Mil: ¶ **~ [sb] in** enrôler; ¶ **~ sb into [sth]** enrôler qn dans [*army*].
■ **muster out** US Mil: **~ [sb] out** rendre [qn] à la vie civile.
muster station *n* point *m* de rassemblement.
mustiness /ˈmʌstɪnɪs/ *n* **1** (of room) odeur *f* de renfermé; (of book, clothing) odeur *f* de moisi; **2** fig (of ideas, thinking) aspect *m* vieux jeu.
mustn't /ˈmʌsnt/ *abrév* = **must not**.
must've /ˈmʌstəv/ = **must have**.
musty /ˈmʌstɪ/ *adj* **1** [*room, area*] qui sent le renfermé; [*book, clothing*] qui a une odeur de moisi; [*smell*] (of room etc) de renfermé; (of book etc) de moisi; **to smell ~** sentir le moisi or le renfermé; **to taste ~** avoir un goût de moisi; **to go ~** moisir; **2** fig [*ideas, thinking*] vieux jeu *inv*.
mutability /ˌmjuːtəˈbɪlətɪ/ *n* mutabilité *f*.
mutable /ˈmjuːtəbl/ *adj* mutable (**into** en).
mutagen /ˈmjuːtədʒən/ *n* substance *f* mutagène.
mutagenic /ˌmjuːtəˈdʒenɪk/ *adj* mutagène.
mutant /ˈmjuːtənt/ *n, adj* mutant/-e (*m/f*).
mutate /mjuːˈteɪt, US ˈmjuːteɪt/ **I** *vtr* faire subir une mutation à.
II *vi* [*cell, organism*] subir une mutation; [*alien, monster*] se métamorphoser (**into** en).
mutation /mjuːˈteɪʃn/ *n* **1** gen, Biol mutation *f*; **2** Ling altération *f*.
mutatis mutandis /muːˌtɑːtɪs muːˈtændɪs/ *adv* mutatis mutandis.
mute /mjuːt/ **I** *n* Mus sourdine *f*.
II *adj* **1** (dumb) muet/-ette; **2** gen, Ling (silent) muet/-ette; **to remain ~** rester muet/-ette; **3** Jur **to stand ~** refuser de plaider.
III *vtr* **1** Mus mettre la sourdine à [*instrument*]; **2** gen tempérer [*enthusiasm, resistance*].

■ Note Attention! Ce mot peut être perçu comme injurieux dans l'acception II 1. Lui préférer *speech impaired*.

muted /ˈmjuːtɪd/ *adj* **1** (subdued) [*response*] tiède; [*celebration, pleasure*] mitigé; [*criticism*] voilé; [*colour*] sourd; [*sound*] assourdi; **2** Mus [*trumpet*] bouché.
mutely /ˈmjuːtlɪ/ *adv* en silence.
mute swan *n* cygne *m* tuberculé.
mutilate /ˈmjuːtɪleɪt/ *vtr* mutiler.
mutilation /ˌmjuːtɪˈleɪʃn/ *n* **1** (of body, property) mutilation *f*; **2** (injury) blessure *f*.
mutineer /ˌmjuːtɪˈnɪə(r)/ *n* mutiné/-e *m/f*.
mutinous /ˈmjuːtɪnəs/ *adj* [*soldier, sailor*] mutiné; [*pupil, behaviour, look*] rebelle; **to turn ~** se rebeller.

mutiny /ˈmjuːtɪnɪ/ *n* mutinerie *f*.

mutt○ /mʌt/ *n* **1** (dog) clébard○ *m*; **2** (person) corniaud○ *m*.

mutter /ˈmʌtə(r)/ **I** *n* marmonnement *m*.
II *vtr* marmonner [*prayer, reply*]; (disagreeably) grommeler [*curse, insult*]; **'too bad,' he ~ed** 'tant pis,' marmonna-t-il; (imitating people conferring) **'~, ~'** 'gna, gna, gna'.
III *vi* marmonner; **to ~ about doing**○ parler de faire; **to ~ to oneself** marmonner; **what are you ~ing about**○**?** qu'est-ce que tu marmonnes?

muttering /ˈmʌtərɪŋ/ *n* ¢ grommellements *mpl* (**about** contre).

mutton /ˈmʌtn/ **I** *n* Culin mouton *m*.
II *modif* [*stew, pie*] de mouton.
IDIOMS **as dead as ~** mort et bien mort; **~ dressed as lamb** habillé trop jeune pour son âge.

mutton: **~ chops** *npl* (whiskers) (favoris *mpl* en) côtelettes *fpl*; **~ head**○ *n* US tête *f* de veau○.

mutual /ˈmjuːtʃʊəl/ *adj* **1** (reciprocal) mutuel/-elle, réciproque; **the feeling is ~** c'est réciproque; **2** (common) commun; **our ~ friend** notre ami commun; **by ~ agreement** d'un commun accord; **it is to their ~ advantage** c'est dans leur intérêt à tous deux; **it's to our ~ advantage to sign** c'est dans notre intérêt commun de signer; **3** Comm [*organization, society*] mutuel/-elle.
IDIOMS **it's a ~ admiration society** ils/elles s'entr'admirent.

mutual aid, **mutual assistance** *n* entraide *f*.

mutual consent *n* gen, Jur consentement *m* mutuel; **to get divorced by ~** divorcer par consentement mutuel; **by ~** d'un commun accord.

mutual fund *n* US Fin fonds *m* commun de placement.

mutuality /ˌmjuːtʃʊˈælətɪ/ *n* gen, Jur réciprocité *f*.

mutually /ˈmjuːtʊəlɪ/ *adv* mutuellement; **~ acceptable** acceptable pour les deux parties; **~ agreed** fixé d'un commun accord; **~ dependent** interdépendant; **~ exclusive options** des options qui s'excluent mutuellement; **I hope we find a ~ acceptable solution** j'espère que nous trouverons une solution qui nous satisfera tous les deux.

Muzak® /ˈmjuːzæk/ *n* péj musique *f* d'ambiance (enregistrée).

muzzle /ˈmʌzl/ **I** *n* **1** (snout) museau *m*; **2** (worn by animal) muselière *f*; **3** (of gun) canon *m*; (of canon) bouche *f*.
II *vtr* lit, fig museler.

muzzle: **~loader** *n* [*gun*] qu'on charge par le canon; [*cannon*] qu'on charge par la bouche; **~ velocity** *n* vitesse *f* initiale.

muzzy○ /ˈmʌzɪ/ *adj* **1** (confused) [*head*] embrumé; **my head's ~** je suis dans les vapes○; **2** (blurred) [*recollection*] brouillé; [*picture*] pas net/nette; **to go ~** gen se brouiller.

MV *n* **1** Naut (*abrév* = **motor vessel**) bateau *m* à moteur; **2** Elec (*abrév* = **megavolt**) MV.

MVP *n* Sport (*abrév* = **Most Valued Player**) vedette *f* de l'équipe.

MW *n* Radio (*abrév* = **medium wave**) ondes *fpl* moyennes.

MX (missile) *n* MX *m*.

my /maɪ/

■ **Note** In French, determiners agree in gender and number with the noun that follows. So *my* is translated by *mon* + masculine singular noun (mon chien), *ma* + feminine singular noun (ma maison) BUT by *mon* + feminine noun beginning with a vowel or mute h (mon assiette) and by *mes* + plural noun (mes enfants).
– When *my* is stressed, *à moi* is added after the noun: MY *house* = ma maison à moi.
– For *my* used with parts of the body see the Usage Note ▶ **1037**.

I *det* **1** gen mon/ma/mes; **2** (used emphatically) MY **house** ma maison à moi.
II *excl* **~ ~!** ça alors!

myalgic /maɪˈældʒɪk/ *adj* myalgique.

myalgic encephalomyelitis, **ME** /maɪˌældʒɪk enˌsefələʊˌmaɪəˈlaɪtɪs/ ▶ **1354** *n* encéphalomyélite *f* myalgique.

Myanmar /mjænˈmɑː(r)/ ▶ **1131** *pr n* **Union of ~** Myanmar *m*.

mycology /maɪˈkɒlədʒɪ/ *n* mycologie *f*.

mycosis /maɪˈkəʊsɪs/ ▶ **1354** *n* mycose *f*.

mynah /ˈmaɪnə/ *n* (also **~ bird**) mainate *m*.

MYOB US (*abrév* = **mind your own business**) occupe-toi de tes affaires.

myopia /maɪˈəʊpɪə/ *n* Med myopie *f* also fig.

myopic /maɪˈɒpɪk/ *adj* **1** Med [*vision*] myope; **2** fig [*attitude, policy*] à courte vue; [*view*] étroit.

myriad /ˈmɪrɪəd/ **I** *n* littér myriade *f* (**of** de).
II *adj* [*problems, opportunities, items*] innombrable; **~ detail** une myriade de détails.

myrmidon /ˈmɜːmɪdən, US -dɒn/ *n* littér péj ou hum sbire *m* pej, homme *m* de main.

myrrh /mɜː(r)/ *n* myrrhe *f*.

myrtle /ˈmɜːtl/ *n* myrte *m*.

myself /maɪˈself, məˈself/

■ **Note** When used as a reflexive pronoun, direct and indirect, *myself* is translated by *me* which is always placed before the verb: *I've hurt myself* = je me suis fait mal.
– When used as an emphatic the translation is *moi-même*: *I did it myself* = je l'ai fait moi-même.
– When used after a preposition *myself* is translated by *moi* or *moi-même*: *I did it for myself* = je l'ai fait pour moi *or* moi-même.
– For particular usages see below.

pron **1** (refl) me, (*before vowel*) m'; **2** (emphatic) moi-même; **I saw it ~** je l'ai vu moi-même; **for ~** pour moi, pour moi-même; **(all) by ~** tout seul; **3** (expressions) **I'm not much of a dog-lover ~** moi personnellement je n'aime pas trop les chiens; **I'm not ~ today** je ne suis pas dans mon assiette aujourd'hui.

mysterious /mɪˈstɪərɪəs/ *adj* **1** (puzzling) mystérieux/-ieuse; **2** (enigmatic) [*person, smile, place*] mystérieux/-ieuse; **to give sb a ~ look** regarder qn d'un air mystérieux; **don't be so ~!** ne fais pas tant de mystères!; **to be ~ about** faire grand mystère de [*person, activity, object*].
IDIOMS **God moves in ~ ways** les voies du Seigneur sont impénétrables.

mysteriously /mɪˈstɪərɪəslɪ/ *adv* [*die, disappear, appear*] mystérieusement; [*say, smile, signal*] d'un air mystérieux.

mystery /ˈmɪstərɪ/ **I** *n* **1** (puzzle) mystère *m*; **to be/remain a ~ to sb** être/rester un mystère pour qn; **it's a ~ to me how/why/where** je n'arrive pas à comprendre comment/pourquoi/où; **it's a ~ how/where** on ne sait pas comment/où; **there is no ~ about her success** ou **about why she is successful** son succès n'a rien de mystérieux; **there's no ~ about it** ce n'est pas un mystère; **to make a great ~ of sth** faire grand mystère de qch; **2** (mysteriousness) mystère *m*; **the ~ surrounding sth** le mystère qui entoure qch; **shrouded in ~** enveloppé de mystère; **3** (book) roman *m* policier; **4** (film) film *m* policier; **5** Relig mystère *m*.
II *modif* [*death, illness, voice*] mystérieux/-ieuse; [*guest, visitor*] mystère; [*prize, tour, trip*] surprise; **the ~ man/woman** l'inconnu/-e.

mystery: **~ play** *n* Theat mystère *m*; **~ tour** *n* voyage *m* surprise.

mystic /ˈmɪstɪk/ **I** *n* Relig mystique *mf*.
II *adj* [*religion, union, beauty*] mystique; [*power*] occulte; [*practice*] ésotérique.

mystical /ˈmɪstɪkl/ *adj* mystique.

mysticism /ˈmɪstɪsɪzəm/ *n* mysticisme *m*.

mystification /ˌmɪstɪfɪˈkeɪʃn/ *n* **1** (of issue, process) mystification *f*; **2** (of person) perplexité *f*; **in some ~, he...** quelque peu perplexe, il...

mystify /ˈmɪstɪfaɪ/ *vtr* laisser [qn] perplexe; **I am completely mystified** je suis tout à fait perplexe; **to be mystified to find** ou **discover that...** découvrir avec perplexité que...

mystifying /ˈmɪstɪfaɪɪŋ/ *adj* intrigant.

mystifyingly /ˈmɪstɪfaɪɪŋlɪ/ *adv* bizarrement.

mystique /mɪˈstiːk/ *n* aura *f* de mystique; **full of/clothed in ~** chargé de/enveloppé de mystère.

myth /mɪθ/ *n* **1** C (story, fallacy) mythe *m*; **2** ¢ (mythology) mythologie *f*.

mythic(al) /ˈmɪθɪk(l)/ *adj* **1** Mythol [*hero, creature, portrayal*] mythique; **2** fig [*proportions*] légendaire.

mythological /ˌmɪθəˈlɒdʒɪkl/ *adj* mythologique.

mythologize /mɪˈθɒlədʒaɪz/ *vtr* mythologiser.

mythology /mɪˈθɒlədʒɪ/ *n* mythologie *f*.

myxomatosis /ˌmɪksəməˈtəʊsɪs/ *n* myxomatose *f*.

n, N /en/ *n* **1** (letter) n, N *m*; **2 n** Math n; **to the power of n** à la puissance n; fig **to the nth degree** au énième degré; **for the nth time** pour la énième fois; **3 N** Geog (*abrév écrite* = **north**) N; **4 'n'** = **and.**

n/a, N/A (*abrév* = **not applicable**) s/o.

NA *n: abrév* ▶ **North America.**

NAACP *n* US (*abrév* = **National Association for the Advancement of Colored People**) association *f* de défense des droits civiques des Noirs.

Naafi /'næfɪ/ *n* GB **1** (*abrév* = **Navy Army and Air Force Institutes**) intendance *f* militaire; **2** (canteen) cantine *f* de l'armée.

nab /næb/ **I** *n* GB (*abrév* = **no alcohol beer**) bière *f* sans alcool.

II *vtr* (*p prés etc* **-bb-**) **1** (catch) pincer○ [*wrongdoer*]; coincer○ [*passer-by*]; **2** (appropriate) mettre le grappin○ sur [*person, object*]; **3** (steal) piquer○.

nablabs /'næblæbs/ *npl* GB (*abrév* = **no alcohol beers and low alcohol beers**) *catégorie de bières sans alcool et à bas taux d'alcool.*

nabob /'neɪbɒb/ *n* nabab *m.*

nacelle /nə'sel/ *n* nacelle *f.*

nacho /'nætʃəʊ/ *n* nacho *m.*

nacre /'neɪkə(r)/ *n* nacre *f.*

nacreous /'neɪkrɪəs/ *adj* nacré.

nadir /'neɪdɪə(r)/ *n* **1** (celestial point) nadir *m*; **2** fig (low point) point *m* le plus bas; **to reach a ~** tomber on ne peut plus bas.

naff○ /næf/ *adj* GB ringard○.

■ **naff off**◑ foutre le camp◑, s'en aller.

naffing◑ /'næfɪŋ/ *adj* GB foutu◑.

NAFTA /næftə/ *n* (*abrév* = **North American Free Trade Agreement**) ALÉNA *m.*

nag /næg/ **I** *n* **1**○ (horse) péj canasson○ *m* pej, vieux cheval *m*; **2**○ (woman) péj mégère *f* pej.

II *vtr* (*p prés etc* **-gg-**) **1** (pester) enquiquiner○ [*person*] (**about** au sujet de); **he's been ~ging me for a new bike** il m'enquiquine○ pour que je lui achète un nouveau vélo; **to ~ sb into doing** enquiquiner○ qn pour qu'il/elle fasse; **2** (niggle) [*pain, discomfort*] lanciner; [*doubt, worry, conscience*] travailler, lanciner.

III *vi* (*p prés etc* **-gg-**) **1** (moan) faire des remarques continuelles; **stop ~ing!** arrête de m'enquiquiner○!; **all you do is ~!** tu n'arrêtes pas de m'enquiquiner○!; **to ~ at sb** enquiquiner○ qn; **to ~ at sb to do** enquiquiner○ qn pour qu'il/elle fasse; **2** (niggle) **to ~ (away) at sb** [*pain*] harceler qn; [*conscience, worry*] travailler qn.

IV nagging *pres p adj* (niggling) [*pain, doubt, suspicion*] tenace; [*problem*] obsédant; **I still had a ~ging doubt** le soupçon continuait à me travailler.

naiad /'naɪæd/ *n* (*pl* **~s** ou **~es**) (all contexts) naïade *f.*

nail /neɪl/ **I** *n* **1** Anat ongle *m*; **to bite one's ~s** se ronger les ongles; **2** Tech clou *m.*

II *vtr* **1** (attach with nails) clouer; **they ~ed planks over the doors** ils ont cloué des planches sur les portes; **to ~ a picture to a wall** clouer un tableau sur un mur; **2**○ (trap, pin down) coincer○ [*wrongdoer*]; démasquer [*liar*]; **3**○ (expose) démentir [*rumour*]; démolir [*myth*].

IDIOMS **a ~ in sb's coffin** un coup dur; **to hit the ~ on the head** mettre le doigt dessus; **cash on the ~** argent *m* comptant; **to be as hard** ou **as tough as ~s** être sans cœur; **to fight tooth and ~** se battre avec acharnement (**against** contre). ▶ **mast.**

■ **nail down**: ¶ **~ down [sth], ~ [sth] down 1** clouer; **2** fig (define) définir [*agreement, policy*]; ¶ **~ [sb] down** coincer○ [*person*]; **to ~ sb down to a time/date/price** obtenir de qn qu'il fixe (*subj*) une heure/une date/un prix.

■ **nail up**: **~ up [sth], ~ [sth] up 1** clouer [*picture, sign*]; **2** (board up) condamner (*avec des planches*) [*doors, windows*]; (seal) clouer [*box, crate*].

nail-biting /'neɪlbaɪtɪŋ/ **I** *n* habitude *f* de se ronger les ongles.

II *adj* [*match, finish*] palpitant; [*wait*] angoissant.

nail: **~ bomb** *n* bombe *f* à clous; **~brush** *n* brosse *f* à ongles; **~ clippers** *npl* coupe-ongles *m inv*; **~ enamel** *n* vernis *m* à ongles; **~ file** *n* lime *f* à ongles; **~ polish** *n* vernis *m* à ongles; **~ polish remover** *n* dissolvant *m*; **~ scissors** *npl* ciseaux *mpl* à ongles; **~ varnish** *n* vernis *m* à ongles; **~ varnish remover** *n* dissolvant *m.*

naïve /naɪ'i:v/ *adj* gen, Art naïf/-ïve.

naïvely /naɪ'i:vlɪ/ *adv* [*believe, say, behave*] naïvement; [*draw, write*] dans un style naïf; **~ forthright/loyal** d'une franchise/loyauté naïve.

naïvety, naïveté /naɪ'i:vtɪ/ *n* naïveté *f*; **in my ~** en toute naïveté.

naked /'neɪkɪd/ *adj* **1** (bare) [*person, body*] nu; **to go ~** se promener tout nu; **you can't go around stark ~!** tu ne peux pas te balader complètement nu or à poil○!; **~ to the waist** torse nu; **2** (exposed) [*flame, light bulb, sword*] nu; **3** (blunt) [*truth*] tout nu; [*facts*] brut; [*aggression, hostility, ambition, terror*] non déguisé; **4** (unaided) **visible to the ~ eye** visible à l'œil nu; **5** Jur (incomplete) **~ agreement** contrat *m* à titre gratuit; **6** Fin (unhedged) **~ option** option *f* découverte; **~ writer** vendeur *m* découvert.

IDIOMS **as ~ as the day he was born** nu comme un ver, nu comme la main.

nakedness /'neɪkɪdnɪs/ *n* nudité *f.*

NALGO /'nælgəʊ/ *n* GB (*abrév* = **National and Local Government Officers' Association**) syndicat *m* des fonctionnaires de l'administration.

NAM *n: abrév* ▶ **New Age Movement.**

namby-pamby○ /ˌnæmbɪ'pæmbɪ/ *n, adj* péj gnangnan○ (*mf*) *inv.*

name /neɪm/ **I** *n* **1** (title) (of person, place, object) nom *m*; (of book, film) titre *m*; **first ~** prénom *m*; **my ~ is Louis** je m'appelle Louis; **what is your ~?** comment vous appelez-vous?; **what ~ shall I say?** (on phone) c'est de la part de qui?; (in person) qui dois-je annoncer?; **a woman by the ~ of Catherine** une femme répondant au nom de Catherine; **he goes by the ~ of Max** il s'appelle Max; **I know it by another ~** je le connais sous un autre nom; **I know my regulars by ~** je connais mes habitués par leurs noms; **I only know the company by ~** je ne connais la société que de nom; **to refer to sb/sth by ~** désigner qn/qch par son nom; **the common/Latin ~ for this plant** le nom vulgaire/latin de cette plante; **in the ~ of God!** au nom de Dieu!; **in the ~ of freedom** au nom de la liberté; **in my ~** en mon nom; **a passport in the ~ of Nell Drury** un passeport au nom de Nell Drury; **she writes under the ~ Eve Quest** elle écrit sous le nom d'Eve Quest; **he's president in ~ only** il n'a de président que le nom; **they are married in ~ only** ils ne sont mariés que sur le papier; **to be party leader in all** ou **everything but ~** être chef du parti sinon en titre, du moins en pratique; **to give/lend one's ~ to sth** donner/prêter son nom à qch; **to put one's ~ to** apposer son nom à [*petition*]; **to take** ou **get one's ~ from** porter le nom de [*relative, flower*]; **to put one's ~ down for** s'inscrire à [*course, school*]; **she put her ~ down to act in the play** elle s'est proposée pour jouer dans la pièce; **the big ~s in showbusiness** les grands noms du monde du spectacle; **2** (reputation) réputation *f*; **a good/bad ~** une bonne/mauvaise réputation; **they have a ~ for efficiency** ils ont la réputation d'être efficaces; **that was the film that made her ~** c'est ce film qui a fait sa réputation or qui l'a rendue célèbre; **to make one's ~ as a writer** se faire un nom comme écrivain; **to make a ~ for oneself as a singer/photographer** se faire un nom dans la chanson/la photo; **to make a ~ for oneself as a coward/liar** péj se faire une réputation de lâche/menteur; **3** (insult) **to call sb ~s** injurier qn; **he called me all sorts of ~s** il m'a traité de tous les noms.

II *vtr* **1** (call) appeler [*person, area*]; baptiser [*boat, planet*]; **they ~d the baby Nadine** ils ont appelé le bébé Nadine; **they ~d her after** GB ou **for** US **her mother** ils l'ont appelée comme sa mère; **we'll ~ him Martin after Martin Luther King** on l'appellera Martin en souvenir de Martin Luther King; **a boy ~d Joe** un garçon nommé Joe; **the product is ~d after its inventor** le produit porte le nom de son inventeur; **2** (cite) citer [*country, name, planet*]; **~ three American States** citez trois États américains; **~ me all the members of the EEC** citez-moi tous les pays membres de la CEE; **France, Spain, Italy, to ~ but a few** la France, l'Espagne, l'Italie, pour n'en citer que quelques-uns; **illnesses? you ~ it, I've had it!** des maladies? je les ai toutes eues!; **hammers, drills, nails, you ~ it, we've got it!** marteaux, perceuses, clous, nous avons tout ce que vous voulez; **3** (reveal identity of) citer [*names*]; révéler [*sources*]; révéler l'identité de [*suspect*]; **to ~ ~s** donner des noms; **naming no ~s** sans vouloir dénoncer personne; **to be ~d as a suspect** être désigné comme suspect; **4** (appoint) nommer [*captain*]; donner la composition de [*team*]; désigner [*heir*]; nommer [*successor*];

he's been ~d actor of the year il a été nommé acteur de l'année; **to ~ sb for** nommer qn à [*post, award*]; **5** (state) indiquer [*place, time*]; fixer [*price, terms*]; **~ your price** fixez votre prix; **to ~ the day** fixer la date du mariage.
IDIOMS **that's the ~ of the game** c'est la règle du jeu; **competitiveness/perfection is the ~ of the game** c'est la compétitivité/la perfection qui prime; **to see one's ~ in lights** devenir célèbre.
name-calling /ˈneɪmkɔːlɪŋ/ *n* injures *fpl*; **to resort to/indulge in ~** en venir/se laisser aller aux injures.
name day *n* **1** Relig fête *f*; **2 Name Day** Fin *deuxième jour d'une transaction en Bourse où le nom de l'acheteur est communiqué au vendeur*.
name-drop /ˈneɪmdrɒp/ *vi* (*p prés etc* **-pp-**) péj citer des gens célèbres (*qu'on prétend connaître*).
name-dropper /ˈneɪmdrɒpə(r)/ *n* **he's a ~** péj il aime bien citer des gens connus (qu'il prétend connaître personnellement).
nameless /ˈneɪmlɪs/ *adj* **1** (anonymous) [*person, grave*] anonyme; **a certain person, who shall remain** ou **be ~** une personne que je ne nommerai pas; **2** (indefinable) [*fear, dread*] inexprimable.
namely /ˈneɪmlɪ/ *adv* à savoir; **two countries, ~ France and Spain** deux pays, à savoir la France et l'Espagne.
name part *n* Theat rôle *m* titre.
name plate *n* (of manufacturer) plaque *f* (de fabrication); (of practitioner) plaque *f* (professionnelle); (of home owner) plaque *f*.
name: **~sake** *n* homonyme *m*; **~ tag** *n* étiquette *f* (*sur laquelle est marqué le nom du propriétaire*); **~ tape** *n* Sewing nom *m* tissé.
Namibia /nəˈmɪbɪə/ ▶ 1131 *pr n* Namibie *f*.
Namibian /nəˈmɪbɪən/ ▶ 1486 **I** *n* Namibien/-ienne *m/f*.
II *adj* namibien.
nan○ /næn/, **nana**○ /ˈnænə/ *n* mamie○ *f*, mémé○ *f*.
nan bread /ˈnɑːn bred/ *n* pain *m* indien au levain (*plat et rond*).
nance○ /næns/, **nancy**○ /ˈnænsɪ/, **nancy-boy**○ /ˈnænsɪbɔɪ/ *n* injur tapette○ *f*, tante○ *f* offensive.
nankeen /næŋˈkiːn/ *n* nankin *m*.
Nanking /ˌnænˈkɪŋ/ ▶ 1818 *pr n* Nankin.
nanny /ˈnænɪ/ *n* GB **1** (nurse) bonne *f* d'enfants, nurse *f*; **2**○ (grandmother) mamie *f*, mémé *f*.
nanny: **~ goat** *n* chèvre *f*, bique○ *f*; **~ state** *n* Pol État *m* hyperprotecteur.
nap /næp/ **I** *n* **1** (snooze) petit somme *m*; **afternoon ~** sieste *f*; **to have** ou **take a ~** faire un petit somme; (after lunch) faire la sieste; **2** Tex (pile) poil *m*; **velvet that has lost its ~** velours râpé or élimé; **3** Tex (direction of cut) sens *m*; **with the ~** dans le sens du tissu; **against the ~** à rebrousse-poil; **4** Games nap *m*; **5** GB Turf favori *m*.
II *vtr* (*p prés etc* **-pp-**) GB Turf **to ~ the winner** donner le cheval gagnant.
III *vi* (*p prés etc* **-pp-**) sommeiller, faire un petit somme.
IDIOMS **to catch sb ~ping**○ (off guard) prendre qn au dépourvu or à l'improviste; **to go ~ (on sth)**○ tout miser (sur qch).
napalm /ˈneɪpɑːm/ **I** *n* napalm *m*.
II *modif* [*bomb, attack*] au napalm.
III *vtr* attaquer [qch] au napalm.
nape /neɪp/ *n* nuque *f*; **the ~ of the neck** la nuque.
naphtha /ˈnæfθə/ *n* naphte *m*.
naphthalene /ˈnæfθəliːn/ *n* Chem naphtalène *m*; Comm naphtaline *f*.
napkin /ˈnæpkɪn/ *n* **1** (serviette) serviette *f* (de table); **~ ring** rond *m* de serviette; **2** GB sout (nappy) couche *f* de bébé.
Naples /ˈneɪplz/ ▶ 1818 *pr n* Naples.
napoleon /nəˈpəʊlɪən/ *n* **1** (coin) napoléon *m*; **2** US Culin ≈ millefeuille *m*; **3** = **nap I 3**.
Napoleon /nəˈpəʊlɪən/ *pr n* Napoléon.
Napoleonic /nəˌpəʊlɪˈɒnɪk/ *adj* napoléonien/-ienne.
nappy /ˈnæpɪ/ *n* GB couche *f* (de bébé).
nappy liner *n* lange *m* fin.
nappy rash *n* GB érythème *m* fessier; **to have ~** avoir les fesses irritées.
narc○ /nɑːk/ *n* US (*abrév* = **narcotics agent**) agent *m* de la brigade des stupéfiants.
narcissi /nɑːˈsɪsaɪ/ *pl* ▶ **narcissus**.
narcissism /ˈnɑːsɪsɪzəm/ *n* narcissisme *m*.
narcissist /ˈnɑːsɪsɪst/ *n* narcisse *m*.
narcissistic /ˌnɑːsɪˈsɪstɪk/ *adj* narcissique.
narcissus /nɑːˈsɪsəs/ **I** *n* (*pl* **-cissi** ou **~es**) Bot, Hort narcisse *m*.
II Narcissus *pr n* Mythol Narcisse.
narcolepsy /ˈnɑːkəlepsɪ/ *n* narcolepsie *f*.
narcosis /nɑːˈkəʊsɪs/ *n* narcose *f*.
narcotic /nɑːˈkɒtɪk/ **I** *n* (soporific) lit, fig narcotique *m*; (illegal drug) stupéfiant *m*; **to be arrested on a ~s charge** être arrêté pour trafic de stupéfiants.
II *adj* lit, fig narcotique.
narcotic: **~s agent** *n* US agent *m* de la brigade des stupéfiants; **~s squad** *n* US brigade *f* des stupéfiants.
narcotize /ˈnɑːkətaɪz/ *vtr* administrer un narcotique à [*person*].
nark○ /nɑːk/ **I** *n* **1** GB (informant) mouchard○ *m*; **2** GB (grumbler) rouspéteur/-euse○ *m/f*; **3** US = **narc**.
II *vtr* GB (annoy) mettre [qn] en boule○, agacer.
III *vi* GB **1** (grumble) rouspéter○ (**about** contre); **2** (inform police) moucharder○.
IV narked○ *pp adj* en rogne○, en boule○; **to get ~ed** se ficher en boule○ or en rogne○.
narky○ /ˈnɑːkɪ/ *adj* GB ronchon/-onne.
narrate /nəˈreɪt/ *vtr* raconter, narrer liter.
narration /nəˈreɪʃn/ *n* récit *m*, narration *f*.
narrative /ˈnærətɪv/ **I** *n* **1** (account, story) récit *m*, histoire *f*; **2** (storytelling) narration *f*; **he is a master of ~** il est maître dans l'art du récit ou de la narration.
II *modif* [*prose, poem*] narratif/-ive; [*skill, talent*] de conteur; **~ writer** narrateur/-trice *m/f*.
narratology /ˌnærəˈtɒlədʒɪ/ *n* narratologie *f*.
narrator /nəˈreɪtə(r)/ *n* Literat narrateur/-trice *m/f*; Mus récitant/-e *m/f*.
narrow /ˈnærəʊ/ ▶ 1412 **I narrows** *npl* goulet *m*.
II *adj* **1** (in breadth) [*street, valley, gap, vase, room, bridge, face*] étroit; **to grow** ou **become ~** [*road, river*] se rétrécir; [*valley*] se resserrer; **to have ~ eyes** avoir des petits yeux; **he is ~ across the shoulders, his shoulders are ~** il est étroit d'épaules; **2** (in scope) [*range, choice*] restreint; [*issue, field, boundaries, group, sense, definition*] étroit; [*vision, life, interests, understanding*] limité; [*views, version*] étriqué pej; **3** (in degree) [*majority, margin*] faible (*before n*); **to have a ~ lead** avoir une légère avance; **to suffer a ~ defeat** perdre de justesse; **to win a ~ victory** gagner de justesse; **to win by the ~est of margins** gagner d'une extrême justesse; **to have a ~ escape** ou **a ~ squeak**○ GB l'échapper belle; **that was a ~ squeak**○! GB on l'a échappé belle!; **4** (in size, shape) [*shoes, jacket, dress, skirt, trousers*] étroit; **5** Ling [*vowel*] tendu; [*transcription*] phonétique.
III *vtr* **1** (limit) limiter [*choice, range, field, options*] (**to** à); restreindre [*sense, definition*] (**to** à); **2** (reduce) réduire [*gap, deficit, margin*] (**from** de; **to** à); **Elliott has ~ed the gap** (in race, poll) Elliott a réduit l'écart; **3** (reduce breadth of) rétrécir [*road, path, arteries*]; **to ~ one's eyes** plisser les yeux.
IV *vi* **1** (in breadth) [*street, lake, corridor*] se rétrécir; [*valley, arteries*] se resserrer; **the road ~ed to a track** la route se rétrécissait au point de devenir un chemin; **her eyes ~ed** elle plissait les yeux; **2** (fall off) [*gap, deficit, margin, lead*] se réduire (**to** à); **3** (in scope) [*choice*] se limiter (**to** à).
V narrowing *pres p adj* [*street, channel, passage*] qui se rétrécit; [*gap, deficit, field*] qui se réduit.
IDIOMS **the straight and ~** le droit chemin; **to keep to/wander from the straight and ~** rester dans le/s'écarter du droit chemin.
■ **narrow down**: ¶ [*investigation, search*] se limiter (**to** à); [*field of contestants, suspects*] se réduire (**to** à); ¶ **~ [sth] down, ~ down [sth]** réduire [*numbers, list, choice*] (**to** à); limiter [*investigation, research*] (**to** à).
narrow: **~ boat** *n* GB péniche *f*; **~ gauge** *n* voie *f* étroite; **~-gauge engine** *n* locomotive *f* pour voie étroite; **~-gauge railway** *n* chemin *m* de fer à voie étroite.
narrowly /ˈnærəʊlɪ/ *adv* **1** (barely) de justesse; **2** (strictly) [*define, interpret*] strictement.
narrow-minded /ˌnærəʊˈmaɪndɪd/ *adj* péj borné; **to be ~ about** avoir des vues étroites sur.
narrow-mindedness /ˌnærəʊˈmaɪndɪdnɪs/ *n* péj étroitesse *f* d'esprit.
narrowness /ˈnærəʊnɪs/ *n* (all contexts) étroitesse *f*.
narwhal /ˈnɑːwəl/ *n* narval *m*.
NAS *n* US (*abrév* = **National Academy of Sciences**) académie *f* des sciences.
NASA /ˈnæsə/ *n* (*abrév* = **National Aeronautics and Space Administration**) NASA *f*.
nasal /ˈneɪzl/ **I** *n* Ling nasale *f*.
II *adj* **1** Ling [*vowel, pronunciation*] nasal; **2** gen [*voice, accent*] nasillard; **to speak with a ~ twang** parler du nez, nasiller.
nasality /neɪˈzælətɪ/ *n* nasalité *f*.
nasalization /ˌneɪzəlaɪˈzeɪʃn/ *n* nasalisation *f*.
nasalize /ˈneɪzəlaɪz/ *vtr* nasaliser.
nasally /ˈneɪzəlɪ/ *adv* [*speak*] d'une voix nasillarde.
nasal spray *n* nébuliseur *m* (*pour le nez*).
nascent /ˈnæsnt/ *adj* **1** gen naissant; **2** Chem (à l'état) naissant.
nastily /ˈnɑːstɪlɪ/ *adv* **1** (unkindly) [*behave, speak, laugh*] d'une façon désagréable; **to say sth ~** dire qch d'un ton sarcastique; **2** (severely) [*leak, crack*] sérieusement.
nastiness /ˈnɑːstɪnɪs/ *n* **1** (spitefulness) méchanceté *f*; **2** (unpleasantness) (of food, medicine) mauvais goût *m*.
nasturtium /nəˈstɜːʃəm/ *n* capucine *f*.
nasty /ˈnɑːstɪ/ **I**○ *n* (in food, water, air) saleté *f*; **video ~** film *m* d'épouvante sur cassette vidéo.
II *adj* **1** (unpleasant) [*crime, experience, sight, taste, surprise, suspicion*] horrible; [*feeling, task*] désagréable; [*habit*] mauvais; [*expression, look*] méchant; [*rumour*] inquiétant; [*stain*] gros/grosse; [*affair, business*] sale (*before n*); **I got a ~ fright** j'ai vraiment eu un choc; **the ~ weather** le mauvais temps; **to smell ~** sentir mauvais; **to taste ~** avoir mauvais goût; **it's ~ and hot** il fait une chaleur désagréable; **things could get ~** les choses pourraient mal tourner; **to turn ~** [*dog*] devenir méchant; [*person*] s'emporter; [*weather*] se gâter; **to be a ~ piece of work** être un sale type/une sale femme; **2** (unkind) [*person*] désagréable; [*trick*] sale (*before n*), vilain; [*gossip, letter*] méchant; **you've got a ~ mind** tu vois toujours le mal partout; **a ~ sense of humour** un humour méchant; **he gets ~ when he's tired** il devient méchant quand il est fatigué; **to be ~ to** être dur envers; **to say ~ things about** dire des choses méchantes au sujet de; **3** (serious) [*cut, bruise*] vilain (*before n*); [*bump, crack*,

Nationalities

Words like French *can also refer to the language (e.g.* a French textbook, ▶ 1402*) and to the country (e.g.* French history ▶ 1131*).*

Note the different use of capital letters in English and French; adjectives never have capitals in French:

a French student = un étudiant français/une étudiante française
a French nurse = une infirmière française/un infirmier français
a French tourist = un touriste français/une touriste française

Nouns have capitals in French when they mean a person of a specific nationality:

a Frenchman = un Français
a Frenchwoman = une Française
French people *or* the French = les Français *mpl*
a Chinese man = un Chinois
a Chinese woman = une Chinoise
Chinese people *or* the Chinese = les Chinois *mpl*

*English sometimes has a special word for a person of a specific nationality; in French, the same word can almost always be either an adjective (*no capitals*) or a noun (*with capitals*):*

Danish = danois
a Dane = un Danois, une Danoise
the Danes = les Danois *mpl*

Note the alternatives using either adjective (il/elle est ... etc.) *or noun* (c'est ...) *in French:*

he is French = il est français *or* c'est un Français
she is French = elle est française *or* c'est une Française
they are French = (*men or mixed*) ils sont français
or ce sont des Français
(*women*) elles sont françaises
or ce sont des Françaises

When the subject is a noun, like the teacher *or* Paul *below, the adjective construction is normally used in French:*

the teacher is French = le professeur est français
Paul is French = Paul est français
Anne is French = Anne est française
Paul and Anne are French = Paul et Anne sont français

Other ways of expressing someone's nationality or origins are:

he's of French extraction = il est d'origine française
she was born in Germany = elle est née en Allemagne
he is a Spanish citizen = il est espagnol
a Belgian national = un ressortissant belge
she comes from Nepal = elle vient du Népal

fall, accident] grave; [*cold*] mauvais (*before n*); **4** (ugly) [*colour, shape, style*] affreux/-euse; **5** (tricky) [*problem, question*] difficile; [*bend*] dangereux/-euse.

NAS/UWT *n* GB (*abrév* = **National Association of Schoolmasters/Union of Women Teachers**) syndicat *m* d'enseignants.

natal /'neɪtl/ *adj* natal; **~ day** littér jour *m* de la naissance.

Natal /nə'tæl/ *pr n* Natal *m*.

natality /nə'tæləti/ *n* natalité *f*.

natch○ /nætʃ/ *excl* US naturellement.

NATFHE *n* GB (*abrév* = **National Association of Teachers in Further and Higher Education**) association *f* nationale des enseignants du troisième cycle.

nation /'neɪʃn/ *n* **1** Pol (entity) nation *f*, pays *m*; **the ~'s past** le passé de la nation; **throughout** ou **across the ~** à travers tout le pays; **2** (people) peuple *m*; **to address the ~** s'adresser à la nation; **a ~ of storytellers** un pays de conteurs.

national /'næʃənl/ **I** *n* **1** Admin (citizen) ressortissant/-e *m/f*; **foreign/EC ~s** ressortissants étrangers/de la CEE; **2**○ GB, Journ (newspaper) **the ~s** les grands quotidiens *mpl*.
II *adj* **1** (concerning country) [*event, news, channel*] national; **the ~ press** ou **newspapers** GB les grands quotidiens *mpl*; **~ affairs** les affaires du pays; **in the ~ interest** dans l'intérêt national; **the ~ government** le gouvernement; **a ~ strike** une grève qui s'étend à l'ensemble du pays; **2** (particular to country) [*dress, flag, game, pastime*] national; **3** (government-run) [*railway, company*] national.

national: **~ anthem** *n* hymne *m* national; **National Assembly** *n* Assemblée *f* nationale; **National Curriculum** *n* GB programme *m* scolaire national; **~ debt** *n* dette *f* publique; **National Enterprise Board**, **NEB** *n* GB ≈ institut *m* de développement industriel britannique; **National Foundation for the Arts and the Humanities** *n* US *institution gouvernementale subventionnant des activités artistiques et culturelles*; **National Front**, **NF** *n* GB *parti britannique d'extrême droite*; cf Front *m* national; **National Geographic Association** *n* US société *f* de géographie des États-Unis; **National Graphical Association**, **NGA** *n* fédération *f* du livre; **~ grid** *n* Elec réseau *m* national haute-tension; **National Guard**, **NG** *n* US *milice de volontaires au service de l'État et de la fédération*.

National Health *n* GB **to get sth on the ~** ≈ se faire rembourser qch par la Sécurité Sociale.

national: **National Health Service**, **NHS** *n* GB services *mpl* de santé britanniques, ≈ Sécurité *f* Sociale; **~ holiday** *n* fête *f* nationale; **~ income** *n* revenu *m* national; **National Insurance**, **NI** *n* GB securité *f* sociale britannique; **National Insurance contributions** *npl* cotisations *fpl* à la sécurité sociale; **National Insurance number** *n* numéro *m* de sécurité sociale.

nationalism /'næʃnəlɪzəm/ *n* nationalisme *m*.

nationalist /'næʃnəlɪst/ *n, adj* nationaliste (*mf*).

nationalistic /ˌnæʃnə'lɪstɪk/ *adj* souvent péj nationaliste.

nationality /ˌnæʃə'nælətɪ/ *n* nationalité *f*; **what ~ is he?** il est de quelle nationalité?

nationalization /ˌnæʃnəlaɪ'zeɪʃn, US -lɪ'z-/ *n* nationalisation *f*.

nationalize /'næʃnəlaɪz/ *vtr* nationaliser [*industry, mine*].

nationally /'næʃnəlɪ/ *adv* **1** (at national level) [*develop, institute, negotiate*] à l'échelon national; **there are problems locally and ~** il y a des problèmes aux plans local et national; **2** (nationwide) [*broadcast, enforce, employ, distribute*] sur l'ensemble du pays; [*known, respected, available*] dans tout le pays.

national: **~ monument** *n* monument *m* historique; **~ park** *n* parc *m* national; **National Power** *n* GB *compagnie d'électricité privée*; **National Rifle Association**, **NRA** *n* US Association *f* nationale des chasseurs à pied (*lobby en faveur du port d'armes*); **National Savings Bank** *n* GB ≈ Caisse *f* d'Épargne; **National Savings Certificate** *n* GB ≈ bon *m* de caisse; **National School**, **NS** *n* (in Ireland) école *f* primaire d'État; **National Science Foundation**, **NSF** *n* US centre *m* national de la recherche scientifique; **~ security** *n* sécurité *f* nationale; **National Security Adviser** *n* US conseiller/-ère *m/f* pour la sécurité auprès du Président américain; **National Security Council** *n* US conseil *m* national de sécurité; **~ service** *n* GB Hist service *m* militaire; **~ socialism** *n* Hist national-socialisme *m*; **National Trust**, **NT** *n* GB commission *f* nationale des sites et monuments historiques.

nationhood /'neɪʃnhʊd/ *n* statut *m* national.

nation-state /ˌneɪʃn'steɪt/ *n* État-nation *m*.

nationwide /ˌneɪʃn'waɪd/ **I** *adj* [*appeal, coverage, scheme, strike*] sur l'ensemble du territoire; [*campaign*] national; [*survey, poll*] à l'échelle nationale.
II *adv* [*broadcast, travel, compete*] dans tout le pays; **showing at cinemas ~** sortie sur tous les écrans.

native /'neɪtɪv/ **I** *n* **1** gen, Bot, Zool (from a particular place) natif/-ive *m/f*; **to be a ~ of** [*person, plant*] être originaire de; **to speak a language like a ~** parler une langue comme si c'était sa langue maternelle; **2** Anthrop (indigenous inhabitant) indigène *mf*; **3** péj (local resident) autochtone *mf*; **the ~s never visit the museum** hum les gens du pays ne vont jamais au musée.
II *adj* **1** (original) [*land*] natal; [*tongue*] maternel/-elle; **his ~ Austria** l'Autriche, son pays natal; **~ German speaker** personne *f* de langue maternelle allemande; **~ English speaker** anglophone *mf*; **~ French speaker** francophone *mf*; **2** Anthrop, Bot, Zool [*labour, peoples, quarter, species*] indigène; **~ to Northern Europe** originaire de l'Europe du Nord; **to go ~** hum adopter les coutumes locales; **3** (natural) [*cunning*] inné; [*wit*] naturel/-elle; **4** (local) [*produce*] du pays.

native: **Native American** *n, adj* amérindien/-ienne (*m/f*); **~ son** *n* enfant *m* du pays.

native speaker *n* locuteur natif/locutrice native *m/f*; **to have ~ fluency** avoir l'aisance d'un locuteur natif; **'we require a ~ of English'** 'recherchons personne de langue maternelle anglaise'.

nativism /'neɪtɪvɪzəm/ *n*: *politique favorisant la population autochtone d'un pays aux dépens des immigrants*.

Nativity /nə'tɪvətɪ/ *n* Relig, Art nativité *f*.

Nativity: **~ Play** *n* mystère *m* de la Nativité; **~ scene** *n* nativité *f*.

Nato, **NATO** *n* (*abrév* = **North Atlantic Treaty Organization**) OTAN *f*.

natter○ /'nætə(r)/ GB **I** *n* causette○ *f* (**about** sur); **to have a ~** faire un brin de causette○.
II *vi* (also **~ on**) papoter (**about** sur; **to** à; **with** avec).

natterer○ /'nætərə(r)/ *n* GB bavard/-e *m/f*.

natterjack (toad) /'nætədʒæk/ *n* calamite *m*, crapaud *m* des joncs.

natty○ /'nætɪ/ *adj* **1** (smart) [*outfit*] chic *inv*; [*person*] chic *inv*, pimpant; **he's a ~ dresser** il est toujours pimpant; **2** (clever) [*machine, tool*] ingénieux/-ieuse, astucieux/-ieuse.

natural /'nætʃrəl/ **I** *n* **1**○ (person) **as an actress, she's a ~** c'est une actrice née; **he's a ~ for the role of Hamlet** il est fait pour jouer Hamlet; **2** Mus (sign) bécarre *m*; (note) note *f* naturelle; **3**‡ (simpleton) imbécile *mf*.
II *adj* **1** (not artificial or man-made) [*phenomenon, force, disaster, harbour, light, resources, process, progression, beauty, material, food*] naturel/-elle; **the ~ world** le monde naturel; **in its ~ state** à l'état naturel; **2** (usual, normal) naturel/-elle, normal; **it's ~ to do/to be** c'est normal de faire/d'être; **it's**

~ **for sb to do** c'est normal que qn fasse; **the ~ thing to do would be to protest** la chose la plus normale serait de protester; **it's only ~** c'est tout à fait naturel; **it's not ~!** ce n'est pas normal!; **to die of ~ causes** mourir de mort naturelle or de sa belle mort; **death from ~ causes** Jur mort naturelle; **for the rest of one's ~ life** Jur à vie; **3** (innate) [*gift, talent, emotion, trait*] inné; [*artist, professional, storyteller*] né; [*affinity*] naturel/-elle; **a ~ advantage** (of person, party, country) un atout; **4** (unaffected) [*person, manner*] simple, naturel/-elle; **try and look more ~** essaie d'avoir l'air plus naturel; **5** (actual, real) [*parent*] naturel/-elle; ‡(illegitimate) [*child*] naturel/-elle; **6** Mus naturel/-elle; **~ horn** cor *m* d'harmonie.

natural: **~ childbirth** *n* accouchement *m* sans douleur, accouchement *m* psychoprophylactique spec; **~ gas** *n* gaz *m* naturel; **~ history** *n* histoire *f* naturelle.

naturalism /ˈnætʃrəlɪzəm/ *n* naturalisme *m*.

naturalist /ˈnætʃrəlɪst/ *n, adj* naturaliste (*mf*).

naturalistic /ˌnætʃrəˈlɪstɪk/ *adj* naturaliste.

naturalization /ˌnætrəlaɪˈzeɪʃn, US -lɪˈz-/ *n* **1** Admin naturalisation *f*; **~ papers** lettres *fpl* or documents *mpl* de naturalisation; **2** Bot, Zool acclimatation *f*.

naturalize /ˈnætʃrəlaɪz/ **I** *vtr* **1** Admin naturaliser [*person*]; **to be ~d** se faire naturaliser; **she's a ~d American** elle est naturalisée Américaine; **2** Bot, Zool acclimater; **3** Ling naturaliser.
II *vi* **1** Bot, Zool s'acclimater; **2** Admin [*person*] se faire naturaliser.

natural: **~ justice** *n*: *principes d'égalité s'appliquant au règlement de disputes*; **~ language** *n* langage *m* naturel; **~ language processing**, **NLP** *n* traitement *m* automatique du langage naturel; **~ logarithm** *n* logarithme *m* naturel.

naturally /ˈnætʃrəlɪ/ *adv* **1** (obviously, of course) naturellement, bien entendu, bien sûr; **~ enough, she refused** naturellement, elle a refusé; **2** (as a logical consequence) naturellement; **I ~ assumed that** j'ai tout naturellement pensé que; **3** (by nature) [*cautious, pale, shy etc*] de nature; **her hair is ~ blonde** elle a des cheveux blond naturel; **~ talented** naturellement doué; **I was doing what comes ~** j'ai fait ce qui me semblait naturel; **politeness comes ~ to him** il est d'un naturel poli; **politeness doesn't come ~ to him** iron on se demande où il a appris la politesse iron; **4** (unaffectedly, unselfconsciously) [*act, behave, speak , smile*] avec naturel; **she expressed herself quite ~** elle s'exprimait avec beaucoup de naturel; **just try and act ~** essaie simplement d'être naturel; **5** (in natural world) à l'état naturel; **~ occurring** présent à l'état naturel.

naturalness /ˈnætʃrəlnɪs/ *n* (of manner, behaviour, person, style etc) naturel *m*.

natural: **~ number** *n* nombre *m* naturel; **~ sciences**† *npl* sciences *fpl* naturelles; **~ selection** *n* sélection *f* naturelle; **~ wastage** *n* ¢ départs *mpl* naturels or volontaires.

nature /ˈneɪtʃə(r)/ **I** *n* **1** (the natural world) nature *f*; **in ~** dans la nature; **the laws/wonders of ~** les lois *fpl*/les merveilles *fpl* de la nature; **it's ~'s way of doing sth** c'est la façon dont la nature fait qch; **let ~ take its course** laissez faire la nature; **contrary to ~**, **against ~** contre nature; **~ versus nurture** l'inné et l'acquis, la nature opposée à la culture; **to obey a call of ~** euph aller se soulager○; **to go back to** ou **return to ~** retourner à la nature; **state of ~** Philos état *m* de nature; **to paint from ~** peindre d'après nature; **one of ~'s gentlemen** un gentleman né; **2** (character, temperament) nature *f*, naturel *m*; **by ~** de or par nature; **it's not in her ~ to be aggressive** elle n'est pas agressive de nature; **he has a very loving ~** il est très affectueux par nature or de nature; **it is in the ~ of animals to kill** c'est dans la nature des animaux de tuer; **3** (kind, sort) nature *f*, sorte *f*; **what is the ~ of the problem?** quelle est la nature du problème?; **nothing of that ~ ever happened here** il ne s'est jamais rien produit de cette nature ici; **matters of a personal/medical ~** des choses d'ordre personnel/médical; **of a serious ~** d'une nature grave; **her letter was something in the ~ of a confession** sa lettre tenait de la confession; **'~ of contents'** Post 'désignation du contenu'; **4** (essential character) nature *f*, essence *f*; **it is in the ~ of things** il est dans l'ordre des choses; **dangerous by its very ~** dangereux/-euse de par sa nature même.
II -natured (*dans composés*) **sweet-/pleasant-~d** d'un naturel doux/agréable.
IDIOMS **~ abhors a vacuum** la nature a horreur du vide.

nature: **~ conservancy** *n* protection *f* de la nature; **Nature Conservancy Council, NCC** *n* ≈ Conseil *m* National de la Protection de la Nature; **~ cure** *n* cure *f* d'air (naturiste); **~-identical** *adj* synthétique; **~ reserve** *n* réserve *f* naturelle; **~ trail** *n* sentier *m* écologique.

naturism /ˈneɪtʃərɪzəm/ *n* naturisme *m*.

naturist /ˈneɪtʃərɪst/ *n, adj* naturiste (*mf*).

naught /nɔːt/ *n*‡ ou littér (nothing) rien *m*; **to bring sth to ~** réduire qch à zéro; **to come to ~** ne mener à rien.

naughtily /ˈnɔːtɪlɪ/ *adv* **1** (disobediently) **to behave ~** [*child*] être vilain; **2** (suggestively) **she winked at him ~** hum elle lui a fait un clin d'œil coquin.

naughtiness /ˈnɔːtɪnɪs/ *n* **1** (of child, pet etc) mauvaise conduite *f*, désobéissance *f*; **2** (of joke, story, picture, suggestion) grivoiserie *f*.

naughty /ˈnɔːtɪ/ *adj* **1** (disobedient) [*child*] vilain; **you ~ boy!** vilain!; **don't be ~!** sois sage!; **a ~ word** un gros mot; **2** (suggestive) [*joke, picture, story*] coquin; **the ~ nineties** ≈ la Belle Époque.

Nauru /nɑːˈuːruː/ ▶ **1131** *pr n* Nauru *f*.

nausea /ˈnɔːsɪə, US ˈnɔːʒə/ *n* nausée *f*; **a wave of ~** une nausée; **to have a feeling of ~** avoir la nausée, avoir envie de vomir; **the idea filled her with ~** l'idée lui donnait la nausée.

nauseate /ˈnɔːsɪeɪt, US ˈnɔːz-/ *vtr* lit, fig écœurer.

nauseating /ˈnɔːsɪeɪtɪŋ, US ˈnɔːz-/ *adj* lit, fig écœurant, nauséabond.

nauseatingly /ˈnɔːsɪeɪtɪŋlɪ, US ˈnɔːz-/ *adv* **~ sweet/rich** d'une douceur/richesse écœurante.

nauseous /ˈnɔːsɪəs, US ˈnɔːʃəs/ *adj* [*taste, smell*] écœurant; [*gas*] qui donne des nausées; **to feel ~** avoir la nausée, avoir mal au cœur.

nautical /ˈnɔːtɪkl/ *adj* [*instrument, term*] nautique, de marine; [*rules*] de navigation; [*almanac*] nautique; [*theme*] marin; [*career*] dans la marine; **~ mile** mile *m* marin or nautique; **~ telescope** lunette *f* marine.

nautilus /ˈnɔːtɪləs/ *n* nautile *m*.

Navaho (Indian) /ˈnævəhəʊ/ *n* Navaho *mf*, Navajo *mf*.

naval /ˈneɪvl/ *adj* naval; [*officer, recruit, uniform, affairs*] de la marine; [*traditions, strength, building*] maritime.

naval: **~ academy** *n* école *f* navale; **~ air force** *n* forces *fpl* aéronavales; **~ air station** *n* station base *f* aéronavale; **~ architect** *n* architecte *m* naval; **~ architecture** *n* construction *f* navale; **~ attaché** *n* attaché naval/attachée navale *m/f*; **~ base**, **~ station** *n* base *f* navale; **~ battle** *n* bataille *f* navale; **~ dockyard** *n* chantier *m* naval; **~ forces** *npl* forces *fpl* navales; **~ stores** *npl* (depot) entrepôt *m* maritime; (supplies) fournitures *fpl* maritimes; **~ warfare** *n* combat *m* naval.

nave /neɪv/ *n* **1** Archit nef *f*; **2** Tech (of wheel) moyeu *m*.

navel /ˈneɪvl/ *n* nombril *m*, ombilic *m* spec.

navel: **~-gazing** *n* péj nombrilisme○ *m*; **~ orange** *n* (orange *f*) navel *f*.

navigable /ˈnævɪgəbl/ *adj* [*river*] navigable; [*balloon*] dirigeable; **a vessel in a ~ condition** un vaisseau en état de naviguer.

navigate /ˈnævɪgeɪt/ **I** *vtr* **1** (sail) parcourir, naviguer; **2** (guide) [*navigator*] piloter [*plane, ship*]; **3** (steer) piloter [*plane*]; gouverner [*ship*]; **~ one's way through** retrouver son chemin dans [*streets*]; se frayer un chemin à travers [*crowd, obstacles, difficulties*].
II *vi* Naut, Aviat naviguer; Aut (in a rally) faire le copilote; (on a journey) [*passenger*] tenir la carte; (without a map) retrouver son chemin; **to ~ by the stars** s'orienter avec les étoiles.

navigation /ˌnævɪˈgeɪʃn/ *n* Naut, Aviat navigation *f*.

navigational /ˌnævɪˈgeɪʃənl/ *adj* [*instruments*] de navigation; [*science*] de la navigation.

navigation: **~ channel** *n* couloir *m* de navigation; **~ laws** *npl* code *m* maritime; **~ lights** *npl* feux *mpl* de navigation.

navigator /ˈnævɪgeɪtə(r)/ *n* Aviat, Naut navigateur/-trice *m/f*; Aut copilote *mf*.

navvy○ /ˈnævɪ/ *n* GB ouvrier *m* du bâtiment.

navy /ˈneɪvɪ/ **I** *n* **1** (fleet) flotte *f*; **2** (fighting force) marine *f*; **to join the ~** s'engager dans la marine.
II *adj* ▶ **1104** **1** (also **~ blue**) (colour) bleu marine *inv*; **2** Mil, Naut [*life, uniform, wife*] de marin.

navy: **~ bean** *n* US haricot *m* blanc; **~ yard** *n* US arsenal *m* de la marine.

nay /neɪ/ ‡ou littér **I** *particle* nenni‡, non.
II *n* (negative vote) non *m*; **the ~s have it** les nons l'ont emporté.
III *adv* et même; **she is pretty, ~ beautiful!** elle est jolie, que dis-je, belle!; **irreverent, ~ immoral** irrévérencieux, voire immoral.

Nazi /ˈnɑːtsɪ/ **I** *n* nazi/-e *m/f*.
II *adj* nazi.

Nazi(i)sm /ˈnɑːtsɪzəm/ *n* nazisme *m*.

NB (*abrév écrite* = **nota bene**) NB.

NBA *n* US **1** (*abrév* = **National Basketball Association**) association *f* nationale de basket-ball; **2** (*abrév* = **National Boxing Association**) association *f* nationale de boxe; **3** *abrév* ▶ **Net Book Agreement**.

NBC *n* US TV (*abrév* = **National Broadcasting Company**) *chaîne nationale de la télévision américaine*.

NC **1** Comm (*abrév* = **no charge**) gratuit; **2** US Post *abrév écrite* = **North Carolina**; **3** ▶ **numerical control**.

NCO *n* Mil (*abrév* = **noncommissioned officer**) sous-officier *m*, gradé *m*.

NCVQ *n* GB (*abrév* = **National Centre for Vocational Qualifications**) conseil *m* national des qualifications professionnelles.

ND US Post *abrév écrite* = **North Dakota**.

NE **1** ▶ **1568** (*abrév* = **northeast**) NE *m*; **2** US Post *abrév écrite* = **Nebraska**.

Neanderthal /nɪˈændətɑːl/ **I** *n* Néandertal *m*.
II *adj* néandertalien/-ienne; **~ man** l'homme *m* de Néandertal.

neap(-tide) /niːp/ *n* (marée *f* de) morte-eau *f*, marée *f* de quadrature.

Neapolitan /nɪəˈpɒlɪtən/ **I** *n* Napolitain/-e *m/f*.
II *adj* napolitain; **~ ice cream** tranche *f* napolitaine.

near /nɪə(r)/ **I** *adv* **1** (nearby) **to live/work quite ~** habiter/travailler tout près; **to move** ou **draw ~** approcher (**to** de); **to move** ou **draw ~er** s'approcher davantage (**to** de); **to bring sth ~er** approcher qch; **2** (close in time) **the exams are drawing ~**

les examens approchent; **the time is ~ when...** dans peu de temps,...; **how ~ are they in age?** combien ont-ils de différence d'âge?; **3** (nearly) **as ~ perfect as it could be** aussi proche de la perfection que possible; **nowhere ~ finished/ready** loin d'être fini/prêt; **he's not anywhere ~ as bright as her** il est loin d'être aussi intelligent qu'elle.

II **near enough** *adv phr* **1** (approximately) à peu près ; **there were 20 yachts ~ enough** il y avait à peu près 20 yachts; **2** (sufficiently close) **that's ~ enough** (not any closer) tu es assez près; (acceptable as quantity) ça ira; **to be ~ enough/come ~ enough to do** être assez près/s'approcher suffisamment pour faire.

III *prep* **1** (in space) près de [*place, person, object*]; **~ here/there** près d'ici/de là; **don't go ~ the fire** ne t'approche pas trop du feu; **don't come ~ me** ne t'approche pas de moi; **2** (in time) **~er the time** quand la date approchera; **it's getting ~ Christmas** Noël approche; **on or ~ the 12th** autour du 12; **their anniversary is ~ ours** leur anniversaire de mariage est à quelques jours du nôtre; **~er 40 than 30** plus proche or plus près de 40 ans que de 30; **3** (in degree) proche de; **~er the truth** plus proche de la vérité; **~er this colour than that** plus proche de cette couleur-ci que de celle-là; **~er what I'm looking for** plus proche de ce que je cherche; **~ the beginning/end of the article** presque au début/à la fin de l'article; **~ the climax of the play** à l'approche du point culminant de la pièce; **I'm no ~er (finding) a solution than I was yesterday** je n'ai pas plus de solution que je n'en avais hier; **he's no ~er (making) a decision** il n'est pas plus décidé; **she's nowhere ~ finishing** elle est loin d'avoir fini; **£400? it cost ~er £600** 400 livres? je dirais plutôt 600; **nobody comes anywhere ~ her** fig personne ne lui arrive à la cheville.

IV **near to** *prep phr* **1** (in space) près de [*place , person , object*]; **~ to where** près de l'endroit où; **~er to** plus près de; **how ~ are we to Dijon?** à quelle distance sommes-nous de Dijon?; **2** (on point of) au bord de [*tears, hysteria, collapse*]; **to be ~ to doing** être sur le point de faire; **how ~ are you to completing...?** est-ce que vous êtes sur le point de finir...?; **3** (in degree) **to come ~est to** s'approcher le plus de [*ideal, conception*]; **to come ~ to doing** faillir faire; **he came ~ to giving up** il a failli abandonner.

V *adj* **1** (close in distance, time) proche; **the ~est tree** l'arbre le plus proche; **our ~est neighbours** nos voisins les plus proches; **in the ~ future** dans un avenir proche; **2** (in degree) **in the ~ darkness** dans la pénombre; **he's the ~est thing to an accountant we've got** c'est lui qui a le plus de connaissances en comptabilité parmi nos employés; **it's the ~est thing** (to article, colour required) c'est ça le plus approchant; **to calculate sth to the ~ whole number** Math arrondir un résultat; **3** (short) **the ~est route** le chemin le plus court.

VI **near+** (*dans composés*) presque; **a ~-catastrophic blunder** une gaffe presque catastrophique; **a ~-perfect exam paper** un examen presque parfait or proche de la perfection.

VII *vtr* **1** (draw close to) approcher de [*place*]; **as we ~ed the city/the harbour** comme nous approchions de la ville/du port; **2** fig approcher de [*peak, record high*]; **to ~ the end of** approcher de la fin de [*season, term*]; **to ~ the end of one's life** lit, fig approcher de sa fin; **to ~ completion** [*project, book*] toucher à sa fin; **to ~ retirement** partir bientôt à la retraite.

nearby /nɪə'baɪ/ **I** *adj* [*person*] qui se trouve/trouvait etc à proximité; [*town, village etc*] d'à côté; **to a ~ bench/garage** jusqu'au banc/garage le plus proche.

II *adv* [*park, wait, stand*] à proximité; **~, there's a village** tout près or juste à côté il y a un village.

Near East *pr n* Proche-Orient *m*.

nearly /'nɪəlɪ/ *adv* **1** (almost) presque; **~ as big** presque aussi grand; **she was ~ crying** elle pleurait presque; **we're ~ there** nous sommes presque arrivés; **I have ~ finished** j'ai presque fini; **it's ~ bedtime** c'est presque l'heure d'aller se coucher; **have you ~ finished?** as-tu bientôt fini?; **~ identical** quasiment or presque identique; **~ a week later** presque une semaine plus tard; **he ~ laughed** il a réprimé un rire; **I very ~ gave up** j'ai bien failli abandonner; **it's the same thing or very ~** c'est du pareil au même; **£1,000 or very ~** 1 000 livres sterling ou presque; **2** (used with negatives) **not ~** loin d'être; **not ~ as talented/surprised as** loin d'être aussi doué/surpris que; **he's not ~ ready** il est loin d'être prêt; **there isn't ~ enough to go around** c'est loin d'être suffisant pour tout le monde; **3** (closely) **the more you look, the more ~ it seems to resemble him** plus on regarde plus on trouve que la ressemblance est frappante.

nearly new *adj* [*clothes*] d'occasion.

near miss *n* Aviat risque *m* de collision; **to have a ~** [*planes*] frôler la collision; [*cars*] faillir se percuter.

near money *n* US valeurs *fpl* réalisables à très court terme.

nearness /'nɪənɪs/ *n* (of person, object, place) proximité *f*; (of event) approche *f*.

nearside /'nɪəsaɪd/ GB Aut, Equit **I** *n* GB côté *m* gauche; (elsewhere) côté *m* droit.

II *modif* GB [*lane*] gauche; (elsewhere) [*lane*] droit.

near: **~-sighted** *adj* myope; **~-sightedness** *n* myopie *f*.

neat /ni:t/ **I** *adj* **1** (tidy) [*person*] (in habits) ordonné; (in appearance) soigné, propre; [*room, house, desk*] bien rangé, ordonné; [*garden*] soigné; [*village*] coquet/-ette; [*handwriting*] soigné; [*accounts, copybook*] bien tenu; **their house is always ~ and tidy** leur maison est toujours impeccable; **she's a ~ worker** elle soigne toujours la présentation de son travail; **in ~ piles** en piles régulières; **2** (adroit) [*theory, explanation, solution*] habile, astucieux/-ieuse; [*formula*] bien trouvé; [*phrase, slogan*] bien tourné, bien trouvé; [*category, division*] bien défini, net/nette; [*summary*] concis; **that's a ~ way of doing it!** c'est astucieux!; **3** (trim) [*figure*] bien fait; [*waist*] fin; [*features*] régulier/-ière; **she has a ~ little figure** elle a une jolie silhouette; **she was wearing a ~ little hat** elle portait un joli petit chapeau; **4**○ US (very good) [*plan, party, car*] super○, formidable; [*profit, sum of money*] joli (*before n*), coquet/-ette; **that's a ~ idea**○**!** c'est une super○ idée!; **5** (unmixed) [*alcohol, spirits*] sans eau, pur; **a ~ vodka** une vodka pure or sans eau.

II *adv* sec, sans eau; **he drinks his whisky ~** il boit son whisky sec or sans eau.

IDIOMS **to be as ~ as a new pin** [*house*] être propre comme un sou neuf.

neaten /'ni:tn/ *vtr* arranger, rajuster [*tie, skirt*]; ranger [*pile of paper*]; **to ~ one's hair** arranger ses cheveux, se recoiffer.

neatly /'ni:tlɪ/ *adv* **1** (tidily) [*arrange, dress, wrap, fold*] avec soin, soigneusement; [*write*] proprement; **his hair was ~ combed** ses cheveux étaient impeccablement peignés; **2** (perfectly) [*link*] habilement; [*illustrate, summarize, match*] parfaitement; **the facts fit together ~** tout s'agence parfaitement; **~ put!** bien or joliment dit!; **the case is designed to fit ~ into your pocket** l'étui est conçu pour rentrer facilement dans la poche.

neatness /'ni:tnɪs/ *n* **1** (tidiness, orderliness) (of person's appearance) aspect *m* soigné; (in habits) méticulosité *f*; (of room, house) propreté *f*, ordre *m*; (of garden) aspect *m* soigné; (of copybook) propreté *f*; (of handwriting) netteté *f*; **extra marks are given for ~** on tiendra compte de la présentation dans la notation; **2** (trimness) (of figure, features) finesse *f*; **3** (adroitness) (of explanation, solution) habileté *f*; (of divisions, categories) précision *f*.

NEB *n* GB *abrév* ▶ **National Enterprise Board**.

nebbish○ /'nebɪʃ/ US **I** *n* empoté/-e○ *m/f*.

II *adj* empoté○.

Nebraska /nɪ'bræskə/ ▶ **1744** *pr n* Nebraska *m*.

Nebuchadnezzar /ˌnebjʊkəd'nezə(r)/ *pr n* Nabuchodonosor.

nebula /'nebjʊlə/ *n* (*pl* **-ae**) nébuleuse *f*.

nebular /'nebjʊlə(r)/ *adj* [*cloud, gas*] des nébuleuses.

nebulous /'nebjʊləs/ *adj* **1** Astron nébuleux/-euse; **2** fig nébuleux/-euse, flou.

NEC *n* (*abrév* = **National Executive Committee**) comité *m* exécutif national.

necessarily /ˌnesə'serəlɪ, 'nesəsərəlɪ/ *adv* **1** (definitely) forcément; **it is not ~ the answer** ce n'est pas forcément la solution; **not ~!** pas forcément!; **2** (of necessity) [*slow, brief*] nécessairement; **a ~ cautious statement** une déclaration prudente par nécessité.

necessary /'nesəsərɪ, US -serɪ/ **I** *n* **1**○ (money) fric○ *m*, argent *m*; **have you got the ~?** tu as le fric?; **2** (needed thing) **to do the ~** faire le nécessaire.

II **necessaries** *npl* Jur minimum *m* vital.

III *adj* **1** (required) [*arrangement, decision, information, skill*] nécessaire; [*qualification*] requis; **if ~, as ~** si besoin est; **it is ~ that you do** il vous faut faire; **'no experience ~'** 'aucune expérience requise'; **2** (essential) [*action*] nécessaire; **a ~ evil** un mal nécessaire; **to become ~** devenir urgent; **to find it ~ to do** éprouver le besoin de faire; **it is ~ for him to do** il faut qu'il fasse; **it is ~ that she should do** il faut vraiment qu'elle fasse; **to do what is ~** faire ce qui est nécessaire; **to do everything (that is) ~** faire tout ce qui est nécessaire; **when ~** quand cela sera nécessaire; **don't spend more time than is ~** n'y consacre pas plus de temps qu'il n'est nécessaire; **circumstances make it ~ for me to do** les circonstances font que je dois faire; **3** (inevitable) [*consequence, result*] nécessaire.

necessitate /nɪ'sesɪteɪt/ *vtr* nécessiter [*cuts, operation, work*]; **the changes were ~d by** ces changements ont été rendus nécessaires par; **the job would ~ your moving** le travail t'obligerait à déménager.

necessitous /nɪ'sesɪtəs/ *adj* sout [*family, person*] nécessiteux/-euse.

necessity /nɪ'sesətɪ/ *n* **1** (need) nécessité *f*; **from** ou **out of ~** par nécessité; **the ~ of doing** la nécessité de faire; **the ~ for** le besoin de; **the ~ of** la nécessité de; **there is a ~ for** il existe un besoin de [*action, change*]; **there is no ~ for** il n'y a pas de réel besoin de [*action, change*]; **there is no ~ for tears** il n'y a pas lieu de pleurer; **the ~ for him to work** la nécessité pour lui de travailler; **there is no ~ for you to do that** tu n'as pas besoin de faire cela; **if the ~ arises** si le besoin se fait sentir; **of ~** nécessairement; **2** (essential item) **the necessities of life** les produits *mpl* de première nécessité; **to be a ~** être indispensable; **the bare necessities** les choses essentielles; **3** (essential measure) impératif *m*; **a political ~** un impératif politique; **to be a ~** être nécessaire; **to be an absolute ~** être indispensable; **4** (poverty) besoin *m*; **to live in ~** vivre dans le besoin; **5** Philos nécessité *f*.

IDIOMS **~ knows no law** nécessité fait loi.

neck /nek/ **I** *n* ▶ **1037** **1** Anat cou *m*; **to wear sth round one's ~** porter qch autour du cou; **to fling one's arms around sb's ~** sauter or se jeter au cou de qn; **to**

drip ou **run down sb's ~** [*liquid*] dégouliner dans le cou de qn; **the back of the ~** la nuque; **2** Zool (of horse, donkey) encolure *f*; **3** Fashn (collar) col *m*; (neckline) encolure *f*; **with a high ~** à or avec un col montant; **with a low ~** décolleté; **4** Culin (of lamb) collet *m*; (of beef) collier *m*; **best end of ~** collet *m*; **5** (narrowest part) (of bottle, flask) goulot *m*, col *m*; (of vase) col *m*; **the ~ of the womb** le col de l'utérus; **6** Mus (of instrument) manche *m*; **7** Geog isthme *m*; **8** Dent collet *m*; **9** Tech (of screw) collet *m*; **10** Geol (of volcano) neck *m*.

II° *vi* se bécoter°.

IDIOMS **to be a pain in the ~**° être casse-pieds°; lit, fig **to be ~ and ~** être à égalité; **he's up to his ~ in it**° il y est enfoncé jusqu'au cou; **he's up to his ~ in debt**° il est endetté jusqu'au cou; **to get** ou **catch it in the ~**° en prendre pour son grade°; **to risk one's ~**° risquer sa peau°; **to stick one's ~ out**° s'avancer; **to win by a ~** [*horse*] gagner d'une encolure; [*person*] gagner de peu; **in this ~ of the woods**° par ici, dans ces parages; **to be dead from the ~ up**° être abruti, n'avoir rien dans la cervelle.

neckband /ˈnekbænd/ *n* **1** (part of garment) bande *f* d'encolure; **2** (choker) ruban *m*.

neckerchief /ˈnekətʃɪf/ *n* foulard *m*.

necking° /ˈnekɪŋ/ *n* ¢ papouilles° *fpl*.

necklace /ˈneklɪs/ **I** *n* collier *m*; (longer) sautoir *m*.

II *vtr* faire subir le supplice du collier à [*victim*].

neck: **~lacing** *n* (torture) supplice *m* du collier; **~let** *n* collier *m*.

neckline /ˈneklaɪn/ *n* encolure *f*; **a plunging ~** un décolleté plongeant.

neck: **~ scarf** *n* foulard *m*; **~tie** *n* US cravate *f*.

necrological /ˌnekrəˈlɒdʒɪkl/ *adj* nécrologique.

necrologist /neˈkrɒlədʒɪst/ *n* nécrologue *mf*.

necrology /neˈkrɒlədʒɪ/ *n* nécrologie *f*.

necromancer /ˈnekrəʊmænsə(r)/ *n* nécromancien/-ienne *m/f*.

necromancy /ˈnekrəʊmænsɪ/ *n* nécromancie *f*.

necrophile /ˈnekrəfaɪl/ *n* = **necrophiliac**.

necrophilia /ˌnekrəˈfɪlɪə/ *n* nécrophilie *f*.

necrophiliac /ˌnekrəˈfɪlɪæk/ *n, adj* nécrophile (*mf*).

necrophobe /ˌnekrəˈfəʊb/ *n* nécrophobe *mf*.

necrophobia /ˌnekrəˈfəʊbɪə/ *n* nécrophobie *f*.

necrophobic /ˌnekrəˈfəʊbɪk/ *adj* nécrophobe.

necropolis /neˈkrɒpəlɪs/ *n* (*pl* **-poles**) nécropole *f*.

nectar /ˈnektə(r)/ *n* (all contexts) nectar *m*.

nectarine /ˈnektərɪn/ *n* (fruit) nectarine *f*, brugnon *m*; (tree) brugnonier *m*.

NEDC *n* GB (*abrév* = **National Economic Development Council**) *organisme consultatif de l'économie britannique*.

Neddy° /ˈnedɪ/ *n* GB (*abrév* = **National Economic Development Council**) ▶ **NEDC**.

née /neɪ/ *adj* née.

need /niːd/

■ **Note** When *need* is used as a verb meaning *to require* or *to want* it is generally translated by *avoir besoin de* in French: *I need help* = j'ai besoin d'aide.

– When *need* is used as a verb to mean *must* or *have to* it can generally be translated by *devoir + infinitive* or by *il faut que + subjunctive*: *I need to leave* = je dois partir, il faut que je parte.

– When *need* is used as a modal auxiliary in the negative to say that there is no obligation it is generally translated by *ne pas être obligé de + infinitive*: *you needn't finish it today* = tu n'es pas obligé de le finir aujourd'hui.

– When *needn't* is used as a modal auxiliary to say that something is not worthwhile or necessary it is generally translated by *ce n'est pas la peine de + infinitive* or *ce n'est pas la peine que + subjunctive*: *I needn't have hurried* = ce n'était pas la peine de me dépêcher *or* ce n'était pas la peine que je me dépêche.

– For examples of the above and further uses of *need*, see the entry below.

I *modal aux* **1** (must, have to) **he didn't ~ to ask permission** il n'était pas obligé de demander la permission; **you needn't wait** tu n'es pas obligé d'attendre; **'I waited'—'you needn't have'** 'j'ai attendu'—'ce n'était pas la peine'; **I needn't have worn a jacket** ce n'était pas la peine que je mette une veste; **you needn't shout!** ce n'est pas la peine de crier!; **~ he reply?** est-ce qu'il faut qu'il réponde?, est-ce qu'il doit répondre?; **~ we discuss it now?** est-ce qu'il faut vraiment en parler maintenant?; **why do you always ~ to complain?** pourquoi faut-il toujours que tu te plaignes? ; **~ I say more?** tu vois ce que je veux dire? ; **I hardly ~ say that...** inutile de dire que...; **I ~ hardly remind you that** inutile de vous rappeler que; **did you ~ to be so unpleasant to him?** est-ce que tu avais besoin d'être si désagréable avec lui?; **'previous applicants ~ not apply'** 'les candidats ayant déjà répondu à l'annonce sont priés de ne pas se représenter'; **2** (be logically inevitable) **~ that be true?** est-ce que c'est forcément vrai?; **it needn't be the case** ce n'est pas forcément le cas; **it needn't follow that** il ne s'ensuit pas forcément que; **it needn't cost a fortune** ça ne coûte pas forcément très cher; **microwaved food needn't be bland** les aliments cuits au micro-onde ne sont pas forcément insipides; **they needn't have died** leur mort aurait pu être évitée.

II *vtr* **1** (require) **to ~ sth** avoir besoin de qch; **to ~ to do** avoir besoin de faire; **my shoes ~ to be polished**, **my shoes ~ polishing** mes chaussures ont besoin d'être cirées; **the proofs ~ careful checking** les épreuves ont besoin d'être vérifiées soigneusement; **I ~ you to hold the ladder** j'ai besoin de toi pour tenir l'échelle; **more money/more time is ~ed** nous avons besoin de plus d'argent/de plus de temps; **everything you ~** tout ce qu'il vous faut, tout ce dont vous avez besoin; **they ~ one another** ils ont besoin l'un de l'autre; **I gave it a much-~ed clean** je l'ai nettoyé, il en avait grand besoin, je l'ai nettoyé et ça n'était pas un luxe; **this job ~s a lot of concentration** ce travail demande beaucoup de concentration; **to raise the money ~ed for the deposit** réunir l'argent nécessaire pour la caution; **they ~ to have things explained to them** il faut tout leur expliquer; **it ~ed six men to restrain him** il a fallu six hommes pour le maîtriser; **you don't ~ me to tell you that...** vous n'êtes pas sans savoir que...; **everything you ~ to know about computers** tout ce que vous devez savoir sur les ordinateurs; **parents—who ~s them**°! les parents—à quoi ça sert?; **2** (have to) **you ~ to learn some manners** il va falloir que tu apprennes à bien te tenir; **you'll ~ to work hard** il va falloir que tu travailles dur; **something ~ed to be done** il fallait faire quelque chose; **why do you always ~ to remind me?** pourquoi faut-il toujours que tu me le rappelles?; **it ~ only be said that** il suffit de dire que; **you only ~ed to ask** il suffisait de demander, tu n'avais qu'à demander; **nothing more ~ be said** on n'en parlera plus; **nobody ~ know** que cela reste entre nous; **nobody ~ know that I did it** ou **that it was me who did it** personne ne doit savoir que c'est moi qui l'ai fait; **3** (want) avoir besoin de; **I ~ a holiday/a whisky** j'ai besoin de vacances/d'un whisky; **she ~s to feel loved** elle a besoin de se sentir aimée; **that's all I ~!** il ne me manquait plus que ça, j'avais bien besoin de ça!

III *n* **1** (necessity) nécessité *f* (**for** de); **the ~ for closer co-operation** la nécessité d'une plus grande collaboration; **I can't see the ~ for it** je n'en vois pas la nécessité; **without the ~ for an inquiry** sans qu'une enquête soit nécessaire; **to feel the ~ to do** éprouver le besoin de faire; **to have no ~ to work** ne pas avoir besoin de travailler; **there's no ~ to wait/hurry** inutile d'attendre/de se dépêcher; **there's no ~ for panic/ anger** ça ne sert à rien de s'affoler/de se mettre en colère; **there's no ~ for you to wait** ce n'est pas la peine que tu attendes; **there's no ~ to worry/shout** ce n'est pas la peine de s'inquiéter/de crier; **if ~ be** s'il le faut, si nécessaire; **if the ~ arises** si le besoin s'en fait sentir; **there's no ~, I've done it** inutile, c'est fait; **2** (want, requirement) besoin *m* (**for** de); **to be in ~ of sth** avoir besoin de qch; **to be in great ~ of sth** avoir grand besoin de qch; **to have no ~ of sth** ne pas avoir besoin de qch; **to satisfy/express a ~** répondre à/exprimer un besoin; **to be in ~ of repair/painting** avoir besoin d'être réparé/repeint; **to meet sb's ~s** répondre aux besoins de qn; **to meet industry's ~ for qualified staff** répondre aux besoins des entreprises en personnel qualifié; **a list of your ~s** une liste de ce dont vous avez besoin; **my ~s are few** j'ai peu de besoins; **manpower/energy ~s** besoins *mpl* en main-d'œuvre/en énergie; **3** (adversity, distress) **to help sb in times of ~** aider qn à faire face à l'adversité; **she was there in my hour of ~** elle était là quand j'ai eu besoin d'elle; **your ~ is greater than mine** tu en as plus besoin que moi; **4** (poverty) besoin *m*; **to be in ~** être dans le besoin; **families in ~** les familles qui sont dans le besoin.

needful /ˈniːdfl/ *adj* sout nécessaire.

neediness /ˈniːdɪnɪs/ *n* indigence *f*.

needle /ˈniːdl/ **I** *n* lit (all contexts) aiguille *f*.

II *vtr* **1** (annoy) harceler [*person*]; **2**° US (increase alcoholic strength of) corser [*drink*].

IDIOMS **as sharp as a ~** rusé comme un singe; **to have pins and ~s** avoir des fourmis; **to get the ~**° GB prendre la mouche°; **to give sb the ~**° mettre qn en rogne°; **to be on the ~**° US argot des drogués se piquer°. ▶ **haystack**.

needle: **~ book**, **~ case** *n* porte-aiguilles *m inv*; **~craft** *n* travaux *mpl* d'aiguille; **~ exchange** *n*: *local où les toxicomanes peuvent échanger des seringues usagées contre des neuves*; **~point** *n* tapisserie *f* au petit point.

needless /ˈniːdlɪs/ *adj* **1** [*anxiety, delay, suffering*] inutile; **2** [*intrusion, intervention*] inopportun; **~ to say** inutile de dire que.

needlessly /ˈniːdlɪslɪ/ *adv* [*worry, suffer, die*] inutilement, pour rien; [*disturbed, upset*] pour rien.

needlessness /ˈniːdlɪsnɪs/ *n* **1** (unnecessary nature) inutilité *f* (**of** de); **2** (tactlessness) inopportunité *f*.

needle: **~woman**† *n* couturière *f*; **~work** *n* couture *f*.

needs /niːdz/ *adv*: IDIOMS **~ must**† il faut bien; **~ must when the devil drives** nécessité fait loi.

need-to-know *adj* **we operate on a ~ basis**, **we have a ~ policy** nous avons pour principe de ne divulguer les informations qu'aux personnes strictement concernées.

needy /ˈniːdɪ/ **I** *n* **the ~** (+ *v pl*) les indigents *mpl*.

II *adj* [*person*] nécessiteux/-euse, dans le dénuement; [*sector, area*] sans ressources.

ne'er‡ /neə(r)/ *adv* (*abrév* = **never**) jamais.

ne'er-do-well† /ˈneəduːwel/ péj **I** *n* bon/bonne *m/f* à rien, propre *mf* à rien.

II *adj* [*person*] bon/bonne or propre à rien.

nefarious /nɪˈfeərɪəs/ *adj* sout abominable.

nefariously /nɪˈfeərɪəslɪ/ *adv* sout de façon ignoble.

negate /nɪˈgeɪt/ *vtr* **1** (cancel out) réduire [qch] à néant [*advantage, effect, work*]; **2** (deny) nier [*concept, existence, fact*]; **3** (contradict) contredire [*theory, results*]; **4** Ling mettre [qch] au négatif [*phrase, meaning*].

negation /nɪˈgeɪʃn/ *n* **1** (contradiction) négation *f*; **2** (denial) réfutation *f*; **3** Ling, Philos négation *f*.

negative /ˈnegətɪv/ **I** *n* **1** (refusal) réponse *f* négative; **to answer** ou **reply in the ~** répondre par la négative; **2** Phot négatif *m*, cliché *m*; **3** Ling négation *f*; **double ~** double négation; **in the ~** à la forme négative; **4** Electron négatif *m*.
II *adj* **1** (saying no) [*answer, decision, statement*] négatif/-ive; **2** Ling négatif/-ive; **3** (pessimistic) [*attitude, response, approach*] negatif/-ive; **to be ~ about sth** être négatif/-ive à l'égard de qch; **don't be so ~!** ne sois pas si négatif!; **4** (harmful) [*effect, influence*] néfaste; **5** (unpleasant) [*association, experience, feeling*] négatif/-ive; **6** Chem, Electron, Med, Phys négatif/-ive; **7** Accts, Math [*amount, answer, number*] négatif/-ive; [*bank balance*] débiteur/-trice; **8** Phot en négatif.
III *excl* Mil, Radio négatif.

negative equity *n*: *moins-value d'une propriété hypothéquée*.

negative income tax *n* Tax impôt *m* négatif.

negatively /ˈnegətɪvlɪ/ *adv* **1** (unenthusiastically) [*react, respond*] négativement; **2** (harmfully) [*affect, influence*] de façon néfaste; **3** Electron, Phys **~ charged** à charge négative.

Negev /ˈnegev/ *pr n* **the ~** (**Desert**) le désert *m* du Néguev.

neglect /nɪˈglekt/ **I** *n* **1** (lack of care) (of person) négligence *f*; (of building, garden) manque *m* d'entretien; (of health, appearance) manque *m* de soin; (of equipment) manque *m* d'entretien; **to fall into ~** être laissé à l'abandon; **to be in a state of ~** être mal entretenu; **2** (lack of interest) indifférence *f* (**of** à l'égard de); **the government's ~ of agriculture** l'indifférence du gouvernement à l'égard de l'agriculture.
II *vtr* **1** (fail to care for) ne pas s'occuper de [*person, dog, plant*]; ne pas entretenir [*garden, house*]; négliger [*health, appearance*]; **2** (ignore) [*person*] négliger [*problem, friend, work*]; [*government*] se désintéresser de [*industry, economy, sector*]; ne pas tenir compte de [*needs, wishes*]; **3** (fail) **to ~ to do** négliger de faire; **4** (overlook) ignorer [*offer, opportunity*]; négliger [*artist, writer, subject*]; **to ~ to mention** omettre de mentionner.
III *v refl* **to ~ oneself** se laisser aller.

neglected /nɪˈglektɪd/ *adj* **1** (uncared for) [*child, pet, appearance*] négligé; [*garden, building*] mal entretenu; **to feel ~** se sentir délaissé; **2** (overlooked) [*writer, subject, masterpiece*] négligé.

neglectful /nɪˈglektfl/ *adj* [*owner, parent*] négligent; **to be ~ of** être peu soucieux/-ieuse de [*appearance, health*]; **to be ~ of sb** négliger qn; **to be ~ of one's duties** avoir peu de conscience professionnelle.

negligee, **négligée** /ˈneglɪʒeɪ, US ˌneglɪˈʒeɪ/ *n* déshabillé *m*.

negligence /ˈneglɪdʒəns/ *n* **1** gen négligence *f*; **through ~** par négligence; **2** Jur **gross ~** faute *f* de nature délictuelle; **criminal ~** négligence *f* criminelle, faute *f* grave; **contributory ~** imprudence *f*; **to sue for (medical) ~** intenter un procès en responsabilité médicale.

negligent /ˈneglɪdʒənt/ *adj* **1** gen, Jur [*person, procedure*] négligent; **to be ~ in doing/failing to do sth** faire preuve de négligence en faisant/en manquant de faire qch; **to be ~ of one's duties** sout manquer à ses devoirs; **2** [*air, manner*] nonchalant.

negligently /ˈneglɪdʒəntlɪ/ *adv* **1** gen, Jur (irresponsibly) négligemment, avec négligence; **2** (nonchalantly) nonchalamment.

negligible /ˈneglɪdʒəbl/ *adj* négligeable.

negotiable /nɪˈgəʊʃəbl/ *adj* **1** [*rate, terms, figure*] négociable; **'salary ~'** 'salaire négociable'; **2** Comm [*cheque, bill of exchange*] négociable; **'not ~'** non à ordre; **3** [*road, pass*] praticable; [*obstacle*] franchissable.

negotiable instrument, **negotiable security** *n* effet *m* de commerce.

negotiate /nɪˈgəʊʃɪeɪt/ **I** *vtr* **1** (discuss) négocier (**with** avec); **'to be ~d'** 'à négocier'; **2** (manoeuvre around) négocier [*bend, turn*]; franchir [*obstacle, rapids*]; **3** (deal with) résoudre [*problem*]; surmonter [*difficulty*]; **4** Fin négocier [*cheque, bond, asset*].
II *vi* négocier (**with** avec; **for** pour obtenir).
III **negotiated** *pp adj* [*settlement, peace, solution*] négocié.

negotiating /nɪˈgəʊʃɪeɪtɪŋ/ *pres p adj* **1** [*ploy, position*] de négociation; [*rights*] à la négociation; **the ~ table** la table des négociations; **2** [*team, committee*] qui conduit les négociations.

negotiation /nɪˌgəʊʃɪˈeɪʃn/ *n* négociation *f* (**between** entre; **with** avec); **to enter into ~(s)** entrer en négociations; **pay/arms ~s** négociations *fpl* salariales/sur le désarmement; **by ~** par la négociation; **to be under ~** être en cours de négociations; **to be open for ~** être négociable; **to be up for ~** être à négocier.

negotiator /nɪˈgəʊʃɪeɪtə(r)/ *n* négociateur/-trice *m/f*.

Negress /ˈniːgrɪs/ *n* injur négresse *f*.

Negro /ˈniːgrəʊ/ **I** *n* (*pl* **-es**) injur nègre *m*.
II *adj* [*descent, race*] noir, nègre.

Negroid /ˈniːgrɔɪd/ *adj* négroïde.

Negro spiritual *n* négro-spiritual *m*.

neigh /neɪ/ **I** *n* hennissement *m*.
II *vi* hennir.

neighbour, **neighbor** US /ˈneɪbə(r)/ **I** *n* **1** (person, country, object) voisin/-e *m/f*; **next-door-~** voisin/-e *m/f* d'à côté; **upstairs/downstairs ~** voisin/-e *m/f* de dessus/de dessous; **she's our next-door ~** elle habite à côté de chez nous; **England's nearest ~ is France** le pays le plus proche de l'Angleterre est la France; **to be a good ~** être un bon voisin; **2** Relig, littér prochain *m*; **love thy ~** aime ton prochain.
II *vi* **to ~ on sth** [*building, site*] avoisiner qch; [*country*] border qch.

neighbourhood GB, **neighborhood** US /ˈneɪbəhʊd/ **I** *n* **1** (district) quartier *m*; **in the ~** dans le quartier; **2** (vicinity) **in the ~** lit dans le voisinage; **in the ~ of the station** au voisinage de la gare.
II *modif* [*facility, shop, office*] du quartier.

neighbourhood: **~ effect** Pol effet *m* de voisinage; **~ television** *n* télévision *f* locale; **~ watch** (**scheme**) *n* surveillance *f* par les gens du quartier.

neighbouring GB, **neighboring** US /ˈneɪbərɪŋ/ *adj* voisin.

neighbourliness GB, **neighborliness** US /ˈneɪbəlɪnɪs/ *n* rapports *mpl* de bon voisinage; **out of good ~** en bon voisin/en bonne voisine *m/f*.

neighbourly GB, **neighborly** US /ˈneɪbəlɪ/ *adj* [*person, act*] gentil/-ille; [*relations*] de bon voisinage; **she is very ~** c'est une bonne voisine.

neighbour states *npl* États *mpl* voisins.

neighing /ˈneɪɪŋ/ *n* hennissement *m*.

neither /ˈnaɪðə(r), ˈniːð-/

■ **Note** When used as co-ordinating conjunctions *neither...nor* are translated by *ni...ni*: *she speaks neither English nor French* = elle ne parle ni anglais ni français; *he is neither intelligent nor kind* = il n'est ni intelligent ni gentil; *neither tea, nor milk* = ni (le) thé, ni (le) lait. Note that the preceding verb is negated by *ne*.
– For examples and further uses see the entry ***neither*** I 1.
– When used as a conjunction to show agreement or similarity with a negative statement, *neither* is translated by *non plus*: *'I don't like him'—'neither do I'* = 'je ne l'aime pas'—'moi non plus'; *'he's not Spanish'—'neither is John'* = 'il n'est pas espagnol'—'John non plus'; *'I can't sleep'—'neither can I'* = 'je n'arrive pas à dormir'—'moi non plus'.
– When used to give additional information to a negative statement *neither* can often be translated by *non plus* preceded by a negative verb: *she hasn't written, neither has she telephoned* = elle n'a pas écrit, et elle n'a pas téléphoné non plus; *I don't wish to insult you, but neither do I wish to lose money* = je ne veux pas vous offenser, mais je ne souhaite pas non plus perdre de l'argent.
– For examples and further uses see the entry ***neither*** I 2.

I *conj* **1** (not either) ni...ni; **I have ~ the time nor the money** je n'ai ni le temps ni l'argent; **I've seen ~ him nor her** je ne les ai vus ni l'un ni l'autre; **2** (nor) **he doesn't have the time, ~ does he have the money** il n'a pas le temps, et il n'a pas l'argent non plus; **you don't have to tell him, ~ should you** tu n'es pas obligé de le lui dire, tu ferais même mieux d'éviter.
II *det* aucun des deux; **~ book is suitable** aucun des deux livres ne convient; **~ girl replied** aucune des deux filles n'a répondu.
III *pron* ni l'un/-e, ni l'autre *m/f*; **~ of them came** ni l'un ni l'autre n'est venu, ils ne sont venus ni l'un ni l'autre; **'which one is responsible?'—'~'** 'lequel des deux est responsable?'—'ni l'un ni l'autre'.

Nelly, **Nellie** /ˈnelɪ/ **I**◑ *pr n* US péj folle *f*.
II◑ *adj* US péj efféminé.
IDIOMS **not on your ~**○ GB jamais de la vie.

nelson /ˈnelsn/ *n* Sport (also **full nelson**) double nelson *m*; **half-~** gen clé *f* au bras; nelson *m*.

nem con /ˌnemˈkɒn/ *adv* (*abrév* = **nemine contradicente**) à l'unanimité.

nemesia /nɪˈmiːʒə/ *n* némésia *f*.

nemesis /ˈneməsɪs/ *n* (punishment) juste punition *f*.

Nemesis /ˈneməsɪs/ *pr n* Mythol Némésis.

neo+ /niːəʊ/ (*dans composés*) néo-.

Neocene /ˈniːəsiːn/ *n* = **Neogene**.

neoclassical /ˌniːəʊˈklæsɪkl/ *adj* néoclassique.

neoclassicism /ˌniːəʊˈklæsɪsɪzəm/ *n* néoclassicisme *m*.

neocolonial /ˌniːəʊkəˈləʊnɪəl/ *adj* néocolonial.

neocolonialism /ˌniːəʊkəˈləʊnɪəlɪzəm/ *n* néocolonialisme *m*.

neocolonialist /ˌniːəʊkəˈləʊnɪəlɪst/ *n* neocolonialiste *mf*.

neoconservative /ˌniːəʊkənˈsɜːvətɪv/ *n*, *adj* néoconservateur/-trice (*m/f*).

neodymium /ˌniːəˈdɪmɪəm/ *n* néodyme *m*.

neofascism /ˌniːəʊˈfæʃɪzəm/ *n* néofascisme *m*.

neofascist /ˌniːəʊˈfæʃɪst/ *n*, *adj* néo-fasciste (*mf*).

Neogene /ˈniːədʒiːn/ **I** *n* **the ~** le néogène.
II *adj* néogène.

neolith /ˈniːəlɪθ/ *n* pierre *f* polie.

Neolithic /ˌnɪːəˈlɪθɪk/ **I** *n* **the ~** le néolithique.
II *adj* néolithique.

neologism /niːˈɒlədʒɪzəm/ *n* néologisme *m*.

neologistic /ˌniːɒləˈdʒɪstɪk/ *adj* néologique.

neologize /niːˈɒlədʒaɪz/ *vi* faire des néologismes.

neomycin /ˌniːəʊˈmaɪsɪn/ *n* néomycine *f*.

neon /ˈniːɒn/ **I** *n* **1** Chem (gas) néon *m*; **2** (type of lighting) néon *m*.
II *modif* [*light, lighting, sign*] au néon; [*atom*] de néon.

neonatal /ˌniːəʊˈneɪtl/ *adj* néo-natal.
neonate /ˈniːəneɪt/ *n* nouveau-né *m*.
neonazi /ˌniːəʊˈnɑːtsɪ/ **I** *n* néonazi *mf*.
II *adj* [*party, group*] néonazi.
neophyte /ˈniːəfaɪt/ *n* (all contexts) néophyte *mf*.
neoplasm /ˈniːəʊplæzəm/ *n* néoplasme *m*.
Neo-Platonic /ˌniːəʊpləˈtɒnɪk/ *adj* néo-platonicien/-ienne.
Neo-Platonism /ˌniːəʊˈpleɪtənɪzəm/ *n* néo-platonisme *m*.
Neo-Platonist /ˌniːəʊˈpleɪtənɪst/ *n* néoplatonicien/-ienne *m/f*.
Neozoic /ˌniːəʊˈzəʊɪk/ *adj* néozoïque.
Nepal /nɪˈpɔːl/ ▶ **1131** *pr n* Népal *m*; **in ~** au Népal.
Nepalese /ˌnepəˈliːz/ ▶ **1486** **I** *n* (person) Népalais/-e *m/f*.
II *adj* népalais.
Nepali /nɪˈpɔːlɪ/ ▶ **1486**, **1402** **I** *n* **1** (person) Népalais/-e *m/f*; **2** (language) népalais *m*.
II *adj* népalais.
nephew /ˈnevjuː, ˈnef-/ *n* neveu *m*.
nephralgia /nɪˈfrældʒɪə/ ▶ **1354** *n* néphralgie *f*.
nephrectomy /nɪˈfrektəmɪ/ *n* néphrectomie *f*.
nephritic /nɪˈfrɪtɪk/ *adj* néphrétique.
nephritis /nɪˈfraɪtɪs/ ▶ **1354** *n* néphrite *f*.
nephrology /nɪˈfrɒlədʒɪ/ *n* néphrologie *f*.
nephrosis /nɪˈfrəʊsɪs/ ▶ **1354** *n* néphrose *f*.
nephrotomy /nɪˈfrɒtəmɪ/ *n* néphrotomie *f*.
nepotism /ˈnepətɪzəm/ *n* népotisme *m*.
Neptune /ˈneptjuːn/ *pr n* **1** Mythol Neptune *m*; **2** Astron Neptune *f*.
nerd◐ /nɜːd/ *n* péj crétin/-e○ *m/f*.
nerdy◐ /ˈnɜːdɪ/ *adj* péj débile○.
Nereid /ˈnɪərɪɪd/ *n* néréide *f*.
Nero /ˈnɪərəʊ/ *pr n* Néron.
nerve /nɜːv/ **I** *n* **1** Anat nerf *m*; Bot nervure *f*; **2** (courage) courage *m*; (confidence) assurance *f*; **to have the ~ to do** avoir le courage or le cran○ de faire; **to keep one's ~** conserver son sang-froid; **to lose one's ~** perdre son courage, se dégonfler○; **to recover one's ~** retrouver son assurance; **3**○ (impudence, cheek) culot○ *m*, audace *f*; **to have the ~ to do** avoir le culot○ de faire; **he's got a ~!** il est gonflé○!, il a du culot○!; **you've got a ~**○**!** tu as un sacré culot○!; **of all the ~!**, **what a ~!** quel culot○!
II nerves *npl* (nervousness) nerfs *mpl*; (stage fright) trac○ *m*; **to have an attack of ~s** faire une crise de nerfs; **she suffers from (her) ~s** c'est une grande nerveuse; **to be in a state of ~s** avoir les nerfs en pelote○; **it's only ~s!** c'est nerveux!; **his ~s were on edge** il était sur les nerfs; **that noise is getting on my ~s** ce bruit me tape sur les nerfs○; **to live on one's ~s** vivre sur les nerfs; **to be all ~s** être un paquet de nerfs; **to calm sb's ~s** calmer qn; **you need strong ~s to do that kind of work** il faut avoir les nerfs solides pour faire ce genre de travail; **to have ~s of steel** avoir des nerfs d'acier; **a war** ou **battle of ~s** une guerre des nerfs.
III *vtr* **to ~ oneself to do** s'armer de courage pour faire.
IDIOMS **to touch** ou **hit a raw ~** toucher un point sensible; **to strain every ~ to do** s'évertuer à faire.
nerve: **~ cell** *n* cellule *f* nerveuse; **~ centre** GB, **~ center** US *n* Anat centre *m* nerveux; fig centre *m* névralgique; **~ ending** *n* terminaison *f* nerveuse; **~ gas** *n* gaz *m* neurotoxique; **~ impulse** *n* influx *m* nerveux.
nerveless /ˈnɜːvlɪs/ *adj* **1** (numb) [*fingers, limbs*] (from cold) engourdi; (from fear, fatigue) inerte; **2** (brave) [*person*] courageux/-euse; **3** (lacking courage, vigour) mou/molle; **4** Anat non innervé; Bot sans nervures.
nerve racking, **~ wracking** *adj* angoissant, insoutenable.
nerviness /ˈnɜːvɪnɪs/ *n* **1** GB (nervousness) nervosité *f*; **2** US (impudence) toupet○ *m*, aplomb *m*.
nervous /ˈnɜːvəs/ *adj* **1** [*person*] (fearful) timide; (anxious) angoissé; (highly strung) nerveux/-euse; [*smile, laugh, habit*] nerveux/-euse; **to be ~ of** GB ou **around** US avoir peur de [*strangers, animals etc*]; **to be ~ of** GB ou **about** US redouter [*change, disagreement*]; **to be ~ about doing** avoir peur de faire; **to feel ~** (apprehensive) gen être angoissé; (before performance) avoir le trac○; (afraid) avoir peur; (ill at ease) se sentir mal à l'aise; **I feel ~ in crowds** les foules m'angoissent; **she makes me feel ~** (intimidates me) elle me met mal à l'aise; (puts my nerves on edge) elle me rend nerveux; **all this talk of war makes me ~** toutes ces rumeurs de guerre m'inquiètent ; **'not suitable for persons of a ~ disposition'** 'ce film est déconseillé aux âmes sensibles'; **2** Anat, Med nerveux/-euse; **~ disease** maladie *f* nerveuse; **~ exhaustion** fatigue *f* nerveuse; **~ tension** tension *f* nerveuse; **3** Fin [*market*] instable.
nervous breakdown *n* dépression *f* nerveuse; **to have a ~** avoir or faire○ une dépression nerveuse.
nervous energy *n* énergie *f*; **to be full of ~** être plein d'énergie.
nervously /ˈnɜːvəslɪ/ *adv* nerveusement.
nervous Nellie○ *n* US péj trouillard/-e○ *m/f*.
nervousness /ˈnɜːvəsnɪs/ *n* **1** (of person) (shyness) timidité *f*; (fear) peur *f*; (anxiety) inquiétude *f*; (stage fright) trac○ *m*; (physical embarrassment) agitation *f*; (tenseness) nervosité *f*; **2** (of smile, laughter) nervosité *f*; **3** Fin (of market) instabilité *f*.
nervous: **~ system** *n* système *m* nerveux; **~ wreck**○ *n* boule *f* de nerfs○.
nervy○ /ˈnɜːvɪ/ *adj* **1** GB (tense, anxious) nerveux/-euse; **2** US (impudent) gonflé○.
nest /nest/ **I** *n* **1** (of animal) nid *m*; **to build** ou **make its ~** faire son nid; **wasps'/ants' ~** nid de guêpes/de fourmis; **2** (group of baby birds, mice) nichée *f* (**of** de); **3** (of criminals, traitors) nid *m*; **4** (of boxes, bowls) série *f*; **~ of tables** tables *fpl* gigognes; **5** (gun site) nid *m*; **machine-gun ~** nid de mitrailleuses.
II *vi* **1** [*bird*] faire son nid; **2** [*tables*] s'insérer; [*boxes, pans*] s'emboîter.
IDIOMS **to flee** ou **fly** ou **leave the ~** fig quitter le nid familial; **to feather one's (own) ~** se remplir les poches; **to foul one's (own) ~** [*polluter*] polluer le milieu dans lequel on vit; [*criminal, adulterer*] éclabousser l'honneur de ses proches; ▶ **viper**.
nested /ˈnestɪd/ *adj* **1** [*pans, bowls*] qui s'emboîtent; **a set of ~ tables** des tables gigognes; **2** Comput [*loop, subroutine*] imbriqué, emboîté; **3** Ling [*phrase, expression*] enchâssé, emboîté.
nest egg *n* magot○ *m*.
nesting /ˈnestɪŋ/ **I** *n* **1** Zool construction *f* de nid, nidification *f* spec; **2** Comput emboîtement *m*, imbrication *f*; **3** Ling enchâssement *m*; **4** = **bird's-nesting**.
II *modif* [*ground, habitat, place*] propice à la construction des nids; [*habit, season*] de construction des nids.
nesting: **~ box** *n* nichoir *m*; **~ site** *n* site *m* de nidification.
nestle /ˈnesl/ **I** *vtr* **to ~ one's head** appuyer sa tête (**on** sur; **against** contre); **to ~ a baby in one's arms** étreindre un bébé.
II *vi* **1** [*person, animal*] se blottir (**against** contre; **under** sous); **to ~ into an armchair** se caler confortablement dans un fauteuil; **2** [*village, house, object*] être niché.
■ **nestle down** s'installer confortablement.
■ **nestle up** se blottir (**against, to** contre).
nestling /ˈneslɪŋ/ *n* oisillon *m*.
net /net/ **I** *n* **1** Fishg, Hort, Hunt filet *m*; **butterfly ~** filet à papillons; **2** Sport (in tennis) filet *m*; **to come (up) to the ~** monter au filet; (in football) filets *mpl*; **in the ~** dans les filets; **to put the ball into (the back of) the ~** mettre la balle dans les filets; **3** fig (trap) piège *m*; **the ~ is closing** l'étau se resserre; **to slip through the ~** passer à travers les mailles du filet; **4** Telecom réseau *m*; **5** Tex (voile *m* de) tulle *m*.
II *adj* (also **nett**) **1** Fin, Comm [*profit, income, price, weight*] net/nette; [*loss*] sec/sèche; **~ of tax** net après impôt; **terms strictly ~** prix nets; **it weighs 20 kilos ~** cela pèse 20 kilos net; **an income of £30,000 ~** un revenu net de 30 000 livres sterling; **2** gen [*result, effect, increase*] net/nette.
III *vtr* (*p prés etc* **-tt-**) **1** Fishg, Hunt prendre [qch] au filet [*fish, butterfly*]; **2** Comm, Fin [*person*] faire un bénéfice de; [*sale, export, deal*] rapporter; **to ~ sb sth** rapporter qch à qn; **3** Sport (in football) marquer, rentrer [*goal*]; **4** fig (catch) [*police*] attraper [*criminal*]; **5** (win) [*sportsman, team*] gagner [*trophy*].
IDIOMS **to cast one's ~ wide** ratisser large.
net: **~ asset value** *n* Fin valeur *f* liquidative; **~ball** *n*: *sport d'équipe proche du basket joué par les femmes*; **Net Book Agreement**, **NBA** *n* GB Comm convention *f* sur le prix unique du livre.
net cord *n* Sport (in tennis) **1** (shot) net *m*; **2** (cord) corde *f* (du filet).
net curtain *n* voilage *m*.
nether‡ /ˈneðə(r)/ *adj* bas/basse; [*garments*] de dessous; **the ~ regions** (hell) les enfers; (lower body) euph hum les parties inférieures euph; (basement) les parties basses.
Netherlander† /ˈneðələndə(r)/ ▶ **1486** *n* Hollandais/-e *m/f*.
Netherlands /ˈneðələndz/ ▶ **1131** **I** *pr n* **the ~** (+ *v sg*) les Pays-Bas *mpl*, la Hollande; **in the ~** aux Pays-Bas, en Hollande.
II *adj* [*tradition, climate*] hollandais, des Pays-Bas.
Netherlands Antilles /ˌneðələndz ænˈtɪliːz/ ▶ **1131** *pr n* Antilles *fpl* néerlandaises.
nethermost‡ /ˈneðəməʊst/ *adj* le plus bas; **the ~ depths** les profondeurs.
net present value, **NPV** *n* Fin valeur *f* actuelle nette, VAN.
nett *adj* GB = **net** II.
netting /ˈnetɪŋ/ *n* **1** (mesh) (of rope) filet *m*; (of metal, plastic) grillage *m*; **side ~** (in football) filets *mpl* latéraux; **2** Tex voile *m*, tulle *m*.
nettle /ˈnetl/ **I** *n* (also **stinging ~**) ortie *f*.
II *modif* [*sting*] d'ortie; [*soup*] aux orties.
III *vtr* agacer.
IDIOMS **to grasp** ou **seize the ~** prendre le taureau par les cornes.
nettle rash *n* urticaire *f*.
net ton ▶ **1883** *n* US tonne *f* courte.
network /ˈnetwɜːk/ **I** *n* (all contexts) réseau *m* (**of** de); **computer/telephone ~** réseau informatique/téléphonique; **radio ~** réseau de radiodiffusion; **rail/road ~** réseau ferroviaire/routier; **TV** ou **television ~** réseau de télévision.
II *vtr* **1** TV, Radio diffuser [*programme*]; **2** Comput interconnecter [*computers*].
III *vi* tisser un réseau de relations.
IV networked *pp adj* [*computer, workstation*] interconnecté.
networking /ˈnetwɜːkɪŋ/ *n* **1** Comm constitution *f* de réseaux; **2** Comput interconnexion *f*; **3** (establishing contacts) **~ is important** c'est important d'avoir des contacts; **I was doing some ~** j'essayais de me faire des contacts.
network: **~ operator** *n* Telecom opérateur *m* de réseau; **~ television** *n* US chaîne *f* nationale.

Neuchâtel /ˌnɜːʃæˈtel/ ▶ 1818, 1776 *pr n* Neuchâtel; **the canton of ~** le canton de Neuchâtel.

neural /ˈnjʊərəl, US ˈnʊ-/ *adj* neuronal.

neuralgia /ˌnjʊəˈrældʒə, US ˌnʊ-/ ▶ 1354 *n* névralgie *f*.

neuralgic /ˌnjʊəˈrældʒɪk, US ˌnʊ-/ *adj* névralgique.

neurasthenia‡ /ˌnjʊərəsˈθiːnɪə, US ˌnʊ-/ *n* neurasthénie *f*.

neurasthenic‡ /ˌnjʊərəsˈθenɪk, US ˌnʊ-/ *n*, *adj* neurasthénique (*mf*).

neuritis /ˌnjʊəˈraɪtɪs, US ˌnʊ-/ ▶ 1354 *n* névrite *f*.

neurogenic /ˌnjʊərəʊˈdʒenɪk, US ˌnʊ-/ *adj* neurogène.

neurological /ˌnjʊərəˈlɒdʒɪkl, US ˌnʊ-/ *adj* neurologique.

neurologist /ˌnjʊˈrɒlədʒɪst, US ˌnʊ-/ ▶ 1692 *n* neurologue *mf*.

neurology /ˌnjʊəˈrɒlədʒɪ, US ˌnʊ-/ *n* neurologie *f*.

neuroma /ˌnjʊəˈrəʊmə, US ˌnʊ-/ *n* (*pl* **~s** ou **-mata**) névrome *m*.

neuromuscular /ˌnjʊərəʊˈmʌskjʊlə(r), US ˌnʊ-/ *adj* neuromusculaire.

neuron /ˈnjʊərɒn, US ˈnʊ-/, **neurone** /ˈnjʊərəʊn, US ˈnʊ-/ *n* neurone *m*.

neuropathic /ˌnjʊərəʊˈpæθɪk, US ˌnʊ-/ *adj* névropathique.

neuropathology /ˌnjʊərəʊpəˈθɒlədʒɪ/ *n* névropathologie *f*.

neuropathy /njʊˈrɒpəθɪ, US nʊ-/ *n* neuropathie *f*.

neurophysiological /ˌnjʊərəʊˌfɪzɪəˈlɒdʒɪkl, US ˌnʊ-/ *adj* neurophysiologique.

neurophysiologist /ˌnjʊərəʊˌfɪzɪɒˈlədʒɪst, US ˌnʊ-/ ▶ 1692 *n* neurophysiologiste *mf*.

neurophysiology /ˌnjʊərəʊˌfɪzɪˈɒlədʒɪ, US ˌnʊ-/ *n* neurophysiologie *f*.

neuropsychiatric /ˌnjʊərəʊˌsaɪkɪˈætrɪk, US ˌnʊ-/ *adj* neuropsychiatrique.

neuropsychiatrist /ˌnjʊərəʊsaɪˈkaɪətrɪst, US ˌnʊ-/ ▶ 1692 *n* neuropsychiatre *mf*.

neuropsychiatry /ˌnjʊərəʊsaɪˈkaɪətrɪ, US ˌnʊ-/ *n* neuropsychiatrie *f*.

neurosis /njʊəˈrəʊsɪs, US nʊ-/ *n* (*pl* **-oses**) névrose *f*; fig **to have a ~ about sth** avoir une idée fixe à propos de qch.

neurosurgeon /ˌnjʊərəʊˈsɜːdʒn, US ˌnʊ-/ ▶ 1692 *n* neurochirurgien *m*.

neurosurgery /ˌnjʊərəʊˈsɜːdʒərɪ, US ˌnʊ-/ *n* neurochirurgie *f*.

neurosurgical /ˌnjʊərəʊˈsɜːdʒɪkl, US ˌnʊ-/ *adj* [*technique, institution, patient*] de neurochirurgie; [*operation*] neurochirurgical.

neurotic /njʊəˈrɒtɪk, US nʊ-/ **I** *n* névrosé/-e *m/f*.
II *adj* névrosé; **to be ~ about sth/about doing** être complètement maniaque en ce qui concerne qch/quand il s'agit de faire.

neurotically /njʊəˈrɒtɪklɪ, US nʊ-/ *adv* de façon obsessionnelle.

neuroticism /njʊəˈrɒtɪsɪzəm, US nʊ-/ *n* tendance *f* à la névrose.

neurovascular /ˌnʊərəʊˈvæskjʊlə(r), US ˌnʊ-/ *adj* neurovasculaire.

neuter /ˈnjuːtə(r), US ˈnuː-/ **I** *n* Ling neutre *m*; **in the ~** au neutre.
II *adj* Bot, Ling, Zool neutre.
III *vtr* Vet châtrer.

neutral /ˈnjuːtrəl, US ˈnuː-/ **I** *n* **1** Mil, Pol neutre *mf*; **2** Aut point *m* mort; **in/into ~** au point mort.
II *adj* (all contexts) neutre (**about** en ce qui concerne); **to have a ~ policy** pratiquer une politique de neutralité; **to have a ~ effect on sth** ne pas avoir d'effet sur qch.

neutralism /ˈnjuːtrəlɪzəm, US ˈnuː-/ *n* neutralisme *m*.

neutralist /ˈnjuːtrəlɪst, US ˈnuː-/ *n*, *adj* neutraliste (*mf*).

neutrality /njuːˈtrælətɪ, US nuː-/ *n* **1** Chem, Pol (status) neutralité *f*; **armed ~** neutralité *f* armée; **2** Pol, gen (attitude) attitude *f* de neutralité (**towards** vis-à-vis).

neutralization /ˌnjuːtrəlaɪˈzeɪʃn, US ˌnuːtrəlɪˈzeɪʃn/ *n* Chem, Mil, aussi euph, Pol neutralisation *f* also euph.

neutralize /ˈnjuːtrəlaɪz, US ˈnuː-/ *vtr* Chem, Mil, aussi euph, Pol neutraliser also euph.

neutrino /njuːˈtriːnəʊ, US nuː-/ *n* (*pl* **~s**) neutrino *m*.

neutron /ˈnjuːtrɒn, US ˈnuː-/ **I** *n* neutron *m*.
II *modif* [*bomb, star*] à neutrons.

neutron number *n* nombre *m* de neutrons.

Nevada /nəˈvɑːdə/ ▶ 1744 *pr n* Nevada *m*; **in/to ~** au Nevada.

Nevadan /nəˈvɑːdən/ **I** *n* habitant/-e *m/f* du Nevada.
II *adj* [*landscape*] du Nevada; [*weather*] au Nevada.

never /ˈnevə(r)/

■ **Note** When *never* is used to modify a verb (*she never wears a hat, I've never seen him*) it is translated *ne...jamais* in French; *ne* comes before the verb, and before the auxiliary in compound tenses, and *jamais* comes after the verb or auxiliary: *elle ne porte jamais de chapeau, je ne l'ai jamais vu*.
– When *never* is used without a verb, it is translated by *jamais* alone: *'admit it!'—'never!'* = 'avoue-le!'—'jamais'.
– For examples and particular usages, see the entry below.

adv **1** (not ever) **I ~ go to London** je ne vais jamais à Londres; **he will ~ forget it** il ne l'oubliera jamais; **she ~ says anything** elle ne dit jamais rien; **I ~ work on Saturdays** je ne travaille jamais le samedi; **I've ~ known him to be late** ce n'est pas le genre à être en retard; **I've ~ seen such a mess** je n'ai jamais vu un désordre pareil; **~ have I seen such poverty** je n'ai jamais vu une telle pauvreté; **'have you ever been to Paris?'—'~'** 'as-tu déjà visité Paris?'—'jamais'; **it's now or ~** c'est le moment ou jamais; **~ again** plus jamais; **~ before has the danger been so great** le danger n'a jamais été aussi grand; **~ in all my life** ou **born days** jamais de la vie; **~ ever lie to me again!** ne me mens plus jamais!; **he ~ ever drinks alcohol** il ne boit absolument jamais d'alcool; **~ one to refuse a free meal, he agreed** il a accepté parce qu'il ne dit jamais non à un repas gratuit; **~ a day passes but he phones me** pas un jour ne passe sans qu'il me téléphone; **better late than ~** mieux vaut tard que jamais; **you ~ know** on ne sait jamais; **2** (as an emphatic negative) **he ~ said a word** il n'a rien dit; **I ~ knew that** je ne le savais pas; **he ~ so much as apologized** il ne s'est même pas excusé; **Bob, ~ a strong swimmer, tired quickly** Bob, qui n'a jamais été un bon nageur, s'est vite fatigué; **she mustn't catch you crying! that would ~ do** il ne faut surtout pas qu'elle te voie pleurer; ▶ **fear**, **mind**; **3** (expressing surprise, shock) **you're ~ 40!** GB ce n'est pas possible, tu n'as pas 40 ans!; **you've ~ gone and broken it have you**○! GB ne me dis pas que tu l'as cassé!; **~!** pas possible!; **'I punched him'—'you ~ (did)○!'** GB 'je lui ai donné un coup de poing'—'c'est pas vrai○!'; **well I ~ (did)!** ça par exemple!

never-ending /ˌnevərˈendɪŋ/ *adj* interminable.

nevermore /ˌnevəˈmɔː(r)/ *adv* plus jamais; **~ will he see his homeland** il ne verra plus jamais sa patrie.

never-never○ /ˌnevəˈnevə(r)/ *n* GB **to buy sth on the ~** acheter qch à crédit.

never-never land *n* pays *m* imaginaire; **to live in ~** ne pas avoir les pieds sur terre.

nevertheless /ˌnevəðəˈles/ *adv* **1** (all the same) quand même, malgré tout; **I like him ~** je l'aime quand même; **he's my friend ~** c'est quand même mon ami; **they go on trying ~** ils continuent quand même à essayer; **thanks ~** merci quand même; **~, I think you should go** je crois que tu devrais y aller quand même; **2** (nonetheless) pourtant, néanmoins; **it's ~ true that** c'est pourtant vrai que..., il est néanmoins vrai que; **so strong yet ~ so gentle** si fort et pourtant si doux; **3** (however) pourtant, toutefois, néanmoins; **he did ~ say that** il a pourtant or toutefois or néanmoins dit que.

never-to-be-forgotten *adj* inoubliable.

new /njuː, US nuː/ *adj* **1** (not known, seen, owned etc before) nouveau/-elle (*before n*); (brand-new) [*car, dress, carpet*] neuf/neuve; **the area is ~ to me** la région m'est inconnue; **the work/subject is ~ to me** je ne connais rien au travail/au sujet; **as good as ~** lit, fig comme neuf; **'as ~'** (in advertisement) 'état neuf'; **that's nothing ~** ce n'est pas nouveau; **I feel like a ~ man** je suis transformé; **'what's ~?'** 'quoi de neuf?'; **that's a ~ one on me** on en apprend tous les jours; **2** (different) [*boyfriend, life, era, approach, design*] nouveau/-elle (*before n*); **the New Left/Right** Pol la Nouvelle Gauche/Droite; **someone/something ~** quelqu'un/quelque chose d'autre; **could I have a ~ plate? This one is dirty** est-ce que je pourrais avoir une autre assiette? Celle-ci est sale; **3** (recently arrived) [*recruit, arrival*] nouveau/-elle (*before n*); **to be ~ to** ne pas être habitué à [*job, way of life*]; **we're ~ to the area** nous sommes nouveaux venus dans la région; **4** (latest) [*book, film, model*] nouveau/-elle (*before n*); [*fashion*] dernier/-ière (*before n*); **5** (harvested early) [*vegetable*] nouveau/-elle (*after n*).

New Age **I** *n* New Age *m*.
II *modif* [*music, ideas, sect*] New Age *inv*.

New Age: ~ Movement, **NAM** *n* New Age *m*; **~ Traveller** *n* voyageur/-euse *m/f* New Age.

new blood *n* sang *m* frais.

newborn /ˈnjuːbɔːn, US ˈnuː-/ *adj* nouveau-né/-née; **~ baby** nouveau-né/-née *m/f*.
IDIOMS **as innocent as a ~ babe** innocent comme l'enfant qui vient de naître.

new: **New Brunswick** *pr n* Nouveau-Brunswick *m*; **New Caledonia** ▶ 1381 *pr n* Nouvelle-Calédonie *f*.

newcomer /ˈnjuːkʌmə(r), US ˈnuː-/ *n* (in place, job, club) nouveau venu/nouvelle venue *m/f*; (in sport, theatre, cinema) nouveau/-elle *m/f*; **to be a ~ to a job/town/team** être nouveau/-elle dans un emploi/une ville/une équipe.

New Deal *n* US Hist New Deal *m*.

New Delhi /ˌnjuː ˈdelɪ/ US /ˌnuː-/ ▶ 1818 *pr n* New Delhi.

newel /ˈnjuːəl, US ˈnuːəl/ *n* **1** (also **~ post**) (on banisters) pilastre *m*; **2** (for spiral stairs) noyau *m*.

new: **New England** ▶ 1744 *pr n* Nouvelle-Angleterre *f*; **~fangled** *adj* péj moderne.

newfound /ˈnjuːˌfaʊnd/ *adj* tout nouveau/toute nouvelle.

Newfoundland /njuːˈfaʊndlənd, US nuː-/ **I** *pr n* Geog Terre-Neuve *f*; **to/in ~** à Terre-Neuve.
II *n* (dog) terre-neuve *m*.
III *modif* [*people*] terre-neuvien/-ienne; [*landscape, industry*] de Terre-Neuve.

Newfoundlander /njuːˈfaʊndləndə(r), US nuː-/ *n* Terre-Neuvien/-ienne *m/f*.

new: **New Guinea** ▶ 1381 *pr n* Nouvelle-Guinée *f*; **New Hampshire** ▶ 1744 *pr n* US New Hampshire *m*; **New Hebrides** ▶ 1131 *pr n* Hist Nouvelles-Hébrides *fpl*.

newish /ˈnjuːɪʃ, US ˈnuː-/ *adj* assez neuf/neuve.

new: **New Jersey** ▶ 1744 *pr n* New Jersey *m*; **~ Jerusalem** *pr n* Relig Nouvelle Jérusalem; **New Latin** *n* latin *m* moderne.

new look **I** *n* (image) (for person, car, house) nouveau style *m*.
II new-look *adj* [*product*] nouvelle version

inv; [*car, team*] nouveau/-elle (*before n*); [*edition, show*] remanié.

New Look *n, modif* Fashn Hist new-look (*m*) (*inv*).

newly /ˈnjuːlɪ, US ˈnuː-/ *adv* **1** (recently) [*built, elected, formed, qualified*] nouvellement; [*washed, shaved*] fraîchement; **2** (differently) [*named, arranged*] différemment.

newlyweds /ˈnjuːlɪwedz, US ˈnuː-/ *npl* jeunes mariés *mpl*.

new: **~ man** *n* homme *m* moderne or nouveau; **~ math** *n* US maths *fpl* modernes; **New Mexico** ▶ 1744 *pr n* Nouveau-Mexique *m*; **~ moon** *n* nouvelle lune *f*; **~-mown** *adj* (*épith*) fraîchement coupé ou fauché (*after n*).

newness /ˈnjuːnɪs, US ˈnuː-/ *n* (of idea, feeling, fashion) nouveauté *f*; (of object, car, clothes) état *m* neuf.

New Orleans ▶ 1818 *pr n* Nouvelle-Orléans *f*.

news /njuːz, US nuːz/ *n* **1** (new political or public information) nouvelle(s) *f(pl)*; **an item of ~** gen une nouvelle; Journ une information; **the latest ~ is that all is quiet** aux dernières nouvelles tout était calme; **the ~ that she had resigned** la nouvelle selon laquelle elle aurait démissionné; **~ of her resignation reached Parliament** la nouvelle de sa démission est parvenue au Parlement; **~ is just coming in of an explosion** on vient juste d'apprendre la nouvelle d'une explosion; **here now with ~ of today's sport is X** et voici maintenant, pour nous parler du sport aujourd'hui, X; **these events are not ~** ces événements n'ont rien de nouveau; **to be in the ~, to make (the) ~** défrayer la chronique; **she's always in the ~** on parle beaucoup d'elle dans les médias; **2** (personal information) nouvelle(s) *f(pl)*; **a bit** ou **piece of ~** une nouvelle; **a sad bit of ~** une triste nouvelle; **have you heard the ~?** tu connais la nouvelle?; **it's wonderful ~ about Louis!** nouvelle formidable à propos de Louis!; **I heard the ~ from Jo** j'ai appris la nouvelle par Jo; **have I got ~ for you**○! j'ai une nouvelle à t'apprendre!; **have you any ~ of her?** est-ce que tu as de ses nouvelles?; **I have no ~ of her** je n'ai aucune nouvelle d'elle; **tell me all your ~!** raconte-moi ce que tu deviens!; **that's ~ to me**○! ça, c'est du nouveau○!; **that's good/bad ~** c'est une bonne/mauvaise nouvelle; **she's bad ~**○! c'est un véritable fléau○!; **this is** ou **spells bad ~ for** c'est une mauvaise nouvelle pour; **bad ~ travels fast** les mauvaises nouvelles circulent vite; **3** Radio, TV (programme) **the ~** les informations *fpl*, les infos○ *fpl*, le journal *m*; **to see sth/sb on the ~** voir qch/qn aux informations; **4** Journ (column title) **'financial ~'** 'chronique *f* financière'; **'Home News'** 'les informations *fpl* nationales'; **'The Baltimore News'** (newspaper title) 'Les Nouvelles *fpl* de Baltimore'.
IDIOMS **no ~ is good ~** pas de nouvelles, bonnes nouvelles.

news: **~ agency** *n* agence *f* de presse; **~agent** ▶ 1692 *n* GB marchand *m* de journaux; **~agent's** ▶ 1692 *n* GB magasin *m* de journaux; **~ analyst** ▶ 1692 *n* US commentateur/-trice *m/f*; **~ blackout** *n* black-out *m*; **~boy** *n* vendeur *m* de journaux; **~ bulletin** GB, **~cast** US *n* Radio, TV bulletin *m* d'information; **~caster** ▶ 1692 *n* présentateur/-trice *m/f* des informations; **~ conference** *n* conférence *f* de presse; **~dealer** ▶ 1692 *n* US marchand *m* de journaux.

news desk *n* (at newspaper) (salle *f* de) rédaction *f*; **now over to our ~ for the headlines** et maintenant les titres de l'actualité.

news: **~ editor** ▶ 1692 *n* rédacteur/-trice *m/f*; **~ flash** *n* flash *m* (d'information); **~gathering** *n* collecte *f* de l'information; **~group** *n* Comput forum *m* de discussion; **~hawk**○ *n* US reporter *m*; **~ headlines** *npl* TV titres *mpl* de l'actualité; **~hound** *n* reporter *m*; **~ item** *n* sujet *m* d'actualité, information *f*; **~letter** *n* bulletin *m*; **~ magazine** *n* magazine *m* d'informations; **~man** ▶ 1692 *n* journaliste *m*.

New South Wales *pr n* Nouvelle-Galles *f* du Sud.

newspaper /ˈnjuːspeɪpə(r), US ˈnuːz-/ **I** *n* **1** (item) journal *m*; **the Sunday ~s** les journaux du dimanche; **2** (substance) papier *m* journal; **wrapped in ~** enveloppé dans du papier journal.
II *modif* [*article, photograph*] de presse; [*archives*] du journal, de la rédaction; [*cuttings*] de journaux, de presse.

newspaper: **~man** ▶ 1692 *n* journaliste *m*; **~ office** *n* bureau *m* de rédaction; **~woman** ▶ 1692 *n* journaliste *f*.

newspeak /ˈnjuːspiːk, US ˈnuː-/ *n* péj jargon *m* administratif péj.

news photographer ▶ 1692 *n* reporter *m* photographe.

newsprint /ˈnjuːzprɪnt, US ˈnuː-/ *n* (paper) papier *m* journal; (ink) encre *f* d'imprimerie.

news: **~reader** ▶ 1692 *n* GB présentateur/-trice *m/f* des informations; **~reel** *n* Cin Hist actualités *fpl*; **~room** *n* (salle *f* de) rédaction *f*.

news service *n* **1** (agency) agence *f* de presse; **2** (service provided by media) service *m* d'information.

news: **~ sheet** *n* bulletin *m*; **~stand** *n* kiosque *m* à journaux.

new: **~-style** *adj* nouveau style *inv*; **New Style** *pr n* nouveau calendrier *m*, calendrier *m* grégorien.

news: **~ value** *n* valeur *f* médiatique; **~ vendor** ▶ 1692 *n* vendeur/-euse *m/f* de journaux; **~woman** ▶ 1692 *n* journaliste *f*; **~worthy** *adj* médiatique.

newsy /ˈnjuːzɪ, US ˈnuː-/ *adj* [*letter*] plein de nouvelles.

newt /njuːt, US nuːt/ *n* triton *m*.
IDIOMS **pissed as a ~**◑ soûl comme une bourrique○.

New Testament, NT *pr n* Bible Nouveau Testament *m*.

newton /ˈnjuːtn, US ˈnuː-/ *n* Phys newton *m*.

Newtonian /njuːˈtəʊnɪən, US nuː-/ *adj* newtonien/-ienne.

new town *n* ville *f* nouvelle.

new wave I *n* nouvelle vague *f*.
II New Wave *pr n* Cin Nouvelle Vague *f*.
III *adj* nouvelle vague *inv*.

New World *n* Nouveau Monde *m*.

New Year *n* **1** (January 1st) le nouvel an *m*; **at (the) ~** au nouvel an; **for** ou **over (the) ~** pour le nouvel an; **closed for ~** ou US **~'s** Comm fermé pour les fêtes du nouvel an; **to celebrate ~** ou US **~'s** célébrer le nouvel an; **to see in** ou **bring in the ~** fêter la Saint-Sylvestre; **Happy ~!** bonne année!; **2** (next year) (whole) l'année *f* prochaine; (the beginning) la nouvelle année; **early in the ~** au début de l'année prochaine.

New Year's day GB, **New Year's** US *n* le jour *m* de l'an.

New Year's Eve *n* la Saint-Sylvestre; **~ party** ou **celebrations** fêtes *fpl* de la Saint-Sylvestre.

New Year: **~'s Honours list** *n* GB liste *f* des décorés du 1er janvier; **~'s resolution** *n* résolution *f* pour la nouvelle année.

new: **New York City** ▶ 1818 *pr n* New York; **New Yorker** *n* New-Yorkais/-e *m/f*; **New York State** ▶ 1744 *pr n* État *m* de New York *m*.

New Zealand /ˌnjuːˈziːlənd, US ˌnuː-/ **I** ▶ 1131 *pr n* Nouvelle-Zélande *f*.
II *adj* néo-zélandais.

New Zealander ▶ 1486 *n* Néo-Zélandais/-e *m/f*.

next /nekst/

■ **Note** When *next* is used as an adjective it is generally translated by *prochain* when referring to something which is still to come or happen and by *suivant* when referring to something which has passed or happened: *I'll be 40 next year* = j'aurai 40 ans l'année prochaine; *the next year, he went to Spain* = l'année suivante il est allé en Espagne.
– For examples and further usages see the entry below.
– See also the usage note on time units ▶ 1807.

I *pron* **after this train the ~ is at noon** le train suivant est à midi; **he's happy one minute, sad the ~** il passe facilement du rire aux larmes; **I hope my ~ will be a boy** j'espère que mon prochain enfant sera un garçon; **from one minute to the ~** d'un instant à l'autre; **take the ~ left** prends la prochaine rue à gauche; **to go from one pub to the ~** aller d'un pub à l'autre; **to survive from one day to the ~** survivre au jour le jour; **the ~ to speak was Emily** ensuite, c'est Emily qui a parlé; **the week/month after ~** dans deux semaines/mois.
II *adj* **1** (in list, order or series) (following) suivant; (still to come) prochain; **the ~ page** la page suivante; **get the ~ train** prenez le prochain train; **he got on the ~ train** il a pris le train suivant; **the ~ person to talk will be punished** la prochaine personne qui parle sera punie; **she's ~ in the queue** GB elle sera la prochaine à être servie; **you're ~ on the list** tu es le prochain sur la liste; **what's ~ on the list?** qu'est-ce qu'on doit faire maintenant?; **the ~ thing to do is** ce qu'il faut faire maintenant c'est; **the ~ thing to do was** ce qu'il fallait faire ensuite c'était; **'~! '** 'au suivant!'; **'who's ~?'** 'c'est à qui le tour?'; **'you're ~'** 'c'est à vous'; **you're ~ in line** la prochaine fois c'est ton tour; **you're ~ but one** plus qu'une personne et c'est à toi; **~ to last** avant-dernier/-ière; **the ~ size (up)** la taille au-dessus; **the ~ size down** la taille en-dessous; **I don't know where my ~ meal is coming from** je vis au jour le jour; **I asked the ~ person I saw** j'ai demandé à la première personne que j'ai croisée; **2** (in expressions of time) (in the future) prochain; (in the past) suivant; **~ Thursday, Thursday ~** jeudi prochain; **~ year** l'année prochaine; **~ month's forecasts** les prévisions pour le mois prochain; **when is the ~ meeting?** quand aura lieu la prochaine réunion?; **~ time you see her** la prochaine fois que tu la vois; **the ~ few hours are critical** les prochaines heures or les heures à venir seront décisives; **I'll phone in the ~ few days** je téléphonerai d'ici quelques jours; **he's due to arrive in the ~ 10 minutes** il est censé arriver d'ici 10 minutes; **this time ~ week** d'ici une semaine; **I'll do it in the ~ two days** je le ferai d'ici 2 jours; **the ~ week she was late** la semaine suivante elle était en retard; **the ~ day** le lendemain; **the ~ day but one** le surlendemain; **the ~ morning** le lendemain matin; **during the ~ few hours he rested** pendant les quelques heures qui ont suivi, il s'est reposé; **the ~ moment** l'instant d'après; **(the) ~ thing I knew, he'd stolen my wallet** il m'a volé mon portefeuille sans que je m'en rende compte; **~ thing you know he'll be writing you love poems!** si ça continue comme ça, il va bientôt t'envoyer des poèmes!; **(the) ~ thing I knew, the police were at the door** la police était à la porte avant que j'aie eu le temps de comprendre ce qui se passait; **we offer a ~-day service** nous proposons un service en 24 heures; **3** (adjacent) [*room, street*] voisin; [*building, house*] voisin, d'à côté.
III *adv* **1** (afterwards) ensuite, après; **what happened ~?** que s'est-il passé ensuite?; **what word comes ~?** quel mot vient après or y a-t-il après?; **whatever ~!** et quoi encore!; **2** (now) **~, I'd like to say...** je

voudrais maintenant dire...; **what shall we do ~?** qu'est-ce qu'on fait maintenant?; **3** (on a future occasion) **when I ~ go there** la prochaine fois que j'irai; **when she ~ comes to visit** la prochaine fois qu'elle viendra nous voir; **when you phone her ~** la prochaine fois que tu lui téléphoneras; **they ~ met in 1981** ils se sont ensuite revus en 1981; **4** (nearest in order) **the ~ tallest is Patrick** ensuite c'est Patrick qui est le plus grand; **she's the ~ oldest after Brigitte** c'est elle la plus âgée après Brigitte; **after 65, 50 is the ~ best score** c'est 65 le meilleur score, ensuite c'est 50; **after champagne, sparkling white wine is the ~ best thing** après le champagne, le mousseux est ce qu'il y a de mieux; **the ~ best thing would be to...** à défaut, le mieux serait de...

IV **next to** *adv phr* presque; **~ to impossible** presque impossible; **~ to nobody** presque personne; **~ to no details/money** presque pas de détails/d'argent ; **to give sb ~ to nothing** ne donner pratiquement rien à qn; **to get sth for ~ to nothing** avoir qch pour quasiment rien; **in ~ to no time it was over** en un rien de temps c'était fini.

V **next to** *prep phr* à côté de; **~ to the bank/table** à côté de la banque/table; **two seats ~ to each other** deux sièges l'un à côté de l'autre; **to wear silk ~ to the skin** porter de la soie à même la peau; **~ to Picasso, my favourite painter is Chagall** après Picasso c'est Chagall mon peintre préféré.

IDIOMS **to get ~ to sb**○ US se mettre bien avec qn○; **I can sing as well as the ~ man** ou **person** je ne chante pas plus mal qu'un autre; **he's as honest as the ~ man** ou **person** il est aussi honnête que n'importe qui.

next door I *n* (people) les voisins *mpl*, les gens *mpl* d'à côté; **~'s cat** le chat des voisins; **~'s garden** le jardin d'à côté.

II *adj* (also **next-door**) [*garden, building*] d'à côté; **the girl ~** lit la fille d'à côté or qui habite à côté; fig une fille très simple.

III *adv* [*live, move in*] à côté; **to live ~ to sth/to sb** habiter à côté de qch/de chez qn; **to pop ~** faire un saut○ chez le/la voisin/-e.

next-door neighbour *n* voisin/-e *m/f* (d'à côté); **we're ~s** nous habitons à côté l'un de l'autre.

next of kin *n* (close relative) **to be sb's ~** être le parent le plus proche de qn; **to inform the ~** (close relative) prévenir le parent le plus proche; (family) prévenir la famille.

nexus /ˈneksəs/ *n* (*pl* **~** ou **-uses**) **1** (link) connexion *f*; **2** (network) réseau *m*.

NF *n* **1** GB Pol (*abrév* = **National Front**) cf FN *m*; **2** Fin (also **N/F**) (*abrév* = **no funds**) défaut *m* de provision.

NFL *n* US (*abrév* = **National Football League**) Fédération *f* américaine de football américain.

NFU *n* GB (*abrév* = **National Farmers' Union**) syndicat *m* agricole britannique.

NG *n* US *abrév* ▶ **National Guard**.

NGA *n* GB *abrév* ▶ **National Graphical Association**.

NGO *n* (*abrév* = **Non-Governmental Organization**) ONG *f*.

NHL *n* US (*abrév* = **National Hockey League**) Fédération *f* américaine de hockey sur glace.

NHS I *n* GB (*abrév* = **National Health Service**) services *mpl* de santé britanniques; **on the ~** ≈ remboursé par la sécurité sociale.

II *modif* [*hospital, bed, ward*] conventionné; [*operation, treatment*] remboursé par la sécurité sociale; **~ waiting list** liste *f* d'attente (*pour une opération prise en charge par la sécurité sociale*).

NI *n* **1** GB *abrév* ▶ **National Insurance**; **2** Geog (*abrév écrite* = **Northern Ireland**) Irlande *f* du Nord.

niacin /ˈnaɪəsɪn/ *n* acide *m* nicotinique.

Niagara /naɪˈægərə/ ▶ **1644** *pr n* Niagara *m*; **~ Falls** chutes *fpl* du Niagara.

nib /nɪb/ I *n* plume *f*.

II **-nibbed** (*dans composés*) **fine-/steel-~bed** à plume fine/en acier.

nibble /ˈnɪbl/ I *n* **1** (snack food) amuse-gueule *m inv*; **2** (action) mordillement *m*; **to have** ou **take a ~ at** grignoter; **3** (small meal) collation *f*; **to feel like** ou **fancy a ~** avoir envie de grignoter quelque chose.

II *vtr* (eat) **1** [*mouse, rabbit, person*] grignoter; [*sheep, goat*] brouter; **2** (playfully) [*person, animal*] mordiller [*ear, neck*].

III *vi* **1** lit [*animal*] mordiller; [*person*] grignoter; **to ~ at** [*mouse, rabbit*] grignoter; [*sheep, goat*] brouter; [*fish*] mordre à [*bait*]; [*person*] manger [qch] du bout des dents; **2** fig **to ~ at** considérer [*idea, proposal*].

nibs○ /nɪbz/ hum **his ~** (+ *v sg*) son altesse hum.

NIC /enaɪˈsiː, nɪk/ *n* (*abrév* = **newly industrialized countries**) NPI *mpl*.

Nicaragua /ˌnɪkəˈrægjʊə/ ▶ **1131** *pr n* Nicaragua *m*.

Nicaraguan /ˌnɪkəˈrægjʊən/ ▶ **1486** I *n* Nicaraguayen/-enne *m/f*.

II *adj* nicaraguayen/-enne.

nice /naɪs/ *adj* **1** (enjoyable, pleasant) [*drive, holiday*] agréable; **it would be ~ to do** ce serait bien de faire; **it would be ~ for him to do** ce serait bien qu'il fasse; **it's not very ~ doing** ce n'est pas très agréable de faire; **did you have a ~ time?** tu t'es bien amusé?; **~ weather isn't it?** beau temps, n'est-ce pas?; **a ~ cool drink** une boisson bien fraîche; **it's ~ and sunny** il fait beau; **to have a ~ long chat** bien bavarder; **~ work if you can get it!** hum il y en a qui ont de la veine○!; **~ to have met you** ravi d'avoir fait votre connaissance; **~ to see you** ça fait plaisir de te voir; **how ~!** comme c'est bien!; **have a ~ day!** bonne journée!; **2** (attractive) [*house, district, painting*] beau/belle; [*place*] agréable ; **a really ~ house** une très belle maison; **Edinburgh is a really ~ place** Édimbourg est vraiment une ville agréable; **you look very ~** tu es très chic; **he has a ~ taste in clothes** il a très bon goût en matière de vêtements; **3** (tasty) bon/bonne; **to taste ~** avoir bon goût; **a ~ cup of tea** une bonne tasse de thé; **4** (kind) sympathique; **to be ~ to** être gentil avec; **it was ~ of her to do** c'était gentil de sa part de faire; **how ~ of you to come** comme c'est gentil d'être venu; **he's a really ~ guy**○ c'est un type très sympa○; **what a ~ man!** quel homme sympathique!; **he says really ~ things about you** il dit beaucoup de bien de toi; **5** (socially acceptable) [*manners, behaviour, neighbourhood, school*] comme il faut *inv*; **it is not ~ to do** ce n'est pas bien de faire; **a ~ girl** une jeune fille bien or comme il faut; **that's not very ~!** ça ne se fait pas!; **6** (used ironically) **~ friends you've got!** ils sont bien tes amis!; **a ~ mess you've got us into!** tu nous as fichus dans un beau pétrin○!; **that's a ~ way to talk to your father!** en voilà une façon de parler à ton père!; **this is a ~ state of affairs!** c'est du propre!; **7** sout (subtle) [*distinction*] subtil; **8** sout (pleasing to the mind) [*coincidence, contrast*] plaisant fml.

IDIOMS **~ one!** (in admiration) bravo!; iron il ne manquait plus que ça.

nice-looking /ˌnaɪsˈlʊkɪŋ/ *adj* beau/belle.

nicely /ˈnaɪslɪ/ *adv* **1** (kindly) [*speak, treat, ask*] gentiment; **2** (attractively) [*decorated, furnished, dressed*] agréablement; **she sings very ~** elle chante très bien; **3** (satisfactorily) bien; **the engine is ticking over ~** le moteur tourne bien; **the building is coming along very ~** la construction avance très bien; **to be ~ chilled** être juste frais/fraîche comme il faut; **to be ~ done** [*steak*] être juste à point; **that will do ~** cela fera l'affaire; **to be ~ placed to do** être bien placé pour faire; **4** (politely) [*eat, speak*] convenablement; [*ask, explain*] poliment; **5** sout (subtly) [*distinguish*] subtilement.

Nicene /ˌnaɪˈsiːn/ *adj* de Nicée.

niceness /ˈnaɪsnɪs/ *n* **1** (kindness) gentillesse *f*; **2** (subtlety) (in distinction, contrast) subtilité *f*.

nicety /ˈnaɪsətɪ/ *n* **1** (subtle detail) subtilité *f*; **the niceties of protocol** les subtilités du protocole; **2** (refinement) **the social niceties** les raffinements *mpl* mondains.

niche /nɪtʃ, niːʃ/ *n* **1** (role, occupation) place *f*; **to find one's ~** trouver sa place; **to carve out one's** ou **a ~** se faire une place; **2** Advertg créneau *m*; **3** (recess) niche *f*; **4** Ecol niche *f* écologique.

niche: **~ market** *n* marché *m* spécialisé; **~ marketing** *n* marketing *m* de créneaux.

Nicholas /ˈnɪkələs/ *pr n* Nicolas.

nick /nɪk/ I *n* **1** (notch) encoche *f* (**in** dans); **to take a ~ out of sth** faire une encoche dans qch; **2**○ GB (condition) **to be in good/bad ~** [*car, machine, carpet etc*] être en bon/mauvais état; [*person*] être/ne pas être en forme; **3**○ GB (jail) taule○ *f*, prison *f*; **in the ~** en taule○; **4**○ GB (police station) poste *m*, commissariat *m*.

II *vtr* **1** (cut) faire une entaille dans [*stick, surface*]; **to ~ one's finger** s'entailler le doigt; **2**○ GB (steal) piquer○, voler; **3**○ GB (arrest) pincer○, arrêter; **he got ~ed (for speeding)** il s'est fait pincer○ (pour excès de vitesse); **4**○ US (strike) donner un coup léger à; **5**◑ US (cheat, overcharge) arnaquer◑; **6** Equit, Vet anglaiser [*horse, tail*].

III *v refl* **to ~ oneself** s'écorcher.

IDIOMS **just in the ~ of time** juste à temps.

■ **nick off**○ GB se tailler○, s'enfuir.

Nick /nɪk/ *pr n* **Old ~**○ le diable.

nickel /ˈnɪkl/ I *n* **1** US (coin) pièce *f* de cinq cents; **2** (metal) nickel *m*.

II *modif* [*coin, knife*] en nickel; [*alloy*] de nickel.

III *vtr* nickeler.

nickel-and-dime○ /ˌnɪklənˈdaɪm/ *adj* US qui ne vaut pas un clou○.

nickelodeon /ˌnɪkəˈləʊdɪən/ *n* US **1** (juke box) juke-box *m*; **2**† (cinema) nickelodeon *m*, cinéma *m*.

nickel: **~-plated** *adj* nickelé; **~ silver** *n* maillechort *m*.

nicker /ˈnɪkə(r)/ I○ *n* (*pl* **~**) GB livre *f* sterling.

II *vi* (neigh) hennir doucement.

nickname /ˈnɪkneɪm/ I *n* surnom *m*.

II *vtr* surnommer.

Nicosia /ˌnɪkəʊˈsiːə/ ▶ **1818** *pr n* Nicosie.

nicotiana /nɪˌkəʊʃɪˈɑːnə/ *n* nicotiana *m*.

nicotine /ˈnɪkətiːn/ I *n* nicotine *f*.

II *modif* [*addiction, poisoning, chewing gum*] à la nicotine; [*stain*] de nicotine; **~ content** teneur *f* en nicotine; **~-stained** taché de nicotine.

nicotinic acid /ˌnɪkəˈtɪnɪk/ *n* acide *m* nicotinique.

NICS *n* GB (*abrév* = **National Insurance Contributions**) cotisations *fpl* d'assurance maladie-retraite.

niece /niːs/ *n* nièce *f*.

Nietzschean /ˈniːtʃɪən/ *adj* nietzschéen/-éenne.

Nièvre ▶ **1163** *pr n* Nièvre *f*; **in/to ~** dans la Nièvre.

niff○ /nɪf/ I *n* GB puanteur *f*.

II *vi* GB puer.

niffy○ /ˈnɪfɪ/ *adj* GB puant.

nifty○ /ˈnɪftɪ/ *adj* **1** (skilful) [*manoeuvre, footwork, player*] habile; **2** (attractive) [*car, clothes, design*] chouette○.

Niger /ˈnaɪdʒə(r)/ ▶ **1131**, **1644** *pr n* (all contexts) Niger *m*.

Nigeria /naɪˈdʒɪərɪə/ ▶ **1131** *pr n* Nigeria *m*.

Nigerian /naɪ'dʒɪərɪən/ ▶ 1486 I *n* Nigérian/-e *m/f*.
II *adj* nigérian.

niggardliness /'nɪgədlɪnɪs/ *n* avarice *f*.

niggardly /'nɪgədlɪ/ *adj* **1** [*person*] avare; **2** [*portion, amount*] mesquin.

nigger◐ /'nɪgə(r)/ *n* injur nègre/négresse *m/f* offensive, noir/-e *m/f*.
IDIOMS **there is a ~ in the woodpile** il y a anguille sous roche.

niggle○ /'nɪgl/ I *n* **1** (complaint) remarque *f*; **2** (worry) **I've a ~ at the back of my mind** il y a quelque chose qui me travaille.
II *vtr* (irritate) tracasser.
III *vi* (complain) se plaindre sans arrêt (**about, over** de; **that** que).

niggling /'nɪglɪŋ/ I *n* chicanerie *f*.
II *adj* **1** [*person*] tatillon/-onne; **2** [*doubt, fear, worry*] insidieux/-ieuse.

nigh /naɪ/ I‡ ou littér *adj, adv* proche; **to draw ~** se rapprocher.
II **well nigh** *adv phr* presque.
III **nigh on** *prep phr* presque.

night /naɪt/ ▶ 1807 *n* **1** (period of darkness) nuit *f*; (before going to bed) soir *m*; **during the ~** pendant la nuit; **in the middle of the ~** au milieu de la nuit; **to travel/hunt by ~** voyager/chasser de nuit; **at ~** la nuit; **all ~ long** toute la nuit; **~ and day** nuit et jour; **Moscow by ~** Moscou la nuit; **to work ~s** travailler de or la nuit; **to be on ~s** être de nuit; **eight o'clock at ~** huit heures du soir; **late at ~** tard le soir; **late into the ~** tard dans la nuit; **he arrived last ~** il est arrivé hier soir; **I slept badly last ~** j'ai mal dormi la nuit dernière; **he arrived the ~ before last** il est arrivé avant-hier soir; **I slept badly the ~ before last** j'ai mal dormi (la nuit d')avant-hier; **she had arrived the ~ before** elle était arrivée la veille; **on the ~ of October 6** la nuit du 6 octobre; **on Tuesday ~s** le mardi soir; **it rained on Tuesday ~** il a plu mardi soir; **to sit up all ~ with sb** veiller toute la nuit avec qn; **to sit up all ~ reading** passer toute la nuit à lire; **to spend** ou **stay the ~ with sb** passer la nuit avec qn; **to have a good/bad ~** bien/mal dormir; **to have a comfortable/restless ~** passer une nuit reposante/agitée; **to have a late ~** se coucher tard; **to get an early ~** se coucher tôt; **to stay out all ~** ne pas rentrer de la nuit; **2** (evening) soir *m*; (evening as a whole) soirée *f*; **it's his ~ out** c'est son soir de sortie; **to take a ~ off** se libérer une soirée; **it's my ~ off** ce soir je suis libre; **a ~ to remember** une soirée mémorable; **a ~ at the opera** une soirée à l'opéra; **the play will run for three ~s** Theat la pièce aura trois représentations; **to make a ~ of it**○ faire la fête○; **3** (darkness) nuit *f*; **he left as ~ was falling** il est parti à la tombée de la nuit; **to disappear into the ~** disparaître dans la nuit; **in our dark ~ of despair** littér au plus profond de notre désespoir.

night bird *n* Zool oiseau *m* de nuit; fig couche-tard *mf inv*.

night blindness *n* héméralopie *f*.

nightcap /'naɪtkæp/ *n* **1** (hat) bonnet *m* de nuit; **2** (drink) **to have a ~** boire quelque chose (avant d'aller se coucher).

night: **~clothes** *npl* vêtements *mpl* pour la nuit; **~club** *n* boîte *f* de nuit.

nightclubbing *n* **to go ~** aller en boîte○.

night: **~dress** *n* chemise *f* de nuit; **~ editor** *n* Journ rédacteur/-trice *m/f* de nuit.

nightfall /'naɪtfɔːl/ *n* tombée *f* de la nuit; **at ~** à la tombée de la nuit.

nightgown† /'naɪtgaʊn/ *n* chemise *f* de nuit.

nighthawk /'naɪthɔːk/ *n* **1** (bird) engoulevent *m* (d'Amérique); **2**○ US (person) couche-tard *mf inv*.

nightie○ /'naɪtɪ/ *n* chemise *f* de nuit.

nightingale /'naɪtɪŋgeɪl, US -tŋg-/*n* rossignol *m*.

night: **~jar** *n* engoulevent *m* (d'Europe); **~ letter** *n* US télégramme *m* de nuit.

nightlife /'naɪtlaɪf/ *n* vie *f* nocturne; **there's not much ~** il n'y a rien à faire le soir.

night-light /'naɪtlaɪt/ *n* veilleuse *f*.

nightlong /ˌnaɪt'lɒŋ, US -'lɔːŋ/ I *adj* [*festivities, vigil*] qui dure toute la nuit.
II *adv* littér [*work, watch*] toute la nuit.

nightly /'naɪtlɪ/ I *adj* [*journey, performance, visit*] de tous les soirs; [*prayers*] du soir; [*revels, visitor, disturbance*] littér nocturne.
II *adv* **1** [*perform, visit*] tous les soirs; **performances ~** Theat représentation tous les soirs; **2** (at night) [*occur, happen*] de nuit.

nightmare /'naɪtmeə(r)/ *n* cauchemar *m*; **to have a ~ about sth** faire un cauchemar à propos de qch; **it was a living ~** c'était un vrai cauchemar; **a ~ journey/experience** un voyage/une expérience cauchemardesque.

night: **~marish** *adj* cauchemardesque; **~-night**○ *excl* lang enfantin bonne nuit; **~ nurse** *n* infirmier/-ière *m/f* de nuit; **~ owl** *n* couche-tard *mf inv*; **~ porter** *n* portier *m* de nuit; **~ safe** *n* coffre *m* de nuit.

night school *n* cours *mpl* du soir; **to study at** ou **go to ~** suivre des cours du soir.

night: **~shade** *n* solanacée *f*; **~ shelter** *n* asile *m* de nuit.

night shift *n* **1** (period) **to be/work on the ~** être/travailler de nuit; **2** (workers) équipe *f* de nuit.

nightshirt /'naɪtʃɜːt/ *n* chemise *f* de nuit (d'homme).

night sky *n* **the ~** le ciel (la nuit).

night: **~ soil** *n* excréments *mpl* (humains); **~ spot**○ *n* boîte○ *f* de nuit; **~stand** *n* US table *f* de nuit; **~stick** *n* US matraque *f*; **~ table** *n* table *f* de nuit.

night-time /'naɪttaɪm/ I *n* nuit *f*; **at ~** la nuit.
II *modif* nocturne.

night: **~ vision** *n* vision *f* nocturne; **~ watchman** ▶ 1692 *n* veilleur *m* de nuit; **~wear** *n* vêtements *mpl* de nuit.

nihilism /'naɪɪlɪzəm, 'nɪhɪl-/ *n* nihilisme *m*.

nihilist /'naɪɪlɪst, 'nɪhɪl-/ *n, adj* nihiliste (*mf*).

nihilistic /ˌnaɪɪ'lɪstɪk, ˌnɪhɪ'l-/ *adj* nihiliste.

nil /nɪl/ *n* **1 to be ~** [*courage, enthusiasm*] être à zéro; [*importance, progress*] être zéro; **2** Sport zéro *m*; **3** (on forms) néant *m*.

Nile /naɪl/ ▶ 1644 *pr n* Nil *m*.

nimbi /'nɪmbaɪ/ *pl* ▶ **nimbus**.

nimble /'nɪmbl/ *adj* [*person, movement*] agile (**at doing** pour faire; **with** de); [*fingers*] habile; [*mind, wits*] vif/vive; **to be ~ on one's feet** avoir le pied agile.

nimble-fingered /ˌnɪmbl'fɪŋgəd/ *adj* habile de ses doigts.

nimbleness /'nɪmblnɪs/ *n* (of person) agilité *f*; (of fingers) habileté *f*.

nimbly /'nɪmblɪ/ *adv* avec agilité.

nimbostratus /ˌnɪmbəʊ'streɪtəs, -'strɑːtəs/ *n* (*pl* **-strati**) nimbostratus *m inv*.

nimbus /'nɪmbəs/ *n* (*pl* **-bi** ou **~es**) **1** Meteorol nimbus *m*; **2** (halo) nimbe *m*.

NIMBY, Nimby /'nɪmbɪ/ *n* (*abrév* = **not in my back yard**) (person) égoïste *mf* (*partisan du 'où vous voulez mais pas chez moi'*).

nincompoop○ /'nɪŋkəmpuːp/ *n* nigaud/-e *m/f*.

nine /naɪn/ ▶ 1505, 1037, 1096 I *n* neuf *m inv*.
II *adj* neuf *inv*; **~ times out of ten** neuf fois sur dix, généralement; **~-hole golf course** parcours *m* de neuf trous; **to dial 999** GB appeler police secours; **a 999 call** GB un appel d'urgence.
IDIOMS **a ~ day(s') wonder** la merveille d'un jour; **to have ~ lives** avoir neuf vies; **to be dressed up to the ~s**○ être sur son trente et un○.

ninepin /'naɪnpɪn/ *n* quille *f*.
IDIOMS **to go down** ou **fall like ~s** tomber comme des mouches.

ninepins ▶ 1282 *n* (+ *v sg*) jeu *m* de quilles.

nineteen /ˌnaɪn'tiːn/ ▶ 1505 *n, adj* dix-neuf (*m*) *inv*.
IDIOMS **to talk ~ to the dozen** parler à n'en plus finir.

nineteenth /ˌnaɪn'tiːnθ/ ▶ 1505, 1150 I *n* **1** (in order) dix-neuvième *mf*; **2** (of month) dix-neuf *m inv*; **3** (fraction) dix-neuvième *m*.
II *adj* dix-neuvième.
III *adv* [*come, finish*] dix-neuvième, en dix-neuvième position.

nineteenth hole○ *n* hum bar *m* (*sur un terrain de golf*).

ninetieth /'naɪntɪəθ/ ▶ 1505 *n, adj, adv* quatre-vingt-dixième (*mf*).

nine-to-five /ˌnaɪntə'faɪv/ I *adj* [*job, routine*] de bureau.
II **nine to five** *adv* [*work*] de neuf à cinq.

ninety /'naɪntɪ/ ▶ 1505, 971 *n, adj* quatre-vingt-dix (*m*) *inv*.

ninny○ /'nɪnɪ/ *n* niais/-e *m/f*.

ninth /naɪnθ/ ▶ 1505, 1150 I *n* **1** (in order) neuvième *mf*; **2** (of month) neuf *m inv*; **3** (fraction) neuvième *m*; **4** Mus neuvième *f*.
II *adj* neuvième.
III *adv* [*come, finish*] neuvième, en neuvième position.

nip /nɪp/ I *n* **1** (pinch) pincement *m*; **2** (bite) morsure *f*; **the dog gave him a ~ on the ankle** le chien l'a (légèrement) mordu à la cheville; **3** fig **there's a ~ in the air** il fait frisquet○, ça pince○; **4**○ (small measure) petit verre *m* (**of** de).
II **Nip**○ *n* injur Jap *m* offensive.
III *vtr* (*p prés etc* **-pp-**) **1** (pinch) pincer; **to ~ one's finger in sth** se pincer le doigt dans qch; **2** (bite) mordre (légèrement), donner un petit coup de dent à; (playfully) mordiller; **he was ~ped on the ankle by a crab** il s'est fait pincer à la cheville par un crabe; **3** [*frost*] brûler [*seedlings*]; **4**○ (steal) piquer○, faucher○.
IV *vi* (*p prés etc* **-pp-**) **1** (bite) [*animal*] mordre; (playfully) mordiller; [*bird*] donner un petit coup de bec à; **2**○ GB (go) **to ~ into a shop** entrer (rapidement) dans un magasin; **to ~ in front of sb** passer devant qn; **to ~ out to the shops** faire un saut jusqu'aux magasins; **to ~ downstairs** descendre rapidement; **to ~ over to France for the weekend** faire un saut en France pour le weekend.
IDIOMS **to ~ sth in the bud** étouffer or tuer qch dans l'œuf; **~ and tuck**○ (cosmetic surgery) chirurgie *f* esthétique; (neck and neck) US au coude à coude; **the race was ~ and tuck**○ **all the way** la course s'est faite au coude à coude.
■ **nip along** [*person, vehicle, train*] aller à bonne allure; **to ~ along to sth** faire un saut○ à [*shops*].
■ **nip in**: **~ in [sth], ~ [sth] in** cintrer [*garment*].
■ **nip off**: ¶ **~ off** [*person*] se sauver; ¶ **~ off [sth], ~ [sth] off** couper [*withered flower*]; pincer [*bud*].

nipper I /'nɪpə(r)/ *n* **1**○ GB (child) gosse○ *mf*, mioche○ *mf*; **2** (of crab) pince *f*.
II **nippers** *npl* (tool) **~s** pince *f*; **a pair of ~s** une pince.

nipple /'nɪpl/ *n* **1** Anat mamelon *m*; **2** (also **grease ~**) Tech graisseur *m*.

nippy○ /'nɪpɪ/ *adj* **1** (cold) [*air*] piquant; [*wind*] froid et vif; **it's a bit ~ today** il fait frisquet○ aujourd'hui, ça pince○ aujourd'hui; **2** GB (quick) [*person*] vif/vive, leste; [*car*] rapide; **be ~ about it!** grouille-toi○!, fais vite!; **3** (strong) [*flavour, cheese*] piquant.

nirvana /nɪə'vɑːnə/ *n* nirvana *m*.

Nisei /'niːseɪ/ *n* US *Américain/-e né/-e d'immigrants japonais*.

nisi /'naɪsaɪ/ *adj* Jur provisoire; **decree ~** jugement *m* provisoire (de divorce).

Nissen hut /'nɪsn/ *n* baraquement *m* en

tôle ondulée (*de forme allongée et semi-cylindrique*).

nit /nɪt/ *n* **1** (egg) lente *f*; (larva) larve *f* de pou; **to have ~s** avoir des poux; **2**○ GB (idiot) imbécile *mf*.

niter *n* US = **nitre**.

nit: **~-pick** *vi* chercher la petite bête○; **~-picker** *n* pinailleur/-euse *m/f*.

nit-picking /ˈnɪtpɪkɪŋ/ **I** *n* pinaillage *m*.
II *adj* pinailleur/-euse.

nitrate /ˈnaɪtreɪt/ *n* **1** Chem nitrate *m*; **sodium ~** nitrate de sodium; **2** (fertilizer) engrais *m* azoté.

nitre GB, **niter** US /ˈnaɪtə(r)/ *n* nitre *m*.

nitric /ˈnaɪtrɪk/ *adj* nitrique.

nitric: **~ acid** *n* acide *m* nitrique; **~ oxide** *n* oxyde *m* nitrique.

nitrogen /ˈnaɪtrədʒən/ *n* azote *m*.

nitrogen dioxide *n* dioxide *m* d'azote.

nitrogenous /naɪˈtrɒdʒɪnəs/ *adj* azoté.

nitroglycerin(e) /ˌnaɪtrəʊˈglɪsəriːn, US -rɪn/ *n* nitroglycérine *f*.

nitrous /ˈnaɪtrəs/ *adj* nitreux/-euse.

nitrous: **~ acid** *n* acide *m* nitreux; **~ oxide** *n* oxyde *m* nitreux.

nitty-gritty○ /ˌnɪtɪˈgrɪtɪ/ **I** *n* **the ~** la réalité pure et dure; **to get down to the ~** passer aux choses sérieuses.
II *adj* pur et dur.

nitwit○ /ˈnɪtwɪt/ *n* imbécile *mf*.

nix○ /nɪks/ US **I** *particle* non.
II *excl* sûrement pas!
III *pron* que dalle◑, rien.
IV *vtr* mettre son veto à.

NJ *abrév* = **New Jersey**.

NLF (*abrév* = **National Liberation Front**) FLN *m*.

NLP *n*: *abrév* ▶ **natural language processing**.

NM *abrév* = **New Mexico**.

NMR *n* (*abrév* = **nuclear magnetic resonance**) RMN *f*.

no /nəʊ/ **I** *particle* non; **'lend me £10'—'~, I won't'** 'prête-moi dix livres'—'non'; **~ thanks** non merci; **oh ~!** (exasperation) oh NON!; (contradicting) non!; (polite reassurance) non non!
II *det* **1** (none, not any) **to have ~ coat/job/money/shoes** ne pas avoir de manteau/de travail/d'argent/de chaussures; **~ intelligent man would have done that** aucun homme intelligent n'aurait fait cela; **~ two dresses are alike** il n'y a pas deux robes pareilles; **~ two people would agree on this** il n'y a pas deux personnes qui seraient d'accord là-dessus; **of ~ interest/importance** sans intérêt/importance; **with ~ help** sans aide; **I have ~ wish to do** je n'ai aucune envie de faire; **he has ~ intention of going** il n'a aucune intention d'y aller; **there's ~ chocolate like Belgian chocolate** il n'y a pas de meilleur chocolat que le chocolat belge; **2** (with gerund) **there's ~ knowing/saying what will happen** impossible de savoir/dire ce qui va arriver; **there's ~ denying that** inutile de nier que; **there's ~ arguing with him** ce n'est pas la peine de discuter avec lui; **3** (prohibiting) **~ smoking** défense de fumer; **~ parking** stationnement interdit; **~ talking!** silence!; **~ surrender!** on ne se rendra pas!; **~ job losses!** non aux licenciements!; **4** (for emphasis) **he's ~ expert** ce n'est certes pas un expert!; **you're ~ friend of mine!** tu n'es pas mon ami!; **this is ~ time to cry** ce n'est pas le moment de pleurer; **at ~ time did I say that** je n'ai jamais dit que; **this is ~ place to stop** ce n'est pas un endroit pour s'arrêter; **it was ~ easy task** ce n'était pas une tâche facile; **5** (hardly any) **in ~ time** en un rien de temps; **it was ~ distance** ce n'était pas loin.
III *n* gen non *m inv*; (vote against) non *m inv*, voix *f* contre.
IV *adv* **1** (not any) **it's ~ further/easier/more interesting than** ce n'est pas plus loin/facile/intéressant que; **I ~ longer work there** je n'y travaille plus; **~ later than Wednesday** pas plus tard que mercredi; **it's ~ different from driving a car** c'est exactement comme conduire une voiture; **~ fewer than 50 people** pas moins de 50 personnes; **they need ~ less than three weeks/£1,000** ils ont besoin d'au moins trois semaines/mille livres sterling; **it was the president, ~ less!** iron c'était le président, rien de moins!; **2** (not) non; **tired or ~, you're going to bed** que tu sois fatigué ou non, tu vas te coucher; **whether it rains or ~** qu'il pleuve ou non.

no., No. (*abrév écrite* = **number**) n°.

no-account○ /ˈnəʊəkaʊnt/ *n, adj* bon/bonne (*m/f*) à rien.

Noah /ˈnəʊə/ *pr n* Noé; **~'s Ark** l'arche *f* de Noé.

nob○ /nɒb/ *n* **1** GB (person) rupin○ *m*; **2**† (head) caboche○ *f*.

no-ball /ˈnəʊbɔːl/ *n* Sport lancer *m* nonvalable.

nobble○ /ˈnɒbl/ *vtr* GB **1** (drug) droguer [*horse*]; **2** (bribe) soudoyer; (threaten) menacer; **3** (catch) pincer○ [*criminal*]; **4** (get the attention of) attraper [qn] au passage; **5** (steal) piquer○.

nobelium /nəʊˈbiːlɪəm/ *n* nobélium *m*.

Nobel prize /nəʊˈbel ˈpraɪz/ **I** *n* prix *m* Nobel (**for** de).
II *modif* **a ~ physicist** un prix Nobel de physique.

Nobel: **~ prizewinner** *n* lauréat/-e *m/f* du prix Nobel; **~ prizewinning** *adj* (person) lauréat/-e du prix Nobel (*after n*).

nobility /nəʊˈbɪlətɪ/ *n* (all contexts) noblesse *f*.

noble /ˈnəʊbl/ **I** *n* noble *m*.
II *adj* **1** [*birth, family, appearance*] noble (*after n*); **the ~ art of** le noble art de; **2** [*spirit, sentiment, character, act*] noble; **that was very ~ of you** c'était très gentil de ta part; **3** [*building, arch, proportions*] imposant; [*tree*] majestueux/-euse; **4** Chem noble.

noble: **~man** *n* aristocrate *m*, noble *m*; **~-minded** *adj* magnanime.

nobleness /ˈnəʊblnɪs/ *n* noblesse *f*.

noble: **~ savage** *n* bon sauvage *m*; **~woman** *n* aristocrate *f*, noble *f*.

nobly /ˈnəʊblɪ/ *adv* **1** [*behave, serve, strive*] noblement; [*give, donate, allow*] généreusement; **2** (aristocratically) noblement; **to be ~ born** être de haute naissance; **3** (of building) **~ proportioned** aux proportions majestueuses.

nobody /ˈnəʊbədɪ/

■ **Note** When *nobody* is used as a pronoun it is almost always translated by *personne*.
– When the pronoun *nobody* is the subject or object of a verb, the French requires *ne* before the verb (or auxiliary): *nobody likes him* = personne ne l'aime; *I heard nobody* = je n'ai entendu personne.
– For examples and particular usages, see the entry below.

I *pron* (also **no-one**) personne; **'who's there?'—'~'** 'qui est là?'—'personne'; **~ saw her** personne ne l'a vue; **there was ~ in the car** il n'y avait personne dans la voiture; **~ but me** personne sauf moi; **it's ~'s business but mine** ça ne regarde personne d'autre que moi.
II *n* **to be a ~** être insignifiant; **they're just nobodies** ils sont complètement insignifiants; **I knew her when she was still a ~** je la connaissais alors qu'elle n'était encore qu'une inconnue.
IDIOMS **to work like ~'s business**○ GB travailler comme un fou/une folle *m/f*; **he's ~'s fool** on ne la lui fait pas○.

no-claim(s) bonus *n* Insur bonus *m*.

nocturnal /nɒkˈtɜːnl/ *adj* (all contexts) nocturne.

nocturne /ˈnɒktɜːn/ *n* nocturne *m*.

nod /nɒd/ **I** *n* signe *m* de (la) tête; **she gave him a ~** gen elle lui a fait un signe de (la) tête; (as greeting) elle l'a salué d'un signe de tête; (indicating assent) elle a fait oui; **to answer with a ~** répondre d'un signe de tête; **with a ~ to his guests he left the room** il a quitté la pièce en saluant ses invités d'un signe de tête.
II *vtr* (*p prés etc* **-dd-**) **to ~ one's head** gen faire un signe de (la) tête; (to indicate assent) hocher la tête; **he ~ded his assent/approval** il a hoché la tête en signe d'assentiment/d'approbation.
III *vi* (*p prés etc* **-dd-**) **1** gen faire un signe de tête; (in assent) faire oui (de la tête); **to ~ to sb** gen faire un signe de tête à qn; (in greeting) saluer qn d'un signe de tête ; **she ~ded to him to sit down** d'un signe de tête, elle l'a invité à s'asseoir; **he ~ded in agreement** il a fait oui d'un signe de tête; **2** (sway) [*flowers, treetops, feathers*] onduler; **3** (be drowsy) sommeiller.
IDIOMS **to get the ~**○ GB [*proposal, project*] avoir le feu vert; **to give sb/sth the ~**○ GB donner le feu vert à qn/qch; **on the ~**○ GB d'un commun accord; **a ~ is as good as a wink (to a blind man)** ne t'en fais pas○, on a compris.
■ **nod off** s'endormir.

nodal /ˈnəʊdl/ *adj* nodal.

noddle○ /ˈnɒdl/ *n* caboche○ *f*.

node /nəʊd/ *n* Astron, Ling, Bot, Phys, Math nœud *m*; (abnormal) Med nodosité *f*.

nodular /ˈnɒdjʊlə(r), US ˈnɒdʒuːlə(r)/ *adj* nodulaire.

nodule /ˈnɒdjuːl, US ˈnɒdʒuːl/ *n* (all contexts) nodule *m*.

Noel /nəʊˈel/ *pr n* Noël *m*.

no: **~-fault divorce** *n* US Jur divorce *m* par consentement mutuel; **~-fault insurance** *n* US Insur assurance *f* sans faute; **~-frills** *adj* [*insurance policy*] de base; [*approach*] simplifié.

noggin† /ˈnɒgɪn/ *n* **1** (drink) petit verre *m*; (cup) pot *m*; **2**○ (head) caboche○ *f*.

no-go○ /ˌnəʊˈgəʊ/ *adj* **it's (a) ~** ça ne sert à rien.

no: **~-go area** *n* quartier *m* chaud (*où la police etc ne s'aventure plus*); **~-good**○ *adj* US bon/bonne à rien; **~-hoper**○ *n* raté/-e○ *m/f*.

noise /nɔɪz/ **I** *n* **1** (sound) bruit *m*; **aircraft/background/traffic ~** bruit des avions/de fond/du trafic; **loud/soft ~** grand/léger bruit; **to make a ~** faire du bruit; **above the ~ of the engine** au-dessus du bruit du moteur; **a grinding/tinkling/rattling ~** un grincement/tintement/cliquetis; **2** (din) bruit *m*, vacarme *m*; (shouting) tapage *m*; **please make less ~!** s'il vous plaît, faites moins de bruit!; **hold your ~**○! ferme-la○!; **3** Elec, Telecom interférences *fpl*; **4** (comment, reaction) tapage *m* (**about** au sujet de); **to make ~s** ou **a ~ about sth** dire qch au sujet de qch; **to make polite/sympathetic ~s** dire des choses polies/compatissantes; **to make the right ~s** dire ce qui convient; **5** Theat **~s off** bruits *mpl* en coulisse.
IDIOMS **to be a big ~ (in sth)**○ être une grosse légume (de qch)○.
■ **noise abroad**†, **noise about**†: **~ [sth] abroad** ébruiter.

noise generator *n* générateur *m* de bruit.

noiseless /ˈnɔɪzlɪs/ *adj* silencieux/-ieuse.

noiselessly /ˈnɔɪzlɪslɪ/ *adv* silencieusement.

noise: **~ level** *n* niveau *m* sonore; **~ nuisance**, **~ pollution** *n* nuisances *fpl* sonores.

noisily /ˈnɔɪzɪlɪ/ *adv* bruyamment.

noisiness /ˈnɔɪzɪnɪs/ *n* (niveau *m* de) bruit *m*.

noisome /ˈnɔɪsəm/ *adj* sout immonde.

noisy /ˈnɔɪzɪ/ *adj* [*person, activity, machine, place, talk*] bruyant; [*argument*] tumultueux/-euse.

no-knock raid *n* US descente *f* de police.

nomad /ˈnəʊmæd/ *n* nomade *mf*.
nomadic /nəʊˈmædɪk/ *adj* nomade.
nomadism /ˈnəʊmædɪzəm/ *n* nomadisme *m*.
no-man's land *n* (all contexts) no man's land *m*.
nom de plume /ˌnɒm də ˈpluːm/ *n* pseudonyme *m*, nom *m* de plume.
nomenclature /nəˈmenklətʃə(r), US ˈnəʊmənkleɪtʃər/ *n* nomenclature *f*.
nominal /ˈnɒmɪnl/ *adj* **1** (in name only) nominal; **2** (small) [*fee, sum*] minimal; [*fine, penalty*] symbolique; [*rent*] dérisoire; **3** Ling nominal.
nominal damages *n* Jur franc *m* symbolique (de dommages et intérêts).
nominalism /ˈnɒmɪnəlɪzəm/ *n* nominalisme *m*.
nominalist /ˈnɒmɪnəlɪst/ *n, adj* nominaliste (*mf*).
nominalization /ˌnɒmɪnəlaɪˈzeɪʃn, US -lɪˈz-/ *n* nominalisation *f*.
nominalize /ˈnɒmɪnəlaɪz/ *vtr* nominaliser.
nominally /ˈnɒmɪnəlɪ/ *adv* (in name) nominalement; (in theory) théoriquement.
nominal: **~ price** *n* prix *m* nominal or théorique; **~ value** *n* valeur *f* nominale.
nominate /ˈnɒmɪneɪt/ *vtr* **1** (propose) proposer; **to ~ sb for a position/for president** proposer qn pour un poste/comme candidat à la présidence; **to ~ sb for a prize** sélectionner qn pour un prix; **2** (appoint) nommer; **to ~ sb (as) chairman/to a position** nommer qn président/à un poste; **to ~ sb to do** désigner qn pour faire.
nomination /ˌnɒmɪˈneɪʃn/ *n* **1** (as candidate) proposition *f* de candidat; **his ~ was approved** sa proposition comme candidat a été approuvée; **the Democratic ~ went to Smith** Smith a été nommé candidat pour le parti démocrate; **2** (appointment) nomination *f* (**to** à); **3** (for award) sélection *f*.
nominative /ˈnɒmɪnətɪv/ *n, adj* nominatif (*m*).
nominator /ˈnɒmɪneɪtə(r)/ *n* personne *f* qui propose un candidat.
nominee /ˌnɒmɪˈniː/ *n* candidat/-e *m/f* désigné/-e.
nominee company *n* Fin fond *m* commun de créances.
non+ /nɒn-/ (*dans composés*) (+ *noun*) non-; (+ *adj*) non.
nonabsorbent /ˌnɒnəbˈsɔːbənt/ *adj* non absorbant.
nonacademic /ˌnɒnækəˈdemɪk/ *adj* [*course*] pré-professionnel/-elle; [*staff*] non enseignant.
nonacceptance /ˌnɒnəkˈseptəns/ *n* nonacceptation *f*.
non-accountability /ˌnɒnəˈkaʊntəbɪlətɪ/ *n* irresponsabilité *f*.
nonaddictive /ˌnɒnəˈdɪktɪv/ *adj* [*substance, drug*] qui ne crée pas de dépendance.
nonadmission /ˌnɒnədˈmɪʃn/ *n* dénégation *f*.
nonaffiliated /ˌnɒnəˈfɪlɪeɪtɪd/ *adj* non affilié.
nonage /ˈnəʊnɪdʒ/ *n* gen immaturité *f*; Jur minorité *f*.
nonagenarian /ˌnɒnədʒɪˈneərɪən/ *n, adj* nonagénaire (*mf*).
nonaggression /ˌnɒnəˈgreʃn/ **I** *n* nonagression *f*.
II *modif* [*pact, treaty*] de non-agression.
nonalcoholic /ˌnɒnælkəˈhɒlɪk/ *adj* non alcoolisé.
nonaligned /ˌnɒnəˈlaɪnd/ *adj* Pol non aligné.
nonalignment /ˌnɒnəˈlaɪnmənt/ *n* Pol nonalignement *m*.
nonappearance /ˌnɒnəˈpɪərəns/ *n* Jur noncomparution *f*.
nonapproved /ˌnɒnəˈpruːvd/ *adj* Fin, Insur non approuvé.
nonarrival /ˌnɒnəˈraɪvl/ *n* (of letter) non-distribution *f*; (of person) absence *f*.
nonattendance /ˌnɒnəˈtendəns/ *n* absence *f*.
nonavailability /ˌnɒnəˌveɪləˈbɪlətɪ/ *n* pénurie *f*.
nonavailable /ˌnɒnəˈveɪləbl/ *adj* non disponible.
nonbank /ˌnɒnˈbæŋk/ *adj* US non bancaire.
nonbeliever /ˌnɒnbɪˈliːvə(r)/ *n* non-croyant/-e *m/f*.
nonbelligerent /ˌnɒnbɪˈlɪdʒərənt/ *adj* non belligérant.
nonbiodegradable /ˌnɒnbaɪəʊdɪˈgreɪdəbl/ *adj* non biodégradable.
nonbreakable /ˌnɒnˈbreɪkəbl/ *adj* incassable.
non-broadcast video *n* enregistrement *m* vidéo à usage non commercial.
non-budgetary /ˌnɒnˈbʌdʒɪtrɪ/ *adj* extrabudgétaire.
non-Catholic /nɒnˈkæθəlɪk/ **I** *n* non-catholique *mf*.
II *adj* non catholique.
nonce /nɒns/ *n* **1**† (present) **for the ~** pour l'instant, pour la circonstance; **2**○ (offender) argot des prisonniers violeur *m*.
nonce word *n* mot *m* de circonstance.
nonchalance /ˈnɒnʃələns/ *n* nonchalance *f*; **an air of ~** un air nonchalant.
nonchalant /ˈnɒnʃələnt/ *adj* nonchalant.
nonchalantly /ˈnɒnʃələntlɪ/ *adv* nonchalamment.
non-chlorine bleached *adj* [*paper*] non blanchi avec des dérivés chlorés.
non-Christian /nɒnˈkrɪstʃən/ **I** *n* non-chrétien/-ienne *m/f*.
II *adj* non chrétien/-ienne.
nonclassified /ˌnɒnˈklæsɪfaɪd/ *adj* [*information*] non confidentiel/-ielle.
noncollegiate student /ˌnɒnkəˈliːdʒɪət/ *n* Univ étudiant/-e *m/f* qui n'appartient à aucun collège.
noncom○ /ˌnɒnˈkɒm/ *n* (*abrév* = **noncommissioned officer**) ≈ sous-off○ *m*.
noncombatant /ˌnɒnˈkɒmbətənt/ **I** *n* noncombattant/-e *m/f*.
II *adj* non combattant.
noncombustible /ˌnɒnkəmˈbʌstəbl/ *adj* incombustible.
non-commercial /ˌnɒnkəˈmɜːʃəl/ *adj* [*event, activity*] à but non lucratif.
noncommissioned officer *n* Mil sous-officier *m*.
noncommittal /ˌnɒnkəˈmɪtl/ *adj* [*person, reply*] évasif/-ive (**about** au sujet de).
noncommittally /ˌnɒnkəˈmɪtəlɪ/ *adv* [*respond*] évasivement.
noncommunicant /ˌnɒnkəˈmjuːnɪkənt/ **I** *n* non-communiant/-e *m/f*.
II *adj* non communiant.
noncommunication /ˌnɒnkəˌmjuːnɪˈkeɪʃn/ *n* non-communication *f*.
noncompletion /ˌnɒnkəmˈpliːʃn/ *n* (of work) inachèvement *m*.
noncompliance /ˌnɒnkəmˈplaɪəns/ *n* (with standards) (of substance, machine) nonconformité *f* (**with** à); (with orders) (of person) non-obéissance *f* (**with** à).
non compos mentis /ˌnɒn ˌkɒmpəs ˈmentɪs/ *adj phr* **to be ~** Jur être en état de démence (au moment des faits); gen ne pas avoir toutes ses facultés.
nonconductor /ˌnɒnkənˈdʌktə(r)/ *n* Elec, Phys mauvais conducteur *m*.
nonconformism /ˌnɒnkənˈfɔːmɪzəm/ *n* **1** gen non-conformisme *m*; **2** GB Relig (also **Nonconformism**) non-conformisme *m*.
nonconformist /ˌnɒnkənˈfɔːmɪst/ **I** *n* nonconformiste *mf*.
II *adj* non conformiste.
nonconformity /ˌnɒnkənˈfɔːmətɪ/ *n* gen, Relig non-conformisme *m*; Tech (with standards) non-conformité *f*.
noncontemporary /ˌnɒnkənˈtemprərɪ, US -pərerɪ/ *adj* non contemporain.
non-contract /nɒnˈkɒntrækt/ *adj* sans contrat.
noncontributory pension scheme /ˌnɒnkənˈtrɪbjʊtərɪ, US -tɔːrɪ/ *n* Soc Admin pension *f* à titre non onéreux.
noncontroversial /ˌnɒnkɒntrəˈvɜːʃl/ *adj* non sujet/-ette à controverse.
noncooperation /ˌnɒnkəʊˌɒpəˈreɪʃn/ *n* refus *m* de coopération.
noncooperative /ˌnɒnkəʊˈɒpərətɪv/ *adj* non coopératif/-ive.
non-core /ˌnɒnˈkɔː(r)/ *adj* [*business*] annexe.
non-corroding /ˌnɒnkəˈrəʊdɪŋ/ *adj* inaltérable.
non-custodial sentence *n* Jur condamnation *f* sans incarcération.
nondairy /ˌnɒnˈdeərɪ/ *adj* sans lait.
nondazzle /ˌnɒnˈdæzl/ *adj* antiaveuglant.
nondemocratic /ˌnɒndeməˈkrætɪk/ *adj* non démocratique.
nondenominational /ˌnɒndɪˌnɒmɪˈneɪʃənl/ *adj* [*church*] œcuménique; [*school*] laïque.
nondescript /ˈnɒndɪskrɪpt/ *adj* [*person, clothes*] insignifiant; [*building*] quelconque; [*colour*] indéfinissable; [*performance, book*] sans intérêt.
nondestructive /ˌnɒndɪˈstrʌktɪv/ *adj* non destructif/-ive.
nondetachable /ˌnɒndɪˈtætʃəbl/ *adj* (from clothing) non amovible; (from equipment) indémontable.
nondirectional /ˌnɒndɪˈrekʃənl, -daɪ-/ *adj* [*method, technique*] non directif/-ive.
nondirective therapy /ˌnɒndɪˈrektɪv, -daɪ-/ *n* Psych psychothérapie *f* non directive.
nondomestic /ˌnɒndəˈmestɪk/ *adj* [*premises*] non résidentiel/-ielle.
nondrinker /ˌnɒnˈdrɪŋkə(r)/ *n* non-buveur/-euse *m/f*.
nondriver /ˌnɒnˈdraɪvə(r)/ *n* personne *f* qui ne conduit pas.
none /nʌn/ **I** *pron* **1** (not any, not one) aucun/-e *m/f*; **~ of us/you/them** aucun de nous/de vous/d'entre eux; **~ of the chairs/houses** aucune des chaises/maisons; **'have you any pens?'—'~ at all'** 'as-tu des stylos?'—'pas un seul'; **~ was more beautiful/interesting than...** il n'y en avait aucun de plus beau/intéressant que...; **he saw three dogs, ~ of which was black** il a vu trois chiens, aucun des trois n'était noir; **he waited for some sign of anger but saw ~** il guettait un signe de colère mais n'en a décelé aucun; **2** (not any, no part) **~ of the wine/milk** pas une goutte de vin/lait; **~ of the bread** pas une miette de pain; **~ of the cheese** pas un morceau de fromage; **'is there any money left?'—'~ at all'** 'est-ce qu'il reste de l'argent?'—'pas du tout'; **'did you have any difficulty?'—'~ whatsoever** ou **at all'** 'as-tu eu des difficultés?'—'aucune'; **we have ~** nous n'en avons pas; **there's ~ left** il n'y en a plus; **~ of it was true/of any interest** il n'y avait rien de vrai/d'intéressant; **he was having ~ of it** il ne voulait rien entendre; **we'll have ~ of that now!** ça suffit comme ça!; **some money is better than ~** un peu d'argent c'est toujours mieux que rien; **3** (nobody, not one person) personne; **~ can sing so well as her** personne ne chante aussi bien qu'elle; **there's ~ so clever/old as Jane** il n'y a personne de plus intelligent/vieux que Jane; **I waited but ~ came** j'ai attendu mais personne n'est venu; **if you need a lawyer, there's ~ better than George** si tu as besoin d'un avocat, il n'y en a pas de meilleur que George; **~ but him/you** personne sauf lui/toi; **I told ~ but him/you** je ne l'ai dit à personne sauf à lui/toi; **~ but a fool would do it** il n'y a qu'un imbécile pour faire une chose pareille; **it was ~**

other than Peter/the prime minister (himself) ce n'était autre que Peter/le premier ministre; **4** (on form, questionnaire) néant *m*.

II *adv* (not, not at all) **it was ~ too easy/pleasant** c'était loin d'être facile/agréable; **it's ~ too warm** il ne fait pas trop chaud; **I was ~ too sure/happy that** je n'étais pas trop sûr/content que (+ *subj*); **'I'm here!'—'and ~ too soon!'** 'je suis là!'—'ce n'est pas trop tôt!'; **he was ~ the worse for the experience** il ne se portait pas plus mal après cette expérience; **the play is long, but ~ the worse for that** la pièce est longue mais ce n'est pas un défaut.

non-EC *adj* [*country*] hors CEE; [*national*] non ressortissant de la CEE.

nonedible /ˌnɒnˈedɪbl/ *adj* non comestible.

nonemergency /ˌnɒnɪˈmɜːdʒənsɪ/ *adj* non urgent.

nonenforcement /ˌnɒnɪnˈfɔːsmənt/ *n* US Jur inapplication *f*.

nonentity /nɒˈnentətɪ/ *n* péj (person) être *m* insignifiant; **a complete** ou **total ~** un personnage complètement insignifiant.

nonessential /ˌnɒnɪˈsenʃl/ *adj* non essentiel/-ielle.

nonessentials /ˌnɒnɪˈsenʃlz/ *npl* (objects) accessoires *mpl*; (details) accessoire *msg*; **forget the ~** oublie l'accessoire.

nonestablished /ˌnɒnɪˈstæblɪʃt/ *adj* non établi.

nonetheless /ˌnʌnðəˈles/ *adv* ▸ **nevertheless**.

nonevent /ˌnɒnɪˈvent/ *n* non-événement *m*.

non-examination course *n* études *fpl* non sanctionnées par un examen.

nonexecutive director *n* consultant/-e *m/f*.

nonexistence /ˌnɒnɪɡˈzɪstəns/ *n* gen inexistence *f*; (of God) non-existence *f*.

nonexistent /ˌnɒnɪɡˈzɪstənt/ *adj* inexistant.

nonexplosive /ˌnɒnɪkˈspləʊsɪv/ *adj* inexplosible.

nonfactual /ˌnɒnˈfæktʃʊəl/ *adj* fictif/-ive.

non-family /ˌnɒnˈfæməlɪ/ *adj* en dehors de la famille.

nonfat /ˌnɒnˈfæt/ *adj* sans matières grasses.

nonfattening /ˌnɒnˈfætnɪŋ/ *adj* qui ne fait pas grossir.

nonferrous /ˌnɒnˈferəs/ *adj* non ferreux/-euse.

nonfiction /ˌnɒnˈfɪkʃn/ **I** *n* œuvres *fpl* non fictionnelles.

II *modif* [*publishing, section, writing*] non fictionnel/-elle.

non-finite form /ˌnɒnˈfaɪnaɪt/ *n* Ling forme *f* impersonnelle.

non-finite verb *n* verbe *m* à un mode impersonnel.

nonflammable /ˌnɒnˈflæməbl/ *adj* ininflammable.

non-fulfilment /ˌnɒnfʊlˈfɪlmənt/ *n* (of contract, obligation) inexécution *f*; (of desire, wish) inaccomplissement *m*.

non-governmental organization /ˌnɒnɡʌvnˈmentl/ *n* organisation *f* non gouvernementale.

nongrammatical /ˌnɒnɡrəˈmætɪkl/ *adj* non grammatical.

non grata /ˌnəʊn ˈɡrɑːtɑ/ *adj* non grata.

nongreasy /ˌnɒnˈɡriːsɪ/ *adj* [*make-up, skin*] non gras/grasse; [*food*] sans graisses.

non-infectious /ˌnɒnɪnˈfekʃəs/ *adj* intransmissible.

noninflammable /ˌnɒnɪnˈflæməbl/ *adj* ininflammable.

noninflationary /ˌnɒnɪnˈfleɪʃnrɪ, US -nerɪ/ *adj* non inflationniste.

noninterference /ˌnɒnɪntəˈfɪərəns/ *n* non-interférence *f*.

nonintervention /ˌnɒnɪntəˈvenʃn/ *n* non-intervention *f*.

nonintoxicating /ˌnɒnɪnˈtɒksɪkeɪtɪŋ/ *adj* non alcoolisé.

noninvolvement /ˌnɒnɪnˈvɒlvmənt/ *n* non-engagement *m*.

noniron /ˌnɒnˈaɪən, US -ˈaɪərn/ *adj* infroissable.

non-Jew /ˌnɒnˈdʒuː/ *n* non-juif/juive *m/f*.

non-Jewish /ˌnɒnˈdʒuːɪʃ/ *adj* non juif/juive.

nonjudgmental /ˌnɒndʒʌdʒˈmentl/ *adj* neutre.

non-league /ˌnɒnˈliːɡ/ *adj* Sport hors division.

nonliability /ˌnɒnlaɪəˈbɪlətɪ/ *n* non-responsabilité *f*.

nonlinear /ˌnɒnˈlɪnɪə(r)/ *adj* non linéaire.

nonlinguistic /ˌnɒnlɪŋˈɡwɪstɪk/ *adj* non linguistique.

nonmember /ˌnɒnˈmembə(r)/ *n* non-membre *m*.

nonmetal /ˌnɒnˈmetl/ *n* métalloïde *m*.

nonmetallic /ˌnɒnmɪˈtælɪk/ *adj* non métallique.

nonmetallic element *n* Chem métalloïde *m*.

nonmilitary /ˌnɒnˈmɪlɪtrɪ, US -terɪ/ *adj* non militaire.

nonnuclear /ˌnɒnˈnjuːklɪə(r), US -ˈnuː-/ *adj* non nucléaire.

no-no○ /ˈnəʊnəʊ/ *n* **that's a ~** ça ne se fait pas.

nonobservance /ˌnɒnəbˈzɜːvəns/ *n* (of law) non-observation *f*.

non obst. (*abrév* = **non obstante**) nonobstant.

no-nonsense /ˌnəʊˈnɒnsəns/ *adj* [*manner, look, tone, attitude, policy*] direct; [*person*] franc/franche.

nonoperational duties /ˌnɒnɒpəˈreɪʃənl/ *npl* (in police force) tâches *fpl* purement administratives.

nonpareil /ˌnɒnpəˈreɪl, US -ˈrel/ **I** *n* (master) **he's the ~ of tragedians** c'est un tragédien sans égal.

II nonpareils *npl* US Culin (decoration) nonpareilles *fpl*.

nonpartisan /ˌnɒnpɑːtɪˈzæn/ *adj* impartial.

nonparty /ˌnɒnˈpɑːtɪ/ *adj* [*issue, decision*] non partisan; [*person*] non affilié au parti.

nonpayer /ˌnɒnˈpeɪə(r)/ *n* Tax récalcitrant/-e *m/f* à l'impôt.

nonpaying /ˌnɒnˈpeɪɪŋ/ *adj* non payant.

nonpayment /ˌnɒnˈpeɪmənt/ *n* non-paiement *m*.

nonperishable /ˌnɒnˈperɪʃəbl/ *adj* non périssable.

nonperson /ˈnɒnˈpɜːsn/ *n* **1** pej (insignificant person) être *m* falot; **2** Pol **officially, he's a ~** officiellement, il n'a jamais existé.

nonplussed /ˌnɒnˈplʌst/ *adj* perplexe.

nonpolitical /ˌnɒnpəˈlɪtɪkl/ *adj* apolitique.

non-practising /ˌnɒnˈpræktɪsɪŋ/ *adj* **1** Relig non pratiquant; **2** [*barrister*] sans cause.

nonproductive /ˌnɒnprəˈdʌktɪv/ *adj* improductif/-ive.

nonprofessional /ˌnɒnprəˈfeʃənl/ *n, adj* amateur (*m*).

nonprofit /ˌnɒnˈprɒfɪt/ *adj* US = **non-profitmaking**.

non-profitmaking /ˌnɒnˈprɒfɪtmeɪkɪŋ/ *adj* [*organization*] à but non lucratif; **on a ~ basis** sans but lucratif; **to be ~** être sans but lucratif.

nonproliferation /ˌnɒnprəlɪfəˈreɪʃn/ *n* non-prolifération *f*.

nonpunitive /ˌnɒnˈpjuːnətɪv/ *adj* non punitif/-ive.

nonreceipt /ˌnɒnrɪˈsiːt/ *n* non-réception *f*.

nonrecurring expenses /ˌnɒnrɪˈkɜːrɪŋ/ *npl* dépenses *fpl* exceptionnelles.

non-redeemable /ˌnɒnrɪˈdiːməbl/ *adj* Fin perpétuel/-elle.

nonrefillable /ˌnɒnriːˈfɪləbl/ *adj* [*lighter, pen*] non rechargeable; [*can, bottle*] non réutilisable.

nonreflective /ˌnɒnrɪˈflektɪv/ *adj* non réfléchissant.

nonrefundable /ˌnɒnrɪˈfʌndəbl/ *adj* Fin non remboursable.

nonreligious /ˌnɒnrɪˈlɪdʒəs/ *adj* laïque.

nonrenewable /ˌnɒnrɪˈnjuːəbl, US -ˈnuː-/ *adj* non renouvelable.

nonrenewal /ˌnɒnrɪˈnuːəl/ *n* (of contract, lease) non-reconduction *f*.

nonresident /ˌnɒnˈresɪdənt/ **I** *n* non-résident/-e *m/f*.

II *adj* **1** [*guest*] de passage; [*student, visitor*] non résident; [*caretaker*] de jour; **2** (also **non-residential**) [*job, course*] sans hébergement; **3** Comput [*routine*] qui ne réside pas en permanence en mémoire centrale.

nonrestrictive /ˌnɒnrɪˈstrɪktɪv/ *adj* Ling [*clause*] explicatif/-ive.

nonreturnable /ˌnɒnrɪˈtɜːnəbl/ *adj* [*bottle*] non consigné.

nonrun /ˌnɒnˈrʌn/ *adj* [*tights*] indémaillable.

nonrunner /ˌnɒnˈrʌnə(r)/ *n* Turf non-partant *m*.

nonsectarian /ˌnɒnsekˈteərɪən/ *adj* non sectaire.

nonsegregated /ˌnɒnˈseɡrɪɡeɪtɪd/ *adj* [*area, arrangement*] sans ségrégation; [*society*] non ségrégationniste.

nonsense /ˈnɒnsns, US -sens/ *n* **1** (foolishness) absurdités *fpl*; **it's a ~ that** c'est absurde que (+ *subj*); **to make (a) ~ of** être en totale contradiction avec [*law, system, claim, hard work*]; **(stuff and) ~!** balivernes! *fpl*; **what utter ~!** c'est complètement absurde!; **to talk/write ~** dire/écrire n'importe quoi; **what's all this ~ about feeling ill/leaving work?** qu'est-ce que c'est que ces histoires de te sentir malade/quitter le travail?; **I won't stand any more ~ from him/you!** j'en ai assez de ses/tes bêtises!; **there's no ~ about him** il ne permet pas de fantaisie; **2** (trifle) petit rien *m*.

nonsense: **~ verse** *n* vers *mpl* fantaisistes; **~ word** *n* mot *m* fantaisiste.

nonsensical /nɒnˈsensɪkl/ *adj* (stupid) absurde.

nonsensically /nɒnˈsensɪklɪ/ *adv* de façon absurde.

non-separation /ˌnɒnsepəˈreɪʃən/ *n* Pol **~ of powers** confusion *f* des pouvoirs.

non sequitur /ˌnɒn ˈsekwɪtə(r)/ *n* **1** gen **to be a ~** être illogique; **2** Philos illogisme *m*.

nonsexist /ˌnɒnˈseksɪst/ *adj* non sexiste.

nonshrink /ˌnɒnˈʃrɪŋk/ *adj* irrétrécissable.

nonsked○ /ˌnɒnˈsked/ **I** *n* US vol *m* spécial.

II non-sked *adj* US [*flight*] spécial.

nonskid /ˌnɒnˈskɪd/, **nonslip** /ˌnɒnˈslɪp/ *n* antidérapant *m*.

nonsmoker /ˌnɒnˈsməʊkə(r)/ *n* (person) non-fumeur/-euse *m/f*.

nonsmoking /ˌnɒnˈsməʊkɪŋ/ *adj* [*area, compartment*] non fumeur *inv*.

nonsolvent /ˌnɒnˈsɒlvənt/ **I** *n* non-dissolvant *m*.

II *adj* non dissolvant.

non-speaking /ˌnɒnˈspiːkɪŋ/ *adj* Cin, Theat [*role*] muet/-ette.

nonspecialist /ˌnɒnˈspeʃəlɪst/ *adj* [*publication*] de vulgarisation; **to the ~ ear** pour le non-spécialiste.

non-specialized /ˌnɒnˈspeʃəlaɪzd/ *adj* généraliste.

nonstandard /ˌnɒnˈstændəd/ *adj* gen, Ling non standard *inv*.

nonstarter /ˌnɒnˈstɑːtə(r)/ *n* fig **to be a ~** [*person*] être hors-course; [*plan, idea*] être voué à l'échec.

nonstick /ˌnɒnˈstɪk/ *adj* [*coating, pan*] anti-adhésif/-ive.

nonstop /ˌnɒnˈstɒp/ **I** *adj* [*flight*] sans escale; [*journey*] sans arrêt; [*train*] direct; [*talk, work, pressure, noise*] incessant;

[*service, show*] permanent; [*coverage*] non-stop *inv*.
II *adv* [*work, talk, drive, argue*] sans arrêt; [*fly*] sans escale.

non-stretch /ˌnɒnˈstretʃ/ *adj* inextensible.

nonstriker /ˌnɒnˈstraɪkə(r)/ *n* non-gréviste *mf*.

nonstudent /ˌnɒnˈstjuːdnt/ *n* non-étudiant/-e *m/f*.

nonsuit /nɒnˈsjuːt, -ˈsuːt/ Jur **I** *n* déboute *m*.
II *vtr* débouter.

nonsupport /ˌnɒnsəˈpɔːt/ *n* US Jur défaut *m* de versement de pension alimentaire.

nonswimmer /ˌnɒnˈswɪmə(r)/ *n* personne *f* qui ne sait pas nager.

non-taxable /ˌnɒnˈtaksabl/ *adj* non imposable.

non-taxpayer /ˌnɒnˈtækspeɪə(r)/ *n* Fin personne *f* non imposable.

nonteaching staff /ˌnɒnˈtiːtʃɪŋ/ *n* Sch personnel *m* non enseignant.

nonthreatening /ˌnɒnˈθretnɪŋ/ *adj* non menaçant.

non-toxic /ˌnɒnˈtɒksɪk/ *adj* non toxique.

non-trading /ˌnɒnˈtreɪdɪŋ/ *adj* **~ partnership** association *f* professionnelle.

non-U○ /ˌnɒnˈjuː/ *adj* (*abrév* = **non upper class**) popu○, trivial.

non-union /ˌnɒnˈjuːnɪən/ *adj* non syndiqué.

nonverbal /ˌnɒnˈvɜːbl/ *adj* [*communication*] non-verbal.

nonviable /ˌnɒnˈvaɪəbl/ *adj* non viable.

non-vintage /nɒnˈvɪntɪdʒ/ *adj* [*champagne*] non-millésimé; [*port*] ordinaire.

nonviolence /ˌnɒnˈvaɪələns/ *n* non-violence *f*.

nonviolent /ˌnɒnˈvaɪələnt/ *adj* nonviolent.

nonvocational /ˌnɒnvəʊˈkeɪʃənl/ *adj* non professionnel/-elle.

nonvoluntary /ˌnɒnˈvɒləntrɪ/ *adj* non bénévole.

nonvoter /ˌnɒnˈvəʊtə(r)/ *n* non-votant/-e *m/f*.

nonvoting share /ˌnɒnˈvəʊtɪŋ/ *n* Fin action *f* sans droit de vote.

non-white, **non-White** /ˌnɒnˈwaɪt/ **I** *n* personne *f* de couleur.
II *adj* [*person*] de couleur; [*immigration*] des personnes de couleur.

non-worker /ˌnɒnˈwɜːkə(r)/ *n* inactif/-ive *m/f*.

non-working /ˌnɒnˈwɜːkɪŋ/ *adj* inactif/-ive.

nonwoven /ˌnɒnˈwəʊvn/ *adj* non tissé.

noodle /ˈnuːdl/ **I** *n* **1**○ US (head) caboche○† *f*, tête *f*; **2**○ † GB (fool) andouille○ *f*, imbécile○ *mf*.
II noodles *npl* Culin nouilles *fpl*; **egg ~s** nouilles aux œufs.

nook /nʊk/ *n* **1** (retreat) coin *m*; **2** (in room) coin *m*; (for ornaments) niche *f*; **breakfast ~** coin-repas *m*.
IDIOMS **every ~ and cranny** tous les coins et recoins.

nookie◑, **nooky**◑ /ˈnʊkɪ/ *n* **nice ~** de jolis petits culs◑; **to get some ~** baiser●, faire l'amour.

noon /nuːn/ **I** *n* midi *m*; **by/about ~** à/vers midi; **at 12 ~** à midi; **at high ~** en plein midi.
II *modif* [*heat, sun, train, deadline*] de midi.
IDIOMS **morning, ~ and night** du matin au soir.

noonday /ˈnuːndeɪ/ **I** *n*† midi *m*.
II *modif* littér **the ~ sun** le soleil de midi.

no-one /ˈnəʊwʌn/ *pron* = **nobody I**.

noose /nuːs/ *n* **1** (loop) nœud *m* coulant; **2** (for hanging) corde *f*; **the hangman's ~** la corde de la potence; **to put a ~ around one's neck** mettre une corde autour de son cou; fig se mettre la corde au cou.
IDIOMS **to put one's head in a ~** se jeter dans la gueule du loup.

nope○ /nəʊp/ *excl* nan○, non.

nor /nɔː(r), nə(r)/

■ **Note** If you want to know how to translate *nor* when used in combination with *neither* look at the entry ***neither***.
– When used as a conjunction to show agreement or similarity with a negative statement, *nor* is very often translated by *non plus*: *'I don't like him'—'nor do I'* = 'je ne l'aime pas'—'moi non plus'; *'he's not Spanish'—'nor is John'* = 'il n'est pas espagnol'—'John non plus'; *'I can't sleep'—'nor can I'* = 'je n'arrive pas à dormir'—'moi non plus'.
– When used to give additional information to a negative statement *nor* can very often be translated by *non plus* preceded by a negative verb: *she hasn't written, nor has she telephoned* = elle n'a pas écrit, et elle n'a pas téléphoné non plus; *I do not wish to insult you, (but) nor do I wish to lose money* = je ne veux pas vous offenser, mais je ne souhaite pas non plus perdre de l'argent.
– For examples and further uses of *nor* see the entry below.

conj **you don't have to tell him, ~ should you** tu n'es pas obligé de le lui dire, tu ferais même mieux d'éviter.

nor' /nɔː(r)/ *adj* nord *inv*; **to sail ~-~-east** naviguer nord-nord-est.

noradrenalin(e) /ˌnɔːrəˈdrenəlɪn/ *n* noradrénaline *f*.

Nord ▶ 1273, 1163 *pr n* Nord *m*; **in/to the ~** dans le Nord.

Nordic /ˈnɔːdɪk/ *adj* [*customs, appearance, country*] nordique; **the ~ peoples** les peuplades nordiques.

Norfolk /ˈnɒːfək/ ▶ 1624 *pr n* Norfolk *m*.

norm /nɔːm/ *n* (all contexts) norme *f* (**for** pour); **it is the ~ to do** c'est la norme de faire; **above/below the ~** au-dessus/en dessous de la norme.

normal /ˈnɔːml/ **I** *n* gen, Math normale *f*; **above/below ~** au-dessus/en dessous de la norme; **to get back** ou **return to ~** revenir à la normale; **a temperature above ~ for May** une température un peu élevée pour le mois de mai; **richer/bigger than ~** plus riche/plus grand que la normale.
II *adj* **1** (usual) [*place, time*] habituel/-elle; [*amount, method, position, service, size, temperature*] normal; [*view*] courant; **it is ~ for sb to do** il est normal pour qn de faire; **it is ~ that** c'est normal que (+ *subj*); **it is ~ for trains to be late in winter** il est normal que les trains aient du retard en hiver; **as ~** comme d'habitude; **in the ~ course of events** si tout va bien; **in ~ circumstances** en temps normal; **2** Psych (conventional) [*person, behaviour*] normal; **3** Math normal; **4** Biol [*control*] sain; **5** Chem neutre.

normalcy /ˈnɔːmlsɪ/ *n* normalité *f*.

normality /nɔːˈmælətɪ/ *n* normalité *f*; **to return to ~** revenir à la normale.

normalization /ˌnɔːməlaɪˈzeɪʃn, US -lɪˈz-/ *n* normalisation *f*.

normalize /ˈnɔːməlaɪz/ **I** *vtr* normaliser.
II *vi* se normaliser.

normalizing /ˈnɔːməlaɪzɪŋ/ *n* Tech (of steel) traitement *m* par trempage.

normally /ˈnɔːməlɪ/ *adv* normalement.

Norman /ˈnɔːmən/ **I** *n* **1** gen, Hist Normand/-e *m/f*; **2** (also **~ French**) ling normand *m*.
II *adj* **1** gen, Hist [*landscape, village*] normand; [*produce*] de Normandie; **2** Archit roman.

Norman Conquest *n* conquête *f* normande.

Normandy /ˈnɔːməndɪ/ ▶ 1273 *pr n* Normandie *f*.

Norman English *n* anglo-normand *m*.

normative /ˈnɔːmətɪv/ *adj* normatif/-ive.

Norse /nɔːs/ **I** *n* ▶ 1486, 1402 **1** (language) norrois *m*; **Old ~** le vieux norrois; **2** (also **~ men**) **the ~** (+ *v pl*) les Scandinaves.
II *adj* [*mythology, saga*] nordique.

north /nɔːθ/ ▶ 1568 **I** *n* (compass direction) nord *m*; **true ~** le nord géographique.
II North *pr n* **1** Pol, Geog, US Hist (part of world, country) **the North** le Nord; **the far North** le Grand Nord; **2** (in cards) nord *m*.
III *adj* [*coast, side, face, wall*] nord *inv*; [*wind*] gen du nord; Meteorol de nord; **in/from ~ London** dans le/du nord de Londres.
IV *adv* [*move*] vers le nord; [*lie, live*] au nord (**of** de); **to go ~ of sth** passer au nord de qch.

North Africa ▶ 1131 *pr n* Afrique *f* du Nord.

North African ▶ 1486 **I** *n* Nord-Africain/-e *m/f*.
II *adj* [*town, custom, climate*] nord-africain.

North America ▶ 1131 *pr n* Amérique *f* du Nord.

North American ▶ 1486 **I** *n* Nord-Américain/-e *m/f*.
II *adj* nord-américain.

Northamptonshire /nɒːˈθæmptənˌʃɪə(r)/ ▶ 1624 *pr n* Northamptonshire *m*.

Northants /nɔːˈθænts/ *n* GB Post *abrév écrite* = **Northamptonshire**.

north: **North Atlantic Drift** *n* dérive *f* nord-atlantique; **North Atlantic Treaty Organization, NATO** *n* Organisation *f* du traité de l'Atlantique Nord.

northbound /ˈnɔːθbaʊnd/ *adj* [*carriageway, traffic*] en direction du nord; **the ~ platform/train** GB (in underground) le quai/la rame direction nord.

North Carolina ▶ 1744 *pr n* Caroline *f* du Nord.

Northd *n* GB Post *abrév écrite* ▶ **Northumberland**.

North Dakota ▶ 1744 *pr n* Dakota *m* du Nord.

northeast /ˌnɔːθˈiːst/ ▶ 1568 **I** *n* nord-est *m*.
II *adj* [*coast, side*] nord-est *inv*; [*wind*] de nord-est.
III *adv* [*move*] vers le nord-est; [*lie, live*] au nord-est (**of** de).

northeaster /ˌnɔːθˈiːstə(r)/ *n* vent *m* de nord-est.

northeasterly /ˌnɔːθˈiːstəlɪ/ **I** *n* vent *m* de nord-est.
II *adj* [*wind*] de nord-est; [*point*] au nord-est; **in a ~ direction** en direction du nord-est.

northeastern /ˌnɔːθˈiːstən/ ▶ 1568 *adj* [*coast, boundary*] nord-est *inv*; [*town, custom, accent*] du nord-est; **~ Scotland** le nord-est de l'Écosse.

northerly /ˈnɔːðəlɪ/ **I** *n* vent *m* du nord.
II *adj* [*wind*] de nord; [*point*] au nord; [*area*] du nord; [*breeze*] venant du nord; **in a ~ direction** en direction du nord.

northern /ˈnɔːðən/ ▶ 1568 *adj* [*coast, boundary*] nord *inv*; [*town, region, custom, accent*] du nord; [*hemisphere*] Nord *inv*; [*latitude*] boréal; **~ England** le nord de l'Angleterre; **~ English** [*landscape etc*] du nord de l'Angleterre.

northerner /ˈnɔːðənə(r)/ *n* **~s** les gens du Nord; **to be a ~** être du Nord.

northern: **Northern Ireland** ▶ 1131 *n* Irlande *f* du Nord; **Northern Irish** *adj* d'Irlande du Nord; **Northern Lights** *npl* aurore *f* boréale; **~most** *adj* à l'extrême nord, le/la plus au nord; **Northern Territory, NT** *n* Territoire *m* du Nord.

north: **~-facing** *adj* exposé au nord; **North Island** *n* Île *f* du Nord (*de la Nouvelle-Zélande*); **North Korea** ▶ 1131 *pr n* Corée *f* du Nord; **Northman** *n* Viking *m*; **North Pole** *n* pôle *m* Nord.

North Sea ▶ 1511 **I** *n* **the ~** la mer du Nord.
II *modif* **~ oil/gas** pétrole/gaz *m* de la mer du Nord.

North Star *n* étoile *f* polaire.

not

When *not* is used without a verb before an adjective, an adverb, a verb or a noun it is translated by *pas*:

it's a cat not a dog = c'est un chat pas un chien
not at all = pas du tout
not bad = pas mal

For examples and particular usages see the entry **not**.

When *not* is used to make the verb *be* negative (*it's not a cat*) it is translated by *ne ... pas* in French; *ne* comes before the verb or the auxiliary in compound tenses and *pas* comes after the verb or auxiliary: *ce n'est pas un chat*; *she hasn't been ill* = elle n'a pas été malade.

When *not* is used with the auxiliary *do* to make a verb negative (*he doesn't like oranges*) do + *not* is translated by *ne ... pas* in French: il n'aime pas les oranges.

When *not* is used in the present perfect tense (*I haven't seen him, she hasn't arrived yet*), *ne ... pas* is again used in French on either side of the appropriate auxiliary (*avoir* or *être*): *je ne l'ai pas vu, elle n'est pas encore arrivée.*

When *not* is used with *will* to make a verb negative (*will not, won't*), *ne ... pas* is used with the *future tense* in French:

she won't come by car = elle ne viendra pas en voiture

When used with a verb in the infinitive *ne pas* are placed together before the verb:

he decided not to go = il a décidé de ne pas y aller
you were wrong not to tell her = tu as eu tort de ne pas le lui dire

When *not* is used in question tags the whole tag can usually be translated by the French *n'est-ce pas*, e.g.

she bought it, didn't she? = elle l'a acheté, n'est-ce pas?

For usages not covered in this note see the entry **not**.

Northumberland /nɒːˈθʌmbələnd/ ▶ **1624** *pr n* Northumberland *m*.

Northumbria /nɔːˈθʌmbrɪə/ ▶ **1624** *pr n* Northumbrie *f* also Hist.

Northumbrian /nɔːˈθʌmbrɪən/ **I** *n* **1** (native) habitant/-e *m/f* de Northumbrie; **2** (dialect) northumbrien *m*.
II *adj* northumbrien/-ienne.

northward /ˈnɔːθwəd/ ▶ **1568** **I** *adj* [*side*] nord *inv*; [*wall, slope*] du côté nord; [*journey, root, movement*] vers le nord; **in a ~ direction** en direction du nord, vers le nord.
II *adv* (also **~s**) vers le nord.

northwest /ˌnɔːθˈwest/ ▶ **1568** **I** *n* nord-ouest *m*.
II *adj* [*coast, side*] nord-ouest *inv*; [*wind*] de nord-ouest.
III *adv* [*move*] vers le nord-ouest; [*lie, live*] au nord-ouest (**of** de).

northwester /ˌnɔːθˈwestə(r)/ *n* vent *m* de nord-ouest, noroît *m*.

northwesterly /ˌnɔːθˈwestəlɪ/ **I** *n* vent *m* de nord-ouest, noroît *m*.
II *adj* [*wind*] de nord-ouest; [*point*] au nord-ouest; **in a ~ direction** en direction du nord-ouest.

northwestern /ˌnɔːθˈwestən/ *adj* [*coast, boundary*] nord-ouest *inv*; [*town, accent, custom*] du nord-ouest; **~ Scotland** le nord-ouest de l'Écosse.

northwest: **Northwest Passage** *pr n* passage *m* du Nord-Ouest; **Northwest Territories** *pr npl* Territoires *mpl* du Nord-Ouest.

North Yorkshire /ˌnɔːθ ˈjɔːkʃɪə(r)/ ▶ **1624** *pr n* North Yorkshire *m*.

Norway /ˈnɔːweɪ/ ▶ **1131** *pr n* Norvège *f*.

Norwegian /nɔːˈwiːdʒən/ ▶ **1486**, **1402** **I** *n* **1** (person) Norvégien/-ienne *m/f*; **2** (language) norvégien *m*.
II *adj* norvégien/-ienne.

no sale *n* non-vente *f*.

nose /nəʊz/ **I** ▶ **1037** *n* **1** Anat nez *m*; **to breathe through one's ~** respirer par le nez; **to speak through one's ~** parler du nez; **the end** ou **tip of the ~** le bout du nez; **to bury one's ~ in a book** plonger le nez dans un livre; **2** (of plane, boat) nez *m*; (of car) avant *m*; **~ to tail traffic** des voitures pare-chocs contre pare-chocs; **to travel ~ to tail** rouler à touche-touche; **3** (sense of smell) gen odorat *m*; (of wine or perfume expert) nez *m*; (of dog) flair *m*; **a dog with a good ~** un chien qui a du flair; **4** (smell of wine) bouquet *m*; **5** fig (instinct) **to have a ~ for sth** avoir du flair pour qch; **to follow one's ~** se fier à son instinct.
II *vtr* **1** (sniff) [*animal*] renifler; [*wine-trader*] sentir; **2** (manœuvre) **to ~ sth in/out** faire entrer/sortir qch avec précaution [*boat, vehicle*]; **the captain ~d the boat out of the harbour** le capitaine a fait sortir le bateau du port avec précaution; **the boat ~d its way out of the harbour** le bateau est sorti du port avec prudence.
III *vi* **to ~ into/out of sth** [*boat, vehicle*] entrer dans/sortir de qch avec prudence; **the car ~d into the traffic** la voiture s'est faufilée dans la circulation.
IDIOMS **it's as plain as the ~ on your face** cela se voit comme le nez au milieu de la figure; **it's six on the ~**○ US il est six heures pile○; **to count ~s**○ compter les personnes présentes; **to get up sb's ~**○ taper sur le système de qn○; **to hit sth on the ~** US taper qch dans le mille; **to keep one's ~ clean**○ se tenir hors du coup○; **to keep one's ~ out of sth**○ ne pas se mêler de qch; **to lead sb by the ~**○ mener qn par le bout du nez; **to look down one's ~ at sb/sth** prendre qn/qch de haut; **to pay through the ~ for sth** payer le prix fort pour qch; **to poke** ou **stick one's ~ into sth**○ fourrer○ son nez dans qch; **to see no further than the end of one's ~** ne pas voir plus loin que le bout de son nez; **to turn one's ~ up at sth** faire le dégoûté/la dégoûtée devant qch; **to turn up one's ~ at the idea of doing** faire le dégoûté/la dégoûtée à l'idée de faire; **(right) under sb's ~** sous le nez de qn; **to win by a ~** Turf gagner d'une courte tête; **with one's ~ in the air** d'un air supérieur. ▶ **joint, rub.**
■ **nose about, nose around** fouiner (**in** dans).
■ **nose at**: **~ at [sth]** [*animal*] renifler.
■ **nose out**: ¶ **~ out** ¶ [*vehicle*] déboîter prudemment; [*boat*] sortir avec prudence; ¶ **~ out [sth], ~ [sth] out 1** lit (sniff out) dépister [*animal, scent*]; **2** fig, péj (discover) dénicher [*facts, truth, secret*]; **3** fig Sport (put in second place) battre [qch] d'un cheveu [*car, horse*].

nose: **~bag** *n* musette *f* mangeoire; **~band** *n* muserolle *f*; **~bleed** *n* saignement *m* de nez; **~-cone** *n* Aerosp, Mil ogive *f*.

nose-dive /ˈnəʊzdaɪv/ **I** *n* **1** Aviat piqué *m*; **to go into a ~** faire un piqué; **2** fig **to go into** ou **take a ~** [*currency, rate*] chuter.
II *vi* [*plane*] descendre en piqué; [*demand, prices, sales*] chuter.

nose: **~ drops** *npl* gouttes *fpl* pour le nez; **~gay** *n* petit bouquet *m*.

nose job *n* **to have a ~** se faire refaire le nez.

nose: **~piece** *n* (on glasses) pont *m*; **~ ring** *n* anneau *m* de nez; **~ wheel** *n* roue *f* avant.

nosey○ *adj* = **nosy**.

nosh○ /nɒʃ/ **I** *n* GB bouffe○ *f*, gueuleton○ *m*; US casse-croûte *m*.
II *vtr* GB bouffer○.
III *vi* **1** GB bouffer○; **2** US **to ~ on** grignoter [*food*].

no-show *n* US *personne ayant fait une réservation qui ne se présente pas à l'hôtel, l'aéroport etc.*

nosh-up○ /ˈnɒʃʌp/ *n* GB bouffe○ *f*, gueuleton○ *m*.

nosily /ˈnəʊzɪlɪ/ *adv* indiscrètement.

nosing /ˈnəʊzɪŋ/ *n* (on stair) rebord *m*; (moulding) moulure *f*.

nosography /nəˈsɒgrəfɪ/ *n* nosographie *f*.

nosological /ˌnɒsəˈlɒdʒɪkl/ *adj* [*book, experience*] de nosologie; [*theory, problem*] nosologique; [*expert*] en nosologie.

nosologist /nəˈsɒlədʒɪst/ ▶ **1692** *n* nosologiste *mf*.

nosology /nəˈsɒlədʒɪ/ *n* nosologie *f*.

nostalgia /nɒˈstældʒə/ *n* nostalgie *f*.

nostalgic /nɒˈstældʒɪk/ *adj* [*feeling, portrayal*] nostalgique; **to feel ~ for** avoir la nostalgie de [*era, place*].

nostalgically /nɒˈstældʒɪklɪ/ *adv* [*talk, look back*] avec nostalgie.

nostril /ˈnɒstrɪl/ *n* (of person) narine *f*; (of horse) naseau *m*.

nostrum† /ˈnɒstrəm/ *n* péj (remedy) remède *m* de bonne femme; fig panacée *f*.

nosy○ /ˈnəʊzɪ/ *adj* fouineur/-euse○.

nosy parker○ /ˈnəʊzɪpɑːkə(r)/ *n* péj fouineur/-euse○ *m/f*.

not /nɒt/ **I** *adv* **1** (negating verb) ne...pas; **she isn't at home** elle n'est pas chez elle; **they didn't like it** ils ne l'ont pas aimé; **we won't need a car** nous n'aurons pas besoin d'une voiture; **has he ~ seen it?** il ne l'a pas vu alors?; **2** (replacing word, clause, sentence etc) **'is he angry?'—'I hope ~'** 'est-il en colère?'—'j'espère que non'; **'is she married?'—'I believe** ou **think ~'** 'est-ce qu'elle est mariée?'—'je ne crois pas, je crois que non'; **I'm afraid ~** je crains que non; **certainly/probably ~** sûrement/probablement pas; **~ only** ou **simply** ou **merely** ou **just** pas seulement; **tired or ~, you're going to bed** fatigué ou non, tu vas te coucher; **do you know whether he's coming or ~?** est-ce que tu sais s'il vient ou pas?; **whether it rains or ~, I'm going** qu'il pleuve ou non, j'y vais; **why ~?** pourquoi pas?; **3** (contrasting) non pas; **they live in caves, ~ in houses, they live ~ in houses, but in caves** ils habitent non pas dans des maisons, mais dans des grottes; **I laughed, ~ because I was amused but from nervousness** je n'ai pas ri parce que je trouvais ça drôle, c'était nerveux; **he's ~ so much aggressive as assertive** il est plutôt sûr de lui qu'agressif; **4** (to emphasize opposite) **it's ~ impossible/cheap** ce n'est pas impossible/bon marché; **she's ~ a dishonest/an aggressive woman** elle n'est pas malhonnête/agressive; **~ without problems/some reservations** non sans problèmes/quelques réserves; **you're ~ wrong** tu n'as pas tort; **a ~** ou **not an (entirely) unexpected response** une réponse prévisible; **5** (less than) moins de; **~ three miles/hours from here** à moins de trois miles/heures d'ici; **~ five minutes ago** il y a moins de cinq minutes; **6** (in suggestions) **hadn't we better pay the bill?** est-ce qu'on ne ferait pas mieux de payer l'addition?; **couldn't we tell them later?** est-ce qu'on ne pourrait pas le leur dire plus tard?; **why ~ do it now?, why don't we do it now?** pourquoi ne pas le faire tout de suite?; **7** (with all, every) **~ all doctors agree, ~ every doctor agrees** tous les docteurs ne sont pas d'accord; **~ everyone likes it** tout le monde ne l'aime pas; **it's ~ everyone that can speak several foreign languages** tout le monde n'est pas capable de parler plusieurs langues; **it's ~ every day that** ce n'est pas tous les jours que; **8** (with a, one) **~ a** ou **one** pas un/-e, pas un/-e seul/-e; **not one** ou **a (single) chair/letter**

pas une seule chaise/lettre; **~ a sound was heard** on n'entendait pas un bruit; **~ one** ou **a single person knew** personne ne le savait.
II not at all *adv phr* gen pas du tout; (responding to thanks) de rien.
III† not but what ▶ not that.
IV not that *conj phr* **(it's) ~ that he hasn't been helpful/friendly** non pas qu'il n'ait pas été serviable/aimable, ce n'est pas qu'il n'ait pas été serviable/aimable; **~ that I know of** pas (autant) que je sache; **if she refuses, ~ that she will...** si elle refuse, je ne dis pas qu'elle le fera...

■ Note Dans la langue parlée ou familière, *not* utilisé avec un auxiliaire ou un modal prend parfois la forme *n't* qui est alors accolée au verbe (eg *you can't go, he hasn't finished*).

notability /ˌnəʊtəˈbɪlətɪ/ *n* (person) notable *m*.
notable /ˈnəʊtəbl/ **I** *n* sout notable *m*.
II *adj* [*person*] remarquable; [*event, achievement, success, difference*] notable; **with a few ~ exceptions** à part quelques exceptions notables; **to be ~ for** être remarquable pour [*clarity, appearance, quality*]; être notoire pour [*incompetence, failure*]; **it is ~ that** il est remarquable or notable que (+ *subj*).
notably /ˈnəʊtəblɪ/ *adv* **1** (in particular) notamment; **most ~** plus or tout particulièrement; **2** (markedly) [*unimpressed, resilient*] remarquablement.
notarial /nəʊˈteərɪəl/ *adj* [*seal, stamp*] notarial; [*status, profession*] de notaire.
notarial deed acte *m* notarié.
notarize /ˈnəʊtəraɪz/ *vtr* [*notary*] certifier; **to be ~d** être certifié devant notaire.
notary /ˈnəʊtərɪ/ **▶ 1692** *n* (also **~ public**) notaire *m*; **before a ~** devant notaire.
notate /nəʊˈteɪt/ *vtr* transcrire.
notation /nəʊˈteɪʃn/ *n* **1** Mus, Math notation *f*; **2** (system) (système *m* de) notation *f*; **3** (record) note *f*.
notch /nɒtʃ/ **I** *n* **1** (nick) (in plank) entaille *f*; (in fabric, belt) cran *m*; (in lid) encoche *f*; **2** (as record) encoche *f*, entaille *f*; **3**○ (degree) cran *m*; **to go up a ~** [*opinion*] monter d'un cran; **to be several ~es above sb** être nettement au-dessus de qn; **4** US Geog (pass) défilé *m*.
II *vtr* **1** (mark) encocher [*stick, surface, edge*]; cranter [*fabric*]; **2**○ (achieve) = **notch up**○.
■ **notch up**○: **~ up [sth]** remporter [*win, point, prize*]; **to ~ up a notable success** se tailler un vif succès.
note /nəʊt/ **I** *n* **1** (written record) note *f*; **to make a ~ in** mettre une note dans [*diary, notebook*]; **to make a ~ of** noter [*date, address*]; **to take ~ of** lit, fig prendre note de; **take ~!** prenez note!; **to take ~s** [*student, secretary*] prendre des notes; **to speak without ~s** parler sans notes; **according to police ~s** selon le rapport de la police; **2** (short letter) mot *m*; **to write sb a ~** écrire un mot à qn; **a ~ of thanks** un mot de remerciement; **3** (explanation, annotation) (in book, on form) note *f*; (accompanying form) notice *f*; (on theatre programme) commentaire *m*; **see ~ below** voir note ci-dessous; **4** fig (tone) ton *m*; **to hit the right ~** trouver le ton juste; **to strike** ou **hit a wrong ~** commettre un impair; **on a less serious ~** en passant à un registre moins sérieux; **to end on an optimistic ~** se terminer sur une note d'optimisme; **to sound a ~ of caution** émettre une mise en garde; **5** Mus (sound, symbol) note *f*; **to play** ou **hit a wrong ~** faire une fausse note; **a high/low ~** une note aiguë/basse; **the black ~s** (on keyboard) les touches *fpl* noires; **6** (tone) (in voice) note *f*; **a ~ of panic** une note de panique; **the engine took on a different ~** le bruit du moteur a changé; **7** (banknote) billet *m*; **£500 in ~s** 500 livres en billets; **a £20 ~** un billet de 20 livres; **8** (diplomatic memo) note *f*.
II of note *adj phr* [*person*] éminent, réputé; [*development, contribution*] digne d'intérêt.
III *vtr* **1** (observe) noter [*change, increase, similarity, absence*]; **to ~ that** noter que; **it is interesting to ~ that** il est intéressant de noter que; **the report ~d that** dans le rapport on a noté or constaté que; **noting the improvements, the minister said...** après avoir noté les améliorations, le ministre a dit...; **as I ~d last week...** comme je l'avais noté la semaine dernière...; **2** (pay attention to) prendre bonne note de [*comment, remarks, complaint, concern*]; **it should be ~d that** il faut noter que; **~ that she didn't mention him!** note bien qu'elle ne l'a pas mentionné!; **aspiring managers, please ~!** managers en puissance, prenez-en de la graine○!; **3** (write down) noter [*date, time, number, symptom*] **(in** dans); **'no change,' he ~d** 'aucun changement,' a-t-il noté.
IV noted *pp adj* [*intellectual, criminal*] célèbre; **to be ~d/not ~d for** être réputé/ne pas être réputé pour [*tact, wit*].
IDIOMS **to compare ~s** échanger ses impressions (**with** avec).
■ **note down**: **~ down [sth]**, **~ [sth] down** noter [*idea, detail*].
notebook /ˈnəʊtbʊk/ *n* **1** gen carnet *m*; **2** Jur, Accts livre *m* de comptes; **3** Journ (column title) **City ~** carnet *m* de la Bourse; **4** Comput agenda *m* électronique.
note: **~book pc** *n* ordinateur-agenda *m*; **~case** *n* portefeuille *m*; **~ issue** *n* émission *f* fiduciaire; **~pad** *n* bloc-notes *m*; **~paper** *n* papier *m* à lettres.
noteworthy /ˈnəʊtwɜːðɪ/ *adj* remarquable.
not guilty *adj* Jur [*person*] non coupable; [*verdict*] d'acquittement; **to plead ~** plaider non coupable; **to find sb ~** acquitter qn.
nothing /ˈnʌθɪŋ/ **I** *pron* **1** (no item, event, idea) rien; (as object of verb) ne...rien; (as subject of verb) rien...ne; **she says ~** elle ne dit rien; **I knew ~ about it** je n'en savais rien; **we saw ~** nous n'avons rien vu; **we can do ~ (about it)** nous n'y pouvons rien; **there's ~ in the fridge** il n'y a rien dans le frigidaire®; **~ can alter the fact that** rien ne peut changer le fait que; **~ could be further from the truth** rien n'est plus faux; **can ~ be done to help?** est-ce qu'on ne peut rien faire pour aider?; **~ happened** il ne s'est rien passé; **they behaved as if ~ had happened** ils ont fait comme si de rien n'était; **there's ~ to drink** il n'y a rien à boire; **I've got ~ to wear** je n'ai rien à me mettre; **you have ~ to lose** vous n'avez rien à perdre; **there's ~ to stop you leaving** rien ne t'empêche de partir; **we've had ~ to eat** nous n'avons rien mangé; **you did ~ at all to stop them** tu n'as absolument rien fait pour les arrêter; **next to ~** presque rien; **~ much** pas grand-chose; **there's ~ much on TV** il n'y a pas grand-chose à la télé○; **~ much happens here** il ne se passe pas grand-chose ici; **I've ~ much to tell** je n'ai pas grand-chose à raconter; **~ more** rien de plus; **we ask for ~ more** nous ne demandons rien de plus; **is there ~ more you can do?** vous ne pouvez rien faire de plus?; **she's just a friend, ~ more or less** c'est une amie, c'est tout; **~ else** rien d'autre; **there's ~ else for us** il n'y a rien d'autre pour nous; **~ else matters** rien d'autre ne compte, il n'y a que ça qui compte; **she thinks about ~ else** elle ne pense à rien d'autre, elle ne pense qu'à cela; **there's ~ else one can say** il n'y a rien d'autre à dire; **if ~ else it will be a change for us** au moins ça nous changera les idées; **to have ~ against sb/sth** ne rien avoir contre qn/qch; **to have ~ to do with** (no connection) ne rien avoir à voir avec; (no dealings, involvement) ne rien avoir à faire avec;

> ## nothing
> When *nothing* is used alone as a reply to a question in English, it is translated by *rien*:
>
> *'what are you doing?' 'nothing'* = 'que fais-tu?' 'rien'
>
> *nothing* as a pronoun when it is the subject of a verb is translated by *rien ne* in French:
>
> *nothing changes* = rien ne change
> *nothing has changed* = rien n'a changé
>
> *nothing* as a pronoun when it is the object of a verb is translated by *ne rien*; *ne* comes before the verb, and before the auxiliary in compound tenses, and *rien* comes after the verb or auxiliary:
>
> *I see nothing* = je ne vois rien
> *I saw nothing* = je n'ai rien vu
>
> When *ne rien* is used with an infinitive the two words are not separated:
>
> *I prefer to say nothing* = je préfère ne rien dire
>
> For examples and particular usages, see **I** in the entry ***nothing***.
>
> For translations of *nothing* as an adverb (*it's nothing like as difficult*) and for the phrases *nothing but, nothing less than, nothing more than*, see **II, V, VI** and **VII** respectively in the entry ***nothing***.

the drop in sales has ~ to do with the scandal la baisse des ventes n'a rien à voir avec le scandale; **it had ~ to do with safety** ça n'avait rien à voir avec la sécurité; **he had ~ to do with the murder** il n'avait rien à voir avec le meurtre, il n'était pour rien dans le meurtre; **I had ~ to do with it!** je n'y étais pour rien!; **that's got ~ to do with it!** ça n'a rien à voir!; **she will have** ou **she wants ~ to do with it/us** elle ne veut rien avoir à faire avec ça/nous; **it's ~ to do with us** ça ne nous regarde pas; **she acts as though it had ~ to do with her** elle fait comme si ça ne la concernait pas; **to come to ~** n'aboutir à rien; **to stop at ~** ne reculer devant rien (**to do** pour faire); **to have ~ on** (no clothes) être nu; (no engagements, plans) n'avoir rien de prévu; **you've got ~ on me**○! (to incriminate) vous n'avez rien contre moi!; **he's got ~ on you**○! (to rival) il ne t'arrive pas à la cheville○!; **Paris has ~ on this**○! Paris ne peut pas rivaliser avec ça!; **2** (emphasizing insignificance) rien; **a fuss about ~** une histoire pour (un) rien; **to get upset over ~** s'énerver pour (un) rien; **we were talking about ~ much** nous parlions de tout et de rien; **to count for ~** ne compter pour rien; **he means** ou **is ~ to me** il n'est rien pour moi; **so all this effort means ~ to you?** alors tout ce travail t'est complètement égal?; **it meant ~ to him** ça lui était complètement égal (**that, whether** que + *subj*); **the names meant ~ to him** les noms ne lui disaient rien; **he cares ~ for convention** sout il se moque des conventions; **to think ~ of doing** (consider normal) trouver tout à fait normal de faire; (not baulk at) ne pas hésiter à faire; **I thought ~ of it until the next day** ça m'a paru tout à fait normal jusqu'au lendemain; **think ~ of it!** ce n'est rien!; **it was ~ to them to walk miles to school** ils trouvaient tout à fait normal de faire des kilomètres à pied pour aller à l'école; **there's ~ to driving a truck** ce n'est rien de conduire un camion; **there's really ~ to it!** c'est tout ce qu'il y a de plus facile!; **3** (very little indeed) lit, fig rien; **she's four foot ~** ≈ elle ne fait pas plus d'un mètre vingt, elle fait un mètre vingt à tout casser○; **it costs next to ~** ça ne coûte presque rien; **for ~** (for free) gratuitement, gratis○; (pointlessly) pour rien; **it's money for ~** c'est de l'argent vite gagné; **all this work for ~** tout ce travail pour rien; **they aren't called skyscrapers for ~** ce n'est pas pour rien qu'on appelle ça des gratte-ciel; **not for ~**

is he known as... ce n'est pas pour rien qu'il est connu comme...; **I'm not English for ~!** hum je ne suis pas anglais pour rien!; **4** (indicating absence of trait, quality) **~ serious/useful** rien de grave/d'utile; **~ too fancy** rien de très compliqué; **~ interesting, ~ of any interest** rien d'intéressant ; **~ new to report** rien de nouveau à signaler; **have they ~ cheaper?** est-ce qu'ils n'ont rien de moins cher?; **there's ~ unusual about doing** il n'y a rien d'extraordinaire à faire; **there's ~ unusual about it** ça n'a rien d'extraordinaire; **it seems easy but it's ~ of the kind** cela paraît facile mais il n'en est rien; **~ of the kind should ever happen again** une chose pareille ne devrait jamais se reproduire; **you'll do ~ of the sort!** tu n'en feras rien!; **5** (emphatic: setting up comparisons) **it's ~ like that at all!** ce n'est pas ça du tout!; **there's ~ like the sea air for doing** il n'y a rien de tel que l'air marin pour faire; **there's ~ like seeing old friends** revoir de vieux amis, il n'y a rien de tel; **there's ~ like it!** il n'y a rien de tel or de mieux!; **there's ~ so embarrassing as doing** il n'y a rien d'aussi gênant que de faire; **I can think of ~ worse than** je ne peux rien imaginer de pire que; **there's ~ more ridiculous than** il n'y a rien de plus ridicule que; **that's ~ to what he'll do if he finds out that** ce n'est rien comparé à or à côté de ce qu'il fera quand il découvrira que; **the hive resembles ~ so much as a business** la ruche ressemble tout à fait à une entreprise; **to say ~ of** sans parler de; **detested by his colleagues to say ~ of the students** détesté par ses collègues sans parler des étudiants; **6** (no element, part) **to know ~ of** ne rien savoir de [*truth, events, plans*]; **he knows ~ of the skill involved** il n'imagine pas la technique que cela implique; **we heard ~ of what was said** nous n'avons rien entendu de ce qui s'est dit; **he has ~ of the aristocrat about him** il n'a rien d'un aristocrate; **there was ~ of the exotic in the place** l'endroit n'avait rien d'exotique; **7** (no truth, value, use) **you get ~ out of it** ça ne rapporte rien; **there's ~ in it for me** ça n'a aucun intérêt pour moi; **there's ~ in it** (in gossip, rumour) il n'y a rien de vrai là-dedans; (in magazine, booklet) c'est sans intérêt.

II *adv* **1** (in no way) **it is ~ like as important/difficult as** c'est loin d'être aussi important/difficile que; **it's ~ like enough!** c'est loin d'être suffisant!; **the portrait looks ~ like her** le portrait ne lui ressemble pas du tout; **she is ~ like her sister** elle ne ressemble pas du tout à sa sœur; **the city is ~ like what it was** la ville n'est plus du tout ce qu'elle était; **2** (emphatic: totally, only) **it's ~ short of brilliant/disgraceful** c'est tout à fait génial/scandaleux; **~ short of a miracle can save them** il n'y a qu'un miracle qui puisse les sauver; **3** (emphatic: decidedly) **she's ~ if not original in her dress** le moins qu'on puisse dire c'est qu'elle s'habille de façon originale; **I'm ~ if not stubborn!** le moins qu'on puisse dire c'est que je suis têtu!

III *adj* **to be ~ without sb/sth** ne rien être sans qn/qch; **he's ~ without you/his career** il n'est rien sans toi/sa carrière.

IV *n* **1** (nothingness) néant *m*; **2** (trivial matter) **it's a mere ~ compared to** ce n'est pratiquement rien par rapport à; ▶ **sweet.**

V nothing but *adv phr* **he's ~ but a coward** ce n'est qu'un lâche; **they've done ~ but moan**○ ils n'ont fait que râler○; **it's caused me ~ but trouble** ça ne m'a valu que des ennuis; **~ but the best for me!** je ne veux que ce qu'il y a de meilleur!; **she has ~ but praise for them** elle ne tarit pas d'éloges sur eux.

VI nothing less than *adv phr* **it's ~ less than a betrayal** c'est une véritable trahison; **they want ~ less than reunification** ils ne seront satisfaits que quand il y aura la réunification; **~ less than real saffron will do** il n'y a que du vrai safran qui fera l'affaire.

VII nothing more than *adv phr* **it's ~ more than a strategy to do** ce n'est qu'une stratégie pour faire; **the stories are ~ more than gossip** ces histoires ne sont rien d'autre que des ragots; **they'd like ~ more than to do** ils ne demandent pas mieux que de faire.

IDIOMS **~ doing**○! (outright refusal) pas question○!; (no chance of success) pas moyen○!; **there's ~ doing at the office**○ il ne se passe rien au bureau; **there was ~ for it but to call the doctor** GB il ne restait plus qu'à faire venir le médecin; **there's ~ for it!** GB il n'y a rien à faire; **you get ~ for ~** on n'a rien sans rien.

nothingness /ˈnʌθɪŋnɪs/ *n* néant *m*.

no throw *n* lancer *m* nonvalable.

notice /ˈnəʊtɪs/ **I** *n* **1** (written sign) pancarte *f*, écriteau *m*; **2** (advertisement) annonce *f*; (announcing birth, marriage, death) avis *m*; **3** (attention) attention *f*; **to take ~** faire attention (**of** à); **they never take any ~ of what I say** ils ne font jamais attention à ce que je dis; **take no ~, don't take any ~** ne fais pas attention; **it was beneath her ~** ça ne méritait pas son attention; **to bring sth to sb's ~** porter qch à l'attention de qn; **it did not escape my ~ that** il n'a pas échappé à mon attention que; **it has come to my ~ that** il m'a été signalé que; **they took absolutely no ~, they didn't take a blind bit** ou **the slightest bit of ~** ils n'en ont tenu aucun compte; **4** Theat, Journ (review) compte-rendu *m*, critique *f*; **5** (advance warning) préavis *m*; **we require a month's ~** nous exigeons un préavis d'un mois; **without ~** sans préavis; **to do sth at short ~/at a moment's ~/at two hours' ~** faire qch au pied levé/sur le champ/dans les deux heures qui suivent; **to give sb ~ of sth** avertir or prévenir qn de qch; **until further ~** jusqu'à nouvel ordre; **two days is very short ~** deux jours, c'est très court comme délai; **I'm sorry it's such short ~** je suis désolé de vous prévenir si tard; **6** Admin, Jur (notification) avis *m*; **to give sb ~ that, serve ~ on sb that** aviser qn que; **7** (notification of resignation, dismissal) **to give in** ou **hand in one's ~** donner sa démission; (domestic staff) donner ses huit jours; **to give sb (their) ~** congédier qn; **to get one's ~** recevoir son congé; **to get** ou **to be given three weeks' ~** recevoir trois semaines de préavis; **8** (to vacate premises) préavis *m*; **to give ~** [*tenant*] donner son préavis; **one month's ~** un mois de préavis; **to give sb ~ to quit** avertir qn qu'il doit évacuer les lieux; **to give the landlord ~** prévenir le propriétaire de son départ.

II *vtr* remarquer, s'apercevoir de [*absence, mark*]; **I ~ that** je vois que; **I ~d you talking to that girl** je t'ai vu parler à cette fille; **to ~ that sth is happening** remarquer que qch se passe; **to get oneself ~d** se faire remarquer, attirer l'attention; **you'll ~ we don't stand on ceremony here!** tu remarqueras que nous ne faisons pas de façons ici!; **not so as you'd ~**○ pas vraiment; **I can't say I ~d** je n'ai pas fait attention.

noticeable /ˈnəʊtɪsəbl/ *adj* [*flaw, scar, improvement, deterioration*] visible.

noticeably /ˈnəʊtɪsəblɪ/ *adv* [*increase, improve*] sensiblement; [*different, better, colder*] nettement.

notice: **~board** *n* panneau *m* d'affichage; **~ to pay** *n* avis *m* de paiement.

notifiable /ˈnəʊtɪfaɪəbl/ *adj* [*disease, crime, incident*] à signaler, à déclarer; **to be ~ to** [*noncompliance, disease*] devoir être signalé à [*authorities*].

notification /ˌnəʊtɪfɪˈkeɪʃn/ *n* **1** ¢ Admin, Jur (communication) notification *f*; **to receive written ~ of sth** recevoir notification écrite de qch; **to receive ~ that** être avisé que; **2** C (of decision, changes) annonce *f*; (of disease) notification *f*; (of fine) rappel *m*; **3** Journ (formal announcement) gen avis *m*; Jur annonce *f*; **'please accept this as the only ~'** 'cet avis ne sera pas répété'.

notify /ˈnəʊtɪfaɪ/ *vtr* **1** GB (give notice of) notifier; **all claims should be notified** toute demande d'indemnité doit être notifiée; **to ~ sb of** ou **about** aviser qn de [*result, incident*]; avertir qn de [*intention*]; **to ~ sth to sb** GB notifier qch à qn; **to ~ sb that** notifier à qn que; **2** (announce formally) **to ~ sb of** informer qn de [*birth, engagement, death*].

notion /ˈnəʊʃn/ **I** *n* **1** (idea) idée *f*; **I had a ~ (that) he was married** j'avais dans l'idée qu'il était marié; **I never had any ~ of asking her** il ne m'est jamais venu à l'idée de lui demander; **this gave him the ~ of going abroad** ceci lui a donné l'idée d'aller à l'étranger; **what gave you the ~ that they were rich?** qu'est-ce qui t'a fait penser qu'ils étaient riches?; **she has some strange ~s** elle a de drôles d'idées; **what a silly ~!** quelle drôle d'idée!; **another one of his silly ~s!** encore une de ses idées à lui!; **he got the ~ that he hadn't been invited** il s'est mis en tête qu'on ne l'avait pas invité; **she got the ~ into her head that** elle s'est mis en tête l'idée que; **what put such ~s into your head?** qu'est-ce qui t'a mis de pareilles idées en tête?; **don't be putting ~s into his head!** ne lui mets pas des idées dans la tête!; **2** (vague understanding) idée *f*, notion *f*; **some ~ of** quelques notions de; **he has no ~ of what is meant by discipline** il n'a aucune notion or idée de ce qu'est la discipline; **she has no ~ of time** elle n'a pas la notion du temps; **3** (whim, desire) idée *f*, envie *f*; **he had** ou **took a sudden ~ to go for a swim** il a eu l'envie soudaine d'aller nager.

II notions *npl* US (haberdashery) (articles *mpl* de) mercerie *f*.

notional /ˈnəʊʃənl/ *adj* **1** (hypothetical) [*element, amount, figure*] hypothétique, théorique; **2** Philos notionnel/-elle, conceptuel/-elle.

notional: **~ grammar** *n* grammaire *f* notionnelle; **~ word** *n* mot *m* lexical, mot *m* plein.

notoriety /ˌnəʊtəˈraɪətɪ/ *n* **1** (reputation) notoriété *f* (**for** pour); **the ~ surrounding sth** la publicité qui entoure qch; **2** GB péj (person) personne *f* ayant une certaine notoriété.

notorious /nəʊˈtɔːrɪəs/ *adj* [*criminal, organization*] notoire (*after n*); [*district, venue*] mal famé; [*feature, opinion*] connu; [*example*] célèbre; [*case*] fameux/-euse; **~ for/as sth** [*person, place*] connu pour/comme qch; **the ~ Mr Brown/Bermuda Triangle** le fameux M. Brown/triangle des Bermudes.

notoriously /nəʊˈtɔːrɪəslɪ/ *adv* [*erratic, difficult*] notoirement; **~ corrupt/inefficient** d'une corruption/inefficacité notoire; **they're ~ unreliable** il est bien connu qu'on ne peut pas compter sur eux.

no trumps *n* sans atout.

Nottinghamshire /ˈnɒtɪŋəmʃɪə(r)/ ▶ **1624** *pr n* Nottinghamshire *m*.

Notts *n* GB Post *abrév écrite* = **Nottinghamshire**.

notwithstanding /ˌnɒtwɪθˈstændɪŋ/ **I**† *adv* néanmoins.

II *prep* **~ the legal difficulties, the legal difficulties ~** en dépit des difficultés légales.

nougat /ˈnuːɡɑː, ˈnʌɡət, US ˈnuːɡət/ *n* nougat *m*.

nought /nɔːt/ **I** *n* **1** (as number) zéro *m*; **three ~s** trois zéros; **2**‡ (nothing) = **naught**.

II *adj* zéro; **~ per cent** zéro pour cent.

noughts and crosses ▶ **1282** *n* (+ *v sg*) (jeu *m* de) morpion *m*.

noun /naʊn/ *n* nom *m*, substantif *m*.

noun: **~ clause** *n* proposition *f* nominale; **~ phrase**, **NP** *n* syntagme *m* nominal.

nourish /ˈnʌrɪʃ/ *vtr* **1** lit nourrir [*person, animal, plant, skin*] (**with** avec; **on** de); enrichir [*soil*] (**with** avec); **2** fig sout nourrir [*dream, illusion, feeling, belief*].

nourishing /ˈnʌrɪʃɪŋ/ *adj* nourrissant.

nourishment /ˈnʌrɪʃmənt/ *n* **1** (nutrition) **there's lots of ~ in it** c'est très nourrissant; **there is no ~ in that** ce n'est absolument pas nourrissant; **2** (food) nourriture *f*; **to take ~** se nourrir; **to give sb ~** donner de la nourriture à qn; **3** fig **intellectual ~** nourritures *fpl* intellectuelles.

nous○ /naʊs/ *n* GB bon sens *m*; **to have the ~ to do** avoir assez de bon sens pour faire; **political ~** intelligence politique.

Nov *abrév écrite* = **November**.

nova /ˈnəʊvə/ *n* (*pl* **-ae** ou **-as**) nova *f*.

Nova Scotia /ˌnəʊvə ˈskəʊʃə/ *pr n* Nouvelle-Écosse *f*.

Nova Scotian /ˌnəʊvəˈskəʊʃn/ **I** *n* Néo-écossais/-e *m/f*.
II *adj* [*accent, climate, flora, village*] de la Nouvelle Écosse.

novel /ˈnɒvl/ **I** *n* **1** (work) roman *m*; **historical/detective ~** roman historique/policier; **2** (genre) **the ~** le roman.
II *adj* original.

novelette /ˌnɒvəˈlet/ *n* **1** (short novel) gen petit roman *m*; péj (over-sentimental) roman *m* à l'eau de rose; (trivial) roman *m* à deux sous pej; **2** Literat (novella) nouvelle *f*.

novelettish○ /ˌnɒvəˈletɪʃ/ *adj* péj [*style*] à l'eau de rose pej.

novelist /ˈnɒvəlɪst/ **▶ 1692** *n* romancier/-ière *m/f*.

novella /nəˈvelə/ *n* Literat nouvelle *f*.

novelty /ˈnɒvəltɪ/ **I** *n* **1** nouveauté *f* (**of doing** de faire); **to be a ~ to sb** avoir l'attrait de la nouveauté pour qn; **to do sth for the ~** faire qch pour l'attrait de la nouveauté; **the ~ soon wore off** l'attrait de la nouveauté a vite passé; **2** (trinket) babiole *f*.
II *modif* [*key ring, mug, stationery*] fantaisie.

November /nəˈvembə(r)/ **▶ 1472** *n* novembre *m*.

novena /nəˈviːnə/ *n* neuvaine *f*.

novice /ˈnɒvɪs/ **I** *n* **1** gen (beginner) débutant/-e *m/f* (**in** en); **a political ~** un débutant en politique; **2** Relig (probationer) novice *mf*; **3** Sport (beginner) débutant/-e *m/f*; **4** Turf (horse) débutant *m*.
II *modif* **1** gen [*writer, driver, salesperson, teacher*] débutant; **~ gardener/workman** apprenti *m* jardinier/ouvrier; **2** Sport [*class, crew*] débutant.

novitiate /nəˈvɪʃɪət/ *n* noviciat *m*.

novocaine® /ˈnəʊvəkeɪn/ *n* novocaïne® *f*.

now /naʊ/ **I** *conj* **~ (that) I know her** maintenant que je la connais; **~ (that) you've recovered** maintenant que tu es guéri.
II *adj* (current) actuel/-elle.
III *adv* **1** (at the present moment) **she's ~ 17** elle a 17 ans à présent; **I'm doing it ~** je suis en train de le faire; **the ~ familiar routine** la routine maintenant habituelle; **the ~ famous court case** l'affaire maintenant célèbre; **2** (these days) maintenant; **they ~ have 5 children** ils ont 5 enfants maintenant; **she's working in Japan ~** elle travaille au Japon maintenant; **business is better ~** les affaires marchent mieux maintenant; **3** (at once) maintenant; **right ~** tout de suite; **do it ~** fais-le maintenant; **I must go ~** il faut que je parte maintenant; **4** (the present time) **you should have phoned him before ~** tu aurais dû lui téléphoner avant; **before** ou **until ~** jusqu'à présent; **he should be finished by ~** il devrait avoir fini maintenant; **between ~ and next Friday** d'ici vendredi prochain; **between ~ and then** entre-temps; **10 days from ~** d'ici 10 jours; **from ~ on(wards)** à partir de maintenant, dorénavant; **that's enough for ~** ça suffit pour le moment; **good-bye for ~** à bientôt; **~ is as good a time as any** le moment n'est pas plus mal choisi qu'un autre; **~ is the best time to do** c'est le meilleur moment pour faire; **5** (in time expressions) **it's a week ~ since she left** cela fait une semaine maintenant qu'elle est partie; **it has been six months ~** cela fait six mois; **some years ago ~** il y a de cela quelques années maintenant; **he won't be long ~** il ne devrait pas tarder maintenant; **he could arrive any time** ou **moment ~** il peut arriver d'un moment à l'autre; **the results will be announced any day ~** les résultats peuvent être annoncés d'un jour à l'autre; **6** (in view of events) maintenant; **I'll never get a job ~** je ne retrouverai plus jamais de travail maintenant; **~ I understand why** maintenant je comprends pourquoi; **how can you trust them ~?** comment peux-tu leur faire confiance maintenant?; **he ~ admits to being wrong** il reconnaît maintenant qu'il a eu tort; **I'll be more careful ~** je serai plus prudent dorénavant; **7** (at that moment, then) **it was ~ 4 pm** il était alors 16 heures; **~ the troops attacked** à ce moment-là, les troupes ont attaqué; **by ~ it was too late** à ce moment-là, il était trop tard; **8** (sometimes) **~ fast, ~ slowly** tantôt vite, tantôt lentement; **~ and then, ~ and again** de temps en temps, de temps à autre; **every ~ and then** de temps en temps; **9** (introducing a change) **~ for the next question** passons à la question suivante; **~ for a drink** si on prenait un verre; **if we can ~ compare...** si nous comparons maintenant...; **~ then, where was I?** bon, où en étais-je?; **10** (introducing information, opinion) **~, this is important because** c'est important parce que; **~ there's a man I can trust!** ah! voilà un homme en qui on peut avoir confiance!; **~ Paul would never do a thing like that** Paul, lui, ne ferait jamais une chose pareille; **~ that would never have happened 10 years ago** ça ne se serait jamais produit il y a dix ans; **11** (in requests, warnings, reprimands) **careful ~!** attention!; **~ let's see** voyons donc; **~! ~!** voyons!; **come ~!** voyons!; **there ~, what did I tell you?** eh bien, qu'est-ce que je t'avais dit?; **~ then, let's get down to work** bon, reprenons le travail maintenant; **~ then! what's all this noise?** bon sang! qu'est-ce que c'est que tout ce bruit?

nowadays /ˈnaʊədeɪz/ *adv* (these days) de nos jours, aujourd'hui; (at present, now) actuellement, maintenant; **I can't afford wine ~** maintenant je n'ai plus les moyens d'acheter du vin.

noway /ˈnəʊweɪ/, **noways** /ˈnəʊweɪz/ US *adv* = **nowise**.

nowhere /ˈnəʊweə(r)/ **I** *adv* nulle part; **~ special** nulle part; **~ but in Scotland** nulle part sauf en Écosse; **she's ~ to be seen** on ne la voit nulle part; **the key is ~ to be found** on ne trouve la clé nulle part; **I've got ~ else to go** je n'ai nulle part où aller; **~ else will you find a better bargain** vous ne trouverez pas de meilleure affaire ailleurs; **to appear** ou **come out of ~** venir de nulle part; **there's ~ better for a holiday** il n'y a pas de meilleur endroit pour passer des vacances; **there's ~ to sit down/park** il n'y a pas d'endroit pour s'asseoir/se garer; **~ is this custom more widespread than in China** c'est en Chine que cette coutume est la plus répandue; **business is good and ~ more so than in Tokyo** les affaires marchent bien, surtout à Tokyo; **these negotiations are going ~** ces négociations ne mènent nulle part; **this company/this team is going ~** l'entreprise/l'équipe ne fait aucun progrès; **£10 goes ~ these days** avec 10 livres sterling on ne va pas loin de nos jours; **all this talk is getting us ~** tout ce bavardage ne nous avance à rien; **flattery will get you ~!** tu n'arriveras à rien en me flattant; **she came out of ~ to win the race** elle a gagné la course contre toute attente.
II nowhere near *adv phr, prep phr* **~ near sufficient/satisfactory** loin d'être suffisant/satisfaisant; **~ near big enough** loin d'être assez grand; **~ near as useful as** loin d'être aussi utile que; **the carpark is ~ near the bank** le parking est loin de la banque; **50 dollars is ~ near enough** 50 dollars, c'est loin d'être assez; **I'm ~ near finished** je ne suis pas près de finir; **we're ~ near finding a solution** nous ne sommes pas près de trouver une solution.
IDIOMS **we're getting ~ fast** nous n'avançons pas du tout; ▶ **middle**.

nowise /ˈnəʊwaɪz/ *adv* aucunement, nullement.

nowt /naʊt/ *n* GB dial rien *m*.
IDIOMS **there's ~ so queer as folk** il faut de tout pour faire un monde.

noxious /ˈnɒkʃəs/ *adj* (all contexts) nocif/-ive, délétère.

nozzle /ˈnɒzl/ *n* **1** (of hose, pipe) ajutage *m*, jet *m*; (of bellows) bec *m*; (of hoover) suceur *m*; (for icing) douille *f*; **2**○ (nose) pif○ *m*, blair○ *m*.

NP *n* Ling *abrév* ▶ **noun phrase**.

NPV *n* Fin (*abrév* = **net present value**) VAN *f*.

nr *abrév écrite* = **near**.

NRA *n* US *abrév* ▶ **National Rifle Association**.

NSPCC *n* GB (*abrév* = **National Society for the Prevention of Cruelty to Children**) *société pour la protection de l'enfance*.

NSW *abrév écrite* = **New South Wales**.

NT 1 Bible *abrév* ▶ **New Testament**; **2** GB *abrév* ▶ **National Trust**; **3** Geog *abrév* ▶ **Northern Territory**.

nth /enθ/ *adj* Math, fig énième; **to the ~ power** ou **degree** à la puissance n; **for the ~ time** pour la énième fois.

NTSC *n* TV (*abrév* = **national television system committee**) NTSC *m*; **~ standard** système *m* NTSC.

nuance /ˈnjuːɑːs, US ˈnuː-/ *n* nuance *f*.

nub /nʌb/ *n* **1** (of problem) fond *m*; **the ~ of the matter** le cœur du sujet; **2** (knob, lump) petit morceau *m*.

nubby /ˈnʌbɪ/ *adj* [*fabric, tweed, silk*] à l'aspect noueux.

Nubia /ˈnjuːbɪə, US ˈnuː-/ *pr n* Nubie *f*.

Nubian /ˈnjuːbɪən, US ˈnuː-/ **I** *n* Nubien/-ienne *m/f*.
II *adj* nubien/-ienne.

nubile /ˈnjuːbaɪl, US ˈnuːbl/ *adj* **1** (attractive) désirable; **2** sout (marriageable) nubile.

nuclear /ˈnjuːklɪə(r), US ˈnuː-/ *adj* [*accident, arsenal, electricity, fission, fusion, fuel, industry, missile, potential, reaction, research, technology*] nucléaire.

nuclear: **~ bomb** *n* bombe *f* atomique; **~ capability** *n* capacité *f* nucléaire; **~ deterrence** *n* dissuasion *f* nucléaire; **~ deterrent** *n* force *f* de dissuasion nucléaire; **~ device** *n* engin *m* nucléaire; **~ disarmament** *n* désarmement *m* nucléaire; **~ energy** *n* énergie *f* nucléaire or atomique; **~ family** *n* famille *f* nucléaire; **~-free zone** *n* GB zone *f* où les expériences nucléaires sont interdites; **~ physicist ▶ 1692** *n* chercheur/-euse *m/f* en physique nucléaire; **~ physics** *n* (+ *v sg*) physique *f* nucléaire.

nuclear power *n* **1** (energy) = **nuclear energy**; **2** (country) puissance *f* nucléaire.

nuclear: **~-powered** *adj* fonctionnant à l'énergie nucléaire; **~ power station** *n* centrale *f* nucléaire; **~ reactor** *n* réacteur *m* nucléaire; **Nuclear Regulatory Commission** *n* US Commission *f* à l'énergie atomique; **~ reprocessing plant** *n* usine *f* de retraitement des déchets nucléaires; **~ scientist** *n* = **nuclear**

physicist; **~ shelter** *n* abri *m* antiatomique; **~ submarine** *n* sous-marin *m* nucléaire or atomique; **~ test** *n* essai *m* nucléaire; **~ testing** *n* expérience *f* nucléaire; **~ umbrella** *n* parapluie *m* nucléaire; **~ warhead** *n* ogive *f* or tête *f* nucléaire; **~ waste** *n* déchets *mpl* nucléaires; **~ weapon** *n* arme *f* nucléaire or atomique; **~ winter** *n* hiver *m* nucléaire.

nuclei /ˈnjuːklɪaɪ, US ˈnuː-/ *pl* ▶ **nucleus**.

nucleic acid /njuːˌkliːɪk ˈæsɪd, US nuː-/ *n* acide *m* nucléique.

nucleus /ˈnjuːklɪəs, US ˈnuː-/ *n* (*pl* **-clei**) (all contexts) noyau *m*; **atomic ~** noyau atomique.

nude /njuːd, US nuːd/ **I** *n* **1** Art nu/-e *m/f*, nudité *f*; **2 in the ~** nu.
II *adj* [*person*] nu; **to do ~ scenes** jouer dans des scènes déshabillées.

nudge /nʌdʒ/ **I** *n* coup *m* de coude, poussée *f*.
II *vtr* (push, touch) pousser du coude, donner un petit coup de coude à; (accidentally) heurter; (brush against) frôler; **to ~ one's way through** se frayer un chemin à travers [qch] à coups de coude.
IDIOMS **~ ~, wink wink**○ tu vois un peu ce que je veux dire.

nudie○ /ˈnjuːdɪ, US ˈnuːdɪ/ *adj* porno○.

nudism /ˈnjuːdɪzəm, US ˈnuː-/ *n* nudisme *m*.

nudist /ˈnjuːdɪst, US ˈnuː-/ **I** *n* nudiste *mf*.
II *modif* [*camp, colony*] de nudistes; [*beach*] nudiste.

nudity /ˈnjuːdətɪ, US ˈnuː-/ *n* nudité *f*.

nudnik○ /ˈnʌdnɪk/ *n* US casse-pieds○ *mf inv*.

nugatory /ˈnjuːgətərɪ, US ˈnuːgətɔːrɪ/ *adj* sout (worthless) sans valeur; (invalid) non valable.

nugget /ˈnʌgɪt/ *n* pépite *f*; **gold ~** pépite d'or; **a ~ of information** une information précieuse.

nuisance /ˈnjuːsns, US ˈnuː-/ *n* **1** (annoyance) désagrément *m*; **the ~ caused by heavy traffic** le désagrément causé par la circulation intense; **the delay/noise was a ~** le retard/le bruit a été très pénible; **2** (annoying person) (child) peste○ *f*; (adult) personne *f* pénible; **children can be little ~s** les enfants sont parfois de véritables pestes; **Mr Jenkins is a real ~** M. Jenkins est vraiment pénible; **~s like him should not be on the committee** des gens aussi pénibles que lui ne devraient pas faire partie du comité; **to be a ~ to sb** [*person*] ennuyer qn; [*action, noise, smell*] gêner qn; **to make a ~ of oneself** embêter tout le monde; **3** (inconvenience) gêne *f*; **to be a ~** être gênant; **to cause a ~ to sb** gêner qn; **it's a ~ that...** c'est ennuyeux que... (+ *subj*); **it's a ~ for me to do** cela me gêne de faire; **it's a ~ doing/having to do** c'est gênant de faire/de devoir faire; **the ~ is that...** l'ennui c'est que...; **what a ~!** que c'est agaçant!; **I'm sorry to be such a ~** excusez-moi de vous déranger tout le temps; **to have a ~ value** servir à embêter○ les gens; **4** Jur nuisance *f*.

nuisance call *n* Telecom appel *m* anonyme.

NUJ *n* GB (*abrév* = **National Union of Journalists**) syndicat *m* des journalistes.

nuke○ /njuːk, US nuːk/ **I** *n* **1** (weapon) arme *f* nucléaire or atomique; **2** US (plant) centrale *f* nucléaire.
II *vtr* US **1** (bomb) détruire [qch] à l'arme atomique; **2** (microwave) passer [qch] aux micro-ondes.

null /nʌl/ *adj* **1** Jur [*document, decision*] nul/nulle; **~ and void** nul et non avenu; **to render ~** annuler, invalider; **2** Math nul/nulle.

null hypothesis *n* Stat hypothèse *f* nulle.

nullification /ˌnʌlɪfɪˈkeɪʃn/ *n* invalidation *f*.

nullify /ˈnʌlɪfaɪ/ *vtr* invalider, annuler.

nullity /ˈnʌlətɪ/ *n* Jur (of act, contract, marriage) nullité *f*, invalidité *f*.

nullity suit *n* demande *f* en nullité de mariage.

NUM *n* GB (*abrév* = **National Union of Mineworkers**) syndicat *m* des mineurs.

numb /nʌm/ **I** *adj* **1** [*limb, face*] (due to cold, pressure) engourdi; (due to anaesthetic) insensible; **to go ~** s'engourdir; **~ with cold** engourdi par le froid, gourd; **2** fig [*person*] hébété; **~ with shock** hébété par le choc; **to feel ~** être comme hébété.
II *vtr* **1** [*cold*] engourdir; [*anaesthetic*] insensibiliser; **to ~ the pain** endormir la douleur; **2** [*news, shock*] laisser [qn] comme hébété.

number /ˈnʌmbə(r)/ ▶ **1505** **I** *n* **1** (figure) nombre *m*; (written) chiffre *m*; **the ~ twelve** le nombre douze; **think of a ~** pensez à un nombre; **a three-figure ~** un nombre à trois chiffres; **odd/even ~** nombre impair/pair; **a list of ~s** une liste de chiffres; **2** gen, Telecom (in series) (of bus, house, account, page, passport, telephone) numéro *m*; **to live at ~ 18** habiter au (numéro) 18; **the ~ 7 bus** le bus numéro 7; **to take a car's ~** relever le numéro d'une voiture; **a wrong ~** un faux numéro; **is that a London ~?** est-ce un numéro à Londres?; **there's no reply at that ~** ce numéro ne répond pas; **to be ~ three on the list** être troisième sur la liste; **to be ~ 2 in the charts** être numéro 2 au hit-parade; **3** (amount, quantity) nombre *m*, quantité *f*; **a ~ of people/times** un certain nombre de personnes/fois, plusieurs personnes/fois; **for a ~ of reasons** pour plusieurs raisons; **a large ~ of** un grand nombre de; **to come in large ~s** venir nombreux or en grand nombre; **to come in such ~s that** venir en si grand nombre que; **large ~s of people** beaucoup de gens; **a small ~ of houses** quelques maisons; **in a small ~ of cases** dans un nombre réduit de cas, dans quelques cas; **on a ~ of occasions** plusieurs fois, un certain nombre de fois; **on a large ~ of occasions** maintes fois, souvent; **a fair ~** un assez grand nombre; **to be due to a ~ of factors** être dû à un ensemble de facteurs; **five people were killed, and a ~ of others were wounded** cinq personnes ont été tuées, et d'autres ont été blessées; **many/few in ~** en grand/petit nombre; **they were sixteen in ~** ils étaient (au nombre de) seize; **in equal ~s** en nombre égal; **any ~ of books** d'innombrables livres; **any ~ of times** maintes fois, très souvent; **any ~ of things could happen** tout peut arriver, il peut se passer beaucoup de choses; **this may be understood in any ~ of ways** cela peut être entendu de plusieurs façons or de diverses façons; **beyond** ou **without ~** littér innombrables, sans nombre; **times without ~** d'innombrables fois, à maintes reprises; **4** (group) **one of our ~** un des nôtres; **three of their ~ were killed** trois d'entre eux or trois des leurs ont été tués; **among their ~, two spoke English** parmi eux, deux parlaient anglais; **5** (issue) (of magazine, periodical) numéro *m*; **the May ~** le numéro de mai; **6** Mus, Theat (act) numéro *m*; (song) chanson *f*; **for my next ~ I would like to sing...** maintenant j'aimerais vous chanter...; **7**○ (object of admiration) **a little black ~** (dress) une petite robe noire; **that car is a neat little ~** elle est épatante○ or chouette○, cette voiture; **a nice little ~ in Rome** (job) un boulot sympa○ à Rome; **she's a cute little ~** elle est mignonne comme tout; **8** Ling nombre *m*; **to agree in ~** s'accorder en nombre.
II numbers *npl* (in company, school) effectifs *mpl*; (of crowd, army) nombre *m*; **a fall in ~s** une diminution des effectifs; **to estimate their ~s** estimer leur nombre; **to win by force** or **weight of ~s** gagner parce que l'on est plus nombreux; **to make up the ~s** faire le compte.
III Numbers *pr n* Bible (livre *m* des) Nombres *mpl*.
IV *vtr* **1** (allocate number to) numéroter; **to be ~ed** [*page, house*] être numéroté; **they are ~ed from 1 to 100** ils sont numérotés de 1 à 100; **2** (amount to) compter; **the regiment ~ed 1,000 men** le régiment comptait 1 000 hommes; **3** (include) compter; **to ~ sb among one's closest friends** compter qn parmi ses amis les plus intimes; **to be ~ed among the great novelists** compter parmi les plus grands romanciers; **4** (be limited) **to be ~ed** [*opportunities, options*] être compté; **his days are ~ed** ses jours sont comptés.
V *vi* **1** (comprise in number) **a crowd ~ing in the thousands** une foule de plusieurs milliers de personnes; **to ~ among the great musicians** compter parmi les plus grands musiciens; **2** = **number off**.
IDIOMS **I've got your ~**○**!** je te connais!; **your ~'s up**○**!** ton compte est bon!, tu es fichu○!; **to do sth by the ~s** US ou **by ~s** faire qch mécaniquement; **to colour** ou **paint by ~s** colorier selon les indications chiffrées (*dans un album de coloriage*); **to play the ~s** ou **the ~s game** (lottery) jouer au loto; **to play a ~s game** ou **racket** US pej (falsify figures) truquer les chiffres; (embezzle money) détourner des fonds.
■ **number off** gen, Mil se numéroter; **they ~ed off from the right** ils se sont numérotés en commençant par la droite.

number: **~-cruncher**○ *n* hum (machine) calculatrice *f*, machine *f* à calculer; **~-crunching**○ *n* hum calcul *m*.

numbering /ˈnʌmbərɪŋ/ *n* (action) numérotage *m*; (sequence of numbers) numérotation *f*.

numbering machine *n* numéroteur *m*.

numberless /ˈnʌmbəlɪs/ *adj* littér innombrable, sans nombre.

number one **I** *n* **1**○ (oneself) **she only thinks about ~** elle ne pense qu'à sa pomme○ or qu'à elle; **to look after** ou **look out for** ou **take care of ~** penser avant tout à son propre intérêt; **2** (most important) numéro un *m* (**in** de); **to be the world ~** Sport être le numéro un mondial; **their record is (at) ~** leur disque est numéro un; **3**○ euph, lang enfantin **to do ~** (urinate) faire pipi○, faire la petite commission○.
II *modif* [*player, expert*] premier/-ière; [*problem, enemy, priority*] numéro un; **the world's ~ tennis player** le numéro un mondial du tennis; **rule ~ is to keep calm** il faut rester calme avant toute chose.

number: **~plate** *n* GB plaque *f* minéralogique or d'immatriculation; **Number Ten** *n* GB Pol 10 Downing Street (*résidence officielle du premier ministre britannique*).

number two *n* **1** (second-in-command) gen, Pol numéro deux *m*; **the party ~** le numéro deux du parti; **to be sb's ~** être le second de qn; **2**○ euph (lang enfantin) **to do ~** faire caca○, faire la grosse commission○.

numbly /ˈnʌmlɪ/ *adv* [*say, look*] avec un air hébété.

numbness /ˈnʌmnɪs/ *n* (physical) engourdissement *m*; (emotional, mental) torpeur *f*.

numbskull○ /ˈnʌmskʌl/ *n* nigaud/-e *m/f*, gourde○ *f*.

numerable /ˈnjuːmərəbl/ *adj* dénombrable.

numeracy /ˈnjuːmərəsɪ, US ˈnuː-/ *n* aptitude *f* au calcul; **to improve pupils' standards of ~** améliorer le niveau des élèves en calcul.

numeral /ˈnjuːmərəl, US ˈnuː-/ **I** *n* chiffre *m*, nombre *m*; **Roman/Arabic ~s** chiffres romains/arabes.
II *adj* numéral.

numerate /ˈnjuːmərət, US ˈnuː-/ *adj* sachant compter; **to be ~** savoir compter; **~ degree, degree in a ~ subject** ≈ licence *f* scientifique.

numeration /ˌnjuːməˈreɪʃn, US ˈnuː-/ *n* numération *f*.

numerator /ˈnjuːməreɪtə(r), US ˈnuː-/ *n* (of fraction) numérateur *m*.

Numbers (1)

Cardinal numbers in French

0	zéro*
1	un†
2	deux
3	trois
4	quatre
5	cinq
6	six
7	sept
8	huit
9	neuf
10	dix
11	onze
12	douze
13	treize
14	quatorze
15	quinze
16	seize
17	dix-sept
18	dix-huit
19	dix-neuf
20	vingt
21	vingt et un
22	vingt-deux
30	trente
31	trente et un
32	trente-deux
40	quarante
50	cinquante
60	soixante
70	soixante-dix septante (*in Belgium, Canada, Switzerland etc.*)
71	soixante et onze septante et un (*etc*)
72	soixante-douze
73	soixante-treize
74	soixante-quatorze
75	soixante-quinze
76	soixante-seize
77	soixante-dix-sept
78	soixante-dix-huit
79	soixante-dix-neuf
80	quatre-vingts‡
81	quatre-vingt-un§
82	quatre-vingt-deux
90	quatre-vingt-dix nonante (*in Belgium, Canada, Switzerland etc.*)
91	quatre-vingt-onze nonante et un
92	quatre-vingt-douze nonante-deux (*etc*)
99	quatre-vingt-dix-neuf
100	cent
101	cent un†
102	cent deux
110	cent dix
111	cent onze
112	cent douze
187	cent quatre-vingt-sept
200	deux cents
250	deux centǁ cinquante
300	trois cents
1 000ǁ	mille
1 001	mille un†
1 002	mille deux
1 020	mille vingt
1 200	mille** deux cents
2 000	deux mille††
10 000	dix mille
10 200	dix mille deux cents
100 000	cent mille
102 000	cent deux mille
1 000 000	un million‡‡
1 264 932	un million deux cent soixante-quatre mille neuf cent trente-deux
1 000 000 000	un milliard‡‡
1 000 000 000 000	un billion‡‡

* *In English 0 may be called* nought, zero *or even* nothing; *French is always* zéro; a nought = un zéro.

† *Note that* one *is* une *in French when it agrees with a feminine noun, so* un crayon *but* une table, une des tables, vingt et une tables, combien de tables? – il y en a une seule *etc.*

‡ *Also* huitante *in Switzerland. Note that when 80 is used as a page number it has no* s, *e.g.* page eighty = page quatre-vingt.

§ *Note that* vingt *has no* s *when it is in the middle of a number. The only exception to this rule is when* quatre-vingts *is followed by* millions, milliards *or* billions, *e.g.* quatre-vingts millions, quatre-vingts billions *etc.*

¶ *Note that* cent *does not take an* s *when it is in the middle of a number. The only exception to this rule is when it is followed by* millions, milliards *or* billions, *e.g.* trois cents millions, six cents billions *etc. It has a normal plural when it modifies other nouns, e.g.* 200 inhabitants = deux cents habitants.

ǁ *Note that figures in French are set out differently; where English would have a comma, French has simply a space. It is also possible in French to use a full stop (period) here, e.g.* 1.000. *French, like English, writes dates without any separation between thousands and hundreds, e.g.* in 1995 = en 1995.

** *When such a figure refers to a date, the spelling* mil *is preferred to* mille, *i.e.* en 1200 = en mil deux cents. *Note however the exceptions: when the year is a round number of thousands, the spelling is always* mille, *so* en l'an mille, en l'an deux mille *etc.*

†† Mille *is invariable; it never takes an* s.

‡‡ *Note that the French words* million, milliard *and* billion *are nouns, and when written out in full they take* de *before another noun, e.g.* a million inhabitants *is* un million d'habitants, a billion francs *is* un billion de francs. *However, when written in figures,* 1,000,000 inhabitants *is* 1 000 000 habitants, *but is still spoken as* un million d'habitants. *When* million *etc. is part of a complex number,* de *is not used before the nouns, e.g.* 6,000,210 people = six millions deux cent dix personnes.

Use of en

Note the use of en *in the following examples:*

there are six	=	il y en a six
I've got a hundred	=	j'en ai cent

En *must be used when the thing you are talking about is not expressed (the French says literally* there of them are six, I of them have a hundred *etc.). However,* en *is not needed when the object is specified:*

there are six apples	=	il y a six pommes

Approximate numbers

When you want to say about ..., *remember the French ending* -aine:

about ten	=	une dizaine
about ten books	=	une dizaine de livres
about fifteen	=	une quinzaine
about fifteen people	=	une quinzaine de personnes
about twenty	=	une vingtaine
about twenty hours	=	une vingtaine d'heures

Similarly une trentaine, une quarantaine, une cinquantaine, une soixantaine *and* une centaine (*and* une douzaine *means* a dozen). *For other numbers, use* environ (about):

about thirty-five	=	environ trente-cinq
about thirty-five francs	=	environ trente-cinq francs
about four thousand	=	environ quatre mille
about four thousand pages	=	environ quatre mille pages

Environ *can be used with any number:* environ dix, environ quinze *etc. are as good as* une dizaine, une quinzaine *etc.*

Note the use of centaines *and* milliers *to express approximate quantities:*

hundreds of books	=	des centaines de livres
I've got hundreds	=	j'en ai des centaines
hundreds and hundreds of fish	=	des centaines et des centaines de poissons
I've got thousands	=	j'en ai des milliers
thousands of books	=	des milliers de livres
thousands and thousands	=	des milliers et des milliers
millions and millions	=	des millions et des millions

Phrases

numbers up to ten	=	les nombres jusqu'à dix
to count up to ten	=	compter jusqu'à dix
almost ten	=	presque dix
less than ten	=	moins de dix
more than ten	=	plus de dix
all ten of them	=	tous les dix
all ten boys	=	les dix garçons

Note the French word order:

my last ten pounds	=	mes dix dernières livres
the next twelve weeks	=	les douze prochaines semaines
the other two	=	les deux autres
the last four	=	les quatre derniers

Calculations in French

	say
10 + 3 = 13	dix et trois font *ou* égalent treize
10 – 3 = 7	trois ôté de dix il reste sept *or* dix moins trois égale sept
10 × 3 = 30	dix fois trois égale trente
30 : 3 = 10	(30 ÷ 3 = 10) trente divisé par trois égale dix

Note how the French division sign differs from the English.

5^2	cinq au carré
5^3	cinq puissance trois
5^4	cinq puissance quatre
5^{100}	cinq puissance cent
5^n	cinq puissance n
$\sqrt{12}$	racine carrée de douze
$\sqrt{25} = 5$	racine carrée de vingt-cinq égale cinq
B > A	B est plus grand que A
A < B	A est plus petit que B

☛ See next page

numerical /njuːˈmerɪkl, US ˈnuː-/ *adj* numérique; **in ~ order** dans l'ordre numérique.

numerical: **~ code** *n* = **numeric code**; **~ control, NC** *n* Ind commande *f* numérique.

numerically /njuːˈmerɪklɪ, US nuː-/ *adv* numériquement; **we were ~ superior to them** nous leur étions supérieurs en nombre.

numeric code *n* Math, Comput code *m* or indicatif *m* numérique.

numerous /ˈnjuːmərəs, US ˈnuː-/ *adj* nombreux/-euse; **on ~ occasions** souvent, maintes fois, en de nombreuses occasions.

numinous /ˈnjuːmɪnəs, US ˈnuː-/ *adj* (holy) sacré; (mysterious) mystérieux/-ieuse.

numismatics /ˌnjuːmɪzˈmætɪks, US ˌnuː-/ *n* (+ *v sg*) numismatique *f*.

numismatist /njuːˈmɪzmətɪst, US nuː-/ **▶ 1692** *n* numismate *mf*.

numskull○ *n* US = **numbskull**.

nun /nʌn/ *n* religieuse *f*, bonne sœur *f*; **to become a ~** entrer au couvent, prendre le voile.

nunciature /ˈnʌnʃətjʊə(r)/ *n* nonciature *f*.

nuncio /ˈnʌnʃɪəʊ/ *n* (*pl* **-cios**) nonce *m*.

nunnery‡ /ˈnʌnərɪ/ *n* couvent *m*.

NUPE *n* GB (*abrév* = **National Union of Public Employees**) syndicat *m* des employés municipaux.

nuptial /ˈnʌpʃl/ *adj* littér ou hum nuptial.

nuptials /ˈnʌpʃlz/ *npl* littér ou hum cérémonie *f* nuptiale, noces *fpl*.

NUR *n* GB (*abrév* = **National Union of Railwaymen**) syndicat *m* des cheminots.

nurd○ *n* = **nerd**.

Numbers (2)

Decimals in French

Note that French uses a comma where English has a decimal point.

	say
0,25	zéro virgule vingt-cinq
0,05	zéro virgule zéro cinq
0,75	zéro virgule soixante-quinze
3,45	trois virgule quarante-cinq
8,195	huit virgule cent quatre-vingt-quinze
9,1567	neuf virgule quinze cent soixante-sept *or* neuf virgule mille cinq cent soixante-sept
9,3456	neuf virgule trois mille quatre cent cinquante-six

Percentages in French

	say
25%	vingt-cinq pour cent
50%	cinquante pour cent
100%	cent pour cent
200%	deux cents pour cent
365%	troix cent soixante-cinq pour cent
4,25%	quatre virgule vingt-cinq pour cent

Fractions in French

	say
½	un demi*
⅓	un tiers
¼	un quart
⅕	un cinquième
⅙	un sixième
⅐	un septième
⅛	un huitième
⅑	un neuvième
⅒	un dixième
1/11	un onzième
1/12	un douzième (*etc.*)
⅔	deux tiers†
⅖	deux cinquièmes
2/10	deux dixièmes (*etc.*)
¾	trois quarts
⅗	trois cinquièmes
3/10	trois dixièmes (*etc.*)
1½	un et demi
1⅓	un (et) un tiers
1¼	un et quart
1⅕	un (et) un cinquième
1⅙	un (et) un sixième
1⅐	un (et) un septième (*etc.*)
5⅔	cinq (et) deux tiers
5¾	cinq (et) trois quarts
5⅘	cinq (et) quatre cinquièmes

45/100ths of a second = quarante-cinq centièmes de seconde

Ordinal numbers in French§

1st	1er‡	premier (*feminine* première)
2nd	2^{e}	second *or* deuxième
3rd	3^{e}	troisième
4th	4^{e}	quatrième
5th	5^{e}	cinquième
6th	6^{e}	sixième
7th	7^{e}	septième
8th	8^{e}	huitième
9th	9^{e}	neuvième
10th	10^{e}	dixième
11th	11^{e}	onzième
12th	12^{e}	douzième
13th	13^{e}	treizième
14th	14^{e}	quatorzième
15th	15^{e}	quinzième
16th	16^{e}	seizième
17th	17^{e}	dix-septième
18th	18^{e}	dix-huitième
19th	19^{e}	dix-neuvième
20th	20^{e}	vingtième
21st	21^{e}	vingt et unième
22nd	22^{e}	vingt-deuxième
23rd	23^{e}	vingt-troisième
24th	24^{e}	vingt-quatrième
25th	25^{e}	vingt-cinquième
30th	30^{e}	trentième
31st	31^{e}	trente et unième
40th	40^{e}	quarantième
50th	50^{e}	cinquantième
60th	60^{e}	soixantième
70th	70^{e}	soixante-dixième septantième (*in Belgium, Canada, Switzerland etc.*)
71st	71^{e}	soixante et onzième septante et unième (*etc.*)
72nd	72^{e}	soixante-douzième
73rd	73^{e}	soixante-treizième
74th	74^{e}	soixante-quatorzième
75th	75^{e}	soixante-quinzième
76th	76^{e}	soixante-seizième
77th	77^{e}	soixante-dix-septième
78th	78^{e}	soixante-dix-huitième
79th	79^{e}	soixante-dix-neuvième
80th	80^{e}	quatre-vingtième¶
81st	81^{e}	quatre-vingt-unième
90th	90^{e}	quatre-vingt-dixième nonantième (*in Belgium, Canada, Switzerland etc.*)
91st	91^{e}	quatre-vingt-onzième nonante et unième (*etc.*)
99th	99^{e}	quatre-vingt-dix-neuvième
100th	100^{e}	centième
101st	101^{e}	cent et unième
102nd	102^{e}	cent-deuxième
196th	196^{e}	cent quatre-vingt-seizième
200th	200^{e}	deux centième
300th	300^{e}	trois centième
400th	400^{e}	quatre centième
1,000th	$1\,000^{e}$	millième
2,000th	$2\,000^{e}$	deux millième
1,000,000th	$1\,000\,000^{e}$	millionième

Like English, French makes nouns by adding the definite article:

the first	=	le premier (*or* la première, *or* les premiers *mpl* *or* les premières *fpl*)
the second	=	le second (*or* la seconde *etc.*)
the first three	=	les trois premiers *or* les trois premières

Note the French word order in:

the third richest country in the world = le troisième pays le plus riche du monde

* *Note that* half, *when not a fraction, is translated by the noun* moitié *or the adjective* demi; *see the dictionary entry.*

† *Note the use of* les *and* d'entre *when these fractions are used about a group of people or things:* two-thirds of them = les deux tiers d'entre eux.

‡ *This is the masculine form; the feminine is* 1re *and the plural* 1ers (*m*) *or* 1res (*f*). *All the other abbreviations of ordinal numbers are invariable.*

§ *All the ordinal numbers in French behave like ordinary adjectives and take normal plural endings where appropriate.*

¶ *Also* huitantième *in Switzerland.*

nurse /nɜːs/ ▶ 1692 **I** *n* **1** Med infirmier/-ière *m/f*; **male ~** infirmier *m*; **school ~** infirmier/-ière scolaire; **2** = **nursemaid**.
II *vtr* **1** Med soigner [*person, cold*]; **to ~ sb through an illness** soigner qn pendant sa maladie; **to ~ sb back to health** soigner qn jusqu'à sa guérison; **to ~ one's pride** s'apitoyer sur son sort; **2** (clasp) serrer [*object*]; **to ~ a baby in one's arms** bercer un bébé dans ses bras; **to ~ one's drink** faire durer sa boisson; **3** (suckle) nourrir, allaiter [*baby*]; **4** (nurture) soigner [*project, young company, constituency*]; **the economy needs nursing** l'économie a besoin d'être gérée avec prudence; **5** (foster) entretenir, nourrir [*grievance, hatred, hope, dream*].
III *vi* **1** (be a nurse) être infirmier/-ière; **2** (feed) [*baby*] téter.

nurseling *n* = **nursling**.

nurse: **~maid** *n* nurse *f*, bonne *f* d'enfants; **~ practitioner** ▶ 1692 *n* US infirmier/-ière *m/f* diplômé/-e d'État (spécialisé/-e).

nursery /ˈnɜːsərɪ/ *n* **1** (also **day ~**) gen crèche *f*; (in hotel, shop) garderie *f*; **2** (room) nursery *f*, chambre *f* d'enfants; **3** Hort pépinière *f*; **4** fig (cradle) pépinière *f*.

nursery: **~ education** *n* éducation *f* maternelle; **~man** ▶ 1692 *n* pépiniériste *m*; **~ nurse** ▶ 1692 *n* puériculteur/-trice *m/f*; **~ rhyme** *n* comptine *f*; **~ school** *n* école *f* maternelle; **~ slope** *n* GB piste *f* pour débutants; **~ (school) teacher** ▶ 1692 *n* instituteur/-trice *m/f* d'école maternelle.

nurse's aide ▶ 1692 *n* US aide-soignant/-e *m/f*.

nursing /ˈnɜːsɪŋ/ ▶ 1692 **I** *n* **1** (profession) profession *f* d'infirmier/-ière; **to enter** ou **go into ~** devenir infirmier/-ière; **2** (care) soins *mpl*; **round-the-clock ~** soins 24 heures sur 24; **3** (breast-feeding) allaitement *m*.
II *adj* **1** [*mother*] qui allaite; **2** Med [*staff*] infirmier/-ière; [*methods, practice*] de soins.

nursing: **~ auxiliary** *n* GB aide-soignant/-e *m/f*; **~ bra** *n* soutien-gorge *m* d'allaitement.

nursing home *n* **1** (old people's) maison *f* de retraite; (convalescent) maison *f* de repos; **2** GB (small private hospital) clinique *f*; (maternity) clinique *f* obstétrique.

nursing: **~ orderly** ▶ 1692 *n* auxiliaire *mf* médical/-e; **~ school** *n* école *f* d'infirmières; **~ sister** *n* GB infirmière *f* chef.

nursling /ˈnɜːslɪŋ/ *n* nourrisson *m*.

nurture /ˈnɜːtʃə(r)/ **I** *n* ¢ soins *mpl*.
II *vtr* **1** lit élever [*child*]; soigner, entretenir [*plant*]; **2** fig nourrir [*hope, feeling, talent*]; veiller au développement de [*project*].
IDIOMS **the nature ~ debate** la question de l'inné et de l'acquis.

NUS *n* GB (*abrév* = **National Union of Students**) syndicat *m* des étudiants.

nut /nʌt/ **I** *n* **1** Culin (walnut) noix *f*; (hazelnut) noisette *f*; (almond) amande *f*; (peanut) cacahuète *f*; **2** Tech écrou *m*; **3**○ (mad person) cinglé/-e○ *m/f*, fou/folle *m/f*; **4**○ (enthusiast) dingue○ *mf*; **a cycling/health food ~** un dingue○ du vélo/de la diététique; **5**○ (head) caboche○ *f*, tête *f*; **use your ~!** fais travailler tes méninges○!, réfléchis donc un peu!; **6** Mus (on bow) chevalet *m*; (on string instrument) sillet *m*; **7** (in climbing) coinceur *m*.
II◑ **nuts** *npl* (testicles) couilles◑ *fpl*, testicules *mpl*.
III○ **nuts** *adj* **1** (crazy) (*jamais épith*) cinglé○, fou/folle; **2**○ (enthusiastic) **to be ~s about sb/sth** être fou/folle de qn/qch.
IV○ *excl* zut○!
V○ *vtr* GB (*p prés etc* **-tt-**) flanquer un coup de boule à○ [*person*].
IDIOMS **~s to you!**○ rien à foutre◑!; **I can't draw/cook for ~s** GB je dessine/cuisine comme un pied○; **he's a hard** ou **tough ~ to crack** il est dur à convaincre; **to be off one's ~** être complètement cinglé○; **to do one's ~** piquer une crise○; **the ~s and bolts** les détails pratiques (**of** de).

NUT *n* GB (*abrév* = **National Union of Teachers**) syndicat *m* des enseignants.

nut-brown /ˈnʌtbraʊn/ ▶ 1104 *adj* [*hair*] châtain *inv*; [*skin*] mat; [*eyes*] noisette *inv*.

nut: **~ burger** *n* steak *m* végétarien (*à base de noisettes*); **~case**○ *n* cinglé/-e○ *m/f*; **~crackers** *npl* casse-noisettes *m inv*; **~ cutlet** *n* côtelette *f* végétarienne (*à base de noisettes*); **~hatch** *n* Zool sittelle *f*.

nuthouse○ /ˈnʌthaʊs/ *n* maison *f* de fous○, asile *m* (d'aliénés); **he's in the ~** il est chez les fous○ or à l'asile.

nutmeg /ˈnʌtmeg/ *n* **1** (tree) muscadier *m*; **2** (fruit) noix *f* de muscade.

nutmeg-grater *n* Culin râpe *f* à muscade.

nutria /ˈnjuːtrɪə, US ˈnuː-/ *n* Zool, Fashn ragondin *m*.

nutrient /ˈnjuːtrɪənt, US ˈnuː-/ **I** *n* substance *f* nutritive, élément *m* nutritif.
II *adj* nutritif.

nutriment /ˈnjuːtrɪmənt, US ˈnuː-/ *n* aliments *mpl*, nourriture *f*.

nutrition /njuːˈtrɪʃn, US nuː-/ *n* **1** (act, process) nutrition *f*, alimentation *f*; **2** (science) diététique *f*.

nutritional /njuːˈtrɪʃənl, US nuː-/ *adj* **1** (good for you) nutritif/-ive; **~ value** valeur *f* nutritive; **2** [*composition, information*] nutritionnel/-elle.

nutritionist /njuːˈtrɪʃənɪst, US nuː-/ *n* nutritionniste *mf*.

nutritious /njuːˈtrɪʃəs, US nuː-/ *adj* nourrissant, nutritif/-ive.

nutritive *adj* = **nutritious**.

nuts-and-bolts *adj* (*épith*) pratique.

nutshell /ˈnʌtʃel/ *n* **1** lit coquille *f* de noix ou noisette; **2** fig **in a ~** en un mot; **to put sth in a ~** résumer qch en un mot.

nutter○ /ˈnʌtə(r)/ *n* GB dingue○ *mf*; **to be a ~** être dingue○.

nutty /ˈnʌtɪ/ *adj* **1** (containing hazelnuts) [*cake, chocolate*] aux noisettes; [*taste*] de noisettes; **2**○ (mad) [*person*] cinglé/-e○; [*idea, plan*] fou/folle.

nutty slack *n* charbonnaille *f*.

nuzzle /ˈnʌzl/ **I** *vtr* [*horse, dog, person*] frotter son nez contre; [*pig*] fouiller avec le groin, fouiner.
II *vi* = **nuzzle up**.
■ **nuzzle up**: **to ~ up against** ou **to sb** se blottir contre qn.

NV US Post *abrév écrite* = **Nevada**.

NVQ *n* GB (*abrév* = **National Vocational Qualification**) qualification *f* nationale professionnelle (*obtenue par formation continue ou initiale*).

NW ▶ **1568** *n* (*abrév* = **northwest**) NW *m*.

NY US *abrév écrite* = **New York**.

Nyasaland /naɪˈæsəlænd/ *pr n* Hist Nyassaland *m*.

NYC US *abrév écrite* = **New York City**.

nylon /ˈnaɪlɒn/ **I** *n* nylon® *m*.
II *modif* [*article*] de or en nylon®.

nylons /ˈnaɪlɒnz/ *npl* bas *mpl* nylon.

nymph /nɪmf/ *n* Mythol, Zool nymphe *f*.

nymphet /nɪmˈfet/ *n* hum nymphette *f*.

nympho○ /ˈnɪmfəʊ/ *n* péj nympho○ *f*, nymphomane *f*.

nymphomania /ˌnɪmfəˈmeɪnɪə/ *n* nymphomanie *f*.

nymphomaniac /ˌnɪmfəˈmeɪnɪæk/ *n, adj* péj nymphomane (*f*).

N Yorkshire *n* GB Post *abrév écrite* ▶ **North Yorkshire**.

NYSE US (*abrév écrite* = **New York Stock Exchange**) Bourse *f* de New York.

NZ *abrév écrite* = **New Zealand**.

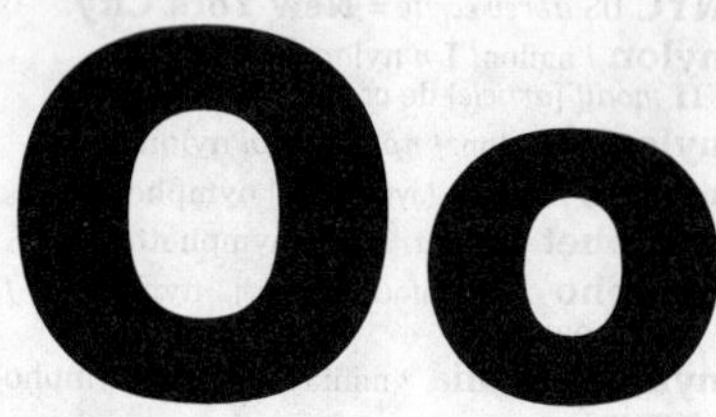

o, O /əʊ/ **I** *n* **1** (letter) o, O *m*; **2 O** (spoken number) zéro.
II O *excl* littér Ô.

o' /ə/ *prep* (*abrév* = **of**) de.

oaf /əʊf/ *n* (clumsy) balourd/-e *m/f*; (loutish) mufle *m*.

oafish /'əʊfɪʃ/ *adj* [*person*] mufle; [*behaviour*] de mufle.

oak /əʊk/ **I** *n* chêne *m*; **light/dark ~** chêne clair/foncé.
II *modif* [*table*] en chêne; [*finish*] imitation chêne *inv*.
IDIOMS **big** or **great ~s from little acorns grow** Prov les petits ruisseaux font les grandes rivières Prov.

oak apple *n* noix *f* de galle, galle *f* du chêne.

oaken /'əʊkən/ *adj* littér en chêne.

oakleaf lettuce *n* feuille *f* de chêne.

oakum /'əʊkəm/ *n* étoupe *f*; **to pick ~** faire de l'étoupe.

OAP *n* GB **1** (*abrév* = **old age pensioner**) retraité/-e *m/f*; **2** (*abrév* = **old age pension**) retraite *f* de la Sécurité Sociale.

oar /ɔ:(r)/ *n* **1** rame *f*, aviron *m*; **2** (person) rameur/-euse *m/f*, nageur/-euse *m/f*.
IDIOMS **to put** ou **shove** ou **stick one's ~ in**○ mettre son grain de sel○.

oar: **~lock** *n* US dame *f* de nage, tolet *m*; **~sman** *n* rameur *m*, nageur *m*; **~swoman** *n* rameuse *f*, nageuse *f*.

OAS *n* US (*abrév* = **Organization of American States**) Organisation *f* des États américains.

oasis /əʊ'eɪsɪs/ *n* (*pl* **oases**) **1** (in desert) oasis *f*; **2** fig (of civilization) oasis *f*; (of peace) havre *m*.

oast /əʊst/ *n* four *m* à houblon.

oasthouse /'əʊsthaʊs/ *n* sécherie *f* à houblon.

oat /əʊt/ **I** *n* (plant) avoine *f*; **~s** avoine *f*.
II *modif* [*biscuit, crop*] d'avoine.
IDIOMS **to be off one's ~s**○ manquer d'appétit; **to feel one's ~s**○ (feel exuberant) être en pleine forme; (be self-important) faire l'important; **to be getting/not getting one's ~**○ ne pas être privé/être privé sexuellement; **to sow one's wild ~s** jeter sa gourme.

oatcake /'əʊtkeɪk/ *n* galette *f* d'avoine.

oath /əʊθ/ *n* **1** Jur serment *m*; **under ~, on ~** GB sous serment; **to take the ~, to swear an ~** prêter serment (**to do** de faire; **that** que); **to administer the ~ to sb, to put sb under ~** faire prêter serment à qn; **she swore on** ou **under ~** elle a juré sous la foi du serment; **I'll take my ~ on it** j'en jurerais; **~ of office** serment; **~ of allegiance** serment d'allégeance; **2** (swearword) juron *m*; **a stream** ou **torrent of ~s** un torrent de jurons; **to let out an ~** lâcher un juron.

oatmeal /'əʊtmi:l/ **I** *n* ¢ **1** (cereal) farine *f* d'avoine; **2** US (porridge) bouillie *f* d'avoine, porridge *m*; **3** (colour) beige *m*, grège *m*.
II ▶ **1104** *adj* [*fabric, garment*] beige, grège.

OAU *n* (*abrév* = **Organization of African Unity**) OUA *f*.

Obadiah /ˌəʊbə'daɪə/ *pr n* Abdias.

obbligato /ˌɒblɪ'gɑ:təʊ/ **I** *n* partie *f* obligée; **with piano ~** avec piano obligé.
II *adj* obligé.

obduracy /'ɒbdjʊrəsɪ, US -dər-/ *n* **1** (stubborness) obstination *f*, entêtement *m*; **2** (hardheartedness) dureté *f* de cœur.

obdurate /'ɒbdjʊrət, US -dər-/ *adj* **1** (stubborn) obstiné, entêté; **2** (hardhearted) endurci.

OBE *n* GB (*abrév* = **Officer of the Order of the British Empire**) officier *m* de l'ordre de l'empire britannique.

obedience /ə'bi:dɪəns/ *n* **1** (to person, rite, law) obéissance *f*, soumission *f* (**to** à); **in ~ to** conformément à [*wish, order*]; **to show ~ to** obéir à; **to owe ~ to** devoir obéissance à; **2** Relig obédience *f* (**to** à).

obedient /ə'bi:dɪənt/ *adj* [*child, dog*] obéissant; **to be ~ to** obéir à; **your ~ servant** (in letters) votre très obéissant serviteur.

obediently /ə'bi:dɪəntlɪ/ *adv* docilement, avec obéissance.

obeisance /əʊ'beɪsns/ *n* sout **1** (homage) hommage *m*; **2** (bow) révérence *f*.

obelisk /'ɒbəlɪsk/ *n* **1** Archit obélisque *m*; **2** Print croix *f*.

obese /əʊ'bi:s/ *adj* obèse.

obesity /əʊ'bi:sətɪ/ *n* obésité *f*.

obey /ə'beɪ/ **I** *vtr* obéir à [*person, order, conscience*]; obéir à, se conformer à [*law*]; observer, se conformer à [*instructions*]; obéir à, suivre [*instinct*]; Jur obtempérer à [*summons, order*].
II *vi* obéir.

obfuscate /'ɒbfəskeɪt/ *vtr* sout obscurcir [*issue, mind*].

obit○ /'ɒbɪt, 'əʊbɪt/ *n* = **obituary**.

obiter dicta /ˌɒbɪtə 'dɪktə/ *npl* Jur opinions *fpl* incidentes.

obituary /ə'bɪtʃʊərɪ, US -tʃʊerɪ/ **I** *n* (also **~ notice**) notice *f* nécrologique, nécrologie *f*.
II *modif* [*column, page*] nécrologique.

object I /'ɒbdʒɪkt/ *n* **1** (item) objet *m*; **everyday ~s** les objets de tous les jours; **2** (goal) but *m* (**of** de); **his ~ was to do** son but était de faire; **the ~ of the exercise** le but de l'exercice; **with the ~ of doing** dans le but de faire; **3** (focus) **to be the ~ of** être l'objet de; **to become the sole ~ of sb's affections** devenir l'unique objet de l'affection de qn; **4** Ling complément *m* d'objet; **direct/indirect ~** complément d'objet direct/indirect; **5** Philos objet *m*.
II /əb'dʒekt/ *vtr* **to ~ that** objecter que; **'it's unfair,' she ~ed** 'c'est injuste,' a-t-elle objecté.
III /əb'dʒekt/ *vi* soulever des objections; **if people ~** si les gens s'y opposent; **the neighbours started to ~** les voisins ont commencé à se plaindre; **'I ~!'** 'je proteste!'; **if you don't ~** si vous n'y voyez pas d'objection; **I won't do it if you ~** je ne le ferai pas si vous y voyez une objection; **would you ~ if...?** cela vous ennuie-t-il que...? (+ *subj*); **they didn't ~ when...** ils n'ont soulevé aucune objection quand...; **to ~ to** s'opposer à [*plan, action, law, attitude*]; se plaindre de [*noise, dirt, delay*]; être contre [*leader, candidate*]; récuser [*witness, juror*]; **to ~ strongly to** s'opposer catégoriquement à; **to ~ to sb as president** être contre qn comme président; **to ~ to sb on grounds of sex/age** objecter à qn son sexe/âge; **to ~ to sb('s) doing** s'opposer à ce que qn fasse; **do you ~ to my** ou **me smoking?** est-ce que cela t'ennuie que je fume?; **to ~ to doing** se refuser à faire; **I don't ~ to signing but...** je veux bien signer mais...
IDIOMS **money is no ~** l'argent n'est pas un problème.

object clause *n* proposition *f* complétive.

objection /əb'dʒekʃn/ *n* **1** gen objection *f* (**to** à; **from** de la part de); **are there any ~s?** y a-t-il des objections? **if you have no ~(s)** si vous n'y voyez pas d'inconvénient; **I've no ~(s)** je n'y vois pas d'inconvénient; **I can't see any ~** je ne vois aucune objection (**to doing** à faire); **the main ~ was to tax increases** l'objection principale concernait l'augmentation des impôts; **to have an ~ to sb** avoir quelque chose contre qn; **to have an ~ to doing** avoir une objection à faire; **have you some ~ to washing up?** iron aurais-tu une objection à faire la vaisselle? iron; **have you any ~ to people taking photos?** est-ce que cela vous dérange que les gens prennent des photos? **I've no ~ to them coming** cela ne me dérange pas qu'ils viennent; **the ~ that** l'objection selon laquelle; **2** Jur **to make ~ to** marquer son opposition à [*argument, statement*]; **~!** objection! (*formule employée par un avocat pour marquer son opposition à une affirmation de la partie adverse*); **~ sustained/overruled** objection retenue/rejetée.

objectionable /əb'dʒekʃənəbl/ *adj* [*remark, allegation*] désobligeant; [*views, behaviour, habit, language*] choquant; [*law, system*] inacceptable; [*person*] insupportable; **there's nothing ~ about him** il n'y a pas d'objection spéciale à son sujet.

objective /əb'dʒektɪv/ **I** *n* **1** gen, Med, Mil, Phot objectif *m*; **to do sth with the ~ of doing** faire qch dans le but de faire; **foreign policy ~s** objectifs *mpl* or visées *fpl* de la politique étrangère; **2** Ling accusatif *m*.
II *adj* **1** (unbiased) objectif/-ive, impartial (**about** en ce qui concerne); **2** Philos objectif/-ive; **3** Ling accusatif/-ive.

objective: **~ case** *n* Ling accusatif *m*, cas *m* régime; **~ complement** *n* Ling complément *m* d'objet direct.

objectively /əb'dʒektɪvlɪ/ *adv* **1** (fairly) objectivement, avec impartialité; **2** Ling, Philos objectivement.

objectivism /əb'dʒektɪvɪzəm/ *n* objectivisme *m*.

objectivity /ˌɒbdʒek'tɪvətɪ/ *n* objectivité *f*, impartialité *f*.

object language *n* langage *m* objet.

object lesson *n* démonstration *f* (**in** de); **an ~ in doing** ou **in how to do** une démonstration sur la façon de faire.

objector /əb'dʒektə(r)/ *n* opposant/-e *m/f*.

object-oriented database *n* Comput base *f* de données orientée objet.

objet d'art /ˌɒbʒeɪ 'dɑː/ *n* objet *m* d'art.

oblate /'ɒbleɪt/ **I** *n* Relig oblat *m*.
II *adj* Math aplati aux pôles.

oblation /əʊ'bleɪʃn/ *n* Relig (offering) oblat *m*; (act) oblation *f*.

obligate /'ɒblɪgeɪt/ *vtr* contraindre (**to do** à faire).

obligation /ˌɒblɪ'geɪʃn/ *n* **1** (duty) devoir *m* (**towards, to** envers); **family/moral ~s** devoirs familiaux/moraux; **to have an ~ to do** avoir le devoir de faire; **to be under (an) ~ to do** être obligé de faire; **to fulfil one's ~s** faire son devoir; **out of a sense of ~** par sens du devoir; **2** (commitment) (contractual) obligation *f* (**to** envers; **to do** de faire); (personal) engagement *m* (**to** envers); **without ~** Comm sans engagement; **there is no ~ to pay** vous n'êtes pas obligé de payer; **'no ~ to buy'** Comm 'sans obligation d'achat'; **to discharge** ou **fulfil one's ~s** remplir ses engagements; **he failed to meet his ~s** il a manqué à ses engagements; **to place sb under (an) ~ to do** mettre qn dans l'obligation de faire; **to be under ~ to do** être obligé de faire; **3** (debt) (financial) dette *f*; (of gratitude) dette *f* de reconnaissance; **to meet one's ~s** honorer ses dettes; **to repay an ~** s'acquitter d'une dette de reconnaissance; **to be under ~ to sb for sth** être redevable à qn de qch.

obligatory /ə'blɪgətrɪ, US -tɔːrɪ/ *adj* **1** (compulsory) obligatoire (**to do** de faire); **to make it ~ for sb to do sth** obliger qn à faire qch; **2** (customary) de rigueur.

oblige /ə'blaɪdʒ/ *vtr* **1** (compel) [*contract, event, law, person*] obliger (**to do** à faire); **to be/feel ~d to do** être/se sentir obligé de faire; **don't feel ~d to pay** ne vous croyez pas obligé de payer; **2** (be helpful) rendre service à [*person*]; **to ~ sb by doing** rendre service à qn en faisant; **could you ~ me with a lift?** auriez-vous l'amabilité de me déposer?; **anything to ~!** à votre service!; **3** (be grateful) **to be ~d to sb** être reconnaissant à qn (**for** de; **for doing** d'avoir fait); **I would be ~d if you'd stop smoking** je vous saurais gré de ne pas fumer; **much ~d!** merci beaucoup!

obliging /ə'blaɪdʒɪŋ/ *adj* [*manner, person*] serviable; **it is ~ of them** c'est aimable de leur part (**to do** de faire).

obligingly /ə'blaɪdʒɪŋlɪ/ *adv* aimablement.

oblique /ə'bliːk/ **I** *n* Print oblique *f*.
II *adj* **1** lit [*line, stroke, look*] oblique; **2** fig [*reference, compliment, method*] indirect; **3** Ling oblique.

oblique angle *n* angle *m* qui n'est pas droit.

obliquely /ə'bliːklɪ/ *adj* **1** lit [*placed, drawn*] obliquement, de biais; **2** fig [*answer, refer*] indirectement.

obliqueness /ə'bliːknɪs/ *n* **1** (of line, look) obliquité *f*; **2** (of reference) indirect *m*.

obliterate /ə'blɪtəreɪt/ *vtr* **1** (rub out, remove) effacer [*trace, print, word*]; **the village was completely ~d** le village a été rayé de la carte; **2** (cover) masquer [*sun, view*]; **3** (erase from mind) effacer [*memory*]; **4** (cancel) oblitérer [*stamp*].

obliteration /əˌblɪtə'reɪʃn/ *n* **1** (of mark, memory, impression) effacement *m*; **2** (of city) destruction *f* totale.

oblivion /ə'blɪvɪən/ *n* **1** (being forgotten) oubli *m*; (being as yet unknown) obscurité *f*; **to rescue sb/sth from ~** sauver qn/qch de l'oubli; **to sink into ~** tomber dans l'oubli; **2** (unconsciousness, nothingness) néant *m*; **to drink oneself into ~** boire jusqu'à sombrer dans le néant; **to long for ~** (death) aspirer au néant; (sleep, drug-induced) aspirer à un état d'inconscience.

oblivious /ə'blɪvɪəs/ *adj* **1** (unaware) inconscient; **to be ~ of** ou **to** ne pas être conscient de [*surroundings, presence, risk, implications*]; **2** (forgetful) oublieux/-ieuse.

oblong /'ɒblɒŋ, US -lɔːŋ/ **I** *n* rectangle *m*.
II *adj* [*table, building*] oblong/-ongue, rectangulaire.

obloquy /'ɒbləkwɪ/ *n* opprobre *m*.

obnoxious /əb'nɒkʃəs/ *adj* [*person, behaviour*] odieux/-ieuse, exécrable; [*smell*] nauséabond.

obnoxiously /əb'nɒkʃəslɪ/ *adv* odieusement.

oboe /'əʊbəʊ/ ▶ **1481** *n* hautbois *m*.

oboist /'əʊbəʊɪst/ ▶ **1692**, **1481** *n* hautboïste *mf*.

obscene /əb'siːn/ *adj* **1** [*film, publication, remark*] obscène; **2** fig [*wealth*] indécent; [*war*] monstrueux/-euse.

obscenely /əb'siːnlɪ/ *adv* [*leer, suggest*] de manière obscène; **to be ~ rich** être tellement riche que c'en est indécent.

obscenity /əb'senətɪ/ *n* **1** (obscene remark) obscénité *f*; **~ laws** Jur lois *fpl* sur l'obscénité; **2** (obscene nature) caractère *m* obscène, obscénité *f*; **the ~ of war** le scandale de la guerre.

obscurantism /ˌɒbskjʊə'ræntɪzəm/ *n* obscurantisme *m*.

obscurantist /ˌɒbskjʊə'ræntɪst/ *n, adj* obscurantiste (*mf*).

obscure /əb'skjʊə(r)/ **I** *adj* **1** (hard to understand) [*meaning, theory, motive, origin*] obscur; **2** (little-known) [*book, writer*] obscur, inconnu; [*village*] inconnu; [*life*] obscur; **3** (indistinct) [*shape, memory*] indistinct; [*feeling*] vague.
II *vtr* **1** (conceal) obscurcir [*truth, meaning*]; **to ~ the issue** embrouiller la question; **2** (cover) cacher [*moon, view*]; **3** (darken) obscurcir, assombrir.

obscurely /əb'skjʊəlɪ/ *adv* obscurément.

obscurity /əb'skjʊərətɪ/ *n* **1** (of argument, reference, origin, life) obscurité *f*; **to fall back into ~** retourner dans l'ombre; **2** (of shape) caractère *m* indistinct; **3** littér (darkness) obscurité *f*, ténèbres *fpl* liter.

obsequies /'ɒbsɪkwɪz/ *npl* sout obsèques *fpl*, funérailles *fpl*.

obsequious /əb'siːkwɪəs/ *adj* obséquieux/-ieuse, servile (**to, towards** devant).

obsequiously /əb'siːkwɪəslɪ/ *adv* obséquieusement, servilement.

obsequiousness /əb'siːkwɪəsnɪs/ *n* obséquiosité *f*, servilité *f*.

observable /əb'zɜːvəbl/ *adj* **1** (discernible) observable; **2** (noteworthy) notable.

observably /əb'zɜːvəblɪ/ *adv* [*move, react*] de façon notable; [*change, improve*] notablement; [*larger, smaller*] nettement.

observance /əb'zɜːvəns/ *n* **1** (of law, rule, right, code) respect *m* (**of** de); (of sabbath, religious festival) observance *f* (**of** de); (of anniversary) célébration *f* (**of** de); **2** (religious rite, ceremony) observance *f*; **religious ~s** observances religieuses.

observant /əb'zɜːvənt/ *adj* **1** [*person, eye, mind, reporter*] observateur/-trice; **2** (of law) respectueux/-euse (**of** de).

observation /ˌɒbzə'veɪʃn/ *n* **1** gen, Sci, Med observation *f* (**of** de); **to be under ~** (in hospital) être en observation; **to keep sb/sth under ~** gen surveiller qn/qch; **powers of ~** dons *mpl* d'observation; **clinical/scientific ~s** observations cliniques/scientifiques; **2** (remark) remarque *f* (**about, on** sur); (critical) observation *f* (**about, on** sur); **to make an ~** faire une remarque; **to make the ~ that** faire observer que.

observation: **~ balloon** *n* ballon *m* d'observation or d'aérostation; **~ car** *n* wagon *m* panoramique; **~ deck** *n* terrasse *f* panoramique; **~ post** *n* poste *m* d'observation; **~ satellite** *n* satellite *m* d'observation; **~ tower** *n* mirador *m*; **~ ward** *n* salle *f* des malades en observation.

observatory /əb'zɜːvətrɪ, US -tɔːrɪ/ *n* observatoire *m*.

observe /əb'zɜːv/ *vtr* **1** (see, notice) observer, remarquer (**that** que); **this was ~d to be true** on a observé or remarqué que cela était vrai; **2** (watch) [*doctor, police*] surveiller; [*scientist, researcher*] observer; **3** (remark) faire observer, faire remarquer (**that** que); **as Sartre ~d** comme le faisait observer Sartre; **'it's raining,' she ~d** 'il pleut,' fit-elle observer; **4** (adhere to) observer [*law, custom, condition, silence*]; **to ~ neutrality** rester neutre; **5** (celebrate) observer [*Sabbath, religious festival*].

observer /əb'zɜːvə(r)/ **I** *n* **1** (of event, phenomenon, election) observateur/-trice *m/f* (**of** de); **to attend as an ~** assister en (tant qu')observateur; **an independent/outside ~** un observateur indépendant/extérieur; **2** Journ, Pol (commentator) spécialiste *mf*, observateur/-trice *m/f* (**of** de); **according to a well-placed ~...** de source bien informée, on sait que...
II *modif* [*delegation, group*] d'observateurs; [*mission*] d'observation; [*status*] d'observateur; [*country*] observateur/-trice.

obsess /əb'ses/ *vtr* obséder; **~ed by** ou **with** obsédé par.

obsession /əb'seʃn/ *n* (state) obsession *f*, manie *f* (**with** de; **with doing** de faire); (object of attention) idée *f* fixe, obsession *f*; **she has an ~ with hygiene/with tidiness** elle a la manie de la propreté/de l'ordre; **sailing is an ~ with him** sa passion pour la voile tient de l'obsession; **to have an ~ with death** être obsédé par l'idée de la mort; **her life was dominated by one great ~** sa vie était dominée par une idée fixe.

obsessional /əb'seʃənl/ *adj* obsessionnel/-elle; **to be ~ about doing** avoir l'obsession de faire.

obsessive /əb'sesɪv/ **I** *n* Psych névrotique *mf* obsessionnel/-elle; fig obsédé/-e *m/f*.
II *adj* [*person*] maniaque; [*neurosis*] obsessionnel/-elle; [*thought, memory*] obsédant; **his ~ fear of illness/death** sa hantise de la maladie/mort.

obsessive-compulsive disorder *n* névrose *f* obsessionnelle compulsive.

obsessively /əb'sesɪvlɪ/ *adv* **~ clean** d'une propreté maniaque; **to be ~ interested in sth** s'intéresser à qch au point d'en être obsédé; **to be ~ concerned with sth** être obsédé par qch; **~ devoted/discreet** d'une dévotion/discrétion presque obsessive.

obsidian /əb'sɪdɪən/ *n* obsidienne *f*.

obsolescence /ˌɒbsə'lesns/ *n* obsolescence *f*; **built-in ~, planned ~** obsolescence planifiée.

obsolescent /ˌɒbsə'lesnt/ *adj* obsolescent.

obsolete /'ɒbsəliːt/ *adj* [*technology*] dépassé; [*custom, idea*] démodé; [*word*] obsolète.

obstacle /'ɒbstəkl/ *n* lit, fig obstacle *m*; **to be an ~ to sth** (accidentally) être un obstacle à qch, entraver qch; (deliberately) faire obstacle à qch; **to put an ~ in the way of sth** faire obstacle à qch; **to put an ~ in sb's way** faire obstacle à qn; **partition is the chief ~ in the talks** la partition constitue la pierre d'achoppement des pourparlers.

obstacle: **~ course** *n* Mil parcours *m* du combattant; fig course *f* d'obstacles; **~ race** *n* course *f* d'obstacles.

obstetric /əb'stetrɪk/ *adj* [*service, technique*] obstétrical; **~ medicine** obstétrique *f*.

obstetrician /ˌɒbstə'trɪʃn/ ▶ **1692** *n* obstétricien/-ienne *m/f*.

obstetrics /əb'stetrɪks/ *n* (+ *v sg*) obstétrique *f*.

obstinacy /'ɒbstənəsɪ/ *n* (of person) obstination *f*, entêtement *m* (**in doing** à faire); (of cough, illnesss) persistance *f*; (of resistance) obstination *f*.

obstinate /'ɒbstənət/ *adj* [*person*] obstiné, têtu (**about** en ce qui concerne); [*behaviour, silence, effort*] obstiné; [*resistance*] acharné; [*illness, cough*] persistant; [*fever, stain*] rebelle; **he's being most ~ about it** il n'en démord pas.

obstinately /'ɒbstənətlɪ/ *adv* [*refuse*] obstinément; [*defend, resist*] avec acharnement;

he ~ clings to the belief that il s'obstine à croire que; **she ~ insisted on paying** elle a absolument tenu à payer.

obstreperous /əbˈstrepərəs/ *adj* [*drunk, child*] tapageur/-euse; [*crowd*] tumultueux/-euse.

obstreperously /əbˈstrepərəslɪ/ *adv* [*act*] de façon tapageuse; [*say*] en rouspétant.

obstruct /əbˈstrʌkt/ **I** *vtr* **1** (block) cacher, obstruer [*view*]; bloquer [*road*]; Med obstruer (**with** de); **2** (impede) bloquer, gêner [*traffic*]; faire obstacle à [*plan*]; gêner, entraver [*progress*]; gêner [*person*]; faire obstruction à [*player*]; entraver le cours de [*justice*]; **to ~ the passage of a bill** Pol faire de l'obstruction pour empêcher le vote d'une loi; **to ~ the police** gêner la police dans l'exercice de ses fonctions.
II *vi* Sport faire obstruction.

obstruction /əbˈstrʌkʃn/ *n* **1** ¢ (act, state) (of road) encombrement *m*; (of pipe, artery) engorgement *m*; Pol obstruction *f*; **to be charged with ~ of the police (in the course of their duties)** être inculpé pour avoir gêné la police dans l'exercice de ses fonctions; **2** (thing causing blockage) (to traffic, progress) obstacle *m*; (in pipe) bouchon *m*; Med obstruction *f*, occlusion *f*; **~ of the bowels** obstruction or occlusion intestinale; **to cause an ~ to traffic** provoquer un bouchon, bloquer la circulation; **3** Sport obstruction *f*; **to commit an ~** faire obstruction.

obstructionism /əbˈstrʌkʃənɪzəm/ *n* obstructionnisme *m*; **to have a policy of ~** pratiquer l'obstruction systématique.

obstructionist /əbˈstrʌkʃənɪst/ *n, adj* obstructionniste (*mf*).

obstructive /əbˈstrʌktɪv/ *adj* **1** (uncooperative) [*policy, tactics*] obstructionniste; [*person*] peu coopératif/-ive, qui fait obstruction; [*behaviour*] récalcitrant; **he's just being ~** il ne cherche qu'à mettre des bâtons dans les roues; **2** Med qui obstrue, obstruant.

obtain /əbˈteɪn/ **I** *vtr* obtenir [*information, permission, degree, visa*]; (for oneself) se procurer [*money, goods*]; acquérir [*experience*]; obtenir, remporter [*prize*]; **to ~ sth for sb** procurer qch à qn; **this effect is ~ed by mixing colours** cet effet s'obtient par le mélange des couleurs; **this chemical is ~ed from zinc** on obtient ce produit chimique à partir du zinc; **our products may be ~ed from any supermarket** vous trouverez nos produits dans tous les supermarchés.
II *vi* sout [*practice, situation*] être courant, avoir cours; [*rule*] être de rigueur.

obtainable /əbˈteɪnəbl/ *adj* **~ in all good bookstores** disponible dans toutes les bonnes librairies; **petrol is easily ~** on peut se procurer de l'essence facilement.

obtrude /əbˈtruːd/ *vi* **1** sout (impinge) **to ~ on** [*person, law*] empiéter sur; **2** sout (become apparent) [*opinion, comedy*] transparaître; **3** (stick out) lit sortir.

obtrusive /əbˈtruːsɪv/ *adj* **1** (conspicuous) [*decor*] choquant; [*stain, object*] visible; [*noise, smell*] gênant; **2** (indiscreet) [*person, behaviour*] importun.

obtrusively /əbˈtruːsɪvlɪ/ *adv* [*behave*] de façon importune; [*stick out*] de façon visible.

obtrusiveness /əbˈtruːsɪvnɪs/ *n* (of person) importunité *f*.

obtuse /əbˈtjuːs, US -ˈtuːs-/ *adj* **1** (stupid) [*person*] obtus; [*remark*] stupide; **he's being deliberately ~** il joue les abrutis; **2** Math [*angle*] obtus.

obtuseness /əbˈtjuːsnɪs, US -ˈtuːs-/ *n* stupidité *f*.

obverse /ˈɒbvɜːs/ **I** *n* **1** (opposite) contraire *m*; **2** (of coin, medal) avers *m*.
II *adj* **1** (contrary) [*argument*] contraire; **2** (of coin) **the ~ side** ou **face** l'avers *m*; **3** Bot [*leaf*] obovale.

obviate /ˈɒbvɪeɪt/ *vtr* sout obvier à [*difficulty*]; éviter [*delay, requirement*]; écarter [*danger*]; **to ~ the need for sth** éviter d'avoir recours à qch; **this would ~ the need to do** cela éviterait d'avoir à faire.

obvious /ˈɒbvɪəs/ **I** *n* **to state the ~** enfoncer les portes ouvertes; **statement of the ~** lapalissade *f*.
II *adj* **1** (evident) évident (**to** pour); **it's ~ that...** il est évident que...; **her anxiety was ~** il était évident qu'elle était inquiète; **his disappointment was ~ to all** sa déception était écrite sur son visage; **it was ~ to everyone that there had been a mistake** il était évident pour tout le monde qu'il y avait eu erreur; **she is the ~ choice for the job** c'est la personne qu'il nous faut pour ce poste; **it was the ~ solution to choose** la solution s'imposait d'elle-même; **it was the ~ thing to do** c'était la chose à faire; **the ~ thing to do would be to...** la chose à faire serait de...; **for ~ reasons, I do not wish to discuss this** pour des raisons évidentes je ne veux pas en parler; **2** (unsubtle) [*lie*] flagrant; [*joke, symbolism*] lourd; **she was too ~ about it** elle a un peu trop manqué de finesse, on la voyait venir avec ses gros sabots○.

obviously /ˈɒbvɪəslɪ/ **I** *adv* manifestement; **she ~ needs help** il est évident qu'elle a besoin d'aide; **he's ~ lying** il est clair qu'il ment; **she's ~ happy/clever** il est évident qu'elle est heureuse/intelligente; **he was ~ in pain** il souffrait visiblement; **'hasn't he heard of them?'— '~ not'** iron 'n'en a-t-il pas entendu parler?'—'on dirait que non'; **he had ~ been taking lessons** il était évident qu'il avait pris des leçons.
II *excl* (indicating assent) bien sûr!, évidemment!

obviousness /ˈɒbvɪəsnɪs/ *n* gen évidence *f*, caractère *m* évident; (of outcome) prévisibilité *f*; (of remark) platitude *f*; (of plot) manque *m* d'originalité.

OC *n* GB (*abrév* = **Officer Commanding**) officier *m* commandant.

ocarina /ˌɒkəˈriːnə/ *n* ocarina *m*.

occasion /əˈkeɪʒn/ **I** *n* **1** (particular time) occasion *f*; **on that ~** à cette occasion, cette fois-là; **on one ~** une fois; **on several ~s** à plusieurs occasions or reprises; **on a previous ~** précédemment; **on rare ~s** rarement, en de rares occasions; **on ~** de temps en temps, à l'occasion; **on the ~ of** à l'occasion de; **when the ~ demands it** lorsque les circonstances l'exigent; **to rise to the ~** se montrer à la hauteur des circonstances; **2** (opportunity) occasion *f*; **to have ~ to do** avoir l'occasion de faire; **it's no ~ for laughter/frivolity** ce n'est pas le moment de rire/d'être frivole; **should the ~ arise** le cas échéant, si l'occasion se présente; **3** (event, function) occasion *f*, événement *m*; **a big ~** une grande occasion, un grand événement; **on special ~s** dans les grandes occasions; **for the ~** pour l'occasion; **the wedding was quite an ~** le mariage a été un événement; **ceremonial ~, state ~** cérémonie *f* officielle; **4** sout (cause) raison *f*; **there was no ~ to be so rude** il n'y avait aucune raison d'être si impoli; **there is no ~ for alarm** il n'y a pas lieu de s'inquiéter; **we have no ~ for complaint** nous n'avons pas lieu de nous plaindre.
II *vtr* sout occasionner, provoquer.

occasional /əˈkeɪʒənl/ *adj* **1** [*event*] qui se produit or qui a lieu de temps en temps; **the ~ letter/cigarette** une lettre/cigarette de temps en temps; **they have the ~ row** ils se disputent de temps en temps; **~ showers** Meteorol averses *fpl* intermittentes; **2** sout [*poem, music*] de circonstance.

occasionally /əˈkeɪʒənəlɪ/ *adv* de temps à autre; **very ~** très rarement, presque jamais.

occasional table *n* petite table *f*.

Occident /ˈɒksɪdənt/ *n* littér **the ~** l'Occident *m*.

occidental /ˌɒksɪˈdentl/ *adj* occidental.

occiput /ˈɒksɪpʌt/ *n* occiput *m*.

occlude /əˈkluːd/ *vtr* occlure; **~d front** Meteorol front *m* occlus.

occlusion /əˈkluːʒn/ *n* occlusion *f*.

occlusive /əˈkluːsɪv/ Ling **I** *n* (consonne *f*) occlusive *f*.
II *adj* occlusif/-ive.

occult **I** /ɒˈkʌlt, US əˈkʌlt/ *n* **the ~** (+ *v sg*) les sciences *fpl* occultes.
II /ɒˈkʌlt/ *adj* [*powers, arts, literature*] occulte.

occultism /ɒˈkʌltɪzəm, US əˈ-/ *n* occultisme *m*.

occupancy /ˈɒkjʊpənsɪ/ *n* occupation *f*; **full ~** pleine occupation; **multiple/sole ~ of a house** occupation d'une maison par plusieurs personnes/par une seule personne; **a change of ~** un changement d'occupant/-e *m/f*; **to have sole ~ of a house** être le seul occupant/la seule occupante *m/f* d'une maison; **available for immediate ~** libre immédiatement.

occupant /ˈɒkjʊpənt/ *n* **1** (of building, bed) occupant/-e *m/f*; **2** (of vehicle) passager/-ère *m/f*; **3** (of post) titulaire *mf*.

occupation /ˌɒkjʊˈpeɪʃn/ **I** *n* **1** (of house) **to be in ~** être installé; **ready for ~** prêt à être habité; **the date of their ~** la date où ils se sont installés dans les locaux; **to take up ~** s'installer (**of** dans); **2** Mil, Pol occupation *f* (**de** of); **to be under ~** être occupé; **to come under ~** être envahi; **an army of ~** une armée d'occupation; Hist **the Occupation** l'occupation *f*; **3** (job) (trade) métier *m*; (profession) profession *f*; **4** (leisure activity) occupation *f*.
II *modif* [*army, forces, troops*] d'occupation.

occupational /ˌɒkjʊˈpeɪʃənl/ *adj* [*accident, disease*] du travail; [*activity, group, opportunity, training*] professionnel/-elle; [*risk*] du métier; [*stress*] dû au travail; [*safety*] au travail.

occupational: **~ hazard** *n* risque *m* professionnel; **~ health** *n* médecine *f* du travail; **~ pension** *n* GB, Soc, Admin retraite *f* professionnelle; **~ pension scheme** *n* GB, Soc, Admin retraite *f* complémentaire; **~ psychologist** ▶ 1692 *n* psychologue *mf* du travail; **~ psychology** *n* psychologie *f* du travail; **~ therapist** ▶ 1692 *n* ergothérapeute *mf*; **~ therapy** *n* ergothérapie *f*.

occupier /ˈɒkjʊpaɪə(r)/ *n* occupant/-e *m/f*.

occupy /ˈɒkjʊpaɪ/ **I** *vtr* **1** (inhabit) occuper [*house, premises*]; **2** (fill) occuper [*bed, seat, room*]; **is this seat occupied?** est-ce que cette place est occupée or prise?; **3** (take over) occuper [*country, building*]; **an occupied territory** un territoire occupé; **the occupied territories** Pol les terres occupées; **the occupied zone** la zone d'occupation; **4** (take up) prendre [*time*]; [*activity*] durer [*day, afternoon*]; **the lecture occupies a whole day** la conférence dure toute une journée; occuper [*area, floor, surface*]; **that table occupies too much space** cette table tient trop de place; **5** (keep busy) occuper [*person*]; capter [*attention*]; **to be occupied in doing** être occupé à faire; **to be occupied with sb/sth** s'occuper de qn/qch; **something to ~ my mind** quelque chose pour m'occuper l'esprit; **6** (hold) remplir [*position, post, office*].
II *v refl* **to ~ oneself** s'occuper; **to keep oneself occupied** s'occuper (**by doing** en faisant).

occur /əˈkɜː(r)/ *vi* (*p prés etc* **-rr-**) **1** (happen) [*change, delay, event, fault, mistake*] se produire; [*epidemic, outbreak*] se déclarer; [*symptom*] apparaître; [*opportunity*] se présenter; [*sale, visit*] s'effectuer; **2** (be present) [*disease, infection*] se produire; [*species, toxin*] se trouver; [*expression, phrase*] se rencontrer; [*misprint, mistake*] se trouver; **3** (suggest itself) **the idea ~red to me that...** l'idée m'est venue à l'esprit que...; **it ~s to me that she's wrong** il me semble qu'elle a tort; **it ~red to me to do** l'idée m'est venue à l'esprit de faire; **it didn't ~ to**

me to do il ne m'est pas venu à l'idée de faire; **it only ~red to me later** cela ne m'a frappé que plus tard; **that she was mistaken never ~red to me** jamais je n'aurais pensé qu'elle se trompait.

occurrence /ə'kʌrəns/ *n* **1** (event) fait *m*; **to be a rare/regular/daily ~** se produire rarement/régulièrement/tous les jours; **an unfortunate ~** une affaire malencontreuse; **2** (instance) occurence *f* (**of** de); **3** (presence) (of disease, phenomenon) cas *m*; (of species) apparition *f*.

ocean /'əʊʃn/ **I** *n* lit océan *m*.
II oceans○ *npl* **~s of** plein de○ [*food, space, time, work etc*].
III *modif* [*voyage, wave*] océanique; **~ bed** fond *m* de l'océan.

oceanarium /ˌəʊʃə'neərɪəm/ *n* (*pl* **~s** ou **-ria**) aquarium *m* d'eau de mer.

ocean-going /'əʊʃngəʊɪŋ/ *adj* [*vessel, ship*] de haute mer; **~ liner** paquebot *m*.

Oceania /ˌəʊʃɪ'eɪnɪə/ *pr n* Océanie *f*.

Oceanian /ˌəʊʃɪ'eɪnɪən/ **I** *n* Océanien/-ienne *m/f*.
II *adj* océanien/-ienne.

oceanic /ˌəʊʃɪ'ænɪk/ *adj* océanique.

oceanographer /ˌəʊʃə'nɒgrəfə(r)/ **▶1692** *n* océanographe *mf*.

oceanographic /ˌəʊʃənə'græfɪk/ *adj* océanographique.

oceanography /ˌəʊʃə'nɒgrəfɪ/ *n* océanographie *f*.

ocelot /'əʊsɪlɒt, US 'ɒsəlɒt/ *n* ocelot *m*.

och /ɒx/ *excl* Scot oh!

ochre GB, **ocher** US /'əʊkə(r)/ **▶1104** **I** *n* (pigment) ocre *f*; (colours) ocre *m*.
II *adj* (colour) ocre.

o'clock /ə'klɒk/ **▶1096** *adv* **at one ~** à une heure; **it's two/three ~** il est deux/trois heures; **12 ~ midday/midnight** midi/minuit; **the 10 ~ screening** la séance de 10 heures; **to catch the six ~** prendre le train/bus etc de six heures.

OCR **I** *n* (*abrév* = **optical character recognition**) ROC *f*;
II *modif* **~ machine** ou **reader** lecteur *m* optique.

Oct *abrév écrite* = **October**.

octagon /'ɒktəgən, US -gɒn/ *n* octogone *m*.

octagonal /ɒk'tægənl/ *adj* octogonal.

octahedron /ˌɒktə'hi:drən, -'hedrən, US -drɒn/ *n* octaèdre *m*.

octal /'ɒktl/ Comput, Math **I** *n* système *m* octal.
II *adj* [*system, notation*] octal; **235 ~** 235 en base huit.

octane /'ɒkteɪn/ *n* octane *m*.

octane number, **octane rating** *n* indice *m* d'octane.

octave /'ɒktɪv/ *n* **1** Mus octave *f*; **2** Literat huitain *m*.

octavo /ɒk'teɪvəʊ/ **I** *n* (*pl* **~s**) in-octavo *m*.
II *modif* [*volume*] in-octavo.

octet /ɒk'tet/ *n* **1** Mus (group, composition) octuor *m*; **2** Comput octet *m*; **3** Literat huitain *m*.

October /ɒk'təʊbə(r)/ **▶1472** *n* octobre *m*; **the ~ Revolution** Hist la Révolution d'octobre.

octogenarian /ˌɒktədʒɪ'neərɪən/ *n, adj* octogénaire (*mf*).

octopus /'ɒktəpəs/ *n* **1** (*pl* **~es** ou **~**) Zool pieuvre *f*; Culin poulpe *m*; **2** (*pl* **~es**) GB (elastic straps) fixe-bagages *m inv*.

octosyllabic /ˌɒktəsɪ'læbɪk/ *adj* [*poem*] en vers octosyllabiques, en octosyllabes; [*word*] octosyllabique.

octosyllable /'ɒktəsɪləbl/ *n* octosyllabe *m*.

ocular /'ɒkjʊlə(r)/ *adj* [*defect*] oculaire; [*muscle*] de l'œil.

oculist /'ɒkjʊlɪst/ **▶1692** *n* ophtalmologiste *mf*.

OD○ /əʊdi:/ **I** *n* = **overdose I**.
II *vi* (*prés* **OD's**; *p prés* **OD'ing**; *prét, pp* **OD'd**, **OD'ed**) (on medicine) prendre une dose mortelle; (on drugs) prendre une overdose; **to ~ on** lit prendre une dose mortelle de [*tablets*]; prendre une overdose de [*drugs*]; fig se gaver de [*chocolate etc*]; s'abrutir de [*television*].

ODA *n* GB *abrév* **▶ Overseas Development Administration**.

odalisque /'əʊdəlɪsk/ *n* odalisque *f*.

odd /ɒd/ **I** *adj* **1** (strange, unusual) [*person, object, occurrence*] bizarre; **there is something ~ about** il y a quelque chose de bizarre dans [*appearance, statement*]; **there is something ~ about her** elle a quelque chose de bizarre; **there is something/nothing ~ about it** il y a quelque chose/il n'y a rien de bizarre; **it is ~ that** c'est bizarre que (+ *subj*); (more formally) il est surprenant que (+ *subj*); **it is ~ to see** c'est bizarre de voir; (more formally) il est surprenant de voir; **it is ~ how people react** c'est bizarre comme les gens réagissent; **it would be ~ if they were to do** il serait surprenant qu'ils fassent; **to be an ~ couple** former un drôle de couple; **that's ~** bizarre; **he's a bit ~** (eccentric) il est un peu loufoque○; **2** (occasional) **I have the ~ drink/ pizza** il m'arrive de boire un verre/manger une pizza; **to write the ~ article** écrire un article de temps en temps; **to pay sb the ~ visit** aller voir qn de temps en temps; **the landscape was bare except for the ~ tree** le paysage était désert à part un arbre ou deux; **3** (not matching) [*socks, gloves*] dépareillé; **4** (miscellaneous) **there were some ~ envelopes/bits of cloth left** il restait encore quelques enveloppes/bouts de tissu; **a few ~ coins** un reste de monnaie; **5** Math [*number*] impair; **6** (different) **spot the ~ man** ou **one out** trouvez l'intrus; **to feel the ~ one out** ne pas se sentir à sa place.
II -odd (*dans composés*) (approximately) **he lost a thousand-~ dollars** il a perdu mille dollars et quelques; **there were sixty-~ people** il y avait soixante et quelques personnes; **twenty-~ years later** une bonne vingtaine d'années après.
IDIOMS **he's as ~ as two left feet**○ il marche à côté de ses pompes○.

odd: **~ball**○ *n* farfelu/-e○ *m/f*; **~ bod**○ *n* GB drôle de mec○/nana○ *m/f*.

oddity /'ɒdɪtɪ/ *n* (odd thing) bizarrerie *f*; (person) excentrique *mf*.

odd job *n* (for money) petit boulot *m*; **to do ~s around the house** bricoler dans la maison.

odd-jobman *n* homme *m* à tout faire.

odd-looking *adj* à l'air bizarre (*after n*); **to be ~** avoir l'air bizarre.

odd lot *n* **1** Comm (merchandise) lot *m* dépareillé; **2** Fin (in stock market) paquet *m* d'actions hors quotité.

oddly /'ɒdlɪ/ *adv* [*dress*] bizarrement; **~ shaped** de forme bizarre; **~ enough**... chose curieuse...

oddment† /'ɒdmənt/ *n* chute *f* de tissu.

oddness /'ɒdnɪs/ *n* bizarrerie *f*.

odds /ɒdz/ *npl* **1** (in betting) cote *f* (**on** sur); **what are the ~?** quelle est la cote?; **the ~ are 20 to 1** la cote est 20 contre 1; **the ~ on Dayjar are 3 to 1** Dayjar est coté à 3 contre 1; **the ~ are six to one on** la cote est de un contre 6; **the ~ are five to two against** la cote est de cinq contre deux; **to give** ou **offer ~ of** proposer une cote de; **to quote ~ of 6 to 1** coter 6 contre 1; **the ~ on X are short/long** X est bien/mal coté; **2** (chance, likelihood) chances *fpl*; **the ~ are against/in favour of sth** qch est improbable/probable; **the ~ are against it** il y a peu de chances; **the ~ against/in favour of sth happening** les chances que qch n'arrive pas/arrive; **the ~ on sth happening are even** il y a une chance sur deux que qch arrive; **the ~ are against us/in our favour** la chance n'est pas/est de notre côté; **the ~ are in favour of her doing** elle a de fortes chances de faire; **the ~ are that she'll do** il y a de fortes chances qu'elle fasse; **to fight against the ~** lutter contre l'adversité; **to win against the ~** gagner contre toute attente; **to shorten/lengthen the ~ on sth** rendre qch plus/moins probable; **to shorten the ~ on sb doing** augmenter les chances que qn fasse.
IDIOMS **it makes no ~** GB ça n'a pas d'importance; **to pay over the ~ for sth** payer qch plus que son prix; **to be at ~** (in dispute) être en conflit; (contradictory, inconsistent) être en contradiction.

odds and ends, odds and sods○ GB *npl* bricoles○ *fpl*.

odds-on /ˌɒdz'ɒn/ *adj* **1**○ (likely) **it is ~ that** il y a de fortes chances que (+ *subj*); **he has an ~ chance of doing** il a de fortes chances de faire; **2** (in betting) **to be the ~ favourite** être le grand favori.

ode /əʊd/ *n* ode *f*.

odious /'əʊdɪəs/ *adj* odieux/-ieuse.

odiously /'əʊdɪəslɪ/ *adv* [*laugh, say*] de façon odieuse; **~ smug** d'une suffisance odieuse.

odiousness /'əʊdɪəsnɪs/ *n* caractère *m* odieux.

odium /'əʊdɪəm/ *n* réprobation *f* générale.

odometer /ɒ'dɒmɪtə(r)/ *n* Aut US odomètre *m*.

odontological /ɒˌdɒntə'lɒdʒɪkl/ *adj* odontologique.

odontologist /ˌɒdɒn'tɒlədʒɪst/ **▶1692** *n* odontologiste *mf*.

odontology /ˌɒdɒn'tɒlədʒɪ/ *n* odontologie *f*.

odor *n* US = **odour**.

odorous /'əʊdərəs/ *adj* littér odorant.

odour GB, **odor** US /'əʊdə(r)/ *n* odeur *f*; **the ~ of sanctity** l'odeur de sainteté.
IDIOMS **to be in bad ~** être mal vu (**with** de).

odourless GB, **odorless** US /'əʊdəlɪs/ *adj* [*gas, chemical*] inodore; [*cosmetic*] non parfumé.

Odysseus /ə'dɪsju:s/ *pr n* Odusseus.

odyssey /'ɒdɪsɪ/ *n* odyssée *f*; **the Odyssey** l'Odyssée *f*.

OE Ling *abrév écrite* = **Old English**.

OECD *n* (*abrév* = **Organization for Economic Cooperation and Development**) OCDE *f*.

oecumenical *adj* = **ecumenical**.

Oceans and seas

Note that the words océan *and* mer *do not have capitals in French.*

the Atlantic Ocean	=	l'océan Atlantique
the Pacific Ocean	=	l'océan Pacifique
the Indian Ocean	=	l'océan Indien
the Caspian Sea	=	la mer Caspienne
the Baltic Sea	=	la mer Baltique

As in English, French often drops the words océan *or* mer*. When this happens, oceans have masculine gender (from the masculine word* océan*) and seas have feminine gender (from the feminine* mer*):*

the Pacific	=	le Pacifique
the Baltic	=	la Baltique

but

the Aegean	=	la mer Égée

If in doubt, look up the name in the dictionary.

Use with other nouns

Here are some useful patterns, using Pacifique *as a typical name:*

the Pacific coast	=	la côte du Pacifique
a Pacific crossing	=	une traversée du Pacifique
a Pacific cruise	=	une croisière dans le Pacifique
Pacific currents	=	les courants du Pacifique
Pacific fish	=	les poissons du Pacifique
the Pacific islands	=	les îles du Pacifique

of

In almost all its uses the preposition *of* is translated by *de*. Exceptions to this are substances (*made of gold*), uses with a personal pronoun (*that's kind of you*), proportions (*some of us, of the 12 of us …*) and time expressions (*of an evening*). For translations of these, see the entry ***of***. Remember that *de + le* always becomes *du* and that *de + les* always becomes *des*.

To find translations for phrases beginning with *of* (*of course, of all, of interest, of late, of old*) you should consult the appropriate noun etc. entry (***course, all, interest, late, old*** etc.).

of also often appears as the second element of a verb (*consist of, deprive of, die of, think of*). For translations, consult the appropriate verb entry.

of is used after certain nouns, pronouns and adjectives in English (*a member of, a game of, some of, most of, afraid of, capable of, ashamed of*). For translations, consult the appropriate noun, pronoun or adjective entry.

When *of it* or *of them* are used for something already referred to they are translated by *en*:

there's a lot of it = il y en a beaucoup
there are several of them = il y en a plusieurs

Note, however, the following expressions used when referring to people:

there are six of them = ils sont six
there were several of them = ils étaient plusieurs

For particular usages see the entry ***of***.

This dictionary contains usage notes on such topics as ***age, capacity measurement, dates, illnesses, length measurement, quantities, towns and cities***, and ***weight measurement***, many of which use *of*.
For the index to these notes ▶ **1919**.

oedema GB, **edema** US /ɪ'di:mə/ *n* œdème *m*.

oedipal, Oedipal /'i:dɪpl/ *adj* Psych œdipien/-ienne.

Oedipus /'i:dɪpəs/ *pr n* Œdipe.

Oedipus complex *n* complexe *m* d'Œdipe.

oenological /ˌi:nə'lɒdʒɪkl/ *adj* œnologique.

oenologist, GB **enologist** US /i:'nɒlədʒɪst/ ▶ **1692** *n* œnologue *mf*.

oenology GB, **enology** US /i:'nɒlədʒɪ/ *n* œnologie *f*.

o'er /ɔ:(r)/ littér = **over**[1].

oesophagus GB, **esophagus** US /ɪ'sɒfəgəs/ *n* œsophage *m*.

oestrogen GB, **estrogen** US /'i:strədʒən/ *n* œstrogène *m*.

oestrone GB, **estrone** US /'i:strəʊn/ *n* folliculine *f*.

oestrous GB, **estrous** US /'i:strəs/ *adj* [*animal, cycle*] œstral.

oestrus GB, **estrus** US /'i:strəs/ *n* œstrus *m*.

œuvre /ɜ:vrə/ *n* **1** (complete works) œuvre *m*; **2** (individual painting etc) œuvre *f*.

of /ɒv, əv/ *prep* **1** (in most uses) de; **the leg ~ the table** le pied de la table; **the difficulty ~ the work** la difficulté du travail; **the king ~ beasts** le roi des animaux; **2** (made or consisting of) **a ring (made) ~ gold** une bague en or; **a plaque (made) ~ grey marble** une plaque en marbre gris; **a will ~ iron** fig une volonté de fer; **a heart ~ stone** fig un cœur de pierre; **3** (indicating an agent) **that's kind ~ you/him** c'est très gentil de votre/sa part, c'est très gentil à vous/à lui; **4** (indicating a proportion or fraction) **some ~ us stayed for dinner** quelques-uns d'entre nous sont restés dîner; **several ~ them were rotten** plusieurs (d'entre eux) étaient pourris; **of the twelve ~ us only nine could swim** sur les douze (que nous étions) neuf seulement savaient nager; **5** GB (in expressions of time) **~ an evening** le soir; **~ a morning** le matin; **I like to play golf ~ an afternoon** j'aime jouer au golf l'après-midi; ▶ **late, old.**

off /ɒf/, US /ɔ:f/

■ **Note** *off* is often found as the second element in verb combinations (*fall off, run off etc*) and in offensive interjections (*clear off etc*). For translations consult the appropriate verb entry (***fall, run, clear*** etc).
– *off* is used in certain expressions such as *off limits, off piste etc* and translations for these will be found under the noun entry (***limit, piste*** etc).
– For other uses of *off* see the entry below.

I○ *n* (start) **the ~** le départ; **just before the ~** (of race) juste avant le départ; **from the ~** fig dès le départ.

II *adv* **1** (leaving) **to be ~** partir, s'en aller; **it's time you were ~** il est temps que tu partes; **they're ~ to the States today** ils partent pour les États-Unis aujourd'hui; **I'm ~** gen je m'en vais; (to avoid sb) je ne suis pas là; **to be ~ to a good start** avoir pris un bon départ; **'...and they're ~!'** Turf '...et les voici partis!'; **he's ~ again talking about his exploits!** fig et voilà c'est reparti, il raconte encore ses exploits!; **2** (at a distance) **to be 30 metres/kilometres ~** être à 30 mètres/kilomètres; **some way/not far ~** assez/pas très loin; **3** (ahead in time) **Easter is a month ~** Pâques est dans un mois; **the exam is still several months ~** l'examen n'aura pas lieu avant plusieurs mois; **4** Theat **shouting/trumpet sound ~** on entend des cris/une trompette dans les coulisses.

III *adj* **1** (free) **to have Monday ~ to do** prendre sa journée de lundi pour faire; **Tuesday's my day ~** je ne travaille pas le mardi; **did you have the morning ~?** est-ce que tu as pris ta matinée?; **I got time ~** on m'a permis de m'absenter; **2** (turned off) **to be ~** [*water, gas*] être coupé; [*tap*] être fermé; [*light, TV*] être éteint; **in the '~' position** en position 'fermé'; **3** (cancelled) **to be ~** [*match, party*] être annulé; **our engagement's ~** nous avons rompu nos fiançailles; **the coq au vin is ~** (from menu) il n'y a plus de coq au vin; **4** (removed) **the lid** ou **top is ~** il n'y a pas de couvercle; **the handle's ~** la poignée s'est cassée; **with her make-up ~** sans maquillage; **with his shoes ~** sans ses chaussures; **to have one's leg ~**○ se faire couper la jambe; **25% ~** Comm 25% de remise; **5**○ (bad) **to be ~** [*food*] être pourri; [*milk*] avoir tourné.

IV off and on *adv phr* par périodes; ▶ **on.**

V *prep* **1** (away from in distance) **~ Rocky Point/the west coast** au large du Rocky Point/de la côte ouest; **three metres ~ the ground** à trois mètres (au-dessus) du sol; **2** (away from in time) **to be a long way ~ doing** être encore loin de faire; **he's only a year ~ retirement** il n'a plus qu'un an avant la retraite; **3** (also **just ~**) juste à côté de [*area*]; **there's a kitchen (just) ~ the dining room** il y a une cuisine juste à côté de la salle à manger; **a house just ~ the path** une maison à quelques mètres du sentier; **just ~ the motorway** juste à la sortie de l'autoroute; **in a street (leading) ~ the main road** dans une rue qui donne sur l'avenue principale; **4** (astray from) **it is ~ the point** ou **subject** là n'est pas la question; **to be ~ centre** être mal centré; **5** (detached from) **to be ~ its hinges/~ its base** être sorti de ses gonds/détaché de son socle; **there's a button ~ your cuff** il manque un bouton à ton poignet de chemise; **6**○ (no longer interested in) **to be ~ drugs** avoir arrêté de se droguer; **to be ~ one's food** ne pas avoir d'appétit; **I'm ~ her/men at the moment!** il ne faut plus me parler d'elle/des hommes!; **7**○ (also **~ of**) **to borrow sth ~ a neighbour** emprunter qch à un voisin; **to eat ~ a tray/a paper plate** manger sur un plateau/dans une assiette en papier; ▶ **street.**

VI *excl* **~! ~!** (as chant) dehors! dehors!; **~ with her head!** qu'on lui coupe la tête!; **(get) ~**○**!** (from wall etc) descends (de là)!

IDIOMS **how are we ~**○ **for flour/sugar etc?** qu'est-ce qu'il nous reste comme farine/sucre etc?; **that's a bit ~**○ GB ça c'est pas juste○; **to feel a bit ~**○**(-colour)** GB ne pas être dans son assiette○; **to have an ~ day** ne pas être dans un de ses bons jours; ▶ **better-off, well-off.**

offal /'ɒfl, US 'ɔ:fl/ *n* abats *mpl*.

offbeat /ˌɒf'bi:t, US ˌɔ:f-/ **I** *n* Mus temps *m* faible.

II *adj* **1** Mus [*rhythm*] à temps faible; **2** (unusual) [*humour, approach, account*] cocasse.

off-Broadway *adj* US Theat **~ production** production expérimentale différente des spectacles de Broadway; **~ theatre** théâtre situé en dehors de Broadway.

off: **~ camera** *adj, adv* hors champ; **~ -centre** GB, **off-center** US /ˌɒf'sentə(r)/ *adj* décentré.

off-chance /'ɒftʃɑ:ns, US -tʃæns/ *n* chance *f*; **there's just an ~ that** il y a une chance pour que (+ *subj*); **on the ~ that** au cas où; **I came just on the ~!** je suis venu au cas où!

off: **~-color** *adj* US [*story, joke*] indécent; **~-colour**○ *adj* GB (unwell) patraque○; **~cuts** *npl* (of fabric) chutes *fpl*; (of pastry) restes *mpl*; (of meat, fish) parures *fpl*.

offence GB, **offense** US /ə'fens/ *n* **1** Jur infraction *f*; **to commit an ~** commettre une infraction; **to charge sb with an ~** inculper qn d'une infraction; **it is an ~ to do** il est illégal de faire; **~s against property/the person/the state** atteintes *fpl* à la propriété/la personne/la sûreté de l'État; **2** (insult) offense *f*; **to cause** ou **give ~ to sb** offenser qn; **to take ~ (at)** s'offenser (de); **to avoid ~** éviter d'offenser; **this building is an ~ to the eye** ce bâtiment choque la vue; **no ~ intended, but...** je ne voudrais pas te vexer, mais...; **no ~ taken** il n'y a pas de mal; **3** (attack) atteinte *f* **(against** à); **4** Mil offensive *f*; **weapons of ~** armes *fpl* offensives; **5** US Sport **the ~** les attaquants *mpl*.

offend /ə'fend/ **I** *vtr* **1** (hurt) [*person*] offenser [*person*]; [*article, remark*] blesser, offenser [*person*]; **to be ~ed by sth** être blessé par [*behaviour, remark*]; **to get ~ed** se vexer; **don't be ~ed** ne soyez pas vexé; **2** (displease) outrager; **the decision ~s my sense of justice** la décision outrage mon sens de la justice; **to ~ the eye** [*building etc*] choquer la vue.

II *vi* Jur commettre une infraction **(against** à); **to ~ again** récidiver.

III offending *pres p adj* **1** (responsible) [*component, object*] en cause; [*person*] responsable; **2** (offensive) [*photo, sentence*] choquant.

■ **offend against**: **~ against [sth] 1** (commit a crime) enfreindre [*law, rule*]; **2** (violate) offenser [*good taste*]; être un outrage à [*common sense*].

offender /ə'fendə(r)/ *n* **1** Jur (against the law) délinquant/-e *m/f*; (against regulations) contrevenant/-e *m/f* **(against** à); **2** (culprit) coupable *mf*; **the press/the police are the worst ~s** la presse/la police est la plus à blâmer.

offense *n* US ▶ **offence.**

offensive /ə'fensɪv/ **I** *n* **1** Mil, Pol, Sport offensive *f* **(against** contre); **to go on/take the ~** passer à/prendre l'offensive; **air/diplomatic ~** offensive aérienne/diplomatique; **to be on the ~** être à l'attaque; **2** Advertg, Comm campagne *f*; **advertising/sales ~** campagne publicitaire/commerciale.

II *adj* **1** (insulting) [*remark, suggestion*] injurieux/-ieuse (**to** pour); [*behaviour*] insultant; **2** (vulgar) [*language*] grossier/-ière; [*behaviour*] choquant; [*gesture*] vulgaire, choquant; **3** (revolting) [*smell*] repoussant; [*behaviour, idea*] répugnant; **4** Mil, Sport, [*action, play*] offensif/-ive.

offensively /əˈfensɪvlɪ/ *adv* **1** (rudely) [*behave*] de manière offensante; [*speak, write*] de façon injurieuse (**about** au sujet de); **2** (aggressively) **to fight ~** attaquer.

offensive weapon *n* Jur arme *f* offensive.

offer /ˈɒfə(r), US ˈɔːf-/ **I** *n* **1** (proposition) gen, Fin offre *f* (**to do** de faire); **an ~ of help/work** une offre d'assistance/de travail; **to make sb an ~** faire une offre à qn; **job ~** offre d'emploi; **an ~ of marriage** une proposition de mariage; **an ~ of £10 per share** une offre à 10 livres sterling l'action; **~s over/around 40,000 dollars** offres supérieures à/autour de 40000 dollars; **that's my final** ou **best ~** c'est mon dernier mot; **to be open to ~s** être ouvert à toute proposition; **to put in** ou **make an ~ on a house** faire une offre sur une maison; **the house is under ~** il y a une promesse d'achat sur cette maison; **or near(est) ~** (in property ad) à débattre; **~s in the region of £80,000** prix 80 000 livres, à débattre; **2** Comm (promotion) promotion *f*; **to be on special ~** être en promotion; **3** (available) **the goods/cases on ~ were dear** les marchandises/valises en vente étaient chères; **there's a lot/nothing on ~** il y a beaucoup/peu de choix; **what's on ~ in the catalogue?** qu'est-ce qu'on propose dans le catalogue?

II *vtr* **1** (proffer) donner [*advice, explanation, information, friendship*]; offrir [*cigarette, help, job, reward, suggestion, support*]; émettre [*opinion*]; faire [*reduction*]; proposer [*service*]; accorder [*discount*]; **to ~ sb sth, to ~ sth to sb** offrir qch à qn; **to ~ to do** se proposer pour faire; **'I'll do it,' she ~ed** 'je le ferai,' proposa-t-elle; **she has a lot to ~ the company** elle peut beaucoup apporter à la société; **he had little to ~ in the way of news/evidence** il n'avait pas beaucoup de nouvelles/preuves à apporter; **2** (provide) offrir [*facilities, advantages, guarantee, resistance*]; donner [*insight*]; **the tree ~s protection from the rain** l'arbre offre une protection contre la pluie; **this vest ~s protection against bullets** ce gilet protège des balles; **3** (possess) posséder [*language*]; avoir [*experience*]; **candidates must ~ two foreign languages** les candidats doivent posséder deux langues étrangères; **4** (sell) offrir [*goods*]; **the radios were being ~ed at bargain prices** les radios étaient vendues à prix réduit; **to ~ sth for sale** mettre qch en vente; **5** (present) présenter; **the army/battleship ~ed its flank to the enemy** l'armée/le cuirassé a présenté son flanc à l'ennemi.

III *vi* (volunteer) se proposer.

IV *v refl* **to ~ oneself** se proposer (**for** pour); **to ~ itself** [*opportunity*] se présenter.

■ **offer up**: **~ [sth] up, ~ up [sth]** offrir [*prayer*]; faire l'offrande de [*animal, sacrifice*]; **to ~ up one's life for sth** s'offrir en victime pour qch.

offeree /ˌɒfəˈriː, US ˌɔːf-/ *n* Jur destinataire *mf* de l'offre.

offering /ˈɒfərɪŋ, US ˈɔːf-/ *n* **1** (act of giving) offre *f*; **the ~ of bribes is unethical** l'offre de pots-de-vin est immorale; **2** (gift) cadeau *m*; **I heard the band's latest ~ yesterday** iron, péj j'ai écouté le dernier album du groupe hier; **3** Relig collecte *f*, quête *f*; **4** (sacrifice) offrande *f*; **to make an ~** faire une offrande.

offeror /ˈɒfərə(r), US ˈɔːf-/ *n* Jur offrant *m*.

offer price *n* Comm prix *m* de vente.

offertory /ˈɒfətrɪ, US ˈɔːfətɔːrɪ/ *n* Relig offertoire *m*.

off-glide *n* Phon métastase *f*.

offhand /ˌɒfˈhænd, US ˌɔːf-/ **I** *adj* (impolite) désinvolte.

II *adv* **~, I don't know** comme ça au pied levé je ne sais pas.

offhandedly /ˌɒfˈhændɪdlɪ, US ˌɔːf-/ *adv* de façon désinvolte.

offhandedness /ˌɒfˈhændɪdnɪs, US ˌɔːf-/ *n* désinvolture *f*.

office /ˈɒfɪs, US ˈɔːf-/ **I** *n* **1** (room or place of work) bureau *m*; **the accounts ~** le service comptable; **doctor's/dentist's ~** US cabinet *m* médical/dentaire; **lawyer's ~** étude *f* or cabinet *m* de notaire; **to work in an ~** travailler dans un bureau, être employé/-e de bureau; **the whole ~ knows** tout le bureau est au courant; **a day at the ~** une journée au bureau; **2** (position) fonction *f*, charge *f*; **public ~** fonctions *fpl* officielles; **to perform the ~ of** remplir les fonctions de; **to be in** ou **hold ~** [*president, mayor*] être en fonction; [*minister*] avoir un portefeuille; [*political party*] être au pouvoir; **to take ~** [*president, mayor*] entrer en fonction; [*political party*] arriver au or prendre le pouvoir; **to go out of ~** ou **leave ~** [*president, mayor*] quitter ses fonctions; [*minister*] perdre son portefeuille; [*political party*] perdre le pouvoir; **to stand** GB ou **run** US **for ~** être candidat aux élections; **to rise to high ~** être promu à un poste élevé; **3** Relig office *m*; **the ~ for the dead** l'office des morts.

II offices *npl* **1** sout (services) offices *mpl*, aide *f*; **through their good ~s** par leurs bons offices; **2** GB (of property) **'the usual ~s'** (including outbuildings) 'cuisine *f* et dépendances *fpl*'; (in smaller house) 'cuisine *f* et salle *f* de bains'.

III *modif* [*equipment, furniture, staff, job*] de bureau; **~ party** soirée *f* réunissant le personnel d'un bureau; **to go on an ~ outing** sortir avec les gens de son bureau.

office automation *n* bureautique *f*.

office bearer *n* **1** (of society) membre *m* du comité directeur; **2** Pol (of party) représentant *m*; **former ~s such as Reagan** des anciens présidents tel que Reagan.

office: **~ block** *n* GB immeuble *m* de bureaux; **~ boy** *n* garçon *m* de bureau; **~ building** *n* = **office block**; **~holder** *n* = **office bearer**; **~ hours** *npl* heures *fpl* de bureau; **~ junior** *n* employé/-e *m/f* de bureau; **~ manager** *n* directeur *m* de bureau; **~ party** *n* fête *f* d'entreprise; **~ politics** *n* intrigues *fpl* de bureau.

officer /ˈɒfɪsə(r), US ˈɔːf-/ **I** *n* **1** Mil, Naut officier *m*; **2** (official) (in a company) responsable *mf*; (in government) fonctionnaire *mf*; (in committee, union, club) membre *m* du comité directeur or du bureau exécutif; **information/personnel ~** responsable de la communication/du personnel; **the Committee shall elect its ~s** le Comité désignera son bureau; **3** (also **police ~**) policier *m*; **'excuse me, ~'** 'excusez-moi, monsieur l'agent'; **Officer Smith** US Agent Smith.

II *vtr* Mil **1** (command) commander; **2** (supply with officers) pourvoir en officiers.

officer: **~ of the day** *n* officier *m* de jour; **~ of the guard**, **OG** *n* officier *m* de la garde; **~ of the law** *n* = **police officer**; **~ of the watch** *n* officier *m* de quart; **~s' mess** *n* mess *m*; **Officers' Training Corps**, **OTC** *n* GB *organisation universitaire extra-scolaire qui donne une formation militaire de base aux futurs officiers.*

office space *n* bureaux *mpl*; **1,500 m² of ~** 1 500 m² de bureaux.

office worker ▶ 1692 *n* employé/-e *m/f* de bureau.

official /əˈfɪʃl/ **I** *n* (of central or local government, of state) fonctionnaire *mf*; (of party, trade union) officiel/-ielle *m/f*; (of police, customs) agent *m*; (at town hall) employé/-e *m/f*.

II *adj* [*statement, reason, document, function, visit, language, candidate, strike*] officiel/-ielle; [*biography*] autorisé; **it's ~!** journ c'est officiel!

officialdom /əˈfɪʃldəm/ *n* bureaucratie *f*.

officialese /əˌfɪʃəˈliːz/ *n* péj jargon *m* administratif.

officially /əˈfɪʃəlɪ/ *adv* [*announce, confirm, celebrate*] officiellement; **~ she has retired** officiellement elle est à la retraite.

Official Receiver *n* administrateur *m* judiciaire.

Official Secrets Act *n* GB loi *f* relative aux secrets d'État; **to have signed the ~** être astreint au secret.

officiate /əˈfɪʃɪeɪt/ *vi* [*official*] présider; [*priest*] officier; [*referee, umpire*] arbitrer; **to ~ as host** remplir les fonctions d'hôte.

officious /əˈfɪʃəs/ *adj* péj trop empressé, zélé.

officiously /əˈfɪʃəslɪ/ *adv* [*say*] du haut de son importance.

officiousness /əˈfɪʃəsnɪs/ *n* péj excès *m* d'empressement.

offing /ˈɒfɪŋ/: **in the offing** *adv phr* (*tjrs épith, après n*) [*storm, war*] imminent; [*promotion, wedding*] en perspective.

off: **~-key** *adj* Mus faux/fausse; **~-licence** *n* GB magasin *m* de vins et de spiritueux; **~-limits** *adj* interdit; **~-line** *adj* Comput [*equipment, system*] autonome; [*processing*] en différé; [*storage*] non connecté.

off-load /ˌɒfˈləʊd, US ˌɔːf-/ *vtr* **1** fig (get rid of) écouler [*goods, stock*]; se dégager de [*investments*]; **to ~ the blame onto sb** rejeter la responsabilité sur qn; **2** Comput décharger.

off-off-Broadway *adj* US Theat [*production*] d'avant-garde.

off-peak /ˌɒfˈpiːk, US ˌɔːf-/ **I** *adj* [*electricity*] au tarif de nuit; [*travel, flight, reductions*] en période creuse; **in the ~ period** en période creuse, en dehors des heures de pointe; **at the ~ rate** [*call*] au tarif réduit.

II *adv* Telecom [*call, cost*] aux heures de tarif réduit.

offprint /ˈɒfprɪnt, US ˈɔːf-/ **I** *n* tiré *m* or tirage *m* à part.

II *vtr* imprimer un tiré à part de [*article*].

off-putting /ˌɒfˈpʊtɪŋ, US ˌɔːf-/ *adj* [*manner*] peu engageant; **it was very ~** c'était déroutant.

off-road /ˈɒf rəʊd/ *vi* rouler en tout terrain.

off-road vehicle *n* véhicule *m* tout terrain.

off-sales /ˌɒfˈseɪlz/ *n* vente *f* d'alcool à emporter.

off-screen /ˌɒfˈskriːn, US ˌɔːf-/ **I** *adj* Cin [*action*] hors-champ; [*voice*] off *inv*; [*relationship*] dans la vie.

II *adv* en privé.

off-season /ˌɒfˈsiːzn, US ˌɔːf-/ Tourism **I** *n* **during the ~** en hors saison.

II *adj* [*cruise*] hors saison; [*losses, deficit*] de basse saison.

offset /ˈɒfset, US ˈɔːf-/ **I** *n* **1** gen **as an ~ to** pour compenser; **2** Bot rejeton *m*; **3** (also **~ pipe**) Tech coude *m*.

II *vtr* (*p prés* **-tt-**; *prét, pp* **offset**) **1** compenser (**by** par); **to ~ sth against sth** mettre qch et qch en balance; **2** Print imprimer [qch] en offset.

offset: **~ litho(graph)** *n* litho *f* en offset; **~ paper** *n* papier *m* offset; **~ press** *n* presse *f* offset; **~ printing** *n* offset *m*.

offshoot /ˈɒfʃuːt, US ˈɔːf-/ *n* (of tree, organization) ramification *f*; (of plant) rejeton *m*; (of idea, decision) conséquence *f*.

offshore /ˌɒfˈʃɔː(r), US ˌɔːf-/ **I** *adj* **1** Naut [*waters*] du large; [*fishing*] au large; **~ wind** brise *f* de terre; **2** Fin [*funds, banking, tax haven*] hors-lieu *inv*, offshore; **3** (in oil industry) [*drilling, oilfield*] en mer, offshore; [*platform*] marin, offshore; **4** fig **~ English** anglais *m* international.

II *adv* **1 to invest/bank ~** faire des investissements/ouvrir un compte hors-lieu; **2** (in oil industry) [*work*] en mer, offshore.

offside /ˌɒfˈsaɪd, US ˌɔːf-/ **I** *n* GB Aut côté *m* conducteur; **on the ~** (du) côté conducteur.
II *adj* **1** GB Aut **the ~ wing/window** l'aile/la vitre côté conducteur; **the ~ rear wheel** la roue arrière côté conducteur; **the ~ lane** gen la voie de gauche; GB la voie de droite; **2** Sport [*position*] hors jeu; **the ~ rule** la règle du hors-jeu.
off-site /ˈɒfsaɪt, US ˈɔːf-/ *adj, adv* hors site *inv*.
offspring /ˈɒfsprɪŋ, US ˈɔːf-/ *n* (*pl* **~**) (of animal) progéniture *f*; (of human) also hum progéniture *f*; **five ~** cinq enfants.
offstage /ˌɒfˈsteɪdʒ, US ˌɔːf-/ *adj, adv* Theat dans les coulisses.
off-street parking *n* emplacement *m* de stationnement.
off-the-cuff I *adj* [*remark, speech*] impromptu.
II off the cuff *adv* spontanément.
off-the-peg I *adj* [*garment*] de prêt-à-porter.
II off the peg *adv phr* **to buy clothes ~** acheter du prêt-à-porter.
off-the-shelf I *adj* **1** Comm [*goods*] disponible en magasin; **2** Comput [*software*] fixe.
II off the shelf *adv phr* [*available*] à vue, sur stock.
off-the-shoulder *adj* **an ~ dress** une robe qui dégage les épaules.
off: **~-the-wall**○ *adj* loufoque○; **~-white** *adj* blanc cassé *inv*; **~ year** *n* US Pol *année sans élections importantes*.
oft /ɒft/ littér **I** *adv* souvent.
II oft- (*dans composés*) **~-quoted/-repeated/-heard** souvent cité/répété/entendu.
Oftel /ˈɒftel/ *n* GB (*abrév* = **Office of Telecommunications**) *organisme de contrôle des télécommunications au service de la clientèle*.
often /ˈɒfn, ˈɒftən, US ˈɔːfn/ *adv* souvent; **very/so/too/less ~** très/si/trop/moins souvent; **more and more ~** de plus en plus souvent; **as ~ as not, more ~ than not** le plus souvent; **it's not ~ you see that** ce n'est pas souvent qu'on voit ça; **you'll ~ find that** tu constateras souvent que; **how ~ do you meet?** vous vous voyez tous les combien○?, vous vous voyez souvent?; **how ~ do the planes depart?** les avions partent tous les combien?; **an ~-repeated remark** une remarque souvent répétée; **it cannot be said too ~ that** on ne répétera jamais assez que; **once too ~** une fois de trop; **every so ~** (in time) de temps en temps; (in distance, space) ça et là.
oftimes /ˈɒftaɪmz/ *adv* littér souvent.
ogival /əʊˈdʒaɪvl/ *adj* ogival.
ogive /ˈəʊdʒaɪv/ *n* (all contexts) ogive *f*.
ogle○ /ˈəʊgl/ *vtr* reluquer○.
ogre /ˈəʊgə(r)/ *n* **1** (giant) ogre *m*; **2** fig (fearsome person) (man) monstre *m*; (woman) dragon○ *m*; **3** (grim vision) spectre *m*.
ogress /ˈəʊgres/ *n* (giant) ogresse *f*; fig (fearsome woman) dragon○ *m*.
oh /əʊ/ *excl* oh!; **~ dear!** (sympathetic) oh là là!; (dismayed, cross) mon Dieu!; **~ damn○/shit●!** zut○/merde●!; **~ (really)?** (interested) ah bon?; (sceptical) tiens donc!; **~ really!** (cross) ah c'est pas possible○!; **~ by the way** ah au fait; **~ Fred, can you lend me £10?** dis-moi Fred, tu peux me prêter 10 livres?; **~ all right** ah bon d'accord; **~ no!** non!; **~ no, not again!** oh non, encore!; **~ no it isn't!** mais non!; **~ yes?** (pleased) ah bon?; (sceptical) tiens donc!; **~ how I hate work!** ah ce que je déteste le travail!; **~ for some sun!** oh si seulement il faisait beau!; **~ to be in Paris!** oh si seulement j'étais à Paris!
OH US Post *abrév écrite* = **Ohio**.
Ohio /əʊˈhaɪəʊ/ **▶1744** *n* Ohio *m*; **in ~** dans l'Ohio.
ohm /əʊm/ *n* ohm *m*.
OHMS GB (*abrév écrite* = **On Her/His Majesty's Service**) au service de sa majesté (*formule apparaissant sur le courrier officiel de l'administration*).
oik○ /ɔɪk/ *n* GB abruti/-e○ *m/f*.
oil /ɔɪl/ **I** *n* **1** (for fuel) pétrole *m*; (for lubrication) huile *f*; **crude ~** pétrole brut; **engine ~** huile de moteur; **heating ~** fioul *m*, mazout *m*; **to check the ~** Aut vérifier le niveau d'huile; **to change the ~** Aut faire la vidange; **to strike ~** lit découvrir du pétrole; fig découvrir une mine d'or; **2** (for cooking) huile *f*; **corn/sunflower ~** huile de maïs/tournesol; **to cook with ~** cuisiner à l'huile; **an ~ and vinegar dressing** une vinaigrette; **3** Art (medium) huile *f* ¢; **to work in ~s** peindre à l'huile; **the portrait is (done) in ~s** c'est un portrait à l'huile; **4** Art (picture) huile *f*; **5** (medicinal, beauty) huile *f*; **essential ~s** huiles *fpl* essentielles; **~ of cloves/lemon** essence *f* de girofle/citron; **6**○ US (flattery) pommade○ *f*, flatterie *f*.
II *modif* [*deposit, exporter, producer*] de pétrole; [*prices*] du pétrole; [*company, crisis, industry, exploration, production, terminal*] pétrolier/-ière; [*imports, reserves*] pétrolier/-ière; **an ~ magnate** un magnat du pétrole.
III *vtr* **1** (lubricate) huiler, lubrifier [*mechanism, parts*]; huiler [*pan*]; **2** Cosmet huiler [*skin, hair*].
IV oiled *pp adj* **1** [*hair, moustache*] huilé; [*pistons, mechanism*] huilé; [*seabird, animal*] mazouté; [*cloth, paper, silk*] huilé; **2**○ (drunk) bien beurré○, ivre.
IDIOMS **~ and water do not mix** on ne peut pas marier l'eau et le feu; **to ~ the wheels** mettre de l'huile dans les rouages. **to pour ~ on troubled waters** apaiser les esprits.
oil: **~-based** *adj* [*paint, plastic, polymer*] à base d'huile; **~-bearing** *adj* bitumeux/-euse; **~-burning** *adj* [*stove, boiler*] à mazout; **~ cake** *n* Agric tourteau *f* (pour bétail); **~can** *n* (applicator) burette *f* (d'huile); (container) bidon *m* (d'huile); **~ change** *n* vidange *f*; **~cloth** *n* toile *f* cirée; **~ colour** GB, **~ color** US *n* peinture *f* à l'huile; **~-cooled** *adj* [*engine*] à refroidissement par l'huile; **~ drill** *n* trépan *m*; **~ drum** *n* citerne *f* à pétrole.
oiler /ˈɔɪlə(r)/ **I** *n* **1** (ship) pétrolier *m*; **2** (worker) pétrolier *m*; **3**○ (oilcan) burette *f*.
II oilers *npl* US Fashn cirés *mpl*.
oil: **~ field** *n* champ *m* pétrolifère; **~ filter** *n* filtre *m* à huile; **~-fired** *adj* [*furnace, heating*] au fuel; **~ gauge** *n* jauge *f* de niveau d'huile; **~ heater** *n* poêle *m* à mazout.
oiliness /ˈɔɪlɪnɪs/ *n* (of food) (taste) goût *m* huileux; (look) aspect *m* huileux.
oil: **~ lamp** *n* lampe *f* à pétrole; **~ level** *n* niveau *m* d'huile; **~ man** *n* pétrolier *m*.
oil paint *n* couleur *f* à l'huile; **to use ~s** peindre à l'huile.
oil painting *n* (picture, activity) peinture *f* à l'huile; **she's no ~!** hum ce n'est pas une beauté.
oil: **~ palm** *n* palmier *m* à huile; **~ pan** *n* US carter *m*; **~ pipeline** *n* oléoduc *m*; **~ pollution** *n* pollution *f* aux hydrocarbures; **~ pressure** *n* pression *f* d'huile; **~-producing** *adj* [*country*] producteur/-trice de pétrole; **~ refinery** *n* raffinerie *f* de pétrole; **~ rig** *n* (offshore) plate-forme *f* pétrolière; (on land) tour *f* de forage; **~seed rape** *n* colza *m*.
oilskin /ˈɔɪlskɪn/ GB **I** *n* (fabric) toile *f* huilée.
II *adj* [*jacket, trousers*] en toile huilée.
III oilskins *npl* Fashn cirés *mpl*.
oil: **~ slick** *n* marée *f* noire; **~ spill** *n* déversement *m* accidentel d'hydrocarbures; **~stone** *n* pierre *f* à aiguiser; **~ stove** *n* poêle *m* à mazout; **~ tank** *n* (domestic) cuve *f*; (industrial) réserve *f* de stockage de pétrole; **~ tanker** *n* pétrolier *m*; **~ technology** *n* technologie *f* du pétrole; **~ well** *n* puits *m* de pétrole.
oily /ˈɔɪlɪ/ *adj* **1** (saturated) [*cloth, stain, food, water, hair, skin*] gras/grasse; **his hands are ~** il a les mains pleines de graisse; **2** (in consistency) [*substance, dressing*] huileux/-euse; [*lotion*] gras/grasse; **3** péj (slimy) [*person, manner, tone*] onctueux/-euse.
oink /ɔɪŋk/ **I** *n* onomat *cri du cochon*.
II *vi* [*pig*] grogner.
ointment /ˈɔɪntmənt/ *n* pommade *f*.
IDIOMS **she's the fly in the ~** c'est elle l'empêcheuse de tourner en rond; **there's one fly in the ~** il y a un os○.
o.i.r.o. GB (*abrév écrite* = **offers in the region of**) **~ £75,000** 75 000 livres à débattre.
Oise **▶1163** *pr n* Oise *f*; **in/to the ~** dans l'Oise.
OK 1 = **okay**; **2** US Post *abrév écrite* = **Oklahoma**.
okapi /əʊˈkɑːpɪ/ *n* okapi *m*.
okay, **OK**○ /ˌəʊˈkeɪ/ **I** *n* accord *m*; **to give one's ~ to sb/sth** donner son accord à qn/qch; **to give sth the ~** donner le feu vert à qch; **to give sb the ~ to do** donner le feu vert à qn pour faire.
II *adj* **1** [*car, colour, party, holiday, job*] pas mal○; [*plumber, babysitter*] bien (*inv*); **it's ~ to do** il n'y a pas de mal à faire; **it's ~ by me/him** ça ne me/le dérange pas; **is it ~ if...?** est-ce que ça va si ...?; **to be ~ for time/money** avoir assez de temps/d'argent; **he's ~** il est sympa○; **'is he a good teacher?'—'yes, he's ~'** 'c'est un bon prof?'—'oui, il est bien'; **to feel ~** aller bien; **'how are you?'—'~'** 'comment vas-tu?'—'ça va'; **'how was the meeting/interview/exam?'—'~'** 'comment as-tu trouvé la réunion/l'entretien/l'examen?'—'ça s'est bien passé'; **'how was the match?'—'~'** 'comment as-tu trouvé le match?'—'pas mal'; **'is my hat/hair ~?'** 'ça va mon chapeau/mes cheveux○?'; **2** (acceptable) **that's ~ for men, but...** ça passe encore pour les hommes, mais...; **that may be ~ in other countries/in your house, but...** ça se passe peut être dans d'autres pays/chez toi, mais...; **it's ~ to call him by his nickname** tu peux l'appeler par son petit nom; **it's ~ to refuse drugs** on a le droit de dire non à la drogue; **3** (in agreement, confirmation) [*reply, signal*] d'accord.
III *adv* [*cope, drive, ski, work out*] (assez) bien.
IV *particle* **1** (giving agreement) d'accord; **2** (seeking consensus) d'accord?, ça va?; **3** (seeking information) bon d'accord; **~, whose idea was this?** bon d'accord, qui a eu cette idée?; **4** (introducing topic) bien; **~, let's move on to...** bien, passons à...; **~, now turn to page 26** bon, prenez la page 26 maintenant.
V *vtr* approuver [*change, plan*].
okey-doke(y)○ /ˌəʊkɪˈdəʊkɪ/ *particle* OK○, d'accord.
Okie○ /ˈəʊkɪ/ *n* US *résident de l'Oklahoma*.
Oklahoma /ˌəʊkləˈhəʊmə/ **▶1744** *pr n* Oklahoma *m*; **in ~** dans l'Oklahoma.
okra /ˈəʊkrə/ *n* Bot, Culin okra *m*, gombo *m*.
old /əʊld/ **▶971** **I** *n* **1** (old people) **the ~** (+ *v pl*) les personnes *fpl* âgées; **~ and young together** jeunes et vieux ensemble; **2** (earlier era) **(in days) of ~** (au temps) jadis; **the knights of ~** les chevaliers d'antan; **I know him of ~** je le connais depuis longtemps.
II *adj* **1** (elderly, not young) vieux/vieille, âgé; **an ~ man** un vieil homme, un vieillard; **~ people** les vieux; **~er people** les personnes âgées; **if I live to be ~** si je vis vieux; **to get** ou **grow ~** vieillir, se faire vieux/vieille; **to look ~** avoir l'air âgé; **~ before one's time** vieux avant l'âge; **grief has made her ~ before her time** le chagrin l'a vieillie avant l'âge; **do you want ~ Mr Salter or young Mr Salter?** est-ce que vous voulez le père ou le fils Salter?; **2** (of a particular age) **how ~ are you/is he?** quel âge as-tu/a-t-il?; **no-one knows how ~ this tree is** personne ne connaît l'âge de

cet arbre; **she is 10 years ~** elle a 10 ans; **a six-year-~ boy** un garçon (âgé) de six ans; **a six-year ~** un enfant (âgé) de six ans; **when you were one year ~** quand tu avais un an; **this bread is a week ~** ce pain est vieux d'une semaine; **a centuries-~ tradition** une tradition vieille de plusieurs siècles; **to be as ~ as sb/as the century** avoir le même âge que qn/que le siècle; **I'm ~er than you** je suis plus âgé que toi; **she is 10 years ~er than him** elle a 10 ans de plus que lui; **the north wing is 100 years ~er than the east wing** l'aile nord a été construite 100 ans avant l'aile est; **my ~er brother/sister** mon frère aîné/ma sœur aînée; **an ~er man/woman** un homme/une femme plus âgé/-e; **the ~er children play here** les grands jouent ici; **I'll tell you when you're ~er** je te le dirai quand tu seras plus grand; **he's going to be handsome when he's ~er** ce sera un beau jeune homme plus tard; **as you get ~er you learn what really matters** en vieillissant on apprend ce qui est vraiment important; **I'm the ~est** c'est moi l'aîné/-e; **the ~est person there was 18** la personne la plus âgée de l'assemblée avait 18 ans; **~ enough to be your father/mother** assez vieux/vieille pour être ton père/ta mère; **to be ~ enough to do** être en âge de faire; **you're ~ enough to know better** à ton âge tu devrais avoir plus de bon sens; **you're too ~ for silly games** ces jeux stupides ne sont plus de ton âge; **he's too ~ for you** il est trop vieux pour toi; **that dress is too ~ for you** cette robe fait trop vieux pour toi; **to be ~ for one's age** être mûr pour son âge; **3** (not new) [*garment, object, car, song, tradition, family*] vieux/vieille; [*story, excuse*] classique; [*joke*] rebattu; **an ~ friend** un vieil ami; **the ~ town** la vieille ville; **an ~ firm** une maison établie depuis longtemps; **4** (former, previous) [*address, school, job, boss, admirer, system*] ancien/-ienne (*before n*); **there's our ~ house** voilà notre ancienne maison; **where is her ~ confidence?** où est passée son ancienne assurance?; **do you see much of the ~ crowd**○? est-ce que tu en vois beaucoup de notre vieille bande○?; **in the ~ days** autrefois, dans le temps; **just like ~ times** comme au bon vieux temps; **in the good ~ days** au bon vieux temps; **5**○ (as term of affection) vieux/vieille; **there was ~ Jim** il y avait ce bon vieux Jim○; **there's ~ Fido** voilà ce brave vieux Fido○; **dear ~ Max** ce cher vieux Max○; **good ~ Jon!** ce bon vieux Jon○!; **good ~ British weather!** iron ce sacré○ climat anglais!; **hello, ~ chap/girl**†! salut, mon vieux/ma vieille○!; **how are you, you ~ devil**○? ça va, vieux○?; **6**○ (as intensifier) **a right ~ battle/mess** une sacrée bataille/pagaille○; **they were having a high** ou **rare ~ time** ils s'amusaient comme des fous○; **just put them down any ~ how/where** mets-les n'importe comment/où; **I don't want just any ~ doctor/any ~ car** je ne veux pas de n'importe quel docteur/n'importe quelle voiture; **any ~ tie will do** n'importe quelle cravate fera l'affaire.

■ Note The irregular form *vieil* of the adjective vieux/vieille is used before masculine nouns beginning with a vowel or a mute 'h'.

old age *n* vieillesse *f*; **in (one's) ~** sur ses vieux jours.

old: **~-age pension** *n* GB Soc Admin pension *f* de retraite; **~-age pensioner, OAP** *n* GB retraité/-e *m/f*; **Old Bailey** *pr n* cour *f* d'assises de Londres; **Old Bill**○ *n* GB police *f*.

old boy *n* **1** (ex-pupil) ancien élève *m*; **2**○ (old man) vieux *m*; **3**○† (dear chap) (mon) vieux *m*.

old: **~ boy network** *n* GB réseau *m* des anciens élèves des écoles privées; **~ country** *n* mère *f* patrie; **Old Dominion** *n* US Virginie *f*.

olden /'əʊldən/ *adj* **in ~ times, in the ~ days** autrefois, jadis; **tell us about the ~ days** parle-nous de l'ancien temps.

old: **Old English** *n* vieil anglais *m*; **Old English sheepdog** *n* bobtail *m*; **~-established** *adj* ancien/-ienne, établi depuis longtemps.

olde-worlde /ˌəʊld'wɜːld/ *adj* hum ou péj pseudo-ancien/-ienne.

old-fashioned /ˌəʊld'fæʃnd/ **I** *n* US cocktail *m* à base de whisky.
II *adj* [*person, ways, manners*] vieux jeu *inv*; [*idea, attitude, garment, machine*] à l'ancienne, démodé pej; **good ~ common sense** le bon vieux sens commun.

old: **~-fashioned look** *n* regard *m* dubitatif; **~ favourite** *n* (song, film) succès *m* de toujours; (book, play) classique *m*; **~ flame**○ *n* ancien béguin *m*; **~ fogey** GB, **~ fogy**○ US *n* vieux/vieille réactionnaire *mf*; **~ folks' home**○ *n* = **old people's home**; **Old French** *n* ancien français *m*.

old girl *n* **1** (ex-pupil) ancienne élève *f*; **2**○ (old lady) (petite) vieille *f*; **3**○† (dear lady) (ma) vieille○.

old: **Old Glory** *pr n* drapeau *m* des États-Unis; **~ gold** *n, adj* vieil or (*m*) *inv*; **~ guard** *n* vieille *f* garde.

old hand *n* vieux routier *m*; **to be an ~ at sth/at doing** s'y connaître en qch/à faire.

old hat○ *adj* dépassé.

oldie○ /'əʊldɪ/ *n* **1** (film, song) vieux succès *m*; **2** (person) ancien/-ienne *m/f*.

old lady *n* **1** (elderly woman) vieille dame *f*; **2**○ (wife) **my/his/the ~** ma/sa/la bourgeoise○; **3**○ (mother) **my ~** ma maternelle○ or vieille○.

old lag○ /ˌəʊld'læg/ *n* **1** (prisoner) récidiviste *mf*; **2** GB (experienced person) vieux routier *m*.

old: **Old Latin** *n* latin *m* classique; **~ maid** *n* péj vieille fille *f* pej.

old man *n* **1** (elderly man) vieil homme *m*, vieillard *m*; **2**○ (husband) **my/her ~** mon/son homme○; **3**○ (father) **my ~** mon paternel○, mon vieux○; **4**○† (dear chap) (mon) vieux○; **5**○ (boss) **the ~** le patron○, le singe○.

old man's beard *n* Bot clématite *f* des haies.

old master *n* **1** (artist) maître *m* ancien; **2** (work) tableau *m* de maître ancien.

old: **Old Nick**○† *n* le Malin; **~ people's home** *n* (state-run) hospice *m*; (private) maison *f* de retraite; **~ rose** *n, adj* vieux rose (*m*) *inv*; **~ school tie** *n* GB lit cravate *f* aux couleurs d'une école; fig copinage *m* des anciens élèves; **~ sod**○ *n* hum mère *f* patrie.

old soldier *n* **1** (former soldier) ancien combattant *m*; **2** (old hand) vieux routier *m*.

old: **Old South** *n* US Hist Sud *m* d'avant la guerre de Sécession; **~ stager**○ *n* GB ancien/-ienne *m/f*.

oldster○ /'əʊldstə(r)/ *n* ancien/-ienne *m/f*.

old: **~ style** *adj* ancien style (*after n*); **Old Style** *adj* [*date*] d'après le calendrier julien; **Old Testament** *n* Ancien Testament *m*; **~-time** *adj* du temps jadis; **~-time dancing** *n* danses *fpl* de salon; **~-timer**○ *n* ancien/-ienne *m/f*; **~ wives' tale** *n* conte *m* de bonne femme.

old woman *n* **1** (elderly lady) vieille femme *f*, vieille *f*; **2** péj (man) **to be an ~** avoir des manies de petite vieille; **3**○ (wife) **my** ou **the ~** la patronne○, la bourgeoise○; **4**○ (mother) **my** ou **the ~** ma maternelle○, ma vieille○.

old: **~-world** *adj* [*cottage, charm, courtesy*] d'autrefois; **Old World** *n* Vieux monde *m*.

ole○ /əʊl/ *adj* = **old**.

oleaginous /ˌəʊlɪ'ædʒɪnəs/ *adj* oléagineux/-euse.

oleander /ˌəʊlɪ'ændə(r)/ *n* laurier-rose *m*.

olefin(e) /'əʊlɪfaɪn/ *n* oléfine *f*.

oleo /'əʊlɪəʊ/ *n* US *abrév* = **oleomargarine**.

oleomargarine /ˌəʊlɪəʊˌmɑːdʒə'riːn, -'mɑːdʒərɪn/ *n* US margarine *f*.

O level *n* GB (*abrév* = **Ordinary level**) *examen que l'on passait en fin de 1er cycle du secondaire, remplacé par le GCSE*.

olfactory /ɒl'fæktərɪ/ *adj* olfactif/-ive.

oligarchic(al) /ˌɒlɪ'gɑːkɪk(l)/ *adj* oligarchique.

oligarchy /'ɒlɪgɑːkɪ/ *n* oligarchie *f*.

Oligocene /'ɒlɪgəsiːn/ *n, adj* oligocène (*m*).

oligopoly /ˌɒlɪ'gɒpəlɪ/ *n* oligopole *m*.

olive /'ɒlɪv/ **I** *n* **1** (fruit) olive *f*; **green/black ~** olive verte/noire; **2** (also **~ tree**) olivier *m*; **3** (colour) vert *m* olive.
II *adj* [*dress, eyes*] vert olive *inv*; [*complexion*] olivâtre.
IDIOMS **to hold out** ou **extend an ~ branch to** fig tendre la main à; **to be intended as an ~ branch** être une main tendue.

olive: **~ drabs** *npl* vert *m* d'armée; **~ green** ▶ **1104** *n, adj* vert (*m*) olive (*inv*); **~ grove** *n* oliveraie *f*; **~ oil** *n* huile *f* d'olive; **~ press** *n* pressoir *m* à olives; **~-skinned** *adj* au teint olivâtre.

Olympia /ə'lɪmpɪə/ *pr n* Olympie *f*.

Olympiad /ə'lɪmpɪæd/ *pr n* Olympiades *fpl*.

Olympian /ə'lɪmpɪən/ *adj* [*god, hero*] de l'Olympe; [*calm*] olympien/-ienne.

Olympic /ə'lɪmpɪk/ **I** *n* **the ~s** les jeux Olympiques.
II *adj* [*torch, athlete, medal*] olympique.

Olympic Games *npl* jeux *m* Olympiques.

Olympus /ə'lɪmpəs/ *pr n* Olympe *m*.

OM *n* (*abrév* = **Order of Merit**) ≈ OM *m*.

Oman /əʊ'mɑːn/ ▶ **1131** *pr n* Oman *m*.

Omani /əʊ'mɑːnɪ/ ▶ **1438** **I** *n* Omanais/-e *m/f*.
II *adj* omanais.

ombudsman /'ɒmbʊdzmən/ *n* Admin médiateur *m*.

omega /'əʊmɪgə, US əʊ'megə/ *n* oméga *m*.

omelette /'ɒmlɪt/ *n* omelette *f*.
IDIOMS **you can't make an ~ without breaking eggs** on ne fait pas d'omelette sans casser d'œufs.

omen /'əʊmən/ *n* présage *m*.

omentum /əʊ'mentəm/ *n* (*pl* **-ta**) Med épiploon *m*.

ominous /'ɒmɪnəs/ *adj* [*presence, shadow, cloud*] menaçant; [*development, news*] inquiétant; [*sign*] de mauvais augure.

ominously /'ɒmɪnəslɪ/ *adv* **1** (threateningly) [*look, gesture, move*] de façon menaçante; [*say*] d'un ton menaçant; **the house was ~ silent** dans la maison régnait un silence menaçant; **2** (worryingly) **~, the child has not yet been found** on n'a pas encore retrouvé l'enfant, ce qui ne présage rien de bon.

omission /ə'mɪʃn/ *n* **1** gen, Jur omission *f*; **2** (from list, team) absence *f*.

omit /ə'mɪt/ *vtr* (*p prés etc* **-tt-**) omettre (**from** de; **to do** de faire).

omnibus /'ɒmnɪbəs/ **I** *n* **1** (also **~ edition**) GB (of TV programme) *rediffusion des épisodes de la semaine*; **2** (also **~ volume**) (book) recueil *m*; **3**† (bus) omnibus† *m*.
II *adj* US de portée générale.
IDIOMS **the man on the Clapham ~** GB† Monsieur tout le monde.

omnibus bill *n* US Pol *projet de loi comprenant des mesures diverses*.

omnidirectional /ˌɒmnɪdɪ'rekʃənl, -daɪ-/ *adj* omnidirectionnel/-elle.

omnipotence /ɒm'nɪpətəns/ *n* omnipotence *f*, toute-puissance *f*.

omnipotent /ɒm'nɪpətənt/ **I** *pr n* **the Omnipotent** le Tout-Puissant.
II *adj* omnipotent, tout-puissant.

omnipresence /ˌɒmnɪ'prezns/ *n* omniprésence *f*.

omnipresent /ˌɒmnɪ'preznt/ *adj* omniprésent.

omniscience /ɒm'nɪsɪəns/ *n* omniscience *f*.

omniscient /ɒmˈnɪsɪənt/ *adj* omniscient.

omnivore /ˈɒmnɪvɔː(r)/ *n* omnivore *mf*.

omnivorous /ɒmˈnɪvərəs/ *adj* **1** lit omnivore; **2** fig [*reader*] curieux/-ieuse de tout.

omphalos /ˈɒmfəlɒs/ *n* littér nombril *m*.

on /ɒn/

■ **Note** When *on* is used as a straightforward preposition expressing position (*on the beach, on the table*) it is generally translated by *sur*: sur la plage, sur la table; *on it* is translated by dessus: *there's a table over there, put the key on it* = il y a une table là-bas, mets la clé dessus.
– *on* is often used in verb combinations in English (*depend on, rely on, cotton on etc*). For translations, consult the appropriate verb entry (***depend, rely, cotton*** etc).
– If you have doubts about how to translate a phrase or expression beginning with *on* (*on demand, on impulse, on top etc*) consult the appropriate noun or other entry (***demand, impulse, top*** etc).
– This dictionary contains Usage Notes on such topics as dates, islands, rivers etc. Many of these use the preposition *on*. For the index to these notes ▶ **1919**.
– For examples of the above and further uses of *on*, see the entry below.

I *prep* **1** (position) sur; **~ the table/the pavement** sur la table/le trottoir; **~ the coast/the lake** sur la côte/le lac; **~ top of the piano** sur le piano; **~ the wall/ceiling/blackboard** au mur/plafond/tableau noir; **~ the floor** par terre; **there's a stain ~ it** il y a une tache dessus; **to live ~ Park Avenue** habiter Park Avenue; **it's ~ Carson Road** c'est sur Carson Road; **~ the M4 motorway** sur l'autoroute M4; **a studio ~ Avenue Montaigne** un studio Avenue Montaigne; **the paintings ~ the wall** les tableaux qui sont au mur; **accidents ~ and off the piste** des accidents sur la piste et en dehors; **to climb/leap ~ to sth** grimper/sauter sur qch; ▶ **get, hang, jump, pin, sew, tie**; **2** (indicating attachment, contact) **to hang sth ~ a nail** accrocher qch à un clou; **~ a string** au bout d'une or attaché à une ficelle; **to put a hand ~ sb's shoulder** mettre la main sur l'épaule de qn; **to punch sb ~ the nose/on the chin** donner un coup dans le nez/sur le menton de qn; ▶ **hit, pat, slap**; **3** (on or about one's person) **I've got no small change ~ me** je n'ai pas de monnaie sur moi; **have you got the keys ~ you?** est-ce que tu as les clés (sur toi)?; **to have a ring ~ one's finger** avoir une bague au doigt; **the finger with the ring ~ it** le doigt qui porte la bague; **a girl with sandals ~ her feet** une fille avec des sandales aux pieds; **to have a smile/to have a frown ~ one's face** sourire/froncer les sourcils; **4** (about, on the subject of) sur; **a book/a programme ~ Africa** un livre/une émission sur l'Afrique; **information ~ the new tax** des renseignements sur le nouvel impôt; **to read Freud ~ dreams** lire ce que Freud a écrit sur les rêves; **have you heard him ~ electoral reform?** est-ce que tu l'as entendu parler de la réforme électorale?; **we're ~ fractions in maths** en maths, nous en sommes aux fractions; **5** (employed, active) **to be ~** faire partie de [*team*]; être membre de [*board, committee, council*]; **to be ~ the Gazette** travailler pour la Gazette; **a job ~ the railways** un travail dans les chemins de fer; **there's a bouncer ~ the door** il y a un videur à la porte; **there are 20 staff ~ this project** il y a 20 personnes qui travaillent sur ce projet; **6** (in expressions of time) **~ 22 February** le 22 février; **~ Friday** vendredi; **~ Saturdays** le samedi; **~ the night of 15 May** la nuit du 15 mai; **~ or about the 23rd** vers le 23; **~ sunny days** quand il fait beau; **~ Christmas Day** le jour de Noël; **~ your birthday** le jour de ton anniversaire; ▶ **dot, hour**; **7** (immediately after) **~ his arrival** à son arrivée; **~ the death of his wife** à la mort de sa femme; **~ hearing the truth she**... quand elle a appris la vérité, elle...; **~ reaching London he**... quand il est arrivé à Londres, il...; **8** (taking, using) **to be ~ tablets/steroids/heroin** prendre des médicaments/des stéroïdes/de l'héroïne; **to be ~ drugs** se droguer; **to be ~ 40 (cigarettes) a day** fumer 40 cigarettes par jour; **to be ~ a bottle of whisky a day** boire une bouteille de whisky par jour; ▶ **antibiotic, pill, tranquillizer**; **9** (powered by) **to work** ou **run ~ batteries** marcher à piles, fonctionner sur piles; **to run ~ electricity** être électrique; **10** (indicating support) sur; **to stand ~ one leg** se tenir sur un pied; **to lie ~ one's back** s'allonger sur le dos; **put it ~ its side** pose-le sur le côté; **11** (indicating a medium) **~ TV/the radio** à la télé/radio; **I heard it ~ the news** j'ai entendu ça au journal; **~ video/cassette** en vidéo/cassette; **~ disk/computer** sur disquette/ordinateur; **~ channel four** sur la quatrième chaîne; **to play sth ~ the piano** jouer qch au piano; **with Lou Luciano ~ drums** avec Lou Luciano à la batterie; **12** (income, amount of money) **to be ~ £20,000 a year** gagner 20 000 livres sterling par an; **to be ~ a salary** ou **income of £15,000** gagner 15 000 livres sterling; **he's ~ more than me** il gagne plus que moi; **to be ~ a low income** avoir un bas salaire; ▶ **dole, grant, live¹, overtime**; **13** (paid for by, at the expense of) **this round is ~ me** c'est ma tournée; **have a beer ~ me** je te paye une bière; ▶ **credit, expenses, house**; **14** (repeated events) **disaster ~ disaster** désastre sur désastre; **defeat ~ defeat** défaite sur défaite; **15** (in scoring) **to be ~ 25 points** avoir 25 points; **Martin is the winner ~ 50 points** Martin est le gagnant avec 50 points; **16** Turf **he's got £10 ~ Easy Rider** il a parié 10 livres sterling sur Easy Rider; **I'll have 50 dollars ~ Rapido** je parie 50 dollars sur Rapido; ▶ **odds**; **17** Transp **to travel ~ the bus/train** voyager en bus/train; **to be ~ the plane/the train** être dans l'avion/le train; **to be ~ the yacht** être sur le yacht; **to be ~ one's bike** être à vélo; **to leave ~ the first train/flight** prendre le premier train/avion; ▶ **foot, horseback**.

II *adj* **1** (taking place, happening) **to be ~** [*event*] avoir lieu; **is the match still ~?** est-ce que le match aura lieu? ; **the engagement is back ~ again** ils sont à nouveau fiancés; **while the meeting is ~** pendant la réunion; **there's a war/recession ~** il y a une guerre/récession; **I've got nothing ~ tonight** je n'ai rien de prévu pour ce soir; **to have something ~** avoir quelque chose de prévu; **I've got a lot ~** je suis très occupé; **2** (being broadcast, performed, displayed) **Euro-express is ~ tonight** il y a Euro-express à la télé ce soir; **the news is ~ in 10 minutes** le journal est dans 10 minutes; **it's ~ at the Rex** ça passe au Rex; **there's an exhibition ~ at the Town Hall** il y a une exposition à la mairie; **what's ~?** (on TV) qu'est-ce qu'il y a à la télé?; (at the cinema) qu'est-ce qui passe au cinéma?; (at the theatre) qu'est-ce qu'il y a à l'affiche or au théâtre?; **there's nothing ~** il n'y a rien de bien; **Hamlet is still ~** Hamlet est toujours à l'affiche; **3** (functional, live) **to be ~** [*TV, oven, heating, light*] être allumé; [*handbrake*] être serré; [*dishwasher, radio, washing machine*] marcher; [*hot tap, gas tap*] être ouvert; **the power is ~** il y a du courant; **the power is back ~** le courant est rétabli; **the switch is in the '~' position** l'interrupteur est en position 'allumé'; ▶ **switch on, turn on**; **4** GB (permissible) **it's just** ou **simply not ~** (out of the question) c'est hors de question; (not the done thing) ça ne se fait pas; (unacceptable) c'est inadmissible; **it's simply not ~ to expect me to do that** c'est inadmissible de penser que je vais faire ça; **5** (attached, in place) **to be ~** [*lid, top, cap*] être mis; **the cap isn't properly ~** le couvercle est mal mis; **once the roof is ~** une fois le toit construit ; ▶ **put, screw**.

III *adv* **1** (on or about one's person) **to have a hat/coat ~** porter un chapeau/manteau; **to have one's glasses ~** porter ses lunettes; **he's got his suit ~** il est en costume; **to have nothing ~** être nu, ne rien avoir sur le dos; **~ with your coats!** allez, mettez vos manteaux!; **to have make-up ~** être maquillé; **with sandals/slippers ~** en sandales/pantoufles; ▶ **put, try**; **2** (ahead in time) **20 years ~ he was still the same** 20 ans plus tard, il n'avait pas changé; **a few years ~ from now** dans quelques années; **from that day ~** à partir de ce jour-là; **to be well ~ in years** ne plus être tout jeune; **the party lasted well ~ into the night** la soirée s'est prolongée tard dans la nuit; ▶ **later, now**; **3** (further) **to walk ~** continuer à marcher; **to walk ~ another 2 km** faire encore 2 km; **to go ~ to Newcastle** continuer jusqu'à Newcastle; **to go to Paris then ~ to Marseilles** aller à Paris et de là à Marseille; **to play/work ~** continuer à jouer/travailler; **a little further ~** un peu plus loin; ▶ **carry, go, move, press, read**; **4** (on stage) **I'm ~ after the juggler** je passe juste après le jongleur; **he's not ~ until Act II** il n'entre en scène qu'au deuxième acte; **you're ~!** en scène!

IV on and off *adv phr* (also **off and on**) **to see sb ~ and off** voir qn de temps en temps; **she's been working at the novel ~ and off for years** ça fait des années que son roman est en chantier; **he lives there ~ and off** il y habite de temps en temps; **to flash ~ and off** clignoter.

V on and on *adv phr* **to go ~ and ~** [*speaker*] parler pendant des heures; [*lectures, speech*] durer des heures; **he went** ou **talked ~ and ~ about the war** il n'a pas arrêté de parler de la guerre; **the list goes ~ and ~** la liste n'en finit pas.

IDIOMS **you're ~** d'accord; **are you still ~ for tomorrow's party?** c'est toujours d'accord pour la soirée de demain?; **to be always ~ at sb** être toujours sur le dos de qn; **she's always ~ at me to get my hair cut** elle est toujours sur mon dos pour que je me fasse couper les cheveux; **what's he ~ about?** GB qu'est-ce qu'il raconte?; **I don't know what you're ~ about** je ne sais pas de quoi tu parles; **he's been ~ to me about the lost files** GB il m'a contacté à propos des dossiers perdus. ▶ **get, go, put**.

onanism /ˈəʊnənɪzəm/ *n* onanisme *m*.

once /wʌns/ **I** *n* **I've only been there the ~** je n'y suis allé qu'une seule fois; **I'll do it just this ~** je le fais pour cette fois; **for ~** pour une fois.

II *adv* **1** (one time) une fois; **~ or twice** une ou deux fois; **~ before** une fois déjà; **more than ~** plus d'une fois, à plusieurs reprises; **I will tell you ~ only** je ne te le dirai qu'une seule fois, je ne te le dirai pas deux fois○; **if I've told you ~ I've told you a hundred times** si je ne te l'ai pas dit cent fois je ne te l'ai pas dit une fois○; **~ is enough** une fois suffit; **~ again** ou **more** encore une fois, une fois de plus; **~ and for all** une bonne fois pour toutes; **never ~ did he offer** ou **he never ~ offered to help** il ne s'est pas une seule fois proposé pour aider; **~ released, he**... une fois libéré, il...; **~ too often** une fois de trop; **~ a day/year** une fois par jour/an; **~ every six months** une fois tous les six mois; **(every) ~ in a while** de temps en temps; **~ in a lifetime** une fois dans la vie; **it was a ~-in-a-lifetime experience** c'était une expérience unique; **you only live ~** on ne vit qu'une fois; **if ~ you forget the code** si jamais vous oubliez le code; **~ a Catholic, always a Catholic** qui a été catholique le restera toute sa vie; **~ a thief, always a thief** qui a volé, volera; **2** (formerly) autrefois, jadis; **she was ~ very**

famous (autrefois) elle a été très célèbre; **a ~ famous actor** un acteur autrefois célèbre; **I'm not as young as I ~ was** je ne suis plus très jeune; **there was ~ a time when he would have said yes** il fut un temps où il aurait dit oui; **~ upon a time there was a queen** il était une fois une reine.

III at once *adv phr* **1** (immediately) tout de suite; **all at ~** tout d'un coup; **2** (simultaneously) à la fois, en même temps; **don't all talk at ~!** ne parlez pas tous en même temps or tous à la fois!

IV *conj* une fois que, dès que; **~ he had eaten he...** une fois qu'il eut mangé il...; **~ he arrives we...** une fois qu'il arrivera nous...

once-over○ /ˈwʌnsəʊvə(r)/ *n* **1** (quick look) **to give sth the ~** jeter un rapide coup d'œil à qch; **to give sb the ~** gen évaluer qn au premier coup d'œil; (check-up) faire un rapide bilan de santé à qn; **2** (quick clean) **to give sth a quick ~** (with duster) donner un coup de chiffon à qch; (with vacuum cleaner) donner un coup d'aspirateur à qch.

oncologist /ɒŋˈkɒlədʒɪst/ *n* oncologue *mf*, oncologiste *mf*.

oncology /ɒŋˈkɒlədʒɪ/ *n* oncologie *f*.

oncoming /ˈɒnkʌmɪŋ/ *adj* **1** [*car, vehicle*] venant en sens inverse; **'beware of ~ traffic'** 'circulation dans les deux sens'; **2** [*event, election*] imminent.

oncosts /ˈɒnkɒsts/ *npl* Comm frais *mpl* généraux.

OND *n* (*abrév* = **Ordinary National Diploma**) *diplôme d'enseignement technique de fin d'études secondaires.*

one /wʌn/ ▶ 1505, 971, 1096

■ **Note** When *one* is used as a personal pronoun it is translated by *on* when it is the subject of the verb: *one never knows* = on ne sait jamais. When *one* is the object of the verb or comes after a preposition it is usually translated by *vous*: *it can make one ill* = cela peut vous rendre malade.
– For more examples and all other uses, see the entry below.

I *det* **1** (single) un/une; **~ car** une voiture; **~ dog** un chien; **twenty-~ flowers** vingt et une fleurs; **to raise ~ hand** lever la main; **no ~ person can do it alone** personne ne peut faire cela tout seul; **2** (unique, sole) seul; **my ~ and only tie** ma seule et unique cravate; **her ~ vice/pleasure** son seul vice/plaisir; **she's the ~ person who can help** c'est la seule personne qui puisse nous aider; **the ~ and only Edith Piaf** l'incomparable Edith Piaf; **she's ~ fine artist** US c'est une très grande artiste; ▶**hell**; **3** (same) même; **in the ~ direction** dans la même direction; **at ~ and the same time** en même temps; **to be ~ and the same thing** être exactement la même chose; **they're ~ and the same person** il s'agit de la même personne; **two offers in the ~ day** deux offres dans la même journée; **to be of ~ mind** être d'accord; **it's all ~ to me** ça m'est égal; **4** (in expressions of time) **~ day/evening** un jour/soir; **~ hot summer's day** par une chaude journée d'été; **~ of these days** un de ces jours; **5** (for emphasis) **~ Simon Richard** un certain Simon Richard.

II *pron* **1** (indefinite) un/une *m/f*; **can you lend me ~?** tu peux m'en prêter un/une?; **~ of them** (person) l'un d'eux/l'une d'elles; (thing) l'un/l'une *m/f*; **she's ~ of my best customers** c'est une de mes meilleures clientes; **~ after the other** l'un/l'une après l'autre; **I can't tell ~ from the other** je ne peux pas les distinguer (l'un de l'autre); **every ~ of them was broken** ils étaient tous cassés sans exception; **~ was grey and the other was pink** l'un était gris et l'autre était rose; **two volumes in ~** deux tomes en un volume; **it's a two-in-~ whisk and blender** cela fait à la fois batteur et mixeur; **Merry Christmas ~ and all** Joyeux Noël à tous; **she's ~ of us** elle est des nôtres; ▶**any**; **2** (impersonal) (as subject) on; (as object) vous; **~ would like to think that** on aimerait penser que; **~ can't help wondering** on ne peut pas s'empêcher de se demander; **if ~ wanted** si on voulait; **it's enough to make ~ despair** cela suffit pour vous démoraliser; **3** (referring to a specific person) **the advice of ~ who knows** les conseils de quelqu'un qui s'y connaît; **for ~ who claims to be an expert** pour quelqu'un qui prétend être expert; **like ~ possessed** comme un possédé; **I'm not ~ for doing** ce n'est pas mon genre de faire; **she's a great ~ for doing** elle est très douée pour faire; **I'm not ~ for football** je ne suis pas amateur de foot; **he's ~ for the ladies** c'est un homme à femmes; **she's a clever ~** elle est intelligente; **you're a ~**○**!** toi alors!; **I for ~ think that** personnellement or pour ma part je crois que; **'who disagrees?'—'I for ~!'** 'qui n'est pas d'accord?'—'moi'; ▶**never**; **4** (demonstrative) **the grey ~** le gris/la grise; **the pink ~s** les roses; **my friend's ~** celui/celle de mon ami; **this ~** celui-ci/celle-ci; **that ~** celui-là/celle-là; **the ~ in the corner** celui/celle qui est dans le coin; **which ~?** lequel/laquelle?; **that's the ~** c'est celui-là/celle-là; **he's the ~ who** c'est lui qui; **buy the smallest ~** achète le/la plus petit/-e; **my new car is faster than the old ~** ma nouvelle voiture est plus rapide que l'ancienne; **5** (in currency) **~-fifty** (in sterling) une livre cinquante; (in dollars) un dollar cinquante; **6**○ (drink) **he's had ~ too many** il a bu un coup○ de trop; **a quick ~** un pot○ en vitesse; **make mine a large ~** sers-moi un grand verre; ▶**road**; **7**○ (joke) **that's a good ~!** elle est bien bonne celle-là!; **have you heard the ~ about...?** est-ce que tu connais l'histoire de...?; **8**○ (blow) **to land** ou **sock sb ~** en coller une à qn○; **9**○ (question, problem) **that's a tough** ou **tricky ~** c'est une colle○; **ask me another ~** pose-moi une autre question; **10** (person one is fond of) **her loved** ou **dear ~s** ceux qui lui sont chers; **to lose a loved ~** perdre un être cher; **the little ~s** les petits; **11** (in knitting) **knit ~, purl ~** une maille à l'endroit, une maille à l'envers; **make ~** faire une augmentation.

III *n* (number) un *m*; **~, two, three, go!** un, deux, trois, partez!; **to throw a ~** (on dice) faire un un; **there are three ~s in one hundred and eleven** il y a trois fois le chiffre un dans cent onze; **~ o'clock** une heure; **to arrive in ~s and twos** arriver par petits groupes.

IV as one *adv phr* [*rise*] comme un seul homme; [*shout, reply*] tous ensemble.

V in one *adv phr* **to down a drink in ~** boire un verre cul sec○; **you've got it in ~** tu as trouvé tout de suite.

VI one by one *adv phr* [*pick up, collect, wash*] un par un/une par une.

IDIOMS **to be ~ up on sb**○ avoir un avantage sur qn; **to be at ~ with sb** être en accord avec qn; **to go ~ better than sb** faire mieux que qn; **to give sb ~**◐ se faire qn◐; **to be a dictionary and grammar all in ~** ou **all rolled into ~** être à la fois un dictionnaire et une grammaire; **all for ~ and ~ for all** un pour tous et tous pour un; **to have a thousand** ou **million and ~ things to do** avoir un tas de choses à faire.

one-act play *n* pièce *f* en un seul acte.

one another

■ **Note** *one another* is very often translated by using a reflexive pronoun (*nous, vous, se, s'*).
– For examples and particular usages see the entry below.

pron **they love ~** ils s'aiment; **to help ~** s'aider mutuellement, s'entraider; **we often use ~'s cars** souvent nous échangeons nos voitures; **to worry about ~** s'inquiéter l'un pour l'autre; **separated from ~** séparés l'un de l'autre; **close to ~** proches l'un de l'autre.

one: **~-armed** *adj* manchot; **~-armed bandit** *n* machine *f* à sous, jackpot *m*; **~-day** *adj* [*international, seminar*] d'une journée.

one-dimensional /ˌwʌndɪˈmenʃənl/ *adj* **1** gen, Math [*array, image*] unidimensionnel/-elle; **2** fig (superficial) [*treatment*] superficiel/-ielle; **to be ~** [*character*] Literat manquer d'épaisseur.

one-eyed /ˈwʌnaɪd/ *adj* borgne; **a ~ man/woman** un/une borgne.

one-for-one *adj* = **one-to-one** 2.

one-handed /ˌwʌnˈhændɪd/ **I** *adj* [*person*] manchot; [*tool*] utilisable d'une seule main.
II *adv* [*catch, hold*] d'une seule main.

one-horse town○ *n* bled○ *m*, trou○ *m*.

one-legged /ˌwʌnˈlegɪd/ *adj* unijambiste; **a ~ man/woman** un/une unijambiste.

one: **~-line** *adj* d'une seule ligne; **~-liner** *n* bon mot *m*.

one-man /ˈwʌnmæn/ *adj* **1** (for one person) [*job*] pour lequel un seul homme suffit; **it's a ~ outfit** ou **operation** ou **company** il est tout seul; **she's a ~ woman** elle est fidèle en amour; **2** Sport [*bobsled*] monoplace.

one-man band *n* homme-orchestre *m*.

one-man show *n* **1** Theat one-man show *m*, spectacle *m* solo; **2** Art exposition *f* consacrée à un seul artiste; **3** fig (in business) **it's a ~**○ il est tout seul.

oneness /ˈwʌnnɪs/ *n* (unity) unité *f*; (uniformity) uniformité *f*.

one-night stand○ /ˌwʌnnaɪt ˈstænd/ *n* **1** (sexual) amour *m* de rencontre, aventure *f* d'un soir; **2** (of comic, singer) représentation *f* unique.

one-off /ˌwʌnˈɒf/ GB **I** *n* **to be a ~** [*TV programme*] ne pas faire partie d'une série; [*issue, magazine*] être un numéro spécial; [*design, order, object*] être unique; **it was a ~** (of event, accident) ça ne se reproduira pas.
II *adj* [*experiment, order, deal, design, performance*] unique; [*event, decision, offer, payment*] exceptionnel/-elle; [*example*] peu courant.

one: **~-on-one** *adj* = **one-to-one**; **~-parent family** *n* famille *f* monoparentale; **~-party system** *n* système *m* à parti unique.

one-piece /ˈwʌnpiːs/ *adj* gen, Tech d'une seule pièce; **~ swimsuit** maillot *m* de bain une pièce.

one: **~-price store** *n* magasin *m* à prix unique; **~-reeler** *n* Cin court-métrage *m*; **~-room flat**, **~-room apartment** *n* studio *m*.

onerous /ˈɒnərəs/ *adj* **1** [*task, workload, responsibility*] lourd; **2** Jur [*conditions, terms*] dur.

one's /wʌnz/

■ **Note** In French determiners agree in gender and number with the noun they qualify. So when *one's* is used as a determiner it is translated by *son* + masculine singular noun (*son argent*), by *sa* + feminine noun (*sa voiture*) BUT by *son* + feminine noun beginning with a vowel or mute h (*son assiette*) and by *ses* + plural noun (*ses enfants*).
– When *one's* is stressed, *à soi* is added after the noun.
– When *one's* is used as a reflexive pronoun it is translated by se or s' before a vowel or mute h: *to brush one's teeth* = se brosser les dents; ▶ 1037.
– For examples and particular usages see the entry below.

I = **one is, one has**.
II *det* son/sa/ses; **to wash ~ hands** se laver les mains; **~ books/friends** ses livres/amis; **one tries to do ~ best** on essaye de faire de son mieux; **it upsets ~ concentration** ça perturbe la concentration;

it limits ~ options ça limite les choix; **a house/car of ~ own** une maison/voiture à soi.

oneself /ˌwʌnˈself/

■ **Note** When used as a reflexive pronoun, direct and indirect, *oneself* is translated by *se* (or *s'* before a vowel): *to hurt oneself* = se blesser; *to enjoy oneself* = s'amuser.
– When used in emphasis the translation is *soi-même*: *to do something oneself* = faire quelque chose soi-même.
– After a preposition, the translation is *soi*.
– For particular usages see the entry below.

pron **1** (refl) se, s'; **to wash/cut ~** se laver/couper; **2** (for emphasis) soi-même; **3** (after prep) soi; **to be sure of ~** être sûr de soi; **to look pleased with ~** avoir l'air content de soi; **to have the house all to ~** avoir la maison pour soi tout seul/toute seule; **to talk to ~** parler tout seul/toute seule; **(all) by ~** tout seul/toute seule; ▶ **ashamed**, **keep**.

one-shot *adj* US = **one-off**.

one-sided /ˌwʌnˈsaɪdɪd/ *adj* **1** (biased) [*account*] partial; **2** (unequal) [*decision*] unilatéral; [*contest, fight, game*] inégal; [*bargain, deal*] inique; [*conversation, relationship*] à sens unique.

one: **~-size** *adj* [*garment*] taille unique; **~-stop shopping** *n*: *possibilité de faire tous ses achats dans le même centre commercial*; **~-time** *adj* ancien/-ienne (*before n*).

one-to-one /ˌwʌntəˈwʌn/ **I** *adj* **1** (private, personal) **~ meeting** tête-à-tête *m inv*; **~ session** gen, Psych face *m* à face; **~ tuition** cours *mpl* particuliers; **to teach on a ~ basis** donner des cours particuliers; **2** Math [*correspondence, mapping*] biunivoque; **3** Sport [*contest, fight*] à deux (*after n*); [*marking*] individuel/-elle.
II *adv* [*discuss*] en tête à tête; **to teach ~** donner des cours particuliers.

one-track /ˌwʌnˈtræk/ IDIOMS **to have a ~ mind** gen avoir une idée fixe; (sexually) être obsédé.

one-two○ /ˌwʌnˈtuː/ IDIOMS **to give sb the old ~** GB donner à qn un crochet de gauche suivi d'un crochet du droit or un une deux.

one-up○ /ˌwʌnˈʌp/ *vtr* (*p prés etc* **-pp-**) US surenchérir sur [*person*].

one-upmanship /ˌwʌnˈʌpmənʃɪp/ *n* art *m* de paraître supérieur aux autres; **to practise ~** faire de la surenchère sur les autres.

one-way /ˌwʌnˈweɪ/ **I** *adj* **1** Transp [*traffic, tunnel*] à sens unique; **~ street** ou **system** sens *m* unique; **2** (single) **~ ticket** aller *m* simple; **the ~ trip costs £300** l'aller simple coûte 300 livres sterling; **3** (not reciprocal) [*process, conversation*] à sens unique; [*friendship*] non partagé; [*transaction*] unilatéral; **4** Elec, Telecom [*cable, circuit*] unidirectionnel/-elle; **5** (nonrefundable) [*bottle*] non consigné; [*glass*] perdu; **6** (opaque in one direction) [*glass*] argus.
II *adv* **it costs £10 ~** l'aller simple coûte 10 livres sterling; **there's no give-and-take with him**○, **it's all ~** aucun échange n'est possible avec lui, c'est toujours à sens unique.

one-woman /ˌwʌnˈwʊmən/ *adj* [*job*] pour lequel une seule femme suffit; **it's a ~ outfit** ou **operation** ou **company** elle est toute seule; **he's a ~ man** il est fidèle en amour.

one-woman show *n* **1** Theat one-woman show *m*, spectacle *m* solo; **2** Art exposition *f* consacrée à une seule artiste; **3** fig (in business) **it's a ~**○ elle est toute seule.

ongoing /ˈɒngəʊɪŋ/ *adj* [*process*] continu; [*battle, saga*] continuel/-elle; **research is ~** des recherches sont en cours.

onion /ˈʌnjən/ *n* oignon *m*.
IDIOMS **to know one's ~s**○ GB connaître son affaire.

onion: **~ dome** *n* Archit dôme *m* bulbeux; **~ gravy** *n* sauce *f* à l'oignon; **~ rings** *npl* oignons *mpl* frits; **~skin** *n* (paper) papier *m* pelure; **~ soup** *n* soupe *f* à l'oignon.

on-line /ˌɒnˈlaɪn/ **I** *adj* Comput [*access*] direct; [*mode*] connecté; [*data processing*] en direct; [*storage*] en ligne; **~ data service** serveur *m* de données; **to be ~** [*computer*] être connecté or en ligne.
II on line *adv phr* **to have sth on line** avoir qch en accès direct or en ligne.

onlooker /ˈɒnlʊkə(r)/ *n* spectateur/-trice *m/f*.

only /ˈəʊnlɪ/ **I** *conj* (but) mais; **you can hold the baby, ~ don't drop him** tu peux tenir le bébé, mais surtout ne le lâche pas; **it's like hang-gliding ~ safer** c'est la même chose que le deltaplane mais en moins dangereux; **it's like a mouse ~ bigger** c'est comme une souris mais en plus gros; **I'd come ~ I'm working tonight** je viendrais bien mais ce soir je travaille; **he needs a car ~ he can't afford one** il a besoin d'une voiture mais il n'a pas les moyens d'en acheter une; ▶ **if II**.
II *adj* **1** (sole) seul; **~ child** enfant unique; **the ~ one left** le seul/la seule *m/f* or le dernier/la dernière *m/f* qui reste; **you're not the ~ one** tu n'es pas le seul; **we're the ~ people who know** nous sommes les seuls à le savoir; **it's the ~ way** c'est le seul moyen; **one and ~** seul; **the ~ thing is, I'm broke**○ le seul problème, c'est que je suis fauché○; **his ~ answer was to shrug his shoulders** pour toute réponse il haussa les épaules; **2** (best, preferred) **skiing is the ~ sport for me** pour moi, aucun sport ne vaut le ski; **champagne is the ~ drink** rien ne vaut le champagne.
III *adv* **1** (exclusively) **I'm ~ interested in European stamps** je ne m'intéresse qu'aux timbres européens; **~ in Italy can one...** il n'y a qu'en Italie que l'on peut...; **he ~ reads science-fiction** il ne lit que des romans de science-fiction; **we're ~ here for the free beer** nous ne sommes là que pour la bière gratuite; **it's ~ harmful if you eat a lot** ce n'est dangereux que si on en mange beaucoup; **I'll go but ~ if you'll go too** je n'irai que si tu y vas aussi ; **I'll lend you money but ~ if you repay me** je ne te prêterai de l'argent que si tu me rembourses; **~ Annie saw her** Annie est la seule à l'avoir vue; **~ an expert can do that** seul un expert peut faire ça; **~ time will tell** seul l'avenir nous le dira; **'men ~'** 'hommes seulement'; **'for external use ~'** 'usage externe'; **2** (nothing more than) **it's ~ fair to let him explain** ce n'est que justice de le laisser s'expliquer; **it's ~ polite** c'est la moindre des politesses; **it's ~ natural for her to be curious** c'est tout à fait normal qu'elle soit curieuse; **3** (in expressions of time) **~ yesterday/last week** pas plus tard qu'hier/que la semaine dernière; **I saw him ~ recently** je l'ai vu très récemment; **it seems like ~ yesterday** j'ai l'impression que c'était hier; **4** (merely) **he's ~ a baby** ce n'est qu'un bébé; **Mark is ~ sixteen** Mark n'a que seize ans; **it's ~ a suggestion** ce n'est qu'une suggestion; **it's ~ 10 o'clock** il n'est que 10 heures; **it ~ took five minutes** ça n'a pris que cinq minutes; **I ~ earn £2 an hour** je ne gagne que deux livres sterling à l'heure; **you ~ had to ask** tu n'avais qu'à demander; **I've ~ met her once** je ne l'ai rencontrée qu'une fois; **he ~ grazed his knees** il s'est juste égratigné les genoux; **~ half the money** juste la moitié de l'argent; **~ twenty people turned up** seules vingt personnes sont venues; **you've ~ got to look around you** il suffit de regarder autour de soi; **she's not ~ charming but also intelligent** elle n'est pas seulement charmante, elle est aussi intelligente ; **I was ~ joking!** je plaisantais!; ▶ **name**; **5** (just) **I ~ wish he would apologize** je voudrais simplement qu'il s'excuse; **I ~ hope she'll realize** j'espère simplement qu'elle s'en rendra compte; **you'll ~ make him angry** tu ne feras que le mettre en colère; **he'll ~ waste the money** il ne fera que gaspiller l'argent; **~ think, you could win the jackpot** imagine, tu pourrais gagner le gros lot; **I can ~ think that Claire did it** ça ne peut être que Claire qui l'a fait; **open up, it's ~ me** ouvre, c'est moi; **I got home ~ to find** ou **discover (that) I'd been burgled** quand je suis rentré à la maison j'ai découvert que j'avais été cambriolé.
IV only just *adv phr* **1** (very recently) **to have ~ just done** venir juste de faire; **I've ~ just arrived** je viens juste d'arriver; **2** (barely) **it's ~ just tolerable** c'est à peine tolérable; **the plank is ~ just long enough** la planche est juste assez longue; **I caught the bus, but ~ just** j'ai eu le bus mais de justesse.
V only too *adv phr* **it's ~ too obvious that** il n'est que trop évident que; **I remember it ~ too well** je m'en souviens trop bien; **they were ~ too pleased to help** ils étaient trop contents de se rendre utiles.
IDIOMS **goodness** ou **God** ou **Heaven ~ knows!** Dieu seul le sait!

o.n.o. GB (*abrév écrite* = **or nearest offer**) à débattre.

on-off *adj* [*button, control*] marche-arrêt.

onomasiology /ˌɒnəmæzɪˈɒlədʒɪ/ *n* onomasiologie *f*.

onomastic /ˌɒnəˈmæstɪk/ *adj* onomastique.

onomastics /ˌɒnəˈmæstɪks/ *n* (+ *v sg*) onomastique *f*.

onomatopoeia /ˌɒnəˌmætəˈpɪə/ *n* onomatopée *f*.

onomatopoeic /ˌɒnəˌmætəˈpiːɪk/ *adj* onomatopéique.

onrush /ˈɒnrʌʃ/ *n* (of water, tears) torrent *m*; (of people) ruée *f*; (of feelings, pain) accès *m*.

on-screen /ˌɒnˈskriːn/ **I** *adj* **1** Comput sur l'écran; **2** Cin [*action etc*] sur l'écran; [*sex, relationship*] à l'écran.
II *adv* Comput [*edit, display*] sur l'écran.

onset /ˈɒnset/ *n* début *m* (**of** de).

onshore /ˈɒnʃɔː(r)/ *adj* **1** [*installation, oil field, work*] à terre; **2** [*wind, current*] du large.

onside /ˌɒnˈsaɪd/ *adj, adv* Sport en jeu.

on-site /ˌɒnˈsaɪt/ **I** *adj* sur place.
II on site *adv phr* sur place.

onslaught /ˈɒnslɔːt/ *n* attaque *f* (**on** contre).

onstage /ˌɒnˈsteɪdʒ/ *adj, adv* sur scène; **to come ~** entrer en scène.

on-target earnings, **OTE** *npl* **'~ £20,000'** 'salaire plus commission pouvant atteindre 20 000 livres sterling'.

Ontario /ɒnˈteərɪəʊ/ ▶ **1818** *pr n* (city, province) Ontario *m*.

on-the-job **I** *adj* [*training*] sur le tas○, sur le lieu de travail.
II on the job *adv phr* **to get one's training** ou **experience on the job** acquérir de l'expérience sur le tas○.

on-the-spot **I** *adj* [*team, reporting*] sur place; [*investigation*] sur les lieux; [*fine*] sur les lieux de l'infraction; [*advice, quotation*] immédiat.
II on the spot *adv phr* **to be on the spot** gen être sur place; (of police) être sur les lieux; **our correspondent on the spot** notre correspondant sur place; **to agree/decide on the spot** donner son accord/décider sur place.

onto /ˈɒntuː/ *prep* (also **on to**) sur; ▶ **get**, **go**, **move**, **open etc**.
IDIOMS **to be ~ something**○ être sur une piste; **I think I'm ~ something big**○ je suis sur un gros coup○; **the police are ~ him**○ la police est après lui; **she's ~ us**○ elle sait ce que nous mijotons○; ▶ **good**.

ontogenic /ˌɒntəˈdʒenɪk/, **ontogenetic** /ˌɒntədʒɪˈnetɪk/ *adj* ontogénique.

ontogeny /ɒnˈtɒdʒənɪ/ *n* ontogénèse *f*.

ontological /ˌɒntəˈlɒdʒɪkl/ *adj* ontologique.

ontology /ɒnˈtɒlədʒɪ/ *n* ontologie *f*.

onus /ˈəʊnəs/ *n* obligation *f*; **the ~ is on sb to do sth** il incombe à qn de faire qch; **to put the ~ on sb to do sth** obliger qn à faire qch.

onward /ˈɒnwəd/ **I** *adj* **~ flight** correspondance *f* (**to** à destination de); **the coach then makes the ~ journey to Cairo** et puis le car continue sa route jusqu'au Caire; **the ~ march of progress** la marche inéluctable du progrès.
II *adv* = **onwards**.

onwards /ˈɒnwədz/ *adv* **1** (forwards) **the journey ~ to Tokyo** le voyage jusqu'à Tokyo; **to fly to Paris then ~ to Geneva** prendre l'avion jusqu'à Paris puis une correspondance pour Genève; **to go** ou **rise ~ and upwards** gravir les échelons de la hiérarchie; **2** (in time phrases) **from tomorrow/next year ~** à partir de demain/de l'année prochaine; **from now ~** à partir d'aujourd'hui; **from that day ~** à dater de ce jour.

onyx /ˈɒnɪks/ **I** *n* onyx *m*.
II *modif* [*brooch, chess piece, paperweight*] en onyx.

oocyte /ˈəʊəsaɪt/ *n* ovocyte *m*.

oodles○ /ˈuːdlz/ *n* des masses○ *fpl*; **to have ~ of** avoir beaucoup de.

ooh /uː/ **I** *excl* oh!; **~s and ahs** des oh et des ah.
II *vi*: **to ~ and ah** pousser des oh et des ah.

oolite /ˈəʊəlaɪt/ *n* oolithe *m*.

oompah /ˈʊmpɑː/ *n* flonflons *mpl*.

oomph○ /ʊmf/ *n* punch○ *m*, dynamisme *m*.

oophorectomy /ˌəʊəfəˈrektəmɪ/ *n* ovariectomie *f*.

oophoritis /ˌəʊəfəˈraɪtɪs/ **▶ 1354** *n* ovarite *f*.

oops○ /uːps, ʊps/ *excl* oh là là!

oosphere /ˈəʊəsfɪə(r)/ *n* oosphère *f*.

oospore /ˈəʊəspɔː(r)/ *n* oospore *f*.

ooze /uːz/ **I** *n* (silt) vase *f*.
II *vtr* **1** [*wound, scab*] suinter; **the wound ~d blood** du sang suintait de la blessure; **to ~ butter** déborder de beurre; **2** fig [*person*] rayonner de [*charm, sexuality*].
III *vi* **to ~ with** déborder de [*butter, cream*]; rayonner de [*charm, sexuality*].
■ **ooze out** s'écouler.

op○ /ɒp/ *n* Med, Comput *abrév* = **operation** 2, 5.

Op. *abrév écrite* = **opus**.

opacity /əˈpæsətɪ/ *n* lit, fig opacité *f*.

opal /ˈəʊpl/ **I** *n* opale *f*.
II *modif* [*ring, brooch*] d'opale(s); [*necklace*] d'opales.

opalescence /ˌəʊpəˈlesns/ *n* opalescence *f*.

opalescent /ˌəʊpəˈlesnt/ *adj* opalescent.

opaque /əʊˈpeɪk/ *adj* lit, fig opaque.

opaqueness /əʊˈpeɪknɪs/ *n* lit, fig opacité *f*.

opaque projector *n* épiscope *m*.

op art *n* op art *m*.

op artist *n* artiste *mf* op art.

Opec, OPEC /ˈəʊpek/ (*abrév* = **Organization of Petroleum Exporting Countries**) **I** *n* OPEP *f*.
II *modif* [*meeting, member, oil*] de l'OPEP; [*price*] pratiqué par l'OPEP.

op-ed page *n* US Journ (*abrév* = **opposite editorial page**) *page contenant des chroniques, des lettres et des commentaires*.

open /ˈəʊpən/ **I** *n* **1** (outside) **the ~** le plein air; **in the ~** dehors, en plein air; **2** (exposed position) terrain *m* découvert; **in/into the ~** en terrain découvert; fig **to be out in the ~** être étalé en plein jour; **to bring sth out into the ~** mettre qch au grand jour; **to come out into the ~ (and say...)** parler franchement (et dire...); **let's get all this out in the ~** mettons cartes sur table; **3** (also **Open**) Sport (tournoi *m*) open *m*; **the US Open** l'open américain.
II *adj* **1** (not closed) [*door, box, parcel, book, eyes, shirt, wound, flower*] ouvert; [*arms, legs*] écarté; (to the public) [*bank, shop, bar, bridge, meeting*] ouvert; **to get sth ~** ouvrir qch; **to burst** ou **fly ~** s'ouvrir brusquement or violemment; **'~ 9 to 5'** 'ouvert de 9 à 5'; **'~ on Sundays'** 'ouvert le dimanche'; **the book lay ~** le livre était ouvert; **the door was partly** ou **slightly** ou **half ~** la porte était entrouverte; **to be ~ for business** ou **to the public** être ouvert au public; **my door is always ~** ma porte est toujours ouverte; **is there a bank ~?** est-ce qu'il y a une banque ouverte?; **2** (not obstructed) **to be ~** [*road*] être ouvert (à la circulation); [*canal, harbour*] être ouvert (à la navigation); [*telephone line, frequency*] être libre; **the ~ air** le plein air; **in the ~ air** en plein air, au grand air; (at night) à la belle étoile; **~ country** la rase campagne; **~ ground** un terrain vague; **the ~ road** la grand-route; **the ~ sea** la haute mer; **an ~ space** un espace libre; **the (wide) ~ spaces** les (grands) espaces libres; **an ~ view** une vue dégagée (**of** de); **~ water** une étendue d'eau dégagée ; **they're trying to keep the bridge/tunnel ~** ils essaient de laisser le pont/tunnel ouvert à la circulation; **3** (not covered)[*car, carriage*] découvert, décapoté; [*tomb*] ouvert; [*mine, sewer*] à ciel ouvert; **an ~ fire** un feu (de cheminée); **4** (susceptible) **~ to the air/to the wind/to the elements** exposé à l'air/au vent/aux éléments; **~ to attack** exposé à l'attaque; **to be ~ to offers/to suggestions/to new ideas/to criticism** être ouvert aux offres/aux suggestions/aux nouvelles idées/à la critique; **to be ~ to persuasion** être prêt à se laisser convaincre; **to lay** ou **leave oneself ~ to criticism/to attack** s'exposer (ouvertement) à la critique/à l'attaque; **it is ~ to doubt** ou **question whether** on peut douter que (+ *subj*); **this incident has left his honesty ~ to doubt** ou **question** cet incident met en doute son honnêteté; **5** (accessible) (*jamais épith*) [*job, position*] libre, vacant; [*access, competition*] ouvert à tous; [*meeting, hearing, session*] public/-ique; **to be ~ to sb** [*competition, service, park, facilities*] être ouvert à qn; **there are several courses of action/choices ~ to us** nous avons le choix entre plusieurs lignes de conduite/plusieurs possibilités; **6** (candid) [*person, discussion, declaration, statement*] franc/franche; **to be ~ (with sb) about sth** être franc/ franche (avec qn) à propos de qch; **7** (blatant) [*hostility, rivalry, attempt, contempt*] non dissimulé; [*disagreement, disrespect*] manifeste; **in ~ rebellion** ou **revolt** en rébellion ouverte; **8** (undecided) [*question*] non résolu, non tranché; **to leave the date/decision ~** laisser la date/décision en suspens; **the race/election is (wide) ~** l'issue de la course/l'élection est indécise; **to have** ou **keep an ~ mind about sth** réserver son jugement sur qch; **~ return/ticket** Transp retour *m*/billet *m* ouvert or open; **she kept my job ~** elle m'a gardé mon travail; **the job is still ~** l'emploi est toujours vacant; **I have an ~ invitation to visit him/Paris** je suis invité chez lui/à Paris quand je veux; **9** (with spaces) [*weave, material*] ajouré; **10** Sport [*tournament, contest*] open; **11** Mus [*string*] à vide; **12** Ling [*vowel, syllable*] ouvert.
III *vtr* **1** (cause not to be closed) ouvrir [*door, envelope, letter, wound, box, shirt, umbrella, button, jar*]; **to ~ one's arms/legs** ouvrir or écarter les bras/jambes; ouvrir, déplier [*map, newspaper*]; dilater [*pores*]; **to ~ a door/window slightly** ou **a little** entrouvrir une porte/fenêtre; **to ~ one's eyes/mouth** ouvrir les yeux/la bouche; **to ~ one's mind (to sth)** s'ouvrir (à qch); **2** (begin) ouvrir, entamer [*discussions, negotiations, meeting*]; entamer, engager [*conversation*]; ouvrir [*account, enquiry*]; **to ~ the score** ou **scoring** Sport ouvrir la marque; **to ~ fire** ouvrir le feu; **she ~ed the show with a song** elle a ouvert le spectacle avec une chanson; **to ~ the door to** ouvrir la porte à [*abuse, corruption*]; **3** Comm (set up) ouvrir [*shop, business, branch*]; **4** (inaugurate) inaugurer [*shop, bridge*]; ouvrir [*exhibition*]; **to ~ parliament** ouvrir la session parlementaire; **5** (make wider) **▶ open up**.
IV *vi* **1** (become open) [*door, window, flower, curtain*] s'ouvrir; **his eyes/mouth ~ed** il a ouvert les yeux/la bouche; **to ~ into** ou **onto sth** [*door, room, window*] donner sur qch; **~ wide!** (at dentist's) ouvrez grand!; **to ~ slightly** ou **a little** [*window, door*] s'entrouvrir; **2** Comm (operate) [*shop, bank, bar*] ouvrir; **3** (begin) [*meeting, conference, discussion, play*] commencer; **to ~ with sth** [*person, meeting, play*] commencer par qch; **to ~ by doing** [*person*] commencer par faire; **4** Art, Cin, Theat (have first performance) [*film*] sortir (sur les écrans); [*exhibition*] ouvrir; **the play ~s in London on the 25th** la première de la pièce aura lieu à Londres le 25; **we ~ on the 25th** nous donnons la première le 25; **5** (be first speaker) [*person*] ouvrir le débat; **to ~ for the defence/the prosecution** Jur prendre la parole au nom de la défense/du ministère public; **6** (become wider) **▶ open up**; **7** Fin [*shares*] débuter.
■ **open out**: ¶ **~ out** (become broader) [*river, passage, path, view*] s'élargir; [*countryside*] s'étendre; [*flower*] s'ouvrir, éclore; **to ~ out into** [*passage, tunnel*] déboucher sur [*room, cave*]; [*stream, river*] se jeter dans [*pool, lake*]; ¶ **~ [sth] out, ~ out [sth]** ouvrir, déplier [*garment, newspaper, map*].
■ **open up**: ¶ **~ up 1** (unlock a building) ouvrir; **I'll ~ up for you** je t'ouvre; **'police! ~ up!'** 'police! ouvrez!'; **2** (become wider) [*gap*] se creuser; [*crack, split, crevice, fissure*] lit, fig se former; **3** (speak freely) s'ouvrir; **4** (develop) [*opportunities, possibilities, market*] s'ouvrir; **5** (become open) [*flower*] s'ouvrir, éclore; **6** Comm (start up) [*shop, business, branch*] ouvrir; **7** Mil (start firing) se mettre à tirer; ¶ **~ [sth] up, ~ up [sth] 1** (make open) ouvrir [*parcel, suitcase, wound*]; **2** (make wider) creuser [*gap*]; **to ~ up a lead** [*athlete, racer*] creuser l'écart; **3** (unlock) ouvrir [*shop, building*]; **4** (start up) ouvrir [*shop, business, branch, mine*]; **to ~ up a plant** ou **factory** s'implanter; **5** (make accessible) ouvrir [*area, road, country*]; exploiter [*forest, desert*]; fig ouvrir [*opportunities, possibilities, career*]; **to ~ up new horizons for sb** ouvrir de nouveaux horizons à qn; **they are trying to ~ the region up to trade** ils essaient de développer le commerce dans cette région.

open admissions (policy) *npl* US Univ *politique d'admission dans le cycle universitaire sans sélection des candidats*.

open-air /ˌəʊpənˈeə(r)/ *adj* [*swimming pool, market, stage*] en plein air; **~ theatre** théâtre *m* de verdure or en plein air.

open: **~-and-shut** *adj* [*case*] transparent, clair; **~cast mining** *n* GB exploitation *f* minière à ciel ouvert; **~ circuit** *n* Elec circuit *m* ouvert; **~ competition** *n* concours *m*.

open court *n* **in ~** en audience publique.

open day *n* journée *f* portes ouvertes.

open door I *n* Econ, Pol porte *f* ouverte.
II open-door *adj* Econ, Pol [*policy*] de la porte ouverte.

open-ended /ˌəʊpənˈendɪd/ *adj* [*policy, strategy*] flexible; [*contract*] modifiable; [*discussion, debate, question*] ouvert; [*relationship, situation*] flou; [*stay*] de durée indéterminée; [*period*] indéterminé; [*phrase, wording*] sujet/-ette à plusieurs interprétations.

opener /ˈəʊpnə(r)/ **I** *n* **1** Sport (in cricket) premier batteur *m*; (in baseball) premier match *m* de la saison; **2** TV, Theat (first act) premier numéro *m*; (first episode) premier épisode *m*; **3** Games (in bridge) (bid) ouverture *f*; (player) ouvreur/-euse *m/f*; **4** (for bottles) décapsuleur *m*; (for cans, tins) ouvre-boîte *m*.

II for openers○ *adv phr* pour commencer.

open-eyed *adj* **1** (alert) alerte; **2** (agog) **to be ~ in wonder/surprise** avoir les yeux écarquillés d'émerveillement/de surprise.

open: **~-faced** *adj* [*person*] à l'air franc; **~-face(d) sandwich** *n* US canapé *m*; **~ government** *n* Pol politique *f* de transparence; **~-handed** *adj* généreux/-euse; **~-hearted** *adj* chaleureux/-euse.

open-heart surgery *n* Med **1** (discipline) chirurgie *f* à cœur ouvert; **2** (operation) opération *f* à cœur ouvert.

open house *n* **1** (be hospitable) **to keep ~** être très hospitalier/-ière; **it's always ~ at the Batemans'** les Bateman sont très hospitaliers; **2** US (open day) journée *f* portes ouvertes.

opening /ˈəʊpnɪŋ/ **I** *n* **1** (start) (of book, piece of music) début *m*; (of business, premises, shop) ouverture *f*; (of exhibition, parliament) ouverture *f*; (of play, film) première *f*; **2** (inauguration) (of building, business, shop etc) inauguration *f*; **3** (gap) (in wall, fence, garment) ouverture *f*, trouée *f*; (in forest) trouée *f*, percée *f*; **door ~** porte *f*; **4** (opportunity) gen occasion *f* (**to do** de faire); Comm (in market etc) débouché *m*, créneau *m*, marché *m* (**for** pour); (for employment) (in company) poste *m* (disponible); (in field) possibilité *f* de travail; **job** ou **career ~** possibilité *f* or offre *f* d'emploi; **5** Games ouverture *f*.

II *adj* [*scene, line, chapter*] premier/-ière (*before n*); [*remarks, speech, statement*] préliminaire; Fin [*price, offer, bid*] de départ; (at Stock Exchange) [*share price*] d'ouverture; [*move, shot*] premier/-ière (*before n*).

opening: **~ balance** *n* Accts (of individual) solde *m* initial; (of company) solde *m* en début d'exercice; **~ ceremony** *n* (cérémonie *f* d') inauguration *f*; **~ gambit** *n* (in chess) gambit *m*; **~ hours** *n* Comm heures *fpl* d'ouverture; **~ night** *n* Cin, Theat (soir *m* de la) première *f*; **~ time** *n* Comm heure *f* d'ouverture.

open: **~ learning** *n*: *formule d'enseignement à distance ou dans un centre ouvert à tous*; **~ letter** *n* lettre *f* ouverte (**to** à).

openly /ˈəʊpənlɪ/ *adv* (all contexts) ouvertement.

open market *n* Econ marché *m* libre; **on the ~** sur le marché libre.

open marriage *n* mariage *m* où l'infidélité est tolérée.

open-minded /ˌəʊpənˈmaɪndɪd/ *adj* à l'esprit ouvert (*épith*), sans préjugés; **to be ~** avoir l'esprit ouvert; **to be ~ about sth** n'avoir aucun préjugé sur qch.

open-mouthed /ˌəʊpənˈmaʊðd/ *adj* bouche bée *inv*; **~ with surprise/with admiration** béat d'étonnement/d'admiration.

open-necked /ˌəʊpənˈnekt/*n* [*shirt*] à col ouvert.

openness /ˈəʊpənnɪs/ *n* **1** (candour) (of person) franchise *f*; (of manner, attitude) caractère *m* franc; (of government, atmosphere, society) transparence *f*; **2** (receptiveness) ouverture *f* d'esprit (**to** en ce qui concerne).

open: **~-plan** *adj* [*office*] paysagé; **~ primary** *n* US Pol élection *f* primaire ouverte à chaque électeur; **~ prison** *n* prison *f* ouverte; **~ sandwich** *n* Culin sandwich *m* ouvert; **~ scholarship** *n* Univ bourse *f* décernée par un concours ouvert à tous; **~ season** *n* Hunt saison *f* de la chasse; **~ secret** *n* secret *m* de Polichinelle; **~ sesame** *n* carte *f* d'entrée fig; **~ shop** *n* Ind, Pol *établissement où on peut être recruté indépendamment de son appartenance à un syndicat*; **Open University, OU** GB Univ *n*: *système d'enseignement universitaire par correspondance ouvert à tous*; **~ verdict** *n* Jur verdict *m* de décès sans cause déterminée.

openwork /ˈəʊpənwɜːk/ **I** *n* **1** Sewing jours *mpl*, ajours *mpl*; **2** Archit claire-voie *f*.

II *modif* **1** Sewing [*gloves, stockings*] ajouré; **2** Archit à claire-voie.

opera /ˈɒprə/ *n* opéra *m*; **do you like ~?** aimez-vous l'opéra?; **tickets for the ~** billets pour l'opéra.

operable /ˈɒprəbl/ *adj* **1** [*plan*] réalisable; [*machine*] en état de marche; [*system*] capable de fonctionner; **2** Med [*case, condition, tumour*] opérable.

opera: **~ company** *n* troupe *f* d'opéra; **~ glasses** *n* jumelles *fpl* de théâtre; **~goer** *n* personne *f* qui va régulièrement à l'opéra; **~ house** *n* opéra *m*.

operand /ˈɒpərænd/ *n* opérande *m*.

opera singer ▶ 1692 *n* (male) chanteur *m* d'opéra; (female) chanteuse *f* d'opéra.

operate /ˈɒpəreɪt/ **I** *vtr* **1** (run) faire marcher [*appliance, machine, vehicle*]; **2** (enforce) pratiquer [*policy, system*]; mettre [qch] en vigueur [*ban, control*]; **3** (manage) gérer, diriger [*service, radio station*]; exploiter [*mine, racket*]; [*bank*] avoir [*pension plan, savings scheme*].

II *vi* **1** (do business, engage in criminal activity) opérer; **they ~ out of London** ils ont Londres comme base d'opérations; **2** (function) marcher, fonctionner; **3** (take effect) agir; **4** Mil opérer; **5** fig (work) [*factor, force, law*] jouer (**in favour of** en faveur de; **against** contre); **6** (run) fonctionner; **does the shuttle service ~ on Saturdays?** est-ce que la navette fonctionne le samedi?; **7** Med opérer; **we shall have to ~** il faudra opérer; **to ~ on** opérer [*person*]; **to be ~d on** être opéré; **to ~ on sb's leg/ear** opérer qn à la jambe/l'oreille; **to ~ on sb for appendicitis** opérer qn de l'appendicite.

operatic /ˌɒpəˈrætɪk/ **I operatics** *npl* opéra *m* d'amateurs.

II *adj* **1** [*voice, career*] de chanteur/-euse d'opéra; [*composer*] d'opéras; [*society*] de chanteurs d'opéra amateurs; **2** (histrionic) [*gesture, tone*] de chanteur/-euse d'opéra.

operating /ˈɒpəreɪtɪŋ/ *adj* [*costs, income*] d'exploitation.

operating: **~ budget** *n* budget *m* d'exploitation; **~ instructions** *npl* mode *m* d'emploi; **~ manual** *n* manuel *m* d'utilisation; **~ room** *n* US salle *f* d'opération; **~ system** *n* système *m* d'exploitation; **~ table** *n* table *f* d'opération; **~ theatre** *n* GB salle *f* d'opération.

operation /ˌɒpəˈreɪʃn/ *n* **1** (working) fonctionnement *m*; **2** Med opération *f*; **to have an ~** se faire opérer, subir une opération; **to have a major/minor ~** subir une grosse/petite opération; **to have an ~ on one's knee/ankle** se faire opérer du genou/de la cheville; **to have a heart/stomach ~** se faire opérer du cœur/de l'estomac; **3** (use, application) (of machinery) utilisation *f*; (of plant, mine) exploitation *f*; (of law, scheme) mise *f* en vigueur; **to be in ~** [*plan, scheme, rule*] être en vigueur; [*oil rig, mine*] être en exploitation; [*machine*] fonctionner; **to come into ~** [*law, scheme*] entrer en vigueur; **to put sth into ~** mettre qch en vigueur [*law, scheme*]; **to put sth out of ~** mettre qch hors service [*equipment, machinery, factory, vehicle*]; **4** (manoeuvres) (by police, armed forces) opération *f*; **5** Comput opération *f*; **6** (undertaking) opération *f*; **a big ~** une grosse opération; **7** (business) **their European ~ is expanding** ils étendent leurs activités en Europe; **8** Fin opération *f*.

operational /ˌɒpəˈreɪʃənl/ *adj* **1** (working) en service, opérationnel/-elle; **to be fully ~** être pleinement opérationnel/-elle; **2** (encountered while working) [*budget, costs*] d'exploitation; **we have had some ~ problems** on a eu des problèmes d'exploitation; **~ requirements** conditions *fpl* de fonctionnement; **3** Mil (ready to operate) opérationnel/-elle.

operational: **~ amplifier** *n* amplificateur *m* opérationnel; **~ manager** *n* chef *m* d'exploitation; **~ research** *n* recherche *f* opérationnelle.

operation code *n* code *m* opération.

operations research *n* US recherche *f* opérationnelle.

operations room *n* **1** Mil salle *f* d'opérations; **2** (police) centre *m* d'opérations.

operative /ˈɒpərətɪv, US -reɪt-/ **I** *n* (worker) employé/-e *m/f*; (secret agent) agent *m*.

II *adj* **1** (effective) [*rule, law, system*] en vigueur; **how soon will the plan be ~?** quand le plan sera-t-il en vigueur?; **2** (important) [*word*] qui compte; **X being the ~ word** X étant le mot qui compte.

operator /ˈɒpəreɪtə(r)/ ▶ 1692 *n* **1** Telecom standardiste *mf*; **2** Comput, Radio, Tech opérateur *m*; **3** Tourism compagnie *f* de voyages organisés; **4** (of equipment) opérateur/-trice *mf*; **5** Comm (of business) entrepreneur *m*; **he's a smooth** ou **shrewd ~** pej il sait s'y prendre.

operetta /ˌɒpəˈretə/ *n* opérette *f*.

ophthalmia /ɒfˈθælmɪə/ *n* ophtalmie *f*.

ophthalmic /ɒfˈθælmɪk/ *adj* GB [*nerve, vein*] ophtalmique; [*surgeon, surgery, clinic, research*] ophtalmologique.

ophthalmic optician ▶ 1692 *n* optométriste *mf*.

ophthalmologist /ˌɒfθælˈmɒlədʒɪst/ ▶ 1692 *n* ophtalmologue *mf*, ophtalmologiste *mf*.

ophthalmology /ˌɒfθælˈmɒlədʒɪ/ *n* ophtalmologie *f*.

ophthalmoscope /ɒfˈθælməskəʊp/ *n* ophtalmoscope *m*.

ophthalmoscopy /ˌɒfθælˈmɒskəpɪ/ *n* ophtalmoscopie *f*.

opiate /ˈəʊpɪət/ **I** *n* **1** lit (derived from opium) opiacé *m*; **2** gen (narcotic) narcotique *m*.

II *adj* littér opiacé.

opine /əʊˈpaɪn/ *vi* littér émettre un avis, opiner liter.

opinion /əˈpɪnɪən/ *n* **1** (belief, view) opinion *f* (**about** de), avis *m* (**about, on** sur); **conflicting ~s** avis contradictoires; **informed ~** opinion des gens informés; **legal/medical ~** avis juridique/médical; **personal ~** opinion personnelle; **public ~** opinion publique; **world ~** opinion mondiale; **to be of the ~ that** estimer que; **in my/his ~** à mon/son avis; **of the same ~** de la même opinion; **to express/venture an ~** exprimer/hasarder une opinion; **what's your ~?** quel est ton avis, qu'en penses-tu?; **that's my ~, for what it's worth** voilà mon avis, pour ce qu'il vaut; **if you want my honest/considered ~** si vous voulez savoir ce que je pense honnêtement /après mûre réflexion; **that's a matter of ~** chacun ses opinions; **in the ~ of experts, in the experts' ~** d'après les experts; **2** (evaluation) (of person, performance, action) opinion *f* (**of** de); **to have a high/low ~ of sb/sth** avoir une bonne/mauvaise opinion de qn/qch; **to seek** ou **get a second ~** gen demander un autre avis; Med consulter un autre médecin; **3** ₵ (range of views) opinions *fpl*; **a range of ~** une variété d'opinions; **a difference of ~** une divergence d'opinions; **~ is divided** les opinions sont partagées; **a programme of news and ~** Radio, TV un programme d'informations et de commentaires; **4** Jur (also **counsel's ~**) avis *m* motivé; **to take counsel's ~** consulter un avocat.

opinionated /əˈpɪnɪəneɪtɪd/ *adj* [*person*] qui a des avis sur tout; [*tone of voice*] dogmatique.

opinion poll *n* sondage *m* d'opinion; **to hold an ~** faire un sondage d'opinion.

opium /ˈəʊpɪəm/ *n* opium *m*; **the ~ of the masses** l'opium du peuple.

opium: **~ addict** *n* opiomane *mf*; **~ den** *n* fumerie *f* d'opium; **~ poppy** *n* pavot *m* somnifère.

opossum /əˈpɒsəm/ *n* opossum *m*.

opponent /ə'pəʊnənt/ *n* **1** gen, Pol, Sport (adversary) adversaire *mf*; **2** gen, Pol (of regime) opposant/-e *m/f* (**of** à); (of project, scheme) adversaire *mf* (**of** de).

opportune /'ɒpətju:n, US -tu:n/ *adj* [*time, moment, occasion*] opportun; **she considers it ~ to do** il lui paraît opportun de faire.

opportunely /'ɒpətju:nlɪ, US -tu:n/ *adv* [*happen, come along*] au moment opportun; [*situated, placed*] à l'endroit idéal.

opportuneness /'ɒpətju:nnɪs, US -tu:n-/ *n* opportunité *f*.

opportunism /ˌɒpə'tju:nɪzəm, US -'tu:n-/ *n* opportunisme *m*.

opportunist /ˌɒpə'tju:nɪst, US -'tu:n-/ *n, adj* opportuniste (*mf*).

opportunistic /ˌɒpətju:'nɪstɪk, US -tu:n-/ *adj* opportuniste.

opportunistically /ˌɒpətju:'nɪstɪklɪ, US -tu:n-/ *adv* de façon opportuniste.

opportunity /ˌɒpə'tju:nətɪ, US -'tu:n-/ *n* **1** (appropriate time, occasion) occasion *f* (**for** de; **to do, of doing, for doing** de faire); **to seek an ~ for discussion/rest** chercher une occasion de or pour discuter/se reposer; **to give sb an** ou **the ~ to do** donner à qn l'occasion de faire; **to give sb every ~** donner à qn toutes les chances (**to do** de faire); **to miss a golden ~** rater une occasion en or; **I should like to take this ~ to say** j'aimerais profiter de cette occasion pour dire; **at the earliest ~** à la première occasion; **2** (good chance, possibility) possibilité *f*; **training/career opportunities** possibilités de formation/de carrière; **export/investment ~** possibilité d'exportation/d'investissement; **a job with opportunities** un travail avec des perspectives; **'ideal ~ in industry for young graduate'** 'occasion idéale pour jeune diplômé de l'université d'entrer dans l'industrie'.

IDIOMS **~ knocks!** la chance frappe à la porte!

opportunity cost *n* coût *m* d'opportunité.

oppose /ə'pəʊz/ **I** *vtr* gen, Pol s'opposer à [*plan, bill*]; faire opposition à [*bail*]; **to be ~d to sth** être contre qch; **to be ~d to doing** être contre l'idée de faire; **to be ~d to sb doing sth** ne pas être d'accord pour que qn fasse qch; **I am not ~d to his coming** je ne m'oppose pas à ce qu'il vienne.

II as opposed to *prep phr* par opposition à.

III opposing *pres p adj* [*force, group, party, team*] adverse; [*army*] ennemi; [*view, style*] opposé; **the opposing voices** les voix contre.

opposite /'ɒpəzɪt/ **I** *n* contraire *m* (**to, of** de); **the exact ~, quite the ~** tout le contraire; **just the ~** exactement le contraire; **fat is the ~ of thin** gros est l'opposé de mince; **it does the ~ to what one expects** cela fait l'inverse de ce à quoi on pourrait s'attendre; **it's the attraction of ~s, ~s attract** les contraires s'attirent.

II *adj* **1** (facing) [*direction, side, pole*] opposé also Math; [*building*] d'en face; [*page*] ci-contre; **at ~ ends of the table/street** aux deux bouts de la table/rue; **to live at ~ ends of the town** habiter dans des coins opposés de la ville; **2** (different) [*attitude, position, viewpoint, camp*] opposé; [*effect, approach*] inverse; [*sex*] autre.

III *adv* [*live, stand*] en face; **directly ~** juste en face.

IV *prep* gen en face de [*building, park, person*]; Naut devant [*port*]; **to be/live/sit ~ sb/sth** être/habiter/être assis en face de qn/qch; **to stop/turn ~ sth** s'arrêter/tourner en face de qch; **to play ~ one another** Sport jouer l'un contre l'autre; Cin, Theat se donner la réplique.

opposite number *n* gen, Pol homologue *m*; Sport adversaire *mf*.

opposition /ˌɒpə'zɪʃn/ **I** *n* **1** gen opposition *f* (**to** à); **to encounter** ou **meet with ~** rencontrer l'opposition; **to put up ~ against** faire opposition à; **to run into** ou **up against ~** se heurter à de l'opposition; **to express ~** exprimer son opposition (**to** à); **2** Pol (also **Opposition**) opposition *f*; **to be/remain in ~** [*party*] être/rester dans l'opposition; **3** Sport **the ~** l'adversaire *m*.

II *modif* Pol [*politician, debate, party etc*] de l'opposition.

Opposition bench *n* GB Pol banc *m* de l'opposition.

oppress /ə'pres/ *vtr* **1** (subjugate) opprimer; **2** [*weather*] oppresser; [*anxiety, responsibility*] accabler.

oppressed /ə'prest/ **I** *n* **the ~** les opprimés *mpl*.

II *adj* **1** [*minority, group*] opprimé; **2** (by pain, emotion) accablé (**by** par).

oppression /ə'preʃn/ *n* oppression *f*.

oppressive /ə'presɪv/ *adj* **1** [*law, regime*] oppressif/-ive; **2** [*heat*] accablant; [*atmosphere*] oppressant.

oppressively /ə'presɪvlɪ/ *adv* [*govern, rule*] de façon oppressive; **it's ~ hot** il fait chaud à étouffer.

oppressor /ə'presə(r)/ *n* oppresseur *m*.

opprobrious /ə'prəʊbrɪəs/ *adj* sout **1** [*language*] méprisant; **2** [*behaviour*] infâme.

opprobrium /ə'prəʊbrɪəm/ *n* sout **1** (censure) mépris *m*; **2** (disgrace) opprobre *m* liter.

opt /ɒpt/ *vi* **to ~ for sth** opter pour qch; **to ~ to do/not to do** choisir de faire/de ne pas faire.

■ **opt out** [*person, country*] décider de ne pas participer (**of** à); [*school, hospital*] renoncer au contrôle de l'État.

optative /'ɒptətɪv, 'ɒpteɪtɪv/ **I** *n* optatif *m*.

II *adj* optatif/-ive.

optic /'ɒptɪk/ **I** *n* GB (in bar) bouchon *m* doseur.

II *adj* [*nerve, disc, fibre*] optique.

optical /'ɒptɪkl/ *adj* (all contexts) optique.

optical: **~ brightener** *n* azurant *m*; **~ character reader, OCR** *n* lecteur *m* optique de caractères; **~ character recognition, OCR** *n* reconnaissance *f* optique des caractères; **~ disk** *n* disque *m* optique; **~ fibre** GB, **~ fiber** US *n* fibre *f* optique; **~ illusion** *n* illusion *f* d'optique; **~ wand** *n* crayon-lecteur *m* optique.

optician /ɒp'tɪʃn/ ▶ **1692** *n* (selling glasses etc) opticien/-ienne *m/f*; (eye specialist) GB optométriste *mf*, réfractionniste *mf*.

optics /'ɒptɪks/ *n* (+ *v sg*) optique *f*.

optimal /'ɒptɪml/ *adj* optimal.

optimism /'ɒptɪmɪzəm/ *n* optimisme *m*.

optimist /'ɒptɪmɪst/ *n* optimiste *mf*.

optimistic /ˌɒptɪ'mɪstɪk/ *adj* optimiste (**about** quant à); **wildly/cautiously ~** exagérément/raisonnablement optimiste; **to be ~ that sth will happen** avoir grand espoir que qch arrivera.

optimistically /ˌɒptɪ'mɪstɪklɪ/ *adv* [*imagine, promise, say*] avec optimisme.

optimization /ˌɒptɪmaɪ'zeɪʃn/ *n* optimisation *f*.

optimize /'ɒptɪmaɪz/ *vtr* optimiser.

optimum /'ɒptɪməm/ **I** *n* optimum *m*; **at its ~** à son optimum.

II *adj* [*age, conditions, level, rate, speed, value*] optimum, optimal (**for** pour).

option /'ɒpʃn/ *n* **1** gen, Comput (something chosen) option *f* (**to do** de faire); **best ~** meilleure option; **easy ~, soft ~** solution *f* facile; **safe ~** solution *f* la plus sûre; **zero ~** option zéro; **to choose/go for an ~** choisir/prendre une option; **it's the only ~ for us** nous n'avons pas d'autre possibilité; **the only ~ open to me** la seule possibilité que j'ai; **to keep one's ~s open** ne pas s'engager; **to consider one's ~s** considérer ses options; **2** (possibility of choosing) choix *m*; **to have the ~ of doing sth** pouvoir choisir de faire qch; **to give sb the ~ of doing sth** donner le choix à qn de faire qch; **with the ~ of doing** avec l'option de faire; **I had no ~ but to leave** je n'avais pas d'autre choix que de partir; **I had little/no ~** je n'avais guère/pas le choix; **3** Comm, Fin option *f* (**on** sur; **to do** pour faire); **call ~** option d'achat; **exclusive ~** option exclusive; **stock ~** option de souscription; **put ~** option de vente; **to take up an ~** lever une option; **with an ~ on sth** avec une option sur qch; **to have first ~** avoir priorité d'option; **to cancel one's ~s** annuler ses options; **4** GB Sch, Univ (course of study) option *f*; **5** Aut option *f*.

optional /'ɒpʃənl/ *adj* [*activity, course, subject*] facultatif/-ive; [*colour, size*] au choix; **'evening dress ~'** 'tenue de soirée facultative'; **~ extras** accessoires *mpl* en option.

option trading *n* marché *m* des options.

optometrist /ˌɒptə'metrɪst/ ▶ **1692** *n* optométriste *mf*.

optometry /ˌɒptə'metrɪ/ *n* optométrie *f*.

opulence /'ɒpjʊləns/ *n* opulence *f*.

opulent /'ɒpjʊlənt/ *adj* [*person, country*] opulent; [*clothing, object*] somptueux/-euse.

opulently /'ɒpjʊləntlɪ/ *adv* avec opulence.

opus /'əʊpəs/ *n* (*pl* **~es** ou **opera**) opus *m*; **magnum ~** œuvre *f* maîtresse.

opuscule /ə'pʌskju:l/ *n* opuscule *m*.

or /ɔ:(r)/

■ **Note** In most uses *or* is translated by *ou*. There are two exceptions to this:
– When used to link alternatives after a negative verb (*I can't come today or tomorrow*). For translations see 3 below.
– When used to indicate consequence (*be careful or you'll cut yourself*) or explanation (*it can't be serious or she'd have called us*) the translation is *sinon*: fais attention sinon tu vas te couper; ça ne peut pas être grave sinon elle nous aurait appelés. See 6 and 7 below.

conj **1** (linking two or more alternatives) ou; **with ~ without sugar?** avec ou sans sucre?; **would you like to eat here ~ in town?** est-ce que tu veux manger ici ou en ville?; **it can be roasted, grilled ~ fried** on peut le faire rôtir, griller ou frire; **any brothers ~ sisters?** tu as des frères et sœurs?; **2** (linking two clear alternatives) ou; **will you ~ won't you be coming?** est-ce que tu viens ou pas?; **either... ~...** soit... soit...; **essays may be either handwritten ~ typed** les dissertations peuvent être soit manuscrites soit dactylographiées; **they'll stay either here ~ at Dave's** ils vont habiter soit ici soit chez Dave, ils vont habiter ici ou chez Dave; **whether he likes it ~ not** que cela lui plaise ou non; **he wants to know whether ~ not you're free** il veut savoir si tu es libre ou pas; **I didn't know whether to laugh ~ cry** je ne savais pas s'il fallait rire ou pleurer; **rain ~ no rain, we're going out** qu'il pleuve ou non nous sortons; **car ~ no car, you've got to get to work** voiture ou pas, il faut que tu ailles travailler; **3** (linking alternatives in the negative) **I can't come today ~ tomorrow** je ne peux venir ni aujourd'hui ni demain; **don't tell Mum ~ Dad!** ne le dis ni à Maman ni à Papa!; **without food ~ lodgings** sans nourriture ni abri; **I couldn't eat ~ sleep** je ne pouvais ni manger ni dormir; **she doesn't drink ~ smoke** elle ne boit pas et ne fume pas non plus; **4** (indicating approximation, vagueness) ou; **once ~ twice a week** une ou deux fois par semaine; **I'll buy him a tie ~ something** je vais lui acheter une cravate ou quelque chose comme ça; **someone ~ other from Personnel** quelqu'un du service du personnel; **in a week ~ so** dans huit jours environ; **5** (introducing qualification, correction, explanation) ou; **I knew her, ~ at least I thought I did!** je la connaissais, ou plutôt je croyais la connaître!; **my daughter, ~ rather our daughter** ma fille, ou plutôt notre fille; **X, ~ should I say, Mr X** X ou bien devrais-je dire M. X; **Rosalind, ~ Ros to her friends**

Rosalind ou Ros pour ses amis; **6** (indicating consequence: otherwise) sinon, autrement; **be careful ~ you'll cut yourself** fais attention sinon or autrement tu vas te couper; **do as you're told—~ else**○! fais ce qu'on te dit—sinon gare○ à toi or attention!; **7** (in explanation, justification) sinon, autrement; **it can't have been serious ~ she'd have called us** ça ne devait pas être très grave sinon or autrement elle nous aurait appelés.

OR US Post *abrév écrite* = **Oregon**.

oracle /ˈɒrəkl, US ˈɔːr-/ *n* **1** gen, Hist, Relig oracle *m*; **2 Oracle** GB TV cf Antiope *f*.

oracular /əˈrækjʊlə(r)/ *adj* **1** fig (wise) d'oracle; (mysterious) sibyllin; **2** (of oracle) oraculaire.

oral /ˈɔːrəl/ **I** *n* GB Sch, US Univ oral *m*.
II *adj* gen oral; [*contraceptive, medicine*] par voie orale; [*cavity, hygiene, thermometer*] buccal; [*history*] transmis oralement; [*evidence*] verbal.

orally /ˈɔːrəlɪ/ *adv* **1** gen [*communicate, testify, examine*] oralement; **2** Med par voie orale.

oral: **~ sex** *n* relations *fpl* sexuelles buccogénitales; **~ skills** *npl* techniques *fpl* d'expression orale; **~ tradition** *n* tradition *f* orale.

orange /ˈɒrɪndʒ, US ˈɔːr-/ **▶1104** **I** *n* **1** (fruit) orange *f*; **2** (drink) boisson *f* à l'orange; **gin and ~** gin à l'orange; **3** (colour) orange *m*.
II *modif* [*drink, pudding, sauce*] à l'orange; [*jam*] d'orange.
III *adj* (colour) orange *inv*.

orangeade /ˌɒrɪndʒˈeɪd, US ˌɔːr-/ *n* orangeade *f*.

orange: **~ blossom** *n* fleur *f* d'oranger; **~ drink** US = **orange squash**; **~ flower water** *n* eau *f* de fleur d'oranger; **Orange Free State** *pr n* État *m* libre d'Orange; **~ grove** *n* orangeraie *f*; **~ juice** *n* jus *m* d'orange.

Orangeman /ˈɒrɪndʒmən, US ˌɔːr-/ *n* orangiste *m* (*protestant d'Irlande du Nord*).

orange peel *n* gen écorce *f* d'orange, peau *f* d'orange; Culin zeste *m* d'orange.

orangery /ˈɒrɪndʒərɪ, US ˌɔːr-/ *n* orangerie *f*.

orange: **~ segment** *n* quartier *m* d'orange; **~ soda** *n* US boisson *f* à l'orange gazeuse; **~ squash** *n* GB ≈ sirop *m* d'orange; **~ stick** *n* bâtonnet *m* de manucure; **~ tree** *n* oranger *m*; **~wood** *n* (bois *m* d')oranger *m*.

orang-outang GB, **orangutan** US /ɔːˌræŋuːˈtæn, US əˌræŋəˈtæn/ *n* orang-outan(g) *m*.

orate /ɔːˈreɪt/ *vi* sout discourir; péj pérorer pej.

oration /ɔːˈreɪʃn/ *n* sout harangue *f*.

orator /ˈɒrətə(r), US ˈɔːr-/ *n* sout orateur *m*.

oratorical /ˌɒrəˈtɒrɪkl, US ˌɔːrəˈtɔːr-/ *adj* sout [*skill, tone*] oratoire; péj déclamatoire pej.

oratorio /ˌɒrəˈtɔːrɪəʊ, US ˌɔːr-/ *n* (*pl* **~s**) oratorio *m*; **Christmas ~** oratorio de Noël.

oratory /ˈɒrətrɪ, US ˈɔːrətɔːrɪ/ *n* **1** sout (public speaking) (skill) art *m* oratoire; (what is said) éloquence *f*; **2** Archit, Relig oratoire *m*.

orb /ɔːb/ *n* littér (all contexts) globe *m*.

orbit /ˈɔːbɪt/ **I** *n* Aerosp, Anat, Astron orbite *f* also fig; **to be in ~ round sth** être en orbite autour de qch; **to go into ~** se mettre en orbite; **to put sth into ~** mettre qch sur orbite; **to make an ~** décrire une orbite.
II *vtr* décrire une orbite autour de.
III *vi* [*moon, planet*] graviter en orbite; [*spacecraft*] orbiter.

orbital /ˈɔːbɪtl/ *adj* gen, Astron orbital; Anat orbitaire; **~ road** rocade *f*.

Orcadian /ɔːˈkeɪdɪən/ **I** *n* habitant/-e *m/f* des Orcades.
II *adj* des Orcades.

orchard /ˈɔːtʃəd/ *n* verger *m*.

orchestra /ˈɔːkɪstrə/ *n* orchestre *m*; **chamber/dance ~** orchestre de chambre/de danse; **string/symphony ~** orchestre à cordes/symphonique; **the full ~** l'orchestre au complet.

orchestral /ɔːˈkestrəl/ *adj* [*concert, music*] orchestral; [*instrument, player*] d'orchestre.

orchestra: **~ pit** *n* fosse *f* d'orchestre; **~ seats** US, **~ stalls** GB *n* fauteuils *mpl* d'orchestre.

orchestrate /ˈɔːkɪstreɪt/ *vtr* lit, fig orchestrer (**for** pour).

orchestration /ˌɔːkɪˈstreɪʃn/ *n* orchestration *f*.

orchid /ˈɔːkɪd/ *n* orchidée *f*.

orchis /ˈɔːkɪs/ *n* orchis *m*.

ordain /ɔːˈdeɪn/ *vtr* **1** (decree) décréter (**that** que); **2** Relig ordonner; **he was ~ed priest** il a été ordonné prêtre.

ordeal /ɔːˈdiːl, ˈɔːdiːl/ *n* gen épreuve *f*; **to go through/come through an ~** passer par/se sortir d'une rude épreuve; **trial by ~** épreuve judiciaire.

order /ˈɔːdə(r)/ **I** *n* **1** (logical arrangement) ordre *m*; **a sense of ~** un sens de l'ordre; **it's in the natural ~ of things** c'est dans l'ordre naturel des choses; **to produce ~ out of chaos** produire de l'ordre à partir du désordre; **to put** ou **set sth in ~** mettre qch en ordre [*affairs*]; **to set** ou **put one's life in ~** remettre de l'ordre dans sa vie; **2** (sequence) ordre *m*; **to be in alphabetical/chronological ~** être dans l'ordre alphabétique/chronologique; **to put sth in ~** classer [*files, record cards*]; **to put the names in alphabetical ~** mettre les noms par ordre alphabétique; **in ~ of priority** par ordre de priorité; **in ascending/descending ~** dans l'ordre croissant/décroissant; **in the right/wrong ~** dans le bon/mauvais ordre; **to be out of ~** [*files, records*] être en désordre, être mélangé; **3** (discipline, control) ordre *m*; **to restore ~** rétablir l'ordre; **to keep ~** [*police, government*] maintenir l'ordre; [*teacher*] maintenir la discipline; **▶law and order**, **public order**; **4** (established state) ordre *m*; **the old/existing ~** l'ordre ancien/actuel; **5** (command) ordre *m*, consigne *f* (**to do** de faire); **to give/issue an ~** donner/lancer un ordre; **to carry out an ~** exécuter un ordre; **to give an ~ for the crowd to disperse** donner à la foule l'ordre de se disperser; **to be under sb's ~s** être sous les ordres de qn; **to have** ou **to be under ~s to do** avoir (l')ordre de faire; **my ~s are to guard the door** j'ai l'ordre de surveiller l'entrée; **I have ~s not to let anybody through** j'ai ordre de ne laisser passer personne; **to take ~s from sb** recevoir des ordres de qn; **they take their ~s from Paris** ils reçoivent leurs ordres de Paris; **I won't take ~s from you** je ne suis pas à vos ordres; **he won't take ~s from anybody** il ne supporte pas que quiconque lui donne des ordres; **on the ~s of the General** sur les ordres du Général; **to act on sb's ~** agir sur l'ordre de qn; **that's an ~!** c'est un ordre!; **~s are ~s** les ordres sont les ordres; **until further ~s** jusqu'à nouvel ordre; **6** Comm (request to supply) commande *f* (**for** de); (in restaurant) commande *f* (**of** de); **to place an ~** passer une commande; **to put in** ou **place an ~ for sth** commander qch; **to place an ~ with sb for sth** commander qch à qn; **a grocery ~** une commande d'épicerie; **a telephone ~** une commande par téléphone; **a rush/repeat ~** une commande urgente/renouvelée; **the books are on ~** les livres ont été commandés; **made to ~** fait sur commande; **cash with ~** payable à la commande; **7** (operational state) **to be in good/perfect ~** être en bon/parfait état; **in working** ou **running ~** en état de marche; **to be out of ~** [*phone line*] être en dérangement; [*lift, machine*] être en panne; **8** (correct procedure) **to call the meeting to ~** déclarer la séance ouverte; **~!** **~!** un peu de silence, s'il vous plaît!; **to call sb to ~** rappeler qn à l'ordre; **to be in ~** [*documents, paperwork*] être en règle ; **the Honourable member is perfectly in ~** GB Pol Monsieur le député n'enfreint aucunement les règles; **the Speaker ruled the question out of ~** le Président de l'Assemblée a déclaré que cela était contraire à la procédure; **it is perfectly in ~ for him to refuse to pay** il a tout à fait le droit de refuser de payer; **would it be out of ~ for me to phone her at home?** est-ce que ce serait déplacé de lui téléphoner chez elle?; **your remark was way out of ~** ta remarque était tout à fait déplacée; **I hear that congratulations are in ~** il paraît que ça se fait de féliciter; **a toast would seem to be in ~** il me semble qu'un toast serait le bienvenu; **the ~ of the day** Mil, Pol l'ordre du jour; **economy is the ~ of the day** fig l'économie est à l'ordre du jour; **9** (taxonomic group) ordre *m*; **10** Relig ordre *m*; **closed/teaching ~** ordre *m* cloîtré/enseignant; **11** (rank, scale) **craftsmen of the highest ~** des artisans de premier ordre; **investment of this ~ is very welcome** les investissements de cet ordre sont tout à fait souhaitables; **talent of this ~ is rare** un tel talent est rare; **the higher/lower ~s** les classes supérieures/inférieures; **of the ~ of 15%** GB, **in the ~ of 15%** US de l'ordre de 15%; **12** Jur (decree) ordre *m*; **an ~ of the Court** un ordre du tribunal; **by ~ of the Minister** par ordre du ministre; **13** Fin **pay to the ~ of T. Williams** (on cheque, draft) payer à l'ordre de T. Williams; **▶banker's order**, **money order**, **postal order**, **standing order**; **14** (on Stock Exchange) ordre *m* (de Bourse); **buying/selling ~** ordre *m* d'achat/de vente; **limit ~** ordre *m* (à cours) limité; **stop ~** ordre *m* stop; **15** GB (honorary association, title) ordre *m* (**of** de); **she was awarded the Order of the Garter** on lui a conféré l'Ordre de la Jarretière; **16** Archit ordre *m*; **17** Mil (formation) ordre *m*; (clothing) tenue *f*; **battle ~** ordre *m* de bataille; **close ~** ordre *m* serré; **short-sleeve ~** tenue *f* d'été.
II orders *npl* Relig ordres *mpl*; **major/minor ~s** les ordres majeurs/mineurs; **to be in Holy ~** être dans les ordres; **to take Holy ~s** entrer dans les ordres.
III in order that *conj phr* (with the same subject) afin de (+ *infinitive*), pour (+ *infinitive*); (with different subjects) afin que (+ *subj*), pour que (+ *subj*); **I've come in ~ that I might help you** je suis venu pour t'aider; **he brought the proofs in ~ that I might check them** il a apporté les épreuves pour que je puisse les vérifier.
IV in order to *prep phr* pour (+ *infinitive*), afin de (+ *infinitive*); **he came in ~ to talk to me** il est venu pour me parler; **I'll leave in ~ not to disturb you** je partirai pour ne pas te déranger.
V *vtr* **1** (command) ordonner [*inquiry, retrial, investigation*]; **to ~ sb to do** ordonner à qn de faire; **to ~ the closure/delivery of sth** ordonner la fermeture/livraison de qch; **to ~ sb home/to bed** donner à qn l'ordre de rentrer chez lui/d'aller se coucher; **to ~ sth to be done** donner l'ordre de faire qch; **to ~ that sth be done** ordonner que qch soit fait; **the council ~ed the building to be demolished** le conseil municipal a ordonné la démolition de ce bâtiment; **the soldiers were ~ed to disembark** les soldats ont reçu l'ordre de débarquer; **'keep quiet,' she ~ed** 'taisez-vous,' a-t-elle ordonné; **2** (request the supply of) commander [*goods, meal*] (**for sb** pour qn); réserver [*taxi*] (**for** pour); **3** (arrange) organiser [*affairs*]; classer [*files, cards*]; mettre [qch] dans l'ordre [*names, dates*].
VI *vi* [*diner, customer*] commander.
IDIOMS **in short ~** tout de suite.
■ **order about**, **order around**: **~ [sb] around** donner des ordres à qn; **he loves**

~ing people around il adore donner des ordres; **you've got no right to ~ me around** je n'ai pas d'ordre à recevoir de vous.

■ **order off** Sport: **~ [sb] off** [*referee*] expulser [*player*]; **to ~ sb off** ordonner à qn de quitter [*land, grass*].

■ **order out**: **~ [sb] out 1** (summon) appeler [*troops*]; [*union*] appeler [qn] à la grève [*members*]; **2** (send out) **to ~ sb out of** faire sortir qn de [*classroom*].

order book *n* carnet *m* de commandes.

ordered /ˈɔːdəd/ *adj* **1** [*list*] méthodique; [*structure*] régulier/-ière; **an ~ whole** un ensemble ordonné; **a well ~ society/life** une société/vie bien ordonnée; **in ~ ranks** en rangs réguliers; **2** Math [*set*] ordonné.

order: **~ form** *n* bon *m* or bulletin *m* de commande; **Order in Council** *n* GB Pol ≈ décret-loi *m*.

orderliness /ˈɔːdəlɪnɪs/ *n* **1** (of life, habits) régularité *f*; **2** (of room, area) ordre *m*.

orderly /ˈɔːdəlɪ/ **I** *n* **1** Mil planton *m*; **2** Med aide-soignant/-e *m/f*.

II *adj* **1** (well-regulated) [*queue, line*] ordonné; [*arrangement, pattern*] régulier/-ière; [*file, row, rank*] régulier/-ière; [*mind, system*] méthodique; [*lifestyle, society*] bien réglé; **in an ~ fashion** ou **manner** [*leave etc*] dans le calme; **2** (calm) [*crowd, demonstration, debate*] calme.

orderly: **~ officer** *n* Mil officier *m* de service; **~ room** *n* Mil salle *f* de or des rapports.

order: **~ number** *n* numéro *m* de commande; **~ of service** *n* Relig office *m*; **~ paper** *n* GB Pol copie *f* de l'ordre du jour; **~ to view** *n* permis *m* de visiter (une maison à vendre).

ordinal /ˈɔːdɪnl, US -dənl/ *n, adj* ordinal (*m*).

ordinance /ˈɔːdɪnəns/ *n* **1** gen, Jur ordonnance *f*; **2** US Jur Admin arrêté *m* municipal.

ordinand /ˈɔːdɪnənd/ *n* ordinand *m*.

ordinarily /ˈɔːdənrəlɪ, US ˌɔːrdnˈerəlɪ/ *adv* d'ordinaire; **~, it would be fatal** d'ordinaire, ce serait fatal; **more than ~ quiet/cautious** plus calme/prudent que d'ordinaire.

ordinariness /ˈɔːdənrɪnɪs, US ˈɔːrdənerɪnɪs/ *n* banalité *f*.

ordinary /ˈɔːdənrɪ, US ˈɔːrdənerɪ/ **I** *n* **1** (normal) **to be out of the ~** sortir de l'ordinaire; **the trip was something out of the ~** c'était un voyage qui sortait de l'ordinaire; **it's nothing out of the ~** ça n'a rien d'extraordinaire; **2** Relig (of mass) ordinaire *m*; **3** US (penny-farthing) grand bi *m*.

II *adj* **1** (normal) [*experience, clothes*] de tous les jours (*after n*); [*citizen, life, family*] ordinaire; **to seem quite ~** paraître tout à fait ordinaire; **to be just ~ people** n'être que des gens bien ordinaires; **most ~ mortals wouldn't understand it** le commun des mortels ne le comprendrait pas; **objects in ~ use** objets d'usage courant; **this is no ~ case** c'est un cas inhabituel; **in the ~ way, I'd have accepted** normalement or en temps ordinaire, j'aurais accepté; **2** (average) [*consumer, family*] moyen/-enne; **the ~ man in the street** monsieur Tout-le-monde; **3** péj (uninspiring) [*place, film, performance, meal, person*] quelconque.

ordinary: **~ degree** *n* GB licence *f* de niveau moyen; **Ordinary Grade** *n* GB *examen officiel passé à l'âge de 16 ans en Écosse sanctionnant la fin des études obligatoires*; **~ seaman**, **OS** *n* Naut ≈ matelot *m* léger; **~ share** *n* Fin action *f* ordinaire.

ordination /ˌɔːdɪˈneɪʃn, US -dnˈeɪʃn/ *n* ordination *f*.

ordnance /ˈɔːdnəns/ *n* **1** ¢ (supplies) matériel *m* (militaire); **2** Admin (department) ≈ intendance *f*; **3** (artillery) artillerie *f*.

ordnance: **~ depot** *n* dépôt *m* de matériel de guerre; **Ordnance Survey**, **OS** *n* GB (body) *institut géographique national de Grande-Bretagne*; **Ordnance Survey map** *n* ≈ carte *f* d'état-major.

Ordovician /ˌɔːdəˈvɪsɪən, ˌɔːdəʊˈvɪʃɪən/ *adj* ordovicien/-ienne.

ordure /ˈɔːdjʊə(r), US -dʒər/ *n* ordure *f*.

ore /ɔː(r)/ *n* minerai *m*; **iron ~** minerai de fer.

oregano /ˌɒrɪˈgɑːnəʊ/ *n* origan *m*.

Oregon /ˈɒrɪgɒn/ *pr n* Oregon *m*; ▶ **state**.

oreo /ˈəʊrɪəʊ/ *n* US *petit gâteau du chocolat fourré à la vanille*.

Orestes /ɒˈrestiːz/ *pr n* Oreste.

organ /ˈɔːgən/ ▶ **1481** **I** *n* **1** Bot, Anat organe *m*; **to donate an ~** donner un organe; **donor ~**, **transplant ~** (sought) don *m* d'organe; (transplanted) transplant *m*; **male ~** membre *m* viril; **reproductive/sexual ~s** organes reproducteurs/génitaux; **vital ~** organe vital; **~s of speech** organes de la parole; **2** (also **pipe ~**) Mus orgue *m*; **on the ~** à l'orgue; **to play the ~** jouer de l'orgue; (as job) tenir l'orgue; **chamber ~** orgue meuble; **church/cinema ~** orgue d'église/de cinéma; **electric/electronic ~** orgue électrique/électronique; **3** fig (publication, organization) organe *m* (**of** de).

II *modif* Mus [*music, composition*] pour orgue; [*component*] d'orgue.

organ: **~ bank** *n* Med banque *f* d'organes; **~ builder** *n* Mus facteur *m* d'orgues.

organdie, **organdy** US /ˈɔːgəndɪ/ *n* organdi *m*.

organ: **~ donor** *n* Med donneur/-euse *m/f* d'organes; **~ gallery** *n* Archit tribune *f* d'orgue; **~ grinder** ▶ **1692** *n* Mus joueur *m* d'orgue de Barbarie.

organic /ɔːˈgænɪk/ *adj* **1** (not artificial) [*cultivation, grower, produce, restaurant*] biologique; [*fertilizer*] naturel/-elle; [*poultry*] élevé biologiquement; [*meat*] provenant de bétail élevé biologiquement; **2** (of body or plant) [*substance, disease, society*] organique; **3** (integral) [*structure, system, society, unit, whole*] intégré (**to** à); [*part*] intrinsèque; [*development*] organique; **~ law** loi organique.

organically /ɔːˈgænɪklɪ/ *adv* **1** [*grown, raised*] biologiquement; **2** (physiologically) organiquement; **3** [*develop, structured*] organiquement.

organic: **~ chemist** ▶ **1692** *n* chimiste *mf* spécialisé/-e en chimie organique; **~ chemistry** *n* chimie *f* organique.

organism /ˈɔːgənɪzəm/ *n* (all contexts) organisme *m*.

organist /ˈɔːgənɪst/ ▶ **1692**, **1481** *n* organiste *mf*; **church/concert ~** organiste d'église/de concert.

organization /ˌɔːgənaɪˈzeɪʃn, US -nɪˈz-/ *n* **1** (group) gen organisation *f*; (bureaucratic) organisme *m*; (voluntary) association *f*; **employers'/charitable ~** organisation patronale/caritative; **government ~** organisme gouvernemental; **voluntary/human rights ~** association de bénévoles/de défense des droits de l'homme; **2** (arrangement) organisation *f* (**of** de); **3** Ind (unionization) syndicalisation *f*.

organizational /ˌɔːgənaɪˈzeɪʃənl, US -nɪˈz-/ *adj* [*ability, skill, role*] d'organisateur/-trice; [*problem, matter*] d'organisation; [*structure*] de l'organisation.

organizationally /ˌɔːgənaɪˈzeɪʃənəlɪ, US -nɪˈz-/ *adv* du point de vue de l'organisation.

organization: **~ and method(s)**, **O & M** *n* organisation *f* et méthode *f*; **~ chart** *n* organigramme *m*; **Organization of African Unity**, **OAU** *n* Organisation *f* de l'unité africaine.

organize /ˈɔːgənaɪz/ **I** *vtr* **1** (arrange) organiser [*event, day, time, life, facts*]; ranger [*books, papers*]; **to ~ sth into groups/chapters** répartir qch en groupes/chapitres; **I'll ~ the drinks** je m'occuperai des boissons; **I have to ~ the children for school** il faut que je prépare les enfants pour l'école; **I had to ~ a babysitter** j'ai dû trouver une babysitter; **they ~d it** ou **things so I don't have to pay** ils se sont arrangés pour que je n'aie pas à payer; **2** Ind (unionize) syndiquer [*workforce, workers*].

II *vi* (unionize) se syndiquer.

III *v refl* **to ~ oneself** s'organiser (**to do** pour faire).

organized /ˈɔːgənaɪzd/ *adj* **1** [*person, thoughts, household, resistance, support*] organisé; **well/badly ~** bien/mal organisé; **to get ~** s'organiser; **2** [*workforce, workers*] syndiqué.

organized: **~ crime** *n* crime *m* organisé; **~ labour** *n* main-d'œuvre *f* syndiquée; **~ religion** *n*: *la religion en tant qu'institution.*

organizer /ˈɔːgənaɪzə(r)/ *n* **1** (person) organisateur/-trice *m/f* (**of** de); **union ~**, **labour ~** militant/-e *m/f* syndicaliste (*recrutant des ouvriers à la sortie des usines*); **2** (also **personal ~**) (agenda *m*) organisateur *m*; **electronic ~** agenda électronique; **3** (container) **desk ~** (pot *m*) range-tout *m inv*; **shoe ~** range-chaussures *m inv*.

organizer: **~ bag** *n* sac *m* multipoches; **~ file** *n* range-dossiers *m inv*.

organizing /ˈɔːgənaɪzɪŋ/ **I** *n* organisation *f*; **she did all the ~** c'est elle qui a tout organisé; **to be good at ~** avoir le sens de l'organisation.

II *adj* [*group, committee*] organisateur/-trice.

organ: **~ loft** = **organ gallery**; **~ screen** *n* Archit jubé *m*.

organ stop *n* Mus (register) jeu *m* d'orgues; (knob) registre *m* d'orgues.

organ transplant *n* Med transplantation *f* d'organe.

organza /ɔːˈgænzə/ *n* organza *m*.

orgasm /ˈɔːgæzəm/ *n* orgasme *m*.

orgasmic /ɔːˈgæzmɪk/ *adj* **1** Physiol orgasmique; **2** fig extatique.

orgiastic /ˌɔːdʒɪˈæstɪk/ *adj* gen orgiaque; [*scene*] d'orgie.

orgy /ˈɔːdʒɪ/ *n* (all contexts) orgie *f*.

oriel /ˈɔːrɪəl/ *n* (also **~ window**) oriel *m*.

orient /ˈɔːrɪənt/ **I** *n* **the Orient** l'Orient *m*; **in the ~** en Orient.

II *adj* littér oriental; **the Orient Express** Rail l'Orient-Express *m*.

III *vtr* **1** fig orienter [*person, society*] (**at** vers; **towards** en faveur de); **to be ~ed at** viser [*campaign, course*]; **2** lit orienter [*building, map*].

IV *v refl* **to ~ oneself** fig s'adapter (**to, in** à); lit s'orienter.

oriental /ˌɔːrɪˈentl/ **I Oriental** *n* souvent péj Oriental/-e *m/f*.

II *adj* gen oriental; [*appearance, eyes*] d'Oriental; [*carpet*] d'Orient; **~ poppy** pavot *m* orientalis.

orientalist /ˌɔːrɪˈentəlɪst/ ▶ **1692** *n* orientaliste *mf*.

orientate /ˈɔːrɪənteɪt/ *vtr, v refl* = **orient** III, IV.

-orientated /-ˈɔːrɪenteɪtɪd/ (*dans composés*) = **-oriented**.

orientation /ˌɔːrɪənˈteɪʃn/ **I** *n* **1** (training) gen, Univ cours *m* d'introduction; **2** (inclination) (political, intellectual) orientation *f*; (sexual) tendance *f*; **3** Archit, Tech orientation *f*.

II *modif* [*course, week*] d'introduction.

-oriented /-ˈɔːrɪentɪd/ (*dans composés*) **customer-/family-~** orienté vers le client/la famille; **politically ~** politiquement orienté.

orienteering /ˌɔːrɪənˈtɪərɪŋ/ *n* course *f* d'orientation.

orifice /ˈɒrɪfɪs/ *n* gen, Anat orifice *m*.

origami /ˌɒrɪˈgɑːmɪ/ *n* origami *m*.

origin /ˈɒrɪdʒɪn/ *n* **1** gen (of custom, idea, person, relics) origine *f*; **his family has its ~s in Scotland** sa famille est d'origine écossaise; **the problem has its ~(s) in...** le problème provient de...; **2** (of goods) provenance *f*; **of unknown ~** d'origine inconnue; **spare parts of European ~** pièces détachées en provenance d'Europe; **prehistoric in ~** d'origine préhistorique; **country of ~** pays d'origine.

original /əˈrɪdʒənl/ **I** *n* **1** (genuine article) original *m*; **this painting is an ~** ce tableau est un original; **to read sth in the ~** lire qch dans le texte original; **2** (unusual person) original/-e *m/f*.
II *adj* **1** (initial) [*inhabitant, owner*] premier/-ière; [*version*] original; [*comment, question, site, strategy*] originel/-elle; [*member*] originaire; **I saw the film in the ~ version** j'ai vu le film en version originale; **2** (not copied) [*manuscript, painting*] original; [*invoice, receipt*] d'origine; **3** (creative) [*design, suggestion, work, writer*] original; **an ~ thinker** un esprit novateur; **4** (unusual) [*character, person*] original; **he's ~** c'est un original.

original: **~ cost** *n* Comm, Econ prix *m* d'achat; **~ evidence** *n* Jur preuve *f* ayant une force probante propre.

originality /əˌrɪdʒəˈnæləti/ *n* originalité *f*; **of great ~** d'une grande originalité.

original jurisdiction *n* US Jur juridiction *f* de première instance.

originally /əˈrɪdʒənəli/ *adv* **1** (initially) au départ; **~ I had refused** au départ j'avais refusé; **2** (in the first place) à l'origine; **this car was ~ built for export** cette voiture a été fabriquée à l'origine pour l'exportation; **I am** ou **come from France ~** je suis originaire de France; **3** (innovatively) [*speak, think, write*] d'une manière originale.

original sin *n* péché *m* originel.

originate /əˈrɪdʒɪneɪt/ **I** *vtr* [*action, artiste, event*] donner naissance à.
II *vi* [*custom, style, tradition*] voir le jour; [*fire*] se déclarer; **to ~ from** ou **with** [*goods*] provenir de; [*proposal*] émaner de; **this custom ~d in Rome/in the fifteenth century** cette tradition a vu le jour à Rome/au XVᵉ siècle.

originator /əˈrɪdʒɪneɪtə(r)/ *n* **1** (of artwork, idea, rumour) auteur *m*; **2** (of invention, system) créateur/-trice *m/f*; **3** Post, Telecom expéditeur/-trice *m/f*.

Orinoco /ˌɒrɪˈnəʊkəʊ/ **▶ 1644** *pr n* l'Orénoque *m*.

oriole /ˈɔːrɪəʊl/ *n* loriot *m*.

Orion /əˈraɪən/ *pr n* **1** Astron Orion *f*; **2** Mythol Orion *m*.

Orkney /ˈɔːknɪ/ **▶ 1381** *n* (also **~ Islands** *pr npl*) (îles *fpl*) Orcades; **in/on ~** dans les Orcades.

Orlon® /ˈɔːlɒn/ *n* orlon® *m*.

ormer /ˈɔːmə(r)/ *n* ormeau *m*.

ormolu /ˈɔːməluː/ **I** *n* or *m* moulu, chrysocale *m*.
II *modif* [*furniture, object*] en or moulu.

ornament /ˈɔːnəmənt/ **I** *n* **1** (+*c*) (trinket) bibelot *m*; **china ~** bibelot en porcelaine; **2** (-*c*) (decoration) ornement *m*; **(only) for ~** (juste) ornemental; **3** Mus ornement *m*.
II *vtr* **1** gen orner (**with** de); **2** Mus ornementer.

ornamental /ˌɔːnəˈmentl/ **I** *n* Hort (tree) arbre *m* ornemental; (plant) plante *f* ornementale.
II *adj* [*plant*] ornemental; [*garden, lake*] d'agrément; [*motif, artwork, button*] décoratif/-ive.

ornamentation /ˌɔːnəmenˈteɪʃn/ *n* ornementation *f*.

ornate /ɔːˈneɪt/ *adj* gen richement orné; Literat [*style*] très fleuri.

ornately /ɔːˈneɪtlɪ/ *adv* gen richement; [*write*] dans un style fleuri.

ornateness /ɔːˈneɪtnɪs/ *n* (of art) style *m* chargé; (of writing) style *m* fleuri.

Orne **▶ 1163** *pr n* Orne *f*; **in/to the ~** dans l'Orne.

ornery○ /ˈɔːnərɪ/ *adj* US (nasty) [*person, comment, joke*] mesquin, méchant; (cantankerous) [*person*] revêche; (self-willed) entêté, têtu; **an ~ trick** un sale tour.

ornithological /ˌɔːnɪθəˈlɒdʒɪkl/ *adj* ornithologique.

ornithologist /ˌɔːnɪˈθɒlədʒɪst/ **▶ 1692** *n* ornithologue *mf*.

ornithology /ˌɔːnɪˈθɒlədʒɪ/ *n* ornithologie *f*.

orogeny /ɔːˈrɒdʒɪnɪ/ *n* orogénèse *f*.

orphan /ˈɔːfn/ **I** *n* orphelin/-e *m/f*; **war ~** orphelin de guerre.
II *adj* orphelin.
III *vtr* rendre orphelin.

orphanage /ˈɔːfənɪdʒ/ *n* orphelinat *m*.

Orpheus /ˈɔːfɪəs/ *pr n* Orphée.

orrery /ˈɒrərɪ/ *n* planétaire *m*.

orris(-)root /ˈɒrɪsruːt, US ˈɔːr-/ *n* rhizome *m* d'iris.

orthodontic /ˌɔːθəˈdɒntɪk/ *adj* orthodontique.

orthodontics /ˌɔːθəˈdɒntɪks/ *n* (+ *v sg*) orthodontie *f*.

orthodontist /ˌɔːθəˈdɒntɪst/ **▶ 1692** *n* orthodontiste *mf*.

orthodox /ˈɔːθədɒks/ *adj* gen, Relig orthodoxe; **Greek/Russian Orthodox church** église orthodoxe grecque/russe.

orthodoxy /ˈɔːθədɒksɪ/ *n* gen, Relig orthodoxie *f*.

orthogonal /ɔːˈθɒgənl/ *adj* Civ Eng, Math orthogonal.

orthographic(al) /ˌɔːθəˈgræfɪk(l)/ *adj* gen orthographique; [*error, problem*] d'orthographe.

orthographically /ˌɔːθəˈgræfɪklɪ/ *adv* **to be ~ correct/different** avoir une orthographe correcte/différente.

orthography /ɔːˈθɒgrəfɪ/ *n* orthographe *f*.

orthopaedic, **orthopedic** US /ˌɔːθəˈpiːdɪk/ *adj* orthopédique; **~ surgeon** chirurgien *m* orthopédiste.

orthopaedics, **orthopedics** US /ˌɔːθəˈpiːdɪks/ *n* (+ *v sg*) orthopédie *f*.

orthopaedist, **orthopedist** US /ˌɔːθəˈpiːdɪst/ **▶ 1692** *n* orthopédiste *mf*.

ortolan /ˈɔːtələn/ *n* ortolan *m*.

Orwellian /ɔːˈwelɪən/ *adj* orwellien/-ienne.

oryx /ˈɒrɪks, US ˈɔːr-/ *n* (*pl* **~**) oryx *m*.

OS **1** Fashn *abrév* **▶ outsize**; **2** GB Geog *abrév* **▶ Ordnance Survey**; **3** Naut *abrév* **▶ ordinary seaman**.

Oscar /ˈɒskə(r)/ *n* Oscar *m*.

Oscar: **~ nomination** *n* nomination *f* à l'Oscar; **~-winning** *adj* lauréat d'un Oscar.

oscillate /ˈɒsɪleɪt/ **I** *vtr* Phys, Tech faire osciller.
II *vi* gen, Phys, Tech osciller (**between** entre).

oscillation /ˌɒsɪˈleɪʃn/ *n* oscillation *f*.

oscillator /ˈɒsɪleɪtə(r)/ *n* oscillateur *m*.

oscillograph /əˈsɪləgrɑːf, US -græf/ *n* oscillographe *m*.

oscilloscope /əˈsɪləskəʊp/ *n* oscilloscope *m*.

osculate /ˈɒskjʊleɪt/ hum **I** *vtr* embrasser.
II *vi* s'embrasser.

osculation /ˌɒskjʊˈleɪʃn/ *n* **1** Math osculation *f*; **2** littér baiser *m*.

OSHA US (*abrév* = **Occupational Safety and Health Administration**) ≈ inspection *f* du travail.

osier /ˈəʊzɪə(r), US ˈəʊʒər/ *n* osier *m*.

Osiris /əʊˈsaɪrɪs/ *pr n* Osiris.

Oslo /ˈɒzləʊ/ **▶ 1818** *pr n* Oslo.

osmium /ˈɒzmɪəm/ *n* osmium *m*.

osmosis /ɒzˈməʊsɪs/ *n* Biol, Chem, fig osmose *f*; **by ~** par osmose.

osmotic /ɒzˈmɒtɪk/ *adj* osmotique.

osprey /ˈɒspreɪ/ *n* balbuzard *m* pêcheur.

osseous /ˈɒsɪəs/ *adj* osseux/-euse.

ossicle /ˈɒsɪkl/ *n* osselet *m*.

ossiferous /ɒˈsɪfərəs/ *adj* ossifère.

ossification /ˌɒsɪfɪˈkeɪʃn/ *n* **1** Anat ossification *f*; **2** fig sclérose *f*.

ossify /ˈɒsɪfaɪ/ **I** *vtr* **1** Anat ossifier; **2** fig scléroser; **to become ossified** se scléroser.
II *vi* **1** Anat s'ossifier; **2** fig se scléroser.

ossuary /ˈɒsjʊərɪ/ *n* ossuaire *m*.

Ostend /ɒsˈtend/ **▶ 1818** *pr n* Ostende.

ostensible /ɒˈstensəbl/ *adj* apparent.

ostensibly /ɒˈstensəblɪ/ *adv* apparemment.

ostensive /ɒˈstensɪv/ *adj* Philos ostensif/-ive.

ostentation /ˌɒstenˈteɪʃn/ *n* ostentation *f*.

ostentatious /ˌɒstenˈteɪʃəs/ *adj* gen ostentatoire liter; [*surroundings, house, person*] prétentieux/-ieuse.

ostentatiously /ˌɒstenˈteɪʃəslɪ/ *adv* avec ostentation.

osteoarthritis /ˌɒstɪəʊɑːˈθraɪtɪs/ *n* ostéoarthrite *f*.

osteoblast /ˈɒstɪəʊblɑːst/ *n* ostéoblaste *m*.

osteogenesis /ˌɒstɪəʊˈdʒenɪsɪs/ *n* ostéogénèse *f*.

osteology /ˌɒstɪˈɒlədʒɪ/ *n* ostéologie *f*.

osteomalacia /ˌɒstɪəʊməˈleɪʃɪə/ **▶ 1354** *n* ostéomalacie *f*.

osteomyelitis /ˌɒstɪəʊmaɪˈlaɪtɪs/ *n* ostéomyélite *f*.

osteopath /ˈɒstɪəpæθ/ **▶ 1692** *n* ostéopathe *mf*.

osteopathy /ˌɒstɪˈɒpəθɪ/ *n* ostéopathie *f*.

osteophyte /ˈɒstɪəʊfaɪt/ *n* ostéophyte *m*.

osteoplasty /ˈɒstɪəplæstɪ/ *n* ostéoplastie *f*.

osteoporosis /ˌɒstɪəʊpəˈrəʊsɪs/ **▶ 1354** *n* ostéoporose *f*.

osteotomy /ˌɒstɪˈɒtəmɪ/ *n* ostéotomie *f*.

ostler /ˈɒslə(r)/ **▶ 1692** *n* garçon *m* d'écurie.

ostracism /ˈɒstrəsɪzəm/ *n* ostracisme *m*.

ostracize /ˈɒstrəsaɪz/ *vtr* mettre [qn] au ban de la société.

ostrich /ˈɒstrɪtʃ/ **I** *n* Zool, fig autruche *f*.
II *modif* [*feather, egg*] d'autruche.

OT *n* **1** Med *abrév* **▶ occupational therapy, occupational therapist**; **2** Relig *abrév* **▶ Old Testament**; **3** Admin *abrév* **▶ overtime**.

OTC **I** *n* GB Mil *abrév* **▶ Officers' Training Corps**.
II *adv* Fin, Pharm *abrév* **▶ over-the-counter**.

OTE *n* Mgmt *abrév* **▶ on-target earnings**.

other /ˈʌðə(r)/ **I** *adj* **1** (what is left, the rest) autre; **the ~ one** l'autre; **the ~ children** les autres enfants; **the ~ 25** les 25 autres; **2** (alternative, additional) autre; **there was one ~ suggestion** il y a eu une autre suggestion; **I only have one ~ shirt** je n'ai qu'une seule autre chemise; **there are ~ possibilities** il y a d'autres possibilités; **▶ hand, word**; **3** (alternate) **every ~ week** toutes les deux semaines; **every ~ year** tous les deux ans; **every ~ Saturday** un samedi sur deux; **4** (different, not the same) autre; **~ people** les autres; **~ people have read it** d'autres l'ont lu; **~ people's children** les enfants des autres; **in most ~ countries** dans la plupart des autres pays; **I wouldn't have him any ~ way** je ne voudrais pas qu'il change; **some ~ day** ou **time, perhaps** une autre fois peut-être; **it must have been some ~ child** ça devait être un autre enfant; **at all ~ times, phone Paul** en dehors de ces heures-là, téléphone à Paul; **the '~ woman'** (mistress) la maîtresse; **5** (opposite) autre; **on the ~ side of the street** de l'autre côté de la rue; **at the ~ end of the garden** à l'autre bout du jardin; **he was going the ~ way** il allait dans l'autre direction; **6** (recent) **she phoned the ~ week** elle a téléphoné la semaine dernière; **I saw them the ~ day** je les ai vus l'autre jour; **7** (in lists) **it is found in, amongst ~ places, Japan** on en trouve, entre autres, au Japon; **pens, paper and ~ office stationery** des stylos, du papier et autres fournitures de bureau.
II other than *prep phr* **1** (except) **~ than**

that, everything's OK à part ça, tout va bien; **all countries ~ than Spain** tous les pays à part l'Espagne; **there's nobody here ~ than Carole** il n'y a personne d'autre ici à part Carole; **nobody knows ~ than you** personne d'autre que toi n'est au courant; **we can't get home ~ than by car** nous ne pouvons pas rentrer autrement qu'en voiture; **I have no choice ~ than to fire her** je n'ai pas d'autre solution que de la renvoyer; **2** (anything or anyone but) **he could scarcely be ~ than relieved** il aurait difficilement pu être autre chose que soulagé; **ask somebody ~ than Catherine** demande à quelqu'un d'autre que Catherine; ▶ **none**.

III *pron* **the ~s** les autres; **~s** (as subject) d'autres; (as object) les autres; **some like red wine, ~s prefer white** certains aiment le vin rouge, d'autres préfèrent le blanc; **some trains are faster than ~s** certains trains sont plus rapides que d'autres; **each one of them distrusts the ~s** chacun d'entre eux se méfie des autres; **one after the ~** l'un après l'autre; **he's cleverer than all the ~s** il est plus intelligent que tous les autres; **nurses, social workers and ~s** les infirmières, les assistantes sociales et autres; **she doesn't like upsetting ~s** elle n'aime pas vexer les autres; **a family like many ~s** une famille comme beaucoup d'autres; **Lucy, among ~s, has been chosen** Lucy a été choisie parmi d'autres; **Rosie and three ~s** Rosie et trois autres; **there are some ~s** il y en a d'autres; **here's one of them, where's the ~?** en voici un, où est l'autre?; **one or ~ of them will phone** un d'entre eux téléphonera; **somebody** ou **someone or ~ recommended Pauline** quelqu'un m'a recommandé Pauline; **I read it in some book or ~** j'ai lu ça dans un livre, je ne sais plus lequel; **some day or ~** un jour ou l'autre; **somehow or ~** d'une manière ou d'une autre; **in some form or ~** sous une forme ou une autre; **for some reason or ~** pour une raison ou une autre; **he's called Bob something or ~** il s'appelle Bob quelque chose; ▶ **somewhere**.

IDIOMS **do you fancy a bit of the ~**○**?** GB hum et si on faisait l'amour?; **my ~ half**○ ma moitié○ *f*.

other-directed *adj* conformiste.

otherness /ˈʌðənɪs/ *n* étrangeté *f*, altérité *f*.

otherwise /ˈʌðəwaɪz/ **I** *adv* **1** (differently, in other ways) **I have no reason to do ~** je n'ai aucune raison de faire autrement; **if you improve or ~ change the design** si vous améliorez ou que vous modifiez d'une manière ou d'une autre le concept; **no woman, married or ~** aucune femme, mariée ou non; **unless we are told ~, we will go ahead with the work** à moins qu'on nous dise le contraire, nous allons poursuivre le travail; **he says he's 29, but I know ~** il dit qu'il a 29 ans, mais je sais que ce n'est pas le cas; **she thinks she's going to be promoted, but I know ~** elle croit qu'elle va avoir une promotion mais je sais qu'elle se trompe; **William ~ known as Bill** William, qu'on connaît aussi sous le nom de Bill; **2** (in other respects) à part cela, par ailleurs; **my lonely but ~ happy childhood** mon enfance solitaire mais à part cela or par ailleurs heureuse; **he was able to say what he would ~ have kept to himself** il a eu l'occasion de dire ce qu'il aurait gardé pour lui autrement; **there was less damage than might ~ have been the case** il y a eu moins de dégâts qu'on aurait pu s'y attendre.

II *conj* (or else, in other circumstances) sinon; **you have to agree to this, ~ I won't sign the contract** il faut que tu me donnes ton accord sinon je ne signe pas le contrat; **it's quite safe, ~ I wouldn't do it** ce n'est pas dangereux du tout, sinon je ne le ferais pas.

otherworldly /ˌʌðəˈwɜːldlɪ/ *adj* **to be ~** [*person*] ne pas avoir les pieds sur terre.

otiose /ˈəʊtɪəʊs, US ˈəʊʃɪəʊs/ *adj* (pointless) oiseux/-euse.

otitis /əˈtaɪtɪs/ *n* otite *f*.

oto(rhino)laryngology /ˌəʊtə(ˌraɪnəʊ)ˌlærɪnˈgɒlədʒɪ/ *n* oto-rhino-laryngologie *f*.

OTT *adj*: *abrév* ▶ **over-the-top**.

Ottawa /ˈɒtəwə/ ▶ **1818** *pr n* Ottawa.

otter /ˈɒtə(r)/ *n* loutre *f*; **sea ~** loutre marine.

ottoman /ˈɒtəmən/ *n* (sofa) ottomane *f*; (footstool) repose-pied *m*; (fabric) ottoman *m*.

Ottoman /ˈɒtəmən/ **I** *n* Ottoman/-e *m/f*.
II *adj* ottoman.

OU *n* GB Univ *abrév* ▶ **Open University**.

ouch /aʊtʃ/ *excl* aïe.

ought /ɔːt/

■ **Note** In virtually all cases, *ought* is translated by the conditional tense of *devoir*: *you ought to go now* = tu devrais partir maintenant; *they ought to arrive tomorrow* ils devraient arriver demain.
– The past *ought to have done/seen etc* is translated by the past conditional of *devoir*: *he ought to have been more polite* = il aurait dû être plus poli. For further examples, including negative sentences, see the entry below.
– The French verb *devoir* is irregular. For its conjugation see the French verb tables.

modal aux **1** (expressing probability, expectation) **that ~ to fix it** ça devrait arranger les choses; **things ~ to improve by next week** la situation devrait s'améliorer d'ici la semaine prochaine; **the train ~ not to have left yet** le train ne devrait pas encore être parti; **he ~ to be back by now** il devrait être rentré depuis longtemps maintenant; **2** (making polite but firm suggestion) **oughn't we to consult them first?** ne devrions-nous pas les consulter d'abord?; **you ~ to be in bed** tu devrais être au lit; **she ~ to see a doctor** elle devrait consulter un médecin; **3** (indicating moral obligation) **we really ~ to say something** nous devrions vraiment dire quelque chose; **you ~ not to say things like that** tu ne devrais pas dire des choses pareilles; **someone ~ to have accompanied her** quelqu'un aurait dû l'accompagner; **I ~ not to have been so direct** je n'aurais pas dû être aussi direct; **he felt he ~ not to be wasting time** il se disait qu'il n'avait pas de temps à perdre; **4** (when prefacing important point) **I ~ to say perhaps that** je devrais peut-être préciser que; **I think you ~ to know that** je pense qu'il vaudrait mieux que tu saches que.

Ouija® /ˈwiːdʒə/ *n* (also **ouija board**) ouija *m inv*.

ounce /aʊns/ ▶ **1883**, **1068** *n* **1** (weight) once *f* (= *28,35 g*); **2** GB (fluid) = *0,028 l*; US = *0,035 l*; **3** fig once *f*.

our /ˈaʊə(r), ɑː(r)/

■ **Note** In French, determiners agree in gender and number with the noun they qualify. So *our* is translated by *notre* + masculine or feminine singular noun (notre chien, notre maison) and *nos* + plural noun (nos enfants).
– When *our* is stressed, *à nous* is added after the noun: OUR house = notre maison à nous.
– For *our* used with parts of the body ▶ **1037**.

det notre/nos; **~ mother** notre mère; **~ children** nos enfants.

ours /aʊəz/

■ **Note** In French, pronouns reflect the number and gender of the noun they are standing for. Thus *ours* is translated by *le nôtre, la nôtre* or *les nôtres* according to what is being referred to: *the blue car is ours* = la voiture bleue est la nôtre; *their children are older than ours* = leurs enfants sont plus âgés que les nôtres.

pron le nôtre/la nôtre/les nôtres; **their car is red but ~ is blue** leur voiture est rouge mais la nôtre est bleue; **which tickets are ~?** lesquels de ces billets sont les nôtres?; **she's a friend of ~** c'est une amie à nous; **he's no friend of ~!** ce n'est pas un ami à nous!; **the book isn't ~ to lend you** nous ne pouvons pas te prêter ce livre, il n'est pas à nous; **~ is not an easy task** fml notre tâche n'est pas facile.

ourself /aʊəˈself, ɑː-/ *pron* sout (royal, editorial) nous-même.

ourselves /aʊəˈselvz, ɑː-/

■ **Note** When used as a reflexive pronoun, direct and indirect, *ourselves* is translated by *nous* in standard French: *we've hurt ourselves* = nous nous sommes fait mal. However, if the more informal *on* is used to translate *we*, the translation of ourselves will be *se* (or *s'* before a vowel): on s'est fait mal.
– When used as an emphatic the translation is *nous-mêmes*: *we did it ourselves* = nous l'avons fait nous-mêmes.
– When used after a preposition *ourselves* is translated by *nous* or *nous-mêmes*.

pron **1** (refl) nous; **2** (emphatic) nous-mêmes; **3** (after prep) **for ~** pour nous, pour nous-mêmes; **(all) by ~** tout seuls/toutes seules.

oust /aʊst/ *vtr* évincer [*person*] (**from** de; **as** comme); forcer [qn] à démissionner [*government*].

out /aʊt/

■ **Note** *out* is used after many verbs in English to alter or reinforce the meaning of the verb (*hold out, wipe out, filter out etc*). Very often in French, a verb alone will be used to translate these combinations. For translations you should consult the appropriate verb entry (***hold***, ***wipe***, ***filter*** etc).
– When *out* is used as an adverb meaning *outside*, it often adds little to the sense of the phrase: *they're out in the garden = they're in the garden*. In such cases *out* will not usually be translated: *ils sont dans le jardin*.
– *out* is used as an adverb to mean *absent* or *not at home*. In this case *she's out* really means *she's gone out* and the French translation is *elle est sortie*.
– For the phrase *out of* see III in the entry below.
– For examples of the above and other uses, see the entry below.

I *vtr* révéler l'homosexualité de [*person*]; ▶ **come out**.

II *adv* **1** (outside) dehors; **to stand ~ in the rain** rester (dehors) sous la pluie; **to be ~ in the garden** être dans le jardin; **~ there** dehors; **~ here** ici; **2** (from within) **to go** ou **walk ~** sortir; **to pull/take sth ~** retirer/sortir qch; **I couldn't find my way ~** je ne trouvais pas la sortie; **'Out'** (exit) 'Sortie'; **(get) ~!** dehors!; **3** (away from land, base) **~ in China/Australia** en Chine/Australie; **two days ~ from port/camp** à deux jours du port/camp; **when the tide is ~** à marée basse; **further ~** plus loin; **4** (in the world at large) **there are a lot of people ~ there looking for work** il y a beaucoup de gens qui cherchent du travail en ce moment; **5** (absent) **to be ~** gen être sorti; [*strikers*] être en grève; **while you were ~** pendant que tu étais sorti; **she's ~ shopping** elle est sortie faire les courses; **6** (in slogans) **'Tories ~!'** 'les conservateurs dehors!'; **7** (for social activity) **to invite sb ~ to dinner** inviter qn au restaurant; **a day ~ at the seaside** une journée au bord de la mer; **let's have an evening ~ this week** si on sortait un soir de la semaine?; **8** (published, now public) **to be ~** [*book, exam results*] être publié; **my secret is ~** mon secret est révélé; **truth will ~** la vérité éclatera; **9** (in bloom) **to be ~** [*tree, shrub*] être en fleurs; **to be fully ~** [*flower*] être épanoui; **10** (in view) **to be ~** [*sun, moon , stars*] briller; **11** (extinguished) **to be ~** [*fire, light*] être éteint; **lights ~ at 10.30 pm** extinction des feux à 22 h 30; **12** Sport, Games **to be ~** [*player*] être éliminé; **'~!'** (of ball) 'out!'; **13** (unconscious) **to be ~ (cold)**○ gen être dans les pommes○; [*boxer*] être K.O.; **14** (over, finished) **before the week is ~** avant la fin de la semaine; **15** GB (incorrect) **to be ~ in one's calculations** s'être trompé dans ses calculs; **to be three degrees ~** se tromper de trois degrés; **my watch is two minutes ~** (slow) ma montre retarde de deux minutes; (fast) ma montre avance de deux minutes; **16**○ (not possible) **no that option is ~** non cette solution est exclue; **17**○ (actively in search of) **to be ~ to do sth** être bien décidé à faire qch; **to be ~ for revenge** ou **to get sb** être bien décidé à se venger de qn; **he's just ~ for what he can get** péj il ne rate aucune occasion○; **18**○ (not in fashion) **to be ~** [*style, colour*] être passé de mode; **19**○ (in holes) **trousers with the knees ~** pantalon troué aux genoux; **20**○ GB (ever) **he's the kindest/stupidest person ~** c'est la personne la plus gentille/stupide qui soit.

III out of *prep phr* **1** (from) **to go** ou **walk** ou **come ~ of the house** sortir de la maison; **get ~ of here!** sors d'ici!; **to jump ~ of bed/of the window** sauter hors du lit/par la fenêtre; **to tear a page ~ of a book** arracher une page d'un livre; **to take sth ~ of a box/of a drawer** retirer qch d'une boîte/d'un tiroir; **to take sth ~ of one's bag/one's pocket** prendre qch dans son sac/sa poche; **2** (expressing ratio) sur; **two ~ of every three people** deux personnes sur trois; **3** (part of whole) **a paragraph ~ of a book** un paragraphe tiré d'un livre; **like something ~ of a horror movie** comme quelque chose qui sort tout droit d'un film d'horreur; **4** Jur **to be ~** [*jury*] être en délibération; **5** (beyond defined limits) hors de [*reach, sight, water*]; en dehors de [*city, compound*]; **6** (free from confinement) **to be ~ of hospital/of prison** être sorti de l'hôpital/de prison; **7** (expressing shelter) à l'abri de [*sun, rain*]; **8** (lacking) **to be (right) ~ of** ne plus avoir de [*item, commodity*]; **9** (made from) en [*wood, plasticine, metal*]; **10** (due to) par [*malice, respect etc*]; **11** Equit, Turf (lineage of horse) **Rapido ~ of Lightning** Rapido par Lightning.

IDIOMS **I want ~**○**!** je ne marche plus avec vous/eux etc○; **go on, ~ with it**○**!** allez, accouche○!, allez, dis ce que tu as à dire; **to be on the ~s**○ **with sb** US être brouillé avec qn; **to be ~ and about** gen sortir; (after illness) être à nouveau sur pied; **to be ~ of it**○ être dans les vapes○; **to feel ~ of it** se sentir exclu; **you're well ~ of it** tu fais bien de ne pas t'en mêler.

outage /ˈaʊtɪdʒ/ *n* **1** Comm (missing goods) marchandises *fpl* perdues; **2** Ind (stoppage) panne *f*; **power ~** panne de courant.

out and away *adv* de loin; **he's ~ the best athlete** c'est de loin le meilleur athlète.

out-and-out /ˌaʊtənˈaʊt/ *adj* [*villain, liar etc*] fieffé (*before n*); [*adherent*] pur et dur; [*success, failure*] total.

outback /ˈaʊtbæk/ *n* **the ~** la brousse (australienne).

outbalance /ˌaʊtˈbæləns/ *vtr* l'emporter sur.

outbid /ˌaʊtˈbɪd/ *vtr* (*p prés* **-dd-**; *prét, pp* **outbid**) surenchérir sur.

outboard /ˈaʊtbɔːd/ **I** *n* (engine) moteur *m* hors-bord; (boat) hors-bord *m inv*.

II *adj* hors-bord *inv*.

outbound /ˈaʊtbaʊnd/ *adj* [*mail, traffic*] sortant de la ville.

outbreak /ˈaʊtbreɪk/ *n* (of war, unrest) déclenchement *m*; (of violence, spots) éruption *f*; (of disease) déclaration *f*; **at the ~ of war** quand la guerre a éclaté; **an ~ of rain** une ondée.

outbuilding /ˈaʊtbɪldɪŋ/ *n* dépendance *f*.

outburst /ˈaʊtbɜːst/ *n* (of laughter) éclat *m*; (of anger) accès *m*; (of weeping) crise *f*; (of energy) bouffée *f*; (of vandalism, trouble) éruption *f*.

outcast /ˈaʊtkɑːst, US -kæst/ *n* exclu/-e *m/f*.

outclass /ˌaʊtˈklɑːs, US -ˈklæs/ *vtr* dominer.

outcome /ˈaʊtkʌm/ *n* résultat *m*.

outcrop /ˈaʊtkrɒp/ *n* affleurement *m*.

outcry /ˈaʊtkraɪ/ *n* tollé *m* (**about, against** contre).

outdated /ˌaʊtˈdeɪtɪd/ *adj* [*idea, theory, practice*] dépassé; [*style, clothing, product*] démodé; [*word, expression*] vieilli.

outdistance /ˌaʊtˈdɪstəns/ *vtr* lit, fig distancer.

outdo /ˌaʊtˈduː/ (*prét* **outdid**, *pp* **outdone**) **I** *vtr* surpasser (**in** en); **not to be outdone he redoubled his efforts** ne voulant pas être en reste, il redoubla ses efforts.

II *v refl* **to ~ oneself** se surpasser.

outdoor /ˈaʊtdɔː(r)/ *adj* [*life, activity, sport*] de plein air; [*cinema, entertainment*] en plein air; [*restaurant, sports facilities*] en plein air; [*centre*] de plein air; [*person*] sportif/-ive; [*plant, clothing*] d'extérieur; [*shoes*] de marche; **to lead an ~ life** vivre au grand air.

outdoors /ˌaʊtˈdɔːz/ **I** *n* **the great ~** (+ *v sg*) la pleine nature.

II *adv* [*be, sit, work*] dehors; [*live*] en plein air; [*sleep*] à la belle étoile; **to go ~** sortir.

outer /ˈaʊtə(r)/ *adj* **1** (furthest) [*limit*] extrême; **2** (outside) gen extérieur; [*clothing*] de dessus.

outermost /ˈaʊtəməʊst/ *adj* **1** (furthest) le/la plus éloigné/-e; **2** (outside) premier/-ière.

outer: **~ office** *n* ≈ réception *f*; **~ space** *n* espace *m* extra-atmosphérique or extérieur; **~ suburbs** *npl* grande banlieue *f*.

outerwear /ˈaʊtəweə(r)/ *n* US vêtements *mpl* d'extérieur.

outface /ˌaʊtˈfeɪs/ *vtr* dévisager.

outfall /ˈaʊtfɔːl/ *n* (of drain) bouche *f* d'évacuation; (of lake, sewer) déversoir *m*; (of river) embouchure *f*.

outfall pipe *n* tuyau *m* d'évacuation.

outfield /ˈaʊtfiːld/ *n* Sport terrain *m* extérieur.

outfit /ˈaʊtfɪt/ **I** *n* **1** (set of clothes) (for men) costume *m*; (for women) tenue *f*; (for fancy dress) panoplie *f*; **a cowboy's ~** une panoplie de cowboy; **riding/tennis ~** tenue *f* d'équitation/de tennis; **2**○ (company) boîte○ *f*, entreprise *f*; **publishing ~** maison *f* d'édition; **3**○ (group) Sport équipe *f*; Mus groupe *m*; Mil unité *f*; **4** (kit) équipement *m*.

II *vtr* (*p prés etc* **-tt-**) **1** (equip) équiper [*company*]; **2** (dress) habiller [*person*].

outfitter /ˈaʊtfɪtə(r)/ ▶ 1692 *n* **1** (supplier) fournisseur *m*; **2** Fashn spécialiste *mf* de la confection; **ladies'/men's ~** spécialiste *mf* de confection pour femmes/hommes; **school/theatrical ~** fournisseur *m* d'uniformes scolaires/de costumes pour le théâtre; **an ~'s** une maison de confection.

outflank /ˌaʊtˈflæŋk/ *vtr* Mil, fig déborder.

outflow /ˈaʊtfləʊ/ *n* (of money) sortie *f*; (of ideas, emigrants) fuite *f*; (of liquid) écoulement *m*.

outfox /ˌaʊtˈfɒks/ *vtr* se montrer plus malin que.

outgoing /ˈaʊtgəʊɪŋ/ *adj* **1** (sociable) ouvert et sociable; **2** (departing) [*government, president, tenant*] sortant; [*mail*] à expédier; [*tide*] descendant; Telecom **~ call** appel téléphonique.

outgoings /ˈaʊtgəʊɪŋz/ *npl* GB sorties *fpl* (de fonds).

outgrow /aʊtˈgrəʊ/ *vtr* (*prét* **outgrew**, *pp* **outgrown**) **1** (grow too big for) devenir trop grand pour; **the population has outgrown its resources** la croissance de la population a rendu ses ressources insuffisantes; **2** (grow too old for) se lasser de [qch] avec le temps; **don't worry he'll ~ it** ne t'inquiète pas ça lui passera; **3** (grow taller than) devenir plus grand que.

outgrowth /ˈaʊtgrəʊθ/ *n* **1** Bot, Med excroissance *f*; **2** (spin-off) retombées *fpl*; (of theory) corollaire *m*.

outguess /ˌaʊtˈges/ *vtr* (anticipate) deviner les intentions de; (outsmart) être plus malin que.

outgun /ˌaʊtˈgʌn/ *vtr* (*p prés etc* **-nn-**) fig dominer.

outhouse /ˈaʊthaʊs/ *n* **1** (separate) dépendance *f*; (adjoining) appentis *m*; **2** US toilettes *fpl* (extérieures).

outing /ˈaʊtɪŋ/ *n* **1** (excursion) sortie *f*; **school ~** sortie avec l'école; **to go on an ~** faire une sortie; **2** (revealing homosexuality) **the ~ of sb** la révélation (au public) de l'homosexualité de qn.

outlandish /aʊtˈlændɪʃ/ *adj* bizarre.

outlast /ˌaʊtˈlɑːst, US -læst/ *vtr* durer plus longtemps que.

outlaw /ˈaʊtlɔː/ **I** *n* hors-la-loi *m inv*.

II *vtr* **1** déclarer illégal [*practice, organization*]; **2** Hist Jur mettre [qn] hors la loi [*criminal*]; **3** US Jur annuler [*contract*].

outlay /ˈaʊtleɪ/ *n* dépenses *fpl* (**on** en); **capital ~** frais *mpl* d'établissement; **initial ~** mise *f* de fonds initiale.

outlet /ˈaʊtlet/ *n* **1** lit (for gas, air, water) tuyau *m* de sortie; **sink ~** tuyau d'écoulement; **2** Comm (market) débouché *m*; (shop) point *m* de vente; **retail ~, sales ~** point *m* de vente; **3** fig (for energy, emotion, talent) exutoire *m*; **4** US Elec prise *f* de courant.

outlet valve *n* soupape *f* d'échappement.

outline /ˈaʊtlaɪn/ **I** *n* **1** (of object) contour *m*; (of house, mountain, tree) contour *m*, profil *m*; (of face) profil *m*; **2** Art (sketch) ébauche *f*, premier jet *m*; **to draw sth in ~** dessiner qch au trait; **3** (general plan, synopsis) (of plan, policy, reasons) idée *f*, bref exposé *m*; (of essay) (sketchy) ébauche *f*; (more structured) plan *m*; **to describe a plan in broad ~** décrire un projet dans ses grandes lignes or à gros traits; **to give a brief ~ of a plan** présenter un projet dans ses grandes lignes; **in ~, the rules are...** en gros or grosso modo, les règles sont...; **'An Outline of World History'** (title) 'Éléments *mpl* de l'histoire du monde'; **4** (in shorthand) sténogramme *m*.

II *vtr* **1** (give general summary of) exposer brièvement [*aims, motives, reasons*]; donner un aperçu de, présenter [qch] dans ses grandes lignes [*plan, solution*]; **2** (draw round, delineate) souligner le contour de [*eye, picture*] (**in, with** en); **to be ~ed against the sky** se découper sur le ciel.

outline: **~ agreement** *n* accord-cadre *m*; **~ map** *n* fond *m* de carte; **~ planning application** *n* GB avant-projet *m* sommaire; **~ planning permission** *n* GB permis *m* de construire provisoire; **~ proposal** *n* GB = **outline planning application**.

outlive /ˌaʊtˈlɪv/ *vtr* **1** (live longer than) survivre à [*person*]; **she ~d her husband by ten years** elle a survécu dix ans à son mari; **2** (outlast) survivre à [*person, era*]; **he/it has ~d his/its usefulness** il a fait son temps.

outlook /ˈaʊtlʊk/ *n* **1** (attitude) conception *f*, vue *f*; **a narrow/positive ~** une conception or vue étroite/positive; **to change one's ~ on life** changer sa conception de la vie; **to be conservative in ~** avoir une conception or vue conservatrice des choses; **2** (prospects) perspectives *fpl* (**for** pour); **the economic ~ is bleak/bright** les perspectives économiques sont sombres/excellentes; **the ~ for tomorrow is rain** Meteorol demain on prévoit un temps pluvieux; **3** (from window, house) vue *f* (**over, onto** sur); **rural ~** vue sur la campagne.

outlying /ˈaʊtlaɪɪŋ/ *adj* (away from city centre) excentré; (remote) isolé.

outmanoeuvre GB, **outmaneuver** US /ˌaʊtməˈnuːvə(r)/ *vtr* déjouer les plans de.

outmoded /ˌaʊtˈməʊdɪd/ *adj* dépassé.

outnumber /ˌaʊtˈnʌmbə(r)/ *vtr* être plus

nombreux que; **they were ~ed by two to one** ils étaient deux fois moins nombreux.

out-of-body experience *n* projection *f* hors du corps.

out of bounds *adj, adv* **1 to be ~** [*area*] être interdit (**to** à); **'Out of bounds'** (on sign) 'Interdit'; **2** US Sport **to be ~** être hors jeu.

out: **~-of-date** *adj* [*ticket, passport*] périmé; [*clothing, custom*] démodé; [*theory, concept*] dépassé; **~ of doors** *adv* = **outdoors**.

out-of-pocket *adj* **1 ~ expenses** frais *mpl* complémentaires; **2 to be out of pocket** être perdant.

out-of-sight○ *adj* **1** (fantastic) fantastique○, super○; **2** (odd) farfelu○.

out-of-the-way **I** *adj* [*places*] à l'écart; **an ~ spot** un trou perdu○.

II out of the way *adv phr* **get out of the way!** pousse-toi!; **I should stay out of the way until tomorrow** à ta place j'éviterais de me montrer jusqu'à demain.

outpace /ˌaʊt'peɪs/ *vtr* lit distancer; fig devancer.

outpatient /'aʊtpeɪʃnt/ *n* malade *mf* externe; **~s' clinic, ~s' department** service *m* de consultation.

outplacement /'aʊtpleɪsmənt/ **I** *n* Comm aide *f* au placement de cadres surnuméraires.

II *modif* [*agency, consultant*] de placement de cadres surnuméraires.

outplay /ˌaʊt'pleɪ/ *vtr* Sport dominer.

outpoint /ˌaʊt'pɔɪnt/ *vtr* Sport (in boxing) battre aux points.

outpost /'aʊtpəʊst/ *n* Mil, gen avant-poste *m*; **the last ~ of imperialism** le dernier bastion de l'impérialisme.

outpouring /'aʊtpɔːrɪŋ/ *n* (of words, emotion etc) débordement *m*.

output /'aʊtpʊt/ **I** *n* **1** Comm, Ind (of land, machine, mine, worker) rendement *m*; (of factory) production *f*; **industrial ~, manufacturing ~** rendement industriel; **2** Electron, Mech (of equipment, engine) puissance *f*; (of monitor) signal *m*; **cardiac ~** débit *m* cardiaque; **3** Comput (données *fpl* de) sortie *f*; **computer ~** sortie *f* d'ordinateur; **4** (of composer, writer) production *f*; **5** Radio, TV production *f*.

II *modif* [*data, device, power*] de sortie.

III *vtr* (*p prés* **-tt-**; *prét, pp* **-put** ou **-putted**) [*computer*] sortir [*data, results*]; **to ~ sth to a printer** sortir qch sur une imprimante.

outrage /'aʊtreɪdʒ/ **I** *n* **1** (anger) indignation *f* (**at** devant); **sense of ~** sentiment de profonde indignation; **2** (horrifying act) attentat *m* (**against** contre); **bomb ~** attentat à la bombe; **3** (scandal) (against decency, morality) outrage *m* (**against** à; **to** à; **to do** de faire); **it's an ~ that** c'est un scandale que (+ *subj*).

II *vtr* outrager [*feelings, morality*]; scandaliser [*person, public*].

III outraged *pp adj* outragé (**by** par).

outrageous /aʊt'reɪdʒəs/ *adj* **1** (disgraceful) scandaleux/-euse (**to do** de faire); **it is ~ that** il est scandaleux que (+ *subj*); **2** (unconventional) [*person, dress*] insensé; [*remark*] outrancier/-ière.

outrageously /aʊt'reɪdʒəslɪ/ *adv* outrageusement.

outrageousness /aʊt'reɪdʒəsnɪs/ *n* caractère *m* outrageant.

outrank /ˌaʊt'ræŋk/ *vtr* avoir un grade supérieur à.

outré /'uːtreɪ, US uː'treɪ/ *adj* outrancier/-ière.

outreach /'aʊtriːtʃ/ **I** *n* **1** Soc Admin assistance *f*; **2** (extent) portée *f*.

II *modif* **1** Soc Admin [*group, work*] d'assistance; **~ worker** bénévole *mf* d'un organisme d'assistance; **2** US [*program*] destiné au grand public.

outrider /'aʊtraɪdə(r)/ *n* (also **motorcycle ~**) motard *m* (*d'une escorte*).

outrigger /'aʊtrɪgə(r)/ *n* outrigger *m*.

outright /'aʊtraɪt/ **I** *adj* **1** (absolute) [*independence*] total; [*control, defiance, lead, majority*] absolu; [*gift, owner, purchase, sale*] inconditionnel/-elle; [*ban, refusal, rejection*] catégorique; [*attack*] direct; **2** (obvious) [*favourite, victory, winner*] incontesté; [*criminal, liar*] invétéré; **3** (unreserved) [*egoism*] sans mélange; [*contempt, disbelief, hostility*] pur et simple.

II *adv* **1** (completely) [*ban, deny, oppose, refuse*] catégoriquement; [*win*] sans contestation possible; [*buy, sell*] comptant; [*kill*] sur le coup; **2** (openly) [*ask, say, tell*] franchement; **to laugh ~ at sb** rire au nez de qn; **he laughed ~ at my idea** mon idée l'a fait éclater de rire.

outrun /ˌaʊt'rʌn/ *vtr* (*p prés* **-nn-**; *prét, pp* **-ran**) **1** lit distancer; **2** fig (exceed) dépasser.

outsell /ˌaʊt'sel/ **I** *vtr* (*prét, pp* **-sold**) être meilleur vendeur que.

II *vtr* [*product*] se vendre mieux que.

outset /'aʊtset/ *n* **at the ~** au début; **from the ~** dès le début.

outshine /ˌaʊt'ʃaɪn/ *vtr* fig éclipser.

outside /aʊt'saɪd, 'aʊtsaɪd/ **I** *n* **1** (of object, building) extérieur *m*; **to be blue/crisp on the ~** être bleu/croustillant à l'extérieur; **on the ~ of** (on surface itself) sur l'extérieur de [*box, file, fabric*]; (in external space) à l'extérieur de [*building*]; **you can't open the door from the ~** on ne peut pas ouvrir la porte de dehors or de l'extérieur; **2** Aut **to overtake on the ~** GB, Austral etc doubler sur la droite; US, Europe etc doubler sur la gauche; **3** (in motor racing) extérieur *m*; **4** (not within company, institution etc) extérieur *m*; **to bring in an expert from (the) ~** faire venir un expert de l'extérieur; **to smuggle sth in from (the) ~** faire entrer qch clandestinement; **5** fig (from objective position) **from (the) ~** de l'extérieur; **6** (maximum) **at the ~** au maximum.

II *adj* **1** (outdoor) [*temperature*] extérieur; [*toilet*] à l'extérieur; TV, Radio [*broadcast*] enregistré hors studio; **2** (outer) [*measurement, edge, wall*] extérieur; **3** Telecom [*line*] extérieur; [*call*] de l'extérieur; **4** (beyond usual environment) [*interests, commitments*] (outside home) en dehors de la maison; (outside work) en dehors de son/votre etc travail; **the ~ world** le monde extérieur; **5** (from elsewhere) [*help*] de l'extérieur; [*influence*] extérieur; **an ~ opinion** l'avis de quelqu'un qui n'est pas impliqué; **6 ~ lane** GB, Austral etc voie *f* de droite; US, Europe etc voie *f* de gauche; (on athletics track) couloir *m* extérieur; **7** (faint) **an ~ chance** une faible chance.

III *adv* [*play, wait*] dehors; [*film*] tourné en extérieur.

IV outside in *adj phr, adv phr* à l'envers.

V *prep* (also **~ of**) **1** (not within) en dehors de [*city, community*]; de l'autre côté de [*boundary*]; à l'extérieur de [*convent, prison*]; au large de [*harbour*]; **2** (in front of) devant [*house, shop*]; **3** (over) **to wear a shirt ~ one's trousers** porter une chemise sur son pantalon; **4** fig (beyond) **~ her family/her work** en dehors de ses proches/son travail; **~ office hours** en dehors des heures de bureau; **~ our jurisdiction** hors de notre juridiction; **it's ~ my experience** je n'ai jamais été confronté à ce problème.

outside: **~ examiner** *n* GB Sch, Univ examinateur/-trice *m/f* qui vient de l'extérieur; **~ left** (in football) ailier *m* gauche.

outsider /ˌaʊt'saɪdə(r)/ *n* **1** (stranger) (in community) étranger/-ère *m/f*; (to organization, company) personne *f* de l'extérieur; **2** (person, horse) (unlikely to win) outsider *m*; **a complete** ou **rank ~** un parfait outsider.

outside right (in football) ailier *m* droit.

outsize /'aʊtsaɪz/ **I** *n* Comm grandes tailles *fpl*.

II *modif* Comm [*department, shop, clothing*] grandes tailles.

III *adj* gen (also **~d**) énorme.

outsized /'aʊtsaɪzd/ *adj* démesuré, gigantesque.

outsize load *n* Transp convoi *m* exceptionnel.

outskirts /'aʊtskɜːts/ *npl* **1** (of town, city) périphérie *f*; **on the ~** à la périphérie (**of** de); **2** (of forest) lisière *f*.

outsmart /ˌaʊt'smɑːt/ *vtr* se montrer plus futé que.

outspoken /ˌaʊt'spəʊkən/ *adj* **1** (frank) [*opponent, support*] déclaré; [*critic*] qui ne mâche pas ses mots; [*criticism*] franc/franche; **to be ~ in one's remarks/criticism** parler/critiquer sans détour; **2** euph (rude) direct.

outspokenly /ˌaʊt'spəʊkənlɪ/ *adv* gen [*honest, feminist etc*] carrément; [*oppose*] catégoriquement.

outspokenness /aʊt'spəʊkənnɪs/ *n* francparler *m*.

outspread /ˌaʊt'spred/ *adj* [*arms*] grand ouvert; [*wings*] déployé; [*fingers*] écarté.

outstanding /ˌaʊt'stændɪŋ/ *adj* **1** (excellent) [*achievement, performance, career*] exceptionnel/-elle, remarquable; **2** (prominent, conspicuous) [*example, feature*] remarquable, frappant; **3** (unresolved) [*problem, issue*] en suspens; [*correspondence, orders*] en souffrance; [*work*] inachevé; [*bill, account*] impayé; [*interest*] échu; **what is the amount ~?** à combien s'élève l'arriéré?; **questions ~ from the previous meeting** des questions qui n'ont pas été résolues lors de la dernière réunion; **~ debts** créances *fpl* à recouvrer; **~ shares** Fin actions *fpl* en circulation.

outstandingly /ˌaʊt'stændɪŋlɪ/ *adv* **1** (particularly) exceptionnellement; **2** (extremely) remarquablement; **~ good** remarquable.

outstay /ˌaʊt'steɪ/ *vtr* **to ~ sb** rester plus longtemps que qn.

IDIOMS **to ~ one's welcome** s'éterniser.

outstretched /ˌaʊt'stretʃt/ *adj* [*hand, arm, fingers*] tendu; [*wings*] déployé; [*legs*] étendu; **to welcome sb with ~ arms** accueillir qn à bras ouverts.

outstrip /ˌaʊt'strɪp/ *vtr* (*p prés etc* **-pp-**) dépasser [*person*]; excéder [*production*]; être supérieur à [*demand, supply*].

outtake /'aʊtteɪk/ *n* Cin chute *f*.

out-tray *n* corbeille *f* départ.

outturn /'aʊttɜːn/ *n* production *f*.

outvote /ˌaʊt'vəʊt/ *vtr* (in election) battre [qn] aux voix; (on issue) mettre [qn] en minorité; **to be ~d** être battu aux voix.

outward /'aʊtwəd/ **I** *adj* **1** (external) [*appearance, sign*] extérieur; [*calm*] apparent; **to all ~ appearances** en apparence; **2** (from port, base) [*freight, ship*] en partance; **~ journey** aller *m*.

II *adv* = **outwards**.

outward bound **I** *adj* [*ship*] en partance.

II *adv* US **to be ~** être en partance (**from** de; **for** pour).

Outward Bound movement *n*: *groupe d'activités en plein air pour adolescents*.

outwardly /'aʊtwədlɪ/ *adv* **1** (apparently) [*calm, confident, indifferent etc*] en apparence; **2** (seen from outside) de l'extérieur.

outwards /'aʊtwədz/ *adv* (also **outward**) [*open, bend, grow*] vers l'extérieur; **to face ~** [*room*] donner sur la rue; [*person*] se tourner vers l'extérieur.

outweigh /ˌaʊt'weɪ/ *vtr* l'emporter sur (*never passive*); **the advantages ~ the disadvantages, the disadvantages are ~ed by the advantages** les avantages l'emportent sur les inconvénients.

outwit /ˌaʊt'wɪt/ *vtr* (*p prés etc* **-tt-**) gen être plus futé que; déjouer la surveillance de [*guard*]; déjouer les manœuvres de [*opponent*].

outwith /aʊt'wɪθ/ *prep* Scot = **outside**.

outwork /'aʊtwɜːk/ *n* GB travail *m* à domicile.

outworker /ˈaʊtwɜːkə(r)/ *n* GB travailleur/-euse *m/f* à domicile.

outworn /ˌaʊtˈwɔːn/ *adj* [*custom, theory, system*] désuet/-ète; [*clothing, expression*] usé.

ouzel /ˈuːzl/ *n* = **ring ouzel**.

ouzo /ˈuːzəʊ/ *n* ouzo *m*.

ova /ˈəʊvə/ *pl* ▶ **ovum**.

oval /ˈəʊvl/ **I** *n* ovale *m*.
II *adj* (also **~-shaped**) ovale; **the Oval Office** US Pol le bureau ovale.

ovarian /əˈveərɪən/ *adj* ovarien/-ienne.

ovaritis /əʊvəˈraɪtɪs/ ▶ **1354** *n* = **oophoritis**.

ovary /ˈəʊvərɪ/ *n* Anat, Bot ovaire *m*.

ovate /ˈəʊveɪt/ *adj* ové.

ovation /əʊˈveɪʃn/ *n* ovation *f*; **to give sb an ~** ovationner qn; **to give sb a standing ~** se lever pour ovationner qn.

oven /ˈʌvn/ **I** *n* four *m*; **electric/gas/microwave ~** four électrique/à gaz/à micro-ondes; **cook in a hot/moderate/slow ~** faites cuire à four chaud/moyen/doux; **it's like an ~ in here!** fig c'est une fournaise ici!
II *modif* [*door, temperature*] du four.

oven: **~ cleaner** *n* nettoyant *m* pour four; **~ dish** *n* plat *m* allant au four; **~ glove** *n* manique *f*; **~proof** *adj* qui va au four; **~ rack** *n* US = **oven shelf**; **~-ready** *adj* prêt à cuire; **~ shelf** *n* GB grille *f*; **~-to-tableware**, **~ware** *n* ¢ plats *mpl* de service allant au four.

over[1] /ˈəʊvə(r)/

■ **Note** *over* is used after many verbs in English (*change over, fall over, lean over etc*). For translations, consult the appropriate verb entry (**change**, **fall**, **lean** etc).
– *over* is often used with another preposition in English (*to, in, on*) without altering the meaning. In this case *over* is usually not translated in French: *to be over in France* = être en France; *to swim over to sb* = nager vers qn.
– *over* is often used with nouns in English when talking about superiority (*control over, priority over etc*) or when giving the cause of something (*delays over, trouble over etc*). For translations, consult the appropriate noun entry (**control**, **priority**, **delay**, **trouble** etc).
– *over* is often used as a prefix in verb combinations (*overeat*), adjective combinations (*overconfident*) and noun combinations (*overcoat*). These combinations are treated as headwords in the dictionary.
– For particular usages see the entry below.

I *prep* **1** (across the top of) par-dessus; **to jump/look/talk ~ a wall** sauter/regarder/parler par-dessus un mur; **to step ~ the cat** passer par-dessus le chat; **a bridge ~ the Thames** un pont sur la Tamise; **2** (from or on the other side of) **my neighbour/the house ~ the road** mon voisin/la maison d'en face; **it's just ~ the road/river** c'est juste de l'autre côté de la rue/rivière; **the noise came from ~ the wall** le bruit venait de l'autre côté du mur; **~ here/there** par ici/là; **come ~ here!** viens (par) ici!; **from ~ the sea/the Atlantic/ the Channel** d'outre-mer/d'outre-atlantique/d'outre-manche; **3** (above but not touching) au-dessus de; **clouds ~ the valley** des nuages au-dessus de la vallée; **they live ~ the shop** ils habitent au-dessus de la boutique; **4** (covering, surrounding) sur; **to spill tea ~ sth** renverser du thé sur qch; **he's spilled tea ~ it** il a renversé du thé dessus; **to carry one's coat ~ one's arm** porter son manteau sur le bras; **to wear a sweater ~ one's shirt** porter un pull par-dessus sa chemise; **shutters ~ the windows** des volets aux fenêtres; **5** (physically higher than) **the water was** ou **came ~ my ankles** j'avais de l'eau jusqu'aux chevilles; **6** (more than) plus de; **children (of) ~ six** les enfants de plus de six ans; **to be ~ 21** avoir plus de 21 ans; **well ~ 200** bien plus de 200; **to take ~ a year** prendre plus d'un an; **temperatures ~ 40°** des températures supérieures à 40°; **7** (in rank, position) **to be ~ sb** gen être supérieur à qn; Mil être plus gradé que qn; **8** (in the course of) **~ the weekend/the summer** pendant le week-end/l'été; **~ a period of** sur une période de; **~ the last decade/few days** au cours des dix dernières années/de ces derniers jours; **he has changed ~ the years** il a changé avec le temps; **to do sth ~ Christmas** faire qch à Noël or pendant les vacances de Noël; **to stay with sb ~ Easter** passer les vacances de Pâques chez qn; **to talk ~ coffee/lunch** parler autour d'une tasse de café/d'un déjeuner; **9** (recovered from) **to be ~** s'être remis de [*illness, operation, loss*]; **she'll be ~ it soon** elle s'en remettra vite; **to be ~ the worst** avoir passé le pire; **10** (by means of) **~ the phone** par téléphone; **~ the radio** à la radio; **11** (everywhere in) **to travel all ~ the world/Africa** voyager partout dans le monde/en Afrique; **to search all ~ the house** chercher partout dans la maison; **to show sb ~ a house** montrer or faire visiter une maison à qn; **I've lived all ~ France** j'ai habité un peu partout en France; **12** (because of) **to laugh ~ sth** rire de qch; **to pause ~ sth** s'arrêter sur qch; **how long will you be ~ it?** combien de temps cela te prendra-t-il?; **13** Math **12 ~ 3 is 4** 12 divisé par 3 égale 4.
II over and above *prep phr* **~ and above that** en plus de cela; **~ and above the minimum requirement** au-delà du minimum requis.
III *adj, adv* **1** (use with verbs not covered in NOTE) **~ she went** elle est tombée; **~ you go!** allez hop!; **does it go under or ~?** est-ce que ça va en dessous ou au-dessus?; **2** (finished) **to be ~** [*term, meeting, incident*] être terminé; [*war*] être fini; **after the war is ~** lorsque la guerre sera finie; **it was all ~ by Christmas** à Noël tout était fini; **when this is all ~** quand tout ceci sera fini; **to get sth ~ with** en finir avec qch; **3** (more) **children of six and ~** ou **six or ~** les enfants de plus de six ans; **it can be two metres or ~** cela peut faire deux mètres ou plus; **temperatures of 40 ° and ~** des températures supérieures à 40°; **4** (remaining) **two biscuits each and one ~** deux biscuits par personne et il en reste un; **six metres and a bit ~** un peu plus de six mètres; **2 into 5 goes 2 and 1 ~** 5 divisé par 2 font 2 et il reste 1; **there's nothing ~** il ne reste rien; ▶ **leave over**; **5** (to one's house, country) **to invite** ou **ask sb ~** inviter qn; **come ~ for lunch** venez déjeuner; **we had them ~ on Sunday/for dinner** ils sont venus dimanche/dîner; **they were ~ for the day** ils sont venus pour la journée; **they're ~ from Sydney** ils sont venus de Sydney; **when you're next ~ this way** la prochaine fois que tu passes dans le coin; **6** Radio, TV **~!** à vous!; **~ to you** à vous; **now ~ to Tim for the weather** laissons la place à Tim pour la météo; **now ~ to our Paris studios** nous passons l'antenne à nos studios de Paris; **7** (showing repetition) **five/several times ~** cinq/plusieurs fois de suite; **to start all ~ again** recommencer à zéro; **I had to do it ~** US j'ai dû recommencer; **to hit sb ~ and ~ (again)** frapper qn sans s'arrêter; **I've told you ~ and ~ (again)**... je t'ai dit je ne sais combien de fois...; **8** GB (excessively) **I'm not ~ keen** je ne suis pas très enthousiaste; **she wasn't ~ pleased** elle n'était pas très contente.

over[2] /ˈəʊvə(r)/ *n* Sport partie *f* d'un match de cricket (*lors de laquelle le serveur lance six balles d'une extrémité du terrain*).

overact /ˌəʊvərˈækt/ **I** *vtr* charger [*rôle*].
II *vi* en faire trop.

overactive /ˌəʊvərˈæktɪv/ *adj* [*imagination*] débordant; **to have an ~ thyroid** souffrir d'hyperthyroïdie.

overage /ˈəʊvərɪdʒ/ *n* US Comm excédent *m* (*de marchandises*).

overall /ˈəʊvərɔːl/ **I** *n* GB (coat-type) blouse *f*; (child's) tablier *m*.
II overalls *npl* GB combinaison *f*; US salopette *f*.
III /ˌəʊvərˈɔːl/ *adj* **1** [*cost, measurement, responsibility*] total; [*figures, improvement, increase, trend, value*] global; [*control, impression, standard*] général; [*ability, effect*] d'ensemble; [*majority*] Pol absolu; **2** Sport [*placing, winner*] au classement général.
IV *adv* **1** (in total) en tout; **2** (in general) dans l'ensemble; **3** Sport **first ~** premier/-ière au classement général; **4** littér (everywhere) partout.

overalled /ˈəʊvərɔːld/ *adj* GB (coat-type) vêtu d'une blouse; (trouser-type) vêtu d'une combinaison; US vêtu d'une salopette.

overanxious /ˌəʊvərˈæŋkʃəs/ *adj* (nervous) trop anxieux/-ieuse; **I'm not ~ to go** je n'ai pas vraiment envie d'y aller.

overarm /ˈəʊvərɑːm/ *adj, adv* Sport [*serve, throw*] par le haut (*inv*); (in swimming) **~ stroke** crawl *m*.

overate /ˌəʊvərˈeɪt/ *prét* ▶ **overeat**.

overawe /ˌəʊvərˈɔː/ *vtr* intimider.

overbalance /ˌəʊvəˈbæləns/ **I** *vtr* déséquilibrer.
II *vi* [*person*] perdre l'équilibre; [*pile of objects*] s'écrouler.

overbearing /ˌəʊvəˈbeərɪŋ/ *adj* [*person, manner*] dominateur/-trice.

overbid /ˌəʊvəˈbɪd/ **I** *n* (at auction) surenchère *f*; (in bridge) annonce *f* exagérée.
II *vtr* (*p prés* **-dd-**; *prét, pp* **~**) (at auction) enchérir sur [*person*]; (in bridge) **to ~ a hand** annoncer au-dessus de ses moyens.
III *vi* (*p prés* **-dd-**; *prét, pp* **~**) (at auction) faire une enchère trop élevée; (in bridge) annoncer au-dessus de ses moyens.

overblown /ˌəʊvəˈbləʊn/ *adj* **1** [*style*] ampoulé; **2** [*flower*] trop ouvert; **3** [*beauty*] trop mûr.

overboard /ˈəʊvəbɔːd/ *adv* par-dessus bord, à l'eau; **to fall/jump ~** tomber à/sauter dans l'eau; **to push/throw sb/sth ~** pousser/jeter qn/qch par-dessus bord; **man ~!** un homme à la mer!; **to go ~**○ fig aller trop loin.

overbook /ˌəʊvəˈbʊk/ *vtr, vi* surréserver.

overbooking /ˌəʊvəˈbʊkɪŋ/ *n* surréservation *f*.

overbuild /ˌəʊvəˈbɪld/ *vtr* (*prét, pp* **-built**) trop bâtir; **to ~a site** trop bâtir sur un terrain.

overburden /ˌəʊvəˈbɜːdn/ *vtr* (with work) surcharger; (with responsibility, debt, guilt) accabler.

overcapacity /ˌəʊvəkəˈpæsətɪ/ *n* Econ surcapacité *f*.

overcapitalize /ˌəʊvəˈkæpɪtəlaɪz/ *vtr* surcapitaliser.

overcast /ˌəʊvəˈkɑːst, US -ˈkæst/ **I** *vtr* (*prét, pp* **overcast**) (in sewing) surfiler.
II *adj* **1** Meteorol couvert; **to become ~** se couvrir; **2** fig [*expression*] sombre.

overcautious /ˌəʊvəˈkɔːʃəs/ *adj* excessivement prudent.

overcautiously /ˌəʊvəˈkɔːʃəslɪ/ *adv* d'une manière excessivement prudente.

overcharge /ˌəʊvəˈtʃɑːdʒ/ **I** *vtr* **1** (in money) faire payer trop cher à; **they ~d him** ils lui ont fait payer trop cher; **they ~d him by £10** ils lui ont fait payer 10 livres de trop; **they ~d him for it** ils le lui ont fait payer au prix fort; **2** Elec surcharger.
II *vi* faire payer au prix fort.

overcoat /ˈəʊvəkəʊt/ *n* pardessus *m*.

overcome /ˌəʊvəˈkʌm/ **I** *vtr* (*prét* **-came**, *pp* **-come**) **1** (defeat) battre [*opponent*]; vaincre [*enemy*]; maîtriser [*nerves*]; surmonter [*dislike, fear, problem*]; **2** (overwhelm) **to be overcome by smoke** être suffoqué par la fumée; **to be overcome by** ou **with jealousy/despair** succomber à la jalousie/au désespoir; **overcome by fear** transi de peur; **tiredness overcame them** la fatigue a eu raison d'eux; **I was over-**

come when I heard the news la nouvelle m'a terrassé.
II *vi* (*prét* **-came**, *pp* **-come**) triompher.

overcompensate /ˌəʊvəˈkɒmpenseɪt/ *vi* **1** gen trop compenser; **to ~ for sth** trop compenser qch (**by doing** en faisant); **2** Psych surcompenser.

overcompensation /ˌəʊvəˌkɒmpenˈseɪʃn/ *n* Psych surcompensation *f*.

overconfidence /ˌəʊvəˈkɒnfɪdəns/ *n* assurance *f* excessive.

overconfident /ˌəʊvəˈkɒnfɪdənt/ *adj* trop sûr de soi (moi, toi etc).

overconsumption /ˌəʊvəkənˈsʌmpʃn/ *n* surconsommation *f*.

overcook /ˌəʊvəˈkʊk/ *vtr* trop cuire.

overcrowded /ˌəʊvəˈkraʊdɪd/ *adj* [*vehicle, shop, room*] (with people) bondé (**with** de); [*road*] surencombré; [*institution, city*] surpeuplé (**with** de); [*class*] surchargé; [*room*] (with furniture) encombré (**with** de); Dent [*teeth*] trop rapproché.

overcrowding /ˌəʊvəˈkraʊdɪŋ/ *n* (in city, institution) surpeuplement *m*; (in transport) surencombrement *m*; **~ in classrooms** les classes surchargées.

overdeveloped /ˌəʊvədɪˈveləpt/ *adj* **1** (physically) [*person*] trop développé; [*muscle*] hypertrophié; **2** [*sense of humour, of importance etc*] excessif/-ive; **3** Phot trop développé; **4** Pol, Econ surdéveloppé.

overdo /ˌəʊvəˈduː/ *vtr* (*prét* **overdid**, *pp* **overdone**) **1** (exaggerate) exagérer [*sentiment, reaction*]; **to ~ it** ou **things** (when describing) exagérer, en rajouter○; (when performing) forcer la note○, en faire trop○; (when working) en faire trop○; **don't ~ the exercises/studying** ne force pas trop○ sur les exercices/les études; **he rather overdoes the devoted nephew** il joue un peu trop au neveu dévoué; **2** (use too much of) avoir la main lourde sur [*flavouring, perfume, makeup*]; **3** (overcook) faire trop cuire [*meat, vegetables*].

overdone /ˌəʊvəˈdʌn/ *adj* **1** (exaggerated) [*effect, emotion*] exagéré; **the comedy was ~** les passages comiques n'étaient pas très subtils; **2** (overcooked) trop cuit.

overdose /ˈəʊvədəʊs/ **I** *n* **1** (large dose) surdose *f*, dose *f* excessive; **radiation/vitamin ~** dose excessive de radiation/vitamines; **2** (lethal dose) (of medicine) dose *f* mortelle; (of drugs) overdose *f*, surdose *f*; **to take an ~ of** prendre une dose mortelle de; **a heroin ~** une overdose d'héroïne.
II /ˌəʊvəˈdəʊs/ *vtr* donner une trop forte dose à [*patient*].
III *vi* (on medicine) prendre une dose mortelle; (on drugs) faire une overdose; **to ~ on** lit prendre une dose mortelle de [*tablets*]; prendre une overdose de [*drugs*]; fig○ se gaver de [*chocolate etc*]; s'abrutir de [*television*].

overdraft /ˈəʊvədrɑːft, US -dræft/ **I** *n* découvert *m*; **to take out an ~** obtenir un découvert; **to have an ~** être à découvert; **agreed ~, ~ arrangement** découvert autorisé.
II *modif* [*facility*] de découvert; [*limit*] de crédit.

overdraw /ˌəʊvəˈdrɔː/ **I** *vtr* (*prét* **overdrew**, *pp* **overdrawn**) **1** Fin tirer à découvert; **I am £100 overdrawn** j'ai un découvert de 100 livres; **you are/your account is £100 overdrawn** vous êtes/votre compte est à découvert de 100 livres; **2** Literat (exaggerate) outrer.
II overdrawn *pp adj* **1** Fin [*account*] à découvert; **2** Literat outré.

overdress /ˌəʊvəˈdres/ **I** *vtr* trop habiller.
II *vi* être trop habillé.

overdrive /ˈəʊvədraɪv/ *n* **1** Aut vitesse *f* surmultipliée; **in ~** en (vitesse) surmultipliée; **to go into ~** passer en (vitesse) surmultipliée; **2** fig s'activer intensivement.

overdue /ˌəʊvəˈdjuː, US -ˈduː/ *adj* [*plane, train, work*] en retard (**by** de); [*bill*] impayé; [*cheque*] présenté tardivement; [*baby, pregnant woman*] dont le terme est dépassé; **the car is ~ for a service** la voiture aurait déjà dû passer à la révision; **this measure is long ~** cette mesure aurait déjà dû être prise; **the book is ~** le livre aurait dû être rendu.

overeager /ˌəʊvəˈiːgə(r)/ *adj* [*person*] trop zélé.

overeat /ˌəʊvərˈiːt/ *vi* (*prét* **overate**, *pp* **overeaten**) manger à l'excès.

overeating /ˌəʊvərˈiːtɪŋ/ *n* excès *mpl* de table.

overemphasize /ˌəʊvəˈemfəsaɪz/ *vtr* accorder trop d'importance à [*aspect, fact*]; exagérer [*importance*]; **I cannot ~ how vital it is** je ne saurais trop souligner combien c'est vital.

overemployment /ˌəʊvəɪmˈplɔɪmənt/ *n* suremploi *m*.

overenthusiastic /ˌəʊvərɪnˌθjuːzɪˈæstɪk, US -ˌθuː-/ *adj* trop enthousiaste; **to be ~ in doing** dépasser la mesure en faisant.

overenthusiastically /ˌəʊvərɪnˌθjuːzɪˈæstɪklɪ, US -ˌθuː-/ *adv* avec trop d'enthousiasme.

overestimate **I** /ˌəʊvərˈestɪmət/ *n* surestimation *f*.
II /ˌəʊvərˈestɪmeɪt/ *vtr* surestimer.

overexcite /ˌəʊvərɪkˈsaɪt/ *vtr* surexciter.

overexcited /ˌəʊvərɪkˈsaɪtɪd/ *adj* surexcité; **he gets ~ very easily** il est vite surexcité.

overexcitement /ˌəʊvərɪkˈsaɪtmənt/ *n* surexcitation *f*.

overexert /ˌəʊvərɪgˈzɜːt/ **I** *vtr* surmener.
II *v refl* **to ~ oneself** se surmener.

overexertion /ˌəʊvərɪgˈzɜːʃn/ *n* surmenage *m*.

overexpose /ˌəʊvərɪkˈspəʊz/ *vtr* **1** Phot surexposer; **2** Cin, TV médiatiser [qn] de façon excessive [*actor*].

overexposure /ˌəʊvərɪkˈspəʊʒə(r)/ *n* **1** Phot surexposition *f*; **2** Cin, TV médiatisation *f* excessive.

overfeed /ˌəʊvəˈfiːd/ *vtr* (*prét, pp* **-fed**) suralimenter [*child, pet*]; donner trop d'engrais à [*plant*].

overfeeding /ˌəʊvəˈfiːdɪŋ/ *n* suralimentation *f*.

overfill /ˌəʊvəˈfɪl/ *vtr* trop remplir.

overfish /ˌəʊvəˈfɪʃ/ **I** *vtr* surexploiter [*river, sea*].
II *vi* surexploiter les fonds de pêche.

overfishing /ˌəʊvəˈfɪʃɪŋ/ *n* surexploitation *f* des fonds de pêche.

overflow **I** /ˈəʊvəfləʊ/ *n* **1** (surplus) **the ~ of students/passengers** les étudiants/les passagers en surnombre; **our school takes in the ~ from other areas** notre école accueille les élèves en surnombre dans les régions voisines; **2** (also **~ pipe**) (from bath, sink) trop-plein *m*; (from dam) déversoir *m*; **3** (spillage) (action) débordement *m*; (liquid spilt) trop-plein *m*; **4** Comput dépassement *m* de capacité.
II /ˌəʊvəˈfləʊ/ *vtr* [*river*] inonder [*banks*]; [*crowd*] déborder de [*stadium, theatre*].
III /ˌəʊvəˈfləʊ/ *vi* [*bath, bin, river, water*] déborder (**into** dans; **onto** sur); [*crowd, refugees*] déborder; **they ~ed onto the steps/into the streets** ils ont débordé sur les marches/dans les rues; **to be full to ~ing** [*bath, bowl*] déborder; [*room, theatre*] être plein à craquer; **to ~ with** fig déborder de [*gratitude, love*].
IV overflowing /ˌəʊvəˈfləʊɪŋ/ *pres p adj* [*school*] saturé; [*prison*] surpeuplé; [*dustbin, bath*] débordant.

overflow car park GB, **overflow parking lot** US *n* parc *m* de stationnement supplémentaire.

overfly /ˌəʊvəˈflaɪ/ *vtr* (*prét* **-flew**, *pp* **-flown**) survoler.

overfull /ˌəʊvəˈfʊl/ *adj* trop plein.

overgenerous /ˌəʊvəˈdʒenərəs/ *adj* trop généreux/-euse (**with** avec); [*amount, dose*] excessif/-ive.

overgrown /ˌəʊvəˈgrəʊn/ *adj* **1** (covered in weeds) envahi par la végétation; **~ with nettles** envahi par les orties; **2** (big) souvent hum géant; **3 to behave like an ~ schoolboy** se conduire comme un collégien.

overhand /ˈəʊvəhænd/ US *adj, adv* par le haut.

overhang **I** /ˈəʊvəhæŋ/ *n* **1** gen (of cliff) surplomb *m*; (of roof) avancée *f*; (of tablecloth, bedcover etc) pan *m*; **2** Fin surplus *m*.
II /ˌəʊvəˈhæŋ/ *vtr* surplomber.
III /ˌəʊvəˈhæŋ/ *vi* être en surplomb.

overhanging /ˌəʊvəˈhæŋɪŋ/ *adj* [*ledge, cliff, rock*] en surplomb; [*tree, branch*] qui surplombe; [*balcony*] faisant saillie.

overhaul **I** /ˈəʊvəhɔːl/ *n* (of machine) révision *f*; fig (of system) restructuration *f*.
II /ˌəʊvəˈhɔːl/ *vtr* **1** réviser [*car, machine*]; refaire [*roof*]; fig restructurer [*system, procedure*]; **2** (overtake) dépasser; (catch up with) rattraper [*rival, ship, vehicle*].

overhead /ˈəʊvəhed/ **I** *n* US frais *mpl* généraux.
II overheads *npl* GB frais *mpl* généraux.
III *adj* **1** Fin **~ charges** ou **costs** ou **expenses** frais *mpl* généraux; **2** [*cable, railway*] aérien/-ienne; **3** Sport [*stroke*] haut.
IV /ˌəʊvəˈhed/ *adv* **1** (in the sky) dans le ciel; **2** (above the head) au-dessus de la tête; **to hold sth ~** tenir qch au-dessus de la tête.

overhead: **~ camshaft** *n* arbre *m* à cames en tête; **~ed price** *n* Fin prix *m* toutes charges comprises; **~ light** *n* plafonnier *m*; **~ locker** *n* Aviat compartiment *m* à bagages; **~ luggage rack** *n* Rail porte-bagages *m inv*; **~ projector** *n* rétroprojecteur *m*; **~ valve** *n* Aut soupape *f* en tête.

overhear /ˌəʊvəˈhɪə(r)/ **I** *vtr* (*p prés, pp* **-heard**) entendre par hasard; **I overheard a conversation between...** j'ai surpris une conversation entre...
II overheard *pp adj* [*conversation, remark*] entendu par hasard.

overheat /ˌəʊvəˈhiːt/ **I** *vtr* surchauffer [*room, economy*]; faire trop chauffer [*sauce, oven*].
II *vi* [*car, equipment*] chauffer; [*oven, furnace*] chauffer trop; [*child*] avoir trop chaud; [*economy*] être en surchauffe.

overheated /ˌəʊvəˈhiːtɪd/ *adj* [*room*] surchauffé; [*debate, person*] emporté; [*imagination*] en ébullition; [*economy*] en surchauffe.

overheating /ˌəʊvəˈhiːtɪŋ/ *n* surchauffe *f*.

overindulge /ˌəʊvərɪnˈdʌldʒ/ **I** *vtr* gâter [*child, pet*].
II *vi* faire des excès (**in** de).

overindulgence /ˌəʊvərɪnˈdʌldʒəns/ *n* **1** (excess) abus *m* (**in** de); **2** (partiality) trop grande indulgence *f* (**of, towards** envers).

overindulgent /ˌəʊvərɪnˈdʌldʒənt/ *adj* trop indulgent (**to, towards** envers).

overinvest /ˌəʊvərɪnˈvest/ *vi* surinvestir (**in** dans).

overjoyed /ˌəʊvəˈdʒɔɪd/ *adj* [*person*] fou/folle de joie (**at** devant); [*cry, smile*] de joie intense; **to be ~ to do** être fou de joie de faire; **I was ~ that she had returned** son retour m'a rendu fou de joie.

overkill /ˈəʊvəkɪl/ *n* **1** Mil capacité *f* de surextermination; **2** fig matraquage *m*; **advertising/media ~** matraquage médiatique/publicitaire.

overland /ˈəʊvəlænd/ **I** *adj* [*route*] terrestre; [*journey*] par route.
II *adv* par route; **to go ~ to India** aller en Inde par route.

overlap **I** /ˈəʊvəlæp/ *n* **1** (of organizations, services, systems, activities) chevauchement *m* (**between** de); (undesirable) empiètement *m* (**between** de); **an ~ between the public and private sectors** un chevauchement du secteur public sur le secteur privé; **an ~ between the two sectors** un chevauche-

ment des deux secteurs; **2** Tech (in sewing) partie *f* qui déborde.
II /ˌəʊvəˈlæp/ *vtr* (*p prés etc* **-pp-**) lit (partly cover) recouvrir partiellement; **the tiles ~ (each other)** les tuiles se recouvrent l'une l'autre.
III /ˌəʊvəˈlæp/ *vi* (*p prés etc* **-pp-**) **1** [*organization, service, sector, system, activity*] chevaucher (**with** avec) ; (undesirably) empiéter (**with** sur); [*events*] coïncider (**with** avec); **the two sectors ~** les deux secteurs se chevauchent; **2** lit [*materials, edges*] se recouvrir partiellement; [*one edge*] dépasser.
IV overlapping /ˌəʊvəˈlæpɪŋ/ *pres p adj* **1** fig [*organizations, services, systems, activities*] qui se chevauchent; [*events*] qui coïncident; **2** [*edges, scales*] qui se recouvrent partiellement; [*one edge*] qui dépasse.

overlay I /ˈəʊvəleɪ/ *n* **1** (clear sheet) transparent *m*; **2** (decoration) revêtement *m*; **3** fig (layer) vernis *m*.
II /ˌəʊvəˈleɪ/ *vtr* (*prét, pp* **-laid**) recouvrir (**with** de).

overleaf /ˌəʊvəˈliːf/ *adv* au verso; **see ~** voir au verso.

overlie /ˌəʊvəˈlaɪ/ *vtr* (*prét* **-lay**; *pp* **-lain**) recouvrir.

overload /ˈəʊvələʊd/ **I** *n* **1** Civ Eng, Electron surcharge *f*; **2** fig surcharge *f*.
II /ˌəʊvəˈləʊd/ *vtr* surcharger [*machine, vehicle, system*] (**with** de).
III overloaded *pp adj* surchargé.

overlong /ˌəʊvəˈlɒŋ/ *adj* trop long/longue.

overlook /ˌəʊvəˈlʊk/ *vtr* **1** (have a view of) [*building, window*] donner sur; **we ~ the sea from the balcony** notre balcon donne sur la mer; **2** (miss) ne pas voir [*detail, error*]; **to ~ the fact that** négliger le fait que; **3** (ignore) laisser passer [*behaviour, fault, mistake*]; ne pas considérer [*candidate, person*]; ignorer [*effect, fact, need, problem*].

overlord /ˈəʊvəlɔːd/ *n* suzerain *m*.

overly /ˈəʊvəlɪ/ *adv* trop, excessivement.

overmanned /ˌəʊvəˈmænd/ *adj* [*factory, office*] en sureffectif.

overmanning /ˌəʊvəˈmænɪŋ/ *n* sureffectif *m*, effectif *m* pléthorique.

overmantel /ˈəʊvəmæntl/ *n*: *étagère située au-dessus d'une cheminée*.

overmuch /ˌəʊvəˈmʌtʃ/ **I** *adj* excessif/-ive.
II *adv* trop.

overnight /ˈəʊvənaɪt/ **I** *adj* **1** (night-time) [*crossing, boat, bus, flight, journey, train*] de nuit; [*stay*] d'une nuit; [*guest*] pour la nuit; [*stop*] pour une nuit; [*party, rain*] pendant toute la nuit; **2** fig (rapid) [*change, result, success*] immédiat.
II /ˌəʊvəˈnaɪt/ *adv* **1** (in the night) dans la nuit; (for the night) pour la nuit; [*drive*] toute la nuit; [*stop*] pour la nuit; [*keep*] jusqu'au lendemain; **to stay ~** rester dormir; **2** fig (rapidly) du jour au lendemain.

overnight bag *n* petit sac *m* de voyage.

overpaid /ˌəʊvəˈpeɪd/ *adj* surpayé.

overparticular /ˌəʊvəpəˈtɪkjʊlə(r)/ *adj* **1** (fussy) trop pointilleux/-euse; **2** (concerned) très soucieux/-ieuse (**about** de); **he's not ~ about his reputation** il n'est pas très soucieux de sa réputation; **I'm not ~** ça m'est égal.

overpass /ˈəʊvəpɑːs, US -pæs/ *n* **1** (for cars) toboggan *m*; **2** (footbridge) passerelle *f*.

overpay /ˌəʊvəˈpeɪ/ *vtr* (*prét, pp* **-paid**) surpayer [*employee*]; **I was overpaid by £500** on m'a versé 500 livres de trop.

overpayment /ˌəʊvəˈpeɪmənt/ *n* **1** (of tax etc) trop-perçu *m*; **2** (excess paid) trop-payé *m*.

overplay /ˌəʊvəˈpleɪ/ *vtr* **1** (exaggerate) exagérer [*benefits, problem, situation*]; **2** (overact) charger [*role, part*].
IDIOMS **to ~ one's hand** aller trop loin.

overpopulated /ˌəʊvəˈpɒpjʊleɪtɪd/ *adj* surpeuplé.

overpopulation /ˌəʊvəpɒpjʊˈleɪʃn/ *n* surpopulation *f*.

overpower /ˌəʊvəˈpaʊə(r)/ *vtr* **1** lit maîtriser [*thief*]; vaincre [*army, nation*]; **2** Sport dominer [*rival*]; **3** fig [*smell, smoke, heat*] accabler.

overpowering /ˌəʊvəˈpaʊərɪŋ/ *adj* [*person*] dominateur/-trice; [*personality*] écrasant; [*desire, urge*] irrésistible; [*heat*] accablant; [*smell*] irrespirable; [*strength*] invincible.

overpraise /ˌəʊvəˈpreɪz/ *vtr* faire trop de compliments sur [*person, achievement*].

overprescribe /ˌəʊvəprɪˈskraɪb/ **I** *vtr* [*doctor*] prescrire trop de [*drugs*].
II *vi* trop prescrire.

overprice /ˌəʊvəˈpraɪs/ *vtr* vendre [qch] trop cher [*goods, services*].

overpriced /ˌəʊvəˈpraɪst/ *adj* **1** gen trop cher/chère; **2** Fin, Econ [*market*] gonflé.

overprint /ˈəʊvəprɪnt/ Print **I** *n* surcharge *f*.
II /ˌəʊvəˈprɪnt/ *vtr* **1** (add) imprimer [qch] en surcharge [*additions*]; surcharger [*stamp*]; **~ed in red** repiqué en rouge; **2** (cover up) recouvrir [*error*].
III *vi* (print too much) faire un surtirage.

overproduce /ˌəʊvəprəˈdjuːs, US -duːs/ **I** *vtr* surproduire.
II *vi* surproduire.

overproduction /ˌəʊvəprəˈdʌkʃn/ *n* surproduction *f*.

overprotect /ˌəʊvəprəˈtekt/ *vtr* surprotéger.

overprotective /ˌəʊvəprəˈtektɪv/ *adj* [*attitude, feelings*] excessivement protecteur/-trice; **an ~ father** un père qui couve ses enfants.

overqualified /ˌəʊvəˈkwɒlɪfaɪd/ *adj* surqualifié.

overrate /ˌəʊvəˈreɪt/ *vtr* surestimer [*person, ability, value*].

overrated /ˌəʊvəˈreɪtɪd/ *adj* surfait.

overreach /ˌəʊvəˈriːtʃ/ *v refl* **to ~ oneself** se fixer des objectifs trop ambitieux.

overreact /ˌəʊvərɪˈækt/ *vi* réagir de façon excessive (**to** à).

overreaction /ˌəʊvərɪˈækʃn/ *n* réaction *f* excessive (**by** de la part de; **to** face à).

overreliance /ˌəʊvərɪˈlaɪəns/ *n* dépendance *f* excessive (**on** vis-à-vis de).

override /ˈəʊvəraɪd/ **I** *n* commande *f* manuelle; **on ~** en (mode) manuel.
II *modif* [*facility, mechanism*] manuel/-elle.
III /ˌəʊvəˈraɪd/ *vtr* (*prét* **-rode**; *pp* **-ridden**) **1** (control) passer [qch] en manuel [*machine*]; **2** (disregard) passer outre à [*consideration, opinion*]; **3** (take precedence) l'emporter sur [*decision, desire, theory*]; **4** (cancel) annuler [*order, law*].

overrider /ˌəʊvəˈraɪdə(r)/ *n* GB butoir *m* de pare-chocs, banane *f*.

overriding /ˌəʊvəˈraɪdɪŋ/ *adj* [*importance*] primordial; [*problem, priority*] numéro un.

overriding commission *n* Fin commission *f* additionnelle.

overripe /ˌəʊvəˈraɪp/ *adj* [*fruit*] trop mûr, blet/blette; [*cheese*] trop fait.

overrule /ˌəʊvəˈruːl/ *vtr* Jur annuler [*decision, judgment*]; rejeter [*conclusion, plan, vote, objection*]; l'emporter sur la décision de [*person, committee*].

overrun /ˈəʊvərʌn/ **I** *n* Fin dépassement *m* (**of** de); **cost ~** dépassement *m* du budget, surcoût *m*.
II /ˌəʊvəˈrʌn/ *vtr* (*p prés* **-nn-**; *prét* **overran**, *pp* **overrun**) **1** (invade) envahir [*country, site*]; **to be overrun with** être envahi par; **2** (exceed) dépasser [*time, budget*]; **3** Aviat, Rail (overshoot) dépasser.
III *vi* [*conference, activity, performer*] dépasser l'horaire (**by** de); **the lecturer overran his time by an hour** le conférencier a dépassé son temps d'une heure; **the lecture overran by an hour** la conférence a duré une heure de plus que prévu.

overseas /ˌəʊvəˈsiːz/ **I** *adj* **1** (from abroad) [*student, visitor, investor, company*] étranger/-ère; **2** (in or to other countries) [*travel, investment*] à l'étranger; [*trade, market*] extérieur; **~ aid** aide *f* aux pays étrangers; **to get an ~ posting** être nommé à l'étranger.
II *adv* (abroad) [*work, retire*] à l'étranger; (across the sea) outre-mer; (across the Channel) outre-manche; **from ~** de l'étranger.

Overseas Development Administration, ODA *n* GB *organisme gouvernemental d'aide aux pays en voie de développement*.

oversee /ˌəʊvəˈsiː/ *vtr* (*prét* **-saw**; *pp* **-seen**) superviser.

overseer /ˈəʊvəsiːə(r)/ *n* **1** (of workers, convicts) contremaître *m*; **2** (of project) responsable *mf*.

oversell /ˌəʊvəˈsel/ **I** *vtr* (*prét, pp* **-sold**) Fin, Econ **1** (sell aggressively) employer des méthodes agressives pour vendre; **2** (exaggerate the merits of) trop vanter [*idea, plan, job*].
II *v refl* **to ~ oneself** exagérer ses propres mérites.

oversensitive /ˌəʊvəˈsensɪtɪv/ *adj* [*personne*] trop susceptible; [*attitude, approach*] très délicat; **to be ~ about public opinion** trop s'attendrir sur l'opinion publique.

oversew /ˈəʊvəsəʊ/ *vtr* (*prét* **-sewed**; *pp* **-sewn**) surjeter.

oversexed○ /ˌəʊvəˈsekst/ *adj* péj **to be ~** être un/une obsédé/-e sexuel/-elle.

overshadow /ˌəʊvəˈʃædəʊ/ *vtr* **1** (tower over) [*mountain*] dominer [*valley*]; **2** (spoil) [*death, news, war*] assombrir [*celebration*]; **3** (eclipse) éclipser [*achievement*].

overshoe /ˈəʊvəʃuː/ *n* (rubber) caoutchouc *m*.

overshoot /ˌəʊvəˈʃuːt/ *vtr* (*prét, pp* **-shot**) dépasser [*junction, runway*]; rater [*traffic lights*]; tirer au-dessus de [*target*]; manquer [*hole*].
IDIOMS **to ~ the mark** se planter○, commettre une erreur de jugement.

oversight /ˈəʊvəsaɪt/ *n* (omission) erreur *f*; (criticized) négligence *f*; **due to** ou **through an ~** par inadvertance.

oversimplification /ˌəʊvəˌsɪmplɪfɪˈkeɪʃn/ *n* schématisation *f*; **it is an ~ to say** c'est simplifier à l'extrême de dire.

oversimplify /ˌəʊvəˈsɪmplɪfaɪ/ **I** *vtr* simplifier [qch] à l'excès.
II oversimplified *pp adj* simpliste, trop simple.

oversize(d) /ˈəʊvəsaɪzd/ *adj* **1** (very big) énorme; (too big) [*shirt, boots, sweater*] trop grand; **2** [*book*] grand format.

oversleep /ˌəʊvəˈsliːp/ *vi* (*prét, pp* **-slept**) se réveiller trop tard; **sorry I'm late—I overslept** désolé d'être en retard—je ne me suis pas réveillé.

oversold /ˌəʊvəˈsəʊld/ *adj* Fin [*market*] saturé.

overspend /ˌəʊvəˈspend/ **I** *n* (in public spending) dépassement *m* budgétaire.
II *vtr* (*prét, pp* **-spent**) dépasser [*budget, income*].
III *vi* (*prét, pp* **-spent**) trop dépenser; **they've overspent by £500** ils ont dépensé 500 livres de plus que prévu.

overspending /ˌəʊvəˈspendɪŋ/ **I** *n* ¢ gen dépense *f* excessive; Fin, Admin dépassement *m* budgétaire.
II *adj* [*council*] qui dépasse son budget.

overspill /ˈəʊvəspɪl/ **I** *n* excédent *m* de population.
II *modif* **an ~ (housing) development** une cité de relogement; **~ population** population *f* excédentaire; **~ town** ≈ ville *f* satellite.

overstaffed /ˌəʊvəˈstɑːft, US -ˈstæft/ *adj* [*company*] au personnel pléthorique; **the section was ~** la section avait du personnel en surnombre.

overstaffing /ˌəʊvəˈstɑːfɪŋ, US -ˈstæfɪŋ/ *n* sureffectif *m*.

overstate /ˌəʊvəˈsteɪt/ *vtr* gen exagérer; **to ~ the case** exagérer; **the importance of this new product cannot be ~d**

l'importance de ce nouveau produit ne saurait être trop soulignée.

overstatement /ˌəʊvəˈsteɪtmənt/ *n* exagération *f*.

overstay /ˌəʊvəˈsteɪ/ *vtr* trop prolonger [*visit*]; **to ~ one's welcome** prolonger indûment son séjour; **to ~ one's visa** dépasser la limite de validité de son visa.

overstayer /ˌəʊvəˈsteɪə(r)/ *n*: *étranger qui a dépassé la limite de validité de son visa*.

oversteer /ˈəʊvəstɪə(r)/ *vi* braquer trop.

overstep /ˌəʊvəˈstep/ *vtr* (*p prés etc* **-pp-**) dépasser [*limits, bounds*]; outrepasser [*authority*]; **to ~ the mark** ou **line** dépasser les bornes.

overstock /ˌəʊvəˈstɒk/ **I** *vtr* surpeupler [*farm enclosure*] (**with** de); approvisionner excessivement [*shop, factory*] (**with** en).
II *vi* surstocker; **the farm was ~ed** la ferme avait un cheptel excessif.
III overstocking *pres p, n* Comm surstockage *m*.

overstocked /ˌəʊvəˈstɒkt/ *adj* [*shop*] avec un stock excessif; Econ surstocké; [*farmland*] au cheptel excessif.

overstrain /ˌəʊvəˈstreɪn/ **I** *vtr* surmener [*heart, animal*]; surexploiter [*resources, reserves*]; fatiguer [*metal*].
II *v refl* **to ~ oneself** se surmener.

overstress /ˌəʊvəˈstres/ *vtr* trop souligner [*importance*]; Ling trop accentuer [*syllable*].

overstressed /ˌəʊvəˈstrest/ *adj* (person) surmené.

overstretched /ˌəʊvəˈstretʃt/ *adj* [*budget*] excessivement serré; [*resources*] surexploité; **she is ~** elle essaie d'en faire trop.

overstrung /ˌəʊvəˈstrʌŋ/ *adj* **~ piano** piano à cordes croisées.

overstuffed /ˌəʊvəˈstʌft/ *adj*: **an ~ armchair** un fauteuil rembourré à craquer.

oversubscribed /ˌəʊvəsəbˈskraɪbd/ *adj* [*offer, tickets*] en excès de demandes; **an ~ share issue** une émission d'actions à couverture excédentaire.

overt /ˈəʊvɜːt, US əʊˈvɜːrt/ *adj* manifeste.

overtake /ˌəʊvəˈteɪk/ (*prét* **-took**, *pp* **-taken**) **I** *vtr* **1** (pass) [*vehicle*] GB dépasser, doubler○; [*person*] dépasser; **2** (catch up with) rattraper; **3** fig [*disaster, change, misfortune*] frapper [*project, country*]; [*fear, surprise*] saisir [*person*]; [*storm*] surprendre [*person*]; **he was overtaken by** ou **with fear** il fut saisi par la peur; **utter weariness overtook me** un complet abattement s'est emparé de moi fml; **to be overtaken by events** être pris de vitesse; **4** fig (take the lead over) dépasser [*team, economy*]; **5** (supplant) [*problem, question*] prendre le pas sur; **his fear was overtaken by embarrassment** sa peur faisait place à de la gêne.
II *vi* GB [*vehicle*] dépasser, doubler○; [*person*] dépasser; **'no overtaking'** 'dépassement interdit'.

overtax /ˌəʊvəˈtæks/ **I** *vtr* **1** (strain) surmener; **2** Fin, Admin surimposer.
II *v refl* **to ~ oneself** se surmener.

over-the-counter /ˌəʊvəðəˈkaʊntə(r)/ **I** *adj* [*medicines*] vendu sans ordonnance; Fin hors cote.
II *adv* **to sell medicines over the counter** vendre des médicaments sans ordonnance.

over-the-top○**, OTT** /ˌəʊvəðəˈtɒp/ *adj* **1** (*épith*) outrancier/-ière; **2** (*après v*) **to go over the top** (with anger) sortir de ses gonds (**about** à propos de); (overreact) avoir une réaction exagérée; **to go over the top with one's hairstyle/clothes** avoir une coiffure/une tenue vestimentaire outrancière.

overthrow /ˈəʊvəθrəʊ/ **I** *n* Pol renversement *m*.
II /ˌəʊvəˈθrəʊ/ *vtr* (*prét* **-threw**; *pp* **-thrown**) Pol renverser [*government, system*]; fig fouler aux pieds [*values, standards*].

overtime /ˈəʊvətaɪm/ **I** *n* **1** (extra hours) heures *fpl* supplémentaires; **to put in** ou **do ~** faire des heures supplémentaires; **2** (also **~ pay**) (extra pay) heures *fpl* supplémentaires; **to earn £50 in ~** gagner 50 livres en heures supplémentaires; **3** US, Sport prolongations *fpl*; **to play ~** jouer les prolongations.
II *adv* **to work ~** [*person*] lit, fig faire des heures supplémentaires; [*imagination*] travailler sans arrêt.

overtime: **~ ban** *n* boycott *m* des heures supplémentaires; **~ rate** *n* tarif *m* des heures supplémentaires.

overtired /ˌəʊvəˈtaɪəd/ *adj* gen épuisé; (baby, child) énervé.

overtly /ˈəʊvɜːtlɪ, US əʊˈvɜːtlɪ/ *adv* ouvertement.

overtone /ˈəʊvətəʊn/ *n* **1** (nuance) sous-entendu *m*, connotation *f*; **~s of racism** des connotations racistes; **2** (similarity) air *m*; **to have ~s of Proust** avoir des airs de Proust; **3** Mus son *m* harmonique.

overtrick /ˈəʊvətrɪk/ *n* (in bridge) levée *f* supplémentaire.

overtrump /ˌəʊvəˈtrʌmp/ *vtr* Games surcouper.

overture /ˈəʊvətjʊə(r)/ *n* **1** Mus ouverture *f* (**to** de); **2** (approach) (*gén pl*) (social) ouverture *f*, offre *f* (**to** à); (business) proposition *f*; **to make friendly ~s** faire des ouvertures d'amitié; **romantic ~s** avances *fpl*.

overturn /ˌəʊvəˈtɜːn/ **I** *vtr* **1** (roll over) renverser [*car, chair*]; faire chavirer [*boat*]; **2** (reverse) faire annuler [*decision, sentence*]; casser [*judgment, ruling*]; faire basculer [*majority*].
II *vi* [*car, chair*] se renverser; [*boat*] chavirer.

overuse I /ˌəʊvəˈjuːs/ *n* **1** (of word, product) abus *m*; **2** (of facility) utilisation *f* excessive; **to be worn through ~** être usé d'avoir trop servi.
II /ˌəʊvəˈjuːz/ *vtr* trop se servir de [*machine*]; abuser de [*chemical, service*]; galvauder [*word*].

overvalue /ˌəʊvəˈvæljuː/ *vtr* Econ, Fin surévaluer [*currency, property*].

overview /ˈəʊvəvjuː/ *n* vue *f* d'ensemble (**of** de).

overweening /ˌəʊvəˈwiːnɪŋ/ *adj* démesuré.

overweight /ˌəʊvəˈweɪt/ *adj* **1** [*person*] obèse; **to be ~** avoir des kilos en trop, être obèse Med; **to be ~ by 10 kilos** avoir 10 kilos de trop; **2** [*parcel, suitcase*] trop lourd; **to be ~** peser trop; **my case is 10 kilos ~** j'ai un excédent de bagages de 10 kilos.

overwhelm /ˌəʊvəˈwelm, US -hwelm/ **I** *vtr* **1** lit [*wave, avalanche*] submerger; [*flood*] inonder; [*enemy*] écraser; **2** fig [*emotion, letters, offers, phone calls*] submerger; [*feeling*] envahir; [*shame, unhappiness, work*] accabler; [*favours, kindness*] combler; **the performance ~ed me** la représentation m'a ébloui.
II overwhelmed *pp adj* (with letters, offers, phone calls, kindness) submergé (**with, by** de); (with shame, unhappiness, work) accablé (**with, by** de); (by sight, experience) ébloui (**by** par).

overwhelming /ˌəʊvəˈwelmɪŋ, US -hwelm-/ *adj* [*defeat, victory, majority, argument, evidence*] écrasant; [*desire, beauty, generosity, welcome*] irrésistible; [*force, effect*] implacable; [*heat, sorrow*] accablant; [*concern, importance, impression*] dominant; [*response, support*] enthousiaste; [*conviction*] absolu.

overwhelmingly /ˌəʊvəˈwelmɪŋlɪ, US -hwelm-/ *adv* [*beautiful, generous, successful*] extraordinairement; [*win, lose*] de manière écrasante; [*vote, accept, reject*] à une écrasante majorité; **the country is ~ Protestant** le pays est presque exclusivement protestant; **the meeting was ~ in favour of the motion** l'assemblée était à une majorité écrasante en faveur du projet.

overwinter /ˌəʊvəˈwɪntə(r)/ **I** *vtr* hiverner [*animal*]; protéger [qch] du froid [*plant*].
II *vi* [*animal*] hiverner.

overwork /ˈəʊvəwɜːk/ **I** *n* surmenage *m*.
II /ˌəʊvəˈwɜːk/ *vtr* surmener [*animal, employee, heart*].
III *vi* se surmener.

overworked /ˌəʊvəˈwɜːkt/ *adj* **1** [*employee, parent*] surmené; **2** [*excuse, word*] éculé.

overwrite /ˌəʊvəˈraɪt/ *vtr* (*prét* **-wrote**; *pp* **-written**) Comput remplacer [*data, memory*].

overwrought /ˌəʊvəˈrɔːt/ *adj* à bout de nerfs; **to get ~ about sth** se mettre dans tous ses états à propos de qch.

overzealous /ˌəʊvəˈzeləs/ *adj* [*person*] trop zélé; [*attitude, use*] excessif/-ive.

Ovid /ˈɒvɪd/ *pr n* Ovide.

oviduct /ˈəʊvɪdʌkt/ *n* oviducte *m*.

oviform /ˈəʊvɪfɔːm/ *adj* Biol oviforme.

ovine /ˈəʊvaɪn/ *adj* ovin.

oviparous /əʊˈvɪpərəs/ *adj* ovipare.

ovoid /ˈəʊvɔɪd/ *n, adj* ovoïde (*m*).

ovulate /ˈɒvjʊleɪt/ *vi* ovuler.

ovulation /ˌɒvjʊˈleɪʃn/ *n* ovulation *f*.

ovule /ˈəʊvjuːl/ *n* ovule *m*.

ovum /ˈəʊvəm/ *n* (*pl* **ova**) ovule *m*.

ow /aʊ/ *excl* aïe!

owe /əʊ/ *vtr* **1** (be indebted for) devoir [*money, invention, life, success*]; **to ~ sth to sb** tenir qch de qn [*good looks, talent*]; devoir qch à qn [*failure, money*]; **I ~ him £10 for the ticket** je lui dois 10 livres pour le billet; **he still ~s us for the ticket** il nous doit encore de l'argent pour le billet; **I've forgotten my purse, can I ~ it to you?** j'ai oublié mon porte-monnaie, est-ce que je peux te le rendre plus tard?; **my mother, to whom I ~ so much** ma mère, à qui je dois tout; **I ~ you one**○ ou **a favour** je te le revaudrai; **he ~s me one**○ ou **a favour** il me doit bien ça; **2** (be morally bound to give) devoir [*apology, duty, loyalty, explanation, thanks*]; **you ~ it to your parents to work hard** tu dois à tes parents de travailler dur; **you ~ it to yourself to try everything** tu te dois de tout essayer; **don't think the world ~s you a living**○**!** ne crois pas que le monde te doive quoi que ce soit!; **3** (be influenced by) **to ~ much/something to sb** devoir beaucoup/quelque chose à qn; **his style ~s much to the Impressionists** son style doit beaucoup aux impressionnistes.

owing /ˈəʊɪŋ/ **I** *adj* (*après n, après v*) à payer, dû (**for** pour); **how much is ~ to you?** combien est-ce qu'on vous doit (encore)?; **£20 is still ~** il y a encore 20 livres à payer; **the amount** ou **sum ~** le montant à payer or dû.
II owing to *prep phr* en raison de; **~ to the fact that** parce que.

owl /aʊl/ *n* hibou *m*; (with tufted ears) chouette *f*.
IDIOMS **a wise old ~** un sage vieillard chenu.

owlet /ˈaʊlɪt/ *n* jeune hibou *m*; (with tufted ears) jeune chouette *f*.

owlish /ˈaʊlɪʃ/ *adj* [*appearance, gaze*] de hibou; [*expression*] solennel/-elle.

own /əʊn/ **I** *adj* **1** (belonging to particular person, group etc) propre; **his ~ car/house** sa propre voiture/maison; **my ~ sister/daughter** ma propre sœur/fille; **his ~ children** ses propres enfants; **to have/start one's ~ business** avoir/lancer sa propre affaire; **the company has its ~ lawyer** l'entreprise a son propre avocat; **he has his ~ ideas about what the truth is** il a sa propre idée sur ce qui s'est vraiment passé; **he is responsible to his ~ government/department** il est responsable devant son gouvernement/service; **don't ask him to do it, he has his ~ problems** ne lui demande pas de le faire, il a assez de problèmes comme ça; **for your/his/their ~ safety** pour ta/sa/leur sécurité; **he's very nice in his ~ way** il est très gentil à sa manière; **the film was, in his ~ words, 'rubbish'** selon ses propres termes, le film était 'nul'; **the house has its ~ garage/garden** c'est une maison avec

garage/jardin (privatif); **with my ~ eyes** de mes propres yeux; **she does her ~ cooking/washing** c'est elle qui se fait à manger/qui fait sa lessive (elle-même); **he makes his ~ decisions** il prend ses décisions tout seul.
II *pron* **I don't have a company car, I use my ~** je n'ai pas de voiture de fonction, j'utilise la mienne; **he didn't borrow it, it's his ~** il ne l'a pas emprunté, c'est le sien; **she borrowed my pen, because she'd lost her ~** elle m'a emprunté mon stylo, parce qu'elle avait perdu le sien; **they have problems of their ~** ils ont assez de problèmes comme ça; **when you have children of your ~** quand tu auras des enfants; **he has a room of his ~** il a sa propre chambre; **I have a suggestion of my ~ to make** j'ai une suggestion personnelle à faire; **a house/a garden of our (very) ~** une maison/un jardin (bien) à nous; **it's his (very) ~** c'est à lui (tout seul); **we've got nothing to call our ~** nous n'avons rien à nous; **my time's not my ~** je n'ai pas une minute à moi.
III *vtr* **1** (possess) avoir; [*car, house, dog*]; **she ~s three shops and a café** elle est propriétaire de trois magasins et d'un café; **who ~s this house/car?** à qui est cette maison/voiture?; **he walks around as if he ~s the place** pej il se conduit comme s'il était chez lui; **2** (admit) reconnaître, avouer; **to ~ that** avouer que.
IV *vi* **to ~ to a mistake** reconnaître son erreur; **he ~ed to having lied/cheated/forgotten** il a avoué or reconnu avoir menti/triché/oublié.
IDIOMS **to come into one's ~** s'épanouir fig; **to do one's ~ thing** être indépendant; **each to his ~** chacun fait ce qu'il veut, chacun son truc○; **to get one's ~ back** se venger (**on sb** de qn); **to hold one's ~** bien se défendre; **on one's ~** tout seul; **to get sb on their ~** voir qn en privé.
■ **own up** avouer; **to ~ up to having done** ou **to doing** avouer or reconnaître avoir fait; **to ~ up to the murder/theft** avouer avoir commis le meurtre/vol.

own brand, **own label** I *n* marque *f* du distributeur.
II **own-brand**, **own-label** *modif* [*product*] vendu sous la marque du distributeur.

owner /ˈəʊnə(r)/ *n* propriétaire *mf*; **car/dog/home ~** propriétaire d'une voiture/d'un chien/d'un logement; **legal ~** propriétaire légitime; **previous ~** ancien/-ienne propriétaire; **proud ~** heureux/-euse propriétaire; **rightful ~** possesseur *m* légitime; **share ~** actionnaire *mf*; **'one careful ~'** (car ad) 'de première main, bien entretenue'.

owner-driver /ˌəʊnəˈdraɪvə(r)/ *n* conducteur/-trice *m/f* propriétaire.

ownerless /ˈəʊnəlɪs/ *adj* [*car*] sans propriétaire; [*dog*] sans maître.

owner: **~-manager** *n* propriétaire-gérant/-e *m/f*; **~-occupied** *adj* occupé par le propriétaire; **~-occupier** *n* propriétaire *mf* occupant/-e.

ownership /ˈəʊnəʃɪp/ *n* propriété *f*; (of land) possession *f*; **foreign ~** propriété étrangère; **home ~** fait *m* d'être propriétaire de son logement; **joint ~** copropriété *f*; **private/public ~** propriété privée/publique; **property ~** propriété immobilière; **share ~** participation *f* dans le capital d'une société; **to be in** ou **under private ~** être en propriété privée; **to take into public ~** nationaliser; **'under new ~'** 'changement de propriétaire'; **under her ~ the club has flourished** depuis qu'elle a racheté le club celui-ci a prospéré; **home ~ is increasing** le nombre de personnes propriétaires de leur logement augmente; **to provide proof of ~** prouver qu'on est propriétaire.

ownsome○ /ˈəʊnsəm/ *n* GB hum **all on one's ~** tout seul.

owt /aʊt/ *n* GB dial quelque chose.

ox /ɒks/ *n* (*pl* **~en**) bœuf *m*.
IDIOMS **as strong as an ~** fort comme un bœuf; **a blow that would have felled an ~** un coup qui aurait assommé un bœuf.

oxalic acid /ˌɒksælɪkˈæsɪd/ *n* acide *m* oxalique.

oxblood /ˈɒksblʌd/ *adj* [*shoes, polish*] rouge foncé *m inv*.

oxbow /ˈɒksbəʊ/ *n* **1** Geog méandre *m* (*de forme arquée*); **2** = **oxbow lake**.

oxbow lake *n* oxbow *m*, bras *m* mort.

Oxbridge /ˈɒksbrɪdʒ/ *n* universités *fpl* d'Oxford et de Cambridge.

ox cart *n* char *m* à bœufs.

oxen /ˈɒksn/ *pl* ▶ **ox.**

oxeye daisy /ˌɒksaɪ ˈdeɪzɪ/ *n* marguerite *f*.

Oxfam /ˈɒksfæm/ *n* (*abrév* = **Oxford Committee for Famine Relief**) Oxfam *m*.

Oxford /ˈɒksfəd/ ▶ 1818 *pr n* Oxford.

Oxford: **~ bags** *npl* Fashn pantalon *m* aux jambes larges; **~ blue** ▶ 1104 *n* bleu *m* marine; **~ movement** *n* Relig mouvement *m* d'Oxford.

oxfords /ˈɒksfədz/ *npl* chaussures *fpl* d'homme (*basses, à lacets et bouts renforcés*).

Oxfordshire /ˈɒksfədʃə(r)/ ▶ 1624 *pr n* Oxfordshire *m*.

oxidase /ˈɒksɪdeɪz/ *n* Physiol oxydase *f*.

oxidation /ˌɒksɪˈdeɪʃn/ *n* oxydation *f*.

oxide /ˈɒksaɪd/ *n* oxyde *m*.

oxidize /ˈɒksɪdaɪz/ I *vtr* oxyder.
II *vi* s'oxyder.

Oxon /ˈɒksən/ **1** GB Post *abrév écrite* = **Oxfordshire**; **2** GB Univ (*abrév écrite* = **Oxoniensis**) d'Oxford.

Oxonian /ɒkˈsəʊnjən/ sout I *n* **1** (graduate) licencié/-e *m/f* de l'université d'Oxford; **2** (inhabitant) Oxfordien/-ienne *m/f*.
II *adj* d'Oxford.

ox: **~tail soup** *n*: *soupe à base de queue de bœuf*; **~ tongue** *n* langue *f* de bœuf.

oxyacetylene /ˌɒksɪəˈsetɪliːn/ *adj* oxyacétylénique.

oxyacetylene burner, **oxyacetylene lamp**, **oxyacetylene torch** *n* chalumeau *m* oxyacétylénique.

oxygen /ˈɒksɪdʒən/ I *n* oxygène *m*; **to be on ~** Med être sous oxygène.
II *modif* [*bottle, cylinder, supply, tank*] d'oxygène; [*mask, tent*] à oxygène.

oxygenate /ɒkˈsɪdʒəneɪt/ *vtr* oxygéner.

oxygenation /ˌɒkɪdʒəˈneɪʃn/ *n* oxygénation *f*.

oxymoron /ˌɒksɪˈmɔːrɒn/ *n* Littérat oxymoron *m*.

oyster /ˈɔɪstə(r)/ I *n* **1** (fish) huître *f*; **2** (colour) gris *m* perle; **3** Culin (part of fowl) sot-l'y-laisse *m inv*.
II *modif* [*knife*] à huîtres; [*sauce*] aux huîtres; [*shell*] d'huître.
IDIOMS **the world's your ~** le monde est à toi.

oyster: **~ bed** *n* banc *m* d'huîtres; **~ catcher** *n* huîtrier *m*; **~ cracker** *n* US petit biscuit *m* salé; **~ farm** *n* parc *m* à huîtres; **~ farmer** ▶ 1692 *n* ostréiculteur/-trice *m/f*; **~man** *n* ostréiculteur *m*; **~ mushroom** *n* pleurote *m*.

oz *abrév écrite* = **ounce(s)**.

Oz○ /ɒz/ *n* GB Australie *f*.

ozone /ˈəʊzəʊn/ *n* **1** Chem, Meteorol ozone *m*; **2**○ (sea air) air *m* pur marin.

ozone: **~-depleting** *adj* [*chemical, gas*] qui détruit la couche d'ozone (*after n*); **~ depletion** *n* destruction *f* de la couche d'ozone; **~ distribution** *n* profil *m* d'ozonité; **~-friendly** *adj* qui protège la couche d'ozone (*after n*); **~ layer** *n* couche *f* d'ozone.

ozonosphere /əʊˈzəʊnəsfɪə/ *n* ozonosphère *f*, couche *f* d'ozone.

Pp

p, P /piː/ *n* **1** (letter) p, P *m*; **2 p** GB (*abrév* = **penny**, **pence**) (nouveau) penny *m*, (nouveaux) pence *mpl*.
IDIOMS **you'd better mind** ou **watch your p's and q's** tu as intérêt à bien te tenir.

pa○ /pɑː/ *n* papa *m*.

p.a. (*abrév écrite* = **per annum**) par an.

PA 1 (*abrév* = **personal assistant**) secrétaire *mf* de direction; **2** (*abrév* = **public address (system)**) système *m* de sonorisation, sono○ *f*; **to announce sth over the ~** annoncer qch par haut-parleurs; **3** US Post *abrév écrite* = **Pennsylvania**.

PAC *n*: *abrév* ▸ **political action committee**.

pace¹ /peɪs/ **I** *n* **1** (step) pas *m*; **to take a ~ backwards/forwards** faire un pas en arrière/en avant; **2** (measure) pas *m*; **the room measures 12 ~s by 14 ~s** la pièce fait 12 pas sur 14; **12 ~s away** à 12 pas; **3** (rate of movement) (of person walking, of life, change) rythme *m*, allure *f*; **at a fast/slow ~** vite/lentement; **at walking ~** au pas; **to quicken one's ~** presser le pas; **at my own ~** à mon propre rythme; **to keep up the ~** lit, fig tenir le rythme; **to keep ~ with sth** lit, fig arriver à suivre qch; **I can't stand the ~** lit, fig je n'arrive pas à suivre; **to step up/slow down the ~** accélérer/ralentir le rythme; **to set the ~** lit imposer le rythme; fig donner le ton; **4** (speed) vitesse *f*; **to have ~** être rapide; **to gather ~** [*vehicle, ball*] prendre de la vitesse; [*athlete*] accélérer; [*process*] prendre de l'ampleur; **his lack of ~ let him down** il a perdu à cause de son manque de rapidité; **5** Mus, Theat rythme *m*.
II *vtr* arpenter [*cage, room*].
III *vi* (also **~ up and down**) (slowly) marcher à pas lents; (impatiently) faire les cent pas; **to ~ up and down sth** arpenter qch.
IV *v refl* **to ~ oneself** (in a race) doser son effort; (at work) se ménager.
IDIOMS **to put sb through their ~s** mettre qn à l'épreuve.

pace² /'peɪsɪ/ *prep* sout n'en déplaise à.

pacemaker /'peɪsmeɪkə(r)/ *n* **1** Med stimulateur *m* cardiaque; **2** Sport lièvre *m*, meneur/-euse *m/f* de train.

pacer /'peɪsə(r)/ *n* **1** Equit amble *m*; **2** Sport lièvre *m*, meneur/-euse *m/f* de train.

pacesetter /'peɪssetə(r)/ *n* **1** Sport (horse) cheval *m* de jeu; (athlete) lièvre *m*, meneur/-euse *m/f* de train; **2** fig (trendsetter) pionnier *m*.

pachyderm /'pækɪdɜːm/ *n* pachyderme *m*.

pacific /pə'sɪfɪk/ *adj* pacifique.

Pacific /pə'sɪfɪk/ ▸ **1511** *pr n* **the ~** le Pacifique *m*.

Pacific: **~ Daylight Time**, **PDT** *n* US heure *f* d'été du Pacifique; **~ Islands** *npl* îles *fpl* du Pacifique; **~ Ocean** *n* océan *m* Pacifique; **~ Rim** *n* ceinture *f* du Pacifique; **~ Standard Time**, **PST** *n* heure *f* du Pacifique.

pacifier /'pæsɪfaɪə(r)/ *n* US (for baby) tétine *f*, sucette *f*.

pacifism /'pæsɪfɪzəm/ *n* pacifisme *m*.

pacifist /'pæsɪfɪst/ *n, adj* pacifiste (*mf*).

pacify /'pæsɪfaɪ/ *vtr* **1** gen apaiser [*person*]; **2** Mil, Pol pacifier [*country*].

pack /pæk/ **I** *n* **1** (container) (box) paquet *m*; (large box) boîte *f*; (bag) sachet *m*; **a cigarette ~** un paquet de cigarettes; **a cornflakes ~** une boîte de cornflakes; **2** (group) (of wolves, people, dogs) bande *f*; (of hounds, in hunting) meute *f*; (of scouts, guides) section *f*; **3** Sport (in rugby) pack *m*; (in race) peloton *m*; **4** Games (of cards) jeu *m* de cartes; **5** (load) (backpack) sac *m* à dos; (carried by animal) fardeau *m*, charge *f*; **6** Med enveloppement *m*; (smaller) compresse *f*.
II -pack (*dans composés*) **a two/four-~** (of cassettes) un lot de deux/quatre; (of beer) un pack de deux/quatre.
III *vtr* **1** (stow) (in suitcase) mettre [qch] dans une valise [*clothes*]; (in box, crate) emballer [*ornaments, books*]; **2** (put things into) emballer [*box, crate*]; **to ~ one's suitcase** faire sa valise; **to ~ one's bags** lit, fig faire ses valises; **to ~ sth with** remplir qch de; **3** (package commercially) emballer, conditionner [*fruit, meat, goods*]; **4** (cram into) [*people, crowd*] remplir complètement [*church, theatre, stadium*]; boucher [*corner, hole, gap*] (**with** avec); **to be ~ed with** être bondé de [*people*]; être plein de [*ideas, sweets*]; **to ~ sth into a hole** bourrer ou boucher un trou avec qch; **5** (press firmly) tasser [*snow, earth*]; **6**○ (carry) avoir [*pistol, gun*]; **7** Pol (influence composition of) s'assurer [*jury*]; rendre [qch] favorable à ses vues [*conference, meeting, committee*].
IV *vi* **1** (get ready for departure) [*person*] faire ses valises; **2** (crowd) **to ~ into** s'entasser dans [*hall, theatre, church, stadium*].
IDIOMS **a ~ of lies** un tissu de mensonges; **to send sb ~ing** envoyer promener qn.
■ **pack away**: **~ [sth] away**, **~ away [sth]** ranger [*clothes, books*].
■ **pack in**: ¶ **~ in**○ (break down) [*car*] tomber en panne; [*machine*] se détraquer○; [*heart, liver*] craquer○; ¶ **~ [sth] in**, **~ in [sth] 1** (cram in) faire tenir [*people*]; **that play is really ~ing them in** cette pièce attire vraiment les foules; **2**○ (give up) plaquer○ [*job, boyfriend*]; **to ~ it all in** tout plaquer○; **I've ~ed in smoking** j'ai arrêté de fumer; **~ it in!** arrête!, ça suffit!
■ **pack off**: **~ [sb] off**, **~ off [sb]** expédier; **to ~ sb off to** expédier qn à [*school, bed*]; expédier qn en [*country*].
■ **pack up**: ¶ **~ up 1** (prepare to go) [*person*] faire ses valises; **2**○ (break down) [*TV, machine*] se détraquer○; [*car*] tomber en panne; [*heart, liver*] craquer○; **3**○ (stop) s'arrêter; ¶ **~ [sth] up**, **~ up [sth] 1** (put away) ranger [*books, clothes*]; (in boxes, crates) emballer [*books, objects*]; **2**○ (stop) **to ~ up doing** arrêter de faire.

package /'pækɪdʒ/ **I** *n* **1** (parcel) paquet *m*, colis *m*; **2** (collection) (of reforms, measures, proposals) ensemble *m* (**of** de); **aid ~** ensemble *m* de mesures d'assistance; **an insurance ~** une assurance; **the sunroof is not part of the ~** le toit ouvrant est en option; **the radio is part of the ~** la radio est comprise dans le prix; **3** US (pack) paquet *m* (**of** de); **4** Comput progiciel *m*; **word-processing ~** progiciel *m* de traitement de texte; **5** = **package holiday**.
II *vtr* **1** (put into packaging) emballer, conditionner [*goods, object*]; **2** (present, design image for) concevoir un conditionnement pour [*product*]; présenter [*policy, proposal*]; concevoir la publicité de [*film, singer, band*].

package: **~ deal** *n* Comm offre *f* globale; **~ holiday** GB, **~ tour**, **~ vacation** US *n* voyage *m* organisé, forfait *m*.

packaging /'pækɪdʒɪŋ/ *n* **1** Comm (materials) emballage *m*; **2** (way thing is presented, promoted) (of product) conditionnement *m*; (of company, policy, film, singer) image *f* publique.

pack animal *n* bête *f* de somme.

pack drill *n* GB Mil punition *f* consistant à faire des tours de caserne avec l'équipement de combat.
IDIOMS **no names, no ~** nous garderons les noms secrets.

packed /pækt/ *adj* **1** (crowded) comble, bondé; **~ with** plein de; **to play to ~ houses** Theat faire salle comble; **2** (after packing) **I'm ~** j'ai fait mes valises.

packed lunch *n* panier-repas *m*.

packer /'pækə(r)/ *n* Ind **1** (person) emballeur/-euse *m/f*, conditionneur/-euse *m/f*; **2** (machine) emballeuse *f*.

packet /'pækɪt/ **I** *n* **1** (container) (box) paquet *m*; (bag) sachet *m*; (for drinks) brique *f*; **2** (parcel) paquet *m*, colis *m*; **3**† Naut paquebot *m*.
II *modif* [*soup*] en sachet; [*drink*] en brique.
IDIOMS **to cost/earn a ~**○ coûter/gagner un argent fou○.

packet switching *n* Comput, Telecom commutation *f* par paquets.

pack: **~ horse** *n* cheval *m* de somme; **~ ice** *n* pack *m*, banquise *f*.

packing /'pækɪŋ/ *n* **1** Comm emballage *m*, conditionnement *m*; **2** (of suitcases) **to do one's ~** faire ses valises; **3** Tech (for making water- or gas-tight) garniture *f* d'étanchéité. ▸ **postage**.

packing: **~ case** *n* caisse *f* d'emballage; **~ density** *n* Comput densité *f* d'enregistrement or de stockage.

pack: **~saddle** *n* bât *m*; **~thread** *n* ficelle *f*.

pact /pækt/ *n* gen, Pol pacte *m*; **to make a ~ with** conclure or signer un pacte avec [*country, government*]; faire un pacte avec [*person*]; **to make a ~ with the devil** pactiser avec le diable; **to make a ~ to do** [*people*] se mettre d'accord pour faire.

pad /pæd/ **I** *n* **1** (of paper) bloc *m*; **2** (to prevent chafing or scraping) protection *f*; **foam/rubber/felt ~** protection *f* de mousse/de caoutchouc/de feutre; **3** (to absorb or distribute liquid) tampon *m*; **make-up remover/scouring ~** tampon *m* démaquillant/à recurer; **4** (to give shape to sth) rembourrage *m*; **foam ~** rembourrage de mousse; **5** (sticky part on object, plant, animal) ventouse *f*; **6** Sport (in general) protection *f*; (for leg in cricket, hockey) jambière *f*; **7** (of paw) coussinet *m*; (of finger) pulpe *f*; **8** (also **launch ~**) rampe *f* de lancement; **9** (sani-

tary towel) serviette *f* hygiénique; **10**○ † (flat) appart○ *m*, piaule◑ *f*; **11**○ US (bribe) pot-de-vin *m*.
II *vtr* (*p prés etc* **-dd-**) **1** (put padding in, on) rembourrer [*chair, shoulders, bra, jacket*] (**with** avec); capitonner [*walls, floor, large surface*]; **to ~ a wound with cotton wool** mettre un tampon de coton sur une plaie; **2** (make longer) = **pad out**.
III *vi* (*p prés etc* **-dd-**) **to ~ along/around** avancer/aller et venir à pas feutrés.
■ **pad out**: **~ out** [**sth**], **~** [**sth**] **out 1** fig étoffer, délayer pej [*essay, book, speech*] (**with** à l'aide de); allonger [*meal, course, dish*] (**with** avec); gonfler○ [*bill, expense account*] (**with** avec); **2** lit rembourrer [*shoulders, bust, costume*].

padded /ˈpædɪd/ *adj* [*armrest, bra, seat, jacket*] rembourré (**with** avec).

padded: **~ cell** *n* cellule *f* capitonnée; **~ envelope** *n* enveloppe *f* matelassée; **~ income**○ *n* US *revenu agrémenté d'à-côtés illicites*; **~ shoulder** *n* épaule *f* rembourrée.

padding /ˈpædɪŋ/ *n* **1** (stuffing, foam) rembourrage *m*; (on wall, large surface) capitonnage *m*; **protective ~** rembourrage de protection; **2** (in speech, essay) remplissage *m*; **3**○ (filling food) plat *m* d'accompagnement bourratif○.

paddle /ˈpædl/ **I** *n* **1** (oar) pagaie *f*; **2** (on waterwheel) aube *f*; **3** (wade) **to go for a ~** faire trempette *f*; **4** Culin spatule *f*; **5** US Sport raquette *f* de ping-pong®.
II *vtr* **1** (row) **to ~ a canoe** pagayer; **2** (dip) patouiller○, agiter [*feet, fingers*] (**in** dans); **3** US (spank) donner une fessée à [*child*].
III *vi* **1** (row) pagayer; **2** (wade) patauger; **3** (swim about) [*duck, swan*] barboter.

paddle: **~ boat** *n* bateau *m* à aubes; **~ steamer** *n* bateau *m* à aubes; **~ wheel** *n* roue *f* à aubes.

paddling pool *n* (public) pataugeoire *f*; (inflatable) piscine *f* gonflable.

paddock /ˈpædək/ *n* **1** (field) enclos *m*, paddock *m*; **2** (in horse racing) paddock *m*; **3** (in motor racing) box *m*.

paddy /ˈpædɪ/ *n* **1** (rice) (riz *m*) paddy *m*; **2** = **paddyfield**; **3**○ GB crise *f* de colère; **to get into a ~** piquer une colère○.

Paddy○ /ˈpædɪ/ *n* injur Irlandais *m*.

paddy: **~field** *n* rizière *f*; **~ wagon**○ *n* US panier *m* à salade○, voiture *f* cellulaire.

padlock /ˈpædlɒk/ **I** *n* gen cadenas *m*; (for bicycle) antivol *m*.
II *vtr* cadenasser [*door, gate*]; mettre un antivol à [*bicycle*].

padre /ˈpɑːdreɪ/ *n* (priest) prêtre *m*; Mil (chaplain) aumônier *m*.

paean /ˈpiːən/ *n* littér péan *m*; fig hymne *m* (**to** à).

paederast *n* = **pederast**.

paediatric *adj* = **pediatric**.

paediatrician *n* = **pediatrician**.

paediatrics *n* = **pediatrics**.

paedophile *n* = **pedophile**.

paedophilia *n* = **pedophilia**.

paella /paɪˈelə/ *n* paella *f*.

pagan /ˈpeɪgən/ *n, adj* païen/païenne (*m/f*).

paganism /ˈpeɪgənɪzəm/ *n* paganisme *m*.

page /peɪdʒ/ **I** *n* **1** (in book, newspaper) page *f*; **on ~ two** à la page deux; **a six ~ letter** une lettre de six pages; **the book is 200 ~s long** le livre a 200 pages; **two ~s on fishing** deux pages consacrées à la pêche; **financial ~** page économique; **sports/women's ~** page des sports/lectrices; **2** Comput page-écran *f*; **3** (attendant) (in hotel) groom *m*, chasseur *m*; US (in Congress) coursier *m*; Hist page *m*; **4** fig (episode) page *f*.
II *vtr* (on pager) rechercher; (over loudspeaker) faire appeler; **'paging Mr Jones'** 'on demande M. Jones'.
IDIOMS **to turn the ~ on sth** tourner la page sur qch.

pageant /ˈpædʒənt/ *n* (play) reconstitution *f* historique; (carnival) fête *f* à thème historique.
IDIOMS **it's all part of life's rich ~** iron tel est notre pain quotidien.

pageantry /ˈpædʒəntrɪ/ *n* pompe *f*.

pageboy /ˈpeɪdʒbɔɪ/ *n* **1** (bride's attendant) garçon *m* d'honneur; **2** (hairstyle) coupe *f* à la Jeanne d'Arc.

page: **~ break** *n* Comput saut *m* de page; **~ number** *n* numéro *m* de page, folio *m* spec; **~ proof** *n* Print tierce *f*.

pager /ˈpeɪdʒə(r)/ *n* Telecom radiomessageur *m*.

page: **~ reference** *n* page *f*; **~ set-up** *n* Comput mise *f* en page; **~ three** *n* GB page *f* des pin-up (*aux seins nus dans certains journaux*); **~ three girl** *n* GB pin-up *f* (*dans un journal*).

paginate /ˈpædʒɪneɪt/ *vtr* paginer.

pagination /ˌpædʒɪˈneɪʃn/ *n* pagination *f*.

paging /ˈpeɪdʒɪŋ/ *n* Comput pagination *f*.

pagoda /pəˈgəʊdə/ *n* pagode *f*.

paid /peɪd/ **I** *prét, pp* ▶ **pay**.
II *adj* [*job*] rémunéré; [*holiday*] payé; **~ assassin** tueur *m* à gages.
IDIOMS **to put ~ to sth** GB mettre un terme à qch.

paid: **~-up** *adj* GB [*payment, instalment*] à jour; [*share, capital*] remboursé; **~-up member** *n* GB adhérent/-e *m/f*.

pail /peɪl/ *n* seau *m* (**of** de).

paillasse *n* = **palliasse**.

pain /peɪn/ **I** *n* **1** (suffering) douleur *f*; **to feel ~, to be in ~** souffrir, avoir mal; **he's caused me a lot of ~** il m'a fait beaucoup souffrir; **the cramps are causing me a lot of ~** les crampes me font très mal; **the ~ of separation/loss** la douleur de la séparation/perte; **to feel no ~** lit ne ressentir aucune douleur; US fig (be drunk) être soûl○; **2** (localized) douleur *f*; **abdominal/chest ~s** douleurs *fpl* abdominales/à la poitrine; **period ~s** règles *fpl* douloureuses; **I have a ~ in my arm** j'ai mal au bras; **where is the ~?** où avez-vous mal?; **3**○ (annoying person, thing) **she can be a real ~** elle peut être très enquiquinante○ or énervante; **he gives me a ~** il m'enquiquine○, il m'énerve; **he's a ~ in the neck**○ il est casse-pieds○; **he's a ~ in the arse**● GB ou **ass**● US il est emmerdant◑; **4 on ~ of death/of excommunication** sous peine de mort/d'excommunication.
II pains *npl* **to be at ~s to do sth** prendre grand soin de faire qch; **I was at ~s to speak very slowly** j'ai pris (grand) soin de parler très lentement; **to take great ~s over** ou **with sth** se donner beaucoup de mal pour faire qch; **for my/his etc ~s** pour ma/sa etc peine; **he got a black eye for his ~s** pour tout remerciement il a eu droit à un œil au beurre noir.
III *vtr* **1** (hurt) **my leg ~s me a little** ma jambe me fait un peu mal; **2** sout (grieve) chagriner; **it ~s me to have to tell you that** cela me chagrine de devoir vous dire que.
IV pained *pp adj* **with a ~ed expression** d'un air affligé.

painful /ˈpeɪnfl/ *adj* **1** (injury, swelling etc) douloureux/-euse; fig [*lesson, memory, reminder*] pénible; [*blow*] dur; **it was ~ to watch** c'était pénible à regarder; **it was too ~ to bear** c'était trop dur or pénible à supporter; **2** (laborious) [*progress, task*] pénible; **3**○ (bad) [*display, performance*] lamentable.

painfully /ˈpeɪnfəlɪ/ *adv* **1** (excruciatingly) **his arm is ~ swollen** son bras est enflé et lui fait mal; **to be ~ shy** être maladivement timide; **I am ~ aware of that** je n'en ai que trop conscience; **2** (laboriously) **progress has been ~ slow** les progrès ont été terriblement lents.

pain: **~killer** *n* analgésique *m*; **~killing** *adj* analgésique.

painless /ˈpeɪnlɪs/ *adj* **1** [*operation, injection*] indolore; [*death*] sans souffrance; **2** (trouble-free) sans peine.

painlessly /ˈpeɪnlɪslɪ/ *adv* **1** (without physical pain) sans douleur; **2** (easily) [*achieved, completed*] sans trop de mal.

painstaking /ˈpeɪnzteɪkɪŋ/ *adj* minutieux/-ieuse.

painstakingly /ˈpeɪnzteɪkɪŋlɪ/ *adv* minutieusement.

paint /peɪnt/ **I** *n* **1** gen, Art peinture *f*; **the ~ on the walls has yellowed** la peinture des murs a jauni; **all it needs is a fresh coat of ~** il suffirait d'un coup de badigeon; **'wet ~'** 'peinture fraîche'; **2** (make-up)† hum fard *m*.
II paints *npl* Art couleurs *fpl*; **why don't you get out your ~s ?** pourquoi ne prends-tu pas ta boîte de couleurs?
III *vtr* **1** lit peindre [*wall, subject*]; peindre le portrait de [*person*]; **to ~ sth blue/green** peindre qch en bleu/en vert; Art **to ~ sth in** peindre [*background, figure*]; **to ~ sth on** appliquer [*varnish, undercoat*]; **to ~ sth out** peindre par-dessus qch [*face, figure, wallpaper*]; **I'm going to ~ a picture** je vais peindre quelque chose; **to ~ one's nails** se vernir les ongles; **2** fig (depict) dépeindre; **to ~ a rather gloomy picture of sth** brosser un tableau assez sombre de qch; **to ~ an unflattering portrait of sb** décrire qn en termes peu élogieux; **3** Med badigeonner [*cut, wound*] (**with** de).
IV *vi* peindre; **to ~ from life/outdoors** peindre d'après nature/en plein air; **to ~ in oils/watercolours** faire de la peinture à l'huile/de l'aquarelle.
IDIOMS **he is not as black as he is ~ed** il n'est pas si méchant qu'on le prétend; **to ~ the town red** faire la noce.

paint: **~box** *n* boîte *f* de couleurs; **~brush** *n* pinceau *m*.

painted lady *n* Zool vanesse *f*.

painter /ˈpeɪntə(r)/ ▶ **1692** *n* **1** (artist, workman) peintre *m*; **~ and decorator** peintre-décorateur *m*; **2** Naut amarre *f*.

painting /ˈpeɪntɪŋ/ *n* **1** ¢ (activity, art form) peinture *f*; **2** (work of art) tableau *m*; (unframed) toile *f*; (of person) portrait *m*; **a ~ by Watteau** un tableau de Watteau; **a ~ of Napoleon by David** un portrait de Napoléon peint par David; **a ~ of Flatford Mill** un tableau qui représente le moulin de Flatford; **3** ¢ (domestic decorating) peintures *fpl*; **finish the ~ before you put the carpets down** finissez les peintures avant de poser les tapis.

painting book *n* album *m* à colorier.

paintpot /ˈpeɪntpɒt/ *n* pot *m* de peinture.

paint remover *n* **1** (for removing stains) solvant *m*; **2** = **paint stripper**.

paint: **~ roller** *n* rouleau *m* à peinture; **~ spray** *n* bombe *f* de peinture, peinture *f* en aérosol; **~ stripper** *n* (chemical) décapant *m*; (tool) racloir *m*; **~ tray** *n* bac *m* à peinture.

paintwork /ˈpeɪntwɜːk/ *n* **1** (on door, window) peintures *fpl*; **2** (on car) peinture *f*.

pair /peə(r)/ **I** *n* **1** (two matching items) paire *f*; **to be one of a ~** faire partie d'une paire; **these candlesticks are sold in ~s** ces bougeoirs sont vendus par paires; **the children arrive in ~s** les enfants arrivent deux par deux; **to work in ~s** travailler en groupes de deux; **to put** ou **arrange sth in ~s** mettre en paires; **these gloves are not a ~** ces gants sont dépareillés; **I've only got one ~ of hands**○! je n'ai pas quatre bras○!; **2** (item made of two parts) paire *f*; **a ~ of glasses/scissors** une paire de lunettes/ciseaux; ▶ **trouser etc**; **3** (two people, animals etc) (sexually involved) couple *m*; (grouped together) paire *f*; **they're a ~ of crooks/fools** ce sont deux escrocs/imbéciles; **the ~ of them**○ **are on very good terms** ils s'entendent très bien tous les deux; **a coach and ~** une voiture à deux

chevaux; **4** GB Pol *parlementaire qui a passé un accord avec un parlementaire du parti opposé pour que tous deux s'abstiennent de voter.*
II **pairs** *modif* Sport [*competition, final*] pour équipes de deux.
III *vtr* apparier [*gloves, socks*]; **to ~ Paul with Julie** mettre Paul avec Julie; **to ~ jeans with a T-shirt** mettre un jean avec un T-shirt; **to ~ each name with a photograph** associer chaque nom à une photo; **to ~ one player against another** faire jouer un joueur contre un autre.
■ **pair off**: **~ off** (as a couple) se mettre ensemble; (for temporary purposes) se mettre par deux; **to ~ Ruth off with Paul** mettre Ruth et Paul ensemble.
■ **pair up**: **~ up** [*dancers, lovers*] former un couple; [*competitors*] faire équipe; **to ~ Frank up with Rita** mettre ensemble Frank et Rita.

pair: **~ bond** *n* Zool union *f* monogame; **~ bonding** *n* Zool union *f* monogame.

paisley /ˈpeɪzlɪ/ I *n* (fabric) tissu *m* à motifs cachemire.
II *modif* [*scarf, skirt*] à motifs cachemire; **~ pattern** motifs *mpl* cachemire.

pajamas *npl* US = **pyjamas**.

Paki◑ /ˈpækɪ/ GB injur I *n* Pakistanais/-e *m/f*.
II *adj* pakistanais.

Paki: **~-basher**◑ *n* GB *personne qui s'attaque aux immigrants pakistanais et indiens*; **~-bashing**◑ *n* GB *violences contre les immigrants pakistanais et indiens.*

Pakistan /ˌpɑːkɪˈstɑːn, ˌpækɪ-/ ▶ 1131 *pr n* Pakistan *m*.

Pakistani /ˌpɑːkɪˈstɑːnɪ, ˌpækɪ-/ ▶ 1486 I *n* Pakistanais/-e *m/f*.
II *adj* pakistanais.

pal○ /pæl/ *n* copain○/copine○ *m/f*; **to be ~s with sb** être copain avec qn; **be a ~!** sois sympa!
■ **pal up** devenir copain (**with** avec).

PAL /pæl/ *n* TV (*abrév* = **phase alternative line**) PAL *m*; **~ standard** système *m* PAL.

palace /ˈpælɪs/ *n* (of monarch) palais *m*; (of bishop) évêché *m*.

palace revolution *n* Pol révolution *f* de palais.

paladin /ˈpælədɪn/ *n* paladin *m*.

palais (de danse)○† *n* GB salle *f* de bal.

palatable /ˈpælətəbl/ *n* [*food*] savoureux; [*solution, law*] acceptable.

palatal /ˈpælətl/ Phon I *n* phonème *m* palatal.
II *adj* palatal.

palatalize /ˈpælətəlaɪz/ *vtr* Phon palataliser.

palate /ˈpælət/ *n* **1** Anat palais *m*; **to have a discriminating ~** fig avoir un palais fin; **2** (sense of taste) goût *m*; **too sweet for my ~** trop sucré à mon goût.

palatial /pəˈleɪʃl/ *adj* immense.

palatinate /pəˈlætɪneɪt, US -tənət/ *n* palatinat *m*.

palaver○ /pəˈlɑːvə(r), US ˈ-læv-/ *n* (bother) bazar○ *m*; **what a ~ doing** ça a été un de ces bazars○ pour faire.

pale /peɪl/ I *adj* [*complexion, colour*] pâle; [*light, dawn*] blafard; **~ blue** bleu pâle; **you look ~** tu es pâle; **to turn** ou **go ~** pâlir; **~ with fright** blanc de peur.
II *vi* **1** [*person, face*] pâlir; **2** fig **to ~ into insignificance** devenir dérisoire.
IDIOMS **to be beyond the ~** [*remark, behaviour*] être inadmissible; [*person*] (socially) être infréquentable.

pale: **~ ale** *n* GB pale-ale *m* (*bière blonde légère*); **~face** *n* Visage pâle *mf*; **~-faced** *adj* pâle.

paleness /ˈpeɪlnɪs/ *n* (of face, person, skin) pâleur *f*.

paleographer /ˌpælɪˈɒgrəfə(r)/ *n* paléographe *mf*.

paleography /ˌpælɪˈɒgrəfɪ/ *n* paléographie *f*.

paleolithic /ˌpælɪəʊˈlɪθɪk/ *adj* paléolithique.

paleontologist /ˌpælɪɒnˈtɒlədʒɪst/ ▶ 1692 *n* paléontologiste *mf*.

paleontology /ˌpælɪɒnˈtɒlədʒɪ/ *n* paléontologie *f*.

Palermo /pəˈlɜːməʊ/ ▶ 1818 *pr n* Palerme.

Palestine /ˈpæləstaɪn/ *pr n* Palestine *f*.

Palestine Liberation Organization, **PLO** *n* Organisation *f* de Libération de la Palestine.

Palestinian /ˌpælɪˈstɪnɪən/ ▶ 1486 I *n* Palestinien/-ienne *m/f*.
II *adj* palestinien/-ienne.

palette /ˈpælɪt/ *n* (object, colours) palette *f*.

palette knife *n* **1** Art couteau *m* à palette; **2** Culin palette *f*.

palfrey‡ /ˈpɔːlfrɪ/ *n* palefroi‡ *m*.

palimony /ˈpælɪmənɪ/ *n* pension *f* alimentaire (*versée à un/-e ex-concubin/-e*).

palimpsest /ˈpælɪmpsest/ *n* palimpseste *m*.

palindrome /ˈpælɪndrəʊm/ *n* palindrome *m*.

paling /ˈpeɪlɪŋ/ I *n* (stake) palis *m*.
II **palings** *npl* (fence) palissade *f*.

palisade /ˌpælɪˈseɪd/ I *n* (fence) palissade *f*.
II **palisades** *npl* US (cliffs) muraille *f* de falaises à pic.

pall /pɔːl/ I *n* **1** (coffin-cloth) drap *m* mortuaire; (coffin) cercueil *m*; **2** (covering) (of smoke, dust) nuage *m*; (of gloom, mystery, silence) manteau *m*.
II *vi* **it never ~s** on ne s'en lasse jamais; **these pleasures soon ~ed** je me suis/il s'est etc vite lassé de ces plaisirs.

Palladian /pəˈleɪdɪən/ *adj* palladien/-ienne.

pallbearer /ˈpɔːlbeərə(r)/ *n* porteur/-euse *m/f* de cercueil.

pallet /ˈpælɪt/ *n* **1** (for loading) palette *f*; **2**† (mattress) paillasse *f*; **3**† (bed) grabat *m*.

pallet truck *n* transpalette *m*.

palliasse† /ˈpælɪæs, US ˌpælɪˈæs/ *n* paillasse *f*.

palliate /ˈpælɪeɪt/ *vtr* sout pallier; **to ~ a crime** atténuer la gravité d'un crime.

palliative /ˈpælɪətɪv/ *adj* I *n* gen, Med palliatif *m*.
II *adj* gen, Med palliatif/-ive *m/f*.

pallid /ˈpælɪd/ *adj* [*skin, light*] blafard.

pallor /ˈpælə(r)/ *n* pâleur *f*.

pally○ /ˈpælɪ/ *adj* GB copain/copine○ (**with** avec).

palm /pɑːm/ I *n* **1** (of hand) paume *f*; **in the ~ of one's hand** dans le creux de la main; **he read my ~** il m'a lu les lignes de la main; **2** Bot (also **~ tree**) (plant) palmier *m*; **3** (branch) branche *f* de palmier; (leaf) palme *f*; **4** Relig rameau *m*.
II *vtr* (hide in trick) escamoter [*card, coin*]; (steal) subtiliser [*money*].
IDIOMS **you have him in the ~ of your hand!** tu pourrais lui faire faire tout ce que tu veux!; **to grease** ou **oil sb's ~** graisser la patte○ à qn; **to cross sb's ~ with silver** donner de l'argent à qn.
■ **palm off**○: **~ [sth] off, ~ off [sth]** faire passer qch (**as** pour); **to ~ sth off on sb, to ~ sb off with sth** refiler○ qch à qn.

palmate /ˈpælmeɪt/ *adj* Bot, Zool palmé.

palmetto /pælˈmetəʊ/ *n* (*pl* **-toes, -tos**) palmier *m* nain.

palm grove *n* palmeraie *f*.

palmist /ˈpɑːmɪst/ ▶ 1692 *n* chiromancien/-ienne *m/f*.

palmistry /ˈpɑːmɪstrɪ/ *n* chiromancie *f*.

palm: **Palm Sunday** *n* dimanche *m* des Rameaux; **~top computer** *n* ordinateur *m* de poche.

palmy /ˈpɑːmɪ/ *adj* **in the ~ days of sth** aux beaux jours de qch; **in my ~ days** pendant mes beaux jours.

palomino /ˌpæləˈmiːnəʊ/ *n* palomino *m*.

palooka○ /pəˈluːkə/ *n* US imbécile○ *m*, cornichon○ *m*.

palpable /ˈpælpəbl/ *adj* [*difference, fear, tension, relief*] palpable; [*lie, error, nonsense*] manifeste.

palpably /ˈpælpəblɪ/ *adv* manifestement.

palpate /ˈpælpeɪt/ *vtr* Med palper.

palpitate /ˈpælpɪteɪt/ *vi* (all contexts) palpiter (**with** de).

palpitation /ˌpælpɪˈteɪʃn/ *n* Med palpitation *f*.

palsied‡ /ˈpɔːlzɪd/ *adj* tremblant.

palsy /ˈpɔːlzɪ/ *n* (paralysis) paralysie *f*; (trembling) tremblement *m*.

palsy-walsy○ /ˌpælzɪˈwælzɪ/ *adj* US = **pally**.

paltry /ˈpɔːltrɪ/ *adj* [*sum*] dérisoire; [*excuse*] piètre.

pampas /ˈpæmpəs, US -əz/ *n* (+ *v sg*) pampa *f*.

pampas grass *n* herbe *f* des pampas.

pamper /ˈpæmpə(r)/ I *vtr* choyer [*person, pet*]; soigner [*skin*].
II *v refl* **to ~ oneself** se bichonner○.

pamphlet /ˈpæmflɪt/ *n* **1** gen brochure *f*; **2** (political) tract *m*; **3** Hist (satirical) pamphlet *m*.

pamphleteer† /ˌpæmflɪˈtɪə(r)/ *n* pamphlétaire *mf*.

pan /pæn/ I *n* **1** Culin (saucepan) casserole *f*; **heavy ~** casserole *f* à fond épais; **a ~ of water** une casserole d'eau; **heat up a ~ of water** faites bouillir de l'eau dans une casserole; **2** (on scales) plateau *m*; **3** (in lavatory) cuvette *f*; **4** (for washing ore) batée *f*.
II *vtr* (*p prés etc* **-nn-**) **1**○ (criticize) éreinter [*performance, production*]; **2** Cin, Phot, TV faire un panoramique de; **3** laver [qch] à la batée [*gravel, silt*]; récolter [*gold*].
III *vi* **1** Phot (*p prés etc* **-nn-**) [*camera*] faire un panoramique; **to ~ around** faire un panoramique de [*room*]; **2** Miner **to ~ for** chercher [*gold*].
IV **Pan+** (*dans composés*) **Pan-American** panaméricain/-aine; **Pan-Slavism** panslavisme *m*; **Pan-African** panafricain/-aine.
■ **pan out** (turn out) marcher; (turn out well) s'arranger.

panacea /ˌpænəˈsiːə/ *n* (all contexts) panacée *f*.

panache /pæˈnæʃ, US pə-/ *n* panache *m*.

Panama /ˈpænəmɑː/ I *n* (also **panama**) (hat) panama *m*.
II ▶ 1131 *pr n* Panama *m*.

Panama Canal *pr n* canal *m* de Panama.

Panama City /ˌpænəmə ˈsɪtɪ/ ▶ 1818 *pr n* Panama.

Panama hat *n* = **Panama** I.

Panamanian /ˌpænəˈmeɪnɪən/ ▶ 1486 I *n* Panaméen/-éenne *m/f*.
II *adj* panaméen/-éenne.

pancake /ˈpæŋkeɪk/ *n* **1** Culin crêpe *f*; **2** Theat Cosmet fond *m* de teint.
IDIOMS **as flat as a ~**○ complètement plat.

pancake: **~ day** *n* mardi *m* gras; **~ filling** *n* garniture *f* pour crêpes; **~ mix** *n* (in packet) préparation *f* pour pâte à crêpes; (batter) pâte *f* à crêpes; **~ race** *n* course *f* du mardi gras (*avec poêle et crêpe*).

panchromatic /ˌpænkrəˈmætɪk/ *adj* panchromatique.

pancreas /ˈpæŋkrɪəs/ *n* pancréas *m*.

pancreatic /ˌpæŋkrɪˈætɪk/ *adj* pancréatique.

panda /ˈpændə/ *n* panda *m*.

panda car○ *n* GB voiture *f* pie.

pandemic /pænˈdemɪk/ Med I *n* pandémie *f*.
II *adj* pandémique.

pandemonium /ˌpændɪˈməʊnɪəm/ *n* tohu-bohu *m*.

pander /ˈpændə(r)/ I‡ *n* souteneur *m*.
II *vi* **to ~ to** céder aux exigences de [*person*]; flatter [*whim, market*].

Pandora /pænˈdɔːrə/ *pr n* Pandore; **~'s box** Mythol, fig boîte *f* de Pandore.

pane /peɪn/ *n* vitre *f*, carreau *m*; **a ~ of glass** une vitre, un carreau.

panegyric /ˌpænɪˈdʒɪrɪk/ *n* littér panégyrique *m* (**on, of** de).

panel /'pænl/ **I** *n* **1** (group) (of experts, judges) commission *f*, comité *m*; TV, Radio (on discussion programme) invités *mpl*; (on quiz show) jury *m*; **to be on a ~** (of experts, judges) être membre d'un comité or d'une commission; TV, Radio faire partie d'un jury; **adjudication/investigating ~** commission *f* d'arbitrage/d'enquête; **2** Archit, Constr (section of wall) panneau *m*; **glass/wooden ~** panneau *m* de verre/en bois; **3** Aut, Tech (section) panneau *m*; (of instruments, switches) tableau *m*; **4** Jur (list) liste *f* (des jurés); (specific jury) jury *m*.
II *vtr* (*p prés etc* **-ll-**, **-l-** US) recouvrir [qch] de panneaux.
III panelled, **paneled** US *pp adj* [*fencing*] en panneaux; [*door, ceiling*] lambrissé; [*walls, bath*] cloisonné.
IV -panelled, **-paneled** US (*dans composés*) **oak-/wood-~led** couvert de panneaux en chêne/en bois.

panel: **~ beater** *n* tôlier *m*; **~-beating** *n* tôlerie *f*; **~ discussion** *n* Radio, TV débat *m*; **~ game** *n* Radio jeu *m* radiophonique; TV jeu *m* télévisé.

panelling, **paneling** US /'pænəlɪŋ/ *n* lambris *m*; **oak/pine ~** lambris *m* de chêne/de pin; **wood ~** boiseries *fpl*.

panellist, **panelist** US /'pænəlɪst/ *n* Radio, TV invité/-e *m/f*.

panel: **~ pin** *n* pointe *f*; **~ truck** *n* US camionnette *f*.

pan-fry /'pænfraɪ/ *vtr* faire sauter.

pang /pæŋ/ *n* **1** (emotional) serrement *m* de cœur; **a ~ of jealousy/regret** une pointe de jalousie/regret; **~s of conscience** ou **guilt** remords *mpl* de conscience; **2** (physical) **~s of hunger**, **hunger ~s** crampes *fpl* d'estomac; **birth ~s** lit douleurs *fpl* de l'enfantement; fig difficultés *fpl* initiales.

panhandle○ /'pænhændl/ US **I** *vtr* demander l'aumône à.
II *vi* mendier.

panhandler○ /'pænhændlə(r)/ *n* US mendiant/-e *m/f*.

panic /'pænɪk/ (*p prés etc* **-ck-**) **I** *n* **1** gen panique *f*, affolement *m*; **in a ~** dans l'affolement; **to get into a ~** s'affoler, être pris de panique (**about** à cause de); **to throw sb into a ~** affoler qn; **the news threw the city into a ~** la nouvelle a semé la panique dans la ville; **2**○ US **she's a ~** elle est impayable○.
II *modif* [*decision*] pris dans un moment de panique; [*reaction*] de panique.
III *vtr* affoler, paniquer○ [*person, animal*]; semer la panique dans [*crowd*]; **to be ~ked into doing** se laisser affoler et faire.
IV *vi* [*person, animal, crowd*] s'affoler, paniquer○; **don't ~!** pas de panique!; **to ~ at the idea/sight of** s'affoler à l'idée/la vue de.

panic attack *n* crise *f* d'angoisse.

panic button *n* signal *m* d'alarme; **to hit** ou **push the ~**○ paniquer○.

panic buying *n* achats *mpl* par crainte de la pénurie.

panicky /'pænɪkɪ/ *adj* paniqué○, affolé.

panic: **~ measure** *n* Pol, Econ disposition *f* précipitée; **~ selling** *n* Fin mouvements *mpl* de panique chez les petits porteurs.

panic stations *n* **it was ~** c'était la panique générale○.

panic-stricken /'pænɪkstrɪkn/ *adj* pris de panique.

pannier /'pænɪə(r)/ *n* **1** (on bike) sacoche *f*; **2** (on mule) panier *m* de bât.

panoply /'pænəplɪ/ *n* panoplie *f*.

panorama /ˌpænə'rɑːmə/ *n* lit, fig panorama *m*.

panoramic /ˌpænə'ræmɪk/ *adj* panoramique.

pan: **~pipes** *npl* flûte *f* de Pan; **~ scourer**, **~ scrubber** *n* tampon *m* à récurer.

pansy /'pænzɪ/ *n* **1** Bot pensée *f*; **2**○ †(weak man) femmelette *f* pej; (homosexual) pédale○ *f*.

pant /pænt/ **I** *n* halètement *m*.
II *vtr* = **pant out**.
III *vi* [*person*] haleter, souffler; [*animal*] haleter; **to be ~ing for breath** être tout essoufflé; **she came ~ing up the stairs** elle est arrivée essoufflée en haut de l'escalier.
■ **pant out**: **~ out [sth]**, **~ [sth] out** dire [qch] d'une voix haletante.

pantaloons† /ˌpæntə'luːnz/ *npl* culottes† *fpl*.

pantechnicon† /pæn'teknɪkən/ *n* GB camion *m* de déménagement.

pantheism /'pænθɪɪzəm/ *n* panthéisme *m*.

pantheist /'pænθɪɪst/ *n, adj* panthéiste (*mf*).

pantheon /'pænθɪən, US -θɪɒn/ *n* (all contexts) panthéon *m*.

panther /'pænθə(r)/ *n* **1** (leopard) panthère *f*; **2** US (puma) puma *m*.

panties /'pæntɪz/ ▶ **1703** *npl* slip *m* (de femme), petite culotte *f*.

pantile /'pæntaɪl/ *n* tuile *f* flamande, tuile *f* panne.

panting /'pæntɪŋ/ **I** *n* halètement *m*.
II *adj* [*person, animal*] essoufflé; [*breath*] haletant.

panto○ /'pæntəʊ/ *n* GB = **pantomime 1**.

pantograph /'pæntəgrɑːf, US -græf/ *n* pantographe *m*.

pantomime /'pæntəmaɪm/ *n* **1** GB Theat spectacle *m* pour enfants (*à Noël*); **2** (mime) mime *m*; **to explain sth in ~** expliquer qch en mimant.

pantry /'pæntrɪ/ *n* **1** (larder) garde-manger *m inv*; **2** (butler's etc) office *m*.

pants /pænts/ ▶ **1703** **I** *npl* **1** US (trousers) pantalon *m*; **he was still in short ~** il était encore en culottes courtes; **2** GB (underwear) slip *m*.
II○ *vtr* US déculotter.
IDIOMS **to beat the ~ off sb**○ mettre la pâtée à qn; **to bore the ~ off sb**○ faire mourir d'ennui qn; **to charm the ~ off sb**○ séduire qn fig; **to scare the ~ off sb**○ flanquer la trouille à qn○; **to catch sb with his/her ~ down**○ prendre qn au dépourvu; **to fly by the seat of one's ~** [*pilot*] naviguer à l'instinct; **a kick in the ~** lit, fig un coup de pied au derrière; **to wear the ~**○ porter la culotte○.

pantsuit /'pæntsuːt, -sjuːt/ *n* US tailleur-pantalon *m*.

panty /'pæntɪ/ *n* ▶ **panties**.

panty: **~ girdle** *n* gaine-culotte *f*; **~ hose** *n pl* US collant *m*; **~-liner** *n* protège-slip *m*.

pap /pæp/ *n* **1** (mush, babyfood) bouillie *f*; **2** ¢ péj (in book, on TV) inepties *fpl*; **3**‡ (nipple) mamelon *m*.

papa /pə'pɑː, US 'pɑːpə/ *n* **1**† père *m*; **2** papa *m*.

papacy /'peɪpəsɪ/ *n* papauté *f*.

papal /'peɪpl/ *adj* [*authority, blessing, residence*] papal, pontifical.

papal: **~ bull** *n* bulle *f* pontificale; **~ nuncio** *n* nonce *m* apostolique; **Papal States** *pr n* États *mpl* pontificaux.

paparazzi /ˌpæpə'rætsɪ/ *npl* paparazzi *mpl*.

papaya /pə'paɪə/ *n* **1** (fruit) papaye *f*; **2** (tree) papayer *m*.

paper /'peɪpə(r)/ **I** *n* **1** (substance) (for writing etc) papier *m*; **a piece/a sheet of ~** un morceau/une feuille de papier; **to get** ou **put sth down on ~** mettre qch par écrit; **it's a good idea on ~** fig c'est une bonne idée en théorie; **the car only exists on ~** la voiture n'existe que sur le papier; **this contract isn't worth the ~ it's written on** ce contrat ne vaut absolument rien; **2** (also **wall~**) papier *m* peint; **3** (newspaper) journal *m*; **local/Sunday ~** journal *m* local/du dimanche; **4** (scholarly article) article *m* (**on** sur); **5** (lecture) communication *f* (**on** sur); (report) exposé *m* (**on** sur); **I'm writing Monday's discussion ~** je prépare le sujet du débat de lundi; **6** (examination) épreuve *f* (**on** de); **the French ~** l'épreuve de français; **7** Fin effet *m* de commerce, papier *m*; **commercial ~** effet *m* de commerce; **financial ~** effet *m* de crédit; **long/short ~** effets *mpl* à long/court terme, papier *m* long/court; **8** (government publication) livre *m*.
II papers *npl* Admin papiers *mpl*; **identification ~** papiers d'identité.
III *modif* **1** lit [*bag, hat, napkin*] en papier; [*plate*] en carton; [*industry, manufacture*] de papier; **2** fig [*loss, profit*] théorique; [*promise, agreement*] sans valeur.
IV *vtr* (also **wall~**) tapisser [*room, wall*].
V *vi* **to ~ over the existing wallpaper** recouvrir le papier actuel; **to ~ over one's differences/problems** passer sur ses différences/problèmes.
IDIOMS **to ~ over the cracks** passer sur les problèmes.

paperback /'peɪpəbæk/ **I** *n* livre *m* de poche; **in ~** en livre de poche.
II *modif* [*edition, version*] de poche, broché; [*copy rights*] en livre de poche; **~ book** livre *m* de poche.

paper: **~ bank** *n* conteneur *m* de récupération de vieux papiers; **~board** *n* papier *m* cartonné; **~bound** *adj* Print, Publg broché; **~ boy** *n* livreur *m* de journaux; **~ chain** *n* guirlande *f* de papier; **~ chase** *n* jeu *m* de piste; **~clip** *n* trombone *m*; **~ cup** *n* gobelet *m* en carton; **~ currency** *n* monnaie *f* de papier; **~ fastener** *n* attache *f* parisienne; **~ feed tray** *n* Comput, Print bac *m* d'alimentation en papier; **~ girl** *n* livreuse *f* de journaux; **~ handkerchief** *n* mouchoir *m* en papier, kleenex® *m*; **~ knife** *n* coupe-papier *m inv*; **~ lantern** *n* lampion *m*.

paperless /'peɪpəlɪs/ *adj* Comput [*office*] électronique; [*system*] informatisé.

paper: **~ mill** *n* papeterie *f*, fabrique *f* de papier; **~ money** *n* monnaie *f* de papier; **~ qualifications** *npl* diplômes *mpl*.

paper round *n* **he has** ou **does a ~** il livre des journaux.

paper: **~ seller** *n* vendeur/-euse *m/f* de journaux; **~ shop** *n* marchand *m* de journaux; **~ shredder** *n* déchiqueteuse *f* à papier; **~ tape** *n* Comput bande *f* perforée; **~ thin** *adj* mince comme du papier à cigarette; **~ tiger** *n* fig tigre *m* de papier; **~ towel** *n* essuie-tout *m inv*, papier *m* absorbant; **~weight** *n* presse-papier *m inv*.

paperwork /'peɪpəwɜːk/ *n* **1** (administration) travail *m* administratif; **2** (documentation) documents *mpl*.

papery /'peɪpərɪ/ *adj* [*texture, leaves*] mince comme du papier; [*skin*] parcheminé.

papilla /pə'pɪlə/ *n* (*pl* **-illae**) papille *f*.

papist /'peɪpɪst/ *n, adj* péj papiste (*mf*) pej.

papoose /pə'puːs/ *n* bébé *m* peau-rouge.

pappy○ /'pæpɪ/ *n* US papa *m*.

paprika /'pæprɪkə, pə'priːkə/ *n* paprika *m*.

Pap smear, **Pap test** *n* US frottis *m* vaginal.

Papuan /'pɑːpʊən, 'pæ-/ ▶ **1486**, **1402** **I** *n* (person) Papou/-e *m/f*.
II *adj* [*culture, language*] papou.

Papua New Guinea /ˌpɑːpʊə njuː 'gɪnɪː, US nuː-/ ▶ **1131** *pr n* Papouasie-Nouvelle-Guinée *f*.

papyrus /pə'paɪərəs/ *n* (*pl* **~es** ou **-pyri**) papyrus *m*.

par /pɑː(r)/ *n* **1** gen **to be on a ~ with** [*performance*] être comparable à; [*person*] être l'égal de; **to be up to ~** être à la hauteur; **to be below** ou **under ~** [*performance*] être en dessous de la moyenne; [*person*] ne pas se sentir en forme; **2** (in golf) par *m*; **two under ~** deux sous le par; **3** Econ, Fin pair *m*; **at ~** au pair; **above/below ~** au-dessus/au-dessous du pair.

IDIOMS **to be ~ for the course** être typique.

para /ˈpærə/ *n* **1** *abrév écrite* = **paragraph**; **2**○ GB Mil (*abrév* = **paratrooper**) para○ *m*.

parable /ˈpærəbl/ *n* Bible parabole *f*.

parabola /pəˈræbələ/ *n* Math parabole *f*.

parabolic /ˌpærəˈbɒlɪk/ *adj* parabolique.

parabolic reflector *n* réflecteur *m* parabolique.

paraboloid /pəˈræbəlɔɪd/ *n* paraboloïde *m*.

paracetamol /ˌpærəˈsetəmɒl, -ˈsiːtəmɒl/ *n* GB paracétamol *m*.

parachute /ˈpærəʃuːt/ **I** *n* parachute *m*.
II *vtr* parachuter; **to ~ sth into a country** parachuter qch dans un pays.
III *vi* descendre en parachute.

parachute: **~ drop** *n* parachutage *m*; **~ jump** *n* saut *m* en parachute; **~ regiment** *n* régiment *m* de parachutistes; **~ silk** *n* soie *f* de parachute.

parachuting /ˈpærəʃuːtɪŋ/ **▶1282** *n* **to go ~** faire du parachutisme.

parachutist /ˈpærəʃuːtɪst/ *n* parachutiste *mf*.

parade /pəˈreɪd/ **I** *n* **1** (procession) parade *f*; **a ~ of floats** une parade de chars; **carnival ~** défilé *m* de carnaval; **circus ~** parade *f* de cirque; **2** Mil (public march) défilé *m*; (review) prise *f* d'armes; (in barracks) appel *m*; **to be on ~** être à l'exercice; **3** (display) (of designs, models) défilé *m*; (of ideas) souvent péj étalage *m*; **new inventions will be on ~** de nouvelles inventions seront exposées; **4 to make a ~ of** péj faire étalage de [*grief, knowledge*]; **5** GB (row) **a ~ of shops/houses** une rangée *f* de magasins/maisons.
II *vtr* **1** (display) souvent péj faire étalage de [*knowledge, morals, wares, wealth*]; **2** (claim) **to ~ sth as sth** présenter qch comme qch; **it was ~ed as the miracle solution** cela a été présenté comme la solution miracle.
III *vi* **1** (march) défiler (**through** dans); **to ~ up and down** [*soldier, model*] défiler; [*child, person*] parader.
■ **parade about, parade around** parader.

parade ground *n* champ *m* de manœuvres.

paradigm /ˈpærədaɪm/ *n* paradigme *m*.

paradigmatic /ˌpærədɪɡˈmætɪk/ *adj* paradigmatique.

paradise /ˈpærədaɪs/ *n* Relig, fig paradis *m*; **in ~** au paradis; **an artist's ~** un paradis pour les peintres; **an island ~** une île paradisiaque.
IDIOMS **to be living in a fool's ~** rêver.

paradox /ˈpærədɒks/ *n* paradoxe *m*.

paradoxical /ˌpærəˈdɒksɪkl/ *adj* paradoxal.

paradoxically /ˌpærəˈdɒksɪklɪ/ *adv* paradoxalement.

paraffin /ˈpærəfɪn/ **I** *n* **1** GB (fuel) pétrole *m*; **2** (also **~ wax**) paraffine *f*.
II *modif* GB [*lamp, heater*] à pétrole.

paraglider /ˈpærəɡlaɪdə(r)/ *n* parapente *m*.

paragliding /ˈpærəɡlaɪdɪŋ/ **▶1282** *n* parapente *m*.

paragon /ˈpærəɡən, US -ɡɒn/ *n* modèle *m* (**of** de); **a ~ of virtue** un parangon de vertu.

paragraph /ˈpærəɡrɑːf, US -ɡræf/ **I** *n* **1** (section) paragraphe *m*; **new ~** (in dictation) à la ligne; **2** Journ (article) entrefilet *m*; **3** Print (also **~ mark**) pied *m* de mouche.
II *vtr* diviser en paragraphes.

Paraguay /ˈpærəɡwaɪ/ **▶1131** *pr n* Paraguay *m*.

Paraguayan /pærəɡwaɪən/ **▶1486** **I** *n* Paraguayen/-enne *m/f*.
II *adj* paraguayen/-enne.

parakeet /ˈpærəkiːt/ *n* perruche *f*.

paralanguage /ˈpærəlæŋɡwɪdʒ/ *n* paralangage *m*.

paralinguistic /ˈpærəlɪŋɡwɪstɪk/ *adj* paralinguistique.

parallactic /ˌpærəˈlæktɪk/ *adj* parallactique.

parallax /ˈpærəlæks/ *n* parallaxe *f*.

parallel /ˈpærəlel/ **I** *n* **1** Math parallèle *f*; **2** Geog parallèle *m*; **3** (comparison) parallèle *m* (**between** entre; **to** avec); **in ~** en parallèle; **to draw/establish a ~ between** faire/établir un parallèle entre; **to be on a ~ with sth** être comparable à qch; **without ~** sans pareil; **4** Electron **in ~** en parallèle.
II *adj* **1** Math parallèle (**to, with** à); **~ lines** lignes *fpl* parallèles; **2** (similar) [*case, example, experience, situation*] analogue (**to, with** à); **to develop along ~ lines** évoluer de manière analogue; **3** (simultaneous) parallèle (**to, with** à); **4** Electron [*circuit, connection*] monté en parallèle; **5** Comput [*printer, transfer, transmission*] parallèle.
III *adv* **~ to, ~with** parallèlement à; **the species evolved ~ to one another** les espèces ont évolué parallèlement.
IV *vtr* (*p prés* GB **-ll-**, US **-l-**) **1** (equal) égaler; **2** (find a comparison) trouver un équivalent à.

parallel bars *npl* barres *fpl* parallèles.

parallelepiped /ˌpærəleˈlepɪped/ *n* parallélépipède *m*.

parallelism /ˈpærəlelɪzəm/ *n* **1** Math parallélisme *m* (**between** entre); **2** fig parallèle *m* (**between** entre).

parallelogram /ˌpærəˈleləɡræm/ *n* parallélogramme *m*.

parallel: **~-park** *vi* Aut faire un créneau; **~ processing** *n* Comput traitement *m* en parallèle; **~ programming** *n* Comput programmation *f* en parallèle; **~ turn** *n* Sport virage *m* parallèle.

paralysation GB, **paralyzation** US /ˌpærəlaɪˈzeɪʃn, US -lɪˈz-/ *n* **1** Med paralysie *f*; **2** (of network) immobilisation *f*.

paralyse GB, **paralyze** US /ˈpærəlaɪz/ *vtr* Med, fig paralyser.

paralysed GB, **paralyzed** US /ˈpærəlaɪzd/ *adj* **1** Med paralysé; **to be ~ from the waist down** être paraplégique; **her right arm is ~** elle est paralysée du bras droit; **2** fig [*network, industry, person*] paralysé (**with, by** par).

paralysis /pəˈræləsɪs/ *n* Med, fig paralysie *f*; **~ of the arm** paralysie du bras.

paralytic /ˌpærəˈlɪtɪk/ **I** *n* paralytique *mf*.
II *adj* **1** Med [*person*] paralytique; [*arm, leg*] paralysé; **2**○ GB (drunk) complètement bourré○, ivre mort.

paramedic /ˌpærəˈmedɪk/ **▶1692** *n* auxiliaire *mf* médical/-e.

paramedical /ˌpærəˈmedɪkl/ *adj* paramédical.

parameter /pəˈræmɪtə(r)/ *n* **1** Math, Comput paramètre *m*; **2** (limiting factor) paramètre *m*; **to define the ~s of** définir les paramètres or les grandes lignes de; **within the ~s of** dans les limites de.

parametric /ˌpærəˈmetrɪk/ *adj* paramétrique.

paramilitary /ˌpærəˈmɪlɪtrɪ, US -terɪ/ **I** *n* membre *m* d'une organisation paramilitaire.
II *adj* paramilitaire.

paramnesia /ˌpæræmˈniːzɪə, US -ˈniːʒə/ *n* paramnésie *f*.

paramount /ˈpærəmaʊnt/ *adj* [*consideration, goal*] suprême; **to be ~, to be of ~ importance** être d'une importance capitale.

paramour‡ /ˈpærəmʊə(r)/ *n* amant/-e *m/f*.

paranoia /ˌpærəˈnɔɪə/ **▶1354** *n* Psych, fig paranoïa *f*.

paranoi(a)c *n, adj* = **paranoid**.

paranoid /ˈpærənɔɪd/ **I** *n* paranoïaque *mf*.
II *adj* **1** Psych paranoïde; **2** (suspicious) paranoïaque, parano○ (**about** au sujet de); **to be ~ about being burgled** avoir une peur maladive d'être cambriolé.

paranoid schizophrenia *n* schizophrénie *f* paranoïde.

paranormal /ˌpærəˈnɔːml/ *n, adj* paranormal (*m*).

parapet /ˈpærəpɪt/ *n* Archit, Mil parapet *m*.

IDIOMS **to stick one's head above the ~** fig se mouiller○, prendre un risque.

paraphernalia /ˌpærəfəˈneɪlɪə/ *n* (+ *v sg*) **1** (articles, accessories) attirail *m*; **2** GB (rigmarole, procedure) comédie○ *f*.

paraphrase /ˈpærəfreɪz/ **I** *n* paraphrase *f*.
II *vtr* paraphraser.

paraplegia /ˌpærəˈpliːdʒə/ *n* paraplégie *f*.

paraplegic /ˌpærəˈpliːdʒɪk/ **I** *n* paraplégique *mf*.
II *adj* [*person*] paraplégique; [*games*] pour les paraplégiques.

parapsychology /ˌpærəsaɪˈkɒlədʒɪ/ *n* parapsychologie *f*.

paraquat® /ˈpærəkwɒt/ *n* paraquat® *m*.

parascending /ˈpærəsendɪŋ/ *n* GB parachutisme *m* ascensionnel; **to go ~** faire du parachute ascensionnel.

parasite /ˈpærəsaɪt/ *n* lit, fig parasite *m*.

parasitic(al) /ˌpærəˈsɪtɪk(l)/ *adj* **1** Bot, Zool, fig parasite (**on** de); **2** Med parasitaire.

parasiticide /ˌpærəˈsɪtɪsaɪd/ *n* parasiticide *m*.

parasol /ˈpærəsɒl, US -sɔːl/ *n* (sunshade) ombrelle *f*; (for table) parasol *m*.

parasympathetic /ˌpærəˌsɪmpəˈθetɪk/ *adj* parasympathique.

parataxis /ˌpærəˈtæksɪs/ *n* parataxe *f*.

parathyroid /ˌpærəˈθaɪrɔɪd/ *n* parathyroïde *f*.

parathyroid gland *n* parathyroïde *f*.

paratrooper /ˈpærətruːpə(r)/ **▶1692** *n* parachutiste *m*.

paratroops /ˈpærətruːps/ *npl* (unités *fpl* de) parachutistes *mpl*.

paratyphoid /ˌpærəˈtaɪfɔɪd/ **▶1354** *n* (also **~ fever**) fièvre *f* paratyphoïde.

parboil /ˈpɑːbɔɪl/ *vtr* faire cuire [qch] à demi.

parcel /ˈpɑːsl/ **I** *n* **1** (package) paquet *m*, colis *m*; **2** (of land) parcelle *f*; **3** Fin (of shares) paquet *m*; **4**○ fig (of people, problems etc) tas○ *m*; **a ~ of lies** un tissu de mensonges.
II *vtr* = **parcel up**.
IDIOMS **to be part and ~ of** faire partie intégrante de.
■ **parcel out**: **~ out [sth], ~ [sth] out** répartir (**among** entre).
■ **parcel up**: **~ up [sth], ~ [sth] up** emballer.

parcel: **~ bomb** *n* colis *m* piégé; **~ office** *n* (bureau *m* des) messageries *fpl*.

parcel post *n* service *m* de colis postaux; **to send sth by ~** envoyer qch par colis postal.

parcels service *n* (company) société *f* d'expédition des colis postaux.

parch /pɑːtʃ/ *vtr* dessécher.

parched /pɑːtʃt/ *adj* **1** [*earth, grass, lips*] desséché; **2**○ (thirsty) **to be ~** mourir de soif.

parchment /ˈpɑːtʃmənt/ *n* **1** Hist (substance, document) parchemin *m*; **2** (paper) papier-parchemin *m*.

pardon /ˈpɑːdn/ **I** *n* **1** (forgiveness) pardon *m*; **to beg sb's ~** demander pardon à qn; **I beg your ~?** pardon?; **2** Jur (also **free ~**) grâce *f*; **royal ~** grâce royale; **3** Relig indulgence *f*.
II *excl* (what?) pardon?; (sorry!) pardon!
III *vtr* **1** (forgive) pardonner; **to ~ sb for sth** pardonner qch à qn; **to ~ sb for doing sth** pardonner à qn d'avoir fait qch; **~ me for asking, but...** pardonnez-moi de vous poser la question, mais...; **~ me!** pardon!; **2** Jur gracier [*criminal*].

pardonable /ˈpɑːdnəbl/ *adj* pardonnable.

pardonably /ˈpɑːdnəblɪ/ *adv* de façon (bien) pardonnable.

pare /peə(r)/ *vtr* **1** (peel) peler [*apple*]; **2** (trim) rogner [*nails*]; **3** (reduce) = **pare down**.
IDIOMS **to ~ sth to the bone** réduire qch au minimum vital.

■ **pare down**: **~ [sth] down, ~ down [sth]** réduire (**to** à).
■ **pare off**: **~ [sth] off, ~ off [sth] 1** peler [*rind, peel*]; **2** réduire [*amount, percentage*].

pared-down /ˌpeəd ˈdaʊn/ *adj* [*budget*] réduit; [*version*] abrégé; [*prose, plot*] dépouillé.

parent /ˈpeərənt/ *n* **1** (of child) parent *m*; **my ~s** mes parents; **as a ~** en ma qualité de parent; **~s are worried** les parents s'inquiètent; **2** Comm (company) maison *f* mère; (organization) organisation *f* mère.

parentage /ˈpeərəntɪdʒ/ *n* ascendance *f*; **of unknown ~** de parents *mpl* inconnus.

parental /pəˈrentl/ *adj* [*rights, authority, involvement*] parental fml, des parents; **his ~ pride** sa fierté paternelle; **to leave the ~ home** quitter la maison de ses parents.

parent: **~ company** *n* maison *f* mère; **~-governor** *n* GB Sch *membre du conseil d'établissement et représentant des parents d'élèves*.

parenthesis /pəˈrenθəsɪs/ *n* (*pl* **-theses**) parenthèse *f*; **in ~** en parenthèse.

parenthetic(al) /ˌpærənˈθetɪk(l)/ *adj* [*comment*] entre parenthèses.

parenthetically /ˌpærənˈθetɪklɪ/ *adv* [*note, observe*] entre parenthèses.

parenthood /ˈpeərənthʊd/ *n* (fatherhood) paternité *f*; (motherhood) maternité *f*; **ready for ~** prêt à fonder une famille; **the joys of ~** iron la joie d'être père/mère.

parenting /ˈpeərəntɪŋ/ *n* éducation *f* des enfants.

parent: **~ organization** *n* organisation *f* mère; **~ power** *n* Sch pouvoir *m* décisionnel des parents d'élèves; **~s' evening** *n* Sch réunion *f* pour les parents d'élèves; **~-teacher association**, **PTA** *n* association *f* des parents d'élèves et des professeurs; **~ tree** *n* arbre *m* étalon; **~ word** *n* Ling mot *m* souche.

parer /ˈpeərə(r)/ *n* épluche-légumes *m inv*.

pariah /pəˈraɪə, ˈpærɪə/ *n* paria *m*.

parietal /pəˈraɪətl/ *n, adj* pariétal (*m*).

parietals /pəˈraɪətlz/ *npl* US Univ *règlement concernant les visites des personnes du sexe opposé dans les résidences universitaires*.

paring /ˈpeərɪŋ/ **I** *n* (process) (of fruit) épluchage *m*; (of budget, economy) dégraissage *m*.
II parings *npl* **1** (of fruit) épluchures *fpl*; **2** (of nails) rognures *fpl*.

paring knife *n* couteau *m* à éplucher.

Paris /ˈpærɪs/ ▶**1818** **I** *pr n* Paris.
II *modif* [*fashion, metro, restaurant*] parisien/-ienne.

parish /ˈpærɪʃ/ **I** *n* **1** Relig paroisse *f*; **2** GB (administrative) commune *f*; **3** US comté *m* (*en Louisiane*).
II *modif* [*church, hall, meeting, register*] paroissial.

parish council *n* Relig conseil *m* paroissial; Pol conseil *m* municipal GB.

parishioner /pəˈrɪʃənə(r)/ *n* paroissien/-ienne *m/f*.

parish priest *n* (Protestant) pasteur *m*; (Catholic) curé *m*.

parish-pump *adj* GB **~ politics** péj politique *f* de clocher pej.

Parisian /pəˈrɪzɪən/ **I** *n* Parisien/-ienne *m/f*.
II *adj* parisien/-ienne.

parity /ˈpærətɪ/ *n* (equality) parité *f* (**with** avec); **nuclear/pay ~** parité des forces nucléaires/des salaires.

park /pɑːk/ **I** *n* **1** (public garden) jardin *m* public, parc *m*; **2** (estate) parc *m*; **3** Comm, Ind parc *m*; **business/industrial/science ~** parc d'affaires/industriel/scientifique; **4** GB (pitch) terrain *m*; US (stadium) stade *m*; **5** (on automatic gearbox) position *f* parking.
II *vtr* **1** Aut garer [*vehicle*]; **2**○ (deposit) laisser [*equipment, boxes, person*].
III *vi* [*driver*] se garer.
IV parked *pp adj* [*car, lorry*] en stationnement; **badly ~ed** mal garé.
V○ *v refl* **to ~ oneself** s'installer.

parka /ˈpɑːkə/ *n* parka *m* or *f*.

park: **~-and-ride** *n* GB Transp *parking situé à l'entrée d'une ville avec service de transport menant au centre*; **~ bench** *n* banc *m* (public).

parkerhouse roll *n* US ≈ petit pain *m* brioché.

parkin /ˈpɑːkɪn/ *n* GB *gâteau à l'avoine et au gingembre*.

parking /ˈpɑːkɪŋ/ **I** *n* **1** (action) stationnement *m*; **'No ~'** 'stationnement interdit'; **2** (space for cars) place *f* de stationnement.
II *modif* [*area, charge, permit, problem, regulations, restrictions*] de stationnement; [*facilities*] pour le stationnement.

parking: **~ attendant** ▶**1692** *n* gardien/-ienne *m/f* de parking; **~ bay** *n* place *f* de stationnement; **~ brake** *n* Aut frein *m* à main, frein *m* de stationnement.

parking garage *n* US (multi-storey) parking *m* aérien; (underground) parking *m* souterrain.

parking: **~ light** *n* Aut feu *m* de position; **~ lot** *n* US parking *m*; **~ meter** *n* parcmètre *m*; **~ offence** GB, **~ offense** US *n* infraction *f* aux règles de stationnement; **~ place**, **~ space** *n* place *f*.

parking ticket *n* **1** (from machine) ticket *m* de stationnement; **2** (fine) contravention *f*, PV○ *m*.

parkinsonism /ˈpɑːkɪnsənɪzəm/ *n* = **Parkinson's disease**.

Parkinson: **~'s disease** ▶**1354** *n* maladie *f* de Parkinson; **~'s law** *n* hum *adage selon lequel tout travail prendra le temps dont on dispose*.

park: **~ keeper** ▶**1692** *n* gardien/-ienne *m/f* de parc; **~land** *n* parc *m* boisé; **~ ranger**, **~ warden** ▶**1692** *n* (on estate) garde *m* forestier; (in game reserve) garde-chasse *m*; **~way** *n* US *route bordée de verdure*.

parky○ /ˈpɑːkɪ/ *adj* GB frisquet○.

parlance /ˈpɑːləns/ *n* langage *m*; **in legal/journalistic/common ~** en langage juridique/journalistique/courant.

parlay /ˈpɑːleɪ/ US **I** *n* remise *f* en jeu des gains.
II *vtr* **1** (bet) remettre ses gains en jeu; **2** (transform) transformer.

parley /ˈpɑːlɪ/ **I** *n* pourparlers *mpl*.
II *vi* parlementer (**with** avec).

parliament /ˈpɑːləmənt/ **I** *n* Pol parlement *m*; **in ~** au parlement.
II Parliament *pr n* GB **1** (institution, members) Parlement *m*; **to get into Parliament** se faire élire député; **2** (parliamentary session) session *f* parlementaire.

parliamentarian /ˌpɑːləmenˈteərɪən/ *n* **1** (member) parlementaire *m*, membre *m* du parlement; **2** (expert in procedure) expert *m* des procédures parlementaires.

parliamentary /ˌpɑːləˈmentrɪ, US -terɪ/ *adj* parlementaire.

parliamentary: **Parliamentary Commissioner** *n* ≈ médiateur *m*; **~ election** *n* élections *fpl* législatives; **~ government** *n* régime *m* parlementaire; **~ private secretary**, **PPS** *n* GB député *m* attaché ministériel (*chargé de la liaison avec les autres députés*); **~ privilege** *n* immunité *f* parlementaire; **~ secretary** *n* GB député *m* attaché ministériel; **~ undersecretary** *n* GB sous-secrétaire *m* d'État.

parlour GB, **parlor** US /ˈpɑːlə(r)/ *n* **1**† (in house) petit salon *m*; **2** (in convent) parloir *m*.

parlour: **~ game** *n* jeu *m* de salon; **~ maid** *n* domestique *f* (*qui sert à table*).

parlous /ˈpɑːləs/ *adj* sout ou hum alarmant.

Parma /ˈpɑːmə/ ▶**1818** *pr n* Parme.

Parma: **~ ham** *n* jambon *m* de Parme; **~ violet** *n* violette *f* de Parme.

Parmesan /ˈpɑːmɪzæn, US ˌpɑːrmɪˈzæn/ *n* (also **~ cheese**) parmesan *m*.

Parnassus /pɑːˈnæsəs/ *pr n* mont *m* Parnasse.

parochial /pəˈrəʊkɪəl/ *adj* **1** péj [*interest, view*] de clocher; **2** US (of parish) paroissial.

parochialism /pəˈrəʊkɪəlɪzəm/ *n* péj esprit *m* de clocher.

parochial school *n* US école *f* religieuse.

parodic /pəˈrɒdɪk/ *adj* parodique.

parodist /ˈpærədɪst/ *n* parodiste *mf*.

parody /ˈpærədɪ/ **I** *n* (all contexts) parodie *f*.
II *vtr* parodier [*person, style*].

parole /pəˈrəʊl/ **I** *n* **1** Jur liberté *f* conditionnelle; **on ~** en liberté conditionnelle; **to release sb on ~** mettre qn en liberté conditionnelle; **he was granted/refused ~** on lui a accordé/refusé la mise en liberté conditionnelle; **to break ~** ne pas respecter les conditions de sa mise en liberté conditionnelle; **2** Mil parole *f* (d'honneur); **on ~** sur parole; **3** Ling parole *f*.
II *vtr* Jur mettre [qn] en liberté conditionnelle.

parole board *n conseil chargé d'étudier les dossiers de mise en liberté conditionnelle*.

parolee /pəˌrəʊˈliː/ *n* US prisonnier/-ière *m/f* libéré/-e sur parole.

parole officer *n* contrôleur *m* judiciaire.

paroxysm /ˈpærəksɪzəm/ *n* crise *f* (**of** de).

parquet /ˈpɑːkeɪ, US pɑːrˈkeɪ/ **I** *n* **1** (floor, flooring) parquet *m*; **to lay ~** poser du or un parquet; **2** US Theat parterre *m*.
II *vtr* parqueter.

parquetry /ˈpɑːkɪtrɪ/ *n* parquetage *m*, parquet *m*.

parr /pɑː(r)/ *n* Zool tacon *m*.

parricidal /ˌpærɪˈsaɪdl/ *adj* parricide.

parricide /ˈpærɪsaɪd/ *n* **1** (crime) parricide *m*; **2** (person) parricide *mf*.

parrot /ˈpærət/ **I** *n* Zool, péj (person) perroquet *m*.
II *vtr* péj répéter comme un perroquet.
IDIOMS **as sick as a ~**○ en rage; **to have a mouth (that tastes) like the bottom of a ~'s cage**○ avoir la bouche pâteuse.

parrot: **~-fashion** *adj* comme un perroquet; **~ fever** ▶**1354** *n* psittacose *f*; **~ fish** *n* perroquet *m* de mer.

parry /ˈpærɪ/ **I** *n* **1** Sport parade *f*; **2** (verbal) riposte *f*.
II *vtr* **1** Sport parer; **2** éluder [*question*].
III *vi* (in fencing, boxing) parer.

parse /pɑːz/ *vtr* Ling, Comput faire l'analyse grammaticale de; **to ~ a sentence** faire l'analyse grammaticale d'une phrase.

parsec /ˈpɑːsek/ *n* parsec *m*.

Parsee /ˌpɑːˈsiː/ *n* Parsi/-e *m/f*.

parser /ˈpɑːzə(r)/ *n* Ling, Comput analyseur *m* (grammatical), parser *m*.

parsimonious /ˌpɑːsɪˈməʊnɪəs/ *adj* sout parcimonieux/-ieuse fml.

parsimoniously /ˌpɑːsɪˈməʊnɪəslɪ/ *adv* sout parcimonieusement.

parsimony /ˈpɑːsɪmənɪ, US -məʊnɪ/ *n* sout parcimonie *f*.

parsing /ˈpɑːzɪŋ/ *n* Ling, Comput analyse *f* grammaticale.

parsley /ˈpɑːslɪ/ *n* persil *m*.

parsley sauce *n* sauce *f* persillée.

parsnip /ˈpɑːsnɪp/ *n* panais *m*.
IDIOMS **fine words butter no ~s** les belles paroles n'arrangent rien.

parson /ˈpɑːsn/ *n* pasteur *m*.

parsonage /ˈpɑːsənɪdʒ/ *n* presbytère *m*.

parson: **~'s nose**○ *n* croupion *m*; **Parsons table** *n* US table *f* basse (*en plastique*).

part /pɑːt/ **I** *n* **1** (of whole) gen partie *f*; (of country) région *f*; **~ of the book/time/district** une partie du livre/temps/quartier; **~ of me hates him** une partie de moi-même le déteste; **in** ou **around these ~s** dans la région; **in ~** en partie; **in ~ it's due to...** c'est dû en partie à...; **~ of the reason is...** c'est en partie parce que...; **to be (a) ~ of** faire partie de; **to feel ~ of** avoir le sentiment de faire partie de; **to form ~ of** faire partie de; **the early ~ of my life** ma jeunesse; **it's all ~ of being young** il faut bien que jeunesse se passe; **the latter ~ of the century** la fin du siècle; **that's the best/hardest ~** c'est ça le meilleur/le plus dur; **that's the ~ I don't understand** voilà ce que je ne comprends pas; **to be good in ~s** GB avoir de bons passages; **in ~s it's very violent** GB il y a des passages très violents; **for the most ~** dans l'ensemble; **my/our ~ of the world** mon/notre pays; **what are you doing in this ~ of the world?** qu'est-ce que tu fais par ici?; **2** (component of car, engine, machine) pièce *f*; **machine/engine ~s** pièces de machine/de moteur; **spare ~s** pièces détachées; **~s and labour** pièces et main-d'œuvre; **3** TV (of serial, programme, part work) partie *f*; **'end of ~ one'** 'fin de la première partie'; **a two-/four-~ series** une série en deux/quatre épisodes; **4** (share, role) rôle *m* (**in** dans); **to do one's ~** jouer son rôle; **to have a ~ in sth** jouer un rôle dans qch; **to have a ~ in deciding to do/in choosing** jouer un rôle dans la décision de faire/dans le choix de; **I want no ~ in it, I don't want any ~ of it** je ne veux pas m'en mêler; **to take ~** participer, prendre part (**in** à); **they took no further ~ in it** ils n'ont rien fait de plus; **5** Theat, TV, Cin rôle *n* (**of** de); **I got the ~!** j'ai le rôle!; **to play the ~ of** jouer le rôle de; **6** (equal measure) mesure *f*; **two ~s tonic to one ~ gin** deux mesures de tonic pour une mesure de gin; **mix X and Y in equal ~s** mélangez une quantité égale de X et Y; **in a concentration of 30,000 ~s per million** dans une concentration de 3%; **7** Mus (for instrument, voice) partie *f*; **the viola/tenor ~** la partie de l'alto/de ténor; **voice ~** partie vocale; **8** Mus (sheet music) partition *f*; **the piano ~** la partition du piano; **9** (behalf) **on the ~ of** de la part de; **it wasn't very nice on your ~** ce n'était pas très gentil de ta part; **for my/his ~** pour ma/sa part; **to take sb's ~** prendre le parti de qn; **10** US (in hair) raie *f*.

II *adv* (partly) en partie; **it was ~ fear, ~ greed** c'était à la fois de la crainte et de la cupidité.

III *vtr* **1** (separate) séparer [*couple, friends, boxers*]; écarter [*legs*]; entrouvrir [*lips, curtains*]; fendre [*crowd, ocean, waves*]; **to be ~ed from** être séparé de; **'till death do us ~'** 'jusqu'à ce que la mort nous sépare'; **2** (make parting in) **to ~ one's hair** se faire une raie; **he ~s his hair on the left** il se fait une raie à gauche.

IV *vi* **1** (take leave, split up) [*partners, husband and wife*] se séparer; **we ~ed friends** nous nous sommes quittés bons amis; **to ~ from** quitter [*husband, wife*]; **2** (divide) [*crowd, sea, lips, clouds*] s'ouvrir; Theat [*curtains*] se lever; **3** (break) [*rope, cable*] se rompre.

IDIOMS **a man/a woman of (many) ~s** un homme/une femme qui a plusieurs cordes à son arc; **to look the ~** avoir la tête de l'emploi; **to take sth in good ~** prendre qch en bonne part.

■ **part with**: **~ with [sth]** se défaire de [*money*]; se séparer de [*object*].

partake /pɑːˈteɪk/ *vi* sout **1 to ~ of** prendre [*food, drink*]; tenir de [*quality, nature*]; **2 to ~ in** participer à.

part-baked *adj* précuit.

part exchange *n* GB reprise *f*; **to take sth in ~** reprendre qch.

parthenogenesis /ˌpɑːθɪnəʊˈdʒenəsɪs/ *n* parthénogénèse *f*.

parthenogenetic /ˌpɑːθɪnəʊdʒɪˈnetɪk/ *adj* parthénogénétique.

parthenogenetically /ˌpɑːθɪnəʊdʒɪˈnetɪklɪ/ *adv* parthénogénétiquement.

Parthenon /ˈpɑːθənɒn/ *pr n* **the ~** le Parthénon.

Parthian shot /ˈpɑːθɪən/ *n* flèche *f* du Parthe.

partial /ˈpɑːʃl/ *adj* **1** [*collapse, deafness, failure, reduction, success, truth, victory, withdrawal*] partiel/-ielle; **2** (biased) [*judgment, attitude*] partial; **3** (fond) **to be ~ to** avoir un faible pour.

partial: **~ disability** *n* invalidité *f* partielle, incapacité *f* partielle; **~ eclipse** *n* éclipse *f* partielle; **~ exchange** *n* US = **part exchange**.

partiality /ˌpɑːʃɪˈælətɪ/ *n* **1** (bias) partialité *f*; **2** (liking) penchant *m* (**to, for** pour).

partially /ˈpɑːʃəlɪ/ *adv* **1** [*controlled, obscured, recovered, severed*] partiellement (*before adj*); en partie (*after adj*); **he was only ~ successful** il n'a eu qu'un succès mitigé; **2** [*treat, judge, regard*] avec partialité.

partially clothed *adj* [*person, body*] à moitié nu.

partially preserved *adj* **~ product** semi-conserve *f*.

partially sighted I *n* **the ~** (+ *v pl*) les malvoyants *mpl*.

II *adj* malvoyant.

partial pressure *n* pression *f* partielle.

participant /pɑːˈtɪsɪpənt/ *n* participant/-e *m/f* (**in** à).

participate /pɑːˈtɪsɪpeɪt/ *vi* participer (**in** à).

participation /pɑːˌtɪsɪˈpeɪʃn/ *n* participation *f* (**in** à); **audience/worker ~** participation de l'audience/des ouvriers.

participatory /pɑːˌtɪsɪˈpeɪtrɪ, US -tɔːrɪ/ *adj* **~ play** pièce avec participation du public; **~ democracy** ≈ démocratie *f* directe.

participial /ˌpɑːtɪˈsɪpɪəl/ *adj* participial.

participle /ˈpɑːtɪsɪpl/ *n* participe *m*; **past/present ~** participe passé/présent.

particle /ˈpɑːtɪkl/ *n* **1** Phys particule *f*; **elementary/subatomic ~** particule élémentaire/subatomique; **2** (of ash, dust, metal, food) particule *f*; **not a ~ of truth/evidence** pas une once de vérité/preuve; **3** Ling particule *f*.

particle: **~ accelerator** *n* accélérateur *m* de particules; **~ board** *n* US (bois *m*) aggloméré *m*; **~ physics** *n* physique *f* des particules.

parti-coloured GB, **parti-colored** US /ˈpɑːtɪkʌləd/ *adj* bariolé.

particular /pəˈtɪkjʊlə(r)/ **I** *n* **1** (detail) détail *m*; **in every ~** dans tous les détails; **in one ~** sur un point précis; **in several ~s** à plus d'un titre; **to go into ~s** entrer dans les détails; **2 in ~** en particulier; **France in general and Paris in ~** la France en général et Paris en particulier; **nothing in ~** rien de particulier; **are you looking for anything in ~?** vous cherchez quelque chose de précis?

II particulars *npl* (information) détails *mpl*, renseignements *mpl*; (description) (of person) (name, address etc) coordonnées *fpl*; (of missing person, suspect) signalement *m*; Admin (of vehicle, stolen goods etc) description *f*; **~s of sale** Jur ≈ cahier *m* des charges; **for further ~s please phone...** pour plus amples renseignements veuillez téléphoner à...

III *adj* **1** (specific) particulier/-ière; **for no ~ reason** sans raison particulière or précise; **in this ~ case** dans ce cas particulier or précis; **this ~ colour doesn't really suit me** cette couleur-là ne me va pas très bien; **I didn't watch that ~ programme** je n'ai pas regardé cette émission-là; **is there any ~ colour you would prefer?** est-ce que vous désirez une couleur en particulier?; **no ~ time has been arranged** on n'a pas fixé d'heure précise; **2** (special, exceptional) particulier/-ière; **to take ~ care over sth** faire qch avec un soin tout particulier; **I have ~ pleasure in welcoming tonight's guest speaker** j'éprouve un plaisir tout particulier à accueillir notre conférencier de ce soir; **this painting is a ~ favourite of mine** j'aime tout particulièrement ce tableau; **he is a ~ friend of mine** c'est un de mes meilleurs amis; **3** (fussy) méticuleux/-euse; **to be ~ about** être exigeant sur [*cleanliness, punctuality*]; faire attention à [*appearance*]; être difficile pour [*food*]; **'any special time?'—'no, I'm not ~'** 'y a-t-il une heure spéciale qui vous convient?'—'non, je n'ai pas de préférence'; **4** sout (exact) [*account, description*] détaillé, circonstancié.

particularity /pəˌtɪkjʊˈlærətɪ/ *n* particularité *f*.

particularize /pəˈtɪkjʊləraɪz/ *vtr, vi* préciser.

particularly /pəˈtɪkjʊləlɪ/ *adv* **1** (in particular) en particulier, particulièrement; **2** (especially) spécialement; **not ~** pas particulièrement, pas spécialement.

parting /ˈpɑːtɪŋ/ **I** *n* **1** (separation) séparation *f*; **the ~ of the Red Sea** le passage de la Mer Rouge; **the ~ of the ways** la croisée des chemins; **2** GB (in hair) raie *f*; **centre/left ~** raie au milieu/à gauche; **side ~** raie sur le côté.

II *adj* [*gift, words*] d'adieu also iron; **~ shot** flèche *f* du Parthe.

partisan /ˈpɑːtɪzæn, ˌpɑːtɪˈzæn, US ˈpɑːrtɪzn/ **I** *n* Mil, gen partisan *m*.

II *adj* **1** (biased) partisan; **2** [*army, attack*] de partisans.

partisanship /ˈpɑːtɪzænʃɪp, ˌpɑːtɪ-, US ˈpɑːrt-/ *n* partialité *f*.

partition /pɑːˈtɪʃn/ **I** *n* **1** (in room, office, house) cloison *f*; **glass/wooden ~** cloison en verre/en bois; **2** Pol (of country) partition *f*; **3** Jur (of property) morcellement *m*.

II *vtr* **1** = **partition off**; **2** Pol diviser, partager [*country*]; **3** Jur morceler [*property*].

■ **partition off**: **~ off [sth], ~ [sth] off** cloisonner [*space, area, room*].

partition wall *n* cloison *f*.

partitive /ˈpɑːtɪtɪv/ *adj* partitif/-ive.

partly /ˈpɑːtlɪ/ *adv* [*explain, justify, funded, dependent, responsible*] en partie; **~, I did it because...** je l'ai fait en partie parce que...

partner /ˈpɑːtnə(r)/ **I** *n* **1** Comm, Jur associé/-e *m/f* (**in** dans); **active ~** associé-gérant *m*, commandité *m*; **business ~** associé/-e *m/f*; **general ~** commandité *m*; **limited ~** commanditaire *m*; **2** Econ, Pol partenaire *m*; **Britain's Nato ~s** les partenaires de la Grande Bretagne au sein de l'OTAN; **3** Sport, Dance partenaire *mf*; **golf/tennis ~** partenaire *mf* de golf/tennis; **4** (in relationship) (married) époux/-se *m/f*; (unmarried) partenaire *mf*; **5** (workmate) collègue *mf*; **6**○ US (form of address) mon pote *m*.

II *vtr* être le collègue de [*workmate*]; être le partenaire de [*dancer*]; faire équipe avec [*player*].

IDIOMS **to be ~s in crime** être complices.

partnership /ˈpɑːtnəʃɪp/ *n* **1** Jur association *f* (**between** entre; **with** avec); **to be in ~ with** être associé avec; **to go into ~ with** s'associer à; **in ~ with** en association avec; **to take sb into ~** prendre qn pour associé/-e *m/f*; **general ~** ≈ société *f* en nom collectif; **limited ~, special ~** ≈ société *f* en commandite (simple); **professional ~, non-trading ~** association *f* professionnelle; **2** (alliance) partenariat *m* (**between** entre; **with** avec); **in ~ with** en partenariat avec; **economic/industrial ~** partenariat *m* économique/industriel; **3** (pairing) association *f*; **acting/sporting ~** association d'acteurs/de sportifs; **a working ~** une équipe *f*; **we make a good ~** nous formons une bonne équipe.

partnership: **~ agreement** *n* Comm Jur acte *m* d'association; **~ certificate** *n* US Comm Jur certificat *m* d'association commerciale; **~ limited by shares** *n* Comm Jur ≈ société *f* en commandite par actions.

part: **~ of speech** *n* partie *f* du discours; **~ owner** *n* copropriétaire *mf*; **~ payment** *n* règlement *m* partiel.

partridge /ˈpɑːtrɪdʒ/ *n* perdrix *f*.

part song *n* chant *m* polyphonique.

part-time /ˌpɑːtˈtaɪm/ **I** *n* temps *m* partiel; **to be on** ou **work ~** travailler à temps partiel.
II *adj, adv* [*work, worker*] à temps partiel.

part-timer /ˌpɑːtˈtaɪmə(r)/ *n* employé/-e *m/f* à temps partiel.

parturition /ˌpɑːtjʊˈrɪʃn, US -tʃʊ-/ *n* parturition *f*.

partway /ˌpɑːtˈweɪ/ *adv* **~ through the evening/film** à un moment de la soirée/du film; **~ down the page** vers le bas de la page; **to drill ~ through the rock** pénétrer en partie dans la roche; **to be ~ through doing** être en train de faire; **I'm ~ through the book** j'en suis à la moitié du livre.

part work *n* GB fascicules *mpl* (*à relier en volumes*).

party /ˈpɑːtɪ/ **I** *n* **1** (social event) fête *f*; (in evening) soirée *f*; (formal) réception *f*; **birthday ~** (fête d')anniversaire *m*; **children's ~** goûter *m* d'enfants; **leaving ~** pot° *m* de départ; **to give** ou **have a ~ for sb** organiser une fête pour qn; **I'm having a ~** je fais une fête; **2** (group) groupe *m*; Mil détachement *m*; **a ~ of tourists/children** un groupe de touristes/d'enfants; **reconnaissance ~** Mil détachement *m* de reconnaissance; **rescue ~** équipe *f* de secouristes; **3** Pol parti *m*; **political ~** parti *m* politique; **the Party** le Parti (Communiste); **4** Jur (individual, group) partie *f*; **a solution acceptable to both/all parties** une solution acceptable pour les deux parties/toutes les parties; **to be a ~ to a contract/treaty** être partie prenante dans un contrat/traité; **a ~ to the suit** Jur une personne en cause; **innocent ~** innocent/-e *m/f*; **5** sout (participant) **to be a ~ to** être complice de [*crime*]; **I won't be ~ to any violence** je ne me ferai complice d'aucune violence; **6**° † hum (person) individu *m*.
II *modif* **1** [*atmosphere, spirit*] de fête; [*game*] de société; **2** Pol [*activist, conference, loyalty, meeting, member, policy*] du parti; **the ~ faithful** les fidèles du parti.
III° *vi* faire la fête.

party animal° *n* fêtard/-e° *m/f*, noceur/-euse *m/f*.

party dress *n* (formal) robe *f* de soirée; **she was wearing her ~** (child) elle avait mis sa belle robe.

party: **~goer** *n* fêtard/-e° *m/f*; **~ hat** *n* chapeau *m* en papier (*que l'on met pour s'amuser*).

party line *n* **1** Pol, fig **the ~** la ligne du parti; **to follow the ~** suivre la ligne du parti; **2** Telecom ligne *f* commune (*à plusieurs abonnés*).

party machine *n* machine *f* du parti.

party piece *n* **to do one's ~**° faire son numéro°.

party: **~ political** *adj* [*issue, point*] exploité à des fins politiques; **~ political broadcast** *n émission dans laquelle un parti expose sa politique*; **~ politics** *n* pej politique *f* politicienne; **~ pooper**° *n* rabat-joie *mf inv*; **~ wall** *n* mur *m* mitoyen.

par value *n* Fin montant *m* nominal.

PASCAL /ˌpæsˈkæl/ *n* Comput (also **Pascal**) Pascal *m*.

paschal /ˈpæskl, ˈpɑːskl/ *adj* pascal.

paschal: **~ candle** *n* cierge *m* pascal; **Paschal Lamb** *n* agneau *m* pascal.

Pas-de-Calais ▶1163 *pr n* Pas-de-Calais *m*; **in/to the ~** dans le Pas-de-Calais.

pass /pɑːs, US pæs/ **I** *n* **1** (permission document) (to enter, leave) laisser-passer *m inv*; (for journalists) coupe-file *m inv*; (to be absent) permission *f* also Mil; (of safe conduct) sauf-conduit *m*; **2** (travel document) carte *f* d'abonnement; **bus/train/monthly ~** carte d'abonnement pour le bus/pour le train/mensuelle; **3** Sch, Univ (success) moyenne *f* (**in** en); **I'll be happy with a ~** je me contenterais de la moyenne; **to get a ~** être reçu; **4** Sport (in ball games) passe *f*; (in fencing) botte *f*; **a backward/forward ~** une passe en arrière/en avant; **to make a ~** faire une passe; **5** Geog (in mountains) col *m*; **mountain ~** col *m* de montagne; **6** Aviat **he flew a low ~** il est passé à basse altitude; **to make a ~ over sth** survoler qch.
II *vtr* **1** (go past) (to far side) passer [*checkpoint, customs*]; franchir [*lips, finishing line*]; (alongside and beyond) passer devant [*building, area*]; [*vehicle*] dépasser [*vehicle*]; dépasser [*level, understanding, expectation*]; **to ~ sb in the street** croiser qn dans la rue; **2** (hand over) (directly) passer; (indirectly) faire passer; **~ me your plate** passe-moi ton assiette; **~ the salt along please** faites passer le sel s'il vous plaît; **to ~ stolen goods/counterfeit notes** faire passer des marchandises volées/des faux billets; **to ~ sth along the line** se passer qch de main en main; **'we'll ~ you back to the studio now'** TV, Radio 'maintenant nous repassons l'antenne au studio'; **3** (move) passer; **~ the rope through/round the ring** passez la corde dans/autour de l'anneau; **he ~ed his hand over his face** il s'est passé la main sur le visage; **4** Sport passer [*ball*]; **to ~ the ball backwards/forwards** passer la balle en arrière/en avant; **5** (spend) passer [*time*] (**doing** à faire); **6** (succeed in) [*person*] réussir [*test, exam*]; [*car, machine etc*] passer [qch] (avec succès) [*test*]; **7** (declare satisfactory) admettre [*candidate*]; approuver [*invoice*]; **to ~ sth (as being) safe/suitable etc** juger qch sans danger/convenable etc; **the censors ~ed the film as suitable for adults only** la censure a jugé que le film ne convenait qu'aux adultes; **8** (vote in) adopter [*bill, motion, resolution*]; **9** (pronounce) prononcer [*judgment, verdict, sentence*]; **to ~ sentence on** Jur prononcer un verdict à l'encontre de [*accused*]; **to ~ a remark about sb/sth** faire une remarque sur qn/qch; **10** Med **to ~ water** uriner; **to ~ blood** avoir du sang dans les urines; **11** Fin surtout US escamoter [*dividend*].
III *vi* **1** (go past) [*person, car*] passer; **let me ~** laissez-moi passer; **2** (move) passer; **to ~ along/over sth** passer le long de/au-dessus de qch; **to ~ through sth** traverser qch; **~ down the bus please** avancez dans le fond s'il vous plaît; **3** fig (go by) [*time, crisis, feeling*] passer; [*memory, old order*] disparaître; **the evening had ~ed all too quickly** la soirée avait passé beaucoup trop vite; **to ~ unnoticed** passer inaperçu; **let the remark ~** laissez couler; **4** (be transferred) passer (**to** à); [*title, property*] passer (**to** à); [*letter, knowing look*] être échangé (**between** entre); **his mood ~ed from joy to despair** son humeur est passée de la joie au désespoir; **deeds which have ~ed into legend** exploits qui sont passés dans la légende; **5** Sport passer; **to ~ to sb** faire une passe à qn; **6** Games passer; **I'm afraid I must ~ on that one** fig (in discussion) je cède mon tour de parole; **7** littér (happen) se passer; **to come to ~** arriver; **it came to ~ that...** Bible il advint que...; **to bring sth to ~** accomplir qch; **8** (succeed) réussir; **she ~ed in both subjects** elle a réussi dans les deux matières; **9** (be accepted) [*person, rudeness, behaviour*] passer; **he'd ~ for an Italian** il pourrait passer pour un Italien; **she ~es for 40** on lui donnerait 40 ans; **10** US, Jur se prononcer (**on** sur); **11** Chem se transformer (**into** en).
IDIOMS **in ~ing** en passant; **to come to such a ~ that...** arriver à un tel point que...; **to make a ~ at sb** faire du plat° à qn; **to ~ the word** passer la consigne; **to sell the ~** trahir la cause.
■ **pass along**: **~ [sth] along, ~ along [sth]** faire passer.
■ **pass around, pass round**: **~ [sth] around, ~ around [sth]** faire circuler [*document, photos*]; faire passer [*food, plates etc*].
■ **pass away** euph décéder.
■ **pass by** [*procession*] défiler; [*person*] passer; **life seems to have ~ed me by** j'ai le sentiment d'être passé à côté de la vie.
■ **pass down**: **~ [sth] down, ~ down [sth]** transmettre [*secret, knowledge, title*] (**from** de; **to** à).
■ **pass off**: ¶ **~ off 1** (take place) [*demonstration*] se dérouler; [*fête*] se passer; **2** (disappear) [*headache, effects*] se dissiper; ¶ **~ [sb/sth] off, ~ off [sb/sth]** faire passer [*person, incident*] (**as** pour).
■ **pass on**: ¶ **~ on** poursuivre; **to ~ on to sth** passer à qch; **let's ~ on to the next question** passons à la question suivante; ¶ **~ [sth] on, ~ on [sth]** transmettre [*good wishes, condolences, message, title*] passer [*book, clothes, cold*]; répercuter [*costs*].
■ **pass out**: ¶ **~ out 1** (faint) gen perdre connaissance; (fall drunk) tomber ivre mort; **2** Mil (complete training) sortir avec ses diplômes (**of, from** de); ¶ **~ [sth] out, ~ out [sth]** distribuer [*leaflets*].
■ **pass over**: ¶ **~ over**† = **pass away**; ¶ **~ [sb] over** délaisser [*employee, candidate*]; **he was ~ed over in favour of another candidate** on lui a préféré un autre candidat; ¶ **~ over [sth]** ne pas tenir compte de [*rude remark, behaviour*].
■ **pass through**: **~ through [sth]** traverser [*substance, place*]; **I'm just ~ing through** je suis de passage.
■ **pass up**°: **~ up [sth]** laisser passer [*opportunity, offer*].

passable /ˈpɑːsəbl, US ˈpæs-/ *adj* **1** (of acceptable standard) [*English, quality, food*] passable; [*knowledge, performance*] assez bon/bonne; **only ~** moyen/-enne sans plus; **to have a ~ knowledge of sth** connaître assez bien qch; **2** (traversable) [*road*] praticable; [*river*] franchissable.

passably /ˈpɑːsəblɪ, US ˈpæs-/ *adv* passablement.

passage /ˈpæsɪdʒ/ *n* **1** (also **~way**) (indoors) corridor *m*; (outdoors) passage *m*; **clear a ~ for the King** livrez passage au roi; **2** Anat conduit *m*; **ear/urinary ~** conduit *m* auditif/urinaire; **nasal ~s** fosses *fpl* nasales; **3** Mus, Literat passage *m*; **selected ~s** Literat morceaux *mpl* choisis; **4** (movement) passage *m*; **the ~ of vehicles/ships** le passage des véhicules/navires; **~ of arms** passe *f* d'armes; **the ~ of time** le passage du temps; **her beauty survived the ~ of time** sa beauté a survécu au temps; **5** Jur (also **right of ~**) droit *m* de passage (**over** sur); **to deny sb ~** refuser le droit de passage à qn; **6** (journey) traversée *f*; **to book/work one's ~** réserver/travailler pour payer sa traversée; **the bill had a stormy ~ through parliament** fig la discussion de ce projet de loi au parlement a été mouvementée.

pass: **~band** *n* Audio bande *f* passante; **~book** *n* Fin livret *m* (bancaire); **~ degree** *n* Univ diplôme *m* avec mention passable.

passé /ˈpæseɪ, US pæˈseɪ/ *adj* péj démodé.

passenger /ˈpæsɪndʒə(r)/ *n* **1** (in car, boat, plane, ship) passager/-ère *m/f*; (in train, bus, coach, tube) voyageur/-euse *m/f*; **2** GB péj (idler) parasite *m*, tire-au-flanc° *m inv*.

passenger: **~ car** *n* US = **passenger coach**; **~ coach** GB *n* voiture *f* or wagon *m* de voyageurs; **~ compartment** *n* GB Aut habitacle *m*; **~ door** *n* portière *f* avant côté passager; **~ ferry** *n* ferry *m*; **~ inquiries** *npl* renseignements *mpl* (*pour les voyageurs*); **~ jet** *n* avion *m* de ligne; **~ list** *n* liste *f* des passagers; **~ plane** *n* = **passenger jet**; **~ seat** *n* place *f* du passager; **~ service** *n* ligne *f*; **~ train** *n* train *m* de voyageurs.

passe-partout /ˌpæspɑːˈtuː, ˌpɑːs-/ *n* (key) passe-partout *m inv*; (frame) sous-verre *m inv*.

passerby /ˌpɑːsəˈbaɪ/ *n* (*pl* **passersby**) passant/-e *m/f*.

pass for press *n* bon *m* à tirer.

passing /ˈpɑːsɪŋ, US ˈpæs-/ **I** *n* **1** (movement) passage *m*; **the ~ of the years/boats** le passage des années/bateaux; **with the ~ of time** avec le temps; **2** (end) fin *f*; **the ~ of traditional customs** la fin des coutumes traditionnelles; **3** euph (death) disparition *f* euph, mort *f*.
II *adj* **1** (going by) [*motorist, policeman*] qui passe; **witnessed by a ~ tourist** vu par un touriste qui passait; **with each ~ day** de jour en jour; **2** (momentary) [*whim*] passager/-ère; **3** (cursory) [*reference*] en passant *inv*; **4** (vague) [*resemblance*] vague (*before n*).

passing: **~ note** *n* Mus note *f* de passage; **~-out parade** *n* Mil défilé *m* de promotion; **~ place** *n* aire *f* de croisement; **~ shot** *n* (in tennis) tir *m* passant.

passion /ˈpæʃn/ **I** *n* **1** (love, feeling) passion *f*; **a ~ for opera** une passion pour l'opéra; **2** (anger) colère *f*; **a fit of ~** un accès de colère.
II Passion *pr n* Relig **the Passion** la Passion; **Saint Matthew's Passion** la Passion selon saint Matthieu.

passionate /ˈpæʃənət/ *adj* [*kiss, person, nature, speech*] passionné; [*advocate, belief, plea*] fervent; [*relationship*] passionnel/-elle.

passionately /ˈpæʃənətlɪ/ *adv* [*love, kiss*] passionnément; [*write, defend*] avec passion; [*believe, want*] ardemment; [*oppose*] farouchement; **to be ~ fond of sb/sth** adorer qn/qch.

passion: **~ flower** *n* passiflore *f*, fleur *f* de la passion; **~ fruit** *n* fruit *m* de la passion.

passion-killer○ *n* **it's a real ~**○ hum ça tue l'amour.

passionless /ˈpæʃənlɪs/ *adj* [*marriage*] sans amour; [*account*] détaché, neutre.

passion: **Passion play** *n* mystère *m* de la Passion; **Passion Sunday** *n* dimanche *m* d'avant les Rameaux; **Passiontide** *n* temps *m* de la Passion; **Passion Week** *n* semaine *f* de la Passion.

passive /ˈpæsɪv/ **I** *n* Ling **the ~** le passif, la voix passive; **in the ~** à la voix passive.
II *adj* (all contexts) passif/-ive.

passive disobedience *n* désobéissance *f* passive.

passively /ˈpæsɪvlɪ/ *adv* **1** [*gaze, stare*] d'un air passif; [*wait, react*] passivement; **2** Ling [*use, express*] au passif.

passive: **~ resistance** *n* résistance *f* passive; **~ smoking** *n* tabagisme *m* passif.

passivity /pæˈsɪvətɪ/, **passiveness** /ˈpæsɪvnɪs/ *n* passivité *f*.

pass: **~key** *n* passe *m*; **~ mark** *n* Sch, Univ moyenne *f*.

Passover /ˈpɑːsəʊvə(r), US ˈpæs-/ *n* Pâque *f* juive.

passport /ˈpɑːspɔːt, US ˈpæs-/ *n* passeport *m*; **false ~** faux passeport; **diplomatic ~** passeport diplomatique; **visitor's ~** GB passeport temporaire; **a ~ to success** fig un passeport pour la réussite.

passport holder *n* détenteur/-trice *m/f* d'un passeport.

pass: **~ the parcel** *n*: *jeu d'enfants*; **~-through** *n* US passe-plat *m*; **~word** *n* (all contexts) mot *m* de passe.

past /pɑːst, US pæst/

■ **Note** For a full set of translations for *past* used in clocktime consult the Usage Note ▶ 1096.

I *n* **1** gen passé *m*; **in the ~** dans le passé, par le passé, autrefois; **she had taught at the school in the ~** elle avait enseigné à l'école par le passé; **I have done things in the ~ that I'm not proud of** j'ai fait des choses dans le passé dont je ne suis pas fier; **there are more students/unemployed people now than in the ~** il y a plus d'étudiants/de chômeurs qu'autrefois or que dans le passé; **in the ~ we have (always) spent our holidays in Greece/taken the train** jusqu'ici nous avons toujours passé nos vacances en Grèce/pris le train; **to live in the ~** vivre dans le passé; **that's a thing of the ~** c'est du passé; **soon petrol-driven cars will be a thing of the ~** les voitures qui fonctionnent à l'essence feront bientôt partie du passé; **he/she has a ~** il/elle a un passé chargé; **2** Ling (also **~ tense**) passé *m*; **in the ~** au passé.
II *adj* **1** (preceding) [*week, days, month etc*] dernier/-ière; **during the ~ few days/months** ces derniers jours/mois; **in the ~ three years/months** dans les trois dernières années/derniers mois; **the ~ two years have been difficult** ces deux dernières années ont été difficiles; **2** (previous, former) [*generations, centuries, achievements, problems, experience*] passé; [*president, chairman, incumbent*] ancien/-ienne (*before n*); [*government*] précédent; **in times ~** autrefois, jadis; **3** (finished) **summer is ~** l'été est fini; **that's all ~** c'est du passé.
III *prep* **1** (moving beyond) **to walk** ou **go ~ sb/sth** passer devant qn/qch; **to drive ~ sth** passer devant qch (en voiture); **to run ~ sth** passer devant qch (en courant); **2** (beyond in time) **it's ~ 6/midnight** il est 6 heures passées/minuit passé; **twenty ~ two** deux heures vingt; **half/quarter ~ two** deux heures et demie/et quart; **he is ~ 70** il a 70 ans passés, il a plus de 70 ans; **3** (beyond in position) après; **~ the church/the park** après l'église/le parc; **4** (beyond or above a certain level) **the temperature soared ~ 40°C** la température est montée brutalement à plus de 40°C; **he didn't get ~ the first chapter** il n'est pas allé plus loin que le premier chapitre; **he didn't get ~ the first interview** (for job) il n'a pas passé la barrière du premier entretien; **she can't count ~ ten** elle ne sait compter que jusqu'à dix; **5** (beyond scope of) **to be ~ understanding** dépasser l'entendement; **to be ~ caring** ne plus s'en faire; **he is ~ playing football/working** ce n'est plus de son âge de jouer au foot/de travailler.
IV *adv* **1** (onwards) **to go** ou **walk ~** passer; **2** (ago) **two years ~** il y a deux ans.
IDIOMS **to be ~ it**○ avoir passé l'âge; **to be ~ its best** [*cheese, fruit etc*] être un peu avancé; [*wine*] être un peu éventé; **I wouldn't put it ~ him/them to do** je ne pense pas que ça le/les gênerait de faire; ▶ **care**.

pasta /ˈpæstə/ *n* ¢ pâtes *fpl* (alimentaires).

paste /peɪst/ **I** *n* **1** (glue) colle *f*; **wallpaper ~** colle *f* à papier peint; **2** (mixture) pâte *f*; **mix to a smooth ~** mélanger jusqu'à l'obtention d'une pâte souple; **3** Culin (fish, meat) pâté *m*; (vegetable, fruit) purée *f*; **salmon ~** pâté *m* de saumon; **tomato ~** purée *f* de tomates; **4** (in jewellery) strass *m*.
II *modif* [*gem, ruby*] en strass.
III *vtr* **1** (stick) coller [*label, paper*] (**onto** sur; **into** dans; **together** ensemble); **2** (coat in glue) encoller [*wallpaper*]; **3**○ (hit) tabasser [*person*]; **4**○ (defeat) battre [qn] à plates coutures○ [*opponent, team*]; **5** Comput coller.
■ **paste up**: **~ [sth] up, ~ up [sth] 1** afficher [*notice, poster*]; **2** Print faire une maquette de [*article, page*].

pasteboard /ˈpeɪstbɔːd/ **I** *n* Print carton *m*.
II *modif* (flimsy) en carton-pâte.

pastel /ˈpæstl, US pæˈstel/ **I** *n* **1** (medium, stick) pastel *m*; **to work in ~s** dessiner au pastel; **2** (drawing) dessin *m* au pastel.
II *modif* [*colour, green, pink, shade*] pastel; [*drawing*] au pastel.

pastern /ˈpæstən/ *n* paturon *m*.

paste: **~-up** *n* Print maquette *f* (*de mise en page*); **~-up artist** ▶ 1692 *n* Print maquettiste *mf*.

pasteurization /ˌpɑːstʃəraɪˈzeɪʃn, US ˌpæstʃərɪˈzeɪʃn/ *n* pasteurisation *f*.

pasteurize /ˈpɑːstʃəraɪz, US ˈpæst-/ *vtr* pasteuriser.

pasteurized /ˈpɑːstʃəraɪzd, US ˈpæst-/ *adj* pasteurisé.

past historic *n* Ling passé *m* simple.

pastiche /pæˈstiːʃ/ *n* (all contexts) pastiche *m*.

pastille /ˈpæstəl, US pæˈstiːl/ *n* pastille *f*; **throat ~** pastille pour la gorge.

pastime /ˈpɑːstaɪm, US ˈpæs-/ *n* passe-temps *m inv*; **America's national ~** le sport national des Américains also iron.

pasting○ /ˈpeɪstɪŋ/ *n* **1** (defeat) gamelle○ *f*, défaite *f*; **to take a (severe) ~** ramasser une (sacrée) gamelle○; **to give sb a ~** battre qn à plates coutures○; **2** (criticism) **to take a ~** se faire descendre en flammes; **to give sb a ~** descendre qn en flammes.

past master *n* **to be a ~ at doing** avoir l'art de faire.

pastor /ˈpɑːstə(r), US ˈpæs-/ ▶ 1692 *n* pasteur *m*.

pastoral /ˈpɑːstərəl, US ˈpæs-/ **I** *n* pastorale *f*.
II *adj* **1** [*life, idyll, scene, poem, society*] pastoral; **2** GB Sch, Univ [*role, work*] de conseiller/-ère; **he looks after students' ~ needs** il s'occupe du bien-être des étudiants; **3** Relig pastoral.

pastoral care *n* GB, Sch, Univ **to be responsible for ~** avoir la charge du bien-être des étudiants.

pastoral letter *n* lettre *f* pastorale.

pastorate /ˈpɑːstərət, US ˈpæs-/ *n* pastorat *m*.

past perfect *n* Ling plus-que-parfait *m*.

pastrami /pæˈstrɑːmɪ/ *n* bœuf *m* fumé.

pastry /ˈpeɪstrɪ/ *n* **1** (mixture, substance) pâte *f*; **to make/to roll out ~** faire/étaler une pâte; **frozen ~** pâte congelée; **2** (item, cake) pâtisserie *f*.

pastry: **~ bag** *n* US Culin poche *f* à douille; **~ board** *n* planche *f* à pâtisserie; **~ brush** *n* pinceau *m* à pâtisserie; **~ case** *n* fond *m* de tarte; **~ cook** *n* pâtissier/-ière *m/f*; **~ cutter** *n* Culin emporte-pièce *m inv*; **~ shell** *n* = **pastry case**.

past tense *n* Ling passé *m*; **to talk about sb in the ~** parler de qn au passé.

pasturage /ˈpɑːstʃərɪdʒ, US ˈpæs-/ *n* ¢ **1** (land) pâturages *mpl*; **2** (right) droit *m* de pacage.

pasture /ˈpɑːstʃə(r), US ˈpæs-/ **I** *n* **1** (land) pré *m*, pâturage *m*; **rich ~** riches pâturages; **permanent ~** pâture *f* permanente; **to put a cow out to ~** mettre une vache au pré; **2** (grass) herbe *f*.
II *vtr* faire paître [*animal*].
III *vi* paître.
IDIOMS **to leave for ~s new** partir vers de nouveaux horizons; **to put sb out to ~** mettre qn au vert or à la retraite.

pastureland /ˈpɑːstʃəlænd, US ˈpæs-/ *n* ¢ pâturages *mpl*.

pasty I /ˈpæstɪ/ *n* GB Culin *petit pâté en croûte à la viande et aux pommes de terre*.
II /ˈpeɪstɪ/ *adj* **1** (white) [*face, skin*] terreux/-euse; **2** (doughy) [*consistency, mixture*] pâteux/-euse.

pasty-faced /ˌpeɪstɪˈfeɪst/ *adj* au teint terreux.

pat /pæt/ **I** *n* **1** (gentle tap) petite tape *f*; **a ~ on the head/the knee** une tape sur la tête/le genou; **2** (of butter) noix *f*; (larger) morceau *m*.
II *adj* **1** (glib) tout prêt; **2** (apt) pertinent.
III *vtr* (*p prés etc* **-tt-**) **1** (tap gently) tapoter [*ball, hand, car*]; **to ~ one's hair into place** arranger ses cheveux; **2** (stroke) caresser [*dog*].
IDIOMS **to have sth off** GB ou **down** US **~** connaître qch par cœur; **to get a ~ on the back** se faire féliciter; **to give oneself a ~ on the back** s'applaudir; **to stand ~** US demeurer inflexible.

Patagonia /ˌpætəˈgəʊnɪə/ *pr n* Patagonie *f*.

patch /pætʃ/ **I** *n* (*pl* **~es**) **1** (for repair) (in clothes) pièce *f*; (on tyre, airbed) rustine® *f*; **2** (protective cover) (on eye) bandeau *m*; (on wound) pansement *m*; **3** (small area) (of snow, ice) plaque *f*; (of colour, damp, rust, sunlight) tache *f*; (of fog) nappe *f*; (of oil) flaque *f*; (of blue sky) coin *m*; **to have a bald ~** être un peu dégarni; **in ~es** par endroits; **4** (area of ground) gen zone *f*; (for planting) carré *m*; **strawberry/vegetable ~** carré *m* de fraises/de légumes; **a ~ of grass** un coin d'herbe; **a ~ of daisies** une touffe de marguerites; **5** Hist, Cosmet mouche *f*; **6** GB○ (territory) (of gangster, salesman) territoire *m*; (of policeman, official) secteur *m*; **7**○ (period) période *f*; **to go through** ou **have a bad ~** traverser une mauvaise passe○; **in ~es** par moments; **8** Electron connexion *f*, raccordement *m*; **9** Comput correction *f* provisoire.
II *vtr* **1** (repair) rapiécer [*hole, trousers*]; réparer [*tyre*]; **2** Electron raccorder [*circuits*]; **3** Comput corriger [*software*].
IDIOMS **he's not a ~ on his father** il n'arrive pas à la cheville de son père; **the film isn't a ~ on the book** le film est loin de valoir le livre.
■ **patch through** Telecom **to ~ a call through** faire un transfert (**to sb** vers qn).
■ **patch together**: **~ [sth] together** rafistoler○ [*pieces, fragments*]; concocter [*deal, report, team*].
■ **patch up**: ¶ **~ up [sth], ~ [sth] up** soigner [*person*]; rapiécer [*hole, trousers*]; réparer [*ceiling, tyre*]; fig rafistoler○ [*marriage*]; ¶ **~ up [sth]** résoudre [*differences, quarrel*]; **we've ~ed it up** nous nous sommes réconciliés.

patch: **~ pocket** *n* poche *f* plaquée; **~ test** *n* Med test *m* cutané.

patchwork /ˈpætʃwɜːk/ **I** *n* **1** Sewing patchwork *m*; **2** fig (of episodes, ideas, groups) patchwork *m*; (of colours, fields) mosaïque *f*.
II *modif* **1** Sewing [*cover, quilt*] en patchwork; **2** (not uniform) [*approach, theory*] hétérogène.

patchy /ˈpætʃɪ/ *adj* [*colour*] inégal; [*essay, novel*] inégal; [*quality, result, safety record*] inégal; [*performance*] de qualité inégale; [*knowledge*] incomplet/-ète; **~ cloud** nuages *mpl* épars; **~ fog** nappes *fpl* de brouillard.

pate /peɪt/ *n*† crâne *m*; **a bald ~** un crâne chauve.

pâté /ˈpæteɪ, US pɑːˈteɪ/ *n* pâté *m*, terrine *f*; **liver/duck ~** pâté de foie/de canard; **salmon ~** terrine de saumon.

patella /pəˈtelə/ *n* (*pl* **~e**) rotule *f*.

paten /ˈpætn/ *n* patène *f*.

patent /ˈpætnt, ˈpeɪtnt, US ˈpætnt/ **I** *n* **1** (document) brevet *m* (**for, on** pour); **to hold/to take out a ~** détenir/obtenir un brevet; **to come out of ~** ou **off ~** tomber dans le domaine public; **~ pending** en cours de brevetage *m*; **2** (patented invention) invention *f* brevetée.
II *adj* **1** (obvious) manifeste; **2** Jur (licensed) breveté.
III *vtr* Jur faire breveter.
IV patented *pp adj* breveté.

patentable /ˈpætntəbl, ˈpeɪt-, US ˈpæt-/ *adj* brevetable.

patent agent GB, **patent attorney** US ▶**1692** *n* juriste *mf* spécialisé/-e en propriété industrielle.

patentee /ˌpeɪtnˈtiː, US ˌpætn-/ *n* titulaire *mf* d'un brevet.

patent leather *n* cuir *m* verni.

patently /ˈpeɪtntlɪ, US ˈpæt-/ *adv* manifestement.

patent: **~ medicine** *n*: *médicament de marque déposée délivré sans ordonnance*; **Patent Office** GB, **Patent and Trademark Office** US *n* ≈ Institut *m* national de la propriété industrielle.

patentor /ˈpeɪtntə(r), US ˈpæt-/ ▶**1692** *n* (person) personne *f* délivrant des brevets; (body) organisme *m* délivrant des brevets.

patent: **~ right** *n* Jur droit *m* exclusif d'exploitation; **Patent Rolls** *n* GB Jur registre *m* des brevets d'invention.

pater† /ˈpeɪtə(r)/ *n* GB hum paternel○ *m*.

paterfamilias /ˌpeɪtəfəˈmɪlɪæs, US ˌpæt-/ *n* sout paterfamilias *m*.

paternal /pəˈtɜːnl/ *adj* (all contexts) paternel/-elle; **to feel ~ towards sb** éprouver des sentiments paternels à l'égard de qn.

paternalism /pəˈtɜːnəlɪzəm/ *n* paternalisme *m*.

paternalist /pəˈtɜːnəlɪst/ *n, adj* paternaliste (*mf*).

paternalistic /pəˌtɜːnəˈlɪstɪk/ *adj* péj paternaliste.

paternalistically /pəˌtɜːnəˈlɪstɪklɪ/ *adv* péj de façon paternaliste.

paternally /pəˈtɜːnəlɪ/ *adv* [*smile, greet*] paternellement.

paternity /pəˈtɜːnətɪ/ *n* paternité *f*; **to deny/acknowledge ~** nier/reconnaître la paternité.

paternity: **~ leave** *n* congé *m* de paternité; **~ suit** *n* recherche *f* de paternité.

paternoster /ˌpætəˈnɒstə(r)/ *n* **1** Relig (also **Paternoster**) Pater (noster) *m inv*; **2** (elevator) pater-noster *m*.

path /pɑːθ, US pæθ/ **I** *n* **1** (track) (also **~way**) chemin *m*; (narrower) sentier *m*; **a mountain ~** un sentier de montagne; **to clear a ~ through the jungle** se frayer un chemin à travers la jungle; **2** (in garden) allée *f*; **3** (course) (of projectile, vehicle) trajectoire *f*; (of planet, river, sun) cours *m*; (of hurricane) passage *m*; **in the ~ of the car** sur la trajectoire de la voiture; **he threw himself in the ~ of the train** il s'est jeté sous le train; **to stand in sb's ~** lit, fig barrer le chemin à qn; **4** (option) voie *f*; **the ~ of least resistance** la voie de la facilité; **5** (means) (difficult) chemin *m* (**to** de); (easy) route *f* (**to** de).
II *n* (*abrév* = **pathology**) pathologie *f*.
IDIOMS **to beat a ~ to sb's door** accourir en foule chez qn.

Pathan /pəˈtɑːn/ **I** *n* Pachtou *mf*, Pathan *mf*.
II *adj* pachtou.

pathetic /pəˈθetɪk/ *adj* **1** (full of pathos) pathétique; **2** pej (inadequate) misérable; **3**○ pej (contemptible) lamentable.

pathetically /pəˈθetɪklɪ/ *adv* **1** [*vulnerable*] pathétiquement; [*grateful*] éperdument; **~ thin** d'une maigreur pathétique; **2**○ pej [*fail*] lamentablement; [*play, perform*] de façon lamentable.

pathetic fallacy *n* ≈ sophisme *m* sentimental.

pathological /ˌpæθəˈlɒdʒɪkl/ *adj* **1** [*fear, hatred, condition*] pathologique; **he's a ~ liar**○ c'est pathologique chez lui, il ment sans arrêt○; **2** [*journal*] médical; [*research*] des causes pathologiques.

pathologically /ˌpæθəˈlɒdʒɪklɪ/ *adv* **he's ~ jealous/mean** sa jalousie/son avarice est pathologique.

pathologist /pəˈθɒlədʒɪst/ ▶**1692** *n* (doing post-mortems) médecin *m* légiste; (specialist in pathology) pathologiste *mf*.

pathology /pəˈθɒlədʒɪ/ *n* pathologie *f*.

pathos /ˈpeɪθɒs/ *n* pathétique *m*, pathos *m*.

patience /ˈpeɪʃns/ *n* **1** patience *f* (**with** avec); **to have no ~ with sth** n'avoir aucune patience avec qch; **to lose ~** (**with sb**) perdre patience (avec qn); **to try** ou **test sb's ~** mettre la patience de qn à l'épreuve; **my ~ is running out** ou **wearing thin** ma patience s'épuise; **2** ▶**1282** (game) réussite *f*, patience *f*; **to play ~** faire une réussite.
IDIOMS **~ is a virtue** la patience est mère de toutes les vertus.

patient /ˈpeɪʃnt/ **I** *n* patient/-e *m/f*; **private ~** patient privé; **heart ~** patient souffrant d'une maladie cardiaque; **mental ~** malade *mf* mental/-e.
II *adj* patient (**with** avec).

patiently /ˈpeɪʃntlɪ/ *adv* avec patience, patiemment.

patina /ˈpætɪnə/ *n* **1** lit (on metal, wood) patine *f*; **2** fig (aura) aura *f*.

patio /ˈpætɪəʊ/ *n* **1** (terrace) terrasse *f*; **2** (courtyard) patio *m*.

patio: **~ doors** *npl* porte-fenêtre *f*; **~ furniture** *n* meubles *mpl* de jardin; **~ garden** *n* patio *m*.

Patna rice /ˈpætnə/ *n*: *variété de riz à long grain*.

patois /ˈpætwɑː/ *n* Ling patois *m*; hum jargon *m*.

patriarch /ˈpeɪtrɪɑːk, US ˈpæt-/ *n* **1** gen patriarche *m*; **2** Relig (also **Patriarch**) patriarche *m*.

patriarchal /ˌpeɪtrɪˈɑːkl, US ˌpæt-/ *adj* **1** [*society, system*] patriarcal; **2** [*figure, beard*] de patriarche.

patriarchate /ˈpeɪtrɪɑːkeɪt, US ˈpæt-/ *n* patriarcat *m*.

patriarchy /ˈpeɪtrɪɑːkɪ, US ˈpæt-/ *n* patriarcat *m*.

patrician /pəˈtrɪʃn/ *n, adj* patricien/-ienne (*m/f*).

patricide /ˈpætrɪsaɪd/ *n* **1** (act) parricide *m*; **2** sout (person) parricide *mf*.

patrimony /ˈpætrɪmənɪ, US -məʊnɪ/ *n* sout patrimoine *m*.

patriot /ˈpætrɪət, US ˈpeɪt-/ *n* patriote *mf*.

patriotic /ˌpætrɪˈɒtɪk, US ˈpeɪt-/ *adj* [*person*] patriote; [*mood, emotion, song*] patriotique.

patriotically /ˌpætrɪˈɒtɪklɪ, US ˌpeɪt-/ *adv* [*react, cheer, say*] en patriote; [*decorated*] de façon patriotique.

patriotism /ˈpætrɪətɪzəm, US ˈpeɪt-/ *n* patriotisme *m*.

patrol /pəˈtrəʊl/ **I** *n* **1** (surveillance, activity) patrouille *f*; **to be/go (out) on ~** être de/aller en patrouille; **air/sea ~** patrouille aérienne/maritime; **foot/traffic/night ~** patrouille à pied/routière/de nuit; **to carry out a ~** faire une ronde; **2** (of group) patrouille *f*; **a military/police ~** une patrouille militaire/de police.
II *modif* [*helicopter, vehicle*] de patrouille.
III *vtr* (*p prés etc* **-ll-**) patrouiller; **a heavily ~led zone** une zone fréquemment patrouillée.
IV *vi* (*p prés etc* **-ll-**) patrouiller.

patrol: **~ boat, ~ vessel** *n* patrouilleur *m*; **~ car** *n* voiture *f* de police; **~ leader** *n* chef *m* de patrouille.

patrolman /pəˈtrəʊlmən/ ▶**1692** *n* **1** US (policeman) agent *m* de police; **2** GB Aut *agent d'un service d'assistance routière privé*.

patrol wagon *n* US fourgon *m* cellulaire.

patron /ˈpeɪtrən/ *n* **1** (supporter) (of artist) mécène *m*; (of person) protecteur/-trice *m/f*; (of cause, charity) bienfaiteur/-trice *m/f*; **~ of the arts** mécène *m*; **to be ~ of an organization** parrainer une organisation; **2** Comm (client) client/-e *m/f* (**of** de); **3** (also **~ saint**) saint/-e *m/f* patron/-onne (**of** de).

patronage /ˈpætrənɪdʒ/ *n* **1** (support) patronage *m*; **under the ~ of** sous le patronage de; **Royal/government ~** patronage royal/de l'État; **~ of the arts** mécénat *m*; **2** Pol (right to appoint) droit *m* de présentation; **3** péj **political ~** copinage *m*; **to get a ~ appointment** obtenir un poste grâce à ses relations; **4** GB Relig droit *m* de disposer d'un bénéfice (ecclésiastique); **5** Comm pratique† *f*.

patronize /ˈpætrənaɪz/ *vtr* **1** péj traiter [qn] avec condescendance; **don't ~ me!** ne prends pas cet air supérieur avec moi!; **2** Comm fréquenter [*restaurant, cinema*]; se fournir chez [*shop*]; **3** (support) protéger [*charity, the arts*].

patronizing /ˈpætrənaɪzɪŋ/ *adj* péj condescendant.

patronizingly /ˈpætrənaɪzɪŋlɪ/ *adv* [*smile, say, treat*] avec condescendance; [*behave*] de façon condescendante.

patron saint *n* saint/-e *m/f* patron/-onne (**of** de).

patronymic /ˌpætrəˈnɪmɪk/ **I** *n* patronyme *m*.
II *adj* patronymique.

patsy° /ˈpætsɪ/ *n* péj pigeon° *m*, dupe *f*.

patter /ˈpætə(r)/ **I** *n* **1** (of raindrops) crépitement *m*; **~ of footsteps** bruit *m* de pas rapides et légers; **we'll soon be hearing the ~ of tiny feet** hum la maison retentira bientôt de rires enfantins; **2**° (of salesman, comedian, magician) baratin° *m*, boniment *m*.
II *vi* [*child, mouse*] trottiner; [*rain, hailstones*] crépiter (**on** sur).

pattern /ˈpætn/ **I** *n* **1** (decorative design) dessin *m*, motif *m*; **striped/floral ~** motif à rayures/de fleurs; **a ~ of roses** un motif de roses; **he drew a ~ in the sand** il a tracé une figure dans le sable; **2** (regular or standard way of happening) **~ of behaviour, behaviour ~** mode *m* de comportement; **working ~s in industry** l'organisation *f* du travail dans l'industrie; **the current ~ of events** la situation actuelle; **the ~ of events leading to the revolution** l'enchaînement des événements qui a conduit à la révolution; **a clear ~ emerges from these statistics** une tendance nette ressort de ces statistiques; **the current scandal is part of a much wider ~ of corruption** le scandale actuel s'inscrit dans un climat de corruption généralisée ; **he could detect a ~ in the plot** il arrivait à discerner une logique dans l'intrigue; **to follow a set ~** se dérouler toujours de la même façon; **traffic ~** distribution *f* de la circulation; **weather ~s** tendances *fpl* climatiques; ▶**trade pattern**; **3** (model, example) modèle *m*; **on the ~ of** sur le modèle de; **to set the ~ for sth** déterminer le modèle de qch; **4** (in dressmaking) patron *m*; (in knitting) modèle *m*; **5** (style of manufacture) style *m*; **6** (sample) (of cloth, wallpaper etc) échantillon *m*; **7** Ling modèle *m*; **8** Tech (for casting metal) modèle *m*.
II *vtr* (model) modeler (**on, after** sur).

pattern book *n* (of fabrics, wallpaper) catalogue *m* d'échantillons; (in dressmaking) catalogue *m* de patrons.

patterned /ˈpætnd/ *adj* [*fabric etc*] à motifs.

patterning /ˈpætnɪŋ/ *n* **1** (patterns) motifs *mpl*; (on animal's coat) (spots) taches *fpl*; (stripes) rayures *fpl*; **2** Psych conditionnement *m*.

patternmaker /ˈpætnmeɪkə(r)/ *n* modeleur/-euse *m/f*.

patty /ˈpætɪ/ *n* **1** US (in hamburger etc) steak *m* haché; **2** (pie) petit feuilleté *m*.

paucity /ˈpɔːsətɪ/ *n* sout (of crops, fuel) pénurie *f*; (of money, evidence, work, information) manque *m*.

Pauline /ˈpɔːlaɪn/ *adj* Relig paulinien/-ienne.

paulownia /pɔːˈləʊnɪə/ *n* Bot paulownia *m*.

paunch /pɔːntʃ/ *n* **1** (of person) ventre *m*, bedaine° *f*; **2** (of ruminant) panse *f*.

paunchy /ˈpɔːntʃɪ/ *adj* péj ventru.

pauper /ˈpɔːpə(r)/ *n* indigent/-e *m/f*; **to die a ~** mourir dans la misère; **~'s funeral** enterrement *m* de pauvre; **~'s grave** fosse *f* commune.

pause /pɔːz/ **I** *n* **1** (brief silence) silence *m*; **an awkward ~** un silence embarrassé; **2** (break) pause *f* (**in** dans; **for** pour); **3** (stoppage) interruption *f*; **there was a ten minute ~ in production** il y a eu une interruption de dix minutes dans la production; **without a ~** sans interruption; **4** Mus point *m* d'orgue; **5** Literat césure *f*.
II *vi* **1** (stop speaking) marquer une pause; **2** (stop) s'arrêter; **to ~ in** interrompre [*activity, work*]; **to ~ for lunch/thought** faire une pause pour déjeuner/réfléchir; **to ~ to do** s'arrêter pour faire; **3** (hesitate) hésiter.
■ **pause over**: **~ over [sth]** s'arrêter sur.

pavane /pəˈvɑːn/ *n* pavane *f*.

pave /peɪv/ *vtr* paver (**with** de).
IDIOMS **to ~ the way for sth** ouvrir la voie à qch.

pavement /ˈpeɪvmənt/ *n* **1** GB (footpath) trottoir *m*; **2** US (roadway) chaussée *f*; (road surface) revêtement *m* (de la chaussée); **3** (paved area) surface *f* pavée; **4** US (material) dallage *m*.

pavement: **~ artist** ▶**1692** *n* GB artiste *mf* qui dessine sur les trottoirs; **~ café** *n* GB ≈ café *m* avec terrasse; **~ stall** *n* GB étalage *m* (dans la rue).

pavilion /pəˈvɪlɪən/ *n* (all contexts) pavillon *m*.

paving /ˈpeɪvɪŋ/ *n* dalles *fpl*.

paving slab, **paving stone** *n* dalle *f*.

pavlova /ˈpævləvə, pævˈləʊvə/ *n* GB, Austral *gâteau meringué aux fruits*.

Pavlovian /pævˈləʊvɪən/ *adj* Psych pavlovien/-ienne; fig [*response, reaction*] conditionné.

paw /pɔː/ **I** *n* (of animal) patte *f*; péj (hand) patte° *f*.
II *vtr* **1** [*animal*] donner des coups de patte à; **to ~ the ground** [*horse*] piaffer; [*bull*] frapper le sol du sabot; **2** péj [*person*] peloter°.

pawky /ˈpɔːkɪ/ *adj* GB pince-sans-rire *inv*.

pawl /pɔːl/ *n* Tech cliquet *m*; Naut linguet *m*.

pawn /pɔːn/ **I** *n* **1** (in chess) pion *m* also fig; **he's just a ~ (in their hands)** il n'est qu'un pion sur l'échiquier; **2** Comm (article deposited) gage *m*, nantissement *m*; **3** Comm **to be in ~** être au mont-de-piété; **to get sth out of ~** dégager qch (du mont-de-piété).
II *vtr* mettre au mont-de-piété.

pawn: **~broker** ▶**1692** *n* prêteur/-euse *m/f* sur gages; **~shop** *n* mont-de-piété *m*, bureau *m* de prêteur sur gages; **~ ticket** *n* reconnaissance *f* du mont-de-piété.

pawpaw GB, **papaw** US /ˈpɔːpɔː/ *n* papaye *f*.

pax /pæks/ **I** *n* Relig baiser *m* de paix.
II°† *excl* GB pouce!

pay /peɪ/ **I** *n* gen salaire *m*; (to manual worker) paie *f*, salaire *m*; (to soldier) solde *f*; (to domestic) gages† *mpl*, salaire *m*; Admin traitement *m*; **back ~** rappel *m* de salaire; **extra ~** prime *f* de salaire; **to be in the ~ of sb** péj être à la solde de qn; **rate of ~** Admin taux de rémunération; **holidays** GB ou **vacation** US **with/without ~** congés payés/sans solde ; **~ and allowances** rémunération principale et indemnités; **what's the ~ like?** est-ce que c'est bien payé?; **the ~ is good** c'est bien payé.
II *modif* [*agreement, claim, negotiations, deal*] salarial; [*rise, cut*] de salaire; [*freeze, structure, policy*] des salaires.
III *vtr* (*prét, pp* **paid**) **1** (for goods, services) payer [*tradesman, creditor*] (**for** pour; **to do** pour faire); payer, régler [*bill, debt, fees*]; payer [*price, sum etc*] (**for** pour); verser [*down payment*] (**on** sur); **to ~ cash** payer comptant; **to ~ £100 on account** verser un acompte de 100 livres; **she paid him £300 to repair the roof** elle l'a payé 300 livres pour réparer le toit; **to ~ sth into** verser qch sur [*account*]; verser qch à [*charity*]; **to ~ sb for his trouble** payer qn de sa peine; **2** (for regular work) payer [*employee*]; **to ~ high/low wages** payer bien/mal; **to be paid weekly/monthly** être payé à la semaine/au mois; **all expenses paid** tous frais payés; **3** Fin (accrue) [*account, bond*] rapporter [*interest*]; **to ~ dividends** fig finir par rapporter; **4** (advantage) (give) **to ~ attention/heed to** faire/prêter attention à; **to ~ a tribute to sb** rendre hommage à qn; **to ~ sb a compliment** faire des compliments à qn; **to ~ sb a visit** rendre visite à qn; **5** (benefit) **it would ~ him/her etc to do** fig il/elle etc y gagnerait à faire; **it would ~ you to find out** tu y gagnerais à te renseigner; **it ~s to be honest** cela paie toujours d'être honnête; **it doesn't ~ to do** cela ne sert à rien de faire; **6** Naut (*prét, pp* **paid** ou **payed**) laisser dériver [*vessel*].
IV *vi* (*prét, pp* **paid**) **1** (hand over money) payer; **she/the insurance will ~** elle/l'assurance paiera; **to ~ for sth** payer qch also fig; **to ~ dearly for sth** fig payer chèrement qch; **I'll make you ~ for this!** fig tu me le paieras!; **I'll ~ for you** (in cinema etc) je vais payer pour toi; **they're paying for him to go to college/to Spain** ils lui paient ses études/son voyage en Espagne; **'~ on entry'** 'paiement à l'entrée'; **you have to ~ to get in** l'entrée est payante; **'~ and display'** (in carpark) 'payez et laissez le ticket en évidence'; **~ on demand** (on cheque) payer à vue; **2** (settle) payer; **to ~ in cash/by cheque/in instalments** payer en espèces/par chèque/à tempérament; **to ~ one's own way** payer sa part; **3** (reward employee) **the work doesn't ~ very well** le travail est mal payé; **4** (bring gain) [*business*] rapporter; [*activity, quality*] payer; **to ~ handsomely** rapporter gros; **crime/dishonesty doesn't ~** le crime/la malhonnêteté ne paie pas; **to ~ for itself** [*business, purchase*] s'amortir; **to make sth ~** rentabiliser qch.
IDIOMS **there'll be hell**° ou **the devil to ~** ça va barder°; **to ~ a visit**° euph aller au petit coin°.
■ **pay back**: ¶ **~ [sb] back** (reimburse) rembourser [*person*]; **I'll ~ him back for the trick he played on me** je lui revaudrai le tour qu'il m'a joué; **he'll ~ you back with interest** fig il te le rendra au centuple; ¶ **~ [sth] back**, **~ back [sth]** rembourser [*money*].
■ **pay down**: **~ [sth] down** verser un acompte de; **I'd like to ~ £100 down** je voudrais verser un acompte de 100 livres.
■ **pay in** GB: **~ [sth] in**, **~ in [sth]** déposer [*cheque, sum*].
■ **pay off**: ¶ **~ off** fig être payant; **his hard work finally paid off** tout le travail qu'il a fourni a finalement été payant; ¶ **~ [sb] off**, **~ off [sb]** **1** (dismiss from work) gen congédier [*worker*]; Naut débarquer [*seaman*]; **2**° (buy silence) acheter le silence de [*possible informer*]; ¶ **~ off [sth]**, **~ [sth] off** rembourser [*mortgage, debt*].
■ **pay out**: **~ out [sth]** **1** (hand over) débourser [*sum*], dépenser [*sum*] (**in** pour); **we've paid out a lot in publicity** on a beaucoup dépensé pour la publicité; **he paid out £300 for his new washing machine** il a payé 300 livres sa nouvelle machine à laver; **2** (release) laisser filer [*rope*].
■ **pay up**° ¶ **~ up** payer; **~ up!** payez!; ¶ **~ up [sth]** payer [*amount*]; **~ up the money you owe me!** paie-moi l'argent que tu me dois!

payable /ˈpeɪəbl/ *adj* **1** (which will be paid) [*amount, interest*] à payer; **the interest ~ on the loan** les intérêts à payer sur le prêt; **to make a cheque ~ to** faire un chèque à l'ordre de; **2** (requiring payment) **to be ~** [*amount, instalment, debt*] être payable; **~ when due** Comm, Fin, Jur payable à l'échéance; **~ on demand** payable à vue; **3** (may be paid) payable; **~ in instalments** payable en plusieurs versements; **4** (profitable) [*proposition, venture*] rentable.

pay-as-you-earn, **PAYE** *n* GB Tax prélèvement *m* de l'impôt à la source.

payback /ˈpeɪbæk/ **I** *n* (of debt) remboursement *m*.
II *modif* [*period*] de remboursement.

pay: **~bed** *n* Med Admin lit *m* payant; **~book** *n* Mil livret *m* de solde; **~ cheque** GB, **pay check** US *n* chèque *m* de paie; **~day** *n* (for wages) jour *m* de paie; (in Stock Exchange) séance *f* de liquidation; **~desk** *n* caisse *f*.

pay dirt *n* US gisement *m* exploitable; **to strike ~**° fig trouver le filon.

PAYE *n* GB Tax *abrév* ▶**pay-as-you-earn**.

payee /peɪˈiː/ *n* bénéficiaire *mf*.

payer /ˈpeɪə(r)/ *n* **1**° gen payeur/-euse *m/f*;

he's a good/bad ~ c'est un bon/mauvais payeur; **2** Comm tireur *m*.

pay gate *n* tourniquet *m*.

paying /ˈpeɪɪŋ/ *adj* [*proposition*] rentable.

paying guest, **PG** *n* hôte *m* payant.

pay: **~ing-in book** GB, **~ing-in deposit book** US *n* carnet *m* de bordereaux de versement; **~ing-in slip** GB, **~ing-in deposit slip** US *n* bordereau *m* de versement.

payload /ˈpeɪləʊd/ *n* **1** (of aircraft, ship) passagers et fret *mpl*; **2** (of bomb) charge *f* explosive; **3** (of spacecraft) charge *f* utile.

paymaster /ˈpeɪmɑːstə(r), US -mæstər/ *n* **1** gen caissier *m*; Naut commissaire *m*; Mil trésorier *m*; **2** péj (employer) commanditaire *m*.

Paymaster General, **PMG** *n* GB trésorier-payeur *m* de l'Échiquier.

payment /ˈpeɪmənt/ *n* gen paiement *m*; (in settlement) règlement *m*; (into account, of instalments) versement *m*; (to creditor) remboursement *m*; fig (for kindness, help) récompense *f* also iron; **to make a ~** faire ou effectuer un paiement; **cash ~** (not credit) paiement comptant; (not cheque) paiement en liquide; **in ~ for the books received** en règlement de ma commande de livres; **in ~ for what I owe** en remboursement de ce que je dois; **~ in full is now requested** un règlement complet est désormais exigé; **in monthly ~s of £30** en mensualités de 30 livres; **~ on** (instalment) traite de [*television, washing machine etc*]; **on ~ of £30** moyennant 30 livres; **Social Security ~s** prestations *fpl* de la Sécurité sociale; **in ~ for your kindness** en récompense de votre gentillesse.

payoff /ˈpeɪɒf/ *n* (reward) récompense *f*; fig bouquet *m*.

payola○ /peɪˈəʊlə/ *n* US (bribe) pot-de-vin *m*; (practice) pratique *f* des pots-de-vin.

pay: **~-packet** *n* enveloppe *f* de paie; fig paie *f*; **~ phone** *n* téléphone *m* public.

payroll /ˈpeɪrəʊl/ *n* (list) fichier *m* des salaires; (sum of money) paie *f* (de tous les employés); (employees collectively) ensemble *m* du personnel; **to be on a company's ~** être employé par une entreprise; **to take sb off the ~** licencier qn; **a ~ of 500 workers** un effectif de 500 ouvriers.

pay: **~round** *n* négociation *f* des salaires; **~slip** *n* bulletin *m* de salaire; **~ television** *n* télévision *f* à péage.

PBX *n* GB Télécom (*abrév* = **private branch exchange**) commutateur *m* privé, standard *m* privé.

pc *n* **1** (also **PC**) *abrév* ▶ **personal computer**; **2** *abrév* ▶ **per cent**; **3** *abrév* ▶ **postcard**; **4** (also **PC**) *abrév* ▶ **political correctness, politically correct**.

p/c *n* **1** (*abrév* = **prices current**) prix *mpl* courants; **2** *abrév* ▶ **petty cash**.

PC *n* GB **1** *abrév* ▶ **Police Constable**; **2** *abrév* ▶ **Privy Council, Privy Councillor**.

PCB *n* (*abrév* = **polychlorinated biphenyl**) polychlorobiphényle *m*.

PCN *n* (*abrév* = **Personal Communications Network**) PCN *m*.

pd (*abrév* = **paid**) payé.

PD *n* US *abrév* ▶ **Police Department**.

pdq○ (*abrév* = **pretty damn quick**) illico○.

PDQ machine *n* TPV *m*, terminal *m* point de vente.

PE *n*: *abrév* ▶ **physical education**.

pea /piː/ *n* **1** Bot pois *m*; **2** Culin (also **green ~**) petit pois *m*.
IDIOMS **to be as like as two ~s in a pod** se ressembler comme deux gouttes d'eau.

peabrain○ /ˈpiːbreɪn/ *n* cervelle *f* d'oiseau.

peace /piːs/ **I** *n* **1** (absence of conflict) paix *f*; **to be at ~** être en paix; **to make ~** faire la paix (**with** avec); **to bring ~ to a country** rétablir la paix dans un pays; **to keep the ~** (between countries, individuals) maintenir la paix; (in town) [*police*] maintenir l'ordre public; [*citizen*] ne pas troubler l'ordre public; **2** (period without war) paix *f*; **a fragile/an uneasy/a negotiated ~** une paix fragile/instable/négociée; **3** (tranquillity) paix *f*, tranquillité *f*; **to live in ~** vivre en paix; **to leave sb in ~/give sb no ~** laisser qn/ne pas laisser qn en paix; **to break the ~ of sth** troubler la paix de qch; **I need a bit of ~ and quiet** j'ai besoin d'un peu de calme; **to find ~ of mind** trouver la paix; **to disturb sb's ~ of mind** troubler qn; **to be at ~** euph (dead) avoir trouvé la paix.
II *modif* [*campaign, march, moves*] pour la paix; [*agreement, conference, initiative, mission, plan, settlement, talks, treaty*] de paix.
IDIOMS **to be a man of ~** être un homme de paix; **to come in ~** venir avec des intentions pacifiques; **to hold one's ~** rester muet; **to make one's ~ with sb** faire la paix avec qn.

peaceable /ˈpiːsəbl/ *adj* [*person*] pacifique.

peaceably /ˈpiːsəblɪ/ *adv* pacifiquement.

peace: **~ campaigner** *n* militant/-e *m/f* pacifiste; **Peace Corps** *n* US Admin *organisation composée de volontaires pour l'aide aux pays en voie de développement*; **~ envoy** *n* négociateur/-trice *m/f* de paix.

peaceful /ˈpiːsfl/ *adj* **1** (tranquil) [*place, holiday, scene*] paisible; **2** (without conflict) [*coexistence, protest, solution, reign*] pacifique.

peacefully /ˈpiːsfəlɪ/ *adv* **1** (without disturbance) [*die, sleep*] paisiblement; [*situated*] à un endroit paisible; **2** (without violence) [*demonstrate*] pacifiquement; **the demonstration passed off ~** la manifestation s'est déroulée dans le calme.

peacefulness /ˈpiːsflnɪs/ *n* **1** (calm) tranquillité *f*; **2** (nonviolent nature) caractère *m* pacifique; **the ~ of her reign** la paix qui caractérisa son règne.

peacekeeping /ˈpiːskiːpɪŋ/ **I** *n* Mil, Pol maintien *m* de la paix.
II *modif* [*force, troops*] de maintien de la paix.

peace: **~ lobby** *n* US *lobby pour la paix et le désarmement nucléaire*; **~-loving** *adj* pacifique.

peacemaker /ˈpiːsmeɪkə(r)/ *n* **1** Pol (statesman, nation) artisan *m* de la paix; **2** (in family) conciliateur *m*.

peace: **Peace Movement** *n* Mouvement *m* pour la paix; **~ offensive** *n* offensive *f* de paix; **~ offering** *n* gage *m* de réconciliation; **~ pipe** *n* calumet *m* de la paix; **~ studies** *n* (+ *v sg* ou *pl*) études *fpl* sur la paix.

peacetime /ˈpiːstaɪm/ **I** *n* temps *m* de paix; **in ~** en temps de paix.
II *modif* [*activity*] qui se pratique en temps de paix; [*army, alliance, training*] en temps de paix; [*planning, government, administration*] de temps de paix.

peach /piːtʃ/ **I** *n* **1** (fruit) pêche *f*; (tree) pêcher *m*; **2** (colour) (couleur *f*) pêche *f*; **3**○ **a ~ of a game**○ un match formidable.
II *modif* [*jam, yoghurt*] aux pêches; [*stone*] de pêche.
III *adj* couleur *f* pêche *inv*.
IV *vi*○ argot des prisonniers **to ~ on sb** moucharder○ qn.

peach: **~ blossom** *n* fleurs *fpl* de pêcher; **~ brandy** *n* eau-de-vie *f* de pêche; **~es and cream** *adj* [*complexion*] de pêche; **~ melba** *n* pêche *f* Melba.

peacock /ˈpiːkɒk/ *n* paon *m*.
IDIOMS **to be as proud as a ~** être fier/fière comme un paon.

peacock: **~ blue** ▶ **1104** *n, adj* bleu (*m*) canard *inv*; **~ butterfly** *n* paon *m* de jour.

pea green *n, adj* vert (*m*) pomme *inv*.

peahen /ˈpiːhen/ *n* paonne *f*.

pea jacket *n* caban *m*.

peak /piːk/ **I** *n* **1** (of mountain) pic *m* (**of** de); **2** (of cap) visière *f*; **3** Stat (of inflation, quantity, demand, price, market) maximum *m* (**in** dans; **of** de); (in hormone, popularity) pic *m*; (on a graph) sommet *m*; **to be at its** ou **a ~** être à son maximum; **4** fig (high point) (of career, achievement, empire, mental powers, creativity) apogée *m* (**of** de); (of fitness, form) meilleur *m* (**of** de); **her success is at its ~, she is at the ~ of her success** son succès a atteint son apogée; **her fitness is at its ~, she is at the ~ of her fitness** elle est au meilleur de sa forme; **at his ~, he earned** ... à l'apogée de sa carrière, il gagnait ...; **in the ~ of condition** en excellente santé; **to be past its** ou **one's ~** avoir fait son temps; **5** (busiest time) gen heure *f* de pointe; Telecom heures *fpl* rouges; **to cost 40 pence ~** Telecom coûter 40p au tarif rouge; **6** (of roof) faîte *m*; (of hair) banane *f*; **'beat the egg white until it forms stiff ~s'** 'battre les blancs jusqu'à ce qu'ils deviennent fermes'.
II *modif* [*demand, figure, level, population, price, risk*] maximum, maximal; [*fitness, form, performance*] meilleur.
III *vi* [*inflation, rate, market, workload*] culminer (**at** à); fig [*career, performance, enthusiasm, interest*] culminer; **to ~ in May/in the morning** culminer en mai/dans la matinée; **to ~ too early** [*runner*] se lancer trop tôt; [*prodigy*] s'épanouir trop tôt; (in career) réussir trop tôt.
■ **peak out**○ [*athlete, prowess, skill, luck*] commencer à décliner; [*inflation, rate*] commencer à décroître.

peak demand *n* gen demande *f* record; Elec période *f* de consommation de pointe.

peaked /piːkt/ *adj* **1** (with peak) [*cap, hat*] à visière; **2** (pointed) [*roof*] pointu; **3** US = **peaky**.

peak hour **I** *n* (on road, in shops) heure *f* de pointe; **at** ou **during ~s** aux heures de pointe.
II *modif* [*delays, problems, traffic*] des heures de pointe.

peak: **~ listening time** *n* Radio heures *fpl* de grande écoute; **~ load** *n* charge *f* maximale.

peak period *n* (on road, in shops) période *f* de pointe; **at** ou **during ~s** en période de pointe.

peak rate *n* Telecom tarif *m* rouge; **at ~** pendant les heures rouges.

peak season *n* haute saison *f*.

peak time **I** *n* **1** (on TV) heures *fpl* de grande écoute; **at** ou **during ~** aux heures de grande écoute; **2** (for switchboard, traffic) heures *fpl* de pointe.
II *modif* [*viewing, programme*] de grande écoute; [*series*] diffusé aux heures de grande écoute.

peaky○ /ˈpiːkɪ/ *adj* pâlot/-otte.

peak year *n* année *f* record.

peal /piːl/ **I** *n* **1** (sound) (of bells) carillonnement *m*; (of doorbell) sonnerie *f*; (of thunder) grondement *m*; (of organ) retentissement *m*; **~s of laughter** éclats *mpl* de rire; **2** Tech (in bell-ringing) (motif, set of bells) carillon *m*.
II *vi* = **peal out**.
III *vtr* sonner (à toute volée) [*bells*].
■ **peal out** [*bells*] carillonner; [*thunder*] gronder; [*organ*] retentir; [*laughter*] éclater.

peanut /ˈpiːnʌt/ **I** *n* (nut) cacahuète *f*; (plant) arachide *f*.
II peanuts○ *npl* (meagre sum of money) clopinettes○ *fpl*; **they're paid ~s** ils sont payés trois fois rien.

peanut: **~ butter** *n* beurre *m* de cacahuètes; **~ gallery** *n* Theat poulailler○ *m*; **~ oil** *n* huile *f* d'arachide.

pea pod *n* cosse *f* de pois.

pear /peə(r)/ *n* **1** (fruit) poire *f*; **~-shaped** en forme de poire, piriforme; **2** (also **~ tree**) poirier *m*.

pearl /pɜːl/ ▶ **1104** **I** *n* **1** (real, imitation) perle *f*; fig (of dew, sweat) perle *f* (**of** de); **natural ~** perle fine ou naturelle; **2** fig (prized person, object) perle *f*; (city, building) joyau *m*; **~s of wisdom** trésors *mpl* de sagesse; **3** (colour) (couleur *f*) perle *f*.

II *modif* [*necklace, brooch, etc*] de perles; [*button*] en nacre; **~ earrings** boucles *fpl* d'oreilles en perles.
III *adj* couleur perle *inv*.
IV *vi* **1** littér [*dew, liquid*] perler; **2** [*diver, fisherman*] pêcher les perles.

pearl: **~ barley** *n* orge *m* perlé; **~ diver** *n* pêcheur/-euse *m/f* de perles; **~ diving** *n* pêche *f* des perles; **~ grey** ▶ **1104** *n, adj* gris (*m*) perle *inv*.

pearl-handled /ˌpɜːlˈhændld/ *adj* [*knife, hairbrush etc*] au manche de nacre; [*revolver*] à la crosse en nacre.

pearl: **~ necklace** *n* collier *m* de perles; **~ oyster** *n* huître *f* perlière.

pearly /ˈpɜːlɪ/ *adj* nacré.

Pearly Gates *npl* **the ~** hum les portes *fpl* du Paradis.

pearly king, pearly queen *n* GB *marchand ou marchande des quatre saisons de l'est londonien dans son costume traditionnel cousu de boutons de nacre*.

peasant /ˈpeznt/ **I** *n* **1** (rustic) paysan/-anne *m/f*; **2** péj plouc◐ *mf*, paysan/-anne *m/f* pej.
II *modif* [*class, custom, cuisine, craft, life*] paysan/-anne; [*costume*] de paysan/-anne.

peasant farmer ▶ **1692** *n* paysan *m*.

peasantry /ˈpezntrɪ/ *n* (+ *v sg ou pl*) paysannerie *f*.

peasant woman *n* paysanne *f*.

pease pudding /ˌpiːzˈpʊdɪŋ/ *n* GB purée *f* de pois cassés.

pea shooter *n* sarbacane *f*.

pea soup *n* **1** lit soupe *f* aux pois; **2** (fog) (also **pea souper**) purée *f* de pois.

peat /piːt/ **I** *n* **1** (substance) tourbe *f*; **to cut** ou **dig ~** extraire de la tourbe; **2** (piece) morceau *m* de tourbe.
II *modif* [*lands, soil*] tourbeux/-euse; [*cutting, shrinkage*] de la tourbe.

peat: **~ bog** *n* tourbière *f*; **~ cutter** *n* tourbier *m*; **~ moss** *n* sphaigne *f*.

peaty /ˈpiːtɪ/ *adj* tourbeux/-euse.

pebble /ˈpebl/ **I** *n* **1** caillou *m*; (on beach) galet *m*; **2** Tech cristal *m* de roche.
II *modif* [*beach*] de galets.
IDIOMS **he's not the only ~ on the beach** il n'y a pas que lui sur terre.

pebbledash /ˈpebldæʃ/ **I** *n* crépi *m*, mouchetis *m*.
II *modif* [*wall*] en crépi, moucheté.
III *vtr* crépir.

pecan /ˈpiːkən, prˈkæn, US prˈkɑːn/ **I** *n* **1** (nut) noix *f* de pecan; **2** (tree) pacanier *m*.
II *modif* [*pie*] aux noix de pecan.

peccadillo /ˌpekəˈdɪləʊ/ *n* (*pl* **~s** ou **~es**) peccadille *f*.

peccary /ˈpekərɪ/ *n* pécari *m*.

peck /pek/ **I** *n* **1** (from bird) coup *m* de bec; **2**○ (kiss) bise *f*; **to give sb a ~ (on the cheek)** faire or donner une bise à qn; **3** Meas ≈ picotin *m*.
II *vtr* **1** (with beak) [*bird*] picorer [*food*]; donner un coup de bec à [*person, animal*]; **the bird ~ed my hand** l'oiseau m'a donné un coup de bec à la main; **to ~ a hole in sth** faire un trou dans qch à (force de) coups de bec; **2**○ (kiss) faire or donner une bise à [*person*].
III *vi* **1** (with beak) **to ~ at** picorer [*food*]; donner des coups de bec contre [*window, tree*]; **the hens were ~ing at the ground in the yard** les poules picoraient dans la cour; **2**○ fig (eat very little) **to ~ at one's food** [*person*] chipoter.
■ **peck out**: **~ [sth] out, ~ out [sth]** arracher [qch] à coups de bec [*kernel, seeds*]; **to ~ sb's eyes out** [*bird*] crever les yeux à qn.

pecker◐ /ˈpekə(r)/ *n* zob *m*◐, pénis *m*.
IDIOMS **to keep one's ~ up** GB ne pas se laisser démonter.

peckerwood /ˈpekəwʊd/ *n* US injur nègre *m* blanc offensive.

pecking order *n* lit, fig ordre *m* hiérarchique.

peckish○ /ˈpekɪʃ/ *adj* GB **to be** ou **feel ~** avoir un petit creux○, avoir un peu faim.

pecs○ /peks/ *npl* pectoraux *mpl*.

pectin /ˈpektɪn/ *n* pectine *f*.

pectoral /ˈpektərəl/ **I** *n* (ornament) pectoral *m*.
II **pectorals** *npl* pectoraux *mpl*.
III *adj* pectoral.

peculate /ˈpekjʊleɪt/ *vtr* Fin détourner [*funds*].

peculation /ˌpekjʊˈleɪʃn/ *n* Fin détournement *m* de fonds publics.

peculiar /prˈkjuːlɪə(r)/ *adj* **1** (odd) bizarre, curieux/-ieuse, étrange (**that** que + *subj*); **to feel ~** se sentir bizarre; **funny ~**○ hum bizarre; **2** (exceptional) [*situation, importance, circumstances*] particulier/-ière; **3** (exclusive to) [*characteristic, language, system*] particulier/-ière; **to be ~ to sb/sth** [*feature, trait*] être particulier/-ière à or propre à qn/qch; **the species is ~ to Asia** on ne trouve cette espèce qu'en Asie; **he has his own ~ way of doing it** il a sa façon bien à lui de le faire.

peculiarity /prˌkjuːlɪˈærətɪ/ *n* **1** (feature) particularité *f*; **2** (strangeness) bizarrerie *f*.

peculiarly /prˈkjuːlɪəlɪ/ *adv* **1** (strangely) de façon étrange; **2** (particularly) particulièrement.

pecuniary /prˈkjuːnɪərɪ, US -ɪerɪ/ *adj* pécuniaire.

pedagogic(al) /ˌpedəˈgɒdʒɪkl/ *adj* pédagogique.

pedagogue /ˈpedəgɒg/ *n* pédagogue *mf*.

pedagogy /ˈpedəgɒdʒɪ/ *n* pédagogie *f*.

pedal /ˈpedl/ **I** *n* (all contexts) pédale *f*; **loud/soft ~** Mus pédale forte/douce.
II *vtr* (*p prés etc* **-ll-** GB, **-l-** US) **to ~ a bicycle** pédaler.
III *vi* (*p prés etc* **-ll-** GB, **-l-** US) **1** (use pedal) pédaler; **to ~ hard** ou **furiously** pédaler dur; **2** (cycle) **to ~ down/up/through** descendre/monter/traverser à vélo; **to ~ along/towards** pédaler le long de/vers.

pedal: **~ bin** *n* GB poubelle *f* à pédale; **~ boat** *n* pédalo® *m*; **~ car** *n* voiture *f* à pédales; **~ cycle** *n* bicyclette *f*.

pedalo /ˈpedələʊ/ *n* surtout GB (*pl* **~s** ou **~es**) pédalo® *m*.

pedal: **~ pushers** *npl* Fashn pantalon *m* corsaire; **~ steel guitar** *n* guitare *f* hawaïenne.

pedant /ˈpednt/ *n* pédant/-e *m/f*.

pedantic /prˈdæntɪk/ *adj* pédant (**about** dans le domaine de).

pedantically /prˈdæntɪklɪ/ *adv* de façon pédante.

pedantry /ˈpedntrɪ/ *n* pédantisme *m*.

peddle /ˈpedl/ **I** *vtr* colporter [*wares, ideas*]; **to ~ drugs** faire du trafic de drogue (*à petite échelle*).
II *vi* faire du colportage.

peddler /ˈpedlə(r)/ *n* **1 drug ~** trafiquant *m*; **street ~** camelot *m*; **2** US = pedlar.

pederast /ˈpedəræst/ *n* pédéraste *m*.

pederasty /ˈpedəræstɪ/ *n* pédérastie *f*.

pedestal /ˈpedɪstl/ *n* (of statue, column, ornament) socle *m*, piédestal *m*; (of washbasin) colonne *f*.
IDIOMS **to put sb on a ~** mettre qn sur un piédestal; **to knock sb off their ~** détrôner qn.

pedestal: **~ desk** *n* bureau *m* ministre; **~ table** *n* guéridon *m*; **~ washbasin** *n* lavabo-colonne *m*.

pedestrian /prˈdestrɪən/ **I** *n* piéton *m*; **for ~s only** réservé aux piétons.
II *modif* [*street, area*] piétonnier/-ière, piéton/-onne.
III *adj* (humdrum) terre à terre *inv*.

pedestrian crossing *n* passage *m* pour piétons, passage *m* clouté.

pedestrianization /prˌdestrɪənaɪˈzeɪʃn, US -nɪˈz-/ *n* transformation *f* en zone piétonnière.

pedestrianize /prˈdestrɪənaɪz/ *vtr* transformer [qch] en zone piétonnière [*street, town centre*].

pedestrian: **~ precinct** *n* GB zone *f* piétonne; **~ traffic** *n* ¢ piétons *mpl*.

pediatric /ˌpiːdɪˈætrɪk/ *adj* [*ward, department*] de pédiatrie; [*illness*] infantile; **~ medicine** pédiatrie *f*; **~ nurse** puéricultrice *f*; **~ nursing** puériculture *f*.

pediatrician /ˌpiːdɪəˈtrɪʃn/ ▶ **1692** *n* pédiatre *mf*.

pediatrics /ˌpiːdɪˈætrɪks/ *n* (+ *v sg*) pédiatrie *f*.

pedicab /ˈpedɪkæb/ *n* cyclo-pousse *m*.

pedicure /ˈpedɪkjʊə(r)/ *n* pédicurie *f*; **to have a ~** se faire soigner les pieds.

pedigree /ˈpedɪgriː/ **I** *n* **1** (ancestry) (of animal) pedigree *m*; (of person, family) (line) ascendance *f*; (tree, chart) arbre *m* généalogique; (background) origines *fpl*; **2** (purebred animal) animal *m* avec pedigree; **my dog is a ~** mon chien a un pedigree; **3** fig (of book, sportsman, artist) antécédents *mpl*.
II *modif* [*animal*] de pure race; **~ registration certificate** pedigree *m*, certificat *m* d'origine.

pediment /ˈpedɪmənt/ *n* fronton *m*.

pedlar /ˈpedlə(r)/ *n* colporteur/-euse *m/f*.

pedological /ˌpedəˈlɒdʒɪkl/ *adj* pédologique.

pedologist /prˈdɒlədʒɪst/ ▶ **1692** *n* pédologue *mf*.

pedology /prˈdɒlədʒɪ/ *n* pédologie *f*.

pedometer /prˈdɒmɪtə(r)/ *n* podomètre *m*.

pedophile /ˈpedəfaɪl/ *n* pédophile *mf*.

pedophilia /ˌpedəˈfɪlɪə/ *n* pédophilie *f*.

pee○ /piː/ **I** *n* pipi○ *m*; **to have** ou **do a ~** faire pipi○.
II *vi* faire pipi○; (more vulgar) pisser◐.

peek /piːk/ **I** *n* coup *m* d'œil furtif; **to have** ou **take a ~ at sb/sth** jeter un coup d'œil furtif à qn/qch.
II *vi* jeter un coup d'œil furtif (**at** à, sur); **she was ~ing out at me from behind the curtains** elle me jetait des coups d'œil de derrière les rideaux; **no ~ing!** on ne regarde pas!

peekaboo /ˌpiːkəˈbuː/ *excl* coucou!; **to play ~** jouer à faire coucou.

peel /piːl/ **I** *n* (before peeling) peau *f*; (after peeling) épluchures *fpl*; **potato ~** épluchures *fpl* de pommes de terre.
II *vtr* éplucher [*vegetable, fruit*]; décortiquer [*prawn, shrimp*]; écorcer [*stick*].
III *vi* [*paint*] s'écailler; [*sunburnt person, skin*] peler; [*fruit, vegetable*] s'éplucher.
■ **peel away** ¶ [*paper, plastic*] se décoller; [*paint*] s'écailler; [*skin*] peler; ¶ **~ away [sth], ~ [sth] away** décoller [*layer, paper, plastic*].
■ **peel back** = **peel away**.
■ **peel off** ¶ **1** (become removed) [*label*] se détacher (**from** de); [*paint*] s'écailler; [*paper*] se décoller; **2**○ hum (undress) se dévêtir; **3** Aviat [*plane*] quitter sa formation; ¶ **~ off [sth], ~ [sth] off** enlever [*clothing, label, leaves*].
■ **peel out** US **1**○ (accelerate) démarrer en trombe○; **2** [*bells*] tinter.

peeler /ˈpiːlə(r)/ *n* **1** Culin (manual) économe *m*; (electric) éplucheur *m* électrique; **potato ~** épluche-légumes *m inv*; **2**○ US (stripper) strip-teaseuse *f*, effeuilleuse○ *f*.

peeling /ˈpiːlɪŋ/ **I** *n* (skin of fruit, vegetable) épluchure *f*; **potato ~s** épluchures *fpl* de pommes de terre.
II *adj* [*walls, paint, surface*] qui s'écaille; [*skin*] qui pèle.

peep /piːp/ **I** *n* **1** (look) (quick) coup *m* d'œil; **to have a ~ at sth** jeter un coup d'œil à qch; (furtively) regarder qch à la dérobée; **can I have a ~?** puis-je jeter un coup d'œil?; **2** (noise) (of chick) pépiement *m*; (of mouse) couinement *m*; (of car horn) coup *m* de klaxon®;

there wasn't a ~ out of him il n'a pas pipé mot; **one more ~ out of you and...** je ne veux plus entendre un mot, sinon...
II *vi* **1** (look) jeter un coup d'œil (**over** par-dessus; **through** par); **to ~ at sth/sb** gen jeter un coup d'œil à qch/qn; (furtively) regarder qch/qn furtivement; **no ~ing!** défense de regarder!; **to ~ round the door** passer la tête dans l'entrebâillement de la porte; **2** littér **daylight was ~ing through the curtains** le jour filtrait à travers les rideaux; **3** (make noise) [*chick*] pépier; [*mouse*] couiner; [*car horn*] klaxonner.
IDIOMS **at the ~ of day** aux premiers feux du jour.
■ **peep out** [*person, animal*] se montrer, apparaître; [*gun, hanky*] dépasser; **she ~ed out from behind the curtains** elle épiait de derrière les rideaux; **the sun ~ed out from behind the clouds** le soleil est apparu derrière les nuages; **to ~ out of** [*gun, hanky, pencil*] dépasser de [*bag, pocket*].

peeper○ /ˈpiːpə(r)/ *n* **1** (eye) quinquet○ *m*, œil *m*; **2** (voyeur) voyeur/-euse *m/f*.

peep: **~hole** /ˈpiːphəʊl/ *n* gen trou *m*; (in door) judas *m*; **Peeping Tom**○ *n* voyeur *m*; **~show** /ˈpiːpʃəʊ/ *n* peep-show *m*; **~toe sandals** *npl* escarpins *mpl* à bouts découpés; **~-toe shoe** *n* chaussure *f* à bout ouvert.

peer /pɪə(r)/ **I** *n* **1** (equal) (in status) pair *m*; (in profession) collègue *mf*; **2** (contemporary) (adult) personne *f* de la même génération; (child) personne *f* du même âge; **to be tried by one's ~s** être jugé par ses pairs; **3** GB Pol (also **~ of the realm**) pair *m*; **4** (person of equal merit) égal/-e *m/f*; **to be without ~** ou **to have no ~ as a surgeon** ne pas avoir d'égal comme chirurgien.
II *vi* **to ~ at** regarder (fixement); **to ~ shortsightedly/anxiously at sth** regarder qch avec des yeux de myope/d'un air inquiet; **to ~ through/over** regarder par/par-dessus; **to ~ into the mist** chercher à discerner quelque chose dans la brume.

peerage /ˈpɪərɪdʒ/ *n* **1** GB Pol (aristocracy) pairie *f*; **2** GB Pol (title) pairie *f*; **to raise sb to the ~** conférer le titre de pair à qn; **to be given a ~** être anobli; **3** (book) nobiliaire *m*.

peeress /ˈpɪəres/ *n* GB Pol pairesse *f*.

peer group *n* **1** (of same status) pairs *mpl*; **2** (contemporary) (adults) personnes *fpl* de la même génération; (children) enfants *mpl* du même âge.

peer group pressure *n* pression *f* du groupe.

peerless /ˈpɪəlɪs/ *adj* hors pair *inv*.

peeve○ /piːv/ **I** *n* bête *f* noire.
II *vtr* mettre [qn] en rogne○, irriter; **it ~s me that** cela m'irrite que (+ *subj*).

peeved○ /piːvd/ *adj* [*person, expression*] irrité, en rogne○.

peevish /ˈpiːvɪʃ/ *adj* grognon.

peevishly /ˈpiːvɪʃlɪ/ *adj* d'un air grognon.

peevishness /ˈpiːvɪʃnɪs/ *n* maussaderie *f*.

peewee /ˈpiːwiː/ *n, adj* US tout petit/toute petite (*m/f*).

peewit /ˈpiːwɪt/ *n* vanneau *m*.

peg /peg/ **I** *n* **1** (to hang garment) patère *f*; **2** GB (also **clothes ~**) pince *f* à linge; **3** (to mark place in ground, game) piquet *m*; (for surveying) piquet *m* d'arpentage; **4** (in carpentry) cheville *f*; **5** (for tuning) cheville *f*; **6** Econ indice *m*; **7** (barrel stop) fausset *m*; **8** (piton) piton *m*; **9** GB (small drink) goutte○ *f*, doigt *m*.
II *vtr* (*p prés etc* **-gg-**) **1** (fasten cloth) **to ~ sth on ou onto a line** accrocher qch sur une corde avec des pinces [*washing*]; **to ~ sth down** ou **in place** fixer qch avec des piquets [*fabric, tent*]; **2** (fasten wood) cheviller (**to** à; **together** ensemble); **3** Econ indexer [*price, currency, rate*] (**to** sur); **to ~ sth at 10%/at present levels** indexer qch à 10%/au niveau actuel; **to ~ sth for 12 months** indexer qch pour une durée de 12 mois; **4** US (characterize) cataloguer [*person*] (**as** comme).
III **pegged** *pp adj* [*price, rate, tax*] indexé.
IDIOMS **to be a square ~ (in a round hole)** ne pas être dans son élément; **to be taken** ou **brought down a ~ (or two)**○ être rabaissé d'un cran (ou deux); **to take** ou **bring sb down a ~ (or two)**○ remettre qn à sa place; **to use sth as a ~ (to hang a discussion/a theory on)** se servir de qch comme prétexte (pour entamer la discussion/exposer une théorie).
■ **peg away**○ travailler ferme, bosser○ (**at** sur).
■ **peg out**: ¶ **~ out**○ (die) claquer○; (collapse) s'écrouler de fatigue; ¶ **~ out [sth]**, **~ [sth] out** **1** GB (hang out) étendre [*washing*]; **2** (stake out) délimiter [*land*]; **3** (spread out) tendre [qch] avec des piquets [*hide*].

Pegasus /ˈpegəsəs/ *pr n* Mythol Pégase.

peg: **~board** *n* Games, gen panneau *m* alvéolé; **~ doll(y)** *n* GB poupée *f* fabriquée à partir d'une pince à linge; **~ leg** *n* jambe *f* de bois; **~(-top) pants** US, **~(-top) trousers** GB *npl* pantalon *m* serré à la cheville.

pejoration /ˌpɪdʒəˈreɪʃn/ *n* péjoration *f*.

pejorative /pɪˈdʒɒrətɪv, US -ˈdʒɔːr-/ *adj* péjoratif/-ive.

peke○ /piːk/ *n* Zool pékinois *m*.

Pekin(g)ese /ˌpiːkɪˈniːz/ ▶ **1402** *n* Ling, Zool pékinois *m*.

Peking /ˌpiːˈkɪŋ/ ▶ **1818** *pr n* Pékin.

Peking duck *n* ≈ canard *m* laqué.

pekoe /ˈpiːkəʊ/ *n* pekoe *m*.

pelagic /pəˈlædʒɪk/ *adj* pélagique.

pelargonium /ˌpeləˈgəʊnɪəm/ *n* pélargonium *m*.

pelf /pelf/ *n* péj lucre *m* pej.

pelican /ˈpelɪkən/ *n* pélican *m*.

pelican crossing *n* GB passage *m* pour piétons.

pellagra /pɪˈlægrə, -ˈleɪg-/ ▶ **1354** *n* pellagre *f*.

pellet /ˈpelɪt/ *n* **1** (of paper, wax, mud) boulette *f*; **2** (of shot) plomb *m*; **3** Zool boulette *f* de résidus regorgés; **4** Pharm cachet *m*; **5** Chem gélule *f*; **6** Agric granulé *m*.

pell-mell /ˌpelˈmel/ *adv* pêle-mêle.

pellucid /peˈluːsɪd/ *adj* pellucide.

pelmet /ˈpelmɪt/ *n* cantonnière *f*.

Peloponnese /ˈpeləpəniːs/ *pr n* Péloponnèse *m*.

Peloponnesian /ˌpeləpəˈniːʃn/ *adj* péloponnésien/-ienne; **the ~ war** la guerre du Péloponnèse.

pelota /pəˈləʊtə/ ▶ **1282** *n* pelote *f* basque.

pelt /pelt/ **I** *n* (fur) fourrure *f*; (hide) peau *f*.
II **at full pelt** *adv phr* à toute vitesse.
III *vtr* bombarder [qn]; **to ~ sb with sth** lancer une volée de qch à qn [*stones*].
IV *vi* **1** (fall) (also **~ down**) [*rain*] tomber à verse; **it's ~ing with rain** il pleut à verse; **the ~ing rain** la pluie battante; **2**○ (run) [*person*] courir à toutes jambes; **to ~ down/across the road** descendre/traverser la rue à toutes jambes.

pelvic /ˈpelvɪk/ *adj* pelvien/-ienne; **~ floor** plancher *m* pelvien; **~ girdle** ceinture *f* pelvienne.

pelvic inflammatory disease, PID ▶ **1354** *n* inflammation *f* pelvienne.

pelvis /ˈpelvɪs/ ▶ **1037** *n* bassin *m*, pelvis *m* spec; **upper/lower ~** grand/petit bassin.

pemmican /ˈpemɪkən/ *n* pemmican *m*.

pen /pen/ **I** *n* **1** (for writing) stylo *m*; **to put** ou **run one's ~ through sth** barrer qch; **to put ~ to paper** (write) écrire, prendre la plume; (give signature) signer; **to live by one's ~** vivre de sa plume; **2** (enclosure) (for animals) parc *m*, enclos *m*; (for child) parc *m*; **3** Zool cygne *m* femelle; **4**○ US (*abrév* = **penitentiary**) taule○ *f*, prison *f*.
II *vtr* (*p prés etc* **-nn-**) **1** (write) écrire [*letter, article*]; **2** (also **~ in**) enfermer, parquer [*sheep, pigs*].

penal /ˈpiːnl/ *n* [*reform, law, code, system*] pénal; [*colony, institution*] pénitentiaire; **~ servitude** Hist travaux *mpl* forcés.

penalization /ˌpiːnəlaɪˈzeɪʃn, US -lɪˈz-/ *n* (all contexts) pénalisation *f*.

penalize /ˈpiːnəlaɪz/ *vtr* (all contexts) pénaliser (**for** pour); **to ~ sb for doing** pénaliser qn pour avoir fait.

penalty /ˈpenltɪ/ *n* **1** Jur, gen (punishment) peine *f*, pénalité *f*; (fine) amende *f*; **on** ou **under ~ of** sous peine de; **the ~ for this offence is...** ce délit est passible d'une peine de...; **2** Tax pénalité *f*; **3** fig (unpleasant result) prix *m* (**for** de); **to pay the ~ for sth** payer le prix de qch, subir les conséquences de qch; **4** Sport (in soccer) penalty *m*, (in rugby) pénalité *f*; **to score (from) a ~** (in soccer) marquer un penalty; **to take a ~** tirer un penalty; **5** Games amende *f*; **a ten-point ~ for a wrong answer** une amende de dix points pour une mauvaise réponse.

penalty: **~ area** *n* Sport surface *f* de réparation; **~ box** *n* (in soccer) surface *f* de réparation; (in ice-hockey) banc *m* des pénalités; **~ clause** *n* Comm, Jur clause *f* pénale; **~ goal** *n* Sport (in rugby) but *m* sur pénalité; **~ kick** *n* Sport (in rugby) coup *m* de pied de pénalité; (in soccer) penalty *m*; **~ miss** *n* Sport (in soccer) penalty *m* raté; **~ shoot-out** *n* tirs *mpl* au but; **~ spot** *n* Sport (in soccer) point *m* de penalty.

penance /ˈpenəns/ *n* gen, Relig pénitence *f*; **to do ~ (for one's sins)** gen, Relig faire pénitence (pour ses péchés).

pen-and-ink drawing *n* dessin *m* à la plume.

pence /pens/ *npl* GB ▶ **penny**.

penchant /ˈpɑːnʃɑːn, US ˈpentʃənt/ *n* penchant *m* (**for** pour); **to have a ~ for doing** avoir tendance *f* à faire.

pencil /ˈpensl/ **I** *n* crayon *m*; **in ~** au crayon; **~ drawing** dessin *m* au crayon; **a ~ of light** fig un pinceau de lumière.
II *vtr* (*p prés etc* **-ll-** GB, **-l-** US) écrire [qch] au crayon [*note*].
■ **pencil in**: **~ [sth] in, ~ in [sth]** lit écrire [qch] au crayon [*word, hyphen*]; fig marquer [qch] comme possibilité [*appointment, date*]; **let's ~ in the second of May** disons le deux mai pour l'instant.

pencil: **~ box** *n* plumier *m*; **~ case** *n* trousse *f* (à crayons); **~ pusher**○ *n* US péj gratte-papier *m inv* pej; **~ sharpener** *n* taille-crayon *m*.

pendant /ˈpendənt/ *n* **1** (necklace) pendentif *m*; **2** (bauble) (on earring, chandelier) pendeloque *f*; (on necklace) pendentif *m*; **3** (ceiling light) lustre *m*.

pending /ˈpendɪŋ/ **I** *adj* **1** (not yet concluded) Jur [*claim, case, charge*] en instance; gen [*deal, matter*] en souffrance; **patent ~** modèle *m* déposé; **2** (imminent) [*election, event, result*] imminent.
II *prep* en attendant; **~ trial/a decision** en attendant le procès/une décision.

pending tray *n* corbeille *f* des affaires en souffrance.

pendulous /ˈpendjʊləs, US -dʒʊləs/ *adj* [*breasts, stomach*] tombant; [*lips, ears*] pendant.

pendulum /ˈpendjʊləm, US -dʒʊləm/ *n* **1** (in clock) pendule *m*, balancier *m*; **2** fig balancier *m*; **the swings of the ~** les mouvements du pendule; **3** Phys pendule *m*; **4** (in climbing) pendule *m*.

peneplain /ˈpiːnɪpleɪn/ *n* pénéplaine *f*.

penetrate /ˈpenɪtreɪt/ **I** *vtr* **1** (enter into or through) pénétrer [*protective layer, territory, skin, surface*]; percer [*cloud, fog, darkness, silence, defences*]; traverser [*wall*]; (sexually) pénétrer [*woman*]; **2** fig (permeate) pénétrer [*consciousness, market, mind, soul, ideas*]; [*spy*] infiltrer [*organization*]; **3** (understand) percer [*disguise, mystery*].
II *vi* **1** (enter) pénétrer [*place, city*] (**into**

dans; **as far as** jusqu'à); **2** (be perceived) [*sound*] parvenir (**to** à); [*understanding*] pénétrer (**to** à); **nothing I say seems to ~** j'ai l'impression de parler à un mur.

penetrating /ˈpenɪtreɪtɪŋ/ *adj* **1** (invasive) [*cold, eyes, gaze, rain, wind*] pénétrant; [*sound, voice*] perçant; **2** (perceptive) [*analysis, criticism, comment, question*] pénétrant.

penetratingly /ˈpenɪtreɪtɪŋlɪ/ *adv* **1** (loudly) [*speak, shout*] d'une voix pénétrante; **2** (perceptively) [*comment, analyse*] avec pénétration.

penetration /ˌpenɪˈtreɪʃn/ *n* **1** (entering) pénétration *f* (**into** de); (by spies) infiltration *f*; (sexual) pénétration *f*; **2** Mil (ability to penetrate) (of bullets, shells) pouvoir *m* de pénétration; **3** (insight) perspicacité *f*.

penetrative /ˈpenɪtrətɪv, US -treɪtɪv/ *adj* [*power*] pénétrant; **~ sex** relations *fpl* sexuelles avec pénétration.

pen friend *n* correspondant/-e *m/f*.

penguin /ˈpeŋgwɪn/ *n* pingouin *m*, manchot *m*.

pen holder *n* porte-plume *m inv*.

penicillin /ˌpenɪˈsɪlɪn/ *n* pénicilline *f*.

peninsula /pəˈnɪnsjʊlə, US -nsələ/ *n* péninsule *f*.

peninsular /pɪˈnɪnsjʊlə(r), US -nsələr/ *adj* péninsulaire; **the Peninsular War** la guerre d'Espagne.

penis /ˈpiːnɪs/ *n* pénis *m*.

penis envy *n* Psych envie *f* du pénis.

penitence /ˈpenɪtəns/ *n* gen, Relig pénitence *f*, repentir *m*; **to show ~** montrer du repentir.

penitent /ˈpenɪtənt/ *n, adj* gen, Relig pénitent/-e (*m/f*).

penitential /ˌpenɪˈtenʃl/ *adj* pénitentiel/-ielle; **the ~ psalms** les Psaumes pénitentiaux.

penitentiary /ˌpenɪˈtenʃərɪ/ *n* **1** US (prison) pénitencier *m*, prison *f*; **federal/state ~** pénitencier fédéral/d'État; **2** Relig (cleric) pénitencier *m*; (tribunal) pénitencerie *f*.

penitently /ˈpenɪtəntlɪ/ *adv* [*look*] d'un air pénitent; [*speak*] d'un ton pénitent.

pen: **~knife** *n* canif *m*; **~manship** *n* calligraphie *f*; **~ name** *n* pseudonyme *m*, nom *m* de plume.

pennant /ˈpenənt/ *n* **1** (flag) (on boat) flamme *f*; (in competition. procession, on car) fanion *m*; **2** US Sport championnat *m*; **~ holder** ou **winner** champion/-ionne *m/f*.

penniless /ˈpenɪlɪs/ *adj* sans le sou, sans ressources; **to be left ~** se retrouver sans le sou or sans ressources.

Pennine /ˈpenaɪn/ *pr n* **the ~s** les Pennines *fpl*; **the ~ chain** la chaîne *f* des Pennines.

pennon /ˈpenən/ *n* (of knight) oriflamme *f*; Naut flamme *f*.

Pennsylvania /ˌpensɪlˈveɪnɪə/ **▶ 1744** *pr n* Pennsylvanie *f*.

Pennsylvanian /ˌpensɪlˈveɪnɪən/ **I** *n* Pennsylvanien/-ienne *m/f*.
II *adj* pennsylvanien/-ienne.

penny /ˈpenɪ/ *n* **1** (*pl* **pennies**) (small amount of money) ≈ centime *m*; **it won't cost you a ~!** ça ne te coûtera pas un centime!; **not a ~ more!** pas un centime de plus!; **when he died she didn't get a ~** quand il est mort elle n'a pas eu un sou; **not to have a ~ to one's name** ou **two pennies to rub together** être sans le sou; **2** GB (*pl* **pence** ou **pennies**) (unit of currency) penny *m*; **fifty pence** ou **p** cinquante pence; **a five pence** ou **five p piece** une pièce de cinq pence; **a 25 pence** ou **25p stamp** un timbre-poste à 25 pence; **3** US (*pl* **pennies**) cent *m*.
IDIOMS **a ~ for your thoughts** ou **for them**○ à quoi penses-tu?; **a ~ saved is a ~ gained** ou **earned** un sou économisé est un sou gagné; **a pretty ~**○ une jolie somme; **in for a ~ in for a pound** lorsque le vin est tiré, il faut le boire; **take care of the pennies and the pounds will take care of themselves** Prov il n'y a pas de petites économies; **the ~ dropped**○ ça a fait tilt○; **they are two** ou **ten a ~** on les ramasse à la pelle○; **to be ~ wise pound foolish** économiser un franc et en prodiguer mille; **to earn** ou **turn an honest ~** gagner honnêtement son pain; **to spend a ~**○ GB euph aller au petit coin euph; **to turn up like a bad ~** revenir continuellement.

■ Note Le pluriel de *penny* est *pence* pour une somme spécifique: *10 pence, 24 pence*. A l'oral et à l'écrit on utilise souvent l'abréviation *p*: *47p, 1p*. Le pluriel de *penny* est *pennies* pour les pièces en tant qu'objets comptables: *a bag of pennies*.

penny: **Penny Black** *n* Penny Black *m* (*premier timbre adhésif apparu en Grande-Bretagne*); **~ dreadful**○† *n* roman *m* à quatre sous; **~-farthing** *n* grand bi *m*; **~-pincher** *n* grippe-sou *m*.

penny-pinching /ˈpenɪpɪntʃɪŋ/ **I** *n* économies *fpl* de bouts de chandelle.
II *adj* grippe-sou *inv*.

penny: **~royal** *n* pouliot *m*; **~ whistle** *n* flûteau *m*; **~wort** *n* ombellifère *f*.

pennyworth /ˈpenɪwəθ/ *n* **a ~ of sweets** un penny de bonbons.

penologist /piːˈnɒlədʒɪst/ **▶ 1692** *n* pénologue *mf*.

penology /piːˈnɒlədʒɪ/ *n* pénologie *f*.

pen: **~ pal**○ *n* correspondant/-e *m/f*; **~ pusher**○ *n* péj gratte-papier○ *m inv* pej; **~ pushing**○ *n* péj travaux *mpl* d'écritures.

pension /ˈpenʃn/ *n* **1** (from state) pension *f*, retraite *f*; **to be** ou **live on a ~** être pensionné; **old age ~** pension *f* vieillesse; **2** (from employer) retraite *f*; **company ~** retraite *f* de société; **3** (in recognition of talent, services) pension *f*; **4** Tourism pension *f*.
■ **pension off**: **~ [sb] off, ~ off [sb]** mettre qn à la retraite.

pensionable /ˈpenʃənəbl/ *adj* [*post, service*] donnant droit à la retraite; [*employee*] ayant droit à la retraite; **to be of ~ age** avoir l'âge de la retraite.

pension book *n* livret *m* de retraite.

pensioner /ˈpenʃənə(r)/ *n* retraité/-e *m/f*.

pension: **~ fund** *n* fonds *m* d'assurance-vieillesse; **~ plan, ~ scheme** *n* plan *m* de retraite; **~ rights** *npl* droit *m* à une retraite complémentaire.

pensive /ˈpensɪv/ *adj* songeur/-euse, pensif/-ive.

pensively /ˈpensɪvlɪ/ *adv* pensivement.

pensiveness /ˈpensɪvnɪs/ *n* humeur *f* songeuse.

pent /pent/ **I** *pp* **▶ pen II 2**.
II *adj* liter renfermé.

pentacle /ˈpentəkl/ *n* pentacle *m*.

pentagon /ˈpentəgən, US -gɒn/ **I** *n* **1** Math pentagone *m*; **2 Pentagon** US Pol **the ~** le Pentagone.
II Pentagon *modif* [*statement, official*] du Pentagone.

pentagonal /penˈtægənl/ *adj* pentagonal.

pentagram /ˈpentəgræm/ *n* pentagramme *m*.

pentahedron /ˌpentəˈhiːdrən, US -drɒn/ *n* pentaèdre *m*.

pentameter /penˈtæmɪtə(r)/ *n* pentamètre *m*.

Pentateuch /ˈpentətjuːk/ *pr n* Pentateuque *m*.

pentathlete /penˈtæθliːt/ *n* pentathlonien/-ienne *m/f*.

pentathlon /penˈtæθlən, -lɒn/ *n* pentathlon *m*; **modern ~** pentathlon *m* moderne.

pentatonic /ˌpentəˈtɒnɪk/ *adj* pentatonique.

Pentecost /ˈpentɪkɒst, US -kɔːst/ *n* Pentecôte *f*.

Pentecostal /ˌpentɪˈkɒstl, US -kɔːstl/ *adj* de la Pentecôte.

Pentecostalism /ˌpentɪˈkɒstəlɪzəm, US -ˈkɔːst-/ *n* Pentecôtisme *m*.

Pentecostalist /ˌpentɪˈkɒstəlɪst, US -ˈkɔːst-/ *n, adj* pentecôtiste (*mf*).

penthouse /ˈpenthaʊs/ **I** *n* **1** (flat) appartement *m* de grand standing (*au dernier étage d'un immeuble*); **2** (roof) auvent *m*.
II *modif* [*accommodation, suite*] de grand standing; [*roof*] en auvent.

pent-up /ˌpentˈʌp/ *adj* [*emotion, energy, frustration*] contenu; [*feelings*] réprimé.

penultimate /penˈʌltɪmət/ **I** *n* Ling pénultième *f*.
II *adj* avant-dernier/-ière.

penumbra /pɪˈnʌmbrə/ *n* Astron, littér pénombre *f*.

penurious /pɪˈnjʊərɪəs, US -ˈnʊr-/ *adj* sout **1** (poor) [*family*] indigent; [*existence*] misérable; [*soil*] infertile; **2** (mean) parcimonieux/-ieuse.

penury /ˈpenjʊrɪ/ *n* indigence *f*.

peon /ˈpiːən/ *n* péon *m*.

peony /ˈpiːənɪ/ *n* pivoine *f*.

people /ˈpiːpl/ **I** *n* (nation) peuple *m*, peuplade *f*; **an ancient ~** un peuple antique; **the English-speaking ~s** les anglophones *mpl*; **Stone Age ~s** les peuplades de l'âge de pierre; **the chosen ~** le peuple des élus.
II *npl* **1** (in general) gens *mpl*; (specified or counted) personnes *fpl*; **disabled/old ~** les personnes handicapées/âgées; **they're nice ~** ce sont des gens sympathiques; **how many ~ are there?** combien y a-t-il de personnes?; **there were several/a few/500 ~** il y avait plusieurs/quelques/500 personnes; **there was a roomful of ~** il y avait une pièce pleine de monde; **there were a lot of ~** il y avait beaucoup de monde; **a lot of/most ~ think that** beaucoup de/la plupart des gens pensent que; **some ~ here think that** certaines personnes ici pensent que; **~ say that** les gens disent que; **what will ~ say?** que vont dire les gens?; **other ~ say that** d'autres disent que; **other ~'s property** la propriété des autres; **he likes helping ~** il aime aider les autres; **you shouldn't do that in front of ~** tu ne devrais pas faire ça en public; **~ at large, ~ in general** le grand public; **what do you ~ want?** que voulez-vous?; **you of all ~!** je n'aurais jamais pensé ça de toi!; **you of all ~ should know that...** tu devrais savoir encore mieux que les autres que...; **I met Jack of all ~ at the party!** à la soirée il y avait Jack, figure-toi!; **2** (inhabitants) (of town) habitants *mpl*; (of a country) peuple *m*; **the ~ of Bath** les habitants de Bath; **the British ~** le peuple britannique, les Britanniques *mpl*; **the good ~ of Oxford** les bonnes gens d'Oxford; **3** (citizens, subjects) **the ~** le peuple; **the common ~** le peuple; **the ~ are protesting** le peuple proteste; **a man of the ~** un homme du peuple; **to address one's ~** s'adresser à son peuple; **4**○ (experts) gens○ *mpl*; **the tax/heating ~** les gens○ des impôts/du chauffage; **5**○ (relations) famille *f*; (parents) parents *mpl*.
III *vtr* littér peupler (**with** de).

■ Note *gens* is masculine plural and never countable (you CANNOT say *'trois gens'*). When used with *gens*, some adjectives such as *vieux, bon, mauvais, petit, vilain* placed before *gens* take the feminine form: *les vieilles gens*.

people carrier *n* monospace *m*.

people management *n* **do you have experience of ~?** est-ce que vous avez déjà dirigé une équipe?

people: **~ mover** *n* US tapis *m* roulant; **~ power** *n* pouvoir *m* populaire; **~'s army** *n* armée *f* populaire; **~'s democracy** *n* démocratie *f* populaire; **~'s front** *n* front *m* populaire; **~'s park** *n* jardin *m* public; **People's Party** *n* US Hist parti *m* populiste; **~'s republic** *n* république *f* populaire; **People's Republic of China**

▶**1131**] *pr n* République *f* populaire de Chine.

pep /pep/ *n* entrain *m*, dynamisme *m*.
■ **pep up**: ¶ **~ up** [*person*] retrouver des forces; [*economy*] repartir; [*business*] reprendre; ¶ **~ [sb/sth] up, ~ up [sb/sth]** remettre [qn] d'aplomb [*person*]; animer [*party, team*].

PEP *n* GB Fin *abrév* ▶**Personal Equity Plan**.

pepper /ˈpepə(r)/ **I** *n* **1** (spice) poivre *m*; **black/white ~** poivre noir/blanc; **2** (vegetable) poivron *m*; **red/green ~** poivron rouge/vert.
II *vtr* **1** lit poivrer [*meal, food*]; **2** fig (sprinkle liberally) parsemer (**with** de); **to be ~ed with** être parsemé de [*swearwords, criticisms*]; **3** (fire at) cribler [*person, wall, area*] (**with** de).

pepper: **~-and-salt** *adj* [*hair*] poivre et sel; [*material*] chiné noir et blanc; **~corn** *n* grain *m* de poivre; **~corn rent** *n* GB loyer *m* symbolique; **~ mill** *n* moulin *m* à poivre.

peppermint /ˈpepəmɪnt/ **I** *n* **1** (sweet) pastille *f* de menthe; **2** (plant) menthe *f* poivrée.
II *modif* (also **~-flavoured**) à la menthe.

pepper pot, **~ shaker** *n* poivrier *m*.

peppery /ˈpepərɪ/ *adj* **1** (spicy) poivré; **2** (irritable) irascible.

pep pill○ *n* excitant *m*.

peppy○ /ˈpepɪ/ *adj* [*person*] plein d'entrain; [*car*] nerveux/-euse.

pep rally *n* US Sch *défilé de supporters avant un match scolaire*.

pepsin /ˈpepsɪn/ *n* pepsine *f*.

pep talk○ *n* laïus○ *m* d'encouragement.

peptic /ˈpeptɪk/ *adj* gen digestif/-ive; **~ ulcer** ulcère *m* de l'estomac.

peptone /ˈpeptəʊn/ *n* peptone *f*.

per /pɜː(r)/ *prep* **1** (for each) par; **~ head** par tête or personne; **~ annum** par an; **~ diem** par jour; **80 km ~ hour** 80 km à l'heure; **to pay sb £5 ~ hour** payer qn 5 livres (de) l'heure; **revolutions ~ minute** tours-minute; **as ~ usual**○ comme d'habitude; **2** (by means of) **~ post** par la poste; **3** Comm **as ~ invoice/specifications** suivant facture/spécifications; **as ~ sample** conformément à l'échantillon; **as ~ your instructions** conformément à vos instructions.

perambulate /pəˈræmbjʊleɪt/ sout **I** *vtr* parcourir.
II *vi* déambuler.

perambulation /pəˌræmbjʊˈleɪʃn/ *n* sout promenade *f*.

perambulator† /pəˈræmbjʊleɪtə(r)/ *n* GB voiture *f* d'enfant, landau *m*.

perborate /pəˈbɔːreɪt/ *n* perborate *m*.

per capita *adj, adv* par habitant.

perceive /pəˈsiːv/ **I** *vtr* percevoir.
II perceived *pp adj* [*need, benefit, success, failure*] perçu/-e comme tel/telle.
III *v refl* **to ~ oneself as (being) sth** se percevoir comme qch.

per cent, **pc** /pəˈsent/ **I** *n* centième *m*.
II *adv* pour cent.

percentage /pəˈsentɪdʒ/ **I** *n* pourcentage *m* (**of** de; **on** sur); **as a ~ of** calculé par rapport à; **a high/small ~** un fort/faible pourcentage; **to get a ~ on** toucher un pourcentage sur [*sale*].
II *modif* [*increase, decrease, change*] en pourcentage.

percentage point *n* Fin point *m*.

perceptible /pəˈseptəbl/ *adj* perceptible (**to** à); **barely ~** à peine perceptible.

perceptibly /pəˈseptəblɪ/ *adv* sensiblement, de façon perceptible.

perception /pəˈsepʃn/ *n* **1** Philos, Psych perception *f*; **visual ~** perception visuelle; **a child's ~ of his environment** la perception qu'a un enfant de son environnement; **2** (view) **my ~ of him/of the problem** l'idée que je me fais de lui/du problème; **the popular ~ of the 1960s as an era of liberation** l'idée que les gens se font des années soixante comme étant une époque de libération; **there is a ~ growing among nationalists that** on voit se répandre parmi les nationalistes l'idée selon laquelle; **3** (insight) (of person) perspicacité *f*; (of essay, novel) finesse *f*; **the psychological ~ of her later novels** la finesse de l'analyse psychologique dans ses derniers romans; **4** Comm, Tax perception *f*.

perceptive /pəˈseptɪv/ *adj* **1** [*person, mind, wit*] perspicace; [*study, account, article*] pertinent; [*vignette, comedy*] spirituel/-elle; **how ~ of you!** quelle perspicacité (de votre part)!; **2** Psych perceptif/-ive.

perceptively /pəˈseptɪvlɪ/ *adv* avec perspicacité; **as she ~ observes...** comme elle le fait très justement remarquer...

perceptiveness /pəˈseptɪvnɪs/ *n* = **perception 3**.

perch /pɜːtʃ/ **I** *n* **1** (for bird) perchoir *m*; **2** fig (vantage point) position *f* élevée; **3** Zool perche *f*; **4**† Meas ≈ 5 mètres.
II *vtr* percher.
III *vi* [*bird, person*] se percher (**on** sur); **to be ~ed on sth** [*bird, person, building*] être perché sur qch.
IDIOMS **to knock sb off their ~**○ détrôner qn.

perchance /pəˈtʃɑːns, US -ˈtʃæns/ *adv* liter (perhaps) peut-être; (by accident) par hasard.

percipient /pəˈsɪpɪənt/ *adj* **1** sout [*person*] perspicace, fin; [*observation, remark*] pertinent; **2** Philos percipient.

percolate /ˈpɜːkəleɪt/ **I** *vtr* passer [*coffee*]; **~d coffee** café fait dans une cafetière à pression.
II *vi* (also **~ through**) [*coffee*] passer; [*water, rain*] passer, filtrer; [*news, idea, information*] filtrer (**into, to** jusqu'à).

percolator /ˈpɜːkəleɪtə(r)/ *n* cafetière *f* à pression.

percussion /pəˈkʌʃn/ **I** *n* **1** Mus percussions *fpl*; **2** (striking together) choc *m*; (sound) percussion *f*.
II *modif* [*board, lesson*] de percussions; [*instrument*] à percussion; **~ player** percussionniste *mf*; **~ section** percussions *fpl*.

percussion: **~ bullet** *n* balle *f* explosive; **~ cap** *n* capsule *f* fulminante; **~ drill** *n* perçeuse *f* à percussion.

percussionist /pəˈkʌʃənɪst/ *n* percussionniste *mf*.

percussion lock *n* percuteur *m*.

percussive /pəˈkʌsɪv/ *adj* percutant.

perdition /pəˈdɪʃn/ *n* Relig perdition *f*.

peregrination /ˌperɪgrɪˈneɪʃn/ *n* littér pérégrination *f*.

peregrine falcon /ˌperɪgrɪn ˈfɔːlkən, US ˈfælkən/ *n* faucon *m* pèlerin.

peremptorily /pəˈremptrəlɪ, US ˈperəmptɔːrəlɪ/ *adv* péremptoirement.

peremptory /pəˈremptərɪ, US ˈperəmptɔːrɪ/ *adj* péremptoire.

perennial /pəˈrenɪəl/ **I** *n* plante *f* vivace; **hardy ~** plante *f* vivace.
II *adj* **1** (recurring) perpétuel/-elle; **2** Bot [*plant*] vivace.

perennially /pəˈrenɪəlɪ/ *adv* (all contexts) perpétuellement.

perestroika /ˌpereˈstrɔɪkə/ *n* perestroïka *f*.

perfect I /ˈpɜːfɪkt/ *n* Ling parfait *m*; **in the ~** au parfait.
II /ˈpɜːfɪkt/ *adj* **1** (flawless) [*arrangement, behaviour, blend, condition, copy, crime, example, French, health, match, performance, shape, score, technique, weather, world*] parfait (**for** pour); [*choice, holiday, moment, name, opportunity, place, partner, solution*] idéal (**for** pour); [*hostess*] exemplaire; **she is ~ for the part/the job** c'est la personne idéale pour le rôle/ce travail; **that screw will be ~ for the job** cette vis fera parfaitement l'affaire; **that recording is less than ~** cet enregistrement laisse franchement à désirer; **that jacket is a ~ fit** cette veste va parfaitement; **to do sth with ~ timing** faire qch au bon moment; **everything is ~** tout est parfait ; **'all right?'—'~!'** 'ça va?'—'parfait!'; **2** (total) [*stranger, fool*] parfait (*before n*); [*pest*] véritable (*before n*); **to have a ~ right to do** avoir parfaitement le droit de faire; **3** Ling **the ~ tense** le parfait.
III /pəˈfekt/ *vtr* perfectionner.

perfectibility /pəˌfektɪˈbɪlətɪ/ *n* perfectibilité *f*.

perfection /pəˈfekʃn/ *n* perfection *f* (**of** de); **to do sth to ~** faire qch à la perfection; **his singing/cooking was ~ (itself)** sa façon de chanter/de cuisiner était la perfection même.

perfectionism /pəˈfekʃənɪzəm/ *n* perfectionnisme *m*.

perfectionist /pəˈfekʃənɪst/ *n, adj* perfectionniste (*mf*).

perfective /pəˈfektɪv/ Ling **I** *n* (verb) verbe *m* perfectif; (aspect) aspect *m* perfectif.
II *adj* perfectif/-ive.

perfectly /ˈpɜːfɪktlɪ/ *adv* **1** (totally) [*acceptable, all right, clear, happy, dreadful, healthy, normal, obvious, reasonable*] tout à fait; [*good*] parfaitement; **to be ~ entitled to do** avoir parfaitement le droit de faire; **2** (very well) [*fit, illustrate*] parfaitement.

perfidious /pəˈfɪdɪəs/ *adj* perfide; **~ Albion** la perfide Albion.

perfidiously /pəˈfɪdɪəslɪ/ *adv* perfidement.

perfidy /ˈpɜːfɪdɪ/ *n* perfidie *f*.

perforate /ˈpɜːfəreɪt/ *vtr* perforer.

perforated ulcer /ˌpɜːfəreɪtɪd ˈʌlsə(r)/ *n* perforation *f* ulcéreuse.

perforation /ˌpɜːfəˈreɪʃn/ *n* (all contexts) perforation *f*.

perforce /pəˈfɔːs/ *adv* sout nécessairement.

perform /pəˈfɔːm/ **I** *vtr* **1** (carry out) exécuter [*task*]; accomplir [*duties*]; procéder à [*operation, abortion, lobotomy*]; **2** (for entertainment) jouer [*piece, play*]; chanter [*song*]; exécuter [*dance, acrobatics, trick*]; **3** (enact) célébrer [*rite, ceremony*].
II *vi* **1** [*actor, musician*] jouer; **to ~ in public** jouer en public; **to ~ on the violin** jouer du violon; **she ~ed brilliantly as Viola** elle a brillamment joué le rôle de Viola; **2** (conduct oneself) **to ~ well/badly** [*team*] bien/mal jouer; [*interviewee*] faire bonne/mauvaise impression; **the students ~ed better than last year** les étudiants ont eu de meilleurs résultats que l'année dernière; **the minister ~s well on television** le ministre fait une bonne performance à la télévision; **3** Comm, Fin [*company, department*] avoir de bons résultats; **sterling ~ed badly** la livre sterling a baissé.

performance /pəˈfɔːməns/ *n* **1** (rendition) interprétation *f* (**of** de); **his ~ of Hamlet** son interprétation du rôle de Hamlet; **her ~ in King Lear** son interprétation dans le Roi Lear; **2** (concert, show, play) représentation *f* (**of** de); **to give a ~ of** donner une représentation de; **to put on a ~** monter un spectacle; **3** (of team, sportsman) performance *f* (**in** à); **4** (economic, political record) performances *fpl*; **sterling's ~** les performances de la livre sterling; **5** (of duties) exercice *m* (**of** de); (of rite) célébration *f* (**of** de); (of task) exécution *f* (**of** de); **6** Aut (of car, engine) performances *fpl*; **7**○ (outburst) scène *f*; (elaborate procedure) affaire *f*; **what a ~!** quelle scène or affaire!; **it's a real ~ doing** c'est toute une affaire de faire; **8** Ling performance *f*.

performance: **~ appraisal** *n* Mgmt évaluation *f* des performances; **~ art** *n* Art art *m* vivant, performance *f*; **~ artist** ▶**1692**] *n* performer *mf*; **~ indicators** *npl* Mgmt tableau *m* de bord; **~ review** *n* = **performance appraisal**.

performative /pəˈfɔːmətɪv/ *adj* performatif/-ive.

performer /pəˈfɔːmə(r)/ *n* **1** (artist) artiste *mf*; **2** (achiever) **the car is a good/bad ~ on hilly terrain** la voiture se comporte bien/mal en terrain vallonné.

performing /pəˈfɔːmɪŋ/ *adj* [*seal, elephant*] savant.

performing arts *npl* arts *mpl* scéniques.

perfume /ˈpɜːfjuːm, US pərˈfjuːm/ **I** *n* parfum *m*.
II *vtr* parfumer.

perfumery /pəˈfjuːmərɪ/ *n* parfumerie *f*.

perfunctorily /pəˈfʌŋktrəlɪ, US -tɔːrəlɪ/ *adv* [*search, bow, greet*] pour la forme; [*kiss, comment*] du bout des lèvres; [*investigate, carry out*] sommairement.

perfunctory /pəˈfʌŋktərɪ, US -tɔːrɪ/ *adj* [*search, bow, greeting*] pour la forme; [*kiss, nod, shrug*] rapide, sans conviction; [*investigation*] sommaire.

pergola /ˈpɜːgələ/ *n* pergola *f*.

perhaps /pəˈhæps/ *adv* peut-être; **~ she's forgotten** elle a peut-être oublié; **~ he has missed the train** peut-être qu'il a manqué le train, peut-être a-t-il manqué le train; **~ I should explain that...** je devrais peut-être expliquer que...; **~ I might have a cup of tea?** pourrais-je avoir une tasse de thé?

perianth /ˈperɪænθ/ *n* périanthe *m*.

pericardium /ˌperɪˈkɑːdɪəm/ *n* (*pl* **-dia**) péricarde *m*.

pericarp /ˈperɪkɑːp/ *n* péricarpe *m*.

peridot /ˈperɪdɒt/ *n* péridot *m*.

perigee /ˈperɪdʒiː/ *n* périgée *m*.

periglacial /ˌperɪˈgleɪʃl/ *adj* périglaciaire.

peril /ˈperəl/ *n* péril *m*, danger *m*; **in ~ (of)** en danger (de); **in ~ of one's life** au péril de sa vie; **at my/your ~** à mes/tes risques et périls.

perilous /ˈperələs/ *adj* périlleux/-euse.

perilously /ˈperələslɪ/ *adv* dangereusement; **to be** ou **come ~ close to** être à deux doigts de○.

perimeter /pəˈrɪmɪtə(r)/ **I** *n* périmètre *m*; **on the ~ of** aux abords de [*park, site*]; **to go round the ~ of** faire le tour de.
II *modif* [*wall*] d'enceinte; [*path*] circulaire.

perimeter fence *n* (also **~ fencing**) clôture *f* grillagée.

perinatal /ˌperɪˈneɪtl/ *adj* périnatal.

perineal /ˌperɪˈniːəl/ *adj* [*tear, damage*] du périnée.

perineum /ˌperɪˈniːəm/ *n* (*pl* **-nea**) périnée *m*.

period /ˈpɪərɪəd/ **I** *n* **1** gen, Geol, Astron, Hist période *f*; (longer) époque *f*; **for a short ~** pendant une courte période; **a ~ of peace and prosperity** une période or une époque de paix et de prospérité; **trial/Christmas ~** période d'essai/de Noël; **the late Roman/pre-war ~** l'époque romaine tardive/l'époque or la période de l'avant-guerre; **cloudy/sunny ~s** Meteorol périodes nuageuses/d'ensoleillement; **bright ~s** Meteorol éclaircies *fpl*; **rainy ~s** Meteorol averses *fpl*; **for/over a two-year ~** pendant/en deux ans; **for a long ~** pendant longtemps; **2** Art période *f*; **Picasso's blue ~** la période bleue de Picasso; **3** US (full stop) lit, fig point *m*; **4** (menstruation) règles *fpl*; **5** Sch (lesson) cours *m*, leçon *f*; **a double ~ of French** deux cours de français à la suite; **to have a free ~** ≈ avoir une heure de libre; **6** Sport période *f* de jeu, manche *f*.
II *modif* (of a certain era) [*costume, furniture, instrument*] d'époque; (reproduction) [*costume, instrument, style, performance*] caractéristique de l'époque; [*furniture*] de style (ancien).

periodic /ˌpɪərɪˈɒdɪk/ *adj* périodique.

periodical /ˌpɪərɪˈɒdɪkl/ *n, adj* périodique (*m*).

periodically /ˌpɪərɪˈɒdɪklɪ/ *adv* périodiquement.

periodicity /ˌpɪərɪəˈdɪsətɪ/ *n* périodicité *f*.

periodic: **~ law** *n* principe *m* de classification périodique des éléments chimiques; **~ table** *n* tableau *m* de classification périodique des éléments.

period: **~ of office** *n* Pol, Admin mandat *m*; **~ pains** *npl* règles *fpl* douloureuses; **~ piece** *n* curiosité *f* d'époque.

periosteum /ˌperɪˈɒstɪəm/ *n* (*pl* **-tea**) périoste *m*.

peripatetic /ˌperɪpəˈtetɪk/ **I** *n* (also **Peripatetic**) Philos péripatéticien/-ienne *m/f*.
II *adj* [*life, existence*] itinérant; [*teacher*] affecté à plusieurs établissements scolaires.

peripheral /pəˈrɪfərəl/ **I** *n* Comput périphérique *m*.
II *adj* [*equipment, vision, suburb*] périphérique; [*issue, business, investment*] annexe; **to be ~ to** être secondaire par rapport à [*activity, issue*].

periphery /pəˈrɪfərɪ/ *n* **1** (edge) périphérie *f*; **2** fig (fringes) **to be on the ~ of** être dans la mouvance de [*party, movement*]; **to remain on the ~ of** rester à l'écart de [*event, movement*].

periphrasis /pəˈrɪfrəsɪs/ *n* (*pl* **-ses**) périphrase *f*.

periscope /ˈperɪskəʊp/ *n* périscope *m*; **at ~ depth** en immersion périscopique.

perish /ˈperɪʃ/ *vi* **1** littér (die) périr (**from** de); **to do sth or ~ in the attempt** hum faire qch coûte que coûte; **~ the thought!** le Ciel nous en préserve!; **2** (rot) [*food*] se gâter; [*rubber*] se détériorer.

perishable /ˈperɪʃəbl/ *adj* périssable; **~ goods** denrées périssables.

perishables /ˈperɪʃəblz/ *npl* denrées *fpl* périssables.

perished○ /ˈperɪʃt/ *adj* **to be ~** [*person*] être gelé○.

perisher○† /ˈperɪʃə(r)/ *n* GB **1** (nuisance) **little ~** petite peste *f*; **2** (child) **poor little ~** pauvre petit/-e *m/f*.

perishing○ /ˈperɪʃɪŋ/ *adj* **1** (cold) **to be ~** (of weather) faire un froid de canard○; **2**† (emphatic) parfait; **~ idiot** parfait imbécile; **what a ~ nuisance!** quelle barbe○!

perishingly○ /ˈperɪʃɪŋlɪ/ *adv* **it's ~ cold** il fait froid à crever○.

peristalsis /ˌperɪˈstælsɪs/ *n* (*pl* **-ses**) péristaltisme *m*.

peristyle /ˈperɪstaɪl/ *n* péristyle *m*.

peritoneum /ˌperɪtəˈniːəm/ *n* (*pl* **-nea** ou **~s**) péritoine *m*.

peritonitis /ˌperɪtəˈnaɪtɪs/ **▶ 1354** *n* péritonite *f*.

periwig /ˈperɪwɪg/ *n* Hist perruque *f*.

periwinkle /ˈperɪwɪŋkl/ **▶ 1104** *n* **1** Bot pervenche *f*; **2** (also **~-blue**) bleu *m* pervenche *inv*; **3** Zool bigorneau *m*.

perjure /ˈpɜːdʒə(r)/ *v refl* **to ~ oneself** Jur faire un faux serment; (morally) se parjurer.

perjured /ˈpɜːdʒəd/ *adj* Jur [*witness*] parjure; [*testimony*] faux/fausse (*before n*).

perjurer /ˈpɜːdʒərə(r)/ *n* Jur parjure *mf*.

perjury /ˈpɜːdʒərɪ/ *n* Jur faux témoignage *m*; **to commit ~** faire un faux témoignage.

perk○ /pɜːk/ **I** *n* gen avantage *m*; (benefit in kind) avantage *m* en nature.
II *vtr* (percolate) passer [*coffee*].
■ **perk up**: ¶ **~ up** [*person*] se ragaillardir; [*business, life, plant*] reprendre; [*weather*] s'adoucir; ¶ **~ [sth] up, ~ up [sth]** revigorer [*person, plant, business*]; égayer [*dress*].

perkily /ˈpɜːkɪlɪ/ *adv* avec entrain.

perkiness /ˈpɜːkɪnɪs/ *n* entrain *m*.

perky /ˈpɜːkɪ/ *adj* guilleret/-ette.

perm /pɜːm/ **I** *n* **1** Cosmet permanente *f*; **to have a ~** se faire faire une permanente; **2** GB Sport (football pools) combinaison *f*.
II *vtr* **1 to ~ sb's hair** faire une permanente à qn; **2** (football pools) **to ~ 8 from 16** faire une combinaison de 8 équipes sur 16.

permafrost /ˈpɜːməfrɒst, US -frɔːst/ *n* permagel *m*, permafrost *m*.

permanence /ˈpɜːmənəns/ *n* permanence *f*.

permanency /ˈpɜːmənənsɪ/ *n* **1** = **permanence**; **2** (job) emploi *m* à titre définitif.

permanent /ˈpɜːmənənt/ **I** *n* US permanente *f*.
II *adj* [*job, disability, exhibition, address, friendship*] permanent; [*premises, closure*] définitif/-ive; [*contract*] à durée indéterminée; [*staff*] ayant un contrat à durée indéterminée; **~ damage** (to property) dégâts *mpl* permanents; (to health, part of body) dommages *mpl* permanents; **to be in a ~ state of depression** être déprimé en permanence; **the payments are a ~ drain on our resources** les versements grèvent nos ressources en permanence; **I'm not ~ in this job** GB je ne suis pas ici à titre définitif; **▶ fixture**.

permanently /ˈpɜːmənəntlɪ/ *adv* (constantly) [*angry, happy, tired*] en permanence; (definitively) [*employed, disabled*] de façon permanente; [*appointed*] à titre définitif; [*close, emigrate, leave, settle*] définitivement; **a ~ high level of unemployment** un taux de chômage constamment élevé; **he will be ~ scarred** lit il aura cette cicatrice pour toujours; fig il sera marqué pour la vie.

permanent: **~ press** *modif* [*trousers*] à pli permanent; [*skirt, fabric*] indéplissable; **~ secretary (of state)** *n* GB Pol Admin directeur/-trice *m/f* de cabinet; **~ under-secretary** *n* GB Pol Admin ≈ conseiller/-ère *m/f*; **~ wave**† *n* permanente *f*; **~ way** *n* Rail voie *f* ferrée.

permanganate /pəːˈmæŋgəneɪt/ *n* permanganate *m*; **potassium ~** permanganate *m* de potassium.

permeability /ˌpɜːmɪəˈbɪlətɪ/ *n* perméabilité *f*.

permeable /ˈpɜːmɪəbl/ *adj* perméable.

permeate /ˈpɜːmɪeɪt/ **I** *vtr* **1** [*liquid, gas*] s'infiltrer dans; [*odour*] pénétrer dans; **2** fig [*ideas*] imprégner.
II permeated *pp adj* **to be ~d with** être imprégné de also fig.

Permian /ˈpɜːmɪən/ **I** *n* **the ~** le permien.
II *adj* permien/-ienne.

permissible /pəˈmɪsɪbl/ *adj* [*level, limit, conduct*] admissible; [*error*] acceptable, tolérable; **it is morally/legally ~ to do** il est moralement/légalement admissible de faire; **to tell sb what is ~** dire à qn ce qui est permis.

permission /pəˈmɪʃn/ *n* gen permission *f*; (official) autorisation *f*; **to have ~ to do** avoir la permission or l'autorisation de faire; **to do sth without ~** faire qch sans permission or sans autorisation; **to get ~ to do** obtenir la permission or l'autorisation de faire; **to give ~ for sb to do, to give sb ~ to do** donner la permission à qn de faire, autoriser qn à faire; **he will not give ~ for any player to miss training** il n'autorisera aucun joueur à manquer l'entraînement; **she will not give ~ for the meeting to take place** elle n'autorisera pas la réunion; **to ask (for) sb's ~ to do** demander la permission à qn de faire; **written ~ to do** l'autorisation écrite de faire; **reprinted by ~ of the author** reproduit avec l'autorisation de l'auteur; **by kind ~ of the management** avec l'aimable autorisation de la direction.

permissive /pəˈmɪsɪv/ *adj* **1** (morally lax) permissif/-ive; **the ~ society** la société permissive; **during the ~ sixties** pendant la période permissive des années 60; **2** (liberal) [*view, law*] libéral; **to take a ~ view on sth** avoir une opinion libérale sur qch.

permissively /pəˈmɪsɪvlɪ/ *adv* libéralement; **some of us view such problems more ~ than others** certains d'entre nous ont des vues plus libérales que d'autres.

permissiveness /pəˈmɪsɪvnɪs/ *n* permissivité *f*.

permit I /ˈpɜːmɪt/ *n* **1** (document) permis *m*; (official permission) autorisation *f*; **to apply for/issue a ~** faire une demande de permis/délivrer un permis; **work/fishing ~** permis *m* de travail/pêche: **2** US Aut permis *m* (de conduire).
II /pəˈmɪt/ *vtr* (*p prés etc* **-tt-**) **1** (allow) permettre [*action, measure*]; **travel by herself? her parents would never ~ it!** voyager toute seule? ses parents ne le permettraient jamais; **smoking is not ~ted** il est interdit de fumer; **to ~ sb to do** permettre à qn de faire; **space does not ~ me to quote at length** l'espace ne me permet pas de citer en entier; **~ me, Madam, to assist you** permettez-moi, Madame, de vous aider; **2** (allow formally, officially) autoriser; **to ~ sb to do** autoriser qn à faire.
III /pəˈmɪt/ *vi* (*p prés etc* **-tt-**) permettre; **weather ~ting** si le temps le permet; **time ~ting** à condition d'en avoir le temps; **as soon as circumstances ~, I will join you** dès que les circonstances le permettront, je vous rejoindrai; **to ~ of two interpretations** sout [*text, phrase*] se prêter à deux interprétations; **to ~ of no delay** sout [*matter*] n'admettre aucun retard; **to ~ of no defence** sout être indéfendable.
IV **permitted** *pp adj* [*additive, level*] autorisé.
V /pəˈmɪt/ *v refl* **to ~ oneself** se permettre [*smile, drink*].

permutation /ˌpɜːmjʊˈteɪʃn/ *n* (all contexts) permutation *f*.

permute /pəˈmjuːt/ *vtr* permuter.

pernicious /pəˈnɪʃəs/ *adj* (all contexts) pernicieux/-ieuse.

pernicious anaemia ▶ 1354 *n* anémie *f* pernicieuse.

perniciously /pəˈnɪʃəslɪ/ *adv* [*damage, spread*] de façon pernicieuse; [*invasive*] pernicieusement.

pernickety° GB /pəˈnɪkətɪ/ *adj* **1** (detail-conscious) pointilleux/-euse (**about** sur); **2** (choosy) péj tatillon/-onne (**about** quant à).

peroration /ˌperəˈreɪʃn/ *n* péroraison *f*.

peroxide /pəˈrɒksaɪd/ *n* **1** Chem peroxyde *m*; **2** (also **hydrogen ~**) Pharm eau *f* oxygénée.

peroxide blonde *n* péj blonde *f* décolorée.

perpend /pəˈpend/ *n* Constr parpaing *m*.

perpendicular /ˌpɜːpənˈdɪkjʊlə(r)/ I *n* **1** gen, Math verticale *f* (**to** à); **to lean from the ~** dévier de la verticale; **2** Archit style *m* perpendiculaire.
II *adj* **1** [*line*] perpendiculaire; **a ~ cliff face** un à-pic; **2** Archit [*style*] perpendiculaire; [*building*] de style perpendiculaire.

perpendicularly /ˌpɜːpənˈdɪkjʊləlɪ/ *adv* perpendiculairement.

perpetrate /ˈpɜːpɪtreɪt/ *vtr* perpétrer [*deed, fraud*]; monter [*hoax*].

perpetration /ˌpɜːpɪˈtreɪʃn/ *n* **1** (carrying out) perpétration *f*; **2**† (crime) forfait *m*.

perpetrator /ˈpɜːpɪtreɪtə(r)/ *n* auteur *m* (**of** de).

perpetual /pəˈpetʃʊəl/ *adj* [*meetings, longing, disloyalty, turmoil*] perpétuel/-elle; [*darkness, stench, state*] permanent; [*banter*] éternel/-elle.

perpetually /pəˈpetʃʊəlɪ/ *adv* perpétuellement.

perpetual motion *n* mouvement *m* perpétuel.

perpetuate /pəˈpetjʊeɪt/ *vtr* perpétuer.

perpetuation /pəˌpetʃʊˈeɪʃn/ *n* perpétuation *f* (**of** de).

perpetuity /ˌpɜːpɪˈtjuːətɪ, US -ˈtuː-/ *n* **1** (eternity) perpétuité *f*; **in ~** gen, Jur à perpétuité; **2** Fin annuité *f* à vie.

perpetuity rule *n* Jur *règle empêchant tout contrat immobilier à perpétuité.*

perplex /pəˈpleks/ *vtr* plonger [qn] dans la perplexité.

perplexed /pəˈplekst/ *adj* perplexe; **to be ~ as to why/how** se demander pourquoi/comment.

perplexedly /pəˈpleksɪdlɪ/ *adv* avec perplexité.

perplexing /pəˈpleksɪŋ/ *adj* [*behaviour*] curieux/-ieuse; [*situation*] confus; [*question*] difficile.

perplexity /pəˈpleksətɪ/ *n* perplexité *f*.

perquisite /ˈpɜːkwɪzɪt/ *n* avantage *m*.

perry /ˈperɪ/ *n* (drink) poiré *m*.

per se /ˌpɜː ˈseɪ/ *adv* en soi.

persecute /ˈpɜːsɪkjuːt/ *vtr* persécuter (**for** pour; **for doing** pour avoir fait); **he was ~d for being a member/for having a different view** on l'a persécuté parce qu'il était membre/parce qu'il avait une conception différente.

persecution /ˌpɜːsɪˈkjuːʃn/ *n* persécution *f* (**of** de; **by** par).

persecution complex, **persecution mania** *n* délire *m* de persécution.

persecutor /ˈpɜːsɪkjuːtə(r)/ *n* persécuteur/-trice *m/f*.

Persephone /pɜːˈsefənɪ/ *pr n* Perséphone.

Perseus /ˈpɜːsjuːs/ *pr n* Persée.

perseverance /ˌpɜːsɪˈvɪərəns/ *n* persévérance *f*.

persevere /ˌpɜːsɪˈvɪə(r)/ *vi* persévérer (**with, at** dans; **in doing** à faire).

persevering /ˌpɜːsɪˈvɪərɪŋ/ *adj* persévérant (**in** dans).

Persia /ˈpɜːʃə/ ▶ 1131 *pr n* Hist Perse *f*.

Persian /ˈpɜːʃn/ ▶ 1486, 1402 I *n* **1** (person) (ancient) Perse *mf*; (from 7th century on) Persan/-e *m/f*; **2** Ling persan *m*.
II *adj* [*person, state*] (ancient) perse; (from 7th century on) persan; [*carpet, cat*] persan.

Persian: **~ Gulf** ▶ 1511 *pr n* Golfe *m* persique; **~ lamb** *n* astrakan *m*.

persiflage /ˈpɜːsɪflɑːʒ/ *n* propos *mpl* frivoles.

persimmon /pɜːˈsɪmən/ *n* **1** (tree) plaqueminier *m*, kaki *m*; **2** (fruit) kaki *m*.

persist /pəˈsɪst/ I *vtr* **'go on,' she ~ed** 'allez-y,' a-t-elle insisté.
II *vi* persister (**in** dans; **in doing** à faire).

persistence /pəˈsɪstəns/, **persistency** /pəˈsɪstənsɪ/ *n* gen persévérance *f*; pej persistance *f* (**in** dans; **in doing** à faire).

persistent /pəˈsɪstənt/ *adj* **1** [*person*] (persevering) persévérant; (obstinate) obstiné pej (**in** dans); **2** (continual) [*rain, denial, unemployment, nuisance*] persistant; [*inquiries, meddling, noise, pressure*] continuel/-elle; [*illness, fears, problem, idea*] tenace.

persistently /pəˈsɪstəntlɪ/ *adv* continuellement.

persistent offender *n* Jur récidiviste *mf*.

persnickety° /pəˈsnɪkətɪ/ *adj* US = **pernickety**.

person /ˈpɜːsn/ *n* **1** (human being) (*pl* **people**, **persons** sout) personne *f*; **there's room for one more ~** il y a de la place pour une autre personne; **you're just the ~ we're looking for!** vous êtes exactement la personne qu'il nous faut; **the average ~ cannot afford to run three cars** une personne ordinaire ne peut pas se permettre d'avoir trois voitures; **the English drink four cups of tea per ~ per day** les Anglais boivent quatre tasses de thé par personne et par jour; **to do sth in ~** faire qch en personne; **he's not the kind of ~ to do** ou **who would do such a thing** ce n'est pas le genre à faire ça; **help appeared in the ~ of passing motorist Jo Ware** le secours s'est manifesté dans la personne de Jo Ware, une automobiliste qui passait; **single ~** célibataire *mf*; **the ~ concerned** l'intéressé/-e *m/f*; **no such ~ as Sherlock Holmes ever existed** Sherlock Holmes n'a jamais existé; **'any ~ who knows of his whereabouts is requested to contact the police'** 'toute personne sachant où il se trouve est priée de contacter la police'; **the accident killed one ~ and injured four more** l'accident a fait un mort et quatre blessés; **a five-~ crew is being sent to the scene** on envoie une équipe de cinq personnes sur les lieux; **the very ~ I was looking for!** c'est justement toi que je cherchais!; **2** (type) **I didn't know she was a horsey ~**°! je ne savais pas que c'était une passionnée de cheval!; **I'm not a wine ~ myself** je ne suis pas amateur de vin; **what's she like as a ~?** en tant que femme, elle est comment?; **he's a very private/discreet ~** il est très réservé/discret; **3** (body) **to have/carry sth about one's ~** avoir/porter qch sur soi; **with drugs concealed about his ~** avec de la drogue cachée sur lui; Jur **offences against the ~** atteintes à la personne; **her ~ was pleasing**† elle était agréable de sa personne†; **4** Ling personne *f*; **the first ~ singular** la première personne du singulier.

persona /pɜːˈsəʊnə/ *n* **1** Theat (*pl* **-ae**) personnage *m*; **dramatis ~e** personnages *mpl* (de la pièce); **2** Psych (*pl* **-ae** GB, **~s** US) personnage *m*.

personable /ˈpɜːsənəbl/ *adj* [*man, woman*] qui présente bien; **to be ~** être bien de sa personne.

personage /ˈpɜːsənɪdʒ/ *n* personnalité *f*; **a royal ~** une personnalité de la famille royale.

persona grata *n* persona grata *inv*.

personal /ˈpɜːsənl/ I *n* US petite annonce *f* personnelle.
II *adj* [*opinion, life, problem, information, attack, remark*] personnel/-elle; [*consumption, freedom, choice, income, profit*] individuel/-elle; [*service*] personnalisé; [*discussion, dispute, matter*] personnel/-elle, privé; **don't be so ~!** ne fais pas d'allusions personnelles!; **the discussion/argument became rather ~** la discussion/dispute a pris un ton personnel; **on** ou **at a ~ level** sur le plan personnel; **for ~ reasons** pour des raisons personnelles; **he doesn't take enough care of his ~ appearance** il ne prend pas assez soin de son apparence; **to make a ~ appearance** venir en personne (**at** à); **he paid them a ~ visit** il leur a rendu visite en personne; **~ call** (on telephone) appel *m* personnel; **~ belongings** ou **effects** effets *mpl* personnels; **~ friend** ami personnel/amie personnelle *m/f*; **~ hygiene** hygiène *f* intime; **~ possessions** effets *mpl* personnels; **~ safety** sécurité *f* individuelle; **my ~ best is 10 seconds** mon meilleur temps est de 10 secondes; **as a ~ favour to you** pour te faire plaisir, spécialement pour toi.

personal: **~ accident insurance** *n* Insur assurance *f* individuelle contre les accidents; **~ ad** *n* petite annonce *f* personnelle; **~ allowance** *n* GB Tax abattement *m* fiscal personnel; **~ assistant** ▶ 1692 *n* (secretary) (also **PA**) secrétaire *mf* de direction; (assistant) assistant/-e *m/f*; **~ chair** *n* GB Univ chaire *f* personnelle; **~ column** *n* petites annonces *fpl* personnelles; **~ computer**, **PC** *n* ordinateur *m* (personnel); **~ damages** *npl* Jur dommages *mpl* individuels; **~ details** *npl* gen renseignements *mpl* d'ordre personnel; (more intimate) détails *mpl* intimes; Admin (on application form) état civil *m* et coordonnées *fpl*; **Personal Equity Plan**, **PEP** *n* GB Fin *plan d'investissement en actions avec abattement fiscal plafonné sur les dividendes et plus-values*; **~ injury** *n* Jur préjudices *m* individuels.

personality /ˌpɜːsəˈnælətɪ/ *n* **1** (character) personnalité *f*; **the study of ~** l'étude de la personnalité; **to have an attractive/extrovert ~** avoir une personnalité séduisante/extravertie; **to dominate others by sheer force of ~** dominer les autres par la seule force de sa personnalité; **she has a very strong ~** elle a une très forte personnalité, elle a beaucoup de caractère; **let's leave personalities out of this!** pas de commentaires personnels!; **2** (person) personnalité *f*; **a well-known local ~** une personnalité locale bien connue; **a sporting ~** une vedette du sport; **a television ~** une vedette de la télévision.

personality: **~ cult** *n* culte *m* de la personnalité; **~ disorder** *n* troubles *mpl* de la personnalité; **~ test** *n* test *m* de personnalité.

personalize /ˈpɜːsənəlaɪz/ **I** *vtr* **1** (tailor to individual) personnaliser [*stationery, number-plate, clothing, car, letter*]; **2** (aim at individual) ramener [qch] à un plan personnel [*issue, discussion, dispute*].
II personalized *pp adj* [*number-plate, badge*] personnalisé.

personal loan *n* Fin (borrowed) emprunt *m* (à titre personnel); (given by bank etc) prêt *m* personnel.

personally /ˈpɜːsənəlɪ/ *adv* personnellement; **~, I'm against the idea** personnellement or pour ma part, je suis contre; **~ speaking** personnellement; **to take sth ~** se sentir visé personnellement par qch.

personal: **~ maid** *n* femme *f* de chambre (*personnelle*); **~ organizer** *n* ≈ agenda *m*; **~ pension plan**, **~ pension scheme** *n* Insur plan *m* de retraite; **~ pronoun** *n* Ling pronom *m* personnel; **~ property** *n* Jur biens *mpl* personnels; **~ stereo** *n* Audio baladeur *m*.

personalty /ˈpɜːsənltɪ/ *n* Jur biens *mpl* mobiliers.

persona non grata *n* persona non grata *inv*.

personate /ˈpɜːsəneɪt/ *vtr* Theat incarner.

personation /ˌpɜːsəˈneɪʃn/ *n* Theat incarnation *f* (**of** de).

personification /pəˌsɒnɪfɪˈkeɪʃn/ *n* **1** (embodiment) incarnation *f* (**of** de); **2** Literat personnification *f*.

personify /pəˈsɒnɪfaɪ/ *vtr* **1** incarner [*ideal, attitude*]; **2** Literat personnifier [*beauty, faith*].

personnel /ˌpɜːsəˈnel/ *n* **1** gen, Mil (staff, troops) personnel *m*; **2** Admin (also **Personnel**) service *m* du personnel; **you'll have to see ~ about that** vous devrez consulter le service du personnel à ce sujet.

personnel: **~ carrier** *n* véhicule *m* de transport de troupes; **~ department** *n* service *m* du personnel; **~ file** *n* dossier *m* personnel; **~ management** *n* gestion *f* du personnel; **~ manager** **▶ 1692** *n* directeur/-trice *mf* du personnel; **~ officer** **▶ 1692** *n* responsable *mf* du personnel.

person-to-person **I** *adj* Telecom [*call*] avec préavis.
II *adv* Telecom [*phone, call*] en préavis.

perspective /pəˈspektɪv/ *n* gen, Art perspective *f*; **new/historical ~** perspective nouvelle/historique; **from one's (own) ~** de son (propre) point de vue; **to keep things in ~** garder un sens de la mesure; **to let things get out of ~** perdre le sens de la mesure; **to put sth in its true ~** ramener qch à ses véritables proportions; **to put sth/things into ~** relativiser qch/les choses; **to see sth from a different ~** appréhender qch sous un angle différent.

perspex® /ˈpɜːspeks/ **I** *n* plexiglas® *m*.
II *modif* [*shield, window*] en plexiglas®.

perspicacious /ˌpɜːspɪˈkeɪʃəs/ *adj* sout perspicace.

perspicacity /ˌpɜːspɪˈkæsətɪ/ *n* sout perspicacité *f*.

perspicuity /ˌpəspɪˈkjuːətɪ/ *n* sout netteté *f*.

perspicuous /pəˈspɪkjʊəs/ *adj* sout clair.

perspiration /ˌpɜːspɪˈreɪʃn/ *n* **1** (sweat) sueur *f*; **2** (sweating) transpiration *f*.

perspire /pəˈspaɪə(r)/ *vi* transpirer.

persuade /pəˈsweɪd/ **I** *vtr* **1** (influence) persuader, convaincre [*person*]; **to ~ sb to do/not to do** persuader or convaincre qn de faire/de ne pas faire; **to be ~d by sb to do** être convaincu par qn de faire; **2** (convince intellectually) convaincre (**of** de); **to ~ sb that** convaincre qn que; **try and ~ her!** essaie de la convaincre!; **you will never ~ the rest of the family** tu ne convaincras jamais le reste de la famille.
II *v refl* **to ~ oneself** réussir à se convaincre; **he ~d himself that it was true** il a réussi à se convaincre que c'était vrai.

persuader○ /pəˈsweɪdə(r)/ *n* US (gun) flingue● *m*.

persuasion /pəˈsweɪʒn/ *n* **1** ¢ (persuading, persuasiveness) persuasion *f*; **they had to use all their powers of ~ to get her to agree** ils ont dû employer toute leur force de persuasion pour l'amener à accepter; **no amount of ~ will make her change her mind** on aura beau essayer de la persuader, rien ne la fera changer d'avis; **to be open to ~** être prêt à se laisser convaincre; **2** Relig confession *f*; **3** (political view) conviction *f*; **people of very different political ~s** des personnes de convictions politiques très différentes; **that depends on your ~** cela dépend de vos convictions; **4** (kind, sort) sorte *f*; **people of that ~** les gens de cette sorte.

persuasive /pəˈsweɪsɪv/ *adj* [*person*] persuasif/-ive, convaincant; [*argument, evidence, words*] convaincant; **he can be very ~** il peut être très persuasif.

persuasively /pəˈsweɪsɪvlɪ/ *adv* [*speak*] d'un ton persuasif; [*prove, demonstrate*] d'une manière convaincante; **this view is ~ developed** ce point de vue est exposé de manière convaincante.

persuasiveness /pəˈsweɪsɪvnɪs/ *n* force *f* de persuasion.

pert /pɜːt/ *adj* [*person, manner*] espiègle; [*hat, nose*] coquin.

pertain /pəˈteɪn/ *vi* **to ~ to** Jur dépendre de; gen se rapporter à.

pertinacious /ˌpɜːtɪˈneɪʃəs, US -tnˈeɪʃəs/ *adj* sout opiniâtre.

pertinaciously /ˌpɜːtɪˈneɪʃəslɪ, US -tnˈeɪʃəs-/ *adv* sout opiniâtrement.

pertinacity /ˌpɜːtɪˈnæsətɪ, US -tnˈæ-/ *n* sout opiniâtreté *f* (**in** dans; **in doing** à faire).

pertinence /ˈpɜːtɪnəns, US -tənəns/ *n* sout pertinence *f*.

pertinent /ˈpɜːtɪnənt, US -tənənt/ *adj* sout [*question, point*] pertinent; **to be ~ to** avoir rapport à; **to be ~ to do** être approprié de faire.

pertinently /ˈpɜːtɪnəntlɪ, US -tənəntlɪ/ *adv* sout pertinemment.

pertly /ˈpɜːtlɪ/ *adv* espiègIement.

pertness /ˈpɜːtnɪs/ *n* espièglerie *f*.

perturb /pəˈtɜːb/ *vtr* [*news, rumour*] perturber; **to be ~ed by** [*person*] être troublé par; (more deeply) être alarmé par.

perturbation /ˌpɜːtəˈbeɪʃn/ *n* **1** (disquiet) agitation *f*; **2** (disturbance) moment *m* d'agitation; **3** Astron, Phys perturbation *f*.

perturbing /pəˈtɜːbɪŋ/ *adj* troublant; (more deeply) alarmant.

pertussis /pəˈtʌsɪs/ **▶ 1354** *n* spéc coqueluche *f*.

Peru /pəˈruː/ **▶ 1131** *pr n* Pérou *m*.

Perugia /pəˈruːdʒə/ **▶ 1818** *pr n* Pérouse.

perusal /pəˈruːzl/ *n* sout lecture *f*.

peruse /pəˈruːz/ *vtr* sout passer en revue.

Peruvian /pəˈruːvɪən/ **▶ 1486** **I** *n* Péruvien/-ienne *m/f*.
II *adj* péruvien/-ienne.

pervade /pəˈveɪd/ *vtr* imprégner; **to be ~d by** être imprégné par.

pervasive /pəˈveɪsɪv/ *adj* [*smell*] pénétrant; [*idea, feeling*] envahissant.

perverse /pəˈvɜːs/ *adj* **1** (twisted) [*person*] retors; [*desire*] pervers; **2** (contrary) [*refusal, attempt, behaviour, attitude*] illogique; [*effect*] contraire; **it is/was ~ of her to do** c'est/c'était illogique de sa part de faire; **to take a ~ pleasure** ou **delight in doing** prendre un malin plaisir à faire.

perversely /pəˈvɜːslɪ/ *adv* avec un malin plaisir.

perverseness /pəˈvɜːsnɪs/ *n* = **perversity 1**.

perverse verdict *n* Jur *verdict en contradiction avec les directives du juge sur un point de droit.*

perversion /pəˈvɜːʃn, US -ʒn/ *n* **1** (deviation) perversion *f* (**of** de); **~ of innocence** perversion de l'innocence; **2** (wrong interpretation) (of facts, justice) travestissement *m* (**of** de).

perversity /pəˈvɜːsətɪ/ *n* **1** (corruptness) (of person) mauvais esprit *m*; (of action) malignité *f*; **2** (perverse thing) caprice *m*.

pervert **I** /ˈpɜːvɜːt/ *n* pervers/-e *m/f*.
II /pəˈvɜːt/ *vtr* **1** (corrupt) corrompre [*person, mind, behaviour*]; **2** (misrepresent) travestir [*truth, facts*]; dénaturer [*meaning, tradition*]; fausser [*values*]; **to ~ the course of justice** Jur entraver l'action de la justice.

perverted /pəˈvɜːtɪd/ *adj* **1** (sexually deviant) [*person*] pervers; **2** (distorted) [*idea*] tordu; [*act*] vicieux/-ieuse.

pervious /ˈpɜːvɪəs/ *adj* **1** [*surface, soil*] perméable (**to** à); **2** fig **~ to** [*person, mind*] ouvert à.

peseta /pəˈseɪtə/ **▶ 1143** *n* peseta *f*.

pesky○ /ˈpeskɪ/ *adj* US (*épith*) satané○ (*before n*).

peso /ˈpeɪsəʊ/ **▶ 1143** *n* peso *m*.

pessary /ˈpesərɪ/ *n* pessaire *m*.

pessimism /ˈpesɪmɪzəm/ *n* pessimisme *m*.

pessimist /ˈpesɪmɪst/ *n* pessimiste *mf*.

pessimistic /ˌpesɪˈmɪstɪk/ *adj* pessimiste.

pessimistically /ˌpesɪˈmɪstɪklɪ/ *adv* avec pessimisme.

pest /pest/ *n* **1** Agric (animal) animal *m* nuisible; (insect) insecte *m* nuisible; **2**○ (person) gen enquiquineur/-euse○ *m/f*; (little boy) garnement *m*; (little girl) chipie○ *f*; **he's such a little ~!** c'est un vrai garnement!

pest control *n* (of insects) désinsectisation *f*; (of rats) dératisation *f*.

pest control officer **▶ 1692** *n* (for insects) employé/-e *m/f* des services de désinsectation; (for rats) employé/-e *m/f* des services de dératisation.

pester /ˈpestə(r)/ *vtr* **1** (annoy) harceler [*person, people*] (**with** de; **for** pour obtenir); [*fly*] harceler [*horse, cow, person*]; **to ~ sb to be allowed to do** harceler qn pour obtenir la permission de faire; **the children ~ed us to let them stay up late** les enfants nous ont harcelés pour qu'on les laisse veiller; **to be ~ed over the telephone** se faire harceler au téléphone; **stop ~ing me!** fiche-moi la paix!○; **to ~ the life out of sb**○ casser les pieds à qn○; **2** (harass sexually) harceler, poursuivre [qn] de ses assiduités.

pesticidal /ˌpestɪˈsaɪdl/ *adj* pesticide.

pesticide /ˈpestɪsaɪd/ **I** *n* pesticide *m*; **crops treated with ~** des cultures traitées aux pesticides.
II *modif* [*level, residue*] de pesticide; [*manufacturer, use*] de pesticides.

pestiferous /peˈstɪfərəs/ *adj* hum satané○.

pestilence‡ /ˈpestɪləns/ *n* littér peste *f*.

pestilent /ˈpestɪlənt/ *adj* sout [*air*] pestilentiel/-ielle.

pestilential /ˌpestɪˈlenʃl/ *adj* **1** hum (annoying) satané○; **get those ~ kids out of here** fais sortir ces satanés gosses○; **2** (unhealthy) sout pestilentiel/-ielle.

pestle /ˈpesl/ *n* pilon *m*.

pet /pet/ **I** *n* **1** (animal) animal *m* de compagnie; **'no ~s'** 'les animaux domestiques ne sont pas acceptés'; **tenants may not keep ~s** les locataires n'ont pas le droit d'avoir des animaux; **2** (favourite) chouchou/chouchoute○ *m/f*; **teacher's ~** le chouchou du professeur○; **3** (sweet person) (used affectedly) chou○ *m*; **he's such a ~!** ce qu'il est

chou○!; 4† (term of endearment) **hello, ~!** bonjour mon chou○!
II *adj* (favourite) [*charity, theory*] favori/-ite; **~ dog/cat** chien/chat.
III *vtr* (*p prés etc* **-tt-**) **1** (spoil) chouchouter○ [*person*]; **2** (caress) caresser [*animal*].
IV *vi* (*p prés etc* **-tt-**) échanger des caresses, se peloter○.
IDIOMS **to be in a ~**○ être de mauvais poil○.

petal /ˈpetl/ *n* pétale *m*.

Pete○ /piːt/ *pr n* (*abrév* = **Peter**) **for ~'s sake, stop it!** mais enfin, arrête!

peter /ˈpiːtə(r)/ *n*◑ US queue● *f*, pénis *m*; **to point ~** pisser◑.
■ **peter out** [*conversation, creativity*] tarir; [*process, story, meeting*] tourner court; [*plan*] tomber à l'eau; [*flame*] mourir; [*road*] s'arrêter; [*supplies*] s'épuiser.

Peter /ˈpiːtə(r)/ *pr n* Pierre.
IDIOMS **to rob ~ to pay Paul** déshabiller Pierre pour habiller Paul.

Peter: **~ principle** *n* principe *m* de Peter; **~'s pence** *npl* Relig denier *m* de Saint-Pierre.

pet: **~ food** *n* aliments *mpl* pour chiens et chats; **~ hate** GB *n* bête *f* noire.

pethidine /ˈpeθɪdiːn/ *n* Med péthidine *f*.

petit bourgeois /ˌpetɪˈbɔːʒwɑː, US -bʊərʒ-/ *n, adj* petit/-e bourgeois/-e (*m/f*).

petite /pəˈtiːt/ I *n* (size) taille *f* petite.
II *adj* [*woman*] menue; [*size*] petite.

petit four /ˌpetɪˈfɔː(r)/ *n* petit four *m*.

petition /pəˈtɪʃn/ I *n* **1** (document) pétition *f* (**to** à); **a ~ protesting against/calling for sth** une pétition protestant contre/réclamant qch; **a ~ signed by 10,000 people** une pétition portant 10000 signatures; **2** (formal request) pétition *f*; **3** Jur demande *f*; **a ~ for divorce** une demande de divorce; **a ~ in bankruptcy** une demande en déclaration de faillite; **to present a ~** (in private bill) soumettre une demande; **to file one's ~** déposer son bilan; **a ~ for reprieve** un recours en grâce.
II *vtr* adresser une pétition à [*person, body, government*]; Jur **to ~ the court for sth** réclamer qch au tribunal.
III *vi* **1** gen faire une pétition; **2** Jur **to ~ for divorce** demander le divorce.

petitioner /pəˈtɪʃnə(r)/ *n* **1** (presenter of petition, signatory) pétitionnaire *mf*; **2** Jur gen requérant/-ante *m/f*; (in divorce) demandeur/-deresse *m/f*.

petit jury *n* US Jur jury *m* d'accusation.

petit mal /ˌpetɪ ˈmæl, ˌpətɪ/ ▶ 1354 *n* petit mal *m*.

petit pois *n* petit pois *m*.

pet: **~ name** *n* petit nom *m*; **~ peeve**○ *n* US bête *f* noire; **~ project** *n* enfant *m* chéri fig.

Petrarch /ˈpetrɑːk/ *pr n* Pétrarque.

Petrarchan sonnet *n* (by poet himself) sonnet *m* de Pétrarque; (of similar style) sonnet *m* pétrarquiste.

petrel /ˈpetrəl/ *n* pétrel *m*.

petrifaction /ˌpetrɪˈfækʃn/ *n* (also **petrification**) pétrification *f*.

petrified /ˈpetrɪfaɪd/ *adj* (all contexts) pétrifié (**with, by** par).

petrify /ˈpetrɪfaɪ/ I *vtr* (all contexts) pétrifier.
II *vi* [*substance*] se pétrifier; [*civilisation, system*] se fossiliser.

petrifying /ˈpetrɪfaɪɪŋ/ *adj* (terrifying) terrifiant.

petro+ /ˈpetrəʊ-/ (*dans composés*) pétro-.

petrochemical /ˌpetrəʊˈkemɪkl/ I *n* produit *m* pétrochimique.
II *adj* [*industry, plant*] pétrochimique; [*worker, expert*] de pétrochimie.

petrodollar /ˈpetrəʊdɒlə(r)/ *n* pétrodollar *m*.

petrographic /ˌpetrəʊˈgræfɪk/ *adj* pétrographique.

petrography /peˈtrɒgrəfɪ/ *n* pétrographie *f*.

petrol /ˈpetrəl/ GB I *n* essence *f*; **to fill up with ~** faire le plein (d'essence); **to run on ~** fonctionner à l'essence; **to run out of ~** [*car*] tomber en panne d'essence; [*garage*] ne plus avoir d'essence.
II *modif* [*prices, coupon, rationing*] d'essence; [*tax*] sur l'essence.

petrol bomb GB I *n* cocktail *m* Molotov.
II **petrol-bomb** *vtr* lancer des cocktails Molotov sur [*building*].

petrol: **~ can** GB *n* bidon *m* à essence; **~ cap** *n* GB bouchon *m* de réservoir (d'essence); **~-driven** *adj* GB à essence; **~ engine** *n* GB moteur *m* à essence.

petroleum /pəˈtrəʊlɪəm/ I *n* pétrole *m*.
II *modif* [*product, industry, engineer*] pétrolier/-ière.

petroleum jelly *n* vaseline® *f*.

petrol gauge *n* GB jauge *f* d'essence.

petroliferous /ˌpetrəʊˈlɪfərəs/ *adj* pétrolifère.

petrology /pəˈtrɒlədʒɪ/ *n* pétrologie *f*.

petrol: **~ pump** *n* GB (at garage, in engine) pompe *f* à essence; **~ station** *n* GB station *f* d'essence; **~ tank** *n* GB réservoir *m* d'essence; **~ tanker** *n* GB (ship) pétrolier *m*; (lorry) camion-citerne *m*.

petro-politics /ˌpetrəʊˈpɒlɪtɪks/ *npl*: *politique menée par les pays exportateurs de pétrole*.

pet: **~ shop** GB, **~ store** US *n* animalerie *f*, magasin *m* d'animaux de compagnie; **~ subject** *n* sujet *m* favori, dada *m*.

petticoat /ˈpetɪkəʊt/ *n* (full slip) combinaison *f*; (half slip) jupon *m*.
IDIOMS **to chase ~s** être coureur de jupons.

pettifogging /ˈpetɪfɒgɪŋ/ *adj* péj pointilleux/-euse.

pettily /ˈpetɪlɪ/ *adv* mesquinement.

pettiness /ˈpetɪnɪs/ *n* mesquinerie *f*.

petting /ˈpetɪŋ/ *n* caresses *fpl*, pelotage○ *m*.

pettish /ˈpetɪʃ/ *adj* grincheux/-euse.

pettishly /ˈpetɪʃlɪ/ *adv* [*speak*] d'un ton grincheux; [*react*] avec mauvaise humeur.

petty /ˈpetɪ/ *adj* [*person, jealousy, squabble*] mesquin; [*detail*] insignifiant; [*regulation*] tracassier/-ière; [*snobbery*] étroit; **~ official** péj petit fonctionnaire *m*.

petty: **~ cash**, **p/c** *n* petite caisse *f*; **~ crime** *n* petite délinquance *f*; **~ criminal** *n* petit/-e délinquant/-e *m/f*; **~ expenses** *npl* menues dépenses *fpl*; **~ larceny** *n* larcin *m*; **~-minded** *adj* mesquin; **~-mindedness** *n* mesquinerie *f*; **~ officer** *n* Naut ≈ maître *m*; **~ sessions** *npl* GB, Jur sessions *fpl* des juges de paix; **~ theft** *n* Jur larcin *m*.

petulance /ˈpetjʊləns, US -tʃʊ-/ *n* irascibilité *f*.

petulant /ˈpetjʊlənt, US -tʃʊ-/ *adj* irascible.

petulantly /ˈpetʊləntlɪ, US -tʃʊ-/ *adv* avec humeur.

petunia /pəˈtjuːnɪə, US -tuː-/ *n* pétunia *m*.

pew /pjuː/ *n* banc *m* (d'église); **have** ou **take a ~**○ hum prenez un siège.

pewter /ˈpjuːtə(r)/ I *n* **1** (metal) étain *m*; **2** (colour) (gris *m*) anthracite *m inv*.
II *modif* [*plate, pot*] en étain.
III *adj* (colour) (gris) anthracite *inv*.

PFC *n* US Mil *abrév* ▶ **private first class.**

PFLP *n* Mil (*abrév* = **Popular Front for the Liberation of Palestine**) FPLP *m*.

PG *n* **1** Cin (*abrév* = **Parental Guidance**) *tous publics avec accord parental suggéré*; **2** *abrév* ▶ **paying guest**.

PGCE *n* (*abrév* = **postgraduate certificate in education**) diplôme *m* de spécialisation dans l'enseignement.

pH /piːˈeɪtʃ/ *n* (*abrév* = **potential of hydrogen**) pH *m inv*.

PH *n* Mil *abrév* ▶ **Purple Heart**.

Phaedra /ˈfiːdrə/ *pr n* Phèdre.

phaeton /ˈfeɪtn/ *n* phaéton *m*.

phagocyte /ˈfægəsaɪt/ *n* phagocyte *m*.

phagocytosis /ˌfægəsaɪˈtəʊsɪs/ *n* phagocytose *f*.

phalange /ˈfælændʒ/ *n* Anat, Mil phalange *f*.

phalanstery /ˈfælənstərɪ/ *n* phalanstère *m*.

phalanx /ˈfælæŋks/ *n* phalange *f*.

phalarope /ˈfælərəʊp/ *n* phalarope *m*.

phallic /ˈfælɪk/ *adj* phallique.

phallus /ˈfæləs/ *n* (*pl* **-luses** ou **-li**) phallus *m*.

phantasm /ˈfæntæzəm/ *n* **1** (ghost) fantôme *m*; **2** Psych fantasme *m*.

phantasmagoria /ˌfæntæzməˈgɒrɪə, US -ˈgɔːrɪə/ *n* fantasmagorie *f*.

phantasmagoric(al) /ˌfæntæzməˈgɒrɪk(l), US -ˈgɔːrɪk(l)/ *adj* fantasmagorique.

phantasmal /fænˈtæzml/ *adj* fantomatique.

phantom /ˈfæntəm/ I *n* **1** (ghost) fantôme *m*; **2** Aviat (also **~ jet**) Phantom *m*.
II *modif* [*army, bell, threat*] fantôme.

phantom pregnancy *n* grossesse *f* nerveuse.

pharaoh /ˈfeərəʊ/ *n* (also **Pharaoh**) pharaon *m*; (title) Pharaon *m*.

Pharaoh ant *n* Zool fourmi *f* pharaon.

Pharisaic(al) /ˌfærɪˈseɪk(l)/ *adj* souvent péj pharisaïque.

Pharisee /ˈfærɪsiː/ *n* Pharisien/-ienne *m/f*.

pharmaceutical /ˌfɑːməˈsjuːtɪkl, US -ˈsuː-/ *adj* pharmaceutique.

pharmaceuticals /ˌfɑːməˈsjuːtɪklz, US -ˈsuː-/ I *npl* produits *mpl* pharmaceutiques.
II *modif* [*industry, factory*] pharmaceutique; [*salesman*] de produits pharmaceutiques.

pharmacist /ˈfɑːməsɪst/ ▶ 1692 *n* (person) pharmacien/-ienne *m/f*; **~'s shop** pharmacie *f*.

pharmacological /ˌfɑːməkəˈlɒdʒɪkl/ *adj* pharmacologique.

pharmacology /ˌfɑːməˈkɒlədʒɪ/ *n* pharmacologie *f*.

pharmacopoeia /ˌfɑːməkəˈpiːə/ *n* pharmacopée *f*, codex *m*.

pharmacy /ˈfɑːməsɪ/ ▶ 1692 *n* **1** (shop) pharmacie *f*; **2** (also **pharmaceutics**) pharmaceutique *f*.

pharyngitis /ˌfærɪnˈdʒaɪtɪs/ ▶ 1354 *n* pharyngite *f*.

pharynx /ˈfærɪŋks/ *n* pharynx *m*.

phase /feɪz/ I *n* (all contexts) phase *f*; **the ~s of the moon** les phases de la lune; **to go through a difficult ~** traverser une phase difficile; **it's just a ~ (she's going through)** ça lui passera; **the war has entered a new ~** on est entré dans une nouvelle phase de la guerre; **the first ~ of the work** Constr la première phase or tranche des travaux; **to be in ~** Elec être en phase; fig être en harmonie; **to be out of ~** Elec être déphasé; fig ne pas être en harmonie.
II *vtr* échelonner [*changes, innovations, modernization*] (**over** sur); **~d withdrawal of troops** retrait progressif de troupes.
■ **phase in**: **~ in [sth]** introduire [qch] progressivement.
■ **phase out**: **~ out [sth]** supprimer [qch] peu à peu.

phatic /ˈfætɪk/ *adj* phatique.

PhD *n* (*abrév* = **Doctor of Philosophy**) doctorat *m*.

pheasant /ˈfeznt/ *n* faisan/-e *m/f*; **~ shooting** chasse *f* aux faisans.

phenix *n* US = **phoenix**.

phenobarbitone /ˌfiːnəʊˈbɑːbɪtəʊn/ *n* phénobarbital *m*, gardénal® *m*.

phenol /ˈfiːnɒl/ *n* phénol *m*.

phenomena /fəˈnɒmɪnə/ *pl* ▶ **phenomenon**.

phenomenal /fəˈnɒmɪnl/ *adj* phénoménal.

phenomenally /fəˈnɒmɪnəlɪ/ *adv* [*grow, increase*] de manière phénoménale; (emphatic) [*stupid, difficult, successful*] extraordinairement.

phenomenological /fəˌnɒmɪnəˈlɒdʒɪkl/ *adj* phénoménologique.

phenomenologist /fəˌnɒmɪˈnɒlədʒɪst/ *n* phénoménologue *mf*.
phenomenology /fəˌnɒmɪˈnɒlədʒɪ/ *n* phénoménologie *f*.
phenomenon /fəˈnɒmɪnən/ *n* (*pl* **-na**) phénomène *m*.
pheromone /ˈferəməʊn/ *n* phéromone *f*.
phew /fjuː/ *excl* (in relief) ouf; (when too hot) pff; (in surprise) oh.
phial /ˈfaɪəl/ *n* fiole *f*.
Phi Beta Kappa /ˌfaɪ biːtə ˈkæpə/ *n* US Univ **1** (group) *association d'anciens étudiants d'élite*; **2** (person) membre *m* de Phi Beta Kappa.
Philadelphia /ˌfɪləˈdelfɪə/ ▶ 1818 *pr n* Philadelphie.
Philadelphia lawyer *n* US péj avocat *m* retors.
philander /fɪˈlændə(r)/ *vi* courir la gueuse○.
philanderer /fɪˈlændərə(r)/ *n* coureur *m* de jupons○.
philandering /fɪˈlændərɪŋ/ *n* batifolage *m*.
philanthropic /ˌfɪlənˈθrɒpɪk/ *adj* philanthropique.
philanthropist /fɪˈlænθrəpɪst/ *n* philanthrope *mf*.
philanthropy /fɪˈlænθrəpɪ/ *n* philanthropie *f*.
philatelic /ˌfɪləˈtelɪk/ *adj* philatélique.
philatelist /fɪˈlætəlɪst/ *n* philatéliste *mf*.
philately /fɪˈlætəlɪ/ *n* philatélie *f*.
philharmonic /ˌfɪlɑːˈmɒnɪk/ **I** *n* (orchestra) **the Liverpool ~** le Philharmonique de Liverpool.
II *adj* [*hall, orchestra*] philharmonique.
Philip /ˈfɪlɪp/ *pr n* Philippe.
philippic /fɪˈlɪpɪk/ *n* philippique *f*.
Philippine /ˈfɪlɪpiːn/ ▶ 1486 *adj* philippin.
Philippines /ˈfɪlɪpiːnz/ ▶ 1131 *pr n* Philippines *fpl*.
philistine /ˈfɪlɪstaɪn/ **I** *n* béotien/-ienne *m/f*; **don't be such a ~!** ne sois pas aussi béotien!
II *adj* [*attitude, article*] béotien/-ienne; [*public*] de béotiens.
philistinism /ˈfɪlɪstɪnɪzəm/ *n* philistinisme *m*.
Phillips screwdriver *n* tournevis *m* cruciforme.
philodendron /ˌfɪləʊˈdendrən/ *n* philodendron *m*.
philological /ˌfɪləˈlɒdʒɪkl/ *adj* philologique.
philologist /fɪˈlɒlədʒɪst/ *n* philologue *mf*.
philology /fɪˈlɒlədʒɪ/ *n* philologie *f*.
philosopher /fɪˈlɒsəfə(r)/ ▶ 1692 *n* lit, fig philosophe *mf*.
philosopher's stone *n* pierre *f* philosophale.
philosophic(al) /ˌfɪləˈsɒfɪk(l)/ *adj* **1** [*knowledge, question, treatise*] philosophique; **2** fig (calm, stoical) philosophe; **to be ~ about sth, to take a ~ view of sth** être philosophe à propos de qch.
philosophically /ˌfɪləˈsɒfɪklɪ/ *adv* philosophiquement; **he took it all very ~** fig il a pris tout ça avec philosophie.
philosophize /fɪˈlɒsəfaɪz/ *vi* philosopher (**about** sur).
philosophy /fɪˈlɒsəfɪ/ *n* philosophie *f*; **my ~ of life** ma philosophie de la vie; **~ of science** philosophie des sciences.
philtre, philter US /ˈfɪltə(r)/ *n* philtre *m*.
phizog○† /ˈfɪzɒg/ *n* hum binette○ *f*, tête *f*.
phlebitis /flɪˈbaɪtɪs/ ▶ 1354 *n* phlébite *f*.
phlebology /flɪˈbɒlədʒɪ/ *n* phlébologie *f*.
phlebotomy /flɪˈbɒtəmɪ/ *n* phlébotomie *f*.
phlegm /flem/ *n* **1** Med mucosité *f*; **2** (calm) flegme *m*.
phlegmatic /flegˈmætɪk/ *adj* flegmatique (**about** au sujet de).
phlegmatically /flegˈmætɪklɪ/ *adv* avec flegme, flegmatiquement.
phlox /flɒks/ *n* phlox *m*.
pH meter *n* pH-mètre *m*.
phobia /ˈfəʊbɪə/ *n* phobie *f*; **to have a ~ about rats/spiders/flying** avoir la phobie des rats/des araignées/de l'avion.
phobic /ˈfəʊbɪk/ **I** *n* phobique *mf*.
II *adj* phobique; **to be ~ about sth** avoir la phobie de qch.
phoenix /ˈfiːnɪks/ *n* phénix *m*; **to rise like a ~ from the ashes** renaître de ses cendres tel le phénix.
phonatory /ˈfəʊnətərɪ, US -tɔːrɪ/ *adj* phonatoire.
phone /fəʊn/ **I** *n* **1** Telecom téléphone *m*; **to be on the ~** (be talking) être au téléphone; (be subscriber) avoir le téléphone; **she's on the ~ to her boyfriend** elle est au téléphone avec son copain; **he told me on** ou **over the ~ that** il m'a dit au téléphone que; **can you order by ~?** est-ce qu'on peut commander par téléphone?; **2** Ling phone *m*.
II *vtr* passer un coup de fil à○, téléphoner à [*person, organization*]; **she ~d her instructions to her lawyer** elle a téléphoné ses instructions à son avocat; **to ~ France** téléphoner en France, appeler la France.
III *vi* téléphoner; **to ~ for a doctor/taxi** appeler un médecin/taxi.
■ **phone in**: ¶ **~ in** [*listener, viewer*] téléphoner; ¶ **~ in [sth]** communiquer [qch] par téléphone [*information, answers*]; **she ~d in sick** elle a téléphoné au bureau pour dire qu'elle était malade.
■ **phone up**: ¶ **~ up** téléphoner; ¶ **~ up [sb], ~ [sb] up** téléphoner à, appeler [*person, organization*].
phone: **~ book** *n* annuaire *m* (du téléphone); **~ booth, ~ box** GB *n* cabine *f* téléphonique.
phone call *n* gen coup *m* de fil○, Admin communication *f* (téléphonique); **to make a ~** passer un coup de fil○ (**to** à).
phone: **~ card** *n* GB télécarte *f*, carte *f* de téléphone; **~-in** *n* émission *f* à ligne ouverte; **~ link** *n* liaison *f* téléphonique.
phoneme /ˈfəʊniːm/ *n* phonème *m*.
phonemic /fəˈniːmɪk/ *adj* phonémique.
phonemics /fəˈniːmɪks/ *n* (+ *v sg*) phonématique *f*.
phone: **~ number** *n* numéro *m* de téléphone; **~ tapping** *n* ¢ écoutes *fpl* téléphoniques.
phonetic /fəˈnetɪk/ *adj* phonétique.
phonetic alphabet *n* alphabet *m* phonétique.
phonetician /ˌfəʊnəˈtɪʃn/ ▶ 1692 *n* phonéticien/-ienne *m/f*.
phonetics /fəˈnetɪks/ *n* **1** (science) (+ *v sg*) phonétique *f*; **2** (transcription) (+ *v pl*) phonétique *f*.
phoney○ /ˈfəʊnɪ/ péj **I** *n* (affected person) poseur/-euse *m/f*; (impostor) charlatan *m*; (forgery, fake) faux *m*; **he's not a real scientist, he's a ~** ce n'est pas un vrai scientifique, c'est un charlatan.
II *adj* [*name, address, accent*] faux/fausse (*before n*); [*company, firm*] bidon○; [*story, excuse*] inventé, bidon○; [*emotion*] faux/fausse (*before n*), simulé; [*jewel*] faux/fausse (*before n*), en toc○; [*Old Master*] faux/fausse (*before n*); [*person*] poseur/-euse; **there's something ~ about her** il y a quelque chose de pas franc chez elle.
phoney war *n* Hist **the ~** la drôle de guerre.
phonic /ˈfɒnɪk/ *adj* phonique.
phonograph /ˈfəʊnəgrɑːf, US -græf/ *n* phono○ *m*, phonographe *m*.
phonological /ˌfəʊnəˈlɒdʒɪkl/ *adj* phonologique.
phonologically /ˌfəʊnəˈlɒdʒɪklɪ/ *adv* phonologiquement.
phonologist /fəˈnɒlədʒɪst/ ▶ 1692 *n* phonologue *mf*.
phonology /fəˈnɒlədʒɪ/ *n* phonologie *f*.
phony○ /ˈfəʊnɪ/ *adj* = **phoney**○.
phony baloney○ /ˌfəʊnɪ bəˈləʊnɪ/ *n* US ¢ conneries● *fpl*, idioties *fpl*.
phooey /ˈfuːɪ/ *excl* peuh!, pfft!
phosgene /ˈfɒzdʒiːn/ *n* phosgène *m*.
phosphate /ˈfɒsfeɪt/ **I** *n* Chem phosphate *m*.
II phosphates *npl* Agric phosphates *mpl*, engrais *mpl* phosphatés.
phosphene /ˈfɒsfiːn/ *n* phosphène *m*.
phosphide /ˈfɒsfaɪd/ *n* phosphure *m*.
phosphine /ˈfɒsfiːn/ *n* phosphine *f*.
phosphoresce /ˌfɒsfəˈres/ *vi* être phosphorescent.
phosphorescence /ˌfɒsfəˈresns/ *n* phosphorescence *f*.
phosphorescent /ˌfɒsfəˈresnt/ *adj* phosphorescent.
phosphoric /fɒsˈfɒrɪk, US -ˈfɔːr-/ *adj* phosphorique.
phosphorous /ˈfɒsfərəs/ *adj* phosphoreux/-euse.
phosphorus /ˈfɒsfərəs/ *n* phosphore *m*.
photo /ˈfəʊtəʊ/ *n* photo *f*; ▶ **photograph**.
photo: **~ album** *n* album *m* de photos; **~ booth** *n* photomaton® *m*; **~call** *n* GB séance *f* de photos.
photocell /ˈfəʊtəʊsel/ *n* cellule *f* photo-électrique.
photochemical /ˌfəʊtəʊˈkemɪkl/ *adj* photochimique.
photochemistry /ˌfəʊtəʊˈkemɪstrɪ/ *n* photochimie *f*.
photocompose /ˌfəʊtəʊkəmˈpəʊz/ *vtr* US photocomposer.
photocomposer /ˌfəʊtəʊkəmˈpəʊzə(r)/ *n* US photocomposeuse *f*.
photocomposition /ˌfəʊtəʊˌkɒmpəˈzɪʃn/ *n* US photocomposition *f*.
photoconductive /ˌfəʊtəʊkənˈdʌktɪv/ *adj* photoconducteur/-trice.
photocopier /ˈfəʊtəʊkɒpɪə(r)/ *n* photocopieuse *f*.
photocopy /ˈfəʊtəʊkɒpɪ/ **I** *n* photocopie *f*.
II *vtr* photocopier.
photodisintegration /ˌfəʊtəʊdɪsˌɪntɪˈgreɪʃn/ *n* photodésintégration *f*.
photodynamic /ˌfəʊtəʊdaɪˈnæmɪk/ *adj* photodynamique.
photodynamics /ˌfəʊtəʊdaɪˈnæmɪks/ *n* (+ *v sg*) photobiologie *f*.
photoelasticity /ˌfəʊtəʊɪˈlæstɪsətɪ/ *n* photoélasticité *f*.
photoelectric(al) /ˌfəʊtəʊɪˈlektrɪk(l)/ *adj* photo-électrique.
photoelectricity /ˌfəʊtəʊɪlekˈtrɪsətɪ/ *n* photo-électricité *f*.
photoelectron /ˌfəʊtəʊɪˈlektrɒn/ *n* photoélectron *m*.
photoengrave /ˌfəʊtəʊɪnˈgreɪv/ *vtr* reproduire [qch] en photogravure.
photoengraving /ˌfəʊtəʊɪnˈgreɪvɪŋ/ *n* photogravure *f*.
photo finish *n* (result) arrivée *f* départagée au photo-finish; (picture) photo-finish *f*.
Photofit® /ˈfəʊtəʊfɪt/ *n* GB portrait-robot *m*.
photo: **~flash** *n* ampoule *f* de flash; **~flood** *n* projecteur *m*.
photogenic /ˌfəʊtəʊˈdʒenɪk/ *adj* photogénique.
photogeology /ˌfəʊtəʊdʒɪˈɒlədʒɪ/ *n* photogéologie *f*.
photograph /ˈfəʊtəgrɑːf, US -græf/ **I** *n* photo *f*; **in the ~** sur la photo; **to take a ~ of sb/sth** prendre qn/qch en photo, prendre une photo de qn/qch; **he takes a good ~** (he is photogenic) il est photogénique, il est bien en photo; (he takes good photographs) il prend de bonnes photos; **I have a ~ of her** je l'ai en photo, j'ai une photo d'elle.
II *vtr* photographier, prendre [qn/qch] en photo.
III *vi* **to ~ well** [*person*] être photogénique, être bien en photo.

photograph album *n* album *m* de photos.

photographer /fə'tɒgrəfə(r)/ **▶1692⌋** *n* photographe *mf.*

photographic /ˌfəʊtə'græfɪk/ *adj* [*method, image, reproduction, art, equipment*] photographique; [*studio*] de photo; [*shop, agency*] de photos; [*exhibition*] de photos, de photographies; **to have a ~ memory** avoir une mémoire visuelle exceptionnelle.

photographically /ˌfəʊtə'græfɪklɪ/ *adv* en termes de photographie.

photographic library *n* photothèque *f.*

photography /fə'tɒgrəfɪ/ *n* photographie *f.*

photogravure /ˌfəʊtəʊgrə'vjʊə(r)/ *n* photogravure *f.*

photojournalism /ˌfəʊtəʊ'dʒɜːnəlɪzəm/ *n* photojournalisme *m.*

photojournalist /ˌfəʊtəʊ'dʒɜːnəlɪst/ **▶1692⌋** *n* photojournaliste *mf.*

photokinesis /ˌfəʊtəʊkaɪ'niːsɪs/ *n* photocinèse *f.*

photolithograph /ˌfəʊtəʊ'lɪθəgrɑːf, US -græf/ *n* reproduction *f* photolithographique.

photolithography /ˌfəʊtəʊlɪ'θɒgrəfɪ/ *n* photolithographie *f.*

photolysis /fəʊ'tɒləsɪs/ *n* photolyse *f.*

photomap /'fəʊtəʊmæp/ *n* photocarte *f.*

photomechanical /ˌfəʊtəʊmɪ'kænɪkl/ *adj* photomécanique.

photometer /fəʊ'tɒmɪtə(r)/ *n* photomètre *m.*

photometric /ˌfəʊtəʊ'metrɪk/ *adj* photométrique.

photometry /fəʊ'tɒmɪtrɪ/ *n* photométrie *f.*

photomontage /ˌfəʊtəʊ'mɒntɑːʒ/ *n* photomontage *m.*

photomultiplier /ˌfəʊtəʊ'mʌltɪplaɪə(r)/ *n* photomultiplicateur *m.*

photon /'fəʊtɒn/ *n* photon *m.*

photo-offset /ˌfəʊtəʊ'ɒfset/ *n* offset *m.*

photo opportunity *n* séance *f* de photos.

photoperiod /ˌfəʊtəʊ'pɪərɪəd/ *n* photopériode *f.*

photoperiodic /ˌfəʊtəʊpɪərɪ'ɒdɪk/ *adj* photopériodique.

photoperiodism /ˌfəʊtəʊ'pɪərɪədɪzəm/ *n* photopériodisme *m.*

photophobia /ˌfəʊtəʊ'fəʊbɪə/ *n* (all contexts) photophobie *f.*

photorealism /ˌfəʊtəʊ'rɪəlɪzəm/ *n* hyperréalisme *m.*

photoreconnaissance /ˌfəʊtəʊrɪ'kɒnɪsns/ *n* reconnaissance *f* photographique.

photosensitive /ˌfəʊtəʊ'sensətɪv/ *adj* photosensible.

photosensitivity /ˌfəʊtəʊˌsensə'tɪvətɪ/ *n* photosensibilité *f.*

photosensitize /ˌfəʊtəʊ'sensətaɪz/ *vtr* rendre [qch] photosensible.

photo session *n* séance *f* de photos.

photoset /'fəʊtəʊset/ *vtr* (*p prés* **-tt-**, *prét, pp* **-set**) photocomposer.

Photostat® /'fəʊtəstæt/ **I** *n* photocopie *f.*
II *vtr* (*p prés etc* **-tt-**) photocopier.

photosynthesis /ˌfəʊtəʊ'sɪnθəsɪs/ *n* photosynthèse *f.*

photosynthetic /ˌfəʊtəʊsɪn'θetɪk/ *adj* photosynthétique.

phototelegram /ˌfəʊtəʊ'telɪgræm/ *n* phototélégramme *m.*

phototelegraphy /ˌfəʊtəʊtɪ'legrəfɪ/ *n* phototélécopie *f.*

phototropic /ˌfəʊtəʊ'trɒpɪk/ *adj* phototropique.

phototropism /ˌfəʊtəʊ'trəʊpɪzəm/ *n* phototropisme *m.*

phototype /'fəʊtəʊtaɪp/ *n* (process) phototypie *f*; (print) phototype *m.*

phototypesetting /ˌfəʊtəʊ'taɪpsetɪŋ/ *n* US photocomposition *f.*

phototypography /ˌfəʊtəʊtaɪ'pɒgrəfɪ/ *n* phototypographie *f.*

phrasal verb *n* verbe *m* à particule.

phrase /freɪz/ **I** *n* **1** (expression) gen expression *f*, Ling locution *f*; **in Rousseau's ~...** pour reprendre l'expression de Rousseau...; **2** Ling (part of clause) syntagme *m*; **noun/verb ~** syntagme nominal/verbal; **3** Mus phrase *f.*
II *vtr* **1** (formulate) exprimer [*idea, notion*]; formuler [*question, sentence, speech*]; **a neatly ~d letter** une lettre bien tournée; **2** Mus phraser.

phrase: **~book** *n* manuel *m* de conversation; **~ marker** *n* marqueur *m* syntagmatique.

phraseology /ˌfreɪzɪ'ɒlədʒɪ/ *n* phraséologie *f.*

phrase structure *n* structure *f* syntagmatique.

phrasing /'freɪzɪŋ/ *n* **1** (of thought) expression *f*, formulation *f*; (of sentence, letter) formulation *f*; **2** Mus phrasé *m.*

phrenic /'frenɪk/ *adj* Anat phrénique.

phrenologist /frə'nɒlədʒɪst/ **▶1692⌋** *n* phrénologiste *mf*, phrénologue *mf.*

phrenology /frə'nɒlədʒɪ/ *n* phrénologie *f.*

Phrygian cap /'frɪdʒɪən/ *n* bonnet *m* phrygien.

phthisiology /ˌθaɪsɪ'ɒlədʒɪ/ *n* phtisiologie *f.*

phthisis /'θaɪsɪs/ **▶1354⌋** *n* phtisie *f.*

phut○ /fʌt/ *adv* **to go ~** [*machine, car*] rendre l'âme; [*plans*] tomber à l'eau○.

phycology /faɪ'kɒlədʒɪ/ *n* phycologie *f.*

phylactery /fɪ'læktərɪ/ *n* Relig phylactère *m.*

phyletic /faɪ'letɪk/ *adj* phylogénétique.

phylloxera /ˌfɪlɒk'sɪərə, fɪ'lɒksərə/ *n* phylloxéra *m.*

phylogenesis /ˌfaɪləʊ'dʒenəsɪs/, **phylogeny** /faɪ'lɒdʒɪnɪ/ *n* phylogénie *f.*

phylogen(et)ic /ˌfaɪləʊ'dʒenɪk/ *adj* phylogénétique.

phylum /'faɪləm/ *n* phylum *m.*

physic‡ /'fɪzɪk/ *n* (art of medicine) médecine *f*; (drug) médicament *m.*

physical /'fɪzɪkl/ **I**○ *n* bilan *m* de santé; **to have a ~** se faire faire un bilan de santé.
II *adj* **1** (of the body) [*strength, pain, violence, handicap, symptom*] physique; **~ abuse** sévices *mpl*; **it's a ~ impossibility** c'est physiquement impossible; **she's very ~** (demonstrative) elle est très démonstrative; **did he get ~?** (become intimate) est-ce qu'il s'est montré entreprenant?; (in quarrel) (become violent) est-ce qu'il en est venu aux mains?; **2** [*chemistry, science, property*] physique.

physical: **~ anthropology** *n* anthropologie *f* physique; **~ culture** *n* culture *f* physique; **~ education, PE** *n* éducation *f* physique; **~ examination** *n* examen *m* médical; **~ fitness** *n* forme *f* physique; **~ geography** *n* géographie *f* physique; **~ jerks**○† *npl* GB gymnastique *f.*

physically /'fɪzɪklɪ/ *adv* physiquement; **it is ~ impossible to...** il est physiquement impossible de...; **to be ~ abused** être victime de sévices.

physically handicapped **I** *n* **the ~** (+ *v pl*) les handicapés *mpl* physiques.
II *adj* **to be ~** être handicapé/-e *m/f* physique.

physical: **~ sciences** *npl* sciences *fpl* physiques; **~ therapist** **▶1692⌋** *n* US Med kinésithérapeute *mf*; **~ therapy** *n* US Med kinésithérapie *f*; **~ training, PT** *n* éducation *f* physique.

physician /fɪ'zɪʃn/ **▶1692⌋** *n* GB†, US médecin *m*; GB spécialiste *mf.*

physicist /'fɪzɪsɪst/ **▶1692⌋** *n* physicien/-ienne *m/f.*

physics /'fɪzɪks/ *n* (+ *v sg*) physique *f*; **theoretical ~** physique théorique; **the ~ of sound/motion** la physique du son/mouvement.

physio○ /'fɪzɪəʊ/ **▶1692⌋** *n* GB **1** (*abrév* = **physiotherapist**) kinési○ *mf*, kinésithérapeute *mf*; **2** (*abrév* = **physiotherapy**) kinési○ *f*, kinésithérapie *f.*

physiognomist /ˌfɪzɪ'ɒnəmɪst, US -'ɒgnəmɪst/ **▶1692⌋** *n* physionomiste *mf.*

physiognomy /ˌfɪzɪ'ɒnəmɪ, US -'ɒgnəʊmɪ/ *n* (all contexts) physionomie *f* (**of** de).

physiological /ˌfɪzɪə'lɒdʒɪkl/ *adj* physiologique.

physiologist /ˌfɪzɪ'ɒlədʒɪst/ **▶1692⌋** *n* physiologiste *mf.*

physiology /ˌfɪzɪ'ɒlədʒɪ/ *n* physiologie *f.*

physiotherapist /ˌfɪzɪəʊ'θerəpɪst/ **▶1692⌋** *n* kinésithérapeute *mf.*

physiotherapy /ˌfɪzɪəʊ'θerəpɪ/ *n* kinésithérapie *f.*

physique /fɪ'ziːk/ *n* physique *m.*

phytogeography /ˌfaɪtəʊdʒɪ'ɒgrəfɪ/ *n* phytogéographie *f.*

phytopathology /ˌfaɪtəʊpə'θɒlədʒɪ/ *n* phytopathologie *f.*

phytoplankton /ˌfaɪtəʊ'plæŋktn/ *n* phytoplancton *m.*

pi /paɪ/ *n* Math pi *m.*

pianissimo /ˌpɪə'nɪsɪməʊ/ *adj, adv* pianissimo (*inv*).

pianist /'pɪənɪst/ **▶1692⌋, 1481⌋** *n* pianiste *mf.*

piano /pɪ'ænəʊ/ **▶1481⌋** **I** *n* piano *m.*
II *modif* [*key, lesson, teacher, tuner*] de piano; [*concerto, music, piece, quartet*] pour piano.
III *adj, adv* piano (*inv*).

piano: **~ accordion** **▶1481⌋** *n* accordéon *m* à clavier; **~ bar** *n* piano-bar *m.*

pianoforte /ˌpɪænəʊ'fɔːtɪ/ **▶1481⌋** *n* sout piano-forte fml *m.*

pianola® /pɪə'nəʊlə/ **▶1481⌋** *n* piano *m* mécanique.

piano: **~ organ** **▶1481⌋** *n* piano *m* mécanique; **~ player** *n* pianiste *mf*; **~ roll** *n* bande *f* perforée (*pour piano mécanique*); **~ stool** *n* tabouret *m* (de piano).

piazza /pɪ'ætsə/ *n* **1** (public square) place *f*; **2** US (veranda) véranda *f.*

pic○ /pɪk/ *n* photo *f.*

pica /'paɪkə/ *n* **1** Print cicéro *m*; **2** Med (craving) pica *m.*

picador /'pɪkədɔː(r)/ *n* picador *m.*

Picardy /'pɪkədɪ/ **▶1273⌋** *pr n* Picardie *f*; **in ~** en Picardie.

picaresque /ˌpɪkə'resk/ *adj* picaresque.

picayune○† /ˌpɪkə'juːn/ *adj* US mesquin.

piccalilli /ˌpɪkə'lɪlɪ/ *n* ¢ pickles *mpl* à la moutarde.

piccaninny○ /ˌpɪkə'nɪnɪ/ *n* injur négrillon/-onne *m/f* offensive.

piccolo /'pɪkələʊ/ **▶1481⌋** *n* piccolo *m.*

pick /pɪk/ **I** *n* **1** (tool) gen pioche *f*, pic *m*; (of miner, geologist) pic *m*; (of climber) piolet *m*; (of mason) smille *f*; **to dig with a ~** creuser à la pioche; **2** (choice) choix *m*; **to have one's ~ of** avoir le choix parmi; **to take one's ~** faire son choix (**of** parmi); **take your ~** choisis; **to get first ~** choisir le/la premier/-ière, être le/la premier/-ière à choisir; **3** (best) meilleur/-e *m/f*; **the ~ of the crop** (fruit) les meilleurs fruits; **the ~ of this month's new films** les meilleurs films sortis ce mois-ci; **the ~ of the bunch** le/la etc meilleur/-e etc du lot.
II *vtr* **1** (choose, select) gen choisir (**from** parmi); Sport sélectionner [*player*] (**from** parmi); former [*team*]; **'~ a card, any card'** 'choisis une carte, n'importe laquelle'; **to be ~ed for England/for the team** être sélectionné pour représenter l'Angleterre/pour faire partie de l'équipe; **you ~ed the right person/a good time to do it** tu as choisi la personne qu'il fallait/le bon moment pour faire cela; **you ~ed the wrong man** ou **person** tu as choisi la mauvaise personne; **he certainly knows how to ~ them!** il sait les choisir! also iron; **to ~ a fight** (physically) chercher à se bagarrer○ (**with** avec); **to ~ a fight** ou **a**

quarrel chercher querelle (**with** à); **2 to ~ one's way through** avancer avec précaution parmi [*rubble, litter*]; **to ~ one's way down** prendre des précautions pour descendre [*mountain, slope*]; **3** (pluck, gather) cueillir [*fruit, flowers*]; **4** (poke at) gratter [*spot, scab, skin*]; **to ~ sth from** ou **off sth** enlever qch de qch; **to ~ one's nose** mettre les doigts dans son nez; **to ~ one's teeth** se curer or se nettoyer les dents; **to ~ a hole in one's sweater** faire un trou dans son pullover à force de tirer les mailles; **to ~ a lock** crocheter une serrure; **to ~ sb's pocket** faire les poches de qn.

III *vi* **1** (choose) choisir; **you can afford to ~ and choose** tu peux te permettre de faire les difficiles or de faire la fine bouche (**among, between** pour choisir parmi); **2** (poke) ▶ **pick at, pick over etc**.

■ **pick at**: ¶ **~ at [sth] 1** [*person*] manger [qch] du bout des dents [*food*]; gratter, tripoter○ [*spot, scab*]; tripoter○ [*fabric, knot*]; **2** [*bird*] picorer [*crumbs*]; ¶ **~ at [sb]** US ▶ **pick on**.

■ **pick off**: ¶ **~ [sb] off, ~ off [sb]** (kill) abattre; **he ~ed them off one by one** il les visait soigneusement et les abattait un à un; **lions ~ off any stragglers** les lions se jettent sur les traînards; ¶ **~ [sth] off, ~ off [sth]** enlever [qch]; ¶ **~ [sth] off sth** cueillir [qch] sur qch [*apple, cherry*]; **to ~ sth off the floor** prendre qch qui était par terre; **to ~ sth off the top of a cake** retirer qch qui était sur un gâteau.

■ **pick on**: **~ on [sb]** (harass, single out) harceler; **stop ~ing on me!** arrête de me harceler comme ça, fiche-moi la paix!○; **~ on someone your own size!** ne t'attaque pas à quelqu'un de plus faible que toi.

■ **pick out**: **~ [sb/sth] out, ~ out [sb/sth] 1** (select) gen choisir; (single out) repérer; **to be ~ed out from the group** être remarqué dans le groupe; **to ~ out three winners** sélectionner trois gagnants (**from** parmi); **2** (make out, distinguish) distinguer [*object, landmark*]; saisir, comprendre [*words*]; reconnaître [*person in photo, suspect*]; repérer [*person in crowd*]; **to ~ out the theme in a variation** reconnaître le thème dans une variation; **3** (highlight) [*person, artist*] mettre en valeur [*title, letter*]; [*torch, beam*] révéler [*form, object*]; **to be ~ed out in red** être mis en valeur en rouge; **4 to ~ out a tune (on the piano)** retrouver un air (au piano).

■ **pick over**: **~ [sth] over, ~ over [sth] 1** lit trier [*articles, lentils, raisins*]; **2** fig analyser [*film, book*].

■ **pick up**: ¶ **~ up 1** (improve) [*trade, market, business*] reprendre; [*weather, performance, health*] s'améliorer; [*ill person*] se rétablir; **things have ~ed up slightly** ça commence à aller mieux; **2** (resume) reprendre; **to pick up (from) where one left off** reprendre là où on s'est arrêté; ¶ **~ [sb/sth] up, ~ up [sb/sth] 1** (lift, take hold of) (to tidy) ramasser [*object, litter, toys, clothes*]; (to examine) prendre; (after fall) relever [*person, child*]; (for cuddle) prendre [qn] dans ses bras [*person, child*]; **to ~ sth up in** ou **with one's left hand** prendre qch de sa main gauche; **to ~ up the telephone** décrocher le téléphone; **the wave ~ed up the boat** la vague a soulevé le bateau; **to ~ up the bill** ou **tab**○ régler l'addition, casquer○; **2** (collect) prendre [*passenger, cargo, hitcher*]; (passer) prendre [*dry-cleaning, ticket, keys*]; aller chercher [*person from airport, station*]; **could you ~ me up?** est-ce que tu peux venir me chercher?; ¶ **~ [sth] up, ~ up [sth] 1** (buy) prendre, acheter [*milk, bread, newspaper*]; dénicher [*bargain, find*]; **could you ~ up some milk on the way home?** peux-tu prendre du lait en rentrant à la maison?; **2** (learn, acquire) apprendre [*language*]; prendre [*habit, accent*]; développer [*skill*]; **where did he ~ up those manners?** où a-t-il pris or attrapé ces manières?; **I'm hoping to ~ up some tips** j'espère obtenir quelques tuyaux; **it's not difficult, you'll soon ~ it up** ce n'est pas difficile, tu t'y mettras vite; **3** (catch) attraper [*illness, cold, infection*]; **4** (notice, register) [*person*] repérer [*mistake, error*]; [*person, machine*] détecter [*defect*]; **5** (detect) [*person, animal*] trouver [*trail, scent*]; [*searchlight, radar*] détecter la présence de [*aircraft, person, object*]; Radio, Telecom capter [*signal, broadcast*]; **6** (gain, earn) gagner [*point, size*]; acquérir [*reputation*]; **to ~ up speed** prendre de la vitesse; **7** (resume) reprendre [*conversation, career*]; **you'll soon ~ up your French again** ton français te reviendra vite; **to ~ up the pieces (of one's life)** recoller les morceaux; ¶ **~ [sb] up, ~ up [sb] 1** (rescue) [*helicopter, ship*] recueillir [*person*]; **2** (arrest) [*police*] arrêter [*suspect*]; **3** (meet) péj ramasser [*person, partner, prostitute*]; **4** (find fault with) faire des remarques à [*person*] (**on** sur); **they'll ~ you up for being improperly dressed** ils vont te faire remarquer que tu n'es pas vêtu correctement; ¶ **~ oneself up 1** lit (get up) se relever; **2** fig (recover) se reprendre.

pickaback /ˈpɪkəbæk/ = **piggyback**.

pickaninny *n* US = **piccaninny**.

pickaxe GB, **pickax** US /ˈpɪkæks/ *n* pioche *f*.

picker /ˈpɪkə(r)/ *n* cueilleur/-euse *m/f*.

picket /ˈpɪkɪt/ **I** *n* **1** (in strike) (group of people) piquet *m* (de grève); (one person) gréviste *mf* (*qui fait partie d'un piquet*); **to be on a ~** faire partie d'un piquet de grève; ▶ **flying picket**; **2** Mil (detachment) détachement *m*; (one soldier) factionnaire *m*; **fire ~** piquet *m* d'incendie; **3** (stake) piquet *m*, pieu *m*.

II *vtr* **1** (to stop work) installer un piquet de grève aux portes de [*factory, site*]; (to protest) former un cordon de protestation devant [*hall, meeting place, embassy*]; **2** (fence in) clôturer, palissader [*land*].

III *vi* organiser un piquet de grève.

picket duty *n* **to be on ~** Ind faire partie d'un piquet de grève; Mil être (de service) de guet.

picket fence *n* palissade *f*.

picketing /ˈpɪkɪtɪŋ/ *n* ¢ piquets *mpl* de grève.

picket line *n* (outside factory etc) (cordon *m* de) piquet *m* de grève; (outside embassy) cordon *m* de protestation; **to cross the ~** traverser les piquets de grève.

picking /ˈpɪkɪŋ/ **I** *n* (of crop) cueillette *f*.

II pickings *npl* (rewards) gains *mpl*; **there'll be slim ~ for us on this job** on ne tirera pas grand-chose de ce travail.

pickle /ˈpɪkl/ **I** *n* **1** ¢ (preserved food) pickles *mpl*, conserves *fpl* au vinaigre; **cheese and ~** fromage et pickles; **2 C** (item) (gherkin) cornichon *m*; **~s** pickles *mpl*; **3** ¢ (preserving substance) (brine) saumure *f*; (vinegar) vinaigre *m*; (marinade) marinade *f*.

II *vtr* (in vinegar) conserver [qch] dans du vinaigre; (in brine) conserver [qch] dans de la saumure.

IDIOMS **to be in a ~** hum être dans le pétrin○.

pickled /ˈpɪkld/ *adj* **1** Culin [*onion, gherkin*] au vinaigre; **2**○ GB (drunk) bourré○.

picklock /ˈpɪklɒk/ *n* **1** (tool) gen crochet *m*; (of burglar) rossignol *m*; **2** (burglar) crocheteur *m*.

pick: **~-me-up** *n* (drink, medicine) remontant *m*; **~pocket** *n* voleur *m* à la tire, pickpocket *m*.

pickup /ˈpɪkʌp/ *n* **1** (of record player) lecteur *m*, pick-up *m inv*; **2** (on electric guitar) capteur *m*; **3** Radio, TV (reception) réception *f*; **4**○ (sexual partner) partenaire *mf* de rencontre; **5** Transp (collection) (of goods) ramassage *m*; (passenger) passager/-ère *m/f* ramassé/-e en route; **the school bus makes about twenty ~s** le bus scolaire s'arrête une vingtaine de fois pour prendre des écoliers; **I've still got a number of ~s to make** je dois encore m'arrêter un certain nombre de fois pour prendre des passagers; **6** Aut (acceleration) reprises *fpl*; **7** (improvement, revival) (in business, economy) reprise *f* (**in** de); **8** = **pickup truck**.

pickup: **~ arm** *n* = **pickup** 1; **~ point** *n* (for passengers) point *m* de ramassage; (for goods) point *m* de chargement; **~ truck**, **~ van** GB *n* pick-up *m inv*, camionnette *f* (à plateau découvert).

picky○ /ˈpɪkɪ/ *adj* difficile (**about** pour ce qui est de); **to be a ~ eater** être difficile pour ce qui est de la nourriture.

pick your own, **PYO** *n* ferme *f* où l'on peut cueillir ses propres fruits ou légumes; (on sign) 'cueillette *f* à la ferme'.

picnic /ˈpɪknɪk/ **I** *n* pique-nique *m*; **to go for** ou **on a ~** aller en pique-nique.

II *vi* (*p prés etc* **-ck-**) pique-niquer.

IDIOMS **it's no ~!** ce n'est pas une partie de plaisir!

picnic: **~ basket** *n* panier *m* à pique-nique; **~ ham** *n* jambonneau *m*; **~ hamper** *n* grand panier *m* à pique-nique.

picnicker /ˈpɪknɪkə(r)/ *n* pique-niqueur/-euse *m/f*.

picnic lunch *n* pique-nique *m*.

Pict /pɪkt/ *n* Picte *m*.

Pictish /ˈpɪktɪʃ/ *n, adj* picte (*m*).

pictogram /ˈpɪktəgræm/ *n* **1** (symbol) pictogramme *m*; **2** (chart) carte *f* thématique.

pictograph /ˈpɪktəgrɑːf, US -græf/ *n* = **pictogram**.

pictorial /pɪkˈtɔːrɪəl/ **I**† *n* (magazine *m*) illustré *m*.

II *adj* **1** (in pictures) [*calendar, magazine*] illustré; [*record, information*] graphique; [*style, technique, means*] artistique; **2** (resembling pictures) [*language, description*] imagé.

pictorially /pɪkˈtɔːrɪəlɪ/ *adv* **1** (by means of pictures) [*portray, show*] par l'image; **2** (from a pictorial point of view) d'un point de vue graphique.

picture /ˈpɪktʃə(r)/ **I** *n* **1** (visual depiction) (painting) peinture *f*, tableau *m*; (drawing) dessin *m*; (in book) gen illustration *f*; (in child's book) image *f*; (in mind) image *f*; **to draw a ~ of sb/sth** faire un dessin de qn/qch; **to paint a ~ of sb/sth** peindre qn/qch; **to paint sb's ~** faire le portrait de qn; **2** fig (description) description *f*, tableau *m*; **to paint a ~ of sb/sth** dépeindre qn/qch; **to paint** ou **draw a gloomy/optimistic ~ of sth** donner une image sombre/optimiste de qch; **to give** ou **present a clear/accurate ~ of sth** dépeindre qch avec clarté/précision; **3** Phot photo *f*, photographie *f*; **to take a ~ (of sb/sth)** prendre une photo (de qn/qch); **4** fig (overview) situation *f*; **to get the ~** comprendre la situation; **to put/keep sb in the ~** mettre/tenir qn au courant; **to be in the ~** être au courant; **5** Cin (film) film *m*; **to make a ~** faire un film; **6** TV image *f*; **the ~ is blurred** l'image est floue.

II pictures○ *npl* **the ~s** le cinéma; **to go to the ~s** aller au cinéma.

III *vtr* **1** (form mental image of) s'imaginer, se représenter [*person, place, scene*]; **2** (show in picture form) **to be ~d** être représenté; **the vase (~d above) is...** le vase (voir photo ci-dessus) est...

IDIOMS **to be the ~ of health** respirer la santé; **to be the ~ of sb** être le portrait tout craché de qn; **to look** ou **be a ~** être ravissant; **her face was a ~!** son expression en disait long!

picture: **~ book** *n* livre *m* d'images; **~ card** *n* Games figure *f* (*carte*); **~ desk** *n* Journ service *m* photo; **~ editor** ▶ **1692** *n* Journ directeur/-trice *m/f* du service photo; **~ frame** *n* cadre *m*; **~ framer** ▶ **1692** *n* encadreur/-euse *m/f*; **~ framing** *n* encadrement *m*; **~ gallery** *n* galerie *f* de peinture; **~ hat** *n* capeline *f*; **~ hook** *n* crochet *m* (à tableaux); **~ house**†, **~ palace**† *n* cinéma *m*; **~ postcard** *n* carte *f* postale; **~ rail** *n* cimaise *f*.

picturesque /ˌpɪktʃəˈresk/ *adj* pittoresque.

picturesquely /ˌpɪktʃəˈresklɪ/ *adv* avec pittoresque.

picture: **~ window** *n* baie *f* vitrée; **~ wire** *n* fil *m* (pour accrocher les tableaux); **~ writing** *n* écriture *f* pictographique.

PID *n*: *abrév* ▶**pelvic inflammatory disease**.

piddle○ /ˈpɪdl/ **I** *n* **to go for a ~** aller faire pipi○, aller pisser◑.
II *vi* (urinate) faire pipi○.
■ **piddle away**: **~ away [sth]**, **~ [sth] away** gaspiller [*time, life*].
■ **piddle down** GB **it's piddling down** il pleut à verse.

piddling○ /ˈpɪdlɪŋ/ *adj* insignifiant.

pidgin /ˈpɪdʒɪn/ *n* **1** (also **~ English**) pidgin *m*; **2** (also **~ French**) (French with Arab) sabir *m*; (French with other language) petit nègre *m*; **3** (other languages spoken incorrectly) charabia *m*.

pie /paɪ/ *n* **1** (savoury) gen tourte *f*; **meat/fish ~** tourte à la viande/au poisson; **pork ~** pâté *m* de porc en croûte; **2** (sweet) tarte *f* (*recouverte de pâte*); **apple/plum ~** tarte aux pommes/prunes.
IDIOMS **it's all ~ in the sky** c'est de l'utopie; **to be as easy as ~** être simple comme bonjour; **to have a finger in every ~** être mêlé à tout; **they all want a piece of the ~** ils veulent tous leur part du gâteau; **to be as sweet** ou **nice as ~** gen être gentil/-ille comme tout, pej être tout sucre tout miel.

piebald /ˈpaɪbɔːld/ **I** *n* cheval *m* pie.
II *adj* pie *inv*.

piece /piːs/ **I** *n* **1** (indeterminate amount) (of fabric, wood, paper, metal) morceau *m*, bout *m*; (of string, ribbon) bout *m*; (of cake, pie, pâté) morceau *m*, tranche *f*; (of meat, cheese, chocolate) morceau *m*; **2** (unit) **a ~ of furniture** un meuble; **a ~ of pottery** une poterie; **a ~ of sculpture** une sculpture; **a ~ of luggage** une valise; **a ~ of advice** un conseil; **a ~ of evidence** une preuve; **a ~ of information** un renseignement; **a ~ of legislation** une loi; **a ~ of news** une nouvelle; **a ~ of work** gen un travail; (referring to book, article etc) une œuvre; **a ~ of luck** un coup de chance; **a ~ of history** une tranche d'histoire; **to be paid by the ~** être payé à la pièce ; **they cost £20 a ~** ils coûtent 20 livres pièce; **3** (component part) (of jigsaw, machine, model) pièce *f*; **~ by ~** pièce par pièce; **in ~s** en pièces (détachées); **to come in ~s** [*kit furniture*] être livré en kit; **to take sth to ~s** démonter qch; **4** (broken fragment) (of glass, cup) morceau *m*, fragment *m*; **in ~s** en morceaux, en miettes; **to fall to ~s** [*machine, object*] tomber en morceaux; fig [*case, argument*] s'effondrer; **it came to ~s in my hands** ça s'est cassé dans mes mains; **to go to ~s** fig [*person*] (from shock) s'effondrer; (emotionally) craquer○; (in interview) paniquer complètement; **5** (artistic work) (of music) morceau *m*; (sculpture) sculpture *f*; (painting) peinture *f*; (article) article *m* (**on** sur); (play) pièce *f*; **he read them a ~ out of the book** il leur a lu un passage du livre; **6** (instance) **a ~ of** un exemple de [*propaganda, materialism, flattery*]; **a wonderful ~ of running/acting/engineering** une très belle course/interprétation/réalisation technique; **7** (coin) pièce *f*; **a 50p ~** une pièce de 50 pence; **30 ~s of silver** 30 pièces d'argent; **8** Games (in chess) pièce *f*; (in draughts) pion *m*; **chess ~** pièce de jeu d'échecs; **9** Mil (gun) fusil *m*; (cannon) pièce *f* (d'artillerie); **10**○ (gun) flingue○ *m*, pistolet *m*; **11**○ (woman) beau brin *m* de fille○.
II -piece (*dans composés*) **a 60-~ cutlery set** un service de couverts de 60 pièces; **a 5-~ band** Mus un groupe de 5 musiciens.
IDIOMS **to be (all) of a ~** [*town, house*] être d'un style homogène; **to be (all) of a piece with sth** [*action, statement, ideas*] s'accorder avec qch; **to be still in one ~** [*object*] être intact; [*person*] être sain et sauf; **to give sb a ~ of one's mind** dire ses quatre vérités or son fait à qn; **to pick sth to ~s** descendre qch en flammes; **to pick up the ~s** recoller les morceaux; **to say one's ~** dire ce qu'on a à dire.
■ **piece together**: **~ [sth] together**, **~ together [sth]** rassembler [*fragments, shreds*]; reconstituer [*vase, garment, letter*]; assembler [*puzzle*]; fig reconstituer [*facts, evidence, event, account*]; **they tried to ~ together what had happened** ils ont essayé de reconstituer ce qui s'était passé.

pièce de résistance /ˌpjes də reˈzɪstɑːns, US -ˌrezɪˈstɑːns/ *n* pièce *f* de résistance.

piecemeal /ˈpiːsmiːl/ **I** *adj* [*approach, reforms, legislation*] fragmentaire; [*story, description*] décousu; [*research, construction, development*] (random) fragmentaire; (at different times) irrégulier/-ière.
II *adv* [*develop, introduce*] petit à petit, par à-coups pej; [*sell off, arrive*] petit à petit.

piecework /ˈpiːswɜːk/ **I** *n* **to be on ~** être payé à la pièce.
II *modif* [*rate*] à la pièce.

pie: **~ chart** *n* diagramme *m* circulaire sectorisé, camembert○ *m*; **~ crust** *n* croûte *f*.

pied /paɪd/ *adj* gen bigarré; Zool pie *inv*.

pied-à-terre /ˌpjeɪd ɑː ˈteə(r)/ *n* pied-à-terre *m inv*.

pie dish *n* moule *m* à tarte.

piedmont /ˈpiːdmɒnt/ *adj* Geol [*plain, glacier*] de piémont.

Pied Piper /ˌpaɪd ˈpaɪpə(r)/ *n* **the ~ (of Hamelin)** le joueur de flûte de Hamelin.

pied wagtail *n* bergeronnette *f* (lavandière).

pie-eyed○ /ˌpaɪˈaɪd/ *adj* rond○, soûl○.

pier /pɪə(r)/ *n* **1** (at seaside resort) jetée *f* (sur pilotis) (*où les gens viennent se promener*); **2** (part of harbour) (built of stone) digue *f*; (landing stage) embarcadère *m*; **3** Constr (of bridge, dam, foundations) pile *f*; (pillar in church, of gateway) pilier *m*; (wall between openings) trumeau *m*.

pierce /pɪəs/ *vtr* **1** lit (make hole in) percer; (penetrate) transpercer [*armour, skin, leather, paper*]; **to ~ a hole in** percer un trou dans; **to have one's ears ~d** se faire percer les oreilles; **to ~ the enemy lines** Mil pénétrer les lignes ennemies; **2** fig (penetrate) [*cry, light*] percer; [*cold, wind*] transpercer.

piercing /ˈpɪəsɪŋ/ *adj* [*noise, scream, voice*] perçant; [*light*] intense; [*cold, wind*] glacial, pénétrant; **his ~ blue eyes** ses yeux bleus perçants.

pier glass *n* glace *f* de trumeau.

pierhead /ˈpɪəhed/ **I** *n* musoir *m*.
II *modif* GB [*show, entertainment*] populaire; [*humour*] troupier pej; **~ comic** comique *m* de foire.

pierrot /ˈpɪərəʊ/ *n* pierrot *m*.

Pietism /ˈpaɪətɪzəm/ *n* Relig piétisme *m*.

Pietist /ˈpaɪətɪst/ *n* Relig piétiste *mf*.

pietistic(al) /ˌpaɪəˈtɪstɪk(l)/ *adj* péj bigot.

piety /ˈpaɪətɪ/ *n* **1** (religiousness) piété *f*; **2** (belief or custom) pratique *f* pieuse.

piezoelectric /piːˌeɪzəʊɪˈlektrɪk/ *adj* [*crystal, effect*] piézoélectrique.

piezoelectricity /piːˌeɪzəʊˌɪlekˈtrɪsətɪ/ *n* piézo-électricité *f*.

piezometer /ˌpaɪɪˈzɒmɪtə(r)/ *n* piézomètre *m*.

piffle○ /ˈpɪfl/ *n* GB ¢ balivernes† *fpl*, fadaises *fpl*.

piffling○ /ˈpɪflɪŋ/ *adj* GB insignifiant.

pig /pɪg/ **I** *n* **1** (animal) porc *m*, cochon *m*; **to be in ~** [*sow*] être grosse; **2**○ fig pej (greedy) goinfre○ *m*; (dirty) cochon/-onne○ *m/f*; (nasty) sale type○ *m*, salaud◑ *m*; **to eat/live like a ~** (dirtily) manger/vivre comme un cochon; **to make a ~ of oneself** manger comme un goinfre○, se goinfrer○; **you ~!** (greedy person) quel goinfre○!; (dirty person) tu es un cochon○!; (nasty person) tu es vache○!; **3**○ pej (policeman) flic○ *m*, poulet○ *m*; **the ~s** les flics○ *mpl*, la flicaille◑ *f*; **4**○ GB (task) **this is a real ~ to do!** c'est vachement○ dur à faire!
II *vi* [*sow*] mettre bas.
III○ *v refl* **to ~ oneself** se goinfrer○, s'empiffrer○ (**on** de).
IDIOMS **to buy a ~ in a poke** acheter chat en poche; **~s might fly** le jour où les poules auront des dents!; **in a ~'s eye**○! US mon œil○!; **to make a ~'s ear of sth** bousiller○ qch; **to ~ it**○ vivre comme un cochon.
■ **pig out** se goinfrer○, s'empiffrer○ (**on** de).

pigeon /ˈpɪdʒɪn/ *n* pigeon *m*.
IDIOMS **that's your ~**○! ça, c'est ton affaire!; **to put** ou **set the cat among the ~s** faire des vagues.

pigeon: **~-breasted**, **~-chested** *adj* à la poitrine bombée; **~ fancier** *n* colombophile *mf*.

pigeonhole /ˈpɪdʒɪnhəʊl/ GB **I** *n* **1** lit (in desk) case *f*, casier *m*; (in wall unit) casier *m*; **2** fig (neat category) catégorie *f*.
II *vtr* **1** (categorize) étiqueter, cataloguer [*person, activity*] (**as** comme); **2** (file) classer [*papers, letters*].

pigeon house, **pigeon loft** *n* pigeonnier *m*.

pigeon post *n* GB **to send sth by ~** envoyer qch par pigeon voyageur.

pigeon: **~ racing** *n* ¢ courses *fpl* de pigeons voyageurs; **~ shooting** *n* tir *m* aux pigeons.

pigeon-toed *adj* **to be ~** marcher les pieds en dedans.

pig: **~ farm** *n* élevage *m* de porcs; **~ farmer** ▶**1692** *n* éleveur/-euse *m/f* de porcs; **~ farming** *n* élevage *m* de porcs.

piggery /ˈpɪgərɪ/ *n* (pigsty) porcherie *f*.

piggish /ˈpɪgɪʃ/ *adj* (greedy) goinfre○; (dirty) sale; (rude) grossier/-ière.

piggy /ˈpɪgɪ/ **I** *n* lang enfantin cochon *m*.
II *adj* [*manners etc*] de cochon; **to have ~ eyes** péj avoir des petits yeux porcins.
IDIOMS **to be ~ in the middle** fig se trouver entre deux chaises, avoir le cul○ entre deux chaises.

piggyback /ˈpɪgɪbæk/ **I** *n* **1** (also **~ ride**) **to give sb a ~** porter qn sur son dos or sur ses épaules; **2** Rail, Aerosp ferroutage *m*.
II *adv* [*ride, carry*] sur le dos.
III *vtr* **1** (carry) porter [qn] sur son dos or sur ses épaules [*person*]; **2** Rail, Aeron ferrouter; **3 to be ~ed on** lit (superposed) être superposé sur; fig [*expenses*] être absorbé par.
IV *vi* **1** [*expenses*] être absorbé or couvert; **2** Rail, Aeron être ferrouté.

piggy bank *n* tirelire *f* (*en forme de cochon*).

pigheaded /ˌpɪgˈhedɪd/ *adj* péj entêté, obstiné.

pigheadedness /ˌpɪgˈhedɪdnɪs/ *n* péj entêtement *m*, obstination *f*.

pig: **~ ignorant**○ *adj* péj d'une ignorance crasse; **~ iron** *n* métal *m* en gueuse; **Pig Latin** *n* langage *m* secret des enfants.

piglet /ˈpɪglɪt/ *n* porcelet *m*, petit cochon *m*.

pigment /ˈpɪgmənt/ *n* Biol, Art pigment *m*.

pigmentation /ˌpɪgmənˈteɪʃn/ *n* pigmentation *f*.

pigmented /ˈpɪgməntɪd/ *adj* pigmenté.

pigmy = **pygmy**.

pigpen *n* US = **pigsty**.

pigskin /ˈpɪgskɪn/ **I** *n* peau *f* de porc.
II *modif* [*bag etc*] en peau de porc.

pigsty /ˈpɪgstaɪ/ *n* (*pl* **-sties**) lit, fig porcherie *f*.

pigswill /ˈpɪgswɪl/ *n* ¢ **1** lit pâtée *f* pour porcs; **2** fig (nasty food) bouillie *f*.

pigtail /ˈpɪgteɪl/ *n* natte *f*; **to wear one's hair in ~s** porter des nattes.

pike /paɪk/ *n* **1** Hist (spear) pique *f*; **2** (fish) brochet *m*; **3** GB (peak) pic *m*; **4** GB Sport (in swimming) plongeon *m* carpé; (in gymnastics) mouvement *m* carpé; **5** = **turnpike**.

pike: **~man** *n* Hist piquier *m*; **~perch** *n* sanche *m*.

piker○ /ˈpaɪkə(r)/ *n* US péj minable *mf*.

pikestaff /ˈpaɪkstɑːf, US -stæf/ *n*: IDIOMS **it's as plain as a ~** ça se voit comme le nez au milieu de la figure.

pilaf(f) /pɪˈlæf, US -ˈlɑːf/ *n* = **pilau**.

pilaster /pɪˈlæstə(r)/ *n* pilastre *m*.

pilau /pɪˈlaʊ/ *n* pilaf *m*; **~ rice** riz *m* pilaf.

pilchard /ˈpɪltʃəd/ *n* pilchard *m*.

pile /paɪl/ **I** *n* **1** (untidy heap) tas *m* (**of** de); (stack) pile *f* (**of** de); **to be in a ~** être en tas or en pile; **to leave sth in a ~** laisser qch en tas; **to sort sth into ~s** trier qch en tas; **put those books into ~s** mettez ces livres en piles; **2** (of fabric, carpet) poil *m*; **deep-~ carpet** tapis *m* au poil épais; **to brush sth with the ~/against the ~** brosser qch dans le sens du poil/à rebrousse-poil; **3**○ (large amount) **a ~** ou **~s of** un tas or des tas de; **to have ~s of money** être plein aux as○; **4** Constr (post) pilier *m*; **5** Elec, Nucl pile *f*; **6** littér ou hum (building) édifice *m*.
II piles *npl* Med hémorroïdes *fpl*.
III *vtr* (in a heap) entasser (**on** sur); (in a stack) empiler (**on** sur); **to be ~d with** [*surface*] être recouvert de piles de [*books, objects*]; **the room was ~d high with boxes** il y avait une montagne de cartons dans la pièce; **a plate ~d high with cakes** une assiette avec une montagne de gâteaux; **to ~ luggage into a car** empiler des bagages dans une voiture.
IV *vi*○ **1** (board) **to ~ on/off** monter dans [qch]/sortir de [qch] en se bousculant [*bus, train*]; **to ~ into** s'engouffrer dans [*vehicle*]; **2** (crash) **to ~ into** [*vehicle*] rentrer dans [*other vehicle*]; **the bus ~d into them** le bus leur est rentré dedans.
IDIOMS **to be at the top/bottom of the ~** être en haut/bas de l'échelle; **to make one's ~**○ faire son beurre○.
■ **pile in**○ monter en se serrant; **the bus came and we all ~d in** le bus est arrivé et nous y sommes montés en nous serrant.
■ **pile on**○: **to ~ on the charm** en faire un peu trop pour séduire; **to ~ it on** mettre le paquet○.
■ **pile up** ¶ [*leaves, snow, rubbish*] s'entasser; [*money*] s'amasser; [*debts, evidence, problems, work*] s'accumuler; [*cars*] (in accident) se rentrer dedans; ¶ **~ [sth] up, ~ up [sth] 1** lit (in a heap) entasser; (in a stack) empiler; **to be ~d up** [*books, plates*] s'empiler (**on** sur); **2** fig accumuler [*debts, evidence, problems, work*].

pile: **~ driver** *n* sonnette *f* de battage; **~ fabric** *n* Tex (velvet) velours *m*; (other) fourrure *f* synthétique; **~ shoe** *n* Tech sabot *m* de pieu; **~up** *n* Aut carambolage *m*.

pilfer /ˈpɪlfə(r)/ **I** *vtr* dérober (**from** dans).
II *vi* commettre des larcins.

pilferage /ˈpɪlfərɪdʒ/ *n* Insur vol *m*.

pilferer /ˈpɪlfərə(r)/ *n* voleur/-euse *m/f*.

pilfering /ˈpɪlfərɪŋ/ *n* vol *m*.

pilgrim /ˈpɪlgrɪm/ *n* pèlerin *m* (**to** de).

pilgrimage /ˈpɪlgrɪmɪdʒ/ *n* Relig, fig pèlerinage *m*; **to go on** ou **make a ~** faire un pèlerinage (**to** à).

Pilgrim Fathers *npl* Hist Pères *mpl* Pèlerins.

pill /pɪl/ **I** *n* **1** Med, Pharm (for general use) comprimé *m*, cachet *m* (**for** contre, pour); **to take a ~** prendre un comprimé or un cachet; ▶ **pep pill**, **sleeping pill**; **2** (contraceptive) **the ~** la pilule; **to be on/to go on the ~** prendre/commencer à prendre la pilule; **to come off the ~** arrêter la pilule; **3**○ (idiot) abruti○ *m*.
II *vi* [*sweater*] boulocher.
IDIOMS **he found it a bitter ~ to swallow** il a trouvé la pilule amère; **to sugar** ou **sweeten** ou **gild the ~** dorer la pilule○.

pillage /ˈpɪlɪdʒ/ **I** *n* pillage *m*.
II *vtr, vi* piller.

pillar /ˈpɪlə(r)/ *n* **1** Archit pilier *m*; **2** (of smoke, fire, rock etc) colonne *f*; **a ~ of salt** Bible une statue de sel; **the ~s of Hercules** Geog les Colonnes d'Hercule; **3** fig (of institution, society) pilier *m* (**of** de); **to be a ~ of strength to sb** être d'un grand soutien à qn; **4** Aut pied *m* de caisse, montant *m*; **5** Mining (as support) pilier *m*.
IDIOMS **to go from ~ to post**○ courir à droite et à gauche○ (**doing** pour faire); **to be sent from ~ to post**○ (for information, papers) se faire renvoyer de service en service○.

pillar: **~ box** *n* GB boîte *f* aux lettres; **~-box red** *n, adj* GB rouge (*m*) vif *inv*.

pillared /ˈpɪləd/ *adj* [*building, arcade*] à colonnades.

pillbox /ˈpɪlbɒks/ *n* **1** (for pills) boîte *f* à pilules; **2** Mil casemate *f*; **3** (also **~ hat**) toque *f*.

pillion /ˈpɪlɪən/ **I** *n* (also **~ seat**) siège *m* de passager.
II *modif* [*passenger*] arrière *inv*.
III *adv* **to ride ~** monter en croupe.

pillock◐ /ˈpɪlək/ *n* GB péj abruti○ *m* pej.

pillory /ˈpɪlərɪ/ **I** *n* Hist pilori *m*.
II *vtr* lit, fig mettre [qn] au pilori (**for** pour).

pillow /ˈpɪləʊ/ **I** *n* **1** (on bed) oreiller *m*; (of moss, grass) coussin *m*; **neck ~** oreiller *m* pour le cou; **2** (in lacemaking) carreau *m*.
II *vtr* **to be ~ed on** [*head*] reposer sur.

pillow: **~case** *n* taie *f* d'oreiller; **~ fight** *n* bataille *f* d'oreillers or de polochons; **~ lace** *n* dentelle *f* au fuseau; **~slip** *n* GB = **pillowcase**; **~ talk**○ *n* confidences *fpl* sur l'oreiller.

pill popping○ *adj* [*person*] qui prend des pilules.

pilot /ˈpaɪlət/ ▶ **1692** **I** *n* **1** Aviat, Aerosp pilote *m*; **2** Radio, TV (programme) émission *f* pilote (**for** pour); **3** (on cooker etc) (also **~ light**) (gas) veilleuse *f*; (electric) voyant *m* lumineux; **4** Naut (navigator) pilote *m*.
II *modif* **1** Comm, Ind [*course, project, study*] pilote; Radio, TV [*programme, series*] expérimental, pilote; **2** Aviat [*instruction, training*] des pilotes; [*error*] de pilotage.
III *vtr* **1** Aviat, Naut (navigate) piloter; **to ~ sb through** fig guider qn à travers [*crowd, streets*]; **to ~ a bill through parliament** assurer le passage d'un projet de loi au parlement; **he ~ed the party to victory** il a mené le parti à la victoire; **2** (test) mettre [qch] au banc d'essai [*course, system*].

pilot: **~ boat** *n* bateau-pilote *m*; **~ burner** *n* (gas) veilleuse *f*; (electric) voyant *m* lumineux; **~ fish** *n* poisson *m* pilote; **~house** *n* poste *m* de pilotage; **~ officer** *n* GB sous-lieutenant *m*; **~ plant** *n* usine-pilote *f*; **~ scheme** *n* projet-pilote *m*; **~'s licence** *n* brevet *m* de pilote.

pimento, **pimiento** /pɪˈmentəʊ/ **I** *n* **1** (vegetable) piment *m* doux; **2** (spice) piment *m* de la Jamaïque; **3** (tree) pimenta *m*.
II *modif* [*cheese*] en piment.

pimp /pɪmp/ **I** *n* proxénète *m*.
II *vi* **1** (control prostitutes) faire du proxénétisme; **2** (find customers) servir d'entremetteur (**for** à).

pimpernel /ˈpɪmpənel/ *n* mouron *m*.

pimping /ˈpɪmpɪŋ/ *n* proxénétisme *m*.

pimple /ˈpɪmpl/ *n* bouton *m*; **to break out in ~s** avoir une éruption de boutons.

pimply /ˈpɪmplɪ/ *adj* boutonneux/-euse also pej.

pin /pɪn/ **I** *n* **1** (for sewing, fastening cloth or paper) épingle *f*; **2** Elec (of plug) fiche *f*; **two-/three-~ plug** prise *f* à deux/trois fiches; **3** Tech (to attach wood or metal) goujon *m*; (machine part) goupille *f*; **4** Med (in surgery) broche *f*; **5** (brooch) barrette *f*; **diamond ~** barrette avec brillant; **6** (in bowling) quille *f*; **7** (in golf) drapeau *m* (de trou).
II pins○ (legs) *npl* quilles○ *fpl*, jambes *fpl*.
III *vtr* (*p prés etc* **-nn-**) **1** (attach with pins) épingler [*dress, hem, curtain*]; **to ~ sth to** épingler qch à; **to ~ sth on(to)** épingler qch sur; (with drawing pin) fixer qch avec une punaise sur [*board, wall*]; **to ~ two things together** épingler deux choses l'une avec l'autre; **to ~ sth with** attacher qch avec [*brooch, grip, pin*]; **2** (trap, press) coincer [*person, part of body*]; **to ~ sb against** ou **to** coincer qn contre [*wall, sofa, floor*]; **her arms were ~ned to her sides** elle avait les bras plaqués au corps; **to be ~ned under** être coincé sous [*fallen tree, wreckage*]; **3**○ (attribute, attach) **to ~ sth on sb** imputer qch à qn, rejeter qch sur qn [*blame, crime*]; **4** Mil, Sport coincer, bloquer; **France were ~ned in their own half** la France a été coincée sur son terrain; **5** (in chess) coincer [*piece*].
IDIOMS **for two ~s I would do** pour un peu je ferais; **to ~ one's ears back**○ ouvrir grand les oreilles○; **you could have heard a ~ drop** on aurait entendu voler une mouche; ▶ **hope**.
■ **pin down**: ¶ **~ down [sb], ~ [sb] down 1** (physically) immobiliser (**to** à); **2** fig coincer; **he won't be ~ned down** il ne se laissera pas coincer; **to ~ sb down to a definite date/an exact figure** arriver à soutirer une date fixe/un chiffre exact à qn; **to ~ sb down to doing** obliger qn à s'engager à faire; ¶ **~ down [sth], ~ [sth] down 1** lit accrocher [*piece of paper, cloth, map*]; épingler [*sheet*]; **2** fig (define) identifier [*concept, feeling*]; **I can't ~ it down** je n'arrive pas à mettre le doigt dessus.
■ **pin up**: **~ up [sth], ~ [sth] up** accrocher [*poster, notice, map*] (**on** à); remonter [*hair*].

PIN /pɪn/ *n* (also **~ number**) (*abrév* = **personal identification number**) code *m* confidentiel (*pour carte bancaire*).

pinafore /ˈpɪnəfɔː(r)/ *n* (apron) tablier *m*; (overall) blouse *f*.

pinafore dress *n* robe-chasuble *f*.

pin: **~ball** ▶ **1282** *n* flipper *m*; **~ball machine** *n* flipper *m*, billard *m* électrique.

pince-nez /ˌpænsˈneɪ/ *n* (*pl* **~**) pince-nez *m inv*.

pincer /ˈpɪnsə(r)/ **I** *n* Zool pince *f*.
II pincers *npl* (tool) tenailles *fpl*; **a pair of ~s** une paire de tenailles.

pincer movement *n* mouvement *m* en tenailles.

pinch /pɪntʃ/ **I** *n* **1** (nip) pincement *m*; **to give sb a ~ on the cheek** pincer la joue de qn; **2** (small quantity) (of salt, spice) pincée *f*; **a ~ of snuff** une prise de tabac.
II *vtr* **1** (with fingers) pincer; **to ~ sb's arm/bottom, to ~ sb on the arm/bottom** pincer le bras/les fesses de qn; **2** [*shoe*] serrer [*foot*]; **3**○ (steal) faucher○ (**from** à); **4** [*crab*] pincer; **5** Hort **to ~ out** ou **off** enlever [*bud, tip*]; **6**○ US (arrest) pincer○.
III *vi* [*shoe*] serrer.
IV *v refl* **to ~ oneself** lit, fig se pincer.
IDIOMS **at** GB ou **on** US **a ~** à la rigueur; **to feel the ~** avoir de la peine à joindre les deux bouts; **to ~ and scrape** rogner sur tout.

pinchbeck /ˈpɪntʃbek/ **I** *n* similor *m*.
II *modif* **1** (of alloy) en similor; **2** fig (sham) en toc.

pinched /pɪntʃt/ *adj* [*nerve*] pincé; **his face looked ~** il avait les traits tirés.

pinch-hit /ˌpɪntʃˈhɪt/ *vi* US **1** Sport jouer à la place de qn; **2** (deputize) **to ~ for sb** remplacer qn au pied levé.

pinch-hitter /ˌpɪntʃˈhɪtə(r)/ *n* US (all contexts) remplaçant/-e *m/f*.

pincushion /ˈpɪnkʊʃn/ *n* pelote *f* à épingles.

pine /paɪn/ **I** *n* **1** (also **~ tree**) pin *m*; **2** (timber) pin *m*; **made of ~** en pin; **stripped ~** pin décapé,.
II *modif* [*branch, log, fragrance*] de pin; [*furniture, plank*] en pin; [*disinfectant*] parfumé au pin.
III *vi* languir (**for** après; **to do** de faire).
■ **pine away** se laisser dépérir.

pineal body, **pineal gland** /ˈpɪnɪəl, paɪˈniːəl/ *n* glande *f* pinéale.

pineapple /ˈpaɪnæpl/ **I** *n* (fruit, plant) ananas *m*.
II *modif* [*juice, flesh, slice*] d'ananas; [*dish, yogurt, cake*] à l'ananas.

pineapple-flavoured GB, **pineapple-flavored** US *adj* parfumé à l'ananas.

pine: **~-clad** *adj* littér couvert de sapins; **~cone** *n* pomme *f* de pin; **~ kernel** *n* pignon *m* de pin; **~ marten** *n* martre *f*; **~-needle** *n* aiguille *f* de pin; **~nut** *n* = **pine kernel**; **~-scented** *adj* [*cleanser, essence*] parfumé au pin; [*forest*] qui sent le pin.

pinewood /ˈpaɪnwʊd/ **I** *n* (forest) forêt *f* de pins; (timber) pin *m*.
II *modif* [*furniture*] en pin.

ping /pɪŋ/ **I** *n* **1** (noise) (of bell) tintement *m*; (of bullet) claquement *m*; US (of car engine) bruit *m* inquiétant; **2** onomat ding.
II *vtr* faire retentir [*bell*]; tirer [*elastic*].
III *vi* [*bell*] tinter; [*bullet*] claquer; [*cash register*] sonner.
IV pinging *pp adj* [*sound*] de ding.

pinger○ /ˈpɪŋə(r)/ *n* minuterie *f*.

ping-pong® /ˈpɪŋpɒŋ/ ▶1282 **I** *n* ping-pong® *m*; **to play ~** jouer au ping-pong®.
II *modif* [*game, equipment, player*] de ping-pong®.

pinhead /ˈpɪnhed/ *n* **1** lit tête *f* d'épingle; **2**○ péj abruti/-e○ *m/f*.

pin: **~hole** *n* trou *m* d'épingle; **~hole camera** *n* appareil *m* à sténopé.

pinion /ˈpɪnɪən/ **I** *n* **1** littér (wing) aile *f*; **2** Zool (feather) rémige *f* primaire; **3** Tech pignon *m*.
II *vtr* **1** (hold firmly) **to ~ sb against** plaquer qn contre [*wall, door*]; **to ~ sb's arms** tenir les bras de qn; **2** Vet rogner les ailes à [*bird*].

pinion wheel *n* roue *f* à pignon.

pink /pɪŋk/ **I** *n* ▶1104 **1** (colour) rose *m*; **a shade of ~** un ton rosé; **2** Bot œillet *m* mignardise; **3** ▶1282 (in snooker) bille *f* rose.
II *adj* ▶1104 **1** rose; **to go** ou **turn ~** rosir; (blush) rougir (**with** de); **2** (leftwing) gauchisant; **3**○ (gay) homosexuel/-elle.
III *vtr* **1** (scallop) denteler [*fabric*]; **2** (prick) toucher [*person*].
IV *vi* GB Aut cliqueter.
IDIOMS **to be in the ~** être en pleine forme.

pink: **~eye** *n* conjonctivite *f* aiguë; **~-footed goose** *n* oie *f* à bec court; **~ gin** *n* cocktail *m* de gin et d'angusture; **~(-fleshed) grapefruit** *n* pamplemousse *m* rose.

pinkie /ˈpɪŋkɪ/ *n* US, Scot petit doigt *m*.

pinking /ˈpɪŋkɪŋ/ *n* GB Aut cliquetis *m*.

pinking shears, **pinking scissors** *npl* ciseaux *mpl* cranteurs.

pinkish /ˈpɪŋkɪʃ/ ▶1104 *adj* **1** [*colour*] rosâtre; **~-white** blanc rosé; **2** (leftwing) gauchisant.

pinko○ /ˈpɪŋkəʊ/ péj **I** *n* (*pl* **~s** ou **~es**) gauchiste *mf*.
II *adj* gauchisant.

pink slip *n* US lettre *f* de licenciement.

pin money *n* argent *m* de poche.

pinnace /ˈpɪnɪs/ *n* chaloupe *f*.

pinnacle /ˈpɪnəkl/ *n* **1** fig sommet *m*, apogée *m* (**of** de); **2** Archit pinacle *m*; **3** (of rock) pic *m*, cime *f*.

pinny○ /ˈpɪnɪ/ *n* **1** GB (apron) tablier *m*; **2** US (singlet) maillot *m* (d'une équipe).

pinochle /ˈpiːnɒkl/ ▶1282 *n*: *jeu de cartes américain se jouant avec 48 cartes*.

pinpoint /ˈpɪnpɔɪnt/ **I** *n* tête *f* d'épingle; **a ~ of light** un point lumineux.
II *vtr* **1** (identify, pick out) indiquer [*problem, risk, causes*]; **2** (place exactly) indiquer [*location, position, site*]; déterminer [*time, exact moment*].

pinprick /ˈpɪnprɪk/ *n* **1** lit coup *m* d'épingle; (feeling caused) sensation *f* de piqûre; **2** fig (of jealousy, remorse) pointe *f*.

pinstripe /ˈpɪnstraɪp/ **I** *n* (stripe) rayure *f* fine.
II pinstripes *npl* (suit) costume *m* à fines rayures.
III *modif* [*fabric, suit*] à fines rayures.

pinstriped *adj* = **pinstripe III**.

pint /paɪnt/ ▶1068 **I** *n* **1** Meas pinte *f* (GB = *0.57 litres*, US = *0.47 litres*); **a ~ of milk** ≈ un demi-litre de lait; **to be sold in ~s** être vendu par pinte; **to cost 50 pence a ~** coûter 50 pence la pinte; **2**○ GB **to go for a ~** aller boire une bière; **he's fond of a ~** il aime bien sa bière.
II *modif* [*carton, jug*] d'une pinte.

pinta○ /ˈpaɪntə/ *n* GB *bouteille de lait d'une pinte*.

pintable† /ˈpɪnteɪbl/ *n* flipper *m*.

pint glass, **pint pot** *n* ≈ chope *f* (d'un demi-litre).

pinto /ˈpɪntəʊ/ **I** *n* US (*pl* **-os** ou **-oes**) cheval *m* pie.
II *adj* [*horse, pony*] pie.

pinto bean *n* haricot *m* pinto.

pint-size(d) /ˈpaɪntsaɪzd/ *adj* petit.

pin tuck *n* Sewing petit pli *m* (cousu), nervure *f*.

pinup /ˈpɪnʌp/ *n* **1** (semi-naked) (woman) pin-up *f inv*; (man) photo *f* d'homme à moitié nu; **2** (poster of star) affiche *f* de vedette; (star) idole *f*.

pinwheel /ˈpɪnwɪəl, US -hwɪəl/ *n* soleil *m* (*feu d'artifice*).

pioneer /ˌpaɪəˈnɪə(r)/ **I** *n* (all contexts) pionnier *m* (**of, in** de).
II *modif* [*research, work*] novateur/-trice; [*life*] de pionnier; [*farm, wagon*] de pionniers; **the ~ spirit** la mentalité de pionnier; **a ~ socialist/immunologist** un pionnier du socialisme/de l'immunologie; **a ~ astronaut** un des premiers astronautes.
III *vtr* mettre [qch] au point [*invention, technique*]; **to ~ the use/study of** être le premier à utiliser/étudier.
IV pioneering *pres p adj* [*scientist, socialist, film-maker, scheme, study*] innovateur/-trice; [*surgery*] d'avant garde; **he did ~ing work in physics** il a fait des recherches jamais entreprises auparavant en physique.

pioneer: **~ farmer** *n* pionnier *m*; **~ settler** *n* colon *m*.

pious /ˈpaɪəs/ *adj* **1** (devout) pieux/pieuse; **2** péj (sanctimonious) plein de componction; (insincere) faussement vertueux/-euse; **~ hope, ~ wish** vœu pieux.

piously /ˈpaɪəslɪ/ *adv* **1** [*worship*] pieusement; **2** [*say, moralize*] avec componction.

pip /pɪp/ **I** *n* **1** (seed) pépin *m*; **2** GB Telecom **the ~s** tonalité *f* (*indiquant qu'il faut introduire à nouveau de l'argent*); **3** Radio top *m* (*signal pour indiquer l'heure*); **4** (on card, dice, domino) point *m*; **5** GB (showing rank) étoile *f*.
II *vtr*○ GB battre; **to ~ sb for sth** souffler○ qch à qn; **to ~ sb at** ou **to the post** souffler la place à qn; **to be ~ped at** ou **to the post** se faire souffler la victoire.
IDIOMS **to give sb the ~**○† énerver qn.

pipe /paɪp/ ▶1481 **I** *n* **1** (conduit) (in building) tuyau *m*; (underground) conduite *f*; **waste/gas ~** tuyau d'écoulement/de gaz; **2** (for smoker) pipe *f*; **to smoke a ~** (habitually) fumer la pipe; **to have a ~** fumer une pipe; **to fill a ~** bourrer une pipe; **3** Mus (on organ) tuyau *m* (d'orgue); **4** Mus (flute) chalumeau *m*; **5** (birdsong) chant *m*; **6** Naut sifflet *m*.
II pipes *npl* Mus cornemuse *f*.
III *vtr* **1** (carry) **to ~ water into a house** alimenter un foyer en eau; **oil is ~d across/under/to** le pétrole est transporté par canalisation à travers/sous/jusqu'à; **~d water** eau courante; **2** (transmit) diffuser [*music*] (**to** dans); **music is ~d throughout the store** la musique est diffusée dans tout le magasin; **3** (sing) [*person*] chanter [qch] d'une voix flûtée [*tune*]; **4** (play) (on bagpipes) jouer [qch] sur sa cornemuse [*tune*]; (on flute) jouer [qch] sur son chalumeau [*tune*]; **5** Sewing passepoiler [*cushion, collar*]; **a cushion ~d with pink** un coussin avec un passepoil rose; **6** Culin **to ~ icing onto a cake** décorer un gâteau; **to ~ sb's name on a cake** décorer un gâteau du nom de qn; **7** Naut siffler [*order*]; **to ~ sb aboard** accueillir qn à bord au son du sifflet; **to ~ 'all hands on deck'** siffler le rassemblement.
IV *vi* siffler.
■ **pipe down**○ (quieten down) faire moins de bruit; **~ down!** tais-toi!
■ **pipe in**: **~ [sth] in, ~ in [sth]** annoncer l'arrivée de [qch] au son d'une cornemuse [*haggis, guests*].
■ **pipe up** [*voice*] se faire entendre; **'it's me!' she ~d up** 'c'est moi!' dit-elle d'une petite voix.

pipe: **~clay** *n* terre *f* de pipe; **~-cleaner** *n* cure-pipe *m*; **~d music** *n* musique *f* d'ambiance; **~-dream** *n* chimère *f*; **~ful** *n* pipée *f*.

pipeline /ˈpaɪplaɪn/ *n* **1** Tech oléoduc *m*, pipeline *m*; **2** fig **to be in the ~** [*change*] être en cours; [*product*] être en route; **she's got a new novel in the ~** elle a un roman en chantier.

pipe: **~ of peace** *n* calumet *m* de la paix; **~ organ** *n* Mus orgue *m*.

piper /ˈpaɪpə(r)/ ▶1692, 1481 *n* **1** (bag-pipe player) joueur/-euse *m/f* de cornemuse; **2** (flute-player) joueur/-euse *m/f* de chalumeau.
IDIOMS **he who pays the ~ calls the tune** Prov l'argent c'est le pouvoir.

pipe: **~ rack** *n* râtelier *m* à pipes; **~-smoker** *n* fumeur/-euse *m/f* de pipe; **~-smoking** *adj* qui fume la pipe (*after n*); **~s of Pan** ▶1481 *npl* flûte *f* de Pan; **~ tobacco** *n* tabac *m* à pipe.

pipette /pɪˈpet/ *n* pipette *f*.

pipework /ˈpaɪpwɜːk/ *n* tuyauterie *f*.

piping /ˈpaɪpɪŋ/ **I** *n* **1** (conduit) tuyau *m*; (system of conduits) canalisations *fpl*; **2** (transportation) transport *m* par canalisation; **3** Sewing passepoil *m*; **4** Culin décoration *f* (en sucre).
II *adj* [*voice, tone*] flûté.

piping: **~ bag** *n* poche *f* à douille; **~ cord** *n* Sewing ganse *f*; **~ hot** *adj* fumant.

pipit /ˈpɪpɪt/ *n* pipit *m*.

pipkin /ˈpɪpkɪn/ *n* poêlon *m*.

pipsqueak○ /ˈpɪpskwiːk/ *n* demi-portion○ *f*, freluquet *m*.

piquancy /ˈpiːkənsɪ/ *n* (of situation) piquant *m*; (of food) goût *m* piquant; **to add ~ to** donner du piquant à [*situation*]; donner un goût piquant à [*food*].

piquant /ˈpiːkənt/ *adj* (all contexts) piquant.

piquantly /ˈpiːkəntlɪ/ *adv* [*remark, describe*] de façon piquante.

pique /piːk/ **I** *n* dépit *m*; **to do sth in ~** ou **out of ~** faire qch par dépit; **in a fit of ~** dans un accès de dépit.
II *vtr* **1** (hurt) froisser; **2** (arouse) piquer [*curiosity, interest*].

piqué /ˈpiːkeɪ/ *n* Tex piqué *m*.

piqued /piːkt/ *adj* vexé (**at, by** par; **to do** de faire).

piquet /pɪˈket/ ▶1282 *n* piquet *m*.

piracy /ˈpaɪərəsɪ/ *n* **1** Naut piraterie *f*; **2** (of tapes, software) duplication *f* pirate (**of** de).

Piraeus /paɪˈrɪəs/ ▶1818 *pr n* le Pirée.

piranha (fish) /pɪˈrɑːnə/ *n* piranha *m*.

pirate /ˈpaɪərət/ **I** *n* **1** Naut pirate *m*; **2** (copy of tape etc) contrefaçon *f*, version *f* pirate; **3** (also **~ station**) station *f* pirate; **4** (entrepreneur) pirate *m*; **5** (copier) contrefacteur *m*.
II *modif* [*video, tape, operator, firm*] pirate; [*ship, raid*] de pirates.
III *vtr* pirater [*tape, video, software*].

pirated /ˈpaɪərətɪd/ *adj* [*video, tape, software, version*] pirate.

pirate: **~ radio** *n* radio *f* pirate; **~ radio ship** *n* bateau *m* émetteur pirate; **~ radio station** *n* (station *f* de) radio *f* pirate.

piratical /ˌpaɪəˈrætɪkl/ *adj* [*appearance, exploit*] de pirate.

pirating /ˈpaɪərætɪŋ/ *n* piratage *m*.

pirogue /pɪˈrəʊg/ *n* pirogue *f*.

pirouette /ˌpɪrʊˈet/ **I** *n* pirouette *f*; **to do ~s** faire des pirouettes.
II *vi* pirouetter.

Pisa /ˈpiːzə/ ▶1818 *pr n* Pise.

Piscean /ˈpaɪsɪən/ ▶1916 **I** *n* **to be a ~** être Poissons.
II *adj* **~ character** caractère/type des Poissons.

Pisces /ˈpaɪsiːz/ ▶1916 *n* (all contexts) Poissons *mpl*.

pisciculture /ˈpɪsɪkʌltʃə(r)/ *n* pisciculture *f*.

piss◑ /pɪs/ **I** *n* **1** lit pisse◑ *f*; **to need a ~** avoir envie de pisser◑; **to have** GB ou **take** US **a ~** aller pisser◑; **2** fig **to go (out) on the ~** GB aller se soûler.
II *vtr* **to ~ blood** pisser◑ du sang; **to ~ one's pants** pisser◑ dans sa culotte.
III *vi* pisser◑; **to ~ with rain** GB pleuvoir comme vache qui pisse◑.
IV *v refl* **to ~ oneself** pisser◑ sur soi; **to ~ oneself (laughing)** pisser◑ de rire.
IDIOMS **it's a piece of ~**◑ GB c'est du gâteau○; **to take the ~ out of sb/sth**◑ se moquer de qn/qch; **it's ~ing in the wind**◑ c'est comme si on pissait◑ dans un violon.
■ **piss about, piss around**◑: ¶ **~ about** glander◑; ¶**~ [sb] about** se foutre de◑.
■ **piss away**◑ US: **~ away [sth]** claquer [*fortune*].
■ **piss down**◑ GB pleuvoir comme vache qui pisse◑.
■ **piss off**◑: ¶ **~ off** se casser○; ¶ **~ [sb] off, ~ off [sb]** (make fed up) emmerder◑; (make angry) foutre [qn] en rogne◑.
■ **piss on**◑: **~ on [sb]** (defeat) GB battre [qn] à plates coutures○; (treat contemptuously) US traiter qn comme de la merde●.

piss artist, pisshead◑ *n* GB pilier *m* de bistrot.

pissed◑ /pɪst/ *adj* **1** GB bourré◑; **to get ~** se soûler la gueule◑; **2** US furieux/-ieuse (**at sb** contre qn).

pissed off◑ /ˌpɪstˈɒf/ *adj* **to be ~** en avoir marre○ (**with, at** de); **I'm ~ that** ça m'agace○ que; **a ~ tone** un ton agacé○.

pisser◑ /ˈpɪsə(r)/ *n* US **1** (job) emmerdement◑ *m*; **2** (remarkable person, thing) merveille *f*.

piss: **~ poor**◑ *adj* [*excuse*] nul/nulle○; [*person*] fauché○, pauvre; **~-take**◑ *n* GB (joke) blague○ *f*; (parody) parodie *f* (**of** de).

piss-up◑ /ˈpɪsʌp/ *n* GB beuverie *f*.
IDIOMS **he couldn't organize a ~ in a brewery** il ne serait même pas foutu◑ de trouver de l'eau dans la mer.

pistachio /pɪˈstɑːʃɪəʊ, US -æʃɪəʊ/ **I** *n* (*pl* **~s**) **1** (nut, flavour) pistache *f*; **2** (tree) pistachier *m*; **3** ▶1104 (colour) (vert *m*) pistache *m*.
II *adj* ▶1104 (colour) (vert) pistache *inv*.

pistachio: **~-coloured** ▶1104 *adj* vert pistache *inv*; **~-flavoured** *adj* à la pistache.

piste /piːst/ *n* piste *f*; **to ski off ~** faire du ski hors piste.

pistil /ˈpɪstɪl/ *n* pistil *m*.

pistol /ˈpɪstl/ *n* pistolet *m*; **automatic/starter's/toy ~** pistolet automatique/de starter/pour enfants.
IDIOMS **to hold a ~ to sb's head** mettre le couteau sous la gorge de qn.

pistol: **~ grip** *n* poignée *f* pistolet; **~-whip** *vtr* frapper [qn] à coups de crosse.

piston /ˈpɪstən/ *n* piston *m*.

piston: **~ engine** *n* moteur *m* à pistons; **~ pin** *n* axe *m* de piston; **~ ring** *n* segment *m* (de piston); **~ rod** *n* tige *f* de piston.

pit /pɪt/ **I** *n* **1** (for storage, weapons, bodies) fosse *f*; **2** Mining mine *f*; **to work at the ~** travailler à la mine; **to go down the ~** aller travailler à la mine; **to work down the ~** être mineur; **3** (hollow) creux *m*; **the ~ of the stomach** le creux du ventre; **a ~ of depravity** fig un abîme de dépravation; **4** (quarry) **gravel ~** carrière *f* de gravier, gravière *f*; **5** (trap) trappe *f*; **6** US (in peach, cherry, olive) noyau *m*; **7** Fin corbeille *f*; **trading ~** parquet *m* de la Bourse; **wheat ~** Bourse *f* du blé; **8** Theat parterre *m*; **orchestra ~** fosse *f* d'orchestre; **9** Aut (at garage) fosse *f*; (at racetrack) stand *m*; **10**○ GB (bed) pieu *m*○, lit *m*.
II *modif* Mining [*closure, fire, gates*] de mine; [*strike, village*] de mineurs; **~ disaster** désastre *m* minier.
III *vtr* (*p prés etc* **-tt-**) **1** (in struggle) **to ~ sb against** opposer qn à [*opponent*]; **the match will ~ Scotland against Brazil** le match opposera l'Écosse au Brésil; **2** (mark) [*tool*] marquer [*surface, stone*]; [*acid*] ronger [*metal*]; **her skin was ~ted by smallpox/acne** elle avait la peau grêlée par la variole/marquée par l'acné; **3** US (remove stones from) dénoyauter [*peach, cherry, olive*].
IV *v refl* **to ~ oneself against sb** se mesurer à qn; **to ~ one's wits against sb** se mesurer à qn.
IDIOMS **it's the ~s**○! (of place, workplace) c'est l'enfer!; **this place is the ~s (of the earth)**○ c'est un des coins les plus moches du globe○; **to dig a ~ for sb** tendre un piège à qn.

pitapat /ˌpɪtəˈpæt/ *n* (of rain, feet) martèlement *m*; (of heart) battement *m*; **to go ~** [*heart, rain*] faire toc-toc.

pit bull terrier *n* pit bull *m*.

pitch /pɪtʃ/ **I** *n* **1** Sport terrain *m*; **football/rugby ~** terrain de foot(ball)/rugby; **on the ~** sur le terrain; **2** (sound level) gen (of note, voice) also Phon hauteur *f*; Mus ton *m*; **to give the ~** Mus donner le ton; **the ~ is too high/low** Mus c'est trop haut/bas; **absolute ~, perfect ~** oreille *f* absolue; **3** (degree) degré *m*; (highest point) comble *m*; **excitement was at its (highest) ~** ou **was at full ~** l'excitation était à son comble; **a ~ of frustration had been reached** on avait atteint le comble de la frustration; **the situation has reached such a ~ that** la situation en est à un tel point que; **4** (sales talk or argument) gen, Comm boniment *m*; **sales ~** boniment de vente; **to make** ou **give** US **a ~ for sth** se prononcer pour [*idea, proposal*]; faire des avances à [*man, woman*]; **5** Constr, Naut (tar) brai *m*; **6** GB (for street trader, entertainer) emplacement *m*; **7** Naut (movement of boat) tangage *m*; **8** Sport (bounce) lancement *m*; **9** Constr (of roof) pente *f*; **10** (in mountaineering) longueur *f* (de corde).
II *vtr* **1** (throw) jeter, balancer○ [*object*] (**into** dans); Sport lancer; **to ~ hay** Agric jeter du foin avec une fourche; **the horse ~ed her off** le cheval l'a désarçonnée; **the carriage turned over and she was ~ed out** le wagon s'est renversé et elle a été éjectée; **the passengers were ~ed forward** les passagers ont été projetés vers l'avant; **2** (aim, adjust) adapter [*campaign, publicity, speech*] (**at** à); (set) fixer [*price*]; **newspaper/programme ~ed at young people** journal/émission qui vise un public jeune; **the exam was ~ed at a high level** l'examen a été ajusté à un haut niveau; **to ~ one's ambitions too high** placer ses ambitions trop haut; **to ~ sth a bit strong**○ y aller trop fort avec qch○; **3** Mus [*singer*] trouver [*note*]; [*player*] donner [*note*]; **to ~ one's voice higher/lower** hausser/baisser le ton de la voix; **the song is ~ed too high for me** cette chanson est trop haute pour moi; **4** (erect) planter [*tent*]; **to ~ camp** établir un camp; **5 to ~ sb a story**○ sortir○ une histoire à qn; **to ~ sb an excuse**○ débiter○ une excuse à qn.
III *vi* **1** gen (be thrown) [*rider, passenger, cyclist*] être projeté; **2** Naut [*boat*] tanguer; **to ~ and roll** ou **toss** tanguer; **3** US (in baseball) lancer (la balle); **4** GB Sport [*ball*] rebondir.
■ **pitch in**○ **1** (on job) (set to work) s'atteler à la tâche; (join in) y mettre du sien○; (help) mettre la main à la pâte○, donner un coup de main○; **everyone ~ed in with contributions** tout le monde a apporté sa contribution; **2**○ (start to eat) attaquer○.
■ **pitch into**: ¶ **~ into [sth]** (attack) lit, fig attaquer [*attacker, opponent, speaker*]; attaquer [*work, meal*]; ¶ **~ [sb] into** (land in new situation) propulser [qn] dans [*situation*]; **the circumstances which ~ed him into the political arena** les circonstances qui l'ont propulsé dans l'arène politique; **the new director was ~ed straight into an industrial dispute** le nouveau directeur s'est retrouvé au beau milieu d'un conflit social.
■ **pitch out**○: **~ out [sb/sth], ~ [sb/sth] out** éjecter [*troublemaker*] (**from** de), se débarrasser de [*object*].
■ **pitch over** culbuter.

pitch: **~-and-putt** *n* mini-golf *m*; **~-black** *adj* tout noir; [*night*] d'un noir d'encre.

pitchblende /ˈpɪtʃblend/ *n* pechblende *f*.

pitch: **~ dark** *adj* tout noir; **~ darkness** *n* nuit *f* noire; **~ed battle** *n* lit, fig bataille *f* rangée; **~ed roof** *n* toit *m* en pente.

pitcher /ˈpɪtʃə(r)/ *n* **1** (jug) cruche *f*; **2** US Sport lanceur *m*.

pitchfork /ˈpɪtʃfɔːk/ **I** *n* fourche *f*.
II *vtr* **1** Agric fourcher; **2** fig **to ~ sb into** parachuter qn dans [*situation*].

pitch: **~ invasion** *n* invasion *f* du terrain; **~-pine** *n* pitchpin *m*; **~ pipe** *n* diapason *m* à bouche.

piteous /ˈpɪtɪəs/ *adj* [*cry, sight, story*] pitoyable; [*condition, state*] piteux/-euse.

piteously /ˈpɪtɪəslɪ/ *adv* piteusement.

pitfall /ˈpɪtfɔːl/ *n* **1** (of action) écueil *m* (**of** de); **the ~s of doing** les écueils qui guettent celui qui fait; **2** (of language) piège *m*; **3** lit (trap) piège *m*.

pith /pɪθ/ *n* **1** (of fruit) peau *f* blanche; **2** (of stem) moelle *f*; **3** fig essence *f* (**of** de).

pit head *n* carreau *m* de mine.

pithecanthropine /ˌpɪθɪkænˈθrəʊpaɪn/ *adj* pithécanthropien/-ienne.

pithecanthropus /ˌpɪθɪkænˈθrəʊpəs/ *n* pithécanthrope *m*.

pith helmet *n* casque *m* colonial.

pithiness /ˈpɪθɪnɪs/ *n* densité *f*; (of remark, style, writing) (incisiveness) piquant *m*; (terseness) concision *f*.

pithy /ˈpɪθɪ/ *adj* **1** [*remark, style, writing*] (incisive) piquant; (terse) concis; **2** [*fruit*] qui a une peau épaisse.

pitiable /ˈpɪtɪəbl/ *adj* **1** (arousing pity) [*appearance, existence, sight*] pitoyable; [*situation*] lamentable; [*salary*] misérable; **a ~ beggar** un pauvre mendiant; **2** (arousing contempt) [*attempt, excuse*] lamentable; [*state*] déplorable.

pitiably /ˈpɪtɪəblɪ/ *adv* **~ poor/weak** d'une pauvreté/faiblesse à faire pitié; **~ thin** maigre à faire peur.

pitiful /ˈpɪtɪfl/ *adj* **1** (causing pity) [*appearance, cry, sight*] pitoyable; [*income*] misérable; [*condition, state*] lamentable; **2** (arousing contempt) [*attempt, excuse, speech, state*] lamentable; [*amount*] ridicule.

pitifully /ˈpɪtɪfəlɪ/ *adv* **1** (arousing pity) [*thin*] à faire peur; [*cry, look, suffer*] pitoyablement; **2** (arousing contempt) [*perform, sing*] lamentablement; [*low, obvious, poor, small*] lamentablement.

pitiless /ˈpɪtɪlɪs/ *adj* impitoyable.

pitilessly /ˈpɪtɪlɪslɪ/ *adv* [*beat, punish, tease*] impitoyablement; [*stare*] sans pitié; **~ cruel** d'une cruauté sans pitié.

piton /'pi:tɒn/ *n* piton *m*.

pit: **~ pony** *n* cheval *m* de mine; **~ prop** *n* étai *m* de mine.

pit stop *n* **1** (in motor racing) (for repairs) arrêt *m* mécanique; (for fuel) arrêt *m* de ravitaillement; **2** fig (quick break) petite pause *f*.

pitta (bread) /'pɪtə/ *n* pitta *f*, pain *m* arabe.

pittance /'pɪtns/ *n* **a ~** trois fois rien; **to live on/earn a ~** vivre avec/gagner trois fois rien.

pitted /'pɪtɪd/ *adj* **1** [*surface*] rongé; [*face, skin*] grêlé (**with** de); **2** [*olive*] dénoyauté.

pitter-patter /'pɪtəpætə(r)/ *n* = **pitapat**.

pituitary /pɪ'tju:ɪtərɪ, US -tu:əterɪ/ *adj* pituitaire; **~ gland** hypophyse *f*, glande *f* pituitaire.

pit worker ▶ **1692** *n* mineur *m* de fond.

pity /'pɪtɪ/ **I** *n* **1** (compassion) pitié *f* (**for** pour); **out of ~** par pitié; **to feel ~** avoir de la pitié; **to have** ou **take ~ on sb** avoir pitié de qn; **to move sb to ~** faire pitié à qn; **2** (shame) dommage *m*; **what a ~!** quel dommage!; **that would be a ~** ce serait dommage; **it's a ~ that**... c'est dommage que (+ *subj*); **it would be a ~ if**... ce serait dommage si... (+ *ind*); **the ~ (of it) is that**... ce qui est vraiment dommage c'est que...; **what a ~ that**... quel dommage que (+ *subj*); **I'm not rich, more's the ~** je ne suis pas riche, c'est bien dommage; **I neglected to warn him, more's the ~** le pire c'est que j'ai négligé de le prévenir.
II *vtr* **1** (feel compassion for) avoir pitié de [*animal, person*]; **he's to be pitied** il faut avoir pitié de lui; **it's the police I pity, not the criminals** c'est la police que je plains, pas les criminels; **2** (feel contempt for) plaindre [*person*].

pitying /'pɪtɪɪŋ/ *adj* **1** (compassionate) plein de pitié; **2** (scornful) méprisant.

pityingly /'pɪtɪɪŋlɪ/ *adv* **1** (compassionately) avec pitié; **2** (scornfully) avec mépris.

Pius /'paɪəs/ *pr n* Pie.

pivot /'pɪvət/ **I** *n* **1** Mech, Mil pivot *m*; **2** fig pivot *m*, centre *m*.
II *vtr* **1** gen (turn) faire pivoter [*lever*]; orienter [*lamp*]; **2** Tech (provide with a bearing) monter [qch] sur pivot.
III *vi* **1** [*lamp, mechanism, device*] pivoter (**on** sur); **to ~ on one's heels** pivoter sur ses talons; **to ~ from the hips** faire pivoter le torse; **2** fig [*outcome, success, discussion*] reposer (**on** sur).

pivotal /'pɪvətl/ *adj* [*factor, role, decision*] essentiel/-ielle, capital; [*moment*] crucial.

pivot joint *n* articulation *f* trochoïde.

pix○ /pɪks/ *npl* (*abrév* = **pictures**) **1** (photos) photos *fpl*; **2** (cinema) ciné○ *m*, cinoche○ *m*.

pixel /'pɪksl/ *n* pixel *m*.

pixie /'pɪksɪ/ **I** *n* lutin *m*.
II *modif* [*hat, hood*] en pointe; [*haircut*] à la garçonne.

pizza /'pi:tsə/ **I** *n* pizza *f*.
II *modif* [*base, oven, pan*] à pizza.

pizza parlour GB, **pizza parlor** US *n* pizzeria *f*.

pizzazz○ /pɪ'zæz/ *n* panache *m*.

pizzeria /,pi:tsə'ri:ə/ *n* pizzeria *f*.

pizzicato /,pɪtsɪ'kɑ:təʊ/ *adv* pizzicato.

placard /'plækɑ:d/ **I** *n* (at protest march) pancarte *f*; (on wall) affiche *f*.
II *vtr* afficher [*slogan, notice*]; placarder [*wall*].

placate /plə'keɪt, US 'pleɪkeɪt/ *vtr* apaiser, calmer.

placatory /plə'keɪtərɪ, US 'pleɪkətɔ:rɪ/ *adj* apaisant.

place /pleɪs/ **I** *n* **1** (location, position) endroit *m*; **to move from ~ to ~** se déplacer d'un endroit à l'autre; **I hope this is the right ~** j'espère que c'est le bon endroit; **we've come to the wrong ~** nous nous sommes trompés d'endroit; **the best ~ to buy sth** le meilleur endroit pour acheter qch; **same time, same ~** même heure, même endroit; **in many ~s** dans de nombreux endroits; **in ~s** [*hilly, damaged, worn*] par endroits; **her leg had been stung in several ~s** elle avait été piquée à la jambe à plusieurs endroits; **a ~ for** un endroit pour [*meeting, party, monument, office*]; **a ~ to do** un endroit pour faire; **a safe ~ to hide** un endroit sûr pour se cacher; **a good ~ to plant roses** un bon endroit pour planter des roses; **a ~ where** un endroit où; **it's no ~ for a child!** ce n'est pas un endroit pour un enfant!; **the perfect ~ for a writer** l'endroit or le lieu idéal pour un écrivain; **this is the ~ for me!** c'est le rêve ici!; **if you need peace and quiet, then this is not the ~!** si tu veux être tranquille, alors ce n'est pas l'endroit rêvé!; **to be in the right ~ at the right time** être là où il faut quand il le faut; **to be in two ~s at once** être au four et au moulin, être partout à la fois; **not here, of all ~s!** surtout pas ici!; **in Oxford, of all ~s!** à Oxford, figure-toi!; **2** (town, hotel etc) endroit *m*; **a nice/strange ~ to live** un endroit agréable/bizarre pour vivre; **a good ~ to eat** une bonne adresse (pour manger); **we stayed at a ~ on the coast** nous étions sur la côte; **a little ~ called**... un petit village du nom de...; **in a ~ like Kent/Austria** dans une région comme le Kent/un pays comme l'Autriche; **this ~ is filthy!** cet endroit est dégoûtant!; **he threatened to burn the ~ down**○ il a menacé d'y mettre le feu; **to be seen in all the right ~s** se montrer dans les lieux qui comptent; **all over the ~** (everywhere) partout; fig○ [*speech, lecture*] complètement décousu; **your hair is all over the ~**○**!** tu es complètement décoiffé!; **3** (for specific purpose) **~ of birth/work/pilgrimage** lieu *m* de naissance/travail/pèlerinage; **~ of residence** domicile *m*; **~ of refuge** refuge *m*; **4** (home) (house) maison *f*; (apartment) appartement *m*; **David's ~** chez David; **a ~ by the sea** une maison au bord de la mer; **a ~ of one's own** un endroit à soi; **your ~ or mine?** chez toi ou chez moi?; **5** (seat, space) (on bus, at table, in queue) place *f*; (setting) couvert *m*; **to keep a ~** garder une place (**for** pour); **to find/lose one's ~** trouver/perdre sa place; **to show sb to his/her ~** conduire qn à sa place; **please take your ~s** veuillez prendre place; **I couldn't find a ~ to park** je n'ai pas trouvé de place pour me garer; **to lay** ou **set a ~ for sb** mettre un couvert pour qn; **is this ~ taken?** cette place est-elle prise?; **6** (on team, with firm) place *f* (**on** dans); (on committee, board) siège *m* (**on** au sein de); **a ~ as** une place comme [*au pair, cook, cleaner*]; **7** GB Univ place *f* (**at** à); **to get a ~ on** obtenir une place dans [*course*]; **she got a ~ on the fashion design course** elle a obtenu une place en cours de stylisme; **she has a ~ on a carpentry course** elle a été acceptée pour suivre des cours de menuiserie; **8** lit (in competition, race) place *f*; **to finish in first ~** terminer premier/-ière or à la première place; **he backed Red Rum for a ~** Turf il a joué Red Rum placé; **to take second ~** fig (in importance) passer au deuxième plan; **to take second ~ to sth** passer après qch; **to relegate sth to second ~** faire passer qch en second; **9** (in argument, analysis) **in the first ~** (firstly) en premier lieu; (at the outset) pour commencer; **how much money did we have in the first ~?** combien d'argent avions-nous pour commencer?; **10** (correct position) **to put sth in ~** mettre qch en place [*fencing, construction*]; **to push sth back into ~** remettre qch en place; **to return sth to its ~** remettre qch à sa place; **everything is in its ~** tout est bien à sa place; **to hold sth in ~** maintenir qch en place; **when the lever is in ~** quand le levier est engagé; **is the lid in ~?** est-ce que le couvercle est mis?; **in ~** [*law, system, scheme*] en place; **to put sth in ~** mettre qch en place [*scheme, system, regime*]; **11** (rank) **sb's/sth's ~ in** la place de qn/qch dans [*world, society, history, politics*]; **to take one's ~ in society** prendre sa place dans la société; **to put sb in his/her ~** remettre qn à sa place; **to know one's ~** rester à sa place; **12** (role) **it's not my ~ to do** ce n'est pas à moi de faire; **to fill sb 's ~** remplacer qn; **to take sb's ~, take the ~ of sb** prendre la place de qn; **to have no ~ in** n'avoir aucune place dans [*organization, philosophy, creed*]; **there is a ~ for someone like her in this company** il y a une place pour une femme comme elle dans cette entreprise; **there are ~s for people like you**○**!** fig péj ça se soigne○!; **13** (situation) **in my/his ~** à ma/sa place; **in your ~, I'd have done the same** à ta place, j'aurais fait la même chose; **to change** ou **trade ~s with sb** changer de place avec qn; **14** (moment) moment *m*; **in ~s** [*funny, boring, silly*] par moments; **this is not the ~ to do** ce n'est pas le moment de faire; **this is a good ~ to begin** c'est un bon moment pour commencer; **there were ~s in the film where**... il y avait des moments dans le film où...; **15** (in book) (in paragraph, speech) **to mark one's ~** marquer sa page; **to lose/find one's ~** (in book) perdre/retrouver sa page; (in paragraph, speech) perdre/retrouver le fil; **16**○ US (unspecified location) **some ~** quelque part; **no ~** nulle part; **he had no ~ to go** il n'avait nulle part où aller; **he always wants to go ~s with us** il veut toujours venir avec nous; **she goes ~s on her bicycle** elle se déplace à bicyclette.
II out of place *adj phr* [*remark, behaviour*] déplacé; [*language, tone*] inapproprié; **to look out of ~** [*building, person*] détonner; **to feel out of ~** ne pas se sentir à l'aise.
III in place of *prep phr* à la place de [*person, object*]; **X is playing in ~ of Y** X remplace Y; **he spoke in my ~** il a parlé à ma place.
IV *vtr* **1** lit (put carefully) placer; (arrange) disposer; **~ the cucumber slices around the edge of the plate** disposez les rondelles de concombre autour de l'assiette; **she ~d the vase in the middle of the table** elle a placé le vase au milieu de la table; **~ the smaller bowl inside the larger one** mets le petit bol dans le grand; **to ~ sth back on** remettre qch sur [*shelf, table*]; **to ~ sth in the correct order** mettre qch dans le bon ordre; **2** (locate) placer; **to be strategically/awkwardly ~d** être bien/mal placé; **the switch had been ~d too high** l'interrupteur avait été placé trop haut; **3** (using service) **to ~ an advertisement in the paper** mettre une annonce dans le journal; **to ~ an order for sth** passer une commande pour qch; **to ~ a bet** parier, faire un pari (**on** sur); **4** fig (put) **to ~ emphasis on sth** mettre l'accent sur qch; **to ~ one's trust in sb/sth** placer sa confiance en qn/qch; **to ~ sb in a difficult situation/in a dilemma** mettre qn dans une situation difficile/devant un dilemme; **to ~ sb at risk** faire courir des risques à qn; **to ~ the blame on sb** rejeter toute la faute sur qn; **two propositions were ~d before those present** deux propositions ont été soumises aux personnes présentes; **5** (rank) (in competition) classer; (in exam) GB classer; **to be ~d third** [*horse, athlete*] arriver troisième; **6** (judge) juger; **to be ~d among the top scientists of one's generation** être jugé comme un des plus grands scientifiques de sa génération; **where would you ~ him in relation to his colleagues?** comment le jugeriez-vous par rapport à ses collègues?; **7** (identify) situer [*person*]; reconnaître [*accent*]; **I can't ~ his face** je ne le reconnais pas; **8** (find home for) placer [*child*]; **9** Admin (send, appoint) placer [*student, trainee*] (**in** dans); **to ~ sb in charge of staff/a project** confier la direction du personnel/d'un projet à qn; **to be ~d in quarantine** être placé en quarantaine.
V placed *pp adj* **1** gen (situated) **to be well**

~d être bien placé (**to do** pour faire); **he is not well ~d to judge** il est mal placé pour juger; **she is well/better ~d to speak on this subject** elle est bien/mieux placée pour parler de ce sujet; **2** Sport, Turf **to be ~d** [*horse*] GB être placé; US terminer en deuxième position.

IDIOMS **that young man is really going ~s**○ voilà un jeune homme qui ira loin; **to have friends in high ~s** avoir des amis haut placés; **corruption in high ~s** la corruption en haut lieu; **to fall** ou **click** ou **fit into ~** devenir clair; ▶ **take place**.

place-bet /ˈpleɪsbet/ *n* pari *m* placé; **to make a ~** jouer placé.

placebo /pləˈsiːbəʊ/ *n* **1** Med placebo *m*; **2** fig os *m* à ronger.

placebo effect *n* Med, fig effet *m* placebo.

place card *n* carton *m* (de table).

placekick /ˈpleɪskɪk/ Sport **I** *n* tir *m* de remise en jeu; **to take a ~** tirer la remise en jeu.

II *vtr* **to ~ the ball** remettre le ballon en jeu.

place mat *n* set *m* de table.

placement /ˈpleɪsmənt/ *n* **1** GB (also **work ~**) (trainee post) stage *m*; **to get a ~** trouver un stage; **2** (in accommodation, employment) (of child, unemployed person) placement *m* (**in** dans); **3** Fin placement *m*.

placement: **~ office** *n* US Univ centre *m* de liaison université-entreprises; **~ test** *n* US Sch (entrance exam) examen *m* d'entrée; (proficiency test) test *m* de niveau.

place-name /ˈpleɪsneɪm/ *n* nom *m* de lieu; **dictionary of ~s** dictionnaire *m* toponymique.

placenta /pləˈsentə/ *n* placenta *m*.

place of safety order *n* GB Jur *ordre émis par un juge permettant de mettre un enfant en lieu sûr pour le soustraire aux mauvais traitements.*

placer /ˈpleɪsə(r)/ *n* Geol placer *m*.

place: **~ setting** *n* couvert *m*; **~-value** *n* position *f* numérique.

placid /ˈplæsɪd/ *adj* [*person, animal, nature, smile*] placide.

placidity /pləˈsɪdətɪ/ *n* placidité *f*.

placidly /ˈplæsɪdlɪ/ *adv* placidement, avec placidité.

placing /ˈpleɪsɪŋ/ *n* **1** (position) (in race, contest, league) classement *m*, place *f*; **2** (of ball, players) (positioning) positionnement *m*; (location) position *f*; **3** Fin placement *m*.

plagal /ˈpleɪɡl/ *adj* plagal.

plagiarism /ˈpleɪdʒərɪzəm/ *n* plagiat *m*.

plagiarist /ˈpleɪdʒərɪst/ *n* plagiaire *mf*.

plagiaristic /ˌpleɪdʒəˈrɪstɪk/ *adj* plagié.

plagiarize /ˈpleɪdʒəraɪz/ **I** *vtr* plagier; **to ~ a chapter/paragraph from sth** plagier un chapitre/paragraphe de qch.

II *vi* plagier; **to ~ from** plagier [*writer, work*].

plague /pleɪɡ/ **I** *n* **1** Med (bubonic) peste *f*; (epidemic) épidémie *f*; **the ~** la peste; **I haven't got the ~!** hum je n'ai pas la gale○!; **a ~ on you!**‡ la peste soit de toi!‡; **2** fig (nuisance) plaie *f*; **the noise is a constant ~ to residents** le bruit est une vraie plaie pour les résidents; **what a ~ that boy is!** quelle plaie ce garçon!; **3** (large number) (of ants, rats, locusts etc) invasion *f*; (of crimes) vague *f*; **to reach ~ proportions** atteindre des proportions astronomiques; **4** Bible plaie *f*.

II *vtr* **1** (beset) **to be ~d by** ou **with** être en proie à, être assailli par [*doubts, remorse, difficulties*]; **he's ~d by ill health** il a sans arrêt des ennuis de santé; **we were ~d by bad weather** le mauvais temps s'est acharné sur nous; **we were ~d by wasps** nous avons été envahis par les guêpes; **2** (harass) harceler; **to ~ sb with questions** harceler qn de questions; **to ~ sb for sth** harceler qn pour obtenir qch; **to ~ the life out of sb**○ empoisonner l'existence de qn.

IDIOMS **to avoid sb/sth like the ~** fuir qn/qch comme la peste.

plague: **~-ridden** *adj* péj pestiféré; **~-stricken** *adj* [*person, village, population*] atteint de la peste.

plaice /pleɪs/ *n* (*pl* **~**) plie *f*, carrelet *m*.

plaid /plæd/ **I** *n* **1** (fabric) tissu *m* écossais; (pattern) motif *m* écossais; **2** (garment) plaid *m*.

II *modif* [*scarf, shirt, design*] écossais.

plain /pleɪn/ **I** *n* **1** Geog plaine *f*; **on the ~** dans la plaine; **the (Great) Plains** US les Grandes Plaines; **2** (knitting stitch) maille *f* à l'endroit; **a row of ~** un rang à l'endroit.

II *adj* **1** (simple) [*dress, decor, food, living, language*] simple; [*building, furniture*] sobre; **~ cooking** cuisine *f* simple; **she's a good ~ cook** elle fait une bonne cuisine simple; **a ~ man** un homme simple; **2** (of one colour) [*background, fabric*] uni; [*envelope*] sans inscription; **a sheet of ~ paper** (unheaded) une feuille de papier libre; (unlined) une feuille de papier non reglé; **a ~ blue dress** une robe toute bleue; **under ~ cover** Post sous pli discret; **3** euph (unattractive) [*woman*] quelconque; **she's rather ~** elle a un visage quelconque, elle n'a rien d'une beauté; **4** (clear) [*line, marking*] net/nette; **in ~ view of sb** sous les yeux de qn; **5** (obvious) évident, clair; **it was ~ to everyone that he was lying** il était évident pour tout le monde qu'il mentait; **it's a ~ fact that** il est bien clair que; **it is ~ from this report that** il est clair d'après ce rapport que; **she's jealous, it's ~ to see** elle est jalouse, ça saute aux yeux; **her suffering was ~ to see** on ne pouvait pas ignorer sa souffrance; **to make it ~ to sb that** faire comprendre clairement à qn que; **let me make myself quite ~, I'm not going** que ce soit bien clair, je n'y vais pas; **do I make myself ~?** suis-je bien clair?; **she made her irritation quite ~** elle n'a pas caché son irritation; **6** (direct) [*answer, language*] franc/franche; **~ speaking** franchise *f*; **there was plenty of ~ speaking** tout le monde a eu son franc-parler; **can't you speak in ~ English?** tu ne peux pas parler en termes simples?; **in ~ English, this means that** en clair, ceci veut dire que; **the ~ truth of the matter is that** la vérité est que; **7** (*tjrs épith*) (downright) [*common sense*] simple (*before n*); [*ignorance, laziness*] pur et simple (*after n*); **8** (ordinary) **I knew him when he was ~ Mr Spencer** je l'ai connu quand il s'appelait M. Spencer tout court; **9** (unflavoured) [*yoghurt, crisps, rice*] nature *inv*; **10** (in knitting) à l'endroit.

III *adv* **1** (completely) [*stupid, wrong*] tout bonnement, tout simplement; **~ lazy** tout bonnement paresseux; **2** (directly) **I can't put it any ~er than that** je ne peux pas être plus clair.

IDIOMS **to be as ~ as day** être clair comme l'eau de roche; **to be ~ sailing** [*project, task etc*] marcher comme sur des roulettes .

plain: **~chant** *n* plain-chant *m*; **~ chocolate** *n* chocolat *m* à croquer.

plain clothes I *npl* **to wear ~, to be in ~** être en civil.

II plain-clothes *adj* (*tjrs épith*) [*policeman, customs officer*] en civil.

plain: **~ dealing** *n* honnêteté *f*; **~ flour** *n* Culin farine *f* (*sans levure*).

plain Jane○ *n* **she's rather a ~** ce n'est pas une beauté.

plainly /ˈpleɪnlɪ/ *adv* **1** (obviously) manifestement; **they were ~ lying** manifestement ils mentaient, il était évident qu'ils mentaient; **that is ~ not the case** cela n'est manifestement pas le cas; **2** (distinctly) [*hear*] distinctement; [*see*] clairement; [*remember*] parfaitement; **the rainbow was ~ visible** on voyait nettement l'arc-en-ciel; **3** (in simple terms) [*explain, state*] clairement; **4** (frankly) [*speak*] franchement; **5** (simply) [*dress, eat*] simplement; [*decorated, furnished*] sobrement.

plainness /ˈpleɪnnɪs/ *n* **1** (simplicity) (of decor, dress) sobriété *f*; (of food, language) simplicité *f*; **2** (unattractiveness) manque *m* de beauté.

plain: **Plains Indian** *n* Indien/-ienne *m/f* des Plaines; **~sman** *n* (*pl* **-men**) homme *m* des plaines; **~song** *n* plain-chant *m*; **~ speaker** *n* personne *f* qui a son franc-parler; **~-spoken** *adj* direct.

plaint /pleɪnt/ *n* **1** littér (complaint) lamentation *f*; **2** Jur demande *f*.

plain text *n* Comput, Telecom texte *m* en clair.

plaintiff /ˈpleɪntɪf/ *n* Jur plaignant/-e *m/f*.

plaintive /ˈpleɪntɪv/ *adj* plaintif/-ive.

plaintively /ˈpleɪntɪvlɪ/ *adv* [*say*] d'un ton plaintif.

plait /plæt/ **I** *n* natte *f*, tresse *f*; **to wear (one's hair in) ~s** avoir des nattes or des tresses.

II *vtr* tresser [*hair, rope, necklace*]; **to ~ one's hair** se faire des nattes or des tresses.

III plaited *pp adj* [*hair, rope, reed*] tressé.

plan /plæn/ **I** *n* **1** (scheme, course of action) plan *m*; **to draw up a six-point ~** dresser un plan en six points; **a ~ of action/of campaign** un plan d'action/de campagne; **the ~ is to leave very early** nous avons prévu de partir très tôt; **the best ~ would be to stay here** le mieux serait de rester ici; **everything went according to ~** tout s'est passé comme prévu; **2** (definite aim) projet *m* (**for** de; **to do** pour faire); **to have a ~ to do** projeter de faire; **3** Archit, Constr, Tech plan *m* (**of** de); **4** (rough outline) (of essay, book) plan *m*; **make a ~ before you start to write** fais un plan avant de commencer à écrire; **5** (map) plan *m*.

II plans *npl* **1** (arrangements) (known, fixed) projet *m*; (vague, not fixed) projets *mpl*; **the ~s for the school trip** le projet de voyage scolaire; **what are your ~s for the future?** quels sont vos projets d'avenir?; **to make ~s** faire des projets; **to make ~s for sth** (organize arrangements) organiser qch; (envisage) projeter qch; **to make ~s to do** projeter de faire; **to have ~s for sth/sb** avoir des projets pour qch/qn; **I have no particular ~s** (for tonight) je n'ai rien de prévu; (for the future) je n'ai pas de projets bien déterminés; **what are your holiday ~s?** quels sont vos projets pour les vacances?; **but Paul had other ~s** mais Paul avait prévu autre chose; **2** Archit, Constr **the ~s** les plans *mpl*; **submit the ~s before the end of the month** soumettez les plans avant la fin du mois.

III *vtr* (*p prés etc* **-nn-**) **1** (prepare, organize) planifier [*future, traffic system, economy, production*]; organiser, préparer [*timetable, meeting, operation, expedition*]; préparer [*retirement*]; organiser [*day*]; faire un plan de [*career*]; **to ~ it so that one can do** s'organiser pour pouvoir faire; **he ~ned it so he could leave early** il s'est organisé pour pouvoir partir tôt; **2** (intend, propose) projeter [*visit, trip*]; prévoir [*new development, factory*]; **to ~ to do** projeter de faire, se proposer de faire; **3** (premeditate) préméditer [*crime*]; **4** Archit, Constr (design) concevoir [*kitchen, garden, city centre, building*]; **5** (give structure to) construire [*essay, book*]; (make notes for) faire le plan de [*essay, book*]; **6** (decide on size of) **to ~ a family** planifier les naissances.

IV *vi* (*p prés etc* **-nn-**) prévoir; **to ~ for** prévoir [*changes, increase*]; **to ~ on doing/on sth** (expect) s'attendre à faire/à qch; (intend) compter faire/sur qch; **I'm not ~ning on losing the election** je ne m'attends pas à perdre les élections; **why don't you ever ~?** pourquoi ne t'organises-tu pas à l'avance?; **the present situation makes it impossible to ~** vu la situation actuelle, on ne peut pas faire de projets à l'avance.

■ **plan ahead** (vaguely) faire des projets; **it**

is impossible to ~ ahead il est impossible de faire des projets; (look, think ahead) prévoir; **in business, you have to ~ ahead** en affaires, il faut savoir prévoir.

■ **plan out**: **~ out [sth]** définir, arrêter [*strategy, policy*]; planifier [*expenditure, traffic system*]; arrêter [*itinerary*].

planchette /plɑːnˈʃet/ *n* planchette *f* (*en spiritisme*).

plane /pleɪn/ **I** *n* **1** Aviat avion *m*; **to travel by ~** voyager en or par avion; **2** (in geometry) plan *m*; **the horizontal/vertical ~** le plan horizontal/vertical; **3** (face of cube, pyramid) face *f*; **4** Tech (tool) rabot *m*; **5** Bot (also **~ tree**) platane *m*.
II *modif* [*ticket, accident*] d'avion.
III *adj* (flat) plan, uni.
IV *vtr* raboter [*wood, edge*]; **to ~ sth smooth** lisser qch au rabot.
V *vi* [*bird, aircraft, glider*] planer.
■ **plane down**: ¶ **~ down** [*bird, hang-glider*] descendre en vol plané; ¶ **~ down [sth], ~ [sth] down** raboter [*surface, wood*].

plane: **~ geometry** *n* géométrie *f* plane; **~ spotter** *n* passionné/-e *m/f* d'avions.

planet /ˈplænɪt/ *n* planète *f*; **Planet Earth** la planète Terre; **to be on another ~**○ (dreaming) être dans les nuages; (weird) marcher à côté de ses pompes○.

planetarium /ˌplænɪˈteərɪəm/ *n* (*pl* **~s** or **-aria**) planétarium *m*.

planetary /ˈplænɪtrɪ, US -terɪ/ *adj* planétaire.

planetology /ˌplænɪˈtɒlədʒɪ/ *n* planétologie *f*.

plangent /ˈplændʒənt/ *adj* littér (plaintive) mélancolique; (resonant) retentissant.

planisphere /ˈplænɪsfɪə(r)/ *n* planisphère *m*.

plank /plæŋk/ **I** *n* **1** lit planche *f*; **to walk the ~** Naut Hist être exécuté par noyade; **2** fig (of policy, argument) point *m*; **to form the main** ou **central ~ of** être la pierre angulaire de.
IDIOMS **to be as thick as two (short) ~s**○ en tenir une couche○.
■ **plank down**: **~ down [sth], ~ [sth] down** faire du bruit en posant [*chair, case, money*].

planking /ˈplæŋkɪŋ/ *n* ¢ gen, Constr planches *fpl*; Naut bordé *m*.

plankton /ˈplæŋktən/ *n* plancton *m*.

planned /plænd/ *adj* [*growth, change, redundancy*] planifié; [*sale, development*] prévu; [*crime*] prémédité.

planned: **~ economy** *n* économie *f* planifiée; **~ parenthood** *n* régulation *f* des naissances.

planner /ˈplænə(r)/ *n* gen planificateur/-trice *m/f*; (in town planning) urbaniste *mf*.

planning /ˈplænɪŋ/ **I** *n* **1** (organization) (of industry, economy, work) planification *f*; (of holiday, party, meeting) organisation *f*; **we need to do some ~** il faut que nous nous organisions; **that was bad ~** c'était mal calculé; **2** Archit (in town) urbanisme *m*; (out of town) aménagement *m* du territoire.
II *modif* **1** gen, Admin [*decision*] prévisionnel/-elle; **at the ~ stage** à l'état de projet; **2** Transp, Constr, Archit [*department, authorities*] de l'urbanisme; [*policy*] d'urbanisme; [*decision*] en matière d'urbanisme.

planning: **~ application** *n* demande *f* de permis de construire; **~ blight** *n* séquelles *fpl* des excès de la planification.

planning board *n* **1** (in town-planning) commission *f* d'urbanisme; **2** Econ commission *f* de planification (économique).

planning: **~ committee** *n* = **planning board 1**; **~ permission** *n* permis *m* de construire; **~ regulations** *npl* règlements *mpl* d'urbanisme.

plant /plɑːnt, US plænt/ **I** *n* **1** Bot, Hort gen plante *f*; (seedling) plant *m*; **tobacco/flowering ~** plante de tabac/à fleurs; **2** Ind (factory) usine *f*; (power station) centrale *f*; **chemical ~** usine chimique; **nuclear ~** centrale nucléaire; **steel ~** aciérie *f*; **3** ¢ Ind (buildings, machinery, fixtures) installations *fpl* industrielles et commerciales; (fixed machinery) installations *fpl*; (movable machinery) matériel *m*; **4** (person) taupe○ *f*; (piece of evidence) faux indice *m*.
II *modif* Bot [*disease, reproduction*] des plantes; [*biologist, geneticist*] spécialisé dans l'étude des plantes.
III *vtr* **1** (put to grow) planter [*seed, bulb, tree*]; semer [*crop*]; **to ~ a field with wheat** semer un champ de blé; **to ~ one's garden with trees** planter des arbres dans son jardin; **2** (illicitly put in place) placer [*bomb, explosive, tape recorder, spy*]; **to ~ drugs/a weapon on sb** placer de la drogue/une arme sur qn pour l'incriminer; **to ~ a story** faire paraître un article (pour influencer l'opinion); **to ~ a question** poser une question (dont on a tacitement convenu auparavant); **3 to ~ a kiss/foot etc on sth** planter un baiser/pied etc sur qch; **to ~ a knife/a spade in sth** planter un couteau/une bêche dans qch; **4** (start, engender) donner [*idea*]; jeter [*doubt*]; **to ~ doubt in sb's mind** jeter le doute dans l'esprit de qn ; **to ~ an idea in sb's mind** mettre une idée dans la tête de qn.
IV *v refl* **to ~ oneself between/in front of** se planter entre/devant.
■ **plant out**: **~ [sth] out, ~ out [sth]** repiquer [*seedlings*].

plantain /ˈplæntɪn/ *n* **1** (tree, plant) plantain *m*; **2** (fruit) banane *f* plantain.

plantar /ˈplæntə(r)/ *adj* plantaire.

plantation /plænˈteɪʃn/ *n* (all contexts) plantation *f*; **tea/rubber ~** plantation de thé/d'hévéas.

plant breeder *n* Hort sélectionneur/-euse *m/f*.

planter /ˈplɑːntə(r), US ˈplænt-/ *n* **1** (person) planteur/-euse *m/f*; (machine) planteuse *f*; **2** (large plantpot) jardinière *f*; (to hold pot) cache-pot *m inv*.

plant: **~ food** *n* engrais *m*; **~ geneticist** ▶ **1692** *n* phytogénéticien/-ienne *m/f*; **~ hire** *n* GB location *f* de machines.

planting /ˈplɑːntɪŋ, US ˈplænt-/ *n* plantation *f*; **tree ~** plantation d'arbres.

plant: **~ kingdom** *n* règne *m* végétal; **~ life** *n* flore *f*; **~ louse** *n* puceron *m*; **~ pot** *n* pot *m* de fleurs.

plaque /plɑːk, US plæk/ *n* **1** (on wall, monument) plaque *f*; **2** Dent plaque *f* dentaire.

plash /plæʃ/ *n, vi* = **splash**.

plasm /ˈplæzəm/ *n* **1** (protoplasm) protoplasme *m*; **2** = **plasma**.

plasma /ˈplæzmə/ *n* Physiol, Med, Phys plasma *m*.

plaster /ˈplɑːstə(r), US ˈplæs-/ **I** *n* **1** Constr, Med, Art plâtre *m*; **to have an arm in ~** avoir un bras dans le plâtre; **to put sb's leg in ~** plâtrer la jambe à qn; **2** GB (bandage) sparadrap *m*; **a (piece of) ~** un pansement; **to put a ~ on a cut** mettre un pansement sur une coupure.
II *modif* [*model, figure, moulding*] en plâtre.
III *vtr* **1** Constr **to ~ the walls of a house** faire les plâtres d'une maison; **2** (cover) (with posters, pictures) couvrir, tapisser (**with** de); (with oil, paint) badigeonner; **the rain had ~ed his clothes to his body** la pluie avait collé ses vêtements à sa peau; **the story was ~ed all over the front page** l'histoire s'étalait en première page; **3** Med plâtrer; **4**† (defeat) battre [qn] comme plâtre.
■ **plaster down**: **~ down [sth], ~ [sth] down** plaquer [*hair*].
■ **plaster over**: **~ over [sth]** Constr boucher [*crack, hole*]; fig masquer.
■ **plaster up**: **~ up [sth], ~ [sth] up** = **plaster over**.

plasterboard /ˈplɑːstəbɔːd, US ˈplæst-/ **I** *n* placoplâtre® *m*.
II *modif* [*wall, ceiling*] de placoplâtre®.

plaster cast *n* Med plâtre *m*; Art (mould) moulage *m*; (sculpture) plâtre *m*.

plastered○ /ˈplɑːstəd, US ˈplæst-/ *adj* beurré○, pinté○; **to get ~** prendre une cuite○.

plasterer /ˈplɑːstərə(r), US ˈplæst-/ ▶ **1692** *n* plâtrier *m*.

plastering /ˈplɑːstərɪŋ, US ˈplæst-/ *n* **to do the ~** faire les plâtres.

plaster: **~ of Paris** *n* plâtre *m* de Paris; **~work** *n* ¢ plâtres *mpl*.

plastic /ˈplæstɪk/ **I** *n* **1** (substance) plastique *m*; **2**○ ¢ (credit cards) cartes *fpl* de crédit.
II plastics *npl* (matières *fpl*) plastiques *mpl*.
III *adj* **1** (of or relating to plastic) [*industry*] des plastiques; [*manufacture*] de plastique; [*bag, bucket, strap, pouch, component*] en plastique; **2** Art plastique; **the ~ arts** les arts *mpl* plastiques; **3**○ (unnatural) péj [*food*] insipide; [*smile, world, environment*] artificiel/-ielle.

plastic bomb I *n* bombe *f* au plastic.
II *modif* **~ bomb attack** plasticage *m* (**on** de), attentat *m* au plastic (**on** de).

plastic: **~ bullet** *n* balle *f* (de) plastique; **~ cup** *n* gobelet *m* en plastique; **~ explosive** *n* plastic *m*; **~ foam** *n* polystyrène *m* expansé.

Plasticine® /ˈplæstɪsiːn/ **I** *n* pâte *f* à modeler.
II *modif* [*model, shape*] en pâte à modeler.

plasticity /plæsˈtɪsətɪ/ *n* plasticité *f*.

plastic: **~ money**○ *n* cartes *fpl* de crédit; **~ surgeon** ▶ **1692** *n* chirurgien *m* esthétique.

plastic surgery *n* Cosmet chirurgie *f* esthétique; Med chirurgie *f* plastique; **to have ~** subir une intervention de chirurgie plastique or esthétique.

plate /pleɪt/ **I** *n* **1** (dish) (for eating) assiette *f*; (for serving) plat *m*; **china/paper ~** assiette *f* en porcelaine/papier; **to hand** ou **present sth to sb on a ~** lit, GB fig apporter/présenter qch à qn sur un plateau; **2** (dishful) assiette *f*; **a ~ of spinach** une assiette d'épinards; **3** (sheet of metal) plaque *f*, tôle *f*; **a metal ~** une plaque de métal, une tôle; **4** (name plaque) plaque *f*; **5** (registration plaque) plaque *f* minéralogique; **foreign ~s** plaques *fpl* minéralogiques étrangères; **6** ¢ (silverware) gen argenterie *f*; Relig trésor *m*; **the church ~ was stolen** on a volé le trésor de l'église; **7** (metal coating) plaqué *m*; **8** (illustration) planche *f*, hors-texte *m inv*; **9** Print planche *f*; **printer's ~** planche *f* d'imprimerie; **10** Photo plaque *f*; **11** Dent dentier *m*; **12** Geol plaque *f*; **13** Zool plaque *f*; **14** Sport (trophy) plaque *f*; (competition) coupe *f*; **15** Med plaque *f*.
II *vtr* plaquer [*bracelet, candlestick*] (**with** avec, de).
III -plated (*dans composés*) **gold-/silver-~d** plaqué or/argent.
IDIOMS **to have a lot on one's ~** avoir beaucoup à faire.

plate armour *n* GB Hist armure *f* de plates.

plateau /ˈplætəʊ, US plæˈtəʊ/ *n* (*pl* **~s** or **~x**) **1** Geog plateau *m*; **2** fig palier *m*; **to reach a ~** atteindre un palier.

plateful /ˈpleɪtfʊl/ *n* assiette *f*.

plate glass I *n* verre *m* à vitre.
II *modif* [*window, door*] en verre à vitre.

platelayer /ˈpleɪtleɪə(r)/ ▶ **1692** *n* GB Rail agent *m* de voie.

platelet /ˈpleɪtlɪt/ *n* plaquette *f*.

platen /ˈplætən/ *n* (on typewriter) rouleau *m*; (in printing press) platine *f*.

plate: **~-rack** *n* (for draining) égouttoir *m*; (for storage) étagère *f* pour assiettes (*à rangement vertical*); **~ tectonics** *n* tectonique *f* des plaques; **~ warmer** *n* chauffe-assiettes *m inv*.

platform /ˈplætfɔːm/ **I** *n* **1** (stage) (for performance) estrade *f*; (at public meeting) tribune *f*; **please address your remarks to the ~** adressez vos remarques à la tribune or aux membres de la tribune; **to share a ~ with sb** partager la tribune avec qn; **to provide a ~ for sb/sth** offrir une tribune à qn/qch; **2** (in oil industry, in scaffolding, on loading vehicle, for guns) plate-forme *f*; (on weighing machine) gen plateau *m*; (for vehicles) plate-forme *f*; **3** Pol (electoral programme) plate-forme *f* électorale; **to come to power on a ~ of economic reform** arriver au pouvoir grâce à une plate-forme de réformes économiques; **4** Rail quai *m*; **5** (springboard) also fig tremplin *m*.

II platforms *npl* = **platform shoes**.

platform: **~ party** *n*: *personnes qui ont une place dans la tribune officielle*; **~ scales** *n* bascule *f*; **~ shoes** *npl* chaussures *fpl* à semelles compensées; **~ ticket** *n* GB Rail ticket *m* de quai.

plating /ˈpleɪtɪŋ/ *n* **1** (metal coating) placage *m*; **silver/nickel ~** placage *m* d'argent/de nickel; **2** (protective casing) tôle *f*; **doors with steel ~** portes blindées.

platinum /ˈplætɪnəm/ **I** *n* platine *m*.
II *modif* [*ring, jewellery*] de or en platine; [*alloy*] de platine; [*hair*] platiné, platine; **~ disc record** disque *m* de platine.

platinum blonde **I** *n* blonde *f* platine or platinée.
II *adj* **~ hair** cheveux *mpl* blond platine or blonds platinés.

platitude /ˈplætɪtjuːd, US -tuːd/ *n* platitude *f*, lieu *m* commun.

platitudinize /ˌplætɪˈtjuːdɪnaɪz, US -tuːd-/ *vi* se répandre en lieux communs (**about** sur).

Plato /ˈpleɪtəʊ/ *pr n* Platon.

Platonic /pləˈtɒnɪk/ *adj* **1** (also **platonic**) [*love, relationship*] platonique; **2** Philos [*archetype, ideal*] platonicien/-ienne.

platoon /pləˈtuːn/ *n* (+ *v sg ou pl*) **1** Mil (of soldiers, police, fireman) section *f*; (in cavalry, armoured corps) peloton *m*; **2** fig (of waiters, followers) régiment *m*.

platoon: **~ commander** ▶1612 *n* GB Mil chef *m* de section; **~ sergeant** ▶1612 *n* US Mil sous-officier *m* adjoint de la section.

platter /ˈplætə(r)/ *n* **1** (serving dish) plat *m* de service; (wooden) plat *m* en bois; **a silver ~** un plat d'argent; **2** (meal) assiette *f*; **the seafood/cold meat ~** l'assiette de fruits de mer/de charcuterie; **to hand sb sth on a ~** lit, fig apporter qch à qn sur un plateau d'argent; **3** US Audio (of turntable) plateau *m*; **4** US Audio (record) disque *m*.

platypus /ˈplætɪpəs/ *n* ornithorynque *m*.

plaudits /ˈplɔːdɪts/ *npl* applaudissements *mpl*.

plausibility /ˌplɔːzəˈbɪlətɪ/ *n* (of story) plausibilité *f*; (of person) crédibilité *f*.

plausible /ˈplɔːzəbl/ *adj* [*story, plot, alibi*] plausible, vraisemblable; [*person*] convaincant; **the characters are not very ~** les personnages manquent de vraisemblance.

plausibly /ˈplɔːzəblɪ/ *adv* [*speak*] avec vraisemblance; **he claims quite ~ that...** il prétend, et c'est vraisemblable, que...

play /pleɪ/ ▶1282, 1481 **I** *n* **1** Theat pièce *f* (**about** sur); **the characters in a ~** les personnages d'une pièce; **a radio ~, a ~ for radio** une pièce radiophonique; **a one-/five-act ~** une pièce en un acte/en cinq actes; **2** (amusement, recreation) **the sound of children at ~** le bruit d'enfants en train de jouer; **the rich at ~** les riches dans leurs moments de loisir; **to learn through ~** apprendre par le jeu; **3** Sport, Games **~ starts at 11** la partie commence à 11 heures; **there was no ~ today** il n'y a pas eu de partie aujourd'hui; **rain stopped ~** la partie a dû être arrêtée à cause de la pluie; **one evening's ~** (in cards) une soirée de jeu; **the ball is out of ~/in ~** la balle est hors jeu/en jeu; **there was some good defensive ~** la défense a été bonne; **there was some fine ~ from the Danish team** l'équipe danoise a bien joué; **4** (movement, interaction) jeu *m*; **to come into ~** entrer en jeu; **it has brought new factors into ~** cela a introduit de nouveaux éléments; **the ~ of light on the water/of shadows against the wall** le jeu de la lumière sur la surface de l'eau/des ombres contre le mur; **the ~ of forces beyond our comprehension** le jeu de forces qui dépassent notre compréhension; **the free ~ of the imagination** le libre jeu de l'imagination; **5** (manipulation) jeu *m*; **a ~ on words** un jeu de mots; **a ~ on the idea of reincarnation** un jeu sur la notion de la réincarnation; **6** US (in football) tactique *f*; **7** Mech (scope for movement) jeu *m* (**between** entre; **in** dans); **there's some ~ in the lock** il y a du jeu dans la serrure; **8** Fishg **to give a line more/less ~** donner du mou à/tendre une ligne.

II *vtr* **1** (for amusement) **to ~ football/bridge** jouer au football/au bridge; **to ~ cards/a computer game** jouer aux cartes/à un jeu électronique; **to ~ sb at chess/at tennis, to ~ chess/tennis with sb** jouer aux échecs/au tennis avec qn; **to ~ a game of chess/of tennis with sb** jouer une partie d'échecs/de tennis avec qn; **I'll ~ you a game of chess** on peut faire une partie d'échecs si tu veux; **she ~s basketball for her country** elle est dans l'équipe nationale de basketball; **to ~ shop/hide and seek** jouer à la marchande/à cache-cache; **to ~ a joke on sb** jouer un tour à qn; **2** Mus jouer [*symphony, chord*]; **to ~ the guitar/the piano** jouer de la guitare/du piano; **to ~ a tune on a clarinet** jouer un air à la clarinette; **to ~ a piece to** ou **for sb** jouer un morceau à qn; **~ them a tune** joue-leur un air; **they will ~ a nationwide tour** ils vont en tournée dans tout le pays; **they're ~ing the jazz club on Saturday** ils jouent au club de jazz samedi; **3** (act out) Theat interpréter, jouer [*role*]; **to ~ (the part of) Cleopatra** interpréter or jouer (le rôle de) Cléopâtre; **Cleopatra, ~ed by Elizabeth Taylor** Cléopâtre, interprétée or jouée par Elizabeth Taylor; **he ~s a young officer** il joue un jeune officier; **to ~ the diplomat/the sympathetic friend** fig jouer au diplomate/à l'ami compatissant; **to ~ a leading role in public affairs** jouer un rôle déterminant dans les affaires publiques; **to ~ a significant part in the creation of a clean environment** jouer un rôle important dans la création d'un environnement propre; **I'm not sure how to ~ things** je ne sais pas trop comment procéder; **that's the way I ~ things**○ c'est ma façon de faire; **to ~ a line for laughs** dire une réplique de façon à faire rire tout le monde; **4** Audio mettre [*tape, video, CD*]; **~ me the record** mets-moi le disque; **to ~ music** écouter de la musique; **the tape was ~ed to the court** on a fait entendre la bande au tribunal; **let me ~ the jazz tape for you** je vais vous faire entendre la cassette de jazz; **5** Sport (in a position) [*coach, manager*] faire jouer [*player*]; **to ~ goal/wing** être gardien de but/ailier; **he ~s goal for Fulchester** il est gardien de but dans l'équipe de Fulchester; **6** Sport (hit, kick) [*golfer, tennis player*] envoyer [*ball*]; [*basketball player*] lancer [*ball*]; **to ~ the ball over the goal** tirer le ballon par-dessus la cage; **to ~ the ball to sb** passer la balle à qn; **to ~ a forehand** délivrer un coup droit; **7** Games (in chess, draughts) déplacer [*piece*]; (in cards) jouer [*card*]; **to ~ a club** jouer du trèfle; **to ~ the tables** (in roulette) miser; **8** Fin **to ~ the stock market** boursicoter○; **9** Fishg épuiser [*fish*].

III *vi* **1** [*children*] jouer (**with** avec); **to ~ together** jouer ensemble; **can Rosie come out to ~?** est-ce que Rosie peut venir jouer?; **to ~ at soldiers/at keeping shop** jouer aux soldats/à la marchande; **to ~ at hide and seek** jouer à cache-cache; **2** fig **she's only ~ing at her job** elle ne travaille pas vraiment; **to ~ at being a manager/an artist** jouer au directeur/à l'artiste; **what does he think he's ~ing at?**○ GB qu'est-ce qu'il fabrique○?; **3** Sport, Games jouer; **do you ~?** est-ce que tu sais jouer?; **have you ~ed yet?** avez-vous joué?; **to ~ out of turn** jouer avant son tour; **I've seen them ~** (team) je les ai vus jouer; **England is ~ing against Ireland** l'Angleterre joue contre l'Irlande; **he ~s for Liverpool** il joue dans l'équipe de Liverpool; **she ~ed for her club in the semifinal** elle a joué dans l'équipe de son club en demi-finale; **to ~ in goal** être dans les buts; **to ~ for money** [*cardplayer*] jouer pour de l'argent; **to ~ fair** jouer franc jeu; **4** Sport (hit, shoot) **to ~ into a bunker/the net** envoyer la balle dans un bunker/le filet; **to ~ to sb's backhand** jouer sur le revers de qn; **5** Mus [*musician, band, orchestra*] jouer (**for** pour); **to ~ on the flute/on the xylophone** jouer de la flûte/du xylophone; **to ~ to large audiences/to small groups** jouer devant un grand public/pour de petits groupes; **6** Cin, Theat [*play*] se jouer; [*film*] passer; [*actor*] jouer; **'Macbeth' is ~ing at the Gate** 'Macbeth' se joue au Gate; **she's ~ing opposite him in 'Macbeth'** elle joue avec lui dans 'Macbeth'; **he's ~ing to packed houses** il joue devant des salles combles; **7** (make noise) [*fountain, water*] couler, jaser littér; **a record ~ed softly in the background** un disque jouait doucement en arrière-fond; **I could hear music/the tape ~ing in the next room** j'entendais de la musique/la bande dans la pièce à côté; **8** (move lightly) **sunlight ~ed over the water** le soleil jouait sur l'eau; **a breeze ~ed across the lake** une brise effleurait la surface du lac; **a smile ~ed around** ou **on her lips** un sourire flottait sur ses lèvres.

IDIOMS **to ~ for time** essayer de gagner du temps; **we have everything to ~ for** rien n'est encore gagné; **to ~ sb false** ne pas jouer franc jeu avec qn; **they ~ed to her strengths** (in interview) il ne lui ont rien demandé de difficile; **he doesn't ~ to his own strengths** il n'utilise pas ses capacités; **all work and no ~ (makes Jack a dull boy)** Prov il n'y a pas que le travail dans la vie; **to make a ~ for sb**○ draguer qn○; **to make great ~ of sth/of the fact that** accorder beaucoup d'importance à qch/au fait que.

■ **play along 1** (acquiesce) entrer dans le jeu; **to ~ along with sb** entrer dans le jeu de qn; **2** (accompany) **I'll sing, you ~ along on the piano** je chante et tu m'accompagnes au piano; **to ~ along with sb/with a song** accompagner qn/une chanson.

■ **play around**○ **1** (be promiscuous) coucher à droite et à gauche○; **2** (act the fool) faire l'imbécile; **to ~ around with** (rearrange, juggle) changer [qch] de place [*chairs, ornaments*]; jongler avec [*dates, figures*]; (fiddle) jouer avec [*paperclips, pens*]; **to ~ around with the idea of doing** caresser vaguement l'idée de faire; **how much time/money do we have to ~ around with?** combien de temps/d'argent avons-nous à notre disposition?

■ **play back**: **~ [sth] back, ~ back [sth]** rejouer [qch] du début [*song*]; repasser [*film, video*]; **to ~ sth back to sb** faire réentendre qch à qn [*record, music*]; repasser qch à qn [*video, film*].

■ **play down**: **~ down [sth]** minimiser [*defeat, disaster, effects*].

■ **play off**: **to ~ sb off against sb** monter qn contre qn (pour en tirer avantage); **they can ~ the companies/buyers off against each other** ils peuvent créer une concurrence entre les sociétés/acheteurs.

■ **play on**: ¶ **~ on 1** [*musicians, footballers*] continuer à jouer; **2** (in cricket) *envoyer la balle sur son propre guichet*; ¶ **~ on [sth]** exploiter [*fears, prejudices*]; jouer avec [*idea*].

■ **play out**: **~ out [sth]** vivre [*fantasy*];

their love affair was ~ed out against a background of war leur histoire d'amour s'est déroulée sur un fond de guerre; **the drama which is being ~ed out in India** le drame qui se joue aux Indes.

■ **play up**: ¶ **~ up**○ [*computer, person*] commencer à faire des siennes○; **the children are ~ing up again** les enfants recommencent à en faire des leurs○; **my rheumatism is ~ing up** mes rhumatismes me taquinent; ¶ **~ up [sth]** mettre l'accent sur [*dangers, advantages, benefits*]; **to ~ up a story** Journ monter une histoire en épingle.

■ **play upon** = **play on**.

■ **play with**: **~ with [sth] 1** (fiddle) jouer avec [*pen, food, paperclip*]; **to ~ with oneself**○ euph (masturbate) se tripoter○; **2** (toy) **to ~ with words** jouer avec les mots; **to ~ with sb's affections** jouer avec les sentiments de qn; **3** (be insincere) **to ~ with sb** jouer avec qn.

playable /ˈpleɪəbl/ *adj* [*shot, pitch*] jouable; **the record is still ~** on peut encore écouter le disque.

play-acting /ˈpleɪæktɪŋ/ *n* comédie *f*, simagrées *fpl*; **stop your ~!** arrête ta comédie○!

play area *n* (outside) aire *f* de jeu; (inside) coin-jeu *m*.

playback /ˈpleɪbæk/ *n* **1** (reproduction of sound, pictures) play-back *m inv*; **2** (device) appareil *m* de play-back.

play: **~back head** *n* tête *f* de lecture (de magnétophone); **~bill** *n* Theat affiche *f*; **~book** *n* US Sport *répertoire de tactiques pratiquées par une équipe de football américain*; **~boy** *n* playboy *m*; **~-by-play** *n* US Sport commentaire *m* suivi; **~-centred learning** *n* Sch apprentissage *m* par le jeu; **~ed-out** *adj* [*emotions, passions*] éteint; [*theories*] éculé.

player /ˈpleɪə(r)/ *n* Sport, Mus joueur/-euse *m/f*; Theat comédien/-ienne *m/f*; fig (in market, negotiations, crisis) protagoniste *mf*; **tennis/chess ~** joueur/-euse *m/f* de tennis/d'échecs; **piano ~** pianiste *mf*.

player-piano /ˈpleɪəpɪænəʊ/ *n* piano *m* mécanique.

playfellow /ˈpleɪfeləʊ/ *n* compagnon *m* de jeu.

playful /ˈpleɪfl/ *adj* [*remark, action*] enjoué; [*mood, person*] gai, enjoué; [*child, kitten*] joueur/-euse; **she's just being ~** elle fait (or elle dit) ça pour s'amuser.

playfully /ˈpleɪfəlɪ/ *adv* [*remark, say*] pour plaisanter; [*tease, push, pinch*] malicieusement, avec espièglerie.

playfulness /ˈpleɪflnɪs/ *n* (of remark, action, mood) caractère *m* enjoué; (of child, kitten) espièglerie *f*; (of person) enjouement *m*.

playground /ˈpleɪgraʊnd/ *n* (in school) cour *f* de récréation; (in park, city) terrain *m* de jeu; **the island is a ~ for the rich** fig l'île est un lieu de divertissement pour les riches.

play: **~group** *n* ≈ halte-garderie *f*; **~house** *n* théâtre *m*.

playing /ˈpleɪɪŋ/ *n* **1** Mus, Theat interprétation *f*; **there was some excellent guitar ~** il y a eu quelques excellentes interprétations à la guitare; **2** Sport jeu *m*.

playing card *n* carte *f* à jouer.

playing field *n* terrain *m* de sport.

IDIOMS **a level ~** l'égalité des chances; **to compete on a level ~** [*companies, individuals*] être sur un pied d'égalité.

playlet /ˈpleɪlɪt/ *n* saynète *f*.

playmaker /ˈpleɪmeɪkə(r)/ *n* Sport, fig stratège *m*.

playmate /ˈpleɪmeɪt/ *n* camarade *mf* de jeu.

play-off /ˈpleɪɒf/ *n* **1** GB (at end of match, game) prolongation *f*; **2** US (contest) match *m* crucial.

play: **~pen** *n* parc *m* (*pour bébé*); **~reading** *n* lecture *f* d'une pièce de théâtre; **~room** *n* salle *f* de jeux; **~school** *n* ≈ halte-garderie *f*; **~suit** *n* ensemble *m* short.

plaything /ˈpleɪθɪŋ/ *n* lit, fig jouet *m*; **the ~s of the gods** les jouets des dieux; **I'm tired of being her ~** j'en ai assez d'être son pantin.

play: **~time** *n* Sch récréation *f*; **~wright** *n* auteur *m* dramatique, dramaturge *m*.

plaza /ˈplɑːzə, US ˈplæzə/ *n* **1** (public square) place *f*; **shopping ~** centre *m* commercial; **2** US Transp (services point) aire *f* de service; (toll point) péage *m*.

plc, PLC (*abrév* = **public limited company**) GB SA.

plea /pliː/ **I** *n* **1** (for tolerance, mercy etc) appel *m* (**for** à); (for money, food) demande *f* (**for** de); **her ~ that the school (should) be kept open** son appel pour que l'école soit maintenue; **to make a ~ for aid** lancer un appel à l'aide; **his ~ for the homeless** son appel en faveur des sans-abri; **she ignored his ~s** elle est restée sourde à ses prières; **2** Jur **to make** ou **enter a ~ of guilty/not guilty** plaider coupable/non coupable; **to make a ~ of self-defence/insanity** plaider la légitime défense/la démence; **3** (excuse) excuse *f*; **on the ~ that** sous prétexte que.

plea bargaining *n* Jur *arrangement entre la défense et l'accusation visant à réduire les charges si l'accusé plaide coupable pour un délit moins grave*.

plead /pliːd/ **I** *vtr* (*prét, pp* **pleaded**, US **pled**) **1** (beg) supplier; **2** (argue) plaider; **to ~ sb's case** Jur, fig plaider la cause de qn; **to ~ insanity** Jur plaider la démence; **3** (give as excuse) **to ~ ignorance** plaider l'ignorance; **she left early, ~ing a headache** elle est partie tôt, en prétextant un mal de tête.

II *vi* (*prét, pp* **pleaded**, US **pled**) **1** (beg) supplier; (more fervently) implorer; **to ~ with sb** supplier, implorer qn (**to do** de faire); **to ~ with sb for mercy/forgiveness** implorer la clémence/le pardon de qn; **to ~ with sb for more time** supplier qn d'accorder plus de temps; **2** Jur plaider; **to ~ guilty/not guilty (to a charge)** plaider coupable/non coupable.

pleading /ˈpliːdɪŋ/ **I** *n* **1** ₵ (requests) supplications *fpl*; **2** Jur (presentation of a case) plaidoirie *f*.

II pleadings *npl* Jur (documents) conclusions *fpl*.

III *adj* [*voice, look*] suppliant.

pleadingly /ˈpliːdɪŋlɪ/ *adv* [*look*] d'un air suppliant; [*say*] d'un ton suppliant.

pleasant /ˈpleznt/ *adj* [*taste, smell, voice, place etc*] agréable; [*person*] agréable, aimable (**to** avec); **it's ~ here** (nice surroundings) c'est agréable ici; (nice weather) il fait bon ici; **to spend a very ~ evening** passer une soirée agréable; **~ to the ear** agréable à l'oreille; **a very ~ place to live** un endroit où il fait bon vivre; **it makes a ~ change from work!** ça change du travail!

pleasantly /ˈplezntlɪ/ *adv* [*say, smile, behave*] aimablement; **~ surprised** agréablement surpris; **it was ~ warm** il faisait bon.

pleasantness /ˈplezntnɪs/ *n* gen caractère *m* agréable; (of climate) clémence *f*; (of person, manner) amabilité *f*; (of voice) charme *m*.

pleasantry /ˈplezntrɪ/ **I** *n* sout (joke) plaisanterie *f*.

II pleasantries *npl* (polite remarks) civilités *fpl*; **to exchange pleasantries** bavarder aimablement.

please /pliːz/ **I** *adv* **1** (with imperative) s'il vous plaît; (to close friend) s'il te plaît; **two teas ~** deux thés s'il vous plaît; **~ call me Mike** s'il vous plaît, appelez-moi Mike; **~ be seated** sout veuillez vous asseoir fml; **'~ do not smoke'** 'prière de ne pas fumer'; **2** (with question, request) s'il vous plaît; (to close friend) s'il te plaît; **can I speak to Jo ~?** est-ce que je pourrais parler à Jo, s'il vous plaît?; **'can I go?'—'say ~!'** 'je peux y aller?'—'dis s'il te plaît!'; **will you ~ be quiet!** tenez vous tranquilles, s'il vous plaît; **3** (accepting politely) **yes ~** oui, s'il vous plaît; **'more tea?'—'(yes) ~!'** 'encore du thé?'—'oui, s'il vous plaît'; **4** (encouraging, urging) je vous en prie; (to close friend) je t'en prie; **~, come in** entrez, je vous en prie; **~, you're my guest!** je vous en prie, vous êtes mon invité!; **'may I?'—'~ do'** 'je peux?'—'oui, je vous en prie'; **'can I take another?'—'~ do!'** 'je peux en prendre un autre?'—'vas-y!'; **~ tell me if you need anything** n'hésitez pas à me dire si vous avez besoin de quelque chose; **5** (in entreaty) **~ stop/don't!** arrête/pas ça, s'il vous plaît!; **~, that's enough** arrêtez, ça suffit; **Tom, ~, they can't help it** Tom, je t'en prie, ils ne le font pas exprès; **~ miss...** s'il vous plaît mademoiselle...; **oh ~!** (exasperated) et quoi encore!; **~ let it be me next!** (praying) mon Dieu, faites que ce soit moi le prochain!

II if you please *adv phr* **1** sout (please) si vous le voulez bien; **2** (indignantly) **he came to the wedding, if you ~!** il est venu au mariage, rien que ça!

III *vtr* **1** (give happiness, satisfaction to) faire plaisir à [*person*]; **the gift ~d him** le cadeau lui a fait plaisir; **it ~d her that** ça lui a plu que (+ *subj*); **she is easy/hard to ~** c'est facile/difficile de lui faire plaisir; **you're easily ~d!** ce n'est pas dur de te faire plaisir!; **there's no pleasing him** il n'est jamais satisfait; **there's no pleasing some people** il y a des gens qui ne sont jamais contents; **you can't ~ all of the people all of the time** on ne peut pas plaire à tout le monde; **2** sout (be the will of) plaire à [*person*]; **it ~d him to refuse** cela lui a plu de refuser; **may it ~ your Majesty** si votre Majesté le permet.

IV *vi* **1** (give happiness or satisfaction) plaire; **to be eager** ou **anxious to ~** être très désireux/-euse de plaire; **this is sure to ~** ceci plaira; **we aim to ~** vous satisfaire est notre priorité; **2** (like, think fit) **do as** ou **what you ~** fais comme il te plaira, fais comme tu veux; **as you ~!** comme il te plaira!, comme tu veux!; **I shall do as I ~** je ferai ce qui me plaît; **come whenever you ~** viens quand ça te plaira or quand tu veux; **take as much as you ~** tu peux en prendre autant que tu veux.

V *v refl* **to ~ oneself** faire comme on veut; **you can ~ yourself what time you start** c'est à toi de décider à quelle heure tu commences; **~ yourself!** comme tu veux!

pleased /pliːzd/ *adj* content (**that** que + *subj*; **about, at** de; **with** de; **for sb** pour qn); **to look** ou **seem ~** avoir l'air content; **to be/look ~ with oneself** être/avoir l'air content de soi; **I was ~ to see her** j'ai été content or ça m'a fait plaisir de la voir; **I'm none too ~** je ne suis pas du tout content; **I am only too ~ to help** je ne suis que trop content de vous aider; **I am ~ to announce that/to inform you that** j'ai le plaisir d'annoncer que/de vous informer que; **I'm ~ to hear it!** quelle bonne nouvelle!; **~ to meet you** enchanté; **I'm ~ to say that we won** je suis content, nous avons gagné; **you've passed, I'm ~ to say** j'ai le plaisir de vous annoncer que vous avez réussi votre examen; **she is ~ to accept the invitation** fml elle a le plaisir d'accepter votre invitation.

pleasing /ˈpliːzɪŋ/ *adj* [*appearance, shape, colour, voice*] agréable; [*manner, smile, personality*] avenant; [*effect, result*] heureux/-euse; **~ to the ear/the eye** agréable à l'oreille/l'œil.

pleasingly /ˈpliːzɪŋlɪ/ *adv* agréablement.

pleasurable /ˈpleʒərəbl/ *adj* agréable.

pleasurably /ˈpleʒərəblɪ/ *adv* agréablement.

pleasure /ˈpleʒə(r)/ **I** *n* **1** ₵ (enjoyment) plaisir *m* (**of** de; **of doing** de faire); **to give/bring ~ to millions** donner/apporter du plaisir à des millions de gens; **to**

watch/listen with ~ regarder/écouter avec plaisir; **to take all the ~ out of** enlever tout le plaisir de; **to take ~ in/in doing** prendre plaisir à/à faire; **to find ~ in** trouver du plaisir à; **to do sth for ~** faire qch par plaisir; **sb's ~ at sth** le plaisir qu'apporte qch à qn; **his ~ at my remark** le plaisir que lui apportait ma remarque; **it gives me no ~ to do** cela ne m'est pas agréable de faire; **to get more ~ out of life** avoir une vie plus agréable; **2 ¢** (sensual enjoyment) plaisir *m*; **sexual/sensual ~** plaisir sexuel/sensuel; **3 C** (enjoyable activity, experience) plaisir *m* (**of** de); **he has few ~s in life** il a peu de plaisirs dans la vie; **it is my only ~** c'est mon seul plaisir; **it is/was a ~ to do** c'est/c'était agréable de faire; **4 ¢** (recreation) plaisir *m*; **to put duty before ~** faire passer le devoir avant le plaisir; **to mix business and ~** joindre l'utile à l'agréable; **are you in Paris for business or ~?** êtes-vous à Paris pour vos affaires ou en voyage d'agrément?; **5** (in polite formulae) **it gives me great ~ to do** c'est avec plaisir que je fais; **'will you come?'—'thank you, with (the greatest) ~'** 'voulez-vous venir?'—'merci, avec (le plus grand) plaisir'; **I look forward to the ~ of meeting you** j'espère avoir prochainement le plaisir de vous rencontrer; **'it's been a ~ meeting you** ou **to meet you' — 'the ~ was all mine'** 'je suis ravi d'avoir fait votre connaissance'—'tout le plaisir est pour moi'; **my ~** (replying to request for help) avec plaisir; (replying to thanks) je vous en prie; **what an unexpected ~!** gen quelle excellente surprise!; iron ça! par exemple!; **may I have the ~ (of this dance)?** m'accorderez-vous cette danse?; **would you do me the ~ of dining with me?** me ferez-vous le plaisir de dîner avec moi?; **'Mr and Mrs Moor request the ~ of your company at their daughter's wedding'** 'M. et Mme Moor vous prient d'assister à la cérémonie de mariage de leur fille'; **6** sout (will, desire) **what is your ~?** gen que désirez-vous?; (offering drink) que prenez-vous?; **at one's ~** à son gré.
II *vtr* (give sexual pleasure to) donner du plaisir à, faire jouir [*partner*].

pleasure: **~ boat** *n* bateau *m* de plaisance; **~ craft** *n* **¢** bateaux *mpl* de plaisance; **~ cruise** *n* croisière *f*.

pleasure-loving *adj* **to be ~** être amateur/-trice de plaisirs.

pleasure: **~ principle** *n* principe *m* de plaisir; **~-seeker** *n* viveur/-euse *m/f*, jouisseur/-euse *m/f*.

pleat /pli:t/ **I** *n* pli *m*.
II *vtr* plisser.
III pleated *pp adj* [*skirt*] plissé; [*trousers*] à plis.

pleb○ /pleb/ *n* GB péj prolo○ *mf*; **the ~s** la populace.

plebeian /plɪ'bi:ən/ **I** *n* Hist ou péj plébéien/-ienne *m/f*; **the ~s** la plèbe.
II *adj* plébéien/-ienne.

plebiscite /'plebɪsɪt, US -saɪt/ *n* plébiscite *m*.

plectrum /'plektrəm/ *n* (*pl* **~s** or **-tra**) médiator *m*.

pled /pled/ US *prét, pp* ▶ **plead**.

pledge /pledʒ/ **I** *n* **1** (promise) promesse *f*, engagement *m*; **to give a ~ to sb** faire une promesse à qn; **to give** ou **make a ~ to do** promettre or prendre l'engagement de faire; **to keep/break one's ~** tenir/rompre son engagement or sa promesse; **to take** ou **sign the ~**† hum faire vœu de tempérance† hum; **2** (thing deposited as security) (to creditor, pawnbroker) gage *m*; **to put/hold sth in ~** mettre/laisser qch en gage; **to take sth out of ~** dégager qch; **3** (token) gage *m*; **as a ~ of her friendship** en gage ou en témoignage de son amitié; **4** (money promised to charity) promesse *f* de don; **make your ~s now!** faites vos dons dès maintenant!; **5**† (toast) toast *m* (**to** à); **6** US Univ *étudiant/-e en période d'initiation à l'entrée d'un club*.
II *vtr* **1** (promise) promettre [*allegiance, aid, support*] (**to** à); **to ~ (oneself) to do, to ~ that one will do** s'engager à faire; **the treaty ~s the signatories to do** le traité engage les signataires à faire; **to be ~d to secrecy** être tenu au secret; **to ~ one's word** donner sa parole; **to ~ money to charity** promettre de faire un don aux œuvres charitables; **to ~ allegiance to the flag** jurer fidélité au drapeau; **2** (give as security) (to creditor, pawnbroker) mettre [qch] en gage; **3**† (toast) porter un toast à; **4** US Univ **to ~ a fraternity/sorority** accepter de subir l'épreuve d'initiation pour entrer dans un club d'étudiants/d'étudiantes.

Pledge of Allegiance *n* US Serment *m* au drapeau.

Pleistocene /'pleɪstəsi:n/ *n, adj* pléistocène (*m*).

plenary /'pli:nərɪ, US -erɪ/ *adj* [*session, meeting, discussion*] plénier/-ière; [*powers*] plein; [*authority*] absolu.

plenipotentiary /ˌplenɪpə'tenʃərɪ, US -erɪ/ **I** *n* plénipotentiaire *m*.
II *adj* [*powers*] plein; [*authority, ambassador*] plénipotentiaire.

plenitude /'plenɪtju:d, US -tu:d/ *n* plénitude *f*.

plenteous /'plentɪəs/ *adj* littér abondant.

plentiful /'plentɪfl/ *adj* [*diet, food, harvest*] abondant; **fish were ~ in this river** il y avait du poisson en abondance dans cette rivière; **a ~ supply of** une abondance de; **in ~ supply** en abondance.

plentifully /'plentɪfəlɪ/ *adv* en abondance.

plenty /'plentɪ/ **I** *quantif* **1** (a lot, quite enough) **to have ~ of** avoir beaucoup de, ne pas manquer de [*time, money, friends*]; **there is ~ of time/money** on a tout le temps/l'argent qu'il faut, on a beaucoup de temps/d'argent; **there are ~ of other reasons/ideas** il y a beaucoup d'autres raisons/idées; **there was wine, and ~ of it!** du vin il y en avait, et en quantité!; **there is ~ more tea** il y a encore beaucoup de thé; **there's ~ more where that came from**○! (of food, joke etc) profites-en, j'en ai toute une réserve!; **to see ~ of sb** voir qn assez souvent; **to have ~ to eat/to do** avoir beaucoup or suffisamment à manger/à faire; **that's ~** c'est bien assez, ça suffit amplement; **£10 is/will be ~** 10 livres sterling suffisent/suffiront largement; **'have you any questions/money?'—'~!'** 'as-tu des questions/de l'argent?'—'tout plein○!', 'des tas○!'; **'do you know anything about cars?'—'~!'** 'est-ce que tu t'y connais en voitures?'—'oui, je m'y connais vraiment'; **2 ¢** (abundance) **a time of ~** une époque prospère; **in ~** en abondance; **3**○ (lots of) beaucoup de [*work, money, friends*].
II○ *adv* **1** (quite) **~ old/tall enough** suffisamment vieux/grand; **that's ~ big enough!** c'est bien assez or largement assez grand!; **2** US (very or very much) **to be ~ thirsty** avoir très soif; **he cried ~** il a beaucoup pleuré.

plenum /'pli:nəm/ *n* plénum *m*.

pleonasm /'pli:ənæzəm/ *n* pléonasme *m*.

pleonastic /ˌplɪə'næstɪk/ *adj* pléonastique.

plethora /'pleθərə/ *n* sout pléthore *f*, surabondance *f*; **there is a ~ of** il y a pléthore de.

plethoric /plɪ'θɒrɪk/ *adj* sout pléthorique.

pleura /'plʊərə/ *n* (*pl* **-ae**) plèvre *f*.

pleurisy /'plʊərəsɪ/ ▶ 1354 *n* pleurésie *f*.

pleuritic /ˌplʊə'rɪtɪk/ *adj* pleurétique.

Plexiglass® /'pleksɪglɑ:s, US -glæs/ *n* plexiglas® *m*.

plexus /'pleksəs/ *n* (*pl* **~es** ou **~**) plexus *m*.

pliability /ˌplaɪə'bɪlətɪ/ *n* (of materials) flexibilité *f*; (of minds) malléabilité *f*.

pliable /'plaɪəbl/ *adj* [*twig, plastic*] flexible; [*person*] malléable.

pliant /'plaɪənt/ *adj* [*branch, plastic*] flexible; [*person*] malléable.

pliers /'plaɪəz/ *npl* pinces *fpl*; **a pair of ~** des pinces.

plight /plaɪt/ **I** *n* **1** (dilemma) situation *f* désespérée; **2** (suffering) détresse *f*; **the ~ of the homeless** la détresse des sans-abri; **to ease sb's ~** soulager la détresse de qn.
II *vtr*‡ **to ~ one's troth** engager sa foi†, se fiancer.

plimsoll /'plɪmsəl/ *n* GB chaussure *f* de tennis.

Plimsoll line /'plɪmsəl laɪn/ *n* ligne *f* de flottaison en charge.

plink /plɪŋk/ **I** *n* bruit *m* métallique.
II *vtr* tirer sur [*tin can*].
III *vi* tirer.

plinth /plɪnθ/ *n* Archit plinthe *f*; (of statue) socle *m*.

Pliny /'plɪnɪ/ *pr n* Pline; **~ the Younger/the Elder** Pline le Jeune/l'Ancien.

Pliocene /'plaɪəʊsi:n/ *n, adj* pliocène (*m*).

PLO *n* (*abrév* = **Palestine Liberation Organization**) OLP *f*.

plod /plɒd/ **I** *n* (slow walk) marche *f* pesante; **it's a long ~ home** c'est une route longue et pénible jusqu'à la maison.
II *vi* (*p prés etc* **-dd-**) (walk) marcher péniblement.
■ **plod along** lit, fig avancer d'un pas lent.
■ **plod away** travailler ferme, bosser○.
■ **plod on** lit continuer à marcher; fig persévérer.
■ **plod through**: **~ through [sth]** fig faire [qch] laborieusement.

plodder /'plɒdə(r)/ *n* bûcheur/-euse○ *m/f*.

plodding /'plɒdɪŋ/ *adj* [*step*] lourd; [*style, performance*] laborieux/-ieuse.

plonk /plɒŋk/ **I** *n* **1** (sound) plouf○ *m*, son *m* creux; **2**○ (wine) vin *m* ordinaire, pinard◑ *m*.
II○ *vtr* planter [*plate, bottle*] (**on** sur).
■ **plonk down**○: ¶ **~ [sth] down** poser [*box, sack*] (**on** sur); **to ~ oneself down on** s'installer dans [*armchair*]; s'installer sur [*sofa*]; **to ~ oneself down in front of sth** s'installer devant [*TV, screen*]; ¶ **~ down [sth]** US (pay) allonger○, payer [*sum*].

plonker /'plɒŋkə(r)/ *n* GB **1**○ (fool) imbécile *mf*; **2**◑ (penis) queue◑ *f*, pénis *m*.

plop /plɒp/ **I** *n* floc *m*.
II *vi* (*p prés etc* **-pp-**) faire floc; **the stone ~ped into the water** le caillou a fait floc en tombant dans l'eau.

plosive /'pləʊsɪv/ **I** *n* (consonne *f*) occlusive *f*.
II *adj* occlusif/-ive.

plot /plɒt/ **I** *n* **1** (conspiracy) complot *m*, conspiration *f* (**against** contre; **to do** pour faire); **an assassination ~** un complot d'assassinat; **2** Cin, Literat (of novel, film, play) intrigue *f*; **the ~ thickens** l'histoire se corse; **3** Agric, Hort (allotment) **~ of land** parcelle *f* de terre; **a vegetable ~** un carré de légumes; **4** Constr (site) terrain *m* à bâtir; **5** (in cemetery) concession *f* funéraire.
II *vtr* (*p prés etc* **-tt-**) **1** (plan) comploter [*murder, attack, return*]; fomenter [*revolution*]; **to ~ to do** comploter de faire; **2** (chart) relever [qch] sur une carte [*course*]; tracer [qch] sur une carte [*progress*]; **we ~ted our position on the map** nous avons pointé notre position sur la carte; **3** Math, Stat (on graph) tracer [qch] point par point [*curve, graph*]; reporter [*figures, points*]; **to ~ the progress/decline of sth** tracer la courbe de progression/déclin de qch; **4** Literat (invent) inventer [*episode, story, destiny*]; **a carefully/thinly ~ted play** une pièce à l'intrigue bien construite/bien mince.
III *vi* (*p prés etc* **-tt-**) (conspire) conspirer (**against** contre); **to ~ together** conspirer ensemble.

plotter /'plɒtə(r)/ *n* **1** (schemer) conspirateur/-trice *m/f*; **2** Comput traceur *m* (de courbes).

plotting /'plɒtɪŋ/ *n* **¢** (scheming) complots

mpl; **to be accused of ~** être accusé d'avoir tramé un complot.

plotting board, **plotting table** *n* table *f* traçante.

plotzed○ /plɒtst/ *adj* US **to be (completely) ~** être (complètement) bourré○.

plough GB, **plow** US /plaʊ/ **I** *n* Agric (implement) charrue *f*; **to come under the ~** [*land*] devenir labourable.
II Plough *pr n* Astron **the ~** le Grand Chariot *m*, la Grande Ourse *f*.
III *vtr* **1** Agric labourer [*land, field*]; creuser [*furrow*]; **2** (invest) **to ~ money into** investir de l'argent dans [*project, company*]; **3**† ○GB (fail) [*candidate*] se faire recaler○ à [*exam*]; [*examiner*] recaler○ [*candidate*].
IV *vi* Agric labourer.
IDIOMS **to put one's hand to the ~** se mettre au travail.
■ **plough back**: **~ [sth] back, ~ back [sth]** réinvestir [*profits, money*] (**into** dans).
■ **plough in**: **~ [sth] in, ~ in [sth]** Agric enterrer [qch] en labourant [*crop, manure*].
■ **plough into**: **~ into [sth] 1** (crash into) [*vehicle*] percuter [*tree, wall*]; **the car skidded and ~ed into the crowd** la voiture a dérapé et a fini sa course dans la foule; **2** US (begin enthusiastically) se lancer à corps perdu dans [*work*].
■ **plough through**: **~ through sth** [*vehicle, driver*] défoncer [*hedge, wall*]; fig [*person*] ramer○ sur [*book, task*]; [*walker*] se frayer un chemin dans [*mud, snow*]; [*vehicle*] avancer péniblement dans [*mud, snow*].
■ **plough under**: ¶ **~ [sth] under, ~ under [sth]** faire disparaître [qch] en labourant [*crop, manure*]; ¶ **~ [sb] under**○ US (thrash) démolir○ [*opponents*].
■ **plough up**: **~ [sth] up, ~ up [sth]** Agric mettre [qch] en labour [*field*]; fig [*car, person*] défoncer [*ground*].

plough horse *n* cheval *m* de labour.

ploughing GB, **plowing** US /ˈplaʊɪŋ/ *n* labourage *m*.

plough: **~land** GB, **plow-land** US *n* terres *fpl* arables or labourables; **~man** GB, **plow-man** US ▶ **1692** *n* laboureur *m*; **~man's lunch** *n* GB *plat servi dans les pubs composé de fromage, de pain et de salade*.

ploughshare GB, **plow-share** US /ˈplaʊʃeə(r)/ *n* soc *m* de charrue.
IDIOMS **to turn** ou **beat (one's) swords into ~s** œuvrer pour la paix.

plover /ˈplʌvə(r)/ *n* pluvier *m*.

plow *n, vtr, vi* US = **plough**.

ploy /plɔɪ/ *n* stratagème *m*; **it is a ~ to attract attention/to disarm his critics** c'est un stratagème pour attirer l'attention/pour désarmer ses détracteurs.

PLR *n* GB *abrév* ▶ **Public Lending Right**.

pluck /plʌk/ **I** *n* **1** (courage) courage *m*, cran○ *m*; **2** Culin fressure *f*.
II *vtr* **1** cueillir [*flower, fruit*]; **to ~ sth from sb's grasp** arracher qch à qn; **to be ~ed from obscurity** être sorti de l'anonymat; **2** Culin plumer [*chicken*]; **3** Mus pincer [*strings*]; pincer les cordes de [*guitar*]; **4 to ~ one's eyebrows** s'épiler les sourcils.
IDIOMS **to ~ up one's courage** prendre son courage à deux mains; **to ~ up the courage to do sth** trouver le courage de faire qch.
■ **pluck at**: **to ~ at sb's sleeve/arm** tirer qn par la manche/le bras.
■ **pluck off**: **~ off [sth], ~ [sth] off** arracher [*feathers, hair*]; enlever [*piece of fluff*].
■ **pluck out**: **~ out [sth], ~ [sth] out** arracher.

pluckily /ˈplʌkɪlɪ/ *adv* vaillamment.

pluckiness /ˈplʌkɪnɪs/ *n* bravoure *f*, cran○ *m*.

plucky /ˈplʌkɪ/ *adj* courageux/-euse; **to be ~** avoir du cran○.

plug /plʌg/ **I** *n* **1** Elec (on appliance) prise *f* (de courant); **to pull out the ~** débrancher la prise; **to be fitted with a ~** avoir une prise; **to pull the ~ on**○ retirer son soutien à [*scheme, project*]; **to pull the ~ on sb**○ Med débrancher le système de survie de qn; US fig trahir qn; **2** Audio, Comput, Electron (connecting device) fiche *f*; **3** Elec (socket) prise *f* (de courant); **a mains ~** une prise secteur; **4** (in bath, sink) bonde *f*; **to pull out the ~** retirer la bonde; **5** Constr (for screw) cheville *f*; **6** (stopper) (in barrel) bonde *f*; (for leak) bouchon *m*; (for medical purpose) tampon *m*; **7** Aut (in engine) (also **spark ~**) bougie *f*; **8** (for chewing) **a ~ of tobacco** une chique de tabac; **9**○ Advertg, Radio, TV (mention) pub○ *f*, publicité *f* (**for** pour); **to give sth a ~, put in a ~ for sth** faire de la pub○ or publicité pour qch; **10** US (fire hydrant) bouche *f* d'incendie; **11** Geol (also **volcanic ~**) culot *m*.
II *vtr* (*p prés etc* **-gg-**) **1** (block) colmater [*leak*] (**with** avec); boucher [*hole*] (**with** avec); **to ~ a gap** lit boucher un trou; fig combler une lacune; **she ~ged a hole in my tooth** elle m'a rebouché une dent; **to ~ one's ears** se boucher le oreilles; **2**○ Advertg, Radio, TV (promote) faire de la pub○ or publicité pour [*book, show, product*]; **to ~ one's record on a programme** faire de la pub○ pour son disque au cours d'une émission; **3** Elec (insert) **to ~ sth into** brancher qch à [*socket*]; connecter qch à [*amplifier, computer*]; **4**○ †US (shoot) abattre, flinguer○.
III *vi* (*p prés etc* **-gg-**) **to ~ into** (be compatible with) se connecter à [*TV, computer*]; **they have ~ged into the national mood**○ journ ils sont au courant de l'état d'esprit général.
■ **plug away**○ s'acharner (**at** sur); **he's ~ging away at his Latin** il bûche○ son latin.
■ **plug in**: ¶ se brancher; ¶ **~ [sth] in, ~ in [sth]** brancher [*appliance*].
■ **plug up**: **~ up [sth], ~ [sth] up** boucher [*hole, gap*] (**with** avec).

plughole /ˈplʌghəʊl/ *n* GB bonde *f*; **to go down the ~** lit [*water*] s'écouler par la bonde; [*ring*] tomber dans le trou de l'évier; fig○ s'en aller à vau-l'eau.

plug: **~-in** *adj* [*appliance*] enfichable; **~-in telephone** *n* téléphone *m* à prise.

plum /plʌm/ ▶ **1104** **I** *n* **1** Bot (fruit) prune *f*; (tree) prunier *m*; **2** (colour) couleur *f* prune *inv*.
II *adj* **1** (colour) (also **~-coloured**) prune *inv*; **2**○ (good) **to get a ~ job/part** décrocher un boulot/rôle en or○.

plumage /ˈpluːmɪdʒ/ *n* plumage *m*.

plumb /plʌm/ **I** *n* **1** (also **~ line**) Constr fil *m* à plomb; Naut sonde *f*; **2** (perpendicular) **to be out of ~** ou **off ~** ne pas être d'aplomb.
II *adv* **1**○ US (totally) [*crazy, wrong*] complètement; **2**○ (precisely) **~ in** ou **down** ou **through the middle** en plein milieu.
III *vtr* **1** fig percer à jour [*mystery, soul*]; **to ~ the depths of** toucher le fond de [*despair, misery*]; atteindre le comble de [*bad taste*]; **2** lit sonder [*sea, depths*].
■ **plumb in**: **~ [sth] in, ~ in [sth]** brancher.

plumbago /plʌmˈbeɪgəʊ/ *n* **1** Miner plombagine *f*; **2** Bot plumbago *m*.

plumber /ˈplʌmə(r)/ *n* plombier *m*.

plumber: **~'s helper**○ *n* US débouchoir *m* à ventouse; **~s' merchant** *n* grossiste *m* en plomberie.

plumbic /ˈplʌmbɪk/ *adj* plombique.

plumbing /ˈplʌmɪŋ/ *n* plomberie *f*; **lead ~** tuyauterie *f* en plomb; **~ system** plomberie *f*.

plum: **~ brandy** *n* eau-de-vie *f* de prunes; **~ cake** *n* (plum-)cake *m*; **~ duff, ~ pudding** *n* (plum-)pudding *m*.

plume /pluːm/ **I** *n* (feather) plume *f*; (of several feathers) panache *m*; fig (of steam, smoke etc) panache *m* (**of** de).
II *v refl* **to ~ oneself** lit [*bird*] se lisser les plumes; fig **to ~ oneself on sth** [*person*] tirer vanité de qch.

plumed /pluːmd/ *adj* [*horse, helmet*] empanaché; [*hat*] à plumes.

plum jam *n* confiture *f* de prunes.

plummet /ˈplʌmɪt/ **I** *n* Tech, Fishg plomb *m*.
II *vi* **1** lit [*bird, aircraft*] tomber à pic; **2** fig [*share prices, birthrate, profits, sales*] s'effondrer; [*temperature, value*] baisser brusquement; [*standards, popularity, morale*] tomber à zéro.

plummy /ˈplʌmɪ/ *adj* **1**○ GB [*voice*] maniéré; [*accent*] affecté; **2** (plum-coloured) (couleur) prune *inv*; **3** (of plums) [*taste*] de prune.

plump /plʌmp/ *adj* [*person, chicken*] dodu; [*cheek, face*] rond, plein; [*arm, leg*] potelé; [*cushion*] bien rembourré.
■ **plump down**○: ¶ **~ down** [*person*] s'asseoir (lourdement) (**into** dans; **onto** sur); ¶ **~ [oneself] down**○ s'asseoir (lourdement); **~ yourself down over there** assieds-toi là-bas; ¶ **~ [sth] down, ~ down [sth]** déposer.
■ **plump for**○: **~ for [sth]** opter pour [*candidate, purchase*]; prendre [*food*].
■ **plump out** [*cheeks*] s'arrondir; [*person, animal*] prendre du poids.
■ **plump up**: **~ up [sth]** redonner du volume à [*cushion*].

plumpness /ˈplʌmpnɪs/ *n* (of person) embonpoint *m*; (of arms, legs etc) rondeur *f*.

plum: **~ tart** *n* tarte *f* aux prunes; **~ tomato** *n* olivette *f*; **~ tree** *n* prunier *m*.

plunder /ˈplʌndə(r)/ **I** *n* **1** (act of stealing) pillage *m*; **2** (booty) butin *m*.
II *vtr* [*soldiers*] piller [*shop, property, possessions*]; [*thieves*] dévaliser; **to ~ a museum of its treasures** piller les trésors d'un musée.
III *vi* se livrer au pillage.

plunderer /ˈplʌndərə(r)/ *n* pillard *m*.

plundering /ˈplʌndərɪŋ/ **I** *n* pillage *m*.
II *adj* [*mob, troops*] pillard.

plunge /plʌndʒ/ **I** *n* **1** (from height) plongeon *m*; **death ~** journ plongeon de la mort; **to take a ~** (dive) piquer une tête; **2** Fin chute *f* libre; **a ~ in share** GB ou **stock** US **prices** une chute libre du prix des actions; **3** gen, fig **the company's ~ into debt** l'endettement subit de l'entreprise; **the ~ in confidence** la perte subite de confiance; **nothing could prevent the country's ~ into chaos** rien ne pouvait empêcher le pays de sombrer dans le chaos.
II *vtr* **1** (thrust) **to ~ sth into sth** plonger qch dans qch; **he ~d the knife into her heart** il lui a plongé le couteau dans le cœur; **she ~d her hand into the water/the bag** elle a plongé sa main dans l'eau/le sac; **to be ~d into** être plongé dans [*crisis, danger, new experience, strike*]; être submergé de [*debt*]; **the house was ~d into darkness** la maison a été plongée dans l'obscurité; **2** (unblock) déboucher [qch] avec une ventouse [*sink*].
III *vi* **1** (fall from height) [*person, waterfall, submarine*] plonger; [*bird, plane*] piquer; [*road, cliff*] fig plonger; **the plane ~d to the ground** l'avion a piqué vers le sol; **the boy ~d over the precipice to his death** l'enfant a fait une chute mortelle dans le précipice; **the car ~d off the road** la voiture est sortie en catastrophe de la route; **2** fig (drop sharply) [*rate, value*] chuter; **3** fig (embark on) **to ~ into** se lancer dans [*activity, career, negotiations*]; sombrer dans [*chaos, crisis, decline*]; se ruer vers [*danger*].
IDIOMS **to take the ~** se jeter à l'eau.
■ **plunge forward** [*person*] s'élancer; [*boat*] piquer de l'avant; [*horse*] se ruer; [*vehicle*] foncer.
■ **plunge in** [*swimmer*] plonger; fig (impetuously) se lancer.

plunge: **~ bath** *n* bain *m*; **~ pool** *n* bassin *m*.

plunger /ˈplʌndʒə(r)/ *n* (for sink) ventouse *f*.

plunging /ˈplʌndʒɪŋ/ *adj* **~ neckline** décolleté *m* plongeant.

plunk○ /plʌŋk/ **I** *n* toc○ *m*, bruit *m* sourd.
II *vtr* **1** (place) planter [*bottle, plate*] (**on**

sur); **2** (strum) pincer les cordes de [*banjo, guitar*].
■ **plunk down**○ = **plonk down**.
pluperfect /ˌpluːˈpɜːfɪkt/ Ling **I** *n* plus-que-parfait *m*.
II *modif* [*tense*] au plus-que-parfait; [*form*] du plus-que-parfait.
plural /ˈplʊərəl/ **I** *n* Ling pluriel *m*; **in the ~** au pluriel.
II *adj* **1** Ling [*noun, adjective*] au pluriel; [*form, ending*] du pluriel; **2** Pol (society, system) pluraliste.
pluralism /ˈplʊərəlɪzəm/ *n* pluralisme *m*.
pluralist /ˈplʊərəlɪst/ **I** *n* partisan/-e *m/f* du pluralisme.
II *adj* [*society, policy, values*] pluraliste.
plurality /plʊəˈrælətɪ/ *n* **1** (multitude) pluralité *f* (**of** de); **2** (diversity) pluralité *f*; **3** (majority) gen majorité *f*; US Pol majorité *f* relative.
plus /plʌs/ **I** *n* **1** Math plus *m*; **2** (advantage) avantage *m*; **with the added ~ that** avec l'avantage supplémentaire que.
II *adj* **1** Math, Elec positif/-ive; **2** (advantageous) **~ factor**, **~ point** atout *m*; **the ~ side** le côté positif; **3** (in expressions of age, quantity) **50 ~** plus de 50; **20 years ~** plus de 20 ans; **the 65-~ age group** les personnes qui ont 65 ans et plus.
III *prep* Math plus; **15 ~ 12** 15 plus 12.
IV *conj* et; **bedroom ~ bathroom** chambre et salle de bains; **two adults ~ a baby** deux adultes et un bébé.
plus-fours /ˈplʌsfɔːz/ *npl* culotte *f* de golf.
plush /plʌʃ/ **I** *n* Tex peluche *f*.
II *adj* **1**○ (luxurious) [*house, room, hotel, surroundings*] somptueux/-euse; [*district, area*] riche; **2** Tex [*curtain, furniture, carpet*] en or de peluche.
plushy○ /ˈplʌʃɪ/ *adj* [*house, room, hotel*] somptueux/-euse.
plus sign *n* Math signe *m* plus.
Plutarch /ˈpluːtɑːk/ *pr n* Plutarque.
Pluto /ˈpluːtəʊ/ *pr n* **1** Mythol Pluton *m*; **2** Astron Pluton *f*.
plutocracy /pluːˈtɒkrəsɪ/ *n* ploutocratie *f*.
plutocrat /ˈpluːtəkræt/ *n* ploutocrate *m*.
plutocratic /ˌpluːtəˈkrætɪk/ *adj* ploutocratique.
plutonium /pluːˈtəʊnɪəm/ *n* plutonium *m*.
pluviometer /ˌpluːvɪˈɒmɪtə(r)/ *n* pluviomètre *m*.
ply /plaɪ/ **I** *n* (thickness) épaisseur *f*; **two/three ~ paper** papier double/triple épaisseur; **two ~ wool** laine deux fils; **three/five ~ wood** contreplaqué trois/cinq plis.
II *vtr* **1** (sell) vendre [*wares*]; **2** (perform) exercer [*trade*]; **3** (manipulate) manier [*pen, oars*]; **to ~ one's needle** tirer l'aiguille; **4** (travel) [*boat*] sillonner [*sea*]; **to ~ the route between two ports** faire la navette entre deux ports; **5** (press) **to ~ sb for** harceler qn pour obtenir [*information*]; **to ~ sb with** assaillir qn de [*questions*]; **to ~ sb with food/drink** ne cesser de remplir l'assiette/le verre de qn.
III *vi* [*boat, bus*] faire la navette (**between** entre).
plywood /ˈplaɪwʊd/ **I** *n* contreplaqué *m*.
II *modif* [*box, boat*] en contreplaqué; [*sheet*] de contreplaqué.
pm ▶ **1096** *adv* (*abrév* = **post meridiem**) **two pm** quatorze heures, deux heures de l'après-midi; **nine pm** vingt-et-une heures, neuf heures du soir.
PM *n* GB *abrév* ▶ **Prime Minister**.
PMG *n* **1** *abrév* ▶ **Paymaster General**; **2** *abrév* ▶ **Postmaster General**.
PMS *n* (*abrév* = **premenstrual syndrome**) SPM *m*.
PMT *n* (*abrév* = **premenstrual tension**) SPM *m*.
PND *n* Med *abrév* ▶ **post-natal depression**.
pneumatic /njuːˈmætɪk, US nuː-/ *adj* **1** Mech [*brakes, system, hammer*] pneumatique; **2**○ GB (rounded) [*woman*] bien roulé○; [*body*] bien fait; **to have a ~ figure** avoir des formes avantageuses.
pneumatic drill *n* marteau *m* piqueur.
pneumatics /njuːˈmætɪks, US nuː-/ *n* (+ *v sg*) pneumatique *f*.
pneumatic tyre GB, **~ tire** US pneu *m*.
pneumoconiosis /ˌnjuːməʊˌkɒnɪˈəʊsɪs, US nuː-/ ▶ **1354** *n* pneumoconiose *f*.
pneumonia /njuːˈməʊnɪə, US nuː-/ ▶ **1354** *n* pneumonie *f*.
po○ /pəʊ/ *n* GB pot *m* de chambre.
PO **1** *abrév* = **post office**; **2** *abrév* ▶ **postal order**.
poach /pəʊtʃ/ **I** *vtr* **1** (hunt illegally) chasser [qch] illégalement [*game*]; pêcher [qch] illégalement [*fish*]; **2** fig (steal) débaucher [*staff, players*] (**from** de); s'approprier [*idea, information*] (**from** de); **3** Culin faire pocher [*fish, eggs*].
II *vi* **1** (hunt) lit braconner; **to ~ on sb's territory** fig empiéter sur le territoire de qn; **2** Sport (in tennis) *renvoyer la balle à la place de son partenaire*.
III poached *pp adj* Culin [*egg, fish*] poché.
poacher /ˈpəʊtʃə(r)/ *n* **1** (hunter) braconnier *m*; **2** Culin (pan) (for eggs) pocheuse *f*; (for fish) US poissonnière *f*.
poaching /ˈpəʊtʃɪŋ/ *n* Hunt braconnage *m*.
pock /pɒk/ *n* = **pockmark**.
pocket /ˈpɒkɪt/ **I** *n* **1** (in garment) poche *f*; **jacket/trouser ~** poche de veste/de pantalon; **with one's hands in one's ~s** les mains dans les poches; **to put one's hand in one's ~** lit, fig mettre sa main dans sa poche; **to go through sb's ~s** faire les poches de qn; **to turn out one's ~s** vider or retourner ses poches; **he paid for it out of his own ~** il l'a payé de sa poche; **prices to suit every ~** fig des prix à la portée de tout le monde; **2** (in car door, suitcase, folder etc) poche *f*; **3** fig (small area) poche *f*; **~ of resistance/of opposition** poche *f* or foyer *m* de résistance/d'opposition; **4** Mining, Geol poche *f*; **air ~** Aviat trou *m* d'air; **5** (in billiards) bourse *f*.
II *modif* [*calculator, flask, diary, dictionary, edition*] de poche.
III *vtr* **1** (put in one's pocket) empocher, mettre [qch] dans sa poche; fig (keep for oneself) empocher [*money, profits*]; **2** US Pol **to ~ a bill** opposer un veto à une loi; **3** (in billiards) blouser.
IDIOMS **to be in ~** GB être en fonds; **to be out of ~** GB en être de sa poche; **I'm £40 out of ~** j'ai 40 livres de moins en poche; **to have sb in one's ~** avoir qn dans sa poche; **to line one's ~s** se remplir les poches; **to live in each other's ~s** être tout le temps l'un sur l'autre; **to ~ one's pride** ravaler sa fierté.
pocket battleship *n* cuirassé *m* de poche.
pocket billiards *npl* **1** ▶ **1282** Games billard *m* américain; **2** fig **to play ~**◑ jouer avec ses boules◑.
pocketbook /ˈpɒkɪtbʊk/ *n* **1** (wallet) portefeuille *m*; **2** US (book) livre *m* de poche; **3** US (bag) sac *m* à main.
pocket calculator *n* calculatrice *f* de poche, calculette *f*.
pocketful /ˈpɒkɪtfʊl/ *n* poche *f* pleine (**of** de).
pocket-handkerchief /ˌpɒkɪtˈhæŋkətʃiːf/ **I** *n* pochette *f*.
II *modif* [*garden, plot*] grand comme un mouchoir de poche.
pocket: **~knife** *n* couteau *m* de poche; **~ money** *n* argent *m* de poche; **~phone** *n* téléphone *m* de poche; **~-size(d)** *adj* [*book, map, edition etc*] de poche; fig (tiny) tout petit; **~ veto** *n* US Pol veto *m* implicite (*lorsque le Président ne signe pas un projet de loi dans les délais prévus*); **~ watch** *n* montre *f* de gousset.
pock: **~mark** *n* cicatrice *f* (*de variole, d'acné etc*); **~marked** *adj* [*skin, face*] grêlé.
pod /pɒd/ **I** *n* **1** Bot (of peas, beans) (intact) gousse *f*; (empty) cosse *f*; (of vanilla) gousse *f*; **2** Aviat (for engine, weapons) nacelle *f*; (for fuel) bidon *m*; **3** Aerosp module *m*.
II *vtr* (*p prés etc* **-dd-**) écosser [*beans, peas*].
podgy○ /ˈpɒdʒɪ/ *adj* grassouillet/-ette.
podiatrist /pəˈdaɪətrɪst/ ▶ **1692** *n* US pédicure *mf*.
podiatry /pəˈdaɪətrɪ/ *n* US podologie *f*.
podium /ˈpəʊdɪəm/ *n* (*pl* **-iums**, **-ia**) (for speaker, conductor) estrade *f*; (for winner) podium *m*.
Podunk /ˈpɒdʌŋk/ *n* US bled○ *m* perdu.
poem /ˈpəʊɪm/ *n* poème *m*.
poet /ˈpəʊɪt/ *n* poète *m*.
poetaster /ˌpəʊɪˈtæstə(r)/ *n* rimailleur *m*.
poetess /ˈpəʊɪtes/ ▶ **1692** *n* péj poétesse *f* pej.
poetic /pəʊˈetɪk/ *adj* poétique.
poetical /pəʊˈetɪkl/ *adj* poétique.
poetically /pəʊˈetɪklɪ/ *adv* avec poésie.
poeticize /pəʊˈetɪsaɪz/ *vtr* poétiser.
poetic: **~ justice** *n* justice *f* immanente; **~ licence** GB, **~ license** US *n* licence *f* poétique.
poetics /pəʊˈetɪks/ *n* (+ *v sg*) poétique *f*.
poet laureate *n* poète *m* lauréat.
poetry /ˈpəʊɪtrɪ/ *n* poésie *f*; **to write/read ~** écrire/lire des poèmes *mpl*; **a collection of ~** un recueil de poèmes; **the ~ of Pope** la poésie de Pope; **~ reading** séance *f* de lecture de poésie.
po-faced○ /ˈpəʊfeɪst/ *adj* GB **to look/be ~** avoir l'air pincé.
pogo /ˈpəʊgəʊ/ *vi* danser le pogo.
pogonip /ˈpəʊgəʊnɪp/ *n* US brouillard *m* glacial (*dans l'Ouest des États-Unis*).
pogo-stick /ˈpəʊgəʊstɪk/ *n* Games échasse *f* à ressort.
pogrom /ˈpɒgrəm, US pəˈgrɒm/ *n* pogrom *m*; **a ~ against Armenians/Palestinians** un pogrom anti-arménien/anti-palestinien.
poignancy /ˈpɔɪnjənsɪ/ *n* (of situation, poem, play) caractère *m* poignant; **a song/moment of great ~** un chant/moment très émouvant; **to add ~ to sth** rendre qch plus poignant.
poignant /ˈpɔɪnjənt/ *adj* poignant.
poignantly /ˈpɔɪnjəntlɪ/ *adv* [*note, feel, describe*] de manière poignante; **the sacrifice was ~ vain** le sacrifice fut d'une futilité poignante.
poinsettia /pɔɪnˈsetɪə/ *n* poinsettia *m*.
point /pɔɪnt/ **I** *n* **1** (tip) (of knife, needle, pencil, tooth) pointe *f*; (of star) branche *f*; **the knife has a sharp ~** le couteau a la pointe très acérée; **the pencil has a sharp ~** le crayon est très bien taillé; **the tree comes to a ~ at the top** l'arbre se termine en pointe; **to threaten sb at knife ~** menacer qn avec un couteau; **2** (place) (precise location, position on scale) point *m*; (less specific) endroit *m*; **boiling ~** point d'ébullition; **compass ~** point de la boussole; **assembly ~** point de rassemblement; **embarkation ~** lieu *m* d'embarquement; **the furthest/highest ~** le point le plus éloigné/le plus élevé; **at the ~ where the path divides** à l'endroit où le chemin bifurque; **the road swings north at this ~** à cet endroit la route se dirige vers le nord; **~ of entry** (into country) point d'arrivée; (of bullet into body) point d'impact; (into atmosphere) point d'entrée; **~ of no return** point de non-retour; **3** (extent, degree) point *m*; **the rope had been strained to breaking ~** la corde avait été tendue au point qu'elle pouvait se rompre; **his nerves were strained to breaking ~** il était très tendu; **to be driven to the ~ of exhaustion** être poussé jusqu'à l'épuisement; **I've got to the ~ where I can't take any more** j'en suis arrivé au point où je n'en peux plus; **to push sth to the ~ of absurdity** pousser qch jusqu'à l'absurde; **she was frank to the ~ of brutality** ou **of being brutal** elle était franche au point d'en être brutale; **to reach a**

Points of the compass

abbreviated as

north	= nord	N
south	= sud	S
east	= est	E
west	= ouest	O

nord, sud, est, ouest *is the normal order in French as well as English.*

northeast	= nord-est	NE
northwest	= nord-ouest	NO
north-northeast	= nord-nord-est	NNE
east-northeast	= est-nord-est	ENE

Where?

Compass points in French are not normally written with a capital letter. However, when they refer to a specific region in phrases such as I love the North *or* he lives in the North, *and it is clear where this North is, without any further specification such as* of France *or* of Europe, *then they are written with a capital letter, as they often are in English, too. In the following examples,* north *and* nord *stand for any compass point word.*

I love the North = j'aime le Nord
to live in the North = vivre dans le Nord

Normally, however, these words do not take a capital letter:

in the north of Scotland = dans le nord de l'Écosse

Take care to distinguish this from

to the north of Scotland
(*i.e. further north than Scotland*) = au nord de l'Écosse
in the south of Spain = dans le sud de l'Espagne*
it is north of the hill = c'est au nord de la colline
a few kilometres north = à quelques kilomètres au nord
due north of here = droit au nord

* *Note that the south of France is more usually referred to as* le Midi.

There is another set of words in French for north, south *etc., some of which are more common than others:*

(north)	septentrion (*rarely used*)	septentrional(e)
(south)	midi	méridional(e)
(east)	orient	oriental(e)
(west)	occident	occidental(e)

Translating northern etc.

a northern town = une ville du Nord
a northern accent = un accent du Nord
the most northerly outpost = l'avant-poste le plus au nord

Regions of countries and continents work like this:

northern Europe = l'Europe du Nord
the northern parts of Japan = le nord du Japon
eastern France = l'est de la France

For names of countries and continents which include these compass point words, such as North America *or* South Korea, *see the dictionary entry.*

Where to?

French has fewer ways of expressing this than English has; vers le *is usually safe:*

to go north = aller vers le nord
to head towards the north = se diriger vers le nord
to go northwards = aller vers le nord
to go in a northerly direction = aller vers le nord
a northbound ship = un bateau qui se dirige vers le nord

With some verbs, such as face, *the French expression changes:*

the windows face north = les fenêtres donnent au nord
a north-facing slope = une pente orientée au nord

If in doubt, check in the dictionary.

Where from?

The usual way of expressing from the *is* du:

it comes from the north = cela vient du nord
from the north of Germany = du nord de l'Allemagne

Note also these expressions relating to the direction of the wind:

the north wind = le vent de nord
a northerly wind = un vent du nord
prevailing north winds = des vents dominants du nord
the wind is in the north = le vent est au nord
the wind is coming from the north = le vent vient du nord

Compass point words used as adjectives

The French words nord, sud, est *and* ouest *are really nouns, so when they are used as adjectives they are invariable.*

the north coast = la côte nord
the north door = la porte nord
the north face (*of a mountain*) = la face nord
the north side = le côté nord
the north wall = le mur nord

Nautical bearings

The preposition by *is translated by* quart *in expressions like the following:*

north by northwest = nord quart nord-ouest
southeast by south = sud-est quart sud

~ in sth when... atteindre un stade dans qch où...; **up to a ~** jusqu'à un certain point; **4** (moment) (precise) moment *m*; (stage) stade *m*; **to be on the ~ of doing** être sur le point de faire; **to be on the ~ of bankruptcy** être au bord de la faillite; **at this ~ I gave up** à ce stade-là j'ai abandonné; **at this ~ in her career** à ce stade-là de sa carrière; **at what ~ do we cease to feel sorry for him?** à quel moment cesse-t-on de le plaindre?; **at some ~ in the future** plus tard; **at one ~** à un moment donné; **the judge intervened at this ~** le juge est intervenu à ce moment-là; **it's at this ~ in the story that** c'est à ce stade de l'histoire que; **there comes a ~ when...** il arrive un moment où...; **when it came to the ~ of deciding** quand il a fallu décider; **at this ~ in time** dans l'état actuel des choses; **5** (question, matter, idea) point *m*; (contribution in discussion) remarque *f*; **to make a ~** faire une remarque (**about** sur); **to make the ~ that** faire remarquer que; **you've made your ~, please let me speak** vous vous êtes exprimé, laissez-moi parler; **to make a ~ of doing** (make sure one does) s'efforcer de faire; (do proudly, insistently) mettre un point d'honneur à faire; (do obviously, to make a point) faire [qch] de manière visible; **to raise a ~ about sth** soulever la question de qch; **my ~ was that** ce que je voulais dire, c'était que; **to take up** ou **return to sb's ~** revenir sur un point soulevé par qn; **this proves my ~** cela confirme ce que je viens de dire; **are we agreed on this ~?** sommes-nous d'accord sur ce point?; **a three/four-~ plan** un plan en trois/quatre points; **to go through a text ~ by ~** examiner un texte point par point; **the ~ at issue** le sujet de la discussion; **that's a good ~** c'est une remarque judicieuse; **I take your ~** (agreeing) je suis d'accord avec vous; **I take your ~, but** je vois bien où vous voulez en venir, mais; **all right, ~ taken!** très bien, j'en prends note; **good ~!** très juste!; **you've got a ~ there** vous n'avez pas tort; **in ~ of fact** en fait; **as a ~ of information** pour information; **6** (central idea) point *m* essentiel; **the ~ is that** le point essentiel, c'est que; **the ~ is, another candidate has been selected** malheureusement, un autre candidat a été sélectionné; **to come straight to the ~** aller droit au fait; **he never got to the ~** il n'est jamais entré dans le vif du sujet; **to keep to** ou **stick to the ~** rester dans le sujet; **to miss the ~** ne pas comprendre; **I missed the ~ of what she said** je n'ai pas compris ce qu'elle a voulu dire; **to the ~** pertinent; **what she said was short and to the ~** ce qu'elle a dit était bref et pertinent; **that's beside the ~** là n'est pas la question; **what you're saying is beside the ~** ce que vous dites est à côté de la question; **to wander off the ~** s'écarter du sujet; **to see the ~** saisir; **to get the ~** comprendre; **that's not the ~** il ne s'agit pas de cela; **7** (purpose) objet *m*; **what was the ~ of her visit?** quel était l'objet de sa visite?; **the exercise does have a ~** l'exercice n'est pas gratuit; **what's the ~?** à quoi bon? ; **what's the ~ of doing...?** à quoi bon faire...?; **there's no ~ in doing** ça ne sert à rien de faire; **I see little ~ in doing, I don't see the ~ of doing** je ne vois pas l'intérêt de faire; **8** (feature, characteristic) point *m*, côté *m*; **his good/bad ~s** ses bons/mauvais côtés; **what ~s do you look for when buying a car?** que recherchez-vous lorsque vous achetez une voiture?; **punctuality is not her strong ~** la ponctualité n'est pas son point fort; **the ~s of similarity/difference between** les points communs/de divergence entre; **it's a ~ in their favour** c'est un point en leur faveur; **it has its ~s** il/elle n'est pas mauvais/-e; **9** Sport, Fin (in scoring) point *m*; **to win/to be beaten by 4 ~s** gagner/être battu à 4 points près; **to win on ~s** (in boxing) remporter une victoire aux points; **the FT 100 was up/down three ~s** Fin l'indice FT 100 a gagné/perdu trois points; **Smurfit gained 4 ~s** Fin les actions Smurfit ont gagné 4 points; **to evaluate sth on a 5-~ scale** évaluer qch d'après une échelle à 5 degrés; **match/championship ~** (in tennis) balle *f* de match/championnat; **10** (dot) point *m*; (decimal point) virgule *f*; (diacritic) signe *m* diacritique; **a ~ of light** un point lumineux; **11** Math (in geometry) point *m*; **12** Print, Comput (also **~ size**) corps *m* (de caractère); **13** Geog (headland) pointe *f*.

II points *npl* **1** GB, Rail aiguillages *mpl*, aiguilles *fpl*; **2** Aut électrodes *fpl*; **3** (in ballet) **to dance on ~(s)** faire des pointes *fpl*.

III *vtr* **1** (aim, direct) **to ~ sth at sb** braquer qch sur qn [*camera, gun*]; **to ~ one's finger at sb** montrer qn du doigt; **to ~ the finger at sb** (accuse) accuser qn; **just ~ the camera and press** tu n'as qu'à viser avec l'appareil photo et appuyer; **to ~ sth towards** (of car, boat) diriger qch vers; **to ~ sb in the right direction** lit, fig mettre qn dans la bonne direction; **2** (show) **to ~ the way to** lit (person, signpost) indiquer la direction de; **to ~ sb the way to** indiquer à qn la direction de; **the report ~s the way to a fairer system** le rapport ouvre la voie à un système plus équitable; **3** (in ballet, gym) **to ~ one's toes** faire des pointes; **4** Constr jointoyer [*wall*].

IV *vi* **1** (indicate) indiquer or montrer (du doigt); **it's rude to ~** ce n'est pas poli de montrer du doigt; **she ~ed over her shoulder** elle a indiqué derrière elle; **she ~ed in the direction of** elle a indiqué du

doigt la direction de; **to ~ at sb/sth** montrer qn/qch du doigt; **he was ~ing with his stick at something** il indiquait quelque chose de son bâton; **to ~ to** désigner; **2** (be directed, aligned) [*signpost, arrow*] indiquer; **to ~ at sb** ou **in sb's direction** [*gun, camera*] être braqué sur qn; **the needle ~s north** l'aiguille indique le nord; **the gun was ~ing straight at me** l'arme était braquée sur moi; **3** (suggest) **to ~ to** [*evidence, facts*] sembler indiquer; **all the evidence ~s to murder** les preuves semblent indiquer qu'il s'agit d'un meurtre; **everything ~s in that direction** tout semble indiquer que c'est ainsi; **4** (cite) **to ~ to** citer; **to ~ to sth as evidence of success** citer qch comme preuve d'une réussite; **5** Comput **to ~ at sth** mettre le pointeur sur qch; **6** [*dog*] se mettre à l'arrêt.
■ **point out**: ¶ **~ out [sth/sb], ~ [sth/sb] out** (show) montrer (**to** à); **can you ~ him out to me?** peux-tu me le montrer?; **to ~ out where/who** montrer l'endroit où/la personne qui; ¶ **~ out [sth]** (remark on) faire remarquer [*fact, discrepancy*]; **to ~ out that** faire remarquer que; **as he ~ed out** comme il l'a fait remarquer.
■ **point up**: **~ up [sth]** mettre [qch] en avant [*contrast, similarity*]; faire ressortir [*lack, incompetence*].

point-blank /ˌpɔɪntˈblæŋk/ **I** *adj* **at ~ range** à bout portant.
II *adv* **1** lit [*shoot*] à bout portant; **2** fig [*refuse, deny*] catégoriquement; [*ask*] à brûle-pourpoint, de but en blanc; [*reply*] de but en blanc.

point duty *n* GB **to be on ~** [*policeman*] être affecté à la circulation.

pointed /ˈpɔɪntɪd/ *adj* **1** (sharp) [*hat, stick, chin*] pointu; [*window*] en pointe; [*arch*] en ogive; **2** [*remark, reference, question*] qui vise quelqu'un; **her ~ remarks were not lost on me** les remarques qui me visaient ne m'ont pas échappé.

pointedly /ˈpɔɪntɪdlɪ/ *adv* [*ignore, look*] ostensiblement; **somewhat ~, he remained silent** assez ostensiblement, il a gardé le silence.

pointer /ˈpɔɪntə(r)/ *n* **1** (piece of information) indication *f*; **a ~ to sth** une indication concernant qch; **to give sb a few ~s to a problem** donner à qn quelques indications quant à l'approche d'un problème; **2** (dog) (breed) pointer *m*; Hunt chien *m* d'arrêt; **3** (for teaching) baguette *f*; **4** (on projector screen) flèche *f*; **5** Comput pointeur *m*.

pointillism /ˈpɔɪntɪlɪzəm, ˈpwæntiːlɪzəm/ *n* pointillisme *m*.

pointing /ˈpɔɪntɪŋ/ *n* Constr jointoiement *m*.

pointless /ˈpɔɪntlɪs/ *adj* [*request, demand, activity*] absurde; [*gesture*] inutile; [*attempt*] vain; **it's ~ to do/for me to do** ça ne sert à rien de faire/que je fasse.

pointlessly /ˈpɔɪntlɪslɪ/ *adv* pour rien.

pointlessness /ˈpɔɪntlɪsnɪs/ *n* absurdité *f*.

point: **~ of contact** *n* contact *m*; **~ of departure** *n* point *m* de départ; **~ of law** *n* point *m* de droit.

point of order *n* question *f* relative à la procédure; **to reject sth on a ~** rejeter qch conformément à la procédure.

point: **~ of principle** *n* point *m* de principe; **~ of reference** *n* point *m* de référence; **~ of sale** *n* point *m* de vente; **~-of-sale advertising** *n* publicité *f* sur les lieux de vente, PLV *f*; **~-of-sale terminal** *n* terminal *m* point de vente, TPV *m*.

point of view *n* point *m* de vue; **to see sth from her ~** voir qch de son point de vue; **it depends on your ~** cela dépend de quel point de vue on se place.

point: **~sman** ▶ **1692** *n* GB Rail aiguilleur *m*; **~(s) system** *n* système *m* de points; **~-to-point** *n* Equit course *f* d'obstacles en extérieur.

pointy /ˈpɔɪntɪ/ *adj* pointu.

poise /pɔɪz/ **I** *n* **1** (aplomb) sang-froid *m inv*; **2** (confidence) assurance *f*; **3** (physical elegance) aisance *f*.
II *vtr* tenir [*javelin, spade*].

poised /pɔɪzd/ *adj* **1** (self-possessed) [*person*] plein d'assurance; [*manner*] posé; **2** (elegant) plein d'aisance; **3** (suspended) [*pen, knife, hand*] en suspens; **~ in mid-air** suspendu dans l'air; **she sat there, pen ~** elle était assise, prête à écrire; **4** (balanced) **to be ~ on** lit se tenir sur [*rock, platform, cliff*]; **the power was ~ between ministers and businessmen** fig les ministres et les hommes d'affaires se partageaient le pouvoir; **~ on the brink of a great discovery** fig à la veille d'une grande découverte; **5** (on the point of) **to be ~ to do** être sur le point de faire; **to be ~ for sth** être prêt pour qch.

poison /ˈpɔɪzn/ **I** *n* **1** lit, fig poison *m*; **to take ~** s'empoisonner; **2**○ †(drink) **what's your ~?** qu'est-ce que tu bois?, tu te soûles○ à quoi?
II *vtr* [*person*] empoisonner [*person, animal*] (**with** avec); [*lead, chemical fumes*] intoxiquer; (make poisonous) empoisonner [*dart, arrowtip*]; mettre du poison dans [*foodstuffs, water*]; Ecol (contaminate) empoisonner [*environment, air, rivers*] (**with** avec); fig (damage) empoisonner [*relationship, life*]; **to have a ~ed finger/toe** avoir une infection au doigt/à l'orteil; **to ~ sb's mind** corrompre l'esprit de qn; **they've ~ed his mind against his family** ils l'ont dressé contre sa famille.
IDIOMS **to hate sb like ~** avoir qn en horreur.

poisoner /ˈpɔɪzənər/ *n* empoisonneur/-euse *m/f*.

poison gas *n* gaz *m* asphyxiant or toxique.

poisoning /ˈpɔɪzənɪŋ/ *n* empoisonnement *m*; **alcoholic/cyanide ~** empoisonnement par l'alcool/au cyanure.

poison ivy, poison oak *n* Bot sumac *m* vénéneux; Med (rash) urticaire *f* (provoquée par le sumac vénéneux).

poisonous /ˈpɔɪzənəs/ *adj* **1** (noxious) [*chemicals, fumes, gas*] toxique; [*plant, mushroom, berry*] vénéneux/-euse, toxique; Zool [*snake, insect, bite, sting*] venimeux/-euse; **the coffee's absolutely ~**○! le café est infect!; **2** fig (vicious) [*rumour, propaganda, ideology*] pernicieux/-ieuse; [*person*] malveillant.

poison: **~-pen letter** *n* lettre *f* anonyme pleine de venin; **~ pill** *n* Fin *tactique qui consiste à décourager d'éventuels acquéreurs d'une société en vendant une OPA très coûteuse*.

Poitou-Charentes ▶ **1273** *pr n* Poitou-Charentes *m*; **in/to ~** dans le Poitou-Charentes.

poke /pəʊk/ **I** *n* **1** (prod) coup *m*; **a ~ in the eye** lit un coup dans l'œil; fig un camouflet; **to give the fire a ~** tisonner le feu; **2** (punch) coup *m* de poing; **to take a ~ at sb** lit envoyer un coup de poing à qn; fig envoyer une pierre dans le jardin de qn; **3●** (sex) coup● *m*; **to have a ~** tirer un coup●.
II *vtr* **1** (jab, prod) pousser [*person*]; donner un coup dans [*pile, substance*]; tisonner [*fire*] **to ~ sb in the ribs/the eye** donner un coup dans les côtes/l'œil de qn; **to ~ oneself in the eye with a pencil** se mettre un crayon dans l'œil; **he ~d his food with his fork** il inspecta le contenu de son assiette avec sa fourchette; **2** (push, put) **to ~ sth into** enfoncer qch dans [*hole, pot*]; **to ~ one's finger into a hole/pot** mettre le doigt dans un trou/pot; **to ~ one's finger up one's nose** se mettre le doigt dans le nez; **to ~ one's head round the door/out of the window** passer la tête par la porte/par la fenêtre; **to ~ food through the bars** passer de la nourriture à travers les barreaux; **3** (pierce) **to ~ a hole in sth** percer qch, faire un trou dans qch (**with** avec).
III *vi* ▶ **poke at, poke out, poke up**.
IDIOMS **it's better than a ~ in the eye (with a sharp stick)** c'est mieux que rien.
■ **poke around, poke about** GB fouiner, farfouiller (**in** dans; **for** pour trouver).
■ **poke at**: **~ at [sth]** chipoter devant [*food, plate*].
■ **poke out**: ¶ **~ out** [*elbow, toe, blade, spring*] dépasser; [*flower*] poindre; **to ~ out through** [*spring, stuffing*] dépasser [*hole, old mattress*]; [*flower*] poindre à travers [*snow, rubble*]; **to ~ out from under** dépasser de dessous [*bed, covers*]; ¶ **to ~ out [sth], to ~ [sth] out** sortir [*head, nose, tongue*]; **to ~ sb's eye out** crever l'œil de qn.
■ **poke up** [*flower, shoot*] poindre (**through** à travers).

poker /ˈpəʊkə(r)/ ▶ **1282** *n* **1** (for fire) tisonnier *m*, pique-feu *m inv*; **2** (cardgame) poker *m*.
IDIOMS **(as) stiff as a ~** raide comme la justice.

poker dice *npl* dés *mpl* de poker d'as; **to play ~** jouer au poker d'as.

poker-faced /ˈpəʊkəfeɪst/ *adj* [*person*] au visage impénétrable; [*look*] impénétrable.

pokerwork /ˈpəʊkəwɜːk/ *n* pyrogravure *f*.

pokey○ /ˈpəʊkɪ/ *n* taule◑ *f*.

poky /ˈpəʊkɪ/ *adj* **1** (small) [*room*] minuscule; **2**○ US (slow) [*waiter*] lambin○.

pol◑ US /pɒl/ *n* politicien/-ienne *m/f*.

Polack○ /ˈpəʊlæk/ *n* injur polaque○ *mf* offensive.

Poland /ˈpəʊlənd/ ▶ **1131** *pr n* Pologne *f*.

polar /ˈpəʊlə(r)/ *adj* Geog, Elec [*icecap, lights, region*] polaire; [*attraction*] (one) du pôle; (both) des pôles; **to be ~ opposites** fig être des pôles opposés.

polar bear *n* ours *m* polaire.

polarimeter /ˌpəʊləˈrɪmɪtə(r)/ *n* polarimètre *m*.

Polaris /pəˈlɑːrɪs/ *n* Mil, Nucl missile *m* Polaris.

polarity /pəˈlærətɪ/ *n* **1** Elec, Phys polarité *f*; **reversed ~** polarité opposée; **2** fig opposition *f*.

polarization /ˌpəʊləraɪˈzeɪʃn, US -rɪˈz-/ *n* **1** Elec, Phys polarisation *f*; **2** fig (split) divergence *f* (**of** de).

polarize /ˈpəʊləraɪz/ **I** *vtr* **1** Elec, Phys polariser; **~d sun glasses** lunettes de soleil polarisantes; **2** (divide) diviser [*opinion*]; **3** (focus) polariser.
II *vi* (divide) [*opinions*] diverger.

Polaroid® /ˈpəʊlərɔɪd/ **I** *n* (photograph) photo *f* polaroïd®; (camera) polaroïd® *m*; (glass) polaroïd® *m*.
II *modif* [*camera, film, glass, photograph*] polaroïd® *inv*.
III Polaroids® *npl* lunettes *fpl* polaroïd®; **a pair of ~s**® une paire de lunettes polaroïd®.

polder /ˈpəʊldə(r)/ *n* polder *m*.

pole /pəʊl/ **I** *n* **1** (stick) gen perche *f*; (for tent, flag) mât *m*; (for athletics, boat, garden) perche *f*; Equit barre *f*; (for skiing) bâton *m*; (piste marker) piquet *m*; (for scaffolding) perche *f*; **2** Geog, Phys pôle *m*; **North/South ~** pôle *m* Nord/Sud; **negative/positive ~** pôle *m* négatif/positif; **to go from ~ to ~** fig faire le tour de la terre; **to be at the opposite ~ from** fig être aux antipodes de; **3** Fishg canne *f* à pêche; **4** Meas ≈ 5 mètres.
II *vtr* pousser [qch] à la perche [*boat*].
IDIOMS **to be up the ~**○ (wrong) se tromper; (mad) être toqué○; **to be ~s apart** [*theories, methods*] être aux antipodes; [*people*] être vraiment différents; [*opinions*] être diamétralement opposés; **I wouldn't touch him with a ten-foot ~** US je ne voudrais rien avoir à faire avec lui; **I wouldn't touch it with a ten-foot ~** US je ne voudrais de cela pour rien au monde.

Pole /pəʊl/ ▶ **1486** *n* Polonais/-e *m/f*.

poleaxe GB, **poleax** US /ˈpəʊlæks/ **I** *n* hache *f* d'armes.
II *vtr* assommer [*person, animal*].

pole-axed○ /ˈpəʊlækst/ *adj* **to be ~** être renversé (par la surprise).

polecat /ˈpəʊlkæt/ *n* **1** (ferret) putois *m*; **2** US (skunk) mouf(f)ette *f*.

polemic /pəˈlemɪk/ *n* polémique *f* (**about** sur); **a ~ against sb/sth** un réquisitoire contre qn/qch; **a ~ on behalf of sb/sth** un plaidoyer en faveur de qn/qch.

polemical /pəˈlemɪkl/ *adj* polémique.

polemicist /pəˈlemɪsɪst/ *n* polémiste *mf*.

polemics /pəˈlemɪks/ *npl* polémique *f* ¢.

pole position *n* pole position *f*; **to be in/to have ~** lit être en/avoir la pole position; **to be in ~** fig être à la meilleure place.

pole star /ˈpəʊlstɑ:(r)/ *n* Astron étoile *f* polaire; fig principe *m* directeur.

pole vault /ˈpəʊlvɔ:lt/ **I** *n* saut *m* à la perche.
II *vi* faire du saut à la perche.

pole: **~ vaulter** /ˈpəʊlvɔ:ltə(r)/ *n* perchiste *mf*; **~ vaulting** ▶ 1282 *n* saut *m* à la perche.

police /pəˈli:s/ **I** *n* **1** (+ *v pl*) (official body) **the ~** gen la police; (in France outside cities) la gendarmerie; **to be in the ~** être dans la police; **to assist the ~ with their enquiries** euph être interrogé par la police; **2** (men and women) policiers *mpl*; (in France, outside cities) gendarmes *mpl*.
II *modif* [*action, involvement, intervention, protection*] de la police; [*raid, car, operation, vehicle*] de police; [*presence, escort*] policier/-ière.
III *vtr* **1** (keep order) maintenir l'ordre dans [*area*]; **2** (patrol) [*area, frontier*] surveiller; **3** (staff with police) **to ~ a demonstration/a match** organiser le service d'ordre pour une manifestation/un match; **4** (monitor) contrôler l'application de [*measures, regulations*].

police: **~ academy** *n* US = **police college**; **~ cell** *n* cellule *f* (dans un poste de police); **~ chief** *n* commissaire *m* divisionnaire; **~ college** *n* centre *m* de formation de la police; **Police Complaints Authority** *n* GB ≈ inspection *f* générale des services; **~ constable, PC** *n* agent *m* de police; (female) femme *f* agent (de police); **~ court** *n tribunal de police et correctionnel*.

police custody *n* garde *f* à vue; **to be in ~** être en garde à vue.

police: **Police Department, PD** *n* US services *mpl* de police (d'une ville); **~ dog** *n* chien *m* policier.

police force *n* police *f*, forces *fpl* de l'ordre; **to join the ~** entrer dans la police.

police: **~ headquarters** *npl* administration *f* centrale de la police; **~man** *n* agent *m* de police, gardien *m* de la paix; (in France, outside cities) gendarme *m*; **~ officer** *n* policier *m*.

police record *n* casier *m* judiciaire; **to have no ~** avoir un casier judiciaire vierge.

police: **~ state** *n* péj État *m* policier; **~ station** *n* poste *m* de police; (larger) commissariat *m*; (in France outside cities) gendarmerie *f*; **~ van** *n* fourgon *m* cellulaire, panier *m* à salade○; **~woman** *n* femme *f* policier; **~ work** *n* (detection) investigations *fpl* policières.

policing /pəˈli:sɪŋ/ **I** *n* **1** (maintaining law and order) maintien *m* de l'ordre; **the ~ of our city streets** le maintien de l'ordre dans nos rues; **2** (patrolling) surveillance *f*; **the ~ of the border** la surveillance de la frontière; **3** (staffing with police) organisation *f* du service d'ordre; **the ~ of football matches/demonstrations** l'organisation du service d'ordre pour les matchs/manifestations; **4** (monitoring) contrôle *m*; **the ~ of the new regulations** le contrôle de l'application des nouveaux règlements.
II *modif* [*measures, system, strategy*] (at strike, demonstration, match) de maintien de l'ordre.

policy /ˈpɒləsɪ/ **I** *n* **1** (political line) politique *f* (**on** sur); **economic/foreign ~** politique *f* économique/étrangère; **government ~** politique *f* du gouvernement; **to make ~** formuler une politique; **2** (administrative rule) politique *f*; **company ~** politique *f* de l'entreprise; **it is our ~ to do** nous avons pour politique de faire; **to have** ou **follow a ~ of doing** avoir politique de faire; **they make it their ~ to do** ils ont pour règle de faire; **it is our ~ that** nous avons pour règle que (+ *subj*); **it's a matter of ~** c'est une question de principe (**to do** que de faire); **our company has a no-smoking ~** notre société a mis en place des mesures de restriction du tabagisme; **3** Insur (type of cover) contrat *m*; (document) police *f*; **to take out a ~** contracter une assurance.
II *modif* [*decision, statement*] de principe; [*discussion, matter, meeting, paper*] de politique générale.

policy: **~holder** *n* Insur assuré/-e *m/f*; **~ maker** *n* décideur *m*.

policy-making /ˈpɒləsɪmeɪkɪŋ/ **I** *n* décisions *fpl*.
II *adj* [*body, group*] de décision (*after n*).

policy unit *n* comité *m* de conseillers politiques.

polio /ˈpəʊlɪəʊ/ ▶ 1354 *n* (*abrév* = **poliomyelitis**) polio *f*.

poliomyelitis /ˌpəʊlɪəʊˌmaɪəˈlaɪtɪs/ ▶ 1354 *n* poliomyélite *f*.

polish /ˈpɒlɪʃ/ **I** *n* **1** (substance) (for wood, floor, furniture) cire *f*; (for shoes) cirage *m*; (for brass, silver) pâte *f* à polir; (for car) lustre *m*; **2** (action) **to give sth a ~** (dust) faire reluire or briller qch; (put polish on) cirer qch; **3** (shiny surface) éclat *m*; **to lose its ~** perdre son éclat; **table with a high ~** table *f* vernie; **4** fig (elegance) (of manner, performance) brio *m*; (of person) chic *m*.
II *vtr* **1** lit cirer [*shoes, wood, floor, furniture*]; astiquer [*leather, car, glass, glasses, silver, brass*]; polir [*stone, jet, marble*]; **2** fig (refine) soigner [*performance, act, image*]; affiner [*manner, style*].
III *vi* cirer.
■ **polish off**○: **~ off [sth], ~ [sth] off 1** (eat, finish) expédier○ [*food, meal, job, task*]; **2** (see off, beat or kill) liquider○ [*opponent, team, rival*].
■ **polish up**: **~ up [sth], ~ [sth] up 1** lit astiquer [*glass, car, cutlery, silver*]; cirer [*wood, floor, table*]; **2**○ (perfect) parfaire [*Spanish, piano playing*]; perfectionner [*sporting skill*]; **to ~ up one's act** fignoler○ son numéro.

Polish /ˈpəʊlɪʃ/ ▶ 1486, 1402 **I** *n* **1** Ling polonais *m*; **2** (people) **the ~** (+ *v pl*) les Polonais.
II *adj* polonais.

polished /ˈpɒlɪʃt/ *adj* **1** lit [*surface, wood*] poli; [*floor, shoes*] ciré; [*silver, brass*] astiqué; **highly ~** reluisant; **2** fig (refined) [*person, manner*] raffiné; **3** (accomplished) [*performance, production, speech*] (bien) rodé.

polisher /ˈpɒlɪʃə(r)/ ▶ 1692 *n* **1** (machine) (for floor) cireuse *f*; (for stones, gems) polisseuse *f*; **2** (person) polisseur *m*.

polite /pəˈlaɪt/ *adj* poli (**to** avec, envers fml); **to be ~ about sth** faire des commentaires polis sur qch; **when I complimented her I was only being ~** quand je l'ai complimentée c'était uniquement par politesse; **to make ~ conversation** échanger des politesses; **I made ~ noises about his present** je l'ai remercié de son cadeau pour la forme; **in ~ company** ou **society** en bonne société; **to keep a ~ distance** rester à une distance respectueuse; **to use the ~ form** Ling utiliser le vouvoiement, vouvoyer.

politely /pəˈlaɪtlɪ/ *adv* poliment.

politeness /pəˈlaɪtnɪs/ *n* politesse *f*; **out of ~** par politesse.

politic /ˈpɒlətɪk/ *adj* sout (wise) **it is** ou **would be ~ to do** il serait avisé de faire; **to find** ou **feel it ~ to do** trouver plus avisé de faire; ▶ **body politic**.

political /pəˈlɪtɪkl/ *adj* politique; **he's a ~ animal** c'est un politicien né.

political: **~ act** *n* acte *m* politique; **~ action committee, PAC** *n* US comité *m* de soutien; **~ analyst** ▶ 1692 *n* commentateur/-trice *m/f* politique; **~ asylum** *n* asile *m* politique; **~ colour** *n* couleur *f* politique; **~ commentator** *n* = **political analyst**; **~ correctness, PC** *n*: *attitude idéologique qui s'applique à n'offenser ni brimer aucune minorité*; **~ economy** *n* économie *f* politique.

political football *n* enjeu *m* politique; **the parties are playing ~** les partis politiques se renvoient la balle.

politically /pəˈlɪtɪklɪ/ *adv* [*motivated, biased*] politiquement; **~ speaking** du point de vue politique.

politically: **~ correct, PC** *adj* politiquement correct; **~-minded** *adj* [*person*] tourné vers la politique; **~-sensitive** *adj* [*issue, problem*] délicat sur le plan politique.

political: **~ prisoner** *n* prisonnier/ière *m/f* politique; **~ refugee** *n* réfugié/-e *m/f* politique; **~ science** *n* sciences *fpl* politiques; **~ scientist** ▶ 1692 *n* spécialiste *mf* en sciences politiques.

politician /ˌpɒlɪˈtɪʃn/ ▶ 1692 *n* **1** Pol (man) homme *m* politique; (woman) femme *f* politique; **2** US péj politicard○ *m*.

politicization /pəˈlɪtɪsaɪˈzeɪʃn/ *n* politisation *f*.

politicize /pəˈlɪtɪsaɪz/ *vtr* politiser.

politicking /ˈpɒlətɪkɪŋ/ *n* péj politique *f* politicienne.

politico /pəˈlɪtɪkəʊ/ **I** *n* (*pl* **~s**) US péj (politician) politicard *m*.
II politico+ (*dans composés*) politico-.

politics /ˈpɒlətɪks/ **I** *n* **1** (+ *v sg*) (political life, affairs) politique *f*; **English/local ~** la politique anglaise/locale; **to talk ~**○ parler politique○; **to make a career in ~** se lancer dans la politique; **2** (+ *v sg*) Sch, Univ sciences *fpl* politiques; **3** (+ *v pl*) (political views) opinions *fpl* politiques; **4** péj (+ *v pl*) (manoeuvering) **office ~** intrigues *fpl* au bureau.
II *modif* Univ, Sch [*exam, student*] en sciences politiques; [*teacher, course*] de sciences politiques.

polity /ˈpɒlətɪ/ *n* (form of government) régime *m* politique; (state) État *m*.

polka /ˈpɒlkə, US ˈpəʊlkə/ *n* polka *f*.

polka dot I *n* pois *m*.
II *modif* [*pattern, garment*] à pois.

poll /pəʊl/ **I** *n* **1** (vote casting) scrutin *m*, vote *m*; (election) élections *fpl*; (number of votes cast) voix *fpl*, suffrages *mpl*; (counting of votes) dépouillement *m* (du scrutin); **to take a ~ on** procéder à un vote sur; **on the eve of the ~** à la veille des élections; **the result of the ~** les résultats du scrutin; **to top** ou **head the ~** arriver en tête du scrutin; **they got 45% of the ~** ils ont obtenu 45% des suffrages exprimés; **a light/heavy ~** une faible/forte participation électorale; **there was a 75% ~** le taux de participation aux élections a été de l'ordre de 75%; **to go to the ~s** se rendre aux urnes; **the party sustained a heavy defeat at the ~s** le parti a subi une lourde défaite aux élections; **2** (list of voters) liste *f* électorale; (list of taxpayers) liste *f* de contribuables; **3** (survey) sondage *m* (**on** sur); **to conduct a ~** effectuer un sondage; **a ~ of teachers/workers** un sondage effectué auprès des enseignants/ouvriers.
II *vtr* **1** (obtain in election) obtenir [*votes*]; **2** (canvass) interroger [*group*]; **a majority of those ~ed were against censorship** une majorité des personnes interrogées étaient contre la censure; **3** Comput interroger.
III *vi* **1** (obtain votes) **to ~ badly/well** recueillir peu de/beaucoup de voix; **2** (cast vote) voter.

pollack, pollock /ˈpɒlək/ *n* Zool lieu *m* jaune.

pollard /ˈpɒləd/ *vtr* étêter [*tree*].

pollen /ˈpɒlən/ *n* pollen *m*.

pollen: **~ count** *n* taux *m* de pollen dans l'atmosphère; **~ sac** *n* sac *m* pollinique.

pollinate /ˈpɒləneɪt/ *vtr* polliniser.

pollination /ˌpɒləˈneɪʃn/ *n* pollinisation *f*.

polling /ˈpəʊlɪŋ/ *n* **1** (voting) vote *m*; (election) élections *fpl*; (turnout) participation *f* électorale; **~ was light/heavy** la participation électorale était faible/forte; **2** Comput interrogation *f*.

polling: **~ booth** *n* isoloir *m*; **~ day** *n* jour *m* des élections; **~ place** *n* US = **polling station**; **~ station** *n* bureau *m* de vote.

pollster /ˈpəʊlstə(r)/ *n* sondeur *m*; **according to the ~s** d'après les instituts de sondage.

poll tax *n* GB ≈ impôts *mpl* locaux.

■ Note Le terme officiel était **community charge**. Il a été remplacé par **council tax** en avril 1993.

pollutant /pəˈluːtənt/ *n* polluant *m*.

pollute /pəˈluːt/ *vtr* **1** Ecol polluer (**with** avec); **2** fig (morally) corrompre; (physically) souiller.

polluter /pəˈluːtə(r)/ *n* pollueur/-euse *m/f*.

pollution /pəˈluːʃn/ **I** *n* **1** Ecol pollution *f* (**of** de); **noise/oil ~** pollution sonore/par les hydrocarbures; **2** fig (moral) corruption *f*.
II *modif* [*level, control, test*] de pollution; [*measures*] contre la pollution.

Pollyanna /ˌpɒlɪˈænə/ *n* US optimiste *f* béate.

polo /ˈpəʊləʊ/ **I** *n* **1** ▶ **1282** Equit, Sport polo *m*; **2** GB (sweater) col roulé *m*.
II *modif* Equit, Sport [*match, player, stick etc*] de polo.

polonaise /ˌpɒləˈneɪz/ *n* Dance, Mus polonaise *f*.

polo: **~ neck** *n* GB (collar, sweater) col *m* roulé; **~ neck sweater** *n* pull *m* à col roulé.

poltergeist /ˈpɒltəgaɪst/ *n* esprit *m* frappeur.

poltroon‡ /pɒlˈtruːn/ *n* littér poltron/-onne *m/f*.

poly /ˈpɒlɪ/ **I**○ *n* GB *abrév* ▶ **polytechnic**.
II poly+ (*dans composés*) poly-.

polyandrous /ˌpɒlɪˈændrəs/ *adj* Bot, Sociol polyandre.

polyandry /ˈpɒlɪændrɪ/ *n* polyandrie *f*.

polyanthus /ˌpɒlɪˈænθəs/ *n* (*pl* **~** ou **-thuses**) primevère *f*.

polyarchy /ˈpɒlɪɑːkɪ/ *n* polyarchie *f*.

polychromatic /ˌpɒlɪkrəʊˈmætɪk/ *adj* polychromatique.

polychrome /ˈpɒlɪkrəʊm/ **I** *n* objet *m* d'art polychrome.
II *adj* polychrome.

polychromy /ˈpɒlɪkrəʊmɪ/ *n* polychromie *f*.

polycotton /ˌpɒlɪˈkɒtn/ **I** *n* polyester *m* et coton *m*.
II *modif* [*sheets*] en polyester et coton.

polyester /ˌpɒlɪˈestə(r)/ **I** *n* polyester *m*.
II *modif* [*garment etc*] en or de polyester.

polyethylene /ˌpɒlɪˈeθəliːn/ *n* = **polythene**.

polygamist /pəˈlɪgəmɪst/ *n* polygame *mf*.

polygamous /pəˈlɪgəməs/ *adj* polygame.

polygamy /pəˈlɪgəmɪ/ *n* polygamie *f*.

polyglot /ˈpɒlɪglɒt/ *n, adj* polyglotte (*mf*).

polygon /ˈpɒlɪgən, US -gɒn/ *n* polygone *m*.

polygonal /pəˈlɪgənl/ *adj* polygonal.

polygraph /ˈpɒlɪgrɑːf, US -græf/ **I** *n* détecteur *m* de mensonges.
II *modif* [*test*] de détection de mensonges.

polyhedral /ˌpɒlɪˈhedrəl/ *adj* [*form*] polyédrique; [*angle*] polyèdre.

polyhedron /ˌpɒlɪˈhiːdrən, US -drɒn/ *n* polyèdre *m*.

polymath /ˈpɒlɪmæθ/ *n* esprit *m* universel.

polymer /ˈpɒlɪmə(r)/ *n* polymère *m*.

polymorphism /ˌpɒlɪˈmɔːfɪzəm/ *n* polymorphisme *m*.

polymorphous /ˌpɒlɪˈmɔːfəs/ *adj* polymorphe.

Polynesia /ˌpɒlɪˈniːʒə/ *pr n* Polynésie *f*.

Polynesian /ˌpɒlɪˈniːʒn/ ▶ **1486**, **1402** **I** *n* **1** (person) Polynésien/-ienne *m/f*; **2** (language) polynésien *m*.
II *adj* polynésien/-ienne.

polynomial /ˌpɒlɪˈnəʊmɪəl/ **I** *n* polynôme *m*.
II *adj* polynomial.

polyp /ˈpɒlɪp/ *n* Med, Zool polype *m*.

polyphase /ˈpɒlɪfeɪz/ *adj* polyphasé.

polyphonic /ˌpɒlɪˈfɒnɪk/ *adj* polyphonique.

polyphony /pəˈlɪfənɪ/ *n* polyphonie *f*.

polypropylene /ˌpɒlɪˈprəʊpɪliːn/ *n* polypropylène *m*.

polypus /ˈpɒlɪpəs/ *n* = **polyp**.

polysemous /ˌpɒlɪˈsiːməs/ *adj* polysémique.

polysemy /ˌpɒlɪˈsiːmɪ/ *n* polysémie *f*.

polystyrene /ˌpɒlɪˈstaɪriːn/ **I** *n* polystyrène *m*; **expanded ~** polystyrène expansé.
II *modif* [*packaging, tile*] en polystyrène.

polystyrene: **~ cement** *n* colle *f* polystyrène; **~ chips** *npl* billes *fpl* de polystyrène.

polysyllabic /ˌpɒlɪsɪˈlæbɪk/ *adj* polysyllabique.

polysyllable /ˈpɒlɪsɪləbl/ *n* polysyllabe *m*.

polytechnic /ˌpɒlɪˈteknɪk/ *n* GB établissement *m* d'enseignement supérieur.

polytheism /ˈpɒlɪθiːɪzəm/ *n* polythéisme *m*.

polytheistic /ˌpɒlɪθiːˈɪstɪk/ *adj* polythéiste.

polythene /ˈpɒlɪθiːn/ GB **I** *n* polyéthylène *m*.
II *modif* [*sheeting*] de polyéthylène; **~ bag** sac *m* en plastique.

polyunsaturated /ˌpɒlɪʌnˈsætʃəreɪtɪd/ *adj* [*fat*] polyinsaturé.

polyunsaturates /ˌpɒlɪʌnˈsætʃərɪts/ *npl* acides *mpl* gras polyinsaturés; **high in ~** riche en acides gras polyinsaturés.

polyurethane /ˌpɒlɪˈjʊərəθeɪn/ *n, modif* polyuréthane (*m*).

polyvalent /ˌpɒlɪˈveɪlənt/ *adj* polyvalent.

polyvinyl /ˌpɒlɪˈvaɪnɪl/ **I** *n* polyvinyle *m*.
II *modif* [*acetate, chloride*] de polyvinyle; [*resin*] polyvinylique.

pom○ /pɒm/ *n* Austral injur = **pommy**.

pomade /pəˈmɑːd/ **I** *n* brillantine *f*.
II *vtr* brillantiner.

pomander /pəˈmændə(r)/ *n* diffuseur *m* de parfum.

pomegranate /ˈpɒmɪgrænɪt/ *n* **1** (fruit) grenade *f*; **2** (tree) grenadier *m*.

pomelo /ˈpʌmələʊ/ *n* (fruit, tree) pomelo *m*.

Pomeranian /ˌpɒməˈreɪnɪən/ *n* (dog) loulou *m* de Poméranie.

pommel /ˈpʌml/ **I** *n* **1** (on saddle, sword) pommeau *m*; **2** (in gymnastics) poignée *f*.
II *vtr* = **pummel**.

pommel horse *n* (in gymnastics) cheval *m* d'arçons.

pommy○ /ˈpɒmɪ/ *n* Austral injur Anglais/-e *m/f*.

pomp /pɒmp/ *n* pompe *f*; **with great ~** en grande pompe; **~ and circumstance** grand apparat.

Pompeii /pɒmˈpeɪiː/ ▶ **1818** *pr n* Pompéi.

Pompey /ˈpɒmpɪ/ *pr n* Pompée.

pompom, **pompon** /ˈpɒmpɒm/ *n* pompon *m*.

pompom girl *n* US majorette *f*.

pomposity /pɒmˈpɒsətɪ/ *n* (of manner) air *m* pompeux; (of voice) ton *m* pompeux.

pompous /ˈpɒmpəs/ *adj* [*person*] plein de suffisance; [*air, speech, style*] pompeux/-euse.

pompously /ˈpɒmpəslɪ/ *adv* [*speak*] d'un ton pompeux; [*behave*] de manière pompeuse.

ponce○† /pɒns/ GB **I** *n* **1** (pimp) souteneur *m*, maquereau○ *m*; **2** péj (homosexual) tapette○ *f*; **he looks a ~** il fait tapette○.
■ **ponce about**○, **ponce around**○ (show off) se pavaner.

poncho /ˈpɒntʃəʊ/ *n* (*pl* **~s**) poncho *m*.

pond /pɒnd/ *n* (large) étang *m*; (in garden) bassin *m*; (stagnant, for ducks) mare *f*.

ponder /ˈpɒndə(r)/ **I** *vtr* considérer [*options, possible action*]; réfléchir à [*past events*].
II *vi* réfléchir (**on** à); (more deeply) méditer (**on** sur).

ponderous /ˈpɒndərəs/ *adj* [*movement*] maladroit, lourd; [*tone*] pesant.

ponderously /ˈpɒndərəslɪ/ *adv* [*move*] lourdement; [*speak, write*] avec lourdeur.

pond: **~ life** *n* vie *f* animale des eaux stagnantes; **~weed** *n* potamot *m*.

pong○ /pɒŋ/ GB **I** *n* puanteur *f*; **what a ~!** ça pue○!
II *vi* puer○.
■ **pong out**○ GB: **~ out [sth]**, **~ [sth] out** empester [*place*].

pons Varolii /ˌpɒns væˈrɒlɪiː/ *n* (*pl* **pontes Varolii**) pont *m* de Varole.

pontiff /ˈpɒntɪf/ *n* pontife *m*; **the Supreme Pontiff** le souverain pontife.

pontifical /pɒnˈtɪfɪkl/ *adj* **1** Relig pontifical; **2** pej [*manner, tone*] pontifiant.

pontificate **I** /pɒnˈtɪfɪkət/ *n* pontificat *m*.
II /pɒnˈtɪfɪˌkeɪt/ *vi* pontifier (**about, on** sur).

Pontius Pilate /ˌpɒntjəs ˈpaɪlət/ *pr n* Ponce Pilate.

pontoon /pɒnˈtuːn/ *n* **1** (pier) ponton *m*; **2** Aviat (float) flotteur *m*; **3** ▶ **1282** GB Games vingt-et-un *m*.

pontoon bridge *n* pont *m* flottant.

pony /ˈpəʊnɪ/ **I** *n* **1** poney *m*; **2**○ GB (£25) vingt-cinq livres sterling.
II *modif* [*ride, trekking*] à poney.

ponytail /ˈpəʊnɪteɪl/ *n* queue *f* de cheval; **in a ~** en queue de cheval.

pooch○ /puːtʃ/ *n* clebs○ *m*, chien *m*.

poodle /ˈpuːdl/ *n* caniche *m*.

poof○ /pʊf/, **poofter**○ /ˈpʊftə(r)/ *n* GB injur (homosexual) tapette◐ *f* offensive, homosexuel *m*.

poofy○ /ˈpʊfɪ/ *adj* GB injur (effeminate) [*person, manner*] efféminé.

pooh /puː/ **I** *n* GB lang enfantin caca○ *m* baby talk.
II *excl* (expressing disgust) berk○!; (expressing scorn) peuh!

pooh-pooh○ /ˌpuːˈpuː/ *vtr* faire peu de cas de [*idea, anxiety*].

pool /puːl/ **I** *n* **1** (pond) étang *m*; (artificial) bassin *m*; (still spot in river) plan *m* d'eau; (underground: of oil, gas) nappe *f*; **2** (also **swimming ~**) piscine *f*; **3** (puddle) flaque *f*; **(to be lying in) a ~ of blood** (être étendu dans) une mare de sang; **a ~ of light** une flaque de lumière; **4** (kitty, in cards) mises *fpl*; gen cagnotte *f*; **5** (common supply) (of money, resources) pool *m*; (of experts) équipe *f* de réserve; (of ideas, experience) réservoir *m*; (of labour) réserve *f*; (of teachers, players, candidates) liste *f*; **6** Sport (billiards) billard *m* américain; **7** US Comm (monopoly trust) trust *m*; **8** US Fin (consortium) pool *m*; ▶ **car pool**, **gene pool etc**.
II pools *npl* GB (also **football ~s**) ≈ loto *m* sportif (*limité aux matchs de football*); **to do the ~s** jouer au loto sportif.
III *vtr* mettre [qch] en commun [*money, resources, information, experience*].
IDIOMS **to play dirty ~**○ US donner des coups en traître.

pool: **~ attendant** ▶ **1692** *n* surveillant/-e *m/f* de baignade; **~ liner** *n* revêtement *m* de piscine; **~ party** *n* réception *f* au bord de la piscine; **~ room** *n* salle *f* de billard américain; **~side** *adj* au bord de la piscine; **~ table** *n* table *f* de billard américain.

poop /puːp/ *n* **I 1** Naut (stern) poupe *f*; **2** (also **~ deck**) dunette *f*; **3**○ (dog's dirt) ¢ crotte *f*.

II○ *vi* US [*dog, child*] faire caca○.

pooped○ /pu:pt/ *adj* **to be ~ (out)** être crevé○.

pooper-scooper○ /'pu:pəsku:pə(r)/ *n* caninette® *f*.

poor /pɔ:(r), US pʊər/ **I** *n* **the ~** (+ *v pl*) les pauvres *mpl*.
II *adj* **1** (not wealthy) [*person, country*] pauvre (*never before n*) (**in** en); **I ended up £100 the ~er** je me suis retrouvé plus pauvre de cent livres; **to become** ou **get ~er** s'appauvrir; **2** (inferior) [*quality, start, result, record*] mauvais; [*work*] (of student, pupil) faible; (of worker, factory) mauvais; [*soldier, manager, performance*] piètre (*before n*), mauvais; [*education, English, communication, planning, advice*] mauvais; [*harvest, weather, forecast, visibility*] mauvais; [*health, eyesight, memory*] défectueux/-euse, mauvais; [*soil*] pauvre (*never before n*); [*appetite*] petit; [*chance, attendance*] faible; [*lighting*] mauvais; [*meal*] (insufficient) maigre; (lacking quality) mauvais; [*consolation*] piètre (*before n*); **to be ~ at** [*person*] être faible en [*maths, French*]; **to be a ~ sailor** ne pas avoir le pied marin; **I'm a ~ traveller** je supporte mal les voyages; **to be a ~ substitute for sth** ne pas valoir qch; **3** (deserving pity) pauvre (*before n*); **the ~ little boy** le pauvre petit garçon; **~ Eric!** pauvre Éric!; **~ you!** pauvre de toi!; **you ~ (old) thing!** mon/ma pauvre!; **she's got a cold, ~ thing** elle a attrapé un rhume, la pauvre; **4** (sorry, pathetic) [*attempt, creature*] pauvre; [*excuse*] piètre (*before n*).
IDIOMS **as ~ as a church mouse** pauvre comme Job; **the ~ man's champagne** le champagne du pauvre.

poor: **~ box** *n* tronc *m* des pauvres; **~ boy (sandwich)** *n* US, Culin sandwich *m*; **~ house** *n* Hist asile *m* de pauvres; **Poor Laws** *npl* GB Hist *lois régissant l'aide aux pauvres dans l'Angleterre victorienne*.

poorly /'pɔ:lɪ, US 'pʊərlɪ/ **I** *adj* malade, souffrant.
II *adv* **1** (not richly) [*live, dress, dressed*] pauvrement; **to be ~ off** être pauvre; **2** (badly) [*written, designed, paid, argued*] mal; **to do ~** [*company, student*] obtenir des résultats médiocres; **3** (inadequately) [*funded, managed, lit*] mal.

poor-mouth○ /'pɔ:maʊθ, US pʊərmaʊθ/ *vi* US se plaindre d'être pauvre.

poorness /'pɔ:nɪs, US 'pʊərnɪs/ *n* (of land, soil, diet) pauvreté *f*; (of education, pay) médiocrité *f*; (of appetite) manque *m*; (of eyesight, hearing) défaillance *f*.

poor: **~ relation** *n* lit, fig parent *m* pauvre; **~-spirited** *adj* timoré; **~ White** *n* US pej Blanc/Blanche *m/f* pauvre du Sud des États-Unis.

pop /pɒp/ **I** *n* **1** (sound) (*aussi onomat*) pan *m*; **to go ~** (explode) éclater; (make a sound) faire pan; **the balloons went ~** les ballons ont fait pan; **2**○ (drink) soda *m*; **3** (popular music) pop *m*, pop music *f*; **4**○ US (dad) (also **~s**) papa *m*; **5**○ GB (punch) coup *m* de poing; **to take a ~ at** envoyer un coup de poing à.
II *modif* [*concert, group, music, song, video*] pop; [*record, singer, star*] de pop.
III *vtr* (*p prés etc* **-pp-**) **1**○ (burst) faire éclater [*balloon, bubble*]; **2** (remove) faire sauter [*cork*]; **3**○ (put) **to ~ sth in(to)** mettre qch dans [*oven, cupboard, mouth*]; **to ~ a letter in the post** mettre une lettre à la poste; **to ~ one's head through the window** passer la tête par la fenêtre; **4**○ (take) prendre [*pills*]; **5**○ GB (pawn) mettre [qch] au clou○.
IV *vi* (*p prés etc* **-pp-**) **1** (go bang) [*balloon*] éclater; [*cork*] sauter; **2** [*ears*] se déboucher brusquement; **3** (bulge, burst) [*buttons*] sauter; **her eyes were ~ping out of her head** les yeux lui sortaient de la tête; **4**○ GB (go) **to ~ across** ou **over to** faire un saut○ dans [*shop, store*]; **to ~ into town/into the bank** faire un saut○ en ville/à la banque; **to ~ home/next door** faire un saut○ chez soi/chez les voisins.
IDIOMS **to ~ the question** faire sa demande en mariage.
■ **pop back**○ GB revenir; **I'll ~ back in 20 minutes** je reviendrai dans 20 minutes.
■ **pop in**○ GB passer; **I'll ~ in later** je passerai plus tard; **I've just ~ped in to say hello** je suis juste passé dire bonjour.
■ **pop off**○ GB **1** (leave) filer○; **2** (die) crever○.
■ **pop out** GB sortir; **I only ~ped out for a couple of minutes** je suis seulement sorti cinq minutes.
■ **pop round** GB, **pop over** GB passer; **to ~ over and see sb** passer voir qn; **~ over if you have time** passe si tu as le temps.
■ **pop up**○ GB (appear suddenly) [*head*] surgir; [*missing person*] refaire surface○.

pop: **~ charts** *npl* hit-parade *m*; **~ corn** pop-corn *m*.

pope /pəʊp/ *n* pape *m*; **Pope Paul VI** le Pape Paul VI.

popery‡ /'pəʊpərɪ/ *n* péj papisme *m* pej.

pop-eyed○ /'pɒpaɪd/ *adj* **1** (permanently) exorbités (*after n*); **to be ~** avoir les yeux exorbités; **2** (with amazement) ébahi.

pop gun *n* pistolet *m* à bouchon.

popish‡ /'pəʊpɪʃ/ *adj* péj papiste pej.

poplar /'pɒplə(r)/ *n* peuplier *m*.

poplin /'pɒplɪn/ **I** *n* popeline *f*.
II *modif* [*dress, blouse*] en popeline.

popover /'pɒpəʊvə(r)/ *n* US Culin chausson *m*.

poppadom, **poppadum** /'pɒpədəm/ *n* poppadum *m* (*fine galette de blé croustillante*).

popper○ /'pɒpə(r)/ *n* **1** GB (press-stud) bouton-pression *m*; **2** US Culin poêle *f* (*pour faire des popcorns*); **3**○ (argot des drogués) nitrite *m* d'amyle.

poppet○† /'pɒpɪt/ *n* GB **my (little) ~** ma puce; **she's a real ~** c'est un amour.

poppy /'pɒpɪ/ **I** *n* **1** Bot pavot *m*; **wild ~** coquelicot *m*; **2** (colour) rouge *m* coquelicot; **3** GB (worn in buttonhole) coquelicot *m* en papier (*porté en commémoration des soldats tombés au champ d'honneur*).
II *modif* [*seeds, fields*] de pavot.
III *adj* rouge coquelicot *inv*.

poppycock○† /'pɒpɪkɒk/ *n* ¢ sornettes○† *fpl*, balivernes *fpl*.

Poppy Day○ *n* GB anniversaire *m* de l'armistice (*de 1918*).

Popsicle® /'pɒpsɪkl/ *n* US glace *f* à l'eau.

pop sock *n* mi-bas *m*.

populace /'pɒpjʊləs/ *n* population *f*.

popular /'pɒpjʊlə(r)/ *adj* **1** (generally liked) [*actor, singer, politician*] populaire (**with, among** parmi); [*profession, hobby, sport*] répandu (**with, among** chez); [*food, dish*] prisé (**with, among** par); [*product, resort, colour, design*] en vogue (**with, among** chez); **John is very ~** John a beaucoup d'amis; **Smith was a ~ choice as chairman** le choix de Smith comme président a été très apprécié; **she's ~ with the boys** elle a du succès auprès des garçons; **I'm not very ~ with my husband at the moment** je n'ai pas tellement la cote○ auprès de mon mari en ce moment; **2** (of or for the people) [*music, song*] populaire; [*entertainment, TV programme*] grand public *inv*; [*science, history etc*] de vulgarisation; [*enthusiasm, interest, support*] du public; [*discontent, uprising*] du peuple; [*movement*] populaire; **to have ~ appeal** avoir du succès auprès du public; **contrary to ~ belief** contrairement à ce qu'on pense généralement; **the ~ image of sth** l'image qu'on se fait généralement de qch; **the ~ view** ou **perception of sth** l'opinion générale sur qch; **by ~ demand** ou **request** à la demande générale; **the ~ press** la presse populaire.

Popular Front *n* Front *m* populaire.

popularist /'pɒpjʊlərɪst/ *adj* gen du grand public; pej des masses.

popularity /ˌpɒpjʊ'lærətɪ/ *n* popularité *f* (**of** de; **with** auprès de); **to lose ~** perdre de sa popularité; **to gain ~** gagner en popularité.

popularization /ˌpɒpjʊləraɪ'zeɪʃn, US -rɪ'z-/ *n* popularisation *f*; (of ideas, science) vulgarisation *f*.

popularize /'pɒpjʊləraɪz/ *vtr* **1** (make fashionable) généraliser; **2** (make accessible) vulgariser.

popularizer /'pɒpjʊləraɪzə(r)/ *n* (of commodity) promoteur/-trice *m/f*; (of ideas, science) vulgarisateur/-trice *m/f*.

popularly /'pɒpjʊləlɪ/ *adv* généralement; **it is a ~ held belief that** les gens croient généralement que.

populate /'pɒpjʊleɪt/ **I** *vtr* peupler.
II populated *pp adj* peuplé (**with, by** de); **densely/sparsely ~d** très/peu peuplé.

population /ˌpɒpjʊ'leɪʃn/ **I** *n* population *f*.
II *modif* [*increase, decrease, figure*] démographique.

population: **~ control** *n* contrôle *m* des naissances; **~ explosion** *n* explosion *f* démographique.

populism /'pɒpjʊlɪzəm/ *n* populisme *m*.

populist /'pɒpjʊlɪst/ *n, adj* populiste (*mf*).

populous /'pɒpjʊləs/ *adj* populeux/-euse.

pop: **~-up book** *n* livre *m* avec découpes en relief; **~-up headlight** *n* Aut phare *m* escamotable; **~-up menu** *n* Comput menu *m* déroulant; **~-up toaster** grille-pain *m inv* vertical.

porcelain /'pɔ:səlɪn/ **I** *n* **1** (ware) porcelaine *f*; **a piece of ~** une porcelaine; **to collect ~** collectionner les porcelaines; **2** (substance) porcelaine *f*.
II *modif* [*cup, plate, doll*] en or de porcelaine; [*clay*] à porcelaine.

porcelain ware *n* vaisselle *f* en or de porcelaine.

porch /pɔ:tʃ/ *n* **1** (of house, church) porche *m*; **2** US (veranda) véranda *f*.

porcine /'pɔ:saɪn/ *adj* porcin.

porcupine /'pɔ:kjʊpaɪn/ *n* porc-épic *m*.

porcupine fish *n* poisson-globe *m*.

pore /pɔ:(r)/ *n* (all contexts) pore *m*.
■ **pore over**: **~ over [sth]** se plonger dans [*book*]; étudier soigneusement [*map, details*]; **she's always poring over her books** elle est toujours plongée dans ses livres.

pork /pɔ:k/ *n* (viande *f* de) porc *m*; **a leg of ~** un jambon.

pork: **~ barrel**○ *n* US Pol magouille○ *f* (*consistant, pour un élu, à faire passer un projet qui profite surtout à sa circonscription*); **~ butcher** ▶ 1692 *n* charcutier/-ière *m/f*; **~ chop** *n* côte *f* de porc.

porker /'pɔ:kə(r)/ *n* goret *m*.

pork: **~ pie** *n* ≈ pâté *m* en croûte; **~ pie hat** *n* feutre *m* rond; **~ sausage** *n* saucisse *f*; **~ scratchings** *npl* GB grattons *mpl*.

porky○ /'pɔ:kɪ/ *adj* gras comme un porc.

porn○ /pɔ:n/ (*abrév* = **pornography**) **I** *n* porno○ *m*; **it's ~** c'est du porno○.
II *modif* [*film, magazine, shop*] porno○ *inv*.

porno○ /'pɔ:nəʊ/ *adj* (*abrév* = **pornographic**) porno○ *inv*.

pornographic /ˌpɔ:nə'græfɪk/ *adj* pornographique.

pornography /pɔ:'nɒgrəfɪ/ *n* pornographie *f*; **child ~** pornographie *f* avec mineurs.

porosity /pɔ:'rɒsətɪ/ *n* porosité *f*.

porous /'pɔ:rəs/ *adj* **1** [*rock, wood, substance*] poreux/-euse; **2 ~ border** ou **frontier** fig frontière-passoire *f*.

porousness /'pɔ:rəsnɪs/ *n* porosité *f*.

porphyry /'pɔ:fɪrɪ/ *n* porphyre *m*.

porpoise /'pɔ:pəs/ *n* Zool marsouin *m*.

porridge /'pɒrɪdʒ, US 'pɔ:r-/ *n* **1** Culin porridge *m* (*bouillie de flocons d'avoine*); **2**○ GB argot des prisonniers **to do ~** faire de la taule○.

port /pɔːt/ I *n* **1** (harbour) port *m*; **in ~** au port; **to come into ~** entrer dans le port; **to put into ~** relâcher; **the ship left ~** le bateau a appareillé; **~ of despatch/embarkation/entry** port *m* d'expédition/d'embarquement/de débarquement; **~ of call** Naut escale *f*; fig (stop) arrêt *m*; **home ~** port *m* d'attache; **2** Wine porto *m*; **3** Aviat, Naut (window) = **porthole**; **4** Mil Naut (gunport) sabord *m*; **5** Aviat, Naut (left) bâbord *m*; **to ~/on the ~ side** à bâbord; **6** Tech (in engine) orifice *m*; **7** Comput port *m*.
II *modif* **1** (harbour) [*area, authorities, facilities, security*] portuaire; [*dues*] de port; **2** Aviat, Naut (left) [*entrance, engine, bow*] de bâbord.
III *vtr* Comput transporter [qch] (d'un système à l'autre).
IDIOMS **any ~ in a storm** nécessité fait loi.

portability /ˌpɔːtəˈbɪlətɪ/ *n* gen, Comput portabilité *f*.

portable /ˈpɔːtəbl/ I *n* portable *m*.
II *adj* **1** gen [*TV, telephone etc*] portatif/-ive, portable; **2** Comput [*software*] portable.

portage /ˈpɔːtɪdʒ/ *n* **1** (transport) port *m*; **2** (costs) frais *mpl* de port.

Portakabin® /ˈpɔːtəkæbɪn/ *n* gen bâtiment *m* préfabriqué; (on building site) baraque *f* (de chantier).

portal /ˈpɔːtl/ *n* portail *m*.

portcullis /ˌpɔːtˈkʌlɪs/ *n* herse *f* (*de forteresse*).

portend /pɔːˈtend/ *vtr* littér présager (**for** pour).

portent /ˈpɔːtent/ *n* littér **1** (omen) présage *m* (**of** de, **for** pour); **a ~ of doom** un présage de malheur; **2** (importance) **a day of ~** un jour décisif.

portentous /pɔːˈtentəs/ *adj* littér **1** (ominous) sinistre; **2** (significant) très important, capital; **3** (solemn) grave; **4** (pompous) pompeux/-euse.

portentously /pɔːˈtentəslɪ/ *adv* littér **1** (ominously) [*say, announce*] d'un ton solennel; **2** (pompously) [*say, announce*] d'un ton pompeux.

portentousness /pɔːˈtentəsnɪs/ *n* littér solennité *f* pej.

porter /ˈpɔːtə(r)/ ▶1692 *n* **1** (in station, airport, hotel) porteur *m*; (in hospital) brancardier *m*; (in market) débardeur *m*; (on expedition) porteur *m*; **2** GB (at entrance) (of hotel) portier *m*; (of apartment block) gardien/-ienne *m/f*; (of school, college) concierge *mf*; **3** US Rail (steward) employé *m* des wagons-lits; **4** (beer) porter *m*, bière *f* brune.

porterage /ˈpɔːtərɪdʒ/ *n* (costs) frais *mpl* de portage.

porterhouse (steak) /ˈpɔːtəhaʊs/ *n* châteaubriant *m*.

portfolio /pɔːtˈfəʊlɪəʊ/ *n* **1** (case) porte-documents *m inv*; (for drawings) carton *m* (à dessins); **2** Art, Phot (sample) portfolio *m* (**of** de); **3** Pol (post) portefeuille *m* (ministériel); **defence/finance ~** portefeuille de la Défense/des Finances; **minister without ~** ministre sans portefeuille; **4** Fin (of investments) portefeuille *m* (**of** de).

portfolio: **~ management** *n* Fin gestion *f* de portefeuille; **~ manager** *n* Fin gestionnaire *mf* de portefeuille.

porthole /ˈpɔːthəʊl/ *n* hublot *m*.

portico /ˈpɔːtɪkəʊ/ *n* portique *m*.

portion /ˈpɔːʃn/ *n* **1** (part, segment) (of house, machine, document, country) partie *f* (**of** de); (of group) part *f* (**of** de); **2** (share) (of money, food item) part *f* (**of** de); (of responsibility, blame) part *f* (**of** de); **3** (at meal) portion *f*; **an extra ~** une portion supplémentaire; **4** littér (fate) destin *m*.
■ **portion out**: **~ out [sth]**, **~ [sth] out** répartir (**among** parmi; **between** entre).

portliness /ˈpɔːtlɪnɪs/ *n* corpulence *f*.

portly /ˈpɔːtlɪ/ *adj* corpulent.

portmanteau /pɔːtˈmæntəʊ/ *n* (*pl* **-teaus** ou **-teaux**) malle *f*.

portmanteau word *n* mot-valise *m*.

portrait /ˈpɔːtreɪt, -trɪt/ *n* **1** Art, fig portrait *m* (**of** de); **family/group ~** portrait de famille/de groupe; **2** Comput portrait *m*.

portrait gallery *n* galerie *f* de portraits.

portraitist /ˈpɔːtreɪtɪst, -trɪtɪst/ ▶1692 *n* portraitiste *mf*.

portrait: **~ lens** *n* objectif *m* à portrait; **~ painter** ▶1692 *n* portraitiste *mf*; **~ photography** *n* photographie *f* de portrait.

portraiture /ˈpɔːtreɪtʃə(r), -trɪtʃə(r), US -treɪtʃʊər/ *n* art *m* du portrait.

portray /pɔːˈtreɪ/ *vtr* **1** (depict) dépeindre, décrire [*place, era, event*] (**as** comme étant); présenter [*person, group, situation*] (**as** comme étant); **2** Cin, Theat [*actor*] interpréter [*figure, character*]; [*film, play*] évoquer [*period*]; **3** Art [*artist*] peindre [*person*]; [*picture, artist*] représenter [*scene*].

portrayal /pɔːˈtreɪəl/ *n* **1** (by actor) interprétation *f* (**of** de); **2** (by author, filmmaker) portrait *m* (**of** de, **as** comme); **the media's ~ of women** le portrait que les médias dressent de la femme; **his ~ of country life** le tableau qu'il brosse de la vie à la campagne.

Portugal /ˈpɔːtʃʊgl/ ▶1131 *pr n* Portugal *m*; **in/to ~** au Portugal.

Portuguese /ˌpɔːtʃʊˈgiːz/ ▶1486, 1402 I *n* **1** (native) Portugais/-e *m/f*; **the ~** (+ *v pl*) les Portugais; **2** Ling portugais *m*.
II *adj* [*lesson, class, course*] de portugais; [*custom, landscape, literature*] portugais; [*ambassador, prime minister*] portugais, du Portugal.

Portuguese: **~ man-of-war** *n* Zool galère *f* portugaise; **~-speaking** *adj* [*person, country*] lusophone.

pose /pəʊz/ I *n* **1** (for portrait, photo) pose *f*; **to adopt a ~** adopter une pose; **2** péj (posture) pose *f*, frime *f*; **it's all a ~** c'est pour épater la galerie○; **to strike a ~** prendre une pose.
II *vtr* (present) poser [*problem*] (**for** pour); présenter [*challenge*] (**to** à); représenter [*threat, risk*] (**to** pour); soulever [*question*] (**about** de).
III *vi* **1** (for artist) poser (**for** pour; **with** avec); **to ~ for one's portrait** se faire faire son portrait; **2** (in front of mirror, audience) prendre des poses; **3** (masquerade) **to ~ as** se faire passer pour [*nurse, salesman*]; **4** péj (posture) frimer.

Poseidon /pɒˈsaɪdn/ *pr n* Poséidon.

poser○ /ˈpəʊzə(r)/ *n* **1** (person) frimeur/-euse○ *m/f*; **2** (question) colle *f*.

poseur /pəʊˈzɜː(r)/ *n* frimeur/-euse○ *m/f*.

posh○ /pɒʃ/ *adj* **1** (high-class) [*person*] huppé○; [*house, resort, clothes, car*] chic *inv*; [*voice, accent*] distingué; [*wedding, party*] mondain; **the ~ part of town** les quartiers chic de la ville; **2** péj (snobbish) [*person*] snob; [*school, district*] de riches, de rupins○; [*clientele, club*] sélect○; **to talk ~**○ parler comme les gens de la haute○.
■ **posh up**○ GB: **to be all ~ed up** [*person*] être tiré à quatre épingles; [*room, flat*] être briqué.

posit /ˈpɒzɪt/ *vtr* sout avancer.

position /pəˈzɪʃn/ I *n* **1** (situation, state) situation *f*; **to be in an awkward/impossible ~** se trouver dans une situation délicate/impossible; **the management is in a strong ~** la direction est en position de force; **to be in a ~ to do** être en mesure de faire; **to be in a good ~ to do** être bien placé pour faire; **to be in no ~ to do** être mal placé pour faire; **to undertake sth from a ~ of strength** entreprendre qch à partir d'une position de force; **to be** ou **find oneself in the happy/unhappy ~ of doing** avoir la chance/malchance de faire; **if I were in your ~** si j'étais à ta place: **put yourself in my ~!** mets-toi à ma place!; **well, what's the ~?** alors, qu'est-ce qui se passe?; **2** (attitude, stance) position *f*; **I understand your ~, but...** je comprends ta position, mais...; **the official/British ~** la position officielle/britannique; **there has been a change in their negotiating ~** ils ont changé leur position dans les négociations; **3** (place, location) position *f*; **to be in ~** (in place) être en place; (ready) être prêt; **to get into ~** se mettre en place, prendre position; **to hold sth in ~** [*glue, string*] maintenir qch en place; **please put everything back in its original ~** veuillez tout remettre à sa place; **I can't see anything from this ~** je ne vois rien d'ici; **the house is in a good ~** la maison est bien située; **4** (posture, attitude of body) position *f*; **the sitting ~** la position assise; **to be in a sitting/kneeling ~** être assis/agenouillé; **5** (of lever, switch) position *f*; **in the on/off ~** sur la position ouvert/fermé; **6** (ranking) place *f*, rang *m*; (in sport, competitive event) position *f*; **can the airline retain its ~ among the leaders?** la compagnie aérienne peut-elle conserver sa place parmi les premières?; **to be in third ~** être en troisième position; **7** Sport poste *m*; **his usual ~ as goalkeeper** son poste habituel de gardien de but; **what ~ does he play?** quel est son poste?; **8** (job) poste *m*; **to hold** ou **occupy a senior ~** occuper un poste responsable; **her ~ as party leader** son poste de chef du parti; **a ~ of responsibility** un poste de responsabilité; **9** (place in society) position *f*, statut *m*; **10** Mil position *f*; **11** (counter) guichet *m*; **'~ closed'** 'guichet fermé'.
II *vtr* **1** (station) poster [*policemen, soldiers*]; **2** (situate) disposer [*flowerbed, house extension*]; **3** (get correct angle) orienter [*telescope, lamp, aerial*].
III *v refl* **to ~ oneself** prendre position.

positive /ˈpɒzətɪv/ I *n* **1** Ling (degré *m*) affirmatif *m*; **in the ~** à la forme affirmative; **2** Phot positif *m*; **3** Math nombre *m* positif; **4** Elec (pôle *m*) positif *m*.
II *adj* **1** (affirmative) [*answer*] positif/-ive; **2** (optimistic) [*message, person, response, attitude, tone*] positif/-ive; **to be ~ about** être enthousiaste à propos de [*idea, proposal*]; **~ thinking** manière *f* de voir les choses de façon positive; **to think ~** voir les choses de façon positive; **3** (constructive) [*contribution, effect, progress*] positif/-ive; [*advantage, good*] réel/réelle; **these measures could do some ~ good** ces mesures pourraient produire un bien réel; **4** (pleasant) [*association, experience, feeling*] positif/-ive; **5** (sure) [*identification, proof*] formel/-elle; [*fact*] indéniable; **to be ~** être sûr (**about** de; **that** que); **~!** certain!; **6** (forceful) [*action, measure*] catégorique; [*kick, shot*] sec/sèche; [*order*] formel/-elle; **7** Med, Sci [*reaction, result, test*] positif/-ive; **8** Chem, Electron, Math, Phot, Phys positif/-ive; **9** (extreme) [*pleasure*] pur (*before n*); [*disgrace, outrage*] véritable (*before n*); [*genius*] véritable (*before n*).

positive discrimination *n* mesures *fpl* antidiscriminatoires.

positively /ˈpɒzətɪvlɪ/ *adv* **1** (constructively) [*contribute, criticize*] de façon constructive; **to think ~** voir les choses de façon positive; **2** (favourably) [*react, refer, respond, speak*] favorablement; **3** (actively) [*participate, prepare, promote*] activement; **4** (definitely) [*identify, prove*] formellement; **5** (absolutely) [*beautiful, dangerous, miraculous, disgraceful, idiotic*] vraiment; [*refuse, forbid*] catégoriquement; **~ not/nothing** absolument pas/rien; **I ~ hated the film** j'ai carrément détesté ce film; **7** Electron, Phys **~ charged** à charge positive.

positiveness /ˈpɒzətɪvnɪs/ *n* positivité *f*.

positive vetting *n* Admin enquête *f* administrative.

positivism /ˈpɒzɪtɪvɪzəm/ *n* positivisme *m*.

positivist /ˈpɒzɪtɪvɪst/ *n* positiviste *mf*.

positron /ˈpɒzɪtrɒn/ *n* posit(r)on *m*.

posse /ˈpɒsɪ/ *n* **1** Hist (sheriff's) détachement *m*; **2** (group) (of pressmen) équipe *f* (**of** de); (of security men) détachement *m* (**of** de).
IDIOMS **to be ahead of the ~** être le premier/les premières.

possess /pəˈzes/ **I** *vtr* **1** (have) posséder [*property, weapon, proof*]; (illegally) détenir [*arms, drugs*]; **2** (be endowed with) posséder [*quality, facility, charm*]; avoir [*power, advantage*]; **to be ~ed of** sout avoir [*charm, feature*]; **3** (take control of) [*anger, fury*] s'emparer de [*person*]; [*devil*] posséder [*person*]; **to be ~ed by** être obsédé par [*idea, illusion*]; être dévoré par [*jealousy*]; **what ~ed you/him to do that?** qu'est-ce qui t'a/lui a pris de faire ça?
II possessed *pp adj* (by demon) possédé; **he was screaming like one ~ed** il hurlait comme un possédé.

possession /pəˈzeʃn/ **I** *n* **1** (state of having) possession *f* (**of** de); **the ~ of certain abilities** le fait d'avoir certaines compétences; **to be in ~ of** être en possession de [*passport, degree, evidence*]; **to come into sb's ~** entrer en la possession de qn; **to come into the ~ of a newspaper** [*information*] tomber en la possession d'un journal; **to have sth in one's ~** avoir qch en sa possession; **to have ~ of sth** posséder qch; **to get ~ of sth** (legally) acquérir qch; (by force) s'approprier qch; **among the documents in our ~** parmi les documents dont nous disposons; **2** Jur (illegal) détention *f* (**of** de); **to be in ~ of** détenir [*arms, drugs*]; **3** Jur (of property) jouissance *f* (**of** de) ; **to come into ~ of** entrer en jouissance or en possession de; **to take ~ of** prendre possession de [*premises, property*]; **to be in ~** occuper les lieux; **4** Sport **to be in** ou **have ~** contrôler le ballon; **to win/lose ~** s'emparer du/perdre le ballon; **5** (by demon) possession *f* (**by** par); **6** (colonial) possession *f*.
II possessions *npl* (belongings) biens *mpl*.
IDIOMS **~ is nine-tenths** ou **nine points of the law** Prov possession vaut titre Prov.

possession order *n* ordonnance *f* de retour en possession.

possessive /pəˈzesɪv/ **I** *n* Ling possessif *m*; **in the ~** à la forme possessive.
II *adj* **1** (jealous) [*person, behaviour*] possessif/-ive (**towards** à l'égard de; **with** avec); **2** (slow to share) possessif/-ive; **he's ~ about his toys** il n'aime pas prêter ses jouets; **3** Ling [*pronoun, adjective*] possessif/-ive.

possessively /pəˈzesɪvlɪ/ *adv* de façon possessive.

possessiveness /pəˈzesɪvnɪs/ *n* (with people) possessivité *f* (**towards** envers); (with things) instinct *m* de possession (**about** vis-à-vis de).

possessor /pəˈzesə(r)/ *n* possesseur *m*; **to be the ~ of** être en possession de [*object*]; **the proud ~ of** l'heureux/-euse propriétaire *m/f* de.

possibility /ˌpɒsəˈbɪlətɪ/ **I** *n* **1** (chance, prospect) possibilité *f*; **he had ruled out the ~ that he might win** ou **of winning** il avait exclu la possibilité de gagner; **there is a definite ~ that he'll come** il y a de très grandes chances qu'il vienne; **there is no ~ of him succeeding** il est impossible qu'il réussisse; **the ~ of him succeeding** ses chances de réussite; **there is no ~ of changing the text** il est impossible de changer le texte; **within the bounds of ~** dans la limite du possible; **beyond the bounds of ~** au delà des limites du possible; **there is little or no ~ of a strike** les chances de grève sont minimes; **2** (eventuality) **the ~ of a refusal/of failure** l'éventualité d'un refus/d'un échec; **the collapse of the company is now a ~** l'effondrement de la société est à présent possible.
II possibilities *npl* (potential) **the idea/the market has possibilities** l'idée/le marché a un fort potentiel; **this invention opens up fantastic possibilities** cette invention ouvre des perspectives fantastiques.

possible /ˈpɒsəbl/ **I** *n* **a list of ~s for the vacancy** une liste de candidats possibles pour le poste; **she's a ~ for the team** c'est une joueuse possible pour l'équipe; **it's within the realms of the ~** c'est dans le domaine du possible.
II *adj* **1** (likely to happen) [*consequence, litigation, risk*] possible; **it's quite ~** c'est tout à fait possible; **2** (that can be achieved) [*strategy, result, improvements*] possible; **to be ~ to do sth** être possible de faire qch; **the experiments are technically ~** les expériences sont techniquement possibles; **if ~, I would like a change** j'aimerais changer, si possible; **he did as much as ~** il a fait tout son possible; **as far as ~** dans la mesure du possible; **I'll do it as soon as ~** je le ferai dès que possible; **as quickly as ~** le plus vite possible; **we interviewed witnesses wherever ~** nous avons interrogé les témoins chaque fois que c'était possible; **to make sth ~** rendre qch possible; **none of this would have been ~ without your help** rien de tout cela n'aurait été possible sans votre aide; **3** (when conjecturing) possible (**to do** de faire; **that** que + *subj*); **it's ~ (that) he took it** il est possible qu'il l'ait pris; **4** (acceptable) [*solution, explanation, candidate*] possible; **5** (for emphasis) **of what ~ interest/benefit can it be to you?** quel intérêt/avantage cela peut-il bien avoir pour toi?; **there can be no ~ excuse for such behaviour** un tel comportement est inexcusable.

possibly /ˈpɒsəblɪ/ *adv* **1** (maybe) peut-être; **pornography is ~ to blame** la pornographie en est peut-être la cause; **the infection is ~ due to contaminated water** l'infection est peut-être due à de l'eau contaminée; **the house was ~ once an inn** autrefois la maison était peut-être une auberge; **'will it rain tonight?'—'~'** 'va-t-il pleuvoir ce soir?'—'peut-être (bien)'; **~, but is there any evidence?** peut-être (bien), mais y a-t-il des preuves?; **2** (for emphasis) **how could they ~ understand?** comment donc pourraient-ils comprendre?; **what can he ~ do to you?** qu'est-ce que tu veux qu'il te fasse?; **we can't ~ afford it** nous n'en avons absolument pas les moyens; **I can't ~ stay here** je ne peux absolument pas rester ici; **I'll do everything I ~ can** je ferai (absolument) tout mon possible; **she'll come as soon as she ~ can** elle viendra dès que cela lui sera possible.

possum○ /ˈpɒsəm/ *n* opossum *m*; **to play ~** faire le mort.

post /pəʊst/ **I** *n* **1** Admin (job) poste *m* (**as** comme; **of** de); **administrative ~** poste *m* administratif; **defence ~** poste *m* à la défense; **management ~** poste *m* de cadre; **party ~** poste *m* au parti; **to hold a ~** occuper un poste; **to have/fill a ~** avoir/remplir un poste; **to take up a ~** prendre un poste; **to offer sb a ~** proposer un poste à qn; **2** GB Post (system) poste *f*; (letters) courrier *m*; (delivery) distribution *f*; **to send sth/notify sb by ~** envoyer qch/avertir qn par la poste; **(to reply) by return of ~** (répondre) par retour du courrier; **to put sth in the ~** mettre qch à la poste; **it was lost in the ~** cela s'est égaré dans le courrier; **to get sth through the ~** recevoir qch par la poste; **your cheque is in the ~** votre chèque est au courrier; **is there any ~ for me?** est-ce que j'ai du courrier?; **has the ~ come yet?** est-ce que le courrier est arrivé?; **to deal with/answer one's ~** s'occuper de/répondre à son courrier; **it came in today's ~** il est arrivé par la poste aujourd'hui; **has the ~ gone yet?** le courrier est-il déjà parti?; **please take this letter to the ~** voulez-vous me poster cette lettre?; **to catch/miss the ~** ne pas manquer/manquer la levée; **3** (duty, station) gen, Mil poste *m*; **at one's ~** à son poste; **to remain at one's** ou **in ~** demeurer à son poste; **4** (pole) gen, Turf poteau *m*; **starting/finishing ~** poteau *m* de départ/d'arrivée; **beaten at the ~** battu au poteau; **to be the first past the ~** Turf être le premier à l'arrivée; fig Pol obtenir la majorité; **5** (in soccer) montant *m* des cages; **6†** (for stagecoach) poste *f*.
II post- (*dans composés*) post-; **~-1992, things changed** après 1992, les choses ont changé; **in ~-1992 Europe** dans l'Europe d'après 1992; **in the ~-Cold War years** dans les années qui ont suivi la guerre froide.
III *vtr* **1** GB (send by post) poster or expédier (par la poste); (put in letterbox) mettre [qch] à la poste; **2** (stick up) afficher [*notice, poster, rules*]; annoncer [*details, results*]; **to be ~ed missing in action** être porté disparu au combat; **~ no bills** défense d'afficher; **3** gen, Mil (send abroad) affecter (**to** à); **to be ~ed overseas/to a unit** être affecté outre-mer/à une unité; **4** (station) gen, Mil poster [*guard, sentry*]; **5** US Jur fournir [*bail*]; **6** Accts inscrire [*entry*]; tenir [qch] à jour [*ledger*].
IV *vi* Hist voyager par la poste.
IDIOMS **to keep sb ~ed (about sth)** tenir qn au courant (de qch); **to be left at the ~** rester sur la touche.
■ **post off** GB: **~ [sth] off, ~ off [sth]** mettre [qch] à la poste.
■ **post on** GB: **~ on [sth], ~ [sth] on** faire suivre; **I will ~ it on to you** je vous le ferai suivre.
■ **post up**: **~ up [sth], ~ [sth] up** afficher [*information, notice*].

postage /ˈpəʊstɪdʒ/ *n* affranchissement *m*, tarif *m* postal; **how much is the ~ for Belgium?** quel est le tarif (postal) pour la Belgique?; **including ~ and packing** frais *mpl* d'expédition inclus; **~ extra** affranchissement en supplément; **£12 plus ~** 12 livres sterling plus affranchissement; **~ free** franc de port.

postage: **~ meter** *n* US machine *f* à affranchir; **~ rates** *npl* tarifs *mpl* postaux; **~ stamp** *n* timbre-poste *m*.

postal /ˈpəʊstl/ *adj* [*charges, district*] postal; [*worker*] des Postes; [*application*] par la poste; [*strike*] des employés des Postes; **~ service** courrier *m*; **US ~ Service** Service *m* des Postes des États-Unis; **~ ballot** vote *m* par correspondance.

postal order, PO *n* GB mandat *m* (**for** de).

postal vote *n* GB (process) vote *m* par correspondance; (paper) bulletin *m* de vote par correspondance.

postbag /ˈpəʊstbæg/ *n* GB **1** lit sac *m* postal; **2** (mail) courrier *m*.

post: **~box** *n* GB boîte *f* aux lettres; **~card, pc** *n* carte *f* postale; **~ chaise** *n* chaise *f* de poste; **~ code** *n* GB code *m* postal.

postdate /ˌpəʊstˈdeɪt/ *vtr* postdater.

postdoctoral /ˌpəʊstˈdɒktərəl/ *adj* [*research, studies*] d'après-doctorat.

poster /ˈpəʊstə(r)/ *n* (for information) affiche *f*; (decorative) poster *m*; **election/Aids ~** affiche *f* électorale/sur le sida; **to put up a ~** mettre une affiche or un poster au mur.

poste restante /ˌpəʊst ˈrestɑːnt, US reˈstænt/ *n, modif, adv* GB poste *f* restante; **to send sth ~** envoyer qch poste restante.

posterior /pɒˈstɪərɪə(r)/ **I** *n* hum (buttocks) derrière *m*.
II *adj* sout postérieur (**to** à).

posterity /pɒˈsterətɪ/ *n* **1** (future generations) postérité *f*; **to go down to ~ as** passer à la postérité en tant que; **2** (descendants) sout postérité *f*.

poster paint *n* gouache *f*.

post-free /ˌpəʊstˈfriː/ *adj, adv* franc de port *inv*.

postgraduate /ˌpəʊstˈgrædʒʊət/ **I** *n* ≈ étudiant/-e *m/f* de troisième cycle.
II *adj* ≈ de troisième cycle.

post: **~ haste**† *adv* GB en toute hâte; **~-horn** *n* cornet *m* de poste; **~-horse** *n* cheval *m* de poste; **~-house** *n* relais *m* de poste.

posthumous /ˈpɒstjʊməs, US ˈpɒstʃəməs/ *adj* posthume.

posthumously /ˈpɒstjʊməslɪ, US ˈpɒstʃəməslɪ/ *adv* [*publish*] après la mort de l'auteur; [*award*] à titre posthume.

postiche /pɒˈstiːʃ/ **I** *n* mascarade *f*.
II *adj* postiche.

postil(l)ion /pɒˈstɪlɪən/ *n* postillon *m*.

postimpressionism /ˌpəʊst ɪmˈpreʃənɪzəm/ *n* post-impressionnisme *m*.

postimpressionist /ˌpəʊstɪmˈpreʃənɪst/ *n, adj* post-impressionniste (*mf*).

postindustrial /ˌpəʊstɪnˈdʌstrɪəl/ *adj* post-industriel/-ielle.

posting /ˈpəʊstɪŋ/ *n* **1** (job) affectation *f* (**to** à); **an overseas ~** une affectation outre-mer; **2** GB Post envoi *m*; **proof of ~** justificatif *m* d'expédition.

post-lingually deaf *adj* sourd post-linguistique.

postman /ˈpəʊstmən/ ▶1692 *n* facteur *m*.

postmark /ˈpəʊstmɑːk/ **I** *n* cachet *m* de la poste; **date as ~** le cachet de la poste faisant foi.
II *vtr* timbrer; **the card was ~ed Brussels** la carte était timbrée de Bruxelles.

post: **~master** ▶1692 *n* receveur *m* des Postes; **Postmaster General**, **PMG** *n* ministre *m* des Postes et Télécommunications; **~mistress** ▶1692 *n* receveuse *f* des Postes.

postmodern /ˌpəʊstˈmɒdn/ *adj* postmoderne.

postmodernism /ˌpəʊstˈmɒdənɪzəm/ *n* postmodernisme *m*.

postmodernist /ˌpəʊstˈmɒdənɪst/ *n, adj* postmoderniste (*mf*).

post-mortem /ˌpəʊstˈmɔːtəm/ **I** *n* Med autopsie *f*; fig autopsie *f*, analyse *f* rétrospective.
II *adj* [*investigation*] rétrospectif/-ive; **~ examination** autopsie *f*.

post-natal /ˌpəʊstˈneɪtl/ *adj* post-natal.

post-natal depression, **PND** *n* dépression *f* post-natale.

post office **I** *n* **1** (building) poste *f*, bureau *m* de poste; **main ~** poste *f* principale; **2** (institution) (also **Post Office**, **PO**) **the ~** la poste, le service des Postes.
II *modif* [*management, staff, strike*] de la poste, des Postes.

Post Office Box *n* boîte *f* postale.

post-operative /ˌpəʊstˈɒpərətɪv, US -reɪt-/ *adj* Med postopératoire.

post paid *adv* port payé.

postpone /pəˈspəʊn/ *vtr* reporter, remettre (**until** à; **for** de).

postponement /pəˈspəʊnmənt/ *n* report *m*, renvoi *m* (**of** de; **until** à).

postposition /ˌpəʊstpəˈzɪʃn/ *n* postposition *f*.

postpositive /ˌpəʊstˈpɒzətɪv/ **I** *n* postpositive *f*.
II *adj* postpositif/-ive.

postprandial /ˌpəʊstˈprændɪəl/ *adj* sout hum (nap, speech etc) (d')après le repas; Med post-prandial.

postscript /ˈpəʊsskrɪpt/ *n* **1** (at end of letter) post-scriptum *m inv* (**to** à); (to book, document) postface *f* (**to** à); fig suite *f* (**to** à); **2** fig (spoken) **can I add a brief ~ to that?** puis-je ajouter un petit quelque chose?

post-tax /ˌpəʊstˈtæks/ *adj, adv* après paiement des impôts.

postulant /ˈpɒstjʊlənt, US -tʃʊ-/ *n* postulant/-e *m/f*.

postulate **I** /ˈpɒstjʊlət, US -tʃʊ-/ *n* postulat *m*.
II /ˈpɒstjʊleɪt, US -tʃʊ-/ *vtr* poser [qch] comme postulat; **to ~ that** postuler que.

posture /ˈpɒstʃə(r)/ **I** *n* **1** (pose) posture *f*; fig (stance) position *f*; **2** (bearing) maintien *m*; **to have good/bad ~** se tenir bien/mal.
II *vi* péj poser, prendre des poses.

posturing /ˈpɒstʃərɪŋ/ *n* péj affectation *f*.

post-viral (fatigue) syndrome ▶1354 *n* encéphalomyélite *f* myalgique.

postvocalic /ˌpəʊstvəˈkælɪk/ *adj* postvocalique.

postwar /ˌpəʊstˈwɔː(r)/ *adj* d'après-guerre; **the ~ period** ou **years** l'après-guerre *m*.

postwoman /ˈpəʊstwʊmən/ ▶1692 *n* préposée *f* (des Postes).

posy /ˈpəʊzɪ/ *n* petit bouquet *m* (de fleurs).

pot /pɒt/ **I** *n* **1** (container) (for jam) pot *m* (**of** de); (for paint, glue) pot *m* (**of** de); **2** (also **tea ~**) théière *f*; **a ~ of tea for two** deux thés; **to make a ~ of tea** faire du thé; **3** (also **coffee ~**) cafetière *f*; **to make a ~ of coffee** faire du café; **4** (saucepan) casserole *f*; **~s and pans** casseroles; **5** (piece of pottery) poterie *f*; **to throw a ~** tourner un pot; **6** (also **plant ~**) pot *m* (**of** de); **7**○ (drug) (marijuana) herbe○ *f*; (hashish) hasch○ *m*; **to smoke ~** fumer de l'herbe○ (or du hasch○); **8** (also **chamber ~**) pot *m* de chambre; (for infant) pot *m*; **9**○ (belly) bedaine *f*; **10** (in billiards) mise *f* en blouse; **11** US (in gambling) (pool) cagnotte *f*; **12**○ (trophy) coupe *f*.
II *vtr* (**-tt-**) **1** mettre [qch] en pot [*jam*]; mettre [qch] en conserve [*shrimps*]; **2** (in billiards) **to ~ the red** blouser la bille rouge; **3** mettre [qn] sur le pot [*baby*]; **4** (also **~ up**) mettre [qch] en pot, empoter [*plant*]; **5**○ (shoot) abattre [*rabbit, pigeon*].
III *vi* **1** [*potter*] faire de la poterie; **2 to ~**○ **at sth** canarder○ qch.
IV potted *pp adj* **1** Culin **~ted meat** GB terrine *f* de viande; **~ted shrimps** crevettes *fpl* conservées (*dans du beurre*); **2** [*palm, plant*] en pot; **3** (condensed) [*biography, history*] bref/brève; [*version*] abrégé.
IDIOMS **to go to ~**○ (person) se laisser aller; (thing) aller à vau-l'eau; **to have/make ~s of money**○ GB avoir/faire un tas○ d'argent; **to keep the ~ boiling** (in children's games) garder le rythme; **a watched ~ never boils** Prov quand on est impatient chaque seconde semble durer une éternité; **to take ~ luck** (for meal) GB manger à la fortune du pot; (for hotel room etc) prendre ce que l'on trouve.

potable /ˈpəʊtəbl/ *adj* potable.

potash /ˈpɒtæʃ/ *n* potasse *f*.

potassium /pəˈtæsɪəm/ **I** *n* potassium *m*.
II *modif* [*carbonate, compound*] de potassium.

potation /pəˈteɪʃn/ *n* sout (act) libations *fpl*; (drink) boisson *f*.

potato /pəˈteɪtəʊ/ *n* (*pl* **-es**) Bot, Culin pomme *f* de terre; **a little more ~?** encore un peu de pommes de terre?

potato: **~ beetle** *n* doryphore *m*; **~ blight** *n* maladie *f* de la pomme de terre; **~ bug** *n* = **potato beetle**; **~ crisps** GB, **~ chips** US *npl* chips *fpl*; **~ masher** *n* presse-purée *m inv*; **~ peeler** *n* éplucheLégumes *m inv*, économe *m*, couteau-éplucheur *m*.

pot: **~ bellied** *adj* [*person*] (from overeating) bedonnant○; (from hunger) au ventre ballonné; [*stove*] renflé; **~ belly** *n* (from overeating) bedaine *f*; (from malnutrition) ventre *m* gonflé; **~boiler** *n* péj œuvre *f* alimentaire; **~-bound** [*plant*] à l'étroit dans son pot; **~ cheese** *n* US fromage blanc *m* (*égoutté*).

poteen /pɒˈtiːn/ *n* whisky *m* (distillé en fraude).

potency /ˈpəʊtnsɪ/ *n* **1** (strength) (of drug, remedy, image, voice) puissance *f*; (of drink) force *f*; **2** (sexual ability) virilité *f*.

potent /ˈpəʊtnt/ *adj* **1** (strong) [*argument, factor, force, weapon, image, symbol, drug, remedy*] puissant; [*alcoholic drink, mixture*] fort; **2** (able to have sex) [*man*] viril.

potentate /ˈpəʊtnteɪt/ *n* potentat *m*.

potential /pəˈtenʃl/ **I** *n* (all contexts) potentiel *m* (**as** en tant que; **for** de); **growth/human/industrial/sales ~** potentiel de croissance/humain/industriel/de vente; **the ~ to do** les qualités nécessaires pour faire; **to have ~** avoir du potentiel or des capacités; **to fulfil one's ~** montrer de quoi on est capable.
II *adj* (possible) [*buyer, danger, energy, disaster, market, target, value, victim*] potentiel/-ielle; [*champion, bestseller, rival*] en puissance; [*bidder, investor*] éventuel/-elle; **he is a ~ leader/musician** il a toutes les qualités d'un futur chef/musicien; **the play is a ~ success** la pièce a toutes les qualités pour réussir.

potential difference *n* Phys différence *f* de potentiel.

potentiality /pəˌtenʃɪˈælətɪ/ *n* capacités *fpl* (**as** comme).

potentially /pəˈtenʃəlɪ/ *adv* potentiellement.

pothead○ /ˈpɒthed/ *n* drogué/-e *m/f* (*à la marijuana*).

pother○ /ˈpɒðə(r)/ *n* agitation *f*; **to be in a ~** être très agité.

pothole /ˈpɒthəʊl/ *n* **1** (in road) fondrière *f*, nid *m* de poule; **2** Geol (in riverbed) marmite *f* torrentielle; (in rock) grotte *f*, gouffre *m*; (system of passages) réseau *m* souterrain (de grottes).

pot: **~holer** *n* GB spéléologue *mf*; **~holing** ▶1282 *n* GB spéléologie *f*; **~hook** *n* crémaillère *f*; **~-hunter** *n* chasseur *m* de trophées.

potion /ˈpəʊʃn/ *n* potion *f*; **magic ~** potion magique; **love ~** philtre *m* (d'amour).

potlatch /ˈpɒtlætʃ/ *n* **1** Anthrop fête *f* des échanges de cadeaux (*chez les Indiens d'Amérique*); **2** US (party) fête *f* à tout casser○.

pot: **~pie** *n* US tourte *f* à la viande; **~ plant** *n* plante *f* d'appartement.

potpourri /ˌpəʊˈpʊərɪ, US ˌpəʊpəˈriː/ *n* (all contexts) pot-pourri *m*.

pot roast /ˈpɒtrəʊst/ **I** *n* rôti *m* (*cuit dans une cocotte*).
II pot-roast *vtr* faire cuire [qch] à la cocotte.

pot: **~ scrub** *n* tampon *m* à récurer; **~sherd** *n* tesson *m* de poterie.

potshot /ˈpɒtʃɒt/ *n* **to take a ~ at sth** tirer à vue sur qch.

potter /ˈpɒtə(r)/ **I** ▶1692 *n* potier *m*.
II *vi* GB = **potter about**.
■ **potter about**, **potter around** GB (do odd jobs) bricoler○; (go about daily chores) suivre son petit train-train○; (pass time idly) traîner.
■ **potter along** GB poursuivre son petit bonhomme de chemin.

potter: **~'s field** *n* US cimetière *m* des pauvres; **~'s wheel** *n* tour *m* de potier.

pottery /ˈpɒtərɪ/ **I** *n* **1** (craft, subject) poterie *f*; **2** ¢ (ware) poteries *fpl*; **a piece of ~** une poterie; **to sell/make ~** vendre/fabriquer des poteries; **3** (factory, workshop) poterie *f*.
II *modif* [*dish*] en terre; **~ class** cours *m* de poterie; **~ town** ville réputée pour ses poteries.

pot: **~ting compost** *n* terreau *m*; **~ting shed** *n* abri *m* de jardin.

potty○ /ˈpɒtɪ/ **I** *n* lang enfantin pot *m* (d'enfant).
II *adj* GB **1** (crazy) dingue○; **to drive sb ~** rendre qn dingue○; **2** (foolish) [*scheme, idea*] farfelu○; **3** (enthusiastic) **to be ~ about sb/sth** être toqué○ de qn/qch.

potty-train /ˈpɒtɪtreɪn/ *vtr* **to ~ a child** apprendre à un enfant à aller sur le pot.

potty-trained /ˈpɒtɪtreɪnd/ *pp adj* [*child*] propre.

pouch /paʊtʃ/ *n* **1** (bag) petit sac *m*; (for tobacco) blague *f* (à tabac); (for ammunition) étui *m* (à munitions); (for cartridges) giberne *f*; (for mail) sac *m* postal; (for money) bourse *f*;

(of clothes, skin) poche *f*; **2** Zool (of marsupials) poche *f* ventrale; (of rodents) abajoue *f*.

pouf(fe) /pu:f/ *n* **1** (cushion) pouf *m*; **2** GB = **poof**.

poulterer /ˈpəʊltərə(r)/ **▶1692** *n* GB volailler/-ère *m*/*f*.

poultice /ˈpəʊltɪs/ **I** *n* cataplasme *m*; **mustard ~** cataplasme à la moutarde.
II *vtr* mettre un cataplasme sur [*head, knee*].

poultry /ˈpəʊltrɪ/ *n* ¢ (birds) volailles *fpl*; (meat) volaille *f*.

poultry: **~ dealer ▶1692** *n* marchand/-e *m*/*f* de volailles; **~ farm** *n* (ferme *f* d'）élevage *m* de volailles; **~ farmer ▶1692** *n* volailleur/-euse *m*/*f*; **~ farming** *n* élevage *m* de volailles, aviculture *f*; **~man ▶1692** *n* US volailleur *m*.

pounce /paʊns/ **I** *n* bond *m*.
II *vi* bondir; **to ~ on** [*animal*] bondir sur [*prey, object*]; [*person*] se jeter sur [*victim*]; **he ~d on my mistake** il s'est jeté sur l'occasion de relever mon erreur.

pound /paʊnd/ **I** *n* **1** Meas **▶1883** livre *f* (*de 453,6 g*); **two ~s of apples** ≈ un kilo de pommes; **pears are 80 pence a** ou **per ~** ≈ les poires sont à 80 pence la livre; **~ for ~ chicken is better value than pork** tout comparé le poulet revient moins cher que le porc; **to lose ten ~s in weight** ≈ perdre quatre kilos et demi; **2** (unit of currency) **▶1143** livre *f*; **the British/Irish/Maltese ~** la livre sterling/irlandaise/maltaise; **£500 worth of traveller's cheques**, (spoken) **five hundred ~s' worth of traveller's cheques** 500 livres sterling en chèques de voyage; **I'll match your donation ~ for ~** je donnerai exactement la même somme que toi; **3** (compound) (for dogs, cars) fourrière *f*.
II *modif* [*weight*] d'une livre, de 453,6 grammes; [*coin, note*] d'une livre; **a £200,000 house**, (spoken) **a two hundred thousand ~ house** une maison de 200 000 livres sterling; **a two million ~ fraud/robbery** une escroquerie/ un hold up de deux millions de livres; **a five/ten ~ note** un billet de cinq/dix livres.
III *vtr* **1** Culin (crush) piler [*spices, grain, salt*]; aplatir [*meat*]; **to ~ sth to** réduire qch en [*powder, paste, pieces*]; **2** (beat) [*waves*] battre [*shore*]; **to ~ one's chest** se frapper la poitrine; **to ~ sth with one's fists** frapper sur qch avec ses poings [*door, table*]; **to ~ a stake into the ground** enfoncer un pieu dans la terre; **3** (bombard) [*artillery*] pilonner [*city*]; **4** (tread heavily) **to ~ the streets** battre le pavé; **to ~ the beat** [*policeman*] faire sa ronde.
IV *vi* **1** (knock loudly) **to ~ on** marteler [*door, wall*]; **2** (beat) [*heart*] battre ; **to ~ on** [*waves*] battre contre [*beach, rocks*]; **3** (run noisily) **to ~ up/down the stairs** monter/descendre l'escalier d'un pas lourd; **to come ~ing down** ou **along the street** descendre la rue d'un pas lourd; **4** (throb) **my head is ~ing, I've got a ~ing headache** j'ai des élancements dans la tête.
■ **pound away**: **~ away at [sth] 1** (strike hard) taper à tour de bras sur [*piano, typewriter*]; **2** (work doggedly) travailler d'arrache-pied sur [*novel, report*].
■ **pound out**: ¶ **~ out** [*music*] retentir; ¶ **~ [sth] out, ~ out [sth] 1** (play) faire ressortir [*rhythm, tune*]; **2**○ (produce) pondre○ [qch] sur une machine à écrire [*script*]; **3** US Culin (flatten) aplatir [*steak*].
■ **pound up**: **~ [sth] up, ~ up [sth]** concasser [*rocks, pepper*].

poundage /ˈpaʊndɪdʒ/ *n* **1** (weight) poids *m*; **2** (tax) taxe *f* perçue par livre sterling.

poundcake /ˈpaʊndkeɪk/ *n* ≈ quatre-quarts *m inv*.

-pounder○ /ˈpaʊndə(r)/ (*dans composés*) **1** gen **a ten~** (fish) ≈ un poisson de quatre kilos et demi; (baby) ≈ un bébé de quatre kilos et demi; **2** Mil **a thirty~** une pièce de trente.

pounding /ˈpaʊndɪŋ/ *n* **1** (sound) (of waves, drums, heart) battement *m*; (of hooves, fists) martèlement *m*; (of guns) pilonnage *m*; **2** (damage, defeat) **to take a ~** [*area, building*] être pilonné; **we took a ~ in the final**○ Sport on s'est pris la pâtée○ en finale; **we gave the other team a ~**○ nous avons donné une bonne raclée○ à l'autre équipe.

pound sign *n* symbole *m* de la livre sterling (£).

pour /pɔ:(r)/ **I** *vtr* **1** verser [*liquid*]; couler [*cement, metal, wax*]; **to ~ sth into/over** verser qch dans/sur; **she ~ed the milk down the sink** elle a versé le lait dans l'évier; **she looks as if she's been ~ed into that dress**○! elle a l'air moulée dans cette robe; **2** (also **~ out**) (serve) servir [*drink*]; **I ~ed him a cup of coffee** je lui ai versé or servi un café; **he ~ed her a drink, he ~ed a drink for her** il lui a servi un verre; **~ me a drink please** sers-moi un verre, s'il te plaît; **can I ~ you some more coffee?** puis-je vous resservir du café?; **to ~ oneself a drink** se servir un verre; **she ~ed herself another whisky** elle s'est resservi un whisky; **3** (supply freely) **to ~ money into industry/education** investir des sommes énormes dans l'industrie/l'éducation; **to ~ one's energies into one's work** mettre toute son énergie dans son travail; **they're still ~ing troops into the region** ils envoient encore beaucoup de troupes dans la région.
II *vi* **1** (flow) [*liquid*] couler (à flots); **to ~ into** [*water, liquid*] couler dans; [*smoke, fumes*] se répandre dans; [*light*] inonder; **to ~ out of** ou **from** [*smoke, fumes*] s'échapper de; [*water*] ruisseler de; **there was blood ~ing from the wound** le sang coulait à flots de la blessure; **perspiration/tears ~ed down her face** la transpiration ruisselait/les larmes ruisselaient sur son visage; **water ~ed down the walls** l'eau coulait le long des murs; **light ~ed through the window** la lumière entrait à flots par la fenêtre; **relief ~ed over me** j'ai été envahi par une sensation de soulagement; **2** fig **to ~ into** [*people*] affluer dans; **to ~ from** ou **out of** [*people, cars*] sortir en grand nombre de; [*supplies, money*] sortir en masse de; **to ~ across** ou **over** [*people*] traverser [qch] en grand nombre [*border, bridge*]; **workers came ~ing through the factory gates** les ouvriers sortaient en masse de l'usine; **3** (serve tea, coffee) **shall I ~?** je sers?, je fais le service?; **4** [*jug, teapot*] verser; **to ~ well/badly** verser bien/mal.
III pouring *pres p adj* **1 in the ~ing rain** sous la pluie battante; **2 to be of ~ing consistency** Culin être liquide.
IV *v impers* **it's ~ing (with rain)** il pleut à verse; **it's ~ing buckets**○ il pleut à seaux.
IDIOMS **to ~ cold water on sth** se montrer peu enthousiaste pour qch; **to ~ it on**○ péj en rajouter○; ▶ **oil**.
■ **pour away**: **~ away [sth], ~ [sth] away** vider [*surplus, dregs*].
■ **pour down** pleuvoir à verse; **the rain was ~ing down** la pluie tombait à verse.
■ **pour forth** littér = **pour out**.
■ **pour in**: ¶ **~ in** [*people*] affluer; [*letters, requests*] pleuvoir; [*money, job offers*] arriver en masse; [*water*] entrer à flots; **invitations came ~ing in** il y a eu une avalanche d'invitations; ¶ **~ in [sth], ~ [sth] in** verser [*water, cream*].
■ **pour off**: **~ off [sth], ~ [sth] off** vider [*excess, fat, cream*].
■ **pour out**: ¶ **~ out** [*liquid, smoke*] se déverser; [*people*] sortir en grand nombre; **all her troubles came ~ing out** elle a vidé son cœur; ¶ **~ out [sth], ~ [sth] out 1** verser, servir [*coffee, wine etc*]; **2** fig donner libre cours à [*ideas, feelings, anger, troubles*] (**to sb** devant qn); rejeter [*fumes, sewage*]; déverser [*music*]; engloutir [*money, funding*] (**on** dans); déverser [*goods, exports*]; **to ~ out one's troubles** ou **heart to sb** s'épancher auprès de qn; **he ended up ~ing out all he knew about...** il a fini par livrer tout ce qu'il savait sur...

pout /paʊt/ **I** *n* moue *f*; **to answer with a ~** répondre en faisant la moue.
II *vtr* **to ~ one's lips** faire la moue.
III *vi* faire la moue.

poverty /ˈpɒvətɪ/ *n* **1** (lack of money) pauvreté *f*; (more severe) misère *f*; **to live in ~** vivre dans la misère; **to be reduced to ~** en être réduit à l'indigence; **2** (of imagination, resources) pauvreté *f* (**of** de).

poverty line, **poverty level** *n* seuil *m* de pauvreté; **below/near the ~** au-dessous du/presque au seuil de pauvreté.

poverty-stricken /ˈpɒvətɪstrɪkn/ *adj* misérable.

poverty trap *n* GB *situation d'une personne assistée qui perd toutes ses aides dès qu'elle gagne un peu d'argent*.

POW *n* (*abrév* = **prisoner of war**) prisonnier/-ière *m*/*f* de guerre.

powder /ˈpaʊdə(r)/ **I** *n* gen, Cosmet poudre *f*; (snow) poudreuse *f*; **face ~** poudre *f*; **washing ~** lessive *f*; **to crush** ou **reduce to a ~** réduire [qch] en poudre; **to grind to a ~** moudre; **in ~ form** en poudre.
II *vtr* **1** (dust) Cosmet poudrer [*face*]; (with snow) saupoudrer (**with** de); **2** (grind up) réduire [qch] en poudre.
III powdered *pp adj* [*egg, milk, coffee*] en poudre.
IDIOMS **to keep one's ~ dry** être paré; **to ~ one's nose** euph hum se refaire une beauté euph hum.

powder: **~ blue ▶1104** *n, adj* bleu (*m*) pastel *inv*; **~ compact** *n* Cosmet poudrier *m*.

powder keg *n* **1** Mil baril *m* de poudre; **2** fig poudrière *f* fig.

powder: **~ magazine** *n* Mil poudrière *f*; **~ puff** *n* houppette *f*; **~ room** *n* euph toilettes *fpl* pour dames; **~ snow** *n* poudreuse *f*.

powdery /ˈpaʊdərɪ/ *adj* **1** (in consistency) poudreux/-euse; [*stone*] friable; **2** (covered with powder) couvert de poudre.

power /ˈpaʊə(r)/ **I** *n* **1** gen, Pol (control) pouvoir *m*; **to take** ou **seize ~** prendre le pouvoir; **to be in/come to ~** être/accéder au pouvoir; **to be returned/swept to ~** être rétabli/propulsé au pouvoir; **~ to the people!** le pouvoir au peuple!; **~ corrupts** le pouvoir corrompt; **to be in sb's ~** être à la merci de qn; **to have sb in one's ~** tenir qn à sa merci; **2** (strength) puissance *f*; **divine ~** la puissance divine; **to wield enormous ~** détenir une puissance énorme; **a poem/speech of great ~** un poème/discours d'une puissance extraordinaire; **3** (influence) influence *f* (**over** sur); **I have no ~ over the committee/over how the money is spent** je n'ai aucune influence sur le comité/sur la façon dont l'argent est dépensé; **4** (capability) pouvoir *m*; **~(s) of concentration/persuasion** pouvoir de concentration/persuasion; **it is in ~** ou **within my ~ to do** il est en mon pouvoir de faire; **it is in** ou **you have it in your ~ to change things** il est en votre pouvoir de changer les choses; **it does not lie within my ~ to help you** sout il n'est pas en mon pouvoir de vous aider; **to do everything in one's ~** faire tout ce qui est en son pouvoir (**to do** pour faire); **to lose the ~ of speech** perdre l'usage de la parole; **to be at the height of one's ~s** gen avoir atteint la plénitude de ses moyens; [*artist*] être au sommet de son art; **5** ¢ (authority) attributions *fpl*; **the act gives new ~s to the taxman** la loi donne de nouvelles attributions au fisc; **the courts/police have the ~ to do sth** il est dans les attributions de la justice/police de faire qch; **6** (physical force) (of person, explosion) force *f*, puissance *f*; (of storm) violence *f*; **7** Phys, Tech gen énergie *f*; (electrical) énergie *f* électrique; (current) courant *m*; **to**

switch on the ~ mettre le courant; **a cheap source of ~** une source d'énergie peu coûteuse; **8** Mech (of vehicle, plane) puissance *f*; **we're losing ~** nous perdons de la puissance; **to be running at full/half ~** fonctionner à plein/mi-régime; **9** Sci (magnification) puissance *f*; **10** Math **8 to the ~ of 3** 8 puissance 3; **to the nth ~** (à la) puissance n; **11** (country) puissance *f*; **the big ~s** les grandes puissances.
II *modif* Tech, Elec [*drill, lathe, circuit, cable*] électrique; [*steering, brakes*] assisté; [*mower*] à moteur; [*shovel*] mécanique.
III *vtr* faire marcher [*engine*]; propulser [*plane, boat*]; **~ed by** propulsé par [*engine*]; alimenté par [*electricity, gas, generator*].
IV -powered (*dans composés*) **electrically-~ed** fonctionnant à l'électricité, électrique; ▶ **nuclear-powered**.
IDIOMS **to do sb a ~ of good** faire à qn un bien fou; **to be the ~ behind the throne** être l'éminence grise, tirer les ficelles○; **the ~s of darkness** les puissances des ténèbres; **the ~s that be** les autorités.

power: **~-assisted** *adj* [*steering*] assisté; **~ base** *n* base *f* politique; **~boat** *n* hors-bord *m inv*; **~ broker** *n*: *celui/celle qui détient les clés du pouvoir*; **~ cut** *n* coupure *f* de courant; **~ dispute** *n* grève *f* dans le secteur de l'électricité; **~ dive** *n* Aviat descente *f* en piqué; **~ dressing** *n* tenue *f* vestimentaire qui en impose (*portée par les femmes cadres au travail*); **~-driven** *adj* [*lawn-mower, bike*] à moteur.

powerful /ˈpaʊəfl/ *adj* [*person, arms, build, athlete, engine, computer, description*] puissant; [*government, regime*] fort; [*bomb*] de forte puissance; [*smell, emotion, impression, light, voice*] fort; [*kick, blow*] bon/bonne; [*argument, evidence*] solide; [*portrayal*] saisissant; [*performance*] magistral.

powerfully /ˈpaʊəfəlɪ/ *adv* [*influenced, affected*] fortement; [*portrayed*] d'une manière saisissante; [*attack, urge*] vivement; [*argue*] avec force; [*reek, smell*] fortement (**of** de); **to be ~ built** avoir une forte carrure.

power game *n* rapport *m* de force.

powerhouse /ˈpaʊəhaʊs/ *n* **1** lit centrale *f* électrique; **2**○ fig (of ideas etc) laboratoire *m*; **3** fig (person) locomotive *f*; **she's a ~!** c'est une vraie locomotive!; **to be a ~ in attack** [*team*] avoir une attaque en béton.

powerless /ˈpaʊəlɪs/ *adj* impuissant (**against** face à); **I was ~ to prevent it** il m'était impossible de l'empêcher; **the police were ~ to intervene** la police n'a pas pu intervenir.

powerlessness /ˈpaʊəlɪsnɪs/ *n* impuissance *f*.

power: **~ line** *n* ligne *f* à haute tension; **~ of attorney** *n* procuration *f*; **~ pack** *n* US Elec bloc *m* d'alimentation; **~ plant** US = **power station**; **~ play** *n* US fig coup *m* de force; **~ point** *n* prise *f* (de courant); **~ politics** *npl* (using military force) politique *f* de la force armée; (using coercion) politique *f* d'intimidation; **~ sharing** *n* partage *m* du pouvoir; **~ station** *n* centrale *f* (électrique); **~ structure** *n* répartition *f* des pouvoirs; **~ surge** *n* Elec surintensité *f*; **~ tool** *n* outil *m* électrique; **~ workers** *npl* ouvriers *mpl* dans les centrales électriques.

powwow /ˈpaʊwaʊ/ *n* **1** Anthrop assemblée *f* (*d'Indiens d'Amérique*); **2**○ fig discussion *f* importante.

Powys /ˈpaʊɪs/ ▶ **1624** *pr n* Powys *m*.

pox /pɒks/ ▶ **1354** *n* **1**‡ (smallpox) variole *f*, petite vérole *f*; **2**○ †(syphilis) syphilis *f*.
IDIOMS **a ~ on you**‡! maudit sois-tu!

poxy○ /ˈpɒksɪ/ *adj* GB [*face, dog, house*] moche○; [*meal*] infect; [*present, reward, salary*] minable○.

pp 1 (on document) (*abrév* = **per procurationem**) po; **2** Mus (*abrév* = **pianissimo**) pp; **3** (*abrév* = **pages**) pp.

p & p *n* (*abrév* = **postage and packing**) frais *mpl* d'expédition.

PPE GB Univ (*abrév* = **philosophy, politics and economics**) philosophie, politique et économie *f*.

PPS *n* GB *abrév* ▶ **Parliamentary Private Secretary**.

Pr *abrév écrite* = **prince**.

PR *n* **1** *abrév* ▶ **public relations**; **2** *abrév* ▶ **proportional representation**; **3** US Post *abrév écrite* = **Puerto Rico**; **4**○ US injur (*abrév* = **Puerto Rican**) portoricain/-e *m/f*.

practicability /ˌpræktɪkəˈbɪlətɪ/ *n* **1** (feasibility) (of proposal, plan) faisabilité *f*; **2** (of roads, access) praticabilité *f*.

practicable /ˈpræktɪkəbl/ *adj* **1** (feasible) [*proposal, plan*] réalisable; **2** (passable) [*road*] praticable.

practical /ˈpræktɪkl/ **I** *n* (exam) épreuve *f* pratique; (lesson) travaux *mpl* pratiques.
II *adj* **1** (concrete, not theoretical) pratique; **for all ~ purposes** en pratique; **in ~ terms** en pratique; **2** [*person*] (sensible) pratique; (with hands) adroit; **to be ~** avoir l'esprit pratique; **3** (functional) [*clothes, shoes, furniture, equipment*] pratique; **4** (viable) [*plan etc*] réalisable; **5** (virtual) **it's a ~ certainty that** c'est pratiquement certain que.

practicality /ˌpræktɪˈkælətɪ/ **I** *n* **1** (of person) esprit *m* pratique; (of clothes, equipment) facilité *f* d'utilisation; **2** (of scheme, idea, project) aspect *m* pratique.
II practicalities *npl* détails *mpl* pratiques.

practical: **~ joke** *n* farce *f*; **~ joker** *n* farceur/-euse *m/f*.

practically /ˈpræktɪklɪ/ *adv* **1** (almost, virtually) pratiquement; **2** (in a practical way) d'une manière pratique.

practicalness /ˈpræktɪklnɪs/ *n* = **practicality I.**

practical nurse ▶ **1692** *n* aide-soignant/-e *m/f*.

practice /ˈpræktɪs/ **I** *n* **1** ¢ (exercises) exercices *mpl*; (experience) entraînement *m*; **it's just a matter of ~** ce n'est qu'une question d'entraînement; **to do one's piano ~** faire ses exercices de piano, travailler son piano; **to have had ~ in** ou **at sth/in** ou **at doing** avoir l'expérience en qch/pour ce qui est de faire; **it's all good ~** cela fait partie de l'entraînement; **to be in ~** (for sport) être bien entraîné; (for music) être bien exercé; **to be out of ~** être rouillé○; **2** (meeting) (for sport) entraînement *m*; (for music, drama) répétition *f*; **I've got football ~ tonight** j'ai un entraînement de football ce soir; **3** (procedure) pratique *f*, usage *m*; **it's standard/common ~ to do** il est d'usage/courant de faire; **against normal ~** contre l'usage; **business ~** usage en affaires; **it's normal business ~ to do** il est courant de faire; **4 C** (habit) habitude *f*; **my usual ~ is to do** j'ai l'habitude de faire; **to make a ~ of doing, to make it a ~ to do** prendre l'habitude de faire; **as is my usual ~** comme je le fais d'habitude; **5** (custom) coutume *f*; **the ~ of doing** la coutume selon laquelle on fait; **they make a ~ of doing, they make it a ~ to do** c'est la coutume chez eux de faire; **6** (business of doctor, lawyer) cabinet *m*; **to have a ~ in London** avoir un cabinet à Londres; **to be in ~** exercer; **to be in ~ in Oxford** exercer à Oxford; **to set up in** ou **go into ~** (as doctor) s'établir en tant que médecin; (in law) s'établir en tant que juriste; **7** ¢ (as opposed to theory) pratique *f*; **in ~** en pratique; **to put sth into ~** mettre qch en pratique.
II *modif* [*game, match*] d'essai; [*flight*] d'entraînement; **~ exam** examen *m* blanc.
III *vtr, vi* US = **practise**.
IDIOMS **~ makes perfect** Prov c'est en forgeant qu'on devient forgeron Prov.

practice: **~ run** *n* essai *m*; **~ teacher** *n* US (secondary) professeur *m* stagiaire; (primary) instituteur/-trice *m/f* stagiaire.

practise GB, **practice** US /ˈpræktɪs/ **I** *vtr* **1** (work at) travailler [*song, speech, French*]; s'exercer à [*movement, shot*]; réviser [*technique*]; répéter [*play, performance*]; **to ~ the piano** travailler le piano; **to ~ one's scales** faire ses gammes; **she's practising what to say to him** elle répète ce qu'elle va lui dire; **to ~ doing** ou **how to do** s'entraîner à faire; **to ~ one's French on sb** essayer son français sur qn; **2** (use) pratiquer [*restraint, kindness, economy*]; utiliser [*method*]; employer [*torture*]; **3** (follow a profession) exercer; **to ~ medicine/law** exercer la médecine/la profession de juriste; **4** (observe) pratiquer [*custom, religion*].
II *vi* **1** (train) (at piano, violin) s'exercer; (for sports) s'entraîner; (for play, concert) répéter; **to ~ for** s'entraîner pour [*match, game*]; répéter [*play, speech*]; **2** (follow a profession) exercer; **to ~ as** exercer la profession de [*doctor, lawyer*].
IDIOMS **to ~ what one preaches** prêcher par l'exemple.

practised GB, **practiced** US /ˈpræktɪst/ *adj* [*player, lawyer, cheat*] expérimenté; [*eye, ear, movement, performance*] expert; **to be ~ in/in doing** être fort dans/pour faire.

practising GB, **practicing** US /ˈpræktɪsɪŋ/ *adj* [*Christian, Muslim*] pratiquant; [*doctor, lawyer*] en exercice; [*homosexual*] actif/-ive.

practitioner /prækˈtɪʃənə(r)/ *n* **1** (of profession) praticien/-ienne *m/f*; **legal ~** juriste *m*; **dental ~** dentiste *mf*; **2** (of art, belief) praticien/-ienne *m/f*; **~ of** adepte *mf* de.

praesidium *n* = **presidium**.

praetorian /priːˈtɔːrɪən/ *adj* prétorien/-ienne.

pragmatic /prægˈmætɪk/ *adj* gen, Philos pragmatique.

pragmatical /prægˈmætɪkl/ *adj* pragmatique.

pragmatically /prægˈmætɪklɪ/ *adv* [*say, accept etc*] avec pragmatisme; [*considered*] d'un point de vue pragmatique.

pragmatics /prægˈmætɪks/ *n* (+ *v sg*) **1** Ling pragmatique *f*; **2** (of scheme, situation) détails *mpl* pratiques.

pragmatism /ˈprægmətɪzəm/ *n* pragmatisme *m*.

pragmatist /ˈprægmətɪst/ *n* gen, Ling pragmatiste *mf*.

Prague /prɑːg/ ▶ **1818** *pr n* Prague.

prairie /ˈpreərɪ/ *n* plaine *f* (herbeuse), prairie *f*.

prairie: **~ chicken** *n* US Zool cupidon *m* des prairies; **~ dog** *n* chien *m* de prairie.

prairie oyster *n* US **1**○ (drink) *mélange à base d'œuf cru utilisé comme remède après des excès d'alcool*; **2** Culin (testicles) testicules *mpl* de veau cuisinés.

prairie: **~ schooner** *n* chariot *m* bâché; **~ wolf** *n* US coyote *m*.

praise /preɪz/ **I** *n* **1** gen éloges *mpl*, louanges *fpl* (**for** de; **for doing** pour avoir fait); **in ~ of sb** à la louange de qn; **in ~ of sth** louant qch; **beyond ~** au-dessus de tout éloge; **worthy of ~** digne d'éloges; **to be loud in one's ~ of sb/sth** ne pas tarir d'éloges sur qn/qch; **to heap ~ on sb** couvrir qn d'éloges; **to be highly ~d** être couvert d'éloges; **faint ~** éloge mesuré; **high ~** éloge enthousiaste; **that's ~ indeed coming from her** venant d'elle c'est un compliment; **2** Relig louange(s) *f(pl)*.
II *vtr* **1** gen faire l'éloge de [*person, book, achievement*]; **to ~ sb for sth/for doing** féliciter qn pour qch/pour avoir fait; **to ~ sb/sth as sth** faire l'éloge de qn/qch en tant que qch; **to ~ sb/sth to the skies** porter qn/qch aux nues; **to sing sb's/sth's ~s** chanter les louanges de qn/qch; **2** Relig louer [*God*] (**for** pour); **Praise be to God!** Dieu soit loué!

praiseworthiness /ˈpreɪzwɜːðɪnɪs/ *n* mérite *m* (**of** de).

praiseworthy /ˈpreɪzwɜːðɪ/ *adj* digne d'éloges, méritoire (**to do** de faire).

pram /præm/ *n* GB landau *m*.

prance /prɑːns, US præns/ *vi* [*horse*] caracoler; [*person*] (gaily) sautiller; (smugly) se pavaner; **to ~ in/out** [*person*] entrer/sortir allègrement.

prang○† /præŋ/ GB **I** *n* accident *m*.
II *vtr* bousiller○ [*car*].

prank /præŋk/ *n* farce *f*; **to play a ~ on sb** faire une farce à qn; **childish ~s** gamineries *fpl*.

prankster /ˈpræŋkstə(r)/ *n* farceur/-euse *m/f*.

praseodymium /ˌpreɪzɪəˈdɪmɪəm/ *n* praséodyme *m*.

prat◑ /præt/ *n* GB abruti/-e○ *m/f*.

prate† /preɪt/ *vi* (also **~ on**) jaser (**about** à propos de).

pratfall◑ /ˈprætfɔːl/ *n* lit, fig peau *f* de banane.

prattle /ˈprætl/ **I** *n* bavardage *m*, papotage○ *m*; (of children) babillage *m*.
II *vi* papoter○; [*children*] babiller; **to ~ on about sth** parler de qch à n'en plus finir.

prawn /prɔːn/ **I** *n* crevette *f* rose, bouquet *m*.
II *modif* [*salad, sandwich*] aux crevettes; **~ cocktail** salade *f* de crevettes.

pray /preɪ/ **I**‡ *adv* also iron je vous prie; **what is that, ~?** qu'est-ce donc, je vous prie?; **~ be seated** asseyez-vous, je vous prie; **~ silence for his lordship** veuillez faire silence pour sa seigneurie.
II *vtr* **1** Relig prier (**that** pour que + *subj*); **to ~ God for forgiveness/mercy** prier Dieu pour son pardon/sa miséricorde; **2**‡ (request) prier; **to ~ sb (to) do sth** prier qn de faire qch.
III *vi* gen, Relig prier (**for** pour); **to ~ to God for sth** prier Dieu pour qch; **to ~ for rain/fair weather** prier pour qu'il pleuve/qu'il fasse beau.

prayer /ˈpreə(r)/ **I** *n* Relig prière *f*; fig (hope) souhait *m*; **in ~** en prière; **to be at ~** ou **at one's ~s** être à la prière; **to say a ~ that** faire une prière pour que (+ *subj*); **to say one's prayers** faire sa prière; **his ~s were answered** lit, fig sa prière a été exaucée; **you are in my ~s** je prie pour vous et votre bien-être; **the Book of Common Prayer** le rituel de l'Église anglicane.
II prayers *npl* (informal) prière *f*; (formal) office *m*; **family/evening ~s** prière *f* en famille/du soir; **Evening/Morning ~s** office *m* du soir/du matin.
III *modif* Relig [*group, meeting*] de prière.
IDIOMS **not to have a ~**○ ne pas avoir la moindre chance; **on a wing and a ~**○ Dieu sait comment.

prayer beads *npl* chapelet *m*.

prayer book *n* gen livre *m* de prières; **the Prayer Book** le rituel de l'Église anglicane.

prayer: **~ mat**, **~ rug** *n* tapis *m* de prière; **~ shawl** *n* taled *m*; **~ wheel** *n* moulin *m* à prière.

praying /ˈpreɪɪŋ/ **I** *n* prières *fpl*.
II *adj* en prière.

praying mantis *n* mante *f* religieuse.

preach /priːtʃ/ **I** *vi* Relig prêcher (**to** à); fig péj sermonner; **to ~ at sb** sermonner qn.
II *vtr* Relig prêcher (**to** à); fig prêcher, prôner [*tolerance, virtue, pacifism etc*]; **to ~ a sermon** faire un sermon, prêcher.
IDIOMS **to practise what one ~es** conformer ses actes à ses paroles; **to ~ to the converted** enfoncer une porte ouverte.

preacher /ˈpriːtʃə(r)/ *n* pasteur *m*.

preachify○ /ˈpriːtʃɪfaɪ/ *vi* péj faire du prêchi-prêcha○, prêcher.

preachy○ /ˈpriːtʃɪ/ *adj* sermonneur/-euse.

preamble /priːˈæmbl/ *n* préambule *m* (**to** à).

preamplifier /priːˈæmplɪfaɪə(r)/ *n* préamplificateur *m*.

prearrange /ˌpriːəˈreɪndʒ/ *vtr* fixer [qch] à l'avance.

prebend /ˈprebənd/ *n* prébende *f*.

prebendary /ˈprebəndərɪ/ *n* prébendier *m*.

precarious /prɪˈkeərɪəs/ *adj* précaire.

precariously /prɪˈkeərɪəslɪ/ *adv* de manière précaire.

precast /ˌpriːˈkɑːst, US -ˈkæst/ *adj* [*concrete*] précoulé.

precaution /prɪˈkɔːʃn/ *n* précaution *f* (**against** contre); **as a ~** par précaution; **to take ~s** (all contexts) prendre des précautions; **to take ~s to ensure/avoid** prendre des précautions pour assurer/éviter; **to take the ~ of doing** prendre la précaution de faire.

precautionary /prɪˈkɔːʃənərɪ, US -nerɪ/ *adj* préventif/-ive; **~ measure** mesure *f* de précaution.

precede /prɪˈsiːd/ *vtr* précéder; **to ~ sb as** précéder qn comme [*president, leader*]; **~d by** précédé de or par; **to ~ a speech with a few words of thanks** faire précéder un discours de quelques mots de remerciement.

precedence /ˈpresɪdəns/ *n* **1** (in importance) priorité *f*; **to take** ou **have ~ over sth/sb** avoir la priorité sur qch/qn; **2** (in rank) préséance *f*; **to have ~ over sb** avoir la préséance sur qn; **in order of ~** par ordre de préséance.

precedent /ˈpresɪdənt/ *n* précédent *m*; **to set a ~** créer un précédent.

preceding /prɪˈsiːdɪŋ/ *adj* précédent.

precentor /prɪˈsentə(r)/ *n* maître *m* de chapelle.

precept /ˈpriːsept/ *n* précepte *m*.

preceptor /ˈpriːseptə(r)/ *n* **1**‡ (teacher) maître *m*; précepteur/-trice‡ *m/f*; **2** US Univ ≈ moniteur/-trice *m/f*.

pre-Christian /prɪˈkrɪstʃən/ *adj* pré-chrétien/-ienne.

precinct /ˈpriːsɪŋkt/ **I** *n* **1** GB (also **shopping ~**) quartier *m* commerçant; **2** GB (also **pedestrian ~**) zone *f* piétonne; **3** US Admin circonscription *f*.
II precincts *npl* **1** (surrounding area) alentours *mpl*; **2** GB (of university, cathedral) enceinte *f*.
III *modif* US Admin [*captain, police station*] de quartier; **~ worker** US Pol militant/-e *m/f* politique de quartier.

precious /ˈpreʃəs/ **I** *n* (as endearment) mon trésor; **Diane come here ~** Diane viens ici mon trésor.
II *adj* **1** (valuable) [*resource, possession, land, time*] précieux/-ieuse; **2** (held dear) [*person*] cher/chère (**to** à); **3**○ iron (beloved) cher/chère; **4** pej (affected) [*person, style*] précieux/-ieuse, affecté.
III *adv* (very) **~ little time/sense** fort peu de temps/de bon sens; **~ little to do** fort peu à faire; **~ few cars/solutions** fort peu de voitures/de solutions.

precious metal *n* métal *m* précieux.

preciousness /ˈpreʃəsnɪs/ *n* **1** (value) (of time, possessions) valeur *f*; **2** (affectedness) préciosité *f*.

precious stone *n* pierre *f* précieuse.

precipice /ˈpresɪpɪs/ *n* lit, fig précipice *m*.

precipitance /prɪˈsɪpɪtəns/ *n* sout précipitation *f*.

precipitant /prɪˈsɪpɪtənt/ **I** *n* Chem agent *m* de précipitation.
II *adj* sout (hasty) précipité.

precipitate I /prɪˈsɪpɪteɪt/ *n* Chem précipité *m*.
II /prɪˈsɪpɪtət/ *adj* (hasty) [*action, decision, departure*] précipité; [*person*] (trop) prompt.
III /prɪˈsɪpɪteɪt/ *vtr* Chem, Meteorol, gen précipiter.
IV /prɪˈsɪpɪteɪt/ *vi* **1** Chem précipiter; **2** Meteorol être précipité.

precipitately /prɪˈsɪpɪtətlɪ/ *adv* sout précipitamment.

precipitation /prɪˌsɪpɪˈteɪʃn/ *n* **1** Chem précipitation *f*; **2** Meteorol précipitations *fpl*.

precipitous /prɪˈsɪpɪtəs/ *adj* **1** sout (steep) [*cliff*] à pic *inv*; [*road*] escarpé; [*steps*] raide; **2** (hasty) = **precipitate II**.

precipitously /prɪˈsɪpɪtəslɪ/ *adv* sout à pic.

précis /ˈpreɪsiː, US preɪˈsiː/ **I** *n* résumé *m*.
II *vtr* faire un résumé de [*text, speech*].

precise /prɪˈsaɪs/ *adj* **1** (exact) [*idea, moment, sum, measurement*] précis; **can you be more ~?** pourriez-vous être plus précis?; **to be ~...** pour être précis...; **not at this ~ moment** pas pour l'instant; **2** (meticulous) [*person, mind*] méticuleux/-euse.

precisely /prɪˈsaɪslɪ/ *adv* **1** (exactly) exactement, précisément; **I saw her ~ four times** je l'ai vue quatre fois exactement; **~ because** précisément parce que; **that's ~ why...** c'est précisément la raison pour laquelle...; **at ten o'clock ~** à dix heures précises; **2** (accurately) [*describe, record*] avec précision.

preciseness /prɪˈsaɪsnɪs/ *n* méticulosité *f*.

precision /prɪˈsɪʒn/ **I** *n* précision *f*; **with ~** avec précision; **with military/surgical ~** avec une précision militaire/chirurgicale.
II *modif* [*engineering, steering, tool*] de précision.

precision bombing *n* bombardement *m* de précision.

preclude /prɪˈkluːd/ *vtr* exclure [*choice, possibility*]; empêcher [*action, involvement*]; **to ~ sb/sth (from) doing** empêcher qn/qch de faire.

precocious /prɪˈkəʊʃəs/ *adj* gen précoce; **a ~ child** péj un petit prodige.

precociously /prɪˈkəʊʃəslɪ/ *adv* précocement.

precociousness /prɪˈkəʊʃəsnɪs/, **precocity** /prɪˈkɒsətɪ/ *n* précocité *f*.

precognition /ˌpriːkɒgˈnɪʃn/ *n* précognition *f*.

pre-Columbian /ˌpriːkəˈlʌmbɪən/ *adj* précolombien/-ienne.

precombustion /ˌpriːkəmˈbʌstʃən/ **I** *n* précombustion *f*.
II *modif* **~ chamber** chambre *f* de précombustion; **~ engine** moteur *m* à précombustion.

preconceived /ˌpriːkənˈsiːvd/ *adj* préconçu.

preconception /ˌpriːkənˈsepʃn/ *n* opinion *f* préconçue (**about** au sujet de).

preconcerted /ˌpriːkənˈsɜːtɪd/ *adj* prévu.

precondition /ˌpriːkənˈdɪʃn/ **I** *n* condition *f* requise.
II *vtr* Psych conditionner.

precook /ˌpriːˈkʊk/ **I** *vtr* précuire.
II precooked *pp adj* précuit.

precool /ˌpriːˈkuːl/ *vtr* préréfrigérer.

precursor /ˌpriːˈkɜːsə(r)/ *n* (person) précurseur *m*; (sign) signe *m* avant-coureur; (prelude) prélude *m* (**to, of** à); (earlier form) ancêtre *m*.

precursory /ˌpriːˈkɜːsərɪ/ *adj* préalable.

predate /ˌpriːˈdeɪt/ *vtr* **1** (put earlier date) antidater [*cheque, document*]; **2** (exist before) [*event, discovery, building*] être antérieur à.

predator /ˈpredətə(r)/ **I** *n* **1** (animal) prédateur *m*; **2** Comm (in takeover) prédateur *m*, attaquant *m*.
II *modif* **~ group**, **~ company** prédateur *m*, attaquant *m*.

predatory /ˈpredətrɪ, US -tɔːrɪ/ *adj* **1** [*animal*] prédateur/-trice; [*habits*] de prédateur; **2** Comm [*consortium, company, raid*] hostile.

predatory: **~ competition** *n* Comm concurrence *f* déloyale or sauvage par dumping; **~ pricing** *n* Comm dumping *m*; **~ stake** *n* Fin participation *f* résultant d'une OPA hostile.

predecease /ˌpriːdɪˈsiːs/ *vtr* sout Jur décéder antérieurement à.

predecessor /ˈpriːdɪsesə(r), US ˈpredə-/ *n* prédécesseur *m*.

predestination /ˌpriːdestɪˈneɪʃn/ *n* prédestination *f*.

predestine /ˌpriːˈdestɪn/ *vtr* [*God, fate*] prédestiner (**to** à; **to do** à faire); **it is** ou **has been ~d that** il est écrit que.

predetermination /ˌpriːdɪtɜːmɪˈneɪʃn/ *n* **1** Relig prédétermination *f*; **2** (of outcome) détermination *f* préalable.

predetermine /ˌpriːdɪˈtɜːmɪn/ *vtr* **1** (fix beforehand) déterminer d'avance; **~d personality/strategy** personnalité/stratégie déterminée d'avance; **2** Relig, Philos prédéterminer.

predicable /ˈpredɪkəbl/ *adj* Philos prédicable.

predicament /prɪˈdɪkəmənt/ *n* situation *f* difficile; **to help sb out of his/her ~** aider qn à se sortir d'un mauvais pas.

predicate I /ˈpredɪkət/ *n* Ling, Philos prédicat *m*.
II /ˈpredɪkət/ *adj* **1** Ling, Philos prédicatif/-ive; **2** Math **~ calculus** calcul des prédicats.
III /ˈpredɪkeɪt/ *vtr* **1** gen (assert) avancer [*theory*]; **to ~ sth to be** poser que qch est; **to ~ that** poser que; **2** Philos (affirm) affirmer (**of** de); **3** (base) fonder (**on** sur); **4 to be ~ed on** (have as condition) impliquer.

predicative /prɪˈdɪkətɪv, US ˈpredɪkeɪtɪv/ *adj* Ling prédicatif/-ive.

predicatively /prɪˈdɪkətɪvlɪ, US ˈpredɪkeɪtɪvlɪ/ *adv* Ling [*use*] en tant que prédicat.

predict /prɪˈdɪkt/ *vtr* prédire [*future, event*]; **to ~ that** prédire que; **to ~ where/when/how** prédire où/quand/la façon dont.

predictability /prɪˌdɪktəˈbɪlətɪ/ *n* prévisibilité *f*.

predictable /prɪˈdɪktəbl/ *adj* prévisible; **you're so ~** tes actions sont si prévisibles.

predictably /prɪˈdɪktəblɪ/ *adv* [*boring, late*] comme prévu; **~, nobody came** comme on pouvait s'y attendre, personne n'est venu.

prediction /prɪˈdɪkʃn/ *n* prédiction *f* (**about** sur; **of** de; **that** selon laquelle); **a ~ that inflation will fall** une prédiction selon laquelle l'inflation va baisser.

predictive /prɪˈdɪktɪv/ *adj* prophétique.

predigested /ˌpriːdaɪˈdʒestɪd/ *adj* prédigéré.

predilection /ˌpriːdɪˈlekʃn, US ˌpredlˈek-/ *n* prédilection *f* (**for** pour).

predispose /ˌpriːdɪˈspəʊz/ *vtr* prédisposer (**to** à; **to do** à faire).

predisposition /ˌpriːdɪspəˈzɪʃn/ *n* prédisposition *f* (**to** à; **to do** à faire).

predominance /prɪˈdɒmɪnəns/ *n* prédominance *f* (**of** de; **over** sur).

predominant /prɪˈdɒmɪnənt/ *adj* prédominant.

predominantly /prɪˈdɒmɪnəntlɪ/ *adv* [*represent, feature*] principalement; [*Muslim, female, French-speaking*] essentiellement; **~ influenced by** influencé principalement par; **the flowers were ~ pink** la plupart des fleurs étaient roses.

predominate /prɪˈdɒmɪneɪt/ *vi* prédominer (**over** sur).

pre-embryo /ˌpriːˈembrɪəʊ/ *n*: *embryon de moins de 14 jours.*

preemie○ /ˌpriːˈemiː/ *n* (also **premie**) US Med prématuré/-e *m/f*.

pre-eminence /ˌpriːˈemɪnəns/ *n* gen suprématie *f*; Sport supériorité *f*.

pre-eminent /ˌpriːˈemɪnənt/ *adj* **1** (distinguished) [*celebrity, scientist*] éminent; **2** (leading) [*nation, cult, company*] dominant.

pre-eminently /ˌpriːˈemɪnəntlɪ/ *adv* **1** (highly) [*successful, distinguished*] particulièrement; **2** (above all) avant tout.

pre-empt /ˌpriːˈempt/ *vtr* **1** (anticipate) anticiper [*question, decision, move*]; devancer [*person*]; **2** (thwart) contrecarrer [*action, plan*]; **3** Jur (appropriate) préempter [*building, land*].

pre-emption /ˌpriːˈempʃn/ I *n* **1** gen action *f* préventive; **2** Jur (of sale) préemption *f*.
II *modif* Jur [*right*] de préemption.

pre-emptive /ˌpriːˈemptɪv/ *adj* **1** Jur [*right*] de préemption; [*purchase*] par préemption; **2** Mil [*strike, attack*] préventif/-ive; **3** Games (in bridge) [*bid*] de barrage.

preen /priːn/ I *vtr* [*bird*] lisser [*feathers*].
II *vi* [*bird*] se lisser les plumes.
III *v refl* **to ~ oneself** [*bird*] se lisser les plumes; [*person*] péj se pomponner.

pre-establish /ˌpriːɪˈstæblɪʃ/ *vtr* préétablir.

pre-exist /ˌpriːɪgˈzɪst/ I *vtr* préexister à.
II *vi* [*situation, phenomenon*] préexister; [*person, soul*] avoir une vie antérieure.
III **pre-existing** *pres p adj* préexistant; **a ~ing medical condition** un antécédent médical.

pre-existence /ˌpriːɪgˈzɪstəns/ *n* **1** (of phenomenon) préexistence *f*; **2** (of person) vie *f* antérieure.

pre-existent /ˌpriːɪgˈzɪstənt/ *adj* préexistant.

prefab /ˈpriːfæb, US ˌpriːˈfæb/ I *n* (bâtiment *m*) préfabriqué *m*.
II *adj* préfabriqué.

prefabricate /ˌpriːˈfæbrɪkeɪt/ *vtr* préfabriquer.

prefabrication /ˌpriːfæbrɪˈkeɪʃn/ *n* préfabrication *f*.

preface /ˈprefɪs/ I *n* (to book) préface *f* (**to** à); (to speech) préambule *m*.
II *vtr* préfacer [*livre*]; **to ~ sth with sth** faire précéder qch de qch; **I would like to ~ my remarks with a word of thanks to...** avant d'aborder mon sujet, je voudrais remercier...

prefaded /ˌpriːˈfeɪdɪd/ *adj* délavé.

prefatory /ˈprefətrɪ, US -tɔːrɪ/ *adj* [*comments*] préliminaire; [*pages, notes*] liminaire.

prefect /ˈpriːfekt/ *n* **1** GB Sch *élève de dernière année chargé de la surveillance*; **2** Pol préfet *m*.

prefecture /ˈpriːfektjʊə(r), US -tʃər/ *n* Pol préfecture *f*.

prefer /prɪˈfɜː(r)/ I *vtr* **1** (like better) préférer, aimer mieux; **to ~ sth to** préférer qch à; **to ~ doing** préférer faire; **I ~ painting to drawing** je préfère peindre que de dessiner; **to ~ to do** préférer faire; **to ~ to walk rather than to take the bus** préférer y aller à pied plutôt que de prendre le bus; **to ~ sb to do/not to do** préférer que qn fasse/ne fasse pas; **to ~ that** préférer que (+ *subj*); **to ~ it if** aimer mieux que (+ *subj*); **I would ~ it if you didn't smoke** j'aimerais mieux que tu ne fumes pas; **2** Jur **to ~ charges** porter plainte; **to ~ charges against sb** engager des poursuites contre qn; **3** (promote) élever [*clergyman*].
II **preferred** *pp adj* (*tjrs épith*) [*term, method, route, option, solution*] préféré; **~red position** journ emplacement *m* privilégié; **~red creditor** Fin créancier/-ière *m/f* prioritaire; **there is a ~red candidate** (in job ad) il y a un candidat prioritaire.

preferable /ˈprefrəbl/ *adj* préférable (**to** à); **it is ~ to do** il est préférable de faire.

preferably /ˈprefrəblɪ/ *adv* de préférence.

preference /ˈprefrəns/ *n* préférence *f* (**for** pour); **in ~ to** de préférence à; **in ~ to doing** plutôt que de faire; **to give ~ to sb (over sb)** donner la préférence à qn (plutôt qu'à qn).

preference share *n* GB Fin action *f* privilégiée.

preferential /ˌprefəˈrenʃl/ *adj* (all contexts) préférentiel/-ielle.

preferment /prɪˈfɜːmənt/ *n* Admin élévation *f*, avancement *m*.

preferred stock *n* US, Fin actions *fpl* privilégiées.

prefiguration /ˌpriːfɪgəˈreɪʃn/ *n* préfiguration *f*.

prefigure /ˌpriːˈfɪgə(r), US -gjər/ *vtr* **1** (be an early sign of) [*event*] préfigurer; [*person*] être le précurseur de; **2** (imagine beforehand) imaginer d'avance.

prefix /ˈpriːfɪks/ I *n* (*pl* **-es**) **1** Ling préfixe *m*; **2** GB Telecom indicatif *m*; **3** GB Aut *première lettre d'une immatriculation automobile.*
II *vtr* préfixer [*word*]; **to ~ X to Y** faire précéder Y de X.

preflight /ˈpriːflaɪt/ *adj* [*checks*] précédant le décollage; **he suffers from ~ nerves** il est très angoissé avant le décollage.

preform /ˌpriːˈfɔːm/ *vtr* préformer [*components*].

preformation /ˌpriːfɔːˈmeɪʃn/ *n* préformage *m*.

prefrontal /ˌpriːˈfrʌntl/ *adj* [*lobe, lobotomy*] préfrontal.

preggers○† /ˈpregəz/ *adj* GB grosse○, enceinte.

pregnancy /ˈpregnənsɪ/ *n* (of woman) grossesse *f*; (of animal) gestation *f*.

pregnancy test *n* test *m* de grossesse.

pregnant /ˈpregnənt/ *n* **1** Med [*woman*] enceinte; [*female animal*] pleine; **to become ~** se retrouver enceinte; **~ mothers** femmes enceintes; **to get ~**○ tomber enceinte○; **to get ~ by sb** se trouver enceinte de qn; **to get sb ~**○ faire un enfant à qn○; **two months ~** enceinte de deux mois; **to be ~ with twins** attendre des jumeaux; **2** fig [*pause*] éloquent; **~ with meaning/danger** lourd de sens/danger.

preheat /ˌpriːˈhiːt/ *vtr* préchauffer [*oven*].

prehensile /ˌpriːˈhensaɪl, US -sl/ *adj* préhensile.

prehistoric /ˌpriːhɪˈstɒrɪk, US -tɔːrɪk/ *adj* Archeol, fig préhistorique; **in ~ times** à l'époque préhistorique.

prehistory /ˌpriːˈhɪstrɪ/ *n* **1** Hist préhistoire *f*; **2** fig (beginnings) débuts *mpl*.

pre-ignition /ˌpriːɪgˈnɪʃn/ *n* autoallumage *m*.

prejudge /ˌpriːˈdʒʌdʒ/ *vtr* juger [qn] d'avance [*person*]; préjuger [*issue*].

prejudice /ˈpredʒʊdɪs/ I *n* **1** (single, specific) préjugé *m* (**against** contre; **in favour of** en faveur de); **to overcome one's ~s** surmonter ses préjugés **2** ¢ préjugés *mpl*; **racial/political ~** préjugés raciaux/en matière de politique; **3** (harm) gen, Jur préjudice *m*; **to the ~ of** au préjudice de; **without ~** sans préjudice (**to** de).
II *vtr* **1** (bias) influencer; **to ~ sb against/in favour of** prévenir qn contre/en faveur de; **2** (harm, jeopardize) porter préjudice à [*claim, case*]; léser [*person*]; compromettre [*chances*]; **to ~ the course of justice** Jur entraver le cours de la justice.

prejudiced /ˈpredʒʊdɪst/ *adj* [*person*] plein de préjugés; [*judge, jury*] partial; [*opinion*] préconçu; [*judgment, account*] tendancieux/-ieuse, partial; **to be ~ against/in favour of** avoir des préjugés contre/en faveur de; **you're ~** tu es partial.

prejudicial /ˌpredʒʊˈdɪʃl/ *adj* sout préjudiciable (**to** à).

prelacy /ˈpreləsɪ/ *n* prélature *f*.

prelate /ˈprelət/ *n* prélat *m*.

prelaw /ˈpriːlɔː/ *adj* US Univ [*studies*] préparatoire aux études de droit; [*student*] en classe préparatoire aux études de droit.

prelim /ˈpriːlɪm/ *n* (*gén pl*) **1** GB Univ examen *m* de passage en deuxième année; **2** GB Sch ≈ bac *m* blanc; **3** Print pièces *fpl* liminaires; **4** Sport épreuve *f* éliminatoire.

preliminary /prɪˈlɪmɪnərɪ, US -nerɪ/ I *n* **1 as a ~ to** en prélude à; **2** Sport épreuve *f* éliminatoire.
II **preliminaries** *npl* préliminaires *mpl* (**to** à).
III *adj* [*comment, data, test*] préliminaire; [*heat, round*] éliminatoire; **~ to** préalable à.

preliminary: **~ hearing** *n* GB Jur audience *f* préliminaire; **~ inquiry**, **~ investigation** *n* Jur enquête *f* préliminaire; **~ ruling** *n* Jur décision *f* préliminaire.

prelude /ˈprelju:d/ **I** *n* gen, Mus prélude *m* (**to** à).
II sout *vtr* préluder à fml, annoncer.

premarital /ˌpri:ˈmærɪtl/ *adj* [*sex, relations*] avant le mariage; [*contract*] de mariage.

premature /ˈpremətjʊə(r), US ˌpri:məˈtʊər/ *adj* **1** gen prématuré; **it is ~ to do, it is ~ to be doing** il est prématuré de faire; **2** Med [*baby, birth, ageing*] prématuré; [*ejaculation, menopause*] précoce; **to be born two weeks ~** naître deux semaines avant terme.

prematurely /ˈpremətjʊəlɪ, US ˌpri:məˈtʊərlɪ/ *adv* [*act, be born, die, flower*] prématurément; [*aged, born, bald, wrinkled*] prématurément; **to retire ~** prendre une retraite anticipée.

premed /ˌpri:ˈmed/ **I** *n* GB Med (*abrév* = **premedication**) prémédication *f*.
II *adj* US Univ (*abrév* = **premedical**) [*studies*] préparatoire aux études de médecine; [*student*] en classe préparatoire aux études de médecine.

premedication /ˌpri:medɪˈkeɪʃn/ *n* Med prémédication *f*.

premeditate /ˌpri:ˈmedɪteɪt/ *vtr* gen, Jur préméditer [*act, attack, crime*].

premeditation /ˌpri:medɪˈteɪʃn/ *n* gen, Jur préméditation *f*.

premenstrual /ˌpri:ˈmenstrʊəl/ *adj* prémenstruel/-elle.

premenstrual: **~ syndrome**, **PMS** *n* spec syndrome *m* prémenstruel; **~ tension**, **PMT** *n* syndrome *m* prémenstruel.

premier /ˈpremɪə(r), US ˈpri:mɪər/ **I** *n* **1** (prime minister) premier ministre *m*; **2** (head of government) chef *m* du gouvernement.
II *adj* premier/-ière.

première /ˈpremɪeə(r), US ˈpri:mɪər/ **I** *n* première *f*; **world/British/London ~** première mondiale/en Grande-Bretagne/à Londres.
II *vtr* donner [qch] en première [*film, play*].
III *vi* [*film*] passer en première.

premiership /ˈpremɪeəʃɪp, US prɪˈmɪərʃɪp/ *n* Pol (of prime minister) fonction *f* de premier ministre; (of head of government) fonction *f* de chef du gouvernement; (period of office) ministère *m*.

premise /ˈpremɪs/ **I** *n* GB (also **premiss** GB) prémisse *f*; **on the ~ that** en supposant que (+ *subj*).
II premises *npl* locaux *mpl*; **business/council ~s** locaux *mpl* commerciaux/de la mairie; **embassy ~s** ambassade *f*; **office ~s** bureaux *mpl*; **on the ~s** sur place; **off the ~s** à l'extérieur; **she asked me to leave the ~s** elle m'a demandé de quitter les lieux; **the accident happened off our ~s** l'accident s'est produit en dehors de nos locaux.

premium /ˈpri:mɪəm/ *n* **1** gen (extra payment) supplément *m*; **to buy/sell at a ~ (price)** acheter/vendre au prix fort; **2** (Stock Exchange) prime *f* d'émission; **to sell shares** ou **stock at a ~** vendre des actions au-dessus du pair; **3** Insur prime *f* (d'assurance); **4** Comm (payment for lease) reprise *f*; **5** fig **to be at a ~** valoir de l'or; **time is at a ~** le temps devient précieux; **to put** ou **place** ou **set a (high) ~ on sth** mettre qch au (tout) premier plan.

premium: **~ bond** GB *n* obligation *f* à lots; **~ fuel** GB, **~ gasoline** US *n* supercarburant *m*; **~ price** *n* prix *m* fort; **~ product** *n* produit *m* de luxe; **~ rent** *n* loyer *m* très cher.

premolar /ˌpri:ˈməʊlə(r)/ *n* prémolaire *f*.

premonition /ˌpri:məˈnɪʃn, ˌpre-/ *n* prémonition *f*; **to have a ~ of/that** avoir la prémonition de/que.

premonitory /prɪˈmɒnɪtərɪ, US -tɔ:rɪ/ *adj* sout prémonitoire.

prenatal /ˌpri:ˈneɪtl/ *adj* surtout US prénatal.

prenuptial /ˌpri:ˈnʌpʃl/ *adj* prénuptial.

preoccupation /ˌpri:ɒkjʊˈpeɪʃn/ *n* préoccupation *f*; **to have a ~ with** se préoccuper de; **his ~ with** son obsession pour.

preoccupied /ˌpri:ˈɒkjʊpaɪd/ *adj* préoccupé (**with, by** par).

preoccupy /ˌpri:ˈɒkjʊpaɪ/ *vtr* (*prét, pp* **-pied**) préoccuper.

pre-op° /ˌpri:ˈɒp/ **I** *n* médicament *m* préopératoire.
II *adj* = **preoperative**.

preoperative /ˌpri:ˈɒpərətɪv, US -reɪt-/ *adj* préopératoire; **~ injection/medication** piqûre *f*/médicament *m* préopératoire.

preordain /ˌpri:ɔ:ˈdeɪn/ **I** *vtr* **1** prescrire [qch] d'avance [*decree, order*]; **2** Relig, Philos prédestiner [*sb's fate*]; préétablir [*shape of world*].
II preordained *pp adj* **1** [*decree, order*] prescrit d'avance; **2** Relig, Philos [*outcome*] prédestiné; [*pattern*] préétabli.

prep° /prep/ **I** *n* **1** GB Sch (homework) devoirs *mpl*; (study period) étude *f*; **2** US Sch (student) élève *mf* d'un lycée privé; **3** US Med (of patient) préparation *f*.
II *vtr* US Med préparer [*patient*].
III *vi* (*p prés etc* **-pp-**) US **1 to ~ for**° se préparer à [*exam, studies*]; **2** Sch être en classe préparatoire.

prepack /ˌpri:ˈpæk/, **prepackage** /ˌpri:ˈpækɪdʒ/ *vtr* pré-emballer.

prepaid /ˌpri:ˈpaɪd/ *adj* gen payé d'avance; **carriage ~** port payé; **~ reply card** carte-réponse *f* avec port payé; **~ envelope** enveloppe *f* affranchie pour la réponse.

preparation /ˌprepəˈreɪʃn/ **I** *n* **1** (of meal, report, lecture, event) préparation *f*; **~s** préparatifs *mpl*; **to make ~s for** faire les préparatifs de; **in ~ for** en vue de [*event, journey, meeting, conflict*]; **to be in ~** être en préparation; **2** (physical, psychological) préparation *f* (**for** pour); (sporting) entraînement *m* (**for** pour); **education should be a ~ for life** l'éducation devrait préparer à la vie; **3** Cosmet, Culin, Med (substance) préparation *f* (**for** pour; **to do** pour faire); **4** GB (homework) ¢ devoirs *mpl*.
II *modif* [*time*] de préparation; [*stage*] préparatoire.

preparatory /prɪˈpærətrɪ, US -tɔ:rɪ/ *adj* [*training, course, studies*] préparatoire; [*meeting, report, research, steps, investigations*] préliminaire, préalable; [*drawing*] préparatoire; **~ to sth** en vue de qch, avant qch; **~ to doing** avant de faire.

preparatory school *n* **1** GB école *f* primaire privée; **2** US lycée *m* privé.

prepare /prɪˈpeə(r)/ **I** *vtr* (plan) préparer [*food, meal, bed, room, class, speech, report, plan*] (**for** pour); préparer [*surprise*] (**for** à); **to ~ to do** se préparer or s'apprêter à faire; **to ~ sb for** préparer qn à [*exam, situation, shock*]; **to ~ one's defence** Jur préparer sa défense; **to ~ the ground** ou **way for sth** préparer le terrain or la voie pour qch.
II *vi* **to ~ for** se préparer à [*trip, talks, exam, election, storm, war*]; se préparer pour [*party, ceremony, game*]; **to ~ for action** Mil se préparer à l'action.
III *v refl* **to ~ oneself** se préparer; **~ yourself for some bad news** prépare-toi à recevoir une mauvaise nouvelle.

prepared /prɪˈpeəd/ *adj* **1** (willing) **to be ~ to do** être prêt à faire; **2** (ready) **to be ~ for** [*disaster, strike, conflict, change*] être prêt à; **to be well-/ill-~** (with materials) être bien/mal équipé; **to come ~** venir bien préparé; **be ~!** soyez prêt!; **to be ~ for the worst** s'attendre au pire; **I really wasn't ~ for this!** je ne m'attendais pas du tout à ça!; **3** (ready-made) [*meal*] tout prêt; [*speech, statement, response, text*] préparé d'avance.

preparedness /prɪˈpeərɪdnɪs/ *n* **1 ~ for** préparation *f* en cas de [*disaster, development*]; **a state of ~** Mil un état d'alerte; **2** (willingness) **her ~ to address major issues** son empressement à aborder des problèmes importants.

prepay /ˌpri:ˈpeɪ/ *vtr* payer [qch] d'avance.

prepayment /ˌpri:ˈpeɪmənt/ *n* paiement *m* d'avance.

preponderance /prɪˈpɒndərəns/ *n* prépondérance *f* (**of** de; **over** sur); **it differs from previous governments in the ~ of ministers below the age of 63** il se distingue des gouvernements précédents par la prépondérance de ministres de moins de 63 ans.

preponderant /prɪˈpɒndərənt/ *adj* prépondérant.

preponderantly /prɪˈpɒndərəntlɪ/ *adv* principalement.

preponderate /prɪˈpɒndəreɪt/ *vi* prédominer (**over** sur).

preposition /ˌprepəˈzɪʃn/ *n* préposition *f*.

prepositional /ˌprepəˈzɪʃənəl/ *adj* prépositionnel/-elle; **~ phrase** (used as preposition) locution *f* prépositive; (introduced by preposition) syntagme *m* prépositionnel.

prepositionally /ˌprepəˈzɪʃənəlɪ/ *adv* comme préposition.

prepossess /ˌpri:pəˈzes/ *vtr* sout **1** (preoccupy) préoccuper; **2** (influence) influencer.

prepossessing /ˌpri:pəˈzesɪŋ/ *adj* avenant.

preposterous /prɪˈpɒstərəs/ *adj* grotesque.

preposterously /prɪˈpɒstərəslɪ/ *adv* ridiculement.

preppie, **preppy** /ˈprepɪ/ US **I** *n* (*pl* **-pies**) (student) élève *mf* d'un lycée privé; fig péj jeune bourgeois/-e *mf* à l'allure bon chic bon genre.
II *adj* bon chic bon genre *inv*, B.C.B.G.

preprogrammed /ˌpri:ˈprəʊgræmd, US -grəmd/ *adj* gen programmé (**to do** pour faire); Comput préprogrammé.

prep school /ˈprepsku:l/ *n* **1** GB école *f* primaire privée; **2** US lycée *m* privé.

prepster° /ˈprepstə(r)/ *n* US Sch élève *mf* d'un lycée privé.

prepuce /ˈpri:pju:s/ *n* prépuce *m*.

Pre-Raphaelite /ˌpri:ˈræfəlaɪt/ **I** *n* préraphaélite *mf*.
II *adj* [*style, sensibility*] préraphaélite; [*face, look*] préraphaélique.

prerecord /ˌpri:rɪˈkɔ:d/ **I** *vtr* TV, Radio enregistrer à l'avance [*programme*].
II prerecorded *pp adj* [*broadcast*] préenregistré, en différé *inv*.

preregister /ˌpri:ˈredʒɪstə(r)/ *vi* US Univ s'inscrire.

preregistration /ˌpri:redʒɪˈstreɪʃn/ *n* US Univ préinscription *f*.

prerelease /ˌpri:rɪˈli:s/ *adj* Cin [*screening, publicity*] d'avant-première *inv*.

prerequisite /ˌpri:ˈrekwɪzɪt/ **I** *n* **1** gen préalable *m* (**of** de; **for** à); **2** US Univ unité *f* de valeur; **to be a ~ for** [*course*] être l'unité de valeur dont l'obtention conditionne l'inscription en [*higher course*].
II *adj* [*condition*] préalable.

prerogative /prɪˈrɒgətɪv/ *n* (official) prérogative *f*; (personal) droit *m*; **~s of the head of State/of the regime** prérogatives du chef de l'État/du régime; **that is your ~** c'est votre droit.

presage /ˈpresɪdʒ/ sout **I** *n* présage *m* (**of** de).
II *vtr* laisser présager [*disaster*].

presbyopia /ˌprezbɪˈəʊpɪə/ *n* presbytie *f*.

Presbyterian /ˌprezbɪˈtɪərɪən/ *n, adj* presbytérien/-ienne (*m/f*).

Presbyterianism /ˈprezbɪˈtɪərɪənɪzəm/ *n* presbytérianisme *m*.

presbytery /ˈprezbɪtrɪ, US -terɪ/ *n* **1** (priest's house) presbytère *m*; **2** (ruling body) (+ *v sg ou pl*) consistoire *m* presbytérien; **3** (part of church) chœur *m*.

preschool /ˌpri:ˈsku:l/ **I** *n* US (kindergarten) école *f* maternelle; **in ~** à l'école maternelle.
II *adj* [*child*] d'âge préscolaire *inv*; [*years*] préscolaire.

preschooler /ˌpri:ˈsku:lə(r)/ *n* US Sch enfant *mf* d'âge préscolaire.

preschool playgroup *n* GB ≈ jardin *m* d'enfants.

prescience /ˈpresɪəns/ *n* prescience *f*.

prescient /ˈpresɪənt/ *adj* prescient.

prescribe /prɪˈskraɪb/ **I** *vtr* **1** Med fig prescrire (**for sb** à qn; **for sth** pour qch); **he was ~d aspirin** on lui a prescrit de l'aspirine®; **what do you ~?** hum qu'est-ce que je peux faire docteur?; **2** (lay down) imposer [*rule*].
II prescribed *pp adj* **1** Med, fig (recommended) [*drug, treatment, course of action*] prescrit; **2** (set) [*rule*] imposé; Sch, Univ [*book*] inscrit au programme.

prescription /prɪˈskrɪpʃn/ **I** *n* **1** Med (paper) ordonnance *f* (**for** pour); **on ~** sur ordonnance; **repeat ~** ordonnance renouvelable; **2** Med (recommendation) prescription *f* (**of** de); **3** fig (formula) recette *f* (**for** de); (set of rules) prescription *f*.
II *modif* Med [*glasses, lenses*] correcteur/-trice; **~ drug** préparation médicinale.

prescription charges *npl* GB Med frais *mpl* d'ordonnance (*payables en pharmacie*).

prescriptive /prɪˈskrɪptɪv/ *adj* **1** gen, Ling (with set rules) normatif/-ive; **2** Jur [*right, title*] prescriptible; **3** gen, sout consacré par l'usage.

prescriptivism /prɪˈskrɪptɪvɪzəm/ *n* normativisme *m*.

presence /ˈprezns/ *n* **1** présence *f*; **in sb's ~, in the ~ of sb** en présence de qn; **in my ~** en ma présence; **to be admitted to sb's ~** être admis auprès de qn; **signed in the ~ of X** Jur signé par-devant X; **your ~ is requested at** vous êtes prié d'assister à; **2** (personal quality) présence *f*, prestance *f*; **stage ~** présence sur scène; **3** (of troops, representatives) présence *f*; **a military/UN ~** une présence militaire/de l'ONU; **to maintain a ~ in a country** maintenir une présence dans un pays; **a heavy police ~** (in streets) une forte présence policière; (at match, demonstration) un important service d'ordre; **4** (human or ghostly) présence *f*; **to sense a ~** sentir une présence; **ghostly ~** présence surnaturelle.
IDIOMS **to make one's ~ felt** ne pas passer inaperçu.

presence of mind *n* présence *f* d'esprit.

present I /ˈpreznt/ *n* **1** (gift) cadeau *m*; **to give sb a ~** offrir un cadeau à qn; **to give sb sth as a ~** offrir qch à qn; **2 the ~** (now) le présent; **the past and the ~** le passé et le présent; **to live in the ~** vivre dans le présent or l'instant; **for the ~** pour le moment, pour l'instant; **3** Ling (also **~ tense**) présent *m*; **in the ~** au présent.
II presents *npl* Jur présentes *fpl*.
III /ˈpreznt/ *adj* **1** (attending) [*person*] présent; **all those ~, everybody ~** toutes les personnes présentes, tous les présents; **half of those ~** la moitié des personnes présentes or des présents; **to be ~ at** assister à; **to be ~ in** [*substance, virus*] être présent dans [*blood, wine, population*]; **there are ladies ~**† il y a des dames dans l'assistance†; **~ company excepted** à l'exception des personnes ici présentes; **all ~ and correct!** tous présents à l'appel!; **2** (current) [*address, arrangement, circumstance, government, leadership, situation*] actuel/-elle; **in the ~ climate** fig dans le climat actuel; **up to the ~ day** jusqu'à ce jour; **at the ~ time** ou **moment** actuellement; **during the ~ year/decade** pendant cette année/décennie; **3** (under consideration) [*case, argument, issue*] présent; **the ~ writer feels that** l'auteur (de cet article) pense que; **4** Ling [*tense, participle*] présent.
IV at present *adv phr* (at this moment) en ce moment; (nowadays) actuellement, à présent.
V /prɪˈzent/ *vtr* **1** (raise) présenter [*problem, challenge, obstacle, risk*]; offrir [*chance, opportunity*]; **2** (proffer, show) présenter [*tickets, documents, sight, picture*]; **to ~ a cheque for payment** présenter un chèque à l'encaissement; **to be ~ed with a choice/dilemma** se trouver face à un choix/dilemme; **to be ~ed with a huge bill/with a splendid view** se retrouver avec une énorme facture/devant un panorama splendide; **3** (submit for consideration) présenter [*plan, report, figures, views, bill, case*]; présenter, soumettre [*petition*]; fournir [*evidence*]; **to ~ sth to sb, to ~ sb with sth** présenter qch à qn; **4** (formally give) remettre [*bouquet, prize, award, certificate, cheque*]; présenter [*apologies, respects, compliments*]; **to ~ sth to sb, to ~ sb with sth** remettre qch à qn; **5** (portray) présenter, représenter [*person, situation*] (**as** comme étant); **to ~ sth in a good/different light** présenter qch sous un jour favorable/différent; **6** TV, Radio présenter [*programme, broadcast, show*]; **~ed by** présenté par; **7** (put on, produce) donner [*production, play, concert*]; présenter [*exhibition, actor, star*]; **we are proud to ~ Don Wilson** nous sommes fiers de vous présenter Don Wilson; **8** sout (introduce) présenter; **may I ~ my son Piers?** permettez-moi de vous présenter mon fils Piers; **to be ~ed at court** être présenté à la Cour; **9** Mil présenter [*arms*]; **~ arms!** présentez armes!
VI *vi* Med [*baby, patient*] se présenter; [*symptom, humour, condition*] apparaître.
VII *v refl* **1 to ~ oneself** se présenter (**as** comme étant; **at** à; **for** pour); **to learn how to ~ oneself** apprendre à mettre en avant ses qualités; **2 to ~ itself** [*opportunity, thought*] se présenter.
IDIOMS **there is no time like the ~** il ne faut jamais remettre au lendemain ce que l'on peut faire le jour même.

presentable /prɪˈzentəbl/ *adj* présentable.

presentation /ˌprezənˈteɪʃn/ *n* **1** (of plan, report, bill, petition etc) présentation *f*; **on ~ of this coupon** Comm sur présentation de ce coupon; **2** (by salesman, colleague, executive etc) exposé *m*; **to do** ou **give** ou **make a ~ on** faire un exposé sur; **3** (of gift, cheque, award) remise *f* (**of** de); **the chairman will make the ~** le président remettra le prix; **there will be a ~ at 5.30** il y aura une cérémonie à 17h 30; **4** (person's way of communicating sth) présentation *f*; **5** (portrayal) représentation (**of** de; **as** comme); **6** Theat représentation *f*; **7** Med (of baby) présentation *f*; **8** (introduction) sout présentation *f*.

presentational skills *npl* = **presentation skills**.

presentation: **~ box** *n* coffret-cadeau *m*; **~ copy** *n* hommage *m* (*de l'auteur ou de l'éditeur*); **~ pack** *n* présentoir *m*.

presentation skills *npl* **to have good ~** avoir le sens de la communication.

present-day /ˌprezəntˈdeɪ/ *adj* actuel/-elle.

presenter /prɪˈzentə(r)/ ▶ 1692 *n* TV, Radio présentateur/-trice *m/f*; **television/radio ~** présentateur/-trice de télévision/de radio.

presentiment /prɪˈzentɪmənt/ *n* sout pressentiment *m*.

presently /ˈprezəntlɪ/ *adv* **1** (currently) à présent, en ce moment; **2** (soon afterwards, in past) peu de temps après; **3** (soon, in future) bientôt; **he will be here ~** il va bientôt arriver.

presentment /prɪˈzentmənt/ *n* **1** Fin présentation *f*; **~ for payment** présentation à l'encaissement; **2** US, Jur déclaration *f* d'accusation (*émise par le jury*).

present perfect *n* passé *m* composé.

preservation /ˌprezəˈveɪʃn/ *n* (of building, wildlife, tradition, peace, dignity) préservation *f* (**of** de); (of food) conservation *f* (**of** de); (of life) protection *f* (**of** de).

preservation order *n* **to put a ~ on sth** classer qch; **there is a ~ on the tree** l'arbre est classé.

preservative /prɪˈzɜːvətɪv/ **I** *n* (for food) agent *m* de conservation; (for wood) revêtement *m* (protecteur).
II *adj* [*mixture, product, effect*] de conservation.

preserve /prɪˈzɜːv/ **I** *n* **1** Culin (jam) (also **~s**) confiture *f*; (pickle) conserve *f*; **peach/cherry ~** confiture *f* de pêche/de cerise; **2** (territory) lit, fig chasse *f* gardée (**of** de); **to be a male ~** être la chasse gardée des hommes, être reservé aux hommes.
II *vtr* **1** (save from destruction) préserver [*land, building, manuscript, memory, tradition, language*] (**for** pour); entretenir [*wood, leather, painting*]; **2** (maintain) préserver [*peace, harmony, standards, rights*]; maintenir [*order*]; **3** (keep, hold onto) [*person*] garder [*sense of humour, dignity, silence, beauty, health*]; **4** (rescue, save life of) préserver; **God ~ us!**† Dieu nous garde!; **heaven** ou **the saints ~ us from that!**† ou hum le ciel nous en préserve!; **5** Culin (prevent from rotting) conserver [*food*]; **6** (make into jam) faire de la confiture de [*fruit*].
III preserved *pp adj* [*food*] en conserve; [*site, castle*] protégé; **~d in vinegar/peat** conservé dans le vinaigre/la tourbe; **~d on film/on tape** conservé sur la pellicule/sur bande.

preserver /prɪˈzɜːvə(r)/ *n* Relig sauveur *m*; gen gardien/-ienne *m/f*.

preserving pan *n* bassine *f* à confiture.

preset /ˌpriːˈset/ *vtr* (*prét, pp* **-set**) régler (à l'avance) [*timer, cooker, video*] (**to do** pour faire).

preshrunk /ˌpriːˈʃrʌŋk/ *adj* [*fabric*] irrétrécissable.

preside /prɪˈzaɪd/ *vi* présider; **to ~ at** présider [*meeting, conference*]; **to ~ over** (chair) présider [*conference, committee*]; (oversee) présider à [*activity, change*].

presidency /ˈprezɪdənsɪ/ *n* présidence *f*.

president /ˈprezɪdənt/ ▶ 1268 *n* **1** gen, Pol président/-e *m/f*; **President Kennedy** le président Kennedy; **to run for ~** être candidat/-e à la présidence; **2** US Comm président-directeur *m* général.

president-elect *n* président/-e *m/f* élu/-e (*avant sa prestation de serment*).

presidential /ˌprezɪˈdenʃl/ *adj* [*election, government, term*] présidentiel/-ielle; [*race, candidate*] à la présidence; [*adviser, office, policy*] du président.

president: **President of the Board of Trade** *n* GB ≈ ministre *m* du Commerce; **Presidents' Day** *n* US *jour férié pour commémorer l'anniversaire de Washington*.

presidium /prɪˈsɪdɪəm/ *n* Pol présidium *m*.

pre-soak /ˌpriːˈsəʊk/ *vtr* faire tremper [*washing*].

presort /ˌpriːˈsɔːt/ *vtr* US trier par codes postaux [*mail*].

press /pres/ **I** *n* **1 the ~, the Press** (+ *v sg* ou *pl*) la presse *f*; **in the ~** dans la presse; **to get a good/bad ~** lit, fig avoir bonne/mauvaise presse; **2** (also **printing ~**) presse *f*; **to come off the ~** sortir des presses; **to go to ~** être mis sous presse; **at** ou **in (the) ~** sous presse; **to pass sth for ~** donner le bon à tirer à qch; **at the time of going to ~** à l'heure où nous mettons or mettions sous presse; **3** (publishing house) maison *f* d'éditon; (print works) imprimerie *f*; **the University Press** les Presses *fpl* Universitaires; **the Starlight Press** les Éditions Starlight; **4** (device for flattening) presse *f*; ▶ **cider press, garlic press etc**; **5** (act of pushing) pression *f*; **to give sth a ~** appuyer sur qch; **at the ~ of a button** en appuyant sur un bouton; **6** (with iron) repassage *m*; **to give sth a ~** repasser qch; **7** (crowd) foule *f* (**of** de); **8** Sport épaulé-jeté *m*, épaulé-développé *m*; **9** GB dial (cupboard) placard *m*.
II *modif* [*acclaim, freedom, criticism*] de la presse; [*campaign, photo, photographer*] de presse; [*announcement, advertising*] par voie de presse; **~ story, ~ report** reportage *m*.
III *vtr* **1** (push) appuyer sur [*button, switch, pedal*]; **to ~ sth in** enfoncer qch; **~ the pedal right down** appuie à fond sur la pédale; **~ the switch down** pousse

l'interrupteur vers le bas; **to ~ sth into** enfoncer qch dans [*clay, mud, ground*]; **to ~ sth into place** appuyer sur qch pour le mettre en place; **to ~ a lid onto sth** mettre le couvercle de qch; **to ~ sth into sb's hand** glisser qch dans la main de qn; **2** (apply) **to ~ one's nose/face against sth** coller son nez/visage contre qch; **to ~ a blotter/cloth onto sth** appliquer un buvard/chiffon sur qch; **to ~ a stamp/a label onto sth** apposer un timbre/une étiquette sur qch; **to ~ one's hands to one's ears** se plaquer les mains contre les oreilles; **to ~ the receiver to one's ear** mettre l'écouteur contre son oreille; **to ~ one's face into the pillow** enfoncer son visage dans l'oreiller; **to ~ one's knees together** serrer les genoux; **to ~ two objects together** presser deux objets l'un contre l'autre; **3** (squeeze) presser [*fruit, flower*]; serrer [*arm, hand, person*]; **to ~ sb to one** presser qn contre soi; **to ~ sb to one's bosom** presser qn contre son cœur; **to ~ the soil flat** aplanir or niveler le sol; **to ~ clay into shape** modeler de l'argile; **4** (iron) repasser [*clothes*]; **to ~ the pleats flat** aplatir les plis; **5** (urge) faire pression sur [*person*]; insister sur [*point*]; mettre [qch] en avant [*matter, issue*]; défendre [qch] avec insistance [*case*]; **to ~ sb to do** presser qn de faire; **to ~ sb for action** presser qn d'agir; **to ~ sb into a role** forcer qn à jouer un rôle; **to ~ sb into doing** forcer qn à faire; **I must ~ you for an answer** je dois avoir une réponse; **when ~ed, he admitted that...** quand on a insisté, il a reconnu que...; **to ~ a point** insister; **to ~ one's suit**† faire une cour insistante; **6** Tech former [*shape, object*]; presser [*record, CD*]; emboutir [*steel, metal, car body*]; **~ed steel** acier embouti; **to ~ out pieces** reproduire des pièces par pression; **7** Naut Hist racoler, enrôler [qn] de force [*recruit, man*]; **8** Sport soulever [*weight*]; **9** Hist (as torture) soumettre [qn] au supplice de l'écrasement.

IV *vi* **1** (push with hand, foot, object) **to ~ down** appuyer; **to ~ (down) on, to ~ against** appuyer sur [*pedal, surface*]; **the blankets are ~ing (down) on my leg** les couvertures pèsent sur ma jambe; **her guilt ~ed down on her** sa culpabilité lui pesait; **2** (throng, push with body) [*crowd, person*] se presser (**against** contre; **around** autour de; **forward** vers l'avant); **to ~ through the entrance** se presser à l'entrée; **to ~ through the crowd** se frayer un chemin à travers la foule.

V *v refl* **to ~ oneself against** se plaquer contre [*wall*]; se presser contre [*person*].

■ **press ahead** aller de l'avant; **to ~ ahead with** [sth] faire avancer [*reform, plan, negotiations*].

■ **press for**: **~ for** [sth] faire pression pour obtenir [*change, support, release*]; **to be ~ed for sth** ne pas avoir beaucoup de qch.

■ **press on**: ¶ **~ on 1** (on journey) continuer; **to ~ on through the rain** continuer sous la pluie; **2** (carry on) aller de l'avant; **to ~ on regardless** continuer malgré tout; **3** (move on, keep moving) fig passer à la suite; **let's ~ on to the next item** passons au point suivant; **to ~ on with** faire avancer [*reform, plan, negotiation, agenda*]; passer à [*next item*]; ¶ **~ [sth] on sb** forcer qn à prendre [*gift, food, drink*].

press: **~ agency** *n* agence *f* de presse; **~ agent** ▶1692 *n* attaché /-e *m/f* de presse; **Press Association** *n* GB agence *f* de presse britannique; **~ attaché** *n* = **press agent**; **~ baron** *n* magnat *m* de la presse; **~ box** *n* tribune *f* de la presse; **~ card** *n* carte *f* de presse; **~ clipping** *n* coupure *f* de presse; **~ conference** *n* conférence *f* de presse; **~ corps** *n* journalistes *mpl*; **~ cutting** *n* coupure *f* de presse; **~ gallery** *n* tribune *f* de la presse.

press-gang /ˈpresgæŋ/ **I** *n* Hist (+ *v sg ou pl*) racoleurs *mpl*.

II *vtr* Hist racoler; **to ~ sb into the navy** recruter qn de force dans la marine; **to ~ sb into doing** fig forcer qn à faire.

pressie○ /ˈprezɪ/ *n* GB cadeau *m*.

pressing /ˈpresɪŋ/ **I** *n* **1** (of olives) pression *f*; **2** (of records) pressage *m*.

II *adj* **1** (urgent) [*need, business, concern, duty*] pressant, urgent; [*issue, problem, question*] urgent; **2** (insistent) [*invitation*] pressant; [*anxiety, feeling*] oppressant.

press lord *n* magnat *m* de la presse.

pressman /ˈpresmən/ ▶1692 *n* **1** (printer) imprimeur/-euse *m/f*; **2** GB (journalist) journaliste *m*.

press: **~mark** *n* GB cote *f*; **~ officer** ▶1692 *n* attaché/-e *m/f* de presse; **~ of sail** *n* Naut force *f* de voiles; **~ pack** *n* dossier *m* de presse; **~ pass** *n* coupe-file *m inv*; **~ release** *n* communiqué *m* de presse; **~room** *n* Print salle *f* des presses or d'imprimerie; Journ, Pol salle *f* de presse; **~ run** *n* tirage *m*; **~ secretary** *n* attaché/e *m/f* de presse; **~-stud** *n* GB (bouton-)pression *m*; **~-up** *n* pompe○ *f*, flexion *f* en appui sur les bras.

pressure /ˈpreʃə(r)/ **I** *n* **1** gen, Tech, Meteorol pression *f*; **to exert/put ~ on sth** exercer une/faire pression sur qch; **to store sth under ~** stocker qch sous pression; **a ~ of 1 kg per cm²** une pression de 1 kg par cm²; ▶**blood pressure**, **high pressure etc**; **2** fig (on person) pression *f*; **the ~ on her to conform** la pression exercée sur elle pour qu'elle se conforme à la norme; **to put ~ on sb** faire pression sur qn (**to do** pour qu'il/elle fasse); **to do sth under ~** faire qch sous la contrainte; **to do sth under ~ from sb** faire qch sous la pression de qn; **to work well/badly under ~** travailler bien/mal sous pression; **he is under ~ from his boss to do** son patron fait pression sur lui pour qu'il fasse; **she has come under a lot of ~ to do** on exerce de fortes pressions sur elle pour l'amener à faire; **to be put under ~ by one's job** être stressé○ par son travail; **due to ~ of work** pour cause d'emploi du temps chargé; **financial ~s** contraintes financières; **the ~s of fame** les tensions amenées par la célébrité; **the ~s of modern life** le stress de la vie moderne; **3** (volume) (of traffic, tourists, visitors) flux *m*.

II *vtr* = **pressurize**.

pressure: **~ cabin** *n* cabine *f* pressurisée; **~-cook** *vtr* cuire [qch] dans un autocuiseur or à la cocotte-minute®; **~ cooker** *n* cocotte-minute *f*®, autocuiseur *m*; **~ gauge** *n* manomètre *m*, indicateur *m* de pression; **~ group** *n* (+ *v sg ou pl*) groupe *m* de pression; **~ point** *n* point *m* de compression; **~ suit** *n* combinaison *f* pressurisée; **~ vessel** *n* Nucl réservoir *m* à pression.

pressurization /ˌpreʃəraɪˈzeɪʃn, US -rɪˈz-/ *n* Aerosp pressurisation *f*.

pressurize /ˈpreʃəraɪz/ *vtr* **1** (maintain pressure in) pressuriser [*cabin, compartment, suit*]; **2** (put under pressure) lit pressuriser [*liquid, gas*]; **~d gas** gaz pressurisé; **3** fig faire pression sur [*person*]; **to be ~d into doing** être contraint de faire.

pressurized water reactor *n* réacteur *m* à eau pressurisée.

presswoman /ˈpreswʊmən/ ▶1692 *n* GB journaliste *f*.

Prestel® /presˈtel/ *n* GB Telecom cf Télétel® *m*.

prestidigitation /ˌprestɪdɪdʒɪˈteɪʃn/ *n* prestidigitation *f*.

prestige○ /preˈstiːʒ/ **I** *n* prestige *m*.

II *modif* [*car, site*] de prestige; [*housing, hotel*] de grand standing.

prestigious /preˈstɪdʒəs/ *adj* prestigieux/-ieuse.

presto /ˈprestəʊ/ **I** *adv* Mus presto.

II *excl* **hey ~!** hop!

prestressed /ˌpriːˈstrest/ *adj* Constr précontraint.

presumably /prɪˈzjuːməblɪ, US -ˈzuːm-/ *adv* sans doute.

presume /prɪˈzjuːm, US -ˈzuːm/ **I** *vtr* **1** (suppose) supposer, présumer (**that** que); **I ~ (that) he's honest** je suppose qu'il est honnête; **I ~d him to be honest** je le croyais honnête; **to be ~d to be** être présumé être; **I ~ it was him** je suppose que c'était lui; **'does he know?'—'I ~ so/I ~ not'** 'le sait-il?'—'probablement/probablement pas'; **you'll come, I ~?** tu viendras, je suppose?; **~d dead/innocent/guilty** présumé mort/innocent/coupable; **2** (presuppose) présupposer (**that** que); **3** (dare) **to ~ to do** se permettre de faire.

II *vi* **to ~ upon** abuser de [*person, kindness*]; **I hope I'm not presuming** j'espère que je ne m'avance pas trop.

presumption /prɪˈzʌmpʃn/ *n* **1** (supposition) supposition *f* (**that** que); Jur présomption *f* (**of** de); **on the ~ that** en supposant que; **to make a ~** supposer; **the ~ is that** on suppose que; **2** (basis) arguments *mpl* (**against** contre; **in favour of** en faveur de); **3** (impudence) audace *f*.

presumptive /prɪˈzʌmptɪv/ *adj* **1** gen par présomption; **2** Jur [*heir*] présomptif/-ive; **~ evidence** présomptions *fpl*.

presumptuous /prɪˈzʌmptʃʊəs/ *adj* audacieux/-ieuse (**of** de la part de; **to do** de faire).

presumptuously /prɪˈzʌmptʃʊəslɪ/ *adv* avec audace.

presumptuousness /prɪˈzʌmptʃʊəsnɪs/ *n* audace *f*.

presuppose /ˌpriːsəˈpəʊz/ *vtr* présupposer (**that** que).

presupposition /ˌpriːsʌpəˈzɪʃn/ *n* présupposition *f* (**that** que).

pre-tax /ˌpriːˈtæks/ *adj* avant impôts *inv*; **a ~ profit of £3m** un bénéfice de 3 millions de livres avant impôts.

preteen /ˌpriːˈtiːn/ **I** *n* préadolescent/-e *m/f*; **the ~s** (period) la préadolescence; (people) les préadolescents.

II *adj* (also **pre-teen**) préadolescent.

pretence GB, **pretense** US /prɪˈtens/ *n* **1** (false show) faux-semblant *m*; **to make a ~ of sth** feindre qch; **to make a ~ of doing** faire semblant de faire; **to make no ~ of sth** ne pas se donner la peine de feindre qch; **on** ou **under the ~ of doing** sous prétexte de faire; **under the ~ that** sous prétexte que; **to keep up/abandon the ~ of doing** entretenir/cesser d'entretenir l'illusion de faire; **he spoke with no ~ at ou of politeness** il a parlé sans même faire semblant d'être poli; **2** (sham) simulacre *m* (**of** de); (of illness) simulation *f* (**of** de); **a ~ of love/sympathy** un amour/une sympathie feint/-e; ▶**false pretences**.

pretend /prɪˈtend/ **I**○ *adj* lang enfantin (make-believe) [*gun, car*] imaginaire; [*jewels*] faux/fausse (*before n*); **it's only ~!** c'est pour rire!

II *vtr* **1** (feign) simuler [*emotion, illness, ignorance*]; **to ~ that** faire comme si; **to ~ to do** faire semblant de faire; **let's ~ (that) it never happened/we are cowboys** faisons comme si cela n'était pas arrivé/nous étions des cowboys; **a thief ~ing to be a policeman** un voleur se faisant passer pour un policier; **2** (claim) **to ~ to know/understand** avoir la prétention de savoir/comprendre; **to ~ to be** prétendre être.

III *vi* **1** (feign) faire semblant; **to play let's ~** jouer à faire semblant; **2** (maintain deception) jouer la comédie; **after 40 years of marriage it is time to stop ~ing** après 40 ans de mariage il faut cesser de se jouer la comédie; **I was only ~ing** c'était pour rire; **3** (claim) **to ~ to** prétendre à [*throne*]; revendiquer son droit à [*title, crown*].

IV pretended *pp adj* [*emotion, ignorance, illness*] simulé.

pretender /prɪ'tendə(r)/ *n* prétendant/-e *m/f* (**to** à).

pretense *n* US = **pretence**.

pretension /prɪ'tenʃn/ *n* prétention *f*; **to have ~s to sth** prétendre à qch; **to have ~s to doing** avoir la prétention de faire.

pretentious /prɪ'tenʃəs/ *adj* prétentieux/-ieuse.

pretentiously /prɪ'tenʃəslɪ/ *adv* avec prétention.

pretentiousness /prɪ'tenʃəsnɪs/ *n* prétention *f*.

preterite /'pretərət/ *n* prétérit *m*; **in the ~** au prétérit.

preternatural /,pri:tə'nætʃərəl/ *adj* surnaturel/-elle.

pretext /'pri:tekst/ *n* prétexte *m* (**for** à; **for doing** pour faire); **under** ou **on the ~ of sth/of doing** sous le prétexte de qch/de faire.

Pretoria /prɪ'tɔ:rɪə/ ▶ **1818** *pr n* Pretoria.

pretrial /,pri:'traɪl/ **I** *n* US Jur *séance qui a lieu avant le procès pour clarifier les détails légaux.*
II *adj* précédant le procès.

prettify /'prɪtɪfaɪ/ *vtr* enjoliver.

prettily /'prɪtɪlɪ/ *adv* [*arrange, dress, decorate, perform, talk*] joliment; [*blush, smile*] de façon charmante; [*apologize, thank*] gentiment.

pretty /'prɪtɪ/ **I** *adj* **1** (attractive) joli; **it was not a ~ sight** ce n'était pas beau à voir; **2** (trite) péj [*speech*] joli; [*music*] joli, petit; **3**○ (considerable) [*sum*] coquet/-ette (*before n*).
II○ *adv* (very) vraiment; (fairly) assez; (almost) pratiquement; **~ certain, ~ sure** pratiquement sûr; **~ good** pas mal du tout; **~ well all, ~ much all** pratiquement tout; **'how are you?'—'~ well'** 'comment ça va?' —'très bien'.
IDIOMS **~ as a picture** ravissant; **I'm not just a ~ face**○ hum j'ai aussi quelque chose dans la tête; **this is a ~ mess** ou **a ~ state of affairs** iron voilà du beau travail iron; **that must have cost you a ~ penny**○ ça a dû te coûter cher; **to be sitting ~** ○ avoir une bonne situation, se la couler douce○; **things have come to a ~ pass when...** ça commence à ne plus aller du tout quand...
■ **pretty up**: **~ [sth] up, ~ up [sth]** enjoliver.

pretty: **~ boy**○ *n* péj minet○ *m* pej; **~-pretty** *adj* péj trop coquet/-ette.

pretzel /'pretsl/ *n* bretzel *m*.

prevail /prɪ'veɪl/ *vi* **1** (win) [*ability, commonsense, vice, virtue*] prévaloir (**against** contre); **2** (be usual) prédominer.
■ **prevail upon**: **~ upon [sb]** persuader (**to do** de faire).

prevailing /prɪ'veɪlɪŋ/ *adj* **1** gen [*custom, attitude, idea, style*] qui prévaut, prévalent; **2** Fin [*rate*] en vigueur; **3** Meteorol [*wind*] dominant.

prevalence /'prevələns/ *n* **1** (widespread nature) fréquence *f*; **2** (superior position) prédominance *f*.

prevalent /'prevələnt/ *adj* **1** (widespread) répandu; **2** (predominant) qui prévaut.

prevaricate /prɪ'værɪkeɪt/ *vi* sout se dérober, tergiverser.

prevarication /prɪ,værɪ'keɪʃn/ *n* sout tergiversation *f*; **after much ~** après bien des tergiversations.

prevent /prɪ'vent/ *vtr* prévenir [*fire, illness, violence*]; éviter [*conflict, disaster, damage*]; faire obstacle à [*marriage*]; **to ~ the outbreak of war/the introduction of reform** empêcher le déclenchement d'une guerre/l'introduction de réformes; **to ~ sb/sth from doing** empêcher qn/qch de faire; **to ~ sb/sth from being criticized** empêcher que qn/qch soit critiqué; **to prevent sb's death** empêcher que qn ne meure.

preventable /prɪ'ventəbl/ *adj* évitable; **the accident was ~** l'accident aurait pu être évité, l'accident était évitable.

preventative /prɪ'ventətɪv/ *adj* = **preventive**.

prevention /prɪ'venʃn/ *n* prévention *f*; **accident ~** gen prévention *f* des accidents; (on road) prévention *f* routière; **crime ~** lutte *f* contre la délinquance; **fire ~** prévention *f* contre les incendies.
IDIOMS **~ is better than cure** Prov mieux vaut prévenir que guérir Prov.

preventive /prɪ'ventɪv/ *adj* préventif/-ive; **~ detention** Jur détention *f* (*à titre préventif*).

preview /'pri:vju:/ **I** *n* **1** (showing) (of film, play) avant-première *f*; (of exhibition) vernissage *m*; **2** (report) (of match, programme) présentation *f* (**of** de).
II *vtr* présenter [*match, programme*].

previous /'pri:vɪəs/ **I** *adj* **1** (before) (*épith*) [*day, meeting, manager, chapter*] gen précédent; (further back in time) antérieur; **the ~ page** la page précédente; **the ~ day** la veille, le jour précédent or d'avant; **the ~ week/year** la semaine/l'année précédente or d'avant; **in a ~ life** dans une vie antérieure; **on a ~ occasion** (une fois) déjà; **on ~ occasions** à plusieurs reprises; **she has two ~ convictions** Jur elle a déjà fait l'objet de deux inculpations; **he has no ~ convictions** Jur il a un casier judiciaire vierge; **to have a ~ engagement** être déjà pris; **'~ experience essential'** 'expérience préalable indispensable'; **2**○ (hasty) (*jamais épith*) [*decision*] hâtif/-ive; [*action*] prématuré; **he was a little ~ in making the decision alone** c'était un peu hâtif de sa part de prendre seul cette décision.
II previous to *prep phr* avant; **~ to living here, he ...** avant de vivre ici, il...

previously /'pri:vɪəslɪ/ *adv* (before) auparavant, avant; (already) déjà; **two years/days ~s** deux ans/jours auparavant; **we've met ~** nous nous sommes déjà rencontrés.

prewar /,pri:'wɔ:(r)/ *adj* d'avant-guerre *inv*; **the ~ period** ou **years** l'avant-guerre *m* or *f*.

prewash /,pri:'wɒʃ/ *n* prélavage *m*.

prexy○ /'preksɪ/ *n* US président *m* (*de l'Université*).

prey /preɪ/ *n* lit, fig proie *f*; **to fall ~ to sth/sb** devenir la proie de qch/qn; **he was ~ to anxiety** il était en proie à l'anxiété.
■ **prey on**: ¶ **~ on [sth] 1** (hunt) [*animal*] chasser, faire sa proie de [*rodents, birds*]; **2** fig (worry) **to ~ on sb's mind** [*accident, exam, problems*] préoccuper qn; **3** (exploit) exploiter [*fears, worries*]; ¶ **~ on [sb]** [*con man*] choisir ses victimes parmi [*the elderly, the gullible*]; [*mugger, rapist*] s'attaquer à [*women, joggers etc*].

prezy○ /'prezɪ/ *n* US Pol président *m*.

prezzie○ /'prezɪ/ *n* GB cadeau *m*.

price /praɪs/ **I** *n* **1** gen, Comm, lit, fig (cost) prix *m*; **the ~ per ticket/kilo/head** le prix du billet/du kilo/par personne; **to sell sth for** ou **at a good ~** vendre qch à un bon prix; **at competitive/attractive ~s** à des prix compétitifs/intéressants; **'we pay top ~s for...'** 'nous payons le prix fort pour...'; **cars have gone up/fallen in ~** les voitures ont augmenté/baissé; **to give sb a ~** (estimate) donner un prix à qn; **what sort of ~ did you have to pay?** à peu près combien est-ce que tu as eu à payer?; **to pay a high ~ for sth** lit payer cher qch; **to pay a high ~ for sth/for doing** fig payer cher qch/d'avoir fait; **loss of independence was a high ~ to pay for peace** perdre son indépendance c'était cher pour obtenir la paix; **no ~ is too high for winning their support** on ferait tout pour obtenir leur soutien; **that's the ~ one pays for being famous** c'est le prix de la célébrité; **he paid a very low ~ for it** lit il l'a acheté à très bas prix; **that's a small ~ to pay for sth/for doing** fig ce n'est pas un gros sacrifice pour obtenir qch/pour faire; **you can achieve success—but at a ~!** tu peux réussir—mais à quel prix!; **that can be arranged—for a ~!** gen, hum ça peut s'arranger, si tu y mets le prix!; **she wants to get on in life, at any ~** ou **whatever the ~** elle veut à tout prix réussir dans la vie; **peace at any ~** la paix à n'importe quel prix; **I wouldn't buy/wear that horrible thing at any ~!** pour rien au monde je n'achèterais/ne porterais cette horrible chose!; ▶ **half price, full price, selling price etc**; **2** gen, Comm, lit, fig (value) valeur *f*; **of great ~** d'une grande valeur; **beyond** ou **above ~** (d'une valeur) inestimable; **to put a ~ on** lit évaluer [*object, antique*]; **to put** ou **set a high ~ on** attacher beaucoup de prix à [*loyalty, hard work*]; **you can't put a ~ on friendship** l'amitié n'a pas de prix; **what ~ all his good intentions now!** qu'en est-il maintenant de ses bonnes intentions!; **3** (in betting) lit cote *f*; **what ~ he'll turn up late?** fig qu'est-ce que tu paries qu'il va arriver en retard?
II *vtr* **1** (fix, determine the price of) fixer le prix de [*product, object*] (**at** à); **a dress ~d at £30** une robe à 30 livres; **this product is reasonably/competitively ~d** ce produit est à un prix raisonnable/compétitif; **a moderately-~d hotel** un hôtel aux tarifs raisonnables; **2** (estimate, evaluate the worth of) estimer la valeur de [*object*]; **3** (mark the price of) marquer le prix de [*product*].
IDIOMS **every man** ou **everyone has his ~** on peut acheter n'importe qui à condition d'y mettre le prix; **to put a ~ on sb's head** mettre à prix la tête de qn; **he has a ~ on his head** sa tête a été mise à prix.
■ **price down**: **~ [sth] down, ~ down [sth]** GB diminuer le prix de.
■ **price out**: **~ oneself** ou **one's goods out of the market** perdre un marché en pratiquant des prix trop élevés; **we've been ~d out of business/the British market** nous avons perdu notre affaire/notre place dans le marché britannique à cause de nos prix trop élevés; **X has ~d Y out of the market** X a évincé Y du marché en pratiquant des prix moins élevés.
■ **price up**: **~ [sth] up, ~ up [sth]** GB augmenter le prix de [qch].

price: **~ bracket** *n* = **price range**; **~ control** *n* contrôle *m* des prix; **~ cut** *n* baisse *f* du prix; **~ cutting** *n* baisse *f* des prix; **~ discrimination** *n* discrimination *f* des prix; **~-earning ratio** *n* coefficient *m* de capitalisation des résultats; **~ fixing** *n* détermination *f* illégale des prix; **~ freeze** *n* blocage *m* des prix; **~ index** *n* indice *m* des prix; **~ inflation** *n* inflation *f* des prix; **~ label** *n* étiquette *f*.

priceless /'praɪslɪs/ *adj* **1** (extremely valuable) [*object, treasure, person, advice, information*] inestimable; **2** (amusing) [*person, joke, speech*] impayable○, tordant.

price list *n* (in shop, catalogue) liste *f* des prix; (in bar, restaurant) tarif *m*.

price range *n* fourchette *f*; **cars in a ~ of £15,000 to £20,000** des voitures dont les prix se situent dans une fourchette allant de 15 000 à 20 000 livres sterling; **that's out of/in my ~** cela n'est pas/est dans mes prix.

price: **~ restrictions** *n* contrôle *m* des prix; **~ rigging** *n* manipulation *f* des prix; **~ ring** *n* cartel *m* de vendeurs; **~ rise** *n* hausse *f* des prix, augmentation *f* des prix; **~s and income policy** *n* politique *f* des prix et des revenus; **~ support** *n* politique *f* de soutien des prix.

price tag *n* **1** (label) étiquette *f*; **2** fig (cost) coût *m* (**on, for** de).

price: **~ ticket** *n* étiquette *f*; **~ war** *n* guerre *f* des prix.

pricey○ /'praɪsɪ/ *adj* cher/chère.

prick /prɪk/ **I** *n* **1** (of needle etc) (feeling) piqûre *f*; (hole) trou *m* (d'épingle); **to give sth a ~** piquer qch; **a ~ of conscience**

fig un petit remords *m*; **2**● (penis) bitte● *f*, pénis *m*; **3**○ (idiot) con/-nne● *m/f*.

II *vtr* **1** (cause pain) [*needle, thorn, person*] piquer (**with** avec); **to ~ one's finger** se piquer le doigt; **to ~ sb's conscience** fig peser sur la conscience de qn; **his conscience ~ed him** fig il avait mauvaise conscience; **2** (pierce) percer [*paper, plastic*] (**with** avec); crever [*bubble, balloon*] (**with** avec); Culin piquer [*potato etc*]; **to ~ a hole in sth** percer un trou dans qch; **3** = **prick up**.

III *vi* **1** (sting) [*eyes*] piquer; [*skin*] picoter; **my eyes are ~ing** j'ai les yeux qui piquent; **my eyes ~ed with tears** les larmes me piquaient les yeux; **2** [*bush, thorn*] piquer.

IV *v refl* **to ~ oneself** se piquer (**on, with** avec).

IDIOMS **to kick against the ~s** s'obstiner pour rien.

■ **prick out**: **~ out [sth], ~ [sth] out** **1** Hort repiquer [*seedlings*]; **2** Art piquer [*design, outline*].

■ **prick up**: **~ up** [*dog's ears*] se dresser; **at that, my ears ~ed up** cela m'a fait dresser l'oreille; **to ~ up its ears** [*dog*] dresser les oreilles; **to ~ up its/one's ears** dresser l'oreille.

pricking /ˈprɪkɪŋ/ **I** *n* (internal feeling) fourmillement *m*; (result of pin etc) picotement *m*.

II *modif* [*sensation, feeling*] de fourmillement.

prickle /ˈprɪkl/ **I** *n* **1** (of hedgehog, thistle, holly) piquant *m*; **2** (feeling) frisson *m*; **to feel ~s down one's spine** avoir des frissons dans le dos; **to feel a ~ of hostility** ressentir une pointe d'hostilité.

II *vtr* [*clothes, jumper*] gratter.

III *vi* [*hairs*] se hérisser (**with** de); **my skin ~d** j'ai eu la chair de poule.

prickly /ˈprɪklɪ/ *adj* **1** (with prickles) [*bush, rose, leaf*] épineux/-euse; [*animal*] armé de piquants; [*thorn*] piquant; **2** (itchy) [*jumper, beard*] qui gratte; **my skin feels ~** j'ai la peau qui me gratte; **3**○ (touchy) irritable (**about** à propos de).

prickly heat *n* fièvre *f* miliaire.

prickly pear *n* **1** (plant) figuier *m* de Barbarie; **2** (fruit) figue *f* de Barbarie.

prick teaser● *n* allumeuse○ *f*.

pride /praɪd/ **I** *n* **1** (satisfaction) fierté *f* (**in sb/sth** éprouvée pour qn/qch); **with ~** avec fierté; **to take ~ in** être fier/fière de [*ability, achievement, talent*]; soigner [*appearence, work*]; **2** (self-respect) amour-propre *m*; péj orgueil *m*; **to hurt** ou **wound sb's ~** blesser l'amour-propre de qn; **her ~ was hurt** elle était blessée dans son amour-propre; **she has no ~** elle n'a aucune fierté; **~ alone prevented him from...** il avait trop d'amour-propre pour...; **family ~** honneur *m* familial; **national ~** sentiment *m* de fierté nationale; **3** (source of satisfaction) fierté *f*; **to be the ~ of** être la fierté de; **to be sb's ~ and joy** être la (grande) fierté de qn; **4** (group of lions) troupe *f* (**of** de).

II *v refl* **to ~ oneself on sth/on doing** être fier/fière de qch/de faire.

IDIOMS **to have ~ of place** être mis en vedette; **to give sth ~ of place** mettre qch en vedette; **~ comes before a fall** Prov péché d'orgueil ne va pas sans danger.

priest /priːst/ *n* prêtre *m*; **parish ~** curé *m*.

priestess /ˈpriːstes/ *n* prêtresse *f*.

priesthood /ˈpriːsthʊd/ *n* (calling) prêtrise *f*; (clergy) clergé *m*; **to enter the ~** entrer dans les ordres.

priestly /ˈpriːstlɪ/ *adj* sacerdotal.

prig /prɪg/ *n* bégueule *mf*.

priggish /ˈprɪgɪʃ/ *adj* bégueule.

priggishness /ˈprɪgɪʃnɪs/ *n* bégueulerie *f*.

prim /prɪm/ *adj* (also **~ and proper**) [*person*] collet monté *inv*, guindé; [*manner, appearance*] guindé, très comme il faut○ *inv*; [*expression*] pincé; [*voice*] affecté; [*clothing*] très convenable.

prima ballerina /ˌpriːmə ˌbæləˈriːnə/ *n* danseuse *f* étoile.

primacy /ˈpraɪməsɪ/ *n* **1** (primary role) (of principle, language, skill) primauté *f* (**of** de, **over** sur); (of party, power) suprématie *f* (**of** de); **to have ~** avoir la primauté; **2** Relig (also **Primacy**) primatie *f*.

prima donna /ˌpriːmə ˈdɒnə/ *n* Theat prima donna *f inv*; fig (difficult person) **to be a (real) ~** jouer les divas.

primaeval *adj* = **primeval**.

prima facie /ˌpraɪmə ˈfeɪʃiː/ **I** *adj* Jur, gen légitime (à première vue); **to make a ~ case** Jur produire des éléments suffisants; **~ evidence** Jur commencement *m* de preuve.

II *adv* Jur, gen de prime abord.

primal /ˈpraɪml/ *adj* [*quality, feeling, myth*] primitif/-ive; [*stage, origins*] premier/-ière (*before n*); [*cause*] premier/-ière (*after n*); **~ scream** Psych cri *m* primal.

primarily /ˈpraɪmərəlɪ, US praɪˈmerəlɪ/ *adv* **1** (chiefly) essentiellement; **2** (originally) à l'origine.

primary /ˈpraɪmərɪ, US -merɪ/ **I** *n* **1** US Pol (also **~ election**) primaire *f*; ▶ **closed primary**, **open primary**; **2** Zool (also **~ feather**) rémige *f* primaire; **3** Sch ▶ **primary school**.

II *adj* **1** (main) [*aim, cause, concern, factor, reason, role, source, task*] principal; [*sense, meaning*] premier/-ière (*after n*); [*importance*] primordial; **of ~ importance** de première importance; **2** Sch (elementary) [*teaching, education*] primaire; [*post*] dans l'enseignement primaire; **3** (initial) [*stage*] premier/-ière (*before n*); **4** Geol [*rock*] primaire; **5** Econ (*épith*) [*commodities, industry, products*] de base.

primary: **~ colour** *n* couleur *f* primaire; **~ evidence** *n* Jur preuve *f* de première main; **~ health care** *n* soins *mpl* de premier recours; **~ infection** *n* primo-infection *f*.

primary school **I** *n* école *f* primaire.

II *modif* **~ children** élèves *mpl* de l'enseignement primaire; **children of ~ age** élèves *mpl* du cycle élémentaire.

primary: **~ sector** *n* Econ secteur *m* primaire; **~ stress** *n* accent *m* tonique (principal); **~ (school) teacher** ▶ **1692** *n* surtout GB instituteur/-trice *m/f*.

primate /ˈpraɪmeɪt/ *n* **1** Zool (mammal) primate *m*; **2** Relig (also **Primate**) primat *m* (**of** de); **the Primate of all England** l'archevêque de Cantorbéry.

prime /praɪm/ **I** *n* **1** (peak period) **in one's ~** (politically, professionally) à son apogée; (physically) dans la fleur de l'âge; **in its ~** [*organization, industry*] à son apogée; **to be past one's ~** [*person*] avoir passé son heure de gloire; **to be past its ~** [*building, institution, car*] avoir connu des jours meilleurs; **in the ~ of life** dans la fleur de l'âge; **2** Math (also **~ number**) nombre *m* premier; **3** Relig prime *f*.

II *adj* **1** (chief) [*aim, candidate, factor, target, suspect*] principal; [*importance*] primordial; **of ~ importance** de première importance; **2** Comm (good quality) (*épith*) [*site, location, land*] de premier ordre; [*meat, cuts*] de premier choix; [*foodstuffs*] d'une parfaite fraîcheur; **in ~ condition** [*machine*] en parfait état; [*livestock*] en parfaite condition; **of ~ quality** de première qualité; **3** (classic) [*example, instance*] excellent (*before n*); **4** Math premier/-ière (*after n*).

III *vtr* **1** (brief) préparer [*witness, interviewee*]; **to ~ sb about** mettre qn au courant de [*details, facts*]; **to ~ sb to say** souffler à qn de dire; **to be ~d for sth** être préparé pour qch; **2** Constr (apply primer to) appliquer un apprêt sur [*wood, metal*]; **3** Mil amorcer [*device, bomb, firearm*]; **4** Tech amorcer [*pump*].

prime: **~ bill** *n* effet *m* de premier ordre; **~ cost** *n* prix *m* de revient; **~ meridian** *n* premier méridien *m*; **~ minister**, **PM** ▶ **1268** *n* Premier ministre *m*; **~-ministerial** *adj* [*power, role, responsibility*] de Premier ministre; **~ ministership** *n* (duties) fonctions *fpl* de Premier Ministre; (term of office) ministère *m*.

prime mover *n* **1** (influential force) (person) promoteur/-trice *m/f*; (drive, instinct) moteur *m* principal; **2** Phys, Tech force *f* motrice; **3** Philos cause *f* première.

primer /ˈpraɪmə(r)/ *n* **1** Constr (first coat) apprêt *m*; **2**† (textbook) (introductory) livre *m* élémentaire; (for reading) abécédaire† *m*; **3** (for detonating) amorce *f*.

prime rate *n* taux *m* d'escompte bancaire.

prime time **I** *n* heures *fpl* de grande écoute, prime-time *m*.

II **prime-time** *modif* [*advertising, programme*] passant aux heures de grande écoute.

primeval /praɪˈmiːvl/ *adj* **1** (ancient) [*condition, force, creative*] primitif/-ive; **the ~ forest** la forêt vierge; **2** (instinctive) [*instinct, innocence, terror*] primitif/-ive.

primeval soup *n* Biol soupe *f* primitive.

priming /ˈpraɪmɪŋ/ *n* **1** Mil (of weapon) amorçage *m*; **2** Constr (of surface) application *f* d'un apprêt.

priming coat *n* couche *f* d'apprêt.

primitive /ˈprɪmɪtɪv/ **I** *n* **1** Art primitif *m*; **2** Anthrop (person) primitif/-ive *m/f*.

II *adj* (all contexts) primitif/-ive.

primly /ˈprɪmlɪ/ *adv* **1** (starchily) [*behave, smile*] d'une manière guindée; [*say, reply*] d'un ton guindé; **2** (demurely) [*behave, sit*] très sagement.

primness /ˈprɪmnɪs/ *n* **1** (prudishness) air *m* collet monté; **2** (demureness) aspect *m* très convenable.

primogeniture /ˌpraɪməʊˈdʒenɪtʃə(r)/ *n* primogéniture *f*.

primordial /praɪˈmɔːdɪəl/ *adj* [*chaos, matter*] primitif/-ive; **~ life** la vie à l'état primitif; **~ soup** soupe *f* primitive.

primp /prɪmp/ *vtr* (also **~ and preen**) se pomponner.

primrose /ˈprɪmrəʊz/ *n* primevère *f* (jaune).

IDIOMS **the ~ path** le chemin de la facilité.

primrose yellow ▶ **1104** *n*, *adj* jaune (*m*) pâle *inv*.

primula /ˈprɪmjʊlə/ *n* primevère *f*.

Primus® /ˈpraɪməs/ *n* (also **~ stove**) réchaud *m* de camping.

prince /prɪns/ ▶ **1268** *n* prince *m* also fig; **Prince Charles** le prince Charles; **Prince Charming** le prince charmant; **the ~ of darkness** le prince des ténèbres.

Prince Edward Island ▶ **1381** *pr n* île *f* du Prince-Édouard.

princeling /ˈprɪnslɪŋ/ *n* (young) jeune prince *m*; (petty) péj principicule *m* pej.

princely /ˈprɪnslɪ/ *adj* [*amount, salary, court, style*] princier/-ière; [*life, rôle*] de prince.

prince regent *n* prince *m* régent.

princess /prɪnˈses/ ▶ **1268** *n* princesse *f*; **Princess Anne** la princesse Anne; **the Princess Royal** la princesse royale (*la fille aînée du souverain*).

principal /ˈprɪnsəpl/ **I** *n* **1** ▶ **1268** (headteacher) (of senior school) proviseur *m*; (of junior school, college) directeur/-trice *m/f*; **2** Theat acteur/-trice *m/f* principal/-e; **3** Mus chef *m* de pupitre; **4** (client) mandant *m*; **5** Fin (interest-bearing sum) capital *m*; (debt before interest) principal *m*; **6** Jur auteur *m* principal (d'un crime ou délit); **7** GB Soc Admin chef *m* de section.

II *adj* **1** (main) principal; **2** Dance, Mus, Theat [*violin, clarinet*] premier/-ière (*before n*); [*dancer*] étoile; **3** Ling [*clause*] principal; **the ~ parts of a verb** les temps primitifs d'un verbe.

principal boy *n* Theat rôle *m* principal masculin (*dans une pantomime tenu par une actrice*).

principality /ˌprɪnsəˈpælətɪ/ *n* principauté *f*.

principally /ˈprɪnsəplɪ/ *adv* principalement.

principle /ˈprɪnsəpl/ *n* **1** (basic tenet) principe *m*; **run on socialist ~s** géré selon des principes socialistes; **2** (rule of conduct) principe *m*; **to be against sb's ~s** être contraire aux principes de qn (**to do** de faire); **to have high ~s** avoir beaucoup de principes; **on ~** par principe; **it's the ~ of the thing, it's a point of ~** c'est pour le principe; **a woman of ~** une femme de principes; **to make it a ~ to do** avoir pour principe de faire; **3** (scientific law) principe *m*; **it relies on the ~ that water evaporates** cela repose sur le principe que l'eau s'évapore; **to get back to first ~s** repartir sur des bases concrètes; **in ~** en principe.

principled /ˈprɪnsəpld/ *adj* [*decision*] de principe; [*person*] de principes; **to be ~** avoir des principes; **to act in a ~ way** agir conformément à des principes.

prink /prɪŋk/ *vi* (also **~ and preen**) se pomponner.

print /prɪnt/ **I** *n* **1** (typeface) ¢ caractères *mpl*; **in small/large ~** en petits/gros caractères; **the ~ is very small** c'est écrit très petit; **the small** ou **fine ~** fig les détails; **don't forget to read the small ~** n'oubliez pas de lire tous les détails; **to set sth up in ~** Print composer qch en lettres d'imprimerie; **2** (published form) **in ~** disponible en librairie; **out of ~** épuisé; **to go into ~** être publié; **to put** ou **get sth into ~** publier qch; **to appear in ~, to get into ~** être publié; **to see sth in ~** voir qch noir sur blanc; **to see oneself in ~** se voir publié; **'at the time of going to ~'** 'à l'heure où nous mettons sous presse'; **3** Art (etching) estampe *f*; (engraving) gravure *f*; **4** Phot (from negative) épreuve *f*; **to make a ~ from a negative** tirer une épreuve d'un négatif; **5** Cin (of film) copie *f*, positif *m* spec; **6** (impression) (of finger, hand, foot) empreinte *f*; (of tyre) trace *f*; **to leave ~s** laisser des empreintes; **to take sb's ~s** prendre les empreintes de qn; **7** Tex tissu *m* imprimé; **8** (handwriting) script *m*.

II *modif* Tex [*blouse, curtains, dress*] en tissu imprimé.

III *vtr* **1** Print imprimer [*poster, document, book, banknote*] (**on** sur); **to ~ sth in italics** imprimer qch en italique; **over 1,000 copies of the book have been ~ed** le livre a été imprimé or tiré à plus de 1 000 exemplaires; **'~ed in Japan'** 'imprimé au Japon'; **2** Journ (publish) publier [*story, report, interview, photo*]; **the article was ~ed in the local press** l'article est paru or a été publié dans la presse locale; **3** Art, Tex imprimer [*pattern, motif, design*] (**in** dans; **on** sur); **4** Phot (from negative) tirer [*copy*]; faire développer [*photos*]; **5** (write) écrire [qch] en script [*detail, letter*] (**on** sur); **'~ your name in block capitals'** 'écrivez votre nom en majuscules'.

IV *vi* **1** (write) écrire en script; **2** Print imprimer.

V printed *pp adj* [*design, fabric, paper*] imprimé; **'~ed matter'** Post 'imprimés' *mpl*; **~ed notepaper** papier *m* à lettres à en-tête; **the power of the ~ed word** le pouvoir de l'écrit.

■ **print off**: **~ off [sth], ~ [sth] off** tirer [*copies*].

■ **print out**: **~ out [sth], ~ [sth] out** gen, Comput imprimer.

printable /ˈprɪntəbl/ *adj* **1** (publishable) publiable; **barely** ou **scarcely ~** difficilement publiable; **2** Print imprimable.

print character *n* caractère *m* d'imprimerie.

printer /ˈprɪntə(r)/ *n* **1** (person, firm) imprimeur *m*; **at the ~'s** ou **~s** chez l'imprimeur; **2** Print, Comput (machine) imprimante *f*.

printer: **~'s devil** *n* apprenti *m* imprimeur; **~'s error** *n* faute *f* d'impression; **~'s ink** *n* encre *f* d'imprimerie; **~'s reader** *n* correcteur/-trice *m/f* (d'épreuves).

print: **~ format** *n* format *m* d'impression; **~head** *n* tête *f* d'impression.

printing /ˈprɪntɪŋ/ **I** *n* **1** Art, Ind, Print (technique) imprimerie *f*; (result) impression *f*; **2** (print run) tirage *m*.

II *modif* **~ business** imprimerie *f*; **~ industry** imprimerie *f*.

printing: **~ frame** *n* châssis-presse *m inv*; **~ house** *n* imprimerie *f*; **~ ink** *n* encre *f* d'imprimerie; **~ press** *n* presse *f* (typographique); **~ works** *n* imprimerie *f*.

print: **~ journalism** *n* (journalisme *m* de) presse *f* écrite; **~maker** *n* graveur/-euse *m/f*; **~making** *n* gravure *f*.

printout /ˈprɪntaʊt/ *n* Comput sortie *f* sur imprimante; (with perforations) listing *m*.

print run *n* tirage *m*.

print shop *n* **1** Print (workshop) imprimerie *f*; **2** (art shop) boutique *f* d'art.

print: **~-through** *n* effet *m* d'empreinte; **~ union** *n* syndicat *m* de l'imprimerie; **~wheel** *n* roue *f* d'impression.

prior /ˈpraɪə(r)/ **I** *n* Relig prieur *m*.

II *adj* **1** (previous) [*appointment, engagement*] préalable; **~ notice** préavis *m*; **2** (more important) prioritaire; **she has a ~ claim on the legacy** elle a (un) droit de priorité sur l'héritage.

III prior to *prep phr* **~ to sth/to doing** avant qch/de faire.

prior charge *n* Fin titre *m* prioritaire.

prioress /ˌpraɪəˈres/ *n* prieure *f*.

priority /praɪˈɒrətɪ, US -ˈɔːr-/ **I** *n* **1** C (main concern) priorité *f*; **the main** ou **highest ~** la priorité absolue; **to get one's priorities right/wrong** définir correctement/mal définir l'ordre de ses priorités; **2** ¢ (prominence) priorité *f*; **to have** ou **take ~ over sth** avoir la priorité sur qch; **to get ~** avoir la priorité; **3** Transp priorité *f*; **~ to the right** priorité à droite.

II *modif* [*case, debt, expense, mail*] prioritaire; [*call*] de priorité; [*appointment*] en priorité.

priority share *n* Fin action *f* privilégiée or prioritaire.

prior preferred stock *n* US Fin actions *fpl* privilégiées or prioritaires.

priory /ˈpraɪərɪ/ *n* prieuré *m*.

prise /praɪz/ *vtr*:

■ **prise apart**: **~ [sth] apart** lit, fig séparer [*layers, planks, people*]; ouvrir [qch] de force [*lips, teeth*].

■ **prise away**: **to ~ sb away from** fig arracher qn à [*TV, work*].

■ **prise off**: **~ [sth] off** enlever [qch] en forçant [*lid*].

■ **prise open**: **~ [sth] open, ~ open [sth]** ouvrir [qch] en forçant [*box, door*].

■ **prise out**: **~ [sth] out** lit retirer [*bullet, nail*] (**of, from** de); **to ~ sth out of sb** arracher qch à qn [*details, information, secret*]; **to ~ sb out of** arracher qn de [*bed, chair*].

■ **prise up**: **~ [sth] up** soulever [qch] en forçant [*floorboard*]; arracher [*nail*].

prism /ˈprɪzəm/ *n* prisme *m*.

prismatic /prɪzˈmætɪk/ *adj* prismatique.

prismatic: **~ binoculars** *npl* jumelles *fpl* prismatiques; **~ compass** *n* boussole *f* à prisme.

prison /ˈprɪzn/ **I** *n* **1** (place) prison *f*; **to be in ~** être en prison; **to go to ~** aller en prison; **to send sb to ~** envoyer qn en prison; **he sent them to ~ for 12 years** il les a condamnés à 12 ans de prison; **to put sb in ~** emprisonner qn; **to have been in ~** avoir fait de la prison; **her house felt like a ~** elle se sentait prisonnière entre ses quatre murs; **2** (punishment) emprisonnement *m*, prison *f*.

II *modif* [*death, life, suicide*] en prison; [*administration, regulation*] pénitentiaire; [*population, reform*] pénal; [*cell, governor, yard*] de prison; [*chapel, kitchen*] de la prison; [*conditions*] de détention.

prison: **~ authorities** *npl* administration *f* pénitentiaire; **~ camp** *n* camp *m* de prisonniers.

prisoner /ˈprɪznə(r)/ *n* gen, fig prisonnier/-ière *m/f*; (in jail) détenu/-e *m/f*; **to hold** ou **keep sb ~** garder qn prisonnier; **they took me ~** ils m'ont fait prisonnier; **~ of war/conscience** prisonnier/-ière *m/f* de guerre/d'opinion; **~ of war camp** camp *m* de prisonniers/-ières de guerre; **I'm a ~ in my own home** je suis prisonnier dans ma propre maison.

IDIOMS **to take no ~s** [*army*] ne faire aucun prisonnier; [*boxer, team*] faire un massacre; [*negotiating team, rival*] ne pas faire de concessions.

prison: **~ guard** ▶ 1692 *n* US surveillant/-e *m/f* de prison; **~ issue** *adj* fourni par la prison; **~ officer** ▶ 1692 *n* GB (officially) surveillant/-e *m/f* de prison; gen gardien/-ienne *m/f* de prison; **~ riot** *n* mutinerie *f*.

prison sentence, prison term *n* peine *f* de prison; **a two-year ~** une peine de deux ans de prison.

prison: **~ service** *n* administration *f* pénitentiaire; **~ van** *n* fourgon *m* cellulaire; **~ visiting** *n* visite *f* de détenus en prison; **~ visitor** *n* visiteur/-euse *m/f* de prison.

prissy /ˈprɪsɪ/ *adj* [*person*] collet monté *inv*; [*style*] surchargé.

pristine /ˈprɪstiːn, ˈprɪstaɪn/ *adj* [*snow, sheets, cloth*] immaculé; **to be in ~ condition** être comme neuf/neuve; **'in ~ condition'** 'état neuf'.

privacy /ˈprɪvəsɪ, ˈpraɪ-/ *n* **1** (private life, freedom from interference) vie *f* privée; **to respect/invade sb's ~** respecter/s'immiscer dans la vie privée de qn; **the right to ~** le droit à la vie privée; **2** (solitude, seclusion) intimité *f*; **in the ~ of your own home** dans l'intimité de votre foyer; **there's no ~ here!** pas moyen d'être seul ici!

privacy laws *npl* Jur lois *fpl* relatives aux atteintes à la vie privée.

private /ˈpraɪvɪt/ **I** *n* ▶ 1612 simple soldat *m*; **Private Taylor** soldat Taylor.

II privates○ *npl* parties○ *fpl*, organes *mpl* génitaux.

III *adj* **1** (not for general public) [*property, land, beach, chapel, jet, vehicle, line, collection, party, viewing*] privé; **room with ~ bath** chambre avec salle de bains particulière; **the funeral/the wedding will be ~** l'enterrement/le mariage aura lieu dans la plus stricte intimité; **2** (personal, not associated with company) [*letter, phone call, use of car*] personnel/-elle; [*life*] privé; [*income, means*] personnel/-elle; [*sale*] de particulier à particulier; **a person of ~ means** une personne qui a des revenus personnels; **she is making a ~ visit** elle est en visite privée; **to act in a ~ capacity** ou **as a ~ person** agir à titre personnel; **the ~ citizen** le (simple) particulier; **3** (not public, not state-run) [*sector, healthcare, education, school, hospital, prison, firm*] privé; [*housing, accommodation, landlord*] particulier/-ière; **~ industry** le (secteur) privé; **~ lessons** cours *mpl* particuliers; **4** (not to be openly revealed) [*conversation, talk, meeting, matter*] privé; [*reason, opinion, thought*] personnel/-elle; **to come to a ~ understanding** s'arranger à l'amiable; **to keep sth ~** préserver l'intimité de qch; **a ~ joke** une plaisanterie pour initiés; **5** (undisturbed) [*place, room, corner*] tranquille; **let's go inside where we can be ~** allons dans la maison, nous y serons tranquilles; **6** (secretive) [*person*] renfermé (sur soi-même).

IV in private *adv phr* en privé.

IDIOMS **to go ~** GB Med se faire soigner dans le (secteur) privé.

private: **~ bar** *n* GB bar *m* (*le plus confortable d'un pub*); **~ bill** *n* projet *m* de loi d'intérêt privé; **~ buyer** *n* particulier *m*; **~ company** *n* société *f* privée; **~ detective** ▶1692 *n* détective *m* privé; **~ enterprise** *n* entreprise *f* privée; **~ eye**○ *n* privé○ *m*, détective *m* privé; **~ first class, PFC** ▶1612 *n* US Mil caporal *m*; **~ hotel** *n* ≈ pension *f* de famille; **~ investigator** ▶1692 *n* = **private detective**; **~ investor** *n* petit porteur *m*, petit actionnaire *m*; **~ law** *n* droit *m* privé.

privately /ˈpraɪvɪtlɪ/ *adv* **1** (in private, not publicly) [*tell, talk, admit, question*] en privé; **2** (out of public sector) [*educate, be treated*] dans le privé; **~ managed** à gestion privée; **~-owned** privé; **~ funded, ~ financed** à financement privé; **3** (secretly, in one's heart) [*feel, believe, doubt*] en mon/son etc for intérieur.

private: **~ member's bill** *n* GB Pol Jur *proposition de loi émanant d'un membre de l'assemblée législative n'appartenant pas au gouvernement*; **~ nuisance** *n* Jur atteinte *f* aux droits de l'individu; **~ parts** *npl* euph parties *fpl* génitales.

private practice *n* GB Med cabinet *m* privé; **to work** ou **be in ~** travailler hors des services de santé de l'État.

private secretary *n* gen secrétaire *mf* particulier/-ière; Pol conseiller/-ère *mf* particulier/-ière.

private soldier *n* simple soldat *m*.

private treaty *n* **by ~** de gré à gré.

private view *n* Art vernissage *m*.

privation /praɪˈveɪʃn/ *n* privations *fpl*; **to suffer ~** subir des privations.

privatization /ˌpraɪvɪtaɪˈzeɪʃn, US -tɪˈz-/ *n* privatisation *f*.

privatize /ˈpraɪvɪtaɪz/ **I** *vtr* privatiser.
II privatized *pp adj* privatisé.

privet /ˈprɪvɪt/ *n* troène *m*; **a ~ hedge** une haie de troènes.

privilege /ˈprɪvəlɪdʒ/ *n* **1** (honour, advantage) privilège *m*; **it's been a great ~ to work with you** travailler avec vous a été un grand privilège; **tax ~s** avantages *mpl* fiscaux; **diplomatic ~** immunité *f* diplomatique; **rights and ~s** droits et privilèges; **2** (prerogative) apanage *m*; **travel was then the ~ of the rich** les voyages étaient alors l'apanage des riches; **3** US Fin option *f*.

privileged /ˈprɪvəlɪdʒd/ **I** *n* (+ *v pl*) **the ~** les privilégiés *mpl*; **the less ~** (economically) les économiquement faibles; (unlucky) les moins privilégiés.
II *adj* [*minority, life, position*] privilégié; [*information*] confidentiel/-ielle; **to be ~ to meet sb/to see sth** avoir le privilège de rencontrer qn/de voir qch; **to be ~ to have had a good education** avoir eu le privilège de recevoir une bonne éducation; **the ~ few** les quelques privilégiés.

privily‡ /ˈprɪvɪlɪ/ *adv* en secret.

privy /ˈprɪvɪ/ **I**† *n* cabinet *m* (d'aisances)†.
II *adj* **to be ~ to sth** être au courant de qch.

Privy Council, PC *n* GB Conseil *m* privé (*du roi ou de la reine*).

Privy Councillor, PC *n* GB Conseiller/-ère *m/f* privé/-e (*du roi ou de la reine*).

privy purse *n* GB cassette *f* royale.

prize /praɪz/ **I** *n* **1** (award) prix *m*; (in lottery) lot *m*; **first ~** premier prix; (in lottery) gros lot *m*; **cash ~** prix en espèces; **to win a ~** remporter un prix; **the ~ for coming first in the test will be a book** le prix accordé au gagnant de l'épreuve sera un livre; **2** littér (valued object) trésor *m*; (reward for effort) récompense *f*; **3** Mil Naut prise *f* (de guerre).
II *modif* **1** [*rose, vegetable, bull etc*] (grown or bred for competitions) de concours; (prize-winning) primé; fig (excellent) [*pupil*] hors-pair *inv*; **a ~ example of** un parfait exemple de; **I felt like a ~ idiot!** j'avais l'air d'un parfait idiot!; **2** [*possession*] précieux/-ieuse.
III *vtr* **1** (value) priser [*independence, possession*]; **2** = **prise**.
IV prized *pp adj* [*possession, asset*] précieux/-ieuse; **to be ~d for sth** être prisé pour qch.
IDIOMS **no ~s for guessing who was there!** il n'est pas difficile de deviner qui était là!

prize: **~ day** *n* jour *m* de la distribution des prix; **~ draw** *n* (for charity) tombola *f*; (for advertising) tirage *m* au sort; **~ fight** *n* combat *m* professionnel; **~ fighter** *n* boxeur *m* professionnel; **~ fighting** *n* boxe *f* professionnelle; **~-giving** *n* remise *f* des prix.

prize money *n* (for one prize) argent *m* du prix; (total amount given out) montant *m* total des prix; **all the ~ was stolen** on a volé tout le montant des prix.

prize: **~ ring** *n* ring *m*; **~winner** *n* (in lottery, draw etc) gagnant/-e *m/f*; (of academic, literary award) lauréat/-e *m/f*; **~-winning** *adj* primé.

pro /prəʊ/ **I** *n* **1**○ (professional) pro○ *mf*; **to turn ~** passer pro○; **golf ~** pro *m* de golf; **2**○ (prostitute) prostitué/-e *m/f*; **3** (advantage) **the ~s and cons** le pour et le contre; **the ~s and cons of sth** les avantages et les inconvénients de qch.
II○ *prep* (in favour of) pour; **are you ~ the plan?** es-tu pour le projet?
III pro- (*dans composés*) **to be ~-democracy/-nuclear power** être pour la démocratie/l'énergie nucléaire; **to be a ~-abortionist/-Marketeer** être partisan/-e de l'avortement/du Marché commun; **to be ~-American/-Smith** être proaméricain/pro-Smith.

PRO *n* **1** *abrév* ▶ **public relations officer**; **2** *abrév* ▶ **Public Records Office**.

proactive /prəʊˈæktɪv/ *adj* **1** Psych proactif/-ive; **2** (dynamic) [*approach, role*] dynamique.

pro-am /prəʊˈæm/ *adj* pro-am *inv*.

probability /ˌprɒbəˈbɪlətɪ/ *n* **1** ¢ (likelihood) (of desirable event) chances *fpl*; (of unwelcome event) risques *mpl*; **in all ~** selon toute probabilité; **the ~ of our getting a pay rise is good** il y a de fortes chances pour qu'on ait une augmentation; **what is the ~ of an avalanche?** quels sont les risques d'avalanche?; **the ~ of winning** les chances de gagner; **the ~ of losing** les risques de perdre; **the ~ of sth happening/taking place** les chances pour que qch se passe/ait lieu; **the ~ of an accident/a wedding is remote** il est peu probable qu'il y ait un accident/un mariage; **2** ¢ (likely result) probabilité *f*; **war/an election is a ~** il est probable qu'il y aura une guerre/une élection; **3** Math, Stat probabilité *f* (**that** pour que + *subj*); **the theory of ~, ~ theory** la théorie des probabilités.

probable /ˈprɒbəbl/ **I** *n* **the ~** le probable.
II *adj* probable (**that** que + *subj*).

probably /ˈprɒbəblɪ/ *adv* probablement; **very ~** (as reply) c'est fort probable; **he's very ~ in Paris** il est certainement à Paris.

probate /ˈprəʊbeɪt/ **I** *n* Jur **1** (process) homologation *f*; **to grant ~ (of a will)** homologuer un testament; **to be in ~** être en cours d'homologation; **2** (document) lettres *fpl* d'homologation; **3** (probate copy of will) copie *f* homologuée d'un testament.
II *vtr* US homologuer [*will*].

probate: **~ action** *n* Jur *action judiciaire qui tend à faire homologuer un testament*; **Probate Registry** *n* GB Jur greffe *m* du tribunal d'homologation des testaments.

probation /prəˈbeɪʃn, US prəʊ-/ *n* **1** Jur (for adult) sursis *m* avec mise à l'épreuve, probation *f* spec; (for juvenile) mise *f* en liberté surveillée; **to put sb on ~** (adult) mettre qn en sursis avec mise à l'épreuve; **2** (trial period) période *f* d'essai; **to be on three months ~** être à l'essai pendant trois mois; **to be on (academic) ~** US Sch, Univ être en période d'essai (*après un avertissement pour indiscipline ou travail insuffisant*).

probationary /prəˈbeɪʃnrɪ, US prəʊˈbeɪʃənerɪ/ *adj* **1** (trial) [*period, year*] d'essai; **2** (training) [*month, period*] probatoire.

probationary teacher *n* GB Sch *professeur en première année d'exercice après le diplôme d'enseignement* ≈ professeur *m* en stage pratique.

probationer /prəˈbeɪʃənə(r), US prəʊ-/ *n* **1** (trainee) stagiaire *mf*; **2** (employee on trial) employé/-e *m/f* engagé/-e à l'essai; **3** Jur (adult) probationnaire *m*; (juvenile) jeune délinquant/-e *m/f* en liberté surveillée.

probation: **~ officer** ▶1692 *n* Jur (for juveniles) délégué/-e *m/f* à la liberté surveillée; (for adults) agent *m* de probation; **~ order** *n* Jur ordonnance *f* de probation or de sursis avec mise à l'épreuve; **~ service** *n* Jur comité *m* de probation.

probe /prəʊb/ **I** *n* **1** (investigation) enquête *f* (**into** sur); **death/drugs ~** enquête *f* sur la mort/la drogue; **2** Dent, Med, Tech (instrument) sonde *f*; (operation) sondage *m*; **3** Aerosp sonde *f*; **space ~** sonde *f* spatiale.
II *vtr* **1** (investigate) enquêter sur [*affair, causes, mystery, scandal*]; **2** Dent examiner [qch] avec une sonde [*tooth*]; **3** Med, Tech sonder [*ground, wound*] (**with** avec); tâter [*swelling*]; **4** Aerosp explorer [*space*]; **5** (explore) explorer [qch] avec soin [*hole, surface*]; [*searchlight*] fouiller [*darkness*]; **'do you still love her?' he ~ed** 'tu l'aimes toujours?' s'enquit-il.
III *vi* faire des recherches; **to ~ for** rechercher, fouiner à la recherche de pej [*details, scandal*].
■ **probe into**: **~ into [sth]** enquêter sur [*suspicious activity*]; regarder [qch] de plus près, fouiller or fouiner dans pej [*private affairs*]; sonder [*mind*]; scruter [*thoughts*]; fouiller dans [*post*].

probing /ˈprəʊbɪŋ/ **I** *n* **1** (examination) exploration *f*; **2** (questions) questions *fpl*.
II *adj* [*look*] inquisiteur/-trice; [*question*] pénétrant; [*study, examination*] très poussé.

probity /ˈprəʊbətɪ/ *n* probité *f*.

problem /ˈprɒbləm/ **I** *n* **1** (difficulty) problème *m*; **to have ~s** avoir des problèmes or des ennuis (**with** avec); **to have a drink/weight ~** avoir un problème d'alcoolisme/de poids; **to cause** ou **present a ~** poser un problème; **it's a real ~** c'est un vrai problème; **it's a bit of a ~** c'est un peu un problème; **what's the ~?** quel or où est le problème?; **the ~ is that...** le problème, c'est que...; **that's the least of my ~s!** c'est le moindre de mes problèmes!; **to be a ~ to sb** poser des problèmes à qn; **their son is becoming a real ~** leur fils leur pose beaucoup de problèmes; **she's a real ~** elle est vraiment difficile à vivre; **it wouldn't be any ~ (to me) to do it** cela ne (me) poserait aucun problème de le faire; **I'll have a ~ explaining that to her** j'aurai des problèmes pour lui expliquer cela; **it was quite a ~ getting him to cooperate** c'était vraiment difficile de le faire coopérer, c'était tout un problème que de le faire coopérer; **it was no ~ parking the car** ce n'était pas un problème de garer la voiture, garer la voiture n'a posé aucun problème; **it's** ou **that's not my ~!** cela ne me regarde pas!, ce n'est pas mon problème!; **it's no ~, I assure you!** cela ne pose aucun problème, je vous assure!; **sure, no ~**○! bien sûr, pas de problème○!; **what's your ~**○? t'as un problème ou quoi○?; **2** gen, Math (of logic) problème *m*; **to solve a ~** résoudre un problème.
II *modif* **1** Psych, Sociol [*child*] difficile, caractériel/-ielle; [*family*] à problèmes; [*group*] qui pose des problèmes; **2** Literat [*play, novel*] à thèse.

problematic(al) /ˌprɒbləˈmætɪk/ *adj* problématique.

problem: **~ case** *n* Sociol cas *m* social; **~ page** *n* courrier *m* du cœur; **~ solver** *n* personne *f* apte à résoudre les problèmes; **~ solving** *n* aptitude *f* à résoudre les problèmes.

proboscis /prəˈbɒsɪs/ *n* **1** Zool trompe *f*; **2** hum (nose) appendice *m* (nasal).

procedural /prəˈsiːdʒərəl/ *adj* [*change, detail, error*] de procédure.

procedural language *n* Comput langage *m* procédural.

procedure /prəˈsiːdʒə(r)/ *n* **1** gen procédure *f* (**for doing** pour faire); **to follow a ~** suivre une procédure; (**the**) **normal ~ is to do** la procédure normale est de faire; **parliamentary ~** procédure *f* parlementaire; **2** Comput procédure *f*.

proceed /prəˈsiːd, prəʊ-/ **I** *vtr* **to ~ to do** entreprendre de faire; **'so...,' he ~ed** 'alors...,' a-t-il continué.

II *vi* **1** (act) [*person, committee*] (set about) procéder; (continue) poursuivre; **to ~ with** poursuivre, donner suite à [*idea, plan, sale*]; procéder à [*ballot, election*]; **to ~ to** passer à [*item, problem*]; **let us ~** (begin) commençons; (continue) poursuivons; **please ~** (begin) veuillez commencer; (continue) poursuivez, je vous en prie; **I'm not sure how to ~** je ne sais pas trop comment procéder; **to ~ with care** ou **caution** procéder avec prudence; **before we ~ any further...** (at beginning of meeting) avant d'aller plus loin...; (in middle of speech) avant de poursuivre...; **we'll arrange a meeting and ~ from there** nous organiserons une réunion et procéderons à partir de là; **2** (be in progress) [*project, work*] avancer; [*interview, talks, trial*] se poursuivre; (take place) [*work, interview, talks*] se dérouler; **to ~ smoothly** se dérouler sans incident; **everything is ~ing according to plan** tout se passe comme prévu; **3** (move along) [*person, road, river*] continuer; [*vehicle*] avancer; **to ~ along/to** [*person*] continuer le long de/jusqu'à; [*car*] avancer sur/jusqu'à; **4** sout (issue) **to ~ from** provenir de; **5** Jur **to ~ against sb** [*police, plaintiff*] engager des poursuites contre qn.

proceeding /prəˈsiːdɪŋ/ **I** *n* (procedure) procédure *f*.

II proceedings *npl* **1** gen (meeting) réunion *f*; (ceremony) cérémonie *f*; (discussion) débats *mpl*; **to direct ~s** diriger les opérations; **2** Jur poursuites *fpl*, procédure *f*; **disciplinary ~s** poursuites disciplinaires; **extradition ~s** procédure d'extradition; **to take** ou **institute ~s** engager des poursuites (**against** contre), intenter un procès (**against** à); **to start divorce ~s** intenter un procès en divorce; **to commence criminal ~s** engager une action pénale (**against** contre); **3** (report, record) gen rapport *m*; (of conference, society) actes *mpl*.

proceeds /ˈprəʊsiːdz/ *npl* (of sale, privatization) produit *m*; (of fair, concert) recette *f*.

process **I** /ˈprəʊses, US ˈprɒses/ *n* **1** gen processus *m* (**of** de); **the peace ~** le processus de paix; **the ~ of doing** le processus consistant à faire; **to begin the ~ of doing** entreprendre de faire; **to be in the ~ of doing** être en train de faire; **in the ~ of doing this, he...** pendant qu'il faisait cela, il...; **in the ~** en même temps ; **it's a long** ou **slow ~** cela prend du temps; **2** (method) procédé *m* (**for** pour; **for doing** pour faire); **manufacturing ~** procédé de fabrication; **3** Jur (lawsuit) procès *m*; (summons) citation *f*; **to bring a ~ against** intenter un procès à qn; **to serve a ~ on** citer [qn] à comparaître; **4** Comput processus *m*, traitement *m*; **5** Bot, Zool excroissance *f*.

II /ˈprəʊses, US ˈprɒses/ *vtr* **1** gen, Admin, Comput traiter [*data, form, application*]; **2** Ind transformer [*raw materials, food product*]; traiter [*chemical, synthetic fibre, waste*]; **3** Phot développer [*film*]; **4** Culin [*person, blender*] (mix) mixer; (chop) hacher; **5** US (straighten) décrêper [*hair*].

III /prəˈses/ *vi* **1** Relig, Hist faire des processions; **2** sout (move) **to ~ down/along** défiler dans/le long de [*road*].

IV processed /ˈprəʊsest/ *pp adj* [*food*] qui a subi un traitement; [*meat, peas*] en conserve; [*steel*] traité; **~ed cheese** fromage *m* fondu en tranches.

process control *n* contrôle *m* de processus industriel, automatisme *m* industriel.

processing /ˈprəʊsesɪŋ, US ˈprɒ-/ *n* **1** (of data, form, application) traitement *m*; **2** Ind (of raw material, food product) transformation *f*; (of chemical, synthetic fibre, waste) traitement *m*; **the food ~ industry** l'industrie alimentaire; **3** Phot développement *m*.

procession /prəˈseʃn/ *n* (of demonstration, carnival) défilé *m*; (for formal occasion) cortège *m*; Relig procession *f*; **carnival ~** défilé de carnaval; **funeral/wedding ~** cortège funèbre/nuptial; **to walk/drive along in ~** marcher/rouler en cortège or en défilé.

processional /prəˈseʃənl/ *n* Relig (book) processionnal *m*; (hymn) hymne *m* processionnel.

processor /ˈprəʊsesə(r), US ˈprɒ-/ *n* **1** Comput unité *f* centrale; **2** = **food processor**.

process: **~ printing** *n* quadrichromie *f*; **~-server** ▶ **1692** *n* Jur ≈ huissier *m*.

pro-choice /prəʊˈtʃɔɪs/ *adj* [*voter, candidate*] favorable à l'avortement; **~ lobby** ou **movement** campagne *f* en faveur du libre choix en matière d'avortement; **~ supporter** partisan/-e *m/f* du libre choix en matière d'avortement.

pro-choicer /ˌprəʊˈtʃɔɪsə(r)/ *n* partisan/-e *m/f* du libre choix en matière d'avortement.

proclaim /prəˈkleɪm/ **I** *vtr* (all contexts) proclamer (**that** que).

II *v refl* **to ~ oneself a Christian/communist** se proclamer chrétien/communiste.

proclamation /ˌprɒkləˈmeɪʃn/ *n* proclamation *f* (**of** de).

proclivity /prəˈklɪvətɪ/ *n* propension *f* (**for, to, towards** à); **sexual proclivities** tendances *fpl* sexuelles.

proconsul /ˌprəʊˈkɒnsl/ *n* Antiq proconsul *m*; (in colony) gouverneur *m*.

procrastinate /prəʊˈkræstɪneɪt/ *vi* atermoyer.

procrastination /prəʊˌkræstɪˈneɪʃn/ *n* ¢ atermoiements *mpl*; **to accuse sb of ~** accuser qn d'atermoyer.

IDIOMS **~ is the thief of time** Prov ne remettez pas à demain ce que vous pouvez faire aujourd'hui.

procrastinator /prəʊˈkræstɪneɪtə(r)/ *n* **to be a ~** (by nature) avoir tendance à toujours remettre au lendemain.

procreate /ˈprəʊkrɪeɪt/ **I** *vtr* procréer [*children, young*].

II *vi* se reproduire.

procreation /ˌprəʊkrɪˈeɪʃn/ *n* (human) procréation *f*; (animal) reproduction *f*.

Procrustean /prəʊˈkrʌstɪən/ *adj* Mythol de Procruste; fig [*measures, solution*] draconien/-ienne.

proctor /ˈprɒktə(r)/ **I** *n* GB Univ responsable *mf* de la discipline (*à Oxford et Cambridge*); US Univ (invigilator) surveillant/-e *m/f* (*d'examen*).

II *vtr* US Univ surveiller [*exam*].

procuration /ˌprɒkjʊˈreɪʃn/ *n* **1** sout (obtaining) obtention *f*; **2** Jur (of prostitutes) proxénétisme *m*.

procurator /ˈprɒkjʊreɪtə(r)/ *n* Antiq procurateur *m*; (in church of Rome) procureur *m*.

procurator-fiscal /ˌprɒkjʊreɪtəˈfɪskl/ *n* Scot Jur procureur *m* général.

procure /prəˈkjʊə(r)/ **I** *vtr* **1** sout (obtain) procurer [*object, arms, supplies*]; **to ~ sth for sb** (directly) procurer qch à qn; (indirectly) faire obtenir qch à qn; **to ~ sth for oneself** se procurer qch; **2** Jur procurer [*prostitutes*].

II *vi* Jur (in prostitution) faire du proxénétisme.

procurement /prəˈkjʊəmənt/ *n* gen obtention *f*; Mil, Comm acquisition *f*; **arms/steel ~** acquisition d'armes/d'acier.

procurement department *n* US Mil, Admin cf service *m* central des approvisionnements.

procurer /prəˈkjʊərə(r)/ *n* **1** Admin, Comm acheteur/-euse *m/f*; **2** Jur (in prostitution) proxénète *m*.

procuress /prəˈkjʊərɪs/ *n* Jur (in prostitution) proxénète *f*.

prod /prɒd/ **I** *n* **1** lit (poke) petit coup *m*; **to give sth/sb a ~** (with implement) donner un petit coup à qch/qn; (with finger) toucher qn/qch; **2**○ fig (encouragement, reminder) **to give sb a ~** secouer○ qn; **he/she needs a ~ to do** il faut le/la pousser pour qu'il/elle fasse; **he needs a gentle ~ to do** il faut lui rappeler gentiment de faire; **3** Agric (also **cattle ~**) aiguillon *m*.

II *vtr* (*p prés etc* **-dd-**) (also **~ at**) **1** (poke) (with foot, instrument, stick) donner des petits coups à, pousser [qch] doucement; (with finger) toucher; (with fork) piquer; **stop ~ding me!** arrête de me bousculer!; **to ~ sb in the stomach** (hard) enfoncer les doigts dans l'estomac de qn; **to ~ sb's stomach** (gently) [*doctor*] tâter le ventre de qn; **2**○ (remind, encourage) pousser, secouer○; **to ~ sb into doing** pousser qn à faire; **the government will have to be ~ded into acting** il faudra pousser le gouvernement pour qu'il agisse; **he needs to be ~ed occasionally** il a besoin d'être secoué de temps en temps○; **3** (interrogate) interroger.

Prod○ /prɒd/ *n* GB injur protestant/-e *m/f*.

prodding /ˈprɒdɪŋ/ *n* **1** (reminding) **after a bit of ~ he agreed** il a fallu insister pour qu'il donne son accord; **she needs a bit of ~** elle a besoin d'être poussée; **2** (interrogation) questions *fpl*.

prodigal /ˈprɒdɪgl/ *adj* littér [*expenditure, generosity*] extravagant; [*government, body*] prodigue; **to be ~ with** ou **of** être prodigue de [*gifts, money*]; **the ~ son** Bible le fils prodigue; fig l'enfant prodigue.

prodigality /ˌprɒdɪˈgælətɪ/ *n* littér prodigalité *f*.

prodigally /ˈprɒdɪgəlɪ/ *adv* [*spend, use*] de façon prodigue; [*give, entertain*] avec prodigalité.

prodigious /prəˈdɪdʒəs/ *adj* prodigieux/-ieuse.

prodigiously /prəˈdɪdʒəslɪ/ *adv* [*eat, drink*] énormément; [*drunk, fat*] extrêmement; [*talented, successful*] prodigieusement; [*increase, grow*] prodigieusement.

prodigy /ˈprɒdɪdʒɪ/ *n* **1** (person) prodige *m*; **child ~** enfant prodige; **music/tennis ~** prodige de la musique/du tennis; **2** (wonder) prodige *m*; **to be a ~ of learning** être une merveille de savoir.

produce **I** /ˈprɒdjuːs, US -duːs/ *n* ¢ produits *mpl*; **agricultural ~** produits agricoles; **'~ of Spain'** 'produit d'Espagne'.

II /prəˈdjuːs, US -ˈduːs/ *vtr* **1** (cause) produire [*effect, agreement, result, success*]; provoquer [*reaction, change*]; **2** Agric, Ind [*region, industry, farmer, company*] produire (**from** à partir de); [*worker, machine*] fabriquer; **3** (biologically) [*gland, animal, plant*] produire; **to ~ young** produire des petits; **to ~ children** donner naissance à des enfants, procréer hum; **4** (generate) produire [*heat, electricity, sound, energy, fumes, gas*]; rapporter [*gains, profits, returns*]; **to ~ electricity from coal** produire de l'électricité à partir du charbon; **5** (form, create) [*school, course, era, country*] produire [*scientist, artist, worker*]; **the country that ~ed Picasso** le pays qui a vu naître Picasso; **to ~ a work of art** produire une œuvre d'art; **6** (present) produire [*passport, voucher, document, report, statement*]; fournir [*evidence, argument, example*]; **to ~ sth from** sortir qch de [*pocket, bag*]; **to ~ sth from behind one's back** faire apparaître qch de derrière son dos; **7** Cin, Mus, Radio, TV produire [*film, programme, show*]; GB Theat mettre [qch] en scène [*play*]; **well-~d** [*film, programme, recording*] bien réalisé; **8** (put together) préparer [*meal*]; mettre au point [*argument, timetable, package, solution*]; éditer [*leaflet, brochure, guide*]; **a well-~d brochure** une brochure bien faite; **9** Sport (achieve) marquer [*goal*]; obtenir [*result*]; **to ~ a fine performance** jouer remarquablement; **10** Math prolonger [*line*].

producer /prəˈdjuːsə(r), US -ˈduːs-/ ▶ 1692 *n* **1** (supplier) (of produce, food) producteur *m*; (of machinery, goods) fabricant *m*; **the world's leading tea ~** le premier producteur du thé du monde; **2** Cin, Radio, TV producteur/-trice *m/f*; GB Theat metteur *m* en scène.

producer: **~ gas** *n* gaz *m* à l'air; **~ goods** *n* biens *mpl* d'équipement; **~ price index** *n* indice *m* des prix à la production.

producing /prəˈdjuːsɪŋ, US -ˈduːs-/ **I** *adj* [*country*] producteur/-trice.

II -producing (*dans composés*) producteur/-trice de; **oil-/cocaine-~ countries** pays producteurs de pétrole/cocaïne; **wine-~ region** région vinicole.

product /ˈprɒdʌkt/ **I** *n* **1** (commercial item) produit *m*; **consumer ~s** produits de consommation; **the finished ~** Comm le produit fini; **2** (result) **to be a ~ of** être un produit de [*period, causes, event, imagination, training*]; **he was the ~ of a certain era** il était le produit d'une certaine époque; **the end ~** le résultat final; **3** Math produit *m* (**of** de).

II *modif* [*design, launch, development, testing*] d'un produit; **~ range** gamme *f* de produits.

product designer ▶ 1692 *n* créateur/-trice *m/f* de produit.

production /prəˈdʌkʃn/ **I** *n* **1** Agric, Ind (of crop, produce, foodstuffs, metal) production *f* (**of** de); (of machinery, furniture, cars) fabrication (**of** de); **to go into** ou **be in ~** être fabriqué; **the model has gone** ou **is out of ~** on ne fabrique plus le modèle; **to be in full ~** [*factory*] tourner à plein rendement; **to take land out of ~** cesser l'exploitation d'une terre; **2** (output) production *f*; **crop ~** production agricole; **~ fell by 5%** la production a baissé de 5%; **3** Biol, Sci (generating) (of cells, antibodies, energy, sound) production *f* (**of** de); **4** (presentation) (of document, ticket, report) présentation *f* (**of** de); (of evidence) production *f* (**of** de); **on ~ of** sur présentation de; **5** (of programme, film, record) production *f*; (of play) mise *f* en scène; **to work in TV ~** être producteur/-trice à la télévision; **6 C** (film, opera, programme, show) production *f* (**of** de); (play) mise *f* en scène (**of** de); **X's ~ of 'Le Cid'** 'Le Cid', mis en scène par X; **to put on a ~ of** Theat mettre en scène [*play, work*].

II *modif* [*costs, difficulties, levels, methods, quota, unit*] de production; [*control, department*] de la production.

production company *n* société *f* de production.

production line *n* chaîne *f* de fabrication; **to come off the ~** sortir de la chaîne de fabrication; **to work on a ~** travailler à la chaîne.

production manager ▶ 1692 *n* directeur/-trice *m/f* de la production.

productive /prəˈdʌktɪv/ *adj* **1** (efficient) [*factory, industry, land, worker*] productif/-ive; [*system, method, use*] efficace; **2** (constructive) [*discussion, collaboration, experience*] fructueux/-euse; [*day, phase, period*] productif/-ive; **3** Econ [*sector, capital, task, capacity*] productif/-ive; **4** (resulting in) **to be ~ of** être générateur/-trice de [*knowledge, tyranny, health*]; **5** Med **~ cough** toux *f* grasse.

productively /prəˈdʌktɪvlɪ/ *adv* [*work, organize*] de façon profitable; [*farm, cultivate*] de façon rentable; [*spend time*] utilement.

productivity /ˌprɒdʌkˈtɪvətɪ/ **I** *n* productivité *f*; **to increase ~** augmenter la productivité.

II *modif* [*agreement, bonus, drive, gains, growth*] de productivité.

product: **~ liability** *n* responsabilité *f* de produits; **~ licence** *n* autorisation *f* de mise sur le marché; **~ manager** ▶ 1692 *n* chef *m* de produit.

prof° /prɒf/ *n* (professor) prof° *mf* (*d'Université*).

Prof *abrév écrite* = **professor**.

profanation /ˌprɒfəˈneɪʃn/ *n* sout profanation *f*.

profane /prəˈfeɪn, US prəʊˈfeɪn/ **I** *adj* **1** (blasphemous) impie; **2** (secular) profane.

II *vtr* profaner [*shrine, tradition, honour*].

profanity /prəˈfænətɪ, US prəʊ-/ *n* sout **1** (behaviour) impiété *f*; **2** (oath) blasphème *m*.

profess /prəˈfes/ *vtr* **1** (claim) prétendre (**to do** de faire; **that** que); **to ~ total ignorance of the matter** prétendre ne rien savoir de l'affaire; **I don't ~ to be a lover of poetry** je ne prétends pas adorer la poésie; **2** (declare openly) faire profession de, professer [*opinion, religion*]; **she ~ed faith in their policies** elle a déclaré sa confiance dans leur politique.

professed /prəˈfest/ *adj* **1** gen [*supporter, atheist, Christian etc*] (genuine) déclaré; (pretended) soi-disant; **2** Relig [*nun, monk*] profès/-esse.

professedly /prəˈfesɪdlɪ/ *adv* sout (avowedly) [*antagonistic, supportive*] de son/leur etc propre aveu; (with notion of insincerity) soi-disant; **~ on business** soi-disant pour affaires.

profession /prəˈfeʃn/ *n* **1** (occupation) profession *f*; **by ~** de profession; **the ~s** les professions libérales; **to enter a ~** embrasser une profession; **the oldest ~ (in the world)** euph le plus vieux métier du monde; **2** (group) profession *f*; **the legal/medical/teaching ~** le corps judiciaire/médical/enseignant; **3** (statement) déclaration *f* (**of** de).

professional /prəˈfeʃənl/ **I** *n* **1** (not amateur) professionnel/-elle *m/f*; **2** (in small ad) salarié/-e *m/f*.

II *adj* **1** (relating to an occupation) [*duty, experience incompetence, qualification, status*] professionnel/-elle; **~ career** carrière *f*; **to seek ~ advice** demander l'avis d'un professionnel; **he needs ~ help** il devrait consulter un professionnel; **they are ~ people** ils exercent une profession libérale; **2** (not amateur) [*footballer, dancer*] professionnel/-elle; [*diplomat, soldier*] de carrière; **to turn ~** [*actor, singer*] devenir professionnel/-elle; [*footballer, athlete*] passer professionnel/-elle; **he's a ~ trouble-maker/gossip** iron c'est un fauteur de troubles/bavard professionnel; **3** (of high standard) [*attitude, work, person*] professionnel/-elle; **he did a very ~ job** il a fait un travail de professionnel.

professional: **~ fee** *n* honoraire *m*; **~ foul** *n* Sport faute *f* délibérée.

professionalism /prəˈfeʃənəlɪzəm/ *n* **1** (high standard) (of person, organization) professionnalisme *m*; (of performance, piece of work) (haute) qualité *f*; **2** Sport professionnalisme *m*.

professionally /prəˈfeʃənəlɪ/ *adv* **1** (expertly) [*decorated, designed*] par un professionnel; **to have sth ~ done** faire faire qch par un professionnel; **~ qualified** diplômé; **he is ~ trained** il a reçu une formation professionnelle; **2** (from an expert standpoint) d'un point de vue professionnel, professionnellement; **3** (in work situation) [*know, meet*] dans un cadre professionnel; **he is known ~ as Tim Jones** dans le métier or la profession, il est connu sous le nom de Tim Jones; **4** (as a paid job) [*play sport*] en professionnel/-elle; **he sings/dances ~** il est chanteur/danseur professionnel; **5** (to a high standard) [*do, work, behave*] de manière professionnelle.

professional school *n* US Univ (business school) école *f* de commerce; (law school) faculté *f* de droit; (medical school) faculté *f* de médecine.

professor /prəˈfesə(r)/ ▶ 1268 *n* **1** Univ (chair holder) professeur *m* d'Université; **Professor Barker** Monsieur le Professeur Barker; **2** US Univ (teacher) professeur *m*.

professorial /ˌprɒfɪˈsɔːrɪəl/ *adj* **1** Univ [*duties, post, salary*] de professeur (d'Université); US professoral; **2** (imposing) [*manner, appearance*] imposant.

professorship /prəˈfesəʃɪp/ *n* **1** (chair) chaire *f*; **to apply for/obtain a ~** postuler pour/obtenir une chaire; **the ~ of Physics** la chaire de physique; **2** US Univ (teaching post) poste *m* de professeur.

proffer /ˈprɒfə(r)/ *vtr* sout **1** (hold out) tendre [*hand, pen, handkerchief*]; **2** (offer) offrir [*advice, friendship*].

proficiency /prəˈfɪʃnsɪ/ *n* (practical) compétence *f* (**in, at** en; **in doing** à faire); (academic) niveau *m* (**in** en); **to show/lack ~** faire preuve de/manquer de compétence.

proficiency test *n* test *m* de niveau.

proficient /prəˈfɪʃnt/ *adj* compétent (**at, in** en; **at doing** pour faire); **she is a highly ~ musician/swimmer** c'est une très bonne musicienne/nageuse.

profile /ˈprəʊfaɪl/ **I** *n* **1** (of face) profil *m* (also fig); **in ~** de profil; **a photo in three-quarter ~** une photo de trois quarts; **to keep** ou **maintain a low ~** fig maintenir or adopter un profil bas; **to have/maintain a high ~** fig occuper/rester sur le devant de la scène; **he enjoys a high ~ in the literary world** il est très en vue dans le monde littéraire; **you have the right ~ for the job** vous avez le bon profil pour ce poste; **to raise one's ~** se rendre plus connu; **2** (of body, mountain) silhouette *f*; **3** Journ (of celebrity) portrait *m* (**of** de); **4** (graph, table, list) profil *m*; **reader ~** profil du lecteur.

II *vtr* Journ dresser le portrait de [*person*].

III profiled *pp adj* (silhouetted) **to be ~d** se profiler (**against** sur).

profit /ˈprɒfɪt/ **I** *n* **1** Comm bénéfice *m*, profit *m*; **gross/net ~** bénéfice brut/net; **~ and loss** pertes et profits; **to make** ou **turn a ~** faire or réaliser un bénéfice (**on** sur); **the banks make handsome ~s** les banques font de jolis bénéfices; **they're only interested in making quick ~s** tout ce qui les intéresse c'est de faire de l'argent rapidement; **to sell sth at a ~** vendre qch à profit or avec un bénéfice; **they sold the house at a ~ of £6,000** ils ont réalisé un bénéfice de 6000 livres sterling en vendant la maison; **to operate at a ~** être rentable; **to bring in** ou **yield a ~** rapporter un bénéfice; **there isn't much ~ in that line of business nowadays** ce genre de métier ne rapporte pas gros aujourd'hui; **with ~s insurance policy** police *f* d'assurance avec participation aux bénéfices; **2** fig (benefit) profit *m*, avantage *m*; **to turn sth to ~** fig mettre qch à profit.

II *vtr* littér profiter à; **it will ~ you nothing to do this** cela ne vous profitera en rien de faire cela.

III *vi* **to ~ by** ou **from sth** tirer profit de qch.

profitability /ˌprɒfɪtəˈbɪlətɪ/ *n* rentabilité *f*.

profitable /ˈprɒfɪtəbl/ *adj* Comm [*business, investment, market*] rentable, lucratif/-ive; fig [*meeting, negotiations*] fructueux/-euse; **it is ~ to do** c'est rentable de faire; **to make ~ use of sth** mettre qch à profit; **a most ~ afternoon** un après-midi très fructueux.

profitably /ˈprɒfɪtəblɪ/ *adv* **1** Fin [*sell*] à profit, avec bénéfice; [*trade*] à profit; [*invest*] avec profit; **2** (usefully) utilement.

profit: **~ and loss account** *n* compte *m* de pertes et profits; **~ balance** *n* solde *m* bénéficiaire; **~ centre** GB, **~ center** US *n* centre *m* de profit.

profiteer /ˌprɒfɪˈtɪə(r)/ *péj* **I** *n* profiteur/-euse

m/f pej; **war ~** profiteur/-euse *m/f* de guerre.
II *vi* faire des bénéfices excessifs.
profiteering /ˌprɒfɪˈtɪərɪŋ/ péj **I** *n* réalisation *f* de bénéfices excessifs; **to engage in ~** faire des bénéfices excessifs.
II *adj* profiteur/-euse.
profit: **~ forecast** *n* prévisions *fpl* de bénéfices; **~ graph** *n* courbe *f* de rentabilité.
profitless /ˈprɒfɪtlɪs/ *adj* inutile.
profit: **~-making organization** *n* organisation *f* à but lucratif; **~ margin** *n* marge *f* bénéficiaire; **~ motive** *n* souci *m* de rentabilité; **~ sharing** *n* intéressement *m* des salariés aux bénéfices; **~ sharing scheme** *n* système *m* d'intéressement des salariés aux bénéfices; **~ squeeze** *n* Fin contraction *f* des marges bénéficiaires; **~ taking** *n* prise *f* de bénéfices.
profligacy /ˈprɒflɪgəsɪ/ *n* sout **1** (extravagance) extrême prodigalité *f*; **2** (debauchery) débauche *f*.
profligate /ˈprɒflɪgət/ *adj* sout **1** (extravagant) [*government, body*] extrêmement prodigue; [*spending*] excessif/-ive; **~ use of taxpayers' money** le gaspillage de l'argent des contribuables; **2** (dissolute) débauché.
pro-form /ˌprəʊˈfɔːm/ *n* proforme *f*.
pro forma invoice /ˌprəʊˌfɔːməˈɪnvɔɪs/ *n* facture *f* pro forma.
profound /prəˈfaʊnd/ *adj* profond.
profoundly /prəˈfaʊndlɪ/ *adv* **1** (emphatic) [*traumatized, unnatural, affected*] profondément; **2** (wisely) [*observe, remark*] avec profondeur.
profundity /prəˈfʌndətɪ/ *n* sout **1** (of understanding, changes) profondeur *f*; **2** (wise remark) remarque *f* profonde also iron.
profuse /prəˈfjuːs/ *adj* [*growth, bleeding*] abondant; [*apologies, praise, thanks*] profus.
profusely /prəˈfjuːslɪ/ *adv* [*sweat, bleed*] abondamment; [*bloom*] à profusion; [*thank*] avec effusion; **to apologize ~** se confondre en excuses.
profusion /prəˈfjuːʒn/ *n* profusion *f* (**of** de); **to grow in ~** pousser à foison.
prog○ /prɒg/ *n* GB TV, Radio émission *f*.
progenitor /prəʊˈdʒenɪtə(r)/ *n* sout (father) père *m*; (mother) mère *f*; (of idea) auteur *m*; (of movement) père *m*.
progeny /ˈprɒdʒənɪ/ *n* sout (+ *v sg* ou *pl*) **1** (children) progéniture *f*; **2** (descendants) descendance *f*; fig successeurs *mpl*.
progesterone /prəʊˈdʒestərəʊn/ *n* progestérone *f*.
prognathous /prɒgˈneɪθəs/ *adj* prognathe.
prognosis /prɒgˈnəʊsɪs/ *n* **1** Med pronostic *m* (**on, about** sur); **2** (prediction) pronostics *mpl* (**for** sur).
prognostic /prɒgˈnɒstɪk/ *adj* pronostique.
prognosticate /prɒgˈnɒstɪkeɪt/ *vtr* pronostiquer (**that** que).
prognostication /prɒgˌnɒstɪˈkeɪʃn/ *n* pronostic *m*.
program /ˈprəʊgræm, US -grəm/ **I** *n* **1** Comput programme *m*; **to run a ~** lancer un programme; **2** US Radio, TV émission *f*.
II *vtr* (**-mm-** GB, **-m-** US) gen, Comput programmer (**to do** pour faire).
III *vi* Comput programmer (**in** en).
programer *n* US = **programmer**.
programing *n* US = **programming**.
programme GB, **program** US /ˈprəʊgræm, US -grəm/ **I** *n* **1** TV, Radio (single broadcast) émission *f* (**about** sur); (schedule of broadcasting) programme *m*; **jazz/news ~s** émissions de jazz/d'actualités; **to do a ~** diffuser or passer une émission (**on** sur); **2** (plan, schedule) programme *m* (**of** de); **research/training ~** programme *m* de recherche/formation; **what's on the ~ (for today)?** qu'y a-t-il au programme (aujourd'hui)?; **3** Mus, Theat (booklet) programme *m*; (plan for season) programme *m*.
II *vtr* (set) programmer [*machine*] (**to do** pour faire); **we are ~d from birth to be social beings** nous sommes programmés dès la naissance pour vivre en société.
programme: **~d learning** *n* enseignement *m* programmé; **~ music** *n* Mus musique *f* à programme; **~ note** *n* commentaire *m* de programme.
programmer GB, **programer** US /ˈprəʊgræmə(r), US -grəm-/ **▶ 1692** *n* programmeur/-euse *m/f*.
programming GB, **programing** US /ˈprəʊgræmɪŋ, US -grəm-/ *n* **1** Comput programmation *f*; **2** TV, Radio programmation *f*.
programming language *n* langage *m* de programmation.
progress I /ˈprəʊgres, US ˈprɒgres/ *n* **1** (advances) progrès *m*; **in the name of ~** au nom du progrès; **~ towards a settlement has been slow** les progrès en vue d'un accord ont été longs; **to make ~ in one's work/in physics** faire des progrès dans son travail/en physique; **to make slow/steady ~** progresser lentement/régulièrement; **to work for ~ on human rights** œuvrer pour progresser dans le domaine des droits de l'homme; **the patient is making ~** l'état de santé du malade s'améliore; **2** (course, evolution) (of person, vehicle, inquiry, event) progression *f*; (of talks, dispute, disease, career) évolution *f*; **we are watching the ~ of the negotiations/of the research with interest** nous assistons avec intérêt à l'évolution des négociations/la progression des recherches; **to make (slow/steady) ~** progresser or avancer (lentement/régulièrement); **to be in ~** [*discussions, meeting, work*] être en cours; **work is already in ~** les travaux sont déjà commencés; **'examination in ~'** 'examen en cours'.
II /prəˈgres/ *vi* **1** (develop, improve) [*work, research, studies, society*] progresser; [*person*] faire des progrès, progresser; **to ~ towards democracy** s'acheminer vers la démocratie; **2** (follow course) [*person, vehicle, discussion*] progresser, avancer; [*storm*] s'intensifier; **as the day ~ed** à mesure que la journée s'écoulait; **as the novel ~es** à mesure que l'on avance dans la lecture du roman.
progression /prəˈgreʃn/ *n* **1** (development) (evolution) évolution *f*; (improvement) progression *f*; **natural/logical ~** suite *f* or progression *f* naturelle/logique; **2** (series) succession *f*, suite *f*; **3** Math suite *f*; **4** Mus progression *f*.
progressive /prəˈgresɪv/ **I** *n* **1** gen, Pol (person) progressiste *mf*; **2** Ling progressif *m*.
II *adj* **1** (gradual) [*increase, change*] progressif/-ive; [*illness*] évolutif/-ive; **~ taxation** impôt progressif; **to show a ~ improvement** s'améliorer progressivement; **2** (radical) [*person, idea, policy*] progressiste; [*school*] parallèle; [*age, period*] progressif/-ive; **~ rock** Mus rock *m* progressiste; **3** Ling progressif/-ive.
progressively /prəˈgresɪvlɪ/ *adv* progressivement.
progressiveness /prəˈgresɪvnɪs/ *n* progressivité *f*.
progress report *n* (on construction work) rapport *m* sur l'état or l'évolution des travaux; (on project) rapport *m* sur l'état or l'évolution du projet; (on patient) bulletin *m* de santé; (on pupil) bulletin *m* scolaire.
prohibit /prəˈhɪbɪt, US prəʊ-/ *vtr* **1** (forbid) interdire; **to ~ sb from doing** interdire à qn de faire; **children are ~ed from using the elevator** il est interdit aux enfants d'utiliser l'ascenseur; **'smoking ~ed'** 'défense de fumer'; **2** sout (make impossible) empêcher (**from doing** de faire); **his poor health ~s him from playing sports** sa mauvaise santé l'empêche de faire du sport.
prohibition /ˌprəʊhɪˈbɪʃn, US ˌprəʊəˈbɪʃn/ **I** *n* **1** (forbidding) interdiction *f*, défense *f* (**of** de); **2** (ban) interdiction *f* (**on, against** de).
II **Prohibition** *pr n* **the Prohibition** US Hist la prohibition.
III *modif* [*law, party*] prohibitionniste; [*America, days, years*] de la prohibition.
prohibitionism /ˌprəʊhɪˈbɪʃənɪzəm, US ˌprəʊə-/ *n* prohibitionnisme *m*.
prohibitionist /ˌprəʊhɪˈbɪʃənɪst, US ˌprəʊə-/ *n* prohibitionniste *mf*.
prohibitive /prəˈhɪbətɪv, US prəʊ-/ *adj* [*cost, price*] prohibitif/-ive.
prohibitively /prəˈhɪbɪtɪvlɪ, US prəʊ-/ *adv* **prices are ~ high** les prix sont prohibitifs.
project I /ˈprɒdʒekt/ *n* **1** (plan, scheme) projet *m* (**to do** pour faire); **a ~ to build a road** un projet de construction d'une route; **2** Sch dossier *m* (**on** sur); Univ mémoire *m* (**on** sur); **research ~** programme *m* de recherches; **3** US (state housing) (large) ≈ cité *f* HLM; (small) ≈ lotissement *m* HLM; **to grow up in the ~s** grandir au milieu des HLM.
II /ˈprɒdʒekt/ *modif* [*budget, funds*] d'un projet; **~ manager** gen directeur/-trice *m/f* de projet; Constr maître *m* d'œuvre; **~ outline** avant-projet *m*.
III /prəˈdʒekt/ *vtr* **1** (throw, send) projeter [*object*]; envoyer [*missile*]; faire porter [*voice*]; **2** (put across) donner [*image*]; **to ~ a new image** donner une nouvelle image; **3** (transfer) projeter [*guilt, doubts, anxiety*] (**onto** sur); **4** (estimate) prévoir [*figures, results*]; **5** Cin, Phys projeter [*light, film, slide*] (**onto** sur); **6** Geog faire la projection de [*earth, map*]; Math projeter [*solid*].
IV /prəˈdʒekt/ *vi* **1** gen (stick out) faire saillie (**from** sur); **to ~ over** surplomber; **2** Theat [*actor*] passer la rampe.
V **projected** *pp adj* [*figure, deficit*] prévu; **their ~ed visit** la visite qu'ils ont prévue; **a ~ed £4 m deficit** un deficit prévu de 4 millions de livres; **the ~ed figures are...** les prévisions pour les chiffres sont...
VI /prəˈdʒekt/ *v refl* **to ~ oneself 1** (make an impression) faire impression; **to ~ oneself as being** donner l'impression d'être; **2 to ~ oneself into the future** se projeter dans l'avenir.
projectile /prəˈdʒektaɪl, US -tl/ *n* projectile *m*.
projecting /prəˈdʒektɪŋ/ *adj* saillant.
projection /prəˈdʒekʃn/ *n* **1** (of object, thoughts, emotions) projection *f*; **2** (estimate) prévision *f*; **3** Cin, Math, Geog projection *f*.
projectionist /prəˈdʒekʃənɪst/ **▶ 1692** *n* projectionniste *mf*.
projection room *n* cabine *f* de projection.
projective /prəˈdʒektɪv/ *adj* projectif/-ive.
projector /prəˈdʒektə(r)/ *n* projecteur *m*.
prolactin /prəʊˈlæktɪn/ *n* prolactine *f*.
prolapse /ˈprəʊlæps/ **I** *n* prolapsus *m*.
II *vi* [*organ*] descendre.
prole○ /prəʊl/ *n* péj prolo○ *mf* pej.
proletarian /ˌprəʊlɪˈteərɪən/ **I** *n* prolétaire *mf*.
II *adj* **1** Pol, Econ [*class, revolution*] prolétarien/-ienne; **2** gen [*decency, life*] ouvrier/-ière.
proletarianize /ˌprəʊlɪˈteərɪənaɪz/ *vtr* prolétariser.
proletariat /ˌprəʊlɪˈteərɪət/ *n* prolétariat *m*.
pro-life /ˌprəʊˈlaɪf/ *adj* [*movement, campaigner, lobby*] contre l'avortement.
pro-lifer /ˌprəʊˈlaɪfə(r)/ *n* adversaire *mf* de l'avortement.
proliferate /prəˈlɪfəreɪt, US prəʊ-/ *vi* proliférer.
proliferation /ˌprəlɪfəˈreɪʃn, US ˌprəʊ-/ *n* prolifération *f* (**of** de).
proliferous /prəˈlɪfərəs/ *adj* sout [*plant*] prolifère; [*animal*] proliférant; [*coral*] bourgeonnant.
prolific /prəˈlɪfɪk/ *adj* **1** (productive) [*writer*] prolifique; [*decade*] fécond; **~ scorer** (of goals) excellent buteur; **2** (in reproduction) [*plant*] prolifique; [*animal, person*] prolifique, fécond; [*growth*] rapide.
prolix /ˈprəʊlɪks, US prəʊˈlɪks/ *adj* sout prolixe.
prolixity /prəʊˈlɪksətɪ/ *n* sout prolixité *f*.

prologue /'prəʊlɒg, US -lɔ:g/ *n* **1** Literat prologue *m* (**to** de); **2** (preliminary) prélude *m* (**to** à).

prolong /prə'lɒŋ, US -'lɔ:ŋ/ *vtr* prolonger.

prolongation /,prəʊlɒŋ'geɪʃn, US -lɔ:ŋ-/ *n* (in time) prolongation *f*; (in space) prolongement *m*.

prolonged /prə'lɒŋd, US -'lɔ:ŋd/ *adj* prolongé.

prom○ /prɒm/ *n* **1** GB (concert) concert *m*; **2** US (at high school) bal *m* de lycéens; (college) bal *m* d'étudiants; **3** GB (at seaside) front *m* de mer.

promenade /,prɒmə'nɑ:d, US -'neɪd/ **I** *n* **1** (path) promenade *f*; (by sea) front *m* de mer; **2** Dance promenade *f*.
II *vtr* sout promener [*virtues etc*].
III *vi* sout se promener.

promenade: **~ concerts** *npl* GB série *f* annuelle de concerts; **~ deck** *n* pont *m* promenade.

Prometheus /prə'mi:θju:s/ *pr n* Prométhée.

promethium /prə'mi:θɪəm/ *n* prométhium *m*.

prominence /'prɒmɪnəns/ *n* **1** (of person, issue) importance *f*; **to rise to ~** devenir connu; **to give ~ to sth** donner or accorder de l'importance à qch; **to come to ~ as a writer** devenir célèbre comme écrivain; **2** (of feature, building, object) proéminence *f*.

prominent /'prɒmɪnənt/ *adj* **1** [*person, figure, activist, campaigner*] très en vue, important; [*artist, intellectual, industrialist*] éminent; **to play a ~ part** ou **role in sth** jouer un rôle de premier plan dans qch; **2** [*position, place, feature*] proéminent, en vue; [*peak, ridge*] saillant; [*marking, mole*] bien visible; **leave the key in a ~ place** laisse la clé en évidence; **3** [*nose, forehead*] proéminent; [*cheekbone*] saillant; [*eye*] exorbité; [*tooth*] en avant.

prominently /'prɒmɪnəntlɪ/ *adv* [*displayed, hung, shown*] en évidence; **to feature** ou **figure ~ in sth** jouer un rôle important dans qch.

promiscuity /,prɒmɪ'skju:ətɪ/ *n* **1** (sexual) vagabondage *m* sexuel; **2** (mixing) sout promiscuité *f*.

promiscuous /prə'mɪskjʊəs/ *adj* péj [*person*] aux mœurs légères; [*behaviour*] léger/-ère.

promise /'prɒmɪs/ **I** *n* **1** (undertaking) promesse *f*; **to make a ~ to sb** faire une promesse à qn; **to break/keep one's ~** manquer à/tenir sa promesse; **they held him to his ~** ils lui ont fait tenir sa promesse; **under a ~ of secrecy** sous la promesse du secret; **'I'll come next time!'—'is that a ~?'** 'je viendrai la prochaine fois!'—'c'est promis?'; **2** ¢ (hope, prospect) espoir *m*; **there seems little ~ of peace** il semble qu'il y ait peu d'espoir de paix; **her early life held little ~ of her future happiness** sa jeunesse ne laissait pas présager de son bonheur futur; **full of Eastern ~** plein des charmes de l'Orient; **3** ¢ (likelihood of success) **she shows great ~** elle promet beaucoup; **a young writer of ~** un jeune écrivain qui promet.
II *vtr* **1** (pledge) **to ~ sb sth** promettre qch à qn; **to ~ to do** promettre de faire; **she ~d me (that) she would come** elle m'a promis qu'elle viendrait; **they ~d him their support/to do** ils lui ont promis leur soutien/de faire; **I can't ~ anything** je ne peux rien promettre; **as ~d** comme promis; **2** (give prospect of) annoncer, promettre; **the clouds ~d rain** les nuages annonçaient de la pluie; **it ~s to be a fine day** la journée s'annonce belle; **3** (assure) assurer; **it won't be easy, I ~ you** cela ne sera pas facile, je te l'assure; **4**‡ **to be ~d in marriage to sb** être promis en mariage à qn.
III *vi* **1** (give pledge) promettre; **do you ~?** c'est promis?; **I ~** je le promets; **but you ~d!** mais tu avais promis!; **2** fig **to ~ well** [*young talent, candidate*] être très prometteur; [*result, situation, event*] s'annoncer bien; **this doesn't ~ well for the future** cela ne présage rien de bon pour le futur.
IV *v refl* **to ~ oneself sth** se promettre qch; **to ~ oneself to do** se promettre de faire.
IDIOMS **to ~ sb the earth** promettre la lune à qn.

Promised Land *n* lit, fig Terre *f* Promise.

promising /'prɒmɪsɪŋ/ *adj* [*situation, sign, result, career, future*] prometteur/-euse; the [*artist, candidate*] qui promet; **the weather/the future looks more ~** le temps/l'avenir s'annonce meilleur; **it doesn't look very ~** [*weather, outlook, scheme*] cela n'a pas l'air très prometteur; [*exam results*] cela n'a pas l'air très encourageant; **'I've been shortlisted for the job'—'that's ~'** 'je suis sur la liste des candidats retenus'—'c'est bon signe'; **the film gets off to a ~ start but...** le film démarre bien mais...; **a ~ young actor** un jeune acteur qui promet.

promisingly /'prɒmɪsɪŋlɪ/ *adv* d'une façon prometteuse; **the talks started off quite ~ but...** les discussions ont plutôt bien commencé mais...

promissory note /'prɒmɪsərɪ, US -sɔ:rɪ/ *n* billet *m* à ordre.

promo○ /'prəʊməʊ/ **I** *n* (publicity) pub○ *f*, publicité *f*; (film) (vidéo-)clip *m*, promo *f*.
II *adj* publicitaire.

promontory /'prɒməntrɪ, US -tɔ:rɪ/ *n* promontoire *m*.

promote /prə'məʊt/ **I** *vtr* **1** (in rank) promouvoir (**to** à); **to be ~d from secretary to administrator** être promu du rang de secrétaire à celui d'administrateur; **she was ~d to manager** elle a été promue directrice; **2** (advertise) faire de la publicité pour [*product*]; (market) promouvoir [*brand, book, town*]; promouvoir [*theory, image*]; **to ~ a candidate** mettre un candidat en avant; **to ~ a bill** Pol présenter un projet de loi; **3** (encourage) promouvoir [*democracy, understanding etc*]; **4** GB (in football) **to be ~d from the fourth to the third division** passer de quatrième en troisième division; **5** US Sch être admis dans la classe supérieure.
II *vtr* **to ~ oneself** se mettre en avant.

promoter /prə'məʊtə(r)/ *n* (all contexts) promoteur/-trice *m/f*.

promotion /prə'məʊʃn/ *n* **1** (of employee) promotion *f*; **her ~ to manager** sa promotion au poste de directrice; **after his ~ from captain to colonel** après sa promotion du grade de capitaine à celui de colonel; **to gain ~** être promu; **to recommend sb for ~** recommander qn pour une promotion; **to apply for ~** demander une promotion; **to be in line for ~** avoir des chances d'être promu; **2** Comm promotion *f* (**of** de); **sales ~** (activity) promotion *f* des ventes; (campaign) campagne *f* de publicité; **3** (encouragement) promotion *f* (**of** de); **4** US Sch admission *f* dans la classe supérieure.

promotional /prə'məʊʃənl/ *adj* **1** Comm promotionnel/-elle; **2** (in workplace) **the ~ ladder** les échelons *mpl*.

promotional video *n* (vidéo-)clip *m*.

promotion prospects *npl* (long-term) perspectives *fpl* d'avenir; (immediate) possibilités *fpl* d'avenir.

promotions manager ▶ 1692 *n* directeur/-trice *m/f* de la publicité.

prompt /prɒmpt/ **I** *n* **1** Comput message *m* guide-opérateur; **2** Comm délai *m* de paiement; **3** gen, Theat **to give sb a ~** souffler une réplique à qn.
II *adj* [*attention, reply, result, refund*] rapide; [*action, recovery*] rapide, prompt; **to be ~ to do** être prompt à faire.
III *adv* pile; **at six o'clock ~** à six heures pile or précises.
IV *vtr* **1** (cause) provoquer [*reaction, decision, anger, action, revolt*]; susciter [*concern, accusation, comment, warning*]; déclencher [*alert, strike*]; **to ~ sb to do sth** inciter or pousser qn à faire qch; **2** (encourage to talk) **'and then what?' she ~ed** 'et puis quoi?' demanda-t-elle; **'... boring?' he ~ed** '... ennuyeux?' suggéra-t-il; **3** gen, Theat (remind) souffler à [*person*].
V *vi* gen, Theat souffler.

prompt box *n* Theat trou *m* du souffleur.

prompter /'prɒmptə(r)/ *n* **1** Theat souffleur/-euse *m/f*; **2** US TV téléprompteur *m*.

prompting /'prɒmptɪŋ/ *n* encouragement *m*; **without any ~** de mon/son etc plein gré.

promptitude /'prɒmptɪtju:d, US -tu:d/ *n* sout **1** (speed) promptitude *f*; **2** (punctuality) ponctualité *f*.

promptly /'prɒmptlɪ/ *adv* **1** (immediately) immédiatement, sur-le-champ; **he lifted it up and ~ dropped it** il l'a soulevé et aussitôt or immédiatement il l'a laissé tomber; **2** (without delay) [*reply, act, pay*] rapidement; **3** (punctually) [*arrive, leave, start*] à l'heure; **~ at six o'clock** à six heures précises.

promptness /'prɒmptnɪs/ *n* **1** (speed) rapidité *f* (**in doing** à faire); **2** (punctuality) ponctualité *f*.

prompt: **~ note** *n* Comm rappel *m* de paiement; **~ side** *n* Theat, GB côté *m* cour; US côté *m* jardin.

promulgate /'prɒmlgeɪt/ *vtr* **1** (promote) répandre [*theory, idea*]; **2** (proclaim) promulguer [*law, doctrine*].

promulgation /,prɒml'geɪʃn/ *n* (promotion) dissémination *f*; (announcement) promulgation *f*.

prone /prəʊn/ **I** *adj* **1** (liable) **to be ~ to** être sujet/-ette à [*migraines, colds*]; être enclin à [*depression, violence*]; **to be ~ to do** ou **to doing** être enclin à faire; **2** (prostrate) **to lie ~** (sleeping, sunbathing) être allongé sur le ventre; (injured) être allongé face contre terre.
II -prone (*dans composés*) **accident-~** sujet/-ette aux accidents; **flood-~** inondable.

prong /prɒŋ, US prɔ:ŋ/ *n* (on fork) dent *f*; (on antler) pointe *f*.

-pronged /prɒŋd, US prɔ:ŋd/ *adj* (*dans composés*) **1** (sided) **two-/three-~ attack** attaque *f* sur deux/trois fronts; **2** [*fork, spear*] **two-/three-~** à deux/trois dents.

pronominal /prəʊ'nɒmɪnl/ *adj* pronominal.

pronoun /'prəʊnaʊn/ *n* pronom *m*.

pronounce /prə'naʊns/ **I** *vtr* **1** Ling prononcer [*letter, word*]; **is the letter 'h' ~d?** est-ce que le 'h' se prononce?; **2** (announce) prononcer [*judgment, sentence*]; rendre [*verdict*]; émettre [*opinion*]; **to ~ sb dead/guilty** déclarer qn mort/coupable; **to ~ sth (to be) genuine/satisfactory** déclarer que qch est authentique/satisfaisant; **to ~ that** déclarer que; **'this is a fake,' she ~d** 'c'est un faux,' déclara-t-elle; **I now ~ you man and wife** je vous déclare unis par les liens du mariage.
II *vi* Jur prononcer; **to ~ for/against sb** rendre un jugement favorable/défavorable à qn.
III *v refl* **to ~ oneself satisfied/bored** se déclarer satisfait/ennuyé; **to ~ oneself for/against sth** se prononcer pour/contre qch.
■ **pronounce on**: **~ on [sth]** se prononcer sur [*case, matter*]; affirmer [*existence, truth*]; juger de [*merits*].

pronounceable /prə'naʊnsəbl/ *adj* prononçable.

pronounced /prə'naʊnst/ *adj* **1** (noticeable) [*accent, limp, tendency*] prononcé; [*stammer*] fort; [*change, difference, increase*] marqué; **2** (strongly felt) [*idea, opinion, view*] arrêté.

pronouncement /prə'naʊnsmənt/ *n* **1** (statement) déclaration *f* (**on** sur, à propos de); **2** (verdict) verdict *m* (**on** sur, à propos de).

pronto○ /'prɒntəʊ/ *adv* illico○.

pronuclear /prəʊ'nju:klɪə(r), US -'nu:-/ *adj* pronucléaire.

pronunciation /prəˌnʌnsɪ'eɪʃn/ *n* prononciation *f*.

proof /pru:f/ **I** *n* **1** ₵ (evidence) preuve *f* **C** (**of** de; **that** que); **I have ~** j'ai une preuve or des preuves; **you have no ~** vous n'avez aucune preuve; **to have ~ that** pouvoir prouver que; **there is no ~ that** rien ne prouve que; **do you have (any) ~?** avez-vous des preuves?, en avez-vous la preuve?; **the ~ is that** la preuve en est que; **this is ~ that** cela prouve que; **to produce sth as ~** produire qch à titre de preuve; **to take sth as ~ that** considérer qch comme la preuve que; **absolute/conclusive ~** preuve absolue/irréfutable; **to fail through lack of ~** échouer faute de preuves; **to be ~ of sb's worth/age/existence** prouver la valeur/l'âge/l'existence de qn; **to be living ~ of sth** être la preuve vivante de qch; **~ of identity** pièce *f* d'identité; **2** Math, Philos preuve *f*; **3** Print épreuve *f*; **at ~ stage** au stade des épreuves; **to read sth in ~** lire qch sur épreuves; **4** Phot épreuve *f*; **5** (of alcohol) niveau *m* étalon; **over/under ~** au-dessus/au-dessous du niveau étalon; **to be 70° ou 70% ~** ≈ titrer 40° d'alcool.
II *adj* **to be ~ against** être à l'épreuve de [*wind, infection, heat, time*]; être à l'abri de [*temptation, charms*].
III -proof (*dans composés*) (resistant to) **vandal-~** protégé contre les vandales; **earthquake-~** antisismique; **toddler-~ toys** jouets résistant aux petits.
IV *vtr* **1** (make waterproof) imperméabiliser [*fabric*]; (make soundproof) insonoriser [*room, house*]; **2** = **proofread**.

proof: **~ of delivery** *n* reçu *m* de livraison; **~ of ownership** *n* titre *m* de propriété; **~ of postage** *n* certificat *m* d'expédition; **~ of purchase** *n* justificatif *m* d'achat.

proofread /'pru:fri:d/ **I** *vtr* (*prét, pp* **-read** /red/) **1** (check copy) corriger; **2** (check proofs) corriger les épreuves de [*novel, article*].
II *vi* (*prét, pp* **-read** /red/) **1** (check copy) corriger; **2** (check proofs) corriger des épreuves.

proof: **~reader** ▶1692 *n* correcteur/-trice *m/f*; **~reading** *n* correction *f* d'épreuves; **~ spirit** *n* GB alcool *m* à 57,1°; US alcool *m* à 50°.

prop /prɒp/ **I** *n* **1** Constr, Tech (support) étai *m*; **2** (supportive person) soutien *m* (**for** pour); **3** Theat (*abrév* = **property**) accessoire *m*; **stage ~** accessoire *m* de théâtre; **4**○ Aviat (*abrév* = **propeller**) hélice *f*; **5** Sport (in rugby) pilier *m*; **6** Hort (for plant) tuteur *m*; (for crop) rame *f*.
II *vtr* (*p prés etc* **-pp-**) **1** (support) étayer [*roof, tunnel, wall*]; **I ~ed his head on a pillow** je lui ai soutenu la tête avec un oreiller; **2** (lean) **to ~ sb/sth against sth** appuyer qn/qch contre qch.
III *v refl* (*p prés etc* **-pp-**) **to ~ oneself against sth** s'appuyer à [*tree, wall*].
■ **prop up**: **~ [sth] up, ~ up [sth]** lit étayer [*beam, wall*]; fig soutenir [*company, currency, economy, person, regime*].

propaganda /ˌprɒpə'gændə/ **I** *n* propagande *f* (**against** contre; **for** pour).
II *modif* [*campaign, exercise, film, war*] de propagande.

propagandist /ˌprɒpə'gændɪst/ *n* propagandiste *mf*.

propagandize /ˌprɒpə'gændaɪz/ *vi* faire de la propagande.

propagate /'prɒpəgeɪt/ **I** *vtr* **1** (spread) propager [*myth, story*]; **2** Hort propager [*plant*] (**from** par).
II *vi* Hort se propager.

propagated error *n* erreur *f* répercutée.

propagation /ˌprɒpə'geɪʃn/ *n* propagation *f*.

propagator /'prɒpəgeɪtə(r)/ *n* (tray) germoir *m*.

propane /'prəʊpeɪn/ *n* propane *m*.

propel /prə'pel/ **I** *vtr* (*p prés etc* **-ll-**) **1** (power) propulser [*vehicle, ship*]; **2** (push) pousser [*person*]; (more violently) propulser [*person*]; **to ~ sb into power/into the limelight** propulser qn au pouvoir/au premier plan.
II -propelled (*dans composés*) **wind-~led** propulsé par le vent; ▶**jet-propelled, rocket-propelled.**

propellant /prə'pelənt/ *n* **1** (in aerosol) gaz *m* propulseur; **2** (in rocket) propergol *m*; **3** (in gun) poudre *f* propulsive.

propeller /prə'pelə(r)/ *n* Aviat, Naut hélice *f*.

propeller: **~ blade** *n* pale *f* (d'hélice); **~ shaft** *n* Aut arbre *m* de transmission; Naut arbre *m* porte-hélice; Aviat arbre *m* de propulsion.

propelling pencil *n* GB portemine *m*.

propensity /prə'pensətɪ/ *n* propension *f* (**to,** **for** à; **to do, for doing** à faire).

proper /'prɒpə(r)/ **I** *n* Relig propre *m*.
II *adj* **1** (right) [*term, spelling*] correct; [*order, manner, tool, choice, response*] bon/bonne; [*sense*] propre; [*precautions*] nécessaire; [*clothing*] qu'il faut (*after n*); **it is only ~ for sb to do** il est tout naturel que qn fasse; **it's only ~ for her to keep the money** il est tout naturel qu'elle garde l'argent; **everything is in the ~ place** tout est à sa place; **to go through the ~ channels** passer par la filière officielle; **in the ~ way** correctement, comme il faut; **2** (adequate) [*funding, recognition*] convenable; [*education, training*] bon/bonne; [*care, control*] requis; **there are no ~ safety checks** il n'y a pas les contrôles de sécurité requis; **we have no ~ tennis courts** nous n'avons pas de courts de tennis convenables; **it has ~ facilities** c'est bien équipé; **3** (fitting) **~ to** sout convenant à [*position, status*]; **to show ~ respect for tradition/for the dead** montrer le respect dû à la tradition/aux morts; **I did as I thought ~** j'ai agi comme je l'ai jugé bon; **4** (respectably correct) [*person*] correct; [*upbringing*] convenable; **it wouldn't be ~ to do** ce ne serait pas convenable de faire; **it is only ~ that he be invited** ce serait correct de l'inviter; **prim and ~** très convenable; **to do the ~ thing by a girl** euph se marier pour régulariser la situation; **5** (real, full) [*doctor, holiday, job*] vrai (*before n*); [*opportunity*] bon/bonne; **he did a ~ job of repairing the car** il a bien réparé la voiture; **6**○ (complete) **I felt a ~ fool!** je me suis senti complètement stupide!; **it was a ~ disaster** c'était un désastre complet; **we're in a ~ mess** ou **pickle now** nous voilà dans de beaux draps; **7** (actual) (*après n*) **in the village ~** dans le village même; **the show/competition ~** le spectacle/concours proprement dit; **8** sout (particular to) **~ to sb/sth** propre à qn/qch.
IDIOMS **to beat sb good and ~** fig battre qn haut la main.

proper fraction *n* fraction *f* proprement dite.

properly /'prɒpəlɪ/ *adv* **1** (correctly) correctement; **I like to do things ~** j'aime faire les choses correctement; **to do one's job ~** faire correctement son travail; **you acted very ~ in reporting the theft** vous avez très bien agi en déclarant le vol; **~ speaking** à proprement parler; **2** (fully) [*completed, shut, open*] complètement; **read the letter ~** lis la lettre correctement; **you're not ~ dressed** tu n'es pas assez habillé; **~ prepared for the interview** bien préparé pour l'entretien; **I didn't have time to thank you ~** je n'ai pas eu le temps de vous remercier; **walk/behave ~!** (to child) marche/tiens-toi comme il faut!; **3** (adequately) [*eat, rest, plan*] convenablement; [*insured, ventilated*] convenablement; **4** (suitably) [*dressed*] correctement; **he was ~ apologetic/grateful** il a fait les excuses/montré la reconnaissance qu'il fallait.

proper: **~ motion** Astron *n* mouvement *m* propre; **~ name, ~ noun** *n* Ling nom *m* propre.

propertied /'prɒpətɪd/ *adj* [*class*] possédant; **a ~ man/woman** un/-e possédant/-e *m/f*.

property /'prɒpətɪ/ **I** *n* **1** ₵ (belongings) propriété *f*, bien(s) *m(pl)*; **government ~** propriété *f* de l'État; **personal ~** bien(s) *m(pl)* personnel(s); **public ~** bien *m* public; **'private ~'** (on sign) 'propriété privée'; **that is not your ~** cela ne vous appartient pas; **2** ₵ (real estate) biens *mpl* immobiliers; **to have ~ abroad** avoir des biens à l'étranger; **to invest in ~** investir dans l'immobilier *m*; **~ was damaged** il y a eu des dégâts matériels; **3** **C** (house) propriété *f*; **the ~ is detached** c'est une maison indépendante; **4** Chem, Phys (characteristic) propriété *f*; **5** Jur (copyrighted work) propriété *f*.
II properties *npl* **1** Fin immobilier *m*; **2** Theat accessoires *mpl*.
III *modif* (real estate) [*company, development, group, law, speculator, value*] immobilier/-ière; [*market, prices*] de l'immobilier.
IDIOMS **to be hot ~** être demandé; **~ is theft** la propriété, c'est le vol.

property: **~ dealer** *n* marchand *m* de biens; **~ developer** *n* promoteur *m* immobilier; **~ insurance** *n* assurance *f* des biens; **~ owner** *n* propriétaire *mf*; **~ sales** *npl* vente *f* immobilière; **~ speculation** *n* spéculation *f* foncière; **~ tax** *n* impôt *m* foncier.

prophecy /'prɒfəsɪ/ *n* prophétie *f* (**that** selon laquelle); **to make a ~ that** prophétiser que.

prophesy /'prɒfəsaɪ/ **I** *vtr* prophétiser (**that** que).
II *vi* faire des prophéties (**about** sur).

prophet /'prɒfɪt/ *n* prophète *m*; **~ of doom** lit, fig prophète de malheur.

Prophet /'prɒfɪt/ *n* Relig **the ~** (Mohammed) le Prophète; **the ~s** Bible les Prophètes *mpl*.

prophetess /'prɒfɪtes/ *n* prophétesse *f*.

prophetic /prə'fetɪk/ *adj* prophétique.

prophetically /prə'fetɪklɪ/ *adv* prophétiquement.

prophylactic /ˌprɒfɪ'læktɪk/ **I** *n* **1** Med (treatment) traitement *m* prophylactique; (measure) mesure *f* prophylactique; **2** (condom) préservatif *m*.
II *adj* prophylactique.

prophylaxis /ˌprɒfɪ'læksɪs/ *n* prophylaxie *f*.

propinquity /prə'pɪŋkwətɪ/ *n* sout **1** (in space) proximité *f*; **2** (in relationship) consanguinité *f*.

propitiate /prə'pɪʃɪeɪt/ *vtr* se concilier [*person, gods*].

propitiation /prəˌpɪʃɪ'eɪʃn/ *n* (sacrifice) sacrifice *m* propitiatoire; (act) acte *m* propitiatoire; **to do sth in ~** faire qch à titre propitiatoire.

propitiatory /prə'pɪʃɪətrɪ, US -tɔ:rɪ/ *adj* Relig propitiatoire; gen conciliateur/-trice.

propitious /prə'pɪʃəs/ *adj* propice (**for** à).

propitiously /prə'pɪʃəslɪ/ *adv* [*start*] sous de bons auspices; [*arrive*] fort à propos; [*disposed*] favorablement.

propjet /'prɒpdʒet/ *n* turbopropulseur *m*.

proponent /prə'pəʊnənt/ *n* partisan/-e *m/f* (**of** de).

proportion /prə'pɔ:ʃn/ **I** *n* **1** (part, quantity) (of group, population etc) proportion *f*, pourcentage *m* (**of** de); (of income, profit, work etc) part *f* (**of** de); **a large/small ~ of the students** une proportion élevée/une faible proportion des étudiants; **a large ~ of the work** une grande part du travail; **in equal ~s** en proportions égales, à parts égales; **2** (ratio) also Math proportion *f*; **the ~ of pupils to teachers** la proportion d'élèves par rapport aux professeurs; **productivity increases in ~ to the incentives offered** l'augmentation de la productivité est directement proportionnelle aux primes de rende-

ment; **tax should be in ~ to income** les contributions devraient être en fonction des revenus; **3** (harmony, symmetry) **out of/in ~** hors de/en proportion; **the door is out of ~ with the rest of the building** la porte est hors de proportion avec le reste du bâtiment or est disproportionnée par rapport au reste du bâtiment; **4** fig (perspective) **to get sth out of all ~** faire tout un drame de qch; **her reaction was out of all ~ to the event** sa réaction était tout à fait disproportionnée par rapport à l'événement; **you've got to have a sense of ~** il faut avoir le sens de la mesure.
II **proportions** *npl* (of building, ship, machine) dimensions *fpl*; (of problem, project) dimensions *fpl*; **a lady of ample ~s** une dame aux proportions généreuses; **to reach alarming/epidemic ~s** atteindre des proportions alarmantes/épidémiques.
III **-proportioned** (*dans composés*) **well-/badly-~ed** bien/mal proportionné.

proportional /prə'pɔːʃənl/ I *n* Math quatrième proportionnelle *f*.
II *adj* proportionnel/-elle (**to** à).

proportional: **~ assessment** *n* péréquation *f*; **~ counter** *n* détecteur *m* de rayonnements ionisants.

proportionally /prə'pɔːʃənəlɪ/ *adv* proportionnellement.

proportional representation, **PR** *n* représentation *f* proportionnelle; **to be elected by ~** être élu à la proportionnelle.

proportionate /prə'pɔːʃənət/ *adj* proportionnel/-elle.

proportionately /prə'pɔːʃənətlɪ/ *adv* [*larger, higher*] proportionnellement; [*distribute*] en proportion.

proposal /prə'pəʊzl/ *n* **1** (suggestion) proposition *f*; **to make/put forward a ~** faire/avancer une proposition; **a ~ for changes/new regulations** une proposition de changements/nouvelle réglementation; **a ~ for doing** ou **to do** une proposition visant à faire; **the ~ that everybody should get a pay rise** la proposition selon laquelle tout le monde devrait recevoir une augmentation; **2** (offer of marriage) demande *f* en mariage; **to receive a ~** être demandé en mariage; **3** Insur (also **~ form**) proposition *f* d'assurance.

propose /prə'pəʊz/ I *vtr* **1** (suggest) proposer [*change, course of action, rule, solution*]; présenter [*motion*]; proposer [*toast*] (**to** en l'honneur de); **to ~ doing** proposer de faire; **to ~ that** proposer que (+ *subj*); **2** (intend) **to ~ doing** ou **to do** proposer de faire; **3 to ~ marriage to sb** demander qn en mariage; **4** (nominate) proposer [*person*] (**as** comme; **for** pour).
II *vi* faire sa demande en mariage (**to** à).
III **proposed** *pp adj* [*action, reform*] envisagé.

proposer /prə'pəʊzə(r)/ *n* **1** (of motion) auteur *m*; **2** (of candidate) *personne proposant un candidat à un poste*; **3** (of member) parrain/marraine *m/f*; **4** GB Insur assuré *m* proposant.

proposition /ˌprɒpə'zɪʃn/ I *n* **1** (suggestion) proposition *f*; **a ~ to do** une proposition visant à faire; **2** (assertion) assertion *f*; **the ~ that** l'assertion selon laquelle; **3** Math, Philos proposition *f*; **4** (enterprise) affaire *f*; **an economic** ou **a paying** ou **a commercial ~** une affaire rentable; **that's quite a different ~** c'est une tout autre affaire; **he's a tough** ou **difficult ~** il n'est pas facile; **5** (sexual overture) proposition *f*.
II *vtr* faire une proposition à [*person*].

propositional /ˌprɒpə'zɪʃənl/ *adj* Math, Comput propositionnel/-elle.

propound /prə'paʊnd/ *vtr* avancer.

proprietary /prə'praɪətrɪ, US -terɪ/ *adj* **1** [*rights, duties, interest*] du propriétaire; [*manner, attitude*] de propriétaire; **2** Comm [*information*] qui est la propriété de la compagnie; [*system*] breveté.

proprietary: **~ brand** *n* marque *f* déposée; **~ colony** *n* colonie *f* (*concédée à un ou plusieurs individus*); **~ hospital** *n* US hôpital *m* privé; **~ medicine** *n* spécialité *f* pharmaceutique.

proprietor /prə'praɪətə(r)/ *n* propriétaire *mf* (**of** de).

proprietorial /prəˌpraɪə'tɔːrɪəl/ *adj* de propriétaire.

proprietorship /prə'praɪətəʃɪp/ *n* (fact of owning) possession *f*; **under his ~** pendant qu'il est/était etc propriétaire.

proprietress /prə'praɪətrɪs/ *n* propriétaire *f* (**of** de).

propriety /prə'praɪətɪ/ *n* **1** (politeness) correction *f*; **2** (morality) décence *f*.

prop root *n* racine *f* aérienne.

prop shaft *n*: *abrév* ▶ **propeller shaft**.

prop: **~s master** *n* Theat accessoiriste *m*; **~s mistress** *n* Theat accessoiriste *f*.

propulsion /prə'pʌlʃn/ *n* propulsion *f*.

propulsive /prə'pʌlsɪv/ *adj* [*force, power*] de propulsion; [*gas*] propulsif/-ive.

prop word *n* Ling (empty word) mot *m* vide; (substitute) pronom *m*, substitut *m*.

pro rata /ˌprəʊ 'rɑːtə/ I *adj* **on a ~ basis** en rapport, au prorata.
II *adv* [*increase*] dans la même proportion; **salary £15,000 ~** salaire 15 000 livres sterling au prorata des heures travaillées.

prorate /ˌprəʊ'reɪt/ I *vtr* **1** (divide) diviser [qch] de façon proportionnelle; **2** (assess) calculer [qch] de façon proportionnelle.
II *vi* affecter au prorata.

prorogation /ˌprəʊrə'geɪʃn/ *n* Pol prorogation *f*.

prorogue /prə'rəʊg/ Pol I *vtr* proroger.
II *vi* se proroger.

prosaic /prə'zeɪɪk/ *adj* [*style, description, existence*] prosaïque.

prosaically /prə'zeɪklɪ/ *adv* prosaïquement.

proscenium /prə'siːnɪəm/ *n* **1** Theat avant-scène *f*; **2** Antiq proscenium *m*.

proscenium arch *n* arc *m* de scène.

proscribe /prə'skraɪb, US prəʊ-/ *vtr* proscrire.

proscription /prə'skrɪpʃn, US prəʊ-/ *n* proscription *f*.

prose /prəʊz/ *n* **1** (not verse) prose *f*; **in ~** en prose; **her elegant ~ style** sa prose élégante; **2** GB Sch, Univ (translation) thème *m*.

prosecute /'prɒsɪkjuːt/ I *vtr* **1** Jur poursuivre [qn] en justice; **to ~ sb for doing** poursuivre qn pour avoir fait; **'trespassers will be ~d'** 'défense d'entrer sous peine de poursuites'; **'shoplifters will be ~d'** 'tout vol est passible de poursuites'; **2** (pursue) poursuivre [*war, research, interests*].
II *vi* engager des poursuites.

prosecuting: **~ attorney** *n* US (lawyer) avocat/-e *m/f* de la partie civile; (public official) procureur *m*; **~ lawyer** *n* avocat/-e *m/f* de l'accusation or de la partie civile.

prosecution /ˌprɒsɪ'kjuːʃn/ *n* **1** Jur (institution of charge) poursuites *fpl* (judiciaires); **to face/result in ~** s'exposer à/entraîner des poursuites; **liable to ~** passible de poursuites; **the ~ process** la procédure d'inculpation; **2** Jur (party) **the ~** (private individual) le/les plaignant/-s; (state, Crown) le ministère public; **Mr Green, for the ~, said...** Maître Green, pour le ministère public, a dit...; **3** (of war, research) poursuite *f* (**of** de); **in the ~ of one's duties** dans l'accomplissement *m* de ses fonctions.

prosecutor /'prɒsɪkjuːtə(r)/ *n* Jur **1** (instituting prosecution) **to be the ~** être chargé des poursuites; **2** (in court) procureur *m*; **3** US (prosecuting attorney) avocat/-e *m/f* de la partie civile; (public official) procureur *m*.

proselyte /'prɒsəlaɪt/ I *n* prosélyte *mf*.
II *vtr, vi* US = **proselytize**.

proselytism /'prɒsəlɪtɪzəm/ *n* prosélytisme *m*.

proselytize /'prɒsəlɪtaɪz/ I *vtr* essayer de convertir.
II *vi* faire du prosélytisme.

proseminar /prəʊ'semɪnɑː(r)/ *n* US Univ séminaire *m* (*pour étudiants de licence de niveau avancé*).

prose: **~ poem** *n* poème *m* en prose; **~ writer** *n* prosateur/-trice *m/f*.

prosodic /prə'sɒdɪk/ *adj* prosodique.

prosody /'prɒsədɪ/ *n* prosodie *f*.

prospect I /'prɒspekt/ *n* **1** (hope, expectation) (of change, improvement, promotion) espoir *m*; (of success) chance *f* (**of doing** de faire); **there is some ~/little ~ of improvement** il y a espoir/ peu d'espoir que cela s'améliore; **a bleak/gloomy ~** une perspective triste/sombre; **there is some ~ that** il y a un espoir que (+ *subj*); **there is no ~ of the strike ending soon/of my** ou **me being released** il n'y a aucun espoir que la grève se termine bientôt/que je sois libéré; **to hold out the ~ of sth** présager qch; **to face the ~ of sth/of doing** faire face à la perspective de qch/de faire; **to face the ~ that** faire face à la perspective que (+ *subj*); **to rule out the ~ of sth** écarter l'espoir de qch; **2** (outlook) perspective *f*; **to have sth in ~** avoir qch en perspective; **to be in ~** [*changes, cuts*] être à prévoir; **3** (good option) (for job) recrue *f* potentielle; (for sports team) espoir *m*; **this new product seems like a good ~ for the company** ce nouveau produit semble ouvrir de bonnes perspectives pour la compagnie; **4** Comm (likely client) client/-e *m/f* potentiel/-ielle; **5** (view) littér vue *f* (**of** sur).
II **prospects** *npl* perspectives *fpl* d'avenir; **she has good career ~s** elle a de bonnes perspectives de carrière; **the ~s for the economy/for growth** les perspectives pour l'économie/de croissance; **what are the ~s of promotion/of being promoted?** quelles sont les perspectives de promotion/les chances d'être promu?; **an industry with excellent ~s** une industrie avec d'excellentes perspectives; **a job with good ~s** un emploi ayant de bonnes perspectives; **to have no ~s** [*person*] ne pas avoir d'avenir; [*job*] être sans avenir; **a young man with ~s** un jeune homme qui a de l'avenir.
III /prə'spekt, US 'prɒspekt/ *vtr* prospecter [*land, region*].
IV /prə'spekt, US 'prɒspekt/ *vi* prospecter; **to ~ for** chercher [*gold, oil, diamonds*].

prospecting /prə'spektɪŋ/ I *n* Comm, Geol prospection *f*; **gold/mineral/oil ~** prospection aurifère/de minéraux/pétrolière.
II *modif* [*rights, licence*] de prospection.

prospective /prə'spektɪv/ *adj* [*buyer, earnings, candidate, use*] potentiel/-ielle; [*son-in-law, mother-in-law*] futur (*before n*).

prospector /prə'spektə(r), US 'prɒspektər/ *n* prospecteur/-trice *m/f*; **oil ~** prospecteur/-trice *m/f* de pétrole; **gold ~** chercheur/-euse *m/f* d'or.

prospectus /prə'spektəs/ *n* (booklet) gen brochure *f*, prospectus *m*; (for shares, flotation) prospectus *m* d'émission; **university ~, college ~** ≈ livret *m* de l'étudiant.

prosper /'prɒspə(r)/ *vi* prospérer.
IDIOMS **cheats never ~** Prov ça ne paie jamais de tricher.

prosperity /prɒ'sperətɪ/ *n* prospérité *f*.

prosperous /'prɒspərəs/ *adj* [*person, farm, country*] prospère; [*appearance*] de prospérité.

prostaglandin /ˌprɒstə'glændɪn/ *n* prostaglandine *f*.

prostate /'prɒsteɪt/ *n* (also **~ gland**) prostate *f*; **to have a ~ operation** se faire opérer de la prostate.

prostatectomy /ˌprɒsteɪt'ektəmɪ/ *n* prostatectomie *f*.

prosthesis /'prɒsθəsɪs, -'θiːsɪs/ *n* Med prothèse *f*.

prosthetic /prɒs'θetɪk/ *adj* Med prothétique.

prosthodontics /ˌprɒsθəˈdɒntɪks/ *n* (+ *v sg ou pl*) prothèse *f* dentaire (*technique*).

prosthodontist /ˌprɒsθəˈdɒntɪst/ **▶1692** *n* prothésiste *mf* dentaire.

prostitute /ˈprɒstɪtjuːt, US -tuːt/ **I** *n* **1** (woman) prostituée *f*; **2 male ~** prostitué *m*.
II *vtr* prostituer [*person, talent*].
III *v refl* **to ~ oneself** lit, fig se prostituer.

prostitution /ˌprɒstɪˈtjuːʃn, US -tuːʃ-/ *n* prostitution *f* (**of** de); **to be forced into ~** être forcé à entrer dans la prostitution.

prostrate **I** /ˈprɒstreɪt/ *adj* **1** (on stomach) [*body, figure*] allongé à plat ventre; **to lie ~** être allongé de tout son long; **2** fig (incapacitated) [*nation, country, sick person*] prostré; **~ with grief** accablé de chagrin; **3** Bot rampant.
II /prɒˈstreɪt, US ˈprɒstreɪt/ *vtr* **to be ~d by** être abattu par [*illness, grief*].
III *v refl* **to ~ oneself** se prosterner (**before** devant).

prostration /prɒˈstreɪʃn/ *n* **1** (in submission, worship) prosternation *f*; **2** (from illness, overwork) prostration *f*.

prosy /ˈprəʊzɪ/ *adj* ennuyeux/-euse.

Prot○ *n* injur (*abrév écrite* = **Protestant**) protestant/-e *m/f*.

protagonist /prəˈtægənɪst/ *n* **1** Literat, Cin protagoniste *mf*; **the main ~** le héros/l'héroïne *m/f*; **2** (advocate) partisan/-e *m/f* (**of** de); (participant) participant/-e *m/f*.

protean /ˈprəʊtɪən, -ˈtiːən/ *adj* littér changeant.

protect /prəˈtekt/ **I** *vtr* **1** (keep safe) protéger [*environment, home, identity, person, data, possessions, skin, surface*] (**against** contre; **from** de, contre); **2** (defend) défendre [*consumer, interests, privilege*] (**against** contre); préserver [*privacy*]; protéger [*investment, standards, economy, industry*] (**against** contre; **from** de, contre).
II *v refl* **to ~ oneself** (against threat) se protéger (**against** contre; **from** de, contre); (against attack) se défendre (**against, from** contre).

protection /prəˈtekʃn/ *n* **1** (safeguard) lit, fig protection *f* (**against, from** contre; **for** pour); **to give** ou **offer sb ~ against sth** [*coat, insurance, police, shelter, vaccine*] protéger qn contre qch; **to need ~ against sth** avoir besoin d'être protégé contre qch; **to use sth as ~ against sth** se servir de qch pour se protéger contre qch; **under the ~ of** sous la protection de; **environmental ~** protection de l'environnement; **for his own ~** (moral) pour son bien; (physical) pour le protéger; **2** Econ (also **trade ~**) protectionnisme *m*; **3** (extortion) **to pay sb ~** payer un impôt à qn (*pour assurer sa protection*) iron; **to buy ~** iron acheter sa tranquillité (*à un racketteur*); **4** Comput protection *f*; **data/file ~** protection *f* de données/fichiers; **memory ~**, **storage ~** protection *f* de mémoire; **5** (protective clothing) **head ~** casque *m*; **eye ~** lunettes *fpl*.

protection factor *n* (of sun cream) indice *m* de protection.

protectionism /prəˈtekʃənɪzəm/ *n* protectionnisme *m*; **agricultural/trade ~** protectionnisme *m* dans le secteur agricole/commercial.

protectionist /prəˈtekʃənɪst/ *n, adj* protectionniste *mf*.

protection: **~ money** *n* euph *argent versé à un racketteur*; **to pay ~ to sb** se faire extorquer par qn; **~ racket** *n* racket *m*.

protective /prəˈtektɪv/ **I** *n* US (condom) préservatif *m*.
II *adj* **1** (providing security) [*clothing, cover, gear, layer*] protecteur/-trice; [*measure*] de protection; **2** (caring) [*attitude, gesture, tone*] protecteur/-trice; **to feel ~ towards** avoir une attitude protectrice envers [*person*]; **to be ~ of** veiller jalousement sur [*car, possessions*]; protéger [*discovery, research*]; **3** Econ [*tarif, system*] protectionniste.

protective coloration *n* Zool homochromie *f*.

protective custody *n* Jur **to place sb in ~** détenir qn pour sa (propre) protection.

protectively /prəˈtektɪvlɪ/ *adv* d'une manière protectrice.

protectiveness /prəˈtektɪvnɪs/ *n* instinct *m* de protection.

protector /prəˈtektə(r)/ *n* **1** (defender) gen protecteur/-trice *m/f*; (of rights) défenseur *m*; **2** (protective clothing) **ear ~s** casque *m* antibruit; **elbow/shin ~** protège-coude/-tibia *m*; **3** GB Hist **the Protector** le Protecteur *m* (*Oliver Cromwell*).

protectorate /prəˈtektərət/ *n* Pol (also **Protectorate**) protectorat *m*.

protectress /prəˈtektrɪs/ *n* protectrice *f*.

protein /ˈprəʊtiːn/ *n* protéine *f*; **high-/low-~** riche/pauvre en protéines.

protein: **~ content** *n* teneur *f* en protéines; **~ deficiency** *n* carence *f* en protéines.

pro tem /ˌprəʊ ˈtem/ **I** *adj* provisoire.
II *adv* provisoirement.

protest **I** /ˈprəʊtest/ *n* **1** **C** (disapproval) protestation *f*; **in ~** en signe de protestation; **without ~** sans protester; **in ~ at** ou **against sth** pour protester contre qch; **I paid/followed him under ~** je l'ai payé/suivi contre mon gré; **2 C** (complaint) réclamation *f*, plainte *f* (**about, at** à propos de; **from** de la part de); **as a ~ against** ou **at sth** pour protester contre qch; **to lodge/register a ~** faire/déposer une réclamation; **3** (demonstration) manifestation *f* (**against** contre); **to stage a ~** organiser une manifestation; **4** Jur protêt *m*.
II /ˈprəʊtest/ *modif* [*march, movement, rally, song*] de protestation.
III /prəˈtest/ *vtr* **1** (declare) affirmer [*truth*]; **to ~ one's innocence** protester de son innocence; **2** (complain) **'that's unfair!' they ~ed** 'c'est injuste!' s'écrièrent-ils; **to ~ that** protester que; **3** US (complain about) protester contre (**to** auprès de); **4** Fin Jur **to ~ a bill** dresser un protêt de non-paiement, protester un effet.
IV /prəˈtest/ *vi* **1** (complain) protester (**about, at, over** à propos de; **to** auprès de); **to ~ at being chosen/ignored** protester contre le fait d'avoir été choisi/ignoré; **2** (demonstrate) manifester (**against** contre).

Protestant /ˈprɒtɪstənt/ **I** *n* protestant/-e *m/f*.
II *adj* protestant; **the ~ Church** gen l'Église protestante; (in official names) l'Église Réformée; **the ~ service** le culte.

Protestantism /ˈprɒtɪstəntɪzəm/ *n* protestantisme *m*.

protestation /ˌprɒtɪˈsteɪʃn/ *n* protestation *f*; **in ~** pour protester.

protester /prəˈtestə(r)/ *n* manifestant/-e *m/f*.

protocol /ˌprəʊtəˈkɒl, US -kɔːl/ *n* gen, Pol, Comput protocole *m*.

proton /ˈprəʊtɒn/ *n* proton *m*.

protoplasm /ˈprəʊtəplæzəm/ *n* protoplasme *m*.

prototype /ˈprəʊtətaɪp/ **I** *n* prototype *m* (**of** de).
II *modif* [*vehicle, aircraft*] prototype.

prototype system *n* Comput maquette *f* système.

prototyping /ˈprəʊtəʊtaɪpɪŋ/ *n* maquettage *m*.

protozoan /ˌprəʊtəˈzəʊən/ **I** *n* protozoaire *m*.
II *adj* du protozoaire.

protozoon /ˌprəʊtəˈzəʊɒn/ *n* (*pl* **-zoa**) protozoaire *m*.

protract /prəˈtrækt, US prəʊ-/ *vtr* prolonger.

protracted /prəˈtræktɪd, US prəʊ-/ *adj* prolongé.

protraction /prəˈtrækʃn, US prəʊ-/ *n* prolongation *f*.

protractor /prəˈtræktə(r), US prəʊ-/ *n* Math rapporteur *m*.

protrude /prəˈtruːd, US prəʊ-/ *vi* gen dépasser (**from** de); [*teeth*] avancer.

protruding /prəˈtruːdɪŋ, US prəʊ-/ *adj* **1** [*rock*] en saillie; [*nail*] qui dépasse; **2** [*eyes*] globuleux/-euse; [*ears*] décollé; [*ribs*] saillant; [*chin*] en galoche○, en avant; **to have ~ teeth** avoir les dents qui avancent.

protrusion /prəˈtruːʒn, US prəʊ-/ *n* sout (on rocks) saillie *f*; (part of building) avancée *f*; (on skin) protubérance *f*.

protrusive /prəˈtruːsɪv, US prəʊ-/ *adj* sout [*eyes, teeth, chin, ears*] proéminent.

protuberance /prəˈtjuːbərəns, US prəʊˈtuː-/ *n* sout protubérance *f*.

protuberant /prəˈtjuːbərənt, US prəʊˈtuː-/ *adj* sout protubérant.

proud /praʊd/ *adj* **1** (satisfied) [*person, parent, winner*] fier/fière (**of** de; **of doing** de faire); [*owner*] heureux/-euse; **to be ~ of oneself** être fier de soi; **I was ~ that I had been chosen** j'étais fier d'avoir été choisi; **she is ~ that he has won** elle est fière qu'il ait gagné; **I'm working-class and ~ of it** j'appartiens à la classe ouvrière et j'en suis fier; **I hope you're ~ of yourself!** iron tu peux être fier de toi! iron; **it was his ~ boast that he had won the gold medal** sa grande fierté était d'avoir gagné la médaille d'or; **2** (self-respecting) [*person, nation, race*] fier/fière; péj orgueilleux/-euse, fier/fière; **3** (great) [*day, moment*] grand (*before n*); **4** GB (protruding) protubérant; **fill the hole ~** bouchez le trou en laissant une protubérance; **to stand ~ of** dépasser [*crack, hole, surface*].
IDIOMS **to do sb ~** (entertain) traiter qn royalement; (praise) faire honneur à qn; **your honesty does you ~** ton honnêteté te fait honneur; **to do oneself ~** ne rien se refuser.

proudly /ˈpraʊdlɪ/ *adv* [*display show*] avec fierté; [*sit, speak, stand, fly, walk*] fièrement; **a ~ independent country** un pays fier de son indépendance; Cin **Disney Studios ~ present 'Bambi'** les studios Disney ont le plaisir de présenter 'Bambi'.

prov (*abrév écrite*) *n* **1** = **province**; **2** = **proverb**.

provable /ˈpruːvəbl/ *adj* démontrable.

prove /pruːv/ **I** *vtr* **1** (show) gen prouver (**that** que); (by argument) prouver (**that** que); (by demonstration) démontrer [*theorem, opposite theory*]; **it remains to be ~d** il reste à prouver; **it all goes to ~ that** tout cela prouve que; **to ~ beyond doubt** prouver sans le moindre doute; **events ~d him right/wrong** les événements lui ont donné raison/tort; **to ~ a point** montrer qu'on a raison; **2** Jur authentifier [*will*]; **3** Culin faire lever [*dough*].
II *vi* **1** (turn out) s'avérer; **to ~ to be difficult/broken** s'avérer être difficile/cassé; **it ~d otherwise** il en est allé autrement; **if I ~ to be mistaken** s'il arrive que j'aie tort; **2** Culin [*dough*] lever.
III *v refl* **to ~ oneself** faire ses preuves; **to ~ oneself (to be)** se révéler; **he ~d himself the best/the winner** il s'est révélé le meilleur/le gagnant.

proven /ˈpruːvn/ *adj* **1** [*competence, reliability, method, talent*] éprouvé; **2** Scot Jur **a verdict of not ~** un non-lieu.

provenance /ˈprɒvənəns/ *n* provenance *f*.

Provençal /ˌprɒvɒnˈsɑːl/ *n, adj* provençal (*m*).

Provence /prɒˈvɑːns/ **▶1273** *n* Provence *f*.

Provence-Alpes-Côte d'Azur **▶1273** *pr n* Provence-Alpes-Côte d'Azur *f*; **in/to ~** en Provence-Alpes-Côte d'Azur.

provender† /ˈprɒvɪndə(r)/ *n* provende† *f*.

proverb /ˈprɒvɜːb/ **I** *n* proverbe *m*.
II Proverbs *pr npl* Proverbes *mpl*.

proverbial /prəˈvɜːbɪəl/ *adj* **1** [*wisdom, saying*] proverbial; **he's got me over the**

~ barrel il me tient, comme on dit; **2** (widely known) légendaire.

proverbially /prəˈvɜːbɪəlɪ/ *adv* **he is ~ stupid/mean** il est d'une stupidité/avarice légendaire.

provide /prəˈvaɪd/ **I** *vtr* **1** (supply) fournir [*opportunity, evidence, jobs, meals*] (**for** à); apporter [*answer, support, understanding*] (**for** à); donner [*satisfaction*] (**for** à); assurer [*service, food, shelter*] (**for** à); **the club ~s a meeting place** le club fournit un lieu de réunion; **to ~ access** [*path*] assurer l'accès; (to records, information) fournir l'accès; **'training ~d'** 'formation assurée'; **to ~ sb with** fournir [qch] à qn [*job, room, opportunity*]; assurer [qch] à qn [*food, shelter, service*]; apporter [qch] à qn [*support, understanding*]; **the course ~d them with a chance to meet people** le stage leur a fourni l'occasion de rencontrer des gens; **to ~ the perfect introduction to** être une introduction parfaite à [*subject, work*]; **to ~ an incentive to do** être un encouragement à faire; **please use the bin ~d** veuillez utiliser la poubelle mise à votre disposition; **write your answer in the space ~d** écrivez votre réponse dans l'espace indiqué; **2** Jur, Admin (stipulate) [*law, clause, agreement*] prévoir (**that** que); **except as ~d** sauf indication contraire.
II *vi* pourvoir aux besoins.
■ **provide against**: **~ against [sth]** parer à [*possibility, hardship, disaster*].
■ **provide for**: ¶ **~ for [sth] 1** (account for) envisager [*contingency, expenses, eventuality*]; **to ~ for sth to be done** envisager de faire qch; **2** Jur [*treaty, agreement, clause*] prévoir; **the law ~s for sth to be done** la loi prévoit que qch sera fait; ¶ **~ for [sb]** [*person, will*] subvenir aux besoins de; **she ~s for her family** ou **her family's needs** elle subvient aux besoins de sa famille; **to be well ~d for** être à l'abri du besoin.

provided /prəˈvaɪdɪd/, **providing** /prəˈvaɪdɪŋ/ *conj* (also **~ that**) à condition que (+ *subj*); **I'll go ~ (that) sth is done** j'irai à condition que qch soit fait; **you can go ~ (that) you do** tu peux y aller à condition de faire; **~ always that** Jur, Admin sous réserve que (+ *subj*).

providence /ˈprɒvɪdəns/ *n* **1** (also **Providence**) (fate) providence *f*; **divine ~** la divine providence; **2** sout (foresight, thrift) prévoyance *f*.

provident /ˈprɒvɪdənt/ *adj* prévoyant.

provident association *n* GB société *f* de prévoyance.

providential /ˌprɒvɪˈdenʃl/ *adj* sout providentiel/-ielle.

providentially /ˌprɒvɪˈdenʃəlɪ/ *adv* sout de manière providentielle.

providently /ˈprɒvɪdəntlɪ/ *adv* sout prudemment.

provider /prəˈvaɪdə(r)/ *n* **1** (in family) **to be a good/bad ~** bien/mal subvenir aux besoins de sa famille; **to be the sole ~** être le/la seul/-e à subvenir aux besoins de la famille; **2** Comm pourvoyeur/-euse *m/f*.

providing /prəˈvaɪdɪŋ/ *conj* = **provided**.

province /ˈprɒvɪns/ *n* **1** (region) province *f*; **in the ~s** en province; **2** fig (field, area) domaine *m*; **that is not my ~** ce n'est pas mon domaine; **3** Relig (of archbishop) archevêché *m*; (of religious order) diocèse *m*.

provincial /prəˈvɪnʃl/ **I** *n* **1** (person from provinces) provincial/-e *m/f* also pej; **2** Relig supérieur *m*.
II *adj* **1** [*doctor, newspaper, capital*] de province; [*life*] provincial; [*tour*] en province; **2** péj (narrow) provincial.

provincialism /prəˈvɪnʃəlɪzəm/ *n* péj provincialisme *m*.

proving ground *n* terrain *m* d'essai.

provision /prəˈvɪʒn/ **I** *n* **1** (supplying) (of housing, information, facility, equipment) mise *f* à disposition (**to** à); (of food) approvisionnement *m* (**to** à); (of service) prestation *f* (**to** à); **health care ~** services *mpl* pour la santé; **to be responsible for the ~ of transport/teachers** être responsable d'assurer le transport/de fournir des enseignants; **2** (for future, old age) précautions *fpl*, dispositions *fpl* (**for** pour; **against** contre); **to make ~ for** prendre des dispositions pour; **3** Jur, Admin (stipulation) (of agreement, treaty) clause *f*; (of bill, act) disposition *f*; **~ to the contrary** stipulation *f* du contraire; **to make ~ for** prévoir; **under the ~s of** aux termes de; **with the ~ that** à la condition que (+*subj*); **within the ~s of the treaty** dans le cadre du traité; **to exclude sth from its ~s** [*act, treaty*] exclure qch de ses termes.
II provisions *npl* (food) provisions *fpl*; **to get ~s in** faire des provisions.
III *vtr* ravitailler [*ship*] (**with** en); approvisionner [*house, person*] (**with** en).

provisional /prəˈvɪʒənl/ *adj* provisoire.

Provisional /prəˈvɪʒənl/ *n* membre *m* de la faction dure de l'IRA.

provisional driving licence *n* GB ≈ permis *m* de conduire d'élève conducteur.

Provisional IRA *n* faction *f* dure de l'IRA.

provisionally /prəˈvɪʒnəlɪ/ *adv* provisoirement, à titre provisoire.

proviso /prəˈvaɪzəʊ/ *n* gen condition *f*; Jur clause *f* conditionnelle; **with the ~ that** à condition que (+ *subj*).

provisory /prəˈvaɪzərɪ/ *adj* [*contract, clause, agreement*] conditionnel/-elle.

Provo○ /ˈprəʊvəʊ/ *n*: *abrév* = **Provisional**.

provocation /ˌprɒvəˈkeɪʃn/ *n* provocation *f*; **at the slightest ~** à la moindre provocation; **he will react under ~** il réagit si on le provoque.

provocative /prəˈvɒkətɪv/ *adj* **1** (causing anger, controversy) [*remark, statement, tactics*] provocant; **to be ~** faire de la provocation; **he is being deliberately ~** il cherche à vous/les etc provoquer; **2** (sexually) [*pose, behaviour, dress*] provocant; **to look ~** avoir l'air provocant; **3** (challenging) [*book, film, title*] qui fait réfléchir.

provocatively /prəˈvɒkətɪvlɪ/ *adv* de manière provocante.

provoke /prəˈvəʊk/ *vtr* **1** (annoy) provoquer [*person, animal*]; **to ~ sb to do** ou **into doing sth** pousser qn à faire qch; **he is harmless, unless ~d** il est gentil, sauf si on le provoque; **2** (cause, arouse) susciter [*anger, complaints*]; provoquer [*laughter, crisis*]; **to ~ a reaction** provoquer une réaction (**in sb** chez qn).

provost /ˈprɒvəst/ *n* **1** GB Univ, Sch principal *m*; **2** US Univ doyen *m*; **3** (in Scotland) maire *m*; **4** Relig prévôt *m*.

provost: **~ court** *n* tribunal *m* prévôtal; **~ guard** *n* cf prévôté *f*; **~ marshal** *n* prévôt *m*.

prow /praʊ/ *n* proue *f*.

prowess /ˈpraʊɪs/ *n* ¢ **1** (skill) prouesses *fpl*; **her ~ as a gymnast** ses prouesses de gymnaste; **2** (bravery) vaillance *f*; **3** hum (sexual) prouesses *fpl*.

prowl /praʊl/ **I** *n* **to be on the ~** rôder (**for** en quête de); **to go on the ~** [*animal*] partir en quête d'une proie; fig [*person*] faire une virée.
II *vtr* **to ~ the streets at night** rôder dans les rues la nuit.
III *vi* (also **~ around**, **~ about** GB) [*animal, person*] gen rôder; (restlessly) [*person*] faire les cent pas; [*animal*] (in cage) tourner.

prowl car *n* US voiture *f* de police.

prowler /ˈpraʊlə(r)/ *n* rôdeur/-euse *m/f*.

proximity /prɒkˈsɪmətɪ/ *n* proximité *f* (**of** de); **in the ~ of** à proximité de; **its close ~ to the station/to London** le fait qu'il se trouve près de la gare/de Londres.

proximity fuse *n* fusée *f* de proximité.

proxy /ˈprɒksɪ/ *n* **1** (person) mandataire *mf*; **to be sb's ~** avoir procuration pour qn; **2** (authority) gen, Pol, Fin procuration *f*; **by ~** par procuration.

proxy: **~ battle**, **~ fight** *n* Mil conflit *m* par adversaires interposés; Fin bataille *f* de procédures; **~ vote** *n* vote *m* par procuration.

prude /pruːd/ *n* bégueule *mf*, prude *mf*; **to be a ~** être bégueule.

prudence /ˈpruːdns/ *n* sout prudence *f*.

prudent /ˈpruːdnt/ *adj* sout [*person, choice*] prudent, avisé; [*decision, policy*] prudent; **it would be ~ to wait** il serait prudent d'attendre.

prudential /pruːˈdenʃl/ *adj* sout prudent.

prudently /ˈpruːdntlɪ/ *adv* sout (with caution) avec circonspection; (wisely) prudemment.

prudery /ˈpruːdərɪ/ *n* pruderie *f*.

prudish /ˈpruːdɪʃ/ *adj* pudibond, prude; **to be ~ about sth/about doing** être pudibond quand il s'agit de qch/de faire.

prudishness /ˈpruːdɪʃnɪs/ *n* pruderie *f*.

prune /pruːn/ **I** *n* **1** Culin pruneau *m*; **2**○ US (prude) sainte-nitouche *f*.
II *vtr* **1** Hort (also **~ back**) (cut back) tailler; (thin out) élaguer; **2** fig élaguer [*essay, article*]; réduire [*budget, expenditure*].

pruning /ˈpruːnɪŋ/ *n* (of bush, tree) taille *f*; **to do the ~** tailler.

pruning shears *npl* cisailles *fpl*.

prurience /ˈprʊərɪəns/ *n* sout lubricité *f*.

prurient /ˈprʊərɪənt/ *adj* sout lubrique.

Prussia /ˈprʌʃə/ *pr n* Prusse *f*.

Prussian /ˈprʌʃn/ **I** *n* Prussien/-ienne *m/f*.
II *adj* prussien/-ienne.

Prussian blue *n* Art, Chem bleu *m* de Prusse.

prussic acid /ˌprʌsɪk ˈæsɪd/ *n* acide *m* prussique.

pry /praɪ/ **I** *n* US levier *m*.
II *vtr* US **1** lit **to ~ sth open** ouvrir qch en faisant levier; **to ~ the lid off a jar** forcer le couvercle d'un pot; **2** fig **to ~ sth out of** ou **from sb** soutirer qch à qn.
III *vi* **to ~ into** mettre son nez dans [*business*].

prying /ˈpraɪɪŋ/ *adj* curieux/-ieuse, indiscret/-ète.

PS (*abrév* = **postscriptum**) PS *m*.

psalm /sɑːm/ *n* psaume *m*; **(the book of) Psalms** Bible le Livre des Psaumes.

psalmbook /ˈsɑːmbʊk/ *n* psautier *m*.

psalmist /ˈsɑːmɪst/ *n* psalmiste *m*.

psalmody /ˈsɑːmədɪ/ *n* psalmodie *f*.

psalter /ˈsɔːltə(r)/ *n* psautier *m*.

PSBR *n*: *abrév* ▸ **Public Sector Borrowing Requirement**.

psephologist /seˈfɒlədʒɪst, US siː-/ ▸ **1692** *n* spécialiste *mf* du comportement électoral.

psephology /seˈfɒlədʒɪ, US siː-/ *n* étude *f* du comportement électoral.

pseud○ /sjuːd, US ˈsuːd/ *n, adj* prétentieux/-ieuse (*m/f*).

pseudo+ /ˈsjuːdəʊ, US ˈsuːdəʊ/ (*dans composés*) pseudo-.

pseudonym /ˈsjuːdənɪm, US ˈsuːd-/ *n* pseudonyme *m* (**of** de); **under a ~** sous un pseudonyme.

pseudonymous /sjuːˈdɒnɪməs, US suː-/ *adj* [*novel, article*] écrit sous un pseudonyme.

psi (*abrév* = **pounds per square inch**) livres *fpl* par pouce carré.

psittacosis /ˌsɪtəˈkəʊsɪs/ ▸ **1354** *n* psittacose *f*.

psoriasis /səˈraɪəsɪs/ ▸ **1354** *n* psoriasis *m*.

PST *abrév* ▸ **Pacific Standard Time**.

PSV GB *abrév* ▸ **public service vehicle**.

psych /saɪk/ **I**○ *n* US Univ psycho○ *f*.
II *vtr* = **psych out**.
III○ *excl* US je t'ai eu○!
■ **psych out**○: **~ [sb/sth] out**, **~ out [sb/sth]**○ **1** (intimidate, unnerve) déstabiliser [*person, opponent*]; **2** US (outguess) deviner

[*intentions, response*]; **I ~ed her out** je l'ai sentie venir○, j'ai deviné ses intentions.
■ **psych up**○: **to ~ oneself up** se préparer (psychologiquement) (**for** pour); **to get** ou **be all ~ed up for** être remonté à bloc○ pour.

psyche /'saɪkɪ/ *n* psychisme *m*, psyché *f* spec.

psychedelia /ˌsaɪkɪ'di:lɪə/ *n* ¢ (objects) objets *mpl* psychédéliques; (music) musique *f* psychédélique.

psychedelic /ˌsaɪkɪ'delɪk/ *adj* psychédélique.

psychiatric /ˌsaɪkɪ'ætrɪk/ *adj* [*hospital, care, nurse, treatment, help*] psychiatrique; [*illness, disorder*] mental; [*patient*] d'un hôpital psychiatrique.

psychiatrist /saɪ'kaɪətrɪst, US sɪ-/ ▶1692 *n* psychiatre *mf*.

psychiatry /saɪ'kaɪətrɪ, US sɪ-/ *n* psychiatrie *f*.

psychic /'saɪkɪk/ **I** *n* médium *m*, voyant/-e *m/f*.
II *adj* **1** (paranormal) [*phenomenon, experience*] parapsychologique, psychique○ controv; (telepathic) [*person*] télépathe; **to have ~ powers** avoir des dons de voyance; **you must be ~**○**!** tu dois être devin!; **2** (psychological) psychologique, psychique.

psychical /'saɪkɪkl/ *adj* = **psychic II.**

psychic: **~ determinism** *n* déterminisme *m* psychique; **~ investigator**, **~ researcher** ▶1692 *n* parapsychologue *mf*; **~ research** *n* parapsychologie *f*; **~ surgery** *n* opération *f* à main nue.

psycho◑ /'saɪkəʊ/ *n* dingue○ *mf*.

psychoanalyse GB, **psychoanalyze** US /ˌsaɪkəʊ'ænəlaɪz/ *vtr* psychanalyser.

psychoanalysis /ˌsaɪkəʊə'næləsɪs/ *n* psychanalyse *f*; **to undergo ~** se faire psychanalyser.

psychoanalyst /ˌsaɪkəʊ'ænəlɪst/ ▶1692 *n* psychanalyste *mf*.

psychoanalytic(al) /ˌsaɪkəʊˌænə'lɪtɪk(l)/ *adj* psychanalytique.

psychobabble /'saɪkəʊbæbl/ *n* péj jargon *m* des psychologues.

psychodrama /'saɪkəʊdrɑ:mə/ *n* psychodrame *m*.

psychokinesis /ˌsaɪkəʊkɪ'ni:sɪs/ *n* psychokinésie *f*.

psychokinetic /ˌsaɪkəʊkɪ'netɪk/ *adj* psychokinétique.

psycholinguistic /ˌsaɪkəʊlɪŋ'gwɪstɪk/ *adj* psycholinguistique.

psycholinguistics /ˌsaɪkəʊlɪŋ'gwɪstɪks/ *n* (+ *v sg*) psycholinguistique *f*.

psychological /ˌsaɪkə'lɒdʒɪkl/ *adj* (all contexts) psychologique.

psychologically /ˌsaɪkə'lɒdʒɪklɪ/ *adv* psychologiquement.

psychological warfare *n* guerre *f* psychologique.

psychologist /saɪ'kɒlədʒɪst/ ▶1692 *n* psychologue *mf*.

psychology /saɪ'kɒlədʒɪ/ *n* (all contexts) psychologie *f* (**of** de); **it is bad ~ to do** ce n'est pas très habile de faire.

psychometric /ˌsaɪkəʊ'metrɪk/ *adj* psychométrique.

psychometrics /ˌsaɪkəʊ'metrɪks/ *n* (+ *v sg*) psychométrie *f*.

psychomotor /'saɪkəʊməʊtə(r)/ *adj* psychomoteur/-trice.

psychoneurosis /ˌsaɪkəʊnjʊə'rəʊsɪs, US -nʊ-/ *n* psychonévrose *f*.

psychopath /'saɪkəʊpæθ/ *n* Psych psychopathe *mf* also fig.

psychopathic /ˌsaɪkəʊ'pæθɪk/ *adj* [*personality*] psychopathique; **he's ~** Psych c'est un psychopathe also fig.

psychopathology /ˌsaɪkəʊpə'θɒlədʒɪ/ *n* psychopathologie *f*.

psychopharmacological /ˌsaɪkəʊ ˌfɑ:məkə'lɒdʒɪkl/ *adj* psychopharmacologique.

psychopharmacology /ˌsaɪkəʊ ˌfɑ:mə'kɒlədʒɪ/ *n* psychopharmacologie *f*.

psychophysical /ˌsaɪkəʊ'fɪzɪkl/ *adj* psychophysique.

psychophysics /ˌsaɪkəʊ'fɪzɪks/ *n* (+ *v sg*) psychophysique *f*.

psychophysiological /ˌsaɪkəʊ ˌfɪzɪə'lɒdʒɪkl/ *adj* psychophysiologique.

psychophysiology /ˌsaɪkəʊˌfɪzɪ'ɒlədʒɪ/ *n* psychophysiologie *f*.

psychosis /saɪ'kəʊsɪs/ *n* psychose *f*.

psychosocial /ˌsaɪkəʊ'səʊʃl/ *adj* psychosocial.

psychosomatic /ˌsaɪkəʊsə'mætɪk/ *adj* psychosomatique.

psychosurgery /ˌsaɪkəʊ'sɜ:dʒərɪ/ *n* psychochirurgie *f*.

psychotherapist /ˌsaɪkəʊ'θerəpɪst/ ▶1692 *n* psychothérapeute *mf*.

psychotherapy /ˌsaɪkəʊ'θerəpɪ/ *n* psychothérapie *f*.

psychotic /saɪ'kɒtɪk/ *n, adj* psychotique (*mf*).

psywar○ /saɪ'wɔ:(r)/ *n* US guerre *f* psychologique.

pt *n: abrév écrite* = **pint**.

Pt *n* (*abrév écrite* = **platinum**) Pt *m*.

PT *abrév* ▶ **physical training**.

PTA *n* (*abrév* = **Parent-Teacher Association**) association *f* de parents d'élèves cf APE *f*.

ptarmigan /'tɑ:mɪgən/ *n* lagopède *m*.

Pte *n: abrév écrite* = **Private**.

pterodactyl /ˌterə'dæktɪl/ *n* ptérodactyle *m*.

PTO (*abrév* = **please turn over**) TSVP.

Ptolemaic /ˌtɒlə'meɪɪk/ *adj* **1** Astron ptoléméen/-éenne; **2** Antiq ptolémaïque.

Ptolemaic system *n* système *m* de Ptolémée.

Ptolemy /'tɒləmɪ/ *n* Ptolémée; **the Ptolemies** Antiq les Ptolémées.

ptomaine /'təʊmeɪn/ *n* ptomaïne *f*.

ptosis /'təʊsɪs/ *n* ptôse *f*; (of eyelid) ptôsis *m*.

ptyalin /'taɪəlɪn/ *n* ptyaline *f*.

PU *excl* US pouah!

pub○ /pʌb/ *n* GB pub *m*; **in the ~** au pub.

pub crawl *n* GB **to go on a ~** faire la tournée des pubs.

pube◑ /pju:b, US pu:b/ *n* poil *m* du pubis.

puberty /'pju:bətɪ/ *n* puberté *f*; **at ~** à la puberté; **the age of ~** l'âge de la puberté.

pubescence /pju:'besns/ *n* **1** (stage) début *m* de la puberté; **2** Zool, Bot (downiness) pubescence *f*.

pubescent /pju:'besnt/ *adj* **1** [*girl, boy*] pubère; **2** Zool, Bot (downy) pubescent.

pub food *n* GB cuisine *f* de pub.

pubic /'pju:bɪk/ *adj* pubien/-ienne.

pubic: **~ bone** *n* symphyse *f* pubienne; **~ hair** (single hair) poil *m* du pubis; (area) poils *mpl* du pubis.

pubis /'pju:bɪs/ *n* pubis *m*.

public /'pʌblɪk/ **I** *n* **the ~** le public; **open to the ~** ouvert au public; **to please/disappoint one's ~** plaire à/décevoir son public; **the theatre-going/racing ~** les amateurs *mpl* de théâtre/de courses.
II *adj* [*call box, health, property, park, footpath, expenditure, inquiry, admission, announcement, execution, image*] public/-ique; [*disquiet, enthusiasm, indifference, support*] général; [*library, amenity*] municipal; [*duty, spirit*] civique; **in the ~ interest** dans l'intérêt public; **to receive ~ acclaim** recevoir les éloges du public; **to be in ~ life** participer à la vie publique; **to be in the ~ eye** être exposé à l'opinion publique; **to make one's views ~, to go ~ with one's views** rendre ses opinions publiques; **she has decided to go ~ (with her story)** elle a décidé de rendre son histoire publique; **the company is going ~** la société va être cotée en Bourse; **the ~ good** le bien public; **it is ~ knowledge that** il est de notoriété publique que; **he's become ~ property** il est devenu une figure publique; **let's go somewhere less ~** allons dans un endroit plus discret; **at ~ expense** aux frais du contribuable.
III in public *adv phr* en public.

public: **~ access channel** *n*: *chaîne de télévision ou station de radio accordant du temps d'antenne au public*; **~ address (system)** *n* (système *m* de) sonorisation *f*.

public affairs *npl* affaires *fpl* publiques; **~ manager, director of ~** responsable *mf* des relations publiques.

publican /'pʌblɪkən/ ▶1692 *n* **1** GB (bar owner) patron/-onne *m/f* de pub; **2** Antiq publicain *m*.

public appearance *n* (of dignitary) apparition *f* publique; (of star, celebrity) apparition *f* en public; **to make a ~** paraître en public.

public assistance *n* US aide *f* sociale.

publication /ˌpʌblɪ'keɪʃn/ *n* **1** (printing) publication *f*; **to accept sth for ~** accepter de publier qch; **date of ~** date *f* de publication or de parution; **on the day of ~** le jour de la sortie or de la parution; **at the time of ~** au moment de la parution or de la publication; **'not for ~'** 'confidentiel'; **2** (book, journal) publication *f*; **'~s'** (on CV) 'articles publiés'.

publications list *n* liste *f* de titres.

public: **~ bar** *n* GB bar *m* (*la salle la plus simplement meublée d'un pub*); **~ bill** *n* projet *m* de loi qui concerne l'ensemble des citoyens; **~ company** *n* société *f* anonyme par actions; **~ convenience** *n* GB toilettes *fpl*; **~ corporation** *n* GB organisme *m* public; **~ debt** *n* dette *f* publique; **~ defender** *n* US avocat *m* commis d'office (*par le bureau d'aide judiciaire*).

public domain *n* Jur, gen domaine *m* public; **in the ~** dans le domaine public; **to fall into the ~** tomber dans le domaine public.

public: **~ domain software** *n* logiciel *m* appartenant au domaine public; **~ enemy** *n* ennemi *m* public; **~ enemy number one**○ *n* ennemi *m* public numéro un; **~ examination** *n* examen *m* ouvert à tous; **~ gallery** *n* tribune *f* réservée au public; **~ holiday** *n* GB jour *m* férié.

public house *n* **1** GB pub *m*; **2** US auberge *f*.

publicist /'pʌblɪsɪst/ *n* (advertiser) agent *m* de publicité; (press agent) attaché/-e *m/f* de presse.

publicity /pʌb'lɪsətɪ/ **I** *n* **1** (media attention) **to attract ~** attirer l'attention *f* des médias; **to shun ~** fuir les médias; **to take place in a blaze of ~** avoir lieu sous les feux des médias; **to receive bad** ou **adverse ~** faire l'objet de critiques dans les médias; **there is no such thing as bad ~** toute publicité est bonne à prendre; **2** (advertising) publicité *f*; **to be responsible for ~** être responsable de la publicité; **to give sth great ~, to be great ~ for sth** faire beaucoup de publicité pour qch; **to be bad ~ for** être une mauvaise publicité pour; **advance ~** promotion *f* (**for** pour); **3** (advertising material) (brochures) brochures *fpl* publicitaires; (posters) affiches *fpl* publicitaires; (films) films *mpl* publicitaires; **I've seen some of their ~** j'ai vu quelques-unes de leurs brochures or affiches.
II *modif* [*bureau, launch*] de publicité, publicitaire.

publicity: **~ agency** *n* agence *f* de publicité; **~ agent** ▶1692 *n* attaché/-e *m/f* de presse; **~ campaign** *n* (to sell product) campagne *f* publicitaire or de publicité; (to raise social issue) campagne *f* de sensibilisation; **~ drive** *n* = **publicity campaign**; **~ machine** *n* machine *f* publicitaire;

~ photograph *n* photo *f* publicitaire; **~ stunt** *n* coup *m* publicitaire or de pub○.

publicize /ˈpʌblɪsaɪz/ *vtr* **1** (raise awareness of) attirer l'attention du public sur, sensibiliser l'opinion publique au sujet de [*issue, event, predicament*]; **well-~d**, **much-~d** [*event*] dont on parle beaucoup dans les médias; [*scandal, controversy*] qui fait or qui a fait la une de tous les journaux; **the event was little ~d** on a peu parlé de l'événement dans les médias; **2** (make public) rendre [qch] public [*intentions, reasons, matter*]; **3** (advertise) faire de la publicité pour; **well-~d, much-~d** [*show, concert*] annoncé à grand renfort de publicité.

public: **~ law** *n* droit *m* public; **Public Lending Right**, **PLR** *n* GB *droits perçus par un auteur pour le prêt public de ses ouvrages*.

publicly /ˈpʌblɪklɪ/ *adv* [*state, announce, renounce, exhibit*] publiquement; **~ owned** (state-owned) public; (floated on market) à actionnaires multiples; **~-funded** [*project, scheme*] realisé à l'aide de fonds publics.

public: **~ nuisance** *n* Jur atteinte *f* aux droits du public; **~ opinion** *n* opinion *f* publique; **~ order** *n* ordre *m* public; **~ order act** *n* loi *f* concernant l'ordre public; **~ order offence** *n* trouble *m* de l'ordre public.

public ownership *n* **to be in/be taken into ~** être nationalisé; **to bring sth under** ou **into ~** nationaliser [*industry*].

public: **~ prosecutor** *n* procureur *m* général; **~ purse** *n* Trésor *m* public; **Public Records Office**, **PRO** *npl* Archives *fpl* nationales.

public relations, **PR** **I** *n* relations *fpl* publiques.
II *modif* [*manager, department*] des relations publiques; [*consultant, expert*] en relations publiques; [*firm*] de relations publiques.

public relations officer, **PRO** *n* responsable *mf* des relations publiques.

public restroom *n* US toilettes *fpl*.

public school *n* **1** GB école *f* privée; **to have a ~ education** faire ses études dans une école privée; **2** US école *f* publique.

public: **~ schoolboy** *n* GB élève *m* d'école privée; **~ sector** *n* secteur *m* public; **Public Sector Borrowing Requirement**, **PSBR** *n* besoins *mpl* de financement du secteur public; **~ servant** *n* fonctionnaire *mf*.

public service *n* **1** C (transport, education, utility etc) service *m* public; **2** ¢ (public administration, civil service) fonction *f* publique; **a career in ~** une carrière dans la fonction publique.

public: **~ service broadcasting** *n* ¢ chaînes *fpl* de télévision et radios *fpl* publiques; **~ service corporation** *n* US service *m* public non étatisé; **~ service vehicle**, **PSV** *n* véhicule *m* de transport en commun.

public speaking *n* **the art of ~** l'art de parler en public; **to be unaccustomed to ~** ne pas avoir l'habitude de parler en public.

public-spirited *adj* à l'esprit civique; **it was ~ of you to do** tu as fait preuve de civisme en faisant.

public: **~ transport** *n* transports *mpl* en commun; **~ utilities** *npl* équipements *mpl* collectifs; **~ utility** *n* service *m* public; **~ works** *npl* travaux *mpl* publics.

publish /ˈpʌblɪʃ/ **I** *vtr* **1** (print commercially) publier [*book, article, letter, guide*]; éditer [*newspaper, magazine*]; **who ~es Amis?** qui est-ce qui édite Amis?; **his novel has just been ~ed** son roman vient de paraître or de sortir; **to be ~ed weekly/monthly** paraître toutes les semaines/tous les mois; **2** (make public) publier [*accounts, figures, findings*]; **3** [*scholar, academic*] **have you ~ed anything?** est-ce que vous avez des publications?
II *vi* [*scholar, academic*] faire une publication or des publications.

publisher /ˈpʌblɪʃə(r)/ ▶ **1692** *n* (person) éditeur/-trice *m/f*; (company) maison *f* d'édition; **newspaper ~** (person) patron *m* de presse; (company) maison *f* de presse.

publishing /ˈpʌblɪʃɪŋ/ **I** *n* édition *f*; **a career in ~** une carrière dans l'édition.
II *modif* [*group, empire*] de presse.

publishing house *n* maison *f* d'édition.

pub lunch *n* GB **to go for a ~** aller déjeuner dans un pub; **do they do ~es?** est-ce qu'ils font à manger à midi dans ce pub?

puce /pjuːs/ ▶ **1104** **I** *n* rouge-brun *m*.
II *adj* rouge-brun *inv*; [*curtains, silk*] cramoisi; **to turn ~** (with rage, embarrassment) devenir cramoisi.

puck /pʌk/ *n* **1** (in ice-hockey) palet *m*; **2** (sprite) lutin *m*.

pucker /ˈpʌkə(r)/ **I** *vi* **1** [*face, mouth*] se plisser; **2** [*fabric*] se plisser; [*skirt*] goder; [*seam, cloth*] froncer.
II puckered *pp adj* [*brow, mouth*] plissé; [*seam*] froncé.

pud /pʊd/ *n* **1**○ GB *abrév* = **pudding 1, 2, 3**; **2**◑ US (penis) zizi○ *m*.

pudding /ˈpʊdɪŋ/ *n* **1** (cooked sweet dish) pudding *m*, pouding *m*; **chocolate/bread-and-butter ~** pudding au chocolat/de pain; **apple ~** gâteau *m* aux pommes; **2** GB (dessert) dessert *m*; **what's for ~?** qu'est-ce qu'il y a pour le dessert?; **3** (cooked savoury dish) pudding *m*; **steak-and-kidney ~** pain *m* de viande au bœuf et aux rognons; **4** GB (sausage) **black/white ~** boudin *m* noir/blanc; **5** pej (fat person) patapouf○ *mf*; (slow person) empoté○/-e *m/f*.
IDIOMS **the proof of the ~ is in the eating** Prov la qualité se révèle à l'usage.

pudding basin, **pudding bowl** **I** *n* jatte *f*.
II *modif* **~ basin** ou **bowl haircut** coupe *f* au bol.

pudding: **~ rice** *n* riz *m* à grains ronds; **~stone** *n* poudingue *m*.

puddle /ˈpʌdl/ *n* flaque *f*.

puddling /ˈpʌdlɪŋ/ *n* Ind puddlage *m*.

pudenda /pjuːˈdendə/ *npl* parties *fpl* génitales.

pudgy○ /ˈpʌdʒɪ/ *adj* = **podgy**○.

pueblo /ˈpwebləʊ/ *n* (*pl* **~s**) village *m*.

Pueblo Indian *n* Pueblo *mf*.

puerile /ˈpjʊəraɪl, US -rəl/ *adj* sout puérile.

puerility /pjʊəˈrɪlətɪ/ *n* sout puérilité *f*.

puerperal /pjuːˈɜːpərəl/ *adj* puerpéral.

Puerto Rican /ˌpwɜːtəʊ ˈriːkən/ ▶ **1486** **I** *n* Portoricain/-e *m/f*.
II *adj* portoricain.

Puerto Rico /ˌpwɜːtəʊ ˈriːkəʊ/ ▶ **1131** *pr n* Porto Rico *f*.

puff /pʌf/ **I** *n* **1** (of air, smoke, steam) bouffée *f*; (of breath: from mouth) souffle *m*; **to blow out the candles in one ~** souffler les bougies d'un seul coup; **to take a ~ at** tirer une bouffée de [*cigarette, pipe*]; **to vanish** ou **disappear in a ~ of smoke** lit disparaître dans un nuage de fumée; fig partir en fumée; **~s of cloud** quelques petits nuages; **2**○ GB (breath) souffle *m*; **to be out of ~**○ être essoufflé, être à bout de souffle; **to get one's ~**○ **back** reprendre son souffle; **3** Culin feuilleté *m*; **jam ~** feuilleté à la confiture; **4** Cosmet = **powder puff**; **5**○ GB injur (homosexual) tante◑ *f* offensive; **6**○ (favourable review) article *m* élogieux; (favourable publicity) battage○ *m*; **to give a ~ to** faire du battage autour de [*play, show*].
II *vtr* **1** tirer sur [*pipe*]; **to ~ smoke** [*person, chimney, train*] lancer des bouffées de fumée; **to ~ smoke into sb's face** envoyer de la fumée à la figure de qn; **2**○ (praise) faire du battage○ autour de [*book, film, play*].
III *vi* **1** souffler; **smoke ~ed from the chimney** des bouffées de fumée s'échappaient de la cheminée; **to ~ (away) at** tirer des bouffées de [*pipe, cigarette*]; **to ~ in/out/along** [*train*] entrer/sortir/avancer en lançant des bouffées de fumée; **2** (pant) souffler, haleter; **he was ~ing hard** ou **~ing and panting** il soufflait comme un bœuf; **she came ~ing and blowing up the hill** elle s'essoufflait en montant la côte.
■ **puff out**: ¶ **~ out** [*sails*] se gonfler; [*sleeve, skirt*] bouffer; ¶ **~ out [sth], ~ [sth] out 1** (swell) gonfler [*sails*]; **to ~ out one's cheeks** gonfler ses joues; **to ~ out one's chest** bomber le torse; **the bird ~ed out its feathers** l'oiseau a hérissé ses plumes; **2** (give out) **to ~ out smoke** [*person, chimney, train*] lancer des bouffées de fumée; ¶ **~ [sb] out**○ essouffler; **the run had ~ed him out**○ il était tout essoufflé d'avoir couru.
■ **puff up**: ¶ **~ up** [*feathers*] se hérisser; [*eyes*] bouffir, se gonfler; [*rice*] gonfler; ¶ **~ up [sth], ~ [sth] up** hérisser [*feathers, fur*]; **her eyes were all ~ed up** elle avait les yeux bouffis; **to be ~ed up with pride** être rempli d'orgueil.

puff: **~-adder** *n* vipère *f* heurtante; **~ball** *n* Bot vesse-de-loup *f*.

puffed /pʌft/ *adj* **1**○ (breathless) [*person*] essoufflé; **2** [*sleeve*] bouffant.

puffer /ˈpʌfə(r)/ *n* **1** Zool poisson-globe *m*; **2**○ (train) locomotive *f* à vapeur.

puffin /ˈpʌfɪn/ *n* macareux *m*.

puffiness /ˈpʌfɪnɪs/ *n* (of face, eyes) boursouflure *f*; **~ around the eyes indicates fatigue** les yeux gonflés peuvent indiquer la fatigue.

puff: **~ing billy**○ *n* locomotive *f* à vapeur; **~ pastry** *n* pâte *f* feuilletée; **~ puff**○ *n* lang enfantin train *m*.

puffy /ˈpʌfɪ/ *adj* [*face*] bouffi, boursouflé; [*eye*] gonflé, bouffi; **face ~ with sleep** visage bouffi de sommeil; **~-lipped** aux lèvres bouffies or boursouflées.

pug /pʌg/ **I** *n* (also **~dog**) (dog) carlin *m*.
II *vtr* (*p prés etc* **-gg-**) pétrir [*clay*].

pugilism /ˈpjuːdʒɪlɪzəm/ *n* sout boxe *f*.

pugilist /ˈpjuːdʒɪlɪst/ *n* pugiliste *m*.

pugnacious /pʌgˈneɪʃəs/ *adj* combatif/-ive; pugnace fml.

pugnaciously /pʌgˈneɪʃəslɪ/ *adv* avec pugnacité fml.

pugnacity /pʌgˈnæsətɪ/ *n* pugnacité *f* fml.

pug: **~ nose** *n* nez *m* camus; **~-nosed** *adj* au nez camus.

puke◑ /pjuːk/ **I** *n* dégueulis◑ *m*.
II *vi* [*adult*] dégueuler◑, gerber◑, vomir; [*baby*] vomir.
■ **puke up**: **~ [sth] up, ~ up [sth]** rendre, vomir.

pukka /ˈpʌkə/ *adj* GB, Indian English (real, genuine) vrai de vrai○ (*before n*).

pulchritude /ˈpʌlkrɪtjuːd, US -tuːd/ *n* littér vénusté *f* liter.

pull /pʊl/ **I** *n* **1** (tug) coup *m*; **one good ~ and the door opened** un bon coup et la porte s'est ouverte; **to give sth a ~** tirer sur qch; **2** (attraction) lit force *f*; fig attrait *m*; **gravitational ~** force gravitationnelle; **the ~ of Hollywood/of the sea** l'attrait d'Hollywood/de la mer; **3**○ (influence) influence *f*; **to exert a ~ over sb** exercer une certaine influence sur qn; **to have a lot of ~ with sb** avoir beaucoup d'influence sur qn; **to have the ~ to do** avoir le bras suffisamment long pour faire; **4**○ (swig) lampée○ *f*; **to take a ~ from the bottle** boire une lampée○ à même la bouteille; **5**○ (on cigarette etc) bouffée *f*; **to take a ~ at** ou **on a cigarette** tirer une bouffée sur une cigarette; **6** Sport (in rowing) coup *m* d'aviron; (in golf) coup *m* hooké; **7** (snag) (in sweater) maille *f* tirée; **there's a ~ in my sweater** il y a une maille tirée sur mon pull; **8** Print épreuve *f*; **9** (prolonged effort) **it was a hard ~ to the summit** cela a été très dur d'arriver jusqu'au sommet; **the next five kilo-**

metres will be a hard ~ les cinq prochains kilomètres vont être durs.

II *vtr* **1** (tug) tirer [*chain, curtain, hair, tail*]; tirer sur [*cord, rope*]; **to ~ the door open/shut** ouvrir/fermer la porte; **to ~ the sheets over one's head** se cacher la tête sous les draps; **to ~ a sweater over one's head** (to put it on) enfiler un pull-over; (to take it off) retirer un pull-over; **2** (tug, move) (towards oneself) tirer (**towards** vers); (by dragging) traîner [*reticent person, heavy object*] (**along** le long de); (to show sth) entraîner par le bras [*person*]; **to ~ sb by the arm/hair** tirer qn par le bras/les cheveux; **to ~ sb/sth through** faire passer qn/qch par [*hole, window*]; **3** (draw) [*vehicle*] tracter [*caravan, trailer*]; [*horse*] tirer [*cart, plough*]; [*person*] tirer [*handcart, sled*]; **4** (remove, extract) extraire [*tooth*]; cueillir [*peas, beans, flowers*]; arracher [*potatoes*]; **to ~ sth off** [*small child, cat*] faire tomber qch de [*shelf, table*]; **he ~ed her attacker off her** il a fait lâcher prise à son assaillant; **to ~ sth out of** tirer qch de [*pocket, drawer*]; **to ~ sb out of** retirer qn de [*wreckage*]; sortir qn de [*river*]; **5**○ (brandish) sortir [*gun, knife*]; **to ~ a gun on sb** menacer qn avec un pistolet; **6** (operate) appuyer sur [*trigger*]; tirer [*lever*]; **7** Med (strain) se faire une élongation à [*muscle*]; **a ~ed muscle** une élongation; **8** (hold back) [*rider*] retenir [*horse*]; **to ~ one's punches** [*boxer*] retenir ses coups; fig **he didn't ~ his punches** il n'a pas mâché ses mots; **9** (steer, guide) **to ~ a boat into the bank** amener une barque jusqu'à la berge; **to ~ a plane out of a dive** redresser un avion; **10** Sport [*golfer, batsman*] hooker [*ball, shot*]; **11** Print tirer [*proof*]; **12**○ GB (pour) tirer [*beer*]; **13**○ (attract) attirer [*audience, voters, girls, men*]; **14** (make) **to ~ a face** faire la grimace; **to ~ faces** faire des grimaces; **to ~ a strange expression** faire une drôle de tête○.

III *vi* **1** (tug) tirer (**at, on** sur); **to ~ at sb's sleeve** tirer qn par la manche; **2** (resist restraint) [*dog, horse*] tirer (**at, on** sur); **3** (move) tirer; **the car ~s to the left** la voiture tire à gauche; **the brakes are ~ing to the left** quand on freine la voiture tire à gauche; **to ~ ahead of sb** [*athlete, rally driver*] prendre de l'avance sur qn; [*company*] avoir de l'avance sur [*competitor*]; **4** (smoke) **to ~ at** tirer une bouffée sur [*cigarette*]; **5** Sport [*golfer, batsman*] hooker; **6** (row) ramer.

IDIOMS **~ the other one (it's got bells on)**○! à d'autres (mais pas à moi)○!; **to be on the ~**◐ draguer○.

■ **pull along**: ¶ **~ [sth] along, ~ along [sth]** tirer [*sled*]; ¶ **~ [sb] along** tirer qn par le bras.

■ **pull apart**: ¶ **~ apart** [*component, pieces*] se séparer; ¶ **~ [sb/sth] apart 1** (dismantle) démonter [*machine, toy*]; **2** (destroy) [*child*] mettre en pièces [*toy*]; [*animal*] déchiqueter [*object, prey*]; **I'll find the key, I don't care if I have to ~ the house apart!** fig je trouverai cette clé, même si je dois mettre la maison sens dessus dessous!; **3** fig (disparage) descendre [qch] en flammes [*essay*]; **4** (separate) séparer [*combattants, dogs, pages*].

■ **pull away**: ¶ **~ away 1** (move away, leave) [*car*] démarrer; [*person*] s'écarter; **2** (become detached) [*component, piece*] se détacher; **3** (open up lead) [*car, horse*] se détacher (**from** de); ¶ **~ away from [sb/sth]** [*car, person*] s'éloigner de [*person, kerb*]; ¶ **~ [sb/sth] away** éloigner [*person*]; retirer [*hand*]; **to ~ [sth] away from sb** arracher [qch] à qn [*held object*]; **to ~ sb/sth away from** éloigner qn/qch de [*danger*]; écarter qn/qch de [*window, wall etc*].

■ **pull back**: ¶ **~ back 1** (withdraw) [*troops*] se retirer (**from** de); **2** (move backwards) [*car, person*] reculer; **3** (close the gap) rattraper mon/son etc retard; **she's ~ing back** (in race) elle est en train de rattraper son retard; ¶ **~ [sb/sth] back, ~ back [sb/sth] 1** (restrain) retenir [*person, object*]; **~ her back, she'll fall** retiens-la, elle va tomber; **2** (tug back) **~ the rope back hard** tire fort sur la corde.

■ **pull down**: ¶ **~ [sth] down, ~ down [sth] 1** (demolish) démolir [*building*]; **2** (lower) baisser [*curtain, blind*]; **to ~ down one's trousers** baisser son pantalon; **3** (reduce) baisser [*prices*]; réduire [*inflation*]; ¶ **~ [sb/sth] down, ~ down [sb/sth]** (drag down) tirer [*person, object*] (**onto** sur); fig entraîner [*person, company*]; **he'll ~ you down with him** il va t'entraîner avec lui.

■ **pull in**: ¶ **~ in** [*car, bus, driver*] s'arrêter; **~ in at the next service station** arrêtez-vous à la prochaine station-service; **the police signalled to the motorist to ~ in** GB la police a fait signe à l'automobiliste de s'arrêter; **to ~ in to the kerb** s'arrêter le long du trottoir; ¶ **~ [sb] in, ~ in [sb] 1** (bring in) [*police*] appréhender qn; **to ~ sb in for questioning** appréhender qn pour l'interroger; **2** (attract) [*exhibition, show*] attirer [*crowds, tourists*]; ¶ **~ [sth] in, ~ in [sth] 1** (retract) [*animal*] rentrer [*antenna, tentacle, claw*]; [*person*] rentrer [*stomach*]; **2**○ (earn) [*appeal, event*] réunir [*sum*]; **3** (steer) [*driver*] arrêter.

■ **pull off**: ¶ **~ off** [*flashgun, lid*] s'enlever; [*handle*] être amovible; ¶ **~ off [sth]** (leave) quitter [*motorway, road*]; ¶ **~ off [sth], ~ [sth] off 1** (remove) ôter [*coat, sweater*]; enlever [*shoes, socks*]; enlever [*lid, wrapping, sticker*]; **2**○ (clinch) réussir [*raid, robbery*]; conclure [*deal*]; réaliser [*coup, feat*]; décrocher [*win, victory*].

■ **pull out**: ¶ **~ out 1** (emerge) [*car, truck*] déboîter; **I got to the platform just as the train was ~ing out** je suis arrivé sur le quai au moment où le train partait; **to ~ out of** quitter [*drive, parking space, station*]; **2** (withdraw) [*army, troops*] se retirer; [*candidate, competitor*] se retirer; **to ~ out of** se retirer de [*negotiations, Olympics, area*]; **3** (come away) [*drawer*] s'enlever; [*component, section*] se détacher; ¶ **~ [sth] out, ~ out [sth] 1** (extract) extraire [*tooth*]; enlever [*splinter*]; arracher [*weeds*]; **2** (take out) sortir [*knife, gun, wallet, handkerchief*]; **3** (withdraw) retirer [*troops, army*].

■ **pull over**: ¶ **~ over** [*motorist, car*] s'arrêter (sur le côté); ¶ **~ [sb/sth] over** [*police*] forcer [qn/qch] à se ranger sur le côté [*driver, car*].

■ **pull through**: ¶ **~ through** [*accident victim*] s'en tirer, s'en sortir; ¶ **~ [sb/sth] through** faire passer [*object, person, wool*]; **~ the thread through to the front** faites passer le fil devant.

■ **pull together**: ¶ **~ together** faire un effort, s'y mettre; **we must all ~ together** il faut que tout le monde fasse un effort ou s'y mette; ¶ **~ [sth] together**: **~ the two ends of the rope together** mettez la corde bout à bout; **~ the two pieces together** mettez les deux morceaux l'un contre l'autre; **to ~ oneself together** se ressaisir, se reprendre.

■ **pull up**: ¶ **~ up 1** (stop) [*car, athlete*] s'arrêter; **2** (regain lost ground) [*athlete, pupil*] rattraper son retard; ¶ **~ up [sth], ~ [sth] up 1** (uproot) arracher [*weeds*]; **2** (lift) lever [*anchor, drawbridge*]; **to ~ up one's trousers/one's socks** remonter son pantalon/ses chaussettes; **to ~ up a chair** prendre une chaise; **3** (stop) [*rider*] arrêter [*horse*]; ¶ **~ [sb] up 1** (lift) hisser; **to ~ sb up a cliff/out of a well** hisser qn en haut d'une falaise/hors d'un puits; **to ~ oneself up** se hisser; **2** (reprimand) réprimander qn; **he ~ed me up for working too slowly** il m'a réprimandé parce que je travaillais trop lentement; **3** (stop) [*policeman*] arrêter [*driver*]; Sport [*official*] disqualifier [*athlete*].

pull-down menu *n* Comput menu *m* déroulant.

pullet /ˈpʊlɪt/ *n* poulette *f*.

pulley /ˈpʊlɪ/ *n* poulie *f*.

pull-in /ˈpʊlɪn/ *n* GB **1**○ (café) routier *m*; **2** (lay-by) aire *f* de stationnement (en bordure de la chaussée).

pulling power *n* pouvoir *m* d'attraction.

Pullman /ˈpʊlmən/ *n* **1** (train) pullman *m*; (carriage) voiture *f* pullman; **2** US (suitcase) valise *f*.

Pullman kitchen *n* US cuisinette *f*.

pull-off /ˈpʊlɒf/ *adj* détachable.

pull-out /ˈpʊlaʊt/ **I** *n* **1** Print encart *m*; **2** (withdrawal) retrait *m*; **~ of the troops** retrait des troupes.

II *adj* [*section, supplement*] détachable; [*map, diagram*] hors-texte *inv*, dépliant.

pullover /ˈpʊləʊvə(r)/ *n* pull-over *m*.

pull-through *n* Mil, Mus écouvillon *m*.

pullulate /ˈpʌljʊleɪt/ *vi* pulluler.

pull-up /ˈpʊlʌp/ *n* Sport traction *f*.

pulmonary /ˈpʌlmənərɪ, US -nerɪ/ *adj* pulmonaire.

pulp /pʌlp/ **I** *n* **1** (soft centre) (of fruit, vegetable) pulpe *f*, chair *f*; (of tooth) pulpe *f*; **2** (crushed mass) pâte *f*; **to reduce** ou **crush to a ~** réduire [qch] en pulpe or en purée [*fruit, vegetable*]; réduire [qch] en pâte [*wood, cloth*]; **to beat sb to a ~**○ réduire qn en bouillie○; **3**○ péj (trashy books) littérature *f* de gare pej.

II *modif* [*novel, literature*] de gare; [*magazine*] à sensation.

III *vtr* **1** (crush) écraser, réduire [qch] en pulpe or en purée [*fruit, vegetable*]; réduire [qch] en pâte [*wood, cloth*]; mettre [qch] au pilon [*newspapers, books*]; **2**○ fig (in fight) écrabouiller○ [*person, head*].

pulp: **~ cavity** *n* cavité *f* pulpaire; **~ fiction** *n* littérature *f* de gare pej.

pulpit /ˈpʊlpɪt/ *n* (in church) chaire *f*.

pulpwood /ˈpʌlpwʊd/ *n* bois *m* à pâte.

pulsar /ˈpʌlsɑː(r)/ *n* pulsar *m*.

pulsate /pʌlˈseɪt, US ˈpʌlseɪt/ **I** *vi* [*vein, heart*] palpiter; [*blood*] circuler.

II **pulsating** *pres p adj* **1** lit (beating) [*heart, vein*] qui palpite; [*beat, rhythm*] entraînant; **2** fig (exciting) [*finale*] palpitant.

pulsation /pʌlˈseɪʃn/ *n* pulsation *f*.

pulse /pʌls/ **I** *n* **1** Anat, Med pouls *m*; **his ~ raced** son cœur battait très vite; **to take/feel sb's ~** prendre/tâter le pouls de qn; **to take the ~ of Europe in the 90s** fig prendre le pouls or la température de l'Europe dans les années 90; **to have one's finger on the ~ of sth** fig être à l'écoute de qch, suivre qch de près; **2** (beat, vibration) (of music) rythme *m*; (of drums) battement *m* rythmique; **3** Audio, Elec, Phys impulsion *f*; **4** Bot, Culin graine *f* de légumineuse.

II *vi* [*blood*] circuler; [*heart*] battre fort; **she could feel the blood pulsing through her body** son cœur battait à tout rompre.

pulse: **~-jet** *n* pulsoréacteur *m*; **~ modulation** *n* modulation *f* d'impulsions; **~ rate** *n* pouls *m*.

pulverization /ˌpʌlvəraɪˈzeɪʃn, US -rɪˈz-/ *n* lit, fig pulvérisation *f*.

pulverize /ˈpʌlvəraɪz/ **I** *vtr* lit, fig pulvériser.

II *vi* se pulvériser.

puma /ˈpjuːmə/ *n* puma *m*.

pumice /ˈpʌmɪs/ *n* (also **~ stone**) pierre *f* ponce.

pummel /ˈpʌml/ *vtr* (*p prés etc* **-ll-** GB, **-l-** US) marteler.

pump /pʌmp/ **I** *n* **1** Tech pompe *f*; **bicycle ~** pompe à bicyclette; **air/vacuum ~** pompe à air/à vide; **to prime the ~** lit amorcer la pompe; fig réamorcer la pompe; **2** (squeeze) **to give sb's hand a ~** donner une poignée de main vigoureuse à qn; **3** (plimsoll) chaussure *f* de sport; **4** GB (flat shoe) ballerine *f*; **5** US (shoe with heel) chaussure *f* à talon; **6**† (dancing shoe) chausson *m* de danse (pour homme); **7** (fire-engine) autopompe *f*.

II *vtr* **1** (push) pomper [*air, gas, water, blood*] (**out of** de); **to ~ oil around the engine** pomper l'huile autour du moteur; **to ~ air into a tyre** injecter de l'air dans un pneu; **to ~ sewage into the sea** déverser les eaux usées dans la mer; **the boiler ~s water to the radiators** la chaudière distribue l'eau dans les radiateurs; **to ~ the hold dry** pomper la cale à sec; **to ~ bullets** cracher des balles; **to ~ sb full of drugs**○ gaver qn de médicaments; **to ~ sb full of lead**○ truffer qn de plomb○, mitrailler qn; **to ~ iron**○ faire de la gonflette○; **2** (move) actionner [*handle, lever*]; **to ~ the brakes** freiner par petits coups successifs; **3** (shake) **to ~ sb's hand** donner une poignée de main vigoureuse à qn; **4**○ (question) cuisiner○ [*person*] (**about** à propos de); **to ~ sb for sth** essayer de soutirer qch à qn [*details, information*]; **to ~ sth out of sb** soutirer qch à qn; **5** Med **to ~ sb's stomach** faire un lavage d'estomac à qn; **to have one's stomach ~ed** avoir un lavage d'estomac.

III *vi* **1** (function) [*machine, piston*] fonctionner; **2** (flow) gicler (**from, out of** de); **3** (beat) [*blood, heart*] battre violemment.

IDIOMS **all hands to the ~s!** il faut que tout le monde s'y mette!

■ **pump out**: **~ out [sth], ~ [sth] out 1** (pour out) débiter [*music, propaganda*]; cracher [*fumes*]; déverser [*sewage*]; **2** (empty) pomper [qch] à sec [*hold, pool*]; **to ~ sb's stomach out** faire un lavage d'estomac à qn.

■ **pump up**: **~ up [sth], ~ [sth] up 1** (inflate) gonfler [*tyre, air bed*]; **2**○ (increase) monter [*volume*].

pump: **~-action** *adj* [*gun*] à pompe; **~ attendant** ▶1692 *n* pompiste *mf*; **~ dispenser** *n* Cosmet vaporisateur *m*.

pumpernickel /ˈpʌmpənɪkl/ *n* pumpernickel *m*, pain *m* noir.

pump house *n* station *f* de pompage.

pumpkin /ˈpʌmpkɪn/ *n* citrouille *f*.

pumpkin: **~head**○ *n* abruti/-e○ *m/f*; **~ pie** *n* tourte *f* à la citrouille.

pump prices *npl* (of petrol) prix *m* à la pompe.

pump priming /ˈpʌmppraɪmɪŋ/ **I** *n* **1** Tech amorçage *m* d'une pompe; **2** Fin injection *f* de crédits.

II pump-priming *modif* [*aid, capital, funds*] de soutien (*after n*).

pump room *n* GB Hist buvette *f* (*d'un établissement thermal*).

pun /pʌn/ **I** *n* jeu *m* de mots, calembour *m* (**on** sur).

II *vi* (*p prés etc* **-nn-**) faire des jeux de mots, faire des calembours.

punch /pʌntʃ/ **I** *n* **1** (blow) coup *m* de poing; **to give sb a ~** donner un coup de poing à qn; **she gave him a ~ on the nose/on the chin** elle lui a donné un coup de poing dans le nez/au menton; **to hit sb in the face with a ~** donner un coup de poing dans la figure de qn; **2** fig (forcefulness) (of person) punch○ *m*; (of style, performance) énergie *f*; **it lacks ~** ça manque de nerf; **a slogan with a bit more ~** un slogan plus frappant; **3** (tool) (for leather) alène *f*; (for metal) perçoir *m*; Comput perforateur *m*; **ticket ~** pince *f* à composter; **4** (drink) punch *m*.

II *vtr* **1** (hit) **to ~ sb in the face** donner un coup de poing dans la figure de qn; **to ~ sb on the nose/on the chin** donner un coup de poing dans le nez/au menton de qn; **to ~ sb hard** frapper qn très fort avec le poing; **he was ~ed and kicked** on lui a donné des coups de poing et des coups de pied; **2** Comput, Telecom perforer [*cards, tape*]; appuyer sur [*key*]; **3** (make hole in) (manually) poinçonner; (in machine) composter [*ticket*]; **to ~ holes in sth** (in paper, leather) faire des trous dans qch; (in metal) perforer qch.

III *vi* cogner, donner des coups de poing.

IDIOMS **to pack a ~**○ [*boxer*] avoir du punch; [*cocktail*] être corsé; [*book, film*] avoir un fort impact; **to pull no ~es** lit, fig ne pas y aller de main morte.

■ **punch in**: **~ in [sth], ~ [sth] in** Comput introduire [*data*].

■ **punch out**: **~ out [sth], ~ [sth] out** (shape) découper qch à l'emporte-pièce; **to ~ out a number on the phone** composer un numéro au téléphone.

Punch /pʌntʃ/ *pr n* Polichinelle.

IDIOMS **to be as pleased as ~** être ravi.

Punch: **~-and-Judy show** *n* ≈ spectacle *m* de guignol *m*.

punch: **~bag** *n* GB Sport sac *m* de sable; (whipping-boy) souffre-douleur *m inv*; **~ ball** *n* punching-ball *m*; **~ bowl** *n* coupe *f* à punch; **~ card** *n* carte *f* perforée; **~-drunk** *adj* (in boxing) abruti par les coups; fig (from tiredness) abruti de fatigue; **~ed card** = **punch card**; **~ed paper tape** *n* bande *f* perforée; **~ed tape** *n* bande *f* perforée; **~ing bag** *n* US = **punchbag**; **~ line** *n* chute *f* (*d'une histoire drôle*); **~-up**○ *n* GB bagarre○ *f*.

punchy○ /ˈpʌntʃɪ/ *adj* **1** [*person, music, style*] énergique; [*article*] percutant; **2** = **punch-drunk**.

punctilio /pʌŋkˈtɪlɪəʊ/ *n* sout (etiquette) formalisme *m*; (point of etiquette) point *m* d'étiquette.

punctilious /pʌŋkˈtɪlɪəs/ *adj* sout [*observance, attention*] scrupuleux/-euse; **to be ~ about (one's) work** être méticuleux/-euse dans son travail.

punctiliously /pʌŋkˈtɪlɪəslɪ/ *adv* sout scrupuleusement.

punctual /ˈpʌŋktʃʊəl/ *adj* [*person, delivery*] ponctuel/-elle; **to be ~ for sth** être à l'heure pour qch; **to be ~ in doing** être ponctuel quand il s'agit de faire.

punctuality /ˌpʌŋktʃʊˈælətɪ/ *n* ponctualité *f*.

punctually /ˈpʌŋktʃʊəlɪ/ *adv* [*start, arrive, leave*] à l'heure; **to arrive ~ at 10** arriver ponctuellement à 10 heures.

punctuate /ˈpʌŋktʃʊeɪt/ **I** *vtr* **1** lit ponctuer [*text, letter*]; **2** (interrupt) ponctuer (**with, by** de).

II *vi* ponctuer.

punctuation /ˌpʌŋktʃʊˈeɪʃn/ *n* ponctuation *f*.

punctuation mark *n* signe *m* de ponctuation.

puncture /ˈpʌŋktʃə(r)/ **I** *n* (in tyre, balloon, airbed) crevaison *f*; (in skin) piqûre *f*; (to lung) perforation *f*; **we had a ~ on the way** on a crevé en chemin.

II *vtr* **1** (perforate) crever [*tyre, balloon, airbed*]; ponctionner [*organ*]; crever [*abscess*]; **to ~ a hole in** faire or percer un trou dans; **to ~ a lung** Med se perforer un poumon; **2** fig (deflate) démolir [*myth*]; **to ~ sb's pride** ou **ego** décontenancer qn, rabattre le caquet○ à qn.

III *vi* [*tyre, balloon*] crever.

puncture: **~ (repair) kit** *n* boîte *f* de rustines®; **~-proof** *adj* increvable; **~ wound** *n* trace *f* de piqûre.

pundit /ˈpʌndɪt/ *n* **1** (expert) expert/-e *m/f*; **2** Relig pandit *m*.

pungency /ˈpʌndʒənsɪ/ *n* **1** (of sauce, dish) goût *m* piquant; (of smoke, smell) âcreté *f*; **2** (of speech, satire) mordant *m*.

pungent /ˈpʌndʒənt/ *adj* **1** (strong) [*flavour*] relevé; [*smell*] fort; [*gas, smoke*] âcre; **2** [*speech, satire*] mordant, virulent.

pungently /ˈpʌndʒəntlɪ/ *adv* Culin **a ~ flavoured sauce** une sauce relevée.

Punic /ˈpjuːnɪk/ *n, adj* punique (*m*).

Punic Wars *npl* guerres *fpl* puniques.

punish /ˈpʌnɪʃ/ *vtr* **1** punir [*person, crime*]; **to ~ sb for sth/for doing** punir qn de qch/pour avoir fait; **a crime ~ed by death** un crime puni de mort; **2**○ (treat roughly) malmener [*opponent*]; fatiguer, ne pas ménager [*car, horse*].

punishable /ˈpʌnɪʃəbl/ *adj* [*offence*] punissable, passible d'une peine; **~ by a fine** passible d'une amende; **to be ~ by law** tomber sous le coup de la loi.

punishing /ˈpʌnɪʃɪŋ/ **I** *n* (act) punition *f*; **to take a ~**○ [*opponent, team*] prendre une raclée○, se faire dérouiller○.

II *adj* [*schedule, pace*] éprouvant; [*defeat*] cuisant.

punishment /ˈpʌnɪʃmənt/ *n* **1** punition *f*; (stronger) châtiment *m*; Jur peine *f*; **as ~ for** en punition de; **as ~, they were sent to bed** pour les punir, on les a envoyés se coucher; **2**○ fig (rough treatment) **to take a lot of ~**○ [*team, car, engine*] être mis à rude épreuve.

punitive /ˈpjuːnətɪv/ *n* [*measure, action*] punitif/-ive; [*taxation*] très sévère; **~ damages** Jur dommages et intérêts à valeur répressive.

Punjab /ˌpʌnˈdʒɑːb/ *pr n* Pendjab *m*.

Punjabi /ˌpʌnˈdʒɑːbɪ/ ▶1402 **I** *n* **1** (language) panjabi *m*; **2** (person) habitant/-e *m/f* du Pendjab.

II *adj* du Pendjab.

punk /pʌŋk/ **I** *n* **1** (music, fashion, movement) punk *m*; **2** (person) punk *mf*; **3**○ US péj (hoodlum) voyou *m*; (presumptuous youth) blanc-bec○ *m*.

II *adj* [*music, record, band, hairstyle, clothes*] punk *inv*.

punk rock *n* (rock *m*) punk *m*.

punnet /ˈpʌnɪt/ *n* GB barquette *f*.

punster /ˈpʌnstə(r)/ *n* faiseur/-euse *m/f* de jeux de mots.

punt /pʌnt/ **I** *n* **1** (boat) barque *f* (*à fond plat*); **2** (Irish pound) livre *f* irlandaise; **3** (bet) mise *f*.

II *vi* **1** (travel by punt) **to go ~ing** faire une promenade en barque; **2** (bet) miser.

punter○ /ˈpʌntə(r)/ *n* GB **1** (at horse races) parieur *m*; (at casino) joueur/-euse *m/f*; **2** (average client) client/-e *m/f*.

puny /ˈpjuːnɪ/ *adj* [*person, body*] chétif/-ive; [*effort*] piteux/-euse.

pup /pʌp/ **I** *n* **1** Zool (dog) chiot *m*; (seal, otter etc) petit *m*; **2**○ (person) **a cheeky young ~** un petit insolent.

II *vi* (*p prés etc* **-pp-**) [*bitch, seal*] mettre bas.

IDIOMS **to be sold a ~**○ se faire avoir◑.

pupa /ˈpjuːpə/ *n* (*pl* **pupae**) pupe *f*.

pupate /pjuːˈpeɪt, US ˈpjuːpeɪt/ *vi* se métamorphoser en pupe.

pupil /ˈpjuːpɪl/ *n* **1** Sch élève *mf*; **2** Anat pupille *f*.

puppet /ˈpʌpɪt/ **I** *n* lit, fig marionnette *f*.

II *modif* [*government, state*] fantoche.

puppeteer /ˌpʌpɪˈtɪə(r)/ ▶1692 *n* marionnettiste *mf*.

puppetry /ˈpʌpɪtrɪ/ *n* art *m* de la marionnette.

puppet: **~ show** = spectacle *m* de marionnettes; **~ theatre** GB, **~ theater** US *n* théâtre *m* de marionnettes.

puppy /ˈpʌpɪ/ *n* chiot *m*; **to have puppies** avoir des chiots.

puppy: **~ fat** *n* rondeurs *fpl* de l'enfance; **~ love** *n* amour *m* d'adolescent/-e.

pup tent *n* tente *f* légère.

purblind /ˈpɜːblaɪnd/ *adj* **1** sout (lacking insight) aveugle fig; **2**‡ (partly blind) presque aveugle, malvoyant.

purchase /ˈpɜːtʃəs/ **I** *n* **1** Comm achat *m*; **to make a ~** faire un achat; **2** (grip) prise *f*; **to get** ou **gain (a) ~ on** [*climber*] trouver une prise or un point d'appui sur; [*vehicle*] adhérer à.

II *vtr* **1** Comm acheter, faire l'acquisition de [*hat, painting, house*]; **to ~ sth from sb/from the butcher's/from Buymore** acheter qch à qn/chez le boucher/chez Buymore; **2** fig acquérir [*victory, liberty*].

purchase: **~ ledger** *n* registre *m* or livre *m* des achats; **~ order** *n* ordre *m* d'achat; **~ price** *n* prix *m* d'achat.

purchaser /ˈpɜːtʃəsə(r)/ *n* acheteur/-euse *m/f*, acquéreur *m*.

purchase tax *n* GB taxe *f* sur les produits de luxe.

purchasing /ˈpɜːtʃəsɪŋ/ *n* achat *m*.

purchasing: **~ department** *n* service *m* des achats; **~ officer** ▶1692 *n* agent *m* des achats; **~ power** *n* pouvoir *m* d'achat.

purdah /ˈpɜːdə/ *n*: *isolement des femmes conformément à certaines religions*; **to go into ~** fig s'isoler.

pure /pjʊə(r)/ *adj* **1** (unadulterated) [*gold, oxygen, air, water*] pur; [*silk, cotton, wool*] pur (*before n*); **~ alcohol** Chem alcool *m* absolu or pur; **~ new wool** laine *f* vierge; **a ~ voice** une voix pure; **2** (chaste) [*person, life*] pur; **to be ~ in mind and body** être sain de corps et d'esprit; **blessed are the ~ in heart** Bible bienheureux les cœurs purs; **3** (sheer) [*happiness, nonsense, malice*] pur (*after n*); **out of ~ curiosity** par pure curiosité; **by ~ chance** par pur hasard; **by ~ accident** de façon purement accidentelle; **~ and simple** pur et simple; **4** (not applied) [*mathematics, science*] pur; **~ research** recherche *f* fondamentale.
IDIOMS **as ~ as the driven snow** innocent comme l'enfant or l'agneau qui vient de naître.

purebred /ˈpjʊəbred/ **I** *n* (horse) pur-sang *m inv*.
II *adj* de race, pur-sang *inv*.

puree /ˈpjʊəreɪ, US pjʊəˈreɪ/ **I** *n* purée *f*; **vegetable ~** purée *f* de légumes; **apple ~** compote *f* de pommes.
II *vtr* écraser [*vegetables, fruit*]; **~d vegetables** purée de légumes.

pure line *n* Zool, Bot lignée *f* pure.

purely /ˈpjʊəlɪ/ *adv* purement; **~ and simply** purement et simplement; **~ to be polite** uniquement pour être poli; **~ as a pretext** uniquement comme prétexte.

pureness /ˈpjʊənɪs/ *n* pureté *f*.

pure vowel *n* monophtongue *f*.

purgation /pɜːˈgeɪʃn/ *n* Relig purgation *f*, purification *f*; Med, Pol purge *f*.

purgative /ˈpɜːgətɪv/ **I** *n* purgatif *m*.
II *adj* purgatif/-ive.

purgatorial /ˌpɜːgəˈtɔːrɪəl/ *adj* [*punishment, test*] du purgatoire; fig [*experience, place*] infernal.

purgatory /ˈpɜːgətrɪ, US -tɔːrɪ/ *n* lit, fig purgatoire *m*; **it was (sheer) ~ to do** c'était un véritable supplice de faire.

purge /pɜːdʒ/ **I** *n* (action) gen purge *f*; Pol purge *f*, épuration *f* (**of** de); Med purge *f*.
II *vtr* **1** gen, Med purger (**of** de); **2** Pol purger [*country, party*] (**of** de), éliminer [*extremists, traitors, dissidents etc*] (**from** de); **3** Relig expier [*sin*]; fig libérer, purger liter [*mind, heart*] (**of** de); **4** Jur **to ~ one's contempt** faire amende honorable; **to ~ an offence** purger une peine.
III *v refl* **~ oneself of** Relig se laver de [*sin*]; **to ~ oneself of a charge** Jur se disculper.

purification /ˌpjʊərɪfɪˈkeɪʃn/ *n* **1** (of water, air, chemicals) épuration *f*; **2** Relig (of person, soul) purification *f*.

purification plant *n* station *f* d'épuration.

purifier /ˈpjʊərɪfaɪə(r)/ *n* (for water) épurateur *m*; (for air) purificateur *m*.

purify /ˈpjʊərɪfaɪ/ *vtr* **1** gen, Tech épurer [*air, water, chemical*]; **2** Relig purifier [*person, soul*].

purism /ˈpjʊərɪzəm/ *n* purisme *m*.

purist /ˈpjʊərɪst/ *n, adj* puriste (*mf*).

puritan /ˈpjʊərɪtən/ *n, adj* fig puritain/-e (*m/f*).

Puritan /ˈpjʊərɪtən/ *pr n, adj* Relig, Hist puritain/-e (*m/f*).

puritanical /ˌpjʊərɪˈtænɪkl/ *adj* gen, Relig puritain.

puritanism /ˈpjʊərɪtənɪzəm/ **I** *n* gen puritanisme *m*.
II Puritanism *pr n* puritanisme *m*.

purity /ˈpjʊərətɪ/ *n* pureté *f*.

purl /pɜːl/ **I** *n* maille *f* à l'envers.
II *adj* [*row, stitch*] à l'envers.
III *vtr* tricoter [qch] à l'envers [*row, stitch*].

purlieus /ˈpɜːljuːz/ *npl* sout abords *mpl*.

purlin /ˈpɜːlɪn/ *n* Constr panne *f*.

purloin /pɜːˈlɔɪn/ *vtr* littér dérober liter.

purple /ˈpɜːpl/ ▶1104 **I** *n* **1** (colour) violet *m*; **2** Relig **the ~** (rank) la pourpre; (bishops) GB évêques *mpl* anglicans.
II *adj* (bluish) violet; (reddish) pourpre; **to turn ~** gen virer au violet; [*person*] (in anger) devenir rouge de colère.

purple heart *n* **1** (pill) argot des drogués comprimé *m* d'amphétamine; **2** Bot bois *m* d'amarante.

purple: **Purple Heart, PH** *n* US Mil *médaille accordée aux blessés ou morts à la guerre*; **~ martin** *n* US hirondelle *f* pourpre; **~ passage, ~ patch** *n* Literat péj passage *m* ampoulé; **~ prose** *n* style *m* ampoulé.

purplish /ˈpɜːplɪʃ/ ▶1104 *adj* violacé.

purport sout **I** /ˈpɜːpət/ *n* sens *m*.
II /pəˈpɔːt/ *vtr* **to ~ to do** prétendre faire; **a woman ~ing to be a social worker** une femme qui prétend/prétendait être visiteuse sociale.

purported /pəˈpɔːtɪd/ *adj* sout prétendu.

purportedly /pəˈpɔːtɪdlɪ/ *adv* prétendument.

purpose /ˈpɜːpəs/ **I** *n* **1** (aim) but *m*; **for the ~ of doing** dans le but de faire; **what was his ~ in coming?** dans quel but est-il venu?; **to have a ~ in life** avoir un but dans la vie; **for cooking/business ~s** pour la cuisine/les affaires; **for our ~s, we can assume that...** dans l'optique qui nous intéresse, on peut considérer que...; **for the ~s of this book, I shall confine myself to the 18th century** pour (les besoins de) ce livre, je me limiterai au XVIIIe siècle; **for all practical ~s** en pratique; **~ unknown** usage *m* inconnu; **this knife will serve the ~** ce couteau fera l'affaire; **this bag is large enough for the ~** ce sac est assez grand; **put it in the bin provided for the ~** mets-le dans la poubelle prévue à cet effet; **to some** ou **good ~** utilement; **to no ~** inutilement; **to the ~** sout à propos; **not to the ~** sout hors de propos; **2** (determination) (also **strength of ~**) résolution *f*; **to have a sense of ~** savoir ce que l'on veut, être déterminé; **lack of ~** indécision *f*.
II on ~ *adv phr* (deliberately) exprès; **I didn't do it on ~** je ne l'ai pas fait exprès; **she said it on ~ to frighten him** elle l'a dit exprès pour l'effrayer.
III *vtr*‡ se proposer liter (**to do** de faire).

purpose-built /ˌpɜːpəsˈbɪlt/ *adj* GB conçu pour un usage déterminé; **a ~ apartment** ≈ un appartement indépendant; **it's not a ~ apartment** ça a été transformé en appartement.

purposeful /ˈpɜːpəsfl/ *adj* résolu.

purposefully /ˈpɜːpəsfəlɪ/ *adv* résolument.

purposeless /ˈpɜːpəslɪs/ *adj* sans but.

purposely /ˈpɜːpəslɪ/ *adv* exprès, intentionnellement; **he said it ~ to annoy her** il l'a dit exprès pour l'agacer.

purpose-made /ˌpɜːpəsˈmeɪd/ *adj* GB fait spécialement (**for** pour).

purr /pɜː(r)/ **I** *n* (of cat, engine) ronronnement *m*.
II *vtr* fig roucouler [*endearments*].
III *vi* [*cat, engine*] ronronner.

purse /pɜːs/ *n* **1** (for money) porte-monnaie *m inv*; **2** US (handbag) sac *m* à main; **3** fig (resources) moyens *mpl*; **it's beyond my ~** c'est au-delà de mes moyens; **4** (prize) somme *f* d'argent, prix *m*.
IDIOMS **to hold/loosen/tighten the ~-strings** tenir/délier/serrer les cordons de la bourse; **to ~ one's lips** faire une moue désapprobatrice.

purse-proud /ˈpɜːspraʊd/ *adj* US fier/fière de sa fortune.

purser /ˈpɜːsə(r)/ ▶1692 *n* commissaire *m* de bord.

purse snatcher *n* US voleur/-euse *m/f* de sacs à main.

pursuance /pəˈsjuːəns, US -ˈsuː-/ *n* Jur **in ~ of** (in accordance with) conformément à [*instructions, clause etc*]; (during the execution of) en exécution de.

pursuant /pəˈsjuːənt, US -ˈsuː-/ *adj* Jur **~ to** conformément à.

pursue /pəˈsjuː, US -ˈsuː-/ *vtr* poursuivre [*person, aim, ambition, studies*]; mener [*policy*]; se livrer à [*occupation, interest*]; rechercher [*excellence*]; **to ~ a career** faire carrière (**in** dans); **to ~ a line of inquiry/of thought** suivre une piste/un raisonnement.

pursuer /pəˈsjuːə(r), US -ˈsuː-/ *n* poursuivant/-e *m/f*.

pursuit /pəˈsjuːt, US -ˈsuː-/ *n* **1** ¢ (following) poursuite *f*; **in ~ of** à la poursuite de; **the ~ of happiness** la recherche du bonheur; **in close ~, in hot ~** à vos/ses etc trousses; **2** (hobby, interest) passe-temps *m inv*; **artistic ~s** travaux *mpl* artistiques; **scientific ~s** recherches *fpl* scientifiques.

pursuit plane *n* avion *m* de chasse.

purulence /ˈpjʊərələns/ *n* purulence *f*.

purulent /ˈpjʊərələnt/ *adj* purulent.

purvey /pəˈveɪ/ *vtr* sout fournir [*goods, services, information*].

purveyance /pəˈveɪəns/ *n* sout fourniture *f*.

purveyor /pəˈveɪə(r)/ *n* sout gen fournisseur/-euse *m/f*; **~ of pornography** pourvoyeur/-euse *m/f* de pornographie.

purview /ˈpɜːvjuː/ *n* gen Jur (of act, law) portée *f*; **to be within the ~ of sb/sth** être du ressort de qn/qch.

pus /pʌs/ *n* pus *m*.

push /pʊʃ/ **I** *n* **1** lit (shove, press) poussée *f*; **to give sb/sth a ~** pousser qn/qch; **the car won't start—we need a ~** la voiture ne veut pas démarrer—il faut la pousser; **at the ~ of a button** en appuyant sur un bouton; **2** (campaign, drive) campagne *f* (**for** en faveur de; **to do** pour faire); **3** fig (stimulus) impulsion *f*; **to give sth/sb a ~** encourager qch/qn; **this gave me the ~ I needed** c'est ça qui m'a décidé à faire quelque chose; **to give sth a ~ in the right direction** faire avancer qch dans la bonne direction; **4** Mil poussée *f* (**to** à; **towards** vers); **the big ~** la grande offensive; **5** (spirit, drive) esprit *m* battant.
II *vtr* **1** (move, shove, press) pousser [*person, animal, chair, door, car, pram*]; appuyer sur [*button, switch, bell*]; **to ~ sb/sth away** repousser qn/qch; **to ~ sth down/up sth** pousser qch en bas/en haut de qch [*hill, street*]; **she ~ed him down the stairs** elle l'a poussé dans l'escalier; **to ~ sb/sth into** pousser qn/qch dans [*lake, ditch, house*]; **to ~ one's finger/a stick into** enfoncer son doigt/un bâton dans; **to ~ sth into sb's hand** mettre qch de force dans la main de qn; **I ~ed her in** je l'ai poussée dedans; **to ~ sth to** pousser qch jusqu'à [*place, garage*]; **to ~ sb/sth out of the way** écarter qn/qch; **to ~ sb/a suggestion aside** écarter qn/une suggestion; **to ~ one's way through sth** se frayer un chemin à travers qch; **to ~ sth off the road** enlever qch de la chaussée; **to ~ the door open/shut** pousser la porte; **to ~ a thought to the back of one's mind** repousser une pensée dans un coin de son esprit; **2** (urge, drive) pousser [*pupil, person*] (**to do, into doing** à faire); **to ~ sb too hard** trop pousser qn; **to ~ sb too far** pousser qn à bout; **don't ~ me!**○ ne me pousse pas à bout!; **to be ~ed**○ (under pressure) être à la bourre○; **to be ~ed for sth**○ (short of) être à court de qch; **3**○ (promote) faire la promotion de [*product*]; promouvoir [*policy, theory*]; **4**○ (sell) vendre [*drugs*].
III *vi* pousser; **to get out and ~** sortir pour pousser; **'Push'** 'Poussez'; **there's no need to ~!** ce n'est pas la peine de pousser!; **to ~ against** s'appuyer contre;

to ~ at sth repousser qch; **to ~ past sb** bousculer qn; **to ~ through** se frayer un chemin à travers [*crowd, room*].
IV *v refl* **to ~ oneself upright** se redresser; **to ~ oneself into a sitting position** se redresser en position assise; **to ~ oneself through the crowd** se frayer un chemin à travers la foule; **to ~ oneself through a gap** passer par un trou; (drive oneself) se pousser (**to do** à faire).
IDIOMS **at a ~**○ GB s'il le faut; **if it comes to the ~** si on en vient à cette extrémité; **to be ~ing 50** friser la cinquantaine; **to give sb the ~**○ GB (fire) virer qn○; (break up with) larguer qn○; **to ~ one's luck, to ~ it**○ forcer sa chance; **that's ~ing it a bit!**○ (cutting it fine) c'est un peu juste or risqué!; **when** ou **if ~ comes to shove**○ au pire.
■ **push ahead** (with plans) persévérer (**with** dans); (on journey) continuer.
■ **push around**○: **~ [sb] around** fig bousculer.
■ **push back**: **~ [sth] back, ~ back [sth]** pousser [*object, furniture*]; repousser [*forest, shoreline*]; ramener [qch] en arrière [*hair*]; repousser [*army, enemy, frontier*]; repousser [*date, meeting*].
■ **push down**: ¶ **~ [sth] down, ~ down [sth]** faire chuter [*price, rate, temperature*]; ¶ **~ down [sb], ~ [sb] down** faire tomber [*person*].
■ **push for**: **~ for [sth]** faire pression en faveur de [*reform, action*].
■ **push forward**: ¶ **~ forward** (with plans) persévérer (**with** dans); (on journey) continuer; ¶ **~ [sth] forward, ~ forward [sth]** faire valoir [*idea, proposal*]; **to ~ oneself forward** se mettre en avant (**as** comme; **for** pour).
■ **push in**: ¶ **~ in** s'introduire dans la file; ¶ **~ [sth] in, ~ in [sth]** enfoncer [*button, door, window*].
■ **push off 1**○ GB filer○; **~ off!** file!; **2** Naut pousser; **~ off from** Naut s'éloigner de qch en poussant [*bank, jetty*].
■ **push on** = **push ahead**.
■ **push over**: ¶ **~ over**○ (move over) se pousser; ¶ **~ over [sth/sb], ~ [sth/sb] over** renverser [*person, table, car*].
■ **push through**: **~ [sth] through, ~ through [sth]** faire voter [*bill, legislation*]; faire passer [*deal*]; **to ~ through a passport application** accélérer l'obtention d'un passeport; **to ~ a bill through parliament** faire voter rapidement un projet de loi.
■ **push up**: **~ up [sth], ~ [sth] up** faire monter [*price, rate, unemployment*].

push-bike○ /ˈpʊʃbaɪk/ *n* vélo *m*.

push-button /ˈpʊʃbʌtn/ **I push button** *n* bouton-poussoir *m*.
II *adj* (*épith*) [*control, tuning, selection*] par bouton-poussoir; [*telephone*] à touches; [*radio*] à boutons-poussoirs; [*dialling*] au clavier; **~ warfare** guerre *f* presse-bouton.

push: **~cart** *n* charrette *f* à bras; **~chair** *n* GB poussette *f*.

pusher /ˈpʊʃə(r)/ *n* **1**○ (also **drug ~**) revendeur/-euse *m/f* de drogue; **2** (aircraft propeller) hélice *f* propulsive.

pushiness /ˈpʊʃɪnɪs/ *n* (ambition) arrivisme *m*; (tenacity) obstination *f*.

pushing /ˈpʊʃɪŋ/ *n* bousculade *f*; **a lot of ~ and shoving** une grosse bousculade.

Pushkin /ˈpʊʃkɪn/ *pr n* Pouchkine.

pushover○ /ˈpʊʃəʊvə(r)/ *n* **1** (easy to do, beat) jeu *m* d'enfant; **the team were no ~** battre cette équipe n'a pas été un jeu d'enfant; **2** (easily convinced) **to be a ~** être facile à convaincre.

push: **~pin** *n* US punaise *f*; **~-pull** *adj* Elec symétrique, push-pull *inv*; **~rod** *n* Mech poussoir *m*.

push-start I /ˈpʊʃstɑːt/ *n* **to give sth a ~** pousser qch pour le/la faire démarrer.
II /ˌpʊʃˈstɑːt/ *vtr* pousser [qch] pour le/la faire démarrer [*vehicle*].

push-up /ˈpʊʃʌp/ *n* Sport pompe○ *f*.

pushy○ /ˈpʊʃɪ/ *adj* (ambitious) arriviste; **she's very ~** (assertive) elle s'impose.

pusillanimity /ˌpjuːsɪləˈnɪmətɪ/ *n* sout pusillanimité *f*.

pusillanimous /ˌpjuːsɪˈlænɪməs/ *adj* sout pusillanime.

puss○ /pʊs/ *n* **1** (cat) minet○ *m*; **2** (girl) nana○ *f*; **3** US (mouth) gueule○ *f*.

pussy /ˈpʊsɪ/ *n* **1** GB (cat) lang enfantin minet *m*; **2**● (female genitals) chatte◑ *f*; (intercourse) baise● *f*.

pussy cat *n* **1** lang enfantin minou *m* baby talk; **2**○ fig **he's a real ~** il est très conciliant.

pussyfoot○ /ˈpʊsɪfʊt/ *vi* (also **~ around, ~ about**) tourner autour du pot○.

pussyfooting○ /ˈpʊʃɪfʊtɪŋ/ **I** *n* ¢ tergiversations *fpl*.
II *adj* [*attitude, behaviour*] timoré.

pussy willow *n* **1** (tree) saule *m* blanc; **2** (catkin) chaton *m* de saule.

pustule /ˈpʌstjuːl, US -tʃuːl/ *n* pustule *f*.

put /pʊt/ **I** *n* Fin = **put option**.
II *vtr* (*p prés* **-tt-**; *prét, pp* **put**) **1** (place) mettre [*object*]; **~ them here please** mettez-les ici s'il vous plaît; **to ~ sth on/under/around etc** mettre qch sur/sous/autour de etc; **to ~ a stamp on a letter** mettre un timbre sur une lettre; **to ~ a lock on the door/a button on a shirt** mettre une serrure sur la porte/un bouton sur une chemise; **to ~ one's arm around sb** mettre son bras autour de qn; **to ~ one's hands in one's pockets** mettre les mains dans ses poches; **to ~ sth in a safe place** mettre qch en lieu sûr; **to ~ sugar in one's tea** mettre du sucre dans son thé; **to ~ more sugar in one's tea** ajouter du sucre dans son thé; **to ~ more soap in the bathroom** remettre du savon dans la salle de bains; **2** (cause to go or undergo) **to ~ sth through** glisser qch dans [*letterbox*]; passer qch par [*window*]; faire passer qch à [*mincer*]; **to ~ one's head through the window** passer la tête par la fenêtre; **to ~ one's fist through the window** casser la fenêtre d'un coup de poing; **to ~ sth through the books** Acct faire passer qch dans les frais généraux; **to ~ sth through a test** faire passer un test à qch; **to ~ sth through a process** faire suivre un processus à qch; **to ~ sb through** envoyer qn à [*university, college*]; faire passer qn par [*suffering, ordeal*]; faire passer [qch] à qn [*test*]; faire suivre [qch] à qn [*course*]; **after all you've put me through** après tout ce que tu m'as fait subir; **to ~ sb through hell** faire souffrir mille morts à qn; **to ~ one's hand/finger to** porter la main/le doigt à [*mouth*]; **3** (cause to be or do) mettre [*person*]; **to ~ sb in prison/on a diet** mettre qn en prison/au régime; **to ~ sb on the train** mettre qn dans le train; **to ~ sb in goal/in defence** GB mettre qn dans les buts/en défense; **to ~ sb in a bad mood/in an awkward position** mettre qn de mauvaise humeur/dans une situation délicate; **to ~ sb to work** mettre qn au travail; **to ~ sb to mending/washing sth** faire réparer/laver qch à qn; **4** (devote, invest) **to ~ money/energy into sth** investir de l'argent/son énergie dans qch; **if you ~ some effort into your work, you will improve** si tu fais des efforts, ton travail sera meilleur; **to ~ a lot into** s'engager à fond pour [*work, project*]; sacrifier beaucoup à [*marriage*]; **to ~ a lot of effort into sth** faire beaucoup d'efforts pour qch; **she ~s a lot of herself into her novels** il y a beaucoup d'éléments autobiographiques dans ses romans; **5** (add) **to ~ sth towards** mettre qch pour [*holiday, gift, fund*]; **~ it towards some new clothes** dépense-le en nouveaux vêtements; **to ~ tax/duty on sth** taxer/imposer qch; **to ~ a penny on income tax** GB augmenter d'un pourcent l'impôt sur le revenu; **6** (express) **how would you ~ that in French?** comment dirait-on ça en français?; **how can I ~ it?** comment dirai-je?; **it was—how can I ~ it—unusual** c'était—comment dire—original; **that's one way of ~ting it!** iron on peut le dire comme ça!; **as Sartre ~s it** comme le dit Sartre; **to ~ it simply** pour le dire simplement; **to ~ it bluntly** pour parler franchement; **let me ~ it another way** laissez-moi m'exprimer différemment; **that was very well** ou **nicely put** c'était très bien tourné; **to ~ one's feelings/one's anger into words** trouver les mots pour exprimer ses sentiments/sa colère; **to ~ sth in writing** mettre qch par écrit; **7** (offer for consideration) présenter [*argument, point of view, proposal*]; **to ~ sth to** soumettre qch à [*meeting, conference, board*]; **to ~ sth to the vote** mettre qch au vote; **I ~ it to you that** Jur j'ai la présomption que; **8** (rate, rank) placer; **where would you ~ it on a scale of one to ten?** où est-ce que tu placerais cela sur une échelle allant de un à dix?; **to ~ sb in the top rank of artists** placer qn au premier rang des artistes; **I ~ a sense of humour before good looks** je place le sens de l'humour avant la beauté; **I ~ a sense of humour first** pour moi le plus important c'est le sens de l'humour; **to ~ children/safety first** faire passer les enfants/la sécurité avant tout; **to ~ one's family before everything** faire passer sa famille avant tout; **9** (estimate) **to ~ sth at** évaluer qch à [*sum*]; **to ~ the value of sth at** estimer la valeur de qch à [*sum*]; **I'd ~ him at about 40** je lui donnerais à peu près 40 ans; **10** Sport lancer [*shot*]; **11** Agric (for mating) **to ~ a heifer/mare to** amener une génisse/jument à [*male*].
III *v refl* (*p prés* **-tt-**; *prét, pp* **put**) **to ~ oneself in a strong position/in sb's place** se mettre dans une position de force/à la place de qn.
IDIOMS **I didn't know where to ~ myself** je ne savais pas où me mettre; **I wouldn't ~ it past him!** je ne pense pas que ça le gênerait! (**to do** de faire); **I wouldn't ~ anything past her!** je la crois capable de tout!; **~ it there**○! (invitation to shake hands) tope là!; **to ~ it about a bit**◑ péj coucher à droite et à gauche◑; **to ~ one over** ou **across** GB **on sb**○ faire marcher qn○.
■ **put about**: ¶ **~ about** Naut virer de bord; ¶ **~ [sth] about, ~ about [sth] 1** (spread) faire circuler [*rumour, gossip, story*]; **to ~ (it) about that** faire courir le bruit que; **it is being put about that** le bruit court que; **2** Naut faire virer de bord [*vessel*].
■ **put across**: **~ across [sth], ~ [sth] across** communiquer [*idea, message, concept, case, point of view*]; mettre [qch] en valeur [*personality*]; **to ~ oneself across** se mettre en valeur.
■ **put aside**: **~ aside [sth], ~ [sth] aside** mettre [qch] de côté [*money, article, differences, divisions, mistrust*].
■ **put away**: ¶ **~ away [sth], ~ [sth] away 1** (tidy away) ranger [*toys, dishes*]; **2** (save) mettre [qch] de côté [*money*]; **3**○ (consume) avaler [*food*]; descendre○ [*drink*]; ¶ **~ away [sb]**○, **~ [sb] away**○ **1** (in mental hospital) enfermer; **he had to be put away** il a fallu l'enfermer; **2** (in prison) boucler○ [*person*] (**for** pour).
■ **put back**: **~ back [sth], ~ [sth] back 1** (return, restore) remettre [*object*]; **to ~ sth back where it belongs** remettre qch à sa place; **2** (postpone) remettre, repousser [*meeting, departure*] (**to** à; **until** jusqu'à); repousser [*date*]; **3** retarder [*clock, watch*]; **remember to ~ your clocks back an hour** n'oubliez pas de retarder votre pendule d'une heure; **4** (delay) retarder [*project, production, deliveries*] (**by** de); **5**○ (knock back) descendre○ [*drink, quantity*].
■ **put by** GB: **~ [sth] by, ~ by [sth]** mettre [qch] de côté [*money*]; **to have a bit (of money) put by** avoir un peu d'argent de côté.
■ **put down**: ¶ **~ down** (land) [*aircraft*]

atterrir (**on** sur); ¶ **~ [sth] down, ~ down [sth] 1** (on ground, table) poser [*object, plane*] (**on** sur); mettre [*rat poison etc*]; **2** (suppress) réprimer [*uprising, revolt, opposition*]; **3** (write down) mettre (par écrit) [*date, time, name*]; **~ down whatever you like** mets ce que tu veux; **4** (ascribe) **to ~ sth down to** mettre qch sur le compte de [*incompetence, human error etc*]; **to ~ sth down to the fact that** imputer qch au fait que; **5** (charge) **to ~ sth down to** mettre qch sur [*account*]; **6** Vet (by injection) piquer; (by other method) abattre; **to have a dog put down** faire piquer un chien; **7** (advance, deposit) **to ~ down a deposit** verser des arrhes; **to ~ £50 down on sth** verser 50 livres d'arrhes sur qch; **8** (lay down, store) mettre [qch] en cave [*wine*]; affiner [*cheese*]; **9** (put on agenda) inscrire [qch] à l'ordre du jour [*motion*]; ¶ **~ [sb] down, ~ down [sb] 1** (drop off) déposer [*passenger*]; **to ~ sb down on the corner** déposer qn au coin de la rue; **2**○ (humiliate) rabaisser [*person*]; **3** gen Sch (into lower group) faire descendre [*pupil, team*] (**from** de; **to, into** à); **4** (classify, count in) **to ~ sb down as** considérer qn comme [*possibility, candidate, fool*]; **I'd never have put you down as a Scotsman!** je ne t'aurais jamais pris pour un Écossais!; **to ~ sb down for** (note as wanting or offering) compter [qch] pour qn [*contribution*]; (put on waiting list) inscrire qn sur la liste d'attente pour [*school, club*]; **~ me down for a meal** compte un repas pour moi; **to ~ sb down for £10** compter 10 livres pour qn; **to ~ sb down for three tickets** réserver trois billets pour qn.

■ **put forth** littér: **~ forth [sth], ~ [sth] forth 1** présenter [*shoots, leaves, buds*]; **2** fig émettre [*idea, theory*].

■ **put forward**: ¶ **~ forward [sth], ~ [sth] forward 1** (propose) avancer [*idea, theory, name*]; soumettre [*plan, proposal, suggestion*]; émettre [*opinion*]; **2** (in time) avancer [*meeting, date, clock*] (**by** de; **to** à); **don't forget to ~ your clocks forward one hour** n'oubliez pas d'avancer votre pendule d'une heure; ¶ **~ [sb] forward, ~ forward [sb]** présenter la candidature de (**for** pour); ¶ **~ sb forward as** présenter qn comme [*candidate*]; **to ~ oneself forward** présenter sa candidature, se présenter; **to ~ oneself forward as a candidate** présenter sa candidature; **to ~ oneself forward for** se présenter pour [*post*].

■ **put in**: ¶ **~ in 1** [*ship*] faire escale (**at** à; **to** dans; **for** pour); **2** (apply) **to ~ in for** [*person*] postuler pour [*job, promotion, rise*]; demander [*transfer, overtime*]; ¶ **~ in [sth], ~ [sth] in 1** (fit, install) installer [*central heating, shower, kitchen*]; **to have sth put in** faire installer qch; **2** (make) faire [*request, claim, offer, bid*]; **to ~ in an application for** déposer une demande de [*visa, passport*]; poser sa candidature pour [*job*]; **to ~ in a protest** protester; **to ~ in an appearance** faire une apparition; **3** (contribute) passer [*time, hours, days*]; contribuer pour [*sum, amount*]; **they are each ~ting in £1m** chacun apporte une contribution d'un million de livres; **to ~ in a lot of time doing** consacrer beaucoup de temps à faire; **to ~ in a good day's work** avoir une bonne journée de travail; **to ~ in a lot of work** se donner beaucoup de mal; **thank you for all the work you've put in** merci pour tout le mal que tu t'es donné; **4** (insert) mettre [*paragraph, word, reference*]; **to ~ in that** mettre que; **to ~ in how/why** expliquer comment/pourquoi; **5** (elect) élire; **that ~s the Conservatives in again** les conservateurs ont donc été élus encore une fois; ¶ **~ [sb] in for** présenter [qn] pour [*exam, scholarship*]; poser la candidature de [qn] pour [*promotion, job*]; recommander [qn] pour [*prize, award*]; **to ~ oneself in for** poser sa candidature pour [*job, promotion*].

■ **put off**: ¶ **~ off** Naut partir; ¶ **~ off from** s'éloigner de [*quay, jetty*]; ¶ **~ off [sth], ~ [sth] off 1** (delay, defer) remettre [qch] (à plus tard) [*wedding, meeting*]; **to ~ sth off until June/until after Christmas** remettre qch à juin/à après Noël; **I should see a doctor, but I keep ~ting it off** je devrais voir un médecin, mais je remets toujours ça à plus tard; **to ~ off visiting sb/doing one's homework** remettre à plus tard une visite chez qn/ses devoirs; **2** (turn off) éteindre [*light, radio*]; couper [*radiator, heating*]; ¶ **~ off [sb], ~ [sb] off 1** (fob off, postpone seeing) décommander [*guest*]; dissuader [*person*]; **to ~ sb off coming with an excuse** trouver une excuse pour dissuader qn de venir; **to be easily put off** se décourager facilement; **2** (repel) [*appearance, smell, colour*] dégoûter; [*manner, person*] déconcerter; **to ~ sb off sth** dégoûter qn de qch; **don't be put off by the colour—it tastes delicious!** ne te laisse pas dégoûter par la couleur—c'est délicieux!; **3** GB (distract) distraire; **stop trying to ~ me off!** arrête de me distraire!; **you're ~ting me off my work** tu me distrais de mon travail; **4** (drop off) déposer [*passenger*].

■ **put on**: ¶ **~ on [sth], ~ [sth] on 1** mettre [*garment, hat, cream, lipstick*]; **2** (switch on, operate) allumer [*light, gas, radio, heating*]; mettre [*record, tape, music*]; **to ~ the kettle on** mettre de l'eau à chauffer; **to ~ the brakes on** freiner; **3** (gain) prendre [*weight, kilo*]; **4** (add) rajouter [*extra duty, tax*]; **5** (produce) monter [*play, exhibition*]; **6** (assume, adopt) prendre [*air, accent, look, expression*]; **he's ~ting it on** il fait semblant; **7** (lay on, offer) ajouter [*extra train, bus service*]; proposer [*meal, dish*]; **8** (put forward) avancer [*clock*]; **9** Turf (bet) parier [*amount*]; **to ~ a bet on** faire un pari; ¶ **~ [sb] on 1** Telecom (connect) passer; **I'll ~ him on** je vous le passe; **2**○ US faire marcher○ [*person*]; **3** (recommend) **to ~ sb on to sth** indiquer qch à qn; **who put you on to me?** qui vous a envoyé à moi?; **4** (put on track of) **to ~ sb on to** mettre qn sur la piste de [*killer, criminal, runaway*].

■ **put out**: ¶ **~ out 1** Naut partir (**from** de); **to ~ out to sea** mettre à la mer; **2**◐ US péj coucher avec n'importe qui○; ¶ **~ out [sth], ~ [sth] out 1** (extend) tendre [*hand, arm, foot, leg*]; **to ~ out one's tongue** tirer la langue; **2** (extinguish) éteindre [*fire, cigarette, candle, light*]; **3** (take outside) sortir [*bin, garbage*]; faire sortir [*cat*]; **4** (issue) diffuser [*description, report, warning*]; faire [*statement*]; propager [*rumour*]; **5** (make available, arrange) mettre [*food, dishes, towels etc*]; **6** (sprout) déployer [*shoot, bud, root*]; **7** (cause to be wrong) fausser [*figure, estimate, result*]; **8** (dislocate) se démettre [*shoulder, ankle*]; **9** (subcontract) confier [qch] en sous-traitance [*work*] (**to** à); ¶ **~ [sb] out 1** (inconvenience) déranger; **to ~ oneself out** se mettre en quatre○ (**to do** pour faire); **to ~ oneself out for sb** se donner beaucoup de mal pour qn; **don't ~ yourself out for us** ne vous dérangez pas pour nous; **2** (annoy) contrarier; **he looked really put out** il avait l'air vraiment contrarié; **3** (evict) expulser.

■ **put over** = **put across**.

■ **put through**: ¶ **~ [sth] through, ~ through [sth] 1** (implement) faire passer [*reform, bill, amendment, plan, measure*]; **2** Telecom (transfer) passer [*call*] (**to** à); **she put through a call from my husband** elle m'a passé mon mari○; ¶ **~ [sb] through** Telecom passer [*caller*] (**to** à); **I'm just ~ting you through** je vous le/la passe; **I was put through to another department** on m'a passé un autre service.

■ **put together**: **~ [sb/sth] together, ~ together [sb/sth] 1** (assemble) assembler [*pieces, parts*]; **to ~ sth back together again**, **to ~ sth back together** reconstituer qch; **more/smarter than all the rest put together** plus/plus intelligent que tous les autres réunis; **2** (place together) mettre ensemble [*animals, objects, people*]; **3** (form) former [*coalition, partnership, group, team, consortium*]; **4** (edit, make) constituer [*file, portfolio, anthology*]; rédiger [*newsletter, leaflet*]; établir [*list*]; faire [*film, programme, video*]; **5** (concoct) improviser [*meal*]; **6** (present) constituer [*case*]; construire [*argument, essay*].

■ **put up**: ¶ **~ up 1** (stay) **to ~ up at sb's** se faire héberger par qn; **to ~ up in a hotel** descendre à l'hôtel; **2 to ~ up with** (tolerate) supporter [*behaviour, person*]; **to have a lot to ~ up with** avoir beaucoup de choses à supporter; ¶ **~ up [sth]** opposer [*resistance*]; **to ~ up a fight/struggle** combattre; **to ~ up a good performance** [*team, competitor*] bien se défendre; ¶ **~ [sth] up, ~ up [sth] 1** (raise) hisser [*flag, sail*]; relever [*hair*]; **to ~ up one's hand/leg** lever la main/la jambe; **~ your hands up!** (in class) levez le doigt!; **~ 'em up**○! (to fight) bats-toi!; (to surrender) haut les mains!; **2** (post up) mettre [*sign, poster, notice, plaque, decorations*]; afficher [*list*]; **to ~ sth up on the wall/on the board** afficher qch sur le mur/au tableau; **3** (build, erect) dresser [*fence, barrier, tent*]; construire [*building, memorial*]; **4** (increase, raise) augmenter [*rent, prices, tax*]; faire monter [*temperature, pressure*]; **5** (provide) fournir [*money, amount, percentage*] (**for** pour; **to do** pour faire); **6** (present) soumettre [*proposal, argument*]; **to ~ sth up for discussion** soumettre qch à la discussion; **7** (put in orbit) placer [qch] en orbite [*satellite, probe*]; ¶ **~ [sb] up, ~ up [sb] 1** (lodge) héberger; **2** (as candidate) présenter [*candidate*]; **to ~ sb up for** proposer qn comme [*leader, chairman*]; proposer qn pour [*promotion, position*]; **to ~ oneself up for** se proposer comme [*chairman*]; se proposer pour [*post*]; **3** (promote) faire passer [qn] au niveau supérieur [*pupil*]; **to be put up** [*pupil, team*] monter (**to** dans); **4** (incite) **to ~ sb up to sth/to doing** pousser [qn] à/à faire; **somebody must have put her up to it** quelqu'un a dû l'y pousser.

■ **put upon**: **~ upon [sb]** abuser de [*person*]; **to be put upon** se faire marcher sur les pieds; **to feel put upon** avoir l'impression de se faire marcher sur les pieds; **I won't be put upon any more** je ne me ferai plus jamais avoir○.

put and call *n* GB Fin double option *f*.

putative /ˈpjuːtətɪv/ *adj* sout putatif/-ive.

put-down /ˈpʊtdaʊn/ *n* remarque *f* humiliante; **it was a real ~** ça l'a vraiment remis à sa place.

put: **~ option** *n* Fin Comm option *f* de vente; **~-out**○ *adj* (offended) contrarié.

putrefaction /ˌpjuːtrɪˈfækʃn/ *n* putréfaction *f*.

putrefy /ˈpjuːtrɪfaɪ/ **I** *vtr* putréfier.
II *vi* se putréfier.

putrescence /pjuːˈtresns/ *n* sout putrescence *f*.

putrescent /pjuːˈtresnt/ *adj* sout putrescent, en voie de putréfaction.

putrid /ˈpjuːtrɪd/ *adj* **1** sout (decaying) putride; **2**○ (awful) dégoûtant.

putsch /pʊtʃ/ *n* putsch *m*.

putt /pʌt/ **I** *n* putt *m*.
II *vtr, vi* putter.

puttee /ˈpʌtɪ/ *n* bande *f* molletière.

putter /ˈpʌtə(r)/ **I** *n* Sport putter *m*.
II *vi* **1 to ~ along/past** avancer/passer dans un ronronnement de moteur; **2** US = **potter II**.

putting green *n* green *m*.

putty /ˈpʌtɪ/ **I** *n* mastic *m*.
II *vtr* mastiquer.
IDIOMS **he's like ~ in my hands** j'en fais ce que je veux.

put: **~-up job**○ *n* coup *m* monté; **~-you-up**○ *n* GB canapé-lit *m*.

putz /pʊts/ *n* US **1**◐ (person) détraqué/-e○ *m/f*; **2**● (penis) bitte● *f*, pénis *m*.

Puy-de-Dôme ▶ 1163 *pr n* Puy-de-Dôme *m*; **in/to the ~** dans le Puy-de-Dôme.

puzzle /ˈpʌzl/ **I** *n* **1** (mystery) mystère *m*; **it's a ~ to me how/why** je n'arrive pas à comprendre comment/pourquoi; **it's a bit of a ~**○ GB c'est un peu mystérieux; **2** Games casse-tête *m inv*; ▶ **crossword, jigsaw**.
II *vtr* [*question, attitude*] déconcerter [*person*].
III *vi* **to ~ over sth** réfléchir à qch.
■ **puzzle out**: **~ out [sth], ~ [sth] out** deviner [*identity, meaning*].

puzzle book *n* livre *m* de jeux.

puzzled /ˈpʌzld/ *adj* [*person, smile*] perplexe; **to be ~ as to why/how** se demander pourquoi/comment.

puzzlement /ˈpʌzlmənt/ *n* perplexité *f*.

puzzler /ˈpʌzlə(r)/ *n* énigme *f*.

puzzling /ˈpʌzlɪŋ/ *adj* curieux/-ieuse.

PVC *n* (*abrév* = **polyvinyl chloride**) PVC *m*.

Pvt *n* Mil *abrév écrite* = **private**.

pw (*abrév* = **per week**) par semaine.

PWR *n* (*abrév* = **pressurized water reactor**) REP *m*.

PX *n* US (*abrév* = **Post Exchange**) coopérative *f* militaire.

pygmy /ˈpɪgmɪ/ **I** *n* **1** Anthrop (also **Pygmy**) pygmée *mf*; **2** péj pygmée *m*.
II *modif* [*feature, tradition, race*] pygmée.

pygmy shrew *n* musaraigne *f* pygmée.

pyjama GB, **pajama** US /pəˈdʒɑːmə/ **I** *modif* [*cord, jacket, trousers*] de pyjama.
II pyjamas *npl* pyjama *m*; **a pair of ~s** un pyjama; **to be in one's ~s** être en pyjama.

pylon /ˈpaɪlən, -lɒn/ *n* Elec, Aviat, Antiq pylône *m*; **electricity ~** pylône *m* électrique.

pylori /paɪˈlɔːraɪ/ *pl* ▶ **pylorus**.

pyloric /paɪˈlɒrɪk/ *adj* pylorique.

pylorus /paɪˈlɔːrəs/ *n* (*pl* **-lori**) pylore *m*.

PYO *n*: *abrév* ▶ **pick your own**.

pyorrhea /ˌpaɪəˈrɪə/ ▶ 1354 *n* pyorrhée *f*.

pyramid /ˈpɪrəmɪd/ **I** *n* pyramide *f*.
II *vi* Fin spéculer en réinvestissant des bénéfices fictifs.

pyramidal /pɪˈræmɪdl/ *adj* pyramidal.

pyramidal tract *n* Anat faisceau *m* pyramidal.

pyramid selling *n* vente *f* en cascade.

pyre /ˈpaɪə(r)/ *n* bûcher *m*.

Pyrenean /ˌpɪrəˈniːən/ *adj* pyrénéen/-éenne.

Pyrenean mountain dog *n* berger *m* des Pyrénées.

Pyrenees /ˌpɪrəˈniːz/ *pr npl* Pyrénées *fpl*.

Pyrénées-Atlantiques ▶ 1163 *pr n* Pyrénées-Atlantiques *fpl*; **in/to the ~** dans les Pyrénées-Atlantiques.

Pyrénées-Orientales ▶ 1163 *pr n* Pyrénées-Orientales *fpl*; **in/to the ~** dans les Pyrénées-Orientales.

pyrethrin /paɪˈriːθrɪn/ *n* pyréthrine *f*.

pyrethrum /paɪˈriːθrəm/ *n* (plant, insecticide) pyrèthre *m*.

pyretic /paɪˈretɪk, pɪ-/ *adj* pyrétique.

Pyrex® /ˈpaɪreks/ **I** *n* Pyrex® *m*.
II *modif* [*dish, jug*] en Pyrex®.

pyrexia /paɪˈreksɪə/ *n* pyrexie *f*.

pyrexic /paɪˈreksɪk/ *adj* pyrétique.

pyrite(s) /paɪˈraɪt(iːz), US pɪˈraɪt(iːz)/ *n* pyrite *f*.

pyritic /paɪˈrɪtɪk/ *adj* pyriteux/-euse.

pyromania /ˌpaɪrəʊˈmeɪnɪə/ *n* pyromanie *f*.

pyromaniac /ˌpaɪrəʊˈmeɪnɪæk/ *n* pyromane *mf*.

pyrotechnic /ˌpaɪrəˈteknɪk/ *adj* pyrotechnique; **~ display** feu *m* d'artifice.

pyrotechnics /ˌpaɪrəˈteknɪks/ *n* **1** (+ *v sg*) (science) pyrotechnie *f*; **2** (+ *v sg*) (display) feu *m* d'artifice; **3** (+ *v pl*) **verbal/intellectual ~** feux *mpl* d'artifice verbaux/intellectuels.

Pyrrhic /ˈpɪrɪk/ *adj* **a ~ victory** une victoire à la Pyrrhus.

Pythagoras /paɪˈθægərəs/ *pr n* Pythagore.

Pythagorean /paɪˌθægəˈriːən/ *adj* [*philosophy*] pythagoricien/-ienne; [*theorem*] de Pythagore; [*number*] pythagorique.

python /ˈpaɪθn, US ˈpaɪθɒn/ *n* python *m*.

pyx /pɪks/ *n* (in church) custode *f*; (for the sick) pyxide *f*.

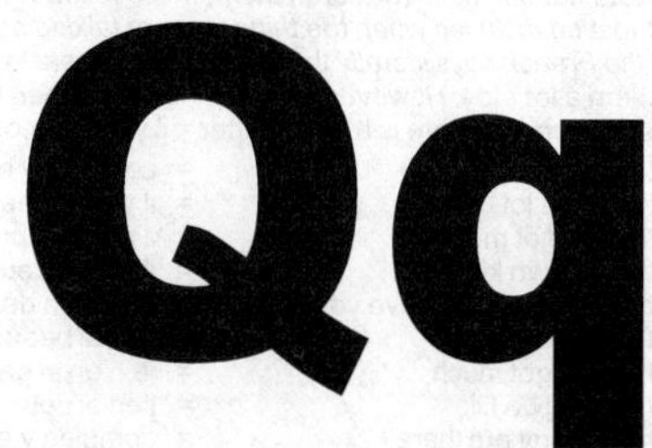

q, Q /kjuː/ *n* q, Q *m*.

Q and A *n* (*abrév* = **question and answer**) questions-réponses *fpl*.

Qatar /kæ'tɑː/ ▶ 1131 *pr n* Qatar *m*.

Qatari /kæ'tɑːrɪ/ ▶ 1486 **I** *n* Qatarien/-ienne *m/f*.
II *adj* quatarien/-ienne.

QC *n* GB, Jur (*abrév* = **Queen's Counsel**) *titre conféré à un avocat éminent*.

QE2 *n* Naut *abrév* = **Queen Elizabeth II**.

QED (*abrév* = **quod erat demonstrandum**) CQFD.

qt° /kjuː'tiː/ *n* (*abrév* = **quiet**) **on the ~** en cachette.

Q-tip® *n* coton-tige® *m*.

qty *n*: *abrév écrite* = **quantity**.

quack /kwæk/ **I** *n* **1** (impostor) charlatan *m*; **2**° GB (doctor) toubib° *m*; **3** onomat coin-coin *m inv*.
II *vi* onomat cancaner.

quackery /'kwækərɪ/ *n* charlatanisme *m*.

quack grass *n* US chiendent *m*.

quad /kwɒd/ *n* **1** *abrév* ▶ **quadrangle**; **2** *abrév* ▶ **quadruplet**.

Quadragesima /ˌkwɒdrə'dʒesɪmə/ *n* quadragésime *f*.

quadrangle /'kwɒdræŋgl/ *n* **1** Math quadrilatère *m*; **2** Archit cour *f* carrée.

quadrangular /kwɒ'dræŋgjʊlə(r)/ *adj* quadrangulaire.

quadrant /'kwɒdrənt/ *n* quadrant *m*.

quadraphonic /ˌkwɒdrə'fɒnɪk/ *adj* quadriphonique.

quadraphonics /ˌkwɒdrə'fɒnɪks/ *n* (+ *v sg*) quadriphonie *f*.

quadraphony /kwɒ'drɒfənɪ/ *n* quadriphonie *f*.

quadrat /'kwɒdrət/ *n* Biol, Ecol quadrat *m*.

quadratic /kwɒ'drætɪk/ *adj* quadratique.

quadratic equation *n* équation *f* du second degré.

quadrature /'kwɒdrətʃə(r)/ *n* Math, Astron, Electron quadrature *f*.

quadriceps /'kwɒdrɪseps/ *n* (*pl* **~**) quadriceps *m*.

quadrilateral /ˌkwɒdrɪ'lætərəl/ **I** *n* quadrilatère *m*.
II *adj* quadrilatéral.

quadrilingual /ˌkwɒdrɪ'lɪŋgwəl/ *adj* quadrilingue.

quadrille /kwɒ'drɪl/ *n* quadrille *m*.

quadrillion /kwɒ'drɪlɪən/ *n* GB quatrillion *m*, US trillion *m*.

quadripartite /ˌkwɒdrɪ'pɑːtaɪt/ *adj* quadripartite.

quadriplegia /ˌkwɒdrɪ'pliːdʒə/ *n* tétraplégie *f*.

quadriplegic /ˌkwɒdrɪ'pliːdʒɪk/ *adj* tétraplégique.

quadroon /kwɒ'druːn/ *n* quarteron/-onne *m/f*.

quadrophonic *adj* = **quadraphonic**.

quadruped /'kwɒdrʊped/ *n*, *adj* quadrupède (*m*).

quadruple I /'kwɒdrʊpl, US kwɒ'druːpl/ *n*, *adj* quadruple (*m*).
II /kwɒ'druːpl/ *vtr*, *vi* quadrupler.

quadruplet /'kwɒdrʊplət, US kwɒ'druːp-/ *n* quadruplé/-e *m/f*; **a set of ~s** des quadruplés.

quadruplicate /kwɒ'druːplɪkət/ *n* **in ~** en quatre exemplaires.

quaff‡ /kwɒf, US kwæf/ *vtr* lamper [*wine, ale*].

quagmire /'kwɒgmaɪə(r), 'kwæg-/ *n* bourbier *m* also fig.

quahog /'kwɔːhɒg/ *n* clam *m*.

quail /kweɪl/ **I** *n* (*pl* **~s** ou *collect* **~**) (bird) caille *f*; **~'s eggs** œufs de caille.
II *vi* fléchir; **he ~ed before her/at the thought of all that work** il a fléchi devant elle/à la pensée de tout ce travail.

quaint /kweɪnt/ *adj* **1** (pretty) [*pub, village, name*] pittoresque; **how ~!** comme c'est pittoresque! also iron; **2** [*manners, ways*] (old-world) d'un charme suranné; (slightly ridiculous) au charme vieillot; **3** (odd) [*reminder, conviction*] bizarre; (unusual) [*title, name*] original.

quaintly /'kweɪntlɪ/ *adv* [*speak, dress*] d'une manière pittoresque.

quaintness /'kweɪntnɪs/ *n* pittoresque *m*.

quake /kweɪk/ **I** *n* (earthquake) tremblement *m* de terre.
II *vi* [*earth, person*] trembler; **to ~ with fear** trembler de peur.

Quaker /'kweɪkə(r)/ *n* Quaker/-eresse *m/f*.

Quaker gun *n* US fusil *m* factice.

Quakerism /'kweɪkərɪzəm/ *n* quakerisme *m*.

Quaker meeting *n* réunion *f* de Quakers.

qualification /ˌkwɒlɪfɪ'keɪʃn/ *n* **1** (diploma, degree etc) diplôme *m* (**in** en); (experience, skills) qualification *f*, compétence *f*; (attribute) qualité *f*; **to have the (necessary** ou **right) ~s for/for doing** ou **to do** (on paper) avoir les titres requis pour/pour faire; (in experience, skills) avoir les qualifications or les compétences pour/pour faire; **2** GB (graduation) **my first job after ~** mon premier travail après avoir reçu mon diplôme; **3** (restriction) restriction *f*; **to accept sth without ~** accepter qch sans restriction; **my only ~ is (that)** ma seule réserve est que; **4** Admin (eligibility) droit *m*; **~ for benefits** droit à des allocations; **5** Ling qualification *f*.

qualification share *n* Fin action *f* de garantie.

qualified /'kwɒlɪfaɪd/ *adj* **1** (for job) (having diploma) diplômé; (having experience, skills) qualifié; **~ homeopath/nurse** homéopathe/infirmier/-ière diplômé/-e; **to be ~ for sth/to do** (on paper) avoir les titres requis pour qch/pour faire; (by experience, skills) être qualifié pour qch/pour faire; **~ teacher** GB *professeur ayant achevé sa formation pédagogique*; **2** (competent) (having authority) qualifié (**to do** pour faire), habilité fml (**to do** à faire); (having knowledge) compétent (**to do** pour faire); **not having read the report, I am not ~ to discuss it** n'ayant pas lu le rapport, je ne suis pas compétent pour en discuter; **3** (modified) [*approval, praise, success*] nuancé, mitigé.

qualifier /'kwɒlɪfaɪə(r)/ *n* **1** Sport (contestant) qualifié/-e *m/f*; (match) éliminatoire *m*; **2** Ling qualificatif *m*.

qualify /'kwɒlɪfaɪ/ **I** *vtr* **1** (make competent) **to ~ sb for a job/to do** [*degree, diploma*] habiliter qn à exercer un emploi/à faire; [*experience, skills*] rendre qn apte à exercer un emploi/à faire; **to ~ to do** avoir les connaissances requises pour faire; **2** Admin **to ~ sb for sth** donner droit à qch à qn [*membership, benefit, legal aid*]; **to ~ sb to do** donner à qn le droit de faire; **to ~ to do** avoir le droit de faire; **3** gen (give authority to) **to ~ sb to do** autoriser qn à faire; **that doesn't ~ you to criticize me** cela ne t'autorise pas à me critiquer; **taking a few family photos hardly qualifies him as a photographer** le fait qu'il prenne quelques photos de famille n'en fait pas pour autant un photographe; **4** (modify) nuancer [*acceptance, approval, opinion*]; préciser [*statement, remark*]; **5** Ling qualifier.
II *vi* **1** (obtain diploma, degree etc) obtenir son diplôme (**as** de, en); (have experience, skill) avoir les connaissances requises (**for** pour); **while she was ~ing as an engineer/teacher** pendant qu'elle faisait ses études d'ingénieur/pour devenir professeur; **2** Admin remplir les conditions (requises); **to ~ for** avoir droit à [*membership, benefit, legal aid*]; **3** (meet standard) **he hardly qualifies as a poet** ce n'est pas vraiment ce que l'on peut appeler un poète; **4** Sport se qualifier (**for** pour).

qualifying /'kwɒlɪfaɪɪŋ/ *adj* **1** gen [*match, exam*] de qualification; **~ round** Sport épreuve de qualification; **~ period** (until trained) (periode *f* de) stage *m*; (until eligible) période *f* d'attente; **2** Ling qualificatif/-ive.

qualitative /'kwɒlɪtətɪv, US -teɪt-/ *adj* qualitatif/-ive.

qualitatively /'kwɒlɪtətɪvlɪ/ *adv* qualitativement.

quality /'kwɒlətɪ/ **I** *n* **1** (worth) qualité *f*; **good/poor ~** bonne/mauvaise qualité; **the ~ of life** la qualité de la vie; **2** (attribute) qualité *f*; **3**† **the ~** (upper classes) les gens de qualité†.
II *modif* [*car, jacket, food, workmanship, newspaper, press*] de qualité.

quality control I *n* contrôle *m* de qualité.
II *modif* [*techniques, procedure*] de contrôle de qualité.

quality controller ▶ 1692 *n* inspecteur/-trice *m/f* chargé/-e du contrôle de la qualité, qualiticien/-ienne *m/f*.

qualm /kwɑːm/ *n* scrupule *m*; **to have no ~s about doing** ne pas avoir le moindre scrupule à faire; **to suffer ~s of guilt** ou **conscience** avoir des scrupules.

quandary /'kwɒndərɪ/ *n* embarras *m*; (serious) dilemme *m*; **to be in a ~** être devant un dilemme (**about, over** à propos de).

quango /'kwæŋgəʊ/ *n* (*pl* **~s**) GB organisme *m* autonome d'État.

quanta /'kwɒntə/ *npl* ▶ **quantum**.

quantifiable /ˌkwɒntɪ'faɪəbl/ *adj* facile à évaluer.

quantifier /'kwɒntɪfaɪə(r)/ *n* Ling, Philos quantificateur *m*.

Quantities

Note the use of en (of it *or* of them) *in the following examples. This word must be included when the thing you are talking about is not expressed* (*the French says literally* there is of it a lot, there is of it two kilos, I have of them a lot *etc.*). *However,* en *is not needed when the commodity is specified e.g.* there is a lot of butter = il y a beaucoup de beurre.

how much is there?	= combien y en a-t-il?
there's a lot	= il y en a beaucoup*
there's not much	= il n'y en a pas beaucoup
there's two kilos	= il y en a deux kilos
how much sugar have you?	= combien de sucre as-tu?
I've got a lot	= j'en ai beaucoup
I've not got much	= je n'en ai pas beaucoup
I've got two kilos	= j'en ai deux kilos
how many are there?	= combien y en a-t-il?
there are a lot	= il y en a beaucoup
there aren't many	= il n'y en a pas beaucoup
there are twenty	= il y en a vingt
how many apples have you?	= combien de pommes as-tu? *or* tu as combien de pommes?
I've got a lot	= j'en ai beaucoup
I haven't many	= je n'en ai pas beaucoup
I've got twenty	= j'en ai vingt
A has got more than B	= A en a plus que B
A has got more money than B	= A a plus d'argent que B
much more than	= beaucoup plus que
a little more than	= un peu plus que
A has got more apples than B	= A a plus de pommes que B
many more apples than B	= beaucoup plus de pommes que B
a few more apples than B	= quelques pommes de plus que B
a few more people than yesterday	= quelques personnes de plus qu'hier
B has got less than A	= B en a moins que A
B has got less money than A	= B a moins d'argent que A
much less than	= beaucoup moins que
a little less than	= un peu moins que
B has got fewer than A	= B en a moins que A
B has got fewer apples than A	= B a moins de pommes que A
many fewer than	= beaucoup moins que

Relative quantities

how many are there to the kilo?	= combien y en a-t-il au kilo?
there are ten to the kilo	= il y en a dix au kilo
you can count six to the kilo	= il faut en compter six au kilo
how many do you get for ten francs?	= combien peut-on en avoir pour dix francs?
you get five for ten francs	= il y en a cinq pour dix francs
how much does it cost a litre?	= combien coûte le litre?
it costs £5 a litre	= ça coûte cinq livres le litre
how much do apples cost a kilo?	= combien coûte le kilo de pommes?
apples cost ten francs a kilo	= les pommes coûtent dix francs le kilo
how much does it cost a metre?	= combien coûte le mètre?
how much does your car do to the gallon?	= combien consomme votre voiture?
it does 28 miles to the gallon	= elle fait dix litres aux cent

(*Note that the French calculate petrol consumption in litres per 100 km. To convert mpg to litres per 100 km and vice versa, simply divide 280 by the known figure.*)

how many glasses do you get to the bottle?	= combien y a-t-il de verres par bouteille?
you get six glasses to the bottle	= il y a six verres par bouteille

* *Never use* très *with* beaucoup.

quantify /ˈkwɒntɪfaɪ/ *vtr* gen évaluer avec précision; Philos, Phys quantifier.

quantitative /ˈkwɒntɪtətɪv, US -teɪt-/ *adj* gen quantitatif/-ive; Literat de quantité; **~ analysis** Chem analyse quantitative.

quantitatively /ˈkwɒntɪtətɪvlɪ/ *adv* quantitativement.

quantity /ˈkwɒntətɪ/ ▶1604 **I** *n* gen, Literat quantité *f*; **in ~** en grande quantité; **a ~ of** une quantité de; **unknown ~** Math, fig inconnue *f*.
II *modif* [*purchase, sale*] en grande quantité; [*production*] en série.

quantity: **~ mark** *n* Literat signe *m* de quantité; **~ surveying** *n* métrage *m*; **~ surveyor** ▶1692 *n* métreur *m*.

quantum /ˈkwɒntəm/ **I** *n* (*pl* **-ta**) quantum *m*.
II *modif* [*mechanics, number, optics, statistics*] quantique.

quantum: **~ leap** *n* Phys saut *m* quantique; fig bond *m* prodigieux; **~ theory** *n* théorie *f* quantique.

quarantine /ˈkwɒrəntiːn, US ˈkwɔːr-/ **I** *n* quarantaine *f*; **in ~** en quarantaine; **to go into/come out of ~** être placé en/sortir de quarantaine; **six months' ~** six mois de quarantaine.
II *modif* [*hospital, kennels, period, laws*] de quarantaine.
III *vtr* mettre [qn/qch] en quarantaine.

quark /kwɑːk/ *n* quark *m*.

quarrel /ˈkwɒrəl, US ˈkwɔːrəl/ **I** *n* **1** (argument) dispute *f* (**between** entre; **over** au sujet de); **to have a ~** se disputer; **2** (feud) brouille *f* (**about, over** au sujet de); **to have a ~ with sb** être brouillé avec qn; **3** (difference of opinion) différend *m*; **to have no ~ with sb** ne rien avoir contre qn; **to have no ~ with sth** ne rien avoir à redire à qch.
II *vi* (*p prés etc* **-ll-**, US **-l-**) **1** (argue) se disputer; **2** (sever relations) se brouiller; **3** (dispute) **to ~ with** contester [*claim, idea, statistics*]; se plaindre de [*price, verdict*].

quarrelling, **quarreling** US /ˈkwɒrəlɪŋ, US ˈkwɔː-/ *n* ¢ disputes *fpl*; **stop your ~!** arrêtez de vous disputer!

quarrelsome /ˈkwɒrəlsəm, US ˈkwɔː-/ *adj* [*person, nature*] querelleur/-euse; [*comment, remark*] agressif/-ive.

quarry /ˈkwɒrɪ, US ˈkwɔːrɪ/ **I** *n* **1** (in ground) carrière *f*; **chalk/slate ~** carrière de craie/d'ardoise; **2** (prey) proie *f*; (in hunting) gibier *m* also fig.
II *vtr* (also **~ out**) extraire [*stone*].
III *vi* **to ~ for** extraire [*stone, gravel*].

quarry: **~man** ▶1692 *n* carrier *m*; **~ tile** *n* carreau *m* de terre cuite; **~-tiled floor** *n* carrelage *m* en terre cuite.

quart /kwɔːt/ ▶1068 *n* ≈ litre *m* (GB = *1.136 litres*, US = *0.946 litres*).
IDIOMS **you can't get a ~ into a pint pot** (ça ne peut pas entrer) il n'y a vraiment pas la place.

quarter /ˈkwɔːtə(r)/ ▶1096, 1143, 1883 **I** *n* **1** (one fourth) (of area, cake, litre, kilometre, tonne) quart *m*; **a ~ of a hectare/of the population** un quart d'hectare/de la population; **2** (15 minutes) **~ of an hour** quart *m* d'heure; **in ~ of an hour** dans un quart d'heure; **3** gen, Fin (three months) trimestre *m*; **4** (district) quartier *m*; **residential/poor/artists' ~** quartier résidentiel/pauvre/des artistes; **5** (group) milieu *m*; **there was criticism in some** ou **certain ~s** il y a eu des critiques dans certains milieux; **don't expect help from that ~** n'attends aucune aide de ce côté-là; **6** (mercy) littér quartier *m* liter, pitié *f*; **to get no ~ from sb** ne recevoir aucune pitié de la part de qn; **to give no ~** ne pas faire de quartier; **7** US (25 cents) vingt-cinq cents *mpl*; **8** GB Meas = 113,4 g; **9** US Meas = 12,7 kg; **10** Culin quartier *m*; **~ of beef** quartier de bœuf; **11** Sport (time period) quart *m* de temps; **12** Astron quartier *m*; **13** gen, Naut **on the port/starboard ~** par la hanche de bâbord/tribord; **a wind from a southerly ~** un vent du sud; **from all ~s of the globe** fig de tous les coins du monde; **14** Herald quartier *m*.
II quarters *npl* Mil quartiers *mpl*, gen logement *m*; **to take up ~s** se loger (**in** dans); **to retire to one's ~s** rentrer dans ses quartiers; **to be confined to ~s** Mil être cantonné dans ses quartiers; **single/married ~s** logements pour célibataires/familles; **servants' ~s** quartiers des domestiques; **we're living in very cramped ~s** nous vivons à l'étroit; **battle** ou **general ~s** Mil poste *m* de combat.
III *pron* **1** (25%) quart *m*; **only a ~ passed** seul le quart a réussi; **you can have a ~ now and the rest later** tu peux en avoir le quart maintenant et le reste plus tard; **2** (in time phrases) **at (a) ~ to 11** GB, **at a ~ of 11** US à onze heures moins le quart; **an hour and a ~** une heure et quart; **3** (in age) **she's ten and a ~** elle a dix ans et trois mois.
IV *adj* **she has a ~ share in the company** elle a un quart des actions de l'entreprise; **a ~ century** (25 years) un quart de siècle; (25 runs at cricket) *25 points au cricket*; **a ~ mile** ≈ *500 m*; **a ~ tonne** ≈ *250 kg*; **three and a ~ years** trois ans et trois mois.
V *adv* **a ~ full** au quart plein; **a ~ as big** quatre fois moins grand; **~ the price/size** quatre fois moins cher/grand.
VI at close quarters *adv phr* de près; **I had never seen a zebra at close ~s** je n'avais jamais vu un zèbre de près; **seen at close ~s, he's ugly** vu de près il est laid; **to fight at close ~s** lutter au corps à corps.
VII *vtr* **1** (divide into four) couper [qch] en quatre [*cake, apple*]; **2** (accommodate) cantonner [*troops*]; loger [*people*]; abriter [*livestock*]; **3** Hist (torture) écarteler [*prisoner*]; **4** Hunt [*dogs*] quêter.

quarter: **~back** *n* US quarterback *m* (*joueur qui dirige l'attaque*); **~-binding** *n* demi-reliure *f* (sans coins); **~-bound** *adj* demi-reliure *f*; [*book, manuscript*] en demi-reliure; **~-day** *n* (jour *m* du) terme *m*.

quarterdeck /ˈkwɔːtədek/ *n* **1** Naut (on ship) plage *f* arrière; **2** (officers) officiers *mpl*.

quarterfinal *n* quart *m* de finale.

quartering /ˈkwɔːtərɪŋ/ *n* **1** Mil cantonnement *m* (**on sb** chez qn); **2** Herald écartelure *f*.

quarter-light *n* Aut déflecteur *m*.

quarterly /ˈkwɔːtəlɪ/ **I** *n* Publg trimestriel *m*.
II *adj* trimestriel/-ielle.
III *adv* tous les trois mois.

quarter: **~master** ▶1612 *n* (in army) intendant *m*; (in navy) maître *m* de timonerie; **~master general** ▶1612 *n* Mil GB commissaire *m*; US commissaire *m* général de division; **~master sergeant** ▶1612 *n* US Mil fourrier *m*; **~-miler** *n* Sport ≈ spécialiste *mf* du 400 m; **~note** *n* US Mus noire *f*; **~-pounder** *n* Culin *hamburger contenant environ 100 grammes de bœuf*; **~staff** *n* Hist, Mil bâton *m*.

quartet /kwɔːˈtet/ *n* gen, Mus quatuor *m*; **piano/string ~** quatuor avec piano/à cordes; **jazz ~** quartette *m*.

quarto /ˈkwɔːtəʊ/ **I** *n* (*pl* **-tos**) in-quarto *m*; **bound in ~** relié in-quarto.
II *modif* [*size, book*] in-quarto.

quartz /kwɔːts/ **I** *n* quartz *m*.
II *modif* [*crystal, deposit, mine*] de quartz; [*clock, lamp, watch*] à quartz.

quartz glass *n* verre *m* de silice.

quartzite /ˈkwɔːtsaɪt/ *n* quartzite *m*.

quasar /ˈkweɪzɑː(r)/ *n* quasar *m*.

quash /kwɒʃ/ *vtr* **1** Jur annuler; **2** gen rejeter [*decision, proposal*]; réprimer [*rebellion*].

quasi+ /ˈkweɪzaɪ, ˈkwɑːzɪ/ (*dans composés*) quasi (+ *adj*), quasi- (+ *noun*); **~-military/-official** quasi militaire/officiel; **a ~-state** un quasi-État.

quatercentenary /ˌkwætəsenˈtiːnərɪ, US -ˈsentənerɪ/ *n* quatrième centenaire *m*.

quaternary /kwəˈtɜːnərɪ/ **I** *n* **1** Math quatre *m*; (set) ensemble *m* de quatre; **2** Geol **the Quaternary** le quaternaire.
II *adj* Chem, Geol quaternaire.

quatrain /ˈkwɒtreɪn/ *n* quatrain *m*.

quaver /ˈkweɪvə(r)/ **I** *n* **1** Mus GB croche *f*; **2** (trembling) tremblement *m* (**in** dans).
II *vtr* **'yes,' he ~ed** 'oui,' dit-il d'une voix tremblotante.
III *vi* trembloter.

quavering /ˈkweɪvərɪŋ/ **I** *n* tremblotement *m*.
II *adj* tremblotant.

quaveringly /ˈkweɪvərɪŋlɪ/ *adv* d'une voix tremblotante.

quavery /ˈkweɪvərɪ/ *adj* = **quavering** II.

quay /kiː/ *n* quai *m*; **at** ou **alongside the ~** à quai; **on the ~** sur le quai.

quayside /ˈkiːsaɪd/ *n* quai *m*; **at the ~** (boat) à quai; (people, cargo) sur le quai.

queasiness /ˈkwiːzɪnɪs/ *n* nausée *f*.

queasy /ˈkwiːzɪ/ *adj* **1** lit **to be** ou **feel ~** avoir mal au cœur; **to have a ~ stomach** (tendency) avoir l'estomac délicat; (temporary) avoir l'estomac un peu dérangé; **2** fig [*conscience*] mauvais; **to have a ~ feeling about sth, to feel ~ about sth** se sentir mal à l'aise en ce qui concerne qch.

Quebec /kwɪˈbek/ **▶ 1818** **I** *pr n* **1** (town) Québec *m*; **in ~** à Québec; **2** (province) Québec *m*; **in ~** au Québec.
II *modif* [*people, architecture, culture*] québécois.

Quebec(k)er /kwɪˈbekə(r)/, **Quebecois** /kwɪˈbekwɑː/ *n* Québécois/-e *m/f*.

Quechua /ˈketʃwə/ **▶ 1402** *n* Ling quechua *m*.

queen /kwiːn/ **I** *n* **▶ 1268** **1** (monarch) lit, fig reine *f*; **the Queen** la Reine; **Queen Anne** la Reine Anne; **2** Zool reine *f*; **3** Games (in chess) reine *f*; (in cards) dame *f*; **4**○ injur (homosexual) tante○ *f* offensive, homosexuel *m*.
II *vtr* (in chess) damer [*pawn*].
IDIOMS **to ~ it over sb** prendre des grands airs avec qn.

queen: **Queen Anne** *modif* [*chair, house*] de l'époque de la Reine Anne (*1702–14*); **Queen Anne's lace** *n* Bot carotte *f* fourragère.

queen bee *n* **1** Zool reine *f* des abeilles; **2** fig **she thinks she's (the) ~ bee** elle se prend pour la reine; **she's (the) ~ around here** c'est elle qui commande ici.

queen: **~ cake** *n* GB *petit gâteau aux raisins secs*; **~ consort** *n* reine *f* (*épouse du roi*); **~ dowager** *n* reine *f* douairière.

queenly /ˈkwiːnlɪ/ *adj* de reine.

queen: **~ mother** *n* Reine mère *f*; **~ post** *n* Constr poinçon *m*; **~ regent** *n* régente *f*; **Queen's Bench (Division)** *n* GB, Jur *division de la Cour Supérieure de Justice*; **Queen's Counsel, QC** *n* GB, Jur avocat *m* éminent (*qui tient son titre de la Reine*).

Queen's English *n* **to speak the ~** parler un anglais correct.

Queen's evidence *n* **to turn ~** GB Jur dénoncer ses complices contre promesse de pardon.

queen-size bed *n* grand lit *m* (*de 1,50 m de large*).

Queensland /ˈkwiːnzlənd/ *pr n* Queensland *m*.

Queen's Regulations *npl* GB Mil code *m* militaire.

Queen's shilling: IDIOMS **to take the ~** s'engager dans l'armée.

Queen's speech *n* GB Pol discours *m* du monarque à l'ouverture de la session parlementaire (*exposant le programme du gouvernement*).

queer /kwɪə(r)/ **I**○ *n* injur (homosexual) pédale○ *f* offensive, homosexuel *m*.
II *adj* **1** (strange) étrange, bizarre; **2** (suspicious) louche, suspect; **3**† GB (ill) patraque○; **to come over**○ ou **feel ~** se sentir mal or patraque○; **4**○ injur (homosexual) pédé◑ offensive, homosexuel/-elle.
IDIOMS **to ~ sb's pitch** contrecarrer les plans de qn; **to be in Queer Street** GB être dans une mauvaise passe.

queer bashing○ *n* injur agression *f* contre des homosexuels.

queerly /ˈkwɪəlɪ/ *adv* singulièrement.

queerness /ˈkwɪənɪs/ *n* singularité *f*, étrangeté *f*.

quell /kwel/ *vtr* étouffer [*anger, anxiety, revolt*]; **to ~ sb with a look** foudroyer qn du regard.

quench /kwentʃ/ *vtr* **1** littér éteindre [*flame*]; étancher [*thirst*]; étouffer [*desire, enthusiasm, hope*]; **2** Tech tremper [*metal*].

quern /kwɜːn/ *n* moulin *m* à bras.

querulous /ˈkwerʊləs/ *adj* grincheux/-euse.

querulously /ˈkwerʊləslɪ/ *adv* d'un ton grincheux.

query /ˈkwɪərɪ/ **I** *n* **1** (request for information) question *f* (**about** au sujet de); **to reply to** ou **answer a ~** répondre à une question; **a ~ from sb** une question venant de qn; **queries from customers/from parents** demandes *fpl* de renseignement venant des clients/des parents; **readers' queries** questions des lecteurs; **2** (expression of doubt) question *f* (**about** à propos de); **to raise a ~ about sth** soulever une question à propos de qch; **I have a ~ about your statement** j'ai une question à propos de votre déclaration; **3** Comput interrogation *f*; **4** (question mark) point *m* d'interrogation.
II *vtr* mettre en doute; **to ~ whether** se demander si; **nobody dares to ~ that** personne n'ose douter du fait que; **to ~ sb's ability** mettre en doute les capacités de qn; **we are ~ing the way the government is handling this matter** nous mettons en doute la façon dont le gouvernement s'occupe de l'affaire; **some may ~ my interpretation of the data** il se peut que certains doutent de mon interprétation des données.

query language *n* Comput langage *m* d'interrogation.

quest /kwest/ *n* quête *f*; **the ~ for sb/sth** la recherche de qn/qch; **his/their ~ to do** son/leur désir de faire; **to abandon/resume one's ~** abandonner/reprendre sa quête.

question /ˈkwestʃən/ **I** *n* **1** (request for information) question *f* (**about** sur); (in exam) question *f*; **to ask sb a ~** poser une question à qn; **answer the ~ about where you were last night** répondez à la question: où étiez-vous la nuit dernière?; **in reply to a ~ from Mr John Molloy** en réponse à une question posée par M. John Molloy; **to ask a ~** poser une question; **to put a ~ to sb** poser une question à qn; **to reply to** ou **to answer a ~** répondre à une question; **to reply to sb's ~** répondre à la question de qn; **to do sth without ~** faire qch sans poser de question; **what a ~!** en voilà une question!; **it's an open ~ as to whether he was innocent** la question reste posée de savoir s'il était innocent; **a ~ from the floor** (in parliament) une question provenant de l'assemblée; **to put down a ~ for sb** GB Pol poser une interpellation à qn; **2** (practical issue) problème *m*; (ethical issue) question *f*; **the Hongkong/Palestinian ~** la question de Hong-Kong/palestinienne; **the ~ of pollution/of military spending** le problème de la pollution/des dépenses militaires; **it's a ~ of doing** il s'agit de faire; **the ~ of animal rights** la question des droits des animaux; **the ~ of how to protect the hostages** le problème de la protection des otages; **the ~ of where to live/of what families want** le problème de savoir où habiter/de savoir ce que veulent les familles; **the ~ of whether** ou **as to whether they can do better** la question de savoir s'ils peuvent faire mieux; **the ~ for him now is how to react** la question pour lui est de savoir comment réagir; **the ~ arises as to who is going to pay the bill** la question se pose à savoir qui va payer la note; **the ~ raised is one of justice** il s'agit ici de justice; **that's another ~** c'est une autre affaire; **the ~ is whether/when** il s'agit ici de savoir si/quand; **there was never any ~ of you paying** il n'a jamais été question que tu paies; **the money/the person in ~** l'argent/la personne en question; **it's out of the ~** il c'est hors de question; **it's out of the ~ for him to leave** il est hors de question qu'il parte; **3** (uncertainty) doute *m*; **to call** ou **bring sth into ~** mettre qch en doute; **to prove beyond ~ that** prouver sans l'ombre d'un doute que; **it's open to ~** cela se discute; **whether we have succeeded is open to ~** qu'on ait réussi ou pas, cela se discute; **his honesty was never in ~** on n'a jamais douté de son honnêteté.
II *vtr* **1** (interrogate) questionner [*suspect, politician*]; **to ~ sb about sth** questionner qn à propos de qch; **to ~ sb closely** interroger qn minutieusement; **2** (cast doubt upon) (on one occasion) mettre en doute [*tactics, methods*]; (over longer period) douter de [*tactics, methods*]; **to ~ whether** douter que (+ *subj*); **he ~ed the use of arms against the people** il a mis en doute l'utilisation des armes contre le peuple.

questionable /ˈkwestʃənəbl/ *adj* (debatable) [*record, motive, decision*] discutable; (dubious) [*virtue, evidence, taste*] douteux/-euse; **it is ~ whether** il est douteux que (+ *subj*).

question-begging *n* Philos pétition *f* de principe.

questioner /ˈkwestʃənə(r)/ *n* interrogateur/-trice *m/f*; **police ~** enquêteur/-euse *m/f* de police; **his ~s asked him if he was going to resign** on lui a démandé s'il allait démissionner.

questioning /ˈkwestʃənɪŋ/ **I** *n* **1** (of person) interrogation *f*; (relentless) interrogatoire *m*; **~ about the scandal continues** on continue à poser des questions à propos du scandale; **to avoid ~ about sth** éviter les questions à propos de qch; **his ~ of his mother** l'interrogatoire auquel il a soumis sa mère; **the ~ of motorists by the police** l'interrogation des automobilistes par la police; **~ by police/reporters** un interrogatoire par la police/les journalistes; **to bring a suspect in for ~** amener un suspect pour interrogatoire; **he is wanted for ~ in connection with the explosion** la police le recherche suite à l'explosion; **to admit sth under ~** avouer qch pendant un interrogatoire; **a line of ~** une série de questions; **what is his line of ~?** quelles questions pose-t-il?; **police ~** interrogatoire *m* policier; **2** (of system, criteria, values) remise *f* en question (**of** de).
II *adj* **1** [*glance, look, tone*] interrogateur/-trice; **2** [*techniques, tactics*] d'interrogation; (by police, judge) d'interrogatoire.

question mark *n* **1** (in punctuation) point *m* d'interrogation; **2** (doubt) **there is a ~ about his honesty** on s'interroge quant à son honnêteté; **there is a ~ about his suitability for the job** on se demande s'il est apte à occuper ce poste; **there is a ~**

hanging over the factory/over his future l'incertitude plane sur l'usine/sur son avenir.

question master *n* animateur/-trice *m/f* de jeu.

questionnaire /ˌkwestʃəˈneə(r)/ *n* questionnaire *m* (**on** sur; **to do** pour faire); **to compile a ~** composer un questionnaire; **to fill in** ou **complete a ~** remplir un questionnaire; **a survey by ~** une étude établie à partir d'un questionnaire.

question: **~ tag** *n* Ling queue *f* de phrase interrogative, tag○ *m*; **~ time** *n* GB Pol *séance pendant laquelle les parlementaires posent des questions au gouvernement*.

queue /kjuː/ **I** *n* GB (of people) queue *f*, file *f* (d'attente); (of vehicles) file *f*; **to stand in a ~** faire la queue; **to join the ~** [*person*] se mettre à la queue; [*car*] se mettre dans la file; **go to the back of the ~!** à la queue!; **to jump the ~**○ passer avant son tour also fig.
II *vi* GB = **queue up**.
■ **queue up** [*people*] faire la queue (**for** pour); [*taxis*] attendre en ligne; **to ~ up to do sth** fig se précipiter pour faire qch.

queue-jump *vi* GB resquiller, passer avant son tour.

queue: **~-jumper** *n* GB resquilleur/-euse *m/f* (*dans une queue*); **~-jumping** *n* GB resquille○ *f* (*dans une queue*).

quibble /ˈkwɪbl/ **I** *n* chicane *f* (**about, over** sur).
II *vi* chicaner (**about, over** sur).

quibbler /ˈkwɪblə(r)/ *n* chicaneur/-euse *m/f*.

quibbling /ˈkwɪblɪŋ/ **I** *n* chicanerie *f*.
II *adj* chicanier/-ière.

quiche /kiːʃ/ *n* quiche *f*.

quick /kwɪk/ **I** *n* Anat, Med chair *f* vive; **to bite one's nails to the ~** se ronger les ongles jusqu'au sang.
II *adj* **1** (speedy) [*pace, train, heartbeat*] rapide; [*solution, reply, profit, result*] rapide; [*storm, shower of rain*] bref/brève; [*meal*] sur le pouce, rapide; **to make a ~ phone call** passer un coup de téléphone rapide; **to have a ~ coffee** prendre un café en vitesse; **I'm going to have a ~ wash** je vais faire une toilette rapide; **the ~est way to get there is**... le chemin le plus rapide pour y aller est...; **she's a ~ worker** elle travaille vite; **the ~est way to lose your friends is to**... le meilleur moyen de perdre ses amis est de...; **she wasn't ~ enough** elle n'a pas été assez rapide; **we'll have to make a ~ decision** il faudra que nous nous décidions rapidement; **we're hoping for a ~ sale** nous espérons que cela se vendra rapidement; **we had a ~ chat about our plans** nous avons rapidement discuté de nos projets; **to make a ~ recovery** se rétablir vite; **to pay a ~ visit to sb** faire une petite visite à qn; **be ~ (about it)!** dépêche-toi!; **a ~ hit** (on drugs) sensation *f* de jouissance brève et forte (*due à la prise de drogue*); **2** (clever) [*child, student*] vif/vive d'esprit; **to be ~ at arithmetic** être bon/bonne en arithmétique; **3** (prompt) **to be ~ to do** être prompt à faire; **to be ~ to anger/take offence/defend one's friends** être prompt à s'emporter/s'offenser/défendre ses amis; **to be ~ to learn, to be a ~ learner** apprendre vite; **to be (too) ~ to criticize/condemn** critiquer/condamner (trop) facilement; **to be ~ to admit one's mistakes** être prêt à reconnaître ses erreurs; **she was ~ to see the advantages** elle a tout de suite vu les avantages; **4** (lively) **to have a ~ temper** s'emporter facilement; **a ~ temper** un tempérament vif; **to have a ~ wit** avoir l'esprit vif.
III *adv* **(come) ~!** (viens) vite!; **(as) ~ as a flash** avec la rapidité de l'éclair.
IDIOMS **a ~ one** = **quickie I 1, 2, 3; the ~ and the dead** les vivants et les morts; **to cut** ou **sting sb to the ~** piquer qn au vif; **to make a ~ buck** gagner de l'argent facile; **to make a ~ killing** faire fortune rapidement.

quick: **~-assembly** *adj* facile à monter; **~ assets** *npl* Fin disponibilités *fpl*; **~-change artist** *n*: *artiste qui change de déguisement rapidement pour interpréter différents personnages*; **~-drying** *adj* qui sèche rapidement.

quicken /ˈkwɪkən/ **I** *vtr* **1** lit accélérer [*pace, rhythm*]; **2** fig, littér stimuler [*interest, excitement*].
II *vi* **1** lit [*pace, rhythm, heartbeat*] s'accélérer; **2** fig, littér [*anger, jealousy*] s'intensifier; **3** [*fœtus*] bouger.

quickening /ˈkwɪkənɪŋ/ *n* **1** lit (of heartbeat) accélération *f*; **2** fig, littér (of interest, life) éveil *m*; **3** (of fœtus) éveil *m*.

quick fire /ˈkwɪkfaɪə/ **I** *n* lit tir *m* rapide.
II quick-fire *modif* [*question, sketch*] rapide.

quick-freeze *vtr* (*prét* **-froze**, *pp* **-frozen**) surgeler.

quickie○ /ˈkwɪkɪ/ *n* **1** (drink) pot○ *m* en vitesse; **2** (question) question *f* rapide; **3**◑ GB **to have a ~** faire l'amour en vitesse; **4** US Cin *film fait rapidement et à petit budget*.

quickie divorce○ *n* divorce *m* à l'amiable.

quicklime *n* chaux *f* vive.

quickly /ˈkwɪklɪ/ *adv* (rapidly) vite, rapidement; (without delay) sans tarder; **the police arrived ~** la police est arrivée très vite, la police est arrivée rapidement; **the problem was ~ resolved** le problème a été vite résolu or résolu rapidement; **we must sort this problem out ~** il nous faut régler ce problème sans tarder; **(come) ~!** (viens) vite!; **as ~ as possible** aussi vite que possible; **I acted ~ on his advice** je me suis dépêché de suivre ses conseils; **I ~ changed the subject** je me suis empressé de changer de sujet; **she dealt with the problem ~ and efficiently** elle s'occupa du problème promptement et efficacement.

quick march Mil **I** *n* ≈ pas *m* cadencé.
II *excl* ≈ pas cadencé marche!

quickness /ˈkwɪknɪs/ *n* **1** (speed) (of person, movement) rapidité *f*; **~ to respond/react** promptitude *f* à répondre/réagir; **2** (nimbleness) (of person, movements) vivacité *f*; **3** (liveliness of mind) vivacité *f* d'esprit.

quick: **~sand** *n* ¢ lit sables *mpl* mouvants; fig bourbier *m*; **~-set hedge** *n* haie *f* vive; **~-setting** *adj* à prise rapide.

quicksilver /ˈkwɪksɪlvə(r)/ **I** *n* Chem mercure *m*, vif-argent† *m*.
II *modif* fig **~ wit** esprit *m* très vif.

quickstep /ˈkwɪkstep/ *n* (dance, dance tune) quickstep *m*; (march tune) musique *f* de cadence.

quick: **~-tempered** *adj* coléreux/-euse, qui s'emporte facilement; **~thorn** *n* aubépine *f*; **~ time** *n* US marche *f* rapide; **~ trick** *n* (in bridge) levée *f* assurée; **~-witted** *adj* [*person*] à l'esprit vif; [*reaction*] vif/vive.

quid /kwɪd/ *n* **1**○ GB (*pl* **~**) livre *f* (sterling); **2** (tobacco) chique *f*.

quiddity /ˈkwɪdətɪ/ *n* Philos quiddité *f*.

quid pro quo /ˌkwɪd prəʊ ˈkwəʊ/ *n* contrepartie *f*.

quiescence /kwaɪˈesns, kwɪˈesns/ *n* (of person) passivité *f*.

quiescent /kwaɪˈesnt, kwɪˈesnt/ *adj* [*person*] passif/-ive; [*mood, state*] tranquille; [*soul, spirit*] en repos.

quiet /ˈkwaɪət/ **I** *n* **1** (silence) silence *m*; **in the ~ of the morning** dans le silence du petit matin; **~ please!** silence, s'il vous plaît!; **2** (peace) tranquillité *f*; **the ~ of the countryside** la tranquillité de la campagne; **let's have some peace and ~** pourrions-nous avoir un peu de calme maintenant; **3**○ (secret) **to do sth on the ~** faire qch discrètement.
II *adj* **1** (silent) [*church, person, room*] silencieux/-ieuse; **to keep** ou **stay ~** garder le silence; **to go ~** [*person, assembly*] se taire; **the room went ~** la salle s'est tue; **to keep sth ~** empêcher [qch] de faire du bruit [*bells, machinery*]; faire taire [*dog, child*]; **be ~** (stop talking) tais-toi; (make no noise) ne fais pas de bruit; **you're ~, are you OK?** tu es bien silencieux, ça va?; **2** (not noisy) [*voice*] bas/basse; [*car, engine*] silencieux/-ieuse; [*music*] doux/douce; [*cough, laugh*] discret/-ète; **in a ~ voice** à voix basse; **that should keep the children ~** cela devrait tenir les enfants tranquilles; **3** (discreet) [*diplomacy, chat*] discret/-ète; [*deal*] en privé; [*confidence, optimism*] serein; [*despair, rancour*] voilé; [*colour, stripe*] sobre, discret/-ète; **I had a ~ laugh over it** j'en ai ri sous cape; **to have a ~ word with sb** parler avec qn en privé; **4** (calm) [*village, holiday, night*] tranquille; **business/the stock market is ~** le marché/la Bourse est calme; **to lead a ~ life** mener une vie tranquille; **OK! anything for a ~ life!** tout ce que tu veux pourvu que je sois tranquille!; **5** (for few people) [*dinner, meal*] intime; [*wedding, funeral*] célébré dans l'intimité; **6** (docile) [*child, pony*] paisible; **7** (secret) **to keep [sth] ~** ne pas divulguer [*plans*]; garder [qch] secret/-ète [*engagement*].
III *vtr* US **1** (calm) calmer [*crowd, class*]; **2** (allay) dissiper [*fears, doubts*]; **3** (silence) faire taire [*person*].

quieten /ˈkwaɪətn/ *vtr* **1** (calm) calmer [*child, crowd, animal*]; **2** (allay) dissiper [*fear, doubts*]; **3** (silence) faire taire [*critics, children*].
■ **quieten down**: ¶ **~ down 1** (become calm) [*person, queue, activity*] se calmer; **I'll wait for things to ~ down** je vais attendre que les choses se calment; **2** (fall silent) se taire; ¶ **~ down [sb/sth], ~ [sb/sth] down 1** (calm) calmer [*baby, crowd, animal*]; **2** (silence) faire taire [*child, class*].

quietism /ˈkwaɪətɪzəm/ *n* quiétisme *m*.

quietist /ˈkwaɪətɪst/ *n, adj* quiétiste (*mf*).

quietly /ˈkwaɪətlɪ/ *adv* **1** (not noisily) [*move, tread*] sans bruit; [*cough, speak, sing, play*] doucement; **2** (silently) [*play, read, sit*] en silence; **3** (discreetly) [*pleased, optimistic, confident*] modérément; **to be ~ confident that** avoir la conviction intime que; **4** (simply) [*live*] simplement; [*get married*] sans cérémonie; **5** (calmly) calmement; **6** (soberly) [*dress, decorate*] de façon discrète.

quietness /ˈkwaɪətnɪs/ *n* **1** (silence) silence *m*, calme *m*; **2** (calmness) (of person) douceur *f*; **3** (lowness) (of voice) faiblesse *f*; **4** (lack of activity) (of village, street) tranquillité *f*.

quietude /ˈkwaɪɪtjuːd, US -tuːd/ *n* littér quiétude *f*.

quiff /kwɪf/ *n* GB (on forehead) toupet *m*; (on top of head) houppe *f*.

quill /kwɪl/ *n* **1** (feather) penne *f*; (stem of feather) tuyau *m* de plume; **2** (on porcupine) piquant *m*; **3** (also **~ pen**) (for writing) plume *f* d'oie.

quilt /kwɪlt/ **I** *n* **1** GB (duvet) couette *f*; **2** (bed cover) dessus *m* de lit.
II *vtr* matelasser.
III quilted *pp adj* [*cover, garment*] matelassé.

quilting /ˈkwɪltɪŋ/ *n* (technique) matelassage *m*; (fabric) matelassure *f*.

quilting bee *n* US groupe *m* de couturières (*de patchwork*).

quim● /kwɪm/ *n* GB chatte● *f*, sexe *m* féminin.

quin /kwɪn/ *n* GB *abrév* = **quintuplet**.

quince /kwɪns/ *n* (fruit) coing *m*; (tree) cognassier *m*.

quincentenary /ˌkwɪnsenˈtiːnərɪ, US -ˈsentənerɪ/ *n* cinq centième anniversaire *m*.

quinine /kwɪˈniːn, US ˈkwaɪnaɪn/ *n* quinine *f*.

Quinquagesima /ˌkwɪŋkwəˈdʒesɪmə/ *n* Quinquagésime *f*.

quinquennial /kwɪnˈkwenɪəl/ *adj* quinquennal.
quinsy /ˈkwɪnzɪ/ *n* abcès *m* periamygdalien.
quint /kwɪnt/ *n* US = **quintuplet**.
quintessence /kwɪnˈtesns/ *n* (perfect example) parfait exemple *m*; (essential part) quintessence *f*.
quintessential /ˌkwɪntɪˈsenʃl/ *adj* [*character, quality*] fondamental; **he is the ~ Renaissance man** c'est l'homme de la Renaissance par excellence.
quintet /kwɪnˈtet/ *n* Mus quintette *m*.
quintuple **I** /ˈkwɪntjʊpl, US kwɪnˈtu:pl/ *adj* quintuple.
II /kwɪnˈtjʊpl/ *vtr* quintupler.
quintuplet /ˈkwɪntju:plet, US kwɪnˈtu:plɪt/ *n* quintuplé/-e *m/f*.
quip /kwɪp/ **I** *n* trait *m* d'esprit.
II *vi* (*p prés etc* **-pp-**) plaisanter.
quire /ˈkwaɪə(r)/ *n* Print (4 folded sheets) cahier *m*; (24 or 25 sheets) main *f*.
quirk /kwɜ:k/ *n* (of person) excentricité *f*; (of fate, nature) caprice *m*.
quirky /ˈkwɜ:kɪ/ *adj* excentrique.
quisling /ˈkwɪzlɪŋ/ *n* péj collaborateur/-trice *m/f* pej.
quit /kwɪt/ **I** *adj* **to be well ~ of sth/sb** être bien débarrassé de qch/qn.
II *vtr* (*p prés* **-tt-**, *prét, pp* **quit** ou **quitted**) (leave) démissionner de, laisser tomber○ [*job*]; quitter [*place, person, profession, school*]; quitter [*politics, teaching*]; **to give a tenant notice to ~** donner congé à un locataire.
III *vi* (*p prés* **-tt-**, *prét, pp* **quit** ou **quitted**) **1** (stop, give up) arrêter (**doing** de faire); **I've had enough, I ~** j'en ai assez, je laisse tomber; **to ~ whilst one is ahead** ou **on top** gen s'arrêter avant que les choses se gâtent; (in career) partir au summum de la gloire; **2** (resign) [*employee, boss*] démissionner; [*politician*] démissionner; **he ~ as chairman** il a démissionné de son poste de président.
quite /kwaɪt/ *adv* **1** (completely) [*new, ready, differently*] tout à fait; [*alone, amazed, empty, exhausted, obnoxious, ridiculous*] complètement; [*impossible*] totalement; [*justified*] entièrement; [*extraordinary, peculiar*] vraiment; **I ~ agree** je suis tout à fait or complètement d'accord; **I ~ understand** je comprends tout à fait; **you're ~ right** vous avez complètement raison; **you're ~ wrong** vous vous trompez complètement; **it's ~ all right** (in reply to apology) c'est sans importance; **it's ~ out of the question** il n'en est pas du tout question, c'est complètement hors de question; **I can ~ believe it** je veux bien le croire; **are you ~ sure?** en êtes-vous certain?; **to be ~ aware of sth/that** être tout à fait conscient de qch/du fait que; **~ frankly** très franchement; **I saw it ~ clearly** je l'ai vu très clairement; **it's ~ clear** c'est parfaitement clair; **it's ~ clear to me that** pour moi il est complètement évident que; **he's ~ clearly mad/stupid** il est manifestement complètement fou/stupide; **and ~ right too!** à juste titre!; **that's ~ enough!** ça suffit!; **have you ~ finished?** iron ce sera tout?; **2** (exactly) **not ~** pas exactement; **it's not ~ what I wanted** ce n'est pas exactement ce que je voulais; **I'm not ~ sure** je ne sais pas exactement; **not ~ so much** un petit peu moins; **not ~ as many as last time** pas tout à fait autant que la dernière fois, un peu moins que la dernière fois; **not ~ as interesting/expensive** pas tout à fait aussi or un peu moins intéressant/cher; **he didn't ~ understand** il ne comprenait pas vraiment; **I don't ~ know** je ne sais pas du tout; **nobody knew ~ what he meant** personne ne savait exactement ce qu'il voulait dire; **it's not ~ that** ce n'est pas tout à fait ça; **that's not ~ all** (giving account of sth) et ce n'est pas tout; **3** (definitely) **it was ~ the best answer/the most expensive seat** c'était de loin la meilleure réponse/la place la plus chère; **he's ~ the stupidest man!** il est vraiment stupide!; **our whisky is ~ simply the best!** Advertg notre whisky est tout simplement le meilleur!; **4** (rather) [*big, wide, easily, often*] assez; **it's ~ small** ce n'est pas très grand; **it's ~ good** ce n'est pas mauvais; **it's ~ cold today** il ne fait pas chaud aujourd'hui; **it's ~ warm today** il fait bon aujourd'hui; **it's ~ likely that** il est très probable que; **I ~ like Chinese food** j'aime assez la cuisine chinoise; **~ a few** ou **~ a lot of people/examples etc** un bon nombre de personnes/d'exemples etc; **~ a lot of money** pas mal d'argent; **~ a lot of opposition** une opposition assez forte; **it's ~ a lot colder/warmer today** il fait nettement plus froid/plus doux aujourd'hui; **I've thought about it ~ a bit** j'y ai pas mal réfléchi; **5** (as intensifier) **~ a difference/drop** une différence/baisse considérable; **that will be ~ a change for you** ça te changera beaucoup; **she's ~ a woman, she's ~ some woman!** quelle femme!; **that was ~ some party!** quelle soirée!; **their house/car is really ~ something**○ leur maison/voiture vaut le coup d'œil○; **it was ~ a sight** iron ça valait le coup d'œil○; **6** (expressing agreement) c'est sûr; **'he could have told us'—'~ (so)'** 'il aurait pu nous le dire'—'c'est sûr'.
quits○ /kwɪts/ *adj* **to be ~** être quitte (**with sb** envers qn); **to call it ~** en rester là; **let's call it ~!** restons-en là!
quitter○ /ˈkwɪtə(r)/ *n* **he's a ~** il n'est pas tenace; **I'm no ~** quand je commence quelque chose je le termine.
quiver /ˈkwɪvə(r)/ **I** *n* **1** (trembling) (of voice, part of body) tremblement *m*; (of leaves) frémissement *m*; **a ~ of excitement** un frémissement d'excitation; **2** (for arrows) carquois *m*.
II *vi* [*hand, voice, lip, animal*] trembler (**with** de); [*leaves*] frémir; [*wings, eyelids*] battre; [*flame*] vaciller.
qui vive /ˌki: ˈvi:v/ *n* **to be on the ~** être sur le qui-vive.
quixotic /kwɪkˈsɒtɪk/ *adj* (chivalrous) chevaleresque; (unrealistic) chimérique.
quixotically /kwɪkˈsɒtɪklɪ/ *adv* de manière chevaleresque.
quiz /kwɪz/ **I** *n* (*pl* **~zes**) **1** (game) jeu *m* de questions-réponses, quiz *m*; (written, in magazine) questionnaire *m* (**about** sur); **a sports/general knowledge ~** un jeu de questions-réponses sur le sport/en culture générale; **2** US Sch interrogation *f*.
II *vtr* (*p prés etc* **-zz-**) questionner (**about** au sujet de).
quiz: **~ game**, **~ show** *n* jeu *m* de questions-réponses; **~ master** *n* animateur *m* de jeu de questions-réponses.
quizzical /ˈkwɪzɪkl/ *adj* interrogateur/-trice.
quizzically /ˈkwɪzɪklɪ/ *adv* d'un air interrogateur.
quod○ /kwɒd/ *n* GB taule○ *f*.
quoin /kɔɪn/ *n* pierre *f* d'angle.
quoit /kɔɪt, US kwɔɪt/ **I** *n* palet *m*.
II **▶ 1282** **quoits** *npl* jeu *m* de palet; **to play ~s** jouer au palet.
quondam /ˈkwɒndæm/ *adj* ancien/-ienne (*before n*).
Quonset hut® /ˈkwɒnsɪt/ *n* US Mil baraquement *m* (*en tôle, de forme allongée et semi-cylindrique*).
quorate /ˈkwɔ:rət, -reɪt/ *adj* GB **the meeting is ~** la réunion a atteint le quorum.
Quorn® /kwɔ:n/ *n* aliment *m* à base de protéines végétales.
quorum /ˈkwɔ:rəm/ *n* quorum *m*; **the ~ is ten** le quorum est fixé à dix; **to have a ~** avoir atteint le quorum.
quota /ˈkwəʊtə/ *n* **1** gen, Comm, EC (prescribed number) quota *m* (**of, for** de); **this year's ~** le quota fixé pour cette année; **milk/export ~s** quotas laitiers/d'exportation; **we haven't got our full ~ of passengers** nous n'avons pas notre quota de passagers; **2** (share) part *f* (**of** de); (officially allocated) quote-part *f*.
quotable /ˈkwəʊtəbl/ *adj* (that may be quoted) que l'on peut citer; (worth quoting) digne d'être cité; **what she said just wasn't ~** ce qu'elle a dit était trop grossier pour être répété.
quota system *n* Comm, EC système *m* de quotas.
quotation /kwəʊˈteɪʃn/ *n* **1** (phrase, passage cited) citation *f*; **2** (estimate) devis *m*; **3** Fin cours *m*, cote *f*.
quotation marks *npl* guillemets *mpl*; **to put sth in ~**, **to put ~ around sth** mettre qch entre guillemets.
quote /kwəʊt/ **I** *n* **1** (quotation) citation *f* (**from** de); **2** (statement to journalist) déclaration *f*; **3** (estimate) devis *m*; **4** Fin cote *f*.
II quotes *npl* = **quotation marks**.
III *vtr* **1** (repeat, recall) citer [*person, passage, proverb*]; rapporter [*words*]; rappeler [*reference number*]; **to ~ Shakespeare/the Bible** citer Shakespeare/la Bible; **to ~ sb/sth as an example** citer qch/qn en exemple; **please ~ this number in all correspondence** veuillez rappeler ce numéro dans toute correspondance; **don't ~ me on this, but...** ne répète pas ce que je dis, mais...; **she was ~d as saying that** elle aurait dit que; **to ~ Plato,...** pour citer Platon,...; **2** Comm (state) indiquer [*price, figure*]; **they ~d us £200 for repairing the car** dans leur devis, ils ont demandé £200 pour la réparation de la voiture; **3** (on stock exchange) coter [*share, price*] (**at** à); **~d company/share** société *f*/valeur *f* cotée en Bourse; **to be ~d on the Stock Exchange** être coté à la Bourse; **4** Turf **to ~ odds of 3 to 1** proposer une cote de 3 à 1; **to be ~d 6 to 1** être coté entre 6 et 1.
IV *vi* (from text, author) faire des citations; **to ~ from Keats/the classics** citer Keats/les classiques; **~ ... unquote** (in dictation) ouvrez les guillemets ... fermez les guillemets; (in lecture, speech) je cite ... fin de citation; **he's in Paris on ~ 'business' unquote** il est à Paris soi-disant pour affaires.
quoth /kwəʊθ/ *vtr*‡ **'alas,' ~ he** 'hélas,' fit-il.
quotient /ˈkwəʊʃnt/ *n* **1** Math quotient *m*; **2** gen niveau *m*.
qv (*abrév écrite* = **quod vide**) voir.
QWERTY, **qwerty** /kwɜ:tɪ/ *adj* **~ keyboard** clavier *m* qwerty.

r, R /ɑ:(r)/ *n* **1** (letter) r, R *m*; **the three R's** l'écriture, la lecture et le calcul; **2 R** *abrév écrite* = **right**; **3 R** *abrév écrite* = **river**; **4 R** GB *abrév* = **Rex, Regina**.

RA *n* GB (*abrév* = **Royal Academy**) membre *m* de l'Académie Royale des Arts.

RAAF *n* (*abrév* = **Royal Australian Air Force**) Armée *f* de l'air australienne.

rabbet /ˈræbɪt/ *n* rainure *f*.

rabbet plane *n* guillaume *m*.

rabbi /ˈræbaɪ/ *n* rabbin *m*; **the Chief Rabbi** le grand rabbin.

rabbinic(al) /rəˈbɪnɪk(l)/ *adj* rabbinique.

Rabbinic /rəˈbɪnɪk/ ▶ **1402** *n* (language) hébreu *m* rabbinique.

rabbit /ˈræbɪt/ **I** *n* gen (male) lapin *m*; (female) lapine *f*; (fur, meat) lapin *m*; **a tame/wild ~** un lapin domestique/de garenne.
II *modif* [*stew, pie*] de lapin; [*jacket*] en lapin.
III *vi* **to go ~ing** aller à la chasse au lapin.
IDIOMS **to breed like ~s** se reproduire comme des lapins; **to pull a ~ out of a hat** fig faire un coup de théâtre.
■ **rabbit on**○ GB parler sans cesse (**about** de).

Rabbit® /ˈræbɪt/ *pr n* Telecom ≈ Bibop® *m*.

rabbit: **~ burrow** *n* terrier *m* de lapin; **~ ears** *n* US (TV aerial) antenne *f* d'intérieur (*en V*); **~ hole** *n* = **rabbit burrow**; **~ hutch** *n* clapier *m*; **~ punch** *n* coup *m* du lapin; **~ warren** *n* lit garenne *f*; fig (maze) labyrinthe *m*.

rabble /ˈræbl/ *n* péj **1** (crowd) foule *f*; **2** (populace) **the ~** la populace pej.

rabble-rouser /ˈræblraʊzə(r)/ *n* agitateur/-trice *m/f*.

rabble-rousing /ˈræblraʊzɪŋ/ **I** *n* incitation *f* à la violence.
II *adj* qui incite à la violence.

Rabelaisian /ˌræbəˈleɪzɪən/ *adj* rabelaisien/-ienne.

rabid /ˈræbɪd, US ˈreɪbɪd/ *adj* **1** Vet enragé; **2** (fanatical) fanatique.

rabidly /ˈræbɪdlɪ, US ˈreɪ-/ *adv* farouchement.

rabies /ˈreɪbi:z/ ▶ **1354** **I** *n* rage *f*; **to have ~** avoir la rage.
II *modif* [*controls, injection, legislation*] antirabique; [*virus*] de la rage.

RAC *n* GB (*abrév* = **Royal Automobile Club**) organisme *m* d'assistance pour les automobilistes.

raccoon /rəˈku:n, US ræ-/ **I** *n* (*pl* **~s** ou **~**) raton *m* laveur.
II *modif* [*garment*] en raton laveur.

race /reɪs/ **I** *n* **1** Sport course *f* (**between** entre; **against** contre); **to come fifth in a ~** arriver cinquième dans une course; **to have a ~** faire la course (**with** avec; **against** contre); **to run a ~** courir (**with** contre); **boat/bicycle ~** course nautique/cycliste; **a ~ against the clock** lit, fig une course contre la montre; **2** fig (contest) course *f* (**for** à; **to do** pour faire); **the ~ to reach the moon** la course à la lune; **presidential/mayoral ~** course à la présidence/à la mairie; **a ~ against time** une course contre la montre; **3** Anthrop, Sociol race *f*; **of an ancient ~** d'une race ancienne; **discrimination on the grounds of ~** discrimination *f* raciale; **4** Bot, Zool espèce *f*; **5** (current) courant *m* fort.
II races *npl* Turf courses *fpl*.
III *modif* [*attack, equality, hatred, law*] racial.
IV *vtr* **1** (compete with) faire la course avec [*person, jockey, car, horse*]; **to ~ sb to sth** faire la course avec qn jusqu'à qch; **2** (rush) **to ~ to do** se précipiter pour faire; **3** (enter for race) faire courir [*horse, dog*]; courir en [*car, bike, boat, yacht*]; courir sur [*Ferrari, Formula One*]; faire voler [qch] en compétition [*pigeon*]; **4** (rev) faire ronfler [*engine*].
V *vi* **1** (compete in race) courir (**against** contre; **at** à; **to** vers; **with** avec); **to ~ around the track** faire le tour de la piste; **2** (rush, run) **to ~ in/out** entrer/sortir en courant; **to ~ after sb/sth** courir après qn/qch; **to ~ down the stairs/the street** dévaler l'escalier/la rue; **to ~ for the house/the train** courir pour atteindre la maison/attraper le train; **to ~ through** faire [qch] rapidement [*exercise, task*]; **3** [*heart, pulse*] battre précipitamment; [*engine*] s'emballer; **my mind started to ~** je me suis mis à imaginer toutes sortes de choses; **4** (hurry) se dépêcher (**to do** de faire); **to ~ against time** courir contre la montre.
■ **race away** partir en courant; **to ~ away from** [*runner*] se détacher de [*pack*]; gen s'éloigner en courant de [*person, place*].
■ **race by** [*time, person, bike*] passer à toute allure.

race: **~ card** *n* Turf programme *m* des courses; **~course** *n* champ *m* de courses; **~goer** *n* Turf turfiste *mf*; **~horse** *n* cheval *m* de course.

raceme /rəˈsi:m, ˈræsi:m, US reɪˈsi:m/ *n* Bot grappe *f*.

race meeting *n* GB réunion *f* de courses.

racer /ˈreɪsə(r)/ *n* **1** (bike) vélo *m* de course; (motorbike) moto *f* de course; **2** (yacht) voilier *m* de course; **3** (car) voiture *f* de course; **4** (dog) chien *m* de course; **5** (horse) cheval *m* de course; **6** (runner, cyclist etc) coureur/-euse *m/f*.

race: **~ relations** *npl* relations *fpl* interraciales; **~ riot** *n* émeute *f* raciale.

racetrack /ˈreɪstræk/ *n* Sport **1** Turf champ *m* de courses; **2** (track) (for cars) circuit *m*; (for dogs, cycles) piste *f*.

raceway /ˈreɪsweɪ/ *n* US (for cars) circuit *m*; (for dogs, harness racing) piste *f*.

Rachmanism /ˈrækmənɪzəm/ *n* pej GB intimidation *f* de locataires (*par un propriétaire pour obtenir leur départ*).

racial /ˈreɪʃl/ *adj* (all contexts) racial.

racialism /ˈreɪʃəlɪzəm/ *n* racisme *m*.

racialist /ˈreɪʃəlɪst/ *n, adj* raciste (*mf*).

racially /ˈreɪʃəlɪ/ *adv* [*mixed, balanced, segregated, tolerant*] racialement; **the attack was ~ motivated** l'attaque avait le racisme pour mobile.

raciness /ˈreɪsɪnɪs/ *n* **1** (lively quality) verve *f*; **2** (risqué quality) audace *f*.

racing /ˈreɪsɪŋ/ **I** *n* **1** Turf hippisme *m*, sport *m* hippique; **did you see the ~?** as-tu vu les courses (de chevaux)?; **2** (with cars, bikes, boats, dogs) course *f*; **motor ~** GB, **car ~** US course automobile; **pigeon ~** concours *m* de pigeons voyageurs.
II *modif* [*car, bike, boat, yacht*] de course; [*fan, commentator*] des courses.

racing: **~ colours** GB, **~ colors** US *n* couleurs *fpl* d'une écurie; **~ cyclist** *n* coureur/-euse *m/f* cycliste; **~ driver** *n* coureur/-euse *m/f* automobile; **~ pigeon** *n* pigeon *m* de compétition; **~ stable** *n* écurie *f* de courses.

racism /ˈreɪsɪzəm/ *n* racisme *m*.

racist /ˈreɪsɪst/ *n, adj* raciste (*mf*).

rack /ræk/ **I** *n* **1** (stand) (for plates) égouttoir *m*; (in dishwasher) panier *m*; (for luggage on train etc) compartiment *m* à bagages; (for clothes) portant *m*; (for cakes) grille *f* (*à gâteau*); (for bottles) casier *m*; (for newspapers) porte-revues *m inv*; (shelving) étagère *f*; ▶ **roof rack**; **2** (torture) chevalet *m*; **to put sb on the ~** mettre qn sur le chevalet; **to be on the ~** fig être au supplice; **3** Culin **~ of lamb** carré *m* d'agneau.
II *vtr* **1** fig (torment) [*pain, guilt, fear*] torturer; [*cough, sobs*] secouer; **to be ~ed with guilt/with sobs** être torturé par le remords/secoué de sanglots; **an industry ~ed by crisis** une industrie très éprouvée par la crise; **2** Wine siphonner.
IDIOMS **to ~ one's brains** se creuser la cervelle○; ▶ **ruin**.
■ **rack up**○ US: **~ up [sth]** décrocher [*victory*]; marquer [*points*]; remporter [*success*].

rack: **~-and-pinion** *n* Aut, Tech crémaillère *f*; **~-and-pinion steering** *n* Aut direction *f* à crémaillère.

racket /ˈrækɪt/ **I** *n* **1** Sport raquette *f*; **2**○ (noise) vacarme *m*, raffut○ *m*; **to make a ~** faire du vacarme, faire du raffut; **3** (swindle) escroquerie *f*; **it's a ~!** c'est de l'escroquerie!; **4** (illegal activity) trafic *m*; **the drugs ~** le trafic des stupéfiants; **he's in on the ~**○ il est dans le coup○; **5**○ (business) métier *m*, boulot○ *m*.
II *modif* Sport [*cover, handle, string, control*] de raquette.
■ **racket around**○ (noisily) faire du vacarme; (having fun) faire la fête.

racket abuse *n* Sport **to be penalized for ~** être pénalisé pour jet de raquette.

racketeer /ˌrækəˈtɪə(r)/ *n* racketteur *m*.

racketeering /ˌrækəˈtɪərɪŋ/ *n* racket *m*.

racket press *n* Sport presse-raquette *m inv*.

rackets /ˈrækɪts/ *n* (+ *v sg*) ≈ squash *m*.

racking /ˈrækɪŋ/ *adj* [*pain*] atroce; [*sobs*] déchirant.

rack railway *n* chemin *m* de fer à crémaillère.

raconteur /ˌrækɒnˈtɜ:(r)/ *n* conteur/-euse *m/f*.

racoon *n* = **raccoon**.

racquet *n* = **racket I 1**.

racquetball /ˈrækɪtbɔ:l/ ▶ **1282** *n* US ≈ squash *m* (*avec raquette à manche court*).

racy /ˈreɪsɪ/ *adj* **1** (lively, spirited) [*account, style, book*] plein de verve; **2** (risqué) osé.

RADA /ˈrɑːdə/ *n* GB (*abrév* = **Royal Academy of Dramatic Art**) Académie *f* d'art dramatique (britannique).

radar /ˈreɪdɑː(r)/ **I** *n* radar *m*; **by ~** par radar.
II *modif* [*beacon, echo, operator, screen, station*] radar.

radar: **~ astronomy** *n* radarastronomie *f*; **~ scanner** *n* déchiffreur *m* de radar.

radar trap *n* contrôle-radar *m inv*; **to get caught in a ~** se faire piéger par un radar; **to go through a ~** passer devant un radar.

raddle /ˈrædl/ Agric **I** *n* (harness) collier *m* marqueur.
II *vtr* marquer [*ram*].

raddled /ˈrædld/ *adj* **1** (worn) [*woman*] au visage marqué par la vie; [*features*] marqué par la vie; **2** (over made-up) péj [*woman*] peinturluré pej.

radial /ˈreɪdɪəl/ **I** *n* (also **~ tyre**) pneu *m* radial.
II *adj* [*lines, roads*] rayonnant; [*engine, layout*] en étoile.

radiance /ˈreɪdɪəns/, **radiancy** /ˈreɪdɪənsɪ/ *n* **1** (brightness) éclat *m*; (softer) lueur *f*; **2** fig (of beauty, smile) éclat *m*, rayonnement *m*.

radiant /ˈreɪdɪənt/ **I** *n* **1** (on electric fire) résistance *f* chauffante; **2** Astron point *m* radiant.
II *adj* **1** fig [*person, beauty, smile*] radieux/-ieuse; **to be ~ with** être rayonnant de [*joy, health*]; **2** (shining) éclatant; **3** Phys [*heat, energy*] radiant.

radiantly /ˈreɪdɪəntlɪ/ *adv* [*shine*] d'un vif éclat; [*smile*] d'un air radieux; **~ beautiful** d'une beauté radieuse.

radiate /ˈreɪdɪeɪt/ **I** *vtr* **1** [*person*] rayonner de [*health, happiness*]; déborder de [*confidence*]; **2** Phys émettre [*heat*].
II *vi* **1 to ~ from sb** [*confidence, happiness*] émaner de qn; **to ~ out from sth** [*roads, buildings etc*] rayonner (à partir) de qch; **2** Phys [*heat*] rayonner; [*light*] irradier.
III radiating *pres p adj* [*roads, lines*] en étoile.

radiation /ˌreɪdɪˈeɪʃn/ **I** *n* **1** Med, Nucl radiation *f*; **to be exposed to ~** être exposé à des radiations; **a high level of ~** un taux élevé de radiations; **a low level of ~** un faible niveau de radiations; **a dose of ~** une dose de radiations; **2** Phys rayonnement *m*.
II *modif* [*levels*] de radiation; [*effects*] des radiations; [*leak*] de radiations.

radiation: **~ exposure** *n* irradiation *f*; **~ processing** *n* traitement *m* des produits radioactifs; **~ sickness** *n* mal *m* or maladie *f* des rayons; **~ therapy** *n* radiothérapie *f*; **~ worker** *n* travailleur/-euse *m/f* de l'industrie nucléaire.

radiator /ˈreɪdɪeɪtə(r)/ **I** *n* **1** (for heat) radiateur *m*; **to put on/turn off a ~** allumer/éteindre un radiateur; **to turn up/down a ~** monter/baisser le chauffage; **2** Aut radiateur *m*.
II *modif* [*cap, thermostat, valve*] de radiateur.

radiator grille *n* Aut calandre *f*.

radical /ˈrædɪkl/ **I** *n* **1** Pol radical/-e *m/f*; **2** Chem **free ~s** radicaux *mpl* libres.
II *adj* gen, Pol radical.

radicalism /ˈrædɪkəlɪzəm/ *n* radicalisme *m*.

radicalize /ˈrædɪkəlaɪz/ *vtr* radicaliser.

radically /ˈrædɪklɪ/ *adv* radicalement.

radices /ˈreɪdɪsiːz/ *pl* ▶ **radix**.

radicle /ˈrædɪkl/ *n* **1** Bot radicule *f*; **2** Chem radical *m*.

radii /ˈreɪdɪaɪ/ *pl* ▶ **radius**.

radio /ˈreɪdɪəʊ/ **I** *n* (*pl* **~s**) **1** Audio radio *f*; **on the ~** à la radio; **she was on the ~ this morning** elle est passée à la radio ce matin; **2** Telecom radio *f*; **to send a message by ~** [*ship, taxi cab*] envoyer un message (par) radio.
II *modif* [*contact, engineer, equipment, operator, receiver, signal, transmitter*] radio *inv*; [*mast, programme*] de radio.
III *vtr* (*3e pers sg prés* **~s**; *prét, pp* **~ed**) **to ~ sb that** envoyer à qn un message radio disant que; **to ~ sb for sth** appeler qn par radio pour demander qch; **to ~ sth (to sb)** communiquer qch par radio (à qn).
IV *vi* (*3e pers sg prés* **~s**; *prét, pp* **~ed**) **to ~ for help** appeler au secours par radio.

radio: **~active** *adj* radioactif/-ive; **~activity** *n* radioactivité *f*; **~ alarm (clock)** *n* radio-réveil *m*; **~ announcer** *n* speaker/-erine *m/f*; **~ astronomy** *n* radioastronomie *f*; **~ beacon** *n* radiophare *m*; **~biology** *n* radiobiologie *f*; **~ broadcast** *n* émission *f* de radio, émission *f* radiophonique; **~ broadcasting** *n* radio *f*; **~ button** *n* Comput case *f* d'option; **~ cab** *n* radio-taxi *m*; **~ car** *n* voiture-radio *f*; **~carbon** *n* radiocarbone *m*; **~carbon dating** *n* datation *f* au carbone quatorze; **~ cassette (recorder)** *n* radiocassette *f*; **~chemistry** *n* radiochimie *f*; **~ communication** *n* contact *m* radio *inv*; **~ compass** *n* radiocompas *m*; **~-controlled** *adj* [*toy, boat*] télécommandé; [*taxi*] radioguidé; **~ documentary** *n* documentaire *m* radiophonique; **~element** *n* radioélément *m*; **~ frequency** *n* radiofréquence *f*.

radiogram† /ˈreɪdɪəʊgræm/ GB *n* combiné *m* radio et pick-up.

radiograph /ˈreɪdɪəʊgrɑːf, US -græf/ *n* radiographie *f*.

radiographer /ˌreɪdɪˈɒgrəfə(r)/ ▶ 1692 *n* manipulateur/-trice *m/f* radiographe.

radiography /ˌreɪdɪˈɒgrəfɪ/ *n* radiographie *f*.

radio: **~ ham○** *n* radio-amateur *m*; **~ interview** *n* entretien *m* radiophonique; **~isotope** *n* isotope *m* radioactif; **~ journalist** *n* journaliste *mf* de radio; **~ link** *n* liaison *f* radio *inv*.

radiological /ˌreɪdɪəˈlɒdʒɪkl/ *adj* radiologique.

radiologist /ˌreɪdɪˈɒlədʒɪst/ ▶ 1692 *n* radiologue *mf*.

radiology /ˌreɪdɪˈɒlədʒɪ/ **I** *n* radiologie *f*.
II *modif* [*department*] de radiologie.

radiolysis /ˌreɪdɪˈɒləsɪs/ *n* radiolyse *f*.

radiometer /ˌreɪdɪˈɒmɪtə(r)/ *n* radiomètre *m*.

radio: **~ microphone**, **~ mike○** *n* micro *m* sans fil; **~-phonograph†** *n* US combiné *m* radio et pick-up; **~ play** *n* pièce *f* pour la radio.

radioscopy /ˌreɪdɪˈɒskəpɪ/ *n* radioscopie *f*.

radio: **~ set†** *n* poste *m* de radio; **~ silence** *n* silence *m* radio; **~ source**, **~ star** *n* radiosource *f*; **~ station** *n* (channel) station *f* de radio; (installation) station *f* émettrice; **~ taxi** *n* radio-taxi *m*; **~telephone** *n* radiotéléphone *m*; **~telephony** *n* radiotéléphonie *f*; **~ telescope** *n* radiotélescope *m*; **~therapist** *n* radiothérapeute *mf*; **~therapy** *n* radiothérapie *f*; **~ wave** *n* onde *f* radio.

radish /ˈrædɪʃ/ *n* radis *m*.

radium /ˈreɪdɪəm/ *n* radium *m*.

radium therapy *n* curiethérapie *f*.

radius /ˈreɪdɪəs/ *n* (*pl* **-dii** ou **-diuses**) **1** Math rayon *m* (**of** de); **2** (distance) rayon *m*; **within a 10 km ~ of here** dans un rayon de 10 km; **3** Anat radius *m*.

radix /ˈreɪdɪks/ *n* (*pl* **-dices**) base *f*.

radon /ˈreɪdɒn/ *n* radon *m*.

RAF *n* GB Mil *abrév* ▶ **Royal Air Force**.

raffia /ˈræfɪə/ **I** *n* raphia *m*.
II *modif* [*basket, mat*] en raphia.

raffish /ˈræfɪʃ/ *adj* littér [*person, behaviour*] libertin; [*figure, look*] canaille; [*place*] mal famé.

raffle /ˈræfl/ **I** *n* tombola *f*; **in a ~** à une tombola.
II *modif* [*prize, ticket*] de tombola.
III *vtr* ▶ **raffle off**.
■ **raffle off**: **~ off [sth]** mettre [qch] en tombola.

raft /rɑːft, US ræft/ *n* **1** (floating) radeau *m*; **2○** US (lot) **~s** ou **a ~ of** un tas de○.

rafter /ˈrɑːftə(r), US ˈræftə(r)/ *n* Constr chevron *m*.

rafting /ˈrɑːftɪŋ, US ˈræftɪŋ/ *n* rafting *m*; **to go ~** faire du rafting.

rag /ræg/ **I** *n* **1** (cloth) chiffon *m*; **a bit of ~** un chiffon; **2○** (newspaper) (local) canard○ *m*; péj (tabloid) torchon○ *m* pej, quotidien *m* populaire; **3** (also **~time**) rag *m*.
II rags *npl* (old clothes) loques *fpl*; **in ~s** en haillons.
III○ *vtr* (*p prés etc* **-gg-**) **to ~ sb** taquiner qn (**about** à propos de).
IDIOMS **it's like a red ~ to a bull** ça a le don de l'exciter; **to be on the ~●** US (menstruate) avoir ses règles; **to feel like a wet ~** se sentir vidé; **to go from ~s to riches** connaître une ascension spectaculaire; **a ~s-to-riches story** une histoire de réussite sociale spectaculaire; **to lose one's ~○** GB sortir de ses gonds○.

ragamuffin /ˈrægəmʌfɪn/ *n* **1†** (urchin) va-nu-pieds *mf inv*; **2** Mus ragamuffin *m*.

rag: **~-and-bone man○†** *n* GB chiffonnier *m*; **~bag** *n* fig (jumble) ramassis *m*; **~ doll** *n* poupée *f* de chiffon.

rage /reɪdʒ/ **I** *n* **1** (anger) rage *f*, colère *f*; **tears of ~** des larmes de rage; **purple with ~** rouge de colère; **trembling with ~** tremblant de rage; **2** (fit of anger) colère *f*; **sudden ~s** des colères soudaines; **to be in/to fly into a ~** être/entrer dans une colère noire; **3○** (fashion) **to be (all) the ~** faire fureur; **it's all the ~ in Paris** ça fait fureur à Paris.
II *vi* **1** [*storm, fire, battle*] faire rage (**across, through** à travers); [*controversy, debate*] se déchaîner (**over, about** à propos de); **2** [*angry person*] tempêter (**at, against** contre); **3○** (party) faire la fête.

ragged /ˈrægɪd/ *adj* **1** (tatty) [*garment, cloth*] en loques; [*cuff, collar*] effiloché; [*person*] dépenaillé; **2** (uneven) [*lawn, hedgerow, fringe, beard*] irrégulier/-ière; [*outline, cloud*] déchiqueté; **3** (motley) [*group, community*] disparate; **4** (in quality) [*performance, race*] inégal.
IDIOMS **to run sb ~○** épuiser qn.

ragged robin *n* Bot coucou *m*.

raging /ˈreɪdʒɪŋ/ *adj* **1** (of feelings) [*passion, argument, hatred*] violent; [*thirst, hunger, pain*] atroce; **a ~ toothache** une rage de dents; **she was absolutely ~** elle était folle de rage; **2** (of forces) [*blizzard, sea*] déchaîné; **there was a ~ storm** la tempête faisait rage.

raglan /ˈræglən/ *adj* raglan *inv*.

rag rug *n* tapis *m* en lirette.

ragtag○ /ˈrægtæg/ *adj* péj [*group, organisation*] désordonné.
IDIOMS **the ~ and bobtail○** la canaille.

ragtime /ˈrægtaɪm/ *n* (also **~ music**) ragtime *m*.

ragtop○ /ˈrægtɒp/ *n* US décapotable *f*.

rag trade○ /ˈrægtreɪd/ *n* **the ~** la confection.

rag: **~weed** *n* Bot ambroisie *f*; **~ week** *n* GB Univ semaine *f* du carnaval étudiant (*au profit d'institutions caritatives*); **~wort** *n* jacobée *f*.

rah /rɑː/ *excl* US hourra!

rah-rah○ /ˈrɑːrɑː/ *adj* US [*response*] hyper-enthousiaste; **~ skirt** jupette *f* à volants.

raid /reɪd/ **I** *n* **1** (attack) (military) raid *m* (**on** sur); (on bank) hold-up *m* (**on** de); (on home) cambriolage *m* (**on** de, dans); (by police, customs) rafle *f* (**on** dans); **to carry out a ~** [*military*] faire un raid; [*robbers*] attaquer; [*police*] faire une rafle; **2** Fin (on stock market) raid *m* (**on** sur).
II *vtr* **1** (attack) [*military*] faire un raid sur [*base, town*]; [*robbers*] attaquer [*bank*]; cambrioler [*house*]; [*police*] faire une rafle dans [*pub, office, house*]; **2** fig hum casser

[*piggybank*]; faire une razzia○ sur [*fridge, orchard*]; **3** Fin [*company*] entamer [*fund, reserves*].

raider /ˈreɪdə(r)/ *n* **1** (thief) pillard *m*; **2** Fin (corporate) raider *m*, attaquant *m*; **3** (soldier) (membre *m* d'un) commando *m*; **4** Mil Naut navire *m* de course.

rail /reɪl/ **I** *n* **1** (for protection, support) (in fence) barreau *m*; (on balcony) balustrade *f*; (on bridge, tower) parapet *m*, garde-fou *m*; (handrail) rampe *f*; (on ship) bastingage *m*; **2** (for display) (in shop) présentoir *m*; **3** (for curtains) tringle *f*; ▶**towel rail**, **picture rail**; **4** Transp (track) rail *m*; **by ~** [*travel, send*] par rail.
II rails *npl* Turf corde *f*; **to come up on the ~s** tenir la corde.
III *modif* [*network, traffic, transport*] ferroviaire; [*journey, travel*] en train; **~ strike** grève *f* des cheminots; **~ ticket** billet *m* de train.
IV *vi* sout **to ~ against** ou **at** s'insurger contre [*injustice, pollution, politician*].
IDIOMS **to go off the ~s** dérailler○.
■ **rail off**: **~ [sth] off, ~ off [sth]** séparer [qch] par un grillage [*areas*]; entourer [qch] d'un grillage [*area*].

rail: **~car** *n* autorail *m*; **~card** *n* GB carte *f* d'abonnement; **~ fence** *n* US palissade *f* de rondins; **~head** *n* tête *f* de ligne.

railing /ˈreɪlɪŋ/ *n* **1** (also **~s**) (in street, park, stadium) grille *f*; **2** (on wall) main courante *f*; (on tower) garde-fou *m*; (on balcony) balustrade *f*.

raillery /ˈreɪlərɪ/ *n* littér raillerie *f* liter.

railroad /ˈreɪlrəʊd/ **I** *n* US Rail **1** (network) chemin *m* de fer; **2** (also **~ track**) voie *f* ferrée; **3** (company) compagnie *f* des chemins de fer.
II *modif* US Rail [*industry, link, tunnel, accident*] ferroviaire; [*bridge, tracks*] de chemin de fer.
III *vtr* **1**○ (push) **to ~ sb into doing** forcer qn à faire; **to ~ the bill through (parliament)** tout faire pour faire adopter le projet de loi (par le parlement); **2** US (send by rail) expédier [qch] par chemin de fer; **3**○ US (imprison) expédier○ [qn] en prison.

railroad car *n* US (for goods) wagon *m*; (for people) voiture *f*, wagon *m*.

rail terminus *n* GB (gare *f*) terminus *m*.

railway /ˈreɪlweɪ/ GB Rail **I** *n* **1** (network) chemin *m* de fer; **to use the ~s** voyager en train; **2** (also **~ line**) ligne *f* (de chemin de fer); **light/high-speed ~** ligne locale/à grande vitesse; **3** (also **~ track**) voie *f* ferrée; **4** (company) compagnie *f* des chemins de fer.
II *modif* [*bridge*] de chemin de fer; [*museum*] des chemins de fer; [*link, tunnel, accident*] ferroviaire.

railway: **~ carriage** *n* GB (for goods) wagon *m*; (for people) voiture *f*, wagon *m*; **~ embankment** *n* remblai *m*; **~ engine** *n* GB locomotive *f*; **~ junction** *n* gare *f* de jonction or de raccordement.

railway line *n* GB **1** (route) ligne *f* de chemin de fer; **2** (tracks) voie *f* ferrée.

railway: **~man** ▶**1692** GB *n* cheminot *m*; **~ station** *n* GB gare *f*.

raiment‡ /ˈreɪmənt/ *n* habits *mpl*.

rain /reɪn/ **I** *n* **1** Meteorol pluie *f*; **the ~ was falling** ou **coming down** la pluie tombait, il pleuvait; **the ~ started/stopped** il a commencé à/il s'est arrêté de pleuvoir; **a light/heavy ~** une pluie fine/battante; **steady/driving/pouring ~** pluie régulière/battante/diluvienne; **in the ~** sous la pluie; **come in out of the ~!** rentre, ne reste pas sous la pluie!; **it looks like ~** le temps est à la pluie; **2** fig (of arrows, ash) pluie *f* (**of** de).
II rains *npl* saison *f* des pluies; **the ~s have failed** la saison a été sèche.
III *modif* [*cloud, hood, water*] de pluie.
IV *vtr* **to ~ blows on sb** [*person*] rouer qn de coups; **to ~ questions/compliments on sb** inonder qn de questions/compliments.
V *v impers* **1** Meteorol pleuvoir; **it's ~ing** il pleut; **it ~ed all night/all summer** il a plu toute la nuit/tout l'été; **it was ~ing hard** il pleuvait à verse; **2** fig = **rain down**.
IDIOMS **come ~ or shine** qu'il pleuve ou qu'il vente; **it never ~s but it pours** un malheur n'arrive jamais seul; **to be (as) right as ~** GB [*person*] se porter comme un charme; [*object*] être en parfait état de marche.
■ **rain down**: ¶ **~ down** [*blows, bullets, ash, insults*] pleuvoir (**on, onto** sur); ¶ **~ down [sth], ~ [sth] down** faire pleuvoir (**on, onto** sur).
■ **rain off** GB **to be ~ed off** (cancelled) être annulé pour cause de pluie; (stopped) être interrompu par la pluie.
■ **rain out** US = **rain off**.

rainbow /ˈreɪnbəʊ/ **I** *n* lit, fig arc-en-ciel *m*.
II *modif* [*colours, stripes*] de l'arc-en-ciel.
IDIOMS **at the ~'s end** du domaine du rêve.

rainbow trout *n* (*pl* **~**) truite *f* arc-en-ciel.

rain chart *n* carte *f* pluviométrique.

rain check *n* US **1** Comm *ticket permettant au client de réserver un article à prix réduit en cas de rupture de stock*; **2** Sport *billet pour un autre match si le premier est annulé pour cause de pluie*.
IDIOMS **to take a ~ on sth** reporter qch.

rain: **~coat** *n* imperméable *m*; **~drop** *n* goutte *f* de pluie.

rainfall /ˈreɪnfɔːl/ *n* niveau *m* de précipitations; **50 cm of ~** un niveau de précipitations de 50 cm; **heavy/low ~** fortes/faibles précipitations.

rain forest *n* forêt *f* tropicale humide; **to save the ~s** sauver la forêt tropicale; **the ~s of Brazil** les forêts tropicales du Brésil.

rain gauge *n* pluviomètre *m*.

rainless /ˈreɪnlɪs/ *adj* sec/sèche.

rain: **~maker** *n* faiseur/-euse *m/f* de pluie; **~making** *n* rites *mpl* pour faire venir la pluie; **~ shadow** *n* zone *f* sous le vent à l'abri de la pluie; **~-soaked** *adj* [*person, garment*] trempé de pluie; [*ground*] détrempé par la pluie; **~storm** *n* trombe *f* d'eau; **~wear** *n* vêtements *mpl* de pluie.

rainy /ˈreɪnɪ/ *adj* [*afternoon, climate, place*] pluvieux/-ieuse; **~ day** jour *m* pluvieux or de pluie; **~ season** saison *f* des pluies.
IDIOMS **to keep** ou **save something for a ~ day** mettre de l'argent de côté; **I'm saving it for a ~ day** je le mets de côté pour le jour où j'en aurai besoin.

raise /reɪz/ **I** *n* **1** US (pay rise) augmentation *f*; **2** Games (in poker) mise *f* supérieure; (in bridge) annonce *f* supérieure.
II *vtr* **1** (lift) lever [*baton, barrier, curtain*]; hisser [*flag*]; soulever [*box, trap door, lid*]; élever [*level, standard*]; renflouer [*sunken ship*]; **to ~ one's hand/head** lever la main/tête; **to ~ one's hands above one's head** lever les mains au-dessus de la tête; **he ~d the glass to his lips** il a porté le verre à ses lèvres; **to ~ a glass to sb** lever son verre à l'honneur de qn; **to ~ one's hat to sb** soulever son chapeau pour saluer qn; **I've never ~d a hand to my children** je n'ai jamais levé la main sur mes enfants; **to ~ an eyebrow** lit froncer les sourcils; **nobody ~d an eyebrow at my suggestion** fig ma suggestion n'a fait sourciller personne; **to ~ sb from the dead** ressusciter qn; **2** (place upright) dresser [*mast, flagpole*]; redresser [*patient*]; **3** (increase) augmenter [*fees, price, offer, salary, volume*] (**from** de; **to** à); élever [*standard*]; reculer [*age limit*] (**for** pour); **to raise sb's awareness** ou **consciousness of** sensibiliser qn à; **to ~ one's voice** (to be heard) parler plus fort; (in anger) élever la voix; **to ~ one's voice against** fig élever la voix contre; **to ~ the temperature** lit, fig faire monter la température; **to ~ sb's hopes** donner de faux espoirs à qn; **to ~ one's sights** augmenter ses prétentions; **4** (cause) faire naître [*doubts, fears, suspicions*]; rappeler [*memories*]; soulever [*dust*]; **to ~ a storm of protest** provoquer une tempête de protestations; **to ~ a cheer** [*speech*] déclencher des hourras; **to ~ a laugh/smile** [*joke*] faire rire/sourire; **to ~ a fuss** faire des histoires○; **to ~ a commotion** faire du vacarme○; **5** (mention) soulever [*issue, objection, problem, possibility*]; **please ~ any queries** ou **questions now** si vous avez des questions, posez-les maintenant; **6** (bring up) élever [*child, family*]; **to be ~d (as) an atheist/a Catholic** être élevé dans l'athéisme/la foi catholique; **7** (breed) élever [*livestock*]; **8** (find) trouver [*capital, money*]; **I need to ~ 3,000 dollars** il faut que je trouve 3 000 dollars; **9** (form) lever [*army*]; former [*team*]; **10** (collect) lever [*tax*]; obtenir [*support*]; collecter [*money*]; **they ~d money for charity** ils ont collecté de l'argent pour une œuvre de charité; **the gala ~d a million dollars** le gala a permis de collecter un million de dollars; **the money ~d from the concert was donated to UNICEF** la recette du concert a été donnée à l'UNICEF; **I ~d £300 against my watch** j'ai engagé ma montre pour 300 livres sterling; **11** (erect) élever [*monument, statue*] (**to sb** en l'honneur de qn); **12** (end) lever [*ban, siege*]; **13** (contact) contacter [*person*]; **I can't ~ her on the phone** je n'arrive pas à la joindre au téléphone; **14** (give) **to ~ the alarm** lit sonner l'alarme; fig donner l'alarme; **she ~d a smile** elle a eu un sourire forcé; **15** (improve) **to ~ the tone** hausser le ton; **to ~ sb's spirits** remonter le moral à qn; **16** (increase the stake) **I'll ~ you 200 dollars!** 200 dollars de mieux!; **to ~ the bidding** (in gambling) monter la mise; (at auction) monter l'enchère; **17** Math **to ~ a number to the power (of) three/four** élever un chiffre à la puissance trois/quatre.
III *v refl* **to ~ oneself** se redresser; **to ~ oneself to a sitting position** se redresser (en position assise); **to ~ oneself up on one's elbows** prendre appui sur ses coudes.

raised /reɪzd/ *pp adj* [*platform, jetty*] surélevé; **I heard ~ voices** j'ai entendu des éclats de voix; **to cause ~ eyebrows** faire froncer les sourcils; **there were ~ eyebrows when I suggested it** ma suggestion a fait froncer les sourcils.

raised: **~ beach** *n* Geol plage *f* soulevée; **~-head** *adj* (*épith*) Tech à tête saillante.

raiser /ˈreɪzə(r)/ *n* Agric éleveur/-euse *m/f*.

raisin /ˈreɪzn/ *n* raisin *m* sec; **seedless ~** raisin sec sans pépins.

raising agent *n* Culin agent *m* de levage.

Raj /rɑːdʒ/ *n* GB Hist **the ~** (gouvernement *m* de) l'empire *m* britannique aux Indes.

rajah /ˈrɑːdʒə/ *n* radjah *m*.

rake /reɪk/ **I** *n* **1** (tool) râteau *m*; (in casino) râteau *m* de croupier; **2**† (libertine) débauché *m*; **3** (slope) inclinaison *f*; **4** (angle) angle *m* d'inclinaison; **5** Naut (of bow) élancement *m*; (of mast) quête *f*.
II *vtr* **1** Agric, Hort ratisser [*earth*]; **to ~ sth into a pile** ratisser qch en tas; **2** (scan) [*gun, beam, soldier*] balayer [*enemy, ground, sky*]; **her eyes ~d the horizon** elle a parcouru l'horizon du regard.
III *vi* **to ~ among** ou **through** fouiller dans [*papers, possessions*].
IV raked *pp adj* incliné.
■ **rake in**○: **~ in [sth]** amasser [*money, profits*]; **he's raking it in**○! il remue l'argent à la pelle○!
■ **rake out**: **~ [sth] out, ~ out [sth]** étouffer [*fire*].
■ **rake over**: **~ over [sth]** **1** lit ratisser [*soil, flowerbed*]; **2** fig remuer [*memories*].
■ **rake up**: **~ up [sth], ~ [sth] up** **1** lit ratisser, ramasser [qch] avec un râteau [*leaves, weeds*]; **2** fig ressusciter [*grievance*]; remuer [*past*].

rake-off○ /ˈreɪkɒf/ *n* (legal) commission *f*; (illicit) ristourne *f* illicite.

rakish /ˈreɪkɪʃ/ *adj* **1**† (dissolute) débauché; **2** (jaunty) désinvolte; **to wear one's hat at a ~ angle** porter son chapeau de façon désinvolte.

rally /ˈrælɪ/ **I** *n* **1** (meeting) rassemblement *m*; **peace ~** rassemblement pour la paix; **2** (car race) rallye *m*; **3** (in tennis) échange *m*; **4** (recovery) gen amélioration *f* (**in** dans); Fin reprise *f*.
II *modif* [*car, circuit, course, driver*] de rallye.
III *vtr* (gather) rassembler [*support, supporters, troops*]; rallier [*public opinion*]; **to ~ one's supporters around** ou **behind one** rassembler ses supporters autour de soi.
IV *vi* **1** (come together) [*people, troops*] se rallier (**to** à); **to ~ to the defence of sb** se porter au secours de qn; **to ~ to the cause** se rallier à la cause; **2** (recover) [*dollar, prices*] remonter; [*patient*] se rétablir; [*sportsperson*] se ressaisir; **her spirits rallied** elle a repris courage.
■ **rally round, rally around**: ¶ **~ round** [*friends, supporters*] se rallier; ¶ **~ round [sb]** soutenir [*person*].

rally driving ▶ 1282 *n* rallye *m*.

rallying /ˈrælɪɪŋ/ *n* rallye *m*; **to go ~** faire des rallyes.

rallying: **~ call, ~ cry** *n* lit, fig cri *m* de ralliement; **~ point** *n* lit, fig point *m* de ralliement.

ram /ræm/ **I** *n* **1** Zool, Astrol bélier *m*; **2** Constr (of pile driver) marteau *m*; Tech (plunger) (piston *m*) plongeur *m*; **hydraulic ~** bélier *m* hydraulique.
II *vtr* (*p prés etc* **-mm-**) **1** (crash into) [*vehicle*] rentrer dans, heurter [*car, boat etc*]; **2** (push) enfoncer [*fist, object*] (**into** dans).
III *vi* (*p prés etc* **-mm-**) **to ~ into sth** [*vehicle*] rentrer dans qch, heurter qch.
■ **ram down**: **~ [sth] down, ~ down [sth]** enfoncer qch.
■ **ram home**: **~ [sth] home, ~ home [sth]** lit placer [*ball, fist*]; fig faire clairement comprendre [*message, point*].

RAM /ræm/ *n* (*abrév* = **random access memory**) RAM *f*.

Ramadan /ˌræməˈdæn, -ˈdɑːn/ *n* ramadan *m*.

ramble /ˈræmbl/ **I** *n* (planned) randonnée *f* (pédestre); (casual) balade *f* (à pied); **to go for a ~** faire une randonnée.
II *vi* **1** (walk) (with itinerary) faire une randonnée; (without itinerary) faire une balade; **2** Hort [*plant*] grimper.
■ **ramble on** (talk) discourir (**about** sur).

rambler /ˈræmblə(r)/ *n* **1** (hiker) randonneur/-euse *m/f*; **2** Hort plante *f* grimpante.

rambling /ˈræmblɪŋ/ **I** *n* randonnée *f*.
II *adj* **1** [*house*] plein de coins et de recoins; [*town*] construit au hasard; **2** [*talk, article*] décousu; **3** Hort grimpant.

rambunctious○ /ræmˈbʌŋkʃəs/ *adj* US exubérant.

RAMC *n* (*abrév* = **Royal Army Medical Corps**) service *m* de santé de l'armée britannique.

ramekin /ˈræməkɪn/ *n* ramequin *m*.

ramification /ˌræmɪfɪˈkeɪʃn/ *n* gen, Anat, Bot ramification *f*.

ramify /ˈræmɪfaɪ/ **I** *vtr* ramifier.
II *vi* se ramifier.

ramjet (engine) /ˈræmdʒet/ *n* Aviat statoréacteur *m*.

ramp /ræmp/ *n* gen rampe *f*; (for wheelchair) rampe *f* d'accès; (in roadworks) GB dénivellation *f*; (to slow traffic) GB ralentisseur *m*; Aut, Tech (for raising vehicle) pont *m* de graissage; Aviat passerelle *f*; US Aut (on, off highway) bretelle *f*; **hydraulic ~** pont *m* élévateur.

rampage **I** /ˈræmpeɪdʒ/ *n* **to be** ou **go on the ~** tout saccager.
II /ræmˈpeɪdʒ/ *vi* se déchaîner (**through** dans).

rampant /ˈræmpənt/ *adj* **1** [*crime, disease, rumour*] endémique; **2** [*plant*] exubérant; **3** Herald rampant.

rampart /ˈræmpɑːt/ *n* lit, fig rempart *m*.

ram-raid /ˈræmreɪd/ **I** *n* casse *m* à la voiture bélier.
II *vtr* **to ~ a shop** dévaliser une boutique à l'aide d'une voiture bélier.

ramrod /ˈræmrɒd/ *n* (for small gun) baguette *f* (*pour une arme*); (for cannon) refouloir *m*.
IDIOMS **straight as a ~** raide comme un piquet.

ramshackle /ˈræmʃækl/ *adj* lit, fig délabré.

ran /ræn/ *prét* ▶ **run**.

RAN *n* (*abrév* = **Royal Australian Navy**) Marine *f* royale australienne.

ranch /rɑːntʃ, US ræntʃ/ *n* ranch *m*.

rancher /ˈrɑːntʃə(r), US ˈræntʃə(r)/ *n* US propriétaire *mf* de ranch.

ranch: **~ hand** *n* garçon *m* de ferme; **~ (style) house** *n* maison *f* style ranch.

ranching /ˈrɑːntʃɪŋ, US ræn-/ *n* élevage *m* en ranch.

rancid /ˈrænsɪd/ *adj* rance; **to go ~** rancir; **to smell ~** sentir le rance.

rancidness /ˈrænsɪdnɪs/, **rancidity** /rænˈsɪdətɪ/ *n* rance *m*.

rancorous /ˈræŋkərəs/ *adj* rancunier/-ière (**towards** envers).

rancour GB, **rancor** US /ˈræŋkə(r)/ *n* rancœur *f* (**against** envers).

rand /rænd/ ▶ 1143 *n* rand *m*.

random /ˈrændəm/ **I** *n* **at ~** au hasard.
II *adj* (fait) au hasard; **on a ~ basis** au hasard.

randomly /ˈrændəmlɪ/ *adv* au hasard.

randy○ /ˈrændɪ/ *adj* (highly-sexed) porté sur la chose; (sexually excited) d'humeur érotique.

rang /ræŋ/ *prét* ▶ **ring**.

range /reɪndʒ/ **I** *n* **1** Comm, gen (choice) (of prices, colours, models, products) gamme *f*; (of activities, alternatives, options) éventail *m*, choix *m*; **a top/bottom of the ~ computer** un ordinateur haut/bas de gamme; **in a wide ~ of prices** à tous les prix; **in a wide ~ of colours** dans un grand choix de couleurs; **2** (spectrum) (of people, abilities, beliefs, emotions) variété *f*; (of benefits, salaries, incentives) éventail *m*; (of issues, assumptions) série *f*; **age ~** tranche *f* d'âge; **price ~** éventail de prix; **salary ~** éventail des salaires; **in the 30–40% ~** dans les 30 à 40%; **in the £50–£100 ~** entre 50 et 100 livres sterling; **what is your price ~?** quel prix voulez-vous y mettre?, dans quel ordre de prix?; **to have a wide ~ of interests** s'intéresser à beaucoup de choses; **a wide ~ of views/opinions** des vues/opinions très diverses; **I teach pupils right across the ability ~** j'enseigne à des élèves de niveaux différents; **3** (assortment) variété *f*; **4** (scope) (of influence, knowledge) étendue *f*; (of investigation, research) domaine *m*; **5** (distance) distance *f*; **at a ~ of 200 m** à une distance de 200 m; **from long ~** de loin; **to shoot sb at close ~** tirer sur qn à bout portant; **within hearing ~** à portée de voix; **6** (capacity) (of radar, weapon, transmitter) portée *f* (**of** de); **to be out of ~** être hors de portée; **7** Aerosp, Aut, Aviat autonomie *f*; **8** US (prairie) prairie *f*; **on the ~** dans les pâturages; **9** (of mountains) chaîne *f*; **10** (stove) (wood etc) fourneau *m*; (gas, electric) cuisinière *f*; **11** Fin limites *fpl*; **the dollar is within its old ~** les fluctuations du dollar sont rentrées dans leurs anciennes limites; **12** (firing area) (for weapons) champ *m* de tir; (for missiles) zone *f* de tir; **13** Theat (of actor) répertoire *m*; **14** Mus (of voice, instrument) tessiture *f*.
II *vtr* **1** (set) opposer (**against** à); **2** (draw up) aligner, ranger [*forces, troops*].
III *vi* **1** (run) aller (**from** de; **to** à); **2** (vary) varier (**between** entre); **3** (cover) **to ~ over sth** couvrir qch; **his speech ~d over a wide variety of subjects** son discours couvrait toute une gamme de sujets; **4** (roam, wander) vagabonder; **5** Mil **to ~ over** [*gun, missile*] avoir une portée de [*20 km*].

rangefinder /ˈreɪndʒfaɪndə(r)/ *n* télémètre *m*.

ranger /ˈreɪndʒə(r)/ *n* **1** Ecol, Agric garde-forestier *m*; **2** US, Mil ranger *m*; **3** GB (in Guides) ≈ éclaireuse *f* aînée.

Rangoon /ræŋˈguːn/ ▶ 1818 *pr n* Rangoun.

rangy /ˈreɪndʒɪ/ *adj* élancé.

rank /ræŋk/ **I** *n* **1** (in military, police) grade *m*; (in company, politics) rang *m*; (social status) rang *m*; **of high/low ~** de haut/bas rang; **to pull ~** abuser de son rang; **2** (line) (of people) rang *m*; (of objects) rangée *f*; **~ upon ~ of soldiers** des rangs de soldats; **to arrange [sth] in ~s** disposer [qch] en rangées [*toy soldiers*]; **to break ~s** lit [*soldiers*] rompre les rangs; fig [*politicians*] se rebeller; **to close ~s (against)** lit, fig serrer les rangs (contre); **3** (for taxis) station *f*; **taxi ~** station de taxis; **4** Ling rang *m*; **5** (in chess) rangée *f*; ▶ 1612.
II ranks *npl* **1** Mil, Pol, Ind rangs *mpl*; **to be in the ~s** Mil être dans les rangs; **to rise through the ~s** sortir du rang; **a leader chosen from the ~s of the party** un dirigeant choisi dans les rangs du parti; **the ~s of the unemployed/of the homeless** les rangs des chômeurs/des sans-abri; **to be reduced to the ~s** Mil être dégradé; **2** (echelons) échelons *mpl*; **to rise through the ~s of the civil service** gravir les échelons de la fonction publique.
III *adj* **1** (absolute) péj (for emphasis) [*outsider, beginner*] complet/-ète; [*favouritism, injustice, stupidity*] flagrant; **2** (foul) [*odour*] fétide; **3** (exuberant) [*ivy, weeds*] envahissant; **to be ~ with weeds** [*garden*] être envahi par les mauvaises herbes.
IV *adv* **to smell ~** avoir une odeur fétide.
V *vtr* **1** (classify) [*person*] classer [*player, novel, restaurant*] (**among** parmi; **above** au-dessus de; **below** au-dessous de); **to be ~ed third in the world** être classé troisième au niveau mondial; **2** US (be senior to) [*officer, colleague*] commander [*person*].
VI *vi* **1** (rate) se classer; **how do I ~ compared to her?** où est-ce que je me classe or situe par rapport à elle?; **to ~ as a great composer** être considéré comme un grand compositeur; **to ~ among** ou **with the champions** être classé parmi les or au nombre des champions; **to ~ above/below/alongside sb** occuper un rang supérieur/inférieur/égal à qn; **this has to** ou **must ~ as one of the worst films I've ever seen** c'est un des films les pires que j'aie jamais vus; **that doesn't ~ very high on my list of priorities** cela ne figure pas très haut dans ma liste de priorités; **2** US Mil (be most senior) [*admiral, general*] commander.

rank and file /ˌræŋkənˈfaɪl/ **I** *n* base *f*.
II rank-and-file *modif* [*opinion*] de la base; [*committee, member, membership, socialist*] de base.

ranker /ˈræŋkə(r)/ *n* Mil **1** (ordinary soldier) simple soldat *m*; **2** (officer) officier *m* sorti du rang.

ranking /ˈræŋkɪŋ/ **I** *n* Sport classement *m*; **to improve one's ~** monter dans le classement.
II -ranking (*dans composés*) **high/low-~** de haut/bas rang.

rankle /ˈræŋkl/ *vi* **to ~ with sb** rester en travers de la gorge de qn○; **there are some things that still ~** il y a encore des choses qui ne sont pas passées; **but it still ~s** mais ça laisse toujours un goût saumâtre.

rankness /ˈræŋknɪs/ *n* **1** (foul smell) odeur *f* fétide; **2** (exuberance) exubérance *f*.

ransack /ˈrænsæk, US rænˈsæk/ *vtr* **1** (search) fouiller (**for** pour trouver); **2** (plunder) mettre [qch] à sac; **to ~ a house** mettre une maison à sac.

ransom /ˈrænsəm/ **I** *n* **1** (sum) (also **~ money**) rançon *f*; **to demand/pay a ~**

Military ranks and titles

The following list gives the principal ranks in the French services. For translations, see the individual dictionary entries.

The Navy = La marine nationale

amiral
vice-amiral d'escadre
vice-amiral
contre-amiral
capitaine de vaisseau
capitaine de frégate
capitaine de corvette
lieutenant de vaisseau
enseigne de vaisseau (1re et 2e classe)
aspirant
major
maître principal
premier maître
maître
second maître
quartier-maître (1re et 2e classe)
matelot

The Army = L'armée de terre

général d'armée
général de corps d'armée
général de division
général de brigade
colonel
lieutenant-colonel
commandant
capitaine
lieutenant
sous-lieutenant
aspirant
major
adjudant-chef
adjudant
sergent-chef
or maréchal des logis-chef (*cavalry*)
sergent
or maréchal des logis (*cavalry*)
caporal-chef
or brigadier-chef (*cavalry*)
caporal
or brigadier (*cavalry*)
soldat
or cavalier (*cavalry*)

The Air Force = L'armée de l'air

général d'armée aérienne
général de corps aérien
général de division aérienne
général de brigade aérienne
colonel
lieutenant-colonel
commandant
capitaine
lieutenant
sous-lieutenant
aspirant
major
adjudant-chef
adjudant
sergent-chef
sergent
caporal-chef
caporal
aviateur

Speaking about someone

he's a colonel	=	il est colonel
to be promoted to colonel	=	être promu colonel
he has the rank of colonel	=	il a le rang de colonel
she's a lieutenant in the Army	=	elle est lieutenant dans l'armée de terre
he's just a private	=	il est simple soldat
Colonel Smith has arrived	=	le colonel Smith est arrivé

Speaking to someone

In the armée de terre, *the* mon *is used to superior officers from* lieutenant *upwards, except for* major. Mon *is never prefixed to ranks in the* marine nationale *or the* armée de l'air *and never used to personnel of inferior rank in any of the three services.*

Service personnel to superior officers

yes, sir	=	oui, mon colonel (*or* mon capitaine, mon lieutenant etc.)
yes, ma'am	=	oui, colonel (*or* capitaine, lieutenant etc.)

Service personnel to someone of lower rank

yes, sergeant	=	oui, sergent

For examples of the use of military titles in letters and on envelopes see the **French correspondence** *section.*

exiger/payer une rançon (**for** pour); **2** to **hold sb to** GB ou **for** US **~** lit garder qn en otage; fig tenir qn en otage.
II *vtr* payer une rançon pour.
IDIOMS **a king's ~** une somme fabuleuse.

rant /rænt/ *vi* déclamer.
IDIOMS **to ~ and rave** tempêter (**at** contre).
■ **rant at**: **~ at** [**sb**] pester contre (**about** à propos de).
■ **rant on** divaguer (**about** sur).

ranting /ˈræntɪŋ/ **I** *n* (also **~s** *npl*) rodomontades *fpl*.
II *adj* déchaîné.

ranunculus /rəˈnʌŋkjʊləs/ *n* (*pl* **-li**) renoncule *f*.

rap /ræp/ **I** *n* **1** (tap) coup *m* sec; **a ~ on the table/at the door** un coup sec sur la table/à la porte; **2** Mus (also **~ music**) rap *m*; **3**○ US (conversation) conversation *f*; **4**○ (accusation) accusation *f*; **to beat the ~** s'en tirer à bon compte; **to hang a murder/burglary ~ on sb** faire endosser un meurtre/cambriolage à qn; **to take the ~** écoper○ (**for** pour).
II *modif* Mus [*artist, poet, record*] rap *inv*.
III *vtr* (*p prés etc* **-pp-**) **1** (tap) frapper sur; **2** (criticize) Journ tancer [*person*] (**for** pour; **for doing** d'avoir fait).
IV *vi* (*p prés etc* **-pp-**) **1** (tap) donner des coups secs (**with** avec); **to ~ on the table/at the door** donner des coups secs sur la table/à la porte; **2** Mus faire du rap; **3**○ US (talk) causer○, parler (**about** de).
■ **rap out**: **~ out** [**sth**] lancer [*order, question*].

rapacious /rəˈpeɪʃəs/ *adj* rapace.

rapaciously /rəˈpeɪʃəslɪ/ *adv* avec rapacité.

rapacity /rəˈpæsətɪ/ *n* rapacité *f*.

rape /reɪp/ **I** *n* **1** Jur, fig viol *m*; **attempted ~** tentative *f* de viol; **2** Agric, Bot colza *m*.
II *modif* Jur [*case, charge*] de viol; **~ counselling** assistance *f* aux victimes d'un viol; **~ victim** (in general) victime *f* d'un viol; (one specific) victime *f* du viol.
III *vtr* violer.

rape(seed) oil *n* huile *f* de colza.

rapid /ˈræpɪd/ *adj* gen rapide; **in ~ succession** coup sur coup.

rapid: **~ deployment force** *n* Mil force *f* d'intervention rapide; **~ eye movement, REM** *n* mouvements *mpl* oculaires rapides; **~ fire** *n* Mil, fig feu *m* roulant.

rapidity /rəˈpɪdətɪ/ *n* rapidité *f*.

rapidly /ˈræpɪdlɪ/ *adv* rapidement.

Rapid Reaction Force *n* Force *f* d'intervention rapide.

rapids /ˈræpɪdz/ *npl* rapides *mpl*; **to shoot** ou **ride the ~** descendre les rapides.

rapid transit *n* US Transp transport *m* public.

rapier /ˈreɪpɪə(r)/ *n* rapière *f*.

rapine /ˈræpaɪn, US ˈræpɪn/ *n* rapine *f*.

rapist /ˈreɪpɪst/ *n* violeur *m*.

rapper /ˈræpə(r)/ *n* **1** Mus chanteur/-euse *m/f* de rap, rappeur/-euse *m/f*; **2** US (door-knocker) heurtoir *m*.

rapping /ˈræpɪŋ/ *n* **1** (knocking) coups *mpl* secs; **2** Mus rap *m*.

rapport /ræˈpɔː(r), US -ˈpɔːrt/ *n* bons rapports *mpl* (**with** avec; **between** entre); **in ~ with** en harmonie avec; **to establish a ~** établir un bon rapport; **a close ~** un rapport étroit.

rapprochement /ræˈprɒʃmɒŋ, ræˈprəʊʃ-, US ˌræprəʊʃˈmɒŋ/ *n* rapprochement *m* (**between** entre).

rapscallion‡ /ræpˈskæljən/ *n* vaurien *m*.

rap sheet○ *n* US casier *m* (judiciaire).

rapt /ræpt/ *adj* gen absorbé; [*smile*] extasié; **~ with wonder** émerveillé; **to watch with ~ attention** regarder très attentivement.

rapture /ˈræptʃə(r)/ *n* ravissement *m*; **with ~, in ~** avec ravissement; **to go into ~s over** ou **about sth** s'extasier sur qch; **to be in ~s over** ou **about sth** être en extase devant qch.

rapturous /ˈræptʃərəs/ *adj* [*delight*] extasié; [*welcome*] enthousiaste; [*applause*] frénétique.

rapturously /ˈræptʃərəslɪ/ *adv* avec extase; [*applaud*] avec frénésie.

rare /reə(r)/ *adj* **1** (uncommon) rare (*before n*); **it is ~ to see** il est rare de voir; **it is ~ for sb to do** il est rare que qn fasse; **with a few ~ exceptions** à quelques rares exceptions près; **on the ~ occasions when**... les rares fois où...; **a ~ event** un événement exceptionnel; **2** [*steak*] saignant; **I like it very ~** je l'aime bleu; **3** [*atmosphere, air*] raréfié; **4**† (wonderful) **to have a ~ old time** bien s'amuser.

rarebit /ˈreəbɪt/ *n* ▶ **Welsh rarebit**.

rarefied /ˈreərɪfaɪd/ *adj* [*atmosphere*] lit raréfié; fig étouffant.

rarely /ˈreəlɪ/ *adv* rarement.

rareness /ˈreənɪs/ *n* rareté *f*.

raring /ˈreərɪŋ/ *adj* **to be ~ to do** être très impatient de faire; **to be ~ to go** piaffer d'impatience.

rarity /ˈreərətɪ/ *n* **1** (plant) plante *f* rare; (bird) oiseau *m* rare; (collector's item) pièce *f* rare; **2** (rare occurrence) phénomène *m* rare; **to be a ~** être rare; **it is a ~ for sb to do** il est rare que qn fasse; **3** (rareness) rareté *f*.

rascal /ˈrɑːskl, US ˈræskl/ *n* **1** (used affectionately) coquin/-e *m/f*; **he's an old ~** c'est un vieux chenapan; **2**† (reprobate) voyou *m*.

rascally /ˈrɑːskəlɪ/ *adj* **her ~ son** son coquin de fils.

rash /ræʃ/ **I** *n* **1** (skin) rougeurs *fpl*; **to have a ~** avoir des rougeurs; **to come out** ou **break out in a ~** se couvrir de rougeurs; **2** fig (spate) vague *f* (**of** de).
II *adj* [*person, decision, move, plan*] irréfléchi; **it was ~ to do** il n'était pas raisonnable de faire; **to be ~ enough to do** avoir l'imprudence de faire; **in a ~ moment** dans un moment d'emballement.

rasher /ˈræʃə(r)/ *n* (of bacon) (slice) tranche *f*; (serving) US portion *f*.

rashly /ˈræʃlɪ/ *adv* sans réfléchir.

rashness /ˈræʃnɪs/ *n* (of person, behaviour) inconséquence *f*.

rasp /rɑːsp, US ræsp/ **I** *n* **1** (of saw, voice) grincement *m*; **2** (file) râpe *f*.
II *vtr* **1** (rub) râper; **2** fig **'no!,' she ~ed** 'non!,' dit-elle d'une voix rauque or râpeuse.
III *vi* [*saw, file*] grincer.
IV rasping *pres p adj* [*voice, sound*] râpeux/-euse.

raspberry /ˈrɑːzbrɪ, US ˈræzberɪ/ **I** *n* **1** (fruit) framboise *f*; **2** (noise) **to blow a ~** faire un bruit de dérision.
II *modif* [*ice cream, tart*] à la framboise; [*jam*] de framboise; **~ cane** Hort framboisier *m*.

Rasta○ /ˈræstə/ *n, adj* Rasta (*mf*).

Rastafarian /ˌræstəˈfeərɪən/ **I** *n* rasta *mf*, rastafari *mf*.
II *adj* rasta.

rat /ræt/ **I** *n* **1** Zool rat *m*; **2**○ péj (person) salaud◑/salope◑ *m/f*; **3** US (informer) mouchard/-e○ *m/f*.

II *vi* (*p prés etc* **-tt-**) **1**○ **to ~ on** moucharder○, dénoncer [*person*]; se dédire de [*deal*]; renoncer à [*belief, commitments*]; **2**† **to go ~ting** faire la chasse aux rats.

III **rats** *excl* mince alors○!

IDIOMS **to look like a drowned ~** être trempé comme une soupe○; **to smell a ~** flairer quelque chose de louche; **~s leave a sinking ship** Prov les rats quittent le navire.

ratable *adj* = **rateable**.

rat-arsed● *adj* GB bourré◑; **to get ~** se bourrer la gueule◑.

rat: **~bag**○ *n* crapule○ *f*; **~catcher** *n* Hist chasseur *m* de rats.

ratchet /ˈrætʃɪt/ I *n* (toothed rack) crémaillère *f*; (wheel) roue *f* à rochet; (tooth) cliquet *m*.

II *vtr* **to ~ (up)** faire augmenter [*prices*].

rate /reɪt/ I *n* **1** (speed) rythme *m*; **the ~ of improvement/of production** le rythme d'amélioration/de production; **the ~ at which children learn** le rythme auquel les enfants apprennent; **to work at a steady ~** travailler à un rythme régulier; **at a ~ of 50 an hour** au rythme de 50 par heure; **at this ~ we'll finish in no time** à ce rythme nous aurons fini en moins de deux; **at this ~ we'll never be able to afford a car** fig à ce rythme-là nous n'aurons jamais les moyens d'acheter une voiture; **at the ~ you're going**... fig au train où tu vas...; **to drive/work at a terrific ~** conduire/travailler à toute vitesse; **2** (number of occurrences) taux *m*; **the divorce/birth/unemployment ~** le taux de divorce/natalité/chômage ; **the pass/failure ~ for that exam is 60%** le taux de réussite/d'échec à l'examen est de 60%; **3** (level) **the interest/mortgage ~** le taux d'intérêt/de l'emprunt-logement; **the ~ of growth/of inflation/of exchange** le taux de croissance/d'inflation/de change; **4** (charge) tarif *m*; **postal/advertising ~s** les tarifs postaux/publicitaires; **translator's ~s** les tarifs des traducteurs; **what is the ~ for a small ad?** quel est le tarif pour une petite annonce?; **telephone calls are charged at several ~s** il existe plusieurs tarifs pour les communications téléphoniques; **at a reduced ~** à tarif réduit; **to get a reduced ~** bénéficier d'un tarif réduit; **what's the going ~ for a Picasso?** quel est le prix moyen d'un Picasso?; **5** (wage) tarif *m*; **his hourly ~ is £12** son salaire horaire est de 12 livres sterling; **to pay sb the going ~ for the job** payer qn au tarif en vigueur; **what's the going ~ for a babysitter?** quel est le tarif actuel pour une babysitter?; **what is your hourly ~ of pay?** combien gagnez-vous de l'heure?, quel est votre salaire horaire?; **6** Fin (in foreign exchange) cours *m*.

II **rates** *npl* GB Tax impôts *mpl* locaux; **business ~s** ≈ taxe *f* professionnelle.

III *modif* GB Econ Fin [*increase, rebate*] des impôts locaux.

IV *vtr* **1** (classify) **I ~ his new novel very highly** j'admire beaucoup son nouveau roman; **how do you ~ this restaurant/him as an actor?** que pensez-vous de ce restaurant/de lui comme acteur?; **how do you ~ the food in that restaurant?** comment trouvez-vous la cuisine de ce restaurant?; **to ~ sb as a great composer** considérer qn comme un grand compositeur; **to ~ sb among the best pianists in the world** classer qn parmi les meilleurs pianistes du monde; **highly ~d** très coté; **2** (deserve) mériter [*medal, round of applause*] **this hotel ~s three stars** cet hôtel mérite trois étoiles; **the joke/the story hardly ~s a mention** la plaisanterie/l'histoire ne mérite pas qu'on en parle; **3** (value) estimer [*honesty, friendship, person*]; **I ~ courage very highly** j'estime beaucoup le courage.

V *vi* (rank) **how did our cheese/wine ~?** où notre fromage/vin s'est-il classé?; **where do I ~ compared to him?** où est-ce que je me classe or situe par rapport à lui?; **she ~s among the best sopranos in Europe** elle compte parmi les meilleures sopranos européennes; **that ~s as the best wine I've ever tasted** c'est le meilleur vin que j'aie jamais goûté; **that doesn't ~ high on my list of priorities** cela ne figure pas très haut dans ma liste de priorités.

VI *v refl* **how do you ~ yourself as a driver?** comment vous jugez-vous en tant que conducteur?; **she doesn't ~ herself very highly** elle n'a pas une très haute opinion d'elle-même.

IDIOMS **at any ~** en tout cas.

rateable GB, **ratable** US /ˈreɪtəbl/ *adj* **1** (liable for local tax) [*property*] imposable; **~ value** GB valeur *f* locative imposable; **2** (assessable) évaluable.

rate-cap /ˈreɪtkæp/ *vtr* (*p prés etc* **-pp-**) GB Pol Econ imposer un plafond aux impôts locaux.

rate: **~-capping** *n* GB Tax plafonnement *m* des impôts locaux; **~ of change** *n* vitesse *f* de changement; **~ of climb** *n* Aviat vitesse *f* ascensionnelle; **~ of flow** *n* Sci débit *m*; **~payer** *n* GB contribuable *mf*.

ratfink◑ /ˈrætfɪŋk/ *n* salaud◑ *m*, crapule *f*.

rather /ˈrɑːðə(r)/ I *adv* **1** (somewhat, quite) plutôt; **it's ~ fun/expensive** c'est plutôt amusant/cher; **he's ~ young** il est plutôt jeune; **it's ~ like an apple** ça ressemble un peu à une pomme; **~ easily/stupidly** plutôt facilement/bêtement; **I ~ like him** je le trouve plutôt sympathique; **I ~ think she's right** j'ai plutôt l'impression qu'elle a raison; **he's ~ a bore** il est plutôt or assez ennuyeux; **he's ~ a cruel man** c'est un homme plutôt or assez cruel; **I'm in ~ a hurry** je suis plutôt or assez pressé; **it's ~ a pity** c'est assez dommage; **it's ~ too/more difficult** c'est un peu trop/plus difficile; **2** (more readily, preferably) **~ than sth** plutôt que qch; **~ than do** plutôt que de faire; **I would** ou **had ~ do** je préférerais faire (**than do** que faire); **I would** ou **had much ~ do** je préférerais de loin faire; **would you ~ wait?** préférez-vous attendre?; **he'd die ~ than admit it** il préférerait mourir plutôt que de l'avouer; **I'd ~ die!** plutôt mourir!; **I'd ~ not** j'aimerais mieux pas; **I'd ~ not say** je préférerais or j'aimerais mieux ne pas dire; **I'd ~ you did/didn't** je préférerais or j'aimerais mieux que tu fasses/ne fasses pas; **3** (more exactly) plutôt; **a tree, or ~ a bush** un arbre, ou plutôt un buisson; **practical ~ than decorative** pratique plutôt que décoratif; **'did it improve?'—'no, ~ it got worse'** 'ça s'est amélioré?'—'non, ça a plutôt empiré'.

II *excl*† GB et comment!

rathskeller○ /ˈrætskelə(r)/ *n* US brasserie *f*.

ratification /ˌrætɪfɪˈkeɪʃn/ *n* ratification *f*; **for ~** pour ratification.

ratify /ˈrætɪfaɪ/ *vtr* ratifier.

rating /ˈreɪtɪŋ/ I *n* **1** (score) cote *f*; **what is her ~ in the polls?** quelle est sa cote dans les sondages?; **she got a good ~ at her appraisal** elle a reçu une mention favorable à son évaluation; **popularity ~** indice or cote de popularité; **IQ ~** GB QI; **2** Fin (status) cote *f*; **share ~** cote en Bourse; **her credit ~ is good** son crédit est bon; **3** GB Tax (local tax due) montant *m* des impôts locaux; (valuation for local tax) valeur *f* imposable; **4** Mil Naut ≈ matelot *m*.

II **ratings** *npl* TV Radio indice *m* d'écoute, audimat® *m*; **to be top/bottom of the ~s** avoir un indice d'écoute maximum/minimum; **the series has gone up/down in the ~s** l'indice d'écoute de la série a augmenté/diminué; **a series with audience ~s of six million** une série regardée par six millions de téléspectateurs.

rating system *n* GB Tax répartition *f* des impôts locaux.

ratio /ˈreɪʃɪəʊ/ *n* rapport *m*; **the pupil/teacher ~** le nombre d'élèves par enseignant; **a ~ of one teacher to 25 pupils** un rapport d'un professeur pour 25 élèves; **the ~ of men to women is two to five** il y a deux hommes pour cinq femmes; **in direct/inverse ~ to** en raison directe/inverse de; **in** ou **by a ~ of 60:40** dans une proportion de 60 à 40.

ratiocination /ˌrætɪˌɒsɪˈneɪʃn, US ˌræʃɪ-/ *n* sout raisonnement *m*.

ration /ˈræʃn/ I *n* **1** (of food, petrol) ration *f* (**of** de); **meat/coal ~** ration de viande/de charbon; **2** fig (of problems, doubts) compte *m* (**of** de); (of TV, music, parties) dose *f* (**of** de).

II **rations** *npl* Mil rations *fpl*; **on short ~s** à rations réduites; **on full ~s** à pleines rations.

III *vtr* rationner [*food, petrol*] (**to** à); limiter la ration de [*person*] (**to** à); **sugar was ~ed to one kilo per family** le sucre était rationné à un kilo par famille.

■ **ration out**: **~ [sth] out, ~ out [sth]** partager [qch] en rations (**among** entre).

rational /ˈræʃənl/ *adj* [*approach, argument, decision, position*] rationnel/-elle; [*person*] sensé; **a ~ being** Philos un être doué de raison; **it is ~ to do** il est logique de faire; **I try to be ~** j'essaie d'être objectif.

rationale /ˌræʃəˈnɑːl, US -ˈnæl/ *n* (*sans pl*) **1** (reasons) raisons *fpl* (**for** pour); **the ~ for doing** les raisons de faire; **2** (logic) (of system, argument) logique *f*; **the ~ behind** la logique de [*decision, treatment*].

rationalism /ˈræʃnəlɪzəm/ *n* rationalisme *m*.

rationalist /ˈræʃnəlɪst/ *n, adj* rationaliste (*mf*).

rationalistic /ˌræʃnəˈlɪstɪk/ *adj* rationaliste.

rationality /ˌræʃəˈnælətɪ/ *n* rationalité *f*.

rationalization /ˌræʃnəlaɪˈzeɪʃn/ *n* **1** (justification) justification *f* (**for** de); **2** GB, Econ (of operation, company, industry) rationalisation *f*.

rationalize /ˈræʃnəlaɪz/ *vtr* **1** (justify) justifier; **2** GB Econ rationaliser [*operation, company, industry*].

rationally /ˈræʃnəlɪ/ *adv* de façon rationnelle, rationnellement.

ration: **~ book** *n* livret *m* de rationnement; **~ card** *n* carte *f* de rationnement.

rationing /ˈræʃnɪŋ/ *n* rationnement *m*; **food/water ~** rationnement *m* de la nourriture/de l'eau.

rat: **~ poison** *n* mort-aux-rats *f inv*; **~ race** *n* péj foire *f* d'empoigne; **~-run** *n* GB Aut *petite rue servant de raccourci*; **~sbane** *n* = **rat poison**.

rattan /ræˈtæn/ I *n* (tree, material) rotin *m*; (stick) canne *f* en rotin.

II *modif* [*chair, table*] en rotin.

rat-tat-tat /ˌrættætˈtæt/ *n* toc-toc *m*.

rattle /ˈrætl/ I *n* **1** (noise) (of bottles, cutlery, chains) cliquetis *m*; (of window, door) vibration *f*; (of car engine) cliquetis *m*; (of car bodywork) fracas *m*, bruit *m* de ferraille; (of rattlesnake) bruit *m* de crécelle; (of machine gun fire) crépitement *m*; **2** (toy) (of baby) hochet *m*; (of sports fan) crécelle *f*; **3** (rattlesnake's tail) cascabelle *f*.

II *vtr* **1** (shake) [*person*] faire s'entrechoquer [*bottles, cutlery, chains*]; [*wind*] faire vibrer [*window, door*]; [*person*] s'acharner sur [*door handle*]; **2**○ (annoy) énerver; **to get ~d** s'énerver.

III *vi* [*bottles, cutlery, chains*] s'entrechoquer; [*window, door*] vibrer; **when I shook the box, it ~d** quand j'ai secoué la boîte, quelque chose a fait du bruit à l'intérieur; **the car ~d along/off etc** la voiture avançait/est partie etc dans un bruit de ferraille.

IDIOMS **to shake sb until their teeth ~** secouer qn comme un prunier.

■ **rattle away**○ = **rattle on**.

■ **rattle off**○: **~ off [sth]** (write) écrire [qch] à toute vitesse; (recite, read) débiter [qch] à toute vitesse.

■ **rattle on**○, **rattle away**○ parler sans discontinuer (**about** à propos de).
■ **rattle through**○: **they ~d through the rest of the meeting** ils ont expédié la fin de la réunion; **she ~d through the list of names** elle a lu la liste des noms à toute vitesse.

rattler○ /ˈrætlə(r)/ *n* = **rattlesnake**.

rattlesnake /ˈrætlsneɪk/ *n* serpent *m* à sonnette, crotale *m*.

rattletrap○† /ˈrætltræp/ *n* vieille guimbarde○ *f*.

rattling /ˈrætlɪŋ/ **I** *n* = **rattle I** 1.
II *adj* **1** (vibrating) [*chain, door, window*] bruyant; [*cough*] rauque; **~ sound** cliquetis *m*; **2** (quick) **at a ~ pace** à vive allure.
III *adv* **a ~**○† **good book/meal** un livre/repas de tout premier ordre.

rat trap *n* piège *m* à rats, ratière *f*.

ratty○ /ˈrætɪ/ *adj* **1** GB (grumpy) [*character*] grincheux/-euse; **2** US (shabby) miteux/-euse; **3** US (tangled) [*hair*] emmêlé.

raucous /ˈrɔːkəs/ *adj* **1** [*laughter, shout, cry*] éraillé; **2** [*person, gathering*] tapageur/-euse, bruyant.

raucously /ˈrɔːkəslɪ/ *adv* [*laugh, call*] d'une voix éraillée; [*behave*] de manière tapageuse.

raucousness /ˈrɔːkəsnɪs/ *n* **1** (of voice, laughter) éraillement *m*; **2** (of person) **he's known for his ~** ses manières tapageuses sont bien connues.

raunch /rɔːntʃ/ *n* US (bawdiness) paillardise *f*.

raunchy○ /ˈrɔːntʃɪ/ *adj* **1** (earthy) [*performer, voice, song*] torride; [*extract, story*] salé○; **2** US (bawdy) paillard; **3** US (dirty, sloppy) dégueulasse◑.

ravage /ˈrævɪdʒ/ **I ravages** *npl* ravages *mpl* (**of** de).
II *vtr* (all contexts) ravager.

rave /reɪv/ **I**○ *n* **1** GB bringue○ *f* (branchée○); **2** (praise) commentaire *m* louangeur; **3** (craze) vogue *f*.
II○ *adj* [*club, restaurant*] en vogue; **a ~ review** une critique dithyrambique.
III *vi* **1** (enthusiastically) s'emballer (**about** au sujet de); **2** (angrily) tempêter (**at, against** contre); **3** (when fevered) délirer also fig.
IDIOMS **to ~ it up**○ GB faire la bringue○.

raven /ˈreɪvn/ *n* grand corbeau *m*.

raven-haired /ˌreɪvnˈheəd/ *adj* aux cheveux de jais.

ravening /ˈrævənɪŋ/ *adj* vorace.

Ravenna /rəˈvenə/ ▶ **1818** *pr n* Ravenne.

ravenous /ˈrævənəs/ *adj* [*animal*] vorace; [*appetite*] féroce; **to be ~** avoir une faim de loup.

ravenously /ˈrævənəslɪ/ *adv* [*eat, look*] voracement, avec voracité; **to be ~ hungry** avoir une faim de loup.

raver○ /ˈreɪvə(r)/ *n* GB **1** (merrymaker) noceur/-euse○ *m/f*; **2** (trendy person) branché/-e *m/f*.

rave-up○ /ˈreɪvʌp/ *n* GB bringue○ *f*, fête *f*.

ravine /rəˈviːn/ *n* ravin *m*.

raving /ˈreɪvɪŋ/ **I ravings** *npl* divagations *fpl*; **the ~s of a lunatic** les divagations d'un fou.
II *adj* **1** (fanatical) enragé; **2 a ~ idiot** ou **lunatic** un fou furieux/une folle furieuse; **3** (tremendous) [*success*] éclatant; **she's a ~ beauty** elle est d'une beauté radieuse.
IDIOMS **to be (stark) ~ mad**○ être complètement dingue○ or fou.

ravioli /ˌrævɪˈəʊlɪ/ *n* ravioli *mpl*.

ravish /ˈrævɪʃ/ *vtr* **1** littér (delight) ravir; **2**‡ (rape) violer.

ravishing /ˈrævɪʃɪŋ/ *adj* ravissant; **to look ~** être ravissant.

ravishingly /ˈrævɪʃɪŋlɪ/ *adv* **to be ~ beautiful** être d'une beauté exquise.

raw /rɔː/ *adj* **1** (uncooked) [*food*] cru; **2** (unprocessed) lit, fig [*cotton, silk, rubber, sugar*] brut; [*data, statistics*] brut; [*sewage*] non traité; [*edge*] (in sewing) non surfilé; (on paper, wood) coupé; **3** (without skin) [*part of body, patch*] à vif; **his hands had been rubbed ~** ses mains avaient été mises à vif; **4** (cold) [*weather, day*] froid et humide; [*air*] cru; [*wind*] pénétrant; **5** (inexperienced) [*novice, recruit, youngster*] inexpérimenté; **6** (realistic) [*description, dialogue, performance*] cru; **7** (undisguised) [*emotion*] à l'état brut; [*energy*] sauvage; **8** US (vulgar) obscène.
IDIOMS **in the ~**○ GB (naked) nu; **life in the ~** la vie dans le vif; **to get sb on the ~** GB toucher qn au vif; **to get** ou **have a ~ deal**○ être défavorisé; **to give sb a ~ deal**○ traiter qn de façon injuste; **to touch a ~ nerve** toucher un point sensible.

rawboned /ˌrɔːˈbəʊnd/ *adj* décharné.

rawhide /ˈrɔːhaɪd/ *n* **1** (leather) cuir *m* brut; **2** (whip) fouet *m* à lanières.

Rawlbolt® /ˈrɔːlbəʊlt/ *n* cheville *f*.

Rawlplug® /ˈrɔːlplʌg/ *n* Constr cheville *f*.

raw: **~ material** *n* lit, fig matière *f* première; **~ material costs** *npl* coûts *mpl* des matières premières.

rawness /ˈrɔːnɪs/ *n* **1** (of language, style) crudité *f*; **2** (realism) brutalité *f*; **3** (naïvety) inexpérience *f*; **4** (of wind) âpreté *f*.

raw score *n* US Sch résultat *m* absolu.

ray /reɪ/ *n* **1** (beam) rayon *m* (**of** de); **a ~ of sunshine** un rayon de soleil; **2** fig **a ~ of hope/of comfort** une lueur d'espoir/de réconfort; **3** (fish) raie *f*; **4** Mus ré *m*.

ray gun *n* pistolet *m* à rayons.

rayon /ˈreɪɒn/ **I** *n* rayonne *f*; **made of ~** en rayonne.
II *modif* [*garment*] en rayonne.

raze /reɪz/ *vtr* raser; **to ~ sth to the ground** raser qch.

razor /ˈreɪzə(r)/ *n* rasoir *m*.
IDIOMS **to live on a ~('s) edge** être au bord de l'abîme.

razor: **~back** *n* US pécari *m*; **~bill** *n* petit pingouin *m*; **~ blade** *n* lame *f* de rasoir; **~ burn** *n* feu *m* du rasoir; **~ clam** *n* US Zool couteau *m*; **~ cut** *n* coupe *f* au rasoir.

razor-sharp /ˌreɪzəˈʃɑːp/ *adj* **1** [*blade, knife, edge*] tranchant comme un rasoir; **2** [*wit, mind*] acéré.

razor: **~-shell** *n* GB Zool couteau *m*; **~ wire** *n* feuillard *m*.

razz○ /ræz/ *vtr* US taquiner.

razzle○ /ˈræzl/ *n* GB **to go on the ~**○ faire la bringue○ or la fête○.

razzledazzle○ /ˌræzlˈdæzl/ **I** *n* éclat *m* (trompeur).
II *modif* [*politics, salesmanship*] accrocheur/-euse○.

razzmatazz○ /ˌræzməˈtæz/ *n* folklore○ *m*, cirque○ *m*.

R & B *n* (*abrév* = **rhythm and blues**) rhythm and blues *m*.

RC *n, adj*: *abrév* ▶ **Roman Catholic**.

RCAF *n* (*abrév* = **Royal Canadian Air Force**) armée *f* de l'air canadienne.

RCMP *n* (*abrév* = **Royal Canadian Mounted Police**) police *f* montée canadienne.

RCN *n* **1** GB (*abrév* = **Royal College of Nursing**) école *f* d'infirmières; **2** (*abrév* = **Royal Canadian Navy**) marine *f* canadienne.

Rd *n*: *abrév écrite* = **road**.

R&D *n*: *abrév* ▶ **research and development**.

RDA *n* (*abrév* = **recommended daily amount**) AQR *mpl*.

re[1] /reɪ/ *n* ré *m*.

re[2] /riː/ *prep* (*abrév* = **with reference to**) (in letter head) 'objet:'; (about) au sujet de; **~ your letter...** suite à votre lettre...

RE *n* **1** GB Sch (*abrév* = **Religious Education**) éducation *f* religieuse; **2** GB Mil (*abrév* = **Royal Engineers**) génie *m* militaire britannique.

reach /riːtʃ/ **I** *n* **1** (physical range) portée *f*; **a long ~** une longue portée; **beyond** ou **out of ~ of** hors de portée; **'keep out of ~ of children'** 'tenir hors de portée des enfants'; **out of my ~** hors de ma portée; **within (arm's) ~** à portée de (la) main; **within easy ~ of** [*place*] à proximité de [*shops, facility*]; **to be within easy ~** être tout près; **2** (capability) **beyond** ou **out of ~ for** hors de portée de [*person*]; **within ~ for** à la portée de [*person*]; **to put sth within/beyond sb's ~** [*price*] mettre qch à la/hors de la portée de qn; **it's still well within her ~** c'est encore tout à fait à sa portée.
II reaches *npl* **1** (of society) **the upper/lower ~es** les échelons *mpl* les plus hauts/les plus bas; **2** Geog (river) **the upper/lower ~es** la partie *f* (*sg*) supérieure/inférieure.
III *vtr* **1** (after travel) [*person, train, river, ambulance*] atteindre [*place, person*]; [*sound, news, letter*] parvenir à [*person, place*]; **to ~ land** toucher terre; **the message took three days to ~ Paris** le message a mis trois jours pour arriver jusqu'à Paris; **the product has yet to ~ Italy/the shops** le produit n'est pas encore arrivé en Italie/dans les magasins; **easily ~ed by bus** facilement accessible par le bus; **2** (on scale, continuum) atteindre [*age, level, position, peak*]; **matters ~ed a point where** les choses en sont arrivées à un point où; **to ~ the finals** parvenir en finale; **3** (come to) arriver à [*decision, compromise, deal, understanding, conclusion*]; **to ~ a verdict** Jur rendre un verdict; **agreement has been ~ed on** on a abouti à un accord sur [*point*]; **4** (by stretching) atteindre [*object, shelf, switch*]; **can you ~ that box for me?** peux-tu me passer cette boîte?; **can you ~ me down that box?** GB peux-tu me descendre cette boîte?; **5** (contact) joindre; **to ~ sb by telephone** joindre qn au téléphone; **to ~ sb on** GB ou **at 514053** joindre qn au numéro 514053; **6** (make impact on) toucher [*audience, public, market*] (**with** avec); **7** (in height, length) arriver à [*floor, ceiling, roof*]; **the snow had ~ed the window** la neige arrivait jusqu'à la fenêtre; **curtains that ~ the floor** des rideaux qui descendent jusqu'au sol; **those trousers don't even ~ your ankles** ce pantalon ne t'arrive même pas aux chevilles; **her feet don't ~ the pedals** ses pieds ne touchent pas les pédales.
IV *vi* **1** (stretch) **to ~ up/down** lever/baisser le bras (**to do** pour faire); **to ~ across and do** étendre le bras et faire; **can you ~ out and close the door?** peux-tu étendre le bras et fermer la porte?; **to ~ for one's gun/a switch** étendre le bras pour saisir son arme/appuyer sur l'interrupteur; **the film will have you ~ing for your hanky!** hum ce film va vous faire sortir votre mouchoir!; **~ for the sky!** les mains en l'air!; **2** (extend) **to ~ (up/down) to** arriver jusqu'à; **her hair ~ed down to her waist** ses cheveux lui arrivaient jusqu'à la taille; **to ~ as far as** [*ladder, rope*] arriver jusqu'à.
■ **reach back**: **~ back to [sth/sb]** remonter à [*era, person*].
■ **reach out**: ¶ **~ out** lit étendre le bras; **to ~ out for** chercher [*affection, success*]; **to ~ out to** (help) aider; (make contact) établir un contact avec; ¶ **~ out [sth], ~ [sth] out** tendre; **to ~ out one's hand** tendre le bras.

react /rɪˈækt/ *vi* **1** (respond) réagir (**to** à; **against** contre); **2** Med (physically) réagir (**to** à); **3** Chem réagir (**with** avec; **on** sur).

reaction /rɪˈækʃn/ *n* **1** (response) réaction *f* (**to** à; **against** contre; **from** de); **2** Med réaction *f* (**to** à); **adverse ~s** effets *mpl* indésirables; **3** Chem réaction *f* (**with** avec; **between** entre); **4** Pol réaction *f*; **the forces of ~** les forces de la réaction.

reactionary /rɪˈækʃənrɪ, US -ənerɪ/ *n, adj* péj réactionnaire pej (*mf*).

reaction engine *n* moteur *m* à réaction.

reactivate /rɪˈæktɪveɪt/ *vtr* remettre [qn/qch] en fonction.

reactive /rɪˈæktɪv/ *adj* **1** Chem réactif/-ive; **2** Psych réactionnel/-elle.

reactor /rɪˈæktə(r)/ *n* **1** (nuclear) réacteur *m* (nucléaire); **2** Electron bobine *f* de réactance; **3** (agent) réacteur *m*; **4** (vat) réacteur *m*.

read **I** /riːd/ *n* surtout GB **to have a ~ of**○ jeter un coup d'œil sur○, lire [*article, magazine*]; **I enjoy a quiet ~** j'aime bien lire tranquillement; **I've already seen the newspaper, do you want a ~?** j'ai déjà regardé le journal, est-ce que tu veux le lire?; **to be an easy/exciting ~** être facile/passionnant à lire; **this book is a good ~** c'est un bon livre.

II /riːd/ *vtr* (*prét, pp* **read** /red/) **1** (in text etc) lire [*book, instructions, map, music, sign*] (**in** dans); **I read somewhere that** j'ai lu quelque part que; **to ~ sth to sb, to ~ sb sth** lire qch à qn; **to ~ sth aloud** lire qch à haute voix; **to ~ sth to oneself** lire qch; **she can ~** elle sait lire; **I can ~ German** je lis l'allemand; **2** (say) **the card ~s 'Happy Birthday Dad'** sur la carte il est écrit 'bon anniversaire Papa'; **the thermometer ~s 20 degrees** le thermomètre indique 20 degrés; **the sentence should ~ as follows** la phrase correcte est; **3** (decipher) lire [*braille, handwriting*]; ▶ **lip-read**; **4** (interpret) reconnaître [*signs*]; interpréter [*intentions, reactions*]; voir [*situation*]; **to ~ sb's thoughts** ou **mind** lire dans les pensées de qn; **to ~ sb's mood** connaître les humeurs de qn; **to ~ sb's tea-leaves** ≈ lire dans le marc de café; **to ~ palms** lire les lignes de la main; **to ~ a remark/statement as** considérer une remarque/déclaration comme; **don't ~ his comments as proof of his sincerity** ne considère pas ses commentaires comme une preuve de sa sincérité; **the book can be read as a satire** le livre peut se lire comme une satire; **to ~ sth into** lire qch derrière [*comment, message, sentence*]; **don't ~ too much into his reply** ne va pas imaginer des choses qu'il n'a pas dites; **5** GB Univ étudier; **she is ~ing history at Oxford** elle fait des études d'histoire à Oxford; **6** (take a recording) relever [*meter*]; lire [*dial, barometer, gauge*]; **I can't ~ what the dial says** je n'arrive pas à lire le cadran; **7** Radio, Telecom recevoir [*person, pilot*]; **I can ~ you loud and clear** je vous reçois cinq sur cinq; **8** Publg lire; **for 'cat' in line 12 ~ 'cart'** au lieu de 'cat' à la ligne 12, (il faut) lire 'cart'; **9** Comput [*computer*] lire [*data, file*].

III /riːd/ *vi* (*prét, pp* **read** /red/) **1** (look at or articulate text) lire (**to sb** à qn); **to ~ aloud** lire à haute voix (**to sb** à qn); **to ~ about sth** lire quelque chose sur [*accident, discovery*]; **I read about it in the 'Times'** j'ai lu quelque chose là-dessus dans le 'Times'; **I read about him yesterday** j'ai lu quelque chose à son sujet hier; **to ~ to sb from sth** lire qch à qn; **2** GB (study) **to ~ for a degree** ≈ préparer une licence (**in** de); **to ~ for the Bar** GB Jur préparer son entrée au barreau; **3** (create an impression) **the document ~s well/badly** le document se lit bien/mal; **the translation ~s like the original** la traduction est aussi bonne que l'original.

IV read /red/ *pp adj* **to take sth as read** considérer qch comme lu [*minutes, report*]; **the press took it as read that he was lying** pour la presse il était évident qu'il mentait; **can we take it as read that everybody will agree?** pouvons-nous considérer que tout le monde sera d'accord?

IDIOMS **to ~ between the lines** lire entre les lignes.

■ **read back**: **~ [sth] back** relire [*message, sentence*] (**to** à).

■ **read in**: **~ [sth] in, ~ in [sth]** [*computer*] enregistrer [*data*].

■ **read off**: **~ off [sth], ~ [sth] off** annoncer [*names, scores*].

■ **read on** continuer à lire.

■ **read out**: **~ [sth] out, ~ out [sth]** lire [qch] à haute voix.

■ **read over, read through**: **~ over** ou **through [sth], ~ [sth] over** ou **through** (for the first time) lire [*article, essay*]; (reread) relire [*notes, speech*].

■ **read up**: **to ~ up on sth/sb** étudier qch/qn à fond, potasser○.

readability /ˌriːdəˈbɪlətɪ/ *n* **1** (legibility) lisibilité *f*; **2** (clarity) clarté *f*.

readable /ˈriːdəbl/ *adj* **1** (legible) lisible; **2** (enjoyable) agréable à lire.

readdress /ˌriːəˈdres/ *vtr* **1** Post changer l'addresse sur [*envelope*]; réexpédier [*mail*]; **2** (take up again) revenir à [*question*].

reader /ˈriːdə(r)/ *n* **1** gen lecteur/-trice *m/f*; **an avid ~ of science fiction** un lecteur passionné de science fiction; **our regular ~s** nos lecteurs (réguliers); **she's a great ~ of French novels** elle aime beaucoup les romans français; **he's a slow ~** il lit lentement; **2** Sch (book) livre *m* de lecture; **3** GB Univ (person) chargé/-e *m/f* de cours; **4** US Univ (person) directeur/-trice *m/f* d'études; **5** (anthology) recueil *m* de textes; **6** Electron lecteur *m*; **7** Publg lecteur/-trice *m/f* dans une maison d'édition.

readership /ˈriːdəʃɪp/ *n* **1** GB Univ poste *m* de chargé/-e *m/f* de cours (**in** en); **2** ¢ Publg lecteurs *mpl*; **he shocked his female ~** il a choqué ses lectrices; **to have a huge ~** [*person*] être énormément lu; **the magazine has a ~ of 35,000** la revue a 35 000 lecteurs.

read head *n* Comput tête *f* de lecture.

readily /ˈredɪlɪ/ *adv* **1** (willingly) [*accept, agree, reply, admit, give*] sans hésiter; [*say*] avec empressement; **2** (easily) [*available, accessible, adaptable, comprehensible*] facilement; [*forget, forgive, understand, achieve, obtain*] facilement.

readiness /ˈredɪnɪs/ *n* **1** (preparedness) niveau *m* de préparation; **in ~ for sth** en prévision de qch; **to be in a state of ~** être (fin) prêt; **2** (willingness) empressement *m* (**to do** à faire); **3** (of response, wit) vivacité *f*.

reading /ˈriːdɪŋ/ *n* **1** (skill, pastime) lecture *f*; **~ is one of my hobbies** la lecture est l'un de mes passe-temps; **~ and writing** la lecture et l'écriture; **his ~ is poor** il lit mal; **2** (books) lecture *f*; **these texts are recommended/required ~** la lecture de ces textes est recommandée/obligatoire; **her novels make light/heavy ~** ses romans sont faciles/difficiles à lire; **a woman of wide ~** une femme très cultivée; **3** (recorded measurement) (on meter) relevé *m* (**on** de); (on instrument) indication *f* (**on** de); **to take a ~** faire or prendre un relevé; **gas ~** relevé du gaz; **barometer ~** indication barométrique; **4** (interpretation) interprétation *f* (**of** de); **5** (spoken extract) lecture *f* (**from** de); **6** (of will, banns) lecture *f*; **7** Bible lecture *f* (**from** de); **8** GB Pol lecture *f* (**of** de); **the bill was defeated at its second ~** le projet de loi a été rejeté en deuxième lecture.

reading age *n* Sch niveau *m* de lecture; **he has a ~ of eight** il a le niveau de lecture d'un enfant de huit ans; **children of ~** les enfants en âge de lire.

reading: **~ glass** *n* loupe *f*; **~ glasses** *npl* lunettes *fpl* (pour lire).

reading knowledge *n* **to have a ~ of German** savoir lire l'allemand; **her ~ of Italian is good** son niveau de lecture en italien est bon.

reading: **~ lamp** *n* (by bed) lampe *f* de chevet; (on desk) lampe *f* de bureau; **~ list** *n* Sch, Univ liste *f* d'ouvrages recommandés.

reading matter *n* **it is not suitable ~ for children** ce n'est pas une lecture pour les enfants; **I've run out of ~** je n'ai plus rien à lire; **I'm looking for ~** je cherche de la lecture.

reading: **~ room** *n* salle *f* de lecture; **~ scheme** *n* GB Sch méthode *f* d'enseignement de la lecture; **~ speed** *n* Comput vitesse *f* de lecture.

readjust /ˌriːəˈdʒʌst/ **I** *vtr* rajuster [*hat*]; régler [qch] de nouveau [*television, lens*]; remettre [qch] à l'heure [*watch*]; réajuster [*salary*].

II *vi* se réadapter (**to** à).

readjustment /ˌrɪːəˈdʒʌstmənt/ *n* **1** (of television, machine) réglage *m*; (of salary) réajustement *m*; **2** (to new situation) réadaptation *f* (**to** à).

read: **~ mode** *n* Comput mode *m* lecture (seulement); **~-only memory**, **ROM** *n* Comput mémoire *f* morte; **~-out** *n* Comput extraction *f*.

readvertise /riːˈædvətaɪz/ **I** *vtr* refaire paraître une annonce pour [*post, sale, item*].

II *vi* refaire paraître une annonce.

readvertisement /ˌriːədˈvɜːtɪsmənt, US ˌriːədvərˈtaɪzmənt/ *n* seconde insertion *f*; **'this is a ~'** Journ 'cette annonce paraît pour la seconde fois'.

read: **~-write access** *n* Comput consultation *f* et mise *f* à jour; **~-write head** *n* Comput tête *f* de lecture-écriture; **~-write memory** *n* Comput mémoire *f* vive.

ready /ˈredɪ/ **I** *n* (**to have**) **a gun/pen at the ~** (être) prêt à tirer/écrire.

II○ **readies** *npl* fric○ *m*, argent *m*.

III *adj* **1** (prepared) [*person, meal, car, product*] prêt (**for sth** pour qch); **~ to do** prêt à faire; **to get ~** se préparer; **to get sth ~** préparer qch; **to make ~ to do** se préparer à faire; **~ for anything** prêt à tout; **~ when you are** quand tu veux; **~, steady, go** Sport à vos marques, prêts, partez!; **~ about!** Naut pare à virer!; **I'm ~, willing and able** je suis à votre service; **~ and waiting** fin prêt; **2** (willing) prêt (**to do** à faire); **more than ~ to do** plus que disposé à faire; **she/the house looked ~ to collapse** elle/la maison semblait prête à s'effondrer; **to be ~ for** avoir besoin de [*meal, vacation*]; **to feel ~ for a rest** avoir besoin de se reposer; **3** (quick) [*answer*] tout prêt; [*wit*] vif/vive; [*smile*] facile; **to be ~ with one's criticism/excuses** être prompt à critiquer/faire des excuses; **4** (available) [*market, supply, source*] à portée (de main); [*access*] direct; **~ to hand** à portée de main; **~ cash**○, **~ money**○ (argent *m*) liquide *m*.

IV *vtr* préparer [*ship, car*] (**for sth** à qch).

V *v refl* **to ~ oneself** se préparer (**for sth** à qch).

ready-made /ˌredɪˈmeɪd/ **I** *n* Art objet *m* trouvé.

II *adj* **1** (for immediate use) [*suit, jacket*] de prêt-à-porter; [*curtains*] prêt à poser; [*furniture*] déjà monté; **2** [*excuse, idea, phrase*] tout fait.

ready: **~-mix** *n* (cement) béton *m* prémélangé; **~ reckoner** *n* barème *m*; **~-to-serve** *adj* [*food*] cuisiné; **~-to-wear** *adj* [*garment*] prêt-à-porter.

reaffirm /ˌriːəˈfɜːm/ *vtr* réaffirmer.

reafforestation GB, **reforestation** US /ˌriːəˌfɒrɪˈsteɪʃn/ *n* reboisement *m*.

reagent /riːˈeɪdʒənt/ *n* réactif *m*.

real /rɪəl/ **I** *n* réel *m*.

II *adj* **1** (actual, not imaginary or theoretical) véritable, réel/réelle; **~ or imagined insults** des injures réelles ou imaginaires; **the threat is very ~** la menace est tout à fait réelle; **there's no real cause for alarm** il n'y a pas vraiment de raison de s'inquiéter; **he has no ~ power** il n'a pas de pouvoir véritable; **in ~ life** dans la réalité; **the ~ world** le monde réel, la réalité; **it's not like that in the ~ world** ce n'est pas comme ça dans la réalité; **in ~ terms** en réalité; **2** (not artificial or imitation) [*champagne, diamond, flower, leather*] vrai (*before n*), authentique; **are these ~ orchids?** est-ce que ce sont de vraies orchidées?; **the ~ thing, the ~ McCoy**○ de l'authentique, du vrai de vrai○; **this time it's the ~ thing** cette fois c'est pour de vrai○; **3** (true, proper) [*Christian,*

Socialist, altruism] véritable, vrai (*before n*); **it's ages since I had a ~ holiday** ça fait très longtemps que je n'ai pas eu de véritables vacances; **he knows the ~ you/me** il connaît ta/ma vraie personnalité; **the ~ France/Africa** la France/l'Afrique profonde; **4** (for emphasis) [*idiot, charmer, stroke of luck, pleasure*] vrai (*before n*); **it's a ~ shame** c'est vraiment dommage; **it was a ~ laugh**○ on s'est bien marré○; **this room is a ~ oven** cette pièce est une vraie fournaise; **5** Fin, Comm [*asset, capital, cost, income, value*] réel/réelle; **in ~ terms** en termes réels; **6** Math réel/réelle.

III *adv*○ US [*good, sorry, soon, fast*] vraiment.

IDIOMS **for ~**○ pour de vrai○; **is he for ~?** US (serious) il est sérieux?; (what a fool) quel idiot○!; **get ~**○! reviens sur terre!

real: **~ accounts** *npl* Comm comptes *mpl* de valeur; **~ ale** *n* GB bière *f* (*de fabrication artisanale*).

real estate *n* **1** Jur Comm (property) biens *mpl* immobiliers; **2** US (selling land, houses) immobilier *m*; **to be in ~** être dans l'immobilier.

real estate: **~ agent** *n* US agent *m* immobilier; **~ developer** *n* US promoteur *m*; **~ office** *n* US agence *f* immobilière.

realign /ˌriːəˈlaɪn/ **I** *vtr* **1** lit remettre [qch] à l'alignement [*objects*]; changer le tracé de [*runway, road*]; **2** fig redéfinir [*views*]; **3** Fin réaligner [*currency*].

II *vi* Pol former de nouvelles alliances; **to ~ with** se réaligner sur.

realignment /ˌriːəˈlaɪnmənt/ *n* **1** (of runway, road) nouveau tracé *m*; **2** fig (of view) redéfinition *f*; Pol (of stance) réalignement *m*; **3** Fin (of currency) réalignement *m*.

realism /ˈriːəlɪzəm/ *n* (all contexts) réalisme *m*; **to lend ~ to sth** donner du réalisme à qch.

realist /ˈriːəlɪst/ *n, adj* (all contexts) réaliste (*mf*).

realistic /ˌrɪəˈlɪstɪk/ *adj* (all contexts) réaliste; **it is not ~ to do** ce n'est pas réaliste de faire.

realistically /ˌrɪəˈlɪstɪklɪ/ *adv* [*look at, think, portray, describe*] de façon réaliste; **~, she can expect**... en réalité, elle peut s'attendre à...

reality /rɪˈælətɪ/ *n* (all contexts) réalité *f* (**of** de); **to be out of touch with ~** vivre hors des réalités; **the economic realities** les réalités économiques; **the ~ is that** la réalité c'est que; **in ~** en réalité.

realizable /ˈrɪəlaɪzəbl/ *adj* (all contexts) réalisable.

realization /ˌrɪəlaɪˈzeɪʃn, US -lɪˈz-/ *n* **1** (awareness) prise *f* de conscience (**of** de; **that** du fait que); **to come to the ~ that** se rendre compte que; **the ~ dawned (on her) that** elle s'est rendu compte que; **there is a growing ~ in society that** la société prend de plus en plus conscience que; **2** (of dream, goal, fear, design, opera) réalisation *f* (**of** de); **3** (of self, potential) épanouissement *m*; **4** Fin conversion *f* en espèces.

realize /ˈrɪəlaɪz/ *vtr* **1** (know, be aware of) se rendre compte de [*error, gravity, significance, fact, extent*]; **I suddenly ~d who he was** tout d'un coup je me suis rendu compte qui c'était; **to ~ that** se rendre compte que; **I ~ you feel differently** je me rends bien compte que vous n'êtes pas du même avis; **to ~ how/why/what** comprendre comment/pourquoi/ce que; **more/less than people ~** plus/moins que les gens n'en ont conscience; **to come to ~ sth** prendre conscience de qch; **I fully realize that**... je comprends complètement que...; **to make sb ~ sth** faire comprendre qch à qn; **I didn't ~!** je ne le savais pas!; **you don't ~ what you're doing** tu es complètement inconscient; **I ~ that!** oui, je sais bien!; **do you ~ that I'm waiting for you?** tu te rends compte que je t'attends?; **you do ~, of course, that** tu as bien sûr conscience que; **I ~ you're busy/it's late, but**... j'ai conscience que vous êtes occupé/qu'il est tard, mais...; **2** (make concrete, real) réaliser [*idea, dream, goal, design*]; **my worst fears were ~d** ce que je craignais le plus est arrivé; **to ~ one's potential** développer ses capacités; **3** Fin (liquidate) réaliser, liquider [*assets*]; **4** Comm [*sale, house, object*] rapporter [*sum*]; [*person, vendor*] faire [*sum*] (**on** en vendant); **to ~ a profit** réaliser un bénéfice.

reallocate /riːˈæləkeɪt/ *vtr* réattribuer [*funds, resources, space, task, time*].

reallocation /ˌriːæləˈkeɪʃən/ *n* réattribution *f*.

really /ˈrɪəlɪ/ **I** *adv* **1** (for emphasis) vraiment, réellement; **they ~ enjoyed the film** le film leur a vraiment plu; **you ~ ought to have ironed them** tu aurais vraiment dû les repasser; **I don't believe it, ~ I don't** je n'y crois vraiment pas; **you ~ must taste it** il faut absolument que tu y goûtes; **I ~ like that colour** j'aime vraiment cette couleur; **2** (very) [*cheap, hot, badly, well*] très, vraiment; **~ big** très grand; **~ good** très bon/bonne; **3** (in actual fact) en fait, réellement; **it was ~ 100 dollars not 50 dollars** en fait, c'était 100 dollars et non pas 50 dollars; **what I ~ mean is that**... en fait, ce que je veux dire c'est que...; **I suppose I did exaggerate ~** en fait, j'ai peut-être exagéré un peu; **he's a good teacher ~** en fait, c'est un bon professeur; **ghosts don't ~ exist** les fantômes n'existent pas; **I'll tell you what ~ happened** je vais te dire ce qui s'est réellement passé; **4** (seriously, in all honesty) vraiment; **I ~ don't know** je ne sais vraiment pas; **do you ~ think he'll apologize?** tu penses vraiment qu'il s'excusera?; **~?** (expressing disbelief) c'est vrai?; **'I'm 45'—'are you ~?'** 'j'ai 45 ans'—'c'est vrai?'; **does she ~?** c'est vrai?

II *excl* (also **well ~**) (expressing annoyance) franchement!

realm /relm/ *n* **1** littér (kingdom) royaume *m*; **2** fig domaine *m*.

real: **~ number** *n* Math nombre *m* réel; **~ presence** *n* Relig présence *f* réelle; **~ tennis** *n* jeu *m* de paume; **~ time** *n* Comput, gen temps *m* réel; **~-time computer** *n* ordinateur *m* exploité en temps réel; **~-time processing** *n* traitement *m* en temps réel; **~-time system** *n* système *m* temps réel.

realtor /ˈriːəltə(r)/ *n* US agent *m* immobilier (*accrédité*).

realty /ˈriːəltɪ/ *n* US biens *mpl* immobiliers; **to be in ~** travailler dans l'immobilier.

ream /riːm/ **I** *n* (of paper) rame *f* (de papier); **she wrote ~s about it** fig elle en a écrit des tonnes○ or toute une tartine○.

II *vtr* Tech fraiser.

reamer /ˈriːmə(r)/ *n* Tech fraise *f*.

reanimate /ˌriːˈænɪmeɪt/ *vtr* ranimer.

reap /riːp/ **I** *vtr* **1** Agric moissonner, recueillir [*crop*]; **2** fig récolter [*benefits, profits*]; **to ~ the rewards of one's efforts** recueillir le fruit de ses efforts.

II *vi* moissonner.

IDIOMS **to ~ what one has sown** récolter ce qu'on a semé.

reaper /ˈriːpə(r)/ *n* **1** (machine) moissonneuse *f*; **2** (person) moissonneur/-euse *m/f*.

reaper-and-binder *n* moissonneuse-lieuse *f*.

reaping /ˈriːpɪŋ/ *n* moisson *f*.

reaping: **~ hook** *n* faucille *f*; **~ machine** *n* moissonneuse *f*.

reappear /ˌriːəˈpɪə(r)/ *vi* reparaître.

reappearance /ˌriːəˈpɪərəns/ *n* réapparition *f*.

reapply /ˌriːəˈplaɪ/ *vi* reposer sa candidature (**for** à).

reappoint /ˌriːəˈpɔɪnt/ *vtr* renommer (**to** à).

reappointment /ˌriːəˈpɔɪntmənt/ *n* renouvellement *m* de nomination (**to** à).

reapportion /ˌriːəˈpɔːʃn/ *vtr* **1** redistribuer, répartir à nouveau [*land, money etc*]; **2** US Pol redécouper [*electoral distribution*].

reapportionment /ˌriːəˈpɔːʃnmənt/ *n* US Pol redécoupage *m* électoral.

reappraisal /ˌriːəˈpreɪzl/ *n* (of question, policy) réexamen *m*; (of writer, work) réévaluation *f*.

reappraise /ˌriːəˈpreɪz/ *vtr* réexaminer [*question, policy*]; réévaluer [*writer, work*].

rear /rɪə(r)/ **I** *n* **1** (of building, car, room etc) arrière *m*; **at the ~ of the house** derrière la maison; **(viewed) from the ~** [*building, monument etc*] vu de l'arrière; [*person*] vu de dos; **'to ~'** (in estate agent's brochure) 'à l'arrière'; **2** (of procession, train) queue *f*; Mil (of unit, convoy) arrière-garde *f*, arrières *mpl*; (of column) queue *f*; **at the ~ of the train** en queue de train; **to attack the enemy in the ~** attaquer l'ennemi à revers; **to bring up the ~** gen, Mil fermer la marche; **3** euph (of person) derrière○ *m*.

II *adj* **1** [*entrance, garden*] de derrière; **2** Aut [*light, seat, suspension*] arrière *inv*.

III *vtr* élever [*child, family, animals*]; cultiver [*plants*]; **to be ~ed on classical music** être nourri de musique classique; ▶ **ugly**.

IV *vi* (also **~ up**) [*horse*] se cabrer; [*snake*] se dresser; fig [*building, tree etc*] s'élever, se dresser.

rear: **~ access** *n* accès *m* arrière; **~ admiral** *n* contre-amiral *m*; **~ bumper** *n* Aut pare-chocs *m inv* arrière *inv*; **~ compartment** *n* Aut arrière *m*; **~ door** *n* (in house) porte *f* de derrière; Aut portière *f* arrière *inv*, porte *f* arrière *inv*; **~-drive** *adj* à traction *f* arrière.

rear end /ˌrɪər ˈend/ **I** *n* **1** (of vehicle) arrière *m*; **2** euph (of person) derrière *m*.

II○ **rear-end** *vtr* US emboutir○ l'arrière de [*person, car*].

rear-engined /ˌrɪərˈendʒɪnd/ *adj* avec moteur à l'arrière.

rearguard /ˈrɪəɡɑːd/ *n* Mil, fig arrière-garde *f*.

rearguard action *n* combat *m* d'arrière-garde; **to fight a ~** mener un combat d'arrière-garde (**against** contre).

rear gunner *n* mitrailleur *m* arrière *inv*.

rearm /ˌriːˈɑːm/ *vtr, vi* réarmer.

rearmament /ˌriːˈɑːməmənt/ *n* réarmement *m*.

rearmost /ˈrɪəməʊst/ *adj* gen tout/-e dernier/-ière; [*carriage*] de queue; [*room*] du fond.

rear: **~-mounted** *adj* installé à l'arrière; **~ projection** *n* (projection *f* par) transparence *f*.

rearrange /ˌriːəˈreɪndʒ/ *vtr* réarranger [*hair, hat*]; redisposer [*furniture*]; réaménager [*room*]; modifier [*plans*]; déplacer [*engagement*].

rearrangement /ˌriːəˈreɪndʒmənt/ *n* (of furniture) redisposition *f*; (of room) réaménagement *m*; (of plans) modification *f*.

rear-view mirror *n* rétroviseur *m*.

rearward /ˈrɪəwəd/ **I** *n* arrière *m*.

II *adj* [*position*] à l'arrière; [*movement*] en arrière.

III (also **rearwards**) *adv* vers l'arrière.

rear wheel *n* Aut roue *f* arrière *inv*.

rear-wheel drive Aut **I** *n* traction *f* arrière.

II *modif* [*vehicle*] à traction arrière.

rear window *n* Aut vitre *f* arrière *inv*.

reason /ˈriːzn/ **I** *n* **1** (cause) raison *f* (**for, behind** de); **for a (good) ~** pour une bonne raison; **for no (good) ~, without good ~** sans raison valable; **not without ~** non sans raison; **for some ~ or other** pour une raison ou pour une autre; **if you are late for any ~** si tu es en retard, pour une raison ou pour une autre; **for ~s best known to herself** pour des raisons connues d'elle seule; **for the (very) good** ou **simple**

~ that pour la simple et bonne raison que; **for ~s of space/time** pour des raisons de place/temps; **for health ~s** pour raisons de santé; **I have ~ to believe that...** j'ai des raisons de croire que...; **by ~ of** sout en raison de; **for that ~ I can't do it** c'est pour cette raison or c'est pour cela que je ne peux pas le faire; **2** (explanation) raison *f*; **the ~ why...** la raison pour laquelle...; **there are several ~s why I have to go** il y a plusieurs raisons qui m'obligent à partir; **I'll tell you the ~ why...** je vais te dire pourquoi...; **and that's the ~ why...** et c'est pourquoi...; **give me one ~ why I should!** et pourquoi donc devrais-je le faire?; **what was his ~ for resigning?** pour quelle raison a-t-il démissionné?; **the ~ for having rules** la raison pour laquelle il y a des règles; **the ~ is that** la raison en est que; **the ~ given is that** la raison invoquée est que; **for some unknown ~** pour une raison inconnue; **3** (grounds) raison *f*; **a good/bad ~ for doing** une bonne/mauvaise raison pour faire; **to have every ~ for doing** ou **to do** avoir tout lieu de faire; **to have good ~ to do** avoir tout lieu de faire; **he had better ~ than most to complain** il avait davantage lieu que d'autres de se plaindre; **I see no ~ to think so** il n'y a pas lieu à mon avis de le penser; **there was no ~ for you to worry** il n'y avait pas de quoi vous inquiéter; **all the more ~ to insist on it** raison de plus pour insister; **she was angry, and with good ~** elle était fâchée, et à juste titre; **4** (common sense) raison *f*; **the power/the voice of ~** le pouvoir/la voix de la raison; **to lose one's ~** perdre la raison; **to listen to** ou **see ~** entendre raison; **it stands to ~ that** il va sans dire que; **within ~** dans la limite du raisonnable; **sweet ~** hum bon sens.

II *vtr* **1** (argue) soutenir (**that** que); **'suppose she killed him,' he ~ed** 'suppose qu'elle l'ait tué,' dit-il; **2** (conclude) déduire (**that** que); **'she must have killed him,' he ~ed** 'elle a dû le tuer,' en a-t-il déduit.

III *vi* **to ~ with sb** raisonner qn.

IV **reasoned** *pp adj* [*argument, approach*] raisonné.

■ **reason out**: **~ out [sth], ~ [sth] out** trouver une solution à [*problem*].

reasonable /ˈriːznəbl/ *adj* **1** (sensible) [*person*] raisonnable; **be ~!** sois raisonnable!; **2** (understanding) [*person*] compréhensif/-ive (**about** au sujet de); **3** (justified) légitime; **it is ~ for sb to do** il est légitime que qn fasse; **it is ~ that he should want to know** son désir de savoir est légitime; **beyond ~ doubt** Jur sans aucun doute possible; **4** (not too expensive) raisonnable; **5**○ (moderately good) convenable; **the food is ~** la cuisine est convenable; **there is a ~ chance that** il est fort possible que.

reasonableness /ˈriːznəblnɪs/ *n* **1** (of remark, argument) bien-fondé *m*; **2** (understanding) réaction *f* posée (**over, about** à propos de).

reasonably /ˈriːznəblɪ/ *adv* **1** (legitimately) légitimement; (sensibly) raisonnablement; **2** (rather) [*comfortable, convenient, confident, satisfied*] assez; **'how are you getting on?'—'~ well'** 'comment ça va?'—'assez bien'.

reasoning /ˈriːznɪŋ/ **I** *n* raisonnement *m*; **powers of ~** capacités de raisonnement; **what is the ~ behind the decision?** quel raisonnement a motivé cette décision?

II *modif* [*skills*] de raisonnement.

reassemble /ˌriːəˈsembl/ **I** *vtr* **1** rassembler [*troops, pupils*]; **2** Tech remonter [*unit, engine etc*].

II *vi* [*people*] se rassembler; **school ~s on 7 January** l'école reprend le 7 janvier.

reassert /ˌriːəˈsɜːt/ **I** *vtr* réaffirmer [*authority, claim*].

II *v refl* **to ~ oneself** [*person*] s'imposer à nouveau; **old habits soon ~ themselves** les vieilles habitudes reprennent vite le dessus.

reassess /ˌriːəˈses/ *vtr* gen réexaminer, reconsidérer [*problem, situation*]; Tax recalculer [*liability*]; Jur réévaluer [*damages*].

reassessment /ˌriːəˈsesmənt/ *n* gen (of situation) réexamen *m*; Tax nouveau calcul *m*; Jur réévaluation *f*.

reassurance /ˌriːəˈʃɔːrəns, US -ˈʃʊər-/ *n* **1** (comfort) réconfort *m*; **2** (security) assurance *f*; **you'll have the ~ of a three-year guarantee** Comm vous aurez la sécurité d'une garantie de trois ans; **3** (official guarantee) **to receive ~s/a ~ from sb that** recevoir de qn des garanties/la garantie que.

reassure /ˌriːəˈʃɔː(r), US -ˈʃʊər-/ *vtr* rassurer (**about** sur).

reassuring /ˌriːəˈʃɔːrɪŋ, US -ˈʃʊər-/ *adj* gen rassurant; Psych sécurisant.

reassuringly /ˌriːəˈʃɔːrɪŋlɪ, US -ˈʃʊər-/ *adv* [*smile*] d'une manière rassurante; [*say*] sur un ton rassurant; **~ familiar** d'une familiarité rassurante.

reawaken /ˌriːəˈweɪkən/ **I** *vtr* **1** sout réveiller à nouveau [*person*]; **2** fig faire renaître [*interest, enthusiasm*].

II *vi* sout [*person*] se réveiller de nouveau.

reawakening /ˌriːəˈweɪkənɪŋ/ *n* sout réveil *m*.

reb, Reb○ /reb/ *n* US Hist (also **Johnny Reb**) soldat *m* confédéré.

rebarbative /rɪˈbɑːbətɪv/ *adj* sout rébarbatif/-ive, rebutant.

rebate /ˈriːbeɪt/ *n* **1** (refund) remboursement *m*; **2** (discount) remise *f*.

rebel **I** /ˈrebl/ *n* révolté/-e *m/f*, rebelle *mf* also fig.

II /ˈrebl/ *modif* [*soldier, group*] rebelle.

III /rɪˈbel/ *vi* (*p prés etc* **-ll-**) lit, fig se rebeller (**against** contre), se révolter (**against** contre).

rebellion /rɪˈbelɪən/ *n* rébellion *f*, révolte *f*; **to rise in ~** se rebeller, se soulever.

rebellious /rɪˈbelɪəs/ *adj* [*nation, people, child*] rebelle, insoumis; [*school, class*] indiscipliné.

rebelliousness /rɪˈbelɪəsnɪs/ *n* (tendency) esprit *m* de rébellion; (behaviour) attitude *f* rebelle.

rebirth /ˌriːˈbɜːθ/ *n* lit, fig renaissance *f*.

reboot /ˌriːˈbuːt/ *vtr* Comput réinitialiser, réamorcer.

rebore **I** /ˈriːbɔː(r)/ *n* réalésage *m*.

II /ˌriːˈbɔː(r)/ *vtr* réaléser.

reborn /ˌriːˈbɔːn/ *adj* **1** Relig **to be ~** renaître (**into** à); **2 to be ~ as sth** réapparaître sous la forme de qch.

rebound **I** /ˈriːbaʊnd/ *n* (of ball) rebond *m*; (in basketball) panier *m*; **he caught the ball on the ~** il a attrapé le ballon après le rebond; **to be on the ~** [*prices*] remonter; **to marry sb on the ~** épouser qn sous le coup d'une déception amoureuse.

II /rɪˈbaʊnd/ *vi* **1** lit (bounce) rebondir; **2** fig **to ~ on** (affect adversely) se retourner contre; **3** (recover) [*prices, interest rates*] remonter.

rebroadcast /ˌriːˈbrɔːdkɑːst, US -kæst/ **I** *n* (repeat) rediffusion *f*; (live) retransmission *f*.

II *vtr* (*prét, pp* **-cast** ou **-casted**) (repeat) rediffuser; (relay live) retransmettre.

rebuff /rɪˈbʌf/ **I** *n* rebuffade *f*; **to meet with a ~** essuyer une rebuffade.

II *vtr* rabrouer [*person*]; repousser [*suggestion, advances*].

rebuild /ˌriːˈbɪld/ *vtr* (*prét, pp* **rebuilt** /riːˈbɪlt/) Constr reconstruire, rebâtir [*building*]; gen reconstruire [*country, business*].

rebuilding /ˌriːˈbɪldɪŋ/ *n* reconstruction *f*.

rebuke /rɪˈbjuːk/ **I** *n* réprimande *f*.

II *vtr* réprimander (**for** pour; **for doing** pour avoir fait).

rebus /ˈriːbəs/ *n* (*pl* **~es**) rébus *m*.

rebut /rɪˈbʌt/ *vtr* (*p prés etc* **-tt-**) réfuter.

rebuttal /rɪˈbʌtl/ *n* réfutation *f*.

rec○ /rek/ *n* GB (*abrév* = **recreation ground**) terrain *m* de jeux.

recalcitrance /rɪˈkælsɪtrəns/ *n* sout esprit *m* récalcitrant.

recalcitrant /rɪˈkælsɪtrənt/ *adj* sout récalcitrant.

recalculate /ˌriːˈkælkjʊleɪt/ *vtr* recalculer [*price, loss etc*].

recall **I** /ˈriːkɔːl/ *n* **1** (memory) mémoire *f*; **he has amazing powers of ~** il a une mémoire extraordinaire; **to have total ~ of sth** se souvenir de qch dans les moindres détails; **lost beyond** ou **past ~** irrévocablement perdu; **2** gen, Mil, Comput (summons) rappel *m*.

II /rɪˈkɔːl/ *vtr* **1** (remember) se souvenir de; **I ~ seeing/what happened** je me souviens d'avoir vu/de ce qui est arrivé; **as I ~** si je m'en souviens bien; **you will ~ that...** comme vous le savez...; **'it was in 1972,' he ~ed** 'c'était en 1972,' se remémora-t-il; **2** (remind of) rappeler; **3** (summon back) gen, Mil, Comput rappeler [*troops, witness, ambassador, faulty product*]; convoquer [*parliament*].

recant /rɪˈkænt/ **I** *vtr* abjurer [*heresy*]; désavouer [*opinion*]; rétracter [*statement*].

II *vi* gen se rétracter; Relig abjurer.

recantation /ˌriːkænˈteɪʃn/ *n* (of statement) rétractation *f*; (of opinion) désaveu *m*; Relig abjuration *f*.

recap **I** *n* **1**○ /ˈriːkæp/ *abrév* ▸**recapitulation**; **2** /ˌriːˈkæp/ US (tyre) pneu *m* rechapé.

II *vtr* (*p prés etc* **-pp-**) **1**○ /ˈriːkæp/ *abrév* ▸**recapitulate**; **2** /ˌriːˈkæp/ US rechaper [*tyre*].

recapitalization /ˌrɪːkæpɪtəlaɪˈzeɪʃən/ *n* Fin recapitalisation.

recapitalization plan *n* Fin plan *m* de recapitalisation.

recapitalize /ˌriːˈkæpɪtəlaɪz/ *vtr* Fin recapitaliser.

recapitulate /ˌriːkəpɪtʃʊleɪt/ sout **I** *vtr* reprendre, récapituler.

II *vi* reprendre, récapituler; **to ~ on sth** reprendre or récapituler qch.

recapitulation /ˌriːkəpɪtʃʊˈleɪʃn/ *n* sout récapitulation *f*.

recapture /ˌriːˈkæptʃə(r)/ **I** *n* (of prisoner, animal) capture *f*; (of town, position) reprise *f*.

II *vtr* **1** (catch) recapturer [*prisoner, animal*]; **2** (get back) Mil reprendre [*town, position*]; Pol reconquérir [*seat*]; **3** fig retrouver [*feeling*]; recréer [*period, atmosphere*].

recast /ˌriːˈkɑːst, US -ˈkæst/ *vtr* (*prét, pp* **recast**) **1** (reformulate) reformuler [*sentence, argument*] (**as** pour en faire); remanier [*text, plan*]; **2** Theat, Cin reprendre [qch] avec d'autres acteurs [*work*]; changer le rôle de [*actor*]; **3** Tech, Ind refondre.

recce○ /ˈrekɪ/ *n* gen, Mil reconnaissance *f*; **to be on a ~** faire une reconnaissance.

recd Comm *abrév écrite* = **received**.

recede **I** /rɪˈsiːd/ *vi* **1** lit, gen s'éloigner; [*tide*] descendre; fig [*hope, memory, prospect*] s'estomper; [*threat*] s'éloigner; [*prices*] baisser; **2** (go bald) [*person*] se dégarnir.

II **receding** /rɪˈsiːdɪŋ/ *pres p adj* [*chin, forehead*] fuyant; **he has a receding hairline** son front se dégarnit; **to have receding gums** avoir les gencives qui s'atrophient.

receipt /rɪˈsiːt/ **I** *n* **1** Comm (in writing) reçu *m*, récépissé *m* (**for** pour); (from till) ticket *m* de caisse; (for rent) quittance *f*; **2** Post (on sending) reçu *m*; (on delivery) accusé *m* de réception (**for** pour); **3** Admin, Comm (of goods, letters) réception *f*; **within 30 days of ~** à 30 jours de la réception; **to acknowledge ~ of sth** accuser réception de qch; **on ~ of sth** dès réception de qch; **to be in ~ of** recevoir [*income, benefits*].

II **receipts** *npl* Comm (takings) recette *f* (**from** de); **net/gross ~s** recette nette/brute.

III *vtr* acquitter [*bill, invoice*].

receipt book *n* livre *m* or carnet *m* de quittances.

receivable /rɪ'si:vəbl/ **I receivables** *npl* comptes *mpl* clients (**on** de).
II *adj* Comm, Fin [*bills*] à recevoir; **accounts ~** comptes *mpl* clients.

receive /rɪ'si:v/ **I** *vtr* **1** (get) recevoir [*letter, money, award, advice, support, treatment, education, training*] (**from** de); subir, essuyer [*setback*]; (wrongfully) receler [*stolen goods*]; recevoir [*bribe, illegal payment*]; **he ~d a 30-year sentence** Jur il a été condamné à 30 ans de prison; **'~d with thanks'** Comm 'pour acquit'; **to ~ its premiere** [*film*] avoir sa première projection; [*composition*] avoir sa première audition; **the bill will ~ its first reading** Pol le projet de loi sera examiné en première lecture; **2** (meet) accueillir, recevoir [*visitor, guest*]; recevoir [*delegation, ambassador*]; recevoir, accueillir [*proposal, article, play*] (**with** avec); **to be warmly ~d** être chaleureusement accueilli; **to be well** ou **positively ~d** être bien reçu; **3 to be ~d into** être reçu or admis dans [*church, order*]; **4** Radio, TV recevoir [*channel, radio message*]; capter, recevoir [*programme, satellite signals*]; **5** Admin (accept) accepter [*application*]; **'all contributions gratefully ~d'** 'merci d'avance de vos dons'; **6** US (in baseball) réceptionner.
II *vi* **1**† sout [*host*] recevoir; **2** GB Jur être coupable de recel.
III received *pp adj* [*ideas, opinions*] reçu.

received: **Received Pronunciation**, **RP** *n* GB prononciation *f* standard (de l'anglais); **Received Standard** *n* US = **Received Pronunciation**; **~ wisdom** *n* opinion *f* générale.

receiver /rɪ'si:və(r)/ *n* **1** (telephone) combiné *m*; **to pick up the ~** décrocher (le combiné); **to put down the ~** raccrocher (le combiné); **2** Radio, TV (equipment) (poste *m*) récepteur *m*; **3** GB Fin Jur (also **Official Receiver**) administrateur *m* judiciaire; **to be in the hands of the ~s** être sous administration judiciaire; **4** GB Jur **~ (of stolen goods)** receleur/-euse *m/f*; **5** Admin (recipient) (of goods, consignment) réceptionnaire *mf*; (of mail) destinataire *mf*; **6** US (in baseball) **(wide) ~** joueur *m* à la réception.

receiver dish *n* antenne *f* parabolique.

receivership /rɪ'si:vəʃɪp/ *n* GB Fin Jur **to go into ~** être placé sous administration judiciaire.

receiving /rɪ'si:vɪŋ/ **I** *n* GB Jur recel *m*.
II *adj* Comm (*épith*) [*department, office*] des réceptions.
IDIOMS **to be on the ~ end of** faire les frais de [*criticism, hostility*]; recevoir [*blow, punch*]; **he'd be a lot less happy if he was on the ~ end** il serait un peu moins ravi si c'était à lui que ça arrivait.

receiving: **~ blanket** *n* US doux nid *m*; **~ clerk** ▶ **1692** *n* Comm réceptionnaire *mf*; **~ line** *n* US *accueil des invités à un mariage*; **~ note** *n* bon *m* à embarquer; **~ order** *n* ordonnance *f* de mise sous séquestre.

recension /rɪ'senʃn/ *n* **1** (act) révision *f*; **2** (text) texte *m* révisé.

recent /'ri:snt/ *adj* [*event, change, arrival, film*] récent; [*acquaintance, development*] nouveau/-elle; **in ~ times** récemment; **in ~ years/weeks** au cours des dernières années/semaines; **to be a ~ graduate** être nouvellement diplômé.

recently /ri:'sntlɪ/ *adv* récemment, dernièrement; **quite/only ~** assez/tout récemment; **as ~ as Monday** pas plus tard que lundi; **until ~** jusqu'à ces derniers temps.

receptacle /rɪ'septəkl/ *n* récipient *m*.

reception /rɪ'sepʃn/ *n* **1** (also **~ desk**) réception *f*; **at ~** à la réception, à l'accueil; **2** (gathering) réception *f* (**for sb** en l'honneur de qn; **for sth** à l'occasion de qch); **3** (public response) accueil *m* (**for** de); **to get** ou **be given a favourable/hostile ~** recevoir un accueil favorable/hostile; **they gave us a great ~** [*fans, audience*] ils nous ont fait un accueil formidable; **4** (of guests, visitors) réception *f*; **5** Radio, TV réception *f* (**on** sur).

reception area *n* réception *f*.

reception camp, **reception centre** *n* centre *m* d'accueil (**for** pour).

reception: **~ class** *n* GB Sch ≈ cours *m* préparatoire; **~ committee** *n* comité *m* d'accueil also fig.

receptionist /rɪ'sepʃənɪst/ ▶ **1692** *n* réceptionniste *mf*.

reception room *n* **1** (in house) (grande) pièce *f*, pièce *f* de réception; **2** (in hotel) salle *f* de réception, salon *m*.

receptive /rɪ'septɪv/ *adj* réceptif/-ive (**to** à); **when he's in a more ~ mood** quand il sera plus disposé à écouter.

receptiveness /rɪ'septɪvnɪs/, **receptivity** /ˌri:sep'tɪvətɪ/ *n* réceptivité *f* (**to** à).

receptor /rɪ'septə(r)/ *n* récepteur *m*.

recess /rɪ'ses, US 'ri:ses/ **I** *n* **1** Jur, Pol (parliamentary) vacances *fpl* parlementaires; (in courts) vacances *fpl* judiciaires; **to be in ~** être en vacances; **2** US (break) (in school) récréation *f*; (during meeting) pause *f*; **3** Constr (for door, window) embrasure *f*; (large alcove) alcôve *f*; (smaller) niche *f*; (very small) recoin *m*.
II recesses *npl* **the ~es of** les recoins *mpl* de [*cupboard, room, building, cave*]; **in the ~es of her mind/her memory** dans les recoins de son esprit/sa mémoire; **in the deepest ~es of his heart** au plus profond de son cœur.
III *vtr* **1** Constr encastrer [*bath, light*]; **2** US (interrupt) suspendre [*meeting, hearing*].
IV *vi* US Jur, Pol suspendre les séances.
V recessed *pp adj* Constr [*bath, cupboard, seat, lighting*] encastré.

recession /rɪ'seʃn/ *n* **1** Econ (slump) récession *f*; **a world ~** une récession mondiale; **to go into ~** entrer dans la récession; **to be in ~** être en récession; **2** (of flood waters) retrait *m*.

recessional /rɪ'seʃənl/ Mus, Relig **I** *n* cantique *m* final.
II *adj* [*hymn*] final.

recessionary /rɪ'seʃənrɪ, US -nerɪ/ *adj* [*effect, measure, period*] de récession.

recessive /rɪ'sesɪv/ *adj* [*characteristic, gene*] récessif/-ive.

recharge /ˌri:'tʃɑ:dʒ/ *vtr* recharger [*battery*]; **to ~ one's batteries** fig recharger ses batteries.

rechargeable /ˌri:'tʃɑ:dʒəbl/ *adj* [*battery*] rechargeable.

recidivism /rɪ'sɪdɪvɪzəm/ *n* récidive *f*.

recidivist /rɪ'sɪdɪvɪst/ *n* récidiviste *mf*.

recipe /'resəpɪ/ *n* **1** Culin recette *f* (**for** de); **2** fig **it's a ~ for disaster/confusion** ça mène tout droit à la catastrophe/confusion; **a ~ for business success** ou **for succeeding in business** une recette pour réussir dans les affaires.

recipe book *n* livre *m* de recettes.

recipient /rɪ'sɪpɪənt/ *n* (receiver) (of mail) destinataire *mf*; (of benefits, aid, cheque) bénéficiaire *mf*; (of prize, award) lauréat/-e *m/f*; (of diploma) récipiendaire *mf*; (of blood, tissue etc) receveur/-euse *m/f*; **welfare ~** bénéficiaire *mf* d'aides sociales.

reciprocal /rɪ'sɪprəkl/ **I** *n* Math inverse *m*.
II *adj* (all contexts) réciproque.

reciprocally /rɪ'sɪprəklɪ/ *adv* réciproquement.

reciprocate /rɪ'sɪprəkeɪt/ **I** *vtr* retourner [*compliment*]; payer [qch] de retour [*love, kindness*]; rendre [*affection, invitation*].
II *vi* rendre la pareille.

reciprocating engine *n* moteur *m* alternatif.

reciprocation /rɪˌsɪprə'keɪʃn/ *n* (exchange) échange *m*; (return) retour *m*.

reciprocity /ˌresɪ'prɒsətɪ/ *n* gen, Math, Phot réciprocité *f*.

recital /rɪ'saɪtl/ **I** *n* **1** (of music, poetry) récital *m*; **to give a piano ~** donner un récital de piano; **in ~** en récital; **2** (narration) gen récit *m*; (tedious) énumération *f*.
II *modif* [*room, hall*] de concert.
III recitals *npl* Jur préambule *m*.

recitation /ˌresɪ'teɪʃn/ *n* Theat, Sch récitation *f*.

recitative /ˌresɪtə'ti:v/ *n* Mus récitatif *m*.

recite /rɪ'saɪt/ **I** *vtr* réciter [*speech, poem, list*]; énumérer [*facts, complaints*].
II *vi* réciter.

reckless /'reklɪs/ *adj* [*person*] (bold) téméraire; (foolish) imprudent; [*promise*] imprudent; **~ behaviour** inconscience *f*; **~ driving** Jur conduite *f* imprudente.

recklessly /'reklɪslɪ/ *adv* [*act*] (dangerously) avec imprudence; [*promise, spend*] de manière inconsciente.

recklessness /'reklɪsnɪs/ *n* (of person, behaviour) imprudence *f*.

reckon /'rekən/ **I** *vtr* **1** (judge, consider) estimer (**that** que); **we ~ that this solution is the best** nous estimons que cette solution est la meilleure; **sb/sth is ~ed to be** on estime que qn/qch est; **the region is ~ed to be uninhabitable** on estime que la région est inhabitable; **she is ~ed (to be) the cleverest** elle est considérée comme la plus intelligente; **he is ~ed among our best salesmen** il est considéré comme l'un de nos meilleurs vendeurs; **2**○ (think) **to ~ (that)** croire que; **I ~ we should leave now** je crois que nous devrions partir maintenant; **3** (estimate) estimer; **the number of part-time workers is ~ed at two million** le nombre des employés à temps partiel est estimé à deux millions; **I ~ he's about 50** à mon avis il a à peu près 50 ans; **what do you ~ our chances of survival are?** quelles sont, à votre avis, nos chances de survie?; **4** (expect) **to ~ to do** compter faire; **we ~ to reach London by midday** nous comptons arriver à Londres avant midi; **5** (calculate accurately) calculer [*charges, amount, number, rent*]; **6**○ (believe to be good) **I don't ~ your chances of success** je doute de vos chances de succès; **7**○ (like) estimer [*person*].
II *vi* calculer.
■ **reckon on**○: ¶ **~ on [sb/sth]** compter sur; ¶ **~ on doing** s'attendre à faire; ¶ **~ on sb** ou **sb's doing** (expect) attendre de qn qu'il fasse; (rely) compter sur qn pour qu'il fasse.
■ **reckon up**: ¶ **~ up** calculer; ¶ **~ [sth] up, ~ up [sth]** calculer.
■ **reckon with**: **~ with [sb/sth]** compter avec; **we had to ~ with a lot of opposition** il nous a fallu compter avec une opposition importante; **a force to be ~ed with** une force avec laquelle il faut compter.
■ **reckon without**: **~ without [sb/sth]** compter sans.

reckoning /'rekənɪŋ/ *n* **1** gen (estimation) estimation *f*; (accurate calculation) calculs *mpl*; **you were £10 out in your ~** vous vous êtes trompé de dix livres dans vos calculs; **by my ~/the president's ~** d'après mes estimations/les estimations du président; **to bring sb/to come into the ~** ramener qn/être dans la course; **2** Naut estime *f*.
IDIOMS **day of ~** Relig jour *m* du Jugement (dernier); **there's bound to be a day of ~ (for him/them etc)** hum, fig il lui/leur etc faudra payer un jour.

reclaim /rɪ'kleɪm/ *vtr* **1** Ecol reconquérir [*coastal land*]; mettre en valeur [*site*]; assécher [*marsh*]; défricher [*forest*]; assainir [*polluted land*]; irriguer [*desert*]; (recycle) récupérer [*glass, metal*]; **2** (get back) récupérer [*possessions, deposit, money*]; **3** littér (redeem) récupérer; **a ~ed drunkard** un alcoolique repenti.

reclaimable /rɪ'kleɪməbl/ *adj* **1** [*waste product*] récupérable; **2** [*expenses*] remboursable.

reclamation /ˌreklə'meɪʃn/ *n* **1** (recycling) récupération *f*; **2** (of land) mise *f* en valeur; (of marsh) assèchement *m*; (of polluted land) assainissement *m*; (of forest) défrichement *m*.

recline /rɪˈklaɪn/ **I** *vtr* appuyer [*head*].
II *vi* **1** [*person*] s'allonger; **2** [*seat*] s'incliner.

reclining /rɪˈklaɪnɪŋ/ *adj* **1** Art [*figure*] allongé; **2** [*seat*] inclinable; [*chair*] réglable.

recluse /rɪˈkluːs/ *n* reclus/-e *m/f*.

reclusive /rɪˈkluːsɪv/ *adj* solitaire.

recognition /ˌrekəgˈnɪʃn/ *n* **1** (identification) reconnaissance *f*; **to avoid ~** pour éviter d'être reconnu; **to change/to improve out of all** ou **beyond ~** changer/s'améliorer jusqu'à en être méconnaissable; **they've changed the town beyond ~** ils ont rendu la ville méconnaissable; **2** (realization) reconnaissance *f* (**of** de); **there is a growing ~ that** il devient de plus en plus apparent que; **3** gen, Pol (acknowledgement) reconnaissance *f*; **to gain international ~** être reconnu mondialement; **he never got the ~ he deserved** il n'a jamais été reconnu comme il le méritait; **union ~** reconnaissance officielle des syndicats; **to give state ~ to sth** reconnaître qch officiellement; **to receive** ou **win ~ for** être reconnu pour [*talent, work, achievement, contribution*]; **in ~ of** en reconnaissance de; **4** Comput (of data) reconnaissance *f*; **voice ~** reconnaissance de la parole; **5** Aviat (identification) identification *f*.

recognizable /ˌrekəgˈnaɪzəbl, ˈrekəgnaɪzəbl/ *adj* reconnaissable; **she is instantly ~ by her hat** on la reconnaît tout de suite à son chapeau.

recognizably /ˌrekəgˈnaɪzəblɪ, ˈrekəgnaɪzəblɪ/ *adv* manifestement.

recognizance /rɪˈkɒgnɪzns/ *n* Jur (promise) engagement *m* (devant un tribunal); (sum) caution *f*; **to enter into ~s for sb** se porter caution pour qn.

recognize /ˈrekəgnaɪz/ **I** *vtr* **1** (identify) reconnaître [*person, voice, sound, place*] (**by** à; **as** comme étant); identifier [*sign, symptom*] (**as** comme étant); **did you ~ each other?** est-ce que vous vous êtes reconnus?; **2** (acknowledge) reconnaître [*problem, fact, value, achievement*]; (officially) reconnaître [*government, authority, claim etc*]; **to ~ that** reconnaître que; **to be ~d as** être reconnu comme étant [*heir, owner*]; **to be ~d by law** être reconnu légalement; **3** US (in debate) donner la parole à [*speaker, debater*].
II recognized *pp adj* **1** (acknowledged) [*expert, organization*] reconnu; **2** Comm (with accredited status) [*firm, supplier*] accrédité; **~d agent** agent *m* accrédité; **~d dealer** concessionnaire *m* attitré.

recoil I /ˈriːkɔɪl/ *n* (of gun) recul *m*; (of spring) détente *f*.
II /rɪˈkɔɪl/ *vi* **1** [*person*] (physically) avoir un mouvement de recul, reculer (**from, at** devant); (mentally) reculer (**from** devant); **to ~ in horror/in disgust** reculer d'horreur/de dégoût; **2** [*gun*] reculer en tirant; [*spring*] se détendre; **3** (affect adversely) **to ~ on sb** retomber sur qn.

recollect /ˌrekəˈlekt/ **I** *vtr* se souvenir de, se rappeler.
II *vi* se souvenir; **as far as I ~** autant qu'il m'en souvienne.
III *v refl* **to ~ oneself** se ressaisir.

recollection /ˌrekəˈlekʃn/ *n* souvenir *m*; **to have some ~ of** se souvenir vaguement de; **to the best of my ~** autant qu'il m'en souvienne.

recommence /ˌriːkəˈmens/ **I** *vtr* recommencer (**doing** à faire).
II *vi* reprendre.

recommend /ˌrekəˈmend/ *vtr* **1** (commend) recommander [*person, company, film, book*] (**as** comme étant); **to ~ sb for a job** recommander qn pour un emploi; **she comes highly ~ed** elle est chaudement recommandée; **2** (advise) conseiller, recommander [*investigation, treatment, policy*]; **the judge ~ed the defendant serve a minimum of 20 years** Jur le juge a requis pour l'accusé une peine minimum de 20 ans; **the scheme is ~ed for approval** c'est un projet qui devrait être approuvé; **'~ed'** Journ [*film etc*] 'à voir'; **3** (favour) **the strategy has much to ~ it** la stratégie présente de nombreux avantages; **the hotel has little to ~ it** on ne peut pas dire grand-chose en faveur de cet hôtel; **her reputation for laziness did not ~ her to potential employers** sa réputation de paresse ne jouait pas en sa faveur auprès d'éventuels employeurs.

recommendable /ˌrekəˈmendəbl/ *adj* **the film is highly ~** c'est un film à recommander vivement.

recommendation /ˌrekəmenˈdeɪʃn/ *n* **1** (by authority, report) recommandation *f* (**to** à; **on** sur); **to make a ~** faire une recommandation; **he was sentenced to life imprisonment with a ~ that he serve at least 30 years** Jur il a été condamné à la réclusion criminelle à perpétuité assortie d'une mesure de sécurité de 30 ans; **his ~ was to lift the ban** il a conseillé de lever l'interdiction; **2** (by colleague, friend) recommandation *f*; **on the ~ of** sur la recommandation de; **we found our plumber by personal ~** notre plombier nous a été recommandé par des gens que nous connaissons; **to speak in ~ of sb/sth** recommander qn/qch; **3** (by employer, referee) **to give sb a ~** recommander qn; **to write sb a ~** donner une lettre de recommandation à qn; **4** (advantage) **the hotel's location is its only ~** l'emplacement de l'hôtel est son seul atout.

recommendatory /ˌrekəˈmenˈdətrɪ, US -tɔːrɪ/ *adj* sout [*letter, remark*] de recommandation.

recommended: **~ed daily amount, RDA** *n* apports *mpl* quotidiens recommandés, AQR; **~ed reading** *n* livres *mpl* conseillés or recommandés; **~ed retail price** *n* prix *m* de vente conseillé.

recommit /ˌriːkəˈmɪt/ *vtr* (*p prés etc* **-tt-**) US Pol renvoyer [qch] en commission [*bill*].

recommittal /ˌriːkəˈmɪtl/ *n* US Pol renvoi *m* en commission.

recompense /ˈrekəmpens/ **I** *n* **1** sout (reward) récompense *f* (**for** de); **as a ~ for** en récompense de; **2** Jur dédommagement *m* (**for** pour).
II *vtr* **1** sout (reward) récompenser (**for** de); **2** gen, Jur dédommager (**for** de).

recompose /ˌriːkəmˈpəʊz/ *vtr* (rewrite) recomposer.

reconcilable /ˈrekənsaɪləbl/ *adj* [*differences*] conciliable; [*views*] compatible (**with** avec).

reconcile /ˈrekənsaɪl/ *vtr* **1** (after quarrel) réconcilier [*people*]; **to be** ou **become ~d** se réconcilier (**with** avec); **2** (see as compatible) concilier [*attitudes, views*] (**with** avec); **3** (persuade to accept) **to ~ sb to sth/to doing** réconcilier qn avec qch/avec l'idée de faire; **to become ~d to sth/to doing** se résigner à qch/à faire.

reconciliation /ˌrekənˌsɪlɪˈeɪʃn/ *n* (of people) réconciliation *f*; (of ideas) conciliation *f*.

recondite /ˈrekəndaɪt/ *adj* sout abstrus.

recondition /ˌriːkənˈdɪʃn/ *vtr* remettre [qch] à neuf.

reconnaissance /rɪˈkɒnɪsns/ **I** *n* Mil reconnaissance *f*; **on ~** en reconnaissance.
II *modif* [*mission, plane, patrol, satellite*] de reconnaissance.

reconnoitre GB, **reconnoiter** US /ˌrekəˈnɔɪtə(r)/ Mil **I** *vtr* reconnaître.
II *vi* faire une reconnaissance.

reconsider /ˌriːkənˈsɪdə(r)/ **I** *vtr* (re-examine) réexaminer [*plan, opinion*].
II *vi* (think further) repenser; (change mind) changer d'avis; **we ask you to ~** nous vous demandons d'y repenser.

reconsideration /ˌriːkənsɪdəˈreɪʃn/ *n* (of decision) remise *f* en cause; (of question) nouvel examen *m*, réexamen *m*.

reconstitute /ˌriːˈkɒnstɪtjuːt, US -tuːt/ *vtr* **1** Admin, Pol reconstituer [*committee, party*]; **2** Culin réhydrater.

reconstitution /ˌriːˌkɒnstɪˈtjuːʃn, US -tuːʃn/ *n* **1** Admin, Pol reconstitution *f*; **2** Culin réhydratation *f*.

reconstruct /ˌriːkənˈstrʌkt/ *vtr* **1** (rebuild) reconstruire [*building*]; réédifier [*system*]; reconstituer [*text*]; **2** (surgically) reconstituer; **3** Cin, TV recréer [*event, period*]; **4** [*police*] faire une reconstitution de [*crime*].

reconstruction /ˌriːkənˈstrʌkʃn/ **I** *n* **1** (of building) reconstruction *f*; (of system) réédification *f*; **2** (of object, event, crime) reconstitution *f*; **3** Med reconstitution *f*.
II Reconstruction *pr n* US **the Reconstruction** la Reconstruction de l'union.

reconstructive /ˌriːkənˈstrʌktɪv/ *adj* [*surgery*] réparateur/-trice.

reconvene /ˌriːkənˈviːn/ **I** *vtr* **to ~ a meeting** fixer une nouvelle réunion.
II *vi* se réunir à nouveau.

record I /ˈrekɔːd, US ˈrekərd/ *n* **1** (written account) (of events) compte-rendu *m*; (of official proceedings) procès-verbal *m*; **to keep a ~ of** noter [*order, calls*]; **I have no ~ of your application** je n'ai aucune trace de votre demande; **the hottest summer on ~** l'été le plus chaud qu'on ait jamais enregistré; **to be on ~ as saying that** avoir déclaré officiellement que; **to say sth off the ~** dire qch en privé; **off the ~, I think it' s a bad idea** entre nous, je crois que c'est une mauvaise idée; **just for the ~, did you really do it?** entre nous, tu l'as vraiment fait?; **I'd like to set the ~ straight** je voudrais mettre les choses au clair; **2** (data) (also **~s**) (historical) archives *fpl*; (personal, administrative) dossier *m*; **~s of births/deaths** registre *m* des naissances/décès; **public ~s** archives *fpl* publiques; **sb's medical ~s** le dossier médical de qn; **official ~s** dossiers officiels; **3** (history) (of individual) passé *m*; (of organization, group) réputation *f*; **to have a good ~ on** avoir une bonne réputation en ce qui concerne [*human rights, recycling, safety*]; **she has a distinguished ~ as a diplomat** son passé en tant que diplomate est remarquable; **service ~** passé *m* militaire; **academic ~** niveau *m* d'études; **4** Audio disque *m* (**by, of** de); **pop/jazz ~** disque de pop/jazz; **to make/to cut a ~** faire/graver un disque; **to put on/to play a ~** mettre/passer un disque; **change the ~○!** change de disque○!; **5** (best performance) record *m* (**for, in** de); **the sprint ~** le record du sprint; **to set/to hold a ~** établir/détenir un record; **6** Comput (collection of data) enregistrement *m*; **7** Jur (also **criminal ~**) casier *m* judiciaire; **to have no ~** avoir un casier judiciaire vierge.
II /ˈrekɔːd, US ˈrekərd/ *modif* **1** Audio [*collection, company, label, producer, sales, shop*] de disques; [*industry*] du disque; **2** (high) [*result, sales, score, speed, time*] record (*inv, after n*); **to do sth in ~ time** faire qch en un temps record; **to be at a ~ high/low** être à son niveau le plus haut/bas.
III /rɪˈkɔːd/ *vtr* **1** (note) noter [*detail, idea, opinion*]; prendre acte de [*transaction*]; **to ~ that** noter que; **to ~ the way in which** prendre note de la façon dont; **2** (on disc, tape) enregistrer [*album, interview, song*] (**on** sur); **to ~ sb doing** enregistrer qn en train de faire; **3** (register) [*equipment*] enregistrer [*temperature, rainfall*]; [*dial, gauge*] indiquer [*pressure, speed*]; **4** (provide an account of) [*diary, report*] rapporter [*event, conditions*]; **to ~ that** rapporter que.
IV *vi* [*video, tape recorder*] enregistrer; **he is ~ing in Paris** il enregistre un disque à Paris.

record book *n* livre *m* des records; **to go down in the ~s** entrer dans le livre des records.

record-breaker /ˈrekɔːdbreɪkə(r), US

'rekərd-/ *n* **to be a ~** avoir battu un record.

record: **~-breaking** *adj* record (*inv, after n*); **~ button** *n* bouton *m* d'enregistrement; **~ card** *n* fiche *f*; **~ deck** *n* platine *f* disques.

recorded /rɪ'kɔ:dɪd/ *adj* **1** (on tape, record) [*interview, message, music*] enregistré; **2** (documented) [*case, sighting*] connu; [*fact*] reconnu.

recorded delivery *n* GB Post recommandé *m*; **to send sth ~** envoyer qch en recommandé.

recorder /rɪ'kɔ:də(r)/ *n* **1** Sci appareil *m* enregistreur; **2** Mus flûte *f* à bec; **3** GB Jur *avocat remplissant temporairement les fonctions d'un juge*.

record-holder /'rekɔ:dhəʊldə(r), US 'rekərd-/ *n* recordman/recordwoman *m/f*.

recording /rɪ'kɔ:dɪŋ/ **I** *n* enregistrement *m*; **a video/sound ~** un enregistrement vidéo/sonore; **to make a ~ of** enregistrer.
II *modif* [*engineer*] du son; [*artist*] qui enregistre (*after n*); [*contract, head, rights, studio*] d'enregistrement.

record: **~ library** *n* discothèque *f* de prêt; **~ player** *n* tourne-disque *m*; **~ sleeve** *n* pochette *f* de disque.

records office *n* **1** (of births, deaths) bureau *m* des archives; **2** Jur (of court records) greffe *m*.

record token *n* chèque-cadeau *m* pour disques.

recount /rɪ'kaʊnt/ *vtr* raconter, conter.

re-count I /'ri:kaʊnt/ *n* Pol deuxième compte *m* des suffrages; **to demand a ~** demander que les suffrages soient recomptés.
II /ˌri:'kaʊnt/ *vtr* recompter.

recoup /rɪ'ku:p/ *vtr* compenser [*losses*]; **to ~ one's costs** rentrer dans ses frais.

recourse /rɪ'kɔ:s/ *n* recours *m*; **to have ~ to** avoir recours à; **without ~ to** sans avoir recours à.

recover /rɪ'kʌvə(r)/ **I** *vtr* **1** (get back) retrouver, récupérer [*money, property, vehicle*]; récupérer [*territory*]; (from water) repêcher, retrouver [*body, wreck*]; **they ~ed the car from the river** ils ont repêché la voiture dans la rivière; **the bodies were ~ed from the wreckage of the car** on a sorti les cadavres de la voiture accidentée; **to ~ one's sight/health** recouvrer la vue/santé; **to ~ one's confidence/one's strength/one's breath** reprendre confiance/des forces/son souffle; **to ~ consciousness** reprendre connaissance; **to ~ one's composure** se ressaisir, se reprendre; **2** (recoup) recouvrer [*loan, debt, taxes, costs*] (**from** auprès de); réparer, compenser [*losses*]; **to ~ damages** Jur obtenir des dommages-intérêts; **the right to ~ damages** Jur le droit à l'allocation de dommages et intérêts; **3** (reclaim for use) récupérer [*waste, bottles, uranium*]; **to ~ land from the sea** reconquérir du terrain sur la mer.
II *vi* **1** gen, Med [*person*] (from illness) se remettre, se rétablir (**from** de); (from defeat, mistake) se ressaisir (**from** après); **2** Econ, Fin [*economy, market*] se redresser; [*shares, currency*] remonter; **3** Jur obtenir gain de cause.
III recovered *pp adj* [*property, uranium*] récupéré.

re-cover /ˌri:'kʌvə(r)/ *vtr* recouvrir [*book, chair*].

recoverable /rɪ'kʌvərəbl/ *adj* **1** Fin recouvrable; **2** Ecol, Ind récupérable.

recovery /rɪ'kʌvərɪ/ *n* **1** (getting better) rétablissement *m*, guérison *f*; fig (of team, player, performer) ressaisissement *m*; **to be on the road to ~** être sur la voie de la guérison; **to make a ~** (from illness) se rétablir, guérir; (from mistake, defeat) se ressaisir; **she has made a full ~** elle est complètement rétablie; **2** Econ, Fin (of economy, country, company, market) redressement *m*, reprise *f*; (of shares, prices, currency) remontée *f*; **the economy has staged a ~** il y a eu une relance de l'économie; **3** (getting back) (of vehicle) rapatriement *m* (**of** de); (of property, money) récupération *f* (**of** de); (of costs, debts) recouvrement *m* (**of** de); (of losses) réparation *f* (**of** de).

recovery: **~ operation** *n* Aerosp, Aviat, Naut opération *f* de récupération; **~ position** *n* Med position *f* latérale de sécurité; **~ room** *n* Med salle *f* de réveil; **~ ship** *n* Aerosp, Naut navire *m* de récupération (*des véhicules spatiaux*); **~ team** *n* Aerosp, Aviat, Naut équipe *f* de récupération; Aut équipe *f* de dépannage; **~ vehicle** *n* Aut (car) voiture *f* de dépannage; (truck) camion *m* de dépannage.

recreate /'rekrɪeɪt, ˌri:krɪ'eɪt/ *vtr* recréer.

recreation /ˌrekrɪ'eɪʃn/ **I** *n* **1** (leisure) loisirs *mpl*; **what do you do for ~?** que faites-vous pour vous détendre?; **2** (pastime) récréation *f*; **3** Sch (break) récréation *f*.
II *modif* [*facilities, centre*] de loisirs; **~ area** (indoor) salle *f* de récréation; (outdoor) terrain *m* de jeux; **~ ground** terrain *m* de jeux; **~ room** US salle *f* de jeux.

re-creation /ˌri:krɪ'eɪʃn/ *n* (historical reconstruction) reconstitution *f*.

recreational /ˌrekrɪ'eɪʃənl/ *adj* [*facilities, amenities*] de loisirs.

recreational: **~ drug** *n*: *drogue que l'on prend de façon occasionnelle*; **~ user** *n* utilisateur/-trice *m/f* occasionnel/-elle de drogue; **~ vehicle**, **RV** *n* US camping-car *m*, autocaravane *f*.

recriminate /rɪ'krɪmɪneɪt/ *vi* récriminer (**against** contre).

recrimination /rɪˌkrɪmɪ'neɪʃn/ *n* récrimination *f* (**against** contre).

rec room○ *n* US salle *f* de jeux.

recrudesce /ˌri:kru:'des/ *vi* littér être en recrudescence.

recrudescence /ˌri:kru:'desns/ *n* littér recrudescence *f*.

recrudescent /ˌri:kru:'desnt/ *adj* littér recrudescent.

recruit /rɪ'kru:t/ **I** *n* **1** Mil, Pol recrue *f* (**to** dans); **2** (new staff member) recrue *f*, personne *f* nouvellement recrutée; **the company is seeking ~s** la société recrute.
II *vtr* **1** Mil, Pol recruter [*soldier, member, agent, spy*] (**from** dans); **to ~ sb as** recruter qn comme [*courier, agent*]; **2** gen recruter, embaucher [*staff, teachers, nurses*]; **to ~ graduates/women** recruter or embaucher des diplômés/des femmes; **to be ~ed to do** être embauché pour faire.
III *vi* recruter.

recruiting /rɪ'kru:tɪŋ/ *n* = **recruitment**.

recruiting officer *n* officier *m* recruteur.

recruitment /rɪ'kru:tmənt/ **I** *n* recrutement *m*.
II *modif* [*agency, drive, ground, office, policy, problem*] de recrutement.

rectal /'rektəl/ *adj* rectal.

rectangle /'rektæŋgl/ *n* rectangle *m*.

rectangular /rek'tæŋgjʊlə(r)/ *adj* rectangulaire.

rectifiable /'rektɪfaɪəbl, ˌrektɪ'faɪəbl/ *adj* rectifiable.

rectification /ˌrektɪfɪ'keɪʃn/ *n* gen, Chem, Math rectification *f*; Elec redressement *m*.

rectifier /'rektɪfaɪə(r)/ *n* Elec redresseur *m*.

rectify /'rektɪfaɪ/ *vtr* **1** rectifier [*error, omission*]; réparer [*oversight*]; **2** Math, Chem rectifier; **3** Elec redresser.

rectilineal /ˌrektɪ'lɪnɪəl/, **rectilinear** /ˌrektɪ'lɪnɪə(r)/ *adj* rectiligne.

rectitude /'rektɪtju:d, US -tu:d/ *n* droiture *f*.

rector /'rektə(r)/ *n* **1** Relig (in Church of England) pasteur *m* anglican; (in seminary) supérieur *m*; (in Episcopal Church) curé *m*; **2** Univ *président élu d'un établissement d'enseignement supérieur*.

rectory /'rektərɪ/ *n* presbytère *m* (anglican).

rectum /'rektəm/ *n* rectum *m*.

recumbent /rɪ'kʌmbənt/ *adj* littér allongé.

recuperate /rɪ'ku:pəreɪt/ **I** *vtr* réparer [*loss*].
II *vi* Med se rétablir (**from** de), récupérer.

recuperation /rɪˌku:pə'reɪʃn/ *n* **1** (of losses) réparation *f*; **2** Med rétablissement *m* (**from** de), récupération *f*.

recuperative /rɪ'ku:pərətɪv/ *adj* réparateur/-trice; **~ powers** pouvoirs de récupération.

recur /rɪ'kɜ:(r)/ *vi* (*p prés etc* **-rr-**) [*event, error, dream*] se reproduire; [*problem, illness, symptom*] réapparaître; [*theme, phrase, thought*] revenir; Math [*number*] se répéter à l'infini.

recurrence /rɪ'kʌrəns/ *n* (of illness) récurrence *f*; (of symptom) réapparition *f*; **let's hope there will be no ~ of the problem** espérons que le problème est définitivement réglé.

recurrent /rɪ'kʌrənt/ *adj* récurrent.

recurring /rɪ'kɜ:rɪŋ/ *adj* **1** (frequent) [*dream, thought, pain*] récurrent, qui revient; **2** Math **~ decimal** suite *f* décimale illimitée.

recursion /rɪ'kɜ:ʃn/ *n* Math récursivité *f*; Comput récursivité *f*, récurrence *f*.

recursive /rɪ'kɜ:sɪv/ *adj* Ling récursif/-ive; Comput récurrent.

recursively /rɪ'kɜ:sɪvlɪ/ *adv* de façon récursive.

recusant /'rekjʊznt/ *n, adj* GB Relig Hist réfractaire (*mf*).

recyclable /ˌri:'saɪkləbl/ *adj* recyclable.

recycle /ˌri:'saɪkl/ *vtr* **1** Ecol recycler [*paper, waste*]; **2** Fin réinvestir [*revenue, profits*].

recycling /ˌri:'saɪklɪŋ/ **I** *n* Ecol recyclage *m*.
II *modif* [*facility, plant, process*] de recyclage.

red /red/ **▶ 1104** **I** *n* **1** (colour) rouge *m*; **I like ~** j'aime le rouge; **~ means 'danger'** le rouge signifie 'danger'; **in ~** en rouge; **a shade of ~** une nuance de rouge; **2**○ pej (also **Red**) (communist) rouge *mf*; **3** (deficit) **to be in the ~** [*individual, account*] être à découvert; [*company*] être en déficit; **to be £500 in the ~** être à découvert de 500 livres; **you've gone into the ~** vous avez un découvert; **4** (wine) rouge *m*; **5** (red ball) bille *f* rouge (*de billard/snooker*); **6** (in roulette) rouge *m*.
II *adj* **1** (in colour) [*apple, blood, lips, sky*] rouge; [*person, face, cheek*] rouge (**with** de); [*hair, curl*] roux/rousse; **to go** ou **turn ~** devenir rouge, rougir; **to paint/dye sth ~** peindre/teindre qch en rouge; **to dye one's hair ~** se teindre les cheveux en roux; **her eyes were ~ with weeping** ses yeux étaient rouges d'avoir pleuré; **his face** ou **he went very ~** il a rougi très fort; **~ in the face** tout rouge; **was my face ~!** comme j'étais gêné!; **there'll be ~ faces when...** certains vont être bien gênés quand...; **2**○ (communist) péj rouge.
IDIOMS **to see ~s under the bed**○ voir un complot communiste partout; **to be caught ~-handed** être pris la main dans le sac○; **to see ~** voir rouge.

red admiral *n* Zool vulcain *m*.

red alert *n* **1** Mil, Nucl alerte *f* rouge; **to be on/to be put on ~** être en/être placé en alerte rouge; **2** gen alerte *f* maximale.

red: **Red Army** *n* Armée *f* rouge; **~ biddy**○ *n* gros rouge *m* qui tache○; **~ blood cell** *n* globule *m* rouge; **~-blooded** *adj* [*male, man*] ardent; **~breast** *n* Zool rouge-gorge *m*; **~-breasted merganser** *n* harle *m* huppé; **~brick university** *n* GB université *f* autre que Cambridge et Oxford; **~-brown ▶ 1104** *adj* brun rouge *inv*; **~ cabbage** *n* chou *m* rouge.

redcap /'redkæp/ *n* **1** GB agent *m* de la police militaire; **2** US porteur *m*.

red card *n* Sport carton *m* rouge; **to be shown the ~** recevoir un carton rouge.

red carpet *n* tapis *m* rouge; **to roll out the ~ for sb** lit, fig sortir le tapis rouge pour qn; **to give sb the ~ treatment** faire un accueil somptueux à qn.

red cent○ *n* US rond○ *m*, sou *m*; **not to have a ~** ne pas avoir le rond○; **not to give sb a ~** ne pas donner un rond○ à qn.

Red China *n* Chine *f* Communiste.

redcoat /'redkəʊt/ *n* **1** GB (at holiday camp) animateur/-trice *m/f*; **2** soldat *m* anglais (*du XVIII*e *siècle*).

red: **~ corpuscle** *n* globule *m* rouge; **Red Crescent** *n* Croissant-Rouge *m*; **Red Cross** *n* Croix-Rouge *f*.

redcurrant /ˌred'kʌrənt/ **I** *n* groseille *f*.
II *modif* [*jam, jelly*] de groseilles.

red deer *n* cerf *m* commun.

redden /'redn/ **I** *vtr* rougir.
II *vi* [*face*] rougir; [*leaves*] roussir.

reddish /'redɪʃ/ *adj* rougeâtre; **~ hair** cheveux tirant sur le roux.

red: **~ duster**○ *n* GB = **Red Ensign**; **~ dwarf** *n* naine *f* rouge.

redecorate /ˌri:'dekəreɪt/ *vtr* (paint and paper) repeindre et retapisser, refaire; (paint only) repeindre.

redecoration /ˌri:dekə'reɪʃn/ *n* travaux *mpl* de peinture; **the house needs ~** toutes les peintures et les papiers sont à refaire.

redeem /rɪ'di:m/ **I** *vtr* **1** (exchange) échanger [*voucher*] (**for** contre); (for cash) convertir [qch] en espèces [*bond, security*]; **2** (pay off) racheter [*pawned goods*]; rembourser [*debt, loan, mortgage*]; **3** (salvage) rattraper [*occasion*]; sauver [*situation*]; racheter [*fault*]; **a mediocre play ~ed by X's performance** une pièce médiocre rachetée par la prestation de X; **4** (satisfy) s'acquitter de [*obligation*]; tenir [*pledge*]; **5** Relig racheter.
II redeeming *pres p adj* **her one ~ing feature** ou **quality is** ce qui la rachète, c'est; **a film without any ~ing social value** un film qu'aucune valeur morale ne rachète.
III *v refl* **to ~ oneself** se racheter (**by doing** en faisant).

redeemable /rɪ'di:məbl/ *adj* **1** Fin [*bond, security*] convertible; [*loan, mortgage*] remboursable; **2** Comm [*voucher*] échangeable; [*pawned goods*] rachetable.

Redeemer /rɪ'di:mə(r)/ *n* Relig Rédempteur *m*.

redefine /ˌri:dɪ'faɪn/ *vtr* (all contexts) redéfinir.

redemption /rɪ'dempʃn/ **I** *n* **1** Fin (of loan, debt, bill) remboursement *m*; (of mortgage) purge *f*; (from pawn) dégagement *m*; **2** Relig rédemption *f*; **beyond** ou **past ~** [*situation*] irrémédiable; [*machine*] irréparable; [*person*] hum irrécupérable.
II *modif* [*date, price, rate, premium*] de remboursement; **~ value** (of bond) valeur *f* de remboursement; (of share) valeur *f* de rachat.

redemptive /rɪ'demptɪv/ *adj* Relig rédempteur/-trice.

Red Ensign /ˌred 'ensən/ *n* pavillon *m* rouge (*de la marine marchande britannique*).

redeploy /ˌri:dɪ'plɔɪ/ *vtr* redéployer [*resources, troops*]; réaffecter [*staff*].

redeployment /ˌri:dɪ'plɔɪmənt/ *n* (of troops, resources) redéploiement *m*; (of staff) réaffectation *f*.

redesign /ˌri:dɪ'zaɪn/ *vtr* transformer [*area, building*]; **to ~ a logo/book jacket** créer un nouveau logo/une nouvelle jaquette.

redevelop /ˌri:dɪ'veləp/ *vtr* réaménager [*site, town centre*]; revaloriser [*run-down district*].

redevelopment /ˌri:dɪ'veləpmənt/ **I** *n* (of site, town) réaménagement *m*; (of run-down area) revalorisation *f*.
II *modif* [*costs, plans*] de réaménagement.

redeye○ /'redaɪ/ *n* US (also **~ flight**) vol *m* de nuit.

red-eyed /'redaɪd/ *adj* aux yeux rouges; **to be ~** avoir les yeux rouges.

red-faced /ˌred'feɪst/ *adj* **1** (with emotion, exertion) rouge; fig (embarrassed) [*officials, ministers*] penaud; **2** (permanently) rougeaud.

red: **~ flag** *n* drapeau *m* rouge; **~ fox** *n* renard *m* roux; **~-gold** ▶ **1104** *adj* blond vénitien *inv*; **~ grouse** *n* grouse *f*, lagopède *m* d'Écosse; **Red Guard** *n* (organization) Garde *f* rouge; (person) Garde *m* rouge; **~-haired** *adj* roux/rousse; **~ hat** *n* Relig chapeau *m* de cardinal; **~head** *n* roux/rousse *m/f*; **~headed** *adj* roux/rousse.

red herring *n* **1** (distraction) faux problème *m*; **2** (cured fish) hareng *m* saur; **3** US Fin prospectus *m* d'émission.

red-hot /ˌred'hɒt/ **I**○ *n* US hot-dog *m*.
II *adj* **1** [*metal, lava, coal, poker*] chauffé au rouge; **2** [*passion, enthusiasm, lover*] ardent; **the ~ favourite** le grand favori; **3** [*news, story*] tout frais/toute fraîche.

redial /ˌri:'daɪəl/ Telecom **I** *vtr* recomposer [*number*].
II *vi* recomposer le numéro.

redial: **~ button** *n* touche *f* bis; **~ facility** *n* rappel *m* du dernier numéro composé.

redid /ˌri:'dɪd/ *prét* ▶ **redo**.

Red Indian *n* injur Peau-Rouge *mf*.

redirect /ˌri:dɪ'rekt/ *vtr* canaliser [*resources*]; dévier [*traffic*]; faire suivre, réexpédier [*mail*].

redirection /ˌri:dɪ'rekʃn/ *n* (of mail) réacheminement *m*, réexpédition *f*.

rediscover /ˌri:dɪ'skʌvə(r)/ *vtr* (find again) retrouver; (re-experience) redécouvrir.

rediscovery /ˌri:dɪ'skʌvərɪ/ *n* redécouverte *f*.

redistribute /ˌri:dɪ'strɪbju:t/ *vtr* redistribuer.

redistribution /ˌri:dɪstrɪ'bju:ʃn/ *n* redistribution *f*.

redistrict /ˌri:dɪs'trɪkt/ *vtr* US Pol faire un redécoupage électoral de.

redistricting /ˌri:dɪs'trɪktɪŋ/ *n* US Pol redécoupage *m* électoral.

red: **~ kidney bean** *n* haricot *m* rouge; **~ lead** *n* minium *m*; **~ lentil** *n* lentille *f* rouge; **~-letter day** *n* jour *m* mémorable.

red light *n* feu *m* rouge; **to go through a ~** brûler un feu rouge.

red light area *n* quartier *m* chaud.

red: **~lining** *n* US *refus d'accorder des prêts hypothécaires dans des quartiers jugés délabrés*; **~man** *n* US injur Peau-Rouge *mf*; **~ meat** *n* viande *f* rouge; **~ mullet** *n* (*pl* **~**) rouget *m*.

redneck /'rednek/ **I** *n* injur péquenaud/-e○ *m/f* offensive.
II *adj* ultraréactionnaire.

redness /'rednɪs/ *n* rougeur *f*.

redo /ˌri:'du:/ *vtr* (3e *pers sg prés* **redoes**; *prét* **redid**; *pp* **redone**) refaire.

redolent /'redələnt/ *adj* littér **to be ~ of sth** lit sentir qch; fig évoquer qch.

redone /ˌri:'dʌn/ *pp* ▶ **redo**.

redouble /ˌri:'dʌbl/ **I** *n* Games surcontre *m*.
II *vtr* **1** gen redoubler; **to ~ one's efforts** redoubler d'efforts; **2** (in bridge) surcontrer.
III *vi* redoubler.

redoubt /rɪ'daʊt/ *n* **1** Mil réduit *m*; **2** (outpost) redoute *f*.

redoubtable /rɪ'daʊtəbl/ *adj* redoutable.

redound /rɪ'daʊnd/ *vi* sout **1** (contribute to) **to ~ to sb's honour** GB ou **honor** US être tout à l'honneur de qn; **2** (recoil) **to ~ (up) on sb/sth** retomber sur qn/qch.

red: **~-pencil** *vtr* corriger; **~ pepper** *n* poivron *m* rouge.

redraft /ˌri:'drɑ:ft/ *vtr* rédiger [qch] à nouveau.

redress /rɪ'dres/ **I** *n* gen, Jur (of wrong) réparation *f*; **to seek/to obtain (legal) ~** demander/obtenir réparation (légale) (**for** pour); **they have no (means of) ~** ils n'ont aucun recours.
II *vtr* réparer [*error, wrong*]; redresser [*situation*]; **to ~ the balance** rétablir l'équilibre.

red: **Red Riding Hood** *n* le Petit Chaperon rouge; **~ salmon** *n* saumon *m* rouge; **Red Sea** *n* mer *f* Rouge; **~ sea bream** *n* dorade *f* rose, rousseau *m*; **~shank** *n* chevalier *m* gambette; **~skin** *n* injur Peau-Rouge *mf*; **~ snapper** *n* vivaneau *m*; **Red Square** *n* place *f* Rouge; **~ squirrel** *n* écureuil *m* roux; **~start** *n* Zool rouge-queue *m*; **~ tape** *n* paperasserie *f*, bureaucratie *f*.

reduce /rɪ'dju:s, US -'du:s/ **I** *vtr* **1** (make smaller) réduire [*inflation, number, pressure, impact*] (**by** de); baisser [*prices, temperature*]; Med résorber [*swelling*]; faire baisser [*fever*]; **the jackets have been ~d by 50%** Comm le prix des vestes a été réduit de 50%; **'~ speed now'** Aut 'ralentir'; **2** (in scale) réduire [*map, drawing*]; (condense) réduire [*chapter, article*]; **3** Mil (in status) rétrograder; **to be ~d to the ranks** être cassé; **4** (alter the state of) **to ~ sth to shreds** (book, document etc) réduire qch en pièces; **to ~ sth to ashes** réduire qch en cendres; **5** (bring forcibly) **to ~ sb to tears** faire pleurer qn; **to be ~d to silence** être réduit au silence; **to be ~d to begging/prostitution** en être réduit à la mendicité/prostitution; **he was ~d to apologizing** il en a été réduit à s'excuser; **6** (simplify) réduire [*argument, existence*] (**to** à); Math réduire [*equation*]; **7** Jur réduire [*sentence*] (**to** à; **by** de); **8** Culin faire réduire [*sauce, stock*].
II *vi* **1** US (lose weight) maigrir (*en suivant un régime*); **2** Culin [*sauce, stock*] réduire; **let the sauce ~ to half its volume** faites réduire la sauce de moitié.
III reduced *pp adj* **1** (in price) réduit; **at a ~d price** à prix réduit; **~d goods** marchandises en solde; **2** [*scale, rate*] réduit; **3** (straitened) **in ~d circumstances** sout dans la gêne.

reducer /rɪ'dju:sə(r), US -'du:sə(r)/ *n* Phot réducteur *m*.

reducible /rɪ'dju:səbl, US -'du:səbl/ *adj* réductible (**to** à).

reductio ad absurdum /rɪˌdʌktɪəʊ æd əb'sɜ:dəm/ *n* raisonnement *m* par l'absurde.

reduction /rɪ'dʌkʃn/ *n* **1** (decrease, diminution) (of volume, speed) réduction *f* (**in** de); (of weight, size, cost) diminution *f* (**in** de); **~ in strength** (of army, workforce) réduction des effectifs; **2** Comm réduction *f*, rabais *m*; **huge ~s!** rabais importants!; **3** (simplification) réduction *f*; **the ~ of life to the basics** la réduction de la vie à l'essentiel; **4** Chem réduction *f*; **5** Mil (in status) rétrogradation *f*.

reductionist /rɪ'dʌkʃənɪst/ **I** *n* **1** gen péj réducteur/-trice; **2** Philos réductionniste.
II *n* Philos réductionniste *mf*.

reductive /rɪ'dʌktɪv/ *adj* [*theory, explanation*] réducteur/-trice, simplificateur/-trice.

redundancy /rɪ'dʌndənsɪ/ **I** *n* **1** GB Ind licenciement *m*; **400 redundancies** 400 licenciements; **to take ~** choisir le licenciement or d'être licencié; **to face ~** être confronté au chômage; **2** Comput, Telecom, Ling redondance *f*.
II *modif* **1** GB [*scheme, pay, notice*] de licenciement; **2 ~ check** Comput contrôle *m* par redondance.

redundant /rɪ'dʌndənt/ *adj* **1** GB Ind [*worker*] licencié; **to be made ~** être licencié, être mis au or en chômage; **2** (not needed, unused) [*information, device*] superflu; [*land, machinery*] inutilisé; **to feel ~** se sentir de trop; **3** GB (outdated) [*technique, practice*] inutile; [*craft*] dépassé; **4** Comput, Ling redondant.

reduplicate I /rɪ'dju:plɪkeɪt, US -'du:-/ *vtr* **1** refaire [*work*]; faire [qch] deux fois [*task*]; **2** Ling redoubler.
II /rɪ'dju:plɪkɪt/ *adj* **1** Bot rédupliqué; **2** Ling redoublé.

reduplication /rɪˌdju:plɪ'keɪʃn, US -'du:-/ *n* gen, Ling redoublement *m*.

reduplicative /rɪˈdjuːplɪkətɪv, US -ˈduː-/ *adj* Ling réduplicatif/-ive.

red: **~ wine** *n* vin *m* rouge; **~ wine vinegar** *n* vinaigre *m* de vin rouge; **~wing** *n* mauvis *m*; **~wood** *n* séquoia *m*.

re-echo /ˌriːˈekəʊ/ (*prét, pp* **~ed**) **I** *vtr* reprendre [*sentiments*].
II *vi* retentir or résonner (à l'infini).

reed /riːd/ **I** *n* **1** Bot roseau *m*; **2** Mus (device) anche *f*; **the ~s** les instruments *mpl* à anche.
II *modif* **1** [*basket, hut*] en roseau; **2** Mus [*instrument*] à anche.
IDIOMS **to be a broken ~** être quelqu'un sur qui on ne peut plus compter.

reed: **~ bunting** *n* Zool bruant *m* des roseaux; **~ stop** *n* jeu *m* d'orgue à anche.

re-educate /ˌriːˈedʒʊkeɪt/ *vtr* rééduquer.

re-education /ˌriːedʒʊˈkeɪʃn/ *n* rééducation *f*.

reedy /ˈriːdɪ/ *adj* [*voice, tone*] aigu/-uë.

reef /riːf/ **I** *n* **1** (in sea) récif *m*, écueil *m* also fig; **coral ~** récif de corail; **2** Mining veine *f*, filon *m*; **3** Naut ris *m*.
II *vtr* Naut prendre un ris dans [*sail*].
III *vi* Naut prendre un ris.

reefer /ˈriːfə(r)/ *n* **1** (also **~ jacket**) caban *m*; **2**○ (joint) argot des drogués joint *m*, cigarette *f* de marijuana; **3**○ US (ship) bateau *m* frigorifique.

reef knot *n* nœud *m* plat.

reek /riːk/ **I** *n* lit puanteur *f*, relent *m*; fig relent *m*; **the ~ of corruption** un relent de corruption.
II *vi* **1** (stink) **to ~ of sth** lit empester or puer qch; fig avoir des relents de qch; **2** dial [*chimney, lamp*] fumer.

reel /riːl/ **I** *n* **1** (for cable, cotton, film, tape) bobine *f*; Fishg moulinet *m*; **~-to-~** [*tape recorder*] à bobines; **a ~ of cotton, a cotton ~** une bobine de coton; **a three-~ film** un film en trois bobines; **2** Dance quadrille *m* écossais.
II *vtr* (wind onto reel) bobiner [*cotton*].
III *vi* (sway) [*person*] tituber; **he ~ed across the room** il a traversé la pièce en titubant; **the blow sent him ~ing** le coup l'a projeté en arrière; **the news sent him ~ing** fig la nouvelle l'a bouleversé; **his mind was ~ing at the thought of** il était dans tous ses états à l'idée de; **the government is still ~ing after its defeat** le gouvernement ne s'est pas encore remis de sa défaite.
IDIOMS **off the ~** US sans hésiter.
■ **reel back** [*person*] reculer en titubant.
■ **reel in** Fishg ramener [*fish*].
■ **reel off**: **~ off [sth]** dérouler [*thread*]; débiter [*list, names*].
■ **reel out**: **~ out [sth]** dérouler.

re-elect /ˌriːɪˈlekt/ *vtr* réélire.

re-election /ˌriːɪˈlekʃn/ *n* réélection *f*; **to stand for** GB ou **run for ~** se représenter (aux élections).

re-embark /ˌriːɪmˈbɑːk/ *vtr, vi* rembarquer.

re-embarkation /ˌriːˌembɑːˈkeɪʃn/ *n* rembarquement *m*.

re-emerge /ˌriːɪˈmɜːdʒ/ *vi* [*person, sun*] réapparaître; [*problem*] resurgir.

re-employ /ˌriːɪmˈplɔɪ/ *vtr* réembaucher.

re-enact /ˌriːɪˈnækt/ *vtr* **1** reproduire [*scene*]; reconstituer [*crime, movements*]; rejouer [*role*]; **to be ~ed** [*scene, drama*] se reproduire; **2** Jur remettre en vigueur.

re-enactment /ˌriːɪˈnæktmənt/ *n* **1** (of scene, movements) reconstitution *f*; **2** Jur remise *f* en vigueur.

re-engage /ˌriːɪnˈgeɪdʒ/ *vtr* **1** Admin réengager [*employee*]; **2** Tech rengrener [*cogwheel*]; **3** Aut rembrayer [*clutch*].

re-engagement /ˌriːɪnˈgeɪdʒmənt/ *n* **1** Admin (of employee) réengagement *m*; **2** Tech rengrènement *m*; **3** Aut (of clutch) rembrayage *m*.

re-enlist /ˌriːɪnˈlɪst/ **I** *vtr* **1** Mil rengager [*soldier*]; **2** fig **to ~ sb's help** s'assurer à nouveau l'aide de qn.
II *vi* se rengager.

re-enter /ˌriːˈentə(r)/ **I** *vtr* revenir dans, entrer à nouveau dans [*room, country etc*]; **to ~ the atmosphere** Aerosp rentrer dans l'atmosphère.
II *vi* **1** (come back in) [*person, vehicle etc*] revenir; **2 to ~ for** se représenter à [*competition, exam*].

re-entry /ˌriːˈentrɪ/ *n* **1** gen, Aerosp rentrée *f*; **2** fig (into politics etc) retour *m* (**into** dans); **~ to the political scene** retour sur la scène politique; **3** Comput réintroduction *f*.

re-entry: **~ point** *n* Aerosp point *m* de rentrée; Comput point *m* de retour; **~ visa** *n* visa *m* aller-retour.

re-erect /ˌriːɪˈrekt/ *vtr* reconstruire [*building, monument*]; remonter [*scaffolding*]; rebâtir [*system*].

re-establish /ˌriːɪˈstæblɪʃ/ *vtr* **1** (restore) rétablir [*contact, order, law*]; remonter [*business*]; **2** (reaffirm status of) réhabiliter [*person, party, art form*].

re-establishment /ˌriːɪˈstæblɪʃmənt/ *n* **1** (of order, business) rétablissement *m*; (of dynasty) restauration *f*; **2** (restoring of status) réhabilitation *f*; **his ~ as a great author** sa réhabilitation comme grand écrivain.

reeve /riːv/ **I** *n* **1** GB Hist (king's agent) bailli *m*; (on estate) intendant *m*; **2** (in Canada) président *m* du conseil municipal.
II *vtr* (*prét* **rove**, **reeved**; *pp* **reeved**) Naut capeler.

re-examination /ˌriːɪgˌzæmɪˈneɪʃn/ *n* **1** (of issue, problem) réexamen *m*; **2** Sch, Univ etc **to present oneself for ~** [*candidate*] se représenter à l'examen or aux examens; **3** gen nouvel interrogatoire *m*.

re-examine /ˌriːɪgˈzæmɪn/ *vtr* **1** réexaminer [*issue, problem*]; **2** gen, Jur (question) interroger à nouveau [*witness, accused, candidate*].

ref /ref/ **I** *n* **1** Comm *abrév écrite* = **reference**; **2**○ Sport (*abrév* = **referee**) arbitre *m*.
II○ *vtr* arbitrer [*match*].
III○ *vi* servir d'arbitre.

refectory /rɪˈfektrɪ, ˈrefɪktrɪ/ *n* réfectoire *m*.

refer /rɪˈfɜː(r)/ (*p prés etc* **-rr-**) **I** *vtr* **1** (pass on) renvoyer [*task, problem, enquiry, matter*] (**to** à); **2** Jur déférer [*case*] (**to** à); **to ~ a dispute to arbitration** soumettre un litige à un arbitrage; **3** Med Admin **to be ~red to a specialist/to a hospital** être envoyé en consultation chez un spécialiste/à un hôpital; **4** (direct) **to ~ sb to** [*person*] envoyer qn à [*department*]; [*critic, text*] renvoyer qn à [*article, footnote*]; **5** Comm, Fin **the cheque has been ~red** le chèque ne peut être honoré pour l'instant.
II *vi* **1** (allude to, talk about) **to ~ to** parler de, faire allusion à [*person, topic, event*]; **I wasn't ~ring to you** je ne parlais pas de toi; **2** (as name, label) **she ~s to him as Bob** elle l'appelle Bob; **this is what I ~ to as our patio** c'est ce que j'appelle notre terrasse; **he's always ~red to as 'the secretary'** quand on parle de lui, on dit toujours 'le secrétaire'; **don't ~ to him as an idiot** ne le traite pas d'imbécile; **3** (signify) **to ~ to** [*number, date, term*] se rapporter à; **what does this date here ~ to?** à quoi se rapporte cette date?; **4** (consult) [*person*] **to ~ to** consulter [*notes, article, system*]; **5** (apply) **to ~ to sb/sth** s'adresser à qn/qch; **this ~s to you in particular** ceci s'adresse particulièrement à toi; **6** Comm Fin **'~ to drawer'** 'voir le tireur'; **'~ to bank'** (in cash machine) 'adressez-vous à votre banque'.
■ **refer back**: ¶ **~ back to** [*speaker*] revenir sur [*issue*]; ¶ **~ [sth] back** renvoyer [*matter, decision, question*] (**to** à).

referable /rɪˈfɜːrəbl/ *adj* **~ to** [*case*] qui peut être soumis à [*court, arbitration*].

referee /ˌrefəˈriː/ **I** *n* **1** Sport arbitre *m*; **2** GB (giving job reference) personne *f* pouvant fournir des références; **to act as a ~ for sb** fournir des références sur qn.
II *vtr, vi* arbitrer.

reference /ˈrefərəns/ **I** *n* **1** (mention, allusion) référence *f* (**to** à), allusion *f* (**to** à); **in a pointed ~ to recent events** dans une allusion claire aux événements récents; **there are three ~s to his son in the article** son fils est mentionné trois fois dans l'article; **few ~s are made to** peu d'allusions sont faites à; **2** (consultation) **to do sth without ~ to sb/sth** faire qch sans consulter qn/qch; **'for ~ only'** (on library book) 'consultation sur place'; **I'll keep this leaflet for future ~** je garde ce prospectus: il pourra me servir plus tard; **for future ~, dogs are not allowed** pour information, je vous signale que les chiens sont interdits ici; **for easy ~, we recommend the pocket edition** nous recommandons l'édition de poche comme ouvrage facile à consulter; **3** (consideration) **without ~ to** sans tenir compte de [*cases, statistics, objectives, needs*]; **4** (allusion) allusion *f* (**to** à); **to make ~ to sb/sth** faire allusion à qn/qch; **5** Print (in book) référence *f*; **6** (also **~ mark**) renvoi *m*; **7** Comm (on letter, memo) référence *f*; **please quote this ~** prière de rappeler cette référence; **8** (testimonial) **a ~** des références *fpl*; **to write** ou **give sb a ~** fournir des références à qn; **9** (referee) personne *f* pouvant fournir des références; **10** Ling référence *f*; **11** Geog **map ~s** coordonnées *fpl*.
II with reference to *prep phr* en ce qui concerne, quant à; **with particular/specific ~ to** particulièrement/spécifiquement en ce qui concerne; **with ~ to your letter/request** suite à votre lettre/demande.
III *vtr* fournir les sources de [*book, article*]; **the book is not well ~d** le livre n'indique pas suffisamment ses sources.

reference: **~ book** *n* ouvrage *m* de référence; **~ library** *n* bibliothèque *f* d'ouvrages de référence; **~ number** *n* numéro *m* de référence; **~ point** *n* fig point *m* de repère.

referendum /ˌrefəˈrendəm/ *n* (*pl* **-da**) référendum *m*; **to hold a ~** organiser un référendum.

referent /ˈrefərənt/ *n* Ling référent *m*.

referential /ˌrefəˈrenʃl/ *adj* référentiel/-ielle.

referral /rɪˈfɜːrəl/ *n* **1** Med Admin (person) patient/-e *m/f* envoyé/-e à un confrère; (system) *fait d'envoyer un malade chez un spécialiste*; **you cannot see a specialist without a ~ from your doctor** il faut passer par votre médecin pour pouvoir consulter un spécialiste; **2** gen (of matter, problem) renvoi *m* (**to** à); **~ to the committee would be time-consuming** soumettre l'affaire au comité prendrait trop longtemps.

refill I /ˈriːfɪl/ *n* **1** (for fountain pen) cartouche *f*; (for ball-point, lighter, perfume) recharge *f*; (for pencil) mine *f* de rechange; (for album, notebook etc) feuilles *fpl* de rechange; **2**○ (drink) **how about a ~?** encore un peu?
II /ˌriːˈfɪl/ *vtr* recharger [*pen, lighter*]; remplir [qch] à nouveau [*glass, bottle*].
III /ˌriːˈfɪl/ *vi* [*tank*] se remplir à nouveau.

refinancing /ˌriːfaɪˈnænsɪŋ, ˌriːˈfaɪnænsɪŋ/ *n* refinancement *m*.

refine /rɪˈfaɪn/ **I** *vtr* **1** Ind raffiner [*oil, sugar etc*]; **2** (improve) peaufiner [*theory, concept*]; raffiner [*manners*]; affiner [*method, taste, language*].
II *vi* **to ~ upon** raffiner sur.

refined /rɪˈfaɪnd/ *adj* **1** (cultured) raffiné; **2** (improved) [*method, model*] très au point; [*theory, concept*] peaufiné; **3** Ind [*oil, sugar etc*] raffiné; [*metal*] affiné.

refinement /rɪˈfaɪnmənt/ *n* **1** (elegance) raffinement *m*; **a man of ~** un homme raffiné; **2** (refined, reworked version) (of plan, joke) version *f* améliorée; **3** (addition, improvement) raffinement *m*.

refiner /rɪˈfaɪnə(r)/ *n* (of oil, foodstuff) raffineur/-euse *m/f*; (of metal) affineur/-euse *m/f*.

refinery /rɪˈfaɪnərɪ/ *n* (for oil, foodstuff) raffinerie *f*.

refining /rɪˈfaɪnɪŋ/ *n* Ind (of oil, sugar etc) raffinage *m*.

refit I /ˈriːfɪt/ *n* (of shop, factory etc) rééquipement *m*; (of ship) réarmement *m*; **the ship is under ~** le navire est au radoub.
II /ˌriːˈfɪt/ *vtr* (*p prés etc* **-tt-**) réarmer [*ship*]; rééquiper [*shop, factory*]; **the liner was ~ted as a warship** le paquebot a été transformé en navire de guerre.
III /ˌriːˈfɪt/ *vi* (*p prés etc* **-tt-**) (ship) être réarmé.

refitment /ˈriːfɪtmənt/ *n* (of shop, factory etc) rééquipement *m*; (of ship) réarmement *m*.

refitting /ˌriːˈfɪtɪŋ/ *n* = **refitment**.

reflate /ˌriːˈfleɪt/ *vtr* Econ relancer.

reflation /ˌriːˈfleɪʃn/ *n* Econ relance *f*.

reflationary /ˌriːˈfleɪʃnrɪ, US -nerɪ/ *adj* Econ [*measure*] de relance; **to be ~** entraîner la relance.

reflect /rɪˈflekt/ I *vtr* **1** lit, fig refléter [*image, face, ideas, views, problems*]; **to be ~ed in sth** lit, fig se refléter dans qch; **he saw himself/her face ~ed in the mirror** il a vu son reflet/le reflet de son visage dans le miroir; **2** (throw back) lit renvoyer, réfléchir [*light, heat, sound*]; **3** (think) se dire, penser (**that** que); **'it's my fault,' he ~ed** 'c'est ma faute,' pensa-t-il or se dit-il.
II *vi* **1** (think) réfléchir (**on, upon** à); **2 to ~ well/badly on sb** faire honneur/du tort à qn; **her behaviour ~s well on her parents** son comportement fait honneur à ses parents; **how is this going to ~ on the school?** quelles vont être les conséquences pour l'école?

reflection /rɪˈflekʃn/ *n* **1** (image) lit, fig reflet *m*, image *f* (**of** de); **2** (thought) réflexion *f*; **on ~** à la réflexion; **lost in ~** perdu dans ses pensées; **this is a time for ~** le temps est à la réflexion; **3** (idea) réflexion *f*, pensée *f* (**on** sur); (remark) remarque *f* (**that** que); **the ~ that** la pensée or l'idée que; **4** (criticism) **it is a sad ~ on our society that...** ce n'est pas à la gloire de notre société que...; **no ~ on you, but...** je ne vous critique pas, mais...

reflective /rɪˈflektɪv/ *adj* **1** (thoughtful) [*mood*] pensif/-ive; [*person*] réfléchi; [*style, piece of music, passage*] profond; **2** (which reflects light, heat) [*material, strip, surface*] réfléchissant.

reflectively /rɪˈflektɪvlɪ/ *adv* d'un air pensif.

reflector /rɪˈflektə(r)/ *n* **1** (on vehicle) cataphote® *m*, catadioptre *m*; **2** (of light, heat) réflecteur *m*.

reflex /ˈriːfleks/ I *n* gen, Physiol réflexe *m*.
II *adj* **1** gen, Physiol réflexe; **a ~ action** un réflexe; **2** Math [*angle*] rentrant; **3** Phys [*light, heat*] réfléchi.

reflex camera *n* reflex *m*.

reflexion *n* = **reflection**.

reflexive /rɪˈfleksɪv/ Ling I *n* **1** (also **~ verb**) verbe *m* pronominal réfléchi; **2** (also **~ form**) forme *f* réfléchie; **in the ~** à la forme réfléchie.
II *adj* réfléchi.

reflexively /rɪˈfleksɪvlɪ/ *adv* Ling à la forme réfléchie.

reflexive verb *n* = **reflexive I 1**.

reflexology /ˌriːflekˈsɒlədʒɪ/ *n* réflexologie *f*.

refloat /ˌriːˈfləʊt/ I *vtr* Naut, Econ renflouer.
II *vi* Naut être renfloué.

reflux /ˈriːflʌks/ *n* reflux *m*.

reforestation /ˌriːˌfɒrəˈsteɪʃn, US -ˌfɔːr-/ *n* reboisement *m*.

reform /rɪˈfɔːm/ I *n* réforme *f*.
II *modif* [*programme, movement*] de réforme.
III *vtr* réformer.
IV *vi* se réformer.
V **reformed** *pp adj* **1** [*state, system*] réformé; [*criminal*] repenti; **he's a ~ed character** il s'est assagi; **2** (in Protestantism) réformé; (in Judaism) libéral.

re-form /ˌriːˈfɔːm/ I *vtr* gen, Mil reformer.
II *vi* **1** Mus [*group*] se reformer; **2** Mil [*troops*] reformer les rangs.

reformat /ˌriːˈfɔːmæt/ *vtr* Comput reformater.

reformation /ˌrefəˈmeɪʃn/ I *n* (of system, person) réforme *f*.
II **Reformation** *pr n* Relig Réforme *f*.

reformative /rɪˈfɔːmətɪv/ *adj* réformateur/-trice.

reformatory /rɪˈfɔːmətrɪ, US -tɔːrɪ/ *n* maison *f* de redressement†.

reformer /rɪˈfɔːmə(r)/ *n* réformateur/-trice *m/f*.

reformist /rɪˈfɔːmɪst/ *n, adj* réformiste (*mf*).

reform: **Reform Judaism** *n* judaïsme *m* réformé; **~ school** *n* US maison *f* de redressement†.

refract /rɪˈfrækt/ *vtr* Phys réfracter.

refracting telescope *n* lunette *f* d'approche.

refraction /rɪˈfrækʃn/ *n* Phys réfraction *f*.

refractive /rɪˈfræktɪv/ *adj* Phys réfringent; **~ index** indice *m* de réfraction.

refractor /rɪˈfræktə(r)/ *n* Phys (substance) milieu *m* réfringent; (object) dispositif *m* de réfraction.

refractory /rɪˈfræktərɪ/ *adj* (all contexts) réfractaire.

refrain /rɪˈfreɪn/ I *n* Mus, Literat, fig refrain *m*.
II *vi* se retenir; **to ~ from doing** s'abstenir de faire; **to ~ from comment** s'abstenir de tout commentaire; **he could not ~ from saying** il ne put s'empêcher de dire; **please ~ from smoking** sout ayez l'obligeance de ne pas fumer fml.

refrangible /rɪˈfrændʒəbl/ *adj* réfrangible.

refresh /rɪˈfreʃ/ I *vtr* **1** (invigorate) [*bath, cold drink*] rafraîchir; [*hot drink*] revigorer; [*holiday, rest*] reposer; **to feel ~ed** se sentir reposé or rafraîchi or revigoré; **2** (renew) rafraîchir [*image, design*]; **to ~ sb's memory** rafraîchir la mémoire à qn.
II *v refl* **to ~ oneself** (with rest) se reposer; (with bath, beer) se rafraîchir.

refresher /rɪˈfreʃə(r)/ *n* GB Jur honoraires *mpl* supplémentaires.

refresher course *n* cours *m* de recyclage.

refreshing /rɪˈfreʃɪŋ/ *adj* **1** (invigorating) [*drink, shower, breeze*] rafraîchissant; [*sleep, rest*] réparateur/-trice; **2** (novel) [*humour, outlook, insight, theme*] original; **it is ~ to see/to hear etc** cela fait du bien de voir/d'entendre etc; **it makes a ~ change** ça change agréablement.

refreshment /rɪˈfreʃmənt/ I *n* (rest) repos *m*; (food, drink) restauration *f*; **to stop for ~** s'arrêter pour se restaurer.
II **refreshments** *npl* (drinks) rafraîchissements *mpl*; **light ~s** (on journey) repas *m* léger; **~s will be served** (at gathering) il y aura un buffet.

refreshment: **~ bar**, **~ stall**, **~ stand** *n* buvette *f*; **~s tent** *n* buvette *f* (sous tente).

refrigerant /rɪˈfrɪdʒərənt/ *n, adj* Tech, Elec, Med réfrigérant (*m*).

refrigerate /rɪˈfrɪdʒəreɪt/ I *vtr* frigorifier; **'keep ~d'** 'conserver au réfrigérateur'.
II **refrigerated** *pp adj* [*product*] frigorifié; [*transport*] frigorifique.

refrigeration /rɪˌfrɪdʒəˈreɪʃn/ I *n* réfrigération *f*; **under ~** au réfrigérateur.
II *modif* [*equipment*] frigorifique; [*engineer*] frigoriste.

refrigerator /rɪˈfrɪdʒəreɪtə(r)/ I *n* (appliance) réfrigérateur *m*, frigidaire® *m*; (room) chambre *f* frigorifique.
II *modif* [*truck, wagon*] frigorifique.

refrigeratory /rɪˈfrɪdʒəreɪtrɪ, US -tɔːrɪ/ *adj* réfrigérant.

refringent /rɪˈfrɪndʒənt/ *adj* réfringent.

refuel /ˌriːˈfjʊəl/ (*p prés etc* **-ll-** GB, **-l-** US) I *vtr* lit ravitailler [qch] en carburant [*plane, boat*]; fig ranimer [*fears, speculation*].
II *vi* se ravitailler en carburant.

refuelling GB, **refueling** US /ˌriːˈfjʊəlɪŋ/ *n* ravitaillement *m* en carburant; **~ stop** Aviat escale *f* technique.

refuge /ˈrefjuːdʒ/ *n* **1** (protection) refuge *m* (**from** contre); **to take ~ from** se mettre à l'abri de [*danger, people*]; s'abriter de [*weather*]; **to take ~ in** se réfugier dans [*place, drink, drugs*]; **to seek/to find ~** (from danger, people) chercher/trouver refuge; (from weather) chercher/trouver un abri; **2** (hostel) foyer *m*.

refugee /ˌrefjʊˈdʒiː, US ˈrefjʊdʒiː/ I *n* réfugié/-e *m/f* (**from** de).
II *modif* [*camp*] de réfugiés; [*status*] de réfugié.

refulgence /rɪˈfʌldʒəns/ *n* littér splendeur *f*.

refulgent /rɪˈfʌldʒənt/ *adj* littér resplendissant.

refund I /ˈriːfʌnd/ *n* remboursement *m*; **to get a ~ on sth** se faire rembourser qch; **did you get a ~?** est-ce que tu t'es fait rembourser?
II /ˌriːˈfʌnd/ *vtr* rembourser [*price, charge, excess paid*]; **your expenses will be ~ed** vos frais vous seront remboursés; **I took the book back and they ~ed the money** j'ai rapporté le livre et ils me l'ont remboursé.

refundable /riːˈfʌndəbl/ *adj* remboursable.

refurbish /ˌriːˈfɜːbɪʃ/ *vtr* rénover.

refurbishment /ˌriːˈfɜːbɪʃmənt/ *n* rénovation *f*.

refurnish /ˌriːˈfɜːnɪʃ/ *vtr* remeubler.

refusal /rɪˈfjuːzl/ *n* **1** (negative response) refus *m* (**to do** de faire); **his ~ of aid** son refus d'être aidé; **her ~ to accept** son refus de [*situation, advice etc*]; **they saw no grounds for ~** ils ne voyaient pas de raison de refuser; **2** (to application, invitation) réponse *f* négative; **3** Comm (option to refuse) **to give sb first ~** donner la priorité à qn; **to give sb first ~ of sth** offrir qch à qn en premier; **she has first ~** elle est la première sur la liste; **4** Jur **~ of justice** déni *m* de justice; **5** Equit refus *m*.

refuse[1] /rɪˈfjuːz/ I *vtr* **1** refuser (**to do** de faire); **to ~ sb sth** refuser qch à qn; **the bank ~d them the loan** la banque leur a refusé le prêt; **I was ~d admittance** on a refusé de me laisser entrer; **2** Equit **to ~ a fence** refuser un obstacle.
II *vi* **1** refuser; **we asked her for a day off but she ~ed** nous lui avons demandé un jour de congé mais elle a refusé; **2** Equit faire un refus.

refuse[2] /ˈrefjuːs/ GB I *n* (household) ordures *fpl*; (industrial) déchets *mpl*; (garden) déchets *mpl* de jardinage.
II *modif* [*collection, burning*] des ordures.

refuse /ˈrefjuːs/: **~ bin** *n* GB poubelle *f*; **~ chute** *n* GB vide-ordures *m inv*; **~ collector** ▶ 1692 *n* GB éboueur *m*; **~ disposal** GB *n* traitement *m* des ordures; **~ disposal service** *n* service *m* de ramassage des ordures; **~ disposal unit** *n* broyeur *m* d'ordures; **~ dump** *n* GB décharge *f* publique; **~ lorry** *n* GB camion *m* des éboueurs, benne *f* de ramassage des ordures.

refusenik /rɪˈfjuːznɪk/ *n* refuznik *m*.

refuse skip /ˈrefjuːs/ *n* GB benne *f* à ordures.

refutable /rɪˈfjuːtəbl, ˈrefjʊtəbl/ *adj* réfutable.

refutation /ˌrefjuːˈteɪʃn/ *n* réfutation *f*.

refute /rɪˈfjuːt/ *vtr* réfuter.

regain /rɪˈgeɪn/ *vtr* **1** (win back) retrouver, recouvrer [*health, strength, sight, freedom*]; reconquérir [*territory, power, seat*]; retrouver [*balance, composure*]; reprendre [*title, lead, control*]; rattraper [*time*]; **to ~ possession of** rentrer en possession de; **to ~ one's footing** reprendre pied; **to ~ consciousness** revenir à soi, reprendre

British regions and counties

The names of British regions and counties usually have the definite article in French, except when used with the preposition en.

In, to and from somewhere

Most counties and regions are masculine; with these, in *and* to *are translated by* dans le, *and* from *by* du:

to live in Sussex	=	vivre dans le Sussex
to go to Sussex	=	aller dans le Sussex
to come from Sussex	=	venir du Sussex

Note however:

Cornwall	=	la Cournouailles
to live in Cornwall	=	vivre en Cornouailles
to go to Cornwall	=	aller en Cornouailles
to come from Cornwall	=	venir de la Cornouailles

Uses with nouns

There are rarely French equivalents for English forms like Cornishmen, *and it is always safe to use* de *with the definite article:*

Cornishmen	=	les habitants *mpl* de la Cornouailles
Lancastrians	=	les habitants du Lancashire

In other cases, du *is often possible:*

a Somerset accent	=	un accent du Somerset
the Yorkshire countryside	=	les paysages du Yorkshire

but it is usually safe to use du comté de:

the towns of Fife	=	les villes du comté de Fife
the rivers of Merioneth	=	les rivières du comté de Merioneth *or* de la région de Merioneth
Grampian cattle	=	le bétail de la région des Grampians

connaissance; **2** (return to) sout regagner [*place*].

regal /ˈriːgl/ *adj* royal.

regale /rɪˈgeɪl/ *vtr* régaler (**with** de).

regalia /rɪˈgeɪlɪə/ *npl* (official) insignes *mpl*; (royal) insignes *mpl* de la royauté; **in full ~** lit, hum en grande tenue.

regally /ˈriːgəlɪ/ *adv* majestueusement.

regard /rɪˈgɑːd/ **I** *n* **1** (consideration) égard *m* fml (**for** pour); **out of ~ for his feelings** par égard pour ses sentiments; **without ~ for the rules/human rights** sans égard pour les règles/les droits humains; **2** (esteem) estime *f* (**for** pour); **to have little ~ for money** faire peu de cas de l'argent; **to hold sb/sth in high ~, to have a high ~ for sb/sth** avoir beaucoup d'estime pour qn/qch; **3** (connection) **with** ou **in ~ to the question of pay, I would like to say that** en ce qui concerne or pour ce qui est de la question de salaires, je voudrais dire que; **his attitude/his policy with ~ to minorities** son attitude/sa politique en ce qui concerne les minorités; **in this ~** à cet égard.
II regards *npl* (good wishes) amitiés *fpl*; **kindest** ou **warmest ~s** avec toutes mes (or nos) amitiés; **with ~s** bien amicalement; **give them my ~s** transmettez-leur mes amitiés.
III as regards *prep phr* concernant; **as ~s the question of pay, I would like to point out that** en ce qui concerne la question de salaires, je voudrais signaler que.
IV *vtr* **1** (consider) considérer; **to ~ sb/sth as sth** considérer qn/qch comme qch; **he is ~ed as** il est considéré comme; **to ~ sb/sth with contempt/dismay** considérer qn/qch avec mépris/consternation; **to ~ sb with suspicion** se montrer soupçonneux à l'égard de qn; **her work is very highly ~ed** son travail est très apprécié; **they ~ him very highly** il est très estimé; **2** (respect) sout tenir compte de; **without ~ing our wishes** sans tenir compte de nos désirs; **3** (look at) **to ~ sb/sth closely** considérer qn/qch avec attention; **4** (concern) sout concerner.

regardful /rɪˈgɑːdfl/ *adj* sout attentif/-ive (**of** à).

regarding /rɪˈgɑːdɪŋ/ *prep* concernant.

regardless /rɪˈgɑːdlɪs/ **I** *prep* **~ of cost/of age/of colour** sans tenir compte du prix/de l'âge/de la couleur; **~ of the weather/the outcome** quel que soit le temps/le résultat.
II *adv* [*continue, press on*] malgré tout.

regatta /rɪˈgætə/ *n* régate *f*.

regency /ˈriːdʒənsɪ/ **I** *n* régence *f*.
II Regency *modif* [*style, furniture*] Regency *inv*.

regenerate /rɪˈdʒenəreɪt/ **I** *vtr* régénérer.
II *vi* se régénérer.

regeneration /rɪˌdʒenəˈreɪʃn/ *n* (economic, political etc) régénération *f*; (urban) restauration *f*.

regenerative /rɪˈdʒenərətɪv/ *adj* régénérateur/-trice.

regent /ˈriːdʒənt/ *n* **1** Pol Hist régent/-e *m/f*; **2** US Univ *membre du conseil d'administration d'une université*.

reggae /ˈregeɪ/ *n* reggae *m*.

regicide /ˈredʒɪsaɪd/ *n* **1** (act) régicide *m*; **2** (person) régicide *mf*.

regime, **régime** /reɪˈʒiːm, ˈreʒiːm/ *n* **1** Pol régime *m*; **2** Med sout régime *m*; **to be on a ~** suivre un régime.

regimen /ˈredʒɪmen/ *n* Med sout régime *m*.

regiment /ˈredʒɪmənt/ *n* Mil, fig régiment *m*.

regimental /ˌredʒɪˈmentl/ **I** *adj* [*colours, band*] du régiment.
II regimentals *npl* uniforme *m*.

Regimental Sergeant-Major, **RSM** **▶ 1612** *n* adjudant-chef *m*.

regimentation /ˌredʒɪmenˈteɪʃn/ *n* discipline *f* excessive.

regimented /ˈredʒɪmentɪd/ *adj* soumis à une discipline toute militaire.

Regina /rəˈdʒaɪnə/ *n* GB Jur **~ v Jones** la Couronne contre Jones.

region /ˈriːdʒən/ **I** *n* **1** Geog région *f*; **in the Oxford ~** dans la région d'Oxford; **in the ~s** GB en province; **the lower ~s** euph les enfers *mpl*; **2** Physiol **in the back/the shoulder ~** dans le dos/l'épaule.
II in the region of *prep phr* environ; **(somewhere) in the ~ of £300** environ 300 livres sterling.

regional /ˈriːdʒənl/ *adj* régional.

regional: **~ council** *n* Scot Admin conseil *m* régional; **~ development** *n* Ind aménagement *m* du territoire.

regionalism /ˈriːdʒənəlɪzəm/ *n* régionalisme *m*.

regionalist /ˈriːdʒənəlɪst/ *n, adj* régionaliste (*mf*).

register /ˈredʒɪstə(r)/ **I** *n* **1** gen, Admin, Comm registre *m*; Sch cahier *m* des absences; **to keep a ~** tenir un registre; **to enter sth in a ~** inscrire qch dans or sur un registre; **to take the ~** Sch remplir le cahier des absences; **~ of births, marriages and deaths** registre public de l'état civil; **missing persons' ~** registre des personnes disparues; **2** Mus, Ling, Comput, Print registre *m*; **lower/middle/upper ~** Mus registre grave/médium/aigu; **3** US (till) caisse *f* enregistreuse; **to ring sth up on the ~** enregistrer qch.
II *vtr* **1** (declare officially) [*member of the public*] déclarer [*birth, death, marriage*]; faire immatriculer [*vehicle*]; faire enregistrer [*luggage*]; déposer [*trademark, patent, invention*]; faire enregistrer [*company*]; déclarer [*firearm*]; déposer [*complaint*]; **to ~ a protest** protester; **2** [*official*] inscrire [*student*]; enregistrer [*name, birth, death, marriage, company, firearm, trademark*]; immatriculer [*vehicle*]; **she has a German-~ed car** elle a une voiture immatriculée en Allemagne; **to be ~ed (as) disabled/unfit for work** être officiellement reconnu handicapé/incapable de travailler; **3** [*measuring instrument*] indiquer [*speed, temperature, pressure*]; (show) [*person, face, expression*] exprimer [*anger, disapproval, disgust*]; [*action*] marquer [*emotion, surprise, relief*]; **the earthquake ~ed six on the Richter scale** le tremblement de terre a atteint la magnitude six sur l'échelle de Richter; **4** (mentally) (notice) remarquer; (realize) se rendre compte; **I ~ed (the fact) that he was late** j'ai remarqué qu'il était en retard; **she suddenly ~ed that, it suddenly ~ed (with her) that** elle s'est soudain rendu compte que; **5** (achieve, record) [*person, bank, company*] enregistrer [*loss, gain, victory, success*]; **6** Post envoyer [qch] en recommandé [*letter*]; enregistrer [*luggage*]; **7** Tech [*person, machine*] faire coïncider [*parts*]; **to be ~ed** [*parts*] coïncider; **8** Print mettre [qch] en registre [*printing press*].
III *vi* **1** (declare oneself officially) [*person*] (to vote, for course, school) s'inscrire; (at hotel) se présenter; (with police, for national services, for taxes) se faire recenser (**for** pour); (for shares) souscrire (**for** à); **to ~ for voting/for a course/for a school** s'inscrire pour voter/à un cours/dans une école; **to ~ with a doctor/dentist** s'inscrire sur la liste des patients d'un médecin/dentiste; **2** (be shown) [*speed, temperature, earthquake*] être enregistré; **3** (mentally) **the enormity of what had happened just didn't ~** on ne se rendait pas compte de l'énormité de ce qui était arrivé; **his name didn't ~ with me** son nom ne me disait rien; **4** Tech [*parts*] coïncider.

registered /ˈredʒɪstəd/ *adj* **1** [*voter*] inscrit; [*vehicle*] immatriculé; [*charity*] ≈ agréé; [*student*] immatriculé; [*firearm*] déclaré; [*company*] inscrit au registre du commerce; [*shares, securities, debentures*] Fin nominatif/-ive; [*design, invention*] déposé; [*childminder*] agréé; **to be ~ (as) disabled/blind** être officiellement reconnu handicapé/aveugle; **a ~ drug addict** *un toxicomane qui suit un programme de désintoxication*; **2** Post [*letter*] recommandé; [*luggage*] enregistré.

registered: **~ general nurse**, **RGN** *n* GB ≈ infirmier/-ière *m/f* diplômé/-e d'État; **~ nurse**, **RN** *n* US ≈ infirmier/-ière *m/f* diplômé/-e d'État.

registered post *n* (service) envoi *m* recommandé; **by ~** en recommandé.

registered: **~ shareholder** *n* actionnaire *mf* inscrit/-e; **~ trademark** *n* nom *m* déposé.

register office *n* = **registry office**.

registrar /ˌredʒɪsˈtrɑː(r), ˈredʒ-/ **▶ 1692** *n* **1** GB Admin officier *m* d'état civil; **2** Univ (for admissions) chef *m* de la division de la scolarité; **3** GB Med adjoint *m*; **4** GB Jur greffier/-ière *m/f* en chef.

Registrar of Companies *n* Comm greffier/-ière *m/f* du tribunal du commerce.

registration /ˌredʒɪˈstreɪʃn/ *n* **1** (of person) (for course, institution) inscription *f*; (for taxes) ≈ déclaration *f*; (for national service) recensement *m* militaire; (of trademark, patent) dépôt *m*; (of firearm) déclaration *f*; (of birth, death, marriage) déclaration *f*; (of company) enregistrement *m*; (of luggage) enregistrement *m*; **2** (entry in register) inscription *f*; **3** Aut année *f* de première immatriculation.

registration: **~ number** *n* numéro *m* d'immatriculation, numéro *m* minéralogique; **~ plate** *n* plaque *f* d'immatriculation, plaque *f* minéralogique.

registry /ˈredʒɪstrɪ/ *n* **1** GB (in church,

university) salle *f* des registres; **2** Naut immatriculation *f*.

registry office *n* GB bureau *m* de l'état civil; **to get married in a ~** se marier civilement; **a ~ wedding** un mariage civil.

regius professor /ˌriːdʒɪəs prəˈfesə(r)/ *n* GB Univ professeur *m* (*titulaire d'une chaire de fondation royale*).

regorge /rɪˈgɔːdʒ/ sout **I** *vtr* régurgiter.
II *vi* refluer (**into** dans).

regress /ˈriːgres/ **I** *n* régression *f*, retour *m* en arrière.
II *vi* Biol, Psych régresser (**to** au stade de); fig [*civilization, economy*] régresser; **to ~ to childhood** retomber en enfance.

regression /rɪˈgreʃn/ *n* **1** Biol, Psych, Stat, fig régression *f*; **2** Med détérioration *f*.

regressive /rɪˈgresɪv/ *adj* **1** Biol, Psych régressif/-ive; **2** péj [*behaviour, measure, policy*] rétrograde; [*effects*] régressif/-ive; **~ tax** *impôt qui favorise les grandes fortunes*.

regret /rɪˈgret/ **I** *n* regret *m* (**about** à propos de; **that** que (+ *subj*)); **my ~ at** ou **for having done** mon regret d'avoir fait; **to have no ~s about doing** ne pas regretter d'avoir fait; **to my great ~** à mon grand regret; **no ~s?** sans regret?
II regrets *npl* (apologies) excuses *fpl*.
III *vtr* (*p prés etc* **-tt-**) **1** (rue) regretter [*action, decision, remark*]; **to ~ that** regretter que (+ *subj*); **to ~ doing** ou **having done** regretter d'avoir fait; **to live to ~ sth** regretter qch toute sa vie; **2** (feel sad about) regretter [*absence, lost youth*]; **I ~ to say that** je suis au regret de dire que; **I ~ to inform you that** j'ai le regret de vous informer que; **it is to be ~ted that** il est regrettable que (+ *subj*).

regretful /rɪˈgretfl/ *adj* [*air, glance, smile*] plein de regrets; **to be ~ about sth** regretter qch.

regretfully /rɪˈgretfəlɪ/ *adv* **1** (with sadness) [*abandon, accept, decide*] à regret; [*announce, smile, wave*] avec regret; **2** (unfortunately) regrettablement.

regrettable /rɪˈgretəbl/ *adj* regrettable; **it is ~ that** il est regrettable que (+ *subj*).

regrettably /rɪˈgretəblɪ/ *adv* **1** (sadly) malheureusement; **~ for him** malheureusement pour lui; **2** (very) [*low, slow, weak*] fâcheusement.

regroup /ˌriːˈgruːp/ **I** *vtr* regrouper.
II *vi* se regrouper.

regrouping /ˌriːˈgruːpɪŋ/ *n* regroupement *m*.

regt *abrév écrite* = **regiment**.

regular /ˈregjʊlə(r)/ **I** *n* **1** (habitual client, visitor etc) habitué/-e *m/f*; **2** GB Mil soldat *m* de métier; **3** US (petrol) ordinaire *m*; **4** US Sport (team member) sociétaire *mf*: **5** US Pol (person loyal to party) fidèle *mf*.
II *adj* **1** (fixed, evenly arranged in time or space) régulier/-ière; **at ~ intervals** à intervalles réguliers; **on a ~ basis** de façon régulière; **to keep ~ hours** avoir un emploi du temps régulier; **to be ~ in one's habits** avoir des habitudes régulières; **~ features** traits réguliers; **~ income** revenu régulier; **to take ~ exercise** prendre de l'exercice régulièrement; **2** (usual) [*activity, customer, dentist, doctor, offender, partner, time, visitor*] habituel/-elle; Comm [*price, size*] normal; **I am a ~ listener to your programme** j'écoute régulièrement votre émission, je suis un de vos auditeurs fidèles; **3** (constant) [*job*] régulier/-ière; **to be in ~ employment** avoir un emploi permanent; **in ~ use** constamment utilisé; **4** GB Admin, Mil [*army, soldier*] de métier; [*army officer, policeman*] de carrière; [*staff*] permanent; **5** Med (breathing, pulse, heartbeat) régulier/-ière; **~ bowel movement** selles *fpl* régulières; **6** (honest) [*procedure, method*] régulier/-ière; **7** Ling [*verb, conjugation, declension etc*] régulier/-ière; **8**○ (thorough) véritable (*before n*); **he's a ~ crook** c'est un véritable escroc; **9**○ US (nice) chic○ *inv*; **he's a ~ guy** c'est un chic type○.

regularity /ˌregjʊˈlærətɪ/ *n* régularité *f*; **with unfailing ~** avec une parfaite régularité.

regularize /ˈregjʊləraɪz/ *vtr* régulariser.

regularly /ˈregjʊləlɪ/ *adv* régulièrement.

regulate /ˈregjʊleɪt/ **I** *vtr* **1** (control) réguler [*behaviour, lifestyle, activity, traffic, tendency*]; contrôler [*money supply*]; réglementer [*use*]; **2** (adjust) régler [*mechanism, temperature, pressure, flow, speed*].
II -regulated *pp adj* (*dans composés*) **well-~d** bien réglé; **state-~d** sous le contrôle de l'État.

regulate: ~d market economy *n* économie *f* dirigée; **~d tenancy** *n* GB location *f* déclarée.

regulation /ˌregjʊˈleɪʃn/ **I** *n* **1** (rule) (for safety, fire) consigne *f*; (for discipline) règlement *m*; (legal requirements) disposition *f* réglementaire (**for** pour); **a set of ~s** une réglementation; **building ~s** normes *fpl* de construction; **college/school ~** règlement *m* du collège/scolaire; **EEC ~s** réglementation *f* communautaire; **fire ~s** (laws) normes *fpl* anti-incendie; (instructions) consignes *fpl* en cas d'incendie; **government ~s** réglementation *f* gouvernementale; **safety ~s** règles *fpl* or normes *fpl* de sécurité; **traffic ~s** règles *fpl* de la circulation; **under the (new) ~s** selon la (nouvelle) réglementation or les (nouvelles) normes; **against** ou **contrary to the ~s** contraire au règlement or aux normes; **to meet the ~s** [*person, company*] se conformer à la réglementation; [*equipment, conditions etc*] être conforme à la réglementation; **2** (act or process of controlling) réglementation *f* (**of** de); **to free sth from excessive ~** libérer qch des réglementations excessives.
II *modif* (legal) [*width, length etc*] réglementaire; hum (standard) [*garment*] de rigueur.

regulator /ˈregjʊleɪtə(r)/ *n* **1** (device) régulateur *m*; **2** (person) régulateur/-trice *m/f*; **3** Econ organisme *m* de contrôle.

regulatory /ˈregjʊleɪtrɪ, US -tɔːrɪ/ *adj* de contrôle.

regulo® /ˈregjʊləʊ/ *n* GB thermostat *m*.

regurgitate /rɪˈgɜːdʒɪteɪt/ *vtr* [*animal, person*] régurgiter; [*drain, pipe*] refluer; [*machine*] rejeter; fig péj ressortir [qch] [*facts, opinions, lecture notes*].

regurgitation /rɪˌgɜːdʒɪˈteɪʃn/ *n* lit régurgitation *f*; fig péj resucée○ *f*.

rehab /ˈriːhæb/ *n* US *abrév* ►**rehabilitation**.

rehabilitate /ˌriːəˈbɪlɪteɪt/ *vtr* **1** (medically) rééduquer; (to society) réinsérer [*handicapped person, ex-prisoner*]; réhabiliter [*addict, alcoholic*]; **2** gen, Pol (reinstate) réhabiliter; **3** (restore) réhabiliter [*building, area*]; assainir [*environment*]; **~d building** US immeuble *m* réhabilité.

rehabilitation /ˌriːəbɪlɪˈteɪʃn/ **I** *n* **1** (of person) (medical) rééducation *f*; (social) réinsertion *f*; **2** gen, Pol (reinstatement) réhabilitation *f*; **3** (restoration) (of building, area) réhabilitation *f*; (of environment) assainissement *m*.
II *modif* [*course, programme*] (for the handicapped) de rééducation; (for alcoholics etc) de réinsertion.

rehabilitation centre GB, **rehabilitation center** US *n* (for the handicapped) centre *m* de rééducation; (for addicts etc) centre *m* de réinsertion (*pour toxicomanes, alcooliques ou anciens détenus*).

rehash péj **I** /ˈriːhæʃ/ *n* resucée○ *f*.
II /ˌriːˈhæʃ/ *vtr* remanier, piller pej.

rehear /ˌriːˈhɪə(r)/ *vtr* (*prét, pp* **reheard**) Jur réviser [*lawsuit*].

rehearsal /rɪˈhɜːsl/ *n* **1** Theat répétition *f* (**of** de); fig préparation *f* (**of** de); **in ~** en répétition; **2** sout (of facts, grievances) énumération *f*.

rehearsal call *n* appel *m* de répétition.

rehearse /rɪˈhɜːs/ **I** *vtr* **1** Theat répéter [*scene*]; faire répéter [*performer*]; fig préparer [*speech, excuse*]; **2** sout (recount) rabâcher [*story*]; énumérer [*grievances*].
II *vi* répéter (**for** pour).

reheat /ˌriːˈhiːt/ *vtr* réchauffer.

rehouse /ˌriːˈhaʊz/ *vtr* reloger.

reign /reɪn/ **I** *n* lit, fig règne *m*; **in the ~ of** sous le règne de [*monarch*]; **during the ~ of Churchill** quand Churchill était au pouvoir; **reign of terror** fig régime *m* de terreur; **the Reign of Terror** Hist la Terreur.
II *vi* lit, fig régner (**over** sur); **to ~ supreme** régner en maître absolu.

reigning /ˈreɪnɪŋ/ *adj* [*monarch*] régnant; [*champion*] en titre.

reimburse /ˌriːɪmˈbɜːs/ *vtr* rembourser; **to ~ sb for sth** rembourser qch à qn, rembourser qn de qch.

reimbursement /ˌriːɪmˈbɜːsmənt/ *n* remboursement *m* (**of** de; **for** pour).

reimpose /ˌriːɪmˈpəʊz/ *vtr* réimposer.

rein /reɪn/ *n* Equit, fig rêne *f*; **to take up/hold the ~s** lit, fig prendre/tenir les rênes; **to keep a horse on a short ~** garder les rênes courtes; **to keep sb on a tight ~** fig tenir qn de près; **to keep a ~ on sth** surveiller qch de près; **to give full** ou **free ~ to** donner libre cours à.
■ **rein back: ~ back [sth] 1** lit faire reculer [*horse*]; **2** fig freiner [*expansion, spending*].
■ **rein in: ~ in [sth] 1** lit freiner [qch] (avec les rênes) [*horse*]; **2** fig contenir [*spending, inflation*]; retenir [*person*].

reincarnate /ˌriːɪnˈkɑːneɪt/ **I** *adj* réincarné.
II *vtr* **to be ~d** se réincarner (**as** en).

reincarnation /ˌriːɪnkɑːˈneɪʃn/ *n* réincarnation *f* (**of** de).

reindeer /ˈreɪndɪə(r)/ *n* (*pl* **~**) renne *m*.

reindeer moss *n* cladonie *f*.

reinforce /ˌriːɪnˈfɔːs/ *vtr* **1** gen, Mil, Constr renforcer; **2** fig renforcer [*feeling, opinion, prejudice, trend*]; conforter [*hopes*]; étayer [*argument, theory*]; **to ~ the belief that** renforcer l'opinion selon laquelle; **this ~s my belief that** ceci me conforte dans mon opinion que.

reinforced concrete *n* béton *m* armé.

reinforcement /ˌriːɪnˈfɔːsmənt/ **I** *n* **1** (action) renforcement *m* (**of** de); **2** (support) renfort *m*.
II reinforcements *npl* Mil, fig renforts *mpl*; **to send for ~s** demander des renforts.

reinforcement rod *n* armature *f*.

reinsert /ˌriːɪnˈsɜːt/ *vtr* réinsérer.

reinstate /ˌriːɪnˈsteɪt/ *vtr* réintégrer [*employee*]; réintégrer [*team*]; rétablir [*legislation, service*]; ranimer [*belief*].

reinstatement /ˌriːɪnˈsteɪtmənt/ *n* (of employee) réintégration *f*; (of legislation, service) rétablissement *m*.

reinstitute /ˌriːˈɪnstɪtjuːt, US -tuːt/ *vtr* rétablir.

reinsurance /ˌriːɪnˈʃɔːrəns, US -ˈʃʊər-/ *n* réassurance *f*.

reinsure /ˌriːɪnˈʃɔː(r), US -ˈʃʊə(r)/ *vtr* réassurer.

reintegrate /ˌriːˈɪntɪgreɪt/ *vtr* réintégrer (**into** dans).

reinvest /ˌriːɪnˈvest/ *vtr* réinvestir (**in** dans).

reinvestment /ˌriːɪnˈvestmənt/ *n* réinvestissement *m* (**in** dans).

reinvigorate /ˌriːɪnˈvɪgəreɪt/ *vtr* revigorer.

reissue /ˌriːˈɪʃuː/ **I** *n* **1** (new version) Mus, Publg réédition *f*; Cin reprise *f*; **2** (act) Publg réédition *f*; Cin redistribution *f*.
II *vtr* rééditer [*book, record*]; ressortir [*film*]; renouveler [*invitation, warning*]; émettre [qch] à nouveau [*share certificates*].

reiterate /riːˈɪtəreɪt/ *vtr* réitérer, répéter.

reiteration /riːˌɪtəˈreɪʃn/ *n* réitération *f*, répétition *f*.

reiterative /riːˈɪtərətɪv/ *adj* réitératif/-ive.

reject I /ˈriːdʒekt/ *n* **1** Comm marchandise *f* de deuxième choix; **2** fig **to be a social ~** [*person*] être un paria.
II /ˈriːdʒekt/ *modif* Comm [*goods, stock*] de deuxième choix.
III /rɪˈdjekt/*vtr* **1** gen rejeter, repousser [*advice, decision, request, application, motion*]; refuser [*invitation, candidate, manuscript*]; démentir [*claim, suggestion*]; repousser [*advances, suitor*]; rejeter [*child, parent*]; **2** Med, Tech, Comput, Psych rejeter.
IV **rejected** /rɪˈdjektɪd/ *pp adj* **to feel ~ed** se sentir rejeté.

rejection /rɪˈdʒekʃn/ *n* **1** gen rejet *m*; (of candidate, manuscript) refus *m*; **to meet with ~** se heurter à un refus; **to experience ~ as a child** se sentir rejeté pendant son enfance; **2** Med, Comput, Tech rejet *m*.

rejection: **~ letter** *n* lettre *f* de refus; **~ slip** *n* Publg avis *m* de refus.

reject shop ▶ **1692** *n* boutique *f* spécialisée dans la vente de marchandises de deuxième choix.

rejig /ˌriːˈdʒɪg/ GB, **rejigger** /ˌriːˈdʒɪgə(r)/ US *vtr* réviser [*plans, timetable*].

rejoice /rɪˈdʒɔɪs/ I *vtr* réjouir; **to ~ that** se réjouir du fait que.
II *vi* se réjouir (**at, over** de); **to ~ in** se réjouir de [*good news, event*]; se régaler de [*joke, story*]; profiter de [*freedom, independence*]; **to ~ in the name of** iron avoir l'insigne honneur de s'appeler iron.

rejoicing /rɪˈdʒɔɪsɪŋ/ I *n* (jubilation) allégresse *f*.
II **rejoicings** *npl* sout (celebrations) réjouissances *fpl*.

rejoin[1] /riːˈdʒɔɪn/ *vtr* **1** (join again) rejoindre [*companion, regiment*]; réintégrer [*team, organization*]; [*road*] rejoindre [*coast, route*]; **to ~ ship** Naut rallier le bord; **2** (put back together) réunir.

rejoin[2] /rɪˈdʒɔɪn/ *vtr* répliquer, riposter.

rejoinder /rɪˈdʒɔɪndə(r)/ *n* gen, Jur réplique *f*.

rejuvenate /rɪˈdʒuːvɪneɪt/ *vtr* lit, fig rajeunir.

rejuvenation /rɪˌdʒuːvɪˈneɪʃn/ *n* lit, fig rajeunissement *m*.

rekindle /ˌriːˈkɪndl/ I *vtr* lit, fig ranimer, raviver.
II *vi* [*fire*] se rallumer; [*emotion*] se ranimer, se raviver.

relapse I /ˈriːlæps/ *n* Med, fig rechute *f*; **to have a ~** avoir or faire une rechute.
II /rɪˈlæps/ *vi* gen retomber (**into** dans); Med rechuter.

relate /rɪˈleɪt/ I *vtr* **1** (connect) **to ~ sth and sth** établir un rapport entre qch et qch; **to ~ sth to sth** associer qch à qch; **2** (recount) raconter, conter [*story*] (**to** à); **to ~ that/how** raconter que/comment.
II *vi* **1** (have connection) **to ~ to** se rapporter à; **the figures ~ to last year** les chiffres se rapportent à l'an dernier; **the two things ~** les deux choses sont liées; **everything relating to** ou **that ~s to him** tout ce qui a un rapport avec lui; **2** (communicate) **to ~ to** s'entendre avec; **the way children ~ to their teachers** la façon dont les enfants communiquent avec leurs professeurs; **to have problems relating (to others)** avoir des difficultés à se lier avec les autres; **3** (respond, identify) **to ~ to** apprécier [*idea, music*]; **I can't ~ to the character/the painting** le personnage/l'œuvre ne me touche pas; **I can to that!** ça, je comprends!

related /rɪˈleɪtɪd/ I *adj* **1** (in the same family) [*person, language*] apparenté (**by, through** par; **to** à); **we are ~ by marriage** nous sommes parents par alliance; **2** (connected) [*subject, matter*] connexe (**to** à); [*area, evidence, idea, information, incident*] lié (**to** à); [*substance, species, type*] similaire (**to** à); **the murders are ~** les crimes sont liés; **plastic and ~ substances** le plastique et ses dérivées; **3** Mus relatif/-ive.
II **-related** (*dans composés*) lié à; **drug/work-~d** lié à la drogue/au travail.

relation /rɪˈleɪʃn/ I *n* **1** (relative) parent/-e *m/f*; **my ~s** ma famille; **Paul Presley, no ~ to Elvis** Paul Presley, qui n'est pas apparenté à or n'a aucun lien de parenté avec Elvis Presley; **2** (connection) rapport *m* (**between** entre; **of** de; **with** avec); **to bear no ~ to** n'avoir aucun rapport avec [*reality, truth*]; **3** (story) récit *m* (**of** de); **4** (comparison) **in ~ to** par rapport à; **with ~ to** en ce qui concerne; **5** Math rapport *m*.
II **relations** *npl* **1** (mutual dealings) relations *fpl* (**between** entre; **with** avec); **to have business ~s with** avoir des relations professionnelles avec; **East-West ~s** les relations Est-Ouest; **2** euph (intercourse) relations *fpl* sexuelles.

relational /rɪˈleɪʃənl/ *adj* Ling, Comput relationnel/-elle.

relational: **~ database** *n* base *f* de données relationnelles; **~ model** *n* modèle *m* relationnel; **~ operator** *n* opérateur *m* relationnel.

relationship /rɪˈleɪʃnʃɪp/ *n* **1** (human connection) relations *fpl* (**with** avec); **to form ~s** se lier (**with** avec); **to have a good ~ with** avoir de bonnes relations avec; **a working ~** des relations professionnelles; **the superpower ~** les relations entre les superpuissances; **a doctor-patient ~** une relation médecin-patient; **a father-son ~** des rapports *mpl* de père à fils; **an actor's ~ with the audience** le contact d'un acteur avec son public; **2** (in a couple) relation *f* (**between** entre; **with** avec); **sexual ~** relation sexuelle; **are you in a ~?** est-ce que vous partagez votre vie avec quelqu'un?; **we have a good ~** nous nous entendons bien; **3** (logical or other connection) rapport *m* (**between** entre; **to, with** avec); **4** (family bond) lien *m* de parenté (**between** entre; **to** avec); **family ~s** liens de parenté.

relative /ˈrelətɪv/ I *n* **1** (relation) parent/-e *m/f*; **my ~s** ma famille; **2** Ling relatif *m*.
II *adj* **1** (comparative) [*comfort, ease, happiness, wealth*] relatif/-ive; **he's a ~ stranger** c'est presque un inconnu; **the ~ merits of X and Y** les mérites respectifs de X et Y; **~ to** (compared to) par rapport à; **supply is ~ to demand** l'offre varie en fonction de la demande; **2** Meas, Sci, Tech [*density, frequency, value, velocity*] relatif/-ive; **3** (concerning) **~ to** relatif/-ive à; **4** Ling [*pronoun, clause*] relatif/-ive; **5** Mus relatif/-ive; **6** Comput relatif/-ive.

relatively /ˈrelətɪvlɪ/ *adv* [*cheap, easy, high, small*] relativement; **~ speaking** toutes proportions gardées.

relativism /ˈrelətɪvɪzəm/ *n* relativisme *m*.

relativist /ˈrelətɪvɪst/ *n, adj* relativiste (*mf*).

relativistic /ˌrelətɪˈvɪstɪk/ *adj* Phys relativiste.

relativity /ˌreləˈtɪvətɪ/ *n* gen, Ling, Phys relativité *f* (**of** de); **the theory of ~** la théorie de la relativité.

relativize /ˈrelətɪvaɪz/ *vtr* relativiser.

relax /rɪˈlæks/ I *vtr* desserrer, relâcher [*grip*]; décontracter [*jaw, muscle, limb*]; relâcher [*concentration, attention, efforts*]; assouplir [*restrictions, discipline, policy*]; détendre [*body, mind*]; défriser [*hair*].
II *vi* **1** (unwind) [*person*] se détendre; **~!** ne t'en fais pas!; **I won't ~ until she arrives** je ne serai tranquille que quand elle sera arrivée; **2** (loosen, ease) [*grip*] se desserrer, se relâcher; [*jaw, muscle, limb*] se décontracter; [*face, features*] se détendre; [*discipline, policy, restrictions*] s'assouplir; **her face ~ed into a smile** son visage s'est détendu et elle a souri.

relaxant /rɪˈlæksnt/ *n* relaxant *m*, décontractant *m*.

relaxation /ˌriːlækˈseɪʃn/ I *n* **1** (recreation) détente *f*; **it's a form of ~** c'est une détente; **her only (form of) ~** sa seule détente; **what do you do for ~?** qu'est-ce que vous faites pour vous détendre?; **2** (loosening, easing) (of grip) relâchement *m*; (of jaw, muscle) décontraction *f*; (of efforts, concentration) relâchement *m*; (of restrictions, discipline, policy) assouplissement *m* (**in** de); (of body, mind) détente *f*, relaxation *f*.
II *modif* [*exercises, technique, session*] de relaxation.

relaxed /rɪˈlækst/ *adj* [*person, manner, atmosphere, discussion*] détendu, décontracté; [*muscle*] décontracté; **he's quite ~ about it** ça ne lui pose aucun problème.

relaxer /rɪˈlæksə(r)/ *n* défrisant *m*.

relaxing /rɪˈlæksɪŋ/ *adj* [*atmosphere, activity, evening*] délassant, relaxant; [*period, vacation*] reposant.

relay I /ˈriːleɪ/ *n* **1** (shift) (of workers) équipe *f* (*de relais*); (of horses) attelage *m*; **to work in ~s** [*rescue workers*] se relayer; [*employees*] travailler par roulement; **2** Radio, TV émission *f* retransmise; **3** (also **~ race**) course *f* de relais; **4** Elec relais *m*.
II *modif* Sport [*team, runner*] de relais.
III *vtr* **1** /ˈriːleɪ, riˈleɪ/ (*prét, pp* **relayed**) Radio, TV retransmettre, relayer (**to** à); fig transmettre [*message, question*] (**to** à); **2** /ˌriːˈleɪ/ (*prét, pp* **relaid**) reposer [*carpet*].

relay station *n* Radio, TV relais *m*.

release /rɪˈliːs/ I *n* **1** (liberation) libération *f*; **the ~ of the hostages (from captivity)** la libération des otages; **on his ~ from prison** à sa sortie de prison; **2** fig (relief) soulagement *m*; **a feeling of ~** un sentiment de soulagement; **death came as a merciful ~** la mort est venue comme une délivrance; **3** Tech, Ind (of pressure) relâchement *m*; (of steam, gas) dégagement *m*; (of liquid, chemicals) déversement *m*; **4** Mil (of missile) lancement *m*; (of bomb) largage *m*; **5** Tech (of mechanism) déclenchement *m*; (handle) manette *f*; **6** Journ (announcement) communiqué *m*; **7** Cin, Video (making publicly available) sortie *f*; **since the ~ of his latest film** depuis la sortie de son dernier film; **the film is now on general ~** le film passe maintenant dans toutes les grandes salles de cinéma; **8** Cin, Video (film, video, record) nouveauté *f*; **9** Transp (from customs, warehouse) sortie *f*; **~ for shipment** autorisation de sortie; **10** (discharge form) décharge *f*; **to sign the ~** signer la décharge; **11** (of employee for training) ▶ **day release**.
II *modif* Tech [*button, mechanism*] d'ouverture; Admin [*documents*] de décharge.
III *vtr* **1** (set free) libérer [*hostage, prisoner*]; dégager [*accident victim*]; relâcher [*animal*]; **2** fig **to ~ sb from** dégager qn de [*promise, obligation*]; **to ~ sb from a debt** faire la remise d'une dette à qn; **to ~ sb to attend a course** accorder un congé à qn pour lui permettre de suivre un stage; **3** Tech (unlock) faire jouer [*safety catch, clasp*]; Phot déclencher [*shutter*]; Aut desserrer [*handbrake*]; **to ~ the clutch (pedal)** embrayer; **4** (launch into flight) décocher [*arrow*]; Mil larguer [*bomb*]; lancer [*missile*]; **5** (let go of) lâcher [*object, arm, hand*]; **to ~ one's grip** lâcher prise; **to ~ one's grip of sth** lâcher qch; **6** Journ communiquer [*news, statement, bulletin*]; publier [*photo, picture*]; **7** Cin, Video, Mus faire sortir [*film, video, record*]; **8** gen, Jur (relinquish) céder [*title, right*]; remettre [*vehicle, keys*]; **9** Med libérer [*hormone, drug*].

relegate /ˈrelɪgeɪt/ *vtr* **1** (downgrade) reléguer [*person, object, issue, information*] (**to** à); **to be ~d to the scrap heap** fig être mis au rebut; **2** GB Sport reléguer (**to** en); **to be ~d** descendre dans la division inférieure; **to be ~d to the third division** être relégué en troisième division; **3** sout (assign) renvoyer (**to** à).

relegation /ˌrelɪˈgeɪʃn/ *n* **1** gen (downgrading) relégation *f* (**to** à); **2** GB Sport relégation *f* (**to** en); **3** sout (of problem, matter) renvoi *m* (**to** à).

relent /rɪˈlent/ *vi* [*person, government*] céder;

[*weather, storm*] se calmer; **the rain showed little sign of ~ing** la pluie ne semblait pas vouloir se calmer.

relentless /rɪ'lentlɪs/ *adj* [*ambition, urge, pressure*] implacable; [*noise, activity*] incessant; [*attack, pursuit, enemy*] acharné; [*advance*] inexorable.

relentlessly /rɪ'lentlɪslɪ/ *adv* **1** (incessantly) [*rain*] sans arrêt; [*shine*] implacablement; [*argue, attack*] sans arrêt; **2** (mercilessly) [*advance*] inexorablement.

relet /ˌriː'let/ *vtr* (*p prés* **-tt-**; *prét, pp* **relet**) relouer.

relevance /'reləvəns/ *n* (of issue, theory, fact, remark, information, resource) pertinence *f*, intérêt *m* (**to** pour); (of art) intérêt *m* (**to** pour); **the ~ of politics to daily life** le rapport entre la politique et la vie quotidienne; **to be of ~ to** être lié à; **of little/great ~** peu/très pertinent; **to have ~ for sb** présenter de l'intérêt pour qn; **this has no ~ to the issue** ceci n'a aucun rapport avec la question.

relevant /'reləvənt/ *adj* **1** (pertinent) [*issue, theory, facts, remark, point, law*] pertinent; [*information, resource*] utile; **to be ~ to** avoir rapport à; **that's not ~ to the subject** cela n'a aucun rapport or n'a rien à voir avec le sujet; **such considerations are not ~** de telles considérations sont hors de propos; **2** (appropriate, corresponding) [*chapter*] correspondant; [*time, period*] en question; **~ document** Jur pièce *f* justificative; **the ~ authorities** les autorités compétentes; **to have ~ experience** avoir une expérience préalable dans le domaine.

reliability /rɪˌlaɪə'bɪlətɪ/ *n* (of friend, witness) honnêteté *f*, intégrité *f*; (of employee, firm) sérieux *m*; (of car, machine) fiabilité *f*; (of information, memory, account) exactitude *f*.

reliable /rɪ'laɪəbl/ *adj* [*friend, neighbour, witness*] digne de confiance, fiable; [*employee, firm*] sérieux/-ieuse; [*car, machine, memory, account*] fiable; [*information*] sûr; **he's not very ~** on ne peut pas lui faire confiance or compter sur lui; **a ~ source of information** une source sûre; **the weather is not very ~** le temps est très variable.

reliably /rɪ'laɪəblɪ/ *adv* [*operate, work*] correctement; **to be ~ informed that** tenir de source sûre que.

reliance /rɪ'laɪəns/ *n* dépendance *f* (**on** vis-à-vis de).

reliant /rɪ'laɪənt/ *adj* **to be ~ on** [*person*] être dépendant de [*drugs, welfare payments*]; [*country*] être tributaire de [*industry, exports*]; [*industry*] être tributaire de [*material*].

relic /'relɪk/ *n* **1** fig (custom, building) vestige *m* (**of** de); (object) relique *f* (**of** de); **2** Relig relique *f*.

relict /'relɪkt/ *n* relique *f*.

relief /rɪ'liːf/ **I** *n* **1** (from pain, distress, anxiety) soulagement *m*; **(greatly) to my ~** à mon grand soulagement; **it was a ~ to them that** ils ont été soulagés que (+ *subj*); **it was a ~ to hear that/to see that** j'ai été soulagé d'apprendre que/de voir que; **to bring** ou **give ~ to sb** apporter du soulagement à qn; **to seek ~ from depression in drink** chercher un soulagement à sa dépression dans la boisson; **that's a ~!** c'est un soulagement!; **2** (alleviation) (of poverty) allégement *m*; **tax/debt ~** allégement fiscal/des dettes; **3** (help) aide *f*, secours *m*; **famine ~** aide aux victimes de la famine; **to come to the ~ of sb** venir à l'aide or au secours de qn; **to send ~ to** envoyer des secours à; **4** US Soc Admin aides *fpl* sociales; **to be on ~** bénéficier des aides sociales; **5** (diversion) divertissement *m*; **to provide light ~** apporter un peu de divertissement; **he reads magazines for light ~** il lit des magazines pour se distraire; **6** Mil (of garrison, troops) délivrance *f* (**of** de); **7** Art, Archit, Geog relief *m*; **high/low ~** haut-/bas-relief; **in ~** en relief; **to bring** ou **throw sth into ~** mettre qch en relief; **to stand out in (sharp) ~ against** se détacher (nettement) sur; **8** (replacement on duty) relève *f*; **9** Jur (of grievance) réparation *f*.

II *modif* [*operation*] de secours; [*programme, project*] d'aide; [*driver, guard*] de relève; [*bus, train, service*] supplémentaire.

relief: **~ agency** *n* organisation *f* humanitaire; **~ effort** *n* effort *m* d'aide; **~ fund** *n* gen fonds *m* d'aide; (in emergency) fonds *m* de secours; **~ map** *n* carte *f* en relief; **~ organization** *n* organisation *f* humanitaire; **~ road** *n* route *f* de délestage; **~ shift** *n* équipe *f* de relève; **~ supplies** *npl* secours *mpl*; **~ valve** *n* soupape *f* de sûreté; **~ work** *n* travail *m* humanitaire; **~ worker** *n* secouriste *mf*.

relieve /rɪ'liːv/ **I** *vtr* **1** (alleviate) soulager [*pain, suffering, distress, anxiety, tension*]; dissiper [*boredom*]; remédier à [*poverty, social conditions, famine*]; alléger [*debt*]; rompre [*monotony*]; **to ~ one's feelings** (when distressed) décharger son cœur; (when angry) décharger sa colère; **to ~ congestion** Med, Aut décongestionner; **2** (brighten) rendre moins sévère; **a black dress ~d by a string of pearls** une robe noire rendue moins sévère par un collier de perles; **3** (take away) **to ~ sb of** débarrasser qn de [*plate, coat, bag*]; soulager qn de [*burden*]; **to ~ sb of a post/command** relever qn de son poste/ses fonctions; **a pickpocket ~d him of his wallet** hum un voleur l'a soulagé de son portefeuille hum; **4** (help) venir en aide à, secourir [*troops, population*]; **5** (take over from) relever [*worker, sentry*]; **to ~ the guard** relever la garde; **6** Mil délivrer, faire lever le siège de [*town*].

II relieved *pp adj* **to feel ~d** se sentir soulagé; **to be ~d to hear that** être soulagé d'apprendre que; **to be ~d that** être soulagé que (+ *subj*); **to be ~d at** être soulagé par [*news, results*].

III *v refl* **to ~ oneself** euph se soulager euph.

religion /rɪ'lɪdʒən/ *n* religion *f*; **what ~ is he?** de quelle religion est-il?; **the Christian/Muslim ~** la religion chrétienne/musulmane; **freedom of ~** liberté *f* de religion or de culte; **it's against my ~ to...** c'est contraire à ma religion de... also hum; **to make a ~ of sth** se faire une religion de qch; **her work is her ~** son travail est une religion pour elle; **to get ~**○ péj devenir bigot; **to lose one's ~** perdre la foi.

religiosity /rɪˌlɪdʒɪ'ɒsətɪ/ *n* péj bigoterie *f*.

religious /rɪ'lɪdʒəs/ **I** *n* religieux/-ieuse *m/f*.

II *adj* **1** [*belief, conversion, faith, fanatic, practice*] religieux/-ieuse; [*war*] de religion; [*person*] croyant; [*art, music*] religieux/-ieuse; **she's very ~** elle est très croyante; **2** fig [*attention, care*] religieux/-ieuse.

religious: **~ affairs** *npl* Journ, Pol affaires *fpl* religieuses; **Religious Education**, **Religious Instruction** *n* instruction *f* religieuse; **~ leader** *n* chef *m* religieux.

religiously /rɪ'lɪdʒəslɪ/ *adv* lit religieusement; fig rituellement.

religiousness /rɪ'lɪdʒəsnɪs/ *n* piété *f*.

reline /ˌriː'laɪn/ *vtr* **1** Sewing redoubler [*garment, curtains*]; **2** Aut changer les garnitures de [*brakes*].

relinquish /rɪ'lɪŋkwɪʃ/ *vtr* sout **1** (surrender) renoncer à [*claim, right, privilege, title*] (**to** en faveur de); céder [*post, task, power*] (**to** à); **2** (abandon) abandonner [*efforts, struggle, responsibility*]; **to ~ one's hold** ou **grip on sth** lâcher qch.

relinquishment /rɪ'lɪŋkwɪʃmənt/ *n* sout (of claim, privilege etc) renonciation *f* (**of** à).

reliquary /'relɪkwərɪ, US -kwerɪ/ *n* reliquaire *m*.

relish /'relɪʃ/ **I** *n* **1 to eat/drink with ~** manger/boire avec un plaisir évident; **2** fig goût *m* (**for** pour); **with ~** [*perform, sing*] avec un plaisir évident; **she announced the news with ~** elle a annoncé la nouvelle avec délectation or (gloatingly) en jubilant; **3** (flavour) saveur *f*; fig (appeal) attrait *m*; **4** Culin condiment *m*.

II *vtr* **1** savourer [*food*]; **2** fig apprécier [*joke, sight*]; se réjouir de [*opportunity, prospect*]; **I don't ~ the thought** ou **prospect of telling her the news** je me passerais bien de lui annoncer la nouvelle.

relive /ˌriː'lɪv/ *vtr* revivre.

relly○ /'relɪ/ *n* GB parent/-e *m/f*; **your rellies** ta famille.

reload /ˌriː'ləʊd/ *vtr* recharger.

relocate /ˌriːləʊ'keɪt, US ˌriː'ləʊkeɪt/ **I** *vtr* muter [*employee*] (**to** à, en); transférer [*offices*] (**to** à, en); Comput translater.

II *vi* [*company*] déménager; [*employee*] être muté.

relocation /ˌriːləʊ'keɪʃn/ **I** *n* (of company) relocalisation *f*, déménagement *m*; (of employee) mutation *f* (**to** à, en); (of population, refugees) transfert *m* (**to** vers); Comput translation *f*.

II *modif* [*costs, expenses*] de déménagement.

relocation: **~ allowance** *n* prime *f* de relogement; **~ package** *n* indemnités *fpl* de déménagement.

reluctance /rɪ'lʌktəns/ *n* **1** gen réticence *f*; (stronger) répugnance *f*; **to show ~ to do** manifester de la réticence or de la répugnance à faire; **with great ~** de mauvaise grâce, à contrecœur; **to do sth with ~** faire qch à contrecœur; **to make a show of ~** se faire prier; **2** Elec réluctance *f*.

reluctant /rɪ'lʌktənt/ *adj* **1** (unwilling) peu enthousiaste; **to be ~ to do** être peu disposé à faire, rechigner à faire; **she is a rather ~ celebrity** elle est devenue une célébrité malgré elle; **2** (lukewarm) [*consent, promise, acknowledgement*] accordé à contrecœur.

reluctantly /rɪ'lʌktəntlɪ/ *adv* [*act, agree, decide*] à contrecœur.

rely /rɪ'laɪ/ *vi* **1** (be dependent) **to ~ on** [*person, place, group*] dépendre de [*industry, subsidy, aid*]; [*economy*] reposer sur [*exports, industry*]; [*system, plant*] reposer sur [*method, technology*]; [*government*] s'appuyer sur [*deterrent, military*]; **he relies on her for everything** il s'en remet à elle pour tout; **2** (count) **to ~ on sb/sth** compter sur qn/qch (**to do** pour faire); **you can ~ on me!** vous pouvez compter sur moi!; **she cannot be relied (up)on to help** on ne peut pas compter sur elle pour aider; **don't ~ on their being on time** ne compte pas sur eux pour être à l'heure; **you can't ~ on the evening being a success** on ne peut pas garantir que la soirée soit une réussite; **3** (trust in) **to ~ on sb/sth** se fier à qn/qch; **he can't be relied (up)on** on ne peut pas lui faire confiance.

REM *n* (*abrév* = **rapid eye movement**) mouvements *mpl* oculaires rapides.

remain /rɪ'meɪn/ **I** *vi* **1** (be left) rester; **not much ~s of the building** il ne reste pas grand-chose du bâtiment; **a lot ~s to be done** il reste beaucoup à faire; **the fact ~s that** il reste que, toujours est-il que; **it ~s to be seen whether** il reste à voir si; **that ~s to be seen** cela reste à voir; **it only ~s for me to say** il ne me reste qu'à dire; **2** (stay) [*person, memory, trace*] rester, demeurer; [*problem, doubt*] subsister; **to ~ standing/seated** rester debout/assis; **to ~ silent** garder le silence; **to ~ hopeful** continuer à espérer; **to let things ~ as they are** laisser les choses en l'état; **to ~ with sb all his/her life** [*memory*] accompagner qn toute sa vie; **if the weather ~s fine** si le temps se maintient au beau; **'I ~, yours faithfully'** 'je vous prie d'agréer mes salutations les meilleures'.

II remaining *pres p adj* restant; **for the ~ months of my life** pendant les mois qu'il me reste à vivre.

remainder /rɪ'meɪndə(r)/ **I** *n* **1** (remaining things, money) reste *m*; (remaining people) autres *mfpl*; (remaining time) reste *m*, restant *m*; **for the ~ of the day** pendant le reste or

le restant de la journée; **2** Math reste *m*; **3** Jur retour *m* en pleine propriété.
II **remainders** *npl* Comm invendus *mpl* soldés.
III *vtr* solder [*books, goods*].

remains /rɪˈmeɪnz/ *npl* **1** (of meal, fortune) restes *mpl*; (of building, city) vestiges *mpl*, restes *mpl*; **literary ~** œuvres *fpl* posthumes; **2** (corpse) restes *mpl*; **human ~** restes humains.

remake I /ˈriːmeɪk/ *n* nouvelle version *f*, remake *m*.
II /ˌriːˈmeɪk/ *vtr* (*prét, pp* **remade**) refaire.

remand /rɪˈmɑːnd, US rɪˈmænd/ Jur I *n* renvoi *m* (*à une audience ultérieure*); **to be on ~** (in custody) être en détention provisoire; (on bail) être en liberté sous caution.
II *vtr* renvoyer, déférer [*case, accused*]; **to be ~ed in custody** être placé en détention provisoire; **to be ~ed on bail** être mis en liberté sous caution; **to ~ sb for trial** renvoyer qn à une audience ultérieure; **to be ~ed to a higher court** être déféré à une instance supérieure; **the case was ~ed for a week** l'affaire a été renvoyée à huitaine.

remand: **~ centre** *n* GB centre *m* de détention (provisoire); **~ home** *n* GB centre *m* de détention (*pour mineurs*); **~ prisoner** *n* GB prisonnier/-ière *m/f* en détention provisoire; **~ wing** *n* GB quartier *m* des prisonniers en détention provisoire.

remark /rɪˈmɑːk/ I *n* **1** (comment, note) remarque *f* (**about** à propos de, sur); **opening ~s** préambule *m*; **closing ~s** conclusion *f*; **2** (casual observation) réflexion *f* (**about** à propos de, sur); **keep your ~s to yourself** garde tes réflexions pour toi; **3** (notice) **worthy of ~** remarquable; **to escape ~** passer inaperçu.
II *vtr* **1** (comment) **to ~ that** faire remarquer que (**to** à); **'strange!' she ~ed** 'étrange!' remarqua-t-elle; **2** (notice) sout remarquer [*change, gesture*]; **to ~ that** remarquer que.
■ **remark on, remark upon**: **~ on** ou **upon [sth]** faire des remarques sur or à propos de [*conduct, dress, weather*] (**to** à).

remarkable /rɪˈmɑːkəbl/ *adj* [*performance, ease, person*] remarquable; **it is ~ that** il est remarquable que (+ *subj*).

remarkably /rɪˈmɑːkəblɪ/ *adv* remarquablement; **~ enough** aussi étonnant que cela paraisse.

remarriage /ˌriːˈmærɪdʒ/ *n* remariage *m*.

remarry /ˌriːˈmærɪ/ I *vtr* se remarier avec.
II *vi* se remarier.

remaster /riːˈmɑːstə(r)/ *vtr* Audio remastériser; **digitally ~ed** remastérisé numériquement.

rematch /ˈriːmætʃ/ *n* Sport gen match *m* de retour; (in boxing) deuxième combat *m*.

remediable /rɪˈmiːdɪəbl/ *adj* réparable, remédiable.

remedial /rɪˈmiːdɪəl/ *adj* **1** gen [*measures*] de redressement; **to take ~ action** prendre des mesures (de redressement); **2** Med [*treatment*] curatif/-ive; **~ exercises** gymnastique *f* corrective; **3** Sch [*class*] de rattrapage, de soutien; **~ French course** cours *m* de rattrapage de français; **~ education** *enseignement pour les élèves en difficulté*.

remedy /ˈremədɪ/ I *n* Med, fig remède *m* (**for** à, contre); Jur recours *m*; **to be beyond (all) ~** être irrémédiable or sans remède.
II *vtr* remédier à; **the situation cannot be remedied** la situation est irrémédiable or sans remède.
IDIOMS **desperate diseases require desperate remedies** aux grands maux les grands remèdes.

remember /rɪˈmembə(r)/ I *vtr* **1** (recall) se souvenir de, se rappeler [*fact, name, place, event*]; se souvenir de [*person*]; **to ~ that** se rappeler que, se souvenir que; **it must be ~ed that** il faut bien se rappeler que; **~ that he was only 20 at the time** n'oublie pas or rappelle-toi qu'il n'avait que 20 ans à l'époque; **to ~ doing** se rappeler avoir fait, se souvenir d'avoir fait; **I ~ him as a very dynamic man** je me souviens de lui comme d'un homme très dynamique; **I ~ a time when** je me souviens de l'époque où; **I don't ~ anything about it** je n'en ai aucun souvenir; **I can never ~ names** je ne retiens jamais les noms; **I can't ~ her name for the moment** je n'arrive pas à me rappeler son nom pour l'instant, son nom m'échappe pour l'instant; **I wish I had something to ~ him by** j'aurais aimé avoir un souvenir de lui; **I've been working here for longer than I care to ~** cela fait une éternité que je travaille ici; **that's longer ago than I care to ~** il y a de cela une éternité; **that's worth ~ing** c'est bon à savoir; **a night to ~** une soirée mémorable; **2** (not forget) **to ~ to do** penser à faire, ne pas oublier de faire; **did you ~ to get a newspaper/feed the cat?** tu as pensé à acheter un journal/donner à manger au chat?; **~ that it's fragile** n'oublie pas que c'est fragile; **~ where you are!** un peu de tenue!; **to ~ sb in one's prayers** ne pas oublier qn dans ses prières; **3** (give money to) euph **he always ~s me on my birthday** il n'oublie jamais mon anniversaire; **she ~ed me in her will** elle ne m'a pas oublié dans son testament; **4** (commemorate) commémorer [*battle, war dead*]; **5** (convey greetings from) **to ~ sb to sb** rappeler qn au bon souvenir de qn; **she asks to be ~ed to you** elle m'a prié de vous transmettre son bon souvenir.
II *vi* se souvenir; **if I ~ correctly** ou **rightly** si je me souviens bien; **not as far as I ~** pas que je sache; **as far as I can ~** pour autant que je me souvienne, autant qu'il m'en souvienne.
III *v refl* **to ~ oneself** se reprendre.

remembrance /rɪˈmembrəns/ *n* **1** (memento) souvenir *m*; **2** (memory) souvenir *m*, mémoire *f*; **in ~ of** en souvenir de.

remembrance: **~ ceremony** *n* cérémonie *f* commémorative; **Remembrance Day, Remembrance Sunday** GB *n jour consacré à la mémoire des soldats tués au cours des deux guerres mondiales*.

remind /rɪˈmaɪnd/ I *vtr* rappeler; **to ~ sb of sth** rappeler qch à qn; **to ~ sb to do** rappeler à qn de faire; **he ~s me of my brother** il me rappelle mon frère, il me fait penser à mon frère; **to ~ sb that** rappeler à qn que; **you are ~ed that** nous vous rappelons que; **I forgot to ~ her about the meeting** je n'ai pas pensé à lui reparler de la réunion; **that ~s me...** à propos...
II *v refl* **to ~ oneself** se dire (**that** que).

reminder /rɪˈmaɪndə(r)/ *n* rappel *m* (**of** de; **that** du fait que); **a ~ to sb to do** un rappel à qn lui demandant de faire; **(letter of) ~** Admin (lettre *f* de) rappel *m*; **to be** ou **to serve as a ~ that** nous rappeler que; **to be** ou **to serve as a ~ of the importance of the treaty** rappeler à tous l'importance du traité; **to be a ~ of the problems faced by parents** rappeler les problèmes auxquels sont confrontés les parents; **~s of the past** des souvenirs du passé; **~s of her status** des signes rappelant sa position.

reminisce /ˌremɪˈnɪs/ *vi* évoquer ses souvenirs (**about** de).

reminiscence /ˌremɪˈnɪsns/ *n* **1** (recalling) réminiscence *f*; **2** (memory) souvenir *m*.

reminiscent /ˌremɪˈnɪsnt/ *adj* **to be ~ of sb/sth** rappeler qn/qch, faire penser à qn/qch.

reminiscently /ˌremɪˈnɪsntlɪ/ *adv* [*smile, look*] avec nostalgie; **to talk ~ of sth/sb** évoquer ses souvenirs de qch/qn.

remiss /rɪˈmɪs/ *adj* négligent; **it was ~ of him not to reply** c'était négligent de sa part de ne pas répondre.

remission /rɪˈmɪʃn/ *n* **1** Jur (of sentence) remise *f*; **2** Med, Relig rémission *f*; **3** (of debt) remise *f*; **fee ~** exonération *f* de frais; **4** (deferment) remise *f* à plus tard.

remit I /ˈriːmɪt/ *n* attributions *fpl* (**to do** pour faire; **for** pour); **it's outside my ~** ce n'est pas dans mes attributions; **to exceed one's ~** aller au-delà de ses attributions.
II /rɪˈmɪt/ *vtr* (*p prés etc* **-tt-**) **1** (send back) renvoyer [*case, problem*] (**to** devant); **2** (reduce) remettre [*penalty, taxation*]; **3** (send) envoyer [*money*]; **4** (postpone) différer [*payment*]; **5** Relig remettre [*sin*].
III /rɪˈmɪt/ *vi* (*p prés etc* **-tt-**) (abate) diminuer.

remittal /rɪˈmɪtl/ *n* Jur remise *f* de peine.

remittance /rɪˈmɪtns/ *n* **1** (payment) versement *m*; **2** (allowance) rente *f*.

remittance advice *n* avis *m* de règlement.

remittent /rɪˈmɪtnt/ *adj* Med rémittent.

remix /ˌriːˈmɪks/ Mus I *n* (version *f*) remix *m*.
II *vtr* remixer.

remnant /ˈremnənt/ *n* (of food, commodity) reste *m*; (of building, past, ideology) vestige *m*; Comm (of fabric) coupon *m*; **the ~s of the crowd/of the army** ce qui restait de la foule/de l'armée.

remodel /ˌriːˈmɒdl/ *vtr* (*p prés etc* GB **-ll-**, US **-l-**) réorganiser, restructurer [*company, institution*]; transformer [*policy*]; remanier [*constitution*]; remodeler [*nose*]; transformer, remodeler [*house, town*].

remonstrance /rɪˈmɒnstrəns/ *n* sout remontrance *f*.

remonstrate /ˈremənstreɪt/ sout I *vtr* faire remarquer (**that** que).
II *vi* protester; **to ~ with sb about sth** faire des remontrances à qn (avec véhémence) au sujet de qch.

remorse /rɪˈmɔːs/ *n* remords *m* (**for** de); **a fit of ~** un accès de remords; **a feeling of ~** un remords; **she felt no ~ for her crime** elle n'éprouvait aucun remords d'avoir commis ce crime.

remorseful /rɪˈmɔːsfl/ *adj* [*person, apology, confession*] plein de remords.

remorsefully /rɪˈmɔːsfəlɪ/ *adv* [*speak*] avec remords; [*cry*] de remords.

remorseless /rɪˈmɔːslɪs/ *adj* **1** (brutal) impitoyable; **2** (relentless) [*ambition, attempt, progress*] implacable; [*enthusiasm, optimism*] perpétuel/-elle.

remorselessly /rɪˈmɔːslɪslɪ/ *adv* implacablement.

remorselessness /rɪˈmɔːslɪsnɪs/ *n* acharnement *m*.

remote /rɪˈməʊt/ I *n* **1** Radio, TV émission *f* en direct (en dehors des studios); **2**○ Audio (gadget) télécommande *f*.
II *adj* **1** (distant) [*era*] lointain; [*antiquity*] haut; [*ancestor, country, planet*] éloigné; **in the ~ future/past** dans un avenir/passé lointain; **in the ~ distance** au lointain; **in the ~st corner of Asia** au fin fond de l'Asie; **2** (isolated) [*area, village*] isolé; **~ from society** à l'écart de la société; **the leaders are too ~ from the people** les dirigeants sont isolés du peuple; **3** fig (aloof) [*person*] distant; **4** (slight) [*chance, connection, resemblance*] vague, infime; **I haven't (got) the ~st idea** je n'en ai pas la moindre idée; **there is only a ~ possibility that they survived** il est très peu probable qu'ils aient survécu; **5** Comput [*printer, terminal*] satellite.

remote: **~ access** *n* Comput téléconsultation *f*, accès *m* à distance; **~ central locking** *n* verrouillage *m* centralisé à distance.

remote control *n* **1** (gadget) télécommande *f*; **2** (technique) télécommande *f*, commande *f* à distance; **to operate sth by ~** télécommander qch.

remote: **~-controlled** *adj* télécommandé; **~ damage** *n* Jur préjudice *m* indirect; ~ **job entry** *n* Comput télésoumission *f* de travaux.

remotely /rɪˈməʊtlɪ/ *adv* **1** (at a distance) [*located, situated*] à l'écart de tout; ~ **operated** télécommandé; **2** (slightly) [*resemble*] vaguement; **he's not ~ interested** ça ne l'intéresse pas du tout; **it is ~ possible that** il est tout juste possible que (+ *subj*); **this does not taste ~ like caviar** ça n'a rien à voir avec le goût du caviar; **I don't look ~ like her** je ne lui ressemble pas le moins du monde; ~ **related events** des événements vaguement liés or ayant un rapport lointain.

remoteness /rɪˈməʊtnɪs/ *n* **1** (isolation) isolement *m* (**from** par rapport à); **his ~ from the electorate** son isolement par rapport à l'électorat; **2** (in time) éloignement *m* (dans le temps) (**from** par rapport à); **3** (of person) attitude *f* distante (**from** envers).

remote: ~ **sensing** *n* télédétection *f*; ~ **surveillance** *n* télésurveillance *f*.

remould GB, **remold** US **I** /ˈriːməʊld/ *n* GB pneu *m* rechapé.
II /ˌriːˈməʊld/ *vtr* **1** GB Aut rechaper [*tyre*]; **2** fig (transform) restructurer [*company, institution*]; corriger [*person, personality*].

remount /ˌriːˈmaʊnt/ **I** *vtr* **1** enfourcher [qch] de nouveau [*bicycle*]; remonter [*hill, stairs*]; grimper de nouveau à [*ladder*]; **to ~ a horse** se remettre en selle; **2** Art remonter [*exhibition*]; encadrer [qch] à nouveau [*picture*].
II *vi* [*cyclist*] remonter à bicyclette; [*rider*] remonter à cheval.

removable /rɪˈmuːvəbl/ *adj* amovible.

removal /rɪˈmuːvl/ **I** *n* **1** (elimination) (of tax, barrier, subsidy, threat) suppression *f*; (of doubt, worry) disparition *f*; **2** (cleaning) **for the ~ of grease stains** pour enlever les taches de graisse; **stain ~** détachage *m*; **3** (withdrawal) (of troops) retrait *m*; **4** Med (excision) ablation *f*; **5** (change of home, location) déménagement *m* (**from** de; **to** à); **6** (dismissal) (of employee, official) renvoi *m*; (of leader) déposition *f*, révocation *f*; **after his ~ from office** à la suite de sa déposition or révocation; **7** (of demonstrators, troublemakers) expulsion *f*; **8** (collecting) **he's responsible for the ~ of the rubbish/boxes** il est chargé d'enlever les ordures/cartons; **9** (transfer) (of patient, prisoner) transfert *m*; **10**○ (killing) euph liquidation *f*.
II *modif* [*costs, firm*] de déménagement.

removal: ~ **expenses** *npl* frais *mpl* de déménagement; ~ **man** *n* déménageur *m*; ~ **order** *n* Jur ordre *m* de déportation; ~ **van** *n* camion *m* de déménagement.

remove /rɪˈmuːv/ **I** *n* sout **to be at one ~ from/at many ~s from** être tout proche de/très loin de; **genius that is (at) only one ~ from madness** le génie qui frise la folie.
II *vtr* **1** enlever [*object*] (**from** de); enlever, ôter [*clothes, shoes*]; enlever, faire partir [*stain*]; enlever, supprimer [*passage, paragraph, word*]; supprimer [*tax, subsidy*]; Med enlever, faire l'ablation de [*tumour, breast, organ*]; **she ~d her hand from his shoulder** elle a enlevé sa main de son épaule; **over 30 bodies were ~d from the rubble** plus de 30 cadavres ont été retirés des décombres; **to ~ a child from a school** retirer un enfant d'une école; **to ~ goods from the market** retirer des marchandises de la vente; **to ~ industry from state control** supprimer le contrôle de l'État sur l'industrie; **to ~ sb's name from a list** rayer qn d'une liste; **to be ~d to hospital** GB être emmené à l'hôpital, être hospitalisé; **to ~ one's make-up** se démaquiller; **to ~ unwanted hair from one's legs** s'épiler les jambes; **2** (oust) démettre, renvoyer [*employee*]; **to ~ sb from office** démettre qn de ses fonctions; **to ~ sb from power** destituer qn; **3** (dispel) dissiper [*suspicion, fears, boredom*]; chasser [*doubt*]; écarter [*obstacle, difficulty*]; supprimer [*threat*]; **4** euph (kill) supprimer, liquider○ [*person*]; **5** Comput effacer.
III *vi* sout déménager; **they have ~d from London to the country** ils ont déménagé de Londres pour aller s'installer à la campagne.
IV *v refl* **to ~ oneself** hum se retirer (**to** à).
V removed *pp adj* **1 to be far ~d from** être très éloigné de [*reality, truth*]; **2** (in kinship) **cousin once/twice ~d** cousin au deuxième/troisième degré.

remover /rɪˈmuːvə(r)/ *n* (person) déménageur *m*; ▶ **stain remover etc.**

REM sleep *n* sommeil *m* paradoxal, sommeil *m* rapide.

remunerate /rɪˈmjuːnəreɪt/ *vtr* rémunérer (**for** pour).

remuneration /rɪˌmjuːnəˈreɪʃn/ *n* sout (all contexts) rémunération *f*.

remunerative /rɪˈmjuːnərətɪv, US -nəreɪtɪv/ *adj* sout rémunérateur/-trice.

renaissance /rɪˈneɪsns, US ˈrenəsɑːns/ *n* (of culture) renaissance *f*; (of interest etc) renouveau *m*.

Renaissance /rɪˈneɪsns, US ˈrenəsɑːns/ **I** *pr n* **the ~** la Renaissance.
II *modif* [*art, palace*] de la Renaissance.

Renaissance man *n* fig esprit *m* universel.

renal /ˈriːnl/ *adj* [*failure, function*] rénal.

renal: ~ **dialysis** *n* hémodialyse *f*; ~ **specialist** ▶ 1692 *n* néphrologue *mf*; ~ **unit** *n* centre *m* de néphrologie.

rename /ˌriːˈneɪm/ *vtr* rebaptiser.

renascent /rɪˈnæsnt/ *adj* renaissant.

rend /rend/ *vtr* (*prét, pp* **rent**) lit, fig déchirer.

render /ˈrendə(r)/ **I** *n* Constr enduit *m*.
II *vtr* **1** (cause to become) **to ~ sth impossible/harmless/lawful** rendre qch impossible/inoffensif/légal; **to ~ sb unconscious/homeless/speechless** laisser qn inconscient/sans abri/sans voix; **2** (provide) rendre [*service*] (**to** à); apporter [*assistance, aid*] (**to** à); **'for services ~ed'** 'pour services rendus'; **3** (give) rendre [*homage, respect, allegiance*] (**to** à); **to ~ one's life for sth** littér se sacrifier pour qch; **4** Art, Literat, Mus rendre [*work, mood, style*]; **5** (translate) rendre [*nuance*]; traduire [*text, phrase*] (**into** en); **6** Comm (submit) remettre [*account*]; présenter [*statement*]; **'for account ~ed'** 'suivant compte remis'; **7** Jur rendre [*judgment, decision*]; **8** Constr enduire, recouvrir [*wall, surface*]; **9** (melt down) ▶ **render down**.
■ **render down**: ~ **[sth] down**, ~ **down [sth]** faire bouillir [qch] pour le/la dégraisser [*carcass, meat*].
■ **render up**: ~ **up [sth]** littér rendre [*soul, arms, treasure*].

rendering /ˈrendərɪŋ/ *n* **1** Art, Literat, Mus interprétation *f* (**of** de); **2** (translation) traduction *f* (**of** de); **3** Constr (plaster) enduit *m*.

rendezvous /ˈrɒndɪvuː/ **I** *n* (*pl* ~) (meeting, place) rendez-vous *m inv*; **to have a ~ with sb** avoir rendez-vous avec qn.
II *vi* (meet) se retrouver; **to ~ with sb** rejoindre qn.

rendition /renˈdɪʃn/ *n* Art, Literat, Mus interprétation *f*.

renegade /ˈrenɪgeɪd/ **I** *n* **1** (abandoning beliefs) renégat/-e *m/f*; **2** (rebel) rebelle *mf*.
II *adj* **1** (abandoning beliefs) renégat; **2** (rebel) rebelle.

renege /rɪˈniːg, -ˈneɪg/ *vi* se rétracter; **to ~ on an agreement** revenir sur sa parole.

renegotiate /ˌriːnɪˈgəʊʃɪeɪt/ *vtr* renégocier [*deal, contract*].

renegotiation /ˌriːnɪˌgəʊʃɪˈeɪʃn/ *n* renégociation *f* (**of** de).

renegue *vi* = **renege**.

renew /rɪˈnjuː, US -ˈnuː/ **I** *vtr* renouveler [*efforts, stock, passport, contract*]; renouer [*acquaintance*]; reprendre [*negotiations*]; changer [*tyres*]; raviver [*courage*]; faire prolonger [*library book*].
II renewed *pp adj* [*interest, optimism*] accru; [*attack, call*] renouvelé.

renewable /rɪˈnjuːəbl, US -ˈnuːəbl/ **I** *n* (*gén pl*) forme *f* d'énergie renouvelable.
II *adj* (all contexts) renouvelable.

renewal /rɪˈnjuːəl, US -ˈnuːəl/ **I** *n* (of subscription, passport, lease) renouvellement *m*; (of hostilities, diplomatic relations) reprise *f*; (of interest) regain *m*; (of premises, drains) rénovation *f*; **to come up for ~** arriver à expiration, expirer.
II *modif* [*date, fee, form*] de renouvellement.

rennet /ˈrenɪt/ *n* présure *f*.

renounce /rɪˈnaʊns/ **I** *vtr* renoncer à [*claim, party, habit, nationality, strategy, violence*]; renier [*faith, family, friend*]; répudier [*succession*]; dénoncer [*agreement, treaty*].
II *vi* Games renoncer.

renovate /ˈrenəveɪt/ *vtr* rénover [*building*]; restaurer [*statue*]; remettre [qch] à neuf [*vehicle, electrical appliance*].

renovation /ˌrenəˈveɪʃn/ **I** *n* (process) rénovation *f*; **property in need of ~** maison à rénover.
II renovations *npl* travaux *mpl* de rénovation.
III *modif* [*scheme, project, work*] de rénovation.

renovation grant *n* GB prime *f* pour l'amélioration de l'habitat.

renown /rɪˈnaʊn/ *n* renommée *f*; **of world/international ~** de renommée mondiale/internationale.

renowned /rɪˈnaʊnd/ *adj* célèbre (**for** pour).

rent /rent/ **I** *prét, pp* ▶ **rend**.
II *n* **1** (for accommodation) loyer *m*; **two months' ~ in advance** deux mois de loyer à l'avance; **for ~** à louer; **2** (rip) lit, fig déchirure *f*.
III *modif* [*control, strike*] des loyers; [*increase*] de loyer.
IV *vtr* **1** (hire) louer [*car, TV, house, apartment*]; **2** (let) = **rent out**.
V *vi* **1** [*tenant*] être locataire; **2** [*landlord*] **he ~s to students** il loue des logements à des étudiants; **3** [*property*] **to ~ for £600 a month** être loué pour 600 livres par mois.
VI rented *pp adj* [*room, villa*] loué; [*car, phone*] de location.
■ **rent out**: ~ **[sth] out**, ~ **out [sth]** louer (**to** à).

rent: ~**-a-crowd**○ *adj* hum pej [*party, event*] *où l'on invite le plus de monde possible pour faire de l'effet*; **Rent Act** *n* GB Jur *décret régissant les relations entre locataires et bailleurs*; ~ **agreement** *n* bail *m*.

rental /ˈrentl/ *n* (of car, premises, equipment) location *f*; (of phone line) abonnement *m*; **monthly/weekly ~** location au mois/à la semaine; **car/video ~** location de voitures/cassettes vidéo; **line ~** abonnement téléphonique; **the weekly ~ for the TV is £2** nous payons 2 livres par semaine pour la location de notre télévision.

rental: ~ **agreement** *n* bail *m*, contrat *m* de location; ~ **building** *n* US immeuble *m* locatif; ~ **company** *n* organisme *m* de location; ~ **income** *n* rapport *m* locatif.

rent: ~**-a-mob**○ *n* péj agitateurs *mpl* (*recrutés*); ~ **arrears** *npl* arriérés *mpl* de loyer; ~ **book** *n* carnet *m* de quittances; ~ **boy** *n* GB jeune prostitué *m*; ~ **collector** *n* personne *f* chargée d'encaisser les loyers; ~**-controlled** *adj* dont le loyer est contrôlé.

renter /ˈrentə(r)/ *n* **1** (tenant) locataire *mf*; **2** (landlord) bailleur/-eresse *m/f*.

rent-free /ˌrentˈfriː/ **I** *adj* [*house*] prêté gratuitement.
II *adv* [*live, use*] sans payer de loyer.

rent: ~ **rebate** *n* remboursement *m* de loyer; ~ **tribunal** *n* GB Jur *organisme chargé de fixer les loyers*.

renumber /ˌriːˈnʌmbə(r)/ *vtr* renuméroter.

renunciation /rɪˌnʌnsɪˈeɪʃn/ *n* (of faith, family, friend) reniement *m* (**of** de); (of pleasures) renoncement *m* (**of** à); (of right, nationality, title) renonciation *f* (**of** à); (of succession) répudiation *f* (**of** de).

reoccupy /ˌriːˈɒkjʊpaɪ/ *vtr* réoccuper [*territory*]; reprendre [*position*].

reopen /ˌriːˈəʊpən/ **I** *vtr* (all contexts) rouvrir; **to ~ old wounds** fig rouvrir de vieilles plaies.
II *vi* [*school, shop*] rouvrir; [*trial, talks, play*] reprendre.

reopening /ˌriːˈəʊpənɪŋ/ *n* réouverture *f*.

reorder /ˌriːˈɔːdə(r)/ **I** *n* nouvelle commande *f*.
II *vtr* commander [qch] à nouveau.
III *vi* passer une nouvelle commande.

reorganization /ˌriːˌɔːɡənaɪˈzeɪʃn/ *n* réorganisation *f*.

reorganize /ˌriːˈɔːɡənaɪz/ **I** *vtr* réorganiser [*office, industry*].
II *vi* se réorganiser.

rep /rep/ ▶1692 *n* **1** Comm, Ind (*abrév* = **representative**) représentant *m* (de commerce); **2** Theat *abrév* ▶**repertory**; **3** Tex reps *m*.

Rep /rep/ *n* **1** US Pol *abrév* ▶**Representative**; **2** US Pol *abrév* ▶**Republican**.

repackage /riːˈpækɪdʒ/ *vtr* **1** Comm reconditionner [*product*]; **2** fig reconditionner [*pay offer*]; modifier l'image publique de [*politician, media personality*].

repaid /ˌriːˈpeɪd/ *prét, pp* ▶**repay**.

repaint /ˌriːˈpeɪnt/ *vtr* repeindre.

repair /rɪˈpeə(r)/ **I** *n* **1** gen réparation *f*; (of clothes) réparation *f*; Naut (of hull) radoub *m*; **to be under ~** [*building*] être en réparation; [*ship*] être au radoub; **the ~s to the roof cost £900** la réparation du toit a coûté 900 livres; **we have carried out the necessary ~s** gen nous avons fait les réparations nécessaires; Constr nous avons fait les travaux nécessaires; **to be (damaged) beyond ~** être irréparable; **'road under ~'** 'travaux'; **'heel ~s while you wait'** 'talon minute'; **2** sout (condition) **to be in good/bad ~, to be in a good/bad state of ~** être en bon/mauvais état; **to keep sth in good ~** (bien) entretenir qch.
II *vtr* **1** lit réparer [*clothes*]; réparer, refaire [*road*]; réparer [*clock, machine*]; Naut radouber [*hull*]; **2** sout fig réparer [*wrong*]; améliorer [*relations*].
III *vi* (go) sout se retirer.

repairable /rɪˈpeərəbl/ *adj* [*article*] réparable; [*wrong, situation*] remédiable.

repairer /rɪˈpeərə(r)/ *n* réparateur/-trice *m/f*.

repair: **~ kit** *n* trousse *f* de réparation; **~man** *n* réparateur *m*.

repaper /ˌriːˈpeɪpə(r)/ *vtr* retapisser.

reparation /ˌrepəˈreɪʃn/ **I** *n* sout réparation *f*; **to make ~ for sth** réparer qch.
II reparations *npl* Pol indemnités *fpl* de guerre.

repartee /ˌrepɑːˈtiː/ *n* **1** (conversation) échange *m* de bons mots; **2** (wit) repartie *f*; **3** (reply) réplique *f*, repartie *f*.

repast /rɪˈpɑːst, US rɪˈpæst/ *n* littér repas *m*.

repatriate /riːˈpætrɪeɪt, US -ˈpeɪt-/ *vtr* gen, Fin rapatrier.

repatriation /ˌriːpætrɪˈeɪʃn, US -peɪt-/ **I** *n* rapatriement *m*.
II *modif* [*scheme*] de rapatriement; [*arrangements*] pour le rapatriement.

repay /rɪˈpeɪ/ *vtr* (*prét, pp* **repaid**) **1** rembourser [*person, sum, loan, debt*]; **2** rendre [*hospitality, favour*]; **to ~ a debt of gratitude** acquitter une dette de reconnaissance; **how can I ever ~ you (for your kindness)**? comment pourrai-je jamais vous remercier (de votre gentillesse)?; **you've been very hospitable, I hope one day I will be able to ~ you** vous m'avez généreusement accordé l'hospitalité, j'espère pouvoir un jour vous rendre la pareille; **3** sout (reward) **this book ~s careful reading** ce livre gagne à être lu attentivement.

repayable /rɪˈpeɪəbl/ *adj* remboursable; **~ in instalments** remboursable par versements échelonnés.

repayment /rɪˈpeɪmənt/ *n* remboursement *m* (**on** de); **to fall behind with one's ~s** accumuler des arriérés de remboursement.

repayment: **~ mortgage** *n* emprunt *m* hypothécaire à remboursements; **~ schedule** *n* échéancier *m* (de remboursement).

repeal /rɪˈpiːl/ **I** *n* Jur abrogation *f* (**of** de).
II *vtr* abroger.

repeat /rɪˈpiːt/ **I** *n* **1** (of event, performance, act) répétition *f*; Theat (in same week) deuxième représentation *f*; **2** Radio, TV rediffusion *f*, reprise *f*; **3** Mus (of movement) reprise *f*.
II *modif* gen [*attack, attempt, offer, order, performance*] répété; **~ offender** Jur récidiviste *mf*; **~ prescription** Med ordonnance *f* renouvelable.
III *vtr* **1** gen répéter [*word, action, success, offer, test*]; Sch redoubler [*year*]; recommencer [*course*]; Radio, TV rediffuser [*programme*]; **to ~ that** répéter que; **to be ~ed** gen [*event, attack*] se répéter; Radio, TV être rediffusé; Comm [*offer*] se représenter, être renouvelé; **2** Mus reprendre [*movement, motif*].
IV *vi* **cucumbers ~ on me** euph je digère mal les concombres.
V *v refl* **to ~ oneself** se répéter; **history is ~ing itself** l'histoire se répète.

repeatable /rɪˈpiːtəbl/ *adj* répétable.

repeated /rɪˈpiːtɪd/ *adj* **1** gen [*warnings, requests, criticisms, refusals*] répété, réitéré; [*efforts, attempts*] répété; [*defeats, difficulties, setbacks*] successif/-ive; **2** Mus [*movement, theme*] repris.

repeatedly /rɪˈpiːtɪdlɪ/ *adv* plusieurs fois, à plusieurs reprises.

repeater /rɪˈpiːtə(r)/ *n* **1** (gun) arme *f* à répétition; **2** (watch) montre *f* à répétition; **3** Elec répétiteur *m* (de signaux électriques); **4** US Sch redoublant/-e *m/f*; **5** US Jur (habitual offender) récidiviste *mf*.

repeating firearm *n* arme *f* à répétition.

repeg /ˌriːˈpeɡ/ *vtr* (*p prés etc* **-gg-**) réaligner.

repel /rɪˈpel/ *vtr* (*p prés etc* **-ll-**) **1** (defeat) repousser [*invader, advances*]; **2** (disgust) dégoûter; **to be ~led by sb** trouver qn repoussant; **3** Electron, Phys [*electric charge*] repousser; [*surface*] résister à [*water*].

repellent /rɪˈpelənt/ *adj* [*idea, image*] repoussant; ▶**insect repellent**.

repent /rɪˈpent/ **I** *vtr* **1** (feel remorse about) se repentir de; **2** (regret) regretter.
II *vi* se repentir.
IDIOMS **marry in haste ~ at leisure** Prov qui se marie promptement s'en repent à loisir.

repentance /rɪˈpentəns/ *n* repentir *m*.

repentant /rɪˈpentənt/ *adj* repentant fml.

repercussion /ˌriːpəˈkʌʃn/ *n* **1** (consequence) répercussion *f* (**of** de; **on** sur; **for** pour); **to have ~s** avoir des répercussions; **2** Phys (recoil) répercussion *f*.

repertoire /ˈrepətwɑː(r)/ *n* (all contexts) répertoire *m*.

repertory /ˈrepətrɪ, US -tɔːrɪ/ *n* **1 to work in ~** jouer avec une troupe de province; **2** = **repertoire**.

repertory company *n* troupe *f* de théâtre de province.

repetition /ˌrepɪˈtɪʃn/ *n* répétition *f*.

repetitious /ˌrepɪˈtɪʃəs/ *adj* répétitif/-ive.

repetitive /rɪˈpetɪtɪv/ *adj* répétitif/-ive.

repetitively /rɪˈpetɪtɪvlɪ/ *adv* de façon répétitive.

repetitiveness /rɪˈpetɪtɪvnɪs/ *n* répétitivité *f*.

repetitive strain injury, **RSI** *n* Med microtraumatismes *mpl* répétés.

rephrase /ˌriːˈfreɪz/ *vtr* reformuler [*remark*].

repine /rɪˈpaɪn/ *vi* littér se plaindre (**at** de).

replace /rɪˈpleɪs/ *vtr* **1** (put back) remettre [*lid, cork*]; remettre [qch] à sa place [*book, ornament*]; **to ~ the receiver** raccrocher; **2** (supply replacement for) remplacer [*goods*] (**with** par); **3** (in job) remplacer [*person*]; **4** euph (dismiss) remplacer; **5** Comput remplacer.

replaceable /rɪˈpleɪsəbl/ *adj* remplaçable.

replacement /rɪˈpleɪsmənt/ **I** *n* **1** (person) remplaçant/-e *m/f* (**for** de); **2** Comm **we will give you a ~** (article) on vous le/la remplacera; **3** (act) remplacement *m*; **4** (spare part) pièce *f* de rechange.
II *modif* [*staff*] intérimaire; [*cost*] de remplacement; [*engine, part*] de rechange.

replant /ˌriːˈplɑːnt/ *vtr* replanter.

replay **I** /ˈriːpleɪ/ *n* Sport match *m* rejoué; fig répétition *f*; **action ~, instant ~** US replay *m*, reprise *f* d'une séquence.
II /ˌriːˈpleɪ/ *vtr* **1** Mus rejouer [*piece*]; **2** Audio écouter [qch] à nouveau [*disc, cassette*]; **3** Sport rejouer [*match*].

replenish /rɪˈplenɪʃ/ *vtr* reconstituer [*stocks*]; remplir [*larder*]; restocker [*shop shelves*]; réapprovisionner [*account*]; **may I ~ your glass?** laissez-moi vous resservir.

replenishment /rɪˈplenɪʃmənt/ *n* (of stocks) reconstitution *f*; (of larder) remplissage *m*; (of shop shelves) restockage *m*; (of account) réapprovisionnement *m*.

replete /rɪˈpliːt/ *adj* **1** (after eating) rassasié (**with** de); **2** (fully supplied) rempli (**with** de).

repletion /rɪˈpliːʃn/ *n* sout satiété *f*.

replica /ˈreplɪkə/ *n* réplique *f*, copie *f* (**of** de).

replicate /ˈreplɪkeɪt/ **I** *vtr* gen renouveler [*success*]; copier [*style, document*]; reproduire [*result*].
II *vi* Med [*virus, chromosome*] se reproduire (par réplication).

replication /ˌreplɪˈkeɪʃn/ *n* Biol réplication *f*; fig (of error, result) reproduction *f*.

reply /rɪˈplaɪ/ **I** *n* gen, Jur réponse *f*; **in ~ to** en réponse à; **to make no ~** ne pas répondre.
II *vtr* répondre.
III *vi* gen, Jur répondre (**to** à).

repoint /ˌriːˈpɔɪnt/ *vtr* rejointoyer [*wall*].

repointing /ˌriːˈpɔɪntɪŋ/ *n* rejointoyage *m*.

repo man○ /ˈriːpəʊ mæn/ *n* = **repossession man**.

report /rɪˈpɔːt/ **I** *n* **1** (written account) rapport *m* (**on** sur); (verbal account, minutes) compte-rendu *m*; **2** (notification) **have you had any ~s of lost dogs this evening?** est-ce qu'on a signalé des chiens perdus ce soir?; **3** Admin (published findings) rapport *m*; (of enquiry) rapport *m* d'enquête; **to prepare/publish a ~** préparer/publier un rapport; **the chairman's/committee's ~** le rapport présidentiel/de la commission; **the Warren commission's ~** le rapport d'enquête de la commission Warren; **4** Journ, Radio, TV communiqué *m*; (longer) reportage *m*; **and now a ~ from our Moscow correspondent** et maintenant un communiqué de notre envoyé spécial à Moscou; **we bring you this special ~** voici un communiqué spécial; **5** GB Sch bulletin *m* scolaire; **6** US Sch (review) critique *f*; **to write a ~** faire une critique; **7** (noise) détonation *f*.
II reports *npl* Journ, Radio, TV, gen (unsubstantiated news) **we are getting ~s of heavy fighting** des combats intensifs auraient lieu; **there have been ~s of understaffing in prisons** les prisons manqueraient de gardiens; **according to ~s, the divorce is imminent** selon certaines sources, le divorce serait imminent; **I've heard ~s that the headmaster is taking early retirement** j'ai entendu dire que le directeur va partir en préretraite.
III *vtr* **1** (relay) signaler [*fact, occurrence*]; **I have nothing to ~** je n'ai rien à signaler; **to ~ sth to sb** transmettre qch à qn [*result, decision, news*]; **the Union ~ed the vote to the management** le syndicat a transmis le résultat du vote à la direction; **did she have anything of interest to ~?** avait-elle quelque chose d'intéressant à

raconter?; **my friend ~ed that my parents are well** mon ami m'a dit que mes parents vont bien; **2** Journ, TV, Radio (give account of) faire le compte-rendu de [*debate*]; **Peter Jenkins is in Washington to ~ the latest developments** Peter Jenkins est à Washington pour nous tenir au courant des dernières nouvelles; **only one paper ~ed their presence in Paris** un seul journal a fait état de leur présence à Paris; **the French press has ~ed that the tunnel is behind schedule** selon la presse française il y aurait du retard dans la construction du tunnel; **3** Admin (notify authorities) signaler, déclarer [*theft, death, accident, case*]; **15 new cases of cholera were ~ed this week** on a signalé 15 nouveaux cas de choléra cette semaine; **five people are ~ed dead** on signale cinq morts; **no casualties have been ~ed** on ne signale pas de victimes; **three people were ~ed missing after the explosion** trois personnes ont été portées disparues après l'explosion; **4** (allege) **it is ~ed that** il paraît que; **she is ~ed to have changed her mind** elle aurait (paraît-il) changé d'avis, il paraît qu'elle a changé d'avis; **5** (make complaint about) signaler [*person*]; péj dénoncer [*person*]; **I shall ~ you to your headmaster** je vais te signaler à ton directeur; **your insubordination will be ~ed** votre insubordination sera signalée; **you will be ~ed to the boss** le directeur sera mis au courant; **the residents ~ed the noise to the police** les habitants se sont plaints du bruit au commissariat.
IV *vi* **1** (give account) **to ~ on** faire un compte-rendu sur [*talks, progress*]; Journ faire un reportage sur [*event*]; **he will ~ to Parliament on the negotiations** il fera un compte-rendu des négociations au parlement; **2** (present findings) [*committee, group*] faire son rapport (**on** sur); **the committee will ~ in June** le comité fera son rapport en juin; **3** (present oneself) se présenter; **~ to reception/to the captain** présentez-vous à la réception/au capitaine; **to ~ for duty** prendre son service; **to ~ sick** se faire porter malade; **to ~ to one's unit** Mil rejoindre son unité; **4** Admin (have as immediate superior) **to ~ to** être sous les ordres (directs) de [*superior*]; **she ~s to me** elle est sous mes ordres.
■ **report back**: **~ back 1** (after absence) [*employee*] se présenter; **2** (present findings) [*committee, representative*] présenter un rapport (**about, on** sur).

reportage /ˌrepɔːˈtɑːʒ/ *n* reportages *mpl*.

report: **~ card** *n* US bulletin *m* scolaire; **~ed clause** *n* proposition *f* indirecte.

reportedly /rɪˈpɔːtɪdlɪ/ *adv* **he is ~ unharmed** il serait indemne; **they are ~ planning a new offensive** selon certaines sources, ils prépareraient une nouvelle offensive.

reported speech *n* style *m* indirect.

reporter /rɪˈpɔːtə(r)/ ▶1692 *n* journaliste *mf*, reporter *mf*.

reporting /ˌrɪˈpɔːtɪŋ/ *n* Journ reportages *mpl*.

report: **~ing restrictions** *npl* Jur, Journ embargo *m* sur l'information; **~ stage** *n* GB Pol *soumission à la Chambre d'un projet de loi après le passage en commission*.

repose /rɪˈpəʊz/ sout **I** *n* (rest) repos *m*; (peace of mind) tranquillité *f*; **in ~** au repos.
II *vtr* placer [*trust*] (**in** dans).
III *vi* (lie buried) reposer; hum (be lying) [*person*] être allongé; [*object*] reposer.

repository /rɪˈpɒzɪtrɪ, US -tɔːrɪ/ *n* **1** (person, institution) (of secret, power, authority) dépositaire *mf*; (of hopes, fears) confident/-e *m/f*; (of learning) gardien/-ienne *m/f*; **2** (place) dépôt *m* (**of, for** de).

repossess /ˌriːpəˈzes/ *vtr* [*bank, building society*] saisir [*house*]; [*landlord, creditor*] reprendre possession de [*property, goods*].

repossession /ˌriːpəˈzeʃn/ *n* saisie *f* immobilière; **to seek ~ of a house** faire saisir une maison.

repossession: **~ man** *n* ≈ huissier *m*; **~ order** *n* ordre *m* de saisie immobilière.

repp *n* = **rep 3**.

reprehend /ˌreprɪˈhend/ *vtr* sout réprimander.

reprehensible /ˌreprɪˈhensɪbl/ *adj* sout répréhensible.

reprehensibly /ˌreprɪˈhensɪblɪ/ *adv* sout [*behave, act*] de façon répréhensible.

reprehension /ˌreprɪˈhenʃn/ *n* sout réprimande *f*.

represent /ˌreprɪˈzent/ **I** *vtr* **1** (act on behalf of) gen, Jur, Pol représenter [*person, group, region*]; **to be under-~ed** être insuffisamment représenté; **to be well ~ed** (numerous) être bien représenté; **2** (present, state to be) présenter [*person, situation, event*] (**as** comme); **3** (convey, declare) exposer [*facts, results, reasons etc*]; **4** (portray) [*painting, sculpture etc*] représenter; **5** (be sign or symbol of) (on map etc) représenter; **6** (correspond to, constitute) représenter; **that ~s an awful lot of work** cela représente une énorme somme de travail; **7** (be typical of, exemplify) représenter; **he ~s the best in the tradition** il représente ce qu'il y a de mieux dans la tradition; **8** Theat jouer [*character*]; interpréter [*role, part*].
II *v refl* **to ~ oneself as** se faire passer pour.

re-present /ˌriːprɪˈzent/ *vtr* présenter de nouveau.

representation /ˌreprɪzenˈteɪʃn/ **I** *n* **1** gen, Pol représentation *f* (**of** de; **by** par); **the right of workers to union ~** le droit des travailleurs à se faire représenter par un syndicat; **2** Theat (of character, scene) représentation *f*; (of role) interprétation *f*.
II representations *npl* **to make ~s to sb** (make requests) faire des démarches auprès de qn; (complain) se plaindre officiellement auprès de qn; **to receive ~s from sb** recevoir les doléances de qn.

representational /ˌreprɪzenˈteɪʃənl/ *adj* **1** gen représentatif/-ive; **2** Art figuratif/-ive.

representative /ˌreprɪˈzentətɪv/ **I** ▶1692 *n* gen représentant/-e *m/f*; Comm représentant/-e *m/f*, agent *m* (commercial); US Pol député *m*.
II *adj* **1** (typical) représentatif/-ive, typique (**of** de); **a ~ cross-section** ou **sample of the population** un échantillon représentatif de la population; **2** Pol [*government, election, institution*] représentatif/-ive.

repress /rɪˈpres/ *vtr* **1** (suppress) réprimer [*reaction, smile etc*]; Psych refouler; **2** (subjugate) opprimer [*people*]; réprimer [*revolt*].

repression /rɪˈpreʃn/ *n* **1** (of people) répression *f*; **2** Psych refoulement *m*.

repressive /rɪˈpresɪv/ *adj* répressif/-ive.

reprieve /rɪˈpriːv/ **I** *n* **1** Jur remise *f* de peine; **2** (delay) sursis *m*; **3** (respite) répit *m*.
II *vtr* **1** Jur accorder une remise de peine à [*prisoner*]; **2 the school was ~d** l'école a été sauvée; (for limited period) l'école a bénéficié d'un sursis.

reprimand /ˈreprɪmɑːnd, US -mænd/ **I** *n* Admin, gen réprimande *f*.
II *vtr* Admin, gen réprimander.

reprint I /ˈriːprɪnt/ *n* réimpression *f*.
II /ˌriːˈprɪnt/ *vtr* réimprimer; **the book is being ~ed** le livre est en réimpression.
III /ˌriːˈprɪnt/ *vi* [*book*] être en réimpression.

reprisal /rɪˈpraɪzl/ **I** *n* représailles *fpl* (**for** à); **in ~ for, in ~ against** en représailles contre.
II reprisals *npl* représailles *fpl* (**for** à; **against** contre); **to take ~s** exercer des représailles.

reprise /rɪˈpriːz/ **I** *n* Mus reprise *f*.
II *vtr* Mus reprendre.

repro /ˈriːprəʊ/ **I** *n* **1** Print *abrév* ▶**reprographics**; **2** Print (also **~ proof**) *abrév* ▶**reproduction proof**; **3**○ *abrév* = **reproduction**.
II○ *adj* [*house*] de style ancien; [*furniture*] de style.

reproach /rɪˈprəʊtʃ/ **I** *n* (all contexts) reproche *m*; **above** ou **beyond ~** irréprochable.
II *vtr* reprocher à [*person*]; **to ~ sb with** ou **for sth** reprocher qch à qn; **to ~ sb for doing** ou **having done** reprocher à qn d'avoir fait.
III *v refl* **to ~ oneself** se reprocher (**for doing** d'avoir fait); **to ~ oneself for** ou **with sth** se reprocher qch.

reproachful /rɪˈprəʊtʃfl/ *adj* [*person, remark, look, expression*] réprobateur/-trice; [*letter, word*] de reproche.

reproachfully /rɪˈprəʊtʃfəlɪ/ *adv* [*look at*] d'un air réprobateur; [*say*] d'un ton réprobateur.

reprobate /ˈreprəbeɪt/ *n* **the old ~** le vieux loustic.

reprobation /ˌreprəˈbeɪʃn/ *n* réprobation *f*.

reprocess /ˌriːˈprəʊses/ *vtr* retraiter.

reprocessing /ˌriːˈprəʊsesɪŋ/ *n* retraitement *m*.

reprocessing plant *n* Nucl usine *f* de retraitement (des déchets nucléaires).

reproduce /ˌriːprəˈdjuːs, US -ˈduːs/ **I** *vtr* (all contexts) reproduire.
II *vi* Biol (also **~ oneself**) se reproduire.

reproducible /ˌriːprəˈdjuːsəbl, US -ˈduːsəbl/ *adj* reproductible.

reproduction /ˌriːprəˈdʌkʃn/ *n* reproduction *f*; **photographic/sound ~** reproduction photographique/sonore.

reproduction: **~ furniture** *n* meubles *mpl* de style; **~ proof** *n* Print contre-épreuve *f*.

reproductive /ˌriːprəˈdʌktɪv/ *adj* [*organ, process*] reproducteur/-trice; **~ cycle** cycle *m* reproductif.

reprogram(me) /ˌriːˈprəʊgræm/ *vtr* reprogrammer.

reprographic /ˌriːprəˈgræfɪk/ *adj* de reprographie (*after n*).

reprographics /ˌriːprəˈgræfɪks/, **reprography** /rɪˈprɒgrəfɪ/ **I** *n* (+ *v sg*) reprographie *f*.
II *modif* [*process, copy*] de reprographie.

reproof /rɪˈpruːf/ *n* réprimande *f*; **in ~** d'un air de réprimande.

re-proof /ˌriːˈpruːf/ *vtr* réimperméabiliser [*coat, tent*].

reprove /rɪˈpruːv/ *vtr* réprimander [*person*] (**for** pour; **for doing** de faire).

reproving /rɪˈpruːvɪŋ/ *adj* réprobateur/-trice (*after n*).

reprovingly /rɪˈpruːvɪŋlɪ/ *adv* [*look, gesture*] d'un air réprobateur; [*say, speak*] d'un ton réprobateur.

reptile /ˈreptaɪl, US -tl/ *n* Zool reptile *m* also fig, pej.

reptile house *n* vivarium *m*.

reptilian /repˈtɪlɪən/ **I** *n* Zool reptile *m*.
II *adj* **1** Zool reptilien/-ienne; **2**○ fig, pej de reptile (*after n*).

republic /rɪˈpʌblɪk/ *n* république *f*.

republican /rɪˈpʌblɪkən/ **I** *n* républicain/-e *m/f*.
II *adj* républicain.

Republican /rɪˈpʌblɪkən/ **I** *n* Pol **1** US Républicain/-e *m/f*; **2** (in Northern Ireland) Républicain/-e *m/f*; (IRA supporter) partisan/-e *m/f* de l'IRA.
II *adj* républicain.

republicanism /rɪˈpʌblɪkənɪzəm/ *n* **1** gen républicanisme *m*; **2 Republicanism** Pol US tendance *f* républicaine; (in Northern Ireland) Républicanisme *m*; (support for IRA) tendance *f* pro-IRA.

republication /ˌriːˌpʌblɪˈkeɪʃn/ *n* réédition *f*.

republish /ˌriːˈpʌblɪʃ/ *vtr* rééditer.

repudiate /rɪˈpjuːdɪeɪt/ *vtr* **1** (reject) gen rejeter; répudier [*spouse*]; **2** (give up) abandonner [*action, violence, aim*]; **3** Jur refuser d'honorer [*treaty, contract, obligation*].

repudiation /rɪˌpjuːdɪˈeɪʃn/ *n* (of charge, claim, violence) rejet *m*; (of spouse) répudiation *f*; (of treaty) refus *m* d'honorer.

repugnance /rɪˈpʌgnəns/ *n* aversion *f* (**for sth** pour qch; **for sb** contre qn).

repugnant /rɪˈpʌgnənt/ *adj* répugnant; **to be ~ to sb** répugner à qn.

repulse /rɪˈpʌls/ **I** *vtr* gen, Mil repousser [*attack, force*].
II repulsed *pp adj* (disgusted) répugné.

repulsion /rɪˈpʌlʃn/ *n* (all contexts) répulsion *f*.

repulsive /rɪˈpʌlsɪv/ *adj* **1** (disgusting) repoussant; **2** Phys répulsif/-ive.

repulsively /rɪˈpʌlsɪvlɪ/ *adv* [*act*] de façon repoussante; **~ ugly/dirty** d'une laideur/saleté repoussante.

repulsiveness /rɪˈpʌlsɪvnɪs/ *n* aspect *m* repoussant.

repurchase /ˌriːˈpɜːtʃɪs/ **I** *n* rachat *m*.
II *vtr* racheter.

repurchase agreement *n* Fin contrat *m* de report.

reputable /ˈrepjʊtəbl/ *adj* [*accountant, firm, shop*] de bonne réputation; [*profession*] honorable.

reputation /ˌrepjʊˈteɪʃn/ *n* réputation *f*; **to have a good/bad ~** avoir bonne/mauvaise réputation; **she has a ~ as a good lawyer** elle a la réputation d'être un bon avocat; **your ~ as** ta réputation de [*lawyer, poet etc*]; **he has a ~ for honesty/arriving late** il a la réputation d'être honnête/d'arriver en retard; **to have the ~ of being** avoir la réputation d'être; **by ~** de réputation; **to live up to one's ~** être à la hauteur de sa réputation.

repute /rɪˈpjuːt/ *n* **of ~** réputé; **to be of high/low ~** avoir bonne/mauvaise réputation; **to hold sb/sth in high ~** tenir qn/qch en haute estime; **a woman of ill ~** euph une femme de mauvaise vie; **a house of ill ~** euph une maison close.

reputed /rɪˈpjuːtɪd/ *adj* **1** (well known) réputé; **2** (alleged) Jur putatif/-ive; **3 to be ~ to be** (have reputation of being) avoir la réputation d'être; **he is ~ to be very rich** à ce que l'on dit il serait très riche.

reputedly /rɪˈpjuːtɪdlɪ/ *adv* à ce que l'on dit.

request /rɪˈkwest/ **I** *n* **1** (comment) demande *f* (**for** de; **to** à), requête *f* (**for** de; **to** à); **to make a ~** faire une demande; **on ~** sur demande; **at the ~ of** sur la demande de; **at your ~** sur votre demande; **by popular ~** à la demande générale; **by special ~** sur demande spéciale; **I have received a ~ that I do/do not do** on m'a demandé de faire/de ne pas faire; **a ~ that we (should) be allowed to do** une demande d'autorisation de faire; **'No flowers by ~'** 'Ni fleurs ni couronnes'; **2** Radio dédicace *f*; **to play a ~ for sb** passer un disque à la demande de qn.
II *vtr* demander [*information, help, money*] (**from** à); **to ~ sb to do** demander à qn de faire; **to ~ sb's help** demander de l'aide à qn; **to ~ that sth be done** demander que qch soit fait; **you are kindly ~ed not to smoke** prière de ne pas fumer; **as ~ed** (in correspondance) conformément à votre demande.

request stop *n* GB arrêt *m* facultatif.

requiem /ˈrekwɪem/ *n* requiem *m*; **Mozart's Requiem** le Requiem de Mozart.

requiem mass *n* messe *f* de requiem.

require /rɪˈkwaɪə(r)/ **I** *vtr* **1** (need) [*person, client, company*] avoir besoin de [*help, money, staff, surgery*]; **this machine ~s servicing** cette machine a besoin d'être révisée; **take the tablets as ~d** en cas de besoin prenez les cachets; **'does Madam ~ tea?'** sout 'Madame désire-t-elle du thé?'; **2** (demand) [*job, law, person, situation*] exiger [*explanation, funds, obedience, qualifications*]; **to be ~d by law** être exigé par la loi; **to ~ that** exiger que (+ *subj*); **to ~ sth of** ou **from** exiger qch de; **to be ~d to do** être tenu de faire; **this job ~s an expert** ce travail nécessite un expert.
II required *pp adj* [*amount, shape, size, qualification*] exigé; **to be ~d reading** [*writer*] être une lecture exigée; **by the ~d date** en temps voulu, avant la date exigée; **~d course** US Univ matière *f* obligatoire.

requirement /rɪˈkwaɪəmənt/ *n* **1** (need) besoin *m* (**for** pour); **to meet sb's ~s** satisfaire les besoins de qn; **market/customer ~s** besoins du marché/client; **performance ~s** critères *mpl* de performance; **2** (condition) condition *f*; **university entrance ~s** conditions d'entrée à l'université; **to fulfil** ou **meet** ou **satisfy the ~s** remplir les conditions; **what are the ~s for membership?** quelles sont les conditions pour devenir membre?; **3** (obligation) obligation *f* (**to do** de faire); **legal ~** obligation légale; **there is no ~ for you to do** vous n'êtes pas obligé de faire; **the ~ for us to do** l'obligation pour nous de faire; **there is a ~ that we do** nous devons faire, nous sommes tenus de faire; **there is a ~ that guns be registered** les armes doivent être déclarées; **4** US Univ (required course) matière *f* obligatoire.

requisite /ˈrekwɪzɪt/ **I** *n* condition *f* (**for** pour).
II requisites *npl* (for artist, office) fournitures *fpl*; **toilet/smokers' ~s** articles *mpl* de toilette/pour fumeurs.
III *adj* exigé, requis.

requisition /ˌrekwɪˈzɪʃn/ **I** *n* **1** Mil réquisition *f*; **2** Admin commande *f*; **the paper is on ~** le papier a été commandé.
II *vtr* **1** Mil réquisitionner [*supplies, vehicle*]; **2** Admin faire une commande de [*equipment, stationery*].

requital /rɪˈkwaɪtl/ *n* sout (reward) récompense *f*; (revenge) punition *f*; **in ~ of** (reward) en récompense de; (revenge) pour se venger de.

requite /rɪˈkwaɪt/ *vtr* sout (repay kindness) récompenser [*person, service*] (**for** de; **with** par); (repay bad deed) se venger de [*person, wrong, injury*]; **~d love** amour partagé.

reran /ˌriːˈræn/ *prét* ▶ **rerun** *vtr*.

reread /ˌriːˈriːd/ *vtr* (*prét, pp* **reread**) relire.

reredos /ˈrɪədɒs/ *n* retable *m*.

reroof /ˌriːˈruːf/ *vtr* refaire la toiture de [*building*].

reroute /ˌriːˈruːt/ *vtr* changer l'itinéraire de [*flight*]; dévier [*traffic, race*].

rerun I /ˈriːrʌn/ *n* (also **re-run**) Cin, Theat reprise *f*; TV rediffusion *f*; fig (of incident, problem) répétition *f*.
II /ˌriːˈrʌn/ *vtr* (*prét* **reran**; *pp* **rerun**) Cin, Theat reprendre [*film, play*]; TV rediffuser; Pol refaire [*election, vote*]; Sport recommencer [*race*].

resale /ˈriːseɪl, riːˈseɪl/ *n* revente *f*; **not for ~** ne peut être vendu.

resat /ˌriːˈsæt/ *prét, pp* ▶ **resit** *vtr*.

reschedule /ˌriːˈʃedjuːl, US -ˈskedʒʊl/ *vtr* **1** gen (change time) changer l'heure de; (change date) changer la date de [*match, performance*]; **2** Fin rééchelonner [*debt, repayment*].

rescheduling /ˌriːˈʃedjuːlɪŋ, US -ˈskedʒʊlɪŋ/ *n* Fin rééchelonnement *m*.

rescind /rɪˈsɪnd/ *vtr* Jur ou sout abroger [*law*]; annuler [*decision, order, treaty*]; résilier [*contract, agreement*]; casser [*judgment*]; retirer [*statement*].

rescission /rɪˈsɪʒn/ *n* Jur ou sout (of law) abrogation *f*; (of decision, order, treaty) annulation *f*; (of contract, agreement) résiliation *f*; (of judgment) cassation *f*; (of statement) retrait *m*.

rescript /ˌriːˈskrɪpt/ *vtr* récrire.

rescue /ˈreskjuː/ **I** *n* **1** (aid) secours *m*; **to wait for ~** attendre les secours; **to come/to go to sb's/sth's ~** venir/aller au secours de qn/qch; **to come/to go to the ~** venir/aller à la rescousse; **X to the ~!** X à la rescousse!; **2** (operation) sauvetage *m* (**of** de); **3** (service) service *m* de secours; **air-sea ~** service aéro-naval de sauvetage.
II *modif* [*bid, helicopter, mission, operation, work*] de sauvetage; [*centre, service, team*] de secours.
III *vtr* **1** (save life of) sauver (**from** de); **2** (aid) porter secours à [*person, company*]; venir à l'aide de [*economy, industry*]; **3** (release) libérer (**from** de); **4** (preserve) (from destruction) sauver [*planet, wildlife*]; (from closure) éviter la fermeture de [*school, museum, factory*]; **5** (salvage) récupérer [*valuables, documents*]; sauver [*plan, game*].

rescue: **~ cover** *n* Insur assurance *f* sauvetage; **~ package** *n* Fin plan *m* de sauvetage; **~ party** *n* équipe *f* de secours.

rescuer /ˈreskjuːə(r)/ *n* sauveteur *m*.

rescue worker *n* secouriste *mf*.

research /rɪˈsɜːtʃ, ˈriːsɜːtʃ/ **I** *n* **1** (academic, medical etc) recherche *f* (**into, on** sur); **to do ~** faire de la recherche; **money for cancer ~** de l'argent pour la recherche sur le cancer; **she's doing some ~ on cancer** elle fait des recherches sur le cancer; **animal ~** expériences *fpl* sur les animaux; **a piece of ~** une recherche; **2** Comm (for marketing) études *fpl*; **~ shows that** les études montrent que; **market ~** étude *f* de marché; **3** Journ, Radio, TV documentation *f* (**into** sur).
II researches *npl* (investigations) recherches *fpl* (**into, on** sur).
III *modif* [*assistant, department, grant, institute, programme, project, unit*] de recherche; [*student*] qui fait de la recherche; [*funding*] pour la recherche; **~ work** recherche *f*; **~ biologist/chemist/physicist/scientist** chercheur/-euse *m/f* en biologie/chimie/physique/science.
IV *vtr* **1** gen, Univ faire des recherches dans [*field*]; faire des recherches sur [*topic*]; préparer [*book, article, play*]; **2** Journ, Radio, TV se documenter sur [*issue, problem*]; **well ~ed** bien documenté; **3** Comm faire une étude sur [*consumer attitudes, customer needs*]; **to ~ the market** faire une étude de marché; **you will be required to ~ techniques for...** votre tâche consistera à mettre au point des techniques de...
V *vi* **to ~ into** faire des recherches sur.

research: **~ and development, R&D** *n* recherche-développement *f*, recherche *f* et développement *m*; **~ assistant** ▶ **1692** *n* GB Univ assistant/-e *m/f* d'un chercheur.

researcher /rɪˈsɜːtʃə(r), ˈriːsɜːtʃə(r)/ ▶ **1692** *n* **1** (academic, scientific) chercheur/-euse *m/f*; **2** TV documentaliste *mf*.

research: **~ establishment** *n* centre *m* de recherches; **~ fellow** *n* GB Univ chercheur/-euse *m/f* universitaire; **~ fellowship** *n* GB Univ poste *m* de chercheur universitaire; **~ laboratory** *n* laboratoire *m* de recherches; **~ worker** ▶ **1692** *n* chercheur/-euse *m/f*.

reseat /ˌriːˈsiːt/ *vtr* **1** faire rasseoir [*person*]; **2** regarnir le fond de [*chair*].

resection /ˌriːˈsekʃn/ *n* Med résection *f*.

reselect /ˌriːsɪˈlekt/ *vtr* Pol réélire [qn] (*à l'intérieur d'un parti*).

reselection /ˌriːsɪˈlekʃn/ *n* Pol réélection *f* (*à l'intérieur d'un parti*); **to stand for ~** se présenter à une réélection.

resell /riːˈsel/ *vtr* (*prét, pp* **-sold**) revendre.

resemblance /rɪˈzembləns/ *n* ressemblance *f* (**between** entre; **to** avec); **family ~** air *m* de famille; **to bear a close ~ to** ressembler fort à; **to bear no ~ to** ne pas ressembler à; **there the ~ ends** la ressemblance s'arrête là.

resemble /rɪˈzembl/ *vtr* ressembler à [*person, building, object*]; **to ~ each other** se ressembler; **she ~s him in manner** elle a les mêmes manières que lui; **he had never had anything resembling a steady job** il n'avait jamais rien eu qui ressemble à un emploi stable; **he ~d nothing so much as a tramp** il avait vraiment l'air d'un clochard.

resent /rɪ'zent/ *vtr* en vouloir à [*person*]; mal supporter [*change, system*]; ne pas aimer [*tone, term*]; **he ~ed her** il lui en voulait (**for doing** d'avoir fait); **to ~ sb's success** en vouloir à qn pour son succès; **to ~ having to do** ne pas supporter de faire; **I ~ that remark** cette réflexion ne me plaît pas du tout; **to ~ sb doing** ne pas supporter que qn fasse; **he ~ed her being better paid** il ne supportait pas qu'elle soit mieux payée que lui; **to ~ the fact that** ne pas supporter le fait que (+ *subj*).

resentful /rɪ'zentfl/ *adj* [*person*] plein de ressentiment (**at** à; **of** à l'égard de); [*look*] de ressentiment; **to be ~ of sb** en vouloir à qn.

resentfully /rɪ'zentfəlɪ/ *adv* [*look, reply*] avec ressentiment.

resentment /rɪ'zentmənt/ *n* ressentiment *m* (**about** au sujet de; **against** envers; **at** à l'égard de); **~ among** mécontentement *m* parmi [*workers, residents, locals*].

reservation /ˌrezə'veɪʃn/ *n* **1** (doubt, qualification) réserve *f*; **mental ~** restriction *f* mentale; **without ~** sans réserve; **with some ~s** avec certaines réserves; **to have ~s about sth** avoir des doutes sur qch; **they expressed some ~s about the plan** ils ont émis des réserves au sujet du projet; **2** (booking) réservation *f*; **to make a ~ at a restaurant** réserver or retenir une table au restaurant; **do you have a ~?** avez-vous réservé?; **3** US (Indian land) réserve *f*; **4** Jur réserve *f* conventionnelle.

reservation desk *n* bureau *m* des réservations.

reserve /rɪ'zɜːv/ **I** *n* **1** (resource, stock) (of commodity) réserve *f*; (of food, parts, ammunition) réserve *f*, stock *m*; **oil/gold ~s** réserves de pétrole/d'or; **capital/currency ~s** réserves de capitaux/de devises; **to have ~s of energy/of patience** avoir des réserves d'énergie/de patience; **to keep** ou **hold sth in ~** tenir qch en réserve; **2** (reticence) réserve *f*; **to break through sb's ~** percer la réserve de qn; **to lose one's ~** perdre sa réserve, sortir de sa réserve; **3** (doubt, qualification) réserve *f*, restriction *f*; **without ~** sans réserve or restriction; **4** Mil **the ~** la réserve; **the ~s** les réservistes, la réserve; **5** Sport remplaçant/-e *m/f*; **6** (area of land) réserve *f*; **wildlife ~** réserve naturelle; **7** Comm = **reserve price**.
II *modif* [*currency, fund, stock, supplies*] de réserve; Sport [*team*] de réserve; [*player*] remplaçant; Mil [*army, forces*] de réserve.
III *vtr* **1** (set aside) réserver, mettre [qch] en réserve or de côté; **she ~s her fiercest criticism for...** elle réserve ses critiques les plus féroces pour...; **to ~ a warm welcome for sb** réserver un accueil chaleureux à qn; **to ~ one's strength** ménager ses forces; **to ~ the right to do sth** se réserver le droit de faire qch; **the management ~s the right to refuse admission** la direction se réserve le droit de refuser l'entrée ; **to ~ judgment** réserver son jugement; **2** (book) réserver [*room, seat*].

reserve bank *n* US banque *f* de réserve.

reserved /rɪ'zɜːvd/ *adj* **1** [*person, manner*] réservé; **to be ~ about sth** rester réservé sur qch; **2** (booked) [*table, room, seat etc*] réservé; **3** Comm **all rights ~** tous droits réservés; **4** Comput **~ word** mot *m* réservé.

reservedly /rɪ'zɜːvɪdlɪ/ *adj* avec réserve.

reserve: **~ list** *n* liste *f* de réserve; **~ petrol tank** *n* réservoir *m* d'essence de secours; **~ price** *n* GB prix *m* minimum, mise *f* à prix.

reservist /rɪ'zɜːvɪst/ *n* réserviste *m*.

reservoir /'rezəvwɑː(r)/ *n* **1** lit réservoir *m*; **2** fig (of funds) réserve *f* (**of** de); (of labour) réservoir *m*.

reset /ˌriː'set/ *vtr* (*p prés* **-tt-**; *prét, pp* **reset**) **1** gen (adjust) régler [*control, machine*]; remettre [qch] à l'heure [*clock*]; remettre [qch] à zéro [*counter*]; **2** Med réduire [*broken bone*]; **3** Comput réinitialiser [*computer*]; **4** Print recomposer [*type*]; **5** [*jeweller*] ressertir [*stone, gem*].

reset: **~ button** *n* Comput, Print bouton *m* de réinitialisation; **~ key** *n* Comput touche *f* de réinitialisation.

resettle /ˌriː'setl/ **I** *vtr* réinstaller [*refugee, worker, immigrant*]; repeupler [*area*].
II *vi* se réinstaller.

resettlement /ˌriː'setlmənt/ *n* (of immigrants, refugees) intégration *f*; (of prisoner, delinquent) réinsertion *f*.

resettlement house *n* US centre *m* de réinsertion.

reshape /ˌriː'ʃeɪp/ *vtr* **1** lit remodeler [*form*]; remodeler [*nose, chin etc*]; **2** (restructure) restructurer, réorganiser [*industry, economy, policy, constitution*]; réorganiser [*life*].

reshuffle /ˌriː'ʃʌfl/ **I** *n* **1** Pol remaniement *m*; **cabinet ~** remaniement ministériel; **2** (of cards) remélange *m*.
II *vtr* **1** Pol remanier [*cabinet*]; **2** Games rebattre [*cards*].

reside /rɪ'zaɪd/ *vi* sout **1** gen, Jur (live) résider, habiter (**with** avec); **2** (be present in) résider (**in** dans).

residence /'rezɪdəns/ *n* **1** (in property ad) maison *f*; (prestigious) maison *f* de standing; **family ~** maison *f* or demeure *f* familiale; **2** sout (dwelling) maison *f*, demeure *f* fml; **3** Admin **official/permanent ~** résidence *f* officielle/permanente; **4** Admin, Jur (in area, country) résidence *f*; **place of ~** lieu de résidence; **to take up ~** [*person, animal*] élire domicile; **she has taken up ~ in France/Paris** elle a élu domicile en France/à Paris; **to be in ~** sout [*monarch*] être au château; **artist/writer in ~** artiste/écrivain résident; ▶ **hall of residence**; **5** US Univ (also **~ hall**) résidence *f* universitaire.

residence permit *n* permis *m* de séjour.

residency /'rezɪdənsɪ/ **I** *n* **1** (for artist, orchestra) tournée *f*; **2** Jur (residence) droit *m* de séjour; **3** US Med (training) internat *m*.
II *modif* [*requirement, right*] de séjour.

resident /'rezɪdənt/ **I** *n* (of city, region, suburbs) résident/-e *m/f*; (of street) riverain/-e *m/f*; (of home, hostel) résident/-e *m/f*; (of guest house) pensionnaire *mf*; **'~s' parking only'** stationnement *m* réservé aux riverains; **the local ~s** les habitants du quartier.
II *adj* **1** (permanent) [*population, species*] local; [*work force*] permanent; **to be ~ in** [*town, district, region*] résider dans; **to be ~ abroad/in the UK/in Paris** résider à l'étranger/au Royaume-Uni/à Paris; **2** (live-in) (*épith*) [*staff, nurse, tutor, caretaker, specialist*] à demeure; **3** [*band, orchestra*] permanent.

resident head *n* US Univ directeur/-trice *m/f* d'une résidence universitaire.

residential /ˌrezɪ'denʃl/ *adj* **1** [*area, district, development*] résidentiel/-ielle; **~ accommodation** logements *mpl*; **2** (living in) [*staff*] à demeure; [*course*] en internat; **~ home** GB (for elderly) maison *f* de retraite; (for disabled) institution *f* pour handicapés; (for youth) foyer *m* d'accueil; **~ school** Sch établissement *m* d'éducation spécialisée; **to be in ~ care** Soc Admin être pris en charge par une institution; **a ~ post** un poste imposant résidence à demeure.

residential qualification *n* quotité *f* d'imposition pour être électeur.

resident: **~s association** *n* association *f* de quartier; **~ student** *n* US Univ *étudiant résidant dans le même état que son université.*

residual /rɪ'zɪdjʊəl, US -dʒʊ-/ **I** *n* **1** Math reste *m*; **2** Chem résidu *m*; **3** Stat écart *m*.
II residuals *npl* Jur *droits d'auteur versés en cas de rediffusion d'un programme télévisé ou d'un film.*
III *adj* **1** gen [*desire, prejudice, need*] persistant; [*income, value*] résiduel/-elle; **a ~ fear of authority** une peur de l'autorité qui persiste; **2** Chem, Phys résiduel/-elle; **3** Geol résiduaire.

residuary /rɪ'zɪdjʊərɪ, US -dʒʊerɪ/ *adj* = **residual III 1.**

residuary: **~ estate** *n* Jur propriété *f* résiduelle; **~ legatee** *n* Jur légataire *m* universel.

residue /'rezɪdjuː, US -duː/ *n* **1** gen, Chem résidu *m* (**of** de); **2** fig reste *m* (**of** de); **3** Jur reliquat *m* d'une succession.

resign /rɪ'zaɪn/ **I** *vtr* démissionner de [*post, job*]; **to ~ one's seat** (on committee) démissionner de son poste; (as MP) démissionner de son mandat parlementaire; **to ~ one's commission** Mil démissionner de l'armée.
II *vi* démissionner (**as** du poste de; **from** de; **over** à cause de); **to be called on to ~** être prié de démissionner.
III *v refl* **to ~ oneself** se résigner (**to** à; **to doing** à faire).

resignation /ˌrezɪg'neɪʃn/ **I** *n* **1** (from post) démission *f* (**from** de; **as** du poste de); **to offer** ou **tender one's ~** présenter sa démission; **to send in** ou **hand in one's ~** donner sa démission; **2** (patience) résignation *f*; **with ~** avec résignation.
II *modif* [*letter*] de démission.

resigned /rɪ'zaɪnd/ *adj* résigné (**to** à; **to doing** à faire).

resignedly /rɪ'zaɪnɪdlɪ/ *adv* [*act, look at*] d'un air résigné; [*speak*] d'un ton résigné.

resilience /rɪ'zɪlɪəns/ *n* **1** (of person, group) (mental) détermination *f*; (physical) résistance *f* physique; **2** (of industry, economy) faculté *f* de reprise; **3** (of substance, material) élasticité *f*.

resilient /rɪ'zɪlɪənt/ *adj* **1** (morally) déterminé; (physically) résistant; **2** [*demand, market*] élastique; **3** [*material, substance*] élastique.

resin /'rezɪn, US 'rezn/ *n* (natural, synthetic) résine *f*.

resinate /'rezɪneɪt/ *vtr* ajouter de la résine à [*wine*].

resinous /'rezɪnəs, US 'rezənəs/ *adj* résineux/-euse.

resist /rɪ'zɪst/ **I** *vtr* **1** (oppose) s'opposer à [*reform, attempt, conscription*]; **2** (struggle against) résister à [*attack, shock*]; **to ~ arrest** refuser de se laisser arrêter; **3** (refrain from) résister à [*temptation, offer, suggestion*]; **to ~ doing** s'empêcher de faire; **4** (to be unaffected by) résister à [*damage, rust, heat*].
II *vi* résister.

resistance /rɪ'zɪstəns/ *n* **1** (to change, enemy) also Psych résistance *f* (**to** à); **to meet with/to overcome ~** se heurter à/vaincre une résistance; **to put up ~** résister; **consumer ~** résistance du consommateur; **fierce ~** résistance acharnée; **2** Physiol résistance *f* (**to** à); **his ~ is low** sa résistance est amoindrie; **to build up a ~ to sth** devenir plus résistant à qch; **the body's ~** la résistance de l'organisme; **3** Elec résistance *f*.
IDIOMS **to take the line** ou **path of least ~** choisir la voie de la facilité.

Resistance /rɪ'zɪstəns/ *n* Pol Hist **the ~** la Résistance.

resistance: **~ fighter** *n* résistant/-e *m/f*; **~ movement** *n* mouvement *m* de résistance.

resistant /rɪ'zɪstənt/ **I** *adj* **1** [*virus, strain*] rebelle (**to** à); **2** (opposed) **~ to** réfractaire à [*change, demands etc*]; **3** [*rock, wall*] résistant (**to** à).
II -resistant (*dans composés*) **heat-/rust-~** résistant à la chaleur/à la rouille; **water-~** imperméable; **fire-~** qui résiste au feu.

resistor /rɪ'zɪstə(r)/ *n* résistance *f*, résistor *m*.

resit GB **I** /'riːsɪt/ *n* session *f* de rattrapage.
II /ˌriː'sɪt/ *vtr* (*prét, pp* **resat**) repasser [*exam, test*].

resold /ˌriː'səʊld/ *prét, pp* ▶ **resell**.

resole /ˌriː'səʊl/ *vtr* ressemeler.

resolute /'rezəluːt/ *adj* [*approach, attitude, person*] résolu; [*action, measure, decision*] ferme; **to remain ~** demeurer résolu; **with a ~ air** d'un air résolu.

resolutely /ˈrezəluːtlɪ/ *adv* [*oppose, persist*] résolument; [*refuse*] fermement; [*independent, objective*] résolument; **to be ~ opposed to sth** être résolument opposé à qch.

resoluteness /ˈrezəluːtnɪs/ *n* résolution *f*, détermination *f*.

resolution /ˌrezəˈluːʃn/ *n* **1** (determination) résolution *f*; **to lack ~** manquer de résolution; **2** (decree) résolution *f* (**against** contre; **that** selon laquelle); **a ~ calling for sth/condemning sth** une résolution appelant à qch/condamnant qch; **to pass a ~** voter une résolution; **3** (promise) résolution *f* (**to do** de faire); **to make a ~ to do** prendre la résolution de faire; **4** (solving of problem) résolution *f* (**of** de); **conflict ~** la résolution des conflits; **5** Chem, Phys résolution *f* (**into** en); **6** Med résolution *f*; **7** Mus résolution *f*; **8** Comput résolution *f*.

resolvable /rɪˈsɒlvəbl/ *adj* [*problem*] soluble; [*crisis, difficulty*] qui peut être résolu.

resolve /rɪˈzɒlv/ **I** *n* **1** (determination) détermination *f*; **to strengthen/weaken sb's ~** rendre qn plus/moins décidé; **to show ~** faire preuve de détermination; **2** (decision) résolution *f*.

II *vtr* **1** (solve) résoudre [*dispute, crisis, contradiction*]; dissiper [*doubts*]; **2** (decide) **to ~ that** décider que; **to ~ to do** résoudre de faire; **3** (break down) résoudre [*problem, argument*] (**into** en); Phys, Chem résoudre (**into** en); **4** Med résoudre [*inflammation*]; **5** Mus résoudre.

III *vi* (decide) [*person, government*] résoudre; **to ~ on doing** résoudre de faire; **to ~ on sth** se décider pour qch.

IV *v refl* **to ~ itself** se résoudre (**into** en).

resolved /rɪˈzɒlvd/ *adj* sout résolu (**to do** à faire; **that** à ce que + *subj*).

resonance /ˈrezənəns/ *n* (all contexts) résonance *f*.

resonant /ˈrezənənt/ *adj* sout **1** [*voice, sound*] sonore; **2** [*place, object*] résonant.

resonate /ˈrezəneɪt/ *vi* sout **1** [*voice, sound*] résonner; **2** [*place*] résonner (**with** de); **3** [*language, word*] résonner (**with** de).

resonator /ˈrezəneɪtə(r)/ *n* résonateur *m*.

resorption /rɪˈzɔːpʃn/ *n* résorption *f*.

resort /rɪˈzɔːt/ **I** *n* **1** (resource) recours *m*; **a last ~** un dernier recours; **as a last ~** en dernier recours; **2 in the last ~** au bout du compte; **3** (recourse) recours *m*; **to have ~ to sth** avoir recours à qch; **4** (holiday centre) lieu *m* de villégiature; **seaside ~** station *f* balnéaire; **ski ~** station *f* de ski; ▶ **health resort**; **5** US (hotel) hôtel-club *m*; **6** sout (haunt) repaire *m*.

II *vi* **to ~ to** recourir à.

resound /rɪˈzaʊnd/ *vi* **1** [*noise*] retentir (**through** partout dans); **2** [*place*] retentir (**with** de); **3** [*fame, reputation, action*] avoir un grand retentissement (**through, throughout** dans).

resounding /rɪˈzaʊndɪŋ/ *adj* **1** [*voice, cheers, crash*] retentissant; **2** [*success, victory*] éclatant; [*failure*] écrasant; **the answer was a ~ 'no'** la réponse a été un 'non' retentissant.

resoundingly /rɪˈzaʊndɪŋlɪ/ *adv* **1** [*echo, crash*] d'une manière retentissante; **2** (thoroughly) **to be ~ successful** connaître un succès éclatant; **to be ~ defeated** subir une défaite écrasante.

resource /rɪˈsɔːs, -ˈzɔːs, US ˈriːsɔːrs/ **I** *n* **1** gen, Econ, Ind, Admin ressource *f*; **natural/energy/financial ~s** ressources naturelles/énergétiques/financières; **the world's ~s of coal/oil** les ressources mondiales en charbon/pétrole; **to put more ~s into sth** investir davantage dans qch; **to draw on one's ~s** mettre en œuvre ses ressources; **he has no inner ~s** fig il n'a pas beaucoup de ressource; **reading is her only ~ against boredom** la lecture est son seul recours contre l'ennui; **to be left to one's own ~s** être livré à soi-même; **2** (facility, service) richesse *f*; **the library is a valuable ~** la bibliothèque est un outil précieux; **3** Comput ressource *f*; **4** sout (cleverness) ressource *f*; **a man of (great) ~** un homme (plein) de ressources; **5** (expedient) ressource *f*.

II *vtr* accorder les ressources nécessaires à [*institution, service*]; **to be under-~d** ne pas disposer de ressources suffisantes.

resource: **~ allocation** *n* Comput allocation *f* des ressources; **~ centre** GB, **~ center** US *n* centre *m* de documentation.

resourceful /rɪˈsɔːsfl, -ˈzɔːsfl, US ˈriːsɔːrsfl/ *adj* [*person*] plein de ressources, débrouillard○; [*adaptation, management*] ingénieux/-ieuse.

resourcefully /rɪˈsɔːsfəlɪ, -ˈzɔːsfəlɪ, US ˈriːsɔːrsfəlɪ/ *adv* d'une manière ingénieuse.

resourcefulness /rɪˈsɔːsflnɪs, -ˈzɔːsflnɪs, US ˈriːsɔːrsflnɪs/ *n* (of person) ressource *f*, débrouillardise○ *f*; (of adaptation) ingéniosité *f*.

resource: **~ management** *n* Comput gestion *f* des ressources; **~(s) room** *n* salle *f* de documentation; **~ sharing** *n* Comput partage *m* des ressources.

respect /rɪˈspekt/ **I** *n* **1** (admiration) respect *m*, estime *f*; **I have the greatest** ou **highest ~ for him/for his works** j'ai infiniment de respect pour lui/pour son œuvre; **to win** ou **earn the ~ of sb** gagner l'estime de qn; **to command ~** imposer le respect; **as a mark** ou **token of his ~** en témoignage de son respect; **2** (politeness, consideration) respect *m*; **out of ~** par respect (**for** pour); **to have no ~ for sb/sth** n'avoir aucun respect pour qn/qch; **you've got no ~!** tu ne respectes rien!; **with (all due** ou **the utmost) ~** sauf votre respect, sauf le respect que je vous dois; **to treat sb with ~** lit traiter qn avec respect or des égards; **to treat sth with ~** fig manipuler qch avec précaution [*machine, appliance*]; **in ~ of** (as regards) pour ce qui est de; (for) pour; **with ~ to** par rapport à; **3** (recognition, regard) (for human rights, privacy, the law) respect *m* (**for** de); **4** (aspect, detail) **in this ~** à cet égard; **in some/all ~s** à certains/tous égards; **in many/in several/in other ~s** à bien des/à plusieurs/à d'autres égards; **in few ~s** à peu d'égards; **in what ~?** à quel égard?

II respects *npl* respects *mpl*; **to offer** ou **pay one's ~s to sb** présenter ses respects à qn; **to pay one's last ~s to sb** rendre un dernier hommage à qn.

III *vtr* (honour, recognize) respecter; **as ~s sth** quant à qch, pour ce qui est de qch.

IV *v refl* **to ~ oneself** se respecter.

respectability /rɪˌspektəˈbɪlətɪ/ *n* respectabilité *f*.

respectable /rɪˈspektəbl/ *adj* **1** (reputable) [*person, home, family*] respectable; [*upbringing*] bon/bonne; **in ~ society** entre gens convenables; **I'm a ~ married man!** hum je suis un homme marié et respectable!; **2** (adequate) [*size, number, crowd*] respectable; [*mark, performance, piece of work*] honorable; **to earn a ~ wage** gagner honorablement sa vie; **to finish a ~ fourth** terminer honorablement quatrième.

respectably /rɪˈspektəblɪ/ *adv* **1** (reputably) [*dress, behave, speak*] convenablement, correctement; **2** (adequately) **a ~ large audience** une assistance plutôt importante; **she finished ~ in fourth place** elle a fini honorablement quatrième; **he plays tennis very ~** il se défend○ très bien au tennis.

respecter /rɪˈspektə(r)/ *n* sout **to be a ~ of sth** être respectueux/-euse de qch; **illness/death is no ~ of persons** nous sommes tous égaux devant la maladie/la mort; **diseases are no ~s of geographical boundaries** les maladies se propagent indépendamment des frontières.

respectful /rɪˈspektfl/ *adj* [*person, behaviour, distance, silence*] respectueux/-euse (**of** de; **to, towards** envers).

respectfully /rɪˈspektfəlɪ/ *adv* respectueusement.

respectfulness /rɪˈspektflnɪs/ *n* attitude *f* respectueuse (**to, towards** envers or à l'égard de qn).

respecting /rɪˈspektɪŋ/ *prep* concernant, ayant trait à.

respective /rɪˈspektɪv/ *adj* respectif/-ive.

respectively /rɪˈspektɪvlɪ/ *adv* respectivement.

respiration /ˌrespɪˈreɪʃn/ *n* (all contexts) respiration *f*; **~ rate** rythme *m* respiratoire.

respirator /ˈrespɪreɪtə(r)/ *n* **1** (artificial) respirateur *m*; **to be on a ~** être sous respirateur; **2** (protective) masque *m* à filtre.

respiratory /rɪˈspɪrətrɪ, US -tɔːrɪ/ *adj* respiratoire; **~ quotient** quotient *m* respiratoire; **~ tract** appareil *m* respiratoire.

respire /rɪˈspaɪə(r)/ *vi* Med, Bot respirer.

respite /ˈrespaɪt, ˈrespɪt/ *n* **1** sout (relief) répit *m* (**from** dans); **a brief ~** un court répit; **2** Comm, Jur (delay) sursis *m*; **a week's ~** un sursis d'une semaine; **to grant a ~ for payment** surseoir au paiement.

resplendent /rɪˈsplendənt/ *adj* sout resplendissant; **to look ~** être resplendissant.

respond /rɪˈspɒnd/ *vi* **1** (answer) répondre (**to** à); **to ~ with a letter/a phone call** répondre par une lettre/en téléphonant; **2** (react) [*patient, organism*] réagir (**to** à); [*engine, car*] répondre; **to ~ to sb's needs** répondre aux besoins de qn; **they ~ed by putting up their prices** ils ont réagi en augmentant les prix; **to ~ to pressure** Pol, Admin céder aux pressions; **3** (listen, adapt) s'adapter; **4** Relig (by singing) chanter les répons; (by speaking) répondre.

respondent /rɪˈspɒndənt/ *n* **1** (to questionnaire) personne *f* interrogée; **2** Jur défendeur/-eresse *m/f*.

response /rɪˈspɒns/ *n* **1** (answer) réponse *f* (**to** à); **in ~ to** en réponse à; **appropriate/lukewarm/official ~** réponse appropriée/peu enthousiaste/officielle; **2** (reaction) réaction *f* (**to** à; **from** de); **to meet with a favourable ~** être bien reçu; **3** Relig **the ~s** les répons.

response time *n* Comput temps *m* de réponse.

responsibility /rɪˌspɒnsəˈbɪlətɪ/ *n* responsabilité *f* (**for** de; **for doing, to do** de faire); **to have a ~ to sb/to sth** avoir une responsabilité envers qn/quant à qch; **to take ~ for sth** prendre la responsabilité de qch; **a sense of ~** le sens des responsabilités; **a great sense of ~** un grand sens des responsabilités; **his responsibilities as chairman include...** ses responsabilités en tant que président comprennent...; **'we take no ~ for loss or damage to possessions'** 'nous déclinons toute responsabilité en cas de perte ou de détérioration de biens personnels'; **the company disclaimed** ou **denied any ~ for the accident** la compagnie a décliné toute responsabilité dans l'accident; **it's not my ~ to do** ce n'est pas à moi de faire; **it's your ~** c'est à vous de vous en occuper; **the terrorists claimed ~ for the attack** les terroristes ont revendiqué l'attaque.

responsible /rɪˈspɒnsəbl/ *adj* **1** (answerable) responsable (**for** de); **for killing ten people/destroying the forest** responsable de la mort de dix personnes/de la destruction de la forêt; **~ for producing the leaflets/looking after the children** chargé de produire les brochures/de s'occuper des enfants; **to be ~ to sb** être responsable devant qn; **to hold sb ~** tenir qn pour responsable (**for** de); **the person ~** la personne responsable; **those ~** les personnes responsables; **I won't be ~ for my actions** je ne réponds plus de moi; **2**

(trustworthy) [*person, organization, attitude*] responsable; **she is very ~** elle a le sens des responsabilités, elle est très responsable; **3** (involving accountability) [*job, task*] à responsabilités.

responsibly /rɪˈspɒnsəblɪ/ *adv* de manière responsable.

responsive /rɪˈspɒnsɪv/ *adj* **1** (alert) [*audience, class, pupil*] réceptif/-ive; **2** (affectionate) affectueux/-euse; **3** (adaptable) [*organization*] dynamique; **a more ~ political system** un système politique plus proche des gens; **4** Aut [*car, engine*] nerveux/-euse; [*brakes, steering*] qui répond bien.

responsiveness /rɪˈspɒnsɪvnɪs/ *n* **1** (of audience, class, pupil) réceptivité *f*; **2** (affection) affection *f*; **3** (of organization) dynamisme *m*.

respray /ˌriːspreɪ/ **I** *n* **the car had been given a ~** on avait refait la peinture de la voiture.
II /ˌriˈspreɪ/ *vtr* refaire la peinture de [*vehicle*].

rest /rest/ **I** *n* **1** (what remains) **the ~** (of food, books, day, story) le reste *m* (**of** de); **you can keep/leave the ~** tu peux garder/laisser le reste or ce qui reste; **I've forgotten the ~** j'ai oublié le reste; **for the ~ of my life** pour le restant de mes jours; **for the ~...** pour ce qui est du reste...; **and all the ~ of it**○ et tout et tout○; **2** (other people) **he is no different from the ~ (of them)** il n'est pas différent des autres; **why can't you behave like the ~ of us?** pourquoi ne peux-tu pas faire comme nous?; **3** (repose, inactivity) repos *m*; **a day of ~** un jour de repos; **to recommend six weeks' ~** conseiller six semaines de repos; **to set** ou **put sb's mind at ~** rassurer qn; **to lay sb/sth to ~** lit, fig enterrer qn/qch; **4** (break) pause *f*; (nap, lie-down) sieste *f*; **to have** ou **take a ~** se reposer; **to have a ~ in the afternoon** faire une sieste dans l'après-midi; **let's have a little ~** et si on faisait une petite pause; **it was a ~ from the serious business of the day** cela nous a reposés des dures tâches de la journée; **he really needs a ~** il a vraiment besoin de se reposer; **5** (object which supports) support *m*; **6** Mus pause *f*; **7** (immobility) **to be at ~** être au repos; **to come to ~** s'arrêter.
II *vtr* **1** (lean) **to ~ sth on** appuyer qch sur [*rock, table*]; **2** (allow to rest) reposer [*legs, feet*]; ne pas utiliser [*injured limb*]; laisser [qch] au repos [*horse*]; **~ your legs!** repose tes jambes!; **3** Agric (leave uncultivated) laisser [qch] en jachère [*land*]; **4** (keep from entering) [*organizer, team*] ne pas faire participer [*competitor*]; **5** Jur **to ~ one's case** conclure; **I ~ my case** fig il n'y a rien à ajouter
III *vi* **1** (relax, lie down) [*person*] se reposer; **I won't ~ until I know** je n'aurai de cesse de savoir; **to ~ easy** être tranquille; **2** (be supported) **to ~ on** [*hand, weight, shelf*] reposer sur; **to be ~ing on** [*elbow, arm*] être appuyé sur; **to ~ on one's spade** s'appuyer sur sa bêche; **I need something to ~ on** j'ai besoin d'un support; **3** euph [*actor*] **to be ~ing** être sans engagement; **4** [*dead person*] **to ~ in peace** reposer en paix; **may he ~ in peace** qu'il repose en paix; **God ~ his soul** Dieu ait son âme; **5** fig (lie) **to let the matter** ou **things ~** en rester là; **you can't just let it ~ there!** tu ne peux pas laisser les choses en l'état!
IDIOMS **a change is as good as a ~** Prov le changement a les mêmes vertus que le repos; **to ~ on one's laurels** se reposer sur ses lauriers; **give it a ~**○! ça suffit comme ça○!; ... **and there the matter ~s** voilà la situation actuelle, voilà où en est l'affaire.
■ **rest in**: **~ in [sth]** [*key, solution*] consister à [*change*]; **to ~ in doing** consister à faire.
■ **rest on**: **~ on [sb/sth]** **1** [*eyes, gaze*] s'arrêter sur [*object, person*]; **2** (depend) reposer sur [*assumption, reasoning*].
■ **rest up** se reposer.
■ **rest with**: **~ with [sb/sth]** [*decision, choice*] être entre les mains de, appartenir à.

rest area *n* aire *f* de repos.

restart /ˈriːstɑːt/ **I** *n* **1** Sport (in football) reprise *f*; (in motor-racing) nouveau départ *m*; **2** GB (retraining) (also **~ scheme**) stage *m* de reconversion.
II /ˌriːˈstɑːt/ *vtr* **1** reprendre [*work, service, talks*]; **2** remettre [qch] en marche [*engine, boiler etc*].
III *vi* [*cycle, activity, person*] recommencer, reprendre; [*engine*] se remettre en marche.

restate /ˌriːˈsteɪt/ *vtr* réaffirmer (**that** que); **he ~d the case for imposing sanctions** il a réaffirmé la nécessité d'imposer des sanctions.

restatement /riːˈsteɪtmənt/ *n* réaffirmation *f*.

restaurant /ˈrestrɒnt, US -tərənt/ *n* restaurant *m*.

restaurant: **~ car** *n* GB wagon-restaurant *m*; **~ owner** *n* restaurateur/-trice *m/f*.

restaurateur /ˌrestərəˈtɜː(r)/ ▶ **1692** *n* restaurateur/-trice *m/f*.

rest cure *n* lit cure *f* de repos; **it wasn't exactly a ~!** hum ce n'était pas vraiment une sinécure!

restful /ˈrestfl/ *adj* [*holiday, hobby, music, colour*] reposant; [*spot, place*] paisible.

rest home *n* maison *f* de retraite.

resting place *n* **his last ~** sa dernière demeure.

restitution /ˌrestɪˈtjuːʃn, US -ˈtuː-/ *n* gen, Jur restitution *f*; **to make ~ of sth** restituer qch; Jur Hist **~ of conjugal rights** ordre *m* de réintégration du domicile conjugal.

restitution order *n* Jur ordonnance *f* de restitution.

restive /ˈrestɪv/ *adj* [*person, crowd*] énervé; [*animal*] rétif/-ive.

restively /ˈrestɪvlɪ/ *adv* nerveusement.

restiveness /ˈrestɪvnɪs/ *n* (of person) énervement *m*; (of animal) agitation *f*.

restless /ˈrestlɪs/ *adj* [*person, animal, movement*] agité; **to get** ou **grow ~** [*audience, person*] commencer à donner des signes d'impatience; [*minority, populace*] commencer à s'agiter; **to feel ~** (on edge) être énervé.

restlessly /ˈrestlɪslɪ/ *adv* nerveusement.

restlessness /ˈrestlɪsnɪs/ *n* **1** (physical) agitation *f*; **2** (of character) instabilité *f*; **3** (in populace, party) mécontentement *m*.

restock /ˌriːˈstɒk/ *vtr* **1** (fill) regarnir [*shelf*] (**with** en); réapprovisionner [*shop*] (**with** en); repeupler [*river, forest*] (**with** de); **2** (reorder) se réapprovisionner en.

restoration /ˌrestəˈreɪʃn/ *n* **1** (of property, territory) restitution *f* (**to** à); **2** (of custom, right) restauration *f*; (of law, order, democracy) rétablissement *m*; (of monarch, dynasty) restauration *f*; **3** (of building, work of art) restauration *f*.

Restoration /ˌrestəˈreɪʃn/ *n* **the ~** la Restauration anglaise.

Restoration drama *n* le théâtre de la Restauration (*en Angleterre*).

restorative /rɪˈstɒrətɪv/ **I** *n* fortifiant *m*.
II *adj* [*tonic*] fortifiant; [*exercises*] de remise en forme; [*sleep*] réparateur/-trice; **~ powers** vertus *fpl* réparatrices.

restore /rɪˈstɔː(r)/ *vtr* **1** (return) restituer, rendre [*property*] (**to** à); **2** (bring back) rétablir [*health*]; rendre [*faculty*]; redonner [*confidence, good humour*] (**to** à); restaurer, rétablir [*right, custom, tradition*] (**to** à); rétablir [*peace, law, tax*] (**to** à); Pol rétablir [*monarch, regime*]; **to ~ sb's sight** rendre la vue à qn; **to be ~d to health** être rétabli; **his sight/health was ~d to him** il a recouvré la vue/la santé; **to ~ sb to life** ramener qn à la vie; **to ~ law and order** rétablir l'ordre; **to ~ sb to power** ramener qn au pouvoir; **to ~ sacked workers to their jobs** réintégrer des travailleurs licenciés; **you ~ my faith in humanity** tu me redonnes confiance dans le genre humain; **3** (repair) restaurer [*work of art, building*]; rénover [*leather*]; **4** Comput redimensionner [*window*].

restorer /rɪˈstɔːrə(r)/ *n* (person) restaurateur/-trice *m/f*; ▶ **hair restorer**.

restrain /rɪˈstreɪn/ **I** *vtr* **1** (hold back) retenir [*person, tears, laughter*]; contenir [*desires*]; maîtriser [*attacker, animal*]; contenir [*crowd*]; **to ~ sb from doing sth** empêcher qn de faire qch; **2** (curb) limiter [*spending, demand*]; maîtriser [*inflation*]; **3** (control) limiter [*demonstration, picketing*]; **4** GB Jur **~ing order** injonction *f*.
II *v refl* **to ~ oneself** se retenir.

restrained /rɪˈstreɪnd/ *adj* **1** (sober) [*style, music, colour*] sobre; [*lifestyle*] simple; [*dress*] discret/-ète; [*writer*] qui a un style dépouillé; [*musician*] qui joue avec sobriété; **2** (kept in check) [*emotion, hysteria*] contenu; [*manner*] réservé; [*protest, argument*] mesuré; [*discussion*] calme.

restraining order *n* injonction *f*.

restraint /rɪˈstreɪnt/ *n* **1** (moderation) modération *f*; **to exercise ~** faire preuve de modération; **he showed remarkable ~** il a fait preuve de beaucoup de modération; **to advocate ~** prôner la modération; **2** (restriction) restriction *f*; **to talk without ~** parler sans retenue; **pay** ou **wage ~s** contrôle *m* des salaires; **to impose price/wage ~s** introduire le contrôle des prix/des salaires; **3** (rule) **social ~s** conventions *fpl* sociales.

restrict /rɪˈstrɪkt/ **I** *vtr* limiter [*activity, choice, growth*] (**to** à); restreindre [*freedom*]; réserver [*access, membership*] (**to** à); **visibility was ~ed to 50 metres** la visibilité était limitée à 50 mètres; **~ed to applicants over 18** réservé aux plus de 18 ans.
II *v refl* **to ~ oneself to sth/to doing** se limiter à qch/à faire.

restricted /rɪˈstrɪktɪd/ *adj* [*budget, growth, movement, powers*] limité; [*hours*] réglementé; [*document, file*] confidentiel/-ielle; [*film*] US interdit aux moins de 17 ans.

restricted: **~ access** *n* accès *m* réservé; **~ area** *n* zone *f* à accès réservé; **~ code** *n* Ling code *m* restreint; **~ language** *n* Ling langage *m* restreint; **~ parking** *n* stationnement *m* réglementé; **~ users group** *n* Comput groupe *m* d'utilisateurs autorisés.

restriction /rɪˈstrɪkʃn/ *n* **1** (rule) limitation *f*; **to impose ~s on sth/sb** imposer des mesures de restriction sur qch/à qn; **the ~s on sb** les mesures de restriction imposées à qn; **~s on arms sales** limitations de ventes d'armes; **credit ~s** encadrement *m* (*sg*) du crédit; **currency ~s** contrôle *m* (*sg*) des devises; **parking ~s** règles *fpl* de stationnement; **price ~s** contrôle *m* (*sg*) des prix; **speed ~s** limitations de vitesse; **travel ~s** restrictions *fpl* à la libre circulation (des citoyens); **weight ~s** (for vehicles) limitations de poids; **2** (limiting) (of amount) limitation *f* (**on** de); (of freedom) restrictions *fpl* (**of** à).

restrictive /rɪˈstrɪktɪv/ *adj* **1** gen [*law, measure*] restrictif/-ive; [*environment, routine*] étouffant; **2** Ling déterminatif/-ive.

restrictive: **~ covenant** *n* Jur servitude *f*; **~ practices** *npl* (by companies) entraves *fpl* à la libre concurrence; (by trade unions) pratiques *fpl* restrictives.

re-string **I** /ˈriːstrɪŋ/ *n* (racket) raquette *f* recordée.
II /ˌriːˈstrɪŋ/ *vtr* (*prét, pp* **re-strung**) changer les cordes de [*instrument*]; recorder [*racket*]; renfiler [*necklace, beads*].

rest room *n* US toilettes *fpl*.

restyle **I** /ˈriːstaɪl/ *n* nouvelle coiffure *f*; **to have a ~** changer de coiffure.
II /ˌriːˈstaɪl/ *vtr* changer la ligne de [*car*]; **to ~ sb's hair** faire une nouvelle coupe (de cheveux) à qn.
III restyled *pp adj* [*car*] nouvelle version *inv*.

result /rɪˈzʌlt/ **I** *n* **1** (consequence) résultat *m*, conséquence *f* (**of** de); **as a ~ of** à la or par suite de; **with the ~ that the company went bankrupt** résultat, la compagnie a fait faillite; **as a ~** en conséquence; **without ~** sans résultat; **2** (of exam, match, election) résultat *m*; **exam(ination) ~s** résultats aux examens; **football ~s** résultats de football; **3**○ (successful outcome) résultat *m*; Sport victoire *f*; **to get ~s** obtenir des résultats; **to need a ~** Sport avoir besoin d'une victoire; **4** Math résultat *m*.
II results *npl* Comm, Fin résultats *mpl*.
III *vi* résulter ; **to ~ from** résulter de; **to ~ in** avoir pour résultat [*death, abolition, re-election, loss*]; **the accident ~ed in him losing his job** l'accident a eu pour résultat de lui faire perdre son emploi.

resultant /rɪˈzʌltənt/ **I** *n* Math résultante *f*.
II *adj* résultant.

resume /rɪˈzjuːm, US -ˈzuːm/ **I** *vtr* reprendre [*flight, work, talks*]; regagner [*seat*]; renouer [*relations*]; **to ~ doing** se remettre à faire.
II *vi* reprendre.

résumé /ˈrezjuːmeɪ, US ˌrezʊˈmeɪ/ *n* **1** (summary) résumé *m*; **2** US (cv) curriculum vitae *m inv*.

resumption /rɪˈzʌmpʃn/ *n* gen reprise *f* (**of** de); (of relations) rétablissement *m* (**of** de).

resurface /ˌriːˈsɜːfɪs/ **I** *vtr* refaire (la surface de) [*road, court*].
II *vi* [*submarine*] faire surface; [*doubt, prejudice, rumour*] réapparaître; [*person, group*] refaire surface.

resurgence /rɪˈsɜːdʒəns/ *n* (of party, danger, tradition) résurgence *f*; (of interest) regain *m*; (of economy) reprise *f*; (of currency) remontée *f*.

resurgent /rɪˈsɜːdʒənt/ *adj* [*country, party*] renaissant; [*economy*] qui redémarre.

resurrect /ˌrezəˈrekt/ *vtr* lit, fig ressusciter.

resurrection /ˌrezəˈrekʃn/ *n* résurrection *f*; Relig **the Resurrection** la Résurrection.

resuscitate /rɪˈsʌsɪteɪt/ *vtr* **1** Med réanimer; **2** fig déterrer [*plan, project*].

resuscitation /rɪˌsʌsɪˈteɪʃn/ **I** *n* réanimation *f*.
II *modif* [*equipment, doll, unit*] de réanimation.

resuscitator /rɪˈsʌsɪteɪtə(r)/ *n* (apparatus) appareil *m* de respiration artificielle.

ret. *abrév écrite* = **retired, returned**.

retail /ˈriːteɪl/ **I** *n* vente *f* au détail.
II *modif* [*business, sector, customer*] de détail.
III *adv* au détail.
IV *vtr* **1** Comm vendre [qch] au détail; **2** (spread) colporter [*gossip*].
V *vi* **to ~ at** se vendre au détail à.

retailer /ˈriːteɪlə(r)/ *n* **1** (company) détaillant *m*; **2** (person) détaillant/-e *m/f*.

retailing /ˈriːteɪlɪŋ/ **I** *n* distribution *f*.
II *modif* [*giant, sector*] de la distribution; [*group, operations*] de distribution.

retail: **~ price** *n* prix *m* de détail; **~ price index, RPI** *n* indice *m* des prix à la consommation; **~ price maintenance, RPM** *n* imposition *f* d'un prix maximum; **~ sales** *npl* ventes *fpl* au détail; **~ space** *n* surface *f* de vente; **~ trade** *n* (companies) détaillants *mpl*; (industry) commerce *m* de détail.

retain /rɪˈteɪn/ *vtr* **1** (keep) garder [*dignity, control, identity, support*]; conserver [*trophy, property*]; **2** (contain) retenir [*water*]; conserver [*heat*]; **3** (remember) retenir [*fact*]; conserver [*image*]; **4** Jur engager [*lawyer*].

retain: **~ed earnings** *n* bénéfices *mpl* non distribués; **~ed object** *n* complément *m* d'objet (d'un verbe au passif).

retainer /rɪˈteɪnə(r)/ *n* **1** (fee) (for services) somme *f* versée à l'avance (*pour s'assurer des services de quelqu'un*); (for lawyer) provision *f*; (for accommodation) loyer *m* réduit (*permettant de conserver son logement en cas d'absence*); **2** Dent appareil *m* dentaire; **3**‡ (servant) domestique *mf*.

retain: **~ing dam** *n* barrage *m* de retenue; **~ing ring** *n* anneau *m* de blocage; **~ing wall** *n* mur *m* de soutènement.

retake **I** /ˈriːteɪk/ *n* Cin nouvelle prise *f* (de vues).
II /ˌriːˈteɪk/ *vtr* (*prét* **retook**; *pp* **retaken**) **1** Cin faire une nouvelle prise de [*scene*]; **2** Sch, Univ repasser [*exam*]; **3** Mil reprendre [*town, island*].

retaliate /rɪˈtælɪeɪt/ *vi* (all contexts) réagir.

retaliation /rɪˌtælɪˈeɪʃn/ *n* représailles *fpl* (**for** de; **against** contre); **in ~** en représailles (**for** de; **against** contre).

retaliatory /rɪˈtælɪətrɪ, US -tɔːrɪ/ *adj* (violent) de représailles; (nonviolent) de rétorsion.

retard /rɪˈtɑːd/ **I**◑ *n* US injur retardé/-e *m/f*.
II *vtr* retarder.

retardation /ˌriːtɑːˈdeɪʃn/ *n* **1** gen retard *m*; **2** Tech accélération *f* négative; **3** US Psych retard *m* mental.

retarded /rɪˈtɑːdɪd/ *adj* **1** Psych retardé; **2**◑ US (stupid) débile○.

retch /retʃ/ **I** *n* haut-le-cœur *m inv*.
II *vi* avoir des haut-le-cœur.

retd *abrév écrite* = **retired**.

retell /ˌriːˈtel/ *vtr* (*prét, pp* **retold**) raconter à nouveau.

retelling /ˌriːˈtelɪŋ/ *n* nouvelle version *f*.

retention /rɪˈtenʃn/ *n* **1** (of right, territory) maintien *m*; **2** (storing of facts) mémoire *f*; **3** Med rétention *f*.

retention money *n* Comm retenue *f* de garantie.

retentive /rɪˈtentɪv/ *adj* **1** [*memory*] fidèle, bon; **2** [*soil*] rétentif/-ive.

rethink **I** /ˈriːθɪŋk/ *n* **to have a ~** repenser.
II /ˌriːˈθɪŋk/ *vtr* (*prét, pp* **rethought**) repenser.
III *vi* (*prét, pp* **rethought**) revoir la question.

reticence /ˈretɪsns/ *n* réticence *f* (**on, about** à propos de), réserve *f* (**on, about** sur).

reticent /ˈretɪsnt/ *adj* réticent, réservé; **to be ~ about sth** ne pas parler beaucoup de qch.

reticently /ˈretɪsntlɪ/ *adv* avec réticence, avec réserve.

reticle /ˈretɪkl/ *n* Tech réticule *m*.

reticulate /rɪˈtɪkjʊlət/ *adj* réticulé.

reticule‡ /ˈretɪkjuːl/ *n* réticule *m*.

retina /ˈretɪnə, US ˈretənə/ *n* rétine *f*.

retinal /ˈretɪnəl, US ˈretənəl/ *adj* rétinien/-ienne; **~ rivalry** Psych rivalité *f* rétinienne.

retinue /ˈretɪnjuː, US ˈretənuː/ *n* escorte *f*.

retire /rɪˈtaɪə(r)/ **I** *vtr* mettre [qn] à la retraite (**on grounds of** pour raisons de); **to be compulsorily ~d** être mis à la retraite d'office.
II *vi* **1** (from work) prendre sa retraite; **to ~ from sth** quitter qch; **to ~ as** se retirer en tant que; **to ~ early** partir en retraite anticipée; **to ~ on £100 a week** prendre sa retraite et toucher 100 livres par semaine; **2** (withdraw) [*jury, person*] se retirer (**from** de); **to ~ to the drawing-room/to one's room** sout se retirer au salon/dans sa chambre; **3**† **to ~ (to bed)** aller se coucher; **to ~ early** (aller) se coucher tôt; **4** Sport abandonner; **to ~ from sth** se retirer de qch; **to ~ with an injury, to ~ injured** abandonner à la suite d'une blessure; **5** Mil se replier (**to** sur).
III retired *pp adj* retraité.
IV retiring *p prés adj* qui prend sa retraite.

retiree /ˌrɪtaɪəˈriː/ *n* US retraité/-e *m/f*.

retirement /rɪˈtaɪəmənt/ *n* **1** (action) départ *m* à la retraite (**of** de); **to announce one's ~** annoncer son départ à la retraite; **to take early ~** partir en retraite anticipée; **2** (state) retraite *f*; **a peaceful ~** une retraite tranquille; **to come out of ~** reprendre ses activités (après avoir pris sa retraite).

retirement: **~ age** *n* âge *m* de la retraite; **~ bonus** *n* prime *f* de départ à la retraite.

retirement home *n* **1** (individual) maison *f* pour la retraite; **2** (communal) maison *f* de retraite.

retirement pension *n* (pension *f* de) retraite *f*.

retiring /rɪˈtaɪərɪŋ/ **I** *p prés* ▶ **retire**.
II *adj* (shy) réservé.

retool /ˌriːˈtuːl/ **I** *vtr* **1** (re-equip) rééquiper [*factory*]; **2** US (reorganize) réorganiser, restructurer [*factory*].
II *vi* **1** (re-equip) se rééquiper (en machines); **2** US (reorganize) se réorganiser, se restructurer.

retort /rɪˈtɔːt/ **I** *n* **1** (reply) riposte *f*; **2** Chem cornue *f*; **3** Tech convertisseur *m*, cornue *f*.
II *vtr* répliquer, rétorquer (**that** que).

retouch **I** /ˈriːtʌtʃ/ *n* retouche *f*.
II /ˌriːˈtʌtʃ/ *vtr* retoucher.

retrace /ˌriːˈtreɪs/ *vtr* reconstituer [*movements*]; **to ~ one's steps** revenir sur ses pas; **to ~ one's path** ou **route** rebrousser chemin.

retract /rɪˈtrækt/ **I** *vtr* **1** (withdraw) rétracter [*statement, allegation*]; retirer [*claim*]; **2** (pull in) escamoter [*landing gear*]; [*animal*] rétracter [*claws etc*].
II *vi* [*landing gear*] s'escamoter; [*horns etc*] se rétracter.

retractable /rɪˈtræktəbl/ *adj* [*landing gear, headlights*] escamotable; [*pen*] à pointe rétractable.

retractile /rɪˈtræktaɪl/ *adj* rétractile.

retraction /rɪˈtrækʃn/ *n* gen rétractation *f*; (of landing gear) escamotage *m*.

retrain /ˌriːˈtreɪn/ **I** *vtr* recycler.
II *vi* se recycler.

retraining /ˌriːˈtreɪnɪŋ/ *n* recyclage *m*.

retransmit /ˌriːtrænzˈmɪt/ *vtr* retransmettre.

retread **I** /ˈriːtred/ *n* pneu *m* rechapé.
II /ˌriːˈtred/ *vtr* (*prét, pp* **~ed**) rechaper [*tyre*].

retreat /rɪˈtriːt/ **I** *n* **1** (withdrawal) retraite *f* (**from** de; **into** dans); **to beat** ou **make a ~** battre en retraite; **to beat a hasty ~** battre en retraite précipitamment; **to sound/beat the ~** Mil sonner/battre la retraite; **to be in ~** [*ideology etc*] reculer; **2** (house) retraite *f*; **mountain ~** refuge *m*; **country ~** retraite campagnarde; **3** Relig retraite *f*; **to go into/go on a ~** entrer en/faire une retraite.
II *vtr* Games ramener [*piece*].
III *vi* **1** gen [*person*] se retirer (**into** dans; **from** de); **to ~ before sth** battre en retraite devant qch; **2** Mil [*army*] se replier (**to** sur; **into** dans; **behind** derrière); **3** fig se retirer (**to** à; **from** de); **to ~ into a dream world/into silence** se réfugier dans un monde imaginaire/dans le silence; **to ~ into oneself** se replier sur soi-même; **4** [*glacier, flood water, desert*] reculer.

retrench /rɪˈtrentʃ/ sout **I** *vtr* restreindre [*expenditure*]; faire des coupures dans [*book*].
II *vi* se restreindre dans ses dépenses.

retrenchment /rɪˈtrentʃmənt/ *n* sout **1** (economizing) restriction *f* (des dépenses); **2** Mil retranchement *m*.

retrial /ˌriːˈtraɪəl/ *n* Jur nouveau procès *m*.

retribution /ˌretrɪˈbjuːʃn/ *n* sout châtiment *m* (**for, against** pour).

retributive /rɪˈtrɪbjʊtɪv/ *adj* sout vengeur/-eresse.

retrievable /rɪˈtriːvəbl/ *adj* **1** gen [*sum*] recouvrable; [*loss, mistake*] récupérable; **2** Comput accessible.

retrieval /rɪˈtriːvl/ *n* **1** gen (of property) récupération *f*; (of money) recouvrement *m*; **2** Comput extraction *f*.

retrieve /rɪˈtriːv/ **I** *vtr* **1** (get back) récupérer [*object*]; **2** (save) redresser [*situation*]; **3** Hunt [*dog*] rapporter [*game*]; **4** Comput extraire [*data*].
II *vi* Hunt [*dog*] rapporter.

retriever /rɪˈtriːvə(r)/ *n* retriever *m*.

retro /ˈretrəʊ/ **I** *n* rétro *m*.

II *modif* [*rock, art, chic*] rétro *inv*.
retroactive /ˌretrəʊˈæktɪv/ *adj* rétroactif/-ive.
retroactively /ˌretrəʊˈæktɪvlɪ/ *adv* de manière rétroactive.
retroengine /ˌretrəʊˈendʒɪn/ *n* rétrofusée *f*.
retrofit /ˈretrəʊfɪt/ *vtr* (*p prés etc* **-tt-**) rééquiper.
retroflex /ˈretrəfleks/ *adj* rétroflexe.
retroflexion /ˌretrəˈflekʃn/ *n* rétroflexion *f*.
retrograde /ˈretrəgreɪd/ *adj* rétrograde.
retrogress /ˌretrəˈgres/ *vi* **1** gen rétrograder (**to** jusqu'à) also fig; **2** Biol, Med régresser.
retrogression /ˌretrəˈgreʃn/ *n* régression *f*.
retrogressive /ˌretrəˈgresɪv/ *adj* **1** gen rétrograde; **2** Biol régressif/-ive.
retropack /ˈretrəʊpæk/ *n* Aerosp faisceau *m* de rétrofusées.
retrorocket /ˈretrəʊrɒkɪt/ *n* rétrofusée *f*.
retrospect /ˈretrəʊspekt/ **in retrospect** *adv phr* rétrospectivement, après coup.
retrospection /ˌretrəˈspekʃn/ *n* examen *m* rétrospectif.
retrospective /ˌretrəˈspektɪv/ **I** *n* (also **~ exhibition** ou **~ show**) Art, Cin rétrospective *f*.
II *adj* **1** gen [*approach, view*] rétrospectif/-ive; **2** Jur, Admin [*regulation, application, rebate*] rétroactif/-ive.
retrospectively /ˌretrəˈspektɪvlɪ/ *adv* **1** Jur, Admin [*apply, validate*] rétroactivement; **2** gen rétrospectivement, après coup.
retrovirus /ˈretrəʊvaɪərəs/ *n* rétrovirus *m*.
retry /ˌriːˈtraɪ/ *vtr* **1** Jur juger à nouveau [*case, person*]; **2** Comput essayer de relancer [*operation*].
retsina /retˈsiːnə, US ˈretsɪnə/ *n* résiné *m*.
retune /ˌriːˈtjuːn, US -ˈtuːn/ *vtr* Mus accorder; Radio, Telecom, Aut régler.
return /rɪˈtɜːn/ **I** *n* **1** lit, fig (getting back, going back) retour *m* (**to** à; **from** de); **my ~ to London** mon retour à Londres; **a ~ to power** un retour au pouvoir; **a ~ to traditional values** un retour aux valeurs traditionnelles; **on my ~ home** (as soon as I return) dès mon retour; (when I return) à mon retour; **on your ~ to work** dès que vous aurez repris votre travail; **2** (recurrence, coming back) retour *m* (**of** de); **I'm hoping for a ~ of the fine weather** j'espère que le beau temps va revenir; **3** (restitution, bringing back) (of law, practice) retour *m* (**of** de); (of object) restitution *f* (**of** de); **I hope for its ~** j'espère qu'on me le/la rendra; **on ~ of the vehicle** à la restitution du véhicule; **4** (sending back of letter, goods) renvoi *m* (**of** de); **5** (reward) récompense *f*; **is this my ~ for helping you?** est-ce là ma récompense pour vous avoir aidé?; **6** Fin (yield on investment) rendement *m*, rapport *m* (**on** de); (on capital) rémunération *f*; **the law of diminishing ~s** la loi des rendements décroissants; **7** Transp (ticket) aller-retour *m inv*; **two ~s to Paris** deux aller-retour pour Paris; **8** Theat (ticket) billet *m* rendu à la dernière minute; **'~s only'** 'complet' (*sous réserve de billets rendus à la dernière minute*); **9** Publg (book) invendu *m*; **10** Sport (of ball) retour *m*.
II returns *npl* Pol résultats *mpl*.
III in return *adv phr* en échange (**for** de).
IV *vtr* **1** (give back) rendre [*book, video, car*]; rembourser [*money*]; **2** (bring back, take back) rapporter [*purchase, library book*] (**to** à); **keep the receipt in case you have to ~ your purchase** gardez votre ticket de caisse en cas de remboursement; **3** (put back) remettre [*file, book*]; **to ~ sth to its place** remettre qch à sa place; **4** (send back) renvoyer [*parcel, sample*]; **'~ to sender'** 'retour à l'expéditeur'; **5** (give, issue in return) rendre [*greeting, invitation*]; **to ~ the compliment** hum retourner le compliment; **to ~ the compliment by doing** remercier qn en faisant; **to ~ the favour** en faire autant; **I'll be glad to ~ the favour** j'en ferai autant pour vous; **6** (reciprocate) répondre à [*love, feelings, affection*]; **7** Mil riposter à [*fire*]; **8** Sport renvoyer [*ball, shot*]; **9** (reply, rejoin) répliquer; **10** Tax **to ~ details of one's income** déclarer ses revenus; **11** Jur prononcer [*verdict*]; **12** Fin (yield) rapporter [*profit*]; **13** Pol (elect) élire [*candidate*]; **to be ~ed** être élu; **14** Telecom **to ~ sb's call** rappeler qn.
V *vi* **1** (come back) revenir (**from** de); **he left never to ~** il est parti pour ne plus jamais revenir; **2** (go back) retourner (**to** à); **3** (come or go back from abroad) rentrer (**from** de); **4** (get back home) rentrer chez soi; **what time did you ~?** à quelle heure êtes-vous rentré?; **5** (resume) **to ~ to** reprendre [*activity*]; **to ~ to one's book** reprendre sa lecture; **to ~ to the point I made earlier** pour reprendre ce que je disais tout à l'heure; **to ~ to power** revenir au pouvoir; **to ~ to sanity** retrouver son équilibre; **6** (recur, come back) [*symptom, feeling, doubt*] réapparaître; [*days, times, season*] revenir.
IDIOMS **by ~ of post** par retour du courrier ; **many happy ~s!** bon anniversaire!
returnable /rɪˈtɜːnəbl/ *adj* [*bottle*] consigné; **~ by 6 April** à rendre avant le 6 avril.
returner /rɪˈtɜːnə(r)/ *n* femme *f* qui reprend le travail (*après avoir élevé ses enfants*).
return: **~ fare** *n* prix *m* d'un billet aller-retour; **~ flight** *n* vol *m* de retour; **~ing officer** *n* GB président/-e *m/f* d'un bureau d'élections.
return journey GB, **return trip** US *n* retour *m*; **on her ~** à son retour.
return: **~ stroke** *n* course *f* retour; **~ ticket** *n* billet *m* aller-retour; **~ visit** *n* retour *m*.
reunification /ˌriːjuːnɪfɪˈkeɪʃn/ *n* réunification *f*.
reunify /ˌriːˈjuːnɪfaɪ/ *vtr* réunifier.
reunion /ˌriːˈjuːnɪən/ *n* **1** (celebration) réunion *f*; **2** (meeting) retrouvailles *fpl* (**with** avec).
Réunion /ˌriːˈjunɪən/ **▶ 1163**, **1381** *pr n* (île *f* de) la Réunion; **in/to ~** à la Réunion.
reunite /ˌriːjuːˈnaɪt/ **I** *vtr* (*gén au passif*) réunir [*family*]; réunifier [*country, party*]; **he was ~d with his family** il a retrouvé sa famille.
II *vi* [*country, party*] se réunifier.
re-up○ /ˌriːˈʌp/ *vi* US argot des soldats rempiler○ soldiers' slang, se rengager.
reusable /ˌriːˈjuːzəbl/ *adj* réutilisable.
reuse I /ˌriːˈjuːs/ *n* réutilisation *f*.
II /ˌriːˈjuːz/ *vtr* réutiliser.
rev○ /rev/ **I** *n* Aut (*abrév* = **revolution** (**per minute**)) tour *m* (par minute).
II *vtr* (*p prés etc* **-vv-**) (also **~ up**) monter le régime de [*engine*].
III *vi* (*p prés etc* **-vv-**) (also **~ up**) [*engine*] monter en régime.
Rev(**d**) *n*: *abrév écrite* = **Reverend**.
revalorization /ˌriːvæləraɪˈzeɪʃn, US -rɪˈz-/ *n* Fin réévaluation *f*.
revalorize /ˌriːˈvæləraɪz/ *vtr* Fin réévaluer.
revaluation /ˌriːvæljuːˈeɪʃn/ *n* Comm, Fin réévaluation *f*.
revalue /ˌriːˈvæljuː/ *vtr* Comm, Fin réévaluer.
revamp /ˌriːˈvæmp/ **I** *n* **1** (process) rajeunissement *m*; **2** (result) nouvelle version *f*.
II *vtr* rajeunir [*image, play*]; réorganiser [*company*]; retaper○ [*building, clothing*].
III revamped *pp adj* [*programme, management, play*] rajeuni; [*building, room, clothing*] retapé○.
revanchism /rɪˈvæntʃɪzəm/ *n* revanchisme *m*.
revanchist /rɪˈvæntʃɪst/ *n, adj* revanchiste (*mf*).
rev counter○ /ˈrev kaʊntə(r)/ GB *n* compte-tours *m inv*.
reveal /rɪˈviːl/ **I** *vtr* **1** (make public) dévoiler [*truth, plan, fault*]; révéler [*secret*]; **to ~ that** révéler que; **to ~ sth to sb** révéler qch à qn; **to ~ sb to be sth** révéler qn comme étant qch; **to ~ sb's identity** révéler l'identité de qn; **to ~ all** (divulge) tout dire; (undress) tout montrer; **2** (make visible) découvrir [*view, picture*]; **~ed religion** religion *f* révélée.
II *v refl* **to ~ oneself** [*person*] se montrer; [*God*] se révéler; **to ~ oneself to be** se révéler être.
revealing /rɪˈviːlɪŋ/ *adj* **1** [*remark, interview, report*] révélateur/-trice; **2** [*dress, blouse*] décolleté.
reveille /rɪˈvælɪ, US ˈrevəlɪ/ *n* Mil réveil *m*.
revel /ˈrevl/ **I** *npl* **~s** festivités *fpl*.
II *vi* (*p prés etc* **-ll-**, **-l-** US) **1** US (celebrate) faire la fête; **2** (enjoy) **to ~ in sth/in doing** se délecter de qch/à faire.
revelation /ˌrevəˈleɪʃn/ *n* gen, Relig révélation *f* (**of** de).
Revelation /ˌrevəˈleɪʃn/ *pr n* Bible Apocalypse *f*.
revelatory /ˌrevəˈleɪtrɪ, US -tɔːrɪ/ *adj* révélateur/-trice.
reveller, US **reveler** /ˈrevələ(r)/ *n* fêtard/-e○ *m/f*.
revelry /ˈrevlrɪ/ *n* (also **revelries**) réjouissances *fpl*.
revenge /rɪˈvendʒ/ **I** *n* **1** (punitive act) vengeance *f*; **in ~** par vengeance; **in ~ for sth** pour venger qch; **to take** ou **get one's ~** se venger (**for** de; **on** sur); **2** (getting even) revanche *f*; **by way of ~** en revanche; **to get one's ~** prendre sa revanche (**on** sur; **for** de).
II *v refl* **to ~ oneself** se venger (**on** sur; **for** de).
IDIOMS **~ is sweet** la vengeance est un plat qui se mange froid.
revengeful /rɪˈvendʒfl/ *adj* [*nature*] vindicatif/-ive; [*mood*] vengeur/-eresse.
revenue /ˈrevənjuː, US -ənuː/ **I** *n* revenus *mpl*; **a source of ~** une source de revenus.
II revenues *npl* **oil ~s** revenus *mpl* pétroliers; **tax ~s** recettes *fpl* fiscales.
Revenue /ˈrevənjuː, US -ənuː/ *n* GB Tax = **Inland Revenue**.
revenue: **~ sharing** *n* US *réattribution partielle des impôts fédéraux aux autorités locales*; **~ stamp** *n* timbre *m* fiscal.
reverberate /rɪˈvɜːbəreɪt/ **I** *vtr* Tech fondre au four à réverbère.
II *vi* [*hills, room*] résonner (**with** de); [*thunder, footsteps*] résonner (**through** dans, par); [*debate, shock wave*] se propager (**through** dans); [*light, heat*] se réverbérer.
reverberation /rɪˌvɜːbəˈreɪʃn/ *n* lit réverbération *f*; fig répercussion *f*.
reverberator /rɪˈvɜːbəreɪtə(r)/ *n* Ind four *m* à réverbère.
revere /rɪˈvɪə(r)/ *vtr* révérer.
reverence /ˈrevərəns/ *n* profond respect *m*.
reverend† /ˈrevərənd/ *adj* vénérable.
Reverend /ˈrevərənd/ **▶ 1268** *n* **1** (person) (Roman Catholic) curé *m*; (Protestant) pasteur *m*; (Anglican) révérend *m*; **2** (as title) **the ~ Jones** (Roman Catholic) l'abbé Jones; (Protestant) le pasteur Jones; (Anglican) le révérend Jones; **the Very ~ X** (Roman Catholic) Monseigneur X; (Anglican) le très révérend X; **the Most ~ X** le Révérendissime X; **~ Mother** Révérende Mère; **~ Father** Révérend Père.
reverent /ˈrevərənt/ *adj* [*hush*] religieux/-ieuse; [*attitude, expression*] de respect.
reverential /ˌrevəˈrenʃl/ *adj* sout [*awe*] révérenciel/-ielle fml; [*tones, attitude*] révérencieux/-ieuse fml.
reverently /ˈrevərəntlɪ/ *adv* [*speak*] très respectueusement; [*listen*] religieusement.
reverie /ˈrevərɪ/ *n* rêverie *f*; **to fall into a ~** se perdre dans une rêverie.
revers /rɪˈvɪə(r)/ *npl* Fashn revers *mpl*.
reversal /rɪˈvɜːsl/ *n* **1** gen (of policy) renversement *m*; (of order, method, trend) inversion *f*; (of fortune) revers *m*; **a ~ of traditional roles** un renversement des rôles traditionnels; **2** Jur annulation *f*.

reverse /rɪ'vɜ:s/ **I** *n* **1** (opposite) **the ~** le contraire; **rather the ~** plutôt le contraire; **quite the ~** bien au contraire; **the truth was exactly the ~** la vérité était tout le contraire; **2** (back) **the ~** (of coin) le revers; (of banknote) le verso; (of fabric, picture) l'envers *m*; **3** (setback) revers *m*; **4** Aut (also **~ gear**) marche *f* arrière; **you're in ~** tu es en marche arrière; **to go into ~** [*driver*] se mettre en marche arrière; fig [*process*] s'inverser; **to put a plan/policy into ~** fig faire marche arrière dans son plan/sa politique; **the same process but in ~** le même procédé mais en sens inverse.
II *adj* **1** (opposite) [*argument, effect, trend*] contraire; [*direction*] opposé; **2** (other) **the ~ side** (of coin, medal) le revers; (of fabric, picture) l'envers *m*; **3** (backwards) [*somersault*] en arrière; **to answer the questions in ~ order** répondre aux questions en commençant par la dernière; **4** Aut **~ gear** marche *f* arrière; **~ turn** virage *m* en marche arrière.
III in reverse *adv phr* [*do, function*] en sens inverse.
IV *vtr* **1** (invert) inverser [*order, trend, process, policy*]; **2** (exchange, switch) renverser [*roles*]; **3** GB Pol retourner [*defeat*]; **4** Tech, Aut faire tourner [qch] à l'envers [*mechanism, machine*]; faire rouler [qch] en marche arrière [*car*]; **to ~ a car out of a garage** sortir une voiture d'un garage en marche arrière; **5** Jur annuler; **6** Telecom **to ~ the charges** appeler en PCV.
V *vi* [*driver*] faire marche arrière; **he ~d into a tree** il a heurté un arbre en faisant marche arrière; **to ~ down the lane/into a parking space** descendre l'allée/se garer en marche arrière.

reverse: **~ charge call** *n* appel *m* en PCV; **~ thrust** *n* poussée *f* inversée.

reversibility /rɪ'vɜ:səbɪlətɪ/ *n* réversibilité *f*.

reversible /rɪ'vɜ:səbl/ *adj* (all contexts) réversible.

reversing light *n* feu *m* de recul.

reversion /rɪ'vɜ:ʃn, US -ʒn/ *n* **1** (process of reverting) retour *m* (**to** à); **~ to its wild state** retour à son état sauvage; **~ to type** (of plant, animal) réversion *f* au type primitif; **2** Jur, Insur réversion *f*.

reversionary /rɪ'vɜ:ʃənərɪ, US -ʒənerɪ/ *adj* gen, Insur [*pension, annuity, bonus*] réversible.

reversionary: **~ characteristic** *n* Biol caractère *m* régressif; **~ rights** *npl* Jur droits *mpl* de retour.

revert /rɪ'vɜ:t/ *vi* **1** (return) **to ~ to** [*person*] reprendre [*habit, name*]; [*area*] redevenir [*moorland, wilderness*]; **to ~ to doing** [*person*] recommencer or se remettre à faire; **to ~ to normal** redevenir normal; **2** Biol, Zool **to ~ to type** retourner or revenir au type primitif; **he ~ed to type** fig le naturel a repris le dessus; **3** (return in speaking, discussing) **to ~ to your first question** pour en revenir à votre première question; **4** Jur retourner, revenir (**to** à).

revet /rɪ'vet/ *vtr* (*p prés etc* **-tt-**) revêtir.

review /rɪ'vju:/ **I** *n* **1** gen, Admin, Jur, Pol (reconsideration) révision *f* (**of** de); (report) rapport *m* (**of** sur); **policy ~** révision de la politique; **to be under ~** [*policy*] être en train d'être réexaminé; [*pay, salaries*] être en train d'être révisé; **to come under ~** être réexaminé; **to keep sth under ~** réviser qch régulièrement; **to set up a ~** établir une révision; **to be subject to ~** pouvoir être reconsidéré; **the week in ~** Radio, TV la semaine passée en revue; **2** Journ, Literat (critical assessment) critique *f* (**of** de); **book ~** critique d'un livre; **music ~** critique musicale; **rave ~**○ revue *f* excellente; **to get a good/bad ~** avoir une bonne/mauvaise critique; **to write a ~** faire une critique; **to send a book for ~** envoyer un livre pour la critique; **3** Journ (magazine) revue *f*; **the Saturday Review** la Revue du Samedi; **4** Mil revue *f*; **to hold a ~** passer les troupes en revue; **5** US Sch, Univ (of lesson) révision *f*.
II *vtr* **1** (re-examine) reconsidérer [*facts, question, situation*]; réviser [*attitude, case, pension, policy, sentence*]; passer [qch] en revue [*performance, progress, success, troops*]; **2** Journ, Literat faire la critique de [*book, film, play etc*]; **to be well/badly ~ed** se faire bien/mal accueillir par la critique; **3** US Sch, Univ réviser [*subject, lesson*].
III *vi* Journ rédiger des critiques (**for sb** pour qn; **in sth** pour qch).

review: **~ article** *n* article *m* de revue; **~ board**, **~ body** *n* Admin comité *m* de révision; **~ copy** *n* Publg exemplaire *m* de service de presse; **~ date** *n* date *f* de révision; **~ document** *n* document *m* de révision.

reviewer /rɪ'vju:ə(r)/ *n* Literat, Mus etc critique *m*; **book/film ~** critique littéraire/de cinéma.

review process *n* Admin processus *m* de révision.

revile /rɪ'vaɪl/ *vtr* sout vilipender fml.

revise /rɪ'vaɪz/ **I** *n* Print seconde *f* (épreuve *f*).
II *vtr* **1** (alter) réviser, modifier [*proposal, treaty, estimate, figures*]; changer [*attitude*]; **to ~ one's position** revenir sur sa position; **to ~ one's opinion of sb/sth** réviser son jugement sur or à propos de qn/qch; **to be ~d upwards/downwards** [*figures, profits etc*] être révisé à la hausse/à la baisse; **2** GB (for exam) réviser, revoir [*subject, notes*]; **3** Print (amend, correct) revoir, réviser [*text*]; **~d edition** édition revue et corrigée.
III *vi* GB réviser; **to ~ for one's exams** réviser pour ses examens; **she's busy revising** elle est en plein dans ses révisions.

revise: **Revised Standard Version**, **RSV** *n*: *traduction américaine de la Bible 1946–52*; **Revised Version**, **RV** *n*: *nouvelle version corrigée de la bible autorisée 1881–85*.

reviser /rɪ'vaɪsə(r)/ **▶1692** *n* (of text, manuscript etc) réviseur/-euse *m/f*; (proofreader) correcteur/-trice *m/f*; Journ réviseur/-euse *m/f*, rewriter *m*.

revision /rɪ'vɪʒn/ *n* révision *f*.

revisionism /rɪ'vɪʒənɪzəm/ *n* révisionnisme *m*.

revisionist /rɪ'vɪʒənɪst/ *n, adj* révisionniste (*mf*).

revisit /ˌri:'vɪzɪt/ *vtr* revisiter [*museum etc*]; retourner voir [*person, childhood home*]; fig (look at again) revoir; **Flaubert ~ed** Flaubert vu sous un jour nouveau.

revitalization /ˌri:vaɪtəlaɪ'zeɪʃn, US -lɪ'z-/ *n* **1** (of economy) relance *f*; **2** (of depressed area) renaissance *f*; **3** Cosmet revitalisation *f*.

revitalize /ri:'vaɪtəlaɪz/ *vtr* **1** relancer [*economy*]; faire démarrer [*company*]; **2** Cosmet revitaliser [*complexion*].

revival /rɪ'vaɪvl/ *n* **1** gen, Med (of person) rétablissement *m*; fig (of economy, trade) reprise *f*, redressement *m*; (of hope, interest) regain *m*; **2** (restoration) (of custom, language, fashion) renouveau *m*; (of law) remise *f* en vigueur; **the Gothic ~** le renouveau de l'art gothique; **3** Theat reprise *f*; **4** Relig (renewal of commitment) renouveau *m* de la foi; (meeting) réunion *f* pour le renouveau de la foi; **5** Mus Hist Revival *m*.

revivalism /rɪ'vaɪvəlɪzəm/ *n* **1** Relig renouveau *m* de la foi; **2** gen, Archit **fifties ~** retour *m* au style des années cinquante; **Gothic ~** esprit *m* de renouveau de l'art gothique.

revivalist /rɪ'vaɪvəlɪst/ **I** *n* **1** Relig prédicateur/-trice *m/f* revivaliste; **2** Archit, Mus etc (of custom, style) partisan/-e *m/f* du retour d'un style; **3** Mus Hist tenant/-e *m/f* du Revival.
II *adj* **1** Relig revivaliste; **2** Archit, Mus etc [*style*] **Greek/Gothic ~** néo-grec/-gothique; **3** Mus Hist [*jazz*] du Revival.

revive /rɪ'vaɪv/ **I** *vtr* **1** gen remonter; (from coma, faint etc) réanimer, faire reprendre connaissance à [*person*]; **the fresh air will ~ you** tu te sentiras mieux quand tu auras respiré un peu d'air frais; **2** fig raviver [*custom, institution, memory*]; ranimer [*anger, fears, enthusiasm, interest, hopes, friendship*]; remettre [qch] à l'ordre du jour [*proposals*]; remettre en vigueur [*law*]; relancer [*debate, career, movement*]; remettre [qch] à la mode [*style, fashion*]; revigorer [*economy*]; faire revivre [*language*]; **to ~ sb's (flagging) spirits** remonter le moral à qn; **to ~ interest in sb/sth** susciter un regain d'intérêt pour qn/qch; **3** Theat reprendre [*play*].
II *vi* [*person*] (from coma, faint) reprendre connaissance; [*wilting flowers*] retrouver leur fraîcheur; [*hopes, interest, enthusiasm*] renaître; [*market, economy*] reprendre; **he ~d once he went outside** il s'est senti mieux dès qu'il est sorti; **our spirits soon ~d** nous avons vite retrouvé le moral.

revivify /rɪ'vɪvɪfaɪ/ *vtr* sout revivifier fml.

revocation /ˌrevə'keɪʃn/ *n* sout ou Jur (of licence, permission) retrait *m*; (of law) abrogation *f*; (of will, offer, edict) révocation *f*; (of decision, order) annulation *f*.

revoke /rɪ'vəʊk/ **I** *n* (in bridge) renonce *f*.
II *vtr* sout ou Jur retirer [*licence, permission, statement*]; révoquer [*will, offer, edict*]; abroger [*law*]; annuler [*decision, order*].
III *vi* (in bridge) faire une renonce.

revolt /rɪ'vəʊlt/ **I** *n* (physical) révolte *f* (**against** contre); (verbal) rébellion *f* (**over** contre); **to be in ~** être en révolte or en rébellion; **they are in ~ over the bill** ils se rebellent contre le projet de loi; **to rise in ~** se soulever (**against** contre); **to be in open ~** être en rébellion ouverte.
II *vtr* dégoûter, révolter; **to be ~ed by sth** être dégoûté or révolté par qch.
III *vi* (physically) se révolter (**against** contre); (verbally) se rebeller (**against, over** contre).

revolting /rɪ'vəʊltɪŋ/ *adj* **1** (morally) révoltant; (physically) répugnant; **2**○ [*food*] infect; [*place, people*] affreux/-euse; **to taste/smell ~** avoir un goût/une odeur exécrable.

revoltingly /rɪ'vəʊltɪŋlɪ/ *adv* affreusement.

revolution /ˌrevə'lu:ʃn/ *n* **1** Pol, fig révolution *f* (**in** dans); **to bring about a ~ in sth** révolutionner qch; **2** Aut, Tech tour *m* (*d'un moteur*); **200 ~s per minute** 200 tours à la minute; **3** Astron révolution *f* (**round** autour de).

revolutionary /ˌrevə'lu:ʃənərɪ, US -nerɪ/ *n, adj* révolutionnaire (*mf*).

revolutionize /ˌrevə'lu:ʃənaɪz/ *vtr* révolutionner.

revolve /rɪ'vɒlv/ **I** *vtr* faire tourner.
II *vi* **1** lit tourner (**on** sur; **around** autour de); **2** fig **to ~ around** (be focused on) être axé sur.

revolver /rɪ'vɒlvə(r)/ *n* revolver *m*.

revolving /rɪ'vɒlvɪŋ/ *adj* [*chair, stand*] pivotant; [*cylinder*] rotatif/-ive; [*heavenly body*] en rotation; [*stage*] tournant.

revolving credit *n* Fin crédit *m* permanent.

revolving door **I** *n* (porte *f* à) tambour *m*.
II○ *modif* [*government, president*] transitoire.

revolving: **~ door sex**○ *n* relations *fpl* sexuelles avec plusieurs partenaires; **~ fund** *n* fonds *m* renouvelable.

revue /rɪ'vju:/ *n* Theat revue *f*.

revulsion /rɪ'vʌlʃn/ *n* dégoût *m* (**against** pour); **to feel ~ at sth/at having to do** être dégoûté par qch/de devoir faire; **to regard sth with ~** considérer qch avec dégoût; **to shudder in ~** frissonner de dégoût.

reward /rɪ'wɔ:d/ **I** *n* **1** (recompense) ré-

compense *f*; **a £50 ~ will be offered** on offre 50 livres sterling de récompense; **a poor ~** fig une maigre récompense; **2** fig (satisfaction) satisfaction *f*.
II *vtr* gen (for efforts, service) récompenser (**for** de, pour); **to ~ sb with a cheque/prize** donner un chèque/prix à qn en récompense.
IDIOMS **virtue is its own ~** Prov la vertu est sa propre récompense.
rewarding /rɪˈwɔːdɪŋ/ *adj* [*experience*] enrichissant; [*job, work*] gratifiant; [*pursuit*] qui en vaut la peine; **a ~ novel** un roman qui vaut la peine d'être lu; **financially ~** rémunérateur/-trice.
rewind /ˌriːˈwaɪnd/ *vtr* (*prét, pp* **rewound**) rembobiner [*tape, film*].
rewind button *n* bouton *m* de retour en arrière.
rewinding /ˌriːˈwaɪndɪŋ/ *n* rembobinage *m*.
rewire /ˌriːˈwaɪə(r)/ *vtr* refaire l'installation électrique.
reword /ˌriːˈwɜːd/ *vtr* reformuler [*paragraph, law, proposal*].
rework /ˌriːˈwɜːk/ *vtr* **1** gen retravailler [*theme, metal*]; **2** Mus, Literat créer une nouvelle version de [*classic*].
reworking /ˌriːˈwɜːkɪŋ/ *n* Mus, Literat nouvelle version *f* (**of** de).
rewound /ˌriːˈwaʊnd/ *prét, pp* ▶ **rewind**.
rewrite I /ˈriːraɪt/ *n* réécriture *f*; **to do three ~s of a story** réécrire une histoire trois fois.
II /ˌriːˈraɪt/ (*prét* **rewrote**; *pp* **rewritten**) *vtr* **1** (rework) ré(é)crire [*story, script*]; **to ~ history** ré(é)crire l'histoire; **to ~ a play as a novel** ré(é)crire une pièce sous la forme d'un roman; **2** US Journ rédiger [*article*].
rewriter /ˌriːˈraɪtə(r)/ ▶ **1692** *n* US Journ rédacteur/-trice *m/f*.
rewrite rule *n* règle *f* de réécriture.
rewritten /ˌriːˈrɪtn/ *pp* ▶ **rewrite**.
rewrote /ˌriːˈrəʊt/ *prét* ▶ **rewrite**.
Rex /reks/ *n* GB Jur **~ v Jones** la Couronne contre Jones.
Reykjavik /ˈreɪkjəvɪk/ ▶ **1818** *pr n* Reykjavik.
RFC *n* Sport (*abrév* = **rugby football club**) club *m* de rugby.
RFD *n* US (*abrév* = **rural free delivery**) *distribution du courrier à la campagne*.
rhapsodic /ræpˈsɒdɪk/ *adj* **1** Mus rhapsodique; **2** Literat [*prose, article*] dithyrambique; **3** fig sout [*welcome*] enthousiaste.
rhapsodize /ˈræpsədaɪz/ *vi* **to ~ about** ou **over sth** s'extasier sur qch.
rhapsody /ˈræpsədɪ/ *n* **1** Mus, Literat rhapsodie *f*; **2** fig **to go into rhapsodies over** ou **about sth** s'extasier sur qch.
rhd *n*: *abrév* ▶ **right-hand drive**.
rhea /ˈrɪə/ *n* nandou *m*.
rheme /riːm/ *n* rhème *m*.
rhenium /ˈriːnɪəm/ *n* rhénium *m*.
rheostat /ˈriːəstæt/ *n* rhéostat *m*.
rhesus: **~ baby** *n* enfant *m* rhésus; **~ factor** *n* facteur *m* rhésus; **~ monkey** *n* rhésus *m*; **~ negative** *adj* [*blood, person*] rhésus négatif *inv*; **~ positive** *adj* [*blood, person*] rhésus positif *inv*.
rhetoric /ˈretərɪk/ *n* **1** Literat rhétorique *f*; **2** gen **the ~ of romanticism** le langage du romantisme; **the ~ of terrorism** le discours terroriste; **empty ~** mots *mpl* creux.
rhetorical /rɪˈtɒrɪkl, US -ˈtɔːr-/ *adj* **1** Literat rhétorique; **~ figure** figure *f* de rhétorique; **~ question** question *f* rhétorique; **2** péj [*style, speech*] ronflant pej.
rhetorically /rɪˈtɒrɪklɪ, US -ˈtɔːr-/ *adv* **1** [*ask*] sans s'attendre à une réponse; **2** (in theory) en théorie; **~ (speaking)** d'un point de vue tout théorique.
rhetorician /ˌretəˈrɪʃn/ *n* **1** Antiq (teacher) rhéteur *m*; **2** (good writer, speaker) rhétoricien/-ienne *m/f*.
rheum /ruːm/ *n* (from eyes) chassie *f*; (from nose) écoulement *m* nasal aqueux.
rheumatic /ruːˈmætɪk/ I *n* (sufferer) rhumatisant/-e *m/f*.
II *adj* [*joints, person*] rhumatisant; [*condition, pain*] rhumatismal.
rheumatic fever ▶ **1354** *n* rhumatisme *m* articulaire aigu.
rheumatics○ /ruːˈmætɪks/ *n* (+ *v sg*) rhumatismes *mpl*.
rheumatism /ˈruːmətɪzəm/ ▶ **1354** *n* rhumatisme *m*; **to suffer from ~** souffrir de rhumatisme(s).
rheumatoid /ˈruːmətɔɪd/ *adj* [*symptom*] rhumatoïde.
rheumatoid arthritis ▶ **1354** *n* polyarthrite *f* rhumatoïde.
rheumatologist /ˌruːməˈtɒlədʒɪst/ ▶ **1692** *n* rhumatologue *mf*.
rheumatology /ˌruːməˈtɒlədʒɪ/ *n* rhumatologie *f*.
rheumy /ˈruːmɪ/ *adj* littér [*eyes*] chassieux/-ieuse.
Rhine /raɪn/ ▶ **1644** *pr n* Rhin *m*.
Rhine: **~land** *n* Rhénanie *f*; **~land Palatinate** *n* Rhénanie-Palatinat *f*.
rhinestone /ˈraɪnstəʊn/ I *n* diamant *m* fantaisie.
II *modif* [*necklace, bracelet*] en strass.
Rhine wine *n* vin *m* du Rhin.
rhino /ˈraɪnəʊ/ *n* (*pl* **~s** ou **~**) rhinocéros *m*.
rhinoceros /raɪˈnɒsərəs/ *n* (*pl* **-eroses, -eri** ou **~**) rhinocéros *m*.
rhinoceros beetle *n* rhinocéros *m* (*insecte*).
rhizome /ˈraɪzəʊm/ *n* rhizome *m*.
Rhode Island red *n* (male) coq *m* Rhode-Island; (female) poule *f* Rhode-Island.
Rhodesia /rəʊˈdiːzjə/ ▶ **1131** *pr n* Hist Rhodésie *f*.
Rhodesian /rəʊˈdiːzjən/ ▶ **1486** Hist I *n* Rhodésien/-ienne *m/f*.
II *adj* rhodésien/-ienne.
rhododendron /ˌrəʊdəˈdendrən/ *n* rhododendron *m*.
rhomb /rɒm/ *n* losange *m*, rhombe† *m*.
rhombic /ˈrɒmbɪk/ *adj* rhombique.
rhomboid /ˈrɒmbɔɪd/ I *n* rhomboïde† *m*.
II *adj* rhomboïdal.
rhombus /ˈrɒmbəs/ *n* (*pl* **-buses** ou **-bi**) losange *m*, rhombe† *m*.
Rhone /rəʊn/ ▶ **1644** I *pr n* Rhône *m*.
II *modif* [*glacier, delta*] du Rhône.
Rhône /rəʊn/ ▶ **1163** *pr n* Rhône *m*; **in/to the ~** dans le Rhône.
Rhône-Alpes ▶ **1273** *pr n* Rhône-Alpes *m*; **in/to the ~** dans le Rhône-Alpes.
rhubarb /ˈruːbɑːb/ I *n* **1** Culin rhubarbe *f*; **it's a ~ plant** c'est de la rhubarbe; **2** GB (nonsense word) **to say '~, ~'** dire 'bla, bla, bla et bla, bla, bla'; **3**○ US prise *f* de bec○.
II *modif* [*pie, pudding*] à la rhubarbe; [*leaf, patch, wine, stem*] de rhubarbe; [*jam*] à la rhubarbe, de rhubarbe.
rhyme /raɪm/ I *n* **1** (poem) vers *mpl*; (children's) comptine *f*; **2** (fact of rhyming) rime *f*; **in ~** en vers *mpl*; **to find a ~ for sth** trouver un mot qui rime avec qch.
II *vtr* faire rimer [*words, lines*] (**with** avec).
III *vi* rimer (**with** avec).
IDIOMS **without ~ or reason** sans rime ni raison.
rhyme: **~ royal** *n*: *strophe composée de sept vers de 10 pieds (avec des rimes ababbcc)*; **~ scheme** *n* agencement *m* des rimes.
rhyming couplet *n* distique *m* rimé.
rhyming slang *n*: *argot consistant à remplacer un mot par une locution qui rime avec ce mot*.
rhymster† /ˈraɪmstə(r)/ *n* péj rimailleur/-euse○ *m/f* pej.
rhythm /ˈrɪðəm/ *n* gen Mus, Literat rythme *m*; **the ~ of the seasons** le rythme des saisons; **to have a sense of ~** avoir le sens du rythme; **to the ~ of** au rythme de [*band, music*]; **in iambic ~** Literat en vers iambiques.
rhythm: **~ and blues** *n* rhythm and blues *m* (*musique influencée par le blues*); **~ band** *n* US orchestre *m* d'instruments de percussion.
rhythmic(al) /ˈrɪðmɪk(l)/ *adj* [*beat, music*] rythmé; [*movement*] rythmique; [*breathing*] régulier/-ière.
rhythmically /ˈrɪðmɪklɪ/ *adv* [*breathe, press*] régulièrement; **he isn't playing/dancing ~** il n'est pas dans le rythme quand il joue/danse; **to move ~ to the music** danser en rythme avec la musique.
rhythmicity /rɪðˈmɪsətɪ/ *n* rythme *m* biologique, biorythme *m*.
rhythm: **~ method** *n* Med méthode *f* des températures; **~ section** *n* section *f* rythmique.
RI *n* **1** Sch (*abrév* = **religious instruction**) ≈ catéchisme *m* (*cours d'instruction religieuse à l'école*); **2** US Post *abrév écrite* = **Rhode Island**.
rib /rɪb/ I *n* **1** Anat, Culin côte *f*; **broken ~** côte cassée; **to give sb a dig in the ~** donner un coup de coude à qn; **2** (structural) (in umbrella) baleine *f*; Bot nervure *f*; Archit nervure *f*; Naut membrure *f*; Aviat nervure *f*; **3** (in knitting) (stitch) côte *f*; **to knit sth in ~** tricoter qch en côtes.
II *vtr*○ (*p prés etc* **-bb-**) (tease) taquiner.
IDIOMS **to stick to one's ~s**○ [*food*] être bourratif○.
ribald /ˈrɪbld/ *adj* paillard.
ribaldry /ˈrɪbldrɪ/ *n* paillardise *f*.
riband† /ˈrɪbənd/ *n* ruban *m*.
ribbed /rɪbd/ *adj* [*garment*] à côtes; [*ceiling, vault*] à nervures; [*seashell*] strié.
ribbing /ˈrɪbɪŋ/ *n* **1** Constr, Archit nervures *fpl*; **2** (in knitting) côtes *fpl*; **3**○ (teasing) **to give sb a ~** taquiner qn.
ribbon /ˈrɪbən/ *n* **1** (for hair, medal, typewriter) ruban *m*; **to tie sth with a ~** attacher qch avec un ruban; **2** fig **a ~ of land/cloud** une étroite bande de terre/nuages; **a ~ of smoke** un filet *m* de fumée; **in ~s** en lambeaux *mpl*; **to tear sth to ~s** mettre qch en lambeaux.
ribbon: **~ development** *n*: *concentration d'habitations le long d'un axe routier*; **~fish** *n* régalec *m*; **~ worm** *n* némertien *m*.
rib cage *n* cage *f* thoracique.
riboflavin /ˌraɪbəʊˈfleɪvɪn/ *n* riboflavine *f*.
ribonucleic acid, **RNA** /ˌraɪbəʊnjuːˈkliːɪk, US -nuː-/ *n* acide *m* ribonucléique, ARN *m*.
rib: **~ roast** *n* côte *f* de bœuf; **~ tickler**○ *n* histoire *f* drôle or tordante○; **~-tickling**○ *adj* drôle, tordant○.
rice /raɪs/ *n* riz *m*; **boiled ~** riz nature.
rice bowl *n* **1** (container) bol *m* à riz; **2** (area) région *f* productrice de riz.
rice: **~field** *n* rizière *f*; **~ paper** *n* Culin galette *f* de pain azyme; Art papier *m* de riz; **~ pudding** *n* riz *m* au lait.
ricer /ˈraɪsə(r)/ *n* US Culin (utensil) presse-purée *m inv*.
rice wine *n* saké *m*.
rich /rɪtʃ/ I *n* (+ *v pl*) **the ~** les riches *mpl*; **to take from the ~ to give to the poor** prendre aux riches pour donner aux pauvres.
II **riches** *npl* richesses *fpl*; ▶ **rag**.
III *adj* **1** [*person, family, country, soil, land, harvest, tradition, life, history*] riche; [*profit*] gros/grosse; **to grow** ou **get ~** s'enrichir; **to make sb ~** enrichir qn; **~ in** riche en [*oil, vitamins, symbolism*]; **2** (lavish) [*costume, furnishings, gift*] riche; **3** (full, strong) [*colour, sound, smell, voice, food, flavour, diet*] riche; **4** Literat **~ rhyme** rime *f* riche.
IV **-rich** (*dans composés*) **oil-/protein-~** riche en pétrole/protéines.
IDIOMS **that's a bit ~**○! GB ça, c'est un

peu fort○! iron; **that's a bit ~ coming from her**○! ça lui va bien○ de dire (or de faire) ça! iron; **to strike it ~** faire fortune.

Richard /ˈrɪtʃəd/ *pr n* Richard; **~ the Lionheart** Richard Cœur de Lion.

richly /ˈrɪtʃlɪ/ *adv* [*dressed, furnished, ornamented, coloured*] richement; [*talented*] extrêmement; **~ deserved** amplement mérité.

richness /ˈrɪtʃnɪs/ *n* **1** (of person, family, country, soil, land, experience, life, history) richesse *f*; (of harvest) abondance *f*; **2** (lavishness) (of costumes, furnishings, meal) richesse *f*; (fullness, vividness) (of colours, voice) richesse *f*.

Richter scale /ˈrɪktə/ *n* échelle *f* de Richter; **on the ~** sur l'échelle de Richter.

rick /rɪk/ **I** *n* (of hay) meule *f*; (of wood) US tas *m* (de petit bois).
II *vtr* **to ~ one's ankle** GB se faire une entorse à la cheville.

rickets /ˈrɪkɪts/ ▶ **1354** *n* (+ *v sg*) rachitisme *m*.

rickety /ˈrɪkətɪ/ *adj* **1** (shaky) [*chair, staircase*] branlant; [*house*] délabré; **2** fig [*coalition, government*] branlant; **3** Med rachitique.

rickey /ˈrɪkɪ/ *n* US ≈ gin-fizz *m*.

rickrack /ˈrɪkræk/ *n* US tresse *f* de galon.

rickshaw /ˈrɪkʃɔː/ *n* pousse-pousse *m inv*; **in a ~** en pousse-pousse.

ricky-tick○ /ˌrɪkɪˈtɪk/ *adj* US démodé.

ricochet /ˈrɪkəʃeɪ, US ˌrɪkəˈʃeɪ/ **I** *n* ricochet *m*; **killed by a ~** tué par une balle qui a ricoché.
II *vi* (*pré, pp* **ricocheted**, **ricochetted** /-ˌʃeɪd/) ricocher (**off** sur).

rictus /ˈrɪktəs/ *n* sout rictus *m*.

rid /rɪd/ **I** *vtr* (*p prés* **-dd-**; *prét, pp* **rid**) **to ~ the house of mice/the streets of cars** débarrasser la maison de souris/les rues de voitures; **to ~ the world of famine/of imperialism** venir à bout de la famine/de l'impérialisme dans le monde; **to ~ sb of his/her illusions** faire perdre ses illusions à qn.
II *v refl* (*p prés* **-dd-**; *prét, pp* **rid**) **to ~ oneself of sth** se débarrasser de qch.
III *pp adj* **to be (well) ~ of** être (bien) débarrassé de; **to get ~ of** se débarrasser de [*waste, old car, guests*]; faire cesser [*pain, famine*]; se défaire de [*prejudice*].

riddance /ˈrɪdns/ *n*: IDIOMS **good ~ (to bad rubbish)**! bon débarras○!

ridden /ˈrɪdn/ **I** *pp* ▶ **ride**.
II -ridden (*dans composés*) **1** (afflicted by) **debt-~** criblé de dettes; **crisis-~** en crise; **guilt-~** rongé par un sentiment de culpabilité; **2** (full of) **flea/snake-~** infesté de puces/de serpents; **famine/drug-~** où règne la famine/la drogue; **cliché-~** bourré d'idées reçues.

riddle /ˈrɪdl/ **I** *n* **1** (puzzle) devinette *f*; **to ask sb/tell sb a ~** poser/raconter une devinette à qn; **to speak in ~s** parler par énigmes; **the ~ of the Sphinx** l'énigme du Sphinx; **2** (mystery) énigme *f*; **he's a ~** c'est une énigme; **3** Hort crible *m*.
II *vtr* **1** (perforate) **to ~ sth with** cribler qch de [*bullets, holes*]; **2** (undermine) **to be ~d with** [*person, organ*] être rongé or miné par [*disease*]; [*person*] être rongé par [*doubt, guilt*]; [*issue, language*] fourmiller de [*problems, ambiguities, errors*]; **it's ~d with corruption** la corruption règne; **3** Hort passer [qch] au crible [*soil*].

ride /raɪd/ **I** *n* **1** (from A to B) trajet *m* (**in, on** en, à); (for pleasure) tour *m*, promenade *f*, balade○ *f*; **bus/train ~** trajet en bus/en train; **horse/bike ~** promenade à cheval/à vélo; **sleigh ~** tour de luge; **it's a short/long ~** le trajet est court/long; **it's a £3 bus ~** ça coûte trois livres en bus; **it's a five-minute ~ by taxi** c'est à cinq minutes en taxi; **to go for a ~** aller faire un tour; **to have a ~ in a steam train/in a cart/on a merry-go-round** faire un tour dans un train à vapeur/sur une charrette/sur un manège; **he took his mother for a nice ~** il a emmené sa mère faire une jolie promenade (en voiture); **to give sb a ~** US emmener qn (en voiture); **give the child a ~ on your shoulders** promène l'enfant sur tes épaules; **2** Equit (in race) course *f*; (for pleasure) promenade *f* à cheval; **the jockey has got three ~s today** Turf le jockey a trois courses aujourd'hui; **3** fig (path) parcours *m*; **an easy ~ to the Presidency** un parcours facile vers la présidence; **he'll have a difficult ~** son parcours sera difficile; **4** Aut **smooth ~** confort *m*; **5** (bridlepath) allée *f* cavalière.
II *vtr* (*prét* **rode**; *pp* **ridden**) **1** (as rider) monter [*animal*]; rouler à [*bike*]; chevaucher [*broomstick, hobby horse*]; courir [*race*]; **can you ~ a bike?** sais-tu faire du vélo?; **to ~ a good race** Turf courir une belle course; **who's riding Pharlap in the 3.30?** Turf qui monte Pharlap dans la course de 15 h 30?; **do you want to ~ my bike/horse?** est-ce que tu veux prendre mon vélo/monter mon cheval?; **he ~s his bike to school** il va à l'école à vélo; **to ~ one's bike up/down the road** monter/descendre la rue à vélo; **2** US (travel on) prendre [*subway, bus*]; parcourir [*prairies, range*]; **3** (float on) [*surfer*] chevaucher [*wave*]; [*bird*] être porté par [*air current*]; **4**○ US (pressure) **to ~ sb about sth** casser les pieds○ à qn à propos de qch; **you're riding them too hard** vous y allez trop fort avec eux; **don't let him ~ you** ne te laisse pas faire par lui.
III *vi* (*prét* **rode**; *pp* **ridden**) **1** (as rider) (to describe position) être; (to express movement) aller; **to ~ astride/side-saddle** être à califourchon/en amazone; **to ~ behind/pillion** être en croupe/derrière; **she was riding on a camel/his shoulders** elle était sur un chameau/ses épaules; **she rode to London on her bike** elle est allée à Londres à vélo; **they had been riding for hours** ils allaient à cheval/à vélo etc depuis des heures; **I can't ~ any further** je ne peux plus avancer; **to ~ across** traverser; **to ~ along sth** longer qch; **to ~ along the lane and back** parcourir l'allée dans les deux sens; **2** (travel) **to ~ in** ou **on** [*passenger*] prendre [*bus, taxi etc*]; [*bird, surfer*] être porté par [*air current, wave*]; **I've never ridden on a bus** je n'ai jamais pris le bus; **riding on a wave of popularity** fig porté par une vague de popularité; **to ~ up and down the escalators** monter et descendre les escaliers mécaniques; **3** Equit, Sport (as leisure activity) faire du cheval; Turf (race) courir; **can you ~?** sais-tu faire du cheval?; **to ~ in the 2.00 race** courir dans la course de 14 h 00; **to ~ well** [*person*] être un bon cavalier/une bonne cavalière; [*horse*] être facile à monter; **4** (be at stake) **to ~ on** [*money, future*] être en jeu dans; **there's a lot riding on this project** beaucoup de choses sont en jeu dans ce projet.
IDIOMS **to be in for a rough** or **bumpy ~** avoir à affronter des temps difficiles; **to be riding for a fall** courir à sa perte; **to be riding high** (of moon) littér être haut dans le ciel; (of person) baigner dans l'euphorie; **to give sb a rough ~** donner du fil à retordre à qn; **to go along for the ~** lit y aller pour le plaisir; fig être là en spectateur; **to let sth** ou **things ~** laisser courir; **to ~ sb on a rail** US chasser qn après l'avoir l'enduit de goudron et de plumes; **to take sb for a ~**○ (swindle) rouler qn○; US euph (kill) emmener qn faire un tour euph.
■ **ride about**, **ride around** se déplacer.
■ **ride back** retourner (**to** à).
■ **ride down**: **~ [sb] down**, **~ down [sb]** **1** (trample) piétiner; **2** (catch up with) rattraper.
■ **ride on** continuer.
■ **ride off**: partir; **to ~ off to** se diriger vers.
■ **ride out**: ¶ **~ out** aller (**to** jusqu'à); ¶ **~ [sth] out**, **~ out [sth]** surmonter [*crisis*]; survivre à [*recession*]; **to ~ out the storm** Naut étaler la tempête; fig surmonter la crise.
■ **ride up** **1** (approach) [*rider*] s'approcher (**to** de); **2** (rise) [*skirt, sweater*] remonter (**over** sur).

ride-off *n* /ˈraɪdɒf/ (in competition) barrage *m*.

rider /ˈraɪdə(r)/ *n* **1** (person) (on horse) cavalier/-ière *m/f*; (on motorbike) motocycliste *mf*; (on bike) cycliste *mf*; (in bike race) coureur/-euse *m/f*; (in horse race) jockey *m*; (in circus) écuyer/-ère *m/f*; **2** (stipulation) (as proviso) correctif *m*; (as addition) Insur, Jur avenant *m*; (to document) annexe *f*; (to contract) clause *f* additionnelle.

ridge /rɪdʒ/ **I** *n* **1** Geog (along mountain top) arête *f*, crête *f*; (on hillside) corniche *f*; (in ocean) dorsale *f*; (mountain range) chaîne *f*; **2** (raised strip) (on rock, metal surface) strie *f*; (on fabric) côte *f*; (in ploughed land) crête *f*, billon *m*; (of potatoes, plants) rang *m*, rangée *f*; (in wet sand) ride *f*; **3** Anat (of nose) arête *f*, (of back) raie *f*; (in skin) ride *f*; **4** Constr (on roof) faîte *m*, faîtage *m*; **5** Meteorol **~ of high pressure** ligne *f* de hautes pressions, dorsale *f* barométrique.
II *vtr* strier [*rock, metal surface*]; rider [*sand*]; enfaîter [*roof*]; Agric billonner [*land*].

ridge: **~ pole** *n* (of roof) faîte *m*, madrier *m* de faîtage; (of tent) barre *f* horizontale (de faîte); **~ tent** *n* (tente *f*) canadienne *f*; **~ tile** *n* (tuile *f*) faîtière *f*, enfaîteau *m*; **~way** *n* GB chemin *m* de faîte.

ridicule /ˈrɪdɪkjuːl/ **I** *n* ridicule *m*; **to hold sb/sth up to ~** tourner qn/qch en ridicule; **to be met with ~** être tourné en ridicule; **to be an object of ~** [*hat, hairstyle*] provoquer la risée de tous; [*person*] être la risée de tous.
II *vtr* tourner [qch] en ridicule [*idea, proposal*].

ridiculous /rɪˈdɪkjʊləs/ *adj* ridicule; **to look ~** avoir l'air ridicule; **he's quite ~** il est parfaitement ridicule; **a ~ price** un prix ridicule.

ridiculously /rɪˈdɪkjʊləslɪ/ *adv* [*dressed*] de façon ridicule; [*cheap, easy, long, expensive*] ridiculement; **~ high prices** des prix ridiculement élevés.

ridiculousness /rɪˈdɪkjʊləsnɪs/ *n* ridicule *m*.

riding /ˈraɪdɪŋ/ ▶ **1282** Equit **I** *n* équitation *f*; **to go ~** faire de l'équitation.
II *modif* [*clothes, equipment, lesson*] d'équitation.

riding: **~ boots** *npl* bottes *fpl* d'équitation; **~ breeches** *npl* culotte *f* d'équitation; **~ crop** *n* cravache *f*; **~ habit** *n* tenue *f* d'amazone; **~ school** *n* centre *m* équestre; **~ stables** *n* manège *m*; **~ whip** *n* = **riding crop**.

rife /raɪf/ *adj* (*après v*) **to be ~** [*crime, disease, drug abuse*] régner; **speculation was ~** les conjectures allaient bon train; **a city ~ with disease/crime** une ville très touchée par la maladie/où règne le crime.

riff /rɪf/ *n* riff *m*; **guitar ~** un riff à la guitare.

riffle /ˈrɪfl/ *vtr* (also **~ through**) feuilleter [*pages*].

riffraff /ˈrɪfræf/ *n* péj populace *f* péj.

rifle /ˈraɪfl/ **I** *n* Mil, Hunt fusil *m*; (at fairground) carabine *f*; **to aim one's ~ at** braquer son fusil sur; **to fire a ~** tirer un coup de fusil (**at** sur).
II *vtr* **1** vider, dévaliser [*house*]; vider [*drawer, safe*]; **2** (make grooves in) rayer [*gun barrel*].
■ **rifle through**: **~ through [sth]** fouiller dans.

rifle: **~ butt** *n* crosse *f* d'un fusil; **~ grenade** *n* grenade *f* à fusil; **~ range** *n* Mil champ *m* de tir; (at fairground) stand *m* de tir; **~ shot** *n* coup *m* de fusil.

rift /rɪft/ *n* **1** (disagreement) désaccord *m* (**between** entre; **with** avec; **about** sur); (permanent) rupture *f* (**between** entre; **with** avec; **about** à propos de); **there is a widening** ou **deepening ~** le fossé se creuse; **2** (split) (in rock) fissure *f*; (in clouds) trouée *f*; **a deep ~**

une crevasse; **3** US (in stream) haut-fond *m* créant des rapides.

rift valley *n* rift *m*.

rig /rɪɡ/ **I** *n* **1** Naut gréement *m*; **2** (for drilling oil) (on land) tour *f* de forage; (offshore) plate-forme *f* pétrolière; **floating ~** plate-forme (pétrolière) flottante; **3** (piece of equipment) appareil *m*; **lighting ~** système *m* d'éclairage; **4** US (carriage) équipage *m*; **5**○ US (lorry) semi-remorque *m*; **6**○ (clothes) ▸**rig-out**.

II *vtr* (*p prés etc* **-gg-**) **1** Naut gréer [*boat*]; **2** (control fraudulently) truquer [*election, result competition, race*]; manipuler [*market*].

■ **rig out**: **~ [sth/sb] out, ~ out [sb/sth] 1** (equip) habiller [*soldier, person*] (**with** de); équiper [*car, house*] (**with** de); **2**○ (dress) **to ~ sb out in sth** habiller qn de qch; **he was ~ged out in his best clothes** il portait ses plus beaux habits.

■ **rig up**: **~ up [sth]** installer [*equipment, system*]; improviser [*clothesline, shelter*].

rigger /ˈrɪɡə(r)/ **▸1692** *n* **1** Naut gréeur *m*; **2** (in rowing) portant *m*; **3** (oil-rig worker) *ouvrier sur une plate-forme pétrolière*.

rigging /ˈrɪɡɪŋ/ *n* **1** Naut gréement *m*; **2** Aviat (of balloon, biplane) haubanage *m*; **3** (fraudulent control) (of election, competition, result) truquage *m*; (of share prices) Fin manipulation *f* illégale; **vote-** ou **poll-~** fraude *f* électorale.

right /raɪt/ **▸1173** **I** *n* **1** (side, direction) droite *f*; **keep to the ~** Aut tenez votre droite; **on** ou **to your ~ is the town hall** à votre droite se trouve la mairie; **he doesn't know his left from his ~** il ne sait pas distinguer sa droite de sa gauche; **take the second ~ after Richmond Road** prenez la deuxième à droite après Richmond Road; **2** Pol (also **Right**) **the ~** la droite; **they are further to the ~ than the Conservatives** ils sont plus à droite que les conservateurs; **3** (morally) bien *m*; **~ and wrong** le bien et le mal; **he doesn't know ~ from wrong** il ne sait pas distinguer le bien du mal; **to be in the ~** avoir raison; **4** (just claim) droit *m*; **to have a ~ to sth** avoir droit à qch; **to have a** ou **the ~ to do** avoir le droit de faire; **the ~ to work/to strike** le droit au travail/de grève; **she has no ~ to treat you like that** elle n'a pas le droit de te traiter comme ça; **he may be the boss, but that doesn't give him the ~ to treat you like that** c'est peut-être lui le patron, mais ça ne lui donne pas le droit de te traiter comme ça; **what ~ have you to criticize me like that?** de quel droit est-ce que vous me critiquez comme ça?; **I've got every ~ to be annoyed** j'ai toutes les raisons d'être agacé; **you have every ~ to do so** c'est tout à fait ton droit; **to know one's ~s** connaître ses droits; **one's ~s as a consumer** ses droits de consommateur; **human ~s** droits de l'homme; **civil ~s** droits civils; **to be within one's ~s** être dans son droit; **you would be quite within your ~s to refuse** tu serais tout à fait dans ton droit de refuser; **the property belongs to him as of ~** la propriété lui revient de plein droit; **her husband is a celebrity in his own ~** son mari est une célébrité à part entière; **the gardens are worth a visit in their own ~** à eux seuls, les jardins méritent la visite; **she is a countess in her own ~** elle est comtesse de par sa naissance; **5** (in boxing) droite *f*; **he hit him a ~ to the jaw** il lui a porté une droite or un direct du droit à la mâchoire.

II rights *npl* **1** Comm, Jur droits *mpl*; **the translation/film ~s of a book** les droits de traduction/d'adaptation cinématographique d'un livre; **mining ~s, mineral ~s** droits miniers; **to have the sole ~s to sth** avoir l'exclusivité des droits de qch; **2** (moral) **the ~s and wrongs of a matter** les aspects *mpl* moraux d'une question; **the ~s and wrongs of capital punishment** les arguments *mpl* pour et contre la peine de mort.

III *adj* **1** (as opposed to left) droit, de droite; **one's ~ eye/arm** son œil/bras droit; **on my ~ hand** (position) sur ma droite; **'eyes ~!'** Mil 'tête droite!'; **2** (morally correct) bien; (fair, just) juste; **it's not ~ to steal** ce n'est pas bien de voler; **you were quite ~ to criticize him** tu as eu tout à fait raison de le critiquer; **it's only ~ that she should know** c'est normal qu'elle soit mise au courant; **I thought it ~ to tell him** j'ai jugé bon de lui dire; **it is ~ and proper that they should be punished** ce n'est que justice qu'ils soient punis; **to do the ~ thing** faire ce qu'il faut; **I hope we're doing the ~ thing** j'espère que nous ne faisons pas une erreur; **you know you're doing the ~ thing** tu sais que c'est la meilleure chose à faire; **to do the ~ thing by sb** faire son devoir envers qn; **3** (correct, true) [*choice, conditions, decision, direction, road etc*] bon/bonne; [*word*] juste; (accurate) [*time*] exact; **to be ~** [*person*] avoir raison; [*answer*] être juste; **I was ~ to distrust him** j'avais raison de me méfier de lui; **you were ~ about her, she's a real gossip** tu avais raison à son sujet, c'est une vraie commère; **you're quite ~!** tu as tout à fait raison!; **that's the ~ answer** c'est la bonne réponse; **she got all the answers ~** elle a répondu juste à toutes les questions; **that's ~** c'est ça; **that's ~, call me a liar!** iron c'est ça, traite-moi de menteur!; **that can't be ~** ça ne peut pas être ça; **what's the ~ time?** quelle est l'heure exacte?; **it's not the ~ time to go away on holiday** GB ou **vacation** US ce n'est pas le bon moment pour partir en vacances; **I hear you're going away on holiday** GB ou **vacation** US, **is that ~?** on m'a dit que tu partais en vacances, est-ce que c'est vrai?; **so you're a student, is that ~?** alors tu es étudiant, c'est ça?; **am I ~ in thinking that...?** ai-je raison de penser que...?; **I think I am ~ in saying that** je pense ne pas me tromper en disant que; **is this the ~ train for Dublin?** c'est bien le train pour Dublin?; **is this the ~ way to the station?** est-ce que c'est la bonne direction pour aller à la gare?; **to do sth the ~ way** faire qch comme il faut; **the ~ side of a piece of material** l'endroit d'un tissu; **make sure it's facing the ~ side** ou **way up** fais bien attention à ce qu'il soit à l'endroit; **to get one's facts ~** être sûr de ce qu'on avance; **you've got the spelling ~** l'orthographe est bonne; **I can't think of the ~ word for it** je n'arrive pas à trouver le mot juste; **they've been rehearsing that scene for weeks and they still haven't got it ~** ils répètent cette scène depuis des semaines et elle n'est toujours pas au point; **let's hope he gets it ~ this time** espérons qu'il y arrivera cette fois-ci; **it's not the ~ size** ce n'est pas la bonne taille; **it wouldn't look ~ if we didn't attend** ça serait mal vu si on n'y assistait pas; **how ~ you are!** comme vous avez raison!; **time proved him ~** le temps lui a donné raison; **4** (most suitable) qui convient; **those aren't the ~ clothes for gardening** ce ne sont pas des vêtements qui conviennent au jardinage; **you need to have the ~ equipment** il te faut le matériel approprié; **when the time is ~** quand le moment sera venu; **you need to choose the model that's ~ for you** il faut que vous choisissiez le modèle qui vous convient; **I'm sure she's the ~ person for the job** je suis sûr que c'est la personne qu'il faut pour le poste; **to be in the ~ place at the ~ time** être là où il faut au bon moment; **to know the ~ people** connaître des gens bien placés; **he was careful to say all the ~ things** il a pris grand soin de dire tout ce qu'il faut dire dans ce genre de situation; **just the ~ combination of humour and pathos** juste le bon équilibre entre l'humour et le pathétique; **5** (in good order) [*machine, vehicle*] en bon état, qui fonctionne bien; (healthy) [*person*] bien portant; **I don't feel quite ~ these days** je ne me sens pas très bien ces jours-ci; **a drink will set you ~** un verre te fera du bien; **the engine isn't quite ~** le moteur ne fonctionne pas très bien; **there's something not quite ~ about him** il a quelque chose de bizarre; **I sensed that things were not quite ~** j'ai senti qu'il y avait quelque chose qui n'allait pas; **things are coming ~ at last** les choses commencent enfin à s'arranger; **6** (in order) **to put** ou **set ~** corriger [*mistake*]; réparer [*injustice*]; arranger [*situation*]; réparer [*machine, engine etc*]; **to put** ou **set one's watch ~** remettre sa montre à l'heure; **they gave him a month to put** ou **set things ~** ils lui ont donné un mois pour arranger les choses; **to put** ou **set sb ~** détromper qn; **I soon put her ~** je l'ai vite détrompée; **this medicine should put** ou **set you ~** ce médicament devrait vous remettre sur pied; **7** Math [*angle, cone*] droit; **at ~ angles to** à angle droit avec, perpendiculaire à; **8**○ GB (emphatic) **he's a ~ idiot!** c'est un idiot fini!; **it's a ~ mess** c'est un vrai gâchis; **9**○ GB (ready) prêt; **are you ~?** tu es prêt?

IV *adv* **1** (of direction) à droite; **to turn ~** tourner à droite; **she looked neither ~ nor left** elle n'a regardé ni à droite ni à gauche; **they looked for him ~, left and centre**○ ils l'ont cherché partout; **they are arresting/killing people ~, left and centre**○ ils arrêtent/tuent les gens en masse; **2** (directly, straight) droit, directement; **it's ~ in front of you** c'est droit or juste devant toi; **I'll be ~ back** je reviens tout de suite; **go ~ home** rentrez directement; **the path goes ~ down to the river** le chemin conduit tout droit à la rivière; **~ before** juste avant; **~ after dinner/Christmas** juste après le dîner/Noël; **the train goes ~ through to Nice** le train va directement à Nice; **he walked ~ up to her** il a marché droit vers elle; **3** (exactly) **~ in the middle of the room** en plein milieu or au beau milieu de la pièce; **he interrupted them ~ in the middle of their dinner** il les a interrompus en plein milieu or au beau milieu de leur dîner; **~ now** (immediately) tout de suite; (at this point in time) en ce moment; **I'm staying ~ here** je ne bougerai pas d'ici; **your book's ~ there by the window** ton livre est juste là à côté de la fenêtre; **he sat down ~ beside me** il s'est assis juste à côté de moi; **the bullet hit him ~ in the forehead** la balle l'a touché en plein front; **they live ~ on the river** ils habitent juste au bord de la rivière; **the house gives ~ onto the street** la maison donne directement sur la rue; **4** (correctly) juste, comme il faut; **you're not doing it ~** tu ne fais pas ça comme il faut; **you did ~ not to speak to her** tu as bien fait de ne pas lui parler; **I guessed ~** j'ai deviné juste; **if I remember ~** si je me souviens bien; **nothing seems to be going ~ for me** rien ne va dans ma vie; **did I hear you ~?** est-ce que je t'ai bien entendu?; **5** (completely) tout; **a wall goes ~ around the garden** il y a un mur tout autour du jardin; **go ~ to the end of the street** allez tout au bout de la rue; **if you go ~ back to the beginning** si vous revenez tout au début; **~ at the bottom** tout au fond; **to turn ~ around** faire demi-tour; **her room is ~ at the top of the house** sa chambre est tout en haut de la maison; **to read a book ~ through** lire un livre jusqu'au bout; **the noise echoed ~ through the building** le bruit a retenti dans tout l'immeuble; **she looked ~ through me** fig elle a fait semblant de ne pas me voir; **to turn the radio/the central heating ~ up** mettre la radio/le chauffage central à fond; **~ up until the 1950s** jusque dans les années 50; **the door handle came ~ off in my hand** la poignée m'est restée dans les mains; **the roof of the house was blown ~ off by the explosion** le toit de la maison a été emporté dans l'explosion; **we're ~ behind you!** nous vous soutenons totalement!; **6** **▸1268** GB (in titles) **the Right Honourable Jasper Pinkerton** le très

honorable Jasper Pinkerton; **the Right Honourable Gentleman** (form of address in parliament) ≈ notre distingué collègue; **the Right Reverend Felix Bush** le très Révérend Felix Bush; **7**† ou GB dial (emphatic) très; **he knew ~ well what was happening** il savait très bien ce qui se passait; **a ~ royal reception** une réception somptueuse; **8** (very well) bon; **~, let's have a look** bon, voyons ça.
V *vtr* **1** (restore to upright position) redresser [*vehicle, ship*]; **2** (correct) réparer [*injustice*]; **to ~ a wrong** redresser un tort.
VI *v refl* **to ~ oneself** [*person*] se redresser; **to ~ itself** [*ship, plane*] se rétablir; [*situation*] se rétablir.
IDIOMS **to see sb ~** (financially) dépanner○ qn; (in other ways) sortir qn d'affaire; **here's £10, that should see you ~** voici 10 livres, ça devrait te dépanner○; **~ you are**○**!**, **~-oh**○**!** GB d'accord!, d'ac○!; **~ enough**○ effectivement; **he's ~ up there!** il est parmi les meilleurs!; **by ~s** normalement, en principe; **by ~s it should belong to me** normalement or en principe, ça devrait m'appartenir; **to put** ou **set sth to ~s** arranger qch.

right: **~ angle** *n* angle *m* droit; **~-angled** *adj* à angle droit; **~-angled triangle** *n* triangle *m* rectangle; **~ away** *adv* tout de suite.

righteous /ˈraɪtʃəs/ **I** *n* **the ~** (+ *v pl*) les justes *mpl*.
II *adj* **1** (virtuous) [*anger*] juste (*before n*); [*thoughts, person*] vertueux/-euse; **to feel ~** se sentir vertueux; **2** (justifiable) [*anger*] juste (*before n*); [*indignation*] vertueux/-euse (*before n*).

righteously /ˈraɪtʃəslɪ/ *adv* de façon vertueuse.

righteousness /ˈraɪtʃəsnɪs/ *n* (rectitude) droiture *f*; Bible (goodness) vertu *f*.

rightful /ˈraɪtfl/ *adj* légitime.

rightfully /ˈraɪtfəlɪ/ *adv* [*mine, yours etc*] légitimement; [*claim, belong*] en droit.

right-hand /ˈraɪthænd/ *adj* du côté *m* droit; **it's on the ~ side** c'est sur la droite.

right-hand drive, **rhd** **I** *n* conduite *f* à droite; **car with ~** voiture avec (la) conduite à droite.
II *modif* [*vehicle*] avec (la) conduite à droite.

right: **~-handed** *adv* [*person*] droitier/-ière; [*blow, stroke*] du droit; Tech [*screw*] à droite; **~-hander** *n* (person) droitier/-ière *m/f*; (blow) coup *m* du droit.

right-hand man *n* bras *m* droit; **he's her ~** c'est son bras droit.

rightism /ˈraɪtɪzəm/ *n* Pol opinions *fpl* de droite, droitisme *m*.

rightist /ˈraɪtɪst/ souvent péj **I** *n* droitiste *mf*.
II *adj* [*party, régime*] de droite.

rightly /ˈraɪtlɪ/ *adv* **1** (accurately) [*describe, guess*] correctement; **2** (justifiably) à juste titre; **and ~ so** et pour cause; **~ or wrongly** à tort ou à raison; **3** (with certainty) au juste; **I can't ~ say** je ne peux pas dire; **I don't ~ know** je ne sais pas au juste.

right: **~-minded** *adj* bien-pensant; **~-of-centre** *adj* Pol centre-droite *inv*; **~ off** *adv* tout de suite.

right of way *n* **1** Aut priorité *f*; **it's your ~** c'est vous qui avez la priorité; **2** (over land, property) (right) droit *m* de passage; (path) sentier *m* public.

right-on○ /ˌraɪtˈɒn/ **I** *adj* péj **they're very ~**○ ils s'appliquent à être idéologiquement corrects sur tout.
II right on *excl* US ça marche!

right: **~s issue** *n* émission *f* de droits de souscription; **~-thinking** *adj* bien-pensant; **~ whale** *n* baleine *f* franche.

right wing **I** *n* **1** Pol (also **Right Wing**) **the ~** la droite; **2** Sport ailier *m* droit.
II right-wing *adj* Pol [*party, policy, attitude*] de droite; **they are very ~** ils sont très à droite.

right-winger *n* **1** Pol personne *f* de droite; **2** Sport ailier *m* droit.

righty-ho○ /ˈraɪtɪhəʊ/ *excl* GB d'accord!, d'ac○!

rigid /ˈrɪdʒɪd/ *adj* **1** (strict) [*rules, system*] rigide; [*controls, adherence, timetable*] strict; **2** (inflexible) [*person, attitude*] rigide; **3** (stiff) [*material, container*] rigide; [*body, bearing*] raide; **to stand ~** se tenir très raide; **to be ~ with fear** être mort de peur.
IDIOMS **to bore sb ~**○ ennuyer qn à mourir; **to shake sb ~**○ GB filer un choc à qn○.

rigidity /rɪˈdʒɪdətɪ/ *n* rigidité *f*; **moral ~** rigidité dans le domaine moral; **the ~ of her bearing** la raideur de son maintien.

rigidly /ˈrɪdʒɪdlɪ/ *adv* **1** [*stand, lie*] de façon très raide; [*stand to attention*] avec beaucoup de raideur; **2** [*opposed*] fermement; [*controlled*] rigoureusement; [*obey*] rigoureusement; [*act, behave*] avec rigidité.

rigmarole /ˈrɪgmərəʊl/ *n* long discours *m* (**about** au sujet de); **to go through a ~** (verbal) se lancer dans un long discours; (procedure) faire tout un circuit○.

rigor *n* US ▶ **rigour**.

rigor mortis /ˌrɪgə ˈmɔːtɪs/ *n* rigidité *f* cadavérique; **~ had set in** la rigidité cadavérique était amorcée.

rigorous /ˈrɪgərəs/ *adj* **1** (strict) [*rules, discipline, controls*] rigoureux/-euse; [*regime*] sévère; [*adherence, observance*] strict; **2** (careful) rigoureux/-euse.

rigorously /ˈrɪgərəslɪ/ *adv* [*test, enforce, interrogate*] rigoureusement.

rigour GB, **rigor** US /ˈrɪgə(r)/ **I** *n* (severity, scrupulousness) rigueur *f*; **academic** ou **intellectual ~** rigueur intellectuelle; **the ~ of the law** l'inflexibilité de la loi.
II rigours *npl* (hardship) rigueurs *fpl*.

rig-out○ /ˈrɪgaʊt/ *n* tenue *f*.

rile○ /raɪl/ *vtr* énerver; **it ~s me that** cela m'énerve que (+ *subj*); **to get ~d** (**up**) s'énerver (**about** à propos de).

rill /rɪl/ *n* **1** littér (stream) ruisselet *m*; **2** (on moon) rainure *f*.

rim /rɪm/ **I** *n* **1** (of container, crater) bord *m*; **a cup with a gold ~** une tasse cerclée d'or; **2** (on wheel) jante *f*; **3** (in basketball) anneau *m*.
II *vtr* (*p prés etc* **-mm-**) [*mountains*] entourer [*valley*].
III -rimmed (*dans composés*) **steel-/gold-~med spectacles** lunettes *fpl* à monture d'acier/d'or.

rime /raɪm/ *n* **1** = **rhyme**; **2** littér ou dial (frost) givre *m*.

rimless glasses /ˈrɪmlɪs/ *n* lunettes *fpl* non cerclées.

rind /raɪnd/ *n* **1** (on cheese) croûte *f*; (on bacon) couenne *f*; **2** (on fruit) peau *f*; **lemon ~** Culin zeste *m* de citron; **3** (bark) écorce *f*.

ring /rɪŋ/ **I** *n* **1** (metal hoop) (for ornament, gymnast, attaching rope) anneau *m*; **to have a ~ in one's/its nose** avoir un anneau au nez; **a diamond/engagement ~** une bague de diamants/de fiançailles; **she wasn't wearing a** (**wedding**) **~** elle ne portait pas d'alliance; **2** (circle) (of people, on page) cercle *m*; **to form a ~** former un cercle: **to put a ~ round** entourer [qch] d'un cercle [*name, ad*]; **to have ~s under one's eyes** avoir les yeux cernés; **3** (sound) (at door) coup *m* de sonnette; (of phone) sonnerie *f*; (of crystal) tintement *m*; **hang up after three ~s** laisse sonner trois fois et puis raccroche; **to have a hollow ~** lit, fig sonner creux; **to have the ~ of truth** sonner vrai; **to have a nice ~ to it** sonner bien; **that story has a familiar ~** (**to it**) j'ai déjà entendu cette histoire quelque part; **4** GB (phone call) coup *m* de téléphone or fil○; **to give sb a ~** passer un coup de fil○ à qn; **5** Sport (for horses, circus) piste *f*; (for boxing) ring *m*; **to retire from the ~ aged 35** se retirer de la boxe à l'âge de 35 ans; **6** (of smugglers, pornographers) réseau *m*; (of dealers, speculators) syndicat *m*; **drugs ~** réseau de trafiquants de drogue; **7** Zool (on swan, bird) bague *f*; **8** Astron anneau *m*; **Saturn's ~s** les anneaux de Saturne; **9** (on cooker) (electric) plaque *f*; (gas) brûleur *m*; **three-~ hob** cuisinière *f* à trois plaques or brûleurs; **10** (set of bells) jeu *m* (**of** de).
II *vtr* **1** (cause to sound) (*prét* **rang**; *pp* **rung**) faire sonner [*bell*]; **to ~ the doorbell** ou **bell** sonner; **2** GB Telecom (*prét* **rang**; *pp* **rung**) appeler [*person, number, station*]; **3** (encircle) (*prét, pp* **ringed**) [*trees, buildings*] entourer; [*police, troops, protesters*] encercler; **to be ~ed in black/by cliffs** être entouré de noir/par des falaises; **4** Zool, Ecol (*prét, pp* **ringed**) baguer [*tree, swan, bird*].
III *vi* (*prét* **rang**; *pp* **rung**) **1** (sound) [*bell, telephone*] sonner; **the doorbell rang** on a sonné à la porte; **it** ou **the number is ~ing** ça sonne; **2** (sound bell) [*person*] sonner; **to ~ at the door** sonner à la porte; **to ~ for sb** sonner qn; **you rang, Sir?** Monsieur a sonné?; **'please ~ for service'** 'prière de sonner'; **3** (resonate) [*footsteps, laughter, words*] résonner; **his words were still ~ing in my ears** ses mots résonnaient encore à mes oreilles; **their steps rang down the corridor** leurs pas résonnaient dans le couloir; **the house rang with laughter** la maison résonnait de rires; **that noise makes my ears ~** ce bruit fait bourdonner mes oreilles; **to ~ true** sonner vrai; **to ~ false** ou **hollow** fig sonner creux/creuse; **4** GB Telecom téléphoner; **to ~ for** appeler [*taxi , ambulance*].
IDIOMS **to ~ down/up the curtain** baisser/lever le rideau; fig **to ~ down the curtain on an era** marquer la fin d'une ère; **to ~ in the New Year** fêter le Nouvel an; **~ out the old, ~ in the new** tournons le dos au passé et faisons confiance à l'avenir; **to run ~s round** éclipser.
■ **ring around** GB (haphazardly) téléphoner un peu partout; (transmitting message) appeler tous les intéressés.
■ **ring back** GB: ¶ **~ back** rappeler; ¶ **~ [sb] back** rappeler [*caller*].
■ **ring in** GB (to work) téléphoner au bureau; **to ~ in sick** téléphoner (au bureau) pour dire qu'on est souffrant.
■ **ring off** GB raccrocher.
■ **ring out**: ¶ **~ out** [*voice, cry*] retentir; [*bells*] sonner; ¶ **~ out [sth]** [*bells*] carillonner [*news, message*].
■ **ring round** = **ring around**.
■ **ring up** GB: ¶ **~ up** téléphoner; ¶ **~ up [sth], ~ [sth] up** **1** (on phone) téléphoner à [*enquiries, station*]; **2** (on cash register) enregistrer [*figure, total*]; ¶ **~ up [sb], ~ [sb] up** téléphoner à [*friend, operator*].

ring: **~-a-ring-a-roses** ▶ 1282 *n*: *ronde et jeu enfantins*; **~ binder** *n* classeur *m* à anneaux.

ringdove /ˈrɪŋdʌv/ *n* **1** (wood pigeon) ramier *m*; **2** (turtle dove) tourterelle *f* rieuse.

ringed plover /ˌrɪŋd ˈplʌvə(r)/ *n* grand gravelot *m*.

ringer○ /ˈrɪŋə(r)/ *n* US imposteur *m*.

ring: **~-fence** *vtr* GB réserver [*funds, grant*]; **~ finger** *n* annulaire *m*.

ringing /ˈrɪŋɪŋ/ **I** *n* **1** (noise of bell, alarm) sonnerie *f*; **2** (in ears) bourdonnement *m*; **3** = **bell-ringing**.
II *adj* lit, fig [*declaration, voice*] retentissant.

ringing tone *n* GB tonalité *f* de sonnerie.

ringleader /ˈrɪŋliːdə(r)/ *n* meneur/-euse *m/f*.

ringlet /ˈrɪŋlɪt/ *n* anglaise *f*.

ring main *n* circuit *m* principal.

ringmaster /ˈrɪŋmɑːstə(r)/ *n* Monsieur Loyal; **the ~ entered** Monsieur Loyal est entré.

ring: **~ ouzel** *n* merle *m* à plastron; **~-pull** *n* anneau *m*; **~-pull can** *n* boîte *f* à ouverture facile.

ringroad /ˈrɪŋrəʊd/*n* GB périphérique *m*; **inner ~** ceinture *f*.

ringside /ˈrɪŋsaɪd/ *n* **at the ~** près du

ring; **our commentator at the ~** notre commentateur en direct du match de boxe.
IDIOMS **to have a ~ seat** fig être aux premières loges.

ring: **~ spanner** *n* clé *f* polygonale; **~-tailed** *adj* à queue rayée.

ringworm /ˈrɪŋwɜːm/ **▶1354** *n* herpès *m* circiné, mycose *f*; **~ on the scalp** teigne *f*.

rink /rɪŋk/ *n* patinoire *f*.

rinky-dink○ /ˌrɪŋkɪˈdɪŋk/ US **I** *n* pacotille *f*.
II *adj* (old-fashioned) ringard○; (broken-down) déglingué○; (cheap quality) de pacotille.

rinse /rɪns/ **I** *n* rinçage *m*; **to give sth a ~** rincer qch [*clothes, dishes*]; **give your mouth/hands a ~** rincez-vous la bouche/les mains.
II *vtr* **1** (to remove soap) rincer [*dishes, clothes*]; **2** (wash) laver; **to ~ the soap off one's hands/out of one's hair** se rincer les mains/les cheveux; **to ~ one's hands/mouth** se rincer les mains/la bouche.
■ **rinse out**: ¶ **~ out** [*colour, dye*] partir au lavage; ¶ **~ [sth] out, ~ out [sth]** rincer [*mouth, glass*].

rinse cycle *n* cycle *m* de rinçage.

Rio de Janeiro /ˌriːəʊ də dʒəˈnɪərəʊ/ **▶1818** *pr n* Rio de Janeiro.

riot /ˈraɪət/ **I** *n* **1** gen (disturbance) émeute *f*, révolte *f*; Jur émeute *f*; **food ~** émeute suscitée par la pénurie alimentaire; **football ~** affrontement *m* de supporters; **prison ~** mutinerie *f*; **race ~** émeute raciale; **2** (profuse display) **a ~ of** une profusion de [*colours, patterns*]; **3**○ **to be a ~** (hilarious) être tordant○.
II *vi* gen se soulever; [*prisoner*] se mutiner.
IDIOMS **to run ~** (behave wildly) lit se déchaîner; fig [*emotion, imagination*] se débrider; [*inflation*] galoper; (grow profusely) [*plant*] proliférer.

Riot Act *n* Jur, Hist loi *f* britannique antiémeutes.
IDIOMS **to read the riot act to sb** chapitrer qn.

riot control *n* contrôle *m* des émeutes.

rioter /ˈraɪətə(r)/ *n* gen émeutier/-ière *m*/*f*; (in prison) mutin *m*.

riot: **~ gear** *n* tenue *f* antiémeutes; **~ gun** *n* mousqueton *m*.

rioting /ˈraɪətɪŋ/ **I** *n* ¢ émeutes *fpl*, bagarres *fpl*.
II *adj* [*people, crowds*] insurgé.

riotous /ˈraɪətəs/ *adj* **1** Jur séditieux/-ieuse; **~ assembly** attroupement *m* séditieux; **2** (boisterous) [*laughter*] exubérant; [*welcome*] délirant; [*play, film*] hilarant; **3** (wanton) [*living, party, evening*] débridé.

riotously /ˈraɪətəslɪ/ *adv* **~ funny** à se tordre or mourir de rire.

riotousness /ˈraɪətəsnɪs/ *n* déchaînement *m*.

riot: **~ police** *n* forces *fpl* d'ordre; **~ shield** *n* bouclier *m* antiémeutes; **~ squad** *n* brigade *f* antiémeutes.

rip /rɪp/ **I** *n* **1** (tear) accroc *m* (**in** dans); **2** = **riptide**.
II *vtr* (*p prés etc* **-pp-**) **1** (tear) déchirer; **to ~ sth with one's bare hands/with one's teeth/with a knife** déchirer qch à mains nues/avec les dents/avec un couteau; **to ~ a hole in sth** faire un trou dans qch; **to ~ sth/sb to pieces** ou **shreds** lit, fig réduire qch/qn en pièces; **2** (snatch, pull) **to ~ sth off** ou **from sth/from sb** arracher qch de qch/à qn.
III *vi* (*p prés etc* **-pp-**) [*fabric*] se déchirer.
IDIOMS **to let ~**○ tempêter○ (**against** contre; **about** à propos de); **to let ~ at sb** engueuler◑ qn; **to let ~ a stream of abuse** lancer un flot d'injures; **let it** ou **her ~**○! (of car) fonce○!
■ **rip apart**: **~ [sth] apart 1** lit [*bomb blast, person*] déchiqueter [*car, building, object*]; **2**○ fig défoncer [*team, team's defences*]; descendre○ [*reputation*].
■ **rip down**: **~ down [sth], ~ [sth] down** arracher [*picture, notice*].
■ **rip off**: ¶ **~ off [sth], ~ [sth] off 1** lit [*person, wind, blast*] arracher [*garment, roof*]; **2**○ (steal) rafler○ [*idea, design, goods*]; ¶ **~ off [sb], ~ [sb] off**○ arnaquer◑; **to get ~ped off** se faire arnaquer◑.
■ **rip into**: **~ into [sth /sb] 1** (enter forcefully) [*knife*] s'enfoncer dans; **2** (attack) [*wind*] frapper [qch] de plein fouet; fig descendre [qn] en flammes [*person*].
■ **rip open**: **~ open [sth], ~ [sth] open** déchirer [*envelope, parcel*]; crever [*bag*].
■ **rip out**: **~ out [sth], ~ [sth] out** arracher [*page, fireplace, heart*].
■ **rip through**: **~ through [sth]** [*bomb blast*] défoncer [*building*]; [*fire*] investir, envahir [*building*].
■ **rip up**: **~ up [sth], ~ [sth] up** déchirer [*letter, paper, contract*]; arracher [*floorboards, carpet*].

RIP (*abrév* = **requiescat** ou **requiescant in pace**) **Anne Smith, ~** ici repose Anne Smith.

riparian /raɪˈpeərɪən/ *n, adj* Jur riverain/-e (*m*/*f*) (*d'un cours d'eau*).

riparian rights *npl* riveraineté *f* ¢.

ripcord /ˈrɪpkɔːd/ *n* poignée *f* d'ouverture.

ripe /raɪp/ *adj* **1** [*fruit*] mûr; [*cheese*] fait; **2** (ready) [*person*] litter mûr (**for** pour); **the time is ~** c'est le bon moment; **the time is ~ for change/reform** c'est le moment d'introduire des changements/des réformes; **a site ~ for development** un terrain bon pour la construction; **3** péj (coarse) [*language*] grossier/-ière; **to smell ~** sentir mauvais.
IDIOMS **to live to a ~ old age** vivre jusqu'à un âge très avancé; **she lived to the ~ old age of 90** elle a vécu jusqu'au bel âge de 90 ans.

ripen /ˈraɪpən/ **I** *vtr* mûrir [*fruit*]; affiner [*cheese*]; **sun-~ed peaches** pêches mûries au soleil.
II *vi* **1** [*fruit*] mûrir; [*cheese*] se faire; **2** littér [*feelings, relationship*] s'épanouir; **their friendship ~ed into love** leur amitié se transforma en amour.

ripeness /ˈraɪpnɪs/ *n* lit, fig maturité *f*.

rip: **~-off**○ *n* (all contexts) arnaque◑ *f*; **~-off artist**○, **~-off merchant**○ *n* arnaqueur/-euse◑ *m*/*f*.

riposte /rɪˈpɒst/ *n* **1** littér riposte *f*; **to make a witty** ou **clever ~** faire une riposte spirituelle; **to make a ~** riposter; **2** (in fencing) riposte *f*.

ripper /ˈrɪpə(r)/ *n* (murderer) éventreur *m*.

ripping†○ /ˈrɪpɪŋ/ *adj* GB épatant, sensationnel/-elle; **~ yarn** histoire *f* sensationnelle.

ripple /ˈrɪpl/ **I** *n* **1** (in water, corn, hair) ondulation *f*; **to make ~s in the water** faire des ondulations dans l'eau; **2** (sound) **a ~ of applause/laughter** une cascade d'applaudissements/de rires; **3** (repercussion) répercussion *f*; **this measure will send ~s through the economy** cette mesure aura des répercussions sur l'économie; **4** (ice cream) glace *f* panachée.
II *vtr* faire onduler [*hair*]; faire des vaguelettes à la surface de [*water*]; **to ~ one's muscles** faire saillir ses muscles.
III *vi* **1** [*water*] (make waves) se rider; (make sound) clapoter; **the water ~d down the pane/over the stones** l'eau coulait sur la vitre/sur les pierres; **2** [*corn*] ondoyer; [*hair, fabric*] onduler; [*muscles*] saillir; **applause/laughter ~d through the room** on entendait des cascades d'applaudissements/de rires dans la salle.

ripple: **~ effect** *n* effet *m* secondaire; **~ mark** *n* ondulation *f* dans le sable.

rip-rap /ˈrɪpræp/ *n* Civ Eng enrochement *m*.

rip-roaring○ /ˈrɪprɔːrɪŋ/ *adj* [*party, show*] délirant; [*success*] dingue○; **to have a ~ time** s'éclater○.

rip: **~saw** *n* scie *f* à refendre; **~tide** *n* courant *m* de marée.

rise /raɪz/ **I** *n* **1** (increase) (in amount, number, inflation, rates) augmentation *f* (**in** de); (in prices, pressure) hausse *f* (**in** de); (in temperature) élévation *f* (**in** de); (in standards) amélioration *f* (**in** de); **to be on the ~** [*crime, inflation, number*] être en augmentation; [*prices*] être en hausse; **2** GB (also **pay ~, wage ~**) augmentation *f* (de salaire); **3** (upward movement) (of plane, balloon) ascension *f*; (of water, liquid, sea) montée *f*; **the ~ and fall of his chest** le mouvement de sa respiration; **4** (progress) (of person) ascension *f*; (of country, company, empire) essor *m*; (of doctrine, ideology) montée *f*; **Hitler's ~ and fall** l'ascension et la chute de Hitler; **the ~ and fall of the Roman Empire** l'essor et le déclin de l'Empire romain; **her ~ to fame** son accession *f* à la gloire; **5** (slope) montée *f*; **there's a slight ~ in the road here** la route monte légèrement ici; **6** (hill) butte *f*; **7** (source) Geog source *f*; **the river has its ~ in...** le fleuve prend sa source dans...; **to give ~ to** fig donner lieu à [*rumours, speculation, suspicion*]; susciter [*happiness, resentment, frustration*]; causer [*problem, increase, unemployment*].
II *vi* (*prét* **rose**; *pp* **risen**) **1** (become higher) [*water*] monter; [*price, rate, number, temperature*] augmenter; [*voice*] devenir plus fort; **to ~ above** [*temperature, amount*] dépasser; **his voice rose to a shout** il a élevé la voix jusqu'à crier; **his voice rose in anger** la colère lui a fait élever la voix; **2** fig (intensify) [*pressure*] augmenter; [*tension*] monter; [*frustration, anger, hopes*] grandir; **3** (get up) [*person*] se lever; (after falling) se relever; **to ~ from the chair** se lever du fauteuil; **to ~ from the dead** ressusciter des morts; **'~ and shine!'** 'debout!'; **'all ~'** Jur 'Messieurs, la cour!'; **4** (ascend) = **rise up**; **5** (rebel) = **rise up**; **6** (meet successfully) **to ~ to** se montrer à la hauteur de [*occasion, challenge*]; **7** (progress) [*person*] réussir; **to ~ to** devenir [*director, manager*]; s'élever à [*rank, position*]; **to ~ to fame** atteindre la célébrité; **he rose from apprentice to manager** il a commencé comme apprenti et est devenu directeur; **she rose from nothing to become** partant de rien elle a réussi à devenir; **to ~ through the ranks** gravir tous les échelons; **8** (slope upwards) [*ground, road*] monter; [*mountain, cliff*] s'élever; **to ~ to a height of** s'élever à une hauteur de; **9** (appear over horizon) [*sun, moon, star*] se lever; **10** Geog (have source) **to ~ in** [*river*] prendre sa source dans [*mountain, area*]; **11** Culin [*dough, cake*] lever; **12** Admin, Jur, Pol [*committee, court, parliament*] lever la séance; **13** Fishg [*fish*] venir nager à la surface.
IDIOMS **to get** ou **take a ~ out of sb**○ faire enrager qn; **to ~**○ **to sth** (react) réagir à qch.
■ **rise above**: **~ above [sth]** (overcome) surmonter [*problems, jealousy, disagreements*].
■ **rise up 1** (ascend) [*ball, balloon, bird, plane*] s'élever; [*smoke, steam*] monter; fig [*building, mountain*] se dresser; **an office building rose up on the site of the old church** un immeuble de bureaux s'est construit à l'emplacement de la vieille église; **a great shout rose up from the crowd** un grand cri a jailli de la foule; **2** (rebel) littér [*people, region, nation*] se soulever (**against** contre); **to ~ up in revolt** se révolter.

risen /ˈrɪzn/ **I** *pp* ▶ **rise**.
II *adj* Relig ressuscité.

riser /ˈraɪzə(r)/ *n* **1** (person) **to be an early/a late ~** être un lève-tôt/un lève-tard; **2** (part of stair) contremarche *f*.

risibility /ˌrɪzəˈbɪlətɪ/ *n* sout ridicule *m*.

risible /ˈrɪzəbl/ *adj* sout ridicule.

rising /ˈraɪzɪŋ/ **I** *n* **1** (of sun, moon) lever *m*; (of tide) montée *f*; **2** (rebellion) soulèvement *m*.
II *adj* **1** (increasing) [*price, costs, inflation,*

Rivers

The English word river *can be either* fleuve *or* rivière *in French. Major rivers, all of which flow into the sea, are* fleuves*: the rest are* rivières. *Here are some examples of* fleuves *in France:* la Garonne, la Loire, la Seine, le Rhin, le Rhône *and* la Somme: *other* fleuves *include:* le Nil, le Danube, le Gange, le Tage, l'Indus, l'Amazone, le Congo, le Mississippi, le Niger *and* le Saint-Laurent.

The following French rivers are rivières: la Marne, l'Oise, l'Allier, la Dordogne, la Saône.

As in English, French uses the definite article with names of rivers:

the Thames	=	la Tamise
to go down the Rhine	=	descendre le Rhin
to live near the Seine	=	habiter près de la Seine
the course of the Danube	=	le cours du Danube

In English you can say the X, the X river *or* the river X. *In French it is always* le X (*or* la X):

the river Thames	=	la Tamise
the Potomac river	=	le Potomac

When the name of the river is used as an adjective, French has de + *definite article:*

Seine barges	=	les péniches de la Seine
a Rhine castle	=	un château des bords du Rhin
the Rhine estuary	=	l'estuaire du Rhin

unemployment, temperature] en hausse; [*demand, sales*] en augmentation; [*activity, tension, expectations*] grandissant; [*optimism, discontent, concern, number*] croissant; **2** (moving upwards) [*sun, moon*] levant; **3** (becoming successful) [*politician, singer*] en pleine ascension; [*talent*] prometteur/-euse; **he's a ~ star** il est en pleine ascension; **4** (moving to maturity) **the ~ generation** la nouvelle génération.

III *adv* **to be ~ twelve/forty** aller sur ses douze/quarante ans.

rising: **~ damp** *n* Constr humidité *f* (*s'élevant du sol*); **~ fives** *npl* GB Sch *enfants sur le point d'avoir cinq ans.*

risk /rɪsk/ **I** *n* **1** gen risque *m* (**of** de; **of doing** de faire); **there's a ~ of him catching the illness** ou **that he'll catch the illness** il risque d'attraper la maladie; **is there any ~ of him catching the illness?** est-ce qu'il risque d'attraper la maladie?; **there's a ~ that the operation will not succeed** l'opération comporte un risque d'échec; **there is no ~ to consumers** il n'y a aucun danger pour le consommateur; **without ~s to health** sans danger pour la santé; **to run the ~ of being injured/ridiculed** courir le risque d'être blessé/tourné en ridicule; **they run a higher ~ of cancer** ils courent un risque supérieur de cancer; **to take ~s** prendre des risques; **it's not worth the ~** le risque est trop grand; **children at ~** enfants menacés de violence; **their jobs are at ~** leurs emplois sont menacés; **the factory is at ~ of closure** l'usine est menacée de fermeture; **to put one's life/health at ~** mettre sa vie/santé en danger; **her health could be at ~** sa santé pourrait être compromise; **at one's own ~** à ses risques et périls; **he saved the child at considerable ~ to himself** il a sauvé l'enfant en prenant des risques considérables; **at the ~ of seeming ungrateful/paradoxical** au risque de paraître ingrat/de sembler paradoxal; **'at owner's ~'** 'aux risques et périls du propriétaire'; **2** Fin, Insur risque *m*; **to be a good/bad ~** être un bon/mauvais risque; **to spread a ~** diviser les risques; **an all-~s policy** Insur une assurance tous risques.

II *vtr* **1** (endanger) **to ~ one's life** risquer sa vie; **to ~ one's health** compromettre sa santé; **to ~ one's neck** (**doing**) lit, fig risquer sa peau (à faire); **2** (venture) **to ~ doing** courir le risque de faire; **we're prepared to ~ cash** nous sommes prêts à risquer de l'argent; **to ~ death** risquer la mort; **to ~ injury** risquer de se blesser; **to ~ one's all** risquer le tout pour le tout; **we decided to ~ it** nous avons décidé de prendre le risque; **let's ~ it anyway** c'est un risque à prendre.

risk: **~ asset ratio** *n* ratio *m* de couverture des risques; **~ capital** *n* Fin capital *m* à risque, capital-risque *m*; **~ factor** *n* facteur *m* de risque.

riskiness /ˈrɪskɪnɪs/ *n* risques *mpl* (**of** de).

risk: **~ management** *n* gestion *f* des risques; **~ manager** ▶ 1692 *n* Insur gestionnaire *mf* des risques.

risk-taker /ˈrɪskteɪkə(r)/ *n* fonceur/-euse○ *m/f*; **he's always been a ~** il a toujours aimé prendre des risques.

risk-taking /ˈrɪskteɪkɪŋ/ *n* **there must be no ~** on ne doit pas prendre de risques; **~ is part of the job** prendre des risques fait partie du travail.

risky /ˈrɪskɪ/ *adj* [*decision, undertaking*] risqué; [*bond, share, investment*] à risques; **it's too ~ to appoint a new director now** il est trop risqué de nommer un nouveau directeur maintenant; **it's ~ to invest so much money in one company** investir autant d'argent dans une seule société est risqué; **it's too ~** c'est trop risqué.

risotto /rɪˈzɒtəʊ/ *n* (*pl* **~s**) risotto *m*.

risqué /ˈriːskeɪ, US rɪˈskeɪ/ *adj* osé.

rissole /ˈrɪsəʊl/ *n* rissole *f*.

rite /raɪt/ *n* rite *m*; **to perform a ~** accomplir un rite; **initiation ~** rite d'initiation; **~ of passage** rite de passage; **the Rite of Spring** Mus le Sacre du printemps.

ritual /ˈrɪtʃʊəl/ **I** *n* rituel *m*, rites *mpl*; **to go through a ~** fig accomplir des gestes *mpl* rituels; **the courtship ~** Zool le cérémonial *m* d'approche; **he went through the ~ of thanking people** fig il a exprimé les remerciements de rigueur.

II *adj* [*dance, gesture, murder*] rituel/-elle; [*visit*] traditionnel/-elle.

ritualism /ˈrɪtʃʊəlɪzəm/ *n* ritualisme *m*.

ritualistic /ˌrɪtʃʊəˈlɪstɪk/ *adj* [*activity*] rituel/-elle; Relig ritualiste.

ritually /ˈrɪtʃʊəlɪ/ *adv* (ceremonially) selon le rituel; fig (routinely) rituellement.

ritzy○ /ˈrɪtzɪ/ *adj* chic *inv*.

rival /ˈraɪvl/ **I** *n* (person) rival/-e *m/f*; (company) concurrent/-e *m/f*; **business ~s** concurrents en affaires; **~s in love** rivaux en amour.

II *adj* [*supporter, suitor, team, bid, business*] rival; [*claim*] opposé.

III *vtr* (*p prés etc* **-ll-, -l-** US) (equal) égaler (**in** en); (compete favourably) rivaliser avec (**in** de); **to ~ sb/sth in popularity** rivaliser de popularité avec qn/qch; **few can ~ his style** son style est sans égal; **his ignorance is ~led only by his obstinacy** son ignorance n'a d'égal que son entêtement.

rivalry /ˈraɪvlrɪ/ *n* rivalité *f* (**between** entre); **bitter/intense ~** rivalité acharnée/intense; **inter-company ~** rivalités entre les compagnies.

riven /ˈrɪvn/ *adj* sout déchiré (**by** par).

river /ˈrɪvə(r)/ ▶ 1644 *n* **1** (flowing into sea) fleuve *m*; (tributary) rivière *f*; **up ~/down ~** en amont/en aval; **2** fig (of lava, mud, oil) fleuve *m*; **~s of blood** des fleuves de sang.

IDIOMS **to sell sb down the ~** trahir qn; **to send sb up the ~** US envoyer qn au pénitentiaire.

riverbank /ˈrɪvəbæŋk/ *n* berge *f*; **along the ~** le long de la rivière.

river: **~ basin** *n* bassin *m* fluvial; **~bed** *n* (going into sea) lit *m* de fleuve; (of tributary) lit *m* de rivière; **~ blindness** ▶ 1354 *n* Med cécité *f* des rivières, onchocercose *f* spec; **~boat** *n* navire *m* à aubes; **~front** *n* quais *mpl*; **~ mouth** *n* embouchure *f*; **~ police** *n* police *f* fluviale.

riverside /ˈrɪvəsaɪd/ **I** *n* rive *f*.

II *adj* [*pub, café*] au bord de la rivière.

river traffic *n* navigation *f* fluviale.

rivet /ˈrɪvɪt/ **I** *n* rivet *m*; **to drive a ~ into sth** poser un rivet dans qch.

II *vtr* **1** (captivate) **to be ~ed by** être captivé par [*performance*]; **2** (fix) **to be ~ed on** [*eyes, gaze*] être rivé sur; **to be ~ed to the spot** [*person*] être cloué sur place; **3** Tech (fasten with rivets) riveter.

riveter /ˈrɪvɪtə(r)/ *n* (machine) riveteuse *f*.

riveting /ˈrɪvɪtɪŋ/ *adj* fascinant.

Riviera /ˌrɪvɪˈeərə/ *n* **the Italian ~** la Riviera; **the French ~** la Côte d'Azur.

rivulet /ˈrɪvjʊlɪt/ *n* **1** Geog (stream) ruisselet *m*; gen **~s of lava** petits ruisseaux *mpl* de lave; **2** fig **~s of water/of sweat/of blood** filets *mpl* d'eau/de sueur/de sang.

Riyadh /rɪˈjɑːd/ ▶ 1818 *pr n* Riyad.

riyal /rɪˈjɑːl/ ▶ 1143 *n* riyal *m*.

RM GB *abrév* ▶ **Royal Marines**.

RN *n* **1** US (*abrév* = **registered nurse**) infirmier/-ière *m/f* diplômé/-e; **2** GB *abrév* ▶ **Royal Navy**.

RNA *n*: *abrév* ▶ **ribonucleic acid**.

RNLI *n* GB (*abrév* = **Royal National Lifeboat Institution**) société *f* nationale de sauvetage en mer.

roach /rəʊtʃ/ *n* **1** (fish) (*pl* **~**) gardon *m*; **2**○ US (insect) cafard *m*; **3**○ argot des drogués filtre *m* de joint.

road /rəʊd/ **I** *n* **1** (between places) route *f* (**from** de; **to** à); **the ~ to Leeds, the Leeds road** la route de Leeds; **the ~ north/inland** la route du nord/qui mène à l'intérieur; **the ~ home** la route qui mène à la maison; **the ~ back to sth** la route du retour à qch; **are we on the right ~ for Oxford?** c'est bien la route pour Oxford?; **follow the ~ round to the right** suivez la route qui tourne à droite; **follow the ~ ahead** allez tout droit; **a dog in the ~** un chien sur la route; **after three hours on the ~** après trois heures de route; **across the ~** de l'autre côté de la route, en face; **along the ~** plus loin; **it's just along the ~** c'est juste un peu plus loin; **down the ~** plus bas, plus loin; **by ~** par la route; **transported by ~** transporté par or sur route; **to hit the ~**○, **to take (to) the ~** prendre la route, se mettre en route; **to be on the ~** [*car*] être en état de rouler; **a bargain at £5,000 on the ~** une occasion à 5 000 livres sterling clés en main; [*driver, person*] être sur la route; [*band, performers*] être en tournée; **to be** ou **get back on the ~** reprendre la route; **I've been on the ~ all night** j'ai roulé toute la nuit; **to go on the ~ with a show** partir en tournée avec un spectacle; **to be off the ~** [*vehicle*] être hors d'usage; **2** (in built-up area) rue *f*; **at the top** ou **end of my ~** au bout de ma rue; **he lives just along** ou **down the ~** il habite un peu plus loin dans la rue; **Tom from down the ~** Tom qui habite plus bas dans la rue; **3** fig (way) voie *f*; **a difficult ~ to follow** une voie difficile à suivre; **to be on the ~ to success/disaster** être sur la voie du succès/désastre; **we think we're on the right ~** nous pensons être sur la bonne voie; **we don't want to go down that ~** nous ne voulons pas suivre cette voie; **they are further down** ou **along the ~ to union** ils sont plus avancés sur la voie de l'union; **somewhere along the ~ she learned** en cours de route elle a appris; **to reach the end of the ~** déboucher sur une impasse; **it's the end of the ~ for us** c'est la fin pour nous; (**get**) **out of my ~**○! dégage○!; **4** Naut rade *f*.

II *modif* [*bridge, condition, congestion, junction, layout, network, map, safety, surface, traffic*] routier/-ière; [*building, construction, maintenance, repair, resurfacing*] des routes; [*accident*] de la route.

IDIOMS **any ~ (up)**○ GB dial n'importe comment○; **let's get this show on the ~!**

c'est parti!; **one for the ~** un dernier verre pour la route.

roadbed /ˈrəʊdbed/ *n* Rail ballast *m*; (of road) empierrement *m*.

roadblock /ˈrəʊdblɒk/ **I** *n* **1** lit barrage *m* routier; **police/army ~** barrage de police/de troupes armées; **to set up/mount a ~** établir/mettre en place un barrage; **2** fig US obstacle *m*.
II *vtr* fig US faire obstacle à.

road fund licence *n* GB Aut **1** (tax) taxe *f* routière; **2** (disc) ≈ vignette *f*.

road: **~ haulage** *n* transports *mpl* routiers; **~ haulier** ▶ 1692 *n* (firm) entreprise *f* de transports routiers; (person) transporteur *m* routier; **~ hog**○ *n* chauffard○ *m*; **~holding** *n* tenue *f* de route.

roadhouse /ˈrəʊdhaʊs/ *n* **1** (inn) relais *m* (routier); **2** US (nightclub) boîte *f* de nuit (*située au bord d'une route de campagne*).

road hump *n* ralentisseur *m*.

roadie○ /ˈrəʊdɪ/ *n* machiniste *mf* (*d'un groupe rock en tournée*).

road: **~man** ▶ 1692 *n* cantonnier *m*; **~ manager** ▶ 1692 *n* organisateur/-trice *m/f* de tournée; **~-mender** ▶ 1692 *n* cantonnier *m*; **~ metal** *n* empierrement *m*; **~ movie** *n* road-movie *m*; **~ racer** *n* (cyclist) routier/-ière *m/f*; **~ racing** ▶ 1282 *n* compétition *f* sur route; **~ rage** *n* violence *f* au volant; **~ rider** *n* = **road racer**; **~roller** *n* rouleau *m* compresseur; **~runner** *n* Zool coucou *m* terrestre; **~ sense** *n* conscience *f* des dangers de la route.

roadshow /ˈrəʊdʃəʊ/ *n* **1** (play, show) spectacle *m* de tournée; **2** (TV, radio programme) émission *f* itinérante en direct; **3** (publicity tour, workshop etc) tour *m* promotionnel.

roadside /ˈrəʊdsaɪd/ **I** *n* bord *m* de la route; **at** ou **by** ou **on the ~** au bord de la route.
II *modif* [*café, inn, meal, hedge, advertising*] au bord de la route; [*breath test, questioning*] sur les lieux; **to carry out ~ repairs** faire des réparations de fortune; **we offer ~ recovery and repairs** nous avons un service de rapatriement or remorquage de véhicules et dépannage.

road: **~sign** *n* panneau *m* de signalisation; **~stead** *n* Naut rade *f*.

roadster /ˈrəʊdstə(r)/ *n* (car) roadster *m*; (bike) vélo *m* de route.

road: **~sweeper** ▶ 1692 *n* (person) balayeur/-euse *m/f*; (machine) balayeuse *f*; **~ tax** *n* taxe *f* routière; **~ tax disc** *n* vignette *f*.

road test **I** *n* essai *m* sur route.
II *vtr* lit tester [qch] sur route [*car*]; US fig tester [*idea*].

road: **~ transport** *n* transports *mpl* routiers; **~ user** *n* usager *m* de la route; **~way** *n* chaussée *f*; **~work** *n* Sport course *f* sur route; **~works** *npl* travaux *mpl* (routiers); **~worthy** *adj* en état de rouler.

roam /rəʊm/ **I** *vtr* parcourir [*world, countryside*]; faire le tour de [*cafés, shops, villages*]; **to ~ the streets** (purposefully) parcourir les rues; (aimlessly) traîner dans les rues.
II *vi* **freedom to ~** la liberté de se promener à sa guise; **to ~ through** parcourir [*region, woods*]; faire le tour de [*building*].
■ **roam around** [*person*] vadrouiller○.

roamer /ˈrəʊmə(r)/ *n* bourlingueur/-euse○ *m/f*.

roaming /ˈrəʊmɪŋ/ *n* vagabondage *m*.

roan /rəʊn/ **I** *n* **1** Equit rouan/rouanne *m/f*; **2** (in bookbinding) basane *f*.
II *adj* [*horse*] rouan/rouanne.

roar /rɔː(r)/ **I** *n* **1** (of lion) rugissement *m*; **to give a ~** rugir; **2** (of person) hurlement *m*; **to give a ~** pousser un hurlement; **3** (vibration) (of engine, machine) vrombissement *m*; (of traffic, waterfall) grondement *m*; **4** (of sea, wind) mugissement *m*; **5** (of crowd) clameur *f*; **a ~ of laughter** un éclat de rire; **a ~ of applause** un tonnerre d'applaudissements.
II *vtr* **1** (shout) **'quiet!' he ~ed** 'silence!' a-t-il vociféré; **to ~ one's approval** hurler son accord; **2** (rev up) faire vrombir [*engine*].
III *vi* **1** [*lion*] rugir; **2** [*person*] vociférer; **to ~ with pain** rugir de douleur; **to ~ at sb** vociférer devant qn; **to ~ with laughter** rire à gorge déployée; **3** (make noise) [*sea, thunder, wind*] mugir; [*fire*] ronfler; [*crowd*] hurler; [*engine, machine*] vrombir; **to ~ past sth** passer devant qch en vrombissant; **the car ~ed into life** la voiture a démarré en vrombissant.
■ **roar out**: **~ out [sth]** hurler [*command*].

roaring /ˈrɔːrɪŋ/ **I** *n* **1** (of lion, person) rugissement *m*; **2** (of storm, wind, sea) mugissement *m*; **3** (of thunder, waterfall) grondement *m*; **4** (of engine, machine) vrombissement *m*; **5** (of crowd) clameur *f*.
II *adj* **1** (loud) [*storm*] rugissant; [*engine, traffic*] grondant; **a ~ fire** une belle flambée; **the ~ forties** Geog les quarantièmes rugissants; **2** [*success*] fou/folle; **to do a ~ trade** faire des affaires en or (**in** dans la vente de); **the ~ Twenties** Hist les Années folles.
III *adv* [*drunk*] complètement.

roast /rəʊst/ **I** *n* **1** Culin rôti *m*; **~ of veal/pork etc** rôti de veau/porc etc; **2** US (barbecue) barbecue *m*; **3**○ US (entertainment) *spectacle amusant où une célébrité se fait éreinter par son entourage*.
II *adj* [*meat, poultry, potatoes*] rôti; **~ beef** rôti *m* de bœuf, rosbif *m*; **~ chestnuts** châtaignes *fpl* grillées.
III *vtr* **1** rôtir [*meat, potatoes*]; (faire) griller [*peanuts, chestnuts*]; torréfier [*coffee beans*]; **dry ~ed peanuts** cacahuètes *fpl* grillées; **to be ~ed alive** fig être grillé vif; **2**○ (criticize severely) descendre [qn] en flammes.
IV *vi* [*meat*] rôtir; [*person*] ○fig (in sun, by fire) rôtir; **I'm ~ing**○**!** je crève de chaud○!

roaster /ˈrəʊstə(r)/ *n* **1** Culin (chicken) poulet *m* à rôtir; **2**○ (hot day) jour *m* de canicule; **3** Culin (oven pan) plat *m* à rôtir; (small oven) US rôtissoire *f*.

roasting /ˈrəʊstɪŋ/ **I**○ *n* (scolding) **to give sb a ~** passer un bon savon à qn○; **the play got a ~ from the critics** la pièce s'est fait éreinter par la critique.
II *adj* **1** Culin [*chicken, cut of meat*] à rôtir; [*pan*] à rôtir; **2**○ [*weather*] chaud à crever○.

rob /rɒb/ *vtr* (*p prés etc* **-bb-**) **1** [*thief*] voler [*person*]; dévaliser [*bank, shop, train*]; **to be ~bed of sth** se faire voler qch; **to ~ the till** voler de l'argent dans la caisse; **2** (deprive) **to ~ sb of sth** priver qn de qch.
IDIOMS **to ~ Peter to pay Paul** déshabiller Pierre pour habiller Paul; **to ~ sb blind** escroquer qn.

robber /ˈrɒbə(r)/ *n* voleur/-euse *m/f*; **train ~** bandit *m* (*qui attaque un train*).

robber baron *n* Hist baron *m* pillard; fig requin *m* de l'industrie.

robbery /ˈrɒbərɪ/ *n* vol *m*; **it's sheer ~!** fig c'est du vol!; **train ~** acte *m* de banditisme ferroviaire; **~ with violence**, **~ and assault** Jur vol *m* avec coups et blessures, vol *m* avec voies de fait.

robe /rəʊb/ **I** *n* **1** (ceremonial garment) robe *f*; **christening/coronation ~** robe de baptême/de sacre; **to wear one's ~ of office** gen porter la robe; [*academic, judge*] porter la toge; **ceremonial ~s** vêtements *mpl* de cérémonie; **2** US (bath robe) peignoir *m*.
II *vtr* vêtir [*dignitary*]; **~d in silk/in white** vêtu de soie/de blanc.

robin /ˈrɒbɪn/ *n* **1** (also **~ redbreast**) rouge-gorge *m*; **2** US merle *m* migrateur.

robot /ˈrəʊbɒt/ **I** *n* (in sci-fi, industry) robot *m* also pej.
II *modif* [*arm*] robotisé; [*method of production, welding*] automatique.

robot bomb *n* bombe-robot *f*.

robotic /rəʊˈbɒtɪk/ *adj* [*movement, voice*] de robot; [*tool, device, machine*] robotisé.

robotics /rəʊˈbɒtɪks/ *n* (+ *v sg*) robotique *f*.

robotization /ˌrəʊbətaɪˈzeɪʃn, US -tɪˈz-/ *n* robotisation *f*.

robotize /ˈrəʊbətaɪz/ **I** *vtr* robotiser.
II **robotized** *pp adj* robotisé.

robot plane *n* avion-robot *m*.

robust /rəʊˈbʌst/ *adj* **1** [*health, person, appetite, furniture, toy*] robuste; [*economy*] solide; **2** [*humour*] fruste; [*defence, reply, attitude, approach, tackle*] énergique; [*common sense*] solide; **3** [*wine, flavour*] corsé.

robustly /rəʊˈbʌstlɪ/ *adv* **1** lit [*constructed, made*] solidement; **2** fig [*answer, deny, defend*] avec force; [*confident, practical*] foncièrement.

robustness /rəʊˈbʌstnɪs/ *n* **1** (of object) robustesse *f*; **2** (of answer, defence) fermeté *f*; (of economy) solidité *f*.

roc /rɒk/ *n* Mythol roc *m*.

rock /rɒk/ **I** *n* **1** ¢ (substance) roche *f*; **solid/molten ~** roche dure/en fusion; **hewn out of solid ~** taillé dans le roc; **2** C (boulder) rocher *m*; **the ship hit the ~s** le bateau a heurté les rochers or les récifs; **on the ~s** lit, Naut sur les récifs; [*drink*] avec des glaçons; **to be on the ~s** fig [*marriage*] aller à vau-l'eau; **3** (stone) pierre *f*; **'falling ~s'** 'chute de pierres'; **4** (also **~ music**) rock *m*; **5** GB (sweet) sucre *m* d'orge; **6**○ (diamond) (*gen pl*) diam○ *m*, diamant *m*; **7**○ argot des drogués (crack) caillou○ *m*, crack *m*.
II **rocks**● *npl* (testicles) couilles● *fpl*; **to get one's ~s off** prendre son pied○.
III *modif* Mus [*band, concert, musician*] rock; [*industry*] du rock.
IV *vtr* **1** (move gently) balancer [*cradle*]; bercer [*baby, boat*]; **she sat ~ing herself in her chair** elle se balançait sur sa chaise; **I ~ed the baby to sleep** j'ai endormi le bébé en le berçant; **2** (shake) [*tremor, bomb*] secouer [*town*]; [*scandal, revelation*] ébranler [*party, government*]; [*waves*] secouer [*vessel*].
V *vi* **1** (sway) [*person, cradle*] se balancer; **to ~ to and fro/back and forth** se balancer de droite à gauche/d'avant en arrière; **to ~ with laughter** être secoué de rire; **2** (shake) [*earth, ground, building*] trembler; **3** (dance) **to ~ (away)** danser le rock; **by midnight, the place is ~ing**○ vers minuit, la fête bat son plein.
IDIOMS **caught between a ~ and a hard place** pris entre le marteau et l'enclume; **as firm** ou **solid as a ~** solide comme le roc; **as hard as a ~** dur comme du fer or le roc.

rockabilly /ˈrɒkəbɪlɪ/ Mus **I** *n* rockabilly *m*.
II *modif* de rockabilly.

rock and roll /ˌrɒkənˈrəʊl/ **I** *n* rock and roll *m*.
II *modif* [*band, singer*] de rock and roll; [*era, music*] du rock and roll.
III *vi* danser le rock and roll.

rock bass *n* crapet *m* de roche.

rock bottom /ˌrɒkˈbɒtəm/ **I** *n* point *m* le plus bas; **to reach** ou **hit ~** toucher le fond; **to be at ~** être au plus bas.
II **rock-bottom** *adj* [*price*] le plus bas.

rockbound /ˈrɒkbaʊnd/ *adj* [*island*] entouré de rochers; [*coast*] bordé de rochers.

rock: **~ bun**, **~ cake** *n* GB *petit gâteau aux raisins secs*; **~ candy** *n* US *friandise à base de sucre candi*; **~ carving** *n* sculpture *f* sur roc; **~ climber** *n* varappeur/-euse *m/f*.

rock climbing ▶ 1282 *n* varappe *f*; **to go ~** faire de la varappe.

rock: **~ crystal** *n* cristal *m* de roche; **~ dash** *n* US crépi *m*.

rocker /ˈrɒkə(r)/ *n* **1** US (chair) fauteuil *m* à bascule; **2** (on cradle, chair) bascule *f*; **3** (also **~ switch**) interrupteur *m* à bascule; **4** GB (biker) rockeur/-euse *m/f*; **5**○ (performer) musicien/-ienne *m/f* rock, rockeur/-euse *m/f*; **6**○ (rock fan) fana○ *mf* de rock.
IDIOMS **to be/go off one's ~**○ débloquer○.

rocker: **~ arm** *n* Tech culbuteur *m*; **~ panel** *n* Aut bas *m* de caisse.

rockery /ˈrɒkərɪ/ *n* GB rocaille *f*.

rocket /ˈrɒkɪt/ **I** *n* **1** (spacecraft, firework) fusée *f*; **distress ~** fusée de détresse; **to take off like a ~** partir en trombe; **2** Mil fusée *f*; **3** Bot, Culin roquette *f*.
II *modif* [*range, base*] de lancement de fusées; [*research, technology*] spatiale.
III *vi* **1** [*price, profit, level, value*] monter en flèche; **to ~ from 10 to 100/by 400%** grimper de 10 à 100/de 400%; **2** [*person, vehicle*] **to ~** ou **go ~ing past sth** passer en trombe devant qch; **to ~ to fame** accéder rapidement à la célébrité.
IDIOMS **to give sb a ~**○ GB sonner les cloches à qn○.

rocket: **~ attack** *n* attaque *f* à la roquette; **~ engine** *n* moteur-fusée *m*; **~ fuel** *n* propergol *m*; **~ launcher** *n* lance-fusées *m inv*; **~-propelled** *adj* autopropulsé; **~ propulsion** *n* autopropulsion *f*.

rocketry /ˈrɒkɪtrɪ/ *n* fuséologie *f*.

rocket ship *n* (spacecraft) vaisseau *m* spatial.

rock: **~ face** *n* paroi *f* rocheuse; **~fall** *n* chute *f* de pierres; **~fish** *n* rascasse *f*; **~ formation** *n* formation *f* rocheuse; **~ garden** *n* rocaille *f*; **~-hard** *adj* extrêmement dur.

Rockies /ˈrɒki:z/ *pr npl* montagnes *fpl* Rocheuses.

rocking /ˈrɒkɪŋ/ **I** *n* (gentle) balancement *m*; (vigorous) ballottement *m*.
II *adj* [*boat*] qui se balance; **a ~ motion** un balancement.

rocking: **~ chair** *n* fauteuil *m* à bascule; **~ horse** *n* cheval *m* à bascule.

rockling /ˈrɒklɪŋ/ *n* loche *f* (de mer).

rock: **~ lobster** *n* homard *m* épineux, langouste *f*; **~'n'roll** = **~ and roll**; **~ painting** *n* peinture *f* rupestre; **~ plant** *n* plante *f* de rocaille; **~ pool** *n* bassin *m* dans les rochers; **~rose** *n* ciste *m*; **~ salmon** *n* GB Culin roussette *f*; **~ salt** *n* sel *m* gemme; **~ star** *n* rock-star *f*; **~-steady** *adj* extrêmement stable; **~ wool** *n* laine *f* minérale.

rocky /ˈrɒkɪ/ *adj* **1** (covered in rocks) [*beach, path, soil*] rocailleux/-euse; [*coast, headland, peninsula*] rocheux/-euse; **a ~ road** lit une route rocailleuse; fig un chemin difficile; **2**○ (unstable) [*personal life, relationship, period, career*] difficile; [*health, business*] précaire; **her marriage is a bit ~** son mariage bat (un peu) de l'aile○.

rocky: **Rocky Mountains** *pr npl* montagnes *fpl* Rocheuses; **Rocky Mountain spotted fever** *n* rickettsiose *f* spec, fièvre *f* pourpre des montagnes Rocheuses.

rococo /rəˈkəʊkəʊ/ *n, adj* rococo (*m*) (*inv*).

rod /rɒd/ *n* **1** (stick) (of wood) tige *f*; (of metal) tringle *f*; Tech tige *f*; **curtain/stair ~** tringle à rideaux/de marche; **steel ~** tige en acier; **2** (for punishment) baguette *f*; **3** Fishg canne *f* à pêche; **to fish with a ~ and line** pêcher à la ligne; **4** (staff of office) bâton *m* de commandement; **5** Meas perche *f*; **6** (in eye) bâtonnet *m* (rétinien); **7**○ US (pistol) flingue○ *m*; **to pack a ~**○ avoir un flingue○ sur soi; **8**● US (penis) bite● *f*.
IDIOMS **to make a ~ for one's own back** s'attirer des ennuis; **to rule with a ~ of iron** gouverner avec une main de fer; **spare the ~ and spoil the child** Prov qui aime bien châtie bien Prov.

rode /rəʊd/ *prét* ▶ **ride**.

rodent /ˈrəʊdnt/ *n* rongeur *m*.

rodent ulcer *n* épithélioma *m* cutané.

rodeo /ˈrəʊdɪəʊ/ *n* (*pl* **~s**) rodéo *m*.

rodomontade /ˌrɒdəmɒnˈteɪd, -tɑ:d/ *n* littér péj rodomontade *f* liter, fanfaronnade *f*.

roe /rəʊ/ *n* **1** ¢ (also **hard ~**) œufs *mpl* (de poisson); **cod's/lumpfish ~** œufs de cabillaud/de lump; **2** (also **soft ~**) laitance *f*.

roebuck /ˈrəʊbʌk/ *n* (*pl* **~**) chevreuil *m*.

roe deer /ˌrəʊˈdɪə(r)/ *n* **1** (generically) chevreuil *m*; **2** (female) chevrette *f*.

Rogation Days /rəʊˈgeɪʃn/ *n* (journées *fpl* des) rogations *fpl*.

rogations /rəʊˈgeɪʃnz/ *npl* rogations *fpl*.

rogatory /ˈrɒgətrɪ/ *adj* rogatoire; **~ letter** commission *f* rogatoire internationale.

roger /ˈrɒdʒə(r)/ **I** *excl* **1** Telecom reçu; **2**○ (OK) d'accord!
II◑ *vtr* GB enfiler◑ [*woman*].

rogue /rəʊg/ **I** *n* **1** hum coquin *m*; **charming/handsome ~** charmante/belle canaille *f*; **2** péj fripouille *f*; **~s' gallery** lit *fichier de photos constitué par la police*; fig hum collection *f* de canailles; **3** (animal) solitaire *m*.
II *modif* **1** (maverick) [*elephant, politician, detective*] solitaire; **2** péj [*builder, landlord, trader*] véreux/-euse.

roguery /ˈrəʊgərɪ/ *n* **1** péj (dishonesty) malhonnêteté *f*; **2** (mischief) espièglerie *f*.

roguish /ˈrəʊgɪʃ/ *adj* espiègle, coquin.

roguishly /ˈrəʊgɪʃlɪ/ *adv* [*smile, say*] avec espièglerie.

roisterer† /ˈrɔɪstərə(r)/ *n* fêtard *m*.

role /rəʊl/ *n* Theat, fig rôle *m* (**as** comme; **in** dans); **in the ~ of** dans le rôle de; **to reverse ~s** permuter les rôles; **to take a ~** interpréter un rôle; **leading/supporting ~** lit, fig rôle principal/secondaire; **title ~** rôle-titre *m*; **vital ~, key ~** fig rôle primordial.

role model *n* gen, Psych modèle *m*.

role-play /ˈrəʊlpleɪ/ **I** *n* Psych psychodrame *m*; Sch jeu *m* de rôle.
II *vtr* jouer [*part, scene*]; imaginer [*situation, feeling*].

role reversal, **role swapping** *n* permutation *f* de rôles.

roll /rəʊl/ **I** *n* **1** (wad) (of paper, cloth) rouleau *m*; (of banknotes) liasse *f*; (of flesh) bourrelet *m*; **a ~ of film** une pellicule; **2** Culin (bread) petit pain *m*; **cheese ~** sandwich *m* au fromage; **chicken/turkey ~** (meat) ≈ galantine *f* de poulet/dinde; **3** (rocking motion) (of ship, train) roulis *m*; **to walk with a ~ of the hips** marcher en balançant les hanches; **4** Sport (in gymnastics) roulade *f*; **forward/backward ~** roulade avant/arrière; **5** Aviat tonneau *m*; **6** Games (of dice) lancer *m*; **7** (deep sound) (of drums) roulement *m*; (of thunder) grondement *m*; **8** (register) liste *f*; **class ~** liste des élèves; **electoral ~** listes électorales; **to have 200 members on the ~** avoir 200 membres inscrits; **to call the ~** faire l'appel; **falling school ~s** baisse *f* des effectifs scolaires; **9** (squirm) **to have a ~ on** [*dog*] se rouler dans [*grass*].
II *vtr* **1** (push) rouler [*ball, barrel, log*]; **to ~ sth away** rouler qch pour l'éloigner (**from** de); **to ~ sth forward** rouler qch en avant; **to ~ sth back a few metres** rouler qch en arrière de quelques mètres; **2** (make) rouler [*cigarette*]; **to ~ one's own** rouler ses cigarettes soi-même; **to ~ sth into a ball** (of paper) faire une boulette de qch; (of dough, clay) faire une boule de qch; (of wool) faire une pelote de qch; **3** (flatten) étendre [*dough*]; rouler [*lawn*]; laminer [*metal*]; **4** (turn) **to ~ one's eyes** rouler des yeux; **~ the patient onto his back** faire rouler le patient sur le dos; **she ~ed her car**○ sa voiture s'est retournée; **5** Cin, Print faire tourner [*camera, presses*]; **6** Games faire rouler [*dice*]; **7** Ling **to ~ one's 'r's** rouler les r.
III *vi* **1** (move) [*ball, coin, rock*] rouler (**onto** sur); [*person, animal*] se rouler; **to ~ backwards** [*car*] reculer; **to ~ down** [*car, rock*] dévaler [*hill*]; [*person*] rouler de haut en bas de [*slope*]; **to ~ into** [*train*] entrer en [*station*]; **to ~ off** [*car*] tomber de [*cliff*]; [*coin, dice*] rouler de [*table*]; [*person*] tomber de [*couch*]; **to ~ out of** [*person*] rouler hors de [*bed*]; **the ball ~ed over the line** la balle a dépassé la ligne; **2** (rotate) [*car, plane*] faire un tonneau; [*eyes*] rouler dans leurs orbites; **3** (sway) [*ship*] tanguer; **to ~ from side to side** [*person*] se balancer; **4** (reverberate) [*thunder*] gronder; [*drum*] rouler; **5** (function) [*camera, press*] tourner.
IV rolled *pp adj* [*steel*] laminé; ▶ **rolled gold**.
V rolling *pres p adj* **1** [*countryside, hills*] valonné; **2** [*walk, gait*] balancé.
IDIOMS **heads will ~!** des têtes vont tomber!; **let the good times ~!** que la fête commence!; **~ on the holidays!** vivement les vacances!; **to be on a ~**○ être dans une période faste; **to be ~ing in it**○ rouler sur l'or; **to be X, Y and Z ~ed into one** être à la fois X, Y et Z.
■ **roll about** GB, **roll around** [*animal, person*] se rouler; [*marbles, tins*] rouler; **to ~ around on the grass** se rouler dans l'herbe.
■ **roll along** [*car*] rouler tranquillement.
■ **roll back**: ¶ **~ back** Comput faire une reprise; ¶ **~ [sth] back, ~ back [sth] 1** (push back) rouler [*carpet*]; **2** fig faire reculer [*years*]; repousser [*frontiers*]; **3** Fin baisser [*prices*].
■ **roll down**: **~ [sth] down, ~ down [sth]** baisser [*blind, sleeve, trouser leg*].
■ **roll in 1** (pour in) [*tourists, money, orders*] affluer; **2** (gather) [*clouds*] se rassembler; **3** (advance) [*tanks, trucks*] avancer; **the tanks ~ed into the city** les chars sont entrés dans la ville; **4**○ (stroll in) s'amener○; **to ~ in 20 minutes late** s'amener 20 minutes en retard.
■ **roll off**: **~ off [sth]** [*cars*] sortir de [*production line*]; [*newspapers*] sortir de [*presses*].
■ **roll on**: ¶ **~ on** [*time, hours*] passer; ¶ **~ [sth] on, ~ on [sth]** enfiler [*stockings*].
■ **roll out**: **~ [sth] out, ~ out [sth]** étirer [*pastry*]; laminer [*metal*]; faire disparaître [*bumps*]; dérouler [*rug*].
■ **roll over**: ¶ **~ over 1** [*car, boat*] se retourner; **2** [*person*] se retourner; **to ~ over on one's back/stomach** rouler sur le dos/ventre; ¶ **~ [sth] over** Accts Fin reconduire [*debt, loan*]; ¶ **~ [sb] over** tourner [*patient, invalid*] (**onto** sur).
■ **roll up**: ¶ **~ up 1**○ (arrive) [*guests, visitors*] s'amener○, arriver; **~ up!** approchez!; **2** (form a cylinder) [*poster, mat*] s'enrouler; ¶ **~ up [sth], ~ [sth] up** enrouler [*rug, poster*]; **to ~ up one's sleeves** retrousser ses manches; **I ~ed his sleeve up** je lui ai retroussé la manche; **to ~ sth/sb up in** enrouler qch/qn dans [*blanket*].

roll: **~away bed** *n* US lit *m* pliant; **~back** *n* US Econ baisse *f* des prix imposée; **~bar** *n* Aut arceau *m* de sécurité; **~-call** *n* Mil appel *m*.

rolled gold **I** *n* or *m* plaqué.
II *modif* [*watch, bracelet*] plaqué or.

roll: **~ed oats** *npl* Culin flocons *mpl* d'avoine; **~ed-up** *pp adj* [*newspaper, carpet*] roulé.

roller /ˈrəʊlə(r)/ *n* **1** Hort, Ind, Tech rouleau *m*; **road/paint ~** rouleau compresseur/de peintre; **2** (curler) bigoudi *m*; **3** (wave) rouleau *m*; **4**○ GB Aut Rolls *f* (Royce).

rollerball /ˈrəʊləbɔ:l/ *n* stylo *m* à bille.

rollerblade /ˈrəʊləbleɪd/ **I** *n* patin *m* en ligne.
II *vi* faire du patin en ligne.

rollerblading /ˈrəʊləbleɪdɪŋ/ *n* patinage *m* en ligne.

roller: **~blind** *n* store *m*; **~ coaster** *n* montagnes *fpl* russes; **~ disco** *n*: *discothèque où l'on danse sur patins à roulettes*; **~drome** *n* piste *f* de patin à roulettes.

roller-skate /ˈrəʊləskeɪt/ **I** *n* patin *m* à roulettes.
II *vi* faire du patin à roulettes; **to ~ to work/round the park** aller au travail/faire le tour du parc en patins à roulettes.

roller-skater /ˈrəʊləskeɪtə(r)/ *n* patineur/-euse *m/f* à roulettes.

roller-skating /ˈrəʊləskeɪtɪŋ/ ▶ **1282** *n*

patinage *m* à roulettes; **to go ~** faire du patin à roulettes.

roller-skating rink *n* patinoire *f*.

roller towel *n* essuie-main *m* à enrouleur.

roll film *n* Phot pellicule *f* en bobine.

rollick○ /ˈrɒlɪk/ *vi* (also **~ about**) faire la java○.

rollicking /ˈrɒlɪkɪŋ/ **I**○ *n* GB savon○ *m*; **to give sb a ~** passer un savon à qn.
II *adj* [*person*] exubérant; [*comedy*] bouffon/-onne; [*party*] délirant.

rolling /ˈrəʊlɪŋ/ *n* Ind laminage *m*.

rolling: **~ mill** *n* laminoir *m*; **~ pin** *n* Culin rouleau *m* à pâtisserie; **~ stock** *n* Rail matériel *m* roulant; **~ stone** *n* fig vagabond/-e *m/f*; **~ strike** *n* Ind grève *f* tournante.

roll: **~mop** *n* Culin rollmops *m*; **~neck** *n* Fashn col *m* roulé.

roll of honour GB, **roll of honor** US *n* **1** Sch, Sport tableau *m* d'honneur; **2** Mil liste *f* des soldats tombés au champ d'honneur.

roll-on /ˈrəʊlɒn/ *n* Cosmet déodorant *m* à bille.

roll-on roll-off, **RORO** **I** *n* roulage *m*.
II *adj* Naut **~ ferry** ou **ship** navire *m* roulier; **the ~ system** le roulage.

roll: **~over** *n* Fin refinancement *m* (d'une obligation arrivée à maturité); **~over credit** *n* Fin crédit *m* renouvelable à taux révisable; **~-top desk** *n* bureau *m* cylindre; **~-up**○ *n* GB (cigarette *f*) roulée○ *f*.

roly-poly /ˌrəʊlɪˈpəʊlɪ/ *n* **1**○ hum patapouf○ *m*; **to be a ~** être potelé; **2** GB Culin roulé *m* à la confiture.

ROM /rɒm/ *n*: *abrév* ▶**read-only memory**.

romaine /rəˈmeɪn/ *n* US (also **~ lettuce**) romaine *f*.

roman /ˈrəʊmən/ *n, adj* Print romain (*m*).

Roman /ˈrəʊmən/ **I** *n* Romain/-e *m/f*; (**the Epistle to the**) **~s** Bible l'Épître *f* aux Romains.
II *adj* [*empire, history, calendar, alphabet, architecture*] romain; [*way of life*] des Romains.

Roman: **~ candle** *n* chandelle *f* romaine; **~ Catholic**, **RC** *n, adj* catholique (*mf*); **~ Catholicism** *n* catholicisme *m*.

romance /rəʊˈmæns/ **I** *n* **1** (of era, way of life, place) charme *m*; (of travel) côté *m* romantique; **2** (love affair) histoire *f* d'amour; (love) amour *m*; **to have a ~** vivre une histoire d'amour; **it was the great ~ of his life** ça a été le grand amour de sa vie; **a holiday** GB ou **vacation** US **~** une aventure de vacances; **3** (entertainment) (novel) roman *m* d'amour; (film) film *m* d'amour; **historical ~** (love story) roman d'amour historique; (heroic) roman de cape et d'épée; **4** Literat (medieval) roman *m* du moyen âge; (Shakespearean) pièce *f* romanesque; **5** Mus romance *f*.
II *vi* idéaliser; **to ~ about sth** idéaliser qch.

Romance /rəʊˈmæns/ *n, adj* Ling roman (*m*).

romancer /rəʊˈmænsə(r)/ *n* conteur/-euse *m/f*; **to be a ~** iron avoir l'imagination fertile.

Romanesque /ˌrəʊməˈnesk/ *adj* roman.

Romania /rəʊˈmeɪnɪə/ **▶1131** *pr n* Roumanie *f*.

Romanian /rəʊˈmeɪnɪən/ **▶1486**, **1402** **I** *n* **1** (person) Roumain/-e *m/f*; **2** Ling roumain *m*.
II *adj* roumain.

romanize /ˈrəʊmənaɪz/ (also **Romanize**) *vtr* Antiq, Ling romaniser.

Roman: **~ law** *n* droit *m* romain; **~ nose** *n* nez *m* aquilin; **~ numerals** *npl* chiffres *mpl* romains; **~ rite** *n* rite *m* romain; **~ road** *n* voie *f* romaine.

Romans(c)h /rəʊˈmænʃ/ *n* romanche *m*.

romantic /rəʊˈmæntɪk/ **I** *n* romantique *mf*.
II *adj* **1** [*place, setting, story, person, idea*] romantique; **2** (involving affair) sentimental; **to form a ~ attachment with sb** nouer une histoire sentimentale avec qn; **3** [*novel, film*] d'amour; **the ~ lead** le rôle du héros romantique.

Romantic /rəʊˈmæntɪk/ *n, adj* romantique (*mf*).

romantically /rəʊˈmæntɪklɪ/ *adv* [*describe, sing, play*] de façon romantique; [*behave*] avec romantisme; **they are ~ involved** il y a quelque chose entre eux.

romantic: **~ comedy** *n* comédie *f* sentimentale; **~ fiction** *n* (genre) romans *mpl* d'amour; (in bookshop) 'sentiment' *m*.

romanticism /rəʊˈmæntɪsɪzəm/ *n* romantisme *m*.

Romanticism /rəʊˈmæntɪsɪzəm/ *n* romantisme *m*.

romanticist /rəʊˈmæntɪsɪst/ *n* romantique *mf*.

romanticize /rəʊˈmæntɪsaɪz/ *vtr* idéaliser [*person, period, childhood*]; présenter [qch] sous un jour romantique [*violence, war*].

Romany /ˈrɒmənɪ/ **▶1402** **I** *n* **1** (gypsy) Tzigane *mf*, Romani *mf*; **2** Ling tzigane *m*, romani *m*.
II *adj* tzigane, romani.

Rome /rəʊm/ **▶1818** *pr n* Rome.
IDIOMS **all roads lead to ~** Prov tous les chemins mènent à Rome Prov; **~ wasn't built in a day** Prov Paris ne s'est pas fait ou Rome ne s'est pas faite en un jour Prov; **when in ~ do as the Romans do** Prov il faut faire comme les gens du pays; **to go over to ~** Relig se convertir au catholicisme.

Romeo /ˈrəʊmɪəʊ/ *pr n* **1** (character) Roméo *m*; **2** fig don Juan *m*.

Romish /ˈrəʊmɪʃ/ *adj* péj papiste pej.

romp /rɒmp/ **I** *n* **1** (frolic) ébats *mpl*; **bedroom ~s** hum ébats amoureux; **the film is an 18th century ~** c'est un film plein d'exubérance qui se passe au XVIIIe siècle; **2** (easy victory) victoire *f* facile; **to come in at a ~** Turf arriver dans un fauteuil.
II *vi* [*children, puppies*] s'ébattre; **to ~ home** l'emporter facilement.
■ **romp away** [*bidding, prices*] s'envoler.
■ **romp through**: **~ through [sth]** gagner [qch] avec une parfaite aisance [*match*]; exécuter [qch] avec une parfaite aisance [*piece, work*].

rompers /ˈrɒmpəz/ *npl* (also **romper suit**) barboteuse *f*.

rondel /ˈrɒndl/ *n* rondeau *m* double.

rondo /ˈrɒndəʊ/ *n* (*pl* **~s**) rondo *m*.

Roneo® /ˈrəʊnɪəʊ/ *vtr* ronéotyper.

rood /ruːd/ *n* **1** Relig crucifix *m*; **2**† GB (unit) quart *m* d'arpent†, ≈ 10 ares.

roodscreen /ˈruːdskriːn/ *n* jubé *m*.

roof /ruːf/ **I** *n* **1** (of building, car, cave, mine) toit *m*; **under one** ou **the same ~** sous le même toit; **a room under the ~** une chambre sous les toits or combles; **to have a ~ over one's head** avoir un toit sur la tête; **the ~ of the world** fig le toit du monde; **2** Anat **the ~ of the mouth** la voûte du palais, la voûte palatine spec.
II *vtr* faire la couverture de [*building*].
III **-roofed** (*dans composés*) **slate-~ed houses** des maisons couvertes en ardoises.
IDIOMS **to go through** ou **hit the ~**○ [*person*] sauter au plafond○; [*prices*] battre tous les records○; **to raise the ~** (be angry) sauter au plafond○; (make noise) faire un boucan de tous les diables○.
■ **roof in**: **~ in [sth]** couvrir [*area*].
■ **roof over**: **~ over [sth]**, **~ [sth] over** couvrir [*area*].

roofer /ˈruːfə(r)/ **▶1692** *n* couvreur *m*.

roof garden *n* jardin *m* aménagé sur le toit.

roofing /ˈruːfɪŋ/ **I** *n* **1** (material) toiture *f*, couverture *f*; **2** (process) pose *f* de la toiture.
II *modif* [*materials*] de couverture.

roofing: **~ contractor** *n* couvreur *m*; **~ felt** *n* carton *m* bitumé.

roof: **~ light** *n* Archit, Constr fenêtre *f* de toit; **~ rack** *n* galerie *f*; **~ tax** *n* GB Hist ≈ taxe *f* d'habitation.

rooftop /ˈruːftɒp/ **I** *n* toit *m*; **to shout sth from the ~s** crier qch sur tous les toits.
II *modif* **~ protest** occupation *f* des toits.

rook /rʊk/ **I** *n* **1** Zool (corbeau *m*) freux *m*; **2** Games tour *f*.
II○ †*vtr* (cheat) avoir○.

rookery /ˈrʊkərɪ/ *n* (colony) (of rooks) colonie *f* de freux; (of seals, penguins) colonie *f*.

rookie○ /ˈrʊkɪ/ US **I** *n* bleu○ *m*.
II *modif* [*player, cop*] débutant.

room /ruːm, rʊm/ **I** *n* **1** (closed area) (for living) pièce *f*; (for sleeping) chambre *f*; (for working) bureau *m*; (for meetings, teaching, operating) salle *f*; **a three ~ apartment** un appartement de trois pièces; **the ~ fell silent** tout le monde se tut; **in the next ~** dans la pièce d'à côté; **'~s to let'** 'chambres à louer'; **~ 159** la chambre 159; **~ and board** chambre avec repas; **he gets ~ and board** il est logé (et) nourri; **2** ¢ (space) place *f* (**for** pour; **to do** pour faire); **to make ~** faire de la place; **to take up ~** prendre de la place; **to be short of ~** manquer de place; **3** (opportunity) **~ for improvement/doubt** possibilité *f* d'amélioration/de doute; **~ for manoeuvre** marge *f* de manœuvre.
II **rooms**† *npl* **1** (rented) meublé *m*; **2** GB Univ chambre *f* d'étudiant.
III *vi* US loger; **to ~ with sb** loger chez qn; **we ~ together** nous habitons ensemble.
IV **-roomed** (*dans composés*) **4-~ed** de 4 pièces.
IDIOMS **there is always ~ at the top** quand on veut réussir dans la vie on peut.

room: **~ clerk** **▶1692** *n* US réceptionniste *mf*; **~ divider** *n* étagère *f* de séparation.

roomer /ˈruːmə(r)/ *n* US locataire *mf*.

roomette /ruːˈmet, rʊ-/ *n* US compartiment *m* de wagon-lit.

roomful /ˈruːmfʊl/ *n* **a ~ of children** une pièce remplie d'enfants; **'have you got many books?'—'a ~'** 'avez-vous beaucoup de livres?'—'une pièce entière'.

roominess /ˈruːmɪnɪs/ *n* (of house) caractère *m* spacieux; (of car) habitabilité *f*.

rooming house *n* immeuble *m* locatif; **to live in a ~** habiter en location.

rooming-in *n* Med *cohabitation de la mère et du nouveau-né*.

roommate /ˈruːmmeɪt/ *n* **1** (in same room) camarade *mf* de chambre; **2** US (flatmate) compagnon/compagne *m/f* d'appartement.

room service *n* service *m* de chambre.

room temperature *n* température *f* ambiante; **to serve a wine at ~** servir un vin chambré.

roomy /ˈruːmɪ/ *adj* [*car, house*] spacieux/-ieuse; [*garment*] large; [*bag, cupboard*] grand.

roost /ruːst/ **I** *n* (perch, tree) perchoir *m*; **the belfry is a ~ for pigeons** le clocher est l'endroit où nichent les pigeons.
II *vi* (in trees) percher (pour la nuit); (in belfry, attic) se nicher.
IDIOMS **his chickens have come home to ~** il a récolté ce qu'il a semé; **to rule the ~** faire la loi.

rooster /ˈruːstə(r)/ *n* coq *m*.

root /ruːt/ **I** *n* **1** Bot, fig racine *f*; **to take ~** [*plant*] prendre racine; [*idea, value, system, feeling*] s'établir; [*company, industry*] s'implanter; **to pull sth up by the ~s** déraciner qch; **to pull sb's hair out by the ~s** arracher les cheveux à qn; **to destroy/reject sth ~ and branch** détruire/rejeter complètement qch; **~ and branch review/opposition** revue/opposition radicale; **2** (origin) (of problem, matter) fond *m*; (of unhappiness, evil) origine *f*; **to get to the ~ of the problem** prendre le problème à la racine; **to be at the ~ of**

sth être à l'origine de qch; **3** Ling racine *f*; **4** Math racine *f*; **the fourth ~ of sth** la quatrième racine de qch.

II roots *npl* **1** (of dyed hair) racines *fpl*; **2** fig racines *fpl*; **to try to get back to one's ~s** essayer de retrouver ses racines; **she has no ~s** elle n'a aucune racine; **to pull up one's ~s** s'arracher à son milieu; **to put down new ~s** se créer de nouvelles racines.

III *modif* **1** fig [*cause*] profond; [*problem*] de base; [*question, issue*] fondamental; **2** Bot [*growth*] des racines; [*system*] radiculaire.

IV *vtr* **1** fig **to be ~ed in sth** [*music, film, person*] être ancré dans qch; **deeply-~ed** lit, fig bien enraciné; **to be/stand ~ed to the spot** ou **the ground** être/rester figé sur place; **2** Bot faire prendre racine [*plant*].

V *vi* **1** Bot prendre racine; **2** (search) [*person, animal*] fouiller (**in, through** dans).

■ **root around**, **root about** [*person, animal*] fouiller (**in** dans).

■ **root for**○: **~ for [sb]** (cheer) encourager [*team, contestant*]; **good luck in the exams—we're all ~ing for you!** bonne chance pour tes examens—nous sommes tous avec toi!.

■ **root out**: ¶ **~ out [sth]**, **~ [sth] out** traquer [*corruption, inefficiency*]; ¶ **~ [sb] out**, **~ out [sb]** déloger.

root: **~ beer** *n* US *boisson pétillante nonalcoolisée aux extraits de plantes*; **~ canal** *n* Dent canal *m* radiculaire; **~ canal treatment**, **~ canal work** *n* Dent dévitalisation *f*; **~ crop** *n* plante *f* à tubercules comestibles; **~ ginger** *n* gingembre *m* frais.

rootless /ˈruːtlɪs/ *adj* [*person, existence*] sans racines.

root: **~ sign** *n* Math radical *m*; **~stock** *n* rhizome *m*.

rootsy○ /ˈruːtsɪ/ *adj* [*music, song, sound*] d'inspiration folklorique.

root: **~ vegetable** *n* légume *m* à racine comestible; **~ word** *n* mot *m* racine.

rope /rəʊp/ **I** *n* **1** gen (also for climbing) corde *f*; **a piece of ~** un bout de corde; **the ~** (hanging) la corde; **to bring back the ~** réintroduire la pendaison; **to be on the ~s** (in boxing) lit être dans les cordes; fig avoir le dos au mur; **2** fig (of pearls) rang *m*; (of hair) tresse *f*.

II *vtr* **1** attacher [*victim, animal*] (**to** à); encorder [*climber*]; nouer [qch] avec une corde [*trunk*]; **a ~d party (of climbers)** une cordée d'alpinistes; **2** US (lasso) prendre [qch] au lasso [*cattle*]; fig○ mettre le grappin sur○ [*husband, job*].

IDIOMS **give him enough ~ and he'll hang himself** si on le laisse faire, il va se casser la figure○ or s'enferrer; **to give sb plenty of ~** laisser à qn toute la liberté qu'il/elle veut; **to know the ~s** connaître les ficelles○; **to show sb the ~s** montrer les ficelles à qn○; **to be at the end of one's ~**○ US être au bout du rouleau○.

■ **rope in**○: **~ [sb], ~ in [sb]** **1** GB (to help with task) embaucher○, mettre [qn] à contribution; **2** US (by trickery) (into situation, deal) embringuer○; **to get ~d in** se faire embringuer○.

■ **rope off**: **~ off [sth], ~ [sth] off** barrer [qch] avec une corde.

■ **rope up** (in climbing) s'encorder.

rope: **~ ladder** *n* échelle *f* de corde; **~-length** *n* Sport longueur *f* de corde; **~maker** *n* cordier/-ière *m/f*; **~ trick** *n* tour *m* de la corde.

rop(e)y○ /ˈrəʊpɪ/ *adj* GB [*food, performance*] minable; **to feel a bit ~** se sentir un peu patraque○.

RORO /ˈrəʊrəʊ/ *abrév* ▸ **roll-on roll-off**.

rosary /ˈrəʊzərɪ/ *n* **1** (prayer) rosaire *m*; **to say the ~** réciter le rosaire; **2** (also **~ beads**) chapelet *m*, rosaire *m*.

rose /rəʊz/ **I** *prét* ▸ **rise**.

II *n* **1** (flower) rose *f*; **2** (shrub) rosier *m*; **3** (colour) rose *m*; **4** (nozzle) (on watering can) pomme *f* d'arrosoir; (on shower) pomme *f* de douche; **5** (gem) pierre *f* taillée en rose; **6** Archit (window) rosace *f*; (on ceiling) rosace *f*; (motif) rose *f*; **7** (girl) **an English ~** une Anglaise au teint de porcelaine; **8** (emblem) rose *f*; GB Hist **the Wars of the Roses** la guerre *f* des Deux-Roses.

IDIOMS **life is not a bed of ~s** ce n'est pas tous les jours la fête; **his life is not all ~s** sa vie n'est pas toujours rose; **everything is coming up ~s** tout se passe merveilleusement bien; **under the ~** en confidence; **to put the ~s back in sb's cheeks** redonner des couleurs à qn; **to come up smelling of ~s** s'en tirer sans tache.

rosé /ˈrəʊzeɪ, US rəʊˈzeɪ/ *n, adj* Wine rosé (*m*).

roseate /ˈrəʊzɪət/ *adj* littér rosé.

rose: **~bay** *n* US Bot rhododendron *m*; **~bay willowherb** *n* Bot épilobe *m* à épi; **~bed** *n* parterre *m* de roses; **~bowl** *n* vase *m* (*spécialement conçu pour les roses*).

rosebud /ˈrəʊzbʌd/ *n* bouton *m* de rose.

rose: **~bud mouth** *n* bouche *f* aux lèvres ourlées; **~bud vase** *n* soliflore *m*; **~ bush** *n* rosier *m*.

rose-coloured GB, **rose-colored** US /ˈrəʊzkʌləd/ ▸ **1104** *adj* **1** (red) vermeil/-eille; **2** (optimistic) [*idea, view*] à l'eau de rose.

IDIOMS **to see the world through ~ spectacles** ou **glasses** voir la vie en rose; **to see sb/sth through ~ spectacles** ne voir que les bons côtés de qn/qch.

rose: **~-cut** *adj* [*gem*] taillé en rose; **~garden** *n* roseraie *f*; **~grower** *n* rosiériste *mf*; **~hip** *n* gratte-cul *m*, cynorhodon *m*; **~hip syrup** *n* sirop *m* d'églantine.

rosemary /ˈrəʊzmərɪ, US -merɪ/ *n* romarin *m*.

rose of Sharon *n* GB millepertuis *m* à grandes fleurs; US hibiscus *m* (syriacus).

roseola /rəʊˈziːələ/ *n* roséole *f*.

rose: **~ petal** *n* pétale *m* de rose; **~ pink** ▸ **1104** *adj* rose; **~-red** ▸ **1104** *adj* vermeil/-eille; **~-tinted** ▸ **1104** *adj* = **rose-coloured**.

rosette /rəʊˈzet/ *n* **1** (for supporter, winner) cocarde *f*; Equit flot *m*; (on gift wrap) faveur *f*, nœud *m*; **2** Bot (of leaves) rosette *f*; **3** Archit (carving) rosette *f*; (window) rosace *f*.

rose: **~-water** *n* eau *f* de rose; **~ window** *n* rosace *f*.

rosewood /ˈrəʊzwʊd/ **I** *n* bois *m* de rose.

II *modif* [*chair, table*] en bois de rose.

Rosicrucian /ˌrəʊzɪˈkruːʃn/ *n, adj* rosicrucien/-ienne (*m/f*).

rosin /ˈrɒzɪn, US ˈrɒzn/ *n* colophane *f*.

ROSPA *n* GB (*abrév* = **Royal Society for the Prevention of Accidents**) association *f* pour la prévention des accidents.

roster /ˈrɒstə(r)/ *n* (also **duty ~**) tableau *m* de service.

rostrum /ˈrɒstrəm/ *n* (*pl* **-trums** ou **-tra**) estrade *f*.

rosy /ˈrəʊzɪ/ *adj* **1** (pink) [*cheek, face, lip, light*] rose; [*dawn*] rosé; **~-cheeked** aux joues roses (*after n*); **2** (favourable) [*future, picture*] prometteur/-euse; **things are looking ~** les choses s'annoncent bien; **our prospects are not ~** nos perspectives ne sont pas bonnes; **to paint a ~ picture of sth** peindre un tableau favorable de qch.

IDIOMS **everything in the garden is ~** tout va très bien.

rot /rɒt/ **I** *n* **1** lit pourriture *f*; fig mal *m*; **the ~ in the system** le mal qui ronge le système; **to stop the ~** fig arrêter le mal or la gangrène; **the ~ set in when...** les choses ont commencé à se gâter quand...; **2**○ †GB (rubbish) balivernes† *fpl*, bêtises *fpl*; **to talk ~** raconter des balivernes†; **3** Vet piétin *m*.

II *vtr* (*p prés etc* **-tt-**) pourrir.

III *vi* (*p prés etc* **-tt-**) (also **~ away**) lit pourrir; fig [*person*] moisir○; **to leave sb to ~ in prison** laisser moisir○ or croupir○ qn en prison.

IV rotting *pres p adj* pourrissant.

rota /ˈrəʊtə/ *n* GB tableau *m* de service; **on a ~ basis** à tour de rôle, par roulement.

Rotarian /rəʊˈteərɪən/ *n* rotarien *m*, membre *m* du Rotary Club.

rotary /ˈrəʊtərɪ/ **I** *n* US Aut rond-point *m*.

II *adj* [*motion*] rotatif/-ive, rotatoire; [*engine, pump, mower*] rotatif/-ive.

rotary: **~ clothes line** *n* séchoir *m* parapluie; **Rotary club** *n* Rotary Club *m*; **~ plough** GB, **~ plow** US *n* motoculteur *m*; **~ (printing) press** *n* rotative *f*.

rotate /rəʊˈteɪt, US ˈrəʊteɪt/ **I** *vtr* **1** faire tourner [*handle, blade*]; faire pivoter [*mirror*]; **2** (alternate) occuper [qch] par roulement, faire [qch] à tour de rôle [*job*]; alterner [*roles*]; **3** Agric alterner [*crops*].

II *vi* [*blade, handle, wings*] tourner.

rotating /rəʊˈteɪtɪŋ, US ˈrəʊteɪtɪŋ/ *adj* **1** (turning) [*blade, globe*] tournant; [*mirror*] pivotant; **2** [*post, presidency*] tournant.

rotation /rəʊˈteɪʃn/ *n* **1** (of blade, wheel, crops) rotation *f*; **2** (taking turns) **job ~** occupation *f* des postes par roulement; **to work in ~** travailler par roulement or à tour de rôle; **in strict ~** [*answer, ask*] à tour de rôle.

rote /rəʊt/ *n* **by ~** [*learn*] par cœur.

rote learning *n* par cœur○ *m*; **to encourage ~** encourager à apprendre par cœur.

rotgut● /ˈrɒtgʌt/ *n* péj tord-boyaux○ *m inv*.

rotisserie /rəʊˈtiːsərɪ/ *n* rôtissoire *f*.

rotogravure /ˌrəʊtəgrəˈvjʊə(r)/ *n* rotogravure *f*.

rotor /ˈrəʊtə(r)/ *n* gen, Elec, Aviat rotor *m*.

rotor: **~ arm** *n* Aut toucheau *m*; **~ blade** *n* pale *f* de rotor.

rotorcraft /ˈrəʊtəkrɑːft, US -kræft/ *n* (*pl* **~**) giravion *m*.

rototill /ˈrəʊtətɪl/ *vtr* US = **rotovate**.

Rototiller® /ˈrəʊtətɪlə(r)/ *n* US motoculteur *m*.

rotovate /ˈrəʊtəveɪt/ *vtr* GB retourner [qch] au motoculteur [*garden*]; passer [qch] au rotavator [*field*].

rotovator® /ˈrəʊtəveɪtə(r)/ *n* GB (for garden) motoculteur *m*; (on farm) rotavator *m*.

rotproof /ˈrɒtpruːf/ *adj* imputrescible.

rotten /ˈrɒtn/ **I** *adj* **1** (decayed) [*produce, wood, vegetation*] pourri; [*teeth*] gâté; [*ironwork*] rongé par la rouille; [*smell*] de pourri, de pourriture; **2** (corrupt) pourri○; **3**○ (bad) [*weather*] pourri; [*food*] infect; [*cook, driver*] exécrable; **what ~ luck!** quel manque de bol○!; **to feel ~** se sentir patraque○; **I feel ~ about it** j'en suis malade; **that was a ~ thing to do!** c'était vraiment un sale coup○!; **a ~ bastard**● un vrai salaud●.

II *adv* **to spoil sb ~**○ pourrir qn○.

IDIOMS **to be ~ to the core** être pourri jusqu'à l'os.

rotten: **~ apple** *n* fig brebis *f* galeuse; **~ borough** *n* GB bourg *m* pourri (*circonscription électorale dépeuplée mais toujours représentée au Parlement*).

rottenness /ˈrɒtnɪs/ *n* pourriture *f*.

rotter○† /ˈrɒtə(r)/ GB *n* chameau○ *m*.

rottweiler /ˈrɒtvaɪlə(r)/ *n* rottweiler *m*.

rotund /rəʊˈtʌnd/ *adj* **1** [*person*] grassouillet/-ette; [*stomach*] rebondi; **2** [*object, building*] aux formes arrondies.

rotunda /rəʊˈtʌndə/ *n* rotonde *f*.

rotundity /rəʊˈtʌndətɪ/ *n* (of person) embonpoint *m*; (of stomach, building) rotondité *f*.

rouble /ˈruːbl/ ▸ **1143** *n* rouble *m*.

roué /ˈruːeɪ/ *n* littér débauché *m*.

rouge† /ruːʒ/ **I** *n* Cosmet rouge *m* à joues.

II *vtr* **to ~ one's cheeks** se mettre du rouge aux joues.

rough /rʌf/ **I** *n* **1** Sport (in golf) rough *m*; **2** (unfinished copy) (draft) brouillon *m*; (sketch)

gen, spec ébauche *f*; **to write sth out in ~** écrire qch au brouillon.
II *adj* **1** (not smooth) [*hand, skin*] rêche; (stronger) rugueux/-euse; [*surface, rock*] rugueux/-euse; [*material, paper*] rêche; [*road, terrain*] cahoteux/-euse; [*landscape*] sauvage; [*grass*] sec/sèche; **to smooth (off) the ~ edges** (of stone, wood, glass etc) polir; **2** (brutal) [*person, treatment, behaviour, sport*] brutal, violent; [*area, district*] dur; **to be ~ with sb/sth** être brutal avec qn/qch; **to get ~ (with sb)** devenir violent (avec qn); **3** (approximate) [*description, map, indication*] sommaire; [*translation, calculation*] sommaire, rapide; [*figure, estimate*] approximatif/-ive; **can you give me a ~ idea of the cost?** est-ce que vous pouvez me donner une idée approximative du coût?; **~ justice** justice *f* sommaire or expéditive; **4** (difficult) [*life, period*] dur, difficile; **to be ~ on sb** [*person*] être dur avec qn; **it's ~ on you/him** c'est dur pour toi/lui; **we're having a ~ time** on traverse une période difficile; **to give sb a ~ ride** rendre la vie dure à qn; **he's had a ~ deal**○ il a été traité injustement; **5** (crude) [*person, manner, behaviour*] grossier/-ière; [*dwelling, shelter, table*] rudimentaire; **6** (harsh) [*voice, sound, taste, wine*] âpre; **7** (stormy) [*sea, crossing*] agité; [*weather*] gros/grosse; (in plane) [*landing*] mouvementé; **8**○ (unwell) **to feel/to look ~** se sentir/avoir l'air patraque○.
III *adv* **1** (outdoors) **to sleep/to live ~** dormir/vivre à la dure; **2** (violently) [*fight, play*] brutalement.
IDIOMS **to cut up ~** s'énerver; **to ~ it** vivre à la dure.
■ **rough in**: **~ in [sth]** (sketch) esquisser; (estimate) ébaucher, donner une idée de [*figures, details*].
■ **rough out**: **~ out [sth]** esquisser, ébaucher [*plan, proposal, drawing*].
■ **rough up**○: **~ [sb] up, ~ up [sb] 1** (manhandle) bousculer euph, malmener; **2** (beat up) tabasser○.

roughage /'rʌfɪdʒ/ *n* fibres *fpl*.

rough-and-ready /ˌrʌfən'redɪ/ *adj* **1** (unsophisticated) [*person, manner*] fruste; [*house, conditions*] rudimentaire; **2** (improvised) [*calculation, method, system*] sommaire.

rough-and-tumble /ˌrʌfən'tʌmbl/ **I** *n* **1** (rough behaviour) chahut *m*; **2** fig (of life, politics, business) mêlée *f* (**of** de).
II *adj* [*life, world, profession*] brutal, impitoyable.

roughcast /'rʌfkɑːst, US -kæst/ Constr **I** *n* crépi *m*.
II *adj* [*wall*] crépi.
III *vtr* (*prét, pp* **-cast**) crépir [*wall*].

rough diamond *n* **1** (jewel) diamant *m* brut; **2** GB (man) brave homme *m*.

roughen /'rʌfn/ **I** *vtr* (make rough) rendre [qch] rêche or rugueux [*skin, hand*]; [*wind, weather*] rendre [qch] rugueux [*rock, stone*].
II *vi* [*hands, skin*] devenir rêche or rugueux.

rough-hewn /'rʌfhjuːn/ *adj* [*wood, stone*] équarri; fig [*features*] buriné.

rough house○ *n* bagarre○ *f*.

roughly /'rʌflɪ/ *adv* **1** (approximately) [*calculate, describe, sketch, indicate*] grossièrement, rapidement; [*equal, equivalent*] à peu près; [*triangular, circular*] à peu près; **~ speaking** en gros, approximativement; **~ 10%/100 people** à peu près or approximativement 10%/100 personnes; **~ the same age/size** à peu près le même âge/la même taille; **2** (with force) [*push, treat, hit*] brutalement; **3** (crudely) [*put together, make, chop, grate*] grossièrement.

roughneck○ /'rʌfnek/ **▶ 1692** *n* **1** (violent person) dur○ *m*; **2** (oil-rig worker) *ouvrier sur une plate-forme pétrolière*.

roughness /'rʌfnɪs/ *n* **1** (lack of smoothness) (of skin, hand, rock, surface, material) rugosité *f*; (of road, terrain) inégalité *f*; **2** (violence) (of person, treatment) brutalité *f*; **3** (lack of sophistication) (of person, manner, voice, appearance) rudesse *f*; (of furniture, house) simplicité *f*; **4** (storminess) **it all depends on the ~ of the sea** tout dépend de l'état de la mer.

rough: **~ paper** *n* feuille *f* de brouillon; **~ puff pastry** *n* Culin pâte *f* feuilletée minute; **~rider** *n* dresseur/-euse *m/f* de chevaux.

roughshod /'rʌfʃɒd/ *adj* IDIOMS **to ride ~ over sb/sth** se moquer (totalement) de qn/qch.

rough: **~-spoken** *adj* grossier/-ière; **~ stuff**○ *n* violence *f*, bagarre○ *f*; **~ trade**○ *n*: *partenaire homosexuel d'un bas niveau social et souvent enclin à la violence*; **~ work** *n* Sch brouillon *m*.

roulette /ruː'let/ *n* roulette *f*.

roulette: **~ table** *n* table *f* de roulette; **~ wheel** *n* roulette *f*.

Roumania *pr n* = **Romania**.

Roumanian *n, adj* = **Romanian**.

round /raʊnd/

■ **Note** *round* often appears after verbs in English (*change round, gather round, pass round*). For translations, consult the appropriate verb entry (***change, gather, pass***).
– For *go round, get round* see the entries ***go, get***.

I *adv* **1** GB (on all sides) **all ~** lit tout autour; **whisky all ~!** du whisky pour tout le monde!; **there were smiles all ~** tout le monde souriait; **to go all the way ~** [*fence, wall, moat*] faire tout le tour; **2** GB (in circular movement) **to go ~ and ~** [*wheel, carousel*] tourner (en rond); [*person*] fig tourner en rond; lit aller et venir; **the tune was going ~ and ~ in my head** j'avais cet air dans la tête; **3** GB (to specific place, home) **to be** ou **go ~ to** passer à [*office, school*]; **to ask sb (to come) ~** dire à qn de passer; **she's coming ~ today** elle passe aujourd'hui; **to invite sb ~ for lunch** inviter qn à déjeuner (chez soi); **I'm just going ~ to Sandra's** je pars chez Sandra; **I'll be ~ in a minute** j'arrive (dans un instant); **4** GB (in circumference) **three metres ~** [*tree trunk*] de trois mètres de circonférence; **5** GB (as part of cycle) **all year ~** toute l'année; **this time ~** cette fois-ci; **as summer comes ~** à l'approche de l'été; **my birthday will soon be ~ again** c'est bientôt mon anniversaire.
II *prep* GB **1** (expressing location) autour de [*table, garden etc*]; **let's sit ~ the table** asseyons-nous autour de la table; **to sit ~ the fire** s'asseoir au coin du feu; **the wall goes right ~ the house** le mur fait le tour de la maison; **he had a scarf ~ his neck** il avait une écharpe autour du cou; **what do you measure ~ the waist?** combien faistu de tour de taille?; **2** (expressing direction) **to go ~ the corner** tourner au coin de la rue; **to go ~ a bend** (in road) prendre un virage; **the baker's is just ~ the corner** la boulangerie est tout près; **to go ~ a roundabout** prendre un rond-point; **to go ~ an obstacle** contourner un obstacle; **3** (on tour, visit) **shall I take you ~ the house?** voulezvous visiter la maison?; **her sister took us ~ Oxford** sa sœur nous a fait visiter Oxford; **to go ~ the shops** faire les magasins.
III round about *adv phr* **1** (approximately) à peu près, environ; **~ about 50 people/9 am** à peu près or environ 50 personnes/9 h; **it happened ~ about here** ça s'est passé par ici; **2** (vicinity) **the people/streets ~ about** les gens/rues des environs; **▶ roundabout**.
IV *n* **1** (set, series) série *f* (**of** de); **the social ~** les réceptions *fpl* mondaines; **the daily ~ of activities** le train-train quotidien; **▶ payround, wage round**; **2** (in competition) rencontre *f*; **qualifying ~** (in football, rugby, tennis) match *m* de qualification; **3** (game of golf, cards) partie *f* (**of** de); (in boxing, wrestling) round *m*; **4** Equit (in event) parcours *m*; **a clear ~** un parcours sans faute; **5** Pol (in election) tour *m*; **6** (of drinks) tournée *f* (**of** de); **it's my ~!** c'est ma tournée!; **to pay for a ~** offrir une tournée; **7** Mil (unit of ammunition) balle *f*; **~ of ammunition** cartouche *f*; **to fire ~ after ~** tirer balle sur balle; **▶ baton round**; **8** Mil (shot fired) salve *f*; **~s of machine-gun fire** des salves de mitrailleuse; **9** (burst) **~ of applause** salve *f* d'applaudissements; **to get a ~ of applause** être applaudi; **let's have a ~ of applause for David!** on applaudit bien fort David!; **10** Culin (of bread) **a ~ of toast** un toast, une tranche de pain grillé; **a ~ of ham sandwiches** des sandwiches *mpl* pain de mie au jambon; **11** (regular route) tournée *f*; **▶ milk round, paper round**; **12** (circular shape) rondelle *f* (**of** de); **13** Mus (canon) canon *m*; **14** Theat **theatre in the ~** théâtre *m* en rond; **15** Art **in the ~** [*sculpture*] en ronde-bosse; **16** Dance ronde *f*; **17** (of cheese) roue *f*; **18** Culin **~ of beef** rond *m*.
V rounds *npl* **to do one's ~s** [*doctor*] visiter ses malades; [*postman, refuse collector*] faire sa tournée; [*security guard*] faire sa ronde; **to be out on one's ~s** [*doctor*] être en visite; **to do** ou **go** ou **make the ~s** [*rumour, joke, document, flu*] circuler; **to go the ~s of** [*story*] faire le tour de [*village, office*]; [*garment, book*] faire le tour de [*relations, family*]; **to do the ~s of** faire le tour de [*employment agencies, relations*].
VI *adj* **1** (circular) [*object, building, glasses, face, head*] rond; **her eyes grew ~** elle a ouvert des yeux ronds; **2** (rounded, curved) [*arch*] arrondi; [*handwriting*] rond; [*cheeks, breasts*] rond; **to have ~ shoulders** avoir le dos voûté; **3** (spherical) rond; **4** (complete) [*figure*] rond; **in ~ figures** en chiffres ronds; **in ~ figures, that's £100** ça fait 100 livres sterling en arrondissant; **a ~ dozen** une douzaine exactement; **a nice ~ sum** une somme appréciable or rondelette○.
VII round+ (*dans composés*) **~-cheeked/-eyed** aux joues rondes/aux yeux ronds; **~-faced** au visage rond; **▶ round-shouldered**.
VIII *vtr* **1** gen, Naut (go round) contourner [*point, headland*]; **to ~ the corner** tourner au coin; **to ~ a bend** prendre un virage; **2** (make round) arrondir [*lips*]; **3** Phon arrondir [*vowels*].
■ **round down**: **~ [sth] down, ~ down [sth]** arrondir [qch] au chiffre inférieur [*figures*].
■ **round off**: **~ off [sth], ~ [sth] off 1** (finish off) finir [*meal, evening, visit, season*] (**with** par) ; conclure [*speech*]; parfaire [*education, process*]; **2** (make smooth) arrondir [*corner, edge*]; **3** (change) arrondir [*figure, number*].
■ **round on** GB: **~ on [sb]** attaquer violemment [*critic, opponent*]; **suddenly she ~ed on me** tout d'un coup elle m'est tombée dessus○.
■ **round out**: **~ [sth] out, ~ out [sth]** compléter [*list, numbers, range*].
■ **round up**: ¶ **~ up [sb], ~ [sb] up** regrouper [*protesters, inhabitants*]; ramasser○ [*thieves, prostitutes, suspects*]; **to be ~ed up** être pris dans une rafle; ¶ **~ up [sth], ~ [sth] up 1** rassembler [*livestock*]; **2** arrondir [qch] au chiffre supérieur [*figure*].

roundabout /'raʊndəbaʊt/ **I** *n* **1** GB (in fairground etc) manège *m*; **2** GB (in playpark) tourniquet *m*; **3** GB Transp rond-point *m*.
II *adj* **to come by a ~ way** ou **route** faire un détour; **by ~ means** par des moyens détournés; **a ~ way of saying sth** une façon détournée or alambiquée○ de dire qch; **he goes about things in rather a ~ way** il se complique la vie.
IDIOMS **it's swings and ~s, what you gain on the swings you lose on the ~s** ce que tu gagnes d'un côté, tu le perds de l'autre.

round: **~ brackets** *npl* GB parenthèses *fpl*; **~ dance** *n* Dance ronde *f*.

rounded /'raʊndɪd/ *adj* **1** [*shape, corner, edge*] arrondi; [*tone, style*] étoffé; **2** Phon [*vowel*] arrondi; **3** (developed) [*phrase*] bien tourné; [*account*] détaillé.

roundel /ˈraʊndl/ *n* **1** Aviat cocarde *f*; **2** Literat rondeau *m*; **3** Mus ronde *f*.

rounders /ˈraʊndəz/ *n* GB Sport (+ *v sg*) ≈ baseball *m*.

round: **Roundhead** *n* GB Hist Tête *f* ronde; **~house** *n* Rail rotonde *f*.

roundly /ˈraʊndlɪ/ *adv* [*condemn, criticize*] sans ambages; [*defeat*] joliment.

round-neck(ed) sweater *n* pull-over *m* ras-de-cou *inv*.

roundness /ˈraʊndnɪs/ *n* rondeur *f*.

round robin *n* **1** (collective statement) lettre *f* de protestation (*où les signatures sont disposées en rond*); **2** (circulated document) circulaire *f*; **3** Sport tournoi *m*.

round-shouldered /ˌraʊndˈʃəʊldəd/ *adj* **to be ~** avoir le dos voûté.

roundsman /ˈraʊndzmən/ *n* (*pl* **-men**) livreur *m*.

round table I *n* table *f* ronde.
II **round-table** *adj* **~ discussions, ~ talks** une table ronde.

Round Table *n* Mythol Table *f* ronde.

round-the-clock I *adj* GB [*care, nursing, surveillance*] 24 heures sur 24; **~ shifts** les trois-huit *m inv*.
II **round the clock** *adv phr* [*work, guard*] 24 heures sur 24.

round-the-world I *adj* [*cruise, trip*] autour du monde; [*sailor*] qui a fait le tour du monde.
II *adv* **to sail round the world** faire le tour du monde à la voile.

round trip I *n* aller-retour *m*.
II **round-trip** *adj* [*price*] tout compris; **~ ticket** billet *m* aller-retour.

roundup /ˈraʊndʌp/ *n* **1** (swoop) rafle *f*; **2** (herding of people, animals) rassemblement *m* (**of** de); **3** (summary) résumé *m* (**of** de); **'news ~'** 'l'actualité en bref'.

roundworm /ˈraʊndwɜːm/ *n* ascaris *m*.

rouse /raʊz/ *vtr* **1** sout (wake) réveiller; **to ~ sb from a deep sleep** tirer qn d'un sommeil profond; **2** (stir) réveiller [*person, troops, nation*]; susciter [*anger, interest*]; **to ~ public opinion** soulever l'opinion publique (**against** contre); **to ~ sb to anger** susciter la colère de qn; **to ~ sb to action** pousser qn à l'action; **when she's ~d** quand elle est en colère.

rousing /ˈraʊzɪŋ/ *adj* [*reception, welcome*] enthousiaste; [*speech, words*] galvanisant; [*song, music*] exaltant.

roustabout /ˈraʊstəbaʊt/ *n* **1** (on oil-rig) manœuvre *m* (de chantier pétrolier); **2** US (docker) débardeur *m*; **3** (in circus) homme *m* à tout faire (*dans un cirque*).

rout /raʊt/ I *n* **1** (defeat) déroute *f*, défaite *f*; **to put sb to ~** mettre qn en déroute; **2** Jur attroupement *m* illicite d'individus.
II *vtr* **1** Mil mettre [qn] en déroute [*enemy*]; **2** fig battre [qn] à plates coutures [*team*].
■ **rout out**: **~ [sth/sb] out, ~ out [sth/sb]** **1** (find) dénicher [*person, animal, object*]; **2** (force out) déloger [*person, animal*] (**of** de).

route /ruːt/ I *n* **1** gen (way) chemin *m*; (to workplace) trajet *m* (**to** pour aller à); **on the ~ to Oxford** sur le chemin d'Oxford; **the main/shortest ~** le chemin le plus direct/le plus court (**to** pour); **escape ~** chemin d'évasion; **to plan a ~** décider d'un itinéraire; **by a different ~** par un chemin différent; **2** Transp route *f*; Aviat, Tourism ligne *f*; **domestic ~s** les lignes intérieures; **shipping ~** route maritime; **bus/rail ~** ligne d'autobus/de chemin de fer; **traffic ~** axe *m* routier; **Route 86** US l'autoroute *f* 86; **the main drug ~s** les principaux circuits de la drogue; **3** (official itinerary) parcours *m*; **they lined the ~** ils se tenaient le long du parcours; **4** fig (to power, success etc) voie *f* (**to** de); **5** US /raʊt/ (**newspaper**) **~** tournée *f* de livraison; **6** Med **~ of infection** mode *m* de transmission.
II *vtr* expédier, acheminer [*goods*] (**to** vers); acheminer [*trains*] (**to** vers, sur); **this flight is ~d to Athens via Rome** ce vol va à Athènes via Rome.

route march *n* marche *f* d'entraînement.

routine /ruːˈtiːn/ I *n* **1** (regular procedure) routine *f* (**of** de); **the daily ~** la routine quotidienne; **office ~** travail *m* de routine; **government ~** les affaires *fpl* courantes du gouvernement; **to establish a ~** (at work) s'organiser; (for spare time) se faire un emploi du temps; **as a matter of ~** systématiquement; **2** (drudgery) routine *f* (**of** de); **it would be a break from ~** ça changerait de la routine; **3** Mus, Theat (act) numéro *m*; **a song and dance ~** un numéro de chant et de danse; **4**○ péj (obvious act) numéro○ *m*; **don't give me that ~!** arrête ton numéro○!; **5** Comput sous-programme *m*; **input/main ~** sous-programme d'introduction/principal; **6** Sport enchaînement *m*.
II *adj* **1** (normal) [*check, enquiry, matter, mission*] de routine; **it's fairly ~** c'est la routine; **~ procedure** la procédure habituelle; **~ maintenance** (of vehicle, building) entretien *m* courant; **2** (uninspiring) [*task, lifestyle, performance*] routinier/-ière.

routinely /ruːˈtiːnlɪ/ *adv* **1** (as part of routine) [*check, contact, review*] systématiquement; **2** (commonly) [*tortured, abused*] régulièrement.

rove /rəʊv/ I *vtr* [*person*] (aimlessly) vagabonder dans [*country*]; (prowl) rôder dans [*streets*].
II *vi* (also **~ around, ~ about**) [*person*] (aimlessly) vagabonder; (prowl) rôder; **his eye ~d around the room** son regard balayait la pièce.

rover /ˈrəʊvə(r)/ *n* **to be a ~** aimer bouger.

roving /ˈrəʊvɪŋ/ *adj* [*ambassador*] itinérant; [*band*] en vagabondage; **~ reporter** hum reporter *m* qui est toujours sur la route; **to have a ~ eye** être toujours à l'affût d'une aventure.

row[1] /rəʊ/ ▶ 1282 I *n* **1** (line) (of people, plants, stitches) rang *m* (**of** de); (of houses, seats, books) rangée *f* (**of** de); **seated in a ~/in ~s** assis en rang/en rangs; **a ~ of cars** une file de voitures; **~s and ~s of** des rangs et des rangs de; **~ after ~ of** rang après rang de; **in the front ~** au premier rang; **2** (succession) **six times in a ~** six fois de suite; **the third time/week in a ~** la troisième fois/semaine d'affilée; **3** (in boat) promenade *f* en barque; **to go for a ~** faire de la barque.
II *vtr* **1** (for transport, pleasure) **to ~ a boat across/up the river** traverser/remonter la rivière à la rame; **to ~ sb across** faire traverser [qch] à qn en barque [*lake, river*]; **2** Sport **to ~ a race** faire une course d'aviron.
III *vi* ramer (**for** pour; **against** contre); **to ~ across/up** traverser/remonter [qch] à la rame [*river, lake*].

row[2] /raʊ/ I *n* **1** (dispute) (public) querelle *f* (**between** entre; **about, over** à propos de; **with** avec); (private) dispute *f* (**between** entre; **about, over** à propos de; **with** avec); **a family ~** une querelle de famille; **to have** ou **get into a ~ with** se disputer avec; **2** (loud noise) tapage *m*; **the ~ from next door** le tapage des voisins; **to make a ~** faire du tapage.
II *vi* se disputer (**with** avec; **about, over** à propos de).

rowan /ˈrəʊən, ˈraʊ-/ *n* **1** (tree) sorbier *m*; **2** (berry) sorbe *f*.

rowboat /rəʊ/ *n* US bateau *m* à rames.

rowdiness /ˈraʊdɪnɪs/ *n* (in streets, at match) (noise) tapage *m*; (violence) bagarre○ *f*; (in classroom) chahut *m*.

rowdy /ˈraʊdɪ/ I *n* (hooligan) voyou *m*; (in classroom) chahuteur/-euse *m/f*.
II *adj* [*youth, behaviour*] (noisy) tapageur/-euse; (violent) bagarreur/-euse; [*pupil*] chahuteur/-euse.

rowdyism /ˈraʊdɪɪzəm/ *n* = **rowdiness**.

rower /ˈrəʊə(r)/ *n* rameur/-euse *m/f*, nageur/-euse *m/f*.

row house /rəʊ/ *n* US maison *f* qui fait partie d'une série de constructions identiques.

rowing /ˈrəʊɪŋ/ ▶ 1282 I *n* aviron *m*; **to like ~** aimer (faire de) l'aviron.
II *modif* [*club, team, star*] d'aviron.

rowing: **~ boat** *n* GB bateau *m* à rames; **~ machine** *n* rameur *m*.

rowlock /rəʊ/ *n* GB dame *f* de nage, tolet *m*.

royal /ˈrɔɪəl/ I *n* **1**○ (person) membre *m* de la famille royale; **2** (paper) cavalier *m*.
II *adj* **1** (also **Royal**) [*couple, palace, visit, prerogative*] royal; **the ~ 'we'** le pluriel de majesté; **2** (splendid) **to give sb a (right) ~ welcome** faire un accueil royal à qn; **3**○ US (thorough) **to be a ~ pain** être le roi des emmerdeurs◑.

royal: **Royal Air Force, RAF** *n* GB armée *f* de l'air britannique; **Royal Assent** *n* GB approbation *f* royale (*d'un projet de loi*); **~ blue** ▶ 1104 *n, adj* bleu (*m*) roi (*inv*); **Royal Commission** *n* GB commission *f* d'enquête parlementaire; **~ family** *n* famille *f* royale; **~ flush** *n* quinte *f* royale.

Royal Highness ▶ 1268 *n* **His/Her ~** Son Altesse *f* royale; **Their ~es** Leurs Altesses *fpl* royales; **Your ~** Votre Altesse *f*.

royal icing *n* GB glaçage *m* aux blancs d'œufs.

royalist, Royalist /ˈrɔɪəlɪst/ *n, adj* royaliste (*mf*).

royal jelly *n* gelée *f* royale.

royally /ˈrɔɪəlɪ/ *adv* [*received, entertained*] royalement.

royal: **Royal Mail** *n* GB service *m* postal britannique; **Royal Marines** *npl* GB fusiliers-marins *mpl* britanniques; **Royal Navy** *n* GB marine *f* britannique; **Royal Society** *n* GB Académie *f* des Sciences.

royalty /ˈrɔɪəltɪ/ *n* **1** ¢ (person) membre *m* d'une famille royale; (persons) membres *mpl* d'une famille royale; **we were treated like ~** on nous a traités comme des rois; **2** (state of royal person) royauté *f*; **3** (money) (to author, musician) droits *mpl* d'auteur (**on** sur); (to publisher) redevance *f* (**on** sur); (on patent, coal deposits) royalties *fpl* (**on** sur); **to receive £100 in royalties** (on book) toucher 100 livres sterling de droits d'auteur.

royal: **Royal Ulster Constabulary, RUC** *n* GB police *f* d'Irlande du Nord; **~ warrant** *n* brevet *m* de fournisseur de la Cour.

rozzer○ /ˈrɒzə(r)/ *n* GB flic○ *m*.

RP *n* GB (*abrév* = **Received Pronunciation**) RP *f* (*prononciation de l'anglais considérée comme standard*).

RPI *abrév* ▶ **retail price index**.

rpm (*abrév* = **revolutions per minute**) tr/min.

RPM *abrév* = **retail price maintenance**.

R & R *n* US Mil (*abrév* = **rest and recuperation**) permission *f* (*récupération entre deux combats*).

RRP GB (*abrév écrite* = **recommended retail price**) prix *m* de détail conseillé.

RSA *n* GB (*abrév* = **Royal Society of Arts**) Académie *f* des Beaux Arts.

RSI *abrév* ▶ **repetitive strain injury**.

RSM (*abrév* = **Regimental Sergeant-Major**) adjudant-chef *m*.

RSPB *n* GB (*abrév* = **Royal Society for the Protection of Birds**) ligue *f* pour la protection des oiseaux.

RSPCA *n* GB (*abrév* = **Royal Society for the Prevention of Cruelty to Animals**) société *f* protectrice des animaux.

RSV *n*: *abrév* ▶ **Revised Standard Version**.

RSVP *abrév écrite* RSVP.

Rt Hon GB *abrév écrite* = **Right Honourable**.

Rt Rev *abrév écrite* = **Right Reverend**.

rub /rʌb/ **I** *n* **1** (massage) friction *f*; **to give [sth] a ~** frictionner [*back*]; bouchonner [*horse*]; **2** (polish) coup *m* de chiffon; **to give [sth] a ~** donner un coup de torchon à [*spoon*]; donner un coup de chiffon à [*table*]; frotter [*stain*]; **3** (liniment) baume *m* pour les muscles; **4** † ou hum (drawback) hic○ *m*, inconvénient *m*; **there's the ~** voilà le hic○.
II *vtr* (*p prés etc* **-bb-**) **1** (touch) se frotter [*chin, eyes, nose*]; **to ~ noses** (in greeting) se frotter le nez; **to ~ one's hands with glee** se frotter les mains de joie; **2** (polish) frotter [*stain, surface*]; **to ~ sth dry** sécher qch avec un torchon; **to ~ sth away** faire disparaître qch [*stain*]; **to ~ a hole in sth** faire un trou dans qch; **3** (massage) frictionner [*back, shoulders*]; **she ~bed my back** elle m'a frictionné le dos; **4** (apply) **to ~ sth on to the skin** appliquer qch sur la peau; **to ~ sth into the skin** faire pénétrer qch dans la peau; **5** (incorporate) **to ~ sth into** Culin incorporer qch à [*flour*]; **~ the cream into your skin** faire pénétrer la pommade en massant; **~ the shampoo into your hair** bien répartir le shampooing en massant; **6** (chafe) [*shoe*] blesser [*heel*]; [*wheel*] frotter contre [*mudguard*].
III *vi* (*p prés etc* **-bb-**) **1** (scrub) frotter; **2** (chafe) **these shoes ~** ces chaussures me blessent.
IV *v refl* (*p prés etc* **-bb-**) **to ~ oneself** se frotter (**against** contre); se frictionner (**with** avec); **to ~ oneself dry** se frictionner pour se sécher.
V rubbed *pp adj* [*furniture*] patiné; [*book cover*] usé.
IDIOMS **to ~ salt into sb's wounds** remuer le couteau dans la plaie; **to ~ sb up the wrong way** prendre qn à rebrousse-poil○; **to ~ shoulders with sb** côtoyer or fréquenter qn; **to ~ sb's nose in it** mettre à qn son nez dans son caca○.
■ **rub along**○: **to ~ along with** s'entendre assez bien avec [*person*].
■ **rub down**: ¶ **~ [sb] down, ~ down [sb]** frictionner [*athlete*]; **to ~ oneself down** se frictionner; ¶ **~ [sth] down, ~ down [sth]** **1** (massage) bouchonner [*horse*]; **2** (smooth) poncer [*plaster, wood*].
■ **rub in**: **~ [sth] in, ~ in [sth]** Culin incorporer [*butter*]; faire pénétrer [*lotion*]; **there's no need to ~ it in**○! fig inutile d'en rajouter○!; **he's always ~bing it in how rich he is** il nous rebat les oreilles avec sa richesse○.
■ **rub off**: ¶ **~ off 1** (come off) [*dye, ink*] déteindre; **the ink ~bed off on my hands** l'encre a déteint sur mes mains; **I hope your integrity ~s off on him** j'espère que ton honnêteté déteindra sur lui; **2** (wipe off) **the chalk/the pencil ~s off easily** la craie/le crayon s'efface facilement; ¶ **~ [sth] off, ~ off [sth]** effacer, faire disparaître [*stain, pattern*].
■ **rub out**: ¶ **~ out** [*chalk, pencil*] s'effacer; ¶ **~ [sth] out, ~ out [sth]** effacer [*word, drawing*]; ¶ **~ [sb] out**○ US fig liquider○ qn.

rubato /ruːˈbɑːtəʊ/ *n, adv* rubato (*m*).

rubber /ˈrʌbə(r)/ **I** *n* **1** (substance) caoutchouc *m*; **made of ~** en caoutchouc; **2** GB (for erasing pencil) gomme *f*; **3** (for cleaning) chiffon *m*; **4**○ US (condom) préservatif *m*, capote○ *f*; **5** Games, Sport partie *f*.
II rubbers *npl* US (galoshes) caoutchoucs *mpl*.
III *modif* [*ball, sole, hose, insulation*] de or en caoutchouc.
IDIOMS **to burn** ou **peel ~**○ US mettre la gomme○.

rubber: **~ band** *n* élastique *m*; **~ bullet** *n* balle *f* de caoutchouc; **~ cement** *n* mastic *m* au caoutchouc; **~ check**○ US chèque *m* en bois○; **~ dinghy** *n* canot *m* pneumatique; **~ glove** *n* gant *m* en or de caoutchouc.

rubberized /ˈrʌbəraɪzd/ *adj* [*fabric, floor surface*] caoutchouté.

rubber johnny◑ *n* préservatif *m*, capote○ *f*.

rubberneck○ /ˈrʌbənek/ **I** *n* **1** (onlooker) curieux/-ieuse *m/f*; **2** (tourist) touriste *mf*.
II *vi* péj regarder d'un air béat.

rubbernecker○ /ˈrʌbənekə(r)/ *n* péj US **1** (onlooker) curieux/-ieuse *m/f*; **2** (tourist) touriste *mf*.

rubber: **~ plant** *n* caoutchouc *m*; **~ plantation** *n* plantation *f* d'hévéas; **~ sheet** *n* alaise *f*; **~-soled** *adj* [*shoes*] à semelles de caoutchouc; **~ solution** *n* dissolution *f*.

rubber stamp **I** *n* **1** lit tampon *m*; **2** fig pej **to be a ~ for sb's decisions** [*body, group*] entériner sans discuter les décisions de qn.
II rubber-stamp *modif* péj [*parliament, assembly*] à l'autorité purement formelle.
III rubber-stamp *vtr* **1** lit (stamp) tamponner [*document, form*]; **2** fig pej entériner [qch] sans discuter [*decision*].

rubber: **~ tapper** *n* personne *f* qui récolte le latex; **~ tapping** *n* récolte *f* du latex par saignée; **~ tree** *n* hévéa *m*.

rubbery /ˈrʌbərɪ/ *adj* [*material, food*] caoutchouteux/-euse.

rubbing /ˈrʌbɪŋ/ *n* **1** (friction) frottement *m*; (in massage) friction *f*; **2** (picture) reproduction *f* par frottement.

rubbish /ˈrʌbɪʃ/ **I** *n* **1** (refuse) (in street) déchets *mpl*; (domestic) ordures *fpl*; (from garden) détritus *mpl*; (on building site) gravats *mpl*; **2** (inferior goods) camelote○ *f*; (discarded objects) saletés○ *fpl*; **3** (nonsense) **to talk ~** raconter n'importe quoi; **this film/book is ~**○! ce film/livre est nul○!; **(what a load of) ~!** n'importe quoi!; **there's nothing but ~ on the TV** il n'y a vraiment rien de bien à la télé.
II *vtr* GB [*critic, article*] descendre [qn/qch] en flammes [*person, work, achievement*].

rubbish: **~ bin** *n* GB poubelle *f*; **~ chute** *n* GB vide-ordures *m inv*; **~ collection** *n* GB ramassage *m* des ordures; **~ dump** GB décharge *f* (publique); **~ heap** *n* gen tas *m* d'ordures; (in garden) tas *m* de saletés○; **~ tip** *n* GB décharge *f* (publique).

rubbishy○ /ˈrʌbɪʃɪ/ *adj* [*article, film, book*] nul/nulle○; **all that ~ food** toutes ces cochonneries○.

rubble /ˈrʌbl/ *n* **1** ¢ (after explosion) décombres *mpl*; (on building site) gravats *mpl*; **the house was reduced to a pile of ~** il ne restait de la maison qu'un tas de décombres; **2** Constr blocaille *f*.

rub-down /ˈrʌbdaʊn/ *n* **to give sb a ~** frictionner qn; **to give [sth] a ~** bouchonner [*horse*]; poncer [*woodwork, plaster*].

Rube Goldberg○ /ˌruːbɪ ˈgəʊldbɜːg/ *adj* US tarabiscoté○.

rubella /ruːˈbelə/ ▶ **1354** **I** *n* rubéole *f*; **to have ~** avoir la rubéole.
II *modif* [*vaccine*] contre la rubéole.

Rubicon /ˈruːbɪkən, US -kɒn/ *pr n* Hist **the ~** le Rubicon.
IDIOMS **to cross the ~** franchir le Rubicon.

rubicund /ˈruːbɪkənd/ *adj* littér rubicond liter.

rubidium /ruːˈbɪdɪəm/ *n* rubidium *m*.

ruble *n* surtout US = **rouble**.

rubric /ˈruːbrɪk/ *n* sout rubrique *f*.

ruby /ˈruːbɪ/ **I** *n* **1** (gem) rubis *m*; **2** ▶ **1104** (colour) rouge *m* rubis.
II *modif* [*bracelet, necklace*] de rubis; **a ~ ring** une bague-rubis.
III *adj* [*liquid, lips*] vermeil/-eille; **~ port** porto *m* (ruby).

ruby: **~-coloured** GB, **~-colored** US ▶ **1104** *adj* rouge rubis *inv*; **~ red** *n, adj* rouge (*m*) rubis (*inv*); **~ wedding** *n* noces *fpl* de vermeil.

RUC *n*: *abrév* ▶ **Royal Ulster Constabulary**.

ruck /rʌk/ **I** *n* **1** (in rugby) mêlée *f* ouverte; **2** pej littér (mass) **the (common) ~** la masse péj; **3** (crease) faux pli *m*.
■ **ruck up** [*dress, skirt*] se plisser.

rucksack /ˈrʌksæk/ *n* sac *m* à dos.

ruckus○ /ˈrʌkəs/ *n* surtout US **a ~** du grabuge○ *m*.

ructions○ /ˈrʌkʃnz/ *npl* GB grabuge○ *m* ¢.

rudder /ˈrʌdə(r)/ *n* (on boat) gouvernail *m*; (on plane) gouverne *f*; **horizontal/vertical ~** Aviat gouverne de direction/de profondeur.

ruddy /ˈrʌdɪ/ *adj* **1** [*cheeks, complexion*] coloré; [*sky, glow*] rougeâtre; **2**○ †GB maudit.

rude /ruːd/ *adj* **1** (impolite) [*comment, question, reply*] impoli; [*person*] mal élevé; **to be ~ to sb** être impoli envers qn; **it is ~ to do** il est impoli or c'est mal élevé de faire; **it was very ~ of him to do** c'était très impoli de sa part de faire; **I don't mean to be ~ but I have to go** je ne veux pas vous vexer mais je dois partir; **2** (indecent) [*joke, gesture*] grossier/-ière; euph ou hum [*book, film, scene*] osé; **a ~ word** un gros mot; **3** (abrupt) [*shock, reminder*] brutal; **4** littér (simple) [*tool, dwelling*] rudimentaire; [*lifestyle, peasant*] rude liter.
IDIOMS **to be in ~ health** littér avoir une santé de fer.

rudely /ˈruːdlɪ/ *adv* **1** (impolitely) de façon impolie; **before I was so ~ interrupted** avant d'être interrompu de façon si impolie; **2** (abruptly) brutalement; **3** littér (simply) [*live*] grossièrement.

rudeness /ˈruːdnɪs/ *n* manque *m* de correction (**to, towards** envers); **she was brusque to the point of ~** elle était d'une brusquerie qui frisait l'impolitesse.

rudimentary /ˌruːdɪˈmentrɪ/ *adj* (all contexts) rudimentaire.

rudiments /ˈruːdɪmənts/ *npl* rudiments *mpl* (**of** de).

rue /ruː/ **I** *n* Bot rue *f*.
II *vtr* se repentir de [*decision, action*]; **you'll ~ the day you joined up** hum tu regretteras le jour où tu t'es engagé.

rueful /ˈruːfl/ *adj* [*smile, look*] attristé; [*thought*] triste.

ruefully /ˈruːfəlɪ/ *adv* tristement.

ruff /rʌf/ **I** *n* **1** (of lace) fraise *f*; **2** (of fur, feathers) collier *m*; **3** (bird) chevalier *m* combattant; **4** (in bridge) coupe *f* (avec un atout).
II *vi* (in bridge) couper (avec un atout).

ruffian† /ˈrʌfɪən/ *n* voyou *m*.

ruffianly /ˈrʌfɪənlɪ/ *adj* littér [*person, manner*] brutal; [*appearance*] de voyou.

ruffle /ˈrʌfl/ **I** *n* **1** (at sleeve) manchette *f*; (at neck) ruche *f*; (on shirt front) jabot *m*; (on curtain) volant *m*; **2** (on water, surface) ride *f*.
II *vtr* **1** (stroke) ébouriffer [*hair, fur*]; **2** hérisser [*feathers*]; **3** [*wind*] rider [*water, cornfield*]; **4** (disconcert) énerver; (upset) froisser; **5** (rumple) froisser [*sheet, cover*].
IDIOMS **to ~ sb's feathers** hum froisser qn.

ruffled /ˈrʌfld/ *adj* **1** [*hair*] ébouriffé; [*feathers*] hérissé; [*waters*] ridé; **2** (disconcerted) énervé; (upset) froissé.
IDIOMS **to smooth ~ feathers** calmer le jeu.

Rufflette (tape)® /ˈrʌflet/ *n* GB ruflette® *f*.

rug /rʌg/ *n* **1** (mat, carpet) tapis *m*; (by bed) descente *f* de lit; **2** GB (blanket) plaid *m*, couverture *f*; **3**○ US (toupee) postiche *m*.
IDIOMS **to be as snug as a bug in a ~**○ être bien au chaud; **to pull the ~ out from under sb's feet** couper l'herbe sous le pied à qn.

rugby /ˈrʌgbɪ/ ▶ **1282** **I** *n* rugby *m*.

II *modif* [*ball, club, match, pitch, player*] de rugby.

rugby international 1 (match) match *m* de rugby international; **2** (player) international *m* de rugby.

rugby: **~ league** *n* rugby *m* à 13; **~ tackle** *n* plaquage *m*; **~ union** *n* rugby *m* à 15.

rugged /ˈrʌɡɪd/ *adj* **1** [*terrain, landscape*] accidenté; [*coastline, cliffs*] déchiqueté; [*mountains, backdrop*] en dents de scie; **2** [*man, features*] rude; **his ~ good looks** sa beauté sauvage; **3** (tough) [*character, personality*] coriace; [*team, defence*] acharné; **4** (durable) [*vehicle, equipment*] solide.

ruggedness /ˈrʌɡɪdnɪs/ *n* **1** (of terrain) caractère *m* accidenté; (of coastline, landscape) caractère *m* sauvage; **2** (of character, appearance) rudesse *f*.

rugger○† /ˈrʌɡə(r)/ **▶ 1282** *n* GB rugby *m*.

Ruhr /rʊə/ *pr n* **the ~** la Ruhr.

ruin /ˈruːɪn/ **I** *n* **1** ¢ (collapse) (physical, financial) ruine *f*; (moral) perte *f*; **in a state of ~** [*town, building*] en ruines; **to fall into ~** tomber en ruines; **to be on the brink of (financial) ~** être au bord de la ruine; **2** (building) ruine *f*.
II ruins *npl* (remains) ruines *fpl* (**of** de); **to be** ou **lie in ~s** lit, fig être en ruines.
III *vtr* **1** (destroy) ruiner [*city, economy, career, person*]; **to ~ one's health** se ruiner la santé; **to ~ one's eyesight** s'abîmer la vue; **to ~ sb's chances of doing** anéantir les espoirs de qn de faire; **2** (spoil) gâcher [*place, holiday, meal, film*]; abîmer [*shoes, clothes*]; fig gâter [*child, pet*]; **it's ~ing our lives** ça nous gâche la vie.
IDIOMS **to go to rack and ~** [*house etc*] se délabrer; [*company, finances etc*] aller à vau-l'eau.

ruination /ˌruːɪˈneɪʃn/ *n* ruine *f*; **you'll be the ~ of me!** hum tu vas me ruiner! hum.

ruined /ˈruːɪnd/ *adj* **1** (derelict) [*building, street, city*] en ruines; **2** (spoilt) [*life, holiday, meal*] gâché; [*clothes, furniture*] abîmé; [*reputation, marriage*] ruiné; (financially) ruiné; **he is ~ politically** c'est un homme politiquement fini.

ruinous /ˈruːɪnəs/ *adj* [*costs, lawsuit*] ruineux/-euse; [*prices*] exorbitant; [*war, dependence, course of action*] désastreux/-euse.

ruinously /ˈruːɪnəslɪ/ *adv* **~ expensive** ruineux/-euse.

rule /ruːl/ **I** *n* **1** (regulation) (of game, sport, language, religion) règle *f*; (of school, company, organization) règlement *m*; **the ~s of the game** lit, fig les règles or la règle du jeu; **school/EC ~s** le règlement de l'école/de la CEE; **to obey/break/bend the ~s** obéir à/violer/contourner les règles or le règlement; **to be against the ~s** être contraire aux règles or au règlement (**to do** de faire); **it is a ~ that** il est de règle que; **under this ~** selon cette règle or le règlement; **~s and regulations** réglementation *f*; **I make it a ~ always/never to do** j'ai pour règle de toujours/de ne jamais faire; **2** (usual occurrence) règle *f*; **hot summers are the ~ here** les étés chauds sont la règle ici; **as a ~** généralement; **as a general ~** en règle générale; **3** ¢ (authority) domination *f*, gouvernement *m*; **colonial ~** domination coloniale; **majority ~** gouvernement majoritaire; **under Tory ~** sous un gouvernement conservateur; **under the ~ of a tyrant** sous la domination d'un tyran; **4** (for measuring) règle *f*; **a metre ~** une règle d'un mètre.
II *vtr* **1** Pol [*ruler, law, convention*] gouverner; [*monarch*] régner sur; [*party*] diriger; [*army*] commander; **2** (control) [*money, appetite*] dominer [*life, character*]; [*person, consideration*] diriger [*behaviour*]; [*factor*] dicter [*strategy*]; **to be ~d by sb**† se laisser diriger par qn; **to let one's heart ~ one's head** laisser son cœur dominer sa raison; **3** (draw) faire, tirer [*line*]; **~d paper** papier réglé; **4** [*tribunal, court, judge, umpire*] **to ~ that** décréter que; **to ~ sth unlawful** décréter que qch est illégal.
III *vi* **1** gen, Pol [*monarch*] régner; [*government*] gouverner; **anarchy ~s** l'anarchie règne; **Leeds United ~ OK**○! vive Leeds United!; **2** [*tribunal, court, judge, umpire*] statuer (**against** contre).
■ **rule off**: **¶ ~ off** faire or tirer un trait; **¶ ~ off [sth], ~ [sth] off** faire or tirer un trait sous [*part of writing*].
■ **rule out**: **~ out [sth], ~ [sth] out 1** (eliminate) exclure [*chance, possibility, candidate*] (**of** de); **to ~ out doing** exclure de faire; **2** (prevent) interdire [*activity*].

rulebook /ˈruːlbʊk/ *n* règlement *m*; **to throw away the ~** fig envoyer promener les conventions.

rule: **~ of law** *n* Pol séparation *f* constitutionnelle de la justice et du pouvoir; **~ of the road** *n* code *m* de la route; **~ of three** *n* règle *f* de trois.

rule of thumb *n* principe *m* de base.

ruler /ˈruːlə(r)/ *n* **1** (leader) dirigeant/-e *m/f* (**of** de); **2** (measure) règle *f*.

ruling /ˈruːlɪŋ/ **I** *n* décision *f* (**against** à l'encontre de; **by** de; **on** sur); **to give a ~** rendre une décision; **a ~ that he must pay** une décision selon laquelle il doit payer.
II *adj* **1** (in power) [*circle, class, body, group, party*] dirigeant; **2** (dominant) [*idea, passion, principle*] dominant.

rum /rʌm/ **I** *n* (alcohol) rhum *m*; **white ~** rhum blanc.
II *adj* ○†GB (odd) bizarre; **a ~ do** hum une affaire louche.

Rumania *pr n* = **Romania**.

Rumanian *adj* = **Romanian**.

rumble /ˈrʌmbl/ **I** *n* **1** (of thunder, artillery, trucks, machines) grondement *m*; (of stomach, pipes) gargouillement *m*; (from unhappy crowd) grondement *m*; **2**○ US (fight) bagarre○ *f* (*entre bandes de jeunes*).
II *vtr* **1**○ GB (unmask) flairer○ [*trick*]; **I ~d your game**○! je t'ai vu venir○!; **we've been ~d!** on nous a démasqués!; **2** (growl) **'well?' he ~d** 'alors?' dit-il en grommelant.
III *vi* **1** (make noise) [*thunder, artillery, machines, voice*] gronder; [*stomach, pipes*] gargouiller; [*person*] grommeler; **2** (trundle) **to ~ in/by** [*vehicle*] entrer/passer bruyamment; **3** (growl) grommeler.
■ **rumble on** [*debate, controversy*] continuer à faire parler beaucoup de monde.

rumble: **~ seat** *n* US Aut spider *m*; **~ strip** *n* bande *f* sonore (*sur l'autoroute*).

rumbling /ˈrʌmblɪŋ/ **I** *n* ¢ (of thunder, vehicles, machines) grondement *m*; (of stomach, in pipes) gargouillement *m*.
II rumblings *npl* (angry) murmures *mpl*; **~s of discontent** des murmures de mécontentement.

rumbustious /rʌmˈbʌstɪəs/ *adj* [*music, game*] bruyant; [*person*] exubérant.

ruminant /ˈruːmɪnənt/ *n, adj* ruminant (*m*).

ruminate /ˈruːmɪneɪt/ *vi* **1** ruminer; **to ~ on** ou **about** ruminer [*event, decision*]; ruminer sur [*meaning of life*]; **2** Zool ruminer.

rumination /ˌruːmɪˈneɪʃn/ *n* (all contexts) rumination *f*.

ruminative /ˈruːmɪnətɪv, US -neɪtɪv/ *adj* littér songeur/-euse.

ruminatively /ˈruːmɪnətɪvlɪ, US -neɪtɪvlɪ/ *adv* littér [*look, stare*] d'un air pensif.

rummage /ˈrʌmɪdʒ/ **I** *n* **1** (look) **to have a ~ in** fouiller dans; **2** US (jumble) vieilleries *fpl*.
II *vi* fouiller (**in, among, through** dans; **for** à la recherche de).
■ **rummage about, rummage around** fouiller (**in** dans).

rummy /ˈrʌmɪ/ **▶ 1282** *n* rami *m*.

rumor US = **rumour**.

rumored US = **rumoured**.

rumour GB, **rumor** US /ˈruːmə(r)/ *n* rumeur *f*, bruit *m* (**about** sur); **to start a ~** faire courir une rumeur or un bruit; **to deny a ~** démentir une rumeur; **~s are circulating that, ~ has it that** le bruit court que; **there is no truth in any of the ~s** les rumeurs sont dénuées de tout fondement; **I heard a ~ about the factory closing** j'ai entendu dire que l'usine allait fermer.

rumoured GB, **rumored** US /ˈruːməd/ *adj* **it is ~ that** il paraît que, on dit que; **she is ~ to be a millionaire** il paraît or on dit qu'elle est millionnaire; **the buyer, ~ to be the Swedish group** l'acheteur qui, selon les rumeurs, serait le groupe suédois.

rumourmonger GB, **rumormonger** US /ˈruːməmʌŋɡə(r)/ *n* personne *f* qui fait courir une rumeur.

rump /rʌmp/ *n* **1** (also **~ steak**) rumsteck *m*; **2** (of animal) croupe *f*; (of bird) croupion *m*; **3** hum (of person) postérieur *m*, derrière○ *m*; **4** (of party, group) vestiges *mpl*; **the Rump Parliament** GB Pol Hist le Parlement Croupion.

rumple /ˈrʌmpl/ **I** *vtr* ébouriffer [*hair*]; froisser [*clothes, sheets, papers*].
II rumpled /ˈrʌmpld/ *pp adj* [*clothes, sheets, papers*] froissé; [*hair*] ébouriffé.

rumpus○ /ˈrʌmpəs/ *n* **1** (noise) boucan○ *m*; **2** (angry protest) esclandre *m* (**about, over** au sujet de); **to kick up a ~** [*protesters*] faire un esclandre; [*child*] faire la comédie○.

rumpus room *n* US salle *f* de jeux.

rum toddy *n* grog *m*.

run /rʌn/ **I** *n* **1** (act or period of running) course *f*; **a two-mile ~** une course de deux miles; **that was a splendid ~ by Reeves** Reeves a fait une course magnifique; **to go for a ~** aller courir; **to take the dog for a ~ in the park** aller faire courir le chien au parc; **to break into a ~** se mettre à courir; **to do sth at a ~** faire qch en courant; **to take a ~ at** prendre son élan pour franchir [*fence, hedge, stream*]; **to give sb a clear ~** fig laisser le champ libre à qn (**at doing** pour faire); **2** (flight) **on the ~** [*prisoner*] en fuite, en cavale○; **to be on the ~ from sb/sth** fuir qn/qch; **to have sb on the ~** lit mettre qn en fuite; fig réussir à effrayer qn; **to make a ~ for it** fuir, s'enfuir; **to make a ~ for the door** se précipiter vers la porte; **3** (series) (of successes, failures, reds, blacks) série *f* (**of** de); **to have a ~ of (good) luck** être en veine; **to have a ~ of bad luck** jouer de malchance; **a ~ of fine weather** une période de beau temps; **we've had a long ~ without any illness** nous avons eu une longue période sans maladie; **the product has had a good ~ but...** le produit a bien marché mais...; **4** Theat série *f* de représentations; **to have a long ~** tenir longtemps l'affiche; **to have a six-month ~** tenir l'affiche pendant six mois; **the play is beginning its Broadway ~** la pièce commence à se jouer à Broadway; **5** (trend) (of events, market) tendance *f*; **the ~ of the cards/dice was against me** le jeu était contre moi; **against the ~ of play** Sport en sens inverse du cours réel du jeu; **in the normal ~ of things** dans l'ordre normal des choses; **out of the common ~** hors du commun; **6** (series of thing produced) (in printing) tirage *m*; (in industry) série *f*; **a paperback ~ of 10,000** un tirage de 10 000 exemplaires en poche; **7** Fin (on Stock Exchange) (rush) ruée *f*; **a ~ on** une ruée sur [*stock market, bank, item*]; **a ~ on sterling/the dollar** une ruée spéculative sur la livre sterling/le dollar; **8** (trip, route) route *f*, trajet *m*; **it's only a short ~ into town** (in car) avec la voiture on est tout de suite en ville; **to go out for a ~ in the car** aller faire un tour en voiture; **the ~ up to York** la route jusqu'à York; **he does the Leeds ~ twice a week** il fait le trajet jusqu'à Leeds deux fois par semaine; **a ferry on the Portsmouth–Caen ~** le ferry faisant la traversée Portsmouth–Caen; **a bombing ~** une mission de bombardement; **9** (in cricket, baseball) point *m*; **to score** ou **make a ~** marquer un point; **10** (for rabbit, chickens) enclos *m*; **11** (in tights, material) échelle *f*; **12** (for skiing etc) piste *f*; **13** (in cards) suite *f*; **a ~ of three** une suite de trois cartes; ▶ **practice run**, **test run**, **trial run**.

II runs○ *npl* **the ~s** la courante○, la diarrhée.

III *vtr* (*prét* **ran**; *pp* **run**) **1** (cover by running) courir [*race, heat, stage, distance, marathon*]; **I ran the rest of the way** j'ai couru le reste du chemin; **she ran a brilliant race/a very fast time** elle a fait une course superbe/un très bon temps; **the race will be run at 10.30** la course se court à 10 h 30; **2** (drive) **to ~ sb to the station/to hospital** conduire qn à la gare/à l'hôpital; **to ~ sb home** ou **back** reconduire qn; **to ~ the car over to the garage** conduire la voiture au garage; **to ~ sth over to sb's house** apporter qch chez qn en voiture; **to ~ the car into a tree** jeter la voiture contre un arbre; **3** (pass, move) **to ~ one's hand over sth** passer la main sur qch; **to ~ one's finger down the list** parcourir la liste du doigt; **to ~ one's eye(s) over sth** parcourir rapidement qch; **to ~ a duster/the vacuum cleaner over sth** passer un coup de chiffon/d'aspirateur sur qch; **to ~ one's pen through sth** rayer qch; **4** (manage) diriger [*business, hotel, store, school, country*]; **a well-/badly-run organization** une organisation bien/mal dirigée; **who is ~ning things here?** qui est-ce qui commande ici?; **I'm ~ning this show**○**!** c'est moi qui commande○!; **stop trying to ~ my life!** arrête de vouloir diriger ma vie!; **5** (operate) faire fonctionner [*machine*]; faire tourner [*motor, engine*]; exécuter [*program*]; entretenir [*car*]; **to ~ sth off the mains/off batteries** faire fonctionner qch sur secteur/avec des piles; **the car is cheap to ~** la voiture est peu coûteuse à entretenir; **to ~ a tape/a film** mettre une cassette/un film; **to ~ tests on sth** effectuer des tests sur qch; **to ~ a check on sb** [*police*] vérifier les antécédents de qn; (generally) prendre des renseignements sur qn; **6** (organize, offer) organiser [*competition, lessons, course*]; mettre [qch] en place [*train, bus, service*]; **7** (extend, pass) (of cable, wire, pipe) **to ~ sth between/from/to/around** faire passer qch entre/de/à/autour de; **to ~ a rope through a ring** faire passer une corde dans un anneau; **8** (cause to flow) faire couler [*water, bath*]; ouvrir [*tap*]; **I'll ~ you a bath** je vais te faire couler un bain; **to ~ water into/over sth** faire couler de l'eau dans/sur qch; **9** Journ [*newspaper*] publier, faire passer○ [*story, article*]; **10** (pass through) franchir [*rapids*]; forcer [*blockade*]; brûler [*red light*]; **11** (smuggle) faire passer [qch] en fraude [*guns, drugs*]; **12** (enter in contest) faire courir [*horse*]; présenter [*candidate*].

IV *vi* (*prét* **ran**; *pp* **run**) **1** (move quickly) [*person, animal*] courir; **to ~ to catch the bus/to help sb** courir pour attraper le bus/pour aider qn; **to ~ to meet sb** courir à la rencontre de qn; **to ~ across/down/up sth** traverser/descendre/monter qch en courant; **to ~ around the house/around (in) the garden** courir dans toute la maison/dans le jardin; **will you ~ over to the shop and get some milk?** peux-tu courir au magasin chercher du lait?; **to ~ for the train** courir pour attraper le train; **to ~ for the exit** courir vers la sortie; **to ~ for one's country** Sport courir pour son pays; **to ~ in the 100 metres/in the 3.30 (race)** courir le 100 mètres/dans la course de 15 h 30; **she came ~ning towards me** elle a couru vers moi; **the customers will come ~ning** fig les clients vont se précipiter; **2** (flee) fuir, s'enfuir; **I dropped everything and ran** j'ai tout jeté et je me suis enfui; **to ~ for one's life** s'enfuir pour sauver sa peau○; **~ for your life!**, **~ for it**○**!** sauve qui peut!, déguerpissons○!; **I had to ~ for it**○ j'ai dû déguerpir○; **there's nowhere to ~ (to)** il n'y a nulle part où aller; **to go ~ning to the police** courir à la police; **to go ~ning to one's parents** se réfugier chez ses parents; **3**○ (rush off) filer○; **sorry—must ~!**○ désolé—il faut que je file!○; **4** (function) [*machine, generator*] marcher; [*engine, press*] tourner; **to leave the engine ~ning** laisser tourner le moteur; **to ~ off** fonctionner sur [*mains, battery*]; **to ~ on** marcher à [*diesel, unleaded*]; **to ~ fast/slow** [*clock*] prendre de l'avance/du retard; **the organization ~s very smoothly** l'organisation fonctionne parfaitement; **5** (continue, last) [*contract, lease*] courir; **to have another month to ~** avoir encore un mois à courir; **to ~ from... to...** [*school year, season*] aller de... à...; **6** Theat [*play, musical*] tenir l'affiche; **this show will ~ and ~!** ce spectacle tiendra l'affiche pendant des mois!; **to ~ for six months** tenir l'affiche pendant six mois; **the film will ~ (for) another week** le film reste à l'affiche une semaine encore; **7** (pass) **to ~ past/through sth** [*frontier, path, line*] passer/traverser qch; **to ~ (from) east to west** aller d'est en ouest, être orienté est-ouest; **the road ~s north for about ten kilometres** la route va vers le nord sur une dizaine de kilomètres; **to ~ parallel to sth** être parallèle à qch; **the stripes ~ vertically** les rayures sont verticales; **the bird has a green stripe ~ning down its back** l'oiseau a une bande verte le long du dos; **a scar ~s down her arm** une cicatrice court le long de son bras; **8** (move) [*sledge, vehicle*] glisser (**on** sur; **forward** vers l'avant; **back** vers l'arrière); [*curtain*] coulisser (**on** sur); **to ~ through sb's hands** [*rope*] filer entre les mains de qn; **a pain ran up my leg** une douleur m'est remontée le long de la jambe; **a wave of excitement ran through the crowd** un frisson d'excitation a parcouru la foule; **his eyes ran over the page** il a parcouru la page des yeux; **the news ran from house to house** la nouvelle s'est transmise de maison en maison; **9** (operate regularly) [*buses, trains*] circuler; **they don't ~ on Sundays** ils ne circulent pas le dimanche; **a taxi service/ferry ~s between X and Y** il existe un service de taxi/un ferry entre X et Y; **the train is ~ning late** le train est en retard; **programmes are ~ning late this evening** (on TV) les émissions ont du retard ce soir; **we are ~ning 30 minutes behind schedule** ou **late** nous avons 30 minutes de retard; **we're ~ning ahead of schedule** nous sommes en avance; **10** (flow) [*water, liquid, stream, tap, bath, nose*] couler; **the tap is ~ning** le robinet coule or est ouvert; **my nose is ~ning** j'ai le nez qui coule; **tears ran down his face** les larmes coulaient sur son visage; **there was water ~ning down the walls** il y avait de l'eau qui coulait le long des murs; **my body was ~ning with sweat** mon corps ruisselait de sueur; **the streets will be ~ning with blood** fig le sang coulera à flots dans les rues; **the river ran red with blood** la rivière est devenue rouge de sang; **the meat juices ran pink/clear** le jus qui est sorti de la viande était rose/incolore; **11** (flow when wet or melted) [*colour, dye, garment*] déteindre; [*ink, makeup, butter, cheese*] couler; **12** Pol (as candidate) se présenter; **to ~ for** être candidat/-e au poste de [*mayor, governor*]; **to ~ for president** être candidat/-e à la présidence; **to ~ against** se présenter or être candidat/-e contre [*person*]; **13** (be worded) [*message, speech*] se présenter, être libellé sout; **the telex ~s...** le télex se présente or est libellé comme suit...; **so the argument ~s** selon l'argument habituellement avancé; **14** (snag) [*tights, material*] filer.

IDIOMS **to have the ~ of sth** avoir qch pour soi; **to give sb the ~ of sth** mettre qch à la disposition de qn; **in the long ~** à la longue, à longue échéance; **in the short ~** à brève échéance.

■ **run about**, **run around**: **~ around 1** (hurrying, playing etc) courir; **I've been ~ning around all over the place looking for you** j'ai couru partout pour essayer de te trouver; **2**○ (have affair with) courir○; **to ~ around**○ **with** voir○, sortir avec [*woman, man*].

■ **run across**○: **~ across [sth/sb]** tomber sur○ [*acquaintance, reference*].

■ **run after**: **~ after [sb]** lit, fig courir après [*thief, woman, man*].

■ **run along** se sauver○, filer○; **~ along!** sauve-toi○!

■ **run at**: **~ at [sth] 1** (charge towards) se précipiter sur [*door, person*]; **2** (be at) [*inflation, unemployment*] atteindre, être de l'ordre de [*percentage, rate, figure*]; **with inflation ~ning at 12%** avec une inflation de l'ordre de 12%.

■ **run away**: ¶ **~ away 1** (flee) s'enfuir (**from sb** devant qn; **to do** pour faire); **to ~ away from home** s'enfuir de chez soi; **to ~ away from one's responsibilities/a situation** fuir ses responsabilités/une situation; **2** (run off) [*water, liquid*] couler; ¶ **~ away with [sth/sb] 1** (flee) partir avec [*profits, object, person*]; **2** (carry off easily) rafler○ [*prizes, title*]; **3** GB dial (use up) [*activity*] engloutir [*money*]; **4** (get into one's head) **to ~ away with the idea** ou **notion that** s'imaginer que; **I don't want him ~ning away with that idea** je ne veux pas qu'il s'imagine ça; **to let one's emotions/one's enthusiasm ~ away with one** se laisser emporter par ses émotions/son enthousiasme.

■ **run back**: **~ back [sth]**, **~ [sth] back** rembobiner [*tape, film*].

■ **run back over**: **~ back over [sth]** revenir sur [*points, plans*].

■ **run down**: ¶ **~ down** [*battery*] se décharger; [*watch*] retarder; [*exports, reserves*] diminuer; [*machine, industry, company*] s'essouffler; ¶ **~ down [sth/sb]**, **~ [sth/sb] down 1** (in vehicle) renverser; **to be** ou **get run down by sth** être renversé par qch; **2** (reduce, allow to decline) réduire [*production, operations, defences, industry, reserves*]; user [*battery*]; **3** (disparage) dénigrer [*person, economy*]; **4** Naut éperonner, heurter [*boat*]; **5** (track down) retrouver [*person*]; dénicher○ [*thing*].

■ **run in**: ¶ **~ in [sth]**, **~ [sth] in** roder [*car, machine*]; **'~ning in—please pass'** 'en rodage'; ¶ **~ [sb] in**○ (arrest) épingler○ [*person*].

■ **run into**: **~ into [sth/sb] 1** (collide with) [*car, person*] heurter, rentrer dans○ [*car, wall*]; **2** (encounter) rencontrer [*person, difficulty, opposition, bad weather*]; **to ~ into debt** s'endetter; **3** (amount to) [*debt, income, sales*] se compter en [*hundreds, millions*]; **the trial could ~ into months** le procès pourrait durer des mois.

■ **run off**: ¶ **~ off 1** [*person, animal*] partir en courant; **to ~ off with** partir avec [*person, savings*]; **2** [*liquid, water*] couler; ¶ **~ off [sth]**, **~ [sth] off 1** (print) sortir [*copy*] (**on** sur); **2** (contest) disputer [*heats*].

■ **run on**: ¶ **~ on** [*meeting, seminar*] se prolonger; ¶ **~ on [sth]** (be concerned with) [*mind*] être préoccupé par; [*thoughts*] revenir sur; [*conversation*] porter sur; ¶ **~ on [sth]**, **~ [sth] on 1** Print faire suivre [qch] sans alinéa; **2** Literat faire enjamber [*line*].

■ **run out**: ¶ **~ out 1** (become exhausted) [*supplies, resources, oil*] s'épuiser; **time is ~ning out** le temps manque; **my money ran out** mes ressources s'étaient épuisées; **my patience is ~ning out** je suis en train de perdre patience; **2** (have no more) [*pen, vending machine*] être vide; **sorry, I've run out** désolé, je n'en ai plus; **quick, before we ~ out** vite, avant que nous n'ayons plus rien; **3** (expire) [*lease, passport*] expirer; ¶ **~ out of** ne plus avoir de [*petrol, time,* *money, ideas*]; **the car ran out of petrol** la voiture est tombée en panne d'essence; **to be ~ning out of** n'avoir presque plus de [*petrol, time, money, ideas*].

■ **run out on**: **~ out on [sb]** abandonner, laisser tomber○ [*family, lover, ally*].

■ **run over**: ¶ **~ over 1** [*meeting, programme*] se prolonger, dépasser l'horaire prévu; **to ~ over by 10 minutes/by an hour** dépasser l'horaire prévu de 10 minutes/d'une heure; **2** (overflow) [*container*] déborder; **my cup ~neth over** Bible la coupe est pleine; ¶ **~ over [sth]** (run through) passer [qch] en revue [*arrangements, main points*]; ¶ **~ over [sth/sb], ~ [sth/sb] over 1** (injure) renverser [*person, animal*]; (kill) écraser [*person, animal*]; **you'll get run over** tu vas te faire écraser; **2** (drive over) passer sur [*log, bump, corpse*].

■ **run through**: ¶ **~ through [sth] 1** (pass through) [*thought, tune, murmur*] courir dans; **2** (be present in) [*theme, concern, prejudice*] se retrouver dans [*work, society*]; **3** (look through) parcourir [*list, article, notes*]; (discuss briefly) passer [qch] en revue [*main points, schedule*]; **4** (use, get through) dépenser [*money, inheritance*]; ¶ **~ through [sth], ~ [sth] through** (rehearse) répéter [*scene, speech*]; ¶ **~ [sb] through** littér (with sword) transpercer [*person*] (**with** avec, de); **to ~ sth through the computer** passer qch dans l'ordinateur; **to ~ sth through a series of tests** faire passer une série de tests à qch.

■ **run to**: **~ to [sth]** (extend as far as) [*book, report*] faire [*number of pages, words*]; **her tastes don't ~ to modern jazz** ses goûts ne vont pas jusqu'au jazz moderne; **his salary doesn't ~ to Caribbean cruises** son salaire ne lui permet pas une croisière aux Caraïbes; **I don't think I can ~ to that** je ne crois pas pouvoir me permettre cela.

■ **run up**: **~ up [sth], ~ [sth] up 1** (accumulate) accumuler [*bill, debt*]; **2** (make) fabriquer [*dress, curtains*]; **3** (raise) hisser [*flag*].

■ **run up against**: **~ up against [sth]** se heurter à [*obstacle, difficulty*].

runabout○ /ˈrʌnəbaʊt/ *n* GB petite voiture *f*.

runaround /ˈrʌnəraʊnd/ *n* **he's giving me/her etc the ~** il se défile○.

runaway /ˈrʌnəweɪ/ **I** *n* (child) fugueur/-euse *m/f*; (slave) fugitif/-ive *m/f*.
II *adj* **1** (having left) [*child, teenager*] fugueur/-euse; [*slave*] fugitif/-ive; [*wife, father*] en fuite; **2** (out of control) [*vehicle*] incontrôlé, fou/folle journ; [*horse*] emballé; [*inflation*] galopant; **3** (great) [*success, victory*] éclatant.

rundown /ˈrʌnˌdaʊn/ **I** *n* **1** (report) récapitulatif *m* (**on** de); **to give sb a quick ~ on sth** donner un récapitulatif rapide de qch à qn; **2** (of industry, factory) réduction *f* de l'activité (**of** de).

run-down /ˌrʌnˈdaʊn/ *adj* **1** (exhausted) [*person*] fatigué, à plat○; **2** (shabby) [*house*, area] décrépit.

rune /ruːn/ *n* rune *f*.

run-flat /ˌrʌnˈflæt/ *n* pneu *m* à affaissement limité.

rung /rʌŋ/ **I** *pp* ▶ **ring**.
II *n* **1** (of ladder) barreau *m*; **the bottom ~** le premier barreau; **2** (in hierarchy) échelon *m*; **to move up a few ~s** gravir quelques échelons.

runic /ˈruːnɪk/ *adj* runique.

run-in○ /ˈrʌnɪn/ *n* prise *f* de bec○.

runner /ˈrʌnə(r)/ *n* **1** (person, animal) coureur *m*; **to be a fast ~** être très rapide à la course; **2** Sport, Turf partant/-e *m/f*; **3** (messenger) Mil estafette *f*; Fin coursier/-ière *m/f*; **4** (for door, seat) glissière *f*; (for drawer) coulisseau *m*; (for curtain) chariot *m*; (on sled) patin *m*; **5** Bot, Hort stolon *m*; **6** (cloth) chemin *m* de table; (carpet) (in hall) chemin *m* de couloir; (on stairs) chemin *m* d'escalier; **7**○ (car) **'good ~'** (in ad) 'en bon état mécanique'.
IDIOMS **to do a ~**○ (from restaurant, taxi) s'esquiver sans payer; (from house etc) déménager à la cloche de bois.

runner bean *n* GB haricot *m* d'Espagne.

runner up /ˌrʌnərˈʌp/ *n* (*pl* **~s up**) second/-e *m/f* (**to** après); **the 50 ~s up** les 50 suivants *mpl*.

running /ˈrʌnɪŋ/ **I** *n* **1** (sport, exercise) course *f* à pied; **to take up ~** se mettre à la course à pied; **2** (management) direction *f* (**of** de).
II *modif* [*gear, shoes, shorts*] de course.
III *adj* **1** (flowing) [*water*] courant; [*tap*] ouvert; [*knot*] coulant; **~ sore** lit plaie *f* suppurante; fig abcès *m*, plaie *f* ouverte; **2** (consecutive) de suite *inv*; **five days ~** cinq jours de suite.
IDIOMS **go take a ~ jump**○! va te faire voir○!; **to be in the ~** être dans la course (**for** pour); **to be out of the ~** ne plus être dans la course (**for** pour); **to make the ~** lit, fig mener la course.

running: **~ battle** *n* éternel conflit *m* (**with** avec, contre); **~ board** *n* marchepied *m*; **~ commentary** *n* commentaire *m* ininterrompu; **~ costs** *n* (of factory, scheme) dépenses *fpl* courantes; (of a machine) coûts *mpl* de fonctionnement; (of car) frais *mpl* d'entretien; **~ head** *n* titre *m* courant; **~ light** *n* Naut, Aviat feu *m* de position.

running mate *n* gen co-candidat/-e *m/f*; (vice-presidential) candidat/-e *m/f* à la vice-présidence.

running order *n* Radio, Theat, TV (of programme) ordre *m* de diffusion; (of items in programme) ordre *m* des titres développés; (of acts in show) ordre *m* des numéros.

running: **~ race** *n* épreuve *f* de course à pied; **~ repairs** *npl* réparations *fpl* courantes; **~-stitch** *n* point *m* devant; **~ time** *n* (of film, cassette) durée *f*; **~ title** *n* = **running head**; **~ total** *n* total *m* cumulé; **~ track** *n* piste *f*.

runny /ˈrʌnɪ/ *adj* [*jam, sauce, icing*] liquide; [*butter, chocolate*] fondu; [*omelette, scrambled eggs*] baveux/-euse; [*fried egg*] avec le jaune à peine cuit; [*poached or boiled egg*] mollet; [*nose, eye*] qui coule; **to have a ~ nose** avoir le nez qui coule.

runoff /ˈrʌnɒf/ *n* **1** (decider) Pol scrutin *m* de ballotage; Sport course *f* finale; **2** (of water, liquid) ruissellement *m*, écoulement *m*.

run: **~-of-the-mill** *adj* ordinaire, banal; **~-on** *adj* Print qui suit sans alinéa; **~-on line** *n* Literat (in poetry) enjambement *m*.

runproof /ˈrʌnpruːf/ *adj* **1** [*stockings, fabric*] indémaillable; **2** [*makeup, mascara*] résistant à l'eau.

runt /rʌnt/ *n* **1** (of litter) *le plus faible d'une portée*; **2** péj (weakling) avorton *m* pej.

run-through /ˈrʌnθruː/ *n* **1** (practice) répétition *f*; **2** (cursory reading, summary) aperçu *m*.

run-up /ˈrʌnʌp/ *n* **1** Sport course *f* d'élan; **to take a ~** prendre son élan pour sauter; **2** (preceding period) **the ~ to** la dernière ligne droite avant [*election, Christmas*].

runway /ˈrʌnweɪ/ *n* Aviat piste *f* d'aviation.

rupee /ruːˈpiː/ ▶ **1143** *n* roupie *f*.

rupture /ˈrʌptʃə(r)/ **I** *n* **1** Med (hernia) hernie *f*; (of blood vessel, kidney) rupture *f*; **2** Tech (in tank, container) rupture *f*; **3** (in relations) rupture *f* (**between** entre).
II *vtr* **1** Med se faire éclater [*kidney, appendix*]; **to ~ oneself** se faire une hernie; **2** rompre [*relations, unity*].
III *vi* **1** Med [*kidney, appendix*] se rompre; **2** Tech [*container*] éclater.
IV ruptured *pp adj* Med éclaté.

rural /ˈrʊərəl/ *adj* **1** [*life, community, industry, tradition*] rural; **~ France** la France rurale; **2** (pastoral) [*scene, beauty*] champêtre.

rural dean *n* GB Relig doyen *m* rural.

ruse /ruːz/ *n* stratagème *m*.

rush /rʌʃ/ **I** *n* **1** (of crowd) ruée *f* (**to do** pour faire); **a ~ of photographers/volunteers** une ruée de journalistes/volontaires; **a ~ for the door/towards the buffet** une ruée vers la porte/vers le buffet; **to make a ~ at/for sth** [*crowd*] se ruer sur/vers qch; [*individual*] se précipiter sur/vers qch; **2** (hurry) **to be in a ~** être pressé (**to do** de faire); **there's no ~** ce n'est pas pressant; **to do sth in a ~** faire qch en vitesse; **what's the ~?** pourquoi faire vite?; **it all happened in such a ~** tout s'est passé si vite; **we had a ~ to finish it** il a fallu qu'on se dépêche pour le terminer; **is there any ~?** y a-t-il urgence?; **3** (peak time) (during day) heure *f* de pointe; (during year) période *f* de pointe; **the morning/evening ~** l'heure de pointe du matin/soir; **the summer/Christmas ~** la période de pointe de l'été/autour de Noël; **beat the ~!** évitez la foule!; **there's a ~ on in the book department** il y a une bousculade au rayon des livres; **4** (surge) (of liquid, energy, adrenalin) montée *f*; (of air) bouffée *f*; (of emotion) vague *f*; (of complaints) flot *m*; **a ~ of blood to one's cheeks/into a limb** un afflux de sang aux joues/dans un membre; **a ~ of blood to the head** fig un coup de tête; **it gives you a ~**○ c'est euphorisant; **5** Bot jonc *m*; **6** US Univ *courte période pendant laquelle les associations d'étudiants essaient d'attirer de nouveaux membres*.
II rushes *npl* Cin rushes *mpl*, épreuves *fpl* de tournage.
III *modif* [*basket, matting, screen*] en jonc.
IV *vtr* **1** (transport urgently) **to ~ sth to** envoyer qch d'urgence à; **troops were ~ed to the scene** des troupes ont été envoyées d'urgence sur les lieux; **to be ~ed to the hospital** être emmené d'urgence à l'hôpital; **'please ~ me my copy'** journ 'envoyez-moi d'urgence mon exemplaire'; **2** (do hastily) expédier [*task, essay, speech*]; **don't try to ~ things** ne va pas trop vite; **3** (pressurize, hurry) presser, bousculer [*person*]; **I don't want to ~ you, but** je ne voudrais pas te bousculer, mais; **the agent ~ed me round the house in five minutes** l'agent m'a fait faire le tour de la maison en cinq minutes; **4** (charge at) sauter sur [*guard, defender, player*]; prendre d'assaut [*building, platform*]; **5** US Univ [*student*] essayer de devenir membre de [*sorority, fraternity*].
V *vi* **1** [*person*] (make haste) se dépêcher (**to do** de faire); (rush forward) se précipiter (**to do** pour faire); **don't ~** ne te précipite pas; **to ~ to explain** se dépêcher d'expliquer; **to ~ up to sb/out of the room** se précipiter vers qn/hors de la pièce; **to ~ at sb/sth** se précipiter sur qn/qch; **to ~ down the stairs/round the house** descendre l'escalier/faire le tour de la maison à toute vitesse; **to ~ along** marcher à toute vitesse; **he ~ed off before I could tell him** il a disparu avant que je n'aie pu le lui dire; **2** (travel) [*train, vehicle*] **to ~ past** passer à toute vitesse; **to ~ along at 120 km/h** filer à 120 km/h; **the stream ~ed down the mountainside** le torrent dévalait le flanc de la montagne; **a ~ing stream** un ruisseau jaillissant; **the sound of ~ing water** le son de l'eau jaillissante.

■ **rush into**: ¶ **~ into [sth]** se lancer dans [*commitment, purchase, sale*]; **to ~ into marriage/a decision** se marier/prendre une décision précipitamment; ¶ **~ [sb] into doing** pousser [qn] à faire; **to ~ sb into marriage/a decision** pousser qn au mariage/à prendre une décision; **don't be ~ed into it** ne te laisse pas bousculer.

■ **rush out**: ¶ **~ out** [*person*] sortir en vitesse; ¶ **~ out [sth], ~ [sth] out** sortir or publier [qch] en vitesse [*pamphlet, edition*].

■ **rush through**: ¶ **~ through [sth]** expédier [*task, agenda*]; parcourir [qch] en vitesse [*book, article*]; ¶ **~ [sth] through, ~ through [sth]** adopter en vitesse [*legislation, bill, amendment*]; traiter en priorité [*order, application*]; **to ~ a bill through parliament** faire passer une loi en vitesse;

¶ **~ [sth] through to** envoyer [qch] d'urgence à [*person, scene*].

rushed /rʌst/ *adj* [*attempt, letter, job*] expédié, bâclé○ pej; [*person, staff*] sous pression.

rush hour /'rʌʃaʊə(r)/ **I** *n* heures *fpl* de pointe; **the morning ~** les heures de pointe du matin; **in** ou **during the ~** aux or pendant les heures de pointe.
II *modif* [*congestion, problems, crowds*] des heures de pointe; [*traffic*] aux heures de pointe; **to get caught in the ~ traffic** être pris dans les embouteillages.

rush job○ *n* travail *m* urgent, urgence *f*; **to have a ~ on** avoir un travail urgent or une urgence.

rush: **~light** *n* GB chandelle *f* à mèche de jonc; **~ order** *n* commande *f* urgente.

rusk /rʌsk/ *n* biscuit *m* pour bébés.

russet /'rʌsɪt/ **I** *n* **1** (colour) brun *m* roux; **2** (apple) canada *f inv*.
II *adj* roussâtre.

Russia /'rʌʃə/ ▶ **1131** *pr n* Russie *f*.

Russian /'rʌʃn/ ▶ **1486**, **1402** **I** *n* **1** (native) Russe *mf*; **2** Ling russe *m*.
II *modif* [*book, class, course*] de russe.
III *adj* russe.

Russian Federation *n* Fédération *f* de Russie.

Russian Orthodox *adj* orthodoxe russe; **the ~ Church** l'Église orthodoxe russe.

Russian: **~ Revolution** *n* révolution *f* russe; **~ roulette** *n* roulette *f* russe; **~ salad** *n* salade *f* russe; **~-speaking** *adj* russophone.

Russky○ GB, **Russki(e)**○ US /'rʌskɪ/ *n* russe *mf*.

Russophile /'rʌsəʊfaɪl/ *n* russophile *mf*.

rust /rʌst/ **I** *n* Agric, Chem, Hort rouille *f*.
II *vtr* **1** lit rouiller; **2** fig altérer.
III *vi* **1** lit se rouiller; **2** fig [*skill*] s'altérer.
IV rusted *pp adj* rouillé; **to become ~ed** se rouiller.
■ **rust away**, **rust out** US, **rust through** être mangé par la rouille.
■ **rust up** se rouiller.

rust-coloured GB, **rust-colored** US /'rʌstkʌləd/ ▶ **1104** *adj* couleur rouille *inv*.

rustic /'rʌstɪk/ **I** *n* campagnard/-e *m/f*; pej rustaud/-e *m/f*.
II *adj* [*furniture, fence, bridge*] rustique; [*charm*] champêtre; [*accent*] rustique.

rusticate /'rʌstɪkeɪt/ **I** *vtr* GB Univ exclure [qn] temporairement.
II *vi* sout se retirer à la campagne.

rustle /'rʌsl/ **I** *n* (of paper, fabric, dry leaves) froissement *m*; (of leaves, silk) bruissement *m*.
II *vtr* **1** froisser [*papers, plastic bag*]; **the wind ~d the leaves** on entendait le bruissement du vent dans les feuilles; **stop rustling your newspaper!** arrête de faire du bruit avec ton journal!; **2** US voler [*cattle, horses*].
■ **rustle up**: **~ up [sth]** préparer [qch] en vitesse [*supper, salad*]; se débrouiller pour trouver [*money*].

rustler /'rʌslə(r)/ *n* US (cattle thief) voleur/-euse *m/f* de bétail; (horse thief) voleur/-euse *m/f* de chevaux.

rustling /'rʌslɪŋ/ *n* **1** (of paper, fabric, dry leaves) froissement *m*; (of leaves, silk) bruissement *m*; (of mice) furètement *m*; **2** US (cattle stealing) vol *m* de bétail; (horses) vol *m* de chevaux.

rust-proof /'rʌstpru:f/ **I** *adj* [*material*] inoxydable; [*paint, coating*] antirouille.
II *vtr* traiter [qch] contre la rouille.

rustproofing /'rʌstpru:fɪŋ/ *n* traitement *m* antirouille.

rusty /'rʌstɪ/ *adj* lit, fig rouillé.

rut /rʌt/ **I** *n* **1** (in ground) ornière *f*; **2** (routine) **to be (stuck) in a ~** être enlisé dans la routine; **to get into a ~** s'enliser dans la routine; **3** Zool (mating) **the ~** le rut.
II *vtr* (*p prés etc* **-tt-**) faire des ornières dans.
III *vi* (*p prés etc* **-tt-**) Zool (mate) être en rut.
IV rutted *pp adj* plein d'ornières.

rutabaga /ˌru:tə'beɪgə/ *n* US rutabaga *m*.

ruthenium /ru:'θi:nɪəm/ *n* ruthénium *m*.

ruthless /'ru:θlɪs/ *adj* impitoyable (**in** dans; **towards** envers).

ruthlessly /'ru:θlɪslɪ/ *adv* impitoyablement.

ruthlessness /'ru:θlɪsnɪs/ *n* caractère *m* impitoyable.

rutting /'rʌtɪŋ/ **I** *n* Zool rut *m*; **~ season** saison du rut.
II *adj* en rut.

RV *n* **1** Bible *abrév* ▶ **Revised Version**; **2** US Aut *abrév* ▶ **recreational vehicle**.

Rwanda /rʊ'ændə/ ▶ **1131** *pr n* Rwanda *m*.

Rwandan /rʊ'ændən/ ▶ **1486** **I** *n* Rwandais/-e *m/f*.
II *adj* rwandais.

Rx US **I** *n* Pharm *symbole signifiant 'ordonnance'*.
II *modif* **~ drug** médicament *m* sur ordonnance.

rye /raɪ/ **I** *n* **1** Agric, Culin seigle *m*; **2** US = **rye whiskey**.
II *modif* [*bread, flour*] de seigle.

rye: **~ grass** *n* ivraie *f* vivace; **~ whiskey** *n* whisky *m* à base de seigle.

Ss

s, **S** /es/ *n* **1** (letter) s, S *m*; **2 S** *abrév écrite* = **South**; **3 S** (*abrév écrite* = **Saint**) St/Ste; **4** *abrév écrite* = **small**.

SA *n* **1** *abrév écrite* = **South Africa**; **2** *abrév écrite* = **South America**; **3** *abrév écrite* = **South Australia**.

Sabbatarian /ˌsæbəˈteərɪən/ **I** *n* observateur/-trice *m/f* du Sabbat.
II *adj* [*family*] qui observe le Sabbat; **~ principles** principes *mpl* d'observance du Sabbat.

sabbath /ˈsæbəθ/ *n* (also **Sabbath**) (Jewish) sabbat *m*; (Christian) jour *m* du seigneur; **to observe/to break the ~** respecter/ne pas respecter le sabbat or le jour du seigneur.

sabbatical /səˈbætɪkl/ **I** *n* congé *m* sabbatique; **to take a ~, to go on ~** prendre un congé sabbatique; **to be on ~** être en congé sabbatique.
II *adj* [*leave, year*] sabbatique.

saber *n* US = **sabre**.

sable /ˈseɪbl/ **I** *n* **1** (fur, animal) zibeline *f*; **2** Herald sable *m*; **3** littér (black) noir *m*.
II *modif* [*hat, garment*] en zibeline; **~ coat/stole** zibeline *f*.
III *adj* littér noir.

sabot /ˈsæbəʊ, US sæˈbəʊ/ *n* sabot *m* (*en bois*).

sabotage /ˈsæbətɑːʒ/ **I** *n* sabotage *m*; **to commit ~** faire du sabotage; **due to ~** causé par un sabotage.
II *vtr* saboter [*equipment, campaign, discussion*]; saper [*economy*].

saboteur /ˌsæbəˈtɜː(r)/ *n* saboteur/-euse *m/f*.

sabre, **saber** US /ˈseɪbə(r)/ *n* Mil, Sport sabre *m*.

sabre: **~ rattling** *n* rodomontade *f*; **~tooth, ~-toothed tiger** *n* machairodonte *m*.

sac /sæk/ *n* **1** Anat, Bot sac *m*; **hernial ~** sac herniaire; **2** Zool (of liquid) poche *f*; **honey ~** poche à miel.

saccharin /ˈsækərɪn/ *n* saccharine *f*.

saccharine /ˈsækəriːn/ *adj* péj **1** [*sentimentality, novel*] à l'eau de rose; [*smile*] mielleux/-euse; **2** [*drink, food*] trop sucré.

sacerdotal /ˌsækəˈdəʊtl/ *adj* sout sacerdotal.

sachet /ˈsæʃeɪ, US sæˈʃeɪ/ *n* (all contexts) sachet *m*.

sack /sæk/ **I** *n* **1** (bag) sac *m*; **potato ~** sac à pommes de terre; **mail ~** sac postal; **2** (contents) sac *m*; **a ~ of flour** un sac de farine; **3**○ (dismissal) **to get the ~** se faire mettre à la porte○; **to give sb the ~** mettre qn à la porte○; **to be threatened with the ~** être menacé de renvoi; **4**○ (bed) **the ~** le lit, le pieu◑; **to hit the ~**○ se coucher, se pieuter◑; **to be great in the ~**◑ bien baiser◑; **5** littér (pillage) sac *m*; **6**‡ Wine *vin blanc d'Espagne*.
II *vtr* **1**○ (dismiss) mettre [qn] à la porte○ [*employee*] (**for** pour; **for doing** pour avoir fait); **to be** ou **get ~ed** se faire mettre à la porte○; **2** littér (pillage) mettre à sac [*town*].
IDIOMS to look like a ~ of potatoes être fagoté comme un sac.
■ **sack out**○ US dormir.

sackbut /ˈsækbʌt/ *n* sacquebute *f*.

sackcloth /ˈsækklɒθ/ *n* toile *f* à sac.
IDIOMS to be in ou **wear ~ and ashes** faire son mea culpa (en public).

sack dress *n* robe *f* sac.

sackful /ˈsækfʊl/, **sackload** /ˈsækləʊd/ *n* sac *m*; **a ~ of toys** un sac de jouets; **cash/letters by the ~** de l'argent/des lettres en quantité.

sacking /ˈsækɪŋ/ *n* **1** Tex (for sacks) toile *f* à sac; (jute) toile *f* de jute; **2**○ (dismissal) licenciement *m*.

sack race *n* course *f* en sac.

sacral /ˈseɪkrəl/ *adj* Anat sacré.

sacrament /ˈsækrəmənt/ *n* (religious ceremony) sacrement *m*.

Sacrament /ˈsækrəmənt/ *n* (Communion bread) Saint sacrement *m*; **to receive the ~(s)** communier.

sacramental /ˌsækrəˈmentl/ *adj* sacramentel/-elle.

sacred /ˈseɪkrɪd/ **I** *n* **the ~ and the profane** le sacré et le profane.
II *adj* **1** (holy) [*place, object*] sacré (**to** pour); **to hold sth ~** tenir qch pour sacré; **2** (revered) [*name*] sacré; [*tradition*] sacro-saint; **is nothing ~?** hum il n'y a rien de sacré?; **'~ to the memory of...'** 'à la mémoire de...'; **3** (binding) [*duty, mission*] sacré; [*trust*] inviolable.

sacred: **~ cow** *n* fig vache *f* sacrée; **Sacred Heart** *n* Sacré Cœur *m*.

sacrifice /ˈsækrɪfaɪs/ **I** *n* **1** (act) Relig, fig sacrifice *m* (**to sb** à qn; **of** de); **to make a ~/many ~s for sb** faire un sacrifice/de nombreux sacrifices pour qn; **2** (offering) Relig sacrifice *m*; **a human ~** un sacrifice humain.
II *vtr* **1** fig sacrifier (**to** à); **to ~ sth for one's friends/for one's principles** sacrifier qch pour ses amis/à ses principes; **principles ~d on the altar of profit** les principes immolés sur l'autel du profit; **2** Relig offrir [qch] en sacrifice (**to** à).
III *v refl* **to ~ oneself** se sacrifier (**for** pour).

sacrificial /ˌsækrɪˈfɪʃl/ *adj* [*victim*] offert en sacrifice; [*knife, robe*] du sacrifice.

sacrificial lamb *n* Relig agneau *m* pascal; fig **to be the ~** être sacrifié.

sacrilege /ˈsækrɪlɪdʒ/ *n* Relig, fig, hum sacrilège *m*; **it's ~ to do** c'est un sacrilège de faire.

sacrilegious /ˌsækrɪˈlɪdʒəs/ *adj* Relig, fig, hum sacrilège.

sacristan /ˈsækrɪstən/ *n* sacristain *m*.

sacristy /ˈsækrɪstɪ/ *n* sacristie *f*.

sacroiliac /ˌsækrəʊˈɪlɪæk/ **I** *n* articulation *f* sacro-iliaque.
II *adj* sacro-iliaque.

sacrosanct /ˈsækrəʊsæŋkt/ *adj* sacro-saint.

sacrum /ˈseɪkrəm/ *n* (*pl* **-cra**) sacrum *m*.

sad /sæd/ *adj* **1** [*person, face, voice, song, film, news*] triste; **to be ~ to do** [*person*] être triste de faire; **it makes me ~** cela me rend triste; **to be ~ that** [*person*] être triste que (+ *subj*); **we are ~ about** ou **at the accident** l'accident nous attriste; **it's ~ that** c'est triste que (+ *subj*); **it's ~ to hear that** il est triste d'apprendre que; **it was a ~ sight** c'était triste à voir; **2** (unfortunate) [*fact, truth*] triste (*before n*); **it is my ~ duty to sentence you to...** c'est mon triste devoir de vous condamner à...; **~ to say,...** c'est malheureux à dire, mais...; **3** (deplorable) [*attitude, situation*] navrant; **a ~ change has come over society** notre société a changé de façon navrante; **it's a ~ state of affairs when one can't/one has to...** c'est triste de ne pas pouvoir/d'avoir à...; **it's a ~ day for democracy/football** c'est un sombre jour pour la démocratie/le football.
IDIOMS to be a ~der but wiser person avoir reçu une leçon dure mais profitable.

SAD /sæd/ *n*: *abrév* ▶ **seasonal affective disorder**.

sadden /ˈsædn/ **I** *vtr* attrister [*person*]; **it ~s me that/to think that** cela m'attriste que (+ *subj*)/de penser que.
II saddened *pp adj* **to be ~ed by sth/to hear sth** être attristé par qch/d'apprendre qch; (stronger) être affligé par qch/d'apprendre qch.
III saddening *pres p adj* **it is ~ing to hear/to think that** c'est désolant d'apprendre/de penser que.

saddle /ˈsædl/ **I** *n* **1** (on horse, bike) selle *f*; **to climb into the ~** Equit se mettre en selle; **2** GB Culin **~ of lamb/venison** selle *f* d'agneau/de chevreuil; **~ of hare** râble *m* de lièvre; **3** Geog (ridge) col *m*.
II *vtr* **1** Equit seller [*horse*]; **2** (impose) **to ~ sb with sth** mettre qch sur les bras de qn [*responsibility, task, debt*]; **he was ~d with the running of the club** on lui a mis l'organisation du club sur les bras; **3** Turf (enter in race) [*trainer*] faire courir [*horse*].
III *v refl* **to ~ oneself with sth** se mettre qch sur les bras.
■ **saddle up**: ¶ **~ up** seller son cheval; ¶ **~ up [sth]** seller [*horse*].

saddle: **~-backed** *adj* ensellé; **~ bag** *n* sacoche *f*; **~bow** *n* pommeau *m*; **~cloth** *n* tapis *m* de selle; **~ horse** *n* cheval *m* de selle.

saddler /ˈsædlə(r)/ ▶ **1692** *n* sellier *m*, bourrelier *m*.

saddlery /ˈsædlərɪ/ *n* sellerie *f*.

saddle: **~ shoes** *n* US chaussures *fpl* d'hommes (*blanches avec une bande noire ou marron*); **~ soap** *n* savon *m* glycériné (*pour nettoyer le cuir*).

saddle sore I *n* plaie *f* causée par le frottement de la selle.
II saddle-sore *adj* **1** (having sores) [*horse, rider*] blessé à cause du frottement de la selle; **2** (sore) [*rider*] **to be ~** avoir mal aux fesses à force d'être resté en selle.

Sadducee /ˈsædjʊsiː/ *n* sadducéen/-éenne *m/f*.

sad: **~-eyed** *adj* [*person*] aux yeux tristes; **~-faced** *adj* [*person*] au visage triste.

sadism /ˈseɪdɪzəm/ *n* sadisme *m*.

sadist /ˈseɪdɪst/ *n* sadique *mf*.

sadistic /səˈdɪstɪk/ *adj* sadique.

sadistically /səˈdɪstɪklɪ/ *adv* [*laugh, say*] sadiquement; [*treated, tortured*] de manière sadique.

sadly /ˈsædlɪ/ *adv* **1** (with sadness) [*sigh, say*] tristement; **he will be ~ missed** il nous manquera beaucoup; **2** (unfortunately) malheureusement; **~, she's right** elle a malheureusement raison; **3** (emphatic) **he is ~ lacking in sense** le bon sens lui fait cruellement défaut; **you are ~ mistaken** vous vous trompez fort.

sadness /ˈsædnɪs/ *n* tristesse *f*.

sadomasochism, S&M /ˌseɪdəʊˈmæsəkɪzəm/ *n* sadomasochisme *m*.

sadomasochist /ˌseɪdəʊˈmæsəkɪst/ *n* sadomasochiste *mf*.

sadomasochistic /ˌseɪdəʊˌmæsəˈkɪstɪk/ *adj* sadomasochiste.

sad sack○ *n* US empoté/-e○ *m/f*.

sae *n*: *abrév* ▶ **stamped addressed envelope**.

safari /səˈfɑːrɪ/ *n* safari *m*; **to go on/to be on ~** aller faire/faire un safari.

safari: **~ hat** *n* casque *m* colonial; **~ jacket** *n* saharienne *f*; **~ park** *n* parc *m* (zoologique) (*où les animaux vivent en semi-liberté*); **~ suit** *n* costume *m* safari.

safe /seɪf/ **I** *n* **1** (for valuables) coffre-fort *m*; **2** (for meat) garde-manger *m inv*.
II *adj* **1** (after ordeal, risk) [*person*] sain et sauf, indemne fml; [*object*] intact; **we know they are ~** nous les savons hors de danger; **to hope for sb's ~ return/arrival** espérer que qn reviendra/arrivera sans encombre; **~ and sound** [*person*] sain et sauf; **2** (free from threat, harm) **to be ~** [*person*] être en sécurité; [*document, valuables*] être en lieu sûr; [*company, job, position, reputation*] ne pas être menacé; **to feel ~/~er** se sentir en sécurité/plus en sécurité; **you're quite ~ here** vous ne risquez rien ici; **is the bike ~ here?** est-ce qu'on peut laisser le vélo ici sans risque?; **he's ~ in bed** il dort tranquillement dans son lit; **have a ~ journey!** bon voyage!; **to keep sb ~** protéger qn (**from** contre, de); **to keep sth ~** (protect) mettre qch à l'abri (**from** de); (store) garder qch en lieu sûr; **to be ~ from** être à l'abri de [*attack, curiosity*]; **no-one is ~ from** personne n'est à l'abri de [*unemployment, infection*]; tout le monde peut être la victime de [*killer, person*]; **to be ~ with sb** ne rien risquer avec qn; **the money is ~ with him** avec lui l'argent ne risque rien; **to be ~ in sb's hands** être en sécurité entre les mains de qn; **3** (risk-free) [*product, toy, level, method*] sans danger; [*place, environment, vehicle, route*] sûr; [*structure, building*] solide; [*animal*] inoffensif/-ive; [*speed*] raisonnable; **the ~st way to do** la façon la plus sûre de faire; **to watch from a ~ distance** observer à distance respectueuse; **in a ~ condition** [*machine, building*] en bon état; **let's go—it's ~** allons-y—il n'y a plus de danger; **it's not ~** c'est dangereux; **to be ~ for sb** être sans danger pour qn; **the drug is ~ for pregnant women** le médicament ne présente pas de risques pour les femmes enceintes; **the toy/park is not ~ for children** le jouet/parc est dangereux pour les enfants; **it's ~ for swimming** ou **to swim in** on peut s'y baigner sans danger; **the meat is ~ for eating** ou **to eat** on peut manger la viande sans danger; **the water is ~ for drinking** l'eau est potable; **it is ~ to do** on peut faire sans danger; **it would be ~r for you to do** ce serait plus sûr ou prudent pour toi de faire; **it is not ~ to do** il est dangereux de faire; **it isn't ~ for you to talk to strangers** tu prends des risques en parlant à des étrangers; **that car is not ~ to drive** cette voiture est dangereuse; **nothing here is ~ to eat** ici rien n'est comestible; **to make sth ~** rendre [qch] (plus) sûr [*premises, beach*]; rendre [qch] inoffensif/-ive [*bomb*]; **to make food ~** rendre la nourriture comestible; **to make a stadium ~ for the public** assurer la sécurité du public dans un stade; **in order to make the world ~ for democracy** pour que la démocratie puisse régner dans le monde; **4** (prudent) [*investment*] sûr; [*estimate, choice, tactic*] prudent; [*topic, question*] anodin; **he's a bit too ~** il est un peu trop timoré; **the ~st thing to do would be to leave** le plus sûr serait de partir; **it would be ~r not to do** il vaudrait mieux ne pas faire; **it is ~ to say/predict that** on peut dire/prédire à coup sûr que; **it's ~ to assume that** on peut raisonnablement penser que; **5** (reliable) [*driver*] prudent; [*companion, guide, confidant*] sûr; **to be in ~ hands** être en bonnes mains; **to have a ~ pair of hands** être adroit; **6**○ GB (great) chouette○, vachement bien○.
IDIOMS **as ~ as houses** GB (secure) [*person*] en sécurité; [*place*] sûr; (risk-free) sans risque; **better ~ than sorry!** mieux vaut prévenir que guérir!; **just to be on the ~ side** simplement par précaution; **to play (it) ~** être prudent, jouer la sécurité○.

safe bet *n* **it's/he's a ~** c'est quelque chose/quelqu'un de sûr; **it's a ~ that** il est certain que.

safe: **~-blower** *n* perceur *m* de coffres-forts (*qui utilise des explosifs*); **~-breaker** *n* perceur *m* de coffres-forts.

safe-conduct /ˌseɪfˈkɒndʌkt/ *n* **1** (guarantee) **to demand/be offered ~ to/from** exiger/obtenir un laissez-passer pour/de; **2** (document) sauf-conduit *m*.

safe: **~-cracker**○ *n* perceur *m* de coffres-forts; **~-deposit box** *n* coffre *m* (à la banque).

safeguard /ˈseɪfgɑːd/ **I** *n* garantie *f* (**for** pour; **against** contre).
II *vtr* protéger (**against, from** contre).

safe house *n* refuge *m*.

safekeeping /ˌseɪfˈkiːpɪŋ/ *n* **in sb's ~** à la garde de qn; **to entrust sth to sb's ~, to give sth to sb for ~** confier qch à la garde de qn, confier la garde de qch à qn.

safely /ˈseɪflɪ/ *adv* **1** (unharmed) [*come back*] (of person) sans encombre; (of parcel, goods) sans dommage; [*land, take off*] sans problème; **I arrived/got back ~** je suis bien arrivé/rentré; **you can walk around quite ~** vous pouvez vous promener en toute sécurité; **to see sb ~ across the road** faire traverser la route à qn; **to be ~ across the border/aboard** être en sécurité de l'autre côté de la frontière/à bord; **2** (without worry or risk) [*leave, do, go*] en toute tranquillité; **you can ~ dispense with that** vous pouvez vous passer de ça sans problème; **we can ~ assume/conclude/say that...** nous pouvons penser/conclure/dire avec certitude que...; **3** (causing no concern) [*locked, hidden, stored*] bien; **to be ~ tucked up in bed** être bien bordé dans son lit; **he's ~ behind bars** heureusement il est sous les verrous; **he's ~ through to the final** il s'est qualifié sans problème pour la finale; **with her parents ~ out of the way**... par chance, ses parents étant absents...; **4** (carefully) prudemment; **drive ~!** conduis prudemment!

safeness /ˈseɪfnɪs/ *n* (of structure, building) solidité *f*; (of method, treatment, product) sécurité *f*; (of investment) sûreté *f*.

safe: **~ passage** *n* laissez-passer *m inv* (**to** pour; **for sb** pour qn); **~ period** *n* période *f* sans danger; **~ seat** *n* Pol siège *m* assuré.

safe sex *n* rapports *mpl* sexuels sans risque; **to practise ~** avoir des rapports sexuels sans risque.

safety /ˈseɪftɪ/ **I** *n* **1** (freedom from harm or hazards) sécurité *f*; **passenger ~** la sécurité des passagers; **to fear for** ou **be concerned about sb's ~** craindre pour la sécurité de qn; **there are fears for her ~** on est inquiet sur son sort; **in ~** en (toute) sécurité; **to help sb to ~** aider qn à se mettre à l'abri; **to flee to ~** courir se mettre à l'abri; **to reach ~** parvenir en lieu sûr; **to transfer sth to ~** transférer qch en lieu sûr; **in the ~ of one's home** chez soi en sécurité; **to watch from the ~ of the hills** observer en sécurité sur les collines; **2** (as public issue) sécurité *f*; **road ~** sécurité routière; **~ in the home** la sécurité domestique; **~ first** la sécurité d'abord; **3**○ US (condom) capote○ *f*, préservatif *m*.
II *modif* [*check, code, level, limit, measure, regulations, test*] de sécurité; [*bolt, blade, strap*] de sûreté; **~ record** résultats *mpl* en matière de sécurité.
IDIOMS **there's ~ in numbers** plus on est nombreux, moins on court de risques; **to play for ~** être prudent, jouer la sécurité○.

safety: **~ belt** *n* ceinture *f* de sécurité; **~ catch** *n* (on gun, knife) cran *m* de sûreté; **~ chain** *n* chaîne *f* de sûreté; **~ curtain** *n* rideau *m* de fer; **~-deposit box** *n* coffre *m* (à la banque); **~ glass** *n* verre *m* de sécurité; **~ helmet** *n* casque *m* de protection; **~ island** *n* US refuge *m* (*pour piétons*); **~ lamp** *n* lampe *f* de sûreté; **~ match** *n* allumette *f* de sûreté.

safety net *n* **1** lit filet *m* (de protection); **2** fig (safeguard) filet *m* de sécurité.

safety: **~ pin** *n* épingle *f* de sûreté; **~ razor** *n* rasoir *m* mécanique; **~ valve** *n* lit, fig soupape *f* de sécurité; **~ zone** *n* US refuge *m* (*pour piétons*).

saffron /ˈsæfrən/ **I** *n* (all contexts) safran *m*.
II *modif* [*flavour, flower*] de safran; [*rice*] au safran.
III ▶ **1104** *adj* [*robes, cloth*] safran.

sag /sæg/ **I** *n* **1** (in ceiling, mattress) affaissement *m*; **2** (in value) baisse *f*.
II *vi* (*p prés etc* **-gg-**) **1** [*ceiling, mattress*] s'affaisser; **to ~ in the middle** [*tent, rope*] ne pas être bien tendu; **2** [*breasts*] pendre; [*flesh*] être flasque; **3** (weaken) **her spirits ~ged** elle a perdu courage; **4** (fall) [*currency, exports*] baisser.

saga /ˈsɑːgə/ *n* **1**○ (lengthy story) histoire *f*; **a domestic ~** une histoire de couple compliquée; **2** Literat saga *f*.

sagacious /səˈgeɪʃəs/ *adj* sout [*person*] sagace; [*advice, decision*] sage (*before n*); [*act, remark*] sensé.

sagaciously /səˈgeɪʃəslɪ/ *adv* sout [*say*] avec sagacité.

sagacity /səˈgæsətɪ/, **sagaciousness** /səˈgeɪʃəsnɪs/ *n* sagacité *f*.

sage /seɪdʒ/ **I** *n* **1** Bot sauge *f*; **2** (wise person) sage *m*.
II *adj* (wise) [*person, comment, air*] avisé; **to give ~ advice** donner de sages conseils.

sage: **~-and-onion stuffing** *n* farce *f* à l'oignon et à la sauge; **~brush** *n* armoise *f*; **Sagebrush State** *n* US Nevada *m*; **~ Derby** *n* GB fromage *m* à la sauge; **~ green** ▶ **1104** *n, adj* vert (*m*) cendré *inv*.

sagely /ˈseɪdʒlɪ/ *adv* [*reply, nod*] avec sagesse.

sagging /ˈsægɪŋ/ *pres p adj* **1** [*beam, roof*] affaissé; [*cable, tent*] mal tendu; **2** [*breast*] tombant; **~ flesh** chairs *fpl* flasques; **3** [*spirits, morale*] défaillant.

Sagittarian /ˌsædʒɪˈteərɪən/ ▶ **1916** **I** *n* (person) sagittaire *m*.
II *adj* [*personality, trait*] du sagittaire.

Sagittarius /ˌsædʒɪˈteərɪəs/ ▶ **1916** *n* Sagittaire *m*.

sago /ˈseɪgəʊ/ *n* sagou *m*.

sago: **~ palm** *n* sagoutier *m*; **~ pudding** *n* bouillie *f* de sagou au lait.

Sahara /səˈhɑːrə/ *pr n* Sahara *m*; **the ~ desert** le désert du Sahara.

Saharan /səˈhɑːrən/ *adj* saharien/-ienne.

sahib /ˈsɑːhɪb/ *n* Monsieur *m*.

said /sed/ **I** *prét, pp* ▶ **say**.
II *pp adj* sout ou Jur dit; **the ~ Mr X** le dit M. X; **on the ~ day** le jour dit.

sail /seɪl/ **I** *n* **1** (on boat) voile *f*; **to take in ~** rentrer des voiles; **2** (navigation) **to set ~** prendre la mer; **to set ~ from/for** partir en bateau de/pour; **to be under ~** être en mer; **to cross the ocean under ~**

traverser l'océan à la voile; **a ship in full ~** un navire toutes voiles dehors; **the age of ~** l'âge de la voile; **3** (on windmill) aile *f*; **4** (journey) **to go for a ~** faire un tour en bateau; **it's two days' ~ from here** c'est à deux jours de bateau d'ici.
II *vtr* **1** (be in charge of) piloter [*ship, yacht*]; faire voguer [*model boat*]; (steer) manœuvrer [*ship, yacht*]; **to ~ a ship between two islands/into the port** manœuvrer un navire entre deux îles/pour entrer au port; **2** (travel across) traverser [qch] en bateau [*ocean, channel*]; **3** (own) avoir [*yacht*]; **I used to ~ a catamaran** j'avais un catamaran.
III *vi* **1** (travel by boat) [*person*] voyager en bateau; **to ~ from... to** voyager en bateau de... jusqu'à; **to ~ around the world** faire le tour du monde en bateau; **to ~ north** voyager en bateau vers le nord; **we flew there and ~ed back** nous avons pris l'avion à l'aller et le bateau au retour; **2** (move across water) [*ship*] **to ~ across** traverser [*ocean*]; **to ~ into** entrer dans [*port*]; **the ship ~ed into Brest** le bateau est entré dans la rade de Brest; **to ~ at 15 knots** filer à 15 nœuds; **to ~ under the Danish flag** naviguer sous pavillon danois; **3** (leave port, set sail) prendre la mer; **the Titanic ~ed on 10 April** le Titanic a pris la mer le 10 avril; **we ~/the boat ~s at 10 am** nous partons/le bateau part à 10 h; **4** (as hobby) faire de la voile; **to go ~ing** faire de la voile; **5** (move smoothly) **to ~ past sb** passer près de qn sans même le/la remarquer; **to ~ into a room** entrer dans une pièce d'un pas nonchalant; **the ball ~ed over the fence** la balle est passée par-dessus la barrière.
IDIOMS **to ~ close to the wind** jouer avec le feu; **to take the wind out of sb's ~s** rabattre le caquet à qn.
■ **sail into**○ US: **~ into [sb]** passer un savon à○.
■ **sail through**: **~ through [sth]** gagner [qch] facilement [*match, election*]; **to ~ through an exam** réussir un examen les doigts dans le nez○; **he ~ed through the interview** il s'en est bien tiré○ à l'entretien.
sail: **~board** *n* planche *f* à voile; **~boarder** *n* véliplanchiste *mf*; **~boarding** *n* planche *f* à voile; **~boat** *n* US voilier *m*; **~cloth** *n* toile *f* à voile.
sailing /ˈseɪlɪŋ/ ▶1282 I *n* **1** (sport) voile *f*; **I love ~** j'adore la voile; **a week's ~** une semaine de voile; **2** (departure) **the next ~** le prochain bateau; **three ~s a day** trois bateaux par jour.
II *modif* [*club, equipment, holiday, instructor*] de voile; [*boat, vessel*] à voiles; [*time, date*] de départ du bateau.
sailing: **~ dinghy** *n* dériveur *m*; **~ ship** *n* voilier *m*.
sail maker ▶1692 *n* fabricant/-e *m/f* de voiles.
sailor /ˈseɪlə(r)/ *n* **1** ▶1612 (seaman) marin *m*; **2** (sea traveller) **to be a good/bad ~** avoir/ne pas avoir le pied marin.
sailor suit *n* costume *m* marin.
sailplane /ˈseɪlpleɪn/ *n* planeur *m*.
sainfoin /ˈseɪnfɔɪn, ˈsæn-/ *n* sainfoin *m*.
saint /seɪnt, snt/ *n* Relig, fig saint/-e *m/f*; **Saint Mark** Saint Marc.
IDIOMS **to have the patience of a ~** avoir une patience d'ange.
sainted /ˈseɪntɪd/ *adj* sanctifié.
Saint Gall ▶1818, 1776 *pr n* Saint-Gall; **the canton of ~** le canton de Saint-Gall.
sainthood /ˈseɪnthʊd/ *n* sainteté *f*.
saintliness /ˈseɪntlɪnɪs/ *n* sainteté *f*.
saintly /ˈseɪntlɪ/ *adj* [*person, manner, expression*] plein de bonté; [*virtue, quality*] de saint.
Saint-Pierre-et-Miquelon ▶1163 *pr n* Saint-Pierre-et-Miquelon; **in/to ~** à Saint-Pierre-et-Miquelon.
saint's day *n* fête *f*.
saithe /seɪθ/ *n* GB Zool, Culin lieu *m* noir.
sake /seɪk/ *n* **1** (purpose) **for the ~ of** pour [*principle, prestige, nation*]; **for the ~ of clarity, for clarity's ~** pour la clarté; **for the ~ of argument** à titre d'exemple; **to kill for the ~ of killing** tuer pour le plaisir de tuer; **to do sth for its own ~** faire qch pour le plaisir; **peace/production for its own ~** la paix/la production pour la paix/la production; **for old times' ~** en souvenir du bon vieux temps; **2** (benefit) **for the ~ of sb, for sb's ~** par égard pour qn; **for my/her/their ~** par égard pour moi/elle/eux; **for all our ~s** dans notre intérêt à tous; **I'm telling you this for your own ~** c'est pour ton bien que je te dis cela; **3** (in anger, in plea) **for God's/heaven's ~!** pour l'amour de Dieu/du ciel!
saki, sake /ˈsɑːkɪ/ *n* sake *m*.
sal /sɑːl/ *n* Chem, Pharm sel *m*.
salaam /səˈlɑːm/ I *n* salut *m* (*chez les musulmans*); **to make a ~** saluer.
II *vi* saluer.
salability *n* US ▶ **saleability**.
salable *adj* US ▶ **saleable**.
salacious /səˈleɪʃəs/ *adj* salace.
salaciousness /səˈleɪʃəsnɪs/ *n* salacité *f*.
salad /ˈsæləd/ *n* salade *f*; **bean/ham ~** salade de haricots/au jambon; **green/mixed ~** salade verte/composée.
salad: **~ bar** *n* buffet *m* de crudités; **~ bowl** *n* saladier *m*; **~ cream** *n* GB ≈ sauce *f* mayonnaise; **~ days** *npl* littér (youth) années *fpl* de jeunesse; **~ dressing** *n* sauce *f* pour salade; **~ oil** *n* huile *f* de table; **~ servers** *npl* couverts *mpl* à salade; **~ shaker** *n* panier *m* à salade; **~ spinner** *n* essoreuse *f* à salade.
salamander /ˈsæləmændə(r)/ *n* Zool, Mythol salamandre *f*.
salami /səˈlɑːmɪ/ *n* saucisson *m* sec.
sal ammoniac /ˌsæləˈməʊnɪæk/ *n* sel *m* ammoniac.
salaried /ˈsælərɪd/ *adj* salarié.
salary /ˈsælərɪ/ I *n* salaire *m*.
II *modif* [*cheque, increase*] de salaire; [*bracket*] de salaires; [*scale*] des salaires.
sale /seɪl/ I *n* **1** (selling) vente *f* (**of** de; **to** à); **for ~** à vendre; **to put sth up** ou **offer sth for ~** mettre qch en vente; **on ~** GB en vente; US en solde; **to go on ~** GB être mis en vente; US être mis en solde; **on ~ or return** en vente avec reprise des invendus; **for general ~** destiné à la vente (au public); **at point of ~** au point de vente; **2** (cut price) solde *f*; **the ~s** les soldes; **in the ~(s)** GB, **on ~** US en solde; **to put sth in the ~** GB ou **on ~** US solder qch; **to have a ~** solder; **the ~s are on** c'est la saison des soldes; **the summer/January ~s** les soldes estivales/de janvier; **3** (event) vente *f*; **book/furniture ~** vente de livres/de meubles; **to have** ou **hold a ~** organiser une vente; **4** (by salesman) vente *f*; **to make a ~** réaliser une vente.
II **sales** *npl* **1** (amount sold) ventes *fpl*; **arms/wine ~s** ventes *fpl* d'armes/de vin; **~s are up/down** les ventes sont en hausse/en baisse; **2** (career) commerce *m*; **3** (department) service *m* des ventes.
III **sales** *modif* [*department, growth*] des ventes.
saleability /ˌseɪləˈbɪlɪtɪ/ *n* qualité *f* marchande.
saleable /ˈseɪləbl/ *adj* vendable, demandé.
sale: **~ item** *n* article *m* soldé; **~ of work** *n* vente *f* de charité; **~ price** *n* prix *m* soldé.
Salerno /səˈleənəʊ/ *pr n* Salerne; **the ~ landings** le débarquement de Salerne.
sale: **~room** *n* hôtel *m* des ventes; **~s assistant** ▶1692 *n* GB vendeur/-euse *m/f*; **~s book** *n* Comm journal *m* des ventes; **~s chart** *n* graphique *m* des ventes; **~sclerk** ▶1692 *n* US vendeur/-euse *m/f*; **~s director** ▶1692 *n* directeur/-trice *m/f* commercial/-e; **~s drive** *n* campagne *f* de vente; **~s executive** ▶1692 *n* cadre *m* commercial; **~s figures** *npl* chiffre *m* de ventes, chiffre *m* d'affaires; **~s force** *n* force *f* de vente; **~s forecast** *n* prévisions *fpl* de vente; **~sgirl** ▶1692 *n* vendeuse *f*; **~slady** ▶1692 *n* US vendeuse *f*.
salesman /ˈseɪlzmən/ ▶1692 *n* (*pl* **-men**) **1** (representative) représentant *m*; **insurance ~** représentant d'assurances; **2** (in shop, showroom) vendeur *m*; **used car ~** revendeur *m* de voitures d'occasion.
sales manager *n* = **sales director**.
salesmanship /ˈseɪlzmənʃɪp/ *n* aptitude *f* à la vente.
sale: **~s office** *n* bureau *m* des ventes; **~sperson** ▶1692 *n* (*pl* **-persons** ou **-people**) vendeur/-euse *m/f*; **~s pitch** *n* baratin○ *m* publicitaire; **~s point** *n* caisse *f*; **~s rep, sales representative** ▶1692 *n* représentant/-e *m/f*; **~s resistance** *n* résistance *f* à l'achat; **~s slip** *n* ticket *m* de caisse; **~s staff** *n* commerciaux *mpl*, équipe *f* commerciale; **~s talk** *n* boniments *mpl*; **~s target** *n* objectif *m* de vente; **~s tax** *n* US taxe *f* à l'achat; **~swoman** ▶1692 *n* (representative) représentante *f*; (in shop) vendeuse *f*; **~ value** *n* valeur *f* marchande.
Salic law /ˈsælɪk lɔː/ *n* loi *f* salique.
salient /ˈseɪlɪənt/ I *n* Mil saillant *m*.
II *adj* (striking) saillant; (principal) essentiel/-ielle.
salina /səˈlaɪnə/ *n* **1** Geog marais *m* salant; **2** (salt works) saline *f*.
saline /ˈseɪlaɪn/ I *n* Med (also **~ solution**) sérum *m* physiologique; **~ drip** perfusion *f* de sérum physiologique.
II *adj* [*liquid, spring*] salé; [*deposit*] salin.
salinity /səˈlɪnətɪ/ *n* salinité *f*.
saliva /səˈlaɪvə/ *n* salive *f*.
salivary /səˈlɪvərɪ, səˈlaɪvərɪ, US ˈsæləverɪ/ *adj* salivaire; **~ gland** glande *f* salivaire.
salivate /ˈsælɪveɪt/ *vi* saliver.
salivation /ˌsælɪˈveɪʃn/ *n* salivation *f*.
sallow /ˈsæləʊ/ I *n* Bot saule *m* marsault.
II *adj* (pale) cireux/-euse.
sallowness /ˈsæləʊnɪs/ *n* pâleur *f* cireuse.
sally /ˈsælɪ/ *n* **1**† Mil sortie *f*; **2** (witty remark) trait *m* d'esprit, saillie *f* liter.
■ **sally forth** hum (set off) se mettre en route avec entrain; (go out) sortir avec entrain.
Sally Army○ *n* GB Armée *f* du Salut.
salmagundi /ˌsælməˈgʌndɪ/ *n* US ragoût *m*.
salmon /ˈsæmən/ I *n* (*pl* **~**) saumon *m*.
II *modif* [*fillet, pâté*] de saumon; [*fishing, sandwich*] au saumon.
salmonella /ˌsælməˈnelə/ *n* (*pl* **-æ** ou **-as**) Biol salmonelle *f*.
salmonella poisoning ▶1354 *n* salmonellose *f*.
salmonellosis /ˌsælməneˈləʊsɪs/ ▶1354 *n* salmonellose *f*.
salmon: **~ pink** ▶1104 *n, adj* rose (*m*) saumon *inv*; **~ steak** *n* darne *f* de saumon; **~ trout** *n* truite *f* saumonée.
Salome /səˈləʊmɪ/ *pr n* Salomé.
salon /ˈsælɒn, US səˈlɒn/ *n* (all contexts) salon *m*; **hairdressing/beauty ~** salon de coiffure/de beauté.
saloon /səˈluːn/ I *n* **1** (also **~ car**) GB Aut berline *f*; **2** (also **~ bar**) GB salle *f* confortable (*d'un pub*); US (in Wild West) saloon *m*, bar *m* (*du Far West américain*); **3** (on boat) salon *m*.
saloon car racing ▶1282 *n* GB courses *fpl* de voitures de tourisme.
Salop *pr n* GB Post *abrév écrite* ▶ **Shropshire**.
salpingitis /ˌsælpɪnˈdʒaɪtɪs/ ▶1354 *n* Med salpingite *f*.
salsa /ˈsælsə/ *n* **1** (dance) salsa *f*; **2** (sauce) sauce *f* pimentée.
salsify /ˈsælsɪfɪ/ *n* salsifis *m*.
salt /sɔːlt/ I *n* **1** Chem, Culin sel *m*; **there's**

too much ~ in the rice le riz est trop salé; **I don't like a lot of ~ on my food** je n'aime pas manger très salé; **~ and pepper** du sel et du poivre; **to put ~ on food/a road** saler les aliments/une route; **2**○† (sailor) **an old ~** un vieux loup de mer.
II salts *npl* Pharm sels *mpl.*
III *modif* [*molecule, crystal, solution*] de sel; [*industry, refining*] du sel; [*production, factory*] de sel; [*water, lake*] salé; [*beef, pork*] salé.
IV *vtr* saler [*meat, fish, road, path*].
IDIOMS **to cry ~ tears** littér verser des larmes amères ; **to be the ~ of the earth** être le sel de la terre; **you should take his remarks with a grain** ou **a pinch of ~** il ne faut pas prendre ses remarques pour argent comptant; **any teacher worth his ~ knows that** tout enseignant digne de ce nom sait cela.
■ **salt away**: **~ away** [**sth**], **~** [**sth**] **away** mettre [qch] de côté.

SALT /sɔ:lt/ *n* (*abrév* = **Strategic Arms Limitation Talks**) négociations *fpl* SALT.

salt: **~box** *n* lit boîte *f* à sel; fig, US *maison ayant deux étages à l'avant et un seul à l'arrière*; **~cellar** *n* salière *f.*

salted /'sɔ:ltɪd/ *adj* [*butter, peanuts*] salé.

salt flat *n* marais *m* salant.

saltine /'sɔ:ltaɪn/ *n* US biscuit *m* salé.

saltiness /'sɔ:ltɪnɪs/ *n* **1** (taste) (of food) goût *m* salé; **2** (salt content) (of solution, water) teneur *f* en sel.

saltings /'sɔ:ltɪŋz/ *npl* GB prés *mpl* salés.

salt: **~ lick** *n* (naturally occurring) pierre *f* salée; Agric bloc *f* de sel; **~ marsh** *n* salin *m.*

saltmine /'sɔ:ltmaɪn/ *n* Mining mine *f* de sel; **it's back to the ~s for me** fig je dois retourner au boulot○.

saltpan /'sɔ:ltpæn/ *n* puits *m* de sel.

saltpetre GB, **saltpeter** US /,sɔ:lt'pi:tə(r)/ *n* salpêtre *m.*

salt: **~shaker** *n* salière *f*; **~ spoon** *n* cuillère *f* à sel; **~ tax** *n* Hist gabelle *f*; **~water** *adj* [*fish*] de mer; [*plant, mammal*] marin; **~works** *npl* salines *fpl.*

salty /'sɔ:ltɪ/ *adj* **1** [*water, food, flavour*] salé; **to taste ~** avoir un goût salé; **2** Miner [*deposit, soil*] salin; **3** fig [*language, humour, slang*] salé.

salubrious /sə'lu:brɪəs/ *adj* lit salubre; fig [*neighbourhood*] tout à fait respectable; **it isn't a very ~ place** c'est un endroit peu recommandable.

salubrity /sə'lu:brətɪ/ *n* sout salubrité *f.*

saluki /sə'lu:kɪ/ *n* sloughi *m.*

salutary /'sæljʊtrɪ, US -terɪ/ *adj* salutaire.

salutation /,sælju:'teɪʃn/ *n* **1** sout (greeting) salutation *f*; **in ~** en guise de salutation; **2** (in letter writing) forme *f* d'adresse.

salutatorian /,sæljuːterˈtɔːrɪən/ *n* US Sch, Univ *étudiant/-e qui se classe deuxième de sa promotion et qui prononce le discours de fin d'année.*

salute /sə'lu:t/ **I** *n* **1** Mil, gen (greeting) salut *m*; **to give a ~** faire un salut; **in ~** en guise de salut; **to take the ~** assister au défilé des troupes; **victory ~** V *m* de la victoire; **2** Mil (firing of guns) salve *f*; **a 21-gun ~** une salve de 21 coups de canon; **3** (tribute) hommage *m* (**to** à).
II *vtr* **1** Mil, gen (greet) saluer; **2** fig (honour) saluer.
III *vi* saluer.

Salvador(e)an /,sælvə'dɔ:rɪən/ **▶ 1486** **I** *pr n* Salvadorien/-ienne *m/f.*
II *adj* salvadorien/-ienne.

salvage /'sælvɪdʒ/ **I** *n* **1** (rescue) sauvetage *m* (**of** de); **2** (goods rescued) biens *mpl* récupérés; **3** (reward) prime *f* de sauvetage.
II *modif* [*operation, team, equipment*] de sauvetage.
III *vtr* **1** (rescue) gen, Naut sauver [*cargo, materials, belongings*] (**from** de); effectuer le sauvetage de [*ship*]; **2** fig sauver [*plan, marriage, reputation*]; sauver [*point, game*]; obtenir [*draw*]; préserver [*pride, memories*]; **3** (save for recycling) récupérer [*metal, paper etc*].

salvation /sæl'veɪʃn/ *n* Relig, gen salut *m*; **national ~** le salut national.

Salvation Army **I** *n* Armée *f* du Salut.
II *modif* [*band, hostel, officer*] de l'Armée du Salut.

salvationist /sæl'veɪʃənɪst/ *n* salutiste *mf.*

salve /sælv, US sæv/ **I** *n* **1** lit, fig (balm) baume *m*; **2** (comfort) **as a ~ to one's/sb's conscience** pour soulager sa conscience/la conscience de qn.
II *vtr* **to ~ one's conscience** soulager sa conscience.

salver /'sælvə(r)/ *n* plateau *m* (à boissons).

salvia /'sælvɪə/ *n* salvia *m.*

salvo /'sælvəʊ/ *n* (*pl* **-os** ou **-oes**) Mil fig salve *f.*

sal volatile /,sælvə'lætəlɪ/ *n* sel *m* volatil.

salvor /'sælvə(r)/ *n* sauveteur *m* en mer.

Salzburg /'sæltsbɜ:g/ **▶ 1818** *pr n* Salzbourg.

SAM *n*: *abrév* ▶ **surface air missile**.

Samaria /sə'meərɪə/ *pr n* Samarie *f.*

Samaritan /sə'mærɪtən/ **I** *n* **1** Geog, Hist Samaritain/-e *m/f*; **the Good ~** le bon Samaritain; **to be a good ~** avoir de la compassion; **2** (organization) **the ~s** les Samaritains *mpl.*
II *adj* Geog, Hist samaritain.

samarium /sə'meərɪəm/ *n* samarium *m.*

samba /'sæmbə/ *n* samba *f.*

sambo○† /'sæmbəʊ/ *n* injur nègre/négresse *m/f* offensive.

Sam Browne belt /,sæmbraʊn'belt/ *n* ceinturon *m* et baudrier *m.*

same /seɪm/ **I** *adj* **1** (identical) même; **to be the ~** être le or la même; **the result was the ~** le résultat était le même; **people are the ~ everywhere** les gens sont partout les mêmes; **you're all the ~!** vous êtes tous les mêmes!; **it's the ~ everywhere** c'est partout la même chose; **it is the ~ for** c'est la même chose pour; **it is the ~ with** il en est de même pour; **to look the ~** être pareil; **they all look the ~ to him** pour lui, ils sont tous pareils; **to be the ~ as sth** être comme qch; **a bag the ~ as the one I lost** un sac comme celui que j'ai perdu; **it is the ~ as doing** c'est comme de faire; **one wine is the ~ as another to him** pour lui un vin en vaut un autre; **the ~ time last week** la semaine dernière à la même heure; **the ~ time last year** l'année dernière à la même époque; **~ time ~ place** même heure même endroit; **in the ~ way** (in a similar manner) de la même manière (**as** que); (likewise) de même; **to do sth (in) the ~ way that sb else does** faire qch comme qn d'autre; **we did it the ~ way as you** on a fait comme toi; **to feel the ~ way about** avoir les mêmes sentiments à l'égard de; **to think the ~ way on** ou **about sth** être du même avis sur qch; **to go the ~ way as** lit aller dans la même direction que; fig connaître le même sort que; **the ~ thing** la même chose; **it's the ~ thing** c'est pareil; **it amounts** ou **comes to the ~ thing** cela revient au même; **it's all the ~ to me** ça m'est complètement égal; **if it's all the ~ to you** si ça ne te fait rien; **2** (for emphasis) (very) même (**as** que); **the ~ one** le/la même; **'ready the ~ day'** 'prêt dans la journée'; **that ~ week** la même semaine; **later that ~ day/week** plus tard dans la journée/semaine; **in that ~ house** dans cette même maison; **those ~ people** ceux-là mêmes; **at the ~ time** (all contexts) en même temps; **they are one and the ~** (**person**) il s'agit d'une seule et même personne; **the very ~** exactement le or la même; **the very ~ day that** le jour même où; **3** (unchanged) même; **it's still the ~ town** c'est toujours la même ville; **she's not the ~ woman** ce n'est plus la même femme; **to be still the ~** être toujours le/la même; **things are just the ~ as before** rien n'a changé; **it's/he's the ~ as ever** c'est/il est toujours pareil; **my views are the ~ as they always were** mes opinions n'ont pas changé; **she's much the ~** elle n'a pas beaucoup changé; **to remain** ou **stay the ~** ne pas changer; **things can't stay the ~ forever** rien n'est immuable; **things were never the ~ again** rien n'était plus comme avant; **it's not the ~ without you** ce n'est pas pareil sans toi; **life wouldn't be the ~ without** la vie ne serait plus la même sans; **the ~ old routine/excuse/clothes** toujours la même routine/la vieille excuse/les mêmes vieux vêtements; **~ old John, always late!** ça c'est bien John, toujours en retard!; ▶ **story**.
II the same *adv phr* [*act, speak, dress*] de la même façon; **they're pronounced the ~** ils se prononcent de la même façon; **to feel the ~** (**as sb**) penser comme qn; **to feel the ~ about** avoir les mêmes sentiments à l'égard de; **life goes on just the ~** la vie continue comme d'habitude; **I love you just the ~** je t'aime toujours autant.
III the same *pron* **1** gen (the identical thing) la même chose (**as** que); **I'll have the ~** je prendrai la même chose; **the ~ applies to** ou **goes for**... il en va de même pour...; **to say the ~ about** en dire autant de; **the ~ cannot be said of** on ne peut pas en dire autant de; **to do the ~ as sb** faire comme qn; **and we're hoping to do the ~** et on espère en faire autant; **I would do the ~ for you** j'en ferais autant pour toi; **I'll do the ~ for you one day** un jour j'en ferai autant pour toi; **I'd do the ~ again** je recommencerais; **the ~ to you!** (in greeting) à toi aussi, à toi de même!; (of insult) et toi-même○!; **(the) ~ again please!** la même chose s'il vous plaît!; **it'll be more of the ~!** péj c'est reparti pour un tour!; **(the) ~ here**○! moi aussi!; **2** Jur celui-ci *m*, celle-ci *f*; **'are you Mrs X?'—'the ~'** 'êtes-vous Mme X?'—'elle-même!'; **3** Accts, Comm le or la même; **to installing ~** installation du même.
IDIOMS **all the ~**..., **just the ~**,... tout de même,...; **thanks all the ~** merci quand même.

same-day /,seɪm'daɪ/ *adj* [*processing, dry-cleaning, service*] effectué dans la journée.

sameness /'seɪmnɪs/ *n* **1** péj (lack of variety) monotonie *f*; **2** (similarity) similitude *f.*

Samoa /sə'məʊə/ **▶ 1381** *pr n* Samoa *m.*

Samoan /sə'məʊən/ **▶ 1486**, **1402** **I** *n* **1** (inhabitant) Samoan/-e *m/f*; **2** (language) samoan *m.*
II *adj* samoan.

samosa /sə'məʊsə/ *n*: *petit pâté épicé en croûte.*

samovar /'sæməvɑ:(r)/ *n* samovar *m.*

sampan /'sæmpæn/ *n* sampan *m.*

sample /'sɑ:mpl, US 'sæmpl/ **I** *n* **1** gen, Comm, Geol (of product, fabric, rock etc) échantillon *m*; **to take a soil ~** prélever un échantillon de sol; **2** Med, Biol (of tissue, DNA) (of individual for analysis) prélèvement *m*; (one of many kept in lab) échantillon *m*; **to take a blood ~** faire une prise de sang; **you should bring a urine ~** ≈ on va vous faire une analyse d'urine; **3** Ecol, Biol (of water etc) prélèvement *m*; **4** Stat (of public, population) panel *m*, échantillon *m*; **representative/limited ~** panel *m* représentatif/restraint.
II *modif* **1** Comm [*cassette, video etc*] de promotion; **~ bottle/packet etc** Comm échantillon *m*; **2** (representative) [*exam question*] type; **~ prices** prix *mpl* donnés à titre d'exemple; **he sent a ~ chapter of his thesis to the publishers** il a envoyé un chapitre de sa thèse aux éditeurs.
III *vtr* **1** goûter (à) [*food, dish, wine etc*]; **to ~ the delights of Paris** goûter aux plai-

sirs de Paris; **2** Comm essayer [*products*]; **3** Sociol, Stat sonder [*opinion, market*].

sampler /'sɑ:mplə(r), US 'sæmplər/ *n* **1** (embroidery) *toile illustrant différents points de broderie*, ≈ abécédaire *m*; **2** (person) échantillonneur/-euse *m/f*; **3** US (box of chocolates) boîte *f* de chocolats assortis.

sample survey *n* sondage *m*.

sampling /'sɑ:mplɪŋ, US 'sæmpl-/ **I** *n* **1** (taking of specimens) prélèvement *m*, échantillonnage *m*; **2** (of population group) échantillonnage *m*; **3** (of wine, cheese) dégustation *f*; **4** Mus échantillonage *m*.

II *modif* **~ procedures** Sociol, Stat méthodes *fpl* de sondage; **~ technique** Med, Geol méthodes *fpl* de prélèvement; Ind (in factory) technique *f* d'échantillonnage.

samurai /'sæmʊraɪ/ *n* (*pl* **~**) samouraï *m*.

San Andreas fault /ˌsænˌændreɪəs'fɔ:lt/ *pr n* **the ~** la faille de San Andreas.

sanatorium /ˌsænə'tɔ:rɪəm/ *n* (*pl* **-riums** ou **-ria**) GB **1** (clinic) sanatorium *m*; **2** (in boarding school) infirmerie *f*.

sanctification /ˌsæŋktɪfɪ'keɪʃn/ *n* sanctification *f*.

sanctify /'sæŋktɪfaɪ/ *vtr* sanctifier.

sanctimonious /ˌsæŋktɪ'məʊnɪəs/ *adj* péj supérieur.

sanctimoniously /ˌsæŋktɪ'məʊnɪəslɪ/ *adv* [*say*] d'un air de supériorité vertueuse.

sanction /'sæŋkʃn/ **I** *n* **1** (authorization) autorisation *f*; (approval) sanction *f*; **with the ~ of** avec l'autorisation de [*court, owner etc*]; **2** Jur (deterrent) **legal ~, criminal ~** sanction *f* pénale; **the ultimate ~** l'ultime sanction; **3** Pol, Econ (punishment, embargo etc) sanction *f*; **powers of ~** pouvoirs *mpl* de sanction.

II sanctions *npl* Pol, Econ sanctions *fpl* (**against** contre); **economic/trade ~s** sanctions économiques/commerciales; **to impose ~s** prendre des sanctions (**on** contre); to break **~s against a country** violer l'embargo contre un pays.

III *vtr* **1** (give permission for) autoriser; **2** (give approval to) sanctionner.

sanctions busting *n* violation *f* de l'embargo.

sanctity /'sæŋktətɪ/ *n* **1** (of life, law) inviolabilité *f*; **2** Relig sainteté *f*.

sanctuary /'sæŋktʃʊərɪ, US -tʃʊerɪ/ *n* **1** (safe place) refuge *m*; **a place of ~** un refuge; **to take ~** trouver asile; **2** (holy place) sanctuaire *m*; **3** (for wildlife) réserve *f*; (for mistreated pets) refuge *m*.

sanctum /'sæŋktəm/ *n* (*pl* **-tums** ou **-ta**) **1** (private place) refuge *m*; **his inner ~** le lieu où il se retire (du monde); **2** Relig **the (inner) ~** (in Jewish temple) le Saint des Saints; gen (holy place) le sanctuaire.

sand /sænd/ **I** *n* **1** (fine grit) sable *m*; **fine/coarse ~** sable fin/grossier; **2**○ US (courage) cran○ *m*, courage *m*.

II sands *npl* **1** (beach) plage *f*; **2** (desert) sables *mpl*; **the shifting ~s of international politics** fig le terrain fragile de la politique internationale.

III *vtr* **1** (also **~ down**) (smooth) poncer [*floor*]; frotter or passer [qch] au papier de verre [*car body, woodwork*]; **2** (put sand on) sabler [*icy road, path*].

IDIOMS **as happy as a ~boy** gai comme un pinson; **to stick** ou **bury one's head in the ~** pratiquer la politique de l'autruche; **the ~s of time run slow** le temps s'écoule lentement; **the ~s of time are running out for the government** les jours du gouvernement sont comptés; **to build on ~** fig bâtir sur le sable.

■ **sand up** [*estuary, river*] s'ensabler.

sandal /'sændl/ *n* sandale *f*.

sandalwood /'sændlwʊd/ **I** *n* (tree) santal *m*; (wood) (bois *m* de) santal *m*.

II *modif* [*oil, soap*] au santal; [*box*] en bois de santal.

sandbag /'sændbæg/ **I** *n* sac *m* de sable.

II *vtr* (*p prés etc* **-gg-**) **1** (protect) (against gunfire) renforcer [qch] avec des sacs de sable [*position*]; (against flood) ériger un mur de sacs de sable contre [*doorway*]; **2** (hit) assommer [qn] avec un sac de sable [*person*]; **3**○ fig (bully) malmener [*person*]; **to ~ sb into doing** contraindre qn à faire.

sand: **~bank** *n* banc *m* de sable; **~ bar** *n* barre *f* de sable.

sandblast /'sændblɑ:st, US -blæst/ *vtr* décaper [qch] à la sableuse.

sand: **~blaster** *n* sableuse *f*; **~blasting** *n* sablage *m*, décapage *m* au jet de sable; **~ castle** *n* château *m* de sable; **~ dollar** *n* Zool oursin *m* plat; **~ dune** *n* dune *f*; **~ eel** *n* anguille *f* de sable, lançon *m*.

sander /'sændə(r)/ *n* ponceuse *f*.

sand: **~ flea** *n* puce *f* de mer, talitre *m* spéc; **~ fly** *n* phlébotome *m*; **~ hopper** *n* = **sand flea**.

Sandhurst /'sændhɜ:st/ *pr n* GB *école militaire de l'armée de terre*.

sanding /'sændɪŋ/ *n* Tech ponçage *m*.

sanding disc *n* disque *m* abrasif.

sandlot /'sændlɒt/ US **I** *n* terrain *m* vague (*où les enfants jouent*).

II *modif* [*baseball, game*] de terrain vague.

sand: **~man** *n* marchand *m* de sable; **~ martin** *n* hirondelle *f* de rivage.

sandpaper /'sændpeɪpə(r)/ **I** *n* papier *m* de verre.

II *vtr* poncer [*plaster, wood*]; polir [*glass, metal*].

sandpiper /'sændpaɪpə(r)/ *n* bécasseau *m* de Baird.

sandpit /'sændpɪt/ *n* **1** (for quarrying) sablière *f*; **2** (for children) bac *m* à sable.

sandshoe† /'sændʃu:/ *n* GB chaussure *f* de sport.

sandstone /'sændstəʊn/ **I** *n* grès *m*; **white/red ~** grès blanc/rose.

II *modif* [*building, façade*] en grès; [*cliff, quarry*] de grès.

sand: **~storm** *n* tempête *f* de sable; **~trap** *n* US Sport (in golf) bunker *m*, obstacle *m* de sable.

sandwich /'sænwɪdʒ, US -wɪtʃ/ **I** *n* **1** sandwich *m*; **cucumber ~** sandwich au concombre; **I just had a ~ for lunch** j'ai déjeuné d'un sandwich; **2** GB (cake) génoise *f* (*fourrée au chocolat, à la confiture etc*).

II *vtr* **to be ~ed between** [*car, building, person*] être pris en sandwich entre, être coincé entre; **her talk was ~ed between two meetings** son discours s'insérait entre deux réunions.

sandwich: **~ bar** *n* sandwich bar *m*; **~ board** *n* panneau *m* publicitaire (*porté par un homme sandwich*); **~ course** *n* GB cours *m* avec stage pratique; **~ loaf** *n* pain *m* en tranches; **~ man** ▶1692 *n* homme-sandwich *m*.

sandworm /'sændwɜ:m/ *n* arénicole *f*.

sandy /'sændɪ/ *adj* **1** Geol [*beach*] de sable; [*path, soil*] sablonneux/-euse; [*sediment, water*] sableux/-euse; **2** (yellowish) [*hair*] blond roux *inv*; [*colour*] sable (*after n*).

sand yacht /'sændjɒt/ **I** *n* char *m* à voile.

II *vi* faire du char à voile.

sane /seɪn/ *adj* **1** (not mad) [*person*] sain d'esprit; **it's the only thing that keeps me ~** c'est la seule chose qui m'empêche de devenir fou; **2** (reasonable) [*policy, judgment*] sensé.

sanely /'seɪnlɪ/ *adv* **1** (not madly) [*behave*] comme quelqu'un qui est sain d'esprit; **2** (wisely) [*judge, decide*] de façon sensée.

Sanforized® /'sænfəraɪzd/ *adj* sanforisé®.

San Francisco /ˌsæn frən'sɪskəʊ/ ▶1818 *pr n* San Francisco.

sang /sæŋ/ *prét* ▶ **sing**.

sangfroid /sɒŋ'frwɑ:/ *n* sang-froid *m inv*.

sangria /sæn'gri:ə/ *n* sangria *f*.

sanguinary /'sæŋgwɪnərɪ, US -nerɪ/ *adj* sout sanguinaire.

sanguine /'sæŋgwɪn/ *adj* sout (hopeful) [*person, remark*] optimiste (**about** au sujet de); **to take a ~ view** voir les choses avec optimisme.

sanguinely /'sæŋgwɪnlɪ/ *adv* de façon optimiste.

sanitarium US = **sanatorium** 1.

sanitary /'sænɪtrɪ, US -terɪ/ *adj* **1** [*facilities, installations*] sanitaire; **2** (hygienic) hygiénique; (clean) propre.

sanitary: **~ engineer** ▶1692 *n* ingénieur *m* sanitaire; **~ protection** *n* garniture *f* périodique; **~ towel** GB, **~ napkin** US *n* serviette *f* hygiénique or périodique; **~ware** *n* équipement *m* sanitaire.

sanitation /ˌsænɪ'teɪʃn/ *n* (toilets) ¢ installations *fpl* sanitaires.

sanitation worker ▶1692 *n* US éboueur *m*.

sanitize /'sænɪtaɪz/ **I** *vtr* **1** péj (tone down) aseptiser [*art, politics*]; expurger [*document*]; **a film that tries to ~ violence** un film qui cherche à rendre la violence plus acceptable; **2** (sterilize) désinfecter.

sanitized /'sænɪtaɪzd/ *adj* péj [*art, politics*] aseptisé pej; [*document*] expurgé.

sanity /'sænətɪ/ *n* **1** (mental health) équilibre *m* mental; **to keep** ou **preserve one's ~** rester sain d'esprit; **to prove one's ~** prouver qu'on est sain d'esprit; **2** (good sense) bon sens *m*; **~ prevailed** le bon sens l'emporta.

sank /sæŋk/ *prét* ▶ **sink** III.

San Marinese /ˌsænˌmærɪ'ni:z/ ▶1486 **I** *n* Saint-Marinais/-e *m/f*.

II *adj* saint-marinais.

San Marino /ˌsæn mə'ri:nəʊ/ ▶1131 *pr n* Saint-Marin *m*.

sansevieria /ˌsænsɪ'vɪərɪə/ *n* sansevière *f*.

Sanskrit /'sænskrɪt/ ▶1402 *n* sanscrit *m*.

Santa (Claus) /'sæntə (klɔ:z)/ *pr n* le père Noël.

Santiago /ˌsæntɪ'ɑ:gəʊ/ ▶1818 *pr n* **1** (also **~ de Compostela**) (in Spain) Saint-Jacques-de-Compostelle; **2** (in Chile) Santiago.

Saone /səʊn/ ▶1644 *pr n* Saône *f*.

Saône-et-Loire ▶1163 *pr n* Saône-et-Loire *f*; **in/to the ~** en Saône-et-Loire.

Sao Tomé and Principe /səʊ ˌtəʊmes ən prɪn'si:p/ ▶1131 *pr n* Sao Tomé-et-Principe *m*.

sap /sæp/ **I** *n* **1** sève *f*; **in spring the ~ rises** lit au printemps la sève monte; fig le printemps est la saison des ébats amoureux; **2**○ US péj abruti○ pej.

II *vtr* (*p prés etc* **-pp-**) (weaken) saper [*strength, courage, confidence*].

saphead○ /'sæphed/ *n* US abruti○ *m*.

sapling /'sæplɪŋ/ *n* jeune arbre *m*.

sapper /'sæpə(r)/ ▶1612 *n* GB Mil soldat *m* du génie.

Sapphic /'sæfɪk/ *adj* (all contexts) saphique.

sapphire /'sæfaɪə(r)/ ▶1104 **I** *n* **1** (stone) saphir *m*; **2** (colour) bleu *m* saphir.

II *adj* (colour) bleu saphir *inv*.

sappy /'sæpɪ/ *adj* **1**○ (silly) bêbête○; **2** [*plant, twig etc*] plein de sève.

sarabande /'særəbænd/ *n* (dance, music) sarabande *f*.

Saracen /'særəsn/ *n* Sarrasin/-e *m/f*.

Saragossa /ˌsærə'gɒsə/ ▶1818 *pr n* Saragosse.

saranwrap® /sə'rænræp/ *n* US ≈ scellofrais® *m*.

sarcasm /'sɑ:kæzəm/ *n* sarcasme *m*.

sarcastic /sɑ:'kæstɪk/ *adj* sarcastique.

sarcastically /sɑ:'kæstɪklɪ/ *adv* [*say, comment*] d'un ton sarcastique.

sarcoma /sɑ:'kəʊmə/ *n* (*pl* **-mata** ou **-mas**) sarcome *m*.

sarcomatosis /sɑ:ˌkəʊmə'təʊsɪs/ ▶1354 *n* sarcomatose *f*.

sarcophagus /sɑ:'kɒfəgəs/ *n* (*pl* **-gi** ou **-guses**) sarcophage *m*.

sardine /sɑːˈdiːn/ **I** *n* Zool, Culin sardine *f*; **to be packed** ou **squashed (in) like ~s** être serrés comme des sardines (en boîte).
II sardines *npl* jeu *m* de cache-cache (*dans lequel les joueurs qui découvrent la personne cachée se cachent avec elle*).
Sardinia /sɑːˈdɪnɪə/ ▶ 1381 *pr n* Sardaigne *f*.
Sardinian /sɑːˈdɪnɪən/ ▶ 1486, 1402 **I** *n* **1** (person) Sarde *mf*; **2** (language) sarde *m*.
II *adj* sarde.
sardonic /sɑːˈdɒnɪk/ *adj* [*laugh, look*] sardonique; [*person, remark*] acerbe.
sardonically /sɑːˈdɒnɪklɪ/ *adv* [*laugh*] sardoniquement; [*comment, say*] de façon acerbe.
sargasso /sɑːˈgæsəʊ/ *n* (also **~ weed**) sargasse *f*.
Sargasso Sea ▶ 1511 *pr n* mer *f* des Sargasses.
sarge○ /sɑːdʒ/ *n*: *abrév* = **sergeant**.
sari /ˈsɑːrɪ/ *n* sari *m*.
Sark /sɑːk/ ▶ 1381 *pr n* Sercq *m*.
sarky○ /ˈsɑːkɪ/ *adj* GB *abrév* = **sarcastic**.
sarnie○ /ˈsɑːnɪ/ *n* GB sandwich *m*.
sarong /səˈrɒŋ/ *n* sarong *m*.
sarsaparilla /ˌsɑːspəˈrɪlə/ *n* US **1** (drink) *boisson gazeuse à la salsepareille*; **2** (plant) salsepareille *f*.
Sarthe ▶ 1163 *pr n* Sarthe *f*; **in/to the ~** dans la Sarthe.
sartorial /sɑːˈtɔːrɪəl/ *adj* sout [*elegance, eccentricity*] vestimentaire.
sartorius /sɑːˈtɔːrɪəs/ *n* (*pl* **-ii**) muscle *m* couturier.
SAS *n* GB (*abrév* = **Special Air Service**) commandos *mpl* britanniques aéroportés.
sash /sæʃ/ *n* **1** (round waist) large ceinture *f* (*en tissu*); **2** (ceremonial) écharpe *f* (*servant d'insigne*); **3** (window frame) châssis *m* d'une fenêtre à guillotine.
sashay○ /ˈsæʃeɪ/ *vi* (walk casually) marcher d'un air dégagé; (walk seductively) marcher de manière aguichante.
sash: **~ cord** *n* corde *f* (*d'une fenêtre à guillotine*); **~lock** *n* serrure *f* à pêne demi-tour; **~ window** *n* fenêtre *f* à guillotine.
Saskatchewan /sæsˈkætʃɪwən/ ▶ 1644 *pr n* Saskatchewan *m*.
sass○ /sæs/ US **I** *n* insolence *f*.
II *vtr* **to ~ sb** être insolent avec qn.
sassafras /ˈsæsəfræs/ **I** *n* sassafras *m*.
II *modif* [*oil, tea*] de sassafras.
Sassenach /ˈsæsənæk/ *n* péj Anglais/-e *m/f* (*expression écossaise*).
sassy○ /ˈsæsɪ/ *adj* US **1** (cheeky) culotté○; **2** (smart) chic.
sat /sæt/ *prét, pp* ▶ **sit**.
Sat ▶ 1883 *abrév écrite* = **Saturday**.
SAT /sæt/ *n* **1** GB Sch *abrév* = **Standard Assessment Task**; **2** US Sch *abrév* ▶ **Scholastic Aptitude Test**.
Satan /ˈseɪtn/ *pr n* Satan.
satanic /səˈtænɪk/ *adj* [*rites*] satanique; [*pride, smile*] démoniaque.
satanic abuse *n*: *violences sexuelles impliquant des enfants au cours de rites sataniques*.
satanically /səˈtænɪklɪ/ *adv* [*laugh, smile*] démoniaquement; **he is ~ charming** il a un charme démoniaque.
satanism, **Satanism** /ˈseɪtənɪzəm/ *n* satanisme *m*.
satanist, **Satanist** /ˈseɪtənɪst/ **I** *n*: *personne qui voue un culte à Satan*.
II *adj* [*ritual, practice*] satanique.
satchel /ˈsætʃəl/ *n* cartable *m* (*à bandoulière*).
Satcom /ˈsætkɒm/ *n* (*abrév* = **Satellite Communications System**) *système de télécommunications par satellite*.
sate /seɪt/ *vtr* sout satisfaire [*appetite*].
sated /ˈseɪtɪd/ *adj* sout (*jamais épith*) [*desire*] assouvi; [*person*] rassasié; [*appetite*] satisfait; **to be ~ with** être repu de.
sateen /sæˈtiːn/ *n* satinette *f*.
satellite /ˈsætəlaɪt/ **I** *n* (all contexts) satellite *m*; **weather/communications ~** satellite météorologique/de télécommunications.
II *modif* [*broadcasting, link, transmission*] par satellite; [*town, country, computer, terminal, photograph*] satellite.
satellite: **~ dish** *n* antenne *f* parabolique; **~ television**, **~ TV** *n* télévision *f* par satellite.
satiate /ˈseɪʃɪeɪt/ **I** *vtr* rassasier [*person*]; satisfaire [*appetite*]; assouvir [*desire*].
II satiated *pp adj* [*person*] rassasié, repu; [*appetite*] satisfait; [*desire*] assouvi; fig [*audience*] repu (**with** de).
satiation /ˌseɪʃɪˈeɪʃn/ *n* assouvissement *m*.
satiety /səˈtaɪətɪ/ *n* satiété *f*.
satin /ˈsætɪn, US ˈsætn/ **I** *n* satin *m*.
II *modif* [*garment, shoe*] de satin; **~ stitch** point *m* de plumetis; **to have a ~ finish** (of paper, paint) être satiné.
satinette /ˌsætɪˈnet/ *n* satinette *f*.
satinwood /ˈsætɪnwʊd, US ˈsætn-/ *n* **1** (tree) chloroxylon *m*; **2** (wood) bois *m* satiné de l'Inde.
satiny /ˈsætɪnɪ, US ˈsætnɪ/ *adj* satiné.
satire /ˈsætaɪə(r)/ *n* satire *f* (**on** sur).
satiric(al) /səˈtɪrɪkl/ *adj* satirique.
satirically /səˈtɪrɪklɪ/ *adv* d'une manière satirique.
satirist /ˈsætərɪst/ *n* satiriste *mf*.
satirize /ˈsætəraɪz/ *vtr* faire la satire de; **~d by** qui a été l'objet de la satire de.
satisfaction /ˌsætɪsˈfækʃn/ *n* ₵ **1** (pleasure) satisfaction *f*; **to express ~ with sth** se déclarer satisfait de qch; **to get** ou **derive ~ from sth** retirer des satisfactions de qch; **to get** ou **derive ~ from doing sth** éprouver du plaisir à faire qch; **the decision was of great ~ to residents** les résidents ont été très satisfaits de la décision; **with great/immense ~** avec une grande/immense satisfaction; **to be a source of ~** être un sujet de satisfaction (**to** pour); **if it gives you any ~, she has been fired** si ça peut te faire plaisir, elle a été licenciée; **he felt he had done the work to his own ~** il était satisfait de son travail; **the conclusions were to everybody's ~** les conclusions ont satisfait tout le monde; **'~ guaranteed'** Comm 'satisfaction garantie'; **2** (fulfilment) satisfaction *f* (**of sth** de qch; **of doing** de faire); **the ~ of basic needs/of human desires** la satisfaction des besoins essentiels/des désirs humains; **an acceptable level of ~** une satisfaction moyenne; **a high level of ~** une grande satisfaction; **3** (compensation) dédommagement *m*; (apology) réparation *f*; **to obtain ~ (for sth)** obtenir satisfaction (pour qch); **he received no ~ from the company** (financial, apology) la compagnie ne lui a pas donné satisfaction.
satisfactorily /ˌsætɪsˈfæktərəlɪ/ *adv* de manière satisfaisante.
satisfactory /ˌsætɪsˈfæktərɪ/ *adj* [*explanation, progress, arrangement*] satisfaisant; **to be ~ to sb** convenir à qn; **the solution is less than ~** la solution est loin d'être satisfaisante; **his work is far from ~** son travail laisse fort à désirer; **her condition was said to be ~** Med son état a été déclaré satisfaisant; **'if this product does not reach you in a ~ condition...'** Comm 'en cas de réclamation...'; **to bring a matter to a ~ conclusion** mener une affaire à bien.
satisfied /ˈsætɪsfaɪd/ *adj* **1** (pleased) satisfait (**with, about** de); **a ~ customer** un client satisfait; **if you are not completely ~** Comm si vous n'êtes pas entièrement satisfait; **not ~ with winning the match, they went on to win the cup** non contents de gagner le match, ils ont aussi remporté la coupe; **now are you ~?** (said angrily) tu es content maintenant?; **2** (convinced) convaincu (**by** par); **to be ~ that** être convaincu que.
satisfy /ˈsætɪsfaɪ/ **I** *vtr* **1** (fulfil) satisfaire [*need, wants, desires, curiosity*]; satisfaire [*person, customer*]; assouvir [*hunger, desire*]; **2** (persuade, convince) convaincre [*critics, police, public opinion*] (**that** que); **I am not satisfied by your explanation** je ne trouve pas votre explication bien convaincante; **3** (meet) satisfaire à [*criteria, demand, regulations, requirements*]; être conforme à [*definition*]; satisfaire à [*conditions*].
II *vi* **to fail to ~** [*book, film etc*] être peu satisfaisant.
III *v refl* **to ~ oneself** s'assurer (**that** que).
satisfying /ˈsætɪsfaɪɪŋ/ *adj* **1** (filling) [*meal*] substantiel/-ielle; [*diet, vegetable, fruit*] nourrissant; **2** (rewarding) [*job*] qui apporte de la satisfaction; [*life*] bien rempli; [*relationship*] heureux/-euse; [*afternoon, evening*] très agréable; **3** (pleasing) [*result, sales, progress, solution*] satisfaisant; **it is ~ to see/know that...** il est satisfaisant de voir/savoir que...
satisfyingly /ˈsætɪsfaɪɪŋlɪ/ *adv* agréablement.
satsuma /ˈsætsuːmə/ *n* satsuma *f*.
saturate /ˈsætʃəreɪt/ *vtr* **1** (soak) gen tremper [*clothes, ground*] (**with** de); fig saturer [*market*] (**with** de); **2** Chem saturer; **3** (bomb) bombarder intensivement (**with** avec).
saturated /ˈsætʃəreɪtɪd/ *adj* **1** gen [*person, clothes*] trempé; [*soil, ground*] détrempé; fig [*market*] saturé (**with** de); **2** Chem saturé; **3** [*fat*] saturé; **4** Art [*colour*] saturé.
saturation /ˌsætʃəˈreɪʃn/ **I** *n* (all contexts) saturation *f*.
II *modif* **1** Advertg [*campaign, coverage, marketing*] de saturation; **2** Mil **~ bombing** bombardement *m* intensif.
saturation point *n* (all contexts) point *m* de saturation; **to reach ~** fig arriver à saturation.
Saturday /ˈsætədeɪ, -dɪ/ ▶ 1883 *n* samedi *m*; **he has a ~ job** GB il a un petit boulot○ le samedi.
Saturday night special○ *n* US revolver *m*.
Saturn /ˈsætən/ *pr n* **1** Mythol Saturne *m*; **2** Astron Saturne *f*.
Saturnalia /ˌsætəˈneɪlɪə/ *n* saturnales *fpl*.
saturnine /ˈsætənaɪn/ *adj* sombre.
satyr /ˈsætə(r)/ *n* lit, fig satyre *m*.
sauce /sɔːs/ **I** *n* **1** Culin sauce *f*; **orange/pepper ~** sauce à l'orange/au poivre; **tomato ~** sauce tomate; US (stewed fruit) compote *f* de fruits; **2**○† (impudence) toupet○ *m*; **3**○ US (alcohol) **the ~** la boisson; **to be on the ~** picoler◑ dur.
II○ *vtr* être insolent avec.
IDIOMS what's ~ for the goose is ~ for the gander ce qui vaut pour l'un vaut pour l'autre.
sauce: **~boat** *n* saucière *f*; **~box**○† *n* impertinent/-e *m/f*.
saucepan /ˈsɔːspən/ *n* casserole *f*.
saucer /ˈsɔːsə(r)/ *n* soucoupe *f*; **with eyes like** ou **as big as ~s** aux yeux ronds comme des soucoupes.
saucily /ˈsɔːsɪlɪ/ *adv* [*speak, behave*] avec impertinence; [*dress*] coquettement.
sauciness /ˈsɔːsɪnɪs/ *n* (cheek) impertinence *f*; (of dress) coquetterie *f*.
saucy† /ˈsɔːsɪ/ *adj* **1** [*person*] (impudent) impertinent; (sexually suggestive) égrillard; **2** [*hat, dress etc*] aguichant.
Saudi /ˈsaʊdɪ/ ▶ 1486 **I** *n* Saoudien/-ienne *m/f*.
II *adj* saoudien/-ienne.
Saudi Arabia /ˌsaʊdɪ əˈreɪbɪə/ ▶ 1131 *pr n* Arabie *f* saoudite.
Saudi Arabian /ˌsaʊdɪ əˈreɪbɪən/ ▶ 1486 *n* = **Saudi**.
sauerkraut /ˈsaʊəkraʊt/ *n* choucroute *f*.
Saul /sɔːl/ *pr n* Bible Saül.

sauna /'sɔːnə, 'saʊnə/ *n* sauna *m*; **it's like a ~ in here!** c'est une étuve ici!

saunter /'sɔːntə(r)/ **I** *n* **1** (stroll) petite balade○ *f*; **to go for a ~** faire une petite balade○; **2** (leisurely pace) allure *f* nonchalante.
II *vi* (also **~ along**) marcher d'un pas nonchalant; **to ~ off** s'éloigner d'un pas nonchalant.

saurian /'sɔːrɪən/ **I** *n* saurien *m*.
II *adj* saurien/-ienne.

sausage /'sɒsɪdʒ, US 'sɔːs-/ *n* (for cooking) saucisse *f*; (ready to eat) saucisson *m*.
IDIOMS **not a ~**○ GB des clopinettes○, rien du tout.

sausage: **~ dog**○ *n* teckel *m*; **~ meat** *n* chair *f* à saucisse; **~ roll** *n* feuilleté *m* à la chair à saucisse.

sauté /'səʊteɪ, US səʊ'teɪ/ Culin **I** *adj* (also **sauté(e)d**) sauté.
II *vtr* (*p prés* **-éing** ou **-éeing**; *prét, pp* **-éd** ou **-éed**) faire sauter.

savage /'sævɪdʒ/ **I** *n* sauvage *mf* also pej.
II *adj* **1** lit [*kick, blow, beating*] violent; [*attacker, rapist*] cruel/-elle; [*attack*] sauvage; [*gunfire, riots*] d'une extrême violence; **2** fig [*temper*] violent; [*mood, humour, satire*] féroce; [*criticism, review*] virulent; [*prison sentence*] lourd; **3** Econ journ [*price increases*] violent; **~ cuts** coupes *fpl* claires (**in** dans).
III *vtr* **1** (physically) [*dog*] attaquer sauvagement [*person, animal*]; [*lion*] déchirer [*person, animal*]; **2** fig descendre [qch/qn] en flammes [*book, film, opponents, critics*].

savagely /'sævɪdʒlɪ/ *adv* **1** lit [*beat, attack*] sauvagement; **2** fig [*criticize, satirize*] férocement; [*hostile, critical*] férocement.

savagery /'sævɪdʒrɪ/ *n* (of war, primitive people) barbarie *f*; (of attack) (physical) sauvagerie *f*; (verbal) férocité *f*; **an act of ~ of the worst kind** un acte d'une épouvantable sauvagerie.

savanna(h) /sə'vænə/ *n* savane *f*.

savant /'sævənt, US sæ'vɑːnt/ *n* sout érudit/-e *m/f*.

save /seɪv/ **I** *n* **1** Sport arrêt *m* de but; **2** Comput sauvegarde *f*.
II *vtr* **1** (rescue) sauver [*person, environment, job, match, film, marriage, sanity*] (**from** de); **to ~ sb's sight/leg** sauver la vue/la jambe à qn; **to ~ sb/sth from doing** empêcher qn/qch de faire; **to ~ sb from himself** protéger qn contre lui-même; **to ~ lives** sauver des vies humaines; **to ~ sb's life** lit, fig sauver la vie à qn; **he can't speak German to ~ his life**○! il est absolument incapable de parler allemand!; **to ~ the day** ou **the situation** sauver la situation (**by doing** en faisant); **to ~ face** sauver la face; **2** (put by, keep) mettre [qch] de côté [*money, food*] (**to do** pour faire); garder [*goods, documents*] (**for** pour); **to have money ~d** avoir de l'argent de côté; **to ~ sth for sb, to ~ sb sth** garder [qch] pour qn [*place, food*]; **to ~ sth for future generations** préserver qch pour les générations à venir; **to ~ a dance/an evening for sb** réserver une danse/une soirée à qn; **to ~ sth until the end** ou **till last** garder qch pour la fin; **3** (economize on) économiser [*money, fuel, energy, water*] (**by doing** en faisant); gagner [*time, space*] (**by doing** en faisant); **to ~ one's energy/voice** ménager ses forces/sa voix; **you'll ~ money/£20** vous ferez des économies/une économie de 20 livres; **to ~ sb sth** faire économiser qch à qn [*money*]; éviter qch à qn [*trouble, expense, journey*]; faire gagner qch à qn [*time*]; **it will ~ us time/money** cela nous fera gagner du temps/de l'argent; **to ~ sb/sth (from) doing** éviter à qn/qch de faire; **to ~ doing** éviter de faire; **4** Sport arrêter [*goal, penalty*]; **5** Relig sauver [*soul, mankind*] (**from** de); **6** Comput sauvegarder, enregistrer [*file, data*] (**on, to** sur); **7** (collect) collectionner [*stamps, cards*].
III *vi* **1** (put by funds) = **save up**; **2** (economize) économiser, faire des économies; **to ~ on** faire des économies de [*energy, paper, heating*].
IV *v refl* **to ~ oneself 1** (rescue oneself) lit, fig s'en tirer (**by doing** en faisant); **to ~ oneself from doing** éviter de faire; **to ~ oneself from drowning** éviter la noyade; **2** (keep energy, virginity) se réserver (**for** pour); **3** (avoid waste) **to ~ oneself money** économiser; **to ~ oneself time** gagner du temps; **to ~ oneself trouble/a journey** s'éviter des tracas/un déplacement.
V‡ *prep* sauf; **~ for** à l'exception de, hormis liter; **~ that he was a friend** s'il n'avait été un ami.
IDIOMS **~ it**○! ça va, à d'autres○!
■ **save up**: ¶ **~ up** faire des économies, mettre de l'argent de côté (**to do** pour faire); **to ~ up for** ou **towards** mettre de l'argent de côté pour s'acheter [*car, house*]; mettre de l'argent de côté pour s'offrir [*holiday, trip*]; ¶ **~ up [sth], ~ [sth] up** mettre [qch] de côté [*money*] (**to do** pour faire); collectionner [*stamps, newspapers*].

save-as-you-earn, SAYE /ˌseɪvəsjuː'ɜːn/ *n* GB *épargne par prélèvement automatique sur salaire*.

saveloy /'sævəlɔɪ/ *n* GB cervelas *m*.

saver /'seɪvə(r)/ *n* épargnant/-e *m/f*.

Savile Row /ˌsævɪl'rəʊ/ *pr n*: *rue de Londres connue pour ses tailleurs, chers et de qualité*.

saving /'seɪvɪŋ/ **I** *n* **1** (reduction) économie *f* (**in** de; **on** sur); **a 25% ~** une économie de 25%; **to make ~s** faire des économies; **2** ¢ Econ, Fin (activity) épargne *f*; **to learn about ~** apprendre à épargner; **3** (conservation) économie *f*; **energy ~** économies *fpl* d'énergie.
II savings *npl* économies *fpl*; **to live off one's ~s** vivre de ses économies; **to lose one's life ~s** perdre les économies de toute une vie.
III -saving (*dans composés*) **energy-/fuel-~** qui réduit la consommation d'énergie/de carburant; ▶ **face-saving, labour-saving etc.**
IV‡ *prep* sout sauf; **~ your presence** sauf votre respect†.

saving clause *n* clause *f* restrictive.

saving grace *n* bon côté *m*; **it's his ~** c'est ce qui le sauve.

savings account *n* **1** GB compte *m* d'épargne; **2** US compte *m* rémunéré.

saving: **~s and loan (association), S&L** *n* US société *f* d'investissement et de crédit immobilier; **~s bank** *n* caisse *f* d'épargne; **~s bond** *n* bon *m* de caisse; **~s book** *n* livret *m* de caisse d'épargne; **~s certificate** *n* bon *m* de caisse; **~s plan** *n* plan *m* d'épargne; **~s stamp** *n* GB timbre-épargne *m*.

saviour GB, **savior** US /'seɪvɪə(r)/ *n* sauveur *m* also Relig.

Savoie ▶ **1163** *pr n* Savoie *f*; **in/to ~** en Savoie.

savoir-faire /ˌsævwɑː'feə(r)/ *n* **1** (social) savoir-vivre *m inv*; **2** (practical) savoir-faire *m inv*.

savor /'seɪvə(r)/ *n* US = **savour**.

savory /'seɪvərɪ/ **I** *n* **1** (herb) sarriette *f*; **2** US = **savoury**.
II *adj* US = **savoury**.

savour GB, **savor** US /'seɪvə(r)/ **I** *n* **1** lit saveur *f*; **to have a (slight) ~ of** avoir un (léger) goût de; **2** fig (enjoyable quality) goût *m*; **life has lost its ~ for her** elle a perdu goût à la vie; **3** (trace, hint) pointe *f*; **a ~ of cynicism** une pointe de cynisme.
II *vtr* lit, fig savourer.
III *vi* **to ~ of** sentir; **to ~ of hypocrisy** sentir l'hypocrisie.

savourless /'seɪvəlɪs/ GB *adj* insipide.

savoury GB, **savory** US /'seɪvərɪ/ **I** *n* (pie, flan, stew) plat *m* salé; (after dessert) GB canapé *m* (*servi après le dessert*).
II *adj* **1** Culin (not sweet) salé; (appetizing) appétissant; (tasty) savoureux/-euse; **~ biscuits** biscuits *mpl* apéritif; **2** fig **not a very ~ individual/area/club** un individu/quartier/club peu recommandable; **not a very ~ reputation** une réputation équivoque; **the less ~ aspects of the matter** le côté plutôt louche de l'affaire.

Savoy /sə'vɔɪ/ ▶ **1273** **I** *pr n* Savoie *f*.
II *modif* [*cuisine, wines*] de Savoie; **the ~ Alps** les Alpes *fpl* savoyardes.

Savoyard /sə'vɔɪɑːd, ˌsævɔɪ'ɑːd/ **I** *n* **1** (person) Savoyard/-e *m/f*; **2** (dialect) savoyard *m*.
II *adj* savoyard.

savoy cabbage *n* chou *m* de Milan.

savvy○ /'sævɪ/ **I** *n* **1** (shrewdness) jugeote○ *f*; **2** (know-how) savoir-faire *m inv*.
II *adj* US calé.
III *vi* (know) savoir; (understand) piger◑.

saw /sɔː/ **I** *pret* ▶ **see**.
II *n* **1** (tool) scie *f*; **electric/power ~** scie électrique/mécanique; **2**† (saying) adage *m*; **an old ~** un vieil adage.
III *vtr* (*prét* **sawed**; *pp* **sawn** GB, **sawed** US) scier; **to ~ through/down/off** scier; **to ~ sth in half** scier qch en deux; **he was ~ing away at the bread** il essayait de couper le pain; **to ~ the air** faire de grands gestes.
■ **saw up**: **~ up [sth], ~ [sth] up** débiter qch à la scie.

saw: **~bones**○† *n* hum chirurgien *m*; **~dust** *n* sciure *f* (de bois).

sawed /sɔːd/ *pp* US ▶ **saw** III.

saw-edged /ˌsɔː'edʒd/ *adj* à lame dentée.

sawed-off /'sɔːdɒf/ *adj* US ▶ **sawn-off**.

saw: **~fish** *n* poisson-scie *m*; **~horse** *n* chevalet *m* (de scieur de bois); **~mill** *n* scierie *f*.

sawn /sɔːn/ *pp* GB ▶ **saw** III.

sawn-off /'sɔːnɒf/ *adj* GB [*gun, shotgun*] à canon scié; **a ~ barrel** un canon scié.

sax○ /sæks/ ▶ **1481** **I** *n* (*pl* **~es**) (*abrév* = **saxophone**) saxo○ *m*.
II *modif* **~ player** saxo○ *m*.

saxhorn /'sækshɔːn/ ▶ **1481** *n* saxhorn *m*.

saxifrage /'sæksɪfreɪdʒ/ *n* saxifrage *f*.

Saxon /'sæksn/ **I** *pr n* **1** (person) Saxon/-onne *m/f*; **2** (language) saxon *m*.
II *adj* saxon/-onne.

Saxony /'sæksənɪ/ *pr n* Saxe *f*.

saxophone /'sæksəfəʊn/ ▶ **1481** *n* saxophone *m*.

saxophonist /sæk'sɒfənɪst/ ▶ **1692**, **1481** *n* saxophoniste *mf*.

say /seɪ/ **I** *n* **to have one's ~** dire ce qu'on a à dire (**on** sur); **to have a ~/no ~ in sth** avoir/ne pas avoir son mot à dire sur qch; **to have no ~ in the matter** ne pas avoir voix au chapitre; **to have a ~ in appointing sb/allocating sth** avoir son mot à dire sur la nomination de qn/l'affectation de qch; **they want more** ou **a bigger ~** ils veulent avoir davantage leur mot à dire; **to have the most** ou **biggest ~** avoir le plus de poids.
II *vtr* (*prét, pp* **said**) **1** [*person*] dire [*words, line, prayer, hello, goodbye, yes, no*] (**to** à); **'hello,' he said** 'bonjour,' dit-il; **~ after me...** répète après moi...; **to ~ one's piece** dire ce qu'on a à dire; **to ~ (that)** dire que; **she ~s he's ill** elle dit qu'il est malade; **he said it was ready** il a dit que c'était prêt; **she said there would be an accident** elle a dit qu'il y aurait un accident; **I just wanted to ~ I'm sorry** je voulais juste te dire que j'étais désolé; **she said we were to wait** ou **we should wait** elle a dit que nous devions attendre; **he said to wait here** il a dit d'attendre ici; **it's my way of ~ing thank you** c'est ma façon de dire merci; **'residents ~ no to nuclear waste'** 'les résidents disent non au stockage des déchets nucléaires'; **I didn't ~ so, but I thought** je ne l'ai pas dit, mais j'ai pensé que; **if he was angry, he didn't ~ so** s'il

était en colère, il ne l'a pas dit; **how nice of you to ~ so** merci, c'est gentil; **didn't I ~ so?** je l'avais bien dit!; **if** ou **though I do ~ so myself!** je ne devrais pas le dire, mais...!; **so they ~** (agreeing) il paraît; **or so they ~** (doubtful) du moins c'est ce qu'on dit; **or so he ~s** du moins c'est ce qu'il prétend; **so to ~** pour ainsi dire; **as you ~**... comme tu le dis...; **as they ~** comme on dit; **what will people ~** ou **they ~** qu'est-ce que les gens diront; **I don't care what anyone ~s** je me moque du qu'en-dira-t-on; **(you can) ~ what you like, I think that**... tu peux dire ce que tu veux, moi je crois que...; **people** ou **they ~ she's very rich, she is said to be very rich** on dit qu'elle est très riche; **some (people) ~ the house is haunted, the house is said to be haunted** certains disent que la maison est hantée; **to have something/to have nothing to ~** avoir quelque chose/ne rien avoir à dire; **to ~ sth about sth/sb** dire qch au sujet de qch/qn; **to ~ sth on a subject** parler d'un sujet; **something was said about that at the meeting** on en a parlé à la réunion; **nothing much was said about that** on n'a pas dit grand-chose à ce sujet; **she'll have something to ~ about that!** elle aura certainement quelque chose à dire là-dessus!; **to ~ sth to oneself** se dire qch; **she said to herself (that) it couldn't be true** elle s'est dit que cela ne pouvait pas être vrai; **what do you ~ to that?** qu'est-ce que tu en dis? **what do you ~ to the argument that...?** que répondez-vous à l'argument selon lequel...?; **what would you ~ to people who think that...?** que répondriez-vous à ceux qui pensent que...?; **what would you ~ to a little walk?** qu'est-ce que tu dirais d'une petite promenade?; **I wouldn't ~ no to another slice** je ne dirais pas non à une autre tranche; **what (do you) ~ we eat now**○? et si on mangeait maintenant?; **to ~ whether/who** dire si/qui; **that's for the committee to ~** c'est au comité de décider; **it's not for me to ~** ce n'est pas à moi de le dire; **you said it**○! tu l'as dit!; **you can ~ that again**○! ça, tu peux le dire○!; **I should ~ it is/they were!** et comment○!; **well said!** bien dit!; **and so ~ all of us!** nous sommes tous d'accord là-dessus!; **~ no more**○ ça va, j'ai compris!○; **let's ~ no more about it** n'en parlons plus; **enough said**○ ça va, j'ai compris○; **there's no more to be said** il n'y a rien à ajouter; **it goes without ~ing that** il va sans dire que; **don't ~ I didn't warn you!** tu ne pourras pas dire que je ne t'avais pas prévenu!; **don't ~ it's raining again!** ne me dis pas qu'il pleut de nouveau!; **you might just as well ~ education is useless** autant dire que l'instruction est inutile; **that is to ~** c'est-à-dire; **that's not to ~ that** cela ne veut pas dire que; **he was displeased, not to ~ furious** il était mécontent, pour ne pas dire furieux; **I'll ~ this for her**... je dois dire à sa décharge que...; **one thing you have to ~ about Liz is**... s'il y a une chose qu'il faut reconnaître à propos de Liz c'est...; **I must ~ (that)** je dois dire que; **it seems rather expensive, I must ~** cela paraît un peu cher, je dois dire; **well, I must ~!** ça alors!; **to have a lot to ~ for oneself** être bavard; **what have you got to ~ for yourself?** qu'est-ce que tu as comme excuse?; **that isn't ~ing much**○ ça ne veut pas dire grand-chose○; **that's ~ing a lot**○ ce n'est pas peu dire; **2** [*writer, book, letter, report, map*] dire; [*painter, painting, music, gift*] exprimer; [*sign, poster, dial, gauge*] indiquer; [*gesture, signal*] signifier; **as Plato ~s** comme le dit Platon; **she wrote ~ing she couldn't come** elle a écrit pour dire qu'elle ne pouvait pas venir; **it ~s on the radio/in the rules that** la radio/le règlement dit que; **it ~s here that** il est dit ici que; **the clock ~s three** la pendule indique trois heures; **the dial ~s 300** le cadran indique 300; **a notice ~ing where to meet** une affiche qui indique le lieu de réunion; **this music ~s something/doesn't ~ anything to me** cette musique me parle/ne me parle pas; **3** (guess) dire **(that** que); **to ~ how much/when/whether** dire combien/quand/si; **that's impossible to ~** c'est impossible à dire; **how high would you ~ it is?** à ton avis, quelle en est la hauteur?; **I'd ~ it was a bargain** à mon avis c'est une bonne affaire; **I'd ~ she was about 25** je lui donnerais environ 25 ans; **he's about six foot, wouldn't you ~?** il mesure environ un mètre quatre-vingts, tu ne crois pas?; **4** (assume) **to ~ (that)** supposer que (+ *subj*), mettre que (+ *indic or subj*); **let's ~ there are 20** mettons ou supposons qu'il y en ait 20; **~ you have an accident** suppose que tu aies un accident; **~ we win, we'll still have to beat Liverpool** à supposer que nous gagnions, il faudra encore battre Liverpool.

III *vi* (*prét, pp* **said**) **1 stop when I ~** arrête quand je te le dirai; **he wouldn't ~** il n'a pas voulu le dire ; **I'd rather not ~** je préfère ne pas le dire; **you don't ~!** iron sans blague!, pas possible!; **~s you**○! (taunting) que tu dis○!; **~s who**○?, **who ~s**○? (sceptical) ah oui?; (on whose authority?) et sur les ordres de qui?; **2**† GB **I ~!** (listen) écoute, dis donc; (shocked) ma parole!; (to hail sb) hé!

IV *adv* disons, mettons; **you'll need, ~, £50 for petrol** tu auras besoin de, disons ou mettons, 50 livres sterling pour l'essence.

V *excl* US dis-donc!; **~, who are you?** dites-donc, qui êtes-vous?

IDIOMS **it doesn't ~ much for their marriage/her commitment** cela en dit long sur leur mariage/son engagement; **it ~s a lot** ou **something about his education that he succeeded** le fait qu'il a réussi en dit long sur son éducation ; **it ~s a lot for sb/sth** c'est tout à l'honneur de qn/qch; **that ~s it all** c'est tout dire, cela se passe de commentaire; **there's a lot to be said for that method** cette méthode est très intéressante à bien des égards; **there's a lot to be said for keeping quiet** il y a intérêt à se taire; **when all is said and done** tout compte fait, en fin de compte.

SAYE *n* GB *abrév* ▶ **save-as-you-earn**.

saying /ˈseɪɪŋ/ *n* dicton *m*, adage *m*; **which proves the old ~ true** ce qui prouve la justesse du vieux dicton; **as the ~ goes** comme on dit.

say-so○ /ˈseɪsəʊ/ *n* permission *f*.

S-bend *n* gen (in road) courbe *f* en S; (in pipe) coude *m* en S.

s/c *adj* (*abrév écrite* = **self-contained**) indépendant.

SC *n* US Post *abrév écrite* = **South Carolina**.

scab /skæb/ *n* **1** Med croûte *f*; **2** Bot, Vet gale *f*; **3**○ péj (strikebreaker) jaune○ *m* pej, briseur *m* de grève.

scabbard /ˈskæbəd/ *n* (for sword) fourreau *m*; (for dagger) gaine *f*.

scabby /ˈskæbɪ/ *adj* **1** [*skin*] couvert de croûtes *fpl*; **2** [*animal, plant*] attaqué par la gale; **3**○ (nasty) moche○.

scabies /ˈskeɪbiːz/ ▶ **1354** *n* gale *f*.

scabious /ˈskeɪbɪəs, US ˈskæb-/ **I** *n* Bot scabieuse *f*.
II *adj* Med scabieux/-ieuse.

scab labour○ *n* péj *personnel qui remplace des travailleurs en grève*.

scabrous /ˈskeɪbrəs, US ˈskæb-/ *adj* **1** (rough) [*bark, skin*] rugueux/-euse; **2** fig (smutty) scabreux/-euse.

scads○ /skædz/ *npl* US **~ of** des tas *mpl* de; **he's got ~ of money** il est plein aux as.

scaffold /ˈskæfəʊld/ *n* **1** (gallows) échafaud *m*; **2** Constr échafaudage *m*.

scaffolder /ˈskæfəʊldə(r)/ ▶ **1692** *n* monteur *m* d'échafaudages.

scaffolding /ˈskæfəldɪŋ/ *n* (structure) échafaudage *m*; (materials) matériel *m* d'échafaudage; **a piece of ~** un tube d'échafaudage.

scag○ /skæg/ *n* US, argot des drogués héroïne *f*.

scalar /ˈskeɪlə(r)/ *n, adj* scalaire (*m*).

scalawag○ /ˈskæləwæg/ *n* US ▶ **scallywag**.

scald /skɔːld/ **I** *n* brûlure *f* (*causée par un liquide bouillant ou par la vapeur*).
II *vtr* **1** (burn) ébouillanter [*person*]; **to ~ one's arm** s'ébouillanter le bras; **2** (heat) ébouillanter [*fruit, vegetable*]; **3** (sterilize) stériliser [qch] à l'eau bouillante [*jar*]; **4** (nearly boil) faire chauffer [qch] sans bouillir [*milk*].
III *v refl* **to ~ oneself** s'ébouillanter.
IDIOMS **to run off like a ~ed cat** prendre ses jambes à son cou.

scalding /ˈskɔːldɪŋ/ **I** *adj* [*heat, tears, water*] brûlant; [*shame*] cuisant; [*criticism, remark*] virulent.
II *adv* **~ hot** brûlant.

scale /skeɪl/ **I** *n* **1** (extent) (of crisis, disaster, success, violence) étendue *f* (**of** de); (of reform, development, defeat, recession, task) ampleur *f* (**of** de); (of activity, operation) envergure *f* (**of** de); (of support, change) degré *m* (**of** de); **on a large/small ~** à grande/petite échelle; **on an unexpected/a modest ~** d'une ampleur inattendue/modeste; **2** (grading system) échelle *f*; **pay ~, salary ~** échelle des salaires; **social ~** échelle sociale; **~ of values** échelle de valeurs; **at the other end of the ~** à l'autre bout de l'échelle; **on a ~ of 1 to 10** sur une échelle allant de 1 à 10; **3** (for maps, models) échelle *f*; **on a ~ of 2 km to 1 cm** à une échelle de 1 cm pour 2 km; **the model is out of** ou **not to ~** la maquette n'est pas à l'échelle; **4** (on thermometer, gauge etc) graduation *f*; **5** (for weighing) balance *f*; **6** Mus gamme *f*; **to play/sing a ~** faire/chanter une gamme; **the ~ of G** la gamme de sol; **7** Zool (on fish, insect) écaille *f*; **8** (deposit) (in kettle, pipes) (dépôt *m*) calcaire *m*; (on teeth) tartre *m*.
II scales *npl* balance *f*.
III *vtr* **1** (climb) escalader [*wall, peak, tower*]; **2** (take scales off) écailler [*fish*].
IDIOMS **the ~s fell from my eyes** tout d'un coup j'ai compris.
■ **scale back** = **scale down** 2.
■ **scale down**: **~ [sth] down, ~ down [sth] 1** (reduce according to scale) réduire l'échelle de [*drawing, map*]; **2** fig (reduce) ralentir [*production*]; réduire [*expenditure, import, involvement, activity*].
■ **scale up**: **~ [sth] up, ~ up [sth] 1** lit augmenter l'échellle de [*drawing, map*]; **2** fig augmenter [*activity, work*].

scale: **~d-down** *adj* réduit; **~ drawing** *n* dessin *m* à l'échelle; **~ model** *n* maquette *f* à l'échelle; **~ pan** *n* plateau *m* de balance.

scallion /ˈskælɪən/ *n* US **1** (spring onion) ciboule *f*; **2** (shallot) échalote *f*; **3** (leek) poireau *m*.

scallop, scollop /ˈskɒləp/ **I** *n* **1** Zool pecten *m*, peigne *m*; **2** Culin coquille *f* Saint-Jacques; **3** Sewing feston *m*.
II *vtr* **1** Sewing festonner [*border*]; **2** Culin servir [qch] en coquille [*seafood*]; **~ed fish** coquille *f* de poisson; **~ed potatoes** ≈ gratin *m* de pommes de terre.

scallop shell *n* coquille *f* Saint-Jacques.

scallywag /ˈskælɪwæg/ *n* **1**○ (rascal) (child) petite canaille *f*; (adult) vaurien/-ienne *m/f*; **2** US Hist péj *Sudiste en faveur de l'émancipation des noirs*.

scalp /skælp/ **I** *n* **1** Anat cuir *m* chevelu; **2** fig (trophy) scalp *m*; **he's after my ~**○ il veut ma peau○.
II *vtr* **1** (remove scalp) scalper; **2**○ fig US (defeat) écraser; **3**○ US (sell illegally) revendre [qch] au marché noir [*tickets*]; **4** US, Fin spéculer sur [*stocks*].

scalpel /ˈskælpl/ *n* Med scalpel *m*.

scalper○ /ˈskælpə(r)/ *n* US vendeur/-euse *m/f* de billets à la sauvette.

scaly /'skeɪlɪ/ *adj* [*wing, fish*] écailleux/-euse; [*skin, fruit, bark*] squameux/-euse; [*plaster, wall*] écaillé.

scam○ /skæm/ **I** *n* escroquerie *f*.
II *vi* (*p prés etc* **-mm-**) faire des escroqueries.

scamp /skæmp/ **I**○ *n* (child) petite canaille *f*; (dog) vilain/-e *m/f*.
II *vtr* bâcler [*work*].

scamper /'skæmpə(r)/ **I** *n* (of child, dog) galopade *f*; (of mouse) trottinement *m*.
II *vi* (also **~ about, ~ around**) [*child, dog*] gambader; [*mouse*] trottiner; **to ~ across/along** [*child*] galoper à travers/le long de; [*mouse*] trottiner à travers/le long de; **to ~ away** ou **off** détaler.

scampi /'skæmpɪ/ *npl* (fresh) langoustines *fpl*; (breaded) scampi *mpl*.

scan /skæn/ **I** *n* **1** Med (CAT) scanner *m*, scanographie *f* spec; (ultrasound) échographie *f*; **to do a ~** faire un scanner; **I had a ~** on m'a fait un scanner; **2** (radar, TV) balayage *m*; (picture resulting) analyse *f*.
II *vtr* (*p prés etc* **-nn-**) **1** (cast eyes over) lire rapidement [*list, small ads*]; **2** (examine) scruter [*face, horizon*]; **3** [*beam of light, radar etc*] balayer [*area*]; **4** Med faire un scanner de [*organ*]; **5** Literat scander.
III *vi* (*p prés etc* **-nn-**) Literat pouvoir se scander.

scandal /'skændl/ *n* **1** (incident, outcry) scandale *m*; **a financial/political ~** un scandale financier/politique; **a drug/prostitution ~** un scandale lié à la drogue/la prostitution; **the Grunard ~** l'affaire *f* Grunard; **the price of coffee is a ~** le prix du café est scandaleux; **2** (gossip) potins○ *mpl*; (shocking stories) histoires *fpl* scandaleuses.

scandalize /'skændəlaɪz/ *vtr* (shock) scandaliser (**by doing** en faisant).

scandalized /'skændəlaɪzd/ *adj* scandalisé (**by** ou **at sth** par qch).

scandalmonger /'skændlmʌŋgə(r)/ **I** *n* mauvaise langue *f*; **~ing** commérage *m*.
II *vi* faire des commérages.

scandalous /'skændələs/ *adj* (all contexts) scandaleux/-euse.

scandalously /'skændələslɪ/ *adv* [*behave, live*] de façon scandaleuse; [*expensive, underpaid*] scandaleusement.

scandal sheet *n* journal *m* à scandales.

Scandinavia /,skændɪ'neɪvɪə/ *pr n* Scandinavie *f*.

Scandinavian /,skændɪ'neɪvɪən/ **I** *n* Scandinave *mf*.
II *adj* scandinave.

scanner /'skænə(r)/ *n* **1** Med (CAT) scanner *m*; **2** (for bar codes, electronic data etc) lecteur *m* optique; **3** (radar) scanner *m*.

scanning /'skænɪŋ/ **I** *n* **1** Med scanner *m*, scanographie *f* spec; **2** (radar) balayage *m*.
II *modif* [*equipment, device, system*] Med de scanographie; [*radar*] de balayage.

scansion /'skænʃn/ *n* scansion *f*.

scant /skænt/ *adj* [*concern, coverage*] maigre; **a ~ five metres** à peine cinq mètres; **he has been given ~ credit for his work** on n'a pas suffisamment reconnu son travail; **to pay ~ attention to sth** ne faire guère attention à qch; **to show ~ regard for sth** n'être guère préoccupé de qch.

scantily /'skæntɪlɪ/ *adv* insuffisamment; **~ clad, ~ dressed** très légèrement vêtu; **~ cut** très échancré.

scantiness /'skæntɪnɪs/ *n* **1** gen insuffisance *f*; **2** (of clothing) minimalisme *m*.

scanty /'skæntɪ/ *adj* [*meal, report, supply*] maigre; [*information*] sommaire; [*knowledge*] rudimentaire; [*swimsuit*] minuscule.

scapegoat /'skeɪpgəʊt/ *n* bouc *m* émissaire (**for** de); **to make a ~ of sb** faire de qn un bouc émissaire.

scapegrace† /'skeɪpgreɪs/ *n* mauvais sujet *m*.

scapula /'skæpjʊlə/ *n* (*pl* **-ae** ou **-as**) omoplate *f*.

scapular /'skæpjʊlə(r)/ **I** *n* Relig scapulaire *m*.
II *adj* Anat scapulaire.

scar /skɑ:(r)/ **I** *n* **1** lit, fig cicatrice *f*; (from knife on face) balafre *f*; **acne ~s** traces *fpl* d'acné; **her years in prison left a permanent ~** ses années de prison l'ont marquée à jamais; **the country still bears the ~s of its violent past** le pays porte toujours la cicatrice de son passé violent; **2** (crag) rocher *m* escarpé.
II *vtr* (*p prés etc* **-rr-**) (physically, psychologically) marquer; (with knife on face) balafrer; fig défigurer [*landscape*]; **to ~ sb for life** lit laisser à qn une cicatrice permanente; fig marquer qn pour la vie; **~red by acne** ravagé par l'acné; **society ~red by crime** société mutilée par le crime.
III *vi* (*p prés etc* **-rr-**) se cicatriser.

scarab /'skærəb/ *n* (all contexts) scarabée *m*.

scarce /skeəs/ **I** *adj* **1** (rare) [*animal, antique, food, plant, water*] rare; **2** (insufficient) [*funds, information, resources*] limité; **to become ~** se faire rare.
II‡ *adv* (hardly) à peine.
IDIOMS **to make oneself ~**○ s'éclipser○.

scarcely /'skeəslɪ/ *adv* **1** (only just) [*credible, noticeable*] à peine; [*know, remember*] à peine; **it ~ matters** il n'importe guère; **the bus was ~ moving** le bus roulait à peine; **~ a week passes without someone telephoning me** presque chaque semaine quelqu'un me téléphone; **to speak ~ a word of French** parler à peine français; **there were ~ 50 people in the room** il y avait à peine 50 personnes dans la salle; **~ anybody believes it** presque personne ne le croit; **there is ~ anything left to be done** il ne reste pratiquement plus rien à faire; **we have ~ any money** nous n'avons pratiquement pas d'argent; **~ ever** presque jamais; **2** (not really) iron difficilement; **I can ~ accuse him** je peux difficilement l'accuser; **3** (not sooner) à peine; **~ had she finished when the door opened** à peine avait-elle fini que la porte s'est ouverte.

scarceness /'skeəsnɪs/ *n* rareté *f*.

scarcity /'skeəsətɪ/ *n* **1** (dearth) pénurie *f* (**of** de); **2** (rarity) rareté *f* (**of** de); **~ value** valeur *f* de rareté.

scare /skeə(r)/ **I** *n* **1** (fright) peur *f*; **to give sb a ~** faire peur à qn; **to get a ~** avoir peur; **2** (alert) alerte *f*; **security ~** alerte; **3** (rumour) bruits *mpl* alarmistes; **food ~** alerte *f* à l'intoxication alimentaire; **bomb/rabies ~** alerte *f* à la bombe/rage.
II *vtr* faire peur à, effrayer [*animal, person*]; **to ~ sb into doing sth** forcer qn à faire qch par intimidation; **to ~ sb out of doing** empêcher qn de faire par intimidation; **to ~ sb stiff**○ ou **stupid**○ paralyser qn de peur.
III *vi* **to ~ easily** s'effrayer facilement.
■ **scare away, scare off: ~ away [sth/sb], ~ [sth/sb] away 1** (put off) dissuader [*burglars, investors, customers*]; **2** (drive away) faire fuir [*animal, attacker*].
■ **scare up**○ US: **~ up [sth], ~ [sth] up** dégoter○ [*food, money, people*].

scarecrow /'skeəkrəʊ/ *n* épouvantail *m*; **to look like a ~** avoir l'air d'un épouvantail.

scared /skeəd/ *adj* [*animal, person*] effrayé; [*look*] apeuré; **to be** ou **feel ~** avoir peur; **to be ~ of** avoir peur de; **to be ~ of doing** avoir peur de faire; **to be ~ about sth** craindre qch; **to be ~ that** avoir peur que (+ *subj*); **to be ~ to do** avoir peur de faire; **to be ~ stiff**○ ou **stupid of/of doing** avoir une peur bleue de/de faire○; **to be running ~** avoir peur; **to be running ~ of sb** éviter qn.

scaredy cat○ /'skeədɪkæt/ *n* lang enfantin poule *f* mouillée○, lâche *mf*.

scare: ~monger *n* alarmiste *mf*; **~mongering** *n* alarmisme *m*; **~ story** *n* rumeur *f* alarmiste; **~ tactic** *n* tactique *f* alarmiste.

scarf /skɑ:f/ *n* (*pl* **scarves**) (long) écharpe *f*; (square) foulard *m*.

scarify /'skeərɪfaɪ/ *vtr* Agric, Hort, Med scarifier.

scarlatina /,skɑ:lə'ti:nə/ **▶1354** *n* scarlatine *f*.

scarlet /'skɑ:lət/ **▶1104** **I** *n* **1** (colour) écarlate *f*; **to blush** ou **go ~** devenir écarlate; **2** (cloth) Relig pourpre *m*; Hist veste *f* écarlate.
II *adj* écarlate.

scarlet: ~ fever ▶1354 *n* scarlatine *f*; **~ pimpernel** *n* mouron *m* rouge; **~ runner** *n* haricot *m* d'Espagne; **~ woman** *n* littér femme *f* de mauvaise vie.

scarp /skɑ:p/ *n* escarpement *m*.

scarper○ /'skɑ:pə(r)/ *vi* GB déguerpir.

scar tissue *n* tissu *m* conjonctif.

scarves /skɑ:vz/ *pl* ▶ **scarf**.

scary○ /'skeərɪ/ *adj* **1** (inspiring fear) [*film, monster, noise*] qui fait peur (*after n*); **to be ~** faire peur; **2** (causing distress) [*experience, moment, situation*] angoissant.

scat /skæt/ **I** *n* scat *m*.
II *excl* ouste!

scathing /'skeɪðɪŋ/ *adj* [*remark, report, tone, wit*] cinglant; [*criticism*] virulent; [*look*] noir; **to be ~ about sb/sth** être cinglant vis-à-vis de qn/qch.

scathingly /'skeɪðɪŋlɪ/ *adv* [*speak, write*] de façon cinglante; **to look ~ at sb** foudroyer qn du regard; **~ honest** d'une honnêteté dévastatrice; **~ witty** d'un humour cinglant.

scatological /,skætə'lɒdʒɪkl/ *adj* scatologique.

scatology /skæ'tɒlədʒɪ/ *n* scatologie *f*.

scatter /'skætə(r)/ **I** *n* **1** (of houses, stars, papers) éparpillement *m* (**of** de); **2** Stat dispersion *f*.
II *vtr* **1** (also **~ around, ~ about**) (throw around) répandre [*seeds, earth*]; éparpiller [*books, papers, clothes*]; disperser [*debris*]; **to be ~ed around** ou **about** [*people, islands, buildings, books*] être éparpillé; **to be ~ed with sth** être jonché de qch; **2** (cause to disperse) disperser [*crowd, animals*]; disperser, faire envoler [*birds*]; **3** Phys disperser [*electrons, light*].
III *vi* [*people, animals, birds*] se disperser.

scatter: ~brain *n* écervelé/-e *m/f*; **~-brained** *adj* [*person*] étourdi; [*idea*] farfelu○; **~ cushion** *n* coussinet *m*; **~ diagram, ~ graph** *n* Stat diagramme *m* de dispersion.

scattered /'skætəd/ *adj* **1** (dispersed) [*houses, villages, trees, population, clouds*] épars; [*books, litter*] éparpillé; [*support, resistance*] clairsemé; **the village is ~** les maisons du village sont dispersées; **2** Meteorol **~ showers** averses *fpl* intermittentes.

scattering /'skætərɪŋ/ *n* (of leaves, papers, people) éparpillement *m*; (of shops, restaurants etc) constellation *f*.

scatter: ~ rug *n* carpette *f*; **~shot** *adj* [*cartridge*] de fusil de chasse; fig [*criticism*] à tout va.

scattiness○ /'skætɪnɪs/ *n* GB étourderie *f*.

scatty○ /'skætɪ/ *adj* GB étourdi.

scavenge /'skævɪndʒ/ **I** *vtr* **1** lit récupérer [*food, scrap metal*] (**from** dans); **2** fig mendier [*funds, subsidies*].
II *vi* **to ~ in** ou **through the dustbins for sth** [*person*] faire les poubelles à la recherche de qch; [*dog*] fouiller les poubelles à la recherche de qch.

scavenger /'skævɪndʒə(r)/ *n* **1** (for food) faiseur *m* de poubelles; **2** (for objects) récupérateur *m*; **3** (animal) charognard *m*.

scavenger: ~ beetle *n* scarabée *m* phytophage; **~ hunt** *n* chasse *f* au trésor.

scenario /sɪ'nɑ:rɪəʊ, US -'nær-/ *n* (*pl* **~s**) **1** Cin scénario *m*; **2** fig scénario *m*; **the worst-case ~** le pire scénario; **a night-**

mare ~ un scénario catastrophe; **this is a ~ for war** cela pourrait bien mener à la guerre.

scenarist /sɪ'nɑːrɪst, US -'nær-/ ▶1692 *n* scénariste *mf*.

scene /siːn/ *n* **1** (in play, film, novel) scène *f*; **act I, ~ 2** acte I, scène 2; **the balcony/seduction ~** la scène du balcon/de séduction; **street/crowd ~** scène de rue/foule; **the ~ is set in a Scottish town** la scène se déroule dans une ville écossaise; **first, let's set the ~: a villa in Mexico** situons le décor d'abord: une villa au Mexique; **this set the ~ for another war/argument** fig ceci a preparé le terrain pour une autre guerre/dispute; **the ~ was set for a major tragedy** fig tous les éléments étaient réunis pour qu'une grande tragédie se produise; **2** Theat (stage scenery) décor *m*; **behind the ~s** lit, fig dans les coulisses *fpl*; **to work behind the ~s** fig travailler en coulisses; **3** (location) lieu *m*; **the ~ of the crime/accident** le lieu du crime/de l'accident; **these streets have been the ~ of violent fighting** ces rues ont été le théâtre de violents affrontements; **to come on the ~** [*police, ambulance*] arriver sur les lieux; fig arriver; **you need a change of ~** tu as besoin de changer d'air or de décor; **4** (sphere, field) scène *f*; **she is a new arrival on the political ~** c'est une nouvelle venue sur la scène politique; **the economic ~** la scène économique; **the jazz/fashion ~** le monde du jazz/de la mode; **it's not my ~** ce n'est pas mon genre; **5** (emotional incident) scène *f*; **there were chaotic/angry ~s in parliament** il y a eu des scènes de désordre/de colère au parlement; **there were ~s of violence after the match** il y a eu des incidents violents après le match; **to make a ~** faire une scène; **he will do anything to avoid a ~** il fera n'importe quoi pour éviter une scène; **6** (image, sight) image *f*; **~s of death and destruction** des images de mort et de destruction; **it's a ~ that will remain with me forever** c'est une image qui demeurera à jamais en moi; **7** (view) vue *f*, tableau *m*; Art scène *f*; **he admired the beauty of the ~** il a admiré la beauté de la vue; **rural/outdoor ~** scène rurale/extérieure.

scene: ~ change *n* Theat changement *m* de décor; **~ designer, ~ painter** *n* ▶1692 Theat décorateur/-trice *m/f*.

scenery /'siːnərɪ/ *n* ¢ **1** (landscape) paysages *mpl*; **mountain ~** paysages de montagne; **a change of ~** fig un changement de décor; **2** Theat décors *mpl*; **a piece of ~** un élément de décor.

scene shifter ▶1692 *n* machiniste *mf*.

scenic /'siːnɪk/ *adj* [*drive, route, walk*] panoramique; [*location, countryside*] pittoresque; **the area is well-known for its ~ beauty** la région est renommée pour la beauté de son panorama.

scenic railway *n* (train) petit train *m* (touristique); (rollercoaster) GB montagnes *fpl* russes.

scenography /siː'nɒgrəfɪ/ *n* Art, Antiq scénographie *f*.

scent /sent/ **I** *n* **1** (smell) odeur *f*; (more positive) parfum *m*; **2** (body smell) (of animal) fumet *m*, odeur *f*; **3** Hunt piste *f*, trace *f*; fig (of scandal, crime, criminal) relents *mpl*; **to pick up the ~** lit, fig trouver la piste; **to throw the dogs/the police off the ~** brouiller la piste aux chiens/à la police; **to be (hot) on the ~ of sth/sb** suivre qch/qn à la trace; **4** (perfume) parfum *m*.

II *vtr* **1** (smell) lit flairer [*prey, animal*]; [*police dog*] flairer [*drugs, explosives*]; fig pressentir [*danger, trouble*]; flairer [*scandal*]; **2** (perfume) parfumer [*air, room*].

■ **scent out: ~ [sth] out, ~ out [sth]** lit, fig flairer.

scented /'sentɪd/ **I** *adj* [*soap, paper, flower, tree*] parfumé; [*air, breeze*] odorant; **~ with** parfumé de.

II -scented (*dans composés*) **1** (with scent added) parfumé à; **rose-~ soap** du savon parfumé à la rose; **2** (natural) à l'odeur de; **honey-~ flowers** des fleurs à l'odeur de miel; **the pine-~ air** l'air qui flaire le pin liter; **sweet-~** à l'odeur suave.

scented orchid *n* orchis *m* moucheron.

scentless /'sentlɪs/ *adj* inodore.

scepter US *n* = **sceptre**.

sceptic GB, **skeptic** US /'skeptɪk/ *n* sceptique *mf*.

sceptical GB, **skeptical** US /'skeptɪkl/ *adj* sceptique (**about, of** en ce qui concerne).

sceptically GB, **skeptically** US /'skeptɪklɪ/ *adv* avec scepticisme *m*.

scepticism GB, **skepticism** US /'skeptɪsɪzəm/ *n* scepticisme *m* (**about** à propos de).

sceptre GB, **scepter** US /'septə(r)/ *n* sceptre *m*.

Schaffhausen ▶1818, 1776 *pr n* Schaffhouse; **the canton of ~** le canton de Schaffhouse.

schedule /'ʃedjuːl, US 'skedʒʊl/ **I** *n* **1** Admin, Comm, Constr programme *m*; (projected plan) prévisions *fpl*; **building ~** programme de construction; **production ~** prévisions de production; **to be ahead of/behind ~** être en avance/en retard sur les prévisions; **to work to a tight ~** travailler selon un programme serré; **to keep to a ~** suivre un programme; **to draw up** ou **make out a ~** établir un programme; **to be on ~ (for July)** progresser comme prévu (pour l'échéance de juillet); **finished on ~** fini à temps; **according to ~** comme prévu; **a ~ of events** un calendrier; **2** (of appointments) programme *m*; **work ~** programme de travail; **a full/crowded ~** gen, Sport un programme chargé/très chargé; **to fit sb/sth into one's ~** intégrer qn/qch dans son programme; **3** TV programme *m*; **autumn/winter ~** programme d'automne/d'hiver; **4** Transp (timetable) horaire *m*; **bus/train ~** horaire des bus/trains; **to arrive on/ahead of/behind ~** arriver à l'heure/en avance/en retard; **5** Comm, Jur (list) (of prices, charges) barème *m*; (of repayments) taux *m*; (of contents, listed buildings) inventaire *m*; (to a contract) annexe *f*; **as per the attached ~** conformément à la liste ci-jointe; **6** GB Tax barème *m* d'imposition.

II *vtr* **1** (plan) prévoir [*activity*]; (arrange) programmer [*holiday, appointment*]; **to do sth as ~d** faire qch comme prévu; **I am ~d to speak at 2.00** je dois parler à 2 h; **the plane is ~d to arrive at 2.00** l'avion est attendu à 2 h; **the station is ~d for completion in 1997** la gare doit être terminée en 1997; **2** GB Archeol, Tourism (list) inventorier [*building, site*].

schedule: ~d building *n* GB immeuble *m* classé; **~d flight** *n* vol *m* régulier; **~d territories** *npl* GB zone *f* sterling.

scheduling /'ʃedjuːlɪŋ, US 'skedʒʊl-/ *n* (of project, work) programmation *f*; (of monument) GB classification *f*.

schema /'skiːmə/ *n* (*pl* **-mata**) schéma *m*.

schematic /skɪ'mætɪk/ *adj* schématique.

schematically /skɪ'mætɪklɪ/ *adv* schématiquement.

scheme /skiːm/ **I** *n* **1** (systematic plan) projet *m*, plan *m* (**to do** pour faire); **a ~ for sth/for doing** un plan pour qch/pour faire; **2** GB Admin (system) système *m*, projet *m*; **discount ~** système de rabais; **insurance ~** projet d'assurance; **road ~** projet de développement routier; **employees under this ~ will earn more** les employés concernés par le projet gagneront plus; **under the government's ~...** conformément au projet gouvernemental...; **3** péj (impractical idea) plan *m*; **to think** ou **dream up a ~** inventer un plan; **I think that's a bad ~** à mon avis, c'est une mauvaise idée; **4** (plot) combine *f* (**to do** pour faire); **5** (design, plan) (for house, garden etc) plan *m*; ▶**colour scheme**.

II *vi* péj comploter (**to do** pour faire; **against sb** contre qn).

IDIOMS **in the ~ of things, this incident is not very important** si on considère la situation dans son ensemble, cet incident n'est pas très grave; **she was unsure how she fitted into the ~ of things** elle ne savait pas où elle se situait; **in the Marxist/Keynesian ~ of things** selon la conception de Marx/Keynes; **in my/his ~ of things** dans mon/son monde.

schemer /'skiːmə(r)/ *n* péj intrigant/-e *m/f*.

scheming /'skiːmɪŋ/ péj **I** *n* ¢ machinations *fpl*.

II *adj* [*person*] intrigant.

scherzando /skeə'tsændəʊ/ **I** *n* (*pl* **-di** ou **-dos**) scherzo *m*.

II *adv* [*play*] scherzando, scherzo.

scherzo /'skeətsəʊ/ *n* (*pl* **-zos** ou **-zi**) scherzo *m*.

schilling /'ʃɪlɪŋ/ ▶1143 *n* schilling *m*.

schism /'sɪzəm/ *n* schisme *m* (**in** au sein de).

schismatic /sɪz'mætɪk/ *n, adj* schismatique (*mf*).

schist /ʃɪst/ *n* schiste *m*.

schizo○ /'skɪtsəʊ/ *n, adj* schizo○ (*mf*).

schizoid /'skɪtsɔɪd/ **I** *n* schizoïde *mf*.

II *adj* **1** Med [*person*] schizoïde; **2** fig [*attitudes, ideas*] contradictoire.

schizophrenia /ˌskɪtsəʊ'friːnɪə/ *n* Med, fig schizophrénie *f*.

schizophrenic /ˌskɪtsəʊ'frenɪk/ **I** *n* schizophrène *mf*.

II *adj* [*behaviour, problems*] schizophrénique; [*patient*] schizophrène.

schlemiel◑, **schlemihl**◑ /ʃlə'miːl/ *n* US (bungler) empoté/-e○ *m/f*; (victim) gogo○ *m*.

schlep(p)◑ /ʃlep/ US **I** *n* **1** (bungler) empoté/-e○ *m/f*; **2** (long journey) trotte○ *f*.

II *vtr* traîner○, trimballer○.

III *vi* (also **~ around**) se traîner○.

schlock◑ /ʃlɒk/ US **I** *n* camelote○ *f*.

II *adj* (also **schlocky**) en toc, qui ne vaut rien.

schlump◑ /ʃlʊmp/ *n* US (person) traîne-savates○ *m inv*.

schmal(t)z○ /ʃmɔːlts/ *n* sensiblerie *f*.

schmal(t)zy○ /'ʃmɔːltsɪ/ *adj* [*lovesong, novel, film*] larmoyant; [*music*] sirupeux/-euse.

schmear◑ /'ʃmɪə(r)/ *n* US **the whole ~** (of details) tout le baratin○; (of people) la troupe entière.

schmo(e)◑ /ʃməʊ/ *n* US andouille○ *f*.

schmooze◑ /ʃmuːz/ **I** *n* ¢ bavardages *mpl*.

II *vi* bavarder.

schmuck◑ /ʃmʌk/ *n* US (jerk) andouille○ *f*; (bastard) salaud◑ *m*.

schnap(p)s /ʃnæps/ *n* schnaps○ *m*.

schnorkel /'ʃnɔːkl/ *n* US = **snorkel**.

schnorrer◑ /'ʃnɔːrə(r)/ *n* US parasite *m*.

schnoz(zle)○ /'ʃnɒzl/ *n* pif○ *m*.

scholar /'skɒlə(r)/ *n* **1** (learned person) érudit/-e *m/f*; **Shakespeare/classical/Hebrew ~** spécialiste *mf* de Shakespeare/de lettres classiques/de l'hébreu; **he's not much of a ~** il est plutôt primaire; **2** (student with scholarship) lauréat/-e *m/f* détenteur/-trice d'une bourse; **3**† (school pupil) élève *mf*.

scholarly /'skɒləlɪ/ *adj* **1** (erudite) [*essay, approach, perspective*] érudit; **2** [*journal, periodical, circles*] (academic) universitaire; (serious) intellectuel/-elle; **3** (like a scholar) [*appearance*] d'intellectuel/-elle.

scholarship /'skɒləʃɪp/ **I** *n* **1** (award) bourse *f* (**to** pour); **to win a ~ to Eton** obtenir une bourse pour Eton; **to award a ~ to sb** décerner une bourse à qn; **2** (meticulous study) érudition *f*; **3** (body of learning) savoir *m*, connaissances *fpl*; (of individual) érudition *f*; **Oxford is a centre of ~** Oxford est un haut-lieu du savoir; **the book is a fine**

piece of ~ c'est un livre d'une grande érudition.

II *modif* [*student*] lauréat/-e *m/f* détenteur/-trice d'une bourse.

scholastic /skəˈlæstɪk/ **I** *n* Philos, Relig scolastique *mf*.

II *adj* **1** Philos scolastique; **2** (of school) scolaire.

Scholastic Aptitude Test, **SAT** *n* US examen *m* d'admission à l'université.

scholasticism /skəˈlæstɪsɪzəm/ *n* Philos scolastique *f*.

school /sku:l/ **I** *n* **1** Sch école *f*; **at ~** à l'école; **to go to/start/leave ~** aller à/commencer/quitter l'école; **to send sb to ~** envoyer qn à l'école; **the whole ~ was there** toute l'école était là; **used in ~s** utilisé à l'école; **broadcasts for ~s** émissions scolaires; **before/after ~** avant/après l'école or la classe; **~ starts/finishes/restarts** les cours commencent/finissent/reprennent; **no ~ today** pas de classe aujourd'hui; **a ~ for the blind/gifted** une école pour aveugles/surdoués; **2** (college) (of music, education etc) école *f*; **to go to medical/law ~** faire des études de médecine/droit; **3** US (university) université *f*; **4** (of painting, literature, thought) école *f*; **5** (of whales , dolphins, porpoises) banc *m*; **6** (group of gamblers, drinkers etc) groupe *m*.

II *modif* gen [*holiday, outing, life, uniform, year*] scolaire; (of particular school) [*canteen, library, minibus, playground, register*] de l'école.

III *vtr* **1** (educate) **to ~ sb in sth** enseigner qch à qn [*art, trick, ways*]; **2** (train) dresser [*horse*].

IV *v refl* **to ~ oneself in** s'enseigner [*patience, prudence*].

IDIOMS **of the old ~** de la vieille école; **to go to the ~ of hard knocks** aller à l'école de la vie; **to grow up/learn sth in a hard ~** grandir/apprendre qch à dure école.

school age I *n* âge *m* scolaire.

II *modif* **~ child** enfant d'âge scolaire.

schoolbag /ˈsku:lbæg/ *n* gen sac *m* de classe; (traditional) cartable *m*.

school board *n* **1** GB Hist *comité élu responsable des écoles publiques locales*; **2** US (of school) comité *m* de gestion d'une école; (of schools) comité *m* de gestion des écoles.

schoolbook /ˈsku:lbʊk/ *n* livre *m* de classe.

schoolboy /ˈsku:lbɔɪ/ **I** *n* (gen) élève *m*; (of primary age) écolier *m*; (secondary) collégien *m*; (sixth former) GB lycéen *m*.

II *modif* **1** [*attitude, behaviour*] de collégien; [*slang, word*] d'élève; [*joke, prank, humour*] de potache○; **2** [*champion, player, championships*] junior.

school: **~ bus** *n* car *m* scolaire; **~ captain** *n* GB Sch *élève responsable de la discipline*; **School Certificate** *n* GB Hist *autrefois certificat de fin d'études à 16 ans*; **~child** *n* écolier/-ière *m/f*; **~ council** *n*: *conseil d'enseignants et de représentants des élèves*; **~ crossing patrol** *n*: *personne remplissant les fonctions d'agent de la circulation à la sortie des écoles*; **~days** *npl* années *fpl* d'école; **~ dinner** *n* = **school lunch**; **~ district** *n* US secteur *m* scolaire; **~ fees** *n* frais *mpl* de scolarité; **~fellow**† *n* camarade *mf* d'école; **~friend** *n* camarade *mf* de classe.

schoolgirl /ˈsku:lgɜ:l/ **I** *n* gen élève *f*; (of primary age) écolière *f*; (secondary) collégienne *f*; (sixth former) GB lycéenne *f*.

II *modif* [*complexion, figure*] de jeune fille; **~ crush** béguin *m* d'adolescence (**on** pour).

school: **~ graduation age** *n* US Sch = **school leaving age**; **~ hours** *npl* heures *fpl* de classe; **~house** *n* école *f*.

schooling /ˈsku:lɪŋ/ *n* **1** (of child) scolarité *f*; **2** Equit (of horse) dressage *m*.

school: **~ inspector** ▶1692 *n* inspecteur/-trice *m/f*; **~-leaver** *n* GB jeune *mf* ayant fini sa scolarité; **~ leaving age** *n* âge *m* de fin de scolarité; **~ lunch** *n* repas *m* de la cantine scolaire; **~man**, **Schoolman** *n* Hist scolastique *m*; **~marm**, **~ma'am** *n* péj maîtresse *f* d'école.

schoolmarmish *adj* **she is ~** elle fait vieille fille pudibonde.

school: **~master** ▶1692 *n* enseignant *m*; **~mate** *n* camarade *mf* d'école; **~ meal** *n* ▶**school lunch**; **~mistress** ▶1692 *n* enseignante *f*; **~ of thought** *n* école *f* (de la pensée); **~ phobia** *n* phobie *f* de l'école; **~ phobic** *n* enfant *mf* qui souffre de la phobie de l'école; **~ prefect** *n* GB Sch *élève de terminale chargé de la discipline*; **~ record** *n* ≈ dossier *m* scolaire; **~ report** GB, **~ report card** US *n* bulletin *m* scolaire; **~room** *n* salle *f* de classe.

schoolteacher /ˈsku:lti:tʃə(r)/ ▶1692 *n* (gen) enseignant/-e *m/f*; (secondary) professeur *m*; (primary) gen instituteur/-trice *m/f*; Admin professeur *m* des écoles.

school: **~teaching** *n* enseignement *m*; **~ time** *n* heures *fpl* de classe.

schoolwork /ˈsku:lwɜ:k/ *n* travail *m* de classe; **to do well in one's ~** bien travailler à l'école.

schooner /ˈsku:nə(r)/ *n* **1** (boat) goélette *f*, schooner *m*; **~-rigged** gréé en goélette; **2** (glass) US grande chope *f* (à bière); GB grand verre *m* à Xérès.

schuss /ʃʊs/ *n* Sport schuss *m inv*.

schwa /ʃwɑ:/ *n* Phon schwa *m*, chva *m*.

Schwyz ▶1818, 1776 *pr n* Schwyz; **the canton of ~** le canton de Schwyz.

sciatic /saɪˈætɪk/ *adj* Med sciatique.

sciatica /saɪˈætɪkə/ ▶1354 *n* Med sciatique *f*; **to have ~** avoir une sciatique.

science /ˈsaɪəns/ **I** *n* **1** science *f*; **~ and technology** la science et la technologie; **~ and the arts** les sciences et les arts; **to teach/study ~** enseigner/étudier les sciences; **the physical/natural ~s** les sciences physiques/naturelles; **sports/military ~** science du sport/militaire; **2** (skill) habileté *f*.

II *modif* [*correspondent, exam, journal, subject*] scientifique; [*department, faculty*] des sciences; [*lecturer, teacher, textbook*] de sciences.

IDIOMS **to blind sb with ~** épater qn avec sa science.

science fiction I *n* science-fiction *f*.

II *modif* [*book, film, writer*] de science-fiction.

science park *n* parc *m* scientifique.

scientific /ˌsaɪənˈtɪfɪk/ *adj* scientifique; **to prove/test sth using ~ method** prouver/tester qch scientifiquement; **it's a very ~ game** c'est un jeu qui exige de l'analyse intellectuelle.

scientifically /ˌsaɪənˈtɪfɪklɪ/ *adv* **1** [*investigate, prove, show*] scientifiquement; **2** [*trained, knowledgeable*] du point de vue scientifique.

scientist /ˈsaɪəntɪst/ ▶1692 *n* gen scientifique *mf*; (eminent) savant *m*.

scientologist /ˌsaɪənˈtɒlədʒɪst/ *n* adepte *mf* de la scientologie.

Scientology /ˌsaɪənˈtɒlədʒɪ/ *n* scientologie *f*.

sci-fi○ /ˈsaɪfaɪ/ **I** *n* (*abrév* = **science fiction**) science-fiction *f*.

II *modif* [*book, film, writer*] de science-fiction.

Scillies /ˈsɪlɪz/, **Scilly Isles** /ˈsɪlɪ aɪlz/ ▶1381 *pr n* (îles *fpl*) Sorlingues *fpl*.

scimitar /ˈsɪmɪtə(r)/ *n* cimeterre *m*.

scintillate /ˈsɪntɪleɪt, US -təleɪt/ *vi* lit scintiller; fig [*person, debate*] briller.

scintillating /ˈsɪntɪleɪtɪŋ, US -təleɪtɪŋ/ *adj* lit scintillant; fig [*person, conversation*] brillant; [*wit*] vif/vive; [*success*] éclatant.

scion /ˈsaɪən/ *n* **1** sout (person) jeune descendant/-e *m/f*; **2** Bot scion *m*.

Scipio /ˈskɪpɪəʊ/ *pr n* Scipion.

scissor /ˈsɪzə(r)/ *vtr* couper avec des ciseaux.

scissor bill *n* bec *m* en ciseaux.

scissors /ˈsɪzəz/ *npl* ciseaux *mpl*; **a pair of ~** une paire de ciseaux; **kitchen/sewing ~** ciseaux de cuisine/de couture; **a ~-and-paste job** un collage; fig péj un tissu d'idées glanées à droite à gauche.

scissors: **~ jump** *n* saut *m* en ciseaux; **~ kick** *n* ciseaux *mpl*.

sclera /ˈsklɪərə/ *n* sclérotique *f*.

sclerosis /sklɪəˈrəʊsɪs/ ▶1354 *n* Med, fig sclérose *f*.

sclerotic /sklɪəˈrɒtɪk/ *adj* scléreux/-euse, sclérosé.

SCM GB *abrév* ▶**State Certified Midwife**.

scoff /skɒf, US skɔ:f/ **I**○ *n* GB (food) bouffe○ *f*.

II **scoffs** *npl* moqueries *fpl*.

III *vtr* **1** (mock) **'love!' she ~ed** 'l'amour!' dit-elle avec dédain; **2**○ GB (eat) engloutir○, bouffer○.

IV *vi* se moquer (**at** de); **the play was ~ed at by the critics** la pièce a été la risée des critiques.

scoffer /ˈskɒfə(r), US ˈskɔ:fə(r)/ *n* moqueur/-euse *m/f*.

scoffing /ˈskɒfɪŋ, US ˈskɔ:fɪŋ/ **I** *n* moqueries *fpl*.

II *adj* moqueur/-euse.

scofflaw○ /ˈskɒflɔ:, US ˈskɔ:f-/ *n* US personne *f* qui se moque de la loi.

scold /skəʊld/ **I**† *n* (woman) mégère *f*.

II *vtr* gronder (**for doing** pour avoir fait).

III *vi* râler○.

scolding /ˈskəʊldɪŋ/ *n* ¢ gronderie *f*; **to give sb a ~** gronder qn; **to get a ~** se faire gronder.

scoliosis /ˌskɒlɪˈəʊsɪs/ ▶1354 *n* scoliose *f*.

scollop *n* = **scallop**.

sconce /skɒns/ *n* applique *f*.

scone /skɒn, skəʊn, US skəʊn/ *n* GB scone *m* (*petit pain rond*).

scoop /sku:p/ **I** *n* **1** (implement) (for shovelling, ladling) pelle *f*; (for measuring coffee etc) mesure *f*; (for ice cream) cuillère *f* à glace; **coffee ~** mesure à café; **2** (scoopful) (of coffee, flour) mesure *f*; (of earth) pelletée *f*; (of ice cream) boule *f*; **3** Journ exclusivité *f*; **to get a ~** avoir une exclusivité.

II○ *vtr* (win, obtain) décrocher○ [*prize, sum, medal*]; journ décrocher○ [*story, interview*].

■ **scoop out**: **~ out [sth]**, **~ [sth] out** creuser [*earth*]; **to ~ out a hole** creuser un trou; **to ~ the flesh out of a tomato** évider une tomate.

■ **scoop up**: **~ [sth] up**, **~ up [sth]** pelleter [*earth, snow*]; recueillir [*water*]; soulever [*child*].

scoopful /ˈsku:pfʊl/ *n* (of coffee, flour, sugar) mesure *f*; (of ice cream) boule *f*.

scoot○ /sku:t/ *vi* filer○; **to ~ in/out** entrer/sortir à fond de train.

scooter /ˈsku:tə(r)/ *n* **1** (child's) trottinette *f*, patinette *f*; **2** (motorized) scooter *m*; **3** US (boat) yacht *m* à glace.

scope /skəʊp/ *n* **1** (opportunity) possibilité *f*; **~ for sth** possibilité(s) de qch; **~ for sb to do** possibilités pour qn de faire; **to have ~ to do** avoir la possibilité de faire; **to give sb ~ to do** laisser toute latitude à qn de faire; **2** (range, extent) (of plan) envergure *f*; (of inquiry, report, study) portée *f*; (of changes, disaster, knowledge, power) étendue *f*; (of textbook) champ *m*, portée *f*; **the research is broad/narrow in ~** le champ de la recherche est large/étroit; **to be within/outside the ~ of the study** faire partie du/sortir du champ de l'étude; **to fall within the ~ of the survey** rentrer dans le champ du sondage; **to extend the ~ of the investigation** élargir le champ de l'enquête; **3** (capacity) compétences *fpl*; **to be within/beyond the ~ of sb** entrer dans/dépasser les compétences de qn; **4** Ling portée *f*.

scorbutic /skɔ:ˈbju:tɪk/ *adj* scorbutique.

scorch /skɔːtʃ/ **I** *n* (also **~ mark**) légère brûlure *f*.
II *vtr* [*fire*] brûler; [*sun*] dessécher [*grass, trees*]; [*sun*] griller [*lawn*]; [*iron etc*] roussir [*fabric*]; **~ed earth policy** Mil tactique *f* de la terre brûlée.
III *vi* **1** [*grass*] se dessécher; [*lawn*] griller; **this fabric ~es easily** ce tissu est fragile au repassage; **2**○ GB (also **~ along**) (speed) [*car, driver, athlete etc*] foncer○.

scorcher○ /ˈskɔːtʃə(r)/ *n* journée *f* de canicule; **yesterday was a real ~!** hier c'était la canicule!

scorching○ /ˈskɔːtʃɪŋ/ *adj* (also **~ hot**) [*heat, conditions, day*] torride; [*sun*] brûlant; [*weather, summer*] caniculaire; [*sand, surface, coffee*] brûlant.

score /skɔː(r)/ **I** *n* **1** (number of points gained) Sport score *m*, marque *f*; (in cards) marque *f*; **to get the maximum ~** obtenir le score maximum; **there is still no ~** le score or la marque est toujours zéro à zéro; **the final ~ was 3–1** le score final était de 3 à 1; **to keep (the) ~** gen marquer les points or les résultats; (in cards) tenir la marque; **what's the ~?** (in game, match) où en est le jeu or le match?; (in cards) quelle est la marque?; fig où en sommes-nous?; **to know the ~** fig savoir où on est; **2** (in exam, test) note *f*, résultat *m*; **his ~ in the test was poor** ou **low** il a obtenu une mauvaise note or un mauvais résultat au test; **3** Mus (written music) partition *f*; (for ballet) musique *f* (du ballet); (for film) musique *f* (du film); **full/short ~** partition intégrale/réduite; **violin ~** partition pour violon; **orchestral ~** partition d'orchestre; **who wrote the ~?** Cin qui a composé la musique (du film)?; **4** (twenty) **a ~** vingt *m*, une vingtaine *f*; **a ~ of sheep** une vingtaine de moutons; **three ~ years and ten** soixante-dix ans; **by the ~** à la pelle; **~s of requests** des tas de demandes; **~s of times** d'innombrables fois; **5** (scratch) gen éraflure *f*; (on rock) strie *f*; **6** (cut, incision) entaille *f*; **7** (account) sujet *m*; **on this ~** à ce sujet, à cet égard; **you need have no worries on that ~** tu n'as aucun souci à te faire à ce sujet.
II *vtr* **1** Sport marquer [*goal, point*]; remporter [*victory, success*]; **to ~ three goals** marquer trois buts; **to ~ 9 out of 10** avoir 9 sur 10; **to ~ a hit** (in swordsmanship) toucher; (in shooting) mettre dans le mille; fig remporter un grand succès; **to ~ a point against** ou **off** ou **over** (in argument, debate) l'emporter sur, marquer un point sur [*opponent*]; **2** Mus (arrange) adapter; (orchestrate) orchestrer (**for** pour); Cin composer la musique de [*film*]; **~d for the piano** écrit pour le piano; **3** (mark) (with chalk, ink) marquer, rayer; **4** (cut) entailler [*wood, metal, leather*]; strier [*rock*]; inciser [*meat, fish*]; **the water had ~d channels into the rock** l'eau avait creusé des rainures dans les rochers; **a face ~d with wrinkles** un visage sillonné de rides.
III *vi* **1** Sport (gain point) marquer un point; (obtain goal) marquer un but; **to ~ twice** marquer deux buts; **they failed to ~** (in match) ils n'ont pas réussi à marquer un but; **to ~ well** ou **highly** obtenir un bon résultat; **to ~ over** ou **against sb** (in argument, debate) prendre le dessus sur qn; **2** (keep score) marquer les points or les résultats; **3**○ (be successful) avoir du succès, l'emporter; (sexually) faire une touche○; **to ~ with a novel/with the critics** avoir du succès avec un roman/auprès de la critique; **you ~d last night!** tu as fait une touche○ hier soir!; **4**○ argot des drogués réussir à se procurer de la drogue.
IDIOMS **to settle a ~** régler ses comptes; **I have an old ~ to settle with her** j'ai un vieux compte à régler avec elle.
■ **score off**: ¶ **~ off [sth], ~ [sth] off** rayer, barrer [*name, figure*]; **to ~ sb's name off a list** rayer qn d'une liste; ¶ **~ off [sb]** (in argument) marquer des points sur [*opponent*].
■ **score out** = **score off**.
■ **score up**: **~ up [sth], ~ [sth] up** inscrire [*debt*]; marquer, dénombrer [*points*].

score: **~board** *n* gen tableau *m* d'affichage; (in billiards) boulier *m*; **~card** *n* gen, Sport carte *f* de score; (in cards) feuille *f* de marque; **~line** *n* score *m*.

scorer /ˈskɔːrə(r)/ *n* **1** (of goal) marqueur/-euse *m/f* (de but); **2** (keeping score) marqueur/-euse *m/f*.

scoresheet /ˈskɔːʃiːt/ *n* feuille *f* de match; **to add one's name to the ~** marquer un but.

scoring /ˈskɔːrɪŋ/ *n* **1** Sport **to open the ~** ouvrir la marque or le score; **2** Mus arrangement *m*; **3** gen, Culin (cuts) incisions *fpl*.

scorn /skɔːn/ **I** *n* mépris *m*, dédain *m* (**for** pour); **she has nothing but ~ for him** elle n'a que du mépris pour lui; **to be held up to ~ by sb** être l'objet des railleries de qn; **to pour** ou **heap ~ on** accabler [qn] de mépris [*person*], dénigrer [*attempt, argument, organization*].
II *vtr* **1** (despise) mépriser [*person, action*]; dédaigner [*fashion, make-up*]; **2** (reject) rejeter [*advice, invitation, offer of help*]; accueillir avec mépris [*claim, suggestion*]; **3** sout **to ~ to do, to ~ doing** ne pas daigner faire.
IDIOMS **hell hath no fury like a woman ~ed** une femme humiliée est capable de tout; **to laugh sth to ~** exprimer son mépris pour qch.

scornful /ˈskɔːnfl/ *adj* méprisant, dédaigneux/-euse; **to be ~ of** manifester du mépris pour.

scornfully /ˈskɔːnfəlɪ/ *adv* avec mépris, dédaigneusement.

Scorpio /ˈskɔːpɪəʊ/ ▶**1916** *n* Scorpion *m*.

scorpion /ˈskɔːpɪən/ *n* scorpion *m*.

scorpion fish *n* rascasse *f*, scorpène *f* spec.

Scot /skɒt/ ▶**1486** *n* Écossais/-e *m/f*.

scotch /skɒtʃ/ *vtr* étouffer [*rumour, revolt*]; contrecarrer [*plans*]; anéantir [*hopes*].

Scotch /skɒtʃ/ **I** *n* (also **~ whisky**) whisky *m*, scotch *m*.
II *adj* écossais.

Scotch: **~ broth** *n* potage *m* écossais (*à base de mouton, d'orge et de légumes*); **~ egg** *n* GB *œuf dur enrobé de chair à saucisse*; **~-Irish** *adj* irlando-écossais; **~ mist** *n* bruine *f*, crachin *m*; **~ pancake** *n* GB petite crêpe *f* épaisse; **~ pine** *n* = **Scots pine**; **~ tape**® *n* US scotch® *m*; **~ terrier** *n* = **Scottish terrier**.

scot-free /ˌskɒtˈfriː/ *adj* **to get off** ou **go ~** (unpunished) s'en tirer sans être inquiété; (unharmed) s'en sortir indemne.

Scotland /ˈskɒtlənd/ ▶**1131** *pr n* Écosse *f*.

Scotland Yard *n* Scotland Yard (*police judiciaire britannique*).

Scots /skɒts/ ▶**1402** *n, adj* Ling écossais (*m*).

Scots: **~man** *n* Écossais *m*; **~ pine** *n* pin *m* sylvestre; **~woman** *n* Écossaise *f*.

Scotticism /ˈskɒtɪsɪzəm/ *n* expression *f* écossaise.

Scottie /skɒtɪ/ *n* scotch-terrier *m*, terrier *m* écossais.

Scottish /ˈskɒtɪʃ/ ▶**1486** *adj* écossais; **the ~ Highlands** les Highlands *mpl* d'Écosse.

Scottish: **~ country dancing** danse *f* folklorique écossaise; **~ Nationalist** *n* membre *m* du Parti national écossais; **~ National Party, SNP** *n* Parti *m* national écossais; **~ Office** *n* Pol ministère *m* des Affaires écossaises; **~ Secretary** *n* Pol ministre *m* chargé des Affaires écossaises; **~ terrier** *n* scotch-terrier *m*, terrier *m* écossais.

scoundrel /ˈskaʊndrəl/ *n* péj gredin *m*; hum chenapan *m*.

scour /ˈskaʊə(r)/ **I** *n* (erosion) erosion *f*.
II *vtr* **1** (scrub) récurer; **2** (erode) [*river, wind*] éroder; **3** (search) parcourir [*area, book, list*] (**for** à la recherche de); lire [qch] d'un bout à l'autre [*book, list*] (**for** à la recherche de); **to ~ the shops for sth** faire le tour des magasins à la recherche de qch; **4** (wash) dégraisser [*wool, cloth*].
■ **scour out**: **~ out [sth], ~ [sth] out** récurer.

scourer /ˈskaʊərə(r)/ *n* **1** (pad) tampon *m* à récurer; **2** (powder) poudre *f* à récurer.

scourge /skɜːdʒ/ **I** *n* lit, fig fléau *m*.
II *vtr* **1** lit fouetter; **2** fig [*ruler*] opprimer; [*famine, disease, war*] frapper.
III *v refl* **to ~ oneself** [*monk, nun*] se donner la discipline.

scouring powder *n* poudre *f* à récurer.

scouse○ /skaʊs/ GB **I** *n* (person) personne *f* originaire de Liverpool; (dialect) dialecte *m* de Liverpool.
II *adj* de Liverpool.

scouser○ /ˈskaʊsə(r)/ *n* GB personne *f* originaire de Liverpool.

scout /skaʊt/ **I** *n* **1** (also **Scout**) (Catholic) scout *m*; (non-Catholic) éclaireur *m*; **2** Mil éclaireur *m*; **to have a ~ around** Mil aller en reconnaissance; fig explorer; **3** (also **talent ~**) découvreur/-euse *m/f* de nouveaux talents; **4** GB Univ (cleaner) domestique *mf*.
II *modif* (also **Scout**) [*camp, leader, movement*] scout; [*uniform*] de scout; [*troop*] de scouts.
III *vi* **1** Mil aller en reconnaissance; **2** Sport (search) **to ~ for talent** prospecter pour trouver des joueurs.
■ **scout around** Mil aller en reconnaissance; gen explorer (**to do** pour faire); **to ~ around for sth** rechercher qch.

scout: **Scout Association** *n* association *f* de scouts; **~ hut** *n* GB local *m* de scouts.

scouting /ˈskaʊtɪŋ/ *n* scoutisme *m*.

scoutmaster /ˈskaʊtmɑːstə(r)/ *n* chef *m* scout.

scow /skaʊ/ *n* chaland *m*.

scowl /skaʊl/ **I** *n* air *m* renfrogné; **with a ~** d'un air renfrogné.
II *vi* prendre un air renfrogné; **she ~ed at me** elle a pris un air renfrogné.

scowling /ˈskaʊlɪŋ/ *adj* maussade.

scrabble /ˈskræbl/ *vi* **1** (also **~ around**) (search) fouiller; **2** (scrape) gratter; **he ~d desperately for a hold** il a cherché désespérément à s'accrocher quelque part.

Scrabble® /ˈskræbl/ *n* Scrabble® *m*.

scrag /skræg/ *n* **1** (also **~ end**) Culin collet *m* de mouton; **2** (thin person) maigrichon *m*.

scraggly /ˈskræglɪ/ *adj* US [*beard*] en bataille.

scraggy /ˈskrægɪ/ *adj* [*person*] maigrichon/-onne; [*part of body*] décharné; [*animal*] famélique.

scram○ /skræm/ *vi* (*p prés etc* **-mm-**) filer○.

scramble /ˈskræmbl/ **I** *n* **1** (rush) course *f* (**for** pour; **to do** pour faire); **the ~ for the best seats** la course pour avoir les meilleurs sièges; **2** (climb) escalade *f*; **3** Sport motocross *m*; **4** Aviat, Mil décollage *m* d'urgence.
II *vtr* **1** (also **~ up**) (jumble) mettre [qch] en désordre [*papers*]; emmêler [*string, wool*]; **2** Culin **to ~ eggs** faire des œufs brouillés; **3** (code) Radio, Telecom brouiller [*signal*]; TV coder, crypter [*signal*]; **4** Mil faire décoller [qch] d'urgence [*aircraft, squadron*].
III *vi* **1** (clamber) grimper; **to ~ up/down** escalader [*slope, wall*]; **to ~ over** escalader [*rocks, debris*]; **to ~ through** se frayer un passage à travers [*bushes*]; **to ~ to one's feet** se lever en sursaut; **2** (compete) **to ~ for** se disputer [*contracts, jobs, prizes*]; **to ~ to do** se dépêcher de faire; **3** (rush) **to ~ for** se précipiter sur [*door, buffet*]; **to ~ to do** se démener pour faire.

scrambled egg *n* **1** (also **~s**) Culin œufs *mpl* brouillés; **2**○ Mil galon *m* d'officier.

scramble net *n* filet *m* d'escalade.

scrambler /ˈskræmblə(r)/ *n* **1** Radio, Telecom brouilleur *m*; **2** GB (motorcyclist) trialiste *mf*.

scrambling /ˈskræmblɪŋ/ ▶ **1282** *n* **1** Sport motocross *m*; **2** Radio, Telecom brouillage *m*; **3** TV cryptage *m*.

scrap /skræp/ **I** *n* **1** (fragment) (of paper, cloth) petit morceau *m*; (of news, information, verse) fragment *m*; (of conversation) bribe *f*; (cutting) coupure *f*; (of land) parcelle *f*; **they devoured every ~ of food** ils ont tout dévoré jusqu'à la dernière miette; **there wasn't a ~ of evidence** il n'y avait pas la moindre preuve; **there isn't a ~ of truth in what they say** il n'y a pas une parcelle or un atome de vérité dans leurs propos; **she never does a ~ of work** elle ne fiche○ jamais rien; **2**○ (fight) bagarre○ *f*; **to get into a ~ with sb** se bagarrer○ avec qn; **3** (discarded goods) (metal) ferraille *f*; **to sell sth for ~** mettre qch à la casse.
II scraps *npl* (of food) restes *mpl*; (in butcher's) déchets *mpl*; (of bread) bouts *mpl*.
III *modif* [*price, value*] à la casse; **~ trade** marché *m* de la ferraille.
IV *vtr* (*p prés etc* **-pp-**) **1**○ (do away with) abandonner [*system, policy, agreement, scheme, talks, tax*]; **2** (dispose of) détruire [*aircraft, weaponry, equipment*].
V○ *vi* (*p prés etc* **-pp-**) (fight) se bagarrer○ (**with** avec).

scrap: **~book** *n* album *m* (de coupures de journaux etc); **~ (metal) dealer** ▶ **1692** *n* marchand *m* de ferraille.

scrape /skreɪp/ **I** *n* **1**○ (awkward situation) **to get into a ~** s'attirer des ennuis; **to get sb into a ~** mettre qn dans le pétrin○; **he's always getting into ~s** il s'attire toujours des ennuis, il se retrouve toujours dans des situations impossibles; **2** (in order to clean) **to give sth a ~** gratter qch; **3** (sound) (of cutlery, shovels, boots) raclement *m*; **4** (small amount) **a ~ of** un petit peu de [*butter, jam*].
II *vtr* **1** (clean) gratter [*vegetables, shoes*]; **to ~ sth clean** nettoyer qch en le grattant; **2** (damage) érafler [*paintwork, car part, furniture*]; **3** (injure) écorcher [*elbow, knee etc*]; **to ~ one's knee** s'écorcher le genou; **4** (making noise) racler [*chair, feet*]; **5**○ (get with difficulty) **to ~ a living** s'en sortir à peine (**doing** en faisant); **she ~d a ten in biology** elle a laborieusement décroché un dix en biologie.
III *vi* **1 to ~ against sth** [*car part*] érafler qch; [*branch*] battre contre qch; **2** (economize) économiser le moindre sou.
IDIOMS **to ~ the bottom of the barrel** gen être réduit à faire avec ce que l'on a sous la main; (when raising money) racler les fonds de tiroir.
■ **scrape back**: **~ [sth] back, ~ back [sth]** tirer [qch] en arrière [*hair*].
■ **scrape by** s'en tirer○; **he manages to ~ by on £80 a week** il réussit à s'en tirer avec 80 livres sterling par semaine.
■ **scrape home** Sport gagner de justesse.
■ **scrape in** (to university, class) entrer de justesse.
■ **scrape off**: **~ off [sth], ~ [sth] off** enlever [qch] en grattant.
■ **scrape out**: **~ out [sth], ~ [sth] out** enlever [qch] en grattant [*contents of jar*]; nettoyer [qch] en grattant [*saucepan*].
■ **scrape through**: ¶ **~ through** s'en tirer de justesse; ¶ **~ through [sth]** réussir [qch] de justesse [*exam, test*].
■ **scrape together**: **~ [sth] together, ~ together [sth]** arriver à amasser [*sum of money*]; arriver à réunir [*people*].
■ **scrape up** = **scrape together**.

scraper /ˈskreɪpə(r)/ *n* (for decorating) couteau *m* de peintre; (for shoes) grattoir *m*.

scrap heap /ˈskræp hiːp/ *n* lit tas *m* de ferraille; **to be thrown on** ou **consigned to the ~** fig être mis au rebut.

scrapie /ˈskreɪpɪ/ *n* scrapie *f*.

scraping /ˈskreɪpɪŋ/ **I** *n* **1** (noise) (of feet, chairs, cutlery) raclement *m* (**on** sur); **2** GB (small amount) **a ~ of** un petit peu de [*butter, jam*]; **3** (scratching) grattement *m*.
II scrapings *npl* GB (of paint, food etc) restes *mpl*.
III *pres p adj* [*noise*] de raclement, de grattement.

scrap: **~ iron** *n* ferraille *f*; **~ merchant** ▶ **1692** *n* marchand *m* de ferraille; **~ metal** *n* ferraille *f*; **~ paper** *n* papier *m* brouillon.

scrappy /ˈskræpɪ/ *adj* **1** (disorganized) [*play, programme, report, essay*] décousu; [*game, playing*] désordonné; [*meal*] de bric et de broc; **2**○ US, péj (pugnacious) [*person*] bagarreur/-euse○.

scrap yard /ˈskræp jɑːd/ *n* chantier *m* de ferraille, casse *f*; **to take sth to/buy sth from the ~** mettre qch/acheter qch à la casse.

scratch /skrætʃ/ **I** *n* **1** (wound) gen égratignure *f*; (from a claw, fingernail) griffure *f*; **to escape without a ~** s'en tirer sans une égratignure; **to get a ~ from a cat** se faire griffer par un chat; **2** (mark) (on metal, furniture) éraflure *f*; (on record, disc, glass) rayure *f*; **3** (action to relieve an itch) **to have a ~** se gratter; **to give one's arm/foot a ~** se gratter le bras/pied; **4** (sound) grattement *m*; **5**○ (satisfaction, standard) **he/his work is not up to ~** il/son travail n'est pas à la hauteur; **to keep sth up to ~** maintenir qch au niveau voulu; **6** (zero) **to start from ~** partir de zéro; **to plan/study sth from ~** concevoir/étudier qch en partant de zéro; **7** Sport **to play off ~** jouer scratch.
II *adj* [*team*] de fortune; [*meal*] improvisé; **he's a ~ golfer** il joue scratch.
III *vtr* **1** (cancel) supprimer [*race, meeting*]; **2** Comput (delete) effacer [*file*]; **3** (trace) **to ~ one's initials on sth** graver ses initiales sur qch; **to ~ a line in the soil** tracer une ligne dans la terre; **4** (wound) [*cat, person*] griffer [*person*]; [*thorns, rosebush*] égratigner [*person*]; **to get ~ed** (by cat) se faire griffer; (by thorns) être égratigné; **to ~ sb's eyes out** arracher les yeux à quelqu'un; **5** (react to itch) gratter [*spot*]; **to ~ one's arm/chin** se gratter le bras/menton; **to ~ an itch** se gratter; **to ~ sb's back** gratter le dos de qn; **to ~ one's head** lit se gratter la tête; fig être perplexe; **6** (damage) [*person, branch*] érafler [*car*]; [*cat*] se faire les griffes sur [*furniture*]; [*person, toy*] érafler [*furniture, wood*]; rayer [*record*]; **the table is all ~ed** la table est toute éraflée; **7** Sport (withdraw) retirer, scratcher [*horse, competitor*].
IV *vi* **1** (relieve itch) [*person*] se gratter; **2** (inflict injury) [*person, cat*] griffer.
V *v refl* **to ~ oneself** [*dog, person*] se gratter.
IDIOMS **to ~ a living from the soil** tirer une maigre subsistance du sol; **you ~ my back and I'll ~ yours** un service en vaut un autre; **~ a translator and you'll find a writer underneath!** dans tout traducteur il y a un écrivain qui sommeille!
■ **scratch around** [*hen*] gratter (**in** dans); **to ~ around to find the money** gratter un peu partout pour trouver l'argent nécessaire.
■ **scratch at**: **~ at [sth]** gratter à [*door*].

scratch: **~card** *n* jeu *m* de grattage; **~ file** *n* fichier *m* de travail; **~ mark** *n* éraflure *f*; **~ pad** *n* bloc-notes *m*; **~ tape** *n* bande *f* de travail; **~ test** *n* Med test *m* cutané; **~ video** *n* cassette *f* de montage.

scratchy /ˈskrætʃɪ/ *adj* [*fabric, wool*] rêche.

scrawl /skrɔːl/ **I** *n* gribouillage *m*.
II *vtr, vi* gribouiller.

scrawny /ˈskrɔːnɪ/ *adj* [*person, animal*] décharné; [*vegetation*] maigre.

scream /skriːm/ **I** *n* **1** (sound) (of person, animal) cri *m* (perçant); (stronger) hurlement *m*; (of brakes) grincement *m*; (of tyres) crissement *m*; **~s of laughter** éclats *mpl* de rire; **2**○ (funny person) **to be a ~** être tordant○.
II *vtr* lit crier, hurler [*words, insult, order*]; fig Journ [*headline*] annoncer (en titre).
III *vi* [*person, animal, bird*] crier, pousser des cris; (stronger) hurler; [*brakes*] grincer; [*tyres*] crisser; fig [*colour*] crier; **to ~ at sb** crier après qn○; **to ~ at sb to do sth** crier à qn de faire qch; **to ~ for sth/sb** réclamer qch/qn avec des cris; **to ~ with** hurler de [*fear, pain, rage*]; pousser des cris de [*excitement, pleasure*]; **to ~ with laughter** rire aux éclats.
IDIOMS **to ~ the place down** pousser des hurlements; **he was kicking and ~ing** il se débattait en criant; **to drag sb kicking and ~ing to the dentist** forcer qn à aller chez le dentiste; **the company was dragged kicking and ~ing into the twentieth century** l'entreprise a été forcée à s'adapter aux exigences du monde moderne.

screamer○ /ˈskriːmə(r)/ *n* US (headline) manchette *f*, gros titre *m*.

screaming /ˈskriːmɪŋ/ **I** *n* (of person, animal, bird) cris *mpl*; (stronger) hurlements *mpl*; (of brakes) grincements *mpl*; (of tyres) crissements *mpl*.
II *adj* fig [*headline*] racoleur/-euse; [*colour*] criard; ▶ **scream III**.

screamingly /ˈskriːmɪŋlɪ/ *adv* **~ funny** à mourir de rire; **~ obvious** absolument évident.

scree /skriː/ *n* éboulis *m*.

screech /skriːtʃ/ **I** *n* gen cri *m* strident; (of tyres) crissement *m*.
II *vtr* hurler.
III *vi* [*person, animal*] pousser un cri strident; [*tyres*] crisser; **to ~ to a halt** s'arrêter dans un crissement de pneus.

screech-owl *n* GB effraie *f*; US petit-duc *m* maculé.

screed /skriːd/ *n* **1** épître *f*; **to write ~s** écrire des pages et des pages; **2** Constr (strip) règle *f*; (surfacing) chape *f* de nivellement.

screen /skriːn/ **I** *n* **1** Cin, Comput, TV écran *m*; **computer/television ~** écran d'ordinateur/de télévision; **on ~** Comput sur l'écran; Cin, TV à l'écran; **the big ~** fig le grand écran, le cinéma; **the small ~** fig le petit écran, la télévision; **the ~** fig le grand écran, le cinéma; **a star of stage and ~** une vedette du théâtre et du cinéma; **he writes for the ~** Cin il écrit pour le cinéma; TV il écrit pour la télévision; ▶ **on-screen**; **2** (panel) (decorative or for getting changed) paravent *m*; (partition) cloison *f* mobile; (to protect) écran *m*; **bullet-proof ~** écran *m* pare-balles; **the hedge formed a ~ which hid the house from the road** la haie formait un écran qui rendait la maison invisible de la route; **a ~ of trees** un rideau d'arbres; **3** fig (cover) couverture *f*; **to act as a ~ for** servir de couverture à [*illegal activity*]; **4** Med visite *f* de dépistage; **5** Mil rideau *m*; **6** (sieve) crible *m*; **7** US (in door) grille *f*.
II *modif* Cin [*actor, star*] de cinéma; [*appearance, debut, performance*] cinématographique, au cinéma.
III *vtr* **1** (show on screen) Cin projeter [*film*]; TV diffuser, transmettre [*programme, film, event*]; **2** (shield) (conceal) cacher, masquer [*person, house*]; (protect) protéger (**from** de); **she wore a hat to ~ her eyes from the sun** elle portait un chapeau pour se protéger les yeux du soleil; **to ~ sth from sight** ou **view** cacher or masquer qch; **3** (subject to test) Admin examiner le cas de [*applicants, candidates*]; contrôler le statut de [*refugees*]; (at airport) contrôler [*baggage*]; Med faire passer des tests de dépistage à [*person, patient*]; **to be ~ed** [*staff*] faire l'objet d'une enquête de sécurité; **to ~ sb for cancer/Aids** faire passer à qn des tests de dépistage du cancer/du sida; **to ~ for cancer/Aids** faire des tests de dépistage du cancer/du sida; **4** (sieve) cribler.
■ **screen off**: **~ off [sth], ~ [sth] off** isoler [*part of room, garden*].
■ **screen out**: ¶ **~ [sb] out, ~ out [sb]**

refuser [*candidate*]; refuser la demande (de statut) de [*refugee*]; ¶ **~ out [sth], ~ [sth] out** filtrer [*unwanted data, nuisance calls*]; filtrer [*light, noise*].

screen: ~ door *n* porte *f* munie d'une moustiquaire; **~ dump** *n* Comput impression *f* d'écran.

screening /'skri:nɪŋ/ *n* **1** (showing) Cin projection *f*; TV diffusion *f*; **the film has already had two ~s this year** le film a été diffusé deux fois déjà cette année; **2** (testing) (of candidates) sélection *f*, tri *m*; Med (of patients) examens *mpl* systématiques, examens *mpl* de dépistage; **blood ~** Med analyse *f* de sang (de dépistage); **cancer ~** dépistage *m* du cancer; **3** (vetting) (of calls, information) filtrage *m*; **4** (sieving) criblage *m*.

screening: ~ room *n* Cin salle *f* de projection; **~ service** *n* Med service *m* de dépistage.

screen: ~play *n* Cin scénario *m*; **~ printing** *n* sérigraphie *f*; **~ rights** *npl* droits *mpl* d'adaptation à l'écran; **~ saver** *n* Comput protecteur *m* d'écran; **~ test** *n* Cin bout *m* d'essai.

screen wash *n* Aut **1** (device) lave-glace *m*; **2** (liquid) liquide *m* lave-glace.

screenwriter /'skri:nraɪtə(r)/ ▶ 1692 *n* Cin, TV scénariste *mf*.

screw /skru:/ **I** *n* **1** Tech vis *f*; **2** Aviat, Naut hélice *f*; **3**○ GB (prison guard) maton/-onne○ *m/f*; **4**● (sex) **to have a ~** tirer un coup●; **to be a good ~** bien baiser●; **5**○ GB (wage) **to earn a fair ~** gagner un bon paquet○.
II *vtr* **1** Tech visser [*object*] (**into** dans); **to ~ sth onto** ou **to a door/to the floor** visser qch sur une porte/au plancher; **he ~ed the top on the bottle** il a vissé le bouchon sur la bouteille; **2**◑ (extort) **to ~ sth out of sb** extorquer qch à qn; **3**◑ (swindle) arnaquer◑ [*person*]; **4**◑ (have sex with) se taper●, baiser● [*person*].
III *vi* **1** Tech **to ~ onto/into sth** [*part, component*] se visser sur/dans qch; **2**◑ (have sex) baiser●.
IDIOMS **~ you**◑**!** va te faire voir○!; **to have a ~ loose**○ avoir une case en moins○; **to have one's head ~ed on** avoir la tête sur les épaules; **to put the ~s on sb**○ forcer la main à qn.
■ **screw around: ~ around 1**◑ (sleep around) coucher à droite et à gauche; **2**○ US (do nothing) glander◑; **3**○ US (refuse to be serious) déconner◑; **quit ~ing around** arrête de déconner◑.
■ **screw down:** ¶ **~ down** [*lid, hatch*] se visser; ¶ **~ [sth] down, ~ down [sth]** visser (à fond) [*lid , screw*].
■ **screw in:** ¶ **~ in** [*attachment*] se visser; ¶ **~ [sth] in, ~ in [sth]** visser [*bolt*].
■ **screw off:** ¶ **~ off** [*cap, lid*] se dévisser; ¶ **~ [sth] off, ~ off [sth]** dévisser [*cap, lid*].
■ **screw on:** ¶ **~ on** [*lid, cap, handle*] se visser; ¶ **~ [sth] on, ~ on [sth]** visser [*lid, cap, handle*].
■ **screw round: to ~ one's head round** tourner la tête.
■ **screw together:** ¶ **~ together** [*parts*] se visser l'un à l'autre; ¶ **~ [sth] together, ~ together [sth]** assembler [qch] avec des vis [*table, model*]; **she ~ed the two parts together** elle a vissé les deux pièces l'une à l'autre.
■ **screw up:** ¶ **~ up**○ (mess up) [*person, company*] merder◑, cafouiller○; ¶ **~ [sth] up, ~ up [sth] 1** (crumple) froisser [*piece of paper, material*]; **to ~ up one's eyes** plisser les yeux; **to ~ up one's face** faire la grimace; **2**○ (make a mess of) faire foirer○ [*plan, preparations, task*]; **3** (summon) **to ~ up one's courage** prendre son courage à deux mains; **to ~ up the courage to do** trouver le courage de faire; ¶ **~ [sb] up**○ perturber [*person*]; **he's really ~ up** il est vraiment perturbé.

screwball○ /'skru:bɔ:l/ **I** *n* cinglé/-e○ *m/f*.
II *modif* [*person*] cinglé○.

screw: ~bolt *n* boulon *m*; **~-cap** *n* bouchon *m* à vis.

screwdriver /'skru:draɪvə(r)/ *n* **1** (tool) tournevis *m*; **2** (cocktail) vodka-orange *f*.

screw: ~-in *adj* [*lightbulb*] à vis; **~-off**○ *n* US fumiste○ *mf*; **~ thread** *n* Tech filetage *m*.

screw top I *n* bouchon *m* à vis.
II screw-top *modif* [*jar*] avec un couvercle à vis; [*bottle*] avec un bouchon à vis.

screwy○ /'skru:ɪ/ *adj* cinglé○.

scribble /'skrɪbl/ **I** *n* gribouillage *m*, griffonnage *m*; **I can't read his ~** je n'arrive pas à lire son gribouillage; **his signature was just a ~** sa signature était illisible.
II *vtr* griffonner, gribouiller; **to ~ a note to sb** griffonner un mot à qn.
III *vi* lit, fig griffonner, gribouiller.
■ **scribble down: ~ [sth] down, ~ down [sth]** griffonner [*message, note*].
■ **scribble out: ~ [sth] out, ~ out [sth]** raturer [*sentence, word*].

scribbler /'skrɪblə(r)/ *n* gen gribouilleur/-euse *m/f*; (author) écrivaillon *m* pej, écrivain *m* de deuxième catégorie.

scribbling /'skrɪblɪŋ/ *n* lit, fig griffonnage *m*, gribouillage *m*.

scribe /skraɪb/ *n* Hist, Bible scribe *m*.

scrimmage /'skrɪmɪdʒ/ *n* **1** US (in football) mêlée *f*; **2** (struggle) bousculade *f*.

scrimp /skrɪmp/ *vi* économiser; **to ~ on sth** lésiner sur qch péj; **to ~ and save** se priver de tout.

scrimshank○ /'skrɪmʃæŋk/ *vi* GB Mil tirer au flanc○.

scrimshanker○ /'skrɪmʃæŋkə(r)/ *n* GB Mil tire-au-flanc○ *m inv*.

scrimshaw /'skrɪmʃɔ:/ *n*: *objets sculptés sur de l'ivoire ou de l'os (par des marins)*.

scrip /skrɪp/ *n* **1** (shares) actions *fpl* gratuites; **2** (certificate) certificat *m* d'actions provisoire.

scrip issue *n* émission *f* d'actions gratuites.

script /skrɪpt/ **I** *n* **1** (text) Cin, Radio, TV script *m*; Theat texte *m*; **2** (handwriting) écriture *f*; (print imitating handwriting) script *m*; **Cyrillic/italic ~** écriture cyrillique/italique; **3** GB Sch, Univ copie *f* (d'examen); **4** Jur document *m* original.
II *vtr* écrire le scénario de [*film etc*].

scripted /'skrɪptɪd/ *adj* Cin, Radio, TV écrit.

scriptural /'skrɪptʃərəl/ *adj* sout biblique.

scripture /'skrɪptʃə(r)/ *n* **1** Relig (also **Holy Scripture, Holy Scriptures**) (Christian) Saintes Écritures *fpl*; (other) textes *mpl* sacrés; **2**† Sch instruction *f* religieuse.

scriptwriter /'skrɪptraɪtə(r)/ ▶ 1692 *n* Cin, Radio, TV scénariste *mf*.

scrofula /'skrɒfjʊlə/ ▶ 1354 *n* scrofule *f*.

scrofulous /'skrɒfjʊləs/ *adj* scrofuleux/-euse (also fig).

scroll /skrəʊl/ **I** *n* **1** (manuscript) rouleau *m* (manuscrit); (painting, commemorative) rouleau *m*; **the Dead Sea Scrolls** les Manuscrits *mpl* de la mer Morte; **2** Archit, Art (on column, violin) volute *f*.
II *vtr* Comput **to ~ sth up/down** faire défiler qch vers le haut/vers le bas.
III *vi* Comput défiler.

scroll arrow *n* Comput flèche *f* de défilement; **up/down/left/right ~** flèche de défilement vers le haut/le bas/la gauche/la droite.

scrolling /'skrəʊlɪŋ/ *n* Comput défilement *m*.

scroll saw *n* scie *f* à ruban de précision.

scrollwork /'skrəʊlwɜ:k/ *n* Art ornementations *fpl* en volute.

Scrooge○ /skru:dʒ/ *n* grippe-sou *m*.

scrotum /'skrəʊtəm/ *n* (*pl* **~s** ou **-ta**) scrotum *m*.

scrounge○ /skraʊndʒ/ **I** *n* **to be on the ~** être toujours en train de mendier.
II *vtr* quémander; **to ~ sth off sb** gen taper○ qn de qch.
III *vi* **1 to ~ off sb** vivre sur le dos de qn; **2 to ~ (around) for sth** chercher qch.

scrounger○ /'skraʊndʒə(r)/ *n* parasite *m*.

scroungy○ /'skraʊndʒɪ/ *adj* US minable.

scrub /skrʌb/ **I** *n* **1** (clean) **to give sth a (good) ~** (bien) nettoyer qch; **2** Bot broussailles *fpl*; **3** Cosmet gommage *m*.
II *vtr* (*p prés etc* **-bb-**) **1** (clean) frotter [*floor, object, back, child*]; nettoyer [*mussel, vegetable*]; **to ~ sth with a brush** brosser qch; **to ~ one's nails/hands** se brosser les ongles/les mains; **to ~ sth clean** nettoyer qch à fond; **2**○ (scrap) laisser tomber○ [*meeting, idea*].
III *vi* (*p prés etc* **-bb-**) nettoyer, frotter.
IV *v refl* (*p prés etc* **-bb-**) **to ~ oneself** se frotter.
■ **scrub down: ~ down [sth/sb], ~ [sth/sb] down** nettoyer [qch/qn] à fond.
■ **scrub off: ~ off [sth], ~ [sth] off** nettoyer, enlever [*stain, graffiti*].
■ **scrub out: ~ out [sth], ~ [sth] out 1** (clean inside) récurer [*pan, oven, sink*]; **2** (rub out) effacer [*mark, word, line*].
■ **scrub up** [*surgeon*] se stériliser les mains (*avant une opération*).

scrubber /'skrʌbə(r)/ *n* **1** Ind (gas purifier) épurateur *m*; **2** (scourer) tampon *m* à récurer; **3**◑ GB Austral injur pouffiasse◑ *f* offensive.

scrubbing brush, scrub brush US *n* brosse *f* de ménage.

scrubby /'skrʌbɪ/ *adj* **1** [*land, hill*] broussailleux/-euse; **2** [*tree, bush*] rabougri.

scrubwoman /'skrʌbwʊmən/ ▶ 1692 *n* US femme *f* de ménage.

scruff /skrʌf/ *n* **1** (nape) **by the ~ of the neck** par la peau du cou; **2**○ GB (untidy person) **he's a bit of a ~**○ il est peu soigné.

scruffily /'skrʌfɪlɪ/ *adv* [*dress*] de façon négligée.

scruffiness /'skrʌfɪnɪs/ *n* **1** (of person) allure *f* négligée; **2** (of clothes) aspect *m* négligé; **3** (of building, district) délabrement *m*.

scruffy /'skrʌfɪ/ *adj* [*clothes, person*] dépenaillé; [*flat, town*] délabré.

scrum /skrʌm/ *n* **1** (in rugby) mêlée *f*; **loose/tight ~** mêlée ouverte/fermée; **2**○ GB (crowd) bousculade *f*.
■ **scrum down** (*p prés etc* **-mm-**) former la mêlée.

scrum half *n* Sport demi *m* de mêlée.

scrummage /'skrʌmɪdʒ/ **I** *n* (in rugby) mêlée *f*.
II *vi* (in rugby) jouer en mêlée.

scrump○ /skrʌmp/ *vtr* GB chiper○ [*apples*].

scrumptious○ /'skrʌmpʃəs/ *adj* délicieux/-ieuse.

scrumpy /'skrʌmpɪ/ *n* GB cidre *m*.

scrunch /skrʌntʃ/ **I** *n* crissement *m*.
II *vi* [*footsteps, tyres*] crisser.
■ **scrunch up:** ¶ **~ up** US se tasser; ¶ **~ [sth] up, ~ up [sth]** faire une boule de.

scruple /'skru:pl/ **I** *n* scrupule *m* (**about** vis à vis de); **without ~** sans aucun scrupule; **to have ~s about doing** avoir des scrupules à faire; **to have no ~s about sth/about doing** n'avoir aucun scrupule vis à vis qch/à faire.
II *vi* **not to ~ to do** n'avoir aucun scrupule à faire.

scrupulous /'skru:pjʊləs/ *adj* [*attention, detail, person*] scrupuleux/-euse; **to be ~ about punctuality/hygiene** être d'une ponctualité/d'une hygiène scrupuleuse.

scrupulously /'skru:pjʊləslɪ/ *adv* [*wash, prepare, avoid*] scrupuleusement; **~ honest/fair/clean** d'une honnêteté/équité/propreté scrupuleuse.

scrutineer /ˌskru:tɪ'nɪə(r), US -tn'ɪər/ *n* scrutateur/-trice *m/f*.

scrutinize /'skru:tɪnaɪz, US -tənaɪz/ *vtr* scruter [*face, motives*]; examiner [qch] minutieusement [*document, plan*]; vérifier [*accounts, votes*]; surveiller [*activity, election*].

scrutiny /'skru:tɪnɪ, US 'skru:tənɪ/ *n* **1** (investigation) examen *m*; **close ~** examen approfondi; **the results are subject to ~** les résultats sont donnés sous réserve de vérification; **to come under ~** être examiné; **to avoid ~** échapper au contrôle; **2** (surveillance) surveillance *f*; **3** (look) regard *m* scrutateur.

SCSI *n* Comput (*abrév* = **small computer systems interface**) *interface pour mini-systèmes informatiques.*

scuba /'sku:bə/ *n* matériel *m* de plongée.

scuba: **~ diver** *n* Sport plongeur/-euse *m/f* sous-marin/-e; **~ diving** ▶1282 *n* plongée *f* sous-marine.

scud /skʌd/ *vi* (*p prés etc* **-dd-**) **1** Naut [*ship*] fuir; **2** [*cloud*] filer; **to ~ across the sky** filer dans le ciel.

scuff /skʌf/ **I** *n* (also **~ mark**) **1** (on leather) éraflure *f*; **2** (on floor, furniture) rayure *f*.
II *vtr* érafler [*shoes*]; rayer [*floor, furniture*]; **to ~ one's feet** traîner les pieds.
III *vi* [*shoes*] s'érafler; [*floor*] se rayer.
■ **scuff up** soulever [*dust*]; abîmer [*lawn*].

scuffle /'skʌfl/ **I** *n* bagarre *f*.
II *vi* se bagarrer.

scull /skʌl/ **I** *n* **1** (boat) outrigger *m*; **single ~** skiff *m*; **double ~** deux *m* de couple; **2** (single oar) godille *f*; **3** (one of a pair of oars) aviron *m*.
II *vtr* **1** (with one oar) faire avancer [qch] à la godille; **2** (with two oars) faire avancer [qch] à l'aviron.
III *vi* **1** (with one oar at stern) godiller; **2** (with two oars) ramer en couple; **to ~ up/down the river** remonter/descendre la rivière à l'aviron.

scullery /'skʌlərɪ/ *n* GB arrière-cuisine *f*.

scullery maid ▶1692 *n* Hist fille *f* de cuisine.

sculpt /skʌlpt/ *vtr, vi* sculpter.

sculptor /'skʌlptə(r)/ ▶1692 *n* sculpteur *m*.

sculptress /'skʌlptrɪs/ ▶1692 *n* sculpteur *m*.

sculptural /'skʌlptʃərəl/ *adj* sculptural.

sculpture /'skʌlptʃə(r)/ **I** *n* sculpture *f*.
II *modif* [*class, gallery*] de sculpture.
III *vtr* sculpter.

scum /skʌm/ *n* **1** (on pond) couche *f*; **2** (on liquid) mousse *f*; **3** (on bath) crasse *f*; **4**◐ injur (worthless person) ordure◐ *f* offensive; (worthless group) racaille *f*; **they're the ~ of the earth** ce sont des moins que rien.

scumbag◐ /'skʌmbæg/ *n* injur salaud◐/salope◐ *m/f* offensive.

scummy /'skʌmɪ/ *adj* **1** (dirty) [*bath, canal, pond*] crasseux/-euse; [*liquid*] mousseux/-euse; **2**◐ injur (rotten) **you ~ bastard**●! espèce de salaud◐! offensive.

scupper /'skʌpə(r)/ **I** *n* Naut dalot *m*.
II *vtr* **1** GB Naut saborder [*ship*]; **2**○ GB (ruin) faire capoter [*attempt, deal, plan*]; **we're ~ed!** nous sommes fichus○!

scurf /skɜ:f/ *n* ¢ **1** (dandruff) pellicules *fpl*; **2** (dead skin) peau *f* morte.

scurfy /'skɜ:fɪ/ *adj* [*hair*] pelliculeux/-euse; [*skin*] squameux/-euse.

scurrility /skə'rɪlətɪ/ *n* sout **1** (viciousness) calomnie *f*; **2** (vulgarity) vulgarité *f*.

scurrilous /'skʌrɪləs/ *adj* **1** (defamatory) calomnieux/-ieuse; **2** (vulgar) scabreux/-euse.

scurrilously /'skʌrɪləslɪ/ *adv* **1** (insultingly) [*abuse, attack*] avec calomnie; **2** (vulgarly) [*describe, write*] de façon scabreuse.

scurry /'skʌrɪ/ **I** *n* (*tjrs sg*) **the ~ of feet** le bruit de pas rapides.
II *vi* (*prét, pp* **-ried**) se précipiter; **to ~ across/along/into** se précipiter à travers/le long de/dans; **to ~ to and fro** courir dans tous les sens; **to ~ to and fro between the kitchen and the living room** courir de la cuisine au salon; **to ~ away, to ~ off** se sauver.

scurvy /'skɜ:vɪ/ **I** *n* Med scorbut *m*.
II‡ *adj* [*knave, fellow*] misérable; [*trick*] perfide.

scut /skʌt/ *n* Zool queue *f*.

scutcheon /'skʌtʃən/ *n* écusson *m*.

scuttle /'skʌtl/ **I** *n* **1** (hatch) écoutille *f*; **2** (basket) panier *m* à fond plat; **3** ▶**coal scuttle**.
II *vtr* lit saborder [*ship*]; fig faire échouer [*talks, project, etc*].
III *vi* courir à toute vitesse; **to ~ across sth** traverser qch à toute vitesse; **to ~ after sb/sth** courir après qn/qch; **to ~ away, to ~ off** filer.

scuttlebutt /'skʌtlbʌt/ *n* **1** Naut Hist charnier *m*; **2**○ US (gossip) ragots *mpl*.

Scylla /'sɪlə/ *pr n*: IDIOMS **to be between ~ and Charybdis** être entre le marteau et l'enclume.

scythe /saɪð/ **I** *n* faux *f inv*.
II *vtr* faucher [*grass*]; [*sword*] fendre [*air*].

SD *n* US Post *abrév* ▶**South Dakota**.

SDI *n* US Mil Hist (*abrév* = **Strategic Defense Initiative**) IDS *f*.

SDLP *n* Pol (in Ireland) (*abrév* = **Social Democratic and Labour Party**) SDLP *m*.

SDP *n* GB Pol Hist (*abrév* = **Social Democratic Party**) parti *m* social démocrate britannique.

SDR *n* Fin (*abrév* = **special drawing rights**) DTS *mpl*.

SE ▶1568 *n* (*abrév* = **southeast**) SE *m*.

sea /si:/ ▶1511 **I** *n* **1** (as opposed to land) gen mer *f*; (distant from shore) large *m*; **beside** ou **by the ~** au bord de la mer; **the open ~** le large; **to look/be swept out to ~** regarder/être entraîné vers le large; **to be at ~** être en mer; **once we get out to ~** une fois qu'on sera en mer; **once out to ~** une fois en pleine mer; **to put (out) to ~** prendre la mer; **to go to ~** [*boat*] prendre la mer; **a long way out to ~** très loin de la côte; **by ~** [*travel*] en bateau; [*send*] par bateau; **to travel over land and ~** littér parcourir océans et continents; **to bury sb at ~** immerger le corps de qn; **2** (surface of water) **the ~ is calm/rough/very rough/choppy** la mer est calme/mauvaise/démontée/agitée; **the ~ was like glass** la mer était d'huile; **3** (also **Sea**) **the Mediterranean/North ~** la mer Méditerranée/du Nord; **the ~ of Galilee** la mer de Galilée; **the Sea of Storms** l'océan des Tempêtes; **4** (as career) **to go to ~** (join Navy) s'engager dans la marine; (join ship) se faire engager comme marin; **after six months at ~** gen après six mois comme marin; (in Navy) après six mois dans la marine; **5** (sailor's life) **the ~** la vie de marin; **to give up the ~** abandonner la vie de marin; **6** fig **a ~ of** une nuée de [*banners, faces*]; **a ~ of troubles** littér une avalanche d'ennuis.
II seas *npl* **the heavy ~s** la tempête; **to sink in heavy ~s** couler par gros temps.
III *modif* gen [*air, breeze, mist*] marin; [*bird, water*] de mer; [*crossing, voyage*] par mer; [*boot, chest*] de marin; [*battle*] naval; [*creature, nymph*] de la mer; [*power*] maritime.
IDIOMS **to be all at ~** être complètement perdu; **to get one's ~ legs** s'habituer au roulis; **worse things happen at ~!** ça aurait pu être pire!

sea: **~ anchor** *n* ancre *f* flottante; **~ anemone** *n* anémone *f* de mer; **~ bag** *n* sac *m* de marin; **~ bass** *n* loup *m* de mer.

seabed /'si:bed/ *n* **the ~** les fonds *mpl* marins; **on the ~** sur les fonds marins.

Seabee /'si:bi:/ *n* US Mil Naut soldat *m* au service du génie maritime.

sea: **~board** *n* côte *f*; **~borne** *adj* [*attack*] venant de la mer; [*algae*] flottant; [*trade*] maritime; **~ bream** *n* dorade *f*; **~ captain** ▶1612 *n* capitaine *m* de la marine marchande; **~ change** *n* transformation *f* radicale; **~ cow** *n* vache *f* marine; **~ defences** GB, **~ defenses** US *npl* digues *fpl*; **~ dog** *n* (vieux) loup *m* de mer, marin *m* chevronné; **~ dumping** *n* déversement *m* de déchets en mer; **~ eagle** *n* aigle *m* de mer; **~ eel** *n* anguille *f* de mer; **~ elephant** *n* éléphant *m* de mer; **~farer** *n* marin *m*.

seafaring /'si:feərɪŋ/ *adj* [*nation*] de marins; **my ~ days** ma vie de marin; **a ~ man** un marin.

sea fish farming *n* aquaculture *f*.

seafood /'si:fu:d/ **I** *n* fruits *mpl* de mer.
II *modif* [*kebab, cocktail, platter*] de fruits de mer; [*sauce*] aux fruits de mer.

seafront /'si:frʌnt/ *n* front *m* de mer, bord *m* de mer; **a hotel on the ~** un hôtel situé sur le front de mer; **to stroll along the ~** se promener sur le front de mer.

sea: **~going** *adj* [*vessel, ship*] pour la navigation maritime; **~-green** ▶1104 *n, adj* vert (*m*) d'eau; **~gull** *n* mouette *f*; **~ horse** *n* hippocampe *m*; **~kale** *n* chou *m* marin.

seal /si:l/ **I** *n* **1** Zool phoque *m*; **2** Jur, gen (insignia) sceau *m*; **to set one's ~ on** lit apposer son cachet sur [*document*]; fig conclure [*championship, match*]; **to set the ~ on** sceller [*friendship*]; confirmer [*trend, regime*]; **I need your ~ of approval** j'ai besoin de votre approbation; **to give sth one's ~ of approval** approuver qch; **look for our ~ of quality** exigez le label de qualité; **3** (integrity mechanism) (on container) plomb *m*; (on package, letter) cachet *m*; (on door) scellés *mpl*; **4** (closing mechanism) fermeture *f*; **the cork provides a tight ~** le bouchon ferme hermétiquement; **cheap envelopes have a poor ~** les enveloppes bon marché se collent mal; **an airtight/watertight ~** une fermeture étanche (à l'air/à l'eau); **the rubber strip forms a ~ around the door** la bande de caoutchouc scelle le tour de la porte.
II *modif* Zool [*hunting*] au phoque; [*meat*] de phoque; [*population*] de phoques.
III *vtr* **1** (authenticate) cacheter [*document, letter*]; **the letter was ~ed with a kiss** un baiser servit de sceau à la lettre; **2** (close) fermer [*envelope, package*]; plomber [*container, lorry*]; sceller [*oil well, pipe*]; boucher [*gap*]; **3** (make airtight, watertight) fermer [qch] hermétiquement [*jar, tin*]; lisser [*plaster*]; rendre [qch] étanche [*roof, window frame*]; **4** (settle definitively) sceller [*alliance, friendship*] (**with** par); conclure [*deal*] (**with** par); **to ~ sb's fate** décider du sort de qn.
IV *vi* Hunt chasser le phoque; **to go ~ing** aller à la chasse au phoque.
V sealed *pp adj* [*envelope*] cacheté; [*package*] scellé; [*bid, instructions, orders*] sous pli cacheté; [*jar*] fermé hermétiquement; [*door, vault*] scellé.
■ **seal in** conserver [*flavour*].
■ **seal off**: **~ [sth] off, ~ off [sth] 1** (isolate) isoler [*corridor, wing*]; **2** (cordon off) boucler [*area, building*]; barrer [*street*].
■ **seal up**: **~ [sth] up, ~ up [sth]** fermer [qch] hermétiquement [*jar*]; boucher [*gap*].

sea lane *n* couloir *m* de navigation.

sealant /'si:lənt/ *n* **1** (coating) enduit *m* d'étanchéité; **2** (filler) mastic *m*.

sea: **~-launched missile** *n* missile *m* mer-sol; **~ lavender** *n* lavande *f* de mer.

seal: **~ cull** *n* Hunt massacre *m* des phoques; **~ culling** *n* massacre *m* de phoques.

sealer /'si:lə(r)/ *n* **1** Hunt (person) chasseur *m* de phoques; (ship) navire *m* chasseur de phoques; **2** Constr enduit *m* d'étanchéité.

sea level *n* niveau *m* de la mer; **above/below ~** au-dessus/en dessous du niveau de la mer; **1,000 m above ~** à 1000 m au-dessus du niveau de la mer; **rising ~s threaten the coastline** la montée du niveau de la mer menace les côtes.

sealing /'si:lɪŋ/ *n* **1** Hunt chasse *f* aux phoques; **2** (closing) (of letter) cachetage *m*; (of container) plombage *m*.

sealing wax *n* cire *f* à cacheter.

Seasons

French never uses capital letters for names of seasons as English sometimes does.

spring = le printemps
summer = l'été *m*
autumn *or* fall = l'automne *m*
winter = l'hiver *m*

in spring = au printemps
in summer = en été
in autumn *or* fall = en automne
in winter = en hiver

In the following examples, summer *and* été *are used as models for all the season names.*
French normally uses the definite article, whether or not English does

I like summer *ou* I like the summer = j'aime l'été
during the summer = pendant l'été *or* au cours de l'été
in early summer = au début de l'été
in late summer = à la fin de l'été
for the whole summer = pendant tout l'été
throughout the summer = tout au long de l'été
last summer = l'été dernier
next summer = l'été prochain
the summer before last = il y a deux ans en été
the summer after next = dans deux ans en été

However, words like chaque, ce *etc. may replace the definite article*

every summer = tous les ans en été
this summer = cet été

There is never any article when en *is used*

in summer = en été
until summer = jusqu'en été

Seasons used as adjectives with other nouns

De alone, without article, is the usual form, e.g.

summer clothes = des vêtements d'été
the summer collection = la collection d'été
the summer sales = les soldes d'été
a summer day = une journée d'été
a summer evening = un soir d'été
a summer landscape = un paysage d'été
summer weather = un temps d'été

sea: **~ lion** *n* lion *m* de mer; **~ loch** *n* loch *m* (*en Écosse, ouvert sur la mer*); **Sea Lord** *n* GB *l'un des deux officiers d'active de la Marine qui tiennent un poste-clé au Ministère de la Défense.*

seal ring *n* bague *f* portant un sceau.

sealskin /ˈsiːlskɪn/ **I** *n* peau *f* de phoque. **II** *modif* [*coat, gloves*] en peau de phoque.

seam /siːm/ **I** *n* **1** Sewing couture *f*; **to be bursting at the ~s** [*building*] être bondé; [*suitcase*] être plein à craquer; **his coat is bursting at the ~s** les coutures de son manteau sont prêtes à craquer; **to come apart at the ~** [*marriage, plan*] s'écrouler; [*garment*] craquer; **2** Ind, Tech (cordon *m* de) soudure *f*; **3** Geol veine *f*; **4** (suture) couture *f*; **5** (in cricket) *couture centrale de la balle de cricket.* **II** *vtr* Sewing coudre.

seaman /ˈsiːmən/ *n* (*pl* **-men**) **1** ▶ **1612** Mil Naut matelot *m*; **2** (amateur) marin *m*.

seaman apprentice *n* US, Mil Naut matelot *m* de seconde classe breveté provisoire.

seamanlike /ˈsiːmənlaɪk/ *adj* **to look ~** avoir l'air d'un vrai marin; **in a ~ manner** comme un vrai marin.

seaman recruit *n* US, Mil Naut matelot *m* de seconde classe sans spécialité.

seamanship /ˈsiːmənʃɪp/ *n* capacités *fpl* de navigateur.

seamed /siːmd/ *pp adj* [*stockings, tights*] à coutures; **a face ~ with wrinkles** un visage sillonné de rides.

sea: **~ mile** *n* mille *m* marin; **~ mist** *n* brume *f*.

seamless /ˈsiːmlɪs/ *adj* [*garment, cloth*] sans coutures; [*transition*] sans heurts; [*process, whole*] continu.

seamstress /ˈsemstrɪs/ ▶ **1692** *n* couturière *f*.

seamy /ˈsiːmɪ/ *adj* [*intrigue, scandal*] sordide; [*area*] malfamé; **the ~ side of sth** le côté peu reluisant de qch.

seance /ˈseɪɑːns/ *n* séance *f* de spiritisme.

sea: **~ otter** *n* loutre *f* de mer; **~ perch** *n* perche *f* de mer; **~plane** *n* hydravion *m*; **~ pollution** *n* pollution *f* marine; **~port** *n* port *m* maritime.

sear /sɪə(r)/ **I** *adj* littér [*plant*] flétri. **II** *vtr* **1** (scorch) calciner; **2** (seal) cautériser [*wound*]; saisir [*meat*]; **3** (wither) flétrir; **4** (brand) lit brûler [*flesh*]; fig graver.

search /sɜːtʃ/ **I** *n* **1** (seeking) recherches *fpl* (**for sb/sth** pour retrouver qn/qch); **in ~ of** à la recherche de; **in the ~ for a solution/for peace** à la recherche d'une solution/de la paix; **2** (examination) (of house, area, bag, cupboard) fouille *f* (**of** de); **house ~** Jur perquisition *f*; **right of ~** Jur, Naut droit *m* de visite; **to carry out a ~ of sth** fouiller qch; **3** Comput recherche *f*; **to do a ~** effectuer une recherche. **II** *vtr* **1** (examine) fouiller [*area, countryside, woods*]; fouiller, perquisitionner dans Jur [*house, office, premises*]; fouiller dans [*cupboard, drawer*]; [*police, customs*] fouiller [*person, luggage*]; [*person*] fouiller dans, chercher dans [*memory*]; examiner (attentivement) [*page, map, records*]; **I ~ed his face for some sign of remorse** j'ai scruté son visage pour y déceler quelque trace de remords; **~ me**○! aucune idée!, j'en sais rien○!; **2** Comput rechercher dans [*file*]. **III** *vi* **1** (seek) chercher; **to ~ for** ou **after sb/sth** chercher qn/qch; **2** (examine) **to ~ through** fouiller dans [*cupboard, bag*]; examiner [*records, file*]; **3** Comput **to ~ for** rechercher [*data, item, file*].

■ **search about, search around** chercher, fouiller (**in** dans); **to ~ around for sb/sth** chercher qn/qch.

■ **search out**: **~ [sb/sth] out, ~ out [sb/sth]** découvrir.

searcher /ˈsɜːtʃə(r)/ *n* sauveteur/-euse *m/f*.

searching /ˈsɜːtʃɪŋ/ *adj* [*look, question*] pénétrant.

searchingly /ˈsɜːtʃɪŋlɪ/ *adv* [*look at, gaze at*] d'un air pénétrant.

search: **~light** *n* projecteur *m*; **~ party** *n* équipe *f* de secours; **~ warrant** *n* Jur mandat *m* de perquisition.

searing /ˈsɪərɪŋ/ *adj* [*heat*] incandescent; [*pace, pain*] fulgurant; [*criticism, indictment*] virulent.

sea: **~ route** *n* voie *f* maritime; **~ salt** *n* Culin sel *m* de mer; Ind sel *m* marin; **~scape** *n* Art marine *f*; **Sea Scout** *n* scout *m* marin; **~ shanty** *n* chanson *f* de marins; **~shell** *n* coquillage *m*.

seashore /ˈsiːʃɔː(r)/ *n* **1** (part of coast) littoral *m*; **the Cornish ~** le littoral de la Cornouailles; **2** (beach) plage *f*; **to go for a walk along the ~** se promener sur la plage.

seasick /ˈsiːsɪk/ *adj* **to be** ou **get** ou **feel ~** avoir le mal de mer.

seasickness /ˈsiːsɪknɪs/ *n* mal *m* de mer; **to suffer from ~** souffrir du mal de mer.

seaside /ˈsiːsaɪd/ **I** *n* **the ~** le bord de la mer; **to go to the ~** aller à la mer ou au bord de la mer. **II** *modif* [*holiday*] à la mer; [*hotel*] en bord de mer; [*town*] maritime.

seaside resort *n* station *f* balnéaire.

season /ˈsiːzn/ **I** *n* **1** (time of year) saison *f*; **in the dry/rainy ~** pendant la saison sèche/des pluies; **the growing/planting ~** la saison de croissance/des semis; **the mating** ou **breeding ~** la saison des amours; **it's the ~ for tulips** c'est la saison des tulipes; **strawberries are out of/in ~** c'est/ce n'est pas la saison des fraises; **when do melons come into ~?** quand est-ce que c'est la saison des melons?; **2** Fashn, Tourism, Sport saison *f*; **the football/hunting ~** la saison de football/de la chasse; **hotels are full during the ~** les hôtels sont complets pendant la saison; **the town is quiet out of ~** la ville est calme hors saison ou pendant la basse saison; **early in the tourist ~** au début de la saison touristique; **late in the ~** dans l'arrière-saison; **the holiday ~** la période des vacances; **the new ~'s fashions** les nouvelles tendances de la saison; **3** (feast, festive period) **the ~ of Advent/of Lent** le temps de l'Avent/du Carême; **the Christmas ~** la période de Noël or des fêtes; **Season's greetings!** (on Christmas cards) Joyeuses fêtes!; **4** Cin, Theat, TV saison *f*; **I played two ~s at Stratford** j'ai joué deux saisons à Stratford; **a ~ of French films** un festival du film français; **a Fellini/Beethoven ~** un festival Fellini/Beethoven; **5** Vet **to be in ~** [*animal*] être en chaleur; **6**† (period of social activity) saison *f*; **her first ~** ses débuts dans le monde; **7** (suitable moment) **there is a ~ for everything** littér il y a un temps pour tout; **a word in ~**† un mot opportun. **II** *vtr* **1** Culin (with spices) relever; (with condiments) assaisonner; **~ with salt and pepper** salez et poivrez; **2** (prepare) sécher [*timber*]; abreuver [*cask*].

seasonable /ˈsiːznəbl/ *adj* [*weather*] de saison.

seasonal /ˈsiːzənl/ *adj* **1** [*change, unemployment, work, rainfall*] saisonnier/-ière; [*fruit, produce*] de saison; **the price/menu varies on a ~ basis** le prix/menu varie selon la saison; **2** (befitting festive period) **he's full of ~ cheer** il déborde de bonne volonté (à la période de Noël).

seasonal affective disorder, **SAD** *n* Med dépression *f* saisonnière.

seasonally /ˈsiːzənəlɪ/ *adv* **1** (periodically) [*change, vary*] selon la saison; **2** Fin **~ adjusted figures** chiffres *mpl* corrigés en fonction des variations saisonnières.

seasoned /ˈsiːznd/ *adj* **1** Constr [*timber*] bien séché; **2** (experienced) [*soldier, veteran*] aguerri; [*traveller*] grand (*before n*); [*politician, leader*] chevronné; [*campaigner, performer*] expérimenté; **3** Culin [*dish*] assaisonné; **highly ~** relevé, épicé; **4** Wine vieilli en fût.

seasoning /ˈsiːznɪŋ/ *n* **1** Culin assaisonnement *m*; **2** (preparation) (of timber) séchage *m*; **3** Wine (of barrel) avinage *m*; (of wine) vieillissement *m* en fût.

season: **~ ticket** *n* Transp carte *f* d'abonnement; Sport, Theat abonnement *m*; **~ ticket holder** *n* Transp détenteur/-trice *m/f* de carte d'abonnement; Sport, Theat abonné/-e *m/f*.

seat /siːt/ **I** *n* **1** (allocated place) place *f*; **I sat down on** ou **in the first ~ I could find** je me suis assis à la première place que j'ai trouvée; **the nearest available ~** la place la plus proche; **to book** ou **reserve a ~** (in theatre, on train) réserver une place; **to keep**

a ~ for sb garder une place pour qn; **to give up one's ~ to sb** céder sa place à qn; **to take sb's ~** prendre sa place à qn; **has everybody got a ~?** est-ce que tout le monde est assis?; **keep your ~s please** nous vous prions de rester assis; **take your ~s please** Theat (before performance) veuillez gagner vos places; (after interval) veuillez regagner vos places; **the best ~s in the house** les meilleures places; **would you prefer a ~ next to the window or next to the aisle?** (on plane) voulez-vous (une place côté) fenêtre ou (une place côté) couloir?; **2** (type, object) gen, Aut siège *m*; (bench-type) banquette *f*; **leather/fabric ~s** sièges en cuir/en tissu; **the back ~** la banquette arrière; **how many ~s do we need to put out in the hall?** combien de sièges est-ce qu'il faut installer dans la salle?; **'take a ~'** (indicating) 'prenez un siège'; **take** ou **have a ~** asseyez-vous; **sit in the front ~** mets-toi devant; **3** GB Pol (in parliament, on committee) siège *m*; **safe/marginal ~** siège sûr/menacé; **to win a ~** gagner un siège; **they won the ~ from the Democrats** ils ont enlevé ce siège aux Démocrates; **the CDU lost seven ~s to the Greens** la CDU a perdu six sièges au profit des Verts; **to keep/lose one's ~** garder/perdre son siège; **to have a ~ on the council** siéger au conseil; **to take up one's ~** entrer en fonction; **4** (part of chair) siège *m*; **5** (location, centre) siège *m*; **~ of government/learning** siège du gouvernement/savoir; **6** (residence) résidence *f* familiale; **country ~** résidence de campagne; **7** Equit **to have a good ~** avoir une bonne assiette; **to keep one's ~** rester en selle; **to lose one's ~** perdre son assiette; **8** euph (bottom) postérieur *m*; **9** (of pants, trousers) fond *m*.

II -seat (*dans composés*) **a 150-~ plane/cinema** un avion/cinéma de 150 places; **a single-~ constituency** GB une circonscription à siège unique.

III *vtr* **1** (assign place to) placer [*person*]; **to ~ sb next to sb** placer qn à côté de qn; **2** (have seats for) **the car ~s five** c'est une voiture à cinq places; **how many does it ~?** (of car) elle a combien de places?; **the table ~s six** c'est une table de six couverts; **the room ~s 30 people** la salle peut accueillir 30 personnes.

IV *v refl* **to ~ oneself** prendre place; **to ~ oneself at the piano/next to sb** prendre place au piano/à côté de qn.

V seated *pp adj* assis; **to be ~ed at** être assis à [*table, desk*]; **is everybody ~ed?** est-ce que tout le monde est assis?; **please remain ~ed** veuillez rester assis.

IDIOMS **to take/occupy a back ~** fig se mettre/se tenir en retrait.

seatbelt /ˈsiːtbelt/ *n* ceinture *f* (de sécurité); **please fasten your ~s** veuillez attacher vos ceintures; **to put on one's ~** mettre sa ceinture; **he wasn't wearing a ~** il n'avait pas mis sa ceinture; **adjustable ~** ceinture réglable.

seat cover *n* Aut housse *f* de siège.

-seater /ˈsiːtə(r)/ (*dans composés*) **a two~** (plane) un avion à deux places; (car) un coupé; **a three/four~** (car) une trois/quatre places; (plane) un trois/quatre places; **a two/three~** (sofa) un (canapé) deux/trois places; **all~ stadium** GB stade *m* sans places debout.

seating /ˈsiːtɪŋ/ **I** *n* **1** (places) places *fpl* assises; **a stadium with ~ for 50,000** un stade de 50 000 places (assises); **to introduce extra ~** ajouter plus de sièges; **2** (arrangement) **I'll organize the ~** je placerai les gens.

II *modif* **~ arrangements** placement *m* des gens; **~ capacity** nombre *m* de places assises; **what is the ~ capacity?** combien y a-t-il de places?; **~ plan** plan *m* de table; **~ requirements** nombre *m* requis de places assises; **the lounge has ~ accommodation for 250 passengers** le hall d'embarquement peut accueillir 250 passagers.

seatmate /ˈsiːtmeɪt/ *n* US voisin/-e *m/f* (*dans les transports en commun*).

sea: **~ trout** *n* truite *f* de mer; **~ urchin** *n* oursin *m*; **~ view** *n* vue *f* sur la mer; **~wall** *n* digue *f*.

seaward /ˈsiːwəd/ **I** *adj* [*side of building*] qui donne sur la mer; [*side of cape, isthmus*] qui fait face au large.

II *adv* (also **~s**) [*fly, move*] vers la mer; [*gaze*] vers le large.

sea: **~way** *n* chenal *m*; **~weed** *n* algue *f* marine; **~worthiness** *n* navigabilité *f*.

seaworthy /ˈsiːwɜːðɪ/ *adj* [*ship, vessel*] qui tient la mer; **to make a vessel ~** vérifier qu'un bateau tient la mer.

sebaceous /sɪˈbeɪʃəs/ *adj* sébacé.

Sebastian /sɪˈbæstɪən/ *pr n* Sébastien.

Sebastopol /sɪˈbæstəpl/ ▶1818 *pr n* Sébastopol.

seborrhoea /ˌsebəˈrɪə/ ▶1354 *n* Med séborrhée *f*.

sebum /ˈsiːbəm/ *n* sébum *m*.

sec /sek/ *n* **1** (*abrév écrite* = **second**) s; **2**○ (short instant) instant *m*; **hang on a ~!** attends un instant!

SEC *n* US (*abrév* = **Securities and Exchange Commission**) commission *f* des opérations de Bourse; cf COB.

SECAM /ˈsiːkæm/ *n* TV (*abrév* = **séquentiel couleur à mémoire**) SECAM *m*; **~ standard** système *m* SECAM.

secant /ˈsiːkənt/ *n* Math sécante *f*.

secateurs /ˌsekəˈtɜːz, ˈsekətɜːz/ *npl* GB sécateur *m*; **a pair of ~** un sécateur.

secede /sɪˈsiːd/ *vi* faire sécession (**from** de).

secession /sɪˈseʃn/ *n* sécession *f* (**from** de).

secessionist /sɪˈseʃənɪst/ *n, adj* sécessionniste (*mf*).

seclude /sɪˈkluːd/ *vtr* isoler (**from** de).

secluded /sɪˈkluːdɪd/ *adj* retiré.

seclusion /sɪˈkluːʒn/ *n* isolement *m* (**from** à l'écart de); **to live in ~** vivre isolé; **in the ~ of one's own home** dans l'intimité de son foyer.

second ▶1096, 1505, 1150 **I** /ˈsekənd/ *n* **1** (unit of time) also Math, Phys seconde *f*; (instant) instant *m*; **the whole thing was over in ~s** tout s'est passé en (l'espace de) quelques secondes; **with (just) ~s to spare** à quelques secondes près; **this won't take a ~** cela ne prendra qu'un instant; **now just a ~!** un instant, là!; **(with)in ~s she was asleep** elle s'est endormie en l'espace de quelques instants; **they should arrive any ~ now** ils devraient arriver d'un instant à l'autre; **we arrived at six o'clock to the ~** nous sommes arrivés à six heures pile; **2** ▶1505 (ordinal number) deuxième *mf*, second/-e *m/f*; **she came a good** ou **close ~** elle ne s'est fait battre que de justesse dans la course; **X was the most popular in the survey, but Y came a close ~** dans le sondage X était le plus populaire mais Y suivait de près; **he came a poor ~** il est arrivé deuxième, mais loin derrière le premier; **his family comes a poor ~ to his desire for success** sa famille passe loin après son désir de réussir; **the problem of crime was seen as ~ only to unemployment** le problème du crime venait juste derrière le chômage; **3** ▶1150 (date) **the ~ of May** le deux mai; **4** GB Univ **upper/lower ~** ≈ licence *f* avec mention bien/assez bien; **5** (also **~ gear**) Aut deuxième *f*, seconde *f*; **in ~** en deuxième or seconde; **6** (defective article) article *m* à défauts; **these plates are (slight) ~s** ce sont des assiettes à défauts; **7** (in boxing, wrestling) soigneur *m*; (in duel) témoin *m*; **~s out (of the ring)!** (in boxing, wrestling) soigneurs, hors du ring!; **8** Mus (interval) seconde *f*.

II○ **seconds** /ˈsekəndz/ *npl* rab○ *m*; **to ask for/have ~s** demander/prendre du rab○.

III /ˈsekənd/ *adj* deuxième, second; **for the ~ time** pour la deuxième fois; **the ~ teeth** les dents définitives; **~ violin** Mus second violon; **he thinks he's a ~ Churchill** il se prend pour un second Churchill; **every ~ day/Monday** un jour/un lundi sur deux; **to have** ou **take a ~ helping (of sth)** reprendre (de qch); **to have a ~ chance to do sth** avoir une nouvelle chance de faire; **you won't get a ~ chance!** (good opportunity) l'occasion ne se représentera pas; (to take exams) tu n'auras pas de deuxième chance; **to ask for a ~ opinion** (from doctor) demander l'opinion d'un autre médecin; (from lawyer) demander l'opinion d'un autre avocat; **I like this one, but can you give me a ~ opinion?** j'aime bien celui-ci, mais qu'en penses-tu?

IV /ˈsekənd/ *adv* **1** (in second place) deuxième; **to come** ou **finish ~** (in race, competition) arriver or finir deuxième or en deuxième position; **I agreed to speak ~** j'ai accepté de parler le deuxième; **to travel ~** voyager en deuxième classe; **the ~ biggest/most beautiful building** le deuxième bâtiment de par sa grandeur/sa beauté; **the ~ oldest in the family** le deuxième de la famille; **his loyalty to the firm comes ~ to** ou **after his personal ambition** sa loyauté envers la société passe après son ambition personnelle; **the fact that he's my father comes ~** le fait qu'il soit mon père est secondaire; **2** (also **secondly**) deuxièmement; **~, I have to say...** deuxièmement, je dois dire...

V *vtr* **1** /ˈsekənd/ (help) gen seconder [*person*]; Sport être le soigneur de [*boxer*]; être le témoin de [*duellist*]; **2** /ˈsekənd/ (support) gen soutenir [*person*]; appuyer [*idea*]; (in debate, election) appuyer [*motion, resolution, vote of thanks*]; **3** /sɪˈkɒnd/ Mil, Comm détacher (**from** de; **to** à).

IDIOMS **every ~ counts** chaque seconde compte; **to be ~ nature** être une seconde nature; **after a while, driving becomes ~ nature** au bout d'un certain temps, conduire devient une seconde nature; **it's ~ nature to him** c'est une seconde nature chez lui; **to be ~ to none** être sans pareil; **to do sth without (giving it) a ~ thought** faire qch sans se poser de questions; **he didn't give them a ~ thought** il ne s'est pas posé de questions à leur sujet; **on ~ thoughts** à la réflexion; **to have ~ thoughts** avoir quelques hésitations or doutes; **to have ~ thoughts about doing** avoir moins envie de faire; **to get one's ~ wind** trouver son second souffle.

secondarily /ˈsekəndrəlɪ, US ˌsekənˈderəlɪ/ *adv* accessoirement.

secondary /ˈsekəndrɪ, US -derɪ/ **I** *n* **1** Med métastase *f*; **2** = **secondary colour**.

II *adj* **1** gen [*consideration, importance, process, effect, cause*] secondaire; [*sense, meaning*] dérivé; **2** Ling [*accent, stress*] secondaire; **3** Psych [*process*] secondaire; **4** Philos [*cause, quality*] second; **~ to sth** moins important que qch; **5** Sch [*education, level*] secondaire; [*teacher*] du secondaire.

secondary: **~ colour** GB, **~ color** US couleur *f* secondaire, couleur *f* binaire; **~ evidence** *n* Jur preuve *f* secondaire; **~ glazing** *n* survitrage *m*; **~ health care** *n* ≈ soins *mpl* hospitaliers; **~ infection** *n* surinfection *f*; **~ modern (school)** *n* GB ≈ collège *m* d'enseignement général; **~ picket** *n* piquet *m* de grève de solidarité; **~ picketing** *n* mise *f* en place de piquets de grève de solidarité; **~ road** *n* route *f* secondaire; **~ school** *n* ≈ école *f* secondaire; **~ sexual characteristic** *n* caractère *m* sexuel secondaire.

second ballot *n* second tour *m*, deuxième tour *m* (du scrutin).

second best **I** *n* **I refuse to settle for** ou **take ~** je refuse de me contenter de pis-aller; **as a ~, I suppose it will do** je suppose que faute de mieux, cela fera l'affaire.

II *adv* **he came off** GB ou **out** US **~** il a été largement battu; **in the choice between quality and price, quality often comes off**

~ quand il faut choisir entre la qualité et le prix, c'est généralement la qualité qui passe après.

second chamber *n* chambre *f* haute.

second class **I** *n* **1** Post ≈ acheminement *m* lent; **2** Rail deuxième classe *f*.

II second-class *adj* **1** Post [*post, mail, stamp*] au tarif lent; **2** Rail [*carriage, ticket*] de deuxième classe; **3** GB Univ **~ degree** ≈ licence *f* obtenue avec mention assez bien; **4** (second rate) [*goods, product, treatment*] de qualité inférieure; **~ citizen** citoyen/-enne *m/f* de seconde zone.

III *adv* Rail [*travel*] en deuxième classe; Post [*send*] au tarif lent.

second: **Second Coming** *n* second avènement *m*; **~ cousin** *n* cousin/-e *m/f* issu/-e de germains; **~ degree** *n* Univ ≈ diplôme *m* de troisième cycle; **~-degree burn** *n* brûlure *f* au deuxième degré; **~-degree murder** *n* US Jur homicide *m* involontaire.

Second Empire **I** *n* Second Empire *m*.

II *modif* [*furniture, decor, style*] Second Empire *inv*.

seconder /ˈsekəndə(r)/ *n* personne *f* qui appuie une motion.

second estate *n* Hist noblesse *f*.

second generation **I** *n* deuxième génération *f*.

II *modif* [*artist, computer*] de la deuxième génération.

second-guess○ /ˌsekəndˈges/ *vtr* anticiper [*thoughts, reaction*]; **to ~ sb** anticiper les actions de qn.

second hand /ˈsekəndhænd/ **I** *n* (on watch, clock) trotteuse *f*.

II second-hand /ˌsekəndˈhænd/ *adj* [*clothes, car, goods*] d'occasion; [*market*] de l'occasion; [*news, information, report*] de seconde main; [*opinion*] d'emprunt; **~ dealer** vendeur/-euse *m/f* d'objets d'occasion; **~ car dealer** ou **salesman** vendeur/-euse *m/f* de voitures d'occasion; **~ value** valeur *f* à la revente.

III *adv* [*buy*] d'occasion; [*find out, hear*] indirectement.

second in command ▶ **1612** *n* **1** Mil commandant *m* en second; **2** gen second *m* adjoint.

second: **~ language** *n* seconde langue *f*; **~ lieutenant** ▶ **1612** *n* Mil sous-lieutenant *m*.

secondly /ˈsekəndlɪ/ *adv* deuxièmement.

second mate ▶ **1612** *n* Naut deuxième lieutenant *m*.

secondment /sɪˈkɒndmənt/ *n* détachement *m* (**from** de; **to** à); **on ~** en détachement.

second mortgage *n* hypothèque *f* de second rang.

second name *n* **1** (surname) nom *m* de famille; **2** (second forename) deuxième prénom *m*.

second officer *n* Naut ▶ **second mate**.

second person *n* Ling deuxième personne *f*; **in the ~ singular/plural** à la deuxième personne du singulier/du pluriel.

second: **~-rate** *adj* [*actor, writer, novel, institution, mind*] de second ordre; [*product*] de qualité inférieure; **~-rater** *n* médiocre *mf*; **~ reading** *n* Pol seconde lecture *f*.

second sight *n* double vue *f*; **to have (the gift of) ~** avoir le don de double vue.

second strike Mil **I** *n* deuxième frappe *f*.

II *modif* [*capability, missile, strategy*] de deuxième frappe.

second string *n* Sport recours *m*.

secrecy /ˈsiːkrəsɪ/ *n* secret *m*; **in ~** en secret; **why all the ~?** pourquoi tous ces secrets?; **the ~ surrounding their finances** le secret qui entoure leurs finances; **there's no need for ~** ce n'est pas un secret; **she's been sworn to ~** on lui a fait jurer le secret; **a veil/an air of ~** un voile/un air de mystère.

secret /ˈsiːkrɪt/ **I** *n* **1** (unknown thing) secret *m*; **to tell sb a ~** confier un secret à qn; **to keep a ~** garder un secret; **to let sb in on a ~** mettre qn dans le secret; **I make no ~ of my membership of the party** je ne fais pas mystère de mon appartenance au parti; **it's an open ~ that...** tout le monde sait que...; **there's no ~ about who/when/how etc** tout le monde sait qui/quand/comment etc; **I have no ~s from my sister** je n'ai pas de secrets pour ma sœur; **2** (key factor) secret *m* (**of** de).

II *adj* [*passage, meeting, ingredient*] secret/-ète; [*contributor*] anonyme; [*admirer, admiration*] secret/-ète; **to keep sth ~ from sb** cacher qch à qn; **to be a ~ drinker** boire en cachette.

III in secret *adv phr* gen en secret; Jur à huis clos.

secret agent *n* agent *m* secret.

secretaire /ˌsekrɪˈteə(r)/ *n* secrétaire *m*.

secretarial /ˌsekrəˈteərɪəl/ *adj* [*course, skills, work*] de secrétaire; [*college*] de secrétariat; **~ staff** personnel *m* de secrétariat.

secretariat /ˌsekrəˈteərɪət/ *n* secrétariat *m*.

secretary /ˈsekrətrɪ, US -rəterɪ/ ▶ **1692** *n* **1** Admin secrétaire *mf* (**to sb** de qn); **general/regional ~** secrétaire général/régional; **party ~** Hist (in USSR) secrétaire du parti (communiste); **personal/private ~** secrétaire personnel/-elle/privé; **2 Secretary** GB Pol **Foreign/Home/Defence ~** ministre *m* des Affaires étrangères/de l'Intérieur/de la Défense; **Environment/Northern Ireland ~** ou **~ of State for the Environment/for Northern Ireland** ministre *m* de l'Environnement/pour l'Irlande du Nord; **3 Secretary** US Pol **Defense Secretary** ministre *m* de la Défense; **Secretary of State** ministre *m* des Affaires étrangères; **4** US (desk) secrétaire *m*.

secretary: **~ bird** *n* serpentaire *m*; **~-general** ▶ **1692** *n* secrétaire *m* général.

secrete /sɪˈkriːt/ *vtr* **1** Biol, Med sécréter [*fluid*]; **2** (hide) cacher.

secretion /sɪˈkriːʃn/ *n* **1** Biol, Med sécrétion *f*; **2** (hiding) action *f* de cacher.

secretive /ˈsiːkrətɪv/ *adj* [*person, nature, organization*] secret/-ète; [*expression, conduct*] mystérieux/-ieuse; [*smile*] énigmatique; **to be ~ about sth** faire un mystère de qch.

secretively /ˈsiːkrətɪvlɪ/ *adv* [*behave, smile*] (mysteriously) énigmatiquement; (furtively) furtivement.

secretiveness /ˈsiːkrətɪvnɪs/ *n* air *m* de mystère.

secretly /ˈsiːkrɪtlɪ/ *adv* secrètement.

secret: **~ police** *n* police *f* secrète; **~ service** *n* services *mpl* secrets; **Secret Service** *n* US services *mpl* chargés de la protection du président; **~ society** *n* société *f* secrète; **~ weapon** *n* lit, fig arme *f* secrète.

sect /sekt/ *n* secte *f*.

sectarian /sekˈteərɪən/ *n, adj* sectaire (*mf*).

sectarianism /sekˈteərɪənɪzəm/ *n* sectarisme *m*.

section /ˈsekʃn/ **I** *n* **1** (part) (of train, aircraft, town, forest, area) partie *f*; (of pipe, tunnel, road, river) tronçon *m*; (of object, kit) élément *m*; (of orange, grapefruit) quartier *m*; (of public, population, group) tranche *f*; **women's ~s** Pol sections *fpl* féminines; **2** (department) (of company, office, department, government) service *m*; (of library, shop) rayon *m*; **computer/consular ~** service *m* informatique/consulaire; **3** (subdivision) (of act, bill, report) article *m*; (of newspaper) rubrique *f*; **under ~ 24** aux termes de l'article 24; **sports/books ~** rubrique *f* sportive/littéraire; **4** (passage) (of book) passage *m* (**on** sur); (larger) partie *f* (**on** qui traite de); **there's a ~ on verbs at the end** il y a un chapitre sur les verbes à la fin; **5** Mil groupe *m*; **6** Biol, Geol lamelle *f*; **7** Math section *f*; **8** Med sectionnement *m*; **9** Rail (part of network) canton *m* (*de voie ferrée*); **10** US Rail (of sleeping car) compartiment-couchettes *m*; **11** US Rail (relief train) train *m* supplémentaire.

II *vtr* **1** (divide) sectionner [*document, text*]; segmenter [*computer screen*]; **2** Med (in surgery) sectionner; **3** GB Med (confine to mental hospital) décider l'internement de [*person*].

■ **section off**: **~ off [sth], ~ [sth] off** séparer [*part, area*].

sectional /ˈsekʃənl/ *adj* **1** (factional) [*interest*] catégoriel/-ielle; [*hatred, discontent*] de groupe; **2** (in section) [*drawing, view*] en coupe; **3** US [*bookcase, sofa*] à éléments.

sectionalism /ˈsekʃənəlɪzəm/ *n* US péj régionalisme *m*.

section: **~ gang** *n* US équipe *f* de cheminots; **~ hand** ▶ **1692** *n* US cantonnier *m*; **~ mark** *n* symbole *m* du paragraphe.

sector /ˈsektə(r)/ *n* (all contexts) secteur *m*; **public/private ~** secteur *m* public/privé.

sectorial /sekˈtɔːrɪəl/ *adj* [*analysis etc*] sectoriel/-ielle.

secular /ˈsekjʊlə(r)/ *adj* [*politics, law, society, education*] laïque; [*belief, music*] profane; [*priest, power*] séculier/-ière.

secularism /ˈsekjʊlərɪzəm/ *n* (doctrine) laïcisme *m*; (political system) laïcité *f*.

secularization /ˌsekjʊləraɪˈzeɪʃn, US -rɪˈz-/ *n* (of society, education) sécularisation *f*, laïcisation *f*; (of church property) sécularisation *f*.

secularize /ˈsekjʊləraɪz/ *vtr* séculariser, laïciser [*society, education*]; séculariser [*church property*].

secure /sɪˈkjʊə(r)/ **I** *adj* **1** (stable, not threatened) [*job, marriage, income, financial position*] stable; [*basis, base, foundation*] solide; [*world record, sporting position*] assuré; [*investment*] sûr; **2** (safe) [*hiding place, route*] sûr; **~ hospital** hôpital-prison *m* de haute sécrité; **to be ~ against sth** être à l'abri de qch; **3** (reliable) [*padlock, bolt, nail, knot*] solide; [*structure, ladder*] stable; [*foothold, handhold*] sûr; [*rope*] bien attaché; [*door, window*] bien fermé; **to make a rope ~** bien attacher une corde; **to make a door ~** bien fermer une porte; **4** Psych [*feeling*] de sécurité; [*family, background*] sécurisant; **to feel ~** se sentir en sécurité; **to be ~ in the knowledge that** avoir la certitude que.

II *vtr* **1** (procure, obtain) obtenir [*agreement, promise, job, majority, money, release, conviction, visa, right, victory*]; atteindre [*objective*]; **2** (make firm, safe) bien attacher [*rope*]; bien fermer [*door, window*]; fixer [*wheel*]; stabiliser [*ladder*]; **3** (make safe) protéger [*house, camp, flank*]; assurer [*position, future, job*]; **4** Fin garantir [*loan, debt*] (**against, on** sur).

secure: **~d bond** *n* obligation *f* garantie; **~d loan** *n* emprunt *m* garanti.

securely /sɪˈkjʊəlɪ/ *adv* **1** (carefully) [*fasten, fix, tie*] solidement; [*wrap, tuck, pin*] soigneusement; **2** (safely) [*lock up, hide, invest, store*] en sûreté; **3** fig [*founded, settled, rooted*] bel et bien; **it is not very ~ founded** ce n'est pas très fermement fondé.

secure unit *n* (in children's home) *section surveillée dans une maison de rééducation*; (in psychiatric hospital) quartier *m* de haute sécurité (*dans un hôpital psychiatrique*).

securities /sɪˈkjʊərətɪz/ **I** *npl* Fin titres *mpl*.

II *modif* Fin [*company, market, trading*] des titres.

securitization /sɪˌkjʊərɪtaɪˈzeɪʃn/ *n* Fin titrisation *f*.

securitize /sɪˈkjʊərɪtaɪz/ *vtr* Fin titriser.

security /sɪˈkjʊərətɪ/ **I** *n* **1** (safe state or feeling) (of person, child, financial position, investment) sécurité *f*; **~ of employment**, **job ~** sécurité de l'emploi; **2** (measures) (for site, prison, nation, VIP) sécurité *f*; **to tighten ~** renforcer la sécurité; **state** ou **national ~** sûreté *f* de l'État; **3** (department) service *m* de sécurité; **to call ~** appeler la sécurité; **4** (guarantee) garantie *f* (**on** sur); **to take/leave sth as ~** prendre/laisser qch en garantie; **to stand ~ for sb** se porter garant de qn; **5** Fin (*souvent pl*) valeur *f* (boursière), titre *m*.

II *modif* [*arrangements, badge, barrier, camera, check, code, device, door, lock, measures, standards*] de sécurité; [*firm, staff*] de surveillance.

security: **~ blanket** *n* Psych doudou○ *m*, objet *m* transitionnel spec; **~ clearance** *n* habilitation *f* sécuritaire; **Security Council** *n* Conseil *m* de sécurité; **~ forces** *npl* forces *fpl* de sécurité; **~ guard** ▶ 1692 *n* garde *m* sécurité, vigile *m*; **~ leak** *n* fuite *f* (*d'information*); **~ officer** ▶ 1692 *n* responsable *mf* de la sécurité; **~ risk** *n* (person) danger *m* pour la sécurité; **~ van** *n* GB fourgon *m* blindé (*pour le transport de fonds*).

sedan /sɪˈdæn/ *n* US berline *f*.

sedan chair *n* chaise *f* à porteurs.

sedate /sɪˈdeɪt/ **I** *adj* [*person*] posé; [*lifestyle, pace*] tranquille; [*décor*] propret/-ette.
II *vtr* mettre [qn] sous calmants [*patient*].
III sedated *pp adj* sous calmants.

sedately /sɪˈdeɪtlɪ/ *adv* tranquillement.

sedateness /sɪˈdeɪtnɪs/ (of attitude) *n* pondération *f*; (of manner) air *m* posé.

sedation /sɪˈdeɪʃn/ *n* Med sédation *f*; **to be under ~** être sous calmants.

sedative /ˈsedətɪv/ **I** *n* sédatif *m*, calmant *m*.
II *adj* [*effect, drug*] sédatif/-ive.

sedentary /ˈsedntrɪ, US -terɪ/ *adj* [*job, lifestyle, population*] sédentaire.

sedge /sedʒ/ *n* laiche *f*, carex *m* spec.

sedge warbler *n* Zool phragmite *m* des joncs.

sediment /ˈsedɪmənt/ *n* gen dépôt *m*; Geol sédiment *m*; Wine lie *f*.

sedimentary /ˌsedɪˈmentrɪ, US -terɪ/ *adj* sédimentaire.

sedimentation /ˌsedɪmenˈteɪʃn/ *n* Geol, Chem sédimentation *f*.

sedition /sɪˈdɪʃn/ *n* sédition *f*.

seditious /sɪˈdɪʃəs/ *adj* [*view, activity*] séditieux/-ieuse.

seduce /sɪˈdjuːs, US -ˈduːs/ *vtr* **1** (sexually) [*person*] séduire; **2** fig [*idea, project etc*] tenter, attirer; **to ~ sb into doing** persuader qn de faire; **to be ~d into doing** se laisser convaincre de faire; **to ~ sb away from sth** détourner qn de qch.

seducer /sɪˈdjuːsə(r), US -ˈduːs/ *n* séducteur *m*.

seduction /sɪˈdʌkʃn/ *n* **1** (act of seducing) séduction *f*; **2** (attractive quality) attrait *m* (**of** de).

seductive /sɪˈdʌktɪv/ *adj* [*person*] séduisant; [*argument, proposal*] alléchant; [*smile*] aguicheur/-euse.

seductively /sɪˈdʌktɪvlɪ/ *adv* [*smile, murmur*] d'une manière séduisante.

seductiveness /sɪˈdʌktɪvnɪs/ *n* pouvoir *m* de séduction.

seductress /sɪˈdʌktrɪs/ *n* séductrice *f*.

sedulous /ˈsedjʊləs, US ˈsedʒʊləs/ *adj* sout [*student*] zélé; [*devotion*] assidu; [*attention*] empressé.

sedulously /ˈsedjʊləslɪ, US ˈsedʒʊləslɪ/ *adv* sout [*strive*] assidûment; [*guard*] avec zèle.

see /siː/ **I** *n* (of bishop) évêché *m*; (of archbishop) archevêché *m*.
II *vtr* (*prét* **saw**, *pp* **seen**) **1** (perceive) voir [*object, person*]; **to ~ sb/sth with one's own eyes** voir qn/qch de ses propres yeux; **to ~ that** voir que; **to ~ where/how etc** voir où/comment etc; **you'll ~ how it's done** tu verras comment c'est fait; **to ~ sb do sth** ou **doing sth** voir qn faire qch; **I saw him steal** ou **stealing a car** je l'ai vu voler une voiture; **we didn't ~ anything** nous n'avons rien vu; **I saw something in the dark** j'ai vu quelque chose dans l'obscurité; **there's nothing to ~** il n'y a rien à voir; **there's nobody to be seen** il n'y a personne en vue; **I couldn't ~ her in the crowd** je ne la voyais pas dans la foule; **can you see him?** est-ce que tu le vois?; **I could ~ (that) she'd been crying** je voyais bien qu'elle avait pleuré; **I can ~ her coming down the road** je la vois qui arrive sur la route; **there was going to be trouble**: **I could ~ it coming** ou **I could ~ it a mile off** il allait y avoir des problèmes: je le sentais venir; **I don't like to ~ you so unhappy** je n'aime pas te voir si malheureux; **I hate to ~ an animal in pain** je déteste voir souffrir les animaux; **I don't know what you ~ in him**○ je ne sais pas ce que tu lui trouves○; **he must ~ something attractive in her**○ il doit lui trouver quelque chose d'attirant; **I must be ~ing things!** j'ai des visions!; **to ~ one's way** voir où on va; **to ~ one's way (clear) to doing sth** trouver le moyen de faire qch; **2** (look at) (watch) voir [*film, programme*]; (inspect) voir [*accounts, work*]; **I've seen the play twice** j'ai vu cette pièce deux fois; **~ page 156** voir page 156; **~ over(leaf)** voir au verso; **3** (go to see, visit) voir [*person, country, building*]; **to ~ the Parthenon** voir le Parthénon; **to ~ a doctor about sth** voir un médecin au sujet de qch; **what did you want to ~ me about?** pourquoi vouliez-vous me voir?; **I'm ~ing a psychiatrist** je vais chez un psychiatre; **to ~ the sights** faire du tourisme; **4** (meet up with) voir [*person*]; **I'll be ~ing him in June** je le verrai en juin; **I happened to ~ her in the post office** je l'ai vue par hasard à la poste; **they ~ a lot of each other** ils se voient souvent; **~ you**○**!** salut○!; **~ you next week/(on) Sunday**○**!** à la semaine prochaine/à dimanche!; **he's ~ing a married woman** il fréquente une femme mariée; **5** (receive) recevoir [*person*]; **the doctor/headmaster will ~ you now** le docteur/directeur va vous recevoir; **6** (understand) voir [*relevance, advantage, problem*]; comprendre [*joke*]; **to ~ sth from sb's point of view** voir qch du point de vue de qn; **can't you ~ that...?** ne vois-tu donc pas que...?; **to ~ how/where...** voir comment/où...; **do you ~ what I mean?** tu vois ce que je veux dire?; **7** (look upon, consider) voir; **I ~ things differently now** je vois les choses différemment maintenant; **to ~ sb as** considérer qn comme [*leader, hero*]; **I ~ it as an opportunity** je pense que c'est une occasion à saisir; **I ~ it as an insult** je prends ça pour une insulte; **not to ~ sb/sth as...** ne pas croire que qn/qch soit...; **I don't ~ it as a problem of poverty** je ne crois pas que ce soit un problème lié à la pauvreté; **I don't ~ him as honest** je ne crois pas qu'il soit honnête; **8** (note, observe) voir (**that** que); **as we have already seen,...** comme nous l'avons déjà vu,...; **it can be seen from this example that...** cet exemple nous montre que...; **9** (envisage, visualize) **I can't ~ sb/sth doing** je ne pense pas que qn/qch puisse faire; **I can't ~ the situation changing** je ne pense pas que la situation puisse changer; **I can ~ a time when this country will be independent** je peux imaginer qu'un jour ce pays sera indépendant; **10** (make sure) **to ~ (to it) that...** veiller à ce que... (+ *subj*); **~ (to it) that the children are in bed by nine** veillez à ce que les enfants soient couchés à neuf heures; **~ that you do!** (angrily) tu as intérêt à le faire!; **11** (find out) voir; **to ~ how/if/when etc** voir comment/si/quand etc; **I'm going to ~ what she's doing/how she's doing** je vais voir ce qu'elle fait/comment elle se débrouille; **I'll have to ~ if I can get permission** il faudra que je voie si je peux obtenir la permission; **it remains to be seen whether** ou **if...** reste à voir si...; **12** (witness) voir; (experience) connaître; **a period which saw enormous changes/the birth of computer science** une période qui a vu d'énormes changements/naître l'informatique; **next year will ~ the completion of the road** la route sera terminée l'année prochaine; **I never thought I'd ~ the day that he'd admit to being wrong!** je ne pensais vraiment pas que je le verrais un jour reconnaître qu'il avait tort!; **we'll never ~ her like again** jamais nous ne reverrons sa pareille; **13** (accompany) **to ~ sb to the door** raccompagner qn (jusqu'à la sortie); **to ~ sb to the station** accompagner qn à la gare; **to ~ sb home** raccompagner qn chez lui; **14** (in betting) **I'll ~ your £10** j'égalise à 10 livres; **I'll ~ you for £10** je parie 10 livres.
III *vi* (*prét* **saw**, *pp* **seen**) **1** (with eyes) voir; **I can't ~** je ne vois rien; **~ for yourself** voyez vous-même; **as you can ~** comme vous pouvez le voir; **to ~ beyond sth** voir au-delà de qch; **try to ~ beyond your own immediate concerns** tâche de voir plus loin que tes préoccupations immédiates; **so I ~** c'est ce que je vois; **move over**: **I can't ~ through you** pousse-toi! tu n'es pas transparent!; **some animals can ~ in the dark** certains animaux y voient la nuit; **you can ~ for miles** on y voit à des kilomètres; **2** (understand) voir; **do you ~?** tu vois?; **yes, I ~** oui, je vois; **now I ~** maintenant, je comprends; **can't you ~?**: **the situation is different now** tu ne vois donc pas que la situation n'est plus la même?; **as far as I can ~** autant que je puisse en juger; **3** (check, find out) **I'll go and ~** je vais voir; **we'll just have to wait and ~** il ne nous reste plus qu'à attendre; **4** (think, consider) **I'll have to ~** il faut que je réfléchisse; **let's ~**, **let me ~** voyons (un peu).
IV *v refl* (*prét* **saw**, *pp* **seen**) **to ~ oneself** lit, fig se voir; **he saw himself already elected** il se voyait déjà élu; **I can't ~ myself as** ou **being...** je ne pense pas que je vais être...; **I can't ~ myself being chosen/as a famous ballerina** je ne pense pas que je vais être choisi/devenir une ballerine célèbre.
IDIOMS **I'll ~ you right**○ je ne te laisserai pas tomber; **now I've seen it all!** j'aurai tout vu!
■ **see about**: **~ about [sth]** s'occuper de; **we'll soon ~ about that**○**!** iron c'est ce qu'on va voir!; **to ~ about doing** penser à faire.
■ **see off**: **~ [sb] off**, **~ [off] sb** **1** (say goodbye to) dire au revoir à qn; **we saw him off at the station** nous lui avons dit au revoir à la gare; **2** (throw out) **the drunk was seen off the premises** on a mis l'ivrogne à la porte; **to ~ sb off the premises** veiller à ce que qn quitte les lieux.
■ **see out**: ¶ **~ [sth] out**, **~ out [sth]** **we have enough coal to ~ the winter out** nous avons assez de charbon pour passer l'hiver; ¶ **~ [sb] out** raccompagner [qn] à la porte; **I'll ~ myself out** (in small building) je m'en vais mais ne vous dérangez pas; (in big building) je trouverai la sortie, ne vous dérangez pas.
■ **see through**: ¶ **~ through [sth]** déceler [*deception, lie*]; **it was easy enough to ~ through the excuse** c'était évident que c'était une fausse excuse; **I can ~ through your little game**○**!** je vois clair dans ton petit jeu!; ¶ **~ through [sb]** percer [qn] à jour; ¶ **~ [sth] through** mener [qch] à bonne fin; ¶ **~ [sb] through**: **there's enough food to ~ us through the week** il y a assez à manger pour tenir toute la semaine; **this money will ~ you through** cet argent te dépannera.
■ **see to**: **~ to [sth]** s'occuper de [*person, task*]; **there is no cake left, the children saw to that!** il ne reste plus de gâteau, les enfants se sont chargés de le faire disparaître!

seed /siːd/ **I** *n* **1** Bot, Agric (of plant) graine *f*; (fruit pip) pépin *m*; **2** ¢ Agric (for sowing) semences *fpl*; Culin graines *fpl*; **to go** ou **run to ~** lit [*plant*] monter en graine; fig [*person*] se ramollir; [*organization, country*] être en déclin; **3** fig (beginning) germes *mpl*; **the ~(s) of discontent/hope** les germes du mécontentement/de l'espoir; **the ~s of doubt were sown in her mind** le doute avait germé dans son esprit; **4** Sport tête *f* de série; **the top ~** la tête de série numéro

un; **the fifth** ou **number five ~** la tête de série numéro cinq; **5‡** (semen) semence *f*; **6‡** (descendants) progéniture *f*.
II *vtr* **1** (sow) ensemencer [*field, lawn*] (**with** de); **2** (also **deseed**) épépiner [*grape, raisin*]; **3** Sport classer [qn] tête de série; **to be ~ed sixth** ou (**number**) **six** être classé tête de série numéro six; **a ~ed player** une tête de série; **4** Meteorol ensemencer [*clouds*].
III *vi* [*plant*] monter en graine.

seedbed /ˈsiːdbed/ *n* **1** lit semis *m*; **2** fig pépinière *f*.

seed: **~ box** *n* = **seed tray**; **~cake** *n* gâteau *m* au carvi; **~ corn** *n* lit blé *m* de semence; fig germes *mpl*.

seeder /ˈsiːdə(r)/ *n* semoir *m*.

seedily /ˈsiːdɪlɪ/ *adv* [*dress, live*] de façon minable.

seediness /ˈsiːdɪnɪs/ *n* **1** (shabbiness) aspect *m* minable; **2** (sordidness) caractère *m* sordide.

seeding /ˈsiːdɪŋ/ *n* **1** Agric ensemencement *m*; **2** Sport classement *m* des têtes de série.

seeding machine *n* semoir *m* mécanique.

seed leaf *n* cotylédon *m*.

seedless /ˈsiːdlɪs/ *adj* sans pépins.

seedling /ˈsiːdlɪŋ/ *n* plant *m*.

seed merchant ▶ **1692** *n* (person) grainetier/-ière *m/f*; **~'s** (**shop**) graineterie *f*.

seed: **~ money** *n* Fin capitaux *mpl* de lancement; **~ oyster** *n* naissain *m* d'huîtres; **~ pearl** *n* perle *f* de très petite dimension; **~ pod** *n* péricarpe *m*; **~ potato** *n* pomme *f* de terre de semence; **~ tray** *n* germoir *m*.

seedy /ˈsiːdɪ/ *adj* **1** (shabby) [*hotel, street*] miteux/-euse; [*person*] minable; **2** (disreputable) [*activity, person*] louche; [*area, club*] mal famé; **3**○ (ill) patraque○, indisposé; **to feel ~** se sentir patraque○.

seeing /ˈsiːɪŋ/ *conj* **~ that**, **~ as** étant donné que, vu que; **~ that** ou **as they can't swim, it's not a good idea** étant donné ou vu qu'ils ne savent pas nager, ce n'est pas une bonne idée; **~ as how she doesn't live here anymore**○ vu qu'elle n'habite plus ici.

seek /siːk/ (*prét, pp* **sought**) **I** *vtr* **1** (try to obtain, wish to have) chercher [*agreement, asylum, confrontation, means, promotion, refuge, solution*]; demander [*advice, help, permission, public inquiry, backing, redress*]; **to ~ revenge** chercher à se venger; **to ~ sb's approval/a second term of office** chercher à obtenir l'approbation de qn/un second mandat; **to ~ to do** chercher à faire, tenter de faire; **I do not ~ to do** je ne cherche pas à faire; **to ~ one's fortune** chercher fortune; **2** (look for) [*police, employer, person*] rechercher [*person, object*]; **'sporty 45-year-old divorcee ~s similar'** Journ 'femme divorcée, 45 ans, sportive, cherche âme sœur'.
II **-seeking** (*dans composés*) en quête de (*before n*).
III *vi* **to ~ for** ou **after sth** rechercher qch.
■ **seek out**: **~ out [sth/sb]**, **~ [sth/sb] out** aller chercher, dénicher; **to ~ out and destroy** Mil repérer et détruire.

seeker /ˈsiːkə(r)/ *n* **~ after** ou **for sth** personne *f* en quête de qch.

seem /siːm/ *vi* **1** (give impression) sembler; (in less formal French) avoir l'air; **he ~s happy/sad** il a l'air heureux/triste; **he ~ed disappointed** il a semblé déçu; **the statistics/experiments ~ to indicate that**... les statistiques/expériences semblent indiquer que...; **there ~s to be a fault in the generator** il semble y avoir un problème dans le générateur; **he ~s to be looking for/to have lost**... on dirait qu'il cherche/qu'il a perdu...; **it would ~ so/not** on dirait que oui/non; **the whole house ~ed to shake** on aurait dit que toute la maison tremblait; **things ~ to be a lot better between them now** ça a l'air d'aller bien mieux entre eux maintenant; **things are not always what they ~** les apparences sont souvent trompeuses; **how does she ~ today?** comment va-t-elle aujourd'hui?; **2** (have impression) **it ~s to me that**... il me semble que... (+ *indic*); **there ~ to me to be two possibilities** il me semble qu'il y a deux possibilités; **it ~s/it very much ~s as if** ou **as though** il semble/semble fort que (+ *subj*); **I ~ to have done** j'ai l'impression que j'ai fait; **I ~ to have offended him** j'ai l'impression que je l'ai vexé; **I ~ to have forgotten my money** je crois que j'ai oublié mon argent; **I ~ to remember I left it on the table** je crois me rappeler que je l'ai laissé sur la table; **it ~s hours since we left** on dirait qu'il y a des heures que nous sommes partis; **that would ~ to be the right thing to do** j'ai l'impression que c'est ce qu'il faut faire; **there doesn't ~ to be any solution** il semble qu'il n'y ait aucune solution; **there ~s to be some mistake** il semble qu'il y ait erreur; **it ~ed like a good idea at the time** cela avait l'air d'une bonne idée; **3** (expressing criticism or sarcasm) **he/she ~s to think that**... il/elle a l'air de croire que...; **they don't ~ to realize that**... ils n'ont pas l'air de se rendre compte que...; **you ~ to have forgotten this point** tu sembles avoir oublié ce détail; (from evidence) **they haven't, it ~s, reached a decision yet** ils ne sont pas encore arrivés à une décision apparemment; **it ~s that sugar is bad for you** apparemment cela vous fait du mal de manger du sucre; **what ~s to be the problem?** quel est le problème?; **4** (despite trying) **he can't ~ to do** on dirait qu'il n'arrive pas à faire; **I just can't ~ to do** je n'arrive pas à faire.

seeming /ˈsiːmɪŋ/ *adj* [*ease, lack*] apparent.

seemingly /ˈsiːmɪŋlɪ/ *adv* [*unaware, oblivious*] apparemment.

seemliness /ˈsiːmlɪnɪs/ *n* sout (of behaviour) bienséance *f*; (of dress) décence *f*.

seemly /ˈsiːmlɪ/ *adj* sout [*conduct*] bienséant; [*dress*] décent; **it would be more ~ to**... ça serait plus convenable de...

seen /siːn/ *pp* ▶ **see**.

seep /siːp/ *vi* suinter; **to ~ out of sth** suinter de qch; **to ~ into/under sth** s'infiltrer dans/sous qch; **to ~ away** s'écouler; **to ~ through sth** [*water, gas*] s'infiltrer à travers qch; [*light*] filtrer à travers qch; **the blood ~ed through the bandages** le sang suintait à travers le pansement.

seepage /ˈsiːpɪdʒ/ *n* (trickle) suintement *m*; (leak) (from container, tank) fuite *f*; (drainage into structure, soil) infiltration *f* (**into** dans).

seer /ˈsiːə(r), sɪə(r)/ *n* voyant/-e *m/f*.

seersucker /ˈsɪəsʌkə(r)/ *n* Tex seersucker *m*.

seesaw /ˈsiːsɔː/ **I** *n* lit tapecul *m*; fig (motion) va-et-vient *m inv*.
II *vi* lit faire du tapecul; fig [*price, rate*] osciller; **the fight/debate ~ed** l'avantage du combat/débat allait de l'un à l'autre.

seethe /siːð/ *vi* **1** [*water, sea*] bouillonner; **2** [*person*] **to ~ with rage/impatience** bouillir de colère/d'impatience; **he was seething** il était furibond; **3** (teem) grouiller; **the streets were seething with tourists** les rues grouillaient de touristes; **to ~ with activity** être en effervescence; **a country seething with unrest** un pays en proie à l'agitation.

see-through /ˈsiːθruː/ *adj* transparent.

segment I /ˈsegmənt/ *n* **1** Anat, Comput, Math, Ling, Zool segment *m*; **2** (of economy, market) secteur *m*; (of population, vote) part *f*; **3** (of orange) quartier *m*.
II /segˈment/ *vtr* segmenter [*market, surface*]; couper [qch] en quartiers [*orange*].

segmental /segˈmentl/ *adj* **1** Zool segmentaire; **2** Ling segmental.

segmentation /ˌsegmenˈteɪʃn/ *n* segmentation *f*.

segregate /ˈsegrɪgeɪt/ *vtr* **1** (separate) [*government, policy*] séparer [*races, sexes, fans*] (**from** de); **to ~ pupils by ability/sex** séparer les élèves en fonction des capacités/du sexe; **2** (isolate) isoler [*patient, prisoner*] (**from** de); **to ~ sb from society** exclure qn de la société.

segregated /ˈsegrəgeɪtɪd/ *adj* [*education, parliament, society*] ségrégationniste; [*area, school*] où la ségrégation raciale (or religieuse) est en vigueur; [*facilities*] séparé.

segregation /ˌsegrɪˈgeɪʃn/ *n* (of races, religions, social groups) ségrégation *f* (**from** de); (of rivals) séparation *f*; (of prisoners) isolement *m* (**from** de).

segregationist /ˌsegrɪˈgeɪʃənɪst/ Pol *n, adj* ségrégationniste (*mf*).

seine /seɪn/ **I** *n* (also **~ net**) Fishg seine *f*, senne *f*.
II **Seine** ▶ **1644** *pr n* Geog **the** (**river**) **Seine** la Seine.

Seine-et-Marne ▶ **1163** *pr n* Seine-et-Marne *f*; **in/to ~** en Seine-et-Marne.

Seine-Maritime ▶ **1163** *pr n* Seine-Maritime *f*; **in/to ~** en Seine-Maritime.

Seine-Saint-Denis ▶ **1163** *pr n* Seine-Saint-Denis *f*; **in/to ~** en Seine-Saint-Denis.

seismic /ˈsaɪzmɪk/ *adj* sismique.

seismograph /ˈsaɪzməgrɑːf, US -græf/ *n* sismographe *m*.

seismography /saɪzˈmɒgrəfɪ/ *n* sismographie *f*.

seismologist /ˌsaɪzˈmɒlədʒɪst/ ▶ **1692** *n* sismologue *mf*.

seismology /saɪzˈmɒlədʒɪ/ *n* sismologie *f*.

seismometer /saɪzˈmɒmɪtə(r)/ *n* = **seismograph**.

seize /siːz/ **I** *vtr* **1** lit (take hold of) saisir [*person, object*]; **to ~ sb around the waist** saisir qn par la taille; **to ~ hold of** se saisir de [*person*]; s'emparer de [*object*]; sauter sur [*idea*]; **2** fig (grasp) saisir [*opportunity, moment*]; prendre [*initiative*]; **to be ~d by** être pris de [*emotion, pain, fit*]; **3** Mil, Pol (capture) s'emparer de [*territory, hostage, prisoner, installation, power*]; prendre [*control*]; **4** Jur saisir [*arms, drugs, property*]; appréhender [*person*].
II *vi* [*engine, mechanism*] se gripper.
■ **seize on**, **seize upon**: **~ on [sth]** sauter sur [*idea, suggestion, offer, error*].
■ **seize up** [*engine, mechanism*] se gripper; [*limb, back*] se bloquer.

seizure /ˈsiːʒə(r)/ *n* **1** (taking) (of territory, installation, power, control) prise *f*; (of arms, drugs, goods, property) saisie *f*; (of person) (legal) arrestation *f*; (illegal) capture *f*; (of hostage) prise *f*; **2** Med, fig attaque *f*; **to have a ~** avoir une attaque.

seldom /ˈseldəm/ *adv* rarement, ne... guère... fml; **I ~ hear from him** j'ai rarement or je n'ai guère fml de ses nouvelles; **~ have I seen such a good film** j'ai rarement vu un aussi bon film; **~ if ever** rarement, pour ne pas dire jamais.

select /sɪˈlekt/ **I** *adj* [*group, audience*] privilégié; [*hotel, restaurant*] chic *inv*, sélect; [*area*] chic *inv*, cossu; **a ~ few** seulement quelques privilégiés.
II *vtr* sélectionner [*team, candidate*] (**from, from among** parmi); choisir, sélectionner [*item, gift etc*] (**from, from among** parmi).
III **selected** *pp adj* [*poems, letters*] choisi; [*candidate, country, question, materials*] sélectionné; [*ingredients*] de premier choix; **in ~ed stores** dans certains magasins; **taxes on ~ed imports** des taxes sur certains produits importés; **to ~ed customers** à un certain nombre de clients privilégiés; **pilot programmes in ~ed areas** des programmes pilotes dans des zones-test.

select committee *n* commission *f* d'enquête.

selectee /ˌsɪlekˈtiː/ *n* US Mil appelé *m* du contingent.

selection /sɪˈlekʃn/ **I** *n* **1** (act) gen sélection *f*, choix *m*; Sport sélection *f*; **to make a ~**

(for display, sale) faire une sélection; (for purchase) faire un choix; ▶ **natural selection**; **2** (assortment) sélection *f*, choix *m*; **~s from Mozart** morceaux *mpl* choisis de Mozart.
II *modif* [*committee, panel, process*] de sélection.

selective /sɪˈlektɪv/ *adj* **1** (positively biased) [*memory*] sélectif/-ive; [*recruitment, school*] sélectif/-ive; [*admission, education*] basé sur la sélection; **she should be more ~ about the friends she makes/about what she reads** elle devrait mieux choisir ses amis/ses lectures; **2** (negatively biased) [*account, perspective*] tendancieux/-ieuse; **the media were very ~ in their coverage of events** les médias ont couvert les événements de façon tendancieuse; **3** Hort [*weedkiller*] sélectif/-ive.

selective breeding *n* sélection *f* artificielle (*en élevage*).

selectively /sɪˈlektɪvlɪ/ *adv* de manière sélective.

selective service *n* US Hist service *m* militaire obligatoire.

selectivity /ˌsɪlekˈtɪvətɪ/ *n* gen sélection *f*; Elec, Radio sélectivité *f*.

selectman /sɪˈlektmən/ ▶ **1692** *n* US conseiller *m* municipal (*en Nouvelle-Angleterre*).

selector /sɪˈlektə(r)/ *n* **1** GB Sport (person) sélectionneur/-euse *m/f*; **2** Tech (device) sélecteur *m*.

selenium /sɪˈliːnɪəm/ *n* sélénium *m*.

self /self/ *n* (*pl* **selves**) **1** gen, Psych moi *m*; **she's looking for her true ~** elle cherche son vrai moi; **the difference between our private and public selves** la différence entre notre moi privé et notre moi public; **tickets for ~ and secretary** (on memo) billets pour ma secrétaire et moi-même; **without thought of ~** sans une pensée pour soi/lui/elle etc; **the conscious ~** le conscient; **he's back to his old ~ again** il est redevenu lui-même; **he's back to his old, miserly ~** il est redevenu aussi avare qu'avant; **your good ~** vous-même; **your good selves** vous-mêmes; **one's better ~** le meilleur de soi/de lui/d'elle etc; **2** Fin (on cheque) moi-même.

self: **~-abasement** *n* autodénigrement *m*; **~-absorbed** *adj* égocentrique; **~-absorption** *n* égocentrisme *m*; **~-abuse** *n* gen autodestruction *f*; (masturbation) masturbation *f*; **~-accusation** *n* autoaccusation *f*; **~-acting** *adj* automatique; **~-addressed envelope**, **SAE**, **sae** *n* enveloppe *f* à mon/votre etc adresse; **~-adhesive** *adj* auto-adhésif/-ive, autocollant; **~-adjusting** *adj* autorégulateur/-trice; **~-advertisement** *n* propagande *f* personnelle; **~-advocacy** *n* Soc Admin plaidoyer *m* pour sa/ma etc propre condition; **~-aggrandizement** *n* autoglorification *f*; **~-analysis** *n* auto-analyse *f*; **~-apparent** *adj* évident, qui coule de source (*after n*); **~-appointed** *adj* [*leader, guardian*] autonommé (*after n*); **~-appraisal** *n* auto-évaluation *f*; **~-assembly** *adj* en kit; **~-assertion** *n* affirmation *f* de soi/de lui-même etc; **~-assertive** *adj* sûr de soi/de lui/d'elle etc; **~-assessment** *n* auto-évaluation *f*; **~-assurance** *n* assurance *f*.

self-assured /ˌselfəˈʃɔːd, US -ˈʃʊərd/ *adj* [*person, performance*] plein d'assurance; **to be very ~** avoir beaucoup d'assurance.

self: **~-aware** *adj* conscient de ma/sa etc personne; **~-awareness** *n* conscience *f* de soi/de lui-même etc; **~-belief** *n* confiance *f* en soi/en elle etc; **~-betterment** *n* amélioration *f* de soi-même/de lui-même etc.

self-catering /ˌselfˈkeɪtərɪŋ/ GB **I** *n* meublé *m*.
II *modif* [*flat, accommodation*] meublé; **~ holiday** vacances *fpl* en location.

self: **~-censorship** *n* autocensure *f*; **~-centred** GB, **~-centered** US *adj* égocentrique; **~-certification** *n* GB certificat *m* de maladie (*signé par le malade*); **~-cleaning** *adj* autonettoyant; **~-closing** *adj* à fermeture automatique; **~-coloured** GB, **~-colored** US *adj* uni; **~-confessed** *adj* avoué; **~-confidence** *n* assurance *f*; **~-confident** *adj* [*person*] sûr de soi/de lui etc; [*attitude, performance*] plein d'assurance; **~-congratulation** *n* autosatisfaction *f*; **~-congratulatory** *adj* plein d'autosatisfaction.

self-conscious /ˌselfˈkɒnʃəs/ *adj* **1** (shy) timide; **to be ~ about sth/about doing** être gêné par qch/de faire; **2** (deliberate) [*style, artistry*] conscient; **3** = **self-aware**.

self-consciously /ˌselfˈkɒnʃəslɪ/ *adv* **1** (shyly) [*behave, dance*] timidement; **2** (deliberately) [*imitate, refer*] consciemment.

self-consciousness /ˌselfˈkɒnʃəsnɪs/ *n* **1** (timidity) gêne *f*; **2** (deliberateness) conscience *f*; **3** = **self-awareness**.

self-contained /ˌselfkənˈteɪnd/ *adj* **1** [*flat*] indépendant; [*project, unit*] autonome; **2** [*person*] réservé.

self: **~-contempt** *n* mépris *m* de soi; **~-contradiction** *n* contradiction *f* en soi; **~-contradictory** *adj* [*statement, argument*] contradictoire; [*person*] qui se contredit (*after n*).

self-control /ˌselfkənˈtrəʊl/ *n* sang-froid *m inv*, maîtrise *f* de soi; **to exercise ~** avoir du sang-froid.

self: **~-controlled** *adj* [*person*] maître/maîtresse de soi/de lui-même/d'elle-même etc; [*behaviour, manner*] contrôlé; **~-correcting** *adj* à système autocorrecteur; **~-critical** *adj* critique à l'égard de soi/de lui-même/d'elle-même etc; **~-criticism** *n* autocritique *f*; **~-deception** *n* aveuglement *m* à son/votre etc propre égard.

self-defeating /ˌselfdɪˈfiːtɪŋ/ *adj* autodestructeur/-trice (*after n*); **that would be ~** cela irait à l'encontre du but recherché.

self-defence GB, **self-defense** US /ˌselfdɪˈfens/ **I** *n* gen autodéfense *f*; Jur légitime défense *f*; **to learn ~** apprendre l'autodéfense; **to shoot sb in ~** tirer sur qn en état de légitime défense; **can I say in ~ that**... est-ce que je peux dire pour ma défense que...
II *modif* [*class, course, instructor*] d'autodéfense.

self: **~-definition** *n* détermination *f* de soi; **~-delusion** *n* aveuglement *m* à son/mon etc propre égard; **~-denial** *n* abnégation *f*; **~-denying** *adj* plein d'abnégation; **~-deprecating** *adj* [*person*] qui se dénigre (*after n*); [*joke, manner, remark*] d'autodénigrement (*after n*); **~-deprecation** *n* autodénigrement *m*.

self-destruct /ˌselfdɪˈstrʌkt/ **I** *adj* [*button, mechanism*] d'autodestruction.
II *vi* s'autodétruire.

self: **~-destructive** *adj* autodestructeur/-trice; **~-determination** *n* gen, Pol autodétermination *f*; **~-determining** *adj* [*country*] autonome; [*action, move*] d'autodétermination; **~-diagnosis** *n* gen, Med autodiagnostic *m*; **~-discipline** *n* autodiscipline *f*; **~-disciplined** *adj* autodiscipliné; **~-discovery** *n* découverte *f* de soi/d'elle-même etc; **~-disgust** *n* dégoût *m* de soi; **~-doubt** *n* doute *m* de soi-même/de lui-même etc; **~-drive** *adj* GB [*car, van*] de location sans chauffeur; [*holiday*] en voiture; **~-educated** *adj* autodidacte; **~-effacement** *n* effacement *m*; **~-effacing** *adj* effacé.

self-elected *adj* lit [*committee*] autoélu; [*leader*] autoproclamé; **he's a ~ expert on**... il se prétend expert en...

self-employed /ˌselfɪmˈplɔɪd/ **I** *n* **the ~** (+ *v pl*) les travailleurs *mpl* indépendants.
II *adj* [*work, worker*] indépendant (*after n*); **to be ~** travailler à son compte.

self: **~-employment** *n* travail *m* indépendant; **~-esteem** *n* amour-propre *m*; **~-evident** *adj* évident, qui coule de source (*after n*); **~-evidently** *adv* de toute évidence.

self-examination /ˌselfɪɡˌzæmɪˈneɪʃn/ *n* **1** (of conscience, motives) examen *m* de conscience; **2** Med auto-examen *m*.

self-explanatory /ˌselfɪkˈsplænətrɪ, US -tɔːrɪ/ *adj* explicite.

self-expression /ˌselfɪkˈspreʃn/ *n* expression *f* de soi/de lui-même etc; **a means of ~** un moyen de s'exprimer.

self: **~-fertilization** *n* autofécondation *f*; **~-fertilizing** *adj* autofertile.

self-financing /ˌselfˈfaɪnænsɪŋ/ **I** *n* autofinancement *m*.
II *adj* autofinancé.

self: **~-fulfilling prophecy** *n* prédiction *f* qui s'accomplit d'elle-même; **~-fulfilment** *n* accomplissement *m* de soi; **~-funded** *adj* autofinancé; **~-glorification** *n* pej autoglorification *f*; **~-governing** *adj* autonome; **~-governing trust** *n* GB *organisme médical qui gère son budget de manière autonome*; **~-government** *n* autonomie *f*; **~-gratification** *n* gratification *f* personnelle; **~-hate**, **~-hatred** *n* haine *f* de soi.

self-help /ˌselfˈhelp/ **I** *n* **to learn ~** apprendre à se débrouiller seul; **~ is a necessity for this country** savoir se débrouiller seul est essentiel pour ce pays.
II *modif* [*group, scheme, meeting*] d'entraide; **~ book** manuel *m* d'aide.

selfhood /ˈselfhʊd/ *n* individualité *f*.

self: **~-hypnosis** *n* autohypnose *f*; **~-ignite** *vi* s'allumer spontanément; **~-ignition** *n* auto-allumage *m*; **~-image** *n* image *f* de soi-même/de lui-même etc; **~-importance** *n* péj suffisance *f*; **~-important** *adj* péj suffisant; **~-imposed** *adj* auto-imposé; **~-improvement** *n* progrès *mpl* personnels; **~-incrimination** *n* incrimination *f* par soi-même; **~-induced** *adj* auto-infligé; **~-induced hypnosis** *n* autohypnose *f*; **~-indulgence** *n* complaisance *f*, laisser-aller *m inv*; **~-indulgent** *adj* complaisant; **~-inflicted** *adj* auto-infligé; **~-interest** *n* intérêt *m* personnel; **~-interested** *adj* [*person, motive*] intéressé; **~-involved** *adj* égocentrique.

selfish /ˈselfɪʃ/ *adj* égoïste (**to do** de faire); **it was ~ of him to do** c'était égoïste de sa part de faire.

selfishly /ˈselfɪʃlɪ/ *adv* égoïstement.

selfishness /ˈselfɪʃnɪs/ *n* égoïsme *m*; **the ~ of her behaviour** son comportement égoïste.

self: **~-justification** *n* autojustification *f*; **~-justifying** *adj* d'autojustification (*after n*); **~-knowledge** *n* connaissance *f* de soi/d'elle-même etc.

selfless /ˈselflɪs/ *adj* [*person*] dévoué; [*action, devotion*] désintéressé.

selflessly /ˈselflɪslɪ/ *adv* [*give, donate*] sans penser à soi/à lui etc; **to be ~ devoted to** être entièrement dévoué à.

selflessness /ˈselflɪsnɪs/ *n* (of person) dévouement *m*; (of action, devotion) désintéressement *m*.

self: **~-loader** *n* arme *f* automatique; **~-loading** *adj* [*gun, rifle*] automatique; **~-loathing** *n* haine *f* de soi/d'elle-même etc; **~-locking** *adj* à verrouillage automatique; **~-love** *n* amour *m* de soi/de lui-même/d'elle-même etc; **~-lubricating** *adj* autolubrifiant.

self-made /ˌselfˈmeɪd/ *adj* [*star, millionaire*] qui s'est fait tout seul (*after n*); **~ man** self-made man *m*.

self: **~-management** *n* Comm autogestion *f*; Psych gestion *f* de sa vie; **~-mastery** *n* maîtrise *f* de soi/d'elle-même etc; **~-mockery** *n* autodérision *f*; **~-mocking** *adj* plein d'autodérision;

~-motivated *adj* très motivé; **~-motivation** *n* motivation *f* personnelle; **~-mutilate** *vi* s'automutiler; **~-mutilation** *n* automutilation *f*; **~-obsessed** *adj* obsédé par sa/ma etc personne; **~-ordained** *adj* autopromu; **~-parody** *n* auto-parodie *f*; **~-perpetuating** *adj* qui se perpétue (*after n*); **~-pity** *n* apitoiement *m* sur soi-même.

self-pitying /ˌselfˈpɪtɪɪŋ/ *adj* [*person*] qui s'apitoie sur son sort (*after n*); [*look, account*] plein de pitié pour soi-même/lui-même etc; **he is in a ~ mood** il est d'humeur à s'apitoyer sur lui-même.

self-portrait /ˌselfˈpɔːtreɪt/ *n* autoportrait *m*.

self-possessed /ˌselfpəˈzest/ *adj* [*person*] maître/maîtresse de soi; **she gave a ~ performance** sa performance témoignait d'une grande maîtrise de soi or d'elle-même.

self: **~-possession** *n* maîtrise *f* de soi/de lui-même etc, sang-froid *m inv*; **~-praise** *n* autosatisfaction *f*; **~-presentation** *n* façon *f* de se présenter.

self-preservation /ˌselfprezəˈveɪʃn/ *n* autoconservation *f*; **the ~ instinct** l'instinct *m* de conservation.

self: **~-proclaimed** *adj* autoproclamé; **~-promotion** *n* promotion *f* personnelle; **~-propelled** *adj* autopropulsé.

self-protection /ˌselfprəˈtekʃn/ *n* autoprotection *f*; **in ~** pour se/me etc protéger.

self: **~-protective** *adj* autoprotecteur/-trice; **~-publicist** *n* péj spécialiste *mf* de la propagande personnelle; **~-punishment** *n* autopunition *f*; **~-raising flour** GB, **~-rising flour** US *n* farine *f* à gâteau; **~-realization** *n* (discovery) prise *f* de conscience de soi/d'elle-même etc; (fulfilment) accomplissement *m*; **~-referential** *adj* autoréférentiel/-ielle; **~-regard** *n* (concern for oneself) égard *m* pour soi-même/lui-même etc; (self-respect) respect *m* de soi/de lui-même etc; **~-regarding** *adj* (concerned for oneself) plein d'égards pour soi-même/lui-même etc; **~-regulating**, **~- regulatory** *adj* autorégulateur/-trice; **~-regulation** *n* autorégulation *f*; **~-reliance** *n* autosuffisance *f*; **~-reliant** *adj* autosuffisant; **~-renewal** *n* (of country, person) renouvellement *m*; **~-replicating** *adj* Biol autoreproducteur/-trice.

self-representation /ˌselfreprɪzenˈteɪʃn/ *n* **1** Soc Admin, Jur (before tribunal) possibilité *f* de se représenter; **2** (self-portrait) autoportrait *m*.

self: **~-reproach** *n* ¢ reproches *mpl* à soi-même/à elle-même etc; **~-respect** *n* respect *m* de soi/de lui-même etc; **~-respecting** *adj* [*teacher, journalist, comedian*] (worthy of that name) qui se respecte (*after n*); [*person*] respectueux/-euse de sa/ma etc personne; **~-restraint** *n* retenue *f*; **~-ridicule** *n* autodérision *f*; **~-righteous** *adj* péj autosatisfait; **~-righteously** *adv* péj [*say, behave*] en se donnant raison; **~-righteousness** *n* péj autosatisfaction *f*; **~-righting** *adj* qui se redresse tout seul; **~-rising flour** *n* US= **self-raising flour**; **~-rule** *n* autonomie *f*; **~-ruling** *adj* autonome; **~-sacrifice** *n* abnégation *f*; **~-sacrificing** *adj* [*person*] plein d'abnégation; [*gesture, act*] d'abnégation; **~same** *adj* même (*after n*); **~-satisfaction** *n* autosatisfaction *f*; **~-satisfied** *adj* péj autosatisfait; **~-sealing** *adj* [*envelope*] autocollant.

self-seeking /ˌselfˈsiːkɪŋ/ **I** *n* égoïsme *m*.
II *adj* égoïste.

self-service /ˌselfˈsɜːvɪs/ **I** *n* libre-service *m*.
II *adj* [*cafeteria*] en libre-service.

self-serving /ˌselfˈsɜːvɪŋ/ *adj* péj intéressé.

self-starter /ˌselfˈstɑːtə(r)/ *n* **1** (person) personne *f* ambitieuse et indépendante; **2**† Aut démarreur *m* automatique.

self: **~-study** *modif* [[*book, aid*]] d'autoéducation; **~-styled** *adj* autoproclamé; **~-sufficiency** *n* (all contexts) autosuffisance *f*; **~-sufficient** *adj* autosuffisant (**in** en matière de); **~-supporting** *adj* (all contexts) indépendant; **~-sustaining** *adj* autosuffisant; **~-taught** *adj* [*person, musician, typist*] autodidacte; **~-torture** *n* torture *f* de soi-même; **~-treatment** *n* gen traitement *m* autoprescrit; (with medicines) automédication *f*; **~-will** *n* volonté *f* inébranlable; **~-willed** *adj* entêté; **~-winding** *adj* à remontage automatique; **~-worth** *n* estime *f* de soi.

sell /sel/ **I**○ *n* (deception, disappointment) déception *f*; **it was a real ~!** qu'est-ce qu'on s'est fait avoir○!; ▶ **hard sell**, **soft sell**.
II *vtr* (*prét, pp* **sold**) **1** gen, Comm vendre [*goods, article, house, car, insurance*]; **to ~ sth at a loss/low price/profit** vendre qch à perte/à bas prix/avec du bénéfice; **shop that ~s clothes/groceries/stamps** magasin qui or où l'on vend des vêtements/de l'épicerie/des timbres; **to ~ sth to sb**, **to ~ sb sth** vendre qch à qn; **I sold her my car**, **I sold my car to her** je lui ai vendu ma voiture; **to ~ sth for £3** vendre qch (pour) 3 livres; **to ~ sth at** ou **for £5 each/a dozen** vendre qch 5 livres pièce/la douzaine; **'stamps/phonecards sold here'** 'ici on vend des timbres/des cartes de téléphone'; **'sold'** (on article, house) 'vendu'; **sold to the lady in the corner** (at auction) adjugé, vendu à la dame dans le coin; **the novel has sold millions (of copies)** le roman s'est vendu à des millions d'exemplaires; **to ~ sth back** revendre qch; **to be sold into slavery** être vendu comme esclave; **2** (promote sale of) [*quality, reputation, scandal*] faire vendre [*product, book, newspaper*]; **her name will help to ~ the film** son nom aidera à promouvoir le film; **3** (put across, make attractive) [*person, campaign, government*] faire accepter, vendre pej [*idea, image, policy, party*]; **to ~ sth to sb**, **to ~ sb sth** faire accepter qch à qn, vendre qch à qn pej; **the party failed to ~ its policies to the electorate** le parti n'a pas réussi à faire accepter or vendre sa politique aux électeurs; **4**○ (cause to appear true) **to ~ sb sth**, **to ~ sth to sb** faire avaler○ qch à qn [*lie, story, excuse*]; **he tried to ~ me some line about losing his diary** il a essayé de me faire avaler je ne sais quelle histoire comme quoi il avait perdu son agenda○; **5** (surrender, betray) trahir [*honour, integrity, reputation, country*].
III *vi* (*prét, pp* **sold**) **1** [*person, shop, dealer*] vendre; **to ~ at a loss/profit/high price** vendre à perte/avec du bénéfice/à un bon prix; **to ~ to sb** vendre à qn; **I'll ~ to the highest bidder** je vendrai au plus offrant; **to ~ for £50** [*dealer, seller*] vendre à 50 livres; **I'll ~ for the best price** je vendrai au meilleur prix; **to ~ as is** Comm vendre en l'état; **'~ by June 27'** 'date limite de vente: 27 juin'; **2** [*goods, product, house, book*] se vendre; **the new model is/isn't ~ing (well)** le nouveau modèle se vend bien/mal; **to ~ in millions/in great quantities** se vendre à des millions d'exemplaires/en grande quantités; **it only ~s to a sophisticated market/to children** cela ne se vend que sur un marché raffiné/qu'aux enfants.
IV *v refl* (*prét, pp* **sold**) **1** (prostitute oneself) **to ~ oneself** lit, fig se vendre (**to** à; **for** pour); **2** (put oneself across) **to ~ oneself** se vendre○; **you've got to ~ yourself at the interview** il faut que tu te vendes○ lors de l'entretien.
IDIOMS **to be sold on** être emballé○ par [*idea, person*]; **you've been sold**○**!** tu t'es fait rouler○ or avoir!
■ **sell off**: **~ [sth] off**, **~ off [sth]** gen liquider [*goods, stock*]; (in sale) solder [*item, old stock*].
■ **sell out**: ¶ **~ out 1** gen, Comm [*merchandise, tickets, newspapers*] se vendre; **they're ~ing out fast!** ils se vendent vite!; **the tickets/today's papers have sold out**, **we've sold out of tickets/today's papers** tous les billets/les journaux du jour ont été vendus; **sorry, we've sold out** désolé, mais nous avons tout vendu or il n'y en a plus; **2** Theat, Cin **the play/show has sold out** la pièce/le spectacle affiche complet; **3** Fin (of company, shares) vendre ses parts (**to** à); **I've decided to ~ out** j'ai décidé de vendre mes parts; **4**○ (betray one's principles) retourner sa veste; **he's sold out to the opposition** il est passé dans l'opposition; ¶ **~ [sth] out**, **~ out [sth] 1** gen, Comm **the concert is sold out** le concert affiche complet; **the book has sold out its initial print run** la première édition du livre est épuisée; **'sold out'** 'en rupture de stock'; **2** Fin vendre [*shares, interest in company*].
■ **sell up**: ¶ **~ up** vendre (tout); **they've sold up** ils ont tout vendu; ¶ **~ up [sth]** vendre [*business, property*].

sell-by date *n* date *f* limite de vente.

seller /ˈselə(r)/ *n* **1** (person) vendeur/-euse *m/f*; **2** (product, book etc) **it's a good/poor ~** cela se vend bien/mal.

seller: **~'s market** *n* Fin marché *m* à la hausse; Comm marché *m* où la demande est forte; **~'s option** *n* Fin prime *f*.

selling /ˈselɪŋ/ *n* ¢ vente *f*; **telephone ~** vente par téléphone; **panic ~** Fin vente(s) précipitée(s).

selling: **~ cost** *n* prix *m* de vente; **~-off** *n* (of company, assets) liquidation *f*; (of stock) écoulement *m*; **~ point** *n* (all contexts) argument *m* de vente; **~ price** *n* prix *m* de vente; **~ rate** *n* taux *m* de vente.

Sellotape® /ˈseləʊteɪp/ **I** *n* scotch® *m*.
II sellotape *vtr* scotcher.

sellout /ˈselaʊt/ **I** *n* **1 the show was a ~** le spectacle affichait complet; **the product has been a ~** le produit s'est très bien vendu; **2**○ (betrayal) revirement *m*; **what a ~!** quel revirement!
II *modif* [*concert, performance, production*] à guichets fermés; **they played to a ~ crowd of 12,000** ils ont joué à guichets fermés devant une foule de 12 000 spectateurs; **the play was a ~ success** la pièce a eu un succès retentissant.

seltzer /ˈseltsə(r)/ *n* (also **~ water**) eau *f* de Seltz.

selvage, **selvedge** /ˈselvɪdʒ/ *n* Tex lisière *f*.

selves /selvz/ *pl* ▶ **self**.

semantic /sɪˈmæntɪk/ *adj* sémantique.

semantically /sɪˈmæntɪklɪ/ *adv* sémantiquement.

semanticist /sɪˈmæntɪsɪst/ *n* sémanticien/-ienne *m/f*.

semantics /sɪˈmæntɪks/ **I** *n* (subject) (+ *v sg*) sémantique *f*.
II *npl* (meaning) (+ *v pl*) sémantique *f*.

semaphore /ˈseməfɔː(r)/ *n* sémaphore *m*.

semblance /ˈsembləns/ *n* semblant *m*; **a** ou **some ~ of** un semblant de [*order, normality, confidence*]; **to give (sb/sth) some ~ of doing** donner (à qn/à qch) l'illusion de faire; **to maintain a ~ of composure** garder un air dégagé.

seme /semeɪ/ *n* sème *m*.

semen /ˈsiːmən/ **I** *n* ¢ sperme *m*.
II *modif* [*donor, sample*] de sperme.

semester /sɪˈmestə(r)/ *n* semestre *m*.

semi /ˈsemɪ/ **I**○ *n* **1** GB (house) maison *f* jumelée; **2** US Aut semi-remorque *f*.
II semi+ (*dans composés*) **1** (half) semi-, demi-; **2** (partly) plus ou moins; **it was a ~-serious suggestion** c'était une idée plus ou moins sérieuse or pas tout à fait sérieuse.

semi: **~annual** *adj* [*publication*] publié deux fois par an; [*event*] qui a lieu deux fois par an; **~aquatic** *adj* semi-aquatique; **~automatic** *n, adj* semi-automatique (*m*); **~autonomous** *adj* semi-autonome; **~basement** *n* GB ≈ rez-de-jardin *m inv*; **~bold** *n* caractère *m* demi-gras; **~breve** *n* GB Mus ronde *f*; **~centenary**, **~centennial** *n, adj* cinquantenaire (*m*);

~circle *n* demi-cercle *m*; **~circular** *adj* semi-circulaire, en demi-cercle; **~circular canal** *n* canal *m* semi-circulaire; **~colon** *n* point-virgule *m*; **~conductor** *n* semi-conducteur *m*; **~conscious** *adj* à peine conscient; **~consciousness** *n* état *m* de demi-conscience; **~consonant** *n* semi-consonne *f*; **~darkness** *n* pénombre *f*, demi-jour *m*.

semidesert /ˌsemɪˈdesət/ **I** *n* zone *f* semi-aride.
II *adj* semi-aride, semi-désertique.

semi: **~-detached (house)** *n* maison *f* jumelée; **~final** *n* demi-finale *f*; **~finalist** *n* demi-finaliste *mf*; **~fluid** *n*, *adj* semi-fluide (*m*); **~literate** *adj* presque illettré; **~lunar** *adj* semi-lunaire.

semimonthly /ˌsemɪˈmʌnθlɪ/ US **I** *n* publication *f* bi-mensuelle.
II *adj* bi-mensuel/-elle.

seminal /ˈsemɪnl/ *adj* **1** gen [*work, thinker, influence*] déterminant; **2** Physiol [*fluid*] séminal.

seminar /ˈsemɪnɑ:(r)/ *n* séminaire *m* (**on** sur).

seminarian /ˌsemɪˈneərɪən/, **seminarist** /ˈsemɪnərɪst/ *n* séminariste *m*.

seminar room *n* salle *f* de séminaire.

seminary /ˈsemɪnərɪ, US -nerɪ/ *n* Relig séminaire *m*.

semiofficial /ˌsemɪəˈfɪʃl/ *adj* semi-officiel/-ielle.

semiology /ˌsemɪˈɒlədʒɪ/ *n* sémiologie *f*.

semiopaque /ˌsemɪəˈpeɪk/ *adj* à demi opaque, semi-opaque.

semiotic /ˌsemɪˈɒtɪk/ *adj* sémiotique.

semiotics /ˌsemɪˈɒtɪks/ *n* (+ *v sg*) sémiotique *f*.

semi: **~permanent** *adj* semi-permanent; **~permeable** *adj* à demi perméable, semi-perméable; **~precious** *adj* [*metal*] semi-précieux/-ieuse; [*stone*] fin, semi-précieux/-ieuse; **~professional** *n*, *adj* semi-professionnel/-elle (*m/f*); **~quaver** *n* GB Mus double croche *f*; **~rigid** *adj* semi-rigide; **~skilled** /ˌsemɪˈskɪld/ *adj* [*work*] d'ouvrier spécialisé; [*worker*] spécialisé; **~skimmed** /ˌsemɪˈskɪmd/ *adj* demi-écrémé; **~solid** *adj* semi-solide.

Semite /ˈsi:maɪt/ *n* Sémite *mf*.

Semitic /sɪˈmɪtɪk/ *adj* **1** gen sémite; **2** Ling sémitique.

semi: **~tone** *n* Mus demi-ton *m*; **~trailer** *n* US (truck) semi-remorque *m*; (trailer) semi-remorque *f*; **~tropical** *adj* semi-tropical; **~vowel** *n* semi-voyelle *f*; **~weekly** *n*, *adj* semi-hebdomadaire (*m*); **~yearly** *adj* = **semiannual**.

semolina /ˌseməˈli:nə/ *n* semoule *f*.

sempiternal /ˌsempɪˈtɜ:nl/ *adj* littér perpétuel/-elle.

Sen 1 *abrév écrite* = **senator**; **2** *abrév écrite* = **senior**.

SEN GB *abrév* ▶ **State Enrolled Nurse**.

senate /ˈsenɪt/ *n* **1** Pol, Hist sénat *m*; **2** Univ conseil *m* (d'université).

senator /ˈsenətə(r)/ ▶ 1268 *n* sénateur *m* (**for** de).

senatorial /ˌsenəˈtɔ:rɪəl/ *adj* sénatorial.

send /send/ *vtr* (*prét, pp* **sent**) **1** (dispatch) gen envoyer [*letter, parcel, goods, message, person*]; Radio envoyer [*signal*]; **to ~ help** envoyer des secours; **to ~ sth to sb, to ~ sb sth** envoyer qch à qn; **to ~ sth to the cleaner's** faire nettoyer qch; **to ~ sb to do sth** envoyer qn faire qch; **she sent him to the supermarket for some milk** elle l'a envoyé au supermarché acheter du lait; **they'll ~ a car for you** ils enverront une voiture vous chercher; **to ~ sb home** (from school, work) renvoyer qn chez lui; **to ~ sb to bed** envoyer qn se coucher; **to ~ sb to prison** mettre qn en prison; **~ her my love!** embrasse-la de ma part; **~ them my regards/best wishes** transmettez-leur mes amitiés/meilleurs vœux; **Kirsten ~s her regards** tu as le bonjour de Kirsten; (more formally) vous avez les amitiés de Kirsten; **to ~ word that** faire dire que; **2** (cause to move) envoyer; **the explosion sent debris in all directions** l'explosion a envoyé des débris dans toutes les directions; **the blow sent him crashing to the ground** le coup l'a envoyé rouler par terre; **the noise sent people running in all directions** le bruit a fait courir les gens dans toutes les directions; **to ~ share prices soaring/plummeting** faire monter/s'effondrer le cours des actions; **the impact sent the car over the cliff** le choc a fait basculer la voiture du haut de la falaise; **the collision sent the car straight into a wall/into a hedge** la collision a été si forte que la voiture a embouti un mur/est rentrée dans une haie; **the fire sent flickers of light across the room** le feu lançait des lueurs à travers la pièce ; **to ~ shivers down sb's spine** donner froid dans le dos à qn; **3** (cause to become) rendre; **to ~ sb mad/berserk** rendre qn fou/fou furieux; **to ~ sb into a rage** mettre qn dans une rage folle; **to ~ sb to sleep** endormir qn; **to ~ sb into fits of laughter** faire éclater de rire qn; **4**○ (excite) **she really ~s me!** elle me botte○ or m'emballe○ vraiment!; **this music really ~s me!** cette musique me botte○ or me plaît vraiment!

IDIOMS **to ~ sb packing**○, **to send sb about her/his business**○ envoyer balader qn○

■ **send along**: **~ [sb/sth] along, ~ along [sb/sth]** envoyer; **~ him/the documents along to room three** envoyez-le/les documents à la salle trois.

■ **send around** US = **send round**.

■ **send away**: ¶ **~ away for [sth]** commander [qch] par correspondance; ¶ **~ [sb/sth] away** faire partir, renvoyer [*person*]; ¶ **to ~ a child away to boarding school** envoyer un enfant en pension; **to ~ an appliance away to be mended** envoyer un appareil chez le fabricant pour le faire réparer.

■ **send down**: ¶ **~ [sb/sth] down, ~ down [sb/sth]** envoyer; **~ him down to the second floor** dites-lui de descendre au deuxième étage; **can you ~ it down to me?** pouvez-vous me le faire parvenir?; ¶ **~ [sb] down 1** GB Univ renvoyer [qn] de l'université (**for** pour; **for doing** pour avoir fait); **2**○ GB (put in prison) mettre or envoyer qn en prison; **he was sent down for ten years for armed robbery** il a été condamné à dix ans pour vol à main armée.

■ **send for**: **~ for [sb/sth]** appeler, faire venir [*doctor, taxi, plumber*]; demander [*reinforcements*]; **the headmaster has sent for you** le directeur te réclame.

■ **send forth**: **~ forth [sb/sth]** littér envoyer [*messenger, army, ray of light*].

■ **send in**: **~ [sb/sth] in, ~ in [sb/sth]** envoyer [*letter, form*]; envoyer [*police, troops*]; faire entrer [*visitor*]; **to ~ in one's application** poser sa candidature.

■ **send off**: ¶ **~ off for [sth]** commander [qch] par correspondance; ¶ **~ [sth] off, ~ off [sth]** (post) envoyer, expédier [*letter, parcel, form*]; ¶ **~ [sb] off, ~ off [sb]** Sport expulser [*player*] (**for** pour; **for doing** pour avoir fait); ¶ **~ [sb] off to** envoyer [qn] à [*shops, school*]; **to ~ [sb] off to do** envoyer [qn] faire.

■ **send on**: ¶ **~ [sb] on (ahead)** Mil (as scout) envoyer [qn] en éclaireur; **~ him on ahead to open up the shop** dites-lui de partir devant ouvrir le magasin; ¶ **~ [sth] on, ~ on [sth] 1** (send in advance) expédier [qch] à l'avance [*luggage*]; **2** (forward) faire suivre [*letter, mail*].

■ **send out**: ¶ **~ out for [sth]** envoyer quelqu'un chercher [*sandwich, newspaper*]; ¶ **~ [sth] out, ~ out [sth] 1** (post) envoyer [*letters, leaflets*]; **2** (emit) émettre [*light, heat, flames*]; (produce) [*tree, plant*] produire [*leaf, bud, creeper*]; ¶ **~ [sb] out** faire sortir [*pupil*]; ¶**~ [sb] out for** envoyer [qn] chercher [*pizza, sandwich*].

■ **send round** GB: **~ [sb/sth] round, ~ round [sb/sth] 1** (circulate) faire circuler [*letter, memo etc*]; **2** (cause to go) envoyer [*person, object*]; **I've sent him round to my neighbour's** je l'ai envoyé chez le voisin.

■ **send up**: ¶ **~ [sth] up** (post) envoyer; **~ your ideas up to the BBC** envoyez vos idées à la BBC; ¶ **~ [sb] up**○ US (put in prison) mettre or envoyer [qn] en prison; ¶ **~ [sb/sth] up, ~ up [sb/sth] 1** (into sky, space) envoyer [*astronaut, probe*]; **2** (to upper floor) **you can ~ him up now** vous pouvez lui dire de monter maintenant; **can you ~ it up to me?** pouvez-vous me le faire parvenir?; **3**○ GB (parody) parodier [*person, institution*].

sender /ˈsendə(r)/ *n* expéditeur/-trice *m/f*.

send-off /ˈsendɒf/ *n* adieux *mpl*; **her family gave her a warm ~** sa famille lui a fait des adieux chaleureux; **the president was given a big ~** une foule nombreuse était venue souhaiter bon voyage au président.

send-up○ /ˈsendʌp/ *n* GB parodie *f*.

Seneca /ˈsenɪkə/ *pr n* Sénèque.

Senegal /ˌsenɪˈgɔ:l/ ▶ 1131 *pr n* Sénégal *m*.

Senegalese /ˌsenɪgəˈli:z/ ▶ 1486 **I** *n* Sénégalais/-e *m/f*.
II *adj* sénégalais.

senile /ˈsi:naɪl/ *adj* sénile also pej.

senile dementia *n* démence *f* sénile.

senility /sɪˈnɪlətɪ/ *n* sénilité *f*.

senior /ˈsi:nɪə(r)/ **I** *n* **1** (older person) aîné/-e *m/f*; **to be sb's ~ by ten years** avoir dix ans de plus que qn; **to be sb's ~** être plus âgé que qn; **2** (superior) supérieur/-e *m/f*; **3** GB Sch élève *mf* dans les grandes classes; **4** US Sch élève *mf* de terminale; **5** US Univ étudiant/-e *m/f* de licence; **6** Sport senior *m*.
II *modif* **1** Sport [*circuit, league, player, tournament*] senior; **2** US Univ [*year, prom*] de fin d'études.
III *adj* **1** (older) [*person*] plus âgé; [*organization*] plus ancien/-ienne; **to be ~ to sb** être plus âgé que qn; **to be ~ to sb by 12 years** avoir 12 ans de plus que qn; **Mr Becket ~** M. Becket père; **2** (superior) [*person*] plus haut placé; [*civil servant, diplomat*] haut (*before n*); [*aide, adviser, employee, minister*] haut placé; [*colleague*] plus ancien/-ienne; [*figure, member*] prédominant; [*job, post*] supérieur; **to be ~ to sb** être le supérieur de qn.

senior: **~ aircraftman** ▶ 1612 *n* GB Mil Aviat ≈ caporal *m*; **~ airman** ▶ 1612 *n* US Mil Aviat ≈ caporal-chef *m*; **~ chief petty officer** ▶ 1612 *n* US Mil Naut ≈ maître *m* principal; **~ citizen** *n* Soc Admin personne *f* du troisième âge.

Senior Common Room *n* GB Univ **1** (staff room) *salle de repos réservée au corps enseignant d'une université*; **2** (college staff) *corps enseignant d'une université*.

senior: **~ editor** ▶ 1692 *n* Journ, Publg rédacteur/-trice *m/f* en chef; **~ executive** *n* cadre *m* supérieur; **~ high school** *n* US Sch ≈ lycée *m*.

seniority /ˌsi:nɪˈɒrətɪ, US -ˈɔ:r-/ *n* **1** (in years) âge *m*; **in order of ~** par ordre d'âge; **2** (in rank) statut *m* supérieur; **~ brings with it certain privileges** un statut supérieur comporte certains privilèges; **in order of ~** par ordre hiérarchique; **3** (in years of service) ancienneté *f*; **in order of ~** par ordre d'ancienneté.

seniority bonus *n* prime *f* d'ancienneté.

senior: **~ lecturer** *n* GB Univ ≈ maître *m* de conférence (de premier échelon); **~ management** *n* Admin direction *f*; **~ manager** *n* cadre *m* supérieur; **~ master** *n* GB Sch ≈ conseiller *m* d'éducation; **~ master sergeant** ▶ 1612 *n* US Mil adjudant *m*; **~ medical officer** ▶ 1612 *n* Mil directeur *m* du service de santé; **~ mistress** *n* GB Sch ≈ conseillère *f* d'éducation.

senior officer *n* **1** (in police) officier *m* de police supérieur; **2** Soc Admin haut/-e fonctionnaire *m/f*; **inform your ~** informez votre supérieur.

senior: **~ official** *n* haut/-e fonctionnaire *m/f*; **~ partner** *n* associé/-e *m/f* principal/-e; **~ registrar** ▶ **1692** *n* GB Med chef *m* de clinique; **~ school** *n* GB (secondary school) lycée *m*; (older pupils) grandes classes *fpl*; **Senior Service** *n* GB Mil Naut marine *f* de guerre britannique.

senior staff *n* **1** Admin cadres *mpl* supérieurs; **2** GB Univ corps *m* enseignant.

senior year *n* **1** GB Sch (year) dernière année *f* de l'enseignement (secondaire); **2** (pupils) élèves *mfpl* de dernière année; **3** US Univ dernière année *f* du cycle universitaire.

senna /'senə/ *n* séné *m*.

sensation /sen'seɪʃn/ *n* **1** (physical feeling) sensation *f* (**of** de); **a burning/choking ~** une sensation de brûlure/d'étouffement; **2** (impression) sensation *f*; **a floating/drowning ~** la sensation de flotter/de se noyer; **3** (stir) sensation *f*; **to cause** ou **create a ~** faire sensation. **4**○ (person) **to be a ~** être formidable.

sensational /sen'seɪʃənl/ *adj* **1** (dramatic) [*discovery, event, development*] sensationnel/-elle; **2** (sensationalist) péj [*allegation, news*] sensationnel/-elle; **~ story/article** histoire *f*/article *m* à sensation pej; **3**○ (emphatic) sensationnel/-elle.

sensationalism /sen'seɪʃənəlɪzəm/ *n* **1** (of tabloids) péj recherche *f* du sensationnel; **2** Philos sensationnisme *m*, sensualisme *m*.

sensationalist /sen'seɪʃənəlɪst/ **I** *n* **1** (person) péj **to be a ~** aimer dramatiser pej; **2** Philos sensationniste *mf*, sensualiste *mf*.
II *adj* **1** Journ péj [*headline, story, writer*] à sensation pej; **it's too ~** c'est dramatisé pej; **2** Philos sensationniste, sensualiste.

sensationalize /sen'seɪʃənəlaɪz/ *vtr* péj faire un reportage à sensation sur [*event, story*].

sensationally /sen'seɪʃənəlɪ/ *adv* **1** (luridly) péj [*write, describe*] en dramatisant pej; **2**○ (emphatic) [*good, beautiful, rich, stylish*] extraordinairement; [*bad, incompetent*] épouvantablement.

sense /sens/ **I** *n* **1** (faculty) sens *m*; **~ of hearing** ouïe *f*; **~ of sight** vue *f*; **~ of smell** odorat *m*; **~ of taste** goût *m*; **~ of touch** toucher *m*; **to dull/sharpen the ~s** émousser/aiguiser les sens; **2** fig (ability to appreciate) **a ~ of** le sens de; **a ~ of direction/of rhythm** le sens de l'orientation/du rythme; **a writer with a ~ of history/the absurd** un écrivain doué du sens de l'histoire/l'absurde; **to have no ~ of style/decency** n'avoir aucun style/aucune notion de la décence; **to lose all ~ of time** perdre toute notion du temps; **3** (feeling) **a ~ of** un sentiment de [*guilt, security, failure, identity*]; **his ~ of having failed/being excluded** son sentiment d'avoir échoué/d'être exclu; **he had the ~ that something was wrong/that he had forgotten something** il avait le sentiment que quelque chose n'allait pas/d'avoir oublié quelque chose; **a ~ of purpose** le sentiment d'avoir un but; **the town has a great ~ of community** la ville a un grand sens de la communauté; **4** (practical quality) bon sens *m*; **to have the (good) ~ to do** avoir le bon sens de faire; **to have more ~ than to do** avoir suffisamment de bon sens pour ne pas faire; **5** (reason) **there's no ~ in doing** cela ne sert à rien de faire; **what's the ~ in getting angry/leaving now?** à quoi sert de se fâcher/partir maintenant?; **to make ~ of sth** comprendre qch; **I can't make ~ of this article/this sentence** je ne comprends rien à cet article/cette phrase; **it makes ~ to do** c'est une bonne idée de faire; **it makes good business ~ to employ an accountant** ce serait profitable d'employer un comptable; **to make ~** [*sentence, film, theory*] avoir un sens; **not to make any ~** [*sentence, film, theory*] n'avoir aucun sens; **what he said didn't make much ~ to me** ce qu'il a dit ne m'a pas semblé très logique; **6** (meaning) gen, Ling sens *m*; **in the literal/strict ~ (of the word)** au sens littéral/strict (du mot); **in all ~s** ou **in every ~ of the word** dans tous les sens du mot; **in the ~ that** en ce sens que; **he is in a** ou **one** ou **some ~ right to complain, but**... dans un certain sens il a raison de se plaindre, mais...; **they are in no ~ democratic** ils ne sont en aucune manière démocratiques; **7** sout (opinion) opinion *f* (générale).
II senses *npl* (sanity) raison *f*; **to bring sb to his ~s** ramener qn à la raison; **to come to one's ~s** revenir à la raison; **to take leave of one's ~s** perdre la raison or l'esprit.
III *vtr* **1** (be aware of) deviner (**that** que); **he ~d her uneasiness/her anger/her sorrow** il devinait son malaise/sa colère/son chagrin; **to ~ where/how etc** deviner où/comment etc; **to ~ danger/hostility** sentir un danger/de l'hostilité; **to ~ sb** ou **sb's presence** sentir la présence de qn; **2** (detect) [*machine*] détecter [*heat, light*]; **3** Comput (detect) détecter [*location*]; (read) lire [*data*].
IDIOMS **to knock** ou **hammer** ou **pound** US **some ~ into sb** ramener qn à la raison; **to see ~** entendre raison; **to talk ~** dire des choses sensées.

sense datum *n* Philos donnée *f* des sens.

senseless /'senslɪs/ *adj* **1** (pointless) [*violence, killing*] gratuit; [*idea, discussion*] absurde; [*act, waste*] insensé; **it is ~ to do** ou **doing** il est insensé de faire; **2** (unconscious) sans connaissance, inconscient; **he lay ~ on the floor** il était étendu sans connaissance par terre; **to knock sb ~** faire perdre connaissance à qn.

senselessly /'senslɪslɪ/ *adv* [*waste, spend*] de manière insensée.

senselessness /'senslɪsnɪs/ *n* **1** (pointlessness) caractère *m* insensé (**of** de); **2** (unconsciousness) inconscience *f*.

sense organ *n* organe *m* sensoriel; **the ~s** les organes des sens.

sensibility /ˌsensə'bɪlətɪ/ **I** *n* **1** sout (sensitivity) sensibilité *f* (**to** à); **2** Bot (of plant) susceptibilité *f*.
II sensibilities *npl* sout **1** (feelings) susceptibilités *fpl*; **2** (capacity to respond) sensibilités *fpl*.

sensible /'sensəbl/ *adj* **1** (showing common sense) [*person, idea, attitude, remark*] raisonnable, sensé; [*policy, solution, reform, investment*] judicieux/-ieuse; [*diet*] intelligent; **it is ~ (for sb) to do** il est raisonnable (de la part de qn) de faire; **2** (practical) [*shoes, coat, underwear*] pratique; **3** (perceptible) sensible; **4** littér (aware) **~ of sth** conscient de qch, sensible à qch.

sensibly /'sensəblɪ/ *adv* [*eat, dress, act, talk*] de façon raisonnable; [*dressed, equipped*] de façon pratique; [*chosen, managed, organised*] de façon judicieuse; **~ priced** à un prix raisonnable.

sensitive /'sensətɪv/ *adj* **1** (easily affected) [*skin, instrument, nerve, plant, area*] sensible (**to** à); **2** fig (easily hurt) [*person, character*] sensible, susceptible (**to** à); **3** (aware, intelligent) [*person, treatment, approach*] sensible; [*portrayal, work of art, artist*] sensible, fin; **4** (delicate) [*situation*] délicat; [*discussions, issue, job*] difficile; **5** (confidential) [*information, material*] confidentiel/-ielle.

sensitively /'sensətɪvlɪ/ *adv* [*speak, act, treat, tackle, react*] avec délicatesse; [*chosen, portrayed*] avec sensibilité.

sensitive plant *n* Hort sensitive *f*; **she's a ~** fig elle est susceptible.

sensitivity /ˌsensə'tɪvətɪ/ *n* (all contexts) sensibilité *f* (**to** à).

sensitize /'sensɪtaɪz/ *vtr* (all contexts) sensibiliser.

sensor /'sensə(r)/ *n* détecteur *m*.

sensory /'sensərɪ/ *adj* [*nerve, organ, impression*] sensoriel/-ielle.

sensory deprivation *n* Psych perte *f* sensorielle.

sensual /'senʃʊəl/ *adj* sensuel/-elle.

sensualism /'senʃʊəlɪzəm/ *n* gen sensualité *f*; Philos sensualisme *m*.

sensualist /'senʃʊəlɪst/ *n* gen, Philos sensualiste *mf*.

sensuality /ˌsenʃʊ'ælətɪ/ *n* sensualité *f*.

sensually /'senʃʊəlɪ/ *adv* [*speak, laugh, move, dance*] avec sensualité; [*evocative, exciting*] sensuellement.

sensuous /'senʃʊəs/ *adj* sensuel/-elle, voluptueux/-euse.

sensuously /'senʃʊəslɪ/ *adv* de façon sensuelle.

sensuousness /'senʃʊəsnɪs/ *n* sensualité *f*, volupté *f*.

sent /sent/ *prét, pp* ▶ **send**.

sentence /'sentəns/ **I** *n* **1** Jur peine *f*, condamnation *f*; **a jail** ou **prison ~** une peine d'emprisonnement; **the death ~** la peine de mort; **a death ~** une condamnation à mort; **to be under ~ of death** être condamné à mort; **to serve a ~** purger une peine; **to pass ~ on sb** prononcer une peine or une condamnation contre qn; **she got a three year ~** elle a été condamnée à trois ans de prison; **2** Ling phrase *f*.
II *vtr* condamner (**to** à; **to do** à faire; **for** pour); **to ~ sb to jail** condamner qn à une peine de prison.

sentence adverb *n* adverbe *m* de phrase.

sententious /sen'tenʃəs/ *adj* sentencieux/-ieuse.

sententiously /sen'tenʃəslɪ/ *adv* [*speak*] d'un ton sentencieux; [*write*] d'un style sentencieux.

sentient /'senʃnt/ *adj* doué de sensations.

sentiment /'sentɪmənt/ *n* **1** (feeling) sentiment *m* (**for** pour, **towards** envers); **public ~** le sentiment général; **2** (opinion) opinion *f*; **what are your ~s about this?** quelle est votre opinion sur cela?; **my ~s exactly!** c'est bien mon avis!; **3** (sentimentality) gen sentimentalité *f*; pej sensiblerie *f*.

sentimental /ˌsentɪ'mentl/ *adj* sentimental also pej; **of (purely) ~ value** de valeur (purement) sentimentale; **to be ~ about** faire du sentiment pour [*children, animals*]; évoquer [qch] avec émotion [*childhood, past*]; **we can't afford to be ~** on ne peut (pas) se permettre de faire du sentiment; **it's too ~** [*book, film*] c'est trop mélo○.

sentimentalism /ˌsentɪ'mentəlɪzəm/ *n* sentimentalisme *m*.

sentimentalist /ˌsentɪ'mentəlɪst/ *n* sentimental/-e *m/f*.

sentimentality /ˌsentɪmen'tælətɪ/ *n* sentimentalité *f*; pej sensiblerie *f*.

sentimentalize /ˌsentɪ'mentəlaɪz/ **I** *vtr* (treat sentimentally) traiter [qn/qch] de façon sentimentale; (be sentimental about) faire du sentiment pour.
II *vi* faire du sentiment (**about, over** pour).

sentimentally /ˌsentɪ'mentəlɪ/ *adv* sentimentalement.

sentinel /'sentɪnl/ *n* **1** (guard) factionnaire *m*; **to stand ~** monter la garde; **2** Comput drapeau *m*, marque *f*.

sentry /'sentrɪ/ *n* sentinelle *f*.

sentry box *n* guérite *f*.

sentry duty *n* faction *f*; **to be on ~** être de faction.

sentry post *n* poste *m* de garde.

Seoul /səʊl/ ▶ **1818** *pr n* Séoul.

Sep *abrév écrite* = **September**.

sepal /'sepl/ *n* sépale *m*.

separable /'sepərəbl/ *adj* séparable (**from** de).

separate I separates /ˈsepərəts/ *npl* Fashn coordonnés *mpl*.

II /ˈsepərət/ *adj* **1** (with singular noun) [*piece, section, organization*] à part; [*discussion, issue, occasion*] autre; [*problem*] à part; [*identity*] propre (*before n*); **she has a ~ room** elle a une chambre à part; **each room has a ~ bathroom** chaque chambre a sa propre salle de bains; **the flat is ~ from the rest of the house** l'appartement est indépendant du reste de la maison; **a ~ appointment for each child** un rendez-vous pour chaque enfant; **I had a ~ appointment** j'avais un autre rendez-vous; **under ~ cover** Post sous pli séparé; **2** (with plural noun) [*pieces, sections, discussions, issues, problems*] différent; [*organizations, agreements, treaties*] distinct; [*dates, appointments*] différent; **they have ~ rooms** ils ont chacun leur chambre; **they dined at ~ tables** ils ont dîné à des tables différentes; **they asked for ~ bills** (in restaurant) ils ont demandé chacun leur addition; **these are two ~ problems** ce sont deux problèmes différents.

III /ˈsepərət/ *adv* **keep the knives ~** rangez les couteaux séparément or à part; **keep the knives ~ from the forks** séparez les couteaux des fourchettes.

IV /ˈsepəreɪt/ *vtr* **1** (divide) [*wall, river*] séparer [*country, community*]; [*intolerance, belief*] diviser [*people*]; séparer [*milk, egg*]; **only five seconds ~d the two athletes** cinq secondes seulement séparaient les deux athlètes; **to be ~d by** être séparé par [*river, wall*]; être divisé à cause de [*prejudice, intolerance*]; **to ~ sth from sth** [*wall, river*] séparer qch de qch; **to ~ the cream from the milk** séparer la crème du lait; **to ~ sb from sb** [*belief, disapproval*] éloigner qn de qn; **her beliefs ~d her from her sister** ses croyances l'ont éloignée de sa sœur; **the child became ~d from his mother** (in crowd etc) l'enfant s'est retrouvé séparé de sa mère; **to ~ the issue of pay from that of working hours** dissocier la question des salaires de celle des heures de travail; **2** (also **~ out**) (sort out) répartir [*people*]; trier [*objects, produce*]; **he ~d (out) the children according to age** il a réparti les enfants selon leur âge.

V /ˈsepəreɪt/ *vi* (all contexts) [*person , couple, component*] se séparer (**from** de).

VI separated *pp adj* [*person, couple*] séparé.

■ **separate out** [*liquid*] se séparer.

separately /ˈsepərətlɪ/ *adv* (all contexts) séparément.

separation /ˌsepəˈreɪʃn/ *n* gen séparation *f* (**from** de); (of couple) séparation *f* (**from** d'avec).

separatism /ˈsepərətɪzəm/ *n* séparatisme *m*.

separatist /ˈsepərətɪst/ *n, adj* séparatiste (*mf*).

separator /ˈsepəreɪtə(r)/ *n* séparateur *m*.

Sephardic /sɪˈfɑːdɪ/ *adj* séfarade.

sepia /ˈsiːpɪə/ **I** *n* **1** ▶ 1104 (colour) sépia *f*; **2** (cuttlefish) seiche *f*.

II *modif* [*photograph, ink*] sépia *inv*; **~ wash** lavis *m* (en) sépia; **~ drawing** sépia *f*.

sepoy /ˈsiːpɔɪ/ *n* cipaye *m*.

sepsis /ˈsepsɪs/ *n* Med septicité *f*.

Sept *abrév écrite* = **September**.

septa /ˈseptə/ *pl* ▶ **septum**.

September /sepˈtembə(r)/ ▶ 1472 *n* septembre *m*.

September Massacre *n* Hist massacres *mpl* de septembre, septembrisades *fpl*.

Septembrist /sepˈtembrɪst/ *n* Hist septembriseur *m*.

septet /sepˈtet/ *n* Mus septuor *m*.

septic /ˈseptɪk/ *adj* infecté, septique spec; **to go** ou **turn ~** s'infecter.

septicaemia /ˌseptɪˈsiːmɪə/ ▶ 1354 *n* septicémie *f*.

septic tank *n* fosse *f* septique.

septuagenarian /ˌseptjʊədʒɪˈneərɪən, US -tʃʊdʒə-/ *n, adj* septuagénaire (*mf*).

septuagesima /ˌseptjʊəˈdʒesɪmə, US -tʃʊdʒə-/ *n* Septuagésime *m*.

septum /ˈseptəm/ *n* (*pl* **-ta**) septum *m*.

septuplet /ˈseptjʊplɪt, sepˈtjuːplɪt/ *n* septuplé/-e *m/f*.

sepulchral /sɪˈpʌlkrəl/ *adj* **1** fig, littér [*atmosphere, tone*] sépulcral liter; **2** sout [*statue, tomb*] funéraire.

sepulchre GB, **sepulcher** US /ˈseplkə(r)/ *n* tombeau *m*.

sequel /ˈsiːkwəl/ *n* (all contexts) suite *f* (**to** à).

sequence /ˈsiːkwəns/ *n* **1** (of problems) succession *f*; (of photos) série *f*; **the ~ of events** la suite des événements; **2** (order) ordre *m*; **in ascending/chronological ~** par ordre ascendant/chronologique; **3** (in film) séquence *f*; **the dream ~** la scène de rêve; **4** (dance) numéro *m* de danse; **5** (of notes, chords) séquence *f*; **6** Comput, Math, Games séquence *f*.

sequence of tenses *n* concordance *f* des temps.

sequencer /ˈsiːkwənsə(r)/ *n* Comput, Electron, Mus (all contexts) séquenceur *m*.

sequential /sɪˈkwenʃl/ *adj* (all contexts) séquentiel/-ielle.

sequential: **~ access** *n* Comput accès *m* séquentiel; **~ control** *n* Comput exécution *f* séquentielle des instructions.

sequester /sɪˈkwestə(r)/ **I** *vtr* **1** Fin, Jur mettre [qch] sous séquestre; **2** sout (lock away) séquestrer.

II sequestered *pp adj* sout [*life*] cloîtré; [*place*] reculé.

sequestrate /ˈsiːkwestreɪt/ *n* Fin Jur mettre [qch] sous séquestre.

sequestration /ˌsiːkwɪˈstreɪʃn/ *n* mise *f* sous séquestre.

sequin /ˈsiːkwɪn/ *n* paillette *f*.

sequin(n)ed /ˈsiːkwɪnd/ *adj* [*garment*] pailleté.

sequoia /sɪˈkwɔɪə/ *n* (tree, wood) séquoia *m*.

seraglio /seˈrɑːlɪəʊ/ *n* (*pl* **~s**) sérail *m*.

serape /seˈrɑːpeɪ/ *n* couverture-habit *f* (mexicaine).

seraph /ˈserəf/ *n* (*pl* **~s** ou **~im**) séraphin *m*.

seraphic /səˈræfɪk/ *adj* littér séraphique.

seraphim /ˈserəfɪm/ *pl* ▶ **seraph**.

Serb /sɜːb/ ▶ 1486, 1402 **I** *n* **1** (person) Serbe *mf*; **2** Ling serbe *m*.

II *adj* serbe.

Serbia /ˈsɜːbɪə/ ▶ 1131 *pr n* Serbie *f*.

Serbian /ˈsɜːbɪən/ *n, adj* = **Serb**.

Serbo-Croat(ian) /ˌsɜːbəʊˈkrəʊæt, -krəʊˈeɪʃn/ ▶ 1402 *n, adj* Ling serbo-croate (*m*).

SERC /sɜːk/ *n* GB (*abrév* = **Science and Engineering Research Council**) centre *m* national de recherches scientifiques.

serenade /ˌserəˈneɪd/ **I** *n* sérénade *f*.

II *vtr* donner une sérénade à.

serendipitous /ˌserənˈdɪpɪtəs/ *adj* sout [*find, meeting*] heureux/-euse.

serendipity /ˌserənˈdɪpətɪ/ *n* sout don *m* de faire des trouvailles; **it was pure ~ that I found this house** c'est par un heureux hasard que je suis tombé sur cette maison.

serene /sɪˈriːn/ *adj* serein; **His/Her Serene Highness** Son Altesse Sérénissime.

serenely /sɪˈriːnlɪ/ *adv* [*say, smile*] sereinement; **~ indifferent** d'une indifférence sereine.

serenity /sɪˈrenətɪ/ *n* sérénité *f*.

serf /sɜːf/ *n* serf/serve *m/f*.

serfdom /ˈsɜːfdəm/ *n* servage *m*.

serge /sɜːdʒ/ **I** *n* serge *f*.

II *modif* [*garment*] en serge.

sergeant /ˈsɑːdʒənt/ ▶ 1612 *n* **1** GB Mil sergent *m*; **2** US Mil caporal-chef *m*; **3** (in police) ≈ brigadier *m*.

sergeant at arms *n* **1** (who keeps order) huissier *m*; (in court) huissier-audiencier *m*; **2** Hist (armed attendant) sergent *m* d'armes.

sergeant: **~ first class** *n* ▶ 1612 US Mil sergent-chef *m*; **~ major** *n* ▶ 1612 adjudant *m*.

serial /ˈsɪərɪəl/ **I** *n* **1** TV, Radio, Publg (story) feuilleton *m*; **radio/TV ~** feuilleton radiophonique/télévisé; **a seven part ~** un feuilleton en sept épisodes; **to broadcast sth as a ~** diffuser qch en feuilleton; **to adapt** ou **make sth into a ~** faire un feuilleton de qch; **2** Publg (publication) périodique *m*.

II *adj* **1** Comput [*access, computer*] séquentiel/-ielle; [*input/output, printer, programming, transfer*] série *inv*; **2** Mus sériel/-ielle.

serialism /ˈsɪərɪəlɪzəm/ *n* Mus sérialisme *m*.

serialization /ˌsɪərɪəlaɪˈzeɪʃn, US -lɪˈz-/ *n* adaptation *f* en feuilleton.

serialize /ˈsɪərɪəlaɪz/ *vtr* adapter [qch] en feuilleton.

serial killer *n* meurtrier *m* en série.

serially /ˈsɪərɪəlɪ/ *adv* **1** TV, Radio, Publg en feuilleton; **2** (in sequence) en série.

serial number *n* (of machine, car etc) numéro *m* de série; US (of soldier) numéro *m* matricule.

serial rights *npl* droits *mpl* d'adaptation en feuilleton.

seriatim /ˌsɪərɪˈeɪtɪm/ *adv* sout l'un après l'autre.

sericulture /ˈserɪkʌltʃə(r)/ *n* sériciculture *f*.

series /ˈsɪəriːz/ **I** *n* (*pl* **~**) **1** (set) série *f* (**of** de); **a ~ of attacks/of measures** une série d'attaques/de mesures; **a ~ of stamps** une série de timbres; **a ~ of books** une collection de livres; **2** Radio, TV, Literat série *f* (**about** sur); **a drama/comedy ~** une série de fiction/de comédie; **this is the last in the present ~** voici la dernière partie de ce programme; **3** Sport championnat *m* (*à plusieurs épreuves*); **4** Elec, Electron série *f*; **in ~** en série.

II *modif* Elec, Electron [*circuit, connection*] série *inv*.

series: **~ winding** *n* Elec enroulement *m* en série; **~-wound** *adj* Elec enroulé en série.

seriocomic /ˌsɪərɪəʊˈkɒmɪk/ *adj* sérieux/-ieuse et comique à la fois.

serious /ˈsɪərɪəs/ *adj* **1** (not frivolous or light) [*person, expression, discussion, approach, issue, offer, purpose*] sérieux/-ieuse; [*work, literature, actor, scientist, survey*] de qualité; [*attempt, concern*] réel/réelle; [*intention*] ferme; **to be ~ about sth** prendre qch au sérieux; **to be ~ about doing** avoir vraiment l'intention de faire; **is he ~ about going to America?** est-ce qu'il a vraiment l'intention d'aller aux États-Unis?; **is he ~ about her?** est-ce qu'il tient vraiment à elle?; **they're ~ about each other** c'est du sérieux entre eux; **to give ~ thought to sth** penser sérieusement à qch; **there's no ~ case for arguing that...** il n'y a pas vraiment lieu de soutenir que...; **this is deadly ~**○ c'est on ne peut plus sérieux; **you can't be ~** tu veux rire○; **they got down to the ~ business of eating** hum ils sont passés aux choses sérieuses: ils se sont mis à manger; **being a parent is a ~ business** être parent est une grande responsabilité; **to make/spend ~ money**○ gagner/dépenser beaucoup d'argent; **if you want to do some ~ shopping/surfing...**○ si tu veux vraiment faire des courses/du surf...; **he's a ~ drinker**○ hum c'est un buveur professionnel; **2** (grave) [*accident, condition, allegation, crime, crisis, error, problem*] grave; [*concern, doubt, misgiving*] sérieux/-ieuse; **nothing ~, I hope** rien de grave, j'espère; **this is a very ~ matter** l'affaire est très grave.

Serious Fraud Office, **SFO** *n* GB Service *m* de répression des fraudes.

seriously /ˈsɪərɪəslɪ/ *adv* **1** (not frivolously) [*speak, write, think, listen*] sérieusement; **to ~ consider doing sth** penser sérieusement à faire qch; **~, do you need help?** sérieusement, avez-vous besoin d'aide?; **are you ~ suggesting that...?** tu veux vraiment dire que...?; **but ~,...** blague à part,...○; **to take sb/sth ~** prendre qn/qch au sérieux; **he takes himself too ~** il se prend trop au sérieux; **police are treating the threat very ~** la police prend la menace très au sérieux; **2** (gravely) [*ill, injured, damaged, divided, at risk, flawed*] gravement; [*mislead, underestimate*] vraiment; **something is ~ wrong** il y a quelque chose qui ne va vraiment pas; **3**○ (extremely) [*boring, funny*] vraiment.

seriousness /ˈsɪərɪəsnɪs/ *n* **1** (of person, film, treatment, study, approach) sérieux *m*; (of tone, air, occasion, reply) gravité *f*; (of intention) sincérité *f*; **in all ~** sérieusement; **2** (of illness, damage, allegation, problem, situation) gravité *f*.

serjeant‡ *n* = **sergeant**.

sermon /ˈsɜːmən/ *n* sermon *m*; **to give/preach a ~** Relig faire un sermon; **to give/preach sb a ~** (lecture) sermonner qn.

sermonize /ˈsɜːmənaɪz/ *vi* péj pérorer (**about** sur).

sermonizing /ˈsɜːmənaɪzɪŋ/ *n* péj péroraisons *fpl*.

seropositive /ˌsɪərəʊˈpɒzɪtɪv/ *adj* séropositif/-ive.

serous /ˈsɪərəs/ *adj* séreux/-euse.

serpent /ˈsɜːpənt/ *n* (all contexts) serpent *m*.

serpentine /ˈsɜːpəntaɪn, US -tiːn/ **I** *n* Miner serpentine *f*.
II *adj* littér [*river, road*] sinueux/-euse.

SERPS /sɜːps/ *n* GB Soc Admin (*abrév* = **state earnings-related pension scheme**) caisse *f* de retraite.

serrated /sɪˈreɪtɪd, US ˈsereɪtɪd/ *adj* dentelé; **~ knife** couteau-scie *m*.

serration /sɪˈreɪʃn/ *n* dentelure *f*.

serried /ˈserɪd/ *adj* serré.

serum /ˈsɪərəm/ *n* sérum *m*; **snake-bite ~** sérum antivenimeux.

servant /ˈsɜːvənt/ *n* **1** ▶ 1692 (in household) domestique *mf*; **to keep a ~** avoir un domestique; **2** fig serviteur *m*; **your ~, sir**†**!** votre serviteur!; **your obedient ~**† (in letter) votre très obéissant serviteur†.

servant: **~ girl** *n* bonne *f*; **~'s hall** *n* office *m*.

serve /sɜːv/ **I** *n* Sport service *m*; **it's my ~** à moi de servir; **to have a big ~** avoir un très bon service.
II *vtr* **1** (work for) servir [*God, King, country, community, cause, ideal, public, company*]; travailler au service de [*employer, family*]; **to ~ sb/sth well** rendre de grands services à qn/qch; **to ~ two masters** fig servir deux maîtres à la fois; **2** (attend to customers) servir; **are you being ~ed?** on vous sert?; **3** Culin servir [*client, guest, meal, dish*]; **to ~ sb with sth** servir qch à qn; **let me ~ you some beef** laissez-moi vous servir du bœuf; **lunch is ~d** le déjeuner est servi; **we can't ~ them chicken again!** nous ne pouvons pas leur resservir du poulet!; **~ it with a salad** servez-le avec une salade; **~ hot** servir chaud; **~s four** (in recipe) pour quatre personnes; **4** (provide facility) [*public utility, power station, reservoir*] alimenter; [*public transport, library, hospital*] desservir [*area, community*]; **the area is well/poorly ~d with transport** la région est bien/mal desservie par les transports; **the area is well ~d with shops** le quartier est très commerçant; **5** (satisfy) servir [*interests*]; satisfaire [*needs*]; **6** (function) être utile à; **this old pen/my sense of direction has ~d me well** ce vieux stylo/mon sens de l'orientation m'a été très utile; **he has been badly ~d by his advisers** ses conseillers ne lui ont pas été très utiles; **if my memory ~s me well** si j'ai bonne mémoire; **to ~ sb as sth** servir de qch à qn; **the table ~s me as a desk** la table me sert de bureau; **to ~ a purpose** ou **function** être utile; **to ~ no useful purpose** ne servir à rien; **what purpose is ~d by separating them?** à quoi sert de les séparer?; **having ~d its purpose, the committee was disbanded** ayant rempli son rôle, la commission a été dissoute; **to ~ the** ou **sb's purpose** faire l'affaire; **this map will ~ the** ou **my purpose** cette carte fera l'affaire; **7** (spend time) **to ~ a term** Pol remplir un mandat; **to ~ one's time** (in army) faire son temps de service; (in prison) purger sa peine; **to ~ a sentence** purger une peine (de prison); **to ~ five years** faire cinq ans de prison; **8** Jur délivrer [*injunction*] (**on sb** à qn); **to ~ a writ** signifier une assignation; **to ~ a writ on sb, to ~ sb with a writ** assigner qn en justice; **to ~ a summons** signifier une citation; **to ~ a summons on sb, to ~ sb with a summons** citer qn à comparaître; **to ~ notice of sth on sb** Jur, fig signifier qch à qn; **9** Sport servir [*ball, ace*]; **10** (mate with) couvrir, saillir [*cow, mare*].
III *vi* **1** (in shop, church) servir; (at table) faire le service; **2** (on committee, in government) exercer ses fonctions (**as** de); **members ~ for two years** les membres exercent leurs fonctions pendant deux ans; **she's serving as general secretary** elle exerce la fonction ou les fonctions de secrétaire général; **to ~ on** être membre de [*committee, board, jury*]; **3** Mil servir (**as** comme; **under** sous); **to ~ in** ou **with a regiment** servir dans un régiment; **I ~d with him** j'étais dans l'armée avec lui; **4** (meet a need) faire l'affaire; **any excuse will ~** n'importe quelle excuse fera l'affaire; **to ~ as sth** servir de qch; **this room ~s as a spare bedroom** cette pièce sert de chambre d'ami; **this should ~ as a warning** cela devrait nous servir d'avertissement; **the photo ~d as a reminder to me of the holidays** la photo me rappelait les vacances; **to ~ to do** servir à faire; **it ~s to show that...** cela sert à montrer que...; **5** Sport servir (**for** pour); **Conti to ~** au service, Conti.
IDIOMS **it ~s you right!** ça t'apprendra!; **it ~s him right for being so careless!** ça lui apprendra à être si négligent!
■ **serve out**: **~ out [sth], ~ [sth] out 1** Culin servir [*meal, food*] (**to** à); distribuer [*rations, provisions*]; **2** (finish) finir [*term of duty*]; purger [*prison sentence*].
■ **serve up** Culin ¶ servir; ¶ **~ up [sth], ~ [sth] up 1** Culin servir; **to ~ sth up again** resservir qch; **2**○ fig, pej resservir [*fashion, idea, programme, policy*]; donner [*excuse*].

serve-and-volley *adj* [*game, player*] service-volée *inv*.

server /ˈsɜːvə(r)/ *n* **1** Sport serveur *m*; **2** Comput serveur *m*; **3** Culin couvert *m* de service; **4** Relig servant *m*.

server-managed *adj* Comput géré par serveur.

servery /ˈsɜːvərɪ/ *n* GB (room) office *m*; (counter) comptoir *m*.

service /ˈsɜːvɪs/ **I** *n* **1** (department) service *m*; **(accident and) emergency ~** service des urgences; **information ~** service d'informations or de renseignements; **2** (facility, work done) service *m*; **advisory ~** service de conseil; **professional ~s** services *mpl* professionnels; **public ~** service public; **for ~s rendered** Comm pour services rendus; **to offer/provide a ~** offrir/fournir un service; **we need the ~s of an accountant** nous avons besoin (des services) d'un comptable; **to dispense with sb's ~s** se passer des services de qn; **she received an award for ~s to the arts/industry** elle a reçu un prix pour les services qu'elle a rendus à la culture/à l'industrie; **it's all part of the ~** (don't mention it) c'est tout naturel; (it's all included) tout est compris; **'normal ~ will be resumed as soon as possible'** Radio, TV 'dans quelques instants la suite de votre programme'; **my ~s don't come cheap!** je me fais payer cher!; **3** (work, period of work done) gen, Admin, Mil service *m* (**in** dans; **to** de); **30 years of ~** 30 ans de service; **a lifetime of ~ to the firm/community** une vie passée au service de l'entreprise/de la communauté; **at sb's ~** au service de qn; **I'm at your ~** je suis à votre service; **to put** ou **place sth at sb's ~** mettre qch à la disposition de qn; **in sb's ~** au service de qn; **in the ~ of humanity** au service de l'humanité; **he travelled a lot in the ~ of his firm** il a beaucoup voyagé pour sa compagnie; **he gave his life in the ~ of his country** il a donné sa vie pour servir son pays; **to be in ~** Hist travailler comme domestique; **to go into ~ with sb** entrer au service de qn; **to see ~ in the army/in Egypt** servir dans l'armée/en Égypte; **4** Comm (customer care) service *m* (**to** à); **to get good/bad ~** être bien/mal servi; **we add on 15% for ~** nous ajoutons 15% pour le service; **'includes ~'** (on bill) 'service compris'; **is the ~ included?** (in restaurant) le service est compris?; **can we have some ~ here please?** est-ce que quelqu'un peut nous servir s'il vous plaît?; **we must improve the quality of ~** nous devons améliorer la qualité du service; **we have a reputation for good ~** nous sommes réputés pour la qualité de notre service; **5** (from machine, vehicle, product) usage *m*; **to give good** ou **long ~** [*machine*] fonctionner longtemps; [*vehicle, product, garment*] faire de l'usage; **I've had years of ~ from that car/typewriter** cette voiture/machine à écrire m'a duré des années; **to be in ~** être en service; **the plane is still in ~ with many airlines** cet avion est encore en service dans de nombreuses compagnies aériennes; **to come into/go out of ~** entrer en/cesser d'être en service; **it went out of ~ years ago** il n'est plus en service depuis des années; **to take sth out of ~** retirer qch du service [*plane, machine*]; **'out of ~'** (on bus) 'hors service'; (on machine) 'en panne'; **6** (transport facility) service *m* (**to** pour); **bus/coach/taxi/train ~** service d'autobus/de cars/de taxi/de trains; **to run a regular ~** assurer un service régulier; **an hourly bus/train ~** un autobus/train toutes les heures; **the number 28 bus ~** la ligne du 28; **7** Aut, Tech (overhaul) révision *f*; **a 15,000 km ~** la révision des 15 000 km; **the photocopier/washing machine is due for a ~** la photocopieuse/machine à laver a besoin d'être révisée; **8** Relig office *m*; **morning/Sunday ~** office du matin/du dimanche; **marriage ~** cérémonie *f* nuptiale; **form of ~** (printed) déroulement *m* de l'office; **9** (crockery) service *m*; **dinner ~** service de table; **tea ~** service à thé; **10** Sport service *m*; **your ~!** à toi de servir!; **return of ~** retour *m* de service; **11** (help, good turn) service *m*; **to do sb a ~** rendre service à qn; **to be of ~ to sb** [*person*] aider qn; [*thing*] être utile à qn; **12** Jur signification *f*; **13** (of female animal) saillie *f*.
II services *npl* **1 the ~s** Mil, Naut les armées; **a career in the ~s** une carrière dans l'armée; **2** (on motorway) aire *m* de services; **'~s 40 km'** 'aire de services à 40 km'.
III *modif* Mil [*gun*] de guerre; [*pay, pension*] militaire; [*personnel*] de l'armée; [*life*] dans l'armée; **~ dress** tenue *f* militaire.
IV *vtr* **1** Aut, Tech (maintain, overhaul) faire la révision de [*vehicle*]; entretenir, assurer l'entretien de [*machine, boiler*]; **to have one's car ~d** faire réviser sa voiture, donner sa voiture à réviser; **2** Fin payer les intérêts de [*debt, loan*]; **3** (mate with) couvrir [*cow, mare*].

serviceable /ˈsɜːvɪsəbl/ *adj* **1** (usable) utilisable; **the vehicle is still ~** le véhicule est encore utilisable; **2** (practical) pratique; **a ~ grey coat** un manteau gris pratique.

service area *n* aire *f* de services.

service break *n* Sport **to have a ~** avoir fait le break.

service centre GB, **service center** US *n* centre *m* de service après-vente.

service charge *n* **1** (in restaurant) service *m*; **there is a ~** le service n'est pas compris; **what is the ~?** le service est de combien?; **2** (in banking) frais *mpl* de gestion de compte; **3** (for property maintenance) charges *fpl* locatives.

service: **~ company** *n* société *f* de service; **~ contract** *n* Comm contrat *m* d'entretien; **~ department** *n* (office) service *m* entretien; (workshop) atelier *m* d'entretien; **~ elevator** *n* US = **service lift**; **~ engineer** ▶1692 *n* technicien *m* de maintenance; **~ entrance** *n* entrée *f* des fournisseurs, livraisons *fpl*; **~ family** *n* famille *f* d'une personne dans l'armée; **~ flat** *n* GB appartement *m* (*dont le ménage est assuré par l'agence de location*); **~ game** *n* service *m*; **~ hatch** *n* passe-plats *m inv*; **~ industry** *n* Comm (company) industrie *f* de services; (sector) secteur *m* tertiaire; **~ lift** *n* GB (in hotel, building) ascenseur *m* de service; (for heavy goods) monte-charge *m*; **~ line** *n* ligne *f* de service; **~man** *n* militaire *m*; **~ module** *n* Aerosp module *m* de service; **~ operation** *n* service *m* commercial; **~ road** *n* GB, gen voie *f* d'accès; Constr voie *f* de service; **~ sector** *n* secteur *m* tertiaire; **~ station** *n* station-service *f*; **~ till** *n* GB (in shop) caisse *f*; (cash dispenser) distributeur *m* automatique de billets de banque; **~woman** *n* femme *f* soldat.

servicing /'sɜːvɪsɪŋ/ *n* Aut, Tech révision *f*; **the machine has gone in for ~** la machine est en révision.

serviette /ˌsɜːvɪ'et/ *n* GB serviette *f* de table.

servile /'sɜːvaɪl, US -vl/ *adj* servile.

servility /sɜː'vɪlətɪ/ *n* servilité *f*.

serving /'sɜːvɪŋ/ **I** *n* (helping) portion *f*; **enough for four ~s** pour quatre personnes.

II *adj* [*officer*] Mil en activité; [*official, chairman*] Admin en exercice.

serving: **~ dish** *n* plat *m* (de service); **~ hatch** *n* passe-plats *m inv*; **~man†** *n* domestique *m*; **~ spoon** *n* cuillère *f* de service.

servitude /'sɜːvɪtjuːd, US -tuːd/ *n* servitude *f*.

servo /'sɜːvəʊ/ *n*: *abrév* ▶ **servomechanism**.

servo: **~ amplifier** *n* servoamplificateur *m*; **~(-assisted) brake** *n* servofrein *m*; **~ control** *n* servocommande *f*; **~mechanism** *n* servomécanisme *m*; **~motor** *n* servomoteur *m*.

sesame /'sesəmɪ/ **I** *n* sésame *m*.

II *modif* [*oil, seed*] de sésame.

sesquipedalian /ˌseskwɪpɪ'deɪlɪən/ *adj* sout [*word*] à rallonge; [*style*] ampoulé.

session /'seʃn/ *n* **1** Pol (term) session *f*; **parliamentary ~** session parlementaire; **2** Admin, Jur, Pol (sitting) séance *f*; **emergency ~** séance exceptionnelle; **the court is in ~** Jur le tribunal tient séance; **to go into closed** ou **private ~** siéger à huis clos; **3** (meeting) réunion *f*; (informal discussion) discussion *f*; **drinking ~**○ beuverie *f*; **4** GB Sch (year) année *f* scolaire; US (term) trimestre *m*; **autumn ~** premier trimestre; (period of lessons) cours *mpl*; **morning/afternoon ~** cours du matin/de l'après-midi; **5** Med, Dent etc séance *f* (**with** chez); **6** Mus, Sport séance *f*; **training ~** Sport séance d'entraînement; **studio ~** Mus séance d'enregistrement; **7** Fin (at stock exchange) séance *f*; **trading ~** séance de Bourse.

session musician ▶1692 *n* musicien/-ienne *m/f* de séance.

set /set/ **I** *n* **1** (collection) (of keys, spanners, screwdrivers) jeu *m*; (of golf clubs, stamps, coins, chairs) série *f*; (of cutlery) service *m*; (of encyclopedias) collection *f*; fig (of data, rules, instructions, tests) série *f*; **a ~ of china** un service de table; **a new/clean ~ of clothes** des vêtements neufs/propres; **they're sold in ~s of 10** ils sont vendus par lots de 10; **a ~ of bills** Comm, Fin un jeu de connaissements; **a ~ of fingerprints** des empreintes *fpl* digitales; **a ~ of stairs** un escalier; **a ~ of traffic lights** des feux *mpl* (de signalisation); **2** (kit, game) **a backgammon/chess ~** un jeu de jacquet/d'échecs; **a magic ~** une mallette de magie; **3** (pair) **a ~ of sheets** une paire de draps; **a ~ of footprints** l'empreinte des deux pieds; **a ~ of false teeth** un dentier; **my top/bottom ~** (of false teeth) la partie supérieure/inférieure de mon dentier; **one ~ of grandparents lives in Canada** deux de mes grands-parents habitent au Canada; **both ~s of parents agreed with us** ses parents comme les miens étaient d'accord avec nous; **4** Sport (in tennis) set *m*; **'~ to Miss Wilson'** 'set Mademoiselle Wilson'; **5** (television) poste *m*; **TV ~, television ~** poste de télévision; **6** (group) (social) monde *m*; (sporting) milieu *m*; **aristocratic/literary ~** monde aristocratique/littéraire; **the racing/yachting ~** le milieu des courses/du yachting; **the smart** ou **fashionable ~** les gens à la mode; **he's not part of our ~** il ne fait pas partie de notre groupe; **7** (scenery) Theat décor *m*; Cin, TV plateau *m*; **on the ~** Cin, TV sur le plateau; **8** Math ensemble *m*; **9** GB Sch (class, group) groupe *m*; **to be in the top ~ for maths** être dans le groupe des meilleurs en maths; **10** (hair-do) mise *f* en plis; **to have a shampoo and ~** se faire faire un shampooing et une mise en plis; **11** Mus concert *m*; **12** (position) (of sails) réglage *m*; **you could tell by the ~ of his jaw that he was stubborn** ça se voyait à sa tête qu'il était têtu; **13** (direction) sens *m*; **the ~ of the tide/wind** le sens de la marée/du vent; **14** (of badger) terrier *m*; **15** Hort plante *f* à repiquer; **16** Hunt (of hound) arrêt *m*.

II *adj* **1** (fixed) (*épith*) [*pattern, procedure, rule, task*] bien déterminé; [*time, price*] fixe; [*menu*] à prix fixe; [*formula*] toute faite; [*idea*] arrêté; **I had no ~ purpose in arranging the meeting** je n'avais pas d'objectif précis quand j'ai organisé cette réunion; **~ phrase, ~ expression** expression *f* consacrée, locution *f* figée; **to be ~ in one's ideas** ou **opinions** avoir des idées bien arrêtées; **to be ~ in one's ways** avoir ses habitudes; **the weather is ~ fair** le temps est au beau fixe; **2** (stiff) [*expression, smile*] figé; **3** Sch, Univ (prescribed) [*book, text*] au programme; **there are five ~ topics on the history syllabus** il y a cinq sujets au programme d'histoire; **4** (ready) (*jamais épith*) prêt (**for** pour); **to be (all) ~ to leave/start** être prêt à partir/commencer; **they're ~ to win/lose** tout laisse à croire qu'ils vont gagner/perdre; **5** (determined) **to be (dead) ~ against sth/doing** être tout à fait contre qch/l'idée de faire; **he's really ~ against my resigning/marrying** il est tout à fait contre ma démission/mon mariage; **to be ~ on sth/on doing** tenir absolument à qch/à faire; **6** (firm) [*jam, jelly, honey*] épais/épaisse, consistant; [*cement*] dur; [*yoghurt*] ferme.

III *vtr* (*p prés* **-tt-**; *prét, pp* **set**) **1** (place, position) placer [*chair, ornament*] (**on** sur); poster [*guard, sentry*]; monter, sertir [*gem*] (**in** dans); **to ~ sth against a wall** mettre qch contre un mur [*bike, ladder*]; **to ~ sth before sb** lit placer qch devant qn [*food, plate*]; fig présenter qch à qn [*proposals, findings*]; **to ~ sth in the ground** enfoncer qch dans le sol [*stake*]; **to ~ sth into sth** encastrer qch dans qch; **to ~ sth straight** lit (align) remettre qch droit [*painting*]; fig (tidy) remettre de l'ordre dans qch [*papers, room*]; **to ~ sth upright** redresser qch; **a house set among the trees** une maison située au milieu des arbres; **to ~ matters** ou **the record straight** fig mettre les choses au point; **a necklace set with rubies** un collier incrusté de rubis; **his eyes are set very close together** ses yeux sont très rapprochés; **2** (prepare) mettre [*table*]; tendre [*trap*]; **~ three places** mets trois couverts; **to ~ the stage** ou **scene for sth** fig préparer le lieu de qch [*encounter, match*]; **the stage is set for the final** tout est prêt pour la finale; **to ~ one's mark** ou **stamp on sth** laisser sa marque sur qch; **3** (affix, establish) fixer [*date, deadline, place, price, target*]; lancer [*fashion, trend*]; donner [*tone*]; établir [*precedent, record*]; **to ~ a good/bad example to sb** montrer le bon/mauvais exemple à qn; **to ~ one's sights on** viser [*championship, job*]; **4** (adjust) mettre [qch] à l'heure [*clock*]; mettre [*alarm clock, burglar alarm*]; mettre [qch] en marche [*timer, video*]; **to ~ the oven to 180°** mettre le four sur 180°; **to ~ the controls to manual** passer au mode manuel; **to ~ the video to record the film** mettre la vidéo en marche pour enregistrer le film; **to ~ the alarm for 7 am** mettre le réveil pour 7 heures; **~ your watch by mine** règle ta montre sur la mienne; **I set the heating to come on at 6 am** j'ai réglé le chauffage pour qu'il se mette en route à six heures; **to ~ the counter back to zero** remettre le compteur à zéro; **5** (start) **to ~ sth going** mettre qch en marche [*machine, motor*]; **to ~ sb laughing/thinking** faire rire/réfléchir qn; **to ~ sb to work doing** charger qn de faire; **the noise set the dogs barking** le bruit a fait aboyer les chiens; **6** (impose, prescribe) [*teacher*] donner [*homework, essay*]; poser [*problem*]; créer [*crossword puzzle*]; **to ~ an exam** préparer les sujets d'examen; **to ~ a book/subject for study** mettre un texte/un sujet au programme; **to ~ sb the task of doing** charger qn de faire; **7** Cin, Literat, Theat, TV situer; **to ~ a book in 1960/New York** situer un roman en 1960/à New York; **the film/novel is set in Munich/in the 1950's** le film/roman se passe à Munich/dans les années 50; **8** Mus **to ~ sth to music** mettre qch en musique [*libretto, lyrics*]; **9** Print composer [*text, type*] (**in** en); **10** Med immobiliser, éclisser spec [*bone, broken leg*]; **11** (style) **to ~ sb's hair** faire une mise en plis à qn; **to have one' s hair set** se faire faire une mise en plis; **12** (cause to harden) faire prendre [*jam, concrete*]; **13** (esteem) **to ~ sb above/below sb** placer qn au-dessus/en dessous de qn; **14** GB Sch grouper [qn] par niveau [*pupils*].

IV *vi* (*p prés* **-tt-**; *prét, pp* **set**) **1** [*sun*] se coucher; **2** (harden) [*jam, concrete*] prendre; [*glue*] sécher; **3** Med [*fracture, bone*] se ressouder.

V *v refl* (*p prés* **-tt-**; *prét, pp* **set**) **to ~ oneself sth** se fixer qch [*goal, target*].

IDIOMS **to be well set-up**○ (financially) avoir les moyens○; (physically) [*woman*] être bien balancé○; **to make a (dead) ~ at sb**○ GB se lancer à la tête de qn○.

■ **set about**: ¶ **~ about [sth]** se mettre à [*work, duties*]; **to ~ about doing** commencer à faire; **to ~ about the job** ou **task** ou **business of doing** commencer à faire; **I know what I want to do but I don't know how to ~ about it** je sais ce que je veux faire mais je ne sais pas comment m'y prendre; ¶ **~ about [sb]**○ attaquer qn (**with** avec); ¶ **~ [sth] about** faire courir [*rumour, story*]; **to ~ it about that**... faire courir le bruit que...

■ **set against**: ¶ **~ [sb] against** monter qn contre [*person*]; **to ~ oneself against sth** s'opposer à qch; ¶ **~ sth against sth** (compare) confronter qch à qch; **you have to ~ his evidence against what you already know** vous devez examiner son témoignage à la lumière de ce que vous savez déjà; **the benefits seem small, set against the risks** par rapport aux risques les bénéfices semblent maigres.

■ **set apart**: **~ [sb/sth] apart** distinguer [*person, book, film*] (**from** de).

■ **set aside**: **~ [sth] aside, ~ aside [sth] 1** (put down) poser [qch] de côté [*book, knitting*]; **2** (reserve) réserver [*area, room, time*] (**for** pour); mettre [qch] de côté [*money, stock*]; **3** (disregard) mettre [qch] de côté [*differences, prejudices*]; **4** Admin, Jur (reject) rejeter [*decision, request, verdict*]; casser [*judgment, ruling*].

■ **set back**: ¶ ~ **[sth] back 1** (position towards the rear) reculer [*chair, table*]; **the house is set back from the road** la maison est située un peu en retrait de la route; **2** (adjust) retarder [*clock, watch*]; ¶ ~ **back [sth]**, ~ **[sth] back** (delay) retarder [*production, recovery, work*]; ¶ ~ **[sb] back**○ coûter les yeux de la tête à○; **that car must have set you back a bit** cette voiture a dû te coûter les yeux de la tête; **it set me back 2,000 dollars** ça m'a coûté 2 000 dollars.
■ **set by**: ~ **[sth] by**, ~ **by [sth]** mettre [qch] de côté.
■ **set down**: ¶ ~ **[sb/sth] down** déposer [*passenger*]; poser [*suitcases, vase*]; ¶ ~ **down [sth]**, ~ **[sth] down 1** (establish) fixer [*code of practice, conditions, criteria*]; **2** (record) enregistrer [*event, fact*]; **to ~ down one' s thoughts (on paper)** consigner ses pensées par écrit; **3** (land) poser [*helicopter*].
■ **set forth**: ¶ ~ **forth** (leave) se mettre en route; ¶ ~ **forth [sth]** exposer [*findings, facts*]; présenter [*argument*].
■ **set in**: ¶ ~ **in** [*infection, gangrene*] se déclarer; [*complications*] survenir; [*winter*] arriver; [*depression, resentment*] s'installer; **the rain has set in for the afternoon** la pluie va durer toute l'après-midi; ¶ ~ **[sth] in** Sewing rapporter [*sleeve*].
■ **set off**: ¶ ~ **off** partir (**for** pour); **to ~ off on a journey/an expedition** partir en voyage/expédition; **to ~ off to do** partir faire; **he set off on a long description/story** il s'est lancé dans une longue description/histoire; ¶ ~ **[off] sth**, ~ **[sth] off 1** (trigger) déclencher [*alarm*]; faire partir [*firework*]; faire exploser [*bomb*]; déclencher [*riot, row, panic*]; **2** (enhance) mettre [qch] en valeur [*colour, dress, tan*]; **3** Fin **to ~ sth off against profits/debts** déduire qch des bénéfices/des dettes; ¶ ~ **[sb] off** faire pleurer [*baby*]; **she laughed and that set me off** elle a ri et ça m'a fait rire à mon tour; **don't mention politics, you know it always ~s him off** ne parle pas de politique tu sais bien que quand il est parti on ne peut plus l'arrêter.
■ **set on**: ¶ ~ **on [sb]** attaquer qn; ¶ ~ **[sth] on sb** lâcher [qch] contre qn [*dog*]; **to ~ sb onto sb** ou **sb's track** mettre qn sur la piste de qn.
■ **set out**: ¶ ~ **out** (leave) se mettre en route (**for** pour; **to do** pour faire); **we set out from Paris/the house at 9 am** nous avons quitté Paris/la maison à 9 heures; **to ~ out on a journey/an expedition** partir en voyage/expédition; **to ~ out to do** (intend) [*book, report, speech*] avoir pour but de faire; [*person*] chercher à faire; (start) commencer à faire; ¶ ~ **[sth] out**, ~ **out [sth] 1** (spread out) disposer [*goods*]; disposer [*food*]; étaler [*books, papers*]; disposer [*chairs*]; préparer [*board game*]; disposer [*chessmen*]; organiser [*information*]; **2** (state, explain) présenter [*conclusions, ideas, proposals*]; formuler [*objections, terms*].
■ **set to** s'y mettre.
■ **set up**: ¶ ~ **up** (establish oneself) [*business person, trader*] s'établir ; **to ~ up on one's own** s'établir à son compte; **to ~ up (shop) as a decorator/caterer** s'établir en tant que décorateur/traiteur; **to ~ up in business** monter une affaire; ¶ ~ **[sth] up**, ~ **up [sth] 1** (erect) monter [*stand, stall*]; assembler [*equipment, easel*]; déplier [*deckchair*]; ériger [*roadblock*]; dresser [*statue*]; **to ~ up home** ou **house** s'installer; **to ~ up camp** installer un campement; **2** (prepare) préparer [*experiment*]; Sport préparer [*goal, try*]; **3** (found, establish) créer [*business, company*]; implanter [*factory*]; former [*support group, charity*]; constituer [*committee, commission*]; ouvrir [*fund*]; lancer [*initiative, scheme*]; **4** (start) provoquer [*vibration*]; susciter [*reaction*]; **5** (organize) organiser [*conference, meeting*]; mettre [qch] en place [*procedures*]; **6** Print composer [*page*]; ¶ ~ **[sb] up 1** (establish in business) **she set her son up (in business) as a gardener** elle a aidé son fils à s'installer comme jardinier; **2** (improve one's health, fortune) remettre [qn] sur pied; **there's nothing like a good vacation to ~ you up** rien de tel que de bonnes vacances pour vous remettre sur pied; **that deal has set her up for life** grâce à ce contrat elle n'aura plus à se soucier de rien; **3**○ GB (trap) [*police*] tendre un piège à [*criminal*]; [*colleague, friend*] monter un coup contre [*person*]; **4** Comput installer, configurer; ¶ ~ **[oneself] up 1** Comm **she set herself up as a financial advisor** elle s'est mise à son compte comme conseiller financier; **to ~ oneself up in business** se mettre à son compte; **2** (claim) **I don't ~ myself up to be an expert** je ne prétends pas être expert; **she ~s herself up as an authority on French art** elle prétend faire autorité en matière d'art français.
■ **set upon**: ~ **upon [sb]** attaquer qn.

set-aside *n* Agric gel *m* des terres.

setback /'setbæk/ *n* **1** gen, Mil revers *m* (**for** pour); **to suffer a ~** essuyer un revers; **this would be a ~ to our plans** cela compromettrait nos projets; **it was a ~ to his hopes of winning** cela a compromis ses chances de gagner; **a temporary ~** un recul passager; **2** Fin recul *m*; **after an early ~ prices rose steadily** Fin après un recul initial les prix ont augmenté régulièrement.

set: ~ **designer** ▶ 1692 *n* Theat décorateur/-trice *m/f*; **~-in sleeve** *n* Sewing manche *f* rapportée.

set piece I *n* **1** Sport coup *m* préparé; **2** Mus morceau *m* célèbre; **3** Theat (piece of scenery) ferme *f*, décor *m* mobile; **4** (firework display) spectacle *m* de feux d'artifice.
II setpiece *modif* [*manoeuvre, offensive*] préparé d'avance.

set: ~ **play** *n* Sport, gen coup *m* préparé; ~ **point** *n* balle *f* de set; ~ **scrum** *n* (in rugby) mêlée *f* ordonnée; ~ **square** *n* GB Tech équerre *f*.

sett /set/ *n* (of badger) tanière *f*.

settee /se'ti:/ *n* canapé *m*.

setter /'setə(r)/ *n* **1** Zool setter *m*; **2** ▶ 1692 (jeweller) sertisseur/-euse *m/f*.

set theory *n* Math théorie *f* des ensembles.

setting /'setɪŋ/ *n* **1** (location) (for a building, event, film, novel) cadre *m*; **a historic/rural/magnificent ~** un cadre historique/rural/magnifique; **a house in a riverside ~** une maison au bord d'une rivière; **it's the perfect ~ for a holiday/romance** c'est le cadre idéal pour des vacances/une histoire d'amour; **Milan will be the ~ for the gala/film** le gala/le film va se passer à Milan; **Dublin is the ~ for her latest novel** l'action de son dernier roman se passe à Dublin; **this street was the ~ for a riot/murder** cette rue a été le théâtre d'une émeute/d'un meurtre; **2** (in jewellery) monture *f*; **3** (position on dial) position *f* (de réglage); **speed ~** vitesse *f*; **put the iron/heater on the highest ~** mets le fer à repasser/radiateur au maximum; **4** (hardening) (of jam) épaississement *m*; (of cement, glue) durcissement *m*; **5** Mus arrangement *m*; **6 the ~ of the sun** le coucher du soleil; **7** Print composition *f*.

setting: ~ **lotion** *n* fixateur *m*; ~ **ring** *n* bague *f* de réglage.

setting-up /ˌsetɪŋ'ʌp/ *n* (of committee, programme, scheme, business) création *f*; (of inquiry) ouverture *f*; (of factory) implantation *f*.

settle /'setl/ **I** *n* banquette *f* coffre.
II *vtr* **1** (position comfortably) installer [*person, animal*]; **to ~ a child on one's lap** asseoir un enfant sur ses genoux; **to get one's guests ~d** installer ses invités; **to get the children ~d for the night** mettre les enfants au lit; **2** (calm) calmer [*stomach, nerves*]; dissiper [*qualms*]; **3** (resolve) régler [*matter, business, dispute*]; aplanir [*conflict, strike*]; régler, résoudre [*problem*]; Sport décider [*match*]; ~ **it among yourselves** réglez ça entre vous; **that's ~d** voilà qui est réglé; **that's one thing ~d** c'est une chose de réglée; **that ~s it! I'm leaving tomorrow!** (making decision) c'est décidé! je pars demain!; (in exasperation) c'en est trop! je pars demain!; **to ~ an argument** (acting as referee) trancher; **4** (agree on) fixer [*arrangements, terms of payment*]; **nothing is ~d yet** rien n'est encore fixé; **5** (put in order) **to ~ one's affairs** (before dying) mettre de l'ordre dans ses affaires; **6** Comm (pay) régler [*bill, debt, claim*]; **7** (colonize) coloniser [*country, island*]; **8**○ (deal with) **we'll soon ~ her!** on va régler ça! or on va lui régler son compte!; **9** (bequeath) **to ~ money on sb** léguer une somme à qn; **10** (keep down) **spray the path to ~ the dust** arrose le chemin pour que la poussière se tasse; **11** US (impregnate) féconder [*animal*].
III *vi* **1** (come to rest) [*bird, insect, wreck*] se poser; [*dust, dregs, tea leaves*] se déposer; **the boat ~d on the bottom** le bateau s'est posé sur le fond; **let the wine ~** laisse le vin décanter; **to let the dust ~** lit laisser retomber la poussière; fig attendre que les choses se calment; **to ~ over** [*mist, clouds*] descendre sur [*town, valley*]; fig [*silence, grief*] s'étendre sur [*community*]; **2** (become resident) gen s'installer; (more permanently) se fixer; **3** (become compacted) [*contents, ground, wall*] se tasser; **4** (calm down) [*child, baby*] gen se calmer; (go to sleep) s'endormir; **5** (become stable) [*weather*] se mettre au beau fixe; **6** (take hold) **to be settling** [*snow*] tenir; [*mist*] persister; **his cold has ~d on his chest** son rhume s'est transformé en bronchite; **7** (be digested) **let your lunch ~!** attends d'avoir digéré ton déjeuner!; **8** Jur (agree) régler; **to ~ out of court** parvenir à un règlement à l'amiable.
IV *v refl* **to ~ oneself in** s'installer dans [*chair, bed*].
IDIOMS **to ~ a score with sb** régler ses comptes avec qn; **to ~ old scores** régler des comptes.
■ **settle back**: ~ **back** s'installer confortablement; **to ~ back in** se caler dans [*chair*].
■ **settle down**: ~ **down 1** (get comfortable) s'installer (**on** sur; **in** dans); **2** (calm down) [*person*] se calmer; [*situation*] s'arranger; ~ **down, children!** du calme, les enfants!; **3** (marry) se ranger; **to ~ down to work** se concentrer sur son travail; **to ~ down to doing** se résoudre à faire.
■ **settle for**: ~ **for [sth]** se contenter de [*alternative, poorer option*]; **why ~ for less?** pourquoi se contenter de moins?; **to ~ for second best** se contenter d'un pis-aller.
■ **settle in 1** (move in) s'installer; **2** (become acclimatized) s'adapter.
■ **settle on**: ~ **on [sth]** choisir [*name, colour*].
■ **settle to**: ~ **to [sth]** se concentrer sur [*work*]; **I can't ~ to anything** je n'arrive pas à me concentrer.
■ **settle up**: ~ **up 1** (pay) payer, régler; **2** (sort out who owes what) faire les comptes; **shall we ~ up?** tu veux qu'on fasse les comptes?; **3 to ~ up with** régler [*waiter, tradesman*].

settled /setld/ *adj* [*alliance*] stable, solide; [*person, weather, future, relationship*] stable; **she's a lot more ~ now** elle est beaucoup plus stable maintenant; **I feel ~ here** (in home) je me sens chez moi.

settlement /'setlmənt/ *n* **1** (agreement) accord *m*; **2** (resolving) règlement *m*; ~ **of industrial disputes** règlement des conflits sociaux; **3** Jur règlement *m*; **4** Fin (of money) constitution *f* (**on** en faveur de); **5** Sociol (social work centre) centre *m* social; **6** (dwellings) village *m*; **to form a ~** créer un village; **7** (creation of new community) implantation *f*; ~ **in the occupied territories** implantation dans les territoires occupés; **8** Constr tassement *m*.

settlement day *n* Fin jour *m* de la liquidation.

settler /'setlə(r)/ *n* colon *m*.

settlor /'setlə(r)/ *n* Jur disposant/-e *m/f*.

set-to○ /'settu:/ *n* prise *f* de bec○, dispute *f*; **to have a ~ with sb** avoir une prise de bec avec qn○, se disputer avec qn.

set-up○ /'setʌp/ **I** *n* **1** (system, organization) organisation *f*; **2** (trick, trap) traquenard○ *m*.
II *modif* [*costs*] initial; [*time*] de préparation.

seven /'sevn/ ▶**1505**, **971**, **1096** **I** *n* sept *m inv*.
II sevens *npl* Sport rugby *m* à sept.
III *adj* sept; **the ~ deadly sins** les sept péchés capitaux; **the ~ wonders of the world** les sept merveilles du monde; **the ~ seas** toutes les mers.

seven league boots *npl* bottes *fpl* de sept lieues.

Seven Sisters *n* US Univ **the ~** les Sept Sœurs *fpl* (*groupement d'universités féminines du nord-est des USA*).

seventeen /ˌsevn'ti:n/ ▶**1505**, **971** *n, adj* dix-sept (*m inv*).

seventeenth /ˌsevn'ti:nθ/ ▶**1505**, **1150** **I** *n* **1** (in order) dix-septième *mf*; **2** (of month) dix-sept *m inv*; **3** (fraction) dix-septième *m*.
II *adj* dix-septième.
III *adv* [*come, finish*] dix-septième, en dix-septième position.

seventh /'sevnθ/ ▶**1505**, **1150** **I** *n* **1** (in order) septième *mf*; **2** (of month) sept *m inv*; **3** (fraction) septième *m*; **4** Mus septième *f*.
II *adj* septième.
III *adv* [*come, finish*] septième, en septième position.
IDIOMS **to be in ~ heaven** être au septième ciel.

seventies /'sevntɪz/ ▶**971**, **1150** *npl* **1 the ~s** les années *fpl* soixante-dix; **2 to be in one's ~** avoir plus de soixante-dix ans; **a man in his ~** un septuagénaire.

seventieth /'sevntɪəθ/ ▶**1505** *n, adj* soixante-dixième (*mf*).

seventy /'sevntɪ/ ▶**1505**, **971** *n, adj* soixante-dix (*m*) *inv*.

seventy-eight /ˌsevəntɪ'eɪt/ *n* Audio **a ~ (record ou disc)** un soixante-dix-huit tours *m inv*.

seven-year itch *n* démon *m* de l'infidélité (après sept ans de mariage).

sever /'sevə(r)/ *vtr* **1** lit sectionner [*wire, limb, head, nerve, artery*]; couper [*rope, branch*]; **to ~ sth from** séparer qch de; **2** fig (break off) rompre [*link, relations*]; couper [*contact, communications*].

severability /ˌsevrə'bɪlətɪ/ *n* Jur caractère *m* facultatif.

severable /'sevrəbl/ *adj* Jur facultatif/-ive.

several /'sevrəl/ **I** *pron* **~ of you/us** plusieurs d'entre vous/d'entre nous; **~ of our group** plusieurs membres de notre groupe.
II *quantif* **1** (a few) plusieurs; **~ books** plusieurs livres; **2** sout (respective) respectif/-ive; **their ~ briefcases** leur mallette respective; **they went their ~ ways** chacun est parti de son côté.

severally /'sevrəlɪ/ *adv* séparément; ▶**jointly**.

severance /'sevərəns/ *n* **1** (separation) rupture *f*; **2** (redundancy) licenciement *m*.

severance pay *n* indemnités *fpl* de licenciement.

severe /sɪ'vɪə(r)/ *adj* **1** (extreme) [*problem, damage, shortage, injury, depression, shock*] grave; [*weather, cold, winter*] rigoureux/-euse; [*headache*] violent; [*loss*] lourd; **2** (harsh) [*person, punishment, criticism*] sévère (**with sb** avec qn); **3** (austere) [*haircut, clothes*] austère, sévère.

severely /sɪ'vɪəlɪ/ *adv* **1** (seriously) [*restrict, damage*] sévèrement; [*affect, shock*] durement; [*disabled*] gravement; [*injured*] grièvement; **2** (harshly) [*treat, speak, punish*] sévèrement; [*beat*] violemment; **3** (austerely) [*dress*] de façon austère.

severity /sɪ'verətɪ/ *n* **1** (seriousness) (of problem, situation, illness) gravité *f*; (of shock, pain) violence *f*; **2** (harshness) (of punishment, sentence, treatment) sévérité *f*; (of climate) rigueur *f*.

Seville /sə'vɪl/ ▶**1818** *pr n* Séville.

Seville: **~ orange** *n* orange *f* amère; **~ orange marmalade** *n* confiture *f* d'oranges amères.

sew /səʊ/ (*prét* **sewed**, *pp* **sewn**, **sewed**) **I** *vtr* coudre; **to ~ sth on to sth** coudre qch; **he ~ed the button back on** il a recousu le bouton; **she ~s all her children's clothes** elle fait tous les vêtements de ses enfants elle-même.
II *vi* coudre, faire de la couture.
■ **sew up**: **~ [sth] up, ~ up [sth] 1** recoudre [*hole, tear*]; faire [*seam*]; (re)coudre [*wound*]; **2**○ (settle) conclure [*deal*]; conclure [qch] victorieusement [*game*]; (control) dominer [*market*]; **they've got the match/election sewn up** ils sont sûrs de gagner le match/les élections; **the deal is all sewn up!** l'affaire est dans le sac○!

sewage /'su:ɪdʒ, 'sju:-/ *n* eaux *fpl* usées.

sewage: **~ disposal** *n* évacuation *f* des eaux usées; **~ farm** *n* = **sewage works**; **~ outfall, ~ outlet** *n* émissaire *m* d'évacuation; **~ sludge** *n* boues *fpl* d'épuration; **~ system** *n* réseau *m* d'égout; **~ treatment** *n* traitement *m* des eaux usées; **~ works** *n* champ *m* d'épandage.

sewer /'su:ə(r), 'sju:-/ *n* égout *m*.

sewerage† /'su:ərɪdʒ, 'sju:-/ *n* = **sewage**.

sewer: **~ gas** *n* gaz *m* d'égout; **~ rat** *n* rat *m* d'égout.

sewing /'səʊɪŋ/ **I** *n* (activity) couture *f*; (piece of work) ouvrage *m*; **I hate ~** je déteste coudre.
II *modif* [*scissors, thread*] à coudre.

sewing: **~ basket** *n* corbeille *f* à ouvrage; **~ bee** *n* réunion *f* de couture; **~ cotton** *n* fil *m* à coudre; **~ machine** *n* machine *f* à coudre; **~ silk** *n* fil *m* de soie.

sewn /səʊn/ *pp* ▶**sew**.

sex /seks/ **I** *n* **1** (gender) sexe *m*; **people of both ~es** des gens des deux sexes; **2** (intercourse) (one act) rapport *m* sexuel; (repeated) rapports *mpl* sexuels; **to have ~ with sb** avoir des rapports sexuels avec qn; **he thinks about nothing but ~** il ne pense qu'à ça○.
II *modif* Biol [*chromosome, hormone, organ, education, hygiene*] sexuel/-elle.
III *vtr* déterminer le sexe de [*animal*].
IV sexed *pp adj* Bot, Zool sexué; **highly ~ed** [*person*] hypersexué.
■ **sex up**○ US: **~ [sb] up** allumer○.

sex: **~ abuse** *n* violence *f* sexuelle; **~ act** *n* acte *m* sexuel.

sexagenarian /ˌseksədʒɪ'neərɪən/ *n* sexagénaire *mf*.

Sexagesima /ˌseksə'dʒesɪmə/ *n* sexagésime *f*.

sex: **~ aid** *n* gadget *m* érotique; **~ appeal** *n* sex-appeal *m*; **~ attack** *n* agression *f* sexuelle; **~ attacker** *n personne ayant commis un acte d'agression sexuelle*.

sex change *n* **to have a ~** changer de sexe.

sex: **~ discrimination** *n* discrimination *f* sexuelle; **~ drive** *n* besoins *mpl* sexuels, libido *f*; **~ education** *n* éducation *f* sexuelle; **~ fiend**○ *n* hum maniaque *m* sexuel; **~ goddess**○ *n* idole *f* sexuelle.

sexism /'seksɪzəm/ *n* sexisme *m*.

sexist /'seksɪst/ *n, adj* sexiste (*mf*).

sex kitten○ *n* minette○ *f* sexy.

sexless /'sekslɪs/ *adj* asexué.

sex: **~ life** *n* vie *f* sexuelle; **~ mad**○ *adj* dingue○ de sexe; **~ maniac**○ *n* maniaque *m* sexuel; **~ object** *n* objet *m* sexuel; **~ offence** *n* GB délit *m* sexuel; **~ offender** *n* délinquant/-e *m/f* sexuel/-elle.

sexologist /sek'sɒlədʒɪst/ ▶**1692** *n* sexologue *mf*.

sexology /sek'sɒlədʒɪ/ *n* sexologie *f*.

sexploitation /ˌseksplɔɪ'teɪʃn/ *n* exploitation *f* sexuelle.

sex: **~pot**○ *n* aguicheuse *f*; **~ scandal** *n* journ scandale *m* sexuel; **~ scene** *n* Cin, Theat scène *f* érotique; **~ shop** *n* sex-shop *m*; **~ show** *n* spectacle *m* érotique, spectacle *m* de cul◑; **~-starved**○ *adj* frustré, en manque○; **~ symbol** *n* symbole *m* sexuel.

sextant /'sekstənt/ *n* sextant *m*.

sextet /sek'stet/ *n* sextuor *m*.

sex: **~ therapist** ▶**1692** *n* sexologue *mf*; **~ therapy** *n* thérapie *f* sexuelle.

sexton /'sekstən/ *n* sacristain *m*.

sextuple /seks'tju:pl/ *vtr, vi* sextupler.

sextuplet /'sekstjʊplɪt, -'tju:plɪt/ *n* sextuplé/-e *m/f*.

sexual /'sekʃʊəl/ *adj* sexuel/-elle.

sexual: **~ abuse** *n* violence *f* sexuelle; **~ conversion** *n* changement *m* de sexe; **~ harassment** *n* harcèlement *m* sexuel; **~ intercourse** *n* rapports *mpl* sexuels.

sexuality /ˌsekʃʊ'ælətɪ/ *n* **1** (sexual orientation) sexualité *f*; **female/male ~** sexualité féminine/masculine; **2** (eroticism) érotisme *m*.

sexually /'sekʃʊəlɪ/ *adv* [*dominant, explicit, mature, normal, violent*] sexuellement; [*attract, repel*] sexuellement; [*discriminate, distinguish*] selon le sexe; [*transmit, infect*] par voie sexuelle; **~ abused** victime de violence sexuelle.

sexually transmitted disease, **STD** *n* maladie *f* sexuellement transmissible, MST.

sex urge *n* pulsion *f* sexuelle.

sexy○ /'seksɪ/ *adj* **1** (erotic) [*book, film, show*] érotique; [*person, clothing*] sexy○ *inv*; **2** Advertg (appealing) [*image, product, slogan etc*] accrocheur/-euse.

Seychelles /seɪ'ʃelz/ ▶**1131**, **1381** *pr n* **the ~** les Seychelles *fpl*; **in the ~** aux Seychelles.

sez○ /sez/ = **says**.

SF *n* (*abrév* = **science fiction**) science-fiction *f*.

SFO *n* GB *abrév* ▶**Serious Fraud Office**.

S Glam *n* GB Post *abrév écrite* ▶**South Glamorgan**.

Sgt. *n* (*abrév écrite* = **sergeant**) sergent *m*.

sh /ʃ/ *excl* chut.

shabbily /'ʃæbɪlɪ/ *adv* [*dressed*] pauvrement, de façon miteuse; [*behave, treat*] de manière peu élégante.

shabbiness /'ʃæbɪnɪs/ *n* (of clothes, place) aspect *m* miteux; (of behaviour) mesquinerie *f*.

shabby /'ʃæbɪ/ *adj* [*person*] habillé de façon miteuse; [*room, furnishings, clothing*] miteux/-euse; [*treatment*] mesquin; **what a ~ trick!** quel sale tour!

shabby: **~-genteel** /ˌʃæbɪdʒen'ti:l/ *adj* [*person*] pauvre mais digne; **~-looking** *adj* [*house, car*] délabré; [*person*] d'apparence miteuse.

shack /ʃæk/ *n* cabane *f*.
■ **shack up**○: **~ up with sb** se maquer◑ avec qn, se mettre en ménage avec qn.

shackle /'ʃækl/ **I** *n* (chain) fer *m*; fig (constraint) chaîne *f*; **to throw off the ~s of sth** briser les chaînes de qch.
II *vtr* mettre [qn] aux fers.
III shackled *pp adj* enchaîné (**to** à).

shad /ʃæd/ *n* alose *f*.

shade /ʃeɪd/ **I** *n* **1** (shadow) ombre *f*; **40° in the ~** 40° à l'ombre; **in the ~ of** à l'ombre de; **to provide ~** donner de l'ombre; **2** (tint) (of colour) ton *m*; fig (of opinion, meaning) nuance *f*; **pastel ~s** tons pastels; **an attractive ~ of blue** un beau bleu; **to turn a deep ~ of red** devenir tout rouge; **this word has several ~s of meaning** ce mot a plusieurs nuances; **a solution that should appeal to all ~s of opinion** une solution qui devrait plaire à toutes les tendances; **3** (small amount, degree) **a ~ too loud** un tout petit peu or un tantinet○ hum

trop fort; **a ~ of envy/resentment** un soupçon de jalousie/ressentiment; **4** (also **lamp ~**) abat-jour *m inv*; ▶ **eyeshade**; **5** US (also **window ~**) store *m*; **6**† littér (ghost) ombre *f*, fantôme *m*.
II shades *npl* **1**○ (sunglasses) lunettes *fpl* de soleil; **2** (undertones) **~s of Mozart/of the sixties** ça fait penser à Mozart/aux années soixante.
III *vtr* **1** (screen) [*tree, canopy, sunshade*] donner de l'ombre à, protéger [qn/qch] du soleil; **the hat ~d her face** le chapeau projetait une ombre sur son visage; **the garden was ~d by trees** le jardin était ombragé par des arbres; **to ~ one's eyes (with one's hand)** s'abriter les yeux de la main; **2** = **shade in**.
IV *vi* (blend) [*colour, tone*] se fondre (**into** en); **the blue ~s off into green** le bleu se fond en vert; **right ~s into wrong** le bien et le mal se confondent.
V shaded *pp adj* **1** (shady) [*place*] ombragé; **2** (covered) [*light, lamp*] avec un abat-jour; **3** Art (also **~-in**) [*area, background*] gen sombre; (produced by hatching) hachuré.
IDIOMS **to put sb in the ~** éclipser qn; **to put sth in the ~** surpasser or surclasser qch.
■ **shade in**: **~ in [sth], ~ [sth] in** [*artist*] ombrer [*drawing*]; (by hatching) hachurer [*area, map*]; [*child*] colorier [*picture*].

shadiness /'ʃeɪdɪnɪs/ *n* **1** (shadow) ombre *f*; **2** (dishonesty) caractère *m* louche.

shading /'ʃeɪdɪŋ/ *n* (in drawing, painting) ombres *fpl*; (hatching) hachures *fpl*.

shadow /'ʃædəʊ/ **I** *n* **1** (shade) lit, fig ombre *f*; **in (the) ~** dans l'ombre; **in the ~ of** à l'ombre de [*tree, wall*]; dans l'ombre de [*doorway*]; **to live in the ~ of** (near) vivre à proximité de [*mine, power station*]; (in fear of) vivre dans la crainte de [*Aids, unemployment, war*]; **to stand in the ~s** se tenir dans l'ombre; **to be afraid of one's own ~** fig avoir peur de son ombre; **to live in sb's ~** fig vivre dans l'ombre de qn; **to cast a ~ over sth** lit projeter une ombre sur qch; fig jeter une ombre sur qch; **she's a ~ of her former self** elle n'est plus que l'ombre d'elle-même; **she casts a long ~** fig son influence se fait toujours sentir; **the war casts a long ~** les effets de la guerre se font toujours sentir; **the remake is only a pale ~ of the original** le remake n'est qu'une pâle imitation de l'original; **to have ~s under one's eyes** avoir les yeux cernés ; **2** (person who follows another) gen ombre *f*; (detective) détective *m* or policier *m* qui file qn; **to put a ~ on sb** faire filer or suivre qn; **to be sb's ~** suivre qn comme son ombre, être l'ombre de qn; **3** (on X ray) ombre *f*, voile *m*; **4** (hint) **not a ~ of truth** pas le moindre soupçon de vérité; **not a ~ of suspicion** pas le moindre soupçon; **without** ou **beyond the ~ of a doubt** sans l'ombre d'un doute.
II shadows *npl* littér (darkness) ténèbres *fpl*.
III *vtr* **1** (cast shadow on) [*wall, tree*] projeter une ombre (or des ombres) sur; **this tragedy ~ed him all his life** fig cette tragédie l'a hanté toute sa vie; **2** (follow) filer, prendre [qn] en filature.

shadow: **~ box** *vtr* boxer à vide; **~ boxing** *n* lit *entraînement de boxe sans adversaire*; fig attaque *f* purement formelle; **~ cabinet** *n* GB Pol cabinet *m* fantôme; **~ minister** *n* GB Pol = **shadow secretary**; **~ play** *n* théâtre *m* d'ombres; **~ puppet** *n* marionnette *f* de théâtre d'ombres.

shadow secretary *n* GB Pol **the ~ for employment/foreign affairs** le porte-parole de l'opposition dans le domaine de l'emploi/des affaires étrangères.

shadowy /'ʃædəʊɪ/ *adj* **1** (dark) [*path, corridor, woods*] sombre; **2** (indistinct) [*image, outline*] flou; [*form*] indistinct, vague; **3** (mysterious) [*group, world*] mystérieux/-ieuse; **he has always been a ~ figure** il a toujours été un peu énigmatique.

shady /'ʃeɪdɪ/ *adj* **1** [*place*] ombragé; **2** (dubious) [*deal, business*] louche, véreux/-euse; [*businessman, financier*] véreux/-euse.

shaft /ʃɑːft, US ʃæft/ **I** *n* **1** (rod) (of tool) manche *m*; (of arrow) tige *f*; (of spear, sword) hampe *f*; (in machine) axe *m*; (on a cart) brancard *m*; (of feather) rachis *m*; (of hair) tige *f*; (of bone) diaphyse *f*; **2** (passage, vent) puits *m*; **3** fig (of wit) trait *m*; **~ of light** rai *m*; **~ of lightning** éclair *m*; **4**● (penis) bite● *f*, pénis *m*.
II *vtr* **1**● (have sex with) baiser●, avoir des rapports sexuels avec; **2**○ US (cheat) escroquer; (treat unfairly) sacquer○, être injuste avec.

shag /ʃæg/ **I** *n* **1** (tobacco) (tabac *m*) gris *m*; **2** (bird) cormoran *m* huppé.
II *adj* [*rug*] à longues mèches.
III *vtr* (*p prés etc* **-gg-**) **1**● GB (have sex with) baiser●, coucher avec; **2**○ US Sport attraper.

shagged◑ /ʃægd/ *adj* GB crevé○.

shaggy /'ʃægɪ/ *adj* [*hair, beard, eyebrows*] en broussailles; [*animal*] poilu; [*carpet*] à longues mèches.

shaggy dog story *n* histoire *f* drôle sans queue ni tête.

shagreen /ʃæ'griːn/ *n* **1** (leather) chagrin *m*, cuir *m*; **2** (skin of shark, ray) galuchat *m*.

Shah /ʃɑː/ *n* shah *m*.

shake /ʃeɪk/ **I** *n* **1 to give sb/sth a ~** secouer qn/qch [*person, pillow, dice, cloth, branch*]; agiter, secouer [*bottle, mixture*]; **with a ~ of the** ou **one's head** avec un hochement de tête; **2** (also **milk-~**) milkshake *m*.
II *vtr* (*prét* **shook**, *pp* **shaken**) **1** [*person*] secouer [*person, pillow, dice, cloth, branch*]; agiter, secouer [*bottle, mixture*]; [*blow, earthquake, explosion*] secouer [*building, town, area*]; **the dog seized the rat and shook it** le chien a attrapé le rat et l'a secoué; **'~ before use'** 'agiter avant emploi'; **he shook the seeds out of the packet/into my hand** il a fait tomber les graines du paquet/dans ma main; **to ~ the snow from** ou **off one's coat** secouer la neige de son manteau; **to ~ powder over the carpet** répandre de la poudre sur le tapis; **to ~ salt over the dish** saupoudrer le plat de sel; **to ~ one's fist/a stick at sb** menacer qn du poing/d'un bâton; **I shook him by the shoulders** je l'ai pris par les épaules et je l'ai secoué; **to ~ one's hands dry** se secouer les mains pour les sécher; **to ~ one's head** hocher la tête; **to ~ hands with sb, to ~ sb's hand** serrer la main de qn, donner une poignée de main à qn; **to ~ hands** se serrer la main, se donner une poignée de main; **she took my hand and shook it vigorously** elle m'a pris la main et l'a secouée vigoureusement; **to ~ hands on the deal** se serrer la main or se donner une poignée de main pour conclure l'affaire; **to ~ hands on it** (after argument) se serrer la main or se donner une poignée de main en signe de réconciliation; ▶ **shake off**; **2** fig (shock) (by undermining) ébranler [*belief, confidence, faith, resolve, argument, person*]; (by surprise occurrence) [*event, disaster*] secouer [*person*]; **an event that shook the world** un événement qui a secoué le monde; **it really shook me to find out that...** cela m'a vraiment donné un choc de découvrir que...; **now this will really ~ you!** (telling story) cela va te faire un coup!; ▶ **shake out**; **3** US (get rid of) = **shake off**.
III *vi* (*prét* **shook**, *pp* **shaken**) **1** (tremble) [*person, hand, voice, leaf, grass*] trembler; [*building, windows, ground*] trembler, vibrer; **to ~ with** [*person, voice*] trembler de [*fear, cold, emotion*]; se tordre de [*laughter*]; **2** (shake hands) **they shook on it** (on deal, agreement) ils se sont serré la main or se sont donné une poignée de main en signe d'accord; (after argument) ils se sont serré la main or se sont donné une poignée de main en signe de réconciliation; **'~!'** 'serrons-nous la main!'
IV *v refl* (*prét* **shook**, *pp* **shaken**) **to ~ oneself** [*person, animal*] se secouer; **to ~ oneself awake** se secouer pour se réveiller; **to ~ oneself free** se débattre pour se dégager.
IDIOMS **in a ~**○ ou **two ~s**○ ou **a couple of ~s**○ en un clin d'œil, en un tour de main; **in two ~s of a lamb's tail**○ en deux coups de cuillère à pot○; **to be no great ~s**○ ne pas valoir grand-chose; **I 'm no great ~s at singing/as a singer** je ne vaux pas grand-chose en chant/comme chanteur; **to get a fair ~**○ décrocher une bonne affaire○; **to have the ~s**○ (from fear, cold, infirmity) avoir la tremblote○; (from alcohol, fever) trembler; **we've got more of these than you can ~ a stick at**○! on en a encore autant qu'un curé pourrait en bénir○.
■ **shake about, shake around**: ¶ **~ about** ou **around** être secoué; ¶ **~ [sth] about** ou **around** secouer [qch] dans tous les sens.
■ **shake down**: ¶ **~ down 1** (settle down) [*contents*] se tasser; **2**○ (to sleep) se coucher, se pieuter◑; ¶ **~ [sb/sth] down, ~ down [sb/sth] 1 to ~ apples down (off a tree)** secouer un arbre pour faire tomber les pommes; **to ~ down the contents of a packet/jar** secouer un paquet/un bocal pour tasser le contenu; **2**○ US (search) fouiller [*person, building, apartment*]; **3**○ US faire chanter, extorquer de l'argent à [*person*].
■ **shake off**: **~ [sb/sth] off, ~ off [sb/sth]** (get rid of, escape from) se débarrasser de [*cough, cold, depression, habit, unwanted person*]; se défaire de [*feeling*]; semer○ [*pursuer*]; **I can't seem to ~ off this flu** je n'arrive pas à me débarrasser de cette grippe.
■ **shake out**: ¶ **~ [sth] out, ~ out [sth]** secouer [*tablecloth, sheet, rug*]; **to ~ some tablets out of a bottle** secouer un flacon pour en faire tomber quelques comprimés; ¶ **~ [sb] out of** secouer [qn] pour le faire sortir de [*depression, bad mood, complacency*]; **in a effort to ~ them out of their lethargy, he...** pour tenter de les faire sortir de leur léthargie, il...
■ **shake up**: ¶ **~ up [sth], ~ [sth] up** secouer [*cushion, pillow*]; agiter, secouer [*bottle, mixture*]; ¶ **~ [sb/sth] up, ~ up [sb/sth] 1** [*car ride, bumpy road*] secouer [*person*]; **2** fig (rouse, stir, shock) secouer [*person*]; **they're too complacent—they need shaking up!** ils sont trop contents d'eux-mêmes—il faut les secouer!; **they were very shaken up by the experience** ils ont été très secoués par cette expérience; **3** (reorganize) Comm réorganiser (radicalement) [*company, department, management*]; Pol remanier [*cabinet*].

shakedown /'ʃeɪkdaʊn/ **I** *n* **1** (improvised bed) lit *m* de fortune; **2**○ US (extorsion) (by verbal intimidation) chantage *m*; (by physical intimidation) racket *m*; **3**○ US (search) fouille *f*; **4** Aviat, Naut essai *m* final.
II *modif* Aviat, Naut [*voyage, flight, run*] des essais finaux.

shaken /'ʃeɪkən/ **I** *pp* ▶ **shake**.
II *adj* (shocked) choqué; (upset) bouleversé.

shake-out /'ʃeɪkaʊt/ *n* **1** Fin, Econ (in securities market) déconfiture *f* des boursicoteurs; (recession) tassement *m* du marché; **2** Comm, Ind (reorganization) réorganisation *f*, restructuration *f* (*souvent accompagnée de licenciements*); **3** Pol remaniement *m*.

shaker /'ʃeɪkə(r)/ *n* (for cocktails) shaker *m*; (for dice) gobelet *m* or cornet *m* à dés; (for salt) salière *f*; (for pepper) poivrière *f*; (for salad) saladier *m*.

Shakespearean /ʃeɪk'spɪərɪən/ *adj* Literat [*drama, role*] shakespearien/-ienne; [*production, quotation*] de Shakespeare.

shake-up /'ʃeɪkʌp/ *n* Comm réorganisation *f* (importante), restructuration *f* (importante); Pol remaniement *m*.

shakily /'ʃeɪkɪlɪ/ *adv* [*say, speak*] d'une voix tremblante; [*walk*] d'un pas chancelant; **he**

writes ~ il écrit en tremblant; **they started rather ~** leur début était chancelant or mal assuré.

shako /ˈʃeɪkəʊ/ *n* (*pl* **~s** ou **~es**) shako *m*.

shaky /ˈʃeɪkɪ/ *adj* **1** (liable to shake) [*chair, ladder, structure*] branlant, peu stable; **my hands are rather ~** j'ai les mains qui tremblent; **I feel a bit ~** je me sens un peu flageolant; **2** fig (liable to founder) [*marriage, relationship, position*] instable; [*evidence, argument, grounds*] peu solide, peu fiable; [*knowledge, memory, prospects*] peu sûr; [*regime, democracy*] chancelant; **3** fig (uncertain) [*start*] chancelant, mal assuré; **we got off to a rather ~ start** (in relationship, business) au début cela a été difficile pour nous; (in performance) nous étions très peu sûrs de nous au début; **my French is a bit ~** mon français est un peu hésitant.

shale /ʃeɪl/ **I** *n* shale *m*.
II *modif* [*beach, quarry*] de shale.

shale oil *n* huile *f* de schiste.

shall /ʃæl, ʃəl/

■ **Note** When *shall* is used to form the future tense in English, the same rules apply as for *will*. You will find a note on this and on question tags and short answers near the entry ***will***.

modal aux **1** (in future tense) **I ~** ou **I'll see you tomorrow** je vous verrai demain; **we ~ not** ou **shan't have a reply before Friday** nous n'aurons pas de réponse avant vendredi; **2** (in suggestions) **~ I set the table?** est-ce que je mets la table?; **~ we go to the cinema tonight?** et si on allait au cinéma ce soir?; **let's buy some peaches, ~ we?** et si on achetait des pêches?; **3** sout (in commands, contracts etc) **you ~ do as I say** tu dois faire ce que je te dis; **the sum ~ be paid on signature of the contract** le montant devra être versé à la signature du contrat; **thou shalt not steal** Bible tu ne voleras point.

shallot /ʃəˈlɒt/ *n* **1** GB échalote *f*; **2** US cive *f*.

shallow /ˈʃæləʊ/ **▶1412** **I shallows** *npl* bas fonds *mpl*.
II *adj* [*container, hollow, water, grave*] peu profond; [*stairs*] aux marches basses; [*breathing, character, response*] superficiel/-ielle; [*writing, conversation*] plat; [*wit*] creux/creuse; **the ~ end of the pool** l'extrémité la moins profonde de la piscine.

shallowness /ˈʃæləʊnɪs/ *n* (of water) peu *m* de profondeur; (of person) manque *m* de profondeur; (of conversation) caractère *m* superficiel.

shalt‡ /ʃælt/ *2nd pers sg* ▶ **shall**.

sham /ʃæm/ **I** *n* (person) imposteur *m*; (organization) imposture *f*; (democracy, election) parodie *f*; (ideas, views) mystification *f*; (activity) supercherie *f*; **his love was a ~** son amour était de la comédie.
II *adj* (*épith*) [*election, democracy*] prétendu (*before n*); [*object, building, idea, view*] factice; [*activity, emotion*] feint; [*organization*] fantoche.
III *vtr* (*p prés etc* **-mm-**) **to ~ sleep/illness/death** faire semblant de dormir/d'être malade/d'être mort.
IV *vi* (*p prés etc* **-mm-**) faire semblant.

shaman /ˈʃeɪmən/ *n* chaman *m*.

shamanism /ˈʃeɪmənɪzəm/ *n* chamanisme *m*.

shamanistic /ˌʃeɪməˈnɪstɪk/ *adj* chamaniste.

shamateur /ˈʃæmətɜː(r)/ *n* GB Sport pseudo-amateur *mf* (*qui se fait payer*).

shamble /ˈʃæmbl/ *vi* aller d'un pas traînant.

shambles○ /ˈʃæmblz/ *n* (of administration, organization, room) pagaille○ *f*; (of meeting etc) désastre *m*.

shambolic○ /ʃæmˈbɒlɪk/ *adj* GB hum [*place, situation*] désorganisé; [*person*] débraillé.

shame /ʃeɪm/ **I** *n* **1** (embarrassment) honte *f*; **to feel ~** ressentir de la honte; **he has no (sense of) ~** il n'a honte de rien; **to feel ~ at** être honteux/-euse de; **2** (disgrace) honte *f*; **to her/our ~** à sa/notre honte; **to my eternal ~** à ma très grande honte; **the ~ of doing** la honte de faire; **the ~ of it!** quelle honte!, la honte○!; **there's no ~ in doing** il n'y a pas de honte à faire; **to bring ~ on** être or faire la honte de; **~ on you!** tu devrais avoir honte!, tu n'as pas honte?; **~ on him for doing** il devrait avoir honte de faire; **~!** c'est un scandale!; **there were cries of '~!'** les gens criaient au scandale; **3** (pity) **it is a ~ that** c'est dommage que (+ *subj*) ; **it seems a ~** il semble dommage; **it was a great** ou **such a ~ (that) she lost** c'est tellement dommage qu'elle ait perdu; **it would be a ~ if he couldn't come** il serait dommage qu'il ne puisse pas venir; **it's a ~ to do** c'est dommage de faire; **it seemed a ~ to do** il semblait dommage de faire; **it's a ~ about the factory closing** c'est dommage que l'usine ait fermé or ferme; **it's a ~ about your father** (if not very serious matter) c'est dommage pour ton père; (if serious) je suis désolé pour ton père; **nice costumes—~ about the play**○! les costumes étaient réussis—mais la pièce○!; **what a ~!** quel dommage!; **isn't it a ~?** c'est vraiment dommage.
II *vtr* **1** (embarrass) faire honte à [*person*]; **I was ~d by her words** ses paroles m'ont fait honte; **to ~ sb into doing** obliger qn à faire en lui faisant honte; **he was ~d into a confession** il avait tellement honte qu'il a avoué; **to ~ sb out of** faire passer [qch] à qn en lui faisant honte [*habit, fault*]; **2** (disgrace) déshonorer [*family, country*] (**by doing** en faisant); **they ~d the nation** ils ont fait la honte de la nation.
IDIOMS **to put sb to ~** faire honte à qn; **your garden puts the others to ~** tous les jardins semblent minables comparés au tien.

shamefaced /ˌʃeɪmˈfeɪst/ *adj* [*person, look*] penaud.

shamefacedly /ˌʃeɪmˈfeɪstlɪ/ *adv* [*return, say*] d'un air penaud.

shameful /ˈʃeɪmfl/ *adj* [*conduct, ignorance, neglect, waste*] honteux/-euse; **it was ~ of her to do** c'était honteux de sa part de faire; **it was ~ of me to do** j'ai honte d'avoir fait; **it is ~ that** c'est une honte que (+ *subj*).

shamefully /ˈʃeɪmfəlɪ/ *adv* [*behave, act*] honteusement; [*mistreated, neglected*] abominablement; **~ ignorant** d'une ignorance crasse.

shameless /ˈʃeɪmlɪs/ *adj* [*person*] éhonté; [*attitude, negligence, request*] effronté; **a ~ display of** un étalage impudique de [*emotion, wealth*]; **to be quite ~ about** n'avoir pas du tout honte de; **she's a ~ hussy†!** péj c'est une dévergondée†!

shamelessly /ˈʃeɪmlɪslɪ/ *adv* [*behave, boast, exploit, lie*] sans vergogne.

shamelessness /ˈʃeɪmlɪsnɪs/ *n* impudence *f*.

shaming /ˈʃeɪmɪŋ/ *adj* [*defeat, behaviour*] humiliant; **it is ~ that** il est humiliant que (+ *subj*).

shammy○ /ˈʃæmɪ/ *n* ▶ **chamois**.

shampoo /ʃæmˈpuː/ **I** *n* (all contexts) shampooing *m*.
II *vtr* (*prés* **-poos**; *prét, pp* **-pooed**) shampouiner [*customer, pet*]; **to ~ one's hair** se faire un shampooing; **to have one's hair ~ed** se faire faire un shampooing.

shampooer /ʃæmˈpuːə(r)/ *n* **1** (person) shampouineur/-euse *m/f*; **2** (carpet cleaner) shampouineuse *f*.

shamrock /ˈʃæmrɒk/ *n* trèfle *m*.

shamus○ /ˈʃeɪməs/ *n* US (policeman) flic○ *m*; (private detective) privé *m*.

shandy /ˈʃændɪ/, **shandygaff** /ˈʃændɪgæf/ US *n* panaché *m*.

shanghai /ʃæŋˈhaɪ/ *vtr* **1** Naut (pressgang) embarquer [qn] de force; **2**○ fig **to ~ sb into doing sth** contraindre qn à faire qch.

Shanghai /ʃæŋˈhaɪ/ **▶1818** *pr n* Shanghai.

Shangri-La /ˌʃæŋgrɪˈlɑː/ *n* paradis *m* terrestre.

shank /ʃæŋk/ *n* **1** Zool jambe *f*; **2** Culin jarret *m*; **3** (of knife) soie *f*; (of golf-club) manche *m*; (of drill-bit) queue *f*; (of screw, door handle) tige *f*; (of shoe) cambrure *f*.
IDIOMS **by ~'s pony** ou **mare** à pied.

shan't /ʃɑːnt/ = **shall not**.

shantung /ʃænˈtʌŋ/ *n* shantung *m*.

shanty /ˈʃæntɪ/ *n* **1** (hut) baraque *f*; **2** (song) chanson *f* de marins.

shantytown /ˈʃæntɪtaʊn/ *n* bidonville *m*.

shape /ʃeɪp/ **I** *n* **1** (form, outline) (of object, building etc) forme *f*; (of person) silhouette *f*; **a square/triangular/star ~** une forme carrée/triangulaire/d'étoile; **what ~ is it?** de quelle forme est-ce?; **to change ~** [*substance*] changer de forme; **to be an odd ~** avoir une drôle de forme; **to be the right/wrong ~** [*object*] avoir/ne pas avoir la forme qu'il faut; [*person*] avoir/ne pas avoir la silhouette qu'il faut; **to be round/square in ~** avoir la forme d'un rond/d'un carré; **it's like a leaf in ~** de forme cela ressemble à une feuille; **in the ~ of a star/a cat** en forme d'étoile/de chat; **to carve/cut/mould sth into ~** donner forme à qch en le sculptant/taillant/modelant; **to keep its ~** [*garment*] garder sa forme; **to keep one's ~** [*person*] garder sa ligne; **to take ~** [*sculpture, building*] prendre forme; **to be out of ~** [*garment*] ne plus avoir de forme; **to go out of ~, to lose its ~** [*garment*] se déformer; **to bend/knock sth out of ~** gauchir/défoncer qch; **in all ~s and sizes** de toutes les formes et de toutes les tailles; **cookers come in all ~s and sizes** il existe des cuisinières de toutes les formes et de toutes les tailles; **the prince took on the ~ of a frog** le prince a pris la forme d'une grenouille; **2** (optimum condition) forme *f*; **to be in/out of ~** être/ne pas être en forme; **to get in/keep in ~** se mettre/se maintenir en forme; **to get/knock/lick**○ **sb in(to) ~** mettre qn en forme; **to get/knock/lick**○**/whip**○ **sth into ~** mettre qch au point or en état [*project, idea, proposal, report, essay*]; **3** fig (character, structure) gen forme *f*; (of organization) structure *f*; **technology that influences the ~ of the labour market** technologie qui influe sur la structure du marché du travail; **he determined the whole ~ of 20th century poetry** il a déterminé la forme de la poésie du vingtième siècle; **to take ~** [*plan, project, idea*] prendre forme; [*events*] prendre tournure; **the likely ~ of currency union** la forme que prendra probablement l'union monétaire; **this will determine the ~ of political developments over the next decade** ceci déterminera l'évolution politique de la prochaine décennie; **my contribution took the ~ of helping/advising...** j'ai contribué en aidant/en conseillant...; **whatever the ~ of the new government** (in composition) quelle que soit la composition du nouveau gouvernement; (in style) quelle que soit la forme que prendra le nouveau gouvernement; **to spell out the ~ of a proposal** expliquer clairement les grandes lignes d'une proposition; **to decide what ~ one's apology should take** décider comment on va présenter ses excuses; **developments which have changed the ~ of our lives** des développements qui ont changé notre mode de vie; **the ~ of things to come** ce que sera or ce que nous réserve l'avenir; **X comes in many ~s and forms** il y a toutes sortes de X; **tips in any ~ or form are forbidden** les pourboires de toutes sortes sont interdits; **I don't condone violence in any ~ or form** je ne pardonne pas la violence, sous quelque forme que ce soit; **I wasn't involved in the matter in**

any way, ~ or form je n'étais, en aucune manière, impliqué dans cette affaire; **4** (guise) **in the ~ of** sous (la) forme de; **help arrived in the ~ of a policeman/a large sum of money** les secours sont arrivés en la personne d'un agent de police/sous (la) forme d'une importante somme d'argent; **he eats a lot of fat in the ~ of chips and burgers** il mange beaucoup de matière grasse sous (la) forme de frites et de hamburgers; **5** (vague, indistinguishable form) forme *f*, silhouette *f*; **the ~ under the bedclothes groaned** la forme sous les couvertures a grogné; **6** Culin (mould for jelly, pastry) moule *m*; **7** Culin (moulded food) (of jelly) gelée *f*; (of pudding, rice) gâteau *m*; (of meat) pâté *m*, terrine *f*.

II *vtr* **1** (fashion, mould) [*person*] modeler [*clay, dough*]; sculpter [*wood, stone*]; [*wind, rain*] façonner, sculpter [*rock, region*]; [*hairdresser*] couper [*hair*]; **he ~d my hair into a bob/into layers** il m'a coupé les cheveux au carré/en dégradé; **we ~d the sand into a mound** nous avons façonné le sable en forme de butte; **the statue had been ~d out of a single block of stone** la statue avait été sculptée dans un seul bloc de pierre; **caves ~d out of the rock by the action of the water** des grottes creusées dans la roche par l'action de l'eau; **~ the dough into balls** faites des boules avec la pâte; **to ~ the material/cardboard into a triangle** faire un triangle dans le tissu/carton; **2** fig [*person, event*] influencer; (stronger) déterminer [*future, idea*]; modeler [*character*]; [*person*] formuler [*policy, project*]; **you could play a part in shaping this country's future** vous pourriez avoir un rôle dans la détermination de l'avenir du pays; **3** Sewing (fit closely) ajuster [*garment*]; **a jacket ~d at the waist** une veste cintrée.

■ **shape up 1** (develop) [*person*] s'en sortir; **she's shaping up really well as a manager** elle s'en sort bien comme directrice; **how are things shaping up at (the) head office?** quelle tournure prennent les choses au siège?; **to be shaping up to be** être en train de devenir; **this game is shaping up to be an enthralling contest** ce jeu est en train de devenir un concours passionnant; **2** (meet expectations) être à la hauteur; **if he doesn't ~ up, fire him** s'il n'est pas à la hauteur, renvoie-le; **~ up or ship out**○! si tu n'es pas à la hauteur prends la porte!; **3** (improve one's figure) se mettre en forme.

SHAPE /ʃeɪp/ *n* (*abrév* = **Supreme Headquarters Allied Powers Europe**) SHAPE *m* (*quartier général des forces alliées de l'OTAN en Europe*).

shaped /ʃeɪpt/ **I** *adj* **to be ~ like sth** avoir la forme de qch; **a teapot ~ like a house** une théière en forme de maison.

II -shaped (*dans composés*) **star-/V-~** en forme d'étoile/de V; **oddly-/delicately-~** de forme étrange/délicate; **egg-~** en forme d'œuf.

shapeless /ˈʃeɪplɪs/ *adj* sans forme, informe.

shapelessness /ˈʃeɪplɪsnɪs/ *n* absence *f* de forme.

shapeliness /ˈʃeɪplɪnɪs/ *n* (of object, leg) galbe *m*; **the ~ of her figure** sa silhouette bien proportionnée.

shapely /ˈʃeɪplɪ/ *adj* [*object, limb, ankle*] bien galbé; [*figure*] bien proportionné; [*woman*] bien fait.

shard /ʃɑːd/ *n* tesson *m*.

share /ʃeə(r)/ **I** *n* **1** (of money, food, profits, blame) part *f* (**of** de); **to have a ~ in** être pour quelque chose dans, contribuer à [*success, result*]; **to have a ~ in doing** contribuer à faire; **she's had more than her (fair) ~ of bad luck** elle a eu plus que sa part de malchance; **to do one's ~ of sth** faire sa part de qch; **you're not doing your ~** tu ne fais pas ta part de travail; **to pay one's (fair) ~** payer sa part; **to take** ou **accept one's ~ of the responsibility** accepter sa part de responsabilité; **a ~ of the market** une part du marché; **to have a ~ in a company** avoir une participation dans une société; **to own a half-~** posséder la moitié; **2** Fin action *f*; **to have ~s in an oil company/in oil/in Grunard** avoir des actions d'une compagnie pétrolière/dans le pétrole/de Grunard; **3** Agric soc *m* (de charrue).

II *modif* Fin [*allocation, capital, certificate, flotation, issue, offer, portfolio, transfer*] d'actions; [*price, value*] des actions.

III *vtr* partager [*money, food, house, room, prize, responsibility, opinion, taxi, enthusiasm, news*] (**with** avec); [*two or more people*] se partager [*task, chore*]; [*one person*] participer à [*task, chore*]; **we ~ a birthday** nous avons notre anniversaire le même jour; **we ~ an interest in animals** nous aimons tous les deux les animaux; **they ~ an interest in history** ils s'intéressent tous les deux à l'histoire.

IV *vi* **to ~ in** prendre part à [*success, happiness, benefits*].

IDIOMS **~ and ~ alike** il faut partager; ▶ **halve**.

■ **share out**: **~ [sth] out, ~ out [sth]** [*people, group*] partager [*food, profits, presents*]; [*person, organization*] répartir [*food, profits, supplies*] (**among, between** entre); **we ~d the money/the cakes out between us** nous nous sommes partagé l'argent/les gâteaux.

share: **~cropper** *n* US métayer/-ère *m/f*; **~cropping** *n* US métayage *m*.

shared /ʃeəd/ *adj* [*office, room, facilities*] commun; [*belief, experience, interest*] commun, partagé; [*grief*] partagé; [*house, flat*] partagé.

shareholder /ˈʃeəhəʊldə(r)/ *n* actionnaire *mf*; **the ~s** l'actionnariat *m*.

shareholder: **~s' equity** *n* fonds *mpl* propres, capital *m* social; **~s' meeting** *n* assemblée *f* des actionnaires.

shareholding /ˈʃeəhəʊldɪŋ/ *n* détention *f* or possession *f* d'actions; **a majority ~** une participation majoritaire.

share: **~ option scheme** *n* plan *m* de participation par achat d'actions; **~-out** *n* partage *m*, répartition *f*; **~ware** *n* Comput logiciel *m* contributif.

shark /ʃɑːk/ *n* requin *m* also fig.

shark: **~-infested** *adj* infesté de requins; **~'s fin soup** *n* soupe *f* aux ailerons de requins; **~skin** *n* Zool galuchat *m*; Tex peau *f* d'ange; **~'s tooth** *adj* [*pattern*] en dents de scie.

sharp /ʃɑːp/ **I** *n* dièse *m*.

II *adj* **1** (good for cutting) [*knife, razor*] tranchant; [*edge*] coupant; [*blade, scissors*] bien aiguisé; [*saw*] bien affûté; **2** (pointed) [*tooth, fingernail*] acéré; [*end, needle, rock, peak*] pointu; [*pencil*] bien taillé; [*point*] acéré, fin; [*features*] anguleux/-euse; [*nose, chin*] pointu; **3** (abrupt) [*angle*] aigu/-uë; [*bend, turning*] brusque, serré; [*movement, reflex*] brusque; [*drop, incline*] fort; Econ, Fin [*fall, rise, change*] brusque, brutal; **4** (acidic) [*taste, smell*] âcre; [*fruit*] acide; **5** (piercing) [*pain*] vif/vive; [*cry*] aigu/-uë; [*blow*] sévère; [*frost*] fort, intense; [*cold, wind*] vif/vive, pénétrant; **6** fig (aggressive) [*tongue*] acéré; [*tone, reply, rebuke*] acerbe; [*disagreement*] vif/vive; **7** (alert) [*person*] vif/vive, dégourdi; [*mind, intelligence*] vif/vive; [*eyesight, eye*] perçant; [*hearing, ear*] fin; **to have a ~ wit** avoir de la repartie; **to keep a ~ lookout** rester sur le qui-vive (**for** pour); **to have a ~ eye for sth** fig avoir l'œil pour qch; **8** (clever) péj [*businessman, person*] malin/-igne; **~ operator** filou *m*; **9** (clearly defined) [*image, outline, picture, sound*] net/nette; [*contrast*] prononcé; [*difference, distinction*] net/nette; **to bring sth into ~ focus** lit cadrer qch avec netteté; fig faire passer qch au premier plan; **10**○ GB [*suit*] tape-à-l'œil (*inv*) pej; **to be a ~ dresser** prendre grand soin de son apparence; **11**○ US (stylish) chic (*inv*); **12** Mus dièse; (too high) aigu/-uë.

III *adv* **1** (abruptly) [*stop, pull up*] net; **to turn ~ left/right** tourner brusquement vers la gauche/la droite; **2** (promptly) **at 9 o'clock ~** à neuf heures pile○ or précises; **3** Mus [*sing, play*] trop haut.

IDIOMS **to be at the ~ end** être en première ligne; **to look ~**○ se dépêcher; **you're so ~ you'll cut yourself** tu te crois vraiment très malin/-igne.

sharpen /ˈʃɑːpən/ **I** *vtr* **1** lit aiguiser, affûter [*blade, knife, razor*]; aiguiser [*scissors, shears*]; tailler [*pencil*]; **to ~ sth to a point** tailler qch en pointe; **to ~ its claws** [*cat etc*] se faire les griffes; **2** (accentuate) rendre [qch] plus net [*line, contrast*]; affiner [*focus*]; régler [*image, picture*]; **3** (make stronger) aviver [*anger, desire, fear, interest*]; accroître [*feeling, loneliness*]; **to ~ sb's appetite** lit, fig aiguiser l'appétit de qn (**for** pour); **to ~ one's wits** se dégourdir l'esprit; **to ~ sb's wits** dégourdir l'esprit de qn; **to ~ sb's reflexes** affiner les réflexes de qn.

II *vi* [*tone, voice, look*] se durcir; [*pain*] s'aviver.

■ **sharpen up**: **~ up [sth]** affiner [*reflexes*]; **to ~ oneself up for** se préparer pour [*race, competition*]; **to ~ up one's wits** se dégourdir l'esprit; **to ~ up one's image** améliorer son image.

sharpener /ˈʃɑːpənə(r)/ *n* (for pencil) taille-crayon *m*; (for knife) fusil *m*, aiguisoir *m*.

sharper /ˈʃɑːpə(r)/ *n* gen escroc *m*; (also **card~**) tricheur/-euse *m/f* professionnel/-elle.

sharp-eyed /ˌʃɑːpˈaɪd/ *adj* **1** (observant) vigilant; **2** (with good eyesight) à la vue perçante.

sharp-featured /ˌʃɑːpˈfiːtʃəd/ *adj* [*person*] aux traits anguleux.

sharpish○ /ˈʃɑːpɪʃ/ *adv* GB [*do, move, leave*] illico○, vite.

sharply /ˈʃɑːplɪ/ *adv* **1** (abruptly) [*turn, change, rise, fall*] brusquement, brutalement; [*stop*] net; **2** (harshly) [*say, speak, reply*] d'un ton brusque; [*criticize, accuse*] vivement, sévèrement; [*look, glare*] durement; **the article was ~ critical of the government** l'article était une critique virulente du gouvernement; **3** (distinctly) [*differ, contrast, stand out*] nettement; [*defined*] nettement; **to bring sth ~ into focus** lit cadrer qch avec netteté; fig faire passer qch au premier plan; **4** (perceptively) [*say*] très justement; [*observe*] avec acuité; [*characterized, drawn*] avec acuité; [*aware*] vivement; **to be ~ intelligent** avoir une intelligence vive.

sharpness /ˈʃɑːpnɪs/ *n* **1** (of blade, scissors) tranchant *m* (**of** de); **2** (pointedness) (of pencil, needle, nail) finesse *f* de la pointe (**of** de); (of peak, rock) aspérités *fpl* (**of** de); **3** (of turn, bend) angle *m* brusque (**of** de); **4** (of image, outline, contrast, sound) netteté *f* (**of** de); **5** (harshness) (of voice, tone) brusquerie *f* (**of** de); (of reproach, criticism) sévérité *f* (**of** de); **6** (of pain, guilt) acuité *f* (**of** de); **7** (acidity) (of taste) piquant *m*; (of smell) âcreté *f*; (of fruit, drink) acidité *f*.

sharp: **~ practice** *n* filouterie *f*; **~ sand** *n* Constr sable *m* liant; **~shooter** *n* tireur/-euse *m/f* d'élite; **~-sighted** *adj* [*person*] à la vue perçante; **~-tempered** *adj* soupe au lait (*after v*); **~-tongued** *adj* [*person*] à la langue acérée; **~-witted** *adj* dégourdi.

shat /ʃæt/ *prét, pp* ▶ **shit**.

shatter /ˈʃætə(r)/ **I** *vtr* **1** lit fracasser [*window, glass*]; **2** fig rompre [*peace, silence*]; briser [*life, confidence, hope, dream*]; démolir [*nerves*]; **to be ~ed by sth** être bouleversé par qch.

II *vi* [*window, glass*] voler en éclats.

shattered /ˈʃætəd/ *adj* **1** [*dream, ideal*] brisé; [*life, confidence*] anéanti; **2** [*person*] (devastated) effondré; (tired)○ crevé○, épuisé.

shattering /ˈʃætərɪŋ/ *adj* [*disappointment,*

blow, effect] accablant; [*experience, news*] bouleversant.

shatterproof /ˈʃætəpru:f/ *adj* [*windscreen*] en verre securit®.

shatterproof glass *n* verre *m* securit® *inv.*

shave /ʃeɪv/ **I** *n* **to have a ~** se raser; **to give sb a ~** raser qn.

II *vtr* (*pp* **~d** ou **shaven**) **1** lit [*barber*] raser [*person*]; **to ~ sb's beard off** raser la barbe de qn; **to ~ one's beard off** se raser la barbe; **to ~ sb's head** raser la tête de qn; **to ~ one's legs/head** se raser les jambes/la tête; **2** (plane) raboter [*wood*]; **3** fig réduire [*prices, profits*].

III *vi* (*pp* **~d** ou **shaven**) [*person*] se raser.

IV shaven, shaved *pp adj* [*head*] rasé.

IDIOMS **to have a close ~** l'échapper belle; **that was a close ~!** je l'ai/il l'a etc échappé belle!

shaver /ˈʃeɪvə(r)/ *n* **1** (also **electric ~**) rasoir *m* électrique; **2**○† (boy) gosse○ *m*, gamin *m*.

shaver point GB, **shaver outlet** US prise *f* pour rasoir électrique.

Shavian /ˈʃeɪvɪən/ *adj* [*wit*] à la Bernard Shaw; [*corpus, scholar*] de Bernard Shaw.

shaving /ˈʃeɪvɪŋ/ *n* **1** (process) rasage *m*; **2** (sliver) (of wood) copeau *m*; (of metal) rognure *f*, copeau *m*.

shaving: **~ brush** *n* blaireau *m*; **~ cream** *n* crème *f* à raser; **~ foam** *n* mousse *f* à raser; **~ gel** *n* gel *m* à raser; **~ kit** *n* nécessaire *m* de rasage; **~ mirror** *n* petit miroir *m*; **~ soap** *n* savon *m* à barbe; **~ stick** *n* bâton *m* de savon à barbe.

shawl /ʃɔ:l/ *n* châle *m*.

shawl collar *n* col *m* châle.

shawm /ʃɔ:m/ ▶ 1481 *n* Mus chalumeau *m*.

she /ʃi:, ʃɪ/

■ **Note** *she* is translated by *elle*: *she closed the door* = elle a fermé la porte. For particular usages, see the entry below.

pron elle; **~'s not at home** elle n'est pas chez elle; **here she is** la voici; **there she is** la voilà; SHE **didn't take it** ce n'est pas elle qui l'a pris; **she's a genius** c'est un génie; **she who, she that** celle qui; **she who sees** celle qui voit; **she whom** celle que; **she's a lovely boat** c'est un beau bateau; **it's a she**○ (of baby) c'est une fille; (of animal) c'est une femelle.

shea /ʃi:/ *n* karité *m*.

shea butter *n* beurre *m* de karité.

sheaf /ʃi:f/ *n* (*pl* **sheaves**) (of corn, flowers) gerbe *f*; (of papers) liasse *f*.

shear /ʃɪə(r)/ **I** *vtr* (*prét* **sheared**, *pp* **shorn**) tondre [*grass, hair, sheep*].

II shorn *pp adj* fig dépouillé (**of** de).

■ **shear off**: ¶ **~ off** [*metal component*] céder; ¶ **~ off [sth]**, **~ [sth] off** tondre [*hair, fleece*]; [*accident, storm*] emporter [*branch, part of building*].

■ **shear through**: **~ through [sth]** cisailler [*metal, screw*]; fig fendre [*water*].

shearer /ˈʃɪərə(r)/ ▶ 1692 *n* (also **sheep-~**) tondeur/-euse *m/f*.

shearing /ˈʃɪərɪŋ/ *n* (also **sheep-~**) tonte *f*.

shearing shed *n* hangar *m* où on tond les moutons.

shearling /ˈʃɪəlɪŋ/ *n* US (material) ≈ peau *f* de mouton.

shears /ʃɪərz/ *npl* **1** Hort cisaille *f*; **2** (for sheep) tondeuse *f*.

sheath /ʃi:θ/ *n* **1** (condom) préservatif *m*; **2** Bot gaine *f*; **3** (case) (of sword) fourreau *m*; (of knife, cable) gaine *f*.

sheath dress *n* robe *f* fourreau.

sheathe /ʃi:ð/ *vtr* rengainer [*sword, dagger*]; rentrer [*claws*]; replier [*wings*]; gainer [*cable*]; **~d in** gainé de [*silk etc*].

sheath knife *n* couteau *m* à gaine.

sheaves /ʃi:vz/ *npl* ▶ **sheaf**.

Sheba /ˈʃi:bə/ *pr n* **the Queen of ~** la reine de Saba.

shebang○ /ʃɪˈbæŋ/ *n* US **the whole ~**○ tout le tremblement○.

shebeen /ʃɪˈbi:n/ *n* Ir **1** (whiskey) whisky *m* (*fabriqué clandestinement*); **2** (still) débit *m* de boissons clandestin.

shed /ʃed/ **I** *n* gen remise *f*, abri *m*; (lean-to) appentis *m*; (bigger) (at factory site, port etc) hangar *m*.

II *vtr* (*prét, pp* **shed**) **1** verser, répandre [*tears*]; perdre [*leaves, petals, blossoms, weight, antlers*]; enlever, se dépouiller de [*clothes*]; se débarrasser de [*inhibitions, reputation, image*]; Constr [*roof*] évacuer [*rainwater*]; [*waterproof*] ne pas retenir [*rain*]; **to ~ hair** [*animal*] perdre ses poils, muer; **to ~ skin** [*snake*] muer; **to ~ blood** (one's own) perdre du sang; **too much blood has been shed in the name of patriotism** trop de sang a coulé au nom du patriotisme; **to ~ jobs** ou **staff** euph supprimer des emplois; **a truck has shed its load on the road** un camion a déversé son chargement sur la route; **2** (transmit) répandre [*light, warmth, happiness*].

III *vi* (*prét, pp* **shed**) [*dog, cat*] perdre ses poils.

she'd /ʃi:d, ʃɪd/ = **she had, she would**.

she-devil *n* sorcière *f* pej.

sheen /ʃi:n/ *n* (of hair) éclat *m*; (of silk) lustre *m*; **to take the ~ off sth** fig ternir l'éclat de qch.

sheep /ʃi:p/ *n* (*pl* **~**) mouton *m*; (ewe) brebis *f*; **black ~** fig brebis *f* galeuse; **lost ~** fig brebis *f* égarée.

IDIOMS **to count ~** fig compter les moutons; **to follow sb/sth like ~** suivre qn/qch comme des moutons; **to make ~'s eyes at sb** faire les yeux doux à qn; **may as well be hung for a ~ as for a lamb** tant qu'à être condamné pour un crime, autant qu'il en vaille la peine; ▶ **goat**.

sheep: **~cote** ▶ **sheepfold**; **~ dip** *n* bain *m* parasiticide (pour les moutons); **~ dog** *n* chien *m* de berger; **~ dog trials** *npl* concours *m* de chiens de berger; **~ farm** *n* ferme *f* d'élevage de moutons; **~ farmer** ▶ 1692 *n* éleveur *m* de moutons; **~ farming** *n* élevage *m* de moutons; **~fold** *n* parc *m* à moutons; **~herder** ▶ 1692 *n* US berger *m*.

sheepish /ˈʃi:pɪʃ/ *adj* penaud.

sheepishly /ʃi:pɪʃlɪ/ *adv* [*answer, admit*] d'un air penaud, d'un air gêné.

sheepishness /ˈʃi:pɪʃnɪs/ *n* air *m* penaud.

sheep: **~man** *n* US = **sheep farmer**; **~ pasture** *n* pâturage *m* à moutons; **~shank** *n* Naut (nœud *m* de) jambe *f* de chien.

sheepshearer ▶ 1692 *n* **1** (person) tondeur/-euse *m/f* (de moutons); **2** (machine) tondeuse *f*.

sheepshearing *n* tonte *f*.

sheepskin /ˈʃi:pskɪn/ **I** *n* **1** peau *f* de mouton; **2**○ US Univ diplôme *m*.

II *modif* [*gloves, jacket*] en peau lainée.

sheep: **~'s milk** *n* lait *m* de brebis; **~'s milk cheese** *n* fromage *m* de brebis; **~ station** *n* élevage *m* de moutons (*en Australie*); **~ stealing** *n* vol *m* de moutons; **~ track** *n* piste *f* à moutons.

sheer /ʃɪə(r)/ **I** *adj* **1** (pure, unadulterated) [*boredom, desperation, hypocrisy, immorality, panic, stupidity*] pur; **it was ~ coincidence/luck** c'était pure coïncidence/chance; **out of ~ malice/stupidity** par pure méchanceté/bêtise; **it is ~ lunacy to do/on his part** c'est pure folie de faire/de sa part; **to cry out in ~ amazement/happiness** pousser un cri de stupeur/bonheur; **to succeed by ~ bravery/determination/hard work** réussir uniquement grâce à son courage/sa détermination/son acharnement au travail; **by ~ accident** tout à fait par accident; **2** (utter) **the ~ immensity/volume of it is incredible** son immensité/volume même est incroyable; **3** (steep) [*cliff, rockface*] à pic; **4** (fine) [*fabric*] léger/-ère, fin; [*stockings*] extra-fin.

II *adv* [*rise, fall*] à pic.

■ **sheer away, sheer off** faire une embardée; **to ~ away** ou **off to the right/left** effectuer un virage à droite/gauche.

sheet /ʃi:t/ **I** *n* **1** (of paper) gen, Print feuille *f*; **blank/loose ~** feuille blanche/volante; **~ of stamps** feuille de timbres; **2** (for bed) drap *m*; (shroud) linceul *m*; **waterproof ~** alaise *f*; **dust ~** housse *f*; **3** Journ (periodical) périodique *m*; (newspaper) journal *m*; **fact** ou **information ~** bulletin *m* d'informations; **scandal ~** feuille *f* à scandales; **4** (of plastic, rubber) feuille *f*; (of canvas, tarpaulin) bâche *f*; (of metal) plaque *f*; (thinner) feuille *f*; (of glass) plaque *f*; (thinner) vitre *f*; **~ of iron** tôle *f*; **baking ~** tôle *f*; **cookie ~** US plaque *f* à gâteaux; **5** (expanse) (of snow, water etc) couche *f*; (of mist, fog) nappe *f*; **a ~ of ice** (thick) une plaque de glace; (thin) une couche de glace; (on road) une plaque de verglas; **a ~ of flame** un rideau de flammes; **the rain was coming down in ~s** il pleuvait à torrents; **6** Naut écoute *f*; **7**○ US Jur casier *m*.

II *vtr* recouvrir [qch] d'une housse [*furniture*]; recouvrir [qch] d'une bâche, bâcher [*cargo*].

IDIOMS **to be as white as a ~** être blanc comme un linge; **to be three ~s to the wind**† avoir du vent dans les voiles○; **to get in between the ~s with sb** sauter au lit avec qn○; **to have a clean ~** Sport avoir un palmarès vierge.

sheet anchor *n* Naut ancre *f* de veille; fig planche *f* de salut.

sheeting /ˈʃi:tɪŋ/ *n* (fabric) toile *f* à draps; Constr (iron) tôle *f*; **plastic/vinyl ~** couvertures *fpl* de plastique/de vinyle.

sheet: **~ iron** *n* tôle *f*; **~ lightning** *n* éclairs *mpl* de chaleur; **~ metal** *n* Aut, Mining tôle *f*; **~ music** *n* partitions *fpl*.

sheik /ʃeɪk, US ʃi:k/ *n* cheik *m*.

sheikdom /ˈʃeɪkdəm, US ʃi:k-/ *n* territoire *m* sous l'autorité d'un cheik.

sheila○ /ˈʃi:lə/ *n* Austral nana○ *f*, femme *f*.

shekel /ˈʃekl/ **I** *n* **1** Bible, Hist sicle *m*; **2** ▶ 1143 (currency of Israel) shekel *m*.

II shekels○ *npl* (money) fric○ *m*, argent *m*.

sheldrake /ˈʃeldreɪk/ *n* tadorne *m* de Belon.

shelduck /ˈʃeldʌk/ *n* femelle *f* du tadorne de Belon.

shelf /ʃelf/ *n* (*pl* **shelves**) **1** (at home) gen étagère *f*; (in oven) plaque *f*; (in fridge) rayon *m*, clayette *f*; (in shop, library) rayon *m*; **top/bottom ~** étagère du haut/du bas; **a set of shelves** une étagère; **a whole ~ of books** toute une étagère de livres; **you won't find it on the supermarket ~** vous ne le trouverez pas en supermarché; **2** Geol (of rock, ice) corniche *f*.

IDIOMS **to be left on the ~** (remain single) rester vieille fille; (be abandoned) être laissé pour compte.

shelfful /ˈʃelfʊl/ *n* (at home) pleine étagère *f* (**of** de); (in shop) plein rayon *m* (**of** de).

shelf-life /ˈʃelflaɪf/ *n* **1** lit (of product) durée *f* de conservation; **2** fig (of technology, pop music) durée *f* de vie; (of politician, star) période *f* de gloire.

shelf mark *n* cote *f*.

shell /ʃel/ **I** *n* **1** Bot, Zool (of egg, nut, sea creature, snail) coquille *f*; (of crab, tortoise, shrimp) carapace *f*; **sea ~** coquillage *m*; **to develop a hard ~** fig [*person*] se forger une carapace; **2** Mil (bomb) obus *m*; (cartridge) cartouche *f*; **to fire ~s at sb** pilonner qn d'obus; **3** Ind, Tech (of vehicle) carcasse *f*; (of building) cage *f*; (of machine) enveloppe *f*; (of nuclear plant) enceinte *f* de confinement; **body ~** Aut carrosserie *f*; **4** (remains) (of building) carcasse *f*; **5** Naut (boat) outrigger *m*.

II *vtr* **1** Mil pilonner [*town, installation*]; **2**

Culin écosser [*peas*]; décortiquer [*prawn, nut*]; écailler [*oyster*].
IDIOMS **to come out of/go back into one's ~** sortir de/rentrer dans sa coquille; **it's as easy as ~ing peas** c'est simple comme bonjour.
■ **shell out**○: ¶ **~ out** casquer○ (**for** pour); ¶ **~ out [sth]** débourser [*sum*] (**for** pour).

she'll /ʃi:l/ = **she will**.

shellac /ʃə'læk, 'ʃelæk/ US **I** *n* (also **~ varnish**) gomme-laque *f*.
II *vtr* (*prét, pp* **-acked**; *p prés* **-acking**) **1** (varnish) laquer; **2**○ US (beat) piler○, battre [qn] à plates coutures.

shellacking○ /ʃə'lækɪŋ, 'ʃelækɪŋ/ *n* US pile○ *f*, défaite *f* complète; **to get a ~** se faire battre à plates coutures○.

shell company *n* société *f* écran.

shellfire /'ʃelfaɪə(r)/ *n* pilonnage *m*; **to come under ~** se faire pilonner.

shellfish /'ʃelfɪʃ/ *npl* **1** Zool (crustacea) crustacés *mpl*; (mussels, oysters) coquillages *mpl*; **2** Culin fruits *mpl* de mer.

shell: **~ game** *n* lit bonneteau *m*; fig escroquerie *f*; **~hole** *n* nid *m* d'obus.

shelling /'ʃelɪŋ/ *n* pilonnage *m*.

shell-like /'ʃellaɪk/ **I**○ *n* GB hum oreille *f*.
II *adj* en forme de coquillage.

shell: **~ pink** ▶ **1104** *adj* nacré; **~-proof** *adj* blindé; **~ shock** *n* traumatisme *m* du soldat (*soumis au bombardement*).

shell-shocked /'ʃelʃɒkt/ *adj* **1** lit [*soldier*] traumatisé (*par un bombardement*); **2** fig [*person*] en état de choc.

shell suit *n* survêtement *m* en nylon®.

shelter /'ʃeltə(r)/ **I** *n* **1** ¢ (protection, refuge) abri *m*; **in the ~ of** à l'abri de; **to take ~ from** se mettre à l'abri de [*people, danger*]; s'abriter de [*weather*]; **to give sb ~** [*person*] donner un abri à qn; [*hut, tree*] offrir un abri à qn; [*country*] donner asile à qn; **2** (covered place against bomb, rain etc) ¢ abri *m* (**from** contre); **underground ~** abri souterrain; **3** (for victims, homeless) refuge *m* (**for** pour); (for fugitive, refugee) asile *m*.
II Shelter *pr n* GB *organisation bénévole pour les sans-logis*.
III *vtr* **1** (protect against weather) abriter (**from, against** de); **the garden is ~ed by walls** le jardin est abrité par des murs; **2** (protect from competition, reality, truth) protéger (**from** de); **3** (give refuge, succour to) accueillir [*neighbour, refugee, criminal*]; **to ~ sb from sb/sth** accueillir qn pour qu'il/elle échappe à qn/qch.
IV *vi* **1** (from weather, bomb) se mettre à l'abri; **to ~ from the storm** s'abriter de l'orage; **to ~ under a tree** s'abriter sous un arbre; **2** [*refugee, fugitive*] se réfugier.

sheltered /'ʃeltəd/ *adj* **1** [*place*] abrité; **2** [*life, child, upbringing*] protégé; **3** [*workshop, work*] protégé.

sheltered accommodation, sheltered housing *n* GB foyer-résidence *m*.

shelve /ʃelv/ **I** *vtr* **1** (postpone) mettre [qch] en suspens [*plan, project*]; **2** (store on shelf) mettre [qch] sur les rayons [*library, book, product*]; **3** (provide with shelves) garnir [qch] d'étagères.
II *vi* [*beach, sea bottom etc*] descendre en pente; **to ~ quickly** être en pente raide; **to ~ gently** descendre en pente douce.

shelves /ʃelvz/ *pl* ▶ **shelf**.

shelving /'ʃelvɪŋ/ *n* ¢ (at home) étagères *fpl*; (in library, shop) rayons *mpl*.

shemozzle○ /ʃɪ'mɒzl/ *n* ramdam○ *m*.

shenanigans○ /ʃɪ'nænɪgənz/ *npl* **1** (rumpus) chahut *m*; **2** (trickery) magouilles○ *fpl*, intrigues *fpl*.

shepherd /'ʃepəd/ ▶ **1692** **I** *n* berger *m*.
II *vtr* **1** [*host, guide, teacher*] escorter [*group, guests, children*]; **to ~ sb into/out of** escorter qn jusque dans/jusqu'à la sortie de [*room*]; **2** [*herdsman*] guider [*animals*]; **to ~ animals into a pen** faire entrer des animaux dans un enclos.

shepherd: **~ boy** *n* jeune berger *m*; **~ dog** *n* chien *m* de berger.

shepherdess /,ʃepə'des, US 'ʃepərdɪs/ ▶ **1692** *n* bergère *f*.

shepherd: **~'s crook** *n* houlette *f*; **~'s pie** *n* hachis *m* Parmentier; **~'s purse** *n* Bot bourse-à-pasteur *f*.

sherbet /'ʃɜ:bət/ *n* **1** GB (powder) confiserie *f* en poudre acidulée; **2** US (sorbet) sorbet *m*.

sheriff /'ʃerɪf/ ▶ **1692** *n* **1** GB Jur (in England) shérif *m*; (in Scotland) juge *m*; **2** US shérif *m*.

sheriff court *n* Jur (in Scotland) ≈ tribunal *m* d'instance.

sherpa /'ʃɜ:pə/ *n* sherpa *m*.

sherry /'ʃerɪ/ *n* xérès *m*, sherry *m*.

she's /ʃi:z/ = **she is, she has**.

Shetland /'ʃetlənd/ ▶ **1381** **I** *pr n* (also **~ Islands**) îles *fpl* Shetland; **in ~, in the ~s** dans les îles Shetland.
II *modif* (also **~ wool**) [*scarf, sweater, gloves*] en shetland.
III *adj* [*crofter, family*] shetlandais.

Shetlander /'ʃetləndə(r)/ *n* Shetlandais/-e *m/f*.

Shetland: **~ pony** *n* poney *m* des Shetland; **~ wool** *n* shetland *m*.

shew‡ /ʃəʊ/ *vtr, vi* = **show**.

shhh /ʃ/ *excl* chut!

Shia(h) /'ʃi:ə/ **I** *n* chiisme *m*.
II *adj* chiite.

shiatsu /,ʃi:'ætsu:/ *n* shiatsu *m*.

shibboleth /'ʃɪbəleθ/ *n* principe *m*.

shied /ʃaɪd/ *prét, pp* ▶ **shy** II, III.

shield /ʃi:ld/ **I** *n* **1** Mil (of warrior, soldier etc) bouclier *m*; Herald écusson *m*; fig protection *f*, bouclier *m* liter (**against** contre); **2** Sport ≈ trophée *m*; **3** Tech (screen) (on machine, against radiation) écran *m* de protection; (around gun) pare-balles *m inv*; (of tunnel) bouclier *m* (d'avancement); **4** US (policeman's badge) insigne *m*; **5** Zool (shell of animal) carapace *f*.
II *vtr* (from weather) protéger, abriter (**from** de); (from danger, discovery, truth) gen protéger (**from** de); (from authorities) (by lying) couvrir; (by harbouring) donner asile à [*suspect, criminal*]; **to ~ one's eyes from the sun** se protéger les yeux du soleil; **to ~ sb with one's body** faire (un) bouclier de son corps à qn.

shieling /'ʃi:lɪŋ/ *n* GB dial cabane *f* de berger.

shift /ʃɪft/ **I** *n* **1** (alteration) changement *m* (**in** de), modification *f* (**in** de); **there has been a ~ in public opinion** l'opinion publique a changé; **a sudden ~ in public opinion** un retournement de l'opinion publique; **a ~ of policy** un changement de politique; **a ~ to the left/right** Pol un glissement vers la gauche/la droite; **the ~ from agriculture to industry** le passage de l'agriculture à l'industrie; **2** Ind (period of time) période *f* de travail (posté); (group of workers) équipe *f*, poste *m*; **to work ~s** ou **be on ~s** faire un travail posté; **to be on day/night ~s** être (d'équipe) de jour/de nuit; **to work an eight-hour ~** faire une période de huit heures (en travail posté), faire les trois-huit; **the next ~ comes on at 10** la prochaine équipe commence à 10 heures; **3** (woman's dress) robe *f* droite or fourreau *inv*; (undergarment)† chemise *f*; **4** Ling mutation *f*; **a ~ in meaning** un glissement de sens; **5** Geol (fault) faille *f*; (movement of rocks) glissement *m*; **6** Comput décalage *m*; **7** US Aut = **gear-shift**; **8** (on keyboard) = **shift key**.
II *vtr* **1** (move) déplacer, changer [qch] de place [*furniture*]; déplacer [*vehicle*]; bouger, remuer [*arm, leg, head*]; Theat changer [*scenery*]; **will somebody help me ~ this piano?** est-ce que quelqu'un peut m'aider à déplacer ce piano?; **I can't ~ this lid** je n'arrive pas à enlever ce couvercle; **to ~ sth from** enlever qch de; **to ~ sth away from** éloigner qch de [*wall, window*]; **to ~ sth into** mettre qch dans [*room, garden*]; **~ your arse**●! GB bouge ton cul●! **to ~ one's ground** ou **position** fig changer de position or d'avis; **2** (get rid of) faire partir, enlever [*stain, dirt*]; **I can't ~ this cold**○! GB je n'arrive pas à me débarrasser de mon rhume; **3** (transfer) (to another department) affecter; (to another town, country) muter [*employee*]; fig rejeter [*blame, responsibility*] (**onto** sur); **to ~ attention away from a problem** détourner l'attention d'un problème; **to ~ one's weight from one foot to another** se dandiner d'un pied sur l'autre; **the company is ~ing production to Asia** l'entreprise va transférer ses usines en Asie; **4** US Aut **to ~ gear** changer de vitesse.
III *vi* **1** (also **~ about**) (move around) [*load, contents*] se déplacer, bouger; [*cargo*] bouger; **to ~ uneasily in one's chair** remuer sur sa chaise l'air mal à l'aise; **to ~ from one foot to the other** se dandiner d'un pied sur l'autre; **2** (move) **the scene ~s to Ireland** Cin, Theat la scène se situe maintenant en Irlande; **this stain won't ~!** cette tache ne veut pas partir!; **can you ~ along** ou **over a little?** peux-tu te pousser un peu?; **~**○! GB pousse-toi○!; **3** (change) [*opinion, attitude*] se modifier; [*wind*] tourner; **opinion has ~ed to the right** l'opinion a glissé vers la droite; **she won't ~** elle ne veut pas changer d'avis; **4**○ GB (go quickly) [*person*] se grouiller○; [*vehicle*] foncer○; **5** US Aut **to ~ into second gear** passer en seconde; **to ~ from first into second** passer de première en seconde.
IV *v refl* **to ~ oneself** se pousser; **~ yourselves**○! poussez-vous○!; **you'll have to ~ yourself into another room** tu vas être obligé de déménager dans une autre pièce.
IDIOMS **to ~ for oneself** se débrouiller tout seul; **to make ~ with†** se débrouiller avec.

shiftily /'ʃɪftɪlɪ/ *adv* [*look*] furtivement; [*behave*] de façon suspecte.

shiftiness /'ʃɪftɪnɪs/ *n* (of person) caractère *m* louche.

shifting /'ʃɪftɪŋ/ *adj* [*light, alliance, belief*] changeant; [*population*] toujours renouvelé.

shifting: **~ cultivation** *n* culture *f* itinérante; **~ sands** *npl* lit sables *mpl* mouvants; fig terrain *m* mouvant.

shift key *n* touche *f* de majuscule.

shiftless /'ʃɪftlɪs/ *adj* **1** (lazy) paresseux/-euse, apathique; **2** (lacking initiative) qui manque d'ambition.

shift: **~ lock** *n* touche *f* de verrouillage des majuscules; **~ register** *n* Comput registre *m* à décalage; **~ system** *n* Ind travail *m* par équipes.

shift work *n* travail *m* posté; **to be on ~** faire un travail posté, travailler par roulement.

shift worker *n* ouvrier/-ière *m/f* qui fait un travail posté or qui fait les trois-huit.

shifty /'ʃɪftɪ/ *adj* [*person, manner*] louche; **to have ~ eyes** avoir le regard fuyant.

Shiite /'ʃi:aɪt/ **I** *n* chiite *mf*.
II *adj* chiite.

shiksa /'ʃɪksə/ *n* US péj jeune fille *f* goy.

shill /ʃɪl/ US **I** *n* complice *mf* qui fait monter les enchères.
II *vi* faire monter les enchères.

shillelagh /ʃɪ'leɪlə, -lɪ/ ▶ **1481** *n* Irish gourdin *m*.

shilling /'ʃɪlɪŋ/ ▶ **1143** *n* shilling *m*.
IDIOMS **to be down to one's last ~** en être à son dernier sou; **to take the King's** ou **Queen's ~** GB partir sous les drapeaux; **to watch the pounds, ~s and pence** être à un sou près.

shillyshally○ /'ʃɪlɪʃælɪ/ *vi* tergiverser.

shillyshallying○ /'ʃɪlɪʃælɪɪŋ/ *n* tergiversations *fpl*.

shimmer /'ʃɪmə(r)/ **I** *n* (of jewels, water) scintillement *m*; (of silk) chatoiement *m*; (of heat) vibration *f*.

II *vi* **1** [*jewels, water*] scintiller; [*silk*] chatoyer; **2** (in heat) [*landscape*] vibrer.

shimmering /ˈʃɪmərɪŋ/ **I** *n* = **shimmer**.
II *adj* [*water, jewels*] scintillant; [*silk*] chatoyant; [*heat*] vibrant.

shimmy /ˈʃɪmɪ/ **I** *n* **1** (dance) shimmy *m*; **2** Aut shimmy *m*.
II *vi* **1** danser le shimmy; **2** Aut vibrer.

shin /ʃɪn/ *n* tibia *m*; **to kick sb in the ~s** donner à qn un coup de pied dans le tibia.
■ **shin up**: **~ up** [**sth**] grimper sur [*tree*].
■ **shin down**: **~ down** [**sth**] descendre [qch] en s'agrippant [*tree, drainpipe*].

shinbone /ˈʃɪnbəʊn/ *n* tibia *m*.

shindig○ /ˈʃɪndɪɡ/, **shindy**○ /ˈʃɪndɪ/ *n* **1** (disturbance) ramdam○ *m*; **to kick up a ~** faire du ramdam○; **2** (party) nouba○ *f*.

shine /ʃaɪn/ **I** *n* (of floor, hair, marble, metal, wood) lustre *m*; (of parquet) brillant *m*; **to give sth a ~** cirer [*floor, shoes*]; rendre [qch] brillant [*hair*]; faire reluire [*silver*].
II *vtr* **1** (*prét, pp* **shone**) braquer [*headlights, spotlight, torch*]; **2** (*prét, pp* **shined**) faire reluire [*brass, silver*]; cirer [*shoes*].
III *vi* (*prét, pp* **shone**) **1** [*hair, light, sun*] briller; [*brass, floor*] reluire; **to ~ through** percer [*mist, gloom*]; **the light is shining in my eyes** j'ai la lumière dans les yeux; **his face shone with exertion** son visage luisait sous l'effort; **2** fig (be radiant) [*eyes*] briller (**with** de); [*face*] rayonner (**with** de); **her courage shone forth** littér elle a montré un courage éclatant; **3** (excel) briller; **to ~ at** être brillant en [*science, languages etc*]; **he never shone at school** il n'a jamais été brillant à l'école; **4** (be very clean) reluire; **the kitchen shone** la cuisine reluisait.
IDIOMS **to get** ou **have a chance to ~** avoir l'occasion de briller; **to ~ up to sb**○ US passer de la pommade○ à qn; **to take a ~ to sb**○ s'enticher○ de qn; fig **to take the ~ off sth** gâcher qch; **where the sun doesn't ~**◑ où je pense◑.
■ **shine in** pénétrer; **to ~ in through** pénétrer par [*window, chink*].
■ **shine through** [*talent*] éclater au grand jour.
■ **shine out** [*light*] briller, apparaître; **the light shone out through the doorway** la porte ouverte laissait passer la lumière.

shiner○ /ˈʃaɪnə(r)/ *n* **1** (black eye) œil *m* poché, œil *m* au beurre noir○; **2** US (fish) petit poisson *m*.

shingle /ˈʃɪŋɡl/ **I** *n* **1** ¢ (pebbles) galets *mpl*; **2** Constr (tile) bardeau *m*; **3**○ US (nameplate) plaque *f*; **4** (hairstyle) coiffure *f* à la garçonne.
II *vtr* **1** Constr couvrir [qch] de bardeaux [*roof*]; **2** (style hair) coiffer [qn] à la garçonne.
III *modif* **1** [*beach*] de galets; **2** Constr [*roof*] de bardeaux.
IV **shingled** *pp adj* [*hair*] à la garçonne.
IDIOMS **to hang up** ou **out one's ~**○ US accrocher sa plaque○.

shingles /ˈʃɪŋɡlz/ ▶1354 *npl* Med zona *m*; **to have ~** avoir un zona.

shingly /ˈʃɪŋɡlɪ/ *adj* [*beach*] de galets.

shinguard, **shinpad** /ˈʃɪnɡɑːd, ˈʃɪnpæd/ *n* jambière *f*.

shininess /ˈʃaɪnɪnɪs/ *n* lustre *m*.

shining /ˈʃaɪnɪŋ/ *adj* **1** (shiny) [*car*] étincelant; [*hair*] brillant, lustré; [*bald spot*] luisant; [*brass, silver*] brillant, luisant [*floor*] reluisant; **2** (glowing) [*eyes*] brillant; [*face*] radieux/-ieuse; **with ~ eyes she tore the ribbon off the present** les yeux brillants, elle a arraché le ruban qui attachait le cadeau; **3** fig [*achievement*] brillant.
IDIOMS **to be a ~ example of sth** être le parfait exemple de qch; **to be a ~ light** Relig répandre de la lumière.

shinny /ˈʃɪnɪ/ **I** *n* US Sport = **shinty**.
II *vi* US grimper.

Shinto(ism) /ˈʃɪntəʊ(ɪzəm)/ *n* shintoïsme *m*.

Shintoist /ˈʃɪntəʊɪst/ *n* shintoïste *mf*.

shinty /ˈʃɪntɪ/ *n* GB Sport hockey *m* (*version simplifiée*).

shiny /ˈʃaɪnɪ/ *adj* **1** [*metal, coin, photographic finish, surface, hair*] brillant; **2** [*shoes, parquet, wood*] bien ciré; **3** [*seat of trousers*] lustré; **a ~ mac** GB un ciré.

ship /ʃɪp/ **I** *n* navire *m*; (smaller) bateau *m*; **passenger ~** paquebot *m*; **Her Majesty's ~ (HMS) Victory** le Victory (*navire faisant partie de la flotte de guerre britannique*); **to travel by ~** voyager par bateau; **to send sth by ~** envoyer qch par bateau; **to take ~ for India**† prendre le bateau pour l'Inde; **a ~ of the line** Hist un bâtiment de ligne; **the good ~ Ivanhoe**† littér l'Ivanhoe.
II *vtr* (*p prés etc* **-pp-**) **1** (send) (by sea) transporter [qch] par mer; (by air) transporter [qch] par avion; (overland) acheminer; **2** (take on board) charger [*cargo, supplies*]; rentrer [*oars*]; **to ~ water** embarquer de l'eau.
IDIOMS **we are like ~s that pass in the night** nous ne faisons que nous croiser; **the ~ of state** le char de l'État; **the ~ of the desert** (camel) le vaisseau du désert; **to run a tight ~** mener tout le monde à la baguette; **when my ~ comes in** quand j'aurai fait fortune.
■ **ship off**: **~ [sth/sb] off, ~ off [sth/sb]** expédier also hum.
■ **ship out**: ¶ **~ out** US (go to sea) embarquer; ¶ **~ [sth] out, ~ out [sth]** = **ship off**.
■ **ship over** US s'engager dans la marine.

ship: **~board** *adj* [*ceremony*] à bord; [*duty*] du bord; **~broker** ▶1692 *n* courtier *m* maritime.

shipbuilder /ˈʃɪpbɪldə(r)/ ▶1692 *n* constructeur *m* naval; **a firm of ~s** une entreprise de construction navale.

ship: **~building** *n* construction *f* navale; **~ canal** *n* canal *m* maritime; **~load** *n* cargaison *f*; **~mate** *n* camarade *m* de bord.

shipment /ˈʃɪpmənt/ *n* **1** (cargo) (by sea) cargaison *f*; (by air, land) chargement *m*; **arms ~** chargement *m* d'armes; **2** (sending) expédition *f*.

ship owner *n* armateur *m*.

shipper /ˈʃɪpə(r)/ *n* expéditeur/-trice *m/f*.

shipping /ˈʃɪpɪŋ/ **I** *n* **1** (boats) navigation *f*, trafic *m* maritime; **a danger to ~** un danger pour la navigation; **open/closed to ~** ouvert/fermé à la navigation; **British ~** marine *f* britannique; **attention all ~!** avis à toutes les embarcations!; **2** (sending) acheminement *m* (par bateau); US (nonmaritime) acheminement *m*; (as profession, industry) transport *m* maritime.
II *modif* [*agent, exchange, industry, office*] maritime.

shipping: **~ charges** *npl* frais *mpl* de transport; **~ clerk** ▶1692 *n* expéditionnaire *mf*; **~ company** *n* (sea) compagnie *f* maritime; (road) entreprise *f* de transport routier; **~ forecast** *n* météo *f* marine; **~ lane** *n* couloir *m* de navigation; **~ line** *n* compagnie *f* de navigation.

ship: **~'s biscuit** *n* biscuit *m* (de ration); **~'s boat** *n* (lifeboat) canot *m* de sauvetage; **~'s chandler** ▶1692 *n* marchand *m* d'équipement pour bateaux; **~'s company** *n* équipage *m*; **~'s doctor** ▶1692 *n* médecin *m* de bord.

shipshape /ˈʃɪpʃeɪp/ *adj* GB bien en ordre; **~ and Bristol fashion** dans un ordre impeccable.

ship: **~'s mate** ▶1612 *n* lieutenant *m*; **~'s papers** *npl* documents *mpl* de bord; **~-to-shore radio** *n* liaison *f* radio avec la côte.

shipwreck /ˈʃɪprek/ **I** *n* (event) naufrage *m*; (ship) épave *f*.
II *vtr* **to be ~ed** faire naufrage; **a ~ed sailor** un marin naufragé.

shipwright /ˈʃɪpraɪt/ ▶1692 *n* constructeur *m* naval.

shipyard /ˈʃɪpjɑːd/ **I** *n* chantier *m* naval.
II *modif* [*worker*] de chantier naval.

shire /ˈʃaɪə(r)/ GB **I** *n* **1**† comté *m* (du centre de l'Angleterre); **2** Pol **the ~s** les provinces.
II *modif* Pol [*county, politician*] de province.

shire horse *n* shire *m*.

shirk /ʃɜːk/ **I** *vtr* esquiver [*task, duty*]; fuir [*responsibility*]; éluder [*problem*]; **to ~ doing sth** éviter de faire qch.
II *vi* se défiler.

shirker /ˈʃɜːkə(r)/ *n* tire-au-flanc○ *m inv*.

shirr /ʃɜː(r)/ **I** *vtr* Sewing froncer [qch] sur élastique [*bodice etc*].
II **shirred** *pp adj* **1** Culin [*eggs*] en cocotte; **2** Sewing [*bodice etc*] froncé sur élastique.

shirring /ˈʃɜːrɪŋ/ *n* Sewing (process) fronçure *f* sur élastique; (result) fronçures *fpl* sur élastique.

shirt /ʃɜːt/ ▶1703 **I** *n* (man's) chemise *f*; (woman's) chemisier *m*; (for sport) maillot *m*; **long-/short-sleeved ~** chemise à manches longues/courtes; **open-necked ~** chemise à col ouvert.
II *modif* [*button, collar, cuff*] de chemise.
IDIOMS **keep your ~ on**○! du calme!; **to lose one's ~**○ laisser jusqu'à sa dernière chemise○; **to put one's ~ on sth**○ tout miser sur qch; **to sell the ~ off one's back** vendre père et mère○.

shirt: **~dress** *n* US = **shirtwaist(er)**; **~front** *n* plastron *m*.

shirting /ˈʃɜːtɪŋ/ *n* shirting *m*.

shirt-sleeve /ˈʃɜːtsliːv/ **I** *n* manche *f* de chemise; **in one's ~s** en manches de chemise; **to roll up one's ~s** remonter les manches (de chemise) also fig.
II *adj* US (plain) [*approach*] direct.

shirttail /ˈʃɜːtteɪl/ *n* **1** (of shirt) pan *m* de chemise; **2**○ US Journ *commentaire en bas d'un article*.

shirt: **~tail cousin** *n* US cousin/-e *m/f* à la mode de Bretagne; **~waist(er)** *n* GB robe-chemisier *f*.

shirty○ /ˈʃɜːtɪ/ *adj* GB [*person*] de mauvais poil○; **to get ~** prendre la mouche○.

shish-kebab /ˈʃiːʃkəbæb/ *n* chiche-kebab *m*.

shit◑ /ʃɪt/ **I** *n* **1** (excrement) merde◑ *f*, crotte○ *f*; **dog ~** crotte de chien; **horse ~** crottin *m*; **2** (act of excreting) **to have** ou **take** US/**need a ~** chier◑/avoir envie de chier◑; **to have the ~s** avoir la chiasse◑; **3** (also **bull~**) conneries◑ *fpl*; **to talk ~** dire des conneries◑; **I've taken all the ~ I'm going to** tu m'as fait assez chier◑ comme ça; **4** (nasty person) emmerdeur/-euse◑ *m/f*; **5** US (things) trucs○ *mpl*, bordel◑ *m*; **6**◑ US (heroin) héroïne *f*; **7**◑ (marijuana) shit◑ *m*, marijuana *f*.
II *adv* (also **~-all**) **he knows ~ about it** il n'y connaît que dalle◑.
III *vtr* (*prét, pp* **shat**) **1** (excrete) chier◑ dans; **to ~ one's pants** chier◑ dans son froc; **2** US (fool) prendre [qn] pour un con◑.
IV *vi* (*prét, pp* **shat**) chier◑.
V *v refl* (*prét, pp* **shat**) **to ~ oneself** chier◑ dans son froc.
VI *excl* merde◑!; **tough ~!** tant pis!
IDIOMS **are you ~ting?** US tu déconnes◑?; **I don't give a ~ for** ou **about sb/sth** je me fous◑ de qn/qch; **no ~?** sans blague○?; **to be in the ~** ou **in deep ~** être dans la merde◑ jusqu'au cou; **to beat** ou **kick** ou **knock the ~ out of sb** rosser○ qn; **to eat ~** en chier◑; **to scare the ~ out of sb** flanquer la frousse○ à qn; **to ~ on sb** traiter qn comme de la merde◑; **when the ~ hits the fan** quand l'affaire éclatera.

shit: **~ ass**◑ US = **shitface**; **~bag**◑ *n* trou-du-cul◑ *m*.

shite◑ /ʃaɪt/ *n* = **shit**.

shit: **~-eating**◑ *adj* US (gloating) [*grin*] satisfait; **~face**◑ *n* connard◑ *m*/connasse◑ *f*; **~faced**◑ *adj* bourré○; **~head**◑ *n* = **shitbag**; **~-hole**◑ *n* trou *m* à rats○; **~-hot**◑ *adj* super○; **~house**◑ *n* chiottes◑ *fpl*.

shitless◑ /ˈʃɪtlɪs/ *adj* **to scare sb ~**

flanquer la frousse○ à qn; **to be scared ~** mouiller son froc de peur○.

shit-list◑ *n* liste *f* noire.

shit scared◑ *adj* **to be ~** mouiller son froc de peur○.

shit-stirrer◑ *n* emmerdeur/-euse◑ *m/f*.

shitter◑ /ˈʃɪtə(r)/ *n* US **1** (toilets) chiottes◑ *fpl*; **2** (also **bull~**) baratineur/-euse○ *m/f*.

shitty◑ /ˈʃɪtɪ/ *adj* **1** lit merdeux/-euse◑; **2** fig [*person*] merdeux/-euse◑; [*situation, object*] merdique◑; **3** US (ill) **to feel ~** être mal foutu◑.

shitwork◑ /ˈʃɪtwɜːk/ *n* US sale boulot○ *m*; **to have to do the ~** devoir faire le sale boulot.

shiv○ /ʃɪv/ **I** *n* US couteau *m*.
II *vtr* (*p prés etc* **-vv-**) poignarder.

shivaree /ˌʃɪvəˈriː/ *n* US charivari *m*.

shiver /ˈʃɪvə(r)/ **I** *n* lit, fig frisson *m*; **to give a ~** avoir un frisson; **to send a ~ down sb's spine** faire courir un frisson dans le dos à qn.
II shivers *npl* frissons *mpl*; **an attack of the ~s** un accès de frissons; **to give sb the ~s** lit donner des frissons à qn; fig donner froid dans le dos à qn.
III *vtr* briser en mille morceaux.
IV *vi* **1** (with cold, fever) grelotter (**with** de); (with fear, excitement) frémir (**with** de); (with emotion, disgust) frissonner (**with** de); **2** (shatter) se briser en mille morceaux; **3** littér [*leaves etc*] frémir.
IDIOMS **~ my timbers**†! que le diable m'emporte†!

shivery /ˈʃɪvərɪ/ *adj* (feverish) fébrile.

shoal /ʃəʊl/ *n* **1** (of fish) banc *m*; **2** fig (of visitors) foule *f*; (of letters, complaints) quantité *f*; **3** Geog (of sand) banc *m* de sable; (shallows) bas-fond *m*.

shock /ʃɒk/ **I** *n* **1** (psychological) choc *m*; **to get** ou **have a ~** avoir un choc; **to give sb a ~** faire un choc à qn; **the ~ of seeing/hearing** le choc de voir/d'entendre; **it came as a bit of a ~** cela m'a fait comme un choc; **her death came as a ~ to us** sa mort a été un choc pour nous; **it's a ~ to the system when...** c'est un vrai choc quand...; **to recover from** ou **get over the ~** surmonter le choc; **a sense of ~** un choc; **he's in for a nasty**○ **~ when he gets the bill** il va avoir un sacré○ choc quand il recevra la note; **to express one's ~** (indignation) exprimer son indignation; (amazement) exprimer sa surprise; **his ~ at their mistreatment** son indignation en apprenant leur mauvais traitement; **her ~ at her surprisingly good results** sa surprise en apprenant ses bons résultats; **~! horror!** journ ou hum scandale épouvantable!; **minister's resignation ~!** journ coup de théâtre: le ministre démissionne!; **2** Med état *m* de choc; **to be in (a state of) ~** être en état de choc; **to go into ~** entrer en état de choc; **to treat sb for ~** soigner qn en état de choc; **in deep ~** en grave état de choc; **to be suffering from ~** souffrir d'un choc; **severe/mild ~** choc grave/léger; **3** Elec décharge *f*; **electric ~** décharge électrique; **to get/receive a ~** prendre/recevoir une décharge; **to give sb a ~** donner une décharge à qn; **4** (physical impact) (of collision) choc *m*; (of earthquake) secousse *f*; (of explosion) souffle *m*; **5** (of corn) gerbe *f*; fig (of hair) tignasse *f*; **6**○ (also **~ absorber**) amortisseur *m*.
II○ *modif* gen, journ [*approach, effect*] de choc; [*announcement, decision, result*] sidérant.
III *vtr* (distress) consterner; (scandalize) choquer.
IV shocked *pp adj* (distressed) consterné; (scandalized) choqué; **to be ~ed at** ou **by sth** être choqué or consterné par qch; **to be ~ed to hear** ou **learn that...** être choqué or consterné d'apprendre que...; **she's not easily ~ed** on ne la choque pas facilement.

shock absorber *n* amortisseur *m*.

shocker○ /ˈʃɒkə(r)/ *n* (person) provocateur/-trice *m/f*; (book, film, programme) provocation *f*.

shocking /ˈʃɒkɪŋ/ *adj* **1** (upsetting) [*sight*] consternant; (scandalous) [*news*] choquant; **2**○ (appalling) désastreux/-euse○.

shockingly /ˈʃɒkɪŋlɪ/ *adv* [*behave*] scandaleusement; [*expensive*] extrêmement; **it was ~ unfair** c'était d'une injustice scandaleuse; **his work is ~ bad** son travail est désastreux.

shocking pink ▶ 1104 *n, adj* rose (*m*) vif *inv*.

shock: **~proof**, **~ resistant** *adj* antichoc *inv*; **~ tactics** *npl* gen, Mil tactique *f* de choc; **~ therapy** *n* thérapie *f* de choc; **~ treatment** *n* Psych traitement *m* par électrochocs; fig traitement *m* de choc; **~ troops** *npl* troupes *fpl* de choc.

shock value *n* **the ~ of the book is the attraction** le côté provocateur du livre est le seul intérêt; **it's just for ~** c'est juste pour choquer.

shock wave *n* **1** lit onde *f* de choc; **2** fig remous *mpl*; **the news has sent ~s through the stock market** la nouvelle a provoqué des remous à la Bourse.

shod /ʃɒd/ **I** *pret, pp* ▶ **shoe III**.
II *pp adj* chaussé; **well/poorly ~** bien/mal chaussé.

shoddily /ˈʃɒdɪlɪ/ *adv* **1 to be ~ made/built** être de fabrication/de construction sommaire; **2** [*behave*] avec bassesse.

shoddiness /ˈʃɒdɪnɪs/ *n* (of work, product etc) mauvaise qualité *f*.

shoddy /ˈʃɒdɪ/ **I** *n* gros drap *m*.
II *adj* **1** [*product*] de mauvaise qualité; [*work*] mal fait; **2** [*behaviour*] mesquin; **a ~ trick** un sale tour.

shoe /ʃuː/ ▶ 1703 **I** *n* **1** (footwear) chaussure *f*; **a pair of ~s** une paire de chaussures; **to take off/put on one's ~s** enlever/mettre ses chaussures; **2** (for horse) fer *m*; **3** Phot (for flash) griffe *f*; **4** Aut (also **brake ~**) sabot *m* de frein; **5** Civ Eng (also **pile ~**) sabot *m* de pieu.
II *modif* [*box, brush, cleaner, cream*] à chaussures; [*factory, manufacturer, retailer, shop*] de chaussures.
III *vtr* (*p prés* **shoeing**; *prét, pp* **shod**) ferrer [*horse*]; chausser [*person*].
IDIOMS **it's a question of dead men's ~s** il s'agit d'attendre la mort de quelqu'un pour prendre sa place; **to be in sb's ~s** être à la place de qn; **what would you have done in my ~s?** qu'aurais-tu fait à ma place?; **to save/wear out ~ leather** ménager/user ses semelles; **to shake** ou **shiver in one's ~s** avoir peur, avoir la frousse○; **to step into** ou **fill sb's ~s** prendre la place de qn.

shoe: **~bill** *n* bec-en-sabot *m*; **~black** *n* ▶ **shoeshine (boy)**; **~horn** *n* chausse-pied *m*.

shoelace /ˈʃuːleɪs/ *n* lacet *m* de chaussure; **to do** ou **tie up one's ~s** lacer ses chaussures.

shoe: **~maker** ▶ 1692 *n* cordonnier/-ière *m/f*; **~ polish** *n* cirage *m*; **~ rack** *n* porte-chaussures *m*; **~ repairer** ▶ 1692 *n* cordonnier *m*; **~ repairs** *npl* cordonnerie *f*; **~ repair shop** ▶ 1692 *n* cordonnerie *f*; **~shine (boy)** *n* cireur *m* de chaussures; **~ shop** ▶ 1692 *n* magasin *m* de chaussures.

shoe size ▶ 1703 *n* pointure *f*; **what's your ~?** quelle pointure fais-tu?

shoestring /ˈʃuːstrɪŋ/ *n* US lacet *m* de chaussure.
IDIOMS **on a ~**○ avec peu de moyens.

shoe: **~string budget**○ *n* budget *m* de misère; **~ tree** *n* embauchoir *m*.

shogun /ˈʃəʊgʊn/ *n* Hist shogun *m*; fig magnat *m*.

shone /ʃɒn/ *prét, pp* ▶ **shine**.

shoo /ʃuː/ **I** *excl* ouste.
II *vtr* (also **~ away**) chasser.

shoo-in /ˈʃuːɪn/ *n* US favori/-ite *m/f*; **Bates is a ~ to win the election** Bates est donné comme favori pour remporter les élections.

shook /ʃʊk/ *prét* ▶ **shake**.

shoot /ʃuːt/ **I** *n* **1** Bot (young growth) pousse *f*; (offshoot) rejeton *m*; **2** GB, Hunt (meeting) partie *f* de chasse; (area of land) (terrain *m* de) chasse *f*; **3** Cin tournage *m*; **4** (rapid) rapide *m*; **5** Geol, Mining couloir *m* (de minerai).
II○ *excl* US **1** (expressing disbelief) oh non alors!; **2** (telling sb to speak) vas-y, parle○!
III *vtr* (*prét, pp* **shot**) **1** (fire) tirer [*bullet*]; lancer [*missile*]; tirer, décocher [*arrow*]; **to ~ sth at sb/sth** (with gun) tirer qch sur qn/qch; (with missiles) lancer qch sur qn/qch; **to ~ one's way out of somewhere** s'échapper de quelque part en tirant de tous côtés; **2** (hit with gun) tirer sur [*person, animal*]; (kill) abattre [*person, animal*]; **she shot him in the leg/back** elle lui a tiré dans la jambe/le dos; **to be shot in the leg/back** recevoir une balle dans la jambe/le dos; **he was shot in the head** on lui a tiré une balle dans la tête; **to ~ sb for desertion/spying** fusiller qn pour désertion/espionnage; **to ~ sb dead** abattre qn; **you'll get shot if someone catches you!** fig tu vas te faire tuer si on te surprend!; **I could ~ him!** je pourrais le tuer!; **to be shot to pieces**○ lit être criblé de balles; fig être réduit à néant; **3** (direct) lancer, décocher [*look*] (**at** à); jeter [*smile*] (**at** à); **to ~ questions at sb** bombarder qn de questions; **4** Cin, Phot (film) tourner [*film, scene*]; prendre [qch] (en photo) [*subject*]; **5** (push) mettre, pousser [*bolt*]; **6** (in canoeing) **to ~ the rapids** franchir les rapides; **7** (in golf) **to ~ 75** faire un score de 75; **8** US Sport, Games jouer à [*pool, craps*]; **to ~ dice** jouer aux dés; **9** Hunt chasser [*pheasant, game*]; chasser sur [*moor*]; **10**○ (inject) ▶ **shoot up**○.
IV *vi* (*prét, pp* **shot**) **1** (fire a gun) tirer (**at** sur); **to ~ to kill/wound** tirer pour tuer/blesser; **2** (move suddenly) **to ~ out of/into/down sth** sortir de/entrer dans/descendre qch en flèche; **to ~ forward/backwards** s'élancer/reculer à toute vitesse; **the car shot past** la voiture est passée en trombe or à toute allure; **the pain shot down** ou **along his arm** ça lui a élancé dans le bras, il a eu une douleur lancinante dans le bras; **to ~ to fame** fig percer, devenir célèbre subitement; **3** Bot (grow) [*plant*] pousser; **4** Cin tourner; **5** Sport (in football, hockey etc) [*player*] tirer, shooter; **6** Hunt [*person*] chasser.
V *v refl* (*prét, pp* **shot**) **to ~ oneself** se tirer une balle dans la tête; **to ~ oneself in the head/leg** se tirer une balle dans la tête/la jambe.
IDIOMS **to ~ a line**○ frimer○; **to ~ oneself in the foot**○ agir contre son propre intérêt; **to ~ the works**○ US dépenser tout son argent; **the whole (bang) ~**○ tout le bataclan○; ▶ **mouth**.

■ **shoot down**: ¶ **~ down [sb/sth]**, **~ [sb/sth] down** Aviat, Mil abattre, descendre○ [*plane, pilot*]; **he was shot down over France** son avion a été abattu quand il volait au-dessus de la France; **to ~ [sb/sth] down in flames** lit, fig descendre [qn/qch] en flammes [*person, plane, argument*]; ¶ **~ [sb] down**, **~ down [sb]** [*gunman*] abattre [*person*].

■ **shoot off**: **his foot was shot off** il a eu un pied emporté par un éclat d'obus.

■ **shoot out**: **~ out** [*flame, water*] jaillir; **the car shot out of a side street** la voiture est sortie en trombe d'une petite rue; **to ~ one's foot/arm out** tendre la jambe/le bras; **the snake shot its tongue out** le serpent a dardé sa langue; **to ~ it out**○ [*gunmen*] régler leurs comptes à coups de feu.

■ **shoot up**: ¶ **~ up 1** [*flames, spray*] jaillir; fig [*prices, profits*] monter en flèche; **2** (grow rapidly) [*plant*] pousser vite; **that boy has really shot up!** fig qu'est-ce que ce

Shops, trades and professions

Shops

In English you can say at the baker's *or* at the baker's shop; *in French the construction with* chez *(at the house or premises of ...) is common but you can also use the name of the particular shop:*

at the baker's = chez le boulanger *or* à la boulangerie
I'm going to the grocer's = je vais chez l'épicier *or* à l'épicerie
I bought it at the fishmonger's = je l'ai acheté chez le poissonnier *or* à la poissonnerie
go to the chemist's = va à la pharmacie *or* chez le pharmacien
at *or* to the hairdresser's = chez le coiffeur/la coiffeuse
to work in a butcher's = travailler dans une boucherie

Chez *is also used with the names of professions:*

at *or* to the doctor's = chez le médecin
at *or* to the lawyer's = chez le notaire
at *or* to the dentist's = chez le dentiste

Note that there are specific names for the place of work of some professions:

the lawyer's office = l'étude *f* du notaire
the doctor's surgery (GB) *or* office (US) = le cabinet du médecin

Cabinet *is also used for architects and dentists. If in doubt, check in the dictionary.*

People

Talking of someone's profession, we could say he is a dentist. *In French this would be either* il est dentiste *or* c'est un dentiste. *Only when the sentence begins with* c'est *can the indefinite article (*un *or* une*) be used.*

Paul is a dentist = Paul est dentiste
she is a dentist = elle est dentiste *or* c'est une dentiste
she's a geography teacher = elle est professeur de géographie *or* c'est un professeur de géographie

With adjectives, only the c'est *construction is possible:*

she is a good dentist = c'est une bonne dentiste

In the plural, if the construction begins with ce sont *then you need to use* des *(or* de *before an adjective):*

they are mechanics = ils sont mécaniciens *or* ce sont des mécaniciens
they are good mechanics = ce sont de bons mécaniciens

Trades and professions

what does he do? = qu'est-ce qu'il fait?
what's your job? = qu'est-ce que vous faites dans la vie?
I'm a teacher = je suis professeur
to work as a dentist = travailler comme dentiste
to work for an electrician = travailler pour un électricien
to be paid as a mechanic = être payé comme mécanicien
he wants to be a baker = il veut devenir boulanger

garçon a grandi!; **3** (inject oneself) argot des drogués se shooter○; ¶ **~ up [sth], ~ [sth] up 1**○ (inject) argot des drogués se shooter à○ [*heroin*]; **2** (with bullets) tirer sur [*person*]; **he was badly shot up** il a été gravement blessé.

shoot'em-up○ *n* US film *m* violent.

shooting /ˈʃuːtɪŋ/ **I** *n* **1** (act) (killing) meurtre *m* (par arme à feu), assassinat *m* (par arme à feu); **the ~ of the prisoner took place at dawn** le prisonnier a été fusillé à l'aube; **2** ¢ (firing) coups *mpl* de feu, fusillade *f*; **3** Hunt chasse *f*; **to go ~** aller à la chasse; **4** ▶ 1282 Sport (at target etc) tir *m*; **5** Cin tournage *m*.
II *pres p adj* [*pain*] lancinant.

shooting: **~ box** *n* Hunt pavillon *m* de chasse; **~ brake**† *n* GB Aut break *m*; **~ gallery** *n* Sport stand *m* de tir; **~ incident** *n* échange *m* de coups de feu; **~ iron**○ *n* US flingue○ *m*, pistolet *m*; **~ party** *n* Hunt groupe *m* de chasseurs; **~ range** *n* stand *m* de tir; **~ script** *n* Cin découpage *m*; **~ star** *n* Astron étoile *f* filante; **~ stick** *n* canne-siège *f*.

shoot-out○ /ˈʃuːtaʊt/ *n* fusillade *f*.

shop /ʃɒp/ **I** *n* **1** (where goods are sold) magasin *m*; (small, fashionable) boutique *f*; **to work in/open a ~** travailler dans/ouvrir un magasin; **to go to the ~s** aller faire les courses; **he's out at the ~s** il est sorti faire les courses; **to set up ~** lit, fig s'installer; **he set up ~ as a photographer** fig il s'est installé comme photographe; **to shut up ~**○ lit, fig fermer boutique; **2** US (in department store) rayon *m*; **gourmet/beauty ~** rayon gastronomique/de beauté; **3** (workshop) atelier *m*; **repair/print ~** atelier de réparation/d'imprimerie; **4** US Sch atelier *m*; **5**○ GB (shopping) **to do the weekly ~** faire les courses pour la semaine; **to do a big ~** faire le plein○.
II○ *vtr* (*p prés etc* **-pp-**) GB (inform on) donner○, vendre [*person*].
III *vi* (*p prés etc* **-pp-**) faire ses courses; **to be ~ping for sth** vouloir acheter qch; **to go ~ping** gen aller faire des courses; (as browser) aller faire les magasins; **to go ~ping for sth** aller acheter qch.
IDIOMS **all over the ~**○ GB fig partout; **to talk ~** parler boutique; **you've come to the wrong ~** GB vous vous trompez d'adresse.
■ **shop around** (compare prices) faire le tour des magasins (**for** pour trouver); fig (compare courses, services etc) bien chercher; **if you ~ around, you'll find the best course** en cherchant bien vous trouverez le meilleur cours.

shop: **~ assistant** ▶ 1692 *n* GB vendeur/-euse *m/f*; **~ fitter** ▶ 1692 *n* GB installateur/-trice *m/f* de magasins; **~ fitting** *n* GB installation *f* de magasins.

shopfloor /ˌʃɒpˈflɔː(r)/ **I** *n* **problems on the ~** des problèmes parmi les ouvriers; **conditions on the ~** les conditions des ouvriers.
II *modif* **~ opinion** l'opinion des ouvriers.

shop: **~ front** *n* devanture *f*; **~ girl** *n* GB vendeuse *f*; **~keeper** ▶ 1692 *n* commerçant/-e *m/f*; **~lift** *vi* voler à l'étalage; **~lifter** *n* voleur/-euse *m/f* à l'étalage; **~lifting** *n* vol *m* à l'étalage.

shopper /ˈʃɒpə(r)/ *n* **the streets were crowded with ~s** il y avait des foules de gens dans les rues en train de faire leurs courses.

shopping /ˈʃɒpɪŋ/ *n* ¢ **1** (activity) courses *fpl*; **to do some/the ~** faire des/les courses; **we are open for lunch-time ~** le magasin est ouvert à l'heure du déjeuner; **2** (purchases) courses *fpl*.

shopping: **~ bag** *n* sac *m* à provisions; **~ basket** *n* panier *m* (à provisions); (in supermarket) panier *m*; **~ centre** GB, **~ center** US *n* centre *m* commercial; **~ complex** *n* centre *m* commercial; **~ list** *n* liste *f* de courses; **~ mall** *n* US centre *m* commercial; **~ precinct** *n* zone *f* commerçante.

shopping trip *n* **to go on a ~** aller faire les magasins.

shopping trolley *n* caddie® *m*.

shop-soiled *adj* **to be ~** [*garment*] être sali.

shop: **~ steward** *n* représentant/-e *m/f* syndical/-e; **~talk**○ *n* conversation *f* professionnelle; **~ window** *n* vitrine *f* also fig; **~worn** *adj* US ▶ **shopsoiled**.

shore /ʃɔː(r)/ **I** *n* **1** (coast, edge) (of sea) côte *f*, rivage *m*; (of lake) rive *f*; (of island) côte *f*; **on the ~** sur le rivage; **off the ~ of** Naut au large de; **2** gen, Naut (dry land) terre *f*; **on ~** à terre; **from ship to ~** en liaison avec la côte; **3** (beach) grève *f*, plage *f*; **down to/on the ~** vers/sur la grève or la plage.
II shores *npl* littér rives *fpl*.
■ **shore up**: **~ up [sth], ~ [sth] up** étayer [*building, river bank*]; fig soutenir [*economy, system*].

shore-based *adj* Tourism **~ vacation** *vacances en mer avec nuit et repas à terre.*

shore: **~ leave** *n* permission *f* de descendre à terre; **~line** *n* côte *f*; **~ patrol** *n* patrouille *f* côtière.

shoreward /ˈʃɔːwəd/ **I** *adj* [*wind, direction*] vers la côte.
II *adv* (also **shorewards**) vers la côte.

shorn /ʃɔːn/ *pp* ▶ **shear**.

short /ʃɔːt/ ▶ 1412 **I** *n* **1** (drink) alcool *m* fort; **2** Elec = **short-circuit**; **3** Cin court métrage *m*; **4** Fin (deficit) manque *m*, déficit *m*; **5** Fin (on stock exchange) vente *f* à découvert.
II shorts *npl* short *m*; (underwear) caleçon *m*; **a pair of (tennis) ~s** un short (de tennis).
III *adj* **1** (not long-lasting) [*time, stay, memory, period*] court (*before n*); [*course*] de courte durée; [*conversation, speech, chapter*] bref/brève; **a ~ time ago** il y a peu de temps; **that was a ~ hour/month** c'était une petite heure/un petit mois; **in four ~ years** en quatre brèves années; **to work ~er hours** travailler moins d'heures; **the days are getting ~er** les jours diminuent or raccourcissent; **to go for a ~ walk** faire une petite promenade or un petit tour; **the meeting was ~ and sweet** la réunion a été brève; **let's keep it ~ (and sweet)** soyons brefs!; **the ~ answer is that** la réponse est tout simplement que; **2** (not of great length) [*hair, dress, distance, stick*] court (*before n*); [*animal's coat, fur*] court (*before n*); (very short) ras; **the suit is too ~ in the sleeves** les manches du costume sont trop courtes; **to have one's hair cut ~** se faire couper les cheveux court; **to win by a ~ head** Turf l'emporter d'une courte tête; **3** (not tall) [*person*] petit; **4** (scarce) [*water, food*] difficile à trouver; **to be in ~ supply** être difficile à trouver; **food/coal is getting ~** la nourriture/le charbon se fait rare; **time is getting ~** le temps presse; **5** (inadequate) [*rations*] insuffisant; **we're ~ by three** il nous en manque trois; **he gave me a ~ measure** (in shop) il a triché sur le poids; **6** (lacking) **I am/he is ~ of sth** il me/lui manque qch; **to be ~ on** [*person*] manquer de [*talent, tact*]; **to go ~ of** manquer de [*clothes, money, food*]; **my wages are £30 ~** il me manque 30 livres sur mon salaire; **I don't want you to go ~** je ne veux pas qu'il te manque quoi que ce soit; **to be running ~ of sth** commencer à manquer de qch; **7** (in abbreviation) **Tom is ~ for Thomas** Tom est le diminutif de Thomas; **this is Nicholas, Nick for ~!** je te présente Nicholas, mais on l'appelle Nick; **8** (abrupt) [*person, personality*] (*jamais épith*) brusque; [*laugh*] bref/brève; **to be ~ with sb** être brusque avec qn; **9** Ling [*vowel*] bref/brève; **10** Fin [*bill*] à courte échéance; [*loan, credit*] à court terme; [*seller*] à découvert; **11** Culin [*pastry*] brisé.
IV *adv* (abruptly) [*stop*] net; **to stop ~ of doing** se retenir pour ne pas faire; ▶ **cut short**.
V in short *adv phr* bref.
VI short of *prep phr* **1** (just before) un peu avant; **the ball landed (just) ~ of the green** la balle est tombée un peu avant le green; **2** (just less than) pas loin de; **a little ~ of £1,000** pas loin de 1 000 livres; **that's**

nothing ~ of blackmail! c'est du chantage, ni plus ni moins!; **3** (except) à moins de; **~ of locking him in, I can't stop him leaving** à moins de l'enfermer à clé, je ne peux pas l'empêcher de partir.
VII *vtr, vi* Elec = **short-circuit**.
IDIOMS **to bring** ou **pull sb up ~** couper qn dans son élan; **to have a ~ temper, to be ~-tempered** être coléreux or soupe au lait○; **to have sb by the ~ hairs**◑ US ou **~ and curlies**○ GB tenir qn à la gorge; **to sell oneself ~** se sous-estimer; **to make ~ work of sth/sb** expédier qch/qn; **to be taken** ou **caught ~** être pris d'un besoin pressant; **the long and ~ of it is that they**... en un mot (comme en cent), ils...

short account *n* Fin position *f* vendeur.

shortage /'ʃɔ:tɪdʒ/ *n* pénurie *f*, manque *m* (**of** de); **a ~ of teachers/food** une pénurie d'enseignants/de vivres; **~s of sth** une pénurie or un manque de qch; **at a time of ~** en période de pénurie; **housing ~** crise *f* du logement; **there is no ~ of applicants/opportunity** les candidats/occasions ne manquent pas or ne font pas défaut.

short: **~-arse**◑ *n* GB bas-du-cul◑ *m*; **~ back and sides** *n* coupe *f* de cheveux masculine (*dégageant la nuque et les oreilles*); **~bread** *n* sablé *m*; **~cake** *n* (shortbread) sablé *m*; (dessert) tarte *f* sablée; **~-change** *vtr* lit [*shop assistant*] ne pas rendre toute sa monnaie à [*shopper*]; fig rouler○ [*associate, investor*].

short circuit /,ʃɔ:t'sɜ:kɪt/ **I** *n* court-circuit *m*.
II short-circuit *vtr* lit, fig court-circuiter.
III short-circuit *vi* faire court-circuit.

short: **~comings** *npl* défauts *mpl*, points *mpl* faibles; **~ covering** *n* Fin rachat *m* (pour couvrir un découvert); **~crust pastry** *n* pâte *f* brisée.

shortcut *n* **1** lit raccourci *m*; **to take a ~ through the park** prendre un raccourci à travers le parc, couper par le parc; **2** fig **to take ~s** bâcler○; **there are no ~s to becoming a musician** on ne s'improvise pas musicien.

short division *n* Math division *f* facile.

shorten /'ʃɔ:tn/ **I** *vtr* abréger [*visit, life*]; raccourcir [*garment*]; réduire [*journey time, list*]; raccourcir, abréger [*draft, talk, book*]; alléger [*syllabus*]; **to ~ sail** Naut réduire la voilure.
II *vi* [*days, nights*] raccourcir, diminuer; [*wait, odds, period of time*] diminuer.

shortening /'ʃɔ:tnɪŋ/ *n* **1** Culin matière *f* grasse; **2** (reduction) réduction *f* (**of** de); **3** (abridging) abrégement *m*.

short exchange *n* Fin papier *m* court.

shortfall /'ʃɔ:tfɔ:l/ *n* (in budget, accounts) déficit *m*; (in earnings, exports etc) manque *m*; **there is a ~ of £10,000 in our budget** il manque 10 000 livres à notre budget; **there is a ~ of several hundred in the expected number of applications** le nombre de demandes est inférieur de plusieurs centaines au nombre attendu; **to meet** ou **make up the ~ between cost and subsidy** combler la différence or le déficit entre le coût et les subventions.

short-haired /,ʃɔ:t'heəd/ *adj* [*person*] aux cheveux courts; [*animal*] à poil ras.

shorthand /'ʃɔ:thænd/ **I** *n* **1** Comm sténographie *f*, sténo○ *f*; **to take sth down in ~** prendre qch en sténo○; **2** fig (euphemism, verbal shortcut) formule *f* consacrée.
II *modif* [*note, notebook, qualification*] sténo.

short-handed /,ʃɔ:t'hændɪd/ *adj* (in company) à court de personnel; (on farm, building site) à court de main-d'œuvre.

shorthand: **~-typing** *n* sténo-dactylo *f*; **~-typist** ▶ **1692** *n* sténo-dactylo *f*.

short: **~-haul** *adj* Aviat court-courrier; **~horn** /'ʃɔ:thɔ:n/ *n* race *f* shorthorn.

shortie○ /'ʃɔ:tɪ/ *n* ▶ **shorty**.

shortlist /'ʃɔ:tlɪst/ **I** *n* liste *f* des candidats sélectionnés.
II *vtr* sélectionner [*applicant*] (**for** pour).

short-lived /,ʃɔ:t'lɪvd, US -'laɪvd/ *adj* [*triumph, success, happiness*] bref/brève, de courte durée; [*effect, phenomenon*] passager/-ère; **to be ~** ne pas durer longtemps.

shortly /'ʃɔ:tlɪ/ *adv* **1** (very soon) bientôt; **she'll be back ~** elle sera bientôt de retour; **volume four will be published ~** le quatrième volume paraîtra prochainement or sous peu; **2** (a short time) **~ after(wards)/before** peu (de temps) après/avant; **~ before/after lunch** peu avant/après le déjeuner; **3** (crossly) [*reply*] sèchement, brusquement.

shortness /'ʃɔ:tnɪs/ *n* (in time) courte durée *f*; **~ of breath** manque *m* de souffle.

short: **~ odds** *npl* faible cote *f*; **~-order cook** ▶ **1692** *n* US *cuisinier préparant des plats rapides dans un établissement modeste*; **~-range** *adj* [*weather forecast*] à court terme; [*missile*] à courte portée; [*aircraft*] à court rayon d'action; **~ sharp shock (treatment)** *n* GB régime *m* pénal sévère (*destiné à la rééducation d'adolescents*); **~ sight** *n* myopie *f*.

shortsighted /,ʃɔ:t'saɪtɪd/ *adj* **1** lit myope; **~ people** les myopes; **2** fig (lacking foresight) [*person*] peu clairvoyant; [*policy, decision*] à courte vue; **it would be very ~ to do** il serait déraisonnable de faire; **to have a ~ attitude** manquer de perspicacité.

shortsightedness /,ʃɔ:t'saɪtɪdnɪs/ *n* **1** lit myopie *f*; **2** fig manque *m* de perspicacité (**about** à propos de).

short-sleeved /,ʃɔ:t'sli:vd/ *adj* à manches courtes.

short-staffed /,ʃɔ:t'stɑ:ft, US -stæft/ *adj* **to be ~** manquer de personnel.

short: **~-stay** *adj* [*car park*] de courte durée; [*hostel, housing*] à court terme; **~ story** *n* Literat nouvelle *f*; **~-tailed** *adj* Zool à queue courte; **~-tempered** *adj* (by nature) coléreux/-euse, soupe au lait○ (*after v*); (temporarily) irritable.

short term I *n* **in the ~** (looking to future) dans l'immédiat; (looking to past) pendant un temps, pour commencer.
II short-term *adj* gen, Fin à court terme.

short time *n* (in industry) chômage *m* partiel; **to be on ~** être en chômage partiel.

shortwave I *n* ondes *fpl* courtes.
II *modif* [*radio*] à ondes courtes; [*broadcast*] sur ondes courtes.

short-winded /,ʃɔ:t'wɪndɪd/ *adj* **to be ~** avoir le souffle court.

shorty○ /'ʃɔ:tɪ/ *n* pej (person) nabot *m*.

shot /ʃɒt/ **I** *prét, pp* ▶ **shoot**.
II *n* **1** (from gun etc) coup *m* (de feu); **to fire** ou **take a ~ at sb/sth** tirer sur qn/qch; **it took several ~s to kill him** il fallu plusieurs balles pour l'achever; **the government fired the opening ~ by saying**... fig le gouvernement a ouvert le feu en disant...; **2** Sport (in tennis, golf, cricket) coup *m*; (in football) tir *m*; **to have** ou **take a ~ at goal** (in football) tirer au but; **'good ~!'** 'bien joué!'; **two ~s up on/behind sb** (in golf) deux coups d'avance/de retard sur qn; **3** Phot photo *f* (**of** de); **4** Cin plan *m* (**of** de); **action ~** scène *f* d'action; **to be in/out of ~** Cin être dans le champ/hors champ; **5** (injection) piqûre *f* (**of** de); **to give sb a ~** faire une piqûre à qn; **6** (attempt) **to have a ~ at doing** essayer de faire qch; **to give it one's best ~** faire de son mieux; **7** (in shotputting) poids *m*; **to put the ~** lancer le poids; **8** (pellet) **C** balle *f*, plomb *m*; (pellets collectively) **¢** plomb *m*; (smaller) cendrée *f*; **9** (person who shoots) **to be a good/poor ~** être un bon/mauvais tireur; **10**○ (dose) **a ~ of whisky/gin** une lampée○ de whisky/gin; **11** Aerosp (of rocket etc) lancement *m*, tir *m*; **a moon ~** un tir lunaire.
III *adj* **1** (also **~ through**) (streaked) [*silk*] changeant; **~ (through) with gold/red etc** [*material*] strié d'or/de rouge etc; **her hair was ~ (through) with grey** ses cheveux étaient parsemés de gris; **2**○ (also **~ away**) (destroyed) **he is ~ (away)** il n'a plus toute sa tête; **his nerves were ~** il était à bout de nerfs; **his confidence is ~** il a perdu toute confiance.
IDIOMS **to call the ~s** dicter la loi; **to be ~ of sb/sth** être débarrassé de qn/qch; **to get ~ of sb/sth** se débarrasser de qn/qch; **to give sth a ~ in the arm** revigorer qch; **the dog was after the cat like a ~** le chien s'est lancé brusquement à la poursuite du chat; **he'd go like a ~, if he had the chance** il partirait sans hésiter, s'il en avait l'occasion; **'I don't care what you think,' was his parting ~** 'je me moque de ce que vous pensez,' a-t-il décoché en partant; **it was a ~ in the dark** ça a été dit au hasard.

shot-blasting *n* Ind grenaillage *m*.

shotgun /'ʃɒtgʌn/ *n* fusil *m*.
IDIOMS **to ride ~**○ être sur le qui-vive.

shot: **~gun wedding** *n* mariage *m* forcé; **~ hole** *n* Ind trou *m* de mine; **~ put** *n* Sport lancer *m* de poids; **~-putter** *n* Sport lanceur/-euse *m/f* de poids.

should /ʃʊd, ʃəd/ *modal aux* (*conditional of* **shall**) **1** (ought to) **you shouldn't smoke so much** tu ne devrais pas fumer autant; **you ~ have told me before** tu aurais dû me le dire avant; **we ~ try and understand him better** nous devrions essayer de mieux le comprendre; **why shouldn't I do it?** pourquoi est-ce que je ne le ferais pas?; **I ~ explain that** je devrais peut-être expliquer que; **we ~ be there by six o'clock** nous devrions arriver vers six heures; **dinner ~ be ready by now** le dîner devrait être prêt maintenant; **it shouldn't be difficult to convince them** ça ne devrait pas être difficile de les convaincre; **that ~ be them arriving now!** ça doit être eux qui arrivent!; **how ~ I know?** comment veux-tu que je le sache?; **everything is as it ~ be** tout est en ordre; **...which is only as it ~ be** ...ce qui est parfaitement normal; **his hearing is not as good as it ~ be** il entend moins bien qu'il (ne) le devrait; **flowers! you shouldn't have!** des fleurs! il ne fallait pas!; **2** (in conditional sentences) **had he asked me, I ~ have accepted** s'il me l'avait demandé, j'aurais accepté; **if they didn't invite me, I ~ be offended** s'ils ne m'invitaient pas, je serais très vexé; **had they invited me, I ~ have gone** s'ils m'avaient invité, j'y serais allé; **I don't think it will happen, but if it ~**... je ne pense pas que cela arrive, mais si toutefois cela arrivait...; **~ you be interested, I can give you some more information** si cela vous intéresse, je peux vous donner plus de renseignements; **if you ~ change your mind, don't hesitate to contact me** si vous changez d'avis n'hésitez pas à me contacter; **~ anybody phone, tell them I'm out** si quelqu'un téléphone, dis que je suis sorti; **~ the opportunity arise** si l'occasion se présente; **3** (expressing purpose) **she simplified it in order that they ~ understand** elle l'a simplifié pour qu'ils comprennent; **he kept it a secret from them so that they ~ not be worried** il le leur a caché pour qu'ils ne se fassent pas de soucis; **we are anxious that he ~ succeed** nous souhaitons vivement qu'il réussisse; **4** (in polite formulas) **I ~ like a drink** je prendrais volontiers un verre; **I ~ like to go there** j'aimerais bien y aller; **5** (expressing opinion, surprise) **I ~ think so!** je l'espère!; **I ~ think not!** j'espère bien que non!; **'how long will it take?'—'an hour, I ~ think'** 'combien de temps est-ce que ça va prendre?'—'une heure, je suppose'; **I ~ think she must be about 40** à mon avis, elle doit avoir 40 ans environ; **'I'll pay you for it'—'I ~ hope so!'** 'je vous le rembourserai'—'je l'espère bien!'; **I ~ say so!** et comment!; **I shouldn't be surprised if she did that!** cela ne m'étonnerait pas

> ## should
> **Meaning *ought to***
> When *should* is used to mean *ought to*, it is translated by the conditional tense of *devoir*:
> *we should leave at seven* = nous devrions partir à sept heures
> The past *should have* meaning *ought to have* is translated by the past conditional of *devoir*:
> *she should have told him the truth* = elle aurait dû lui dire la vérité
> The same verb is used in negative sentences:
> *you shouldn't do that* = vous ne devriez pas faire ça
> *he shouldn't have resigned* = il n'aurait pas dû démissionner
> For the conjugation of *devoir*, see the French verb tables.
> **In conditional sentences**
> When *should* is used as an auxiliary verb to form the conditional, *should* + verb is translated by the conditional of the appropriate verb in French:
> *I should like to go to Paris* = j'aimerais aller à Paris
> *I should have liked to go to Paris* = j'aurais aimé aller à Paris
> **As a subjunctive in purpose clauses**
> When *should* is used as an auxiliary verb in *that* clauses, *should* + verb is translated by the subjunctive of the appropriate verb in French:
> *in order that they should understand* = pour qu'ils comprennent
> For particular usages see the entry ***should***.

qu'elle le fasse!; **I shouldn't worry about it if I were you** moi à ta place je ne m'en ferais pas○, si j'étais toi je ne m'inquiéterais pas; **I ~ have thought he'd be glad of a holiday** j'aurais pensé qu'il serait content de partir en vacances; **who ~ walk in but John!** devine qui est arrivé—John!; **and then what ~ happen, but it began to rain!** et devine quoi—il s'est mis à pleuvoir!

shoulder /ˈʃəʊldə(r)/ **I** *n* **▶ 1037** **1** Anat épaule *f*; **on** ou **over one's ~** à l'épaule; **on** ou **over one's ~s** sur les épaules; **this jacket is too tight across the ~s** cette veste est trop étroite d'épaules; **to put one's ~s back** rejeter les épaules en arrière; **to straighten one's ~s** redresser les épaules; **to look over sb's ~** regarder par-dessus l'épaule de qn; **to cry on sb's ~** pleurer sur l'épaule de qn; **I am always there if you need a ~ to cry on** je suis toujours là si tu as besoin d'une épaule pour pleurer; **his ~s shook with laughter/sobs** il était secoué de rire/de sanglots; **to have round ~s** avoir le dos rond; **to look (back) over one's ~** lit, fig regarder derrière soi; **the burden/responsibility is** ou **falls on my ~s** la charge/la responsabilité m'incombe; **to stand ~ to ~** lit [*two people*] être côte à côte; **to work ~ to ~** travailler coude à coude or côte à côte; **2** (on mountain) replat *m*; **3** Sewing épaule *f*; **4** (on road) bas-côté *m*; **5** Culin épaule *f*.
II *vtr* **1** lit mettre [qch] sur l'épaule [*bag, implement*]; **to ~ one's gun** mettre son fusil sur l'épaule; **to ~ arms** Mil se mettre au port d'armes; **~ arms!** Mil l'arme sur l'épaule!; **2** fig se charger de [*burden, expense, task*]; endosser [*responsibility*]; **3** (push) **to ~ one's way through** se frayer un chemin à coups d'épaules à travers [*crowd*]; **to ~ sb aside** écarter qn d'un coup d'épaule.
III - shouldered (*dans composés*) **to be round-~ed** avoir le dos rond; **to be narrow/square-~ed** avoir les épaules étroites/carrées.
IDIOMS **to be** ou **stand head and ~s above sb** lit dépasser qn d'une bonne tête; fig laisser qn loin derrière; **to have a good head on one's ~s** avoir la tête sur les épaules; **to have an old head on young ~s** être mûr avant l'âge; **to put one's ~ to the wheel** s'atteler à la tâche; **to rub ~s with sb** côtoyer qn; **straight from the ~**○ [*comment, criticism*] franc/franche; **to give it to sb straight from the ~**○ dire qch à qn sans détours.

shoulder: **~ bag** *n* sac *m* à bandoulière; **~ belt** *n* US Aut sangle *f* transversale (*d'une ceinture de sécurité*); **~ blade** *n* omoplate *f*.

shoulder-high /ˌʃəʊldəˈhaɪ/ *adj* [*crop*] à hauteur d'homme; **to carry sb ~** porter qn en triomphe.

shoulder: **~ holster** *n* étui *m* de revolver (*qui se porte à l'épaule*); **~ joint** *n* articulation *f* de l'épaule; **~-length** *adj* [*veil*] qui arrive jusqu'aux épaules; [*hair*] milong; **~ pad** *n* épaulette *f*; **~ patch** *n* US Mil écusson *m*.

shoulder strap *n* (of garment) bretelle *f*; (of bag) bandoulière *f*.

shouldn't /ˈʃʊdnt/ = **should not**.

shout /ʃaʊt/ **I** *n* **1** (cry) cri *m* (**of** de); **to give a ~ of warning/joy** pousser un cri d'avertissement/de joie; **there were ~s of 'bravo!'** on cria 'bravo!'; **2**○ GB (round of drinks) tournée *f*.
II *vtr* **1** (cry out) crier; (stronger) hurler; **'stop!' she ~ed** 'arrêtez!' cria-t-elle; **2**○ GB (buy) **to ~ a round (of drinks)** payer une tournée.
III *vi* crier; **to ~ at sb** crier après qn; **to ~ at** ou **to sb to do** crier à qn de faire; **to ~ with excitement/anger** crier d'excitation/de colère; **to ~ for help** crier pour demander de l'aide; **what are they ~ing about?** pourquoi crient-ils?
IDIOMS **I'll give you a ~** je te ferai signe; **it's nothing to ~ about** ça n'a rien d'extraordinaire.
■ **shout down**: **~ down [sb], ~ [sb] down** faire taire [qn] (en criant plus fort que lui).
■ **shout out**: ¶ **~ out** pousser un cri; ¶ **~ out [sth]** lancer [qch] à haute voix [*names, answers*].

shouting /ˈʃaʊtɪŋ/ *n* cris *mpl*.
IDIOMS **it's all over bar the ~** c'est pratiquement terminé.

shouting match○ *n* engueulade○ *f*.

shove○ /ʃʌv/ **I** *n* **to give sb/sth a ~** pousser qn/qch; **she gave me a ~ in the back** elle m'a poussé dans le dos; **the door needs a good ~** il faut pousser fort la porte.
II *vtr* **1** (push) pousser (**against** contre; **towards** vers); **to ~ sth through** pousser qch dans [*letterbox*]; pousser qch par [*gap*]; **to ~ sth about** ou **around** déplacer qch; **to ~ sb/sth back** repousser qn/qch; **to ~ sb/sth aside** ou **out of the way** écarter qn/qch en le poussant; **they ~d him down the stairs/out of the window** ils lui ont fait descendre l'escalier en le poussant/l'ont poussé par la fenêtre; **to be ~d into**○ être flanqué○ dans [*room, institution*]; être flanqué○ à [*street*]; **to be ~d out of** être viré○ de [*building*]; **to ~ sth in sb's face** fourrer○ qch sous le nez de qn [*camera, microphone*]; **to ~ sth down sb's throat** fig imposer qch à qn; **2** (stuff hurriedly, carelessly) fourrer; **to ~ sth into** fourrer qch dans [*container, pocket, room, gap*]; **she ~d the clothes back in the drawer** elle a remis les vêtements dans le tiroir n'importe comment; **3** (jostle, elbow) bousculer [*person*]; **to ~ (one's way) past sb** passer devant qn en le bousculant; **he ~d his way to the front of the crowd** il s'est frayé un chemin à travers la foule.
III *vi* pousser; **to ~ past sb** passer devant qn en le bousculant; **people were pushing and shoving** les gens poussaient et se bousculaient.
IDIOMS **if push comes to ~** au pire; **tell him to ~ it**○ ou **he can ~ it**○**!** dis-lui qu'il peut se le mettre où je pense○!
■ **shove off** GB **1**○ (leave) se tirer○; **(why don't you) just ~ off!** tire-toi○! fiche-moi le camp○!; **2** (in boat) déborder.
■ **shove over**○: ¶ **~ over** se pousser; ¶ **~ [sth] over, ~ over [sth]** passer [*object, foodstuff*]; **~ it over here!** passe-le moi○!
■ **shove up**○ se pousser.

shove halfpenny /ˌʃʌvˈheɪpnɪ/ **▶ 1282** *n* GB ≈ jeu *m* de palet (sur table).

shovel /ˈʃʌvl/ **I** *n* **1** (spade) pelle *f*; **2** (mechanical digger) pelleteuse *f*.
II *vtr* (*p prés etc* **-ll-** GB, **-l-** US) enlever [qch] à la pelle [*dirt, snow*] (**off** de); **to ~ sth into sth** verser qch dans qch à l'aide d'une pelle; **to ~ food into one's mouth**○ s'enfourner○ la nourriture dans la bouche.
■ **shovel up**: **~ up [sth], ~ [sth] up** ramasser [qch] à la pelle [*dirt, leaves, snow*].

shoveler /ˈʃʌvlə(r)/ *n* Zool canard *m* souchet.

shovelful /ˈʃʌvlfʊl/ *n* pelletée *f* (**of** de).

show /ʃəʊ/ **I** *n* **1** (as entertainment) Theat, gen spectacle *m*; (particular performance) représentation *f*; Cin séance *f*; Radio, TV émission *f*; (of slides) projection *f*; **live ~** Radio, TV émission en direct; US (sex show) spectacle érotique; **to put on** ou **stage a ~** monter un spectacle; **family ~** spectacle pour tous; **on with the ~ !** (as introduction) place au spectacle!; (during performance) que la représentation continue!; **the ~ must go on** lit la représentation doit avoir lieu vaille que vaille; fig il faut continuer vaille que vaille; **to do**○ ou **take in**○ **a ~** s'offrir un spectacle; **2** Comm (as promotion, display) (of cars, boats etc) salon *m*; (of fashion) défilé *m*; (of flowers, crafts) exposition *f*; **motor/boat ~** salon de l'auto/de la navigation; **flower ~** exposition florale; **to be on ~** être exposé; **3** (outward display) (of feelings) semblant *m* (**of** de); (of strength) démonstration *f* (**of** de); (of wealth) étalage *m* (**of** de); **a ~ of affection/defiance** un semblant d'affection/de rébellion; **a ~ of unity** une démonstration d'unité; **to make** ou **put on a (great) ~ of doing** s'évertuer pour la galerie à faire; **to put on a ~** poser pour la galerie; **he made a ~ of gratitude/concern** il a affiché sa gratitude/sa sollicitude; **to be all ~** n'être que de la comédie; **to be all for** ou **just for ~** être de l'esbroufe○; **the glitter and ~ of the circus** l'éclat et la splendeur du cirque; **the roses make a splendid ~** les roses sont un véritable ravissement pour l'œil; **4** (performance) **he put up a good/poor ~** c'était parfait/lamentable; **it was a poor ~ not to thank them** ce n'était pas très adroit de ne pas les remercier; **good ~ old chap**† bravo mon ami†; **5**○ (business, undertaking) affaire *f*; **she runs the whole ~** c'est elle qui fait marcher l'affaire; **to run one's own ~** avoir sa propre affaire; **it's not his ~** ce n'est pas lui qui prend les décisions; **6** Med (at onset of labour) perte *f* du bouchon muqueux.
II *vtr* (*prét* **showed**, *pp* **shown**) **1** (present for viewing) montrer [*person, object, photo*] (**to** à); présenter [*ticket, fashion collection*] (**to** à); [*TV channel, cinema*] passer [*film*]; **the explosion was shown on the evening news** ils ont montré l'explosion aux informations du soir; **to ~ sb sth** montrer qch à qn; **~ him your book** montre-lui ton

livre; **to ~ sb reclining/being arrested** montrer qn étendu/en train d'être arrêté; **to be shown on TV/at the cinema** passer à la télé/au cinéma; **2** (display competitively) présenter [*animal*]; exposer [*flower, vegetables*]; **3** (reveal) montrer [*feeling, principle, fact*]; [*garment*] laisser voir [*underclothes, dirt, stain*]; [*patient*] présenter [*symptoms*]; **to ~ interest in** montrer de l'intérêt pour; **to ~ that** bien montrer que; **to ~ how/why/when etc** montrer comment/pourquoi/quand etc; **4** (indicate) montrer [*object, trend, loss, profit, difficulty*]; indiquer [*time, direction, area*]; **to ~ sb where to go** indiquer à qn où aller; **the lights are ~ing red** les feux sont au rouge; **5** (demonstrate, express) [*person, action*] montrer [*skill, principle*]; [*writing*] montrer [*originality*]; [*reply*] témoigner de [*wit, intelligence*]; [*gesture, gift*] témoigner de [*respect, gratitude*]; **~ them what you can do** montre-leur ce que tu sais faire; **to ~ consideration/favouritism towards sb, to ~ sb consideration/favouritism** être gentil avec/favoriser qn; **to ~ sb that...** montrer à qn que...; **just to ~ there's no ill-feeling** juste pour montrer qu'il n'y a pas de rancune; **to ~ one's age** accuser son âge; **as shown in diagram 12/scene two** comme on le voit figure 12/dans la deuxième scène; **6** (prove) démontrer [*truth, validity, guilt*]; **to ~ that** [*document*] prouver que; [*findings*] démontrer que; [*facial expression*] montrer que; **this ~s him to be a liar** cela montre qu'il est menteur; **it all goes to ~ that...** ça prouve que...; **7** (conduct) **to ~ sb to their seat** [*host, usher*] placer qn; **to ~ sb to their room** accompagner qn à sa chambre; **to ~ sb up/down the stairs** accompagner qn en haut/en bas; **to ~ sb to the door** reconduire qn; **8**○ (teach a lesson to) **I'll ~ you/him!** (as revenge) je vais t'apprendre/lui apprendre○; (when challenged) je te/lui ferai voir○.

III *vi* (*prét* **showed**; *pp* **shown**) **1** (be noticeable) [*stain, label*] se voir; [*fear, anger, distress*] (by actions, appearance) se voir; (in eyes) se lire; **2** (be exhibited) [*artist*] exposer; [*film*] passer; **to ~ to advantage** [*colour, object*] faire bel effet; **3**○ (turn up) se montrer○; **he didn't ~ after all** il ne s'est pas montré finalement; **4** US Turf (be placed) être placé; **to ~ ahead** être en tête.

IV *v refl* (*prét* **showed**; *pp* **shown**) **to ~ oneself** [*person, animal*] se montrer; **to ~ oneself to be** prouver qu'on est.

IDIOMS **it just goes to ~** c'est ça la vie; **~ a leg**○! debout!; **to have nothing to ~ for sth** ne rien avoir tiré de qch; **to ~ one's face**○ montrer son nez○; **to ~ one's hand** abattre son jeu; **to ~ the way** montrer la voie; **to ~ the way forward** ouvrir la voie; **to steal** ou **stop the ~** être l'attraction; ▶ **door**.

■ **show in**: **~ [sb] in** faire entrer.

■ **show off**: ¶ **~ off**○ faire le fier/la fière; **to ~ off to** ou **in front of sb** faire l'intéressant/-e devant qn; ¶ **~ [sb/sth] off, ~ off [sb/sth]** mettre [qch] en valeur [*figure, special feature*]; faire admirer [*skill, talent*]; exhiber [*baby, boyfriend, car*].

■ **show out**: **~ [sb] out** accompagner [qn] à la porte.

■ **show round**: **~ [sb] round** faire visiter.

■ **show through**: ¶ **~ through** [*courage, determination*] transparaître; ¶ **~ through [sth]** se voir à travers.

■ **show up**: ¶ **~ up 1** (be visible) [*dust, mark*] se voir; [*pollution, signs, symptoms*] se manifester; [*details, colour*] ressortir; **2**○ (arrive) se montrer○; ¶ **~ up [sth]** révéler [*fault, mark*]; ¶ **~ [sb] up 1** (let down) faire honte à [*person*]; **2** (reveal truth about) **research has shown him up for what he is** des recherches ont montré sa vraie nature.

show: **~ biz**○ *n* = **show business**; **~boat** *n* US bateau-théâtre *m*; **~ business** *n* industrie *f* du spectacle.

showcase /ˈʃəʊkeɪs/ **I** *n* lit vitrine *f*; fig (for products, paintings, inventions, ideas etc) vitrine *f* (**for** de); (for new artists, actors etc) tremplin *m* (**for** pour).

II *modif* [*village, prison*] modèle.

III *vtr* servir de tremplin à [*actor, musician, band*].

showdown /ˈʃəʊdaʊn/ *n* (between people) confrontation *f*; (between factions) affrontement *m*.

shower /ˈʃaʊə(r)/ **I** *n* **1** (for washing) douche *f*; **to have** ou **take a ~** prendre une douche; **to be in the ~** être sous la douche; **2** Meteorol averse *f*; **light/heavy ~** petite/grosse averse; **3** (of confetti, sparks, fragments) pluie *f* (**of** de); (of praise, blessings, gifts) avalanche *f* (**of** de); **4** US **bridal/baby ~** *fête donnée à l'occasion d'un mariage/d'une naissance où chaque invité apporte un cadeau*; **5**○ GB péj (gang) bande *f*.

II *modif* [*cubicle, curtain, head, rail, spray*] de douche.

III *vtr* **1** (wash) doucher [*dog, child*]; **2 to ~ sth on** ou **over sb/sth, to ~ sb/sth with sth** [*fire, explosion, volcano*] faire pleuvoir qch sur qn/qch; [*person*] asperger qn/qch de qch [*water, champagne etc*]; **sparks ~ed me** je me suis trouvé sous une pluie d'étincelles; **3** fig **to ~ sb with sth, to ~ sth on sb** couvrir qn de [*gifts, blessings, compliments*]; **I was ~ed with praise** on m'a couvert de louanges.

IV *vi* **1** [*person*] prendre une douche; **2 petals/sparks ~ed on me** une pluie de pétales/d'étincelles est tombée sur moi; **ash ~ed down** une pluie de cendres est retombée.

shower: **~ attachment** *n* douchette *f* de lavabo; **~ cap** *n* bonnet *m* de douche; **~proof** *adj* imperméabilisé; **~ room** *n* (private) salle *f* de bains (avec douche); (public) douches *fpl*; **~ unit** *n* douche *f*.

showery /ˈʃaʊərɪ/ *adj* [*day, weather*] pluvieux/-ieuse; **it will be ~ tomorrow** demain le temps sera pluvieux.

show: **~ flat** *n* GB appartement-témoin *m*; **~girl** *n* girl *f*; **~ground** *n* gen champ *m* de foire; Equit terrain *m* de concours; **~ house** *n* maison-témoin *f*.

showily /ˈʃəʊɪlɪ/ *adv* péj [*dressed, decorated*] d'une façon ostentatoire.

showing /ˈʃəʊɪŋ/ *n* **1** Cin (individual screening) séance *f*; **there are two ~s daily** il y a deux séances par jour; **2** ¢ Cin (putting on) présentation *f* (**of** de); **3** (performance) gen prestation *f*; Sport performance *f*; **if his last ~ is anything to go by** si l'on en croit sa dernière prestation.

showing-off○ /ˌʃəʊɪŋˈɒf/ *n* esbroufe○ *f*.

showjumper /ˈʃəʊdʒʌmpə(r)/ *n* **1** (person) cavalier/-ière *m/f* de saut; **2** (horse) cheval *m* de saut.

showjumping /ˈʃəʊdʒʌmpɪŋ/ ▶ **1282** *n* saut *m* d'obstacles.

showman /ˈʃəʊmən/ *n* **to be a ~** fig avoir le sens du spectacle.

showmanship /ˈʃəʊmənʃɪp/ *n* sens *m* du spectacle.

shown /ʃəʊn/ *pp* ▶ **show II, III, IV**.

show: **~-off**○ *n* m'as-tu-vu○/-e *m/f*; **~ of hands** *n* vote *m* à mains levées.

showpiece /ˈʃəʊpiːs/ *n* **1** (exhibit) œuvre *f* exposée; (in trade fair) objet *m* exposé; **that picture is a real ~** fig ce tableau est une véritable pièce de musée; **this hospital is a ~** fig cet hôpital est un modèle du genre; **2** (popular piece of music) morceau *m* classique.

showplace /ˈʃəʊpleɪs/ *n* US (for tourists) haut lieu *m* touristique.

showroom /ˈʃəʊruːm, -rʊm/ *n* exposition *f*; **to look at cars/kitchens in a ~** regarder les voitures/les cuisines exposées; **in ~ condition** [*furniture, car*] dans un état impeccable.

show: **~stopper**○ *n* clou○ *m* d'un spectacle; **~ trial** *n* procès *m* pour l'exemple.

showy /ˈʃəʊɪ/ *adj* péj [*clothing, style*] tape-à-l'œil○ *inv*.

shrank /ʃræŋk/ *prét* ▶ **shrink II, III**.

shrapnel /ˈʃræpnl/ *n* éclats *mpl* d'obus; **a piece of ~** un éclat d'obus.

shred /ʃred/ **I** *n* **1** fig (of evidence, emotion, sense, truth) parcelle *f*; **2** (of paper, fabric) lambeau *m*; **to be** ou **hang in ~s** être en lambeaux.

II *vtr* (*p prés etc* **-dd-**) déchiqueter [*documents, paper*]; râper [*vegetables*]; **~ded newspaper** déchirures *fpl* de journaux; **~ding attachment** Culin accessoire-râpe *m*.

shredder /ˈʃredə(r)/ *n* **1** (for paper) déchiqueteuse *f*; **to put papers through the ~** faire passer des papiers à la déchiqueteuse; **2** Culin râpe *f*.

shrew /ʃruː/ *n* **1** Zool musaraigne *f*; **2**† (woman) péj mégère *f*; **'The Taming of the Shrew'** 'La Mégère Apprivoisée'.

shrewd /ʃruːd/ *adj* [*person*] habile; [*face*] plein d'astuce; [*move, assessment, investment*] astucieux/-ieuse; **to have a ~ idea that** être porté à croire que; **to make a ~ guess** deviner juste.

shrewdly /ˈʃruːdlɪ/ *adv* [*act, say*] habilement; [*decide, assess*] avec perspicacité.

shrewdness /ˈʃruːdnɪs/ *n* (of person, decision) perspicacité *f*; (of move, suggestion) astuce *f*.

shrewish /ˈʃruːɪʃ/ *adj* acariâtre.

shriek /ʃriːk/ **I** *n* **1** (of pain, fear) cri *m* perçant, hurlement *m*; (of delight) cri *m*; **~s of laughter** éclats *mpl* de rire; **2** (of bird) cri *m*.

II *vtr* crier, hurler; **'no!' he ~ed** 'non!' a-t-il crié.

III *vi* (with pain, fear) crier, hurler (**in, with** de); (with pleasure) crier (**with** de); **to ~ with laughter** hurler de rire.

IV shrieking *pres p adj* criard.

shrift /ʃrɪft/ *n* **to give sb/sth short ~** expédier qn/qch sans ménagements; **to get** ou **receive short ~ from** se faire expédier sans ménagements par.

shrike /ʃraɪk/ *n* pie-grièche *f*.

shrill /ʃrɪl/ **I** *adj* **1** [*voice, cry, laugh*] perçant; [*whistle, tone*] strident; **2** péj [*criticism, protest*] vigoureux/-euse.

II *vi* [*bird*] pousser un cri aigu; [*telephone*] retentir.

shrillness /ˈʃrɪlnɪs/ *n* **1** (of voice, cry) ton *m* perçant; (of whistle, tone) stridence *f*; **2** péj (of criticism, protest) vigueur *f*.

shrilly /ˈʃrɪlɪ/ *adv* **1** [*laugh, scream, shout*] d'une voix perçante; **2** péj [*demand, protest*] avec vigueur.

shrimp /ʃrɪmp/ *n* **1** Zool, Culin crevette *f* grise; **2**○ (small person) gringalet *m*.

shrimping /ˈʃrɪmpɪŋ/ *n* pêche *f* à la crevette; **to go ~** aller à la pêche à la crevette.

shrine /ʃraɪn/ *n* **1** (place of worship) lieu *m* de pèlerinage (**to** consacré à); **2** (in catholicism: alcove) autel *m*; (building) chapelle *f*; **3** (tomb) tombeau *m*.

shrink /ʃrɪŋk/ **I**○ *n* (psychoanalyst) psychanalyste *mf*; (psychiatrist) psy○ *mf*, psychiatre *mf*.

II *vtr* (*prét* **shrank**; *pp* **shrunk** ou **shrunken**) faire rétrécir [*fabric*]; contracter [*wood*]; Anthrop réduire [*head*].

III *vi* (*prét* **shrank**; *pp* **shrunk** ou **shrunken**) **1** [*fabric*] rétrécir; [*timber*] se contracter; [*piece of dough, meat*] réduire; [*forest, area of land*] reculer; [*boundaries*] se rapprocher; [*economy, sales*] être en recul; [*resources, funds*] s'amenuiser; [*old person, body*] se tasser; **the staff has shrunk from 200 to 50** les effectifs sont tombés de 200 à 50; **to have shrunk to nothing** [*team, household*] être quasiment réduit à néant; [*person*] n'avoir plus que la peau sur les os; **2** (recoil) (physically) reculer; **to ~ from** se dérober devant [*conflict, responsibility*]; **to ~ from doing** hésiter à faire; **he didn't**

~ **from the task** il n'a pas rechigné à la tâche.
■ **shrink back** reculer; **to ~ back in horror** reculer d'horreur.

shrinkage /'ʃrɪŋkɪdʒ/ *n* (of fabric) rétrécissement *m*; (of timber) contraction *f*; (of economy, trade) recul *m*; (of resources, profits) diminution *f*; (of forest, area) diminution *f*, recul *m*.

shrinking /'ʃrɪŋkɪŋ/ *adj* [*amount, numbers*] qui diminue; [*population, market, revenue*] en baisse; [*resource, asset*] qui se raréfie; [*audience*] qui s'amenuise.

shrinking violet○ *n* hum personne *f* timorée; **she's no ~!** elle n'a pas froid aux yeux○!

shrink-wrap /'ʃrɪŋkræp/ **I** *n* film *m* plastique (thermo-rétractable).
II *vtr* (*p prés etc* **-pp-**) emballer [qch] sous film plastique, pré-emballer [*food*].

shrive‡ /ʃraɪv/ *vtr* (*prét* **shrived** ou **shrove**, *pp* **shrived** ou **shriven**) Relig confesser et absoudre.

shrivel /'ʃrɪvl/ **I** *vtr* [*sun, heat*] flétrir [*skin*]; dessécher [*plant, leaf*].
II *vi* (*p prés etc* **-ll-**, **-l-** US) (also **~ up**) [*fruit, vegetable*] se ratatiner; [*skin*] se flétrir; [*plant, leaf, meat*] se dessécher.

shrivelled, **shriveled** US /'ʃrɪvld/ *adj* [*fruit, vegetable*] ratatiné; [*skin, body, face*] flétri; [*plant, leaf, meat*] desséché.

shriven /'ʃrɪvn/ *pp* ▸ **shrive**.

Shropshire /'ʃrɒpʃə(r)/ ▸ **1624** *pr n* Shropshire *m*.

shroud /ʃraʊd/ **I** *n* **1** (cloth) linceul *m*, suaire *m*; **2** fig (of fog, secrecy) voile *m* (**of** de); **3** Naut (rope) hauban *m*; **4** (also **~ line**) (on parachute) suspente *f*.
II *vtr* envelopper [*body, person*] (**in** dans); **to be ~ed in** être enveloppé de [*mist, mystery, secrecy*].

shrove /ʃrəʊv/ *prét* ▸ **shrive**.

shrove: **Shrovetide** *n* Relig carême-prenant *m*; **Shrove Tuesday** *n* Relig Mardi *m* gras.

shrub /ʃrʌb/ *n* arbuste *m*.

shrubbery /'ʃrʌbərɪ/ *n* **1** GB **C** (in garden) massif *m* d'arbustes; **2** ₵ (shrubs collectively) arbustes *mpl*.

shrub rose *n* rosier *m* arbuste.

shrug /ʃrʌg/ **I** *n* (also **~ of the shoulders**) haussement *m* d'épaules; **to give a ~** hausser les épaules.
II *vtr* (*p prés etc* **-gg-**) (also **~ one's shoulders**) hausser les épaules *fpl*.
■ **shrug off**: **~ off [sth]**, **~ [sth] off** ignorer [*problem, rumour*].

shrunk /ʃrʌŋk/ *pp* ▸ **shrink** II, III.

shrunken /'ʃrʌŋkən/ *adj* [*person, body*] rabougri; [*apple*] ratatiné; [*budget*] réduit; **~ head** Anthrop tête *f* réduite.

shtick○ /ʃtɪk/ *n* US Theat numéro *m*.

shuck /ʃʌk/ **I** *n* US (of nut) écale *f*; (of bean, pea) cosse *f*; (of corn) enveloppe *f*, spathe *f* spec; (of oyster) coquille *f*.
II *vtr* US écaler, décortiquer [*nut*]; écosser [*pea*]; effeuiller [*corn*]; ouvrir [*oyster*]; [*person*] ôter [*clothes*].
IDIOMS **it's not worth ~s**○ US ça ne vaut pas tripette○.

shucks○ /ʃʌks/ *excl* US **1** (in irritation) zut○, mince○; **2** (in embarrassment) allons donc.

shudder /'ʃʌdə(r)/ **I** *n* **1** (of person) frisson *m* (**of** de); **the news sent a ~ of terror through them** à l'annonce de la nouvelle, un frisson de terreur les parcourut; **to give a ~** frissonner; **with a ~** en frissonnant; **2** (of vehicle) secousse *f*; **to give a ~** avoir une secousse.
II *vi* **1** [*person*] frissonner; **to ~ with fear/pleasure/cold** frissonner de peur/plaisir/froid; **to ~ at the sight/thought of sth** frissonner à la vue/l'idée de qch; **I ~ to think!** j'en ai des frissons rien que d'y penser!; **2** [*vehicle*] (once) avoir un soubresaut; **to ~ to a halt** avoir quelques soubresauts et s'arrêter.
III shuddering *pres p adj* **to come to a ~ing halt** avoir quelques soubresauts et s'arrêter.

shuffle /'ʃʌfl/ **I** *n* **1** (way of walking) pas *mpl* traînants; **2** (sound of walk) bruit *m* de pas traînants; **3** Games **to give the cards a ~** battre les cartes; **4** Dance *danse à petits pas glissés*; **5** US (confusion) confusion *f*.
II *vtr* **1** (also **~ about**) (change position of) déplacer [*furniture, objects, people*]; **2 to ~ one's feet (in embarrassment)** agiter ses pieds (par embarras); **3** (mix together) brasser [*papers*]; mélanger [*data*]; **4** Games battre [*cards*].
III *vi* traîner les pieds; **to ~ along/in** marcher/entrer en traînant les pieds.
■ **shuffle off**: ¶ **~ off** partir en traînant les pieds; ¶ **~ off [sth]** se décharger de [*responsibility, blame, guilt*] (**on(to) sb** sur qn).

shuffleboard /'ʃʌflbɔ:d/ *n* Games **1** ▸ **1282** (game) (jeu *m* de) palets *mpl*; **2** (court) *espace aménagé pour le jeu de palets*.

shufty○ /'ʃʊftɪ/ *n* GB coup *m* d'œil; **to take** ou **have a ~ at sth** jeter un coup d'œil sur qch.

shun /ʃʌn/ *vtr* (*p prés etc* **-nn-**) **1** (avoid) fuir [*contact, people, publicity, responsibility, temptation*]; dédaigner [*work*]; **2** (reject) rejeter [*job, person, offer, suggestion*].

shunt /ʃʌnt/ **I** *n* Med, Electron shunt *m*.
II *vtr* **1**○ (send) expédier○; **to be ~ed from place to place** être expédié d'un endroit à l'autre; **to ~ sb back and forth** ballotter qn d'un côté à l'autre; **we were ~ed from one official to the next** on a été ballottés d'un responsable à l'autre; **2**○ (marginalize) expédier○; **to ~ sb into another department** expédier qn dans un autre service; **to ~ sb into a siding** fig mettre qn sur une voie de garage; **3** Rail (move) aiguiller [*wagon, engine*] (**into** sur).
III *vi* [*train*] changer de voie; **to ~ back and forth** manœuvrer.

shunter /'ʃʌntə(r)/ *n* locomotive *f* de manœuvre.

shunting /'ʃʌntɪŋ/ *n* manœuvres *fpl* d'aiguillage.

shunting: **~ engine** *n* locomotive *f* de manœuvre; **~ yard** *n* gare *f* de manœuvre.

shush /ʃʊʃ/ **I** *excl* chut!
II○ *vtr* faire taire [*person*].

shut /ʃʌt/ **I** *adj* **1** (closed) [*door, book, box, mouth*] fermé; **my eyes were ~** j'avais les yeux fermés; **to slam the door ~** claquer la porte (pour bien la fermer); **to slam ~** se refermer en claquant; **to keep one's mouth ~**○ se taire; **2** (of business) fermé; **it's ~ on Fridays** c'est fermé le vendredi.
II *vtr* (*p prés* **-tt-**; *prét, pp* **shut**) **1** (close) fermer [*door, book, box, mouth*]; **she shut her eyes** elle a fermé les yeux; **~ your mouth** ou **trap** ou **face**○! ferme-la○!, ta gueule●!; **2** (of business) fermer [*office, school, factory*]; **to ~ the shop for a week** fermer le magasin pendant une semaine; **3** (confine) = **shut up 2**.
III *vi* (*p prés* **-tt-**; *prét, pp* **shut**) **1** [*door, book, box, mouth*] se fermer; **to ~ with a bang** se refermer en claquant; **2** [*office, factory*] fermer; **the shop ~s at five** le magasin ferme à cinq heures.
IDIOMS **put up or ~ up**○! prouve ce que tu dis ou alors tais-toi.
■ **shut away**: ¶ **~ [sb/sth] away**, **~ away [sb/sth]** **1** (lock up) enfermer [*person*]; mettre [qch] sous clé [*valuables, medicine*]; **2** (keep at bay) tenir [qn] à distance [*person*]; écarter [*difficulties*]; ¶ **~ [oneself] away** se mettre à l'écart (**from** de).
■ **shut down**: ¶ **~ down** [*business*] fermer; [*plant, machinery*] s'arrêter; ¶ **~ [sth] down**, **~ down [sth]** fermer [*business, amenity, factory*]; arrêter [*service, reactor, machinery, power*].
■ **shut in**: **~ [sb/sth] in** enfermer [*person, animal*]; **to feel shut in** fig se sentir étouffé; **to ~ oneself in** s'enfermer.
■ **shut off**: ¶ **~ [sth] off**, **~ off [sth]** couper [*supply, motor*]; arrêter [*oven, heater, fan*]; fermer [*access, valve*]; ¶ **~ [sb/sth] off** isoler (**from** de); **to ~ oneself off** s'isoler (**from** de).
■ **shut out**: **~ out [sth/sb]**, **~ [sth/sb] out 1** (keep out) laisser [qch] dehors [*animal, person*]; éliminer [*noise, draught*]; **to be shut out** être à la porte; **2** (keep at bay) chasser [*thought , memory, image*]; **3** (reject) repousser [*person, world*]; **to feel shut out** se sentir exclu; **4** (block) empêcher [qch] d'entrer [*light, sun*]; bloquer [*view*]; **5** US Sport empêcher [qn] de marquer.
■ **shut up**: ¶ **~ up**○ se taire (**about** au sujet de); **I wish she'd ~ up!** j'aimerais bien qu'elle la boucle○!; **~ up!** (brisk) taistoi!; (aggressive) boucle-la○!, ferme-la○!; (brutal) ta gueule●!; ¶ **~ [sb] up**, **~ up [sb] 1**○ (silence) faire taire [*person, animal*]; **that soon shut her up!** ça lui a cloué le bec○!; **2** (confine) enfermer [*person, animal*] (**in** dans); **to ~ oneself up** s'enfermer (**in** dans); **3** (close) fermer [*house, business*]; **to ~ up shop**○ lit, fig fermer boutique○.

shutdown /'ʃʌtdaʊn/ *n* gen fermeture *f*; Nucl arrêt *m* (du réacteur).

shut-eye○ /'ʃʌtaɪ/ *n* **to get some ~** (short sleep) piquer un roupillon○; (go to bed) aller se coucher.

shut: **~off valve** *n* dispositif *m* d'arrêt automatique; **~out** *n* US victoire *f* écrasante (*l'équipe perdante ne marquant aucun point*).

shutter /'ʃʌtə(r)/ *n* **1** (on window) (wooden, metal) volet *m*; (on shopfront) store *m*; **to put up the ~s** lit fermer le magasin; fig fermer boutique○; **2** Phot (camera) obturateur *m*.

shuttered /'ʃʌtəd/ *adj* [*houses, windows*] aux volets fermés; **the house was ~ (up)** la maison avait les volets fermés.

shutter speed *n* vitesse *f* d'obturation.

shuttle /'ʃʌtl/ **I** *n* **1** Transp navette *f*; **2** Aerosp (also **space ~**) navette *f* spatiale; **3** (in sewing machine, loom) navette *f*; **4** (in badminton) volant *m*.
II *vtr* transporter [*passengers*].
III *vi* **to ~ between** faire la navette entre [*terminals*].

shuttle: **~ bus** *n* navette *f*; **~cock** *n* volant *m*; **~ diplomacy** *n* Pol démarches *fpl* diplomatiques; **~ mission** *n* Aerosp mission *f* de la navette spatiale; **~ programme** GB, **~ program** US *n* Aerosp programme *m* de la navette spatiale; **~ service** *n* Transp service *m* de navette.

shy /ʃaɪ/ **I** *adj* **1** (timid) [*person*] timide (**with, of** avec); [*animal*] farouche (**with, of** avec); **2** (afraid) **to be ~ of sb/of doing** avoir peur de qn/de faire; **to make sb feel ~** intimider qn; **3** (avoid) **to fight ~ of** fuir devant; **to fight ~ of doing** éviter à tout prix de faire; **4** US (short) **I'm 10 cents ~ of a dollar** il me manque 10 cents pour faire un dollar; **he's two years ~ of 40** dans deux ans il aura 40 ans.
II *vtr* (throw) **to ~ sth at** jeter qch à.
III *vi* [*horse*] faire un écart (**at** devant).
■ **shy away** se tenir à l'écart (**from** de); **to ~ away from doing** répugner à faire.

shyly /'ʃaɪlɪ/ *adv* timidement.

shyness /'ʃaɪnɪs/ *n* timidité *f*.

shyster○ /'ʃaɪstə(r)/ *n* US escroc *m*.

si /si:/ *n* Mus **1** (in fixed-doh system) si *m*; **2** (in solmization system) (note *f*) sensible *f*.

SI *n* (*abrév* = **Système International**) SI *m*.

Siam /,saɪ'æm/ ▸ **1131** *pr n* Hist Siam *m*.

Siamese /,saɪə'mi:z/ ▸ **1486**, **1402** **I** *n* **1** (person) Siamois/-e *m/f*; **2** (language) siamois *m*; **3** (cat) siamois/-e *m/f*.
II *adj* siamois.

Siamese: **~ cat** *n* chat/chatte *m/f* siamois/-e; **~ twins** *npl* Med frères/sœurs *mpl/fpl* siamois/-es.

SIB *n* GB Fin (*abrév* = **Securities and**

Investments Board) commission *f* des opérations de Bourse.

Siberia /saɪˈbɪərɪə/ ▶1131 *pr n* Sibérie *f*.

Siberian /saɪˈbɪərɪən/ ▶1486 I *n* Sibérien/-ienne *m/f*.
II *adj* sibérien/-ienne.

sibilant /ˈsɪbɪlənt/ I *n* Ling sifflante *f*.
II *adj* **1** Ling [*consonant, sound*] sifflant; **2** fig **a ~ sound** un sifflement.

sibling /ˈsɪblɪŋ/ *n* frère/sœur *m/f*.

sibling rivalry *n* rivalité *f* entre frères et sœurs.

Sibyl /ˈsɪbl/ *n* Antiq sibylle *f*.

sibylline /ˈsɪbəlaɪn, sɪˈbɪlaɪn, US also ˈsɪbəliːn/ *adj* sibyllin.

sic /sɪk/ I *adv* sic.
II *excl* US (to dog) attaque!
III *vtr* (*p prés etc* **-ck-**) US **to ~ a dog on sb** lancer un chien sur qn.

Sicilian /sɪˈsɪlɪən/ ▶1486 I *n* **1** (person) Sicilien/-ienne *m/f*; **2** (dialect) sicilien *m*.
II *adj* sicilien/-ienne.

Sicily /ˈsɪsɪlɪ/ ▶1381 *pr n* Sicile *f*.

sick /sɪk/ I *n* **1 the ~** (+ *v pl*) les malades *mpl*; **2**○ GB (vomit) vomi *m*.
II *adj* **1** (ill) malade; **to feel ~** ne pas se sentir bien; **to fall** ou **take ~** GB tomber malade; **to be off ~** GB être absent pour cause de maladie; **to go ~**○ se faire porter malade; **2** (nauseous) **to be ~** vomir; **to feel ~** avoir mal au cœur, avoir envie de vomir; **rhubarb makes him ~** il ne supporte pas la rhubarbe; **you'll make yourself ~ if you eat all that chocolate** tu vas te rendre malade si tu manges tout ce chocolat; **to have a ~ feeling in one's stomach** (from nerves) avoir l'estomac noué; (from food) avoir l'estomac barbouillé; **3** (tasteless) [*joke, story*] malsain, de mauvais goût; **he has a really ~ sense of humour** son sens de l'humour est plus que douteux; **4** (disturbed) [*mind, imagination*] malsain; **what a ~ thing to do!** il faut avoir l'esprit dérangé pour faire une chose pareille!; **5** (disgusted) écœuré, dégoûté; **you make me ~!** tu m'écœures!; **it's enough to make you ~!** il y a de quoi vous rendre malade!; **it makes me ~ to think of how they treated him** ça me rend malade de voir comment ils l'ont traité; **6**○ (fed-up) **to be ~ of sth/sb**○ en avoir assez or marre○ de qn/qch; **to be ~ and tired of sth/sb**○ en avoir ras le bol○ de qch/qn; **to be ~ to death of sth/sb**○ en avoir par-dessus la tête de qch/qn; **to be ~ of the sight of sth/sb**○ ne plus supporter qch/qn.
IDIOMS **to be ~ at heart** avoir la mort dans l'âme; **to be worried ~**○ **about sth** être malade d'inquiétude au sujet de qch.
■ **sick up**○ GB: **~ up [sth], ~ [sth] up**○ vomir, dégueuler◑ [*food*].

sick: **~ bag** *n* sac *m* en papier (*mis à la disposition des voyageurs qui sont malades*); **~ bay** *n* infirmerie *f*.

sickbed /ˈsɪkbed/ *n* lit *m* de malade; **to rise from** ou **leave one's ~** quitter son lit de malade.

sick: **~ building** *n* construction *f* insalubre; **~ building syndrome** *n* syndrome *m* causé par un milieu de travail insalubre.

sicken /ˈsɪkən/ I *vtr* rendre [qn] malade; fig dégoûter, écœurer.
II *vi* **1** littér [*person, animal*] tomber malade, dépérir; **to be ~ing for something** couver quelque chose; **2** fig (grow weary) **to ~ of** se lasser de, en avoir assez de.

sickening /ˈsɪkənɪŋ/ *adj* **1** (nauseating) écœurant; [*sight*] qui soulève le cœur; [*smell*] nauséabond, écœurant; fig [*cruelty, violence*] écœurant; **2**○ (annoying) [*person, behaviour*] insupportable.

sickeningly /ˈsɪkənɪŋlɪ/ *adv* **~ sweet** écœurant; **he is ~ smug** il est d'une suffisance écœurante.

sickie◑ /ˈsɪkɪ/ *n* US = **sicko**.

sickle /ˈsɪkl/ *n* faucille *f*.

sick leave *n* congé *m* de maladie; **to be on ~ leave** être en congé de maladie.

sickle cell anaemia ▶1354 *n* Med anémie *f* à hématies falciformes.

sickliness /ˈsɪklɪnɪs/ *n* **1** (of person) état *m* maladif, mauvaise santé *f*; (of plant) étiolement *m*; (of complexion) pâleur *f* maladive; **2** (nauseousness) (of taste, colour) fadeur *f*; **the ~ of the smell** l'odeur nauséabonde.

sick list *n* **to be on the ~** être porté malade.

sickly /ˈsɪklɪ/ *adj* **1** (unhealthy) [*baby, person, pallor*] maladif/-ive; [*plant*] mal en point; [*complexion*] blafard; **2** (nauseating) [*smell, taste*] écœurant; [*colour*] fadasse; **~ sentimental** mièvre; **~ sweet** douceâtre; **she gave a ~ smile** elle a souri faiblement.

sick-making○ *adj* écœurant.

sickness /ˈsɪknɪs/ *n* **1** (illness) maladie *f*; **to be absent because of ~** être absent pour cause de maladie; **there has been a lot of ~ in the school lately** il y a eu beaucoup de malades à l'école récemment; **the ~ of the economy** la faiblesse de l'économie; **in ~ and in health** ≈ pour le meilleur et pour le pire; **2** ¢ (nausea) vomissements *mpl*; **to suffer bouts of ~** avoir des vomissements; **3** (distasteful nature) (of joke, story) goût *m* douteux.

sickness: **~ benefit** *n* ¢ GB prestations *fpl* de l'assurance-maladie; **~ insurance** *n* assurance *f* maladie.

sick note○ *n* (for school) mot *m* d'excuse; (for work) certificat *m* médical.

sicko◑ /ˈsɪkəʊ/ GB *n* malade○ *mf*, débile○ *mf*.

sick: **~pay** *n* indemnité *f* de maladie; **~room** *n* (in school, institution) infirmerie *f*; (at home) chambre *f* de malade.

side /saɪd/ I *n* **1** (part) (of person's body, object, table) côté *m*; (of animal's body, of hill, boat) flanc *m*; (of ravine, cave) paroi *f*; (of box), (outer) flanc *m*; (inner) paroi *f*; **the right/left ~ of the road** le côté droit/gauche de la route; **on my left/right ~** à ma gauche/droite; **by my/her ~** à côté de moi/d'elle; **on one's/its ~** sur le côté; **~ by ~** côte à côte; **he never leaves her ~** il ne la quitte jamais; **don't leave my ~** reste près de moi; **from every ~** de tous côtés; **on the mountain/hill ~** à flanc de montagne/de coteau; **go round the ~ of the building** contournez le bâtiment; **the south ~ of the mountain** le versant sud de la montagne; **the north/south ~ of town** le nord/sud de la ville; **'this ~ up'** (on package, box) 'haut'; **2** (surface of flat object) (of paper, cloth) côté *m*; (of record) face *f*; **the right ~** (of cloth) l'endroit *m*; (of coin) l'avers *m*; (of paper) le recto *m*; **the wrong ~** (of cloth) l'envers *m*; (of coin) le revers *m*; (of paper) le verso *m*; **3** (edge) (of lake, road) bord *m*; (of building) côté *m*; **at** ou **by the ~ of** au bord de [*lake, road*]; à côté de [*building*]; **4** (aspect) (of person, argument) côté *m*; (of problem, question) aspect *m*; (of story, case) version *f*; **there are two ~s to every question** chaque question a deux aspects; **whose ~ are we to believe?** quelle version faut-il croire?; **try to see it from my ~** essayez de comprendre mon point de vue; **she's on the science/arts ~** (academically) elle a opté pour les sciences/arts; **he's on the marketing/personnel ~** (in company) il fait partie du service de marketing/du service du personnel; **5** (opposing group) côté *m*, camp *m*; **to change ~s** changer de camp; **to take ~s** prendre position; **6** Sport (team) équipe *f*; **which ~ does he play for?** il joue dans quelle équipe?; **you've really let the ~ down** fig tu nous as laissés tomber; **7** (page) page *f*; **8** (line of descent) côté *m*; **on his mother's ~** du côté de sa mère; **9**○ (TV channel) chaîne *f*; **10** Sport (spin) (in snooker) **to put ~ on the ball** donner de l'effet à la boule.
II *modif* [*door, window, entrance*] latéral.
III **-sided** (*dans composés*) **four/six-~d figure** figure *f* à quatre/six côtés; **glass-~d container** récipient *m* à parois de verre; **many-~d problem** problème *m* complexe.
IV **on the side** *adv phr* **a steak with salad on the ~** un steak avec de la salade; **to do sth on the ~** (in addition) faire qch à côté; (illegally) faire qch au noir.
V *vi* (of car, skier) déraper; (of plane) glisser sur l'aile.
IDIOMS **he's/she's like the ~ of a house** il/elle est énorme; **to have a bit on the ~**○ avoir une liaison; **time is on our ~** le temps travaille pour nous; **to be on the safe ~** (allowing enough time) pour calculer large; (to be certain) pour être sûr; **to be (a bit) on the big/small ~** être plutôt grand/petit; **to be on the wrong/right ~ of 40** avoir/ne pas avoir dépassé la quarantaine; **to get on the wrong ~ of sb** prendre qn à rebrousse-poil; **to have no ~** ne pas être prétentieux/-ieuse; **to have right on one's ~** être dans son droit; **to get/keep on the right ~ of sb** se mettre/rester bien avec qn; **to put/leave sth to one ~** mettre/laisser [qch] de côté [*object, task*]; **to take sb to one ~** prendre qn à part.
■ **side with** se mettre du côté de [*person*].

side: **~ arm** *n* (weapon) arme *f* de protection; **~board** *n* buffet *m*; **~boards** GB, **sideburns** *npl* (on face) pattes *fpl*; **~car** *n* side-car *m*; **~ dish** *n* Culin plat *m* d'accompagnement; **~ drum** ▶1481 *n* Mus caisse *f* claire; **~ effect** *n* lit (of drug) effet *m* secondaire; fig (of action) répercussion *f*; **~ elevation** *n* Archit élévation *f* de profil; **~ issue** *n* question *f* annexe; **~kick**○ *n* acolyte *m*.

sidelight /ˈsaɪdlaɪt/ *n* **1** Aut feu *m* de position; **2** Naut (to port) feu *m* rouge de babord; (to starboard) feu *m* vert de tribord; **3** (window) (in house) lucarne *f*; (in car) déflecteur *m*.

sideline /ˈsaɪdlaɪn/ I *n* **1** (extra) à-côté *m*; **he sells clothes as a ~** il vend des vêtements comme à-côté; **2** Sport ligne *f* de touche; **to kick the ball over the ~** envoyer la balle en touche; **to be on the ~s** lit, fig être sur la touche.
II *vtr* US Sport remplacer [*player*]; fig **to be ~d** être mis sur la touche.

side: **~long** *adj* [*glance, look*] oblique; **~man** *n* Mus instrumentiste *mf*; **~ order** *n* Culin portion *f*; **~ plate** *n* petite assiette *f*.

sidereal /saɪˈdɪərɪəl/ *adj* sidéral.

side road *n* petite route *f*.

side saddle I *n* selle *f* d'amazone.
II *adv* **to ride ~** monter en amazone.

side: **~ shoot** *n* Bot pousse *f* latérale; **~ show** *n* (at fair) attraction *f*.

sideslip /ˈsaɪdslɪp/ I *n* (of car, skier) dérapage *m*; (of plane) glissement *m* sur l'aile.
II *vi* (*p prés etc* **-pp-**) [*car, skier*] déraper; [*plane*] glisser sur l'aile.

side: **~sman** *n* (in church) ≈ sacristain *m*; **~splitting**○ *adj* très drôle, tordant○.

sidestep /ˈsaɪdstep/ I *n* pas *m* de côté.
II *vtr* (*p prés etc* **-pp-**) lit éviter [*opponent, tackle*]; fig éluder [*question, issue*].

side: **~ street** *n* petite rue *f*; **~ stroke** *n* (in swimming) brasse *f* indienne.

sideswipe /ˈsaɪdswaɪp/ I *n* coup *m* sur le côté.
II *vtr* emboutir [qch] sur le côté.

side table *n* desserte *f*.

sidetrack /ˈsaɪdtræk/ I *n* Rail voie *f* secondaire.
II *vtr* fig fourvoyer [*person*]; **to get ~ed** se fourvoyer.

side: **~ view** *n* (of object) vue *f* latérale; **~walk** *n* US trottoir *m*.

sideways /ˈsaɪdweɪz/ I *adj* [*look, glance*] de travers; **a ~ move in his career** une bifurcation dans sa carrière.
II *adv* [*move*] latéralement; [*carry*] sur le côté; [*park*] de biais; [*look at*] de travers; **to**

be turned ~ [*person*] être de profil; **~ on** de profil.

IDIOMS **to knock sb ~** fig sidérer qn.

side: **~-wheel** *n* roue *f* à aubes; **~-wheeler** *n* Naut navire *m* à aubes; **~-whiskers** *npl* favoris *mpl*.

sidewinder /ˈsaɪdwaɪndə(r)/ *n* **1** Zool crotale *m* des sables; **2** Mil missile *m* air-air guidé par infra-rouge, missile *m* sidewinder; **3** US (in boxing) (violent) crochet *m*; **left ~** crochet du gauche.

siding /ˈsaɪdɪŋ/ *n* **1** Rail voie *f* de garage; **2** US (weatherproof coating) revêtement *m* extérieur.

sidle /ˈsaɪdl/ *vi* **to ~ into/out of/along...** se faufiler dans/hors de/le long de...; **to ~ up to sb/sth** s'avancer furtivement vers qn/qch.

SIDS /sɪdz/ *n* Med *abrév* ▶ **sudden infant death syndrome**.

siege /siːdʒ/ *n* siège *m*; **to lay ~ to sth** lit, fig assiéger qch; **to come under ~** être assiégé.

IDIOMS **to suffer from** ou **have a ~ mentality** être toujours sur la défensive.

siege warfare *n* guerre *f* de siège.

Siena /sɪˈenə/ *pr n* Sienne.

sienna /sɪˈenə/ *n* terre *f* de Sienne.

sierra /sɪˈerə/ *n* Geog sierra *f*.

Sierra Leone /sɪˌerəlɪˈəʊn/ ▶ **1131** *pr n* Sierra Leone *f*.

Sierra Leonean /sɪˈerə lɪˈəʊnɪən/ ▶ **1486** I *n* Sierra-Léonais/-e *m/f*.

II *adj* [*art, custom*] sierra-léonais.

siesta /sɪˈestə/ *n* sieste *f*; **to have a ~** faire la sieste.

sieve /sɪv/ I *n* (for draining) passoire *f*; (for sifting) tamis *m*; (for coal, stones) crible *m*; (for wheat) van *m*; **to put sth through a ~** passer qch au tamis.

II *vtr* tamiser [*earth, flour, sugar*]; passer [qch] au crible [*coal*]; vanner [*wheat*].

IDIOMS **to have a head/memory like a ~** avoir la tête/la mémoire comme une passoire; **to leak like a ~** être une vraie passoire.

sift /sɪft/ I *vtr* **1** (sieve) tamiser, passer [qch] au tamis [*flour, soil*]; passer [qch] au crible [*coal*]; vanner [*wheat*]; **2** fig (sort) passer [qch] au crible [*data, evidence, information*].

■ **sift out**: ¶ **~ [sb] out, ~ out [sb]** (dispose of) éliminer [*troublemakers*]; ¶ **~ [sth] out, ~ out [sth]** extraire [*gold etc*].

■ **sift through**: **~ through [sth]** explorer [*applications, ashes, rubble*].

sifter /ˈsɪftə(r)/ *n* saupoudreuse *f*.

sigh /saɪ/ I *n* soupir *m*; **to breathe** ou **give** ou **heave a ~** pousser un soupir.

II *vtr* **'how beautiful!' she ~ed** 'comme c'est beau!' soupira-t-elle.

III *vi* **1** (exhale) [*person*] soupirer, pousser un soupir; **to ~ with relief** pousser un soupir de soulagement; **2** (pine) **to ~ for sth** regretter qch; **3** (complain) **to ~ over sth** se lamenter sur qch; **4** (whisper) [*wind*] gémir; [*trees*] bruisser.

sight /saɪt/ I *n* **1** (faculty) vue *f*; **to have good/poor ~** avoir une bonne/mauvaise vue; **her ~ is failing** elle perd la vue; **2** (act of seeing) vue *f*; **at first ~** à première vue; **at the ~ of** à la vue de [*blood, uniform, luxury, injustice*]; **at the ~ of her** en la voyant; **she felt misgivings at the ~** en voyant cela, elle fut saisie d'un doute; **this was my first ~ of** c'était la première fois que je voyais; **to have ~ of** Jur voir [*correspondence, will, document*]; **to catch ~ of sb/sth** apercevoir qn/qch; **to lose ~ of sb/sth** lit, fig perdre qn/qch de vue; **we mustn't lose ~ of the fact that** fig nous ne devons pas perdre de vue que; **to know sb by ~** connaître qn de vue; **to shoot sb on ~** tirer à vue sur qn; **I took a dislike to him on ~** je l'ai détesté dès que je l'ai vu; **I can't stand the ~ of him!** je ne peux pas le voir (en peinture)!; **3** (range of vision) **to be in ~** [*town, land, border*] être en vue; [*peace, victory, freedom, new era*] être proche; **the end/our goal is in ~!** on approche de la fin/du but!; **there's no solution in ~** on n'a pas encore trouvé de solution; **the war goes on with no end in ~** la guerre continue sans aucun espoir de paix; **there wasn't a soldier/boat in ~** il n'y avait pas un soldat/bateau en vue; **in the ~ of God** sout devant Dieu; **to come into ~** apparaître; **to be out of ~** (hidden) être caché; (having moved) ne plus être visible; **to do sth out of ~ of** faire qch sans être vu par [*observer, guard*]; **to keep** ou **stay out of ~** rester caché; **to keep sb/sth out of ~** cacher qn/qch; **don't let her out of your ~!** ne la quitte pas des yeux!; **4** (thing seen) spectacle *m*; **a familiar/sorry ~** un spectacle familier/triste; **a ~ to behold** un spectacle à voir; **it was not a pretty ~!** iron ce n'était pas beau à voir!; **5** (a shock to see) (place) porcherie *f*; (person) **you're a ~!** tu n'es pas présentable!; **I look such a ~** je ne suis pas présentable; **she looked a ~ in that hat** elle avait une de ces allures avec ce chapeau.

II **sights** *npl* **1** (places worth seeing) attractions *fpl* touristiques (**of** de); **to see the ~s** visiter; **to show sb the ~s** faire visiter à qn; **the ~s and sounds of a place** l'ambiance d'un lieu; **2** (on rifle, telescope) viseur *m*; **3** fig **to have sth in one's ~s** avoir qch dans la mire; **to have sb in one's ~s** avoir qn dans le collimateur○; **to set one's ~s on sth** viser qch; **to set one's ~s too high** viser trop haut; **to raise/lower one's ~s** viser plus haut/plus bas; **to have one's ~s firmly fixed on sth** se fixer qch pour but.

III *vtr* apercevoir [*land, plane, ship, rare bird*]; **to ~ a gun** (aiming) viser; (adjusting) régler le viseur de son fusil.

IDIOMS **a damned** ou **jolly** GB **~ better/harder** beaucoup mieux/plus dur; **out of ~, out of mind** Prov loin des yeux, loin du cœur Prov; **out of ~○!** fantastique○!

sight bill *n* effet *m* payable à vue.

sighted /ˈsaɪtɪd/ I *npl* **the ~** (+ *v pl*) les voyants (*mpl*).

II *adj* [*person*] doué de la vue; ▶ **far-sighted**, **near-sighted**, **partially sighted etc**.

sighting /ˈsaɪtɪŋ/ *n* **there have been a number of reported ~s of the animal/the escaped prisoner** plusieurs personnes ont déclaré avoir vu l'animal/le prisonnier en fuite.

sight: **~-read** *vtr, vi* déchiffrer; **~-reading** *n* déchiffrage *m*; **~-screen** *n* GB Sport (in cricket) *écran blanc qui permet aux joueurs de voir la balle*.

sightseeing /ˈsaɪtsiːɪŋ/ *n* tourisme *m*; **to go ~** faire du tourisme.

sightseer /ˈsaɪtsiːə(r)/ *n* **1** (visitor) touriste *mf*; **2** (drawn to scene of disaster) badaud/-e *m/f*, curieux/-ieuse *m/f*.

sight unseen *adv* Comm [*buy*] sur description.

sign /saɪn/ I *n* **1** (symbolic mark) signe *m*, symbole *m*; **the pound/dollar ~** le symbole de la livre/du dollar; **2** (object) (roadsign, billboard) panneau *m* (**for** pour); (smaller, indicating opening hours) pancarte *f*; (outside inn, shop) enseigne *f*; **3** (gesture) geste *m*; **to make a rude ~** faire un geste grossier; **to give sb a V ~** faire un geste obscène à qn; **to make the ~ of the cross** faire le signe de la croix; **4** (signal) signal *m*; **that will be the ~ for us to leave** ce sera le signal du départ or pour que nous partions; **5** (visible evidence) signe *m* (**of** de); **the first ~s of global warming** les premiers signes du réchauffement de la planète; **there was no ~ of any troops** il n'y avait pas l'ombre d'un soldat; **there was no ~ of life at the Smiths'** il n'y avait aucun signe de vie chez les Smith; **there was still no ~ of them at midday** à midi, ils n'étaient toujours pas arrivés; **6** (indication, pointer) signe *m* (**of** de); **it's a ~ of age** c'est un signe qu'on vieillit; **it's a good/bad ~** c'est bon/mauvais signe; **this is a ~ that** c'est signe que, ça indique que; **it's a sure ~ that** c'est la preuve que; **the ~s are that** tout indique que; **there is no ~** ou **there are no ~s of** il n'y a rien qui annonce [*improvement, change, recovery, solution*]; **there is little ~ of an improvement** il n'y a rien qui annonce vraiment une amélioration; **to show ~s of** montrer des signes de [*stress, weakness, growth, talent*]; **to show no ~s of sth** ne montrer aucun signe de qch; **to show ~s of doing** sembler faire; **she shows no ~s of changing her mind** rien ne laisse penser qu'elle va changer d'avis; **a ~ of the times** un signe des temps; **7** ▶ **1916** Astrol (of zodiac) signe *m*; **what ~ are you?** tu es de quel signe?

II *vtr* **1** (put signature to) signer [*agreement, letter, document*]; **to ~ one's own death warrant** signer son arrêt de mort; **~ed, sealed and delivered** lit dûment signé et remis à qui de droit; fig terminé; **2** (on contract) engager [*footballer, musician, band*].

III *vi* **1** [*person*] signer; **~ for** signer un reçu pour [*key, parcel*]; **2** Sport [*player*] signer son contrat (**with** avec; **for** pour); **3** (signal) **to ~ to sb to do** faire signe à qn de faire; **4** (communicate in sign language) communiquer en langage des sourds-muets.

■ **sign away**: **~ away [sth]**, **~ [sth] away** renoncer à [qch] par écrit [*rights, inheritance*].

■ **sign in**: ¶ **~ in** signer le registre (à l'arrivée); ¶ **~ in [sb]**, **~ [sb] in** inscrire [*guest*].

■ **sign off**: **~ off 1** (on radio ou TV show) terminer; **this is X ~ing off and wishing you...** c'était X qui vous souhaite...; **2** (end letter) terminer.

■ **sign on**: ¶ **~ on 1** GB Soc Admin pointer au chômage; **2** (commit oneself) (to training period, time in forces) s'engager; (for course of study) s'inscrire (**for** à, dans); ¶ **~ on [sb]** engager [*player, employee*].

■ **sign out** signer le registre (au départ); **to ~ out a library book** GB signer quand on emprunte un livre dans une bibliothèque.

■ **sign over**: **~ over [sth]**, **~ [sth] over** céder [qch] par écrit [*estate, property*].

■ **sign up**: ¶ **~ up 1** (in forces, by contract) s'engager; **2** (for course) s'inscrire (**for** à, dans); ¶ **~ up [sb]** engager [*player, filmstar*].

signal /ˈsɪgnl/ I *n* **1** (cue) signal *m* (**for** de); **to be the ~ for violent protest** être le signal de violentes protestations; **to give the ~ to leave/to attack** donner le signal du départ/de l'attaque; **this is a ~ to do** cela indique qu'il faut faire; **2** (sign, indication) signe *m* (**of** de); **danger ~** signe de danger; **to be a ~ that** être signe que, indiquer que; **to send a ~ to sb that** indiquer (clairement) à qn que; **3** Rail signal *m*; **4** Radio, TV, Electron signal *m*; **to pick up a radar ~** capter un signal radar; **5** fig (message) **to send out conflicting ~s** envoyer des messages contradictoires; **to read the ~s** comprendre.

II *adj* sout (*épith*) [*triumph, achievement, success*] éclatant; [*honour*] véritable (*before n*); [*failure*] notoire.

III *vtr* (*p prés etc* **-ll-** GB, **-l-** US) **1** lit (gesture to) **to ~ (to sb) that** faire signe (à qn) que; **to ~ sb to do** faire signe à qn de faire; **I ~led John to get the car** j'ai fait signe à John d'aller chercher la voiture; **2** fig (indicate) indiquer [*shift, determination, reluctance, disapproval, support*]; annoncer [*release*]; **to ~ one's intention to do** annoncer son intention de faire; **to ~ one's readiness to do** annoncer qu'on est prêt à faire; **to ~ that** indiquer que; **3** (mark) marquer [*end, beginning, decline*].

IV *vi* (*p prés etc* **-ll-** GB, **-l-** US) faire des signes; **he was ~ling frantically** il faisait des signes désespérés; **to ~ with one's arm/head** faire signe du bras/de la tête.

signal: **~ box** *n* Rail poste *m* d'aiguillage; **~ generator** *n* Elec générateur *m* de fréquence.

signally /ˈsɪgnəlɪ/ *adv* [*fail*] de façon notoire.

signalman /ˈsɪgnlmən/ ▶ 1692 *n* **1** Rail aiguilleur *m*; **2** Naut sémaphoriste *m*.

signal strength *n* intensité *f* de réception.

signatory /ˈsɪgnətrɪ, US -tɔːrɪ/ *n, adj* signataire (*mf*).

signature /ˈsɪgnətʃə(r)/ *n* signature *f*; **to put** ou **set one's ~ to** apposer sa signature à [*letter, document*]; **please return the document to us for ~** veuillez nous renvoyer le document pour que nous puissions le signer.

signature tune *n* indicatif *m*.

signboard /ˈsaɪnbɔːd/ *n* panneau *m* d'affichage.

signer /ˈsaɪnə(r)/ *n*: *personne qui traduit en langage des sourds-muets*.

signet /ˈsɪgnət/ *n* sceau *m*.

signet ring /ˈsɪgnɪtrɪŋ/ *n* chevalière *f*.

significance /sɪgˈnɪfɪkəns/ *n* **1** (importance) importance *f*; **not of any ~, of no ~** sans aucune importance; **2** (meaning) signification *f*.

significant /sɪgˈnɪfɪkənt/ *adj* **1** (substantial) [*amount, influence, impact, increase, saving*] considérable; **2** (important) [*event, aspect, role, victory*] important; **statistically ~** statistiquement important; **3** (meaningful) [*gesture*] éloquent; [*name, figure*] significatif/-ive; [*phrase*] lourd de sens; **it is ~ that** il est significatif que (+ *subj*).

significantly /sɪgˈnɪfɪkəntlɪ/ *adv* **1** (considerably) sensiblement; **not ~ bigger/faster** pas vraiment plus grand/plus rapide; **2** (meaningfully) [*entitle, name*] de façon significative; [*smile, look, nod*] d'un air sous-entendu; **~, he arrived late** fait révélateur, il est arrivé en retard.

signification /ˌsɪgnɪfɪˈkeɪʃn/ *n* signification *f*.

signifier /ˈsɪgnɪfaɪə(r)/ *n* Ling signifiant *m*.

signify /ˈsɪgnɪfaɪ/ **I** *vtr* **1** (denote) [*symbol*] indiquer; [*dream*] signifier; [*clouds*] annoncer [*rain*]; **2** (imply) [*fact, gesture, statement*] indiquer; **3** (display) exprimer [*affection, disapproval, joy, willingness*]; **to ~ that** indiquer que.
II *vi* sout (matter) importer; **it doesn't ~** cela importe peu.

signing /ˈsaɪnɪŋ/ *n* (of treaty, agreement) signature *f*; (of footballer etc) signature *f*; **Liverpool's latest ~, James Addyman** la dernière recrue de Liverpool, James Addyman.

sign language *n* code *m* or langage *m* gestuel; **to talk in ~** communiquer par signes.

signpost /ˈsaɪnpəʊst/ **I** *n* **1** (old free-standing type) poteau *m* indicateur; **2** (any direction sign) panneau *m* indicateur; **3** fig (indication, pointer) indice *m*, indication *f*.
II *vtr* indiquer [*place, direction*]; **to be ~ed** être indiqué.

signposting /ˈsaɪnpəʊstɪŋ/ *n* signalisation *f* routière.

sign: **~ test** *n* test *m* des signes; **~ writer** ▶ 1692 *n* peintre *m* d'enseignes.

Sikh /siːk/ *n, adj* sikh (*mf*).

silage /ˈsaɪlɪdʒ/ *n* fourrage *m* ensilé, ensilage *m*.

silage making *n* ensilage *m*.

silence /ˈsaɪləns/ **I** *n* **1** (quietness) silence *m*; **in ~** en silence; **~ please!** silence, s'il vous plaît!; **~ fell** le silence se fit; **~ reigns** le silence règne; **to call for ~** demander le silence; **to break the ~** rompre le silence; **to reduce sb to ~** réduire qn au silence; **2** (pause) silence *m*; **a two-minute ~** un silence de deux minutes; **3** (absence of communication) silence *m* (**about, on, over** sur); **to break one's ~** sortir de son silence; **right of ~** Jur *droit pour un accusé de se taire avant ou pendant son procès*; **4** (discretion) silence *m*; **to buy sb's ~** acheter le silence de qn.
II *vtr* **1** (quieten) réduire [qn] au silence [*crowd, child*]; **to ~ the enemy's guns** faire taire le feu de l'ennemi; **2** (gag) faire taire [*critic, press*].

silencer /ˈsaɪlənsə(r)/ *n* Mil, GB Aut silencieux *m*.

silent /ˈsaɪlənt/ *adj* **1** (quiet) [*engine, person, room*] silencieux/-ieuse; **to be ~** se taire; **to keep** ou **remain** ou **stay ~** rester silencieux; **to fall ~** se taire; **2** (taciturn) taciturne; **3** (uncommunicative) [*person, official, report*] muet/muette; **the minister remains ~ about** ou **on the matter of** le ministre reste muet au sujet de; **the law is ~ on this point** la loi est muette sur ce point; **4** (unexpressed) [*accusation, disapproval, oath, prayer*] muet/muette; **5** Cin muet/muette; **the ~ screen** le cinéma muet; **6** Ling muet/muette.
IDIOMS **as ~ as the grave** muet comme une tombe.

silently /ˈsaɪləntlɪ/ *adv* [*appear, leave, move*] silencieusement; [*listen, pray, stare, work*] en silence.

silent: **~ majority** *n* majorité *f* silencieuse; **~ partner** *n* Comm, Jur commanditaire *m*.

Silesia /saɪˈliːzɪə/ ▶ 1131 *pr n* Silésie *f*.

silex /ˈsaɪleks/ *n* silex *m*.

silhouette /ˌsɪluːˈet/ **I** *n* silhouette *f*; **in ~** en silhouette; **the ~ of a tree against the sky** la silhouette d'un arbre se détachant sur le ciel.
II *vtr* **to be ~d against sth** se détacher sur qch.

silica /ˈsɪlɪkə/ *n* silice *f*.

silica gel *n* gel *m* de silice.

silicate /ˈsɪlɪkeɪt/ **I** *n* silicate *m*.
II *modif* **~ rock, ~ mineral** silicate *m*.

siliceous /sɪˈlɪʃəs/ *adj* siliceux/-euse.

silicon /ˈsɪlɪkən/ *n* silicium *m*.

silicon chip *n* Comput puce *f* électronique.

silicone /ˈsɪlɪkəʊn/ *n* Chem silicone *f*; Pharm silicone *m*.

silicone rubber *n* silicone *m* élastomère.

Silicon Valley *pr n* Silicon Valley *f*, zone *f* d'industries électroniques.

silicosis /ˌsɪlɪˈkəʊsɪs/ ▶ 1354 *n* silicose *f*.

silk /sɪlk/ **I** *n* **1** (fabric) soie *f*; **2** (thread) fil *m* de soie; **3** (clothing) (*gén pl*) soierie *f*; **4** (of spider) soie *f*; **5** GB, Jur avocat *m* de la couronne; **to take the ~** être nommé avocat de la couronne.
II *modif* [*garment, flower, sheet*] de soie; [*industry, production*] de la soie.
IDIOMS **as soft** ou **smooth as ~** doux comme de la soie.

silken /ˈsɪlkən/ *adj* **1** (shiny) [*hair, sheen, skin*] soyeux/-euse; **2** (made of silk) de soie; **3** (soft) [*voice*] (pleasant) doux/douce; péj doucereux/-euse.

silk: **~ factory** *n* soierie *f*; **~ farming** *n* sériciculture *f*.

silk finish **I** *n* **a fabric with a ~** un tissu soyeux; **a paint with a ~** une peinture satinée.
II *modif* [*fabric*] soyeux/-euse; [*paint*] satiné.

silk hat *n* haut-de-forme *m*.

silkiness /ˈsɪlkɪnɪs/ *n* **1** (of hair, fabric, skin) aspect *m* soyeux; **2** (of voice) (pleasant) douceur *f*; péj ton *m* doucereux.

silk: **~ route** *n* route *f* de la soie; **~-screen printing** *n* sérigraphie *f*; **~ square** *n* carré *m* de soie.

silk stocking **I** *n* **1** lit bas *m* de soie; **2** US fig (rich person) aristocrate *mf*, riche *mf*.
II *modif* US (rich) [*district*] chic; [*party*] mondain.

silk: **~ weaving** *n* Ind soierie *f*; **~worm** *n* ver *m* à soie.

silky /ˈsɪlkɪ/ *adj* **1** (like silk) [*fabric, hair, skin*] soyeux/-euse; **2** (soft) [*tone, voice*] (pleasant) doux/douce; péj doucereux/-euse.

silky smooth *adj* [*hair, skin*] soyeux/-euse.

sill /sɪl/ *n* (of door) seuil *m*; (of window) (interior) rebord *m*; (exterior) appui *m*; (of car) bas *m* de caisse.

silliness /ˈsɪlɪnɪs/ *n* sottise *f*, stupidité *f*; **I've had enough of this ~!** j'en ai assez de ces sottises!

silly /ˈsɪlɪ/ **I**○ *n* lang enfantin idiot/-e *m/f*.
II *adj* [*person*] idiot; [*question, mistake, story, game*] stupide; [*behaviour, clothes*] ridicule; [*price*] astronomique; **don't be ~** ne dis pas de bêtises; **you are a ~ boy!** tu es idiot!; **you ~ fool!** espèce d'idiot/-e!; **what a ~ thing to do!** quelle bêtise!; **he made me feel really ~!** à cause de lui je me suis senti complètement idiot!; **to do something ~** faire une bêtise; **to make sb look ~** faire passer qn pour un/-e idiot/-e.
III *adv* (senseless) **he knocked him ~** il l'a mis KO○; **to drink oneself ~** s'abrutir d'alcool; **to bore sb ~** assommer qn.

silly: **~ billy**○ *n* idiot/-e *m/f*; **Silly Putty**® *n* US Silly Putty® *m*, pâte *f* à modeler; **~ season** *n* GB Journ période *f* creuse (*où il y a une pénurie d'informations et la presse se contente de frivolités*).

silo /ˈsaɪləʊ/ *n* (*pl* **~s**) Agric, Mil silo *m*; **missile ~** silo à missiles.

silt /sɪlt/ **I** *n* limon *m*, vase *f*.
II *vi* (also **~ up**) [*mud, sand*] se déposer; [*river*] (with mud) s'envaser; (with sand) s'ensabler.
■ **silt up**: ¶ **~ up** = **silt** II; ¶ **~ [sth] up, ~ up [sth]** [*mud*] envaser [*estuary*]; [*sand*] ensabler [*river*].

Silurian /saɪˈlʊərɪən/ *adj* silurien/-ienne.

silver /ˈsɪlvə(r)/ ▶ 1104 **I** *n* **1** (metal, colour) argent *m*; **2** (items) (silverware) argenterie *f*; (cutlery) couverts *mpl* en argent; (coins) monnaie *f*; **£10 in ~** 10 livres sterling en monnaie; **3** (medal) médaille *f* d'argent.
II *adj* **1** [*ring, cutlery, coin*] en argent; **2** (colour) [*hair, decoration, moon, lake*] argenté; [*paint*] gris métallisé *inv*.
III *vtr* argenter [*cutlery, dish*]; étamer [*mirror*].

silver birch *n* bouleau *m* argenté.

silvered /ˈsɪlvəd/ *adj* argenté.

silver: **~ fir** *n* sapin *m* argenté; **~fish** *n* (insect) petit poisson *m* d'argent, lépisme *m*; **~ foil** *n* GB papier *m* d'aluminium.

silver fox *n* **1** Zool renard *m* argenté; **2** (fur) fourrure *f* de renard argenté.

silver-gilt *n* plaqué *m* argent.

silver-grey ▶ 1104 **I** *n* gris *m* argenté.
II *adj* [*hair, silk*] gris-argent *inv*; [*paint*] gris métallisé *inv*.

silver: **~-haired** *adj* aux cheveux argentés; **~ jubilee** *n* (date) vingt-cinquième anniversaire *m*; **~ mine** *n* mine *f* d'argent; **~ paper** *n* papier *m* d'argent; **~ plate** *n* métal *m* argenté; **~ plated** *adj* plaqué argent, en métal argenté; **~ plating** *n* argenture *f*; **~ polish** *n* crème *f* pour polir l'argenterie; **~ screen** *n* Cin écran *m*; **~ service** *n* service *m* stylé; **~side** *n* Culin gîte *m*; **~smith** ▶ 1692 *n* orfèvre *mf*; **~-tongued** *adj* à la parole facile; **~ware** *n* (solid) argenterie *f* massive; (plate) métal *m* argenté; **~ wedding** *n* noces *fpl* d'argent.

silvery /ˈsɪlvərɪ/ *adj* **1** [*hair, water*] argenté; **2** [*voice, sound*] argentin.

silviculture /ˈsɪlvɪkʌltʃə(r)/ *n* sylviculture *f*.

simian /ˈsɪmɪən/ **I** *n* simien *m*.
II *adj* **1** Zool [*family, characteristic*] simien/-ienne; **2** fig [*expression, grin*] simiesque.

similar /ˈsɪmɪlə(r)/ *adj* **1** [*object, number, taste, problem, situation*] similaire, analogue; **something ~** quelque chose de similaire; **10 ~ offences** 10 délits similaires; **~ to** analogue à, comparable à; **it's ~ to riding a bike** c'est comme faire du vélo; **~ in size/price** comparable pour ce qui est des

since

as a preposition

In time expressions

since is used in English after a verb in the present perfect or progressive present perfect tense to indicate when something that is still going on started. To express this French uses a verb in the present tense + *depuis*:

I've been waiting since Saturday = j'attends depuis samedi
I've lived in Rome since 1988 = j'habite à Rome depuis 1988

When *since* is used after a verb in the past perfect tense, French uses the imperfect + *depuis*:

I had been waiting since nine o'clock = j'attendais depuis neuf heures

In negative time expressions

Again *since* is translated by *depuis*, but in negative sentences the verb tenses used in French are the same as those used in English:

I haven't seen him since Saturday = je ne l'ai pas vu depuis samedi
I hadn't seen him since 1978 = je ne l'avais pas vu depuis 1978

As a conjunction

In time expressions

When *since* is used as a conjunction, it is translated by *depuis que* and the tenses used in French parallel exactly those used with the preposition *depuis* (see above):

since she's been living in Oxford = depuis qu'elle habite à Oxford
since he'd been in Paris = depuis qu'il était à Paris

Note that in time expressions with *since* French native speakers will generally prefer to use a noun where possible when English uses a verb:

I haven't seen him since he left = je ne l'ai pas vu depuis son départ
she's been living in Nice since she got married = elle habite à Nice depuis son mariage

For particular usages see the entry ***since***.

Meaning because

When *since* is used to mean *because* it is translated by *comme* or *étant donné que*:

since she was ill, she couldn't go = comme elle était malade *or* étant donné qu'elle était malade, elle ne pouvait pas y aller

As an adverb

When *since* is used as an adverb it is translated by *depuis*:

he hasn't been seen since = on ne l'a pas vu depuis.

For particular usages see **III** in the entry ***since***.

dimensions/du prix; **it is ~ in appearance to...** ça ressemble à...; **~ in colour** dans les mêmes tons; **2** Math [*triangle*] semblable.

similarity /ˌsɪmɪˈlærətɪ/ *n* **1** (fact of resembling) ressemblance *f*, similarité *f* (**to, with** avec; **in** dans); **there the ~ ends** la ressemblance s'arrête là; **2** (aspect of resemblance) ressemblance *f*, similitude *f* (**to, with** avec; **in** dans); **there are certain similarities** il y a certaines ressemblances or similitudes.

similarly /ˈsɪmɪləlɪ/ *adv* [*behave, react, dressed, arranged*] de la même façon, de façon similaire; [*elaborate, hostile, distasteful*] aussi (*before adj*); **and ~,...** et de même,...

simile /ˈsɪmɪlɪ/ *n* comparaison *f*.

similitude /sɪˈmɪlɪtjuːd, US -tuːd/ *n* sout **1** (likeness) similitude *f*; **2** (simile) comparaison *f*.

simmer /ˈsɪmə(r)/ **I** *n* ébullition *f* lente.
II *vtr* faire cuire [qch] à feu doux [*soup, vegetables etc*]; laisser frémir [*water*].
III *vi* **1** [*soup, vegetables etc*] cuire à feu doux, mijoter; [*water*] frémir; **2** fig [*person*] (with discontent) bouillonner (**with** de); (with passion, excitement) frémir (**with** de); [*quarrel, revolt, violence*] couver; **3**○ (in sunshine, heat) [*person, car, city*] cuire○.
■ **simmer down**○ [*person*] se calmer; [*quarrel, riots, violence*] s'apaiser.

simmering /ˈsɪmərɪŋ/ *adj* [*conflict, tension, revolt, etc*] latent.

simnel cake /ˈsɪmnl ˌkeɪk/ *n* GB *cake enrobé de pâte d'amandes servi à Pâques.*

Simon says /ˈsaɪmən ˌsez/ **▶ 1282** *n* pigeon *m* vole; **to play ~** jouer à pigeon vole.

simony /ˈsaɪmənɪ/ *n* Relig simonie *f*.

simper /ˈsɪmpə(r)/ **I** *n* péj sourire *m* affecté.
II *vi* péj minauder.

simpering /ˈsɪmpərɪŋ/ **I** *n* péj minauderie *f*.
II *adj* péj [*person*] minaudier/-ière; [*smile*] affecté.

simperingly /ˈsɪmpərɪŋlɪ/ *adv* péj [*smile*] en minaudant; [*speak*] avec affectation.

simple /ˈsɪmpl/ *adj* **1** (not complicated) [*task, method, instructions, solution, answer*] simple; **it's quite ~** c'est très simple; **it's a ~ matter to change a wheel** c'est très simple de changer une roue; **the ~ truth** la vérité pure et simple; **for the ~ reason that** pour la simple raison que; **I can't make it any ~r** je ne peux pas simplifier davantage; **the ~st thing would be to...** la solution la plus simple serait de...; **what could be ~r?** rien de plus facile!; **computing made ~** l'informatique à la portée de tous; **2** (not elaborate) [*dress, furniture, design, style*] sobre; [*food, lifestyle, tastes*] simple; **3** (unsophisticated) [*pleasures, people*] simple; **her parents were ~ shopkeepers** ses parents étaient de simples commerçants; **I'm a ~ soul** iron j'ai des goûts simples; **4** (dimwitted) simplet/-ette○, simple d'esprit; **5** (basic) [*structure*] simple; [*life-form*] primaire; [*sentence, tense*] simple.

simple: **~ equation** *n* équation *f* du premier degré; **~ fraction** *n* fraction *f*; **~ fracture** *n* fracture *f* simple; **~-hearted** *adj* sincère; **~ interest** *n* intérêts *mpl* simples; **~-minded** *adj* péj [*person*] simple d'esprit; [*view, attitude, solution*] naïf/naïve; **~-mindedness** *n* péj (of person) simplicité *f* d'esprit; (of view, solution) naïveté *f*; **Simple Simon** *n* nigaud○ *m*; **~ time** *n* mesure *f* simple.

simpleton /ˈsɪmpltən/ *n* simple *mf* d'esprit, nigaud/-e○ *m/f*.

simplicity /sɪmˈplɪsətɪ/ *n* **1** (of task, method, instructions, solution, answer) simplicité *f*; **it's ~ itself** c'est la simplicité même; **2** (of dress, furniture, design) simplicité *f*, sobriété *f*; **3** (of food, lifestyle, tastes) simplicité *f*.

simplification /ˌsɪmplɪfɪˈkeɪʃn/ *n* simplification *f* (**of** de).

simplify /ˈsɪmplɪfaɪ/ *vtr* simplifier; **this should ~ matters** cela devrait simplifier les choses.

simplistic /sɪmˈplɪstɪk/ *adj* simpliste.

Simplon Pass /ˈsɪmplən/ *pr n* col *m* du Simplon.

simply /ˈsɪmplɪ/ *adv* **1** [*explain, write, dress, live, eat*] simplement, avec simplicité; **to put it ~...** en deux mots...; **2** (just, merely) simplement; **it's ~ a question of concentrating** c'est simplement une question de concentration; **it's ~ a question of explaining** il suffit d'expliquer; **3** (absolutely) absolument; **the concert was ~ wonderful** le concert était absolument merveilleux; **I ~ must dash!** il faut absolument que je m'en aille!; **her latest novel is, quite ~, magnificent** son dernier roman est, tout simplement, magnifique.

simulacrum /ˌsɪmjʊˈleɪkrəm/ *n* (*pl* **-acra**) sout simulacre *m*.

simulate /ˈsɪmjʊleɪt/ *vtr* **1** (feign) simuler [*anger, death, illness, grief*]; affecter [*indifference, interest*]; **2** (reproduce) simuler [*behaviour, conditions, effect, flight*]; imiter [*blood, hair, sound*]; **computer-~d** simulé sur ordinateur.

simulated /ˈsɪmjʊleɪtɪd/ *adj* **1** (fake) [*fur, pearls, snakeskin*] artificiel/-ielle; **2** (feigned) [*anger, grief*] simulé, feint.

simulation /ˌsɪmjʊˈleɪʃn/ *n* **1** Comput, Med, Psych, Sci simulation *f*; **2** Zool mimétisme *m*.

simulator /ˈsɪmjʊleɪtə(r)/ *n* simulateur *m*; **flight ~** simulateur de vol; **driving** ou **road ~** simulateur de conduite.

simulcast /ˈsɪmlkɑːst, US -kæst/ **I** *n* émission *f* diffusée simultanément à la radio et à la télévision.
II *vtr* diffuser [qch] simultanément à la radio et à la télévision.

simultaneity /ˌsɪmltəˈniːətɪ, US ˌsaɪm-/ *n* simultanéité *f*.

simultaneous /ˌsɪmlˈteɪnɪəs, US ˌsaɪm-/ *adj* simultané; **to be ~** avoir lieu en même temps (**with** que).

simultaneous equations *npl* système *m* d'équations.

simultaneously /ˌsɪmlˈteɪnɪəslɪ, US ˌsaɪm-/ *adv* simultanément; **~ with** en même temps que.

sin /sɪn/ **I** *n* **1** Relig péché *m*; fig crime *m*; **to live in ~** vivre dans le péché; **it's a ~ to steal** voler est un péché; **it's a ~ to waste food** gaspiller la nourriture est un crime; **2** Math (*abrév* = **sine**) sinus *m*.
II *vi* (*p prés etc* **-nn-**) pécher (**against** contre).
IDIOMS **to be more ~ned against than ~ning** être plus victime que coupable; **for my/his ~s** hum malheureusement pour moi/lui.

Sinai /ˈsaɪnaɪ/ *pr n* Sinaï *m*; **Mount ~** le mont Sinaï.

Sinai desert *pr n* désert *m* du Sinaï.

sin-bin /ˈsɪnbɪn/ *n* (in ice-hockey) prison *f*; fig hum cendrier *m*.

since /sɪns/ **I** *prep* depuis; **he's been in France ~ March** il est en France depuis le mois de mars; **she'd been a teacher ~ 1965** elle était professeur depuis 1965; **she's been waiting ~ 10 am** elle attend depuis 10 heures; **I haven't spoken to her ~ yesterday** je ne lui ai pas parlé depuis hier; **I haven't seen him ~ then** je ne l'ai pas vu depuis; **~ arriving** ou **~ his arrival he...** depuis son arrivée or depuis qu'il est arrivé, il...; **~ when do you open other people's mail?** depuis quand est-ce que tu ouvres le courrier des autres?
II *conj* **1** (from the time when) depuis que; **~ he's been away** depuis qu'il est absent; **ever ~ I married him** depuis que nous nous sommes mariés, depuis notre mariage; **I've known him ~ I was 12** je le connais depuis que j'ai 12 ans; **it's 10 years ~ we last met** cela fait 10 ans que nous ne nous sommes pas revus; **2** (because) comme, étant donné que; **~ it was raining I stayed at home** comme il pleuvait or étant donné qu'il pleuvait je suis resté à la maison; **~ you ask, I'm fine** puisque tu poses la question, je vais bien; **~ you're so clever, why don't you do it yourself?** puisque tu es tellement malin, pourquoi ne le fais-tu pas toi-même?
III *adv* (subsequently) **she has ~ qualified** depuis elle a obtenu son diplôme; **we've**

kept in touch ever ~ nous ne nous sommes pas perdus de vue depuis; **I haven't phoned her ~** je ne lui ai pas téléphoné depuis; **they've long ~ left** ils sont partis il y a longtemps; **not long ~** il y a peu de temps.

sincere /sɪn'sɪə(r)/ *adj* [*person, apology, belief*] sincère; [*attempt*] réel/réelle; **~ thanks** sincères or profonds remerciements *mpl*; **to be ~ in one's wish/plan** être sincère dans son désir/projet; **it is my ~ belief that** je crois sincèrement que.

sincerely /sɪn'sɪəlɪ/ *adv* sincèrement; **Yours ~, Sincerely yours** US (end of letter) Veuillez agréer, Monsieur/Madame etc, l'expression de mes sentiments les meilleurs; (less formally) cordialement (vôtre).

sincerity /sɪn'serətɪ/ *n* sincérité *f*; **in all ~** en toute sincérité; **with ~** sincèrement.

sine /saɪn/ *n* Math sinus *m*.

sinecure /'saɪnɪkjʊə(r), 'sɪn-/ *n* sinécure *f*.

sine die /ˌsaɪnɪ 'daɪɪ, ˌsɪneɪ 'di:eɪ/ *adj, adv* sine die.

sine qua non /ˌsɪneɪ kwɑ: 'nəʊn/ *n* condition *f* sine qua non.

sinew /'sɪnju:/ *n* Anat tendon *m*.

sine wave *n* onde *f* sinusoïdale.

sinewy /'sɪnju:ɪ/ *adj* **1** [*person, animal*] (mince et) musclé; **2** [*meat*] tendineux/-euse.

sinfonietta /ˌsɪnfən'jetə/ *n* Mus sinfonietta *f*.

sinful /'sɪnfl/ *adj* [*behaviour, pleasure, thought, waste*] immoral; [*place*] de perdition; [*world*] impie; **a ~ man/woman** un pécheur/une pécheresse.

sinfully /'sɪnfəlɪ/ *adv* [*act, think*] d'une façon immorale; [*waste*] scandaleusement.

sinfulness /'sɪnflnɪs/ *n* (of person) péchés *mpl*; (of action, behaviour) caractère *m* immoral.

sing /sɪŋ/ **I** *n* US = **sing-along**.
II *vtr* (*prét* **sang**; *pp* **sung**) [*person*] chanter [*song, note*]; **to ~ a role** chanter dans un rôle; **to ~ the part of...** chanter dans le rôle de...; **to ~ sth to/for sb** chanter qch à/pour qn; **~ him something** chante-lui quelque chose; **to ~ sth in front of** ou **for an audience** chanter qch devant un public; **to ~ sb to sleep** chanter pour endormir qn; **'Happy birthday!' they sang** 'bon anniversaire!' ont-ils chanté; **to ~ sb's praises** chanter les louanges de qn.
III *vi* (*prét* **sang**; *pp* **sung**) **1** [*person*] chanter (**in** dans; **to sb** à qn; **for sb** pour qn); **you can't ~** tu ne sais pas chanter; **to ~ well** chanter bien; **to ~ in/out of tune** chanter juste/faux; **to ~ in front of** ou **for an audience** chanter devant un public; **to ~ to an accompaniment** chanter avec un accompagnement; **he ~s about love** il parle d'amour dans ses chansons; **she sang of her country** littér sa chanson parlait de son pays; **2** [*bird, cricket, instrument, kettle*] chanter; [*wind*] siffler; [*ears*] siffler; **to make sb's ears ~** faire siffler les oreilles de qn; **3**○ (confess) se mettre à table○.
IDIOMS **to ~ a different** ou **another song** changer d'avis.
■ **sing along** chanter en même temps (**with** que).
■ **sing out**: ¶ **~ out** (sing loud) entonner; (call out) appeler; ¶ **~ out [sth]** (shout) crier.
■ **sing up** chanter plus fort.

sing. *abrév écrite* = **singular**.

sing-along /'sɪŋəlɒŋ/ *n* US **to have a ~** chanter ensemble.

Singapore /ˌsɪŋə'pɔ:(r)/ **▶ 1131**, **▶ 1818** *pr n* Singapour *f*; **in/to ~** à Singapour.

Singaporean /ˌsɪŋə'pɔ:rɪən/ **▶ 1486** **I** *n* Singapourien/-ienne *m/f*.
II *adj* singapourien/-ienne.

singe /sɪndʒ/ **I** *n* (also **~ mark**) gen légère brûlure *f*; (from iron) roussissure *f*.
II *vtr* (*p prés* **singeing**) **1** gen brûler [qch] légèrement [*hair, clothing*]; (when ironing) roussir [*clothes*]; **2** Culin flamber [*feathers, poultry*].

singer /'sɪŋə(r)/ *n* chanteur/-euse *m/f*; **he's a ~ in a band** il est chanteur dans un groupe; **she's a good ~** elle chante bien; **▶ opera**.

Singhalese *n, adj* = **Sinhalese**.

singing /'sɪŋɪŋ/ **I** *n* **1** Mus chant *m*; **to teach ~** enseigner le chant; **opera ~** chant d'opéra; **I love ~** j'adore chanter; **to hear ~** entendre chanter; **there was ~ in the bar** on chantait au bar; **2** (sound) (of kettle) sifflement *m*; (in ears) bourdonnement *m* (**in** dans); (of wind) sifflement *m*.
II *modif* [*lesson, teacher*] de chant; [*role, part*] chantant; [*group*] de chanteurs; [*career*] dans la chanson.

singing voice *n* voix *f*.

single /'sɪŋgl/ **I** *n* **1** Transp (also **~ ticket**) aller *m* simple; **2** Tourism (also **~ room**) chambre *f* à une personne; **3** Mus (record) 45 tours *m*; **4** Theat **we only have ~s left** vous ne serez pas ensemble.
II *adj* **1** (sole) seul; **a ~ rose/vote** une seule rose/voix; **in a ~ day** en une seule journée; **2** (not double) [*sink*] à un bac; [*unit*] simple; [*door*] à un battant; [*wardrobe*] à une porte; [*sheet, duvet*] pour une personne; **inflation is in ~ figures** Econ l'inflation est inférieure à 10%; **3** (for one) [*bed, tariff, portion*] pour une personne; **4** (unmarried) célibataire; **the ~ homeless** les personnes seules et sans abri; **5** (used emphatically) **every ~ day** tous les jours sans exception; **every ~ one of those people** chacune de ces personnes; **there isn't a ~ word of truth in it** il n'y a pas un seul mot de vrai dans cela; **there wasn't a ~ person there** il n'y avait absolument personne; **not a ~ thing was left** il ne restait pas la moindre chose; **6** (describing main cause, aspect) **the ~ most important event/factor** l'événement/le facteur principal; **the ~ most important reason for the decline is...** la cause majeure du déclin est...; **heart disease is the ~ biggest killer in Britain** les maladies cardiaques sont la cause majeure de décès en Grande-Bretagne.
■ **single out**: **~ [sb/sth] out, ~ out [sb/sth]** [*person*] choisir; **to be ~d out for** faire l'objet de [*special treatment, praise*]; être l'objet de [*attention*]; être la proie de [*criticism*]; **to ~ sb out for criticism** prendre qn pour cible de ses critiques.

single: **~-action** *adj* [*gun*] à un coup; **~-breasted** *adj* [*jacket*] droit; **~-celled** *adj* unicellulaire; **~ combat** *n* combat *m* singulier; **~ cream** *n* ≈ crème *f* fraîche liquide; **~ currency** *n* monnaie *f* unique; **~ decker** *n* autobus *m* sans impériale.

single entry **I** *n* comptabilité *f* en partie simple.
II *modif* **single-entry** [*bookkeeping, account*] en partie simple.

single file *adv* (also **in ~**) [*walk, move*] en file indienne.

single-handed /ˌsɪŋgl'hændɪd/ **I** *adj* **it was a ~ effort on her part** elle a fait ça toute seule.
II *adv* [*do, cope*] tout seul; [*sail, fly*] en solitaire.

single-handedly /ˌsɪŋgl'hændɪdlɪ/ *adv* [*manage, cope*] tout seul; **he ruined the company ~** il a ruiné la société à lui seul.

single: **~-lens reflex**, **SLR** *n* reflex *m* à un objectif; **~ market** *n* marché *m* unique.

single-minded /ˌsɪŋgl'maɪndɪd/ *adj* [*determination, pursuit*] farouche; [*person*] tenace, résolu; **to be ~ about doing** être résolu à faire.

single: **~-mindedness** *n* ténacité *f*; **~ mother** *n* mère *f* qui élève ses enfants seule.

singleness /'sɪŋglnɪs/ *n* **~ of purpose** ténacité *f*.

single parent **I** *n* parent *m* isolé.
II **single-parent** *modif* [*family*] monoparental.

single-party /ˌsɪŋgl'pɑ:tɪ/ *adj* [*government, rule*] à parti unique.

singles /'sɪŋglz/ **I** *n* **1** Sport (event) **the women's/men's ~** le simple dames/messieurs. **2** (people) célibataires *mpl*; **for ~** [*club, vacation*] pour célibataires.
II *modif* **1** Sport [*final*] du simple; **2** [*club, vacation*] pour célibataires.

singles: **~ bar** *n* bar *m* de rencontres pour célibataires; **~ charts** *npl* palmarès *m* des 45 tours.

single: **~ seater** *n* avion *m* monoplace; **~-sex** *adj* [*school, hostel*] non mixte; **~-sided disk** *n* disquette *f* simple face.

single spacing *n* interligne *m* simple; **typed in ~** tapé avec un interligne simple.

single-storey /ˌsɪŋgl'stɔ:rɪ/ *adj* [*house*] de plain-pied.

singlet /'sɪŋglɪt/ *n* GB **1** Sport maillot *m*; **2** (vest) maillot *m* de corps.

singleton /'sɪŋgltən/ *n* **1** gen exemple *m* unique; **2** Math, Games singleton *m*.

single-track /ˌsɪŋgl'træk/ *adj* **1** Transp [*line, road*] à une voie; **2** fig [*commitment*] entier/-ière.

single: **~ transferable vote** *n* vote *m* unique transférable; **~ yellow line** *n* GB *marquage au sol autorisant le stationnement à certaines heures*.

singly /'sɪŋglɪ/ *adv* **1** (one by one) un à un; **2** (alone) individuellement.

singsong /'sɪŋsɒŋ/ GB **I** *n* **to have a ~** chanter ensemble; **how about a ~?** si on chantait?
II *adj* [*voice, language, dialect*] chantant.

singular /'sɪŋgjʊlə(r)/ **I** *n* Ling singulier *m*; **in the ~** au singulier.
II *adj* **1** Ling [*form*] du singulier; [*noun, verb*] au singulier; **2** (strange, exceptional) singulier/-ière.

singularity /ˌsɪŋgjʊ'lærətɪ/ *n* singularité *f*.

singularly /'sɪŋgjʊləlɪ/ *adv* singulièrement.

Sinhalese /ˌsɪnhə'li:z/ **▶ 1486**, **1402** **I** *n* **1** (*pl inv*) (person) Cingalais/-e *m/f*; **2** Ling cingalais *m*.
II *adj* cingalais.

sinister /'sɪnɪstə(r)/ *adj* **1** [*person, place, plot, look, sign, silence*] sinistre; **2** Herald sénestre.

sink /sɪŋk/ **I** *n* **1** (basin) (in kitchen) évier *m*; (in bathroom) lavabo *m*; **double ~** évier à deux bacs; **2** (cesspit) lit fosse *f* d'aisance; fig cloaque *m*; **3** (also **~hole**) Geol doline *f*.
II *vtr* (*prét* **sank**; *pp* **sunk**) **1** Naut (by scuttling) couler [*ship*]; (by torpedo) torpiller [*ship*]; **2** (bore) forer [*oilwell, shaft*]; creuser [*foundations*]; **3** (embed) enfoncer [*post, pillar*] (**into** dans); **to ~ one's teeth into** mordre à pleines dents dans [*sandwich etc*]; **the dog sank its teeth into my arm** le chien a planté ses crocs dans mon bras; **to ~ a knife into** enfoncer un couteau dans [*cake*]; **4**○ GB (drink) descendre○ [*drink*]; **5** Sport mettre [qch] dans le trou [*billiard ball*]; rentrer [*putt*]; **6** (destroy) [*scandal*] faire couler [*party*]; **without capital/a leader we're sunk** sans capital/chef nous sommes perdus; **7** Fin amortir [*debt*]; **8** (invest heavily) **to ~ money into sth** investir de l'argent dans [*project, company*].
III *vi* (*prét* **sank**; *pp* **sunk**) **1** (fail to float) [*ship, object, person*] couler; **to ~ without a trace** fig [*idea, project etc*] tomber dans les oubliettes; **2** (drop to lower level) [*sun*] baisser; [*cake*] se dégonfler; [*pressure, temperature, water level*] baisser; **the sun ~s in the West** le soleil disparait à l'ouest; **to ~ to the floor** s'effondrer; **to ~ to one's knees** tomber à genoux; **to ~ into a chair** s'affaler dans un fauteuil; **to ~ into a deep sleep/coma** sombrer dans un profond sommeil/dans le coma; **3** fig (fall) [*profits, production*] baisser; **he has sunk in my estimation** il a baissé dans mon estime; **my heart** ou **spirits sank** j'ai eu un serrement de cœur; **I wouldn't ~ so low as to beg from him** je ne m'abaisserais pas à lui

demander de l'argent; **4** (subside) [*building, wall*] s'effondrer; **to ~ into** [*person, feet*] s'enfoncer dans [*mud*]; [*country, person*] sombrer dans [*anarchy, apathy*]; [*celebrity*] sombrer dans [*obscurity*]; **to ~ under the weight of** [*shelf*] plier sous le poids de [*boxes etc*]; [*person, company*] crouler sous le poids de [*debt*].

IDIOMS **to ~ one's differences** oublier ses différences.

■ **sink in 1** [*lotion, water*] pénétrer; **let the lotion ~ in** laisse la crème pénétrer; **2** fig [*news, announcement*] faire son chemin; **it took several minutes for the good news/truth to ~ in** il m'a fallu plusieurs minutes pour réaliser la bonne nouvelle/accepter la vérité; **the result hasn't sunk in yet** je n'ai encore pas réalisé les conséquences du résultat.

sinker /'sɪŋkə(r)/ *n* **1** Fishg plomb *m*; **2** US Culin ≈ beignet *m*.

IDIOMS **he fell for the story hook, line and ~** il a gobé○ toute mon histoire.

sinkhole /'sɪŋkhəʊl/ *n* Geol doline *f*.

sinking /'sɪŋkɪŋ/ **I** *n* **1** Naut (accidental) naufrage *m*; (by torpedo) torpillage *m*; (by flooding) sabordage *m*; **2** Constr, Mining forage *m*; **3** Fin (of debt) amortissement *m*.

II *adj* [*feeling*] angoissant.

sink: **~ing fund** *n* Fin fonds *m* d'amortissement; **~ tidy** *n* égouttoir *m* pour brosses et éponges à vaisselle; **~ unit** *n* évier *m* encastré.

sinless /'sɪnlɪs/ *adj* sans péché.

sinner /'sɪnə(r)/ *n* pécheur/-eresse *m/f*.

Sinn Féin /ʃɪn 'feɪn/ *n* Sinn Féin *m* (*en Irlande: parti républicain nationaliste, branche politique de l'IRA*).

Sinologist /saɪ'nɒlədʒɪst/ ▶ **1692** *n* sinologue *mf*.

Sinology /saɪ'nɒlədʒɪ/ *n* sinologie *f*.

sin tax○ *n* impôt *m* sur l'alcool et le tabac.

sinuosity /ˌsɪnjʊ'ɒsətɪ/ *n* sinuosité *f*.

sinuous /'sɪnjʊəs/ *adj* sinueux/-euse.

sinuously /'sɪnjʊəslɪ/ *adv* sinueusement.

sinus /'saɪnəs/ *n* (*pl* **~es**) sinus *m inv*; **to have ~ trouble** avoir de la sinusite.

sinusitis /ˌsaɪnə'saɪtɪs/ ▶ **1354** *n* sinusite *f*.

Sioux /suː/ **I** *n* **1** (*pl inv*) (person) Sioux *mf*; **2** Ling sioux *m*.

II *adj* sioux *inv*.

sip /sɪp/ **I** *n* petite gorgée *f*.

II *vtr* (*p prés etc* **-pp-**) gen boire [qch] à petites gorgées; (with pleasure) siroter○.

siphon /'saɪfn/ **I** *n* siphon *m*.

II *vtr* **1** siphonner [*petrol, water*]; **to ~ petrol out of a car** siphonner de l'essence dans le réservoir d'une voiture; **2** Fin détourner [*money*] (**out of, from** de; **into** au profit de).

■ **siphon off**: **~ [sth] off**, **~ off [sth] 1** siphonner [*petrol, water*]; **2** fig péj détourner [*money*]; récupérer [*resources, workforce*].

sir /sɜː(r)/ ▶ **1268** *n* **1** (form of address) Monsieur; **yes ~** gen oui, Monsieur; (to president) oui, Monsieur le président; (to headmaster) oui, Monsieur le directeur; Mil oui, mon commandant or mon lieutenant etc; **my dear ~** iron mon cher Monsieur; **Dear Sir** (in letter) Monsieur; **2** GB (in titles) **Sir James** Sir James; **3**○ US (emphatic) **yes/no ~** ça oui/non!

sire /'saɪə(r)/ **I** *n* **1** (of animal) père *m*; **2** ▶ **1268** ‡(form of address) (to king) Sire; (to lord) seigneur *m*.

II *vtr* engendrer.

siree○ /ˌsɜː'riː/ *n* US **yes/no ~** ça oui/non○!

siren /'saɪərən/ **I** *n* **1** (alarm) sirène *f*; **2** Mythol sirène *f* also fig.

II *modif* fig [*song, call, charms*] irrésistible.

sirloin /'sɜːlɔɪn/ *n* aloyau *m*.

sirloin steak *n* biftek *m* dans l'aloyau.

sirocco /sɪ'rɒkəʊ/ *n* sirocco *m*.

sis○ /sɪs/ *n* (*abrév* = **sister**) sœurette *f*.

sisal /'saɪsl/ **I** *n* sisal *m*.

II *modif* [*leaf, fibre*] de sisal; [*rope*] en or de sisal.

siskin /'sɪskɪn/ *n* tarin *m*.

sissy○ /'sɪsɪ/ **I** *n* pej (coward) poule *f* mouillée○; **he's a real ~!** (effeminate) c'est une vraie fille!

II *adj* **that's a ~ game!** c'est un jeu de fille!; **that's a ~ sweater** ce pull-over fait fille.

sister /'sɪstə(r)/ **I** *n* **1** (sibling) sœur *f*; **older** ou **elder/younger ~** sœur aînée/cadette; **big/little ~** grande/petite sœur; **she's like a ~ to me** elle est une sœur pour moi; **2** GB Med infirmière *f* chef; **yes, ~** oui, Madame; **3** (also **Sister**) Relig sœur *f*; **yes, ~** oui, ma sœur; **4** (fellow woman) sœur *f*; **5**○ US (form of address) ma vieille○.

II *modif* [*company, institution, organization*] sœur; [*newspaper, publication*] apparenté; **~ country**, **~ state** pays frère; **~ nation** nation sœur.

sisterhood /'sɪstəhʊd/ *n* **1** Relig (foundation) communauté *f* religieuse; **2** (being sisters) fraternité *f*; **3** (in feminism) solidarité *f* féminine; **the ~** le mouvement *m* de la libération de la femme.

sister-in-law *n* (*pl* **sisters-in-law**) belle-sœur *f*.

sisterly /'sɪstəlɪ/ *adj* **1** [*feeling, affection, kiss*] fraternel/-elle; **~ rivalry** rivalité *f* entre sœurs; **2** [*solidarity*] féminin.

sister ship *n* sister-ship *m*.

Sistine /'sɪstiːn, 'sɪstaɪn/ *adj* **the ~ Chapel** la chapelle Sixtine.

Sisyphus /'sɪsɪfəs/ *pr n* Sisyphe.

sit /sɪt/ (*p prés* **-tt-**; *prét, pp* **sat**) **I** *vtr* **1** (put) **to ~ sb in/on/near sth** asseoir qn dans/sur/près de qch; **to ~ sth in/on/near sth** placer qch dans/sur/près de qch; **2** GB Sch, Univ [*candidate*] se présenter à, passer [*exam*].

II *vi* **1** (take a seat) s'asseoir (**at** à; **in** dans; **on** sur); **to ~ on the floor** s'asseoir par terre; **2** (be seated) [*person, animal*] être assis (**around** autour de; **at** à; **in** dans; **on** sur); [*bird*] être perché (**on** sur); **to be ~ting reading/knitting** être assis à lire/tricoter; **I like to ~ and read/watch TV** j'aime bien m'asseoir et lire/regarder la télé; **to ~ over sth** être penché sur [*accounts, books*]; **to ~ for two hours** rester assis pendant deux heures; **to ~ quietly/comfortably** être tranquillement/confortablement assis; **to ~ still** se tenir tranquille; **to ~ at home** rester à la maison; **don't just ~ there!** ne reste pas là à ne rien faire!; **3** (meet) [*committee, court*] siéger; **4** (hold office) **to ~ for** [*MP*] représenter [*constituency*]; **to ~ as** être [*judge, magistrate*]; **to ~ on** faire parti de [*committee, jury*]; **5** (fit) **to ~ well/badly (on sb)** [*suit, jacket*] bien/mal tomber (sur qn); **the jacket ~s well across the shoulders** la veste tombe bien aux épaules; **success/power ~s lightly on her** fig le succès/le pouvoir ne lui pèse guère; **6** (remain untouched) **the books/keys were still ~ting on the desk** les livres/clés étaient toujours sur le bureau; **the car is ~ting rusting in the garage** la voiture reste à rouiller dans le garage; **7** GB Jur **to ~ for the Bar** se présenter au barreau; **8** Agric, Zool **to ~ on** [*bird*] couver [*eggs*].

IDIOMS **to make sb ~ up and take notice** faire réagir qn.

■ **sit about, sit around** rester assis à ne rien faire; **to ~ around waiting** rester assis à attendre.

■ **sit back**: **~ back 1** (lean back) se caler dans son fauteuil; **2** (relax) se détendre; **to ~ back in** se caler dans [*chair*]; **to ~ back on one's heels** s'asseoir sur les talons.

■ **sit by** rester là à ne rien faire.

■ **sit down**: ¶ **~ down** s'asseoir (**at** à; **in** dans; **on** sur); **it's time we sat down and discussed your ideas** il est temps que nous nous voyions pour discuter de vos projets; **to ~ down to dinner** ou **a meal** se mettre à table; ¶ **~ [sb] down** lit asseoir qn; fig **he sat me down and told me what he thought of me** il m'a emmené à l'écart et m'a dit ce qu'il pensait de moi; **to ~ oneself down** s'asseoir.

■ **sit in**: **to ~ in** [*observer*] assister; **to ~ in on sth** assister à [*meeting*].

■ **sit on**○: **~ on [sth/sb] 1** (not deal with) garder [qch] sous le coude○ [*application form, letter*]; **2** (bring to heel) remettre [qn] à sa place.

■ **sit out**: ¶ **~ out** s'asseoir dehors; ¶ **~ [sth] out 1** (stay to the end) rester jusqu'à la fin de [*lecture*]; **2** (not take part in) ne pas jouer [*game*]; fig attendre la fin de [*crisis, war*]; **I'll ~ the next one out** (dance) je ne danserai pas la prochaine.

■ **sit through**: **~ through [sth]** devoir assister à [*lecture, concert*].

■ **sit up**: ¶ **~ up 1** (raise oneself upright) se redresser; **to be ~ing up** être assis; **he was ~ting up in bed reading** il était assis dans son lit à lire; **~ up straight!** tiens-toi droit!; **2** (stay up late) rester debout (**doing** pour faire); **to ~ up with sb** veiller qn; ¶ **~ [sb/ sth] up** redresser.

sitar /'sɪtɑː(r), sɪ'tɑː(r)/ ▶ **1481** *n* sitar *m*.

sitcom○ /'sɪtkɒm/ *n* (*abrév* = **situation comedy**) sitcom *m*.

sit-down /'sɪtdaʊn/ **I** *n* GB **to have a ~** s'asseoir; **I could do with a ~** je m'assoirais avec plaisir.

II *modif* [*lunch, meal*] assis.

sit-down strike *n* grève *f* sur le tas.

site /saɪt/ **I** *n* **1** Constr (also **building ~**, **construction ~**) (before building) terrain *m*; (during building) chantier *m*; **on ~** sur le chantier; **2** (land for specific activity) terrain *m*; **caravan ~** terrain de caravaning; **3** (of building, town) emplacement *m*; Archeol site *m*; **4** (of recent event, accident) lieux *mpl*.

II *vtr* construire [*building*]; **to be ~d** être situé.

site: **~ measuring** *n* arpentage *m*; **~ office** *n* baraque *f* de chantier; **~-specific** *adj* Art in situ.

sit-in /'sɪtɪn/ *n* sit-in *m inv*, manifestation *f* avec occupation des locaux.

siting /'saɪtɪŋ/ *n* (of building) emplacement *m*; (of weaponry) installation *f*.

sitter /'sɪtə(r)/ *n* **1** Art, Phot modèle *m*; **2** (babysitter) babysitter *mf*.

sitting /'sɪtɪŋ/ **I** *n* **1** Admin, Art, Phot (session) séance *f*; **an all-night ~** Admin une séance de nuit; **I read it at one ~** je l'ai lu d'un seul trait; **2** (period in which food is served) service *m*; **3** (incubation period) couvaison *f*.

II sittings *npl* GB Jur *les quatre sessions de l'année judiciaire*.

III *adj* **1** (seated) **to be in a ~ position** être assis; **2** Agric [*hen*] couveuse *f*.

sitting: **~ duck**○ *n* cible *f* or victime *f* facile; **~ member** *n* GB Pol député *m* en exercice; **~ room** *n* salon *m*; **~ target** *n* lit, fig cible *f* facile; **~ tenant** *n* Jur locataire *mf* dans les lieux; **~ trot** *n* Equit trot *m* assis.

situate /'sɪtjʊeɪt, US 'sɪtʃʊeɪt/ *vtr* **1** situer [*building, town, factory etc*]; **to be ~d** être situé, se trouver; **conveniently ~d** bien situé; **well/badly ~d** bien/mal situé; **2** fig **to be well ~d to do** [*person*] être bien placé pour faire; **she is rather badly ~d at the moment** fig (in difficulties) elle se trouve dans une situation assez défavorable en ce moment; (financially) elle a des ennuis d'argent en ce moment; **how are you ~d for money?** comment est-ce que ça va pour l'argent?; **3** (put into context) situer [*idea, problem, event*].

situation /ˌsɪtjʊ'eɪʃn, US ˌsɪtʃʊ-/ *n* **1** (set of circumstances) situation *f*; **to save the ~** sauver la situation; **in the present economic ~** dans la conjoncture économique or la situation économique actuelle; **the human rights ~** la situation des droits de l'homme; **in an interview/exam ~** lors

Sizes

In the following tables of equivalent sizes, French sizes have been rounded up, where necessary. (It is always better to have clothes a little too big than a little too tight.)

Men's shoe sizes

in UK & US	in France
6	39
7	40
8	42
9	43
10	44
11	45
12	46

Women's shoe sizes

in UK	in US	in France
3	6	35
3½	6½	36
4	7	37
5	7½	38
6	8	39
7	8½	40
8	9	41

Men's clothing sizes

in UK & US	in France
28	38
30	40
32	42
34	44
36	46
38	48
40	50
42	52
44	54
46	56

Women's clothing sizes

in UK	in US	in France
8	4	34
10	6	36
12	8	38–40
14	10	42
16	12	44–46
18	14	48
20	16	50

Men's shirt collar sizes

in UK & US	in France	in UK & US	in France
14	36	16½	41
14½	37	17	42
15	38	17½	43
15½	39	18	44
16	40		

Note that for shoe and sock sizes French uses pointure, *so a size 37 is* une pointure 37. *For all other types of garment (even stockings and tights) the word* taille *is used, so a size 16 shirt is* une chemise taille 40, *etc.*

what size are you? = quelle taille faites-vous? *or* quelle pointure faites-vous?
I take size 40 (*in clothes*) = je prends du 40 *or* je fais du 40
I take a size 7 (*in shoes*) = je chausse du 40 *or* je fais du 40
my collar size is 15 = je porte un 38 *or* je porte du 38
I'm looking for collar size 16 = je cherche un 40
his shoe size is 39 = il chausse du 39
a pair of shoes size 39 = une paire de chaussures pointure 39
have you got the same thing in a 16? = avez-vous ce modèle en 40?
have you got this in a smaller size? = avez-vous ce modèle dans une plus petite taille (*or* pointure)? *or* avez-vous ce modèle en plus petit?
have you got this in a larger size? = avez-vous ce modèle dans une plus grande taille (*or* pointure)? *or* avez-vous ce modèle en plus grand?
they haven't got my size = ils n'ont pas ma taille (*or* ma pointure)

d'un entretien/d'un examen; **the housing/food ~ is worsening** la crise du logement/de l'alimentation s'aggrave; **he doesn't know how to behave in social ~s** il ne sait pas se conduire en société; **2** (location) (of house, town etc) situation *f*; **to be in a beautiful ~** être magnifiquement situé; **3** sout ou † (job) situation *f*, emploi *m*; **'~s vacant'** 'offres *fpl* d'emploi'; **'~s wanted'** 'demandes *fpl* d'emploi'.

situational /ˌsɪtjʊˈeɪʃənl, US ˌsɪtʃʊ-/ *adj* situationnel/-elle.

situation comedy *n* comédie *f* de situation.

sit-ups /ˈsɪtʌps/ *npl* abdominaux *mpl*.

SI units *npl* unités *fpl* du Système International.

six /sɪks/ ▶ 1505, ▶ 971, ▶ 1096 **I** *n* six *m inv*.
II *adj* six *inv*.
IDIOMS **to be (all) at ~es and sevens** [*person*] ne pas savoir où donner de la tête; [*thing, affairs*] être sens dessus dessous; **it's ~ of one and half a dozen of the other** c'est bonnet blanc et blanc bonnet, c'est du pareil au même; **to be ~ foot** ou **feet under** être enterré; **to get ~ of the best** GB recevoir une correction; **to hit** ou **knock sb for ~**○ GB laisser qn KO○.

sixain /ˈsɪkseɪn/ *n* Literat sizain *m*.

six: **Six Counties** *pr npl* six comtés *mpl* de l'Irlande du Nord; **Six Day War** *pr n* guerre *f* des Six Jours; **~-eight time** *n* mesure *f* à six-huit.

six-footer○ /ˌsɪksˈfʊtə(r)/ *n* personne *f* grande d'au moins un mètre quatre-vingts; **they were both ~s** ils faisaient tous les deux plus d'un mètre quatre-vingts.

six: **~-gun**○ /ˈsɪksgʌn/ *n* six-coups *m inv*; **~-pack** *n* pack *m* de six; **~pence** *n* GB (ancienne) pièce *f* de six pence; **~penny** *adj* GB (*épith*) à six pence; **~-shooter** *n* revolver *m* à six coups.

sixteen /ˌsɪkˈstiːn/ *n*, *adj* ▶ 1505, ▶ 971 seize (*m inv*).
IDIOMS **she's sweet ~ (and never been kissed)** elle a la fraîcheur de ses seize ans.

sixteenth /sɪkˈstiːnθ/ ▶ 1505, 1150 **I** *n* **1** (in order) seizième *mf*; **2** (of month) seize *m inv*; **3** (fraction) seizième *m*.
II *adj* seizième.
III *adv* [*come, finish*] seizième, en seizième position.

sixth /sɪksθ/ ▶ 1505, 1150 **I** *n* **1** (in order) sixième *mf*; **2** (of month) six *m inv*; **3** (fraction) sixième *m*; **4** Mus sixième *f*; **5** GB Sch (lower) ≈ première *f*; (upper) ≈ terminale *f*.
II *adj* sixième.
III *adv* [*come, finish*] sixième, en sixième position.

sixth chord *n* accord *m* de sixte.

sixth form GB Sch **I** *n* (lower) ≈ classes *fpl* de premières; (upper) ≈ classes *fpl* terminales; **to be in the ~** ≈ être en première or en terminale.
II *modif* [*pupil, lesson*] ≈ de terminale.

sixth: **~ form college** *n* GB Sch lycée *m* (*n'ayant que des classes de première et terminale*); **~ former** *n* ≈ élève *mf* de terminale.

sixthly /ˈsɪksθlɪ/ *adv* sixièmement, en sixième lieu.

sixth: **~ sense** *n* sixième sens *m*; **~ year** *n* Scot Sch ≈ terminale *f*.

sixties /ˈsɪkstɪz/ ▶ 971, 1150 *npl* **1** (decade) **the ~** les années *fpl* soixante; **2** (age) **to be in one's ~** avoir la soixantaine; **a man in his ~** un sexagénaire.

sixtieth /ˈsɪkstɪəθ/ ▶ 1505 **I** *n* **1** (in sequence) soixantième *mf*; **2** (fraction) soixantième *m*.
II *adj* soixantième.
III *adv* [*come, finish*] soixantième, en soixantième position.

sixty /ˈsɪkstɪ/ ▶ 1505, 971 *n*, *adj* soixante (*m*) *inv*.

sixty: **~-fourth note** *n* US quadruple croche *f*; **~-four thousand dollar question**○ *n* question *f* à mille francs○; **~-fourth rest** *n* US seizième *m* de soupir; **~ nine**○ *n* soixante-neuf○ *m inv*.

six: **~ yard area**, **~ yard box** *n* (in soccer) zone *f* de la surface de but; **~ yard line** *n* (in soccer) limite *f* de la surface de but.

sizable = **sizeable**.

size /saɪz/ ▶ 1703 **I** *n* **1** (dimensions) (of person, head, hand, nose) taille *f*; (of box, glass, plate, stamp) grandeur *f*; (of building, room, garden) grandeur *f*, dimensions *fpl*; (of tree) taille *f*, grandeur *f*; (of apple, egg, bead) grosseur *f*, calibre *m*; (of carpet, chair, bed, machine) dimensions *fpl*; (of book, parcel) grosseur *f*, dimensions *fpl*; (of paper, envelope, picture) taille *f*, dimensions *fpl*; (of country, island, estate) étendue *f*; **a town of some ~** une ville assez importante or assez grande; **chairs of all ~s** des chaises de toutes les grandeurs; **it's about the ~ of an egg/of this room** c'est à peu près de la grosseur d'un œuf/de la grandeur de cette pièce; **he 's about your ~** il est à peu près de ta taille; **to increase in ~** [*plant, tree*] pousser, s'accroître; [*company, town*] s'agrandir; **to cut sth to ~** découper qch à la dimension voulue; **to be of a ~** [*people*] être de la même taille; [*boxes*] être de la même grandeur; **2** (number) (of population, audience) importance *f*; (of class, school, company) effectif *m*; **to increase in ~** [*population*] augmenter; **3** ▶ 1703 Fashn (of jacket, dress, trousers, bra) taille *f*; (of shirt collar) encolure *f*; (of shoes, gloves) pointure *f*; **what ~ are you?**, **what ~ do you take?** (in jacket, trousers, dress) quelle taille faites-vous?; (in shoes) quelle pointure faites-vous?; **what ~ waist are you?** quel est votre tour de taille?; **what ~ shoes do you take?** quelle pointure faites-vous?, vous chaussez du combien?; **to take ~ X** (in clothes) faire du X; **to take ~ X shoes** chausser or faire du X; **I think you need a ~ bigger** je crois qu'il vous faut la taille or la pointure au-dessus; **that jacket is two ~s too big** ce veston est deux tailles trop grand; **'one ~'** 'taille unique'; **try this for ~** lit essayez ceci pour voir si c'est votre taille; fig essayez ceci pour voir si cela vous convient; **4** Tech (substance) (for paper, textiles) apprêt *m*; (for plaster) colle *f*.
II *vtr* **1** classer [qch] selon la grosseur or le calibre, calibrer [*eggs, fruit*]; **2** Tech apprêter [*textile, paper*]; encoller [*plaster*]; **3** [*jeweller*] (make bigger) agrandir [*ring*]; (make smaller) rétrécir [*ring*]; **4** Comput dimensionner [*window*].
IDIOMS **that's about the ~ of it!** c'est à peu près ça!; **to cut sb down to ~** remettre qn à sa place, rabattre le caquet à qn○.
■ **size up**: **~ up [sb/sth]**, **~ [sb/sth] up** jauger, juger [*person*]; évaluer [qch] du regard [*room, surroundings*]; évaluer [*situation*]; mesurer [*problem, difficulty*]; **they seemed to be sizing each other up** ils avaient l'air de se mesurer des yeux.

sizeable /ˈsaɪzəbl/ *adj* [*proportion, section, chunk*] non négligeable; [*amount, sum, salary*] assez important; [*fortune*] assez gros/grosse; [*house, field, town*] assez grand; **to have a ~ majority** avoir assez largement la majorité.

sizeism /ˈsaɪzɪzəm/ *n* discrimination *f* en fonction de la taille des individus.

sizzle /ˈsɪzl/ **I** *n* grésillement *m*.
II *vi* grésiller.

sizzler○ /ˈsɪzlə(r)/ *n* journée *f* caniculaire.

sizzling /ˈsɪzlɪŋ/ *adj* **1** [*fat, sausage*] qui grésille; **a ~ sound** un grésillement; **2**○ (also **~ hot**) [*day, weather*] brûlant, caniculaire; **3**○ (erotic) [*love scene*] osé; [*film*] avec des scènes osées; [*look*] aguichant.

SJ *n*: *abrév* ▶ **Society of Jesus**.

sjambok /ˈʃæmbɒk/ **I** *n* gros fouet *m* en cuir.
II *vtr* fouetter.

ska /skɑː/ *n* Mus ska *m*.

skat /skɑːt/ ▶ 1282 *n*: *jeu de cartes.*

skate /skeɪt/ **I** *n* **1** Sport (ice) patin *m* à glace; (roller) patin *m* à roulettes; **2** Zool (fish) raie *f*.
II *vtr* exécuter [*figure*].
III *vi* patiner (**on, along** sur); **to ~ across** ou **over** traverser [qch] en patins [*pond, lake*].
IDIOMS **get your ~s on**○! grouille-toi○!; **we'd better get our ~s on**○! il va falloir qu'on se grouille○!; **to be skating on thin ice** s'aventurer sur un terrain glissant.
■ **skate over**: **~ over [sth]** fig glisser sur [*problem, issue, fact*].
■ **skate round, skate around**: **~ round [sth]** fig contourner [*requirement, issue*].

skateboard /ˈskeɪtbɔːd/ **I** *n* skateboard *m*, planche *f* à roulettes.
II *vi* faire du skateboard.

skateboarder /ˈskeɪtbɔːdə(r)/ *n* skateur/-euse *m/f*.

skateboarding /ˈskeɪtbɔːdɪŋ/ ▶ 1282 *n* skateboard *m*, planche *f* à roulettes; **to go ~** faire du skateboard.

skater /ˈskeɪtə(r)/ *n* patineur/-euse *m/f*.

skating /ˈskeɪtɪŋ/ ▶ 1282 **I** *n* Sport patinage *m*; **to go ice/roller ~** faire du patin à glace/à roulettes.
II *modif* [*championship, club, competition*] de patinage.

skating: **~ boots** *npl* GB patins *mpl* à glace; **~ rink** *n* (ice) patinoire *f*; (roller-skating) piste *f* de patins à roulettes.

skedaddle○ /skɪˈdædl/ *vi* décamper○, déguerpir.

skeet /skiːt/ ▶ 1282 *n* Sport skeet *m*.

skein /skeɪn/ *n* **1** (of wool) écheveau *m*; **2** (of birds) vol *m*.

skeletal /ˈskelɪtl/ *adj* **1** Anat squelettique; **the ~ structure** le squelette; **~ remains** Med restes de squelette(s); **2** fig squelettique.

skeletal code *n* Comput séquence *f* paramétrable.

skeleton /ˈskelɪtn/ **I** *n* **1** Anat, Constr squelette *m*; **a living** ou **walking ~** un squelette ambulant; **to be reduced to a ~** ne plus avoir que la peau et les os; **2** fig (of plan, novel) grandes lignes *fpl*.
II *modif* fig [*army, staff*] réduit au strict minimum; [*service*] minimum.
IDIOMS **to have a ~ in the cupboard** GB ou **closet** US avoir un cadavre dans le placard○.

skeleton key *n* passe-partout *m inv*.

skep /skep/ *n* (basket) panier *m*; (beehive) ruche *f* (en osier).

skeptic *n, adj* US = **sceptic**.

skeptical *adj* US = **sceptical**.

skeptically *adv* US = **sceptically**.

skepticism *n* US = **scepticism**.

sketch /sketʃ/ **I** *n* **1** (drawing, draft) esquisse *f*; (hasty outline) croquis *m*; **rough ~** ébauche *f*; **2** (comic scene) sketch *m*; **to write ~es** écrire des sketches; **3** (brief account) aperçu *m*; **to give a ~ of sth** donner un aperçu de qch; **a character ~ of sb** une ébauche du personnage de qn.
II *vtr* **1** (make drawing of) faire une esquisse de; (hastily) faire un croquis de; **to ~ the outline of sth** esquisser les contours de qch; **2** (describe briefly) ébaucher [*plans, story*].
III *vi* (as art, hobby) faire des esquisses.
■ **sketch in**: **~ in [sth], ~ [sth] in** (by drawing) ajouter l'esquisse de [*detail, background, trees*]; fig (by describing) donner un aperçu de [*detail, background, reasons*]; **to be hastily/superficially ~ed in** fig être rapidement/superficiellement ébauché.
■ **sketch out ~ out [sth], ~ [sth] out** esquisser [*layout, plan*]; fig ébaucher [*policy, plan, agenda*].

sketchbook /ˈsketʃbʊk/ *n* (for sketching) carnet *m* à croquis; (book of sketches) carnet *m* de croquis.

sketchily /ˈsketʃɪlɪ/ *adv* [*treat, analyze, describe*] superficiellement; [*remember*] vaguement.

sketch: **~ map** *n* carte *f* faite à main levée; **~pad** *n* bloc *m* à dessin.

sketchy /ˈsketʃɪ/ *adj* [*information, details, evidence, report*] insuffisant; [*memory*] vague; [*work*] rapide.

skew /skjuː/ **I** *n* **on the ~** de travers.
II *adj* de travers.
III *vtr* **1** (distort) [*false data, bias*] fausser [*result, survey*]; (deliberately) déformer [*result, report*]; **2** (angle) incliner [*object*]; **3** (divert) faire obliquer [*vehicle, vessel*].
IV *vi* (also **~ round**) [*vehicle, ship*] obliquer.
V skewed *pp adj* **1** (distorted) [*result, research*] faussé (**by** par); (deliberately) déformé (**by** par); **2** [*object*] de travers.

skew: **~ arch** *n* Archit (vault) voûte *f* biaise; (arch) arche *f* biaise; **~bald** *n* cheval *m* pie alezan.

skewer /ˈskjuːə(r)/ **I** *n* (for kebab) brochette *f*; (for joint) broche *f*.
II *vtr* lit embrocher [*joint, carcass*]; mettre [qch] en brochette [*kebab*].

skew: **~-nail** *vtr* clouer [qch] en biais; **~ symmetry** *n* symétrie *f* oblique.

skew-whiff○ /ˌskjuːˈwɪf/ *adj* GB de guingois○.

ski /skiː/ **I** *n* **1** Sport (for snow) ski *m*; (for water) ski *m* (nautique); **cross-country ~s** skis *mpl* de fond; **downhill ~s** skis *mpl* alpins; **on ~s** à ski; **to put on one's ~s** mettre ses skis; **2** Aviat patin *m*.
II *vi* (*prét, pp* **ski'd** ou **skied**) (as hobby) faire du ski; (move on skis) skier; **he ~ed over to the instructor** il a skié vers le moniteur; **to ~ across/down a slope** traverser/descendre une pente à skis; **I ~ a lot** je fais beaucoup de ski.

ski binding *n* fixation *f* (de ski).

skibob /ˈskiːbɒb/ ▶ 1282 **I** *n* ski-bob *m*.
II *vi* faire du ski-bob.

skibobbing /ˈskiːbɒbɪŋ/ ▶ 1282 *n* ski-bob *m*.

ski: **~ boot** *n* chaussure *f* de ski; **~ club** *n* club *m* de ski.

skid /skɪd/ **I** *n* **1** (of car etc) dérapage *m*; **to go** ou **get into a ~** déraper; **to correct a ~** redresser or contrôler un dérapage; **front-wheel ~** dérapage des roues avant; **2** fig (of prices) dérapage *m*; **3** (plank to help move sth) traîneau *m*; **4** (on wheel) patin *m* or sabot *m* d'enrayage.
II *vi* (*p prés etc* **-dd-**) **1** [*car, person, animal*] déraper (**on** sur); **to ~ all over the road** [*car*] déraper en travers de la route; **to ~ into a wall/off the road** déraper et aller se cogner contre un mur/et sortir de la route; **to ~ across the floor** [*person, object*] glisser sur le sol; **to ~ to a halt** [*vehicle*] s'arrêter dans un dérapage; **2** fig [*prices*] déraper.
IDIOMS **to be on** ou **hit** US **the ~s** être sur le déclin; **to put the ~s under sb/sth** (pressurize) obliger qn à faire vite; (wreck, undermine) faire échouer qn/qch.

skid: **~lid**○† *n* casque *m* de moto; **~ mark** *n* trace *f* de pneus; **~pan** *n* GB piste *f* de dérapage; **~proof** *adj* antidérapant.

skid road *n* US **1** (in lumbering) voie *f* de glissement (*pour le transport du bois*); **2** = **skid row**.

skid row○ *n* US *quartier pauvre et délabré de la ville*; **to be/end up on ~** fig être/finir clochard○.

skier /ˈskiːə(r)/ *n* skieur/-euse *m/f*.

skies /skaɪz/ *pl* ▶ **sky**.

skiff /skɪf/ *n* Naut gen petite embarcation *f* légère; (working boat) youyou *m*; (for racing) skiff *m*.

skiffle /ˈskɪfl/ *n*: *musique pop des années 50.*

ski hat *n* bonnet *m* de ski.

skiing /ˈskiːɪŋ/ ▶ 1282 **I** *n* ski *m*; **to go ~** faire du ski; **cross country ~** ski *m* de fond; **downhill ~** ski *m* alpin.
II *modif* [*lesson, equipment*] de ski.

skiing: **~ holiday** *n* vacances *fpl* de neige; **~ instructor** ▶ 1692 *n* moniteur/-trice *m/f* de ski.

ski jump **I** *n* **1** (jump) saut *m* à skis; **2** (ramp) tremplin *m* (de skis); **3** (event) compétition *f* de saut à skis.
II *vi* (once) faire un saut à skis; (as activity) faire du saut à skis.

ski: **~ jumper** *n* Sport concurrent *m* au saut à skis; **~ jumping** *n* ▶ 1282 saut *m* à skis.

skilful GB, **skillful** US /ˈskɪlfl/ *adj* **1** (clever) [*person, team*] habile, adroit; [*performance, portrayal, speech*] excellent; [*leadership*] compétent; **~ at sth** habile en qch; **~ at doing** habile à faire; **~ with his hands/feet** adroit de ses mains/pieds; **2** (requiring talent) [*operation, manoeuvre*] délicat.

skilfully GB, **skillfully** US /ˈskɪlfəlɪ/ *adv* **1** (with ability) [*play, rule, write*] habilement; [*written, painted*] de façon habile; **2** (with agility) adroitement.

skilfulness GB, **skillfulness** US /ˈskɪlflnɪs/ *n* (mental) habileté *f*; (physical) adresse *f*; **her ~ at negotiating** son habileté à négocier; **his ~ at riding** son adresse à cheval; **my ~ as a negotiator/writer** mes talents de négociateur/d'écrivain.

ski lift *n* remontée *f* mécanique.

skill /skɪl/ **I** *n* **1** ¢ (flair) (intellectual) habileté *f*, adresse *f*; (physical) dextérité *f*; **~ at** habileté or adresse à; **~ in** ou **at doing** habileté à faire; **to have ~** être doué; **with ~** avec talent; **a writer of great ~** un écrivain de talent; **2** C (special ability) (acquired) compétence *f*, capacités *fpl*; (innate) aptitude *f*; (practical) technique *f*; (gift) talent *m*; **carpentry is a useful ~** la menuiserie est une compétence utile; **your ~(s) as** vos talents de [*linguist, politician, mechanic*]; **~ at** ou **in doing** talent à faire; **~ at** ou **in sth** compétence en qch.
II skills *npl* (training) connaissances *fpl*; **computer/management ~s** connaissances en informatique/gestion.

Skillcentre /ˈskɪlsentə(r)/ *n* GB centre *m* de formation professionnelle (*pour la réinsertion des demandeurs d'emploi*).

skilled /skɪld/ *adj* **1** (trained) [*labour, worker, job, work*] qualifié; **semi-~** spécialisé; **2** (talented) [*angler, actress, cook, negotiator*] consommé; **to be ~ as** avoir des talents de [*writer, diplomat*]; **to be ~ at doing** savoir faire; **to be ~ in the use of** savoir utiliser [*technique, computers*]; **to be ~ at translation** savoir traduire, être un bon traducteur.

skillet /ˈskɪlɪt/ *n* poêle *f* (à frire).

skillful *adj* US ▶ **skilful**.

skillfully *adv* US ▶ **skilfully**.

skillfulness *n* US ▶ **skilfulness**.

skill: **~ level** *n* niveau *m* de compétence; **~ sharing** *n* Mgmt échange *m* d'expériences; **~s shortage** *n* manque *m* de main-d'œuvre qualifiée.

skim /skɪm/ (*p prés etc* **-mm-**) **I** *vtr* **1** (remove cream) écrémer [*milk*]; (remove scum) écumer [*liquid*]; (remove fat) dégraisser [*sauce, soup*]; **to ~ the fat from the surface of the soup, to ~ the soup to remove the fat** dégraisser la soupe; **to ~ oil from the sea** enlever le pétrole de la surface de la mer par écumage; **2** (touch lightly) [*plane, bird*] raser, frôler [*surface, treetops*]; **the article only ~s the surface of the problem** l'article ne fait qu'effleurer le problème; **3** (read quickly) parcourir [*letter, page*]; **4** (throw on water) faire des ricochets avec [*piece of glass, object*]; **to ~ stones** faire des ricochets avec des cailloux; **5**○ US Tax ne pas déclarer [*part of income*].
II *vi* **1** [*plane, bird*] **to ~ over** ou **across** ou **along sth** raser qch; **2** [*reader*] **to ~ through** ou **over sth** parcourir qch; **in his speech he ~med over the unpalatable**

facts dans son discours il est passé rapidement sur les faits désagréables.
■ **skim off**: **~ off** [**sth**], **~** [**sth**] **off** retirer, enlever [*cream, fat, scum, dross*]; **to ~ off the fat from the sauce** dégraisser la sauce; **~ off the cream from the milk** écrémer le lait.

ski mask *n* cagoule *f* de ski.

skimmer /ˈskɪmə(r)/ *n* **1** Culin écumoire *f*; **2** (bird) bec-en-ciseaux *m*; **3** (for oil spill) écumoire *f*.

skim milk, **skimmed milk** *n* lait *m* écrémé.

skimming /ˈskɪmɪŋ/ *n* écumage *m*.

ski mountaineering ▶1282 *n* ski *m* de haute-montagne.

skimp /skɪmp/ *vi* lésiner; **to ~ on** lésiner sur [*expense, food, materials*]; économiser [*effort, money*]; être avare de [*praise*].

skimpily /ˈskɪmpɪlɪ/ *adv* [*eat*] chichement; [*work, make*] à la va-vite; **~ dressed** en tenue minimale; **a ~ stocked larder** un garde-manger maigrement approvisionné.

skimpiness /ˈskɪmpɪnɪs/ *n* (of portion, allowance, income) maigreur *f*; (of piece of work) insuffisance *f*; **the ~ of her dress** sa tenue minimale.

skimpy /ˈskɪmpɪ/ *adj* [*garment*] minuscule; [*portion, allowance, income*] maigre (*before n*); [*work*] maigre.

skin /skɪn/ **I** *n* **1** (of person) peau *f*; **to have dry/greasy/sensitive ~** avoir la peau sèche/grasse/sensible; **to wear cotton next to the ~** porter du coton à même la peau; **2** (of animal) peau *f*; **leopard/rabbit ~** peau de léopard/de lapin; **3** Culin (of fruit, vegetable, sausage) peau *f*; (of onion) pelure *f*; **remove the ~ before cooking** (of fruit, vegetable) éplucher avant de faire cuire; **4** (on hot milk, cocoa) peau *f*; **5** (of ship, plane) revêtement *m*; **6**○ US (in handshake) paluche○ *f*, pince○ *f*; **give** ou **slip me some ~!** serrons-nous la pince○!; **7**◑ (cigarette paper) papier *m* à cigarette.
II *vtr* (*p prés etc* **-nn-**) **1** Culin dépecer [*animal*]; **2** (graze) **to ~ one's knee/elbow** s'écorcher le genou/coude; **3**○ US (swindle) plumer○; **4**○ US (cut hair) scalper.
IDIOMS **to be nothing but ~ and bones** n'avoir que la peau sur les os; **to get under sb's ~** taper sur les nerfs de qn; **I've got you under my ~** je t'ai dans la peau○; **to have a thick/thin ~** avoir une peau d'éléphant○/l'épiderme sensible○; **to jump out of one's ~** sauter au plafond○; **to save one's (own) ~** sauver sa peau○; **to be** ou **get soaked to the ~** être trempé jusqu'aux os○; **to ~ sb alive** écorcher qn vif; **it's no ~ off my nose** ou **back**○ je m'en balance○; **to keep one's eyes ~ned** rester attentif or vigilant; **by the ~ of one's teeth** [*manage, pass, survive*] de justesse; **to escape** ou **avoid disaster by the ~ of one's teeth** l'échapper belle.

skin cancer ▶1354 *n* cancer *m* de la peau.

skin care I *n* soins *mpl* pour la peau.
II *modif* [*product, range*] de soins pour la peau.

skin cream *n* crème *f* pour la peau.

skin-deep /ˌskɪnˈdiːp/ *adj* superficiel/-ielle.
IDIOMS **beauty is only ~** Prov la beauté est superficielle.

skin: **~ disease** *n* maladie *f* de peau; **~ diver** *n* plongeur/-euse *m/f*; **~ diving** ▶1282 *n* plongée *f* sous-marine; **~ flick**○ *n* film *m* porno○; **~flint** *n* radin/-e○ *m/f*; **~ food** *n* crème *f* nourrissante pour la peau.

skinful○ /ˈskɪnfʊl/ *n* **he's had a ~** il est complètement bourré○.

skin game○ *n* US arnaque◑ *f*.

skin graft *n* **1** ¢ (also **~ grafting**) greffe *f* de la peau; **2** (grafted area) greffon *m* de peau.

skinhead /ˈskɪnhed/ *n* **1** GB (youth) skinhead *m*; **2** US (bald person) chauve *m*; (with close cropped hair) tondu *m*.

skin: **~ lotion** *n* lotion *f* pour la peau; **~ magazine** *n* revue *f* porno○.

skinner /ˈskɪnə(r)/ *n* **1** (dealer) pelletier *m*; **2** (processor) peaussier *m*.

skinny○ /ˈskɪnɪ/ *adj* maigre.
IDIOMS **to get the ~ on sb** US obtenir les ragôts○ sur qn.

skinny: **~-dipping**○ *n* baignade *f* à poil○; **~-ribbed sweater** *n* pull-chaussette *m*.

skin-popping○ /ˈskɪnpɒpɪŋ/ *n* argot des drogués injection *f* sous-cutanée de drogue.

skint○ /skɪnt/ *adj* GB fauché○.

skin: **~ test** *n* cuti-réaction *f*; **~tight** *adj* moulant.

skip /skɪp/ **I** *n* **1** (jump) petit bond *m*; **he gave a little ~** il a fait un petit bond; **2** GB (rubbish container) benne *f*.
II *vtr* (*p prés etc* **-pp-**) **1** (not attend) sauter [*meeting, lunch, bath, class, school*]; **2** (leave out) sauter [*pages, chapter*]; **you can ~ the formalities** vous pouvez sauter les formalités; **~ it**○**!** laisse tomber!; **3**○ (leave) **to ~ town/the country** filer○ de la ville/du pays.
III *vi* (*p prés etc* **-pp-**) **1** (jump) (once) bondir; (several times) sautiller; **to ~ out of the way of sth** ou **out of sth's way** bondir pour éviter qch; **2** (with rope) sauter à la corde; **3** (travel, move) **to ~ from town to town** courir d'une ville à l'autre; **she ~ped from Paris to Lyons** elle a fait un saut de Paris à Lyon; **to ~ from one idea/chapter to another** sauter d'une idée/d'un chapitre à l'autre.
■ **skip over** sauter [*passage, paragraph*].

ski: **~ pants** *n* fuseau *m* (de ski); **~ pass** *n* forfait-skieur *m*.

skipjack /ˈskɪpdʒæk/ *n* (also **~ tuna**) Zool bonite *f* à ventre rayé; (canned) ≈ thon *m* blanc.

ski: **~ plane** *n* avion *m* à skis; **~ pole** *n* = **ski stick**.

skipper /ˈskɪpə(r)/ **I** *n* **1** Naut (of merchant ship) capitaine *m*; (of fishing boat) patron *m*; (of yacht) skipper *m*; **2** gen (leader) chef *m*.
II *vtr* commander.

skipping /ˈskɪpɪŋ/ *n* saut *m* à la corde.

skipping: **~ rhyme** *n* comptine *f* (*pour sauter à la corde*); **~ rope** *n* corde *f* à sauter.

ski: **~ racer** *n* skieur/-euse *m/f* alpin/-e; **~ racing** ▶1282 *n* ski *m* alpin; **~ rack** *n* porte-skis *m inv*; **~ resort** *n* station *f* de ski.

skirl /skɜːl/ *n* son *m* aigu (de la cornemuse).

skirmish /ˈskɜːmɪʃ/ **I** *n* **1** (fight) gen accrochage *m*; Mil escarmouche *f*; **2** (argument) prise *f* de bec○.
II *vi* **1** (fight) gen avoir un accrochage (**with** avec); Mil s'engager dans une escarmouche (**with** avec); **2** (argue) avoir une prise de bec○.

skirt /skɜːt/ ▶1703 **I** *n* **1** Fashn (garment, of dress) jupe *f*; (of frock coat) basques *fpl*; **full/long/straight ~** jupe ample/longue/droite; **2** (of vehicle, machine) jupe *f*; (of sofa) volant *m*; **3**○ (woman) minette○ *f*; **a bit of ~** une sacrée minette○; **to chase ~s** courir le jupon; **4** GB (of beef) hampe *f*; **5** Equit petit quartier *m*.
II skirts *npl* = **outskirts**.
III *vtr* **1** contourner [*wood, village, city*]; **2** esquiver [*problem*].
IDIOMS **to cling to one's mother's ~s** s'accrocher aux jupes de sa mère.
■ **skirt round**, **skirt around**: **~ round** [**sth**] (all contexts) contourner.

skirting /ˈskɜːtɪŋ/ *n* **1** (in room) plinthe *f*; **2** (fabric) tissus *mpl* pour jupes.

skirting board *n* plinthe *f*.

skirt length *n* (piece of fabric) hauteur *f* de jupe; (measurement) longueur *f* d'une jupe; **~s vary** la longueur des jupes varie.

ski: **~ run** *n* piste *f* de ski; **~ slope** *n* piste *f*; **~ stick** *n* bâton *m* de ski; **~ suit** *n* combinaison *f* de ski.

skit /skɪt/ *n* (parody) parodie *f* (**on** de); (sketch) sketch *m* (satirique) (**on, about** sur).

ski: **~ touring** ▶1282 *n* randonnée *f* à skis; **~ tow** *n* téléski *m*; **~ trousers** *n pl* fuseau *m* (de ski).

skitter /ˈskɪtə(r)/ *vi* **1** (also **~ around, ~ about**) (scamper) [*mouse*] trottiner; [*person, horse*] s'agiter; **2** (skim) **to ~ across the water/ground** [*bird, leaf*] voltiger au ras de l'eau/du sol.

skittish /ˈskɪtɪʃ/ *adj* **1** (difficult to handle) capricieux/-ieuse; **2** (playful) joueur/-euse.

skittishly /ˈskɪtɪʃlɪ/ *adv* **1** (unpredictably) d'une manière capricieuse; **2** (playfully) de façon joueuse.

skittle /ˈskɪtl/ ▶1282 **I** *n* quille *f*.
II skittles *npl* (jeu *m* de) quilles *fpl*.

skittle alley *n* piste *f* de jeu de quilles.

skive○ /skaɪv/ GB **I** *n* (easy job) planque○ *f*.
II *vtr* (also **~ off**) **1** (shirk) tirer au flanc○; **2** (be absent) (from school) sécher l'école○; (from work) ne pas aller au boulot○; **3** (leave early) se tirer○.

skiver○ /ˈskaɪvə(r)/ *n* GB (lazy person) tire-au-flanc○ *m inv*; **I was a real ~ (when I was at school)** (quand j'étais à l'école) je n'arrêtais pas de sécher les cours.

skivvy /ˈskɪvɪ/ **I**○ *n* GB lit, fig bonne *f* à tout faire.
II skivvies *npl* US Fashn sous-vêtements *mpl* (masculins).
III○ *vi* GB faire la bonne (**for** pour).

ski: **~ wax** *n* fart *m*; **~ wear** *n* vêtements *mpl* de ski.

skua /ˈskjuːə/ *n* stercoraire *m*; **arctic ~** stercoraire parasite; **great ~** grand stercoraire.

skulduggery○ /skʌlˈdʌɡərɪ/ *n* ¢ magouille○ *f*; **a piece of (political) ~** une magouille○ (politique).

skulk /skʌlk/ *vi* rôder; **he's ~ing around the house** il rôde autour de la maison; **to ~ in/out/off** entrer/sortir/s'éloigner furtivement.
■ **skulk around**, **skulk about** rôder.

skull /skʌl/ *n* **1** Anat crâne *m*; **2**○ (brain) crâne *m*; **get that into your (thick) ~!** mets-toi ça dans le crâne!

skull: **~ and crossbones** *n* (emblem) tête *f* de mort; (flag) pavillon *m* à tête de mort; **~ cap** *n* (Catholic) calotte *f*; (Jewish) kippa *f*.

skunk /skʌŋk/ **I** *n* **1** Zool moufette *f*; **2** (fur) sconse *m*; **3**◑ fig, pej (person) salopard◑ *m*.
II *vtr* US (defeat) battre [qn] à plates coutures○ [*team, opponent*].

sky /skaɪ/ **I** *n* ciel *m*; **clear ~** ciel dégagé; **morning ~** ciel du matin; **night ~** ciel nocturne; **open ~** ciel dégagé; **to scud across the ~** filer dans le ciel; **in(to) the ~** dans le ciel; **the ~ over Paris** le ciel de Paris; **a patch of blue ~** une trouée de ciel bleu; **there are blue skies ahead** fig il y a une éclaircie à l'horizon; **to sleep under the open ~** dormir à la belle étoile.
II skies *npl* Meteorol ciel *m*; fig, littér cieux *mpl*; Art ciels *mpl*; **summer skies** ciel d'été; **a day of rain and cloudy skies** un jour pluvieux et couvert; **the sunny skies of Italy** les cieux ensoleillés d'Italie; **Turner's dramatic skies** les ciels dramatiques de Turner; **to take to the skies** [*plane*] décoller.
III *vtr* Sport **to ~ a ball** faire une chandelle.
IDIOMS **out of a clear blue ~** de façon tout à fait inattendue; **the ~'s the limit** tout est possible; **reach for the ~**○**!** haut les mains!

sky: **~-blue** ▶1104 *n, adj* bleu (*m*) ciel *inv*; **~-blue pink**○ *n, adj* hum bleu (*m*) cerise *inv*; **~cap** *n* US porteur *m* (*dans un aéroport*); **~dive** *vi* faire du saut en chute libre; **~diver** *n* parachutiste *mf* (en chute libre);

~diving ▶1282 *n* parachutisme *m* (en chute libre).

Skye /skaɪ/ ▶1381 *pr n* Skye *f*.

Skye terrier *n* skye-terrier *m*.

sky-high /ˌskaɪˈhaɪ/ **I** *adj* [*prices, rates*] exorbitant.
II *adv* **to rise ~** monter en flèche; **to blow sth ~** faire voler qch en éclats.

skyjack○ /ˈskaɪdʒæk/ **I** *n* (also **~ing**) détournement *m* d'avion.
II *vtr* détourner.

skyjacker /ˈskaɪdʒækə(r)/ *n* pirate *m* de l'air.

skylark /ˈskaɪlɑːk/ **I** *n* alouette *f* des champs.
II○ *vi* chahuter.

sky: **~larking**○ *n* chahut *m*; **~light** *n* fenêtre *f* à tabatière; **~light filter** *n* filtre *m* UV; **~line** *n* (in countryside) ligne *f* d'horizon; (in city) ligne *f* des toits; **~ marshal** *n* US Aviat *agent fédéral chargé de prévenir le détournement des vols commerciaux*; **~ pilot**○† *n* aumônier *m* militaire.

skyrocket /ˈskaɪrɒkɪt/ **I** *n* fusée *f*.
II *vi* [*price, inflation*] monter en flèche.

sky: **~scape** *n* vue *f* du ciel; **~scraper** *n* gratte-ciel *m inv*.

Sky Television *n*: *chaîne privée de télévision britannique transmise par satellite*.

sky: **~ train** *n* aérotrain *m*; **~walk** *n* Archit passerelle *f* aérienne; **~ward(s)** *adj, adv* vers le ciel; **~ways** *npl* US Aviat couloirs *mpl* aériens; **~writing** *n* publicité *f* tracée dans le ciel (*par un avion*).

S & L *n* US *abrév* ▶ **savings and loan (association)**.

slab /slæb/ *n* **1** (piece) (of stone, wood, concrete) dalle *f*; (of meat, cheese, cake) pavé *m*; (of ice) plaque *f*; (of chocolate) (large) plaque *f*; (small) tablette *f*; **butcher's/fishmonger's ~** étal *m* de boucher/de poissonnier; **2**○ (operating table) billard○ *m*, table *f* d'opération; (mortuary table) table *f* d'autopsie.

slab cake *n* pavé *m* (*grand gâteau rectangulaire*).

slack /slæk/ **I** *n* **1** lit (in rope, cable) mou *m*; **to take up the ~ in a rope** tendre une corde; **to take up the ~** fig (take over) prendre le relais; **2** fig (in schedule etc) marge *f*; **3** (coal) poussier *m*; **4** (drop in trade) ralentissement *m* des affaires.
II slacks *npl* pantalon *m*; **a pair of ~s** un pantalon.
III *adj* **1** (careless) [*worker*] peu consciencieux/-ieuse; [*management*] négligent; [*student*] peu appliqué; [*work*] peu soigné; **to be ~ about sth/about doing** négliger qch/négliger de faire; **to get** ou **grow ~** [*worker, discipline, surveillance*] se relâcher; **2** (not busy) [*period, season*] creux/creuse (*after n*); [*demand, sales*] faible; **business is ~** les affaires tournent au ralenti; **the trading** ou **market is ~** le marché est peu actif; **3** (loose, limp) [*cable, rope, body, mouth*] détendu; **to go ~** se détendre.
IV *vi* [*worker*] se relâcher dans son travail.
■ **slack off**: ¶ **~ off** [*business, trade*] diminuer; [*rain*] se calmer; ¶ **~ [sth] off, ~ off [sth]** donner du mou à [*rope*]; desserrer [*nut*].
■ **slack up** [*person*] se relâcher dans son travail.

slacken /ˈslækən/ **I** *vtr* **1** (release) donner du mou à [*rope, cable*]; lâcher [*reins*]; relâcher [*grip, hold, pressure*]; desserrer [*nut*]; **he ~ed his grip on the rope** il a relâché sa prise sur la corde; **2** (reduce) réduire [*pace, speed*]; **3** (loosen) assouplir [*control, rule*].
II *vi* **1** (loosen) [*grip, hold, pressure, rope*] se relâcher; [*nut, bolt*] se desserrer; **his grip on the rope ~ed** il a relâché sa prise sur la corde; **2** (ease off) [*activity, momentum, pace, speed, business, sales, trade*] ralentir; [*pressure, interest*] diminuer; [*rain, gale*] se calmer.
■ **slacken down** [*driver*] ralentir.
■ **slacken off**: ¶ **~ off** [*business, trade, demand*] diminuer; [*gale, rain*] se calmer; ¶ **~ off [sth], ~ [sth] off** donner du mou à [*rope, cable*]; desserrer [*nut, bolt*].
■ **slacken up** [*person*] se relâcher dans son travail.

slackening /ˈslækənɪŋ/ *n* (of grip, discipline, rope, reins, skin) relâchement *m*; (of pace, speed, business, trade, demand, economy) ralentissement *m*; (of tension) diminution *f*.

slacker /ˈslækə(r)/ *n* gen fainéant/-e *m/f*, tire-au-flanc○ *m inv*.

slackness /ˈslæknɪs/ *n* (of worker, student) laisser-aller *m inv*; (in trade, business, economy) stagnation *f*; (in discipline, security) relâchement *m*.

slack: **~ side** *n* brin *m* mou; **~ water** *n* (in lake, river) eaux *fpl* mortes; (at sea) mer *f* étale.

slag /slæg/ *n* **1** (from coal) GB stériles *mpl*; (from metal) scories *fpl*; **2**◐ GB, injur (promiscuous woman) traînée◐ *f* offensive.
■ **slag off**◐: **~ off [sb/sth], ~ [sb/sth] off** GB casser du sucre sur○ [*person*]; critiquer [*government, book, place*].

slag heap *n* terril *m*; **it's ready for the ~** fig c'est bon pour la casse.

slag hole *n* chiot *m* à laitier.

slain /sleɪn/ **I** *pp* ▶ **slay**.
II *n* **the ~** (+ *v pl*) gen les morts *mpl*; (soldiers) les soldats *mpl* tombés au champ d'honneur.

slake /sleɪk/ *vtr* **1** (quench) étancher [*thirst*]; fig assouvir [*desire*]; **2** Chem éteindre [*lime*].

slaked lime *n* chaux *f* éteinte.

slalom /ˈslɑːləm/ ▶1282 *n* slalom *m*; **~ course** piste *f* de slalom; **giant/special ~** slalom géant/spécial; **~ event** épreuve *f* de slalom.

slam /slæm/ **I** *n* **1** (of door) claquement *m*; **to shut sth with a ~** claquer qch; **2** Games chelem *m*; **grand/little** ou **small ~** grand/petit chelem; **3**◐ US (jail) taule◐ *f*.
II *vtr* (*prés p etc* **-mm-**) **1** (shut loudly) [*person*] claquer [*door*]; [*wind*] faire claquer [*door*]; **to ~ sth shut** fermer brutalement qch; **to ~ the door behind one** sortir en claquant la porte derrière soi; **to ~ the door in sb's face** lit, fig claquer la porte au nez de qn; **2** (with violence) **to ~ one's fist/a cup onto the table** taper du poing/poser brutalement une tasse sur la table; **to ~ the ball into the net** renvoyer brutalement la balle dans le filet; **to ~ sb into a wall** jeter qn contre le mur; **to ~ the brakes on, to ~ on the brakes**○ freiner à mort○; **3**○ (criticize) critiquer [qn] violemment (**for** pour; **for doing** pour avoir fait); **to ~ a policy as useless** critiquer violemment une politique pour son inutilité; **to ~ sb as a dictator** critiquer violemment qn comme étant un dictateur; **to be ~med by sb** se faire critiquer violemment par qn; **4**○ (defeat) écraser.
III *vi* (*p prés etc* **-mm-**) **1** [*door, window*] claquer (**against** contre); **to hear the door ~** entendre claquer la porte; **to ~ shut** se refermer en claquant; **2 to ~ into sth** [*vehicle*] s'écraser contre qch; [*boxer, body*] heurter violemment qch.
■ **slam down**: ¶ **~ down** [*heavy object, lid*] s'écraser (**onto** sur); ¶ **~ down [sth], ~ [sth] down** raccrocher violemment [*receiver, phone*]; refermer violemment [*lid, car bonnet*]; jeter brutalement [*object, book*] (**on, onto** sur).

slam-bang○ /ˌslæmˈbæŋ/ **I** *adj* US **1** (loud) bruyant; **2** (all-out) [*effort*] maximum.
II *adv* **to walk** ou **go ~ into sth** enfoncer violemment qch.

slam-dunk○ /ˈslæmdʌŋk/ *n* US Sport lancer *m* coulé.

slammer○ /ˈslæmə(r)/ *n* **the ~** la taule○. ▶ **tequila slammer**.

slander /ˈslɑːndə(r), US ˈslæn-/ **I** *n* **1 C** (slanderous statement) calomnie *f* (**on** sur); **2** ¢ Jur diffamation *f* orale; **to sue sb for ~** intenter un procès en diffamation contre qn.
II *vtr* gen calomnier; Jur diffamer.

slanderer /ˈslɑːndərə(r), US ˈslæn-/ *n* gen calomniateur/-trice *m/f*; Jur diffamateur/-trice *m/f*.

slanderous /ˈslɑːndərəs, US ˈslæn-/ *adj* gen calomnieux/-ieuse; Jur diffamatoire.

slanderously /ˈslɑːndərəslɪ, US ˈslæn-/ *adv* gen calomnieusement; Jur de façon diffamatoire.

slang /slæŋ/ **I** *n* argot *m*; **army/school ~** argot des casernes/des écoles.
II *modif* **~ phrase, ~ expression** argotisme *m*.
III○ *vtr* injurier.

slanginess /ˈslæŋɪnɪs/ *n* caractère *m* argotique.

slanging match *n* GB prise *f* de bec○.

slangy○ /ˈslæŋɪ/ *adj* [*style*] argotique.

slant /slɑːnt, US slænt/ **I** *n* **1** (perspective) point *m* de vue (**on** sur); **with a European ~** d'un point de vue européen; **to give a new ~ on sth** offrir un angle nouveau sur qch; **2** péj (bias) tendance *f*; **with a definite/right-wing ~** avec une tendance marquée/de droite; **3** (slope) pente *f*; **the floor has a ~** le plancher est en pente; **to hang at** ou **on a ~** [*painting*] être de travers; **4** Print barre *f* oblique.
II *vtr* **1** (twist) présenter [qch] avec parti pris [*story, facts*]; **2** (lean) incliner [*object*].
III *vi* [*floor, ground*] être en pente; [*handwriting*] pencher (**to** vers); [*painting*] être de travers; **rays of sun ~ed through the trees/the window** des rayons de soleil passaient obliquement à travers les arbres/la fenêtre.
IV slanting *pres p adj* [*roof, floor*] en pente; **~ing rain** pluie *f* qui tombe en oblique; **~ing eyes** yeux *mpl* bridés.

slanted /ˈslɑːntɪd, US ˈslæn-/ *adj* **1** (biased) orienté (**to, towards** vers); **2** (sloping) en pente.

slant-eyed○ /ˌslɑːntˈaɪd, US ˌslæn-/ *adj* injur chinetoque○ offensive.

slantwise /ˈslɑːntwaɪz, US ˈslæn-/ **I** *adj* **in a ~ direction** de biais.
II *adv* (also **slantways**) en biais.

slap /slæp/ **I** *n* **1** (blow) tape *f* (**on** sur); (stronger) claque *f* (**on** sur); **a ~ on the face** une gifle; **the ~ of the waves against sth** le clapotis des vagues contre qch; **it was a real ~ in the face for him** fig il a reçu une claque; **to give sb a ~ on the back** (friendly gesture) donner à qn une tape dans le dos; fig (in congratulation) féliciter qn; **2** (sound of blow) (bruit *m* d'une) claque *f*.
II *adv* = **slap bang**.
III *vtr* (*p prés etc* **-pp-**) **1** (hit) donner une tape à [*person, animal*]; **to ~ sb for/for doing** gifler qn pour/pour avoir fait; **to ~ sb on the arm/leg, to ~ sb's arm/leg** donner une tape à qn sur le bras/la jambe; **to ~ sb across the face** gifler qn; **to ~ a child's bottom** donner une tape sur les fesses d'un enfant; **to ~ sb on the back** (in friendly way) donner une (grande) claque or tape dans le dos de qn; fig (congratulate) féliciter qn; **to ~ one's thighs** se taper sur les cuisses; **to ~ sb in the face** lit gifler qn; fig donner une claque à qn; **to ~ sb on the wrist** fig taper sur les doigts de qn; **2** (put) **he ~ped the money (down) on the table** il a flanqué○ l'argent sur la table; **he ~ped some paint on the wall** il a flanqué○ quelques coups de pinceau sur le mur; **she ~ped some make-up on her face** elle s'est maquillée en vitesse; **they ~ped**○ **50p on the price** ils ont gonflé○ le prix de 50 pence.
■ **slap around**○: **~ [sb] around** donner quelques coups à [*person*].
■ **slap down**: ¶ **~ [sth] down, ~ down [sth]** (put) poser brusquement [*book, money*]; **to ~ sth down on** flanquer○ qch sur [*table, counter*]; ¶ **~ [sb] down** rembarrer.
■ **slap on**○: **~ [sth] on, ~ on [sth] 1** (apply) flanquer○ [*paint*]; mettre [qch] en

vitesse [*make-up*]; **2** (add to price) **they ~ped on 50p** ils ont gonflé○ le prix de 50 pence.

slap bang○ /ˌslæpˈbæŋ/ *adv* **he ran ~ into the wall** il s'est cogné en plein dans le mur en courant; **~ in the middle (of)** au beau milieu (de).

slapdash○ /ˈslæpdæʃ/ *adj* [*person*] brouillon/-onne○; [*work*] bâclé○, fait à la va-vite; **in a ~ way** à la va-vite.

slaphappy○ /ˌslæpˈhæpɪ/ *adj* **1** (careless) insouciant; **2** (punch-drunk) sonné○, groggy.

slaphead○ /ˈslæphed/ *n* péj, hum chauve *m*.

slapstick /ˈslæpstɪk/ **I** *n* comique *m* tarte à la crème, slapstick *m*.
II *modif* [*comedy, routine*] tarte à la crème *inv*.

slap-up○ /ˈslæpʌp/ *adj* GB [*meal*] bon/bonne; **to go out for a ~ meal** aller faire un bon gueuleton○.

slash /slæʃ/ **I** *n* **1** (wound) balafre *f* (**on** à); **2** (cut) (in fabric, seat, tyre) lacération *f*; (in painting, wood) entaille *f*; **3** Print barre *f* oblique; **4** Comm, Fin réduction *f*; **a 10% ~ in prices** une réduction de 10% sur les prix; **5** Fashn (in skirt) fente *f*; (in sleeve) crevé *m*; **6**○ GB **to have/go for a ~** (urinate) pisser○/aller pisser○, uriner/aller uriner; **7** (sword stroke) coup *m* d'épée.
II *vtr* **1** (wound) balafrer [*cheek*]; faire une balafre à [*person*]; couper [*throat*]; [*knife*] entailler [*face*]; **he ~ed me across the face** il m'a balafré le visage; **to ~ one's wrists** se tailler les veines; **2** (cut) taillader [*painting, fabric, tyres*]; trancher [*cord*]; **to ~ one's way through** se tailler un chemin à travers [*undergrowth*]; **3** (reduce) réduire [qch] (considérablement), sacrifier [*price*]; réduire [qch] (considérablement) [*amount, bill, cost, spending, size*]; **to ~ 40% off the price** réduire le prix de 40%; **4** Fashn faire des crevés dans [*sleeve*]; fendre [*skirt*]; **a ~ed sleeve** une manche à crevés; **5**○ (criticize) démolir○, critiquer [*book, plan*].
III *vi* **to ~ at** cingler [*grass*]; frapper [qch] d'un grand coup [*ball*]; **to ~ at sb with a sword** donner un grand coup d'épée à qn; **to ~ through** trancher [*cord*]; taillader [*fabric*].
■ **slash down**: **~ [sth] down, ~ down [sth]** faucher [*grass*]; faire tomber [*opponent*].
■ **slash open**: **~ [sth] open, ~ open [sth]** balafrer [*face*]; éventrer [*packet, sack*].

slash: **~-and-burn cultivation** *n* Agric culture *f* sur brûlis; **~-and-burn method** *n* Agric brûlis *m*; **~er film, ~er movie** US○ *n* film *m* d'horreur sanglant; **~ pocket** *n* poche *f* fendue.

slat /slæt/ *n* **1** (of shutter, blind) lamelle *f*; (of table, bench, bed) lame *f*; **2** Aviat bec *m* de sécurité.

slate /sleɪt/ **I** *n* **1** (rock) ardoise *f*; **made of ~** en ardoise; **2** (piece, tablet) ardoise *f*; **a roof ~** une ardoise; **3** US Pol liste *f* de candidature.
II *modif* [*roof, floor*] d'ardoises; [*quarry, mining*] d'ardoise.
III *vtr* **1** lit couvrir [qch] d'ardoises [*roof*]; **2**○ GB (criticize) [*press, critic*] taper sur○ [*play, film, politician, policy*] (**for** pour); [*boss, teacher*] blâmer [*worker, pupil*] (**for** pour); **3** US Pol mettre [qn] sur la liste [*candidate*]; **4** US (be expected) **to be ~d to go far** [*person*] avoir de fortes chances d'aller loin.
IDIOMS **to put sth on the ~**○ mettre qch sur l'ardoise○; **to start again with a clean ~** repartir à zéro; **to wipe the ~ clean** faire table rase.

slate: **~ blue** ▶ 1104 *n, adj* bleu (*m*) ardoise *inv*; **~-coloured** GB, **~-colored** US ▶ 1104 *adj* (couleur) ardoise *inv*; **~ grey** GB, **~ gray** US ▶ 1104 *n, adj* gris (*m*) ardoise *inv*.

slater /ˈsleɪtə(r)/ ▶ 1692 *n* **1** (roofer) couvreur-ardoisier *m*; **2** (quarrier) ardoisier *m*; **3** Zool cloporte *m*.

slating /ˈsleɪtɪŋ/ *n* **1** (laying slates) pose *f* des ardoises; **2** (material) couverture *f* d'ardoises; **3**○ GB (criticism) **to give sb a ~** [*critic*] démolir qn○; [*boss*] passer un savon à qn○; **to get a ~ from sb** (from critic) se faire démolir par qn○; (from boss) recevoir un savon de la part de qn○.

slatted /ˈslætɪd/ *adj* [*shelving, table*] en lames; [*blind, shutter*] à lamelles.

slattern† /ˈslætən/ *n* péj souillon *f*.

slatternly† /ˈslætənlɪ/ *adj* péj [*woman, appearance*] négligé; [*behaviour, clothes*] de souillon.

slaty /ˈsleɪtɪ/ *adj* **1** [*colour, blue, grey*] ardoise *inv*; **2** (containing slate) qui contient de l'ardoise.

slaughter /ˈslɔːtə(r)/ **I** *n* **1** (in butchery) abattage *m*; **to send sth for ~** envoyer qch à l'abattage; **to go to ~** aller à l'abattoir; **2** (massacre) massacre *m*, boucherie○ *f*; **~ on the roads** carnage *m* sur les routes; **3** Sport fig massacre *m*.
II *vtr* **1** (in butchery) abattre; **2** (massacre) massacrer; **3**○ Sport journ écraser.
IDIOMS **like a lamb to the ~** comme un agneau à l'abattoir.

slaughterer /ˈslɔːtərə(r)/ ▶ 1692 *n* (in butchery) abatteur *m* de bétail.

slaughterhouse /ˈslɔːtəhaʊs/ *n* abattoir *m*.

Slav /slɑːv, US slæv/ **I** *n* Slave *mf*.
II *adj* slave.

slave /sleɪv/ **I** *n* **1** (servant) esclave *mf*; **2** fig (victim) **to be a ~ to** ou **of** être l'esclave de [*fashion, habit*]; **a ~ to convention** l'esclave des conventions.
II *modif* **1** [*colony, owner, revolt*] d'esclaves; [*market*] aux esclaves; **2** Comput [*computer, station*] asservi.
III *vi* (also **~ away**) travailler comme un forçat, trimer○; **to ~ away from morning to night** trimer○ du matin au soir; **to ~ (away) at housework/at one's job** s'escrimer à faire le ménage/sur son travail; **to ~ over** s'escrimer sur [*accounts, housework*].
IDIOMS **to work like a ~** travailler comme un forçat.

slave: **~ ant** *n* fourmi *f* cendrée; **Slave Coast** *pr n* Hist Côte *f* des Esclaves; **~ cylinder** *n* cylindre *m* de frein (hydraulique); **~ driver** *n* lit Hist surveillant *m* d'esclaves; fig négrier/-ière *m/f* fig; **~holder** *n* propriétaire *mf* d'esclaves.

slave labour *n* (activity) travail *m* de forçat; (manpower) main-d'œuvre *f* esclave.

slaver[1] /ˈsleɪvə(r)/ *n* Hist **1** (dealer) négrier *m*; **2** (ship) navire *m* négrier.

slaver[2] /slævə(r)/ **I** *n* salive *f*.
II *vi* (drool) baver; **to ~ over** [*animal*] saliver devant [*meat, bone*]; péj ou hum [*person*] baver devant [*dish*]; **to ~ over the prospect of doing** baver à l'idée de faire; **he was ~ing over her** il bavait d'envie en la regardant.

slavery /ˈsleɪvərɪ/ *n* **1** (practice, condition) esclavage *m*; **to be sold into ~** être vendu comme esclave; **2** fig (devotion) **~ to** asservissement à [*fashion, convention, passion*].

slave: **~ ship** *n* (vaisseau *m*) négrier *m*; **Slave State** *n* US Hist État *m* esclavagiste.

slave trade *n* commerce *m* des esclaves; **the African ~** la traite des Noirs.

slave: **~-trader** *n* marchand *m* d'esclaves, pej négrier *m*; **~-trading** *n* commerce *m* des esclaves; (in Africa) traite *f* des Noirs.

slavey○ /ˈsleɪvɪ/ *n* GB bon(n)iche○ *f*.

Slavic /ˈslɑːvɪk, US ˈslæv-/ *adj* [*country, name*] slave.

slavish /ˈsleɪvɪʃ/ *adj* **1** (servile) [*devotion, adherence, person*] servile; **2** (unoriginal) [*imitation, translation, reworking*] servile.

slavishly /ˈsleɪvɪʃlɪ/ *adv* servilement.

Slavonic /sləˈvɒnɪk/ ▶ 1402 *n, adj* slave (*m*).

slaw /slɔː/ *n* US = **coleslaw**.

slay /sleɪ/ *vtr* (*prét* **slew**, **slayed**; *pp* **slain**) **1** (*prét* **slew**; *pp* **slain**) littér (kill) faire périr [*enemy*]; pourfendre [*dragon*]; **2**○ (*prét, pp* **slayed**) fig (impress) emballer○ [*audience*]; (amuse) faire mourir de rire [*audience, crowd*].

slayer /ˈsleɪə(r)/ *n* tueur *m*; **dragon ~** pourfendeur *m* de dragon.

SLD GB Pol (*abrév* = **Social and Liberal Democrat**) **I** *n* parti *m* Démocrate Socio-Libéral.
II *modif* [*MP*] du parti Démocrate Socio-Libéral; [*voter*] pour le parti Démocrate Socio-Libéral.

sleaze○ /sliːz/ *n* péj **1** (pornography) pornographie *f*; **2** (corruption) corruption *f*; **3** (sordid nature) (of newspaper, novel) caractère *m* scabreux; (of place) caractère *m* sordide.

sleazebag◑ /ˈsliːzbæg/, **sleazeball**◑ /ˈsliːzbɔːl/ *n* US péj fumier◑ *m*, ordure◑ *f*.

sleazy○ /ˈsliːzɪ/ *adj* péj [*club, area, character*] louche; [*story, aspect*] scabreux/-euse; [*café, hotel*] borgne; **a ~ joint**○ un bouiboui○.

sled /sled/ **I** *n* luge *f*; (pulled) traîneau *m*.
II *vi* (*p prés etc* **-dd-**) faire de la luge; **to go ~ding** faire de la luge.
IDIOMS **it was hard ~ding** US c'était dur.

sled dog *n* US chien *m* de traîneau.

sledge /sledʒ/ **I** *n* **1** GB luge *f*; **2** (pulled) traîneau *m*.
II *vtr* **1** lit transporter [qch] en traîneau; **2**○ fig Austral (rubbish) descendre [qn/qch] en flammes.
III *vi* GB faire de la luge; **to go sledging** faire de la luge.

sledgehammer /ˈsledʒhæmə(r)/ *n* masse *f*.
IDIOMS **to take a ~ to crack a nut** écraser une mouche avec un gant de boxe.

sleek /sliːk/ *adj* **1** (glossy) [*hair*] lisse et brillant; [*animal*] au poil lisse et brillant; **2** (smooth) [*elegance*] raffiné; [*shape*] élégant; [*figure, body*] mince et harmonieux/-ieuse; **3** (prosperous-looking) [*person*] à l'air cossu.
■ **sleek back**: **~ back [sth], ~ [sth] back** lisser [qch] en arrière [*hair*].

sleekness /ˈskiːknɪs/ *n* (of hair) brillant *m*; (of line) pureté *f*.

sleep /sliːp/ **I** *n* **1** sommeil *m*; **to go** ou **get to ~** s'endormir; **to go back to ~** se rendormir; **to send** ou **put sb to ~** [*heat, speech, tablet*] endormir qn; **to get some ~** ou **to have a ~** gen dormir; (have a nap) faire un petit somme; **my leg has gone to ~**○ j'ai la jambe engourdie; **to be in a deep ~** dormir profondément; **I didn't get any ~** ou **a wink of ~ last night** j'ai passé une nuit blanche, je n'ai pas fermé l'œil de la nuit; **I need my ~** il me faut beaucoup de sommeil; **how much ~ did you get last night?** tu as dormi combien d'heures la nuit dernière?; **to have a good night's ~** passer une bonne nuit, bien dormir; **you'll feel much better after a ~** ça te fera du bien de dormir; **to sing/rock a baby to ~** chanter une chanson à/bercer un bébé jusqu'à ce qu'il s'endorme; **to talk in one's ~** parler dans son sommeil; **to walk in one's ~** marcher en dormant; **I could do it in my ~!** je pourrais le faire les yeux fermés!; **she's losing ~ over it** ça l'empêche de dormir; **I'm not going to lose any ~ over that!** ce n'est pas ça qui va m'empêcher de dormir!; **don't lose any ~ over it!** ne t'en fais pas pour ça!, il ne faut pas que ça t'empêche de dormir!; **he rubbed the ~ from his eyes** il a frotté ses paupières collées par le sommeil; **2** Vet **to put an animal to ~** euph faire piquer un animal.
II *vtr* (*prét, pp* **slept**) **the house ~s six (people)** on peut loger or coucher six personnes dans la maison; **the caravan ~s four (people)** on peut coucher à quatre (personnes) dans la caravane; **'apartment, ~s 6'** (in ad) appartement 6 personnes.
III *vi* (*prét, pp* **slept**) **1** dormir; **to ~ deeply** ou **soundly** dormir profondément; **to ~ soundly** (without worry) dormir tranquille, dormir sur ses deux oreilles; **to ~ around the clock** faire le tour du

cadran; **to ~ on one's feet** dormir debout; **~ tight!** dors bien!; **2** (stay night) coucher; **to ~ at a friend's house** coucher chez un ami; **you'll have to ~ on the sofa** il va falloir que tu dormes or couches sur le canapé; **to ~ with sb** euph (have sex) coucher avec qn.

IDIOMS **the big ~** le dernier sommeil, le sommeil des morts; **to cry oneself to ~** pleurer jusqu'à épuisement; **to ~ like a log** ou **top** dormir comme une souche or un loir.

■ **sleep around**○ coucher à droite et à gauche○.

■ **sleep in 1** (stay in bed late) faire la grasse matinée; (oversleep) dormir trop tard; **2** US (live in) [*maid, servant*] être logé sur place.

■ **sleep off**: **~ off [sth], ~ [sth] off** dormir pour faire passer [*headache, hangover*]; **to ~ it off**○ cuver son vin○.

■ **sleep on**: **~ on** continuer à dormir; **she slept on until midday** elle a fait la grasse matinée or elle a dormi jusqu'à midi; **Louis slept on for two more hours** Louis a dormi encore deux heures; **to ~ on a decision/problem** attendre le lendemain pour prendre une décision/résoudre un problème; **it's a tricky decision to make and I'd like to ~ on it** c'est une décision difficile à prendre, et j'aimerais bien dormir dessus; **don't decide now, ~ on it first** ne décide pas maintenant, attends jusqu'à demain, la nuit te portera conseil.

■ **sleep out 1** (in the open) dormir or coucher à la belle étoile; **2** US (live out) [*servant*] ne pas loger sur place.

■ **sleep through**: **I slept through until midday** j'ai dormi jusqu'à midi; **she slept (right) through the storm** l'orage ne l'a pas réveillée.

■ **sleep over** passer la nuit, coucher; **to ~ over at sb's house** passer la nuit or coucher chez qn.

sleeper /ˈsliːpə(r)/ **I** *n* **1** dormeur/-euse *m/f*; **to be a sound ~** avoir le sommeil profond; **the baby is not a good ~** le bébé se réveille beaucoup; **2** Rail (berth) couchette *f*; (sleeping car) wagon-lit *m*, voiture-lit *f*; (train) train-couchettes *m inv*; **3** GB (on railway track) traverse *f*; **4** GB (earring) dormeuse *f*; **5**○ US (successful book, film etc) succès *m* à retardement; **6** (spy) espion/-ionne *m/f* en sommeil.

II sleepers *npl* US grenouillière *f*, pyjama *m* pour bébé.

sleepily /ˈsliːpɪlɪ/ *adv* [*say*] d'un ton endormi; [*look, move*] d'un air endormi.

sleepiness /ˈsliːpɪnɪs/ *n* (of person) envie *f* de dormir, sommeil *m*; (of village, town) somnolence *f*, torpeur *f*.

sleeping /ˈsliːpɪŋ/ *adj* [*person, animal*] qui dort, endormi; **what are the ~ arrangements for our visitors?** où est-ce que nos invités vont dormir?

IDIOMS **let ~ dogs lie** il ne faut pas réveiller le chat qui dort.

sleeping: **~ bag** *n* sac *m* de couchage; **~ car** *n* voiture-lit *f*, wagon-lit *m*; **~ draught**† *n* soporifique *m*; **~ partner** *n* GB Comm commanditaire *mf*; **~ pill** *n* somnifère *m*; **~ policeman**○ *n* GB ralentisseur *m*, gendarme *m* couché; **~ quarters** *npl* (in house) chambres *fpl*; (in barracks) chambrée *f*; (dormitory) dortoir *m*; **~ sickness** ▶ 1354 *n* maladie *f* du sommeil; **~ tablet** *n* somnifère *m*.

sleep learning *n* hypnopédie *f*.

sleepless /ˈsliːplɪs/ *adj* [*person*] incapable de trouver le sommeil; [*vigil, hours*] sans sommeil; **to pass a ~ night** passer une nuit blanche; **she had spent many ~ nights worrying about it** elle avait passé plus d'une nuit blanche à s'inquiéter.

sleeplessly /ˈsliːplɪslɪ/ *adv* sans dormir, sans réussir à trouver le sommeil.

sleeplessness /ˈsliːplɪsnɪs/ *n* insomnie *f*.

sleep: **~walk** *vi* marcher en dormant, être somnambule; **~walker** *n* somnambule *mf*; **~walking** *n* somnambulisme *m*; **~wear** *n* ¢ vêtements *mpl* de nuit.

sleepy /ˈsliːpɪ/ *adj* [*person*] qui a sommeil, qui a envie de dormir; [*voice, town, village*] endormi, somnolent; **to feel** ou **be ~** avoir envie de dormir, avoir sommeil; **to make sb ~** [*fresh air*] donner envie de dormir à qn; [*wine*] endormir qn, assoupir qn.

sleepyhead○ /ˈsliːpɪhed/ *n* endormi/-e *m/f*; **'get up, ~!'** 'debout, paresseux/-euse!'

sleepyheaded○ /ˌsliːpɪˈhedɪd/ *adj* à moitié endormi.

sleet /sliːt/ **I** *n* neige *f* fondue.

II *v impers* **it's ~ing** il tombe de la neige fondue.

sleety /ˈsliːtɪ/ *adj* [*showers, rain*] mêlé de neige.

sleeve /sliːv/ **I** *n* **1** (of garment) manche *f*; **to pull** ou **tug at sb's ~** tirer qn par la manche; **to roll up one's ~s** lit, fig retrousser ses manches; **2** (of record) pochette *f*; (of CD) boîtier *m*; **3** Tech (inner) chemise *f*; (outer) gaine *f*; (short outer) manchon *m*.

II -sleeved (*dans composés*) **long-/short-~d** à manches longues/courtes.

IDIOMS **to laugh up one's ~** rire sous cape; **to wear one's heart on one's ~** laisser voir ses sentiments; **to have an ace up one's ~** fig avoir un atout en réserve; **to have something up one's ~** avoir quelque chose en réserve; **to have a proposal up one's ~** fig avoir une proposition en réserve; **to have a few tricks up one's ~** fig avoir plus d'un tour dans son sac; **what's he got up his ~?** qu'est-ce qu'il nous réserve?

sleeve: **~ board** *n* jeannette *f*; **~ coupling** *n* Tech accouplement *m* à manchon; **~ design** *n* maquette *f* de pochette de disque; **~ designer** ▶ 1692 *n* maquettiste *mf*; **~ joint** *n* Tech assemblage *m* à manchon.

sleeveless /ˈsliːvlɪs/ *adj* sans manches.

sleeve: **~ notes** *npl* texte *m* (sur la pochette d'un disque); **~ valve** *n* soupape *f* à chemise.

sleigh /sleɪ/ **I** *n* traîneau *m*.

II *vi* aller en traîneau.

sleigh: **~ bell** *n* grelot *m* de traîneau; **~ ride** *n* promenade *f* en traîneau.

sleight of hand /ˌslaɪtəvˈhænd/ *n* **1** (dexterity) dextérité *f*; **2** (cunning) agilité *f*; **3** (trick) tour *m* de passe-passe.

slender /ˈslendə(r)/ *adj* **1** (thin) [*person*] mince; [*waist*] fin; [*finger*] effilé; [*neck*] gracile; [*stem, arch*] élancé; **2** (slight) [*majority, margin*] faible (*before n*); **to win by a ~ margin** gagner de justesse; **3** (meagre) [*income, means*] modeste, maigre (*before n*).

slenderize /ˈslendəraɪz/ US **I** *vtr* amincir.

II *vi* mincir.

slenderly /ˈslendəlɪ/ *adv* **~ built** mince.

slenderness /ˈslendənɪs/ *n* **1** (of person) sveltesse *f*; (of part of body) minceur *f*; **2** (of majority, margin) étroitesse *f*.

slept /slept/ *prét, pp* ▶ **sleep**.

sleuth /sluːθ/ *n* limier *m*, détective *m*.

S-level *n* GB Sch (*abrév* = **Special Level**) *épreuve optionnelle d'un niveau supérieur que l'on passe à l'âge de dix-huit ans.*

slew /sluː/ **I** *pp* ▶ **slay**.

II *n* **1**○ (pile) **a ~ of** un tas de○; **2** (bog) marécage *m*.

III *vtr* faire déraper [*vehicle*]; faire pivoter [*mast*].

IV *vi* [*vehicle*] déraper; [*mast*] pivoter.

slewed○ /sluːd/ *adj* soûl○.

slice /slaɪs/ **I** *n* **1** (portion) (of bread, meat, cheese, fish) tranche *f*; (of pie, tart) part *f*; (of lemon, cucumber, sausage) rondelle *f*; **to cut sth into ~s** couper qch en tranches [*loaf, meat*]; couper qch en rondelles [*cucumber, sausage*]; **2** (proportion) (of income, profits, market, aid) part *f*; (of territory, population) partie *f*; **3** Culin (utensil) spatule *f*; **4** Sport (stroke, shot) slice *m*; **forehand ~** coup *m* droit; **back-hand ~** revers *m* slicé.

II *vtr* **1** (section) couper [qch] (en tranches) [*loaf, roast, onion*]; couper [qch] en rondelles [*lemon, sausage, cucumber*]; **2** (cleave) fendre [*water, air*]; **to ~ sb's throat/cheek** trancher la gorge/joue à qn; **3** Sport (as tactic) slicer, couper [*ball*].

III *vi* [*knife, blade, fin, shape*] **to ~ through** fendre [*water, air*]; trancher [*timber, rope, meat*]; **the metal ~d into her ankle** le métal lui a pénétré la cheville.

IV sliced *pp adj* [*meat, peaches*] coupé en tranches; [*cucumber, salami*] coupé en rondelles; **thinly/thickly ~d** [*meat, bread*] en tranches minces/épaisses; **50g mushrooms, thinly ~d** 50 g de champignons, finement émincés.

■ **slice off**: **~ off [sth], ~ [sth] off** détacher [*bodypart, section*]; **the propeller ~d his arm/head off** il a eu le bras coupé/la tête tranchée par l'hélice.

■ **slice up**: **~ [sth] up, ~ up [sth]** couper [qch] en tranches [*meat, cheese, vegetable*]; couper [qch] en rondelles [*salami, lemon*].

slice bar *n* ringard *m* (de chaufferie).

sliced bread *n* pain *m* en tranches.

IDIOMS **it's the best** ou **greatest thing since ~○!** hum on n'a pas fait mieux depuis l'invention du fil à couper le beurre.

sliced loaf *n* pain *m* en tranches.

slice of life Cin, Theat **I** *n* tranche *f* de vie.

II slice-of-life *modif* [*play, naturalism*] réaliste.

slick /slɪk/ **I** *n* **1** (oil) (on water) nappe *f* de pétrole; (on shore) marée *f* noire; **2** (also **~ tyre** GB, **~ tire** US) slick *m*; **3** US (magazine) magazine *m* de luxe.

II *adj* **1** (adeptly executed) [*production, performance, campaign, handling*] habile; [*operation, deal, takeover*] mené rondement; **it's a ~ piece of work** c'est du travail vite fait bien fait○; **2** péj (superficial) [*programme, publication, production*] qui a un éclat plutôt superficiel; **3** péj (insincere) [*person*] roublard○; [*answer, chat*] astucieux/-ieuse; [*excuse*] facile; **~ salesman** vendeur qui a du bagou○; **a ~ operator**○ un rusé, un malin; **4** surtout US (slippery) [*road, surface*] glissant; [*hair*] lissé.

■ **slick back**: **~ [sth] back, ~ back [sth]** lisser [qch] en arrière [*hair*]; **~ed-back hair** des cheveux gominés.

■ **slick down**: **~ [sth] down, ~ down [sth]** (with hand, comb) se lisser [*hair*]; (with cream) se gominer [*hair*].

slicker /ˈslɪkə(r)/ *n* US (raincoat) ciré *m*.

slickly /ˈslɪklɪ/ *adv* parfois péj **1** (cleverly) [*presented, produced*] de manière habile; [*worded, formulated*] habilement; **2** (smoothly) [*carried out, performed*] efficacement; **3** (stylishly) [*dressed*] de manière branchée○.

slickness /ˈslɪknɪs/ *n* **1** (cleverness) (of film, production, style) brillant *m*; (of answer, person) habileté *f*; (of salesman) bagou○ *m*; **2** (smoothness) (of magician) dextérité *f*; (of operation) efficacité *f*.

slide /slaɪd/ **I** *n* **1** (chute) (in playground, factory) toboggan *m*; (for logs) glissoir *m*; (on ice) glissoire *f*; **escape/water ~** toboggan d'évacuation/aquatique; **2** Phot diapositive *f*; **holiday ~s** diapositives de vacances; **lecture with ~s** conférence avec projections; **3** (microscope plate) lame *f* porte-objet; **4** GB (hair clip) barrette *f*; **5** Mus (slur) coulé *m*; **6** Mus (trombone) coulisse *f*; **7** fig (decline) baisse *f* (**in** de).

II *vtr* (*prét, pp* **slid**) (move) faire glisser [*bolt, component*]; **to ~ sth forward** faire glisser quelque chose vers l'avant; **they slid the boat into the water** ils ont fait glisser le bateau dans l'eau; **to ~ a letter into an envelope/under the door** glisser une lettre dans une enveloppe/sous la porte; **to ~ a key into one's pocket** glisser une clé dans sa poche; **to ~ a sword out of its scabbard** sortir une épée de son fourreau.

III *vi* (*prét, pp* **slid**) **1** (also **~ about** GB, **~ around**) (slip) [*car, person*] glisser, partir en glissade (**into** dans; **on** sur); **to ~ off** glisser de [*roof, table, deck*]; sortir de [*road*]; **2** (move) **to ~ down** dévaler [*slope*]; glisser le long de [*bannister*]; **to ~ in and out** [*drawer, component*] coulisser; **to ~ up and down** [*window*] coulisser de bas en haut; **to ~ out of/into** [*person*] se glisser hors de/dans [*seat, room*]; **3** (decline) [*prices, shares*] baisser; **the economy is sliding into recession** l'économie est sur la pente de la récession; **to let sth ~** laisser qch aller à la dérive; **after his wife's death he let things ~** après la mort de sa femme il a tout laissé aller à la dérive.
■ **slide away** [*person*] s'éclipser○.
■ **slide back**: **~ [sth] back, ~ back [sth]** reculer [*car seat*]; tirer [*bolt*]; refermer [*hatch, sunroof*].
■ **slide out** [*drawer, component*] coulisser.

slide: **~-action** *adj* [*gun*] à culasse mobile; **~ fastener** *n* US fermeture *f* à glissière, fermeture *f* éclair®; **~ guitar** ▶1481 *n* Mus bottleneck *m*; **~-in** *adj* Tech coulissant; **~ projector** *n* projecteur *m* de diapositives; **~ rule** GB, **~ ruler** US *n* règle *f* à calcul; **~ show** *n* (at exhibition) diaporama *m*; (at lecture, at home) séance *f* de projection; **~ trombone** ▶1481 *n* trombone *m* à coulisse; **~ valve** *n* soupape *f* à tiroir.

sliding /ˈslaɪdɪŋ/ *adj* [*door*] coulissant; [*roof*] ouvrant.

sliding: **~ friction** *n* Mech frottement *m* de glissement; **~ scale** *n* échelle *f* mobile; **~ seat** *n* (in car) siège *m* réglable; (in boat) banc *m* à glissière.

slight /slaɪt/ **I** *n* affront *m* (**on** à; **from** de la part de); **to suffer a ~** subir un affront.
II *adj* **1** [*change, delay, exaggeration, improvement, injury, movement, rise, shock, stroke*] léger/-ère (*before n*); [*risk, danger*] faible (*before n*); [*pause, hesitation*] petit (*before n*); **the improvement/her interest is ~** l'amélioration/son intérêt est faible; **the chances of it happening are ~** il y a de faibles chances pour que cela arrive; **not to have the ~est difficulty/idea** ne pas avoir la moindre difficulté/idée; **at the ~est provocation** à la moindre provocation; **not in the ~est** pas le moins du monde; **2** [*figure, physique, person*] mince; **to be ~ of build** être mince; **3** (lightweight) [*book, article, film*] superficiel/-ielle.
III *vtr* **1** (offend) humilier [*person*]; **2** US (underestimate) sous-estimer.
IV slighted *pp adj* [*person*] humilié.

slighting /ˈslaɪtɪŋ/ *adj* [*remark, reference*] offensant.

slightingly /ˈslaɪtɪŋlɪ/ *adv* [*describe, speak*] de manière offensante.

slightly /ˈslaɪtlɪ/ *adv* [*change, fall, rise*] légèrement; [*more, less, different, dear, damaged*] légèrement; [*embarrassed, uneasy, unfair*] un peu; **~ built** mince.

slightness /ˈslaɪtnɪs/ *n* **1** (of build) minceur *f*; **2** (of argument, film, work) superficialité *f*; **3** (of change, chance, risk) caractère *m* négligeable.

slim /slɪm/ **I** *adj* **1** (shapely) [*person, waist, figure*] mince; [*ankle, wrist, leg, finger*] fin, mince; **of ~ build** mince; **to get ~** devenir mince, s'amincir; **2** (thin) [*book, volume*] mince; [*watch, calculator*] plat; **3** (slight) [*chance, hope, margin, majority*] mince.
II *vtr* (*p prés etc* **-mm-**) réduire les effectifs de, dégraisser○ [*business*]; réduire [*budget, workforce*].
III *vi* (*p prés etc* **-mm-**) GB (lose weight) maigrir; **I'm ~ming** je fais un régime.
■ **slim down**: ¶ **~ down 1** [*person*] maigrir, perdre du poids; **2** [*company, organization*] réduire ses effectifs; ¶ **~ [sth] down, ~ down [sth]** réduire les effectifs de, dégraisser○ [*industry, company*]; réduire [*portfolio, workforce*].

slime /slaɪm/ *n* gen dépôt *m* gluant; (on riverbed) vase *f*; (in tank) dépôt *m* visqueux; (on beach) algues *fpl*; (of slug, snail) bave *f*.

slimebag◑ /ˈslaɪmbæg/, **slimeball**◑ /ˈslaɪmbɔːl/ *n* US fumier◑ *m*, ordure◑ *f*.

sliminess /ˈslaɪmɪnɪs/ *n* **1** lit viscosité *f*; **2** GB (of person) servilité *f*.

slimline /ˈslɪmlaɪn/ *adj* **1** [*garment*] amincissant; **2** [*drink*] diététique; **3** [*organization*] aux effectifs réduits; **4** [*object, gadget*] mini (*before n*).

slimmer /ˈslɪmə(r)/ *n* GB personne *f* suivant un régime amaigrissant; **~s' magazine** magazine *m* de diététique; **~s' disease**○ anorexie *f* mentale.

slimming /ˈslɪmɪŋ/ GB **I** *n* fait *m* de suivre un régime amaigrissant.
II *modif* [*club, group*] d'amaigrissement; [*pill, product*] pour maigrir.
III *adj* [*garment*] amincissant.

slimness /ˈslɪmnɪs/ *n* **1** (of person) sveltesse *f*; **2** (of book) minceur *f*; **3** (of chance) minceur *f*.

slimy /ˈslaɪmɪ/ *adj* **1** [*weed, mould, monster*] visqueux/-euse; [*plate, fingers*] gluant; [*wall*] suintant; **2** GB péj (obsequious) servile; **3** US péj (sleazy) louche.

sling /slɪŋ/ **I** *n* **1** (weapon) fronde *f*; (smaller) lance-pierres *m inv*; **2** (for support) Med écharpe *f*; (for carrying baby) porte-bébé *m*; (for carrying a load) élingue *f*; **3** Sport (in climbing) boucle *f* d'assurance.
II *vtr* (*prét, pp* **slung**) **1**○ (throw) lit, fig lancer [*object, insult*] (**at** à); **to ~ a shawl around one's shoulders** se mettre un châle sur les épaules; **to ~ a bag over one's shoulder** mettre son sac sur son épaule; **2** (carry or hang loosely) suspendre [*hammock, rope*]; **to ~ sth over one's shoulder** ou **across one's body** porter [qch] en bandoulière [*bag, rifle*]; **to ~ sth from** suspendre qch à [*beam, branch, hook*]; **to be slung over/across/round sth** être jeté par dessus/en travers de/autour de qch.
IDIOMS **to ~ one 's hook**○† GB ficher le camp○.
■ **sling away**○: **~ [sth] away, ~ away [sth]** jeter, se débarrasser de [*object*].
■ **sling out**○: ¶ **~ [sth] out, ~ out [sth]** jeter, se débarrasser de; ¶ **~ [sb] out** flanquer○ [qn] à la porte.

slingback /ˈslɪŋbæk/ **I** *n* escarpin *m* à bride.
II *modif* [*shoe, sandal*] à bride.

slingshot /ˈslɪŋʃɒt/ *n* lance-pierres *m inv*.

slink /slɪŋk/ *vi* (*prét, pp* **slunk**) **to ~ in/out** entrer/sortir furtivement; **to ~ off** [*person*] s'éloigner furtivement; [*dog*] s'en aller la queue basse.

slinkily○ /ˈslɪŋkɪlɪ/ *adv* [*walk*] en roulant les hanches; **~ dressed** habillé sexy.

slinky○ /ˈslɪŋkɪ/ *adj* [*dress*] moulant; [*music, vocals*] sexy○.

slip /slɪp/ **I** *n* **1** (error) gen erreur *f*; (by schoolchild) faute *f* d'étourderie; (faux pas) gaffe○ *f*; **to make a ~** faire une erreur or une faute d'étourderie; **to make a ~ in one's calculations** faire une erreur de calcul; **a ~ of the tongue/a ~ of the pen** un lapsus; **2** (piece of paper) bout *m* de papier; (receipt) reçu *m*; (for salary) bulletin *m*; **credit card ~** reçu *m* de carte de crédit; **a ~ of paper** un bout de papier ; **3** (act of slipping) glissade *f* involontaire; (stumble) faux pas *m*; **4**○† (slender person) **a ~ of a girl/child** une fille/un enfant frêle; **5** Fashn (petticoat) (full) combinaison *f*; (half) jupon *m*; **6** ¢ (clay) engobe *m*; **7** Hort bouture *f*; **8** (landslide) glissement *m* de terrain; **9** Aviat (also **side ~**) glissade *f*; **10** Geol charriage *m*, chevauchement *m*.
II slips *npl* Naut **the ~s** = **slipway**.
III *vtr* (*p prés etc* **-pp-**) **1** (slide) **to ~ sth into** glisser qch dans [*note, coin, joke, remark*]; passer qch dans [*hand, foot, arm*]; **to ~ one's feet into one's shoes** enfiler ses chaussures; **to ~ sth out of** sortir qch de [*object, foot, hand*]; **she ~ped the shirt over her head** (put on) elle a enfilé la chemise; (take off) elle a retiré la chemise; **to ~ a shawl around one's shoulders** passer un châle autour de ses épaules; **to ~ sth onto sb's finger** passer qch au doigt de qn; **to ~ sth into place** mettre qch en place; **to ~ a car into gear** embrayer; **2**○ (give surreptitiously) **to ~ sb sth, to ~ sth to sb** glisser qch à qn; **3** (escape from) [*dog*] se dégager de [*leash, collar*]; Naut [*boat*] filer [*moorings*]; **it ~ped my notice** ou **attention that** je ne me suis pas aperçu que; **it ~ped his/my notice** ou **attention** fig ça lui a/m'a échappé; **it had ~ped my mind** ou **memory (that)** fig j'avais complètement oublié (que); **to let ~ an opportunity** ou **a chance (to do)** laisser échapper une occasion (de faire); **to let ~ a remark** laisser échapper une remarque; **to let (it) ~ that** laisser entendre que; **4** (release) **to ~ the dog's leash** défaire la laisse du chien; **to ~ a stitch** (in knitting) glisser une maille; **5** Med **to ~ a disc** avoir une hernie discale; **6** Aut **to ~ the clutch** faire patiner l'embrayage; ▶ **disc**.
IV *vi* (*p prés etc* **-pp-**) **1** (slide quickly) **~ into** passer [*dress, costume*]; s'adapter à [*rôle*]; tomber dans [*coma*]; sombrer doucement dans [*confusion, madness*]; **to ~ into sleep** littér s'assoupir; **to ~ into bad habits** fig prendre de mauvaises habitudes; **to ~ out of** enlever [*dress, coat, costume*]; **2** (slide quietly) **to ~ into/out of** [*person*] se glisser dans/hors de [*room, building*]; **he ~ped through the fence** il est passé à travers la clôture; **the boat ~ped through the water** le bateau glissait sur l'eau; **to ~ over** ou **across the border** passer la frontière en cachette; **3** (slide accidentally) [*person, animal, object, vehicle*] glisser (**on** sur; **off** de); [*knife, razor*] glisser, déraper; [*pen*] déraper; [*load*] tomber; **the glass ~ped out of his hand/through his fingers** le verre lui a échappé des mains/des doigts; **to ~ through sb's fingers** fig filer entre les doigts de qn; **4**○ (lose one's grip) **I must be ~ping!** je baisse○!; **it's not like you to miss something like that, you're ~ping!** ça ne te ressemble pas de manquer quelque chose de ce genre! tu n'y es plus○!; **5** Aut [*clutch*] patiner.
IDIOMS **to give sb the ~** semer○ qn.
■ **slip away 1** (leave unnoticed) partir discrètement; **to ~ away to Paris** faire un saut○ à Paris; **2** (die) euph s'éteindre doucement.
■ **slip back**: ¶ **~ back** [*person*] revenir discrètement (**to** à); [*boat*] retourner doucement, revenir doucement (**into** dans; **to** à); **I'll just ~ back and ask her** je retourne vite le lui demander; ¶ **~ [sth] back** glisser, remettre.
■ **slip by** [*life, weeks, months*] s'écouler; [*time*] passer.
■ **slip down 1** (fall over) [*person*] glisser et tomber; **2** (taste good) **this wine ~s down well** ce vin descend bien.
■ **slip in**: ¶ **~ in** (enter quietly) [*person*] entrer discrètement; [*animal*] entrer furtivement; **I'll just ~ in and get it** je vais juste entrer le prendre; **a few errors have ~ped in** il y a quelques erreurs; ¶ **~ [sth] in, ~in [sth]** glisser [*remark*]; **to ~ in the clutch** embrayer.
■ **slip off**: ¶ **~ off** [*person*] partir discrètement; ¶ **~ [sth] off, ~ off [sth]** enlever [*coat, gloves, ring*].
■ **slip on**: **~ [sth] on, ~ on [sth]** passer, enfiler [*coat, gloves, ring*].
■ **slip out 1** (leave quietly) [*person*] sortir discrètement; **I have to ~ out for a moment** il faut que je sorte un instant; **he's just ~ped out to the supermarket** il a juste fait un saut○ au supermarché; **2** (come out accidentally) **the words just ~ped out before he could think** les mots lui ont échappé avant même qu'il ait eu le temps de réfléchir; **it just ~ped out!** ça m'a échappé!
■ **slip over** [*person*] glisser et tomber.
■ **slip past** = **slip by**.

■ **slip through**: **a few errors have ~ped through** il y a encore quelques erreurs.
■ **slip up**○ (make mistake) faire une gaffe○ (**on, about** à propos de).

slip: **~case** *n* emboîtage *m*; **~cover** *n* housse *f*; **~ gauge** *n* Tech cale *f* étalon; **~knot** *n* nœud *m* coulant; **~noose** *n* nœud *m* coulant; **~-on (shoe)** *n* mocassin *m*; **~over** *n* Fashn pull-over *m* sans manches.

slippage /ˈslɪpɪdʒ/ *n* **1** (delay) (in production etc) retard *m*; **2** (discrepancy) décalage *m*; **3** Tech (power loss) pertes *fpl* d'énergie.

slipped disc *n* Med hernie *f* discale.

slipper /ˈslɪpə(r)/ **I** *n* **1** (houseshoe) pantoufle *f*; **2**† (evening shoe) escarpin *m*.
II *vtr* battre [qn] avec une pantoufle.

slipper baths† *npl* bains *mpl* publics.

slippery /ˈslɪpərɪ/ *adj* **1** (difficult to grip) [*road, path, fish, material*] glissant; **2** (difficult to deal with) [*subject, situation*] délicat; **3**○ (untrustworthy) [*person*] fuyant; **a ~ customer**○ un personnage suspect.
IDIOMS **to be on the ~ slope** être sur une pente savonneuse.

slippy○ /ˈslɪpɪ/ *adj* **1** (slippery) [*path, surface*] glissant; **2** (quick) **look ~ about it!** grouilletoi○!

slip: **~ road** *n* Transp bretelle *f* d'accès à l'autoroute; **~shod** *adj* [*person, worker*] négligent (**about, in** dans); [*appearance, workmanship, work*] négligé, peu soigné.

slip stitch **I** *n* Sewing point *m* de côté.
II *vtr* coudre [qch] à points de côté.

slipstream /ˈslɪpstriːm/ **I** *n* sillage *m*.
II *vtr* Sport (in motor racing) rouler dans le sillage de [*car*].

slip: **~-up**○ *n* bourde○ *f*; **~ware** *n* céramique *f* façonnée à l'engobe; **~way** *n* Naut cale *f* de construction.

slit /slɪt/ **I** *n* **1** fente *f* (**in** dans); **to make a ~ in sth** faire une fente dans qch; **his eyes narrowed to ~s** il plissa les yeux; **2**● (vagina) con● *m*, vagin *m*.
II *modif* [*eyes*] bridé; [*skirt*] fendu.
III *vtr* (*prét, pp* **slit**) (on purpose) faire une fente dans; (by accident) déchirer; **to ~ a letter open** ouvrir une lettre; **to ~ sb's throat** égorger qn; **to ~ one's (own) throat** s'égorger; **to ~ one's wrists** s'ouvrir les veines.

slither /ˈslɪðə(r)/ *vi* [*person, snake*] glisser; **to ~ about on** avoir du mal à garder son équilibre sur [*ice, surface*]; **to ~ down the bank** glisser jusqu'au bas du talus; **to ~ into one's seat** se glisser dans son fauteuil.

slit: **~ pocket** *n* poche *f* passepoilée; **~ trench** *n* tranchée *f*.

sliver /ˈslɪvə(r)/ *n* (of glass) éclat *m*; (of soap) reste *m*; (of food) mince tranche *f*; **just a ~!** une toute petite tranche!

Sloane /sləʊn/ *n* GB péj (also **~ Ranger**) *femme BCBG*○.

slob○ /slɒb/ *n* (lazy) flemmard/-e○ *m/f*; (with messy habits) cochon/-onne○ *m/f*; **get up, fat ~!** debout, gros lard○!

slobber○ /ˈslɒbə(r)/ **I** *n* bave *f*.
II *vi* baver.
■ **slobber over**○: **~ over [sb/sth]** baver d'attendrissement devant.

slobbery○ /ˈslɒbərɪ/ *adj* péj [*kiss*] mouillé.

sloe /sləʊ/ *n* **1** (fruit) prunelle *f*; **2** (bush) prunellier *m*.

sloe: **~-eyed** *adj* aux yeux de biche; **~ gin** *n* liqueur *f* à base de gin et de prunelles.

slog○ /slɒg/ **I** *n* **1** (hard work) **a hard ~** un travail de Romain○, un travail dur; **it was a real ~** c'était vraiment dur; **it's a long, hard ~ to the village** il faut un long effort pour atteindre le village; **setting the economy right will be a long hard ~** il faudra un long effort pour redresser l'économie; **2**○ (hard stroke) coup *m* violent; **to have** ou **take a ~ at the ball** taper de toutes ses forces dans la balle.
II *vtr* (*p prés etc* **-gg-**) **1** (hit hard) frapper [qn] violemment [*opponent*]; taper de toutes ses forces dans [*ball*]; **to ~ it out** lit, fig se battre; **2** (progress with difficulty) **to ~ one's way through/towards** se frayer un chemin à travers/vers.
III *vi* (*p prés etc* **-gg-**) **1** (work hard) travailler dur, bosser○; **2** (progress with difficulty) **we ~ged up/down the hill** nous avons escaladé/descendu la colline avec effort; **3** (hit hard) **to ~ at** cogner [*person*]; taper de toutes ses forces dans [*ball*].
■ **slog away** travailler dur (**at** sur).

slogan /ˈsləʊgən/ *n* slogan *m*.

slogger /ˈslɒgə(r)/ *n* **1** (person who hits hard) cogneur/-euse *m/f*; **2** (hard worker) bûcheur/-euse○ *m/f*.

sloop /sluːp/ *n* sloop *m*.

sloop-rigged /ˈsluːprɪgd/ *adj* gréé en sloop.

slop /slɒp/ **I** *n* **1** Agric (pigswill) pâtée *f*; **2**○ péj (food) bouillie *f*; **3**○ péj (sentimentality) sentimentalité *f*.
II slops *npl* **1** (liquid food) aliment *m* liquide; **2** (dirty water) eaux *fpl* sales.
III *vtr* (*p prés* etc **-pp-**) renverser [*liquid*] (**onto** sur; **into** dans).
IV *vi* (*p prés* etc **-pp-**) (also **~ over**) déborder (**into** dans).
■ **slop around, slop about** [*person*] traînasser.
■ **slop out** vider sa tinette (*en prison*).

slop: **~ bucket, ~ pail** *n* (in prison) seau *m* hygiénique, tinette *f*; **~ chest** *n* cambuse *f*.

slope /sləʊp/ **I** *n* **1** (incline) gen pente *f*; (of writing) inclinaison *f*; **to be on a ~** être en pente; **the ~ on the road is considerable** la pente de la route est importante; **a 40° ~, a ~ of 40°** une pente de 40°; **a steep/gentle ~** une pente raide/douce; **2** (hillside) flanc *m*; **north/south ~** versant *m* nord/sud; **uphill ~** montée *f*; **downhill ~** descente *f*; **upper ~s** sommet *m* de la montagne; **halfway up** ou **down the ~** (road) à mi-côte; (mountain) à mi-pente.
II *vtr* Mil **~ arms!** portez armes!
III *vi* [*road, path, roof, garden etc*] être en pente (**towards** vers); [*writing*] pencher (**to** vers); **to ~ down** ou **away** descendre en pente (**to** vers); **to ~ to the left/right** descendre vers la gauche/la droite. ▶ **slippery**.
■ **slope off**○ se barrer○.

sloping /ˈsləʊpɪŋ/ *adj* [*ground, roof*] en pente; [*ceiling*] incliné; [*shoulders*] tombant; [*writing*] penché.

sloppily /ˈslɒpɪlɪ/ *adv* [*made, dressed*] n'importe comment; **~ run** mal administré.

sloppiness /ˈslɒpɪnɪs/ *n* (of thinking, discipline) manque *m* de rigueur; (of work) manque *m* de soin; (of dress) débraillé *m*.

slopping out *n* GB vidage *m* de la tinette (*en prison*).

sloppy /ˈslɒpɪ/ *adj* **1**○ (careless) [*personal appearance*] débraillé; [*language, workmanship*] peu soigné; [*management, administration*] laxiste; [*discipline, procedure*] relâché; [*method, thinking*] qui manque de rigueur; Sport [*defence*] mou/molle; **to be a ~ dresser** être toujours débraillé; **to be a ~ worker** travailler n'importe comment; **to be a ~ eater** manger salement; **2**○ (sentimental) [*person, film*] sentimental; **3** GB (baggy) [*sweater*] ample.

sloppy joe○ /ˌslɒpɪˈdʒəʊ/ *n* **1** GB grand pull *m*; **2** US viande *f* hachée à la sauce tomate.

slopwork /ˈslɒpwɜːk/ *n* confection *f* (*de vêtements de qualité inférieure*).

slosh /slɒʃ/ **I** *vtr* **1**○ (spill) répandre (en éclaboussant) [*liquid*]; **2**◑ GB (hit) flanquer un coup○ à [*person*].
II○ *vi* (also **~ about**) clapoter.
III○ **sloshed** *pp adj* bourré○; **to get ~ed** prendre une cuite○.

slot /slɒt/ **I** *n* **1** (slit) (for coin, ticket) fente *f*; (for letters) ouverture *f*; **2** (groove) rainure *f*; **3** (in TV, radio, airline schedule, school timetable) créneau *m*; **a prime-time ~** une tranche horaire de grande écoute; **4** (position, job) place *f*.
II *vtr* (*p prés etc* **-tt-**) **to ~ sth into a machine/groove** insérer qch dans une machine/rainure; **to ~ a film into the timetable** trouver un créneau pour un film dans le programme; **I've decided to ~ her into the newly created position** j'ai décidé de la placer au poste nouvellement créé.
III *vi* (*p prés etc* **-tt-**) **to ~ into** [*coin, piece, component*] s'insérer dans [*groove, machine*]; **she has ~ted into her new position very well** elle s'est très bien adaptée à son nouveau poste; **to ~ into place** ou **position** s'encastrer; **the two parts ~ into each other** les deux éléments s'encastrent l'un dans l'autre.
■ **slot in**: ¶ **~ in** [*coin, piece, component*] se mettre en place; ¶ **~ [sth] in, ~ in [sth]** insérer [*coin, piece, component*]; trouver un créneau pour [*film, programme*]; placer [*person*].
■ **slot together**: ¶ **~ together** s'emboîter; ¶ **~ [sth] together** emboîter [*parts*].

slot: **~ aerial, ~ antenna** *n* antenne *f* à fente; **~ car** *n* US petite voiture-jouet *f* (*de circuit électrique*).

sloth /sləʊθ/ *n* **1** Zool paresseux *m*; **2** sout (idleness) paresse *f*.

sloth bear *n* ours *m* lippu.

slothful /ˈsləʊθfl/ *adj* sout paresseux/-euse.

slot: **~ machine** *n* Games machine *f* à sous; (for vending) distributeur *m* automatique; **~ meter** *n* (for gas, electricity) compteur *m* à pièces; (parking meter) parcmètre *m*; **~ted spoon** *n* ≈ écumoire *f*.

slouch /slaʊtʃ/ **I** *n* **1 to walk with a ~** gen marcher le dos voûté; [*fashion model*] US marcher d'une façon indolente; **she's got a terrible ~** elle a l'air complètement avachie; **2**○ (lazy person) traîne-savates *m inv*; **he's no ~** il n'a rien d'un traîne-savates; **he's no ~ at sth** il se défend pas mal en qch○.
II *vi* **1** (sit or stand badly) être avachi; **2** (also **~ around**) traînasser.
■ **slouch forward** être avachi.

slouch hat *n* chapeau *m* mou.

slough[1] /slaʊ, US also sluː/ *n* **1** fig (of despair) abîme *m*; **2** (bog) marécage *m*.

slough[2] /slʌf/ *n* (of snake, worm) mue *f*.
■ **slough off**: **~ off [sth], ~ [sth] off 1** Zool perdre [*skin*]; **2** fig se débarrasser de.

Slovak(ian) /sləˈvækɪən/ ▶ 1486, 1402 **I** *n* **1** (person) Slovaque *mf*; **2** (language) slovaque *m*.
II *adj* slovaque.

Slovakia /sləˈvækɪə/ ▶ 1131 *pr n* Slovaquie *f*.

Slovene /ˈsləʊviːn/, **Slovenian** /sləˈviːnɪən/ ▶ 1486, 1402 **I** *n* **1** (person) Slovène *mf*; **2** (language) slovène *m*.
II *adj* slovène.

Slovenia /sləˈviːnɪə/ ▶ 1131 *pr n* Slovénie *f*.

slovenliness /ˈslʌvnlɪnɪs/ *n* laisser-aller *m inv*.

slovenly /ˈslʌvnlɪ/ *adj* **1** (unkempt) [*person, dress, appearance*] négligé; [*habits*] malpropre; **2** (sloppy) [*work*] bâclé; [*speech, style*] négligé.

slow /sləʊ/ **I** *adj* **1** (not quick) [*runner, vehicle, gesture, movement, progress, process, development*] lent; **the pace of life is ~ here** on vit au ralenti ici; **to fall into a ~ decline** tomber lentement dans le déclin; **to make ~ progress/a ~ recovery** avancer/se remettre lentement; **the ~ movement** Mus le mouvement lent; **to be ~ to do** tarder à faire; **attitudes are ~ to change** les attitudes changent lentement; **he is ~ to anger** il lui en faut beaucoup pour se mettre en colère; **to be ~ in doing** être lent à faire; **2** (dull) [*film, novel, play, plot*] lent; **3** (slack) [*business, demand, trade, market*] stagnant; [*economic growth*] lent; **4** (intellectually unresponsive) [*child, pupil,*

learner] lent (d'esprit); **~ at sth** faible en qch; **5** (showing incorrect time) [*clock, watch*] **to be ~** retarder; **to be 10 minutes ~** retarder de 10 minutes; **6** (not too hot) [*oven, flame*] doux/douce; **7** Sport [*pitch, court*] lourd.
II *adv* [*go, drive, travel*] gen lentement; **to go ~** [*workers*] freiner la production; **~-acting** à action lente; **~-cooked dish** plat mijoté. ▶ **go-slow**.
III *vtr, vi* ▶ **slow down**.
■ **slow down**: ¶ **~ down** [*train, runner, pulse, output, economy*] ralentir; **to ~ (down) to a crawl** rouler au pas; **to ~ (down) to 20 km/h** ralentir à 20 km/h; **to ~ (down) to 2%** tomber à 2%; **at your age you should ~ down** à ton âge tu devrais ralentir (tes activités); ¶ **~ down [sth/sb]**, **~ [sth/sb] down** ralentir [*car, traffic, runner, progress, production*]; **the illness has ~ed her down** la maladie l'a diminuée.
■ **slow up** = **slow down**.

slow-burning /ˌsləʊˈbɜːnɪŋ/ *adj* **1** lit [*fuse, wire, fuel*] à combustion lente; **2** fig [*anger, rage*] froid.

slow: **~coach**○ *n* GB traînard/-e○ *m/f*; **~ cooker** *n* mijoteuse *f* électrique.

slowdown /ˈsləʊdaʊn/ *n* ralentissement *m*; **~ in demand/in the housing market** ralentissement de la demande/du marché immobilier.

slow: **~ handclapping** *n*: *applaudissements exprimant l'impatience ou le mécontentement*; **~ lane** *n* (in UK, Australia) voie *f* de gauche; (elsewhere) voie *f* de droite.

slowly /ˈsləʊlɪ/ *adv* lentement; **~ but surely** lentement mais sûrement.

slow march *n* Mil marche *f* lente; **'slow…MARCH!'** 'pas ralenti…MARCHE!'

slow match *n* mèche *f* à combustion lente.

slow motion *n* ralenti *m*; **in ~** au ralenti.

slow-moving /ˌsləʊˈmuːvɪŋ/ *adj* lent.

slowness /ˈsləʊnɪs/ *n* **1** (of motion, vehicle, progress, pace, plot) lenteur *f*; **2** Sport (of pitch, court) lourdeur *f*; **3** (of mind, intelligence) lourdeur *f*.

slow: **~poke**○ *n* US = **slowcoach**; **~ puncture** *n* crevaison *f* (*où l'air s'échappe lentement du pneu*); **~ train** *n* omnibus *m*; **~-witted** *adj* à l'esprit lent; **~worm** *n* orvet *m*.

SLR *n* Phot *abrév* = **single-lens reflex**.

sludge /slʌdʒ/ *n* **1** (also **sewage ~**) eaux *fpl* usées; **2** (mud) vase *f*; (in drain) dépôt *m*; **3** Aut, Tech cambouis *m*.

sludgeworks /ˈslʌdʒwɜːks/ *n* station *f* de recyclage des eaux usées.

sludgy /ˈslʌdʒɪ/ *adj* bourbeux/-euse.

slug /slʌg/ **I** *n* **1** Zool limace *f*; **2**○ (bullet) balle *f*, pruneau○*m*; **3** (of alcohol) lampée○ *f*; **4**○ (blow) coup *m*; **5**○ US jeton *m* trafiqué.
II○ *vtr* (*p prés etc* **-gg-**) **1**◑ (hit) cogner [*person*]; **to ~ sb one**○ en envoyer une à qn○; **2**○ US Sport taper○ dans [*ball*]; **3**○ (drink) descendre [*whisky etc*].
IDIOMS **to ~ it out**◑ se tabasser○.

slug bait *n*, **slug pellets** *npl* granulés *mpl* antilimaces.

slugfest○ /ˈslʌgfest/ *n* US bagarre○ *f*.

sluggard /ˈslʌgəd/ *n* paresseux/-euse *m/f*.

slugger○ /ˈslʌgə(r)/ *n* cogneur *m*.

sluggish /ˈslʌgɪʃ/ *adj* **1** [*person, animal*] léthargique; [*circulation, reaction*] lent; [*traffic*] engorgé; [*river*] stagnant; **2** Fin [*demand, economy, market, trade*] qui stagne; **after a ~ start** après un démarrage difficile.

sluggishly /ˈslʌgɪʃlɪ/ *adv* lentement.

sluggishness /ˈslʌgɪʃnɪs/ *n* lenteur *f*.

sluice /sluːs/ **I** *n* (also **~way**) canal *m*.
II *vtr* US (float) faire flotter [*logs*].
■ **sluice down**: ¶ **~ down** se déverser; ¶ **~ down [sth]**, **~ [sth] down** laver [qch] à grande eau.
■ **sluice out**: ¶ **~ out** jaillir; ¶ **~ out [sth]**, **~ [sth] out** laver [qch] à grande eau.

sluice gate *n* vanne *f*.

slum /slʌm/ **I** *n* **1** (poor area) bidonville *m*; **the ~s** les bas-quartiers *mpl* (**of** de); **2**○ (messy house, room) taudis *m*.
II *modif* [*area, housing, house*] misérable; [*child, children*] des bidonvilles; [*conditions*] dans les bidonvilles.
III *vi*○ (*p prés etc* **-mm-**) (also **~ it**) s'encanailler, zoner○.

slumber /ˈslʌmbə(r)/ **I** *n* sommeil *m*.
II *vi* lit, fig sommeiller.

slumber party *n* US *soirée où tous les invités sont en pyjama*.

slum: **~ clearance** *n* démolition *f* de taudis; **~ dwelling** *n* taudis *m*.

slumgullion○ /ˌslʌmˈgʌlɪən/ *n* US ragoût *m*.

slumlord○ /ˈslʌmlɔːd/ *n* US péj vautour○ *m*, propriétaire *m* sans scrupules.

slummy○ /ˈslʌmɪ/ *adj* [*area, house, background*] misérable; **what a ~ kitchen**○! c'est infâme, cette cuisine!

slump /slʌmp/ **I** *n* **1** (fall in trade, price, profit etc) effondrement *m* (**in** de); **retail/shares ~** effondrement de la vente au détail/des valeurs boursières; **~ in the property market** l'effondrement du marché immobilier; **to experience a ~** [*economy, market*] s'effondrer; **2** (in popularity) chute *f* (**in** de); (in support) baisse *f* (**in** de); **the team/party is experiencing a ~** l'équipe/le parti est en déclin.
II *vi* **1** [*demand, trade, value, price*] chuter (**from** de; **to** à; **by** de); **2** [*economy, market*] s'effondrer; **3** [*support, popularity*] être en forte baisse; **4** [*person, body*] s'affaler○; **to ~ into an armchair/to the ground** s'affaler○ dans un fauteuil/sur le sol; **5** [*player, team*] chuter (**to** à).
III slumped *pp adj* [*person, body*] affalé○; **~ed over the steering wheel/across the table/in a chair** affalé○ sur le volant/en travers de la table/dans un fauteuil.

slung /slʌŋ/ *prét, pp* ▶ **sling**.

slunk /slʌŋk/ *prét, pp* ▶ **slink**.

slur /slɜː(r)/ **I** *n* **1** (aspersion) calomnie *f*; **to cast a ~ on sb/sth** répandre des calomnies sur qn/qch; **to be a ~ on sb/sth** porter atteinte à qn/qch; **an outrageous ~** une odieuse calomnie; **a racial ~** une diffamation raciale; **2** Mus liaison *f*; **3** (indistinct utterance) marmonnement *m*.
II *vtr* (*p prés etc* **-rr-**) **1** marmonner [*remark*]; **'goodnight,' he ~red** 'bonne nuit,' marmonna-t-il; **to ~ one's speech** ou **words** gen manger ses mots; [*drunkard*] bafouiller; **2** Mus lier [*notes*].
III *vi* (*p prés etc* **-rr-**) [*speech, voice, words*] être inarticulé.
IV slurred *pp adj* [*voice , words, speech*] inarticulé.
■ **slur over**: **~ over [sth]** éluder [*problem, question, fact*]; passer rapidement sur [*incident, error, discrepancy*].

slurp /slɜːp/ **I** *n* aspiration *f* bruyante.
II *vtr* aspirer [qch] bruyamment.

slurry /ˈslʌrɪ/ *n* **1** (of cement) gâchis *m*; **2** (waste products) (from animals) purin *m*; (from factory) déchets *mpl*.

slush /slʌʃ/ *n* **1** (melted snow) neige *f* fondue; **2**○ péj (sentimentality) sensiblerie *f*; **3** US Culin granité *m*.

slush fund *n* caisse *f* noire.

slushy /ˈslʌʃɪ/ *n* **1** lit [*snow*] fondu; [*street*] couvert de neige fondue; **2**○ fig [*novel, film*] à l'eau de rose, sentimental.

slut /slʌt/ *n* **1**◑ injur (promiscuous woman) traînée◑ *f* offensive, dévergondée *f*; **2**○ (dirty woman) souillon *f*, marie-salope◑ *f* offensive.

sluttish /ˈslʌtɪʃ/ *adj* **1**◑ injur (promiscuous) [*woman, behaviour*] dévergondé; **2**○ (dirty) malpropre.

sly /slaɪ/ *adj* **1** (cunning) [*person, animal, trick, look*] rusé, sournois pej; **2** (secretive) [*smile, wink, look, remark*] entendu; **a ~ (old) dog**○ un fin renard.
IDIOMS **on the ~**○ en douce○, en cachette.

slyboots○ /ˈslaɪbuːts/ *n* US malin/-igne *m/f*.

slyly /ˈslaɪlɪ/ *adv* **1** (with cunning) [*behave, say, ask*] avec malice, malicieusement; [*hide, conceal*] malicieusement; [*persuade*] par la ruse; **2** (secretively) [*say*] d'un ton entendu; [*smile, look*] d'un air entendu.

slyness /ˈslaɪnɪs/ *n* (of smile, look, remark) malice *f*; (of person, act) fourberie *f*.

S & M *abrév* ▶ **sadomasochism**.

smack /smæk/ **I** *n* **1** (blow) (with hand) claque *f*; (on face) gifle *f*; (with bat) coup *m*; **2** (sound of blow) (of object) bruit *m* sec; (of waves) clapotis *m*; (by hand or person) coup *m*; **3** (loud kiss) gros baiser *m*; **4** Naut barque *f* de pêche; **5**◑ argot des drogués (heroin) héroïne *f*, héro◑ *f*.
II *adv*○ (also **~ bang**, **~ dab** US) en plein○; **~ in the middle of** en plein milieu de; **~ in front of** en plein devant.
III *excl* paf!
IV *vtr* **1** taper [*object*] (**on** sur; **against** contre); écraser [*car, aeroplane*] (**on** sur; **against** contre); **2** (have suggestion of) **to ~ of** sentir; **it ~s of incompetence** ça sent l'incompétence.
V *vi* (hit) **to ~ into** ou **against sth** taper contre qch.
IDIOMS **to ~ one's lips** se lécher les babines (**at sth** à l'idée de qch); **a ~ in the eye** un coup dur (**for** pour).

smacker○ /ˈsmækə(r)/ *n* **1** (kiss) (grosse) bise *f*; **2** (money) GB livre *f*; US dollar *m*.

smacking /ˈsmækɪŋ/ *n* fessée *f*; **to get a ~** recevoir une fessée.

small /smɔːl/ **▶ 1703** **I** *n* **the ~ of the back** le creux du dos, les reins *mpl*; **in the ~ of her back** dans le creux du dos.
II○ **smalls** *npl* GB euph petit linge *m*.
III *adj* **1** (not big) [*house, car, book, coin, dog, bag*] petit (*before n*); [*change, job, mistake, matter*] petit (*before n*); [*increase, majority, proportion, quantity, amount, stake*] faible (*before n*); [*sum, number*] petit (*before n*); **the dress is too ~ for her** la robe est trop petite pour elle; **a ~ sweatshirt** un sweatshirt de petite taille; **the change was ~** le changement était sans importance; **his influence was ~** son influence était négligeable; **it would cost a ~ fortune**○ ça me coûterait une petite fortune; **the ~ matter of the £1,000 you owe me** iron la bagatelle de 1 000 livres que tu me dois iron; **it is written with a ~ letter** ça s'écrit avec une minuscule; **in his** ou **her own ~ way** gen à sa façon; (financially) dans la mesure de ses modestes moyens; **~ amount of** ajoutez un peu de; **to cut sth up ~** couper qch en petits morceaux; **to fold sth up ~** plier qch plusieurs fois; **everybody, great and ~, will be affected** riches et pauvres, tout le monde sera touché; **the ~est room**○ euph le petit coin○ euph; **it's a ~ world!** que le monde est petit!; **2** (petty) [*person, act*] mesquin; **3** (not much) **to have ~ cause** ou **reason for worrying** ou **to worry** n'avoir guère de raisons de s'inquiéter ; **it is ~ comfort** ou **consolation to sb** c'est une piètre consolation pour qn; **it is of ~ consequence** c'est sans importance; **it is of no ~ consequence** c'est loin d'être sans importance; **~ wonder he left!** pas étonnant qu'il soit parti!; **4** (quiet) [*voice, noise*] petit; [*sound*] faible; **5** (humiliated) **to feel** ou **look ~** être dans ses petits souliers○; **to make sb feel** ou **look ~** humilier qn; **'I did it,' she said in a ~ voice** 'c'est moi qui l'ai fait' a-t-elle dit d'une petite voix.
IV *adv* [*write*] petit.
IDIOMS **he's ~ beer**○ ou **potatoes**○ US il est insignifiant; **it's ~ beer** ou **potatoes** US c'est de la petite bière○.

small: **~ ad** *n* GB petite annonce *f*; **~ arms** *npl* armes *fpl* légères; **~ arms fire** *n* tirs *mpl* à l'arme légère; **~ business** *n* petite entreprise *f*; **~ businessman** **▶ 1692** *n* petit entrepreneur *m*;

~ change *n* petite monnaie *f*; **~ claims court** *n* GB, Jur ≈ tribunal *m* d'instance; **~ fry** *npl* menu fretin *m*; **~holder** ▶ 1692 *n* GB Agric, Jur petit exploitant *m*; **~holding** *n* GB Agric petite exploitation *f*.

small hours *npl* petit matin *m*; **in the (wee) ~** au petit matin.

small intestine *n* intestin *m* grêle.

smallish /'smɔ:lɪʃ/ *adj* assez petit.

small: **~-minded** *adj* mesquin; **~-mindedness** *n* mesquinerie *f*.

smallness /'smɔ:lnɪs/ *n* (of object, person, group) petite taille *f*; (of sum) modicité *f*.

smallpox /'smɔ:lpɒks/ ▶ 1354 *n* variole *f*.

small print *n* **1** Print petits caractères *mpl*; **2** fig **to read the ~** lire tout jusque dans les moindres détails; **to read the ~ of a contract** éplucher un contrat.

small print condition *n* clause *f* restrictive (*imprimée en petits caractères*).

small-scale /ˌsmɔ:l'skeɪl/ *adj* [*model*] réduit; [*map, plan*] à petite échelle; [*industry*] petit (*before n*).

small: **~ screen** *n* petit écran *m*; **~ shopkeeper** ▶ 1692 *n* petit commerçant *m*.

small talk *n* banalités *fpl*; **to make ~** faire la conversation.

small-time /'smɔ:ltaɪm/ *adj* [*actor, performer*] médiocre; **~ crook** petit escroc *m*.

small-town /'smɔ:ltaʊn/ *adj* péj provincial.

smarm○ /smɑ:m/ *vi* GB **to ~ over sb** lécher les bottes à qn○.

smarmy○ /'smɑ:mɪ/ *adj* GB [*manner, person*] obséquieux/-ieuse; [*tone, voice*] doucereux/-euse; **to be ~** être lèche-bottes○; **he's a ~ git**◑ il est visqueux.

smart /smɑ:t/ **I** *adj* **1** (elegant) élégant; **to look ~** avoir l'air élégant; **you're looking very ~ today** tu es très élégant aujourd'hui; **2**○ (intelligent) [*child, decision*] malin, futé; (shrewd) [*politician, journalist*] habile; **to be ~ at doing** être habile à faire; **it was definitely the ~ choice** c'est certainement ce qu'il fallait choisir; **he's a ~ kid**○ c'est un enfant futé; **would he be ~ enough to spot the error?** serait-il assez futé○ pour repérer l'erreur?; **if you're ~ you'll book in advance** ce serait futé○ de ta part de réserver à l'avance; **are you trying to be ~?** tu veux faire le malin?; **you think it's ~ to smoke** tu penses que c'est malin de fumer; **he thinks he's so ~** il se croit malin; **3** [*restaurant, hotel, street*] chic *inv*; **the ~ set** le beau monde; **4** (stinging) [*blow*] vif/vive; [*rebuke, retort*] cinglant; **5** (brisk) **to set off/walk at a ~ pace** partir/marcher à vive allure; **that was ~ work!** ça a été vite fait!; **6** Comput [*system, terminal*] intelligent.

II *vi* **1** [*graze, cut, cheeks*] brûler; **his eyes were ~ing from the smoke** la fumée lui brûlait les yeux; **her cheek ~ed from the slap** elle avait la joue brûlante sous l'effet de la gifle; **2** fig (emotionally) être piqué au vif; **he ~ed under** ou **at the insult** il a été piqué au vif par l'insulte, l'insulte l'a piqué au vif; **they are ~ing over** ou **from their defeat** ils sont sous le coup de leur défaite.

smart alec(k)○ /ˌsmɑ:t'ælɪk/ *n* gros malin○/grosse maligne○ *m/f*.

smartarse◑ /'smɑ:tɑ:s/ GB **I** *n* (person) grande gueule◑ *f*.

II *modif* [*comments, attitude*] à la con◑ *inv*.

smart: **~ass**◑ *n* US = **smartarse**; **~ bomb** *n* bombe *f* intelligente; **~ card** *n* Comput, Fin carte *f* à puce.

smarten /'smɑ:tn/: ■ **smarten up**: **~ [sth/sb] up, ~ up [sth/sb]** embellir [*premises, room*]; **we'll have to ~ you up** il va falloir qu'on te fasse beau; **he's really ~ed himself up** il s'est beaucoup arrangé.

smartly /'smɑ:tlɪ/ *adv* **1** [*dressed*] (neatly) soigneusement; (elegantly) élégamment; **2** (quickly) [*retort, rebuke*] sèchement; **she slapped him ~ on the cheek** elle l'a giflé sèchement; **she tapped him ~ on the head** elle lui a donné un petit coup sec sur la tête; **3** (briskly) [*step, turn, walk*] vivement; **4** (cleverly) [*answer*] avec malice.

smart money○ *n* **the ~ was on Desert Orchid** Desert Orchid était une mise sûre; **the ~ is on our shares** nos actions sont un investissement.

smartness /'smɑ:tnɪs/ *n* **1** (of clothes) élégance *f*; (of appearance) aspect *m* soigné; **2** (cleverness) pej malice *f*; **3** (of pace) rapidité *f*.

smarty-pants○ /'smɑ:tɪpænts/ *n* = **smart alec(k)**.

smash /smæʃ/ **I** *n* **1** (crash) (of glass, china) bruit *m* fracassant; (of vehicles) fracas *m*; **I heard the ~ of breaking glass** j'ai entendu des bruits de verre; **~! there goes another plate!** crac! encore une assiette cassée!; **2**○ (also **~-up**) (accident) collision *f*; **'rail ~'** 'collision ferroviaire'; **3**○ (also **~ hit**) Mus tube○ *m*; Cin film *m* à grand succès; **to be a ~** faire un tabac○; **4** Fin (collapse) débâcle *f*; (on stock exchange) krach *m*; **5** Sport (tennis) smash *m*.

II *adv* **the motorbike ran ~ into a wall** la motocyclette est allée se fracasser contre un mur; **to go ~** Fin faire faillite.

III *vtr* **1** briser [*glass, door, car etc*] (**with** avec); (more violently) fracasser; **to ~ sb's skull/leg** fracasser le crâne/la jambe de qn; **to ~ sth to bits** ou **pieces** briser or casser qch en mille morceaux; **the boat was ~ed against the rocks** le bateau s'est fracassé sur les rochers; **thieves ~ed their way into the shop** les voleurs sont entrés dans la boutique en cassant tout; **he ~ed my arm against the door** il m'a écrasé le bras contre la porte; **she ~ed the car into a tree** elle est rentrée dans un arbre; **~ing his fist into his attacker's face** écrasant son poing sur la figure de son agresseur; **he ~ed the hammer down on the vase** il a fracassé le vase à coups de marteau; **2** (destroy) écraser [*demonstration, protest, opponent*]; démanteler [*drugs ring, gang*]; enrayer [*inflation*]; **3** Sport (break) pulvériser○ [*record*]; **4** Sport **to ~ the ball** faire un smash.

IV *vi* **1** (disintegrate) se briser, se fracasser (**on** sur, **against** contre); **2** (crash) **to ~ into** [*vehicle, aircraft*] aller s'écraser contre [*wall, vehicle*]; **the raiders ~ed through the door** les cambrioleurs ont enfoncé la porte; **the waves ~ed through the dyke** les vagues ont rompu la digue; **3** Fin faire faillite.

■ **smash down**: **~ [sth] down, ~ down [sth]** enfoncer [*door, fence, wall*].

■ **smash in**: **~ [sth] in** défoncer [*door, skull*]; **I'll ~ your face** ou **head in**○! je te casse la gueule◑!

■ **smash open**: **~ [sth] open, ~open [sth]** défoncer [*door, safe, container*].

■ **smash up**: **~ [sth] up, ~ up [sth]** démolir [*vehicle, building, furniture*]; **they'll ~ the place up!** ils vont tout casser!; **he got ~ed up**○ **in a car crash** il a été amoché○ dans un accident de voiture.

smash-and-grab○ GB *n* (also **~ raid**) cambriolage *m* (*avec destruction de vitrine*).

smashed /smæʃt/ *adj* **1**○ (intoxicated) (on alcohol) bourré○; (on drugs) défoncé○ (**on** à); **to get ~** se soûler la gueule◑; **2** (shattered) [*limb, vehicle*] écrasé; [*window*] fracassé.

smasher○ /'smæʃə(r)/ *n* GB **1** (attractive man) beau mec○ *m*; (woman) belle nana○ *f*; **2** (term of approval) **you're a ~!** tu es un chou○!; **her car's a real ~** sa bagnole est vraiment sensass○!

smashing○ /'smæʃɪŋ/ *adj* GB épatant○.

smattering /'smætərɪŋ/ *n* notions *fpl*, rudiments *mpl* (**of** de); **to have a ~ of Russian** avoir quelques connaissances en russe; **to have a ~ of culture** avoir quelques bribes de culture.

SME *n* (*abrév* = **small and medium enterprise**) PME *f inv*.

smear /smɪə(r)/ **I** *n* **1** (mark) (spot) tache *f*; (streak) traînée *f*; **a ~ of grease** une tache de graisse; **2** (defamation) propos *m* diffamatoire; **a ~ on sb's character** une tache sur la réputation de qn; **he dismissed the rumour as a ~** il a rejeté la rumeur comme diffamatoire; **3** Med = **smear test**.

II *vtr* **1** (dirty) faire des taches sur [*glass, window*]; **to ~ the walls with paint, to ~ paint on the walls** barbouiller les murs de peinture; **the baby ~ed his food over his face** le bébé s'est barbouillé le visage avec sa nourriture; **her face was ~ed with jam** elle avait le visage barbouillé de confiture; **2** (slander) diffamer [*person*]; salir, entacher [*reputation*]; **3** (spread) étaler [*butter, ink, paint*]; appliquer [*sunoil, lotion*] (**on** sur); **she ~ed eyeshadow on her eyelids** elle s'est appliquée du fard sur les paupières; **4**○ (defeat) US écraser [*opposition, rival*].

III *vi* [*ink, paint*] s'étaler; [*lipstick, make-up*] couler.

smear: **~ campaign** *n* campagne *f* de diffamation (**against** contre); **~ tactics** *npl* manœuvres *fpl* diffamatoires; **~ test** *n* Med frottis *m*.

smeary /'smɪərɪ/ *adj* [*glass, window*] couvert de traces; [*face*] sale.

smell /smel/ **I** *n* **1** (odour) gen odeur *f*; (unpleasant) (mauvaise) odeur *f*; **a ~ of cooking/burning** une odeur de cuisine/de brûlé; **there's a bit of a ~ in here** il y a une drôle d'odeur ici; **what a ~!** comme ça sent mauvais!; **2** (sense) odorat *m*; **sense of ~** odorat, sens *m* olfactif; **3** (action) **to have a ~ of** ou **at sth** sentir un peu qch; **4** fig (of absence, fraud, dishonesty) relents *mpl*.

II *vtr* (*prét, pp* **smelled**, **smelt** GB) **1** lit (notice, detect) sentir; (sniff deliberately) [*person*] sentir; [*animal*] renifler, sentir; **I could ~ alcohol on his breath** je sentais à son haleine qu'il avait bu; **I can ~ lemons/burning** ça sent le citron/le brûlé; **2** fig (detect) flairer [*danger, problem, success, change, good worker*]; repérer [*liar, cheat*]; **a good reporter can always ~ a good story** un bon journaliste flaire toujours une bonne histoire.

III *vi* (*prét, pp* **smelled**, **smelt** GB) **1** (have odour) gen sentir; (unpleasantly) sentir (mauvais); **that ~s nice/horrible** ça sent bon/très mauvais; **this gas/flower doesn't ~** ce gaz/cette fleur ne sent rien; **to ~ of roses/garlic** sentir la rose/l'ail; **that ~s like curry** ça sent le curry; **2** fig **to ~ of racism/complacency/corruption** sentir le racisme/la complaisance/la corruption; **3** (have sense of smell) avoir de l'odorat.

■ **smell out**: **~ [sth] out, ~ out [sth] 1** (sniff out, discover) lit [*dog*] flairer [*drugs, explosives*]; **2** fig [*person*] découvrir [*plot, treachery, corruption*]; démasquer [*spy, traitor*]; **3** (cause to stink) empester, empuantir [*room, house*].

smelliness /'smelɪnɪs/ *n* mauvaise odeur *f*.

smelling salts *npl* Med sels *mpl*.

smelly /'smelɪ/ *adj* **1** lit [*animal, person, clothing*] qui sent mauvais; [*breath*] fétide; **2**○ fig [*idea, place, person*] vilain.

smelt /smelt/ **I** *pret, pp* ▶ **smell**.

II *n* Zool (*pl* **~** ou **~s**) éperlan *m*.

III *vtr* extraire [qch] par fusion [*metal*]; fondre [*ore*].

smelter /'smeltə(r)/ *n* (also **smeltery**) fonderie *f*.

smelting /'smeltɪŋ/ *n* extraction *f* par fusion.

smidgen, smidgin○ /'smɪdʒən/ *n* (of flavouring) soupçon *m*; (of alcohol) goutte *f*, doigt *m*; (of emotion) brin *m*; **just a ~** un tout petit peu.

smile /smaɪl/ **I** *n* sourire *m*; **a ~ of welcome/approval** un sourire de bienvenue/d'approbation; **to give a ~** sourire; **to give sb a ~** adresser un sourire à qn; **with a ~** en souriant; **to have a ~ on one's face** sourire; **take that ~ off your**

face il n'y a pas de quoi sourire; **to wipe the ~ off sb's face** faire passer l'envie de sourire à qn; **to be all ~s** être tout sourire; **to crack a ~**○ US consentir à sourire.
II *vtr* **1 to ~ one's consent/thanks** acquiescer/remercier d'un sourire; **to ~ a greeting** saluer d'un sourire; **'Of course,' he ~d** 'bien sûr,' dit-il en souriant; **2 to ~ a grateful/sad smile** avoir un sourire reconnaissant/triste.
III *vi* sourire (**at sb** à qn; **with** de); **we ~d at the idea/his confusion** cette idée/sa confusion nous a fait sourire; **to ~ to think of sth/that** sourire à la pensée de qch/que; **to ~ to oneself** sourire intérieurement; **keep smiling!** garde le sourire!
■ **smile on**: **~ on [sb/sth]** [*luck, fortune, weather*] sourire à; [*person, police, authority*] être favorable à.

smiling /ˈsmaɪlɪŋ/ *adj* souriant.

smilingly /ˈsmaɪlɪŋlɪ/ *adv* en souriant.

smirk /smɜːk/ **I** *n* (self-satisfied) petit sourire *m* satisfait; (knowing) sourire *m* en coin.
II *vi* (in a self-satisfied way) avoir un petit sourire satisfait; (knowingly) avoir un sourire en coin.

smite‡ /smaɪt/ *vtr* (*prét* **smote**; *pp* **smitten**) **1** (strike) frapper; **2** littér (punish) châtier liter.

smith /smɪθ/ ▶ 1692 *n* maréchal-ferrant *m*.

smithereens /ˌsmɪðəˈriːnz/ *npl* **in ~** en mille morceaux; **to smash to ~** voler en éclats; **to smash sth to ~** faire voler qch en éclats.

smithy /ˈsmɪðɪ/ *n* forge *f*.

smitten /ˈsmɪtn/ **I**‡ *pp* ▶ **smite**.
II *adj* **1** (afflicted) **~ by** rongé par [*guilt, regret*]; terrassé par [*illness*]; **2** (in love) fou/folle d'amour; **to be ~ by** ou **with sb** être fou amoureux/folle amoureuse de qn.

smock /smɒk/ **I** *n* blouse *f*, sarrau *m*.
II *vtr* faire des smocks à.

smocking /ˈsmɒkɪŋ/ *n* smocks *mpl*.

smog /smɒg/ *n* smog *m*.

smog mask *n* masque *m* antipollution.

smoke /sməʊk/ **I** *n* **1** (fumes) fumée *f*; **full of tobacco ~** plein de fumée de tabac; **a cloud/a wisp of ~** un nuage/une volute de fumée; **to go up in ~**○ lit brûler, partir en fumée; fig tomber à l'eau○; **to vanish in a puff of ~** disparaître dans un nuage de fumée; **2**○ (cigarette) clope○ *f*, cigarette *f*; **to have a ~** fumer; **she went out for a quick ~** elle est sortie pour fumer or pour en fumer une○; **3**○ **the ~** la ville; **the big Smoke** GB Londres.
II *vtr* **1** (use) fumer [*cigarette, pipe, marijuana*]; **2** Culin fumer [*fish, meat*].
III *vi* **1** (use tobacco, substances) fumer; **when did you start smoking?** quand est-ce que tu as commencé à fumer?; **2** (be smoky) [*fire, lamp, fuel*] fumer.
IV smoked *pp adj* [*food*] fumé; [*glass*] fumé.
IDIOMS **there's no ~ without fire, where there's ~ there's fire** il n'y a pas de fumée sans feu; **stick that in your pipe and ~ it!** si ça ne te plaît pas c'est le même prix!; **to ~ like a chimney**○ fumer comme un pompier○.
■ **smoke out**: ¶ **~ [sth] out, ~ out [sth]** enfumer [*animal*]; ¶ **~ [sb] out, ~ out [sb]** lit déloger qn en l'enfumant [*fugitive, sniper*]; fig débusquer [*traitor, culprit*]; ¶ **~ [sth] out** enfumer [*room, house*]; **you'll ~ the place out!** tu vas enfumer toute la pièce!

smoke: **~ alarm** *n* détecteur *m* de fumée; **~ bomb** *n* grenade *f* fumigène; **~ detector** *n* détecteur *m* de fumée; **~-dried** *adj* fumé; **~-dry** *vtr* fumer; **~-filled** *adj* enfumé.

smokeless /ˈsməʊklɪs/ *adj* [*fuel*] non polluant; [*zone*] où l'utilisation de combustibles polluants est interdite.

smoker /ˈsməʊkə(r)/ *n* **1** (person) fumeur/-euse *m/f*; **a heavy ~** un grand fumeur; **a light ~** une personne qui fume peu; **a ~'s cough** une toux de fumeur; **2** (on train) compartiment *m* fumeurs.

smoke screen *n* **1** Mil écran *m* de fumée; **2** fig diversion *f*; **to create** ou **throw up a ~** faire diversion.

smoke signal *n* signal *m* de fumée.

smokestack /ˈsməʊkstæk/ *n* (chimney) cheminée *f* d'usine; (funnel) cheminée *f*.

smokestack industries *n* industries *fpl* traditionnelles.

smokey = **smoky**.

smoking /ˈsməʊkɪŋ/ **I** *n* Med tabac *m*; **~ and drinking** le tabac et l'alcool; **'~ damages your health'** 'le tabac nuit à la santé'; **to give up ~** arrêter de fumer; **to cut down on one's ~** fumer moins; **a ban on ~** une interdiction de fumer; **'no ~'** 'défense de fumer'; **they want to reduce ~ among pupils** ils veulent réduire la consommation du tabac parmi les élèves.
II *adj* (*épith*) **1** (emitting smoke) [*chimney, volcano*] qui fume; [*cigarette*] allumé; **2** (for smokers) [*compartment, section*] fumeurs (*after n*).

smoking: **~ ban** *n* interdiction *f* de fumer; **~ compartment** GB, **~ car** US *n* compartiment *m* fumeurs; **~ jacket** *n* veste *f* d'intérieur; **~-related** *adj* [*disease*] associé au tabac; **~ room** *n* fumoir *m*.

smoky /ˈsməʊkɪ/ **I**○ *n* US flic *m* motard○.
II *adj* **1** [*atmosphere, room*] enfumé; **it's a bit ~ here** c'est un peu enfumé ici; **2** [*fire*] qui fume; **3** Culin [*cheese, ham, bacon*] fumé; **4** [*glass*] fumé.

smolder *vi* US = **smoulder**.

smoldering *adj* US = **smouldering**.

smooch○ /smuːtʃ/ **I** *n* **1** (kiss and cuddle) pelotage○ *m*; **to have a ~** [*couple*] se peloter○; **2** GB (slow dance) slow *m*.
II *vi* **1** (kiss and cuddle) se peloter○; **2** GB Dance danser un slow.

smoochy○ /ˈsmuːtʃɪ/ *adj* GB langoureux/-euse; **a ~ record** un slow.

smooth /smuːð/ **I** *adj* **1** lit (even, without bumps) [*stone, sea, surface, skin, hair, fabric*] lisse; [*road*] plan; [*curve, line, breathing*] régulier/-ière; [*sauce, gravy, paste*] homogène; [*crossing, flight*] sans heurts, calme; [*movement*] aisé; [*music, rhythm, playing*] fluide; **the tyres are worn ~** les pneus sont (devenus) lisses; **to have a ~ landing** atterrir en douceur; **bring the car to a ~ stop** arrêtez la voiture en douceur; **the engine is very ~** le moteur tourne parfaitement rond; **2** fig (problem-free) [*journey, flight, life*] paisible; **such a change is rarely ~** un tel changement se fait rarement en douceur; **the bill had a ~ passage through Parliament** la loi a été adoptée sans difficultés par le Parlement; **3** (pleasant, mellow) [*taste, wine, whisky*] moelleux/-euse; **4** (suave) gen, pej [*person*] mielleux/-euse; [*manners, appearance*] onctueux/-euse; **to be a ~ talker** être enjôleur/-euse; ▶ **operator**.
II *vtr* **1** lit (flatten out) lisser [*clothes, paper, hair, surface*]; (get creases out) défroisser [*fabric, paper*]; **to ~ the creases from sth** défroisser qch; **she ~ed her skirt over her hips** elle a lissé sa jupe au niveau des hanches; **to ~ one's hair back** se lisser les cheveux en arrière; **~ the cream into your skin/over your face** étalez la crème sur votre peau/visage; **this cream ~s rough skin** cette crème adoucit les peaux desséchées; **2** fig (make easier) faciliter [*process, transition, path*]; **talks to ~ the path towards peace** des pourparlers pour faciliter la voie vers la paix.
IDIOMS **to take the rough with the ~** prendre les choses comme elles viennent; **the course of true love never did run ~** l'amour vrai n'a jamais été facile à vivre; ▶ **silk**, **baby**, **ruffled**.
■ **smooth away**: **~ away [sth]**, **~ [sth] away** lit, fig faire disparaître [*wrinkles, creases, problems*].
■ **smooth down**: **~ [sth] down, ~ down [sth]** gen lisser [*clothes, hair, fabric*]; polir [*wood, rough surface*] (to get creases out) défroisser [*clothes, fabric*].
■ **smooth out**: **~ [sth] out, ~ out [sth]** **1** lit (lay out) étendre [*map, paper, cloth*]; (remove creases) défroisser [*paper , cloth*]; **2** fig aplanir [*difficulties*]; faire disparaître [*imperfections*]; **to ~ out the impact of sth** diminuer l'impact de qch.
■ **smooth over**: **~ [sth] over, ~ over [sth]** fig atténuer [*differences, awkwardness*]; aplanir [*difficulties, problems*]; tempérer [*bad feelings*]; améliorer [*relationship*]; **to ~ things over** arranger les choses.

smooth-cheeked, **smooth-faced** *adj* glabre.

smoothie○, **smoothy**○ /ˈsmuːðɪ/ *n* **1** péj (person) charmeur/-euse *m/f*, beau parleur *m*; **2** US (milk-shake) ≈ milk-shake *m*.

smoothly /ˈsmuːðlɪ/ *adv* **1** (easily) lit [*move, flow, glide*] doucement; [*start, stop, brake, land*] en douceur; [*write, spread*] de façon unie; fig (without difficulties) sans heurts, sans problèmes; **the key turned ~ in the lock** la clé a tourné facilement dans la serrure; **to run ~** [*engine, machinery*] tourner rond; fig [*business, department*] marcher bien; [*holiday*] se dérouler sans problèmes; **things are going very ~ for me** tout va bien or marche bien pour moi; **2** (suavely) [*speak, say, persuade, lie*] gen en douceur; pej mielleusement.

smoothness /ˈsmuːðnɪs/ *n* **1** lit (of surface, skin, hair) aspect *m* lisse; (of crossing, flight) tranquillité *f*; (of car, machine, engine) régularité *f*; (of music, rhythm, playing) fluidité *f*; (of movement) aisance *f*; **2** fig (absence of problems) (of operation, process, transition, journey) harmonie *f*; **3** (mellowness) (of wine, whisky, taste) douceur *f*; **4** (suaveness) (of person, manner, speech) onctuosité *f*.

smooth running **I** *n* (of machinery, engine) bon fonctionnement *m*; (of organization, department, event) bonne marche *f*.
II smooth-running *adj* [*machinery, engine*] qui tourne bien; [*organization, department, event*] qui marche bien.

smooth-tongued *adj* péj enjôleur/-euse.

smoothy○ *n* = **smoothie**○

smorgasbord /ˈsmɔːgəsbɔːd/ *n* **1** Culin buffet *m* (*à la scandinave*); **2** fig assortiment *m* (**of** de).

smote‡ /sməʊt/ *prét* ▶ **smite**.

smother /ˈsmʌðə(r)/ **I** *vtr* **1** (stifle) étouffer [*person, fire, flames, laugh, yawn, doubts, opposition, scandal, emotion*]; **2** (cover) couvrir (**with** de); **to ~ sb with kisses** couvrir qn de baisers; **a cake ~ed in cream** un gâteau recouvert de crème; **her face was ~ed in powder** son visage était recouvert d'une épaisse couche de poudre; **to be ~ed in blankets/furs** être tout emmitouflé dans des couvertures/des fourrures; **3** (overwhelm) (with love, kindness etc) étouffer.
II *vi* [*person*] être étouffé.

smoulder GB, **smolder** US /ˈsməʊldə(r)/ *vi* **1** lit [*fire, cigarette, ruins*] se consumer; **2** fig [*hatred, resentment, jealousy*] couver; **to ~ with** se consumer de [*resentment, jealousy*].

smouldering GB, **smoldering** US /ˈsməʊldərɪŋ/ *adj* **1** lit [*fire, cigarette*] qui se consume; [*ashes, ruins*] fumant; **2** fig (intense) [*hatred, resentment, jealousy*] sourd; **3** (sexy) [*eyes, look*] ardent.

smudge /smʌdʒ/ **I** *n* **1** (mark) trace *f*; **2** US Agric feu *m* de fumigation.
II *vtr* étaler [*make-up, print*]; faire des traces sur [*paper, paintwork*]; étaler [*ink, wet paint*].
III *vi* [*paint, ink, print, make-up*] s'étaler.
IV smudged *pp adj* [*paint, make-up*] qui a coulé (*after n*); [*writing, letter*] maculé; [*paper, cloth*] taché; **your make-up/the paint is ~d** ton maquillage/la couleur a coulé.

smudgy /ˈsmʌdʒɪ/ *adj* **1** (marked) [*paper,*

face] taché; [*writing, letter*] à moitié effacé; **2** (indistinct) [*photograph, image*] voilé; [*outline*] estompé.

smug /smʌg/ *adj* suffisant; **don't be so ~!** ne prends pas cet air suffisant!; **to be ~ about winning** être fier d'avoir gagné; **I can't afford to be ~** je ne peux pas m'endormir sur mes lauriers.

smuggle /ˈsmʌgl/ **I** *vtr* gen faire passer [qch] clandestinement [*message, food*] (**into** dans); faire du trafic de [*arms, drugs*]; (to evade customs) faire passer [qch] en contrebande [*watches, cigarettes, alcohol*]; **to ~ sth/sb in** faire entrer qch/qn clandestinement; **to ~ sb into a** ou **the country** faire entrer qn clandestinement; **to ~ sb into Britain/into the club** faire entrer qn clandestinement en Grande-Bretagne/dans le club; **to ~ sth/sb out (of)** (faire) sortir qch/qn clandestinement (de); **to ~ sth through** ou **past customs** faire passer qch en fraude or en contrebande.
II *vi* faire de la contrebande.
III smuggled *pp adj* [*cigarettes, diamonds*] de contrebande; **~d goods** produits *mpl* de contrebande.

smuggler /ˈsmʌglə(r)/ *n* contrebandier/-ière *m/f*; **drug/arms ~** passeur/-euse *m/f* de drogue/d'armes.

smuggling /ˈsmʌglɪŋ/ *n* gen contrebande *f*; **drug/arms ~** trafic *m* de drogue/d'armes.

smuggling ring *n* gen réseau *m* de contrebandiers; (of drugs, arms) réseau *m* de trafiquants.

smugly /ˈsmʌglɪ/ *adv* [*smile, act*] d'un air suffisant; [*say*] d'un ton suffisant.

smugness /ˈsmʌgnɪs/ *n* suffisance *f*.

smut /smʌt/ *n* **1** ¢ (vulgarity) grivoiseries *fpl*; **2** (stain) tache *f*; **3** Hort, Agric charbon *m*.

smuttiness /ˈsmʌtɪnɪs/ *n* grivoiserie *f*.

smutty /ˈsmʌtɪ/ *adj* **1** (crude) grivois; **2** (dirty) [*face, object*] noir, sale; [*mark*] noirâtre.

snack /snæk/ **I** *n* **1** (small meal) (in café, pub) repas *m* léger; (between meals, instead of meal) casse-croûte *m inv*; **to have** ou **eat a ~** manger quelque chose; **2** (crisps, peanuts etc) amuse-gueule *m inv*.
II *vi* grignoter, manger légèrement; **to ~ on sth** faire un léger repas de qch.

snack bar *n* snack-bar *m*.

snaffle /ˈsnæfl/ **I** *n* (also **~ bit**) mors *m* de filet.
II○ *vtr* GB (steal) barboter○.

snafu◐ /snæˈfuː/ **I** *n* **1** US (mistake) connerie◐ *f*; **2** (mess) pagaille○ *f*.
II *vtr* (*prés* **~es**; *prét, pp* **~ed**) semer la pagaille dans.
III *vi* (*prés* **~es**; *prét, pp* **~ed**) **1** US (make a mistake) faire une connerie◐; **2** (cause havoc) semer la pagaille.

snag /snæg/ **I** *n* **1** (hitch) inconvénient *m* (**in** de); **there's just one ~** il y a un problème or un os○; **that's the ~** voilà le problème or le hic○; **the ~ is that...** l'inconvénient or le problème, c'est que...; **to hit** ou **run into a ~** [*person*] avoir des problèmes, tomber sur un os○; [*plan*] se heurter à des obstacles; **2** (tear) accroc *m* (**in** à); **3** (projection) aspérité *f* (**in** sur).
II *vtr* (*prés p etc* **-gg-**) **1** (tear) filer [*tights, stocking*] (**on** contre); accrocher [*sleeve, garment, fabric*] (**on** à); se casser [*fingernail*] (**on** sur); s'égratigner [*hand, finger*] (**on** sur); **2**○ US (take) piquer○, dérober.
III *vi* (*prés p etc* **-gg-**) (catch) **to ~ on** [*rope, fabric*] s'accrocher à; [*propeller, part*] frotter contre.

snail /sneɪl/ *n* escargot *m*; **at a ~'s pace** à une allure d'escargot.

snail: **~ farm** *n* escargotière *f*; **~ farming** *n* héliciculture *f*; **~ shell** *n* coquille *f* d'escargot.

snake /sneɪk/ **I** *n* **1** Zool serpent *m*; **2** péj (person) traître/traîtresse *m/f*.
II *vi* [*road*] serpenter (**through** à travers); **the road ~d down the mountain** la route descendait la montagne en serpentant.
IDIOMS a ~ in the grass péj un traître/une traîtresse.

snake: **~bite** *n* morsure *f* de serpent; **~ charmer** *n* charmeur/-euse *m/f* de serpent; **~ eyes** *n* Games double un *m* (*aux dés*).

snakelike /ˈsneɪklaɪk/ *adj* [*movement*] ondulant; [*expression*] impénétrable; [*eyes, skin*] de serpent (*after n*).

snake: **~ oil** *n* US remède *m* de charlatan; **~ pit** *n* fosse *f* aux serpents; **~s and ladders ▶ 1282** *n* (+ *v sg*) GB Games ≈ jeu *m* de l'oie.

snakeskin /ˈsneɪkskɪn/ **I** *n* peau *f* de serpent.
II *modif* [*bag, shoes*] en (peau de) serpent.

snap /snæp/ **▶ 1282** **I** *n* **1** (cracking sound) (of branch) craquement *m*; (of fingers, lid, elastic) claquement *m*; **2** (bite) claquement *m*; **with a sudden ~ of his jaws, the fox...** d'un brusque claquement des mâchoires, le renard...; **3**○ Phot photo *f*; **holiday** GB ou **vacation** US **~** photo *f* de vacances; **4** Games ≈ bataille *f*; **5**○ US (easy thing) **it's a ~!** c'est du gâteau○!; **6**○ (vigour) vigueur *f*, nerf○ *m*; **put a bit of ~ into it!** mettez-y un peu de vigueur or nerf○!; **7** Sewing = **snap fastener**; **▶ cold snap**.
II *adj* [*decision, judgment, vote*] rapide.
III *vtr* (*prés p etc* **-pp-**) **1** (click) faire claquer [*fingers, jaws, elastic*]; **to ~ sth shut** fermer qch avec un bruit sec; **2** (break) (faire) casser net [qch]; **3** (say crossly) dire [qch] hargneusement; **'stop it!' she ~ped** 'arrête!' a-t-elle dit or répondu hargneusement; **4**○ Phot prendre une photo de [*person, building etc*].
IV *excl* **1** Games ≈ bataille!; **2**○ **~! we're wearing the same tie!** coïncidence! nous portons la même cravate!
V *vi* (*prés p etc* **-pp-**) **1** lit (break) [*branch, bone, pole*] se casser; [*elastic, rope, wire*] (se) casser; **the mast ~ped in two** le mât s'est cassé en deux; **2** fig (lose control) [*person*] être à bout, craquer○; **suddenly something just ~ped in me** tout à coup, j'ai craqué○; **my patience finally ~ped** ma patience était arrivée à bout; **3** (click) **to ~ open/shut** s'ouvrir/se fermer d'un coup sec; (louder) s'ouvrir/se fermer avec un claquement; **the attachment ~ped into place** l'accessoire s'est encastré avec un claquement; **4** (speak sharply) parler hargneusement.
IDIOMS ~ out of it○! cesse de faire la tête or la gueule◐!; **~ to it**○! et plus vite que ça○!; **to ~ to attention** Mil se figer au garde-à-vous.
■ **snap at**: **~ at [sth/sb] 1** (speak sharply) parler hargneusement à [*person*]; **2** (bite) [*dog, fish etc*] essayer de mordre.
■ **snap off**: ¶ **~ off** [*branch, knob, protrusion*] casser net; ¶ **~ off [sth]**, **~ [sth] off** casser [qch] net.
■ **snap out**: **~ out [sth]** glapir [*order, reply*].
■ **snap up**: **~ up [sth]** arracher [*bargain, opportunity*].

snap: **~dragon** *n* Bot muflier *m*; **~ fastener** *n* bouton-pression *m*; **~-on** *adj* [*lid, attachment*] à pression.

snapper /ˈsnæpə(r)/ *n* Zool lutjanidé *m*.

snappily /ˈsnæpɪlɪ/ *adv* **1** (crossly) hargneusement; **2** (smartly) [*dress*] de façon tapageuse.

snappish /ˈsnæpɪʃ/ *adj* hargneux/-euse.

snappy /ˈsnæpɪ/ *adj* **1** (bad-tempered) [*person, animal*] hargneux/-euse; **2** (lively) [*rhythm, reply, item*] rapide; (punchy) [*advertisement, feature*] accrocheur/-euse; **3**○ (smart) [*clothing*] chic *inv*; **he's a ~ dresser** il s'habille chic.
IDIOMS make it ~○! grouille-toi○!

snapshot /ˈsnæpʃɒt/ *n* photo *f*.

snare /sneə(r)/ **I** *n* piège *m* also fig.
II *vtr* prendre [qn/qch] au piège [*animal, person*].
IDIOMS a ~ and a delusion un miroir aux alouettes.

snare drum ▶ 1481 *n* tambour *m* à timbre.

snarl /snɑːl/ **I** *n* **1** (growl) (of animal) grondement *m*; (of traffic) bourdonnement *m*; **'you'd better watch out!' he said with a ~** 'tu ferais mieux de faire attention!' dit-il d'un ton hargneux; **2** (grimace) mine *f* hargneuse; **3** (tangle) (in single rope, flex) nœud *m*; (of several ropes, flexes) enchevêtrement *m*.
II *vtr* rugir [*order, insult, threat*] **'don't be so stupid,' he ~ed** 'ne sois pas si stupide,' dit-il d'un ton hargneux.
III *vi* (growl) [*animal*] gronder férocement; [*person*] grogner; **the dog ~ed at me** le chien m'a montré les dents; **he ~s at the new recruits** il grogne après les nouvelles recrues.
■ **snarl up**: ¶ **~ up** [*rope, wool*] s'emmêler; ¶ **~ up [sth]** bloquer [*traffic, road*]; **to be ~ed up** [*road, network, traffic*] être bloqué; [*economy, system*] être paralysé; [*plans, negotiations*] être bloqué; **I got ~ed up in the traffic** j'ai été pris dans les embouteillages; **the hook got ~ed up in the net** l'hameçon s'est pris dans le filet.

snarl-up /ˈsnɑːlʌp/ *n* (in traffic) embouteillage *m*; (in distribution network) blocage *m*.

snatch /snætʃ/ **I** *n* (*pl* **~es**) **1** (fragment) (of conversation) bribe *f*; (of poem, poet) quelques vers *mpl*; (of concerto, composer) quelques mesures *fpl*; (of tune) quelques notes *fpl*; **I only caught a ~ of the conversation** je n'ai entendu que des bribes de la conversation; **he remembers odd ~es of the song** il ne se souvient que de quelques bribes de la chanson; **2** (grab) **to make a ~ at sth** essayer d'attraper qch; **3** (theft) vol *m*; **bag ~** vol à l'arraché; **£100,000 was stolen in a wages ~** 100 000 livres ont été volées lors de l'attaque d'un fourgon qui contenait la paie des salariés; **4** Sport (in weightlifting) arraché *m*; **5**● US (vulva) chatte● *f*.
II *vtr* **1** (grab) attraper [*book, key*]; saisir [*opportunity*]; arracher [*victory*]; prendre [*lead*]; **to ~ sth from sb** arracher qch à qn; **she ~ed the letter out of my hands** elle m'a arraché la lettre des mains; **to be ~ed from the jaws of death** être arraché aux griffes de la mort; **2**○ (steal) piquer○, voler [*handbag, jewellery*] (**from** à); kidnapper [*baby*]; voler [*kiss*] (**from** à); **3** (take hurriedly) **try to ~ a few hours' sleep** essaie de dormir quelques heures; **have we got time to ~ a meal?** a-t-on le temps de manger quelque chose en vitesse?; **we managed to ~ a week's holiday** nous avons réussi à grapiller une semaine de vacances.
III *vi* **to ~ at sth** tendre vivement la main vers [*rope, letter*].
■ **snatch away**: **~ [sth] away** arracher qch (**from sb** à qn).
■ **snatch up**: **~ up [sth]** ramasser [qch] en vitesse [*clothes, papers*]; saisir [*child*]; **to ~ up a bargain** faire une affaire.

snatch squad *n* GB forces *fpl* d'intervention antiémeutes.

snazzy○ /ˈsnæzɪ/ *adj* [*clothing, colour*] criard; [*car*] tape-à-l'œil○ *inv*.

sneak /sniːk/ **I**○ *n* péj **1** GB (tell-tale) rapporteur/-euse *m/f*, mouchard/-e○ *m/f*; **2** (devious person) sournois/-e *m/f*.
II *modif* [*attack, raid*] en traître; [*visit*] furtif/-ive.
III *vtr* **1**○ (have secretly) manger [qch] en cachette [*chocolate etc*]; fumer [qch] en cachette [*cigarette*]; **2**○ (steal) piquer○, voler (**out of, from** dans); **I ~ed some brandy from the cupboard** j'ai piqué○ du cognac dans le placard; **they ~ed him out by the back door** ils l'ont fait sortir discrètement par la porte de derrière; **to ~ a look at sth** jeter un coup d'œil furtif à qch.
IV *vi* **1** (move furtively) **to ~ away** s'éclipser discrètement; **to ~ around** rôder; **to ~ in/out** entrer/sortir furtivement; **to ~ into** se faufiler dans [*room, bed*]; **to ~ past sth/sb** passer furtivement devant qch/qn;

to ~ up on sb/sth s'approcher sans bruit de qn/qch; **he ~ed up behind me** il s'est approché de moi par derrière sans bruit; **she ~ed out of the room** elle s'est glissée hors de la pièce; **2**○ GB (tell tales) rapporter, moucharder○; **to ~ on sb** dénoncer qn.

sneaker /'sni:kə(r)/ *n* US basket *f*, (chaussure *f* de) tennis *f*.

sneaking /'sni:kɪŋ/ *adj* [*suspicion*] vague; **I have a ~ suspicion that I've made a mistake** j'ai le vague sentiment d'avoir fait une erreur; **she has a ~ suspicion that he's lying** elle a le vague sentiment qu'il ment; **I have a ~ admiration/respect for her** je ne peux m'empêcher de l'admirer/d'avoir du respect à son égard.

sneak preview *n* Cin, fig avant-première *f*; **to give sb a ~ of sth** montrer qch à qn en avant-première.

sneak thief *n* chapardeur/-euse *m/f*.

sneaky /'sni:kɪ/ *adj* **1** péj (cunning) [*act, behaviour, move, person*] sournois; [*method, plan*] rusé; **2** (furtive) **to have a ~ look at sth** regarder qch en cachette.

sneer /snɪə(r)/ **I** *n* **1** (expression) sourire *m* méprisant; **to say sth with a ~** dire qch avec un sourire méprisant; **2** (remark) raillerie *f*.
II *vi* **1** (smile) sourire avec mépris; **2** (speak) railler; **to ~ at sb** railler qn.

sneering /'snɪərɪŋ/ **I** *n* railleries *fpl*.
II *adj* [*remark*] railleur/-euse; [*smile*] méprisant.

sneeringly /'snɪərɪŋlɪ/ *adv* [*say, watch*] avec un sourire méprisant.

sneeze /sni:z/ **I** *n* éternuement *m*.
II *vi* éternuer.
IDIOMS **it is not to be ~d at** ce n'est pas à dédaigner.

snick○ /snɪk/ **I** *n* **1** (small cut) encoche *f*; **2** (knot) nœud *m*.
II *vtr* **1** (cut) faire une encoche à; **2** Sport donner un petit coup oblique à [*ball*].

snicker /'snɪkə(r)/ **I** *n* **1** (whinny) hennissement *m*; **2** US = **snigger**.
II *vi* **1** (neigh) [*horse*] hennir doucement; **2** US = **snigger**.

snide /snaɪd/ *adj* sournois.

sniff /snɪf/ **I** *n* **1** (of person with cold, person crying) reniflement *m*; (of disgust, disdain) grimace *f*, moue *f*; **2** (inhalation) inhalation *f*; **a single ~ of this substance can be fatal** une seule inhalation de cette substance peut être mortelle; **to take a ~ of** sentir [*perfume, cheese*]; **let me have a ~** laisse-moi sentir; **3** fig (slight scent) **there was a ~ of corruption in the air** cela sentait la corruption; **there has never been a ~ of scandal** il n'y a jamais eu le moindre soupçon de scandale; **I didn't get a ~ of the profits** je n'ai pas vu la couleur des bénéfices; **I didn't get a ~ of the ball** je n'ai pas eu le ballon une seule fois.
II *vtr* [*dog*] flairer [*trail, lamppost*]; [*person*] humer [*air*]; sentir [*perfume, food, flower*]; inhaler, sniffer○ [*glue, cocaine*]; respirer [*smelling salts*].
III *vi* lit [*person*] renifler; [*dog*] renifler, flairer; fig [*person*] faire une moue; **to ~ at sth** lit renifler [*food, liquid*]; fig faire la grimace à [*suggestion, idea*]; faire la fine bouche devant [*dish, food*]; **a free car/a 10% pay rise is not to be ~ed at** une voiture gratuite/une augmentation de 10%, ça ne se refuse pas.
■ **sniff out**: **~ out [sth]** [*dog*] flairer [*explosives, drugs*]; fig [*journalist*] flairer [*scandal*]; [*police*] dénicher [*culprit*]; [*shopper*] flairer [*bargain*].

sniffer dog *n*: *chien policier entraîné pour détecter la drogue ou les explosifs*.

sniffle○ /'snɪfl/ **I** *n* **1** (sniff) reniflement *m*; **2** (slight cold) petit rhume *m*; **to have the ~s**○ être enrhumé.
II *vi* renifler.

sniffy○ /'snɪfɪ/ *adj* dédaigneux/-euse; **to be ~ about sth** faire la fine bouche au sujet de qch.

snifter /'snɪftə(r)/ *n* **1**○ (drink) petit coup○ *m*, petit verre *m*; **2** US (glass) (verre *m*) ballon *m*.

snigger /'snɪgə(r)/ **I** *n* ricanement *m*; **with a ~** en ricanant.
II *vi* ricaner; **to ~ at [sb/sth]** se moquer de [*person*]; ricaner en entendant [*remark*]; ricaner en voyant [*appearance, action*].

sniggering /'snɪgərɪŋ/ **I** *n* ¢ ricanements *mpl*; **stop your ~** cessez de ricaner.
II *adj* [*person*] qui ricane.

snip /snɪp/ **I** *n* **1** (action) petit coup *m* (de ciseaux etc); **2** (onomat) cliquetis *m*; **3** (piece) (of fabric) échantillon *m*; **4**○ (bargain) (bonne) affaire *f*; **5** Turf gagnant *m* sûr.
II *vtr* (*p prés etc* **-pp-**) découper (à petits coups de ciseaux etc) [*fabric, paper*]; tailler [*hedge*].
■ **snip off**: **~ [sth] off**, **~ off [sth]** couper [*nail, twig, corner*].

snipe /snaɪp/ **I** *n* Zool bécassine *f*.
II *vtr* **'rubbish,' he ~d** 'balivernes,' lança-t-il.
III *vi* **to ~ at** (shoot) tirer sur, canarder○ [*person, vehicle*]; (criticize) envoyer des piques à [*person*].

sniper /'snaɪpə(r)/ *n* Mil tireur *m* embusqué.

sniper fire *n* Mil tir *m* de tireurs embusqués.

sniping /'snaɪpɪŋ/ *n* ¢ piques *fpl*.

snippet /'snɪpɪt/ *n* (*gén pl*) (of conversation, information) bribe *f*; (of text, fabric, music) fragment *m*.

snitch○ /snɪtʃ/ **I** *n* **1** (nose) nez *m*, pif○ *m*; **2** (telltale) (adult) mouchard○ *m*; (child) rapporteur/-euse *m/f*.
II *vtr* (steal) faucher○, voler.
III *vi* (reveal secret) moucharder○; **to ~ on sb** dénoncer qn, balancer○ qn.

snivel /'snɪvl/ *vi* (*p prés etc* **-ll-**) pleurnicher.

sniveller○ /'snɪvlə(r)/ *n* péj pleurnicheur/-euse *m/f*.

snivelling /'snɪvlɪŋ/ **I** *n* ¢ pleurnicheries *fpl*.
II *adj* [*child, coward*] pleurnicheur/-euse.

snob /snɒb/ **I** *n* snob *mf*.
II *modif* [*value, appeal*] pour les snobs.

snobbery /'snɒbərɪ/ *n* snobisme *m*.

snobbish /'snɒbɪʃ/ *adj* snob *inv*.

snobbishness /'snɒbɪʃnɪs/ *n* snobisme *m*.

snobby○ /'snɒbɪ/ *adj* snobinard○.

snog○ /snɒg/ **I** *n* bécotage○ *m*.
II *vi* (*p prés etc* **-gg-**) se bécoter○.

snogging○ /'snɒgɪŋ/ *n* bécotage○ *m*.

snood /snu:d/ *n* Hist résille *f*; (modern) cagoule *f*.

snook /snu:k/ *n* (fish) brochet *m* de mer.
IDIOMS **to cock a ~ at sb** faire la nique à qn.

snooker /'snu:kə(r)/ **▶ 1282** **I** *n* **1** (game) snooker *m* (*variante du billard*); **2** (shot) coup *m* fumant.
II *modif* [*ball, cue, tournament, player*] de snooker.
III *vtr* **1** Sport, fig coincer [*player, person*]; **I'm ~ed** fig je suis coincé; **2** US (deceive) avoir○, tromper [*person*]; **we've been ~ed** on nous a eus○.

snoop○ /snu:p/ **I** *n* = **snooper**.
II *vi* espionner; **to ~ into sth** mettre son nez○ dans qch; **to ~ on sb** espionner qn.
■ **snoop around**○ fouiner, fureter.

snoop around○ *n* **to have a ~** jeter un coup d'œil.

snooper○ /'snu:pə(r)/ *n* péj fouineur/-euse○ *m/f*.

snooping○ /'snu:pɪŋ/ **I** *n* (by state, police, journalist) espionnage *m*.
II *adj* fouineur/-euse○.

snoot /snu:t/ *n* Phot réflecteur *m*.

snooty○ /'snu:tɪ/ *adj* [*restaurant, club, college*] huppé; [*tone, person*] prétentieux/-ieuse.

snooze○ /snu:z/ **I** *n* petit somme *m*; **to have a ~** faire un petit somme.
II *vi* sommeiller.

snooze button *n* bouton *m* de répétition de l'alarme.

snore /snɔ:(r)/ **I** *n* ronflement *m*.
II *vi* ronfler.

snorer○ /'snɔ:rə(r)/ *n* ronfleur/-euse *m/f*.

snoring /'snɔ:rɪŋ/ *n* ¢ ronflements *mpl*.

snorkel /'snɔ:kl/ **I** *n* (US **schnorkel**) **1** (for swimmer) tuba *m*, tube *m* respiratoire; **2** (on submarine) schnorchel *m*.
II *vi* (*p prés etc* **-ll-**) faire de la plongée avec tuba.

snorkelling /'snɔ:klɪŋ/ **▶ 1282** *n* Sport plongée *f* avec tuba.

snort /snɔ:t/ **I** *n* **1** (of horse, bull) ébrouement *m*; (of person, pig) grognement *m*; **to give a ~** [*horse, bull*] s'ébrouer; [*person, pig*] grogner; **2** (of cocaine) argot des drogués sniff *m*; **3**○ (drink) petit coup *m*.
II *vtr* **1** **'hooligans!' he ~ed** 'voyous!' grogna-t-il; **2** argot des drogués sniffer [*drug*].
III *vi* [*person, pig*] grogner; [*horse, bull*] s'ébrouer; **to ~ with laughter** rire comme un cheval.

snorter○ /'snɔ:tə(r)/ *n* **1** (drink) **to have a quick ~** boire un petit coup; **2** (horror) **the exam/speech was a real ~** l'examen/le discours était carabiné○; **a ~ of a letter/question** une lettre/question carabinée.

snot○ /snɒt/ *n* **1** (mucus) morve *f*; **2** péj (child) morveux/-euse *m/f*; (adult) péteux/-euse○ *m/f*.

snotty○ /'snɒtɪ/ **I** *n* (in Navy) midshipman *m*.
II *adj* **1** [*nose*] plein de morve; **~-nosed child** enfant avec de la morve au nez; **2** (of person) prétentieux/-ieuse.

snout /snaʊt/ *n* **1** (of most animals) museau *m*; (of pig) groin *m*; **2** fig, hum (of person) museau○ *m*; **keep your ~ out of this** ne mets pas ton museau dedans; **3** argot des prisonniers (tobacco) perlot○ *m*; (cigarettes) sèches○ *fpl*; **4** argot des policiers (informer) indic○ *m*.
IDIOMS **to have one's ~ in the trough** avoir sa part du gâteau.

snow /snəʊ/ **I** *n* **1** Meteorol neige *f*; **a fall of ~** une chute de neige; **2** Radio, TV neige *f*; **3**○ argot des drogués (cocaine) neige○ *f*, cocaïne *f*.
II **snows** *npl* neiges *fpl*; **the ~s of Siberia** les neiges de Sibérie.
III *vtr*○ US emberlificoter○ [*person*].
IV *v impers* neiger; **it's ~ing** il neige.
■ **snow in** (also **~ up**): **to be ~ed in** être bloqué par la neige; **we were ~ed in for three days** on est resté bloqué à l'intérieur pendant trois jours à cause de la neige.
■ **snow under**: **to be ~ed under** lit [*car, house*] être couvert de neige; fig (with work, letters) être submergé (**with** de).

snowball /'snəʊbɔ:l/ **I** *n* **1** lit boule *f* de neige; **2** (drink) *cocktail*; **3**○ argot des drogués (drug cocktail) mélange *m* de cocaïne et d'héroïne.
II *vtr* bombarder [qn] de boules de neige.
III *vi* fig [*profits, problem, plan, support*] faire boule de neige.
IDIOMS **it hasn't got a ~'s chance in hell**○ c'est perdu d'avance; **he hasn't got a ~'s chance in hell**○ il n'a pas la moindre chance.

snowball fight *n* bataille *f* de boules de neige.

snow: **~bank** US *n* congère *f*; **~belt** *n* US *États américains qui connaissent des hivers rigoureux*; **~ blindness** *n* cécité *f* des neiges.

snowboard /'snəʊbɔ:d/ Sport **I** *n* surf *m* des neiges.
II *vi* faire du surf des neiges.

snow: **~boot** *n* Fashn, Sport après-ski *m inv*; **~bound** *adj* [*house, person, vehicle, village*] bloqué par la neige; [*region*] paralysé par la neige; **~ bunting** *n* Zool bruant *m* des neiges; **~ chains** *npl* Aut chaînes *fpl*.

Snowdon /ˈsnəʊdən/ *pr n* le (mont) Snowdon *m*.

Snowdonia /snəʊˈdəʊnɪə/ *pr n* massif *m* du Snowdon.

snow: **~drift** *n* congère *f*; **~drop** *n* Bot perce-neige *m inv*; **~fall** *n* chute *f* de neige; **~field** *n* champ *m* de neige; **~flake** *n* flocon *m* de neige; **~ goose** *n* oie *f* des neiges; **~ job**○ *n* US baratin○ *m*; **~ leopard** *n* léopard *m* des neiges, once *f*; **~ line** *n* limite *f* des neiges éternelles; **~man** *n* bonhomme *m* de neige; **~ mobile** *n* Aut motoneige *f*; **~ plough** GB, **~ plow** US *n* Aut, Sport chasse-neige *m inv*; **~ report** *n* Meteorol bulletin *m* d'enneigement; **~ shoe** *n* raquette *f*; **~slide**, **~slip** *n* Meteorol mini-avalanche *f*; **~storm** *n* tempête *f* de neige; **~ suit** *n* combinaison *f* de ski; **~ tyre** GB, **~ tire** US *n* pneu-neige *m*, pneu *m* clouté; **Snow White** *pr n* Blanche Neige *f*.

snowy /ˈsnəʊɪ/ *adj* **1** lit (after a snowfall) [*landscape, peak, slope*] enneigé, couvert de neige; (usually under snow) [*region, range*] neigeux/-euse; **it will be ~ tomorrow** il neigera demain; **2** ▶**1104** fig (white) [*beard, cloth*] blanc/blanche (comme neige); **a ~-haired old man** un vieil homme aux cheveux blancs.

snowy owl *n* harfang *m*.

SNP *n* GB Pol *abrév* ▶**Scottish National Party**.

Snr. *abrév écrite* = **Senior**.

snub /snʌb/ **I** *n* rebuffade *f*.
II *vtr* (*p prés etc* **-bb-**) rembarrer; **to be ~bed** essuyer une rebuffade (**by** de la part de).

snub: **~ nose** *n* nez *m* retroussé; **~-nosed** *adj* au nez retroussé.

snuck○ /snʌk/ *prét, pp* ▶**sneak**.

snuff /snʌf/ **I** *n* tabac *m* à priser.
II *vtr* **1** (put out) moucher [*candle*]; **2** (sniff) humer [*air*].
IDIOMS **to ~ it**○ casser sa pipe○.
■ **snuff out**: **~ [sth] out, ~ out [sth] 1** moucher [*candle*]; **2** fig éteindre [*hope, interest*]; étouffer [*rebellion, enthusiasm*]; **3**○ (kill) descendre○ [*person*].

snuffbox /ˈsnʌfbɒks/ *n* tabatière *f*.

snuffer /ˈsnʌfə(r)/ **I** *n* (also **candle ~**) éteignoir *m*.
II snuffers *npl* mouchettes *fpl*.

snuffle /ˈsnʌfl/ **I** *n* (of animal, person) reniflement *m*; **to have the ~s** renifler parce qu'on est enrhumé.
II *vi* [*animal, person*] renifler.
■ **snuffle around** renifler.

snuff movie *n*: *film pornographique avec meurtre non simulé*.

snug /snʌg/ **I** *n* GB *petite arrière-salle d'un bar*.
II *adj* [*bed, room*] douillet; [*coat*] chaud; **we were ~ in our new coats/the kitchen** nous étions bien au chaud dans nos nouveaux manteaux/la cuisine. ▶**rug**.

snuggery /ˈsnʌgərɪ/ *n* GB = **snug** I.

snuggle /ˈsnʌgl/ *vi* se blottir, se pelotonner (**into** dans; **against** contre); **to ~ together** se blottir or se pelotonner l'un contre l'autre; **to ~ down in one's bed** se pelotonner dans son lit.
■ **snuggle up** se blottir (**against, beside** contre); **to ~ up to sth/sb** se blottir contre qch/qn.

snugly /ˈsnʌglɪ/ *adv* **the coat fits ~** le manteau est parfaitement ajusté; **the lid of the box should fit ~** le couvercle de la boîte devrait s'adapter parfaitement; **the pieces of the jigsaw fit ~ together** les pièces du puzzle s'emboîtent parfaitement; **the card fits ~ into the envelope** l'enveloppe est exactement de la bonne taille pour la carte; **the baby was ~ wrapped up in a blanket** le bébé était douillettement enveloppé dans une couverture; **he's ~ tucked up in bed** il est bien au chaud dans son lit.

so /səʊ/ **I** *adv* **1** (so very) si, tellement; **~ stupid/quickly** si or tellement stupide/vite; **he's ~ fat he can't get in** il est tellement or si gros qu'il ne peut pas rentrer; **~ thin/tall etc that** si or tellement maigre/grand etc que; **what's ~ funny?** qu'est-ce qu'il y a de si drôle?; **not ~**○ **thin/tall as** pas aussi maigre/grand que [*person*]; **he's not ~ stern a father as yours** ce n'est pas un père aussi sévère que le tien; **not ~ good a plumber** pas un aussi bon plombier; **not nearly ~ expensive as your pen** pas du tout aussi cher que ton stylo; **I'm not feeling ~ good**○ je ne me sens pas très bien; ▶**as**; **2** littér (also **~ much**) tellement; **she loved him/worries ~** elle l'aimait/s'inquiète tellement; **3** (to limited extent) **we can only work ~ fast and no faster** nous ne pouvons vraiment pas travailler plus vite; **you can only do ~ much (and no more)** tu ne peux rien faire de plus; **4** (in such a way) **~ arranged/worded that** organisé/rédigé d'une telle façon que; **walk ~** marchez comme ça; **and ~ on and ~ forth** et ainsi de suite; **just as X is equal to Y, ~ A is equal to B** soit X égale Y, A égale B; **just as you need him, ~ he needs you** tout comme tu as besoin de lui, il a besoin de toi; **just as in the 19th century, ~ today** tout comme au XIXe siècle, aujourd'hui; **~ be it!** soit!; **she likes everything to be just ~** elle aime que les choses soient parfaitement en ordre; **5** (for that reason) **~ it was that** c'est ainsi que; **she was young and ~ lacked experience** elle était jeune et donc sans expérience; **she was tired and ~ went to bed** elle était fatiguée donc elle est allée se coucher; **6** (true) **is that ~?** c'est vrai?; **if (that's) ~** si c'est vrai ou le cas; **7** (also) aussi; **~ is she/do I etc** elle/moi etc aussi; **if they accept ~ do I** s'ils acceptent, j'accepte aussi; **8**○ (thereabouts) environ; **20 or ~** environ 20; **a year or ~ ago** il y a environ un an; **9** (as introductory remark) **~ there you are** te voilà donc; **~ that's the reason** voilà donc pourquoi; **~ you're going are you?** alors tu y vas?; **10** (avoiding repetition) **he's conscientious, perhaps too much ~** il est consciencieux, peut-être même trop; **he's the owner or ~ he claims** c'est le propriétaire du moins c'est ce qu'il prétend; **he dived and as he did ~...** il a plongé et en le faisant...; **he opened the drawer and while he was ~ occupied...** il a ouvert le tiroir et pendant qu'il était en train de le faire...; **perhaps ~** c'est possible; **I believe ~** je crois; **~ I believe** c'est ce que je crois; **I'm afraid ~** j'ai bien peur que oui or si; **~ it would appear** c'est ce qu'il semble; **~ to speak** si je puis dire; **I told you ~** je te l'avais bien dit; **~ I see** je le vois bien; **I think/don't think ~** je pense/ne pense pas; **who says ~?** qui dit ça?; **he said ~** c'est ce qu'il a dit; **we hope ~** nous espérons bien; **only more ~** mais encore plus; **the question is unsettled and will remain ~** la question n'est pas résolue et ne le sera pas; **11** sout (referring forward or back) **yes if you ~ wish** oui si vous le voulez ; **if you ~ wish you may...** si vous le souhaitez, vous pouvez...; **12** (reinforcing a statement) **'I thought you liked it?'—'~ I do'** 'je croyais que ça te plaisait'—'mais ça me plaît'; **'it's broken'—'~ it is'** 'c'est cassé'—'je le vois bien!'; **'I'd like to go to the ball'—'~ you shall'** 'j'aimerais aller au bal'—'tu iras'; **'I'm sorry'—'~ you should be'** 'je suis désolé'—'j'espère bien'; **it just ~ happens that** il se trouve justement que; **13**○ (refuting a statement) **'he didn't hit you'—'he did ~!'** 'il ne t'a pas frappé?'—'si, il m'a frappé'; **I can ~ make waffles** si, je sais faire les gaufres; **14**○ (as casual response) et alors; **'I'm leaving'—'~?'** 'je m'en vais'—'et alors?'; **~ why worry!** et alors, il n'y pas de quoi t'en faire!
II so (that) *conj phr* **1** (in such a way that) de façon à ce que (+ *subj*); **she wrote the instructions ~ that they'd be easily understood** elle a rédigé les instructions de façon à ce qu'elles soient faciles à comprendre; **2** (in order that) pour que; **she fixed the party for 8 ~ that he could come** elle a prévu la soirée pour 8 heures pour qu'il puisse venir; **be quiet ~ I can work** tais-toi que je puisse travailler.
III so as *conj phr* pour; **~ as to attract attention/not to disturb people** pour attirer l'attention/ne pas déranger les gens.
IV so much *adv phr, pron phr* **1** (also **~ many**) (such large quantity) tant de [*sugar, friends*]; **~ much of her life** une si grande partie de sa vie; **~ many of her friends** un si grand nombre de ses amis; **~ much of the information** une large partie des renseignements; ▶**ever**; **2** (also **~ many**) (in comparisons) **to behave like ~ many schoolgirls** se conduire comme des écolières; **tossed like ~ much flotsam** balloté comme des épaves flottantes; **3** (also **~ many**) (limited amount) **I can only make ~ much bread** ou **~ many loaves** je ne peux pas faire plus de pains; **I can pay ~ much** je peux payer tant; **there's only ~ much you can take** il y a des limites à ce qu'on peut supporter; **4** (to such an extent) tellement; **~ much worse** tellement pire; **to like/hate sth ~ much that** aimer/détester qch tellement que; **she worries ~ much** elle s'inquiète tellement; **he was ~ much like his sister** il ressemblait tellement à sa sœur; **~ much ~ that** à un tel point que; **thank you ~ much** merci beaucoup; **5** (in contrasts) **not ~ much X as Y** moins X que Y; **it wasn't ~ much shocking as depressing** c'était moins choquant que déprimant; **it doesn't annoy me ~ much as surprise me** ça m'agace moins que ça ne me surprend; ▶**much**.
V so much as *adv phr* (even) même; **he never ~ much as apologized** il ne s'est même pas excusé; ▶**without**.
VI so much for *prep phr* **1** (having finished with) **~ much for that problem, now for...** assez parlé de ce problème, parlons maintenant de...; **2**○ (used disparagingly) **~ much for equality/liberalism** bonjour l'égalité/le libéralisme○; **~ much for saying you'd help** c'était bien la peine de dire que tu aiderais.
VII so long as○ *conj phr* ▶**long**.
IDIOMS **~ long**○! (goodbye) à bientôt!; **~ much the better/the worse** tant mieux/pis; **~ ~** comme ci comme ça; **~ there!** d'abord!; **I did it first, ~ there!** c'est moi qui l'ai fait le premier, d'abord!

soak /səʊk/ **I** *n* **1 to give sth a ~** GB faire or laisser tremper qch; **to have a ~** [*person*] prendre un long bain; **2**○ (drunk) poivrot/-ote○ *m/f*, ivrogne *mf*.
II *vtr* **1** (wet) tremper [*person, clothes*]; **to get ~ed** se faire tremper; **2** (immerse) laisser or faire tremper [*clothes, dried foodstuff*]; **3**○ fig (drain) faire casquer○ [*customer, taxpayer*].
III *vi* **1** (be immersed) tremper; **to leave sth to ~** mettre qch à tremper [*clothes*]; **2** (be absorbed) **to ~ into** [*water*] être absorbé par [*earth, paper, fabric*]; **to ~ through** [*blood*] traverser [*bandages*]; [*rain*] traverser, transpercer [*coat*].
IV *v refl* **to ~ oneself** (get wet) se tremper; (in bath) prendre un long bain.
V soaked *pp adj* [*person, clothes, shoes*] trempé; **to be ~ed through** ou **~ed to the skin** être trempé jusqu'aux os.
VI -soaked *dans composés* **blood-~ed bandages** des pansements imbibés de sang; **sweat-~ed** trempé de sueur; **rain-~ed** [*pitch, track*] détrempé; **sun-~ed** ensoleillé.
■ **soak away** [*water*] être absorbé.
■ **soak in** [*water, ink*] pénétrer; **let the**

stain remover ~ in laisse le détachant pénétrer.

■ **soak off**: ¶ **~ off** [*label, stamp*] se décoller; **the label on the bottle ~s off** l'étiquette se décolle quand on fait tremper la bouteille dans l'eau; ¶ **~ [sth] off, ~ off [sth]** décoller [qch] en le mouillant [*label*].

■ **soak out**: ¶ **~ out** [*dirt, stain*] partir; ¶ **~ [sth] out, ~ out [sth]** faire partir [qch] en le laissant tremper [*stain*].

■ **soak up**: ¶ **~ [sth] up, ~ up [sth]** [*earth, sponge*] absorber, boire [*water*]; ¶ **~ up [sth]** [*person*] s'imprégner de [*atmosphere*]; **to ~ up the sun** faire le plein○ de soleil.

soakaway /ˈsəʊkəweɪ/ *n* Constr puisard *m*.

soaking /ˈsəʊkɪŋ/ **I** *n* GB douche○ *f*; **to get a ~** prendre une bonne douche○; **to give sb a ~** tremper qn.
II *adj* trempé; **a ~ wet towel/sock** une serviette/chaussette complètement trempée; **I'm ~ wet** je suis trempé jusqu'aux os.

soap /səʊp/ **I** *n* **1** (for washing) savon *m*; **a bar of ~** un savon; **with ~ and water** avec de l'eau et du savon; **2**○ (flattery) (also **soft ~**) pommade○ *f*, flatterie *f*; **3**○ = **soap opera**.
II *vtr* savonner; **to ~ sb's back** savonner le dos à qn.
III *v refl* **to ~ oneself** se savonner.

soapbox /ˈsəʊpbɒks/ *n* (for speeches) tribune *f* improvisée; **to get on one's ~** enfourcher son cheval de bataille.

soapbox: **~ orator** *n* harangueur/-euse *m/f*; **~ oratory** *n* harangue *f* de démagogue.

soap: **~dish** *n* porte-savon *m*; **~flakes** *npl* savon *m* en paillettes; **~ opera** *n* Radio, TV péj feuilleton *m*; **~ powder** *n* lessive *f* (en poudre); **~ star** *n* vedette *f* de feuilleton; **~stone** *n* stéatite *f*; **~suds** *npl* (foam) mousse *f* de savon; (water) eau *f* savonneuse.

soapy /ˈsəʊpɪ/ *adj* **1** lit [*water*] savonneux/-euse; [*hands, face*] plein de savon; [*taste*] de savon; **2** (cajoling) [*compliment, voice, tone*] mielleux/-euse; [*manner*] onctueux/-euse.

soar /sɔː(r)/ *vi* **1** (rise sharply) [*popularity, price, temperature, costs*] monter en flèche; [*hopes, spirits, morale*] s'accroître considérablement; **2** gen, Fin (rise) **to ~beyond/above/through** dépasser; **the index ~ed through 2,000** l'indice a dépassé les 2000; **to ~ to** [*figures, shares, popularity*] atteindre; **inflation has ~ed to a new level** l'inflation a atteint un niveau record; **to ~ from X to Y** passer de X à Y; **3** (rise up) = **soar up**; **4** (glide) [*bird, plane*] planer; **5** littér [*flames, sound*] s'élever; [*tower, cliffs*] se dresser.

■ **soar up** [*bird, plane*] prendre son essor; [*ball*] filer.

soaring /ˈsɔːrɪŋ/ *adj* [*inflation, demand, profits*] en forte progression; [*prices, temperatures*] en forte hausse; [*hopes, popularity*] croissant; [*spire, skyscraper*] élancé.

sob[1] /sɒb/ **I** *n* sanglot *m*; **'forgive me,' he said with a ~** 'pardonne-moi,' dit-il en sanglotant.
II *vtr* (*p prés etc* **-bb-**) **'it hurts,' he ~bed** 'ça fait mal,' dit-il en sanglotant; **to ~ oneself to sleep** s'endormir à force de sangloter.
III *vi* (*p prés etc* **-bb-**) sangloter.
IDIOMS **to ~ one's heart out** pleurer toutes les larmes de son corps.

■ **sob out**: **~ out [sth]** raconter [qch] en sanglotant [*story*].

sob[2]○, **SOB** /esəʊˈbiː/ *n* injur (*abrév* = **son of a bitch**) **you ~!** espèce d'enfoiré●!

sobbing /ˈsɒbɪŋ/ **I** *n* ¢ sanglots *mpl*; **the sound of ~** un bruit de sanglots.
II *adj* [*child*] sanglotant.

sober /ˈsəʊbə(r)/ **I** *adj* **1** (not drunk) **I'm ~** je n'ai pas bu d'alcool; (in protest) je ne suis pas ivre; **2** (no longer drunk) dessoûlé; **don't drive until you're ~** ne prend pas le volant tant que tu n'as pas dessoûlé; **3** (serious) [*person*] sérieux/-ieuse; [*mood*] grave; **4** (realistic) [*estimate, judgment, statement*] modéré; [*reminder*] réaliste; **5** (discreet) [*colour, decor, style*] sobre; [*tie, suit, pattern*] sobre, discret/-ète.
II *vtr* **1** (after alcohol) dessoûler [*person*]; **2** (make serious) [*news, reprimand*] calmer [*person*]. ▶**judge**.

■ **sober up**: ¶ **~ up** dessoûler; ¶ **~ [sb] up** [*fresh air, coffee*] dégriser [*person*].

sobering /ˈsəʊbərɪŋ/ *adj* **it was a ~ thought/reminder** cette pensée/ce rappel donnait à réfléchir; **it is ~ to think that we will all be out of work soon** l'idée que nous allons tous être sans emploi bientôt donne à réfléchir.

soberly /ˈsəʊbəlɪ/ *adv* **1** (seriously) [*speak*] avec modération; [*describe*] avec sobriété; [*estimate*] sérieusement; **2** (discreetly) [*dress, dressed*] discrètement; [*decorate, decorated*] sobrement.

soberness /ˈsəʊbənɪs/ *n* **1** (seriousness) sérieux *m*; **2** (plainness of decor etc) sobriété *f*.

sober sides† *n* hum rabat-joie *mf inv*.

sobriety /səˈbraɪətɪ/ *n* **1** (moderation) sobriété *f*; **2** (seriousness) sérieux *m*; **3** (simplicity of dress, decor) sobriété *f*.

sobriquet /ˈsəʊbrɪkeɪ/ *n* sout sobriquet *m*.

sob /sɒb/: **~ sister**○ *n* US Journ journaliste *mf* qui se spécialise dans le courrier du cœur; **~ story**○ *n* mélo○ *m*, histoire *f* larmoyante; **~ stuff**○ *n* péj sensiblerie *f* pej.

soca /ˈsəʊkə/ *n* Mus calypso *m* soul.

soccer /ˈsɒkə(r)/ ▶**1282** **I** *n* football *m*.
II *modif* [*player, team, club*] de football; [*star*] du football; **~ violence** violence *f* dans les tribunes.

sociability /ˌsəʊʃəˈbɪlətɪ/ *n* sociabilité *f*.

sociable /ˈsəʊʃəbl/ *adj* [*person*] sociable; [*village*] accueillant; **a ~ way to shop/relax** une façon agréable de faire les courses/se détendre.

sociably /ˈsəʊʃəblɪ/ *adv* [*behave*] de façon amicale; [*chat*] amicalement.

social /ˈsəʊʃl/ **I** *n* (party) soirée *f*; (gathering) réunion *f*.
II *adj* **1** (relating to human society) [*background, class, ladder, mobility, structure, system*] social; **~ contract** contrat *m* social; **2** (in the community) [*custom, function, group, problem, status, unrest, unit*] social; **3** (recreational) [*activity*] de groupes; [*call, visit*] amical; **he's a ~ drinker** il boit de l'alcool en société; **he's a ~ smoker** c'est un fumeur occasionnel; **he's got no ~ skills** il ne sait pas se comporter en société; **4** (gregarious) [*animal*] social, sociable.

social: **~ accounting** *n* Econ, Fin comptabilité *f* nationale; **~ anthropology** *n* anthropologie *f* sociale; **~ charter** *n* charte *f* sociale; **~ climber** *n* (still rising) arriviste *mf*; (at his/her peak) parvenu/-e *mf*; **~ club** *n* club *m*; **~ column** *n* carnet *m* mondain, rubrique *f* mondaine.

social conscience *n* **to have a ~** être conscient des injustices sociales.

social: **~ contact** *n* contact *m*; **~ democracy** *n* social-démocratie *f*; **~ democrat** *n* social-démocrate *mf*; **~ democratic** *n* social-démocrate; **~ disease** *n* euph maladie *f* honteuse euph; **~ duty** *n* devoir *m* de citoyen; **~ engagement** *n* obligation *f* sociale; **~ engineering** *n* manipulation *f* des structures sociales; **~ evening** *n* soirée *f*; **~ event** *n* événement *m* mondain; **Social Fund** *n* GB Soc Admin *fonds national de solidarité sous forme de prêt*; **~ gathering** *n* réunion *f* entre amis; **~ historian** ▶**1692** *n* historien/-ienne *m/f* spécialisé/-e dans les faits de société; **~ history** *n* histoire *f* sociale; **~ housing** *n* logements *mpl* sociaux; **~ insurance** *n* US Soc Admin ≈ sécurité *f* sociale.

socialism /ˈsəʊʃəlɪzəm/ *n* socialisme *m*.

socialist /ˈsəʊʃəlɪst/ *n, adj* (also **Socialist**) socialiste (*mf*).

socialistic /ˌsəʊʃəˈlɪstɪk/ *adj* péj socialisant.

socialite /ˈsəʊʃəlaɪt/ *n* mondain/-e *m/f*.

socialization /ˌsəʊʃəlaɪˈzeɪʃn, US -lɪˈz-/ *n* socialisation *f*.

socialize /ˈsəʊʃəlaɪz/ **I** *vtr* (adapt to society) socialiser [*child*].
II *vi* (mix socially) rencontrer des gens; **to ~ with sb** fréquenter qn.

socializing /ˈsəʊʃəlaɪzɪŋ/ *n* **we don't do much ~** on ne sort pas beaucoup.

social life *n* (of person) vie *f* sociale; (of town) vie *f* culturelle.

socially /ˈsəʊʃəlɪ/ *adv* [*meet, mix*] en société; [*acceptable*] en société; [*inferior, superior*] du point de vue social; [*oriented*] vers le social; **I know him ~, not professionally** je le connais personnellement, mais pas sur le plan professionnel.

social: **~ marketing** *n* Advertg promotion *f* d'une cause sociale; **~ misfit** *n* inadapté/-e *m/f*; **~ outcast** *n* paria *m*; **~ rank** *n* position *f* dans la société; **~ realism** *n* Art, Cin, Literat réalisme *m* social; **~ register** *n* US carnet *m* mondain, rubrique *f* mondaine.

social scene *n* **she's well known on the London ~** elle est très connue dans la société londonienne; **what's the Oxford ~ like?** qu'est-ce qu'il y a à faire à Oxford?

social science **I** *n* science *f* sociale.
II *modif* [*faculty*] des sciences sociales; [*degree*] de or en sciences sociales; [*exam*] de sciences sociales.

social: **~ scientist** ▶**1692** *n* spécialiste *mf* des sciences sociales; **~ secretary** *n* (of celebrity) secrétaire *mf* particulier/-ière; (of club) secrétaire *mf* (du club).

social security **I** *n* Soc Admin (benefit) aide *f* sociale; **to live off ~** vivre de l'aide sociale; **to be on ~** recevoir l'aide sociale.
II *modif* [*budget, claimant*] d'aide sociale; [*payment*] de l'aide sociale; [*minister*] des affaires sociales.

social: **Social Security Administration, SSA** *n* US Soc Admin *service de gestion de la retraite et des pensions*; **~ service** *n* US ▶ **social work**.

Social Services GB **I** *npl* services *mpl* sociaux.
II *modif* [*secretary, director*] des affaires sociales; [*department, office*] de l'aide sociale.

social studies *n* (+ *v sg*) sciences *fpl* humaines.

social welfare **I** *n* Soc Admin protection *f* sociale.
II *modif* [*system*] de protection sociale; [*organization, group*] à caractère social.

social work **I** *n* travail *m* social.
II *modif* [*specialist*] du travail social; [*qualifications, skills*] de travailleur social.

social worker ▶**1692** *n* travailleur/-euse *m/f* social/-e.

societal /səˈsaɪətl/ *adj* sociétal.

society /səˈsaɪətɪ/ **I** *n* **1** ¢ (the human race) société *f*; **2** **C** (individual social system) société *f*; **a civilized/closed/multi-cultural ~** une société civilisée/fermée/multiculturelle; **3** (group) (for social contact) association *f*; (for mutual hobbies) club *m*; (for intellectual, business, religious contact) société *f*; **drama/music ~** société de théâtre/de musique; **4** (upper classes) (also **high ~**) haute société *f*; **London ~** la haute société londonienne; **fashionable ~** le beau monde; **5** (company) sout société *f*; **I like the ~ of young people** j'apprécie la société des jeunes.
II *modif* [*artist, columnist, photographer, wedding*] mondain; [*hostess*] des soirées mondaines; **~ gossip** les échos mondains.

society: **~ column** *n* carnet *m* mondain; **Society of Friends** *pr n* Relig Société *f* des Amis; **Society of Jesus, SJ** *pr n* Relig Société *f* de Jésus, S.J.

sociobiology /ˌsəʊsɪəʊbaɪˈɒlədʒɪ/ *n* sociobiologie *f*.

socioeconomic /ˌsəʊsɪəʊˌiːkəˈnɒmɪk/ *adj* socio-économique.

sociolinguistic /ˌsəʊsɪəʊlɪŋˈgwɪstɪk/ **I** *adj* sociolinguistique.
II sociolinguistics *n* (+ *v sg*) sociolinguistique *f*.

sociological /ˌsəʊsɪəˈlɒdʒɪkl/ *adj* [*study, research, issue*] sociologique; [*studies*] de sociologie.

sociologically /ˌsəʊsɪəˈlɒdʒɪklɪ/ *adv* sociologiquement; (sentence adverb) **~ (speaking),...** du point de vue sociologique,...

sociologist /ˌsəʊsɪˈɒlədʒɪst/ **▶ 1692** *n* sociologue *mf*.

sociology /ˌsəʊsɪˈɒlədʒɪ/ **I** *n* sociologie *f*.
II *modif* [*studies, teacher*] de sociologie.

sociometry /ˌsəʊsɪˈɒmətrɪ/ *n* sociométrie *f*.

sociopath /ˈsəʊsɪəpæθ/ *n* US sociopathe *mf*.

sociopathic /ˌsəʊsɪəˈpæθɪk/ *adj* US [*report, study*] sociopathique; [*patient*] sociopathe.

sociopolitical /ˌsəʊsɪəʊpəˈlɪtɪkl/ *adj* sociopolitique.

sock /sɒk/ **▶ 1703** **I** *n* (US *pl* **~s** ou **sox**) **1** (footwear) chaussette *f*; **2** Aviat (also **wind ~**) manche *f* à air; **3**○ (punch) beigne○ *f*.
II○ *vtr* flanquer une beigne○ à [*person*]; **~ him one!** flanque-lui une beigne.
IDIOMS **to put a ~ in it**○ la boucler○; **I wish he'd put a ~ in it**○ si seulement il la bouclait○; **to ~ it to them**○ donner le maximum; **to pull one's ~s up**○ se remuer.

socket /ˈsɒkɪt/ *n* **1** Elec (for plug) prise *f* (de courant); (for bulb) douille *f*; **2** Anat (of joint) cavité *f* articulaire; (of eye) orbite *f*; (of tooth) alvéole *m*; **he nearly pulled my arm out of its ~** il a failli me déboiter le bras; **3** Tech (carpentry joint) mortaise *f*; (of spanner) douille *f*.

Socrates /ˈsɒkrətiːz/ *pr n* Socrate.

Socratic /səˈkrætɪk/ *adj* socratique.

sod /sɒd/ **I** *n* **1**◑ (person) salopard/salope◑ *m/f*; (task) chierie◑ *f*; **you stupid ~** espèce de connard◑; **poor ~** le pauvre; **poor little ~s** (of children) pauvres petits; **2** (turf) motte *f* (de gazon); **3** littér étendue *f* d'herbe.
II◑ *excl* **~ it!** merde◑!; **~ him** qu'il aille se faire voir◑; **~ this typewriter** cette machine à écrire m'emmerde◑.
■ **sod off**◑ dégager◑, partir; **why don't you just ~ off!** tu veux pas dégager◑!

soda /ˈsəʊdə/ **I** *n* **1** Chem soude *f*; **2** (also **washing ~**) soude *f* ménagère; **3** (also **~ water**) eau *f* de seltz; **whisky and ~** whisky *m* soda; **4** (also **~ pop**) US soda *m*.
II *modif* [*bottle*] de soda; [*crystals*] de soude.

soda: **~ ash** *n* Chem soude *f* ménagère; **~ biscuit** *n* biscuit *m* digestif; **~ bread** *n* pain *m* au lait (*et à la levure chimique*); **~ cracker** *n* US = **soda biscuit**; **~ fountain** *n* US distributeur *m* de soda.

sodality /səʊˈdælətɪ/ *n* sout gen, Relig confrérie *f*.

sod all◑ /ˌsɒdˈɔːl/ *pron* des clopinettes○ *fpl*; **what did I get out of it? ~!** et qu'ai-je gagné? des clopinettes○!; **he knows ~ about it** il n'y connaît que dalle◑; **to do ~** glander◑.

soda siphon /ˈsəʊdə saɪfn/ *n* siphon *m* d'eau de seltz.

sodden /ˈsɒdn/ *adj* **1** (wet through) [*towel, clothing*] trempé; [*ground*] détrempé; **2** fig **~ with drink** abruti d'alcool.

sodding◑ /ˈsɒdɪŋ/ *adj* foutu◑.

sodium /ˈsəʊdɪəm/ *n* sodium *m*.

sodium: **~ bicarbonate** *n* bicarbonate *m* de soude; **~ carbonate** *n* carbonate *m* de sodium; **~ chloride** *n* chlorure *m* de sodium; **~ hydroxide** *n* hydroxyde *m* de sodium; **~ hypochlorite** *n* hypochlorite *m* de sodium; **~ lamp**, **~ light** *n* lampe *f* au sodium; **~ nitrate** *n* nitrate *m* de sodium; **~ sulphate** *n* sulfate *m* de sodium.

Sodom /ˈsɒdəm/ *pr n* Sodome.

sodomite /ˈsɒdəmaɪt/ *n* sodomite *m*.

sodomize /ˈsɒdəmaɪz/ *vtr* sodomiser.

sodomy /ˈsɒdəmɪ/ *n* sodomie *f*.

Sod's Law○ /ˌsɒdzˈlɔː/ *n* hum loi *f* de l'emmerdement◑ maximum.

sofa /ˈsəʊfə/ *n* canapé *m*; **convertible ~** canapé convertible.

sofa bed *n* canapé-lit *m*.

Sofia /ˈsəʊfɪə/ **▶ 1818** *pr n* Sofia.

soft /sɒft, US sɔːft/ **I** *adj* **1** (yielding, not rigid or firm) [*ground, soil, clay*] meuble; Sport, Turf lourd; [*rock, metal*] tendre; [*snow*] léger/-ère; [*bed, cushion, pillow*] moelleux/-euse; [*fabric, fur, skin, hand, cheek*] doux/douce; [*brush, hair, leather*] souple; [*muscle*] flasque; [*mixture, dough, butter*] mou/molle; [*pencil*] doux/douce; **to get ~** [*soil, ground, butter, mixture*] s'amollir; [*mattress*] devenir mou; [*muscle*] se ramollir; **to make sth ~** amollir qch [*ground*]; ramollir qch [*butter, mixture*]; assouplir qch [*fabric*]; adoucir qch [*hard water, skin*]; **~ to the touch** doux au toucher; **~ ice cream** glace *f* italienne; **2** (muted) [*colour, glow, light, tone, sound, laugh, music, note, voice, accent*] doux/douce; [*step, knock*] feutré; **~ lighting** éclairage *m* tamisé; **3** (gentle, mild) [*air, climate, rain, breeze, look, words*] doux/douce; [*reply*] apaisant; [*impact, pressure, touch*] léger/-ère; [*eyes, heart*] tendre; [*approach*] gen diplomatique; Pol modéré; **the ~ left** la gauche modérée; **to take a ~ line with sb** adopter une ligne modérée avec qn; **4** (not sharp) [*outline, shape*] flou; [*fold*] souple; **5** Econ [*market, prices*] instable à la baisse; [*loan*] privilégié; **6** (lenient) [*parent, teacher*] (trop) indulgent; **to be ~ on sb/sth** être (trop) indulgent envers qn/qch; **7**○ (in love) **to be ~ on sb** en pincer○ pour qn; **8** Chem [*water*] doux/douce; **9** (idle, agreeable) [*life, job*] peinard○; **10**○ (cowardly) trouillard○; **11**○ (stupid) stupide; **to be ~ in the head** être ramolli du cerveau; **12** Ling [*consonant*] doux/douce.
II *adv* = **softly**.

soft: **~back** *n* Publg livre *m* à couverture plastifiée; **~ball** *n* US *variante du baseball*; **~-boiled** *adj* [*egg*] à la coque; **~ centre** *n* (chocolate) chocolat *m* fourré (*de matière fondante*); **~-centred** *adj* [*chocolate*] fourré; **~ cheese** *n* fromage *m* à pâte molle; **~ copy** *n* Comput visualisation *f* sur écran; **~-core** *adj* érotique; **~ currency** *n* Fin monnaie *f* faible; **~ drink** *n* boisson *f* nonalcoolisée; **~ drug** *n* drogue *f* douce.

soften /ˈsɒfn, US ˈsɔːfn/ **I** *vtr* **1** lit (make less firm or rough) amollir [*ground, metal*]; adoucir [*skin, hard water*]; ramollir [*butter*]; assouplir [*fabric*]; **2** fig atténuer [*blow, impact, image, impression, shock, pain, resistance*]; adoucir [*personality, refusal*]; assouplir [*approach, attitude, position, rule, view*]; minimiser [*fact*]; **3** (make quieter) adoucir [*sound, voice*]; baisser [*music*]; **4** (make less sharp) adoucir [*contour, form, outline, light*].
II *vi* **1** lit [*light, outline, music, colour*] s'adoucir; [*skin*] devenir plus doux; [*substance, ground*] se ramollir; [*consonant*] devenir doux; **2** fig [*person, character, approach, attitude, position, view*] s'assouplir (**towards sb** vis-à-vis de qn); **3** Econ [*currency, economy, market*] fléchir.
■ **soften up**: ¶ **~ up** [*butter, malleable substance*] amollir; ¶ **~ up [sb]**, **~ [sb] up** fig affaiblir [*enemy, opponent*]; attendrir [*customer*].

softener /ˈsɒfnə(r), US ˈsɔːf-/ *n* **1** (also **fabric ~**) (produit *m*) assouplissant *m*; **2** (also **water ~**) adoucisseur *m*.

softening /ˈsɒfnɪŋ, US ˈsɔːf-/ *n* **1** (becoming soft) lit (of substance, surface) ramollissement *m*; fig (of light, colour, outline, consonant, water) adoucissement *m*; (of character, attitude, view) assouplissement *m* (**towards sb/sth** vis-à-vis de qn/qch); (of sound) atténuation *f*; **2** Fin (of economy) fléchissement *m*; **3** Med **~ of the brain** ramollissement *m* cérébral.

soft focus *n* flou *m* artistique; **in ~** en flou artistique.

soft focus lens *n* lentille *f* diffusante.

soft-footed /ˌsɒftˈfʊtɪd, US sɔːft-/ *adj* lit **to be ~** marcher d'un pas feutré; fig **a ~ approach** une attitude diplomatique.

soft: **~ fruit** *n* ¢ fruits *mpl* charnus; **~ furnishings** *npl* tapis et tissus *mpl* d'ameublement; **~ goods** *npl* Comm biens *mpl* non durables.

soft-headed /ˌsɒftˈhedɪd, US ˌsɔːft-/ *adj* **1**○ (silly) fêlé○; **2** Mil [*bullet*] à pointe creuse expansive.

soft: **~-hearted** *adj* [*person*] qui se laisse facilement apitoyer or attendrir; **~-heartedness** *n* (extrême) gentillesse *f*.

softie○ *n* = **softy**.

softish○ /ˈsɒftɪʃ, US ˈsɔːft-/ *adj* **1** [*consistency, bed*] assez mou/molle; **2** Sport [*ground*] assez lourd.

soft landing *n* Aviat, Econ atterrissage *m* en douceur.

softly /ˈsɒftlɪ, US ˈsɔːft-/ *adv* [*speak, touch, play, tread, laugh, blow, shine, shut*] doucement; [*fall*] en douceur.
IDIOMS **~ ~ catchee monkey**† hum il faut être prudent.

softly-softly /ˌsɒftlɪˈsɒftlɪ, US ˌsɔːftlɪˈsɔːftlɪ/ *adj* [*approach*] ultraprudent; **to take a ~ approach** prendre des gants.

softness /ˈsɒftnɪs, US ˈsɔːft-/ *n* (of texture, surface, skin, colour, light, outline, character, sound) douceur *f*; (of substance) consistance *f* molle; fig (of attitude, approach, view) modération *f*; (in economy) fléchissement *m*.

soft option *n* facilité *f*; **to take the ~** choisir la facilité.

soft palate *n* voile *m* du palais.

soft-pedal /ˌsɒftˈpedl, US ˌsɔːft-/ **I soft pedal** *n* Mus pédale *f* douce.
II *vi* (*p prés etc* **-ll-** GB, **-l-** US) **1** Mus mettre la pédale douce; **2** fig mettre un bémol○ fig (**on** à).

soft: **~ porn**○ *n* soft○ *m*; **~ sell** *n* (méthode *f* de) vente *f* persuasive; **~-shell crab** *n* crabe *m* à carapace molle; **~ shoulder** *n* accotement *m* non stabilisé.

soft soap **I** *n* **1** lit savon *m* semi-liquide; **2**○ fig flagornerie○ *f*.
II soft-soap *vtr* fig passer de la pommade○ à [*person*].
III soft-soap *vi* flagorner○.

soft-spoken /ˌsɒftˈspəʊkn US ˌsɔːft-/ *adj* **1** lit à la voix douce; **to be ~** avoir une voix douce; **2** fig beau parleur/belle parleuse.

soft spot○ *n* **to have a ~ for sb** avoir un faible○ pour qn.

soft: **~ target** *n* Mil, fig cible *f* vulnérable; **~ tissue** *n* Med parties *fpl* charnues; **~-top** *n* Aut décapotable *f*; **~ touch**○ *n* poire○ *f*; **~ toy** *n* peluche *f*; **~ verge** *n* accotement *m* non stabilisé; **~-voiced** *adj* à la voix douce.

software /ˈsɒftweə(r), US ˈsɔːft-/ **I** *n* logiciel *m*; **computer ~** logiciel *m* (informatique).
II *modif* [*development, engineering, protection*] informatique; [*company, designer, manufacturer, project, publishing*] de logiciels; [*industry, market*] du logiciel; **~ product** logiciel *m*.

software: **~ house** *n* fabricant *m* de logiciels; **~ package** *n* progiciel *m*; **~ piracy** *n* piratage *m* de logiciels.

softwood /ˈsɒftwʊd, US ˈsɔːft-/ *n* **1** (timber) bois *m* tendre; **2** (tree) conifère *m*.

softy○ /ˈsɒftɪ, US ˈsɔːftɪ/ *n* **1** péj (weak person) mauviette○ *f*; **2** (indulgent person) bonne pâte○ *f*.

SOGAT, **Sogat** /ˈsəʊgæt/ *n* GB (*abrév* = **Society of Graphical and Allied Trades**) confédération *f* des métiers graphiques et associés.

soggy /ˈsɒgɪ/ *adj* [*ground*] détrempé; [*clothes*] trempé; [*food*] ramolli.

soh /səʊ/ *n* Mus sol *m*.

soil /sɔɪl/ I *n* sol *m*, terre *f*; **on British/foreign ~** en territoire britannique/étranger.
II *vtr* lit, fig salir.
IDIOMS **to ~ one's hands with sth/by doing** iron se salir les mains avec qch/à faire.

soiled /sɔɪld/ *adj* **1** (dirty) lit, fig sali; **2** (also **shop-~**) Comm [*clothing, stock, items*] vendu avec défaut.

soil pipe *n* tuyau *m* d'écoulement.

soiree /ˈswɑːreɪ, US swɑːˈreɪ/ *n* soirée *f*.

sojourn /ˈsɒdʒən, US səʊˈdʒɜːrn/ sout I *n* séjour *m*.
II *vi* séjourner.

solace /ˈsɒləs/ I *n* **1** (feeling of comfort) consolation *f*; **to seek** ou **find ~ in sth** chercher sa consolation dans qch; **to draw ~ from sth** se consoler de qch; **2** (source of comfort) réconfort *m*; **to be a ~ to sb** être d'un grand réconfort pour qn.
II *vtr* consoler (**for** de).

solanum /səˈleɪnəm/ *n* solanacée *f*.

solar /ˈsəʊlə(r)/ *adj* [*battery, energy, furnace, ray, system, year*] solaire; [*warmth*] du soleil.

solar: **~ cell** *n* pile *f* solaire, photopile *f*; **~ collector** *n* capteur *m* solaire; **~ eclipse** *n* éclipse *f* de soleil; **~ flare** *n* Astron éruption *f* solaire; **~ heated** *adj* chauffé à l'énergie *f* solaire; **~ heating** *n* chauffage *m* solaire.

solarium /səˈleərɪəm/ *n* (*pl* **-riums** ou **-ria**) (all contexts) solarium *m*.

solar: **~ panel** *n* panneau *m* solaire; **~ plexus** *n* (*pl* **-uses**) plexus *m* solaire; **~ power** *n* énergie *f* solaire; **~ powered** *adj* qui fonctionne à l'énergie solaire; **~ wind** *n* Meteorol vent *m* solaire.

sold /səʊld/ *prét, pp* ▶ **sell**.

solder /ˈsəʊldə(r), ˈsɒ-, US ˈsɒdər/ I *n* **1** (alloy) soudure *f*; **soft ~** soudure *f* à l'étain; **brazing** ou **hard ~** brasure *f*; **2** (join) soudure *f*, cordon *m* de soudure.
II *vtr* souder (**onto, to** à).
III *vi* souder.
■ **solder on**: **~ [sth] on, ~ on [sth]** souder.

soldering iron *n* fer *m* à souder.

soldier /ˈsəʊldʒə(r)/ **▶1692** I *n* soldat *m*/femme soldat *f*, militaire *m*; **to be a ~** être soldat; **to play at ~s** jouer aux soldats; **old ~** ancien combattant *m*; **~ of fortune**† mercenaire *m*; **regular ~** militaire *m* de carrière; **woman ~** femme *f* soldat.
II *vi* être militaire or dans l'armée.
IDIOMS **to come the old ~ with sb** GB prendre des airs supérieurs avec qn; **old ~s never die** la vieille garde reste fidèle au poste.
■ **soldier on** persévérer malgré tout; **to ~ on with doing** persévérer à faire.

soldier: **~ ant** *n* fourmi *f* soldat; **~ boy** *n* Hist, Mil enfant *m* soldat.

soldiering /ˈsəʊldʒərɪŋ/ *n* **1** (army) armée *f*; **2** (army life) vie *f* militaire.

soldierly /ˈsəʊldʒəlɪ/ *adj* [*person*] à l'allure militaire; [*appearance, bearing*] militaire.

soldiery† /ˈsəʊldʒərɪ/ *n* (*pl* **~**) soldatesque† *f* also pej.

sole /səʊl/ I *n* **1** Zool sole *f*; **2** (of shoe, sock, iron) semelle *f*; **3** Anat plante *f*; **the ~ of the foot** la plante du pied.
II *adj* **1** (single) [*aim, concern, duty, reason, source, supporter, survivor*] seul, unique; **for the ~ purpose of doing** uniquement pour faire; **2** (exclusive) [*agent, distributor, importer, right*] exclusif/-ive; [*trader*] indépendant; **for the ~ use of** pour l'usage exclusif de; **to have the ~ agency for** Comm être le concessionnaire exclusif de; **to be in ~ charge of sth** être seul responsable de qch.
III *vtr* ressemeler [*shoe*].
IV **-soled** (*dans composés*) **rubber/leather ~d shoes** chaussures à semelle de caoutchouc /cuir.

sole beneficiary *n* Jur légataire *m* universel.

solecism /ˈsɒlɪsɪzəm/ *n* **1** Ling solécisme *m*; **2** (social) bévue *f*.

solely /ˈsəʊlɪ/ *adv* **1** (wholly) entièrement; **you are ~ responsible** vous êtes entièrement responsable; **2** (exclusively) uniquement; **I'm saying this ~ for your benefit** je dis ça uniquement dans votre intérêt.

solemn /ˈsɒləm/ *adj* **1** (serious) [*face, occasion, person, statement, voice*] solennel/-elle; [*duty, warning*] formel/-elle; **2** (reverent) [*celebration, procession, tribute*] solennel/-elle.

solemnity /səˈlemnətɪ/ I *n* solennité *f*; **with all due ~** dans la plus grande solennité.
II **solemnities** *npl* cérémonial *m* ¢.

solemnization /ˌsɒləmnaɪˈzeɪʃn, US -nɪˈz-/ *n* sout célébration *f* solennelle.

solemnize /ˈsɒləmnaɪz/ *vtr* célébrer [*marriage*]; ratifier [*treaty*].

solemnly /ˈsɒləmlɪ/ *adv* **1** [*bless, move, speak*] solennellement; [*look*] d'un air solennel; **2** (sincerely) [*promise*] solennellement; **I do ~ swear to tell the truth** Jur je jure de dire toute la vérité.

solenoid /ˈsəʊlənɔɪd/ *n* solénoïde *m*.

soleus /ˈsəʊlɪəs/ *n* (*pl* **-lei**) muscle *m* soléaire.

sol-fa /ˌsɒlˈfɑː, US ˌsəʊl-/ *n* solfège *m*.

solicit /səˈlɪsɪt/ I *vtr* **1** (request) solliciter [*attention, information, money, help, opinion, vote*]; rechercher [*business, investment, orders*]; **2** Jur [*prostitute*] racoler [*client*].
II *vi* **1** Jur [*prostitute*] racoler; **2** (request) **to ~ for** solliciter [*votes, support*]; Comm rechercher [*orders*].

solicitation /ˌsəlɪsɪˈteɪʃn/ *n* **1** Jur racolage *m*; **2** liter (request) sollicitations *fpl*.

soliciting /səˈlɪsɪtɪŋ/ *n* Jur racolage *m*.

solicitor /səˈlɪsɪtə(r)/ **▶1692** *n* **1** GB Jur (for documents, oaths) ≈ notaire *m*; (for court and police work) ≈ avocat/-e *m/f*; **the family ~** le notaire de famille; **the company ~** l'avocat de la société; **a firm of ~s** ≈ un cabinet d'avocats; **you'll be hearing from my ~** (menacingly) vous aurez affaire à mon avocat; **2** US Jur (chief law officer) *chargé des affaires juridiques auprès de la municipalité* (or *du département d'État*); **3** US Comm démarcheur/-euse *m/f*; **telephone ~** télévendeur/-euse *m/f*.

solicitor: **Solicitor General** *n* GB adjoint *m* du Procureur général; US *conseiller auprès du Ministre de la Justice*; **~'s fees** *npl* GB Jur frais *mpl* notariés.

solicitous /səˈlɪsɪtəs/ *adj* sout [*expression, person*] plein de sollicitude; [*enquiry, letter, response*] attentionné (**about** sur); **~ about** soucieux/-ieuse de; **to be ~ for** ou **of sth** se soucier de qch.

solicitously /səˈlɪsɪtəslɪ/ *adv* avec sollicitude.

solicitude /səˈlɪsɪtjuːd, US -tuːd/ *n* **1** (concern) sollicitude *f*; **to show ~ for sb/sth** faire preuve de sollicitude envers qn/pour qch; **2** sout (worry) souci *m*.

solid /ˈsɒlɪd/ I *n* Chem, Math solide *m*.
II **solids** *npl* (food) aliments *mpl* solides; **to be on ~s** [*baby*] manger des aliments solides.
III *adj* **1** (not liquid or gaseous) solide; **to go** ou **become ~** se solidifier; **2** (of one substance) [*teak, gold, marble, granite*] massif/-ive; [*tyre*] plein; **the gate was made of ~ steel** le portail était tout en acier; **a tunnel cut through ~ rock** un tunnel taillé dans la masse rocheuse; **3** (dense, compact) [*crowd*] compact, dense; [*earth*] compact; **a ~ bank of cloud** une masse nuageuse dense; **4** (unbroken) [*line, expanse*] continu; **a ~ area of red** une surface rouge unie; **5** (uninterrupted) **five ~ days, five days ~** cinq jours entiers; **I worked for three ~ hours** j'ai travaillé pendant trois heures entières; **a ~ day's work** un jour entier de travail; **6** (strong) [*structure, foundation, basis*] solide; [*building*] massif/-ive; [*relationship, argument*] solide; **a ~ grounding in grammar** une base solide de grammaire; **to be on ~ ground** fig être en terrain sûr; **7** (reliable) [*evidence, information*] solide; [*advice*] sérieux/-ieuse; [*investment*] sûr; [*worker*] sérieux/-ieuse; **I have ~ grounds for** j'ai de solides raisons pour; **she's a very ~ person** c'est quelqu'un de très solide; **a ~ piece of work** un travail sérieux; **8** (firm) [*grip*] ferme; [*punch*] fort; **to have the ~ support of** avoir le soutien massif de; **the strike has remained ~** la grève n'a pas fléchi; **a ~ Republican area** (uniformly) une zone entièrement républicaine; (staunchly) un bastion du républicanisme; **9** (respectable) [*citizen, family, tax payer*] modèle.
IV *adv* [*freeze*] complètement; fig [*vote*] massivement; **the lake was frozen ~** le lac était complètement gelé; **the play is booked ~** la pièce affiche complet.

solid angle *n* angle *m* solide.

solidarity /ˌsɒlɪˈdærətɪ/ *n* solidarité *f*; **to feel ~ with sb** se sentir solidaire de qn; **to do sth out of ~ with sb** faire qch par solidarité envers qn; **to show ~ with** ou **towards sb** manifester sa solidarité envers qn.

solidarity fund *n* caisse *f* de solidarité.

solid compound *n* Ling composé *m* en un seul mot.

solid fuel I *n* combustible *m* solide.
II **solid-fuel** *modif* [*central heating*] à combustibles solides.

solid geometry *n* géométrie *f* dans l'espace.

solidification /ˌsəlɪdɪfɪˈkeɪʃn/ *n* solidification *f* (**of** de).

solidify /səˈlɪdɪfaɪ/ I *vtr* solidifier.
II *vi* [*liquid, semiliquid*] se solidifier; [*honey, oil*] se figer; **to ~ into a jelly** se transformer en gelée.

solidity /səˈlɪdətɪ/ *n* (of construction, relationship, currency) solidité *f* (**of** de); (of research, arguments) sérieux *m* (**of** de).

solidly /ˈsɒlɪdlɪ/ *adv* **1** (strongly) [*built*] solidement; **2** (densely) **~ packed** [*crowd*] compact; [*earth*] très tassé; **3** (continuously) [*work, rain*] sans interruption; **4** (staunchly) [*conservative, socialist*] à cent pour cent; [*respectable*] parfaitement; **they are ~ behind him** ils le soutiennent massivement; **it's a ~ working-class area** c'est une zone essentiellement ouvrière.

solid-state /ˌsɒlɪdˈsteɪt/ *adj* [*stereo, microelectronics*] à semi-conducteur(s); **~ physics** physique *f* des solides.

solidus /ˈsɒlɪdəs/ *n* (*pl* **-di**) barre *f* oblique.

solid word *n* Ling mot *m* simple.

soliloquize /səˈlɪləkwaɪz/ *vi* littér soliloquer.

soliloquy /səˈlɪləkwɪ/ *n* soliloque *m*.

solipsism /ˈsɒlɪpsɪzəm/ *n* solipsisme *m*.

solitaire /ˌsɒlɪˈteə(r), US ˈsɒlɪteər/ **▶1282** *n* **1** (ring) solitaire *m*; **2** US (with cards) réussite *f*; **to play ~** faire une réussite; **3** (board game) solitaire *m*.

solitary /ˈsɒlɪtrɪ, US -terɪ/ I *n* **1** (loner) solitaire *mf*; **2**○ (isolation) mitard○ *m* prisoners' slang, isolement *m* cellulaire; **to be in ~** être au mitard○, être en isolement cellulaire.
II *adj* **1** (unaccompanied) [*drinking, occupation, walk, walker*] solitaire; **2** (lonely) [*person*] très seul, esseulé; **3** (isolated) [*farm, village*] isolé; **4** (single) [*example, incident, person, question*] seul; **with the ~ exception of** à la seule exception de; **a ~ case of** un cas unique de.

solitary confinement *n* Jur, Mil isolement *m* cellulaire; **to put** ou **place sb in ~** placer qn en isolement cellulaire.

solitude /ˈsɒlɪtjuːd, US -tuːd/ *n* solitude *f*; **to eat/work in ~** manger/travailler seul.

solmization /ˌsɒlmɪˈzeɪʃn/ *n* solmisation *f*.

solo /ˈsəʊləʊ/ I *n* gen, Mus solo *m*; **to play a ~** faire un solo; **trumpet ~** solo de trompette.
II *adj* **1** Mus (unaccompanied) **for ~ piano**

pour piano solo; **for ~ voice** pour voix seule; **for ~ violin** (with orchestra) pour violon et orchestre; **a ~ piece** un solo; **2** (single-handed) [*album, appearance, flight, pilot*] en solo.
III *adv* [*dance, fly, perform, play*] en solo; **to go ~** faire cavalier seul.
soloist /'səʊləʊɪst/ *n* soliste *mf*; **a soprano/trumpet ~** un/-e soprano/trompettiste soliste.
Solomon /'sɒləmən/ *pr n* Salomon; **as wise as ~** sage comme Salomon.
Solomon Islands ▶ **1381** *pr npl* Îles *fpl* Salomon.
solon /'səʊlɒn/ *n* surtout US législateur/-trice *m/f*.
Solothurn ▶ **1818**, **1776** *pr n* Soleune; **the canton of ~** le canton de Soleune.
solstice /'sɒlstɪs/ *n* solstice *m*; **the summer/winter ~** le solstice d'été/d'hiver.
solubility /,sɒljʊ'bɪlətɪ/ *n* Chem solubilité *f*.
soluble /'sɒljʊbl/ *adj* **1** (dissolving) soluble; **water-~** soluble dans l'eau; **2** (having an answer) soluble.
solution /sə'lu:ʃn/ *n* **1** (answer) solution *f* (**to** de); **2** Chem, Pharm (act of dissolving) dissolution *f*; (mixture) solution *f* (**of** de); **in ~** en solution.
solvable /'sɒlvəbl/ *adj* soluble; **the problem is ~** ce problème peut être résolu.
solve /sɒlv/ *vtr* (resolve) résoudre [*equation, problem*]; élucider [*crime*]; trouver la solution de [*mystery*]; trouver la solution à [*clue, crossword*]; trouver une solution à [*crisis, poverty, unemployment*].
solvency /'sɒlvənsɪ/ *n* Fin solvabilité *f*.
solvent /'sɒlvənt/ **I** *n* Chem solvant *m*; **water is a ~ for** ou **of salt** l'eau dissout le sel.
II *adj* **1** Chem [*cleaner, liquid*] dissolvant; **2** Fin solvable.
solvent abuse *n* usage *m* de solvants hallucinogènes.
soma /'səʊmə/ *n* (*pl* **~s, -ata**) soma *m*.
soma cell *n* cellule *f* somatique.
Somali /sə'mɑ:lɪ/ ▶ **1486**, **1402** **I** *n* **1** (person) Somalien/-ienne *m/f*; **2** (language) somali *m*.
II *adj* [*person, word*] somali/-e; [*currency, custom, politics*] somalien/-ienne.
Somalia /sə'mɑ:lɪə/ ▶ **1131** *pr n* Somalie *f*.
somatic /səʊ'mætɪk/ *adj* somatique.
sombre GB, **somber** US /'sɒmbə(r)/ *adj* (all contexts) sombre; **to be in ~ mood** être d'humeur sombre.
sombrely GB, **somberly** US /'sɒmbəlɪ/ *adv* [*stare*] d'un air sombre; [*dress, paint*] de manière sombre; [*speak*] d'une voix lugubre.
sombreness GB, **somberness** US /'sɒmbənɪs/ *n* **1** (of clothes, room) aspect *m* sombre; **2** fig (of events, news, prediction) côté *m* sombre.
sombrero /sɒm'breərəʊ/ *n* sombrero *m*.
some /sʌm/

■ **Note** When *some* is used as a quantifier to mean an unspecified amount of something, it is translated by *du, de l'* before vowel or mute h, *de la* or *des* according to the gender and number of the noun that follows: *I'd like some bread* = je voudrais du pain; *have some water* = prenez de l'eau; *we've bought some beer* = nous avons acheté de la bière; *they've bought some peaches* = ils ont acheté des pêches.
– But note that where *some* is followed by an adjective preceding a plural noun, *de* alone is used in all cases: *some pretty dresses* = de jolies robes.
– For particular usages see I below.
– When *some* is used as a pronoun it is translated by *en* which is placed before the verb in French: *would you like some?* = est-ce que vous en voulez?; *I've got some* = j'en ai.
– For particular usages see II below.

I *det, quantif* **1** (an unspecified amount or number) **~ cheese** du fromage; **~ money** de l'argent; **~ apples** des pommes; **~ old/new socks** de vieilles/nouvelles chaussettes; **~ red/expensive socks** des chaussettes rouges/chères; **we need ~ help/support/money** nous avons besoin d'aide/de soutien/d'argent; **2** (certain: in contrast to others) certains; **~ shops won't sell this product** certains magasins ne vendent pas ce produit; **~ children like it** certains enfants aiment ça; **~ tulips are black** certaines tulipes sont noires; **~ people work, others don't** certaines personnes travaillent, d'autres non; **in ~ ways, I agree** d'une certaine façon, je suis d'accord; **in ~ cases, people have to wait 10 years** dans certains cas les gens doivent attendre 10 ans; **~ people say that** certaines personnes disent que; **in ~ parts of Europe** dans certaines parties de l'Europe; **3** (a considerable amount or number) **he has ~ cause for complaint/disappointment** il a des raisons de se plaindre/d'être déçu; **she managed it with ~ ease/difficulty** elle a réussi sans problèmes/avec difficulté; **his suggestion was greeted with ~ indifference/hostility** sa suggestion a été accueillie avec indifférence/hostilité; **it will take ~ doing** ça ne va pas être facile à faire; **we stayed there for ~ time** nous sommes restés là assez longtemps; **we waited for ~ years/months/hours** nous avons attendu plusieurs années/mois/heures; **he hadn't seen her for ~ years** ça faisait plusieurs années qu'il ne l'avait pas vue; **4** (a little, a slight) **the meeting did have ~ effect/~ value** la réunion a eu un certain effet/une certaine importance; **the candidate needs to have ~ knowledge of computers** le candidat doit avoir certaines or un minimum de connaissances en informatique; **there must be ~ reason for it** il doit y avoir une raison; **you must have ~ idea where the house is** tu dois avoir une idée de l'endroit où la maison se trouve; **this money will go ~ way towards compensating her for her injuries** cet argent compensera un peu ses blessures; **the agreement will go ~ way towards solving the difficulties between the two countries** cet accord aidera à résoudre les difficultés entre les deux pays; **to ~ extent** dans une certaine mesure; **well that's ~ consolation anyway!** c'est toujours ça○!; **5** péj (an unspecified, unknown) **~ man came to the house** un homme est venu à la maison; **he' s doing ~ course** il suit des cours; **she's bought ~ cottage in Spain** elle a acheté une maison en Espagne; **a car/computer of ~ sort, ~ sort of car/computer** une sorte de voiture/d'ordinateur; **6**○ (a remarkable) **that was ~ film/car!** ça c'était un film/une voiture!; **that's ~ woman/man!** c'est quelqu'un!; **7**○ (not much) **~ help you are/he is!** iron c'est ça que tu appelles/qu'il appelle aider!; **~ mechanic/doctor he is!** tu parles d'un mécanicien/d'un médecin!; **~ dictionary/pen that is!** tu parles d'un dictionnaire/d'un stylo!; **'I'd like the work to be finished by Monday'—'~ hope!'** 'j'aimerais que le travail soit fini avant lundi'—'tu rêves○!'
II *pron* **1** (an unspecified amount or number) **I'd like ~ of those** j'en voudrais quelques-uns comme ça; **(do) have ~!** servez-vous!; **(do) have ~ more!** reprenez-en!; **2** (certain ones: in contrast to others) **~ (of them) are blue** certains sont bleus; **~ (of them) are French, others Spanish** (people) certains d'entre eux sont des Français, d'autres des Espagnols; **~ say that** certaines personnes disent que; **I agree with ~ of what you say** je suis d'accord avec une partie de ce que tu dis; **~ (of them) arrived early** certains d'entre eux sont arrivés tôt.
III *adv* **1** (approximately) environ; **~ 20 people/buses** environ 20 personnes/autobus; **~ 20 years ago** il y a environ 20 ans; **~ £50** autour de 50 livres (sterling); **~ 70% of the population** environ 70% de la population; **2**○ US (somewhat , a lot) un peu; **to wait/work ~** attendre/travailler un peu; **from here to the town center in 5 minutes, that's going ~**○ aller d'ici au centre ville en 5 minutes, il faut le faire.
IDIOMS **and then ~**○**!** et pas qu'un peu○!; **~ people!** ah vraiment, il y a des gens!
somebody /'sʌmbədɪ/ *pron* **1** (unspecified person) quelqu'un; **~ famous/important** quelqu'un de célèbre/d'important; **~ came to see me** quelqu'un est venu me voir; **we need ~ who speaks Japanese/who can repair cars** on a besoin de quelqu'un qui parle (*subj*) japonais/qui sache réparer les voitures; **Mr Somebody(-or-other)** M. Machin; **ask John or Henry or ~** demande à John, à Henry ou à n'importe qui d'autre; **2** (important person) **he (really) thinks he's ~** il ne se prend pas pour n'importe qui; **they think they're ~** ils se prennent pour des gens importants, ils se croient importants; **she's really ~ in the film industry** c'est vraiment quelqu'un d'important dans le monde du cinéma.
IDIOMS **~ up there likes me** il y a quelqu'un là-haut qui veille sur moi; **~ up there doesn' t like me** je n'ai jamais eu de chance.
somehow /'sʌmhaʊ/ *adv* **1** (by some means) (also **~ or other**) (of future action) d'une manière ou d'une autre; (of past action) je ne sais comment; **we'll get there ~** on y arrivera d'une manière ou d'une autre; **we managed it ~** nous avons réussi je ne sais comment; **he ~ broke his leg** il s'est cassé la jambe, je ne sais comment; **it has ~ disappeared** ça a disparu, sans qu'on sache comment; **2** (for some reason) **~ it doesn't seem very important** en fait, ça ne semble pas très important; **~ he never seems to get it right** il semble que rien ne lui réussisse jamais; **it was ~ shocking/amusing to see...** c'était un peu choquant/amusant de voir...
someone /'sʌmwʌn/ *pron* = **somebody**.
someplace /'sʌmpleɪs/ *adv* = **somewhere**.
somersault /'sʌməsɒlt/ **I** *n* **1** (of gymnast) roulade *f*; (of child) galipette *f*; (of diver) saut *m* périlleux; (accidental) culbute *f*; **to turn ~s** [*gymnast*] faire des roulades; [*child*] faire des galipettes; **2** (of vehicle) tonneau *m*; **to do** ou **turn a ~** faire un tonneau.
II *vi* [*gymnast*] faire une roulade; [*diver*] faire un saut périlleux; [*vehicle*] faire un tonneau; **the car ~ed into the ravine** la voiture a fait des tonneaux jusqu'au fond du ravin.
Somerset /'sʌməsət/ ▶ **1624** *pr n* Somerset *m*.
something /'sʌmθɪŋ/ **I** *pron* **1** (unspecified thing) quelque chose; **~ to do/eat** quelque chose à faire/manger; **to say ~** dire quelque chose; **~ made him laugh** quelque chose l'a fait rire; **~ new/interesting** quelque chose de nouveau/d'intéressant; **he's always trying to get ~ for nothing** il est radin○; **there's ~ wrong** il y a un problème; **there's ~ odd about her** elle a quelque chose de bizarre; **there's ~ funny going on** il se passe quelque chose (de bizarre); **~ or other** quelque chose; **she's ~ (or other) in the army/motor trade** elle est je ne sais quoi dans l'armée/l'industrie automobile; **2** (thing of importance, value etc) **it proves ~** ça prouve quelque chose; **to make ~ of oneself** ou **one's life** réussir sa vie; **he got ~ out of it** il en a tiré quelque chose; **he is quite** ou **really ~!** c'est vraiment un numéro!; **do you want to make ~ out of it?** tu veux te battre?; **that house/car is quite** ou **really ~!** cette maison/voiture c'est quelque chose!; **there's ~ in what he says** il y a du vrai dans ce qu'il dit; **you've got ~ there!** là, tu n'as pas tort!; **he has a certain ~** il a un petit quelque chose; **'I've found the key'—'well that's ~ anyway'** 'j'ai trouvé la clé'—'c'est

déjà ça or quelque chose'; **we gave him ~ for his trouble** (a tip) nous lui avons donné un petit quelque chose pour le dérangement; **3** (forgotten, unknown name, amount etc) **his name's Andy ~** il s'appelle Andy quelque chose; **in nineteen-sixty-~** en mille neuf cent soixante et quelques; **he's six foot ~** ≈ il fait à peu près 2 mètres; **she's gone shopping/swimming or ~** elle est allée faire les courses/nager ou quelque chose comme ça; **are you deaf/stupid or ~?** tu es sourd/bête ou quoi○?

II *adv* **1** (a bit) un peu; **~ over/under £20/50 people** un peu plus de/en dessous-de 20 livres sterling/50 personnes; **~ around £50/100 kilos** environ 50 livres sterling/100 kilos; **2**○ (a lot) **he was howling ~ awful** ou **terrible** ou **shocking** il n'arrêtait pas de hurler. ▶ **else**, **nothing**.

III something of *adv phr* (rather, quite) **he is (also) ~ of an actor/writer** il est aussi un assez bon acteur/écrivain; **she is ~ of an expert on**... elle est assez experte en...; **it was ~ of a surprise/mystery** c'était assez étonnant/mystérieux ; **it was ~ of a disaster/disappointment** c'était plutôt désastreux/décevant.

sometime /ˈsʌmtaɪm/ **I** *adv* (at unspecified time) **we'll have to do it ~** il va falloir qu'on le fasse un jour ou l'autre; **I'll pay you ~** je te paierai plus tard; **all holidays have to end ~** toutes les vacances ont une fin; **I'll tell you about it ~** je te raconterai ça un de ces jours; **I'll phone you ~ tomorrow/next week/next month** je te téléphonerai demain dans la journée/dans le courant de la semaine prochaine/dans le courant du mois prochain.

II *adj* **1** (former) [*president, chairman, captain etc*] ancien/-ienne (*before n*); **2** US (occasional) [*employee, event*] occasionnel/-elle.

sometimes /ˈsʌmtaɪmz/ *adv* parfois, quelquefois, de temps en temps; (in contrast) **~ angry, ~ depressed** tantôt en colère, tantôt déprimé.

somewhat /ˈsʌmwɒt/ *adv* (with adj) plutôt; (with verb) un peu; (with adverb) un peu, quelque peu; **~ disturbed/discouraging** plutôt dérangé/décourageant; **~ faster/happier** un peu plus vite/plus heureux; **things have changed ~** les choses ont un peu changé; **~ differently/reluctantly/defensively** un peu différemment/à contre-cœur/sur la défensive; **~ ironically/improbably/surprisingly** de façon quelque peu ironique/improbable/surprenante; **~ to her disappointment/surprise** à sa grande déception/surprise; **they were more than ~ surprised/disappointed to hear that** ils étaient plus que surpris/déçus d'apprendre que.

somewhere /ˈsʌmweə(r)/ *adv* **1** (some place) quelque part; **she's ~ about** ou **around** elle est quelque part par là; **it's ~ in this chapter** c'est quelque part dans ce chapitre; **I read ~ that** j'ai lu quelque part que; **~ hot/special** un endroit chaud/spécial; **he needs ~ to sleep/stay** il a besoin d'un endroit pour dormir/passer la nuit; **~ or other** je ne sais où; **~ (or other) in Asia** quelque part en Asie; **he's often in the pub or ~**○ on le trouve souvent au pub; **they live in Manchester or ~**○ ils habitent à Manchester ou quelque chose comme ça; **2** (at an unspecified point in range) **~ between 50 and 100 people** entre 50 et 100 personnes; **~ around 10 o'clock/£50** autour de 10 heures/cinquante livres sterling; **they paid ~ around £20,000** ils ont payé à peu près 20 000 livres sterling.

IDIOMS **now we're getting ~!** (in questioning) voilà enfin des informations utiles!; (making progress) on arrive enfin à quelque chose!

Somme /sɒm/ ▶ **1163**, **1644** *pr n* **1** (river) Somme *f*; **the (battle of the) ~** la bataille de la Somme; **2** (department) Somme *f*; **in/to the ~** dans la Somme.

somnambulism /sɒmˈnæmbjʊlɪzəm/ *n* sout somnambulisme *m*.

somnambulist /sɒmˈnæmbjʊlɪst/ *n* sout somnambule *mf*.

somniferous /sɒmˈnɪfərəs/ *adj* sout soporifique.

somnolence /ˈsɒmnələns/ *n* sout somnolence *f*.

somnolent /ˈsɒmnələnt/ *adj* sout somnolent; **to feel ~** avoir envie de dormir.

son /sʌn/ *n* **1** (male child) fils *m* (**of** de); **an only ~** un fils unique; **he's like a ~ to me** il est comme un fils pour moi; **my ~ and heir** mon héritier; **he's his father's ~** c'est bien le fils de son père; **2** littér (descendant) fils *m*; **the ~s of the revolution** les fils de la révolution; **Scotland's favourite ~** l'un des enfants chéris de l'Écosse; **3**○ (as form of address) (kindly) fiston○ *m*; (patronizingly) mon gars *m*.

IDIOMS **every mother's ~ (of them)** tous autant qu'ils sont.

sonar /ˈsəʊnɑː(r)/ *n* sonar *m*.

sonata /səˈnɑːtə/ *n* sonate *f*; **violin ~** sonate pour violon.

sonata form *n* forme *f* sonate.

sonatina /ˌsɒnəˈtiːnə/ *n* Mus sonatine *f*.

sonde /sɒnd/ *n* Meteorol sonde *f*.

sone /səʊn/ *n* sone *m*.

son et lumière /ˌsɒneɪluːˈmjeə(r)/ *n* (spectacle *m*) son et lumière *m*.

song /sɒŋ/ *n* **1** Mus chanson *f*; **to sing/write a ~** chanter/écrire une chanson; **give us a ~** chante-nous quelque chose; **to burst into ~** se mettre à chanter; **2** (of bird) chant *m* (**of** de); **3** Literat poème *m*.

IDIOMS **for a ~**○ pour rien; **they're going for a ~** ils se vendent pour rien; **on ~**○ GB en forme.

song and dance *n* Theat chanson *f* dansée; **~ routine**, **~ act** numéro *m* de chansons dansées.

IDIOMS **to give sb the same old ~**○ US resservir les mêmes excuses à qn; **to make a ~ about sth**○ GB faire toute une histoire de qch.

song: **~bird** *n* oiseau *m* chanteur; **~book** *n* recueil *m* de chansons; **~ cycle** *n* cycle *m* de chansons; **~fest** *n* US festival *m* de chansons; **Song of Solomon** *n* Cantique *m* des Cantiques; **Song of Songs** *n* Cantique *m* des Cantiques; **~smith**† *n* parolier compositeur *m*.

songster† /ˈsɒŋstə(r)/ *n* chanteur *m*.

songstress† /ˈsɒŋstrɪs/ *n* cantatrice *f*.

song thrush /ˈsɒŋθrʌʃ/ *n* grive *f* musicienne.

songwriter /ˈsɒŋraɪtə(r)/ ▶ **1692** *n* (of words) parolier/-ière *m/f*; (of music) compositeur *m* de chansons; (of both) auteur-compositeur *m* de chansons.

songwriting /ˈsɒŋraɪtɪŋ/ *n* composition *f* de chansons.

sonic /ˈsɒnɪk/ *adj* [*vibration*] sonore; **~ interference** parasites *mpl*.

sonic: **~ bang** *n* GB bang *m*; **~ barrier** *n* mur *m* du son; **~ boom** *n* US bang *m*; **~ depth finder** *n* sondeur *m* à ultrasons; **~ mine** *n* Mil mine *f* acoustique.

sonics /ˈsɒnɪks/ *n* (+ *v sg*) acoustique *f*.

son-in-law /ˈsʌnɪnlɔː/ *n* gendre *m*.

sonnet /ˈsɒnɪt/ *n* sonnet *m*.

sonny○ /ˈsʌnɪ/ *n* (kindly) fiston *m*; (patronizing) mon gars○ *m*.

sonny boy, **sonny Jim** *n* **look here, ~** écoute, mon gars○.

son-of-a-bitch◑ /ˌsʌnəvəˈbɪtʃ/ **I** *n* US **1** péj salaud◑ *m*; **2** (jocular) vieille branche○ *f*; **how are you, you old ~◑?** comment vas-tu vieille branche○?; **3** (difficult task) vacherie○ *f*, saleté○ *f*.

II *excl* merde◑!

son-of-a-gun○† /ˌsʌnəvəˈgʌn/ *n* US **you old ~!** espèce de vieux filou○!

sonority /səˈnɒrətɪ, US -ˈnɔːr-/ *n* sonorité *f*.

sonorous /ˈsɒnərəs, səˈnɔːrəs/ *adj* [*language, note, tone, voice*] sonore; [*name*] ronflant; [*chime*] éclatant.

sonorously /ˈsɒnərəslɪ, səˈnɔːrəslɪ/ *adv* [*speak, sing*] d'une voix sonore; [*chime, toll*] de façon éclatante.

sonorousness /ˈsɒnərəsnɪs, səˈnɔːrəsnɪs/ *n* sonorité *f*.

soon /suːn/ *adv* **1** (in a short time) bientôt; **the book will be published ~** le livre sera bientôt publié; **~ there will be no snow left** il n'y aura bientôt plus de neige; **I'll see you very ~** je te verrai très bientôt; **it will ~ be three years since we met** voici bientôt trois ans que nous nous sommes rencontrés; **see you ~!** à bientôt!; **2** (quickly) vite; **write ~** écris-moi vite; **the plan was ~ abandoned** le projet fut vite abandonné; **it ~ became clear that** il est vite devenu évident que; **3** (early) tôt; **we arrived too ~** nous sommes arrivés trop tôt; **~ enough** assez tôt; **the ~er the better** le plus tôt sera le mieux; **the ~er we leave, the ~er we'll get there** plus nous partirons tôt et plus nous y serons vite; **as ~ as possible** dès que possible; **I spoke too ~!** j'ai parlé trop vite!; **as ~ as you can** dès que tu pourras; **as ~ as he arrives** dès qu'il arrivera; **she didn't arrive as ~ as we had hoped** elle n'est pas arrivée aussi vite que nous l'espérions; **~er or later** tôt ou tard; **all too ~ the summer was over** l'été est passé bien trop vite; **tomorrow at the ~est** demain au plus tôt; **and not a moment too ~!** il était temps!; **4** (not long) **they left ~ after us** ils sont partis peu après nous; **~ after breakfast** peu après le petit déjeuner; **~ afterwards** peu après; **no ~er had I done sth than**... j'avais à peine fait qch que...; **5** (rather) **he would just as ~ do** il aime autant faire; **I would just as ~ do X as do Y** j'aime autant faire X que faire Y; **I would ~er not do** j'aime autant ne pas faire; **~er him than me!** plutôt lui que moi!; **he would ~er die than do** il préférerait mourir que de faire.

IDIOMS **least said ~est mended** Prov moins on en dit, mieux ça vaut; **no ~er said than done** aussitôt dit aussitôt fait.

soot /sʊt/ *n* suie *f*.

■ **soot up**: **~ [sth] up**, **~ up [sth]** [*coal*] couvrir de suie [*chimney, hearth*].

sooth‡ /suːθ/ *n* **in ~** en vérité.

soothe /suːð/ **I** *vtr* calmer [*anger, crowd, fear, nerves, pain, person*]; apaiser [*sunburn*]; détendre [*muscles*].

II *vtr* **'don't worry,' she ~d** 'ne t'en fais pas,' dit-elle d'un ton rassurant.

III *vi* [*voice*] rassurer; [*lotion, massage*] faire du bien.

■ **soothe away**: **~ away [sth]**, **~ [sth] away** calmer [*anger, anxiety, fear, pain*].

soothing /ˈsuːðɪŋ/ *adj* [*cream, music, person, presence, voice*] apaisant; [*effect*] calmant; [*word*] rassurant.

soothingly /ˈsuːðɪŋlɪ/ *adv* [*stroke*] de façon apaisante; [*speak*] de façon rassurante.

soothsayer‡ /ˈsuːθseɪə(r)/ *n* devin/-eresse *m/f*.

soothsaying /ˈsuːθseɪɪŋ/ *n* divination *f*.

sooty /ˈsʊtɪ/ *adj* **1** (covered in soot) [*face, hands, room*] couvert de suie; [*air*] chargé de suie; **2** (black) [*cat, fur*] tout noir; **~ black** noir comme du charbon.

sop /sɒp/ **I** *n* **1** (of bread) morceau *m* de pain trempé; **he lives off ~s** il ne mange plus que de la bouillie; **2** (concession) concession *f* symbolique; **as a ~ to public opinion** en guise de concession à l'opinion publique; **as a ~ to her pride** pour flatter son orgueil; **to offer sth as a ~ to sb** offrir qch pour amadouer qn; **to throw a ~ to sb** essayer d'amadouer qn; **3**○ (sissy) mauviette○ *f*.

II *vtr* (*p prés etc* **-pp-**) tremper [*bread, cake*] (**in** dans).

■ **sop up**: **~ up [sth]**, **~ [sth] up** éponger, absorber [*spillage, water*]; **he**

~ped up his soup with some bread il a essuyé son assiette de soupe avec du pain.

sophism /ˈsɒfɪzəm/ *n* sophisme *m*.

sophist /ˈsɒfɪst/ *n* lit, fig sophiste *mf*.

sophistic(al) /səˈfɪstɪk(l)/ *adj* **1** Philos sophistique; **2** fig (specious) [*argument, reasoning*] fallacieux/-ieuse.

sophisticate /səˈfɪstɪkət/ *n* raffiné/-e *m/f*.

sophisticated /səˈfɪstɪkeɪtɪd/ *adj* **1** (smart) [*person*] (worldly, cultured) raffiné, sophistiqué pej; (elegant) chic *inv*; [*clothes, fashion*] recherché; [*restaurant, resort*] chic *inv*; [*magazine*] sophistiqué; **she thinks it's ~ to smoke** elle pense que ça fait chic de fumer; **she was looking very ~ in black** elle était très chic en noir; **2** (discriminating) [*mind, taste*] raffiné; [*audience, public*] averti; **a book for the more ~ student** un livre pour les étudiants plus avancés; **3** (advanced) [*civilization*] évolué; **4** (elaborate, complex) [*equipment, machinery, technology*] sophistiqué; [*argument, discussion, joke*] subtil; [*style*] recherché.

sophistication /səˌfɪstɪˈkeɪʃn/ *n* **1** (smartness) (of person) (in lifestyle, habits) raffinement *m*, sophistication *f* pej; (in judgment, intellect) finesse *f*; (in appearance) chic *m*; (of clothes, fashion) recherche *f*; (of restaurant, resort, magazine) chic *m*; (finesse) (of mind, tastes) raffinement *m*; **lack of ~** simplicité *f*; **2** (of audience, public) caractère *m* averti; **3** (of civilization) raffinement *m*; **4** (complexity) (of equipment, machinery, technology) sophistication *f*; (of argument, discussion, joke) subtilité *f*.

sophistry /ˈsɒfɪstrɪ/ *n* (all contexts) sophisme *m*.

Sophocles /ˈsɒfəkli:z/ *pr n* Sophocle.

sophomore /ˈsɒfəmɔ:(r)/ *n* US Univ *étudiant/-e en deuxième année d'université*; Sch *étudiant/-e en deuxième année de lycée*.

soporific /ˌsɒpəˈrɪfɪk/ I *n* somnifère *m*.
II *adj* **1** (sleep-inducing) soporifique; **2** (sleepy) somnolent.

soppiness /ˈsɒpɪnəs/ *n* mièvrerie *f*.

sopping /ˈsɒpɪŋ/ *adj* (also **~ wet**) trempé.

soppy○ /ˈsɒpɪ/ *adj* péj sentimental.

sopranino /ˌsɒprəˈni:nəʊ/ *n, adj* sopranino (*m*).

soprano /səˈprɑ:nəʊ, US -ˈpræn-/ **▶1868** I *n* (*pl* **~s**) **1** (person) soprano *mf*; **2** (voice, instrument) soprano *m*.
II *adj* [*voice, register, singer*] de soprano; [*part, aria*] pour soprano.

sorb /sɔ:b/ *n* **1** (tree) sorbier *m*; **2** (fruit) sorbe *f*.

Sorb /sɔ:b/ **▶1486**, **1402** *n* Sorabe *mf*.

sorbet /ˈsɔ:beɪ, ˈsɔ:bet/ *n* sorbet *m*; **lemon ~** sorbet au citron.

Sorbian /ˈsɔ:bɪən/ **▶1486**, **1402** I *n* **1** (person) Sorabe *mf*; **2** (language) sorabe *m*.
II *adj* sorabe.

sorbic acid /ˌsɔ:bɪkˈæsɪd/ *n* acide *m* sorbique.

sorbitol /ˈsɔ:bɪtɒl/ *n* sorbitol *m*.

sorcerer /ˈsɔ:sərə(r)/ *n* sorcier *m*.

sorceress /ˈsɔ:sərɪs/ *n* sorcière *f*.

sorcery /ˈsɔ:sərɪ/ *n* **1** (witchcraft) sorcellerie *f*; **2** fig magie *f*.

sordid /ˈsɔ:dɪd/ *adj* [*affair, conditions, life, motive, subject*] sordide; **to go into all the ~ details of sth** hum raconter qch dans tous ses détails.

sordidly /ˈsɔ:dɪdlɪ/ *adv* [*live, behave*] de façon sordide.

sordidness /ˈsɔ:dɪdnɪs/ *n* **1** (of room, film) saleté *f*; **2** (of motive, behaviour) bassesse *f*.

sore /sɔ:(r)/ I *n* plaie *f*.
II *adj* **1** (sensitive) [*eyes, throat, nose, gums*] irrité; [*muscle, tendon, arm, foot*] endolori; **to have a ~ throat/head** avoir mal à la gorge/à la tête; **to be** ou **feel ~ (all over)** avoir mal (partout); **my leg is still a bit ~** ma jambe me fait encore un peu mal; **to be ~ from exercise/running** être endolori d'avoir fait de l'exercice/de la course; **you'll only make it ~ by scratching** tu vas t'irriter encore plus si tu te grattes; **2**○ surtout US (peeved) vexé; **to be ~ about** ou **over sth** être vexé par qch; **to be ~ at sb** en vouloir à qn; **to get ~** se vexer; **3** littér (extreme) **to be in ~ need of sth** avoir grand besoin de qch; **4** (delicate) (*épith*) [*subject, point*] délicat.
IDIOMS **to be like a bear with a ~ head** être d'une humeur massacrante○; **she/it is a sight for ~ eyes** ça réjouit le cœur de la voir/de voir cela.

sorely /ˈsɔ:lɪ/ *adv* [*tempted*] fortement; **~ tried, ~ tested** [*patience, friendship*] mis à rude épreuve; [*person*] soumis à rude épreuve; **volunteers are/medical aid is ~ needed** on a grandement besoin de volontaires/d'aide médicale; **~ needed funds** des fonds bien nécessaires.

soreness /ˈsɔ:nɪs/ *n* douleur *f*.

sorghum /ˈsɔ:gəm/ *n* **1** (plant, foodstuff) sorgho *m*; **2** (syrup) sirop *m* de sorgho.

sorority /səˈrɒrətɪ, US -ˈrɔ:r-/ *n* **1** US Univ (club) association *f* d'étudiantes; **2** (sisterhood) confrérie *f* féminine.

sorrel /ˈsɒrəl, US ˈsɔ:rəl/ **▶1104** I *n* **1** Bot, Culin (edible plant) oseille *f*; **2** (also **wood ~**) Bot oxalis *m*, petite oseille *f*; **3** Equit (horse, colour of horse) alezan *m*; **4** (colour) brun *m* roux.
II *adj* [*horse*] alezan.

sorrow /ˈsɒrəʊ/ I *n* **1** (grief) chagrin *m*; **to feel ~** éprouver du chagrin; **to my ~** à mon grand chagrin; **it was said more in ~ than in anger** cela a été dit avec plus de tristesse que de colère; **I am writing to express my ~ at your sad loss** c'est avec beaucoup de peine que j'ai appris le deuil qui vient de vous frapper; **2** (misfortune) chagrin *m*, peine *f*; **we share each other's joys and ~s** nous partageons nos joies et nos peines.
II *vi* littér se lamenter.
III **sorrowing** *pres p adj* [*widow, mourner*] accablé de douleur or de chagrin.
IDIOMS **one for ~, two for joy** (of magpies) une pie tant pis, deux pies tant mieux.

sorrowful /ˈsɒrəʊfl/ *adj* [*occasion, look*] douloureux/-euse; [*voice*] triste; **to be in ~ mood** hum être d'humeur chagrine.

sorrowfully /ˈsɒrəʊfəlɪ/ *adv* [*say*] avec tristesse, tristement.

sorry /ˈsɒrɪ/ I *adj* **1** (apologetic) désolé; (for emphasis) navré; **I'm terribly ~** je suis vraiment désolé, je suis navré; **(I'm) ~, I haven't a clue**○ ou **I've no idea** je suis désolé mais je n'en ai pas la moindre idée; **to be ~ that** être désolé que (+ *subj*); **to be ~ if** être désolé si; **I'm ~ that things didn't work out/if I was rude** je suis désolé que ça n'ait pas marché/si j'ai été grossier; **I'm ~ I'm late** je suis désolé d'être en retard; **I'm ~ for the delay** je suis désolé du retard, je m'excuse pour le retard; **to be ~ for doing/to do** être désolé d'avoir fait/de faire; **I'm ~ for keeping you waiting** excusez-moi de vous avoir fait attendre; **I'm ~ to be a nuisance but...** excusez-moi de vous embêter, mais...; **to be ~ about** s'excuser de [*behaviour, mistake, change*]; **I'm ~ about this!** je suis désolé!, excusez-moi!; **~ about that!** (je suis) désolé!; **to say ~** s'excuser; **he didn't look the slightest bit ~!** il n'avait pas du tout l'air désolé!; **2** (sympathetic) **to be ~ to hear of sth/to hear that** être désolé d'apprendre qch/d'apprendre que; **I'm very ~ about your uncle** j'ai été désolé d'apprendre pour ton oncle; **3** (regretful) **to be ~ to do** regretter de faire; **we are ~ to inform you that** nous regrettons or nous avons le regret de vous informer que; **will you be ~ to go back?** est-ce que tu auras des regrets en rentrant?; **no-one will be ~ to see him go!** personne ne regrettera son départ!; **and, I'm ~ to say** et malheureusement; **I'm ~ that I didn't come/that you didn't come** je regrette de ne pas être venu/que tu ne sois pas venu; **she was ~ (that) she'd raised the subject** elle regrettait d'avoir abordé le sujet; **I felt ~ about it afterwards** j'ai eu des remords par la suite; **do it now or you'll be ~!** fais-le maintenant ou tu t'en repentiras!; **4** (pitying) **to be** ou **feel ~ for sb** plaindre qn also iron; **5** péj (self-pitying) **to feel ~ for oneself** s'apitoyer sur soi-même or sur son sort; **6** (pathetic, deplorable) [*state, sight, business*] triste; [*person*] minable; **they're a ~ lot!** ils sont minables!; **to be in a ~ state** être dans un triste état or en piteux état; **this is a ~ state of affairs!** c'est vraiment lamentable!
II *excl* **1** (apologizing) désolé!; **2** (failing to hear) **~?** pardon?; **3** (contradicting) **~, Sarah, that isn't true!** désolé, Sarah, mais cela est faux!; **4** (interrupting others) **~, time is running out** je suis désolé, mais nous n'avons plus beaucoup de temps; **5** (adding a comment) **~, may I just say that** excusez-moi, je voudrais simplement ajouter que; **6** (requesting clarification) **~, I'm not with you** pardon, mais je ne vous suis pas; **7** (correcting self) **so we have two, ~, three options** nous avons donc deux, pardon, trois options; **8** (being adamant) **~, but that's the way it is!** désolé, mais c'est comme ça!

sort /sɔ:t/ I *n* **1** (kind, type) sorte *f*, genre *m*; **this ~ of novel/fabric** ce genre de roman/tissu; **this ~ of rabbit/person** ce genre de lapin/personne; **all ~s of reasons/people/colours** toutes sortes de raisons/gens/couleurs; **machines of all ~s** des machines de toutes sortes; **different ~s of cakes** différentes sortes de gâteaux; **I like board games, backgammon, that ~ of thing** j'aime les jeux de société, le jaquet, ce genre de jeu; **books, records—that ~ of thing** des livres, des disques, ce genre de choses; **that's my ~ of holiday** GB ou **vacation** US c'est le genre de vacances que j'aime; **I'm not that ~ of person** ce n'est pas mon genre; **it's some ~ of computer** c'est une sorte d'ordinateur; **there must by some ~ of mistake** il doit y avoir une erreur; **this must be some ~ of joke** ça doit être une plaisanterie; **he must be some ~ of madman** ce doit être un fou; **I need a bag of some ~** j'ai besoin d'un sac quelconque; **you must have some ~ of idea** tu dois avoir une idée; **an odd** ou **strange ~ of chap** un drôle de type; **radiation of any ~ is harmful** toutes les sortes de radiation sont dangereuses; **any ~ of knife will do** n'importe quel couteau fera l'affaire; **what ~ of person would do such a thing?** qui pourrait faire une chose pareille?; **what ~ of person does she think I am?** pour qui me prend-elle?; **what ~ of thing does she like/read?** qu'est-ce qu'elle aime/lit?; **what ~ of a reply/an excuse is that?** qu'est-ce que c'est que cette réponse/excuse?; **you know the ~ of thing (I mean)** tu vois ce que je veux dire; **the same ~ of thing** la même chose; **a liar of the worst ~** un menteur de la pire or de la plus belle espèce; **in an embarrassed ~ of way** d'une façon plutôt embarrassée; **something of that** ou **the ~** quelque chose comme ça; **I didn't say anything of the ~!** je n'ai jamais dit une chose pareille!; **nothing of the ~** (not in the least) pas du tout; **'this milk is off'—'it's nothing of the ~!'** 'ce lait est tourné'—'mais non, pas du tout!'; **'I'll pay'—'you'll do nothing of the ~!'** 'je vais payer'—'il n'en est pas question!'; **'you're being awkward'—'I'm being nothing of the ~'** 'tu es vraiment exigeant'—'ce n'est pas vrai du tout!'; **2** (in vague description) espèce *f*, sorte *f*; **some ~ of bird** une sorte or espèce d'oiseau; **a ~ of blue uniform** une sorte or espèce d'uniforme bleu; **a ~ of elephant without a trunk** une sorte or espèce d'éléphant sans trompe; **3** (type of person) **I know your/his ~** je connais les gens de votre/son espèce; **people of her ~** les gens de son espèce;

he's not the ~ to betray his friends ce n'est pas le genre à trahir ses amis; **she's the ~ who would cheat** c'est le genre or elle est du genre à tricher; **we see all ~s here** on voit toutes sortes de gens ici; **he's a good ~** c'est un brave type; **she's a good ~** c'est une brave fille; **4** Comput tri *m*.
II **of sorts, of a sort** *adv phr* **a duck of ~s** ou **of a ~** une sorte de canard; **a hero of ~s** une sorte de héros; **progress of ~s** un semblant de progrès; **an answer of ~s** un semblant de réponse.
III **sort of** *adv phr* **1** (a bit) **~ of cute/eccentric/embarrassed** plutôt mignon/excentrique/gêné; **to ~ of understand/sympathize** comprendre/compatir plus ou moins; **'is it hard?'—'~ of'** 'est-ce que c'est difficile?'—'plutôt, oui'; **'did you enjoy the film?'—'~ of'** 'est-ce que le film t'a plu?'—'oui, c'était pas mal'; **2** (approximately) **~ of blue-green** dans les bleu-vert; **it just ~ of happened** c'est arrivé comme ça; **he was just ~ of lying there** il était étendu par terre comme ça.
IV *vtr* **1** (classify, arrange) classer [*data, files, stamps*]; trier [*letters, apples, potatoes*]; **to ~ books into piles** ranger des livres en piles; **to ~ buttons by colour** ranger des boutons par couleur; **to ~ the apples according to size** classer les pommes selon leur taille; **2** (separate) séparer; **to ~ the good potatoes from the bad** séparer les bonnes pommes de terre des mauvaises; **to ~ the old stock from the new** séparer les vieux stocks des nouveaux.
IDIOMS **to be** ou **feel out of ~s** (ill) ne pas être dans son assiette; (grumpy) être de mauvais poil○; **it takes all ~s (to make a world)** Prov il faut de tout pour faire un monde Prov.
■ **sort out**: ¶ **~ [sth] out, ~ out [sth] 1** (resolve) régler [*problem, matter*]; **to ~ out the confusion** dissiper un malentendu; **it will take me hours to ~ this mess out** il va me falloir des heures pour remettre de l'ordre dans tout ça; **I'll ~ it out** je m'en occuperai; **they have ~ed out their differences** ils ont réglé leurs différends; **go and ~ it out elsewhere** allez vous expliquer ailleurs; **it's time to ~ this thing out** il est temps de tirer cette affaire au clair; **2** (organize) s'occuper de [*details, arrangements*]; clarifier [*ideas*]; **I'll ~ something out with Tim** j'arrangerai quelque chose avec Tim; **Rex will ~ something out for you** Rex arrangera quelque chose pour vous; **I'll ~ out with him what I have to do** je verrai avec lui ce que j'ai à faire; **3** (tidy up, put in order) ranger [*cupboard, desk*]; classer [*files, documents*]; mettre de l'ordre dans [*finances, affairs*]; **to ~ out one's life** mettre de l'ordre dans sa vie; **4** (select) trier [*photos, clothes*]; **5** (find) trouver [*replacement, stand-in*]; **6** (mend) réparer [*clutch, fault*]; ¶ **~ out [sth] 1** (separate) **to ~ out the clean socks from the dirty** séparer les chaussettes propres des chaussettes sales; **to ~ out the truth from the lies** démêler le vrai du faux; **2** (establish) **to ~ out who is responsible** établir qui est responsable; **we're still trying to ~ out what happened** nous essayons toujours de comprendre ce qui s'est passé; ¶ **~ [sb] out**○ **1** (punish) régler son compte à qn○; **2** (help) [*representative, receptionist, organizer*] aider [*person*]; **the doctor will soon ~ you out** le médecin te remettra sur pied; ¶ **~ [oneself] out** (get organized) s'organiser; (in one's personal life) résoudre ses problèmes; **to get oneself ~ed out** s'organiser; **things will ~ themselves out** les choses vont s'arranger d'elles-mêmes; **the problem ~ed itself out** le problème s'est résolu de lui-même.
■ **sort through**: **~ through [sth]** regarder, passer [qch] en revue [*files, invoices*]; **~ through the cards until you find the ace of clubs** regarde toutes les cartes une par une pour trouver l'as de trèfle.

sort code *n* code *m* d'agence.

sorter /'sɔːtə(r)/ ▶ **1692** *n* **1** (person) trieur/-euse *m/f*; **2** (machine) Agric trieur *m*; Mining, Post, Tex trieuse *f*.

sortie /'sɔːtɪ/ *n* **1** Mil sortie *f*; **2** fig, hum **to make a ~ to** faire un saut○ à [*shops, beach*].

sorting /'sɔːtɪŋ/ *n* **1** gen triage *m*, tri *m*; **2** Post tri *m* postal.

sorting: **~ machine** *n* = **sorter 2**; **~ office** *n* Post centre *m* de tri.

sort-out○ /'sɔːtaʊt/ *n* GB **to have a ~** faire du rangement; **to give sth a ~** ranger qch [*bedroom, cupboard*].

SOS *n* **1** Naut, Aviat SOS *m*; **2** fig appel *m* (au secours).

so-so○ /,səʊ'səʊ/ I *adj* moyen/-enne.
II *adv* comme ci comme ça○.

sot /sɒt/ *n* GB péj poivrot○ *m*.

sotto voce /,sɒtəʊ 'vəʊtʃɪ/ *adv* [*say, add*] à mi-voix.

sou' /suː/ *adj* Naut = **south**.

soubriquet /'suːbrɪkeɪ/ *n* sout sobriquet *m*.

souchong /,suː'tʃɒŋ/ *n* souchong *m*.

soufflé /'suːfleɪ, US suː'fleɪ/ *n* soufflé *m*.

sough /saʊ/ littér I *n* murmure *m*.
II *vi* [*wind*] murmurer.

soughing /'sʌfɪŋ, US saʊɪŋ/ *n* littér (of wind in trees) bruissement *m*; (of sea) murmure *m*.

sought /sɔːt/ *pp* ▶ **seek**.

sought-after /'sɔːtɑːftə(r), US -æf-/ *adj* [*expert, type of employee, guest, skill*] demandé, recherché; [*job, role, brand, garment, village, area*] prisé; **thatched cottages are much ~** les chaumières sont très recherchées; **the most ~ item was the portrait of Napoleon** l'article le plus convoité était le portrait de Napoléon.

soul /səʊl/ *n* **1** Relig (immortal) âme *f*; **to sell one's ~ (to the devil)** vendre son âme (au diable); **to sell one's ~** fig donner n'importe quoi (**for** pour; **to do** pour faire); **bless my ~†!, upon my ~†!** grand Dieu!; **2** (innermost nature) âme *f*; **a ~ in torment** littér une âme en peine; **to have the ~ of a poet** avoir l'âme d'un poète, être poète dans l'âme; **3** (essence) âme *f*; **the ~ of the British middle classes** l'âme de la bourgeoisie britannique; **to be the ~ of kindness/discretion** être la gentillesse/discrétion même; **4** ¢ (emotional appeal or depth) **to lack ~** [*performance, rendition*] être plat; [*building, city*] ne pas avoir d'âme; **he has no ~!** hum il est trop terre à terre!; **5** (character type) **a sensitive ~** une âme sensible; **she's a motherly ~** elle est très maternelle; **6** (person) **you mustn't tell a ~!** ne le dis à personne!; **you can drive miles without seeing a ~** on peut faire des kilomètres sans voir personne or sans voir âme qui vive; **'many people there?'—'not a ~'** 'il y avait du monde?'—'personne, pas un chat○'; **she's too old, poor ~!** elle est trop vieille, la pauvre!; **some poor ~ will have to pay** hum quelque malheureux devra payer!; **7** sout ou hum (inhabitant) habitant *m*; **8** ¢ US (black solidarity) soul *m*; **9** Mus (also **~ music**) (musique *f*) soul *m*.
IDIOMS **it's good for the ~** hum ça forme le caractère; **to be the life and ~ of the party** être un or une boute-en-train; **to throw oneself into sth heart and ~** se donner corps et âme à qch; **you can't call your ~ your own here** on n'est pas libre de faire ce qu'on veut ici.

soul: **~ brother** *n* US frère *m* (*terme que les Afro-Américains utilisent entre eux*); **~-destroying** *adj* [*occupation, role*] abrutissant; **~ food** *n* US *cuisine traditionnelle des Afro-Américains*.

soulful /'səʊlfl/ *adj* (all contexts) mélancolique.

soulfully /'səʊlfəlɪ/ *adv* [*look*] d'un air mélancolique; [*speak*] avec mélancolie.

soulless /'səʊllɪs/ *adj* [*building, office block*] sans âme; [*job*] abrutissant; [*interpretation*] plat.

soul mate *n* âme *f* sœur.

soul-searching /'səʊlsɜːtʃɪŋ/ *n* débat *m* intérieur; **to do some ~** se poser des questions.

soul: **~ sister** *n* US sœur *f* (*terme que les Afro-Américaines utilisent entre elles*); **~-stirring** *adj* [*music*] très émouvant.

sound /saʊnd/ I *n* **1** Phys son *m*; **to fly at the speed of ~** voler à la vitesse du son; **2** TV, Radio, Video son *m*; **he works in ~** il est ingénieur du son; **3** (noise) (of storm, sea, wind, car, machinery, footsteps) bruit *m* (**of** de); (of bell, instrument, voice) son *m* (**of** de); **a grating** ou **rasping ~** un grincement; **the ~ of voices/footsteps** un bruit de voix/pas; **without a ~** sans bruit; **4** (volume) son *m*; **to turn the ~ up/down** monter/baisser le son or le volume; **her television has very good ~** le son de sa télévision est très bon; **5** Mus (distinctive style) **the Motown ~** le style de Motown; **6** fig (impression from hearsay) **a 24 hour flight? I don't like the ~ of that!** un vol de 24 heures? cela ne me tente pas! or ça ne me dit rien; (when situation is threatening) **a reorganization? I don't like the ~ of that** une restructuration? ça m'inquiète or ça ne me dit rien qui vaille; **by the ~ of it, we're in for a rough crossing** d'après ce qu'on a dit, la traversée va être mauvaise; **he was in a bad temper that day, by the ~ of it** il semble que ce jour-là il ait été de mauvaise humeur; **7** Med sonde *f*; **8** Geog détroit *m*; **Plymouth Sound** le détroit de Plymouth.
II *modif* TV, Radio [*engineer, technician*] du son.
III *adj* **1** (in good condition) [*roof, foundations, building, heart, constitution*] solide; [*lungs, physique*] sain; [*health*] bon/bonne; **to be of ~ mind** être sain d'esprit; **2** (solid, well-founded) [*argument, basis, education, knowledge*] solide; [*judgment*] sain; **let me give you some ~ advice** permettez-moi de vous donner un bon conseil; **he has a ~ grasp of the basic grammar** il a une bonne compréhension des bases grammaticales; **a ~ move** une décision or démarche avisée; **3** (of good character) **he's very ~** on peut avoir confiance en lui; **4** Fin, Comm [*investment*] bon/bonne, sûr; [*management*] sain; **5** (thorough) **to give sb a ~ thrashing** donner une bonne raclée○ à qn; **6** (deep) [*sleep*] profond; **7** (correct, acceptable) **that is ~ economics, that makes ~ economic sense** du point de vue économique, c'est très sensé; **our products are ecologically ~** nos produits ne nuisent pas à l'environnement; **she's politically ~, her ideas are politically ~** elle a des idées politiques de bon ton.
IV *vtr* **1** (use) [*person, ship*] faire retentir [*siren, foghorn*]; **to ~ one's horn** klaxonner; lit, fig **to ~ the alarm** sonner or donner l'alarme; **2** Mus, Mil sonner [*trumpet, bugle, reveille, the retreat*]; frapper [*gong*]; **3** Ling prononcer [*letter*] (**in** de); **4** Med ausculter [*chest*]; sonder [*body cavity*]; **5†** Rail sonder [*wheels*]; **6** Naut sonder [*depth*]; **7** (give, express) donner [*warning*] (**about** au sujet de); **to ~ a note of caution** lancer un appel à la prudence.
V *vi* **1** (seem) sembler; **the salary certainly ~s good** le salaire semble vraiment intéressant; **it ~s as if he's really in trouble** il semble qu'il ait vraiment des ennuis; **it ~s to me as though the best plan would be to cancel** il me semble que le mieux serait d'annuler; **it ~s like she's had enough of him** il semble qu'elle en ait assez de lui; **it ~s like it might be dangerous** ça a l'air dangereux; **it ~s like it should be fun!** ça promet d'être amusant!; **it doesn't ~ to me as if she's interested** je ne pense pas qu'elle soit intéressée; **that ~s like a good idea!** ça m'a l'air d'une bonne idée; **a stream in the garden—that ~s nice!** un ruisseau dans le jardin! ça doit être

agréable!; **2** (give impression by voice or tone) **to ~ banal/boring** [*comment, idea*] paraître banal/ennuyeux; **Anne phoned—she ~ed in good form** Anne a téléphoné—elle avait l'air en forme; **you make it ~ interesting** à t'écouter ça a l'air intéressant; **you ~ fed up/as if you've got a cold** on dirait que tu en as marre○/que tu es enrhumé; **it ~s as if he's choking/crying** on dirait qu'il étouffe/pleure; **he ~s like an American** on dirait un américain, il a un accent américain; **that ~s like a flute** on dirait une flûte; **you ~ like my mother!** on dirait ma mère qui parle!; **I don't want to ~ pessimistic** je ne voudrais pas avoir l'air pessimiste; **spell it as it ~s** écris-le comme ça se prononce; **the dawn chorus ~ed wonderful** le chant matinal des oiseaux était merveilleux; **the singer did not ~ in top form** le chanteur n'était pas au mieux de sa forme; **in foggy weather, everything ~s closer** quand il y a du brouillard, tous les bruits paraissent plus proches; **3** (convey impression) faire; **she calls herself Geraldine—it ~s more sophisticated** elle se fait appeler Géraldine—ça fait plus sophistiqué; **it may ~ silly, but...** ça a peut-être l'air idiot, mais...; **4** (make a noise) [*trumpet, bugle, horn, alarm, buzzer*] sonner; [*siren, foghorn*] hurler; **5** Zool [*whale*] plonger en profondeur.
VI *adv* **to be ~ asleep** dormir à poings fermés.
■ **sound off**○: **~ off** rebattre les oreilles aux gens○ (**about** au sujet de).
■ **sound out**: **~ out [sb], ~ [sb] out** sonder, interroger [*colleague, partner, investor*].

sound: **~-absorbent** *adj* antibruit; **~ archives** *npl* archives *fpl* sonores.

sound barrier *n* mur *m* du son; **to break the ~** dépasser le mur du son.

sound: **~ bite** *n*: *bref extrait d'une interview enregistrée*; **~ box** *n* caisse *f* de résonance; **~ change** *n* modification *f* du son; **~ effect** *n* effet *m* sonore.

sound head *n* **1** Cin lecteur *m* de son, tête *f* d'enregistrement du son; **2** (on tape recorder) tête *f* de lecture du son.

sound hole *n* (of violin) ouïe *f*; (of zither, lute) rosace *f*; (of guitar) bouche *f*.

sounding /ˈsaʊndɪŋ/ **I** *n* **1** Sci, Naut (measurement of depth) sondage *m*; **to take ~s** faire des sondages; **2** fig (questioning, probing) sondage *m*; **3** Mus, Mil **the ~ of the retreat** le signal de la retraite; **the ~ of the trumpets announced the Queen's arrival** les trompettes annoncèrent l'arrivée de la reine.
II -sounding (*dans composés*) **a grand-~/English-~ name** un nom qui fait bien/qui fait anglais; **unlikely-~** bizarre.

sounding-board /ˈsaʊndɪŋbɔːd/ *n* **1** (above stage) abat-voix *m inv*; (on instrument) table *f* d'harmonie; **2** fig (person) personne *f* sur qui on peut tester ses idées; **can I use you as a ~?** est-ce que je peux tester mes idées sur toi?

sounding: **~ lead** *n* plomb *m* de sonde; **~ line** *n* ligne *f* de sonde.

sound insulation *n* isolation *f* acoustique.

soundless /ˈsaʊndlɪs/ *adj* silencieux/-ieuse.

soundlessly /ˈsaʊndlɪslɪ/ *adv* [*move, signal, open, shut*] sans bruit, sans faire de bruit.

sound: **~ level** *n* niveau *m* sonore; **~ library** *n* sonothèque *f*.

soundly /ˈsaʊndlɪ/ *adv* **1** (deeply) [*sleep*] à poings fermés; **we can sleep ~ in our beds, now that...** nous pouvons dormir tranquilles, maintenant que...; **2** (thoroughly) [*beat, defeat*] à plates coutures; **3** (firmly) [*built, based*] solidement.

soundness /ˈsaʊndnɪs/ *n* **1** (correctness) sûreté *f*; **I would question the ~ of his judgment** je mets en doute la sûreté de son jugement; **2** (of horse) bonne condition *f*.

sound post *n* âme *f* (*d'un violon, violoncelle*).

sound-proof /ˈsaʊndpruːf/ **I** *adj* [*wall, room*] insonorisé; [*material*] insonorisant.
II *vtr* insonoriser [*room*].

sound-proofing /ˈsaʊndpruːfɪŋ/ *n* insonorisation *f*.

sound recording *n* **1** gen enregistrement *m* du son; **2** Cin prise *f* de son.

sound: **~ shift** *n* mutation *f* phonétique; **~ system** *n* (hi-fi) stéréo○ *f*; (bigger: for disco etc) sono○ *f*.

sound-track /ˈsaʊndtræk/ *n* Mus, TV, Cin **1** (of film) bande *f* sonore; (on record etc) bande *f* originale; **2** (on spool of film) piste *f* son.

sound: **~ truck** *n* US camionnette *f* munie d'un haut-parleur; **~ wave** *n* onde *f* sonore.

soup /suːp/ *n* **1** Culin soupe *f*, potage *m*; **fish ~** soupe *f* de poisson; **mushroom ~** soupe *f* aux champignons; **creamy tomato ~** velouté *m* de tomates; **2** (messy mixture) bouillie *f* (**of** de).
IDIOMS **to land sb/be in the ~** mettre qn/être dans le pétrin○.
■ **soup up**: **~ up [sth], ~ [sth] up** gonfler [*car, engine*].

soupçon /ˈsuːpsɒn, US suːpˈsɒn/ *n* sout soupçon *m*.

soup: **~ed-up** *adj* [*car, engine, version*] gonflé; **~ kitchen** *n* soupe *f* populaire; **~ plate** *n* assiette *f* creuse or à soupe; **~spoon** *n* cuillère *f* à soupe; **~ tureen** *n* soupière *f*.

soupy /ˈsuːpɪ/ *adj* **1** (dense) [*fog*] dense; **2**○ US péj (sentimental) sentimental, mélo○ pej.

sour /ˈsaʊə(r)/ **I** *n* (cocktail) sour *m*.
II *adj* **1** (bitter) [*wine, taste*] acide, aigre; [*unripe fruit*] aigre, âpre; [*cherry*] aigre; **to taste ~** avoir un goût aigre; **2** (off) [*milk*] aigre; [*smell*] aigre, âpre; **to go ~** lit tourner; **to go** ou **turn ~** fig se dégrader; **3** (bad-tempered) [*person, look*] revêche; **to have a ~ look on one's face** avoir un air revêche.
III *vtr* gâter [*relations, atmosphere*].
IV *vi* [*attitude, outlook*] s'aigrir; [*friendship, relationship*] se dégrader.

source /sɔːs/ **I** *n* **1** (origin) source *f* (**of** de); **~ of income, ~ of revenue** source de revenu; **~s of supply** sources d'approvisionnement; **energy/food ~s** ressources *fpl* énergétiques/alimentaires; **at ~** [*affect, cut off, deduct*] à la source; **2** (cause) **~ of** source *f* de [*anxiety, resentment, satisfaction*]; cause *f* de, origine *f* de [*problem, error, infection, pollution*]; origine *f* de [*rumour*]; **3** Journ (informant) source *f* (**close to** proche de); **to hear sth from a reliable ~** tenir qch de source sûre; **one ~ said the king had always known that** le roi aurait toujours su que; **4** Geog (of river) source *f*; **5** Literat (of writer, work) source *f*.
II sources *npl* Univ (reference materials) sources *fpl*.
III *vtr* Ind se procurer [*products, energy*]; **to be ~d from** provenir de [*region, country*].

source: **~ book** *n* livre *m* source; **~ code** *n* Comput code *m* source; **~ language** *n* langue *f* source; **~ material** *n* ¢ sources *fpl*; **~ program** *n* programme *m* source.

sour cream /ˈsaʊə(r)/ *n* crème *f* aigre.

sourdine /ˌsʊəˈdiːn/ *n* sourdine *f*.

sour: **~dough** *n* US levain *m*; **~ dough bread** *n* US ≈ pain *m* au levain; **~-faced** *adj* [*person*] à la mine revêche.

sour grapes *npl* dépit *m*; **it's (a touch of) ~!** c'est du dépit!

sourish /ˈsaʊərɪʃ/ *adj* (all contexts) aigrelet/-ette.

sourly /ˈsaʊəlɪ/ *adv* [*say, answer*] aigrement.

sourness /ˈsaʊənɪs/ *n* lit, fig aigreur *f*.

sourpuss○ /ˈsaʊəpʊs/ *n* hum grincheux/-euse○ *m/f*.

sousaphone /ˈsuːzəfəʊn/ **▶ 1481** *n* hélicon *m*.

souse /saʊs/ **I** *vtr* **1** (soak) tremper [*person, object*]; **2** Culin faire mariner [*herring*].
II soused *pp adj* **1** Culin mariné; **2**○ (drunk) cuité○, pinté○.

south /saʊθ/ **▶ 1568** **I** *n* sud *m*; **the ~ of France** le sud de la France, le Midi.
II South *pr n* **1** Pol, Geog, US Hist **the South** le Sud; **2** (in cards) sud.
III *adj* [*side, face, wall*] sud *inv*; [*wind*] gen du sud; Meteorol de sud; [*coast*] sud *inv*.
IV *adv* [*move*] vers le sud; [*lie, live*] au sud (**of** de); **to go ~ of sth** passer au sud de qch.

South Africa **▶ 1131** *pr n* Afrique *f* du Sud.

South African **▶ 1486** **I** *n* Sud-Africain/-e *m/f*.
II *adj* sud-africain, d'Afrique du Sud.

South America **▶ 1131** *pr n* Amérique *f* du Sud.

South American **I** *n* Sud-Américain/-e *m/f*.
II *adj* sud-américain, d'Amérique du Sud.

South Australia *pr n* Australie-Méridionale *f*.

southbound /ˈsaʊθbaʊnd/ *adj* [*carriageway, traffic*] en direction du sud; **the ~ platform/train** GB (in underground) le quai/la rame direction sud.

south: **South Carolina** **▶ 1744** *pr n* Caroline *f* du Sud; **South China Sea** **▶ 1511** *pr n* mer *f* de Chine méridionale; **South Dakota** **▶ 1744** *pr n* Dakota *m* du Sud.

southeast /ˌsaʊθˈiːst/ **▶ 1568** **I** *n* sud-est *m*.
II *adj* [*coast, side*] sud-est *inv*; [*wind*] de sud-est.
III *adv* [*move*] vers le sud-est; [*lie, live*] au sud-est (**of** de).

South East Asia *pr n* le Sud-Est asiatique.

southeaster /ˌsaʊθˈiːstə(r)/ *n* vent *m* de sud-est.

southeasterly /ˌsaʊθˈiːstəlɪ/ **I** *n* vent *m* de sud-est.
II **▶ 1568** *adj* [*wind*] de sud-est; [*point*] au sud-est; **in a ~ direction** en direction du sud-est.

southeastern /ˌsaʊθˈiːstən/ **▶ 1568** *adj* [*coast, boundary*] sud-est *inv*; [*town, accent, custom*] du sud-est; **~ England** le Sud-est de l'Angleterre.

southerly /ˈsʌðəlɪ/ **I** *n* vent *m* du sud.
II **▶ 1568** *adj* [*wind*] de sud; [*point*] au sud; [*area*] du sud; [*breeze*] venant du sud; **in a ~ direction** en direction du sud.

southern /ˈsʌðən/ **▶ 1568** *adj* **1** [*coast, boundary*] sud *inv*; [*state, region, town, accent*] du sud; **~ France** le sud de la France, le Midi; **~ English** [*landscape etc*] du Sud de l'Angleterre; **~ French** [*landscape etc*] du Midi, méridional; **2** US Hist (also **Southern**) sudiste.

southern: **Southern Alps** *pr npl* Alpes *fpl* néo-zélandaises; **Southern Belle** *n* belle femme *f* du Sud des États-Unis; **Southern Comfort**® *n*: *variété de bourbon*; **Southern Cross** *n* Astron Croix *f* du Sud.

southerner /ˈsʌðənə(r)/ *n* **1** **~s** les gens *mpl* du Sud; **to be a ~** être du Sud; **2** US Hist (also **Southerner**) sudiste *mf*.

southern: **~-fried chicken** *n* US Culin *poulet frit servi avec une sauce épicée*; **~ hemisphere** *n* hémisphère *m* Sud *inv* or austral; **Southern Lights** *npl* aurore *f* australe; **~most** *adj* à l'extrême sud, le/la plus au sud.

south: **~-facing** *adj* exposé au sud; **South Georgia** **▶ 1381** *pr n* Géorgie *f* du Sud.

South Glamorgan /ˌsaʊθ ɡləˈmɔːɡən/ **▶ 1624** *pr n* South Glamorgan *m*.

south: **South Island** **▶ 1381** *pr n* île *f* du Sud; **South Korea** **▶ 1131** *pr n* Corée *f* du Sud.

South Korean ▶1486 **I** *n* Sud-Coréen/-éenne *m/f*.
II *adj* sud-coréen/-éenne.
south: **~paw**○ *n* gen (left-handed person) gaucher/-ère *m/f*; (in boxing) fausse-garde *f*; **South Pole** *pr n* pôle *m* Sud; **South Sea Islands** ▶1381 *pr npl* Océanie *f*; **South Seas** ▶1511 *pr npl* mers *fpl* du Sud; **South Vietnam** ▶1131 *pr n* Vietnam *m* du Sud.
southward /ˈsaʊθwəd/ ▶1568 **I** *adj* [*side*] sud *inv*; [*wall, slope*] du côté sud; [*journey, route, movement*] vers le sud; **in a ~ direction** en direction du sud, vers le sud.
II *adv* (also **~s**) vers le sud.
southwest /ˌsaʊθˈwest/ ▶1568 **I** *n* sud-ouest *m*.
II *adj* [*coast, side*] sud-ouest *inv*; [*wind*] de sud-ouest.
III *adv* [*move*] vers le sud-ouest; [*lie, live*] au sud-ouest (**of** de).
South West Africa *pr n* Afrique *f* du Sud-Ouest.
southwester /ˌsaʊθˈwestə(r)/ *n* vent *m* de sud-ouest, suroît *m*.
southwesterly /ˌsaʊθˈwestəlɪ/ **I** *n* vent *m* de sud-ouest, suroît *m*.
II ▶1568 *adj* [*wind*] de sud-ouest; [*point*] au sud-ouest; **in a ~ direction** en direction du sud-ouest.
southwestern /ˌsaʊθˈwestən/ ▶1568 *adj* [*coast, boundary*] sud-ouest *inv*; [*town, accent, custom*] du sud-ouest; **~ England** le Sud-ouest de l'Angleterre.
South Yorkshire /ˌsaʊθ ˈjɔːkʃə(r)/ ▶1624 *pr n* South Yorkshire *m*.
souvenir /ˌsuːvəˈnɪə(r), US ˈsuːvənɪər/ *n* (object) souvenir *m* (**of, from** de).
souvenir: **~ hunter** *n* amateur *m* de souvenirs; **~ shop** *n* magasin *m* de souvenirs.
sou'wester /ˌsaʊˈwestə(r)/ *n* (hat) suroît *m*.
sovereign /ˈsɒvrɪn/ **I** *n* **1** (monarch) souverain/-e *m/f*; **2** Hist (coin) souverain *m*.
II *adj* **1** (absolute) [*power, authority, state*] souverain (*after n*); [*rights*] de souveraineté; **2** (utmost) [*contempt, indifference*] souverain (*before n*).
sovereignty /ˈsɒvrəntɪ/ *n* souveraineté *f*; **to claim ~ over** revendiquer la souveraineté de [*region, country*].
soviet /ˈsəʊvɪət, ˈsɒ-/ *n* Pol soviet *m*.
Soviet /ˈsəʊvɪət, ˈsɒ-/ ▶1486 Hist **I Soviets** *npl* (people) Soviétiques *mpl*.
II *adj* [*Russia, system, history, bloc*] soviétique.
sovietize /ˈsəʊvɪətaɪz/ *vtr* soviétiser.
Soviet Union /ˌsəʊvɪət ˈjuːnɪən/ ▶1131 *pr n* Hist Union *f* soviétique.
sow[1] /saʊ/ *n* truie *f*.
IDIOMS **you can't make a silk purse out of a ~'s ear** Prov la caque sent toujours le hareng Prov.
sow[2] /səʊ/ *vtr* (*prét* **sowed**, *pp* **sowed, sown**) **1** semer [*seeds, corn*]; **2** ensemencer [*field, garden*] (**with** de); **3** fig (stir up) semer [*discontent, discord*]; **to ~ the seeds of doubt** faire germer le doute (**in sb** dans l'esprit de qn).
sower /ˈsəʊə(r)/ *n* semeur/-euse *m/f* (**of** de).
sowing /ˈsəʊɪŋ/ *n* ¢ semailles *fpl*.
sowing machine /ˈsəʊɪŋ/ *n* semoir *m*.
sown /səʊn/ *pp* ▶ **sow**[2].
sox○ /sɒks/ *npl* US chaussettes *fpl*.
soya /ˈsɔɪə/ **I** *n* soja *m*.
II *modif* [*bean, burger, flour, milk*] de soja.
soya sauce, **soy sauce** *n* sauce *f* soja.
sozzled○ /ˈsɒzld/ *adj* pinté○, cuité○.
spa /spɑː/ *n* **1** (town) station *f* thermale; **2** US (health club) club *m* de remise en forme.
space /speɪs/ **I** *n* **1** ¢ (room) place *f*, espace *m*; **to take up a lot of ~** prendre or occuper beaucoup de place; **to make ~ for sb/sth** faire de la place pour qn/qch; **a car with plenty of luggage ~** une voiture avec beaucoup de place or d'espace pour les bagages; **there is ample ~ for parking** il n'y a aucun problème de stationnement; **to buy/sell (advertising) ~ in a newspaper** acheter/vendre des espaces publicitaires dans un journal; **to give sb ~** fig laisser de la liberté à qn; **to need (one's own) ~** avoir besoin de liberté; **to invade sb's (personal) ~** empiéter sur l'espace vital de qn; **2 C** (gap, blank area) gen espace *m* (**between** entre); Mus interligne *m*; Print (between letters, words) espace *f*; (between lines) interligne *m*, espace *m*; **there is a ~ of ten centimetres between...** il y a un espace de dix centimètres entre...; **enclosed ~s** les espaces fermés; **in the ~ provided** (on application form etc) dans l'espace prévu à cet effet, dans la case prévue à cet effet; **'watch this ~!'** 'à suivre'; **3 C** (area of land) espace *m*; **open ~s** espaces *mpl* libres; **the freedom of the wide open ~s** la liberté des grands espaces; **4** (interval of time) intervalle *m*; **after a ~ of fifteen minutes/two weeks** après un intervalle de quinze minutes/deux semaines; **in** ou **within the ~ of five minutes/a week** en l'espace de cinq minutes/d'une semaine; **in a short ~ of time** en très peu de temps; **5** Aerosp, Phys espace *m*; **the exploration of ~, ~ exploration** l'exploration de l'espace or du cosmos.
II *modif* Aerosp, Phys [*research, programme, exploration, vehicle, rocket*] spatial.
III *vtr* espacer; **the pylons were ~d 100 metres apart** les pylônes étaient espacés de 100 mètres.
IDIOMS **to stare into ~** regarder dans le vide or l'espace.
■ **space out**: **to ~ out [sth], ~ [sth] out** espacer [*objects, rows, words, visits, events*]; échelonner [*payments*]; **to ~ out one's days off throughout the year** répartir ses jours de congé sur toute l'année.
space age I *n* ère *f* spatiale.
II space-age *modif* [*design*] de l'ère spatiale.
space: **Space Agency** *n* Agence *f* spatiale; **~-bar** *n* barre *f* d'espacement; **~ blanket** *n* couverture *f* de survie; **~ cadet**○ *n* US hum cinglé/-e○ *m/f*; **~ capsule** *n* Aerosp capsule *f* spatiale; **~craft** *n* Aerosp (*pl* **~**) vaisseau *m* spatial.
spaced out○ *adj* **he's completely ~**○ il plane○ complètement.
space flight *n* Aerosp **1** (activity) voyages *mpl* interplanétaires; **2** (single journey) vol *m* spatial.
space: **~ heating** *n* chauffage *m*; **~ helmet** *n* Aerosp casque *m* de cosmonaute; **Space Invaders**® *n* (+ *v sg*) *jeu électronique de combats dans l'espace*; **~ lab** *n* Aerosp laboratoire *m* spatial; **~man** *n* Aerosp cosmonaute *m*, spationaute *m*; **~ opera** *n* Cin space opéra *m* (*œuvre ou genre de science-fiction sur le thème des voyages interplanétaires*); **~plane** *n* Aerosp navette *f* spatiale; **~ platform** *n* Aerosp station *f* spatiale; **~port** *n* Aerosp base *f* de lancement; **~ probe** *n* Aerosp sonde *f* spatiale; **~ race** *n* Aerosp, Pol course *f* pour la conquête de l'espace; **~-saving** *adj* qui gagne de la place, compact; **~ science** *n* Aerosp science *f* de l'espace, spatiologie *f*; **~ scientist** ▶1692 *n* Aerosp spécialiste *mf* en spatiologie; **~ship** *n* Aerosp vaisseau *m* spatial; **~ shuttle** *n* Aerosp navette *f* spatiale; **~ sickness** *n* Aerosp, Med mal *m* de l'espace; **~ station** *n* Aerosp station *f* orbitale or spatiale; **~suit** *n* Aerosp combinaison *f* spatiale; **~-time (continuum)** *n* Phys Espace-Temps *m*; **~ travel** *n* Aerosp voyages *mpl* dans l'espace.
spacewalk /ˈspeɪswɔːk/ Aerosp **I** *n* sortie *f* dans l'espace.
II *vi* sortir dans l'espace.
spacewoman /ˈspeɪswʊmən/ *n* Aerosp cosmonaute *f*.
spacey○ /ˈspeɪsɪ/ *adj* US **1** (bewildered or on drugs) **he's ~** il plane○ complètement; **2** (odd) farfelu○.
spacing /ˈspeɪsɪŋ/ *n* **1** Print espacement *m*; **in single/double ~** en simple/double interligne; **2** (also **~ out**) (of objects, buildings, rows, visits, events) espacement *m*; (of payments) échelonnement *m*.
spacious /ˈspeɪʃəs/ *adj* spacieux/-ieuse.
spaciousness /ˈspeɪʃəsnɪs/ *n* ¢ grandeur *f*, grandes dimensions *fpl*.
spade /speɪd/ ▶1282 *n* **1** (tool) bêche *f*, pelle *f*; (toy) pelle *f*; **2** (in cards) pique *m*; **the four of ~s** le quatre de pique; **3**◑ (black person) injur nègre *m*, négresse *f* offensive.
IDIOMS **to call a ~ a ~** appeler un chat un chat; **to have energy/charm in ~s** avoir de l'énergie/du charme à revendre.
spadeful /ˈspeɪdfʊl/ *n* pelletée *f*; **by the ~** en grande quantité, à la pelle.
spadework /ˈspeɪdwɜːk/ *n* fig travail *m* de base.
spaghetti /spəˈgetɪ/ *n* ¢ spaghetti *mpl inv*.
spaghetti: **~ junction**○ *n* GB Transp échangeur *m* à niveaux multiples; **~ western**○ *n* western *m* spaghetti.
Spain /speɪn/ ▶1131 *pr n* Espagne *f*.
spake‡ /speɪk/ = **spoke I**.
spam® /spæm/ *n* viande *f* de porc en conserve.
span /spæn/ **I** *n* **1** (period of time) durée *f*; **the ~ of sb's life/career** la durée de la vie/la carrière de qn; **a short ~ of time** une courte période; **time ~** espace *m* de temps; **over a ~ of several years** sur une période de plusieurs années; **to have a short concentration ~** avoir une capacité de concentration de courte durée; **2** (width) (across hand, arms, wings) envergure *f*; (of bridge) travée *f*; (of arch) portée *f*; **the bridge crosses the river in a single ~** le pont enjambe la rivière d'une seule travée; **3** fig (extent) **the whole ~ of human history** la totalité or l'ensemble de l'histoire de l'humanité; **4**† Meas ≈ empan† *m*; ▶ **wingspan**.
II *vtr* (*p prés* etc **-nn-**) **1** [*bridge, arch*] enjamber; Constr [*person*] construire un pont sur [*river*]; **2** fig (encompass) s'étendre sur; **her life ~ned most of the nineteenth century** sa vie s'est étendue sur la presque totalité du dix-neuvième siècle; **his career ~ned several decades** sa carrière s'est étendue sur or a couvert plusieurs décennies; **a group ~ning the age range 10 to 14** un groupe comprenant les enfants âgés de 10 à 14 ans.
III‡ *pp* ▶ **spin**.
Spandex® /ˈspændeks/ *n* tissu *m* extensible.
spangle /ˈspæŋgl/ *n* paillette *f*.
spangled /ˈspæŋgld/ *adj* pailletté (**with** de).
Spaniard /ˈspænjəd/ ▶1486 *n* Espagnol/-e *m/f*.
spaniel /ˈspænjəl/ *n* épagneul *m*.
Spanish /ˈspænɪʃ/ ▶1486, 1402 **I** *n* **1** (people) **the ~** (+ *v pl*) les Espagnols *mpl*; **2** Ling espagnol *m*.
II *adj* [*custom, people, landscape, literature*] espagnol; [*king, embassy, army*] d'Espagne.
Spanish America *pr n* Amérique *f* espagnole.
Spanish American I *n* Hispano-américain/-e *m/f*.
II *adj* hispano-américain.
Spanish Armada /ˌspænɪʃɑːˈmɑːdə/ *n* **the ~** l'Invincible Armada *f*.
Spanish chestnut *n* **1** (nut) chataîgne *f*; **2** (tree) chataîgnier *m*.
Spanish: **~ Civil War** *n* Hist guerre *f* civile d'Espagne; **~ fly** *n* cantharide *f*; **~ guitar** ▶1481 *n* guitare *f* classique; **~ Main** *pr n*‡ mer *f* des Antilles; **~ moss** *n* Bot tillandsie *f*; **~ omelette** *n* omelette *f* espagnole; **~ onion** *n* oignon *m* espagnol; **~ rice** *n* riz *m* à l'espagnole; **~-speaking** *adj* hispanophone.

spank /spæŋk/ **I** *n* fessée *f*; **to give sb a ~** donner une fessée à qn.
II *vtr* donner une fessée à, fesser [*person*].

spanking /ˈspæŋkɪŋ/ **I** *n* fessée *f*; **to give sb a ~** donner une fessée à qn.
II○ *adj* **at a ~ pace** à une belle allure.
III○ *adv* **a ~ new car/kitchen** une voiture/une cuisine flambant neuve.

spanner /ˈspænə(r)/ *n* GB clé *f* (*de serrage*); **adjustable ~** clé à molette.
IDIOMS **to put** ou **throw a ~ in the works** mettre du sable dans l'engrenage.

spar /spɑː(r)/ **I** *n* **1** Naut espar *m*; **2** Geol, Miner spath *m*.
II *vi* (*p prés etc* **-rr-**) [*boxers*] échanger des coups; fig [*debaters*] se livrer à des joutes oratoires; **to ~ with** s'entraîner à la boxe avec [*partner*]; fig se bagarrer pour rire avec [*child, boyfriend etc*]; gen [*politician*] s'affronter à [*opponent*].

spare /speə(r)/ **I** *n* Tech, gen (part) pièce *f* de rechange; (wheel) roue *f* de secours; **a set of ~s** un jeu de pièces de rechange; **use my pen, I've got a ~** prends mon stylo, j'en ai un autre.
II *adj* **1** (surplus) [*cash, capacity*] restant; [*capital, land, chair, seat*] disponible; [*copy*] en plus; **I've got a ~ ticket** j'ai un ticket en trop; **a ~ moment** un moment de libre; **2** (in reserve) [*component, fuse, bulb*] de rechange; [*wheel*] de secours; **3** (lean) [*person, build*] élancé; [*design, building, style*] simple; **4** (meagre) [*diet, meal*] frugal; **5**○ GB (mad) dingue○; **to go ~** devenir dingue○.
III *vtr* **1 to have sth to ~** avoir qch de disponible; **have my pen, I've got one to ~** prends mon stylo, j'en ai un autre; **to catch the train with five minutes to ~** prendre le train avec cinq minutes d'avance; **to have time to ~ at the airport** avoir du temps d'attente à l'aéroport; **I have no time to ~ for doing** je n'ai pas de temps à perdre à faire; **the project was finished with only days to ~** le projet a été terminé seulement quelques jours avant la date limite; **I have no energy to ~ for the housework** je n'ai plus d'énergie pour les travaux domestiques; **enough and to ~** bien assez et plus qu'il n'en faut; **2** (treat leniently) épargner [*person, animal*]; **to ~ sb sth** épargner qch à qn; **to ~ sb's life** épargner la vie de qn; **~ my life!** ne me tuez pas!; **I will ~ you the details** je vous épargnerai les détails; **we were ~d the full story** hum on a été dispensé du récit complet; **see you next year if I'm ~d** hum à l'année prochaine, si Dieu me prête vie; **3** (be able to afford) avoir [*money, time*]; **can you ~ a minute/a pound/a cigarette?** as-tu un moment/une livre/une cigarette?; **to ~ a thought for** penser à; **4** (manage without) se passer de [*person*]; **I can't ~ him today** je ne peux pas me passer de lui aujourd'hui; **to ~ sb for** se passer de qn pour [*job, task*].
IV *v refl* **to ~ oneself sth** s'épargner qch; **to ~ oneself the trouble of doing** s'épargner l'ennui de faire; **to ~ oneself the expense of** faire l'économie de.
IDIOMS **to ~ no effort** faire tout son possible; **to ~ no pains** se donner du mal.

spare part *n* Aut, Tech pièce *f* de rechange.
IDIOMS **to feel like a ~** se sentir de trop.

spare: **~ part surgery** *n* chirurgie *f* de remplacement; **~ rib** *n* Culin travers *m* de porc; **~ room** *n* chambre *f* d'amis.

spare time *n* ¢ loisirs *mpl*; **to do sth in one's ~** faire qch pendant ses loisirs.

spare tyre GB, **spare tire** US *n* **1** Aut pneu *m* de rechange; **2**○ (fat) bourrelet *m*.

spare wheel *n* Aut roue *f* de secours.

sparing /ˈspeərɪŋ/ *adj* [*person, use*] parcimonieux/-ieuse; **to be ~ with** (economical) économiser [*food, rations, medicine*]; (mean) être avare de [*advice, help*]; (careful) utiliser [qch] avec parsimonie [*flavouring, colour*].

sparingly /ˈspeərɪŋlɪ/ *adv* [*use, add*] en petite quantité.

spark /spɑːk/ **I** *n* **1** gen, Elec étincelle *f*; **2** fig (hint) (of originality) éclair *m*; (of enthusiasm) étincelle *f*; (of intelligence) lueur *f*; **the ~ of interest/mischief in her eyes** la lueur d'intérêt/de malice dans ses yeux; **the ~ has gone out of their relationship** leur relation a perdu tout son piment.
II *vtr* = **spark off**.
III *vi* [*fire*] jeter des étincelles; [*wire, switch*] faire des étincelles.
IDIOMS **~s will fly!** ça va faire des étincelles!
■ **spark off**: **~ off [sth]** susciter [*interest, anger, fear*]; provoquer [*controversy, speculation, reaction, panic*]; être à l'origine de [*friendship, affair*]; déclencher [*war, riot*]; entraîner [*growth, change*]; lancer [*movement*].

spark gap *n* Elec, Aut écartement *m* des électrodes.

sparkle /ˈspɑːkl/ **I** *n* (of light, star, tinsel) scintillement *m*; (of jewel) éclat *m*; (in eye) éclair *m*; fig (of performance) éclat *m*; **she's lost her ~** elle a perdu sa joie de vivre; **there was a ~ in his eye** ses yeux brillaient; **to add ~ to sth** [*product*] donner du brillant à [*glasses etc*].
II *vi* **1** (flash) [*flame, light*] étinceler; [*jewel, frost, metal, water*] scintiller; [*eyes*] briller; **to ~ with** [*eyes*] briller de [*excitement, fun*]; fig [*conversation*] être émaillé de [*wit, anecdotes*]; [*person*] rayonner de [*happiness*]; **2** (fizz) [*drink*] pétiller.

sparkler /ˈspɑːklə(r)/ *n* **1** (firework) cierge *m* magique; **2**○ (jewel) caillou○ *m*.

sparkling /ˈspɑːklɪŋ/ **I** *adj* **1** (twinkling) [*light, flame*] étincelant; [*jewel, metal, water*] scintillant; [*eyes*] brillant (**with** de); **2** (witty) [*conversation, wit*] plein de brio; **~ with wit/humour** étincelant d'esprit/d'humour; **3** [*drink*] pétillant.
II *adv* (for emphasis) **~ clean** étincelant de propreté; **~ white** d'un blanc étincelant.

spark plug *n* Elec, Aut bougie *f*.

sparks○ /spɑːks/ *n* **1** GB (electrician) électricien/-ienne *m/f*; **2** Naut (radio operator) radio○ *m*.

sparky /ˈspɑːkɪ/ **I**○ *n* GB (electrician) électricien/-ienne *m/f*.
II *adj* [*person, performance, humour*] vivace.

spar: **~ring match** *n* (in boxing) combat *m* d'entraînement; fig prise *f* de bec○; **~ring partner** *n* (in boxing) sparring-partner *m*; fig adversaire *mf*.

sparrow /ˈspærəʊ/ *n* moineau *m*.

sparrowhawk /ˈspærəʊhɔːk/ *n* épervier *m*.

sparse /spɑːs/ *adj* [*population, vegetation, hair*] clairsemé; [*furnishings*] rare; [*resources, supplies*] maigre (*before n*); [*information*] épars; [*use*] modéré; **trading was ~** la Bourse était calme.

sparsely /ˈspɑːslɪ/ *adv* peu; **~ wooded/attended** peu boisé/fréquenté; **~ populated** (permanently) à faible population; (temporarily) peu fréquenté.

sparseness /ˈspɑːsnɪs/ *n* rareté *f*.

Sparta /ˈspɑːtə/ ▶ **1818** *pr n* Sparte.

Spartan /ˈspɑːtən/ **I** *n* Spartiate *mf*.
II *adj* **1** (from Sparta) [*tradition, soldier*] spartiate; **2** fig (also **spartan**) [*life, regime*] spartiate.

spasm /ˈspæzəm/ *n* **1** Med spasme *m*; **muscular ~** spasme musculaire; **2** (of pain) spasme *m* (**of** de); (of anxiety, panic, activity, rage, coughing) accès *m* (**of** de).

spasmodic /spæzˈmɒdɪk/ *adj* **1** (intermittent) [*activity*] intermittent; **2** (occurring in spasms) [*coughing, cramp*] spasmodique.

spasmodically /spæzˈmɒdɪklɪ/ *adv* [*work, operate*] par à-coups.

spastic /ˈspæstɪk/ **I** *n* **1** Med handicapé/-e *m/f* moteur; **2**○ injur empoté/-e○ *m/f*.
II *adj* **1** Med handicapé moteur; **2**○ injur empoté○.

spastic colon *n* côlon *m* spasmodique.

spasticity /ˌspæsˈtɪsətɪ/ *n* paralysie *f* spasmodique.

Spastics Society *n Société britannique pour les handicapés moteurs.*

spat /spæt/ **I** *pp, prét* ▶ **spit**.
II *n* **1**○ (quarrel) prise *f* de bec○ (**with** avec); **2** (on shoe) demi-guêtre *f*; **3** Zool naissain *m*.

spatchcock /ˈspætʃkɒk/ **I** *n* volaille *f* grillée à la crapaudine.
II *vtr* **1** Culin griller [qch] à la crapaudine [*fowl*]; **2** (interpolate) interpoler.

spate /speɪt/ *n* **1 in full ~** GB (river) en pleine crue; (person) en plein discours; **2 a ~ of** une série de [*incidents*].

spatial /ˈspeɪʃl/ *adj* spatial.

spatial awareness, spatial intelligence *n* perception *f* spatiale.

spatiotemporal /ˌspeɪʃəʊˈtempərəl/ *adj* spatio-temporel/-elle.

spatter /ˈspætə(r)/ **I** *n* **1** (of liquid) éclaboussure *f*; **a ~ of rain** une petite pluie; **2** (sound) crépitement *m*; **3** US (small amount) un petit peu (**of** de).
II *vtr* **to ~ sb/sth with sth, to ~ sth over sb/sth** (splash) éclabousser qn/qch de qch; (deliberately sprinkle) asperger qn/qch de qch.
III *vi* crépiter (**on** sur; **against** contre).
IV spattered *pp adj* éclaboussé; **blood-/paint-~ed** éclaboussé de sang/de peinture.

spatula /ˈspætʃʊlə/ *n* **1** gen spatule *f*; **2** (doctor's) abaisse-langue *m inv*.

spavin /ˈspævɪn/ *n* Vet éparvin *m*.

spawn /spɔːn/ **I** *n* **1** (of frog, fish) frai *m*; **2** (of fungi) mycélium *m*.
II *vtr* souvent péj engendrer [*product, imitation etc*].
III *vi* **1** Zool frayer; **2** (multiply) se multiplier.

spawning /ˈspɔːnɪŋ/ *n* **1** Zool frai *m*; **2** souvent péj prolifération *f* (**of** de).

spawning ground *n* frayère *f*.

spay /speɪ/ *vtr* enlever les ovaires de; **to have one's cat ~ed** faire opérer sa chatte.

SPCA *n* US (*abrév* = **Society for the Prevention of Cruelty to Animals**) société *f* américaine pour la protection des animaux; cf SPA *f*.

SPCC *n* US (*abrév* = **Society for the Prevention of Cruelty to Children**) *société pour la protection de l'enfance.*

speak /spiːk/ **I -speak** (*dans composés*) jargon *m*; **computer-/management-~** jargon informatique/jargon de gestion.
II *vtr* (*prét* **spoke**, *pp* **spoken**) **1** parler [*language*]; **can you ~ English?** parlez-vous (l')anglais?; **'French spoken'** (sign) 'on parle français'; **English as it is spoken** l'anglais tel qu'on le parle; **people who ~ the same language** lit, fig des gens qui parlent le même langage; **2** (tell, utter) dire [*truth, poetry*]; prononcer [*word, name*]; **to ~ one's mind** dire ce qu'on pense.
III *vi* (*prét* **spoke**; *pp* **spoken**) **1** (talk) parler (**to** à; **about, of** de); **to ~ in a soft/deep voice** parler bas/d'une voix profonde; **to ~ in German/Russian** parler (en) allemand/russe; **to ~ in a whisper** parler tout bas, chuchoter; **to ~ ill/well of sb** dire du mal/du bien de qn; **to ~ through** parler par l'intermédiaire de [*medium, interpreter*]; **to ~ with one's mouth full** parler la bouche pleine; **~ when you're spoken to!** réponds quand on te parle!; **I've spoken to them severely and they've apologized** je leur ai parlé sévèrement et ils se sont excusés; **who's ~ing please?** (on phone) qui est à l'appareil s'il vous plaît?; (**this is**) **Camilla ~ing** c'est Camilla, Camilla à l'appareil; **'is that Miss Durham?'—'~ing!'** 'Mademoiselle Durham?'—'c'est moi!'; **I'm ~ing from a phone box** j'appelle d'une cabine téléphonique; **this is your captain ~ing** Aviat ici le commandant de bord; **~ing of which, have you booked a table?** tiens, ça m'a fait

penser, as-tu réservé une table?; **~ing of lunch, Nancy**... à propos du déjeuner, Nancy...; **she is well spoken of in academic circles** elle est bien considérée dans le milieu universitaire; **he spoke very highly of her/her talents** il a parlé d'elle/de ses talents en termes très élogieux; **he spoke of selling the house/leaving the country** il a parlé de vendre la maison/de quitter le pays; **to ~ as sth** (parler) en tant que qch; **~ing as a layman**... en tant que non-spécialiste...; **~ing personally, I hate him** personnellement, je le déteste; **~ing personally and not for the company** parlant en mon nom et pas en celui de l'entreprise; **generally ~ing** en règle générale; **roughly ~ing** en gros; **strictly ~ing** à proprement parler; **relatively ~ing** relativement parlant; **ecologically/politically ~ing** écologiquement/politiquement parlant, sur le plan écologique/politique; **metaphorically ~ing** pour employer une métaphore; **we've had no trouble to ~ of** nous n'avons pas eu de problème spécial; **they've got no money to ~ of** ils n'ont pour ainsi dire pas d'argent; **'what did you see?'—'nothing to ~ of'** 'qu'est-ce que vous avez vu?'—'rien de spécial'; **not to ~ of his poor mother/the expense** sans parler de sa pauvre mère/du coût; **so to ~** pour ainsi dire; **2** (converse) parler (**about, of** de; **to, with** à); **they're not ~ing (to each other)** ils ne se parlent pas; **I can't remember when we last spoke** je ne me rappelle plus quand nous nous sommes parlé pour la dernière fois ; **I know her by sight but not to ~ to** je la connais de vue mais je ne lui ai jamais parlé; **3** (make a speech) parler; (more formal) prendre la parole; **to ~ from the floor** Pol parler or prendre la parole de sa place; **to ~ about** ou **on** parler de [*topic*]; **to ~ for** parler en faveur de [*view, opinion, party*]; **4** (express) littér **to ~ of** témoigner de [*suffering, effort, emotion*]; **all creation spoke to me of love** toute la création me parlait d'amour; **that look spoke louder than words** ce regard était plus expressif que des mots; **the poem/music ~s to me in a special way** le poème/la musique me touche profondément; **5** fig (make noise) [*gun*] parler; **this clarinet ~s/does not ~ easily** il est facile/difficile de faire sortir un son de cette clarinette.

■ **speak for**: **~ for [sth/sb] 1** (on behalf of) parler pour lit; parler de fig; **it ~s well for their efficiency that they answered so promptly** leur réponse rapide montre bien or prouve bien leur efficacité; **to ~ for oneself** s'exprimer; **let him ~ for himself** laissez-le s'exprimer; **~ing for myself**... pour ma part...; **~ for yourself!** parle pour toi!; **the facts ~ for themselves** les faits parlent d'eux-mêmes; **2** (reserve) **to be spoken for** [*object*] être réservé or retenu; [*person*] ne pas être libre; **that picture's already spoken for** ce tableau est déjà réservé or retenu.

■ **speak out** se prononcer (**against** contre; **in favour of** en faveur de); **don't be afraid! ~ out!** n'aie pas peur! exprime-toi!

■ **speak to**: **~ to [sth]** Admin commenter [*item, motion*]; **please ~ to the point** tenez-vous en au sujet s'il vous plaît.

■ **speak up 1** (louder) parler plus fort; **2** (dare to speak) intervenir; **to ~ up for sb/sth** intervenir or parler en faveur de qn/qch.

speakeasy /ˈspiːkiːzɪ/ *n* US Hist bar *m* clandestin.

speaker /ˈspiːkə(r)/ *n* **1** (person talking) personne *f* qui parle; (orator, public speaker) orateur/-trice *m/f*; (invited lecturer) conférencier/-ière *m/f*; (one of several conference lecturers) intervenant/-e *m/f*; **a ~ from the floor** un intervenant dans le public; **the crowd was too big to identify the ~** la foule était trop importante pour pouvoir identifier celui qui parlait; **2** (of foreign language) **an Italian/an English/a French ~** un/-e italophone/anglophone/francophone *mf*, quelqu'un qui parle l'italien/l'anglais/le français; **a Japanese/Russian ~** quelqu'un qui parle le japonais/le russe; **3** (also **Speaker**) GB Pol président/-e *m/f* des Communes; **Mr Speaker** monsieur le Président; **4** Elec, Mus haut-parleur *m*.

speaking /ˈspiːkɪŋ/ **I** *n* (elocution) élocution *f*; (pronunciation) prononciation *f*.

II -speaking (*dans composés*) **English-/French-~** [*person*] anglophone/francophone, parlant anglais/français; [*area, country*] anglophone/francophone, de langue anglaise/française.

speaking clock *n* horloge *f* parlante.

speaking engagement *n* **to have a ~** devoir prononcer un discours; **I must cancel all my ~s** je dois annuler tous les discours que je devais prononcer.

speaking part, **speaking role** *n* rôle *m*.

speaking terms *npl* **we're not on ~** nous ne nous adressons pas la parole; **he's on ~ with Anne again** il adresse de nouveau la parole à Anne.

speaking tour *n* tournée *f* de conférences; **to be on a ~ of the USA** être en tournée de conférences aux États-Unis.

speaking tube *n* tube *m* acoustique.

speak-your-weight machine *n* pèse-personne *m* parlant.

spear /spɪə(r)/ **I** *n* **1** (weapon) lance *f*; **2** (of plant) tige *f*; (of asparagus) pointe *f*; (of broccoli) branche *f*.

II *vtr* **1** harponner [*fish*]; transpercer (d'un coup de lance) [*person, part of body*]; **2** (with fork etc) piquer [*food*] (**with** avec).

spear carrier *n* figurant/-e *m/f*.

spearfish /ˈspɪəfɪʃ/ *n* **I** *n* marlin *m*.

II *vi* pêcher au harpon.

speargun /ˈspɪəgʌn/ *n* fusil *m* à harpon.

spearhead /ˈspɪəhed/ **I** *n* lit, fig fer *m* de lance (**of** de).

II *vtr* mener [*campaign, offensive, revolt, reform*].

Spearhead Battalion *n* GB Mil *bataillon d'intervention immédiate*.

spear: **~mint** *n* menthe *f* verte; **~ side** *n* branche *f* mâle.

spec○ /spek/ **I** *n* **1** (*abrév* = **specification**) spécification *f*; **to ~** selon les spécifications fournies; **2** (*abrév* = **speculation**) **on ~** à tout hasard.

II specs○ *npl* (*abrév* = **spectacles**) binocles○ *mpl*.

special /ˈspeʃl/ **I** *n* **1** (in restaurant) plat *m* du jour; **the chef's ~** la spécialité du chef; **2**○ (discount offer) promotion *f*; **to be on ~** être en promotion; **3** (extra broadcast) émission *f* spéciale; **an election ~** une émission spéciale élections; **4** (additional transport) (bus) car *m* spécial; (train) train *m* spécial; **holiday/football ~** train spécial vacances/pour les supporters; **5** GB = **special constable**.

II *adj* **1** (for a specific purpose) [*equipment, procedure, paint, clothing, correspondent*] spécial; **2** (marked) [*criticism, affection, interest*] tout/-e particulier/-ière; **3** (official) [*commission, edition, envoy, meeting, power*] spécial; **4** (particular) [*reason, motive, significance, treatment*] particulier/-ière; **'why?'—'no ~ reason'** 'pourquoi?'—'pas de raison spéciale'; **I've nothing ~ to report** je n'ai rien de particulier à signaler; **to make a ~ effort** faire un effort; **to pay ~ attention to** prêter une attention toute particulière à; **5** (unique) [*offer, deal, package, skill*] spécial; [*case, quality*] particulier/-ière; **to be ~ to a region** être particulier/-ière à une région; **what is so ~ about this computer?** qu'est-ce que cet ordinateur a de particulier?; **she has a ~ way with animals** elle sait s'y prendre avec les animaux; **I want to make this Christmas really ~** je voudrais que ce Noël sorte de l'ordinaire; **6** (out of the ordinary) [*announcement, guest, occasion*] spécial; **as a ~ treat you can do** à titre de faveur spéciale tu peux faire; **going anywhere ~?** est-ce que tu sors quelque part?; **you're ~ to me** tu m'es très cher/chère; **the wine is something ~** le vin est exceptionnel; **the wine is nothing ~** le vin n'a rien d'extraordinaire; **what's so ~ about him/that?** qu'est-ce qu'il a/qu'est-ce que cela a de si extraordinaire?; **by ~ request, Julie will sing** à titre exceptionnel, Julie accepte de chanter; **7** (personal) [*chair, recipe*] personnel/-elle; [*friend*] très cher/chère.

special: **~ agent** *n* agent *m* secret; **Special Branch** *n* GB service *m* de contre-espionnage et de lutte contre la subversion interne; **~ constable** *n* GB civil/-e *m/f* habilité/-e à remplir les fonctions d'un officier de police en cas d'urgence.

special delivery *n* Post service *m* exprès; **to send sth (by) ~** envoyer qch en exprès.

special: **~ drawing rights** *n* Fin droits *mpl* de tirage spéciaux; **~ education** *n* enseignement *m* pour les élèves souffrant de difficultés d'apprentissage.

special effect I *n* Cin, TV effet *m* spécial.

II special effects *modif* [*specialist, team*] des effets spéciaux; [*department*] effets spéciaux.

special hospital *n* GB hôpital *m* psychiatrique (*pour malades dangereux*).

special interest group *n* **1** Pol groupe *m* défendant des intérêts particuliers; **2** gen groupe *m* d'intérêt commun.

special interest holiday *n* vacances *fpl* à thème.

specialism /ˈspeʃəlɪzəm/ *n* spécialité *f*.

specialist /ˈspeʃəlɪst/ **I** *n* **1** ▶ 1692 Med spécialiste *mf*; **heart ~** cardiologue *m*; **cancer ~** cancérologue *m*; **2** (expert) spécialiste *mf* (**in** de); **she's our Nietzsche ~** c'est notre spécialiste de Nietsche.

II *adj* [*area, shop, knowledge, care, equipment, service, staff*] spécialisé; [*advice, advisor, help*] d'un spécialiste; [*work*] de spécialiste.

speciality GB /ˌspeʃɪˈælətɪ/, **specialty** US /ˈspeʃəltɪ/ **I** *n* **1** (special service, product, food) spécialité *f*; **a local ~** une spécialité de la région; **pizza's his ~** la pizza est sa spécialité; **2** (special skill, interest) spécialité *f*; **his ~ is telling bad jokes** il a la manie de raconter de mauvaises plaisanteries; **3** Jur contrat *m* formel sous seing privé.

II *modif* [*product, chemical*] spécialisé; **a ~ recipe** ou **dish** une spécialité *f*.

speciality: **~ act** GB, **specialty number** US *n* Theat numéro *m* spécial; **~ holiday** GB, **specialty vacation** US *n* Tourism vacances *fpl* à thème.

specialization /ˌspeʃəlaɪˈzeɪʃn, US -lɪˈz-/ *n* spécialisation *f*.

specialize /ˈspeʃəlaɪz/ **I** *vi* se spécialiser; **to ~ in** se spécialiser en [*subject, field*]; **to ~ in maintenance/construction** se spécialiser dans l'entretien/la construction; **we ~ in repairing computers/training staff** notre spécialité consiste à réparer les ordinateurs/former le personnel; **a company specializing in machinery/chemicals** une entreprise spécialisée dans les machines/les produits chimiques.

II specialized *pp adj* spécialisé.

special licence *n* GB Jur dispense *f* de bans.

specially /ˈspeʃəlɪ/ *adv* **1** (specifically) [*come, make, wait*] spécialement, exprès; [*designed, trained, chosen, created*] spécialement; **I made it ~ for you** je l'ai fait exprès pour toi; **2** (particularly) [*interesting, kind, useful*] particulièrement; [*like, enjoy*] surtout; **I like animals, ~ dogs** j'aime les animaux, surtout les chiens; **why do you want that one ~?** pourquoi veux-tu celui-là en particulier?

special needs *npl* **1** Sociol problèmes *mpl*; **2** Sch difficultés *fpl* d'apprentissage scolaire; **children with ~** enfants *mpl* souffrant de difficultés d'apprentissage scolaire.

special needs group *n* catégorie *f* sociale spécifique.

special: **~ pleading** *n* argumentation *f* spéciale; **~ relationship** *n* Pol lien *m* privilégié; **~ school** *n* GB établissement *m* médico-éducatif pour enfants handicapés.

specialty /ˈspeʃəltɪ/ *n* US = **speciality**.

specie /ˈspiːʃiː/ *n* Fin espèces *fpl*; **in ~** en espèces.

species /ˈspiːʃiːz/ *n* (*pl* **~**) (all contexts) espèce *f*.

specific /spəˈsɪfɪk/ **I** *n* Med médicament *m* or remède *m* spécifique (**for** contre).
II specifics *npl* éléments *mpl* spécifiques; **to get down to (the) ~s** entrer dans les détails.
III *adj* **1** (particular) [*instruction, information, charge, case, example*] précis; **2** (unique) **~ to sb/sth** spécifique de qn/qch.

specifically /spəˈsɪfɪklɪ/ *adv* **1** (specially) [*designed, written*] spécialement (**for** pour); **2** (explicitly) [*ask, demand, forbid, tell, state*] explicitement; **3** (in particular) [*mention, criticize, address*] en particulier; **more ~** plus particulièrement.

specification /ˌspesɪfɪˈkeɪʃn/ **I** *n* **1** (also **specifications**) (of design, building) spécification *f* (**for, of** de); **standard ~** la norme; **built to sb's ~s** fabriqué selon les spécifications or le cahier des charges de qn; **to comply with ~s** être conforme aux spécifications or au cahier des charges; **2** gen, Jur (stipulation) stipulation *f* (**that** que); **~ of the invention** (for patent) description *f* de l'invention.
II specifications *npl* (features of job, car, computer) caractéristiques *fpl*.

specification sheet *n* fiche *f* technique.

specific: **~ code** *n* Comput langage *m* machine; **~ duty** *n* droit *m* spécifique; **~ gravity**† *n* densité *f* relative; **~ heat capacity** *n* capacité *f* thermique.

specificity /spəˈfɪsətɪ/ *n* **1** (of symptom, disease, phenomenon) spécificité *f* (**to** à); **2** (of detail, allegation, report) précision *f*.

specific: **~ performance** *n* Jur exécution *f* en nature; **~ volume** *n* volume *m* massique or spécifique.

specify /ˈspesɪfaɪ/ **I** *vtr* **1** [*law, contract, rule, will*] stipuler (**that** que; **where** où; **who** qui); **as specified above** comme stipulé ci-dessus; **unless otherwise specified** sauf indication contraire; **not elsewhere specified** non dénommé ailleurs; **2** [*person*] préciser (**that** que).
II specified *pp adj* [*amount, date, day, value, way*] spécifié.

specimen /ˈspesɪmən/ **I** *n* (of rock, urine, handwriting) échantillon *m* (**of** de); (of blood, tissue) prélèvement (**of** de); (of species, plant) spécimen *m* (**of** de); **a fine ~ of manhood** hum un beau spécimen masculin.
II *modif* [*page, copy, signature*] spécimen *inv*.

specimen charge, specimen count *n* Jur chef *m* d'accusation typique.

specimen jar *n* **1** (for urine) récipient *m*; **2** (on field trip) pot *m* à échantillon.

specious /ˈspiːʃəs/ *adj* sout **1** [*argument, reasoning*] spécieux/-ieuse; **2** [*glamour, appearance*] trompeur/-euse.

speciously /ˈspiːʃəslɪ/ *adv* sout **1** [*argue, reason*] de manière spécieuse; **2** [*convincing, attractive*] faussement.

speciousness /ˈspiːʃəsnɪs/ sout *n* **1** (of argument, logic) caractère *m* spécieux; **2** (of attractiveness) caractère *m* trompeur.

speck /spek/ **I** *n* **1** (small piece) (of dust, soot) grain *m* (**of** de); (of metal) éclat *m* (**of** de); **2** (small shape, mark) (of dirt, mud) petite tache *f* (**of** de); (of blood, ink, light) point *m* (**of** de); **a ~ on the horizon** un petit point à l'horizon.
II *vtr* moucheter [*cloth, surface*] (**with** de).

speckle /ˈspekl/ **I** *n* (on person's skin, egg) petite tache *f*; (on bird, animal, fabric) moucheture *f*.
II *vtr* **1** [*rain*] tacheter [*surface*]; **2** [*sun*] marquer [qch] de petites taches [*skin*]; **3** [*spots, flecks*] moucheter [*fabric, feathers*].

speckled /ˈspekld/ *adj* [*hen, animal, feather, skin*] tacheté (**with** de); [*egg*] moucheté.

spec sheet /ˈspek ʃiːt/ *n* fiche *f* technique.

spectacle /ˈspektəkl/ **I** *n* spectacle *m*; **to make a ~ of oneself** se donner en spectacle.
II *modif* [*case*] à lunettes; [*frame, lens*] de lunettes.
III spectacles† *npl* lunettes *fpl*; **a pair of ~s** une paire de lunettes.

spectacled /ˈspektəkld/ *adj* [*person*] portant des lunettes; [*animal*] à lunettes.

spectacular /spekˈtækjʊlə(r)/ **I** *n* superproduction *f*.
II *adj* spectaculaire.

spectacularly /spekˈtækjʊləlɪ/ *adv* [*win, collapse, rise, fail*] de façon spectaculaire; **it was ~ successful** cela a été une réussite spectaculaire.

spectate /spekˈteɪt/ *vi* être spectateur/-trice.

spectator /spekˈteɪtə(r)/ *n* spectateur/-trice *m/f*; **to be present as a ~** assister en tant que spectateur/-trice.

spectator sport *n* sport *m* qui attire beaucoup de spectateurs.

specter *n* US = **spectre**.

spectra /ˈspektrə/ *pl* ▶ **spectrum**.

spectral /ˈspektrəl/ *adj* spectral; **~ analysis** analyse *f* spectrale.

spectre GB, **specter** US /ˈspektə(r)/ *n* spectre *m*.

spectrogram /ˈspektrəgræm/ *n* spectrogramme *m*.

spectrograph /ˈspektrəgrɑːf, US -græf/ *n* spectrographe *m*.

spectrometer /spekˈtrɒmɪtə(r)/ *n* spectromètre *m*.

spectroscope /ˈspektrəskəʊp/ *n* spectroscope *m*.

spectroscopic /ˌspektrəˈskɒpɪk/ *adj* spectroscopique.

spectroscopy /spekˈtrɒskəpɪ/ *n* spectroscopie *f*.

spectrum /ˈspektrəm/ (*pl* **-tra, -trums**) *n* **1** Phys spectre *m*; **2** (range) gamme *f*; **at the other end of the ~** à l'autre bout de la gamme; **a broad ~ of views** une large gamme d'opinions; **people across the political ~** des gens de toutes les tendances politiques.

speculate /ˈspekjʊleɪt/ **I** *vtr* **to ~ that** supposer que (+ *indic*); **it has been widely ~d that** on a beaucoup spéculé sur le fait que.
II *vi* **1** gen spéculer, faire des spéculations (**on** sur; **about** à propos de); **to ~ as to why** spéculer sur les raisons pour lesquelles; **2** Fin spéculer (**in, on** sur); **to ~ on the Stock Exchange** spéculer à la Bourse; **to ~ for** ou **on a rise/fall** spéculer à hausse/baisse.
IDIOMS **one must ~ to accumulate** qui ne risque rien n'a rien.

speculation /ˌspekjʊˈleɪʃn/ **I** *n* **1** ¢ gen spéculations *fpl*, conjectures *fpl*; **~ about** ou **over who will win** spéculations sur le gagnant probable; **~ about his future** spéculations sur son avenir; **~ that sth will happen** spéculations sur la possibilité que qch se produise; **~ as to why** spéculations sur les raisons pour lesquelles; **to give rise to** ou **be the subject of ~** donner lieu à des spéculations or conjectures; **2** Fin spéculation *f* (**in** sur).
II speculations *npl* spéculations *fpl* (**about** sur).

speculative /ˈspekjʊlətɪv, US also ˈspekjəleɪtɪv/ *adj* (all contexts) spéculatif/-ive.

speculatively /ˈspekjʊlətɪvlɪ, US also ˈspekjəleɪtɪvlɪ/ *adv* [*ask, think, build, invest*] de façon spéculative.

speculator /ˈspekjʊleɪtə(r)/ *n* Fin spéculateur/-trice *m/f* (**in** en).

speculum /ˈspekjʊləm/ *n* (*pl* **-la** ou **-lums**) spéculum *m*.

sped /sped/ *prét, pp* ▶ **speed** II, III.

speech /spiːtʃ/ *n* **1** (oration) discours *m* (**on** sur; **about** à propos de); Theat tirade *f*; **farewell/opening ~** discours d'adieu/d'ouverture; **in a ~** dans un discours; **to give/make/deliver a ~** tenir/faire/prononcer un discours; **the Speech from the Throne** GB Pol le Discours du Trône; **2** (faculty) parole *f*; (spoken form) langage *m*; **direct/indirect ~** Ling discours *m* or style *m* direct/indirect; **in ~** par le langage; **to express oneself in ~ rather than writing** s'exprimer oralement plutôt que par écrit; **the power of ~** le pouvoir de la parole; **3** (language) langage *m*; **everyday ~** le langage de tous les jours; **4** US Sch, Univ (subject) expression *f* orale; **to teach ~** enseigner l'expression orale.

speech: **~ act** *n* Philos acte *m* de parole; **~ and drama** *n* Sch, Univ art *m* dramatique; **~ clinic** *n* centre *m* d'orthophonie; **~ community** *n* Ling communauté *f* linguistique; **~ day** *n* GB Sch (jour *m* de la) distribution *f* des prix; **~ defect** *n* = **speech impediment**; **~ difficulty** *n* difficulté *f* d'élocution; **~ disorder** *n* trouble *m* d'élocution.

speechify /ˈspiːtʃɪfaɪ/ *vi* péj pérorer.

speechifying /ˈspiːtʃɪfaɪɪŋ/ *n* péj belles paroles *fpl*.

speech: **~ impaired** *adj* (not having speech) muet/-ette; (having a speech impediment) qui a un défaut d'élocution; **~ impediment** *n* défaut *m* d'élocution.

speechless /ˈspiːtʃlɪs/ *adj* [*person, emotion*] muet/-ette; **to be ~ with** rester muet de [*joy, horror, rage*]; **I was ~ at the sight/the news** le spectacle/la nouvelle m'a laissé sans voix; **I'm ~**○! je suis soufflé○!

speech: **~ maker** *n* orateur/-trice *m/f*; **~ organ** *n* organe *m* de la parole; **~ pattern** *n* Ling schéma *m* linguistique; **~ recognition** *n* Comput reconnaissance *f* de la parole; **~ sound** *n* Ling phonème *m*; **~ synthesis** *n* Comput synthèse *f* de la parole; **~ synthesizer** *n* Comput synthétiseur *m* de parole; **~ therapist** ▶ 1692 *n* orthophoniste *mf*; **~ therapy** *n* orthophonie *f*; **~ training** *n* cours *m* de diction; **~writer** ▶ 1692 *n* personne *f* qui écrit des discours.

speed /spiːd/ **I** *n* **1** (velocity of vehicle, wind, record) vitesse *f*; (rapidity of response, reaction) rapidité *f*; **at (a) great ~** à toute vitesse; **at a ~ of 100 km per hour** à une vitesse de 100 km à l'heure; **winds reaching ~s of** des vents atteignant une vitesse de; **car with a maximum ~ of** voiture avec une vitesse maximale de; **at ~** [*go, run*] à toute vitesse; [*work, read*] en quatrième vitesse; **to pick up/lose ~** prendre/perdre de la vitesse; **at the ~ of light** à la vitesse de la lumière; **'full ~ ahead!'** Naut 'en avant toute!'; **what ~ were you doing?** à quelle vitesse est-ce que tu roulais or étais-tu?; **reading/typing ~** vitesse de lecture/frappe; **to make all ~** littér faire diligence liter; **2** (gear) vitesse *f*; **three-~ bicycle** vélo *m* à trois vitesses; **3** Phot (of film) sensibilité *f*; (of shutter) vitesse *f* d'obturation; **4**○ (drug) speed○ *m*, amphétamines *fpl*.
II *vtr* (*prét, pp* **sped** ou **speeded**) hâter [*process, recovery*]; rendre [qch] plus fluide [*traffic*]; **to ~ sb on his/her way** souhaiter bon voyage à qn.
III *vi* **1** (*prét, pp* **sped**) (move swiftly) **to ~ along** aller à toute allure or à toute vitesse, foncer○; **to ~ away** partir à toute vitesse; **the train sped past** le train est passé à toute vitesse; **2** (*prét, pp* **speeded**) (drive too fast) conduire trop vite; **he was caught**

~ing il a eu une contravention (pour excès) de vitesse; **3**○ (on drugs) **to be ~ing** être speedé○.

IDIOMS **that's about my ~** US c'est à peu près de mon niveau; **to be up to ~** être au niveau.

■ **speed up**: ¶ **~ up** [*walker, train*] aller plus vite; [*athlete, car*] accélérer; [*worker*] accélérer l'allure, travailler plus vite; ¶ **~ up [sth]**, **~ [sth] up** accélérer [*work, process, production*]; rendre [qch] plus fluide [*traffic*].

speed: **~ball**○ *n* argot des drogués mélange *m* d'héroïne et de cocaïne; **~boat** *n* hors-bord *m*; **~ bump** *n* = **speed hump**; **~ camera** *n* ≈ cinémomètre *m*.

speeder /ˈspiːdə(r)/ *n* Aut fou *m* du volant.

speed: **~ freak**○ *n* accro○ *mf* au speed; **~ hump** *n* ralentisseur *m*.

speedily /ˈspiːdɪlɪ/ *adv* rapidement.

speediness /ˈspiːdɪnɪs/ *n* rapidité *f*.

speeding /ˈspiːdɪŋ/ *n* Aut excès *m* de vitesse.

speeding offence *n* excès *m* de vitesse.

speed limit *n* limitation *f* de vitesse; **to drive within the ~** conduire en respectant la limitation de vitesse; **to exceed** ou **break the ~** dépasser la limitation de vitesse; **the ~ is 80 km/h** la vitesse est limitée à 80 km/h.

speed merchant○ *n* péj fou *m* du volant.

speedo○ /ˈspiːdəʊ/ *n* = **speedometer**.

speedometer /spɪˈdɒmɪtə(r)/ *n* compteur *m* (de vitesse), indicateur *m* de vitesse.

speed: **~ reading** *n* lecture *f* rapide; **~ restriction** *n* limitation *f* de vitesse; **~ skating** ▶ **1282** *n* patinage *m* de vitesse.

speedster○ /ˈspiːdstə(r)/ *n* (fast driver) fou *m* du volant.

speed: **~ trap** *n* Aut contrôle *m* de vitesse; **~-up** *n* accélération *f*; **~way** *n* (course) piste *f* de vitesse; **~way racing** ▶ **1282** *n* course *f* de vitesse à moto.

speedwell /ˈspiːdwel/ *n* Bot véronique *f*.

Speedwriting® /ˈspiːdraɪtɪŋ/ *n*: *méthode de sténographie*.

speedy /ˈspiːdɪ/ *adj* rapide; **to wish sb a ~ recovery** souhaiter à qn un prompt rétablissement.

speed zone *n* US zone *f* à vitesse limitée.

speleologist /ˌspiːlɪˈɒlədʒɪst/ *n* spéléologue *mf*.

speleology /ˌspiːlɪˈɒlədʒɪ/ ▶ **1282** *n* spéléologie *f*.

spell /spel/ **I** *n* **1** (period) moment *m*, période *f*; **a ~ of sth** une période de qch; **for a ~** pendant un certain temps; **for a long/short ~** pendant une longue/courte période; **a ~ as director/as minister** une brève période comme directeur/ministre; **she had a ~ at the wheel/on the computer** elle a passé un certain temps au volant/à l'ordinateur; **a ~ in hospital/in prison** un séjour à l'hôpital/en prison; **a warm/cold ~** une période de beau temps/de froid; **rainy ~** ondée *f*; **sunny ~** éclaircie *f*; **to go through a bad ~** traverser une mauvaise passe; **2** (magic words) formule *f* magique; **evil ~** maléfice *m*; **to be under a ~** être envoûté; **to cast** ou **put a ~ on sb** lit, fig jeter or lancer un sort à qn; **to break a ~** rompre un sortilège; **to break the ~** fig rompre le charme; **to be/fall under sb's ~** fig être/tomber sous le charme de qn.

II *vtr* (*pp, prét* **spelled** ou **spelt**) **1** (aloud) épeler; (on paper) écrire; **the word is spelt like this** le mot s'écrit comme ça; **she ~s her name with/without an e** son nom s'écrit avec/sans e; **to ~ sth correctly** ou **properly** orthographier qch correctement; **the word is correctly/wrongly spelt** le mot est bien/mal orthographié; **C-A-T ~s cat** les lettres C-A-T forment le mot cat; **will you ~ that please?** (on phone) pouvez-vous l'épeler, s'il vous plaît?; **2** (imply) représenter [*danger, disaster, ruin*]; sonner [*end*]; annoncer [*fame*]; **her letter spelt happiness** sa lettre était une perspective de

Speed

Speed of road, rail, air etc. travel

In French, speed is measured in kilometres per hour:

100 kph = approximately 63 mph
100 mph = approximately 160 kph
50 mph = approximately 80 kph

X miles per hour	=	X miles à l'heure
X kilometres per hour	=	X kilomètres à l'heure *or* X kilomètres-heure
100 kph	=	100 km/h
what speed was the car going at?	=	à quelle vitesse la voiture roulait-elle?
it was going at 150 kph	=	elle roulait à 150 km/h (*cent cinquante kilomètres-heure*)
it was going at fifty (*mph*)	=	elle roulait à quatre-vingts à l'heure (*i.e. at 80 kph*)
the speed of the car was 200 kph	=	la vitesse de la voiture était de 200 km/h (*the de must not be omitted here*)
what was the car doing?	=	la voiture faisait du combien?
it was doing ninety (*mph*)	=	elle faisait du 150 (*du cent cinquante: i.e. 150 kph*)
it was going at more than 200 kph	=	elle roulait à plus de 200 km/h
it was going at less than 40 kph	=	elle roulait à moins de 40 km/h
A was going at the same speed as B	=	A roulait à la même vitesse que B
A was going faster than B	=	A roulait plus vite que B
B was going slower than A	=	B roulait moins vite que A *or* B roulait plus lentement que A

Speed of light and sound

sound travels at 330 metres per second	=	le son se déplace à 330 m/s (*trois cent trente mètres-seconde* or *mètres à la seconde*)
the speed of light is 186,300 miles per second	=	la vitesse de la lumière est de 300,000 km/s (*trois cent mille kilomètres-seconde* or *kilomètres à la seconde*) (*note that the de must not be omitted here*)

bonheur; **the defeat spelt the end of a civilization/for our team** la défaite a sonné la fin d'une civilisation/pour notre équipe.

III *vi* (*pp, prét* **spelled** ou **spelt**) [*person*] connaître l'orthographe; **he can't ~** il ne connaît pas l'orthographe; **he ~s badly/well** il a une mauvaise/bonne orthographe; **to learn (how) to ~** apprendre l'orthographe.

■ **spell out**: **~ out [sth]**, **~ [sth] out** **1** lit épeler [*word*]; **2** fig expliquer [*qch*] clairement [*consequences, demands, details, implications, policy*]; **I had to ~ it out to him** j'ai dû le lui expliquer clairement; **do I have to ~ it out (to you)?** est-ce qu'il faut que je te fasse un dessin?

spell: **~binder** *n* (person) orateur/-trice *m/f* charismatique; (book, film) œuvre *f* envoûtante; **~binding** *adj* envoûtant.

spellbound /ˈspelbaʊnd/ *adj* envoûté (**by** par); **to hold sb ~** tenir qn sous le charme.

spellcheck(er) /ˈspeltʃek(ə(r))/ *n* Comput correcteur *m* orthographique.

speller /ˈspelə(r)/ *n* **1** (person) **a good/bad ~** une personne bonne/mauvaise en orthographe; **2** (book) manuel *m* d'orthographe.

spelling /ˈspelɪŋ/ **I** *n* orthographe *f*.

II *modif* [*lesson, book, mistake, test*] d'orthographe.

spelling: **~ bee** *n* concours *m* d'orthographe; **~ out** *n* fig explication *f* détaillée; **~ pronunciation** *n* Ling prononciation *f* orthographique.

spelt /spelt/ **I** *pp, prét* ▶ **spell II, III**.

II *n* Bot épeautre *m*.

spelunker /spɪˈlʌŋkə(r)/ *n* spéléologue *mf*.

spelunking /spɪˈlʌŋkɪŋ/ ▶ **1282** *n* spéléologie *f*.

spencer /ˈspensə(r)/ *n* **1** (short jacket) spencer *m*; **2**† GB (vest) tricot *m* de corps.

spend /spend/ **I** *n* Accts frais *mpl*.

II *vtr* (*prét, pp* **spent**) **1** (pay out) dépenser [*money, salary*]; **to ~ money on clothes/food/rent** dépenser son argent en vêtements/en nourriture/en loyer; **how much do you ~ on food?** combien est-ce que tu dépenses en nourriture?; **to ~ money on one's house/children/hobbies** dépenser de l'argent pour la maison/les enfants/les loisirs; **to ~ a fortune on books** dépenser une fortune en livres; **he didn't ~ a penny on his son's education** il n'a pas dépensé un sou pour l'éducation de son fils; **2** passer [*time*]; **I spent three weeks in China** j'ai passé trois semaines en Chine; **they will ~ a day in Rome** ils passeront une journée à Rome; **he spent the night with me** il a passé la nuit avec moi; **I spent two hours on my essay** j'ai passé deux heures sur ma dissertation; **to ~ hours/one's life doing** passer des heures/sa vie à faire; **I want to ~ some time with my family** je veux passer un peu de temps avec ma famille; **3** (exhaust) épuiser [*ammunition, energy, resources*].

III *vi* (*prét, pp* **spent**) dépenser.

IV *v refl* (*prét, pp* **spent**) **to ~ itself** [*storm*] s'apaiser.

spender /ˈspendə(r)/ *n* **to be a big ~** être dépensier/-ière; **he's the last of the big ~s** iron il est d'une avarice princière.

spending /ˈspendɪŋ/ *n* ¢ dépenses *fpl*; **~ on education/defence** dépenses d'éducation/militaires or de défense; **credit-card ~** achats *mpl* sur carte de crédit; **defence ~** dépense *f* en matière de défense; **government ~**, **public ~** dépense *f* publique.

spending: **~ cut** *n* gen réduction *f* des dépenses; Pol restriction *f* budgétaire; **~ money** *n* argent *m* de poche; **~ power** *n* Fin pouvoir *m* d'achat.

spending spree *n* folie○ *f* (de dépense); **to go on a ~** faire des folies.

spendthrift /ˈspendθrɪft/ **I** *n* **to be a ~** être dépensier/-ière.

II *adj* [*person*] dépensier/-ière; [*habit, policy*] dispendieux/-ieuse.

spent /spent/ **I** *prét, pp* ▶ **spend**.

II *adj* **1** (used up) [*bullet*] perdu; [*battery*] déchargé; [*match*] utilisé; [*fuel rod*] épuisé; **2** (exhausted) [*person, athlete*] fourbu; [*passion, emotion*] éteint; **their passions/emotions were ~** leurs passions/émotions s'étaient éteintes; **to be a ~ force** fig avoir perdu toute force; **3** Jur [*conviction*] effacé.

sperm /spɜːm/ *n* **1** (cell) spermatozoïde *m*; **2** (semen) sperme *m*.

spermaceti /ˌspɜːməˈsetɪ/ *n* blanc *m* de baleine, spermaceti *m* spec.

spermatic /spɜːˈmætɪk/ *adj* spermatique.

spermatozoa /ˌspɜːmətəˈzəʊə/ *pl* ▶ **spermatozoon**.

spermatozoon /ˌspɜːmətəˈzəʊɒn/ *n* (*pl* **-zoa**) spermatozoïde *m*.

sperm: **~ bank** *n* banque *f* de sperme; **~ count** *n* taux *m* de spermatozoïdes; **~ donation** *n* don *m* de sperme; **~ donor** *n* donneur *m* de sperme.

spermicidal /ˌspɜːmɪˈsaɪdl/ *adj* spermicide.

spermicide /ˈspɜːmɪsaɪd/ *n* spermicide *m*.

sperm: **~ oil** *n* huile *f* de baleine; **~ whale** *n* cachalot *m*.

Spelling and punctuation

The alphabet and accents

The names of the letters are given below with their pronunciation in French and, in the right-hand column, a useful way of clarifying difficulties when you are spelling names etc. A comme Anatole *means* A for Anatole, *and so on.*

		When spelling aloud ...
A	[ɑ]	A comme Anatole
B	[be]	B comme Berthe
C	[se]	C comme Célestin
ç	[sesedij]	c cédille
D	[de]	D comme Désiré
E	[ə]	E comme Eugène
é	[eaksɑ̃tegy] *or* [əaksɑ̃tegy]	e accent aigu
è	[eaksɑ̃gʀav] *or* [əaksɑ̃gʀav]	e accent grave
ê	[ɛaksɑ̃siʀkɔ̃flɛks] *or* [əaksɑ̃siʀkɔ̃flɛks]	e accent circonflexe
ë	[ətʀema]	e tréma
F	[ɛf]	F comme François
G*	[ʒe]	G comme Gaston
H	[aʃ]	H comme Henri
I	[i]	I comme Irma
J*	[ʒi]	J comme Joseph
K	[ka]	K comme Kléber
L	[ɛl]	L comme Louis
M	[ɛm]	M comme Marcel
N	[ɛn]	N comme Nicolas
O	[o]	O comme Oscar
P	[pe]	P comme Pierre
Q	[ky]	Q comme Quintal
R	[ɛʀ]	R comme Raoul
S	[ɛs]	S comme Suzanne
T	[te]	T comme Thérèse
U	[y]	U comme Ursule
V	[ve]	V comme Victor
W	[dubləve]	W comme William
X	[iks]	X comme Xavier
Y	[igʀɛk]	Y comme Yvonne
Z	[zɛd]	Z comme Zoé

Spelling

capital B	=	B majuscule
small b	=	b minuscule
it has got a capital B	=	cela s'écrit avec un B majuscule
in small letters	=	en minuscules
double t	=	deux t [døte]
double n	=	deux n [døzɛn] (*note the liaison which would also be used in* deux l, deux r *etc.*)
apostrophe	=	apostrophe [apɔstʀɔf]
d apostrophe	=	d apostrophe [deapɔstʀɔf]
hyphen	=	trait d'union
rase-mottes has got a hyphen	=	*rase-mottes* s'écrit avec un trait d'union

Dictating punctuation

.	point *or* un point (*full stop*)
,	virgule (*comma*)
:	deux points (*colon*)
;	point-virgule (*semicolon*)
!	point d'exclamation† (*exclamation mark*)
?	point d'interrogation†
	à la ligne (*new paragraph*)
(	ouvrez la parenthèse (*open brackets*)
)	fermez la parenthèse (*close brackets*)
()	entre parenthèses (*in brackets*)
[]	entre crochets (*in square brackets*)
—	tiret (*dash*)
...	points de suspension (*three dots*)
« *ou* "	ouvrez les guillemets (*open inverted commas*)
» *ou* "	fermez les guillemets (*close inverted commas*)
«» *ou* ""	entre guillemets (*in inverted commas*)

The use of inverted commas in French

In novels and short stories, direct speech is punctuated differently from English:

The inverted commas lie on the line, e.g. «Tiens, dit-elle, en ouvrant les rideaux, les voilà !»

This example also shows that the inverted commas are not closed after each stretch of direct speech. In modern texts they are often omitted altogether (though this is still sometimes frowned on):

Il l'interrogea:

– Vous êtes arrivé quand ?
– Pourquoi cette question ? Je n'ai rien fait de mal.
– C'est ce que nous allons voir.

Note the short dash in this case that introduces each new speaker. Even if inverted commas had been used in the above dialogue, they would have been opened before vous *and closed after* voir, *and not used at other points.*

English-style inverted commas are used in French to highlight words in a text:
Le ministre a voulu "tout savoir" sur la question.

* *Note the difference between English and French pronunciation of* g *and* j.
† *Note that, unlike English, French has a space before* ! *and* ? *and* : *and* ;, *e.g.* Jamais !, Pourquoi ? *etc. This is not usual, however, in dictionaries, where it would take up too much room.*
‡ *Single inverted commas are not much used in French.*

spew /spjuː/ **I** *vtr* **1** (also **~ out**) vomir [*smoke, lava, propaganda*]; cracher [*insults, coins, paper*]; **2**○ (also **~ up**) dégobiller○ [*food, drink*].
II *vi* **1** (also **~ out**, **~ forth**) [*lava, smoke, insults*] jaillir; **2**○ (also **~ up**) dégobiller○.

sphagnum /ˈsfægnəm/ *n* (also **~ moss**) sphaigne *f*.

sphere /sfɪə(r)/ *n* **1** (shape) sphère *f*; **2** Astron sphère *f* céleste; **the music of the ~s** la musique des sphères célestes; **3** (field) domaine *m* (**of** de); **~ of influence** sphère d'influence; **4** (social circle) milieu *m*.

spherical /ˈsferɪkl/ *adj* sphérique.

spherical: **~ aberration** *n* aberration *f* sphérique; **~ angle** *n* angle *m* sphérique; **~ coordinate** *n* coordonnée *f* sphérique; **~ geometry** *n* géométrie *f* sphérique; **~ triangle** *n* triangle *m* sphérique.

spheroid /ˈsfɪərɔɪd/ *n, adj* sphéroïde (*m*).

sphincter /ˈsfɪŋktə(r)/ *n* sphincter *m*.

sphinx /sfɪŋks/ *n* (*pl* **~es** ou **sphinges**) **1** (statue) sphinx *m*; **2** Mythol **the Sphinx** le Sphinx; **3** (enigma) sphinx *m*.

sphinx: **~like** *adj* énigmatique; **~ moth** *n* Zool sphinx *m*.

sphygmomanometer /ˌsfɪgməʊməˈnɒmɪtə(r)/ *n* Med tensiomètre *m*, sphygmomanomètre *m*.

spic◐, **spick**◐ /spɪk/ *n* US injur hispano○ *mf*.

spice /spaɪs/ **I** *n* **1** Culin épice *f*; **herbs and ~s** herbes et épices; **mixed ~** épices mélangées; **2** fig piment *m*; **to add/lack ~** ajouter du/manquer de piment.
II *modif* [*jar, rack*] à épices; [*trade, route*] des épices.
III *vtr* **1** Culin épicer [*food*]; **2** (also **~ up**) pimenter [*life, story*] (**with** de); **to ~ up one's sex life** mettre du piment dans sa vie sexuelle.
IV spiced *pp adj* **1** Culin épicé (**with** de); **2** fig pimenté (**with** de).
IDIOMS **variety is the ~ of life** la diversité est le sel de la vie.

Spice Islands ▶ 1381 *pr npl* Hist **the ~** les Moluques *fpl*.

spiciness /ˈspaɪsɪnɪs/ *n* **1** (of food) goût *m* épicé; **2** (of story) piquant *m*.

spick◐ /spɪk/ *n* ▶ **spic**.

spick-and-span *adj* impeccable.

spicy /ˈspaɪsɪ/ *adj* **1** [*food*] épicé; **2** [*story*] croustillant.

spider /ˈspaɪdə(r)/ *n* **1** Zool araignée *f*; **2** GB (elastic straps) fixe-bagages *m inv*; **3** US poêle *f* (munie de pieds); **4** (snooker rest) râteau *m*.

spider: **~ crab** *n* araignée *f* de mer; **~ monkey** *n* singe-araignée *m*, atèle *m* spéc; **~ plant** *n* chlorophytum *m*; **~'s web**, **~web** US *n* toile *f* d'araignée.

spidery /ˈspaɪdərɪ/ *adj* [*shape, form*] d'araignée, arachnéen/-éenne liter; [*writing*] en pattes de mouche.

spiel○ /ʃpiːl, US spiːl/ **I** *n* souvent péj baratin○ *m*; **to give sb a ~** faire du baratin à qn (**about** sur).
II *vi* baratiner○.
■ **spiel off** US: **~ off [sth]** débiter [*facts etc*].

spieler○ /ˈʃpiːlə(r)/ *n* US baratineur/-euse○ *m/f*.

spiffing○† /ˈspɪfɪŋ/ GB, **spiffy**○ /ˈspɪfɪ/ US *adj* épatant○.

spigot /ˈspɪgət/ *n* **1** (of barrel) fausset *m*; **2** US (faucet) robinet *m*.

spike /spaɪk/ **I** *n* **1** (pointed object) pointe *f*; **2** Sport (on shoe) pointe *f*; **a set of ~s** un jeu de pointes; **3** Bot (of flower) hampe *f*; (of corn) épi *m*; **4** Phys (variation) pointe *f* de courant; (on graph) pointe *f*; **5** Sport (in volleyball) smash *m*; **6** Zool (antler) dague *f*.
II spikes *npl* Sport chaussures *fpl* à pointes.
III *vtr* **1** (pierce) embrocher [*person, meat*]; **2**○ (add alcohol to) corser [*drink*] (**with** de); **3** Journ (reject) mettre [qch] au panier [*story*]; **4** Sport (in volleyball) **to ~ the ball** faire un smash; **5** (thwart) contrecarrer [*scheme*]; étouffer [*rumour*].
IV *vi* Sport (in volleyball) smasher.
IDIOMS **to ~ sb's guns** déjouer les plans de qn; **to hang up one's ~s**○ [*sportsman*] se retirer.

spike: **~ heel** *n* talon *m* aiguille; **~ lavender** *n* lavande *f* aspic.

spikenard /ˈspaɪknɑːd/ *n* nard *m*.

spiky /ˈspaɪkɪ/ *adj* **1** (having spikes) [*hair*] en brosse *inv*; [*branch*] piquant; [*object*] acéré; **2**○ GB (short-tempered) [*person, temperament*] revêche.

spill /spɪl/ **I** *n* **1** (accidental) (of oil, etc) déversement *m* accidentel; **2** (fall) (from bike, motorcycle) accrochage *m*; (from horse) chute *f*; **to have** ou **take a ~** [*cyclist*] avoir un accrochage; [*horse-rider*] faire une chute; **3** (for lighting candles) allume-feu *m inv*.
II *vtr* (*prét, pp* **spilt** ou **~ed**) **1** (pour) (overturn) renverser [*liquid*]; (drip) laisser tomber [*liquid*]; **to ~ sth from** ou **out of a bottle/cup** renverser une bouteille/tasse; **to ~ sth on(to)** ou **over** renverser qch sur [*surface, object, person*]; **2** (disgorge) déverser [*oil, rubbish, chemical*] (**into** dans; **on(to)** sur); **to ~ wind from a sail** Naut étouffer une voile.
III *vi* (*prét, pp* **spilt** ou **~ed**) (empty out) [*contents, liquid, light, chemicals*] se répandre (**onto** sur; **into** dans); **to ~ from** ou **out of** couler de [*container*]; **tears ~ed down her cheeks** les larmes coulaient sur ses joues; **to ~ (out) into** ou **onto the street** fig [*crowds, people*] se répandre dans la rue; **the wind ~ed from the sail** Naut la voile s'est déventée.
IDIOMS **(it's) no use crying over spilt milk** ça ne sert à rien de pleurer sur ce qui est

fait; **to ~ the beans**○ vendre la mèche○; **to ~ blood** verser le sang; ▶ **thrill**.

■ **spill down** [*rain*] tomber à grosses gouttes.

■ **spill out**: ¶ **~ out** [*liquid, lava, contents*] se répandre ; **all their secrets came ~ing out** fig tous leurs secrets ont été étalés au grand jour; ¶ **~ out [sth]**, **~ [sth] out** laisser échapper [*contents*]; fig révéler [*secrets*]; débiter [*story*].

■ **spill over** lit déborder (**onto** sur); **to ~ over into** fig s'étendre à [*area of activity, relationship, street, region*]; dégénérer en [*looting, hostility*].

spillage /ˈspɪlɪdʒ/ *n* **1** (spill) (of oil, chemical, effluent) déversement *m* accidentel; **oil ~** déversement *m* accidentel d'hydrocarbures; **2** (spilling) ¢ déversement *m*.

spillikins /ˈspɪlɪkɪnz/ ▶ **1282** *n* (jeu *m* de) jonchets *mpl*.

spillover /ˈspɪləʊvə(r)/ *n* **1** US, Can (overflow) (of traffic) excédent *m*; (of liquid) débordement *m*; **2** Econ (consequence) retombée *f*.

spillway /ˈspɪlweɪ/ *n* déversoir *m*.

spilt /spɪlt/ *prét, pp* ▶ **spill** II, III.

spin /spɪn/ **I** *n* **1** (turn) (of wheel) tour *m*; (of dancer, skate) pirouette *f*; **to give sth a ~** faire tourner qch; **to do a ~ on the ice** exécuter une pirouette sur la glace; **2** Sport effet *m*; **to put ~ on a ball** donner de l'effet à une balle; **3** (in spin-drier) **to give the washing a ~** donner un coup d'essorage au linge; **4** Aviat (descente *f* en) vrille *f*; **to go into a ~** descendre en vrille; **5** (pleasure trip) tour *m*; **to go for a ~** aller faire un tour; **6** US (interpretation) **to put a new ~ on sth** aborder qch sous un nouvel angle.

II *vtr* (*p prés* **-nn-**; *prét, pp* **spun**) **1** (rotate) lancer [*top*]; faire tourner [*globe, wheel*]; [*bowler*] donner de l'effet à [*ball*]; **2** (flip) **to ~ a coin** tirer à pile ou face; **to ~ a coin for sth** tirer qch à pile ou face; **3** Tex filer [*wool, thread*]; **to ~ cotton into thread** filer le coton; **4** Zool [*spider*] tisser [*web*]; **5** (wring out) essorer qch à la machine [*clothes*]; **6** (tell) raconter [*tale*]; **to ~ sb a yarn** raconter des salades à qn; **he spun me some tale about missing his train** il a prétendu qu'il avait raté son train.

III *vi* (*p prés* **-nn-**; *prét, pp* **spun**) **1** (rotate) [*wheel*] tourner; [*weathercock, top*] tournoyer; [*dancer*] pirouetter; **to go ~ning through the air** [*ball, plate*] aller valser○; **the car spun off the road** la voiture est allée valser○ dans la nature; **2** fig tourner; **my head is ~ning** j'ai la tête qui tourne; **the room was ~ning** les murs de la pièce tournaient; **3** (turn wildly) [*wheels*] patiner; [*compass*] s'affoler; **4** (nose dive) [*plane*] descendre en vrille; **5** Tex filer; **6** Fishg pêcher à la cuillère.

IDIOMS **to be in a ~** être dans tous ses états; **to ~ one's wheels** US fig ne pas avancer fig.

■ **spin along** [*car*] filer.

■ **spin around** = **spin round**.

■ **spin off** US Fin: ¶ **~ off [sth]** **1** créer [*new company*]; **2** convertir [*company, business*].

■ **spin out**: **~ [sth] out**, **~ out [sth]** prolonger, faire durer [*visit*]; faire traîner [qch] en longueur [*speech*]; ménager or faire durer [*money*]; **he spun the whole business out** il a fait traîner l'affaire.

■ **spin round**: ¶ **~ round** [*person*] se retourner rapidement; [*dancer, skater*] pirouetter; **she spun round in her chair** elle a pivoté sur sa chaise; [*car*] faire un tête-à-queue; ¶ **~ [sb/sth] round** faire tourner [*wheel*]; faire tournoyer [*dancer, weathercock, top*].

spina bifida /ˌspaɪnə ˈbɪfɪdə/ ▶ **1354** **I** *n* spina-bifida *m inv*.

II *modif* [*baby, sufferer*] atteint de spina-bifida.

spinach /ˈspɪnɪdʒ, US -ɪtʃ/ *n* **1** (plant) épinard *m*; **2** ¢ (vegetable) épinards *mpl*.

spinal /ˈspaɪnl/ *adj* [*injury, damage*] de la colonne vertébrale; [*nerve, muscle*] spinal; [*disc, ligament*] vertébral.

spinal: **~ anaesthesia** *n* rachianesthésie *f*; **~ canal** *n* canal *m* rachidien; **~ column** *n* colonne *f* vertébrale; **~ cord** *n* moelle *f* épinière; **~ fluid** *n* liquide *m* céphalo-rachidien; **~ meningitis** ▶ **1354** *n* méningite *f* cérébro-spinale; **~ tap** *n* ponction *f* lombaire.

spin bowler *n* Sport (in cricket) *lanceur qui donne de l'effet à la balle*.

spindle /ˈspɪndl/ *n* **1** (on spinning wheel) fuseau *m*; **2** (on spinning machine, machine tool) broche *f*.

spindle: **~-legged**, **~-shanked** *adj* aux jambes grêles; **~ tree** *n* fusain *m*.

spindly /ˈspɪndlɪ/ *adj* [*tree, plant*] haut et dégarni; [*legs*] grêle.

spin: **~ doctor** *n* Pol *consultant en communication attaché à un parti politique*; **~-drier**, **~ dryer** *n* essoreuse *f*.

spindrift /ˈspɪndrɪft/ *n* **1** ¢ (sea spray) embruns *mpl*; **2** (snow) *chute de neige poudreuse et fine*.

spin-dry /ˌspɪnˈdraɪ/ *vtr* essorer [qch] (à la machine).

spine /spaɪn/ *n* **1** (spinal column) colonne *f* vertébrale; **it sent shivers up and down my ~** (of fear) cela m'a donné des frissons dans le dos; (of pleasure) cela m'a fait frissonner; **2** fig (backbone) nerf *m*; **3** (prickle) (of plant) épine *f*; (of animal) piquant *m*; **4** (of book) dos *m*; **5** (of hill) arête *f*.

spine: **~-chiller** *n* (film) film *m* qui donne la chair de poule; (book) livre *m* qui donne la chair de poule; **~-chilling** *adj* qui donne la chair de poule.

spineless /ˈspaɪnlɪs/ *adj* **1** Zool invertébré; **2** péj (weak) mou/molle.

spinelessly /ˈspaɪnlɪsnɪs/ *adv* péj lâchement.

spinelessness /ˈspaɪnlɪsnɪs/ *n* péj lâcheté *f*.

spinet /spɪˈnet, US ˈspɪnɪt/ ▶ **1481** *n* épinette *f*.

spine-tingling *adj* [*song, voice, atmosphere*] saisissant.

spinnaker /ˈspɪnəkə(r)/ *n* spinnaker *m*, spi *m*.

spinner /ˈspɪnə(r)/ *n* **1** ▶ **1692** Tex fileur/-euse *m/f*; **2** (in cricket) (bowler) lanceur *m* qui donne de l'effet à la balle; (ball) balle *f* avec de l'effet; **3**○ = **spin-drier**; **4** Fishg cuillère *f*.

spinneret /ˈspɪnəret/ *n* Ind, Zool filière *f*.

spinney /ˈspɪnɪ/ *n* GB bosquet *m*.

spinning /ˈspɪnɪŋ/ **I** *n* **1** Tex filage *m*; **2** Fishg pêche *f* à la cuillère.

II *modif* Tex [*thread, wool*] à filer.

spinning jenny *n* Hist Tex jenny *f*.

spinning: **~ machine** *n* métier *m* à filer; **~ mill** *n* filature *f*; **~ top** *n* toupie *f*; **~ wheel** *n* rouet *m*.

spin-off /ˈspɪnɒf/ **I** *n* **1** (incidental benefit) retombée *f* favorable; **the new plant will have ~s for the area** la nouvelle usine aura des retombées favorables pour la région; **2** (by-product) sous-produit *m* (**of, from** de); **a ~ from space research** un sous-produit de la recherche spatiale; **3** TV, Cin adaptation *f*; **TV ~ from the film** adaptation télévisée du film.

II *modif* [*effect, profit*] secondaire; [*technology, product*] dérivé; **~ series** TV feuilleton télévisé adapté d'un film.

spin setting *n* touche *f* essorage.

spinster /ˈspɪnstə(r)/ *n* Jur célibataire *f*; péj vieille fille *f*.

spinsterish /ˈspɪnstərɪʃ/ *adj* péj [*habit, life*] de vieille fille péj.

spiny /ˈspaɪnɪ/ *adj* [*plant*] épineux; [*animal*] couvert de piquants.

spiny: **~ anteater** *n* échidné *m*; **~-finned** *adj* à nageoires soutenues par des rayons épineux; **~ lobster** *n* langouste *f*.

spiracle /ˈspaɪərəkl/ *n* **1** (vent, blowhole) évent *m*; **2** (of insect) stigmate *m*.

spiraea /ˌspaɪəˈriːə/ *n* spirée *f*.

spiral /ˈspaɪərəl/ **I** *n* **1** (shape) gen, Math, Aviat spirale *f*; **in a ~** [*object, spring, curl*] en forme de spirale; **2** (trend) spirale *f*; **inflationary ~** spirale inflationniste; **the wage-price ~** la spirale des prix et des salaires; **a ~ of violence** une escalade de violence; **a downward/upward ~** une descente/montée en spirale.

II *modif* [*motif, spring, structure*] en spirale.

III *vi* (*p prés etc* **-ll-** GB, **-l-** US) **1** Econ [*costs, interest rates etc*] monter en flèche; **to ~ downwards** tomber en flèche; **2** (of movement) **to ~ up(wards)/down(wards)** (gently) monter/descendre en spirale or en tournoyant; (rapidly) monter/descendre en vrille.

IV spiralling GB, **spiraling** US *pres p adj* [*costs, interest rates, rents*] qui montent en flèche.

spiral: **~ binding** *n* (reliure *f* à) spirales *fpl*; **~ galaxy** *n* galaxie *f* spirale; **~ notebook** *n* cahier *m* à spirales; **~ staircase** *n* escalier *m* en colimaçon.

spire /ˈspaɪə(r)/ *n* **1** Archit flèche *f*; **a church ~** la flèche d'une église; **the church ~** la flèche de l'église; **2** (of plant) pointe *f*.

spirit /ˈspɪrɪt/ **I** *n* **1** (essential nature) (of law, game, era) esprit *m*; **the ~ of the original** l'esprit de l'original; **it's not in the ~ of the agreement** ce n'est pas conforme à l'esprit de l'accord; **2** (mood, attitude) esprit *m* (**of** de); **community/team ~** esprit communautaire/d'équipe; **in a ~ of friendship** dans un esprit amical; **a ~ of forgiveness/of reconciliation** une intention d'indulgence/de réconciliation; **a ~ of optimism** une tendance à l'optimisme; **I am in a party ~** je me sens prêt à faire la fête; **there is a party ~ about** il y a une atmosphère de fête; **to do sth in the right/wrong ~** faire qch de façon positive/négative; **to take a remark in the right/wrong ~** bien/mal prendre une remarque; **to enter into the ~ of sth** se conformer à l'esprit de qch; **there was a great** ou **good ~ among the men** il y avait un excellent état d'esprit entre les hommes; **that's the ~**○! c'est ça!; **3** (courage, determination) courage *m*, énergie *f*; **to show ~** se montrer courageux/-euse; **to break sb's ~** briser la résistance or la volonté de qn; **a performance full of ~** une interprétation pleine de brio; **with ~** [*play, defend*] avec détermination; **4** (soul) gen, Mythol, Relig esprit *m*; **the life of the ~** la vie spirituelle; **evil ~** esprit du mal; **the Holy Spirit** le Saint-Esprit; **5** (person) esprit *m*; **he was a courageous ~** c'était un esprit courageux; **a leading ~ in the movement** l'âme *f* du mouvement; **6** (drink) alcool *m* fort; **wines and ~s** Comm vins et spiritueux *mpl*; **7** Chem, Pharm alcool *m*.

II spirits *npl* **to be in good/poor ~s** être de bonne/mauvaise humeur; **to be in high ~s** être d'excellente humeur; **to keep one's ~s up** garder le moral; **to raise sb's ~s** remonter le moral de qn; **my ~s rose/sank** j'ai repris/perdu courage.

III *modif* [*lamp, stove*] à alcool.

IV *vtr* **to ~ sth/sb away** faire disparaître qch/qn; **to ~ sth in/out** introduire/sortir discrètement qch.

spirited /ˈspɪrɪtɪd/ **I** *adj* [*horse, debate, reply*] fougueux/-euse; [*music, performance*] plein d'entrain; [*attack, defence*] vif/vive.

II -spirited (*dans composés*) **free-~** indépendant; **high-~** excité.

spirit: **~ guide** *n* guide *m* des esprits; **~ gum** *n* colle *f* à postiche.

spiritless /ˈspɪrɪtləs/ *adj* [*person*] qui manque d'entrain.

spirit level *n* niveau *m* à bulle.

spiritual /ˈspɪrɪtʃʊəl/ **I** *n* Mus spiritual *m*.

II *adj* (all contexts) spirituel/-elle; **~ adviser** ou **director** directeur *m* de conscience.

spiritualism /ˈspɪrɪtʃʊəlɪzəm/ *n* **1** (occult) spiritisme *m*; **2** Philos spiritualisme *m*.

spiritualist /ˈspɪrɪtʃʊəlɪst/ *n, adj* **1** (occult) spiritiste (*mf*); **2** Philos spiritualiste (*mf*).

spirituality /ˌspɪrɪtʃʊˈælətɪ/ *n* spiritualité *f*.

spiritually /ˈspɪrɪtʃʊəlɪ/ *adv* [*impoverished, uplifting*] sur le plan spirituel; **to be ~ inclined** avoir une inclination pour les choses spirituelles.

spirituous /ˈspɪrɪtʃʊəs/ *adj* spiritueux/-euse; **~ liquors** spiritueux *mpl*.

spirit world *n* monde *m* des esprits.

spirograph /ˈspaɪərəgrɑːf, US -græf/ *n* Med spiromètre *m*.

spiroid /ˈspaɪərɔɪd/ *adj* spiroïdal.

spirometer /spaɪˈrɒmɪtə(r)/ *n* Med spiromètre *m*.

spit /spɪt/ **I** *n* **1** (saliva) (in mouth) salive *f*; (on ground) crachat *m*; **2** (expectoration) **'I hate you' he said with a ~** 'je te déteste' dit-il en crachant; **to give a ~** cracher; **3** Culin broche *f*; **cooked on a ~** rôti à la broche; **rotating ~** tournebroche *m*; **4** Geol flèche *f*; **5** GB (spade depth) **two ~s deep** à deux fers de profondeur.
II *vtr* (*p prés* **-tt-**, *prét, pp* **spat**) **1** lit [*person*] cracher [*blood, food*] (**into** dans; **onto** sur); **2** fig [*volcano*] cracher [*lava*]; [*pan*] projeter [*oil*]; **3** (utter) proférer [*oath, venom*] (**at** en direction de).
III *vi* (*p prés* **-tt-**, *prét, pp* **spat**) **1** lit [*cat, person*] cracher (**at, on** sur; **into** dans; **out of** de); **to ~ in sb's face** lit, fig cracher à la figure de qn; **2** (be angry) **to ~ with** écumer de [*rage, anger*]; **3** (crackle) [*oil, sausage*] grésiller; [*logs, fire*] crépiter.
IV *v impers* (*p prés* **-tt-**, *prét, pp* **spat**) **it's ~ting (with rain)** il bruine.
IDIOMS **~ and polish** huile *f* de coude; **to be the (dead) ~ of sb** être le portrait tout craché de qn.
■ **spit out**: **~ [sth] out, ~ out [sth]** lit cracher [*blood, drink*] (**into** dans ; **onto** sur); fig proférer [*phrase, word*]; **~ it out**○! crache le morceau○!
■ **spit up**: **~ [sth] up, ~ up [sth]** [*patient*] cracher [*blood*]; US [*baby*] vomir [*milk, food*].

spite /spaɪt/ **I** *n* (malice) méchanceté *f*, malveillance *f*; (vindictiveness) rancune *f*; **out of (pure) ~** (malice) par (pure) méchanceté; (vindictiveness) par (pure) rancune.
II in spite of *prep phr* malgré [*circumstances, event*]; malgré, en dépit de [*advice, warning*]; **in ~ of the fact that** bien que (+ *subj*), malgré le fait que (+ *subj*).
III *vtr* faire du mal à, blesser; (less strong) ennuyer.
IDIOMS **to cut off one's nose to ~ one's face** se punir soi-même.

spiteful /ˈspaɪtfl/ *adj* [*person*] (malicious) malveillant, méchant; (vindictive) rancunier/-ière; [*remark*] méchant, malveillant; [*article*] fielleux/-euse; **~ gossip** commérages *mpl*.

spitefully /ˈspaɪtfəlɪ/ *adv* méchamment.

spitefulness /ˈspaɪtflnɪs/ *n* (malice) méchanceté *f*, malveillance *f*; (vindictiveness) rancune *f*.

spit: **~fire**○ *n* soupe au lait○ *mf*; **~roast** *vtr* faire rôtir [qch] à la broche.

spitting /ˈspɪtɪŋ/ *n* **~ is a dirty habit** cracher est une habitude dégoûtante; **'~ prohibited'** 'interdiction de cracher'.
IDIOMS **to be the ~ image of sb** être le portrait tout craché de qn; **to be within ~ distance of** être à deux pas de.

spitting snake *n* serpent *m* cracheur.

spittle /ˈspɪtl/ *n* **1** (of person) (in mouth) salive *f*; (on surface) crachat *m*; **2** (of animal) bave *f*.

spittoon /spɪˈtuːn/ *n* crachoir *m*.

spitz /spɪts/ *n* loulou *m* (de Poméranie).

spiv○ /spɪv/ *n* GB péj petit truand *m*.

spivvy○ /ˈspɪvɪ/ *adj* GB péj [*appearance, clothes*] tape-à-l'œil *inv*; **to be** ou **look ~** [*person*] avoir une allure tapageuse.

splash /splæʃ/ **I** *n* **1** (sound) plouf *m*; **with a ~** avec un plouf; **to make a big ~** lit faire un grand plouf; fig faire sensation; **2** (drop, patch) (of mud) tache *f*; (of water, oil) éclaboussure *f*; (of colour) touche *f*; (of tonic, soda: in drink) goutte *f*.
II *vtr* **1** (spatter, spray) éclabousser [*person, surface*]; **to ~ sth over sb/sth** éclabousser qn/qch de qch; **to ~ one's way through sth** traverser qch en pataugeant; **2** (sprinkle) **to ~ water on to one's face** s'asperger de l'eau sur le visage; **to ~ one's face with water** s'asperger le visage d'eau; **3** (maliciously) **to ~ water/acid onto** envoyer de l'eau/de l'acide sur; **4** Journ mettre [qch] à la une [*story, picture*]; **the news was ~ed across the front page** la nouvelle a fait la une des journaux.
III *vi* **1** (spatter) [*coffee, paint, wine*] faire des éclaboussures (**onto, over** sur); **water was ~ing from the tap** l'eau giclait du robinet; **2** (move) **to ~ through sth** [*person*] traverser qch en pataugeant; [*car*] traverser qch en faisant des éclaboussures; **3** (in sea, pool) faire des éclaboussures (**in** dans).
■ **splash around**: ¶ **~ around** barboter (**in** dans); ¶ **~ [sth] around** envoyer [qch] partout [*water, paint*]; **to ~ money around**○ claquer○ son argent.
■ **splash down** amerrir.
■ **splash out**○ (spend money) faire des folies; **~ out on** faire la folie de s'offrir [*dress, hat, book*].

splash: **~back** *n* revêtement *m* (*autour d'un évier, d'une baignoire*); **~board** *n* Aut garde-boue *m inv*; **~down** *n* amerrissage *m*; **~guard** *n* = **splashboard**.

splashing /ˈsplæʃɪŋ/ *n* (of sea, waves) clapotis *m*; **a sound of ~** un bruit de clapotis; **the ~ of the shower** le bruit de l'eau dans la douche.

splat /splæt/ **I** *n* **there was a ~** il y a eu un splash○; **he landed with a ~** il a atterri en faisant splash.
II *excl* splash!

splatter /ˈsplætə(r)/ **I** *n* (of rain, bullets) crépitement *m*.
II *vtr* **to ~ sb/sth with sth, to ~ sth over sb/sth** éclabousser qn/qch de qch; **the car ~ed mud everywhere** la voiture a fait gicler de la boue partout.
III *vi* **1** [*ink, paint, mud*] **to ~ onto** ou **over sth** gicler sur qch; **2** [*body, fruit etc*] s'écraser (**on, against** sur).
IV splattered *pp adj* **1 ~ed with** éclaboussé de; **blood-/mud-~ed** éclaboussé de sang/de boue; **2** (squashed) écrasé.

splay /spleɪ/ **I** *n* Archit ébrasement *m*.
II *vtr* évaser [*end of pipe etc*]; ébraser [*side of window, door*]; écarter [*legs, feet, fingers*].
III *vi* (also **~ out**) [*end of pipe*] être évasé; [*window*] être ébrasé.
IV splayed *pp adj* [*feet, fingers, legs*] écarté.

splay: **~foot** *npl* pieds *mpl* plats; **~footed** *adj* [*person*] qui a les pieds plats; [*horse*] panard.

spleen /spliːn/ *n* **1** Anat rate *f*; **2** fig (bad temper) mauvaise humeur *f*; **to vent one's ~ on sb** décharger sa mauvaise humeur or sa bile sur qn; **3**‡ (melancholy) spleen *m*.

splendid /ˈsplendɪd/ *adj* [*building, scenery, view, collection, ceremony*] splendide; [*idea, achievement, holiday, performance, victory*] formidable○, merveilleux/-euse; [*opportunity*] fantastique○; **we had a ~ time!** on s'est vraiment bien amusé!; **she did a ~ job** elle a fait un travail remarquable or formidable○; **~!** (c'est) formidable○!

splendidly /ˈsplendɪdlɪ/ *adv* magnifiquement, merveilleusement; **everything is going ~** tout marche merveilleusement bien.

splendiferous /splenˈdɪfərəs/ *adj* hum magnifique, somptueux/-euse.

splendour GB, **splendor** US /ˈsplendə(r)/ *n* splendeur *f*; **to live/dine in ~** vivre/dîner fastueusement; **the ~s of** les splendeurs de.

splenetic /splɪˈnetɪk/ *adj* [*person, temperament*] acariâtre; [*letter*] plein de fiel.

splice /splaɪs/ **I** *n* (in rope) épissure *f*; (in tape, film) raccord *m*; (in carpentry) enture *f*.
II *vtr* gen coller [*tape, film*]; Naut épisser [*ends of rope*]; fig amalgamer, réunir [*styles, images*].
IDIOMS **to get ~d**○ hum se marier, convoler en justes noces hum; **to ~ the main brace** Naut hum (have a drink) boire un coup○.

splicer /ˈsplaɪsə(r)/ *n* colleuse *f*.

spliff○ /splɪf/ *n* joint○ *m*.

spline /splaɪn/ *n* clavette *f* (linguiforme).

splint /splɪnt/ **I** *n* **1** Med attelle *f*, éclisse *f*; **to put sb's leg in a ~** éclisser la jambe de qn; **2** (sliver of wood) allume-feu *m inv*.
II *vtr* éclisser, poser une attelle à [*arm, leg*].

splinter /ˈsplɪntə(r)/ **I** *n* (of glass, metal) éclat *m*; (of wood) éclat *m*, écharde *f*; (of bone) esquille *f*; **to get a ~ in one's finger** s'enfoncer une écharde dans le doigt.
II *vtr* lit faire voler [qch] en éclats [*glass, windscreen etc*]; fendre [*wood*]; fig scinder [*party, group*].
III *vi* lit [*glass, windscreen*] se briser, voler en éclats; [*wood*] se fendre; fig [*party, alliance etc*] se scinder, se fragmenter.

splinter: **~ group** *n* groupe *m* dissident; **~proof glass** *n* verre *m* sécurit® *inv*.

split /splɪt/ **I** *n* **1** lit (in fabric, garment) déchirure *f*; (in rock, wood) fissure *f*, crevasse *f*; (in skin) crevasse *f*; **2** (in party, movement, alliance) scission *f* (**in** de); (stronger) rupture *f* (**between** entre; **in** dans; **into** dans); **a three-way ~ in the party executive** une scission en trois groupes de la direction du parti; **3** (share-out) (of money, profits, jobs) partage *m*; **a (four-way) ~ of the profits** un partage (en quatre) des bénéfices; **4** US (small bottle) (of soft drink) petite bouteille *f*; (of wine) demi-bouteille *f*; **5** Culin (dessert) ≈ coupe *f* glacée; **6** Fin surtout US marge *f* différentielle, différence *f*; **income/wage ~** éventail *m* des revenus/salaires.
II splits *npl* grand écart *m*; **to do the ~s** faire le grand écart.
III *adj* [*fabric, garment*] déchiré; [*seam*] défait; [*log, pole, hide, lip*] fendu.
IV *vtr* (*p prés* **-tt-**; *prét, pp* **split**) **1** (cut, slit) fendre [*wood, log, rock, slate, seam*] (**in, into** en); déchirer [*fabric, garment*]; **to ~ one's lip** se fendre la lèvre; **to ~ the atom** fissionner l'atome; [*lightning, thunder, noise*] déchirer [*sky, silence*]; **2** (cause dissent) diviser, provoquer une scission dans [*party, movement, alliance*]; **to ~ the vote** diviser l'électorat; **the dispute has split the alliance in two/into two factions** le conflit a divisé l'alliance en deux/en deux factions; **the committee was (deeply) split on** or **over this issue** la commission était (extrêmement) divisée or partagée sur cette question; **3** (divide) ▶ **split up**; **4** (share) partager [*cost, payment*] (**between** entre); **shall we ~ a bottle of wine (between us)?** si on partageait une bouteille de vin?; **to ~ sth three/four ways** partager qch en trois/en quatre [*profits, cost*]; **5** Ling **to ~ an infinitive** *introduire un adverbe au milieu d'un infinitif, entre 'to' et le verbe*; **6** Comput fractionner [*window*].
V *vi* (*p prés* **-tt-**; *prét, pp* **split**) **1** [*wood, log, rock, slate*] se fendre (**in, into** en); [*fabric, garment*] se déchirer; [*seam*] se défaire ; **to ~ in(to) two** [*stream, road*] se diviser en deux; **my head's ~ting** fig j'ai horriblement mal à la tête; **2** gen, Pol [*party, movement, alliance*] se diviser; (stronger) se scinder; **the leadership split on** ou **over (the question of) the voting system** la direction était divisée à propos du système électoral; **to ~ along party lines** se séparer en fonction des différents partis; **3** (divide) ▶ **split up**; **4**○ GB (tell tales) cafarder○; **to ~ on sb** rapporter○ sur qn (**to** à); **5**○ (leave) filer○.
IDIOMS **to ~ the difference** couper la poire en deux; **to ~ one's sides**○ **(laughing)** se tordre de rire.
■ **split off**: ¶ **~ off** [*branch, piece, end*] se détacher (**from** de); [*path*] bifurquer; [*poli-*

tical group] faire scission; [*company*] se séparer (**from** de); ¶ **~** [**sth**] **off** détacher [*branch, piece*]; **to ~ sth off from** détacher qch de [*branch, piece*]; séparer qch de [*company, section, department*].

■ **split open**: ¶ **~ open** [*bag, fabric*] se déchirer; [*seam*] se défaire; ¶ **~** [**sth**] **open** fendre [*box, coconut*]; **to ~ one's head open** se fendre le crâne.

■ **split up**: ¶ **~ up** [*band, couple, members, parents*] se séparer; [*crowd, demonstrators*] se disperser; [*alliance, consortium*] éclater; [*federation*] se scinder (**into** en); **to ~ up with** quitter, se séparer de [*partner, husband, girlfriend*]; **to ~ up into groups of five** se mettre en groupes de cinq; ¶ **~** [**sb**] **up** séparer [*friends, partners, group members*] (**from** de); **everyone tried to ~ the couple up** tout le monde a essayé de les écarter l'un de l'autre; **to ~ the children up into groups** répartir les enfants en petits groupes; ¶ **~** [**sth**] **up, ~ up** [**sth**] partager, répartir [*money, profits, work*] (**into** en); diviser [*area, group*] (**into** en); **to ~ a novel up into chapters** diviser un roman en chapitres; **to ~ sth up into its component parts** séparer les différentes parties qui composent qch.

split cane I *n* osier *m*.
II *modif* [*basket, furniture*] en osier.

split: **~ decision** *n* Sport décision *f* partagée; **~ ends** *npl* cheveux *mpl* fourchus; **~ infinitive** *n*: *erreur de grammaire consistant à introduire un adverbe au milieu d'un infinitif, entre 'to' et le verbe.*

split level I *n* **the flat is on ~s** l'appartement a des demi-étages.
II **split-level** *adj* [*cooker*] à plaques de cuisson et four indépendants; [*room, apartment*] sur deux niveaux.

split: **~ peas** *npl* pois *mpl* cassés; **~ personality** *n* double personnalité *f*; **~ pin** *n* goupille *f* fendue; **~ ring** *n* anneau *m* brisé.

split screen I *n* écran *m* divisé, split screen *m*.
II **split-screen** *adj* [*technique, sequence, film*] (projeté) sur écran divisé; [*facility*] écran divisé.

split second I *n* fraction *f* de seconde; **in/for a ~** en/pendant une fraction de seconde.
II **split-second** *modif* [*decision*] éclair *inv*; [*reflex*] extrêmement rapide; **the success of the mission depends on ~ timing** pour réussir il faut que la mission suive un programme fixé à la seconde près; **the jokes require ~ timing** il faut que les blagues soient minutées à la seconde près.

split shift *n* poste *m* fractionné; **to work ~s** travailler en postes fractionnés.

split: **~-site** *adj* [*factory, school*] dont les locaux sont dispersés; **~ ticket** *n* US Pol vote *m* pour une liste panachée; **~ tin** (**loaf**) *n* GB ≈ pain *m* moulé.

splitting /ˈsplɪtɪŋ/ I *n* (division) (of wood, stone) fendage *m*; (of profits, proceeds) partage *m*, répartition *f*; (of group) répartition *f*.
II *adj* **to have a ~ headache** avoir horriblement mal à la tête.

splodge○ /splɒdʒ/ GB I *n* (of ink, paint, grease, mud etc) éclaboussure *f*, (grosse) tache *f*.
II *vtr* **to ~ sth with paint, to ~ paint on sth** éclabousser qch de peinture.

splotch○ /splɒtʃ/ *n*, *vtr* US = **splodge**.

splurge○ /splɜːdʒ/ I *n* folie○ *f*; **I went on** ou **had a ~ and bought a stereo** j'ai fait une folie○ et je me suis payé une chaîne stéréo.
II *vtr* claquer○ [*money*] (**on** pour).
III *vi* (also **~ out**) claquer○ (**on** pour).

splutter /ˈsplʌtə(r)/ I *n* (of person) (spitting) crachotement *m*; (stutter) bafouillement *m*; (of engine) crachotement *m*; (of fire, sparks) grésillement *m*.
II *vtr* (also **~ out**) bafouiller, bredouiller [*excuse, apology, words*].
III *vi* [*person*] (stutter) bafouiller, bredouiller; (spit) crachoter, postillonner; [*fire, fat, candle, match, sparks*] grésiller, crépiter; **the engine ~ed to a stop** le moteur s'est arrêté dans un crachotement.

spode /spəʊd/ *n* porcelaine *f* de spode.

spoil /spɔɪl/ I *n* ¢ (from excavation) déblais *mpl*.
II **spoils** *npl* **1** (of war, victory) butin *m* (**of** de); **to get a share of the ~s** Mil avoir sa part de butin; fig avoir sa part de gâteau○; **2** (political, commercial) profits *mpl* (**of** de); (sporting) gains *mpl*.
III *vtr* (*pp* **~ed** ou **~t** GB) **1** (mar) gâcher [*event, evening, view, game*] (**by doing** en faisant); gâter [*place, taste, effect*]; **it will ~ your appetite** ça va te couper l'appétit; **to ~ sth for sb** gâcher qch à qn; **it'll ~ the film for us** ça nous gâchera tout le plaisir du film; **they ~ it** ou **things for other people** ils gâchent le plaisir des autres; **to ~ sb's enjoyment of sth** empêcher qn de profiter de qch; **why did you go and ~ everything?** pourquoi as-tu tout gâché?; **to ~ sb's fun** (thwart) contrarier qn; **2** (ruin) abîmer [*garment, toy, crop, food*] (**by doing** en faisant); **to ~ one's chances of doing** gâcher ses chances de faire (**by doing** en faisant); **to ~ sb's plans** gâcher les projets or les plans de qn; **3** (pamper, indulge) gâter [*person, pet*] (**by doing** en faisant); **to ~ sb rotten**○ pourrir qn; **to ~ sb with** gâter qn en lui offrant [*gift, trip*]; **we've been ~ed living so close to the sea** nous avons été privilégiés de vivre si près de la mer; **4** Pol rendre [qch] nul/nulle [*vote, ballot paper*].
IV *vi* (*pp* **~ed** ou **~t** GB) [*product, foodstuff*] s'abîmer; [*meat*] se gâter; **your dinner will ~!** ça ne va plus être bon!
V *v refl* (*pp* **~ed** ou **~t** GB) **to ~ oneself** se faire un petit plaisir; **let's ~ ourselves and eat out!** faisons-nous plaisir en allant au restaurant!
IDIOMS **to be ~ing for a fight** chercher la bagarre○.

spoilage /ˈspɔɪlɪdʒ/ *n* **1** (decay) détérioration *f*; **2** ¢ (wastage) déchets *mpl*.

spoiled, **spoilt** GB /spɔɪlt/ I *prét, pp* ▶ **spoil**.
II *adj* **1** péj [*child, dog*] gâté; **he's terribly ~** il est horriblement gâté; **to be ~ rotten**○ être pourri; **a ~ brat**○ un gamin pourri○; **2** Pol [*ballot paper, vote*] nul/nulle.
IDIOMS **to be ~ for choice** avoir l'embarras du choix.

spoiler /ˈspɔɪlə(r)/ *n* **1** Aut becquet *m*; **rear ~** becquet arrière; **2** Aviat aérofrein *m*.

spoil heap *n* monceau *m* de déblais.

spoilsport○ /ˈspɔɪlspɔːt/ *n* péj rabat-joie *mf inv* pej; **to be a ~** faire son rabat-joie.

spoils system *n* US Pol système *m* des dépouilles.

spoilt /spɔɪlt/ GB I *prét, pp* ▶ **spoil**.
II *adj* = **spoiled**.

spoke /spəʊk/ I *pret* ▶ **speak**.
II *n* (in wheel) rayon *m*; (on ladder) barreau *m*.
IDIOMS **to put a ~ in sb's wheel** mettre des bâtons dans les roues à qn.

spoken /ˈspəʊkən/ I *pp* ▶ **speak**.
II *adj* [*word, dialogue, language*] parlé.

spoke: **~shave** *n* wastringue *f*; **~sman** *n* porte-parole *m inv*; **~sperson** *n* porte-parole *m inv*; **~swoman** *n* porte-parole *m inv*.

spoliation /ˌspəʊlɪˈeɪʃn/ *n* spoliation *f*.

spondaic /spɒnˈdeɪɪk/ *adj* spondaïque.

spondee /ˈspɒndiː/ *n* spondée *m*.

spondulix○, **spondulicks**○ /spɒnˈdjuːlɪks/ *n* hum fric○ *m*, argent *m*.

sponge /spʌndʒ/ I *n* **1** (for cleaning) éponge *f*; **bath ~** éponge *f* de bain; **to soak up water like a ~** absorber l'eau comme une éponge; **at that age, a child's mind is like a ~** à cet âge, le cerveau d'un enfant assimile tout; **2** ¢ (material) éponge *f*; **3** Zool éponge *f*; **to dive for ~s** pêcher les éponges; **4** (wipe) coup *m* d'éponge; **to give sth a ~** donner un coup d'éponge à qch; **5** (also **~ cake**) génoise *f*; **jam/cream ~** génoise *f* fourrée à la confiture/à la crème; **6** Med (pad) compresse *f*.
II *vtr* **1** (wipe) frotter [qch] avec une éponge [*material, garment, stain*]; éponger [*wound, excess liquid*]; laver [qch] avec une éponge [*surface*]; **to ~ one's face** s'essuyer le visage avec une éponge; **2**○ péj (scrounge) **to ~ sth off** ou **from sb** taper○ qch à qn.
III *vi*○ péj **to ~ off** ou **on** vivre sur le dos de [*family, friend, State*].

■ **sponge down**: **~** [**sth**] **down, ~ down** [**sth**] laver [qch] avec une éponge [*car, surface*]; **to ~ oneself down** se laver avec une éponge.

■ **sponge off**: **~** [**sth**] **off, ~ off** [**sth**] faire partir [qch] avec une éponge [*mark, stain*].

sponge: **~ bag** *n* GB trousse *f* de toilette; **~ bath** *n* toilette *f* (à l'éponge); **~ cloth** *n* tissu *m* éponge; **~ diver** ▶ **1692** *n* pêcheur/-euse *m/f* d'éponges; **~ diving** *n* pêche *f* aux éponges.

sponge-down *n* **to have a ~** faire une toilette rapide; **to give sth/sb a ~** donner un coup d'éponge à qch/qn.

sponge: **~ finger** *n* GB biscuit *m* à la cuiller; **~ mop** *n* balai-éponge *m*; **~ pudding** *n* GB *gâteau cuit au bain-marie et servi chaud.*

sponger○ /ˈspʌndʒə(r)/ *n* péj parasite *m* pej.

sponge: **~ roll** *n* GB biscuit *m* roulé; **~ rubber** *n* caoutchouc *m* mousse.

sponginess /ˈspʌndʒɪnɪs/ *n* (of terrain, ground) caractère *m* spongieux; (of texture, material) caractère *m* moelleux.

spongy /ˈspʌndʒɪ/ *adj* [*terrain, ground, moss, rotten wood*] spongieux/-ieuse; [*material, texture, mixture*] moelleux/-euse; [*flesh*] mou/molle.

sponson /ˈspɒnsən/ *n* **1** Naut (for gun) encorbellement *m*; **2** Aviat (on fuselage) flotteur *m*.

sponsor /ˈspɒnsə(r)/ I *n* **1** Advertg, Fin (advertiser, backer) sponsor *m*; **2** (patron) mécène *m*; **3** (guarantor) garant/-e *m/f*; **to act as ~ for sb** être le garant de qn; **4** Relig (godparent) parrain/marraine *m/f*; **5** (for charity) *personne qui parraine un participant à une épreuve sportive organisée dans un but caritatif*; **6** Pol (of bill, motion, law) initiateur/-trice *m/f*.
II *vtr* **1** Advertg, Fin (fund) sponsoriser [*sporting event, team, TV programme*]; financer [*student, study, course, conference, enterprise*]; **government-~ed** financé par le gouvernement; **2** (support) soutenir [*violence, invasion*]; **UN-~ed** soutenu par l'ONU; **3** Pol (advocate) présenter [*bill, motion*]; **4** (for charity) parrainer [*person*] (*pour une épreuve sportive organisée dans un but caritatif*).
III **sponsored** *pp adj* **1** (for charity) **~ed swim** épreuve *f* de natation parrainée; **2** Advertg, Radio, TV [*programme*] sponsorisé.

sponsorship /ˈspɒnsəʃɪp/ *n* **1** Advertg, Fin (corporate funding) parrainage *m*, sponsorat *m* (**from** de); **to seek/raise ~ for sth** chercher/trouver des sponsors pour qch; **2** (backing) (financial) sponsorat *m*; (cultural) patronage *m*; (moral, political) parrainage *m*; **3** C (also **~ deal**) contrat *m* de parrainage; **4** Pol (of bill, motion) soutien *m*; **5** (by guarantor) caution *f* morale.

spontaneity /ˌspɒntəˈneɪətɪ/ *n* spontanéité *f*.

spontaneous /spɒnˈteɪnɪəs/ *adj* spontané.

spontaneous: **~ combustion** *n* combustion *f* spontanée; **~ generation** *n* génération *f* spontanée.

spontaneously /spɒnˈteɪnɪəslɪ/ *adv* spontanément.

spontaneous recovery *n* Psych guérison *f* spontanée.

spoof○ /spuːf/ I *n* **1** (parody) parodie *f* (**on** de); **2** (hoax, trick) blague○ *f*, canular *m*.
II *modif* (parody) **a ~ horror film/crime novel** une parodie de film d'horreur/de roman policier.

III *vtr* **1** (parody) parodier [*book, film*]; **2** (trick) faire marcher, mettre [qn] en boîte○ [*person*].

spook○ /spu:k/ **I** *n* **1** (ghost) fantôme *m*; **2** US (spy) barbouze○ *m*, espion/-ionne *m/f*; **3**◐ US injur (black person) nègre/négresse *m/f* offensive.
II *vtr* surtout US **1** (frighten) effrayer, donner la trouille○ or la frousse○ à [*person*]; **2** (haunt) hanter.

spookiness○ /'spu:kɪnɪs/ *n* caractère *m* sinistre.

spooky○ /'spu:kɪ/ *adj* [*house, atmosphere*] sinistre; [*story*] qui fait froid dans le dos.

spool /spu:l/ **I** *n* (reel: of thread, tape, film) bobine *f*; (for fishing line) bobine *f*, tambour *m*.
II *vtr* **1** dévider [*thread*]; **2** Comput traiter [qch] en différé.

spoon /spu:n/ **I** *n* **1** (utensil) cuiller *f*, cuillère *f*; (for tea, coffee) petite cuiller *f*; **soup-/dessert spoon** cuillère à soupe/à dessert; **2** (measure) cuillerée *f*, cuillère *f*; **two ~s of sugar** deux cuillères de sucre; **3** (golf club) spoon *m*, bois trois *m*; **4** Mus (as instrument) **to play the ~s** jouer des cuillers.
II *vtr* **1** (in cooking, serving) **to ~ sth into a dish/bowl** mettre qch dans un plat/bol avec une cuillère; **to ~ sauce over sth** arroser qch de sauce à la cuillère; **to ~ sth up/out** ramasser/servir qch à la cuillère; **2** Sport (in golf) prendre [qch] en cuiller [*ball*].
III○† *vi* (kiss) se faire des mamours†, flirter.
IDIOMS **to be born with a silver ~ in one's mouth** naître dans la soie.

spoonbill /'spu:nbɪl/ *n* spatule *f*; **common/roseate ~** spatule blanche/rose.

spoonerism /'spu:nərɪzəm/ *n* contrepèterie *f* (involontaire).

spoon-feed /'spu:nfi:d/ *vtr* **1** nourrir [qn] à la petite cuillère [*baby, invalid*]; **2** fig péj [*teacher*] mâcher le travail à [*students*]; **to ~ the public with sth** faire ingurgiter qch au public.

spoonful /'spu:nfʊl/ *n* (*pl* **~fuls** ou **~sful**) cuillerée *f*, cuiller *f*.

spoor /spɔ:(r), US spʊər/ *n* Hunt piste *f*, trace *f*.

sporadic /spə'rædɪk/ *adj* sporadique.

sporadically /spə'rædɪklɪ/ *adv* sporadiquement.

spore /spɔ:(r)/ *n* spore *f*.

sporran /'spɒrən/ *n* sporran *m* (*bourse en cuir ou en fourrure portée sur le devant du kilt*).

sport /spɔ:t/ ▶1282 **I** *n* **1** (physical activity) sport *m*; **to be good/bad at ~** être bon/mauvais en sport; **to do a lot of ~** faire beaucoup de sport; **to play a lot of ~s** pratiquer plusieurs sports; **team ~s** sports *mpl* d'équipe; **indoor/outdoor ~s** sports *mpl* en salle/de plein air; **2** Sch (subject) activités *fpl* sportives; **3** sout (fun) **to have great ~** s'amuser beaucoup; **to do sth for ~** faire qch pour s'amuser; **to make ~ of sb** taquiner qn; **4**○ (person) **to be a good/bad ~** (in games) être beau/mauvais joueur; (when teased) bien/mal prendre les plaisanteries; **5**○ Austral (term of address) **how's it going, ~?** comment ça va, mon pote○?; **6** Biol variant *m*.
II *vtr* arborer [*hat, rose, moustache*].
III *vi* littér (frolic) batifoler.

sport coat *n* US = **sports jacket**.

sportiness /'spɔ:tɪnɪs/ *n* amour *m* du sport.

sporting /'spɔ:tɪŋ/ *adj* **1** [*fixture, event*] sportif/-ive; **~ contacts** relations *fpl* dans le milieu sportif; **the ~ year** la saison sportive; **2** (fair, generous) [*offer*] généreux/-euse; **it's very ~ of you/him to do** c'est très généreux de votre/sa part de faire; **a ~ gesture** un geste généreux; **to give sb/have a ~ chance of winning** donner à qn/avoir de bonnes chances de gagner; **there is a ~ chance that they'll win** ils ont une bonne chance de gagner.

sporting house† *n* US **1** (brothel) maison *f* de passe; **2** (for gambling) maison *f* de jeu.

sportingly /'spɔ:tɪŋlɪ/ *adv* sportivement, généreusement.

sportive† /'spɔ:tɪv/ *adj* littér allègre.

sport: **~s car** *n* voiture *f* de sport; **~scast** *n* US émission *f* sportive; **~scaster** ▶1692 *n* US journaliste *mf* sportif/-ive; **~s centre** GB, **~s center** US *n* centre *m* sportif; **~s club** *n* club *m* sportif; **~s day** *n* GB fête *f* des sports; **~s desk** *n* service *m* des sports; **~s ground** *n* (large) stade *m*; (in school, club etc) terrain *m* de sports; **~s hall** *n* salle *f* omnisports; **~s jacket** *n* GB veste *f* en tweed; **~sman** *n* sportif *m*; **~smanship** *n* (skill in sports) sportivité *f*; (generous behaviour) sout fair-play *m*; **~s page** *n* page *f* sport; **~s shirt** *n* maillot *m* de sport; **~swear** *n* sportswear *m*; **~swoman** *n* sportive *f*; **~s writer** ▶1692 *n* journaliste *mf* sportif/-ive (de la presse écrite).

sporty○ /'spɔ:tɪ/ *adj* **1** (fond of sport) sportif/-ive; **I'm not the ~ type** je ne suis pas du genre sportif; **2** [*trousers, shirt*] pimpant.

spot /spɒt/ **I** *n* **1** (dot) (on animal) tache *f*; (on fabric, wallpaper) pois *m*; (on dice, domino, card) point *m*; **a red dress with white ~s** une robe rouge à pois blancs; **to see ~s before one's eyes** voir trouble; **2** (stain) tache *f*; **a grease/rust ~** une tache de graisse/rouille; **3** (pimple) bouton *m*; **to have ~s** avoir des boutons; **to come out in ~s** être couvert de boutons; **chocolate brings me out in ~s** le chocolat me donne des boutons; **4** (place) endroit *m*; **to be on the ~** gen être en place; (of police) être sur les lieux; **our correspondent on the ~, Paula Cox** notre correspondant sur place, Paula Cox; **to decide/agree on the ~** décider/donner son accord sur-le-champ; **that whisky hit the ~ nicely**○ ce whisky a été le bienvenu; **5**○ (small amount) **a ~ of cream/whisky/exercise/sightseeing** un peu de crème/de whisky/d'exercice/de tourisme; **would you like a ~ of lunch?** et si on mangeait un petit quelque chose?; **to have** ou **be in a ~ of bother (with)** avoir quelques petits ennuis (avec); **6** (drop) goutte *f*; **7**○ (difficulty) situation *f* embêtante; **to be in a (tight) ~** être dans une situation embêtante; **to put sb on the ~** (in an awkward situation) mettre qn en mauvaise posture; (by asking a difficult question) mettre qn dans l'embarras; **8** Advertg spot *m* publicitaire; **9** TV, Radio (regular slot) temps *m* d'antenne; **10** (position) **this record has been on the top ~ for two weeks** ce disque a été numéro un pendant deux semaines; **this book has the number one ~ on the bestseller list** ce livre est en tête de la liste des bestsellers; **11** (moral blemish) tache *f*; **the scandal is a ~ on his reputation** le scandale a entaché sa réputation; **12** (light) Cin, Theat projecteur *m*; (in home, display) spot *m*; **13** Sport (for penalty kick) point *m* de pénalty; (for snooker ball) mouche *f*; **14**○ US (nightclub) boîte *f* de nuit.
II *vtr* (*p prés etc* **-tt**) **1** (see) apercevoir [*person*]; voir [*car, roadsign, book*]; **to ~ sb doing** apercevoir qn en train de faire; **to ~ that...** s'apercevoir que ...; **he was ~ted boarding a plane to Japan** il a été vu en train de prendre l'avion pour le Japon; **well ~ted!** bien vu!; **2** (recognize) reconnaître [*car, person, symptoms, opportunity*]; repérer [*defect, difference, bargain, talent*]; observer [*birds, trains*]; **you'll ~ him by his black beard** tu le reconnaîtras à sa barbe noire; **3**○ US (concede an advantage) **to ~ sb sth** concéder qch à qn [*points*]; **he ~ted me 20 metres** il m'a concédé 20 mètres d'avance; **4** (stain) tacher [*carpet, shirt*]; **the cloth is ~ted with grease** la nappe est couverte de taches de graisse.
III *v impers* (*p prés etc* **-tt-**) (rain) **it's ~ting** il tombe quelques gouttes.
IV -spot (*dans composés*) **1** US (banknote) **a ten/five-~** un billet de dix/cinq dollars; **2** (billiard ball) **the three/five-~** la boule numéro trois/cinq.
IDIOMS **to change one's ~s** changer son caractère; **to knock ~s off sth/sb** être bien meilleur que qch/qn; **this car knocks ~s off other models**○ cette voiture est bien meilleure que les autres modèles; **she knocked ~s off the champion**○ elle a battu la championne à plates coutures○; **to hit the high ~s** US n'évoquer que les grandes lignes.

spot cash *n* Fin argent *m* comptant or spot.

spot check I *n* (unannounced) contrôle *m* surprise (**on** sur); (random) contrôle *m* fait au hasard (**on** sur); **to carry out a ~** effectuer un contrôle au hasard or un contrôle surprise.
II spot-check *vtr* (randomly) effectuer un contrôle sur [*goods*]; (without warning) effectuer un contrôle surprise sur [*passengers*].

spot: **~ delivery** *n* Fin livraison *f* immédiate; **~ fine** *n* amende *f* à régler sur le lieu de l'infraction; **~ goods** *npl* Fin marchandises *fpl* disponibles immédiatement; **~ height** *n* Geog point *m* coté.

spotless /'spɒtlɪs/ *adj* **1** (clean) impeccable; **2** (beyond reproach) [*name, reputation*] irréprochable.

spotlessly /'spɒtlɪslɪ/ *adv* **~ clean** d'une propreté impeccable.

spotlessness /'spɒtlɪsnɪs/ *n* propreté *f* impeccable.

spotlight /'spɒtlaɪt/ **I** *n* **1** (light) Cin, Theat projecteur *m*; (in home) spot *m*; **2** fig (focus of attention) **to be in** ou **under the ~** [*person*] être sur la sellette; [*topic, issue*] faire la une; **the ~ is on Aids** le sida fait la une; **to turn** ou **put the ~ on sb/sth** attirer l'attention sur qn/qch; **the media ~ has fallen on her** l'attention des médias s'est focalisée sur elle.
II *vtr* (*prét, pp* **-lit** ou **-lighted**) **1** Cin, Theat diriger les projecteurs sur [*actor, area*]; **2** fig (highlight) mettre [qch] en lumière [*problem, corruption*].

spot market *n* Fin marché *m* au comptant.

spot-on /ˌspɒt'ɒn/ GB **I** *adj* exact; **he was absolutely ~** il a mis dans le mille.
II *adv* [*guess*] sans se tromper; **he hit the target ~** il a touché la cible en plein dans le mille.

spot: **~ price** *n* Fin prix *m* sur place; **~ rate** *n* Fin cours *m* au comptant; **~ remover** *n* détachant *m*; **~ sale** *n* Fin vente *f* en disponible.

spotted /'spɒtɪd/ *adj* [*tie, fabric*] à pois (*after n*); [*plumage, dog*] tacheté.

spot: **~ted dick** *n* GB Culin pudding *m* aux raisins secs; **~ted fever** ▶1354 *n* méningite *f* cérébrospinale; **~ted flycatcher** *n* gobe-mouches *m* gris.

spotter /'spɒtə(r)/ *n* Mil (for artillery fire) observateur/-trice *m/f*; (for aircraft) guetteur *m*. ▶ **plane spotter**, **train spotter**.

spotter plane *n* Mil Aviat avion *m* d'observation.

spot test *n* interrogation *f* surprise.

spotting /'spɒtɪŋ/ *n* ¢ Med pertes *fpl* de sang.

spot: **~ trader** *n* Fin opérateur *m* au comptant; **~ transaction** *n* Fin opération *f* au comptant.

spotty /'spɒtɪ/ *adj* **1** (pimply) [*adolescent, skin*] boutonneux/-euse; **he's very ~** il est plein de boutons; **2** (patterned) [*dress, fabric*] à pois (*after n*); [*dog*] tacheté.

spot-weld /'spɒtweld/ **I** *n* (action) soudage *m* par points; (result) soudure *f* par points.
II *vtr* souder [qch] par points.

spot-welding /'spɒtweldɪŋ/ *n* soudage *m* par points.

spouse /spaʊz, US spaʊs/ *n* époux/épouse *m/f*.

spout /spaʊt/ **I** *n* **1** (of kettle, teapot) bec *m* verseur; (of tap) brise-jet *m*; (of hose) orifice

m; (of fountain) jet *m*; (of gutter) gargouille *f*; **2** (spurt) (of liquid) jet *m*.
II *vtr* **1** (spurt) [*pipe, fountain, geyser*] faire jaillir; **2** péj (recite) débiter [*poetry, statistics, theories, advice*] (**at** à); **he's always ~ing rubbish about the economy** il est toujours en train de débiter des âneries sur l'économie.
III *vi* **1** (spurt) [*liquid*] jaillir (**from, out of** de); **2**○ GB péj (also **~ forth**) (talk) discourir (**about** sur); **stop ~ing at me!** arrête de me casser les oreilles○!; **3** [*whale*] souffler.
IDIOMS **to be up the ~**○ GB [*plan, scheme, life*] être fichu○; [*woman*] être enceinte, être en cloque◐.
■ **spout out** jaillir (**of, from** de).

sprain /spreɪn/ I *n* entorse *f*; (less severe) foulure *f*.
II *vtr* **to ~ one's ankle/wrist** se faire une entorse à la cheville/au poignet; (less severely) se fouler la cheville/le poignet; **to have a ~ed ankle** avoir une entorse à la cheville.

sprang /spræŋ/ *prét* ▶ **spring**.

sprat /spræt/ *n* sprat *m*.
IDIOMS **to use a ~ to catch a mackerel** se servir de quelqu'un (or de quelque chose) comme appât.

sprawl /sprɔːl/ I *n* (of suburbs, buildings etc) étendue *f*; **the ~ of Paris** l'agglomération parisienne; **suburban ~** banlieues *fpl* tentaculaires.
II *vi* [*person*] (casually) s'étaler, se vautrer pej; (exhaustedly) s'affaler; [*town, suburb, forest, handwriting*] s'étaler; **she lay ~ed across the sofa** elle était étalée or vautrée pej sur le canapé; **they sent him ~ing into the mud** ils l'ont envoyé s'étaler dans la boue.

sprawling /ˈsprɔːlɪŋ/ *adj* [*suburb, city*] tentaculaire; [*handwriting*] qui s'étale dans tous les sens; [*sentence*] interminable; [*position*] avachi.

spray /spreɪ/ I *n* **1** ¢ (seawater) embruns *mpl*; **clouds of ~** nuages *mpl* d'embruns; (other liquid) nuages de (fines) gouttelettes; **2** (container) (for perfume) vaporisateur *m*; (for antifreeze, deodorant, paint etc) bombe *f*; (for inhalant, throat, nose) pulvérisateur *m*; **garden ~** pulvérisateur de jardin; **3** (shower) (of sparks) gerbe *f*; (of bullets) pluie *f*; **4** (of flowers) (bunch) gerbe *f*; (single branch) rameau *m*; (single flowering stem) branche *f*.
II *modif* [*deodorant*] en spray; [*paint, polish, starch*] en atomiseur.
III *vtr* **1** vaporiser [*water, liquid*]; asperger [*person*] (**with** de); arroser [*demonstrator, oilslick*] (**with** de); **to ~ sth onto sth** (onto fire) projeter qch sur qch [*foam, water*]; (onto surface, flowers etc) vaporiser qch sur qch [*paint, insecticide, water*]; **to ~ sth over sb/sth** asperger qn/qch de qch [*champagne, water*]; **to ~ on perfume** se parfumer; **2** fig **to ~ sb/sth with** arroser qn/qch de [*bullets*].
IV *vi* gicler; (more violently) jaillir; **to ~ over/out of sth** gicler sur/de qch.

spray: **~ attachment** *n* buse *f*; **~ can** *n* bombe *f*, aérosol *m*; **~ compressor** *n* compresseur *m* à injection d'eau.

sprayer /ˈspreɪə(r)/ *n* pulvérisateur *m*.

spray: **~ gun** *n* pistolet *m* à peinture; **~-on** *adj* [*conditioner, glitter*] en vaporisateur.

spread /spred/ I *n* **1** (dissemination) (of disease, drugs) propagation *f*; (of news, information) diffusion *f*; (of democracy, infection, weapons) progression *f*; (of education) généralisation *f*; **the ~ of sth to** l'extension *f* de qch à [*group, area, place*]; **2** (extent, range) (of wings, branches) envergure *f*; (of arch) ouverture *f*, portée *f*; (of products, services) éventail *m*; **the ~ in terms of age in the class is quite wide** les membres de la classe sont d'âge varié; **the ~ of the festival is enormous** le programme du festival est très étendu; **~ of sail** ou **canvas** Naut déploiement *m* de voile; **3** Journ **a three-column ~** trois colonnes *fpl*; **double-page ~** page *f* double; **4** Culin pâte *f* à tartiner; **chocolate ~** pâte *f* à tartiner au chocolat; **salmon/shrimp ~** beurre *m* de saumon/crevette; **low-fat ~** (margarine) margarine *f* allégée; **fruit ~** confiture *f* à teneur en sucre réduite; **5** (assortment of dishes) festin *m*; **they laid on a magnificent ~** ils ont servi un véritable festin; **6** US Agric grand ranch *m*.
II *adj* Ling [*lips*] rétracté.
III *vtr* (*prét, pp* **spread**) **1** (open out, unfold) étendre [*cloth, map, rug, newspaper*] (**on, over** sur); (lay out) étaler [*cloth, newspaper, map*] (**on, over** sur); (put) mettre [*cloth, sheet, newspaper*]; **we spread dust sheets over the furniture** nous avons mis des housses sur les meubles; **to ~ a cloth on the table** mettre une nappe sur la table; **she spread her arms wide in greeting** elle a ouvert grand les bras en signe de bienvenue; **the peacock spread its tail/its wings** le paon a fait la roue/a déployé ses ailes; **~ 'em**○**!** (police command) écartez les bras et les jambes!; ▶ **wing**; **2** (apply in layer) étaler [*butter, jam, paste, glue*] (**on, over** sur); **~ the butter thinly on the bread** étaler une mince couche de beurre sur le pain; **3** (cover with layer) **to ~ some bread with jam** tartiner du pain avec de la confiture; **to ~ a surface with glue** enduire une surface de colle; **a biscuit spread with honey** un biscuit recouvert de miel; **the table was spread for lunch** la table était mise pour le déjeuner; **the path had been spread with gravel** le chemin avait été recouvert de gravillons; **4** (distribute over area) disperser [*forces, troops*]; étaler [*cards, documents*]; épandre [*fertilizer*]; répartir, partager [*workload, responsibility*]; **to ~ grit** ou **sand** sabler; **to ~ mud everywhere** mettre de la boue partout; **the resources must be evenly spread between the two projects** les ressources doivent être réparties or partagées de façon égale entre les deux projets; **we have to ~ our resources very thin(ly)** nous devons ménager nos ressources; **my interests are spread over several historical periods** je m'intéresse à plusieurs périodes historiques; **5** (also **~ out**) (distribute in time, space out) étaler, échelonner [*payments, meetings, visits, cost*] (**over** sur); **I'd like to ~ the course (out) over two years** j'aimerais étaler les cours sur deux ans; **6** (diffuse, cause to proliferate) propager [*disease, infection, germs, fire*]; propager [*religion*]; répandre, semer [*fear, confusion, panic*]; faire courir, faire circuler [*rumour, story, lie, scandal*]; **a strong wind helped to ~ the blaze** un vent fort a contribué à propager l'incendie; **to ~ sth to sb** transmettre [qch] à qn [*infection, news*]; **wind spread the fire to neighbouring buildings** le vent a poussé l'incendie vers les bâtiments voisins; **can you ~ the word?** tu peux faire passer?; **to ~ the word that** annoncer que; **word had been spread among the staff that** le bruit courait parmi les membres du personnel que; **to ~ the Word** Relig prêcher la bonne parole.
IV *vi* (*prét, pp* **spread**) **1** [*butter, margarine, jam, glue*] s'étaler; **'~s straight from the fridge'** 's'étale facilement même au sortir du réfrigérateur'; **2** (cover area or time, extend) [*forest, desert, drought, network*] s'étendre (**over** sur); [*experience*] s'étendre (**over** sur); **training can ~ over several months** la formation peut s'étendre sur plusieurs mois; **3** (proliferate, become more widespread) [*disease, infection, germs*] se propager, gagner du terrain; [*fire*] s'étendre, gagner du terrain; [*fear, confusion, panic*] se propager; [*rumour, story, scandal*] circuler, se répandre; [*stain*] s'étaler; [*pain*] se propager; **the rumour was ~ing that** le bruit courait que; **to ~ over sth** [*epidemic, disease*] se propager dans, s'étendre à [*area*]; **the news spread rapidly over the whole town** la nouvelle s'est vite répandue dans toute la ville; **the stain/the damp has spread over the whole wall** la tache/l'humidité s'est étalée sur tout le mur; **to ~ to** [*fire, disease, rioting, strike*] s'étendre à, gagner [*building, region*]; **the panic spread to the people in the street** la panique a gagné les gens qui se trouvaient dans la rue; **the fire spread from one room to another** l'incendie s'est propagé d'une pièce à l'autre; **the disease spread from the liver to the kidney** la maladie s'est propagée du foie aux reins; **the weeds spread from the garden to the path** les mauvaises herbes du jardin ont gagné le chemin; **rain will ~ to the north/to most regions during the night** la pluie va s'étendre vers le nord/à la plupart des régions pendant la nuit.
V *v refl* (*prét, pp* **spread**) **to ~ oneself** (take up space) prendre ses aises; (talk, write at length) s'étendre; **he spread himself over the sofa** il s'est étalé sur le canapé; **to ~ oneself too thin** fig faire trop de choses à la fois.
■ **spread around**, **spread about**: **~ [sth] around** faire circuler [*rumour*]; **he's been ~ing it around that** il a fait courir le bruit que.
■ **spread out**: ¶ **~ out** [*group*] se disperser (**over** sur); [*wings, tail*] se déployer; [*landscape, town, woods*] s'étendre; **~ out!** dispersez-vous!; ¶ **~ [sth] out**, **~ out [sth]** **1** (open out, unfold) étendre [*cloth, map, rug, newspaper*] (**on, over** sur); (lay, flatten out) étaler [*cloth, newspaper, map*] (**on , over** sur); **she lay spread out on the carpet** elle était étendue (de tout son long) sur la moquette; **the whole town was spread out below them** la ville tout entière s'étendait à leurs pieds; **2** (distribute over area) étaler [*cards, maps, trinkets*]; disperser [*forces, troops*]; **the houses were spread out all over the valley** les maisons étaient dispersées or disséminées dans toute la vallée; **you're too spread out, I can't get you all in the photo** vous êtes trop éloignés les uns des autres, vous n'êtes pas tous dans le cadre.

spread: **~ eagle** *n* Herald aigle *f* éployée; **~-eagled** *adj* étendu de tout son long.

spreader /ˈspredə(r)/ *n* Agric épandeur *m*, épandeuse *f*.

spreadsheet /ˈspredʃiːt/ *n* Comput tableur *m*.

spree /spriː/ *n* **to go on a ~** (drinking) faire la bringue○; **to go on a shopping ~** aller faire des folies dans les magasins; **to go on a spending ~** dépenser des sommes folles; **a drinking ~** une beuverie○; **crime ~** série *f* de délits (perpétrés par les mêmes personnes); **to go on a killing ~** être pris d'une folie meurtrière.

sprig /sprɪɡ/ *n* (of thyme, parsley, lavender etc) brin *m*; (of holly, mistletoe) petite branche *f*.

sprigged /sprɪɡd/ *adj* [*fabric, curtains*] à fleurs.

sprightliness /ˈspraɪtlɪnɪs/ *n* vivacité *f*.

sprightly /ˈspraɪtlɪ/ *adj* alerte, gaillard.

spring /sprɪŋ/ I *n* ▶ **1671** **1** (season) printemps *m*; **in the ~** au printemps; **~ is in the air** ça sent le printemps; **~ has sprung** le printemps est arrivé; **2** Tech (coil) ressort *m*; **to be like a coiled ~** fig (ready to pounce) être prêt à bondir; (tense) être tendu; **3** (leap) bond *m*; **with a ~** d'un bond; **4** (elasticity) élasticité *f*; **there's not much ~ in this mattress** ce matelas manque d'élasticité; **to have a ~ in one's step** marcher d'un pas allègre; **the good news put a ~ in his step** la bonne nouvelle lui donnait une démarche dynamique; **5** (water source) source *f*.
II *modif* [*weather, flowers, shower, sunshine*] printanier/-ière; [*day, equinox*] de printemps; [*election*] du printemps.
III *vtr* (*prét* **sprang**; *pp* **sprung**) **1** (set off) déclencher [*trap, lock*]; faire sauter [*mine*]; **2** (develop) **to ~ a leak** [*tank, barrel*] commencer à fuir; **the boat has sprung a leak** une voie d'eau s'est déclarée sur le bateau; **3** (cause to happen unexpectedly) **to ~**

sth on sb annoncer qch de but en blanc à qn [*news, plan*]; **to ~ a surprise** faire une surprise (**on** à); **I hope they don't ~ anything on us at the meeting** j'espère qu'ils ne vont pas nous faire de surprises au cours de la réunion; **4**○ (liberate) aider [qn] à faire la belle○, libérer [*prisoner*]; **5** Hunt lever [*bird, game*].

IV *vi* (*prét* **sprang**; *pp* **sprung**) **1** (jump) bondir; **to ~ across sth** traverser qch d'un bond; **to ~ at sb** [*dog, tiger*] sauter à la gorge de qn; [*person*] se jeter sur qn; **to ~ from/over sth** sauter de/par-dessus de qch; **she sprang onto the stage/up the steps** d'un bond léger elle est montée sur scène/a gravi les marches; **to ~ to one's feet** se lever d'un bond; **to ~ to fame** devenir célèbre du jour au lendemain; **2** (move suddenly) **to ~ open/shut** [*door, panel*] s'ouvrir/se fermer brusquement; **to ~ into action** [*team, troops*] passer à l'action; **to ~ to attention** [*guards*] se mettre brusquement au garde-à-vous; **to ~ to sb's defence/aid** se précipiter pour défendre/aider qn; **to ~ to sb's rescue** se précipiter au secours de qn; **tears sprang to his eyes** les larmes lui sont montées aux yeux; **the first name that sprang to mind was Rosie** le premier prénom qui m'est venu à l'esprit a été (celui de) Rosie; **to ~ into** ou **to life** [*machine, motor*] se mettre en marche or route; **3** (originate) **to ~ from** naître de [*jealousy, fear, idea, suggestion, prejudice*]; **where did these people ~ from?** d'où sortent ces gens?; **where do these files/boxes ~ from?** d'où viennent ces dossiers/cartons?

■ **spring back 1** (step back) [*person*] reculer d'un bond; **he sprang back in surprise** il a reculé de surprise; **2** (return to its position) [*lever, panel*] reprendre sa place.

■ **spring for** US: **~ for** [**sth**] payer qch.

■ **spring up 1** (get up) [*person*] se lever d'un bond; **2** (appear) [*problem*] surgir; [*weeds, flowers*] sortir de terre; [*building*] apparaître; [*wind, storm*] se lever; [*craze, trend*] apparaître; **to ~ up out of nowhere** [*celebrity, building*] surgir de nulle part.

spring: **~ balance** *n* balance *f* à ressort; **~ binder** *n* classeur *m* à anneaux; **~board** *n* Sport, fig tremplin *m* (**to, for** vers); **~bok** *n* Zool springbok *m*.

spring chicken *n* Culin jeune poulet *m*, poulette *f*.

IDIOMS **he's no ~** il n'est plus tout jeune.

spring: **~-clean** *vtr* nettoyer [qch] de fond en comble [*house*]; **~-cleaning** *n* grand nettoyage *m* de printemps.

springe /sprɪndʒ/ *n* Hunt collet *m*.

spring: **~ fever** *n* fièvre *f* printanière; **~ greens** *npl* GB Culin chou *m* de printemps; **~ gun** *n* fusil *m* piégé.

springiness /ˈsprɪŋɪnɪs/ *n* souplesse *f*.

spring: **~-like** *adj* printanier/-ière; **~-loaded** *adj* tendu par un ressort; **~ lock** *n* serrure *f* demi-tour; **~ onion** *n* GB Culin ciboule *f*; **~ roll** *n* Culin rouleau *m* de printemps; **~tide**† *n* littér printemps *m*; **~ tide** *n* Naut, Meteorol grande marée *f*, marée *f* de vive eau.

springtime /ˈsprɪŋtaɪm/ *n* lit, fig printemps *m*; **in the ~** au printemps.

spring: **~ vegetable** *n* légume *m* primeur; **~ water** *n* eau *f* de source.

springy /ˈsprɪŋɪ/ *adj* [*mattress, seat*] élastique; [*floorboards, ground, curls*] souple.

sprinkle /ˈsprɪŋkl/ **I** *n* (of salt, herb, flour) pincée *f* (**of** de); **a ~ of rain** une petite averse *f*.

II sprinkles *npl* Culin (decoration) nonpareilles *fpl*.

III *vtr* **1 to ~ sth with sth, to ~ sth on** ou **over sth** saupoudrer qch de [*salt, sugar*]; parsemer qch de [*herbs*]; **to ~ sth with water** humecter qch; **to ~ a cake with brandy** humecter un gâteau de cognac; **to ~ oneself with talc** se saupoudrer de talc; **to ~ a speech with quotations** parsemer un discours de citations; **2** (water) arroser [*lawn*].

IV sprinkled *pp adj* **~d with** saupoudré de [*salt, sugar*]; parsemé de [*herbs, flowers, quotations, mistakes*].

sprinkler /ˈsprɪŋklə(r)/ *n* **1** (for lawn) arroseur *m*; **2** (for field) (large, rotating) canon *m* arroseur; (smaller) asperseur *m*; **3** (to extinguish fires) diffuseur *m*.

sprinkler: **~ ban** *n* interdiction *f* d'arroser dans les champs; **~ system** *n* (of building) système *m* d'extinction automatique.

sprinkling /ˈsprɪŋklɪŋ/ *n* **1** (of salt, sugar, powder) petite pincée *f* (**of** de); (of snow) fine couche *f*; **a ~ of rain** une petite averse; **a ~ of an audience** fig une petite assistance; **2** (of lawn) arrosage *m*; **to need a ~** avoir besoin d'être arrosé.

sprint /sprɪnt/ **I** *n* (race) sprint *m*, course *f* de vitesse; **the final ~** lit, fig la dernière ligne droite (avant l'arrivée).

II *vi* Sport sprinter; gen piquer un sprint, faire une pointe de vitesse; **he ~ed past them** il les a dépassés en courant à toute vitesse.

sprinter /ˈsprɪntə(r)/ *n* sprinter *m*.

sprit /sprɪt/ *n* livarde *f*, baleston *f*.

sprite /spraɪt/ *n* lutin *m*, elfe *m*.

spritzer /ˈsprɪtsə(r)/ *n*: *vin blanc additionné d'eau gazeuse*.

sprocket /ˈsprɒkɪt/ *n* **1** (also **~ wheel**) gen pignon *m*; (of cinema projector) débiteur *m*; **2** (cog) dent *f* (d'engrenage).

sprog○ /sprɒg/ *n* GB **1** (child) bambin○ *m*, enfant *m*; **2** argot des militaires (new recruit) nouvelle recrue *f*, bleu○ *m*.

sprout /spraʊt/ **I** *n* **1** Bot (on plant, tree) pousse *f*; (on potato) germe *m*; **2** (also **Brussels ~**) chou *m* de Bruxelles.

II *vtr* se laisser pousser [*beard, moustache*]; **to ~ shoots** germer; **the trees are ~ing new growth** les arbres bourgeonnent; **the city has ~ed several small cinemas** plusieurs petits cinémas sont apparus dans la ville du jour au lendemain.

III *vi* **1** Bot, Hort [*bulb, tuber, onion, seed, shoot*] germer; [*grass, weeds*] pousser; **buds are ~ing on the trees** les arbres bourgeonnent; **grass was ~ing out of cracks in the path** l'herbe poussait dans les fissures de l'allée; **2** (develop) [*antlers, horns*] pousser; fig [*child*] pousser vite; **he has hair ~ing from his ears** il a des poils qui lui sortent des oreilles; **3** fig (appear) = **sprout up**.

■ **sprout up** [*plants*] surgir de terre; fig [*buildings, suburbs*] pousser comme des champignons.

spruce /spru:s/ **I** *n* **1** (also **~ tree**) épicéa *m*; **white/black ~** épinette *f* blanche/noire; **2** (wood) bois *m* d'épicéa.

II *adj* [*person*] bien soigné, pimpant; [*clothes*] impeccable, soigné; [*house, garden*] coquet/-ette, bien tenu.

■ **spruce up**: **~ up** [**sth/sb**], **~** [**sth/sb**] **up** faire beau/belle [*person*]; astiquer [*house*]; nettoyer [*garden*]; **to ~ oneself up** se mettre sur son trente et un○, se faire beau/belle; **you need to ~ yourself up a bit!** tu as besoin de t'arranger un peu!; **all ~d up** [*person*] tiré à quatre épingles; [*house, garden*] impeccable.

spruce beer *n* sapinette *f*, bière *f* d'épinette.

sprucely /ˈspru:slɪ/ *adv* **~ dressed** pimpant, tiré à quatre épingles.

spruceness /ˈspru:snɪs/ *n* (of person, clothes) élégance *f*; (of house, garden) propreté *f*.

spruce pine *n* sapinette *f*.

sprue /spru:/ *n* **1** Tech (part of mould) trou *m* de coulée; (of metal or plastic residue) carotte *f*; **2** Med sprue *f*, psilosis *m*.

sprung /sprʌŋ/ **I** *pp* ▶ **spring III, IV**.

II *adj* [*chair, mattress*] à ressorts; **a well-~ chair/bed** un fauteuil/lit souple.

sprung rhythm /sprʌŋ/ *n* Literat *type de versification à la rythmique irrégulière*.

spry /spraɪ/ *adj* alerte, gaillard.

SPUC *n* GB (*abrév* = **Society for the Protection of the Unborn Child**) *société contre l'avortement*.

spud○ /spʌd/ *n* patate○ *f*, pomme *f* de terre.

spud bashing○ *n* GB argot des militaires corvée *f* de patates○.

spume /spju:m/ *n* écume *f*.

spun /spʌn/ **I** *pret, pp* ▶ **spin II, III**.

II *adj* [*glass, gold, sugar*] filé; **hair like ~ gold** littér des cheveux d'or.

spunk /spʌŋk/ *n* **1**○ (courage, spirit) cran○ *m*, courage *m*; **2**● GB (semen) foutre● *m*.

spunky○ /ˈspʌŋkɪ/ *adj* plein de cran○ or d'audace.

spun: **~ silk** *n* schappe *f*; **~ yarn** *n* bitord *m*.

spur /spɜ:(r)/ **I** *n* **1** fig (stimulus) motif *m*; **to be the ~ for** ou **of sth** être la raison de qch; **to act as a ~ to** être une incitation à [*crime, action*]; **2** (for horse, on dog's or cock's leg) éperon *m*; **to wear ~s** porter des éperons; **to dig in one's ~s** donner de l'éperon; **3** Geol contrefort *m*; **4** Rail (also **~ track**) embranchement *m*.

II *vtr* (*p prés etc* **-rr-**) **1** (stimulate) encourager [*economic growth, increase, advance*]; inciter [*action, reaction, response*]; **to ~ sb to sth/to do** inciter qn à qch/à faire; **to ~ sb into action** inciter qn à agir; **~red by this event,...** encouragé par cet événement ,...; **2** [*rider*] éperonner [*horse*]; **to ~ one's horse into a gallop** éperonner son cheval et partir au galop.

III *vi* littér (*prés etc* **-rr-**) (ride hard) **to ~ towards sth** piquer des éperons en direction de qch.

IDIOMS **on the ~ of the moment** sur l'impulsion du moment; **a ~-of-the-moment decision** une décision du moment; **to win one's ~s** faire ses preuves.

■ **spur forward** = **spur on**.

■ **spur on**: ¶ **~ on**† [*rider*] piquer des éperons; ¶ **~** [**sth**] **on**, **~ on** [**sth**] [*rider*] lancer [qch] d'un coup d'éperon [*horse*] (**towards** vers); ¶ **~ on** [**sb**], **~** [**sb**] **on** [*success, good sign, legislation, government*] encourager; [*fear, threat, example , hero*] stimuler; **to ~ sb on to greater efforts** inciter qn à redoubler d'efforts; **~red on by their success** encouragés par leur réussite.

spurge /spɜ:dʒ/ *n* euphorbe *f*.

spur gear *n* engrenage *m* droit.

spurge laurel *n* daphné *m* lauréolé, bois *m* gentil.

spurious /ˈspjʊərɪəs/ péj *adj* [*argument, notion, allegation, claim*] fallacieux/-ieuse; [*excuse*] inventé; [*evidence, documents, credentials*] faux/fausse; [*sentiment*] feint; [*glamour, appeal*] faux/fausse, superficiel/-ielle.

spuriously /ˈspjʊərɪəslɪ/ *adv* péj de façon fausse or douteuse.

spuriousness /ˈspjʊərɪəsnɪs/ *n* péj caractère *m* faux or douteux.

spurn /spɜ:n/ *vtr* refuser [qch] (avec mépris) [*advice, offer, help, gift*]; éconduire [*suitor*].

spur road *n* GB embranchement *m*.

spurt /spɜ:t/ **I** *n* **1** (gush) (of water, oil, blood) giclée *f*; (of flame) jaillissement *m*; (of steam) jet *m*; **to come out in ~s** [*liquid*] sortir en giclant; **2** (burst) (of energy) sursaut *m*; (of activity, enthusiasm) regain *m*; (in growth) poussée *f*; **to put on a ~** [*runner, cyclist*] pousser une pointe de vitesse; [*worker*] donner un coup de collier○; **to do sth in ~s** faire qch par à-coups.

II *vtr* **to ~ flames** cracher or vomir du feu; **the wound was ~ing blood** le sang giclait de la blessure; **the pipes are ~ing water** l'eau jaillit des tuyaux.

III *vi* **1** (gush) [*liquid*] jaillir, gicler (**from, out of** de); [*flames*] jaillir (**from, out of** de); **2** (speed up) [*runner, cyclist*] pousser une pointe de vitesse.

■ **spurt out**: ¶ **~ out** [*flames, liquid*] jaillir; ¶ **~ out [sth]**, **~ [sth] out** = **spurt** II.

spur ~ track *n* Rail embranchement *m*; **~ wheel** *n* roue *f* droite.

sputnik /ˈspʊtnɪk/ *n* spoutnik *m*.

sputter /ˈspʌtə(r)/ *n, vtr, vi* = **splutter**.

sputum /ˈspjuːtəm/ *n* ¢ crachat *m*, expectorations *fpl*.

spy /spaɪ/ **I** *n* (political, industrial) espion/-ionne *m/f*; (for police) indicateur/-trice *m/f*, indic○ *mf*; **to work as a ~ for sb** être un espion à la solde de qn.
II *modif* [*film, novel, network, scandal*] d'espionnage; [*trial*] pour espionnage.
III *vtr* remarquer, discerner [*figure, object*]; **she spied them approaching the window** elle les a remarqués qui s'approchaient de la fenêtre.
IV *vi* **1** Pol **to ~ on** [*army, military, manoeuvres, weapons*] espionner; **to ~ for sb** faire de l'espionnage pour le compte de qn; **2** fig (observe) **to ~ on** espionner [*person*]; épier [*movements*].
IDIOMS **I ~ with my little eye...** (game) *jeu de devinette*.
■ **spy out**: **~ out [sth]**, **~ [sth] out** découvrir [*plan, activity*]; **to ~ out the land** s'enquérir de la situation.

spy: **~ glass** *n* longue-vue *f*; **~hole** *n* judas *m*.

spying /ˈspaɪɪŋ/ *n* espionnage *m*.

spy: **~-in-the-cab**○ *n* tachygraphe *m*; **~-in-the-sky**○ *n* satellite-espion *m*; **~master** *n* maître-espion *m*; **~ ring** *n* réseau *m* d'espionnage; **~ satellite** *n* satellite-espion *m*.

sq. (*abrév écrite* = **square**) Math carré; **10 ~ m** 10 m^2.

Sq *abrév écrite* = **Square**.

Sqn Ldr *n* GB *abrév écrite* = **squadron leader**.

squab /skwɒb/ *n* **1** Zool pigeonneau *m*; **2**○ hum ou péj (fat person) pot *m* à tabac○; **3** GB (cushion) coussin *m*.

squabble /ˈskwɒbl/ **I** *n* dispute *f*, prise *f* de bec○.
II *vi* se disputer, se chamailler○ (**over, about** à propos de).

squabbler /ˈskwɒblə(r)/ *n* chamailleur/-euse○ *m/f*, querelleur/-euse *m/f*.

squabbling /ˈskwɒblɪŋ/ *n* ¢ chamailleries○ *fpl*, disputes *fpl*.

squad /skwɒd/ *n* gen, Mil escouade *f*; Sport (from which team is selected) sélection *f*; **the Olympics ~** les athlètes sélectionnés pour les Jeux olympiques; **the England/Germany ~** (in football etc) la sélection britannique/allemande.

squad car *n* voiture *f* de police.

squaddie○ /ˈskwɒdɪ/ *n* GB bidasse○ *m*, soldat *m*.

squadron /ˈskwɒdrən/ *n* GB Mil (of armoured regiment) escadron *m*; Aviat, Naut escadrille *f*.

squadron leader ▶ 1612 *n* GB Aviat, Mil commandant *m* (*de l'armée de l'air*).

squadroom /ˈskwɒdruːm, -rʊm/ *n* US salle *f* d'un poste de police.

squalid /ˈskwɒlɪd/ *adj* [*house, street, surroundings*] sordide, misérable; [*furnishings, clothes*] crasseux/-euse; [*business, affair, story*] sordide.

squall /skwɔːl/ **I** *n* **1** Meteorol bourrasque *f*, rafale *f* (**of** de); (at sea) grain *m*; **2** fig (quarrel) dispute *f* (violente); **3** (cry) hurlement *m*.
II *vi* [*baby*] hurler, brailler.

squall line *n* Meteorol ligne *f* de grains.

squally /ˈskwɔːlɪ/ *adj* [*wind*] qui souffle en rafales; [*day*] avec des bourrasques fréquentes.

squalor /ˈskwɒlə(r)/ *n* (of house, street, conditions, surroundings, life) caractère *m* sordide, misère *f* (noire); **to live in ~** (great poverty) vivre dans la misère (noire).

squander /ˈskwɒndə(r)/ *vtr* dilapider [*money, fortune, inheritance*] (**on** en); gaspiller [*opportunities, talents, resources, time*]; gâcher, dissiper liter [*youth, health*].

squanderer /ˈskwɒndərə(r)/ *n* gaspilleur/-euse *m/f*.

square /skweə(r)/ **I** *n* **1** (in town) place *f*; (in barracks) cour *f*; **main ~** grand-place *f*; **town ~** place *f* (de la ville); **village ~** place *f* du village; **2** (four-sided shape) carré *m*; (in board game, crossword) case *f*; (of glass, linoleum) carreau *m*; **to arrange/fold sth into a ~** disposer/plier qch en carré; **to divide a page up into ~s** quadriller une feuille; **a pattern of blue and white ~s** un motif à carreaux bleus et blancs; **3** Math (self-multiplied) carré *m*; **9 is the ~ of 3** 9 est le carré de 3; **4** Math, Tech (for right angles) équerre *f*; **5**○ (old-fashioned) ringard/-e *m/f*.
II on the square *adv phr* **1** (at 90°) au carré, à angle droit; **to cut sth on the ~** couper qch au carré or à angle droit; **2**○ (honest) honnête, réglo○ *inv*; **is the business on the ~○?** l'affaire est réglo?; **to do things on the ~** faire les choses dans les règles.
III *adj* **1** (right-angled) [*shape, hole, building, box, jaw, face, shoulders*] carré; (correctly aligned) bien droit; **the photo should be ~ with the frame** il faut mettre la photo bien droit dans le cadre; **the shelf isn't ~ with the sideboard** l'étagère est de travers par rapport au buffet; **a man of ~ build** un homme trapu; **2** ▶ 1771 Math, Meas [*metre, mile, kilometre, centimetre*] carré; **four ~ metres** quatre mètres carrés ; **an area four metres/kilometres ~** une surface de quatre mètres/kilomètres sur quatre; **the Square Mile** GB Econ la City (*cœur financier de Londres*); **3** fig (balanced, level, quits) **to be (all) ~** [*books, accounts*] être équilibré; [*people*] être quitte; [*teams, players*] être à égalité; **I'll give you £5 and we'll be ~** je te donnerai cinq livres et nous serons quittes; **they're all ~ at two all, it's all ~ at two all** ils sont à égalité or il y a égalité à deux partout; **to get the accounts ~** balancer les comptes; **4** (honest) [*person, transaction*] honnête (**with** avec); **a ~ deal** une proposition honnête; **to give sb a ~ deal** traiter qn de façon honnête; **5**○ (boring) vieux jeux *inv* (*after verb*), ringard.
IV *adv* (directly) [*fall, hit, strike*] en plein milieu; **he hit me ~ on the jaw** il m'a frappé en plein dans la mâchoire; **she looked me ~ in the eye** elle m'a regardé droit dans les yeux.
V *vtr* **1** lit (make right-angled) équarrir [*stone, timber*]; couper [qch] au carré or à angle droit [*corner, end, section*]; **to ~ one's shoulders** redresser les épaules; **2** (settle) régler [*account, debt, creditor*]; **to ~ one's account(s) with sb** lit, fig régler ses comptes avec qn; **3** Sport (equalize) égaliser [*score, series*]; **4** (win over) (by persuasion) s 'occuper de [*person*]; (by bribery) graisser la patte à○ [*person*]; **I'll ~ him** je m'occuperai de lui; **go home early, I'll ~ it with the boss** pars avant l'heure, j'arrangerai ça avec le patron; **I have problems ~ing this with my conscience/my beliefs** j'ai du mal à concilier cette action avec ma conscience/mes croyances.
VI squared *pp adj* **1** [*paper*] quadrillé; **2** Math [*number*] au carré; **6 ~d is 36** 6 au carré égale 36.
IDIOMS **to go back to ~ one** retourner à la case départ, recommencer; **to be back at ~ one** se retrouver au point de départ; **to be on the ~○** GB être franc-maçon; **to be out of ~** ne pas être d'équerre; ▶ **circle**.
■ **square off**: **~ off [sth]**, **~ [sth] off** équarrir [*end, edge, section*].
■ **square up**: ¶ **~ up 1** (prepare to fight) lit se mettre en garde (**to** face à); fig faire face (**to** à); **to ~ up for** se préparer pour [*fight, row*]; **2** (settle accounts) régler ses comptes; **I'll ~ up with you tomorrow** nous règlerons nos comptes demain; ¶ **~ up [sth]**, **~ [sth] up 1** (cut straight) couper [qch] au carré [*paper, wood, corner*]; **2** (align correctly) mettre [qch] bien droit; **~ the picture up with the mirror** mets le tableau bien droit par rapport au miroir.
■ **square with**: **~ with [sth]** (be consistent with) correspondre à, cadrer avec [*evidence, fact, statement, theory*].

square-bashing○ *n* GB Mil exercices *mpl*.

square bracket *n* crochet *m*; **in ~s** entre crochets.

square: **~ dance** *n* quadrille *m*; **~ dancing** *n* ¢ quadrille *m* américain; **~-faced** *adj* au visage carré; **~-jawed** *adj* à la mâchoire carrée; **~ knot** *n* US nœud *m* plat.

squarely /ˈskweəlɪ/ *adv* **1** (directly) [*strike, hit, land*] lit en plein milieu; **to look ~ at** regarder [qch] bien en face [*problem, situation*]; **to look at sb ~** regarder qn droit dans les yeux; **to position oneself ~ behind sth** se mettre directement derrière qch; **2** (honestly) honnêtement; **3** (fully) **the blame rests ~ on his shoulders** la responsabilité repose entièrement sur lui; **to knock sth ~ on the head** se débarrasser définitivement de [*racism, prejudice*]; **to fit ~ into the liberal mould** ou **tradition** s'inscrire parfaitement dans la tradition libérale.

square meal *n* bon repas *m*, vrai repas *m*; **three ~s a day** trois bons repas par jour; **she hasn't had a ~ for weeks** elle n'a pas fait un vrai repas depuis des semaines.

square: **~ measure** *n* mesure *f* de superficie; **~-rigged** *adj* gréé (en) carré; **~ root** *n* racine *f* carrée; **~-shouldered** *adj* aux épaules carrées; **~-toed** *adj* [*shoes*] à bout carré.

squash /skwɒʃ/ **I** *n* **1** Sport ▶ 1282 (also **~ rackets**) squash *m*; **2** (drink) sirop *m*; **3** (vegetable) courge *f*; **4** (crush) cohue *f*; **it will be a bit of a ~** on va être un peu entassé.
II *modif* Sport [*club, court, player, racket*] de squash.
III *vtr* **1** (crush) écraser [*fruit, insect, person*] (**against** contre; **between** entre); aplatir [*hat*]; **to be ~ed out of shape** [*car, toy*] être complètement écrasé; [*box*] être complètement déformé; **2** (force) **to ~ sth/sb into** entasser qch/qn dans [*box, car*]; **3** (put down) rabattre le caquet à○ [*person*]; écraser [*revolt, rebellion*]; stopper [*rumour*]; **to feel ~ed** se sentir humilié; **4** (reject) rejeter [*idea, proposal*].
IV *vi* **1** (become crushed) s'écraser; **to ~ easily** s'écraser facilement; **2** (pack tightly) [*people*] s'entasser (**into** dans); **to ~ through a gap** réussir à se glisser par une ouverture.
■ **squash in**○: ¶ **~ in** se faire de la place; ¶ **~ in [sth/sb]**, **~ [sth/sb] in** trouver de la place pour.
■ **squash up**○: **~ up** [*person*] se tasser (**against** contre); [*crowd*] se serrer (**against** contre); **if I ~ up you can fit in** si je me serre ça te fera de la place; **to ~ sb up against** écraser qn contre; **to ~ oneself up against** s'aplatir contre.

squashy○ /ˈskwɒʃɪ/ *adj* mou/molle.

squat /skwɒt/ **I** *n* **1** (position) position *f* accroupie; **2**○ (home) squat○ *m*.
II *adj* [*person, structure, object*] trapu.
III○ *vtr* (*p prés etc* **-tt-**) squattériser○, squatter○ [*house, building*].
IV *vi* (*p prés etc* **-tt-**) **1** (crouch) être accroupi; **2** (also **~ down**) s'accroupir; **3** (inhabit) **to ~ in** squattériser○, squatter○ [*building*].

squatter /ˈskwɒtə(r)/ *n* **1** squatter○ *m*; **2** Austral squatter *m* (*éleveur de moutons utilisant des terrains loués au gouvernement*).

squatter's rights *npl*: *possibilité de devenir propriétaire d'un terrain après l'avoir occupé un certain nombre d'années.*

squatting /ˈskwɒtɪŋ/ **I** *n* squat○ *m*.
II *adj* **1** [*position, person*] accroupi; **2**○ [*homeless person, teenager*] qui squattérise○ or squatte○.

squaw /skwɔː/ *n* **1** injur (North American Indian

woman) squaw *f*, Indienne *f* d'Amérique du Nord; **2**○ (woman) péj femme *f*.

squawk /skwɔ:k/ **I** *n* (of hen) gloussement *m*; (of duck, parrot, crow etc) cri *m* rauque; fig péj (of person) cri *m* aigu.
II *vtr* péj [*person*] crier; **'what?' he ~ed** 'quoi?' cria-t-il.
III *vi* [*hen*] pousser des gloussements; [*duck, parrot, crow etc*] pousser des cris rauques; [*baby*] brailler; [*person*] crier d'une voix hystérique.

squawk box○ *n* (loudspeaker) haut-parleur *m*.

squaw man *n* US péj *mari nonindien d'une Indienne d'Amérique du Nord*.

squeak /skwi:k/ **I** *n* **1** (noise) (of door, wheel, mechanism, chalk) grincement *m*; (of mouse, soft toy) couinement *m*; (of furniture, shoes) craquement *m*; (of infant) vagissement *m*; **to let out** ou **give a ~ (of surprise)** pousser un petit cri (d'étonnement); **without a ~**○ [*accept, give in*] sans broncher; **there wasn't a ~ from her**○ elle n'a pas émis le moindre mot; **2**○ (escape) **that was a narrow ~** on l'a échappé belle○.
II *vtr* **to ~ (out)** glapir; **'No!,' he ~ed** 'Non!,' glapit-il.
III *vi* **1** (make noise) [*child*] glapir; [*door, wheel, mechanism, chalk*] grincer; [*mouse, bat, soft toy*] couiner; [*shoes, furniture*] craquer (**on** sur); **2**○ (with minimal success) **to ~ through** réussir de justesse [*selection, process, trial*].

squeaky /'skwi:kɪ/ *adj* [*voice*] aigu/-uë; [*gate, hinge, wheel*] grinçant; **~ shoes** des chaussures qui craquent.

squeaky-clean○ *adj* **1** [*hair, dishes, house*] propre et net; **2** fig péj [*person*] trop parfait; [*company*] à l'image trop soignée; **a ~ (public) image** une image de marque trop soignée.

squeal /skwi:l/ **I** *n* (of animal, person) cri *m* aigu; (of brakes) grincement *m*; (of tyres) crissement *m*; **a ~ of pain/excitement** un cri aigu de douleur/d'excitation; **~s of laughter** des rires perçants; **to give** ou **let out a ~** pousser un cri aigu.
II *vtr* **'let go!' she ~ed** 'lâche-moi!' cria-t-elle d'une voix perçante.
III *vi* **1** [*person, animal*] pousser des cris aigus (**in, with** de); **to ~ with delight** pousser des cris de joie; **to ~ with laughter** rire d'une voix aiguë; **2**○ (inform) cafarder○, vendre la mèche○; **to ~ on sb** balancer○ qn; **someone ~ed to the police!** quelqu'un nous a balancés○ à la police!

squealer○ /'skwi:lə(r)/ *n* péj mouchard/-e *m/f*.

squeamish /'skwi:mɪʃ/ *adj* **1** (easily sickened) qui a l'estomac délicat; (by screen violence etc) impressionnable; **don't be so ~!** ne fais pas le délicat!; **he's too ~ to be a surgeon** il est trop émotif pour devenir chirurgien; **he's ~ about snakes** les serpents le dégoûtent; **this film is not for the ~** ce film n'est pas pour les âmes sensibles; **2** (prudish) prude.

squeamishness /'skwi:mɪʃnɪs/ *n* **1** (quality of being easily sickened) (about unpleasant sights, topics etc) trop grande délicatesse *f*; (about violence, bloodshed) émotivité *f*; **2** (prudishness) pruderie *f*.

squeegee /'skwi:dʒi:/ *n* **1** Phot raclette *f*; **2** (cleaning device) (for windows) raclette *f*; (for floor) balai-éponge *m*.

squeeze /skwi:z/ **I** *n* **1** (application of pressure) **to give sth a ~** presser qch [*hand, tube*]; **to give sb a ~** serrer qn dans ses bras; **2** (small amount) **a ~ of lemon** quelques gouttes de citron; **a ~ of glue/toothpaste** un peu de colle/dentifrice; **3** Econ, Fin resserrement *m* (**on** de); **wage ~** resserrement *m* des salaires; **to feel the ~** [*person, company, family*] se sentir coincé financièrement; **to put the ~ on**○ [*lenders*] faire pression sur [*debtors*]; **4**○ (crush) **we can all get in the car but it will be a (tight) ~** on peut tous monter dans la voiture mais on sera serré; **I can get past, but it will be a tight ~** je peux passer mais ce sera un peu juste; **5** Games squeeze *m*.
II *vtr* **1** (press) presser [*lemon, bottle, tube*]; serrer [*arm, hand*]; appuyer sur [*bag, parcel, trigger*]; percer [*spot*]; **to ~ glue/toothpaste onto sth** mettre de la colle/du dentifrice sur qch; **to ~ juice out of a lemon** extraire le jus d'un citron; **to ~ water out of** faire sortir de l'eau de [*cloth*]; **2** fig (manage to get) **he ~d three meals out of one chicken** fig il a tiré trois repas d'un seul poulet; **I ~d £10/a loan out of dad** j'ai réussi à obtenir 10 livres/un prêt de papa; **to ~ the truth/a confession out of sb** arracher la vérité/un aveu à qn; **3** (fit) **we can ~ a few more people into the room/van** on a encore de la place pour quelques personnes dans la salle /la camionnette; **I ~d a couple more lines onto the page** j'ai fait tenir quelques lignes en plus sur la page; **I managed to ~ the car through the gap** j'ai tout juste réussi à faire passer la voiture par l'ouverture; **I can just ~ into that dress** je tiens tout juste dans cette robe; **to ~ behind/between/under sth** se glisser derrière/entre/sous qch; **4** Econ, Fin resserrer [*profit, margins*]; **small businesses are being ~d by high interest rates** les petites sociétés sont asphyxiées par des taux d'intérêt élevés.
■ **squeeze in**: ¶ **~ in** [*person*] se glisser; **if you make room I can ~ in** si vous faites de la place je pourrai tenir; **she ~d in between her brothers** elle s'est glissée entre ses frères; ¶ **~ [sb] in** (give appointment to) [*doctor etc*] faire passer [qn] entre deux rendez-vous.
■ **squeeze out**: ¶ **~ out** [*person*] arriver à sortir; ¶ **~ [sth] out** extraire [*juice, water*]; **to ~ water out of** essorer [*cloth, sponge*]; ¶ **~ [sb] out (of the market)** Comm pousser qn hors du marché.
■ **squeeze past**: ¶ **~ past** [*car, person*] passer; ¶ **~ past [sth/sb]** passer à côté de [*obstacle, person*].
■ **squeeze up** [*people*] se serrer.

squeeze: **~ bottle** *n* US bouteille *f* en plastique souple; **~ box**○ *n* Mus accordéon *m*.

squelch /skweltʃ/ **I** *n* (noise) bruit *m* de succion; **to fall to the ground with a ~** tomber par terre avec un grand floc; **the ~ of water in their boots** le flic flac de l'eau dans leurs bottes.
II *vi* [*water, mud*] glouglouter, faire un bruit de succion; **to ~ along/in/out** avancer/entrer/sortir en pataugeant; **they ~ed through the swamp** ils pataugeaient dans le marécage.

squelchy /'skweltʃɪ/ *adj* [*ground, mud*] boueux/-euse; [*fruit, tomato*] mou/molle, ramolli; [*noise*] de succion.

squib /skwɪb/ *n* pétard *m*.
IDIOMS **to be a damp ~**○ GB [*event*] tomber à plat, être décevant; [*venture, revelation*] être un pétard mouillé○.

squid /skwɪd/ *n* calmar *m*, encornet *m*.

squidgy○ /'skwɪdʒɪ/ *adj* GB moelleux/-euse.

squiffy○ /'skwɪfɪ/ *adj* GB pompette○, éméché○.

squiggle /'skwɪgl/ **I** *n* (wavy line) gen ligne *f* ondulée; (written) gribouillis *m*.
II *vi* gribouiller, faire des gribouillis.

squint /skwɪnt/ **I** *n* **1** Med (strabismus) strabisme *m*; **to have a ~** loucher, être affecté de strabisme spec; **2**○ (look) **to have a/take a ~ at sth** jeter un coup d'œil sur qch, zieuter● qch.
II *vi* **1** gen (look narrowly) **to ~** plisser les yeux; **to ~ at sb/sth** regarder qn/qch en plissant les yeux; **to ~ through** lorgner par [*window, peephole*]; lorgner dans [*viewfinder*]; **2** Med loucher.

squirarchy *n* = **squirearchy**.

squire /'skwaɪə(r)/ **I** *n* **1** (country gentleman) ≈ châtelain *m*; **2** Hist (knight's retainer) écuyer *m*; **3**○ GB (form of address) **cheerio ~**○! GB hum salut, chef○ *m*!; **4** US (judge) juge *m* (de paix), magistrat *m*; (lawyer) avocat *m*.
II† *vtr* accompagner, escorter [*woman*].

squirearchy /'skwaɪərɑ:kɪ/ *n* aristocratie *f* terrienne, hobereaux *mpl* pej.

squirm /skwɜ:m/ *vi* (wriggle) [*snake, worm etc*] se tortiller; [*fish*] frétiller; [*kitten, puppy*] remuer; [*person*] (in pain, agony) se tordre; fig (with embarrassment) [[*person*]] être très mal à l'aise, être au supplice; (with revulsion) être écœuré, avoir la nausée; **to make sb ~** (with embarrassment) rendre qn mal à l'aise; (with revulsion) écœurer qn; **he ~ed on his chair** il se tortillait sur sa chaise tellement il était gêné.

squirrel /'skwɪrəl, US 'skwɜ:rəl/ **I** *n* écureuil *m*.
II *modif* [*garment*] en petit-gris.
■ **squirrel away**○: **~ [sth] away, ~ away [sth]** mettre [qch] de côté.

squirrel: **~-cage** *adj* [*motor, rotor*] à cage d'écureuil; **~ monkey** *n* saïmiri *m*.

squirrel(l)y○ /'skwɪrəlɪ, US 'skwɜ:rəlɪ/ *adj* US bizarre.

squirt /skwɜ:t/ **I** *n* **1** (jet) (of water, oil) jet *m*, giclée *f*; (of paint) jet *m*; **2** (small amount) goutte *f*; **3**○ pej (person) **a little ~** un petit morveux○.
II *vtr* faire gicler [*liquid*] (**from, out of** de); **he ~ed some soda water into the glass** il a versé une giclée d'eau de Seltz dans le verre; **she ~ed some oil into the lock** elle a injecté de l'huile dans la serrure; **to ~ water/ink at sb, ~ sb with water/ink** asperger qn d'eau/d'encre; **she ~ed some perfume onto her wrist** elle s'est vaporisé du parfum sur le poignet.
III *vi* [*liquid*] jaillir (**from, out of** de).
■ **squirt out**: ¶ **~ out** [*water, oil*] jaillir (**of , from** de); ¶ **~ [sth] out, ~ out [sth]** faire gicler [*liquid, paste, paint*] (**of** de).
■ **squirt up** [*liquid*] jaillir.

squirt: **~ gun** *n* US, Can pistolet *m* à eau; **~ing cucumber** *n* concombre *m* d'âne.

Sr 1 *abrév écrite* = **Senior**; **2** *abrév écrite* = **Sister**.

Sri Lanka /ˌsri: 'læŋkə/ **▶ 1131** *pr n* Sri Lanka *m*.

Sri Lankan /ˌsri: 'læŋkən/ **▶ 1486** **I** *n* Sri-Lankais/-e *m/f*.
II *adj* sri-lankais.

SRN *n* GB *abrév* ▶ **State Registered Nurse**.

SS 1 Naut (*abrév* = **steamship**) **the ~ Titanic** le Titanic; **2** Mil Hist **the ~** les SS *mpl*; **3** Relig *abrév écrite* = **Saints**.

SSA *n* US *abrév* ▶ **Social Security Administration**.

SSSI *n* GB (*abrév* = **Site of Special Scientific Interest**) site *m* d'intérêt scientifique.

st *n* GB *abrév écrite* = **stone**.

St *n* **1** *abrév écrite* = **Saint**; **2** *abrév écrite* = **Street**.

stab /stæb/ **I** *n* **1** (act) coup *m* de couteau; **a ~ in the back** fig un coup en traître; **2** fig (of pain) élancement *m* (**of** de); (of anger, jealousy, guilt) accès *m* (**of** de); **a ~ of fear** une peur soudaine; **3**○ (attempt) essai *m*, tentative *f*; **to make** ou **take a ~ at sth/at doing** s'essayer à qch/à faire; **go on, have a ~ at it!** vas-y, essaye!
II *vtr* (*p prés etc* **-bb-**) **1** (pierce) donner un coup de couteau à, poignarder [*person*]; piquer dans [*meat, piece of food*]; **to ~ sb to death** poignarder qn à mort, tuer qn à coups de couteau; **to ~ sb in the heart** plonger or planter un poignard dans le cœur de qn; **to ~ sb in the back** lit, fig poignarder qn dans le dos; **2** (poke hard) frapper [*person, object*]; **to ~ at sth with one's finger** frapper qch du doigt.
III *v refl* (*p prés etc* **-bb-**) **to ~ oneself** (accidentally) se blesser avec un couteau; (deliberately) se donner un coup de couteau; **to ~**

oneself in the arm se blesser le bras avec un couteau.

stabbing /ˈstæbɪŋ/ **I** *n* agression *f* au couteau.
II *adj* [*pain*] lancinant.

stabile /ˈsteɪbaɪl, -bɪl/ **I** *n* stabile *m*.
II *adj* gen, Chem stable.

stability /stəˈbɪlətɪ/ *n* **1** (steadiness) gen stabilité *f*; (of character) constance *f*; **to give** ou **lend ~ to** apporter une stabilité à; **2** Chem stabilité *f*.

stabilization /ˌsteɪbəlaɪˈzeɪʃn, US -lɪˈz-/ **I** *n* stabilisation *f*.
II *modif* [*measure, policy, programme*] de stabilisation.

stabilize /ˈsteɪbəlaɪz/ **I** *vtr* gen stabiliser; Med rendre [qch] plus stable [*medical condition*].
II *vi* (all contexts) se stabiliser.
III stabilizing *pres p adj* [*effect, influence*] stabilisateur/-trice.

stabilizer /ˈsteɪbəlaɪzə(r)/ *n* **1** Aviat, Naut, Tech (device) stabilisateur *m*; **horizontal/vertical ~** US Aviat empennage *m* horizontal/vertical; **2** (substance) stabilisant *m*.

stabilizer bar *n* US barre *f* stabilisatrice (antiroulis).

stable /ˈsteɪbl/ **I** *n* **1** (building) écurie *f*; **2** Turf (of racehorses) écurie *f* (de courses); **3** fig (of companies, publications) empire *m*; (of people) équipe *f*; (of racing cars) écurie *f*.
II stables *npl* écurie *f*; **riding ~s** manège *m*.
III *adj* **1** (steady) [*economy, situation, background, relationship, construction, job*] stable; [*medical condition*] stable, stationnaire; **his condition is said to be ~** son état a été déclaré stationnaire; **2** (psychologically) [*person, temperament, character*] équilibré, stable; **3** Chem, Phys [*substance, compound*] stable.
IV *vtr* mettre [qch] à l'écurie [*horse*].

stable: **~ block** *n* écuries *fpl*; **~ boy** ▶ **1692** *n* gen garçon *m* d'étable, palefrenier/-ière *m/f*; Turf lad *m*; **~ companion** *n* cheval *m* de la même écurie.

stable door *n* porte *f* d'écurie.
IDIOMS **to close** ou **lock the ~ after the horse has bolted** fermer la cage quand les oiseaux se sont envolés.

stable: **~ fly** *n* mouche *f* des étables; **~ girl** ▶ **1692** *n* palefrenière *f*; **~ lad** = **stable boy**; **~man** ▶ **1692** *n* palefrenier *m*; **~mate** *n* cheval *m* de la même écurie; fig membre *m* de la même organisation; **~ yard** *n* cour *f* de l'écurie.

stabling /ˈsteɪblɪŋ/ *n* ₵ écuries *fpl*.

stab wound *n* coup *m* de couteau (*blessure*).

staccato /stəˈkɑːtəʊ/ **I** *adj* **1** Mus [*notes, vocals*] staccato *inv*; **2** gen [*gasps, shots*] saccadé.
II *adv* [*play*] staccato.

stack /stæk/ **I** *n* **1** (pile) (of hay, straw) meule *f*; (of books, papers, plates, wood) tas *m*, pile *f*; (of chairs) pile *f*; (of rifles) faisceau *m*; **2** (chimney) cheminée *f*; **3** Geol (in sea) cheminée *f*; **4** Comput pile *f*.
II stacks *npl* **1** (in library) rayons *mpl*; **2**○ **~s of** des tas de○, plein de○; **~s**○ **of food** des tas○ de or plein○ de choses à manger; **I've got ~s**○ **of work to do** j'ai plein○ de travail à faire; **we've got ~s**○ **of time** nous avons tout notre temps; **he has ~s**○ **of money** il est bourré de fric○.
III *vtr* **1** Agric mettre [qch] en meule [*hay, straw*]; **2** (also **~ up**) (pile) empiler [*boxes, books, plates, chairs*]; **~ing chairs** chaises *fpl* superposables; **3** (fill) remplir [*shelves*]; **4** Aviat, Telecom mettre [qch] en attente [*planes, calls*]; **5** (in cards) piper; **6**○ US péj sélectionner [qch] de manière partiale [*jury, committee*] (**against** afin de défavoriser, **for** afin de favoriser).
IDIOMS **to blow one's ~**○ se mettre en boule○; **to be well-~ed**○ US être bien roulé○; **to have the odds** ou **cards ~ed against one** ne pas avoir tous les atouts dans son jeu, être défavorisé.
■ **stack up**: ¶ **~ up**○ US (compare) se comparer (**against, with** avec); ¶ **~ up [sth], ~ [sth] up** empiler [*objects*].

stacker /ˈstækə(r)/ *n* (person, device) chargeur *m*.

stacking /ˈstækɪŋ/ *n* Aviat mise *f* en attente (*en altitude*).

stadium /ˈsteɪdɪəm/ *n* (*pl* **-iums** ou **-ia**) stade *m*.

staff /stɑːf, US stæf/ **I** *n* **1** (*pl* **staves** /steɪvz/ ou **~s**) (stick) (for walking) canne *f*; (crozier) crosse *f*; (as weapon) bâton *m*; **to lean on one's ~** prendre appui sur sa canne; **2** (*pl* **~s**) (employees) personnel *m*; **clerical/kitchen ~** personnel de bureau/de cuisine; **to be on the ~ of a company** faire partie du personnel d'une entreprise; **a small business with a ~ of ten** une petite entreprise de dix employés; **to join/leave the ~** (of a company) entrer dans/quitter l'entreprise; **3** ₵ (also **teaching ~**) Sch, Univ personnel *m* enseignant; **member of ~** enseignant/-e *m/f*; **to join the ~** prendre un poste de professeur; **to be on the ~** faire partie du corps enseignant; **a ~ of 50** un effectif de 50 enseignants; **4** ₵ Mil état-major *m*; **5** (*pl* **staves** /steɪvz/ ou **~s**) Mus portée *f*.
II *vtr* [*owner*] trouver du personnel pour [*company, business*]; **to ~ a company** [*recruitment agency*] pourvoir une société en personnel; **how are we going to ~ our school?** où allons-nous trouver du personnel enseignant?; **the restaurant is entirely ~ed by Italians** tout le personnel du restaurant est italien; **the school is under-~ed** l'école manque d'enseignants.

staff: **~ association** *n* association *f* du personnel; **~ college** *n* Mil ≈ école *f* supérieure de guerre; **~ discount** *n* rabais *m* accordé au personnel.

staffing /ˈstɑːfɪŋ, US ˈstæf-/ *n* **the company is having ~ problems** la société a des problèmes de recrutement.

staffing levels *npl* nombre *m* d'employés.

staff: **~ meeting** *n* Sch réunion *f* du personnel enseignant; **~ nurse** *n* infirmier/-ière *m/f*; **~ officer** ▶ **1612** *n* officier *m* d'état-major; **~ of life** *n* littér aliment *m* de la vie; **~ of office** *n* bâton *m* de commandement.

Staffordshire /ˈstæfədʃə(r)/ ▶ **1624** *pr n* Staffordshire *m*.

staff: **~-pupil ratio** *n* rapport *m* élève-enseignant; **~ room** *n* Sch salle *f* des professeurs.

Staffs *n* GB Post *abrév écrite* = **Staffordshire**.

staff: **~ sergeant** ▶ **1612** *n* GB, US Mil (in army) sergent-chef *m*; (in US air force) sergent *m*; **~-student ratio** *n* rapport *m* étudiant-enseignant; **~ training** *n* formation *f* du personnel.

stag /stæg/ **I** *n* **1** Zool cerf *m*; **2** GB Fin loup *m* de la finance.
II *adj* (all male) réservé aux hommes.

stag beetle *n* cerf-volant *m*, lucane *m*.

stage /steɪdʒ/ **I** *n* **1** (phase) (of illness, career, life, development, match) stade *m* (**of, in** de); (of project, process, plan) phase *f* (**of, in** de); (of journey, negotiations) étape *f* (**of, in** de); **the first ~ of our journey** la première étape de notre voyage; **the first ~ in the process** la première phase or le premier stade du procédé; **the next ~ in the project/his research** la prochaine phase du projet/de ses recherches; **a difficult ~ in the negotiations** une étape difficile des négociations; **the next ~ of a baby's development** le prochain stade du développement d'un bébé; **the baby has reached the talking/walking ~** le bébé commence à parler/marcher; **what ~ has he reached in his education?** il en est à quel stade dans ses études?; **a/the ~ where** un/le stade où; **I've reached the ~ where I have to decide** je suis arrivé au stade où il faut que je décide; **we're at a ~ where anything could happen** nous sommes arrivés à un stade où tout est possible; **at this ~** (at this point) à ce stade; (yet, for the time being) pour l'instant; **I can't say at this ~** pour l'instant je ne peux rien dire; **that's all I can say at this ~** c'est tout ce que je peux dire pour l'instant; **at this ~ in** ou **of your career** à ce stade de votre carrière; **at a late ~** à un stade avancé; **at an earlier/later ~** à un stade antérieur/ultérieur; **at an early ~ in our history** vers le début de notre histoire; **at every ~** à chaque étape; **she ought to know that by this ~** ça fait longtemps qu'elle devrait le savoir; **by ~s** par étapes; **~ by ~** étape par étape; **in ~s** en plusieurs étapes; **in easy ~s** par petites étapes; **the project is still in its early ~s** le projet en est encore à ses débuts; **we're in the late ~s of our research** nous arrivons à la fin de nos recherches; **the project is at the halfway ~** le projet est à mi-chemin; **the project is entering its final ~** le projet touche à sa fin or entre dans sa phase finale; **she's going through a difficult ~** elle traverse une période difficile; **it's just a ~!** (in babyhood, adolescence) ça passera!; **2** (raised platform) gen estrade *f*; Theat scène *f*; **he was on ~ for three hours** il a été en or sur scène pendant trois heures; **to go on ~** monter sur or entrer en scène; **I've seen her on the ~** je l'ai vue jouer; **live from the ~ of La Scala** en direct de La Scala; **a long career on ~ and screen** une longue carrière à la scène et à l'écran; **to hold the ~** lit, fig être le point de mire; **to set the ~** Theat monter le décor; **to set the ~ for sth** fig préparer qch; **the ~ is set for the contest** tout est prêt pour le combat; **3** Theat **the ~** le théâtre; **to go on the ~** faire du théâtre; **to write for the ~** écrire des pièces de théâtre; **after 40 years on the ~** après 40 ans de théâtre or sur les planches; **the decline of the English ~** le déclin du théâtre anglais; **the play never reached the ~** la pièce n'a jamais été jouée; **4** fig (setting) (actual place) théâtre *m*; (backdrop) scène *f*; **Geneva has become the ~ for many international conferences** Genève est devenue le théâtre de nombreuses conférences internationales; **her appearance on the ~ of world politics** son apparition sur la scène politique internationale; **5** Aerosp étage *m*; **6** GB Transp (on bus route) section *f*; **7** (on scaffolding) plate-forme *f* d'échafaudage; **8** (on microscope) platine *f*; **9** Hist Transp = **stagecoach**.
II *modif* Theat [*play, equipment, furniture, lighting, equipment*] de théâtre; [*production*] théâtral; [*appearance, career, performance*] au théâtre.
III *vtr* **1** (organize) organiser [*ceremony, competition, demonstration, event, festival, rebellion, reconstruction, strike*]; fomenter [*coup*]; **2** (fake) simuler [*quarrel, scene*]; **the whole thing was ~d** ce n'était qu'une mise en scène; **3** Theat monter, mettre [qch] en scène [*play, performance*].

stage: **~coach** *n* diligence *f*; **~craft** *n* technique *f* scénique; **~ designer** ▶ **1692** *n* décorateur/-trice *m/f* de théâtre; **~ direction** *n* indication *f* scénique; **~ door** *n* entrée *f* des artistes; **~ fright** *n* trac *m*; **~hand** ▶ **1692** *n* machiniste *m*; **~ left** *adv* côté *m* cour; **~-manage** *vtr* fig orchestrer.

stage-management *n* Theat régie *f*; fig orchestration *f*.

stage: **~-manager** ▶ **1692** *n* régisseur/-euse *m/f*; **~ name** *n* nom *m* de théâtre.

stager /ˈsteɪdʒə(r)/ *n* **old ~** vétéran *m*.

stage: **~ right** *adv* côté *m* jardin; **~ show** *n* ▶ **stage production**; **~-struck** *adj* passionné de théâtre; **~ whisper** *n* Theat, fig aparté *m*.

stagey *adj* = **stagy**.

stagflation /ˌstægˈfleɪʃn/ *n* stagflation *f*.

stagger /ˈstæɡə(r)/ **I** *n* (movement) **with a ~** (weakly) d'un pas chancelant; (drunkenly) en titubant.
II staggers *npl* Vet (disease) (in horses) vertigo *m*; (in sheep) tournis *m*.
III *vtr* **1** (astonish) stupéfier, bouleverser; **2** (spread out) échelonner [*holidays, journeys, timetable, payments, strikes*]; **the closure will be ~ed over five years** la fermeture s'échelonnera sur cinq ans; **3** Tech disposer [qch] en quinconce [*bolts, rivets, spokes*]; **4** Aviat décaler [*wings*].
IV *vi* [*person*] (from weakness, illness) chanceler; (drunkenly) tituber; (under load) chanceler; [*animal*] vaciller; **to ~ in/out/off** entrer/sortir/s'en aller en chancelant or d'un pas chancelant; **to ~ to the door/car** aller vers la porte/la voiture en chancelant; **she ~ed back and fell** elle a reculé en chancelant et elle est tombée; **to ~ to one's feet** se relever en chancelant.
V staggered *pp adj* **1** (astonished) bouleversé, renversé; **to be ~ed to hear that** être bouleversé or renversé d'apprendre que; **we were ~ed by the news** nous avons été renversé par la nouvelle; **2** (carefully timed) **~ed holidays** vacances *fpl* échelonnées; **~ed hours** horaires *mpl* décalés; **~ed start** Sport départ *m* décalé; **3** Transp **~ed junction** croisement *m* en quinconce.

staggering /ˈstæɡərɪŋ/ *adj* [*amount, increase, loss*] prodigieux/-ieuse; [*news, revelation*] renversant; [*event*] bouleversant; [*achievement, contrast, transformation*] stupéfiant; [*success*] étourdissant; **it was a ~ blow to his self-esteem** son amour-propre en a pris un coup.

staggeringly /ˈstæɡərɪŋlɪ/ *adv* incroyablement.

stag: **~horn** *n* Bot lycopode *m*; **~ hunt** *n* chasse *f* au cerf; **~ hunting** *n* chasse *f* au cerf.

staging /ˈsteɪdʒɪŋ/ *n* **1** Theat mise *f* en scène; **2** Constr échafaudage *m*; (for spectators) gradins *mpl* provisoires.

staging area *n* Mil zone *f* de transit.

staging post *n* Mil poste *m* de ravitaillement; fig point *m* de transition.

stagnancy /ˈstæɡnənsɪ/ *n* stagnation *f*.

stagnant /ˈstæɡnənt/ *adj* (all contexts) stagnant.

stagnate /stæɡˈneɪt, US ˈstæɡneɪt/ *vi* **1** fig [*economy, sales, party*] être en stagnation; [*person, mind, society*] stagner; **2** lit [*water, pond*] stagner, croupir.

stagnation /stæɡˈneɪʃn/ *n* stagnation *f*.

stag: **~ night, ~ party** *n* soirée *f* pour enterrer une vie de garçon; **~ show**○ *n* US spectacle *m* porno○.

stagy /ˈsteɪdʒɪ/ *adj* péj [*person*] prétentieux/-ieuse; [*behaviour, manner*] théâtral.

staid /steɪd/ *adj* [*person, character*] posé, guindé pej; [*place*] solennel/-elle; [*appearance, image, society, attitude*] guindé pej.

staidness /ˈsteɪdnɪs/ *n* (of character, person) gravité *f*; (of society, attitudes) austérité *f*.

stain /steɪn/ **I** *n* **1** (mark) lit, fig tache *f*; **blood/coffee ~** tache de sang/de café; **stubborn ~** tache rebelle; **to remove a ~ from sth** enlever une tache sur or de qch; **it will leave a ~** ça fera une tache; **without a ~ on one's character** sans tache pour sa réputation; **2** (dye) (for wood, fabric etc) teinture *f*.
II *vtr* **1** (soil) tacher [*clothes, carpet, table etc*]; **the cherries had ~ed his hands red** les cerises avaient fait des taches rouges sur ses mains; **2** Biol, Tech teindre [*wood, fabric, specimen*].
III *vi* [*fabric*] se tacher.
IV -stained (*dans composés*) **oil/ink-~ed** taché d'huile/d'encre; **tear-~ed** trempé de larmes.

stain: **~ed glass** *n* (glass) verre *m* coloré; (windows collectively) vitraux *mpl*; **~ed glass window** *n* vitrail *m*.

stainless /ˈsteɪnlɪs/ *adj* [*reputation, past etc*] sans tache.

stainless steel I *n* acier *m* inoxydable.
II *modif* [*cutlery, sink*] en acier inoxydable.

stain: **~ remover** *n* détachant *m*; **~-resistant** *adj* antitaches *inv*.

stair /steə(r)/ **I** *n* **1** (step) marche *f* (d'escalier); **the top/bottom ~** la marche du haut/du bas; **2** (staircase) sout escalier *m*, escaliers *mpl* fml.
II stairs *npl* (staircase) **the ~** l'escalier *m*; **a flight of ~** un escalier, une volée *f* d'escalier; **to climb** ou **go up the ~** monter l'escalier; **to come** ou **go down the ~** descendre l'escalier; **to run up the ~** monter l'escalier en courant; **to fall down the ~** tomber dans l'escalier.

stair: **~ carpet** *n* tapis *m* d'escalier; **~case** *n* escalier *m*; **~head** *n* haut *m* d'escalier; **~ rod** *n* tringle *f* d'escalier; **~way** *n* escalier *m*; **~well** *n* cage *f* d'escalier.

stake /steɪk/ **I** *n* **1** Games, Turf, fig (amount risked) enjeu *m*; **to put a ~ on** miser sur [*horse*]; **high/low ~s** enjeux élevés/faibles; **to play for high ~s** lit, fig jouer gros; **to raise the ~s** lit augmenter l'enjeu; fig monter la mise; **to be at ~** fig être en jeu; **there is a lot at ~** fig ce n'est pas à prendre à la légère; **he has a lot at ~** fig il a gros à perdre; **to put sth at ~** lit, fig mettre qch en jeu; **2** (investment) participation *f* (**in** dans); **a large/small ~** une forte/faible participation; **to have a 30% ~ in** avoir une participation de 30% dans [*company*]; **3** (pole) (support) pieu *m*; (thicker) poteau *m*; (marker) piquet *m*; **4** Hist (for execution) bûcher *m*; **to go to the ~** monter au bûcher; **to be burnt at the ~** être brûlé sur le bûcher.
II stakes *npl* Turf montant *m* du prix; **the Diamond Stakes** la course des Diamond Stakes; **'France top in pay ~s'** fig journ 'la France en tête dans la compétition salariale'.
III *vtr* **1** (gamble) miser [*money, property*]; risquer [*reputation*]; **to ~ one's all on** tout miser sur; **I would ~ my life on it** j'en mettrais ma tête à couper○; **2** Hort mettre un tuteur à [*plant, tree*]; **3** US (back) financer [*person*].
IDIOMS **to ~ one's claim to** fig exposer ses revendications sur; **to (pull) up ~s** larguer les amarres○.
■ **stake out**: **~ out [sth], ~ [sth] out 1** [*police*] surveiller [*hide-out*]; **2** lit délimiter [qch] avec des pieux [*land*]; **3** fig (claim) revendiquer [*interest, area of study*].

stake: **~holder** *n* Turf parieur/-ieuse *m/f*; **~out**○ *n* planque○ *f*.

stalactite /ˈstæləktaɪt, US stəˈlæk-/ *n* stalactite *f*.

stalagmite /ˈstæləɡmaɪt, US stəˈlæɡ-/ *n* stalagmite *f*.

stale /steɪl/ **I** *adj* **1** (old) [*bread, cake, biscuit*] rassis; [*beer*] éventé; [*cheese*] desséché; [*air, odour*] vicié; **the smell of ~ cigarette smoke** l'odeur de cigarette refroidie; **the food is ~** la nourriture n'est pas fraîche; **to go ~** [*bread*] se rassir; **the loaf has gone ~** le pain est rassis; **to taste ~** [*beer*] être éventé; [*cheese*] être desséché; **to smell ~** [*room, house*] sentir le renfermé; **2** (hackneyed) [*jokes, ideas, vocabulary*] éculé; [*style, ideal, convention*] usé; **~ news** des nouvelles qui n'en sont pas; **3** (tired) [*player, performer*] usé; **to feel ~** se sentir usé; **to get ~ in a job** s'user dans un travail; **their marriage had gone ~** leur mariage avait perdu de son charme; **4** Fin [*cheque*] périmé; [*market*] inactif/-ive.
II *vi* [*pleasure, delight*] s'affadir; [*pastime*] perdre son charme.

stalemate /ˈsteɪlmeɪt/ **I** *n* **1** (in chess) pat *m*; **2** (deadlock) impasse *f* (**in** dans); **military/political ~** impasse militaire/politique; **industrial ~** impasse entre les partenaires sociaux; **to break a/reach (a) ~** sortir de/être dans l'impasse.
II *vtr* **1** (in chess) faire pat [*opponent*]; **2** (block) bloquer [*negotiations, progress*]; neutraliser [*person*].

staleness /ˈsteɪlnɪs/ *n* **1** (of food) manque *m* de fraîcheur; (of air) caractère *m* vicié; fig (of ideas) banalité *f*; **2** (of performer, athlete) usure *f*; **feeling of ~** sensation d'usure.

Stalin /ˈstɑːlɪn/ *pr n* Staline.

Stalinism /ˈstɑːlɪnɪzəm/ *n* stalinisme *m*.

Stalinist /ˈstɑːlɪnɪst/ *n, adj* stalinien/-ienne (*m/f*).

stalk /stɔːk/ **I** *n* **1** Bot, Culin (of grass, rose, broccoli) tige *f*; (of leaf, apple, pepper) queue *f*; (of mushroom) pied *m*; (of cabbage) trognon *m*; **2** Zool (organ) pédicule *m*.
II *vtr* **1** (hunt) [*hunter*] chasser [qch] à l'approche; [*animal*] chasser; [*murderer, rapist*] suivre; **2** (affect, haunt) [*fear, danger*] régner sur; [*disease, famine*] sévir; [*killer*] rôder dans [*place*]; **3** Comm, Fin (in takeover bid) essayer de prendre le contrôle de [*company*].
III *vi* **1** (walk) **to ~ up/down the corridor** (stiffly) marcher avec raideur dans le couloir; **to ~ out of the room** (angry) quitter la pièce d'un air digne; **2** (prowl) **to ~ through** rôder dans [*countryside, streets*].
IDIOMS **my eyes were out on ~s**○ j'avais les yeux qui sortaient des orbites.

stalking horse *n* Pol homme *m* de paille.

stall /stɔːl/ **I** *n* **1** (at market, fair) stand *m*; (newspaper stand) kiosque *m*; **cake ~** stand des pâtisseries; **to run a ~** tenir un stand; **to set up/take down a ~** installer/démonter un stand; **to buy sth from a ~** acheter qch à un stand; **2** (in stable) stalle *f*; **3** Equit starting-gate *m*, barrière *f* de départ; **4** Aviat décrochage *m*; **5** Archit (in church) stalle *f*; **6** (cubicle) (for shower) compartiment *m*; US (for toilet) cabinet *m*; **7** US (parking space) stalle *f*, place *f* de parking.
II stalls *npl* GB Theat orchestre *m*; **in the ~s** à l'orchestre.
III *vtr* **1** Aut caler [*engine, car*]; **2** (hold up) bloquer [*talks, negotiations, action, process*]; faire patienter [*person*]; **I managed to ~ him** j'ai réussi à le faire patienter.
IV *vi* **1** [*car, driver, engine*] caler; **2** [*plane, pilot*] décrocher; **3** (play for time) temporiser; **to ~ for time** chercher à gagner du temps; **stop** ou **quit** US **~ing!** arrête de temporiser!; **4** (stop, stagnate) [*market, industry*] stagner; [*talks, diplomacy*] se bloquer.
V stalled *pp adj* [*negotiations*] bloqué; [*market, industry*] stagnant.
■ **stall off**: **~ off [sb]** tenir [qn] à distance [*creditors*].

stall: **~-fed** *adj* Agric de batterie; **~ feed** *vtr* Agric engraisser [qch] en batterie; **~holder** *n* marchand/-e *m/f*; **~ing angle** *n* incidence *f* de décrochage; **~ing tactic** *n* tactique *f* pour gagner du temps.

stallion /ˈstælɪən/ *n* étalon *m*.

stalwart /ˈstɔːlwət/ **I** *n* fidèle *mf*; **a party ~** un/une fidèle du parti.
II *adj* (loyal) [*defender, member, supporter*] loyal; [*support*] inconditionnel/-elle; [*defence, resistance*] vaillant; **to do ~ work** fournir un travail solide.

stamen /ˈsteɪmən/ *n* (*pl* **~s** ou **-mina**) étamine *f*.

stamina /ˈstæmɪnə/ *n* résistance *f*, endurance *f*; **to have ~** avoir de l'endurance, être résistant; **to lack ~** manquer d'endurance; **to have the ~ for/to do** avoir la résistance pour/de faire.

stammer /ˈstæmə(r)/ **I** *n* bégaiement *m*; **to have a ~** avoir un bégaiement; **to speak with a ~** bégayer.
II *vtr* bégayer [*apology, excuse*]; **to ~ that** bégayer que; **'n-no,' he ~ed** 'n-non,' a-t-il bégayé.
III *vi* bégayer.

stammerer /ˈstæmərə(r)/ *n* bègue *mf*.

stammering /ˈstæmərɪŋ/ **I** *n* bégaiement *m*.
II *adj* bégayant.

stamp /stæmp/ **I** *n* **1** Post timbre *m*; **a 3 franc ~** un timbre à 3 francs; **first/second-class ~** timbre tarif rapide/lent; **postage ~** timbre-poste *m*; **'no ~ needed'** 'ne pas affranchir'; **2** (token) (for free gift) vignette *f*, timbre *m*; (towards bill, TV licence) bon *m*; **3** (marking device) (made of rubber) tampon *m*; (made of metal) cachet *m*; (for marking metals) étampe *f*; (for marking gold) poinçon *m*; **date ~** timbre *m* dateur; **to give sth one's ~ of approval** fig donner son accord à qch; **4** fig (hallmark) marque *f*; **to bear the ~ of** avoir la marque de [*person, artist*]; **to set one's ~ on** imposer sa marque sur [*play, company, era*]; **5** (calibre) trempe *f*; **men of his ~** des hommes de sa trempe; **6** (sound of feet) piétinement *m*; **the ~ of the horse's hooves** le bruit des sabots des chevaux; **with a ~ of her foot** en tapant du pied; **7†** GB (contribution) cotisation *f* à la sécurité sociale.
II *modif* [*album, collection*] de timbres.
III *vtr* **1** (mark) apposer [qch] au tampon [*date, name, number*] (**on** sur); tamponner [*card, ticket, library book*]; marquer [*goods, boxes*]; viser [*document, ledger, passport*]; **to be ~ed with the official seal** être visé avec le sceau officiel; **to be ~ed 'confidential'** porter la mention 'confidentiel'; **to ~ a book with the date** marquer la date dans un livre; **to ~ one's authority/personality on** imprimer son autorité/sa personnalité sur [*project, enterprise, match*]; **2** (with foot) **to ~ one's foot** (in anger) frapper ou taper du pied; **to ~ one's feet** (rhythmically) taper des pieds; (for warmth) battre la semelle; **to ~ sth flat** tasser qch; **to ~ sth into the ground** enfoncer qch dans le sol du pied; **3** Post affranchir [*envelope*].
IV *vi* **1** (thump foot) [*person*] taper du pied; [*horse*] piaffer; **to ~ on** écraser (du pied) [*toy, foot*]; écraser [*brakes*]; **to ~ the mud off one's boots** ôter la boue de ses bottes en tapant des pieds; **2** (walk heavily) marcher en tapant des pieds; **to ~ into/out of sth** entrer dans/sortir de qch en tapant des pieds; **3** (crush) **to ~ on** lit piétiner [*soil, ground*]; fig écarter [*idea, suggestion*].
■ **stamp out**: **~ out [sth], ~ [sth] out 1** (put out) éteindre [qch] en piétinant [*fire, flames*]; **2** (crush) éradiquer [*cholera, disease*]; réprimer [*terrorism, fraud*]; écraser [*uprising*]; supprimer [*crime*]; **3** (cut out) découper [qch] à la presse [*component*].

stamp: **~-collecting** *n* philatélie *f*; **~-collector** *n* philatéliste *mf*; **~-dealer** ▶ **1692**, **1692** *n* marchand/-e *m/f* philatéliste; **~ duty** *n* Jur droit *m* de timbre; **~ed addressed envelope, sae** *n* enveloppe *f* timbrée à votre/son etc adresse.

stampede /stæm'piːd/ **I** *n* **1** (rush) (of animals) débandade *f*; (of humans) ruée *f*; **there was a ~ for the exit** on s'est rué vers la sortie; **2** (rodeo) rodéo *m*.
II *vtr* **1** lit jeter la panique parmi [*animals, spectators*]; semer la panique dans [*crowd*]; **2** fig (force sb's hand) brusquer [*person*]; **to ~ sb into doing** forcer qn à faire.
III *vi* [*animals*] courir en troupeau; [*people, crowd*] se précipiter; **to ~ towards** se ruer or se précipiter vers [*doors, exit*]; **a stampeding elephant** un éléphant qui se déchaîne.

stamp: **~ing ground**○ *n* GB lit, fig domaine *m*; **~ing mill** *n* Mining bocard *m*; **~ing press** *n* Ind presse *f* à emboutir; **~ machine** *n* Post distributeur *m* de timbres-poste.

stance /stɑːns, stæns/ *n* **1** (attitude) position *f*; **to take** ou **adopt a ~** adopter une position; **her ~ on** sa position sur [*defence, inflation, issue*]; **2** (way of standing) position *f*; **to adopt a ~** prendre une position; **3** (in mountaineering) relais *m*.

stanch *vtr* US = **staunch**.

stanchion /'stænʃən, US 'stæntʃən/ *n* poteau *m* métallique.

stand /stænd/ **I** *n* **1** (piece of furniture) (for coats) portemanteau *m*; (for hats) porte-chapeau *m*; (for plant, trophy) guéridon *m*; (for sheet music) pupitre *m* à musique; **2** Comm (stall) (on market) éventaire *m*; (kiosk) kiosque *m*; (at exhibition, trade fair) stand *m*; **news(paper) ~** kiosque à journaux; **3** Sport (in stadium) tribunes *fpl*; **4** Jur (witness box) barre *f*; **to take the ~** aller à la barre; **5** (stance) position *f*; **to take** ou **make a ~ on sth** prendre position sur qch; **6** (resistance to attack) résistance *f*; (**to make**) **a last ~** (livrer) une dernière bataille; **7** (in cricket) **a ~ of 120 runs** une série ininterrompue de 120 runs; **8** (standstill) **to come to a ~** s'arrêter; **the traffic was brought to a ~** la circulation a été paralysée; **9** (area) (of corn) champ *m*; (of trees) groupe *m*.
II *vtr* (*prét, pp* **stood**) **1** (place) mettre [*person, object*]; **~ it over there** mets-le là-bas; **to ~ sb on/in etc** mettre qn sur/dans etc; **to ~ sth on/in/against etc** mettre qch sur/dans/contre etc; **2** (bear) supporter [*person, insects, certain foods*]; **I can't ~ liars** je ne supporte pas les menteurs; **he can't ~ to do** ou **doing** il ne supporte pas de faire; **I can't ~ him doing** je ne supporte pas qu'il fasse; **she won't ~ any nonsense/bad behaviour** elle ne tolère pas qu'on fasse des bêtises/qu'on se conduise mal; **it won't ~ close scrutiny** il ne faut pas le regarder en détail; **3**○ (pay for) **to ~ sb sth** payer qch à qn; **to ~ sb a meal/a drink** payer un repas/à boire à qn; **4** Jur **to ~ trial** passer en jugement; **to ~ security for sb, to ~ bail for sb** se porter garant de qn; **5** (be liable) **to ~ to lose sth** risquer de perdre qch; **she ~s to gain a million pounds if the deal goes through** elle peut gagner un million de livres si l'affaire marche.
III *vi* (*prét, pp* **stood**) **1** (also **~ up**) se lever; **let's ~, we'll see better** mettons-nous debout, nous verrons mieux; **2** (be upright) [*person*] se tenir debout; [*object*] tenir debout; **they were ~ing at the bar/in the doorway** ils se tenaient debout au bar/dans l'embrasure de la porte; **they were ~ing talking near the car** ils étaient en train de parler près de la voiture; **to remain ~ing** rester debout; **only a few houses were left ~ing** seules quelques maisons sont restées debout; **there's not much of the cathedral still ~ing** il ne reste que des ruines de la cathédrale; **don't just ~ there, do something!** ne reste pas planté○ là! fais quelque chose!; **3** (be positioned) [*building, village etc*] être; (clearly delineated) se dresser; **the house/tree stood on top of the hill** la maison/l'arbre était or se dressait au sommet de la colline; **'the train now ~ing at platform one...'** 'le train au départ du quai numéro un...'; **the train was ~ing at the platform for half an hour** le train est resté une demi-heure à quai; **4** (step) **to ~ on** marcher sur [*insect, foot*]; **5** (be) **to ~ empty** [*house*] rester vide; **to ~ accused of sth** être accusé de qch; **to ~ ready** être prêt; **as things ~...** étant donné l'état actuel des choses...; **I want to know where I ~** fig je voudrais savoir où j'en suis; **where do you ~ on abortion/capital punishment?** quelle est votre position sur l'avortement/la peine de mort?; **nothing ~s between me and getting the job** rien ne s'oppose à ce que j'obtienne ce poste; **my savings are all that ~ between us and poverty** la seule chose qui nous préserve de la misère ce sont mes économies; **to ~ in sb's way** lit bloquer le passage à qn; fig faire obstacle à qn; **to ~ in the way of progress** fig faire obstacle au progrès; **6** (remain valid) [*offer, agreement, statement*] rester valable; **the record still ~s** le record n'est toujours pas battu; **7** (measure in height) **he ~s six feet** il mesure or fait six pieds de haut; **the tower/hill ~s 500 metres high** la tour/colline fait 500 mètres de haut; **8** (be at certain level) **the record/total ~s at 300** le record/total est de 300; **the score ~s at 3-0** le score est 3-0; **9** (be a candidate) se présenter; **to ~ as** se présenter comme [*candidate*]; **to ~ for parliament/president** se présenter aux élections législatives/présidentielles; **10** (act as) **to ~ as godfather for sb** être parrain de qn; **to ~ as guarantor for sb** se porter garant de qn; **11** (not move) [*water, mixture*] reposer; **to let sth ~** laisser reposer qch; **let the tea ~** laissez infuser le thé; **12** Naut **to ~ for** mettre le cap sur [*port, Dover etc*].
IDIOMS **to leave sb ~ing** [*athlete, student, company*] devancer qn; **as a cook, she leaves me ~ing** elle est beaucoup plus douée que moi en cuisine; **to ~ up and be counted** se faire entendre.
■ **stand about, stand around** rester là (**doing** à faire).
■ **stand aside** s'écarter (**to do** pour faire).
■ **stand back**: **1** (move back) [*person, crowd*] reculer (**from** de); fig prendre du recul (**from** par rapport à); **2** (be situated) [*house*] être en retrait (**from** par rapport à).
■ **stand by**: ¶ **~ by 1** (be prepared) se tenir prêt; [*doctor, army, emergency services*] être prêt à intervenir; **to be ~ing by to do** [*services*] être prêt à faire; **'~ by for take-off!'** Aviat 'prêt pour le décollage!'; **2** (refuse to act) rester là; **he stood by and did nothing** il est resté là sans intervenir; **how can you ~ by and let that happen?** comment est-ce que tu peux laisser faire ça sans rien dire?; ¶ **~ by [sb/sth]** (be loyal to) soutenir [*person*]; s'en tenir à [*principles, offer, decision*]; assumer [*actions*].
■ **stand down 1** (resign) [*president, chairman, candidate*] démissionner (**in favour of** en faveur de); **2** Jur quitter la barre.
■ **stand for**: **~ for [sth] 1** (represent) [*party, person*] représenter [*ideal*]; **2** (denote) [*initials*] vouloir dire [qch]; [*company, name*] être un gage de [*quality etc*]; **3** (tolerate) [*person*] tolérer [*cut, reduction, insubordination*]; **I wouldn't ~ for that** je ne le tolérerais pas; **don't ~ for him being so rude to you!** ne le laisse pas te parler comme ça!
■ **stand in**: **to ~ in for sb** remplacer qn.
■ **stand off**: ¶ **~ off 1** (reach a stalemate) aboutir à une impasse; **2** Naut courir au large; ¶ **~ [sb] off**○, **~ off [sb]**○ (lay off) licencier [*workers*].
■ **stand out 1** (be noticeable) [*person*] sortir de l'ordinaire; [*building, design*] se détacher, ressortir (**against** sur); [*work, ability, achievement, person*] être remarquable; **to ~ out from** [*person*] se distinguer de [*group*]; **2** (protrude) [*veins*] saillir; **3** (take a stance) résister; [*person*] **to ~ out for** revendiquer [*right, principle*]; **to ~ out against** se prononcer contre [*change, decision*].
■ **stand over**: ¶ **~ over** (be postponed) être remis à plus tard; ¶ **~ over [sb] 1** (supervise) être sur le dos de○ [*employee etc*]; **2** (watch) **don't ~ over me!** ne reste pas dans mes pattes○!
■ **stand to** Mil: ¶ **~ to** être en état d'alerte; **to ~ to to do** se tenir prêt à faire; ¶ **~ [sb] to** mettre [qn] en état d'alerte.
■ **stand up**: ¶ **~ up 1** (rise) se lever (**to do** pour faire); **2** (stay upright) se tenir debout; **3** (withstand investigation) [*argument, theory, story*] tenir debout; **to ~ up to** résister à [*scrutiny, investigation*]; **4** (resist) **to ~ up to** tenir tête à [*person*]; **5** (defend) **to ~ up for** défendre [*person, rights*]; **to ~ up for oneself** se défendre; ¶ **~ [sb/sth] up 1** (place upright) mettre [qn] debout [*person*]; redresser [*object*]; **to ~ sth up against/on** mettre qch contre/sur; **2**○ (fail to meet) poser un lapin à○ [*girlfriend, boyfriend*].

stand-alone /'stændələʊn/ *adj* Comput autonome.

standard /'stændəd/ **I** *n* **1** (level of quality) niveau *m*; **the ~ of education/hygiene/candidates is good** le niveau d'éducation/d'hygiène/des candidats est bon; **~s of service have declined** la qualité du service a baissé; **our drinking water is of a very high ~** notre eau potable est d'excellente qualité; **the candidates were of a very high ~** les candidats étaient de très haut niveau; **this wine is excellent by any ~s** ce vin est excellent à tout point de vue; **to have high/low ~s** [*person*] être très/peu consciencieux; [*school, institution*] être d'un bon/mauvais niveau; **to have double ~s** faire deux poids deux mesures; **2** (official specification) norme *f* (**for** de); **products must comply with EC ~s** les produits doivent être conformes aux normes de la CE; **3** (requirement) (of student, work) niveau *m* requis (**for** pour); (of hygiene, safety) critères *mpl*; **this work/student is not up to ~** ce travail/cet étudiant n'a pas le niveau requis; **above/below ~** au-dessus du/en dessous du niveau requis; **to set the ~ for others to follow** imposer un modèle à suivre; **by today's ~s** selon les critères actuels; **4** (banner) étendard *m*; **5** (classic song) standard *m*; **a rock/blues ~** un standard du rock/du blues.

II *adj* **1** (normal) [*size, equipment, rate, pay*] standard; [*plan, style*] habituel/-uelle; [*image*] traditionnel/-elle; [*procedure*] habituel/-uelle, normal; [*ton, measurement*] standard; **it's ~ practice to do** il est d'usage de faire; **~ English/French** l'anglais/le français standard; **this model includes a car radio as ~** ce modèle est équipé en série d'une autoradio; **2** (authoritative) [*work, manual*] de référence; **3** (also **~ class**) GB Rail [*ticket*] de seconde classe; [*single, return*] en seconde classe; **4** Bot [*cherry, rose*] (greffé) sur tige.

standard: **~ amenities** *npl* confort *m* minimum; **Standard Assessment Task** *n* GB Sch test *m* d'aptitude scolaire (*par tranches d'âge*); **~-bearer** *n* Mil, fig porte-drapeau *m*; **~-bred** *n* US Equit trotteur *m* américain; **~ cost** *n* Accts prix *m* standard; **~ deviation** *n* Stat écart-type *m*; **~ gauge** *n* Rail écartement *m* de voie normal (1,435 m); **~ gauge railway** *n* Rail voie *f* à écartement normal (1,435 m); **~-issue** *adj* réglementaire.

standardization /ˌstændədaɪˈzeɪʃn, US -dɪˈz-/ *n* normalisation *f*, standardisation *f*.

standardize /ˈstændədaɪz/ **I** *vtr* normaliser, standardiser [*component, laws, procedures, spelling, size, tests*].

II standardized *pp adj* normalisé, standardisé.

standard: **~ lamp** *n* GB lampadaire *m*; **~ normal distribution** *n* Stat loi *f* normale centrée réduite; **~ of living** *n* niveau *m* de vie; **~ time** *n* heure *f* légale.

standby /ˈstændbaɪ/ **I** *n* **1** gen (for use in emergencies) (person) remplaçant/-e *m/f*; (food, ingredient) remplacement *m*; **to be on ~** [*army, emergency services*] être prêt à intervenir; (for airline ticket) être sur la liste d'attente, être en stand-by; **to be put on ~** [*army, emergency services*] être mis en état d'alerte; **2** Telecom veille *f*.

II *modif* **1** (emergency) [*system, circuit, battery*] de secours; **2** Tourism [*ticket*] en stand-by; [*passenger*] sur la liste d'attente, en stand-by.

standee /stænˈdiː/ *n* (spectator) spectateur/-trice *m/f* debout; (passenger) voyageur/-euse *m/f* debout.

stand-in /ˈstændɪn/ **I** *n* gen remplaçant/-e *m/f*; Cin, Theat doublure *f*.

II *adj* remplaçant.

standing /ˈstændɪŋ/ **I** *n* **1** (reputation) réputation *f*, rang *m* (**among** parmi; **with** chez); **academic/professional ~** réputation *f* académique/professionnelle; **social ~** position *f* sociale; **financial ~** situation *f* financière; **of high** ou **considerable ~** très réputé; **2** (length of time) **of long ~** de longue date; **of ten years' ~** vieux/vieille de dix ans.

II *adj* **1** (permanent) [*army, committee, force*] actif/-ive; **2** (continuing) [*rule, invitation*] permanent; **his absent-mindedness is a ~ joke among his friends** sa distraction est un constant sujet de plaisanterie pour ses amis; **it's a ~ joke that she always forgets her key** tout le monde sait qu'elle oublie toujours sa clé; **3** Sport (from standing position) [*jump*] sans élan; **to make a jump from a ~ start** sauter sans élan.

standing: **~ charge** *n* frais *mpl* d'abonnement *m*; **~ order** *n* Fin virement *m* automatique; **~ ovation** *n* ovation *f* debout, standing ovation *f*; **~ room** *n* ¢ places *fpl* debout; **~ stone** *n* pierre *f* levée.

stand-off /ˈstændɒf/ *n* **1** (stalemate) impasse *f*; **2** (counterbalancing of forces) contrepartie *f*; **3** Sport = **stand-off half**.

stand: **~-off half** *n* Sport demi *m* d'ouverture; **~-offish**○ *adj* [*person, manner, attitude*] distant; **~-offishly**○ *adv* [*act, behave*] de manière distante; [*say, reply*] d'un ton distant; **~-offishness**○ *n* froideur *f*; **~-off missile** *n* Mil, Tech missile *m* tiré à distance de sécurité; **~pipe** *n* colonne *f* d'alimentation; **~point** *n* point *m* de vue.

standstill /ˈstændstɪl/ *n* **1** (stop) (of traffic, produciton) arrêt *m*; (of economy, growth) point *m* mort; **to be at a ~** [*traffic*] être à l'arrêt; [*factory, port, rail services*] être au point mort; **to come to a ~** [*person, car*] s'arrêter; [*work, production*] être arrêté; [*negotiations, talks*] arriver à une impasse; **to bring sth to a ~** paralyser qch [*traffic, factory, service, city*]; **2** (on wages, taxes etc) gel *m*.

standstill agreement *n* statu quo *m*.

stand-to /ˈstændtuː/ *n* Mil alerte *f*.

stand-up /ˈstændʌp/ **I** *n* (also **~ comedy**) one man show *m* comique.

II *adj* **1** Theat, TV **~ comedian** comique *mf*; **2** (eaten standing) [*buffet, meal*] debout *inv*; **3** (aggressive) [*fight, argument*] en règle.

stank /stæŋk/ *prét* ▶ **stink**.

Stanley knife® /ˈstænlmaɪf/ *n* cutter *m*.

stannic /ˈstænɪk/ *adj* stannique.

stannous /ˈstænəs/ *adj* stanneux/-euse.

stanza /ˈstænzə/ *n* strophe *f*.

stapes /ˈsteɪpiːz/ *n* Anat (*pl* **~** ou **-pedes**) étrier *m*.

staphylococcus /ˌstæfɪləˈkɒkəs/ *n* (*pl* **-cocci**) staphylocoque *m*.

staple /ˈsteɪpl/ **I** *n* **1** (for paper) agrafe *f*; **2** Constr (U-shaped) clou *m* cavalier; **3** (basic food) aliment *m* de base; **4** Econ (crop) culture *f* principale; (product) principale fabrication *f*; (industry) industrie *f* de base; **5** fig (topic, theme) sujet *m* principal; **6** Tex (fibre) fibre *f*.

II *adj* (*épith*) [*product, industry, food, diet*] de base; [*crop, meal*] principal.

III *vtr* **1** gen (attach) agrafer (**to** à; **onto** sur); **to ~ sheets together** agrafer des feuilles; **2** Med **to have one's stomach ~d** se faire rétrécir l'estomac chirurgicalement.

staple gun *n* agrafeuse *f*.

stapler /ˈsteɪplə(r)/ *n* agrafeuse *f*.

staple remover *n* otagraf® *m*.

star /stɑː(r)/ **I** *n* **1** Astron, Astrol étoile *f*; **the ~s are out** les étoiles brillent; **to navigate by the ~s** naviguer aux étoiles; **born under a lucky ~** né sous une bonne étoile; **2** (person) vedette *f*, star *f*; **a ~ of stage and screen** une vedette de la scène et de l'écran; **a tennis/soccer ~** une vedette du tennis/du football; **to make sb a ~** faire une star de qn; **3** (asterisk) astérisque *m*; **4** (award) (to hotel, restaurant) étoile *f*; (to pupil) bon point *m*; **5** Mil (mark of rank) étoile *f*.

II stars *npl* Astrol horoscope *m*; **what do the ~s foretell?** qu'est-ce que l'horoscope prédit?; **it's written in the ~s** c'est le destin.

III *modif* [*billing, quality*] de vedette.

IV -star (*dans composés*) **1** Tourism **three-/four-~ hotel/restaurant** restaurant/hôtel (à) trois/quatre étoiles; **2** Mil **four-/five-~ general** général à quatre/cinq étoiles.

V *vtr* (*p prés etc* **-rr-**) **1** [*film, play*] avoir [qn] pour vedette [*actor*]; **the play ~s Alan Bates and Maggie Smith as the uncle and aunt** la pièce a pour vedettes Alan Bates dans le rôle de l'oncle et Maggie Smith dans le rôle de la tante; **a comedy ~ring Lenny Henry** une comédie avec Lenny Henry en vedette; **2** (mark with star) (*gén au passif*) marquer [qch] d'un astérisque; **the ~red items/dishes are...** les articles/plats marqués d'un astérisque sont...; **3** (decorate) parsemer; **~red with** parsemé de [*flowers, dots*].

VI *vi* (*p prés etc* **-rr-**) [*actor*] jouer le rôle principal (**in** dans); **Bela Lugosi ~s as Dracula** ou **in the role of Dracula** Bela Lugosi joue (le rôle de) Dracula; **Meryl Streep also ~s** Meryl Streep est également à l'affiche.

IDIOMS **to reach for the ~s** vouloir décrocher la lune; **to see ~s** voir trente-six chandelles. ▶ **all-star**, **ill-starred**.

star anise /ˌstɑːrəˈniːz/ *n* anis *m* étoilé.

starboard /ˈstɑːbəd/ **I** *n* **1** Naut tribord *m*; **to turn to ~** virer sur la droite; **hard a-~!** la barre à droite toute!; **2** Aviat droite *f*; **to bank to ~** virer à droite.

II *modif* [*engine, gun, wing*] tribord; **on the ~ side** à tribord.

starch /stɑːtʃ/ **I** *n* **1** ¢ (carbohydrate) féculents *mpl*; **wheat ~** amidon *m* de blé; **potato ~** fécule *f* de pomme de terre; **corn ~** US fécule *f* de maïs; **2** (for clothes) amidon *m*; **to put ~ on sth** amidonner qch.

II *vtr* amidonner, empeser.

III starched *pp adj* [*sheet, collar*] amidonné, empesé.

Star Chamber *n* **1** GB Hist Jur Chambre *f* étoilée (*conseil qui siégeait comme cour de justice, aboli en 1641*; **2** péj (also **star chamber**) cour *f* de justice arbitraire; **3** GB Pol *conseil des ministres réglant les différends en matière de dépenses gouvernementales.*

star chart *n* carte *f* du ciel.

starch-reduced *adj* [*product, food*] appauvri en féculents.

starchy /ˈstɑːtʃɪ/ *adj* **1** [*food, diet*] riche en féculents; **2** [*substance*] amylacé; **3**○ péj [*person, tone*] guindé.

star: **~ connection** *n* Elec montage *m* en étoile; **~-crossed** *adj* littér maudit.

stardom /ˈstɑːdəm/ *n* vedettariat *m*, célébrité *f*; **to rise to ~** devenir une vedette.

stardust /ˈstɑːdʌst/ *n* fig sensation *f* de rêve.

stare /steə(r)/ **I** *n* regard *m* fixe; **an insolent/a hard ~** un regard insolent/sévère; **she gave me a ~** son regard s'est posé or ses yeux se sont posés sur moi.

II *vtr* **to ~ sb into silence/submission** faire taire/obéir qn du regard; **the truth/solution was staring us in the face** fig la vérité/solution nous crevait les yeux○; **the book I'd been looking for was there all the time, staring me in the face** le livre que je cherchais n'avait pas bougé, il était là juste sous mes yeux; **disaster was staring me in the face** j'étais au bord de la catastrophe.

III *vi* regarder fixement; **to ~ at sb** dévisager qn, regarder qn fixement; **to ~ at sth** regarder qch fixement; **to ~ at sb in surprise/disbelief** regarder qn d'un air surpris/incrédule; **to ~ into space** regarder dans le vide; **to ~ straight ahead** regarder droit devant soi; **to ~ up at sb/sth** lever les yeux pour regarder qn/qch; **to ~ down at sb/sth** baisser les yeux sur qn/qch; **to ~ back at sb** rendre son regard à qn; **to stop and ~** s'arrêter pour regarder; **what are you staring at?** qu'est-ce que tu regardes comme ça?; **to ~ out of the window** regarder par la fenêtre.

■ **stare down** = **stare out**.

■ **stare out**: **~ [sb] out, ~ out [sb]** faire baisser les yeux à [*enemy, rival*].

star: **~fish** *n* étoile *f* de mer; **~flower** *n* ornithogale *m*; **~ fruit** *n* carambole *f*.

stargazer /ˈstɑːgeɪzə(r)/ *n* **1** (astrologer) astrologue *mf*; **2** (astronomer) astronome *mf*.

staring /ˈsteərɪŋ/ *adj* [*eyes*] fixe; [*people, crowd*] curieux/-ieuse; **to look at sb with ~ eyes** regarder qn fixement.

stark /stɑːk/ *adj* **1** (bare) [*landscape, building, appearance*] désolé; [*room, decor*] nu; [*lighting*] cru; [*beauty*] âpre; **2** (unadorned) [*statement, fact*] brut; [*warning, reminder*] sévère; **a ~ choice** un dilemme; **the ~ reality** la réalité pure et simple; **3** (total) [*contrast*] saisissant; **~ terror** terreur *f* folle; **in ~ contrast to** en opposition totale avec.
IDIOMS **to be ~ naked** être complètement nu; **~ raving mad**○, **~ staring mad**○ GB complètement dingue○ or cinglé○.

starkers○ /ˈstɑːkəz/ *adj* GB hum à poil○, nu comme un ver.

starkly /ˈstɑːklɪ/ *adv* **1** (bluntly) [*simple, clear, demonstrated*] carrément; **to contrast ~ with** former un contraste saisissant avec; **2** (barely) [*decorated*] de manière dépouillée; [*lit*] de manière crue.

starkness /ˈstɑːknɪs/ *n* (of landscape) aspect *m* désolé; (of decor, room) nudité *f*.

starless /ˈstɑːlɪs/ *adj* sans étoiles.

starlet /ˈstɑːlɪt/ *n* starlette *f*.

starlight /ˈstɑːlaɪt/ *n* lumière *f* des étoiles.

starling /ˈstɑːlɪŋ/ *n* étourneau *m*.

star: **~lit** *adj* [*night*] étoilé; **~-of-Bethlehem** *n* Bot (also **starflower**) étoile *f* de Bethléem, ornithogale *m*; **Star of Bethlehem** *n* Relig étoile *f* des rois mages; **Star of David** *n* Étoile *f* de David.

starry /ˈstɑːrɪ/ *adj* **1** (with stars) [*night, sky*] étoilé; **2** (shining) [*eyes*] brillant; **3** (in shape of star) [*flower, leaf, design*] en forme d'étoile; **4** [*cast, occasion*] rassemblant des stars.

starry-eyed *adj* [*person*] qui s'émerveille de tout; **~ about sb/sth** ébloui par qn/qch; **with ~ affection** avec une affection débordante.

star: **Stars and Bars** *n* US (+ *v sg*) *drapeau des sept États confédérés durant la guerre de Sécession*; **Stars and Stripes** *n* (+ *v sg*) bannière *f* étoilée; **~ shell** *n* fusée *f* éclairante; **~ sign** *n* signe *m* astrologique; **Star-spangled Banner** *n* bannière *f* étoilée.

starstruck /ˈstɑːstrʌk/ *adj* impressionné par la célébrité.

star-studded *adj* [*cast, line-up*] avec de nombreuses vedettes.

star system *n* **1** Astron système *m* stellaire; **2** (in films) star-system *m*.

start /stɑːt/ **I** *n* **1** (beginning) début *m*; **at the ~ of the war/season** au début de la guerre/saison; **(right) from the start** dès le début; **it would be a ~** ce serait déjà un début; **to make a ~ on doing** se mettre à faire; **to make a ~ on the gardening/one's homework/the dinner** aller faire le jardinage/faire ses devoirs/préparer le dîner; **to make an early ~** (on journey) partir tôt; (on work) commencer tôt; **that's a good ~** lit c'est un bon début; iron ça commence bien; **it was a bad ~ to the day** la journée commençait mal; **to make a fresh** ou **new ~** prendre un nouveau départ; **from ~ to finish** d'un bout à l'autre; **for a ~** pour commencer; **the ~ of a new school year** la rentrée scolaire; **the 'Start' button** le bouton 'Marche'; **2** Sport, gen (advantage) avantage *m*; (in time, distance) avance *f*; **you have a 20 metre/five minute ~** vous bénéficiez d'une avance de 20 mètres/de cinq minutes d'avance; **to give sb a ~ in business** aider qn à démarrer dans les affaires; **3** Sport (departure line) ligne *f* de départ; **lined up at the ~** sur la ligne de départ; **4** (movement) (of surprise, fear) **to give a ~ of surprise** sursauter; **to give sb a ~** faire sursauter qn; **with a ~** en sursaut.
II *vtr* **1** (begin) commencer [*day, exercise, activity*]; entamer [*bottle, packet*]; **to ~ doing** ou **to do** commencer à faire, se mettre à faire; **he's just ~ed a new job** il vient juste de changer de travail; **the butterfly ~s life as a caterpillar** le papillon est d'abord une chenille; **to ~ a new page** prendre une nouvelle page; **don't ~ that again!** ne recommence pas!; **2** (put to work) mettre [qn] au travail [*person*]; **to ~ sb on, to get sb ~ed on** mettre qn à [*typing, cleaning etc*]; **3** (cause, initiate) déclencher [*quarrel, war*]; instaurer [*custom*]; mettre [*fire*]; être à l'origine de [*trouble, rumour*]; lancer [*fashion, enterprise*]; **to ~ a family** avoir des enfants; **4** Mech (activate) faire démarrer [*car*]; mettre [qch] en marche [*machine*]; **5** Tech (cause to loosen) faire jouer [*rivet, screw*]; **6** Hunt lever [*game*]; **to ~ a hare** lit, fig lever un lièvre.
III to start with *adv phr* **1** (firstly) d'abord, premièrement; **2** (at first) au début; **I didn't understand to ~ with** au début je n'ai pas compris; **3** (at all) **I should never have told her to ~ with** pour commencer, je n'aurais jamais dû lui en parler.
IV *vi* **1** (begin) gen commencer; (in job) débuter (**as** comme); **to ~ at 8 o'clock/with the living room** commencer à huit heures/avec le salon; **to ~ again** ou **afresh** recommencer; **to ~ with smoked salmon** commencer par du saumon fumé; **it all ~ed when...** tout a commencé quand...; **prices ~ at around 50 dollars** les prix commencent autour de 50 dollars; **she ~ed up the stairs/down the corridor** elle s'est mise à monter l'escalier/longer le couloir; **to ~ by doing** commencer par faire; **to ~ on** commencer [*memoirs, journey*]; **to ~ on a high salary** commencer avec un salaire élevé; **let's get ~ed** (on work) allez, on commence; (on journey) allez, on y va; **let's get ~ed on the washing-up** allez! on fait la vaisselle; **he got ~ed in the clothes trade** il a débuté dans la vente de vêtements; **don't ~ on me** (in argument) ne recommence pas avec moi; **the day will ~ cloudy** il fera nuageux en début de journée; **~ing Wednesday...** à compter de mercredi...; **2** (depart) partir; **to ~ in good time** partir de bonne heure; **3** (jump nervously) sursauter (**in** de); **she ~ed at the sudden noise** le bruit soudain l'a fait sursauter; **4** (bulge) **her eyes almost ~ed out of her head** les yeux lui sont presque sortis de la tête; **5** Aut, Mech (be activated) [*car, engine, machine*] démarrer; **6** Tech (work loose) jouer.
IDIOMS **~ as you mean to go on** prenez tout de suite les choses en main; **the ~ of something big** un début prometteur; **to ~ something**○ semer la zizanie○.
■ **start back 1** (begin to return) prendre le chemin du retour; **2** (step back) faire un bond en arrière.
■ **start off**: ¶ **~ off 1** (set off) [*train, bus*] démarrer; [*person*] partir; **2** (begin) [*person*] commencer (**by doing** par faire; **with** par); [*matter, business, employee*] débuter (**as** comme; **in** dans); **he ~ed off thinking he could convince them** à l'origine il croyait pouvoir les convaincre; ¶ **~ off for** se mettre en route pour [*place*]; ¶ **~ [sb/sth] off, ~ off [sb/sth] 1** (begin) commencer [*visit, talk*] (**with** par); mettre [qch] en route [*programme*]; **2**○ GB (cause to do) **don't ~ her off laughing/crying** ne la fais pas rire/pleurer; **don't let anybody ~ you (off) smoking** ne laisse personne t'entraîner à fumer; **don't ~ him off** ne le provoque pas; **3** (put to work) mettre [qn] au travail [*worker*]; mettre [qch] en marche [*machine*]; **~ them off in the factory** mettez-les au travail à l'usine; **we'll ~ you off on simple equations** on va commencer avec les équations simples; **4** Sport faire partir [*competitors*].
■ **start out 1** (set off) (on journey) partir; **he ~ed out with the aim of...** fig il avait d'abord pour but de...; **2** (begin) [*matter, business, employee*] débuter (**as** comme; **in** dans).
■ **start over** recommencer (à zéro).
■ **start up**: ¶ **~ up** [*engine*] démarrer; [*noise*] retentir; [*person*] débuter; **he's ~ed up on his own** il a débuté tout seul; ¶ **~ [sth] up, ~ up [sth]** faire démarrer [*car*]; ouvrir [*shop*]; créer [*business*].

starter /ˈstɑːtə(r)/ *n* **1** Sport (participant) partant/-e *m/f*; **to be a fast ~** être rapide au départ; **2** Sport (official) starter *m*; **to be under ~'s orders** [*horse*] être sous les ordres du starter; [*competitor*] être aux ordres du starter; **3** Aut, Tech démarreur *m*; **4** Culin hors d'œuvre *m inv*; **5** (in quiz) première question *f*.
IDIOMS **for ~s**○ pour commencer.

start: **~ing block** *n* Sport bloc *m* de départ, starting-block *m*; **~ing gate** *n* Sport starting-gate *m*; **~ing grid** *n* (in motor racing) grille *f* de départ; **~ing handle** *n* Aut manivelle *f* (de démarrage); **~ing line** *n* Sport ligne *f* de départ; **~ing pistol** *n* Sport pistolet *m* de starter; **~ing point** *n* point *m* de départ; **~ing price** *n* Turf cote *f* au départ; **~ing salary** *n* salaire *m* de départ.

startle /ˈstɑːtl/ *vtr* **1** (take aback) [*reaction, tone, event, discovery*] surprendre; **2** (alarm) [*sight, sound, person*] effrayer; **you ~d me!** tu m'as fait sursauter!

startled /ˈstɑːtld/ *adj* **1** (taken aback) surpris (**at** de; **to do** de faire); **2** (alarmed) [*person, animal, voice, expression*] effrayé; **a ~ cry** un cri d'effroi.

startling /ˈstɑːtlɪŋ/ *adj* [*resemblance, contrast*] saisissant; **a ~ white** un blanc éclatant.

startlingly /ˈstɑːtlɪŋlɪ/ *adv* [*different*] étonnamment; **to be ~ beautiful** être d'une beauté saisissante; **to be ~ similar** se ressembler d'une manière saisissante.

start: **~-up costs** *npl* Comm frais *mpl* de mise en route; **Start-Up scheme** *n* GB *programme gouvernemental d'aide à la création de petites entreprises*.

star turn *n* **1** (act) clou *m* fig; **2** (person) vedette *f*.

starvation /ˌstɑːˈveɪʃn/ **I** *n* famine *f*; **to face ~** être menacé de famine; **to die of ~** mourir de faim.
II *modif* [*rations*] de survie; [*wages*] de misère.

starvation diet *n* **to go on a ~** suivre un régime draconien; **the soldiers were on a ~** les soldats n'avaient presque rien à manger.

starve /stɑːv/ **I** *vtr* **1** (deliberately) priver [qn] de nourriture [*population, prisoners*]; **it's pointless starving yourself** ça ne sert à rien de ne pas t'alimenter; **to ~ oneself/sb to death** se laisser mourir/laisser qn mourir de faim; **to ~ sb into doing** affamer qn pour l'obliger à faire; **to ~ a city into submission** faire la siège d'une ville en affamant la population; **2** (deprive) **to ~ sb/sth of** priver qn/qch de [*investment, cash, oxygen, light, affection*]; **to be ~d for** être en mal de [*choice, company, conversation*].
II *vi* Med (be malnourished) être gravement sous-alimenté, souffrir de malnutrition; **to ~ (to death)** mourir de faim; **to let sb ~** laisser qn mourir de faim.
■ **starve out**: **~ [sb] out, ~ out [sb]** affamer [*enemy, inhabitants*].

starveling /ˈstɑːvlɪŋ/ *n* littér (person) affamé/-e *m/f*; (animal) animal *m* affamé.

starving /ˈstɑːvɪŋ/ *adj* **1**○ (hungry) **to be ~** mourir or crever○ de faim; **I'm ~!** je suis mort de faim○!, j'ai l'estomac dans les talons○!; **2** (hunger-stricken) [*person, animal*] affamé; **the ~ people of the third world** les affamés du Tiers-Monde.

Star Wars, star wars○ *n* US Mil (+ *v sg*) guerre *f* des étoiles.

stash○ /stæʃ/ **I** *n* **1** (hiding place) cachette *f*, planque○ *f*; **2** (hidden supply) provision *f*.
II *vtr* planquer○ [*money, drugs*] (**in** dans; **under** sous).
■ **stash away**○: **~ [sth] away, ~ away [sth]** mettre [qch] de côté, planquer○ [*money,*

US states

In some cases, there is a French form of the name, but not always (if in doubt, check in the dictionary). Each state has a gender in French and is used with the definite article, except after the preposition en*, e.g.:*

Arkansas	=	l'Arkansas *m*
California	=	la Californie
Texas	=	le Texas

So:

Arkansas is beautiful	=	l'Arkansas est beau
I like California	=	j'aime la Californie
do you know Texas?	=	connaissez-vous le Texas?

In, to and from somewhere

For in *and* to *use* en *for feminine states and for masculine ones beginning with a vowel, e.g.:*

in Alaska	=	en Alaska
to Alaska	=	en Alaska
in California	=	en Californie
to California	=	en Californie

For in *and* to *use* au *for masculine states beginning with a consonant, e.g.:*

in Texas	=	au Texas
to Texas	=	au Texas

For from *use* de *for feminine states and for masculine ones beginning with a vowel, e.g.:*

from California	=	de Californie
from Alaska	=	d'Alaska

For from *use* du *for masculine states beginning with a consonant, e.g.:*

from Texas	=	du Texas

Coming from somewhere: uses with another noun

There are a few words e.g. californien, newyorkais, texan *used as adjectives and as nouns (with a capital letter) referring to the inhabitants. In other cases it is usually safe to use* de *for feminine states, and to use* de l' *or* du *for masculine states, e.g.:*

the Florida countryside	=	les paysages de Floride
Illinois representatives	=	les représentants de l'Illinois

but

a Louisiana accent	=	l'accent de la Louisiane
New-Mexico roads	=	les routes du Nouveau-Mexique

drugs]; **to have money ~ed away** avoir de l'argent mis de côté.

stasis /ˈsteɪsɪs, ˈstæsɪs/ *n* **1** (stagnation) stagnation *f*; **2** (*pl* **-es**) Med stase *f*.

state /steɪt/ **I** *n* **1** (condition) état *m*; **~ of health/mind** état de santé/d'esprit; **look at the ~ of the kitchen!** regarde un peu l'état de la cuisine!; **what ~ is the car in?** dans quel état est la voiture?; **she left the house in a terrible ~** (untidy, dirty) elle a laissé la maison dans un état épouvantable; **the present ~ of affairs** l'état actuel des choses; **my financial ~** ma situation financière; **a shocking/odd ~ of affairs** une situation scandaleuse/très étrange; **to be in a good/bad ~** être en bon/mauvais état; **in a good/bad ~ of repair** bien/mal entretenu; **in a poor ~ of health** en mauvaise santé; **he's in a confused ~ of mind** il ne sait plus où il en est; **to be in no ~ to do** ne pas être en état de faire; **he's not in a fit ~ to drive** il n'est pas en état de conduire; **in a liquid/solid ~** à l'état liquide/solide; **a ~ of alert/emergency/siege/war** un état d'alerte/d'urgence/de siège/de guerre; **a ~ of chaos/crisis/shock** un état chaotique/de crise/de choc; **to be in a ~ of despair** être au désespoir; **what's the ~ of play?** gen où en êtes-vous?; (in match) où en est le match?; (in negotiations) où en sont les négociations?; **2** Pol (nation) (also **State**) État *m*; **the State of Israel** l'État d'Israël; **the Baltic States** les États baltes; **to be a ~ within a ~** former un État dans l'État; **3** Admin, Geog (region, area) État *m*; **the ~ of Kansas** l'État du Kansas, le Kansas; **4** Pol (government) État *m*; **the State** l'État; **matters** ou **affairs of ~** les affaires de l'État; **Church and State** l'Église et l'État; **5** (ceremonial) pompe *f*; **in ~** en grande pompe, en grand apparat; **to live in ~** mener grand train; **she will lie in ~** sa dépouille sera exposée au public; **robes of ~** tenue *f* d'apparat; **6‡** (social class) rang *m*.

II States *npl* **the States** les États-Unis *mpl*; **to go to the States** aller aux États-Unis; **to live in the States** vivre aux États-Unis.

III *modif* **1** (government) [*school, sector*] public/-ique; [*enterprise, pension, radio, TV, university, railways, secret*] d'État; [*budget, spending, subsidy*] de l'État; [*army, tax*] national; **~ aid** aide *f* de l'État or étatique; **~ election** (at a national level) élection *f* nationale; US élection *f* au niveau d'un État; **2** (ceremonial) [*coach, occasion, opening*] d'apparat; [*banquet*] de gala; [*funeral*] national; [*visit*] officiel/-ielle; **to go on a ~ visit to Tokyo** se rendre en visite officielle à Tokyo.

IV *vtr* **1** (express, say) exposer [*fact, opinion, position, truth, view*]; (provide information) indiquer [*age, income*]; **to ~ that** [*person*] déclarer que; **'I have no intention of resigning' he ~d** 'je n'ai pas l'intention de démissionner' a-t-il déclaré; **applicants must ~ where they live** les candidats doivent indiquer où ils habitent; **the document ~s clearly the conditions necessary for acceptance** le document présente or indique clairement les conditions requises pour l'acceptation; **to ~ the obvious** énoncer une évidence; **to ~ one's case** gen exposer son cas; Jur présenter son dossier; **as ~d above/below** comme mentionné ci-dessus/ci-dessous; **2** (specify) spécifier [*amount, conditions, place, time, terms*]; exprimer [*preference*]; **the ~d time/amount, the time/amount ~d** l'heure/la somme spécifiée; **at ~d times/intervals** à dates/intervalles fixes; **on ~d days** à jours fixes.

IDIOMS **to be in/get oneself into a ~** être/se mettre dans tous ses états.

state: **~ bank** *n* US banque *f* d'État; **State capital** *n* US capitale *f* d'État; **~ capitalism** *n* capitalisme *m* d'État; **State Capitol** *n* US Pol assemblée *f* législative d'État; **State Certified Midwife**, **SCM** **▶ 1692** *n* sage-femme *f* diplômée.

state control *n* étatisation *f* (**of** de); **to bring sth under ~** étatiser qch.

state: **~-controlled** *adj* contrôlé par l'État; **~craft** *n* capacité *f* à gérer les affaires publiques; **State Department** *n* US, Pol ministère *m* américain des affaires étrangères; **State Enrolled Nurse**, **SEN** **▶ 1692** *n* GB Med ≈ infirmier/-ière *m/f* diplômé/-e d'État; **~-funded** *adj* subventionné par l'État.

statehood /ˈsteɪthʊd/ *n* **our aim is ~** notre objectif est de devenir un État; **to achieve ~** devenir un État.

State house *n* US (for legislature) siège *m* du Parlement; (for public events) édifice *m* public.

stateless /ˈsteɪtlɪs/ *adj* apatride; **~ persons** les apatrides.

statelessness /ˈsteɪtlɪsnɪs/ *n* condition *f* d'apatride.

Stateline /ˈsteɪtlaɪn/ *n* US frontière *f* (entre États).

stateliness /ˈsteɪtlɪnɪs/ *n* aspect *m* imposant.

stately /ˈsteɪtlɪ/ *adj* imposant.

stately home *n* GB demeure *f* ancestrale, château *m*.

statement /ˈsteɪtmənt/ *n* **1** (expression of view) déclaration *f* (**by** de; **on, about** à propos de; **to** à; **of** de); **official ~** communiqué *m* officiel; **~ of belief** profession *f* de foi; **~ of intent/principle** déclaration d'intention/de principe; **~ of fact** exposé *m* des faits; **to make/issue a ~** faire/publier une déclaration; **to release a ~** faire une déclaration; **the Minister's ~ said...** dans son communiqué le Ministre a fait savoir que...; **in a ~ the Minister said...** dans un communiqué or une déclaration le Ministre a fait savoir...; **2** Fin (of bank account) relevé *m* de compte; **a financial ~** un état de la situation financière; **3** Jur déclaration *f*; **to make a false ~** faire une fausse déclaration; **to take a ~** [*police officer*] prendre une déclaration.

statement of claim *n* GB Jur exposé *m* détaillé du demandeur.

state: **~ of the art** *adj* [*equipment, tool, device, laboratory*] ultramoderne; [*technology*] de pointe; **State of the Union Address** *n* US Pol discours *m* public annuel du Président des États-Unis; **~-owned** *adj* [*company*] étatique; **State police** *n* US police *f* d'État; **~ prison** *n* US prison *f* d'État (*pour les peines de longue durée*); **State Registered Nurse**, **SRN** **▶ 1692** *n* GB Med ≈ infirmier/-ière *m/f* diplômé/-e d'État; **State representative** *n* député/-e *m/f* d'État; **~room** *n* Naut cabine *f* particulière; **~ room** *n* salle *f* de réceptions officielles; **~-run** *adj* [*newspaper, radio, television*] contrôlé par l'État; [*company, factory*] géré par l'État; **State's attorney** *n* US Jur avocat/-e *m/f* représentant l'État; **State senator** *n* US Pol sénateur/-trice *m/f* d'État.

State's evidence *n* US Jur **to turn ~** dénoncer ses complices.

States General *npl* **1** Pol Parlement *m* des Pays-Bas; **2** Hist États *mpl* généraux.

stateside /ˈsteɪtsaɪd/ **I** *adj* des États-Unis. **II** *adv* aux États-Unis.

statesman /ˈsteɪtsmən/ *n* (*pl* **-men**) homme *m* d'État.

statesmanlike /ˈsteɪtsmənlaɪk/ *adj* digne d'un homme d'État.

statesmanship /ˈsteɪtsmənʃɪp/ *n* ¢ qualités *fpl* d'homme d'État.

state: **~ socialism** *n* socialisme *m* d'État; **~-sponsored terrorism** *n* terrorisme *m* d'État; **~ trooper** *n* US policier *m* d'État; **State university** *n* US université *f* d'État; **~wide** *adj, adv* US dans tout l'État.

static /ˈstætɪk/ **I** *n* **1** (also **~ electricity**) électricité *f* statique; **2** Radio, TV (interference) (bruit *m* de) friture *f*, parasites *mpl*; **3**° US ¢ (trouble) embêtements *mpl*.

II *adj* **1** (stationary) [*scene, actor, display*] statique; [*image*] fixe; [*traffic*] bloqué; **2** (unchanging) [*society, way of life, values*] immuable; [*style, ideas*] statique; **3** (stable) [*population, prices, demand*] stationnaire; **4** Phys [*force, pressure*] statique; **5** Comput [*memory*] statique; [*data*] fixe.

statics /ˈstætɪks/ *n* (+ *v sg*) statique *f*.

station /ˈsteɪʃn/ **I** *n* **1** Rail gare *f*; **in** ou **at the ~** à la gare; **the train came into the ~** le train est entré en gare; **2** Radio, TV (service) Radio station *f* de radio; TV station *f* de télévision; (frequency) station *f*; **jazz ~** station *f* de jazz; **local/national radio ~** radio *f* locale/nationale; **television ~, TV ~** station *f* de télévision; **3** Mil, Naut (base) base *f*; **air ~** base *f* aérienne; **naval/RAF ~** base *f* navale/de la RAF; **4** Mil, Naut, gen (post) poste *m*; **at one's ~** à son poste; **5** (also **police ~**) commissariat *m*; (small) poste *m* de police; **6** Agric élevage *m*; **cattle/sheep ~** élevage *m* bovin/de moutons; **7†** (rank) condition *f*; **one's ~ in life** sa condition dans la société; **to get ideas above one's ~** ne pas avoir les moyens de ses ambitions; **8** Relig **the Stations of the Cross** les Stations *fpl* de la croix; **to do the Stations of the Cross** faire le chemin de la croix.

II *modif* [*facilities, hotel, platform, staff*] de la gare.

III *vtr* gen, Mil poster [*officer, guard, steward*]; stationner [*troops*]; déployer [*ship, tank*]; **to be ~ed in Germany/at Essen** être en garnison en Allemagne/à Essen.
IV *v refl* **to ~ oneself** se poster.

stationary /ˈsteɪʃənrɪ, US -nerɪ/ *adj* **1** gen [*queue, vehicule*] à l'arrêt; [*traffic*] bloqué; [*prices*] stable; **2** Meteorol [*front*] stationnaire.

station break *n* US Radio, TV pubs○ *fpl*; **'we're going to take a ~'** 'et tout de suite quelques pages de publicité'.

stationer /ˈsteɪʃnə(r)/ **▶ 1692** *n* **1** (person) papetier/-ière *m/f*; **2** (also **~'s**) (shop) papeterie *f*.

stationery /ˈsteɪʃnərɪ, US -nerɪ/ **I** *n* **1** (writing materials) papeterie *f*; (for office) fournitures *fpl* (de bureau); **2** (writing paper) papier *m* à lettres.
II *modif* [*cupboard*] à fournitures; [*department*] des fournitures.

stationery shop GB, **stationery store** US **▶ 1692** *n* papeterie *f*.

station: **~master ▶ 1692** *n* chef *m* de gare; **~ wagon** *n* US break *m*.

statistic /stəˈtɪstɪk/ *n* statistique *f*; **official** ou **government ~s** statistiques officielles; **unemployment ~s** chiffres *mpl* du chômage; **the ~s on** les statistiques de [*prices, crime*]; **~s show that...** d'après les statistiques,...

statistical /stəˈtɪstɪkl/ *adj* statistique.

statistically /stəˈtɪstɪklɪ/ *adv* [*reliable, representative, random*] statistiquement.

statistician /ˌstætɪˈstɪʃn/ **▶ 1692** *n* statisticien/-ienne *m/f*.

statistics /stəˈtɪstɪks/ *n* **1** (subject) (+ *v sg*) statistique *f*; **2** (facts) (+ *v pl*) statistiques *fpl*.

stative /ˈsteɪtɪv/ *adj* Ling [*verb*] d'état.

stats○ /stæts/ *npl* = **statistics**.

statuary /ˈstætʃʊərɪ/ *n* **1** ¢ (collection) statues *fpl*; **2** (art) statuaire *f*.

statue /ˈstætʃuː/ *n* statue *f*.

statuesque /ˌstætʃʊˈesk/ *adj* sculptural.

statuette /ˌstætʃʊˈet/ *n* statuette *f*.

stature /ˈstætʃə(r)/ *n* **1** (height) stature *f*, taille *f*; **small/tall of** ou **in ~** de petite/grande taille or stature; **2** (status) stature *f*, envergure *f*; **his/her ~ as sth** sa réputation de qch; **to give sb ~** donner de l'envergure à qn; **intellectual ~** stature intellectuelle.

status /ˈsteɪtəs/ *n* (*pl* **-uses**) **1** (position) position *f*; **cult ~** qualité *f* de personnage culte; **social ~** position *f* sociale; **her (official) ~ as manager** sa position (officielle) de manager; **2** ¢ (prestige) prestige *m*; **to have ~** avoir du prestige; **3** Admin, Jur statut *m* (**as** de); **to be given equal ~** bénéficier du même statut; **charitable ~** statut d'œuvre charitable; **employment ~** situation *f* professionnelle; **financial ~** état *m* financier; **legal ~** statut légal; **professional ~** statut professionnel; **refugee ~** statut de réfugié.

status: **~ bar** *n* Comput barre *f* d'état; **~ inquiry** *n* Fin enquête *f* sur la situation financière; **~ meeting** *n* réunion *f* de bilan; **~ quo** *n* statu quo *m*; **~ symbol** *n* signe *m* de prestige.

statute /ˈstætʃuːt/ *n* **1** Jur, Pol texte *m* de loi; **by ~** par la loi; **2** Admin règlement *m* (interne); **the University ~s** les statuts *mpl* de l'université.

statute book *n* lois *fpl* en vigueur; **to be on the ~** être en vigueur; **to reach the ~** devenir texte de loi, entrer en vigueur.

statute: **~ law** *n* législation *f*; **~ of limitations** *n* Jur ≈ prescription *f*.

statutory /ˈstatʃʊtərɪ, US -tɔːrɪ/ *adj* [*duty, powers, requirements, sick pay*] légal; [*authority, agency, body*] officiel/-ielle; **~ offence** GB, **~ offense** US infraction *f* à la loi.

statutory: **~ instrument** *n* instrument *m* législatif; **~ rape** *n* US détournement *m* de mineure.

staunch /stɔːntʃ/ **I** *adj* [*supporter, ally, defence*] loyal; [*defender*] ardent.
II *vtr* **staunch, stanch** US /stɑːntʃ, stɔːntʃ/ **1** lit étancher [*wound, flow, bleeding*]; **2** fig arrêter [*decline*].

staunchly /ˈstɔːntʃlɪ/ *adv* [*defend, oppose*] fermement; [*Catholic, Communist*] résolument.

stave /steɪv/ *n* **1** Mus (staff) portée *f*; **2** (of barrel) douve *f*; **3** (stick) bâton *m*; **4** (stanza) strophe *f*.
■ **stave in** (*prét, pp* **staved** ou **stove**): **~ in [sth], ~ [sth] in** défoncer.
■ **stave off** (*prét, pp* **staved**): **~ off [sth]** tromper [*hunger, thirst, fatigue*]; empêcher [*bankruptcy, defeat, crisis*]; écarter [*attack, threat*].

staves /steɪvz/ *pl* ▶ **staff I 1, 5**.

stay /steɪ/ **I** *n* **1** (visit, period) séjour *m*; **a ~ in hospital** un séjour à l'hôpital; **a two-week ~** un séjour de deux semaines; **to have an overnight ~ in Athens** passer la nuit à Athènes; **the bad weather ruined our ~** le mauvais temps a gâché notre séjour; **'enjoy your ~!'** 'bon séjour!'; **2** Naut hauban *m*; **3** Jur sursis *m*; **~ of execution** (of death penalty) sursis (à l'exécution de la peine capitale); (of other sentence) sursis *m*; fig (delay, reprieve) répit *m*.
II stays *npl* corset *m*.
III *vtr* **1** Jur surseoir à [*proceedings*]; **2** Turf [*horse*] tenir [*distance*].
IV *vi* **1** (remain) rester; **~ a few days** restez quelques jours; **to ~ for lunch** rester (à) déjeuner; **to ~ in bed/at home** rester au lit/à la maison; **to ~ calm/faithful** rester calme/fidèle; **I'm not ~ing another minute** je ne resterai pas une minute de plus; **to ~ in Britain** rester en Grande-Bretagne; **to ~ in teaching** rester dans l'enseignement; **to ~ in nursing** continuer comme infirmier/-ière; **to ~ in farming** continuer à travailler dans l'agriculture; **to ~ in business** (not go under) rester à flot; **to ~ put** ne pas bouger; **'~ tuned!'** (on radio) 'restez avec nous!'; **computers are here to ~** les ordinateurs font maintenant partie de la vie; **2** (have accommodation) loger; **where are you ~ing?** où loges-tu?; **to ~ in a hotel/at a friend's house/with Gill** loger à l'hôtel/chez un ami/chez Gill; **3** (spend the night) passer la nuit; **it's very late, why don't you ~?** il est très tard, tu pourrais passer la nuit ici; **I had to ~ in a hotel** j'ai dû passer la nuit à l'hôtel; **to ~ overnight in Philadelphia** passer la nuit à Philadelphie; **4** (visit for unspecified time) **to come to ~** (for a few days) venir passer quelques jours (**with** chez); (for a few weeks) venir passer quelques semaines (**with** chez); **do you like having people to ~?** tu aimes avoir des gens chez toi?; **5** Scot (live) habiter.
■ **stay away 1** (not come) ne plus venir; **when hotels are too dear, tourists ~ away** quand les hôtels sont trop chers, les touristes ne viennent plus; **go away and ~ away!** va-t-en et ne reviens plus!; **to ~ away from** éviter [*town centre, house*]; ne pas s'approcher de [*cliff edge, window, strangers*]; **~ away from my sister/husband!** laisse ma sœur/mon mari tranquille!; **2** (not attend) **to ~ away from school/work** s'absenter de l'école/de son travail.
■ **stay behind** rester; **she ~ed behind after the concert** elle est restée à la fin du concert.
■ **stay in 1** (not go out) rester à la maison, ne pas sortir; **2** (remain in cavity) [*hook, nail*] tenir.
■ **stay on 1** GB Sch rester à l'école; **2** (not leave) rester; **3** (continue in post) rester; **to ~ on as** garder son poste de [*chief accountant, head chef*]; **4** (not fall off) [*handle, label*] tenir.
■ **stay out 1** (remain away) **to ~ out late/all night** rentrer tard/ne pas rentrer de la nuit; **to ~ out of** ne pas entrer dans [*room, house*]; **to ~ out of sight** rester caché; **to ~ out of trouble** éviter les ennuis; **to ~ out of sb's way** éviter qn; **~ out of this!** ne t'en mêle pas!; **2** (continue strike) continuer la grève.
■ **stay over** rester.
■ **stay up 1** (as treat, waiting for sb) veiller (**to do** pour faire; **until** jusqu'à); **2** (as habit) se coucher tard; **he likes to ~ up late** il aime se coucher tard; **3** (not fall down) tenir.

stay-at-home *n, adj* GB casanier/-ière (*m/f*).

stayer /ˈsteɪə(r)/ *n* **1** Sport (athlete, horse) qui a du fond; **2** fig (worker) **to be a ~** ne pas abandonner facilement, avoir de la persévérance.

staying-power *n* endurance *f*; Sport **to have ~** avoir du fond.

stay stitching *n* couture *f* de maintien.

St Bernard /sənt'bɜːnəd/ *n* saint-bernard *m*.

St Christopher-Nevis /sənt,krɪstəfə'niːvɪs/ *pr n* Saint-Christophe-et-Niévès *m*.

STD *n* **1** Med (*abrév* = **sexually transmitted disease**) MST *f*; **2** GB Telecom (*abrév* = **subscriber trunk dialling**) automatique *m*.

STD (area) code *n* GB indicatif *m*.

stead /sted/ *n* **in sb's ~** à la place de qn; **she went in my ~** elle est allée à ma place.
IDIOMS **to stand sb in good ~** s'avérer utile pour qn, être utile à qn.

steadfast /ˈstedfɑːst, US -fæst/ *adj* [*friend*] dévoué; [*supporter*] résolu; [*determination, belief, refusal*] tenace; [*gaze*] franc/franche; **to be ~ in adversity/in one's belief** être ferme dans l'adversité/dans sa croyance.

steadfastly /ˈstedfɑːstlɪ, US -fæstlɪ/ *adv* fermement.

steadfastness /ˈstedfɑːstnɪs, US -fæst-/ *n* ténacité *f*.

steadily /ˈstedɪlɪ/ *adv* **1** (gradually) [*deteriorate, increase, rise*] progressivement; **2** (regularly) [*bang, pump*] régulièrement; **3** (without interruption) [*work, rain*] sans interruption; **4** [*look, gaze*] sans détourner le regard; **to look ~ at sb** regarder qn sans détourner le regard.

steadiness /ˈstedɪnɪs/ *n* **1** (of table, chair) stabilité *f*; (of hand) fermeté *f*; **2** (of voice) fermeté *f*; (of gaze) calme *m*; **3** (in temperament) fermeté *f*; **I admire his ~** j'admire la fermeté de son caractère.

steady /ˈstedɪ/ **I** *adj* **1** (gradual) [*increase, accumulation, decline*] progressif/-ive; **2** (even, continual) [*pace, progress, stream*] régulier/-ière, constant; [*rain*] incessant; [*breathing, drip, thud*] régulier/-ière; **a ~ stream of cars/callers** un flot constant de voitures/visiteurs; **to drive at a ~ 80 kmh** rouler à une vitesse régulière de 80 kmh; **progress has been ~** les progrès ont été réguliers; **3** (firm, unwavering) [*hand*] ferme; fig [*trust, faith*] immuable; **is the ladder/the chair ~?** est-ce que l'échelle/la chaise est stable?; **to keep** ou **hold sth ~** tenir fermement qch; **he isn't very ~ on his feet** (from age) il n'est plus très ferme sur ses jambes; (from drunkenness) il titube; **to hold ~** Fin [*share prices, interest rates*] se maintenir; **to hold ~ at 270 francs** Fin se maintenir à 270 francs; **4** (calm) [*voice*] ferme; [*look, gaze*] calme; **to have ~ nerves** avoir les nerfs solides; **5** (reliable) [*job, income*] fixe; [*boyfriend, relationship*] régulier/-ière; [*company, worker*] fiable.
II○ *excl* GB **~!** doucement!; **~ on!** (reprovingly) ça suffit!
III *vtr* **1** (keep still) tenir [*ladder, camera*]; **she tried to ~ her hand** elle a essayé d'empêcher sa main de trembler; **2** (control) **to ~ one's nerves** se calmer les nerfs; **to ~ one's voice** maîtriser le tremblement de sa voix.
IV *vi* **1** [*hand*] cesser de trembler; [*boat*] cesser de bouger; [*voice, nerves*] se calmer; **2** [*prices, interest rates*] se stabiliser.

V *v refl* **to ~ oneself** (physically) rétablir son équilibre; (mentally) se calmer.
IDIOMS **~ as she goes** Naut en avant toute; **to go ~ with sb**○† sortir avec qn.

steady state theory *n* théorie *f* de la création continue.

steak /steɪk/ *n* Culin (of beef) steak *m*; **~ and chips** steak frites; **cod ~** escalope *f* de colin; **salmon/tuna ~** darne *f* de saumon/thon.

steak: **~ and kidney pie**, **~ and kidney pudding** *n* GB tourte *f* au bœuf et aux rognons; **~house** *n* (restaurant *m*) grill *m*; **~ knife** *n* couteau *m* à steak; **~ sandwich** *n* steak *m* dans un sandwich.

steal /sti:l/ **I**○ *n* (bargain) **the watch was a ~!** cette montre était une super affaire○!; **5 dollars, that's a ~!** 5 dollars, c'est donné!
II *vtr* (*prét* **stole**; *pp* **stolen**) **1** (thieve) voler (**from sb** à qn); **2** fig (take surreptitiously) **to ~ a few minutes sleep/peace** s'offrir en douce quelque minutes de sommeil/de paix; **to ~ the credit for sth** s'attribuer le mérite de qch; **to ~ a glance at sth** jeter un coup d'œil à qch; **to ~ a kiss** voler un baiser; **to ~ a scene from sb** Theat, Cin voler la vedette à qn.
III *vi* (*prét* **stole**; *pp* **stolen**) **1** (thieve) voler; **to ~ from sb** voler qn; **to ~ from a car/house** cambrioler une voiture/maison; **our luggage was stolen from the car** on nous a volé nos bagages dans la voiture; **2** (creep) lit **to ~ into/out of the room** entrer dans/quitter la pièce subrepticement; **to ~ up on sb** s'approcher de qn subrepticement; fig **a sad expression stole across her face** une expression triste passa furtivement sur son visage; **the light stole through the curtains** la lumière filtrait à travers les rideaux.
IDIOMS **to ~ a march on sb** prendre qn de vitesse; **to ~ the show** Theat éclipser tout le monde; **she stole the show** on n'a eu d'yeux que pour elle.
■ **steal away** [*person*] s'esquiver (**from** de).

stealing /'sti:lɪŋ/ *n* vol *m*.

stealth /stelθ/ *n* (of cat, prowler) discrétion *f*; **by ~** furtivement.

Stealth bomber *n* avion *m* furtif.

stealthily /'stelθɪlɪ/ *adv* furtivement.

stealthy /'stelθɪ/ *adj* [*step, glance*] furtif/-ive; [*cat*] silencieux/-ieuse.

steam /sti:m/ **I** *n* **1** (vapour) vapeur *f*; (in room, on window) buée *f*; **vegetables cooked in ~** légumes cuits à la vapeur; **machines/trains powered by ~** machines/trains à vapeur; **~ rose from the ground** la vapeur montait du sol; **my breath turned to ~ in the cold** je faisais de la buée en respirant dans le froid; **2** Mech Eng (from pressure) pression *f*; **to get up** ou **raise ~** mettre la chaudière sous pression; **the locomotive is under ~** la locomotive est sous pression; **full ~ ahead!** Naut, fig en avant toute!
II *modif* [*bath, cloud*] de vapeur; [*cooking*] à la vapeur; [*boiler, iron, railway*] à vapeur.
III *vtr* Culin faire cuire [qch] à la vapeur [*vegetables*]; **~ed carrots** carottes à la vapeur; **~ed pudding** GB pudding cuit à la vapeur.
IV *vi* **1** (give off vapour) [*kettle, pan, soup*] fumer; [*water*] bouillir; [*engine, machine*] fumer; [*horse, ground, volcano*] fumer; **2** Rail **the trains used to ~ across** ou **through the countryside** autrefois les trains traversaient la campagne en crachant des nuages de fumée; **3**○ (move fast) se précipiter.
IDIOMS **to get up** ou **pick up ~** [*machine, vehicle*] prendre de la vitesse; [*campaign*] prendre de l'importance; **to run out of ~** [*athlete, orator, economy*] s'essouffler; [*worker*] peiner; **to let** ou **blow off ~** (use excess energy) se défouler○; (lose one's temper) se mettre en colère; **to get somewhere under one's own ~** se rendre or aller quelque part par ses propres moyens.
■ **steam ahead** fig **to ~ ahead in the polls** progresser dans les sondages; **she's ~ing ahead with her thesis** sa thèse avance bien.
■ **steam off**: ¶ **~ off** [*train*] s'éloigner dans un nuage de vapeur; [*person*] (in anger) partir furieux/-ieuse; ¶ **~ [sth] off**, **~ off [sth]** décoller [qch] à la vapeur [*stamp, wallpaper*].
■ **steam open**: **~ [sth] open**, **~ open [sth]** décacheter [qch] à la vapeur [*envelope, letter*].
■ **steam up**: ¶ **~ up** [*window, glasses*] s'embuer; ¶ **~ [sth] up** embuer [*window*]; **to get ~ed up** fig [*person*] se mettre dans tous ses états (**over** à propos de).

steam: **~boat** *n* bateau *m* à vapeur; **~ cleaner** *n* Tech dispositif *m* de nettoyage à vapeur; **~ engine** *n* locomotive *f* à vapeur.

steamer /'sti:mə(r)/ *n* **1** (boat) vapeur *m*; **2** Culin (pan) cuiseur-vapeur *m*; (trivet) panier *m* pour cuisson à la vapeur.

steaming /'sti:mɪŋ/ *adj* **1** (hot) [*bath*] très chaud; [*soup, tea*] brûlant; [*spring*] bouillant; **2**○ (furious) furax○ (*inv*); **3**○ (drunk) bourré○, ivre.

steam: **~ locomotive** *n* = **steam engine**; **~ museum** *n* Hist, Rail musée *m* du chemin de fer à vapeur; **~ power** *n* vapeur *f*.

steamroller /'sti:mrəʊlə(r)/ **I** *n* Constr rouleau *m* compresseur.
II *vtr* briser [*opposition, rival*]; **to ~ a bill/a plan through** imposer un projet de loi/un projet à [*Parliament, committee*].

steam: **~ room** *n* bain *m* de vapeur; **~ship** *n* gen navire *m* à vapeur; (for passengers) paquebot *m*; **~ship company** *n* compagnie *f* maritime; **~ shovel** *n* pelleteuse *f*; **~ stripper** *n* décolleuse *f* (de papier peint).

steamy /'sti:mɪ/ *adj* **1** (full of vapour) [*bathroom, window*] embué; **2** (humid) [*jungle, day, climate*] chaud et humide; [*heat*] humide; **3**○ (erotic) [*affair, film, scene*] torride.

steed /sti:d/ *n*‡ destrier *m*.

steel /sti:l/ **I** *n* **1** (metal) acier *m*; **made of ~** en acier; **2** (knife sharpener) aiguisoir *m*; **3** fig (in character) acier *m*; **nerves of ~** nerfs *mpl* d'acier.
II *modif* **1** [*bodywork, girder, cutlery, pan*] en acier; [*sheet, plate, pipe*] d'acier; **2** [*city, strike*] de l'acier; [*production, manufacturer*] d'acier.
III *v refl* **to ~ oneself** s'armer de courage (**to do** pour faire; **for** contre).

steel: **~ band** *n* steel band *m* (*ensemble musical dont les instruments sont des bidons et des récipients de récupération*); **~ blue** ▶**1104** *n, adj* bleu (*m*) acier (*inv*); **~ engraving** *n* gravure *f* sur acier; **~ grey** ▶**1104** *n, adj* gris (*m*) plombé (*inv*); **~ guitar** ▶**1481** *n* guitare *f* hawaïienne; **~ industry** *n* sidérurgie *f*; **~ mill** *n* aciérie *f*; **~-stringed guitar** ▶**1481** *n* guitare *f* à cordes d'acier; **~ tape** *n* mètre *m* à ruban; **~ wool** *n* (all contexts) paille *f* de fer; **~worker** ▶**1692** *n* sidérurgiste *mf*; **~works**, **~yard** *n* installations *fpl* sidérurgiques.

steely /'sti:lɪ/ *adj* **1** [*determination, willpower, nerves*] inébranlable; **with ~ eyes**, **~-eyed** au regard d'acier; **2** ▶**1104** [*sky, clouds*] gris plombé *inv*; [*blue, grey*] acier *inv*.

steep /sti:p/ **I** *adj* **1** (sloping) [*path, street, stairs*] raide; [*slope, cliff*] à pic; [*roof, hill*] pentu; [*ascent, climb*] abrupt; **a ~ drop** un à-pic; **2** (sharp) [*increase, rise, fall*] fort (*before n*); [*recession, decline*] profond; **3**○ (excessive) [*price, fees*] exorbitant; [*bill*] salé○.
II *vtr* (soak) **to ~ sth in** faire tremper qch dans.
III *vi* tremper (**in** dans).
IDIOMS **that's a bit ~!**○ GB c'est un peu raide○ or fort○!

steeped /sti:pt/ *adj* **to be ~ in** être imprégné de [*history, tradition, lore*]; être nourri de [*prejudice*]; être pénétré de [*nostalgia*]; **a history ~ in violence** une histoire baignant dans la violence.

steeple /'sti:pl/ *n* (tower) clocher *m*; (spire) flèche *f*.

steeplechase /'sti:pltʃeɪs/ *n* Turf steeplechase *m* (*course d'obstacles*); (in athletics) 3000m steeple *m* (*course d'obstacles*).

steeplechasing /'sti:pltʃeɪsɪŋ/ ▶**1282** *n* Turf steeple-chase *m*; (in athletics) steeple *m*.

steeplejack /'sti:pldʒæk/ *n* réparateur/-trice *m/f* de clochers (et de hautes cheminées).

steeply /'sti:plɪ/ *adv* **1** [*rise, climb, descend*] à pic, abruptement; [*drop, slope*] abruptement; **2** Econ, Fin [*rise*] en flèche; [*fall*] fortement.

steepness /'sti:pnɪs/ *n* (of slope, climb) raideur *f*.

steer /stɪə(r)/ **I** *n* **1** Agric, Zool bouvillon *m*; **2**○ US (tip) tuyau○ *m*; **a bum ~** un mauvais tuyau○.
II *vtr* **1** (control direction of) piloter, conduire [*car*]; piloter, gouverner [*boat, ship*]; **2** (guide) lit diriger, guider [*person*]; fig orienter [*person, conversation*]; conduire [*team, country*]; **to ~ one's way through/towards** lit, fig se frayer un passage à travers/vers; **to ~ a course through/between** fig manœuvrer délicatement à travers/entre; **to ~ a company out of its difficulties** sortir une société de ses difficultés; **to ~ a bill through parliament** faire aboutir un projet de loi.
III *vi* **1** gen **to ~ towards sth** se diriger vers qch; **to ~ away from sth** s'écarter de qch; **the car ~s well/badly** la direction (de la voiture) répond bien/mal; **2** Naut gouverner; **to ~ towards** ou **for** mettre le cap sur; **to ~ by the stars** se guider sur les étoiles.
IDIOMS **to ~ clear of sth/sb** se tenir à l'écart de qch/qn; **to ~ a middle course** adopter une position médiane.

steerage /'stɪərɪdʒ/ *n* Naut **1** (accommodation) entrepont *m*; **to travel ~** voyager dans l'entrepont; **2** (steering) pilotage *m*.

steerageway /'stɪərɪdʒweɪ/ *n* Naut erre *f* suffisante pour gouverner.

steering /'stɪərɪŋ/ *n* **1** (mechanism) direction *f*; **2** (action) conduite *f*.

steering: **~ column** *n* Aut colonne *f* de direction; **~ committee** *n* Admin comité *m* directeur; **~ gear** *n* Aut, Aviat, Naut direction *f*; **~ lock** *n* Aut Neiman® *m*, blocage *m* de direction; **~ system** *n* Aut système *m* de direction; **~ wheel** *n* Aut volant *m*.

steersman /'stɪəzmən/ *n* Naut timonier *m*.

stellar /'stelə(r)/ *adj* Astron stellaire; fig [*talent, cast*] brillant.

St Elmo's Fire /snt,elməʊz 'faɪə(r)/ *n* feu *m* de Saint-Elme.

stem /stem/ **I** *n* **1** (of flower, leaf) tige *f*; (of fruit) queue *f*; **2** (of glass, vase) pied *m*; (of feather, pipe) tuyau *m*; (of letter, note) queue *f*; **3** Ling radical *m*; **4** (of ship) étrave *f*; **from ~ to stern** de la poupe à la proue.
II *vtr* (*p prés etc* **-mm-**) **1** (restrain) arrêter [*bleeding, flow*]; fig enrayer [*advance, tide, increase, inflation*]; contenir [*protest*]; **2** Naut [*ship*] avancer contre [*tide*]; **3** Culin équeuter [*fruit*].
III *vi* (*p prés etc* **-mm-**) **1** (originate) **to ~ from** provenir de; **2** (in skiing) faire un (virage) stem.

stem ginger *n* gingembre *m* confit.

stemmed /stemd/ *adj* [*plant*] à tige; [*glass*] à pied; **long-/short-~** à longue/courte tige.

stem: **~ stitch** *n* point *m* de tige; **~ turn** *n* (in skiing) (virage *m*) stem *m*; **~ware** *n* ¢ US verres *mpl* à pied; **~ winder** *n* montre *f* à remontoir.

stench /stentʃ/ *n* puanteur *f*; fig odeur *f* nauséabonde.

stencil /'stensɪl/ **I** *n* **1** (card) pochoir *m*; **2** (pattern) dessin *m* au pochoir; **3** (in typing) stencil *m*.
II *vtr* (paint) peindre [qch] au pochoir; (draw) dessiner [qch] au pochoir [*motif, flowers*]; décorer [qch] au pochoir [*fabric, surface*].

stencilling, stenciling US /'stensɪlɪŋ/ *n* (technique) technique *f* du pochoir; **to do (some) ~** faire du pochoir.

steno○ /'stenəʊ/ US = **stenographer, stenography**.

stenographer /sten'ɒgrəfə(r)/ ▶**1692** *n* US sténographe *mf*.

stenography /ste'nɒgrəfɪ/ *n* US sténographie *f*.

stentorian /sten'tɔ:rɪən/ *adj* sout [*voice*] de stentor.

step /step/ **I** *n* **1** (pace) pas *m*; **to take a ~** faire un pas; **to walk** ou **keep in ~** marcher au pas or en cadence; **to change ~** changer le pas; **I was a few ~s behind her** je la suivais de près or de quelques pas; **to fall into ~ with sb** se mettre au même pas que qn; **to break ~** rompre le pas; **one ~ out of line and you're finished!**○ fig un pas de travers et t'es cuit○!; **to be out of ~ with the times/the rest of the world** fig être déphasé par rapport à l'époque actuelle/au reste du monde; **to be in ~ with sth** fig être en phase avec qch; **to watch one's ~** lit faire attention où on met les pieds; **you'd better watch your ~**○**!** fig tu ferais mieux de faire attention!; **to be two ~s away from victory** fig être à deux doigts de la victoire; **to be one ~ ahead of the competition** fig avoir une longueur d'avance sur ses concurrents; **I'm with you every ~ of the way** fig je ne te laisserai pas tomber; **2** (sound of footsteps) pas *m*; **I can hear the sound of his ~ on the stair** j'entends ses pas dans l'escalier; **to hear the sound of ~s** entendre des pas; **3** fig (move) pas *m* (**towards** vers); **a ~ forwards/backwards** un pas en avant/en arrière; **it's a ~ in the right direction** c'est un pas dans la bonne voie; **to be a ~ towards doing** être un premier pas pour faire; **the first ~ is the hardest** il n'y a que le premier pas qui coûte; **to be one ~ closer to winning/finishing** approcher de la victoire/de la fin; **the first ~ is to...** la première chose à faire c'est de...; **promotion to headteacher would be a ~ up for him** être nommé directeur lui permettrait de gravir un échelon; **4** fig (measure) mesure *f*; (course of action) démarche *f*; **to take ~s** prendre des mesures; **a positive ~** une mesure positive; **a serious ~** une démarche sérieuse; **to take the ~ of doing** prendre l'initiative de faire; **to take ~s to do** prendre des mesures pour faire; **it's an unusual ~ to take** c'est une initiative surprenante; **to take legal ~s** avoir recours à la justice; **5** fig (stage) étape *f* (**in** dans); **to go one ~ further** aller plus loin; **6** (way of walking) pas *m*; **to have a jaunty ~** marcher d'un pas vif; **7** Dance pas *m*; **to know the ~s to the tango** savoir danser le tango; **8** (stair) marche *f*; **a flight of ~s** (to upper floor) un escalier *m*; (outside building) des marches *fpl*.
II steps *npl* **1** (small ladder) escabeau *m*; **2** (stairs) (to upper floor) escalier *m*; (in front of building) marches *fpl*.
III *vtr* (*p prés etc* **-pp-**) échelonner.
IV *vi* (*p prés etc* **-pp-**) marcher (**in** dans; **on** sur); **to ~ into** entrer dans [*house, lift, room*]; monter dans [*car, dinghy*]; **to ~ into sb's office** entrer dans le bureau de qn; **if you would just like to ~ this way** si vous voulez bien me suivre; **it's like ~ping into another world/century** on a l'impression de se retrouver dans un autre monde/siècle; **to ~ off** descendre de [*bus, plane, pavement*]; **to ~ onto** monter sur [*scales, log, pavement*]; **to ~ over** enjamber [*fence, log, hole*]; **to ~ through** passer sous [*arch*]; passer derrière [*curtains*]; **to ~ through the door** passer la porte; **to ~ out of** sortir de [*house, room*]; **to ~ out of line** lit [*soldier*] sortir des rangs; fig faire un pas de travers; **to ~ up to** s'approcher de [*microphone, lectern*].
IDIOMS **to ~ on it**○ se grouiller○, se dépêcher; **to ~ on the gas**○ appuyer sur le champignon○, se dépêcher; **one ~ at a time** chaque chose en son temps.
■ **step aside** **1** (physically) s'écarter (**in order to** pour); **2** (in job transfer) céder sa place; **to ~ aside in favour of sb** ou **for sb** céder la place à qn.
■ **step back** **1** lit reculer; **to ~ back from** s'écarter de [*microphone*]; **2** fig prendre du recul (**from** par rapport à).
■ **step down**: ¶ **~ down** gen se retirer; (as electoral candidate) se désister; ¶ **~ down [sth]** reduire [qch] petit à petit [*production, imports*].
■ **step forward** s'avancer.
■ **step in** intervenir; **to ~ in to do, to ~ in and do** intervenir pour faire.
■ **step out** **1** (show talent) montrer son talent; **2**† US **to ~ out with sb** sortir avec.
■ **step outside**: ¶ **~ outside** sortir; **would you like to ~ outside** (as threat) est-ce que vous voulez régler ça dehors?; ¶ **~ outside [sth]** sortir de [*house, room*].
■ **step up**: **~ up [sth]** augmenter, accroître [*production*]; intensifier [*fighting, campaign, action, efforts*]; augmenter [*spending, voltage*]; renforcer [*surveillance*].

step: **~ aerobics** ▶**1282** *n* (+ *v sg*) step *m*; **~brother** *n* demi-frère *m*.

step-by-step **I** *adj* [*description*] détaillé; [*guide*] complet/-ète; [*policy, programme, reduction*] progressif/-ive.
II step by step *adv* [*analyse*] point par point; [*explain*] étape par étape; **to take sb through sth ~** expliquer qch à qn étape par étape; **to take things step by step** procéder méthodiquement.

step: **~child** *n* beau-fils/belle-fille *m/f*; **~daughter** *n* belle-fille *f*; **~-down transformer** *n* Tech transformateur *m* dévolteur; **~father** *n* beau-père *m*.

Stephen /'sti:vn/ *pr n* Stéphane, Étienne.

step: **~ladder** *n* escabeau *m*; **~mother** *n* belle-mère *f*; **~parent** *n* beau-père/belle-mère *m/f*.

steppe /step/ *n* steppe *f*.

stepped-up /ˌstept'ʌp/ *adj* [*production*] accru; [*pace*] accéléré.

stepping stone *n* lit pierre *f* de gué; fig tremplin *m*; **a ~ to the Presidency** un tremplin pour parvenir à la Présidence.

step: **~sister** *n* demi-sœur *f*; **~son** *n* beau-fils *m*.

stereo /'sterɪəʊ/ **I** *n* **1** (technique) stéréo *f*; **broadcast in ~** transmis en stéréo; **2** (set) chaîne *f* stéréo; **car ~** autoradio *m* stéréo; **personal ~** baladeur *m*.
II *modif* [*disc, cassette, effect*] stéréo *inv*; [*recording, broadcast*] en stéréo.

stereochemistry /ˌsterɪəʊ'kemɪstrɪ/ *n* stéréochimie *f*.

stereogram /'sterɪəgræm/, **stereograph** /'sterɪəgrɑ:f, US -græf/ *n* stéréogramme *m*.

stereophonic /ˌsterɪə'fɒnɪk/ *adj* stéréophonique.

stereo radio-cassette player *n* radio cassette *m* or *f* stéréo.

stereoscope /'sterɪəskəʊp/ *n* stéréoscope *m*.

stereoscopic /ˌsterɪə'skɒpɪk/ *adj* (all contexts) stéréoscopique.

stereoscopy /ˌsterɪ'ɒskəpɪ/ *n* (all contexts) stéréoscopie *f*.

stereo system *n* chaîne *f* stéréo.

stereotype /'sterɪətaɪp/ **I** *n* **1** (person, idea) stéréotype *m*; **2** Print (plate) stéréotype *m*; (process) clichage *m*.
II *vtr* gen stéréotyper [*image, person*]; Print clicher [*document*].

stereotyping /'sterɪətaɪpɪŋ/ *n* ⊄ formules *fpl* stéréotypées.

stereovision /'sterɪəvɪʒn/ *n* vision *f* stéréoscopique.

sterile /'steraɪl, US 'sterəl/ *adj* (all contexts) stérile.

sterility /stə'rɪlətɪ/ *n* (all contexts) stérilité *f*.

sterilization /ˌsterəlaɪ'zeɪʃn, US -lɪ'z-/ *n* (all contexts) stérilisation *f*.

sterilize /'sterəlaɪz/ *vtr* stériliser [*instrument, utensil, container*]; stériliser [*person, animal*]; rendre [qch] stérile [*land*].

sterling /'stɜ:lɪŋ/ **I** *n* ▶**1143** Fin livre *f* sterling *inv*; **~ rose/fell** la livre sterling a monté/a baissé; **~ was up/down** la livre sterling était en hausse/en baisse; **to quote ~ prices** annoncer des prix en livres sterling; **payable in ~** payable en livres sterling; **£100 ~** 100 livres sterling.
II *modif* Fin [*payment, cheque*] en livres sterling; **~ crisis** crise *f* de la livre sterling.
III *adj* (*épith*) (excellent) [*effort, quality*] remarquable; **to do ~ service** rendre de bons et loyaux services also fig.

sterling: **~ area** *n* zone *f* sterling; **~ silver** *n* argent *m* fin.

stern /stɜ:n/ **I** *n* Naut poupe *f*.
II *adj* [*face, look, parent, measure, warning*] sévère; [*message*] grave; [*challenge, opposition*] sérieux/-ieuse; [*choice*] difficile.
IDIOMS **to be made of ~er stuff** être plus solide qu'on ne pense.

sternly /'stɜ:nlɪ/ *adv* [*say, speak*] sévèrement; [*gaze, look*] d'un air sévère; [*opposed*] sérieusement.

sternness /'stɜ:nnɪs/ *n* sévérité *f*.

sternum /'stɜ:nəm/ *n* sternum *m*.

steroid /'stɪərɔɪd, 'ste-/ *n* (*gén pl*) Pharm, Med stéroïde *m*; **to be on ~s** prendre des stéroïdes; **anabolic ~** anabolisant *m*.

stertorous /'stɜ:tərəs/ *adj* sout [*breathing*] ronflant; [*snoring*] sonore.

stet /stet/ Print bon.

stethoscope /'steθəskəʊp/ *n* stéthoscope *m*.

stetson /'stetsn/ *n* chapeau *m* de cow-boy.

stevedore /'sti:vədɔ:(r)/ ▶**1692** *n* docker *m*.

stew /stju:, US stu:/ **I** *n* Culin gen ragoût *m*; (with game) civet *m*; (with veal, chicken) blanquette *f*.
II *vtr* gen cuire [qch] en ragoût; cuire [qch] en civet [*game*]; faire cuire [*fruit, vegetables*]; **~ed apples** compote *f* de pommes; **~ed lamb** ragoût *m* d'agneau.
III *vi* **1** Culin [*meat*] cuire à l'étouffée; [*fruit*] cuire (dans son jus); [*tea*] infuser trop longtemps; **2**○ [*person*] (in heat) crever de chaud○.
IDIOMS **to be/get in a ~**○ (worry) être/se mettre dans tous ses états, (trouble) être/se mettre dans le pétrin○; **to ~ in one's own juice**○ mijoter dans son jus○.

steward /stjʊəd, US 'stu:ərd/ ▶**1692** *n* (on plane, ship) steward *m*; (of estate, club) intendant/-e *m/f*; (at races) organisateur/-trice *m/f*.

stewardess /'stjʊədes, US 'stu:ərdəs/ ▶**1692** *n* (on plane) hôtesse *f* (de l'air); (on ship) hôtesse *f*.

stewardship /'stjʊədʃɪp, US 'stu:ərdʃɪp/ *n* (management) gestion *f*; (leadership) direction *f*.

stg *n*: *abrév écrite* = **sterling I**.

St Helena /ˌsnt'helənə/ ▶**1381** *pr n* Sainte-Hélène *f*.

stich /stɪk/ *n* Literat vers *m*.

stick /stɪk/ **I** *n* **1** (piece of wood) bâton *m*; (for kindling) bout *m* de bois; (for ice cream, lollipop) bâton *m*; Mil bâton *m*; **2** (also **walking ~**) canne *f*; **3** (rod-shaped piece) **a ~ of rock** ou **candy/chalk/dynamite** un bâton de sucre d'orge/craie/dynamite; **a ~ of celery** une branche de céléri; **a ~ of rhubarb** une tige de rhubarbe; **a ~ of (French) bread** une baguette; **4** Sport (in hockey) crosse *f*; (in polo) maillet *m*; **5** (conductor's baton) baguette *f*; **6** Mil **a ~ of bombs** un chapelet de bombes;

7○ (piece of furniture) meuble *m*; **a few ~s (of furniture)** quelques meubles; **we haven't got a ~ of furniture** nous n'avons pas un seul meuble; **8**○ GB (person) **a funny old ~** un drôle de bonhomme/une drôle de bonne femme *m/f*; **he's a dry old ~** il manque d'humour; **9**○ (criticism) critique *f*; **to get** ou **take (some) ~** se faire critiquer; **to give sb (some) ~** critiquer qn violemment; **10** Aviat manche *m* à balai; **11** US Aut levier *m* (de changement) de vitesse.

II○ **sticks** *npl* **in the ~s** en pleine cambrousse○, dans la campagne; **to be from the ~s** être de la campagne.

III *vtr* (*prét, pp* **stuck**) **1** (stab) égorger [*pig*]; **to ~ a pin/spade/knife into sth** planter une épingle/une pelle/un couteau dans qch; **he stuck a knife into the man's back** il a planté un couteau dans le dos de l'homme; **she stuck her fork into the meat** elle a piqué sa fourchette dans la viande; **to ~ a pin/knife through sth** faire un trou dans qch avec une épingle/un couteau; **a board stuck with pins** un tableau hérissé d'épingles; **2** (put) **he stuck his head round the door/through the window** il a passé sa tête par la porte/la fenêtre; **she stuck her hands in her pockets** elle a enfoncé ses mains dans ses poches; **~ your coat on the chair/the money in the drawer**○ mets ton manteau sur la chaise/l'argent dans le tiroir; **to ~ an advert in the paper**○ mettre une annonce dans le journal; **to ~ sb in a home**○ mettre qn dans une maison de retraite; **you know where you can ~ it** ou **that**◑**!** tu sais où tu peux te le mettre◑!; **~ it up your ass**●**!** va te faire foutre●!; **3** (fix in place) coller [*label, stamp*] **(in** dans; **on** sur; **to** à); coller [*poster, notice*] **(in** dans; **on** à); **'~ no bills'** 'défense d'afficher'; **4**○ GB (bear) supporter [*person, situation*]; **I can't ~ him** je ne peux pas le supporter; **I don't know how he ~s it** je ne sais pas comment il tient le coup○; **I can't ~ it any longer** je n'en peux plus; **5**○ (impose) **he stuck me with the bill** il m'a fait payer la note; **to ~ an extra £10 on the price** augmenter le prix de 10 livres; **I was stuck with Frank** je me suis retrouvé avec Frank; **6**○ (accuse falsely of) **to ~ a murder/a robbery on sb** mettre un meurtre/un cambriolage sur le dos de qn○.

IV *vi* (*prét, pp* **stuck**) **1** (be pushed) **the nail stuck in my finger/foot** je me suis planté un clou dans le doigt/le pied; **there was a dagger ~ing in his back** il avait un poignard planté dans le dos; **2** (be fixed) [*stamp, glue*] coller; **this glue/stamp doesn't ~** cette colle/ce timbre ne colle pas; **to ~ to** se coller à [*page, wall, skin, surface*]; **to ~ to the pan** [*sauce, rice*] coller au fond de la casserole, attacher○; **3** (jam) [*drawer, door, lift*] se coincer; [*key, valve, catch*] se bloquer, se coincer; fig [*price*] être bloqué; **4** (remain) [*name, habit*] rester; **to ~ in sb's memory** ou **mind** rester gravé dans la mémoire de qn; **we've caught the murderer, but now we have to make the charges ~** nous avons attrapé le meurtrier, maintenant nous devons prouver sa culpabilité; **to ~**○ **in the house/one's room** rester dans la maison/sa chambre; **5** (in cards) garder la main.

IDIOMS **to be on the ~**○ US être compétent; **to get on the ~**○ US s'y mettre; **to have** ou **get hold of the wrong end of the ~** mal comprendre; **to up ~s**○ **and leave** plier bagages et partir.

■ **stick around**○ **1** (stay) rester; **~ around!** reste là!; **2** (wait) attendre.

■ **stick at**: **~ at [sth]** persévérer dans [*task*]; **~ at it!** persévère!

■ **stick by**: **~ by [sb]** soutenir.

■ **stick down**: **~ [sth] down, ~ down [sth] 1** (fasten) coller [*stamp*]; **2**○ (write down) écrire [*answer, name, item*].

■ **stick on**: **~ [sth] on, ~ on [sth]** coller [*label, stamp*].

■ **stick out**: **¶ ~ out** [*nail, sharp object*] dépasser; **his ears ~ out** il a les oreilles décollées; **his stomach ~s out** il a un gros ventre; **her teeth ~ out** elle a les dents qui avancent; **to ~ out of sth** [*screw, nail, feet*] dépasser de qch; **to ~ out for** revendiquer [*pay-rise, shorter hours*]; **¶ ~ [sth] out, ~ out [sth] 1** (cause to protrude) **to ~ out one's hand/foot** tendre la main/le pied; **to ~ out one's chest** bomber le torse; **to ~ one's tongue out** tirer la langue; **2** (cope with) **to ~ it out**○ tenir bon○.

■ **stick to**: **~ to [sth/sb] 1** (keep to) s'en tenir à [*facts, point, plan, diet*]; **he stuck to his version of events** il n'a pas changé sa version des faits; **~ to what you know** tiens-toi en à ce que tu sais; **'no whisky for me, I'll ~ to orange juice'** 'pas de whisky pour moi, je m'en tiens au jus d'orange'; **2** (stay close to) rester près de [*person*]; **3** (stay faithful to) rester fidèle à [*brand, shop, principles*].

■ **stick together**: **¶ ~ together 1** (become fixed to each other) [*pages*] se coller; **2**○ (remain loyal) se serrer les coudes○, être solidaire; **3**○ (not separate) rester ensemble; **¶ ~ [sth] together, ~ together [sth]** coller [*objects, pieces*].

■ **stick up**: **¶ ~ up** (project) [*pole, mast*] se dresser; **his hair ~s up** ses cheveux se dressent sur sa tête; **to ~ up from sth** dépasser de qch; **to ~ up for sb** (defend) défendre qn; (side with) prendre le parti de qn; **to ~ up for oneself** défendre ses intérêts; **¶ ~ [sth] up, ~ up [sth]** (put up) mettre [*poster, notice*]; **to ~ up one's hand** lever la main; **to ~ one's legs up in the air** lever les jambes en l'air; **~ 'em up**○**!** haut les mains!

■ **stick with**○: **¶ ~ with [sb]** rester avec [*person*]; **¶ ~ with [sth]** rester dans [*job*]; s'en tenir à [*plan*]; rester fidèle à [*brand*]; **I'm ~ing with my current car for now** je garde la voiture que j'ai pour l'instant.

stickball /ˈstɪkbɔːl/ *n* US *sorte de base-ball joué dans les rues.*

sticker /ˈstɪkə(r)/ *n* autocollant *m*.

sticker price *n* Comm Aut prix *m* affiché.

stick float *n* Fishg flotteur *m* (*long et réglable*).

stickiness /ˈstɪkɪnɪs/ *n* **1** (state of being adhesive) (of tape, plaster) adhésivité *f*; (of substance) viscosité *f*; **2** (of weather) chaleur *m* moite; **3** (awkwardness) (of situation) difficulté *f*.

stick: **~ing plaster** *n* sparadrap *m*; **~ing point** *n* point *m* de désaccord or de friction; **~ insect** *n* phasme *m*; **~-in-the-mud**○ *n* routinier/-ière○ *m/f*.

stickleback /ˈstɪklbæk/ *n* épinoche *f*.

stickler /ˈstɪklə(r)/ *n* **1** (person) **to be a ~ for sth** être à cheval sur qch; **2** (problem, puzzle) casse-tête *m inv*.

stick-on /ˈstɪkɒn/ *adj* [*label*] adhésif/-ive.

stick pin *n* **1** US (tie-pin) épingle *f* de cravate; **2** (brooch) broche *f*.

stick: **~seed** *n* lappula *m*; **~ shift** *n* US Aut levier *m* de (changement de) vitesse; **~ sulphur** *n* soufre *m* en canon; **~tight** *n* Bot bidens *m*; **~-up**○ *n* braquage○ *m*, hold-up *m*; **~weed** *n* Bot ambroisie *f*.

sticky /ˈstɪkɪ/ *n* **1** (tending to adhere) [*hand, floor, substance*] collant; [*label*] adhésif/-ive; **2** (hot and humid) [*weather, day*] lourd; **3** (sweaty) [*hand, palm*] moite; **to feel** ou **be hot and ~** transpirer; **4** (difficult) [*situation, problem, period*] difficile; **to be ~ about sth/doing** ne pas être très conciliant pour qch/faire.

IDIOMS **to have ~ fingers** avoir tendance à voler; **to come to a ~ end** mal finir. ▶ **wicket**.

sticky: **~ bun**○ *n* GB *petit pain enrobé de sucre*; **~ tape**○ *n* GB Scotch® *m*, ruban *m* adhésif.

stiff /stɪf/ **I**○ *n* **1** (corpse) macchabée○ *m*; **2** US (humourless person) rabat-joie *mf inv*; **3** US (man) **a working ~** un travailleur; **4** US (drunk) poivrot○ *m*; **5** US (hobo) clochard *m*.

II *adj* **1** (restricted in movement) gen raide; (after sport, sleeping badly) courbaturé; **to feel ~ after riding/sleeping on the floor** se sentir courbaturé après avoir fait du cheval/dormi par terre; **to have a ~ neck** avoir un torticolis; **to have ~ legs** (after sport) avoir des courbatures dans les jambes; (from old age etc) avoir les jambes ankylosées; **2** (hard to move) [*drawer, door*] dur à ouvrir; [*lever*] dur à manier; [*gear*] dur à passer; **3** (rigid) [*cardboard, fabric, collar*] raide; **4** Culin [*mixture*] consistant, ferme; **beat the egg whites until ~** battre les œufs en neige ferme; **5** (not relaxed) [*manner, person, style*] compassé; **6** (harsh) [*letter, warning, penalty, sentence*] sévère; **7** (difficult) [*exam, climb*] difficile; [*competition*] rude; [*opposition*] fort; **8** (high) [*charge, fine*] élevé; **9** (strong) [*breeze*] fort; **I need a ~ drink** j'ai besoin d'un verre bien tassé○; **10**○ US (drunk) bourré.

III○ *vtr* US **1** (cheat) arnaquer [*person*]; **2** (fail to tip) ne pas laisser de pourboire à [*person*].

IV *adv*○ **to be bored ~** s'ennuyer à mourir; **to bore sb ~** ennuyer qn mortellement; **to be frozen ~** être frigorifié○; **to be scared ~** avoir une peur bleue; **to scare sb ~** faire une peur terrible à qn.

IDIOMS **to keep a ~ upper lip** encaisser○ sans broncher.

stiff-arm /ˈstɪfɑːm/ *vtr* US écarter [qn] avec les bras.

stiffen /ˈstɪfn/ **I** *vtr* **1** renforcer [*card*]; raidir [*structure*]; empeser [*fabric*]; donner de la consistance à [*mixture*]; **2** fig affermir [*resolve, determination*].

II *vi* **1** (grow tense) [*person*] se raidir; **2** Culin [*egg whites*] devenir ferme; [*mixture*] prendre de la consistance; **3** [*joint*] s'ankyloser; [*limbs*] se raidir.

stiffener /ˈstɪfnə(r)/ *n* (in collar) baleine *f* (de col); (in waistband) gros-grain *m*.

stiffly /ˈstɪflɪ/ *adv* **1** [*say*] avec froideur; **2** [*walk, move*] avec raideur; **3 ~ conventional/polite** d'un conformisme/d'une politesse rigide.

stiff-necked /ˈstɪfnekt/ *adj* péj guindé.

stiffness /ˈstɪfnɪs/ *n* **1** (physical) raideur *f*, ankylose *f*; **2** (of manner) froideur *f*; **3** (of fabric, substance) raideur *f*; **4** Culin consistance *f*.

stifle /ˈstaɪfl/ **I** *n* Anat grasset *m*.

II *vtr* étouffer [*person, debate, yawn, opposition, revolt, impulse*]; briser [*business*].

III stifled *pp adj* [*laughter, sigh*] étouffé; **to feel ~d** fig se sentir étouffé (**by** par).

stifling /ˈstaɪflɪŋ/ *adj* étouffant also fig; **it's ~!** on étouffe!

stigma /ˈstɪgmə/ *n* (*pl* **-mas** ou **-mata**) **1** Bot stigmate *m*; **2** (disgrace) stigmate *m* (**of** de).

stigmata /stɪgˈmɑːtə, ˈstɪgmətə/ *npl* stigmates *mpl* also fig.

stigmatic /stɪgˈmætɪk/ *n, adj* Relig stigmatisé/-e (*m/f*).

stigmatize /ˈstɪgmətaɪz/ *vtr* stigmatiser; **to be ~d as sth** être stigmatisé en tant que qch.

stile /staɪl/ *n* **1** (in wall, hedge) échalier *m*; **2** Constr montant *m*.

stiletto /stɪˈletəʊ/ *n* (*pl* **-tos**) **1** (shoe, heel) talon *m* aiguille; **2** (dagger) stylet *m*.

stiletto heel *n* (shoe, heel) talon *m* aiguille.

still[1] /stɪl/ *adv* **1** (up to and including a point in time) toujours, encore; **she ~ doesn't like eggs** elle n'aime toujours pas les œufs; **he's ~ as crazy as ever!** il est toujours aussi fou!; **that's ~ not good enough for you!** tu n'es toujours pas content!; **we're ~ waiting for a reply** nous attendons toujours une réponse; **they're ~ in town** ils sont encore en ville; **you have to eat this bread while it's ~ fresh** il faut manger ce pain pendant qu'il est encore frais; **you're ~**

too young tu es encore trop jeune; **the ruins are ~ to be seen** on peut encore voir les ruines; **I ~ have some money left** il me reste encore de l'argent; **2** (expressing surprise) toujours, encore; **he ~ hasn't come back** il n'est toujours pas revenu; **I ~ can't believe it!** je n'arrive toujours pas à le croire!; **are you ~ here?** tu es toujours or encore là?; **3** (referring to something yet to happen) encore; **it has ~ to be decided** c'est encore à décider; **I have four exams ~ to go** j'ai encore quatre examens à passer; **~ to come, a report on...** Radio, TV dans quelques instants, un reportage sur...; **4** (expressing probability) encore; **you could ~ be a winner** vous pouvez encore gagner; **there is ~ a chance that** il est encore possible que (+ *subj*); **prices are ~ expected to rise** on prévoit encore une augmentation des prix; **if I'm ~ alive** si je suis encore en vie; **5** (nevertheless) quand même; **he's unarmed but he's ~ dangerous** il n'est pas armé mais il est quand même or toujours dangereux; **it ~ doesn't explain why** cela n'explique quand même or toujours pas pourquoi; **it was very dear, ~ it was worth it** c'était très cher, ça valait quand même le coup○; **~, it's the thought that counts** enfin, c'est l'intention qui compte; **~ and all**○ quand même; **6** (with comparatives: even) encore; **faster ~, ~ faster** encore plus rapide; **stranger ~ was the fact that** ce qui était encore plus étrange c'était que; **~ more surprising** encore plus étonnant; **~ more money was spent** on a dépensé encore plus d'argent; **~ less** encore moins; **there is little sense of an objective, ~ less how to achieve it** on n'a pas une idée très précise de l'objectif et encore moins de la manière d'y arriver; **better/worse ~** encore mieux/pire; **7** (emphasizing quantity, numbers: yet) encore; **~ another way to do** encore une autre façon de faire; **many died, ~ more/~ others emigrated** beaucoup sont morts mais beaucoup plus encore/beaucoup d'autres encore ont émigré.

still[2] /stɪl/ **I** *n* **1** (for making alcohol) (apparatus) alambic *m*; (distillery) distillerie *f*; **2** Cin, Phot photographie *f* or photo *f* de plateau; **a ~ from a film** une photo extraite d'un film; **3** (calmness) (lack of motion) calme *m*; (lack of noise) tranquillité *f*; **the ~ of the night/forest** le silence de la nuit/forêt.
II *adj* **1** (motionless) [*air, day, water*] calme; [*hand, person*] immobile; **absolutely** ou **totally ~** immobile; **2** (peaceful) [*countryside, house, streets*] tranquille; **3** Culin, Wine [*drink, fruit juice*] nongazeux/-euse; [*water*] plat; [*wine*] tranquille.
III *adv* **1** (immobile) [*lie, stay*] immobile; **to hold [sth] ~** ne pas bouger [*camera, mirror, plate*]; **2** (calmly) **to sit ~** se tenir tranquille; **to keep** ou **stand ~** ne pas bouger.
IV *vtr* **1** (silence) faire taire [*critic, voice*]; **2** (calm) calmer [*crowd, doubt, fear*].
IDIOMS **~ waters run deep** il faut se méfier de l'eau qui dort.

stillbirth /ˈstɪlbɜːθ/ *n* Med **1** (event) mort *f* à la naissance; **2** (foetus) mort-né/-e *m/f*.

stillborn /stɪl/ *adj* lit, fig mort-né/-e.

still life *n* (*pl* **-lifes**) nature *f* morte; **a ~ painting** ou **drawing** une nature morte.

stillness /ˈstɪlnɪs/ *n* (of lake, evening) calme *m*.

still /stɪl/: **~(s) photographer**, **~ man** ▶ **1692** *n* Cin photographe *m* de plateau; **~(s) photography** *n* Cin photographie *f* de tournage or de plateau; **~ video camera** *n* appareil *m* photo magnétique.

stilt /stɪlt/ *n* **1** (pole) échasse *f*; **on ~s** monté sur des échasses; **2** Constr pilotis *m*.

stilted /ˈstɪltɪd/ *adj* guindé.

Stilton /ˈstɪltən/ *n* stilton *m* (*fromage*).

stimulant /ˈstɪmjʊlənt/ *n* (all contexts) stimulant *m* (**to** de).

stimulate /ˈstɪmjʊleɪt/ *vtr* **1** gen stimuler [*appetite, creativity, person*]; encourager [*demand*]; **2** Med stimuler.

stimulating /ˈstɪmjʊleɪtɪŋ/ *adj* (all contexts) stimulant.

stimulation /ˌstɪmjʊˈleɪʃn/ *n* (all contexts) stimulation *f* (**of** de); **to need intellectual ~** avoir besoin d'être stimulé intellectuellement.

stimulus /ˈstɪmjʊləs/ (*pl* **-li**) *n* **1** Physiol stimulus *m*; **2** fig (boost) impulsion *f*; **the ~ given to the economy** l'impulsion donnée à l'économie; **3** fig (incentive) stimulant *m*; **the ~ of competition** le stimulant de la concurrence.

sting /stɪŋ/ **I** *n* **1** Zool (organ) (of insect) dard *m*, aiguillon *m*; (of scorpion) aiguillon *m*; **2** (wound) (of insect, plant) piqûre *f*; **bee/wasp/nettle ~** piqûre d'abeille/de guêpe/d'orties; **3** (pain) sensation *f* de brûlure; **4** US (in law enforcement) coup *m* monté; **5**○ US (rip-off) arnaque *f*.
II *vtr* (*prét, pp* **stung**) **1** [*insect, antiseptic, plant*] piquer; **2** [*wind, hail*] cingler; **3** fig [*criticism, rebuke*] blesser, piquer [qn] au vif; **4**○ (rip off) arnaquer○; **they really ~ you in that place** on se fait arnaquer là-bas; **5**○ (get money from) **to ~ sb for £10** taper○ dix livres à qn.
III *vi* (*prét, pp* **stung**) [*eyes*] piquer; [*cut*] cuire; [*antiseptic*] piquer; **it ~s!** ça pique!; **my knee ~s** mon genou me cuit.
IDIOMS **a ~ in the tail** une mauvaise surprise; **to ~ sb into action** pousser qn à agir en le piquant au vif; **to take the ~ out of** rendre [qch] moins blessant [*remark, criticism*], atténuer l'effet de [*measure, action*].

stinger○ /ˈstɪŋə(r)/ *n* US (remark) pique○ *f*.

stingily /ˈstɪndʒɪlɪ/ *adv* chichement.

stinginess /ˈstɪndʒɪnɪs/ *n* radinerie○ *f*.

stinging /ˈstɪŋɪŋ/ *adj* **1** [*criticism, attack, remark*] blessant; **2** [*sensation*] de brûlure; [*pain*] cuisant.

stinging nettle *n* ortie *f*.

stingray /ˈstɪŋreɪ/ *n* (raie *f*) pastenague *f*.

stingy /ˈstɪndʒɪ/ *adj* péj [*person*] radin○; [*firm*] près de ses sous○; [*amount, allowance*] mesquin; **to be ~ with** être radin○ avec [*grant, allowance*]; lésiner sur [*food, paint*].

stink /stɪŋk/ **I** *n* **1** (stench) (mauvaise) odeur *f*; **the ~ of death/of rotten fish** l'odeur de mort/de poisson pourri; **there's an awful ~ in here!** ça pue ici!; **2**○ (row) esclandre *m*; **there'll be a (hell of a) ~ over this!** ça va faire un esclandre or du grabuge○!; **to kick up** ou **cause a ~ about sth** causer un esclandre à propos de qch.
II *vi* (*prét* **stank**, *pp* **stunk**) **1** (smell) puer; **to ~ of petrol/garlic** puer l'essence/l'ail; **the room is filthy—it ~s** la pièce est sale—ça pue (là-dedans); **2**○ fig (reek) **to ~ of corruption/injustice** sentir la corruption/l'injustice à plein nez; **the city stank of war/death** la ville puait la guerre/la mort; **the contract ~s!** le contrat pue○!; **we don't want your justice—it ~s!** on s'en fout○ de votre justice—elle pue○!
■ **stink out**: **~ [sth] out, ~ out [sth]** empester [*room, house*].
■ **stink up** US: **~ [sth] up, ~ up [sth]** empuantir.

stink: **~-bomb** *n* boule *f* puante; **~ bug** *n* US punaise *f* des bois.

stinker○ /ˈstɪŋkə(r)/ *n* **1** (difficult problem) casse-tête *m inv*; **the test was a real ~** l'interrogation était vachement○ dure; **2** péj (person) (male) sale type○ *m*; (female) sale bonne femme○ *f*; **he's been a real little ~ today** (child) il est vraiment enquiquinant○ aujourd'hui!; **3** GB (bad cold) rhume *m* carabiné.

stink horn *n* Bot phallus *m* impudique.

stinking /ˈstɪŋkɪŋ/ *adj* **1** (foul-smelling) [*place, person, clothes, water, sewage*] puant; **2**○ péj (emphatic) (*épith*) [*town, place, car, house*] infect; **a ~ cold** un rhume carabiné.
IDIOMS **to be ~ rich** être bourré de fric○.

stink: **~pot**○† *n* galeux/-euse○† *m/f*; **~weed** *n* diplotaxis *m*.

stint /stɪnt/ **I** *n* **1** (period of work) **to do a three-year ~ in Africa/with a company** travailler trois ans en Afrique/pour une entreprise; **to do a six-month ~ as president/as a teacher** être président/professeur pendant six mois; **to do one's ~ at the wheel** conduire à son tour; **during my three-day ~ as a secretary** pendant la période de trois jours où j'étais secrétaire; **I've done my ~ for today** j'en ai assez fait pour aujourd'hui; **2** (limitation) **without ~** généreusement.
II *vtr* priver [*person*] (**of** de).
III *vi* lésiner; **to ~ on** lésiner sur [*drink, presents*].
IV *v refl* **to ~ oneself** se priver (**of** de).

stipend /ˈstaɪpend/ *n* gen, Relig traitement *m* (*salaire*).

stipendiary /staɪˈpendɪərɪ, US -dɪerɪ/ **I** *n* personne *f* recevant un traitement.
II *adj* rémunéré.

stipendiary magistrate *n* GB Jur magistrat *m* professionnel.

stipple /ˈstɪpl/ *vtr* Tech pointiller; **a ~d effect** un effet granité.

stipulate /ˈstɪpjʊleɪt/ *vtr* stipuler (**that** que).

stipulation /ˌstɪpjʊˈleɪʃn/ *n* gen condition *f*; Jur stipulation *f*; **X's ~ that** la condition posée par X que.

stir /stɜː(r)/ **I** *n* **1** (act of mixing) **to give the tea/sauce a ~** remuer le thé/la sauce; **2** (commotion) agitation *f*; **to cause** ou **make a ~** faire du bruit; **to cause quite a ~** faire sensation; **3**○ argot des prisonniers (prison) **in ~** en taule○.
II *vtr* (*p prés etc* **-rr-**) **1** (mix) remuer [*liquid, sauce*]; mélanger [*paint, powder*]; **have you ~red it?** est-ce que tu as bien remué?; **to ~ sth into sth** incorporer qch à qch; **2** (move slightly) [*breeze*] agiter, faire bouger [*leaves, papers*]; **3** (move, arouse) [*music, sight, story*] émouvoir [*person*]; exciter [*curiosity, passions*]; stimuler [*imagination*]; éveiller [*emotions*]; **to ~ sb to pity/compassion** inspirer de la pitié/compassion à qn; **I was ~red by her story** son histoire m'a ému; **a speech which ~s the blood** un discours qui fouette le sang; **4** (incite) **to ~ sb into doing** inciter qn à faire; **to ~ sb to action/revolt** inciter qn à agir/à la révolte.
III *vi* (*p prés etc* **-rr-**) **1** (move gently) [*leaves, papers*] trembler; [*curtains*] remuer; [*person*] bouger; **to ~ in one's sleep** bouger en dormant; **the audience were ~ring in their seats** le public s'agitait dans la salle; **2** (awaken) bouger; **3** (budge) bouger; **do not ~ from that spot** ne bouge pas de l'endroit où tu es; **4** littér (awake) [*love, hope*] naître; [*memories*] se réveiller; **5**○ (cause trouble) [*person*] faire des histoires.
IV *v refl* (*p prés etc* **-rr-**) **to ~ oneself** se secouer○.
IDIOMS **he's always ~ring it**○ c'est un emmerdeur○.
■ **stir in**: **~ [sth] in, ~ in [sth]** incorporer [*flour, powder*]; ajouter [*eggs, milk*].
■ **stir up**: ¶ **~ [sth] up, ~ up [sth] 1** (whip up) [*wind*] faire voler [*dust, leaves*]; [*propeller*] aspirer [*mud*]; **2** fig provoquer [*trouble*]; attiser [*hatred, unrest*]; éveiller [*feelings*]; susciter [*emotions*]; remuer [*past*]; réveiller [*memories*]; rassembler [*support*]; **to ~ things up**○ envenimer les choses; ¶ **~ [sb] up, ~ up [sb]** travailler [*workers*]; exciter [*person, crowd*].

stir crazy○ US *adj* rendu fou/folle par la réclusion.

stir-fry /ˈstɜːfraɪ/ **I** *n* Culin sauté *m*; **a beef/vegetable ~** un sauté de bœuf/de légumes.
II *modif* [*beef, chicken*] sauté.
III *vtr* (*prét, pp* **-fried**) faire sauter [*beef, vegetable*].

stirrer○ /ˈstɪrə(r)/ *n* semeur/-euse *m/f* de zizanie.

stirring /ˈstɜːrɪŋ/ **I** *n* **1** (feeling) **to feel a ~ of hope/desire** avoir une lueur d'espoir/une bouffée de désir; **2** (sign) **the first ~s of revolt/of nationalism** les premières manifestations de la révolte/du nationalisme.
II *adj* [*era, story*] passionnant; [*music, performance, speech*] enthousiasmant; [*victory*] grisant; **the opera was ~ stuff**○ l'opéra était passionnant.
stirrup /ˈstɪrəp/ *n* (all contexts) étrier *m*; **to lose one's ~s** perdre les étriers; **to stand up in the ~s** se dresser sur ses étriers.
stirrup: **~ cup** *n* coup *m* de l'étrier; **~ leather** *n* étrivière *f*; **~ pump** *n* pompe *f* à main portative.
stitch /stɪtʃ/ **I** *n* **1** (in sewing, embroidery) point *m*; (single loop in knitting, crochet) maille *f*; (style of knitting, crochet) point *m*; **to drop a ~** lâcher une maille; **embroidery/knitting ~** point de broderie/tricot; **30 different ~es** 30 sortes de points différents; **2** Med point *m* de suture; **to have ~es** se faire recoudre; **I had ~es** on m'a recousu; **she had 10 ~es** on lui a fait 10 points de suture (**in, to** à); **he needs ~es (in his head)** il faut lui faire des points de suture (à la tête); **to have one's ~es out** se faire retirer les fils; **3** (pain) point *m* de côté; **to have/get a ~** avoir/attraper un point de côté; **4**○ US **to be a ~** [*person, film etc*] être tordant○.
II *vtr* **1** coudre (**to, onto** à); **hand-~ed** cousu à la main; **machine-~ed** piqué à la machine; **2** Med recoudre [*wound, face*]; **to have a cut ~ed** se faire recoudre une coupure.
IDIOMS **a ~ in time saves nine** un point à temps en vaut cent; **to be in ~es**○ rire aux larmes; **to have sb in ~es**○ faire rire aux larmes qn; **to not have a ~ on** être tout nu/toute nue; **I haven't got a ~ to wear** je n'ai rien à me mettre.
■ **stitch down**: **~ [sth] down, ~ down [sth]** fixer [qch] avec des points de couture.
■ **stitch together**: **~ [sth] together** lit assembler [*garment*]; fig assembler rapidement [*coalition, package*]; concocter rapidement [*compromise, proposal*].
■ **stitch up**: ¶ **~ up [sth], ~ [sth] up** lit recoudre [*hem, seam, wound, hand*]; ¶ **~ up [sb], ~ [sb] up**○ GB fig monter un coup contre qn○.
stitching /ˈstɪtʃɪŋ/ *n* couture *f*.
St: **~ John Ambulance** *n* GB *organisation bénévole qui assure les premiers soins dans les manifestations publiques*; **~ John's wort** *n* millepertuis *m*; **~ Lawrence Seaway** *pr n* voie *f* maritime du Saint-Laurent; **~ Lucia** ▶ 1131, 1381 *pr n* Sainte-Lucie *f*.
stoat /stəʊt/ *n* Zool hermine *f*.
stock /stɒk/ **I** *n* **1** ¢ (in shop, warehouse) stock *m*; **to have sth in ~** (in shop) avoir qch en magasin; (in warehouse) avoir qch en stock; **to be out of ~** [*product, model*] être épuisé; [*shop, warehouse*] être en rupture de stock; **the smaller size is out of ~** il n'y a plus de petites tailles; **2** (supply, store, accumulation) (on large scale) stock *m* (**of** de); (on domestic scale) provisions *fpl*; **a massive ~ of unsold homes** un grand stock de maisons invendues; **~s of coal/fish** des stocks de charbon/poisson; **~s are running low** les stocks sont presque épuisés; **we need to replenish our ~s** il faut renouveler les stocks; **to get in** ou **lay in a ~ of provisions** s'approvisionner or faire des provisions; **while ~s last** jusqu'à épuisement des stocks; **a ~ of knowledge** un réservoir de connaissances; **3** Fin (capital) ensemble *m* du capital or des actions d'une société; **4** (descent) souche *f*, origine *f*; **to be of/from peasant/immigrant ~** être de souche or d'origine paysanne/immigrée; **to come from farming ~** venir d'une famille d'agriculteurs; **only the paternal ~ concerns us** seule la branche or lignée paternelle nous intéresse; **5** (personal standing) cote *f*; **his ~ has risen since**... sa cote a monté depuis...; **6** Culin bouillon *m*; **beef ~** bouillon *m* de bœuf; **7** (of gun) fût *m*; **8** Bot giroflée *f*; **9** Games (in cards) talon *m*; **10** Fashn (huntsman's cravat) lavallière *f*; (part of clerical robes) étole *f*; **11** Agric, Zool, Bot (+ *v pl*) (cattle) bétail *m*, cheptel *m* bovin; (bloodstock) chevaux *mpl* de race; (young plants) porte-greffe(s) *m*; **~ rearing** élevage du bétail.
II stocks *npl* **1** Hist, Jur **the ~s** le pilori; **2** Fin valeurs *fpl*, titres *mpl*; **short/medium/long-dated ~** titres à courte/moyenne/longue échéance; **government ~** fonds *mpl* d'État; **~s closed higher/lower** la Bourse a clôturé en hausse/en baisse; **~s and shares** valeurs *fpl* mobilières; **3** Naut **to be on the ~s** [*boat*] être sur cale; fig [*project, product, book*] être en cours.
III *adj* [*size*] courant; [*answer*] classique, banal; [*character, figure*] stéréotypé.
IV *vtr* **1** Comm (sell) avoir, vendre; **I'm sorry, we don't ~ it** je suis désolé, mais nous n'en faisons pas or nous ne vendons pas cela; **2** (fill with supplies) remplir [*larder, fridge*]; garnir [*shelves*]; approvisionner [*shop*]; **to ~ a lake with fish** peupler un lac de poissons; **well-~ed** [*garden, library*] bien fourni.
IDIOMS fig **to take ~** faire le point (**of** sur).
■ **stock up** s'approvisionner (**with, on** en).
stockade /stɒˈkeɪd/ **I** *n* **1** (fence, enclosure) palissade *f*; **2** US Mil prison *f* militaire.
II *vtr* entourer [qch] d'une palissade.
stock: **~-breeder** ▶ 1692 *n* éleveur/-euse *m/f*; **~-breeding** *n* élevage *m*; **~broker** ▶ 1692 *n* agent *m* de change; **~broker belt** *n* GB banlieue *f* cossue; **~broker Tudor** *adj* GB [*style*] faux Tudor des banlieues cossues.
stockbroking /ˈstɒkbrəʊkɪŋ/ **I** *n* commerce *m* de titres en Bourse.
II *modif* [*firm, group*] spécialisé dans le commerce de titres en Bourse.
stock car *n* **1** Aut stock-car *m*; **2** US, Rail wagon *m* à bestiaux.
stock: **~-car racing** ▶ 1282 *n* course *f* de stock-cars; **~ clearance** *n* Comm liquidation *f* de stock; **~ company** *n* Fin société *f* par actions; **~ control** *n* Comm gestion *f* des stocks; **~-cube** *n* bouillon-cube® *m*; **~ dividend** *n* dividende *m* (en) actions.
stock exchange *n* (also **Stock Exchange**) **the ~** la Bourse; **on the Hong Kong Stock Exchange** à la Bourse de Hongkong; **to work on the ~** travailler à la Bourse; **to be listed on the ~** être coté en Bourse.
stock: **~ exchange listing** *n* Fin entrée *f* or admission *f* à la cote; **~fish** *n* stockfisch *m*.
stockholder /ˈstɒkhəʊldə(r)/ *n* actionnaire *mf*.
stock: **~holders' equity** *n* US capital *m* propre, fonds *mpl* propres; **~holders' report** *n* rapport *m* aux actionnaires.
Stockholm /ˈʃtɒkhəʊm/ ▶ 1818 *pr n* Stockholm.
stockily built *adj* [*person*] trapu.
stockiness /ˈstɒkɪnɪs/ *n* (of person) aspect *m* trapu; (of animal) aspect *m* râblé.
stockinet(te) /ˌstɒkɪˈnet/ *n* Tex jersey *m*.
stocking /ˈstɒkɪŋ/ ▶ 1703 *n* **1** Fashn bas *m*; **a pair of ~s** une paire de bas; **silk/woollen ~** bas de soie/de laine; **in one's ~(ed) feet** en chaussettes; **2** (also **Christmas ~**) ≈ soulier *m* de Noël; **what do you want in your ~?** qu'est-ce que tu veux pour Noël?
stocking: **~ cap** *n* bonnet *m* de laine; **~ filler** *n* petit cadeau *m* de Noël.
stocking mask *n* **terrorists wearing ~s** des terroristes le visage masqué d'un bas.
stocking stitch *n* point *m* de jersey.
stock-in-trade *n* spécialité *f*; **irony is part of the ~ of any teacher** l'ironie fait partie de la panoplie de tout professeur.
stock issue *n* Fin émission *f* d'actions.
stockist /ˈstɒkɪst/ *n* Comm, Fashn dépositaire *mf*; **'sole ~s'** 'dépositaire exclusif'.
stock: **~ jobber** ▶ 1692 *n* marchand *m* de titres, négociant *m* en valeurs; **~ list** *n* Comm liste *f* des marchandises en stock.
stockman /ˈstɒkmən/ ▶ 1692 *n* **1** Agric (for cattle) gardien *m* de bétail; (for sheep and cattle) gardien *m* de bestiaux; **2** US (warehouseman) magasinier *m*.
stock market /ˈstɒkmɑːkɪt/ **I** *n* **1** (stock exchange) Bourse *f* des valeurs; **to be quoted** ou **listed on the ~** être coté en Bourse; **2** (prices, trading activity) marché *m* des valeurs.
II *modif* [*analyst*] boursier/-ière de marché; [*crash, rumours, trading, slump, raid*] boursier/-ière; [*quotation, flotation*] en Bourse; **in ~ circles** dans les milieux boursiers; **~ price** ou **value** cote *f*.
stock option *n* option *f* d'achat de titres.
stockpile /ˈstɒkpaɪl/ **I** *n* réserves *fpl*.
II *vtr* stocker [*weapons*]; faire des stocks or des réserves de [*food, goods*].
stock: **~piling** *n* stockage *m*; **~pot** *n* marmite *f*; **~ room** *n* Comm magasin *m*; **~ sheet** *n* fiche *f* d'inventaire; **~ shortage** *n* rupture *f* de stock; **~ split** *n* division *f* des actions (*avec réduction de leur valeur unitaire*).
stock-still /ˌstɒkˈstɪl/ *adv* **to stand ~** rester cloué sur place.
stocktake /ˈstɒkteɪk/ *n* inventaire *m*; **to do a ~** faire l'inventaire.
stocktaking /ˈstɒkteɪkɪŋ/ *n* **1** Comm inventaire *m*; **'closed for ~'** 'fermé pour inventaire'; **to do ~** faire l'inventaire; **2** fig faire le point.
stock: **~ warrant** *n* Fin bon *m* de souscription de titres; **~whip** *n* fouet *m* (pour le bétail).
stocky /ˈstɒkɪ/ *adj* [*person*] trapu; [*animal*] râblé; **of ~ build** de forte carrure.
stockyard /ˈstɒkjɑːd/ *n* parc *m* à bestiaux.
stodge○ /stɒdʒ/ *n* ¢ GB (food) aliments *mpl* bourratifs; (writing) littérature *f* indigeste; (speech) discours *m* indigeste.
stodginess /ˈstɒdʒɪnɪs/ *n* (of food) lourdeur *f*; (of book, style) lourdeur *f*; (of speech) ennui *m*.
stodgy /ˈstɒdʒɪ/ *adj* [*food*] bourratif/-ive; [*person, speech*] ennuyeux/-euse; [*book*] indigeste; [*style*] lourd.
stogie /ˈstəʊgɪ/ *n* US cigare *m*.
stoic /ˈstəʊɪk/ *n, adj* stoïque (*mf*).
Stoic /ˈstəʊɪk/ **I** *n* stoïcien *m*.
II *adj* stoïcien/-ienne.
stoical /ˈstəʊɪkl/ *adj* stoïque.
stoically /ˈstəʊɪklɪ/ *adv* stoïquement.
stoicism /ˈstəʊɪsɪzəm/ *n* stoïcisme *m*.
stoke /stəʊk/ *vtr* (also **~ up**) alimenter [*fire, furnace, engine*]; fig entretenir [*enthusiasm, interest, anger*].
stokehole /ˈstəʊkhəʊl/ *n* **1** (also **stokehold**) Naut chaufferie *f*; **2** Ind porte *f* de chauffe.
stoker /ˈstəʊkə(r)/ ▶ 1692 *n* Naut, Ind, Rail chauffeur *m*.
STOL (*abrév* = **short take off and landing**) avion *m* à décollage et atterrissage courts, ADAC.
stole /stəʊl/ **I** *prét* ▶ **steal** II, III.
II *n* étole *f*.
stolen /ˈstəʊlən/ *pp* ▶ **steal** II, III.
stolid /ˈstɒlɪd/ *adj* [*person, character*] flegmatique; [*book, style*] sans relief.
stolidity /ˌstɒˈlɪdətɪ/ *n* = **stolidness**.
stolidly /ˈstɒlɪdlɪ/ *adv* imperturbablement.
stolidness /ˈstɒlɪdnɪs/, **stolidity** /stəˈlɪdətɪ/ *n* (of person, speech, behaviour) impassibilité *f*; (of nation) flegme *m*.
stollen /ˈstɒlən/ *n* US pain *m* brioché aux fruits.
stomach /ˈstʌmək/ **I** *n* estomac *m*; (belly)

ventre *m*; **to have a pain in one's ~** avoir mal au ventre or à l'estomac; **to lie on one's ~** être à plat ventre; **to do sth on a full/empty ~** faire qch le ventre plein/vide; **the pit of one's ~** le creux de l'estomac; **to be sick to one's ~** être profondément dégoûté; **I'm sick to my ~ of politics** la politique me dégoûte or me donne la nausée; **to have a strong ~** lit avoir un estomac d'autruche○; fig avoir l'estomac bien accroché○; **to turn sb's ~** écœurer qn.
II *modif* [*ulcer, operation*] à l'estomac; [*cancer, disease*] de l'estomac; **to have (a) ~ ache** avoir mal au ventre; **to have ~ trouble** avoir des troubles gastriques.
III *vtr* digérer [*food*]; fig encaisser○, supporter [*person, attitude, behaviour, violence*]; **I can't ~ oysters** je ne digère pas les huîtres; **I can't ~ that guy!** je ne peux pas encaisser○ ce type○!
IDIOMS **an army marches on its ~** il faut nourrir son homme; **to have no ~ for a fight** n'avoir aucune envie de se battre; **your eyes are bigger than your ~** tu as les yeux plus grands que le ventre.

stomach: **~ powder** *n* médicament *m* contre les lourdeurs d'estomac; **~ pump** *n* pompe *f* stomacale.

stomatologist /ˌstəʊməˈtɒlədʒɪst/ ▶ 1692 *n* stomatologue *mf*.

stomatology /ˌstəʊməˈtɒlədʒɪ/ *n* stomatologie *f*.

stomp /stɒmp/ **I** *n* **1** (of feet) bruit *m* de pas lourds; **2** US (dance) danse *f* très rythmée.
II *vi* **1** (walk heavily) **to ~ in/out** entrer/sortir d'un pas lourd; **he ~ed off in a rage** il est parti à grands pas furieux.

stomper○ /ˈstɒmpə(r)/ *n* US écrase-merde● *m*.

stomping ground *n* endroit *m* préféré; (bar) bar *m* favori; (neighbourhood) quartier *m* favori.

stone /stəʊn/ ▶ 1883 **I** *n* **1** ¢ (material) pierre *f*; **(made) of ~** en pierre; **to turn into ~** se changer en pierre; **to have a heart of ~** fig avoir un cœur de pierre; **to be as hard as ~** lit être dur comme de la pierre; fig avoir un cœur de pierre; **2** (small rock) pierre *f*, caillou *m*; **3** (for particular purpose) gen pierre *f*; (standing vertically) menhir *m*; (engraved) stèle *f*; **to lay a ~** poser une pierre; **to erect a ~** ériger une stèle; **they totally destroyed the town, not a ~ was left standing** ils ont complètement détruit la ville, tout était dévasté; **4** (also **precious ~**) (gem) pierre *f*; **5** Bot (in fruit) noyau *m*; **to take the ~ out of a peach** dénoyauter une pêche; **6** Med calcul *m*; **kidney ~** calcul *m* rénal; **7** GB Meas = *6,35 kg*.
II *modif* [*wall, statue, floor, building, step*] en pierre; [*jar, pot, pottery*] en grès; **~ cladding** revêtement *m* de pierre.
III *vtr* **1** (throw stones at) lapider [*person*]; **to ~ sb to death** lapider qn; **2** (remove stone from) dénoyauter [*peach, cherry*].
IDIOMS **~ me†!** GB ça alors!; **to leave no ~ unturned** ne négliger aucun détail; **it's a ~'s throw from here** c'est à deux pas d'ici; **to be set in (tablets of) ~** être gravé dans le marbre; **to cast the first ~** jeter la première pierre **(at** à); **to sink like a ~** couler à pic; ▶ **glasshouse**.

Stone Age I *n* Âge *m* de pierre.
II *modif* (also **stone age**) [*tool, village, society, man*] (datant) de l'Âge de pierre.

stone: **~chat** *n* traquet *m* pâtre; **~ circle** *n* enceinte *f* de monolithes, cromlech *m*.

stone-cold /ˌstəʊnˈkəʊld/ **I** *adj* glacé.
II *adv* **~ sober** parfaitement sobre.

stone: **~crop** *n* Bot orpin *m*; **~ curlew** *n* œdicnème *m* criard.

stoned○ /stəʊnd/ *adj* défoncé; **to get ~** se défoncer○ **(on** à).

stone: **~-dead** *adj* mort et bien mort; **~-deaf** *adj* sourd comme un pot○; **~ fruit** *n* fruit *m* à noyau; **~ground** *adj* moulu à la meule; **~ mason** ▶ 1692 *n* tailleur/-euse *m/f* de pierre; **~ saw** *n* scie *f* de tailleur de pierre.

stonewall /ˌstəʊnˈwɔːl/ **I** *vtr* éluder les questions de [*person*].
II *vi* **1** Sport jouer un jeu défensif; **2** (filibuster) faire de l'obstruction.

stonewalling /ˌstəʊnˈwɔːlɪŋ/ *n* obstructionnisme *m*.

stoneware /ˈstəʊnweə(r)/ **I** *n* poterie *f* en grès.
II *modif* [*jar, pot*] en grès.

stone: **~washed** *adj* Fashn délavé, stonewashed; **~work** *n* maçonnerie *f*.

stonily /ˈstəʊnɪlɪ/ *adv* [*look at, stare*] d'un air glacial; [*say, answer*] d'un ton glacial.

stonking○ /ˈstɒŋkɪŋ/ *adj* (also **~ great**) monstre○.

stony /ˈstəʊnɪ/ *adj* **1** (rocky) [*ground, path, riverbed, beach*] pierreux/-euse; **2** (of or resembling stone) [*colour, texture, appearance*] de (la) pierre; **3** fig (cold) [*look, silence*] glacial.
IDIOMS **to fall on ~ ground** tomber dans le vide.

stony: **~-broke**○ /ˌstəʊnɪˈbrəʊk/ *adj* GB fauché○, à sec○; **~-faced** *adj* impassible.

stood /stʊd/ *prét, pp* ▶ **stand II, III**.

stooge /stuːdʒ/ **I** *n* **1**○ péj (subordinate) larbin *m*; **2** Theat faire-valoir *m inv*.
II *vi* **1**○ péj faire le larbin; **to ~ for sb** être le larbin de qn; **2** Theat servir de faire-valoir à qn.
■ **stooge about, stooge around** aller au hasard.

stook /stuːk, stʊk/ GB **I** *n* moyette *f*.
II *vtr* gerber; **to ~ the sheaves** gerber les moyettes.

stool /stuːl/ **I** *n* **1** (furniture) tabouret *m*; **high/bar/piano ~** tabouret haut/de bar/de piano; **2** (faeces) selle *f*; **3** Bot pied *m* (de plante); **4** US (toilet) toilettes *fpl*.
II○ *vi* moucharder○.
IDIOMS **to fall between two ~s** être ni chair ni poisson.

stoolie○ /ˈstuːlɪ/ *n* = **stool pigeon**.

stool pigeon○ *n* mouchard/-e *m/f*.

stoop /stuːp/ **I** *n* **1** (curvature) **to have a ~** avoir le dos voûté; **to walk with a ~** marcher courbé; **2** US (veranda) perron *m*; **3** (of hawk) descente *f* en piqué.
II *vi* **1** (be bent over) être voûté; **2** (lean forward) se pencher; **to ~ down** se baisser; **to ~ over sth** se pencher sur qch; **3** (debase oneself) **to ~ to** s'abaisser à [*blackmail, lies*]; **to ~ so low as to do sth** s'abaisser jusqu'à faire qch; **4** (plunge) [*bird*] piquer.
III stooping *pres p adj* [*person*] courbé; **~ing shoulders** épaules voûtées.

stoop labour *n* US *travail agricole au ras du sol.*

stop /stɒp/ **I** *n* **1** (halt, pause) arrêt *m*; (short stay) gen halte *f*; Aviat, Naut escale *f*; **to have** ou **make a ten-minute ~ for coffee** faire un arrêt de dix minutes pour prendre un café; **to make an overnight ~** gen faire une halte d'une nuit; Aviat, Naut faire une escale d'une nuit; **the train makes three ~s before London** le train fait trois arrêts or s'arrête trois fois avant Londres; **our next ~ will be (in) Paris** (on tour, trip) notre prochaine halte sera Paris; **there are ~s in Bruges and Mons** on fait halte à Bruges et à Mons; **next ~ Dover/home** le prochain arrêt à Douvres/à la maison; **we've had too many ~s and starts on this project** nous avons dû arrêter et reprendre ce projet trop souvent; **to be at a ~** [*traffic, production*] être arrêté; **to bring sth to a ~** arrêter qch; **to come to a ~** [*vehicle, work, progress*] s'arrêter; **to put a ~ to** mettre fin à; **I'll soon put a ~ to that!** je vais bientôt mettre fin à ça!; **2** (stopping place) (for bus) arrêt *m*; (for train) gare *f*; (for tube, subway) station *f*; **from X to Y is three ~s on the bus** de X à Y il y a trois arrêts (de bus); **I've missed my ~** (on bus) j'ai loupé mon arrêt; (on train) j'ai loupé ma gare; **3** (punctuation mark) (in telegram) stop *m*; (in dictation) point *m*; **4** (device) (for door) butoir *m*; (on window, typewriter) taquet *m*; (for drawer) butée *f*; **5** Mus (on organ) (pipes) jeu *m* d'orgues; (knob) registre *m* d'orgues; **6** Phot (aperture) diaphragme *m*; **7** Phon occlusive *f*.
II *modif* [*button, lever, signal*] d'arrêt.
III *vtr* (*p prés etc* **-pp-**) **1** (cease) [*person*] arrêter, cesser [*work, activity*]; **~ what you're doing/that noise** arrêtez or cessez ce que vous faites/ce bruit; **~ it!** arrête!; (that's enough) ça suffit!; **to ~ doing** arrêter or cesser de faire; **to ~ smoking** arrêter or cesser de fumer; **he never ~s talking** il n'arrête pas de parler; **I can't ~ thinking about her** je n'arrête pas de penser à elle, je ne cesse de penser à elle; **he couldn't ~ laughing** il ne pouvait pas s'arrêter de rire; **it's ~ped raining** il a arrêté ou cessé de pleuvoir; **~ writing please** (in exam) veuillez poser vos stylos s'il vous plaît; **2** (bring to a halt) (completely) [*person, mechanism*] arrêter [*person, vehicle, process, match, trial*]; [*strike, power cut*] entraîner l'arrêt de [*activity, production*]; (temporarily) [*person, rain*] interrompre [*process, match, trial*]; [*strike, power cut*] provoquer une interruption de [*activity, production*]; **rain ~ped play** la pluie a interrompu la partie; **~ the clock!** arrêtez le chronomètre!; **something to ~ the bleeding** quelque chose pour arrêter le sang de couler; **to ~ a bullet, to ~ one**○ recevoir or choper○ une balle; **the pistol will ~ a man at 30 metres** le pistolet étendra un homme à 30 mètres; **3** (prevent) empêcher [*war, publication*]; empêcher [qch] d'avoir lieu [*event, ceremony*]; arrêter [*person*]; **I'm leaving and you can't ~ me!** je pars et tu ne pourras pas m'en empêcher or m'arrêter!; **what's to ~ you?, what's ~ping you?** qu'est-ce qui t'en empêche or t'arrête?; **to ~ sb (from) doing** empêcher qn de faire; **she ~ped me (from) making a fool of myself** elle m'a empêché de me rendre idiot; **you won't be able to ~ the marriage (from taking place)** tu ne pourras pas empêcher le mariage or empêcher que le mariage ait lieu; **there's nothing to ~ you (from) doing** rien ne t'empêche de faire; **4** (refuse to provide) (definitively) supprimer [*grant, allowance*]; arrêter [*payments, deliveries, subscription*]; couper [*gas, electricity, water*]; (suspend) suspendre [*grant, payment, subscription, gas*]; **to ~ a cheque** faire opposition à un chèque; **to ~ £50 out of sb's pay** GB retenir 50 livres sur le salaire de qn; **all leave has been ~ped** toutes les permissions ont été suspendues; **5** (plug) boucher [*gap, hole, bottle*]; **to ~ a leak** arrêter une fuite; **to ~ one's ears** se boucher les oreilles; **6** Mus bloquer [*string*]; boucher [*hole*].
IV *vi* (*p prés etc* **-pp-**) **1** (come to a standstill, halt) [*person, vehicle, clock, machine, heart*] s'arrêter; **to ~ somewhere for lunch** s'arrêter quelque part pour déjeuner; **everything ~ped** tout s'est arrêté; **2** (cease) [*person, discussion, bleeding, breathing*] s'arrêter; [*pain, worry, enjoyment, battle*] cesser; [*noise, music, rain*] s'arrêter, cesser; **to ~ for questions** s'arrêter pour répondre aux questions; **not to know when to ~** ne pas savoir s'arrêter; **this is going to have to ~** il va falloir que cela cesse; **without ~ping** sans arrêt; **to ~ to do** s'arrêter pour faire; **you didn't ~ to think** tu n'as pas pris le temps de réfléchir; **3**○ GB (stay) rester; **to ~ for dinner** rester dîner; **to ~ the night with sb** passer la nuit chez qn.
V *v refl* (*p prés etc* **-pp-**) **to ~ oneself** (restrain oneself) s'en empêcher, se retenir; **I nearly fell but I ~ped myself** j'ai failli tomber mais je me suis rattrapé; **to ~ oneself (from) doing** s'empêcher de faire;

he tried to ~ himself (from) telling her il a essayé de ne rien lui dire.
IDIOMS to pull out all the ~s frapper un grand coup (to do pour faire).
■ stop away○ GB: ~ away (not go) ne pas aller (from à); (not come) ne pas venir (from à).
■ stop behind○ GB rester.
■ stop by○: ¶ ~ by passer; to ~ by at Eric's place passer chez Éric; ¶ ~ by [sth] passer à [*bookshop, café*].
■ stop down Phot fermer le diaphragme.
■ stop in○ GB (stay in) rester chez soi; I'm ~ping in je vais rester chez moi.
■ stop off faire un arrêt; to ~ off in Bristol faire un arrêt à Bristol; to ~ off at Paul's house passer chez Paul.
■ stop on○ GB rester; to ~ on at school rester à l'école.
■ stop out○ GB to ~ out late rentrer tard; to ~ out all night ne pas rentrer de la nuit.
■ stop over (at sb's house) rester; to ~ over in Athens gen faire une halte à Athènes; Aviat, Naut faire escale à Athènes.
■ stop up: ¶ ~ up○ GB veiller; ¶ ~ [sth] up, ~ up [sth] boucher [*hole, gap*]; to be ~ped up with être bouché par.

stop: ~ bath *n* Phot bain *m* de rinçage; ~cock *n* robinet *m* d'arrêt; ~ consonant *n* occlusive *f*.

stopgap /'stɒpgæp/ I *n* bouche-trou *m*.
II *modif* [*leader*] bouche-trou; [*measure*] provisoire.

stop: ~-go *adj* Econ [*policy*] d'oscillation; ~ lamp *n* US = stop light; ~ light *n* (on vehicle) feu *m* stop; (traffic light) feu *m* rouge; ~-off *n* (quick break) arrêt *m*; (longer) halte *f*; ~ order *n* Fin ordre *m* stop; ~over *n* gen halte *f*; Aviat, Naut escale *f*.

stoppage /'stɒpɪdʒ/ *n* 1 Ind (strike) interruption *f* (de travail); a 24-hour ~ une interruption de 24 heures du travail; 2 GB (deduction from wages) retenue *f* (sur salaire).

stop: ~ payment *n* Fin opposition *f* (à un chèque); ~ payment order *n* contre-ordre *m*.

stopper /'stɒpə(r)/ I *n* (for bottle, jar) bouchon *m*; (for bath, basin) bonde *f*.
II *vtr* boucher [*bottle*].

stopping /'stɒpɪŋ/ I *n* 'no ~' 'arrêt *m* interdit'; all this ~ and starting is stupid tous ces arrêts et ces redémarrages sont stupides.
II *modif* Aut [*distance, time*] d'arrêt.

stopping: ~ place *n* endroit *m* pour s'arrêter; ~ train *n* omnibus *m*.

stop-press /,stɒp'pres/ I *n* dernières nouvelles *fpl*.
II *modif* [*news, item*] de dernière heure or minute.

stop: ~ sign *n* (panneau *m* de) stop *m*; ~watch *n* chronomètre *m*.

storage /'stɔ:rɪdʒ/ I *n* 1 (keeping) (of food, fuel, goods) stockage *m* (of de); (of furniture) entreposage *m* (of de); (of document, file) classement *m* (of de); (of heat, energy, electricity) accumulation *f* (of de); to be in ~ [*food, fuel, goods*] être entreposé; [*furniture*] être au garde-meuble; to put sth in(to) ~ entreposer [*goods*]; mettre qch au garde-meuble [*furniture*]; 2 (space) Comm entrepôt *m*; gen espace *m* de rangement; 3 Comput (facility) mémoire *f*; (process) mise *f* en mémoire.
II *modif* [*container*] Comm de stockage; [*compartment, space*] de rangement; ~ area Comm entrepôt *m*; ~ costs gen frais *mpl* de stockage; (for furniture) frais *mpl* de garde-meuble.

storage: ~ battery *n* accumulateur *m*; ~ capacity *n* Comput capacité *f* de mémoire; ~ device *n* Comput mémoire *f*; ~ heater *n* Elec radiateur *m* électrique à accumulation; ~ jar *n* (glass) bocal *m* (de rangement); (ceramic) pot *m* de rangement; ~ tank *m* (for oil, chemicals) réservoir *m*, tank *m*; (for rainwater) citerne *f*.

storage unit *n* 1 (cupboard) meuble *m* de rangement; 2 Comm (area of storage space) unité *f* de stockage.

store /stɔ:(r)/ I *n* 1 ▶ 1692 (shop) magasin *m*; (smaller) boutique *f*; the big ~s les grands magasins; 2 (supply) (of food, fuel, paper) réserve *f*, provision *f* (of de); (of knowledge, information) fonds *mpl* (of de); to keep/lay in a ~ of sth avoir/constituer une réserve or provision de qch; 3 (place of storage) (for food, fuel) réserve *f*; (for furniture) garde-meuble *m*; Comm entrepôt *m*, magasin *m*; Mil magasin *m*; (for nuclear waste) réservoir *m* de stockage; 4 (storage) to put sth in(to) ~ mettre qch au garde-meuble [*furniture*]; mettre qch en magasin, entreposer [*goods*]; fig there's a surprise/a nasty shock in ~ for him une surprise/une mauvaise surprise l'attend; I wonder what the future has in ~ (for us) je me demande ce que l'avenir nous réserve.
II stores *npl* 1 (supplies) provisions *fpl*; to take on ~s Naut ravitailler; 2 (storage area) magasin *m*.
III *vtr* 1 (put away) conserver [*food*]; ranger [*objects, furniture*]; stocker [*nuclear waste, chemicals*]; conserver [*information*]; Agric engranger [*crops, grain*]; 2 (accumulate) faire des provisions de [*food, supplies, fuel*]; accumuler [*energy, heat, water*]; 3 (hold) [*cupboard, fridge, freezer*] contenir [*food, objects*]; 4 Comput mettre [qch] en mémoire, mémoriser [*data, records*] (on sur).
IV stored *pp adj* [*food, wine, supplies*] gen mis de côté; Comm stocké; fig [*troubles, unhappiness*] accumulé.
IDIOMS to set great ~ by sth attacher beaucoup d'importance à qch; not to set great ~ by sth, to set little ~ by sth ne pas attacher beaucoup d'importance à qch.
■ store away: ~ [sth] away, ~ away [sth] mettre de côté, ranger [*clothes, furniture, objects*].
■ store up: ~ up [sth] accumuler [*food, supplies, energy, heat*]; fig accumuler [*hatred, resentment, unhappiness*]; you're storing up trouble/problems for yourself tu ne fais qu'accumuler les ennuis/les problèmes.

store: ~card *n* Comm Fin carte *f* de crédit (*d'un grand magasin*); ~ cupboard *n* armoire *f* de rangement; ~ detective ▶ 1692 *n* surveillant/-e *m/f* (*dans un magasin*); ~front *n* US Comm vitrine *f* (*d'un magasin*); ~house *n* entrepôt *m*; ~keeper ▶ 1692 *n* US commerçant/-e *m/f*; ~man *n* Comm magasinier *m*; ~ manager ▶ 1692 *n* Comm directeur/-trice *m/f* de (grand) magasin; ~room *n* (in house, school, office) réserve *f*; (in factory, shop) magasin *m*.

storey GB, **story** US /'stɔ:rɪ/ *n* (*pl* -reys GB, -ries US) étage *m*; on the top ~ au dernier étage; on the third ~ GB au troisième étage; US au quatrième étage; a three-storeyed building GB, a three storied building US un bâtiment à or de trois étages; single-~ building bâtiment *m* de plain-pied.
IDIOMS to be a bit weak in the top ~○ être bête comme ses pieds○.

stork /stɔ:k/ *n* cigogne *f*.

storksbill /'stɔ:ksbɪl/ *n* érodium *m*.

storm /stɔ:m/ I *n* 1 (violent weather) tempête *f*; (thunderstorm) orage *m*; to get caught in a ~ se faire prendre dans une tempête; the ~ broke la tempête a éclaté; to weather a ~ lit résister à la tempête; fig surmonter une mauvaise passe; 2 Meteorol (gale) vent *m* de tempête; 3 (irresistible attack) to take a town by ~ Mil prendre une ville d'assaut; she took Broadway by ~ fig elle a remporté un succès foudroyant à Broadway; 4 (outburst) tempête *f*; a ~ of criticism/protest une tempête de critiques/protestations; a ~ of applause/laughter un tonnerre d'applaudissements/d'éclats de rire; a ~ of violence une vague de violence; to bring a ~ down about one's ears s'attirer de violentes critiques.
II *vtr* 1 (invade) prendre [qch] d'assaut [*citadel, prison*]; looters ~ed the shops les pillards ont pris les magasins d'assaut; 2 (roar) 'get out!' he ~ed 'sortez!' cria-t-il dans un accès de colère.
III *vi* 1 [*wind, rain*] faire rage; 2 (move angrily) to ~ into a room entrer avec fracas dans une pièce; to ~ off partir avec fracas; he ~ed off in a temper il est parti furibond; 3 (get angry) tempêter; to ~ at sb tempêter contre qn.

storm: ~ belt *n* zone *f* de tempêtes; ~bound *adj* retenu par la tempête; ~ cellar *n* cave-refuge *f*; ~ centre GB, ~ center US *n* Meteorol œil *m* du cyclone; fig cœur *m* des problèmes; ~cloud *n* lit nuage *m* orageux; fig nuage *m* noir; ~ damage *n* dégâts *mpl* causés par la tempête; ~ door *n* double porte *f*; ~ drain *n* collecteur *m* d'eaux pluviales; ~ force wind *n* vent *m* de tempête.

storming /'stɔ:mɪŋ/ *n* prise *f*; the ~ of the palace la prise du palais.

storm: ~ lantern *n* lampe-tempête *f*; ~-lashed *adj* battu par les tempêtes; ~ petrel *n* pétrel-tempête *m*.

storm-tossed *adj* [*waters*] agité par la tempête; [*ship*] ballotté par la tempête.

storm: ~ trooper *n* membre *m* de section d'assaut; ~ warning *n* avis *m* de tempête; ~ window *n* double fenêtre *f*.

stormy /'stɔ:mɪ/ *adj* 1 [*weather, sky, night*] orageux/-euse; [*sea, waves*] houleux/-euse; 2 (turbulent) [*meeting, debate, period*] houleux/-euse; [*relationship*] orageux/-euse; ~ scenes éclats *mpl*; there was a ~ scene when he came back late il y a eu un éclat lorsqu'il est rentré tard.

stormy petrel = storm petrel.

story /'stɔ:rɪ/ *n* 1 (account) histoire *f* (of de); to tell a ~ raconter une histoire; the ~ of Elvis Presley l'histoire d'Elvis Presley; it's a true ~ c'est une histoire vécue; based on a true ~ inspiré par une histoire vécue; to stick to/change one's ~ maintenir/changer sa version des faits; what is the real ~? où est la vérité?; they all have similar stories, they all tell the same ~ ils sont tous passés par là; 2 (tale) gen histoire *f* (about, of de); Literat conte *m* (of de); to tell an entertaining ~ raconter une histoire divertissante; a detective/ghost ~ une histoire policière/de fantômes; tell us a ~ about when you lived in London during the war racontez-nous comment c'était pendant la guerre à Londres; read us a (bedtime) ~! tu nous lis une histoire?; 3 Journ article *m* (on, about sur); exclusive ~ reportage *m* exclusif; to carry or run a ~ publier un article; to kill a ~ ne pas publier un article; a front-page ~ un article à la une; the inside ~ les dessous de l'affaire; 4 (lie) histoire *f*; to make up a ~ inventer une histoire (about à propos de); she made up some ~ about her train being late elle a inventé une histoire de train en retard; 5 (rumour) rumeur *f* (about sur); all sorts of stories are going round the office toutes sortes de rumeurs circulent dans le bureau; 6 (also ~ line) (of novel, play) intrigue *f*; (of film) scénario *m*; the ~ was taken from a Russian novel l'histoire est tirée d'un roman russe; there was no ~! il n'y avait pas d'histoire!; 7 (unfolding of plot) action *f*; the ~ is set in Normandy l'action or l'histoire se passe en Normandie; 8 US (floor) étage *m*; first ~ rez-de-chaussée *m*; second ~ premier étage *m*; ▶ storey.
IDIOMS but that's another ~ mais ça c'est une autre histoire; to cut a long ~ short bref; that's not the whole ~, that's only half the ~ ce n'est qu'une partie de l'histoire, ce n'est pas tout; that's the ~ of my life! c'est toujours la même chose, avec moi!; it's always the same ~, it's the same old ~ c'est toujours la même chose; every picture tells a ~ ça se passe de commentaires; a likely ~! elle est bien

bonne, celle-là○!; **the ~ goes/has it that** on raconte/dit que; **or so the ~ goes** du moins c'est ce qu'on dit; **what's the ~**○**?** qu'est-ce qui se passe?; ▶ **two**.

storyboard /ˈstɔːrɪbɔːd/ *n* maquette *f* préparatoire.

storybook /ˈstɔːrɪbʊk/ *n* livre *m* de contes. IDIOMS **it's a ~ ending** ça finit comme dans les romans.

storyteller /ˈstɔːrɪtelə(r)/ *n* **1** (writer) conteur/-euse *m/f*; **2** (liar) menteur/-euse *m/f*.

stoup /stuːp/ *n* **1** Relig bénitier *m*; **2**† (drinking vessel) gobelet *m*.

stout /staʊt/ **I** *n* (drink) stout *f*.
II *adj* **1** (fat) [*person*] corpulent; [*animal*] gros/grosse; **to grow ~** avoir tendance à l'embonpoint; **2** (strong) [*fence, wall*] épais/-aisse; [*branch, shoe, stick*] gros/grosse (*before n*); **3** (valiant) [*defence, resistance, supporter*] acharné; [*support*] inconditionnel/-elle.

stout-hearted /ˌstaʊtˈhɑːtɪd/ *adj* littér au courage valeureux liter.

stoutly /ˈstaʊtlɪ/ *adv* **1** (strongly) **~ made** solide; **~ constructed**, **~ built** de construction *f* solide; **2** (valiantly) [*defend, fight*] résolument; [*deny, resist*] avec acharnement; **~ held beliefs** des croyances tenaces.

stoutness /ˈstaʊtnɪs/ *n* **1** (of person, animal) corpulence *f*; **2** (of shoe, stick) solidité *f*; **3** (of defence, resistance) acharnement *m*; **4** (of intention, purpose) fermeté *f*.

stove /stəʊv/ **I** *prét, pp* ▶ **stave**.
II *n* **1** (cooker) cuisinière *f*; **electric/gas ~** cuisinière électrique/à gaz; **2** (heater) poêle *m*; **3** Ind (kiln) four *m*.
III *vtr* Ind cuire.
IDIOMS **to slave over a hot ~** hum trimer à ses fourneaux.

stove: **~d moulding** GB, **~ molding** US *n* moulage *m* cuit; **~ enamel** *n* émail *m* au four; **~-enamelled** *adj* émaillé au four.

stovepipe /ˈstəʊvpaɪp/ **I** *n* **1** (flue) tuyau *m* de poêle; **2** (also **~ hat**) (chapeau *m* en) tuyau *m* de poêle.
II stovepipes○ *npl* GB pantalon *m* moulant; US pantalon *m* droit.

stoving /ˈstəʊvɪŋ/ *n* Ind cuisson *f*.

stow /stəʊ/ *vtr* **1** (pack) ranger [*baggage, ropes, tarpaulin*]; plier [*sail*]; **to ~ cargo in the hold** Naut arrimer la cargaison dans la cale; **2**○ GB (shut) **~ it**○! ferme-la○!
■ **stow away**: ¶ **~ away** [*passenger, escapee*] voyager clandestinement; ¶ **~ [sth] away**, **~ away [sth]** ranger [*provisions, ropes, baggage*]; plier [*sail*].

stowage /ˈstəʊɪdʒ/ *n* **1** gen (of baggage, load) rangement *m*; Naut (of cargo, equipment) arrimage *m*; **2** (space) place *f* pour le rangement. **3** Comm (cost) frais *mpl* d'arrimage.

stowaway /ˈstəʊəweɪ/ *n* passager/-ère *m/f* clandestin/-e.

St Patrick's Day /sntˈpætrɪks deɪ/ *n* la Saint-Patrick.

str *n* GB (*abrév écrite* = **street**) rue *f*.

Str *n* (*abrév écrite* = **Strait**) détroit *m*.

strabismus /strəˈbɪzməs/ *n* Med strabisme *m*.

straddle /ˈstrædl/ **I** *n* (also **~ jump**) Sport rouleau *m* (ventral).
II *vtr* **1** (in position) [*person*] enfourcher [*horse, bike*]; s'asseoir à califourchon sur [*chair, person*]; enjamber [*ditch, stream*]; **he was straddling his bike** il chevauchait son vélo; **he was straddling the ditch** il se tenait les jambes écartées au-dessus du fossé; **2** (in location) [*bridge*] enjamber [*road, river*]; [*town, country*] être à cheval sur [*counties, continents*]; [*village, town*] être traversé par [*road, border*]; **3** fig (in debate) **to ~ the line between two things** être à mi-chemin entre deux choses; **to ~ (both sides of) an issue** péj essayer de ménager les deux parties.

strafe /strɑːf, streɪf/ *vtr* **1** Mil Aviat mitrailler [qn] en rase-mottes; **2**○ fig passer un savon à.

strafing /ˈstrɑːfɪŋ, ˈstreɪf-/ *n* **1** Mil Aviat mitraillage *m* en rase-mottes; **2**○ fig savon○ *m*; **I got a real ~!** quel savon on m'a passé○!

straggle /ˈstrægl/ **I** *n* (loose group) (of buildings) rangée *f* irrégulière; (of people) groupe *m* désordonné.
II *vi* **1** (spread untidily) **to ~ along** s'étendre au hasard le long de [*road, beach, railtrack*]; **huts ~d down the mountainside** des refuges étaient disséminés sur le flanc de la montagne; **his hair was ~d over his eyes** des mèches folles tombaient sur ses yeux; **2** (dawdle) traîner; **they were straggling behind the other walkers** ils étaient à la traîne derrière les autres promeneurs.
III straggling *pres p adj* [*hedge*] broussailleux/-euse; [*hair, moustache*] en désordre; [*plant*] qui pousse dans tous les sens; **a ~ village/suburb** un village/une banlieue s'étendant au hasard.
■ **straggle in** [*latecomers, runners*] arriver petit à petit.
■ **straggle off** [*crowd, group*] se disperser peu à peu.

straggler /ˈstræglə(r)/ *n* traînard/-e *m/f*.

straggly /ˈstræglɪ/ *adj* [*hair, beard*] en désordre; [*bush, hedge*] broussailleux/-euse; [*plant*] qui pousse dans tous les sens.

straight /streɪt/ **I** *n* **1** Sport ligne *f* droite; **back ~** côté *m* opposé de la piste; **home ~** dernière ligne droite; **into the ~** dans la ligne droite; **2** Games suite *f*; **3**○ (heterosexual) hétéro○ *mf*.
II *adj* **1** (not bent or curved) [*line, cut, edge, road, stretch*] droit; [*chair*] à dossier droit; [*hair*] raide; **dead ~** gen tout droit; [*hair*] très raide; **in a ~ line** en ligne droite; **2** (level, upright) [*fixture, post, shelf, hem, edge, wall*] bien droit; [*garment, bedclothes, rug, tablecloth*] bien mis; **is the picture ~ now?** est-ce que le tableau est droit maintenant?; **the picture/your tie isn't ~** le tableau/ta cravate est de travers; **to put** ou **set sth ~** mettre qch (bien) droit [*furniture, picture, mirror*]; ajuster [*tie, hat*]; **to have a ~ back** avoir le dos droit; **a ~(-sided) glass** un verre droit; **3** (tidy, in order) en ordre; **to get** ou **put sth ~** lit, fig mettre qch en ordre; **I must get the house ~ before Sunday** il faut que je mette la maison en ordre avant dimanche; **the lawyer will put things ~** l'avocat va mettre les choses en ordre; **4** (clear) **to get sth ~** comprendre qch; **have you got that ~?** c'est compris?; **let's get this ~, you're paying half** entendons-nous bien, tu paies la moitié; **now let's get one thing ~** que ce soit bien clair; **to put** ou **set sb ~ about sth** éclairer qn sur qch; **to set matters ~** mettre les choses en clair; **to put** ou **set the record ~** établir la vérité; **5** (honest, direct) [*person*] honnête, loyal; [*answer, question*] clair; [*advice, tip*] sûr; **to be ~ with sb** jouer franc jeu avec qn; **I want a ~ answer to a ~ question** je veux une réponse claire à une question claire; **it's time for ~ talking** il est temps de parler franchement; **6** (unconditional) [*contradiction, majority, profit*] net/nette; [*choice*] simple; [*denial, refusal, rejection*] catégorique; **to do a ~ swap** faire simplement l'échange; **a ~ fight** GB Pol une élection à deux candidats; **that's ~ dishonesty** c'est de la malhonnêteté pure et simple; **7** (undiluted) [*spirits, drink*] sec, sans eau; **8** (consecutive) [*wins, defeats*] consécutif/-ive; **she got ~ 'A's** Sch elle a eu A partout; **to win/lose in ~ sets** Sport gagner/perdre en plusieurs sets consécutifs; **to vote a ~ ticket** US Pol voter pour la liste d'un parti; **9** Theat [*actor, play, role*] classique; **10** (quits) **to be ~** être quitte; **to get oneself ~** régler ses dettes; **11**○ [*person*] (conventional) conventionnel/-elle; (not on drugs) qui ne se drogue pas; (heterosexual) hétéro○ *inv*.
III *adv* **1** (not obliquely or crookedly) [*walk, stand up, grow, fly, steer, hang, cut, throw, hit*] droit; [*shoot*] juste; **stand up ~!** tenez-vous droit!; **sit up ~!** asseyez-vous convenablement!; **she held her arm out ~** elle a tendu son bras tout droit; **she was stretched ~ out on the floor** elle était étendue toute raide sur le sol; **to go ~ ahead** aller tout droit; **to look ~ ahead** regarder droit devant soi; **to look sb ~ in the eye** ou **face** regarder qn droit dans les yeux; **can you see ~?** est-ce-que tu vois bien?; **he headed ~ for the bar** il s'est dirigé droit vers le bar; **he went ~ for me** il s'est jeté sur moi; **he walked ~ across the road** il a traversé la route tout droit; **the car was coming ~ at** ou **towards me** la voiture se dirigeait droit sur moi; **she was looking ~ at me** elle regardait droit dans ma direction; **~ above our heads** juste au-dessus de nos têtes; **~ down into the ground** droit dans le sol; **~ up in the air** droit en l'air; **the bullet went ~ through his body** la balle lui a traversé le corps de part en part; **we went ~ through the book** nous avons lu le livre de bout en bout; **he fired ~ into** ou **through the crowd** il a tiré en plein dans la foule; **they drove ~ through the red light** ils ont brûlé le feu rouge; **they drove ~ past me** ils sont passés droit devant moi; **she drove ~ into a tree** elle est rentrée droit dans un arbre; **keep ~ on, it's on the left** continuez tout droit, c'est sur la gauche; **his poems speak ~ to our hearts** ses poèmes nous vont droit au cœur; **2** (without delay) directement; **to go ~ home** rentrer directement à la maison; **to go ~ to bed** aller directement au lit; **she went ~ back to Paris** elle est rentrée directement à Paris; **shall we go ~ there?** nous y allons directement?; **she wrote ~ back** elle a répondu immédiatement; **to come ~ to the point** aller droit au fait; **he went ~ to the heart of the matter** il est rentré directement dans le vif du sujet; **~ after** tout de suite après; **I went out ~ after phoning you** je suis sorti tout de suite après t'avoir téléphoné; **~ away**, **~ off** tout de suite; **I saw ~ away** ou **off that it was impossible** j'ai vu tout de suite que c'était impossible; **he sat down and read/played it ~ off** il s'est assis et l'a lu/joué d'une seule traite; **I can tell you the dates/prices ~ off** je peux vous donner les dates/prix de mémoire; **she told him ~ out that...** elle lui a dit carrément or sans ambages que...; **it seemed like something ~ out of a horror film/the Middle Ages** cela semblait sortir tout droit d'un film d'horreur/du Moyen Âge; **3** (frankly) tout net; **I'll tell you ~, I'll give it to you ~**○ je vous le dirai tout net; **give it to me ~**○ dis-moi la vérité; **~ out** carrément; **I told him ~ out that he was wrong** je lui ai dit carrément qu'il se trompait; **to play ~ with sb** fig jouer franc jeu avec qn; **4** Theat (conventionally) [*act, produce*] de manière classique; **5** (neat) **to drink one's whisky ~** boire son whisky sec or sans eau.
IDIOMS **to keep a ~ face** garder son sérieux; **to keep to the ~ and narrow** suivre le droit chemin; **to stray from the ~ and narrow** s'écarter du droit chemin; **to go ~**○ [*criminal*] se ranger; **~ up**○**?** GB sans blague○?

straight arrow *n* US personne *f* réglo○.

straightaway /ˈstreɪtəweɪ/ **I** *n* US (part of racetrack, highway) ligne *f* droite.
II *adv* tout de suite.

straightedge /ˈstreɪtedʒ/ *n* règle *f* plate graduée.

straighten /ˈstreɪtn/ **I** *vtr* **1** tendre [*arm, leg*]; redresser [*picture, teeth*]; ajuster [*tie, hat*]; refaire (en ligne droite) [*road*]; défriser [*hair*]; arrondir [*hem*]; **to ~ one's back** ou **shoulders** se redresser; **to have one's nose ~ed** se faire refaire le nez; **to have one's teeth ~ed** se faire redresser les dents; **2** (also **~ up**) (tidy) mettre [qch] en ordre [*room*]; mettre de l'ordre sur [*desk*].
II *vi* **1** = **straighten out**; **2** [*person*] se redresser.

IDIOMS **to ~ up and fly right** US marcher droit.

■ **straighten out**: ¶ **~ out** [*road*] devenir droit; ¶ **~ out [sth], ~ [sth] out 1** lit redresser [*sth crooked*]; refaire (en ligne droite) [*road*]; **2** fig (clarify) tirer [qch] au clair [*misunderstanding, problem*]; organiser [*life*]; **to ~ things out** organiser or arranger les choses.

■ **straighten up**: ¶ **~ up 1** lit [*person*] se redresser; **2** fig (tidy up) mettre de l'ordre; ¶ **~ up [sb/sth], ~ [sb/sth] up 1** lit mettre droit [*leaning object*]; redresser [*crooked object*]; **2** (tidy) ranger [*objects, room*]; **to ~ oneself up** s'arranger; **go and ~ yourself up**○! va t'arranger un peu!

straight: **~-faced** *adj* à l'air sérieux; **~ flush** *n* quinte *f* floche.

straightforward /ˌstreɪt'fɔːwəd/ *adj* **1** (honest) [*answer, person*] franc/franche; [*business*] honnête; **2** (simple) [*account, explanation, case, question*] simple; [*rudeness, abuse*] pur et simple (*after n*); [*performance, production*] simple et direct; [*version*] fidèle.

straightforwardly /ˌstreɪt'fɔːwədlɪ/ *adv* **1** (honestly) [*reply, speak*] franchement; [*deal*] honnêtement; **2** (simply) [*describe, explain*] simplement; Mus, Theat [*play, perform, produce*] de façon simple et directe.

straightforwardness /ˌstreɪt'fɔːwədnɪs/ *n* **1** (frankness) (of reply) franchise *f*; (of character) droiture *f*; **2** (simplicity) simplicité *f*.

straight: **~-laced** *adj* collet-monté *inv*; **~ left** *n* Sport direct *m* du gauche; **~-line depreciation** *n* amortissement *m* constant; **~ man** *n* Theat faire-valoir *m inv*.

straightness /'streɪtnɪs/ *n* **1** (honesty) (of reply) franchise *f*; (of character) droiture *f*; **2** (of line, shoulders) raideur *f*.

straight: **~-out** *adj* (frank) franc/franche; **~ right** *n* Sport direct *m* du droit; **~way**† *adv* littér tout de suite.

strain /streɪn/ **I** *n* **1** Phys (weight) effort *m*, contrainte *f* (**on** sur); (from pulling) tensions *fpl* (**on** de); **to put a ~ on** soumettre [qch] à des efforts or à des sollicitations [*beam, bridge, rope*]; fatiguer [*heart, lungs*]; faire travailler [*muscles*]; **to be under ~** [*bridge, structure*] être soumis à des efforts or des sollicitations; **to grimace/sweat under the ~** grimacer/suer sous l'effort; **to take the ~** [*beam, bracket, rope*] être soumis à des efforts or des sollicitations; **the rope/shelf can't take the ~** la corde/l'étagère ne résistera pas; **2** (pressure) (on person) stress *m*; (in relations) tension *f*; **mental** ou **nervous ~** tension *f* nerveuse; **to put a ~ on** avoir un effet néfaste sur [*relationship*]; créer des tensions au sein de [*group, alliance*]; surcharger [*system, network*]; provoquer une crise dans [*sector, prison system*]; grever [*economy, finances*]; mettre [qch] à rude épreuve [*patience, goodwill*]; **to be under ~** [*person*] être stressé; [*relations*] être tendu; [*network, system*] être surchargé; **to take the ~** [*person*] supporter la pression; **he can't take the ~** il supporte mal le stress or la pression; **to crack under the ~** [*person*] craquer sous la pression; **to take the ~ out of** faciliter [*climb, management, organization*]; **to show signs of ~** [*person*] montrer des signes de fatigue; **the ~ (on him) was beginning to tell** il montrait des signes de fatigue; **the ~s within the coalition** les tensions au sein de la coalition; **it's a ~ talking to him** c'est pénible de lui parler; **it's getting to be a ~** ça commence à devenir pénible; **3** (injury) muscle *m* froissé; **a calf/thigh ~** un muscle du mollet/de la cuisse froissé; **4** (breed) (of animal) race *f*; (of plant, seed) variété *f*; (of virus, bacteria) souche *f*; **5** (recurring theme) (of melancholy, etc) courant *m* (**of** de); **6** (tendency) (in family, nation, group) tendance *f* (**of** à); **7** (style) veine *f*, ton *m*; **the rest of the speech was in the same ~** le reste du discours était dans la même veine.

II strains *npl* (tune) littér (of piece of music, song) air *m*; **to the ~s of**... aux accents de...

III *vtr* **1** (stretch) tendre [*rope, cable*]; **to ~ one's eyes** (to see) plisser les yeux; **to ~ one's ears** tendre l'oreille; **to ~ one's muscles/every muscle** tendre ses muscles/tous ses muscles (**to do** pour faire); ▶**nerve**; **2** fig grever [*resources, finances, economy*]; compromettre [*relationship, alliance*]; surcharger [*network, system*]; mettre [qch] à rude épreuve [*patience, credulity, understanding*]; **it would be ~ing the truth to say**... ce serait exagéré de dire...; **the writer has ~ed the possibilities of conventional language** l'écrivain a dépassé or sublimé les possibilités du langage conventionnel; **3** (injure) **to ~ a muscle** se froisser un muscle; **to ~ one's thigh/groin/shoulder** se froisser un muscle de la cuisse/l'aine/l'épaule; **to ~ one's eyes/heart** se fatiguer les yeux/le cœur; **to ~ one's voice** forcer sa voix; **to ~ one's back** se faire un tour de reins; **4** (sieve) passer [*tea, sauce*]; égoutter [*vegetables, pasta, rice*].

IV *vi* **to ~ against sth** pousser de toutes ses forces contre qch; **to ~ at** tirer sur [*leash, rope*]; **to ~ to see/hear** faire un gros effort pour voir/entendre; **to ~ forward** se pencher en avant.

V *v refl* **to ~ oneself 1** (injure) se blesser; **2** (tire) se fatiguer; **don't ~ yourself!** iron ne te fatigue surtout pas!

■ **strain off**: **~ [sth] off, ~ off [sth]** faire égoutter [*water, liquid, fat*].

strained /streɪnd/ *adj* **1** (tense) [*atmosphere, expression, silence, relations, voice*] tendu; [*smile*] forcé; **to look ~** avoir l'air tendu; **2** (injured) [*muscle*] froissé; **to have a ~ thigh/shoulder** s'être froissé un muscle à la cuisse/à l'épaule; **3** (sieved) [*baby food*] en purée; [*soup, sauce*] passé.

strainer /'streɪnə(r)/ *n* passoire *f*.

strait /streɪt/ **I** *n* Geog détroit *m*; **the Straits of Gibraltar** le détroit de Gibraltar.

II straits *npl* difficultés *fpl*; **to be in difficult ~s** connaître de graves difficultés; **to be in dire ~s** être aux abois.

III‡ *adj* étroit.

straitened /'streɪtnd/ *adj* **in ~ circumstances** dans la gêne.

straitjacket /'streɪtdʒækɪt/ **I** *n* **1** lit camisole *f* de force; **2** fig carcan *m*.

II *vtr* **1** lit mettre la camisole à; **2** fig entraver.

strait-laced /ˌstreɪt'leɪst/ *adj* collet monté *inv* (**about** en ce qui concerne).

strand /strænd/ **I** *n* **1** (of hair) mèche *f*; (of fibre, web, wire) fil *m*; (of beads) rangée *f*; **2** fig (of argument, thought, plot) fil *m*; (of activity, life) aspect *m*; **3** littér (beach) grève *f*.

II *vtr* **to be ~ed** être bloqué; **to leave sb ~ed** laisser qn en rade○.

III stranded *pp adj* [*climber, traveller*] bloqué.

strange /streɪndʒ/ *adj* **1** (unfamiliar) inconnu; **you shouldn't talk to ~ men** il ne faut pas parler à des inconnus; **he can't sleep in a ~ bed** il ne peut pas dormir dans un lit qu'il ne connaît pas; **2** (odd) bizarre; **it's ~ to do** ou **be doing** c'est bizarre de faire; **it is ~ (that)**... c'est bizarre que... (+ *subj*); **it feels ~ to be back again** cela fait une drôle d'impression d'être de retour; **there's something ~ about her/this place** elle/cet endroit a quelque chose de bizarre; **in a ~ way**... curieusement...; **~ as that might seem** aussi bizarre que cela puisse paraître; **~ but true** incroyable mais vrai; **~ to say, we never met again** c'est curieux à dire, mais nous ne nous sommes plus jamais rencontrés; **3** (unwell) **to look/feel ~** avoir l'air/se sentir drôle or bizarre; **4** sout (new) **to be ~ to** être étranger/-ère à [*place, customs, work*].

strangely /'streɪndʒlɪ/ *adj* [*behave, act, react, smile*] d'une façon étrange; [*quiet, calm, empty, beautiful*] étrangement; **~ shaped** d'une forme étrange; **she looks ~ familiar** c'est curieux, son visage ne m'est pas étranger; **~ enough,**... chose étrange,...

strangeness /'streɪndʒnɪs/ *n* (of place, routine, thought, feeling) étrangeté *f*; **I like both its familiar aspects and its ~** j'aime son caractère à la fois étrange et familier.

stranger /'streɪndʒə(r)/ *n* **1** (unknown person) étranger/-ère *m/f*; **a complete** ou **total ~** un parfait étranger; **he's a complete ~ to us** c'est pour nous un parfait étranger; **I'm a ~ in my own home** je suis comme un étranger chez moi; **don't take lifts from ~s** ne monte jamais en voiture avec un inconnu; **'hello, ~○!'** 'tiens, voilà un revenant○!'; **2** (newcomer) étranger/-ère *m/f*; **she's a ~ to the town** elle ne connaît pas la ville; **to be no ~ to** avoir l'habitude de [*success, controversy, adversity*]; **they're no ~s to Thailand** ils connaissent bien la Thaïlande.

strangers' gallery *n* GB tribune *f* réservée au public.

strangle /'stræŋgl/ *vtr* **1** (throttle) [*person*] étrangler; **to ~ sb to death** tuer qn par strangulation; **to ~ an idea at birth** étouffer une idée dans l'œuf; **I could cheerfully have ~d him** hum je l'aurais étranglé de bon cœur; **2** (choke) [*collar*] étrangler [*person*]; [*weed*] envahir [*plant*]; **in a ~d voice** d'une voix étranglée; **3** (curb) étouffer [*creativity, project*]; entraver [*development, growth*]; étrangler [*economy*]; **4** (repress) réprimer [*cry, protest, sob*].

stranglehold /'stræŋglhəʊld/ *n* **1** (in combat) étranglement *m*; **to have sb in a ~** tenir qn avec un étranglement; **2** fig (control) mainmise *f*; **to have a ~ on** avoir la mainmise sur; **3** fig (curb) **to put a ~ on** étrangler [*growth, inflation*].

strangler /'stræŋglə(r)/ *n* étrangleur/-euse *m/f*.

strangles /'stræŋglz/ *n* (+ *v sg*) Vet gourme *f*.

strangling /'stræŋglɪŋ/ *n* strangulation *f*.

strangulate /'stræŋgjʊleɪt/ *vtr* gen, Med étrangler.

strangulation /ˌstræŋgjʊ'leɪʃn/ *n* **1** (of person) strangulation *f*; **2** Med étranglement *m*; **3** fig (of activity, economy) étranglement *m*.

strap /stræp/ **I** *n* **1** gen (band of cloth, leather) (on shoe, cap) bride *f*; (on bag, case, container, harness) courroie *f*; (on watch) bracelet *m*; (on handbag) bandoulière *f*; (on bus, train) poignée *f*; **2** Fashn (on dress, bra, overalls, lifejacket) bretelle *f*; **the ~ has broken** la bretelle a lâché; **3** Tech courroie *f*; **to tighten a ~** resserrer une courroie; **4** Med (on ankle) chevillère *f*; (on wrist) poignet *m* de contention; **5**† (punishment) **the ~** le fouet; **to get the ~** avoir le fouet.

II *vtr* (*p prés etc* **-pp-**) **1** (secure) **to ~ sth to** attacher qch à [*surface, roof, seat, wing*]; **to have a pistol ~ped to one's waist** avoir un pistolet attaché à la ceinture; **to ~ sb into** attacher qn dans [*seat, cockpit, pram*]; **2** Med, Sport (bandage) bander; **to ~ sb's ankle (up)** bander la cheville à qn; **to have one's thigh ~ped (up)** se faire bander la cuisse; **3**† (punish) fouetter.

■ **strap down**: **~ [sth/sb] down, ~ down [sth/sb]** attacher [*prisoner, patient, equipment*].

■ **strap in**: **~ [sb] in, ~ in [sb]** attacher [*passenger, child*]; **to ~ oneself in** s'attacher.

■ **strap on**: **~ [sth] on, ~ on [sth]** attacher [*watch, goggles, skis*].

strap: **~ fastening** *n* fermeture *f* à lanière; **~hang**○ *vi* voyager debout (en se tenant aux poignées); **~hanger**○ *n* voyageur/-euse *m/f* debout (*inv*); **~ hinge** *n* gond *m* à penture.

strapless /'stræplɪs/ *adj* [*bra, dress*] sans bretelles.

strapped○ /stræpt/ *adj* **to be ~ for** être à court de [*cash, staff*].

strapping /ˈstræpɪŋ/ **I** *n* ¢ gen sangles *fpl*; Ind cerclage *m*.
II *adj* parfois hum **a ~ fellow** un costaud; **a big ~ girl** une fille bien balancée○.

strapwork /ˈstræpwɜːk/ *n* entrelacs *m*.

Strasbourg /ˈstræzbɜːg/ ▶ 1818 *pr n* Strasbourg.

strata /ˈstrɑːtə, US ˈstreɪtə/ *pl* ▶ **stratum**.

stratagem /ˈstrætədʒəm/ *n* stratagème *m*.

strategic /strəˈtiːdʒɪk/, **strategical** /strəˈtiːdʒɪkl/ *adj* (all contexts) stratégique.

Strategic Air Command *n* US Mil Aviat Commandement *m* des Forces Aériennes Stratégiques.

strategically /strəˈtiːdʒɪklɪ/ *adv* [*plan, develop*] stratégiquement; [*important, placed, relevant*] du point de vue stratégique.

strategics /strəˈtiːdʒɪks/ *n* (+ *v sg*) stratégie *f*.

strategist /ˈstrætədʒɪst/ *n* gen, Mil, Pol stratège *m*; **armchair ~** péj stratège *m* en chambre pej.

strategy /ˈstrætədʒɪ/ *n* stratégie *f*; **business/company ~** stratégie des affaires/de l'entreprise; **financial/marketing ~** stratégie financière/commerciale.

Strathclyde /stræθˈklaɪd/ ▶ 1624 *pr n* (also **~ Region**) Strathclyde *m*.

stratification /ˌstrætɪfɪˈkeɪʃn/ *n* gen, Geol stratification *f*.

stratificational /ˌstrætɪfɪˈkeɪʃənl/ *adj* Ling stratificationnel/-elle.

stratify /ˈstrætɪfaɪ/ **I** *vtr* stratifier.
II *vi* [*rock*] se stratifier; [*society*] se cliver; **a stratified society** une société pleine de clivages.

stratocumulus /ˌstrætəʊˈkjuːmjʊləs/ *n* strato-cumulus *m*.

stratosphere /ˈstrætəsfɪə(r)/ *n* stratosphère *f*.

stratospheric /ˌstrætəˈsferɪk/ *adj* stratosphérique.

stratum /ˈstrɑːtəm, US ˈstreɪtəm/ *n* (*pl* **-ta**) **1** Geol strate *f*; **rock ~** strate *f* rocheuse; **2** Biol couche *f*; **3** (social) couche *f*.

straw /strɔː/ **I** *n* **1** gen (substance) paille *f*; (single stem) fétu *m* or brin *m* de paille; **bedding ~** paille *f* à litière; **2** (for thatching) chaume *m*; **3** (for drinking) paille *f*; **to drink sth with a ~** boire qch avec une paille or à la paille.
II *modif* [*bag, hat*] de paille.
IDIOMS **to draw ~s** tirer à la courte paille; **to draw the short ~** tirer le mauvais numéro; **to grasp** ou **clutch at ~s** se raccrocher à une chimère; **it's not worth a ~** cela ne vaut pas un clou○; **I don't care a ~**○ je m'en moque éperdument; **the last** ou **final ~** la goutte qui fait déborder le vase; **a man of ~** un homme de paille; **a ~ in the wind** un indice; **to make bricks without ~** faire avec ce que l'on a.

strawberry /ˈstrɔːbrɪ, US -berɪ/ **I** *n* Bot, Culin **1** (plant) fraisier *m*; **2** (berry) fraise *f*; **wild ~** fraise des bois; **strawberries and cream** fraises à la crème; **3** ▶ 1104 (colour) fraise *f*.
II *modif* [*flan, tart*] aux fraises; [*ice cream*] à la fraise; [*liqueur*] de fraise; [*jam*] de fraises; [*crop, field*] de fraises.

strawberry bed *n* carré *m* de fraises.

strawberry blonde **I** *n* femme *f* aux cheveux blond vénitien.
II ▶ 1104 *adj* [*hair*] blond vénitien *inv*.

strawberry: **~ bush** *n* Bot fusain *m*; **~ mark** *n* tache *f* de vin; **~ roan** *n, adj* Equit aubère (*mf*).

straw: **~board** *n* carton-paille *m*; **~-coloured** ▶ 1104 *adj* paille *inv*; **~ man** *n* US homme *m* de paille fig; **~ mat** *n* natte *f* (de paille); **~ poll** *n* Pol sondage *m* nonofficiel; **~ wine** *n* vin *m* de paille.

stray /streɪ/ **I** *n* **1** (animal) animal *m* égaré; (dog) chien *m* errant; (cat) chat *m* vagabond; **2** (bullet) balle *f* perdue.
II strays *npl* Electron parasites *mpl*.
III *adj* **1** (lost) [*dog*] errant; [*cat*] vagabond; [*child*] perdu; [*sheep, goat*] égaré; **2** (isolated) [*bullet*] perdu; [*car, tourist*] isolé; [*coin, crumb, pencil*] qui traîne○.
IV *vi* **1** lit (wander) [*animal, person, hand*] s'égarer; **to ~ from the road** s'écarter de la route; **to ~ from sb/from the house** s'éloigner de qn/de la maison; **to ~ onto the road** [*animal*] divaguer sur la route; **to ~ into a shop** entrer par hasard dans un magasin; **2** fig [*eyes, mind*] errer; [*thoughts*] vagabonder; **to ~ from the point** [*person*] s'écarter du sujet; **to ~ onto sth** (in telling) en venir par hasard à parler de qch; **to let one's thoughts ~** laisser errer ses pensées; **to let one's thoughts ~ to sth** en venir à penser à qch; **3** Relig pécher; **to ~ from the path of righteousness** s'écarter du droit chemin; **4** euph (commit adultery) avoir une aventure.

streak /striːk/ **I** *n* **1** (in character) côté *m*; **a cruel/mean ~, a ~ of cruelty/meanness** un côté cruel/mesquin; **2** (period) passe *f*; **to be on a winning/losing ~** être dans une bonne/mauvaise passe; **3** (mark) (of paint, substance, water) traînée *f*; (of light) rai *m*; **~ of lightning** lit, fig éclair *m*; **4** Cosmet mèche *f*; **to have ~s done** se faire faire des mèches.
II *vtr* **1** [*light, red*] strier [*sea, sky*]; **2** Cosmet **to ~ sb's hair** faire des mèches à qn; **to get one's hair ~ed** se faire faire des mèches.
III *vi* **1** (move fast) **to ~ past** passer comme une flèche; **to ~ across** ou **through sth** traverser qch comme une flèche; **2**○ (run naked) courir nu, courir à poil○.
IV streaked *pp adj* (with tears) sillonné (**with** de); (with dirt) maculé (**with** de); (with colour, light) strié (**with** de); **tear-~ed** sillonné de larmes; **sweat-~ed** dégoulinant de sueur.

streaker○ /ˈstriːkə(r)/ *n* streaker○ *m* (*personne qui court nue*).

streak lightning *n* trainée *f* d'éclairs.

streaky /ˈstriːkɪ/ *adj* [*surface*] couvert de traînées; [*paint*] avec des traînées; [*pattern*] en forme de traînees; **~ mark** traînée *f*.

streaky bacon *n* GB bacon *m* entrelardé.

stream /striːm/ **I** *n* **1** (small river) ruisseau *m*; **underground/trout ~** ruisseau souterrain/à truites; **2** (flow) **a ~ of** un flot de [*traffic, customers, questions, jokes*]; un torrent de [*insults, invective*]; un jet de [*light, flames*]; une coulée de [*lava*]; un écoulement de [*water*]; **a ~ of abuse** un torrent d'insultes; **3** (current) courant *m*; **to drift with the ~** [*leaves, particles*] flotter au gré du courant; **4** GB, Sch groupe *m* de niveau; **the top/middle/bottom ~** le groupe des élèves forts/moyens/faibles; **the A ~** ≈ le groupe des élèves forts; **to divide a class into ~s** répartir une classe en groupes de niveau.
II *vtr* GB, Sch répartir [qch/qn] en groupes de niveau [*class, children*].
III *vi* **1** (flow) [*tears, blood, water*] ruisseler; **blood was ~ing from the wound** le sang ruisselait de la blessure; **water was ~ing down the walls** l'eau ruisselait sur les murs; **sunlight was ~ing into the room** le soleil entrait à flots dans la pièce; **tears were ~ing down his face** ses larmes coulaient à flots; **2** (move) [*traffic, cars, people*] (into a place) affluer; (out of a place) [*traffic, cars*] sortir à flots; [*people*] sortir en foule; **they ~ed through the gates** ils ont franchi le portail en foule; **3** (flutter, blow) [*banners, hair*] flotter; **to ~ in the wind** flotter au vent; **4** [*eyes, nose*] couler; **my eyes were ~ing** j'avais les yeux qui coulaient; **pollen makes his nose ~** le pollen lui fait couler le nez.
IDIOMS **to come on ~** [*factory, oil field*] entrer en activité.

streamer /ˈstriːmə(r)/ **I** *n* **1** (flag, ribbon of paper) banderole *f*; **2** Journ (headline) manchette *f*; **3** Astron (corona) couronne *f* solaire.
II streamers *npl* Astron aurore *f* boréale.

streaming /ˈstriːmɪŋ/ **I** *n* GB, Sch répartition *f* par groupes de niveau.
II○ *adj* **a ~ cold** un très gros rhume.

streamline /ˈstriːmlaɪn/ *vtr* **1** Aut, Aviat, Naut caréner; **2** (make more efficient) rationaliser [*distribution, production, procedures*]; euph (cut back) dégraisser [*company*].

streamlined /ˈstriːmlaɪnd/ *adj* **1** gen [*cooker, bathroom, furniture*] aux lignes modernes; Aut, Aviat, Naut [*hull, body*] caréné; **2** fig [*procedures, production, system*] simplifié.

streamlining /ˈstriːmlaɪnɪŋ/ *n* **1** (of cars, boats) carénage *m*; **2** (of procedures, production, work methods) rationalisation *f*; (of company) euph dégraissage.

stream of consciousness *n* courant *m* de conscience.

street /striːt/ **I** *n* rue *f*; **in** ou **on the ~** dans la rue; **across** ou **over** GB **the ~** de l'autre côté de la rue; **to go down/go across the ~** descendre/traverser la rue; **to put** ou **turn sb out on the ~** mettre or jeter qn à la rue; **to be on the** ou **walk the ~s** [*homeless person*] être à la rue; [*prostitute*] faire le trottoir; **to keep people off the ~s** éviter que les gens ne se retrouvent à la rue; **to keep trouble off the ~s** maintenir l'ordre dans la rue; **to take to the ~s** [*population, rioters*] descendre dans la rue; [*prostitute*] faire le trottoir; **the man in the ~** l'homme de la rue.
II *modif* **1** [*accident*] de la circulation; [*directory, plan, musician*] des rues; **2** [*style, drug, culture*] de la rue.
IDIOMS **it's right up my/your ~**○ c'est exactement ce qu'il me/vous faut; **they are ~s apart** GB un abîme les sépare; **to be in Queer Street**○† GB être dans la panade◑; **to be ~s ahead of**○ GB être bien meilleur que.

street: **~ arab**○† *n* petit/-e va-nu-pieds *m/f*; **~car** *n* US tramway *m*; **~ cleaner** ▶ 1692 *n* (person) balayeur *m*; (machine) balayeuse *f*; **~ cleaning, ~ cleansing** GB *n* nettoyage *m* or balayage *m* des rues; **~ clothes** *npl* US habits *mpl* de tous les jours.

street cred○ /ˌstriːt ˈkred/ *n* **to do sth to gain ~** faire qch pour montrer qu'on est dans le coup○; **it gives him ~** cela montre qu'il est dans le coup○.

street: **~ credibility** *n* = **street cred**; **~ door** *n* porte *f* d'entrée; **~ fighting** *n* ¢ combats *mpl* de rue; **~ furniture** *n* mobilier *m* urbain; **~ guide** *n* indicateur *m* des rues; **~lamp** *n* (old gas-lamp) réverbère *m*; (modern) lampadaire *m*.

street level **I** *n* rez-de-chaussée *m*; **at ~** au rez-de-chaussée.
II street-level *adj* [*exit*] au rez-de-chaussée; [*parking*] au niveau de la rue.

street: **~light** *n* réverbère *m*; **~ lighting** *n* éclairage *m* des rues; **~ market** *n* marché *m* en plein air; **~ plan** *n* ▶ **street guide**; **~ sweeper** ▶ 1692 *n* = **street cleaner**; **~ theatre** GB, **~ theater** US *n* théâtre *m* de rue; **~ value** *n* valeur *f* à la revente; **~walker** *n* prostituée *f*; **~wise**○ *adj* [*person*] dégourdi○; [*image*] déluré.

strength /streŋθ/ *n* **1** (power) (of person, wind) force *f*; (of lens, magnet, voice) puissance *f*; **to summon up/save one's ~** rassembler/ménager ses forces; **his ~ failed him** ses forces l'ont trahi; **with all one's ~** de toutes ses forces; **to find/have the ~ to do** avoir/trouver la force de faire; **to have great ~** être très fort; **to build up one's ~** lit développer ses muscles; (after illness) reprendre des forces; **2** (toughness) (of structure, equipment) solidité *f*; (of material, substance) résistance *f*; **3** (concentration) (of solution) titre *m*; (of dose, medicine) concentration *f*; **taste the ~ of the mixture/coffee** goûtes le mélange/café pour voir s'il est fort; **the alcoholic ~ of a drink** la teneur en alcool d'une boisson; **4** (capability) force *f*; **to test the ~ of the government/team** mettre la force du gouvernement/de l'équipe à l'épreuve; **to be in a position of ~** être en position de forces; **economic/military ~** puissance *f* économique/militaire; **5** (intensity) (of bond) force *f*; (of feeling, reaction) intensité; (of bulb) puissance *f*; (of current) intensité *f*; **6** Fin fermeté *f*; **the ~ of the dollar against the pound** la fermeté du dollar par rapport à la livre; **to gain ~** se raffermir; **7** (resolution) force *f*; **~ of character** force de caractère; **inner/moral ~** force intérieure/morale; **~ of will** volonté *f*; **~ of purpose** détermination *f*; **8** (credibility) (of argument) force *f*; (of case, claim) solidité *f*; **to give** ou **lend ~ to** [*evidence*] renforcer [*argument, theory*]; **he was convicted on the ~ of the evidence** on l'a condamné sur la base des témoignages; **I got the job on the ~ of my research/his recommendation** j'ai obtenu le poste grâce à mes recherches/sa recommandation; **9** (asset) (of person, team) qualité *f*; (of novel, play) qualité *f*; **his patience is his greatest ~** sa patience est sa meilleure qualité; **10** (total size) **the team is below ~** l'équipe n'est pas au complet; **the workforce is at full ~** la main-d'œuvre est au complet; **to bring the team up to ~** compléter l'équipe; **his fans were present in ~** ses fans étaient là en foule.

IDIOMS **to go from ~ to ~** se porter de mieux en mieux; **give me ~**○! c'est pas possible○!

strengthen /ˈstreŋθn/ **I** *vtr* **1** (reinforce) renforcer [*building, material, wall*]; consolider [*equipment, machine*]; **2** (increase the power of) renforcer [*government, party, team*]; renforcer [*argument, claim, position*]; consolider [*bond, links*]; **3** (increase) renforcer [*belief, determination, love*]; affirmer [*power, role*]; **to ~ sb's hand** fig consolider la position de qn; **to ~ one's lead** renforcer sa position de leader; **4** (build up) fortifier [*muscles*]; raffermir [*dollar, economy*].
II *vi* [*muscles*] se fortifier; [*current, wind*] augmenter (de force); [*economy, yen*] se raffermir (**against** par rapport à).

strengthening /ˈstreŋθnɪŋ/ **I** *n* (of building, equipment) consolidation *f*; (of solution) concentration *f*; (of numbers of people) renforcement *m*; **the rioting called for a ~ of the police presence** l'émeute a nécessité un renforcement des forces de police.
II *adj* [*current, wind*] qui augmente de forces (*after n*); [*currency, pound*] qui se consolide (*after n*); **the dollar fell today against a ~ pound** le dollar a chuté aujourd'hui alors que la livre s'est consolidée; **the news had a ~ effect on the market** la nouvelle a raffermi le marché.

strenuous /ˈstrenjʊəs/ *adj* **1** (demanding) [*exercise*] énergique; [*walk*] difficile; [*day, schedule*] chargé; [*work, activity, job*] ardu; **2** (determined) [*protest, disagreement*] vigoureux/-euse; **to put up ~ opposition to sth** s'opposer vigoureusement à qch; **to make ~ efforts to do** faire des efforts acharnés pour faire.

strenuously /ˈstrenjʊəslɪ/ *adv* [*deny, protest, oppose*] vigoureusement; [*try, work*] avec acharnement.

strenuousness /ˈstrenjʊəsnɪs/ *n* (of work, activity) caractère *m* épuisant; (of protest, resistance) vigueur *f*.

streptococcal /ˌstreptəˈkɒkl/ *adj* Med streptococcique.

streptococcus /ˌstreptəˈkɒkəs/ *n* (*pl* **-cci**) streptocoque *m*.

streptomycin /ˌstreptəʊˈmaɪsɪn/ *n* streptomycine *f*.

stress /stres/ **I** *n* **1** (nervous) tension *f*, stress *m*; **emotional/mental ~** tension émotionnelle/nerveuse; **signs of ~** signes *mpl* de tension; **to suffer from ~** être stressé; **to be under ~** être stressé; **to put sb under ~, to put ~ on sb** soumettre qn au stress; **in times of ~** en période de stress; **the ~es and strains of modern life** les agressions *fpl* de la vie moderne; **2** (emphasis) **~ on** insistance *f* sur [*aspect, point*]; **to lay** ou **put ~ on** mettre l'accent *m* sur, insister sur [*fact, problem, feature*]; **there is not enough ~ (laid) on vocational skills** on ne met pas assez l'accent sur les aptitudes pratiques; **3** Civ Eng, Phys effort *m*; **subject to high ~es** soumis à des efforts importants; **a ~ of 500 kg** une charge de 500 kg; **to put** ou **impose ~ on sth** soumettre qch à un effort; **the ~ on the fuselage** l'effort subi par le fuselage; **to be in ~** travailler; **the ~ produced in a structure** le travail d'une structure; **4** Ling, Phon (phenomenon) accentuation *f*; (instance) accent *m*; **the ~ falls on...** l'accent tombe sur...; **to put** ou **place the ~ on sth** mettre or placer l'accent sur qch; **5** Mus accent *m*.
II *vtr* **1** (emphasize) mettre l'accent *m* or insister sur [*commitment, issue, difficulty, advantage*]; **to ~ the importance of sth** souligner l'importance *f* de qch; **to ~ the need for sth/to do** souligner la nécessité de qch/de faire; **to ~ the point that** insister sur le fait que; **to ~ (that)** souligner que; **2** Ling, Mus accentuer [*note, syllable*]; **3** Civ Eng, Tech (experimentally) soumettre [qch] à des efforts *mpl* [*structure, component*]; (in practice) faire travailler [*structure, metal*].
■ **stress out**○: **~ [sb] out** stresser [qn].

stressed /strest/ *adj* **1** (also **~ out**) (emotionally) stressé; **to feel ~** se sentir stressé; **2** Mech, Phys, Tech (*épith*) [*components, covering, structure*] travaillant; **3** Ling, Phon accentué.

stress: **~ factor** *n* Med facteur *m* de stress; **~ fracture** *n* Med fracture *f* de fatigue; Civ Eng crique *f* de fatigue.

stressful /ˈstresfl/ *adj* [*lifestyle, situation, circumstances, work*] stressant; **it's very ~ living with them** c'est très stressant de vivre avec eux.

stress: **~ limit** *n* limite *f* de fatigue; **~ mark** *n* accent *m*; **~-related** *adj* [*illness*] dû au stress; **~ relief** *n* détente *f*; **~ unit** *n* unité *f* de charge.

stretch /stretʃ/ **I** *n* **1** (extending movement) (in gymnastics) extension *f*; **to have a ~** s'étirer; **to give sth a ~** étirer [*arm, leg*]; tirer sur [*elastic*]; **to be at full ~** lit (taut) [*rope, elastic*] être tendu au maximum; fig (flat out) [*factory, office*] être à plein régime; **to work at full ~** [*factory, machine*] travailler à plein régime; [*person*] travailler au maximum de ses capacités; **at a ~** à la rigueur; **2** (elasticity) élasticité *f*; **3** (section) (of road, track) tronçon *m*; (of coastline, river) partie *f*; **a clear/dangerous ~ of road** un tronçon de route dégagé/dangereux; **the ~ of track/road between Oxford and Banbury** le tronçon de voie/route entre Oxford et Banbury; **to be on the home** ou **finishing ~** [*athlete, racehorse*] être sur la ligne d'arrivée; **4** (expanse) (of water, countryside) étendue *f*; **a ~ of land** une étendue de terre; **5** (period) période *f*; **a short/long ~** une longue/courte période; **he was often left alone for long ~es** on le laissait souvent seul des heures durant; **a three-hour ~** trois heures; **I did an 18-month ~ in Tokyo** j'ai travaillé 18 mois à Tokyo; **to work for 12 hours at a ~** travailler 12 heures d'affilée; **6**○ (prison sentence) peine *f*; **a five-year ~** une peine de cinq ans; **to do a long ~** servir une longue peine.
II *adj* (*épith*) [*cover, fabric, waist*] extensible; [*limousine*] à carrosserie allongée, longue.
III *vtr* **1** (extend) tendre [*rope, net*] (**between** entre); **to ~ one's neck/arms/legs** lit s'étirer le cou/les bras/les jambes; **to ~ one's legs** fig se dégourdir or se dérouiller les jambes; **to ~ one's wings** lit, fig déployer ses ailes; **the fabric was ~ed tight across his shoulders/buttocks** le tissu lui moulait les épaules/les fesses; **2** (increase the size) lit tendre [*spring*]; étirer [*elastic*]; tirer sur [*fabric*]; (deliberately) élargir [*shoe*]; (distort) déformer [*garment, shoe*]; fig **they ~ed their lead to 5-0** ils ont conforté leur position de leader en menant 5-0; **3** (bend) déformer [*truth*]; contourner [*rules, regulations*]; **to ~ a point** (make concession) faire une exception; (exaggerate) aller trop loin; **4** (push to the limit) abuser de [*patience, tolerance*]; utiliser [qch] au maximum [*budget, resources*]; pousser [qn] au maximum de ses possibilités [*pupil, employee, competitor*]; **to be fully ~ed** [*person, company*] être à son maximum; **the system is ~ed to the limit** le système est exploité au maximum de ses possibilités; **you're ~ing my credulity to the limit** n'abuse pas trop de ma crédulité; **I need a job that ~es me** j'ai besoin d'un travail qui me motive à fond; **she isn't ~ed at school** l'école ne la pousse pas assez; **isn't that ~ing it a bit**○? vous ne poussez pas un peu○?; **5** (eke out) économiser [*budget*]; faire durer [*supplies*].
IV *vi* **1** (extend one's limbs) s'étirer; **2** (spread) [*road, track*] s'étaler (**for** sur); [*forest, water, beach, moor*] s'étendre (**for** sur); **the road ~es for 200 km** la route s'étale sur 200 km; **to ~ over** [*empire*] couvrir [*Europe*]; [*festivities, course*] s'étaler sur [*fortnight, month*]; **to ~ to** ou **as far as sth** [*flex, string*] aller jusqu'à qch; **how far does the queue/traffic jam ~?** jusqu'où va la queue/l'embouteillage?; **the weeks ~ed into months** les semaines devenaient des mois; **3** (become larger) [*elastic*] s'étendre; [*shoe*] s'élargir; [*fabric, garment*] se déformer; **this fabric ~es** ce tissu se déforme; **4**○ (afford) **I think I can ~ to a bottle of wine** je pense que je peux me permettre une bouteille de vin; **the budget won't ~ to a new computer** le budget ne peut pas supporter l'achat d'un nouvel ordinateur.
V *v refl* **to ~ oneself** s'étirer; fig faire un effort.
■ **stretch back**: **the queue ~es back for 100 metres** la queue s'étend sur 100 mètres; **to ~ back for centuries** [*tradition*] remonter à plusieurs siècles; **to ~ back to** [*problem, tradition*] remonter à [*1970, last year*]; [*traffic jam, queue*] remonter à [*place, corner*].
■ **stretch out**: ¶ **~ out 1** (lie down) s'étendre, s'allonger; **2** (extend) [*plain, countryside, road*] s'étaler, s'étendre; ¶ **~ out [sth], ~ [sth] out** (extend) tendre [*hand, foot*] (**towards** vers); étendre [*arm, leg*]; étaler [*nets, sheet*]; **I ~ed my speech out to an hour** j'ai fait durer mon discours pendant une heure.

stretcher /ˈstretʃə(r)/ *n* **1** Med civière *f*, brancard *m*; **2** (for hat) conformateur *m*; (for shoes) forme *f*; (for canvas) châssis *m*; **3** (strut) (on chair) barreau *m*; (on umbrella) baleine *f*; **4** Constr (wooden) traverse *f*.
■ **stretcher off**: **~ [sb] off** Sport emmener [qn] sur une civière [*injured player*].

stretcher: **~-bearer** ▶ 1692 *n* brancardier/-ière *m/f*; **~ case** *n* blessé/-e *m/f* grave (*incapable de se déplacer*).

stretch mark *n* vergeture *f*.

stretchy /ˈstretʃɪ/ *adj* extensible.

strew /struː/ *vtr* (*prét* **strewed**; *pp* **strewed** ou **strewn**) éparpiller [*clothes, litter, paper*] (**on, over** sur); répandre [*sand, straw, wreckage*] (**on, over** sur); semer [*flowers*] (**on, over** sur); **to ~ the floor with clothes** éparpiller des vêtements par terre; **strewn with** parsemé de; **leaf-strewn** parsemé de feuilles; **rock-strewn** caillouteux/-euse.

strewth◑ /struːθ/ *excl* GB bon sang○!

stria /ˈstraɪə/ *n* (*pl* **-ae**) **1** Biol, Geol strie *f*; **2** Archit cannelure *f*.

striate /straɪˈeɪt, US ˈstraɪeɪt/ *vtr* strier.

striation /straɪˈeɪʃn/ *n* striation *f*.

stricken /ˈstrɪkən/ *adj* **1** (afflicted) [*face, look, voice*] affligé; **2** (affected) [*area*] sinistré; **~ with, ~ by** frappé par [*fear, illness, poverty*]; accablé par [*doubt, guilt*]; atteint de [*chronic illness*]; **guilt-~** accablé par la culpabilité; **drought-/famine-~** frappé par la sécheresse/la famine; **3** (incapacitated) [*plane, ship*] en détresse.

strict /strɪkt/ *adj* **1** (not lenient) [*person, rule, upbringing, discipline, school*] strict, sévère; [*view, principle*] rigide; [*Methodist, Catholic*] de stricte observance; **to be ~ with sb** être strict or sévère avec qn; **he is very ~ about discipline** il est très strict sur la discipline; **2** (stringent) [*law, order, instructions*] formel/-elle, strict; [*meaning, criterion*] strict (*after n*); [*interpretation, observance, limit*] strict (*before n*); (absolute) [*truth, accuracy*] strict (*before n*), absolu; [*silence, privacy*] absolu; **in the ~ sense of the word** au sens strict du terme; **they have to work to ~ deadlines** ils doivent respecter des délais très stricts; **in ~ confidence** à titre strictement confidentiel; **in ~ secrecy** dans le plus grand secret; **on the ~ understanding that** à la condition expresse que (+ *subj*).

strict liability *n* Jur responsabilité *f* sans faute intentionnelle.

strictly /ˈstrɪktlɪ/ *adv* **1** (not leniently) [*deal with, treat*] avec sévérité, sévèrement; **2** (absolutely) [*confidential, private, functional*] strictement; **'camping is ~ prohibited'** 'camping strictement interdit'; **~ speaking** à proprement parler; **~ between ourselves...** que ceci reste entre nous...; **that is not ~ true** ceci n'est pas tout à fait vrai.

strictness /ˈstrɪktnɪs/ *n* (of person, upbringing, regime) sévérité *f*; (of rule, law) sévérité *f*, rigueur *f*; (of views, principles) rigueur *f*, rigidité *f*.

stricture /ˈstrɪktʃə(r)/ *n* **1** (censure) condamnation *f* (**against, on** de); **to pass ~s on sb/sth** critiquer qn/qch sévèrement, condamner qn/qch; **2** (restriction) contrainte *f*; **3** Med rétrécissement *m*, sténose *f* spec.

stridden /ˈstrɪdn/ *pp* (rare) ▶ **stride** III, IV.

stride /straɪd/ **I** *n* **1** (long step) enjambée *f*; **to cross a room in two ~s** traverser une pièce en deux enjambées; **a few ~s from sth** à quelques pas de qch; **2** (gait) démarche *f*; **to have a confident/elegant ~** avoir une démarche assurée/élégante; **to have a long ~** marcher à grandes enjambées; **to lengthen one's ~** allonger le pas.
II strides○ *npl* Austral pantalon *m*.
III *vtr* (*prét* **strode**, *pp* rare **stridden**) (cover) parcourir [qch] à grands pas [*distance*].
IV *vi* (*prét* **strode**, *pp* rare **stridden**) **1 to ~ across/out/in** traverser/sortir/ entrer à grands pas ; **to ~ off** ou **away** s'éloigner à grands pas; **to ~ up and down sth** arpenter qch; **2** (cross in a stride) **to ~ over** ou **across sth** enjamber qch.
IDIOMS **to get into one's ~** trouver son rythme; **to make great ~s** faire de grands progrès; **to put sb off his/her ~** faire perdre le rythme à qn; **to take sth in one's ~** (cope practically) prendre qch calmement; (cope emotionally) accepter qch avec sérénité.

stridency /ˈstraɪdnsɪ/ *n* **1** (of sound, voice) stridence *f*; **2** (of claim, protest) véhémence *f*.

strident /ˈstraɪdnt/ *adj* **1** (harsh) [*sound, voice*] strident; **~ with anger** vibrant de colère; **2** (vociferous) [*statement, group*] véhément.

stridently /ˈstraɪdntlɪ/ *adv* **1** (harshly) [*speak, play*] de façon stridente; **2** (vociferously) [*protest, shout*] avec véhémence.

stridulate /ˈstrɪdjʊleɪt, US ˈstrɪdʒʊleɪt/ *vi* Zool striduler.

strife /straɪf/ *n* **1** (conflict) conflits *mpl* (**among** au sein de; **in** dans); **ethnic/industrial ~** conflits ethniques/industriels; **in a state of ~** en conflit; **2** (dissent) querelles *fpl*; **domestic ~** querelles domestiques.
IDIOMS **my trouble and ~**○ GB argot des Cockney ma bourgeoise○.

strife-torn, strife-ridden *adj* déchiré par les conflits.

strike /straɪk/ **I** *n* **1** Ind, Comm grève *f*; **to be/come out on ~** être/se mettre en grève; **2** gen, Mil (attack) attaque *f* (**on, against** contre); **air/pre-emptive ~** attaque aérienne/préventive; **3** Mining (discovery) découverte *f* (d'un gisement); **to make a ~** trouver or découvrir un gisement; **diamond ~** découverte d'un gisement de diamants; **lucky ~** fig coup *m* de chance; **4** (clock mechanism) sonnerie *f*; **5** Sport (in baseball) bonne balle *f*, strike *m*; (in ten-pin bowling) double honneur *m*; **6** Fishg touche *f*.
II *modif* Ind, Comm [*committee, notice*] de grève; [*leader*] des grévistes.
III *vtr* (*prét, pp* **struck**) **1** (hit) [*person, stick, bat*] frapper [*person, object, ball*]; [*torpedo, missile*] frapper, toucher [*target, vessel*]; [*ship, car, person*] heurter [*rock, tree, pedestrian*]; **to ~ sb on the head/in the face** [*person*] frapper qn à la tête/au visage; [*object*] heurter qn à la tête/au visage; **to ~ sth with** taper qch avec [*stick, hammer*]; **she struck the table with her fist** (deliberately) elle a frappé du poing sur la table; **he struck his head on the table** il s'est cogné la tête contre la table; **his head struck the table** sa tête a heurté la table; **lightning struck the house/struck him** la foudre est tombée sur la maison/l'a frappé; **to be struck by lightning** [*tree, house, person*] être touché par la foudre; **to ~ sb to the ground** (with fist) faire tomber qn d'un coup de poing; (with stick) faire tomber qn d'un coup de bâton; **to ~ sb a blow** lit, fig porter un coup à qn; **to ~ the first blow** lit, fig porter le premier coup; **to ~ sb dead** [*lightning, God*] foudroyer qn; [*person*] porter un coup mortel à qn; **to be struck blind/dumb** litér être frappé de cécité/de mutisme; **to be struck dumb with amazement** être frappé d'étonnement; **2** (afflict) [*quake, famine, disease, storm, disaster*] frapper [*area, people*]; **'earthquake ~s San Francisco'** journ 'San Francisco secoué par un tremblement de terre'; **the pain ~s when I bend down** je ressens cette douleur lorsque je me baisse; **to ~ terror into sb** ou **sb's heart** frapper qn de terreur; **3** (make impression on) [*idea, thought*] venir à l'esprit de [*person*]; [*resemblance*] frapper [*person*]; **to be struck by** être frappé par; **an awful thought struck me** une horrible pensée m'est venue à l'esprit; **a terrible sight struck my eyes** un horrible spectacle s'est présenté à mes yeux; **it ~s me as funny/stupid that** je trouve drôle/bête que (+ *subj*); **it ~s me as mean of them to do** je trouve que c'est méchant de leur part de faire; **to ~ sb as odd/absurd** paraître or sembler étrange/absurde à qn; **he ~s me as an intelligent man** il me paraît intelligent; **it ~s me as a good idea to do** cela me paraît or me semble une bonne idée de faire; **did anything ~ you as odd?** as-tu remarqué quelque chose de bizarre?; **how does the idea ~ you?** qu'est-ce que vous pensez de cette idée?; **how did he ~ you?** quelle impression vous a-t-il faite?; **it ~s me (that)** à mon avis; **it struck him that here was the opportunity** il s'est dit soudain que c'était l'occasion; **I was struck**○ **with him/it** il/ça m'a plu; **she wasn't very struck**○ **with it** ça ne lui a pas beaucoup plu; **to be struck on**○ GB être entiché○ de; **4** (discover, come upon) découvrir, tomber sur○ (*oil, gold*); trouver, tomber sur○ [*road*]; rencontrer, tomber sur○ [*rock, concrete, obstacle*]; **to ~ a rich vein of humour** trouver une riche source d'humour; **5** (achieve) conclure [*accord, bargain*]; **to ~ a balance** trouver le juste milieu (**between** entre); **6** (ignite) frotter [*match*]; **to ~ a spark from a flint** produire une étincelle en frottant un silex; **7** [*clock*] sonner [*time*]; **the clock struck six** la pendule a sonné six heures; **it had just struck two** deux heures venaient de sonner; **8** (delete) supprimer, rayer [*word, sentence, comment*]; **to order sth to be struck from the record** ordonner que qch soit supprimé or rayé du procès-verbal; **9** (dismantle) démonter [*tent, scaffolding*]; **to ~ camp** lever le camp; **to ~ one's colours** Mil abaisser les couleurs; **to ~ the set** Theat démonter le décor; **10** Fin (mint) frapper [*coin*]; **11** Hort planter [*cutting*]; **to ~ root** prendre racine; **12** Fishg [*fisherman*] ferrer [*fish*]; [*fish*] mordre [*bait*].
IV *vi* (*prét, pp* **struck**) **1** (deliver blow) [*person*] frapper; (collide) [*bomb, shell*] tomber; **to ~ short of the target** tomber à côté de la cible; **my head struck against a beam** ma tête a heurté une poutre, je me suis cogné la tête contre une poutre; **to ~ at** attaquer; **2** (attack) [*killer, rapist, disease, storm*] frapper; [*army, animal, snake*] attaquer; **the terrorists have struck again** les terroristes ont encore frappé; **disaster struck** la catastrophe s'est produite; **'when pain ~s, take Calmaways'** 'en cas de douleur, prenez des Calmaways'; **to ~ at** attaquer [*target*]; **this ~s at the heart of the democratic system** cela frappe au cœur du système démocratique; **to ~ at the root of the problem** s'attaquer à la racine du problème; **Henry ~s again**○! hum Henry nous en a fait encore une○; **3** Ind, Comm faire (la) grève; **to ~ for/against** faire (la) grève pour obtenir/pour protester contre; **4** [*match*] s'allumer; **5** [*clock, time*] sonner; **six o'clock struck** six heures ont sonné; **6** (proceed) **to ~ north/inland** prendre au nord/vers l'intérieur des terres; **to ~ across** prendre à travers [*field, country*]; **7** Hort [*cutting, plant*] prendre (racine); **8** Fishg [*fish*] mordre.
IDIOMS **to have two ~s against one** US être désavantagé.
■ **strike back** (retaliate) riposter (**at** à).
■ **strike down**: **~ [sb] down, ~ down [sb]** [*person*] faire tomber, terrasser; **to be struck down by** (affected) être frappé par [*illness*]; (incapacitated) être terrassé par [*illness*]; être abattu de [*bullet*].
■ **strike off**: ¶ **~ off** (go off) prendre (**across** à travers; **towards** vers); ¶ **~ [sth] off, ~ off [sth] 1** (delete) rayer [*item on list, name*]; **2** Print tirer [*copy*]; **3** sout (cut off) couper [*branch, flowerhead*]; ¶ **~ [sb] off** radier [*doctor*]; **he's been struck off** il a été radié; ¶ **~ [sb/sth] off** rayer [qn/qch] de [*list*]; **to be struck off the roll** [*doctor*] être radié de l'ordre des médecins; [*barrister*] être rayé du barreau.
■ **strike out**: ¶ **~ out 1** (hit out) frapper; **he struck out blindly** il a frappé à l'aveuglette; **to ~ out at** lit attaquer [*adversary*]; fig s'en prendre à [*critics, rival*]; **2** (proceed) **to ~ out towards** s'élancer vers; fig **to ~ out in new directions** adopter de nouvelles orientations; **to ~ out on one's own** gen voler de ses propres ailes; (in business) s'établir à son compte; **3** US (in baseball) être éliminé; **4**○ US (fail) ne pas parvenir à ses fins; ¶ **~ [sth] out, ~ out [sth]** (delete) rayer, supprimer [*name, mention, paragraph*].
■ **strike up**: ¶ **~ up** [*band, orchestra*] commencer à jouer; [*singer, choir*] commencer à chanter; **the band struck up with a waltz** l'orchestre a attaqué une valse; ¶ **~ up [sth]** (start) [*band, orchestra*] attaquer [*tune, piece*]; [*singer, choir*] entamer [*song, tune*]; **to ~ up an acquaintance with** faire connaissance avec; **to ~ up a conversation with** engager la conversation avec; **to ~ up a friendship with** se lier d'amitié avec; **they struck up a friendship** ils sont devenus amis; **to ~ up a relationship with** établir des rapports avec.

strike: **~ ballot** *n* vote *m* au sujet de la grève; **~bound** *adj* [*factory, area*] victime d'une grève, paralysé par la grève;

~breaker *n* briseur/-euse *m/f* de grève; **~breaking** *n* (refusal to strike) refus *m* de faire grève; (work during strike) retour *m* au travail; **~ force** *n* Mil détachement *m* d'intervention; **~ fund** *n* caisse *f* de grève; **~ pay** *n* indemnité *f* de grève.

striker /'straɪkə(r)/ *n* **1** Ind, Comm gréviste *mf*; **2** Sport (in football) attaquant/-e *m/f*; **3** Mech (in clock) marteau *m*; (in gun) percuteur *m*.

striking /'straɪkɪŋ/ **I** *n* **1** (of clock) sonnerie *f*; **2** (of coin) frappe *f*.
II *adj* **1** [*person, clothes, pictures*] que l'on remarque (*after n*); [*pattern, design*] qui se remarque (*after n*); [*similarity, contrast*] frappant; **2** [*clock*] qui sonne les heures (*after n*); **3** Ind, Comm [*worker*] gréviste, en grève.

striking distance *n* **to be within ~** [*army, troops*] être à portée de canon (**of** de); **to be within ~ for sb** [*agreement, success*] être à la portée de qn; **we are within ~ of winning** la victoire est à notre portée.

strikingly /'straɪkɪŋlɪ/ *adv* [*beautiful, different, similar*] remarquablement; [*stand out, differ*] de manière frappante.

string /strɪŋ/ **I** *n* **1** ¢ (twine) ficelle *f*; **a ball/a piece of ~** une pelote/un bout de ficelle; **to tie sth up with ~** attacher qch avec de la ficelle; **tied up with ~** ficelé; **2** (length of cord) (for packaging) ficelle *f*; (on garment, medal) cordon *m*; (on bow, racket) corde *f*; (on puppet) fil *m*; **hanging on a ~** suspendu à une ficelle; **to tie a ~ round sth** attacher or mettre une ficelle autour de qch; **to pull the ~s** lit, fig tirer les ficelles; **3** (series) **a ~ of** un défilé de [*visitors, ministers, boyfriends*]; une série de [*crimes, convictions, scandals, takeovers, novels*]; une succession de [*victories, successes, awards*]; une chaîne de [*shops, businesses*]; une kyrielle de [*complaints, insults*]; **4** (set) **~ of garlic** tresse *f* d'ail; **~ of onions** chapelet *m* d'oignons; **~ of pearls** collier *m* de perles; **~ of beads** collier *m* de perles (fantaisie); **~ of islands** chapelet *m* d'îles; **~ of light bulbs** guirlande *f* d'ampoules; **5** Equit, Turf **a ~ of racehorses** une écurie (de courses); **6** Mus (on instrument) corde *f*; **C-~** la corde de do; **to tighten/break a ~** tendre/casser une corde; **7** Comput chaîne *f*; **numeric/character ~** chaîne numérique/de caractères; **8** Bot, Culin (in bean) fil *m*; **to remove the ~s from the beans** effiler les haricots; **9** Ling suite *f*; **10** (also **~board**) Constr limon *m* (d'escalier).
II strings *npl* Mus **the ~s** les cordes *fpl*.
III *vtr* (*prét, pp* **strung**) **1** Mus, Sport corder [*racket*]; monter [*guitar, violin*]; garnir [qch] d'une corde [*bow*]; **to ~ [sth] tightly** faire un cordage tendu à [*racket*]; **2** (thread) enfiler [*beads, pearls*] (**on** sur); **3** (hang) **to ~ sth (up) above/across** suspendre qch au-dessus de/en travers de [*street*]; **to ~ sth up on** accrocher qch à [*lamppost, pole*]; **to ~ sth between** suspendre qch entre [*trees, supports*].
IV *vi* (*prét, pp* **strung**) Journ **to ~ for a newspaper** travailler comme correspondant free-lance pour un journal.
V -stringed (*dans composés*) **a six-~ed instrument** un instrument à six cordes.
IDIOMS **to have sb on a ~** mener qn à la baguette; **to pull ~s**○ faire jouer le piston○; **to pull ~s for sb**○ pistonner○ qn; **without ~s** ou **with no ~s attached** sans conditions. ▶ **bow**[1].
■ **string along**○ GB: ¶ **~ along** suivre; **to ~ along with sb** suivre qn; ¶ **~ [sb] along** péj mener qn en bateau pej.
■ **string out**: ¶ **~ out** s'échelonner; ¶ **~ [sth] out**, **~ out [sth]** échelonner; **to be strung out along** [*vehicles, groups*] s'échelonner le long de [*road*]; **to be strung out across** [*people*] se déployer dans [*field, zone*].
■ **string together**: **~ [sth] together**, **~ together [sth]** aligner [*sentences, words*]; enchaîner [*songs, rhymes*]; **unable to ~ two sentences together** péj incapable de mettre deux phrases bout à bout.
■ **string up**○: **~ [sb] up** pendre [qn] haut et court; **he was strung up by the heels** il a été pendu par les pieds.

string: **~ bag** *n* filet *m* à provisions; **~ band** *n* orchestre *m* à cordes; **~ bass** ▶ 1481 *n* contrebasse *f*; **~ bean** *n* haricot *m* à écosser; **~course** *n* bandeau *m*, cordon *m*.

stringency /'strɪndʒənsɪ/ *n* **1** (of criticism, law, measure) sévérité *f*; **2** (of control, regulation, test) rigueur *f*; **economic ~**, **financial ~** austérité *f*.

stringent /'strɪndʒənt/ *adj* [*measure, standard*] rigoureux/-euse; [*ban, order*] formel/-elle.

stringently /'strɪndʒəntlɪ/ *adv* [*observe, respect*] scrupuleusement; [*apply, treat*] avec rigueur; [*examine, test*] rigoureusement; [*critical*] rigoureusement.

stringer /'strɪŋə(r)/ ▶ 1692 *n* **1** Journ correspondant/-e *m/f* free-lance; **2** Archit longeron *m*.

string: **~ instrument**, **~ed instrument** ▶ 1481 *n* instrument *m* à cordes; **~ orchestra** *n* orchestre *m* à cordes; **~ player** *n* musicien/-ienne *m/f* qui joue d'un instrument à cordes; **~-pulling**○ *n* piston○ *m*; **~ puppet** *n* marionnette *f* à fils; **~ quartet** *n* quatuor *m* à cordes; **~ variable** *n* variable *f* alpha-numérique; **~ vest** *n* tricot *m* de corps à larges mailles.

stringy /'strɪŋɪ/ *adj* **1** péj Culin [*meat, beans, celery*] filandreux/-euse; **2** péj (thin) [*hair*] plat et sec; **3** (wiry) littér [*person, build*] filiforme liter.

strip /strɪp/ **I** *n* **1** (narrow piece) (of material, paper, carpet) bande *f* (**of** de); (of land, sand) bande *f*, langue *f* (**of** de); (of bacon) tranche *f* (of de); **a ~ of garden/beach** un jardin/une plage tout/-e en longueur; **metal/paper ~** bande de métal/de papier; **centre** GB ou **median** US **~** (on motorway) terre-plein *m* central; **2** (striptease) strip-tease *m*; **3** Sport (clothes) tenue *f*; **the Germany ~** la tenue de l'équipe allemande or d'Allemagne.
II *vtr* (*p prés etc* **-pp-**) **1** (also **~ off**) (remove) enlever [*clothes, paint*]; **to ~ sth from** ou **off sth** enlever or arracher qch de qch; **the storm had ~ped all the leaves from** ou **off the tree** la tempête avait dépouillé l'arbre de toutes ses feuilles; **2** (remove everything from) déshabiller [*person*]; [*person*] vider [*house, room*]; [*thief*] vider, dévaliser [*house*]; [*wind, animal*] dépouiller [*tree, plant*]; [*person*] défaire [*bed*]; (remove paint or varnish from) décaper [*window, door, table*]; (dismantle) démonter [*gun, engine*]; **to ~ a room of furniture** vider une pièce de ses meubles; **to ~ sb of** dépouiller qn de [*belongings, rights*]; **to ~ sb of his** ou **her rank** dégrader [*soldier, civil servant*]; **he was ~ped of his medal/his title** on lui a retiré sa médaille/son titre; **3** (damage) faire foirer [*nut, screw*]; **to ~ the gears** Aut arracher les dents de l'engrenage.
III *vi* (*p prés etc* **-pp-**) (take off one's clothes) se déshabiller, enlever ses vêtements (**for** pour); **to ~ to the waist** se déshabiller jusqu'à la ceinture; **to ~ naked** se mettre tout nu.
IV stripped *pp adj* [*pine, wood*] décapé.
IDIOMS **to tear sb off a ~**, **to tear a ~ off sb**○ enguirlander○ qn.
■ **strip down**: ¶ **~ down** se déshabiller; **to ~ down to one's underwear** se déshabiller en ne gardant que ses sous-vêtements; ¶ **~ [sth] down**, **~ down [sth]** (dismantle) démonter [*gun, engine*]; (remove linen from) défaire [*bed*]; (remove paint or varnish from) décaper [*door, window, woodwork*].
■ **strip off**: ¶ **~ off** [*person*] se déshabiller; ¶ **~ [sth] off**, **~ off [sth]** (remove) enlever [*paint, wallpaper, clothes*]; arracher [*leaves*].
■ **strip out**: **~ [sth] out**, **~ out [sth] 1** Fin, Stat (disregard) décompter; **2** (remove everything from) extirper [*plants, vegetation*]; retirer [*fixtures, fittings etc*]; **3** Comput supprimer [*tags, data*].

strip: **~ cartoon** *n* bande *f* dessinée; **~ club** *n* boîte○ *f* de strip-tease.

stripe /straɪp/ **I** *n* **1** (on fabric, wallpaper) rayure *f*; **with blue and white ~s** à rayures bleues et blanches; **2** (on crockery) filet *m*; **3** (on animal) (isolated) rayure *f*; (one of many) zébrure *f*; **4** Mil galon *m*; **to win one's ~s** gagner ses galons; **to lose one's ~s** être dégradé.
II striped *pp adj* rayé; **blue ~d** rayé de bleu, à rayures bleues.

strip: **~ joint**○ *n* = **strip club**; **~ light** *n* lampe *f* au néon; **~ lighting** *n* éclairage *m* au néon *m*.

stripling /'strɪplɪŋ/ *n* littér, péj jouvenceau *m*.

strip mining /'strɪpmaɪnɪŋ/ *n* exploitation *f* (minière) à ciel ouvert.

stripper /'strɪpə(r)/ ▶ 1692 *n* strip-teaseur/-euse *m/f*; **male ~** strip-teaseur *m*.

stripping /'strɪpɪŋ/ *n* **1** (strip-tease) strip-tease *m*; **2** Med (of veins) éveinage *m*, stripping *m*.

strip poker /ˌstrɪp'pəʊkə(r)/ ▶ 1282 *n* Games strip-poker *m*.

strip-search /'strɪpsɜːtʃ/ **I** *n* fouille *f* corporelle.
II *vtr* faire subir une fouille corporelle à.

strip: **~ show** *n* strip-tease *m*; **~tease** *n* strip-tease *m*; **~tease artist** ▶ 1692 *n* strip-teaseur/-euse *m/f*.

strip-wash /'strɪpwɒʃ/ **I** *n* toilette *f* complète.
II *vtr* faire une toilette complète à [*patient*].

stripy /'straɪpɪ/ *adj* rayé, à rayures.

strive /straɪv/ *vi* (*prét* **strove**; *pp* **striven**) **1** (try) s'efforcer; **to ~ to do** s'efforcer de faire; **to ~ for** ou **after sth** rechercher qch; **2** (fight) lit se battre (**against** contre); fig lutter (**against** contre).

strobe /strəʊb/ *n* (also **~ light**) lumière *f* stroboscopique.

strobe lighting *n* éclairage *m* stroboscopique.

stroboscope /'strəʊbəskəʊp/ *n* stroboscope *m*.

strode /strəʊd/ *prét* ▶ **stride III, IV**.

stroke /strəʊk/ **I** *n* **1** (blow) gen coup *m*; (in tennis, golf) coup *m*; **to have a 3-~ lead** avoir 3 coups d'avance; **to win by 2 ~s** gagner avec 2 coups d'avance; **to be 4 ~s behind** avoir 4 coups de retard; **20 ~s of the cane** 20 coups de trique; **2** fig (touch) coup *m*; **it was a brilliant/master ~** c'était un coup brillant/de maître; **at one** ou **at a single ~** d'un seul coup; **a ~ of luck** un coup de chance; **a ~ of bad luck** une malchance; **a ~ of genius** un trait de génie; **3** Sport (swimming, movement) mouvement *m* des bras; (style) nage *f*; ▶ **breast stroke etc**; **Tim can swim a few ~s** Tim sait un peu nager; **4** Sport (in rowing) (movement) coup *m* d'aviron; (person) chef *m* de nage; **5** Art (mark of pen) trait *m*; (mark of brush) touche *f*; (stroking action) coup *m* de pinceau/crayon etc; **6** (in punctuation) barre *f* oblique; **7** (of clock) coup *m*; **on the ~ of four** à quatre heures sonnantes; **at the ~ of midnight** à minuit sonnant; **at the third ~ the time will be...** au troisième top il sera exactement...; **8** Med congestion *f* cérébrale, attaque *f*; **9** Tech (in engine, pump) course *f*; **a 2 ~ engine** un moteur à 2 temps; **10** (caress) caresse *f*; **to give sb/sth a ~** caresser qn/qch.
II *modif* Med **~ victim**, **~ patient** malade *mf* atteint/-e de congestion cérébrale.
III *vtr* **1** (caress) caresser [*person, animal*]; **to ~ sb's back** caresser le dos de qn; **to ~ one's beard** se caresser la barbe; **2** Sport (in rowing) **to ~ an eight** être le chef de nage d'un huit.
IV *vi* Sport (in rowing) être chef de nage.
IDIOMS **not to do a ~ of work** ne rien

faire, ne pas en ficher une rame○; **to put sb off their ~** (upset timing) faire perdre le rythme à qn; fig (disconcert) faire perdre les pédales○ à qn.

strokeplay /ˈstrəʊkpleɪ/ **I** *n* Sport concours *m* par coups.
II *modif* [*title*] en concours par coups; [*championship*] par coups.

stroll /strəʊl/ **I** *n* promenade *f*; **to go for** ou **take a ~** (aller) faire un tour; **to take sb for a ~** emmener qn faire un tour.
II *vi* **1** (also **~ about**, **~ around**) (walk) se promener; (more aimlessly) flâner; **to ~ along the beach** se promener le long de la plage; **to ~ in/out** entrer/sortir sans se presser; **2**○ (also **~ home**) (win easily) gagner facilement.

stroller /ˈstrəʊlə(r)/ *n* **1** (walker) promeneur/-euse *m/f*; (more aimless) flâneur/-euse *m/f*; **2** US (pushchair) poussette *f*.

strolling /ˈstrəʊlɪŋ/ *adj* [*shopper, tourist*] en promenade.

strolling: **~ minstrel** *n* ménestrel *m*; **~ player** ▶**1692** *n* comédien/-ienne *m/f* ambulant/-e.

stroma /ˈstrəʊmə/ *n* (*pl* **-mata**) Biol stroma *m*.

strong /strɒŋ, US strɔːŋ/ *adj* **1** (powerful) [*arm, person*] fort; [*army, country, state, lens, magnet*] puissant; [*runner, swimmer*] puissant; [*current, wind*] fort; **2** (sturdy) lit [*fabric, rope, shoe, table*] solide; [*heart, constitution, nerves*] solide; fig [*bond*] puissant; [*relationship*] solide; [*alibi, argument*] bon/bonne; [*evidence*] solide; [*cast, candidate, team*] bon/bonne; [*industry*] solide; [*currency, market*] ferme; **the pound remained ~ against the dollar** Fin la livre est restée ferme face au dollar; **to have a ~ stomach**○ fig avoir l'estomac bien accroché○; **3** (concentrated) [*bleach, glue*] fort; [*medicine, pain-killer*] fort; [*coffee*] serré; [*tea*] fort; **4** (alcoholic) [*drink*] alcoolisé; **would you like tea or something ~er?** voulez-vous un thé ou un apéritif?; **5** (noticeable) [*smell*] fort (*before n*); [*taste, light*] fort; [*colour*] vif/vive; **6** (heartfelt) [*conviction*] intime (*before n*); [*desire, feeling*] profond; [*believer, supporter*] acharné; [*opinion*] arrêté; [*criticism, opposition, reaction*] vif/vive; **to have a ~ belief in sth** croire fermement en qch; **the article aroused ~ feelings** l'article a provoqué de vives réactions; **I have a ~ feeling that she won't come** je suis pratiquement sûr qu'elle ne viendra pas; **I told him so in the ~est possible terms** je le lui ai dit sans détours; **7** (resolute) [*ruler, leadership*] à poigne (*after n*); [*action, measure, sanction*] sévère; **8** (pronounced) [*resemblance*] fort (*before n*); [*accent*] fort (*before n*); [*rhythm*] cadencé; **9** (brave) [*person*] fort (*after n, after v*); **try to be ~** essaie d'être fort; **10** (definite) [*chance, possibility*] fort (*before n*); **there's a ~ possibility that it's true** il y a de fortes chances que ce soit vrai; **11** (good) **to be ~ on military history/physics** être fort en histoire militaire/en physique; **he finished the race a ~ second** il a fini la course juste derrière le premier; **tact/spelling is not my ~ point** ou **suit** le tact/l'orthographe n'est pas mon fort; **what are your ~ points?** quels sont vos points forts?; **maths is my ~ subject** les maths sont la matière où je suis le plus fort; **12** (immoderate) **~ language** mots *mpl* grossiers; **13** Ling [*verb*] fort; [*syllable*] accentué; **14** (in number) **the workforce is 500 ~** la main-d'œuvre est forte de 500 personnes; **a 2000-~ crowd** une foule (forte) de 2000 personnes.
IDIOMS **to be still going ~** [*person, company*] se porter toujours très bien or à merveille; **to come on ~**○ (make sexual advances) faire des avances; (be severe) être sévère.

strong-arm /ˈstrɒŋɑːm, US ˈstrɔːŋ-/ **I** *adj* [*measure, method*] brutal; **~ tactics** la manière forte.
II *vtr* **to ~ sb into doing** forcer qn à faire.

strongbox /ˈstrɒŋbɒks, US ˈstrɔːŋ-/ *n* coffre-fort *m*.

stronghold /ˈstrɒŋhəʊld, US ˈstrɔːŋ-/ *n* (bastion) lit forteresse *f*; fig fief *m*; **a nationalist/socialist ~** un fief nationaliste/socialiste.

strongly /ˈstrɒŋlɪ, US ˈstrɔːŋlɪ/ *adv* **1** (with force) lit [*blow*] fort; [*defend oneself*] vigoureusement; fig [*criticize, attack, object, oppose, advise*] vivement; [*protest, deny*] énergiquement; [*suggest, suspect*] fortement; [*believe*] fermement; **to feel ~ about sth** avoir des idées arrêtées sur qch; **I feel ~ that...** je crois fermement que...; **~ held beliefs** des croyances fortement ancrées; **to be ~ in favour of/against sth** être absolument pour/contre qch; **2** (solidly) [*fixed, made, reinforced*] solidement; **3** (in large numbers) [*supported, represented, defended*] fortement; **4** (powerfully) **to smell ~** dégager une forte odeur; **~ flavoured** très relevé.

strongly-worded *adj* virulent.

strongman /ˈstrɒŋmæn, US ˈstrɔːŋ-/ ▶**1692** *n* (in circus) hercule *m* de foire; fig (leader) homme *m* fort.

strong: **~-minded** *adj* obstiné; **~-mindedness** *n* obstination *f*; **~room** *n* chambre *f* forte; **~-willed** *adj* obstiné.

strontium /ˈstrɒntɪəm/ *n* strontium *m*; **~ 90** strontium *m* 90.

strop /strɒp/ **I** *n* cuir *m* (à rasoir).
II *vtr* (*p prés etc* **-pp-**) repasser [qch] sur le cuir [*razor*].

strophe /ˈstrəʊfɪ/ *n* strophe *f*.

strophic /ˈstrəʊfɪk/ *adj* strophique.

stroppy○ /ˈstrɒpɪ/ *adj* GB ronchon/-onne○; **to be** ou **get ~** se mettre en pétard○ (**about** à propos de; **with** contre).

strove /strəʊv/ *prét* ▶ **strive**.

struck /strʌk/ *prét, pp* ▶ **strike** II, III.

structural /ˈstrʌktʃərəl/ *adj* **1** (fundamental) [*problem, change, reform*] structurel/-elle; **2** Anat, Bot, Geol, Phys structural; **3** Ling structurel/-elle, structural; **4** Econ structurel/-elle; **5** Constr [*defect*] de construction; **~ alterations** transformations *fpl*; **~ damage** dégâts *mpl* matériels.

structural: **~ analysis** *n* Ling analyse *f* structurale or structurelle; **~ engineer** ▶**1692** *n* ingénieur *m* des ponts et chaussées; **~ engineering** *n* génie *m* civil; **~ formula** *n* formule *f* développée.

structuralism /ˈstrʌktʃərəlɪzəm/ *n* structuralisme *m*.

structuralist /ˈstrʌktʃərəlɪst/ *n, adj* structuraliste (*mf*).

structural linguistics *n* (+ *v sg*) linguistique *f* structurale or structurelle.

structurally /ˈstrʌktʃərəlɪ/ *adv* gen, Anat, Bot, Geol, Phys structurellement, du point de vue de la structure; Constr du point de vue de la construction; **~ sound** de construction solide.

structural: **~ psychology** *n* psychologie *f* structurale; **~ steel** *n* acier *m* de construction; **~ survey** *n* GB inspection *f* d'expert-immobilier (*pour déterminer la solidité de la construction d'un bâtiment, lors d'une vente*); **~ unemployment** *n* chômage *m* structurel.

structure /ˈstrʌktʃə(r)/ **I** *n* **1** (overall shape, organization) structure *f*; **political/social ~** structure politique/sociale; **wage ~** échelle *f* des salaires; **price ~** Econ échelle *f* des prix; **career ~** plan *m* de carrière; ▶ **power structure**; **2** Constr (building) construction *f*, édifice *m*; (manner of construction) construction *f*.
II *vtr* **1** (organize) structurer [*argument, essay, novel*]; organiser [*day, life, timetable*]; **2** Constr construire.

structured /ˈstrʌktʃəd/ *adj* structuré.

structuring /ˈstrʌktʃərɪŋ/ *n* structuration *f*.

struggle /ˈstrʌgl/ **I** *n* **1** (battle, fight) lit, fig lutte *f* (**against** contre; **between** entre; **for** pour; **over** au sujet de; **to do** pour faire); **the ~ for democracy/for survival** la lutte pour la démocratie/pour survivre; **armed/non-violent ~** lutte *f* armée/non violente; **class ~** lutte *f* des classes; **power ~** lutte *f* pour le pouvoir; **to give up** ou **abandon the ~** abandonner la lutte or la partie; **to put up a (fierce) ~** se défendre (avec acharnement); **they gave up without a ~** lit, Mil ils ont abandonné sans opposer de résistance; fig ils ont abandonné sans lutter; **2** (scuffle) rixe *f*, bagarre○ *f*; **two people were injured in** ou **during the ~** deux personnes ont été blessées pendant la rixe or la bagarre○; **3** (difficult task, effort) **it was a ~ but it was worth it** on a eu du mal or cela a été dur mais cela en valait la peine; **learning to read was a great ~ for him** apprendre à lire lui a coûté de gros efforts; **he finds everything a real ~** il trouve que tout est très dur; **I find it a real ~ to do** ou **doing** cela m'est très difficile de faire; **they had a ~ to do** ou **doing** ils ont eu du mal à faire; **to succeed after years of ~** réussir après des années d'efforts; **after a long ~ he managed to contact her** après s'être donné beaucoup de mal il est parvenu à la joindre; **she managed it but not without a ~** elle a réussi mais non sans mal.
II *vi* **1** lit (put up a fight) [*person, animal*] se débattre (**to do** pour faire); (tussle, scuffle) [*people, animals*] lutter, se battre; [*armies, forces*] se battre; **he ~d with his attacker** il s'est débattu pour se dégager de l'emprise de son agresseur; **they ~d with each other** ils ont lutté or se sont battus (**for** pour); **they ~d for the gun** ils se sont battus pour le revolver; **to ~ free** se dégager; **2** fig (try hard) se battre, lutter; (stronger) se démener; **a young artist struggling for recognition** un jeune artiste qui lutte or se démène pour faire reconnaître son talent; **to ~ to do sth** lutter or se battre pour faire; **the firm has had to ~ to survive** (try hard) la société a dû lutter or se battre pour survivre; **to ~ with a problem/ one's conscience** être aux prises avec un problème/sa conscience; **3** (have difficulty) (at school, with job, in market) [*person, company*] éprouver des difficultés; **to ~ to keep up/to survive/with one's homework** avoir du mal à suivre/à survivre/à faire ses devoirs; **4** (move with difficulty) **he ~d into/out of his jeans** il a enfilé/enlevé péniblement son jean; **to ~ to one's feet** se lever avec peine; **we ~d up the steep path** nous avons monté péniblement la côte raide.

■ **struggle along** lit avancer à grand-peine; fig persévérer.

■ **struggle back** revenir à grand-peine or avec peine.

■ **struggle on** lit continuer à grand-peine; fig persévérer.

■ **struggle through**: ¶ **~ through** s'en sortir tant bien que mal; ¶ **~ through** [sth] se frayer péniblement un chemin dans [*snow, jungle, crowd*]; se débattre avec [*book, task*]; **the bill ~d through Parliament** le projet de loi a été adopté non sans peine par le Parlement.

struggling /ˈstrʌglɪŋ/ *adj* [*writer, artist*] qui essaie de percer.

strum /strʌm/ (*p prés etc* **-mm-**) **I** *vtr* **1** (carelessly) gratter [*guitar, tune*]; **2** (gently) jouer doucement de [*guitar*]; **to ~ a tune** jouer doucement un air.
II *vi* **1** (carelessly) gratter (**on** sur); **2** (gently) jouer doucement (**on** de).

strumming /ˈstrʌmɪŋ/ *n* accords *mpl* légers.

strumpet‡ /ˈstrʌmpɪt/ *n* péj catin‡ *f*.

strung /strʌŋ/ *prét, pp* ▶ **string** III, IV.

strung out○ /ˌstrʌŋˈaʊt/ *adj* **1** (addicted) **to be ~ on** être accro○ or accroché à [*drug*]; **2** (physically wasted) **to be ~** (from drugs) être en état de manque; (generally) être au bout du rouleau○.

strung up○ /ˌstrʌŋˈʌp/ *adj* nerveux/-euse;

to get (all) ~ about sth être dans tous ses états à l'idée de qch.

strut /strʌt/ **I** *n* **1** (support) montant *m*; **2** (swagger) démarche *f* orgueilleuse.
II *vi* (also **~ about**, **~ around**) (*p prés etc* **-tt-**) se pavaner; **to ~ along** marcher en se pavanant.
IDIOMS **to ~ one's stuff**○ s'exhiber.

strychnine /'strɪkni:n/ *n* strychnine *f*.

stub /stʌb/ **I** *n* **1** (end, stump) (of pencil, stick, lipstick) bout *m*; (of cigarette) mégot *m*, bout *m*; (of tail) moignon *m*; **2** (counterfoil) (of cheque, ticket) talon *m*.
II *vtr* (*p prés etc* **-bb-**) **to ~ one's toe** se cogner l'orteil.
■ **stub out**: **~ [sth] out**, **~ out [sth]** écraser [*cigarette*].

stubble /'stʌbl/ *n* **1** (straw) chaume *m*; **2** (beard) barbe *f* de plusieurs jours.

stubbly /'stʌblɪ/ *adj* [*chin*] non rasé.

stubborn /'stʌbən/ *adj* [*person, animal, government*] entêté, têtu; [*attitude, behaviour*] obstiné; [*affection, independence*] tenace; [*resistance, refusal*] opiniâtre; [*stain, lock, illness*] rebelle; **to be ~ about** ou **over sth/doing sth** s'entêter sur qch/à faire qch.

stubbornly /'stʌbənlɪ/ *adv* [*refuse, deny, resist*] obstinément; [*behave, act*] de manière têtue.

stubbornness /'stʌbənnɪs/ *n* entêtement *m*.

stubby /'stʌbɪ/ *adj* [*finger, pencil, tail*] court; [*person*] trapu.

stucco /'stʌkəʊ/ **I** *n* (*pl* **~s** ou **~es**) (outside plasterwork) enduit *m*; (decorative work) stuc *m*.
II *vtr* stuquer.

stuck /stʌk/ **I** *prét, pp* ▶ **stick III, IV**.
II *adj* **1** (unable to move) bloqué, coincé; **to get ~ in** s'enliser dans [*mud, sand*]; **to be ~ at home** être bloqué ou coincé chez soi; **to be ~ with**○ se farcir [*task*]; ne pas pouvoir se débarrasser de [*possession, person*]; **2**○ (stumped) **to be ~** sécher○; **3** (in a fix) **to be ~** être coincé; **to be ~ for a babysitter/cash** ne pas avoir de babysitter/d'argent; **to be ~ for something to say/do** ne pas savoir quoi dire/faire.
IDIOMS **to be ~ on sb**○ avoir qn dans la peau○; **to squeal like a ~ pig** crier comme un cochon égorgé; **to get ~ into sb**○ engueuler qn◑.

stuck-up○ /,stʌk'ʌp/ *adj* bêcheur/-euse○.

stud /stʌd/ **I** *n* **1** (metal) (on jacket) clou *m*; (on door) clou *m* à grosse tête; **2** (earring) clou *m* d'oreilles; **3** (for grip) (on shoe) clou *m*; (on football boot) crampon *m*; **4** (fastener) **collar ~** bouton *m* de col; **press-~** GB bouton-pression *m*; **5** Transp (in road) clou *m* à catadioptre; **6** (also **~ farm**) haras *m*; **7** (for breeding) **he's now at ~** il est devenu reproducteur; **to put a horse out to ~** mettre un cheval au haras or à la reproduction; **8**○ (man) mâle *m*; **he's a real ~** il se défend bien au lit○; **9** Aut (wheel bolt) goujon *m* de roue; (in tyre) clou *m*; **10** Constr (for wall) montant *m*; **11** Tech (bolt) goujon *m*; **12** = **stud poker**.
II studded *pp adj* **1** lit [*jacket*] garni de clous; [*door, beam*] clouté; **~ed boots**, **~ed shoes** Sport chaussures *fpl* à crampons; **~ed tyres** Aut pneus *mpl* cloutés; **2** (sprinkled) **~ed with** parsemé de [*stars, flowers, islands*]; constellé de [*diamonds, jewels*].

studbook /'stʌdbʊk/ *n* stud-book *m*, registre *m* des pur-sang.

student /'stju:dnt, US 'stu:-/ **I** *n* **1** gen, US, Sch élève *mf*; Univ étudiant/-e *m/f*; **medical/art ~** étudiant/-e *m/f* en médecine/d'art; **he's a very good ~** c'est un excellent élève; **2** (person interested in a subject) **a ~ of** une personne qui étudie or s'intéresse à [*literature, history*].
II *modif* Univ [*life, unrest*] étudiant; [*population*] d'étudiants.

student: **~ driver** *n* US *personne qui apprend à conduire*; **~ grant** *n* Univ bourse *f* d'études; **~ ID card** *n* US Univ carte *f* d'étudiant; **~ loan** *n* Univ *prêt bancaire pour étudiants*; **~ nurse** *n* élève *mf* infirmier/-ière.

studentship /'stju:dntʃɪp, US 'stu:-/ *n* Univ bourse *f* universitaire.

student teacher *n* enseignant/-e *m/f* stagiaire.

student union *n* **1** (union) syndicat *m* étudiant; **2** (also **~ building**) maison *f* des étudiants.

stud: **~ fee** *n* prix *m* de la saillie; **~horse** *n* étalon *m*.

studied /'stʌdɪd/ *adj* [*negligence*] faux/fausse (*before n*); [*elegance, simplicity*] artificiel/-ielle.

studio /'stju:dɪəʊ, US 'stu:-/ *n* (*pl* **~s**) **1** (of photographer, dancer, film or record company) studio *m*; (of painter) atelier *m*; **2** (also **~ apartment**, **~ flat** GB) studio *m*; **3** (film company) compagnie *f* de cinéma.

studio audience *n* public *m* du studio; **recorded in front of a ~** enregistré publiquement en studio.

studio: **~ couch** *n* canapé-lit *m*; **~ portrait** *n* Phot portrait *m* d'art; **~ recording** *n* enregistrement *m* en studio; **~ set** *n* décor *m* de studio; **~ theatre** GB, **~ theater** US *n* théâtre *m* de poche.

studious /'stju:dɪəs, US 'stu:-/ *adj* **1** (hard-working) [*person*] studieux/-ieuse; **2** (deliberate) [*calm, indifference*] étudié, délibéré.

studiously /'stju:dɪəslɪ, US 'stu:-/ *adv* (deliberately) [*avoid, ignore*] délibérément; **~ calm/~ indifferent** d'un calme étudié/d'une indifférence étudiée.

studiousness /'stju:dɪəsnɪs, US 'stu:-/ *n* assiduité *f* (à l'étude).

stud: **~ mare** *n* (jument *f*) poulinière *f*; **~ poker** ▶ **1282** *n* poker *m* ouvert, stud poker *m*.

study /'stʌdɪ/ **I** *n* **1** (gaining of knowledge) étude *f*; **2** (piece of research) étude *f* (**of, on** de); **to make a ~ of sth** faire une étude de qch, étudier qch; **3** (room) bureau *m*, cabinet *m* de travail; **4** Art, Mus étude *f*; **5** (model) **a ~ in incompetence/in bigotry** un modèle d'incompétence/de bigoterie.
II studies *npl* études *fpl*; **computer studies** informatique *f*; **social studies** sciences *fpl* humaines.
III *modif* [*group, visit*] d'étude; **~ leave** congé *m* d'étude; **~ period** heure *f* d'étude; **~ tour** ou **trip** voyage *m* d'études.
IV *vtr* (all contexts) étudier; Univ also faire des études de [*French, Law, Physics*]; **to ~ to be a teacher/lawyer/nurse** faire des études pour être enseignant/juriste/infirmière; **she's ~ing to be a doctor** elle fait des études de médecine.
V *vi* **1** (revise) réviser; **to ~ for an exam** réviser pour un examen; **2** (get one's education) faire ses études (**under sb** avec qn).
IDIOMS **his face was a ~!** il fallait voir sa tête!

study aid *n* outil *m* pédagogique (destiné à l'élève).

study hall *n* US **1** (room) salle *f* d'étude; **2** (period) heure *f* d'étude.

study hall teacher *n* US enseignant/-e *m/f* chargé/-e de l'étude.

stuff /stʌf/ **I** *n* ¢ **1** (unnamed substance) truc○ *m*, chose *f*; **what's that ~ in the box/on the table?** qu'est-ce que c'est que ce truc○ dans la boîte/sur la table?; **what's that ~ in the bottle?** qu'est-ce que c'est dans la bouteille?; **there's some black ~ stuck to my shoe** il y a un truc○ noir collé à ma chaussure; **I don't eat pre-packaged ~ if I can help it** j'évite autant que possible de manger des trucs○ pré-emballés; **this ~ stinks!** ça pue ce truc!○; **have we got any more of that cement ~?** est-ce qu'on a encore de cette espèce de ciment?; **she loves the ~** elle adore ça; **acid is dangerous ~** l'acide est (un truc○) dangereux; **gin? never touch the ~**○ le gin? je n'y touche jamais; **expensive ~**, **caviar** ça coute cher, le caviar; **we've sold lots of the ~** nous en avons vendu beaucoup; **it's strong ~** (of drink, drug, detergent) c'est costaud○; **2**○ (unnamed objects) trucs○ *mpl*; (implying disorder) bazar○ *m*; (personal belongings) affaires *fpl*; **what's all this ~ in the hall?** qu'est-ce que c'est que ces trucs○ or ce bazar○ dans l'entrée?; **she brought down a load of ~ from the attic** elle a descendu un tas de trucs○ du grenier; **don't leave your ~ all over the floor** ne laisse pas traîner les affaires or ton bazar○ par terre; **3**○ (content of speech, book, film, etc) **the sort of ~ you read in the newspapers** le genre de chose or de truc○ qu'on lit dans les journaux; **who wrote this ~?** gen qui a écrit ça?; pej qui a écrit cette chose?; **there's some good ~ in this article** il y a de bonnes choses dans cet article; **this poem is good ~** c'est un bon poème; **have you read much of her ~?** as-tu lu beaucoup de ce qu'elle a écrit?; **this ~ is excellent/absolute rubbish** c'est excellent/complètement nul○; **it's not my kind of ~** ce n'est pas mon truc○; **it's romantic/terrifying ~** c'est romantique/terrifiant; **I sent him a tape of my ~** je lui ai envoyé une cassette de ce que je fais; **do you believe all that ~ about his private life?** tu crois à tout ce qu'on dit sur sa vie privée?; **there was a lot of ~ about the new legislation in his speech** il a beaucoup parlé de la nouvelle législation dans son discours; **he likes painting and drawing and ~ like that**○ il aime la peinture et le dessin et tout ce genre de trucs○; **the book's all about music and ~** le livre parle de la musique et tout ça; **4** (fabric) lit étoffe *f*; fig essence *f*; **such conflicts are the very ~ of drama** de tels conflits sont l'essence même du drame; **this is the ~ that heroes/traitors are made of** c'est l'étoffe dont on fait les héros/les traîtres; **the ~ that dreams are made of** la substance (même) des rêves; **her husband was made of somewhat coarser/finer ~** son mari était plus grossier/plus raffiné de nature; **5**○ (drugs) came○ *f*, drogue *f*; **6**○ (stolen goods) marchandise○ *f*.
II *vtr* **1** (fill, pack) garnir, rembourrer [*cushion, pillow, furniture*] (**with** de); (implying haste, carelessness) bourrer [*pocket, cupboard, suitcase*] (**with** de); (block up) boucher [*hole, crack*] (**with** avec); **a book ~ed with useful information** un livre bourré d'informations utiles; **they ~ed his head with useless information** ils lui ont bourré la tête de faits inutiles; **to ~ one's face**○ bâfrer, s'empiffrer◑; **get ~ed**◑**!** va te faire voir◑!; **~ the system**◑**!** au diable○ le système!; **~ you**◑**!** va te faire voir◑!; **2** (pack in) fourrer○ [*objects, clothes, paper*] (**in, into** dans); **we ~ed paper into the cracks** nous avons fourré du papier dans les fissures; **she ~ed the papers/ some clothes into a bag** elle a fourré les papiers/des vêtements dans un sac; **to ~ one's hands in one's pockets** se fourrer les mains dans les poches; **to ~ sth up one's jumper** cacher qch sous son pull; **to ~ sth under the bed** fourrer qch sous le lit; **to ~ food into one's mouth** se bâfrer○; **you know where you can ~ it**◑**!** tu sais où tu peux te le mettre●; **tell him he can take his precious plan and ~ it**◑**!** dis-lui que son projet il peut se le mettre où je pense●!; **3** Culin farcir [*turkey, tomato, olive*]; **4** [*taxidermist*] empailler [*animal, bird*].
III stuffed *pp adj* [*tomato, vine leaf, olive*] farci; [*toy animal*] en peluche; [*bird, fox*] empaillé.
IV○ *v refl* **to ~ oneself** bâfrer○, s'empiffrer◑.
IDIOMS **a bit of ~**○ péj une gonzesse○ pej, une nana○; **to do one's ~**○ faire ce qu'on a à faire; **go on—do your ~**○**!** vas-y—fais ce que tu as à faire, vas-y—à toi de jouer; **to know one's ~**○ connaître son affaire○; **that's the ~**○**!** c'est bon!, c'est ça!; **that's the ~ to give them** ou **to give the**

troops○! c'est ce que demande le peuple!; **I don't give a ~**○! je m'en fiche○!, je m'en fous◑!

■ **stuff up**; **~ [sth] up**, **~ up [sth]** boucher [*crack, hole*] (**with** avec); **I'm all ~ed up, my nose is ~ed up** j'ai le nez bouché.

stuffed shirt○ *n* péj **to be a ~** être pompeux et suffisant.

stuffily /ˈstʌfɪlɪ/ *adv* péj [*say, speak*] d'un ton pincé; [*behave, refuse*] d'un air pincé.

stuffiness /ˈstʌfɪnɪs/ *n* **1** (airlessness) atmosphère *f* étouffante; **2** (staidness) (of person, institution, attitude) raideur *f*.

stuffing /ˈstʌfɪŋ/ *n* **1** Culin farce *f*; **chestnut ~** farce aux marrons; **2** (of furniture, pillow) rembourrage *m*; (of stuffed animal) paille *f*.
IDIOMS **to knock the ~ out of sb**○ [*punch*] désarçonner qn; [*illness*] mettre qn à plat○; [*defeat, loss, event*] démoraliser qn.

stuffy /ˈstʌfɪ/ *adj* **1** [*room, atmosphere*] étouffant; **it's very ~ in here** on étouffe ici; **2** (staid) [*person, institution, remark*] guindé; **3** (blocked) [*nose*] bouché.

stultify /ˈstʌltɪfaɪ/ *vtr* abrutir [*person, mind, senses*].

stultifying /ˈstʌltɪfaɪɪŋ/ *adj* abrutissant.

stumble /ˈstʌmbl/ **I** *n* faux pas *m*; **without a ~** sans trébucher.
II *vi* **1** (trip) trébucher (**against** contre; **on, over** sur); **2** (stagger) **to ~ in/out/off** entrer/sortir/s'en aller en chancelant; **he ~d around the room** il a fait le tour de la pièce en chancelant; **3** (in speech) hésiter; **to ~ over** [*phrase, word*] buter sur; **he ~d through his farewell speech** il a prononcé son discours d'adieu en bafouillant.
■ **stumble across**: **~ across [sth]** tomber par hasard sur [*person, information, fact*].
■ **stumble on**: ¶ **~ on** [*walkers, travellers*] avancer en trébuchant; fig [*undertaking, leadership*] continuer tant bien que mal; ¶ **~ on [sth]**, **~ upon [sth]** tomber par hasard sur [*person, place, date, event, item*].

stumblebum○ /ˈstʌmblbʌm/ *n* US abruti/-e○ *m/f*.

stumbling block /ˈstʌmblɪŋblɒk/ *n* obstacle *m*; **the main ~ is...** le principal obstacle est... ; **that's the main ~** c'est ça la pierre d'achoppement; **to be** ou **prove a ~ to** faire obstacle à.

stump /stʌmp/ **I** *n* **1** (of tree) souche *f*; **the ~ of a tree** une souche; **2** (of candle, pencil, cigar, tail, tooth) bout *m*; **3** (of limb) moignon *m*; **4** (in cricket) piquet *m*; **5** US Pol (rostrum) tribunal *m*.
II *vtr* **1**○ (perplex) déconcerter [*person, expert*]; **to be ~ed by sth** être en peine d'expliquer qch; **to be ~ed for an answer/a solution** ne pas trouver de réponse/de solution; **the question had me ~ed** je n'ai pas su répondre à la question; **I'm ~ed** (in quiz) je sèche○; (nonplussed) aucune idée; **2** Sport (in cricket) éliminer, mettre [qn] hors jeu [*batsman*]; **3** US Pol faire une tournée électorale dans [*state, region*].
III *vi* **1** (stamp) **to ~ in/out** entrer/sortir d'un air mécontent; **to ~ up/down** monter/descendre lourdement; **to ~ off** partir d'un air mécontent; **2** US Pol faire une tournée électorale; **to ~ for sb/sth** faire campagne pour qn/qch.
IDIOMS **to be on the ~** US être en tournée électorale; **to be up a ~**○ US être troublé; **to stir one's ~s**○ se remuer un peu○.
■ **stump up**○ GB: ¶ **~ up** débourser (**for** pour); ¶ **~ up [sth]**, **~ [sth] up** débourser [*money, amount*].

stumpy /ˈstʌmpɪ/ *adj* [*person, legs*] courtaud.

stun /stʌn/ *vtr* (*p prés etc* **-nn-**) **1** (physically) assommer; **2** (shock, amaze) stupéfier.

stung /stʌŋ/ *prét, pp* ▶ **sting II**, **III**.

stun: **~ grenade** *n* grenade *f* catapleXiante; **~ gun** *n* fusil *m* hypodermique.

stunk /stʌŋk/ *pp* ▶ **stink II**.

stunned /stʌnd/ *adj* **1** (dazed) assommé; **2** (amazed, shocked) [*person*] stupéfait, sidéré○; [*silence*] figé.

stunner○ /ˈstʌnə(r)/ *n* (person) **to be a ~** être fantastique.

stunning /ˈstʌnɪŋ/ *adj* **1** (beautiful) sensationnel/-elle; **2** (amazing) stupéfiant; **3** [*blow*] étourdissant.

stunningly /ˈstʌnɪŋlɪ/ *adv* extrêmement; **~ attractive** éblouissant.

stunt /stʌnt/ **I** *n* **1** parfois péj (for attention) coup *m* organisé, truc○ *m*; **publicity ~** coup *m* de publicité, truc○ *m* publicitaire; **2** Cin, TV (with risk) cascade *f*; **to do a ~** exécuter une cascade; **aerial ~s** acrobaties *fpl* aériennes; **3**○ US numéro○ *m*.
II *vtr* empêcher [*economic growth, progress, development*]; rabougrir [*plant growth, crops*]; empêcher [*personal growth, development*].
IDIOMS **to pull a ~**○ faire le malin○; **if you pull a ~ like that again**○ si tu (me) refais ce coup-là○.

stunted /ˈstʌntɪd/ *adj* **1** (deformed) [*tree, plant*] rabougri; [*body*] chétif/-ive; **2** (blighted) [*mentality, personality, growth*] retardé; [*life*] appauvri.

stunt: **~man** ▶ **1692** *n* cascadeur *m*; **~ pilot** ▶ **1692** *n* pilote *m* de voltige; **~ rider** ▶ **1692** *n* cascadeur/-euse *m/f* à moto; **~woman** ▶ **1692** *n* cascadeuse *f*.

stupefaction /ˌstjuːpɪˈfækʃn/ *n* (all contexts) stupeur *f*.

stupefy /ˈstjuːpɪfaɪ, US ˈstuː-/ *vtr* **1** (astonish) stupéfier; **2** (make torpid) abrutir.

stupefying /ˈstjuːpɪfaɪɪŋ, US ˈstuː-/ *adj* (all contexts) stupéfiant.

stupendous /stjuːˈpendəs, US stuː-/ *adj* [*achievement, idea, film, size, amount*] prodigieux/-ieuse; [*building, view*] fantastique; [*loss, stupidity, folly*] incroyable.

stupendously /stjuːˈpendəslɪ, US stuː-/ *adv* [*rich*] prodigieusement; **to be ~ successful/powerful** avoir un succès/pouvoir prodigieux.

stupid /ˈstjuːpɪd, US ˈstuː-/ **I**○ *n* imbécile *mf*; **don't do that, ~!** ne fais pas ça, imbécile!
II *adj* **1** (unintelligent) [*person, animal*] stupide, bête; **2** (foolish) [*person*] idiot; [*idea, remark, behaviour, clothes, mistake*] stupide; **it is ~ of sb to do** c'est idiot de la part de qn de faire; **I've done something ~** j'ai fait une bêtise; **don't be ~!** arrête tes bêtises!; **the ~ car won't start!** cette idiote de voiture ne veut pas démarrer!; **you ~ idiot!** espèce d'imbécile!; **3** (in a stupor) abruti (**with** de); **to drink oneself ~** s'abrutir d'alcool; **to be knocked ~ by sth** être abruti par qch.

stupidity /stjuːˈpɪdətɪ, US stuː-/ *n* **1** (foolishness) (of person, idea, remark, action) bêtise *f*; **2** (lack of intelligence) stupidité *f*.

stupidly /ˈstjuːpɪdlɪ, US stuː-/ *adv* bêtement.

stupor /ˈstjuːpə(r), US ˈstuː-/ *n* stupeur *f*; **to be in a ~** être à moitié hébété; **in a drunken ~** hébété par l'alcool.

sturdily /ˈstɜːdɪlɪ/ *adv* solidement.

sturdiness /ˈstɜːdɪnɪs/ *n* (of object, plant, animal) robustesse *f*; (of character) solidité *f*.

sturdy /ˈstɜːdɪ/ *adj* [*person, animal, plant, object*] robuste; [*independence, intelligence, loyalty*] solide (*before n*).

sturgeon /ˈstɜːdʒən/ *n* esturgeon *m*.

stutter /ˈstʌtə(r)/ **I** *n* bégaiement *m*; **to have a ~** bégayer.
II *vtr, vi* bégayer.

stuttering /ˈstʌtərɪŋ/ **I** *n* bégaiement *m*.
II *adj* bégayant.

STV *n*: *abrév* ▶ **single transferable vote**.

St Valentine's Day *n* la Saint-Valentin.

St Vincent and the Grenadines /sənt ˌvɪnsnt ən ðə ˈgrenədiːnz/ ▶ **1131** *pr n* Saint-Vincent- et-les Grenadines *m*.

St Vitus's dance /səntˈvaɪtəsəʒˌdaːns/ *n* ▶ **1354** danse *f* de Saint-Guy.

sty /staɪ/ *n* **1** (for pigs) porcherie *f*; **2** (also **stye**) Med orgelet *m*.

Stygian /ˈstɪdʒɪən/ *adj* **1** Mythol du Styx; **2** [*gloom, darkness*] profond.

style /staɪl/ **I** *n* **1** (manner) style *m*; **a building in the neoclassical ~** un bâtiment de style néoclassique; **built/decorated in the neo-classical ~** bâti/aménagé dans le or en style néo-classique; **in the ~ of Van Gogh** dans le style de Van Gogh; **an opera in the Italian ~** un opéra dans le style italien; **his paintings are very individual in ~** ses tableaux ont un style très personnel; **a ~ of teaching/living** un style d'enseignement/de vie; **my writing/driving ~** ma façon d'écrire/de conduire; **that's the ~!** bravo!, c'est bien; **2** Literat style *m*; **he has a very good ~** il a un très bon style; **3** (elegance) classe *f*, chic *m*; **to have ~** avoir de la classe; **to bring a touch of ~ to** ajouter de la classe à; **the performance had great ~** c'était une représentation de grande classe; **to marry in ~** se marier en grande pompe; **to live in ~** mener grand train; **to travel in ~** voyager princièrement; **to win in ~** gagner haut la main; **she likes to do things in ~** elle aime faire les choses en grand; **4** (design) (of car, clothing) modèle *m*; (of house) type *m*; **to come in several ~s** exister en plusieurs modèles; **5** (fashion) mode *f*; **minis are the latest ~ in skirts** la minijupe est la toute dernière mode; **to wear the newest ~s** s'habiller à la toute dernière mode; **to have no sense of ~** n'avoir aucun sens de la mode; **6** (approach) genre *m*, style *m*; **I don't like your ~** je n'aime pas ton genre; **that's not my ~** ce n'est pas mon genre; **7** (hairstyle) coupe *f*; **8** Publg, Journ style *m*; **9** Bot style *m*.
II -style (*dans composés*) **alpine/Californian-~** de style alpin/californien; **Chinese/Italian-~** à la chinoise/l'italienne; **leather-~ case** valise imitation cuir.
III *vtr* **1** (design) concevoir [*car, kitchen, building*]; créer [*collection, dress*]; **a superbly ~d car** une voiture superbement conçue; **2** (cut) couper [*hair*]; **her hair is ~d by Giorgio** elle est coiffée par Giorgio.
IV *v refl* **to ~ oneself sth** se donner le titre de qch.

style: **~ book**, **~ guide**, **~ manual** *n* Publg manuel *m* de rédaction; **~ sheet** *n* Comput feuille *f* de style.

styling /ˈstaɪlɪŋ/ **I** *n* **1** (design) conception *f*; **2** (contours) ligne *f*; **3** (in hairdressing) coupe *f*.
II *modif* [*gel, mousse, product*] fixant; [*equipment*] de coiffure.

styling: **~ brush** *n* brosse *f* ronde; **~ tongs** *n* US fer *m* à friser.

stylish /ˈstaɪlɪʃ/ *adj* **1** (smart) [*car, coat, flat*] beau/belle (*before n*); [*person*] élégant; [*resort, restaurant*] chic *inv*; **2** (accomplished) [*director, performance, player*] de grande classe (*after n*); [*thriller, writer*] de grand style.

stylishly /ˈstaɪlɪʃlɪ/ *adv* **1** (fashionably) [*designed, dressed*] avec élégance; **2** (with panache) [*perform, write*] avec panache.

stylishness /ˈstaɪlɪʃnɪs/ *n* (of dress, person) élégance *f*; (of performance) style *m*.

stylist /ˈstaɪlɪst/ ▶ **1692** *n* **1** (hairdresser) coiffeur/-euse *m/f*; **2** (writer) maître/-esse *m/f* du style; **3** Fashn styliste *mf*; **4** Advertg, Ind concepteur/-trice *m/f*.

stylistic /staɪˈlɪstɪk/ *adj* **1** Literat [*detail, variety*] stylistique; [*question*] de style (*after n*); **2** Archit, Art [*quality, similarity*] de style; [*detail, development*] stylistique.

stylistically /ˌstaɪˈlɪstɪklɪ/ *adv* stylistiquement; (sentence adverb) **~ (speaking),...** du point de vue stylistique,...

stylistic: **~ device** *n* Literat procédé *m* stylistique; **~ marker** *n* Ling indicateur *m* de niveau de langue.

stylistics /staɪˈlɪstɪks/ *n* (+ *v sg*) Literat stylistique *f*.

stylized /ˈstaɪlaɪzd/ *adj* **1** (non-realist) stylisé; **2** (sober) simple.

stylus /ˈstaɪləs/ *n* (*pl* **-li** ou **-luses**) **1** Audio pointe *f* de lecture; **2** (for writing) style *m*.

stymie /ˈstaɪmɪ/ **I** *n* (in golf) trou *m* barré.
II *vtr* **1**○ contrecarrer [*plan, attempt*]; contrecarrer les desseins de [*person*]; **2** (in golf) barrer le trou à [*opponent*].

stymied○ /ˈstaɪmɪd/ *adj* (thwarted) coincé.

styptic /ˈstɪptɪk/ *n, adj* styptique (*m*).

styptic pencil *n* crayon *m* hémostatique.

Styrofoam® /ˈstaɪrəfəʊm/ *n* polystyrène *m* expansé.

suave /swɑːv/ *adj* [*person*] mielleux/-euse; [*words, manner, smile*] onctueux/-euse.

suavely /ˈswɑːvlɪ/ *adv* [*talk, smile*] avec onctuosité; [*dress*] avec une élégance apprêtée.

suaveness /ˈswɑːvnɪs/ *n* (of manner) onctuosité *f*.

sub /sʌb/ **I** *n* **1** Sport *abrév* = **substitute**; **2** Naut *abrév* = **submarine**; **3** *abrév* = **subscription**; **4** US *abrév* = **substitute teacher**.
II○ *vi* (*p prés etc* **-bb-**) (as teacher) faire des remplacements; **to ~ for sb** remplacer qn.

subagent /ˈsʌbeɪdʒənt/ *n* sous-agent *m*.

subalpine /ˌsʌbˈælpaɪn/ *adj* subalpin.

subaltern /ˈsʌbltən, US səˈbɔːltərn/ ▶ **1612** **I** *n* **1** GB Mil ≈ officier *m* subalterne; **2** (subordinate) subalterne *m*.
II *adj* (all contexts) subalterne.

subaqua /ˌsʌbˈækwə/ *adj* [*club*] de plongée.

subaqueous /ˌsʌbˈeɪkwɪəs/ *adj* subaquatique.

subarctic /ˌsʌbˈɑːktɪk/ *adj* subarctique.

subassembly /ˌsʌbəˈsemblɪ/ *n* Mech sous-ensemble *m*.

subatomic /ˌsʌbəˈtɒmɪk/ *adj* subatomique.

subclass /ˈsʌbklɑːs/ *n* sous-classe *f*.

subcommittee /ˈsʌbkəmɪtɪ/ *n* sous-comité *m*.

subconscious /ˌsʌbˈkɒnʃəs/ **I** *n* **the ~** le subconscient.
II *adj* gen inconscient; Psych subconscient.

subconsciously /ˌsʌbˈkɒnʃəslɪ/ *adv* gen inconsciemment; Psych de façon subconsciente.

subcontinent /ˌsʌbˈkɒntɪnənt/ *n* sous-continent *m*.

subcontract **I** /ˈsʌbkɒntrækt/ *n* contrat *m* de sous-traitance.
II /ˌsʌbkənˈtrækt/ *vtr* sous-traiter (**to, out to** à).

subcontracting /ˌsʌbkənˈtræktɪŋ/ *n* sous-traitance *f*.

subcontractor /ˌsʌbkənˈtræktə(r)/ ▶ **1692** *n* sous-traitant *m*.

subculture /ˈsʌbkʌltʃə(r)/ *n* **1** Sociol subculture *f*; **2** Biol repiquage *m*.

subcutaneous /ˌsʌbkjuːˈteɪnɪəs/ *adj* sous-cutané.

subdeacon /ˌsʌbˈdiːkən/ *n* sous-diacre *m*.

subdivide /ˌsʌbdɪˈvaɪd/ **I** *vtr* subdiviser [*house, site*].
II *vi* se subdiviser.

subdivision /ˌsʌbdɪˈvɪʒn/ *n* **1** (process, part) subdivision *f*; **2** US (housing development) lotissement *m*.

subdominant /ˌsʌbˈdɒmɪnənt/ *n* **1** Mus sous-dominante *f*; **2** Ecol subdominant *m*, espèce *f* subdominante.

subdue /səbˈdjuː, US -ˈduː/ *vtr* **1** (conquer) soumettre [*people, nation*]; mater [*rebellion*]; **2** (hold in check) contenir [*anger, fear, delight*].

subdued /səbˈdjuːd, US -ˈduːd/ *adj* **1** (downcast) [*person*] maussade; [*mood*] morose; [*voice*] terne; **2** (muted) [*excitement, enthusiasm, reaction*] contenu; [*voices, conversation*] bas/basse; [*lighting*] tamisé; [*colour*] atténué.

subedit /ˌsʌbˈedɪt/ *vtr* GB corriger [*text*].

subeditor /ˌsʌbˈedɪtə(r)/ ▶ **1692** *n* GB Publg, Journ correcteur/-trice *m/f*.

subentry /ˈsʌbentrɪ/ *n* **1** (in account) subdivision *f* de compte; **2** Comput sous-rubrique *f*.

subfamily /ˈsʌbfæmɪlɪ/ *n* (all contexts) sous-famille *f*.

subfield /ˈsʌbfiːld/ *n* sous-zone *f*.

subgroup /ˈsʌbgruːp/ *n* sous-groupe *m*.

subheading /ˈsʌbhedɪŋ/ *n* (in text) sous-titre *m*.

subhuman /ˌsʌbˈhjuːmən/ *adj* [*behaviour*] monstrueux/-euse.

subject **I** /ˈsʌbdʒɪkt/ *n* **1** (topic) sujet *m*; **let's get back to the ~** revenons au sujet or à nos moutons○; **to change** ou **drop the ~** parler d'autre chose, changer de sujet; **to raise a ~** soulever une question; **while we're on the ~ of bonuses**... pendant que nous en sommes aux primes...; **2** (branch of knowledge) (at school, college) matière *f*; (for research, study) sujet *m*; **my favourite ~ is English** l'anglais est ma matière préférée; **her ~ is genetics** elle est spécialisée en génétique; **3** Art, Photo sujet *m*; **4** Sci (in experiment) sujet *m*; **5** (focus) objet *m*; **to be the ~ of an inquiry** faire l'objet d'une enquête; **it has become a ~ for complaints** cela fait l'objet de beaucoup de plaintes; **6** Ling sujet *m*; **7** (citizen) sujet/-ette *m/f*; **British ~s** les sujets britanniques.
II /ˈsʌbdʒɪkt/ *adj* **1** (subservient) [*people, race*] asservi; **2** (obliged to obey) **to be ~ to** être soumis à [*law, rule*]; **3** (liable) **to be ~ to** être sujet/-ette à [*flooding, fits*]; être passible de [*tax*]; **prices are ~ to increases** les prix peuvent subir des augmentations; **flights are ~ to delay** les vols sont susceptibles d'être en retard; **4** (dependent) **to be ~ to** dépendre de [*approval*]; **you will be admitted ~ to producing a visa** vous serez admis à condition de présenter un visa; **'~ to alteration'** 'sous réserve de modification'; **'~ to availability'** (of flights, tickets) 'dans la limite des places disponibles'; (of goods) 'dans la limite des stocks disponibles'.
III /səbˈdʒekt/ *vtr* **1** (expose) **to ~ sb to sth** faire subir qch à qn [*stress, insults, torture*]; **to be ~ed to** devoir supporter [*noise*]; faire l'objet de [*attacks*]; être soumis à [*torture*]; **to ~ sth to heat/light** exposer qch à la chaleur/lumière; **2** (subjugate) littér assujettir [*race, country*].

subject: **~ heading** *n* sujet *m*; **~ index** *n* (in book) index *m* des sujets traités; (in library) fichier *m* par sujets.

subjection /səbˈdʒekʃn/ *n* sujétion *f* (**to** à); **to keep sb in a state of ~** maintenir qn dans la sujétion.

subjective /səbˈdʒektɪv/ **I** *n* Ling cas *m* sujet, nominatif *m*.
II *adj* **1** (personal or biased) subjectif/-ive; **2** Ling [*case, pronoun*] sujet/-ette; [*genitive*] subjectif/-ive.

subjectively /səbˈdʒektɪvlɪ/ *adv* [*perceive, exist*] subjectivement; [*assess, talk, view*] de façon subjective.

subjectivism /səbˈdʒektɪvɪzəm/ *n* subjectivisme *m*.

subjectivity /ˌsʌbdʒekˈtɪvətɪ/ *n* subjectivité *f*.

subject: **~ matter** *n* sujet *m*; **~ pronoun** *n* Ling pronom *m* sujet.

sub judice /ˌsʌb ˈdʒuːdɪsɪ, sʊb ˈjuːdɪkeɪ/ *adj* [*case*] devant les tribunaux.

subjugate /ˈsʌbdʒʊgeɪt/ *vtr* **1** (oppress) subjuguer [*country, people*]; **2** (suppress) dompter [*desire*]; soumettre [*will*].

subjugation /ˌsʌbdʒʊˈgeɪʃn/ *n* assujettissement *m*.

subjunctive /səbˈdʒʌŋktɪv/ **I** *n* subjonctif *m*; **in the ~** au subjonctif.
II *adj* [*form, tense*] du subjonctif; [*mood*] subjonctif/-ive.

subkingdom /ˌsʌbˈkɪŋdəm/ *n* Biol embranchement *m*.

sublease /ˈsʌbliːs/ = **sublet**.

sublet /ˈsʌblet/ **I** *n* sous-location *f*.
II /ˌsʌbˈlet/ *vtr, vi* (*p prés* **-tt-**; *prét, pp* **-let**) [*owner, tenant*] sous-louer.

sublibrarian /ˌsʌblaɪˈbreərɪən/ ▶ **1692** *n* bibliothécaire *mf* adjoint/-e.

sublieutenant /ˌsʌblefˈtenənt, US -luːt-/ ▶ **1612** *n* GB enseigne *m* de vaisseau.

sublimate /ˈsʌblɪmeɪt/ **I** *n* Chem sublimé *m*.
II *vtr* Chem, Psych sublimer.

sublimation /ˌsʌblɪˈmeɪʃn/ *n* Chem, Psych sublimation *f*.

sublime /səˈblaɪm/ **I** *n* **the ~** le sublime.
II *adj* **1** [*genius, beauty, heroism, art*] sublime; **2**○ [*food, clothes, person*] fantastique; **3** [*indifference, contempt, egoism*] suprême.
III *vtr* Chem sublimer.
IDIOMS **to go from the ~ to the ridiculous** passer du sublime au grotesque.

sublimely /səˈblaɪmlɪ/ *adv* **1** [*play, perform, sing*] d'une façon sublime; **~ beautiful/heroic** d'une beauté/d'un héroïsme sublime; **2** [*indifferent, contemptuous, confident*] suprêmement.

subliminal /səbˈlɪmɪnl/ *adj* [*advertising, message, level*] subliminal.

subliminally /səbˈlɪmɪnəlɪ/ *adv* à un niveau subliminal.

sublimity /səbˈlɪmətɪ/ *n* sublimité *f*.

sublingual /ˌsʌbˈlɪŋgwəl/ *adj* sublingual.

submachine gun /ˌsʌbməˈʃiːn/ *n* mitraillette *f*.

submarine /ˌsʌbməˈriːn, US ˈsʌb-/ **I** *n* **1** Naut sous-marin *m*; **2** (also **~ sandwich**) US sandwich *m*.
II *modif* Mil [*base, warfare, detection, accident*] de sous-marins; [*captain, commander*] de sous-marin.
III *adj* [*plant, life, cable*] sous-marin.

submarine: **~ chaser** *n* chasseur *m* de sous-marins; **~ pen** *n* abri *m* pour sous-marins.

submariner /ˌsʌbˈmærɪnə(r), US ˈsʌb-/ ▶ **1612** *n* sous-marinier *m*.

submaxillary /ˌsʌbmækˈsɪlərɪ/ *adj* sous-maxillaire.

submediant /ˌsʌbˈmiːdɪənt/ *n* Mus sus-dominante *f*.

submenu /ˈsʌbmenjuː/ *n* Comput sous-menu *m*.

submerge /səbˈmɜːdʒ/ **I** *vtr* [*sea, flood, tide*] submerger; [*person*] immerger (**in** dans); **to remain ~d for several days** [*submarine*] rester en plongée pendant plusieurs jours.
II submerged *pp adj* lit, fig [*wreck, person*] submergé.
III *v refl* **to ~ oneself in** se plonger dans [*work*].

submergence /səbˈmɜːdʒəns/ *n* submersion *f*.

submersible /səbˈmɜːsəbl/ *n, adj* submersible (*m*).

submersion /səbˈmɜːʃn, US -mɜːrʒn/ *n* (action) immersion *f*; (fact of being submerged) submersion *f*.

submission /səbˈmɪʃn/ *n* **1** (obedience, subjection) soumission *f* (**to** à) also Sport; **to beat/frighten/starve sb into ~** réduire qn par la force/la peur/la famine; **2** (of application, document, proposal, report) soumission *f* (**to** à); **3** (report) rapport *m*; **4** Jur (closing argument) conclusions *fpl*; **the ~ that** les suggestions selon lesquelles; **to make a ~ that** suggérer que; **5** sout (opinion) thèse *f*.

submissive /səbˈmɪsɪv/ *adj* [*person, attitude*] soumis; [*behaviour*] docile.

submissively /səbˈmɪsɪvlɪ/ *adv* [*behave*] avec docilité; [*react, accept, say*] docilement.

submissiveness /səbˈmɪsɪvnɪs/ *n* docilité *f*.

submit /səbˈmɪt/ (*p prés etc* **-tt-**) **I** *vtr* **1** (send, present) soumettre [*report, proposal, budget, accounts, plan*] (**to** à); présenter [*bill, application, resignation, nomination*] (**to** à); déposer [*claim, estimate*] (**to** à); soumettre [*entry, script, sample*] (**to** à); **2** sout gen, Jur

(propose) **to ~ that** suggérer que; **I would ~ that** je me permets de suggérer que fml.
II *vi* se soumettre; **to ~ to** subir [*humiliation, injustice, pain*]; céder à [*will, demand, discipline*]; subir [*medical examination, treatment*]; Jur se soumettre à [*jurisdiction, decision*].
III *v refl* **to ~ oneself to** Jur se soumettre à [*jurisdiction, decision*]; subir [*medical examination*].
subnormal /sʌbˈnɔːml/ *adj* **1** pej [*person*] arriéré; **2** [*temperature*] au-dessous de la normale.
suborder /ˈsʌbɔːdə(r)/ *n* Biol sous-ordre *m*.
subordinate I /səˈbɔːdɪnət, US -dənət/ *n* subalterne *mf*.
II /səˈbɔːdɪnət/ *adj* [*officer, rank, position*] subalterne; [*issue, matter, question*] secondaire (**to** par rapport à); **to be ~ to sb** être le subalterne de qn.
III /səˈbɔːdɪneɪt/ *vtr* gen, Ling subordonner (**to** à); **subordinating conjunction** Ling conjonction *f* de subordination.
subordinate clause *n* Ling proposition *f* subordonnée.
subordination /səˌbɔːdɪˈneɪʃn/ *n* subordination *f*.
suborn /səˈbɔːn/ *vtr* suborner.
subparagraph /ˈsʌbpærəgrɑːf/ *n* sous-paragraphe *m*.
subplot /ˈsʌbplɒt/ *n* intrigue *f* secondaire.
subpoena /səˈpiːnə/ **I** *n* assignation *f* à comparaître; **to serve a ~ on sb** assigner qn à comparaître.
II *vtr* (*3ᵉ pers sg prés* **~s**; *prét, pp* **~ed**) assigner [qn] à comparaître.
subpopulation /ˌsʌbpɒpjʊˈleɪʃn/ *n* Stat échantillon *m*.
sub-post office *n* GB bureau *m* de poste (*de quartier ou de village*).
subregion /ˈsʌbriːdʒən/ *n* sous-région *f*.
subrogation /ˌsʌbrəˈgeɪʃn/ *n* subrogation *f*.
sub rosa /ˌsʌb ˈrəʊzə/ *adv* en secret.
subroutine /ˈsʌbruːtiːn/ *n* Comput sous-programme *m*.
subscribe /səbˈskraɪb/ **I** *vtr* **1** (pay) souscrire [*sum, amount*] (**to** à); **2** sout (sign) signer; **to ~ one's name to sth** apposer sa signature sur qch fml.
II *vi* **1** (agree with) **to ~ to** partager [*view, values*]; souscrire à [*opinion, principle, theory, doctrine, belief*]; **2** (buy) s'abonner; **to ~ to** être abonné à [*magazine, TV, channel*]; **3** Fin (apply) **to ~ for** souscrire à [*shares*]; **4** (contribute) **to ~ to** donner (de l'argent) à [*charity, fund*].
subscriber /səbˈskraɪbə(r)/ *n* **1** Comm, Journ (to periodical etc) abonné/-e *m/f* (**to** de); **2** Telecom abonné/-e *m/f* (du téléphone); **3** (to fund) souscripteur *m* (**to** à); **4** Fin (to shares) souscripteur *m*; **5** (to doctrine) partisan/-e *m/f* (**to** de).
subscript /ˈsʌbskrɪpt/ *adj* souscrit.
subscription /səbˈskrɪpʃn/ *n* **1** (magazine) abonnement *m* (**to** à); **to take out/cancel/renew a ~** prendre/annuler/renouveler un abonnement; **2** GB (fee) (to association, scheme) cotisation *f* (**to** à); (TV) abonnement *m* (**to** à); **annual ~** cotisation annuelle; **3** (to fund) don *m* (**to** à); **4** (system) souscription *f*; **by ~** par souscription; **available on ~** disponible par souscription; **5** Fin (to share issue) souscription *f* (**to** à).
subscription: **~ concert** *n* concert *m* pour abonnés; **~ fee**, **~ rate** *n* tarif *m* d'abonnement; **~ magazine** *n* magazine *m* vendu par abonnement; **~ service** *n* service *m* d'abonnement.
subsection /ˈsʌbsekʃn/ *n* Jur alinéa *m*; gen paragraphe *m*.
subsequent /ˈsʌbsɪkwənt/ *adj* [*event, problem, success, work*] (in past) ultérieur; (in future) à venir.
subsequently /ˈsʌbsɪkwəntlɪ/ *adv* par la suite.
subserve /səbˈsɜːv/ *vtr* sout favoriser.
subservience /səbˈsɜːvɪəns/ *n* servilité *f* (**to** envers).
subservient /səbˈsɜːvɪənt/ *adj* **1** péj servile pej (**to** envers); **2** (subordinate) subordonné (**to** à); **3** sout (useful) profitable (**to** à).
subset /ˈsʌbset/ *n* Math sous-ensemble *m*.
subside /səbˈsaɪd/ *vi* **1** (die down) [*storm, wind, applause, noise*] s'apaiser; [*anger, pain, fear*] se calmer; [*laughter, fever, excitement*] retomber; [*threat*] diminuer; [*flames*] reculer; **2** (sink) [*water, river, flood*] se retirer; [*building, road, land*] s'affaisser; **3** (sink down) [*person*] s'effondrer (**into, onto** sur).
subsidence /səbˈsaɪdns, ˈsʌbsɪdns/ *n* affaissement *m*.
subsidiarity /səbˌsɪdɪˈærətɪ/ *n* EC subsidiarité *f*.
subsidiary /səbˈsɪdɪərɪ, US -dɪerɪ/ **I** *n* (also **~ company**) filiale *f* (**of** de); **banking/insurance ~** filiale d'une banque/compagnie d'assurances.
II *adj* [*reason, character, question*] secondaire (**to** par rapport à).
subsidize /ˈsʌbsɪdaɪz/ *vtr* subventionner.
subsidy /ˈsʌbsɪdɪ/ *n* subvention *f* (**to, for** à).
subsist /səbˈsɪst/ *vi* subsister.
subsistence /səbˈsɪstəns/ *n* subsistance *f*.
subsistence: **~ allowance** *n* GB Admin ≈ indemnité *f* de subsistance; **~ farming** *n* agriculture *f* de subsistance; **~ level** *n* niveau *m* minimum pour vivre; **~ wage** *n* minimum *m* vital.
subsoil /ˈsʌbsɔɪl/ *n* sous-sol *m*.
subsonic /ˌsʌbˈsɒnɪk/ *adj* subsonique.
subspecies /ˈsʌbspiːʃiːz/ *n* sous-espèce *f*.
substance /ˈsʌbstəns/ *n* **1** Chem (matter) substance *f*; **illegal ~s** substances illicites; **2** (essence) (of argument, talks, protest) essentiel *m* (**of** de); (of book, plot) substance *f* (**of** de); **the ~ of what he says** l'essentiel de ce qu'il dit; **in ~** en substance; **3** (solidity, reality) (of argument, point) poids *m*; (of claim, accusation) fondement *m*; (of play, book) fond *m*; **to lack ~** [*argument*] manquer de poids; [*book*] manquer de fond; **there is no ~ to the allegations** les allégations sont dénuées de fondement; **is there any ~ to these claims?** est-ce que ces réclamations sont bien fondées?; **to lend ~ to** donner du poids ā [*claim, allegation*]; **4** sout (significance) **something of ~** quelque chose d'important; **talks/matters of ~** des entretiens importants/affaires importantes; **the meeting yielded little of ~** la réunion n'a pas donné grand-chose; **5** (tangible quality) substance *f*; **6** sout †(wealth) **a person of ~** un nanti/une nantie *m/f*.
substance abuse *n* abus *m* de substances toxiques.
substandard /ˌsʌbˈstændəd/ *adj* **1** [*goods, housing*] de qualité inférieure; [*essay, performance*] insuffisant; [*workmanship*] défectueux/-euse; **2** Ling [*language, usage*] incorrect.
substantial /səbˈstænʃl/ *adj* **1** (in amount) [*sum, payment, fee, income, quantity*] important; [*imports, loss*] considérable; [*majority, number, proportion*] appréciable; [*meal*] substantiel/-ielle; **~ damages** Jur dommages et intérêts substantiels; **2** (in degree) [*change, improvement, difference, increase, fall, impact, risk, damage*] considérable; [*role*] important; **to be in ~ agreement (over sth)** être largement d'accord (sur qch); **3** (solid) [*chair, lock, wall*] solide; [*evidence, proof*] solide; **4** (wealthy) [*business, company*] financièrement solide; [*businessman, landowner*] riche, aisé; **5** sout (tangible) [*being*] réel/réelle.
substantially /səbˈstænʃəlɪ/ *adv* **1** (considerably) [*increase, change, fall, reduce*] considérablement; [*higher, lower, better, less*] nettement; **2** (mainly) [*true, correct, unchanged*] en grande partie, en gros; **the team will not be ~ different from last week's** l'équipe ne différera pas de beaucoup de celle de la semaine dernière.
substantiate /səbˈstænʃɪeɪt/ *vtr* sout justifier, prouver [*allegation, complaint*]; établir [*charge*]; appuyer [qch] par des preuves, justifier [*statement, view*].
substantiation /səbˌstænʃɪˈeɪʃn/ *n* sout justification *f*.
substantival /ˌsəbstænˈtaɪvl/ *adj* Ling substantif/-ive.
substantive /ˈsʌbstəntɪv/ **I** *n* Ling substantif *m*.
II *adj* **1** sout (significant) [*discussion*] positif/-ive; [*change, decision*] important; [*progress*] considérable; [*issues*] d'importance; **2** Ling substantif/-ive.
substantive law *n* Jur droit *m* positif.
substation /ˈsʌbsteɪʃn/ *n* Elec sous-station *f*.
substitute /ˈsʌbstɪtjuːt, US -tuːt/ **I** *n* **1** (person) gen, Sport remplaçant/-e *m/f*; **to come on as a ~** Sport jouer comme remplaçant; **their dog is a child ~** leur chien remplace l'enfant qu'ils n'ont pas eu; **2** (product, substance) produit *m* de substitution, succédané *m*, ersatz *m* pej; **chocolate/coffee ~** succédané de chocolat/de café, produit de substitution pour le chocolat/le café; **sugar ~** édulcorant *m* de synthèse; **there is no ~ for analysis/a good education** rien ne remplace l'analyse/une bonne éducation; **there is no ~ for real leather** rien ne vaut le cuir véritable; **it's a poor ~ for a glass of wine!** ça ne vaut pas un verre de vin!; **3** Ling substitut *m*.
II *modif* [*machine, device*] de remplacement; [*family, parent*] adoptif/-ive; Sport [*player*] de remplacement; **~ teacher** US remplaçant/-e *m/f*, suppléant/-e *m/f*; **to work as a ~ teacher** US faire des remplacements.
III *vtr* substituer (**for** à); **to ~ X for Y** substituer X à Y, remplacer X par Y; **honey can be ~d for sugar in this recipe** on peut remplacer le sucre par du miel dans cette recette.
IV *vi* **to ~ for sb/sth** remplacer qn/qch.
substitute: **~'s bench** *n* Sport banc *m* de touche; **~ teacher** *n* Sch remplaçant/-e *m/f*, suppléant/-e *m/f*.
substitution /ˌsʌbstɪˈtjuːʃn, US -ˈtuː-/ *n* gen substitution *f*, remplacement *m*; Chem, Math, Ling, Psych substitution *f*; **the ~ of X for Y** la substitution de X à Y.
substratum /ˌsʌbˈstrɑːtəm, US ˈsʌbstreɪtəm/ *n* (*pl* **-strata**) **1** gen (basis) fond *m*; **2** Geol (subsoil) sous-sol *m*; (bedrock) substratum *m*; **3** Sociol couche *f*; **4** Ling, Philos substrat *m*.
substructure /ˈsʌbstrʌktʃə(r)/ *n* substructure *f*.
subsume /səbˈsjuːm, US -ˈsuːm/ *vtr* subsumer (**into, under** sous).
subsystem /ˈsʌbsɪstəm/ *n* Comput sous-système *m*.
subteen /ˈsʌbtiːn/ *n* US jeune *mf* de moins de treize ans.
subtemperate /ˌsʌbˈtempərət/ *adj* tempéré froid.
subtenancy /ˈsʌbtenənsɪ/ *n* sous-location *f*.
subtenant /ˈsʌbtenənt/ *n* sous-locataire *mf*.
subtend /səbˈtend/ *vtr* (all contexts) sous-tendre.
subterfuge /ˈsʌbtəfjuːdʒ/ *n* subterfuge *m* (**of doing** de faire).
subterranean /ˌsʌbtəˈreɪnɪən/ *adj* souterrain.
subtext /ˈsʌbtekst/ *n* Literat thème *m* sous-jacent; fig message *m* sous-jacent.
subtilize /ˈsʌtɪlaɪz/ sout **I** *vtr* purifier.
II *vi* Literat raffiner.
subtitle /ˈsʌbtaɪtl/ **I** *n* sous-titre *m*.
II *vtr* sous-titrer.
subtitling /ˈsʌbtaɪtlɪŋ/ *n* sous-titrage *m*.
subtle /ˈsʌtl/ *adj* **1** (barely perceptible) [*distinction, pressure*] subtil; [*change, shift, form*] imperceptible; **2** (finely tuned) [*argument, analysis, allusion, decision*] subtil; [*strategy, tactic, idea*] astucieux/-ieuse, habile;

[*humour, irony*] très fin; [*performance, plot, characterization*] habile; [*hint*] voilé; **in a ~ way** d'une façon subtile; **you weren't very ~ about it!** tu n'as pas été très subtil!; **3** (perceptive) [*observer, analyst*] perspicace; [*person, mind*] subtil; **4** (delicate) [*blend, colour, fragrance*] subtil; [*lighting*] nuancé.

subtlety /ˈsʌtltɪ/ *n* **1** (of film, book, music, style) complexité *f*; (of expression, feeling, tone, idea) subtilité *f*; **2** (fine point) subtilité *f*; **3** (of actions, reaction, approach, manner) subtilité *f*; **4** (of flavour) délicatesse *f*; (of lighting) caractère *m* nuancé.

subtly /ˈsʌtlɪ/ *adv* **1** (imperceptibly) [*change, alter, shift, influence*] imperceptiblement; [*different, humorous*] légèrement; **2** (in a complex way) [*argue, mock, evoke*] avec subtilité; [*analyse, act*] avec finesse; **3** (delicately) [*flavoured, coloured*] délicatement; [*lit*] de manière nuancée.

subtonic /ˌsʌbˈtɒnɪk/ *n* (note *f*) sensible *f*.

subtopic /ˈsʌbtɒpɪk/ *n* sous-rubrique *f*.

subtotal /ˈsʌbtəʊtl/ *n* sous-total *m*.

subtract /səbˈtrækt/ **I** *vtr* Math soustraire (**from** de).
II *vi* faire des soustractions.

subtraction /səbˈtrækʃn/ *n* soustraction *f*.

subtropical /ˌsʌbˈtrɒpɪkl/ *adj* subtropical.

subtropics /ˌsʌbˈtrɒpɪks/ *npl* zones *fpl* subtropicales.

suburb /ˈsʌbɜːb/ **I** *n* gen banlieue *f*; **inner ~** faubourg *m*; **an expensive ~** une banlieue chère.
II suburbs *npl* **the ~s** la banlieue; **the outer ~s** la grande banlieue; **the ~s of London** la banlieue de Londres or londonienne.

suburban /səˈbɜːbən/ *adj* **1** [*street, shop, train*] de banlieue; [*development*] suburbain; US [*shopping mall*] à l'extérieur de la ville; **~ sprawl** (phenomenon) développement *m* des banlieues; (one suburb) banlieue *f* gigantesque or tentaculaire; **2** péj [*outlook*] étroit; [*values*] de petit-bourgeois.

suburbanite /səˈbɜːbənaɪt/ *n* souvent péj banlieusard/-e *m/f*.

suburbanize /səˈbɜːbənaɪz/ *vtr* transformer [qch] en banlieue.

suburbia /səˈbɜːbɪə/ *n* ¢ la banlieue; **to live in ~** habiter en banlieue.

subvention /səbˈvenʃn/ *n* **1 C** (subsidy) subvention *f*; **2 ¢** (financing) subventions *fpl*.

subversion /səˈbɜːʃn, US -ˈvɜːrʒn/ *n* subversion *f*.

subversive /səbˈvɜːsɪv/ **I** *n* (person) élément *m* subversif.
II *adj* (all contexts) subversif/-ive.

subvert /səbˈvɜːt/ *vtr* déstabiliser [*government, establishment*]; ébranler [*belief, idea, ideology*]; corrompre [*diplomat, agent*]; faire échouer [*negotiations, talks*].

subway /ˈsʌbweɪ/ **I** *n* **1** GB (for pedestrians) passage *m* souterrain; **2** US (underground railway) métro *m*.
II *modif* US [*station*] de métro; [*train*] souterrain.

sub-zero /ˌsʌbˈzɪərəʊ/ *adj* [*temperature*] inférieur à zéro.

succeed /səkˈsiːd/ **I** *vtr* succéder à [*person*]; succéder à, suivre [*event*]; **to ~ sb as king** succéder à qn sur le trône; **she ~ed him as president** elle lui a succédé à la présidence.
II *vi* **1** (achieve success) [*person, plan, technique*] réussir; **to ~ in doing** réussir or parvenir à faire; **to ~ in business** réussir or avoir du succès en affaires; **to ~ in life/in one's exams** réussir dans la vie/aux examens; **2** (accede) succéder; **to ~ to** succéder à [*throne, presidency*].
IDIOMS **nothing ~s like success** un succès en appelle un autre.

succeeding /səkˈsiːdɪŋ/ *adj* (in past) suivant; (in future) à venir; **~ generations have done** les générations suivantes ont fait; **~ generations will do** les générations à venir feront; **with each ~ year** d'année en année.

success /səkˈses/ *n* **1** succès *m*, réussite *f*; **without ~** sans succès; **to meet with ~** avoir du succès; **to stand the best chance of ~** [*candidate, applicant*] avoir la meilleure chance de réussir; **to make a ~ of** réussir [*dish, life, career*]; faire un succès de [*business, venture*]; **sb's ~ in** le succès de qn à [*exam, election*]; **despite her ~ in doing** bien qu'elle ait réussi à faire; **he never had much ~ with women** il n'a jamais eu beaucoup de succès auprès des femmes; **wishing you every ~** avec tous mes vœux de succès or de réussite; **2** (person, thing that succeeds) succès *m*, réussite *f*; **to be a huge ~** [*party, film*] être un grand succès, avoir un succès retentissant; **to be a ~ with** avoir du succès auprès de [*critics, children*]; **to be a ~ as** avoir du succès comme [*teacher, actor*].
IDIOMS **to enjoy the sweet smell of ~** savourer son succès; **to scent the sweet smell of ~** sentir que l'on va réussir.

successful /səkˈsesfl/ *adj* **1** (that achieves its aim) [*attempt, operation*] réussi; [*plan, campaign, summit*] couronné de succès; [*treatment, policy*] efficace; **the operation was not entirely ~** l'opération n'a pas complètement réussi; **to be ~ in** ou **at doing** réussir à faire; **2** (that does well) [*film, book, writer*] (profitable) à succès; (well regarded) apprécié; [*businessman, company*] prospère; [*career*] brillant; **to be ~** réussir; **to be ~ in business/in a profession** réussir en affaires/dans une profession; **the film was less ~** le film a eu moins de succès; **3** (that wins, passes) [*candidate*] heureux/-euse (*before n*); [*applicant*] retenu; [*team, contestant*] victorieux/-ieuse; **to be ~ in an exam** réussir à un examen; **her application was not ~** sa candidature n'a pas été retenue; **4** (happy) [*marriage, partnership*] réussi; [*outcome*] heureux/-euse.

successfully /səkˈsesfəlɪ/ *adv* [*try, campaign, argue*] avec succès.

succession /səkˈseʃn/ *n* **1** (sequence) (of attempts, events, people) série *f*, succession *f* (**of** de); **in ~** de suite; **for five years in ~** pendant cinq années de suite; **in close** ou **quick** ou **swift ~** coup sur coup; **three explosions in rapid ~** trois explosions coup sur coup; **the days followed each other in quick ~** les jours s'enchaînaient rapidement; **2** (act, right of inheriting) succession *f* (**to** à); (line of descent) héritiers *mpl*; **to be fifth in ~ to the throne** être le cinquième dans la succession au trône.

successive /səkˈsesɪv/ *adj* [*attempt, victory, generation, government*] successif/-ive; [*day, week, year*] consécutif/-ive; **for five ~ years** pendant cinq années consécutives or de suite; **with each ~ season/disaster...** à chaque nouvelle saison/catastrophe...

successively /səkˈsesɪvlɪ/ *adv* successivement, tour à tour.

successor /səkˈsesə(r)/ *n* **1** (person) successeur *m* (**of sb, to sb** de qn; **to sth** à qch); **to be sb's ~** être le successeur de qn; **to be sb's ~ as** succéder à qn en tant que [*monarch, minister*]; **a worthy ~ to sb** un successeur digne de qn; **2** (invention, concept) remplaçant/-e *m/f*; **it is a possible ~ to silicon** cela pourrait succéder à or remplacer le silicum.

success: **~ rate** *n* taux *m* de réussite; **~ story** *n* réussite *f*.

succinct /səkˈsɪŋkt/ *adj* [*statement, phrase*] succinct; [*person*] concis.

succinctly /səkˈsɪŋktlɪ/ *adv* succinctement.

succinctness /səkˈsɪŋktnɪs/ *n* concision *f*.

succor *n* US ▶ **succour**.

succotash /ˈsʌkətæʃ/ *n* US plat *m* de maïs et de fèves.

succour GB, **succor** US /ˈsʌkə(r)/ sout **I** *n* secours *m*.
II *vtr* secourir.

succulence /ˈsʌkjʊləns/ *n* succulence *f*.

succulent /ˈsʌkjʊlənt/ **I** *n* plante *f* grasse.
II *adj* gen, Bot succulent.

succumb /səˈkʌm/ *vi* (all contexts) succomber (**to** à).

such /sʌtʃ/ **I** *pron* **1** (this) **~ is life** c'est la vie; **she's a good singer and recognized as ~** c'est une bonne chanteuse et elle est reconnue comme telle; **she's talented and recognized as ~** elle a du talent et son talent est reconnu; ▶ **as**; **2** = **suchlike**.
II *det* **1** (of kind previously mentioned) (replicated) tel/telle; (similar) pareil/-eille; (of similar sort) de ce type (*after n*); **~ a situation** une telle situation; **~ individuals** de tels individus; **in ~ a situation** dans une situation pareille; **at ~ a time** dans un moment pareil; **many ~ proposals** de nombreuses propositions de ce type; **and other ~ arguments** et autres arguments de ce type; **all ~ basic foods** tous les aliments de base de ce type; **potatoes, bread and all ~ basic foods** les pommes de terre, le pain et tous les autres aliments de base; **doctors, dentists and all ~ people** les docteurs, les dentistes et toutes les personnes qui exercent ce type de métier; **a mouse or some ~ animal** une souris ou un animal semblable; **he said 'so what!' or some ~ remark** il a dit 'et alors!' ou quelque chose comme ça; **there was some ~ case last year** il s'est produit la même chose l'année dernière; **there's no ~ person** il/elle n'existe pas; **there was ~ a man I believe** je crois que cet homme a existé; **there's no ~ thing** ça n'existe pas; **I've never heard of ~ a thing** je n'ai jamais entendu parler d'une chose pareille; **I didn't say any ~ thing** je n'ai jamais dit une chose pareille; **you'll do no ~ thing!** il n'en est pas question! ; **I 've been waiting for just ~ an opportunity** j'attendais justement que l'occasion se présente; **2** (of specific kind) **to be ~ that** être tel/telle que; **my hours are ~ that I usually miss the last train** mes horaires sont tels que je rate habituellement le dernier train; **his movements were ~ as to arouse suspicion** il se conduisait de telle façon qu'il éveillait les soupçons; **in ~ a way that** d'une telle façon que; **3** (any possible) **~ money as I have** le peu d'argent or tout l'argent que j'ai; **until ~ time as** jusqu'à ce que (+ *subj*); **4** (so great) tel/telle; **there was ~ carnage!** il y avait un tel carnage!; **to be having ~ problems** avoir de tels problèmes; **~ was his admiration/anger that** son admiration/sa colère était telle que; **his fear was ~ that** il avait tellement peur que; **to be in ~ despair/in ~ a rage** être tellement désespéré/dans une telle colère; **5** iron (of such small worth, quantity) **you can borrow my boots ~ as they are** ces bottes ne sont pas géniales○ mais tu peux les emprunter; **we picked up the apples ~ as there were** nous avons ramassé les rares pommes qu'il y avait par terre.
III such as *det phr, conj phr* comme, tel/telle que; **~ a house as this, a house ~ as this** une maison comme celle-ci; **it was on just ~ a night as this that** c'est par une nuit exactement comme celle-ci que; **~ cities as** or **cities ~ as Manchester and Birmingham** des villes telles que or comme Manchester et Birmingham; **a person ~ as her** une personne comme elle; **~ as?** (as response) gen quoi par exemple?; (referring to person) qui par exemple?; **there are no ~ things as giants** les géants n'existent pas; **have you ~ a thing as a screwdriver?** auriez-vous un tournevis par hasard?; **inflation ~ as occurred last year** l'inflation telle qu'elle s'est manifestée l'année dernière.
IV *adv* **1** (to a great degree) (with adjectives) si, tellement; (with nouns) tel/telle; **in ~ a persuasive way** d'une façon si convaincante; **~ a nice boy!** un garçon si

gentil!, un si gentil garçon!; **~ excellent meals** de si bons plats; **~ good quality as this** une telle qualité; **I hadn't seen ~ a good film for years** je n'avais pas vu un aussi bon film depuis des années; **don't be ~ an idiot** ne sois pas si stupide; **she's not ~ an idiot as she seems** elle n'est pas aussi stupide que l'on croit; **only ~ an idiot (as him) would do** il n'y a qu'un imbécile (comme lui) qui ferait; **it was ~ (a lot of) fun** on s'est tellement amusé; **~ a lot of problems** tant de problèmes; (**ever**○) **~ a lot of people** beaucoup de gens; **thanks ever ~ a lot**○ merci mille fois.

such and such *det* tel/telle; **on ~ a topic** sur tel sujet; **at ~ a time** à telle heure.

suchlike○ /ˈsʌtʃlaɪk/ **I** *pron* **and ~** (of people) et autres; **lions, tigers and ~** les lions, les tigres et autres fauves.
II *adj* de ce type; **caviar, smoked salmon and ~ delicacies** le caviar, le saumon fumé et autres mets raffinés de ce type.

suck /sʌk/ **I** *n* **to give sth a ~** sucer qch; **to have a ~ of sth** goûter à qch (en suçant); **to give ~**† donner la tétée.
II *vtr* **1** (drink in) [*person, animal, machine*] aspirer [*liquid, air*] (**from** de; **through** avec); (extract) sucer (**from** de); **to ~ milk through a straw** aspirer du lait avec une paille; **to ~ poison from a wound** sucer le poison d'une plaie; **to ~ blood** sucer le sang; **to ~ sb dry** fig (of affection) vampiriser qn; (of money) pomper○ qn jusqu'au dernier sou; **2** (lick) sucer, suçoter [*bottle, fruit, pencil, pipe, thumb, cut*]; [*baby*] téter [*breast*]; **to ~ one's teeth** claquer des lèvres (en signe de désapprobation); **3** (pull) [*current, wind, mud*] entraîner [*person*]; **to be ~ed down** ou **under** être entraîné au fond; **to get ~ed into** fig être entraîné dans.
III *vi* **1** [*baby*] téter; **to ~ at** sucer [*bottle, ice*]; **to ~ on** tirer sur [*pipe, cigar, tube*]; **2**◑ US **it ~s!** c'est nul○!, c'est de la foutaise◑!
IV sucking *pres p adj* [*noise*] de succion.
IDIOMS **~s to you**○! GB tu l'as dans le baba○!; **to ~ it up**○ US affronter une situation difficile.
■ **suck in**: **~ in [sth], ~ [sth] in** [*sea, wind*] engloutir; [*person, machine*] aspirer [*air, dirt, liquid*]; **to ~ in one's cheeks** creuser les joues; **to ~ in one's stomach** rentrer l'estomac.
■ **suck off**◑: **~ [sb] off, ~ off [sb]** tailler une pipe◑ à [*man*]; faire minette◑ à [*woman*].
■ **suck out**: **~ [sth] out, ~ out [sth]** aspirer [*air, liquid, dirt*] (**from** de); sucer [*poison, blood*] (**from** de); **to be ~ed out of a plane** être aspiré hors d'un avion.
■ **suck up**: ¶ **~ up**○ faire de la lèche○; **to ~ up to sb** cirer les pompes à qn○; ¶ **~ [sth] up, ~ up [sth]** pomper [*liquid*]; aspirer [*dirt*].

sucker /ˈsʌkə(r)/ **I** *n* **1**○ (dupe) bonne poire○ *f*; **he's a ~ for compliments** les compliments le font craquer○; **2** Bot, Hort surgeon *m*; **3** (animal's pad, rubber pad) ventouse *f*.
II○ *vtr* (dupe) entuber○.
III *vi* Bot, Hort surgeonner.

sucking pig *n* cochon *m* de lait.

suckle /ˈsʌkl/ **I** *vtr* allaiter [*baby*].
II *vi* téter.

suckling /ˈsʌklɪŋ/ **I** *n* **1**† [*child*] enfant *mf* au sein; **2** [*act*] allaitement *m*.
II *adj* [*animal*] à la mamelle.
IDIOMS **out of the mouths of babes and ~s** la vérité sort de la bouche des enfants.

suckling pig *n* cochon *m* de lait.

sucrase /ˈsuːkreɪz/ *n* sucrase *f*.

sucrose /ˈsuːkrəʊz, -rəʊs/ *n* saccharose *f*.

suction /ˈsʌkʃn/ *n* succion *f*; **by ~** par succion.

suction: **~ pad** *n* ventouse *f*; **~ pump** *n* pompe *f* aspirante; **~ valve** *n* clapet *m* d'aspiration.

Sudan /suːˈdɑːn/ **▶1131** *pr n* (also **the ~**) Soudan *m*.

Sudanese /ˌsuːdəˈniːz/ **▶1486** **I** *n* (person) Soudanais/-e *m/f*.
II *adj* soudanais.

Sudanic /suːˈdænɪk/ **▶1402** **I** *n* Ling soudanais *m*.
II *adj* soudanais.

sudden /ˈsʌdn/ *adj* [*impulse, death*] soudain, subit; [*movement*] brusque; **all of a ~** tout à coup, tout d'un coup; **it's all a bit ~** c'est un peu trop soudain; **it was all very ~** ça s'est passé très vite.

sudden: **~ death overtime** *n* US Sport *prolongation d'un match pour départager deux équipes*; **~ death play-off** *n* GB Sport *penalties pour départager deux équipes*; **~ infant death syndrome**, **SIDS** *n* Med mort *f* subite du nourrisson.

suddenly /ˈsʌdnlɪ/ *adv* gen subitement; (all of a sudden) tout à coup, tout d'un coup.

suddenness /ˈsʌdnnɪs/ *n* gen soudaineté *f*; (of death, illness) caractère *m* subit.

suds /sʌdz/ *npl* **1** (also **soap ~**) (foam) mousse *f* (de savon); (soapy water) eau *f* savonneuse; **2**○ US (beer) bière *f*; (foam) mousse *f*.

sudsy /ˈsʌdzɪ/ *adj* [*water*] savonneux/-euse.

sue /suː, sjuː/ **I** *vtr* Jur intenter un procès à; **to ~ sb for divorce/libel** intenter un procès en divorce/en diffamation à qn; **to ~ sb for damages** poursuivre qn en dommages-intérêts.
II *vi* **1** Jur intenter un procès; **to ~ for divorce/damages** intenter un procès pour obtenir le divorce/des dommages-intérêts; **2** littér **to ~ for pardon/peace** solliciter le pardon/la paix.

suede /sweɪd/ **I** *n* daim *m*; **imitation ~** suédine *f*.
II *modif* [*shoe, glove*] en daim.

suet /ˈsuːɪt, ˈsjuːɪt/ *n* graisse *f* de rognon de bœuf; **~ pudding** GB gâteau *m* à la graisse de rognon.

Suez /ˈsuːɪz/ *n* **1** Geog Suez *m*; **the ~ Canal** le Canal de Suez; **2** Pol Hist (also **the ~ crisis**) l'affaire *f* de Suez.

suffer /ˈsʌfə(r)/ **I** *vtr* **1** (undergo) subir [*punishment, defeat, loss, delay, consequences*]; souffrir de [*hunger*]; **she ~ed a great deal of pain** elle a beaucoup souffert; **he ~ed a severe neck injury** il a été gravement blessé au cou; **to ~ a heart attack/a stroke** avoir une crise cardiaque/une attaque; **the roof ~ed storm damage** le toit a été endommagé par la tempête; **ports have ~ed a drop in trade** les ports ont enregistré un ralentissement de l'activité commerciale; **the region has ~ed severe job losses** la région a enregistré d'importantes pertes d'emplois; **2** sout (tolerate) supporter; **I won't ~ this a moment more** je ne supporterai pas cela plus longtemps.
II *vi* **1** (with illness) **to ~ from** souffrir de [*malnutrition, rheumatism, heat, cold*]; avoir [*headache, blood pressure*]; **she was ~ing from a cold** elle avait un rhume; **to ~ from agoraphobia/depression** être agoraphobique/dépressif/-ive; **2** (experience pain) souffrir; **I hate to see him ~ like that** j'ai horreur de le voir souffrir comme cela; **they ~ed a lot in the war** ils ont beaucoup souffert pendant la guerre; **to ~ for one's beliefs** souffrir à cause de ses convictions; **to ~ for one's sins** expier ses péchés; **you'll ~ for it later** vous le regretterez plus tard; **you'll ~ for this!** tu t'en repentiras!; **3** (do badly) [*company, profits, popularity*] souffrir; [*health, quality, work*] s'en ressentir; **the country ~s from its isolation** le pays souffre de son isolement; **she keeps late hours and her work is beginning to ~** elle veille tard la nuit et son travail s'en ressent or en pâtit; **the project ~s from a lack of funds** le problème du projet, c'est qu'il est insuffisamment financé.

sufferance /ˈsʌfərəns/ *n* **I'm only here on ~** je suis tout juste toléré ici.

sufferer /ˈsʌfərə(r)/ *n* victime *f*; **the families are the worst ~s** les familles sont les véritables victimes; **leukemia ~s, ~s from leukemia** les leucémiques, les personnes atteintes de leucémie.

suffering /ˈsʌfərɪŋ/ **I** *n* ¢ souffrances *fpl* (**of** de).
II *adj* souffrant.

suffice /səˈfaɪs/ sout **I** *vtr* suffire à.
II *vi* suffire, être suffisant (**to do** à faire); **~ it to say (that)** qu'il suffise de dire (que).

sufficiency /səˈfɪʃnsɪ/ *n* (adequate quantity) quantité *f* suffisante.

sufficient /səˈfɪʃnt/ *adj* suffisamment de, assez de; **~ money/time/books** suffisamment d'argent/de temps/de livres; **a ~ amount** une quantité suffisante; **a ~ number** un nombre suffisant; **to be ~** suffire, être suffisant; **this food/an hour will be ~** cette nourriture/une heure suffira or sera suffisante; **to be more than ~** être plus que suffisant; **to be quite ~** suffire largement; **to be ~ to do** suffire pour faire; **one match was ~ to show her talent** un match a suffi pour démontrer son talent; **to have ~ to drink/to live on** avoir suffisamment à boire/pour vivre; **to be ~ for sb to do** suffire à qn pour faire; **this salary is ~ for me to live on** ce salaire me suffit pour vivre; **to be ~ unto oneself** sout se suffire à soi-même.
IDIOMS **~ unto the day (is the evil thereof)** Prov à chaque jour suffit sa peine.

sufficiently /səˈfɪʃntlɪ/ *adv* suffisamment, assez (**to do** pour faire); **~ for sb to do** suffisamment pour que qn fasse.

suffix **I** /ˈsʌfɪks/ *n* suffixe *m*.
II /səˈfɪks/ *vtr* pourvoir [qch] d'un suffixe.

suffocate /ˈsʌfəkeɪt/ **I** *vtr* **1** lit [*smoke, fumes*] asphyxier; [*person, pillow*] étouffer; **2** fig [*rage, anger*] étouffer; [*fright*] paralyser; **she felt ~d by her family** elle se sentait étouffée par sa famille.
II *vi* **1** lit (by smoke, fumes) (in enclosed space, crowd) être asphyxié; (by pillow) être étouffé; **2** fig suffoquer (**with** de).

suffocating /ˈsʌfəkeɪtɪŋ/ *adj* [*smoke, fumes*] asphyxiant; [*atmosphere*] étouffant; [*heat*] suffocant; **a ~ rage** une fureur noire; **it's ~** on étouffe.

suffocation /ˌsʌfəˈkeɪʃn/ *n* (by smoke, fumes, enclosed space, crowd) asphyxie *f*; (by pillow) étouffement *m*.

Suffolk /ˈsʌfək/ **▶1624** *pr n* Suffolk *m*.

suffragan /ˈsʌfrəgən/ *n, adj* suffragant (*m*).

suffrage /ˈsʌfrɪdʒ/ *n* **1** (right) droit *m* de vote; **women's ~** droit *m* de vote pour les femmes; **2** (system) suffrage *m*; **universal ~** suffrage *m* universel.

suffragette /ˌsʌfrəˈdʒet/ **I** *n* suffragette *f*.
II *modif* [*movement*] des suffragettes.

suffragist /ˈsʌfrədʒɪst/ *n* partisan *m* du droit de vote pour les femmes.

suffuse /səˈfjuːz/ sout **I** *vtr* se répandre sur.
II suffused *pp adj* **~d with** [*style, writing*] imprégné de; [*person*] envahi de [*joy, melancholy*]; inondé de [*light*]; teint de liter [*colour*].

sugar /ˈʃʊgə(r)/ **I** *n* **1** Culin sucre *m*; **to take ~** prendre du sucre; **'how many ~s?'** 'combien de sucres?'; **brown/white ~** sucre *m* roux/blanc; **no ~, thanks** sans sucre, merci; **2**○ (as endearment) chéri/-e *m/f*.
II *modif* [*industry, prices*] du sucre; [*production, refinery*] de sucre; [*spoon, canister*] à sucre.
III○ *excl* zut○!
IV *vtr* sucrer [*tea, coffee*].
IDIOMS **to ~ the pill (for sb)** dorer la pilule (à qn).

sugar: **~ beet** *n* betterave *f* à sucre; **~ bowl** *n* sucrier *m*; **~ cane** *n* canne *f* à sucre; **~-coated** *adj* lit enrobé de sucre, fig édulcoré; **~ content** *n* teneur *f* en sucre; **~ cube** *n* morceau *m* de sucre; **~ daddy** *n* vieux protecteur *m* (d'une jeune fille); **~ diabetes** ▶1354 *n* Med diabète *m* sucré; **~ed almond** *n* dragée *f*; **~-free** *n* sans sucre.

sugariness /ˈʃʊgərɪnɪs/ *n* fig douceur *f* mielleuse.

sugarless /ˈʃʊgəlɪs/ *adj* sans sucre.

sugar: **~ loaf** *n* pain *m* de sucre; **~ lump** *n* morceau *m* de sucre; **~ maple** *n* Bot érable *m* à sucre; **~ mouse** *n* souris *f* en sucre; **~ pea** *n* mange-tout *m inv*; **~ plantation** *n* plantation *f* de canne à sucre.

sugarplum /ˈʃʊgəplʌm/ *n* **1** (piece of candy) bonbon *m*; **2** (as endearment) mon chou.

sugar: **~plum fairy** *n* fée *f* Dragée; **~ sifter** *n* saupoudreuse *f*; **~ soap** *n* décapant *m* alcalin pour peinture; **~ sprinkler** *n* = **sugar sifter**; **~ tongs** *n* pince *f* à sucre.

sugary /ˈʃʊgərɪ/ *adj* **1** lit [*food, taste*] sucré; **2** fig [*person, image, smile*] mielleux/-euse; [*sentimentality*] mièvre.

suggest /səˈdʒest, US səgˈdʒ-/ *vtr* **1** (put forward for consideration) suggérer [*solution, possibility*]; **to ~ that** suggérer que; **I ~ to you that** je vous suggère que; **can you ~ how/why/where...?** comment/pourquoi/où, selon vous...?; **why, do you ~, did he do it?** pourquoi, selon vous, l'a-t-il fait? **he did it, I ~, because...** je pense qu'il l'a fait parce que...; **it would be wrong to ~ that** il serait faux de prétendre que; **to ~ otherwise is ludicrous** prétendre qu'il en est autrement serait ridicule; **what are you ~ing?** qu'est-ce que vous insinuez?; **I venture to ~ that** je me risquerais à dire que; **2** (recommend, advise) suggérer; **can you ~ a place to meet/eat?** peux-tu suggérer un endroit où nous retrouver/où manger? ; **where do you ~ we go?** où nous suggères-tu d'aller?; **to ~ sb/sth for sth** suggérer qn/qch pour qch; **they ~ed that I (should) leave** ils m'ont suggéré de partir; **I ~ that you leave at once** je suggère que vous partiez tout de suite; **the committee ~s that steps be taken** le comité suggère que des mesures soient prises; **I ~ waiting** je suggère d'attendre; **an idea ~ed itself (to me)** une idée m'est venue à l'esprit; **3** (indicate) [*evidence, test, result, poll, calculation*] sembler indiquer (**that** que); **there is nothing to ~ that** rien ne semble indiquer que; **it was more difficult than the result might** ou **would ~** ce fut plus difficile que le résultat ne semble l'indiquer; **4** (evoke) [*painting, image, sound*] évoquer; **what does it ~ to you?** qu'est-ce que cela évoque pour vous?

suggestible /səˈdʒestəbl, US səgˈdʒ-/ *adj* influençable.

suggestion /səˈdʒestʃn, US səgˈdʒ-/ *n* **1** (proposal) suggestion *f* (**about** à propos de; **as to** en ce qui concerne; **that** que); **to make** ou **put forward a ~** faire une suggestion; **if I may make a ~** si je peux me permettre de faire une suggestion; **any ~s?** y-a-t-il des suggestions? **my ~ is that...** je suggère que... (+ *subj*); **there is no ~ that** on n'a jamais dit que (+ *subj*); **there is no ~ of fraud** rien ne laisse suggérer qu'il y a eu fraude; **at** ou **on sb's ~** sur ou suivant le conseil de qn; **there was some ~ that** il a été suggéré que; **2** (hint) (of cruelty, racism, pathos) soupçon *m* (**of** de); (of smile) pointe *f* (**of** de); **3** Psych suggestion *f*; **the power of ~** la force de suggestion.

suggestions box *n* boîte *f* à idées.

suggestive /səˈdʒestɪv, US səgˈdʒ-/ *adj* (all contexts) suggestif/-ive; **to be ~ of sth** évoquer qch.

suggestively /səˈdʒestɪvlɪ, US səgˈdʒ-/ *adv* de façon suggestive.

suggestiveness /səˈdʒestɪvnɪs, US səgˈdʒ-/ *n* caractère *m* suggestif.

suicidal /ˌsuːɪˈsaɪdl, ˌsjuː-/ *adj* lit, fig suicidaire; **to feel ~** être suicidaire; **that would be ~!** fig ce serait un véritable suicide!

suicidally /ˌsuːɪˈsaɪdəlɪ, sjuː-/ *adv* [*depressed*] jusqu'au suicide; [*behave, decide, drive*] de manière suicidaire.

suicide /ˈsuːɪsaɪd, ˈsjuː-/ **I** *n* (action) lit, fig suicide *m*; (person) suicidé/-e *m/f*; **it would be political ~ to do that** faire cela serait un véritable suicide politique; **to attempt ~** tenter de se suicider; **to commit ~** se suicider.

II *modif* [*attempt, bid, rate*] de suicide.

suicide: **~ bomber** *n* (person) bombardier *m* suicide; **~ mission** *n* mission *f* suicide; **~ note** *n* lettre *f* de suicide; **~ pact** *n* engagement *m* de se suicider ensemble; **~ sale** *n* GB, Comm soldes *fpl* monstres○.

suit /suːt, sjuːt/ **I** *n* **1** Fashn (man's) costume *m*; (woman's) tailleur *m*; **two-/three-piece ~** costume deux/trois pièces; **to be wearing a ~ and tie** être en costume cravate; **a ~ of clothes** une tenue; **a ~ of armour** une armure complète; ▶**bathing suit, diving suit etc**; **2** Jur (lawsuit) procès *m*; **civil/libel ~** procès civil/en diffamation; **to file a ~ against** intenter or faire un procès à; **to file a ~ for damages** intenter un procès pour dommages et intérêts; **3** (in cards) couleur *f*; **short ~** couleur courte; **long** ou **strong ~** couleur longue; **to be sb's strong ~** fig être le point fort de qn; **to follow ~** lit fournir de la couleur; fig faire de même.

II *vtr* **1** (flatter) [*colour, outfit*] aller à [*person*]; **does it ~ me?** est-ce que cela me va?; **red doesn't ~ your complexion** le rouge ne te va pas (au teint); **short hair really ~ed her** les cheveux courts lui allaient très bien; **to ~ sb down to the ground**○ [*garment, arrangement, job*] aller à qn comme un gant; **2** (be convenient) [*date, arrangement*] convenir à [*person*]; **does Sunday ~ you?** est-ce que dimanche te convient?; **it ~s me fine** ça me convient or me va très bien; **~s me**○! ça me va!; **she's liberal when it ~s her** elle est libérale quand ça l'arrange; **we'll go when it ~s us!** on partira quand cela nous arrangera!; **we stay here because it ~s us** on reste parce qu'on est bien ici; **it ~s us to do** cela nous convient de faire; **it ~s him to live alone** ça lui plaît de vivre seul; **it ~s me that** cela me convient que (+ *subj*); **3** (be appropriate) [*part, job*] convenir à [*person*]; **the role didn't ~ me** le rôle ne me convenait pas or n'était pas fait pour moi; **a loan that ~s your needs** un prêt qui répond parfaitement à vos besoins; **you should find something to ~ you** tu devrais trouver quelque chose qui te convienne; **the house ~ed me fine** la maison me convenait parfaitement; **4** (be beneficial) [*sea air, change*] convenir à [*person*]; **5** (adapt) **to ~ sth to** adapter qch à [*need, occasion*]; **to ~ the action to the word** joindre le geste à la parole.

III *vi* convenir ; **does that ~?** est-ce que ça (vous) convient?

IV *v refl* **to ~ oneself** faire comme on veut; **~ yourself!** fais comme tu veux!; **they twist the facts to ~ themselves** ils manipulent les faits à leur convenance.

suitability /ˌsuːtəˈbɪlətɪ, ˌsjuːt-/ *n* (of person) (professional) aptitude *f* (**for** pour); (personal) capacité *f* (**for** pour); (of place, route) commodité *f*; **the ~ of a plant to** ou **for a climate** l'adéquation *f* d'une plante à un climat.

suitable /ˈsuːtəbl, ˈsjuː-/ *adj* [*accommodation, clothing, employment, qualification, venue*] adéquat; [*candidate*] apte; [*treatment, gift, gesture*] approprié; **did you see anything ~?** as-tu vu quelque chose qui (te) convienne?. **to be ~ for** convenir à [*person*]; se prêter bien à [*climate, activity, occasion*]; être fait pour [*role*]; être apte à [*job, position*]; **not ~ for human consumption** impropre à la consommation; **to be a ~ model for sb** être un exemple convenable pour qn; **is it a ~ setting for the film?** est-ce que le lieu convient bien pour le film?; **to be ~ to** convenir à [*person, age-group, culture*]; **the book isn't ~ to use with beginners** le livre ne convient pas à des débutants; **now seems a ~ time to discuss it** il semble que ce soit le moment opportun pour en discuter.

suitably /ˈsuːtəblɪ, ˈsjuː-/ *adv* **1** (appropriately) [*dressed, equipped, qualified*] convenablement; **2** (to the right degree) aussi hum [*austere, futuristic*] suffisamment; [*chastened, impressed*] dûment.

suitcase /ˈsuːtkeɪs, ˈsjuː-/ *n* valise *f*.

IDIOMS **to be living out of a ~** passer sa vie à se déplacer.

suite /swiːt/ *n* **1** (furniture) mobilier *m*; **dining-room/bathroom ~** mobilier *m* de salle à manger/de salle de bains; **2** (rooms) suite *f*; **a ~ of rooms** une suite; **3** Mus suite *f*; **4** littér (retinue) suite *f*.

suited /ˈsuːtɪd, ˈsjuː-/ *adj* **to be ~ to** [*place, vehicle, clothes*] être commode pour; [*class, game, format, style*] convenir à; [*person, personality*] être fait pour; **they are ideally ~ (to each other)** ils sont faits l'un pour l'autre; **to be ideally ~ for a post** être fait pour un emploi.

suiting /ˈsuːtɪŋ, ˈsjuː-/ *n* tissu *m* pour tailleurs.

suitor /ˈsuːtə(r), ˈsjuː-/ *n* **1**† (admirer) prétendant *m*, soupirant† *m*; **2** Fin (company) prétendant *m*.

sulcus /ˈsʌlkəs/ *n* (*pl* **-ci**) Anat scissure *f*.

sulfa *n* US ▶ **sulpha**.

sulfate *n* US ▶ **sulphate**.

sulfide *n* US ▶ **sulphide**.

sulfonamide *n* US ▶ **sulphonamide**.

sulfur *n* US ▶ **sulphur**.

sulfureous *adj* US ▶ **sulphureous**.

sulfuric *adj* US ▶ **sulphuric**.

sulfurous *adj* US ▶ **sulphurous**.

sulk /sʌlk/ **I** *n* **to be in a ~** bouder; **to go into a ~** se mettre à bouder.

II sulks *npl* **to have (a fit of) the ~s** bouder.

III *vi* bouder (**about, over** à cause de).

sulkily /ˈsʌlkɪlɪ/ *adv* [*say, reply*] d'un ton boudeur.

sulkiness /ˈsʌlkɪnɪs/ *n* **1** (characteristic) caractère *m* maussade; **2** (behaviour) bouderies *fpl*.

sulky /ˈsʌlkɪ/ *adj* (all contexts) boudeur/-euse; **to look ~** faire la tête.

sullen /ˈsʌlən/ *adj* [*person, expression*] renfrogné; [*resentment*] morne; [*day, sky, indifference, mood*] maussade; [*silence*] obstiné.

sullenly /ˈsʌlənlɪ/ *adv* [*watch, stare*] d'un air renfrogné; [*reply*] d'un ton maussade.

sullenness /ˈsʌlənnɪs/ *n* [*of look*] air *m* maussade; [*of mood*] humeur *f* maussade.

sully /ˈsʌlɪ/ *vtr* littér souiller fml.

sulpha drug GB, **sulfa drug** US /ˈsʌlfə/ *n* sulfamide *m*.

sulphate GB, **sulfate** US /ˈsʌlfeɪt/ *n* sulfate *m* (**of** de); **copper ~** sulfate *m* de cuivre.

sulphide GB, **sulfide** US /ˈsʌlfaɪd/ *n* sulphure *m*; **hydrogen/silver ~** sulphure *m* d'hydrogène/d'argent.

sulphonamide GB, **sulfonamide** US /sʌlˈfɒnəmaɪd/ *n* sulfamide *m*.

sulphur GB, **sulfur** US /ˈsʌlfə(r)/ *n* soufre *m*.

sulphur dioxide /ˌsʌlfə daɪˈɒksaɪd/ *n* anhydride *m* sulfureux.

sulphureous GB, **sulfureous** US /sʌlˈfjʊərɪəs/ *adj* sulfureux/-euse.

sulphuric GB, **sulfuric** US /sʌlˈfjʊərɪk/ *adj* sulfurique.

sulphuric acid *n* acide *m* sulfurique.

sulphurous GB, **sulfurous** US /ˈsʌlfərəs/ *adj* sulfureux/-euse.

sulphur spring *n* source *f* sulfureuse.

sultan /ˈsʌltən/ *n* sultan *m*.

sultana /sʌlˈtɑːnə, US -ˈtænə/ *n* **1** Culin

raisin *m* de Smyrne; **2** (wife of sultan) sultane *f*.

sultanate /'sʌltəneɪt/ *n* sultanat *m*.

sultriness /'sʌltrɪnɪs/ *n* (of atmosphere) lourdeur *f*; (of woman) sensualité *f*.

sultry /'sʌltrɪ/ *adj* **1** [*day, place*] étouffant; [*weather*] lourd; **2** [*voice*] voluptueux/-euse; [*woman, look*] sensuel/-elle.

sum /sʌm/ *n* **1** (amount of money) somme *f*; **a considerable/paltry ~** une somme considérable/dérisoire; **a large/small ~ of money** une grosse/petite somme; **2** (calculation) calcul *m*; **to be good at ~s** être bon en calcul or en arithmétique; **to do one's ~s** fig faire ses comptes; **3** (total) lit somme *f*, total *m*; **the ~ of** fig la somme de [*experience, happiness*]; l'ensemble *m* de [*achievements*]; **the whole is greater than the ~ of its parts** l'ensemble est plus grand que la somme de ses parties; **4** (summary) **in ~** en somme.

■ **sum up**: ¶ **~ up 1** gen [*person*] récapituler; **to ~ up, I'd like to say**... pour récapituler or en résumé, je voudrais dire...; **2** Jur [*judge*] résumer; ¶ **~ up [sth] 1** (summarize) résumer [*argument, point of view*]; **that ~s it up exactly** ça résume parfaitement la situation; **2** (judge accurately) apprécier [*situation*]; se faire une idée de [*person*].

IDIOMS **the ~ and substance of sth** l'essentiel de qch.

sumac(h) /'ʃuːmæk, suː-, sjuː-/ *n* sumac *m*.

Sumatra /sʊ'mɑːtrə/ **▶ 1381** *pr n* Sumatra.

summa cum laude /ˌsʊmə kʊm 'laʊdeɪ/ *n* US Univ ≈ mention *f* très bien.

summarily /'sʌmərəlɪ, US sə'merəlɪ/ *adj* sommairement.

summarize /'sʌməraɪz/ *vtr* résumer [*book, problem, argument, speech*]; récapituler [*argument, speech*].

summary /'sʌmərɪ/ **I** *n* résumé *m*; **news ~** résumé des informations; **in ~** en résumé.

II *adj* gen, Jur [*statement, judgment, justice*] sommaire.

summary: **~ jurisdiction** *n* Jur juridiction *f* sommaire; **~ offence** GB, **~ offense** US *n* Jur infraction *f* (punissable par procédure) sommaire.

summat○ /'sʌmət/ *n* GB dial = **something**.

summation /sə'meɪʃn/ *n* sout **1** (summary) (of facts) résumé *m*; (of work, ideas) récapitulation *f*; **2** (addition) total *m*; **3** US Jur conclusions *fpl*.

summer /'sʌmə(r)/ **I ▶ 1671** *n* été *m*; **in ~** en été; **in the ~ of 1991** pendant l'été de 1991; **a lovely ~('s) day** une belle journée d'été; **a youth of sixteen ~s** littér un jeune de seize printemps.

II *modif* [*weather, evening, resort, clothes, vacation*] d'été; **~ tourist** ou **visitor** estivant/-e *m/f*.

III *vtr* US Agric estiver [*cattle*].

IV *vi* passer l'été.

IDIOMS **the ~ of discontent** *été de 1982 au cours duquel des émeutes ont eu lieu dans plusieurs villes d'Angleterre*.

summer: **~ camp** *n* US colonie *f* de vacances; **~ holiday** GB, **~ vacation** US gen vacances *fpl* (d'été); Sch, Univ grandes vacances *fpl*; **~house** *n* pavillon *m* d'été; **~ lightning** *n* ₵ (one flash) éclair *m* de chaleur; (storm) éclairs *mpl* de chaleur; **~ pudding** *n* GB gâteau *m* aux fruits rouges; **~ resort** *n* station *f* estivale; **~ sausage** *n* US saucisse *f* sèche fumée; **~ school** *n* université *f* d'été; **~ solstice** *n* solstice *m* d'été; **~ squash** *n* US petite courge *f* d'été; **~ term** *n* Sch, Univ troisième trimestre *m*.

summertime /'sʌmətaɪm/ **I** *n* **1** (period) été *m*; **2** GB **summer time** (by clock) heure *f* d'été.

II *modif* d'été.

summery /'sʌmərɪ/ *adj* estival; **it's quite ~** on se croirait en été.

summing-up /ˌsʌmɪŋ'ʌp/ *n* gen récapitulation *f*; Jur résumé *m*.

summit /'sʌmɪt/ **I** *n* **1** Pol sommet *m* (**on** sur); **Paris/Nato ~** sommet de Paris/de l'OTAN; **economic/peace ~** sommet *m* économique/pour la paix; **2** (of mountain) sommet *m*, cime *f*; **3** fig (of career, influence) sommet *m*, apogée *m*.

II *modif* Pol [*meeting, talks, conference, nation*] au sommet.

summiteer /ˌsʌmɪ'tɪə(r)/ *n* Pol participant *m* d'un sommet.

summitry /'sʌmɪtrɪ/ *n* US politique *f* diplomatique basée sur les rencontres au sommet.

summon /'sʌmən/ *vtr* **1** (call for) faire venir [*doctor, employee, servant, police, waiter*]; convoquer [*ambassador*]; **to ~ sb to sb's office/to a meeting** convoquer qn dans le bureau de qn/à une réunion; **to ~ sb in** faire entrer qn; **to ~ sb to do sth** sommer qn de faire qch; **to ~ help** chercher de l'aide; **to ~ reinforcements/a taxi** appeler des renforts/un taxi; **2** (summons) citer; **to be ~ed (to appear) before the court** être cité à comparaître devant la cour (**for** pour; **for doing** pour avoir fait); **3** (convene) convoquer [*parliament, meeting, conference*] (**to do** pour faire); **4** Mil sommer [*troops*] (**to do** de faire); **5** = **summon up**.

■ **summon up**: **~ up [sth]** (gather) rassembler [*energy, courage, support, resources*] (**to do** pour faire); (evoke) évoquer [*memory, thought, image, scenario*]; **to ~ up spirits** appeler les esprits.

summons /'sʌmənz/ **I** *n* **1** Jur citation *f* (**to do** à faire; **for** pour); **a ~ to appear** une citation à comparaître; **to serve a ~** signifier or notifier une citation; **to serve sb with a ~** citer qn à comparaître; **2** gen (order) injonction *f* (**from** de; **to** à); **to answer sb's ~** obéir à l'injonction de qn.

II *vtr* citer (**to** à; **to do** à faire; **for** pour).

sumo /'suːməʊ/ **▶ 1282** *n* (also **~ wrestling**) sumo *m*; **~ wrestler** lutteur *m* de sumo.

sump /sʌmp/ *n* **1** (for draining water) puisard *m*; **2** Aut carter *m*.

sump oil *n* huile *f* de carter.

sumptuary /'sʌmptʃʊərɪ/ *adj* sout somptuaire.

sumptuous /'sʌmptʃʊəs/ *adj* (all contexts) somptueux/-euse.

sumptuously /'sʌmptʃʊəslɪ/ *adv* [*decorate, design*] somptueusement; [*attired, arrayed*] de manière somptueuse.

sumptuousness /'sʌmptʃʊəsnɪs/ *n* somptuosité *f*.

sum total *n* (of money) montant *m* total; (of achievements) ensemble *m*; **is that the ~ of your achievements?** iron c'est tout ce que tu as fait?

sun /sʌn/ **I** *n* gen, Astron soleil *m*; **the midday/August ~** le soleil de midi/d'août; **the ~ is shining** le soleil brille; **to have the ~ in one's eyes** avoir le soleil dans les yeux; **in the ~** au soleil; **don't lie right in the ~** ne vous allongez pas en plein soleil; **you should come out of the ~** vous devriez vous mettre à l'ombre; **a place in the ~** (position) un endroit ensoleillé; (house) une maison dans le sud; fig une place au soleil; **it's the most beautiful place under the ~** c'est l'endroit le plus beau du monde; **they sell everything under the ~** ils vendent de tout; **to be up before the ~** être levé avant l'aube.

II US *vi* (*p prés etc* **-nn-**) [*person*] prendre le soleil; [*animal*] se chauffer au soleil.

III *v refl* (*p prés etc* **-nn-**) **to ~ oneself** [*person*] prendre le soleil; [*animal*] se chauffer au soleil.

IDIOMS **there's nothing new under the ~** il n'y a rien de nouveau sous le soleil.

Sun *abrév écrite* = **Sunday**.

sun: **~baked** *adj* brûlé par le soleil; **~bath** *n* bain *m* de soleil.

sunbathe /'sʌnbeɪð/ **I** GB *n* = **sunbath**.

II *vi* se faire bronzer.

sun: **~bather** *n* personne *f* qui prend un or des bain(s) de soleil; **~bathing** *n* bains *mpl* de soleil; **~beam** *n* lit, fig rayon *m* de soleil; **~bed** *n* (lounger) chaise *f* longue ; (with sunlamp) lit *m* solaire; **Sunbelt** *n* US *les États du Sud et de l'Ouest des États-Unis*; **~ blind** *n* GB store *m*; **~ block** *n* crème *f* écran total; **~bonnet** *n* bonnet *m* (de coton); **~burn** *n* coup *m* de soleil.

sunburned, **sunburnt** /'sʌnbɜːnt/ *adj* (burnt) brûlé par le soleil; (tanned) GB bronzé; **to get ~** (burn) attraper un coup de soleil; (tan) GB bronzer.

sun: **~burst** *n* éclaircie *f*; **~burst clock** *n* pendule *f* soleil; **~ cream** *n* = **suntan cream**.

sundae /'sʌndeɪ, US -diː/ *n* sundae *m*, coupe *f* glacée.

sun dance *n* danse *f* du soleil.

Sunday /'sʌndeɪ, -dɪ/ **▶ 1883** **I** *n* dimanche *m*.

II Sundays *pr npl* **the ~s** les journaux *mpl* du dimanche.

III *modif* [*service, Mass, newspaper, painter, walk, lunch*] du dimanche; **a ~ driver** péj un chauffeur du dimanche.

IDIOMS **he'll never do it, not in a month of ~s** il ne le fera jamais.

Sunday best *n* (**dressed**) **in one's ~** endimanché.

Sunday: **~ driver** *n* chauffeur *m* du dimanche; **~-go-to-meeting**○ *adj* US hum [*dress, suit*] du dimanche; **~ observance** *n* observance *f* du repos dominical; **~ opening** *n* ouverture *f* dominicale (*des commerces et des bars*); **~ school** *n* école *f* du dimanche; **~ school teacher** *n* catéchiste *mf* à l'école du dimanche; **~ trading** *n* commerce *m* dominical; **~ trading laws** *npl* réglementation *f* du commerce dominical.

sundeck /'sʌndek/ *n* (on ship) pont *m* supérieur; (in house) terrasse *f*.

sunder /'sʌndə(r)/ littér **I** *n* **in ~** en morceaux.

II *vtr* séparer.

sun: **~dial** *n* cadran *m* solaire; **~down** *n* = **sunset**.

sundowner /'sʌndaʊnə(r)/ *n* **1** GB (drink) cocktail *m*; **2** Austral (tramp) clochard *m*.

sun: **~drenched** *adj* inondé de soleil; **~dress** *n* robe *f* bain de soleil; **~-dried** *adj* séché au soleil.

sundry /'sʌndrɪ/ **I sundries** *npl* articles *mpl* divers.

II *adj* [*items, objects, occasions*] divers; (**to**) **all and ~** gen (à) tout le monde; (critical) (à) n'importe qui.

sun: **~-filled** *adj* ensoleillé; **~fish** *n* (saltwater) poisson *m* lune; (freshwater) centrarchidé *m*.

sunflower /'sʌnflaʊə(r)/ **I** *n* tournesol *m*.

II *modif* [*oil, seed*] de tournesol; [*margarine*] au tournesol.

sung /sʌŋ/ *pp* ▶ **sing**.

sun: **~glasses** *npl* lunettes *fpl* de soleil; **~-god** *n* dieu *m* soleil; **~-goddess** *n* déesse *f* du soleil; **~ hat** *n* chapeau *m* de soleil.

sunk /sʌŋk/ *pp* ▶ **sink** II, III.

sunken /'sʌŋkən/ *adj* **1** (under water) [*treasure, wreck*] immergé; [*vessel*] englouti; **2** (recessed) [*cheek*] creux/creuse; [*eye*] cave; **3** (low) [*bath*] encastré; [*garden, living area*] en contrebas.

Sun King *n* **the ~** le Roi Soleil.

sun: **~-kissed** *adj* littér [*beach, water, mountain*] baigné par le soleil; [*face, limbs*] hâlé par le soleil; [*hair*] éclairci par le soleil; **~lamp** *n* (for tanning) lampe *f* à bronzer; Med lampe *f* à rayons ultraviolets.

sunless /'sʌnlɪs/ *adj* sans soleil.

sunlight /'sʌnlaɪt/ *n* lumière *f* du soleil; **in**

the ~ au soleil; **in direct ~** en plein soleil.

sun: **~lit** *adj* ensoleillé; **~ lotion** *n* = **suntan lotion**; **~ lounge** GB, **~ parlor** US, **~ room** US *n* gen verrière *f*; (in hospital, rest home) solarium *m*; **~lounger** *n* chaise *f* longue.

Sunni /ˈsʌnɪ/ *n* Relig **1** (branch of Islam) sunnisme *m*; **2** (adherent) (also **~ Muslim**) sunnite *mf*.

sunny /ˈsʌnɪ/ *adj* **1** lit [*weather, morning, period*] ensoleillé; [*place, side, garden, room*] (facing the sun) exposé au soleil; (sunlit) ensoleillé; **~ interval** période *f* ensoleillée; **it's going to be ~** il va faire (du) soleil; **the outlook is ~** on prévoit du soleil; **2** fig [*person, disposition, temperament*] joyeux/-euse; **to look on the ~ side (of things)** regarder or voir le bon côté des choses; **~ side up** [*egg*] sur le plat.

sun: **~ oil** *n* = **suntan oil**; **~ parlor** *n* US = **sun lounge**; **~ porch** *n* petite véranda *f*; **~ray lamp** *n* = **sunlamp** Med; **~ray treatment** *n* héliothérapie *f*; **~rise** *n* lever *m* du soleil; **~rise industry** *n* US industrie *f* en pleine expansion; **~roof** *n* toit *m* ouvrant; **~screen** *n* filtre *m* solaire; **~seeker** *n* fanatique *mf* du soleil.

sunset /ˈsʌnset/ **I** *n* lit coucher *m* du soleil; fig crépuscule *m*.
II *adj* **1** US Admin, Jur [*law, bill, clause*] de durée d'application limitée; **2** fig **in her ~ years** dans son grand âge.

sunset industry *n* US industrie *f* en déclin.

sun: **~ shade** *n* (parasol) parasol *m*; (awning) auvent *m*; (in car) pare-soleil *m inv*; (eyeshade) visière *f*; **~shield** *n* pare-soleil *m inv*.

sunshine /ˈsʌnʃaɪn/ **I** *n* **1** gen soleil *m*; Meteorol ensoleillement *m*; **in the morning/summer ~** au soleil du matin/d'été; **12 hours of ~** 12 heures d'ensoleillement; **you're a real ray of ~!** tu respires la joie de vivre! also iron; **2**○ (addressing someone) coco/cocotte○ *m/f*; **hi, ~!** salut, coco○!
II *adj* US Admin, Jur [*law, bill, clause*] sur la transparence.
IDIOMS **life's not all ~ and roses** la vie n'est pas toujours rose.

sunshine roof *n* = **sunroof**.

sun: **~specs**○ *npl* = **sunglasses**; **~spot** *n* Astron tache *f* solaire.

sunstroke /ˈsʌnstrəʊk/ *n* insolation *f*; **to get ~** attraper une insolation.

sunsuit /ˈsʌnsuːt, -sjuːt/ *n* barboteuse *f*.

suntan /ˈsʌntæn/ *n* bronzage *m*; **to get a ~** bronzer; **to have a good** ou **nice ~** être bien bronzé.

sun: **~tan cream**, **~ cream** *n* crème *f* solaire; **~tan lotion**, **~ lotion** *n* lotion *f* solaire; **~tanned** *adj* bronzé; **~tan oil**, **~ oil** *n* huile *f* solaire; **~trap** *n* coin *m* ensoleillé; **~ umbrella** *n* parasol *m*; **~up**○ *n* US = **sunrise**; **~ visor** *n* (in car) pare-soleil *m inv*; (for eyes) visière *f*; **~ worship** *n* gen, Relig culte *m* du soleil; **~ worshipper** *n* gen fanatique *mf* du soleil; Relig adorateur/-trice *m/f* du soleil.

sup /sʌp/ **I** *n* petite gorgée *f*.
II *vtr* (*p prés etc* **-pp-**) **1** (drink slowly) boire [qch] à petites gorgées; **2**○ GB dial (drink) boire [*drink*].
III *vi* (*p prés etc* **-pp-**) (have supper) US souper.
■ **sup up**○ GB dial: **~ up [sth]** finir [qch]; **~ up!** finis de boire!

super /ˈsuːpə(r), ˈsjuː-/ **I** *n* **1** US (petrol) super (carburant) *m*; **2** argot des policiers *abrév* = **superintendent**.
II○ *adj, excl* formidable; **it's ~ to...** c'est formidable de...
III super+ (*dans composés*) super-.

superabundance /ˌsuːpərəˈbʌndəns, ˌsjuː-/ *n* surabondance *f*.

superabundant /ˌsuːpərəˈbʌndənt, ˌsjuː-/ *adj* surabondant.

superannuate /ˌsuːpərˈænjʊeɪt, ˌsjuː-/ **I** *vtr* mettre [qn] à la retraite.
II superannuated *pp adj* lit mis à la retraite; fig suranné.

superannuation /ˌsuːpərˌænjʊˈeɪʃn, ˌsjuː-/ **I** *n* (pension) retraite *f* complémentaire.
II *modif* **~ fund** caisse *f* de retraite; **~ plan**, **~ scheme** régime *m* de retraite.

superb /suːˈpɜːb, sjuː-/ *adj* superbe.

superbly /suːˈpɜːblɪ, sjuː-/ *adv* superbement.

Super Bowl *n* US Sport *championnat de football américain*.

supercargo /ˈsuːpəkɑːgəʊ, ˈsjuː-/ *n* subrécargue *m*.

supercharged /ˈsuːpətʃɑːdʒd, ˈsjuː-/ *adj* Tech, Aut surcomprimé.

supercharger /ˈsuːpətʃɑːdʒə(r), ˈsjuː-/ *n* compresseur *m*.

supercilious /ˌsuːpəˈsɪlɪəs, ˌsjuː-/ *adj* dédaigneux/-euse.

superciliously /ˌsuːpəˈsɪlɪəslɪ, ˌsjuː-/ *adv* dédaigneusement.

superciliousness /ˌsuːpəˈsɪlɪəsnɪs, sjuː-/ *n* caractère *m* dédaigneux.

superclass /ˈsuːpəklɑːs, ˈsjuː-, US -klæs/ *n* superclasse *f*.

superconducting /ˌsuːpəkənˈdʌktɪŋ, ˌsjuː-/, **superconductive** /ˌsuːpəkənˈdʌktɪv, ˌsjuː-/ *adj* supraconducteur/-trice.

superconductivity /ˌsuːpəˌkɒndʌkˈtɪvətɪ, ˌsjuː-/ *n* supraconductivité *f*.

super-duper○ /ˌsuːpəˈduːpə(r), ˌsjuː-/ *adj, excl* sensass○.

superego /ˈsuːpəregəʊ, ˈsjuː-, US -iːgəʊ/ *n* sur-moi *m*.

supererogation /ˌsuːpərˌerəˈgeɪʃn, ˌsjuː-/ *n* sout surérogation *f*.

superficial /ˌsuːpəˈfɪʃl, ˌsjuː-/ *adj* (all contexts) superficiel/-ielle.

superficiality /ˌsuːpəˌfɪʃɪˈælətɪ, ˌsjuː-/ *n* gen caractère *m* superficiel; pej manque *m* de profondeur.

superficially /ˌsuːpəˈfɪʃəlɪ, ˌsjuː-/ *adv* superficiellement.

superficies /ˌsuːpəˈfɪʃiːz, ˌsjuː-/ *n* (*pl* **~**) superficie *f*.

superfine /ˈsuːpəfaɪn, ˈsjuː-/ *adj* **1** [*flour, chocolate, needle*] extra-fin; [*quality*] surfin; **~ sugar** US sucre *m* en poudre; **2** [*distinction*] très subtil.

superfluity /ˌsuːpəˈfluːətɪ, ˌsjuː-/ *n* **1** (overabundance) surabondance *f*; **2** = **superfluousness**.

superfluous /suːˈpɜːflʊəs, sjuː-/ *adj* superflu (**to** pour; **to do** de faire); **~ hair(s)** poils *mpl* superflus; **to feel (rather) ~** se sentir de trop.

superfluously /suːˈpɜːflʊəslɪ, sjuː-/ *adv* de manière superflue.

superfluousness /suːˈpɜːflʊəsnɪs, sjuː-/ *n* caractère *m* superflu.

supergiant /ˈsuːpədʒaɪənt, ˈsjuː-/ *n* supergéante *f*.

superglue® /ˈsuːpəgluː, ˈsjuː-/ **I** *n* superglue® *f*.
II *vtr* coller [qch] avec de la super-glue®.

supergrass○ /ˈsuːpəgrɑːs, ˈsjuː-/ *n* indicateur/-trice *m/f* de police.

superhighway /ˈsuːpəhaɪweɪ, ˈsjuː-/ *n* US autoroute *f*.

superhuman /ˌsuːpəˈhjuːmən, ˌsjuː-/ *adj* surhumain.

superimpose /ˌsuːpərɪmˈpəʊz, ˌsjuː-/ *vtr* superposer [*picture, soundtrack*] (**on** à); **~d images** images en surimpression.

superintend /ˌsuːpərɪnˈtend, ˌsjuː-/ *vtr* surveiller [*person, work*]; diriger [*organization, research*].

superintendent /ˌsuːpərɪnˈtendənt, ˌsjuː-/ *n* **1** (supervisor) responsable *mf*; **2** (also **police ~**) cf commissaire *m* de police; **3** US (in apartment house) concierge *mf*; **4** US (also **school ~**) inspecteur/-trice *m/f*.

superior /suːˈpɪərɪə(r), sjuː-, sʊ-/ **I** *n* gen, Relig supérieur/-e *m/f*; **as an actor he has few ~s** il y a peu d'acteurs qui lui soient supérieurs.
II *adj* **1** (better than average) [*intelligence, power, knowledge, person, team*] supérieur (**to** à; **in** en); [*product*] de qualité supérieure; (better than another) meilleur; **their forces attacked in ~ numbers** leurs forces ont attaqué en plus grand nombre; **2** (higher in rank) [*officer*] supérieur; **3** (condescending) [*person, look, smile, air*] condescendant, suffisant; **4** Biol, Bot, Print supérieur.

superior court *n* US *cour subalterne* or *cour d'appel inférieure à la cour d'appel suprême*.

superiority /suːˌpɪərɪˈɒrətɪ, sjuː-, US -ˈɔːr-/ *n* (all contexts) supériorité *f* (**over, to** sur; **in** en).

superiority complex *n* complexe *m* de supériorité.

superjacent /ˌsuːpəˈdʒeɪsnt, ˌsjuː-/ *adj* susjacent.

superlative /suːˈpɜːlətɪv, sjuː-/ **I** *n* Ling superlatif *m*; **in the ~** au superlatif; **a review full of ~s** une critique pleine de superlatifs.
II *adj* [*performance, service*] superbe; [*physical condition*] exceptionnel/-elle; [*match, player*] de toute première classe.

superlatively /suːˈpɜːlətɪvlɪ, sjuː-/ *adv* parfaitement; **a ~ polished performance** une représentation absolument impeccable; **a ~ fit athlete** un athlète au summum de sa forme.

superman /ˈsuːpəmæn, ˈsjuː-/ *n* (*pl* **-men**) surhomme *m*.

supermarket /ˈsuːpəmɑːkɪt, ˈsjuː-/ *n* supermarché *m*.

supernal /suːˈpɜːnl, sjuː-/ *adj* littér céleste, divin.

supernatural /ˌsuːpəˈnætʃrəl, ˌsjuː-/ **I** *n* surnaturel *m*.
II *adj* surnaturel/-elle.

supernaturally /ˌsuːpəˈnætʃrəlɪ, ˌsjuː-/ *adv* de manière surnaturelle.

supernormal /ˌsuːpəˈnɔːml, ˌsjuː-/ *adj* audessus de la normale.

supernova /ˌsuːpəˈnəʊvə, ˌsjuː-/ *n* (*pl* **-vae** ou **-vas**) supernova *f*.

supernumerary /ˌsuːpəˈnjuːmərərɪ, ˌsjuː-, US -ˈnuːmrerɪ/ **I** *n* **1** Admin surnuméraire *mf*; **2** Cin, Theat (extra) figurant/-e *m/f*.
II *adj* (all contexts) surnuméraire.

superorder /ˈsuːpərɔːdə(r), ˈsjuː-/ *n* superordre *m*.

superordinate /ˌsuːpərˈɔːdɪnət, ˌsjuː-/ **I** *n* **1** sout (in rank) supérieur/-e *m/f*; **2** Ling hyperonyme *m*.
II *adj* **1** sout [*person*] supérieur (**to** à); **2** Ling hyperonymique (**to** par rapport à).

superphosphate /ˌsuːpəˈfɒsfeɪt, ˌsjuː-/ *n* superphosphate *m*.

superpose /ˌsuːpəˈpəʊz, ˌsjuː-/ *vtr* superposer (**on** à).

superpower /ˈsuːpəpaʊə(r), ˈsjuː-/ **I** *n* superpuissance *f*.
II *modif* [*talks, summit*] des superpuissances.

supersaturated /ˌsuːpəˈsætʃəreɪtɪd, ˌsjuː-/ *adj* sursaturé.

superscript /ˈsuːpəskrɪpt, ˈsjuː-/ *adj* [*number, letter*] en exposant.

supersede /ˌsuːpəˈsiːd, ˌsjuː-/ *vtr* remplacer [*model, service, arrangement, agreement*]; supplanter [*belief, theory*].

supersensitive /ˌsuːpəˈsensətɪv, ˌsjuː-/ *adj* hypersensible.

supersonic /ˌsuːpəˈsɒnɪk, ˌsjuː-/ *adj* supersonique.

supersonically /ˌsuːpəˈsɒnɪklɪ, ˌsjuː-/ *adv* [*fly, travel*] à une vitesse *f* supersonique.

superstar /ˈsuːpəstɑː(r), ˈsjuː-/ **I** *n* superstar *f*; **a pop/football ~** une superstar de la pop/du football.
II *modif*: **a ~ designer/footballer** GB un

grand de la mode/du football; **to achieve ~ status** devenir une grande vedette.

superstition /ˌsuːpəˈstɪʃn, ˌsjuː-/ *n* superstition *f*.

superstitious /ˌsuːpəˈstɪʃəs, ˌsjuː-/ *adj* superstitieux/-ieuse.

superstitiously /ˌsuːpəˈstɪʃəslɪ, ˌsjuː-/ *adv* [*believe, repeat*] par superstition.

superstore /ˈsuːpəstɔː(r), ˈsjuː-/ *n* **1** (large supermarket) hypermarché *m*; **2** (specialist shop) grande surface *f*; **a furniture/electrical ~** une grande surface de l'ameublement/l'électroménager.

superstratum /ˈsuːpəstrɑːtəm, ˈsjuː-/ *n* (*pl* **-ta**) **1** Geol couche *f* supérieure; **2** Ling superstrat *m*.

superstructure /ˈsuːpəstrʌktʃə(r), ˈsjuː-/ *n* Constr, Naut superstructure *f*.

supertanker /ˈsuːpətæŋkə(r), ˈsjuː-/ *n* Naut supertanker *m*.

supertax /ˈsuːpətæks, ˈsjuː-/ *n* Fin *impôt supplémentaire sur les très hauts revenus*.

supervene /ˌsuːpəˈviːn, ˌsjuː-/ *vi* sout [*change, election, decision, illness*] survenir; [*cut, reduction*] intervenir.

supervention /ˌsuːpəˈvenʃn, ˌsjuː-/ *n* (of illness) apparition *f*; (of disaster) arrivée *f*; (of event) survenue *f* sout.

supervise /ˈsuːpəvaɪz, ˈsjuː-/ **I** *vtr* **1** (watch over) superviser [*activity, area, staff, student, work*]; surveiller [*child, patient*]; diriger [*thesis*]; **2** (control) diriger [*department, investigation, project*].
II *vi* [*supervisor*] superviser; [*doctor, parent*] surveiller; [*manager*] diriger.
III supervised *pp adj* [*facility, playground*] surveillé.

supervision /ˌsuːpəˈvɪʒn, ˌsjuː-/ *n* **1** (of staff, work) supervision *f*; **to work under sb's ~** travailler sous la supervision de qn; **with/without the ~ of** sous/sans la supervision de qn; **she is responsible for the ~ of two students** Univ elle dirige les recherches de deux étudiants; **2** (of child, patient, prisoner) surveillance *f*; **to be under 24 hour ~** être sous surveillance 24 heures sur 24.

supervisor /ˈsuːpəvaɪzə(r), ˈsjuː-/ ▶ **1692** *n* **1** Admin, Comm responsable *m*; **canteen ~** gérant/-e *m/f* de cantine; **factory ~** ≈ contremaître *m*; **shop ~** chef *m* de rayon; **2** Civ Eng, Constr contremaître *m*; **site ~** chef *m* de chantier; **3** GB Univ (for thesis) directeur/-trice *m/f* de thèse; **4** US Sch directeur/-trice *m/f* d'études.

supervisory /ˈsuːpəvaɪzərɪ, ˈsjuː-, US ˌsuːpəˈvaɪzərɪ/ *adj* [*body, board, duty, role, work*] de supervision; **she's a ~ officer** elle fait partie du personnel d'encadrement; **the work is mainly ~** c'est essentiellement un travail de supervision; **in a ~ capacity** en qualité de superviseur.

superwoman /ˈsuːpəwʊmən, ˈsjuː-/ *n* (*pl* **-women**) superwoman© *f*.

supine /ˈsuːpaɪn, ˈsjuː-/ **I** *n* Ling supin *m*.
II *adj* **1** lit [*person*] étendu sur le dos; **to be ~** être allongé sur le dos; **2** [*complacency, submission*] mou/molle.
III *adv* [*lie*] sur le dos.

supper /ˈsʌpə(r)/ *n* **1** (evening meal) dîner *m*; **we had beef for ~** nous avons eu du bœuf au dîner; **what's for ~?** qu'est-ce qu'on mange ce soir?; **to have** ou **eat ~** dîner; **2** (late snack) collation *f* (*du soir*); **do you fancy a bite of ~** tu veux manger un petit quelque chose avant de te coucher?; **3** (after a show) souper *m*; **to have** ou **eat ~** souper; **4** Relig **the Last Supper** la Cène *f*.
IDIOMS **to sing for one's ~** se donner du mal pour mériter des avantages; **you'll have to sing for your ~** on n'a rien pour rien.

supper: **~ club** *n* US restaurant *m* (*souvent avec bar*); **~ licence** *n* GB Jur *autorisation de vendre de l'alcool après l'heure légale avec un repas*; **~ time** *n* heure *f* du dîner.

supplant /səˈplɑːnt/ *vtr* évincer [*lover, rival*]; supplanter [*doctrine, method, person, product, system, trend*].

supple /ˈsʌpl/ *adj* [*body, leather, person*] souple; [*mind*] délié; **the ~ grace of the dancer** la souplesse gracieuse de la danseuse.

supplement **I** /ˈsʌplɪmənt/ *n* **1** (to diet, income) complément *m* (**to** à); **vitamin ~** complément *m* en vitamines; **2** Tourism supplément *m* (**of** de); **a first class/single room ~** un supplément de première classe/pour chambre à un lit; **balcony available for** ou **at a ~** balcon avec supplément; **flight ~** supplément *m* de vol; **3** Journ supplément *m*; **business/job ~** supplément des affaires/de l'emploi.
II *vtr* augmenter [*income, staff*] (**with** de); compléter [*diet, knowledge, resources, service, training*] (**with** de).

supplementary /ˌsʌplɪˈmentrɪ, US -terɪ/ **I** *n* GB Pol question *f* annexe.
II *adj* [*heating, income, pension*] d'appoint; [*charge, payment*] additionnel/-elle; [*angle, comment, evidence, question, staff, vitamins*] supplémentaire.

supplementary benefit *n* GB Soc Admin *autrefois allocation versée aux personnes n'ayant pas droit au chômage*.

suppleness /ˈsʌplnɪs/ *n* (all contexts) souplesse *f*; **to improve the ~ of** assouplir [*joint, leather*].

suppletion /səˈpliːʃn/ *n* Ling suppléance *f*.

suppletive /səˈpliːtɪv/ *adj* Ling supplétif/-ive.

supplicant /ˈsʌplɪkənt/, **suppliant** /ˈsʌplɪənt/ sout **I** *n* suppliant/-e *m/f*.
II *adj* [*attitude*] de supplication; [*person*] suppliant.

supplicate /ˈsʌplɪkeɪt/ sout **I** *vtr* supplier; **to ~ sb for sth** implorer qch de qn.
II *vi* implorer; **to ~ for pardon** implorer le pardon.

supplication /ˌsʌplɪˈkeɪʃn/ *n* supplication *f*; **in ~** en signe de supplication.

supplier /səˈplaɪə(r)/ *n* (all contexts) fournisseur *m* (**of, to** de).

supply /səˈplaɪ/ **I** *n* **1** (stock) réserves *fpl*; **a plentiful ~ of bullets/money** des réserves abondantes de balles/d'argent; **in short/plentiful ~** difficile/facile à obtenir or se procurer; **a plentiful ~ of workers** un grand nombre de travailleurs; **to get in a ~ of sth** s'approvisionner en qch; **win a year's ~ of wine!** gagnez du vin pour toute une année!; **2** (source) (of fuel, gas, water, blood, oxygen) alimentation *f* (**of** en); (of food) approvisionnement *m*; **the ~ has been cut off** l'alimentation a été coupée; **the ~ of oxygen to the tissues** l'alimentation des tissus en oxygène; **the blood ~ to the legs/the heart** le sang qui alimente les jambes/le cœur; **the blood ~ to the baby** le sang transfusé au bébé; **3** (action of providing) fourniture *f*, approvisionnement *m* (**to** à); **to control the ~ of alcoholic drinks** contrôler la fourniture de boissons alcoolisées; **4** GB Sch = **supply teacher**.
II supplies *npl* **1** (food, equipment) réserves *fpl*; **food supplies** ravitaillement *m*; **to cut off sb's supplies** couper les vivres à qn; **2** (for office, household) (machines, electrical goods) matériel *m*; (stationery, small items) fournitures *fpl*; **3** GB Pol, Admin crédits *mpl*.
III *modif* [*ship, train, truck*] ravitailleur/-euse; [*problem, route*] (for industry) d'approvisionnement; (for population) de ravitaillement; **~ company** fournisseur *m*.
IV *vtr* **1** (provide) fournir [*goods, arms, fuel, water, oxygen, calories, drugs, word, phrase, information, recipe*] (**to, for** à); apporter [*love, companionship, affection*] (**to** à); **to ~ arms/details to sb, to ~ sb with arms/details** fournir des armes/des détails à qn; **to ~ a name to the police, to ~ the police with a name** donner un nom à la police; **to keep sb supplied with** approvisionner régulièrement qn en [*parts, equipment*]; **to keep a machine supplied with fuel** assurer l'alimentation d'un appareil en combustible; **to keep sb supplied with information/gossip** tenir qn au courant de ce qui se passe/des potins; **2** (provide food, fuel for) ravitailler [*area, town*] (**with** en); **3** (provide raw materials for) approvisionner [*factory, company*] (**with** en); **4** (satisfy, fulfil) subvenir à [*needs, wants, requirements*]; répondre à [*demand, need*].

supply: **~ and demand** *n* l'offre *f* et la demande; **~ line** *n* voie *f* de ravitaillement; **~-side economics** *n* (+ *v sg*) économie *f* de l'offre; **~ teacher** *n* GB suppléant/-e *m/f*, remplaçant/-e *m/f*.

support /səˈpɔːt/ **I** *n* **1** (moral, financial, political) soutien *m* (**for sth** en faveur de qch; **for sb** à qn); **financial/state ~** soutien financier/de l'État; **there is considerable public ~ for the strikers** les grévistes bénéficient du soutien d'une grande partie de la population; **there is little public ~ for this measure** il y a peu de gens favorables à cette mesure; **socialist/Green party ~** soutien en faveur des socialistes/verts; **~ for the party is increasing** le parti a de plus en plus de partisans; **air/land/sea ~** Mil appui *m* aérien/terrestre/maritime; **to give sb/sth (one's) ~** apporter son soutien à qn/qch; **to get ~ from sb/sth** obtenir le soutien de qn/qch; **to have the ~ of sb/sth** avoir le soutien de qn/qch; **in ~ of sb/sth** [*campaign, intervene*] en faveur de qn/qch; **he spoke in ~ of the motion** il a parlé en faveur de la motion; **the workers went on strike in ~ of their demands** les ouvriers se sont mis en grève pour soutenir leurs revendications; **the students demonstrated in ~ of the strikers** les étudiants ont manifesté pour montrer leur solidarité avec les grévistes; **in ~ of this point of view/theory** pour appuyer ce point de vue/cette théorie; **a collection in ~ of war victims** une collecte au profit des victimes de guerre; **with ~ from sb** avec l'appui or le soutien de qn; **to win** ou **gain ~ from sb** trouver du soutien auprès de qn; **they need ~ to raise enough money** ils ont besoin d'aide pour rassembler des fonds suffisants; **the theatre**[GB] **closed for lack of ~** le théâtre a fermé faute de public; **strong ~** fig ferme soutien; **means of ~** (financial) moyens *mpl* de subsistance; **2** (physical, for weight) gen, Constr support *m*; Med (for limb) appareil *m* de maintien; **athletic ~** coquille *f*; **neck ~** Med minerve *f*; **he used his stick as a ~** il s'appuyait sur sa canne; **he had to lean on a chair for ~** il a dû s'appuyer sur une chaise; **3** (person) soutien *m* (**to** de); **Paul was a great ~ when she died** Paul a été (d')un soutien précieux quand elle est morte; **4** (singer etc not topping the bill) (individual) artiste *mf* qui assure la première partie; (band) groupe *m* de la première partie.
II *vtr* **1** (provide moral, financial backing) soutenir [*person, cause, campaign, party, reform, team, venture, price, currency*]; donner à [*charity*]; **to ~ sb/sth by doing** aider or soutenir qn/qch en faisant; **the museum is ~ed by public funds** le musée est subventionné par l'État; **2** (physically) supporter [*weight*]; soutenir [*person*]; **3** (validate) confirmer, corroborer fml [*argument, case, claim, story, theory*]; **4** (maintain) [*breadwinner*] faire vivre, avoir [qn] à charge [*family*]; [*land, farm*] faire vivre [*inhabitants*]; [*charity*] aider [*underprivileged*]; **he has a wife and children to ~** il a une femme et des enfants à charge; **she ~ed her son through college** elle a payé les études de son fils; **5** (put up with) sout endurer [*adverse conditions, bad behaviour*]; **6** Comput prendre en charge.
III *v refl* **to ~ oneself** subvenir à ses propres besoins.

supportable /səˈpɔːtəbl/ *adj* supportable.

support: **~ act** *n* ▶ **support** I 4; **~ area** *n* Mil zone *f* de soutien logistique; **~ band** *n* Mus groupe *m* de la première partie.

supporter /səˈpɔːtə(r)/ *n* gen partisan *m*; Pol sympathisant/-e *m/f*; Sport supporter *m*; **football ~** supporter de foot○.

support: **~ group** *n* Soc Admin groupe *m* de soutien; **~ hose** = **support stockings**.

supporting /səˈpɔːtɪŋ/ *adj* **1** Cin, Theat [*actor, role*] de second plan also fig; **'best ~ actor/actress'** 'meilleur second rôle masculin/féminin'; **~ cast** les seconds rôles; **'with full ~ cast'** Cin (in publicity) 'avec de prestigieux seconds rôles'; **~ programme** Cin avant-programme *m*; **2** Constr [*wall, beam*] de soutènement; **3 ~ evidence** Jur preuves *fpl* à l'appui; **~ document** document *m* annexe.

supportive /səˈpɔːtɪv/ *adj* [*person, organization*] d'un grand secours; [*role, network*] de soutien.

support: **~ personnel** *n* Mil (personnel *m* de) soutien *m* logistique; **~ scheme** *n* GB Soc Admin système *m* de soutien mutuel; **~ services** *n* services *mpl* d'assistance technique; **~ slot** *n* Mus avant-programme *m*; **~ staff** *n* personnel *m* d'assistance technique; **~ stockings** *npl* bas *mpl* de maintien or de contention spec; **~ system** *n* gen réseau *m* de soutien; Comput programme *m* de soutien; **~ team** *n* équipe *f* de renfort; **~ tights** *npl* collant *m* anti-fatigue or de contention spec; **~ troops** *npl* renforts *mpl*; **~ vessel** *n* bâtiment *m* de soutien.

suppose /səˈpəʊz/ **I** *vtr* **1** (think) **to ~ (that)** penser or croire que; **I ~ (that) she knows** je pense qu'elle est au courant; **I don't ~ (that) she knows** je ne pense pas qu'elle soit au courant; **do you ~ (that) he's guilty?** est-ce que tu crois qu'il est coupable? **to ~ sb to be sth** croire qn qch; **I ~d him to be a friend** je le croyais un ami; **2** (assume) supposer [*existence, possibility*]; **to ~ (that)** supposer que; **I ~ (that) you've checked** je suppose que tu as vérifié; **let us ~ that it's true** supposons que ce soit vrai; **I ~ it's too late now?** je suppose qu'il est trop tard maintenant?; **it is generally ~d that** tout le monde croit que; **I ~ so/not** je suppose que oui/non; **even supposing he's there** même en supposant qu'il soit là; **3** (admit) **to ~ (that)** supposer que; **I ~ you're right** je suppose que tu as raison; **I ~ that if I'm honest...** si je veux être honnête je dois avouer que...; **4** (imagine) **when do you ~ (that) he'll arrive?** quand penses-tu qu'il arrivera? **who do you ~ I saw yesterday?** devine un peu qui j'ai vu hier; **~ (that) it's true, what will you do?** imagine que ça soit vrai, qu'est-ce que tu feras?; **~ (that) he doesn't come?** et s'il ne vient pas?; **I don't ~ you can do it?** je suppose que tu ne peux pas le faire?; **5** (making a suggestion) **~ we go to a restaurant?** et si on allait au restaurant? **~ we take the car?** et si on prenait la voiture?

II supposed *pp adj* **1** (putative) [*father, owner, witness*] présumé (*before n*), putatif/-ive; [*advantage, benefit*] prétendu (*before n*); **2** (expected, required) **to be ~d to do** être censé faire; **to be ~d to be at work** être censé être au travail; **there was ~d to be a room for us** nous étions censés avoir une chambre; **you're not ~d to do** tu n'es pas censé faire; **3** (alleged) **this machine is ~d to do** il paraît que cette machine fait; **it's ~d to be a good hotel** il paraît que c'est un bon hôtel.

supposedly /səˈpəʊzɪdlɪ/ *adv* **to be ~ rich/intelligent** être censé être riche/intelligent; **the ~ developed nations** les pays soi-disant développés; **a ~ wealthy widow** une veuve réputée riche; **~ she's very shy** il paraît qu'elle est très timide.

supposing /səˈpəʊzɪŋ/ *conj* **~ (that) he says no?** et s'il dit non?; **~ your income is X, you pay Y** supposons que ton revenu soit de X, tu paieras Y.

supposition /ˌsʌpəˈzɪʃn/ *n* **1** (guess, guesswork) supposition *f*; **2** (assumption) hypothèse *f*; **to be based on the ~ that sth is available** reposer sur l'hypothèse de la disponibilité de qch.

suppositious /ˌsʌpəˈzɪʃəs/ *adj* (hypothetical) hypothétique; (false) fallacieux/-ieuse.

suppository /səˈpɒzɪtrɪ, US -tɔːrɪ/ *n* suppositoire *m*.

suppress /səˈpres/ *vtr* **1** (prevent) réprimer [*smile, urge, doubt*]; étouffer [*yawn*]; contenir [*anger, excitement*]; refouler [*sexuality*]; supprimer [*report, evidence, information, fact*]; interdire [*newspaper*]; abolir [*party, group*]; réprimer [*opposition, riot, rebellion*]; étouffer [*criticism, scandal*]; dissimuler [*truth*]; mettre fin à [*activity*]; retenir [*tears*]; **to ~ a cough/sneeze** se retenir de tousser/d'éternuer; **2** (reduce, weaken) empêcher [*growth*]; affaiblir [*immune system*]; tuer [*weeds*]; **3** Med inhiber [*symptom, reaction*]; **4** Radio, Electron antiparasiter.

suppressant /səˈpresənt/ *n* (drug etc) inhibiteur *m*.

suppression /səˈpreʃn/ *n* **1** (of party) abolition *f*; (of truth) dissimulation *f*; (of newspaper) interdiction *f*; (of activity, demonstration, evidence, information, report, facts) suppression *f*; (of revolt) répression *f*; (of scandal) étouffement *m*; Psych (of feeling) (deliberate) répression *f*; (involuntary) refoulement *m*; **2** (retardation) (of growth, development) retard *m*; **3** Radio, Electron antiparasitage *m*.

suppressive /səˈpresɪv/ *adj* répressif/-ive.

suppressor /səˈpresə(r)/ *n* Radio, Electron antiparasite *m*.

suppurate /ˈsʌpjʊreɪt/ *vi* suppurer.

suppuration /ˌsʌpjʊˈreɪʃn/ *n* suppuration *f*.

supranational /ˌsuːprəˈnæʃənl/ *adj* supranational.

suprarenal /ˌsuːprəˈriːnl/ *adj* surrénal.

suprasegmental /ˌsuːprəsegˈmentl/ *adj* suprasegmental.

supremacist /suːˈpreməsɪst, sjuː-/ *n* Pol *personne qui croit à la supériorité d'un groupe ou d'une race*.

supremacy /suːˈpreməsɪ, sjuː-/ *n* **1** (power) suprématie *f*; **2** (greater ability) supériorité *f*.

supreme /suːˈpriːm, sjuː-/ *adj* [*ruler, power, achievement, courage*] suprême; [*importance*] capital; [*stupidity, arrogance*] extrême; **to reign ~** fig régner; **to make the ~ sacrifice** mourir pour la patrie.

supreme: **Supreme Being** *n* Relig Être *m* suprême; **Supreme Commander** *n* Mil Commandant *m* en chef; **Supreme Court** *n* US, Can, Jur Cour *f* suprême.

supremely /suːˈpriːmlɪ, sjuː-/ *adv* [*difficult*] extrêmement; [*happy, important*] suprêmement; [*confident*] absolument.

Supreme Soviet *n* Pol Hist Soviet *m* suprême.

supremo /suːˈpriːməʊ, sjuː-/ *n* (*pl* **-mos**) leader *m*.

Supt *abrév écrite* = **Superintendent**.

sura /ˈsʊərə/ *n* surate *f*.

surcharge /ˈsɜːtʃɑːdʒ/ **I** *n* **1** gen supplément *m*; **2** Elec, Post surcharge *f*.

II *vtr* faire payer un supplément à [*person*].

surd /sɜːd/ **I** *n* **1** Math nombre *m* irrationnel; **2** Ling (consonne *f*) sourde *f*.

II *adj* **1** Math irrationnel/-elle; **2** Ling sourd.

sure /ʃɔː(r), US ʃʊər/ **I** *adj* **1** (certain) sûr **(about, of de)**; **I feel ~ that...** je suis sûr que...; **I'm quite ~ (that) I'm right** je suis tout à fait sûr que j'ai raison or d'avoir raison; **'are you ~?'—'yes, I'm ~'** 'en es-tu sûr?'—'oui, j'en suis sûr'; **I'm not ~ when he's coming/how old he is** je ne sais pas trop quand il viendra/quel âge il a; **I'm not ~ if** ou **whether he's coming or not** je ne sais pas trop s'il va venir ou pas; **I'm not ~ that he'll be able to do it** je ne suis pas sûr qu'il puisse le faire; **(are you) ~ you're all right?** t'es sûr que ça va?; **to be ~ of one's facts** être sûr de son fait; **you can be ~ of a warm welcome/of succeeding** vous pouvez être sûr d'être bien accueilli/de réussir; **she'll be on time, of that you can be ~** elle sera à l'heure, tu peux en être sûr; **one thing you can be ~ of...** une chose est sûre...; **I couldn't be ~ I had locked the door** je n'étais pas vraiment sûr d'avoir fermé la porte; **'did you lock it?'—'I'm not ~ I did'** 'tu l'as fermé?'—'je n'en suis pas sûr'; **I'm ~ I don't know, I don't know I'm ~** je n'en ai pas la moindre idée; **we can never be ~** on n'est jamais sûr de rien; **I wouldn't be so ~ about that!** ça m'étonnerait!; **I won't invite them again, and that's for ~**○! une chose est sûre, je ne les inviterai plus!; **we 'll be there next week for ~!** on y sera la semaine prochaine sans faute!; **we can't say for ~** nous n'en sommes pas vraiment sûrs; **nobody knows for ~** personne ne (le) sait au juste; **there' s only one way of finding out for ~** il n'y a qu'une seule façon de s'en assurer or d'en avoir la certitude; **he is, to be ~, a very charming man** c'est certes un homme très charmant; **to make ~ that** (ascertain) s'assurer que (+ *indic*); (ensure) faire en sorte que (+ *subj*); **make ~ all goes well** fais en sorte que tout se passe bien; **make ~ you phone me** n'oublie pas de m'appeler; **be** ou **make ~ to tell him that...** surtout n'oublie pas de lui dire que...; **she made ~ to lock the door behind her** elle a fait bien attention de fermer la porte derrière elle; **in the ~ and certain knowledge of/that** avec la profonde conviction de/que; **he's a ~ favourite (to win)** Sport c'est le grand favori; **2** (bound) **he's ~ to fail** il va sûrement échouer; **she' s ~ to be there** elle y sera sûrement; **if I am in the shower, the phone is ~ to ring** si je suis sous la douche, le téléphone va sûrement se mettre à sonner; **3** (confident) sûr; **to be/feel ~ of oneself** être/se sentir sûr de soi; **I never feel quite ~ of her** je me méfie toujours un peu d'elle; **4** (reliable) [*friend*] sûr; [*method, remedy*] infaillible; **the ~st route to success** le moyen le plus sûr de réussir; **the ~st way to do** le moyen le plus efficace de faire; **she was chain -smoking, a ~ sign of agitation** elle fumait sans arrêt, ce qui montrait bien qu'elle était agitée; **to have a ~ eye for detail/colour** avoir l'œil pour les détails/la couleur; **5** (steady) [*hand, footing*] sûr; **with a ~ hand** d'une main sûre; **to have a ~ aim** bien viser.

II *adv* **1**○ (yes) bien sûr; **'you're coming?'—'~!'** 'tu viens?'—'bien sûr!'; **2**○ (certainly) **it ~ is cold** ça oui, il fait froid; **'is it cold?'—'it ~ is!'** 'fait-il froid?'—'ça oui○!'; **that ~ smells good**○! US qu'est-ce que ça sent bon○!; **3 ~ enough** effectivement; **I said he'd be late and ~ enough he was!** j'ai dit qu'il serait en retard et effectivement il l'était!

IDIOMS **as ~ as eggs is eggs**○, **as ~ as fate, as ~ as I'm standing here** aussi sûr que deux et deux font quatre; **~ thing**○! US d'accord!; **to be ~**†! certes!

sure: **~-fire**○ *adj* [*success, method*] garanti; **~-footed** *adj* agile; **~-footedness** *n* agilité *f*; **~-handed** *adj* habile.

surely /ˈʃɔːlɪ, US ˈʃʊərlɪ/ *adv* **1** (expressing certainty) sûrement, certainement; **I am ~ correct** j'ai sûrement raison; **~ we've met before?** nous nous sommes déjà rencontrés, n'est-ce pas?, il me semble que nous nous sommes déjà rencontrés?; **you noted his phone number, ~?** tu as noté son numéro de téléphone, j'imagine?; **~ you can understand that?** c'est quelque chose que tu peux comprendre, n'est-ce-pas?; **2** (expressing surprise) tout de même, quand même; **you're ~ not going to eat that!** tu ne vas tout de même pas manger ça!; **that ~ can't be right!** ça ne peut tout de même pas être vrai!; **~ you don't think that's true!** tu ne penses quand même pas que c'est vrai!; **~ not!** pas possible!; **~ to God** ou **good-**

ness you've written that letter by now! ne me dis pas que tu n'as pas encore écrit cette lettre!; **3** (expressing disagreement) **'it was in 1991'—'1992, ~'** 'c'était en 1991'—'1992, tu veux dire'; **4** (yes) bien sûr; **'will you meet me?'—'~'** 'tu viendras me chercher?'—'bien sûr'.

sureness /'ʃɔːnɪs, US 'ʃʊərnɪs/ *n* (of technique) précision *f*; (of intent) certitude *f*.

surety /'ʃɔːrətɪ, US 'ʃʊərtɪ/ *n* Fin Jur **1** (money) dépôt *m* de garantie, caution *f*; **2** (guarantor) garant/-e *m/f*; **to stand ~ for sb** se porter garant de qn.

surf /sɜːf/ **I** *n* **1** (waves) vagues *fpl* (déferlantes); **2** (foam) écume *f*.
II *vtr* Comput surfer [*Internet*].
III *vi* **1** Sport faire du surf; **2** Comput surfer l'Internet.

surface /'sɜːfɪs/ **I** *n* **1** lit (of water, land, object) surface *f*; **on** ou **at the ~** (of liquid) à la surface; **on the ~** (of solid) sur la surface; **to work at the ~** Mining travailler en surface or au jour; **2** fig apparence *f*; **to skim the ~ of** effleurer [*issue*]; **on the ~ it was a simple problem** en apparence le problème était simple; **beneath the ~ he's very shy** au fond il est très timide; **violence is never far below the ~** la violence est toujours latente; **to come** ou **rise to the ~** [*tensions, feelings*] se manifester; **3** Math (of solid, cube) côté *m*, face *f*; **4** (worktop) plan *m* de travail.
II *modif* **1** lit [*vessel, fleet, transport*] de surface; [*work, worker*] en surface, au jour; [*wound*] superficiel/-ielle; **~ measurements** superficie *f*; **2** fig [*problem, resemblance*] superficiel/-ielle; **3** Ling [*structure, grammar, analysis*] de surface.
III *vtr* faire le revêtement de [*road, ground*]; **to ~ sth with** revêtir qch de.
IV *vi* **1** lit [*object, animal, person*] remonter à la surface; [*submarine*] faire surface; **2** fig (come to surface) [*tension, anxiety, racism*] se manifester; [*problem, evidence, scandal*] apparaître; **3** (reappear) [*person*] (after absence) refaire surface○, réapparaître; (from bed) se lever; [*object*] réapparaître.

surface: **~ air missile, SAM** *n* missile *m* S.A.; **~ area** *n* superficie *f*, surface *f*; **~ mail** *n* courrier *m* par voie de surface; **~ noise** *n* bruit *m* de surface; **~ tension** *n* tension *f* superficielle; **~-to-air** *adj* sol-air; **~-to-surface** *adj* sol-sol.

surfactant /sɜː'fæktənt/ *n* tensioactif *m*.

surf: **~board** *n* planche *f* de surf; **~boarder** *n* surfeur/-euse *m/f*; **~boarding ▶ 1282** *n* surf *m*; **~boat** *n* surf-boat *m*; **~casting ▶ 1282** *n* pêche *f* au lancer sur une plage.

surfeit /'sɜːfɪt/ **I** *n* excès *m* (**of** de).
II *vtr* **to be ~ed with** être repu de [*food, pleasure*].
III *v refl* **to ~ oneself with** faire des excès de [*food, wine*]; se repaître de [*pleasure*].

surfer /'sɜːfə(r)/ *n* **1** Sport surfeur/-euse *m/f*; **2** Comput internaute *mf*.

surfing /'sɜːfɪŋ/ **▶ 1282** *n* surf *m*; **to go ~** aller faire du surf.

surf: **~ride** *vi* faire du surf; **~rider** *n* surfeur/-euse *m/f*; **~riding ▶ 1282** *n* surf *m*.

surge /sɜːdʒ/ **I** *n* **1** (rush) (of water) brusque montée *f*; (of blood, energy, adrenalin) montée *f* (**of** de); fig (of anger, desire) accès *m* (**of** de); (of optimism, enthusiasm) élan *m* (**of** de); (of pity, relief, happiness, resentment) sentiment *m* (**of** de); **2** Fin, Pol (increase) (in prices, unemployment, inflation, immigration) hausse *f* (**in** de); (in borrowing, demand, imports) accroissement *m* (**in** de); **3** Elec (also **power ~**) surtension *f*; **4** (increase in speed) Sport remontée *f*.
II *vi* **1** (rise) [*water, waves*] déferler; [*blood, energy*] monter; fig [*emotion*] monter (**in sb** en qn); **the crowd ~d into the stadium/theatre** la foule s'est engouffrée dans le stade/le théâtre; **the crowd ~d (out) onto the streets/the square** la foule a déferlé dans les rues/sur la place; **to ~ forward** [*crowd*] avancer en masse; [*car*] démarrer en trombe○; **2** Fin (increase) [*prices, profits, shares, demand*] monter en flèche; **3** Sport (increase speed) [*runner, swimmer, team*] s'élancer; **to ~ through (to win)** remonter (pour gagner).
III surging *pres p adj* Fin [*market, rates, prices*] en hausse.

surgeon /'sɜːdʒən/ **▶ 1692** *n* chirurgien *m*.

surgeon general *n* **1 ▶ 1612** Med Mil médecin-chef *m*; **2** US ≈ ministre *m* de la Santé.

surgery /'sɜːdʒərɪ/ *n* **1** Med (operations) chirurgie *f*; **to have ~, to undergo ~** se faire opérer; **to need ~** avoir besoin d'une opération; **2** GB Med (building) cabinet *m*; **doctor's/dentist's ~** cabinet médical/dentaire; **3** GB (consultation time) (of doctor) (heures *fpl* de) consultation *f*; (of MP) permanence *f*; **to take ~** assurer la consultation; **4** US (operating room) salle *f* d'opération.

surgical /'sɜːdʒɪkl/ *adj* [*mask, instrument, treatment*] chirurgical; [*boot, stocking*] orthopédique; **with ~ precision** fig avec une précision scientifique.

surgical: **~ appliance** *n* appareil *m* orthopédique; **~ clamp** *n* clamp *m*; **~ dressing** *n* pansement *m*.

surgically /'sɜːdʒɪklɪ/ *adv* [*treat*] par opération; **to remove sth ~** opérer qch.

surgical: **~ shock** *n* Med choc *m* opératoire; **~ spirit** *n* alcool *m* (à 90 degrés); **~ strike** *n* Mil frappe *f* chirurgicale; **~ ward** *n* service *m* de chirurgie.

Surinam /ˌsʊərɪ'næm/ **▶ 1131** *pr n* Suriname *m*.

Surinamese /ˌsʊərɪnə'miːz/ **▶ 1486** **I** *n* Surinamais/-e *m/f*.
II *adj* surinamais.

surliness /'sɜːlɪnɪs/ *n* caractère *m* revêche.

surly /'sɜːlɪ/ *adj* revêche.

surmise /sə'maɪz/ sout **I** *n* conjecture *f*.
II *vtr* conjecturer (**that** que).

surmount /sə'maʊnt/ *vtr* **1** lit (be on top of) surmonter; **to be ~ed by** être surmonté de [*statue, tower*]; **2** fig (overcome) surmonter [*difficulty, challenge*]; résoudre [*problem*].

surmountable /sə'maʊntəbl/ *adj* surmontable.

surname /'sɜːneɪm/ *n* nom *m* de famille.

surpass /sə'pɑːs, US -pæs/ **I** *vtr* (be better or greater than) surpasser; (go beyond) dépasser [*expectations*]; **to ~ sb/sth in sth** surpasser qn/qch en qch; **to ~ sth in size/height** être plus grand/haut que qch; **to ~ sth/sb in numbers** être plus nombreux que qch/qn.
II *v refl* **to ~ oneself** se surpasser.

surpassing /sə'pɑːsɪŋ, US -'pæs-/ *adj* sout exceptionnel/-elle.

surplice /'sɜːplɪs/ *n* surplis *m*.

surplus /'sɜːpləs/ **I** *n* (*pl* **~es**) gen surplus *m*; Econ, Comm excédent *m*; **to be in ~** être excédentaire; **oil/food ~** excédent de pétrole/de produits agricoles; **trade/budget ~** excédent commercial/budgétaire.
II *adj* (*tjrs épith*) gen [*milk, bread, clothes*] en trop (*after n*); **~ to requirements** de trop; Econ, Comm [*money, food, labour*] excédentaire.

surplus value *n* **1** Comm valeur *f* additionnelle or de boni; **2** (in Marxism) plus-value *f*.

surprise /sə'praɪz/ **I** *n* **1** (unexpected event) surprise *f*; **there are more ~s in store** ou **to come** il y a d'autres surprises en réserve; **the result came as** ou **was no ~** le résultat n'a surpris personne; **that's a bit of a ~** c'est surprenant; **it comes as** ou **is no ~ that** ce n'est pas surprenant que (+ *subj*); **it came as something of a ~ that people were so pleased** c'était surprenant de voir combien les gens étaient contents; **it would come as no ~ if** ce ne serait pas surprenant que (+ *subj*) or si (+ *indic*); **it comes as** ou **is a ~ to hear/to see that** c'est une surprise d'apprendre/de voir que; **it came as no ~ to us to hear that** nous n'avons pas été surpris d'apprendre que; **it came as** ou **was a complete ~ to me** cela m'a vraiment étonné; **to spring a ~ on sb** préparer une surprise à qn; **~, ~!** ô surprise!; **is he in for a ~!** ça va être la surprise!; **and, ~, ~, they agreed** iron et, surprise, ils étaient d'accord; **2** (experience, gift) surprise *f*; **what a nice ~!** quelle bonne surprise!; **she wants it to be a ~** elle veut que ce soit une surprise; **3** (astonishment) surprise *f*, étonnement *m*; **there was some ~ at the news** la nouvelle a provoqué une certaine surprise; **to express ~ at sth** se déclarer surpris par qch; **to express ~ that** se déclarer surpris que (+ *subj*); **to my (great) ~** à ma (grande) surprise; **much to my ~** à ma grande surprise; **with ~** avec étonnement; **'are you sure?' she said in ~** 'en es-tu sûr?' dit-elle, surprise; **4** Mil, Pol, gen (as tactic) surprise *f*; **the element of ~** l'effet de surprise; **to take sb by ~** gen prendre qn au dépourvu; Mil surprendre qn.
II *modif* **1** (unexpected) [*announcement, closure, result*] inattendu; [*visit, guest, holiday, party*] surprise (*after n*); [*attack, invasion*] surprise (*after n*); **~ tactics** lit, fig tactique *f* fondée sur l'effet de la surprise; **to pay sb a ~ visit** aller voir qn sans le prévenir.

Surface area measurements

Note that French has a comma where English has a decimal point.

1 sq in = 6,45 cm² (*centimètres carrés*)*		1 acre = 40,47 ares
1 sq ft = 929,03 cm²		= 0,4 ha (*hectares*)
1 sq yd = 0,84 m² (*mètres carrés*)		1 sq ml = 2,59 km² (*kilomètres carrés*)

* *There are three ways of saying* 6,45 cm², *and other measurements like it:*
six virgule quarante-cinq centimètres carrés,
or (*less formally*) six centimètres carrés virgule quarante-cinq,
or six centimètres carrés quarante-cinq.
For more details on how to say numbers, **▶ 1505**.

how big is your garden?	= quelle est la superficie de votre jardin?
what's its area?	= il a quelle superficie?
it's 200 square metres	= il mesure 200 mètres carrés
its surface area is 200 square metres	= il mesure 200 mètres carrés de superficie
it's 20 metres by 10 metres	= il mesure 20 mètres sur 10 mètres *or* il fait 20 mètres sur 10 mètres
sold by the square metre	= vendu au mètre carré
there are 10,000 square centimetres in a square metre	= il y a 10 000 centimètres carrés dans un mètre carré
10,000 square centimetres make one square metre	= 10 000 centimètres carrés font un mètre carré
A is the same area as B	= A a la même superficie que B
A and B are the same area	= A et B ont la même superficie

Note the French construction with de, *coming after the noun it describes:*

a 200-square-metre plot	= un terrain de 200 mètres carrés

III *vtr* **1** (astonish) surprendre; **he ~d everyone by winning** il a surpris tout le monde par sa victoire; **to be ~d by sth** être surpris par qch; **what ~s me most is**... ce qui me surprend le plus c'est...; **it ~d them that** ils étaient surpris que (+ *subj*); **it wouldn't ~ me if** cela ne me surprendrait pas que (+ *subj*) or si (+ *indic*); **it might ~ you to know that** tu seras peut-être surpris d'apprendre que; **would it ~ you to learn that he's 60?** ça te surprendrait d'apprendre qu'il a 60 ans?; **nothing ~s me any more!** je ne m'étonne plus de rien!; **you (do) ~ me!** iron tu m'étonnes! **go on, ~ me** allez, dis toujours!; **2** (come upon) surprendre [*intruder, thief*]; attaquer [qch] par surprise [*garrison*].

surprised /sə'praɪzd/ *adj* [*person*] surpris, étonné; [*expression, look*] étonné; **I was really ~** j'étais vraiment étonné or surpris; **I'm not ~** ça ne m'étonne pas; **don't look so ~** ne prends pas cet air surpris; **to be ~ to hear/to see** être surpris d'apprendre/de voir; **to be ~ at sth** être étonné par qch; **I would/wouldn't be ~ if** cela m'étonnerait/ne m'étonnerait pas que (+ *subj*) or si (+ *indic*); **don't be ~ if he's late** ne t'étonne pas s'il est en retard; **you'd be ~ (at) how many cars there are/how expensive they are** tu serais étonné par le nombre de voitures/par leur prix élevé; **'there'll be no-one'—'oh, you'd be ~'** 'il n'y aura personne'—'détrompe-toi'; **I'm ~ at him!** je ne m'attendais pas à cela de sa part!

surprising /sə'praɪzɪŋ/ *adj* étonnant, surprenant; **it would be ~ if** ce serait étonnant que (+ *subj*) or si (+ *indic*); **it is ~ (that)** c'est étonnant que (+ *subj*); **I find it ~ that** je trouve étonnant que (+ *subj*); **it's hardly ~ they didn't come** ce n'est pas étonnant qu'ils ne soient pas venus; **it is ~ to see/find** c'est étonnant de voir/trouver; **what is even more ~ is that he**... plus surprenant encore, il...

surprisingly /sə'praɪzɪŋlɪ/ *adv* [*accurate, calm, cheap, dense, high, realistic, strong*] incroyablement; [*bad*] très; [*well, quickly*] étonnamment; **~ beautiful/frank** d'une beauté/franchise étonnante; **~ few people know about it** c'est étonnant que si peu de gens le sachent; **~**, ... cela peut paraître étonnant, mais...; **they didn't know her, ~ enough** chose étonnante, ils ne la connaissaient pas; **not ~**, ... (ce n'est) pas étonnant que... (+ *subj*); **more ~**, ... ce qui est plus étonnant, c'est que...

surreal /sə'rɪəl/ *adj* surréaliste.

surrealism, **Surrealism** /sə'rɪəlɪzəm/ *n* surréalisme *m*.

surrealist /sə'rɪəlɪst/ *n, adj* surréaliste (*mf*).

surrealistic /ˌsərɪə'lɪstɪk/ *adj* surréaliste.

surrender /sə'rendə(r)/ **I** *n* **1** Mil (of army) capitulation *f* (**to** devant); (of soldier, town, garrison) reddition *f* (**to** à); **no ~!** nous ne nous rendrons pas!; **2** (renouncing, giving up) (of territory) abandon *m*, cession *f* (**to** à); (of liberties, rights, power) abandon *m* (**to** à); (of insurance policy) rachat *m*; **3** (handing over) (of weapons, ticket, document) remise *f* (**to** à); **4** fig (of self) (to joy, despair) abandon *m* (**to** à).

II *vtr* **1** Mil livrer [*town, garrison*] (**to** à); **2** (give up) céder, abandonner [*liberty, rights, power*] (**to** à); racheter [*insurance policy*]; céder [*lease*]; **3** (hand over) remettre [*firearm*] (**to** à); donner, remettre [*ticket*] (**to** à); rendre [*passport*] (**to** à).

III *vi* **1** (give up) [*army, soldier*] se rendre (**to** à); [*country*] capituler (**to** devant); **I ~** Mil je me rends; fig je cède; **2** (give way) **to ~ to** se livrer à [*passion, despair*].

IV *v refl* **to ~ oneself to** se livrer à [*emotion*]; (sexually) se donner à [*person*].

surrender value *n* valeur *f* de rachat.

surreptitious /ˌsʌrəp'tɪʃəs/ *adj* [*glance, gesture*] furtif/-ive; [*search, exit*] discret/-ète.

surreptitiously /ˌsʌrəp'tɪʃəslɪ/ *adv* [*look, examine*] furtivement; [*take, put*] subrepticement.

Surrey /'sʌrɪ/ **▶1624** *pr n* Surrey *m*.

surrogacy /'sʌrəgəsɪ/ *n* pratique *f* des mères porteuses.

surrogate /'sʌrəgeɪt/ **I** *n* **1** (substitute) substitut *m* (**for** de); **2** GB Relig official *m*; **3** US Jur *juge chargé d'homologuer les testaments*; **4** (also **~ mother**) mère *f* porteuse.

II *adj* [*sibling, father, religion*] de substitution, de remplacement.

surrogate motherhood *n* pratique *f* des mères porteuses.

surround /sə'raʊnd/ **I** *n* GB **1** (for fireplace) encadrement *m*; **2** (border) bordure *f*; (between carpet and wall) *la partie du sol comprise entre le tapis et les murs*.

II *vtr* lit [*fence, trees*] entourer [*village, garden*]; [*police*] encercler [*building*]; cerner [*person*]; fig [*secrecy, confusion*] entourer [*plan, event*]; **~ed by, ~ed with** lit, fig entouré de.

III *v refl* **to ~ oneself with** s'entourer de.

surrounding /sə'raʊndɪŋ/ *adj* [*countryside, hills, villages*] environnant; **the ~ area** ou **region** les environs *mpl*.

surroundings /sə'raʊndɪŋz/ *npl* gen cadre *m*; (of town) environs *mpl*; **in their natural ~** dans leur milieu naturel.

surtax /'sɜːtæks/ *n* (on income) impôt *m* supplémentaire; (additional tax) surtaxe *f*.

surveillance /sɜː'veɪləns/ **I** *n* surveillance *f*; **to keep sb under ~** garder qn sous surveillance.

II *modif* [*officer, team*] chargé de la surveillance des suspects; [*equipment, device*] de surveillance; [*camera, photograph, film*] de surveillance vidéo.

survey **I** /'sɜːveɪ/ *n* **1** (of trends, prices, reasons) gen enquête *f* (**of** sur); (by questioning people) sondage *m*; (study, overview of work) étude *f* (**of** de); **to carry out** ou **conduct** ou **do a ~** gen effectuer or faire une enquête; (by questioning people) effectuer or faire un sondage; **a ~ of five products** une enquête sur cinq produits; **a ~ of intentions/of 500 young people** un sondage sur les intentions/effectué parmi 500 jeunes gens; **2** GB (in housebuying) (inspection) expertise *f* (**on** de); (report) rapport *m* d'expertise; **to do** or **carry out a ~** effectuer or faire une expertise; **to get a ~ done** faire faire une expertise; **3** Geog, Geol (action) (of land) étude *f* topographique; (of sea) étude *f* hydrographique; **4** Geog, Geol (map) (of land) levé *m* topographique; (of sea) levé *m* hydrographique; **5** (rapid examination) (of crowd, faces, town, room) rapide examen *m*.

II /sə'veɪ/ *vtr* **1** (investigate) gen faire une étude de [*market, prices, trends*]; (by questioning people) faire un sondage parmi [*people*]; faire un sondage sur [*opinions, intentions*]; **2** GB (in housebuying) faire une expertise de [*property, house*]; **3** Geog, Geol (inspect) faire l'étude topographique de [*area*]; faire l'étude hydrographique de [*sea*]; **4** gen (look at) contempler [*scene, picture, audience*].

survey course *n* US Univ cours *m* d'introduction.

surveying /sə'veɪɪŋ/ **I** *n* **1** GB (in housebuying) expertise *f* (immobilière); **2** Geog, Geol (science) (for land) topographie *f*; (for sea) hydrographie *f*.

II *modif* [*instrument*] (for land) d'arpentage; (for sea) d'hydrographie.

surveyor /sə'veɪə(r)/ **▶1692** *n* **1** GB (in housebuying) expert *m* (en immobilier); **2** Geog, Geol (for map-making) topographe *mf*; (for industry, oil) ingénieur *m* topographique.

survey ship *n* Naut bateau *m* de recherche hydrographique.

survival /sə'vaɪvl/ **I** *n* **1** (act, condition) (of person, animal, plant) survie *f* (**of** de); (of custom, belief) survivance *f* (**of** de); **the ~ of the fittest** la survie des plus forts; **2** (remaining person, belief etc) vestige *m*.

II *modif* [*kit, equipment, course*] de survie.

survive /sə'vaɪv/ **I** *vtr* **1** (live through) lit survivre à [*winter, operation, heart attack*]; réchapper de [*accident, fire, explosion*]; fig surmonter [*recession, crisis, divorce*]; [*government, politician*] survivre à [*vote*]; **2** (live longer than) survivre à [*person*]; **he is ~d by a son and a daughter** son fils et sa fille lui survivent; **to ~ sb by 10 years** survivre à qn de 10 ans.

II *vi* lit, fig survivre; **to ~ on sth** vivre de qch; **to ~ on £20 a week** survivre avec 20 livres sterling par semaine; **I'll ~** je m'en tirerai.

surviving /sə'vaɪvɪŋ/ *adj* survivant; **the longest ~ patient** le patient qui a vécu le plus longtemps.

survivor /sə'vaɪvə(r)/ *n* **1** (of accident, attack etc) rescapé/-e *m/f*; **2** Jur survivant/-e *m/f*; **3** (resilient person) **to be a ~** avoir de la ressource.

susceptibility /səˌseptə'bɪlətɪ/ **I** *n* **1** (vulnerability) (to flattery, pressure) sensibilité *f* (**to** à); (to disease) prédisposition *f* (**to** à); **2** (impressionability) impressionnabilité *f*.

II susceptibilities *npl* susceptibilité *f*.

susceptible /sə'septəbl/ *adj* **1** (vulnerable) (to cold, heat, flattery, pressure, persuasion) sensible (**to** à); (to disease) prédisposé (**to** à); **2** (impressionable) impressionnable; **3** sout **~ of** (amenable to) susceptible de.

sushi /'suːʃɪ/ *n* Culin (+ *v sg*) sushi *m*.

sus law○ /'sʌslɔː/ *n* GB *loi permettant d'appréhender tout vagabond suspecté de vouloir commettre un délit*.

suspect **I** /'sʌspekt/ *n* suspect/-e *m/f*.

II /'sʌspekt/ *adj* [*claim, person, notion, vehicle*] suspect; [*practice*] douteux/-euse; [*item, valuable*] d'authenticité douteuse; [*foodstuff, ingredient, water, smell*] douteux/-euse.

III /sə'spekt/ *vtr* **1** (believe) soupçonner [*murder, plot, sabotage, fraud*]; **to ~ that** penser que; **there is reason to ~ that**... il y a des raisons de penser que...; **we strongly ~ that**... nous avons de bonnes raisons de croire que...; **I ~ she didn't want to leave** je pense or j'ai le sentiment qu'elle ne voulait pas partir; **it isn't, I ~, a very difficult task** ce n'est pas, à mon avis, une tâche très difficile; **2** (doubt) douter de [*truth, validity, sincerity, motives*]; **she ~s nothing** elle ne se doute de rien; **3** (have under suspicion) soupçonner [*person, organization*] (**of** de); **she was ~ed of stealing money** elle était soupçonnée d'avoir volé de l'argent.

IV suspected *pp adj* (*épith*) [*sabotage, food-poisoning, pneumonia*] présumé; **a ~ed war criminal/terrorist** une personne soupçonnée de crimes de guerre/de terrorisme.

suspend /sə'spend/ *vtr* **1** (hang) suspendre (**from** à); **to be ~ed in midair/time** être suspendu dans le vide/le temps; **2** (float) **to be ~ed in** [*balloon, feather*] flotter dans [*air*]; [*particles*] être en suspension dans [*gel*]; **3** (call off) suspendre [*talks, hostilities, aid, trade, trial*]; interrompre [*transport services, meeting*]; **to ~ play** Sport interrompre le match; **4** (reserve) réserver [*comment, judgment*]; **to ~ disbelief** accepter les invraisemblances; **to ~ (one's) judgment** réserver son jugement; **5** (remove from activities) suspendre [*employee, official*] (**from** de); suspendre [*footballer, athlete*] (**from** de); exclure [qn] temporairement [*pupil*] (**from** de); **to be ~ed from duty** être suspendu de ses fonctions; **6** Fin **to ~ shares** suspendre la cotation d'un titre; **7** Jur **her sentence was ~ed** elle a été condamnée avec sursis; **he was given an 18 month sentence ~ed for 12 months** il a été condamné à 18 mois de prison avec un an de sursis.

suspended animation *n* lit engourdissement *m*; **to be in a state of ~** fig [*service, business*] végéter.

suspended sentence *n* condamnation *f* avec sursis; **to give sb a two-year ~**

condamner qn à deux ans de prison avec sursis.

suspender belt *n* GB porte-jarretelles *m inv.*

suspenders /sə'spendəz/ *npl* **1** GB (for stockings) jarretelles *fpl*; (for socks) fixe-chaussettes *mpl*; **2** US (for pants) bretelles *fpl*.

suspense /sə'spens/ *n* **1** (tension) suspense *m*; **to wait in ~ for sth** attendre qch avec une vive impatience; **to break the ~** mettre fin au suspense; **to keep** ou **leave sb in ~** laisser qn dans l'expectative; **I'd prefer to keep them in ~** je préfère ménager mes effets; **the ~ is killing me!** je n'en peux plus d'attendre!; **2** Comm, Fin **to be/remain in ~** être/rester en suspens.

suspense: **~ account** *n* compte *m* d'ordre; **~ drama, ~ thriller** *n* film *m* à suspense.

suspenseful /sə'spensfl/ *adj* plein de suspense.

suspension /sə'spenʃn/ *n* **1** (postponement) (of meeting, trial, services) interruption *f*; (of talks, hostilities, payments, quotas) suspension *f*; **~ of play** Sport interruption *f*; **2** (temporary dismissal) (of employee) suspension *f* **(from** de); (of footballer, athlete) suspension *f* **(from** de); (of pupil) exclusion *f* temporaire **(from** de); **~ from duty** suspension de fonctions; **after her ~ from duty, she...** après avoir été suspendue de ses fonctions, elle...; **she wants to appeal against her ~** elle veut faire appel contre la mesure de suspension prise contre elle; **3** Aut suspension *f*; **4** Chem suspension *f*; **in ~** en suspension.

suspension: **~ bridge** *n* pont *m* suspendu; **~ cable** *n* suspente *f*; **~ points** *npl* points *mpl* de suspension.

suspensory /sə'spensərɪ/ *adj* [*muscle, ligament*] suspenseur; **~ bandage** suspensoir *m*.

suspicion /sə'spɪʃn/ *n* **1** (mistrust) méfiance *f* **(of** de); **to view sb/sth with ~** se méfier de qn/qch; **to arouse ~** éveiller des soupçons; **2** (of guilt) **to be arrested on ~ of murder/theft** être arrêté sur présomption de meurtre/de vol; **he is under ~** il est considéré comme suspect; **to fall under ~** devenir l'objet de soupçons; **to be above ~** être à l'abri de tout soupçon; **3** (idea, feeling) **to have a ~ that** soupçonner que; **I have a strong ~ that she is lying** je suis presque sûr qu'elle ment; **to have ~s about sb/sth** avoir des doutes quant à qn/qch; **to share sb's ~s** partager les doutes de qn; **nobody knows who did it, although I have my ~s** personne ne sait qui l'a fait, bien que j'aie ma théorie or ma petite idée là-dessus; **his ~s that all was not well were confirmed** son pressentiment que tout n'allait pas pour le mieux s'est avéré juste; **4** fig (hint) soupçon *m*; **a ~ of garlic** un soupçon d'ail.

suspicious /sə'spɪʃəs/ *adj* **1** (wary) méfiant; **to be ~ of** se méfier de [*person, motive, scheme*]; **to be ~ that...** soupçonner que...; **we became ~ when...** on a commencé à se douter que quelque chose n'allait pas or on a commencé à se poser des questions quand...; **2** (suspect) [*person, character, object, vehicle, incident, death, circumstances*] suspect; [*behaviour, activity*] louche; **it is/I find it ~ that...** c'est/je trouve suspect que (+ *subj*); **a ~-looking individual** un individu à l'air louche; **you should report anything ~** il faut signaler la moindre chose suspecte.

suspiciously /sə'spɪʃəslɪ/ *adv* **1** (warily) [*say, ask, watch, stare, approach*] d'un air soupçonneux; **2** (oddly) [*behave, act*] de façon suspecte; [*quiet, heavy, keen*] étrangement; [*clean, tidy*] iron étonnamment; **it looks ~ like a plot** cela ressemble étrangement à un complot; **it sounded ~ like a heart attack to me** cela m'avait tout l'air d'être une crise cardiaque.

suspiciousness /sə'spɪʃəsnɪs/ *n* méfiance **(of** à l'égard de).

suss○ /sʌs/ GB **I** *vtr* résoudre; **to have it ~ed** avoir tout compris; **to have sb ~ed** avoir percé qn à jour.
II sussed *pp adj* astucieux/-ieuse.
■ **suss out**○: **~ [sth/sb] out, ~ out [sth/sb]** comprendre.

sustain /sə'steɪn/ **I** *vtr* **1** (maintain) maintenir [*interest, mood, growth, success, quality*]; poursuivre [*campaign, war, policy*]; **2** Mus soutenir, tenir [*note*]; **3** (provide strength) (physically) donner des forces à; (morally) soutenir; **4** (support) soutenir [*regime, economy, market, system*]; **to ~ life** rendre la vie possible; **5** (suffer) recevoir [*injury, blow, burn*]; éprouver [*loss*]; subir, essuyer [*defeat*]; **to ~ severe damage** subir d'importants dégâts; **6** (bear) supporter [*weight*]; **7** Jur (uphold) faire droit à [*claim*]; admettre [*objection*]; **objection ~ed!** objection accordée!
II sustained *pp adj* [*attack, criticism, development, effort*] soutenu; [*applause, period*] prolongé; [*note*] tenu.
III sustaining *pres p adj* [*drink, meal*] nourrissant.

sustainable /səs'teɪnəbl/ *adj* **1** Ecol [*development, forestry*] durable; [*resource*] renouvelable; **2** Econ [*growth*] viable.

sustaining pedal *n* Mus pédale *f* forte.

sustenance /'sʌstɪnəns/ *n* **1** (nourishment) valeur *f* nutritive; **there isn't much ~ in those meals** ces repas ne sont pas très nutritifs; **2** (food) nourriture *f*; **to provide ~ for sb** [*foodstuff*] être une nourriture pour qn; **the slaughter of animals for ~** l'abattage des bêtes pour l'alimentation; **I need some ~!** hum j'ai besoin de me sustenter! hum; **spiritual ~** fig nourriture *f* spirituelle.

suttee /sʌ'ti:, 'sʌtɪ/ *n* Relig, Hist **1** (custom) sati *m*; **2** (widow) (veuve *f*) sati *f*.

suture /'su:tʃə(r)/ *n* suture *f*.

suzerain /'su:zərən/ *n* suzerain/-e *m/f*.

svelte /svelt/ *adj* svelte.

SW *n* **1** **▶ 1568** Geog (*abrév* = **southwest**) SO *m*; **2** Radio (*abrév* = **short wave**) OC *fpl*.

swab /swɒb/ **I** *n* **1** Med (for cleaning) tampon *m*; **2** Med (specimen) prélèvement *m*; **to take a ~** faire un prélèvement; **3** (mop) serpillière *f*; Naut faubert *m*.
II *vtr* (*p prés etc* **-bb-**) **1** Med nettoyer [qch] avec un tampon, tamponner [*wound*]; **2** Naut, gen (also **~ down**) laver [*deck, floor*].

swaddle /'swɒdl/ *vtr* **1** (in swaddling bands) emmailloter [*baby*]; **2** (wrap up) emmitoufler [*person, baby*] **(in** dans).

swaddling bands, swaddling clothes *npl* langes *mpl*.

swag /swæg/ **I** *n* **1**† ○(stolen property) butin *m*; **2**○ Austral baluchon *m*; **3** (on curtains) fronce *f*; **4** US = **swag lamp**.
II *vtr* (*p prés etc* **-gg-**) froncer [*curtain*].
III swagged *pp adj* [*curtain*] à fronces.

swagger /'swægə(r)/ **I** *n* démarche *f* arrogante; **with a ~** en se pavanant.
II *vi* **1** (walk) se pavaner; **to ~ in/out** entrer/sortir en se pavanant; **2** (boast) fanfaronner **(about** à propos de).
III swaggering *pres p adj* arrogant.

swagger: **~ cane** *n* GB Mil badine *f*; **~ coat** *n* manteau *m* court; **~ stick** *n* badine *f*.

swag: **~ lamp** *n* US suspension *f*; **~man**○ *n* Austral vagabond *m*.

Swahili /swə'hi:lɪ/ **▶ 1486, 1402** *n* **1** Ling swahili *m*; **2** (people) **the ~s** les Swahilis *mpl*.

swain /sweɪn/ *n*‡ ou hum (admirer) soupirant *m*.

swallow /'swɒləʊ/ **I** *n* **1** Zool hirondelle *f*; **2** (gulp) gorgée *f*; **in one ~** [*drink*] d'un trait, d'une seule gorgée; [*eat*] d'une seule bouchée.
II *vtr* **1** (eat) avaler [*food, drink, pill*]; gober [*oyster*]; **2** (believe) avaler○ [*story, explanation*]; **I find that hard to ~** je trouve cela dur à avaler○; **3** (suffer) encaisser○ [*insult, sarcasm*]; ravaler [*pride, anger, disappointment*]; **4** fig (consume) = **swallow up**.
III *vi* avaler; (nervously) avaler sa salive; **to ~ hard** avaler sa salive avec difficulté.
IDIOMS **one ~ doesn't make a summer** Prov une hirondelle ne fait pas le printemps.
■ **swallow back**: **~ back [sth], ~ [sth] back** ravaler [*bile, anger, vomit*].
■ **swallow down**: **~ down [sth], ~ [sth] down** avaler [*drink, medicine, meal*].
■ **swallow up**: **~ up [sth], ~ [sth] up** lit, fig engloutir [qch]; **to be ~ed up in the crowd** se noyer dans la foule; **I wanted the ground to ~ me up** j'avais envie de disparaître sous terre.

swallow: **~ dive** *n* GB Sport saut *m* de l'ange; **~tail (butterfly)** *n* machaon *m*; **~tailed coat** *n* queue-de-pie *f*, habit *m* de soirée.

swam /swæm/ *prét* ▶ **swim** II, III.

swami /'swɑ:mɪ/ *n* swami *mf*.

swamp /swɒmp/ **I** *n* marais *m*, marécage *m*.
II *vtr* inonder; **to be ~ed with** ou **by** être inondé de [*applications, mail*]; être débordé de [*work*]; être envahi par [*tourists*].

swamp buggy *n* voiture *f* amphibie.

swampy /'swɒmpɪ/ *adj* marécageux/-euse.

swan /swɒn/ **I** *n* cygne *m*.
II○ *vi* (*p prés etc* **-nn-**) GB **to ~ around** ou **about** se pavaner; **to ~ in** arriver comme une fleur○; **she's ~ned off to a conference** elle est partie se la couler douce○ à un congrès.

swan dive *n* saut *m* de l'ange.

swank○ /swæŋk/ **I** *n* **1** (boastful behaviour) frime○ *f*; **2** GB (boastful person) frimeur/-euse○ *m/f*; **3** US (style) classe *f*.
II *adj* US ▶ **swanky**.
III *vi* frimer○.

swanky○ /'swæŋkɪ/ *adj* **1** (posh) [*car, hotel*] rupin○, luxueux/-euse; **2** (boastful) [*person*] frimeur/-euse○, fanfaron/-onne.

Swan Lake *n* le Lac *m* des cygnes.

swan neck *n* Tech **with a ~** [*pipe*] en S.

swan-necked *adj* [*person*] au cou de cygne.

swannery /'swɒnərɪ/ *n* colonie *f* de cygnes.

swan: **~sdown** *n* (feathers) duvet *m* de cygne; (fabric) molleton *m*; **~song** fig *n* chant *m* du cygne; **~-upping** *n* GB *recensement annuel des cygnes de la Tamise par marquage du bec.*

swap○ /swɒp/ **I** *n* échange *m*.
II *vtr* (*p prés etc* **-pp-**) échanger [*object, stories, news*]; **to ~ sth for sth/with sb** échanger qch contre qch/avec qn; **to ~ places (with sb)** changer de place (avec qn); **they have ~ped jobs/cars** ils ont échangé leurs postes/leurs voitures; **I'll ~ you A for B** je te donne A en échange de B.
■ **swap around**: **~ [sth] around, ~ around [sth]** permuter.
■ **swap over** GB: ¶ **~ over** échanger; ¶ **~ [sth] over, ~ over [sth]** permuter [*players, objects*]; échanger [*jobs*].

SWAPO /'swɒpəʊ/ *n* Pol (*abrév* = **South-West Africa People's Organization**) SWAPO *f*.

sward /swɔ:d/ *n* Agric, liter gazon *m*.

swarm /swɔ:m/ **I** *n* (of bees) essaim *m*; (of flies, locusts) nuée *f*; **a ~ of people, ~s of people** une masse de personnes.
II *vi* **1** (move in swarm) [*bees*] essaimer; **2** [*people*] **to ~ into/out of** entrer/sortir en masse; **to ~ around sb/sth** se presser autour de qn/qch; **to be ~ing with** grouiller de [*ants, tourists*]; **3** (climb) **to ~ up** monter [qch] en vitesse [*cliff, hill*].

swarthy /'swɔ:ðɪ/ *adj* basané.

swashbuckling /'swɒʃbʌklɪŋ/ *adj* [*adventure, tale*] de cape et d'épée; [*hero, appearance*] bravache.

swastika /'swɒstɪkə/ *n* svastika *m*.

swat /swɒt/ **I** *n* **1** (object) tapette *f* à mouches; **2** (action) tape *f*.

II *vtr* (*p prés etc* **-tt-**) écraser [*fly, wasp*] (**with** avec).

SWAT /swɒt/ *n* (also **~ team**) (*abrév* = **Special Weapons and Tactics**) forces *fpl* de l'ordre, cf CRS *f*.

swatch /swɒtʃ/ *n* (sample) échantillon *m*.

swath(e) /swɔːθ, sweɪð/ *n* **1** (band) (of grass, corn) andain *m*; (of land) bande *f*; **2** (cloth) drapé *m*.

IDIOMS **to cut a ~ through** se frayer un chemin au milieu de [*obstacles, difficulties*].

swathe /sweɪð/ *vtr* envelopper (**in** dans); **~d in** enveloppé de [*bandages*]; emmitouflé dans [*blankets, clothes*].

sway /sweɪ/ **I** *n* **1** (of tower, bridge, train) oscillation *f*; (of boat) balancement *m*; **2** (power) **under the ~ of** sous la domination de; **to hold ~** avoir une grande influence; **to hold ~ over** dominer [*person, country*].

II *vtr* **1** (influence) influencer [*person, jury, voters*]; **to ~ sb in favour of doing** déterminer qn à faire; **to ~ the outcome in sb's favour** faire pencher la balance en faveur de qn; **she would not be ~ed** elle ne se laissait pas influencer; **I was almost ~ed by** j'ai failli être emporté par; **2** (rock) osciller [*trees, building*]; **to ~ one's hips** se déhancher; **to ~ one's body** se balancer.

III *vi* [*tree, building, bridge*] osciller; [*vessel, carriage*] tanguer; [*robes*] flotter; [*person, body*] (from weakness, inebriation) chanceler; (to music) se balancer; **to ~ from side to side** [*person*] se balancer de droite à gauche; **to ~ along the path** avancer le long du chemin en chancelant.

IV swaying *pres p adj* [*building, train*] oscillant; **the ~ing palms/dancers** les palmiers/danseurs qui se balancent.

swayback /ˈsweɪbæk/ *n* Equit dos *m* ensellé.

Swazi /ˈswɑːzɪ/ ▶ **1486**, **1402** *n* **1** Ling swazi *m*; **2** (people) **the ~s** les Swazis *mpl*.

Swaziland /ˈswɑːzɪlænd/ ▶ **1131** *pr n* Swaziland *m*.

swear /sweə(r)/ (*prét* **swore**, *pp* **sworn**) **I** *vtr* **1** gen, Jur (promise) jurer [*loyalty, allegiance, revenge*]; **to ~ (an oath of) allegiance** to faire serment d'allégeance à; **I ~!, I ~ it!** fml je le jure!; **I ~ to God, I didn't know** je ne le savais pas, je le jure; **to ~ to do** jurer de faire; **to ~ (that)** jurer que; **he swore he'd never write again/never to write again** il a juré qu'il n'écrirait plus jamais/de ne plus jamais écrire; **I could have sworn she was there** j'aurais juré qu'elle y était; **to ~ to sb that** jurer à qn que; **I ~ by all that I hold dear that** je jure sur la tête de tous ceux que j'aime que; **to ~ blind (that)**○ jurer sur sa tête que; **2** (by solemn oath) **to ~ sb to secrecy** faire jurer le secret à qn; **she had been sworn to secrecy** on lui avait fait jurer le secret; **to be sworn to do** avoir prêté serment de faire; **to be sworn into office** prêter serment; **3** (curse) **'damn!' he swore** 'bon Dieu!' jura-t-il; **to ~ at** pester contre; **to be** ou **get sworn at** se faire injurier.

II *vi* **1** (curse) jurer; **she swore loudly** elle a lâché un juron; **he never ~s** il ne dit jamais de gros mots; **to ~ in front of** dire de gros mots devant; **stop ~ing!** arrête de jurer!, ne sois pas si grossier!; **2** (attest) **to ~ to having done** jurer d'avoir fait; **would he ~ to having seen them?** est-ce qu'il pourrait jurer de les avoir vus?; **I wouldn't** ou **couldn't ~ to it** je n'en jurerais pas; **to ~ on** jurer sur [*Bible, honour*].

■ **swear by**○: **~ by [sth/sb]** ne jurer que par [*remedy, electrician*].

■ **swear in**: **~ in [sb], ~ [sb] in** faire prêter serment à [*jury, witness*]; **to be sworn in** prêter serment.

■ **swear off**: **~ off [sth]** renoncer à [*alcohol, smoking*].

■ **swear out** US Jur **to ~ out a warrant for sb's arrest** accuser qn sous serment pour obtenir un mandat d'arrêt.

swearing /ˈsweərɪŋ/ *n* (words, curses) jurons *mpl*; **I'm sick of his ~** j'en ai marre○ de ses grossièretés *fpl*.

swearing-in ceremony *n* cérémonie *f* d'investiture.

swearword /ˈsweəwɜːd/ *n* juron *m*, gros mot *m*.

sweat /swet/ **I** *n* **1** (perspiration) sueur *f*; **to be in a ~** être en sueur; **to be covered in ~** être couvert de sueur; **to be dripping** ou **pouring with ~** être en nage; **to break out into a ~** se mettre à suer; **to work up a (good) ~** se prendre une bonne suée; **in a cold ~** lit dans une sueur froide; **to be in a cold ~ about sth** fig avoir des sueurs froides à l'idée de qch; **beads** ou **drops of ~** gouttes *fpl* de sueur; **night ~s** Med suées *fpl* nocturnes; **2** littér (hard work) labeur *m*; **by the ~ of his brow** à la sueur de son front; **3**○ (old soldier) vieux *m* de la vieille○.

II sweats *npl* US survêtement *m*.

III *vtr* **1** Culin faire suer [*vegetables*]; **2**○ (interrogate) cuisiner○ [*suspect*].

IV *vi* **1** lit [*person, animal*] suer; [*hands, feet*] transpirer; [*cheese*] transpirer; **the ~ing horses/runners** les chevaux/coureurs en sueur; **2**○ fig (wait anxiously) **to let** ou **make sb ~** laisser mariner○ qn.

IDIOMS **no ~**○! pas de problème!; **to be/get in a ~**○ être/se mettre dans tous ses états; **to ~ blood over sth** suer sang et eau sur qch.

■ **sweat off**: **~ [sth] off, ~ off [sth]** perdre [qch] à force de transpirer [*calories, weight*].

■ **sweat out**: **to ~ it out 1** lit, Med se faire transpirer beaucoup pour faire tomber la fièvre; **2**○ fig s'armer de patience.

■ **sweat over**○: **~ over [sth]** en suer○ pour faire [*homework, task*]; en suer○ pour écrire [*letter, essay*].

sweat: **~band** *n* Sport bandeau *m*; (on hat) cuir *m* intérieur; **~ bath** *n* bain *m* de sueur; **~ duct** *n* conduit *m* sudorifère; **~ed goods** *npl* produits *mpl* fabriqués par une main-d'œuvre exploitée; **~ed labour** *n* main-d'œuvre *f* exploitée.

sweater /ˈswetə(r)/ ▶ **1703** *n* (pullover) pull *m*; (any knitted top) lainage *m*.

sweat: **~ gland** *n* glande *f* sudoripare; **~ pants** *npl* pantalon *m* de survêtement; **~shirt** *n* sweatshirt *m*; **~shop** *n* atelier *m* où on exploite le personnel; **~-soaked** *adj* trempé de sueur; **~stained** *adj* maculé de sueur; **~suit** *n* survêtement *m*.

sweaty /ˈswetɪ/ *adj* **1** (sweat-stained) [*person*] en sueur; [*hand, palm*] moite; [*foot*] qui transpire; [*clothing*] couvert de sueur; [*cheese*] qui transpire; **2** (hot) [*atmosphere*] étouffant; [*place, climate*] moite; [*clothing*] qui fait transpirer; [*climb, work*] laborieux/-ieuse.

swede /swiːd/ *n* GB rutabaga *m*.

Swede /swiːd/ ▶ **1486** *n* Suédois/-e *m/f*.

Sweden /ˈswiːdn/ ▶ **1131** *pr n* Suède *f*.

Swedish /ˈswiːdɪʃ/ ▶ **1486**, **1402** **I** *n* **1** Ling suédois *m*; **2** (people) **the ~** les Suédois *mpl*.

II *adj* suédois.

sweep /swiːp/ **I** *n* **1** (also **~ out**) coup *m* de balai; **to give sth a (good/quick) ~** donner un (bon/petit) coup de balai à qch; **2** (movement) **with a ~ of the scythe/the paintbrush** d'un coup de faux/de pinceau; **with a ~ of his arm** d'un grand geste du bras; **to make a wide ~ south to avoid the mountains** faire un grand crochet vers le sud pour éviter les montagnes; **3** (tract, stretch) (of land, woods, hills, cliffs) étendue *f*; (of lawn) surface *f*; (of fabric) drapé *m*; **4** (scope, range) (of events, history, novel, country) ampleur *f*; (of opinion) éventail *m*; (of telescope, gun) champ *m*; **the broad ~ of left-wing opinion** le large éventail d'opinions qui composent la gauche; **5** (search) (on land) exploration *f*, fouille *f*; (by air) survol *m*; (attack) sortie *f*; (to capture) ratissage *m*; **to make a ~ of** (search) (on land) explorer, fouiller; (by air) survoler; (to capture) ratisser; **a ~ for bugs** une fouille à la recherche de micros; **a ~ for mines** un dragage des mines; **6** (also **chimney ~**) ramoneur *m*; **7** (of electron beam) balayage *m*; **8** = **sweepstake**.

II *vtr* (*prét, pp* **swept**) **1** (clean) balayer [*floor, room, path*]; ramoner [*chimney*]; **to ~ the carpet** (with vacuum cleaner) passer l'aspirateur (sur le tapis); **to ~ a channel clear** dégager un chenal; **to ~ sth free of mines** déminer qch; **2** (clear away, remove with brush) **to ~ sth up** ou **away** balayer [*dust, leaves, glass*]; **to ~ leaves into a corner/a heap** balayer des feuilles et les pousser dans un coin/et en faire un tas; **to ~ the crumbs onto the floor** balayer les miettes sur le sol; **to ~ the crumbs off a table** ramasser les miettes d'une table; **3** (move, push) **to ~ sth off the table** faire tomber qch de la table (d'un grand geste de la main); **to ~ sb into one's arms** prendre qn dans ses bras; **to ~ sb off his/her feet** [*sea, wave*] emporter qn, faire perdre pied à qn; fig (romantically) faire perdre la tête à qn; **to ~ sb overboard/out to sea** entraîner qn par-dessus bord/vers le large; **to be swept over a waterfall** être entraîné dans une chute d'eau; **a wave of nationalism which ~s all before it** une vague de nationalisme qui balaye tout devant elle; **a wave of public euphoria swept him into office** une vague d'euphorie générale l'a amené à ses fonctions; **to be swept into power** être porté au pouvoir avec une majorité écrasante; **4** (spread through) [*disease, crime, panic, fashion, craze*] déferler sur; [*storm, fire*] ravager; [*rumour*] se répandre dans; **cold winds are ~ing the country** des vents froids balayent le pays; **the party swept the country** Pol le parti a remporté un immense succès dans le pays; **5** (search, survey) [*beam, searchlight*] balayer; [*person*] parcourir [qch] des yeux; Mil [*vessel, submarine*] sillonner; [*police*] ratisser (**for** à la recherche de); **to ~ sth for mines** déminer qch; **to ~ sth for bugs** fouiller qch à la recherche de micros.

III *vi* (*prét, pp* **swept**) **1** (clean) = **sweep up**; **2** lit, fig (move with sweeping motion) **to ~ in/out** (quickly) entrer/sortir rapidement; (majestically) entrer/sortir majestueusement; **the plane swept (down) low over the fields** l'avion survolait les champs à basse altitude; **the wind swept in from the east** le vent soufflait de l'est; **to ~ into** [*person*] entrer majestueusement dans [*room*]; [*invaders, enemy*] envahir [*region*]; **to ~ (in)to power** Pol être porté au pouvoir (avec une majorité écrasante); **to ~ to victory** remporter une victoire écrasante; **to ~ through** [*disease, crime, panic, fashion, craze, change, democracy*] déferler sur; [*fire, storm*] ravager; [*rumour*] se répandre dans; **to ~ over** [*beam, searchlight*] balayer; [*gaze*] parcourir; **fear/pain swept over him** la peur/la douleur l'a envahi; **the feeling swept over me that** j'ai été pris de la sensation que; **3** (extend) **the road ~s north/around the lake** la route décrit une large courbe vers le nord/autour du lac; **the river ~s north/around the town** la rivière continue vers le nord/contourne la ville en décrivant une large boucle; **the mountains ~ down to the sea** les montagnes descendent majestueusement jusqu'à la mer; **a flight of steps ~s up to the entrance** un perron majestueux mène à l'entrée.

IDIOMS **to ~ sth under the carpet** GB ou **rug** US escamoter qch, occulter qch.

■ **sweep along**: **~ [sb/sth] along** [*current, water*] entraîner ; **to be swept along by** être emporté par [*crowd*]; être entraîné par [*public opinion*].

■ **sweep aside**: **~ [sb/sth] aside, ~ aside [sb/sth]** lit, fig écarter [*person, objection, protest*]; repousser [*offer*]; balayer [*inhibition*].

■ **sweep away**: **~ [sb/sth] away, ~**

away [sb/sth] **1** lit [*river, flood*] emporter [*person, bridge*]; **2** fig éliminer, faire disparaître [*restrictions, limits*]; balayer [*obstacle, difficulty*]; **to be swept away by** se laisser entraîner par [*enthusiasm, optimism*]; être emporté par [*passion*].

■ **sweep out**: **~ [sth] out**, **~ out [sth]** balayer [*room, garage*].

■ **sweep up**: ¶ **~ up** balayer; ¶ **~ up [sth]**, **~ [sth] up** **1** (with broom) balayer [*leaves, litter*]; **2** (with arms) ramasser [qch] d'un geste large; **3** fig **to be swept up in** être entraîné dans [*revolution*]; être entraîné par [*wave of nationalism, of enthusiasm*].

sweepback /ˈswiːpbæk/ *n* Aviat flèche *f*.

sweeper /ˈswiːpə(r)/ *n* **1** (cleaner) (person) balayeur/-euse *m/f*; (machine) balayeuse *f*; **2** Sport libero *m*.

sweeper system *n* Sport tactique *f* 1-4-2-3.

sweep hand *n* (on clock) trotteuse *f*.

sweeping /ˈswiːpɪŋ/ **I sweepings** *npl* balayures *fpl*.

II *adj* **1** (wide, far reaching) [*change, reform, review*] radical; [*legislation, power*] d'une portée considérable; [*cut, reduction*] considérable; [*victory*] éclatant; **~ gains/losses** Pol une progression/un recul considérable; **2** (over-general) [*assertion*] péremptoire; [*statement*] trop général; **~ generalization** généralisation *f* à l'emporte-pièce; **3** [*movement, gesture, curve*] large; [*bow, curtsy*] profond; [*glance*] circulaire; [*skirt*] qui balaie le sol.

sweepstake /ˈswiːpsteɪk/ *n* sweepstake *m*.

sweet /swiːt/ **I** *n* **1** GB (candy) bonbon *m*; (dessert) dessert *m*; **2**○ (term of endearment) chou *m*, ange *m*.

II *adj* **1** lit [*food, tea*] sucré; [*fruit*] (not bitter) doux/douce; (sugary) sucré; [*wine, cider*] (not dry) doux/douce; (sugary) sucré; [*taste*] sucré; [*scent, perfume*] (pleasant) doux/douce; (sickly) écœurant; **to like ~ things** aimer tout ce qui est sucré; **to have a ~ tooth** aimer les sucreries; **2** (kind, agreeable) [*person*] gentil/-ille; [*nature*] sympathique; [*face, smile, voice*] doux/douce; **to be ~ to** être gentil avec; **it was ~ of him/you to do** c'était gentil de sa/ta part de faire; **3** (pure, fresh) [*water, breath, smell*] bon/bonne; [*sound, song, note*] mélodieux/-ieuse; **4** (pretty, cute) [*baby, animal, cottage*] mignon/-onne; [*old person*] adorable; **5** (pleasurable) [*certainty, hope, solace*] doux/douce; **6** iron (for emphasis) **to go one's own ~ way** agir comme ça lui/leur etc plaît; **he'll do it in his own ~ time** il le fera quand ça lui plaira; **all he cares about is his own ~ self** tout ce qui le préoccupe c'est sa petite personne.

III *adv* **to taste ~** avoir un goût sucré; **to smell ~** sentir bon.

IDIOMS **~ f. a.**◑, **~ Fanny Adams**◑ que dalle◑, rien; **to be ~ on sb**† avoir le béguin○ pour qn; **to keep sb ~** amadouer qn; **to whisper ~ nothings into sb's ear** susurrer des douceurs à l'oreille de qn.

sweet: **~-and-sour** *adj* aigre-doux/-douce; **~ basil** *n* basilic *m*; **~bread** *n* (of veal) ris *m* de veau; (of lamb) ris *m* d'agneau; **~briar**, **~brier** *n* églantier *m*.

sweet chestnut *n* **1** (nut) châtaigne *f*, marron *m*; **2** (tree) châtaignier *m*.

sweet: **~corn** *n* maïs *m*; **~ course** *n* GB dessert *m*.

sweeten /ˈswiːtn/ *vtr* **1** sucrer [*food, drink*] (**with** avec); **~ed with** sucré à; **2** parfumer [*air, room*]; **3** Comm rendre [qch] plus tentant [*offer, deal*]; **4** = **sweeten up**.

■ **sweeten up**: **~ [sb] up**, **~ up [sb]** amadouer [*person*].

sweetener /ˈswiːtnə(r)/ *n* **1** lit édulcorant *m*; **2** Comm, Fin (legal) incitation *f*; (illegal) pot-de-vin○ *m*.

sweetening /ˈswiːtnɪŋ/ *n*, *modif* édulcorant (*m*).

sweet factory *n* GB confiserie *f*.

sweetheart /ˈswiːthɑːt/ *n* (boyfriend) petit ami *m*; (girlfriend) petite amie *f*; **to be a real ~** être un ange; **hello ~** bonjour mon ange; **childhood ~** amour *m* d'enfance.

sweetie○ /ˈswiːtɪ/ *n* **1** GB (to eat) bonbon *m*; **2** (person) ange *m*; **hello ~** bonjour mon ange.

sweetly /ˈswiːtlɪ/ *adv* [*say, smile*] gentiment; [*sing*] d'une voix mélodieuse; [*dressed, decorated*] joliment; **the engine's running ~** le moteur tourne rond○.

sweet: **~ marjoram** *n* marjolaine *f*; **~meal** *adj* GB [*biscuit*] ≈ à la farine non blutée; **~meat**† *n* sucrerie *f*; **~-natured** *adj* ▶ **sweet-tempered**.

sweetness /ˈswiːtnɪs/ *n* **1** (sugary taste) (of food, drink) goût *m* sucré; **2** (pleasantness, charm) (of air, perfume, smile) douceur *f*; (of sound) harmonie *f*; (of music, voice) son *m* mélodieux; (of person, character) gentillesse *f*.

IDIOMS **to be all ~ and light** [*person*] être tout conciliant; **it hasn't been all ~ and light recently** tout n'a pas été rose récemment.

sweet: **~ pea** *n* pois *m* de senteur; **~ potato** *n* patate *f* douce; **~ shop** ▶ 1692 *n* GB confiserie *f*; **~-smelling** *adj* parfumé.

sweet-talk○ /ˈswiːttɔːk/ **I** *n* baratin○ *m*.

II *vtr* baratiner○; **to ~ sb into doing** baratiner○ qn pour lui faire faire.

sweet: **~-tempered** *adj* [*person*] doux/douce; **~ trolley** *n* GB chariot *m* des desserts; **~ william** *n* œillet *m* de poète.

swell /swel/ **I** *n* **1** (of waves) houle *f*; **a heavy ~** une forte houle; **2** Mus crescendo *m* et diminuendo *m*; **3** (of organ) boîte *f* expressive; **4**†○ (fashionable person) personne *f* huppée○; **the ~s** (+ *v pl*) le grand monde; **5** (bulge) (of belly) rondeur *f*; (of chest) largeur *f*; (of muscles) grosseur *f*.

II○ *adj* US **1** (smart) [*car, outfit*] classe○ (*inv*); [*restaurant*] chic (*inv*); **to look ~** faire chic (*inv*); **2** (great) formidable; **he's a ~ guy** c'est un type formidable; **we had a ~ time** on s'est bien amusés.

III *vtr* (*prét* **swelled**; *pp* **swollen** ou **swelled**) **1** (increase) gonfler [*population, crowd*]; augmenter [*membership, number*]; gonfler [*bank balance, figures, funds, total*]; **students ~ed the ranks of the demonstrators** les étudiants ont gonflé les rangs des manifestants; **2** (fill) [*wind*] gonfler [*sail*]; [*floodwater*] grossir [*river*].

IV *vi* (*prét* **swelled**; *pp* **swollen** ou **swelled**) **1** (expand) [*balloon, bud, fruit, tyre, sail, stomach*] se gonfler; [*dried fruit, wood*] gonfler; [*ankle, gland*] enfler; [*river*] grossir; **her heart ~ed with pride** elle était gonflée d'orgueil; **2** (increase) [*crowd, population, membership*] s'accroître; [*demand, prices*] augmenter (**to** jusqu'à); **to ~ to 20,000** [*total*] atteindre 20 000; [*crowd, number of people*] atteindre 20 000 personnes; **3** (grow louder) [*music*] devenir plus fort; [*note, sound*] monter; **the cheers ~ed to a roar** les applaudissements sont devenus des clameurs; **4** (ooze) [*blood, liquid*] s'écouler (**from, out of** de).

IDIOMS **to have a swollen head**○ avoir la grosse tête○; **you'll make his head ~** il va avoir la grosse tête.

■ **swell out**: **~ [sth] out**, **~ out [sth]** [*wind*] gonfler [*sails*].

■ **swell up** [*ankle, finger*] enfler.

swell: **~ box** *n* Mus boîte *f* expressive; **~head**○ *n* US prétentieux/-ieuse *m/f*; **~headed**○ *adj* US prétentieux/-ieuse.

swelling /ˈswelɪŋ/ **I** *n* **1** ¢ (bump) gen enflure *f*; (on head) bosse *f*; **I have a ~ on my ankle** j'ai la cheville enflée; **2** ¢ (enlarging) (of limb, skin) enflure *f*; (of fruit) grossissement *m*; (of sails) gonflement *m*; (of crowd, population) accroissement *m*.

II *adj* [*river*] en crue; [*crowd, minority, number*] croissant; **a ~ tide** fig une poussée; **the ~ sound** ou **note of the horns** le crescendo des cors.

swelter○ /ˈsweltə(r)/ *vi* étouffer de chaleur.

sweltering○ /ˈsweltərɪŋ/ *adj* [*conditions*] accablant; [*day, heat, climate*] torride; **it's ~ in here** on étouffe ici.

swept /swept/ *prét, pp* ▶ **sweep** II, III.

swept: **~-back** *adj* [*hair*] coiffé en arrière; Aviat [*wing*] en flèche; **~-wing** *adj* [*aircraft*] à aile en flèche.

swerve /swɜːv/ **I** *n* écart *m*.

II *vtr* [*driver*] faire faire un écart à [*vehicle*].

III *vi* **1** lit [*person, vehicle*] faire un écart; **to ~ around sb/sth** faire un écart pour éviter qn/qch; **to ~ into sth** aller s'écraser contre qch; **to ~ off the road** sortir de la route; **2** fig **to ~ from** s'écarter de [*plan, course of action*].

swift /swɪft/ **I** *n* Zool martinet *m*.

II *adj* **1** rapide, prompt; **to be ~ to do/in doing** être prompt à faire; **to have a ~ half**○ GB boire un verre en vitesse; **2**○ US (shrewd) malin/-igne.

swiftly /ˈswɪftlɪ/ *adv* rapidement, vite.

swiftness /ˈswɪftnɪs/ *n* (of change, movement) rapidité *f*; (of answer, response) promptitude *f*.

swig○ /swɪɡ/ **I** *n* gorgée *f* (**of** de).

II *vtr* (*p prés etc* **-gg-**) descendre○, boire à grands traits.

■ **swig down**, **swig back**: **~ [sth] down**, **~ down [sth]** avaler [qch] d'un trait, descendre○.

swill /swɪl/ **I** *n* **1** (food) pâtée *f* (des porcs); **2** (act of swilling) lavage *m*.

II○ *vtr* (drink) écluser○, boire.

■ **swill around**, **swill about** [*liquid*] se répandre.

■ **swill down**: **~ [sth] down**, **~ down [sth]** **1**○ (drink) descendre○, avaler; **2** (wash) laver [qch] à grande eau.

swim /swɪm/ **I** *n* baignade *f*; **to go for a ~** aller se baigner; **we had a lovely ~** nous nous sommes bien baignés; **to have another ~** retourner se baigner; **a good ~ by Evans** Sport une bonne performance de la part d'Evans.

II *vtr* (*p prés* **-mm-**; *prét* **swam**; *pp* **swum**) nager [*mile, length, stroke*]; traverser [qch] à la nage [*Channel, river*]; faire [qch] à la nage [*race*]; **the race is swum over 10 lengths** la course se fait sur 10 longueurs.

III *vi* (*p prés* **-mm-**; *prét* **swam**; *pp* **swum**) **1** [*person, fish, animal*] nager (**in** dans; **out to** vers, jusqu'à); **she can ~** elle sait nager; **to ~ on one's back** nager sur le dos; **to ~ across sth** traverser qch à la nage; **to ~ away** s'éloigner à la nage; **to ~ in the team** faire partie de l'équipe de natation; **2** (be floating, bathed) **to be ~ming in** nager or baigner dans [*cream, syrup, sauce*]; **the kitchen was ~ming in water** la cuisine était inondée; **her eyes were ~ming in** ou **with tears** ses yeux étaient baignés de larmes; **3** (wobble) [*scene, room, head*] tourner; [*mirage*] flotter; **my head is ~ming** j'ai la tête qui tourne.

IDIOMS **to be in the ~** être dans le coup○; **sink or ~** marche ou crève○; **to leave sb to sink or ~** laisser qn se débrouiller tout seul.

swim bladder *n* vessie *f* natatoire.

swimmer /ˈswɪmə(r)/ *n* nageur/-euse *m/f*; **a strong ~** un bon nageur/une bonne nageuse; **a poor ~** un nageur inexpérimenté.

swimming /ˈswɪmɪŋ/ ▶ 1282 **I** *n* natation *f*; **I love ~** j'adore la natation; **to go ~** (in sea, river) aller se baigner; (in pool) aller à la piscine.

II *modif* [*contest, gala, lessons, course*] de natation.

swimming: **~ baths** *npl* piscine *f*; **~ cap** *n* GB bonnet *m* de bain; **~ costume** *n* GB maillot *m* de bain; **~ instructor** ▶ 1692 *n* maître-nageur *m*.

swimmingly† /ˈswɪmɪŋlɪ/ *adv* à merveille.

swimming pool *n* piscine *f*.

swimming trunks *npl* slip *m* de bain; **a pair of ~** un slip de bain.

Swiss cantons

All names of cantons are masculine, and the definite article is normally used:

Ticino = le Tessin
Valais = le Valais
Graubünden = les Grisons

So:

I like Ticino = j'aime le Tessin
the Valais is beautiful = le Valais est beau
do you know Graubünden? = connaissez-vous les Grisons?

Many cantons have names which are also names of towns. If you are not sure of the name in French, le canton de X *is usually safe, and in some cases this is the only form available, as, for instance,* le canton de Vaud *(because* le Vaud *sounds like* le veau *= the calf). Similarly it is usual to say* le canton de Lucerne, le canton de Berne, le canton de Fribourg *to distinguish them from the towns bearing those names).*

In, to and from somewhere

For in *and* to *use* dans le *or* dans les, *and for* from *use* du *or* des:

to live in the Valais = vivre dans le Valais
to go to the Valais = aller dans le Valais
to come from the Valais = venir du Valais
to live in Graubünden = vivre dans les Grisons
to go to Graubünden = aller dans les Grisons
to come from Graubünden = venir des Grisons
to live in the Vaud = vivre dans le canton de Vaud
to go to the Vaud = aller dans le canton de Vaud
to come from the Vaud = venir du canton de Vaud

Uses with other nouns

There are a number of words used as adjectives and as nouns referring to the people of the canton, e.g.: bernois, valaisan, vaudois. *When nouns, these start with a capital letter.*

However, it is always safe to make a phrase with du, de l' *or* des:

a Valais accent = un accent du Valais
the Graubünden area = la région des Grisons
the Vaud countryside = les paysages du canton de Vaud

swimsuit /ˈswɪmsuːt, -sjuːt/ *n* maillot *m* de bain.

swindle /ˈswɪndl/ **I** *n* escroquerie *f*; **a tax ~** une fraude fiscale.
II *vtr* escroquer; **to ~ sb out of sth** soutirer or escroquer qch à qn.

swindler /ˈswɪndlə(r)/ *n* escroc *m*.

swine /swaɪn/ *n* **1** (pig) (*pl* **~**) porc *m*; **2**◐ péj (*pl* **~s**) salaud◑ *m*.
IDIOMS **to cast pearls before ~** jeter des perles aux pourceaux, donner de la confiture aux cochons○.

swineherd /ˈswaɪnhɜːd/ *n* porcher/-ère *m/f*.

swing /swɪŋ/ **I** *n* **1** (action, movement) (of pendulum, pointer, needle) oscillation *f*; (of hips, body) balancement *m*; (in golf) swing *m*; (in boxing) swing *m*, coup *m* de poing; **to aim** ou **take a ~ at** (with fist) essayer de donner un coup de poing à [*person, head, stomach*]; **to take a ~ at sb with an iron bar** essayer de frapper qn avec une barre de fer; **to take a wild ~ at the ball** faire un mouvement désespéré pour frapper la balle; **2** (fluctuation, change) (in voting, public opinion) revirement *m* (**in** de); (in prices, values, economy) fluctuation *f* (**in** de); (in business activity) variation *f* (**in** de) ; (in mood) saute *f* (**in** de); **a ~ to the left/right** Pol un revirement vers la gauche/la droite; **a 10% ~** Pol une variation de 10% (**to** en faveur de); **market ~s** les fluctuations du marché; **a ~ away from/towards** (in opinions) un mouvement contre/vers; (in behaviour, buying habits) un rejet de/retour vers [*method, product*]; **there has been a ~ to the left in the party** on a observé un mouvement vers la gauche chez les membres du parti; **a ~ away from/towards religion** un rejet de/un retour vers la religion; **to get a far bigger ~ than the polls predicted** avoir un nombre de voix nettement supérieur à celui prédit par les sondages; **3** (in playground, garden) balançoire *f*; **to give sb a ~** pousser qn sur une balançoire *f*; **4** Mus swing *m*; **5** (drive, rhythm) (of music, dance) rythme *m*.
II *modif* Mus [*band*] de swing; [*era*] du swing.
III *vtr* (*prét, pp* **swung**) **1** (move to and fro) balancer [*object*]; **to ~ one's arms/legs** balancer les bras/les jambes; **to ~ a bucket from the end of a rope** balancer un seau au bout d'une corde; **2** (move around, up, away) **to ~ sb onto the ground** poser qn sur le sol (d'un geste vif); **to ~ a bag onto one's back** mettre un sac sur son dos (d'un geste vif); **he swung the child into the saddle** d'un geste vif il a mis l'enfant en selle; **to ~ a child around and around** faire tournoyer un enfant; **he swung the car around** il a fait demi-tour; **to ~ a car around a corner** tourner brusquement à un coin de rue; **she swung him around to face her** elle l'a fait se retourner pour qu'il lui fasse face; **he swung his chair around** il a retourné sa chaise; **she swung the telescope through 180°** elle a fait pivoter le télescope de 180°; **to ~ one's bat at the ball** faire un mouvement de sa batte pour frapper la balle; **3** (cause to change) **to ~ a match/a trial sb's way** ou **in sb's favour** faire basculer un match/un procès en faveur de qn; **to ~ the voters** [*speech, incident*] faire changer les électeurs d'opinion (**towards** en faveur de; **away from** contre); **4**○ (cause to succeed) remporter [*election, match*]; **to ~ a deal** emporter une affaire; **can you ~ it for me?** tu peux arranger ça pour moi?; **to ~ it for sb to do** s'arranger pour que qn fasse.
IV *vi* (*prét, pp* **swung**) **1** (move to and fro) [*object, rope*] se balancer; [*pendulum*] osciller; **she sat on the branch with her legs ~ing** elle était assise sur la branche et balançait ses jambes; **to ~ on the gate** se balancer sur le portillon; **to ~ by one's hands from** se suspendre or se balancer à; **to leave sth ~ing from** laisser qch suspendu à; Naut **to ~ at anchor** se balancer sur son ancre; **2** (move along, around) **to ~ from branch to branch** se balancer de branche en branche; **to ~ onto the ground** (with rope) s'élancer sur le sol; **to ~ along a rope (hand over hand)** avancer en se suspendant à la corde; **to ~ up into the saddle** se mettre en selle d'un geste vif; **to ~ back to zero** [*needle*] revenir brusquement vers le zéro; **to ~ open/shut** s'ouvrir/se fermer; **the car swung into the drive** la voiture s'est engagée dans l'allée ; **the camera swung to the actor's face** la caméra s'est tournée brusquement vers le visage de l'acteur; **to ~ around** [*person*] se retourner (brusquement); **to ~ around in one's chair** pivoter sur sa chaise; **the road ~s around the mountain/towards the east** la route contourne la montagne/continue vers l'est; **the army swung towards the east** l'armée a dévié vers l'est; **the regiment swung along the street** le régiment s'avançait dans la rue d'un pas rythmé; **3 to ~ at** (with fist) lancer un coup de poing à; **to ~ at the ball** faire un grand mouvement pour frapper la balle; **4** fig (change) **to ~ from optimism to despair** passer de l'optimisme au désespoir; **the party swung towards the left** le parti basculait vers la gauche; **the mood of the voters has swung towards** l'état d'esprit des électeurs a connu un revirement en faveur de; **opinion swung between indifference and condemnation** l'opinion hésitait entre l'indifférence et le blâme; **5** [*music, musician*] avoir du rythme; **6**○ (be lively) **a club which really ~s** une boîte qui est vraiment branchée○; **the party was ~ing** la soirée marchait du tonnerre○; **7**○ ou † **to ~ for** lit (be hanged) être pendu pour; **the boss will make sure I ~ for that!** fig le patron va me le faire payer!
IDIOMS **to go with a ~**○ [*party*] marcher du tonnerre○; **to get into the ~ of things**○ se mettre dans le bain○; **they soon got into the ~ of the competition**○ ils sont vite entrés dans l'esprit de la compétition; **to be in full ~** [*party, meeting, strike, inquiry*] battre son plein○.

swing: **~bin** *n* poubelle *f* à couvercle basculant; **~boat** *n* balançoire *f*; **~bridge** *n* pont *m* tournant; **~ door** GB, **~ing door** US *n* porte *f* battante.

swingeing /ˈswɪndʒɪŋ/ *adj* [*cuts, increases, sanctions*] drastique; [*attack*] violent.

swinger†○ /ˈswɪŋə(r)/ *n* **to be a ~** (trendy) être branché○; **an ageing ~** péj un ringard○.

swinging /ˈswɪŋɪŋ/ *adj* [*music, step*] rythmé; [*band, musician*] qui swingue (*after n*); [*rhythm*] entraînant; [*place, nightlife*] branché○; **the ~ sixties** les années soixante.

swingometer /ˌswɪŋˈɒmɪtə(r)/ *n* indicateur *m* de tendances.

swing: **~ shift** *n* US roulement *m* d'une équipe de travailleurs (*entre 16 h et minuit*); **~ wing** *n* Aviat aile *f* à flèche variable.

swipe /swaɪp/ **I** *n* **to take a ~ at** (try to hit) essayer de frapper [*ball, person*]; (criticize) attaquer [*person, government*].
II○ *vtr* (steal) piquer○, voler.
III *vi* **to ~ at 1** (try to hit) essayer de frapper [*person, object*]; **2** (criticize) attaquer [*person, government*].

swipe card *n* carte *f* à piste magnétique.

swirl /swɜːl/ **I** *n* **1** (shape) tourbillon *m* (**of** de); **2** (action) tournoiement *m*.
II *vi* [*water*] tourbillonner; [*skirt, snow, fog*] tournoyer, tourbillonner.
III swirling *pres p adj* [*skirt, snow, fog*] tournoyant, tourbillonnant; [*water*] tourbillonnant; [*pattern*] ondoyant.

swish /swɪʃ/ **I** *n* onomat (of water, skirt, grass) bruissement *m*; (of whip, racket) sifflement *m*.
II○ *adj* chic.
III *vtr* **1** [*person*] faire siffler [*whip, cane, golf club*]; **2** [*person, wind*] faire bruire [*skirt, branch, long grass*].
IV *vi* **1** [*skirt, curtain, fabric*] bruire; **2** [*sword, whip, racket*] siffler; **to ~ through the air** siffler dans l'air.

swishy○ /ˈswɪʃɪ/ *adj* = **swish** II.

Swiss /swɪs/ ▶ 1486 **I** *n* Suisse/-esse *m/f*.
II *adj* suisse.

Swiss: **~ Alps** *n* Alpes *fpl* suisses; **~ Army knife** *n* couteau *m* suisse; **~ bank account** *n* compte *m* en Suisse; **~ chard** *n* bette *f*; **~ cheese** *n* gruyère *m*, emmenthal *m*; **~ French** ▶ 1486, ▶ 1402 *adj* suisse français, suisse romand.

Swiss German ▶ 1486, 1402 **I** *n* **1** (person) Suisse allemand/-e *m/f*; **2** (language) suisse *m* allemand.
II *adj* suisse allemand.

Swiss: **~ Guard** *n* (corps) garde *f* suisse; (person) garde *m* suisse; **~ Italian** ▶ 1486, 1402 *adj* suisse italien/-ienne; **~ roll** *n* GB gâteau *m* roulé; **~ steak** *n* US *steak, bifteck fariné et braisé*.

switch /swɪtʃ/ **I** *n* **1** (change) (in weather, policy, behaviour, method, practice, allegiance) changement *m* (**in** de); **the ~ (away) from gas to electricity** le passage du gaz à l'électricité; **a ~ to the Conservatives** un glissement en faveur des conservateurs; **2** Elec (for light) interrupteur *m*; (on radio, appliance) bouton *m*; **on/off ~** interrupteur *m*

marche-arrêt; **ignition ~** Aut démarreur *m*; **the ~ is on/off** c'est allumé/éteint; **3** US Rail (points) aiguillage *m*; (siding) voie *f* de garage; **4** (stick, whip) badine *f*; **(riding) ~** cravache *f*; **5** (hairpiece) postiche *m*.
II *vtr* **1** (change) changer de [*brands, products, currencies, parties, flights, seats etc*]; reporter [*support, attention*] (**to** sur); transférer [*bank account*] (**to** dans); **to ~ lanes** Aut changer de voie; **to ~ the conversation to another topic** changer de sujet de conversation; **the organization has ~ed its support from amateurs to professionals** l'organisation a reporté son soutien des amateurs aux professionnels; **she ~ed her support to the other party** elle a reporté son soutien sur l'autre parti; **she ~ed from the violin to the viola** elle est passée du violon à l'alto; **to ~ the emphasis to** remettre l'accent sur; **he ~ed his allegiance back to Labour** il est revenu au parti travailliste; **could you ~ the TV over?** est-ce que tu pourrais changer de chaîne?; **2** (also **~ round**) (change position or order of) intervertir [*objects, roles, jobs*]; **I've ~ed the furniture round** j'ai changé la disposition des meubles; **~ the players round at half-time** permutez les joueurs à la mi-temps; **3** (whip) donner un coup de badine à [*horse*]; **4** Rail aiguiller [*train*].
III *vi* **1** (change) lit, fig changer; **to ~ between two languages/brands** alterner entre deux langues/marques; **I can't ~ from German to French** je n'arrive pas à passer de l'allemand au français; **we have ~ed (over) from oil to gas** nous sommes passés du mazout au gaz; **he has ~ed (over) from Labour to the Green party** il est passé du parti travailliste au parti écologiste; **in the end she ~ed back to teaching/to her original brand** finalement elle est revenue à l'enseignement/à sa marque d'avant; **can we ~ back to BBC 2?** est-ce qu'on peut remettre BBC 2?; **I ~ed from shopping on Saturdays to shopping on Mondays** j'ai cessé de faire mes courses le samedi pour les faire le lundi; **2** (also **~ over** ou **round**) [*people*] (change positions) changer, alterner; (change scheduling) (in work rota) permuter (**with** avec); **I'm tired, can we ~ (over** ou **round)?** je suis fatigué, on peut changer or alterner?; **3** Comput **to ~ to sth** basculer vers qch.
■ **switch off**: ¶ **~ off 1** Elec [*appliance, light, supply*] s'éteindre; [*person*] éteindre; **2**○ (stop listening) décrocher○; ¶ **~ off [sth]**, **~ [sth] off 1** Aut, Elec éteindre [*appliance, light*]; couper [*supply*]; éteindre, couper [*car engine*]; **the kettle ~es itself off** la bouilloire s'éteint toute seule or automatiquement; **2** fig **to ~ off the charm** cesser de faire du charme.
■ **switch on**: ¶ **~ on** Elec [*appliance, light, supply*] s'allumer; [*person*] allumer; ¶ **~ on [sth]**, **~ [sth] on 1** Aut, Elec allumer [*appliance, light, supply*]; allumer, mettre [qch] en marche [*car engine*]; **2** fig **to ~ on the charm** faire du charme; **3**○ **to be ~ed on** gen (excited) être émoustillé○; (on drugs) planer○.
■ **switch over** TV, Radio changer de programme.

switchback /ˈswɪtʃbæk/ **I** *n* **1** GB (rollercoaster) montagnes *fpl* russes; fig (in road) alternance *f* vertigineuse; **2** (twisty) (road) route *f* en lacet; (railway track) voie *f* ferrée en lacet; (bend) virage *m* en épingle à cheveux.
II *modif* [*road, track*] en lacet.

switchblade /ˈswɪtʃbleɪd/ *n* US (couteau *m* à) cran *m* d'arrêt.

switchboard /ˈswɪtʃbɔːd/ *n* (installation) standard *m*; (staff) standardistes *mfpl*; **you have to go through the ~** vous devez passer par le standard.

switchboard operator ▶ 1692 *n* standardiste *mf*.

switcheroo○ /ˈswɪtʃəruː/ *n* US tromperie *f* sur la marchandise.

switch-hitter○ /ˈswɪtʃhɪtə(r)/ *n* US (in baseball) joueur *m* ambidextre; fig (bisexual) bisexuel/-elle *m/f*; **he's a ~** fig il marche à voile et à vapeur○.

switchover /ˈswɪtʃəʊvə(r)/ *n* passage *m* (**from** de; **to** à); **the ~ to computers** le passage à l'informatique.

switch-yard /ˈswɪtʃjɑːd/ *n* US Rail gare *f* de triage.

Switzerland /ˈswɪtzəlænd/ ▶ 1131 *pr n* Suisse *f* ; **French/German/Italian speaking ~** la Suisse romande/allemande/italienne.

swivel /ˈswɪvl/ **I** *n* **1** Fishg émerillon *m*; **2** (movement) pivotement *m*.
II *modif* [*arm, lamp, tap*] pivotant, orientable.
III *vtr* (*p prés etc* **-ll-** GB , **-l-** US) faire pivoter [*chair, camera, telescope*]; tourner [*eyes, head, body*]; **to ~ one's hips** se déhancher.
IV *vi* (*p prés etc* **-ll-** GB, **-l-** US) [*person, head, chair, gun*] pivoter (**on** sur); [*eyes*] tourner.
■ **swivel round**: ¶ **~ round** pivoter; ¶ **~ [sth] round, ~ round [sth]** faire pivoter [qch].

swivel chair, swivel seat *n* fauteuil *m* tournant, chaise *f* tournante.

swiz(z)○ /swɪz/ *n* GB arnaque○ *f*.

swizzle○ /ˈswɪzl/ *n* GB = **swiz(z)**.

swizzle stick *n* cuillère *f* à cocktail or à soda.

swollen /ˈswəʊlən/ **I** *pp* ▶ **swell III**, **IV**.
II *adj* [*ankle, gland*] enflé; [*eyes*] gonflé; [*river*] en crue; **my eyes are ~ with crying** j'ai les yeux gonflés d'avoir pleuré.
IDIOMS **to have a ~ head**○, **to be ~headed**○ avoir la grosse tête○.

swoon /swuːn/ **I** *n* littér pâmoison *f*; **in a ~** en pâmoison.
II *vi* lit défaillir (**with** de; **at** à); fig se pâmer (**with** de; **at** à); **to ~ over sb** se pâmer d'admiration devant qn.

swoop /swuːp/ **I** *n* **1** (of bird, plane) descente *f* en piqué; **2** (police raid) rafle *f*; **arrested in a ~** arrêté lors d'une rafle.
II *vi* **1** [*bird, bat, plane*] plonger; **to ~ above the crowd** plonger vers la foule; **to ~ down** descendre en piqué; **to ~ down on** fondre sur; **2** [*police, raider*] faire une descente; **to ~ on** fondre or s'abattre sur.

swoosh /swʊʃ/ onomat **I** *n* bruissement *m*.
II *vi* [*tall grass, leaves*] bruire.

swop /swɒp/ *n, vtr* = **swap**.

sword /sɔːd/ **I** *n* épée *f*; **to put sb to the ~** passer qn au fil de l'épée; **to put up one's ~** remettre l'épée au fourreau.
II *modif* [*blade, hilt*] d'épée.
IDIOMS **to be a double-edged** ou **two-edged ~** être une arme à double tranchant; **he who lives by the ~ will die by the ~** qui se sert de l'épée périra par l'épée; **to cross ~s with sb** croiser le fer avec qn.

sword: **~ belt** *n* baudrier *m*; **~ dance** *n* danse *f* du sabre; **~fish** *n* espadon *m*; **~play** *n* maniement *m* de l'épée; **~sman** *n* épéiste *m*; **~smanship** *n* art *m* de manier l'épée; **~stick** *n* canne-épée *f*; **~ swallower** *n* avaleur/-euse *m/f* de sabres.

swore /swɔː(r)/ *prét* ▶ **swear**.

sworn /swɔːn/ **I** *pp* ▶ **swear**.
II *adj* **1** Jur (under oath) [*statement*] fait sous serment; **he said in ~ evidence** ou **testimony that** il a témoigné sous serment que; **2** (avowed) [*enemy*] juré; [*ally*] pour la vie; **we are ~ enemies** on s'est juré une haine éternelle.

swot○ /swɒt/ **I** *n* bûcheur/-euse○ *m/f*.
II *vi* (*p prés etc* **-tt-**) bûcher○; **to ~ for an exam** potasser○ un examen.
■ **swot up**: ¶ **~ [sth] up, ~ up [sth]** potasser qch; ¶ **~ up on [sth]** potasser qch.

swum /swʌm/ *pp* ▶ **swim** II, III.

swung /swʌŋ/ *prét, pp* ▶ **swing** III, IV.

swung dash *n* tilde *m*.

sybarite /ˈsɪbəraɪt/ *n* sout sybarite *mf*.

sybaritic /ˌsɪbəˈrɪtɪk/ *adj* sout sybarite.

sycamore /ˈsɪkəmɔː(r)/ *n* sycomore *m*.

sycophancy /ˈsɪkəfənsɪ/ *n* flagornerie *f*.

sycophant /ˈsɪkəfænt/ *n* flagorneur/-euse *m/f*.

sycophantic /ˌsɪkəˈfæntɪk/ *adj* flagorneur/-euse.

Sydney /ˈsɪdnɪ/ ▶ 1818 *pr n* Sydney.

syllabary /ˈsɪləbərɪ, US -berɪ/ *n* syllabaire *m*.

syllabic /sɪˈlæbɪk/ *adj* syllabique.

syllabification /sɪˌlæbɪfɪˈkeɪʃn/ *n* syllabation *f*.

syllabify /sɪˈlæbɪfaɪ/ *vtr* diviser [qch] en syllabes.

syllable /ˈsɪləbl/ *n* syllabe *f*; **in words of one ~** en termes simples; **not one ~** pas un seul mot.

syllabub /ˈsɪləbʌb/ *n* crème *f* fouettée (*parfumée au cognac et au citron*).

syllabus /ˈsɪləbəs/ *n* (*pl* **-buses** ou **-bi**) programme *m*; **on the ~** au programme.

syllogism /ˈsɪlədʒɪzəm/ *n* syllogisme *m*.

syllogistic /ˌsɪləˈdʒɪstɪk/ *adj* syllogistique.

syllogize /ˈsɪlədʒaɪz/ *vi* raisonner par syllogismes.

sylph /sɪlf/ *n* (fairy) sylphe/sylphide *m/f*; fig (slender woman) sylphide *f*.

sylphlike /ˈsɪlflaɪk/ *adj* [*woman, movements*] d'une grâce ethérée; **~ figure** souvent hum silhouette de sylphide.

sylvan /ˈsɪlvən/ *adj* littér sylvestre liter.

sylviculture /ˈsɪlvɪkʌltʃə(r)/ *n* sylviculture *f*.

symbiosis /ˌsɪmbaɪˈəʊsɪs, ˌsɪmbɪ-/ *n* symbiose *f*; **in ~** en symbiose.

symbiotic /ˌsɪmbaɪˈɒtɪk, ˌsɪmbɪ-/ *adj* symbiotique.

symbol /ˈsɪmbl/ *n* (all contexts) symbole *m* (**of, for** de); **chemical/phallic ~** symbole chimique/phallique.

symbolic(al) /sɪmˈbɒlɪk(l)/ *adj* symbolique (**of** de).

symbolically /sɪmˈbɒlɪklɪ/ *adv* symboliquement.

symbolism /ˈsɪmbəlɪzəm/ *n* (all contexts) symbolisme *m*.

symbolist /ˈsɪmbəlɪst/ *n, adj* symboliste (*mf*).

symbolization /ˌsɪmbəlaɪˈzeɪʃn/ *n* symbolisation *f* (**of** de; **by** par).

symbolize/ˈsɪmbəlaɪz/ *vtr* symboliser (**by** par).

symmetric(al) /sɪˈmetrɪk(l)/ *adj* symétrique.

symmetrically /sɪˈmetrɪklɪ/ *adv* symétriquement.

symmetry /ˈsɪmətrɪ/ *n* symétrie *f*.

sympathetic /ˌsɪmpəˈθetɪk/ *adj* **1** (compassionate) [*person*] compatissant (**to, towards** envers); [*smile, remark, words, gesture*] compatissant; (understanding) [*person*] compréhensif/-ive; (kindly) gentil/-ille, bienveillant; (well-disposed) [*person, government, organization*] bien disposé (**to, towards** à l'égard de), favorable (**to, towards** à); **he is ~ to their cause** il est solidaire de leur cause, il est de leur côté; **2** (pleasant, friendly) [*person, manner*] sympathique; **3** (environmentally) [*building, development*] qui s'harmonise bien avec l'environnement; **4** Med (ortho)sympathique; **~ nervous system** système *m* sympathique; **~ pregnancy** grossesse *f* nerveuse.

sympathetically /ˌsɪmpəˈθetɪklɪ/ *adv* **1** (compassionately) avec compassion; **2** (kindly) avec bienveillance; **3** (favourably) favorablement.

sympathize /ˈsɪmpəθaɪz/ *vi* **1** (feel compassion) témoigner de la sympathie (**with** à); **they called to ~ with the widow** ils sont allés présenter leurs condoléances or témoigner de leur sympathie à la veuve; **I ~ with you in your grief** je compatis or m'associe à votre douleur; **we ~ with your feelings, but...** nous comprenons vos sentiments, mais...; **I ~, I used to be a teacher** je comprends, moi aussi j'ai été professeur; **2** (support) **to ~ with** être solidaire de [*cause, organization*]; souscrire à, être d'accord avec [*aims, views*].

sympathizer /ˈsɪmpəθaɪzə(r)/ *n* **1** gen, Pol (supporter) sympathisant/-e *m/f* (**of** de); **they are Communist ~s** ce sont des sympathisants communistes; **2** (at funeral etc) personne *f* qui témoigne de la compassion.

sympathy /ˈsɪmpəθɪ/ **I** *n* **1** (compassion) compassion *f*; **to feel ~ for sb** éprouver de la compassion pour qn; **to do sth out of ~ for sb** faire qch par compassion pour qn; **he pressed my hand in ~** il m'a serré la main en signe de compassion; **she could show a bit more ~!** elle pourrait se montrer un peu plus compatissante!; **'with deepest ~'** 'avec notre or ma profonde sympathie', 'avec nos or mes sincères condoléances'; **2** (solidarity) solidarité *f*; **to be in ~ with sb** être d'accord avec qn, être du côté de qn; **I am in ~ with their aims** je suis d'accord avec leurs objectifs; **I have little ~ for their cause** j'ai peu de sympathie pour leur cause; **the workers have come out on strike in ~ with the students** les ouvriers se sont mis en grève par solidarité avec les étudiants; **the programme aroused public ~ for victims of the famine** le public a été profondément ému par cette émission sur les victimes de la famine; **3** (affinity, empathy) affinité *f*; **there is a deep ~ between them** il y a une grande affinité entre eux.
II sympathies *npl* gen, Pol **what are her political ~s?** quelles sont ses tendances *fpl* politiques?; **to have left-wing/right-wing ~s** être de gauche/de droite; **my ~s lie entirely with the workers** je suis entièrement du côté des ouvriers.

sympathy strike *n* grève *f* de solidarité.

symphonic /sɪmˈfɒnɪk/ *adj* symphonique.

symphonic poem *n* poème *m* symphonique.

symphonist /ˈsɪmfənɪst/ *n* symphoniste *mf*.

symphony /ˈsɪmfənɪ/ *n* lit, fig symphonie *f*.

symphony orchestra *n* orchestre *m* symphonique.

symposium /sɪmˈpəʊzɪəm/ *n* (*pl* **-sia**) **1** (conference) symposium *m*; **2** (collection) recueil *m*.

symptom /ˈsɪmptəm/ *n* (all contexts) symptôme *m*; **to show ~s of sth** présenter des symptômes de qch.

symptomatic /ˌsɪmptəˈmætɪk/ *adj* symptomatique (**of** de).

synagogue /ˈsɪnəgɒg/ *n* synagogue *f*.

sync(h) /sɪŋk/ *n* (*abrév* = **synchronization**) synchronisation *f*; **in/out of ~** [*watch, system, machine*] bien/mal synchronisé; **to be in/out of ~ with** [*person, government*] être en phase/déphasé par rapport à [*public opinion*]; **the soundtrack is out of ~ with the picture** la bande sonore et l'image ne sont pas synchronisées.

synchromesh /ˌsɪŋkrəʊˈmeʃ/ *adj* **a ~ gearbox** une boîte de vitesses synchronisées.

synchronic /sɪŋˈkrɒnɪk/ *adj* **1** Ling synchronique; **2** = **synchronous**.

synchronicity /sɪŋˌkrɒnˈɪsətɪ/ *n* synchronisme *m*.

synchronism /ˈsɪŋkrənɪzəm/ *n* synchronisme *m*.

synchronization /ˌsɪŋkrənaɪˈzeɪʃn/ *n* synchronisation *f*; **in/out of ~** bien/mal synchronisé.

synchronize /ˈsɪŋkrənaɪz/ **I** *vtr* synchroniser.
II *vi* être synchrone.
III synchronized *pp adj* synchronisé.

synchronized swimming ▶ **1282** *n* natation *f* synchronisée.

synchronous /ˈsɪŋkrənəs/ *adj* synchrone.

synchronous: **~ converter** *n* convertisseur *m* synchrone; **~ motor** *n* moteur *m* synchrone; **~ orbit** *n* orbite *f* synchrone.

syncline /ˈsɪŋklaɪn/ *n* synclinal *m*.

syncopate /ˈsɪŋkəpeɪt/ *vtr* syncoper.

syncopation /ˌsɪŋkəˈpeɪʃn/ *n* syncope *f*.

syncope /ˈsɪŋkəpɪ/ *n* Med, Ling syncope *f*.

syncretism /ˈsɪŋkrətɪzəm/ *n* syncrétisme *m*.

syncretize /ˈsɪŋkrətaɪz/ *vtr* opérer le syncrétisme de.

syndeton /sɪnˈdiːtən/ *n* syndète *f*.

syndic /ˈsɪndɪk/ *n* GB Univ contrôleur *m* de gestion.

syndicalism /ˈsɪndɪkəlɪzəm/ *n* syndicalisme *m*.

syndicalist /ˈsɪndɪkəlɪst/ *n* syndicaliste *mf*.

syndicate I /ˈsɪndɪkət/ *n* **1** Comm, Fin (of people) syndicat *m*; (of companies) consortium *m*; **to form a ~** [*investors*] se constituer en syndicat; **financial ~** syndicat financier; **banking ~** consortium bancaire; **to be a member of a ~** [*industrialist*] être syndicataire; [*banker*] faire partie d'un consortium; **2** Journ (agency) syndicat *m* de distribution; (for cartoons) syndicat *m*; **3** surtout US (association) (of criminals) association *f* de malfaiteurs; (for lottery) association *f* de joueurs *(de loterie)*; **crime ~** syndicat du crime; **drug(s) ~** cartel de la drogue.
II /ˈsɪndɪkeɪt/ *vtr* **1** Journ [*agency, person*] vendre [qch] par l'intermédiaire d'un syndicat de distribution [*column, photograph, comic strip*]; **~d in over 50 newspapers** publié simultanément dans plus de 50 journaux; **2** US Radio, TV (sell) distribuer [qch] sous licence [*programme*]; **3** (assemble) syndiquer [*workers*]; regrouper [qn] au sein d'un consortium [*bankers*].
III syndicated *pp adj* **1** Journ [*columnist*] d'agence; **2** Fin [*loan*] participatif, en participation; [*shares*] syndiqué.

syndrome /ˈsɪndrəʊm/ *n* (all contexts) syndrome *m*.

synecdoche /sɪˈnekdəkɪ/ *n* synecdoque *f*.

synergy /ˈsɪnədʒɪ/ *n* synergie *f*.

synod /ˈsɪnəd/ *n* synode *m*; **the General Synod** le Synode Général (*corps exécutif de l'Église anglicane*).

synonym /ˈsɪnənɪm/ *n* synonyme *m* (**of, for** de).

synonymous /sɪˈnɒnɪməs/ *adj* synonyme (**with** de).

synonymy /sɪˈnɒnəmɪ/ *n* synonymie *f*.

synopsis /sɪˈnɒpsɪs/ *n* (*pl* **-ses**) (of play, film) synopsis *m*; (of book) résumé *m*.

synoptic /sɪˈnɒptɪk/ *adj* synoptique.

synovia /saɪˈnəʊvɪə/ *n* synovie *f*.

synovial /saɪˈnəʊvɪəl/ *adj* synovial.

syntactic(al) /sɪnˈtæktɪk(l)/ *adj* [*accuracy, analysis, link*] syntaxique; **~ errors** erreurs de syntaxe.

syntactically /sɪnˈtæktɪklɪ/ *adv* syntaxiquement.

syntactics /sɪnˈtæktɪks/ *n* (+ *v sg*) syntactique *f*.

syntagm(a) /sɪnˈtægm(ə)/ *n* syntagme *m*.

syntagmatic /ˌsɪntægˈmætɪk/ *adj* syntagmatique.

syntax /ˈsɪntæks/ *n* syntaxe *f*.

synth /sɪnθ/ *n* Mus (*abrév* = **synthesizer**) synthé○ *m*.

synthesis /ˈsɪnθəsɪs/ *n* (*pl* **-ses**) (all contexts) synthèse *f*.

synthesize /ˈsɪnθəsaɪz/ *vtr* **1** Chem, Ind produire [qch] par synthèse; **2** Literat, Philos (fuse) synthétiser; **3** Electron, Mus synthétiser.

synthesizer /ˈsɪnθəsaɪzə(r)/ *n* synthétiseur *m*.

synthetic /sɪnˈθetɪk/ **I** *n* (textile) (fibre *f*) synthétique *m*; (substance) produit *m* synthétique.
II *adj* **1** (man-made) synthétique; **2** péj (false) [*smile, emotion*] factice; [*smell, taste*] synthétique pej.

synthetically /sɪnˈθetɪklɪ/ *adv* synthétiquement.

S Yorkshire *n* GB Post *abrév écrite* = **South Yorkshire**.

syphilis /ˈsɪfɪlɪs/ ▶ **1354** *n* syphilis *f*.

syphilitic /ˌsɪfɪˈlɪtɪk/ *n, adj* syphilitique (*mf*).

syphon *n* = **siphon**.

Syria /ˈsɪrɪə/ ▶ **1131** *pr n* Syrie *f*.

Syrian /ˈsɪrɪən/ **I** *n* Syrien/-ienne *m/f*.
II *adj* syrien/-ienne.

syringa /sɪˈrɪŋgə/ *n* seringa(t) *m*.

syringe /sɪˈrɪndʒ/ **I** *n* seringue *f*.
II *vtr* **1** Med seringuer [*wound*]; **to have one's ears ~d** se faire déboucher les oreilles (avec une seringue); **2** Hort seringuer (**with** de).

syrup /ˈsɪrəp/ *n* (all contexts) sirop *m*; **cough ~** sirop *m* contre la toux.

syrup of figs *n* sirop *m* de figues.

syrupy /ˈsɪrəpɪ/ *adj* sirupeux/-euse also fig, pej.

system /ˈsɪstəm/ *n* **1** Admin (way of organizing) système *m* (**for doing, to do** pour faire); **filing ~** système de classement; **we need a ~** il faut organiser ça de manière systématique; **to lack ~** manquer d'organisation; **2** Comput système *m* (**for doing, to do** pour faire); **to store sth in the ~** mettre qch en mémoire; **3** Econ, Jur, Ling, Philos, Pol (set of principles) système *m*; **banking/educational ~** système bancaire/éducatif; **a gambling ~** un système de probabilités; **4** (electrical, mechanical) système *m*; **public address ~** système de sonorisation; **stereo ~** chaîne *f* stéréo; **braking ~** dispositif *m* de freinage; **5** Pol (established structures) **the ~** le système *m*; **to work within the ~** agir de l'intérieur du système; **to beat the ~** contourner le système; **6** (network) réseau *m*; **telephone/road ~** réseau téléphonique/routier; **traffic ~** système *m* de circulation; **7** Anat, Med (digestive, nervous, respiratory) système *m*; **reproductive ~** appareil *m* reproducteur; **8** Physiol (human, animal) organisme *m*; **to damage/get into the ~** nuire à/s'introduire dans l'organisme; **to get sth out of one's ~** lit rendre qch; fig○ oublier qch; **9** Geog, Geol, Meteorol (of features) système *m*; **high-pressure ~** roue *f* de hautes pressions (atmosphériques); **river ~** réseau *m* fluvial; **10** Chem, Math, Meas (for classification, measurement) système *m*.

systematic /ˌsɪstəˈmætɪk/ *adj* **1** (efficient) [*person, approach, training, planning*] méthodique; [*method, way*] rationnel/-elle; **to be ~ in** être méthodique dans; **2** (deliberate) [*attempt, abuse, torture, destruction*] systématique; **3** Biol, Bot, Zool systématique.

systematically /ˌsɪstəˈmætɪklɪ/ *adv* **1** (in ordered way) [*list, work, process, study*] méthodiquement; [*arrange, construct*] systématiquement; **2** (deliberately) [*destroy, undermine, spoil, cut*] systématiquement.

systematize /ˈsɪstəmətaɪz/ *vtr* systématiser.

systemic /sɪˈstemɪk/ **I** *n* insecticide *m* systémique.
II *adj* **1** gen, Econ, Pol [*change, collapse*] du système; **2** Physiol [*poison, disease*] de l'organisme; **3** Agric, Hort [*pesticide, insecticide*] systémique; **4** Ling systémique.

systemic: **~ circulation** *n* circulation *f* générale; **~ grammar** *n* grammaire *f* systémique; **~ infection** *n* infection *f* généralisée.

system: **~s analysis** *n* analyse *f* de systèmes; **~s analyst** ▶ **1692** *n* analyste *mf* de systèmes; **~s design** *n* conception *f* de systèmes; **~s disk** *n* disque *m* système; **~s diskette** *n* disquette *f* système; **~s engineer** ▶ **1692** *n* ingénieur *m* système; **~s engineering** *n* architecture *f* des systèmes; **~(s) software** *n* logiciel *m* de base; **~s programmer** ▶ **1692** *n* programmeur *m* d'étude; **~s theory** *n* théorie *f* des systèmes.

systole /ˈsɪstəlɪ/ *n* systole *f*.

t, T /tiː/ *n* (letter) t, T *m*.
IDIOMS **it suits me to a T** [*job, situation*] ça me convient à la perfection; [*garment, role*] ça me va comme un gant; **that's Robert to a T** c'est signé Robert.
t. *abrév écrite* = **tempo**.
ta○ /tɑː/ *excl* GB merci.
TA *n* **1** GB (*abrév* = **Territorial Army**) armée *f* territoriale; **2** *abrév* ▶ **transactional analysis**; **3** US Univ *abrév* ▶ **teaching assistant**.
tab /tæb/ **I** *n* **1** (on garment) (decorative) patte *f*; (loop) attache *f*; GB (on military uniform) écusson *m*; GB (on shoelace) ferret *m*; **2** (on can) languette *f*; **3** (on files) onglet *m*; **4** (for identification) étiquette *f*; **5** Aviat (on wing etc) compensateur *m*; **6** US (bill) note *f*, addition *f*; **to pick up the ~** lit, fig payer la note; **7**○ (tablet) comprimé *m*; **8** Comput (tabulator) tabulatrice *f*; **9** (of word processor, typewriter) (device) tabulateur *m*; (setting) marque *f* de tabulation; **to set ~s** placer des marques de tabulation; **10** Theat rideau *m* à l'italienne.
II *modif* [*character, key, stop*] de tabulation.
III *vtr* (*p prés etc* **-bb-**) **1** (label) marquer [*garment, file*]; **2** US (single out) désigner.
IDIOMS **to keep ~s on sb**○ tenir qn à l'œil○; **to keep ~s on sth**○ avoir l'œil sur qch.
TAB (*abrév* = **typhoid-paratyphoid A and B** (**vaccine**)) vaccin *m* TAB.
tabard /ˈtæbəd/ *n* tabar(d) *m*.
Tbasco® /təˈbæskəʊ/ *n* Tabasco® *m*.
tabby (**cat**) /ˈtæbɪ/ *n* chat/chatte *m*/*f* tigré/-e.
tabernacle /ˈtæbənækl/ *n* **1** Bible, Relig tabernacle *m*; **2** US (church) grande église *f*.
table /ˈteɪbl/ **I** *n* **1** (piece of furniture) table *f*; **garden/kitchen ~** table de jardin/de cuisine; **at ~** à table; **to lay** ou **set the ~** mettre le couvert or la table; **to put sth on the ~** fig GB (propose) avancer [*proposal, offer*]; US (postpone) ajourner [*proposal, offer*]; **the proposal is now on the ~** GB la proposition est à présent déposée; **the offer is still on the ~** l'offre tient toujours; **the UN is trying to get the warring parties round the ~** l'ONU tente de réunir les parties en conflit autour de la table de négociations; **he keeps a good ~** fig on mange bien chez lui; **2** (list) table *f*, tableau *m*; **to present sth in ~ form** présenter qch sous forme de table; **3** Math table *f*; **the six-times ~** Math la table de six; **to learn one's ~s** Math apprendre ses tables de multiplication; **conversion ~** table de conversion; **multiplication ~** table de multiplication; **4** Sport (also **league ~**) classement *m*; **to be at the top/bottom of the ~** être en tête/en bas du classement; **5** Geog plateau *m*; **6** Hist (tablet) table *f*; **the Tables of the Law** les Tables de la Loi.
II *vtr* **1** GB (present) présenter [*bill, amendment, proposal*]; **to ~ sth for discussion** soumettre qch au débat; **2** US (postpone) ajourner [*motion, bill, amendment*].
IDIOMS **I can drink you under the ~** je tiens mieux l'alcool que toi; **she drank everyone under the ~** quand tous les autres étaient soûls, elle se tenait toujours debout; **to do sth under the ~** faire qch sous le manteau; **to turn the ~s on sb** renverser les rôles aux dépens de qn; **to lay** ou **put one's cards on the ~** jouer cartes sur table.
tableau /ˈtæbləʊ/ *n* (*pl* **~x** ou **~s**) **1** Theat (also **~ vivant**) tableau *m* vivant; **2** gen (scene) tableau *m*.
table: **~cloth** *n* nappe *f*; **~ d'hôte** *adj* à prix fixe; **~ football** ▶ 1282 *n* baby-foot *m*; **~-hop** *vi* US faire le tour des tables; **~ lamp** *n* lampe *f* de table; **~land** *n* Geog haut plateau *m*; **~ leg** *n* pied *m* de table; **~ linen** *n* linge *m* de table.
table manners *npl* **to have good/bad ~** savoir/ne pas savoir se tenir à table.
table: **~ mat** *n* (under plate) set *m* de table; (under serving-dish) dessous-de-plat *m inv*; **Table Mountain** *pr n* la montagne de la Table; **~ napkin** *n* serviette *f* (de table); **~ salt** *n* sel *m* fin or de table.
tablespoon /ˈteɪblspuːn/ *n* **1** (object) cuillère *f* de service; **2** Meas, Culin (also **~ful**) cuillerée *f* à soupe (GB = *18 ml*, US = *15 ml*).
tablet /ˈtæblɪt/ *n* **1** (medicine) comprimé *m* (**for** pour); **sleeping ~s** somnifères *mpl*; **2** (commemorative) plaque *f* (commémorative); **3** Archeol (for writing) tablette *f*; **4** (bar) (of chocolate) tablette *f*; **a ~ of soap** une savonnette; **5** Comput (pad) tablette *f*; **6** US (writing pad) bloc-notes *m*.
IDIOMS **engraved in ~s of stone** gravé dans la pierre.
table talk *n* propos *mpl* de table.
table tennis I *n* tennis *m* de table, ping-pong® *m*.
II table-tennis *modif* [*bat, player, table*] de ping-pong®.
table: **~ top** *n* dessus *m* de table; **~-turning** *n* spiritisme *m* par les tables tournantes; **~ware** *n* vaisselle *f*; **~ wine** *n* vin *m* de table.
tabloid /ˈtæblɔɪd/ **I** *n* **1** (also **~ newspaper**) quotidien *m* populaire, tabloïde *m* pej; **the ~s** la presse populaire; **2** (format) tabloïd(e) *m*.
II *modif* **1** péj [*journalism, journalist, press*] populaire; **2** [*format, size*] tabloïd(e).
taboo /təˈbuː/ **I** *n* **1** gen tabou *m*; **there's a ~ on discussing sex** parler de sexe est tabou; **2** Anthrop tabou *m* (**on** de).
II *adj* [*word, subject, function*] tabou.
tabour /ˈteɪbɔː(r)/ ▶ 1481 *n* tambourin *m*.
tabular /ˈtæbjʊlə(r)/ *adj* tabulaire.
tabulate /ˈtæbjʊleɪt/ *vtr* **1** (present) présenter [qch] sous forme de tableau [*figures, data, results*]; **2** (in typing) tabuler.
tabulation /ˌtæbjʊˈleɪʃn/ *n* **1** (of data, results) disposition *f* en tableaux; **2** (in typing) tabulation *f*.
tabulator /ˈtæbjʊleɪtə(r)/ *n* **1** (device) (on typewriter) tabulateur *m*; (on computer) tabulatrice *f*; **2** (person) tableautier *m*.
tache○ /tæʃ, tɑːʃ/ *n* GB moustache *f*, bacchantes○ *fpl*.
tacheometer /ˌtækeɪˈɒmɪtə(r)/ *n* tachéomètre *m*.
tachograph /ˈtækəgrɑːf, US -græf/ *n* tachygraphe *m*.
tachometer /təˈkɒmɪtə(r)/ *n* tachymètre *m*.
tachycardia /ˌtækɪˈkɑːdɪə/ *n* tachycardie *f*.
tachycardiac /ˌtækɪˈkɑːdɪæk/ *adj* tachycardiaque.
tachymeter /təˈkɪmɪtə(r)/ *n* tachéomètre *m*.
tacit /ˈtæsɪt/ *adj* **1** gen tacite; **by ~ agreement** par consentement tacite; **2** Ling **~ knowledge** connaissance implicite du langage.
tacitly /ˈtæsɪtlɪ/ *adv* tacitement.
taciturn /ˈtæsɪtɜːn/ *adj* taciturne.
taciturnity /ˌtæsɪˈtɜːnətɪ/ *n* taciturnité *f*.
taciturnly /ˈtæsɪtɜːnlɪ/ *adv* d'une manière taciturne.
Tacitus /ˈtæsɪtəs/ *pr n* Tacite.
tack /tæk/ **I** *n* **1** (nail) clou *m*, semence *f* (de tapissier); **2** US (drawing pin) punaise *f*; **3** (approach) tactique *f*; **to take** ou **try another ~** opter pour une autre tactique; **to change ~** changer de tactique; **4** Naut bordée *f*; **a ~ to port/starboard** une bordée de bâbord/tribord; **on the port/starboard ~** bâbord/tribord amures; **5** Equit sellerie *f*; **6** Sewing (stitch) point *m* de bâti.
II *vtr* **1** (nail) **to ~ sth to** clouer qch à [*wall, door*]; **to ~ sth down** clouer qch avec des semences; **2** Sewing bâtir, faufiler.
III *vi* [*sailor*] faire or tirer une bordée; [*yacht*] louvoyer; **to ~ to port/starboard** [*sailor*] faire or tirer une bordée de bâbord/tribord; [*yacht*] virer sur bâbord/tribord; **they ~ed towards the mainland** ils sont rentrés vers la terre en louvoyant.
■ **tack on**: **~ [sth] on, ~ on [sth]** Sewing fixer [qch] à points de bâti; fig ajouter [qch] après coup [*clause, ending, building*] (**to** à).
■ **tack up**: **~ [sth] up, ~ up [sth]** fixer [*poster*].
tack hammer *n* marteau *m* de tapissier.
tacking /ˈtækɪŋ/ *n* Sewing bâti *m*, faufil *m*.
tacking: **~ stitch** *n* point *m* de bâti; **~ thread** *n* fil *m* à bâtir.
tackle /ˈtækl/ **I** *n* **1** Sport (in soccer, hockey) tacle *m* (**on** sur); (in rugby, American football) plaquage *m* (**on** sur); **2** gen (equipment) équipement *m*; (for fishing) articles *mpl* or matériel *m* de pêche; **3** Naut, Tech ₵ (on ship) gréement *m*; (for lifting) palan *m*.
II *vtr* **1** (handle) s'attaquer à [*task, problem, subject, challenge*]; essayer de maîtriser [*fire*]; attaquer○ [*food*]; **to ~ sth head-on** s'attaquer de front à qch; **2** (confront) **to ~ sb** prendre qn de front; **to ~ sb about** parler à qn de [*subject, grievance, problem*]; **3** Sport (intercept) (in soccer, hockey) tacler; (in rugby, American football) plaquer; **4** (take on) [*person*] maîtriser [*intruder, criminal*].
III *vi* (in soccer, hockey) tacler; (in rugby, American football) plaquer.
tackle block *n* moufle *f*.
tackler /ˈtæklə(r)/ *n* tacleur *m*.
tackling /ˈtæklɪŋ/ *n* (in rugby) plaquage *m*; (in soccer) tacle *m*.
tack room *n* sellerie *f*.
tack weld I *n* point *m*.
II *vtr* pointer.

tack welding *n* pointage *m*.

tacky /'tækɪ/ *adj* **1** (sticky) [*surface, putty*] collant; **the paint is still ~** la peinture n'est pas encore tout à fait sèche; **2**○ péj [*place, garment, object*] tocard○ pej; [*person*] rustaud○ pej; [*remark*] de mauvais goût.

taco /'tɑːkəʊ/ *n*: *crêpe de maïs farcie et frite*.

tact /tækt/ *n* tact *m*; **to have ~** avoir du tact; **to have the ~ to do** avoir le tact de faire.

tactful /'tæktfl/ *adj* [*person, suggestion*] plein de tact, délicat; [*reply, words, letter, intervention*] plein de tact, diplomatique; [*enquiry*] discret/-ète; [*attitude, approach*] diplomatique; **be a bit more ~** sois un peu plus diplomate; **to be ~ with sb** user de tact avec qn; **it wasn't very ~ to laugh** ce n'était pas très délicat de rire.

tactfully /'tæktfəlɪ/ *adv* [*say, behave, reply, refuse*] avec tact; [*ask, enquire*] avec diplomatie; [*decide, refuse, refrain*] par tact; [*worded, phrased, called*] avec diplomatie.

tactfulness /'tæktfʊlnɪs/ *n* tact *m*.

tactic /'tæktɪk/ *n* (stratagem) tactique *f*; **~s** tactique *f*; **a delaying/scare ~** une tactique dilatoire/alarmiste; **bullying/questionable ~s** méthodes brutales/douteuses; **to change ~s** changer de tactique; **his ~ of doing, his ~s of doing** sa tactique de faire; **strong-arm ~s** pej la manière forte.

tactical /'tæktɪkl/ *adj* (all contexts) tactique.

tactically /'tæktɪklɪ/ *adv* [*astute, sound, unwise, successful*] tactiquement; [*vote, proceed*] en fonction de considérations tactiques; **~ the plan was perfect** du point de vue tactique le plan était parfait.

tactical voting *n* vote *m* utile.

tactician /tæk'tɪʃn/ *n* tacticien/-ienne *m/f*.

tactile /'tæktaɪl, US -tl/ *adj* tactile.

tactile: **~ feedback** *n* sensation *f* de déclic; **~ keyboard** *n* clavier *m* tactile.

tactless /'tæktlɪs/ *adj* [*person, suggestion, attitude, behaviour*] peu délicat; [*question, enquiry*] indiscret/-ète; [*reply, words*] peu diplomatique; **it was ~ of him/her to do** c'était indélicat de sa part de faire.

tactlessly /'tæktlɪslɪ/ *adv* [*say, behave, ask*] sans tact; [*worded, phrased, expressed*] indélicatement.

tactlessness /'tæktlɪsnɪs/ *n* manque *m* de tact.

tad○ /tæd/ *n* US **1** (quantity) **a ~** un peu; **2** (child) bambin○ *m*.

tadpole /'tædpəʊl/ *n* têtard *m*.

Tadzhiki /tɑː'dʒiki:/ **▶ 1402** *n* tadjik *m*.

Tadzhikistan /tɑːˌdʒɪkɪ'stɑːn/ **▶ 1131** *pr n* Tadjikistan *m*.

Tadzhik /'tɑːdʒɪk/ **▶ 1486** **I** *n* Tadjik *m*.
II *adj* tadjik.

tae kwon do /'taɪ'kwɒn'dəʊ/ *n* taekwondo *m*.

taffeta /'tæfɪtə/ **I** *n* taffetas *m*.
II *modif* [*dress, gown, curtains*] en or de taffetas.

taffrail /'tæfreɪl/ *n* lisse *f* de couronnement.

taffy /'tæfɪ/ *n* US ≈ barbe *f* à papa.

Taffy○ /'tæfɪ/ *n* GB injur Gallois/-e *m/f*.

tag /tæg/ **I** *n* **1** (label) (on goods) étiquette *f*; (on luggage) étiquette *f*; (on cat, dog) plaque *f*; (on file) onglet *m*; **luggage ~** étiquette à bagages; **name ~** étiquette; **price ~** étiquette; **to put a ~ on sth** attacher une étiquette à [*suitcase*]; mettre une étiquette sur [*coat*]; **2** (for hanging) bride *f*; **hang the coat up by the ~** accroche le manteau par la bride; **3** Games (jeu *m* de) chat *m*; **to play ~** jouer à chat; **4** Ling tag *m*; **5** (quotation) gen citation *f*; (hackneyed) lieu *m* commun; **a Latin ~** une citation latine; **6** (signature) argot des graffistes tag○ *m*, griffe *f*; **7** Jur marqueur *m*; **electronic ~** marqueur *m* électronique; **8**○ US (registration plate) plaque *f* d'immatriculation; **9** (name) étiquette *f* also pej; **his work earned him the ~ 'subversive'** son œuvre lui a valu l'étiquette d'auteur subversif; **10** (on shoelace) ferret *m*; **11** Comput balise *f*, étiquette *f*.
II *vtr* (*p prés etc* **-gg-**) **1** (label) étiqueter [*goods*]; marquer [*clothing*]; apposer un onglet sur [*file*]; **2** Jur marquer [*criminal*]; **3** (name) étiqueter; **the film/novel was ~ged 'surreal'** le film a été qualifié de 'surréaliste '; **4**○ US Aut coller un papillon○ or une contravention sur [*car*]; **he was ~ged for speeding** il a eu une contravention pour excés de vitesse; **5** Comput baliser, étiqueter [*data item*]; **6** Games crier 'chat' en touchant [*player*]; **7** US (in baseball) = **tag out**.
III *vi* (*p prés etc* **-gg-**) **1** (follow) **to ~ after** gen suivre [*person*]; [*detective*] filer [*suspect*].
■ **tag along** venir aussi; **to ~ along behind** ou **after sb** suivre qn.
■ **tag on**: ¶ **~ on** [*person*] venir aussi; **whenever I go out, he ~s on** chaque fois que je sors il vient aussi; ¶ **~ [sth] on** rajouter [*paragraph, phrase*]; **to ~ sth onto sth** attacher qch à qch [*label, note*].
■ **tag out** US: **~ [sb] out** (in baseball) mettre qn hors jeu.

tag: **~ board** *n* papier *m* cartonné (*de bonne qualité*); **~ day** *n* US jour *m* de collecte (*au profit d'une œuvre caritative*); **~ end** *n* US restes *mpl*.

tagging /'tægɪŋ/ *n* **1** Jur marquage *m*; **electronic ~ of criminals** marquage *m* électronique des criminels; **2** Comput balisage *m*, étiquetage *m*.

tagliatelle /ˌtæljə'telɪ, ˌtæglɪə'telɪ/ *n* tagliatelles *fpl*.

tag line *n* (of entertainer) slogan *m*; (in play) mot *m* de la fin; (of poem) dernier vers *m*.

tagmeme /'tægmiːm/ *n* tagmème *m*.

tagmemics /tæg'miːmɪks/ *n* (+ *v sg*) tagmémique *f*.

tag question *n* Ling queue *f* de phrase interrogative, tag○ *m*.

Tagus /'teɪgəs/ **▶ 1644** *pr n* **the ~** le Tage.

tag: **~ wrestler** *n* catcheur *m* (de catch à quatre); **~ wrestling** **▶ 1282** *n* Sport catch *m* à quatre.

tahini /tə'hiːniː/, **tahina** /tə'hiːnə/ *n* tahina *m*.

Tahiti /tɑː'hiːtɪ/ **▶ 1381** *pr n* Tahiti *m*; **in/to ~** à Tahiti.

Tahitian /tə'hiːʃn/ **▶ 1486** **I** *n* Tahitien/-ienne *m/f*.
II *adj* tahitien/-ienne.

t'ai chi (ch'uan) /'taɪdʒiː('tʃwɑːn)/ *n* taichi(-chuan) *m*.

tail /teɪl/ **I** *n* **1** Zool (of mammal, bird, fish) queue *f*; **2** (end piece) (of aircraft, comet, kite) queue *f*; **at the ~ of the procession** à la queue du cortège; **3**○ (police observer) **to put a ~ on sb** faire filer qn, prendre qn en filature; **4**○ (buttocks) postérieur○ *m*.
II tails *npl* **1** (tailcoat) habit *m*; **wearing ~s** en habit; **white tie and ~s** queue-de-pie *f*; **2** (of coin) pile *f*; **heads or ~s?** pile ou face?; **~s you win** pile tu gagnes.
III○ *vtr* filer○, suivre [*suspect, car*] (**to** jusqu'à); **we're being ~ed** on est pris en filature.
IDIOMS **I can't make head (n)or ~ of this** je ne comprends rien du tout à cela; **we couldn't make head or ~ of his reply** sa réponse n'avait ni queue ni tête; **to be on sb's ~** suivre qn de près, talonner○ qn; **to go off with one's ~ between one's legs** partir la queue basse; **to turn ~** péj tourner les talons pej.
■ **tail away** (fade) [*voice, noise*] s'éteindre; **her voice ~ed away to a whisper** elle a baissé la voix et s'est mise à chuchoter.
■ **tail back** GB **to ~ back from** [*traffic jam*] remonter de; **to ~ back to** [*traffic jam*] s'étirer jusqu'à; **the traffic ~s back for miles** le bouchon s'étire sur des kilomètres.
■ **tail off** **1** (reduce) [*percentage, figures, demand*] diminuer; [*acceleration*] baisser; **2** (fade) [*remarks*] cesser; [*voice*] s'éteindre; **he ~ed off into silence** sa voix s'est éteinte.

tail: **~ assembly** *n* empennage *m* (*de queue*); **~back** *n* GB bouchon *m*, ralentissement *m*; **~board** *n* hayon *m*; **~bone** *n* coccyx *m*; **~coat** *n* habit *m*.

tail end *n* **1** (last piece) (of joint, roast) dernier morceau *m*; (of film, conversation) fin *f*; **to catch the ~ of the film** voir les toutes dernières minutes du film; **2**○ (buttocks) derrière○ *m*.

tail: **~ feather** *n* penne *f* rectrice; **~ fin** *n* Zool nageoire *f* caudale.

tailgate /'teɪlgeɪt/ **I** *n* hayon *m*.
II○ *vtr* coller○ au pare-chocs de [*car*].
III○ *vi* US **do not ~** ne suivez pas de trop près la voiture de devant.

tail: **~gate party** *n* US pique-nique *m* improvisé près des voitures; **~-heavy** *adj* [*aircraft*] centré à l'arrière; **~light** *n* feu *m* arrière; **~-off** *n* diminution *f* (**in** de).

tailor /'teɪlə(r)/ **▶ 1692** **I** *n* tailleur *m*.
II *vtr* **1** (adapt) (*souvent au passif*) **to ~ sth to** adapter qch à [*needs, requirements, circumstances, person*]; **to ~ sth for** concevoir qch pour [*user, market*]; **a programme ~ed to meet specific needs** un programme adapté à des besoins spécifiques; **2** (make) confectionner.
III tailored *pp adj* [*garment*] ajusté.

tailorbird /'teɪləbɜːd/ *n* fauvette *f* couturière.

tailoring /'teɪlərɪŋ/ *n* **1** (workmanship) ouvrage *m* de tailleur; **2** (occupation) métier *m* de tailleur; **3** (sewing) confection *f*; **4** (cut, style) coupe *f*.

tailor-made /ˌteɪlə'meɪd/ *adj* **1** (perfectly suited) [*scheme, solution, system, mortgage, training*] fait sur mesure; **to be ~ for sth/sb** [*machine, system, building, course*] être conçu spécialement pour qch/qn; **the part is ~ for her** le rôle est fait pour elle; **2** (made to measure) [*suit, jacket*] fait sur mesure.

tailor: **~'s chalk** *n* craie *f* de tailleur; **~'s dummy** *n* mannequin *m*; **~'s tack** *n* point *m* de bâti.

tailpiece /'teɪlpiːs/ *n* **1** (in book) cul-de-lampe *m*; **2** Mus (on viola, violin) cordier *m*; **3** (extension) extrémité *f*.

tail: **~pipe** *n* tuyau *m* d'échappement; **~plane** *n* empennage *m* arrière; **~race** *n* galerie *f* d'évacuation; **~ rotor** *n* rotor *m* anticouple; **~ section** *n* Aviat partie *f* arrière; **~skid** *n* patin *m* arrière.

tailspin /'teɪlspɪn/ *n* **1** Aviat vrille *f*; **to go into a ~** descendre en vrille; **2** fig (recession) dégringolade○ *f*; **to be in a ~** être en dégringolade○.

tail: **~ wheel** *n* roulette *f* de queue; **~ wind** *n* vent *m* arrière.

tain /teɪn/ *n* tain *m*.

taint /teɪnt/ **I** *n* **1** (defect) (of crime, corruption, cowardice) souillure *f*; (of insanity, heresy) tare *f*; **2** (trace) (of contamination, infection, bias) trace *f*.
II *vtr* **1** (sully) souiller [*public figure, organization, reputation*]; entacher [*lineage*]; altérer [*motive*]; entacher [*opinion*]; **2** (poison) polluer [*air, water*]; gâter [*meat, food*].

tainted /'teɪntɪd/ *adj* **1** (poisoned) [*meat*] avarié; [*foodstuffs*] gâté; [*water, air*] infecté, pollué (**with** par); **2** (sullied) [*reputation, organization, opinions*] entaché (**with** de); [*motives*] impur; [*money*] mal acquis.

Taiwan /taɪ'wɑːn/ **▶ 1381** *pr n* Taiwan *m*.

Taiwanese /ˌtaɪwə'niːz/ **▶ 1486**, **1402** **I** *n* Taiwanais/-e *m/f*.
II *adj* taiwanais.

Tajik /'tɑːdʒɪk/ *n, adj* ▶ **Tadzhik**.

Tajiki /tɑː'dʒɪkiː/ *n* ▶ **Tadzhiki**.

Tajikistan /tɑːˌdʒɪkɪ'stɑːn/ *pr n* ▶ **Tadzhikistan**.

take /teɪk/ **▶ 1703** **I** *n* **1** Cin prise *f* (de vues); **'it's a ~!'** 'elle est bonne!'; **2** Fishg, Hunt (of fish) prise *f*; (of game) tableau *m* de chasse; **3**○ Comm (amount received) recette *f*.

II *vtr* (*prét* **took**; *pp* **taken**) **1** (take hold of) prendre [*object, money*]; **to ~ sb by the arm/hand/throat** prendre qn par le bras/par la main/à la gorge; **to ~ sb's arm/hand** prendre le bras/la main de qn; **to ~ sth from** prendre qch sur [*shelf, table*]; prendre qch dans [*drawer, box*]; **to ~ sth out of sth** sortir qch de qch; **the passage is taken from his latest book** le passage est tiré de son dernier livre; **2** (use violently) **to ~ a knife/an axe to sb** attaquer qn avec un couteau/une hache; **3** (have by choice) prendre [*bath, shower, holiday*]; **to ~ lessons** prendre des leçons (**in** de); **we ~ a newspaper/three pints of milk every day** nous prenons le journal/trois pintes de lait tous les jours; **we ~ the Gazette** nous recevons la Gazette; **I'll ~ a pound of apples, please** donnez-moi une livre de pommes, s'il vous plaît; **~ a seat!** asseyez-vous!; **to ~ a wife/a husband**† prendre femme/un mari†; **4** (carry along) emporter, prendre [*object*]; emmener [*person*]; **to ~ sb to school/to work/to the hospital** emmener qn à l'école/au travail/à l'hôpital; **to ~ a letter/a cheque to the post office** porter une lettre/un chèque à la poste; **to ~ chairs into the garden** porter des chaises dans le jardin; **to ~ the car to the garage** emmener la voiture au garage; **the book? he's taken it with him** le livre? il l'a emporté; **to ~ sb sth**, **to ~ sth to sb** apporter qch à qn; **to ~ sb dancing/swimming** emmener qn danser/se baigner; **to ~ sth upstairs/downstairs** monter/descendre qch; **you can't ~ him anywhere!** hum il n'est pas sortable!; **5** (lead, guide) **I'll ~ you through the procedure** je vous montrerai comment on procède; **to ~ the actors through the scene** faire travailler la scène aux acteurs; **I'll ~ you up to the second floor/to your room** je vais vous conduire au deuxième étage/à votre chambre; **6** (transport) **to ~ sb to** [*bus*] conduire or emmener qn à [*place*]; [*road, path*] conduire or mener qn à [*place*]; **his work ~s him to many different countries** son travail l'appelle à se déplacer dans beaucoup de pays différents; **what took you to Brussels?** qu'est-ce que vous êtes allé faire à Bruxelles?; **7** (use to get somewhere) prendre [*bus, taxi, plane etc*]; prendre [*road, path*]; **~ the first turn on the right/left** prenez la première à droite/à gauche; **8** (negotiate) [*driver, car*] prendre [*corner, bend*]; [*horse*] sauter [*fence*]; **9** (accept) accepter, recevoir [*bribe, money*]; prendre [*patients, pupils*]; accepter [*job*]; prendre [*phone call*]; [*machine*] accepter [*coin*]; [*shop, restaurant etc*] accepter [*credit card, cheque*]; [*union, employee*] accepter [*reduction, cut*]; **will you ~ £10 for the radio?** je vous offre 10 livres sterling en échange de votre radio; **that's my last offer, ~ it or leave it !** c'est ma dernière proposition, c'est à prendre ou à laisser!; **whisky? I can ~ it or leave it!** le whisky? je peux très bien m'en passer; **10** (require) [*activity, course of action*] demander, exiger [*patience, skill, courage*]; **it ~s patience/courage to do** il faut de la patience/du courage pour faire; **it ~s three hours/years etc to do** il faut trois heures/ans etc pour faire; **it won't ~ long** ça ne prendra pas longtemps; **it took her 10 minutes to repair it** elle a mis 10 minutes pour le réparer; **the wall won't ~ long to build** le mur sera vite construit; **it won't ~ long to do the washing-up** la vaisselle sera vite faite; **it would ~ a genius/a strong person to do that** il faudrait un génie/quelqu'un de robuste pour faire ça; **to have what it ~s** avoir tout ce qu'il faut (**to do** pour faire); **typing all those letters in two hours will ~ some doing!** ce ne sera pas facile de taper toutes ces lettres en deux heures! ; **she'll ~ some persuading** ce sera dur de la convaincre; **11** Ling [*verb*] prendre [*object*]; [*preposition*] être suivi de [*case*]; **12** (endure) supporter [*pain, criticism*]; accepter [*punishment, opinions*]; **I find their attitude hard to ~** je trouve leur attitude difficile à accepter; **he can't ~ being criticized** il ne supporte pas qu'on le critique; **she just sat there and took it!** elle est restée là et ne s'est pas défendue; **he can't ~ a joke** il ne sait pas prendre une plaisanterie; **go on, tell me, I can ~ it!** vas-y, dis-le, je n'en mourrai pas○!; **I can't ~ any more!** je suis vraiment à bout!; **13** (react to) prendre [*news, matter, criticism, comments*]; **to ~ sth well/badly** bien/mal prendre qch; **to ~ sth seriously/lightly** prendre qch au sérieux/à la légère; **to ~ things one** ou **a step at a time** prendre les choses une par une; **14** (assume) **I ~ it that** je suppose que; **to ~ sb for** ou **to be sth** prendre qn pour qch; **what do you ~ me for?** pour qui est-ce que tu me prends?; **what do you ~ this poem to mean?** comment est-ce que vous interprétez ce poème?; **15** (consider as example) prendre [*person, example, case*]; **~ John (for example), he has brought up a family by himself** prends John, il a élevé une famille tout seul; **let us** ou **if we ~ the situation in France** prenons la situation en France; **~ Stella, she never complains!** regarde Stella, elle ne se plaint jamais!; **16** (adopt) adopter [*view, attitude, measures, steps*]; **to ~ a soft/tough line on sb/sth** adopter une attitude indulgente/sévère à l'égard de qn/qch; **to ~ the view** ou **attitude that** être d'avis que, considérer que; **17** (record) prendre [*notes, statement*]; [*doctor, nurse*] prendre [*pulse, temperature, blood pressure*]; [*secretary*] prendre [*letter*]; **to ~ sb's measurements** (for clothes) prendre les mesures de qn; **to ~ a reading** lire les indications; **18** (hold) [*hall, bus*] avoir une capacité de, pouvoir contenir [*50 people, passengers etc*]; [*tank, container*] pouvoir contenir [*quantity*]; **the tank/bus will ~...** le réservoir/bus peut contenir...; **the cupboard/the suitcase won't ~ any more clothes** il est impossible de mettre plus de vêtements dans ce placard/cette valise; **19** (consume) prendre [*sugar, milk, pills, remedy*]; **to ~ tea/lunch with sb** GB sout prendre le thé/déjeuner avec qn; ▶ **drug**; **20** (wear) (in clothes) faire [*size*]; **to ~ a size 4** (in shoes) ≈ faire○ or chausser du 37; **21** Phot prendre [*photograph*]; **22** Math (subtract) soustraire [*number, quantity*] (**from** de); **23** (study) prendre, faire [*subject*]; suivre [*course*]; **24** Sch, Univ (sit) passer [*exam, test*]; **25** (teach) [*teacher, lecturer*] faire cours à [*students, pupils*]; **to ~ sb for Geography/French** faire cours de géographie/de français à qn; **26** (officiate at) [*priest*] célébrer [*service, prayer, wedding*]; dire [*mass*]; **27** (capture) [*army, enemy*] prendre [*fortress, city*]; (in chess) [*player*] prendre [*piece*]; (in cards) faire [*trick*]; [*person*] remporter [*prize*]; ▶ **hostage**, **prisoner**; **28**○ (have sex with) prendre [*woman*].

III *vi* (*prét* **took**; *pp* **taken**) **1** (have desired effect) [*drug*] faire effet; [*dye*] prendre; (grow successfully) [*plant*] prendre; **2** Fishg [*fish*] mordre.

IDIOMS **I'll ~ it from here** fig je prendrai la suite; **to be on the ~**○ toucher des pots-de-vin; **to ~ it** ou **a lot out of sb** fatiguer beaucoup qn; **to ~ it upon oneself to do** prendre sur soi de faire; **to ~ sb out of himself** changer les idées à qn; **you can ~ it from me,...** croyez-moi,...

■ **take aback**: **~ [sb] aback** interloquer [*person*].

■ **take after**: **~ after [sb]** tenir de [*father, mother etc*].

■ **take against**: **~ against [sb]** prendre [qn] en grippe.

■ **take along**: **~ [sb/sth] along**, **~ along [sb/sth]** emporter [*object*]; emmener [*person*].

■ **take apart**: ¶ **~ apart** se démonter; **does it ~ apart?** est-ce que ça se démonte?; ¶ **~ [sb/sth] apart 1** (separate into parts) démonter [*car, machine*]; **2**○ fig (defeat) [*player, team*] massacrer○ [*opponent, team*]; **3**○ (criticize) [*person, critic, teacher*] descendre [qch] en flammes○ [*essay, film, book*].

■ **take aside**: **~ [sb] aside** prendre [qn] à part.

■ **take away**: **~ [sb/sth] away**, **~ away [sb/sth] 1** (remove) enlever, emporter [*object*] (**from** de); emmener [*person*] (**from** de); supprimer [*pain, fear, grief*] (**from** de); **'two hamburgers to ~ away, please'** GB 'deux hamburgers à emporter, s'il vous plaît'; **to ~ away sb's appetite** faire perdre l'appétit à qn; **2** fig (diminish) **that doesn't ~ anything away from his achievement** ça n'enlève rien à ce qu'il a accompli; **3** (subtract) soustraire [*number*] (**from** à, de); **ten ~ away seven is three** dix moins sept égalent trois.

■ **take back**: ¶ **~ [sth] back**, **~ back [sth] 1** (return to shop) [*person , customer*] rapporter [*goods*] (**to** à); **2** (retract) retirer [*statement, words*]; **I ~ it back** je retire ce que j'ai dit; ¶ **~ [sb] back** (cause to remember) rappeler des souvenirs à [*person*]; **this song ~s me back to my childhood** cette chanson me rappelle mon enfance; ¶ **~ [sb/sth] back**, **~ back [sb/sth]** (accept again) reprendre [*partner, employee*]; reprendre [*gift, ring*]; [*shop*] reprendre [*goods*].

■ **take down**: **~ [sth] down**, **~ down [sth] 1** (remove) descendre [*book, vase, box*]; enlever [*picture, curtains*]; **2** (lower) baisser [*skirt, pants*]; **3** (dismantle) démonter [*tent, scaffolding*]; **4** (write down) noter [*name, statement, details*].

■ **take hold**: **~ hold** [*disease, epidemic*] s'installer; [*idea, ideology*] se répandre; [*influence*] s'accroître; **to ~ hold of** (grasp) prendre [*object, hand*]; fig (overwhelm) [*feeling, anger*] envahir [*person*]; [*idea*] prendre [*person*].

■ **take in**: ¶ **~ [sb] in**, **~ in [sb] 1** (deceive) tromper, abuser [*person*]; **he was taken in** il s'est laissé abuser; **don't be taken in by appearances!** ne te fie pas aux apparences!; **I wasn't taken in by him** je ne me suis pas laissé prendre à son jeu; **2** (allow to stay) recueillir [*person, refugee*]; prendre [*lodger*]; ¶ **~ in [sth] 1** (understand) saisir, comprendre [*situation*]; **I can't ~ it in!** je n'arrive pas à le croire!; **2** (observe) noter [*detail*]; embrasser [*scene*]; **3** (encompass) inclure [*place, developments*]; **4** (absorb) [*root*] absorber [*nutrients*]; [*person, animal*] absorber [*oxygen*]; fig s'imprégner de [*atmosphere*]; **5** Naut [*boat*] prendre [*water*]; **6** Sewing reprendre [*dress, skirt etc*]; **7** (accept for payment) faire [qch] à domicile [*washing, mending*]; **8**○ (visit) aller à [*play, exhibition*].

■ **take off**: ¶ **~ off 1** (leave the ground) [*plane*] décoller; **2** fig [*idea, fashion*] prendre; [*product*] marcher; [*sales*] décoller; **3**○ (leave hurriedly) filer○; ¶ **~ [sth] off 1** (deduct) **to ~ £10 off (the price)** réduire le prix de 10 livres, faire une remise de 10 livres; **2** (have as holiday) **to ~ two days off** prendre deux jours de congé; **I'm taking next week off** je suis en congé la semaine prochaine; **3** (make look younger) **that hairstyle ~s 15 years off you!** cette coiffure te rajeunit de 15 ans!; ¶ **~ [sth] off**, **~ off [sth] 1** (remove) enlever, ôter [*clothing, shoes*]; enlever [*lid, feet, hands*] (**from** de); supprimer [*dish, train*]; **to ~ sth off the market** retirer qch du marché; **2** (amputate) amputer, couper [*limb*]; **3** (withdraw) annuler [*show, play*]; ¶ **~ [sb] off**, **~ off [sb] 1**○ (imitate) imiter [*person*]; **2** (remove) **to ~ sb off the case** [*police*] retirer l'affaire à qn; **to ~ oneself off** partir, s'en aller (**to** à).

■ **take on**: ¶ **~ on** (get upset) **don't ~ on so** (stay calm) ne t'énerve pas; (don't worry) ne t'en fais pas; ¶ **~ [sb/sth] on**, **~ on [sb/sth] 1** (employ) embaucher, prendre [*staff, worker*]; **2** (compete against) [*team, player*] jouer contre [*team, player*]; (fight) se battre contre [*person, opponent*]; **to ~ sb on at chess/at tennis** jouer aux échecs/au tennis contre qn; **3** (accept) accepter, prendre [*work, task*]; prendre [*responsibilities*]; **4** (acquire) prendre [*look, significance, colour, meaning*].

■ **take out**: ¶ **~ out** s'enlever; **does this ~ out?** est-ce que ça s'enlève?; ¶ **~ [sb/sth] out, ~ out [sb/sth] 1** (remove) sortir [*object*] (**from, of** de); [*dentist*] extraire, arracher○ [*tooth*]; [*doctor*] enlever [*appendix*]; (from bank) retirer [*money*] (**of** de); **~ your hands out of your pockets!** enlève tes mains de tes poches!; **2** (go out with) sortir avec [*person*]; **to ~ sb out to dinner/for a walk** emmener qn dîner/se promener; **3** (eat elsewhere) emporter [*fast food*]; **'two hamburgers to ~ out, please!'** 'deux hamburgers à emporter, s'il vous plaît!; **4** (deduct) déduire [*contributions, tax*] (**of** de); **5**○ (kill, destroy) éliminer [*person*]; détruire [*installation, target*]; **6 to ~ sth out on sb** passer qch sur qn [*anger, frustration*]; **to ~ it out on sb** s'en prendre à qn.

■ **take over**: ¶ **~ over 1** (take control) (of town, country, party) [*army, faction*] prendre le pouvoir; **he's always trying to ~ over** il veut toujours tout commander; **2** (be successor) [*person*] prendre la suite (**as** comme); **to ~ over from** remplacer, succéder à [*predecessor*]; ¶ **~ over [sth] 1** (take control of) prendre le contrôle de [*town, country*]; reprendre [*business*]; **shall I ~ over the driving for a while?** veux-tu que je prenne un peu le volant?; **2** Fin racheter, prendre le contrôle de [*company*].

■ **take part** prendre part; **to ~ part in** participer à [*production, activity*].

■ **take place** avoir lieu.

■ **take to**: **~ to [sb/sth] 1** (develop liking for) **he has really taken to her/to his new job** elle/son nouvel emploi lui plaît vraiment beaucoup; **2** (begin) **to ~ to doing**○ se mettre à faire; **he's taken to smoking/wearing a hat** il s'est mis à fumer/porter un chapeau; **3** (go) se réfugier dans [*forest, hills*]; **to ~ to one's bed** se mettre au lit; **to ~ to the streets** descendre dans la rue.

■ **take up**: ¶ **~ up** (continue story etc) reprendre; **to ~ up where sb/sth left off** reprendre là où qn/qch s'était arrêté; **to ~ up with** s'attacher à [*person, group*]; ¶ **~ up [sth] 1** (lift up) enlever [*carpet, pavement, track*]; prendre [*pen*]; **2** (start) se mettre à [*golf, guitar*]; prendre [*job*]; **to ~ up a career as an actor** se lancer dans le métier d'acteur; **to ~ up one's duties** ou **responsibilities** entrer dans ses fonctions; **3** (continue) reprendre [*story, discussion*]; reprendre [*cry, refrain*]; **4** (accept) accepter [*offer, invitation*] relever [*challenge*]; **to ~ up sb's case** Jur accepter de défendre qn; **5 to ~ sth up with sb** soulever [qch] avec qn [*matter*]; **6** (occupy) prendre, occuper [*space*]; prendre, demander [*time, energy*]; **7** (adopt) prendre [*position, stance*]; **8** Sewing (shorten) raccourcir [*skirt, curtains etc*]; **9** (absorb) [*sponge, material, paper*] absorber [*liquid*]; ¶ **~ [sb] up 1** (adopt) fig **she was taken up by the surrealists** elle a été adoptée par les surréalistes; **2 to ~ sb up on** (challenge) reprendre qn sur [*point, assertion*]; (accept) **to ~ sb up on an invitation/an offer** accepter l'invitation/l'offre de qn.

take-away /'teɪkəweɪ/ **I** *n* GB **1** (meal) repas *m* à emporter; **2** (restaurant) restaurant *m* qui fait des plats à emporter.
II *modif* [*food*] à emporter.

takedown /'teɪkdaʊn/ *adj* US démontable.

take-home pay *n* salaire *m* net.

taken /'teɪkən/ **I** *pp* ▶ **take**.
II *adj* **1** (occupied) **to be ~** [*seat, room*] être occupé; **2** (impressed) **to be ~ with** être emballé par [*idea, person*]; **she's quite/very ~ with him** il lui plaît assez/beaucoup.

take-off /'teɪkɒf/ *n* **1** Aviat décollage *m*; **2**○ (imitation) imitation *f*.

take-out /'teɪkaʊt/ **I**○ *n* GB (from pub) boisson *f* à emporter.
II *adj* **1** US [*food, meal, pizza*] à emporter; **2** (in bridge) **~bid** réponse *f* de faiblesse.

takeover /'teɪkəʊvə(r)/ *n* **1** Fin rachat *m*, prise *f* de contrôle; **2** Pol (of country) prise *f* de pouvoir.

takeover bid *n* Fin offre *f* publique d'achat, OPA *f*.

taker /'teɪkə(r)/ *n* preneur/-euse *m/f*; **any ~s?** il y a des preneurs?

take-up /'teɪkʌp/ *n* **1** (claiming) (of benefit, rebate, shares) demande *f* (**of** de); **2** (number of claimants) (also **~ rate**) **an increase in ~ of shares/unemployment benefit** une augmentation du pourcentage d'actions vendues/de personnes qui reçoivent effectivement l'allocation chômage.

take-up spool *n* GB bobine *f* réceptrice.

taking /'teɪkɪŋ/ **I** *n* (act) prise *f*; **it was his for the ~** il n'avait qu'à se donner la peine de le prendre; **the money was there for the ~** il n'y avait plus qu'à encaisser l'argent.
II takings *npl* recette *f*.

talc /tælk/, **talcum (powder)** /'tælkəm (ˌpaʊdə(r))/ *n* (all contexts) talc *m*.

tale /teɪl/ *n* **1** (story) histoire *f* (**about** sur); (fantasy story) conte *m* (**about** sur); (narrative, account) récit *m* (**about** sur); (legend) légende *f* (**about** de); **to tell a ~** raconter une histoire; **to tell a ~ of woe** (about oneself) raconter ses malheurs; (about others) raconter une histoire pathétique; **the figures tell the same/another ~** les chiffres disent la même chose/tout autre chose; **the recent events tell their own ~** les événements récents parlent d'eux-mêmes; **2** (hearsay) histoire *f*; (gossip) cancan *m*; **to spread** ou **tell ~s** raconter des histoires (**about sb** sur qn).
IDIOMS **a likely ~!** et puis quoi encore!; **dead men tell no ~s** les morts ne parlent pas; **to live to tell the ~** être encore là pour en parler; **to tell ~s out of school** révéler des choses indiscrètes.

tale: **~bearer** *n* rapporteur/-euse *m/f*, cafardeur/-euse○ *m/f*; **~bearing** *n* rapportage *m*, cafardage○ *m*.

talent /'tælənt/ *n* **1** (gift) don *m*, talent *m*; **her ~(s) as a speaker/teacher** ses talents d'oratrice/de professeur; **she has a remarkable ~ for music** elle est remarquablement douée pour la musique; **a man of many ~s** un homme très doué; **2** (ability) talent *m* (**for doing** pour faire); **to have ~** avoir du talent, être doué; **a musician/painter of ~** un musicien/un peintre de talent; **there's a lot of ~ in that team** il y a beaucoup de gens de talent dans cette équipe; **employers on the look-out for new ~** des employeurs qui sont à l'affût de gens de talent or de nouveaux talents; **a scheme to encourage young ~** un projet pour encourager les jeunes talents or les jeunes espoirs; **3**○ GB (sexually attractive people) (boys) beaux mecs○ *mpl*; (girls) belles nanas○ *fpl*; **to eye up the (local) ~**○ (male) reluquer○ les beaux mecs○ (du coin); (female) reluquer○ les belles gonzesses◑ (du coin); **4** Hist (unit of money) talent *m*.

talent contest *n* concours *m* de jeunes talents or d'amateurs (*pour découvrir de futures vedettes*).

talented /'tæləntɪd/ *adj* [*person*] doué, talentueux/-ueuse.

talentless /'tæləntlɪs/ *adj* sans talent, dépourvu de talent.

talent: **~ scout** *n* découvreur/-euse *m/f* de nouveaux talents; **~ show** *n* = **talent contest**; **~ spotter** *n* = **talent scout**; **~-spotting** *n* recherche *f* de nouveaux talents.

tale: **~teller** = **talebearer**; **~telling** = **talebearing**..

tali /'teɪlaɪ/ *pl* ▶ **talus**.

talisman /'tælɪzmən, 'tælɪs-/ *n* talisman *m*.

talismanic /ˌtælɪz'mænɪk, ˌtælɪs-/ *adj* talismanique.

talk /tɔːk/ **I** *n* **1** (talking, gossip) ¢ propos *mpl*; **there is ~ of sth/of doing** il est question de qch/de faire, on parle de qch/de faire; **there is ~ of me doing** il est question que je fasse; **there is ~ that** on dit que, le bruit court que; **there is (a lot of) ~ about sth** il est (beaucoup) question de qch; **he's all ~** il parle beaucoup mais agit peu; **it's nothing but** ou **a lot of ~** ce ne sont que de belles paroles; **it's just ~** ce ne sont que des paroles en l'air; **such ~ is dangerous/ridiculous** de tels propos sont dangereux/ridicules; **he dismissed ~ of problems/defeat** il a refusé de parler des problèmes/de la défaite; **they are the ~ of the town** on ne parle que d'eux; **2** (conversation) conversation *f*, discussion *f*; **to have a ~ with sb** parler à qn; **to have a ~ about sth/sb** parler de qch (**with** avec), avoir une discussion à propos de qch (**with** avec); **3** (speech) exposé *m* (**about, on** sur); (more informal) causerie *f*; **to give a ~** faire un exposé; **radio ~** exposé *m* à la radio.
II talks *npl* (formal discussions) (between governments) discussions *fpl* (**between** entre); (between several groups, countries) conférence *f*; (between management and unions) négociations *fpl*, discussions *fpl* (**beween** entre); **to hold ~s** tenir une conférence; **arms ~s** conférence sur le désarmement; **pay ~s** négociations salariales; **trade ~s** négociations commerciales; **~s about ~s** négociations pour mettre sur pied une conférence.
III *vtr* **1** (discuss) **to ~ business/sport** parler affaires/de sport; **2** (speak) parler [*French, Spanish etc*]; **to ~ nonsense** raconter n'importe quoi; **she's ~ing sense** ce qu'elle dit est plein de bon sens; **we're ~ing £2 million/three years**○ il faut compter deux millions de livres sterling/trois ans; **we're ~ing a huge investment/a major project**○ il s'agit d'un investissement énorme/d'un projet important; **3** (persuade) **to ~ sb into doing** persuader qn de faire; **to ~ sb out of doing** dissuader qn de faire; **you've ~ed me into it!** vous m'avez convaincu!; **to ~ one's way out of doing** s'en tirer sans avoir à faire.
IV *vi* **1** (converse) parler , discuter; **to ~ to** ou **with sb** parler à or avec qn; **to ~ to oneself** parler tout seul; **to ~ about sth/about doing** parler de qch/de faire; **to ~ at sb** parler à qn sans l'écouter; **to keep sb ~ing** faire parler qn aussi longtemps que possible; **I'm not ~ing to him** (out of pique) je ne lui parle plus; **~ing of films/tennis...** à propos de films/tennis...; **he knows/he doesn't know what he's ~ing about** il sait/il ne sait pas de quoi il parle; **it's easy** ou **all right for you to ~, but you don't have to do it!** tu peux parler, mais ce n'est pas toi qui dois le faire!; **who am I to ~?** remarque, je peux parler!; **look** ou **listen who's ~ing!, you're a fine one to ~!, you can ~!** tu peux parler!; **now you're ~ing!** eh bien voilà!; **~ about stupid/expensive**○! comme idiotie/comme prix élevé, ça se pose un peu là○!; **~ about laugh/work**○! qu'est-ce qu'on a ri/travaillé!; **2** (gossip) parler, bavarder; péj jaser; **to give people sth to ~ about** donner aux gens matière à jaser; **3** (give information) [*person, prisoner, suspect*] parler.

■ **talk back** répondre (insolemment) (**to** à).

■ **talk down**: ¶ **~ down to sb** parler à qn avec condescendance; ¶ **~ [sb/sth] down 1** Aviat aider [qn/qch] à atterrir en le guidant par radio [*pilot, plane*]; **2** (denigrate) dénigrer.

■ **talk out**: **~ [sth] out, ~ out [sth] 1** (discuss) discuter or parler de [qch] à fond; **2** GB Pol (prevent passing of) **to ~ out a bill** prolonger la discussion d'un projet de loi (*de manière à ce que le vote n'ait pas lieu*).

■ **talk over**: ¶ **~ [sth] over** (discuss) discuter de, parler de [*matter, issue*]; ¶ **~ [sb] over** (persuade) faire changer [qn] d'avis.

■ **talk round**: ¶ **~ round** [sth] tourner autour de [*subject*]; ¶ **~** [sb] **round** faire changer [qn] d'avis.
■ **talk through**: **~** [sth] **through** discuter de [qch] tranquillement; **to ~ it through** en discuter tranquillement.
■ **talk up**: **~** [sb/sth] **up**, **~ up** [sb/sth] vanter (les mérites de) [*candidate, product*].

talkathon /ˈtɔːkəθɒn/ *n* US débat-marathon *m*.

talkative /ˈtɔːkətɪv/ *adj* [*person*] bavard, volubile.

talkativeness /ˈtɔːkətɪvnɪs/ *n* loquacité *f*.

talk: **~back** *n* TV, Radio intercommunication *f*; **~box** *n* larynx *m*.

talked-about /ˈtɔːktəbaʊt/ *adj* **the much ~ love affair/resignation** (recently) la liaison/la démission dont on a beaucoup parlé dernièrement; (in the past) la liaison/la démission dont on a beaucoup parlé à l'époque.

talker /ˈtɔːkə(r)/ *n* **to be a good ~** avoir de la conversation; **he's not a great ~** il n'est pas bavard; **to be a slow/fluent ~** parler lentement/avec aisance.

talkie○† /ˈtɔːkɪ/ *n* Cin film *m* parlant.

talking /ˈtɔːkɪŋ/ **I** *n* **there's been enough ~** assez de paroles!; **I'll do the ~** c'est moi qui parlerai; **'no ~!'** 'silence!'
II *adj* [*bird, doll*] qui parle.

talking: **~ book** *n* livre *m* enregistré (*à l'usage des non-voyants*); **~ heads** *npl* interlocuteurs/-trices *m/fpl*; **~ point** *n* sujet *m* de conversation; **~ shop** *n* (lieu *m* de) parlotte *f*○.

talking-to /ˈtɔːkɪŋtuː/ *n* savon○ *m*, réprimande *f*; **to give sb a ~** passer un savon○ à qn, réprimander qn.

talk show *n* TV talk-show *m* (*émission où un présentateur s'entretient avec des invités*).

tall /tɔːl/ *adj* [*person*] grand; [*building, tree, grass, chimney, mast*] haut; **how ~ are you?** tu mesures combien?; **he's six feet ~** ≈ il mesure un mètre quatre-vingts; **she's four inches ~er than me** ≈ elle fait dix centimètres de plus que moi; **to get** ou **grow ~(er)** grandir; **he was ~ dark and handsome** c'était un beau ténébreux.
IDIOMS **it's a ~ order** c'est une tâche difficile; **that's a bit of a ~ order!** c'est beaucoup demander!; **a ~ story** ou **tale** une histoire à dormir debout; **to stand ~** être résolu; **to walk ~** marcher la tête haute; **to feel (about) ten feet ~** se sentir tout fier.

tallboy /ˈtɔːlbɔɪ/ *n* commode *f* (haute).

tallness /ˈtɔːlnɪs/ *n* (of person) grande taille *f*; (of building, tree, chimney, mast) hauteur *f*.

tallow /ˈtæləʊ/ *n* suif *m*.

tallow candle *n* chandelle *f*.

tall ship *n* grand voilier *m*.

tally /ˈtælɪ/ **I** *n* **1** (record) compte *m*; **to keep a ~** tenir le compte (**of** de); **to make a ~** faire le compte; **2** (amount accumulated) gen nombre *m* total; Sport (score) score *m*; **3** (identification ticket) contremarque *f*; **4** (counterfoil) souche *f*; **5** Hist (stick) taille *f*.
II *vtr* (also **~ up**) tenir le compte de [*expenses*]; compter [*points*].
III *vi* **1** (correspond) correspondre (**with** à); **2** (be the same) concorder (**with** avec); **his view tallies with mine** nos vues concordent.

tally clerk, **tally keeper** *n* pointeur/-euse *m/f* de marchandises.

tally-ho /ˌtælɪˈhəʊ/ *excl* taïaut!

Talmud /ˈtælmʊd, US ˈtɑːl-/ *pr n* Talmud *m*.

talmudic /tælˈmʊdɪk, US tɑːl-/ *adj* talmudique.

talon /ˈtælən/ *n* **1** Zool serre *f*; **2** Games, Archit talon *m*.

talus /ˈteɪləs/ *n* (*pl* **tali**) astragale *m*.

tamarin /ˈtæmərɪn/ *n* tamarin *m*.

tamarind /ˈtæmərɪnd/ *n* **1** (fruit) tamarin *m*; **2** (tree) tamarinier *m*.

tamarisk /ˈtæmərɪsk/ *n* tamaris *m*.

tambour /ˈtæmbʊə(r)/ *n* (all contexts) tambour *m*.

tambourine /ˌtæmbəˈriːn/ ▶ 1481 *n* tambourin *m*.

tame /teɪm/ **I** *adj* **1** [*animal*] apprivoisé; [*person*] hum complaisant; **to become** ou **grow ~** [*animal*] s'apprivoiser; **2** (unadventurous) [*story, party, contest*] sans relief; [*reform, decision*] timide; [*reply, remark, ending of book, film*] plat; [*ending of match*] décevant; [*cooperation, acquiescence*] docile.
II *vtr* **1** (domesticate) apprivoiser [*animal*]; **2** (train) dompter [*lion, tiger*]; dresser [*horse, dog*]; **3** fig (curb) maîtriser [*river, land, nature*]; soumettre [*person, country, opposition*]; contenir [*interest rates*]; juguler [*inflation*]; dompter [*hair*].

tamely /ˈteɪmlɪ/ *adv* [*abandon, accept, submit, decide*] docilement; [*reply, end, worded, phrased*] platement.

tameness /ˈteɪmnɪs/ *n* **1** (domestication) (of animal) docilité *f*; **2** (lack of initiative) (of story, party, contest) médiocrité *f*; (of reform, decision) timidité *f*; (of reply, remark, ending) platitude *f*; (of co-operation, acquiescence) docilité *f*.

tamer /ˈteɪmə(r)/ *n* (of lions, tigers) dompteur/-euse *m/f*.

Tamil /ˈtæmɪl/ ▶ 1486, 1402 **I** *n* **1** (person) Tamoul/-e *m/f*; **2** Ling tamoul *m*, tamil *m*.
II *adj* tamoul, tamil.

taming /ˈteɪmɪŋ/ *n* **1** (making less wild) (of animal, person) apprivoisement *m*; **2** (training) (of lion, tiger) domptage *m*; (of horse, dog) dressage *m*; **3** fig (of river, land, nature) maîtrise *f*; (of people, country, opposition) soumission *f*; (of inflation, interest rates) maîtrise *f*.

Tammany /ˈtæmənɪ/ *adj* US Pol corrompu.

tam-o'-shanter /ˌtæməˈʃæntə(r)/ *n* béret *m* écossais.

tamp /tæmp/ *vtr* bourrer (**with** à).
■ **tamp down**: **~** [sth] **down**, **~ down** [sth] (over explosive) damer [*earth*] (**in, into** dans); tasser [*tobacco*] (**in, into** dans).

tamper /ˈtæmpə(r)/ *vi* **to ~ with** tripoter, manipuler [qch] en douce [*car, safe, machinery, lock*]; altérer [*text*]; trafiquer [*accounts, records, evidence, food*]; altérer [*nature*].

tampering /ˈtæmpərɪŋ/ *n* **food/product ~** altération *f* de nourriture/de produits.

tamper-proof /ˈtæmpəpruːf/ *adj* [*lock, machine, jar, ballot box*] de sécurité.

tampon /ˈtæmpɒn/ *n* tampon *m*.

tan /tæn/ **I** *n* **1** (also **sun~**) gen bronzage *m*; (weather-beaten) hâle *m*; **to get a ~** bronzer; **2** (colour) (of leather) fauve *m*; (of fabric, paper) terre *f* de sienne; **3** Math (*abrév* = **tangent**) tan.
II *adj* [*leather*] fauve; [*fabric, paper*] terre de sienne *inv*.
III *vtr* (*p prés etc* **-nn-**) **1** [*sun*] gen bronzer; [*sun, wind*] (make weather-beaten) tanner; **to ~ one's back/face** se bronzer le dos/le visage; **2** tanner [*animal hide*]; **3**○ (beat) rosser○ [*personne*]; **I'll ~ your hide**○ **(for you)!** je vais te flanquer une raclée○!
IV *vi* (*p prés etc* **-nn-**) bronzer.

tandem /ˈtændəm/ *n* tandem *m*; **in ~** en tandem.

tandoori /tænˈdʊərɪ/ *n, modif* tandoori (*m*).

tang /tæŋ/ *n* **1** (taste) goût *m* acidulé; (smell) odeur *f* piquante; **the salty ~ of the sea** la saveur vivifiante de l'air marin; **with a ~ of lemon** avec une pointe de citron; **2** (of knife, chisel) soie *f*.

Tanganyika /ˌtæŋgəˈniːkə/ ▶ 1131, 1400 *pr n* Hist Tanganyika *m*; **Lake ~** le lac Tanganyika.

tangent /ˈtændʒənt/ **I** *n* (all contexts) tangente *f*; **to fly off at a ~** [*object, ball*] dévier; **to go off at** ou **on a ~** (in speech) partir dans une digression.
II *adj* tangent (**to** à).

tangential /tænˈdʒenʃl/ *adj* **1** Math tangentiel/-ielle; **2** fig secondaire (**to** par rapport à).

tangerine /ˈtændʒəriːn/ **I** *n* (fruit, colour) mandarine *f*.
II *adj* mandarine *inv*.

tangibility /ˌtændʒəˈbɪlətɪ/ *n* tangibilité *f*.

tangible /ˈtændʒəbl/ *adj* tangible.

tangible assets *npl* valeurs *fpl* matérielles.

tangibly /ˈtændʒəblɪ/ *adv* (clearly) manifestement.

Tangier /tænˈdʒɪə/ ▶ 1818 *pr n* Tanger *m*.

tangle /ˈtæŋgl/ **I** *n* **1** (of hair, string, wires, weeds) enchevêtrement *m*; (of clothes, sheets) fouillis *m*; **in a ~** tout embrouillé; **to get in** ou **into a ~** s'embrouiller; **2** fig (political, legal, emotional) imbroglio *m*; **a ~ of problems/motives** un embrouillamini de problèmes/motifs; **in a ~** très embrouillé; **to get in** ou **into a ~** [*person*] s'empêtrer (**with** avec); **3** (quarrel) prise *f* de bec.
II *vtr* = **tangle up**.
III *vi* **1** [*hair, string, cable*] s'emmêler (**around** autour de); **2** = **tangle up**.
■ **tangle up**: ¶ **~ up** s'embrouiller; ¶ **~ up** [sth], **~** [sth] **up** embrouiller, emmêler; **to get ~d up** [*hair, string, wires*] s'emmêler (**in** dans); [*clothes*] s'entortiller (**in** dans); [*person*] fig s'empêtrer (**in** dans).
■ **tangle with**: **~ with** [sb/sth] se frotter à.

tangled /ˈtæŋgld/ *adj* **1** [*hair, wool, wire*] emmêlé; [*brambles, wires, wreckage*] enchevêtré; **2** [*situation*] embrouillé.
IDIOMS **what a ~ web we weave (when first we practise to deceive)** la vie devient compliquée lorsque l'on commence à mentir.

tangly /ˈtæŋglɪ/ *adj* enchevêtré.

tango /ˈtæŋgəʊ/ **I** *n* tango *m*.
II *vi* danser le tango.
IDIOMS **it takes two to ~** tous les torts ne peuvent pas être du même côté.

tangy /ˈtæŋɪ/ *adj* acidulé.

tank /tæŋk/ **I** *n* **1** (container) (for storage) réservoir *m*; (for heating oil) cuve *f*; (for water) citerne *f*; (for hot water) ballon *m*; (for processing) cuve *f*; (small) bac *m*; (for fish) aquarium *m*; (in fish-farming) vivier *m*; Aut réservoir *m*; **gas/oxygen ~** réservoir *m* à gas/oxygène; **fuel ~** GB, **petrol ~** GB, **gas ~** US réservoir *m* à essence; **fill the ~!** faites le plein!; **2** (contents) (of water) citerne *f* pleine (**of** de); (of petrol) réservoir *m* plein; **3** Mil char *m* (de combat).
II *modif* Mil [*battle, column, tracks*] de chars; [*regiment, warfare*] de chars, de blindés.
■ **tank up** **1** US Aut faire le plein; **2**○ **to get ~ed up**○ se bourrer○, se soûler.

tankard /ˈtæŋkəd/ *n* chope *f* (*souvent en métal*).

tank: **~ car** *n* wagon-citerne *m*; **~ engine**, **~ locomotive** *n* locomotive *f* à vapeur.

tanker /ˈtæŋkə(r)/ *n* **1** Naut navire-citerne *m*; **oil ~**, **petrol ~** pétrolier *m*; **2** (lorry) camion-citerne *m*; **water ~** camion-citerne *m*.

tanker: **~ aircraft** *n* avion *m* ravitailleur, avion-citerne *m*; **~ lorry** GB *n* camion-citerne *m*.

tank farming *n* Agric culture *f* hydroponique.

tankful /ˈtæŋkfʊl/ *n* **1** (of petrol) réservoir *m* plein, plein *m* (**of** de); **this car does 100 km on a ~ of petrol** cette voiture fait 100 km avec un plein d'essence; **2** (of water) citerne *f* pleine (**of** de).

tank: **~ top** *n* débardeur *m*, pull *m* sans manches; **~ trap** *n* Mil fossé *m* antichar; **~ truck** *n* US camion-citerne *m*.

tanned /tænd/ *adj* (also **sun~**) bronzé; (weather-beaten) tanné.

tanner /ˈtænə(r)/ *n* **1** (person) tanneur *m*; **2**○ GB Hist (sixpence) *ancienne pièce de six pence*.

tannery /ˈtænərɪ/ *n* tannerie *f*.

tannic /ˈtænɪk/ *adj* tannique.

tannic acid *n* acide *m* tannique.

tannin /ˈtænɪn/ *n* tanin *m*.

tanning /ˈtænɪŋ/ I *n* **1** (by sun) bronzage *m*; **2** (of hides) tannage *m*; **3**○ (beating) raclée○ *f*; **to give sb a (good) ~** flanquer une (bonne) raclée à qn.
II *modif* [*lotion, product*] de bronzage; **~ center** US, **~ salon** GB salon *m* de beauté (avec équipement UV).

Tannoy® /ˈtænɔɪ/ *n* GB **the ~** système *m* de haut-parleurs; **over the ~** par les haut-parleurs.

tansy /ˈtænzɪ/ *n* tanaisie *f*.

tantalite /ˈtæntəlaɪt/ *n* tantalite *f*.

tantalize /ˈtæntəlaɪz/ *vtr* allécher.

tantalizing /ˈtæntəlaɪzɪŋ/ *adj* [*suggestion*] tentant; [*possibility*] séduisant; [*glimpse*] excitant, qui fait envie; [*smell*] alléchant; [*smile*] énigmatique.

tantalizingly /ˈtæntəlaɪzɪŋlɪ/ *adv* **to be ~ close to victory** être à deux doigts de la victoire; **the truth was ~ elusive** la vérité était cruellement insaisissable.

tantalum /ˈtæntələm/ *n* tantale *m*.

tantalus /ˈtæntələs/ I *n* GB coffret *m* à bouteilles.
II **Tantalus** *pr n* Mythol Tantale.

tantamount /ˈtæntəmaʊnt/ *adj* **to be ~ to** équivaloir à, être équivalent à.

tantrum /ˈtæntrəm/ *n* crise *f*; **to throw** ou **have a ~** [*child*] faire un caprice; [*adult*] piquer une colère○.

Tanzania /ˌtænzəˈnɪə/ **▶ 1131** *pr n* Tanzanie *f*.

Tanzanian /ˌtænzəˈnɪən/ **▶ 1486**, **1402** I *n* (person) Tanzanien/-ienne *m/f*.
II *adj* tanzanien/-ienne.

Tao /taʊ, tɑːəʊ/ *pr n* Tao *m*.

Taoiseach /ˈtiːʃəx/ *pr n* premier ministre *m* de la République d'Irlande.

Taoism /ˈtaʊɪzəm, ˈtɑːəʊ-/ *n* taoïsme *m*.

Taoist /ˈtaʊɪst/ *n, adj* taoïste (*mf*).

tap /tæp/ I *n* **1** (device to control flow) (for water, gas) robinet *m*; (on barrel) robinet *m*, bonde *f*; **the cold/hot ~** le robinet d'eau froide/chaude; **to run one's hands under the ~** se passer les mains sous le robinet; **to turn the ~ on/off** ouvrir/fermer le robinet; **on ~** [*beer*] pression *inv*; [*wine*] en fût; fig disponible; **2** (blow) petit coup *m*, petite tape *f*; **he felt a ~ on his shoulder** il a senti une tape sur son épaule; **she heard a ~ at the door** elle a entendu frapper à la porte; **a soft ~** un léger coup; **a sharp ~** un coup sec; **to give sth a ~** donner un petit coup or une tape à qch; **3** (listening device) **to put a ~ on a phone** mettre un téléphone sur écoute; **4** Dance (also **~ dancing**) claquettes *fpl*; **5** US Elec connexion *f*; **6** Tech (also **screw ~**) taraud *m*.
II **taps** *npl* (+ *v sg*) (bugle call) (for lights out) sonnerie *f* d'extinction des feux; (at funeral) sonnerie *f* aux morts.
III *vtr* (*p prés etc* **-pp-**) **1** (knock) [*person*] taper, tapoter (**on** sur; **against** contre); **to ~ sth with sth** taper or frapper qch de qch; **to ~ sb on the shoulder/the arm** taper qn sur l'épaule/le bras; **to ~ one's feet** (**to the music**) taper du pied (en rythme); **to ~ a rhythm** battre la mesure (**with sth** de qch); **to ~ one's fingers on the table** pianoter sur la table; **to ~ data into the computer** introduire des données dans l'ordinateur; **2** (extract) exploiter [*talent, resources, market, energy*]; **to ~ sb for money**○ demander de l'argent à qn, taper qn○; **3** (install listening device) mettre [qch] sur écoute [*telephone*]; mettre les téléphones de [qch] sur écoute [*house, embassy*]; **4** (breach) mettre une cannelle à [*barrel*]; percer [*furnace*]; **5** (for sap) gemmer, inciser [*tree*] (**for** pour en extraire); **6** (collect resin) recueillir [qch] par incision [*rubber*]; **7** Tech (cut thread of) tarauder; **8** US (designate) désigner (**as** comme; **for** pour; **to do** pour faire).
IV *vi* (*p prés etc* **- pp-**) [*person, finger, foot*] taper; **to ~ on** ou **at the window/door** taper à la fenêtre/porte; **to ~ against sth** taper or battre contre qch.
■ **tap in**: **~ [sth] in, ~ in [sth]** enfoncer [*nail, peg*]; Comput taper [*information, number*].
■ **tap out**: **~ [sth] out, ~ out [sth]** transmettre [*message*].

tap dance I *n* claquettes *fpl*.
II *vi* faire des claquettes.

tap: **~ dancer** *n* danseur/-euse *m/f* de claquettes; **~ dancing** *n* claquettes *fpl*.

tape /teɪp/ I *n* **1** (substance) (for recording) bande *f*; **to put sth on ~** enregistrer qch sur bande; **2** (item) (cassette) cassette *f*; (reel) bande *f* magnétique; (for computer) bande *f*; (for video) vidéocassette *f*; **to play a ~** mettre une cassette; **on ~** en cassette; **3** (recording) enregistrement *m*; **to make a ~ of** faire un enregistrement de; **to edit a ~** mettre au point un enregistrement; **4** (strip of material) ruban *m*; **tied with ~** attaché avec du ruban; **5** (for sticking) (also **adhesive ~**, **sticky ~**) scotch® *m*, ruban *m* adhésif ; **a roll of ~** un rouleau de scotch®; **6** (marking off something) (in race) fil *m* d'arrivée; (in ceremony) ruban *m*; (put by police) cordon *m*; **to cut the ~** couper le ruban; **7** (for teleprinter) bande *f* de téléscripteur; **8** gen (for measuring) mètre *m* ruban; Sewing mètre *m* de couturière; (retractable) mètre *m* enrouleur.
II *vtr* **1** (on cassette, video) enregistrer; **to ~ sth from** enregistrer qch transmis à [*radio, TV*]; **2** (stick) attacher [*parcel, article*]; **to ~ sb's hands together** attacher les mains de qn avec du scotch®; **to ~ sb's mouth shut** fermer la bouche de qn avec du scotch®; **to ~ sth to** coller qch à [*surface, door*].
III **taped** *pp adj* [*message, conversation*] enregistré.
IDIOMS **to have sb ~d**○ savoir ce que vaut qn; **to have sth ~d**○ connaître qch comme sa poche.
■ **tape up**: **~ [sth] up, ~ up [sth]** recoller [qch] avec du scotch® [*parcel, box*]; **to ~ sth up with** recoller qch avec.

tape: **~ cassette** *n* cassette *f*; **~ deck** *n* platine *f* cassette; **~ drive** *n* dérouleur *m* de bande magnétique; **~-edit** *n* montage *m* (d'un enregistrement); **~-editing** *n* montage *m*; **~ head** *n* tête *f* de lecture; **~ machine** *n* téléscripteur *m*.

tape measure *n* gen mètre *m* ruban; Sewing mètre *m* de couturière; (retractable) mètre *m* enrouleur.

taper /ˈteɪpə(r)/ I *n* **1** (spill) longue allumette *f*, mèche *f* (*pour allumer les bougies*); **2** (candle) cierge *m*; **3** (narrow part) **to have a ~** [*trousers*] être en forme de fuseau; [*column, spire*] être effilé; [*blade*] se terminer en pointe.
II *vtr* tailler [qch] en pointe [*stick, fabric*].
III *vi* [*sleeve, trouser leg*] se resserer; [*column, spire*] s'effiler; **to ~ to a point** se terminer en pointe; **a loan of £400 ~ing to £200 in the final year** un prêt de 400 livres sterling qui diminue progressivement pour atteindre 200 livres la dernière année.
■ **taper off**: ¶ **~ off** diminuer, aller en s'amenuisant; ¶ **~ off [sth], ~ [sth] off** diminuer or réduire [qch] progressivement.

tape: **~-record** *vtr* enregistrer; **~ recorder** *n* magnétophone *m*; **~ recording** *n* enregistrement *m*.

tapered /ˈteɪpəd/ *adj* = **tapering**.

tapering /ˈteɪpərɪŋ/ *adj* [*trousers*] en forme de fuseau; [*sleeves*] aux poignets étroits; [*column, leg, wing*] fuselé; [*flame*] qui file; [*finger*] effilé, fuselé.

taper pin *n* goupille *f* conique.

tapestry /ˈtæpəstrɪ/ *n* tapisserie *f*.
IDIOMS **it's all part of life's rich ~** c'est la vie.

tapeworm /ˈteɪpwɜːm/ *n* ver *m* solitaire, ténia *m*.

taphole /ˈtæphəʊl/ *n* Ind trou *m* de coulée.

tapioca /ˌtæpɪˈəʊkə/ *n* **1** (cereal) tapioca *m*; **2** (also **~ pudding**) gâteau *m* de tapioca.

tapir /ˈteɪpə(r)/ *n* tapir *m*.

tappet /ˈtæpɪt/ *n* poussoir *m* de soupape.

tapping /ˈtæpɪŋ/ *n* **1** (knocking) battement *m*; **2** Telecom (also **telephone ~**) mise *f* sur écoute; **3** GB Elec connexion *f*.

tap: **~room**† *n* bar *m*; **~root** *n* Bot racine *f* pivotante; **~ water** *n* eau *f* du robinet.

tar /tɑː(r)/ I *n* **1** gen goudron *m*; (on roads) bitume *m*; **2**○ ‡(sailor) matelot *m*.
II *modif* [*road*] goudronné; **~ paper** papier *m* goudronné; **~ content** (of cigarette) taux *m* de goudron; **low-/high-~ cigarette** cigarette *f* à faible/forte teneur en goudrons.
III *vtr* (*p prés etc* **-rr-**) goudronner [*road, roof, fence, timber*].
IDIOMS **to ~ and feather sb** enduire qn de goudron et de plumes; **to ~ everyone with the same brush** mettre tout le monde dans le même sac; **they're ~red with the same brush** ils sont à mettre dans le même sac; **to spoil the ship for a ha'p'orth of ~** tout gâcher pour s'économiser quelques sous.

taramasalata /ˌtærəməsəˈlɑːtə/ *n* tarama *m*.

tarantella /ˌtærənˈtelə/ *n* tarentelle *f*.

tarantula /təˈræntjʊlə, US -tʃələ/ *n* tarentule *f*.

tarboosh, **tarbush** /tɑːˈbuːʃ/ *n* tarbouch *m*.

tardily /ˈtɑːdɪlɪ/ *adv* littér tardivement.

tardiness /ˈtɑːdɪnɪs/ *n* **1** (slowness) manque *m* d'empressement (**in doing** à faire); **2** (lateness) retard *m*.

tardy /ˈtɑːdɪ/ *adj* littér **1** (slow) lent (**in doing** à faire); **2** (late) tardif/-ive.

tardy slip *n* US Sch billet *m* de retard.

tare /teə(r)/ *n* **1** Bot ivraie *f*; **2** Meas tare *f*.

target /ˈtɑːgɪt/ I *n* **1** (in archery, shooting practice) cible *f*; **2** Mil (of bomb, missile) objectif *m*; **to be a soft ~** être une cible facile; **to be right on ~** être en plein dans la cible; **3** (goal, objective) objectif *m*, but *m*; **production ~** cible *f* de production; **to meet one's ~** atteindre son but; **to be on ~** réaliser ses objectifs; **the figures are way off** ou **below ~** les chiffres sont très insuffisants; **4** (butt) cible *f*; **to be the ~ of** être objet de [*abuse, ridicule*]; **an easy** ou **soft ~** une cible facile; **to be right on ~** [*jibe, criticism*] mettre en plein dans le mille○.
II *modif* [*date, figure*] prévu; [*audience, group*] visé, ciblé.
III *vtr* **1** Mil (aim) diriger [*weapon, missile*] (**at, on** sur); (choose as objective) prendre [qch] pour cible [*city, site, factory*]; **2** fig (in marketing) viser, cibler [*group, sector*]; **to be ~ed at** [*product, publication*] viser, cibler [*group*].

target group *n* groupe *m* cible.

targeting /ˈtɑːgɪtɪŋ/ *n* **1** Comm ciblage *m* (**of** de); **2** Mil **the ~ of enemy bases** la prise de bases ennemies comme objectif.

target: **~ language** *n* langue *f* cible, langue *f* d'arrivée; **~ man** *n* GB Sport grand avant-centre *m*; **~ practice** *n* ¢ exercices *mpl* de tir sur cible; **~ price** *n* prix *m* indicatif or de référence.

tariff /ˈtærɪf/ I *n* **1** (price list) tarif *m*; **2** (customs duty) droit *m* de douane.
II *modif* [*agreement, barrier, cut, exemption, heading, union*] tarifaire; [*reform*] des tarifs douaniers.

tarmac /ˈtɑːmæk/ I *n* **1** (also **Tarmac**®) macadam *m*; **2** GB (of airfield) piste *f*.
II *modif* [*road, footpath*] goudronné.
III *vtr* (*p prés etc* **-ck-**) goudronner.

tarn /tɑːn/ *n* petit lac *m* de montagne.

Tarn **▶ 1163** *pr n* Tarn *m*; **in/to the ~** dans le Tarn.

tarnation○ /tɑːˈneɪʃn/ *n* US **what in ~ is that?** qu'est-ce que c'est que ça?; **what in**

~ are you doing? qu'est-ce que tu fabriques○?

Tarn-et-Garonne ▶1163 *pr n* Tarn-et-Garonne *m*; **in/to the ~** dans le Tarn-et-Garonne.

tarnish /ˈtɑːnɪʃ/ lit, fig **I** *n* ternissure *f*.
II *vtr* ternir also fig.
III *vi* se ternir also fig.

taro /ˈtɑːrəʊ/ *n* taro *m*.

tar oil *n* huile *f* de goudron.

tarot /ˈtærəʊ/ ▶1282 *n* tarot *m*.

tarpaulin /tɑːˈpɔːlɪn/ *n* **1** (material) toile *f* de bâche; **2** (sheet) bâche *f*.

tarpon /ˈtɑːpɒn/ *n* tarpon *m*.

tarragon /ˈtærəgən/ **I** *n* estragon *m*.
II *modif* [*vinegar, sauce*] à l'estragon; [*leaf*] d'estragon.

tarring /ˈtɑːrɪŋ/ *n* goudronnage *m*.

tarry I /ˈtɑːrɪ/ *adj* [*substance*] goudronneux/-euse; [*beach, feet, rock*] plein de goudron.
II /ˈtærɪ/ ‡ ou littér *vi* **1** (delay) s'attarder; **2** (stay) demeurer.

tarsal /ˈtɑːsl/ **I** *n* os *m* tarsien.
II *adj* tarsien/-ienne.

tarsus /ˈtɑːsəs/ *n* (*pl* **tarsi**) tarse *m*.

Tarsus /ˈtɑːsəs/ *pr n* Tarse *f*.

tart /tɑːt/ **I** *n* **1** (individual pie) tartelette *f*; **2** GB (large pie) tarte *f*; **3**◑ péj pute◑ *f*.
II *adj* [*flavour*] acide; [*remark*] acerbe.
■ **tart up**○ GB: ¶ **~ [sth] up, ~ up [sth]** retaper○ [*house, room*]; arranger [*garden, brochure*]; **to be ~ed up** [*person*] être pomponné○; ¶ **~ oneself up** se pomponner○.

tartan /ˈtɑːtn/ **I** *n* (pattern, cloth) écossais *m*; **to wear the ~** porter le kilt.
II *adj* [*fabric, jacket*] écossais, à carreaux.

tartar /ˈtɑːtə(r)/ *n* **1** Dent, Wine tartre *m*; **2** (formidable person) (man) croque-mitaine *m*; (woman) virago *f*.

Tartar /ˈtɑːtə(r)/ ▶1486, 1402 **I** *n* **1** (person) Tatare *mf*; **2** (language) tatar *m*.
II *adj* tatar.

tartaric /tɑːˈtærɪk/ *adj* tartrique.

tartaric acid *n* acide *m* tartrique.

tartar sauce *n* sauce *f* tartare.

tartly /ˈtɑːtlɪ/ *adv* [*say*] d'un ton acerbe.

tartness /ˈtɑːtnɪs/ *n* lit, fig aigreur *f*.

Tashkent /tæʃˈkent/ ▶1818 *pr n* Tachkent.

task /tɑːsk, US tæsk/ **I** *n* **1** (piece of work) travail *m*; **2** (unpleasant duty) tâche *f* (**of doing** de faire); **a hard ~** une lourde tâche; **to have the ~ of doing** avoir pour tâche de faire; **he finds writing reports a hard ~** écrire des rapports est une tâche qu'il trouve difficile; **painting the ceiling will be no easy ~** ce ne sera pas facile de peindre le plafond.
IDIOMS **to take sb to ~** réprimander qn (**about, for, over** pour).

task-based learning *n* apprentissage *m* pratique.

task force *n* **1** Mil corps *m* expéditionnaire; **2** (of police) détachement *m* spécial; **3** (committee) groupe *m* de travail.

taskmaster /ˈtɑːskmɑːstə(r), US ˈtæsk-/ *n* tyran *m*; **to be a hard ~** être très exigeant.

Tasmania /tæzˈmeɪnɪə/ ▶1381 *pr n* Tasmanie *f*.

Tasmanian /tæzˈmeɪnɪən/ **I** *n* Tasmanien/-ienne *m/f*.
II *adj* tasmanien/-ienne.

Tasmanian devil *n* Zool diable *m* de Tasmanie.

Tasman Sea /ˌtæzmən ˈsiː/ ▶1511 *pr n* mer *f* de Tasman.

Tass /tæs/ *pr n* Tass; **the ~ news agency** l'agence *f* Tass.

tassel /ˈtæsl/ *n* (ornamental) gland *m*; (on corn etc) barbe *f*.

tasselled /ˈtæsld/ *adj* à gland(s).

Tasso /ˈtæsəʊ/ *pr n* le Tasse.

taste /teɪst/ **I** *n* **1** (flavour) gen goût *m*; (pleasant) saveur *f*; **a strong ~ of garlic** un fort goût d'ail; **a delicate ~** une saveur délicate; **to leave a bad** ou **nasty ~ in the mouth** lit laisser un goût déplaisant dans la bouche; fig laisser un arrière-goût d'amertume; **it leaves a nasty ~ in the mouth** fig cela laisse de l'amertume or du degoût; **I was left with a nasty ~ in the mouth** fig j'en ai gardé de l'amertume; **2** (sense) le goût *m*; **the sense of ~** le sens du goût; **to be bitter/sweet to the ~** avoir un goût amer/sucré; **this cold has taken my (sense of) ~ away** avec ce rhume je ne sens plus le goût de rien; **3** (small quantity) petit peu *m*; **have a ~ of this** goûtes-en un peu; **add just a ~ of brandy** ajoutez une goutte de cognac; **4** fig (brief experience) gen expérience *f*, aperçu *m*; (foretaste) avant-goût *m*; **a ~ of life in a big city** un aperçu de la vie dans une grande ville; **they were experiencing their first ~ of sth** c'était leur première expérience de qch; **this was just a ~ of the violence to come** ce n'était qu'un avant-goût de la violence qui allait suivre; **a ~ of things to come** un avant-goût de l'avenir; **the ~ of freedom** le goût de la liberté; **she's not used to the ~ of defeat/success** elle n'est pas habituée à (l'idée de) l'échec/la réussite; **5** (liking, preference) goût *m*; **to acquire** ou **develop a ~ for sth** prendre goût à qch; **he has strange ~s** ou **a strange ~ in music/clothes etc** il a des goûts bizarres en matière de musique/de vêtements etc; **it wasn't to her ~** ce n'était pas à son goût; **is this to your ~?** est-ce que ceci vous convient?; **it was too violent for my ~(s)** c'était trop violent pour mon goût; **the resort has something to suit all ~s** la station convient à tous les goûts; **sweeten/add salt to ~** sucrer/saler à volonté; **6** (sense of beauty, appropriateness, etc) goût *m*; **she has exquisite/awful ~ in clothes** elle s'habille avec un goût exquis/épouvantable; **to have good ~ in sth** avoir (bon) goût en matière de qch; **the room had been furnished in** ou **with excellent ~** la pièce avait été meublée avec beaucoup de goût; **the joke was in poor ~** la plaisanterie était de mauvais goût; **that's a matter of ~** ça dépend des goûts; **it would be in bad** ou **poor ~ to do** ce serait de mauvais goût de faire.
II *vtr* **1** (perceive flavour) sentir (le goût de); **I can ~ the brandy in this coffee** je sens le (goût du) cognac dans ce café; **I can't ~ a thing with this cold** je trouve que rien n'a de goût avec ce rhume; **2** (eat or drink) (to test flavour) goûter; **would you like to ~ the wine?** voulez-vous goûter le vin?; **that's the best stew/coffee I've ever ~d** c'est le meilleur ragoût que j'aie jamais mangé/le meilleur café que j'aie jamais bu; **he's never ~d meat** il n'a jamais mangé de viande; **3** fig (experience) goûter à, connaitre [*freedom, success, power*]; connaitre [*failure, defeat, hardship*].
III *vi* **1** (have flavour) **to ~ sweet/salty** avoir un goût sucré/salé; **to ~ good/horrible** avoir bon/mauvais goût; **the milk ~s off to me** je crois que ce lait est tourné; **to ~ like sth** avoir le goût de qch; **what does it ~ like?** quel goût cela a-t-il?; **to ~ of sth** avoir un goût de qch; **it ~s of pineapple** cela a un goût d'ananas; **2** (perceive flavour) avoir du goût; **I can't ~** j'ai perdu le goût.
IDIOMS **there's no accounting for ~s!** chacun ses goûts. ▶**medicine**.

taste bud *n* papille *f* gustative; **a menu/meal to tempt the ~s** un menu/un repas qui vous met l'eau à la bouche.

tasteful /ˈteɪstfl/ *adj* [*clothes, choice, design*] de bon goût; **a ~ room** une pièce meublée avec goût.

tastefully /ˈteɪstfəlɪ/ *adv* [*furnish, dress, decorated*] avec goût.

tastefulness /ˈteɪstflnɪs/ *n* bon goût *m* (**of** de).

tasteless /ˈteɪstlɪs/ *adj* **1** [*remark, joke, garment, furnishings*] de mauvais goût; **a delightfully ~ black comedy** une comédie noire d'un mauvais goût achevé; **2** (without flavour) [*food, drink*] insipide; [*medicine, powder*] qui n'a aucun goût.

tastelessly /ˈteɪstlɪslɪ/ *adv* avec mauvais goût.

tastelessness /ˈteɪstlɪsnɪs/ *n* **1** (of joke, remark, behaviour) mauvais goût *m*; **2** (of food, drink) manque *m* de saveur.

taster /ˈteɪstə(r)/ *n* **1** (person) (to check quality) dégustateur/-trice *m/f*; (to check for poison) goûteur/-euse *m/f*; **2** (foretaste) avant-goût *m* (**of, for** de).

tastiness /ˈteɪstɪnɪs/ *n* goût *m* (délicieux), saveur *f* (agréable).

tasting /ˈteɪstɪŋ/ **I** *n* dégustation *f*; **cheese/wine ~** dégustation *f* de fromages/de vins.
II -tasting (*dans composés*) **sweet-~** (au goût) sucré; **pleasant-~** (au goût) agréable.

tasty /ˈteɪstɪ/ *adj* **1** (full of flavour) [*food*] savoureux/-euse, succulent; **a ~ morsel/dish** un morceau/un plat succulent; **2**○ (attractive) [*price, discount*] intéressant; [*garment*] attrayant; **he's ~** il est beau gosse○.

tat /tæt/ **I**○ *n* GB **1** (junk) camelote○ *f*; **2** (clothing) fripes *fpl*.
II *vtr* (*p prés etc* **-tt-**) **to ~ lace** faire de la dentelle.
III *vi* (*p prés etc* **-tt-**) faire de la frivolité, faire de la dentelle à la navette.

ta-ta /təˈtɑː/ *excl* lang enfantin au revoir!

Tatar *n, adj* = **Tartar**.

tattered /ˈtætəd/ *adj* lit [*coat, clothing*] dépenaillé; [*book, document*] en lambeaux; [*person*] déguenillé; [*reputation*] en miettes; **my hopes are ~** mes espoirs sont presque réduits à néant; **~ and torn** en loques.

tatters /ˈtætəz/ *npl* lambeaux *mpl*; **to be in ~** [*clothing*] être en lambeaux; [*career, life, reputation*] être en ruines; [*hopes*] réduit à néant.

tattersall /ˈtætəsɔːl/ *n* tissu *m* à grands carreaux.

tatting /ˈtætɪŋ/ *n* frivolité *f*, dentelle *f* à la navette.

tattle /ˈtætl/ **I** *n* (also **tittle-tattle**) ¢ commérages *mpl*.
II *vi* jaser (**about** sur); **to ~ on sb** cafarder○ sur qn.

tattler /ˈtætlə(r)/ *n* commère *f*.

tattletale /ˈtætlteɪl/ *n* rapporteur/-euse *m/f*.

tattoo /təˈtuː, US tæˈtuː/ **I** *n* **1** (on skin) tatouage *m*; **2** Mil (on drum, bugle) *signal qui rappelle les soldats vers leurs quartiers*; **to beat/sound the ~** Mil battre le tambour/sonner le clairon (*pour rappeler les soldats vers leurs quartiers*); **3** (parade) parade *f* militaire; **4** fig (drumming noise) roulement *m*, tambourinement *m*; **the rain beat a ~ on the roof** la pluie tambourinait sur le toit; **he was beating a ~ on the table with his fingers** il pianotait or tambourinait sur la table.
II *vtr* tatouer (**on** sur).

tattoo artist ▶1692 *n* tatoueur/-euse *m/f*.

tattooist /təˈtuːɪst, US tæˈtuːɪst/ ▶1692 *n* tatoueur/-euse *m/f*.

tatty○ /ˈtætɪ/ **I** *n* Culin, Scot patate○ *f*, pomme *f* de terre.
II *adj* GB [*appearance*] négligé; [*carpet, garment, curtain*] miteux/-euse; [*book, shoes*] en mauvais état; [*area, building, furniture*] délabré; **a ~ piece of paper** un bout de papier.

taught /tɔːt/ *prét, pp* ▶**teach**.

taunt /tɔːnt/ **I** *n* raillerie *f*.
II *vtr* railler [*person*] (**about, over** à propos de); **to ~ sb into doing sth** provoquer qn pour lui faire faire qch.

taunting /ˈtɔːntɪŋ/ **I** *n* ¢ railleries *fpl*.
II *adj* railleur/-euse, moqueur/-euse.

tauntingly /ˈtɔːntɪŋlɪ/ *adv* [*speak, criticize*]

d'un ton railleur; [*stare, smile*] d'un air railleur.

Taurean /'tɔ:rɪən/ **▶ 1916** I *n* Taureau *m*. II *modif* [*trait*] du Taureau.

taurine /'tɔ:ri:n, -raɪn/ *adj* sout taurin.

tauromachy /tɔ:'rɒməkɪ/ *n* sout tauromachie *f*.

Taurus /'tɔ:rəs/ **▶ 1916** *n* Taureau *m*.

taut /tɔ:t/ *adj* (all contexts) tendu.

tauten /'tɔ:tn/ I *vtr* tendre.
II *vi* se tendre.

tautly /'tɔ:tlɪ/ *adv* **1 a ~-strung racket** une raquette aux cordes tendues; **2** [*say, reply*] d'un air tendu.

tautness /'tɔ:tnɪs/ *n* tension *f*.

tautological /,tɔ:tə'lɒdʒɪkl/ *adj* tautologique.

tautology /tɔ:'tɒlədʒɪ/ *n* tautologie *f*.

tavern /'tævən/ *n* taverne *f*.

taverna /tə'vɜ:nə/ *n* taverne *f* (grecque).

TAVR *n* GB (*abrév* = **Territorial and Army Volunteer Reserve**) armée *f* de réservistes volontaires.

tawdriness /'tɔ:drɪnɪs/ *n* (of clothes) caractère *m* criard; (of jewellery) clinquant *m*; (of furnishings, house, pub) mauvais goût *m*; fig (of motives, method) petitesse *f*; (of affair) médiocrité *f*.

tawdry /'tɔ:drɪ/ *adj* [*clothes*] voyant; [*jewellery*] clinquant; [*furnishings, house*] de mauvais goût; fig [*motives, methods*] bas/basse; [*affair*] minable.

tawny /'tɔ:nɪ/ *adj* fauve.

tawny owl *n* **1** Zool chouette *f* hulotte; **2** (Brownie leader) assistante *f* (de la cheftaine).

tawse /tɔ:z/ *n* Scot martinet *m*, fouet *m*.

tax /tæks/ I *n* gen taxe *f* (**on** sur); (on individual) impôt *m*; **sales ~** taxe à l'achat; **to collect/levy a ~** percevoir un impôt; **to increase** ou **raise ~es** augmenter les impôts; **to cut ~es** diminuer les impôts; **before ~** brut; **after ~** après déduction des impôts; **~ is deducted at source** les impôts sont retenus à la source; **to pay ~, be liable for ~** être imposable; **to pay £1,000 in ~** verser 1000 livres sterling d'impôts; **to pay a substantial sum in ~** verser une grosse somme au fisc; **to pay ~ on one's earnings** être imposé sur ce qu'on gagne.
II *vtr* **1** taxer [*profits, earnings*]; imposer [*person*]; **to be ~ed at a rate of 18%** [*person*] être imposé au taux de 18%; [*sum, income, profit*] être taxé à 18%; **luxury goods are heavily ~ed** les articles de luxe sont lourdement taxés; **to be ~ed at a higher/lower rate** être soumis à un taux d'imposition plus élevé/moins élevé; **2** Aut **to ~ a vehicle** payer la vignette (de l'impôt sur les automobiles); **the car is ~ed till November** la vignette est valable jusqu'en novembre; **3** fig (strain, stretch) mettre [qch] à l'épreuve [*patience, goodwill, wits*]; **this will ~ your wits!** ceci mettra tes méninges à l'épreuve!
■ **tax with: ~ [sb] with** accuser qn de [*misdeed*].

taxable /'tæksəbl/ *adj* [*earnings, profit*] imposable.

tax: **~ accountant** *n* conseiller *m* fiscal; **~ adjustment** *n* redressement *m*; **~ advantage** *n* avantage *m* fiscal; **~ allowance** *n* abattement *m*; **~ arrears** *npl* arriérés *mpl* fiscaux.

taxation /tæk'seɪʃn/ *n* **1** (imposition of taxes) taxation *f*, imposition *f*; **2** (revenue from taxes) impôts *mpl*, contributions *fpl*.

tax: **~ avoidance** *n* évasion *f* fiscale; **~ band** *n* = **tax bracket**; **~ base** *n* assiette *f* de l'impôt; **~ bite** *n* ponction *f* fiscale; **~ bracket** *n* tranche *f* d'imposition du revenu; **~ break** *n* réduction *f* d'impôt, avantage *m* fiscal; **~ burden** *n* charge *f* fiscale; **~ code** *n* code *m* d'imposition; **~ collection** *n* perception *f* des impôts; **~ collector** *n* percepteur *m*; **~ credit** *n* crédit *m* d'impôt; **~ cut** *n* réduction *f* d'impôt; **~-deductible** *adj* déductible des impôts; **~ demand** *n* avis *m* d'imposition; **~ disc** *n* vignette *f* (automobile); **~ dodge**○ *n* combine○ *f* pour éviter l'impôt; **~ dodger** *n* fraudeur/-euse *m/f* fiscal/-e.

taxeme /'tæksi:m/ *n* taxème *m*.

tax: **~ evader** *n* fraudeur/-euse *m/f* fiscal/-e; **~ evasion** *n* fraude *f* fiscale; **~-exempt** *adj* exonéré d'impôt; **~ exemption** *n* exonération *f* d'impôt; **~ exile** *n*: *personne qui s'est expatriée pour raisons fiscales*; **~ form** *n* feuille *f* d'impôts; **~ fraud** *n* fraude *f* fiscale; **~-free** *adj* [*income*] exempt d'impôt; **~ haven** *n* paradis *m* fiscal.

taxi /'tæksɪ/ I *n* taxi *m*; **by ~** en taxi; **we took a ~ to the station** nous avons pris un taxi pour aller à la gare.
II *vi* [*airplane*] rouler doucement; **the plane was ~ing along the runway** l'avion avançait doucement sur la piste.

taxi: **~cab** *n* = **taxi**; **~ dancer** *n* taxi-girl *f*, entraîneuse *f*.

taxidermist /'tæksɪdɜ:mɪst/ **▶ 1692** *n* taxidermiste *mf*.

taxidermy /'tæksɪdɜ:mɪ/ *n* taxidermie *f*.

taxi: **~ driver ▶ 1692** *n* chauffeur *m* de taxi; **~ fare** *n* prix *m* de la course (*de taxi*); **~ man**○ *n* = **taxi driver**; **~meter** *n* taximètre *m*, compteur *m* (de taxi).

tax: **~ immunity** *n* immunité *f* fiscale; **~ incentive** *n* incitation *f* fiscale.

taxing /'tæksɪŋ/ *adj* [*job, role*] épuisant, fatigant.

tax inspector ▶ 1692 *n* inspecteur/-trice *m/f* des impôts.

taxi: **~plane** *n* US avion-taxi *m*; **~ rank** GB, **~ stand** *n* station *f* de taxis; **~way** *n* taxiway *m*.

tax: **~ levy** *n* prélèvement *m* d'impôt; **~ liability** *n* (personal position) assujetissement *m* à l'impôt; (amount payable) montant *m* dû au fisc; **~ loophole** *n* faille *f* dans la législation fiscale.

taxman○ /'tæksmæn/ *n* **the ~** le fisc; **to owe the ~ £500** devoir 500 livres sterling au fisc.

tax office *n* perception *f*.

taxonomist /tæk'sɒnəmɪst/ *n* taxinomiste *mf*.

taxonomy /tæk'sɒnəmɪ/ *n* taxinomie *f*.

taxpayer /'tækspeɪə(r)/ *n* contribuable *mf*.

tax purposes *npl* **to declare a sum for ~** déclarer une somme au fisc; **his income for ~ is £20,000** son revenu imposable est de 20 000 livres sterling.

tax: **~ rate** *n* taux *m* d'imposition; **~ rebate** *n* remboursement *m* d'impôt; **~ relief** *n* dégrèvement *m*.

tax return *n* **1** (form) feuille *f* d'impôts; **2** (declaration) déclaration *f* de revenus; **to file a ~** faire sa déclaration d'impôts.

tax: **~ shelter** *n* (place) paradis *m* fiscal; (stratagem) moyen *m* d'échapper au fisc; **~ year** *n* année *f* fiscale.

Tayside /'teɪsaɪd/ **▶ 1624** *pr n* (also **~ Region**) Tayside *m*.

TB *n*: *abrév* **▶ tuberculosis**.

t: **T-bar** *n* (for skiers) remonte-pente *m*, tire-fesses○ *m inv*; **T-bone steak** *n* steak *m* américain.

tbsp *n*: *abrév écrite* = **tablespoon**.

TCE *n* (*abrév* = **ton coal equivalent**) TEC *f*.

Tchaikovsky /tʃaɪ'kɒfskɪ/ *pr n* Tchaïkovski.

TCP® *n* désinfectant *m*.

TD *n* **1** US *abrév* = **touchdown**; **2** US *abrév* **▶ Treasury Department**; **3** *abrév* **▶ technical drawing**.

te /ti:/ *n* Mus (also **ti**) si *m*.

tea /ti:/ *n* **1** (drink, substance, shrub) thé *m*; **jasmine ~** thé au jasmin; **I'll make a pot of ~** je vais faire du thé; **2** (cup of tea) thé *m*; **two ~s please** deux thés s'il vous plaît; **3** GB (in the afternoon) thé *m*; (for children) goûter *m*; (evening meal) repas *m* du soir, dîner *m*; **they had ~ in the garden** ils ont pris le thé au jardin; **4**○ US (marijuana) marijuana *f*.
IDIOMS **it's not my cup of ~** ce n'est pas mon truc○; **he's not my cup of ~** il ne me plaît pas tellement; **that's just his cup of ~** c'est tout à fait son truc○; **to give sb ~ and sympathy** hum réconforter qn.

tea: **~ bag** *n* sachet *m* de thé; **~ ball** *n* boule *f* à thé; **~ break** *n* GB ≈ pause-café *f*; **~ caddy** *n* boîte *f* à thé; **~ cake** *n* GB brioche *f* aux raisins; **~ cart** *n* US = **tea-trolley**.

teach /ti:tʃ/ (*prét, pp* **taught**) I *vtr* **1** (instruct) enseigner à [*children, adults*]; **to ~ sb about sth** enseigner qch à qn; **to ~ a dog obedience** apprendre à un chien à obéir; **to ~ sb (how) to do** apprendre à qn à faire; **he taught me (how) to drive** il m'a appris à conduire; **to ~ sb what to do** apprendre à qn ce qu'il faut faire; **2** (impart) enseigner [*subject, skill*]; **to ~ Russian/biology** enseigner le russe/la biologie; **to ~ sth to sb, to ~ sb sth** enseigner qch à qn; **to ~ adults French** enseigner le français aux adultes; **to ~ sb the basics of** apprendre à qn les rudiments de; **she could ~ us a thing or two about** elle pourrait nous donner des leçons en matière de; **3** (as career) enseigner [*subject, skill*]; **she ~es swimming** elle est professeur de natation; **to ~ school** US être instituteur/-trice; **4**○ (as correction) **to ~ sb a lesson** [*person*] donner une bonne leçon à qn; [*experience*] servir de leçon à qn; **he needs to be taught a lesson** il a besoin qu'on lui donne une bonne leçon; **to ~ sb to do** apprendre à qn à faire; **I'll/that will ~ you to lie!** je vais t'apprendre/ça t'apprendra à mentir!; **5** (advocate) enseigner [*doctrine, creed, virtue*]; **to ~ that** enseigner que; **to ~ sb to do** enseigner à qn à faire.
II *vi* enseigner.
III *v refl* **to ~ oneself to do** s'apprendre à faire; **to ~ oneself Spanish** apprendre l'espagnol tout seul.
IDIOMS **you can't ~ an old dog new tricks** il est difficile de déranger les vieilles habitudes.

teacher /'ti:tʃə(r)/ **▶ 1692** I *n* (in general) enseignant/-e *m/f*; (secondary) professeur *m*; (primary) instituteur/-trice *m/f*; (special needs) éducateur/-trice *m/f*; **women ~s** femmes *fpl* enseignantes; **French/music ~** professeur de français/de musique; **to be a qualified** ou **certified** US **~** être professeur certifié; **to be a ~ of English** enseigner l'anglais.
II *modif* [*morale, recruitment*] des enseignants; [*numbers, shortage*] d'enseignants.

teacher: **~ certification** *n* US diplôme *m* d'enseignement; **~ education** *n* US formation *f* pédagogique; **~ evaluation** *n* évaluation *f* des enseignants; **~-pupil ratio** *n* taux *m* d'encadrement; **~'s aide** *n* US assistant/-e *m/f* d'instituteur; **~s' centre** GB, **~s' center** US *n* centre *m* de documentation pédagogique; **~'s pet**○ *n* péj chouchou/-te○ *m/f* du professeur pej; **~ training** *n* formation *f* pédagogique; **~-training college** *n* centre *m* de formation pédagogique.

tea chest *n* caisse *f* à thé.

teach-in /'ti:tʃɪn/ *n* groupe *m* de discussion.

teaching /'ti:tʃɪŋ/ I *n* **1** (instruction) enseignement *m*; **the ~ of history, history ~** l'enseignement de l'histoire; **to go into** ou **enter ~** entrer dans l'enseignement; **to have 22 hours ~ per week** avoir 22 heures de cours par semaine; **to do some ~ in the evenings** donner quelques cours le soir; **2** (doctrine) enseignement *m*; **the ~s of Gandhi** les enseignements de Gandhi.

II *modif* [*career, post, union*] d'enseignant; [*ability, materials, method, qualification, strategy, skill*] pédagogique; [*staff*] enseignant.

teaching aid *n* support *m* pédagogique.

teaching assistant, TA ▶ 1692 *n* **1** US Univ chargé/-e *m/f* d'enseignement; **2** GB Sch *personne sans diplôme d'enseignement qui aide l'instituteur.*

teaching: **~ fellow** *n* attaché/-e *m/f* d'enseignement; **~ fellowship** *n* poste *m* d'attaché d'enseignement; **~ hospital** *n* centre *m* hospitalo-universitaire, CHU.

teaching practice *n* GB stage *m* de formation pédagogique; **to be on** ou **be doing ~** être en stage.

teaching profession *n* **1** (teaching body) **the ~** les enseignants *mpl*; **2** (career) **the ~** l'enseignement *m*.

teachware /ˈtiːtʃweə(r)/ *n* Comput didacticiel *m*.

tea: **~ cloth** *n* GB (for drying) torchon *m* (à vaisselle); (for table) nappe *f*; (for tray) napperon *m*; **~ cosy** GB, **~ cozy** US *n* couvre-théière *m inv*.

teacup /ˈtiːkʌp/ *n* tasse *f* à thé.
IDIOMS **a storm in a ~** une tempête dans un verre d'eau.

tea dance *n* thé *m* dansant.

tea garden *n* **1** (café) salon *m* de thé en plein air; **2** (plantation) plantation *f* de thé.

tea: **~ gown** *n* robe *f* d'après-midi (*portée dans les années 1920 et 1930*); **~house** *n* salon *m* de thé (*au Japon ou en Chine*); **~ infuser** *n* boule *f* or infuseur *m* à thé.

teak /tiːk/ I *n* **1** (wood) teck *m*; **2** (tree) teck *m*.
II *modif* [*furniture, construction*] en teck.

tea kettle *n* bouilloire *f*.

teal /tiːl/ *n* sarcelle *f*.

tea lady ▶ 1692 *n* GB *employée qui distribue du thé dans les bureaux.*

tea leaf *n* feuille *f* de thé; **to read the tea-leaves** ≈ lire dans le marc de café; **to read sb's tea-leaves** ≈ lire l'avenir de qn dans le marc de café.

team /tiːm/ I *n* **1** Mgmt, Sport (of people) équipe *f*; **rugby/management ~** équipe de rugby/de direction; **a ~ of advisers/doctors** une équipe de conseillers/de médecins; **to work well as a ~** faire un bon travail d'équipe; **2** (of horses, oxen, huskies) attelage *m*.
II *modif* [*captain, competition, effort, event, games, leader, sport*] d'équipe; [*colours, performance*] d'une équipe.
III *vtr* **1** (coordinate) associer [*garment*] (**with** à); **2** (bring together) ▶ **team up**.
■ **team up**: ¶ **~ up** [*people*] faire équipe (**against** contre; **with** avec); [*organizations*] s'associer (**with** avec); ¶ **~ [sb] up** associer (**with** avec).

team: **~ manager** *n* directeur/-trice *m/f* d'une équipe; **~-mate** *n* coéquipier/-ière *m/f*; **~ member** *n* équipier/-ière *m/f*; **~ player** *n* personne *f* ayant l'esprit d'équipe; **~ spirit** *n* esprit *m* d'équipe.

teamster /ˈtiːmstə(r)/ *n* US routier *m*.

team: **~ teaching** *n* enseignement *m* en équipe; **~work** *n* collaboration *f*.

tea: **~ party** *n* thé *m*; (for children) goûter *m*; **~ plant** *n* arbre *m* à thé, théier *m*; **~ plantation** *n* plantation *f* de thé; **~ planter** *n* planteur *m* de thé; **~ plate** *n* petite assiette *f*.

teapot /ˈtiːpɒt/ *n* théière *f*.
IDIOMS **a tempest in a ~** US une tempête dans un verre d'eau.

tear[1] /teə(r)/ I *n* **1** gen (from strain) déchirure *f* (**in** dans); (done on nail, hook etc) accroc *m* (**in** à or dans); **2** Med (**perineal**) **~** déchirure *f* (du périnée).
II *vtr* (*prét* **tore**, *pp* **torn**) **1** (rip) déchirer [*garment, paper*] (**on** sur); mettre [qch] en pièces [*flesh, prey*]; **to ~ sth from** ou **out of** arracher qch de [*book, notepad*]; **to ~ a hole in sth** faire un trou dans qch; **I've torn a hole in my coat** j'ai fait un accroc à mon manteau; **to ~ sth in half** ou **in two** déchirer qch en deux; **to ~ sth in(to) pieces/strips** déchirer qch en morceaux/lambeaux; **to ~ sth to pieces** ou **bits** ou **shreds** fig démolir [*proposal, argument, book, film*]; lit déchirer [*fabric*]; démolir [*objet*]; **to ~ sb to pieces** fig descendre qn en flammes; lit écharper qn; **to ~ one's hair (out)** lit, fig s'arracher les cheveux; **to ~ a muscle/ligament** se claquer○ or se déchirer un muscle/ligament; **'~ along the dotted line'** 'déchirer en suivant le pointillé'; **2** (remove by force) **to ~ sth from** ou **off** arracher qch de [*roof, surface, object*]; **to ~ sth from sb's hands** ou **grasp** arracher qch des mains de qn; **he was torn from his mother's arms** il a été arraché des bras de sa mère; **to ~ sth out of** arracher qch de [*ground*]; **you nearly tore my arm out of its socket!** tu as failli m'arracher le bras!; **3** (emotionally) (*tjrs au passif*) **to be torn between** être tiraillé entre [*options, persons*]; **she's torn between keeping on her job and going to college** elle hésite entre garder son emploi et faire des études; **4** (divided) **to be torn by war/racism** être déchiré par la guerre/le racisme.
III *vi* (*prét* **tore**, *pp* **torn**) **1** (rip) se déchirer; **to ~ into** déchirer [*flesh, cloth*]; **2** (rush) **to ~ out/off/past** sortir/partir/passer en trombe; **to ~ up/down the stairs** monter/descendre les escaliers quatre à quatre; **she came ~ing into the yard/house** elle est entrée en trombe dans la cour/maison; **she went ~ing (off) down the road** elle a filé à toute allure; **they were ~ing along at 150 km/h** ils filaient à 150 km/h; **the car came ~ing around the corner** la voiture a pris le tournant à toute allure; **they're ~ing around the streets** ils passent en trombe dans les rues; **I tore through the book in two days** j'ai dévoré le livre en deux jours; **3** (pull forcefully) **to ~ at** [*animal*] déchiqueter [*flesh, prey*]; [*person*] s'attaquer à [*rubble*]; **4**○ (criticize) **to ~ into** engueuler◑ [*person*] (**about** à cause de); démolir○ [*play, film, book*].
IV **tearing** *pres p adj* **1 a ~ing sound** un craquement; **2**○ **to be in a ~ing hurry** GB être terriblement pressé (**to do** de faire); **she was in a ~ing hurry** elle avait le feu aux trousses○.
IDIOMS **that's torn it**○! GB il ne manquait plus que ça!
■ **tear apart**: ¶ **~ [sth] apart, ~ apart [sth]** **1** (destroy) lit mettre [qch] en pièces [*prey, game*]; démolir [*building*]; fig déchirer [*relationship, organization, country*]; démolir [*film, novel, essay*]; **2** (separate) séparer [*connected items*]; ¶ **~ [sb] apart** **1** fig (torment) déchirer; **2**○ criticize) descendre [qn] en flammes; **3** lit (dismember) mettre [qn] en pièces; (separate) séparer [*two people*].
■ **tear away**: ¶ **~ away** [*paper, tape*] se déchirer; ¶ **~ away [sth]** arracher [*wrapping, bandage*]; ¶ **~ [sb] away** arracher [*person*] (**from** à); **to ~ one's gaze away** détacher ses yeux; **to ~ oneself away from sth/sb** s 'arracher à qch/qn (**to do** pour faire) also iron.
■ **tear down**: **~ [sth] down, ~ down [sth]** démolir [*building, wall, statue*]; **to ~ sth down from** arracher qch de [*wall, lamppost*].
■ **tear off**: **~ [sth] off, ~ off [sth]** **1** (remove) (carefully) détacher [*coupon, strip, petal*]; (violently) arracher [*aerial, wiper*]; déchirer [*wrapping paper*]; **to ~ sb's clothes off** arracher les vêtements de qn; **2**○ (write)○ torcher [*letter, memo*].
■ **tear open**: **~ open [sth], ~ [sth] open** ouvrir [qch] en le/la déchirant.
■ **tear out**: **~ [sth] out, ~ out [sth]** détacher [*coupon, cheque*]; arracher [*page, picture*].
■ **tear up**: **~ [sth] up, ~ up [sth]** **1** (destroy) déchirer [*page, letter, document*] (**into, in** en); **2** (remove) déraciner [*tree*]; arracher [*tracks, tramlines*]; défoncer [*street, pavement*]; **3** fig (reject) dénoncer [*treaty, legislation, contract*].

tear[2] /tɪə(r)/ *n* (*gén pl*) larme *f*; **close to ~s** au bord des larmes; **in ~s** en larmes; **to burst/dissolve into ~s** éclater/fondre en larmes; **to reduce sb to ~s** réduire qn aux larmes; **to shed ~s of rage/laughter** verser des larmes de rage/de rire; **it brings ~s to the eyes** cela fait venir les larmes aux yeux; **it brought ~s to her eyes, it moved her to ~s** elle en avait les larmes aux yeux; **there were ~s in his eyes** il avait les larmes aux yeux; **French/gardening without ~s** le français/le jardinage sans peine.
IDIOMS **to end in ~s** [*game, party*] finir par des pleurs; [*campaign, experiment*] mal se terminer.

tearaway /ˈteərəweɪ/ *n* casse-cou *m inv*.

tear /tɪə(r)/: **~drop** *n* larme *f*; **~ duct** *n* conduit *m* lacrymal.

tearful /ˈtɪəfl/ *adj* **1** (weepy) [*person, face*] en larmes; [*voice*] larmoyant; **to feel ~** avoir envie de pleurer; **2** (marked by tears) [*speech, conversation*] ému, larmoyant pej; **a ~ reunion** des retrouvailles émues; **a ~ farewell** des adieux éplorés.

tearfully /ˈtɪəfəlɪ/ *adv* [*say, tell*] les larmes aux yeux.

tear gas /tɪə(r)/ *n* gaz *m* lacrymogène.

tear-jerker /ˈtɪədʒɜːkə(r)/ *n* hum, péj **this film is a real ~** ce film est un vrai mélo○.

tear-off /ˈteərɒf/ *adj* [*coupon, slip*] détachable; **~ perforations** Comput pointillés *mpl* de séparation.

tear-off calendar /teə(r)/ *n* éphéméride *f*.

tea: **~room** *n* salon *m* de thé; **~ rose** *n* rose-thé *f*.

tear-stained /ˈtɪəsteɪnd/ *adj* [*face*] barbouillé de larmes; [*pillow, letter*] mouillé de larmes.

teary /ˈtɪərɪ/ *adj* US = **tearful**.

tease /tiːz/ I *n* **1** (joker) taquin/-e *m/f*; **2** (woman) péj allumeuse *f* pej.
II *vtr* **1** (provoke) taquiner [*person*] (**about** à propos de); tourmenter [*animal*]; **2** Tex (separate) carder; (brush) peigner; **3** (backcomb) crêper [*hair*].
III *vi* taquiner.
■ **tease out**: **~ out [sth], ~ [sth] out** **1** démêler [*knots, strands*]; **2** fig clarifier [*information*]; démêler [*significance*].

teasel /ˈtiːzl/ *n* **1** Bot cardère *f*; **2** Tex carde *f*.

teaser /ˈtiːzə(r)/ *n* **1**○ (puzzle) colle○ *f*; **2** (person) taquin/-e *m/f*; **3** Comm, TV (ad) aguiche *f*.

tea: **~ service, ~ set** *n* service *m* à thé; **~ shop** *n* GB salon *m* de thé.

teasing /ˈtiːzɪŋ/ I *n* **1** gen taquineries *fpl*; **2** (in advertising) aguichage *m*.
II *adj* taquin, moqueur/-euse.

teasingly /ˈtiːzɪŋlɪ/ *adv* [*say*] d'un air taquin; [*name*] par taquinerie.

Teasmade®, **Teasmaid**® /ˈtiːzmeɪd/ *n* machine *f* à faire le thé.

tea: **~spoon** *n* petite cuillère *f*, cuillère *f* à café; **~spoonful** *n* cuillerée *f* à café; **~ strainer** *n* passe-thé *m inv*, passoire *f* (à thé).

teat /tiːt/ *n* **1** (of cow, goat, ewe) trayon *m*, tette *f* spec; **2** GB (on baby's bottle) tétine *f*.

tea table *n* (in the afternoon) table *f* mise pour le thé; (for evening meal) table *f* mise pour le dîner; **they were sitting around the ~** ils étaient assis autour de la table.

tea: **~time** *n* (in the afternoon) l'heure *f* du thé; (in the evening) l'heure *f* du dîner; **~ towel** *n* GB torchon *m* (à vaisselle); **~ tray** *n* plateau *m* (à thé); **~-trolley** *n* GB table *f* roulante; **~ urn** *n* grande bouilloire *f* (*pour faire le thé*).

TEC *n* GB (*abrév* = **Training and Enterprise Council**) *organisme local de forma-*

tion professionnelle établi par le gouvernement et géré par le secteur privé.

tech° /tek/ *n* GB *abrév* ▶ **technical college**.

technetium /tek'ni:ʃm/ *n* technétium *m*.

technical /'teknɪkl/ *adj* **1** (mechanical, technological) technique; **a ~ hitch** un incident technique; **the ~ staff** les techniciens; **2** (specialist) technique; **~ terms** mots *mpl* techniques; **3** Jur (in law) [*point, detail, defect*] de procédure; **~ offence** quasi-délit *m*; **4** Mus, Sport technique.

technical: **~ college** *n* institut *m* d'enseignement technique; **~ drawing** *n* dessin *m* industriel.

technicality /ˌteknɪ'kælətɪ/ *n* **1** gen (technical detail) détail *m* technique (**of** de); **2** gen, Admin point *m* de détail; **a mere ~** un détail sans importance; Jur formalité *f*; **the case was dismissed on a ~** l'affaire a été renvoyée pour vice de forme; **3** (technical nature) technicité *f*.

technical knock-out *n* Sport knock-out *m* technique.

technically /'teknɪklɪ/ *adv* **1** (strictly speaking) théoriquement, en principe; **~ speaking** théoriquement parlant; **2** (technologically) [*advanced, backward, difficult, possible*] techniquement; **3** (in technique) [*good, bad*] sur le plan technique.

technical sergeant *n* US sergent-chef *m*.

technician /tek'nɪʃn/ ▶ **1692** *n* **1** Ind, Tech (worker) technicien/-ienne *m/f*; **laboratory ~** technicien/-ienne *m/f* de laboratoire; **2** (performer) technicien/-ienne *m/f*.

Technicolor® /'teknɪkʌlə(r)/ *n* technicolor® *m*.

technicolour GB, **technicolor** US /'teknɪkʌlə(r)/ *adj* hum en technicolor.

technique /tek'ni:k/ *n* **1** (method) technique *f* (**for doing** pour faire); **marketing/printing ~s** techniques de marketing/d'impression; **2** (skill) technique *f*.

techno /'teknəʊ/ Mus **I** *n* techno *f*.
II *adj* techno *inv*.

technocracy /tek'nɒkrəsɪ/ *n* technocratie *f*.

technocrat /'teknəkræt/ *n* technocrate *mf*.

technocratic /ˌteknə'krætɪk/ *adj* technocratique.

technological /ˌteknə'lɒdʒɪkl/ *adj* technologique.

technologically /ˌteknə'lɒdʒɪklɪ/ *adv* [*advanced, refined*] sur le plan technologique.

technologist /tek'nɒlədʒɪst/ ▶ **1692** *n* technologue *mf*.

technology /tek'nɒlədʒɪ/ *n* **1** (applied science) technologie *f*; **information ~** informatique *f*; **2** (method) technologie *f*; **new technologies** les nouvelles technologies; **~ transfer** transfert *m* de technologie.

tectonic /tek'tɒnɪk/ *adj* tectonique.

tectonics /tek'tɒnɪks/ *n* (+ *v sg*) tectonique *f*.

ted /ted/ **I**° *n* GB = **teddy boy**.
II *vtr* Agric (*p prés etc* **-dd-**) faner.

tedder /'tedə(r)/ *n* Agric faneuse *f*.

teddy /'tedɪ/ *n* **1** (also **~ bear**) lang enfantin ours *m* en peluche, nounours *m* baby talk; **2** (garment) teddy *m*.

teddy boy /'tedɪ bɔɪ/ *n* GB *adolescent rebelle des années 50 imitant les idoles du rock and roll.*

tedious /'ti:dɪəs/ *adj* [*lecture, conversation, person*] ennuyeux/-euse; [*job, task*] fastidieux/-ieuse.

tediously /'ti:dɪəslɪ/ *adv* [*say, play, repeat*] d'une façon ennuyeuse; **a ~ repetitive task** une tâche fastidieuse et répétitive; **~ familiar** d'une banalité ennuyeuse.

tediousness /'ti:dɪəsnɪs/ *n* manque *m* d'intérêt.

tedium /'ti:dɪəm/ *n* **1** (boredom) ennui *m*; **2** (tediousness) manque *m* d'intérêt.

tee /ti:/ **I** *n* **1** (peg) tee *m*; **2** (on golf course) tee *m*, départ *m*; **on the sixth ~** au sixième tee, au départ du six.
II *vtr* = **tee up**.
■ **tee off**: ¶ **~ off** Sport partir du tee, jouer le départ; fig commencer; ¶ **~ [sb] off**° US casser les pieds à°; **to look ~d off** avoir l'air d'en avoir marre°.
■ **tee up** placer la balle sur le tee.

tee-hee /ti:'hi:/ **I** *excl* hi-hi!
II *vi* ricaner.

teem /ti:m/ **I** *vi* **to ~ with, to be ~ing with** regorger de [*people*]; abonder en [*wildlife*]; fourmiller de [*ideas*].
II *v impers*: **it was ~ing (with rain)** il pleuvait des cordes.
III teeming *pres p adj* **1** (swarming) [*city, continent, ocean*] grouillant (**with** de), fourmillant (**with** de) liter; [*masses, crowds*] grouillant, pullulant pej; **2** (pouring) [*rain*] battant, diluvien/-ienne.
■ **teem down**: **the rain was ~ing down** il pleuvait des cordes.

teen° /ti:n/ *adj* [*fashion, magazine*] pour les jeunes or adolescents; [*idol, problem*] des jeunes or adolescents; **pre-~** des enfants en-dessous de treize ans; **the ~ years** l'adolescence.

teenage /'ti:neɪdʒ/ *adj* [*daughter, son, sister*] qui est adolescent/-e; [*actor, singer, player*] jeune (*before n*); [*illiteracy, drug-taking*] chez les adolescents; [*pregnancy*] précoce; [*life, fashion, problem*] des adolescents, des jeunes; **~ boy** adolescent *m*; **~ child** adolescent/-e *m/f*; **~ girl** adolescente *f*; **the ~ years** l'adolescence.

teenager /'ti:neɪdʒə(r)/ *n* jeune *mf*, adolescent/-e *m/f*.

teens /ti:nz/ *npl* adolescence *f*; **to be in one's ~** être adolescent/-e; **to be in one's early/late ~** être au début/à la fin de l'adolescence; **a girl barely out of her ~** une fille à peine sortie de l'adolescence; **children in their mid-~** des jeunes de quinze ans.

teensy (**weensy**)° /ˌti:nzɪ ('wi:nzɪ)/ *adj* = **teeny** (**weeny**).

teeny (**weeny**)° /ˌti:nɪ ('wi:nɪ)/ *adj* minuscule; **a ~ bit** un tout petit morceau°.

teeny-bopper° /'ti:nɪbɒpə(r)/ *n* souvent péj petit minet°/petite minette° *m/f*.

teepee /'ti:pi:/ *n* tipi *m*.

tee-shirt /'ti:ʃɜ:t/ *n* tee-shirt, T-shirt *m*.

teeter /'ti:tə(r)/ *vi* vaciller; **to ~ on the edge** ou **brink of sth** fig être au bord de qch.

teeter-totter /'ti:tətɒtə(r)/ *n* US bascule *f*.

teeth /ti:θ/ *npl* ▶ **tooth**.

teethe /ti:ð/ *vi* faire ses dents.

teething /'ti:ðɪŋ/ *n* poussée *f* des dents.

teething: **~ ring** *n* anneau *m* de dentition; **~ troubles** *npl* fig difficultés *fpl* initiales.

teetotal /ti:'təʊtl, US 'ti:təʊtl/ *adj* [*person*] qui ne boit pas d'alcool; **I'm ~** je ne bois jamais d'alcool.

teetotaler *n* US = **teetotaller**.

teetotalism /ti:'təʊtəlɪzəm/ *n* abstention *f* de toute boisson alcoolique.

teetotaller /ti:'təʊtələ(r)/ *n* GB personne *f* qui ne boit jamais d'alcool.

TEFL /'tefl/ *n* (*abrév* = **Teaching of English as a Foreign Language**) enseignement *m* de l'anglais langue étrangère.

Teflon® /'teflɒn/ *n* téflon® *m*.

Teheran /ˌteə'rɑ:n/ ▶ **1818** *pr n* Téhéran.

tel *n* (*abrév écrite* = **telephone**) tél.

Tel Aviv /ˌtel ə'vi:v/ ▶ **1818** *pr n* Tel-Aviv.

tele+ /'telɪ-/ (*dans composés*) télé-

tele-ad /'telɪæd/ *n* petite annonce *f* placée par téléphone.

telecamera /'telɪkæmrə, -mərə/ *n* caméra *f* de télévision.

telecast /'telɪkɑ:st, US -kæst/ **I** *n* émission *f* de télévision.
II *vtr* (*prét, pp* **telecast(ed)**) diffuser [qch] à la télévision.

telecommunications /ˌtelɪkəˌmju:nɪ'keɪʃnz/ **I** *n* (+ *v sg ou pl*) télécommunications *fpl*.
II *modif* [*expert*] en télécommunications; [*firm, satellite*] de télécommunications; [*industry*] des télécommunications.

telecommute /ˌtelɪkə'mju:t/ *vi* faire du télétravail.

telecommuter /ˌtelɪkə'mju:tə(r)/ *n* télétravailleur/-euse *m/f*.

telecommuting /ˌtelɪkə'mju:tɪŋ/ *n* télétravail *m*.

telecoms /'telɪkɒmz/ *n* = **telecommunications**.

teleconference /'telɪkɒnfərəns/ *n* téléconférence *f*.

teleconferencing /ˌtelɪ'kɒnfərənsɪŋ/ *n* téléconférence *f*.

telefax /'telɪfæks/ *n* télécopie *f*, fax *m*; **by ~** par fax.

telefilm /'telɪfɪlm/ *n* téléfilm *m*.

telegenic /ˌtelɪ'dʒenɪk/ *adj* télégénique.

telegram /'telɪgræm/ *n* télégramme *m*.

telegraph /'telɪgrɑ:f, US -græf/ **I** *n* **1** Telecom télégraphe *m*; **2** Naut transmetteur *m* d'ordres.
II *modif* [*pole, post, wire*] télégraphique; [*office*] du télégraphe.
III *vtr* télégraphier.

telegrapher /tɪ'legrəfə(r)/ ▶ **1692** *n* télégraphiste *mf*.

telegraphese /ˌtelɪgrə'fi:z/ *n* style *m* télégraphique.

telegraphic /ˌtelɪ'græfɪk/ *adj* télégraphique.

telegraphically /ˌtelɪ'græfɪklɪ/ *adv* télégraphiquement.

telegraphist /tɪ'legrəfɪst/ ▶ **1692** *n* télégraphiste *mf*.

telegraphy /tɪ'legrəfɪ/ *n* télégraphie *f*.

telekinesis /ˌtelɪkaɪ'ni:sɪs, -kɪ'ni:sɪs/ *n* psychokinésie *f*.

telekinetic /ˌtelɪkaɪ'netɪk, -kɪ'netɪk/ *adj* psychokinétique.

telemarketer /telɪ'mɑ:kɪtə(r)/ *n* téléprospecteur/-trice *m/f*.

telemarketing /'telɪmɑ:kɪtɪŋ/ *n* télémarketing *m*.

telematics /ˌtelɪ'mætɪks/ *n* (+ *v sg*) télématique *f*.

telemessage /'telɪmesɪdʒ/ *n* GB télégramme *m*.

telemeter /'telɪmi:tə(r), tɪ'lemɪtə(r)/ *n* télémètre *m*.

telemetric /ˌtelɪ'metrɪk/ *adj* télémétrique.

telemetry /tɪ'lemətrɪ/ *n* télémétrie *f*.

teleological /ˌtelɪə'lɒdʒɪkl, ˌti:-/ *adj* téléologique.

teleology /ˌtelɪ'ɒlədʒɪ, ˌti:-/ *n* téléologie *f*.

telepath /'telɪpæθ/ *n* télépathe *mf*.

telepathic /ˌtelɪ'pæθɪk/ *adj* [*communication*] télépathique; [*person*] télépathe.

telepathist /tɪ'lepəθɪst/ *n* télépathe *mf*.

telepathy /tɪ'lepəθɪ/ *n* télépathie *f*.

telephone /'telɪfəʊn/ **I** *n* téléphone *m*; **on** ou **over the ~** au téléphone; **to be on the ~** (connected) avoir le téléphone; (talking) être au téléphone; **to book by ~** réserver par téléphone; **an interview conducted by ~** une interview au téléphone; **to answer the ~** répondre au téléphone; **to reach sb on the ~** joindre qn au téléphone; **'Get Mr Smith on the ~ for me, would you'** 'Appelez-moi M. Smith au téléphone, s'il vous plaît'.
II *modif* [*conversation, equipment, message, survey*] téléphonique; [*engineer*] du téléphone.
III *vtr* téléphoner à, appeler [*person, organization*]; téléphoner [*instructions, message*]; **to ~ France** téléphoner en France, appeler la France; **to ~ sb to do** US téléphoner à qn de faire; **to ~ sb that** appeler qn pour dire que.
IV *vi* appeler, téléphoner.

telephone: **~ answering machine** *n* répondeur *m* téléphonique; **~ banking** *n*

Fin transactions *fpl* bancaires télématiques; **~ book** *n* = **telephone directory**; **~ booth, ~ box** GB *n* cabine *f* téléphonique; **~ call** *n* appel *m* téléphonique; **~ directory** *n* annuaire *m* (du téléphone); **~ exchange** *n* centrale *f* téléphonique; **~ kiosk** *n* GB = **telephone booth**; **~ line** *n* ligne *f* de téléphone; **~ number** *n* numéro *m* de téléphone; **~ operator** **▶ 1692** *n* standardiste *mf*; **~ service** *n* service *m* des téléphones; **~ subscriber** *n* abonné/-e *m/f* au téléphone; **~-tapping** *n* mise *f* sur écoute téléphonique.

telephonic /ˌtelɪˈfɒnɪk/ *adj* téléphonique.

telephonist /tɪˈlefənɪst/ **▶ 1692** *n* GB standardiste *mf*.

telephony /tɪˈlefənɪ/ *n* téléphonie *f*.

telephotographic /ˌtelɪˌfəʊtəˈɡræfɪk/ *adj* téléphotographique.

telephotography /ˌtelɪfəˈtɒɡrəfɪ/ *n* téléphotographie *f*.

telephoto lens /ˈtelɪfəʊtəʊ lenz/ *n* téléobjectif *m*.

teleplay /ˈtelɪpleɪ/ *n* télépièce *f*.

Telepoint /ˈtelɪpɔɪnt/ *n* Telecom Pointel *m*.

teleprint /ˈtelɪprɪnt/ *vtr* transmettre [qch] par téléscripteur.

teleprinter /ˈtelɪprɪntə(r)/ *n* téléscripteur *m*.

teleprocessing /ˌtelɪˈprəʊsesɪŋ/ *n* télétraitement *m*.

teleprompter /ˈtelɪprɒmptə(r)/ *n* télésouffleur *m*.

telerecording /ˈtelɪrɪkɔːdɪŋ/ *n* télé-enregistrement *m*.

telesales /ˈtelɪseɪlz/ *n* (+ *v sg*) télévente *f*.

telesales operator *n* télévendeur/-euse *m/f*.

telescope /ˈtelɪskəʊp/ **I** *n* (for astronomy) télescope *m*; (hand-held) lunette *f* d'approche; **visible through a ~** visible au moyen d'un télescope.
II *vtr* lit replier [*stand, umbrella*]; fig condenser [*content, series*] (**into** en).
III *vi* [*stand, umbrella*] être télescopique; [*car, train*] se télescoper.

telescopic /ˌtelɪˈskɒpɪk/ *adj* [*aerial, stand, umbrella*] télescopique; **~ lens** Phot téléobjectif *m*; **~ sight** (on gun) lunette *f* de visée.

teleshopping /ˈtelɪʃɒpɪŋ/ *n* téléachat *m*.

Teletex® /ˈtelɪteks/ *n* Télétex® *m*.

teletext /ˈtelɪtekst/ **I** *n* télétexte *m*.
II *modif* [*service, equipment*] de télétexte.

telethon /ˈtelɪθɒn/ *n* téléthon *m*.

Teletype® /ˈtelɪtaɪp/ **I** *n* télétype® *m*.
II *vtr* transmettre [qch] par téléscripteur.

teletypewriter /ˌtelɪˈtaɪpraɪtə(r)/ *n* téléscripteur *m*.

televangelism /ˌtelɪˈvændʒəlɪzəm/ *n* télévangélisation *f*.

televangelist /ˌtelɪˈvændʒəlɪst/ **▶ 1692** *n* télévangéliste *mf*.

televise /ˈtelɪvaɪz/ **I** *vtr* téléviser.
II televised *pp adj* télévisé.

television /ˈtelɪvɪʒn, -ˈvɪʒn/ **I** *n* **1** (medium) télévision *f*; **on ~** à la télévision; **for ~** pour la télévision; **a job in ~** un travail à la télévision; **to watch ~** regarder la télévision; **live on ~** en direct à la télévision; **it makes good ~** ça marche à la télévision; **2** (set) téléviseur *m*, poste *m* de télévision.
II *modif* [*actor, broadcast, camera, channel, equipment, producer, studio*] de télévision; [*documentary, news, play*] télévisé; [*film, script*] pour la télévision; [*interview*] à la télévision.

television: **~ cabinet** *n* meuble-télévision *m*; **~ dinner** *n* plateau-télévision *m*; **~ licence** *n* redevance *f* télévision; **~ lounge** *n* salle *f* de télévision; **~ picture** *n* image *f*; **~ programme** *n* émission *f* de télévision; **~ room** *n* = **television lounge**; **~ screen** *n* écran *m* de télévision; **~ set** *n* téléviseur *m*, poste *m* de télévision.

televisual /ˌtelɪˈvɪʒʊəl/ *adj* télévisuel/elle.

teleworker /ˈtelɪwɜːkə(r)/ *n* télétravailleur/-euse *m/f*.

telex /ˈteleks/ **▶ 1692** **I** *n* télex *m*; **by ~** par télex.
II *modif* [*number*] de télex; **~ machine** télex *m*; **~ operator** télexiste *mf*.
III *vtr* télexer.

tell /tel/ (*prét, pp* **told**) **I** *vtr* **1** gen (give information to) [*person*] dire; [*manual, instruction, gauge etc*] indiquer, dire; **to ~ sb sth, to ~ sth to sb** [*person*] dire qch à qn; [*map, instructions*] indiquer qch à qn; **to ~ sb how to do/what to do** expliquer à qn comment faire/ce qu'il faut faire; **she told him what had happened/where to go** elle lui a dit or expliqué ce qui était arrivé/où il fallait aller; **he told me how unhappy he was** il m'a dit or il m'a confié combien il était malheureux; **to ~ the time** [*clock*] indiquer or marquer l'heure; [*person*] lire l'heure; **can you ~ me the time please?** peux-tu me dire l'heure (qu'il est), s'il te plaît?; **something ~s me he won't come** quelque chose me dit qu'il ne viendra pas, j'ai le pressentiment qu'il ne viendra pas; **his behaviour ~s us a lot about his character** son comportement nous en dit long sur sa personnalité; **I can't ~ you how happy I am to...** je ne saurais vous dire combien je suis heureux de...; **I am pleased to ~ you that** je suis heureux de pouvoir vous dire or annoncer que; **(I'll) ~ you what**○, **let's get a video out!** tiens, si on louait une vidéo?; **I told you so!**, **what did I ~ you!** je te l'avais bien dit!; **you're ~ing me!** à qui le dis-tu!; **don't ~ me you've changed your mind!** tu ne vas pas me dire que tu as changé d'avis!; **you'll regret this, I can ~ you!** permets-moi de te dire que tu vas le regretter!; **it's true, I ~ you!** puisque je te dis que c'est vrai!; **I won't stand for it, I ~ you!** je ne le permettrai pas, je te préviens!; **2** (narrate, recount) dire, raconter [*joke, story*]; **to ~ sb sth, to ~ sth to sb** dire or raconter qch à qn; **to ~ sb about** ou **of sth** parler de qch à qn, raconter qch à qn; **from what the newspapers ~ us, they're likely to lose the election** d'après ce que disent les journaux, ils risquent de perdre les élections; **~ me all about it!** racontez-moi tout!; **~ me about it!** iron ne m'en parle pas!; **~ me more about yourself** parlez-moi encore un peu de vous; **I told her the news** je lui ai dit or annoncé la nouvelle; **their victims ~ a different story** leurs victimes ont une autre version de l'histoire; **he's very handsome—or so I've been told** il est très beau—du moins c'est ce qu'on m'a dit; **'my life as a slave girl,' as told to Celia Irving** Journ 'ma vie d'esclave,' propos recueillis par Celia Irving; **I could ~ you a thing or two about her!** je pourrais vous en dire long sur elle!; **3** (ascertain, deduce) **you can/could ~ (that)** ça se voit/se voyait que; **I/he can ~ (that)** je sais/il sait que; **who can ~ what will happen next?** qui peut dire or savoir ce qui va se passer ensuite?; **you can ~ a lot from the clothes people wear** la façon dont les gens s'habillent est très révélatrice; **I could ~ that he was in love from the look in his eyes** je lisais dans ses yeux qu'il était amoureux; **4** (distinguish) distinguer; **to ~ sb from sb** distinguer qn de qn; **to ~ sth from sth** sentir or voir la différence entre qch et qch; **he can't ~ right from wrong** il ne sait pas distinguer le bien du mal; **can you ~ the difference?** est-ce-que vous voyez or sentez la différence?; **how can you ~ which is which?**, **how can you ~ them apart?** comment peut-on les distinguer l'un de l'autre?; **the dog can ~ him from his footsteps** le chien le reconnaît à ses pas; **5** (order) dire, ordonner; **to ~ sb to do** dire à qn de faire; **to ~ sb not to do** défendre à qn de faire; **do as you are told!** fais ce qu'on te dit!; **she just won't be told!** elle refuse d'obéir!; **you can't ~ me what to do!** ce n'est pas toi qui vas me dire ce que je dois faire!; **he didn't need ~ing twice!** GB, **he didn't need to be told twice!** il n'y a pas eu besoin de le lui dire deux fois! **6**† (count, enumerate) compter, dénombrer [*votes*]; **to ~ one's beads** Relig dire or réciter son chapelet.
II *vi* **1** (reveal secret) **promise me you won't ~!** promets-moi de ne pas le répéter; **that would be ~ing!** ce serait rapporter or cafarder○!; **2** (be evidence of) **to ~ of** témoigner de; **the lines on his face told of years of hardship** son visage buriné témoignait d'années de misère; **3** (know for certain) savoir, dire; **as** ou **so far as I can ~** pour autant que je sache; **how can you ~?** comment le sais-tu?; **it's very hard to ~** c'est très difficile à dire or de savoir; **you never can ~** on ne sait jamais; **4** (produce an effect) **her age is beginning to ~** elle commence à sentir or à accuser son âge; **every blow told** tous les coups se faisaient sentir or portaient; **her inexperience told against her at the interview** son inexpérience a joué contre elle lors de son entretien.
III *v refl* **to ~ oneself** se dire (**that** que).
IDIOMS **~ me another**○! à d'autres○!; **to ~ sb where to get off** ou **where he gets off**○ envoyer promener qn, envoyer qn sur les roses○; **you ~ me!** je n'en sais rien!, à ton avis?; **to ~ it like it is** parler net; **to ~ the world about sth** raconter qch à tout le monde; **don't ~ the world about it!** ne le crie pas sur les toits!; **more than words can ~** plus qu'on ne peut dire; **time (alone) will ~** Prov (seul) l'avenir le dira, qui vivra verra; **time will ~ which of us is right** l'avenir dira qui de nous a raison; **to ~ one's love**† littér déclarer sa flamme† liter.
■ **tell off**: **~ [sb] off** (scold) disputer○, passer un savon○ à [*person*]; **she got told off for leaving early/arriving late** elle s'est fait disputer○ or passer un savon○ parce qu'elle était partie tôt/arrivée en retard.
■ **tell on**: **~ on [sb] 1** (reveal information about) dénoncer [*person*] (**to** à); **he's always ~ing on people!** il est toujours en train de rapporter or cafarder○!; **2** (have visible effect on) **the strain is beginning to ~ on him** on commence à voir sur lui les effets de la fatigue; **her age is beginning to ~ on her** elle commence à sentir or accuser son âge.

teller /ˈtelə(r)/ **▶ 1692** *n* **1** (in bank) caissier/-ière *m/f*; **2** (in election) scrutateur/-trice *m/f*; **3** (also **story-teller**) conteur/-euse *m/f*.

telling /ˈtelɪŋ/ **I** *n* récit *m*, narration *f*; **a funny story that lost nothing in the ~** une histoire drôle qui ne perdait rien à être racontée; **her adventures grew more and more fantastic in the ~** ses aventures devenaient de plus en plus fantastiques à mesure qu'elle les racontait.
II *adj* **1** (effective) [*blow*] bien porté; [*argument, speech, statement*] efficace; **2** (revealing) [*remark, detail, omission*] révélateur/-trice, éloquent.
IDIOMS **there's no ~ what will happen next** personne ne peut dire ce qui va se passer maintenant.

tellingly /ˈtelɪŋlɪ/ *adv* **1** (effectively) [*argue, speak etc*] efficacement, avec efficacité; **2** (revealingly) **~, he did not allude to this** fait révélateur, il n'y a pas fait allusion; **most ~ of all, no money had been taken** on n'avait pas volé d'argent, ce qui était très révélateur.

telling-off /ˌtelɪŋˈɒf/ *n* réprimande *f*, engueulade○ *f*; **to give sb a (good) ~** disputer qn, engueuler○ qn.

telltale /ˈtelteɪl/ **I** *n* péj rapporteur/-euse *m/f*.
II *adj* [*sign, stain, blush*] révélateur/-trice.

telly○ /ˈtelɪ/ *n* GB télé○ *f*.

Temperature

Temperatures in French are written as in the tables below. Note the space in French between the figure and the degree sign and letter indicating the scale. When the scale letter is omitted, temperatures are written thus: 20°; 98,4° etc. (*French has a comma, where English has a decimal point*).

Note also that there is no capital on 'centigrade in French; capital C *is however used as the abbreviation for* Celsius *and* centigrade *as in* 60 °C.

For how to say numbers in French, **▶ 1505**.

Celsius or centigrade (C)	**Fahrenheit (F)**	
100 °C	212 °F	température d'ébullition de l'eau (boiling point)
90 °C	194 °F	
80 °C	176 °F	
70 °C	158 °F	
60 °C	140 °F	
50 °C	122 °F	
40 °C	104 °F	
37 °C	98,4 °F	
30 °C	86 °F	
20 °C	68 °F	
10 °C	50 °F	
0 °C	32 °F	température de congélation de l'eau (freezing point)
–10 °C	14 °F	
–17,8 °C	0 °F	
–273,15 °C	–459,67 °F	le zéro absolu (absolute zero)

–15°C = –15 °C (moins quinze degrés Celsius)
the thermometer says 40° = le thermomètre indique quarante degrés
above 30°C = plus de trente degrés Celsius
over 30° Celsius = plus de trente degrés Celsius
below 30° = en dessous de trente degrés

People

body temperature is 37°C = la température du corps est de* 37 °C (trente-sept degrés Celsius)
what is his temperature? = quelle est sa température?
his temperature is 38° = il a trente-huit (de* température)

** The* de *is obligatory here.*

Things

how hot is the milk?
ou what temperature is the milk? = à quelle température est le lait?
it's 40°C = il est à 40 °C
what temperature does water boil at? = à quelle température l'eau bout-elle?
it boils at 100°C = elle bout à 100 °C
at a temperature of 200° = à une température de deux cents degrés
A is hotter than B = A est plus chaud que B
B is cooler than A = B est moins chaud que A
B is colder than A = B est plus froid que A
A is the same temperature as B = A est à la même température que B
A and B are the same temperature = A et B sont à la même température

Weather

what's the temperature today? = quelle température fait-il aujourd'hui? (*this French phrase is also the equivalent of both* how hot is it? *and* how cold is it?)
it's 65°F = il fait 65 °F (*soixante-cinq degrés Fahrenheit*)
it's 40 degrees = il fait 40 degrés
Nice is warmer (*or hotter*) than London = il fait plus chaud à Nice qu'à Londres
it's the same temperature in Paris as in London = il fait la même température à Paris qu'à Londres

temerity /tɪˈmerətɪ/ *n* audace *f*; **to have the ~ to do** avoir l'audace de faire.

temp○ /temp/ GB **I** *n* intérimaire *mf*.
II *modif* [*agency*] d'intérimaires.
III *vi* travailler comme intérimaire.

temper /ˈtempə(r)/ **I** *n* **1** (mood) humeur *f*; **to be in a good/bad ~** être de bonne/mauvaise humeur; **to be in a ~** piquer une crise○; **to have a ~** se mettre facilement en colère; **to keep** ou **control one's ~** se contrôler; **to lose one's ~** se mettre en colère (**with** contre); **to fly into a ~** exploser; **~s flared** ou **frayed** les esprits se sont emportés (**over** sur); **in a fit of ~** dans un accès de colère; **you'll only put him into a worse ~** tu vas le mettre encore plus en colère; **~! ~!** on se calme!; **2** (nature) caractère *m*; **to have an even/sweet ~** être d'un caractère égal/doux; **to have a hot** ou **quick ~** être irascible; **to have a nasty ~** avoir un sale caractère; **3** Ind trempe *f*.
II *vtr* **1** (moderate) tempérer; **2** Ind tremper [*steel*]; **~ed steel** acier trempé.

tempera /ˈtempərə/ *n* détrempe *f*.

temperament /ˈtemprəmənt/ *n* **1** (nature) tempérament *m*; **calm by ~** de tempérament calme; **the artistic ~** le tempérament artiste; **2** (excitability) humeur *f*; **an outburst** ou **display of ~** une saute d'humeur; **3** Mus tempérament *m*; **equal ~** tempérament égal.

temperamental /ˌtemprəˈmentl/ *adj* **1** (volatile) [*person, animal, machine*] capricieux/-ieuse; **2** (natural) [*aversion*] viscéral; [*affinity, inclination*] naturel/-elle; [*differences*] de tempérament; [*inability*] physique.

temperamentally /ˌtemprəˈmentəlɪ/ *adv* **1** (by nature) psychologiquement; **they were ~ unsuited** il y avait entre eux incompatibilité de caractère; **he was ~ unsuited to teaching** il n'était pas fait pour l'enseignement; **2** (in volatile manner) [*behave*] de façon capricieuse.

temperance /ˈtempərəns/ **I** *n* **1** (moderation) modération *f*; **2** (teetotalism) sobriété *f*, tempérance *f*.
II *modif* [*league*] antialcoolique; [*society*] de tempérance; [*restaurant*] où l'on ne sert pas de boissons alcoolisées.

temperate /ˈtempərət/ *adj* [*climate, zone*] tempéré; [*person, habit*] modéré.

temperature /ˈtemprətʃə(r), US ˈtempərtʃʊər/ **I** *n* **1** Meteorol, Phys température *f*; **high/low ~** température *f* haute/basse; **storage ~** température *f* de stockage; **at a ~ of 100°C** à une température de 100°C; **at room ~** à température ambiante; **2** Med température *f*; **to be running** ou **have a ~** avoir de la température or de la fièvre; **to have a ~ of 39°** avoir 39° de fièvre; **to take sb's ~** prendre la température de qn; **to have a high/slight ~** avoir beaucoup/un peu de température or fièvre; **3** fig température *f*; **to raise/lower the political ~** faire monter/baisser la température politique.
II *modif* [*change, graph, gauge*] de température; **~ chart** Med feuille *f* de température; **~ level** température *f*.

temperature-controlled *adj* à température constante.

temper tantrum *n* caprice *m*; **to throw** ou **have a ~** faire un caprice.

tempest /ˈtempɪst/ *n* littér lit, fig tempête *f*.

tempestuous /temˈpestʃʊəs/ *adj* [*quarrel, relationship*] tempétueux/-euse; [*music, person*] impétueux/-euse; [*sea, wind*] tempétueux/-euse.

tempestuously /temˈpestʃʊəslɪ/ *adv* **1** lit (of wind, sea) littér tempétueusement; **2** fig (of person) impétueusement.

tempi /ˈtempi:/ *npl* ▶ **tempo**.

temping /ˈtempɪŋ/ *n* intérim *m*.

temping job *n* intérim *m*.

Templar /ˈtemplə(r)/ *n* (also **Knight ~**) Hist Templier *m*.

template /ˈtempleɪt/ *n* **1** Sewing, Tech gabarit *m*; **2** Comput modèle *m*; **3** Constr traverse *f*.

temple /ˈtempl/ **I** *n* **1** Archit temple *m*; **2** Anat tempe *f*.
II Temple *pr n* GB Jur *bâtiment à Londres qui abrite deux des instituts judiciaires d'études.*

tempo /ˈtempəʊ/ *n* (*pl* **~s** ou **tempi**) **1** Mus tempo *m*; **at a fast ~** sur un tempo rapide; **2** fig rythme *m*.

tempo marking *n* indication *f* de tempo.

temporal /ˈtempərəl/ *adj* **1** (secular) temporel/-elle; **2** (concerning time) temporel/-elle; **3** Anat temporal.

temporarily /ˈtempərəlɪ, US -pərerɪlɪ/ *adv* (for a limited time) temporairement; (provisionally) provisoirement.

temporary /ˈtemprərɪ, US -pərerɪ/ *adj* [*job, worker, contract, visa*] temporaire; [*manager, teacher, secretary*] intérimaire; [*arrangement, solution, accommodation, respite*] provisoire; [*improvement*] passager/-ère; **on a ~ basis** à titre provisoire.

temporize /ˈtempəraɪz/ *vi* atermoyer.

tempt /tempt/ *vtr* tenter (**to do** de faire); **to be ~ed** être tenté (**to do** de faire; **by sth** par qch); **to ~ sb with sth** attirer qn avec qch; **to ~ sb into doing sth** inciter qn à faire qch; **to ~ sb back to work** inciter qn à retourner au travail; **can I ~ you to a whisky?** puis-je vous offrir un whisky?; **don't ~ me!** n'essayez pas de me tenter!; **half/sorely ~ed** à moitié/fortement tenté.
IDIOMS **to ~ fate** ou **providence** tenter le destin or sort.

temptation /tempˈteɪʃn/ *n* tentation *f* (**to do** de faire); **to give in to/to resist ~** céder à/résister à la tentation; **to feel a ~ to do** être tenté de faire; **to put ~ in sb's way** exposer qn à la tentation.

tempter /ˈtemptə(r)/ *n* tentateur *m*.

tempting /ˈtemptɪŋ/ *adj* [*offer, discount, suggestion*] alléchant; [*food, smell*] appétissant; [*idea*] tentant; **it is ~ to conclude/think that** il est tentant de conclure/penser que.

temptingly /ˈtemptɪŋlɪ/ *adv* [*describe, speak*] d'une manière tentante; **~ cheap** à un prix attrayant; **~ cool** d'une fraîcheur attrayante.

temptress /ˈtemptrɪs/ *n* tentatrice *f*.

ten /ten/ **▶ 1505**, **971**, **1096** **I** *n* **1** (number) dix *m inv*; **in ~s** [*sell*] par dizaines; [*count*] de dix en dix; **~s of thousands** des dizaines de milliers; **2**○ US (also **~-dollar bill**) billet *m* de dix dollars.
II *adj* dix *inv*.
IDIOMS **~ to one (it'll rain/he'll forget)**

dix contre un○ (qu'il va pleuvoir/qu'il va oublier).

tenable /ˈtenəbl/ *adj* **1** (valid) [*theory, suggestion*] défendable; **2** (available) **the job/scholarship is ~ for a year** le poste/la bourse est accordé/-e pour un an.

tenacious /tɪˈneɪʃəs/ *adj* [*person*] tenace, obstiné pej; [*memory*] tenace.

tenaciously /tɪˈneɪʃəslɪ/ *adv* avec ténacité.

tenacity /tɪˈnæsətɪ/ *n* ténacité *f*.

tenancy /ˈtenənsɪ/ *n* location *f*; **six-month/life ~** bail *m* de six mois/à vie; **to take on** ou **over/give up a ~** prendre/résilier un bail; **terms of ~** conditions de bail.

tenancy agreement *n* bail *m*.

tenant /ˈtenənt/ *n* locataire *mf*.

tenant: **~ farmer** ▶ 1692 *n* métayer/-ère *m/f*; **~ farming** *n* métayage *m*.

tenantry /ˈtenəntrɪ/ *n* ¢ ensemble *m* des métayers.

ten-cent store /ˌtensent ˈstɔː(r)/ *n* US bazar *m*, magasin *m* à prix unique.

tench /tentʃ/ *n* tanche *f*.

tend /tend/ **I** *vtr* soigner [*patient*]; garder [*animals*]; entretenir [*garden*]; surveiller [*fire*]; s'occuper de [*stall, store*].
II *vi* **1** (incline) **to ~ to do** [*person, event*] avoir tendance à faire; **to ~ upwards/downwards** avoir tendance à monter/baisser; **to ~ towards sth** [*tastes, views*] pencher vers qch; **I ~ to think that** j'inclinerais à penser que; **it ~s to be the case** c'est en général le cas; **things are ~ing in that direction** les choses vont dans cette direction; **to ~ the other way** prendre le contrepied; **2** (look after) **to ~ to** soigner [*patient*]; s'occuper de [*guests*]; **to ~ to sb's needs** veiller aux besoins de qn.
III -tended (*dans composés*) **well-~ed** bien soigné; **carefully-~ed** bien entretenu.

tendency /ˈtendənsɪ/ *n* tendance *f* (**to, towards** à; **to do** à faire); **to have** ou **show a ~ to do** avoir tendance à faire; **there is a ~ for people to arrive late** les gens ont tendance à arriver en retard; **upward/downward ~** tendance à la hausse/à la baisse.

tendentious /tenˈdenʃəs/ *adj* tendancieux/-ieuse.

tendentiously /tenˈdenʃəslɪ/ *adv* tendancieusement.

tender /ˈtendə(r)/ **I** *n* **1** (currency) ▶ **legal tender**; **2** Rail tender *m*; **3** Naut (for people) embarcation *f*; (for supplies) ravitailleur *m*; **4** (fire engine) camion *m* de pompiers; **5** Econ, Fin offre *f*, soumission *f* (**for** pour); **to put work/a contract out to tender** mettre un ouvrage/contrat en adjudication; **to put in** ou **make a ~ for a contract** soumissionner à une adjudication; **to invite ~s** faire un appel d'offres; **to sell by ~** vendre par adjudication.
II *adj* **1** (soft) [*food*] tendre; [*bud, shoot*] fragile; **2** (loving) [*kiss, love, smile*] tendre; **~ care** sollicitude *f*; **she needs ~ loving care** elle a besoin d'être dorlotée; **to leave sb to the ~ mercies of the jury** iron abandonner qn aux mains sévères du jury; **3** (sensitive) [*bruise, skin*] sensible; **4** littér (young) **at the ~ age of two** à l'âge tendre de deux ans; **a child of ~ years** un enfant dans la tendresse de l'âge.
III *vtr* offrir [*money*]; présenter [*apology, fare, thanks*]; donner [*resignation*].
IV *vi* soumissionner, faire une soumission; **to ~ for a contract** soumissionner à une adjudication; **an invitation to ~** un appel d'offres; **to offer a contract for ~** faire un appel d'offres pour un contrat.

tenderer /ˈtendərə(r)/ *n* Fin soumissionnaire *mf*; **successful ~** adjudicataire *mf*.

tenderfoot /ˈtendəfʊt/ *n* (*pl* **-foots** ou **-feet**) US **1** (beginner) novice *mf*; **2** (newcomer) nouveau/-elle *m/f*.

tenderhearted /ˌtendəˈhɑːtɪd/ *adj* sensible.

tenderheartedness /ˌtendəˈhɑːtɪdnɪs/ *n* sensibilité *f*.

tendering /ˈtendərɪŋ/ *n* Fin soumission *f*; **the contract was awarded by ~ procedure** le contrat a été accordé par voie d'adjudication.

tenderize /ˈtendəraɪz/ *vtr* attendrir.

tenderizer /ˈtendəraɪzə(r)/ *n* (all contexts) attendrisseur *m*.

tender: **~loin** *n* Culin milieu *m* de filet de porc; **~loin district** *n* US quartier *m* malfamé.

tenderly /ˈtendəlɪ/ *adv* tendrement.

tenderness /ˈtendənɪs/ *n* **1** (gentleness) tendresse *f*; **2** (soreness) sensibilité *f*; **3** (texture) (of shoot) fragilité *f*; (of meat) tendreté *f*.

tender offer *n* US Fin émission *f* par soumission.

tendon /ˈtendən/ **I** *n* tendon *m*.
II *modif* [*injury, operation*] du tendon; [*problem*] de tendon.

tendril /ˈtendrəl/ *n* **1** (of plant) vrille *f*; **2** (of hair) mèche *f* folle.

tenebrous /ˈtenɪbrəs/ *adj* littér ténébreux/-euse.

tenement /ˈtenəmənt/ *n* (also **~ block** ou **~ building** GB, **~ house** US) immeuble *m* ancien (*souvent délabré et insalubre*).

tenement flat *n* GB appartement *m* dans un immeuble ancien.

Tenerife /ˌtenəˈriːf/ ▶ 1381 *pr n* Tenerife *f*.

tenet /ˈtenɪt/ *n* **1** Philos, Pol, Relig dogme *m*; **2** gen principe *m*.

tenfold /ˈtenfəʊld/ **I** *adj* décuple; **a ~ increase** un décuplement.
II *adv* **to increase** ou **multiply ~** décupler.

ten four /ˌten ˈfɔː(r)/ US **I** *n* **that's a ~** c'est exact.
II *excl* message reçu!

ten: **~-gallon hat** *n* chapeau *m* de cowboy à haute forme; **~-metre line** GB, **~-meter line** US *n* ligne *f* des dix mètres.

tenner○ /ˈtenə(r)/ *n* GB (note) billet *m* de dix livres; **I got it for a ~** je l'ai payé dix livres.

Tennessee /ˌtenəˈsiː/ ▶ 1744 *pr n* Tennessee *m*.

tennis /ˈtenɪs/ ▶ 1282 **I** *n* tennis *m*; **a game of ~** une partie de tennis; **men's ~** tennis *m* masculin.
II *modif* [*ball, match, player, racket, skirt*] de tennis.

tennis: **~ court** *n* court *m* or terrain *m* de tennis, tennis *m inv*; **~ elbow** *n* tennis-elbow *m*, épicondylite *f* spec.

tennis shoe *n* chaussure *f* de tennis; **a pair of ~s** une paire de tennis.

tennis whites *npl* tenue *f* de tennis blanche.

tenon /ˈtenən/ *n* Tech tenon *m*.

tenon saw *n* scie *f* à onglets.

tenor /ˈtenə(r)/ ▶ 1868 **I** *n* **1** Mus (singer) ténor *m*; (voice) voix *f* de ténor; **2** (tone) ton *m*; **3** (course) cours *m*; **4** Jur (exact wording) teneur *f*; (copy) copie *f* conforme; **5** Fin échéance *f*.
II *modif* Mus [*part, voice*] de ténor; [*aria, solo*] pour ténor; [*horn, recorder, saxophone*] ténor.

tenpin bowling /ˌtenpɪn ˈbəʊlɪŋ/ GB, **tenpins** US ▶ 1282 *n* bowling *m* (à dix quilles).

tense /tens/ **I** *n* Ling temps *m*; **the present ~** le présent (**of** de); **in the past ~** au passé.
II *adj* **1** (strained) [*atmosphere, conversation, person, relationship, silence*] tendu; [*moment, hours*] de tension; **I get ~ easily** un rien me rend nerveux; **it makes me ~** ça me rend nerveux; **~ with fear** paralysé par la peur; **2** (exciting) tendu; **3** (taut) tendu.
III *vtr* tendre [*muscle*]; raidir [*body*]; **to ~ oneself** se raidir.
IV *vi* se raidir.
■ **tense up**: **1** (stiffen) [*muscle*] se tendre; [*body*] se raidir; **2** (become nervous) [*person*] se crisper; **you're all ~d up!** tu es tout tendu!

tensely /ˈtenslɪ/ *adv* [*listen, sit, wait, watch*] (avec) les nerfs tendus; **to smile ~** avoir un sourire crispé.

tenseness /ˈtensnɪs/ *n* tension *f*.

tensile /ˈtensaɪl, US ˈtensl/ *adj* [*material, plastic, rubber*] extensible; [*metal*] ductile.

tensile strength *n* Phys résistance *f* à la traction.

tension /ˈtenʃn/ *n* **1** (unease) tension *f* (**within** au sein de; **over** au sujet de); **2** Civ Eng, Mech Eng tension *f*; **3** Electron tension *f*; **high ~ wires** fils *mpl* à haute tension; **4** (suspense) suspense *m*.

tension headache *n* mal *m* de tête (à la tension nerveuse), céphalée *f* hypertensive spec.

tent /tent/ *n* tente *f*; **a four-man ~** une tente quatre places.

tentacle /ˈtentəkl/ *n* **1** Bot, Zool tentacule *m*; **2** (influence) ramification *f*.

tentative /ˈtentətɪv/ *adj* **1** (hesitant) [*inquiry, smile, start, stroke, suggestion*] timide; [*movement, person*] hésitant; **2** (provisional) [*booking, conclusion, offer, plan*] provisoire; [*scheme*] expérimental.

tentatively /ˈtentətɪvlɪ/ *adv* **1** (provisionally) [*agree, conclude, plan*] provisoirement; **2** (cautiously) [*smile, speak, step*] timidement; [*decide, suggest, taste*] prudemment.

tentativeness /ˈtentətɪvnɪs/ *n* **1** (hesitancy) hésitation *f*; **2** (provisional nature) caractère *m* provisoire.

tenterhooks /ˈtentəhʊks/ *npl* IDIOMS **to be on ~** être sur des charbons ardents; **to keep sb on ~** faire languir qn.

tenth /tenθ/ ▶ 1505, 1150 **I** *n* **1** (in order) dixième *mf*; **2** (of month) dix *m inv*; **3** (fraction) dixième *m*; **a ~ of a second** un dixième de seconde; **nine-~s of** les neuf dixièmes de [*work, information*]; **it's nine-~s finished** c'est pratiquement terminé; **4** Mus dixième *f*.
II *adj* dixième.
III *adv* [*come, finish*] dixième, en dixième position.

tenth-rate○ /ˌtenθˈreɪt/ *adj* minable○.

tent: **~ peg** *n* piquet *m* de tente; **~ pole** GB, **~ stake** US *n* mât *m* de tente.

tenuous /ˈtenjʊəs/ *adj* **1** lit, fig (thin) [*bond, thread*] ténu; **2** (unconvincing) [*argument, logic*] faible; [*distinction, evidence, plot, theory*] mince; [*connection*] fragile; **3** (precarious) [*position, situation*] précaire.

tenuously /ˈtenjʊəslɪ/ *adv* [*connect*] de manière fragile.

tenuousness /ˈtenjʊəsnɪs/ *n* (of thread, connection) fragilité *f*; (of plot) minceur *f*; (of position, situation) précarité *f*; (of argument, evidence) faiblesse *f*.

tenure /ˈtenjʊə(r), US tenjər/ **I** *n* **1** (right of occupancy) **~ of land/property** jouissance *f* d'un droit à un terrain/une propriété; **to grant security of ~** accorder le maintien dans les lieux; **tenants do not have security of ~** les locataires n'ont pas de bail assuré; **2** Univ (job security) titularisation *f* d'emploi; **to have ~** être titulaire; **to get ~** être titularisé; **3** (period of office) fonction *f*; **a four-year ~** une fonction de quatre ans.
II tenured *pp adj* [*professor*] titulaire; [*job*] de titulaire.

tenure-track position *n* US Univ poste *m* avec possibilité de titularisation.

tepee *n* = **teepee**.

tepid /ˈtepɪd/ *adj* tiède.

tepidity /tɪˈpɪdətɪ/, **tepidness** /ˈtepɪdnɪs/ *n* lit, fig tiédeur *f*.

tepidly /ˈtepɪdlɪ/ *adv* tièdement.

tequila /təˈkiːlə/ *n* tequila *f*.

tequila slammer /ˌtəkiːlə ˈslæmə(r)/ *n* tequila *f* frappée.

Ter *n*: *abrév écrite* = **Terrace**.

tercentenary /ˌtɜːsenˈtiːnərɪ, tɜːˈsentənerɪ/ *n* tricentenaire *m*.

tercet /ˈtɜːsɪt/ *n* tercet *m*.

Teresa /təˈriːzə/ *pr n* Thérèse.

term /tɜːm/ **I** *n* **1** (period of time) gen période *f*, terme *m*; Sch, Univ trimestre *m*; Jur (period when courts are in session) session *f*; (duration of lease) durée *f* (de bail); **he was elected for a four-year ~** il a été élu pour une période or durée de quatre ans; **during the president's first ~ of office** pendant le premier mandat du président; **~ of imprisonment** peine *f* de prison; **to have reached (full) ~** (of pregnancy) être à terme; **in** ou **during ~(-time)** Sch, Univ pendant le trimestre; **autumn/spring/summer ~** Sch, Univ premier/deuxième/troisième trimestre; **2** (word, phrase) terme *m*; **legal/technical ~** terme *m* juridique/technique; **~ of abuse** injure *f*; **she condemned their action in the strongest possible ~s** elle a condamné leur action très fermement; **3** Math terme *m*; **4** (limit) terme *m*, limite *f*; **to set** ou **put a ~ to sth** fixer or mettre un terme à qch.
II terms *npl* **1** (conditions) (of agreement, treaty, contract) termes *mpl*, conditions *fpl*; (of will) dispositions *fpl*; Comm conditions de paiement; **under** ou **by the ~s of the agreement/of the contract** aux termes de l'accord/du contrat; **under the ~s of the will** Jur selon les dispositions testamentaires (du défunt); **name your own ~s** fixez vos conditions; **~s and conditions** Jur modalités *fpl*; **~s of sale/payment** conditions de vente/paiement; **~s of trade** Comm, Econ termes de l'échange international; **credit ~s** conditions de crédit; **on easy ~s** Comm avec facilités *fpl* de paiement; **peace ~s** Pol conditions de paix; **~s of surrender** Pol conditions de la reddition; **~s of reference** attributions *fpl*; **that question is not within our ~s of reference** cette question n'est pas dans nos attributions; **2 to come to ~s with** (accept) assumer [*identity, past, condition, disability*]; accepter [*death, defeat, failure*]; (confront) affronter [*issue*]; **to come to ~s with the idea that** se faire à l'idée que, accepter l'idée que; **she is still trying to come to ~s with what happened** elle essaie toujours de comprendre ce qui s'est passé; **3** (relations) termes *mpl*; **to be on good/bad ~s with sb** être en bons/mauvais termes avec qn; **they are on friendly ~s** ils sont en bons termes, ils ont des relations *fpl* amicales; **they are on first-name ~s** ils s'appellent par leurs prénoms; **4** (point of view) **in his/their etc ~s** selon ses/leurs etc critères.
III in terms of *prep phr* **1** gen, Math (as expressed by) en fonction de; **to express sth in ~s of cost/of colour** exprimer qch en fonction du prix/de la couleur; **2** (from the point of view of) du point de vue de, sur le plan de; **they are equals in ~s of age and experience** ils sont égaux du point de vue de l'âge et de l'expérience; **the novel is weak in ~s of plot/of style** ce roman est faible sur le plan de l'intrigue/du style; **they own very little in ~s of real property** ils ne possèdent pas grand-chose en fait de biens immobiliers; **I was thinking in ~s of how much it would cost/how long it would take** j'essayais de calculer combien cela coûterait/combien de temps cela prendrait.
IV *vtr* appeler, nommer; **to ~ sth sth** appeler or nommer qch qch.

termagant /ˈtɜːməgənt/ *n* littér mégère *f*.

term deposit *n* dépôt *m* à terme.

terminal /ˈtɜːmɪnl/ **I** *n* **1** (at bus or railway station) terminus *m*; Aviat aérogare *f*, terminal *m*; **rail ~** terminus *m*; **oil ~** terminal *m* pétrolier; **ferry ~** gare *f* maritime; **container** ou **freight ~** terminal *m* à container; **2** Comput terminal *m*; **3** Elec borne *f*.
II *adj* **1** (last) [*stage, point*] terminal; Bot [*bud*] terminal; Med [*illness, patient*] (incurable) incurable; (at final stage) en phase terminale; fig [*boredom*] mortel/-elle○; **she is suffering from ~ cancer** elle est atteinte d'un cancer incurable; **to be in ~ decline** subir un déclin irréversible; **the ~ crisis of capitalism/communism** les derniers soubresauts or la crise finale du capitalisme/communisme; **2** Comm, Sch (occurring each term) trimestriel/-ielle; **3** Ling [*element, symbol*] terminal.

terminally /ˈtɜːmɪnəlɪ/ *adv* **the ~ ill** les mourants *mpl*, les malades *mpl* condamnés.

terminal: **~ point, ~ station** *n* Rail terminus *m*; **~ ward** *n* Med ≈ unité *f* de soins palliatifs.

terminate /ˈtɜːmɪneɪt/ **I** *vtr* **1** (put an end to) terminer, mettre fin à [*arrangement, discussion, meeting, phase*]; mettre fin à [*relationship*]; résilier [*contract*]; interrompre [*pregnancy*]; annuler [*agreement*]; arrêter [*treatment*]; **2** US (make redundant) renvoyer [*employee*]; **3**○ US argot des espions liquider○.
II *vi* **1** (end) [*agreement, meeting, commercial contract*] se terminer; [*employment, offer, work contract*] prendre fin; [*speaker, programme*] terminer; [*path, road*] s'arrêter; **2** (end route) s'arrêter; **'this train ~s in Oxford'** 'Oxford, terminus du train'.

termination /ˌtɜːmɪˈneɪʃn/ *n* **1** (ending) (of contract) résiliation *f*; (of service) interruption *f*; (of discussion, relations, scheme) fin *f*; **2** Med interruption *f* de grossesse; **3** Ling terminaison *f*.

termini /ˈtɜːmɪnaɪ/ *pl* ▶ **terminus**.

terminological /ˌtɜːmɪnəˈlɒdʒɪkl/ *adj* terminologique.

terminologist /ˌtɜːmɪˈnɒlədʒɪst/ *n* terminologue *mf*.

terminology /ˌtɜːmɪˈnɒlədʒɪ/ *n* terminologie *f*.

term insurance *n* ≈ assurance-vie *f* à durée limitée.

terminus /ˈtɜːmɪnəs/ *n* (*pl* **-ni** ou **-nuses**) GB Transp terminus *m*.

termite /ˈtɜːmaɪt/ *n* termite *m*.

term loan *n* prêt *m* à terme.

termly /ˈtɜːmlɪ/ *adj* Sch, Univ trimestriel/-ielle.

term paper *n* US Sch, Univ dissertation *f* trimestrielle.

termtime /tɜːmtaɪm/ *n* **during** ou **in ~** durant le trimestre.

tern /tɜːn/ *n* sterne *f*, hirondelle *f* de mer.

ternary /ˈtɜːnərɪ/ *adj* Chem, Math, Mus ternaire.

terrace /ˈterəs/ **I** *n* **1** (of café, house) terrasse *f*; **2** (on hillside) terrasse *f*; **3** Archit alignement *m* de maisons (*identiques et contiguës*).
II terraces *npl* (in stadium) gradins *mpl*.
III *vtr* arranger [qch] en terrasses [*garden, hillside*].
IV terraced [*garden, hillside*] en terrasses.

terrace: **~ cultivation** *n* culture *f* en terrasses; **~ garden** *n* jardin *m* en terrasses.

terrace(d) house *n* Archit maison *f* (*située dans un alignement de maisons identiques et contiguës*).

terracotta /ˌterəˈkɒtə/ **I** *n* **1** (earthenware) terre *f* cuite; **2** (colour) ocre brun *m*.
II *modif* [*pot, tile*] en terre cuite; [*hue, paint*] ocre brun *inv*.

terra firma /ˌterə ˈfɜːmə/ *n* terre *f* ferme.

terrain /ˈtereɪn/ *n* gen, Mil terrain *m*; **all-~ vehicle/tyre** véhicule *m*/pneu *m* tout terrain or tous terrains.

terrapin /ˈterəpɪn/ *n* **1** Zool tortue *f* peinte; **2** (building) baraquement *m* préfabriqué.

terrarium /təˈreərɪəm/ *n* (*pl* **~s** ou **-ia**) **1** (for plants) serre *f* miniature; **2** (for animals) terrarium *m*.

terrazzo /təˈrætsəʊ/ *n* granito *m*.

terrestrial /təˈrestrɪəl/ *adj* terrestre.

terrible /ˈterəbl/ *adj* **1** (awful) épouvantable; **to be ~ at** être nul en [*rugby, maths*]; **to be ~ at writing/driving** écrire/conduire très mal; **to have a ~ time doing** avoir un mal de chien○ à faire; **2** (guilty) **I feel terrible** je suis ennuyé; **to feel ~ about** culpabiliser à cause de [*accident, mistake*]; **3** (ill) **I feel ~** je ne me sens pas bien du tout; **4** (ugly) **you look ~ in that hat** ce chapeau ne te va absolument pas; **5** (for emphasis) [*liar, optimist*] invétéré; **to be a ~ fool** se conduire comme le dernier des imbéciles; **it was/it would be a ~ shame** c'était/ce serait vraiment dommage.

terribly /ˈterəblɪ/ *adv* **1** (very) [*flattered, pleased, obvious*] très; [*clever, easy, hot, polite*] extrêmement; **~ well/badly** fort bien/mal; **I'm ~ sorry** je suis navré; **2** (badly) [*limp, suffer*] horriblement; [*worry*] terriblement; [*sing, drive, write*] affreusement mal; [*deformed, injured*] horriblement.

terrier /ˈterɪə(r)/ *n* Zool terrier *m*.

terrific /təˈrɪfɪk/ *adj* **1** (huge) [*amount, incentive, pleasure, size*] énorme; [*pain, heat, noise*] épouvantable; [*argument*] violent; [*speed*] fou/folle; [*accident, problem, shock, worry*] terrible; [*struggle*] acharné; **2**○ (wonderful) formidable; **to feel ~** se sentir en pleine forme○; **to look ~** (healthy) avoir l'air en pleine forme○; (attractive) être superbe; **we had a ~ time** on s'est vraiment bien amusé.

terrifically /təˈrɪfɪklɪ/ *adv* **1** (extremely) [*difficult, gifted, kind, large*] extrêmement; [*expensive, hot, noisy*] épouvantablement; **2**○ [*sing, write*] formidablement bien○.

terrified /ˈterɪfaɪd/ *adj* [*animal, face, person*] terrifié; [*scream*] de terreur; **to be ~ of** avoir une terreur folle de [*heights, spiders*]; **he's ~ of what might happen** il a une terreur folle de ce qui pourrait se passer; **to be ~ that/to do** être terrifié à l'idée que/à l'idée de faire; **to be too ~ to do** être trop terrifié pour faire.

terrify /ˈterɪfaɪ/ *vtr* terrifier; **guns/threats do not ~ me** les armes/menaces ne me font pas peur.
IDIOMS **to ~ the life out of sb**○ donner une peur bleue à qn○.

terrifying /ˈterɪfaɪɪŋ/ *adj* **1** (frightening) terrifiant; **2** (alarming) effroyable.

terrifyingly /ˈterɪfaɪɪŋlɪ/ *adv* [*fast, normal, real*] effroyablement; [*addictive, dangerous, large, pragmatic*] terriblement; [*shake, tilt*] de façon terrifiante; [*drop, plunge*] terriblement; **to come ~ close to death** friser la mort.

Territoire de Belfort ▶ **1163** *pr n* Territoire *m* de Belfort; **in/to ~** dans le Territoire de Belfort.

territorial /ˌterəˈtɔːrɪəl/ *adj* **1** Geog, Pol territorial; **2** Zool [*behaviour, instinct*] territorial; **to be very ~** avoir un instinct territorial très développé.

Territorial /ˌterəˈtɔːrɪəl/ *pr n* GB Mil membre *m* de l'armée de réservistes volontaires.

territorial: **Territorial Army** *pr n* GB armée *f* de réservistes volontaires; **~ waters** *npl* Jur Naut eaux *fpl* territoriales.

territory /ˈterətrɪ, US ˈterɪtɔːrɪ/ *n* **1** (land owned) territoire *m*; **2** Pol (dependency) territoire *m*; **3** (of animal, inhabitant, team) territoire *m*; **her home ~** son territoire; **4** (of salesperson) secteur *m*; **5** (area of influence, knowledge) domaine *m*; **I'm on familiar ~** je suis sur mon terrain; **6** US Sport (of pitch) camp *m*.
IDIOMS **to go with the ~** faire partie du boulot○.

terror /ˈterə(r)/ **I** *n* **1** (fear) terreur *f*; **to scream with ~** crier de terreur; **to flee in ~** s'enfuir terrifié; **frozen by** ou **with ~** paralysé par la terreur; **to live** ou **go in ~ of** vivre dans la terreur de [*muggers, blackmail*]; **to have a ~ of** être terrifié par; **to strike ~ into (the heart of) sb** semer la terreur chez qn; **2** (unruly person) terreur *f*; **a little/holy ~**○ une petite/vraie terreur; **3** Hist **the Terror** la Terreur.
II *modif* [*bombing*] à la bombe; [*gang*] de

terroristes; [*tactic*] d'intimidation; **a ~ campaign** une vague terroriste.

terrorism /ˈterərɪzəm/ *n* terrorisme *m*; **an act of ~** un acte de terrorisme.

terrorist /ˈterərɪst/ **I** *n* terroriste *mf*.
II *modif* [*attack, bomb, group, plot*] terroriste; [*bombing*] à la bombe.

terrorize /ˈterəraɪz/ *vtr* terroriser [*person, rival, town*]; **to ~ sb into doing** terroriser qn jusqu'à ce qu'il/qu'elle fasse.

terror-stricken /ˈterəstrɪkən/ *adj* frappé de terreur.

terry /ˈterɪ/ **I** *n* (also **~ towelling** GB, **~ cloth** US) tissu *m* éponge.
II *modif* [*nappy, bathrobe*] en tissu éponge.

terse /tɜːs/ *adj* [*novel, style*] succinct; [*person, report, statement*] laconique.

tersely /ˈtɜːslɪ/ *adv* laconiquement.

terseness /ˈtɜːsnɪs/ *n* laconisme *m*.

tertiary /ˈtɜːʃərɪ, US -ʃɪerɪ/ *adj* [*era, industry, sector*] tertiaire; [*education, college*] supérieur; [*burn*] au troisième degré; [*syphilis*] au stade tertiaire.

Tertiary /ˈtɜːʃərɪ, US -ʃɪerɪ/ *n* Geol **the ~** le tertiaire *m*.

Terylene® /ˈterəliːn/ **I** *n* tergal® *m*.
II *modif* [*dress, sheet*] en tergal®.

TESL /tesl/ *n* (*abrév* = **Teaching English as a Second Language**) enseignement *m* de l'anglais à des non-anglophones.

Tessa *n* GB Fin (*abrév* = **Tax Exempt Special Savings Account**) *compte d'épargne bloqué net d'impôt*.

tessellated /ˈtesəleɪtɪd/ *adj* Constr [*floor, pavement*] en mosaïque.

tessellation /ˌtesəˈleɪʃn/ *n* Constr mosaïque *f*.

test /test/ **I** *n* **1** (of person, ability, resources) gen épreuve *f*, Psych test *m*; Sch, Univ (written) contrôle *m*, interrogation *f* écrite; (oral) interrogation *f* orale, épreuve *f* orale; **to put sb/sth to the ~** mettre qn/qch à l'épreuve; **a ~ of strength** une épreuve de force; **to stand the ~ (of time)** résister à l'épreuve (du temps); **a method that has stood the ~ of time** une méthode éprouvée; **intelligence/personality ~** test d'aptitude intellectuelle/de personnalité; **it was a severe ~ of his patience/physical strength** cela mettait sa patience/force physique à rude épreuve; **the crisis was a real ~ of their relationship** cette crise a vraiment mis leurs rapports à l'épreuve; **tomorrow's match should be a good ~ of the team's capabilities** le match de demain devrait permettre de savoir de quoi l'équipe est capable; **Tuesday's poll should be a good ~ of popular opinion** le scrutin de mardi devrait permettre de se faire une idée de l'état de l'opinion publique; **the best ~ of a good novel/car is...** le meilleur critère pour juger de la valeur d'un roman/d'une voiture est...; **2** Comm, Ind, Tech (of equipment, machine, new model) essai *m*; (of new product) contrôle *m*, essai *m*; **3** Med (of blood, urine) analyse *f*; (of organ) examen *m*; (to detect virus, cancer) test *m* de dépistage; Chem, Pharm analyse *f*; **eye/hearing ~** examen des yeux/de l'ouïe; **blood ~** analyse de sang; **Aids ~** test de dépistage du sida; **to have a blood ~** se faire faire une analyse de sang; **the iodine ~ for starch** le test à l'iode pour détecter la présence d'amidon; **4** Aut (also **driving ~**) examen *m* du permis de conduire; **to pass/fail one's ~** être reçu à/échouer son (examen du) permis de conduire; **5** GB Sport = **test match**.
II *vtr* **1** (assess, examine) gen évaluer [*intelligence, efficiency*]; Sch (in classroom) interroger [*student*] (**on** en), (at exam time) contrôler [*student*]; Psych tester; **during the interview they ~ed him on his knowledge of French/current affairs** au cours de l'entretien ils lui ont posé des questions pour évaluer ses connaissances en français/sur les problèmes d'actualité; **to ~ sb's intelligence** gen évaluer l'intelligence de qn, (formally) faire subir un test d'aptitude intellectuelle à qn; **2** Comm, Tech essayer, tester [*vehicle, product*]; Med, Pharm analyser, faire une analyse (or des analyses) de [*blood, urine, sample*]; expérimenter [*new drug, vaccine*]; Chem analyser; **to have one's eyes ~ed** se faire faire un examen des yeux; **to ~ sb for steroids** faire subir une analyse à qn pour déterminer la présence de stéroïdes; **he was ~ed for Aids/leukemia** on lui a fait subir un test de dépistage du sida/de la leucémie; **the water was ~ed for pollution** on a analysé l'eau pour voir si elle était polluée; **to ~ drugs on animals** expérimenter des médicaments sur les animaux; **all the new equipment has been ~ed for faults** le nouveau matériel a été entièrement testé et essayé; **to ~ the water** lit [*swimmer*] prendre la température de l'eau, Chem analyser l'eau, fig tâter le terrain, se faire une idée de la situation; **well-~ed** [*method, formula, model*] éprouvé, qui a fait ses preuves; **3** (tax, strain) mettre [qch] à l'épreuve [*endurance, strength, patience, courage, effectiveness*]; **her patience was severely ~ed** sa patience a été mise à rude épreuve.
III *vi* **to ~ for starch/for alcohol** (in laboratory) faire une recherche d'amidon/d'alcool; **to ~ for an infection/allergy** faire des analyses pour trouver la cause d'une infection/allergie; **his blood ~ed negative** son analyse de sang a été négative; **'one, two, three, ~ing'** (when trying out microphone) ≈ 'un, deux, trois, un, deux, trois'.

testament /ˈtestəmənt/ *n* **1** Jur testament *m*; **last will and ~** dernières volontés et testament; **2** (proof) témoignage *m* (**to sth** de qch); **3** (tribute) hommage *m*; **4** littér (legacy) testament *m*; **5 Testament** Testament *m*; **the Old/the New Testament** l'Ancien/le Nouveau Testament.

testamentary /ˌtestəˈmentrɪ, US -terɪ/ *adj* Jur [*bequest, disposition*] testamentaire.

testamentary capacity *n* capacité *f* de disposer par testament.

testator /teˈsteɪtə(r), US ˈtesteɪtər/ *n* Jur testateur *m*.

testatrix /teˈsteɪtrɪks/ *n* Jur (*pl* **-es**) testatrice *f*.

test: **~ ban** *n* interdiction *f* d'essais nucléaires; **~ bay** *n* zone *f* d'essais; **~-bed, ~-bench** *n* banc *m* d'essai; **~ bore** *n* prospection *f* pétrolière (*par sondage*); **~ card** *n* GB TV mire *f*; **~ case** *n* Jur procès *m* qui fait jurisprudence; **~ data** *n* données *fpl* d'essai; **~ drill** *vi* faire des sondages (pour trouver du pétrole).

test-drive /ˈtestdraɪv/ **I** *n* essai *m* de route.
II *vtr* faire faire un essai de route à, essayer [*car*].

tester /ˈtestə(r)/ *n* **1** (person) contrôleur/-euse *m/f*; (device) testeur *m*, appareil *m* de contrôle; **2** Cosmet (sample) échantillon *m*; **3** (bed canopy) baldaquin *m*.

testes /ˈtestiːz/ *pl* ▶ **testis**.

test: **~ flight** *n* vol *m* d'essai; **~-fly** *vtr* essayer [*plane*].

testicle /ˈtestɪkl/ *n* testicule *m*.

testify /ˈtestɪfaɪ/ *vi* **1** (state solemnly) témoigner; **to ~ in court/under oath** témoigner au tribunal/sous serment; **to ~ against/for** témoigner contre/en faveur de; **to ~ that** attester que; **to ~ to** attester [*fact, hostility, presence*]; **2** (prove) **to ~ to sth** témoigner de qch.

testily /ˈtestɪlɪ/ *adv* [*say, reply*] avec irritation.

testimonial /ˌtestɪˈməʊnɪəl/ *n* **1**† (reference) lettre *f* de recommandation; **2** (tribute) témoignage *m*; **as a ~ to** en témoignage de [*courage, loyalty*]; **3** GB Sport (also **~ match** ou **game**) jubilé *m*.

testimony /ˈtestɪmənɪ, US -məʊnɪ/ *n* **1** (true statement) gen témoignage *m*; Jur déposition *f*; **to give ~** faire une déposition; **2** (evidence) témoignage *m*; **to be a ~ to sb's talent/courage** témoigner du talent/courage de qn; **to bear ~ to sth** être la preuve de qch.

testing /ˈtestɪŋ/ **I** *n* ¢ (of equipment, vehicle, machine, system) essai *m*, mise *f* à l'essai; (of drug, cosmetic) expérimentation *f*; Chem, Med, Pharm (of blood, water etc) analyse *f*; (of person) gen mise *f* à l'épreuve; Med examen *m*; Psych tests *mpl*; Sch contrôles *mpl* (des connaissances); **nuclear (bomb) ~** essais *mpl* nucléaires.
II *adj* [*question, situation, work, period*] éprouvant; **a ~ time** une période éprouvante.

testing: **~-bench** *n* banc *m* d'essai; **~ ground** *n* Mil site *m* d'essais (nucléaires); Ind, Tech banc *m* d'essai; fig terrain *m* d'essai.

testis /ˈtestɪs/ *n* (*pl* **-tes**) testicule *m*.

test market /ˈtestˈmɑːkɪt/ **I** *n* marché *m* test.
II *vtr* commercialiser [qch] à titre expérimental [*product*].

test: **~ marketing** *n* test *m* de marché, marketing *m* à titre expérimental; **~ match** *n* match *m* international (*de cricket*).

testosterone /teˈstɒstərəʊn/ *n* testostérone *f*.

test paper *n* **1** Chem (papier *m*) réactif *m*; **2** GB Sch, Univ interrogation *f* écrite.

test: **~ pattern** *n* US TV mire *f*; **~ piece** *n* Mus morceau *m* de concours; **~ pilot** *n* pilote *m* d'essai; **~ run** *n* essai *m*; **~ strip** *n* Phot bande *f* d'essai; **~ tube** *n* éprouvette *f*; **~-tube baby** *n* bébé-éprouvette *m*.

testy /ˈtestɪ/ *adj* [*person*] irritable; [*comment, reply*] irrité.

tetanus /ˈtetənəs/ ▶ **1354** **I** *n* tétanos *m*.
II *modif* [*injection, vaccine*] antitétanique; [*symptoms*] du tétanos; [*spasm*] tétanique.

tetchily /ˈtetʃɪlɪ/ *adv* [*insist, refuse, speak*] avec emportement.

tetchiness /ˈtetʃɪnɪs/ *n* irritabilité *f*.

tetchy /ˈtetʃɪ/ *adj* [*comment, mood, person, voice*] grincheux/-euse; [*behaviour*] emporté.

tête-à-tête /ˌteɪtɑːˈteɪt/ **I** *n* (*pl* **-têtes** ou **-tête**) tête-à-tête *m inv*.
II *adv* [*dine, meet, talk*] en tête à tête.

tether /ˈteðə(r)/ **I** *n* longe *f*.
II *vtr* attacher (**to** à).
IDIOMS **to be at the end of one's ~** être au bout du rouleau○.

tetherball /ˈteðəbɔːl/ *n* US Sport ballon *m* captif.

tetragon /ˈtetrəgən, US -gɒn/ *n* quadrilatère *m*.

tetrahedron /ˌtetrəˈhiːdrən, -ˈhedrən/ *n* tétraèdre *m*.

tetrameter /təˈtræmɪtə(r)/ *n* tétramètre *m*.

Teutonic /tjuːˈtɒnɪk, US tuː-/ *adj* germanique.

Texan /ˈteksn/ **I** *n* Texan/-e *m/f*.
II *adj* texan.

Texas /ˈteksəs/ ▶ **1744** *pr n* Texas *m*.

Tex Mex○ *adj* Tex-Mex *inv* (*mélange des styles mexicain et texan*).

text /tekst/ *n* texte *m* (**by** de).

textbook /ˈtekstbʊk/ **I** *n* manuel *m* (**about, on** sur); **a German ~** un manuel d'allemand.
II *adj* [*case, landing, pregnancy*] exemplaire; [*example*] parfait.

text editor *n* Comput éditeur *m* de texte.

textile /ˈtekstaɪl/ **I** *n* textile *m*.
II textiles *npl* textile *m*; **to work in ~s** travailler dans le textile.
III *modif* [*prices, sector, technician*] du textile; [*exporter, manufacturer*] de textile; [*worker*] dans le textile; [*fibre, group, industry*] textile.

text processing *n* Comput traitement *m* de texte.

textual /ˈtekstʃʊəl/ *adj* [*analysis, criticism, study*] de texte.

that

As a determiner

In French, determiners agree in gender and number with the noun they precede; *that* is translated by *ce* + masculine singular noun (*ce monsieur*), *cet* + masculine singular noun beginning with a vowel or mute 'h' (*cet homme*) and *cette* + feminine singular noun (*cette femme*); *those* is translated by *ces*.

Note, however, that the above translations are also used for the English *this* (plural *these*). So when it is necessary to insist on *that* as opposed to another or others of the same sort, the adverbial tag *-là* is added to the noun:

I prefer THAT version = je préfère cette version-là

For particular usages, see the entry ***that***.

As a pronoun meaning *that one, those ones*

In French, pronouns reflect the gender and number of the noun they are referring to. So *that* is translated by *celui-là* for a masculine noun, *celle-là* for a feminine noun and *those* is translated by *ceux-là* for a masculine noun and *celles-là* for a feminine noun:

I think I like that one (dress) best = je crois que je préfère celle-là

For other uses of *that, those* as pronouns (e.g. *who's that?*) and for adverbial use (e.g. *that much, that many*) there is no straightforward translation, so see the entry ***that*** for examples of usage.

When used as a relative pronoun, *that* is translated by *qui* when it is the subject of the verb and by *que* when it is the object:

the man that stole the car = l'homme qui a volé la voiture
the film that I saw = le film que j'ai vu

Remember that in the present perfect and past perfect tenses, the past participle will agree with the noun to which *que* as object refers:

the apples that I bought = les pommes que j'ai achetées

When *that* is used as a relative pronoun with a preposition it is translated by *lequel* when standing for a masculine singular noun, by *laquelle* when standing for a feminine singular noun, by *lesquels* when standing for a masculine plural noun and by *lesquelles* when standing for a feminine plural noun:

the chair that I was sitting on = la chaise sur laquelle j'étais assise
the children that I bought the books for = les enfants pour lesquels j'ai acheté les livres

Remember that in cases where the English preposition used would normally be translated by *à* in French (e.g. *to, at*), the translation of the whole (prep + rel pron) will be *auquel, à laquelle, auxquels, auxquelles*:

the girls that I was talking to = les filles auxquelles je parlais

Similarly, where the English preposition used would normally be translated by *de* in French (e.g. *of, from*), the translation of the whole (prep + rel pron) will be *dont* in all cases:

the Frenchman that I received a letter from = le Français dont j'ai reçu une lettre

When used as a conjunction, *that* can almost always be translated by *que* (*qu'* before a vowel or mute 'h'):

she said that she would do it = elle a dit qu'elle le ferait

In certain verbal constructions, *que* is followed by a subjunctive in French. If you are in doubt about the construction to use, consult the appropriate verb entry. For particular usages see the entry ***that***.

textually /'tekstʃʊəlɪ/ *adv* [*alter, analyse*] au niveau du texte.

texture /'tekstʃə(r)/ *n* **1** lit (of cream, paint, soil, surface, cloth) texture *f*; **2** fig (of life, writing) texture *f*; (of music) caractère *m*.

textured /'tekstʃəd/ *adj* [*fabric, paint, wall paper*] texturé; **rough-~** de texture grossière.

textured vegetable protein, TVP *n* Culin protéines *fpl* végétales texturées.

TGWU *n* GB (*abrév* = **Transport and General Workers' Union**) *un des principaux syndicats britanniques*.

Thai /taɪ/ **▶ 1486** **I** *n* **1** (person) Thaïlandais/-e *m/f*; **2** (language) Thaï *m*.
II *adj* thaïlandais/-e.

Thailand /'taɪlænd/ **▶ 1131** *pr n* Thaïlande *f*.

thalamus /'θæləməs/ *n* Anat thalamus *m*.

thalassemia /θælə'siːmɪə/ **▶ 1354** *n* thalassémie *f*.

thalidomide /θə'lɪdəmaɪd/ **I** *n* thalidomide *f*.
II *modif* [*scandal, victim*] de la thalidomide; [*baby*] victime de la thalidomide.

Thames /temz/ **▶ 1644** **I** *pr n* **the** (**river**) **~** la Tamise.
II *modif* [*estuary, docks*] de la Tamise.
IDIOMS **he'll never set the ~ on fire** GB il ne fera jamais d'étincelles.

than /ðæn, ðən/

■ **Note** When *than* is used as a preposition in expressions of comparison, it is translated by *que* (or *qu'* before a vowel or mute 'h'): *he's taller than me* = il est plus grand que moi; *London is bigger than Oxford* = Londres est plus grand qu'Oxford.
– For expressions with numbers, temperatures etc see the entry below.
– See also the entries ***more***, ***less***, ***hardly***, ***soon***, ***rather***, ***other***.
– When *than* is used as a conjunction, it is translated by *que* and the verb following it is preceded by *ne*: *it was farther than I thought* = c'était plus loin que je ne pensais. However, French speakers often try to phrase the comparison differently: *it was more difficult than we expected* = c'était plus difficile que prévu. For other uses see the entry below.
– See also the entries ***hardly***, ***rather***, ***soon***.

I *prep* **1** (in comparisons) que; **thinner ~ him** plus mince que lui; **he has more ~ me** il a plus que moi; **faster by plane ~ by boat** plus rapide en avion qu'en bateau; **I was more surprised ~ annoyed** j'étais plus étonné qu'ennuyé; **it's more difficult for us ~ for them** c'est plus difficile pour nous que pour eux; **2** (expressing quantity, degree, value) de; **more/less ~ 100** plus/moins de 100; **more ~ half** plus de la moitié; **temperatures lower ~ 30 degrees** des températures de moins de 30 degrés.
II *conj* **1** (in comparisons) que; **he's older ~ I am** il est plus âgé que moi; **it took us longer ~ we thought it would** ça nous a pris plus de temps que prévu; **it was further away ~ I remembered** c'était plus loin que dans mon souvenir; **there's nothing better/worse ~ doing** il n'y a rien de mieux/de pire que de faire; **2** (expressing preferences) **I'd sooner** ou **rather do X ~ do Y** je préférerais faire X que (de) faire Y; **3** (when) **hardly** ou **no sooner had he left ~ the phone rang** à peine était-il parti que le téléphone a sonné; **4** US (from) **to be different ~ sth** être différent de qch.

thank /θæŋk/ *vtr* remercier [*person*] (**for** de, pour; **for doing** d'avoir fait); **we've got Cath to ~ for that** c'est à Cath que nous devons cela also iron; **you've only got yourself to ~ for that!** tu ne peux t'en prendre qu'à toi-même!; **I'll ~ you to do** je te serais reconnaissant de faire; **he won't ~ you for doing** il ne va pas apprécier que tu fasses; **~ God!, ~ goodness** ou **heavens!** Dieu merci!; **~ God you're here!** Dieu merci tu es là!; **there's the bus, ~ goodness** heureusement, voilà le bus.

thankful /'θæŋkfl/ *adj* (grateful) reconnaissant (**to** envers; **for** de); (relieved) soulagé (**to do** de faire; **for** de); **to be ~ (that)** être soulagé que (+ *subj*); **that's something to be ~ for!** c'est déjà un soulagement!

thankfully /'θæŋkfəlɪ/ *adv* **1** (luckily) heureusement; **2** (with relief) [*sit down, eat*] avec soulagement; (with gratitude) [*smile*] avec gratitude.

thankfulness /'θæŋkflnɪs/ *n* reconnaissance *f*.

thankless /'θæŋklɪs/ *adj* [*task, person*] ingrat.

thanks /θæŋks/ **I** *npl* remerciements *mpl* (**for** pour; **to** à); **with ~** avec mes/nos etc remerciements; **'received with ~'** Comm 'avec nos remerciements'; **~ be to God** Dieu soit loué; **this is the ~ I get!** voilà les remerciements que j'en ai!; **a letter of ~** une lettre de remerciement.
II thanks to *prep phr* grâce à; **we did it, no ~ to you!**° on a réussi, mais tu n'y es pour rien°!
III° *excl* merci!; **~ for that/for doing** merci pour ça°/d'avoir fait; **~ a lot** merci beaucoup; **~ a lot** ou **a bunch** ou **a bundle!** iron merci beaucoup!, grand merci!; **no ~** non merci.

thanks: **~giving** *n* Relig action *f* de grâces; **Thanksgiving** (**Day**) *n* US jour *m* d'Action de Grâces; **~ offering** *n* action *f* de grâces.

thank you /'θæŋkjuː/ **I** *n* (also **thank-you**, **thankyou**) merci *m*; **to say ~ to sb, to say one's ~s to sb** dire merci à qn.
II *modif* (also **thank-you**, **thankyou**) [*letter, gift*] de remerciement.
III *adv* merci; **~ for that/for doing** merci pour cela/d'avoir fait; **~ very much** aussi iron merci beaucoup also iron; **no ~** non merci.

that **I** /ðæt, ðət/ *det* (*pl* **those**) ce/cet/cette/ces; **~ chair/~ man over there** cette chaise/cet homme là-bas; **I said THAT dress!** j'ai dit cette robe-là!; **I prefer ~ colour to this one** je préfère cette couleur-là à celle-ci; **not ~ one!** pas celui-là!; **~ same day** ce même jour; **you can't do it ~ way** tu ne peux pas le faire comme ça; **he went ~ way** il est allé par là; **those patients** (**who are**) **able to walk** les patients qui sont capables de marcher; **~ train crash last year** la collision ferroviaire qui a eu lieu l'an dernier; **~ lazy son of yours/theirs** ton/leur paresseux de fils; **~ car of his is always breaking down** sa fichue° voiture n'arrête pas de tomber en panne; **it's ~ Mr Jones from down the road** c'est M. Jones qui habite en bas de la rue; **at ~ moment** à ce moment-là; **at ~ time** à cette époque-là.
II /ðæt/ *dem pron* (*pl* **those**) **1** (that one) celui-/celle-/ceux-/celles-là; **we prefer this to ~** nous préférons celui-ci à celui-là; **'which boys?'—'those over there'** 'quels garçons?'—'ceux qui sont là-bas'; **not this, THAT!** pas celui-ci, celui-là!; **it's a more expensive wine than ~ produced by X** c'est un vin plus cher que celui produit par X; **2** (the thing or person observed or mentioned) cela, ça, ce; **what's ~?** qu'est-ce que c'est que ça?; **who's ~?** gen qui est-ce?; (on phone) qui est à l'appareil?; **is ~ John?** c'est John?; **is ~ you John?** c'est toi John?; **who told you ~?** qui t'a dit ça?; **~' s not true/fair** ce n'est pas vrai/ juste; **~'s what he said** c'est ce qu'il a dit; **~'s how/why he did it** c'est comme ça/pour ça qu'il l'a fait; **what did he mean by ~?** qu'est-ce qu'il entendait par là?; **~'s**

the

In French, determiners agree in gender and number with the noun they precede; *the* is translated by *le* + masculine singular noun (*le chien*), by *la* + feminine singular noun (*la chaise*), by *l'* + masculine or feminine singular noun beginning with a vowel or mute 'h' (*l'auteur, l'homme, l'absence, l'histoire*) and by *les* + plural noun (*les hommes, les femmes*).

When *the* is used after a preposition in English, the two words (prep + *the*) are often translated by one word in French. If the preposition would normally be translated by *de* in French (*of, about, from* etc.) the prep + *the* is translated by *du* + masculine noun (*du chien*), by *de la* + feminine noun (*de la femme*), by *de l'* + singular noun beginning with a vowel or mute 'h' (*de l'auteur, de l'histoire*) and by *des* + plural noun (*des hommes, des femmes*). If the preposition would usually be translated by *à* (*at, to* etc.) the prep + *the* is translated according to the number and gender of the noun, by *au* (*au chien*), *à la* (*à la femme*), *à l'* (*à l'enfant*), *aux* (*aux hommes, aux femmes*).

Other than this, there are few problems in translating *the* into French. The following cases are, however, worth remembering as not following exactly the pattern of the English:

the good, the poor etc. = les bons, les pauvres *etc.*
Charles the First, Elizabeth the Second etc. = Charles Premier, Elizabeth Deux *etc.*
she's THE violinist of the century = c'est LA violoniste du siècle *or* c'est la plus grande violoniste du siècle
the Tudors, the Batemans etc. = les Tudor, les Bateman *etc.*

For expressions such as *the more, the better*, see the entry **the**.

This dictionary contains usage notes on such topics as ***weight measurement, days of the week, rivers, illnesses, aches and pains, the human body***, and ***musical instruments***, many of which use *the*; for the index to these notes ▶ 1919.

For other particular usages of *the* see the entry **the**.

bureaucrats for you! c'est ça les bureaucrates!; **~'s the man I was talking about/to** voilà or c'est l'homme dont/auquel je parlais; **~'s the house we used to live in** voilà or c'est la maison dans laquelle on vivait; **those are the books I wanted** voilà or ce sont les livres que je voulais; **before ~, he had always lived in London** avant cela, il avait toujours vécu à Londres; **he never went there again after ~** il n'y est jamais retourné après cela; **after ~ we had lunch** après cela or ensuite, nous avons déjeuné; **I might just do ~!** c'est peut-être ce que je vais faire!; **he 's not as greedy as (all) ~!** il n'est pas si avare que ça!; **3** (before relative pronoun) **those who...** ceux qui...
III /ðət/ *rel pron* (subject) qui; (object) que; (with preposition) lequel/laquelle/lesquels/lesquelles; **the woman ~ won** la femme qui a gagné; **the book ~ I bought** le livre que j'ai acheté; **the house ~ they live in** la maison dans laquelle ils vivent; **the reason ~ I phoned** la raison pour laquelle j'ai téléphoné; **the man ~ I received the letter from** l'homme dont j'ai reçu la lettre; **the way ~ she works** la façon dont elle travaille; **the day ~ she arrived** le jour où elle est arrivée; **and fool ~ I am, I believed him** et bête comme je suis, je l'ai cru.
IV /ðət/ *conj* **1** gen que; **he said ~ he had finished** il a dit qu'il avait fini; **it's likely ~ they are out** il est probable qu'ils sont sortis; **it's important ~ they should realize** il est important qu'ils se rendent compte que; **it's just ~ I'm a bit scared** c'est simplement que j'ai un peu peur; **2** (expressing wish) **oh ~ I could fly!** si je pouvais voler!; **oh ~ he would come** s'il pouvait venir; (expressing surprise) **~ she should treat me so badly!** comment peut-elle me traiter comme ça!; **~ it should come to this!** comment peut-on en arriver là!
V /ðæt/ *adv* **1** (to the extent shown) **it's about ~ thick** c'est à peu près épais comme ça; **he's ~ tall** il est grand comme ça; **she's ~ much smaller than me** elle est plus petite que moi de ça; **I can't do ~ much work in one day** je ne peux pas faire autant de travail dans une journée; **he can't swim ~ far** il ne peut pas nager aussi loin; **you're not ~ stupid** tu n'es pas aussi bête que ça; **2** GB dial (so very) tellement; **he was ~ ill that he had to go into hospital** il était tellement malade qu'il a dû aller à l'hôpital.
IDIOMS **...and (all) ~** ...et tout ça; **...and he's very nice at ~!** ...et en plus il est très gentil!; **I might well go at ~!** en fait, je pourrais bien y aller!; **at ~, he got up and left** en entendant cela, il s'est levé et est parti; **with ~ he got up and left** sur ce il s'est levé et est parti; **~ is (to say)...** c'est-à-dire...; **~'s it!** (that's right) c'est ça!; (that's enough) ça suffit!; **I'll give you £10 but ~'s it!** je te donnerai 10 livres sterling mais pas plus!; **I don't want to see you again and ~'s ~!** je ne veux pas te revoir point final or et il n'y a pas à discuter!; **well, ~'s it then!** il n'y a rien de plus à faire!

thatch /θætʃ/ **I** *n* **1** Constr chaume *m*; **2** fig (of hair) tignasse *f*.
II *vtr* couvrir [qch] de chaume [*cottage, roof*]; **a roof ~ed with reeds** un toit couvert de chaume.
III *vi* faire des toitures en chaume.
IV thatched *pp adj* couvert de chaume.

thatch: **~ed cottage** *n* chaumière *f*; **~ed roof** *n* toit *m* de chaume.

thatcher /ˈθætʃə(r)/ *n* couvreur *m* spécialiste des toitures en chaume.

Thatcherism /ˈθætʃərɪzəm/ *n* Pol thatchérisme *m*.

thaw /θɔː/ **I** *n* **1** Meteorol dégel *m*; **the ~ had set in** le dégel avait commencé; **2** fig (detente) (political) détente *f*; **a ~ in her attitude towards me** (social) une amélioration *f* dans son attitude envers moi.
II *vtr* **1** [*heat, sun*] faire fondre [*ice, snow*]; **2** [*person*] décongeler [*frozen food*].
III *vi* **1** lit [*snow*] fondre; [*ground, frozen food*] se décongeler; **2** fig [*person, relations*] se détendre.
IV *v impers* dégeler; **it's ~ing today** ça dégèle aujourd'hui.
■ **thaw out**: ¶ **~ out** [*frozen food, ground*] dégeler; [*person, fingers*] se réchauffer; ¶ **~ [sth] out, ~ out [sth]** [*person*] décongeler [*frozen food*]; [*sun*] dégeler [*ground*].

the /ðiː, ðɪ, ðə/ *det* **1** (specifying, identifying etc) le/la/l'/les; **two chapters of ~ book** deux chapitres du livre; **I met them at ~ supermarket** je les ai rencontrés au supermarché; **2** (best etc) **she's THE violinist of the century** c'est LA violoniste du siècle, c'est la plus grande violoniste du siècle; **~ book of the year** le meilleur livre de l'année; **THE French restaurant** le meilleur restaurant français; **THE way of losing weight** la façon la plus efficace de perdre des kilos; **do you mean THE William Blake?** tu veux dire LE William Blake?; **3** (with family names) **~ Hapsburgs/the Buntings** les Habsbourg/les Bunting; **4** (with genre) **~ opera** l'opéra; **~ ballet** le ballet; **5** (enough) **he hadn't ~ courage to refuse** il n'a pas eu le courage de refuser; **we don't have ~ money for a holiday** nous n'avons pas les moyens de partir en vacances; **can you spare ~ time to help me?** est-ce que tu as du temps pour m'aider?; **6** (with era) **~ fifties** les années cinquante; **7** (with adj) **~ impossible** l'impossible; **she buys only ~ best** elle n'achète que ce qu'il y a de mieux; **8** (with adj forming group) **~ French** les Français; **~ wounded** les blessés ; **~ handicapped** les handicapés; **9** (with comparative adj) **the news made her all ~ sadder** la nouvelle n'a fait que la rendre encore plus triste; ▶ **all, better, more, none, wise, worse etc**; **10** (in double comparatives) **~ more I learn ~ less I understand** plus j'apprends moins je comprends; **~ longer I do it ~ more difficult it becomes** plus je le fais plus ça devient difficile; **~ sooner ~ better** le plus tôt sera le mieux; **~ longer he waits ~ harder it will be** plus il attendra plus ce sera difficile; **11** (with superlatives) **~ fastest train** le train le plus rapide; **~ prettiest house in the village** la maison la plus jolie du village.

theatre, theater US /ˈθɪətə(r)/ **I** *n* **1** (place) théâtre *m*; **to go to the ~** aller au théâtre; **2** (art form) théâtre *m*; **the ~ of cruelty/the absurd** le théâtre de la cruauté/l'absurde; **he works in ~** il travaille dans le théâtre; **3** US (cinema) cinéma *m*; **4** (also **lecture ~**) amphithéâtre *m*; **5** GB (also **operating ~**) salle *f* d'opération; **the patient is in ~** le malade est en salle d'opération; **6** Mil théatre *m*; **a ~ of war** le théâtre d'une guerre; **~ of operations** théâtre *m* d'opérations.
II *modif* **1** Theat [*audience, lover, owner, seat, ticket*] de théâtre; [*company, production, programme, stage, workshop*] théâtral; [*manager, staff*] du théâtre; [*visit*] au théâtre; **2** GB Med [*nurse*] au bloc *m* opératoire; [*equipment*] du bloc *m* opératoire; **3** US (cinema) [*owner, seat*] de cinéma; [*manager*] du cinéma.

theatre: **~goer** *n* amateur/-trice *m/f* de théâtre; **~ group** *n* troupe *m* de théâtre; **~-in-the-round** *n* théâtre *m* en rond; **~land** *n* quartier *m* des théâtres; **~ weapon** *n* Mil arme *f* de moyenne portée.

theatrical /θɪˈætrɪkl/ *adj* [*figure, star*] du théâtre; [*group, photographer*] de théâtre; [*agency, family, gesture, production, technique*] théâtral.

theatrically /θɪˈætrɪklɪ/ *adv* **1** Theat [*gifted*] pour le théâtre; [*effective, striking*] du point de vue théâtral; **2** (dramatically) [*cry, enter, laugh, wave*] de façon théâtrale.

theatricals /θɪˈætrɪklz/ *npl* théâtre *m*; **amateur ~** théâtre *m* d'amateurs.

Thebes /θiːbz/ ▶ 1818 *pr n* Thèbes.

thee‡ /ðiː/ *pron* = **you**.

theft /θeft/ *n* vol *m* (**of** de); **art/car ~** vol *m* d'œuvres d'art/de voitures; **~s from tourists/cars/shops** des vols commis sur des touristes/sur des voitures/dans les magasins.

their /ðeə(r)/

■ **Note** In French, determiners agree in gender and number with the noun they precede. So *their* is translated by *leur* + masculine or feminine singular noun (*leur chien, leur maison*) and by *leurs* + plural noun (*leurs enfants*).
– When *their* is stressed *à eux* is added after the noun: THEIR house = leur maison à eux.
– For *their* used with parts of the body ▶ 1037.

det leur/leurs.

theirs /ðeəz/

■ **Note** In French, possessive pronouns reflect the gender and number of the noun they are standing for; *theirs* is translated by *le leur, la leur, les leurs*, according to what is being referred to.
– For examples and particular usages see below.

pron **my car is red but ~ is blue** ma voiture est rouge mais la leur est bleue; **the green hats are ~** les chapeaux verts sont à eux or elles; **which house is ~?** c'est

them

When used as a direct object pronoun, referring to people, animals or things, *them* is translated by *les*:

I know them = je les connais

Note that the object pronoun normally comes before the verb in French and that in compound tenses like the present perfect and past perfect, the past participle agrees in gender and number with the direct object pronoun:

he's seen them
(them being masculine or of mixed gender) = il les a vus
(them being all feminine gender) = il les a vues

In imperatives, the direct object pronoun is translated by *les* and comes after the verb:

catch them! = attrape-les! (*note the hyphen*)

When used as an indirect object pronoun, *them* is translated by *leur*:

I gave them it or *I gave it to them* = je le leur ai donné

In imperatives, the indirect object pronoun is translated by *leur* and comes after the verb:

phone them! = téléphone-leur! (*note the hyphen*)

After prepositions and the verb *to be*, the translation is *eux* for masculine or mixed gender and *elles* for feminine gender:

he did it for them = il l'a fait pour eux *or* pour elles
it's them = ce sont eux *or* ce sont elles

For particular usages see the entry ***them***.

laquelle leur maison?; **I'm a friend of ~** je suis un ami à eux; **it's not ~** il or elle n'est pas à eux; **the money wasn't ~ to give away** ils or elles n'avaient pas à donner cet argent; **~ was not an easy task** leur tâche n'était pas facile; **I saw them with that dog of ~** péj je les ai vus avec leur sale chien○.

theism /ˈθiːɪzəm/ *n* théisme *m*.

theist /ˈθiːɪst/ *n* théiste *mf*.

theistic /θiːˈɪstɪk/ *adj* théiste.

them /ðem, ðəm/ *pron* **both of ~** tous/toutes les deux; **both of ~ work in London** ils/elles travaillent à Londres tous/toutes les deux, tous/toutes les deux travaillent à Londres; **some of ~** quelques-uns d'entre eux or quelques-unes d'entre elles; **take ~ all** prenez-les tous/toutes; **none of ~ wants it** aucun d'entre eux or aucune d'entre elles ne le veut; **every single one of ~** chacun/-e d'entre eux/elles.

thematic /θɪˈmætɪk/ *adj* thématique.

theme /θiːm/ *n* **1** (topic, motif) thème *m*; **on the ~ of** sur le thème de; **2** Mus (melodic unit) thème *m*; **3** Radio, TV (also **~ song, ~ tune**) indicatif *m*; **4** Ling thème *m*; **5** US (essay) rédaction *f*.

theme: **~ park** *n* parc *m* de loisirs (à thème); **~ song ~ tune** *n* Cin musique *f*; Radio, TV indicatif *m*; fig rengaine *f*.

themselves /ðəmˈselvz/

■ **Note** When used as a reflexive pronoun, direct and indirect, *themselves* is translated by *se* (or *s'* before a vowel or mute h).

– When used as an emphatic the translation is *eux-mêmes* in the masculine and *elles-mêmes* in the feminine: *they did it themselves* = ils l'ont fait eux-mêmes or elles l'ont fait elles-mêmes.

– After a preposition the translation is *eux* or *elles* or *eux-mêmes* or *elles-mêmes*: *they bought the painting for themselves* = (*masculine or mixed gender*) ils ont acheté le tableau pour eux *or* pour eux-mêmes; (*feminine gender*) elles ont acheté le tableau pour elles *or* pour elles-mêmes.

pron **1** (refl) se/s'; **2** (emphatic) eux-mêmes/elles-mêmes; **3** (after prep) eux/elles, eux-mêmes/elles-mêmes; **(all) by ~** tous seuls/toutes seules.

then /ðen/

■ **Note** When *then* is used to mean *at that time*, it is translated by *alors* or *à ce moment-là*: *I was working in Oxford then* = je travaillais alors à Oxford *or* je travaillais à Oxford à ce moment-là. Note that *alors* always comes immediately after the verb in French.

– For particular usages see I 2 in the entry below.

– For translations of *by then, since then, from then, until then* see the entries ***by, since, from, until***.

– When *then* is used to mean *next* it can be translated by either *puis* or *ensuite*: *a man, a horse and then a dog* = un homme, un cheval puis *or* et ensuite un chien.

– For particular usages see I 2 in the entry below.

– When *then* is used to mean *in that case* it is translated by *alors*: *then why worry?* = alors pourquoi s'inquiéter?

– For all other uses see the entry below.

I *adv* **1** (at that point in time) alors, à ce moment-là; (implying more distant past) en ce temps-là; **we were living in Dublin ~** nous habitions alors à Dublin; **her books were ~ enjoying a lot of success** ses livres se vendaient alors très bien; **X, ~ leader of the party** X, alors chef du parti; **I thought so ~ and I still think so** c'est ce que je pensais alors et je le pense encore; **the company will ~ receive funding** l'entreprise recevra alors une aide financière; **what ~?** et alors?, que feront-ils/ferons-nous etc alors?; **just ~ she heard a noise** à ce moment-là elle a entendu un bruit; **a large sum of money even ~** une grosse somme d'argent même à cette époque; **people were idealistic ~** en ce temps-là les gens étaient idéalistes; **from ~ on, life became easier** à partir de ce moment-là la vie est devenue plus facile; **since ~ there has been little news** depuis on a eu peu de nouvelles; **by ~ the damage had been done** le mal était déjà fait; **he was by ~ running his own company** à ce moment-là il dirigeait déjà sa propre entreprise; **they will let us know by ~** nous aurons la réponse à ce moment-là; **if things haven't changed by ~** si d'ici là les choses n'ont pas changé; **we won't be in contact until ~** nous ne serons pas en contact avant (ce moment-là); ▶**there**; **2** (in sequences: afterwards, next) puis, ensuite; **~ came the big news** puis or ensuite on nous a annoncé la grande nouvelle; **she was an editor ~ a teacher** elle a été rédactrice puis or ensuite professeur; **wash ~ slice finely** laver puis couper finement; **we will ~ start the next project** ensuite nous commencerons le projet suivant; **~ after that...** ensuite...; **and ~ what?** (with bated breath) et ensuite?; **3** (in that case) alors; **I saw them if not yesterday ~ the day before** je les ai vus hier ou avant-hier; **if it's a problem for you ~ say so** si ça te pose un problème dis-le; **if they're so nice ~ why not stay with them?** s'ils sont si agréables pourquoi ne pas rester avec eux?; **if x = 3, ~ 6x = 18** si x = 3 alors 6x = 18; **when we know what the problem is ~ we can find a solution** quand nous saurons quel est le problème alors nous pourrons trouver une solution; **~ why did you tell her?** mais alors pourquoi est-ce que tu le lui as dit?; **how about tomorrow ~?** et demain ça irait?; **well try this ~** et bien alors essaie ça; **well ~ we'll have to start again** et bien alors il faudra recommencer; **~ what DO they want?** mais alors qu'est-ce qu'ils veulent?; **4** (summarizing statement: therefore) donc; **these ~ are the results of the policy** voici donc les résultats de cette politique; **overall ~ it would seem that** en résumé il semble donc que; **5** (in addition, besides) puis...aussi; **and ~ there's the fare to consider** et puis il faut aussi tenir compte du prix de billet; **6** (modifying previous statement: on the other hand) d'un autre côté; **she's good but ~ so is he** elle est bonne mais lui aussi; **they said it would rain but ~ they're often wrong** ils ont prévu de la pluie mais ils se trompent souvent; **but ~ again if you're too quiet, no-one will notice you** mais d'un autre côté si tu es trop discret personne ne te remarquera; **he looks anxious but ~ he always does** il a l'air inquiet mais de toute façon il a toujours cet air-là; **7** (rounding off a topic: so) alors; **it's all arranged ~?** tout est arrangé alors?; **that's all right ~** ça va alors; **till Tuesday ~** à mardi alors; **do you think they'll stay here ~?** tu crois qu'ils vont rester ici alors?; **someone told him already ~** quelqu'un le lui a déjà dit alors; **8** (focusing on topic) bon; **now ~ what's all this?** bon, qu'est-ce qui se passe?; **all right ~ who'd like some coffee?** bon, qui veut du café alors?; **what's the problem ~?** alors quel est le problème?

II *adj* (*épith*) **the ~ prime minister** le premier ministre de l'époque; **the ~ mayor of New York, Mr X** M. X, qui était alors maire de New York; **they took over the ~ state-owned sugar factory** ils ont racheté la sucrerie qui était alors une propriété de l'État.

thence /ðens/ *adv* **1** (from there) de là; **2** (therefore) de cela.

thenceforth /ðensˈfɔːθ/, **thenceforward** /ðensˈfɔːwəd/ à dater de ce moment.

theocracy /θɪˈɒkrəsɪ/ *n* théocratie *f*.

theocratic /θɪəˈkrætɪk/ *adj* théocratique.

theodolite /θɪˈɒdəlaɪt/ *n* Civ Eng théodolite *m*.

theologian /ˌθɪəˈləʊdʒən/ *n* théologien/-ienne *m/f*.

theological /ˌθɪəˈlɒdʒɪkl/ *adj* [*debate, issue, thought, writing*] théologique; [*book, college, faculty, study*] de théologie; [*student*] en théologie.

theology /θɪˈɒlədʒɪ/ **I** *n* théologie *f*.
II *modif* [*faculty, lecture, lecturer*] de théologie.

theorem /ˈθɪərəm/ *n* théorème *m*.

theoretical /ˌθɪəˈretɪkl/ *adj* théorique.

theoretically /ˌθɪəˈretɪklɪ/ *adv* [*propound, prove, speak*] théoriquement; [*new, possible, sound*] théoriquement, en théorie (*after adj*); **you are, ~, responsible** théoriquement, vous êtes responsable; **~ speaking** en théorie.

theoretician /ˌθɪərɪˈtɪʃn/, **theorist** /ˈθɪərɪst/ *n* théoricien/-ienne *m/f*.

theorize /ˈθɪəraɪz/ *vi* théoriser, émettre des théories (**about** sur).

theory /ˈθɪərɪ/ *n* **1** (general principles) théorie *f*; **political/music ~** la théorie politique/de la musique; **in ~** en théorie; **2** (hypothesis) théorie *f*; **I have a ~ that** ma théorie est que.

theosophical /ˌθiːəˈsɒfɪkl/ *adj* théosophique.

theosophist /θiːˈɒsəfɪst/ *n* théosophe *mf*.

theosophy /θiːˈɒsəfɪ/ *n* théosophie *f*.

therapeutic /ˌθerəˈpjuːtɪk/ *adj* thérapeutique.

therapeutics /ˌθerəˈpjuːtɪks/ *n* (+ *v sg*) thérapeutique *f*.

therapist /ˈθerəpɪst/ *n* thérapeute *mf*; **dance/music ~** spécialiste *mf* de la thérapie par la danse/la musique.

therapy /ˈθerəpɪ/ **I** *n* Med, Psych thérapie *f*; **to have** ou **be in ~** suivre une thérapie; **to write as a form of ~** écrire en guise de thérapie; **music/relaxation ~** thérapie *f* par la musique/la relaxation.

II *modif* [*group, session*] de thérapie.

there /ðeə(r)/

■ **Note** *there* is generally translated by *là* after prepositions: *near there* = près de là etc and when emphasizing the location of an object/point etc visible to the speaker: *put them there* = mettez-les là.
– Remember that *voilà* is used to draw attention to a visible place/object/person: *there's my watch* = voilà ma montre, whereas *il y a* is used for generalizations: *there's a village nearby* = il y a un village tout près.
– *there* when unstressed with verbs such as *aller* and *être* is translated by *y*: *we went there last year* = nous y sommes allés l'année dernière, but not where emphasis is made: *it was there that we went last year* = c'est là que nous sommes allés l'année dernière.
– For examples of the above and further uses of *there* see the entry below.

I *pron* (as impersonal subject) il; **~ seems** ou **appears to be** il semble y avoir; **~ is/are** il y a; **~ are many reasons** il y a beaucoup de raisons; **~ is some left** il en reste; **once upon a time ~ was** il était une fois; **~'ll be a singsong later** on va chanter plus tard; **~'s no denying that** personne ne peut nier que; **suddenly ~ appeared a fairy** littér soudain est apparue une fée; **~ arose cries from the audience** littér des cris sont montés de la salle.

II *adv* **1** (that place or point) là; **far from/near/two kilometres from ~** loin de/près de/à deux kilomètres de là; **up to ~, down to ~** jusque là; **put it in ~** mettez-le là-dedans; **in ~ please** (ushering sb) par là s'il vous plaît; **we left ~ on Thursday** nous sommes partis de là jeudi; **2** (at or to that place) là; **stop ~** arrêtez-vous là; **sign ~ please** veuillez signer là s'il vous plaît; **stand ~** mettez-vous là; **go over ~** va là-bas; **are you still ~?** (on phone) est-ce que tu es toujours là?; **since we were last ~** depuis la dernière fois que nous y sommes allés; **it's ~ that** gen c'est là que; (when indicating) c'est là où; **to go ~ and back in an hour** faire l'aller et retour en une heure; **take the offer while it's ~** fig profite de l'occasion pendant que c'est possible; **3** (to draw attention) (to person, activity etc) voilà; (to place) là; **what have you got ~?** qu'est-ce que tu as là?; **~ they go** les voilà qui s'en vont; **~ goes the coach** voilà le car qui s'en va; **~ you go again** fig ça y est c'est reparti; **~ you are** (seeing sb arrive) vous voilà; (giving object) tenez, voilà; (that's done) et voilà; **~ is a hammer/are some nails** voilà un marteau/des clous; **~'s a bus coming** voilà un bus; **listen, ~'s my sister calling** tiens, voilà ma sœur qui appelle; **that paragraph/sales assistant ~** ce paragraphe/vendeur; **my colleague ~ will show you** mon collègue va vous montrer; **which one? this one or that one ~?** lequel? celui-ci ou celui-là?; **what does it say ~?** qu'est-ce qui est marqué là?; **~'s why!** ça explique tout!; **4** (indicating arrival) là; **will she be ~ now?** est-ce qu'elle y est maintenant?; **when do they get ~?** quand est-ce qu'ils arrivent là-bas?; **~ I was at last** j'étais enfin là-bas; **the train won't be ~ yet** le train ne sera pas encore là; **we get off ~** c'est là qu'on descend; **5** (indicating juncture) là; **~ we must finish** nous devons nous arrêter là; **I'd like to interrupt you ~** là je me permets de vous interrompre; **~ was our chance** c'était notre chance; **I think you're wrong ~** je crois que là tu te trompes; **so ~ we were in the same cell** et comme ça on s'est retrouvés dans la même cellule; **6**○ (emphatic) **that ~ contraption** ce truc-là○; **hello ~!** salut!; **hey you ~!** eh toi là-bas!

III there and then *adv phr* directement.

IV there again *adv phr* (on the other hand) d'un autre côté.

V *excl* **~ ~!** (soothingly) allez! allez!; **~!** (triumphantly) voilà!; **~, I told you!** voilà, je te l'avais bien dit!; **~, you've woken the baby!** c'est malin, tu as réveillé le bébé!; ▶ **so**.

thereabouts /ðeərəbaʊts/ GB, **thereabout** /ˈðeərəbaʊt/ US *adv* **1** (in the vicinity) par là; **2** (roughly) **100 dollars or ~** 100 dollars environ.

thereafter /ðeərˈɑːftə(r)/ *adv* par la suite.

thereat‡ /ðeərˈæt/ *adv* là-dessus.

thereby /ðeəˈbaɪ, ˈðeə-/ *conj* ainsi; **~ compromising further negotiations** compromettant ainsi de futures négociations; **the patient is ignored ~ adding to his distress** le patient est tenu à l'écart ce qui ne fait qu'ajouter à son désarroi.

IDIOMS **~ hangs a tale** c'est toute une histoire.

there'd /ðeəd/ = **there had, there would**.

therefore /ˈðeəfɔː(r)/ *adv* donc, par conséquent.

therein /ðeərˈɪn/ *adv* **1** (in that) **~ lies...** c'est en cela que réside...; **the aircraft and the persons ~** l'avion et les personnes qui sont/étaient à l'intérieur; **2** Jur (in contract) **contained ~** ci-inclus.

there'll /ðeəl/ = **there will**.

thereof /ðeərˈɒv/ *adv* **1** Jur de cela; **2**‡ **he partook ~** il en mangea.

thereon‡ /ðeərˈɒn/ *adv* = **thereupon**.

there's /ðeəz/ = **there is, there has**.

thereto /ðeəˈtuː/ *adv* Jur y; **the matters pertaining ~** les questions qui s'y rattachent.

theretofore /ˌðeətʊˈfɔː(r)/ *adv* jusque là.

thereunder /ðeərˈʌndə(r)/ *adv* sout en-dessous.

thereupon /ˌðeərəˈpɒn/ *adv* sout sur ce.

therewith /ðeəˈwɪð/ *adv* **1** sout (attached) avec cela; **2** littér (at once) sur ce.

therm /θɜːm/ *n* thermie *f*.

thermal /ˈθɜːml/ **I** *n* courant *m* ascendant.

II *adj* [*spring, treatment*] thermal; [*garment*] thermique; [*analysis, barrier, energy, insulation, printing, reactor, unit*] thermique.

thermal: **~ baths** *npl* thermes *mpl*; **~ efficiency** *n* rendement *m* thermique; **~ imaging** *n* Sci thermographie *f*.

thermic /ˈθɜːmɪk/ *adj* Sci, Tech thermique.

thermionic /ˌθɜːmɪˈɒnɪk/ *adj* thermoélectrique, thermoïonique.

thermionics /ˌθɜːmɪˈɒnɪks/ *n* (+ *v sg*) thermoélectronique *f*.

thermionic valve GB, **~ tube** US tube *m* thermoïonique.

thermocouple /ˈθɜːməʊkʌpl/ *n* thermocouple *m*, couple *m* thermoélectrique.

thermodynamic /ˌθɜːməʊdaɪˈnæmɪk/ *adj* thermodynamique.

thermodynamics /ˌθɜːməʊdaɪˈnæmɪks/ *n* (+ *v sg*) thermodynamique *f*.

thermoelectric /ˌθɜːməʊɪˈlektrɪk/ *adj* thermoélectrique.

thermograph /ˈθɜːməgrɑːf, US -græf/ *n* thermographe *m*.

thermography /θɜːˈmɒgrəfɪ/ *n* thermographie *f*.

thermoluminescence /ˌθɜːməʊˌluːmɪˈnesns/ *n* thermoluminescence *f*.

thermoluminescence dating *n* datation *f* par thermoluminescence.

thermometer /θəˈmɒmɪtə(r)/ *n* thermomètre *m*.

thermonuclear /ˌθɜːməʊˈnjuːklɪə(r), US -ˈnuː-/ *adj* thermonucléaire.

thermopile /ˈθɜːməʊpaɪl/ *n* thermopile *f*.

thermoplastic /ˌθɜːməʊˈplæstɪk/ *n, adj* thermoplastique (*m*).

Thermopylae /θɜːˈmɒpɪliː/ *pr n* Thermopyles *fpl*.

Thermos® /ˈθɜːməs/ *n* thermos® *m* or *f inv*.

thermosetting /ˌθɜːməʊˈsetɪŋ/ *adj* thermodurcissable.

thermos flask *n* bouteille *f* thermos®.

thermosiphon /ˌθɜːməʊˈsaɪfən/ *n* thermosiphon *m*.

thermostat /ˈθɜːməstæt/ *n* thermostat *m*.

thermostatic /ˌθɜːməˈstætɪk/ *adj* thermostatique.

thesaurus /θɪˈsɔːrəs/ *n* (*pl* **-ri** ou **-ruses**) **1** (of synonyms etc) dictionnaire *m* analogique or des synonymes; **2** (of particular field) lexique *m*.

these /ðiːz/ *pl* ▶ **this**.

Theseus /ˈθiːsjuːs, ˈθiːsjəs/ *pr n* Thésée.

thesis /ˈθiːsɪs/ *n* (*pl* **theses**) **1** Univ (doctoral) thèse *f* (**on** sur); (master's) mémoire *m* (**on** sur); **2** (theory) thèse *f*.

thespian /ˈθespɪən/† ou hum **I** *n* homme/femme *m/f* de théâtre.

II Thespian *adj* dramatique, du théâtre.

Thessalonians /ˌθesəˈləʊnɪənz/ *n* (+ *v sg*) Bible Epître *f* aux Thessaloniciens.

they /ðeɪ/

■ **Note** *they* is translated by *ils* (masculine) or *elles* (feminine). For a group of people or things of mixed gender *ils* is always used. The emphatic form is *eux* (masculine) or *elles* (feminine). For examples and exceptions, see below.

pron **~ have already gone** (masculine or mixed) ils sont déjà partis; (feminine) elles sont déjà parties; **here ~ are!** les voici!; **there ~ are!** les voilà!; **THEY won't be there** eux, ils ne seront pas là, eux or elles ne seront pas là, elles; **she bought one but ~ didn't** elle en a acheté un mais eux pas.

they'd /ðeɪd/ = **they had, they would**.

they'll /ðeɪl/ = **they will**.

they're /ðeə(r)/ = **they are**.

they've /ðeɪv/ = **they have**.

thiamine /ˈθaɪəmɪn, -ˌmiːn/ *n* thiamine *f*.

thick /θɪk/ **I** *adj* **1** [*piece, layer, material, garment, liquid, paste, snow, hair, eyebrows, lips, features, make-up*] épais/épaisse; [*forest, vegetation, fog*] dense, épais/épaisse; [*beard*] touffu; [*accent*] fort (*before n*); [*voice*] (from sore throat, cold) voilé, enroué; (from alcohol) pâteux/-euse; **to be 6 cm ~** faire 6 cm d'épaisseur; **how ~ is the wall/this piece of steel?** quelle est l'épaisseur du mur/de ce morceau d'acier?; **a 6 cm-~ piece of wood** un morceau de bois de 6 cm d'épaisseur; **to make [sth] ~er** épaissir [*soup, sauce*]; **to be ~ with** être plein de [*smoke, noise*]; être chargé de [*emotion*]; **a river ~ with rubbish** une rivière pleine de détritus; **fields ~ with poppies** des champs couverts de coquelicots; **the air was ~ with insults** les insultes fusaient; **the table was ~ with dust** la table était couverte d'une épaisse couche de poussière; **the ground was ~ with ants** le sol grouillait de fourmis; **to have a ~ head** (from hangover) avoir la gueule de bois; (from cold, flu) avoir le cerveau embrumé; **a fog so ~ you could cut it with a knife** un brouillard à couper au couteau; **2**○ (stupid) bête; **I can't get it into his ~ head** ou **skull**○ **that** je n'arrive pas à lui enfoncer dans la tête or le crâne que; **3**○ (friendly) **they're very ~ (with each other)** ils sont très liés; **Tom is very ~ with Anne** Tom et Anne sont très liés; **4**○ (unreasonable) **it's a bit ~ expecting me to do that!** c'est un peu fort or raide○ d'espérer que je ferai ça!

II *adv* **don't spread the butter on too ~** ne mets pas trop de beurre; **the bread was sliced ~** le pain était coupé en tranches épaisses; **her hair fell ~ and straight to her shoulders** ses cheveux épais et raides

tombaient sur ses épaules; **the snow lay ~ on the ground** il y avait une épaisse couche de neige sur le sol.
IDIOMS **to lay it on ~**○ forcer la dose○; **offers of help are coming in ~ and fast** des propositions d'aide affluent de toutes parts; **his tears fell ~ and fast** de grosses larmes lui coulaient sur les joues; **through ~ and thin** contre vents et marées; **to be in the ~ of** être au plus fort or au beau milieu de [*battle, fighting*]; être au beau milieu de [*crowd*]; **when the riots broke out I found myself in the ~ of things** quand les émeutes ont éclaté je me suis retrouvé pris au milieu. ▶ **blood**, **brick**, **ground**, **plank**, **thief**.

thicken /ˈθɪkən/ **I** *vtr* (all contexts) épaissir.
II *vi* [*sauce, soup, fog, snow, cloud, waistline*] s'épaissir; [*accent*] devenir plus fort; [*voice*] s'enrouer; [*traffic*] devenir plus dense.
IDIOMS **the plot ~s!** l'affaire se corse!

thickening /ˈθɪkənɪŋ/ *n* gen, Culin épaississant *m*.

thicket /ˈθɪkɪt/ *n* fourré *m*.

thick: **~head**○ *n* idiot/-e *m/f*; **~-headed**○ *adj* bête.

thickie○, **thicky**○ /ˈθɪkɪ/ *n* idiot/-e *m/f*.

thickly /ˈθɪklɪ/ *adv* [*spread*] en une couche épaisse; [*cut*] en morceaux épais; [*say, speak*] d'une voix enrouée; **the snow was falling ~** la neige tombait dru; **the grass grew ~** l'herbe poussait dru; **the books were ~ covered in** ou **with dust** les livres étaient couverts d'une épaisse couche de poussière; **bread ~ spread with jam** du pain avec une épaisse couche de confiture; **a ~-wooded landscape** un paysage très boisé.

thickness /ˈθɪknɪs/ *n* **1** (of piece, material, liquid, snow, hair, features, make-up) épaisseur *f*; (of fog, vegetation) épaisseur *f*, densité *f*; **6 cm in ~** de 6 cm d'épaisseur; **the ~ of his accent makes him hard to understand** son accent est si fort qu'on a de la peine à le comprendre; **2** (layer) épaisseur *f*.

thicko○ /ˈθɪkəʊ/ *n* idiot/-e *m/f*.

thick: **~set** *adj* [*person*] trapu; [*hedge*] touffu; **~-skinned** *adj* blindé○, endurci; **~-witted**○, **~-skulled**○ *adj* bête.

thief /θi:f/ *n* (*pl* **thieves**) voleur/-euse *m/f*; **car/jewel ~** voleur de voitures/de bijoux; **stop ~!** au voleur!
IDIOMS **set a ~ to catch a ~** seul un voleur peut en attraper un autre; **to be as thick as thieves** s'entendre comme larrons en foire; **like a ~ in the night** comme un voleur; **a den of thieves**, **a thieves' kitchen** un repaire de brigands.

thieve /θi:v/ *vtr*, *vi* voler.

thievery /ˈθi:vərɪ/ *n* vol *m*.

thieves /θi:vz/ *pl* ▶ **thief**.

thieving /ˈθi:vɪŋ/ **I** *n* vol *m*.
II *adj* **~ children** enfants qui volent; **get your ~ hands out!** enlève tes mains de là, voleur!

thigh /θaɪ/ **I** *n* cuisse *f*.
II *modif* [*injury*] à la cuisse; [*muscle*] de la cuisse.

thigh: **~bone** *n* fémur *m*; **~boot** *n* cuissarde *f*.

thimble /ˈθɪmbl/ *n* dé *m* à coudre; ▶ **hunt the thimble**.

thimbleful /ˈθɪmblfʊl/ *n* (of liquor) doigt *m*.

thin /θɪn/ **I** *adj* **1** (in width) [*nose, lips, stick, wall*] mince; [*line, stripe, string, wire*] fin; [*strip*] étroit; **2** (in depth) [*slice, layer*] fin, mince; **the ice is ~** la couche de glace n'est pas très épaisse; **3** (in consistency) [*mud, mixture*] liquide; [*soup, liquid, sauce*] clair; [*oil*] fluide; **4** (lean) [*person, face, arm, leg*] maigre; **he looks ~ and haggard** il est hâve et maigre; **to get ~** maigrir; **5** (fine) [*card, paper*] fin; [*fabric, garment*] léger/-ère; [*mist, smoke*] léger/-ère; **the mist is getting ~ner** la brume se dissipe; **6** (in tone) (high-pitched) aigre; (weak) fluet/fluette; **7** Fin **~ trading** marché *m* calme; **8** (sparse) [*population, crowd, hair, beard*] clairsemé; **9** fig (unconvincing) [*excuse*] peu convaincant; [*evidence*] insuffisant; [*plot*] squelettique; **to wear ~** [*joke, excuse*] être usé; **my patience is wearing ~** je commence à perdre patience; **10** [*air*] (at altitude) raréfié.
II○ *adv* [*slice*] en tranches *fpl* fines; [*spread*] en couche mince.
III *vtr* (*p prés etc* **-nn-**) **1** (also **~ down**) (dilute) diluer [*paint*]; allonger [*sauce, soup*]; **2** (disperse) = **thin out**.
IV *vi* (*p prés etc* **-nn-**) (also **~ out**) [*fog, mist*] se dissiper; [*crowd*] se disperser; [*hair*] se raréfier.
V **thinning** *pres p adj* [*hair, crowd*] clairsemé.
IDIOMS **as ~ as a rake** ou **lath** maigre comme un clou; **to be ~ on the ground** être rare; **to get ~ on top** (bald) se dégarnir; **to have a ~ time of it** traverser une période difficile.
■ **thin down** US maigrir.
■ **thin out**: **~ [sth] out**, **~ out [sth]** éclaircir [*seedlings, hedge*]; réduire [*population*].

thine‡ /ðaɪn/ **I** *pron* = **yours**.
II *det* = **your**.

thing /θɪŋ/ **I** *n* **1** (object) chose *f*, truc○ *m*; **she likes beautiful ~s** elle aime les belles choses; **he was wearing an old yellow ~** il portait un vieux truc○ jaune; **it's a ~ you use for opening envelopes** c'est un truc○ pour ouvrir les enveloppes, ça sert à ouvrir les enveloppes; **any old ~ will do** n'importe quel vieux truc○ fera l'affaire; **what's that ~?** qu'est-ce que c'est que ce truc○?; **what's that ~ on the table?** qu'est-ce c'est que ce truc○ sur la table?; **what's this ~ for?** à quoi sert ce truc○?; **there isn't a ~ to eat in the house!** il n'y a rien à manger dans cette maison!; **I haven't got a ~ to wear!** je n'ai rien à me mettre!; **the one ~ he wants for his birthday is a bike** tout ce qu'il veut pour son anniversaire, c'est un vélo; **it was a big box ~** c'était une espèce de grosse boîte; **2** (action, task, event) chose *f*; **I've got ~s to do** j'ai des choses à faire; **she'll do great ~s in life** elle ira loin dans la vie; **I wouldn't dream of such a ~** une telle chose ne me viendrait jamais à l'esprit; **who would do such a ~?** qui ferait une telle chose?; **how could you do such a ~?** comment as-tu pu faire une chose pareille?; **an awful ~ happened to me** il m'est arrivé une chose épouvantable; **that's the worst ~ you could have said/done** c'était (vraiment) la chose à ne pas dire/faire; **the best ~ (to do) would be to go and see her** le mieux serait d'aller la voir; **that was a silly/dangerous ~ to do** c'était stupide/dangereux d'avoir fait cela; **that was a lovely/horrible ~ to do** c'était gentil/ horrible d'avoir fait cela; **it was a difficult ~ to do** cela n'a pas été facile à faire, cela a été difficile à faire; **there wasn't a ~ I could do** je ne pouvais rien y faire; **it's a good ~ you came** heureusement que tu es venu, c'est une bonne chose que tu sois venu; **the ~ to do is to listen carefully to him** ce qu'il faut faire c'est l'écouter attentivement; **I'm sorry, but I haven't done a ~ about it yet** je suis désolé, mais je ne m'en suis pas encore occupé; **the heat does funny ~s to people** la chaleur a de drôles d'effets sur les gens; **3** (matter, fact) chose *f*; **we talked about lots of ~s** nous avons discuté de beaucoup de choses; **we talked about politics and ~s (like that)** nous avons discuté de la politique et de choses comme ça; **the ~ to remember is**... ce dont il faut se souvenir c'est...; **I couldn't hear a ~ (that) he said** je n'ai rien entendu de ce qu'il a dit; **I said/did no such ~!** je n'ai rien dit/fait de tel!; **I couldn't think of a ~ to say** je n'ai rien trouvé à dire; **one ~ is obvious/certain** une chose est évidente/certaine; **the first ~ we must consider is**... la première chose à considérer, c'est...; **if there's one ~ I hate it's**... s'il y a une chose que je déteste c'est...; **I found the whole ~ a bore** j'ai trouvé tout cela très ennuyeux; **the whole ~ is crazy!** c'est idiot tout cela!; **the ~ is, (that)**... ce qu'il y a, c'est que...; **the only ~ is**,... la seule chose, c'est que...; **the funny/amazing/dreadful ~ is**... le plus drôle/étonnant/épouvantable c'est que...; **the good ~ (about it) is**... ce qu'il y a de bien, c'est que...; **the best/ worst ~ (about it) is**... le mieux/le pire c'est que...; **the ~ about him is that he's very honest** ce qu'il faut lui reconnaître, c'est qu'il est très honnête; **the ~ about him is that he can't be trusted** le problème avec lui c'est qu'on ne peut pas lui faire confiance; **the good/best/worst ~ about her is (that)** ce qu'il y a de bien/de mieux/de pire avec or chez elle c'est (que); **4** (person, animal) **she's a pretty little ~** c'est une jolie petite fille; **he's a funny little ~** c'est un drôle de petit gamin○; **how are you, old ~**○? comment ça va, mon vieux○?; **you lucky ~**○! veinard/-e○!; **you stupid ~**○! espèce d'idiot○!; **(the) stupid ~**○ (of object) sale truc○!; **there wasn't a living ~ to be seen** il n'y avait pas âme qui vive.
II things *npl* **1** (personal belongings, equipment) affaires *fpl*; **have you tidied your ~s?** as-tu rangé tes affaires?; **~s to be washed/ironed** des affaires à laver/repasser; **to wash up the breakfast ~s** faire la vaisselle du petit déjeuner; **2** (situation, circumstances, matters) les choses *fpl*; **to take ~s too seriously/too lightly** prendre les choses trop au sérieux/trop à la légère; **to see ~s as they really are** voir les choses en face; **to take ~s as they come** prendre les choses comme elles viennent; **~s don't look too good** les choses ne se présentent pas trop bien; **~s are getting better/worse** cela s'améliore/empire; **how are ~s with you?**, **how are ~s going?** comment ça va?; **why do you want to change ~s?** pourquoi est-ce que tu veux tout changer?; **to spoil ~s** tout gâcher; **to worry about ~s** se faire du souci; **as ~s are** ou **stand** dans l'état actuel des choses; **as ~s turned out** en fin de compte; **all ~s considered** tout compte fait; **in all ~s** en toute chose; **she's fascinated by ~s Chinese** elle est fascinée par tout ce qui est chinois; **~s eternal and ~s temporal** l'éternel et le temporel; **3** Jur biens *mpl* (immobiliers et mobiliers).
IDIOMS **it's not the done ~ (to do)** ça ne se fait pas (de faire); **it's the in ~**○ c'est à la mode; **she was wearing the latest ~ in hats** elle portait un chapeau dernier cri; **she's got the latest ~ in stereos** elle a une chaîne stéréo dernier cri; **it's all right if you like that sort of ~** c'est pas mal quand on aime ça; **that's just the ~** ou **the very ~!** c'est tout à fait or exactement ce qu'il me/te/lui etc faut; **it's become quite the ~ (to do)** c'est devenu à la mode (de faire); **it was a close** ou **near ~** c'était juste; **he's on to a good ~** il a trouvé le bon filon○; **he likes to do his own ~**○ il aime faire ce qui lui plaît; **for one ~...(and) for another ~**... premièrement...et deuxièmement...; **to have a ~ about**○ (like) craquer pour○ [*blondes, bearded men*]; adorer, avoir la folie de [*emeralds, old cars*]; (hate) ne pas aimer [*dogs*]; **he's got a ~ about flying**○ il n'aime pas l'avion; **to make a big ~ (out) of it**○ en faire toute une histoire or tout un plat○; **to know a ~ or two about sth**○ s'y connaître en qch; **we certainly showed them a ~ or two**○ nous leur avons certainement appris une ou deux choses!; **she can tell you a ~ or two about car engines**○! elle s'y connaît en mécanique; **I could tell you a ~ or two about him**○! je pourrais vous en raconter sur son compte!; **he gave her a snake of all ~s!** il n'a rien trouvé de mieux à lui donner qu'un serpent!; **and**

then, of all ~s, she... et alors, allez savoir pourquoi○, elle...; I must be seeing/hearing ~s! je dois avoir des visions/entendre des voix!; it's ou it was (just) one of those ~s ce sont des choses qui arrivent, c'est la vie; it's one (damned) ~ after another○! les embêtements○ n'en finissent plus!; one ~ led to another and... et, de fil en aiguille...; taking one ~ with another tout bien considéré; what with one ~ and another, I haven't had time to read it avec tout ce que j'ai eu à faire je n'ai pas eu le temps de le lire; ~s aren't what they used to be les choses ne sont plus ce qu'elles étaient; (to try) to be all ~s to all men (essayer de) faire plaisir à tout le monde.

thingumabob○ /'θɪŋəməbɒb/, **thingumajig**○ /'θɪŋəmədʒɪg/ *n* truc○ *m*, machin○ *m*; Mr ~ M. Machin○.

thingummy○ /'θɪŋəmɪ/, **thingy**○ /'θɪŋɪ/ *n* = thingumabob.

think /θɪŋk/ I *n* to have a ~ about sth GB réfléchir à qch; I'll have another ~ and let you know j'y réfléchirai encore et je vous le ferai savoir.

II *vtr* (*prét, pp* thought) 1 (hold view, believe) croire (that que); I ~ this is their house je crois que c'est leur maison; when do you ~ he will come? quand crois-tu qu'il viendra?; we'd better be going, don't you ~? il vaudrait mieux que nous partions, tu ne crois pas?; I ~ so je crois; I don't ~ so, I ~ not sout je ne crois pas; 'the wine is free, isn't it?'—'I don't ~ so!' 'le vin est gratuit, n'est-ce pas?'—'ça m'étonnerait!'; 'can I stay out till midnight?'—'no, I ~ not!' 'je peux sortir jusqu'à minuit?'—'non, sûrement pas!'; 'is he reliable?'—'I'd like to ~ so but...' 'peut-on lui faire confiance?'—'j'espère bien mais...'; to ~ it best to do/that penser qu'il serait préférable de faire/que (+ *subj*); to ~ it better to do/that... penser qu'il vaudrait mieux faire/que... (+ *subj*); I ~ it better to wait, what do you ~? je pense qu'il vaudrait mieux attendre, qu'est-ce que tu en penses?; I ~ it's going to rain j'ai l'impression qu'il va pleuvoir; what do you ~ it will cost? combien ça va coûter à ton avis?; him, a millionnaire? I don't ~! iron lui un millionnaire? sans blague!; 2 (imagine) imaginer, croire; just ~! yesterday we were slaving away○ in the office and today... imagine! hier encore on bossait○ au bureau et aujourd'hui...; just ~ what might happen! imagine ce qui pourrait arriver!; who'd have thought it! qui l'aurait cru?, qui l'eût cru? hum; I'd never have thought it! je n'aurais jamais cru ça!; I never thought you meant it! je ne t'ai jamais pris au sérieux!; I can't ~ how/why etc je n'ai aucune idée comment/pourquoi etc; I can't ~ who did it/what it's about je n'ai aucune idée qui a pu faire ça/de quoi il s'agit; I can't ~ where I've put my keys je ne sais pas du tout où j'ai mis mes clés; I really don't know what to ~ je ne sais vraiment pas quoi penser; who do you ~ you are? injur pour qui vous prenez-vous?; what on earth do you ~ you're doing? mais qu'est-ce que tu fais?; I thought as much! je m'en doutais!; six weeks' holiday! that's what you ~! six semaines de vacances! tu te fais des idées!; and to ~ that I believed him/that I once thought him charming! GB et dire que je le croyais/que je lui trouvais du charme!; 3 (have thought, idea) penser (that que; to do à faire); I didn't ~ to phone/check je n'ai pas pensé à appeler/vérifier; did you ~ to bring a corkscrew/to ring him to confirm? as-tu pensé à apporter un tire-bouchon/à l'appeler pour confirmer?; I ~ I'll take the car/go for a swim je pense que je vais prendre la voiture/me baigner; to ~ beautiful thoughts penser à de belles choses; to ~ deep thoughts avoir des pensées profondes; I was just ~ing: suppose we sold the car? je me posais la question: si nous vendions la voiture?; we're ~ing money/sex here○ c'est de fric○/sexe qu'il s'agit; let's ~ thin/Green○! pensons minceur/écolo○!; 'what a horrible man,' she thought 'quel horrible individu,' s'est-elle dit; 'oh do come in!' (~s) 'oh God not him again○!' 'oh entrez donc!' (à part) 'bon dieu encore lui!'; 4 (rate, assess) to ~ a lot/not much of penser/ne pas penser beaucoup de bien de [*person, work*]; what do you ~ of him/his work? que penses-tu de lui/son œuvre?; 5 (remember) penser (to do à faire); to ~ where/how se rappeler où/comment; I'm trying to ~ just where the house was/what her husband's called j'essaie de me rappeler où était la maison/le nom de son mari.

III *vi* (*prét, pp* thought) 1 (engage in thought) gen penser (about, of à); (before acting or speaking) réfléchir (about à); animals cannot ~ les animaux ne pensent pas; I'll have to ~ about it il faudra que j'y réfléchisse; to ~ constructively penser positivement; ~ before you act réfléchis avant d'agir; what are you ~ing about? à quoi penses-tu?; I was ~ing of you je pensais à toi; let me ~ a moment laissez-moi réfléchir un instant; his remarks made us all ~ ses remarques nous ont tous fait réfléchir; to ~ hard bien réfléchir; to ~ clearly ou straight avoir les idées claires; to ~ for oneself avoir des opinions personnelles; I'm sorry, I wasn't ~ing je m'excuse, je ne sais pas où j'avais la tête; we are ~ing in terms of economics nous voyons les choses du point de vue économique; let's ~: three people at £170 each, plus the plane fare voyons: trois personnes à 170 livres chacune, plus le billet d'avion; come to ~ of it... maintenant que j'y pense...; 2 (take into account) to ~ about ou of sb/sth penser à qn/qch; I can't ~ of everything! je ne peux pas penser à tout!; ~ of your family/about the future pense à ta famille/à l'avenir; she only ~s of herself elle ne pense qu'à elle; 3 (consider) to ~ of sb as considérer qn comme [*brother, friend, ally*]; he ~s of himself as an expert il se prend pour un spécialiste; 4 (have in mind) to ~ of doing envisager de faire; he's ~ing of resigning il envisage de démissionner; she's ~ing of computing as a career elle envisage de faire carrière dans l'informatique; to ~ about doing penser à faire; he's ~ing about a career in the Navy il pense faire carrière dans la marine; whatever were you ~ing of? qu'est-ce qui t'a pris?; 5 (imagine) to ~ of penser à; just ~ of the expense! pense seulement à ce que cela va coûter!; a million pounds, ~ of that! un million de livres, t'imagines○!; and to ~ of her dying just like that! quand on pense qu'elle est morte, là, comme ça!; 6 (tolerate idea) (*tjrs nég*) not to ~ of doing ne pas penser à faire; I couldn't ~ of letting you pay/of making an exception for her il n'est pas question que je te laisse payer/que je fasse une exception pour elle; 7 (remember) to ~ of se rappeler; I just can't ~ of his name je n'arrive pas à me rappeler son nom; if you ~ of anything else si autre chose vous vient à l'esprit.

IDIOMS he thought better of it il est revenu sur sa décision; to have another ~ coming○ GB se tromper lourdement; to ~ on one's feet réfléchir vite et bien; to ~ well of sb penser du bien de qn.

■ **think again** (reflect more) se repencher sur la question; (change mind) changer d'avis; if that's what you ~, you can ~ again si c'est ça que tu penses, tu te trompes.

■ **think ahead** bien réfléchir (à l'avance); you need to ~ ahead and plan what you're going to do il faut que tu réfléchisses bien à ce que tu vas faire; ~ing ahead to our retirement,... quand nous serons à la retraite,...; in tennis it is essential to ~ ahead au tennis il est essentiel d'anticiper.

■ **think back** se reporter en arrière (to à).

■ **think out**: ~ out [sth], ~ [sth] out bien réfléchir à; you must ~ out what you're going to do il faut que tu réfléchisses bien à ce que tu vas faire; well/badly thought out bien/mal conçu.

■ **think over**: ~ over [sth], ~ [sth] over réfléchir à [*proposal*]; I'd like time to ~ it over j'ai besoin de temps pour y réfléchir.

■ **think through**: ~ through [sth], ~ [sth] through bien réfléchir à [*proposal, action*]; faire le tour de [*problem, question*].

■ **think up**: ~ up [sth] inventer [*plan*]; what can we ~ up for her 21st birthday? qu'est-ce qu'on pourrait faire d'original pour ses vingt-et-un ans?

thinkable /'θɪŋkəbl/ *adj* pensable, imaginable; it is hardly/not ~ that il est à peine/n'est pas pensable que (+ *subj*).

thinker /'θɪŋkə(r)/ *n* penseur/-euse *m/f*; a great ~ un grand penseur.

thinking /'θɪŋkɪŋ/ I *n* 1 (thought, reflection) réflexion *f*; this is going to need some ~ cela demande réflexion; to do some (hard) ~ (beaucoup) réfléchir; 2 (way one thinks) pensée *f*; to influence sb's ~ GB influencer la pensée de qn; what's your ~ on immigration? GB quelle est votre opinion sur l'immigration?; current ~ is that GB la tendance actuelle de l'opinion est que; to my way of ~ à mon avis.

II *adj* [*person*] réfléchi; the ~ person's pin-up/sports car le sex symbol/la voiture de sport des intellectuels.

IDIOMS to put on one's ~ cap hum cogiter sout or hum.

think-tank /'θɪŋktæŋk/ *n* groupe *m* de réflexion.

thin-lipped /ˌθɪn'lɪpt/ *adj* [*person*] aux lèvres minces; [*smile*] pincé; she watched in ~ disapproval elle regardait, les lèvres pincées.

thinly /'θɪnlɪ/ *adv* 1 (sparingly) [*slice*] en tranches fines; [*spread*] en couche mince; [*butter*] légèrement; 'apply paint ~' 'appliquez la peinture en couches minces'; 2 (weakly) to smile ~ avoir un sourire pincé; 3 (sparsely) a ~ inhabited/wooded area une région à la population clairsemée/aux arbres clairsemés; 4 fig (scarcely) ~ disguised/veiled à peine déguisé/voilé.

thinner /'θɪnə(r)/ I *comp adj* ▶ thin.

II *n* (also thinners + *v sg*) diluant *m*.

thinness /'θɪnnɪs/ *n* (all contexts) minceur *f*.

thin-skinned /ˌθɪn'skɪnd/ *adj* susceptible.

third /θɜːd/ ▶ 1505, 1150 I *n* 1 (in order) troisième *mf*; 2 (of month) trois *m inv*; 3 (fraction) tiers *m*; 4 (also ~-class degree) GB Univ ≈ *licence avec mention passable*; 5 Mus tierce *f*; 6 (also ~ gear) Aut troisième *f*.

II *adj* troisième.

III *adv* 1 (in sequence) [*come, finish*] troisième, en troisième position; 2 (in list) troisièmement.

IDIOMS never mind— ~ time lucky! ne t'en fais pas, la troisième fois sera la bonne!

third-class /ˌθɜːd'klɑːs/ I *adj* 1 [*carriage, ticket*] de troisième classe; ~ mail Post ≈ plis *mpl* non urgents; 2 GB Univ ~ degree = third I 4.

II **third class** *adv* [*travel*] en troisième classe; to send sth ~ envoyer qch en pli non urgent.

third degree○ /ˌθɜːdə'griː/ *n* interrogatoire *m* musclé; to give sb the ~ lit [*interrogator, captor*] soumettre qn à un interrogatoire musclé; fig [*father, headteacher*] soumettre qn à une interrogation.

third: **~-degree burns** *npl* Med brûlures *fpl* au troisième degré; **Third Estate** *n* Tiers État *m*.

thirdhand /ˌθɜːd'hænd/ I *adj* 1 (not new) [*vehicle, garment*] d'occasion; 2 (indirect) [*report, evidence*] indirect.

II *adv* [*hear, learn*] de manière indirecte.

thirdly /'θɜːdlɪ/ *adv* troisièmement.

third party /ˌθɜːd'pɑːtɪ/ **I** *n* Insur, Jur tiers *m*.

II third-party *modif* Insur **~ insurance** assurance *f* au tiers; **~ liability** responsabilité *f* civile; **cover for ~, fire and theft** assurance au tiers, contre le feu et le vol.

third person /ˌθɜːd'pɜːsən/ *n* troisième personne *f*; **in the ~ singular/plural** à la troisième personne du singulier/pluriel.

third-rate /ˌθɜːd'reɪt/ *adj* péj [*actor, hotel, book*] de troisième ordre pej; [*work*] médiocre.

Third World /ˌθɜːd 'wɜːld/ **I** *n* tiers-monde *m*.

II *modif* [*country, debt, economy*] du tiers-monde.

thirst /θɜːst/ **I** *n* lit, fig soif *f* (**for** de); **it's given me a ~** ça m'a donné soif; **to quench one's ~** se désaltérer.

II *vi*† ou littér avoir soif (**after, for** de).

thirstily /'θɜːstɪlɪ/ *adv* [*drink*] à grands traits.

thirst quencher *n* boisson *f* désaltérante.

thirsty /'θɜːstɪ/ *adj* lit, fig assoiffé; **to be ~** lit, fig avoir soif (**for** de); **to make sb ~** donner soif à qn; **oh, I'm so ~!** oh, que j'ai soif!; **it's ~ work!** c'est un travail qui donne soif!

thirteen /ˌθɜː'tiːn/ ▶ 1505, 1150, 971 **I** *n* treize *m inv*.

II *adj* treize *inv*.

thirteenth /ˌθɜː'tiːnθ/ ▶ 1505, 1150 **I** *n* **1** (in order) treizième *mf*; **2** (of month) treize *m inv*; **3** (fraction) treizième *m*.

II *adj* treizième.

III *adv* [*come, finish*] treizième, en treizième position.

thirtieth /'θɜːtɪəθ/ ▶ 1505, 1150 **I** *n* **1** (in order) trentième *mf*; **2** (of month) trente *m inv*; **3** (fraction) trentième *m*.

II *adj* trentième.

thirty /'θɜːtɪ/ ▶ 1505, 971, 1096 **I** *n* trente *m inv*; **at seven-thirty** à sept heures trente.

II *adj* trente; **the Thirty Years' War** Hist la guerre de Trente Ans.

thirty: **~-second note** *n* US Mus triple croche *f*; **~ something** *n* yuppie *mf* vieillissant/-e.

this /ðɪs/ (*pl* **these**) **I** *det* **~ paper is too thin** ce papier est trop mince; **~ man is dangerous** cet homme est dangereux; **~ lamp doesn't work** cette lampe ne marche pas; **all these books belong to Josephine** tous ces livres appartiennent à Josephine; **do it ~ way not that way** fais-le comme ça et pas comme ça; **~ woman came up to me**○ une femme est venue vers moi○.

II *pron* **what's ~?** qu'est-ce que c'est?; **who's ~?** gen qui est-ce?, c'est qui?; (on telephone) qui est à l'appareil?; **whose is ~?** à qui appartient ceci?, ceci est à qui?; **~ is the dining room** voici la salle à manger; **where's ~?** (on photo) c'est où?; **after ~ we'll have lunch** après ceci nous allons déjeuner; **perhaps he'll be more careful after ~** peut-être qu'il fera plus attention maintenant; **before ~ he'd never been out of France** avant cela il n'était jamais sorti de France; **you should have told me before ~** tu aurais dû me le dire avant; **~ is my sister Pauline** (introduction) voici ma sœur Pauline; (on photo) c'est ma sœur, Pauline; **~ is the book I was talking about** c'est or voici le livre dont je parlais; **~ is not the right one** ce n'est pas le bon; **what did you mean by ~?** qu'est-ce que tu voulais dire par là?; **~ was not what she had intended** ce n'était pas ce qu'elle avait prévu; **who did ~?** qui a fait ça?; **we'll need more than ~** il nous en faudra plus (que ça); **it happened like ~** ça s'est passé comme ça; **what's all ~ about?** qu'est-ce que c'est que cette histoire?; **what's all ~ about Frank resigning?** qu'est-ce que c'est que cette histoire, il paraît que Frank démissionne; **at ~ he got up and left** en entendant cela il s'est levé et il est parti;

> **this**
>
> **As a determiner**
>
> In French, determiners agree in gender and number with the noun they precede; *this* (plural *these*) is translated by *ce* + masculine singular noun (*ce monsieur*) BUT by *cet* + masculine singular noun beginning with a vowel or mute 'h' (*cet arbre, cet homme*), by *cette* + feminine singular noun (*cette femme*) and by *ces* + plural noun (*ces livres, ces histoires*).
>
> Note, however, that the above translations are also used for the English *that* (plural *those*). So when it is necessary to insist on *this* as opposed to another or others of the same sort, the adverbial tag *-ci*, giving the idea of *this one here*, is added to the noun:
>
> *I prefer THIS version* = je préfère cette version-ci
>
> For particular usages see the entry ***this***.
>
> This dictionary contains usage notes on such topics as ***time units, days of the week*** and ***months of the year***. For the index to these notes ▶ 1919.
>
> **As a pronoun meaning *this one***
>
> In French, pronouns reflect the gender and number of the noun they are referring to. So *this* is translated by *celui-ci* for a masculine noun, *celle-ci* for a feminine noun; *those* is translated by *ceux-ci* for a masculine plural noun, *celles-ci* for a feminine plural noun:
>
> *of all the dresses this is the prettiest one* = de toutes les robes celle-ci est la plus jolie
>
> For other uses of *this* used as a pronoun (*who's this?, this is my brother, this is wrong* etc.) and for *this* used as an adverb (*it was this big* etc.), see the entry ***this***.

hold it like ~ tiens-le comme ça; **I never thought it would come to ~** je ne pensais pas qu'on en arriverait là; **~ is what happens when you press the red button** voilà ce qui se passe quand on appuie sur le bouton rouge; **~ is what happens when you disobey your parents!** voilà ce qui arrive quand on désobéit à ses parents!

III *adv* **it's ~ big** c'est grand comme ça; **when she was only ~ high** quand elle était haute comme ça; **having got ~ far it would be a pity to stop now** lit, fig maintenant qu'on est arrivé jusque-là ce serait dommage de s'arrêter; **I can't eat ~ much** je ne peux pas manger tout ça; **I didn't realize it was ~ serious/difficult** je ne m'étais pas rendu compte que c'était sérieux/difficile à ce point-là; ▶ **much**.

IDIOMS **we talked about ~, that and the other** on a parlé de choses et d'autres; **we sat around talking about ~ and that** nous avons parlé de tout et de rien; **'what have you been up to?'—'oh, ~ and that'** 'qu'est-ce que tu as fait?'—'pas grand-chose'; **to run ~ way and that** courir dans tous les sens.

thistle /'θɪsl/ *n* chardon *m*.

thistledown /'θɪsldaʊn/ *n* duvet *m* de chardon.

thistly /'θɪslɪ/ *adj* [*ground*] couvert de chardons.

thither† /'ðɪðə(r)/ *adv* par là.

tho' *abrév écrite* = **though**.

tholepin /'θəʊlpɪn/ *n* tolet *m*.

Thomas /'tɒməs/ *pr n* Thomas.

thong /θɒŋ/ **I** *n* **1** (on whip) lanière *f*; **2** (on shoe, garment) lacet *m*; **3** (underwear) string *m* ficelle.

II thongs *npl* US (sandals) tongs *fpl*.

thoracic /θɔː'ræsɪk/ *adj* thoracique.

thorax /'θɔːræks/ *n* (*pl* **-axes** ou **-aces**) thorax *m*.

thorium /'θɔːrɪəm/ *n* thorium *m*.

thorn /θɔːn/ *n* **1** (on flower, shrub) épine *f*; **crown of ~s** Relig couronne *f* d'épines; **2** (bush) buisson *m* épineux; (hawthorn) aubépine *f*.

IDIOMS **to be a ~ in sb's flesh** ou **side** être une source d'irritation pour qn.

thorn: **~ apple** *n* stramoine *f*; **~bush** *n* (hawthorn) aubépine *f*; (other) buisson *m* épineux; **~ hedge** *n* haie *f* d'épines.

thornless /'θɔːnlɪs/ *adj* sans épines.

thornproof /'θɔːnpruːf/ *adj* résistant aux épines.

thorny /'θɔːnɪ/ *adj* lit, fig épineux/-euse.

thorough /'θʌrə, US 'θʌrəʊ/ *adj* **1** (detailed) [*analysis, examination, investigation, knowledge, research*] approfondi; [*preparation, search, work*] minutieux/-ieuse; **to give sth a ~ cleaning** nettoyer qch à fond; **he did a ~ job on the repair work** il a fait toutes les réparations nécessaires; **to have a ~ grasp of sth** maîtriser parfaitement qch; **2** (meticulous) [*person*] minutieux/-ieuse; **3** (utter) **to make a ~ nuisance of oneself** se rendre totalement insupportable.

thoroughbred /'θʌrəbred/ **I** *n* pur-sang *m*.

II *adj* de pure race.

thoroughfare /'θʌrəfeə(r)/ *n* rue *f*; **main ~** voie *f* principale; **public ~** voie *f* publique; **'no ~'** 'passage interdit'.

thoroughgoing /'θʌrəgəʊɪŋ/ *adj* [*analysis, conviction*] profond.

thoroughly /'θʌrəlɪ, US 'θʌrəʊlɪ/ *adv* **1** (meticulously) [*clean, cook, discuss, examine, read*] à fond; [*check, prepare, search, test*] minutieusement; **2** (completely) [*convincing, dangerous, clean, reliable*] tout à fait; [*depressing, confusing, unpleasant*] profondément; [*beaten*] complètement; [*deserved*] tout à fait; **to ~ enjoy sth/doing** être tout à fait ravi de qch/de faire; **3** (without reservation) [*agree, approve, understand*] parfaitement; [*recommend*] chaleureusement; **to be ~ in favour of** être tout à fait favorable à.

thoroughness /'θʌrənɪs, US 'θʌrəʊnɪs/ *n* (all contexts) minutie *f*.

those /ðəʊs/ *pl* ▶ **that**.

thou **I**○ /θaʊ/ *n* US *abrév* = **thousand**.

II /ðaʊ/ *pron* ‡ou dial tu.

though /ðəʊ/ **I** *conj* **1** (emphasizing contrast: although) bien que (+ *subj*); **we enjoyed the trip (even) ~ it was very hot** nous avons apprécié le voyage bien qu'il ait fait très chaud or malgré la chaleur; **~ she's clever** ou **clever ~ she is, she's not what we're looking for** bien qu'elle soit intelligente or aussi intelligente soit-elle, elle n'est pas ce que nous cherchons; **strange ~ it may seem** si bizarre que ça puisse paraître; **talented ~ he is, I don't like him** il a beau être doué, je ne l'aime pas; **2** (modifying information: but) bien que (+ *subj*), mais; **I think she knows ~ I can't be sure** je pense qu'elle le sait, mais je n'en suis pas sûr; **you can still cancel ~ you'll be charged £10** vous pouvez toujours annuler mais vous devrez payer 10 livres; **the house was small ~ well-designed** la maison était petite mais elle était bien conçue or quoique bien conçue; **a foolish ~ courageous act** un acte stupide quoique courageux; **that was delicious ~ I say so myself!** sans me vanter, c'était délicieux!; ▶ **even**[1].

II *adv* quand même, toutefois; **fortunately, ~, they survived** heureusement ils s'en sont sortis; **in all, ~, we had a good time** tout compte fait, nous nous sommes quand même amusés; **she's probably not home, I'll keep trying ~** elle n'est sûrement pas chez elle mais j'essaie quand même de la joindre; **'travelling abroad's expensive'—'it's worth it, ~'** 'le voyage à l'étranger revient cher'—'ça vaut quand même la dépense', 'n'empêche que ça vaut la dépense○'.

thought /θɔːt/ **I** *prét, pp* ▶ **think** II, III.

II *n* **1** (idea) idée *f*, pensée *f*; **the ~ of**

doing l'idée de faire; **at the ~ of doing** à l'idée de faire; **the mere ~ of doing** la seule idée de faire; **the ~ has just occurred to me** cette pensée vient juste de me venir à l'esprit; **the ~ that** l'idée que; **what a ~!** quelle idée!; **that's a ~!** ça c'est une idée!; **it was just a ~** ce n'était qu'une idée comme ça; **what a kind ~!** comme c'est gentil!; **2** ¢ (reflexion) pensée *f*; **deep in ~** plongé dans ses pensées; **after much ~** après mûre réflexion; **3** (consideration) considération *f*; **with little ~** sans beaucoup de considération pour; **without ~ of the consequences** sans considérer les conséquences; **with no ~ for her own life** sans considération pour sa propre vie; **to give ~ to sth** considérer qch; **little ~ has been given to how/why** on n'a pas assez considéré comment/pourquoi; **more ~ should have been given to it** il aurait fallu l'examiner de plus près; **we never gave it much ~** nous n'y avons pas beaucoup réfléchi; **don't give it another ~** n'y pense plus; **to put a lot of ~ into a gift** choisir un cadeau avec beaucoup de soin; **4** (intention) **to have no ~ of doing** n'avoir aucune intention de faire; **I've given up all ~s of moving** j'ai abandonné toute idée de déménagement; **it's the ~ that counts** c'est l'intention qui compte; **5** Philos (thinking) pensée *f*; **freedom of ~** liberté de pensée.

III thoughts *npl* **1** (mind) pensées *fpl* (**about** au sujet de); **to read sb's ~s** lire (dans) les pensées de qn; **to collect** ou **gather one's ~s** rassembler ses esprits; **alone with one's ~s** seul avec ses pensées; **our ~s turn to the future** nos pensées se tournent vers l'avenir; **my ~s were elsewhere/still on the film** je pensais à autre chose/encore au film; **2** (opinions) opinion *f* (**about, on** sur); **I'd like to hear your ~s** j'aimerais bien connaître votre opinion; **to have some ~s on how sth could be improved** avoir des idées sur la façon d'améliorer qch.

thoughtful /ˈθɔːtfl/ *adj* **1** (reflective) [*expression, mood, smile*] pensif/-ive; [*silence*] profond (*before n*); **to look ~** avoir l'air pensif; **2** (considerate) [*person, gesture*] prévenant; [*letter, gift*] gentil/-ille; **it was ~ of her to do** c'était gentil de sa part de faire; **3** (well thought-out) [*analysis, study*] riche en réflexion.

thoughtfully /ˈθɔːtfəlɪ/ *adv* **1** (considerately) [*behave, treat*] avec prévenance; [*chosen, worded*] avec attention; **tea was ~ provided** on a eu la prévenance de servir le thé; **2** (pensively) [*stare, smile*] d'un air pensif; **3** (reflectively) [*write, describe*] de façon réfléchie.

thoughtfulness /ˈθɔːtflnɪs/ *n* **1** (kindness) prévenance *f* (**towards** à l'égard de); **2** (of expression, character) sérieux *m*.

thoughtless /ˈθɔːtlɪs/ *adj* [*person, remark, act*] irréfléchi; **it was ~ of him to do** c'était irréfléchi de sa part de faire; **to be ~ towards** manquer de considération pour; **how can you be so ~?** comment peux-tu avoir si peu d'égards?

thoughtlessly /ˈθɔːtlɪslɪ/ *adv* (insensitively) sans considération; (unthinkingly) sans réfléchir.

thoughtlessness /ˈθɔːtlɪsnɪs/ *n* manque *m* de considération.

thought-out /ˌθɔːtˈaʊt/ *adj* **well/badly ~** bien/mal conçu.

thought process *n* mécanismes *mpl* de la pensée.

thought-provoking /ˌθɔːtprəˈvəʊkɪŋ/ *adj* [*essay, film*] qui fait réfléchir; **it was very ~** cela m'a fait beaucoup réfléchir.

thought transference *n* transmission *f* de pensée.

thousand /ˈθaʊznd/ ▶ **1505** **I** *n* (figure) mille *m inv*; **a ~ and two** mille deux; **three ~** trois mille; **about a ~** un millier; **by the ~** (exactly) par mille; (roughly) par milliers.

II thousands *npl* (large numbers, amounts) milliers *mpl* (**of** de); **in their ~s** par milliers; **to earn/lose ~s** gagner/perdre une fortune; **a cast of ~s** des milliers de figurants.

III *adj* mille *inv*; **four ~ pounds** quatre mille livres; **about a ~ people** un millier de personnes; **a ~ times** mille fois; **a ~ times better** mille fois mieux.

IDIOMS **to die a ~ deaths** mourir de honte.

thousandfold /ˈθaʊzndfəʊld/ *adv* **a ~** un millier de fois.

Thousand Island dressing *n* sauce *f* salade (*à base de mayonnaise avec des tomates, poivrons et piments*).

thousandth /ˈθaʊzndθ/ ▶ **1505** **I** *n* **1** (fraction) millième *m*; **2** (in order) millième *mf*.

II *adj* millième.

Thrace /θreɪs/ *pr n* Thrace *f*.

Thracian /ˈθreɪʃn/ ▶ **1402** **I** *n* (person) Thrace *mf*; (language) thrace *m*.

II *adj* thrace.

thraldom GB, **thralldom** US /ˈθrɔːldəm/ *n* littér servitude *f*.

thrall /θrɔːl/ *n* littér **to hold sb in ~** fasciner qn; **to be in ~ to sth** être sous l'emprise de qch.

thrash /θræʃ/ **I** *n* **1**○ GB (party) grande fête *f*; **2** Mus thrash *m*.

II *vtr* **1** (whip) rouer [qn] de coups; **2**○ Mil, Sport écraser, piler○ [*enemy, opposition*].

IDIOMS **to ~ the living daylights out of sb** donner une bonne correction à qn.

■ **thrash about, thrash around**: ¶ **~ about, ~ around** se débattre; ¶ **~ [sth] around** agiter; **to ~ one's arms/legs around** agiter les bras/jambes.

■ **thrash out**: **~ out [sth]** venir à bout de [*difficulties, problem*]; réussir à élaborer [*plan, compromise*].

thrashing /ˈθræʃɪŋ/ *n* lit, fig raclée *f*; **to give sb a good ~** donner une bonne raclée à qn.

thread /θred/ **I** *n* **1** Sewing fil *m*; **gold/silver ~** fil *m* d'or/d'argent; **cotton/silk ~** fil *m* de coton/soie; **to be hanging by a ~** lit, fig ne tenir qu'à un fil; **2** fig (of argument, story) fil *m*; **to follow/lose the ~** suivre/perdre le fil; **central ~** fil *m* conducteur; **common ~** point *m* commun; **to pull all the ~s together** faire la synthèse; **to pick up the ~ of** reprendre le fil de [*conversation, story*]; **to pick up the ~s of** reprendre le cours de [*career, life*]; **to pick up the ~ of a relationship with sb** renouer avec qn; **3** Tech (of screw) filetage *m*.

II threads○ *npl* US (clothes) fringues○ *fpl*.

III *vtr* **1** lit enfiler [*bead, needle*]; introduire [*film, tape*] (**into** dans); **2** fig (move) **to ~ one's way through** se faufiler entre [*tables, obstacles*].

IV *vi* [*beads, needle*] s'enfiler; [*film, tape*] passer.

■ **thread up**: **~ up [sth]** enfiler le fil de [*sewing machine*].

thread: **~bare** *adj* lit, fig usé jusqu'à la corde; **~like** *adj* filiforme; **~worm** *n* oxyure *m*.

threat /θret/ *n* **1** (verbal abuse) menace *f*; **to make ~s against sb** lancer des menaces contre qn; **to give in to ~s** céder à la menace; **2** (danger) menace *f* (**to** pour); **to pose a ~ to** être une menace pour; **to be under ~** être menacé (**from** par); **under ~ of** sous la menace de [*death, injury, punishment*]; **3** (risk, possibility) menace *f*, risque *m* (**of** de); **because of the ~ of more rain** à cause du risque qu'il pleuve encore plus.

threaten /ˈθretn/ **I** *vtr* **1** (warn) menacer (**to do** de faire); **to be ~ed with death/prison** être menacé d'être tué/emprisonné; **2** (endanger) menacer [*planet, wildlife, peace, stability*]; **to be ~ed with starvation/extinction** risquer de mourir de faim/de disparaître.

II *vi* [*danger, bad weather*] menacer; **to ~ to do** risquer de faire.

III threatened *pp adj* menacé; **to feel ~ed** se sentir menacé.

threatening /ˈθretnɪŋ/ *adj* [*gesture, expression, atmosphere*] menaçant; [*letter, phone call*] de menaces.

threateningly /ˈθretnɪŋlɪ/ *adv* [*gesture, look, speak, approach*] de façon menaçante.

three /θriː/ ▶ **1505**, **971**, **1096** **I** *n* trois *m inv*; **to play the best of ~** Sport jouer la revanche et la belle.

II *adj* trois *inv*.

three: **~-card monte** *n* bonneteau *m*; **~ card trick** *n* tour *m* de passe-passe; **~-colour** GB, **~-color** US *adj* trichrome.

three-cornered /ˌθriːˈkɔːnəd/ *adj* [*object*] triangulaire; [*discussion*] tripartite; **~ hat** tricorne *m*.

three-D /ˌθriːˈdiː/ **I** *n* **in ~** en trois dimensions.

II *adj* en trois dimensions.

three: **~-day event** *n* concours *m* complet; **~-day eventing** *n* concours *m* complet; **~-decker** *n* (boat) bateau *m* à trois ponts, trois-ponts *m*; **~-dimensional** *adj* en trois dimensions.

threefold /ˈθriːfəʊld/ **I** *adj* triple; **a ~ increase** un triplement.

II *adv* triplement; **to increase ~** tripler.

three-four time *n* Mus mesure *f* à trois quatre; **in ~** à trois-quatre.

three: **~-legged** *adj* [*object*] à trois pieds; [*animal*] à trois pattes; [*race*] à trois jambes; **~pence** *n* GB trois pence.

threepenny /ˈθrəpənɪ, ˈθrʌpənɪ/ *adj* GB à trois pence; **the Threepenny Opera** l'Opéra de quat' sous.

three: **~penny bit**† *n* GB (ancienne) pièce *f* de trois pence; **~-phase** *adj* triphasé; **~-piece suit** *n* (costume *m*) trois-pièces *m inv*; **~-piece suite** *n* salon *m* trois pièces; **~-ply, ~-ply wool** *n* laine *f* triple; **~-point landing** *n* atterrissage *m* trois points; **~-point turn** *n* demi-tour *m* en trois manœuvres.

three-quarter /ˌθriːˈkwɔːtə(r)/ **I** *n* Sport trois-quarts *m*.

II *adj* [*portrait*] de trois-quarts; [*sleeve*] trois-quarts.

three-quarter-length /ˌθriːˈkwɔːtəleŋθ/ *adj* **~ coat** trois-quarts *m*.

three-quarter line *n* Sport ligne *f* de trois-quarts.

three-quarters /ˌθriːˈkwɔːtəz/ ▶ **1807** **I** *n* trois-quarts *mpl*; **~ of an hour** trois-quarts d'heure; **~ of all those who...** (les) trois-quarts de ceux qui...

II *adv* [*empty, full, done*] aux trois-quarts.

three: **~-ring circus** *n* US lit cirque *m* à trois pistes; fig péj cirque *m*; **~ R's** *n* Sch les trois disciplines *fpl* fondamentales (*lecture, écriture, calcul*); **~score**‡ *n, adj* soixante (*m*); **~-sided** *adj* [*object*] à trois côtés; [*discussion*] tripartite; **~some** *n* gen groupe *m* de trois; (for sex) partouze○ *f* à trois; **~-star** *adj* Tourism à trois étoiles; **~-way** *adj* [*junction*] à trois voies; [*split*] en trois; [*discussion, battle*] tripartite; **~-wheeler** *n* (car) voiture *f* à trois roues; (bicycle) tricycle *m*; (motorcycle) moto *f* à trois roues; **~-year-old** *n* enfant *mf* de trois ans.

threnody /ˈθrenədɪ/ *n* mélopée *f*.

thresh /θreʃ/ **I** *vtr* battre.

II *vi* battre le blé.

thresher /ˈθreʃə(r)/ *n* **1** (machine) batteuse *f*; **2** (person) batteur/-euse *m/f*.

threshing /ˈθreʃɪŋ/ *n* battage *m*.

threshing: **~ floor** *n* aire *f* de battage; **~ machine** *n* batteuse *f*.

threshold /ˈθreʃəʊld, -həʊld/ *n* **1** lit seuil *m*; **to cross the ~** franchir le seuil; **2** fig seuil *m*; **pain ~** seuil de tolérance à la douleur; **on the ~ of** au seuil de [*discovery, career, new era*]; **3** Fin, Tax seuil *m*; **tax ~** seuil d'imposition, minimum *m* imposable; **wage ~** GB *seuil à partir duquel les salaires indexés sur le coût de la vie sont augmentés.*

threshold price *n* Agric, EC prix *m* de seuil.

threw /θruː/ *prét* ▶ **throw** II, III, IV.

thrice‡ /θraɪs/ *adv* trois fois.

thrift /θrɪft/ **I** *n* **1** (frugality) économie *f*; **2** Bot armeria *f*.
II thrifts *npl* US Fin (also **~ institutions**) établissements *mpl* de crédit.

thriftiness /ˈθrɪftɪnɪs/ *n* esprit *m* économe.

thriftless /ˈθrɪftlɪs/ *adj* dépensier/-ière.

thrift shop *n* boutique *f* d'articles d'occasion (*dont les bénéfices sont versés à des œuvres*).

thrifty /ˈθrɪftɪ/ *adj* [*person*] économe (**in** dans); [*life, meal*] économique.

thrill /θrɪl/ **I** *n* **1** (sensation) frisson *m*, frémissement *m*; **a ~ of pleasure** un frisson de plaisir; **to feel** ou **experience a ~ (of joy)** frissonner (de joie); **2** (pleasure) plaisir *m* (**of doing** de faire); **it was a ~ to meet her** cela a été un grand plaisir de la rencontrer; **to get a ~** ou **one's ~s** se donner des sensations fortes (**from** ou **out of doing** en faisant); **his victory gave me a ~** sa victoire m'a vraiment fait plaisir; **what a ~!** quelle émotion!
II *vtr* (with joy) transporter [qn] de joie; (with admiration) transporter [qn] d'admiration [*person, audience*]; passionner [*readers, viewers*].
III *vi* frissonner (**at, to** à).
IV thrilled *pp adj* ravi, enchanté (**with** de; **to do** de faire; **that** que (+ *subj*); **~ed to do** ravi de faire; **~ed that** ravi que (+ *subj*); **~ed with** enchanté de.
IDIOMS **the ~s and spills of sth** les sensations fortes que procure qch; **to be ~ed to bits**○ être absolument ravi, être aux anges; **~ed to bits**○ **with sth** absolument enchanté de qch.

thriller /ˈθrɪlə(r)/ *n* **1** Cin, Literat, TV thriller *m*; **comedy/political ~** thriller *m* comique/politique; **spy ~** (book) roman *m* d'espionnage; (film) film *m* d'espionnage; **crime ~** (book) roman *m* noir; (film) film *m* noir; **2** (exciting event) **the match was a ~** le match était palpitant.

thrilling /ˈθrɪlɪŋ/ *adj* [*adventure, match, story, victory*] palpitant; [*concert, moment, sensation*] exaltant.

thrive /θraɪv/ *vi* (*prét* **throve** ou **thrived**; *pp* **thriven** ou **thrived**) **1** lit [*person, animal, virus*] se développer; [*plant*] pousser; **failure to ~** atrophie *f*; **2** fig [*market, business, community*] prospérer; **to ~ on sth/on doing** [*person*] se complaire dans qch/à faire; **to ~ on** [*idea, thing*] se nourrir de.

thriving /ˈθraɪvɪŋ/ *adj* [*business, industry, town, community*] florissant; [*person*] prospère; [*plant, animal*] en pleine santé.

throat /θrəʊt/ **I** *n* **1** Anat gorge *f*; **sore ~** mal *m* de gorge; **to clear one's ~** s'éclaircir la gorge; **to cut/slit sb's ~** couper/entailler la gorge de qn; **to have a lump in one's ~** avoir la gorge nouée; **to stick in sb's ~** lit se coincer dans la gorge de qn; **it sticks in my ~ that**... le fait que... me reste en travers de la gorge; **2** Tech étranglement *m*.
II *modif* [*infection, injury, disease*] de la gorge; [*medicine*] pour la gorge.
IDIOMS **my belly** ou **stomach thinks my ~'s cut**○ j'ai l'estomac dans les talons; **to be at each other's** ou **one another's ~s**○ se disputer; **to cut one's own ~** travailler à sa propre ruine; **to jump down sb's ~**○ s'en prendre à qn; **to ram**○ ou **thrust sth down sb's ~** casser les oreilles○ de qn avec qch.

throaty /ˈθrəʊtɪ/ *adj* **1** (husky) guttural; **2**○ (with sore throat) enroué.

throb /θrɒb/ **I** *n* **1** (of engine, machine) vibration *f*; (of music) rythme *m*; **2** (of heart, pulse) battement *m*; (of pain) élancement *m*.
II *vi* (*p prés etc* **-bb-**) **1** [*heart, pulse*] battre; **my head is ~bing** j'ai des élancements dans la tête; **2** [*motor*] vibrer; [*music, drum, building*] résonner; **~bing with life** fourmillant d'activité.

throbbing /ˈθrɒbɪŋ/ **I** *n* **1** (of heart, pulse, blood) battement *m*; (of pain) élancement *m*; **2** (of motor) vibration *f*; (of music, drum) rythme *m*.
II *adj* **1** [*pain, ache, sound, music*] lancinant; [*head, finger*] souffrant de douleurs lancinantes; **2** [*engine, motor*] qui vibre.

throes /θrəʊz/ *npl* **1 death ~** agonie *f* also fig; **to be in one's/its death ~** être à l'agonie; **2 to be in the ~ of sth/of doing** être au beau milieu de qch/de faire.

thrombocyte /ˈθrɒmbəsaɪt/ *n* thrombocyte *m*.

thrombosis /θrɒmˈbəʊsɪs/ ▶ **1354** *n* thrombose *f*.

throne /θrəʊn/ *n* trône *m*; **on the ~** sur le trône.
IDIOMS **the power behind the ~** l'éminence grise.

throne room *n* salle *f* du trône.

throng /θrɒŋ, US θrɔːŋ/ **I** *n* foule *f* (**of** de).
II *vtr* envahir [*street, square, town*].
III *vi* **to ~ to** ou **towards** converger vers; **to ~ around** se masser autour de; **to ~ to do** se rassembler pour faire.
IV thronged *pp adj* bondé; **~ed with** envahi de.
V thronging *pres p adj* [*people, crowd*] qui se rassemble; [*street, town*] bondé; **~ing with** envahi de.

throttle /ˈθrɒtl/ **I** *n* **1** (also **~ valve**) pointeau *m*; **2** (accelerator) accélérateur *m*; **at full ~** à toute vitesse.
II *vtr* lit étrangler (**with** avec); fig asphyxier [*growth, project*].

through /θruː/ **I** *prep* **1** (from one side to the other) à travers; **to see ~ the curtain/mist** voir à travers le rideau/la brume; **to feel the stones ~ one's shoes** sentir les cailloux à travers ses chaussures; **to cut ~ the fields** couper à travers champs; **the nail went right ~ the wall** le clou a traversé le mur; **to drive ~ the forest/desert** traverser la forêt/le désert (en voiture); **to stick one's finger ~ the slit** passer son doigt dans la fente; **to poke sth ~ a hole** enfoncer qch dans un trou; **to drill ~ a cable** toucher un fil électrique avec une perceuse; **he was shot ~ the head** on lui a tiré une balle dans la tête; **it has a crack running ~ it** il est fêlé; **2** (via, by way of) **to go ~ a tunnel** passer par un tunnel; **to go ~ London/the town centre** passer par Londres/le centre-ville; **to travel ~ Germany to Poland** aller en Pologne en passant par l'Allemagne; **the path goes ~ the woods** le chemin passe par le bois; **to come in ~ the hole/door** entrer par le trou/la porte; **go straight ~ that door** passez cette porte; **to jump ~ the window** sauter par la fenêtre; **to look ~** regarder avec [*binoculars, telescope*]; regarder par [*hole, window, keyhole*]; **to hear sth ~ the wall** entendre qch à travers le mur; **you have to go ~ her secretary** il faut passer par sa secrétaire; **3** (past) **to go ~** brûler [*red light*]; **to get** ou **go ~** passer à travers [*barricade*]; passer [*customs*]; **to push one's way ~** se frayer un chemin à travers [*crowd, undergrowth*]; **the water poured ~ the roof** l'eau passait à travers le toit; **4** (among) **to fly ~ the clouds** voler au milieu des nuages; **to leap ~ the trees** sauter de branche en branche; **to fly ~ the air** [*acrobat*] voler dans les airs; [*arrow, bullet*] fendre l'air; ▶ **go, search, sort**; **5** (expressing source or agency) **I heard ~ a friend** j'ai appris par un ami; **I met my husband ~ her** c'est par elle que j'ai rencontré mon mari; **it was ~ her that I got this job** c'est par son intermédiaire que j'ai eu ce travail; **to speak ~ an interpreter** parler par l'intermédiaire d'un interprète; **to send sth ~ the post** envoyer qch par la poste; **to book sth ~ a travel agent** réserver qch dans une agence de voyage; **to order sth ~ a mail order firm** commander qch à une société de vente par correspondance; **I only know her ~ her writings** je ne la connais qu'à travers ses écrits; **6** (because of) **~ carelessness/inexperience** par négligence/manque d'expérience; **~ illness** pour cause de maladie; **~ no fault of mine, we were late** ce n'était pas à cause de moi que nous étions en retard; **7** (until the end of) **to work ~ the night** travailler toute la nuit; **all** ou **right ~ the day** toute la journée; **he talked right ~ the film** il a parlé pendant tout le film; **to stay ~ until Sunday** rester jusqu'à dimanche; **to work ~ the lunchhour** travailler pendant l'heure du déjeuner; ▶ **live, see, sleep**; **8** (up to and including) jusqu'à; **from Friday ~ to Sunday** de vendredi jusqu'à dimanche; **1939 ~ 1945** US de 1939 jusqu'à 1945; **open April ~ September** US ouvert d'avril à fin septembre.
II *adj* **1**○ (finished) fini; **I'm ~** j'ai fini; **I'm not ~ with you yet!** je n'en ai pas encore fini avec toi!; **are you ~ with the paper?** as-tu fini de lire le journal?; **I'm ~ with men!** les hommes—c'est fini!; **we're ~** (of a couple) c'est fini entre nous; **Claire and I are ~** c'est fini entre Claire et moi; **2** (direct) [*train, ticket*] direct; [*freight*] à forfait; [*bill of lading*] direct; **a ~ route to the station** un chemin direct pour aller à la gare; **'no ~ road'** 'voie sans issue'; **'~ traffic'** (on roadsign) 'autres directions'; **~ traffic uses the bypass** pour contourner la ville on prend la rocade; **3** (successful) **to be ~ to the next round** être sélectionné pour le deuxième tour; ▶ **get, go**; **4** GB (worn) **your trousers are ~ at the knee** ton pantalon est troué au genou.
III *adv* **1** (from one side to the other) **the water went right ~** l'eau est passée à travers; **to let sb ~** laisser passer qn; **can you fit** ou **squeeze** ou **get ~?** est-ce que tu peux passer?; ▶ **pass**; **2** (completely) **wet** ou **soaked ~** [*coat, cloth*] trempé; [*person*] trempé jusqu'aux os; **mouldy right ~** complètement pourri; **cooked right ~** bien cuit; **3** (from beginning to end) **to read/play sth right ~** lire/jouer qch jusqu'au bout; **I'm halfway ~ the article** j'ai lu la moitié de l'article; ▶ **carry, get, go, run, see**; **4** Telecom **you're ~** je vous passe votre correspondant; **you're ~ to Ms Wilkins** je vous passe Madame Wilkins; ▶ **get, go, put**.
IV through and through *adv phr* **to know sth ~ and ~** connaître qch comme sa poche [*area, city*]; **I know him ~ and ~** je le connais comme si je l'avais fait○; **rotten ~ and ~** pourri jusqu'à l'os; **English ~ and ~** anglais jusqu'au bout des ongles; **selfish ~ and ~** d'un égoïsme foncier.
IDIOMS **to have been ~ a lot** en avoir vu des vertes et des pas mûres○; **you really put her ~ it** tu lui en as vraiment fait voir de toutes les couleurs○; ▶ **hell**.

throughout /θruːˈaʊt/ **I** *prep* **1** (all over) **~ Europe/France** dans toute l'Europe/la France; **~ the country** dans tout le pays; **~ the world** dans le monde entier; **scattered ~ the house** éparpillés partout dans la maison; **2** (for the duration of) tout au long de; **~ the interview** tout au long de l'entretien; **~ her career** tout au long de sa carrière; **~ his life** toute sa vie; **~ the year** tout au long de l'année; **~ the winter/April** pendant tout l'hiver/le mois d'avril; **~ history** à travers l'histoire.
II *adv* **printed in italics ~** entièrement imprimé en italique(s); **lined/repainted ~** entièrement doublé/repeint; **the offices are**

carpeted ~ il y a de la moquette dans tous les bureaux.

throughput /ˈθru:pʊt/ *n* **1** Comput débit *m*, capacité *f* de traitement; **2** Ind (of machinery) débit *m*; **the plant has a ~ of 10 tonnes per day** l'usine peut traiter 10 tonnes par jour.

throughway /ˈθru:weɪ/ *n* US Transp voie *f* rapide or express.

throve /θrəʊv/ *prét* ▶ **thrive**.

throw /θrəʊ/ **I** *n* **1** Sport, Games (in football) touche *f*, remise *f* en jeu; (of javelin, discus etc) lancer *m*; (in judo, wrestling etc) jeté *m*; (of dice) coup *m*; **a ~ of 70 m** un lancer de 70 m; **he won with a ~ of six** il a gagné avec un six; **whose ~ is it?** (in ball game) c'est à qui de lancer?; (with dice) c'est à qui le tour?; **2**○ (each) **CDs £5 a ~!** les compacts à cinq livres pièce!; **3** US (blanket) jeté *m* (de lit or de canapé); **4** US (rug) carpette *f*.

II *vtr* (*prét* **threw**; *pp* **thrown**) **1** gen, Games, Sport (project) (with careful aim) lancer (**at** sur); (downwards) jeter; (with violence) [*explosion, impact*] projeter; **she threw the ball in(to) the air/across the pitch/over the wall** elle a lancé la balle en l'air/de l'autre côté du terrain/par-dessus le mur; **he threw the javelin 80m** il a lancé le javelot à 80m; **~ the ball up high** lance la balle en hauteur; **~ the ball back to me!** relance-moi la balle!; **he was thrown across the street/to the floor by the explosion** l'explosion l'a projeté de l'autre côté de la rue/à terre; **he threw a log on the fire/his coat on a chair** il a jeté une bûche sur le feu/son manteau sur une chaise; **she threw her apron over her head** elle s'est couvert la tête avec son tablier; **she threw her arms around my neck** elle s'est jetée à mon cou; **the police threw a cordon around the house** fig la police a encerclé la maison; **he was thrown clear and survived** il a été éjecté et a survécu; **two jockeys were thrown** deux jockeys ont été désarçonnés; **he threw his opponent in the third round** à la troisième reprise il a envoyé son adversaire au tapis; **to ~ a six** (in dice) faire un six; **2** fig (direct) lancer [*punch, question*] (**at** à); jeter [*glance, look*] (**at** à); envoyer [*kiss*]; projeter [*image, light, shadow*] (**on** sur); faire [*shadow*] (**on** sur); **we are ready for all the challenges/problems that Europe can ~ at us** fig nous somme prêts à affronter tous les défis que l'Europe nous lance/tous les problèmes que l'Europe nous pose; **to ~ money at a project/problem** claquer○ de l'argent dans un projet/problème; **there's no point in just ~ing money at it** ce n'est pas l'argent qui résoudra le problème; **to ~ suspicion on sb/sth** faire naître des soupçons sur qn/qch; **to ~ doubt on sb/sth** jeter un doute sur qn/qch; **the company has thrown the full weight of its publicity machine behind the case** la société a investi tout le poids de sa machine publicitaire dans l'affaire; **3** fig (disconcert) désarçonner; **the question completely threw me** la question m'a complètement désarçonné; **I was thrown by the news** j'ai été désarçonné par la nouvelle; **to ~ [sth/sb] into confusion** ou **disarray** semer la confusion dans [*meeting, group*]; semer la confusion parmi [*people*]; **4** Tech (activate) actionner [*switch, lever*]; **the operator threw the machine into gear/reverse** l'opérateur a embrayé l'engin/passé la marche arrière; **5**○ (indulge in, succumb to) **to ~ a fit/tantrum** fig piquer une crise○/colère○; **6**○ (organize) **to ~ a party** faire une fête○; **7** (in pottery) **to ~ a pot** tourner un pot; **8** Archit, Constr jeter [*bridge*] (**over** sur); **9** Vet (give birth to) mettre bas [*calf*].

III *vi* (*prét* **threw**; *pp* **thrown**) lancer.

IV *v refl* (*prét* **threw**; *pp* **thrown**) **to ~ oneself** (onto floor, bed, chair) se jeter (**onto** sur); **to ~ oneself to the ground** se jeter à plat ventre; **to ~ oneself off a building/in front of a train** se jeter du haut d'un immeuble/sous un train; **to ~ oneself at sb's feet** se jeter aux pieds de qn; **to ~ oneself at sb** lit, fig se jeter dans les bras de qn; **to ~ oneself into** lit se jeter dans [*river, sea*]; fig se plonger dans [*work, project*].

IDIOMS **it's ~ing it down**○! GB ça dégringole○!; **to ~ in one's lot with sb** rejoindre qn; **to ~ in the sponge** ou **towel** jeter l'éponge.

■ **throw around**, **throw about**: ¶ **~ [sth] around 1 to ~ a ball around** s'envoyer un ballon; **2** fig lancer au hasard [*ideas, names, references*]; **to ~ money around** jeter l'argent par les fenêtres; ¶ **~ oneself around** se débattre.

■ **throw aside**: ¶ **~ aside [sth]**, **~ [sth] aside 1** lit lancer [qch] sur le côté [*books, documents*]; **2** fig rejeter [*moral standards, principles*]; ¶ **~ [sb] aside** laisser tomber.

■ **throw away**: ¶ Games jeter une carte; ¶ **~ [sth] away**, **~ away [sth] 1** lit jeter [*rubbish, unwanted article*]; **2** fig (waste) gâcher [*chance, opportunity, life*]; gaspiller [*money*]; **he threw away any advantage he might have had** il n'a pas su profiter de son avantage; **she's really thrown herself away on him** c'est vraiment du gâchis qu'elle l'ait épousé; **3** fig (utter casually) lancer [qch] négligemment [*remark, information*].

■ **throw back**: **~ back [sth]**, **~ [sth] back** rejeter [*fish*]; relancer [*ball*]; **we have been thrown back on our own resources** fig nous avons dû recourir à nos propres ressources; **~ your shoulders back** rejetez les épaules.

■ **throw in**: **~ in [sth]**, **~ [sth] in 1** Comm (give free) faire cadeau de [*extra product*]; **a vacuum cleaner with the attachments thrown in** un aspirateur avec les accessoires en cadeau; **2** (add) ajouter; **~ in a few herbs** Culin ajoutez quelques herbes; **thrown in for good measure** (ajouté) pour faire bonne mesure; **3** (contribute) faire [*remark, suggestion*].

■ **throw off**: ¶ **~ off [sth]**, **~ [sth] off 1** (take off) ôter [qch] en vitesse [*clothes*]; écarter [*bedclothes*]; **2** fig (cast aside) se débarrasser de [*cold, handicap, pursuers*]; se soulager de [*burden*]; se libérer de [*tradition*]; sortir de [*depression*]; **3** fig (compose quickly) faire [qch] en cinq minutes [*poem, music*]; ¶ **~ off [sb]**, **~ [sb] off** (eject from train, bus, plane) expulser [*person*].

■ **throw on**: **~ on [sth]**, **~ [sth] on** (put on) enfiler [qch] en vitesse [*clothing*].

■ **throw open**: **~ open [sth]**, **~ [sth] open 1** ouvrir grand [*door, window*]; **2** fig (to public) ouvrir [*facility, tourist attraction*]; **to ~ a discussion open** déclarer une discussion ouverte.

■ **throw out**: ¶ **~ out [sb/sth]**, **~ [sb/sth] out** (eject) jeter [*rubbish*]; (from bar etc) jeter dehors [*person*] (**of** de); (from membership) renvoyer [*person*] (**of** de); **to be thrown out of work** être licencié; ¶ **~ out [sth]**, **~ [sth] out 1** (extend) **~ your arms out in front of you** lancez les bras devant vous; **~ your chest out** sortez la poitrine; **2** (reject) gen Jur rejeter [*application, case, decision, plan*]; Pol repousser [*bill*]; **3** (utter peremptorily) lancer [*comment*]; (casually) **he just threw out some comment about wanting...** il a juste dit qu'il voulait...; ¶ **~ [sb] out** (mislead) déconcerter; **that's what threw me out** c'est ce qui m'a fait me tromper.

■ **throw over**○ GB: **~ over [sb]**, **~ [sb] over** laisser tomber○, plaquer○; **she's thrown him over for another man** elle l'a laissé tomber○ or l'a plaqué○ pour un autre.

■ **throw together**: ¶ **~ [sb] together** [*fate, circumstances*] réunir [*people*]; ¶ **~ [sth] together** improviser [*artefact, meal, entertainment*]; mélanger [*ingredients*].

■ **throw up**: ¶ **~ up**○ vomir; ¶ **~ up [sth]**, **~ [sth] up 1**○ (abandon) laisser tomber [*job, post*]; **2** (reveal) faire apparaître [*fact*]; créer [*idea, problem, obstacle*]; engendrer [*findings, question, statistic*]; **3** (emit) cracher [*smoke*]; émettre [*spray*]; vomir [*lava*]; **4** (toss into air) [*car*] projeter [*stone*]; [*person*] lever [*arms*]; lancer [*ball*]; **to ~ up one's hands in horror** lever les bras d'horreur; **5** (open) ouvrir grand [*window*]; **6** (vomit) vomir [*meal*].

throwaway /ˈθrəʊəweɪ/ *adj* **1** (discardable) [*goods, object, packaging*] jetable; **2** (wasteful) [*society*] de consommation; **3** (casual) [*remark*] désinvolte; [*entertainment, style*] à l'emporte-pièce.

throw-back /ˈθrəʊbæk/ *n* **1** Anthrop, Zool survivant/-e *m/f*; **2** fig survivance *f* (**to** de).

thrower /ˈθrəʊə(r)/ *n* Sport, gen lanceur/-euse *m/f*; **javelin/stone ~** lanceur/-euse de javelot/de pierres.

throw-in /ˈθrəʊɪn/ *n* Sport touche *f*, remise *f* en jeu.

throwing /ˈθrəʊɪŋ/ *n* **1** gen, Sport (of javelin, knives) lancer *m*; (of stones) jet *m*; **2** gen **the ~ of litter is forbidden** il est interdit de jeter des détritus.

thrown /θrəʊn/ *pp* ▶ **throw** II, III, IV.

thru *prep* US = **through**.

thrum /θrʌm/ **I** *n* (sound) bourdonnement *m*; (louder) vrombissement *m*.

II *vtr, vi* = **strum**.

thrush /θrʌʃ/ *n* **1** Zool grive *f*; **2** ▶ **1354** Med (oral) muguet *m* (buccal); (vaginal) mycose *f* vaginale, mycose *f* à candida albicans spec.

thrust /θrʌst/ **I** *n* **1** lit, gen, Mil, Tech, Archit poussée *f*; **sword/dagger ~** coup *m* d'épée/de poignard; **2** (main aim) (of argument, essay, narrative) portée *f*; **3** (attack) pointe *f* (**at** dirigé contre).

II *vtr* (*prét, pp* **thrust**) **to ~ sth towards** ou **at sb** mettre brusquement qch sous le nez de qn; **to ~ sth into sth** enfoncer qch dans qch; **he thrust the letter/a glass into my hands** il m'a brusquement mis la lettre/un verre dans les mains; **to ~ one's head through the window/round the door** passer brusquement la tête par la fenêtre/dans l'entrebâillement de la porte; **to ~ sb/sth away** ou **out of the way** pousser violemment qn/qch; **to ~ sb out of the room/towards the door** pousser qn violemment hors de la salle/vers la porte; **to ~ one's way to the front of the queue** se frayer un passage jusqu'au début de la file d'attente.

III *v refl* (*prét, pp* **thrust**) **he thrust himself to the front of the crowd** il s'est frayé un passage jusqu'au premier rang de la foule; **to ~ oneself forward** lit se lancer en avant; fig se mettre en avant; **to ~ oneself on** ou **onto sb** (impose oneself) imposer sa présence à qn; (pounce on) se jeter sur qn.

■ **thrust aside**: **~ [sth/sb] aside**, **~ aside [sth/sb]** lit repousser [*object, person*]; fig rejeter [*protest, argument*].

■ **thrust back**: **~ [sth] back**, **~ back [sth]** repousser [*object, person, enemy*].

■ **thrust forward**: ¶ **~ forward** [*crowd*] se précipiter en avant; ¶ **~ [sth] forward**, **~ forward [sth]** pousser [qch] en avant [*person, object*].

■ **thrust on**, **thrust onto** = **thrust upon**.

■ **thrust out**: **~ [sth] out**, **~ out [sth]** tendre brusquement [*hand*]; lancer [*leg*]; projeter [qch] en avant [*jaw, chin*]; sortir [qch] (d'un geste brusque) [*implement*]; **to ~ sb out** pousser qn brusquement dehors; **she opened the door and thrust her head out** elle a ouvert la porte et a passé brusquement sa tête à l'extérieur; **to ~ sb/sth out of the way** pousser (violemment) qn/qch.

■ **thrust upon**: **~ [sth] upon sb** imposer [qch] sur qn [*idea, job, responsibility*]; **the job was thrust upon him** il s'est retrouvé avec le travail sur les bras, on lui a imposé le travail; **some have greatness thrust upon them** parfois ce sont les circonstances qui font les grands hommes.

■ **thrust up** [*seedlings, plant*] pousser vigoureusement.

thrust bearing, **thrust block** *n* palier *m* de butée.

thruster /ˈθrʌstə(r)/ *n* **1** Aerosp propulseur *m*; **2** péj arriviste *mf*.

thrust fault *n* faille *f* de compression, faille *f* inverse.

thrusting /ˈθrʌstɪŋ/ *adj* gen, péj [*person, campaign*] agressif/-ive; [*ambition*] puissant.

thrust stage *n* scène *f* ouverte (*entourée de trois côtés par le public*).

thruway /ˈθruːweɪ/ *n* US voie *f* rapide or express.

thud /θʌd/ **I** *n* bruit *m* sourd.
II *vi* (*p prés etc* **-dd-**) faire un bruit sourd; **the body ~ded to the floor** le corps est tombé lourdement sur le sol; **she ~ded on the door** elle a frappé à la porte à coups sourds; **they ~ded up the stairs** ils ont monté l'escalier à pas lourds; **her heart was ~ding** son cœur battait à tout rompre.

thug /θʌg/ *n* (hooligan) voyou *m*; (wrecker, paid muscle) casseur *m*.

thuggery /ˈθʌgərɪ/ *n* pej sauvagerie *f*.

thuja /ˈθuːjə/ *n* thuya *m*.

Thule /ˈθjuːliː/ *pr n* Geog, Hist Thulé *m*.

thumb /θʌm/ **I** *n* pouce *m*.
II *vtr* **1** feuilleter [*book, magazine*]; **a well-~ed book** un livre fatigué; **2**○ (hitchhiking) **to ~ a lift** ou **a ride** faire du stop○ or de l'autostop; **I ~ed a lift from a truck driver** je me suis fait prendre en stop○ par un routier; **they ~ed a lift home** ils sont rentrés en stop○.
III *vi* **to ~ at** ou **towards sth** indiquer qch du pouce.
IDIOMS **to be all ~s** être très maladroit; **to be under sb's ~** être sous la domination de qn; **she's got him under her ~** elle le mène à la baguette○; **to ~ one's nose at sb** lit faire un pied de nez à qn; **to ~ one's nose at sb/sth** fig faire la nique○ à qn/qch; **to stick out like a sore ~** faire tache pej, détonner.
■ **thumb through**: **~ through [sth]** feuilleter [*book, magazine*].

thumb: **~ index** *n* répertoire *m* à onglets; **~-indexed** *adj* avec onglets; **~nail** *n* ongle *m* du pouce; **~nail sketch** *n* lit (drawing) croquis *m* sur le vif; fig (description) (of person) esquisse *f* (de caractère); (of scene, event) aperçu *m* (**of** de).

thumbscrew /ˈθʌmskruː/ *n* **1** Hist (for torture) coins *mpl*; **2** Tech vis *f* à oreilles.

thumbs down○ /ˌθʌmzˈdaʊn/ *n* (signal) **to give sb/sth the ~** fig rejeter [*candidate, proposal, idea*]; **to get the ~** [*candidate, proposal, idea*] être rejeté; [*new product, experiment*] être mal accueilli; **his pizza got the ~ from his guests** ses invités n'ont pas apprécié sa pizza; **as soon as I give you the ~, stop the machine** arrête la machine dès que je te fais signe.

thumbstall /ˈθʌmstɔːl/ *n* poucier *m*.

thumbs up○ /ˌθʌmzˈʌp/ *n* **to give sb/sth the ~** (approve) approuver [*candidate, plan, suggestion*]; **to get the ~** [*plan, person, idea*] être approuvé; **start the car when I give you the ~** démarre quand je te fais signe; **she gave me the ~ as she came out of the interview** elle m'a fait signe que l'entretien s'était bien passé.

thumbtack /ˈθʌmtæk/ **I** *n* punaise *f*.
II *vtr* fixer [qch] avec des punaises.

thump /θʌmp/ **I** *n* **1** (blow) (grand) coup *m*; **to give sb a ~** donner un (grand) coup de poing à qn (**in** dans); **2** (sound) bruit *m* sourd; **~!—the body hit the floor** boum! le corps est tombé par terre.
II *vtr* donner un coup de poing à [*person*]; donner un coup de poing sur [*table*]; **he ~ed the ball into the net** il a envoyé le ballon dans le filet de toutes ses forces; **to ~ sb in the jaw/stomach** envoyer un coup dans la mâchoire/l'estomac de qn; **do that again and I'll ~ you!** ne recommence pas ou je te frappe!
III *vi* **1** (pound) [*heart*] battre violemment; [*music, rhythm*] résonner; **my head is ~ing** j'ai la tête qui m'élance; **to ~ on** marteler [*door, piano, floor*]; **2** (clump) **to ~ upstairs/along the landing** monter l'escalier/marcher dans le couloir à pas lourds.
■ **thump out**: **~ out [sth]** marteler [*tune, rhythm*].

thumping /ˈθʌmpɪŋ/ **I** *n* **1** (of drums, percussion) battement *m*; **2**○ (beating) raclée○ *f*; **to get a ~** prendre une raclée○.
II *adj* **1**○ (emphatic) **~ big**, **~ great** énorme; **2** (loud) [*noise*] sourd; [*rhythm, sound*] lancinant; [*headache*] lancinant.

thunder /ˈθʌndə(r)/ **I** *n* **1** Meteorol tonnerre *m*; **a clap** ou **peal of ~** un coup de tonnerre; **there's ~ in the air** il y a de l'orage dans l'air; **2** (noise) (of hooves) fracas *m* (**of** de); (of traffic) grondement *m* (**of** de); (of cannons, applause) tonnerre *m* (**of** de).
II *vtr* (shout) (also **~ out**) hurler [*command, order*]; **'silence!,' he ~ed** 'silence!,' dit-il d'une voix tonnante; **the crowd ~ed their applause** la foule a fait éclater un tonnerre d'applaudissements.
III *vi* **1** (roar) [*person, cannon*] tonner; [*hooves*] faire un bruit de tonnerre (**on** sur); **to ~ at** ou **against sb/sth** tempêter contre qn/qch; **2** (rush) **to ~ along** ou **past** passer dans un vacarme assourdissant ou un bruit de tonnerre; **he came ~ing down the stairs** il a descendu l'escalier dans un vacarme assourdissant.
IV *v impers* tonner.
IDIOMS **to steal sb's ~** couper l'herbe sous le pied de qn; **with a face like ~**, **with a face as black as ~** l'air furieux.

thunder: **~bolt** *n* Meteorol foudre *f*; fig coup *m* de tonnerre; **~box**○ *n* GB WC *m* chimique portable; **~clap** *n* coup *m* de tonnerre; **~cloud** *n* nuage *m* porteur d'orage.

thundering /ˈθʌndərɪŋ/ **I** *adj* **1** (angry) [*rage, temper*] noir; **2** (huge) [*success*] énorme; [*nuisance*] véritable (*before n*); [*noise, shout*] assourdissant.
II○ *adv* GB (intensifier) **a ~ great skyscraper** un gratte-ciel gigantesque; **a ~ good book/film** un livre/film excellent.

thunderous /ˈθʌndərəs/ *adj* **1** (loud) [*welcome*] tonitruant; [*crash, music, noise*] assourdissant; **~ applause** tonnerre *m* d'applaudissements; **2** (angry) [*face, expression*] orageux/-euse; [*look*] furieux/-ieuse; [*tone*] grondeur/-euse; **3** (powerful) [*kick, punch*] fulgurant.

thunder: **~storm** *n* orage *m*; **~struck** *adj* abasourdi.

thundery /ˈθʌndərɪ/ *adj* [*weather, shower*] orageux/-euse; **it's ~** le temps est à l'orage.

Thur (*abrév écrite* ▶ **Thursday**) jeudi *m*.

Thurgau ▶ **1776** *pr n* **the canton of ~** le canton de Thurgovie.

thurible /ˈθjʊərəbl/ *n* encensoir *m*.

thurifer /ˈθjʊərɪfə(r)/ *n* thuriféraire *m*.

Thurs *abrév écrite* = **Thursday**.

Thursday /ˈθɜːzdeɪ, -dɪ/ ▶ **1883** *n* jeudi *m*.

thus /ðʌs/ *adv* (in this way) ainsi; (consequently) ainsi, par conséquent; **she summed it up ~** elle l'a résumé ainsi; **it was ever ~** il en a toujours été ainsi; **~ far** jusqu'à présent.

thwack /θwæk/ **I** *n* (blow) coup *m*; (with hand) claque *f*; (sound) coup sec; **~!** paf!
II *vtr* frapper (vigoureusement) [*ball, person, animal*].

thwart /θwɔːt/ **I** *n* Naut banc *m* de nage.
II *vtr* contrecarrer, contrarier [*plan, bid*]; contrecarrer les desseins de [*person*]; contrer [*candidature, nomination*]; **to ~ sb in sth** contrarier qn dans qch.
III thwarted *pp adj* [*ambition, love, person, plan*] contrarié (**in** dans).

thy‡ /ðaɪ/ *det* = **your**.

thyme /taɪm/ **I** *n* Bot, Culin thym *m*; **sprig of ~** branche *f* de thym; **wild ~** thym sauvage.
II *modif* [*dressing, sauce, stuffing*] au thym; [*leaf, flower*] de thym.

thymus /ˈθaɪməs/ *n* (*pl* **~es** ou **thymi**) (also **~ gland**) thymus *m*.

thyroid /ˈθaɪrɔɪd/ **I** *n* (also **~ gland**) thyroïde *f*.
II *modif* [*artery, cartilage, disorder*] thyroïdien/-ienne; [*cancer*] de la glande thyroïde.

thyroxin /ˌθaɪˈrɒksɪn/ *n* thyroxine *f*.

thyself‡ /ðaɪˈself/ *pron* = **yourself**.

ti /tiː/ *n* Mus si *m*.

tiara /tɪˈɑːrə/ *n* (woman's) diadème *m*; (Pope's) tiare *f*.

Tiber /ˈtaɪbə(r)/ ▶ **1644** *pr n* Tibre *m*.

Tiberias /taɪˈbɪərɪəs/ ▶ **1400** *pr n* **Lake ~** le lac *m* de Tibériade.

Tiberius /taɪˈbɪərɪəs/ *pr n* Tibère.

Tibet /tɪˈbet/ ▶ **1131** *pr n* Tibet *m*.

Tibetan /tɪˈbetn/ ▶ **1486**, **1402** **I** *n* **1** (person) Tibétain/-e *m/f*; **2** Ling tibétain *m*.
II *adj* tibétain.

tibia /ˈtɪbɪə/ ▶ **1037** *n* (*pl* **~e** ou **~s**) tibia *m*.

tic /tɪk/ *n* tic *m*.

tichy *adj* GB = **titchy**.

Ticino ▶ **1776** *pr n* **the** (**canton of**) **~** le canton du Tessin, le Tessin.

tick /tɪk/ **I** *n* **1** (of clock) tic-tac *m*; **2** (mark on paper) coche *f*; **to put a ~ against sth** cocher qch; **3** Vet, Zool tique *f*; **4**○ GB (short time) minute *f* fig, seconde *f* fig; **I'll be with you in a ~/two ~s** je suis à toi dans une seconde/deux secondes; **I won't be a ~** j'en ai (juste) pour une seconde; **it won't take a ~/two ~s** ça ne prendra qu'une seconde/que deux secondes; **5**○ GB (credit) **on ~** à crédit.
II *vtr* (make mark) cocher [*box, name, answer*].
III *vi* lit [*bomb, clock, watch*] faire tic-tac; **I know what makes him ~** je sais ce qui le motive.
■ **tick away** [*hours, minutes, time*] passer; [*clock, meter*] tourner.
■ **tick by** [*hours, minutes*] passer.
■ **tick off**: **~ [sth/sb] off**, **~ off [sth/sb]** **1** (mark) cocher [*name, item*]; **2**○ GB (reprimand) passer un savon à○, réprimander [*person*]; **3**○ US (annoy) embêter [*person*].
■ **tick over** GB **1** Aut [*car, engine, meter*] tourner; **2** fig [*company, business*] tourner; (not doing really well) tourner au ralenti; [*mind, brain*] travailler.

ticker /ˈtɪkə(r)/ *n* **1** US (on stock exchange) téléscripteur *m*; **2**○ (heart) palpitant○ *m*, cœur *m*; **3**○ (watch) toquante○ *f*, montre *f*.

ticker tape /ˈtɪkəteɪp/ *n* bande *f* de téléscripteur; **to give sb a ~ welcome** ou **reception** accueillir qn par une pluie de serpentins.

ticker tape parade *n* défilé *m* sous une pluie de serpentins.

ticket /ˈtɪkɪt/ **I** *n* **1** (as proof of entitlement) (for bus, underground) ticket *m*; (for plane, train, coach) billet *m*; (for cinema, theatre, game, exhibition) billet *m* (**for** pour); (for cloakroom, laundry, left-luggage) ticket *m*; (for library) carte *f*; (for pawn shop) reconnaissance *f* (du mont-de-piété); **a bus/left-luggage ~** un ticket de bus/de consigne; **admission by ~ only** entrée sur présentation d'un billet; **for him, football was a ~ to a better life** fig le football lui a permis d'accéder à une vie meilleure; **2** (tag, label) étiquette *f*; **3**○ Aut (for fine) PV○ *m*; **a speeding ~** un PV○ pour excès de vitesse; **4** US, Pol (of political party) liste *f* (électorale); (platform) programme *m*; **to run on the Republican ~** se présenter sur la liste des Républicains; **to be elected on an environmental ~** être élu grâce à un programme écologiste; **5** Aviat, Naut (licence) brevet *m*; **to get one's ~** passer capitaine.

II *modif* [*prices, sales*] de billets.
III *vtr* **1** (label) étiqueter [*goods, baggage*]; **2** US (fine) **to be ~ed** avoir un PV○; **he was ~ed for illegal parking** il a eu un PV○ pour stationnement illégal.
IDIOMS **that's (just) the ~**○! voilà (exactement) ce qu'il nous faut!
ticket: **~ agency** *n* agence *f* de spectacles; **~ agent** ▶ 1692 *n* responsable *mf* d'une agence de spectacles; **~ booth** *n* billetterie *f*; **~ clerk** *n* GB Rail guichetier/-ère *m/f*; **~ collector** *n* GB contrôleur *m*.
ticket holder *n* (customer) personne *f* munie d'un billet; **'~s only'** 'réservé aux personnes munies d'un billet'.
ticket: **~ inspector** ▶ 1692 *n* contrôleur *m*; **~ machine** *n* distributeur *m* de billets; **~ office** *n* (office) bureau *m* de vente (des billets); (booth) guichet *m*; **~ punch** *n* poinçonneuse *f*; **~ tout** *n* GB revendeur/-euse *m/f* de billets au marché noir.
tickety-boo○ /ˌtɪkətɪˈbuː/ *adj* GB† ou hum **everything is ~** tout va bien.
tick fever *n* Vet fièvre *f* des montagnes rocheuses.
ticking /ˈtɪkɪŋ/ I *n* **1** (of clock) tic-tac *m*; **2** Tex (material) toile *f* à matelas; (cover) housse *f*; **mattress ~** housse *f* à matelas; **pillow ~** taie *f* d'oreiller.
II *adj* [*clock, meter*] qui fait tic-tac; **a ~ sound** ou **noise** un tic-tac.
ticking-off○ /ˌtɪkɪŋˈɒf/ *n* **to give sb a ~** GB passer un savon à qn○, réprimander qn.
tickle /ˈtɪkl/ I *n* chatouillement *m*; **to give sb a ~** faire des chatouilles à qn; **I've got a ~ in my throat** j'ai la gorge qui me chatouille.
II *vtr* **1** [*person, feather*] chatouiller; **to ~ sb in the ribs/on the tummy** chatouiller les côtes/le ventre de qn; **to ~ sb under the chin** chatouiller qn sous le menton; **2** [*wool, garment*] gratter; **3**○ fig (gratify) chatouiller [*palate, vanity*]; exciter [*senses*]; (amuse) amuser [*person*]; **to ~ sb's fancy** (amuse sb) amuser qn; (appeal to sb) faire envie à qn.
III *vi* [*blanket, garment*] gratter; [*feather*] chatouiller.
IDIOMS **~d pink** ou **to death** ravi; **to have a (bit of) slap and ~**○† GB se bécoter○.
tickling /ˈtɪklɪŋ/ I *n* **1** (act) chatouillement *m*; **2** (feeling) (sensation *f* de) chatouillement *m*.
II *adj* [*feeling*] de chatouillement.
ticklish /ˈtɪklɪʃ/ *adj* **1** [*person*] chatouilleux/-euse; **to have ~ feet** être chatouilleux des pieds; **2** (tricky) [*situation, problem*] épineux/-euse.
tickly /ˈtɪklɪ/ *adj* **1** [*cough*] irritatif/-ive, irritant; **2** [*garment, cloth*] qui gratte.
tick: **~-over** *n* Aut GB ralenti *m*; **~tack** *n* GB *langage gestuel des bookmakers*; **~tack man** *n* assistant *m* de bookmaker; **~-tack-toe** *n* US (jeu *m* de) morpion *m*; **~tock** *n* tic-tac *m*.
ticky-tacky○ /ˈtɪkɪtækɪ/ US péj I *n* pacotille *f*.
II *adj* de pacotille.
tidal /ˈtaɪdl/ *adj* [*river*] à marée (*after n*); [*current, flow*] de marée; [*energy, power*] marémoteux/-trice; **the Thames is ~** la Tamise a des marées.
tidal: **~ basin** *n* bassin *m* de marée; **~ power station** *n* usine *f* marémotrice; **~ waters** *npl* eaux *fpl* de marée; **~ wave** *n* lit, fig raz-de-marée *m inv*.
tidbit /ˈtɪdbɪt/ *n* US (of food) gâterie *f*; (of gossip) cancan○ *m*.
tiddler /ˈtɪdlə(r)/ *n* GB **1** (stickleback) épinoche *f*; (any small fish) petit poisson *m*; **2**○ hum (person) petit mioche○ *m*, petite mioche○ *f*.
tiddly○ /ˈtɪdlɪ/ *adj* GB **1** (drunk) pompette○; **2** (tiny) minuscule.
tiddlywinks /ˈtɪdlɪwɪŋks/ ▶ 1282 *n* (+ *v sg*) jeu *m* de puce.
tide /taɪd/ *n* **1** Naut marée *f*; **the ~ is in/out** c'est la marée haute/basse; **the ~ is turning** la marée change; **the ~ is going out/coming in** la marée monte/descend; **at high/low ~** à marée haute/basse; **2** fig (trend) (of emotion) vague *f*; (of events) cours *m*; **a rising ~ of sympathy/nationalism** une vague montante de sympathie/nationalisme; **the ~ of history/events** le cours de l'histoire/des événements; **to go/swim with the ~** fig aller/nager dans le sens du courant; **to go/swim against the ~** fig aller/nager à contre-courant; **the ~ has turned** la chance a tourné (du bon côté); **to turn the ~ of history** renverser le cours de l'histoire; **the ~ has turned against him/in his favour** la chance s'est retournée contre lui/a tourné en sa faveur; **to stem the ~ of pessimism/anarchy** endiguer la vague de pessimisme/d'anarchie; **3** fig (of complaints, letters, refugees) afflux *m*.
IDIOMS **time and ~ wait for no man** on ne peut pas arrêter le temps.
■ **tide over**: **~ [sb] over** dépanner.
tide: **~ gate** *n* écluse *f* de marée; **~ gauge** *n* marégraphe *m*; **~land** *n* laisse *f*, terre *f* inondée à marée haute; **~less** *adj* sans marée (*after n*); **~ line** *n* ligne *f* de marée; **~ lock** *n* écluse *f* de bassin; **~mark** *n* lit ligne *f* de marée haute; GB fig (line of dirt) marque *f* de crasse○, marque *f* de saleté; **~ race** *n* mascaret *m*; **~ table** *n* annuaire *m* des marées; **~water** *n* (eaux *fpl* de) marée *f*; **~way** *n* Geog, Naut chenal *m* de marée.
tidily /ˈtaɪdɪlɪ/ *adv* [*arrange, fold, write*] soigneusement; [*dress*] de façon soignée; [*fit*] impeccablement.
tidiness /ˈtaɪdɪnɪs/ *n* (of house, room, desk) ordre *m*; (of person, appearance) aspect *m* soigné; (of habits) sens *m* de l'ordre.
tidings /ˈtaɪdɪŋz/ *npl* littér nouvelles *fpl*; **good/bad ~** de bonnes/de mauvaises nouvelles.
tidy /ˈtaɪdɪ/ I *n* GB = **tidy-up**.
II *adj* **1** [*house, room, desk*] bien rangé; [*garden, writing, work, person, appearance*] soigné; [*habits, nature*] ordonné; [*hair*] bien coiffé; [*division, category*] net/nette, bien défini; **to get a room ~** ranger une pièce; **to make oneself ~** s'arranger, ajuster sa toilette; **to have a ~ mind** avoir l'esprit méthodique; **2**○ [*amount, salary, portion*] beau/belle.
III *vtr* = **tidy up**.
IV *vi* = **tidy up**.
■ **tidy away**: **~ [sth] away, ~ away [sth]** ranger [*toys, plates*].
■ **tidy out**: **~ [sth] out, ~ out [sth]** vider [qch] pour ranger [*cupboard, drawer*].
■ **tidy up**: ¶ **~ up** faire du rangement; **to ~ up after** ranger derrière [*person*]; ¶ **~ up [sth], ~ [sth] up 1** lit ranger [*house, room, objects*]; mettre de l'ordre dans [*garden, area, town*]; arranger [*appearance, hair*]; soigner [*handwriting*]; **2** fig résoudre [*problem*]; mettre de l'ordre dans [*finances*]; ¶ **~ oneself up** s'arranger, ajuster sa toilette.
tidy-minded /ˌtaɪdɪˈmaɪndɪd/ *adj* à or ayant l'esprit méthodique.
tidy-out /ˈtaɪdɪaʊt/, **tidy-up** /ˈtaɪdɪʌp/ *n* GB rangement *m*; **to have a ~** faire du rangement.
tie /taɪ/ I *n* **1** (piece of clothing) (also **neck ~**) cravate *f*; **regimental/school ~** GB cravate d'un régiment/d'une école; ▶ **old school tie**; **2** (fastener) (for bags, plants) attache *f*; Constr entretoise *f*; Rail traverse *f*; **3** (bond) (*gén pl*) lien *m*; **family ~s** liens *mpl* familiaux; **to strengthen/sever ~s with** resserrer/rompre les liens avec; **4** (constraint) contrainte *f*; **pets can be a ~** les animaux familiers peuvent être une contrainte; **5** (draw) Sport match *m* nul; **to end in a ~** [*game*] se terminer sur un score nul; **there was a ~ for second place** il y a eu exaequo pour la deuxième place; **there was a ~ between the candidates** les candidats ont obtenu le même nombre de voix; **6** Sport (arranged match) match *m*; **cup/first round ~** match *m* de coupe/de premier tour; **7** Mus liaison *f*.
II *vtr* (*p prés* **tying**) **1** (attach, fasten closely) attacher [*label, animal, prisoner*] (**to** à); ligoter [*hands, ankles*] (**with** avec); ficeler [*parcel, chicken*] (**with** avec); **~ the apron round your waist** attache-toi le tablier autour de la taille; **2** (join in knot) nouer [*scarf, cravate*]; attacher [*laces*]; **~ a bow in the ribbon** fais un nœud avec le ruban; **~ a knot in the string** fais un nœud à la ficelle; **3** fig (link) associer; **to ~ sb/sth to sth** associer qn/qch à qch; **to be ~d to** (linked to) être lié à [*belief, growth, activity*]; Fin être indexé sur [*inflation, interest rate*]; (constrained by) [*person*] être lié par des obligations à [*party, group*]; [*person*] être sous contrat à [*company*]; être rivé à [*job*]; être cloué à [*house*]; [*person, business*] être soumis à [*limitations, market forces*]; **4** Mus lier [*notes*].
III *vi* (*p prés* **tying**) **1** (fasten) s'attacher; **the ribbons ~ at the back** les rubans s'attachent derrière; **the laces/rope won't ~** il n'y a pas moyen d'attacher les lacets/la corde; **2** Sport, gen (draw) (in match) faire match nul (**with** avec); (in race) être ex aequo (**with** avec); (in vote) [*candidates*] obtenir le même nombre de voix; **to ~ for second/third place** être deuxième/troisième ex aequo; **to ~ on 20 points** être ex aequo 20 à 20.
IV *v refl* (*p prés* **tying**) **to ~ oneself to** lit s'attacher à [*railings, etc*]; fig s'astreindre à [*job, commitment*].
IDIOMS **my hands are ~d** j'ai les mains liées.
■ **tie back**: **~ [sth] back, ~ back [sth]** nouer [qch] derrière [*hair*]; attacher [qch] sur le côté [*curtain*].
■ **tie down**: **~ [sb/sth] down, ~ down [sb/sth]** (hold fast) amarrer [*hot air balloon*]; immobiliser [*hostage*]; **she feels ~d down** fig elle a l'impression d'être clouée; **to ~ sb down to sth** (limit) imposer qch à qn; **to ~ sb down to an exact date/price** arriver à soutirer une date/une prix exacte à qn; **to ~ oneself down** s'astreindre (**to** à).
■ **tie in with**: ¶ **~ in with [sth] 1** (tally) concorder avec [*fact, event*]; **it all ~s in with what we've been saying** tout cela concorde avec ce que nous venons de dire; **2** (have link) être en rapport avec; **does this fact ~ in with the murder?** est-ce que cet élément est en rapport avec le meurtre?; ¶ **~ [sth] in with sth, ~ in [sth] with sth 1** (combine) combiner [qch] avec qch; **2** (connect) relier [qch] avec qch [*fact, information*].
■ **tie on**: **~ [sth] on, ~ on [sth]** attacher [*label, ribbon, bauble*].
■ **tie together**: ¶ **~ together** [*facts, information*] s'enchaîner; ¶ **~ [sth] together, ~ together [sth]** attacher [*bundles, objects*]; **we ~d his hands together** on lui a attaché les mains.
■ **tie up**: ¶ **~ [sb/sth] up, ~ up [sb/sth] 1** (secure) ligoter [*prisoner*]; ficeler [*parcel*]; fermer [*sack*]; attacher [*animal*]; amarrer [*boat*]; **2** Fin (freeze) immobiliser [*capital*] (**in** dans); bloquer [*shares*]; **3** (finalize) régler [*details, matters*]; conclure [*deal*]; **to ~ up the loose ends** régler les derniers détails; **4** (hinder) bloquer [*procedure*]; US bloquer [*traffic, route*]; US suspendre [*production*]; **to get ~d up** [*traffic, route*] se bloquer; [*production*] être suspendu; [*person*] être pris; ¶ **to be ~d up** (be busy) être pris; **he's ~d up in a meeting/with a client** il est pris par une réunion/avec un client; **I'm a bit ~d up right now** je suis assez pris.
tie: **~back** *n* (for curtain) embrasse *f*; **~ break(er)** *n* (in tennis) tie-break *m*; jeu *m* décisif; (in quiz) question *f* subsidiaire; **~ clasp, ~ clip** *n* pince *f* à cravate.

tied /taɪd/ *adj* [*accommodation*] fourni par l'employeur.

tied: **~ agent** *n* Insur courtier *m* agréé; Aut concessionnaire *mf*; **~ house** *n* GB (pub) pub *m* qui appartient à une brasserie.

tie-dye /ˈtaɪdaɪ/ **I** *n* chinage *m* par teinture.
II *vtr* chiner par teinture.

tie in /ˈtaɪn/ *n* **1** gen (link) lien *m*; **2** US Comm (sale) vente *f* conditionnée par une autre; (item) article *m* dont l'achat conditionne une vente.

tie: **~ line** *n* Telecom ligne *f* directe; **~ pin** *n* épingle *f* de cravate.

tier /tɪə(r)/ **I** *n* (of cake, sandwich) étage *m*; (of organization, system) niveau *m*; (of seating) gradin *m*; **to rise in ~s** s'étager; ▶ **two-tier**.
II *vtr* disposer [qch] en étages [*cake*]; constituer [qch] en niveaux [*organization, system*]; disposer [qch] en gradins [*seating*].
III tiered *pp adj* [*seating*] en gradins; [*system*] à plusieurs niveaux.

tie: **~ rack** *n* porte-cravates *m*; **~ rod** *n* Aut barre *f* d'accouplement (de la direction); Archit tirant *m*.

Tierra del Fuego /tɪˌerə del ˈfweɪgəʊ/ *pr n* Terre *f* de Feu.

tie tack *n* US = **tie pin**.

tie-up /ˈtaɪʌp/ *n* **1** gen (link) lien *m*; **2** US (stoppage) (of work) suspension *f*; (of traffic) bouchon *m*; **3**○ US (mooring) point *m* d'amarrage.

tiff /tɪf/ *n* (petite) querelle *f*; **a lovers' ~** une querelle d'amoureux; **to have a ~** se chamailler○.

tig /tɪg/ ▶ **1282** *n* Games jeu *m* de chat.

tiger /ˈtaɪgə(r)/ *n* tigre *m*.
IDIOMS **to fight like a ~** [*man*] se battre comme un lion; [*woman*] se battre comme une tigresse.

tiger: **~ cub** *n* bébé tigre *m*; **~ lily** *n* lis *m* tigré; **~ moth** *n* Zool écaille *f* martre; **~'s eye** *n* Miner œil-de-tigre *m*; **~ shark** *n* requin *m* tigre.

tight /taɪt/ ▶ **1703** **I tights** *npl* GB collant(s) *m(pl)*.
II *adj* **1** (firm) [*lid, screw*] serré; [*grip*] ferme; [*knot*] serré; **to hold sb in a ~ embrace** tenir qn serré dans ses bras; **2** (taut) [*rope, string, strap*] tendu; [*voice*] tendu; **3** (constrictive) [*space*] étroit, étriqué; [*clothing*] serré; (closefitting) [*jacket, shirt*] ajusté; **my shoes are too ~** mes chaussures sont trop étroites, mes chaussures me serrent; **a pair of ~ jeans** un jean moulant; **there were six of us in the car—it was a ~ squeeze** on était six dans la voiture—c'était très serré; **4** (strict) [*security, deadline*] strict; [*discipline*] rigoureux/-euse; [*budget, credit*] serré; **to exercise ~ control over sth/sb** contrôler strictement qch/qn; **to be ~ (with one's money)** être près de ses sous, être radin○; **money is a bit ~ these days** (one's own) je suis (or on est) un peu juste ces temps-ci; Econ l'argent se fait rare ces temps-ci; **~ money** Econ argent rare or cher; **5** (packed) [*schedule, timetable*] serré; **6** Sport (close) [*finish, match*] serré; **7** (compact) [*group, bunch*] serré; **they were sitting in a ~ circle around her** ils étaient assis en cercle serré autour d'elle; **8**○ GB (drunk) pompette○, ivre; **to get ~** se soûler; **9** (sharp, oblique) [*angle, turn*] aigu/-uë.
III *adv* **1** (firmly) [*hold, grip*] fermement; **to fasten/close sth ~** bien attacher/fermer qch; **you've screwed the lid too ~** tu as trop serré le couvercle; **to hold sth ~ against one's chest** tenir qch serré contre sa poitrine; **he shut his eyes ~** il a fermé les yeux en plissant les paupières; **2** (closely) **she pulled the collar ~ about her throat** elle a resserré le col autour de son cou; **stand ~ against the wall** appuyez-vous contre le mur; **3** (fast) **hold ~!** cramponne-toi!; **sit ~!** ne bouge pas!; **I just sat ~ and waited for the scandal to pass** fig je suis resté tranquillement dans mon coin en attendant que le scandale passe.
IDIOMS **to be in a ~ spot** ou **situation** ou **corner** être dans une situation difficile; **to run a ~ ship** tout avoir à l'œil.

tight-arsed◑ GB, **tight-assed**◑ US /ˈtaɪtɑːst, ˈtaɪtæst/ *adj* péj [*person, behaviour*] coincé○.

tighten /ˈtaɪtn/ **I** *vtr* serrer [*lid, screw, strap*]; resserrer [*grip*]; tendre [*spring, bicycle chain*]; fig renforcer [*security, restrictions*]; durcir [*legislation, policy*]; **they ~ed their grip on the land** ils ont renforcé leur emprise sur la terre; **to ~ the tension** (in sewing, knitting) augmenter la tension.
II *vi* **1** (contract) [*lips*] se serrer; [*muscle*] se contracter; **her mouth ~ed** elle serrait les lèvres; **she felt her throat ~** elle sentait sa gorge se serrer; **2** [*screw, nut*] se resserrer; **3** (become strict) [*laws, credit controls*] se durcir.
IDIOMS **to ~ one's belt** fig se serrer la ceinture.
■ **tighten up**: **~ up [sth]**, **~ [sth] up** resserrer [*screw, hinge*]; renforcer [*security*]; durcir [*legislation*]; **to ~ up on** durcir la réglementation en matière de [*immigration, fiscal policy etc*].

tight end US ailier *m*.

tightening /ˈtaɪtnɪŋ/ *n* (of screw, lid) resserrement *m*; fig (also **~ up**) (of legislation, security) renforcement *m*, durcissement *m*; **to feel a ~ of one's jaw/stomach muscles** sentir sa mâchoire/les muscles de son estomac se contracter.

tight: **~-fisted**○ *adj* péj radin○; **~-fitting** *adj* Fashn ajusté; **~-knit** *adj* fig uni.

tight-lipped /ˌtaɪtˈlɪpt/ *adj* **they are remaining ~ about the events** ils se refusent à tout commentaire sur les événements; **he watched, ~** il a regardé d'un air pincé or d'un air réprobateur.

tightly /ˈtaɪtlɪ/ *adv* **1** (firmly) [*grasp, grip, hold*] fermement; [*embrace*] bien fort; [*tied, fastened, bound*] bien; **her hair was drawn back ~ in a bun** ses cheveux étaient attachés en chignon serré; **2** (closely) **the ~ packed crowd** la foule dense et serrée; **the sweets are packed ~ in the box** les bonbons sont serrés dans la boîte; **3** (taut) **a ~ stretched rope** une corde très tendue; **4** (precisely) [*scheduled, coordinated*] bien; [*controlled*] bien, strictement.

tightness /ˈtaɪtnɪs/ *n* **1** (contraction) (of muscles, jaw) contraction *f*; **there was a sudden ~ in her chest** elle ressentit soudain un serrement dans sa poitrine; **2** (strictness) (of restrictions, security) rigueur *f* (**of** de); **3** (smallness) (of space, garment) étroitesse *f*; **because of the ~ of his shoes** parce que ses souliers lui serraient.

tightrope /ˈtaɪtrəʊp/ *n* corde *f* raide; **to walk the ~** marcher sur une corde raide; **to be on a ~** fig marcher sur la corde raide; **I'm walking the ~ between my family and my job** je suis tiraillé entre ma famille et mon travail.

tight: **~rope walker** *n* funambule *mf*; **~wad**○ *n* US péj radin/-e○ *m/f*.

tigress /ˈtaɪgrɪs/ *n* tigresse *f*.

Tigris /ˈtaɪgrɪs/ ▶ **1644** *pr n* Tigre *m*.

tilde /ˈtɪldə/ *n* tilde *m*.

tile /taɪl/ **I** *n* (for roof) tuile *f*; (for floor, wall) carreau *m*.
II *vtr* poser des tuiles sur [*roof*]; carreler [*floor, wall*].
III tiled *pp adj* [*roof*] couvert de tuiles; [*floor, wall*] carrelé.
IDIOMS **to go out** ou **have a night on the ~s**○ GB faire la noce○.

tiler /ˈtaɪlə(r)/ *n* (of roofs) couvreur *m*; (of floors, walls) carreleur *m*.

tiling /ˈtaɪlɪŋ/ *n* **1** ¢ (covering of tiles) (of roof) tuiles *fpl*; (of floor, wall) carrelage *m*; **2** (process) (for roof) pose *f* des tuiles; (for floor, wall) pose *f* du carrelage.

till[1] /tɪl/ ▶ **until**.

till[2] /tɪl/ **I** *n* caisse *f*.
II *vtr* labourer.
IDIOMS **to have one's hand in the ~** piocher dans la caisse.

tillage† /ˈtɪlɪdʒ/ *n* (process) labourage *m*; (land) labour *m*.

tiller /ˈtɪlə(r)/ *n* **1** Naut barre *f*; **2** Hort (machine) motoculteur *m*.

till receipt /tɪl/ *n* ticket *m* (de caisse).

tilt /tɪlt/ **I** *n* **1** (incline) inclinaison *f*; **to have a (slight) ~** pencher (un peu); **2** fig (attack) attaque *f* (**at** de); **to have** ou **take a ~ at** attaquer, critiquer [*person, trend, organization*]; s'essayer à [*championship, event*]; se mesurer à [*champion*]; **3** Hist (in jousting) (contest) joute *f*; (thrust) coup *m* (de lance), lancer *m*; **to take a ~ at** porter un coup à [*opponent, competitor*]; **4** Aut, Naut (cover) bâche *f*.
II *vtr* **1** (slant) pencher [*table, chair, sunshade*]; incliner [*head, face, container*]; pencher [qch] sur le côté [*hat, cap*]; **to ~ one's head to the left/back/forward** incliner la tête sur la gauche/en arrière/en avant; **he ~ed his cap over his eyes** il a rabattu sa casquette sur les yeux; **2** fig (influence) **to ~ the balance in favour of/away from** faire pencher la balance en faveur de/contre [*politician, party, measure*].
III *vi* **1** (slant) [*building, spire, tree, table*] pencher; [*floor, ground*] bouger; **to ~ to the left/forward/to one side** pencher vers la gauche/en avant/sur le côté; **2** Hist (joust) jouter; **to ~ at** Hist jouter contre [*opponent*]; fig porter un coup à [*person, organization*].

tilt: **~-and-turn window** *n* fenêtre *f* basculante; **~ angle** *n* angle *m* d'inclinaison.

tilted /ˈtɪltɪd/ *adj* [*spire, head*] penché; **~ to the right/to one side** penché vers la droite/sur le côté; **his head was ~ back/forward** il avait la tête penchée en arrière/en avant.

tilt: **~ hammer** *n* marteau *m* pilon; **~head** *n* Photo (mechanical) rotule *f*; (hydraulic) tête *f* fluide; **~-top table** *n* table *f* à plateau inclinable.

timbal, **tymbal** /ˈtɪmbl/ *n* timbale *f*.

timber /ˈtɪmbə(r)/ **I** *n* **1** (for building) bois *m* (de construction); (for furniture) bois *m* (d'œuvre); **seasoned/green ~** bois séché/vert; **roof ~s** bois de charpente; **2** (lumber) troncs *mpl* d'arbre; **to fell ~** abattre des arbres; **'Timber!'** 'Attention (à l'arbre qui tombe)!'; **3** (forest) bois *mpl*; **land under ~** futaie *f*; **4** (beam) poutre *f*, madrier *m* spec.
II *modif* [*importer, exporter*] de bois; [*treatment, preservative, trade*] du bois; [*building, frame*] en bois; **~ plantation** futaie *f*.
III timbered *pp adj* [*slopes*] boisé; [*house*] en bois; **~ed ceiling** plafond à poutres apparentes; **half-~ed house** maison *f* à colombage.

timber: **~-clad** *adj* revêtu de bois; **~ cladding** *n* revêtement *m* en bois; **~-framed** *adj* [*building*] à colombage.

timbering /ˈtɪmbərɪŋ/ *n* revêtement *m* en bois.

timber: **~land** *n* US terrain *m* forestier exploitable; **~ line** *n* limite *f* des arbres; **~ merchant** *n* GB négociant *m* en bois, marchand *m* de bois; **~ wolf** *n* loup *m* gris; **~ yard** *n* scierie *f*.

timbre /ˈtɪmbə(r), ˈtæmbrə/ *n* timbre *m*.

Timbuktu /ˌtɪmbʌkˈtuː/ ▶ **1818** *n* Tombouctou *m*.

time /taɪm/ ▶ **1807**, **1096** **I** *n* **1** (continuum) temps *m*; **~ and space** le temps et l'espace; **in** ou **with ~**, **in the course of ~** avec le temps; **as ~ goes/went by** avec le temps; **at this point in ~** à l'heure qu'il est; **for all ~** à jamais; **the biggest drugs haul of all ~** la plus importante saisie de drogue de tous les temps; **2** (specific duration) temps *m*; **most of the ~** la plupart du temps; **he was ill for some of**

Time units

Lengths of time

a second = une seconde
a minute = une minute
an hour = une heure
a day = un jour
a week = une semaine
a month = un mois
a year = un an/une année
a century = un siècle

For time by the clock, ▶ 1096*; for days of the week,* ▶ 1883*; for months,* ▶ 1472*; for dates,* ▶ 1150.

How long?

Note the various ways of translating take *into French.*

how long does it take? = combien de temps faut-il?
it took me a week = cela m'a pris une semaine *or* il m'a fallu une semaine
I took an hour to finish it = j'ai mis une heure pour le terminer
the letter took a month to arrive = la lettre a mis un mois pour arriver
it'll take at least a year = il faudra une bonne année *or* il faudra au moins un an
it'll only take a moment = c'est l'affaire de quelques instants

Translate both spend *and* have *as* passer:

to have a wonderful evening = passer une soirée merveilleuse
to spend two days in Paris = passer deux jours à Paris

Use dans *for* in *when something is seen as happening in the future:*

I'll be there in an hour = je serai là dans une heure
she said she'd be there in an hour = elle a dit qu'elle serait là dans une heure
in three weeks' time = dans trois semaines

Use en *for* in *when expressing the time something took or will take:*

he did it in an hour = il l'a fait en une heure

The commonest translation of for *in the 'how long' sense is* pendant:

I worked in the factory for a year = j'ai travaillé à l'usine pendant un an

But use pour *for* for *when the length of time is seen as being still to come:*

we're here for a month = nous sommes là pour un mois
they'll take the room for a week = ils vont prendre la chambre pour huit jours

And use depuis *for* for *when the action began in the past and is or was still going on:*

she has been here for a week = elle est ici depuis huit jours
she had been there for a year = elle était là depuis un an
I haven't seen her for years = je ne l'ai pas vue depuis des années

Note the use of de *when expressing how long something lasted or will last:*

a two-minute delay = un retard de deux minutes
a six-week wait = une attente de six semaines
an eight-hour day = une journée de huit heures
six weeks' sick leave = un congé de maladie de six semaines
five weeks' pay = cinq semaines de salaire

When?

In the past

when did it happen? = quand est-ce que c'est arrivé?
two minutes ago = il y a deux minutes
a month ago = il y a un mois
years ago = il y a des années
it'll be a month ago on Tuesday = ça fera un mois mardi
it's years since he died = il y a des années qu'il est mort
a month earlier = un mois plus tôt
a month before = un mois avant *or* un mois auparavant
the year before = l'année d'avant *or* l'année précédente
the year after = l'année d'après *or* l'année suivante
a few years later = quelques années plus tard
after four days = au bout de quatre jours
last week = la semaine dernière
last month = le mois dernier
last year = l'année dernière
a week ago yesterday = il y a eu huit jours hier
a week ago tomorrow = il y aura huit jours demain
the week before last = il y a quinze jours
over the past few months = au cours des derniers mois

In the future

when will you see him? = quand est-ce que tu le verras?
in a few days = dans quelques jours (*see also above, the phrases with* in *translated by* dans)
any day now = d'un jour à l'autre
next week = la semaine prochaine
next month = le mois prochain
next year = l'année prochaine
this coming week = la semaine qui vient *or* (*more formally*) au cours de la semaine à venir
over the coming months = au cours des mois à venir
a month from tomorrow = dans un mois demain

How often?

how often does it happen? = cela arrive tous les combien?
every Thursday = tous les jeudis
every week = toutes les semaines
every year = tous les ans
every second day = tous les deux jours
every third month = tous les trois mois
day after day = jour après jour
year after year = année après année
the last Thursday of the month = le dernier jeudi du mois
five times a day = cinq fois par jour
twice a month = deux fois par mois
three times a year = trois fois par an
once every three months = une fois tous les trois mois

How much an hour (etc)?

how much do you get an hour? = combien gagnez-vous de l'heure?
I get $20 = je gagne 20 dollars de l'heure
to be paid $20 an hour = être payé 20 dollars de l'heure

but note:

to be paid by the hour = être payé à l'heure
how much do you get a week? = combien gagnez-vous par semaine?
how much do you earn a month? = combien gagnez-vous par mois?
$3,000 a month = 3 000 dollars par mois
$40,000 a year = 40 000 dollars par an

Forms in *-ée: an/année, matin/matinée* etc.

The -ée forms are often used to express a rather vague amount of time passing or spent in something, and so tend to give a subjective slant to what is being said, as in:

a long day/evening/year = une longue journée/soirée/année
a whole day = toute une journée *or* une journée entière
we spent a lovely day there = nous y avons passé une journée merveilleuse
a painful evening = une soirée pénible

When an exact number is specified, the shorter forms are generally used, as in:

it lasted six days = cela a duré six jours
two years' military service = deux ans de service militaire
she spent ten days in England = elle a passé dix jours en Angleterre

However there is no strict rule that applies to all of these words. If in doubt, check in the dictionary.

the ~ il a été malade pendant une partie du temps; **she talked (for) some of the ~, but most of the ~ she was silent** elle a parlé par moments, mais pendant la plupart du temps elle a gardé le silence; **all the ~** tout le temps; **I was waiting for you here all the ~** je t'attendais ici pendant tout ce temps-là; **she was lying all the ~** elle mentait depuis le début; **you've got all the ~ in the world, you've got plenty of ~** tu as tout ton temps; **to find/have/take the ~ to do** trouver/avoir/prendre le temps de faire; **to spend one's ~ doing** passer son temps à faire; **to take one's ~** prendre son temps; **take your ~ over it!** prends ton temps!; **writing a novel takes ~, it takes ~ to write a novel** il faut du temps pour écrire un roman; **do I have (enough) ~ to go to the shops?** est-ce que j'ai le temps d'aller aux magasins?; **half the ~ he isn't even listening** la moitié du temps il n'écoute même pas; **some ~ before/after** quelque temps avant/après; **that's the best film I've seen for a long ~** c'est le meilleur film que j'aie vu depuis longtemps; **he has been gone for a long ~** cela fait longtemps or un bon moment qu'il est parti; **it'll be a long ~ before I go back there!** je n'y retournerai pas de sitôt!; **you took a long ~!, what a (long) ~ you've been!** tu en a mis du temps!; **we had to wait for a long ~** nous avons dû attendre longtemps; **I've been living in this country for a long ~** j'habite dans ce pays depuis longtemps, cela fait longtemps que j'habite dans ce pays; **it takes a long ~ for the car to start** la voiture met du temps à démarrer; **she would regret this for a long ~ to come** elle allait le regretter pendant longtemps; **a long ~ ago** il y a longtemps; **a short ~ ago** il y a peu de temps; **some ~ ago** il y a un moment, il y a quelque temps; **we haven't heard from her for some ~** ça fait un moment qu'on n'a pas eu de ses nouvelles; **it continued for some (considerable) ~** ça a continué pendant un bon moment or pendant pas mal de temps; **it won't happen for some ~ yet** ça ne se produira pas de sitôt or avant longtemps; **she did it in half the ~ it had taken her colleagues** elle l'a fait en deux fois moins de temps que ses collègues; **in no ~ at all, in next to no ~** en moins de deux; **in five days'/weeks' ~** dans cinq jours/semaines; **within the agreed ~** dans les délais convenus; **in your own ~** (at your own pace) à ton rythme; (outside working hours) en dehors des heures de travail; **on company ~** pendant les heures de bureau; **my ~ isn't my own** je n'ai plus une minute à moi; **my ~ is my own** je suis maître de mon temps; **3** (hour of the day, night) heure *f*; **what ~ is it?, what's the ~?** quelle heure est-il?; **she looked at the ~** elle a regardé l'heure; **the ~ is 11 o'clock** il est 11 heures; **10 am French ~**

10 heures, heure française ; **tomorrow, at the same ~** demain, à la même heure; **this ~ next week** la semaine prochaine à la même heure; **this ~ next year** l'année prochaine à la même date or époque; **this ~ last week/year** il y a exactement huit jours/un an; **by this ~ next week/year** d'ici huit jours/un an; **on ~** à l'heure; **the trains are running on** ou **to ~** les trains sont à l'heure; **the bus/train ~s** les horaires *mpl* or les heures des bus/des trains; **the ~s of trains to Montreal** les heures or les horaires des trains pour Montréal; **it's ~ to go!** c'est l'heure de partir!; **it's ~ for school/bed** c'est l'heure d'aller à l'école/au lit; **it's ~ for breakfast** c'est l'heure du petit déjeuner; **it's ~, your ~ is up** c'est l'heure; **it's ~ we started/left** il est temps de commencer/partir; **to lose ~** [*clock*] retarder; **that clock keeps good ~** cette horloge est toujours à l'heure; **about ~ too!** ce n'est pas trop tôt!; **not before ~!** il était (or il est) grand temps!; **you're just in ~ for lunch/a drink** tu arrives juste à temps pour déjeuner/boire quelque chose; **to arrive in good ~** arriver en avance; **to be in plenty of ~** ou **in good ~ for the train** être en avance pour prendre le train; **I want to have everything ready in ~ for Christmas** je veux que tout soit prêt à temps pour Noël; **to be behind ~** avoir du retard; **twenty minutes ahead of ~** vingt minutes avant l'heure prévue; **six months ahead of ~** six mois avant la date prévue; **4** (era, epoch) époque *f*; **in Victorian/Roman ~s** à l'époque victorienne/romaine; **in Dickens' ~s** du temps de Dickens; **at the ~** à l'époque; **at that ~** à cette époque, en ce temps-là; **~ was** ou **there was a ~ when one could...** à une certaine époque on pouvait...; **to be ahead of** ou **in advance of the ~s** [*person, invention*] être en avance sur son époque; **to be behind the ~s** être en retard sur son époque; **to keep up** ou **move with the ~s** être à la page; **~s are hard** les temps sont durs; **those were difficult ~s** c'étaient des temps difficiles; **in ~s past, in former ~s** autrefois; **in happier ~s** en un temps plus heureux, à une époque plus heureuse; **it's just like old ~s** c'est comme au bon vieux temps; **in ~s of war/peace** en temps de guerre/paix; **peace in our ~** la paix de notre vivant; **at my ~ of life** à mon âge; **I've seen a few tragedies in my ~** j'en ai vu des drames dans ma vie; **she was a beautiful woman in her ~** c'était une très belle femme dans son temps; **it was before my ~** (before my birth) je n'étais pas encore né; (before I came here) je n'étais pas encore ici; **if I had my ~ over again** si je pouvais recommencer ma vie; **to die before one's ~** mourir prématurément; **to be nearing one's ~**† (pregnant woman) approcher de son terme; **5** (moment) moment *m*; **at ~s** par moments; **it's a good/bad ~ to do** c'est le bon/mauvais moment pour faire; **the house was empty at the ~** la maison était vide à ce moment-là; **at the ~ I didn't notice** à ce moment-là je ne l'avais pas remarqué; **at the right ~** au bon moment; **this is no ~ for jokes** ce n'est pas le moment de plaisanter; **at all ~s** à tout moment; **at any ~** à n'importe quel moment; **at any ~ of the day or night** à n'importe quelle heure du jour ou de la nuit; **we're expecting him any ~ now** il doit arriver d'un moment à l'autre; **at no ~ did I agree** à aucun moment je n'ai accepté; **come any ~ you want** viens quand tu veux; **the ~ has come for change/action** l'heure est venue de changer/d'agir; **at ~s like these you need your friends** dans ces moments-là on a besoin de ses amis; **by the ~ I finished the letter the post had gone** le temps de finir ma lettre et le courrier était parti; **by the ~ she had got downstairs he had gone** avant qu'elle n'arrive en bas il était déjà parti; **by this ~ most of them were dead** la plupart d'entre eux étaient déjà morts; **some ~ this week** dans la semaine; **some ~ next month** dans le courant du mois prochain; **for the ~ being** pour l'instant, pour le moment; **from that** ou **this ~ on** à partir de ce moment; **from the ~ (that) I was 15** depuis l'âge de 15 ans; **there are ~s when** il y a des moments où; **when the ~ comes** le moment venu; **in ~s of danger** dans les moments de danger; **in ~s of crisis/high inflation** dans les périodes de crise/forte inflation; **no more than 12 people at any one ~** pas plus de 12 personnes à la fois; **until such ~ as he does the work** jusqu'à ce qu'il fasse le travail; **at the same ~** en même temps; **I can't be in two places at the same ~** je ne peux pas être partout à la fois; **now's our ~ to act!** c'est maintenant qu'il faut agir!; **6** (occasion) fois *f*; **nine ~s out of ten** neuf fois sur dix; **three ~s a month** trois fois par mois; **hundreds of ~s** des centaines de fois; **the first/last/next ~** la première/dernière/prochaine fois; **~ after ~, ~ and ~ again** maintes fois; **each** ou **every ~ that** chaque fois que; **some other ~ perhaps** une autre fois peut-être; **three at a ~** trois à la fois; **there were ~s when** il y avait des fois où; **many's the ~ when I refused** bien des fois j'ai refusé; **she passed her driving test first ~ round/third ~ round** elle a eu son permis du premier coup/à la troisième fois; **do you remember the ~ when...?** tu te rappelles quand...?, tu te rappelles la fois où...?; **from ~ to ~** de temps en temps; **10 dollars a ~** 10 dollars le coup; **for months at a ~** pendant des mois entiers; **(in) between ~s** entre-temps; **7** (experience) **to have a tough** ou **hard ~ doing** avoir du mal à faire; **they gave him a rough** ou **hard** ou **tough ~ of it** ils lui en ont fait voir (de toutes les couleurs○); **he's having a rough** ou **hard** ou **tough ~** il traverse une période difficile; **I'm having a bad ~ at work** en ce moment j'ai des problèmes au travail; **we had a good ~** on s'est bien amusé; **have a good ~!** amusez-vous bien!; **to have an easy ~ (of it)** se la couler douce○; **the good/bad ~s** les moments heureux/difficiles; **she enjoyed her ~ in Canada** elle a beaucoup aimé son séjour au Canada; **during her ~ as ambassador** pendant qu'elle était ambassadeur; **8** Admin, Ind (hourly rate) **to work/be paid ~** travailler/être payé à l'heure; **to be paid ~ and a half** être payé une fois et demie le tarif normal; **on Sundays we get paid double ~** le dimanche on est payé double; **9** (length of period) **cooking ~** temps *m* de cuisson; **flight/journey ~** durée du vol/voyage; **10** Mus mesure *f*; **to beat** ou **mark ~** battre la mesure; **to stay in** ou **keep ~** rester en mesure; **to be in/out of ~** être/ne pas être en mesure; **in waltz/march ~** sur un rythme de valse/marche; **11** Sport temps *m*; **a fast ~** un bon temps; **in record ~** en (un) temps record; **to keep ~** chronométrer; **12** Math, fig **one ~s two is two** une fois deux, deux; **three ~s four** trois fois quatre; **ten ~s longer/stronger** dix fois plus long/plus fort; **eight ~s as much** huit fois autant.

II *vtr* **1** (schedule) prévoir [*attack*] (**for** pour); prévoir, fixer [*holiday, visit*] (**for** pour); fixer [*appointment, meeting*]; **the demonstration is ~d to coincide with the ceremony** l'heure de la manifestation est prévue pour coïncider avec la cérémonie; **we ~ our trips to fit in with school holidays** nous faisons coïncider nos voyages avec les vacances scolaires; **the bomb is ~d to go off at midday** la bombe est réglée pour exploser à midi; **to be well-/badly-timed** être opportun/inopportun; **the announcement was perfectly ~d** la déclaration est tombée à point nommé; **2** (judge) calculer [*blow, stroke, shot*]; **to ~ a remark/joke** choisir le moment pour faire une remarque/plaisanterie; **3** (measure speed, duration) chronométrer [*athlete, cyclist*]; mesurer la durée de [*journey, speech*]; minuter la cuisson de [*egg*]; **to ~ sb over 100 metres** chronométrer qn sur 100 mètres.

III *v refl* **to ~ oneself** se chronométrer.

IDIOMS **from ~ out of mind** depuis la nuit des temps; **there is a ~ and place for everything** il y a un temps pour tout; **there's always a first ~** il y a un début à tout; **there's a first ~ for everything** il y a une première fois pour tout; **he'll tell you in his own good ~** il te le dira quand il en aura envie; **all in good ~** chaque chose en son temps; **only ~ will tell** seul l'avenir nous le dira; **to pass the ~ of day with sb** échanger quelques mots avec qn; **I wouldn't give him the ~ of day** je ne lui dirais même pas bonjour; **to have ~ on one's hands** (for brief period) avoir du temps devant soi; (longer) avoir beaucoup de temps libre; **~ hung heavy on his hands** il trouvait le temps long; **to have a lot of ~ for sb** apprécier beaucoup qn; **I've got a lot of ~ for people who work with the sick** j'admire beaucoup les personnes qui soignent les malades; **I've got no ~ for pessimists/that sort of attitude** je ne supporte pas les pessimistes/ce genre d'attitude; **to do ~**○ (prison) faire de la taule○; **to make ~ with sb**○ US (chat up) draguer○ qn; (have sex with) s'envoyer○ qn; **give me France/Lauren Bacall every ~!** rien ne vaut la France/Lauren Bacall!; **long ~ no see**○**!** ça fait un bail○ (qu'on ne s'est pas vu)!; **~ please!** GB (in pub) on ferme!

time: **~-and-motion expert** ▶ 1692 *n* spécialiste *mf* de l'organisation scientifique du travail; **~-and-motion study** *n* étude *f* scientifique de l'organisation du travail; **~ bomb** *n* lit, fig bombe *f* à retardement; **~ capsule** *n* capsule *f* témoin (*contenant des documents représentatifs d'une époque*); **~-card** *n* carte *f* de pointage; **~ check** *n* Radio annonce *f* de l'heure; **~ clause** *n* Ling proposition *f* temporelle; **~ clock** *n* pendule *f* de pointage; **~ code** *n* Audio, TV, Video code *m* temporel; **~ constant** *n* Electron constante *f* de temps.

time-consuming /ˈtaɪmkənˈsjuːmɪŋ, US -ˈsuː-/ *adj* qui prend du temps (*after n*); **to be ~** prendre du temps.

time: **~ delay** *n* délai *m*; **~ deposit** *n* US Fin dépôt *m* à terme; **~ difference** *n* décalage *m* horaire; **~ dilatation, ~ dilation** *n* Sci dilatation *f* des temps; **~ draft** *n* US Fin effet *m* à terme; **~ exposure** *n* Phot (temps de) pose *f*; **~-frame** *n* (period envisaged) calendrier *m*; (period allocated) délai *m*; **~ fuse** *n* détonateur *m* à retardement; **~-honoured** *adj* consacré par l'usage.

timekeeper /ˈtaɪmkiːpə(r)/ *n* **1** Sport chronométreur *m*; **2** (punctual person) **he's a good ~** il est toujours à l'heure; **3** (watch, clock) **this watch is a good ~** cette montre est toujours à l'heure.

time-keeping /ˈtaɪmkiːpɪŋ/ *n* **1** (punctuality) ponctualité *f*; **2** Sport chronométrage *m*.

time: **~-lag** *n* décalage *m*; **~ lapse photography** *n* prise *f* de vue image par image.

timeless /ˈtaɪmlɪs/ *adj* éternel/-elle.

time-limit /ˈtaɪmlɪmɪt/ *n* **1** (deadline) date *f* limite; **to put a ~ on** fixer une date limite pour [*work, delivery, improvements*]; **to set a ~ for** fixer une date limite pour [*work, completion*]; **within the ~** dans les délais; **2** (maximum duration) durée *f* maximum; **there's a 20 minute ~ on speeches** les discours ne doivent pas dépasser 20 minutes.

timeliness /ˈtaɪmlɪnɪs/ *n* opportunité *f*.

time: **~ loan** *n* Fin emprunt *m* à terme; **~ lock** *n* fermeture *f* commandée par une minuterie.

timely /ˈtaɪmlɪ/ *adj* opportun.

time machine *n* machine *f* à explorer le temps.

time off /ˌtaɪm ˈɒf/ *n* **1** (leave) **ask your**

boss for ~ demande un congé à ton patron; **to take ~** prendre un congé; **to take ~ from work to go to the dentist's** prendre du temps sur son travail pour aller chez le dentiste; **to take ~ from teaching** se mettre en disponibilité; **2** (free time) temps *m* libre; **how much ~ do you get a week?** combien de temps libre avez-vous par semaine?; **what do you do in your ~?** que fais-tu quand tu ne travailles pas?; **3** Jur **to get ~ for good behaviour** avoir sa peine réduite pour bonne conduite.

time: **~out** *n* Comput dépassement *m* du temps imparti, timeout *m*; **~-out** *n* Sport temps *m* mort; (break) temps *m* de repos; **~piece** *n* (watch) montre *f*; (clock) horloge *f*; **~ policy** *n* Insur police *f* à terme.

timer /ˈtaɪmə(r)/ *n* (for cooking) minuteur *m*; (on bomb) minuterie; (for controlling equipment) minuterie *f*; programmateur *m*.

timesaver /ˈtaɪmseɪvə(r)/ *n* **a dishwasher is a real ~** un lave-vaisselle fait vraiment gagner du temps.

time-saving /ˈtaɪmseɪvɪŋ/ *adj* qui fait gagner du temps.

time-scale /ˈtaɪmskeɪl/ *n* période *f* (de temps); **within a 6 month ~** dans une période de 6 mois; **over a 2 year ~** sur une période de 2 ans.

time: **~ series** *n* Stat série *f* chronologique; **~-served** *adj* qualifié; **~-server** *n* péj opportuniste *mf*; **~-serving** *n* péj opportunisme *m*.

timeshare /ˈtaɪmʃeə(r)/ **I** *n* (house) maison *f* en multipropriété; (apartment) appartement *m* en multipropriété.
II *modif* [*apartment, complex, studio*] en multipropriété.

time-sharing /ˈtaɪmʃeərɪŋ/ *n* **1** Comput travail *m* en temps partagé; **2** Tourism multipropriété *f*.

time: **~-sheet** *n* feuille *f* de présence; **~-signal** *n* signal *m* horaire; **~ signature** *n* indication *f* de la mesure; **~-slice** *n* Comput tranche *f* de temps; **~ slot** *n* Telecom créneau *m* temporel.

timespan /ˈtaɪmspæn/ *n* durée *f*; **over a 600 year ~** sur une durée de 600 ans.

time-switch /ˈtaɪmswɪtʃ/ *n* minuterie *f*.

timetable /ˈtaɪmteɪbl/ **I** *n* **1** (agenda, schedule) Sch, Univ, Admin emploi *m* du temps; (for plans, negotiations) calendrier *m*; **to set up a ~ of meetings/negotiations** établir un calendrier des réunions/négociations; **a ~ for monetary union/reform** un calendrier de l'union monétaire/de réformes; **to work to a strict ~** suivre un programme de travail très stricte; **2** Transp horaire *m*; **bus/train ~** horaires des autobus/des trains.
II *vtr* fixer l'heure de [*class, lecture*]; fixer la date de [*meeting, negotiations*]; **~ the meeting for 9 am** fixez la réunion pour 9 heures; **the meeting is ~d for Friday** la réunion est fixée à vendredi; **the bus is ~d to leave at 11.30 am** le bus doit partir à 11 h 30.

time: **~ travel** *n* voyage *m* dans le temps; **~ trial** *n* Sport (in cycling) épreuve de sélection contre la montre; (in athletics) épreuve *f* de sélection; **~ value** *n* valeur *f*.

time warp /ˈtaɪm wɔːp/ *n* (in science fiction) faille *f* spatio-temporelle; **the village seems to be caught in a 1950s ~** le village semble ne pas avoir évolué depuis les années 50.

time-waster /ˈtaɪmweɪstə(r)/ *n* **1** (idle person) fainéant/-e *m/f*, flemmard/-e○ *m/f*; **2** (casual inquirer) **'no ~s'** (in advert) 'pas sérieux s'abstenir'.

time-wasting /ˈtaɪmweɪstɪŋ/ **I** *n* perte *f* de temps.
II *modif* [*practice, tactic*] qui fait perdre du temps.

time: **~ work** *n* travail *m* (rémunéré) à l'heure; **~-worn** *adj* consacré par l'usage; **~ zone** *n* fuseau *m* horaire.

timid /ˈtɪmɪd/ *adj* [*animal*] craintif/-ive; [*person, smile, decision, reform*] timide.

timidity /tɪˈmɪdətɪ/ *n* timidité *f*.

timidly /ˈtɪmɪdlɪ/ *adv* timidement.

timing /ˈtaɪmɪŋ/ *n* **1** (scheduling) **the ~ of the announcement was unfortunate** le moment choisi pour la déclaration était inopportun; **there is speculation about the ~ of the election** la date choisie pour l'élection donne lieu à bien des conjectures; **to get one's ~ right/wrong** bien/mal choisir son moment; **2** Theat débit *m*; **to have a good sense of ~** avoir un bon débit; **3** Aut réglage *m* de l'allumage; **4** Mus sens *m* du rythme.

timorous /ˈtɪmərəs/ *adj* timoré.

Timothy /ˈtɪməθɪ/ *pr n* Timothée.

timothy grass *n* fléole *f* des prés.

timpani /ˈtɪmpənɪ/ ▶1481 *npl* timbales *fpl*.

timpanist /ˈtɪmpənɪst/ ▶1692, 1481 *n* timbalier/-ière *m/f*.

tin /tɪn/ **I** *n* **1** Miner (metal) étain *m*; **2** GB (can) boîte *f* (de conserve); **a ~ of soup** une boîte de soupe; **to eat out of ~s** se nourrir de conserves; **to come out of a ~** être de la conserve; **3** (container) (for biscuits, cake) boîte *f*; (for paint) pot *m*; **a biscuit ~** une boîte à biscuits; **a ~ of biscuits** une boîte de biscuits; **4** Culin (for baking) moule *m*; (for roasting) plat *m* (à rôtir); **5** GB (for donations) tirelire *f* (*pour faire la quête*).
II *modif* [*mug, bath*] en étain.
III *vtr* GB (*p prés etc* **-nn-**) mettre [qch] en boîte or en conserve.
IV tinned *pp adj* GB [*meat, fruit*] en boîte, de conserve.
IDIOMS **to have a ~ ear** ne pas avoir d'oreille.

tin can *n* boîte *f* en fer-blanc.

tincture /ˈtɪŋktʃə(r)/ **I** *n* **1** Pharm teinture *f*; **~ of iodine** teinture d'iode; **2** (tinge) trace *f*; **3** Herald émail *m*.
II *vtr* teinter (**with** de).

tinder /ˈtɪndə(r)/ *n* amadou *m*, petit bois *m*; **to be the ~ for** fig être le ferment de.
IDIOMS **as dry as ~** sec comme une allumette.

tinderbox /ˈtɪndəbɒks/ *n* **1** lit boîte *f* d'amadou; **the barn was a (real) ~** fig la grange était sèche comme une allumette; **2** (tense situation, area) poudrière *f* fig.

tine /taɪn/ *n* (of rake, fork) fourchon *m*; (of antler) andouiller *m*.

tin foil /ˈtɪnfɔɪl/ *n* papier *m* (d')aluminium, papier *m* alu○.

ting /tɪŋ/ **I** *n* tintement *m*.
II *vtr* faire tinter [*bell*].
III *vi* tinter.

ting-a-ling /ˌtɪŋəˈlɪŋ/ *n* onomat ding ding *m*.

tinge /tɪndʒ/ **I** *n* (all contexts) nuance *f*.
II *vtr* teinter (**with** de).

tingle /ˈtɪŋgl/ **I** *n* (physical) picotement *m*; (psychological) frisson *m*.
II *vi* **1** (physically) [*fingers, toes, body, neck*] picoter; **a cold shower leaves you tingling all over** une douche froide fait circuler le sang; **2** (psychologically) frissonner; **to ~ with** vibrer de [*excitement*].

tingling /ˈtɪŋglɪŋ/ *n* picotements *mpl*.

tingly /ˈtɪŋglɪ/ *adj* **my fingers/legs have gone all ~** j'ai des picotements dans les doigts/jambes.

tin: **~ god** *n* péj petit chef *m*; **~ hat** *n* casque *m*.

tinker /ˈtɪŋkə(r)/ **I** *n* **1**† (odd-job man) rétameur *m* (itinérant); GB dial (traveller) mendiant *m* itinérant; **2**○ GB fig (child) coquin/-e *m/f*; **3** (attempt to mend) **to have a ~ with sth** bricoler qch.
II *vi* **1** (also **to ~ about** ou **around**) bricoler; **to ~ with** (try and repair) bricoler [*car, machine*]; (fiddle with) tripoter [*watch, pen, keys*]; **who's been ~ing with the computer?** qui a touché à l'ordinateur?; **2** fig (tamper) **to ~ with** faire des retouches à [*wording, document*]; (illegally) falsifier, truquer.
IDIOMS **I don't give a ~'s curse** ou **damn**○! je m'en fiche○ éperdument! ; **it's not worth a ~'s curse** ou **damn**○! ça ne vaut pas un clou○!

tinkle /ˈtɪŋkl/ **I** *n* **1** (of glass, bell, ice) tintement *m*; (of water) murmure *m*; (of telephone) sonnerie *f*; (of piano) bruit *m* léger; **give us a ~ (on the piano)** hum joue-nous un petit air au piano; **to give sb a ~**○ GB passer un coup de fil à qn○; **2**○ lang enfantin pipi○ *m*.
II *vtr* faire tinter [*glass, bell, ice*].
III *vi* [*glass, bell, ice*] tinter; [*water*] murmurer; [*telephone*] sonner.
IDIOMS **to ~ the ivories**† hum pianoter○, jouer du piano.

tinkling /ˈtɪŋklɪŋ/ *n* (of glass, bell, ice) tintement *m*; (of water) murmure *m*; (of telephone) sonnerie *f*; (of piano) notes *fpl* légères.

tin: **~ mine** *n* mine *f* d'étain; **~ned food** *n* GB ¢ conserves *fpl*.

tinnitus /tɪˈnaɪtəs/ ▶1354 *n* bourdonnements *mpl* d'oreilles, acouphène *m* spec.

tinny /ˈtɪnɪ/ *adj* **1** [*sound, music*] grêle; [*piano*] qui fait un bruit de casserole○; **2** (badly made) [*radio, car*] de camelote.

tin: **~ opener** *n* GB ouvre-boîte *m*; **Tin Pan Alley**○† *n* le monde *m* du music-hall; **~ plate** *n* Miner fer-blanc *m*; **~ plated** *adj* étamé; **~pot**○ *adj* GB péj [*dictatorship, organization*] de pacotille.

tinsel /ˈtɪnsl/ **I** *n* **1** ¢ (decoration) guirlandes *fpl*; **2** (sham brilliance) clinquant *m*.
II *modif* [*material, costume*] clinquant.

Tinseltown○ /ˈtɪnsltaʊn/ *n* Hollywood *m*.

tin: **~smith** *n* étameur *m*; **~ soldier** *n* soldat *m* de plomb.

tint /tɪnt/ **I** *n* **1** (trace) nuance *f*; (pale colour) teinte *f*; **blue with a purple ~** bleu tirant légèrement sur le pourpre or avec une nuance de pourpre; **2** (hair colour) shampooing *m* colorant.
II *vtr* **1** gen teinter [*paint, colour, glass*]; **to ~ sth blue/pink** teinter qch en bleu/rose; **2** Cosmet teinter [*hair*]; **to ~ one's hair brown/blonde** se brunir/blondir les cheveux; **to get one's hair ~ed** se faire faire un shampooing colorant.
III tinted *pp adj* **1** [*paint, colour*] teinté; [*glass, window, spectacles*] fumé; **blue-~ed glass, glass ~ed with blue** verre teinté en bleu; **2** [*hair*] teint.

Tintoretto /ˌtɪntəˈretəʊ/ *pr n* le Tintoret.

tin whistle *n* Mus flageolet *m* (*en métal*).

tiny /ˈtaɪnɪ/ *adj* [*person, object, house*] tout petit; [*budget, improvement*] très faible.

tip /tɪp/ **I** *n* **1** (end) (of stick, branch, shoot, leaf, sword, pen, shoe, nose, tongue, finger, wing) bout *m*, pointe *f*; (of tail, feather, cue) bout *m*; (of ski, spire, island, landmass) pointe *f*; **to stand on the ~s of one's toes** être sur la pointe des pieds; **at the southernmost ~ of Italy** à la pointe la plus au sud de l'Italie; **2** (protective cover on end) (of cane, umbrella) pointe *f*; (of shoe heel) bout *m* (ferré); **3** GB (waste dump) (for rubbish) décharge *f*; (at mine) crassier *m*; **4**○ GB (mess) fouillis *m*; **his office is a ~** son bureau est un vrai fouillis; **5** (gratuity) pourboire *m*; **to give/leave a ~** donner/laisser un pourboire; **a £5 ~** 5 livres de pourboire; **6** (hint) truc○ *m*, conseil *m*; **sewing/safety ~s** conseils pour la couture/de sécurité; **a ~ for doing** ou **on how to do** un conseil pour faire; **I'll give you a ~, let me give you a ~** un conseil d'ami; **take a ~ from me, take my ~** suis mon conseil; **take a ~ from your sister** prends exemple sur ta sœur; **7** (in betting) tuyau○ *m*; **to have a hot ~ for sth** avoir un bon tuyau pour qch○.
II -tipped (*dans composés*) **silver-/pink-/spiky-~ed** à bout argenté/rose/pointu.
III *vtr* (*p prés etc* **-pp-**) **1** (tilt, incline) incliner [*object, bowl, seat*]; **to ~ sth forward/back/to one side** incliner qch vers l'avant/vers l'arrière /sur le côté; **to ~ sth onto its side** mettre qch sur le côté;

to ~ one's chair back se balancer sur sa chaise; **to ~ sb off his** ou **her chair** faire tomber qn de sa chaise; **to ~ one's hat** soulever son chapeau (**to sb** pour saluer qn); **to ~ the scales at 60 kg** peser 60 kilos; **2** (pour, empty) **to ~ sth into/onto/out of sth** verser qch dans/sur/de qch; **to ~ sth upside down** retourner qch; **to ~ sth down the sink** verser qch dans l'évier; **to ~ sth away** jeter qch; **3** fig (push, overbalance) **to ~ sth over 50%** faire passer à qch la barre des 50%; **to ~ the economy into recession** faire basculer l'économie dans la récession; **to ~ sb over the edge** (mentally) faire basculer qn; **to ~ the balance** ou **scales** faire pencher la balance (**in favour of** en faveur de); **to ~ the result the other way** inverser les résultats; **4** (throw away, dump) [*person, lorry*] déverser [*waste*]; **to ~ sth by the roadside/in the countryside** déverser qch le long de la route/dans la campagne; **to ~ sth into a pit** verser qch dans un trou; **5** (forecast, predict) **to ~ sb/sth to win** prédire que qn/qch va gagner; **to ~ sb as the next president** prédire que qn sera le prochain président; **to ~ sb for a job** prédire que qn aura un poste; **to be ~ped as a future champion/for promotion** être donné comme futur champion/candidat à une promotion; **to be ~ped for the top** se voir prédire un avenir brillant; **6** (give money to) donner un pourboire à [*waiter, driver*]; **to ~ sb £5** donner 5 livres de pourboire à qn; **how much should I ~ (the porter)?** combien dois-je laisser de pourboire (au porteur)?; **7** (put something on the end of) recouvrir le bout de [*sword, cane, heel*] (**with** avec); **to ~ sth with red paint** peindre le bout de qch en rouge; **to be ~ped with red paint** avoir le bout peint en rouge; **to ~ an arrow with poison** empoisonner la pointe d'une flèche; **8** Sport (touch, gently push) **to ~ the ball over the net/past the goalkeeper** frapper la balle délicatement pour l'envoyer de l'autre côté du filet/dans le but.

IV *vi* (*p prés etc* **-pp-**) **1** (tilt) [*seat, object*] s'incliner; **to ~ forward/back/onto one side** pencher vers l'avant/vers l'arrière/sur le côté; **2** fig [*balance, scales*] pencher (**in favour of sb, in sb's favour** en faveur de qn).

■ **tip down**○ GB dial: **it** ou **the rain is tipping (it) down** il tombe des cordes○.

■ **tip off**: **~ off [sb], ~ [sb] off** avertir, donner un tuyau○ à [*person, police*]; **to ~ sb off about sth** avertir qn de qch; **to be ~ped off** être averti.

■ **tip out**: **~ out [sth], ~ [sth] out** vider [*drawer, contents*].

■ **tip over**: ¶ **~ over** [*chair, cupboard*] basculer; [*cup, bucket, stack, pile*] se renverser; ¶ **~ over [sth], ~ [sth] over** faire basculer [*chair, cupboard*]; renverser [*bucket, cup, stack, pile*].

■ **tip up**: ¶ **~ up** s'incliner, se pencher; ¶ **~ up [sth], ~ [sth] up** incliner [*cup, bottle*]; pencher [*chair, wardrobe*].

tip cart *n* remorque *f* à benne basculante.

tip-off /ˈtɪpɒf/ *n* dénonciation *f*; **to act on a/receive a ~** agir à la suite d'une/recevoir une dénonciation.

tipper /ˈtɪpə(r)/ *n* **1** Transp = **tipper lorry**; **2** (person leaving a tip) **to be a generous/mean ~** laisser des pourboires généreux/peu généreux.

tipper lorry GB, **tipper truck** *n* camion *m* à benne basculante.

tippet /ˈtɪpɪt/ *n* (of garment) étole *f*; (of judge) collet *m*; (of clergyman) étole *f*.

Tipp-Ex® /ˈtɪpeks/ GB **I** *n* Tipp-Ex® *m*.
II *vtr* (also **~ out, ~ over**) effacer [qch] au Tipp-Ex®.

tipple /ˈtɪpl/ **I** *n* **1**○ (drink) boisson *f* alcoolisée; **to have a quiet ~** siroter tranquillement; **sb's favourite ~** la boisson préférée de qn; **2** US Mining culbuteur *m*.
II○ *vi* siroter.

tippler○† /ˈtɪplə(r)/ *n* **to be a bit of a ~** être un peu porté sur la boisson.

tipsily /ˈtɪpsɪlɪ/ *adv* [*walk*] en chancelant; [*speak, laugh*] en vasouillant○.

tipstaff /ˈtɪpstɑːf, US -stæf/ *n* huissier *m*.

tipster /ˈtɪpstə(r)/ *n* pronostiqueur/-euse *m/f*.

tipsy /ˈtɪpsɪ/ *adj* pompette○.

tipsy cake *n* GB *dessert au biscuit imprégné de sherry et aux fruits confits*.

tiptoe /ˈtɪptəʊ/ **I** *n* **on ~** sur la pointe des pieds.
II *vi* marcher sur la pointe des pieds; **to ~ in/out** entrer/sortir sur la pointe des pieds.

tip-top○ /ˌtɪpˈtɒp/ *adj* excellent; **to be in ~ condition** [*horse*] être en excellente forme; [*athlete*] être en excellente condition physique.

tip-up seat *n* (at cinema, theatre) siège *m* rabattable; (in taxi, on bus, train) strapontin *m*.

tip-up truck *n* camion *m* à benne basculante.

tirade /taɪˈreɪd, US ˈtaɪreɪd/ *n* tirade *f*.

tire /ˈtaɪə(r)/ **I** *n* US pneu *m*.
II *vtr* (make tired) fatiguer.
III *vi* **1** (get tired) se fatiguer; **2** (get bored) **to ~ of** se lasser de [*person, place, activity*]; **as they never ~ of telling us** comme ils ne se lassent pas de nous le dire.

■ **tire out**: **~ [sb] out** épuiser; **to be ~d out** être éreinté; **I'm ~d out!** je n'en peux plus!; **to ~ oneself out** se fatiguer (**doing** à faire).

tired /ˈtaɪəd/ *adj* **1** (weary) [*person, animal*] fatigué; [*face, eyes, legs*] fatigué; [*voice*] las/lasse; **it makes me ~** ça me fatigue; **~ of protesting, she agreed** elle a donné son accord de guerre lasse; **~ and emotional**○ euph hum ivre; **2** (bored) **to be ~ of sth/of doing** en avoir assez de qch/de faire; **to grow** ou **get ~** se lasser (**of** de; **of doing** de faire); **3** (hackneyed) [*cliché, formula, idea, image*] rebattu; **4** (worn out) [*machine*] usé; [*clothes, curtains, sofa*] défraîchi; **5** (wilted) [*lettuce, flower*] fané.

tiredly /ˈtaɪədlɪ/ *adv* [*say, reply, gaze*] d'un air las, avec lassitude.

tiredness /ˈtaɪədnɪs/ *n* fatigue *f*.

tireless /ˈtaɪəlɪs/ *adj* [*advocate, campaigner, worker*] inlassable, infatigable; [*dedication, efforts, quest*] constant.

tirelessly /ˈtaɪəlɪslɪ/ *adv* [*campaign, work*] sans relâche.

tiresome /ˈtaɪəsəm/ *adj* [*person, habit*] agaçant; [*problem, task, duty*] fastidieux/-ieuse; **it's a ~ business!** c'est une affaire fâcheuse!

tiresomely /ˈtaɪəsəmlɪ/ *adv* [*behave*] de façon agaçante.

tiring /ˈtaɪərɪŋ/ *adj* fatigant (**to do** de faire).

tiro = **tyro**.

Tirol *pr n* = **Tyrol**.

tisane /tɪˈzæn/ *n* tisane *f*.

tissue /ˈtɪʃuː/ *n* **1** Anat, Bot tissu *m*; **2** (handkerchief) mouchoir *m* en papier, kleenex® *m*; **3** (also **~ paper**) papier *m* de soie; **4** fig tissu *m*; **a ~ of lies** un tissu de mensonges.

tissue: **~ culture** *n* Biol, Med culture *f* de tissus; **~ sample** *n* prélèvement *m* de tissu.

tit /tɪt/ *n* **1** Zool mésange *f*; **2**◑ (breast) néné◑ *m*; **3**◑ (idiot) enfoiré◑ *m*.
IDIOMS **~ for tat** un prêté pour un rendu; **~ for tat killings** meurtres en représailles (d'autres meurtres).

Titan /ˈtaɪtn/ *n* Mythol, Astron Titan *m* also fig.

titanic /taɪˈtænɪk/ *adj* **1** gen titanesque; **2** Chem de titane.

titanium /tɪˈteɪnɪəm/ *n* titane *m*.

titbit /ˈtɪtbɪt/ *n* GB (of food) gâterie *f*; (of gossip) cancan○ *m*.

titch○ /tɪtʃ/ *n* petit bonhomme○ *m*.

titchy○ /ˈtɪtʃɪ/ *adj* GB minuscule.

titfer†○ /ˈtɪtfə(r)/ *n* GB galurin○ *m*.

tithe /taɪð/ *n* dîme *f*.

tithe barn *n* grange *f* aux dîmes.

titian /ˈtɪʃn/ *adj* littér [*hair*] d'un blond vénitien.

titillate /ˈtɪtɪleɪt/ *vtr* titiller.

titillating /ˈtɪtɪleɪtɪŋ/ *adj* affriolant.

titillation /ˌtɪtɪˈleɪʃn/ *n* titillation *f*.

titivate /ˈtɪtɪveɪt/ *vtr* bichonner; **to ~ oneself** se pomponner.

title /ˈtaɪtl/ **I** *n* **1** (of book, film, play) titre *m*; **a book/film with the ~ 'Rebecca'** un livre/film intitulé 'Rebecca'; **the film appeared under the ~ of 'Rebecca'** le film est sorti sous le titre de 'Rebecca'; **2** Sport titre *m*; **to win/hold the ~** remporter/détenir le titre; **women's/men's ~** Sport titre *m* féminin/masculin; **world ~** titre *m* mondial; **1500m ~** titre *m* sur 1500m; **3** (rank) titre *m*; **a man with a ~** un homme titré; **to have a ~** être titré; **to be given a ~** être anobli; **to take a ~** se voir conférer un titre de noblesse; **4** (name) gen, Jur titre *m*; **it earned him the ~ 'King of Rock'** cela lui a valu le titre 'le roi du rock'.
II titles *npl* Cin générique *m*.
III *modif* [*song, track*] titre.
IV *vtr* intituler [*book, play*].

titled /ˈtaɪtld/ *adj* titré.

title: **~ deed** *n* titre *m* constitutif de propriété; **~ fight** *n* combat *m* pour le titre; **~holder** *n* tenant/-e *m/f* du titre; **~ page** *n* page *f* de titre; **~ role** *n* rôle *m* titre.

titmouse /ˈtɪtmaʊs/ *n* (*pl* **-mice**) mésange *f*.

titrate /ˈtaɪtreɪt, ˈtɪ-/ *vtr* titrer.

titter /ˈtɪtə(r)/ **I** *n* ricanement *m*; **a nervous ~** un petit rire nerveux.
II *vtr* **'oh!' she ~ed** 'oh!' glousса-t-elle.
III *vi* ricaner.

tittle /ˈtɪtl/ *n* **1** Print (sign) signe *m* diacritique; **2** (small amount) iota *m*.
IDIOMS **to change sth not one jot or ~** ne pas changer qch d'un iota.

tittle-tattle /ˈtɪtltætl/ **I** *n* potins *mpl* (**about** sur).
II *vi* jaser (**about** sur).

titular /ˈtɪtjʊlə(r), US -tʃʊ-/ *adj* [*president, head*] nominal; [*professor, status*] titulaire.

tizzy○ /ˈtɪzɪ/ *n* **to be in/get into a ~** être dans/se mettre dans tous ses états; **don't get into a ~** ne t'affole pas.

T-junction /ˈtiːdʒʌŋkʃn/ *n* intersection *f* en T.

TM *n* **1** (*abrév* = **trademark**) marque *f* de fabrique; **2** *abrév* ▶ **transcendental meditation**.

TN *n* US Post *abrév écrite* = **Tennessee**.

TNT *n* (*abrév* = **trinitrotoluene**) TNT *m*.

to /tə, before a vowel tʊ, tuː, emphat. tuː/ ▶ **1150**
I *infinitive particle* **1** (expressing purpose) pour; **to do sth ~ impress one's friends** faire qch pour impressionner ses amis; **2** (expressing wish) **oh ~ be in England!** littér ô être en Angleterre!; **oh ~ be able to stay in bed!** hum ô pouvoir rester au lit!; **3** (linking consecutive acts) **he looked up ~ see...** en levant les yeux, il a vu...; **he woke up (only) ~ find** en se réveillant il a découvert; **4** (after superlatives) à; **the youngest ~ do** le or la plus jeune à faire; **5** (avoiding repetition of verb) **'did you go?'—'no I promised not ~'** 'tu y es allé?'—'non j'avais promis de ne pas le faire'; **'are you staying?'—'I want ~ but...'** 'tu restes?'—'j'aimerais bien mais...'; **6** (following impersonal verb) **it is interesting/difficult etc ~ do sth** il est intéressant/difficile de faire qch; **it's hard ~ understand why he did it** il est difficile de comprendre pourquoi il l'a fait.
II *prep* **1** (in direction of) à [*shops, school etc*]; (with purpose of visiting) chez [*doctor's, dentist's etc*]; **she's gone ~ Mary's** elle est partie chez Mary; **to Paris** à Paris; **to Spain** en Espagne; **~ the country** à la campagne;

~ town en ville; **the road ~ the village** la route qui mène au village; **trains ~ and from** les trains à destination et en provenance de [*place*]; **~ your positions!** à vos positions!; **children ~ the front, adults ~ the back** les enfants devant, les adultes derrière; **2** (facing towards) vers; **turned ~ the wall** tourné vers le mur; **with his back ~ them** en leur tournant le dos; **3** (against) contre; **holding the letter ~ his chest** tenant la lettre contre sa poitrine; **back ~ back** dos à dos; **4** (up to) jusqu'à; **to count ~ 100** compter jusqu'à 100; **~ the end/this day** jusqu'à la fin/ce jour; **from this post ~ that tree it's 100 metres** de ce poteau à cet arbre il y a 100 mètres; **50 ~ 60 people** entre 50 et 60 personnes; **in five ~ ten minutes** d'ici cinq à dix minutes; **~ Manchester, it takes 20 minutes** pour aller à Manchester ça prend 20 minutes; **cheque ~ the value of** chèque d'un montant de; **5** (used as dative) [*give, offer, hand*] à; **give the book ~ Sophie** donne le livre à Sophie; **she 's given the meat ~ the dog/dogs** elle a donné la viande au chien/aux chiens; **'give the letter ~ her'—'~ who?'—'~ her over there!'** 'donne-lui la lettre'—'à qui?'—'à elle là-bas!'; **6** (with respect to) **personal assistant ~ the director** assistant du directeur; **ambassador ~ Japan** ambassadeur au Japon; **7** (in attitude to) **be nice ~ your brother** sois gentil avec ton frère; **8** (in the opinion of) **~ me/my daughter it's just a minor problem** pour moi/ma fille ce n'est qu'un problème mineur; **it looks ~ me like rain** à mon avis il va pleuvoir; **9** (in toasts, dedications) à; **~ Steve/prosperity** à Steve/la prospérité; (on tombstone) **~ our dear son** à notre cher fils; **10** (in accordance with) **is it ~ your taste?** c'est à ton goût?; **to dance ~ the music** danser sur la musique; **11** (in relationships, comparisons) **to win by three goals ~ two** gagner par trois buts à deux; **five ~ the square metre/~ the dollar** cinq par mètre carré/pour un dollar; **perpendicular ~ the ground** perpendiculaire au sol; **next door ~ the school** à côté de l'école; **X is ~ Y as A is ~ B** Math X est à Y ce que A est à B; **12** (showing accuracy) **three weeks ~ the day** trois semaines jour pour jour; **~ scale** à l'échelle; **~ time** à l'heure; **13** (showing reason) **to invite sb ~ dinner** inviter qn à dîner; **~ this end** à cette fin, dans ce but; **14** (belonging to) de; **the key ~ the safe** la clé du coffre ; **a room ~ myself** une chambre pour moi tout seul; **there's no sense ~ it** ça n'a aucun sens; **15** (on to) [*tied*] à; [*pinned*] à [*noticeboard etc*]; sur [*lapel, dress etc*]; **16** (showing reaction) à; **~ his surprise/dismay** à sa grande surprise/consternation; **~ the sound of the drums** au son du tambour; **17** Comm **~ repairing/delivering etc** à réparer/livrer etc.

III /tuː/ *adv* **1**○ (closed) **to push the door ~** fermer la porte; **when the curtains are ~** quand les rideaux sont fermés.

IDIOMS **that's all there is ~ it** (it's easy) c'est aussi simple que ça; (not for further discussion) un point c'est tout; **there's nothing ~ it** ce n'est pas compliqué; **what a ~-do**○! quelle histoire○! ; **they made such a ~-do**○ ils en ont fait toute une histoire○; **what's it ~ you**○? qu'est-ce que ça peut te faire?

toad /təʊd/ *n* **1** (animal) crapaud *m*; **2**○ (term of insult) salaud◑ *m*.

toad: **~-in-the-hole** *n* GB *morceaux de saucisse cuits au four dans de la pâte à crêpes*; **~stool** *n* champignon *m* vénéneux.

toady /ˈtəʊdɪ/ péj **I** *n* flagorneur/-euse *m/f*.
II *vi* péj **to ~ to** flagorner [*minister, patron, boss*] pej.

toadying /ˈtəʊdɪɪŋ/ *n* flagornerie *f*.

to and fro /ˌtuː ən ˈfrəʊ/ *adv* [*swing*] d'avant en arrière; **to go ~** [*person*] ne pas arrêter d'aller et venir.

> **to**
>
> This dictionary contains usage notes on such topics as ***the clock***, ***weight measurement***, ***games and sports*** etc. Many of these use the preposition *to*. For the index to these notes **▶ 1919**.
>
> When *to* is used as a preposition with movement verbs (*go*, *travel* etc.) it is often translated by *à* but remember to use *en* with feminine countries (*en France*) and *au* with masculine countries (*au Portugal*); **▶ 1131**.
>
> Remember when using *à* in French that *à* + *le* always becomes *au* and *à* + *les* always becomes *aux*.
>
> When *to* forms the infinitive of a verb taken alone (by a teacher, for example) it needs no translation:
>
> *to go* = aller
> *to find* = trouver etc.
>
> However, when *to* is used as part of an infinitive giving the meaning *in order to*, it is translated by *pour*:
>
> *he's gone into town to buy a shirt* = il est parti en ville pour acheter une chemise
>
> *to* is also used as part of an infinitive after certain adjectives: *difficult to understand*, *easy to read* etc. Here *to* is usually translated by *à*: *difficile à comprendre*, *facile à lire*:
>
> *it's easy to read* = c'est facile à lire
>
> However, when the infinitive has an object *to* is usually translated by *de*:
>
> *it's easy to lose one's way* = il est facile de perdre son chemin
>
> To check translations, consult the appropriate adjective entry: ***difficult***, ***easy*** etc.
>
> *to* is also used as part of an infinitive after certain verbs: *she told me to wash my hands*, *I'll help him to tidy the room* etc. Here the translation, usually either *à* or *de*, depends on the verb used in French. To find the correct translation, consult the appropriate verb entry: ***tell***, ***help*** etc. For all other uses see the entry ***to***.

toast /təʊst/ **I** *n* **1** (grilled bread) toast *m*, pain *m* grillé; **a piece** ou **slice of ~** un toast, une tranche de pain grillé; **cheese/mushrooms on ~** toast *m* au fromage/aux champignons; **to make (some) ~** faire des toasts; **2** (tribute) toast *m*; **to drink a ~** lever son verre (**to sth** à qch); **to drink a ~ to sb** porter un toast à qn; **to propose a ~** proposer un toast (**to sb** en l'honneur de qn; **to sth** à qch); **'join me in a ~ to the bride and groom'** 'buvons à la santé des nouveaux mariés'; **3** (popular person) **the ~ of** l'idole de [*group*]; **she's the ~ of the town** on ne parle que d'elle.
II *vtr* **1** Culin toaster, faire griller [*bread, roll*]; faire griller [*sandwich*]; faire dorer [*cheese, topping*]; (faire) griller [*sesame seeds, nuts*]; **to ~ one's toes in front of the fire** se chauffer les orteils devant le feu; **2** (propose a toast to) porter un toast à [*person, success, victory*]; (drink a toast to) [*guests*] boire à la santé de [*person*]; lever son verre à [*success, freedom*].
III *v refl* **to ~ oneself in front of the fire** se chauffer devant le feu.
IV toasted *pp adj* [*sandwich, chestnuts, sesame seeds, marshmallows*] grillé.
IDIOMS **to be as warm as ~** [*person*] être bien au chaud; [*bed, room*] être bien chaud.

toaster /ˈtəʊstə(r)/ *n* grille-pain *m inv*.

toastie /ˈtəʊstɪ/ *n* GB sandwich *m* grillé.

toast: **~ing fork** *n* fourchette *f* à griller; **~master** *n* (*personne chargée du protocole dans les banquets officiels*); **~ rack** *n* porte-toasts *m inv*.

tobacco /təˈbækəʊ/ **I** *n* (*pl* **~s**) (product, plant) tabac *m*.
II *modif* [*company, farm, leaf, plantation, smoke*] de tabac; [*industry*] du tabac; **~ advertising** publicité *f* pour le tabac; **~ tin** GB, **~ can** US boîte *f* à tabac; **~ plant** tabac *m*.

tobacco brown **▶ 1104** *n, adj* tabac (*m*) *inv*.

tobacconist /təˈbækənɪst/ **▶ 1692** *n* GB (person) buraliste *mf*; **~'s (shop)** bureau *m* de tabac.

Tobago /təˈbeɪgəʊ/ **▶ 1381** *pr n* Tobago *f*.

toboggan /təˈbɒgən/ **I** *n* luge *f*, toboggan *m*.
II *vi* **to ~ down a hill** descendre une pente en luge.

tobogganning /təˈbɒgənɪŋ/ **▶ 1282** *n* luge *f*; **to go ~** faire de la luge.

toboggan: **~ race** *n* course *f* de luge; **~ run** *n* piste *f* de luge.

toby jug /ˈtəʊbɪ dʒʌg/ *n* chope *f* (*en forme de bonhomme à tricorne*).

toccata /təˈkɑːtə/ *n* toccata *f*.

tocsin /ˈtɒksɪn/ *n* lit, fig tocsin *m*.

tod○ /tɒd/ *n* GB: IDIOMS **(all) on one's ~** tout seul.

today /təˈdeɪ/ **▶ 1150**, **1883** **I** *n* **1** lit aujourd'hui *m*; **what's ~'s date?** on est le combien aujourd'hui○?, quel jour sommes-nous aujourd'hui?; **~ is Monday** (aujourd'hui) nous sommes lundi; **~ is my birthday** c'est mon anniversaire aujourd'hui; **~'s newspaper** le journal d'aujourd'hui; **2** fig aujourd'hui *m*; **the computers/teenagers of ~** les ordinateurs/adolescents d'aujourd'hui.
II *adv* **1** lit aujourd'hui; **he's arriving ~** il arrive aujourd'hui; **~ week, a week from ~** dans une semaine aujourd'hui, aujourd'hui en huit; **a month ago ~** il y a un mois aujourd'hui; **30 years ago ~** voici 30 ans aujourd'hui; **it's the fifth of April ~** aujourd'hui nous sommes le cinq avril; **all day ~** toute la journée d'aujourd'hui; **earlier/later ~** plus tôt/tard dans la journée; **2** fig (nowadays) de nos jours.
IDIOMS **he's here ~, gone tomorrow** il va et il vient; **these fashions are here ~ gone tomorrow** ces modes sont éphémères.

toddle /ˈtɒdl/ *vi* **1** (walk) [*child*] faire ses premiers pas; **to ~ to the door** aller d'un pas chancelant vers la porte; **to ~ off** partir d'un pas chancelant; **2**○ (go) **to ~ into town** faire un tour en ville; **to ~ over to Bob's house** aller chez Bob; **to ~ down to the shop** aller au magasin.
■ **toddle about, toddle around** [*child*] trottiner.
■ **toddle off**○ s'en aller, partir; **I've got to ~ off now** il faut que j'y aille○.

toddler /ˈtɒdlə(r)/ *n* bébé *m* (*qui fait ses premiers pas*).

toddy /ˈtɒdɪ/ *n* grog *m*; **hot ~** grog *m* au whisky.

toe /təʊ/ **▶ 1037** *n* **1** Anat (human) orteil *m*, doigt *m* de pied; (animal) orteil *m*; **big/little ~** gros/petit orteil; **to stand** ou **tread** ou **step on sb's ~s** lit marcher sur les pieds de qn; **to tread on sb's ~s** fig marcher sur or piétiner les plates-bandes de qn○; **the ~ of Italy** Geog la Calabre; **2** (of sock, shoe) bout *m*.
IDIOMS **to keep sb on their ~s** forcer qn à être vigilant; **to ~ the line** marcher droit; **to ~ the party/management line** suivre exactement la ligne du parti/de la direction; **from top to ~** de la tête aux pieds; **from the top of one's head to the tip of one's ~s** de la racine des cheveux à la pointe des pieds.

TOE *n* (*abrév* = **ton oil equivalent**) TEP *f*.

toe: **~ cap** *n* bout *m* renforcé or rapporté (*de chaussure*); **~ clip** *n* cale-pied *m inv*.

toehold /ˈtəʊhəʊld/ *n* **1** (in climbing) prise *f*; **2** fig (access) **to get** ou **gain a ~ in** s'introduire dans [*market, organization*].

toe: **~nail** *n* ongle *m* des orteils or de pied; **~ piece** *n* butée *f*; **~rag**○ *n* GB injur minable○ *mf* offensive.

toff○† /tɒf/ *n* GB aristo○† *m*; **they're ~s** ce sont des gens de la haute○.

toffee /ˈtɒfɪ, US ˈtɔ:fɪ/ *n* (mixture, sweet) caramel *m* (au beurre).

IDIOMS **he can't sing/write for ~**○ GB il est incapable de chanter/d'écrire.

toffee: **~ apple** *n* pomme *f* d'amour (*caramélisée*); **~-nosed**○ *adj* GB péj snobinard○ péj.

tofu /ˈtəʊfu:/ *n* tofu *m*.

tog /tɒg/ **I** *n* (also **~ rating**) GB Tex ≈ indice *m* d'isolation du garnissage (*d'une couette*).

II○ **togs** *npl* GB fringues○ *fpl*, vêtements *mpl*; **swimming ~s** maillot *m* de bain.

■ **tog out**○ GB (*p prés etc* **-gg-**): **~ [sb] out** habiller; **they were (all) ~ged out in tennis gear** ils étaient tous en tenue de tennis; **to ~ oneself out** se saper○.

toga /ˈtəʊgə/ *n* toge *f*.

together /təˈgeðə(r)/

■ **Note** *together* in its main adverbial senses is almost always translated by *ensemble*.
– *together* frequently occurs as the second element in certain verb combinations (*get together*, *pull together*, *put together*, *tie together etc*). For translations for these, see the appropriate verb entry (***get***, ***pull***, ***tie*** etc).
– For examples and further uses, see the entry below.

I *adv* **1** (as a pair or group) ensemble; **they're always ~** ils sont toujours ensemble; **we were in school ~** nous étions à l'école ensemble; **let's go there ~** allons-y ensemble; **they're not married but they're living ~** ils ne sont pas mariés mais ils vivent ensemble; **to get back ~ again** se remettre ensemble; **to be close ~** [*objects, trees, plants etc*] être rapprochés; **his eyes are too close ~** ses yeux sont trop rapprochés; **she's cleverer than all the rest of them put ~** elle est plus intelligente que tous les autres réunis; **acting ~, they could have prevented the invasion** en agissant conjointement, ils auraient pu empêcher l'invasion; **she kept the family ~ during the war** c'est grâce à elle que la famille s'en est sortie pendant la guerre; **we're all in this ~** nous sommes tous impliqués dans cette affaire; **they belong ~** (objects) ils vont ensemble; (people) ils sont faits l'un pour l'autre; **these two documents, taken ~, provide crucial evidence** à eux deux, ces documents fournissent des preuves décisives; **these findings, taken ~, indicate that** ces conclusions, considérées dans leur ensemble, indiquent que; **2** (so as to be joined) ensemble; **he nailed the two planks ~** il a cloué les deux planches ensemble; **his argument doesn't hold ~ very well** son argument ne tient pas vraiment debout; **3** (in harmony) **those colours don't go ~** ces couleurs ne vont pas ensemble; **the talks brought the two sides closer ~** les négociations ont rapproché les deux parties; **the soprano and the orchestra weren't quite ~** la soprano et l'orchestre n'étaient pas à l'unisson; **4** (at the same time) à la fois, en même temps; **they were all talking ~** ils parlaient tous à la fois or tous en même temps; **all my troubles seem to come ~** tous mes ennuis semblent arriver en même temps; **all ~ now!** tous ensemble maintenant!; **5** (without interruption) d'affilée; **for four days/three weeks ~** pendant quatre jours/trois semaines d'affilée.

II○ *adj* équilibré; **he's a very ~ guy** c'est un mec○ très équilibré, c'est un mec○ qui est bien dans sa peau○.

III together with *prep phr* (as well as) ainsi que, avec; (in the company of) avec; **he put his wallet, ~ with his passport, in his pocket** il a mis son portefeuille, ainsi que son passeport, dans sa poche; **I went there ~ with George** j'y suis allé avec George; **taken ~ with the rest of the evidence, this proves that he is guilty** si on ajoute ça aux autres preuves, cela prouve qu'il est coupable.

IDIOMS **to get one's act ~, to get it ~**○ s'organiser.

togetherness /təˈgeðənɪs/ *n* (in team, friendship) camaraderie *f*; (in family, couple) intimité *f*.

toggle /ˈtɒgl/ *n* **1** (fastening) bouton *m* de duffel-coat; **2** Naut (pin) cabillot *m*.

toggle: **~ joint** *n* genouillère *f*, levier *m* articulé; **~ switch** *n* Comput, Elec interrupteur *m* à bascule.

Togo /ˈtəʊgəʊ/ **▶ 1131** *pr n* Togo *m*.

toil /tɔɪl/ **I** *n* labeur *m*; **years of ~** des années de labeur.

II toils *npl* fig littér rets *mpl* liter; **to be caught in the ~ of the law** être pris dans les rets des hommes de loi.

III *vi* **1** (also **toil away**) (work) peiner (**at** sur; **to do** pour faire); **2** (struggle)[*person, horse*] **to ~ up the hill** monter péniblement la côte.

toilet /ˈtɔɪlɪt/ **I** *n* **1** (lavatory) toilettes *fpl*, cabinets *mpl*; **to go to the ~** aller aux toilettes ou aux cabinets; **to sit on the ~** s'asseoir sur le siège des cabinets; **2** (room) toilettes *fpl*, cabinets *mpl*; **in the ~** aux toilettes or cabinets; **public ~(s)** toilettes publiques; **men's/women's ~(s)** toilettes *fpl* pour hommes/pour dames; **3**‡ (washing and dressing) toilette *f*.

II *modif* [*bowl, cistern*] de la toilette.

toilet: **~ bag** *n* trousse *f* de toilette; **~ paper, ~ tissue** *n* papier *m* toilette, papier *m* hygiénique.

toiletries /ˈtɔɪlɪtrɪz/ *npl* articles *mpl* de toilette.

toilet roll *n* **1** (roll) rouleau *m* de papier toilette or hygiénique; **2** (tissue) papier *m* toilette, papier *m* hygiénique.

toilet: **~ seat** *n* lunette *f* de WC; **~ soap** *n* savon *m* de toilette.

toilette‡ /twɑ:ˈlet/ *n* toilette *f*.

toilet-train /ˈtɔɪlɪttreɪn/ *vtr* **to ~ a child** apprendre à un enfant à être propre; **he's not yet ~ed** il n'est pas encore propre.

toilet: **~ training** *n* apprentissage *m* de la propreté; **~ water** *n* eau *f* de toilette.

toing and froing /ˌtu:ɪŋ ən ˈfrəʊɪŋ/ *n* **all this ~** toutes ces allées et venues.

toke○ /təʊk/ **I** *n* bouffée *f* (d'une cigarette de marijuana).

II *vi* **to ~ on** tirer une bouffée de [*joint*].

token /ˈtəʊkən/ **I** *n* **1** (for machine, phone) jeton *m*; **2** (product) point *m*; **'collect 12 Luxa ~s'**; 'collectionnez 12 points Luxa'; **book/record ~** chèque-cadeau *m* pour livre/pour disque; **3** (symbol) témoignage *m*; **a ~ of** un signe de [*esteem, gratitude, affection*]; **as a ~ of our esteem** en signe de notre estime; **but by the same ~**... mais de la même façon...; **and by the same ~**... et donc...; **4** Ling occurrence *f*.

II *adj* gén péj [*army, payment, punishment, strike*] symbolique; **to make a ~ effort/gesture** faire un effort/un geste pour la forme; **she's the ~ woman/Left winger** c'est la femme/gauchiste de service.

tokenism /ˈtəʊkənɪzəm/ *n* péj **policy of ~** politique *f* de coopération symbolique; **he has been accused of ~** (performer) on l'a accusé de faire cela pour la forme.

token money *n* Fin monnaie *f* fiduciaire.

Tokyo /ˈtəʊkjəʊ/ **▶ 1818** *pr n* Tokyo.

told /təʊld/ *prét, pp* **▶ tell**.

Toledo /təˈleɪdəʊ, təˈli:dəʊ/ **▶ 1818** *pr n* Tolède.

tolerable /ˈtɒlərəbl/ *adj* **1** (bearable) tolérable; **2** (adequate) acceptable.

tolerably /ˈtɒlərəblɪ/ *adv* [*well*] plutôt, assez; [*certain, confident, content, comfortable*] assez, relativement.

tolerance /ˈtɒlərəns/ *n* **1** (broad-mindedness) tolérance *f* (**of, for** de; **towards** à l'égard de); (understanding, patience) indulgence *f* (**towards** pour, envers); **to show ~** faire preuve de tolérance or d'indulgence; **2** (resistance) tolérance *f* (**of** de); **~ to** tolérance à [*alcohol, cold*]; **3** Med (of body) tolérance *f* (**to** à); **drug ~** accoutumance *f* à une drogue; **4** Phys, Tech (endurance) résistance *f*; **5** Math, Stat (variation) (marge *f* de) tolérance *f*.

tolerant /ˈtɒlərənt/ *adj* **1** (in attitude) tolérant (**of** vis à vis de; **towards** à l'égard de); **a racially ~ society** une société sans préjugés racistes; **2** (resilient) [*plant, substance*] résistant (**of** à).

tolerantly /ˈtɒlərəntlɪ/ *adv* [*accept, treat*] avec tolérance; [*smile*] avec indulgence.

tolerate /ˈtɒləreɪt/ *vtr* **1** (permit) tolérer [*attitude, difference, person, action*]; **2** (put up with) supporter [*temperature, isolation, trait, treatment*]); **to ~ doing** supporter de faire; **3** Med tolérer, supporter [*drug, treatment*]; **4** Hort (withstand) résister à [*frost etc*].

toleration /ˌtɒləˈreɪʃn/ *n* tolérance *f*.

toll /təʊl/ **I** *n* **1** (number) **the ~ of** le nombre de [*victims, incidents, cases*]; **death ~** nombre *m* de victimes (**from** de); **accident ~** nombre *m* d'accidentés; **2** (levy) (on road, bridge) gen, Transp péage *m*; **to pay a ~** acquitter un péage; **to collect ~s** percevoir le péage; **3** (of bell) gen son *m*; (for funeral) glas *m*; **4** US Telecom taxe *f* d'appel.

II *vtr* sonner [*bell*].

III *vi* sonner; **the bell ~ed for the dead** le glas sonnait pour les morts.

IDIOMS **to take a heavy ~** (on lives) faire beaucoup de victimes; (on industry, environment) causer beaucoup de dégâts; **to take its** ou **their ~** [*earthquake, disease, economic factors*] faire des ravages; **the trip/the experience took its ~ on them** le voyage/l'expérience les a rudement mis à l'épreuve.

toll: **~booth** *n* poste *m* de péage; **~ bridge** *n* pont *m* à péage; **~ call** *n* US communication *f* interurbaine.

toll-free /ˌtəʊlˈfri:/ US **I** *adj* [*call, number*] gratuit; [*journey, crossing*] gratuit.

II toll free *adv* [*phone*] gratuitement.

toll: **~ gate** *n* barrière *f* de péage; **~house** *n* péage *m*; **~ keeper** *n* Hist péager/-ère *m/f*; **~ road** GB, **~way** US *n* route *f* à péage.

tom /tɒm/ *n* **1** Zool matou *m*; **2**○ US injur (black person) bon nègre○ *m* offensive.

Tom /tɒm/ *pr n*: IDIOMS **every ~, Dick and Harry**○ n'importe qui; **to go out with every ~, Dick and Harry**○ frayer avec Pierre, Paul et Jacques○.

tomahawk /ˈtɒməhɔ:k/ *n* tomahawk *m*, hache *f* de guerre.

tomato /təˈmɑ:təʊ, US təˈmeɪtəʊ/ **I** *n* (*pl* **~es**) **1** (fruit) tomate *f*; **2** (also **~ plant**) tomate *f*.

II *modif* [*puree, skins*] de tomate; [*juice, salad*] de tomates; [*sandwich, soup*] à la tomate; **~ ketchup** ketchup *m*; **~ sauce** sauce *f* tomate.

tomb /tu:m/ *n* tombeau *m*.

tombac /ˈtɒmbæk/ *n* tombac *m*, laiton *m*.

tombola /tɒmˈbəʊlə/ *n* tombola *f*.

tomboy /ˈtɒmbɔɪ/ *n* garçon *m* manqué; **to be something of a ~** être un peu garçon manqué.

tomboyish /ˈtɒmbɔɪɪʃ/ *adj* [*behaviour*] garçonnier/-ière; [*clothes*] de garçon manqué; [*haircut*] à la garçonne; **to be ~** être garçon manqué.

tombstone /ˈtu:mstəʊn/ *n* pierre *f* tombale.

tomcat /ˈtɒmkæt/ **I** *n* **1** Zool matou *m*; **2**○ US (promiscuous man) cavaleur○ *m*.

II○ *vi* US (*p prés etc* **-tt-**) courir les filles.

tome /təʊm/ *n* gros volume *m*.

tomfool /tɒmˈfu:l/ *adj* [*idea, plan*] absurde.

tomfoolery /tɒmˈfu:lərɪ/ *n* pitreries *fpl*, âneries *fpl*.

Tommy○† /'tɒmɪ/ *n* GB simple soldat *m* (de l'armée britannique).

Tommy gun○† *n* mitraillette *f*.

tommyrot○† /'tɒmɪrɒt/ *n* balivernes *fpl*, inepties *fpl*.

tomorrow /tə'mɒrəʊ/ ▶1150, 1883 **I** *n* **1** lit demain *m*; **~'s Monday** demain c'est lundi; **~'s newspaper** le journal de demain; **what's ~'s date?** on sera le combien demain○?, quel jour serons-nous demain?; **~ will be a difficult day** la journée de demain sera difficile; **who knows what ~ may bring?** de quoi demain sera-t-il fait?; **I'll do it by ~** je le ferai d'ici demain; **2** fig **~'s world/citizens** le monde/les citoyens de demain.

II *adv* **1** lit demain; **see you ~!** à demain!; **~ week, a week ~** demain en huit, dans une semaine demain; **he came a month ago ~** il est venu cela fera un mois demain; **all day ~** toute la journée demain; **early/late ~** tôt/tard dans la journée de demain; **as from ~** à partir de demain, dès demain; **first thing ~** dès demain; **2** fig demain.

IDIOMS **~ is another day** demain il fera jour; **never put off till ~ what can be done today** Prov il ne faut jamais remettre au lendemain ce qu'on peut faire le jour même Prov; **to live like there was no ~** vivre comme si demain on devait mourir.

tomorrow: **~ afternoon** *n*, *adv* demain après-midi; **~ evening** *n*, *adv* demain soir; **~ morning** *n*, *adv* demain matin.

Tom Thumb /ˌtɒm 'θʌm/ *n* Tom Pouce.

tomtit /'tɒmtɪt/ *n* GB mésange *f*.

tom-tom /'tɒmtɒm/ *n* tam-tam *m*.

ton /tʌn/ ▶1883, 1068 *n* **1** (in weight) GB (also **gross** ou **long ~**) ≈ *1016 kg*; US (also **net** ou **short ~**) ≈ *907 kg*; **metric ~** tonne *f*, 1000 kg; **a three-~ truck** un camion de trois tonnes; **to weigh a ~** ou **be a ~ weight** GB fig peser une tonne; **2** Naut (in volume) tonneau *m*; **freight/register ~** tonneau *m* d'affrètement/de jauge; **displacement ~** tonne *f* de déplacement; **3**○ (a lot) **a ~ of** plein de○, un tas de○ [*books, papers etc*]; **~s of** des tas de○, plein de○ [*food, paper, bands*]; **we've ~s left** il nous en reste plein○; **her new car is ~s better than the other one** sa nouvelle voiture est mille fois mieux que l'autre.

IDIOMS **they'll come down on us like a ~ of bricks** ils vont nous tomber dessus○; **to do a ~**○ GB faire du cent soixante à l'heure○.

tonal /'təʊnl/ *adj* tonal.

tonality /tə'næləti/ *n* tonalité *f*.

tonally /'təʊnəlɪ/ *adv* tonalement.

tondo /'tɒndəʊ/ *n* (*pl* **-di**) (painting) tondo *m*; (carving) médaillon *m*.

tone /təʊn/ **I** *n* **1** Mus, gen (quality of sound) timbre *m*; (of radio, TV) son *m*; **2** (character of voice) ton *m*; **his ~ of voice** son ton; **in a defiant ~** d'un ton provocant; **don't speak to me in that ~ (of voice)** ne me parle pas sur ce ton; **in angry/serious ~s** avec colère/avec sérieux; **3** (character) (of letter, speech, meeting) ton *m*; **to set the ~** donner le ton à (**for** à); **to lower the ~ of** rabaisser le niveau de [*conversation*]; dégrader l'image de [*area*]; **4** (colour) ton *m*, couleur *f*; **5** Telecom tonalité *f*; **6** Physiol tonus *m*; **7** Mus (interval) ton *m*; **8** Ling ton *m*.

II *vtr* **1** Physiol (also **~ up**) donner du tonus à, tonifier [*body, muscle, thigh*]; **2** Cosmet tonifier [*skin*].

III *vi* (also **~ in**) (blend) [*colours*] s'harmoniser (**with** avec).

■ **tone down**: **~ [sth] down, ~ down [sth]** lit atténuer [*colours*]; fig atténuer [*criticism, remark*] adoucir le ton de [*letter, statement*]; adoucir [*policy, attitude*].

tone: **~ arm** *n* Audio bras *m* de lecture; **~ colour** GB, **~ color** US *n* Mus timbre *m*; **~ control (button)** *n* Audio bouton *m* de réglage de la tonalité.

toned-down /ˌtəʊnd'daʊn/ *adj* lit, fig atténué.

tone-deaf /ˌtəʊn'def/ *adj* Mus **to be ~** ne pas avoir l'oreille musicale.

tone language *n* langue *f* à tons.

toneless /'təʊnlɪs/ *adj* atone.

tonelessly /'təʊnlɪslɪ/ *adv* [*say*] d'une voix atone.

tone poem *n* Mus poème *m* symphonique.

toner /'təʊnə(r)/ *n* **1** (for photocopier) encre *m*; **2** Cosmet lotion *f* tonique.

Tonga /'tɒŋgə/ ▶1131, 1381 *pr n* Tonga *fpl*; **the ~ islands** les îles Tonga.

Tongan /'tɒŋgən/ ▶1486, 1402 **I** *n* **1** (native) Tonguien/-ienne *m/f*; **2** (language) tongan *m*.

II *adj* tonguien/-ienne.

tongs /tɒŋz/ *npl* (for coal) pincettes *fpl*; (in laboratory) pince *f*; (for hair) fer *m* à friser; (for salad) pinces *fpl* à salade; (for sugar) pince *f* (à sucre); **a pair of (coal) ~** des pincettes.

IDIOMS **to go at it hammer and ~** se disputer violemment.

tongue /tʌŋ/ **I** *n* **1** Anat, fig langue *f*; **to poke** ou **stick out one's ~ at sb** tirer la langue à qn; **his ~ was hanging out** il tirait la langue; **to click one's ~** faire claquer sa langue; **to lose/find one's ~** avaler/retrouver sa langue; **the tip of the ~** le bout de la langue; **2** (language) langue *f*; **mother ~** langue *f* maternelle; **native ~** langue *f* d'origine; **to speak in ~s** Relig parler en langues; **to speak in a foreign ~** parler une langue étrangère; **3** Culin langue *f*; **ox ~** langue *f* de bœuf; **4** (flap) (on shoe) languette *f*; **5** (of flame, land) langue *f*.

II *vtr* Mus détacher [*note, passage*].

IDIOMS **to bite one's ~** se mordre la langue; **has the cat got your ~**○**?** tu as avalé ta langue?; **to get the rough side** ou **edge of sb's ~** subir les paroles désobligeantes de qn; **to give sb a ~-lashing** faire des remarques cinglantes à qn; **I have his name on the tip of my ~** j'ai son nom sur le bout de la langue; **to trip off the ~** [*name, lie*] venir tout seul; **to loosen sb's ~** délier la langue de qn; **I can't get my ~ round it** je n'arrive pas à le prononcer; **a slip of the ~** un lapsus; **hold your ~**○**!** tiens ta langue!; **watch your ~!** surveille tes paroles!; **keep a civil ~ in your head** sois poli.

tongue-and-groove /ˌtʌŋən'gruːv/ *adj* à rainure et languette.

tongue-in-cheek /ˌtʌŋɪn'tʃiːk/ *adj*, *adv* au deuxième degré.

tongue: **~-tied** *adj* muet/-ette; **~-twister** *n*: *phrase amusante pour exercice de diction*; **~-twisting** *adj* difficile à articuler.

tonic /'tɒnɪk/ **I** *n* **1** (drink) Schweppes® *m*; **a gin and ~** un gin tonic; **2** Med, fig remontant *m*, tonique *m*; **he's a real ~** il est plein d'entrain; **to be a ~ for sb** [*news, praise*] remonter le moral de qn; **3** Mus tonique *f*; **4** Ling (syllabe *f*) tonique *f*.

II *adj* tonique; **~ wine** vin *m* tonique.

tonicity /tə'nɪsətɪ/ *n* tonicité *f*.

tonic: **~ sol-fa** *n* Mus *méthode de solfège chanté*; **~ water** *n* eau *f* tonique, tonic *m*, Schweppes® *m*.

tonight /tə'naɪt/ **I** *n* **~'s concert/events/programme** le concert/les événements/le programme de ce soir.

II (this evening) *adv* ce soir; (after bedtime) cette nuit; **you'll sleep well ~!** tu vas bien dormir cette nuit!

toning /'təʊnɪŋ/ **I** *adj* [*colours, furniture, clothes*] harmonisé.

II *modif* [*gel, cream*] tonifiant.

toning-down /ˌtəʊnɪŋ'daʊn/ *n* atténuation *f*.

tonnage /'tʌnɪdʒ/ *n* **1** (ship's capacity) tonnage *m* (**of** de); **gross (register) ~** jauge *f* brute; **register ~** tonnage *m* de jauge; **2** (amount of shipping) tonnage *m*; **3** (total weight) volume *m*.

tonnage dues *npl* droits *mpl* de tonnage.

tonne /tʌn/ ▶1883 *n* tonne *f*.

tonneau /'tɒnəʊ/ *n* (*pl* **~s** ou **~x**) (also **~cover**) capote *f*, bâche *f*.

tonner /'tʌnə(r)/ *n* (*dans composés*) **1** Naut **a one-~** un yacht d'un tonneau; **a 1,000-~** un navire de 1000 tonneaux; **2** Transp **a 40-~** un camion de 40 tonnes.

tonometer /tə'nɒmɪtə(r)/ *n* **1** Mus diapason *m* chromatique; **2** Med tonomètre *m*.

tonsil /'tɒnsl/ *n* amygdale *f*; **to have one's ~s out** se faire opérer des amygdales.

tonsillectomy /ˌtɒnsɪ'lektəmɪ/ *n* amygdalectomie *f*.

tonsillitis /ˌtɒnsɪ'laɪtɪs/ ▶1354 *n* amygdalite *f*; **to have ~** avoir une amygdalite.

tonsure /'tɒnsʃə(r)/ *n* tonsure *f*.

tonsured /'tɒnʃəd/ *adj* tonsuré.

tontine /tɒn'tiːn/ *n* tontine *f*.

Tony /'təʊnɪ/ *n* US Tony *m* (*palmarès de théâtre décerné à Broadway*).

too /tuː, tʊ, tə/ *adv*

■ **Note** When *too* means *also* it is generally translated by *aussi*: *me too* = moi aussi; *can I have some too?* = est-ce que je peux en avoir aussi?

– When *too* means *to an excessive degree* (*too high, too dangerous*) it is translated by *trop*: trop haut, trop dangereux.

– For examples of the above and further usages, see the entry below.

---

1 (also, as well) aussi; **you ~ could be a winner!** vous aussi, vous pourriez réussir!; **'I love you'—'I love you ~'** 'je t'aime'—'moi aussi, je t'aime'; **have you been to India ~?** (like me) est-ce que toi aussi tu es allé en Inde?; (as well as other countries) est-ce que tu es allé en Inde aussi?; **he speaks French, German ~** il parle français et allemand aussi; **the town has changed, so ~ have the inhabitants** la ville a changé, les habitants aussi; **'have a nice evening'—'you ~!'** 'bonne soirée'—'toi aussi!'; **she's kind but she's strict ~** elle est gentille mais elle est stricte; **2** (reinforcing an opinion) **you should talk to someone—and soon ~** il faudrait que tu en parles à quelqu'un et sans tarder; **Marie cooked the meal—and very tasty it is ~!** Marie a préparé le repas—c'est vraiment très bon!; **'she was very annoyed and quite right ~!'** 'elle était vraiment agacée et il y avait de quoi!'; **they sacked him and quite right ~!** ils l'ont viré et ils ont bien fait!; **3** (expressing indignation, annoyance) **'they're here'—'about time ~!'** 'ils sont là'—'il est bien temps!'; **'I'm sorry'—'I should think so ~!'** 'je m'excuse'—'j'espère bien!'; **it was such a smart jacket, expensive ~** c'était une si belle veste, et chère en plus; **...and in front of your mother ~!** ...et devant ta mère en plus or par-dessus le marché!; **4** (excessively) trop; **the coat is ~ big for him** le manteau est trop grand pour lui; **just ~ big/nosy** bien trop grand/curieux; **it's ~ early to leave** il est trop tôt pour partir; **it's ~ early for them to leave** il est trop tôt pour qu'ils partent (*subj*); **the tray was ~ heavy for me to carry** le plateau était trop lourd pour moi; **it's ~ easy (for them) to criticize** c'est trop facile (pour eux) de critiquer; **I was ~ shocked to speak** j'étais trop choqué pour parler; **it's ~ hot a day for walking** il fait trop chaud pour marcher aujourd'hui; **it's ~ fast a game for me** c'est un jeu trop rapide pour moi; **~ many/~ few people** trop de/trop peu de gens; **~ much traffic** trop de circulation; **I ate ~ much** j'ai trop mangé; **it's ~ much of a strain** c'est trop stressant; **she's ~ much of a feminist/a diplomat to do** elle est trop féministe/diplomate pour faire; **he was in ~ much of a hurry to talk** il était trop pressé pour parler; **~ silly for words** d'une bêtise sans nom; **it was ~ little ~ late** c'était trop peu trop tard; **the**

measures were ~ little ~ late les mesures étaient insuffisantes et avaient été prises trop tard; **5** (emphatic: very) trop; **you're ~ kind!** vous êtes trop aimable!; **they'll be only ~ pleased to help** ils seront trop contents or ils seront ravis de rendre service; **he's only ~ ready to criticize** il ne rate pas une occasion de critiquer; **she hasn't been ~ well recently** elle n'est pas vraiment en forme ces temps-ci; **that's ~ bad!** (a pity) c'est tellement dommage!; (tough) tant pis!; **'so you're annoyed'—'~ right (I am)!'** 'alors tu es fâché'—'et comment!'; ▶ **all, only**; **6** (in negatives) trop; **he's not ~ mad about jazz** il n'aime pas trop le jazz; **he didn't do ~ bad a job** il ne s'est pas trop mal débrouillé; **it wasn't ~ bad** [*film, trip*] ce n'était pas trop mal; **he wasn't ~ bad** (in health) il n'allait pas trop mal; (in appearance) il n'était pas trop mal; (in his reactions) il n'était pas trop désagréable; **we're not ~ thrilled** on ne peut pas dire que nous soyons ravis; **I'm not ~ sure about that** je n'en suis pas si sûr; **it's not ~ far removed from blackmail** c'est presque du chantage; **'they've arrived'—'none ~ soon!'** 'ils sont arrivés'—'ce n'est pas trop tôt'; **7**○ (contradicting: so) **'you don't know how to swim'—'I do ~!'** 'tu ne sais pas nager'—'bien sûr que si je sais!'; **'he didn't pinch you'—'he did ~!'** 'il ne t'a pas pincé'—'si d'abord○!'

took /tʊk/ *prét* ▶ **take**.

tool /tu:l/ **I** *n* **1** gen, Comput outil *m*; **a set of ~s** un outillage, un jeu d'outils; **garden ~s** outils de jardinage; **2** (aid) outil *m*, instrument *m*; **an essential ~ in the classroom** un outil essentiel pour la classe; **management ~s** instruments *mpl* de gestion; **3** péj (puppet) instrument *m*; **to be a mere ~ in the hands of** être un simple instrument au service or entre les mains de; **4**◑ (penis) engin◑ *m*, pénis *m*.
II *vtr* travailler, repousser [*leather*].
III *vi*○† (also **~ along**) rouler tranquillement.
IV tooled *pp adj* [*leather, metal*] travaillé, repoussé.
IDIOMS **the ~s of the trade** les outils du métier; **to down ~s** GB (go on strike) se mettre en grève; (take break from work) arrêter de travailler.
■ **tool up**: ¶ **~ up** s'équiper (**to do** pour faire); ¶ **~ up [sth], ~ [sth] up** équiper [*plant, factory*].

tool: **~ bag** *n* trousse *f* à outils; **~ bar** *n* Comput barre *f* d'outils; **~box** *n* boîte *f* à outils; **~ case** *n* petite boîte *f* à outils; **~ chest** *n* caisse *f* à outils; **~house** *n* US = **tool shed**.

tooling /'tu:lɪŋ/ *n* ¢ (on leather) repoussage *m*; (on book cover) dorure *f*.

tool: **~ kit** *n* trousse *f* à outils; **~maker** *n* outilleur *m*; **~ making** *n* outillage; **~room** *n* atelier *m* d'outillage; **~ shed** *n* cabane *f* à outils.

toot /tu:t/ **I** *n* **1** (sound) (of car-horn) coup *m* de klaxon®; (of train whistle) coup *m* de sifflet; **2** onomat **~! ~!** tut! tut!; **3**○ US (snort of cocaine) sniff○ *m*, prise *f* de cocaïne; **4**○ US (drinking spree) beuverie *f*; **to go on a ~**○ se prendre une cuite○.
II *vtr* **to ~ one's horn** donner un coup de klaxon® (**at** à).
III *vi* [*car horn*] klaxonner; [*train*] donner un coup de sifflet.

tooth /tu:θ/ **I** *n* (*pl* **teeth**) (of person, animal, comb, zip, saw) dent *f*; **set of teeth** (one's own) denture *f*, dentition *f*; (false) dentier *m*; **to bare** ou **show one's teeth** lit, fig montrer les dents; **to mutter between one's teeth** marmonner entre ses dents; **to flash one's teeth at sb** sourier à qn de toutes ses dents; **to cut one's teeth** lit faire or percer ses dents; **to cut one's teeth on** fig se faire les dents sur.
II -toothed (*dans composés*) **fine-/wide-~ed comb** peigne *m* fin/à dents larges.
IDIOMS **to be a bit long in the ~** ○ n'être plus tout jeune; **to be fed up to the back teeth** en avoir marre○ or ras le bol○ (**of, with** de); **to do sth in the teeth of** faire qch malgré or en dépit de; **to have teeth** avoir du pouvoir; **to give sth teeth** donner plus de poids à qch; **to get one's teeth into sth** s'investir (à fond) dans qch; **it's a job she can get her teeth into** c'est un travail dans lequel elle peut s'investir; **to lie through one's teeth** mentir effrontément or comme un arracheur de dents○; **to set sb's teeth on edge** taper sur les nerfs○ de qn, agacer qn; **to throw sth in sb's teeth** reprocher qch à qn.

toothache /'tu:θeɪk/ *n* mal *m* de dents; (severe) rage *f* de dents; **to have (a) ~** avoir mal aux dents.

tooth: **~brush** *n* brosse *f* à dents; **~ decay** *n* carie *f* dentaire; **~ fairy** *n* petite souris *f*; **~ glass** *n* verre *m* à dents.

toothless /'tu:θlɪs/ *adj* **1** [*grin, person*] édenté; **2** fig (ineffectual) [*law, organisation*] inefficace.

tooth: **~ mug** *n* = **tooth glass**; **~paste** *n* dentifrice *m*; **~pick** *n* cure-dents *m*; **~powder** *n* poudre *f* dentifrice.

toothsome /'tu:θsəm/ *adj* hum [*dish, food*] savoureux/-euse, succulent; [*person*] beau/belle à croquer○.

toothy /'tu:θɪ/ *adj* **to give a ~ grin** sourire de toutes ses dents.

tootle○ /'tu:tl/ *vi* **1** GB (go) faire un petit tour; **I'll just ~ into town/down to the shops** je vais faire un petit tour en ville/jusqu'aux magasins; **2** (on musical instrument) gen jouer un petit air (**on** sur).

toots○ /tʊts/ *n* ma belle.

tootsy○, **tootsie**○ /'tʊtsɪ/ *n* **1** lang enfantin (toe) doigt *m* de pied; (foot) peton○ *m*, pied *m*; **2** = **toots**.

top /tɒp/ **I** *n* **1** (highest or furthest part) (of page, ladder, stairs, wall) haut *m*; (of list) tête *f*; (of mountain, hill) sommet *m*; (of garden, field) (autre) bout *m*; **eight lines from the ~** à la huitième ligne à partir du haut de la page; **at the ~ of** en haut de [*page, stairs, street, scale*]; au sommet de [*hill*]; en tête de [*list*]; **at the ~ of the building** au dernier étage de l'immeuble; **at the ~ of the table** à la place d'honneur; **to be at the ~ of one's list** fig venir en tête de sa liste; **to be at the ~ of the agenda** fig être une priorité; **2** fig (highest echelon, position) **to aim for the ~** viser haut; **to be at the ~ of one's profession** être tout en haut de l'échelle fig; **life can be tough at the ~** il n'est pas toujours facile d'être en haut de l'échelle; **to get to** ou **make it to the ~** réussir; **to be ~ of the class** être le premier/la première de la classe; **to be ~ of the bill** Theat être la tête d'affiche; **3** (surface) (of table, water) surface *f*; (of box, cake) dessus *m*; **to float to the ~** flotter à la surface; **4** (upper part) partie *f* supérieure; **the ~ of the façade/of the building** la partie supérieure de la façade/du bâtiment; **the ~ of the milk** la crème du lait; **5** (cap, lid) (of pen) capuchon *m*; (of bottle) gen bouchon *m*; (with serrated edge) capsule *f*; (of paint-tin, saucepan) couvercle *m*; ; **6** Fashn haut *m*; **a sleeveless summer ~** un haut sans manches pour l'été; **7** Aut (also **~ gear**) (fourth) quatrième (vitesse) *f*; (fifth) cinquième (vitesse) *f*; **to be in ~** être en quatrième or cinquième; **8** Bot (of vegetable) fane *f*; **carrot ~s** fanes de carottes; **9** (toy) toupie *f*.
II *adj* **1** (highest) [*step, storey*] dernier/-ière; [*bunk*] de haut; [*button, shelf*] du haut; [*division*] Sport premier/-ière; [*layer*] supérieur; [*concern, priority*] fig majeur; **in the ~ left-hand corner** en haut à gauche; **the ~ corridor** le couloir du dernier étage; **the ~ notes** Mus les notes les plus hautes; **the ~ tax band** la catégorie des plus imposables; **to pay the ~ price for sth** [*buyer*] acheter qch au prix fort; **'we pay the ~ prices'** 'nous achetons aux meilleurs prix'; **to be in the ~ class at primary school** être en cours moyen 2ème année; **to get ~ marks** Sch avoir dix sur dix ou vingt sur vingt; fig **~ marks to the company for its initiative** vingt sur vingt à l'entreprise pour son initiative; **2** (furthest away) [*field, house*] du bout; **3** (leading) [*adviser, authority, agency*] plus grand; [*job*] élevé; **one of their ~ chefs/soloists** l'un de leurs plus grands chefs/solistes; **it's one of the ~ jobs** c'est un des postes les plus élevés; **~ people** les gens importants; (bureaucrats) les hauts fonctionnaires; **to be in the ~ three** être dans les trois premiers; **4** (best) [*wine, choice, buy, restaurant*] meilleur; **5** (upper) [*lip*] supérieur; **the ~ half of the body** le haut du corps; **on her ~ half, she wore...** comme haut elle avait mis...; **6** (maximum) [*speed*] maximum; **we'll have to work at ~ speed** nous allons devoir travailler le plus vite possible.
III on top of *prep phr* **1** lit sur [*cupboard, fridge, layer*]; **2** fig (close to) **the car was suddenly right on ~ of me**○ soudain la voiture était sur moi; **to live on ~ of each other** vivre les uns sur les autres; **3** fig (in addition to) en plus de [*salary, workload*]; **on ~ of everything else I have to do** en plus de tout ce que j'ai à faire; **4** fig (in control of) **to be on ~ of a situation** contrôler la situation; **to get on ~ of inflation** maîtriser l'inflation; **you can never really feel on ~ of this job** dans ce métier on se sent toujours un peu dépassé; **things are getting on ~ of her** (she's depressed) elle est déprimée; (she can't cope) elle ne s'en sort plus.
IV *vtr* (*p prés etc* **-pp-**) **1** (head) être en tête de [*charts, polls*]; **2** (exceed) dépasser [*sum, figure, contribution*]; **3** (cap) renchérir sur [*story, anecdote*]; **4** (finish off) gen compléter [*building, creation*] (**with** par); Culin recouvrir [*cake, dish, layer*] (**with** de); **cake ~ped with frosting** gâteau recouvert d'un glaçage; **each cake was ~ped with a cherry** chaque petit gâteau avait une cerise dessus; **a mosque ~ped with three domes** une mosquée surmontée de trois coupoles; **5**○ (kill) dégommer○, tuer [*person*].
V○ *v refl* (*p prés etc* **-pp-**) **to ~ oneself** se suicider.
IDIOMS **on ~ of all this, to ~ it all** (after misfortune) par-dessus le marché○; **from ~ to bottom** de fond en comble; **not to have very much up ~**○ n'avoir rien dans le ciboulot○; **to be over the ~** ou **OTT**○ (in behaviour, reaction) être exagéré; **he's really over the ~**○! il exagère! il pousse○!; **to be the ~s**○† être formidable; **to be/stay on ~** avoir/garder le dessus; **to be ~ dog** être le chef; **to come out on ~** (win) l'emporter; (survive, triumph) s'en sortir; **to feel on ~ of the world** être aux anges; Mil **to go over the ~** monter à l'assaut; **to say things off the ~ of one's head** (without thinking) dire n'importe quoi; **I'd say £5,000, but that's just off the ~ of my head** (without checking) moi, je dirais £5 000, mais c'est approximatif; **to shout at the ~ of one's voice** crier à tue-tête; **to sleep like a ~** dormir comme un loir.
■ **top out**: **~ out [sth]** mettre la dernière pierre à [*building*].
■ **top off**: **~ off [sth], ~ [sth] off** compléter [*meal, weekend, outing, creation*] (**with** par); **shall we ~ off our evening with a glass of champagne?** si on complétait la soirée par un verre de champagne?
■ **top up** ¶ **to ~ up with petrol** faire le plein; ¶ **~ up [sth], ~ [sth] up** remplir (à nouveau) [*tank, glass*]; ajouter de l'eau à [*battery*]; **may I ~ you up?** je vous en remets?

top-and-tail /ˌtɒpən'teɪl/ *vtr* équeuter [*currants, gooseberries*]; effiler [*beans*].

topaz /'təʊpæz/ *n, adj* topaze (*f*) *inv*.

top: **~ banana**○ *n* US gros bonnet *m*; **~-boot** *n* botte *f*; **~ brass**○ *n* (+ *v pl*) huiles○ *fpl*; **~ class** *adj* [*race, athletics,* *professional*] de premier ordre; **~coat** *n* pardessus *m*; **~ copy** *n* original *m*.

top-down /ˈtɒpdaʊn/ *adj* **1** Comput [*design*] de haut en bas; **2** fig [*management*] directif/-ive.

top-drawer○† /ˌtɒpˈdrɔː(r)/ *adj* [*family*] très bourgeois; **to be ~** faire partie de la haute.

top: **~-dress** *vtr* fumer [qch] en surface [*soil*]; **~dressing** *n* (substance) engrais *m* de surface; (process) fumure *f* en surface.

toper○† /ˈtəʊpə(r)/ *n* soiffard/-e○† *m/f*.

top: **~-flight** *adj* de premier ordre; **~ hat** *n* haut-de-forme *m*.

top-heavy /ˌtɒpˈhevɪ/ *adj* **1** [*structure, object*] lourd du haut, déséquilibré; **2** fig [*firm, bureaucracy*] mal équilibré (*ayant trop de cadres par rapport aux employés subalternes*).

top-hole○† /ˈtɒphəʊl/ *adj* GB formidable.

topiary /ˈtəʊpɪərɪ, US -ɪerɪ/ **I** *n* topiaire *f*.
II *modif* [*bush, conifer*] taillé; [*garden*] d'arbustes taillés.

topic /ˈtɒpɪk/ *n* **1** (subject) (of conversation, discussion, conference) sujet *m*; (of essay, research, project) thème *m*; **2** Sch (project) projet *m*.

topical /ˈtɒpɪkl/ *adj* d'actualité; **she made a ~ allusion to the problem** elle a fait référence à l'actualité en parlant du problème; **of ~ interest** d'actualité.

topicality /ˌtɒpɪˈkælətɪ/ *n* actualité *f*.

topic sentence *n* US phrase *f* d'introduction.

topknot /ˈtɒpnɒt/ *n* chignon *m* (haut sur la tête).

topless /ˈtɒplɪs/ *adj* [*model*] aux seins nus; [*bar*] où les serveuses ont les seins nus; **'~ bathing forbidden'** 'le topless est interdit'; **~ swimsuit** monokini *m*.

top: **~-level** *adj* [*talks, negotiations*] au plus haut niveau; **~-loader** *n* machine *f* à laver à charger par le dessus; **~ management** *n* (haute) direction *f*; **~ mast** *n* mât *m* de hune; **~most** *adj* [*branch, fruit*] le/la plus haut/-e; **~-notch** *adj* [*business, executive*] de premier ordre; **~-of-the-range** *adj* [*model*] haut de gamme *inv*.

topographer /təˈpɒgrəfə(r)/ *n* topographe *mf*.

topographic(al) /ˌtɒpəˈgræfɪk(l)/ *adj* topographique.

topography /təˈpɒgrəfɪ/ *n* topographie *f*.

topper○ /ˈtɒpə(r)/ *n* **1** (hat) chapeau *m* haut-de-forme; **2** (success) **chart ~** premier *m* au hit-parade; **3** US (joke etc) **that's a ~!** c'est le comble!

topping /ˈtɒpɪŋ/ **I** *n* (of jam, cream) nappage *m*; **with a ~ of bread crumbs** recouvert d'une couche de chapelure.
II○ †GB *adj* chouette○.

topple /ˈtɒpl/ **I** *vtr* renverser, faire tomber [*object*]; détruire [*building*]; fig renverser [*leader, government*].
II *vi* (sway) [*vase, pile of books*] vaciller; (fall) (also **~ over**) [*vase*] basculer, se renverser; [*pile of books*] s'effondrer; [*person*] basculer, tomber; fig [*government, regime*] tomber; **he ~d over the edge** il a basculé dans le vide; **to ~ over the edge of** tomber de [*cliff, table*].

top: **~-ranking** *adj* important; **~sail** *n* hunier *m*; **~ secret** *adj* ultrasecret; **~ security** *adj* [*prison, wing, building*] de haute sécurité; **~side** *n* Culin gîte *m* à la noix; **~soil** *n* couche *f* arable; **~ spin** *n* lift *m*.

topsy-turvy○ /ˌtɒpsɪˈtɜːvɪ/ *adj, adv* sens dessus dessous; **our plans have been thrown ~** nos projets ont été chamboulés○; **it's a ~ world** on vit vraiment dans un drôle de monde.

top ten /ˌtɒpˈten/ *n* les dix premiers au hit-parade.

top-up○ /ˈtɒpʌp/ *n* **who's ready for a ~?** qui en veut encore?

top-up loan /ˈtɒpʌp ləʊn/ *n* prêt *m* complémentaire.

toque /təʊk/ *n* toque *f*.

tor /tɔː(r)/ *n* tor *m*.

torch /tɔːtʃ/ **I** *n* (burning) flambeau *m*, torche *f*; GB (flashlight) torche *f* or lampe *f* (électrique), lampe *f* de poche; **she shone the ~ into the room** elle a éclairé la pièce de sa torche; **to be turned into a human ~** être transformé en torche vivante.
II *vtr* mettre le feu à [*building*].
IDIOMS **to carry a ~ for sb** avoir un faible pour qn; **to carry the ~ for democracy/freedom** porter le flambeau de la démocratie/la liberté; **to put sth to the ~** incendier [*castle, city*].

torchbearer /ˈtɔːtʃbeərə(r)/ *n* porteur/-euse *m/f* de flambeau.

torchlight /ˈtɔːtʃlaɪt/ **I** *n* **by ~** (burning torches) à la lueur des flambeaux; GB (electric) à la lueur d'une lampe électrique or de poche.
II *modif* (also **torchlit**) [*vigil, walk*] aux flambeaux; **~ procession** retraite *f* aux flambeaux.

torch song *n* US chanson *f* d'amour triste.

tore /tɔː(r)/ *prét* ▶ **tear**[1] II, III.

toreador /ˈtɒrɪədɔː(r), US ˈtɔːr-/ *n* toréador *m*.

torero /tɒˈreərəʊ/ *n* torero *m*.

torment **I** /ˈtɔːment/ *n* tourment *m* liter, supplice *m*; **to suffer ~s of jealousy/remorse** endurer les tourments de la jalousie/du remords; **to be in ~** être au supplice; **to suffer ~(s)** souffrir le martyre.
II /tɔːˈment/ *vtr* (cause suffering to) tourmenter; (tease, annoy) tourmenter, harceler; **to be ~ed by jealousy/remorse** être rongé par la jalousie/les remords.
III /tɔːˈment/ *v refl* **to ~ oneself** se tourmenter.

tormentor /tɔːˈmentə(r)/ *n* persécuteur/-trice *m/f*, bourreau *m*.

torn /tɔːn/ **I** *pp* ▶ **tear**[1] **II, III**.
II *adj* (all contexts) déchiré.

tornado /tɔːˈneɪdəʊ/ *n* (*pl* **~es** ou **~s**) **1** Meteorol tornade *f*; **2** (also **Tornado**) Mil Aviat avion *m* de combat Tornado.

Toronto /təˈrɒntəʊ/ **▶ 1818** *pr n* Toronto.

torpedo /tɔːˈpiːdəʊ/ **I** *n* **1** Mil torpille *f*; **2** Zool (poisson *m*) torpille *f*; **3**○ US (gunman) tueur *m* à gages; **4** US Culin gros sandwich *m*.
II *modif* [*attack*] à la torpille.
III *vtr* lit, fig torpiller.

torpedo: **~ boat** *n* torpilleur *m*, vedette *f* lance-torpilles; **~ tube** *n* tube *m* lance-torpilles *m inv*.

torpid /ˈtɔːpɪd/ *adj* sout torpide fml.

torpor /ˈtɔːpə(r)/ *n* torpeur *f*.

torque /tɔːk/ **I** *n* **1** Phys moment *m* de torsion; **2** Aut couple *m* moteur; **3** Hist torque *m*.
II *vtr* Tech serrer.

torque: **~ converter** *n* Aut, Mech convertisseur *m* de couple; **~ wrench** *n* clé *f* dynamométrique.

torrent /ˈtɒrənt, US ˈtɔːr-/ *n* **1** (of water, rain) torrent *m*; **the rain is falling in ~s** il pleut à torrents; **2** fig flot *m*.

torrential /təˈrenʃl/ *adj* torrentiel/-ielle.

torrid /ˈtɒrɪd, US ˈtɔːr-/ *adj* torride.

torsion /ˈtɔːʃn/ *n* torsion *f*.

torsion: **~ balance** *n* balance *f* de torsion; **~ bar** *n* barre *f* de torsion; **~ test** *n* essai *m* de torsion.

torso /ˈtɔːsəʊ/ *n* (*pl* **~s**) torse *m*.

tort /tɔːt/ *n* préjudice *m*.

tortilla /tɔːˈtiːjə/ *n* tortilla *f*, crêpe *f* mexicaine.

tortoise /ˈtɔːtəs/ *n* tortue *f*.

tortoiseshell /ˈtɔːtəsʃel/ **I** *n* **1** (shell) écaille *f*; **2** (butterfly) vanesse *f*; **3** (cat) chatte *f* écaille de tortue.
II *modif* [*clip, comb*] en écaille; **glasses with ~ frames** des lunettes à monture d'écaille.

tortuous /ˈtɔːtʃʊəs/ *adj* **1** [*path, road*] tortueux/-euse, sinueux/-euse; **2** fig [*argument, explanation*] tortueux/-euse; [*essay*] alambiqué.

tortuously /ˈtɔːtʃʊəslɪ/ *adv* tortueusement.

torture /ˈtɔːtʃə(r)/ **I** *n* lit torture *f*; fig supplice *m*; **under ~** sous la torture; **the long wait was absolute ~!** cette longue attente a été un véritable supplice!
II *vtr* lit torturer; fig tourmenter; **to be ~d by** être travaillé par [*guilt, jealousy*].
III tortured *pp adj* fig [*mind, existence, country*] tourmenté.

torture chamber *n* chambre *f* de torture.

torturer /ˈtɔːtʃərə(r)/ *n* lit tortionnaire *m*; fig bourreau *m*.

Tory /ˈtɔːrɪ/ **I** *n* GB Tory *mf*, conservateur/-trice *m/f*.
II *modif* [*government, party, MP*] tory *inv*; [*attempts, attack*] des Tories.

Toryism /ˈtɔːrɪzəm/ *n* GB torysme *m*.

tosh○ /tɒʃ/ GB **I** *n* fadaises *fpl*.
II *excl* allons donc!

toss /tɒs/ **I** *n* (*pl* **~es**) **1** (turn) **to give sth a ~** tourner qch [*salad*]; faire sauter qch [*pancake*]; **2** (of coin) **to win/lose the ~** remporter/perdre le tirage au sort (à pile ou face); **to decide sth on the ~ of a coin** décider qch à pile ou face; **3** (throw) jet *m*; **4** (jerky movement) **a ~ of the head** un mouvement brusque de la tête; **5**○ (fall) **to take a ~**○ faire une chute (de cheval).
II *vtr* **1** (throw) lancer [*ball, stick*]; **to ~ sth into the air** lancer qch en l'air; **to ~ sb sth** lancer qch à qn; **to ~ sth towards/into/over sth** lancer qch en direction de/dans/par-dessus qch; **2**○ (chuck) **~ me the newspaper** balance-moi○ le journal; **3** (flip) faire sauter [*pancake*]; lancer [*dice*]; **to ~ a coin** tirer à pile ou face; **I'll ~ you for the last piece of cake** tirons le dernier morceau de gâteau à pile ou face; **4** Culin (stir) tourner [*salad*]; faire sauter [*vegetables, meat*] **(in** dans); **~ed in olive oil** sauté dans l'huile d'olive; **5** (throw back) [*animal*] secouer [*head, mane*]; **to ~ one's head** [*person*] rejeter la tête en arrière; **to ~ one's hair back** rejeter les cheveux en arrière; **6** (unseat) [*horse*] désarçonner [*rider*]; **7** (move violently) [*wind*] agiter [*branches, leaves*]; [*waves*] ballotter [*boat*]; **to be ~ed about** ou **to and fro** [*person, boat*] être ballotté; **a storm-~ed sea** littér une mer agitée par la tempête.
III *vi* **1** (turn restlessly) [*person*] se retourner; **I ~ed and turned all night** je me suis tourné et retourné toute la nuit; **2** (flip a coin) [*referee*] tirer à pile ou face; **to ~ for first turn/service** tirer le premier tour/service à pile ou face.
IDIOMS **I'm not prepared to argue the ~** je n'ai pas envie d'en discuter; **I don't** ou **couldn't give a ~**○ je m'en fiche pas mal○; **he couldn't give a ~**○ **if you're tired/about his kids**○ il se fiche pas mal○ que tu sois fatigué/de ses gosses○; **who gives a ~**○**?** on n'en a rien à fiche○!

■ **toss about, toss around** ¶ [*boat, person*] être ballotté; ¶ **~ [sth] around** lit [*people*] se faire des passes avec [*ball*]; fig retourner [*ideas*]; **to get ~ed around** (in vehicle) se faire brinquebaler.

■ **toss away**: **~ [sth] away, ~ away [sth]** jeter [*rubbish*]; fig rater [*opportunity*].

■ **toss back**: **~ [sth] back, ~ back [sth]** renvoyer [*ball, object*].

■ **toss off**○: ¶ **~ off**● se branler●; ¶ **~ [sth] off, ~ off [sth]** expédier [*article, letter*]; lamper○ [*drink*].

■ **toss out**: ¶ **~ [sth] out, ~ out [sth]** jeter [*newspaper, empty bottles*]; ¶ **~ sb out** éjecter qn **(from** de).

■ **toss up** (flip a coin) tirer à pile ou face; **to ~ up**○ **whether to do sth** se tâter○ pour faire qch; **to ~ up**○ **when/where**... se tâter○ pour savoir quand/où...

tosser◑ /ˈtɒsə(r)/ *n* connard◑ *m*.

toss-up○ /ˈtɒsʌp/ *n* **1** (flip of a coin) **let's have a ~ to decide** décidons à pile ou face; **2** (two-way choice) **it's/it was a ~ between a pizza and a sandwich** il faut/il a fallu choisir entre une pizza et un sandwich; **3** (even chance) **who'll win?—it's a ~!** qui va gagner?—ça sera pile ou face!; **it was a ~ who would be chosen** les chances étaient partagées pour la sélection.

tot /tɒt/ *n* **1**○ (toddler) tout/-e petit/-e enfant *m/f*; **2** GB (of whisky, rum) petite dose *f*, doigt *m*.

■ **tot up** GB: ¶ **~ up** [*person*] additionner; **~ up to** [*bill, expenses*] s'élever à; ¶ **~ up [sth], ~ [sth] up** faire le total de [qch].

total /ˈtəʊtl/ **I** *n* total *m*; **£200 in ~** £200 au total; **a ~ of £200** un total de £200; **it comes to a ~ of £200** cela fait £200 en tout.

II *adj* **1** (added together) [*number, cost, amount, loss, profit*] total; **2** (complete) [*effect*] global; [*attention, disaster, eclipse, failure, war*] total; [*ignorance*] complet/-ète; **the ~ debts come to £3,000** le montant total des dettes s'élève à 3 000 livres sterling.

III *vtr* (*p prés etc* **-ll-** GB, **-l-** US) **1** (add up) additionner [*amounts, figures*]; **2** (reach) [*debts, costs, sales, income*] se monter à [*sum*]; **their votes ~led two million** ils ont eu deux millions de voix; **3**○ US (destroy) bousiller○ [*car*].

total allergy syndrome *n* Med absence *f* totale des défenses immunitaires.

totalitarian /ˌtəʊtælɪˈteərɪən/ *n, adj* totalitaire (*mf*).

totalitarianism /ˌtəʊtælɪˈteərɪənɪzəm/ *n* totalitarisme *m*.

totality /təʊˈtælətɪ/ *n* totalité *f*.

totalizator /ˈtəʊtəlaɪzeɪtə(r), US -lɪz-/ *n* Turf totalisateur *m* de paris.

totalize /ˈtəʊtəlaɪz/ *vtr* totaliser.

totalizer *n* = **totalizator**.

totally /ˈtəʊtəlɪ/ *adv* [*blind, deaf, paralysed, at ease*] complètement; [*stupid, unacceptable, opposed, convinced*] totalement; [*agree, change, new, different*] entièrement.

total recall *n* (Psych) ecmnésie *f*.

tote○ /təʊt/ **I** *n* Turf = **totalizator**.

II *vtr* trimballer○ [*bag, gun*]; **gun-toting hooligans** des voyous armés.

tote: **~ bag** *n* US sac *m* fourre-tout; **~ board** *n* Turf tableau *m* d'affichage.

totem /ˈtəʊtəm/ *n* **1** (pole) totem *m*; **2** (symbol) symbole *m*.

totemic /təʊˈtemɪk/ *adj* totémique.

totem pole *n* totem *m*; mât *m* totémique.

totter /ˈtɒtə(r)/ *vi* [*person*] chanceler, vaciller; (drunkenly) tituber; [*baby*] trébucher; [*pile of books, building*] chanceler, vaciller; fig [*regime, government*] chanceler; **to ~ in/out** entrer/sortir en vacillant; **a country ~ing on the brink of civil war** un pays qui bascule dans la guerre civile.

tottering /ˈtɒtərɪŋ/ *adj* [*step, movement*] mal assuré; [*person*] chancelant; [*pile of books, building*] chancelant; fig [*regime, government*] chancelant.

toucan /ˈtuːkæn, -kən, US *also* tʊˈkɑːn/ *n* toucan *m*.

touch /tʌtʃ/ **I** *n* **1** (physical contact) contact *m* (physique); **the ~ of her hand** le contact de sa main; **at the slightest ~** (of hand) au plus petit contact; (of button) à la simple pression; **to long for/dread sb's ~** désirer/appréhender le contact physique de qn; **I felt a ~ on my shoulder** j'ai senti qu'on me touchait l'épaule; **he managed to get a ~ on the ball** (in football) il a réussi à toucher le ballon; **2** (sense) toucher *m*; **a highly-developed sense of ~** un sens très développé du toucher; **soft to the ~** doux au toucher; **by ~** au simple toucher; **3** (style, skill) main *f*; **the ~ of a master** la main d'un maître; **to lose one's ~** perdre la main; **a fine ~ at the net** (in tennis) un toucher délicat au filet; **he handles the children with a firm ~** il s'y prend avec les enfants avec fermeté; **the Spielberg ~** le style Spielberg; **4** (element) gen touche *f*; (underlying tone) note *f*; (tiny amount) pointe *f*; **this room needs the feminine ~** cette pièce aurait besoin d'une note féminine; **he lacks the human ~** il manque de chaleur humaine; **with a ~ of sadness in her voice** avec une note de tristesse dans sa voix; **a ~ of colour/of sarcasm/of garlic** une pointe de couleur/de raillerie/d'ail; **to add** ou **put the finishing ~es to sth** mettre la touche finale à qch; **a clever ~** un trait spirituel; **her gift was a nice ~** son cadeau était un geste délicat; **there's a ~ of class/of genius about her** elle a quelque chose d'élégant/de génial; **he's got a ~ of flu** il est un peu grippé; **there's a ~ of frost in the air** il y a du gel dans l'air○; **5** (little) **a ~** un petit peu; **a ~ colder/heavier** un petit peu plus froid/plus lourd; **just a ~ (more)** un tout petit peu (plus); **6** (communication) contact *m*; **to get/stay in ~ with** se mettre/rester en contact avec; **to lose ~ with** perdre contact avec; **to put sb in ~ with** mettre qn en contact avec; **he's out of ~ with reality** il est déconnecté de la réalité; **she's out of ~ with the times** elle n'est plus dans la course○ or dans le coup○; **7** Sport (area) touche *f*; **in(to) ~** en touche.

II *vtr* **1** (come into contact with) toucher; **he ~ed her hand/the paint** il a touché sa main/la peinture; **to ~ sb on the arm/the shoulder etc** toucher le bras/l'épaule etc de qn; **we ~ed ground at 8 o'clock** on a atterri à 8 heures ; **he ~ed his hat politely** il a porté poliment la main à son chapeau; **did you ~ the other car?** (in accident) tu as accroché l'autre voiture?; **2** (interfere with) toucher à; **don't ~ that/my things** ne touchez pas à ça/à mes affaires; **I never ~ed him** je ne lui ai rien fait; **the police can't ~ me** la police ne peut rien contre moi; **she wouldn't let him ~ her** elle ne lui permettait pas de s'approcher d'elle; **3** (affect) gen toucher; (with pleasure) toucher; (with sadness) bouleverser; (adversely) affecter; (as matter of concern) concerner; **matters which ~ us all** des questions qui nous concernent tous; **inflation has not ~ed the well-off** l'inflation n'a pas affecté les gens aisés; **the paintings were not ~ed by the fire** les tableaux n'ont pas été touchés par les flammes; **to ~ the hearts of** toucher les cœurs de; **we were most ~ed** nous avons été très touchés; **this product won't ~ the stains** ce produit n'agit pas sur les taches; **4** (consume) manger [*meat, vegetables*]; prendre [*drink, drugs*]; fumer [*cigarettes*]; **I never ~ alcohol** je ne prends jamais d'alcool; **you've hardly ~ed your meal** tu as à peine touché à ton repas; **5** (deal in) toucher à; **he'll sell most things but won't ~ drugs** il vend de tout mais ne touche pas à la drogue; **6**○ (ask for) **to ~ sb for sth** taper qch à qn○; **7** (equal) égaler; **when it comes to cooking, no-one can ~ him** pour la cuisine, personne ne peut l'égaler; **8** (reach) [*price, temperature*] atteindre [*level*].

III *vi* **1** (come together) [*wires, hands*] se toucher; **2** (with hand) toucher; **'do not ~'** 'ne pas toucher'.

IDIOMS **to be an easy** ou **soft ~**○ être un pigeon○; **it's ~ and go** ce n'est pas évident; **to lose one's ~** perdre la main.

■ **touch down**: ¶ **~ down 1** Aviat, Aerosp atterrir; **2** Sport (in rugby) marquer un essai; ¶ **~ [sth] down, ~ down [sth]** Sport **he ~ed the ball down** il a marqué un essai.

■ **touch off**: **~ [sth] off, ~ off [sth]** faire partir [*firework*]; fig déclencher [*riot, debate*].

■ **touch (up)on**: **~ (up)on [sth]** effleurer [*subject, matter*].

■ **touch up**: **~ [sb/sth] up, ~ up [sb/sth] 1** (re-do) retoucher [*paint, photograph, scratch, hair roots*]; reteindre [*hair roots*]; **2**○ (touch sexually) peloter○ [*person*].

touchdown /ˈtʌtʃdaʊn/ *n* **1** Aviat, Aerosp atterrissage *m*; **'we have ~!'** 'atterrissage!'; **2** Sport essai *m*.

touché /tuːˈʃeɪ, ˈtuːʃeɪ, US tuːˈʃeɪ/ *excl* (in fencing) touché!; gen juste!.

touched /tʌtʃt/ *adj* **1** (emotionally) touché; **~ by** touché de [*kindness*]; touché par [*words, letter*]; **~ to hear/receive etc** touché d'apprendre/de recevoir etc; **2**○ (mad) dérangé○, anormal.

touch: **~ football** *n* Sport *variante du football*; **~hole** *n* Hist (in cannon) culasse *f*.

touchily /ˈtʌtʃɪlɪ/ *adv* avec susceptibilité.

touchiness /ˈtʌtʃɪnɪs/ *n* (of person) susceptibilité *f*; (of issue) délicatesse *f*.

touching /ˈtʌtʃɪŋ/ *adj* touchant.

touchingly /ˈtʌtʃɪŋlɪ/ *adv* [*speak, write*] de façon touchante.

touch: **~ judge** *n* Sport juge *m* de touche; **~ line** *n* Sport ligne *f* de touche; **~-me-not** *n* Bot balsamine *f*; **~paper** *n* papier *m* nitraté; **~-sensitive** *adj* [*screen*] tactile; [*key*] à effleurement; **~stone** *n* lit, fig pierre *f* de touche; **~ system** *n* (typing) dactylographie *f* au toucher; **~-tone** *adj* US [*telephone*] à touches; **~-type** *vi* taper au toucher; **~-typing** *n* dactylographie *f* au toucher; **~-typist** ▶ 1692 *n* dactylo *f* qui tape au toucher; **~wood** *n* amadou *m*.

touchy /ˈtʌtʃɪ/ *adj* **1** (edgy) [*person*] susceptible (**about** sur la question de); **2** (difficult) [*subject, issue*] délicat.

tough /tʌf/ **I** *n* (person) dur *m*.

II *adj* **1** (ruthless) [*businessman*] coriace; [*criminal*] endurci; **a ~ guy** ou **customer**○ un dur○; **2** (severe) [*policy, stance, measure, law*] strict, sévère; [*opposition, competition, criticism*] rude (*before n*); [*sport*] rude (*after n*); **to take a ~ line** se montrer dur (**on sth** à propos de qch; **with sb** envers qn); **you were a bit ~ on him** tu as été un peu dur envers or avec lui; **to get ~ with sb** se montrer dur avec qn; **~ talk** propos *mpl* inflexibles (**about** au sujet de; **on sur**); **3** (difficult) [*way of life, conditions, situation*] difficile, pénible; [*problem, task, match, decision*] difficile; [*challenge*] redoutable; **to have a ~ time** avoir des difficultés (**doing** pour faire); **she's having a ~ time** elle traverse une période difficile; **4** (hardy) [*person, animal*] robuste; [*plant*] résistant; **5** (durable) [*material, skin, layer*] résistant; péj [*meat, vegetable*] coriace pej; **6** (rough) [*area, school*] dur; **7**○ (unfortunate) **~ break** déveine *f*; **that's ~** manque de pot○!; **~ luck!** manque de pot○!; (unsympathetically) tant pis pour toi!; **~ shit**◑**!** tant pis pour toi!; **it was ~ on them** c'était vache○ pour eux; **8**○ US (great) génial ○.

III○ *excl* tant pis pour toi!

IDIOMS **this meat is as ~ as old boots**○ cette viande c'est de la semelle○; **she's as ~ as old boots**○ elle est coriace○; **to hang ~**○ US tenir bon; **hang ~!** accroche-toi○!

■ **tough out**○: **~ [sth] out** surmonter [*crisis*]; faire face à [*recession*]; **to ~ it out** tenir le coup○.

toughen /ˈtʌfn/ *vtr* **1** (make stronger) renforcer [*leather, plastic*]; tremper [*glass, steel*]; durcir [*skin*]; consolider [*wall*]; endurcir [*person*]; **2** (make stricter) (also **~ up**) renforcer [*law, regulation, penalty*]; durcir [*stance, position*].

■ **toughen up**: ¶ **~ up** [*person*] s'endurcir; ¶ **~ [sb] up, ~ up [sb]** endurcir [*person*]; ¶ **~ [sth] up, ~ up [sth]** durcir [*legislation*].

toughie○ /ˈtʌfɪ/ *n* **1** (person) dur *m* à cuire○; **2** (question, problem) colle○ *f*; **that's a ~!** c'est gratiné○!

tough: **~ly-worded** *adj* sans concessions; **~-minded** *adj* ferme et résolu.

toughness /ˈtʌfnɪs/ *n* **1** (ruthlessness) (of businessman, criminal) dureté *f*; **2** (severity) (of law, measure, penalty) sévérité *f*; (of opposition, competition) acharnement *m*; **3** (harshness) (of way of life, conditions) difficulté *f*; **4** (robustness) (of person, animal) endurance *f*; (of plant) résistance *f*; **5** (durability) (of material, glass, leather) robustesse *f*; pej [*of meat, vegetable*] dureté *f*; **6** (difficulty) (of work, question) difficulté *f*.

toupee /ˈtuːpeɪ, US tuːˈpeɪ/ *n* postiche *m*.

tour /tʊə(r), tɔː(r)/ **I** *n* **1** Tourism (of country) circuit *m* (**of** de); (of city) tour *m* (**of** de); (of building) visite *f* (**of** de); (trip in bus, etc) excursion *f*; **bus ~**, **coach ~** excursion *f* en autocar; **cycling/walking ~** randonnée *f* cycliste/pédestre; **to go on a ~ of** visiter [*one thing*]; faire le circuit de [*several things*]; **to take sb on a ~ of sth** faire visiter qch à qn; **he took me on a ~ of his house** il m'a fait visiter sa maison; **a two-week ~** un circuit de quinze jours; **a ~ of inspection** une tournée d'inspection; **'on ~'** (sign on bus) 'en excursion'; **the Grand Tour** Hist le tour d'Europe; **2** Mus, Sport, Theat, Univ tournée *f*; **concert/lecture/rugby ~** tournée *f* de concerts/de conférences/de rugby; **spring/summer ~** tournée *f* printanière/estivale; **to be on/go on ~** être/partir en tournée; **to do a ~** faire une tournée; **to take a play on ~** donner une pièce en tournée; **a ~ of duty** Mil une période de service.
II *vtr* **1** Tourism visiter [*building, country, gallery, sight*]; **2** Mus, Sport être en tournée en [*country*]; Theat [*company*] faire tourner [*production*]; [*production*] tourner en [*country*].
III *vi* **1** Tourism faire du tourisme; **to go ~ing** faire du tourisme; **2** Mus, Sport, Theat [*orchestra, play, team*] être en tournée; **to go ~ing** partir en tournée.

tourer /ˈtʊərə(r), tɔːrə(r)/ *n* (sports car) cabriolet *m* décapotable; GB (caravan) camping-car *m*; (bicycle) vélo *m* de randonnée.

tour guide *n* guide *mf*.

touring /ˈtʊərɪŋ, ˈtɔːr-/ **I** *n* **1** Tourism tourisme *m*; **to like ~** aimer faire du tourisme; **2** Mus, Sport, Theat tournée *f*.
II *modif* **1** Art, Tourism [*exhibition, holiday*] itinérant; **2** Mus, Sport, Theat [*band, company, show, team*] en tournée; [*production*] de tournée.

touring: **~ bindings** *npl* (skiing) fixations *fpl* de randonnée; **~ car** *n* voiture *f* de randonnée.

tourism /ˈtʊərɪzəm, ˈtɔːr-/ *n* tourisme *m*.

tourist /ˈtʊərɪst, ˈtɔːr-/ **I** *n* **1** gen touriste *mf*; **2** Sport visiteur/-euse *m/f*; **the ~s won** l'équipe visiteuse a gagné.
II *modif* [*area, authority, centre, development, guide, map, resort, route, season*] touristique; **the ~ trade** le tourisme.

tourist: **~ bus** *n* car *m* de tourisme; **~ class** *n* Aviat classe *f* touriste.

tourist (information) office *n* (in town) syndicat *m* d'initiative; (national organization) bureau *m* or office *m* de tourisme.

tourist trap *n* piège *m* à touristes.

touristy○ /ˈtʊərɪstɪ, ˈtɔːr-/ *adj* péj envahi par les touristes.

tournament /ˈtɔːnəmənt, US ˈtɜːrn-/ *n* tournoi *m*.

tourney /ˈtʊənɪ/ *n* **1**‡ Hist tournoi *m* (de chevalerie); **2** US Sport tournoi *m*.

tourniquet /ˈtʊənɪkeɪ, US ˈtɜːrnɪkət/ *n* garrot *m*, tourniquet *m*.

tour operator *n* voyagiste *mf*, tour-opérateur *m*.

tousle /ˈtaʊzl/ **I** *vtr* ébouriffer [*hair*].
II tousled *pp adj* [*hair*] ébouriffé; [*person, appearance*] débraillé.

tout /taʊt/ **I** *n* **1** GB (selling tickets) revendeur *m* de billets au marché noir; **2** Comm (person soliciting custom) racoleur/-euse○ *m/f* pej; **3** Turf vendeur *m* de tuyaux.
II *vtr* **1** [*street merchant*] vendre (en faisant du boniment); **2** GB (illegally) revendre [qch] au marché noir [*tickets*]; **3** (publicize loudly) vanter les mérites de [*product, invention*]; claironner [*good results*]; **much ~ed** tant vanté.
III *vi* (solicit) racoler○ pej; **to ~ for business** racoler○ la clientèle; **to ~ for votes** racoler○ des électeurs.

tow /təʊ/ **I** *n* **1** Aut **to be on ~** être en remorque; **to give sb a ~** remorquer qn; **to need a ~** avoir besoin d'être remorqué; **2** fig hum (following) **to have sb in ~** être accompagné de qn; **a father with two children in ~** un père accompagné de deux enfants; **3** (ski lift) téléski *m*; **4** Tex filasse *f*.
II *vtr* remorquer, tracter [*trailer, caravan*].
■ **tow away**: **~ away [sth]**, **~ [sth] away** [*police*] emmener [qch] à la fourrière; [*recovery service*] remorquer.

towage /ˈtəʊɪdʒ/ *n* (charges) frais *mpl* de remorquage; (act) remorquage *m*.

toward(s) /təˈwɔːd(z), tɔːd(z)/

■ **Note** When *towards* is used to talk about direction or position, it is almost always translated by *vers*: *she ran toward(s) him* = elle a couru vers lui. For particular usages see the entry below.
– When *toward(s)* is used to mean *in relation to*, it is translated by *envers*: *his attitude toward(s) his parents* = son attitude envers ses parents. For particular usages see the entry below.

prep **1** (in the direction of) vers; **~ the east** vers l'est; **she ran ~ him** elle a couru vers lui; **he was standing with his back ~ me** il était dos à moi, il me tournait le dos; **the first steps ~** fig les premiers pas vers [*solution, system etc*]; **the country is moving ~ democracy/independence** le pays se dirige vers la démocratie/l'indépendance; **he is moving ~ the idea that** il commence à penser or à se dire que; **2** (near) vers; **~ the end of** vers la fin de [*day, month, life*]; **~ the rear of the plane** à l'arrière de l'avion; **3** (in relation to) envers; **their attitude/policy ~ Europe** leur attitude/politique envers l'Europe; **to be friendly/hostile ~ sb** se montrer cordial/hostile envers qn; **4** (as a contribution to) **the money will go ~ the cost of a new roof** l'argent servira à payer un nouveau toit; **we are saving ~ a holiday** nous faisons des économies pour partir en vacances; **you should put the money ~ the children's education** tu devrais mettre l'argent de côté pour l'éducation des enfants; **new hostels have gone some way ~ easing the accommodation problem** de nouveaux foyers ont contribué à alléger la crise du logement; **management have gone some way ~ meeting the strikers' demands** la direction a fait quelques concessions pour répondre aux revendications des grévistes.

tow: **~away zone** *n* zone *f* rouge (*de stationnement interdit sous peine de mise en fourrière*); **~ bar** *n* (on car) crochet *m* d'attelage; (on recovery vehicle) barre *f* de remorquage; **~boat** *n* remorqueur *m*.

towel /ˈtaʊəl/ **I** *n* serviette *f* (de toilette); ▶ **bath towel, tea towel**.
II *vtr* (*p prés etc* **-ll-**, US **-l-**) essuyer (avec une serviette); **to ~ one's hair** s'essuyer les cheveux.
IDIOMS **to throw** ou **chuck**○ **in the ~** jeter l'éponge.

towelette /ˌtaʊəˈlet/ *n* US lingette *f* rince-doigts.

towelling /ˈtaʊəlɪŋ/ **I** *n* **1** Tex tissu *m* éponge; **2** (rubbing) **to give sb a good ~ (down)** frictionner qn un bon coup avec une serviette.
II *modif* [*garment*] en tissu éponge.

towel: **~ rail** *n* porte-serviettes *m inv*; **~ ring** *n* anneau *m* porte-serviettes.

tower /ˈtaʊə(r)/ **I** *n* tour *f*.
II *vi* **1** (dominate) **to ~ above** ou **over** dominer [*village, countryside*]; **to ~ above** ou **over sb** gen être plus grand que qn; (menacingly) dominer qn de toute sa hauteur; **2** (outstrip) **to ~ above** dominer [*rival, peer*].
IDIOMS **to be a ~ of strength** être solide comme un roc; **she's been a ~ of strength to me** elle a été d'un grand soutien pour moi.

tower block *n* GB tour *f* (d'habitation).

towering /ˈtaʊərɪŋ/ *adj* (*épith*) **1** [*cliff, building etc*] imposant; **2** (tremendous) **a ~ performance** (by musician) une exécution fantastique; (by actor) une interprétation fantastique; **to be in a ~ rage** être dans une colère noire.

Tower of Babel /ˌtaʊərəvˈbeɪbl/ *pr n* tour *f* de Babel.

tow: **~-haired**, **~headed** *adj* péj blond, filasse pej; **~line** *n* câble *m* de remorquage.

town /taʊn/ *n* ville *f*; **to go into ~** aller en ville; **the whole ~ knows about it** toute la ville est au courant; **she's out of ~ at the moment** elle n'est pas là en ce moment; **he comes from out of ~** US il n'est pas d'ici; **to leave** ou **skip**○ **~** US quitter la ville; **guess who's back in ~**○! devine qui est au retour!; **look me up next time you're in ~** viens me voir la prochaine fois que tu passeras à Londres (or à Paris or à New York etc); **she's in ~ to publicize her film** elle est à Londres (or à Paris or à New York etc) pour faire de la publicité pour son film○.
IDIOMS **to go out on the ~**, **to have a night (out) on the ~** faire la noce or la bombe○; **to go to ~ on** (be extravagant with) ne pas lésiner sur; mettre le paquet○ sur [*decor, catering*]; (make much of) exploiter [qch] à fond [*story, scandal*]; **he's the talk of the ~** on ne parle que de lui; **~ and gown** GB les citadins *mpl* et les universitaires *mpl* ▶ 1818.

town: **~-and-country planning** *n* aménagement *m* du territoire; **~ centre** *n* centre-ville *m*; **~ clerk** *n* GB secrétaire *mf* de mairie; **~ council** *n* GB conseil *m* municipal; **~ councillor** *n* GB conseiller/-ère *m/f* municipal/-e; **~ crier** *n* crieur *m* public.

townee *n* US = **townie**.

town hall *n* mairie *f*, hôtel *m* de ville.

town house *n* **1** (as opposed to country seat) hôtel *m* particulier; **2** (urban terrace) *maison en centre ville avec garage au rez-de-chaussée*.

townie○ /ˈtaʊnɪ/ *n* péj citadin/-e *m/f*.

town: **~ meeting** *n* US assemblée *f* générale des habitants d'une commune; **~ planner** ▶ 1692 *n* GB urbaniste *mf*; **~ planning** *n* GB urbanisme *m*; **~scape** *n* paysage *m* urbain; **~sfolk** *npl*† ou dial = **townspeople**.

township /ˈtaʊnʃɪp/ *n* **1** gen commune *f*, municipalité *f*; **2** (in South Africa) township *m*, ghetto *m* noir; **3** US ≈ canton *m* (*division administrative d'un comté*).

townspeople /ˈtaʊnzpiːpl/ *npl* citadins *mpl*.

tow: **~path** *n* chemin *m* de halage; **~rope** *n* = **towline**.

tow-start /ˌtəʊˈstɑːt/ *n* **to give sb a ~** faire démarrer qn en le remorquant.

tow truck *n* US dépanneuse *f*.

toxaemia, **toxemia** US /tɒkˈsiːmɪə/ ▶ 1354 *n* toxémie *f*.

toxic /ˈtɒksɪk/ *adj* toxique.

toxicity /tɒkˈsɪsətɪ/ *n* toxicité *f*.

toxicological /ˌtɒksɪkəˈlɒdʒɪkl/ *adj* toxicologique.

toxicologist /ˌtɒksɪˈkɒlədʒɪst/ *n* toxicologue *mf*.

toxicology /ˌtɒksɪˈkɒlədʒɪ/ *n* toxicologie *f*.

toxic: **~ shock syndrome**, **TSS** *n* Med syndrome *m* du choc toxique, SCT; **~ waste** *n* déchets *mpl* toxiques.

Towns and cities

Occasionally the gender of a town is clear because the name includes the definite article, e.g. Le Havre *or* La Rochelle. *In most other cases, there is some hesitation, and it is always safer to avoid the problem by using* la ville de:

Toulouse is beautiful	=	la ville de Toulouse est belle

In, to and from somewhere

For in *and* to *with the name of a town, use* à *in French; if the French name includes the definite article,* à *will become* au, à la, à l' *or* aux:

to live in Toulouse	=	vivre à Toulouse
to go to Toulouse	=	aller à Toulouse
to live in Le Havre	=	vivre au Havre
to go to Le Havre	=	aller au Havre
to live in La Rochelle	=	vivre à La Rochelle
to go to La Rochelle	=	aller à La Rochelle
to live in Les Arcs	=	vivre aux Arcs
to go to Les Arcs	=	aller aux Arcs

Similarly, from *is* de, *becoming* du, de la, de l' *or* des *when it combines with the definite article in town names:*

to come from Toulouse	=	venir de Toulouse
to come from Le Havre	=	venir du Havre
to come from La Rochelle	=	venir de La Rochelle
to come from Les Arcs	=	venir des Arcs

Belonging to a town or city

English sometimes has specific words for people of a certain city or town, such as Londoners, New Yorkers *or* Parisians, *but mostly we talk of* the people of Leeds *or* the inhabitants of San Francisco. *On the other hand, most towns in French-speaking countries have a corresponding adjective and noun, and a list of the best-known of these is given at the end of this note.*

The noun forms, spelt with a capital letter, mean a person from X:

the inhabitants of Bordeaux	=	les Bordelais *mpl*
the people of Strasbourg	=	les Strasbourgeois *mpl*

The adjective forms, spelt with a small letter, are often used where in English the town name is used as an adjective:

Paris shops	=	les magasins parisiens

However, some of these French words are fairly rare, and it is always safe to say les habitants de X, *or, for the adjective, simply* de X. *Here are examples of this, using some of the nouns that commonly combine with the names of towns:*

a Bordeaux accent	=	un accent de Bordeaux
Toulouse airport	=	l'aéroport de Toulouse
the La Rochelle area	=	la région de La Rochelle
Limoges buses	=	les autobus de Limoges
the Le Havre City Council	=	le conseil municipal du Havre
Lille representatives	=	les représentants de Lille
Les Arcs restaurants	=	les restaurants des Arcs
the Geneva road	=	la route de Genève
Brussels streets	=	les rues de Bruxelles
the Angers team	=	l'équipe d'Angers
the Avignon train	=	le train d'Avignon
but note		
Orleans traffic	=	la circulation à Orléans

Names of cities and towns in French-speaking countries and their adjectives

Remember that when these adjectives are used as nouns, meaning a person from X or the people of X, they are spelt with capital letters.

Aix-en-Provence	=	aixois(e)
Alger	=	algérois(e)
Angers	=	angevin(e)
Arles	=	arlésien(ne)
Auxerre	=	auxerrois(e)
Avignon	=	avignonnais(e)
Bastia	=	bastiais(e)
Bayonne	=	bayonnais(e)
Belfort	=	belfortain(e)
Berne	=	bernois(e)
Besançon	=	bisontin(e)
Béziers	=	biterrois(e)
Biarritz	=	biarrot(e)
Bordeaux	=	bordelais(e)
Boulogne-sur-Mer	=	boulonnais(e)
Bourges	=	berruyer(-ère)
Brest	=	brestois(e)
Bruges	=	brugeois(e)
Bruxelles	=	bruxellois(e)
Calais	=	calaisien(ne)
Cannes	=	cannais(e)
Carcassonne	=	carcassonnais(e)
Chambéry	=	chambérien(ne)
Chamonix	=	chamoniard(e)
Clermont-Ferrand	=	clermontois(e)
Die	=	diois(e)
Dieppe	=	dieppois(e)
Dijon	=	dijonnais(e)
Dunkerque	=	dunkerquois(e)
Fontainebleau	=	bellifontain(e)
Gap	=	gapençais(e)
Genève	=	genevois(e)
Grenoble	=	grenoblois(e)
Havre, Le	=	havrais(e)
Lens	=	lensois(e)
Liège	=	liégeois(e)
Lille	=	lillois(e)
Lourdes	=	lourdais(e)
Luxembourg	=	luxembourgeois(e)
Lyon	=	lyonnais(e)
Mâcon	=	mâconnais(e)
Marseille	=	marseillais(e) *or* phocéen(ne)
Metz	=	messin(e)
Modane	=	modanais(e)
Montpellier	=	montpelliérain(e)
Montréal	=	montréalais(e)
Moulins	=	moulinois(e)
Mulhouse	=	mulhousien(ne)
Nancy	=	nancéien(ne)
Nantes	=	nantais(e)
Narbonne	=	narbonnais(e)
Nevers	=	nivernais(e)
Nice	=	niçois(e)
Nîmes	=	nîmois(e)
Orléans	=	orléanais(e)
Paris	=	parisien(ne)
Pau	=	palois(e)
Périgueux	=	périgourdin(e)
Perpignan	=	perpignanais(e)
Poitiers	=	poitevin(e)
Pont-à-Mousson	=	mussipontain(e)
Québec	=	québécois(e)
Reims	=	rémois(e)
Rennes	=	rennais(e)
Roanne	=	roannais(e)
Rouen	=	rouennais(e)
Saint-Étienne	=	stéphanois(e)
Saint-Malo	=	malouin(e)
Saint-Tropez	=	tropézien(ne)
Sancerre	=	sancerrois(e)
Sète	=	sétois(e)
Sochaux	=	sochalien(ne)
Strasbourg	=	strasbourgeois(e)
Tarascon	=	tarasconnais(e)
Tarbes	=	tarbais(e)
Toulon	=	toulonnais(e)
Toulouse	=	toulousain(e)
Tours	=	tourangeau(-elle)
Tunis	=	tunisois(e)
Valence	=	valentinois(e)
Valenciennes	=	valenciennois(e)
Versailles	=	versaillais(e)
Vichy	=	vichyssois(e)

toxin /ˈtɒksɪn/ *n* toxine *f*.

toxoplasmosis /ˌtɒksəʊplæsˈməʊsɪs/ **▶ 1354** *n* toxoplasmose *f*.

toy /tɔɪ/ **I** *n* jouet *m*.
II *modif* [*plane, railway*] miniature; [*car, boat*] petit; [*gun, telephone*] d'enfant.
III *vi* **to ~ with** jouer avec [*object, feelings*]; caresser [*idea*]; **to ~ with one's food** chipoter.

toy: **~box** *n* coffre *m* à jouets; **~ boy**○ *n* GB péj gigolo *m*; **~ dog** *n* chien *m* d'appartement; **~ poodle** *n* caniche *m* nain; **~shop** *n* magasin *m* de jouets; **~ soldier** *n* petit soldat *m*; **~ spaniel** *n* épagneul *m* nain.

toytown /ˈtɔɪtaʊn/ **I** *n* petite ville *f* de carte postale.
II *modif* [*village*] de carte postale; péj [*intellectual, politician, politics*] de pacotille pej.

toy train *n* train *m* miniature; (electric) train *m* électrique.

trace /treɪs/ **I** *n* **1** (evidence) trace *f*; **to find ~s of** trouver les traces de [*building*]; **to remove all ~(s) of** retirer toute trace de; **no ~ remains of** ou **there is no ~ of** il ne reste aucune trace de; **2** (hint) (of feeling, irony, humour, flavour, garlic) soupçon *m*; (of accent) pointe *f*; (of chemical, drug) trace *f*; **with/without a ~ of** avec une/sans la moindre trace de [*irony, irritation*]; **with/without a ~ of a smile** avec un léger/sans l'ombre d'un sourire; **without a ~ of make-up** sans aucun maquillage; **3** (aiding retrieval) trace *f*; **without ~** [*disappear, sink*] sans laisser de traces; **they found no ~ of him/the money** ils n'ont trouvé aucune trace de lui/l'argent; **to lose all ~ of** perdre toute trace de; **4** (of harness) trait *m*; **5** (in angling) bas *m* de ligne.
II *vtr* **1** (locate) localiser [*thief, fugitive, call*]; retrouver [*witness, weapon, car, file, source*]; dépister [*fault, malfunction*]; trouver des traces de [*chemical*]; **to ~ sb to** retrouver la trace de qn dans [*hideout*]; **to ~ the cause of** déterminer la cause de; **the call was ~d to a London number** on a pu établir que le coup de téléphone venait d'un numéro à Londres; **2** (follow development) faire l'historique de [*development, growth*]; retracer [*life, story, progress, friendship*]; faire remonter [*origins, ancestry*] (**to** jusqu'à); **to ~ the history of** faire l'historique de; **3** (draw) = **trace out**.
IDIOMS **to kick over the ~s** ruer dans les brancards.
■ **trace back**: **~ [sth] back**, **~ back [sth]** faire remonter (**to** à).
■ **trace out**: **~ out [sth]**, **~ [sth] out** **1** (copy) décalquer [*map, outline*] (**onto** sur); **2** (form) tracer [*pattern, letters*] (**in, on** sur).

traceable /ˈtreɪsəbl/ *adj* [*connection, relationship*] clair; **easily ~** [*file, fault*] facile à retrouver; **to be ~ to** provenir de [*malfunction*]; remonter à [*work, theory*].

trace element, **trace mineral** *n* oligo-élément *m*.

tracer /ˈtreɪsə(r)/ **I** *n* **1** Mil (bullet) balle *f* traçante; (shell) obus *m* traçant; **2** Chem, Med (substance) traceur *m*; **3** (of pattern) (person) traceur/-euse *m/f*; (instrument) traceur *m*.
II *modif* [*bullet, shell*] traçant.

tracery /ˈtreɪsərɪ/ *n* **1** Archit (of window) remplage *m*; **2** gen (of pattern, frost, foliage, veins) fin réseau *m*.

trachea /trəˈkiːə, US ˈtreɪkɪə/ *n* trachée *f*.

tracheotomy /ˌtrækɪˈɒtəmɪ/ *n* trachéotomie *f*.

tracheotomy tube *n* canule *f* à trachéotomie.

trachoma /trəˈkəʊmə/ **▶ 1354** *n* trachome *m*.

tracing /ˈtreɪsɪŋ/ *n* **1** (of map, motif, diagram) calque *m*; **to make a ~ of** faire un calque de; **2** (procedure) calquage *m*; **3** (graph) tracé *m* de courbe.

tracing: **~ paper** *n* papier-calque *m*; **~ wheel** *n* roulette *f* de couturière.

track /træk/ **I** *n* **1** (print) (of animal, person) empreintes *fpl*, traces *fpl*; (of vehicle) traces *fpl*; **we followed his ~(s) to the bank of**

the river nous avons suivi ses traces or ses empreintes jusqu'au bord de la rivière; **the (tyre) ~s led to the lake** les traces (de pneu) menaient au lac; **2** lit, fig (course, trajectory) (of person) trace *f*; (of missile, aircraft, storm) trajectoire *f*; **to be on the ~ of** être sur la trace or piste de [*person*]; être sur la voie de [*discovery*]; **she knew the police were on her ~** elle savait que la police était sur sa trace or piste; **to cover one's ~s** brouiller les pistes; **the negotiations were on ~** les négociations se déroulaient comme prévu; **to be on the right ~** être sur la bonne piste; **to put sb on the right ~** mettre qn sur la bonne piste; **to be on the wrong ~** faire fausse route; **to set sb on the wrong ~** faire faire fausse route à qn; **to keep ~ of** [*person*] se tenir au courant de [*developments, events*]; suivre le fil de [*conversation*]; [*company, authority*] se tenir au courant de la situation de [*customer, taxpayer*]; [*police, race official*] suivre les mouvements de [*criminal, competitor*]; [*computer*] tenir à jour [*bank account, figures*]; tenir à jour les détails concernant [*person*]; **we have to keep ~ of the houses we rent out** nous devons tenir à jour les fichiers des maisons que nous louons; **it's hard to keep ~ of all one's old colleagues** il est difficile de ne pas perdre de vue tous ses anciens collègues; **I must keep ~ of the time** il ne faut pas que j'oublie l'heure; **to lose ~ of** perdre de vue [*friend*]; perdre la trace de [*document, aircraft, suspect*]; perdre le fil de [*conversation*]; **to lose ~ of (the) time** perdre la notion du temps; **to make ~s for sth** se diriger vers qch; **we'd better be making ~s** il est temps de partir; **to stop dead in one's ~s** s'arrêter net; **3** (path, rough road) sentier *m*, chemin *m*; **4** Sport piste *f*; **16 laps of the ~** 16 tours de piste; **athletics/speedway ~** piste d'athlétisme/de vitesse; **(motor-)racing ~** (open-air) circuit *m*; (enclosed) autodrome *m*; **cycling ~** vélodrome *m*; **dog-racing ~** cynodrome *m*; **5** Rail voie *f* ferrée; US (platform) quai *m*; **to leave the ~(s)** [*train*] dérailler; **6** Mus (of record, tape, CD) morceau *m*; (song) chanson *f*; **a 16-~ CD** un disque compact qui a 16 morceaux; **7** Audio, Comput (band) piste *f*; **8** Aut (on wheel of tank, tractor) chenille *f*; (distance between wheels) voie *f*, écartement *m* de voie; **9** (rail) (for curtain) tringle *f*; (for sliding door) rail *m*; **10** US Sch (stream) groupe *m* de niveau; **the top/middle/bottom ~** le groupe des élèves forts/moyens/faibles; **the first ~** ≈ le groupe des élèves forts; **to place students in ~s** répartir les élèves en groupes de niveau.

II *modif* Sport [*event, championship, race*] de vitesse; **~ meet** US épreuves *fpl* de vitesse.

III *vtr* (follow path of) suivre la trace de [*person, animal*]; suivre la progression de [*storm, hurricane*]; suivre la trajectoire de [*rocket, plane, comet, satellite*]; **the police ~ed the terrorists to their hideout** la police a suivi la trace des terroristes jusqu'à leur cachette.

IV *vi* Cin faire un travelling.

IDIOMS **to come from the wrong side of the ~s** venir des quartiers pauvres; **three years down the ~** (in future) dans trois ans; (in present) ça fait trois ans.

■ **track down**: **~ [sb/sth] down, ~ down [sb/sth]** retrouver [*person, object, file*]; **they finally ~ed the gang down to their hideout** ils ont fini par suivre la trace de la bande jusqu'à sa cachette.

track and field events *npl* compétition *f* d'athlétisme.

tracked /trækt/ *adj* [*vehicle*] chenillé, à chenilles.

tracker /'trækə(r)/ *n* (of animal) traqueur *m*; (of person) poursuivant/-e *m/f*.

tracker: **~ ball** *n* Comput, Tech boule *f* de commande; **~ dog** *n* chien *m* policier (*entraîné à la recherche de personnes ou d'objets*).

tracking /'trækɪŋ/ **I** *n* **1** US Sch système *m* de classes de niveau; **2** (monitoring) (of person, plane, storm) localisation *f*; (of satellite) poursuite *f*, localisation *f*; **3** Video alignement *m*.

II *modif* [*device, equipment, system*] de poursuite, de localisation.

track: **~ing shot** *n* Cin travelling *m*; **~ing station** *n* station *f* de poursuite; **~layer**, **~man** *n* US Rail poseur *m* de rails; **~laying** *adj* [*vehicle*] chenillé.

trackless /'træklɪs/ *adj* **1** [*vehicle*] sans chenilles; **2** litér [*desert, waste*] sans pistes; [*forest*] sans chemins.

track: **~ lighting** *n* rampe *f* de spots d'éclairage; **~ maintenance** *n* Rail entretien *m* des voies ferrées.

trackman /'trækmən/ ▶ **1692** *n* US **1** = **tracklayer**; **2** Sport coureur *m*.

track record *n* gen (of government, company) antécédents *mpl*; (of professional person) antécédents *mpl* professionnels; **to have a good/poor ~** gen avoir de bons/mauvais antécédents; [*professional person*] avoir de bons/mauvais antécédents professionnels; **this firm has a poor ~ on pollution control** cette société a une mauvaise réputation pour ce qui est du contrôle de la pollution; **a candidate with a proven ~ in sales** un candidat ayant une bonne expérience commerciale.

track: **~ rod** *n* GB Aut barre *f* d'accouplement; **~ shoe** *n* chaussure *f* de course à pointes; **~suit** *n* survêtement *m*; **~ system** *n* US Sch système *m* de groupes de niveaux.

tract /trækt/ *n* **1** (of land, forest) étendue *f*; **2** Anat **digestive/respiratory ~** appareil *m* digestif/respiratoire; **3** (pamphlet) pamphlet *m*, traité *m*; **4** US (housing development) lotissement *m*.

tractable /'træktəbl/ *adj* [*person, animal, engine*] docile; [*substance*] malléable; [*problem*] soluble.

Tractarian /ˌtræk'teərɪən/ *n, adj* Tractarien/-ienne (*m/f*).

Tractarianism /træk'teərɪənɪzəm/ *n* tractarianisme.

traction /'trækʃn/ *n* **1** (pulling action) traction *f*; **in ~** Med en traction; **2** (of wheel on surface) adhérence *f*.

traction: **~ control system** *n* régulateur *m* de traction; **~ engine** *n* locomobile *f*.

tractive /'træktɪv/ *adj* de traction.

tractor /'træktə(r)/ **I** *n* (all contexts) tracteur *m*.

II *modif* [*driver, engine*] de tracteur.

tractor feed /'træktə(r) fiːd/ *n* Comput dispositif *m* d'entraînement à picols.

tractor mower *n* tondeuse *f* tractée.

tractor-trailer *n* US semi-remorque *m*.

trad○ /træd/ GB Mus **I** *n* le (jazz) traditionnel.

II *adj* traditionnel/-elle.

tradable /'treɪdəbl/ *adj* Fin [*asset, security, currency*] commercialisable.

trade /treɪd/ **I** *n* **1** (activity) commerce *m*; **to do ~ with sb** faire du commerce avec qn; **to do a good ~** faire de bonnes affaires; **2** (sector of industry) industrie *f*; **car/book ~** industrie automobile/du livre; **she's in the furniture ~** elle travaille dans l'ameublement; **3** (profession) (manual) métier *m*; (intellectual) profession *f*; **by ~** de métier; **in the ~ we call it**... dans la profession or le métier on appelle cela...; **as we say in the ~**... comme on dit dans le métier...; **4** (swap) échange *m*, troc *m*; **to do** GB ou **make** US **a ~ with sb** faire un échange or un troc avec qn; **5** Meteorol ▶ **trade wind**; **6**● (male prostitute) prostitué *m*.

II *modif* [*negotiations, route, agreement, restrictions*] commercial; [*sanctions, embargo*] économique; [*press, journal*] professionnel/-elle.

III *vtr* (swap) échanger [*objects*] (**for** contre); échanger [*insults, compliments, blows*]; **the two countries ~d hostages** les deux pays ont échangé des otages.

IV *vi* **1** Comm (buy and sell) faire du commerce (**with** avec; **at** US dans); **the company ~s as Grunard's** la société fait du commerce sous le nom de Grunard's; **to ~ in sth with sb** vendre qch à qn; **to ~ at a profit/loss** vendre à profit/perte; **2** Fin (on financial markets) [*share, commodity*] s'échanger; **to ~ at $10** s'échanger à $10; **3** (exploit) **to ~ on** exploiter, se servir de [*name, reputation, image*].

■ **trade in**: **~ [sth] in, ~ in [sth]** Comm **he ~d in his old car/washing-machine** on lui a repris sa vieille voiture/machine à laver.

■ **trade off**: **~ [sth] off against sth, ~ off [sth] against sth 1** (weigh up) peser le pour et le contre entre [qch] et qch; **2** (exchange) échanger [qch] contre qch.

■ **trade up** US = **trade in**.

trade: **~ acceptance** *n* Comm acceptation *f* commerciale; **Trade and Industry Secretary** *n* GB Pol ministre *m* du commerce et de l'industrie; **~ association** *n* association *f* professionnelle; **~ balance** *n* Econ balance *f* commerciale; **~ barrier** *n* Comm barrière *f* douanière; **~ credit** *n* crédit *m* commercial; **~ cycle** *n* Econ cycle *m* économique; **~ deficit** *n* Econ déficit *m* commercial; **~ description** *n* Comm désignation *f* de marchandise; **Trade Descriptions Act** *n* GB Comm Jur *loi qui protège le consommateur des désignations mensongères de marchandise*; **~ discount** *n* Comm remise *f* professionnelle; **~ dispute** *n* conflit *m* social; **~ fair** *n* Comm salon *m*; **~ figures** *npl* résultats *mpl* financiers; **~ gap** *n* Econ déficit *m* commercial.

trade-in /'treɪdɪn/ **I** *n* Comm reprise *f* (*d'un article usagé à l'achat d'un article neuf*).

II *adj* Comm [*price*] avec reprise; [*value*] de reprise.

trademark /'treɪdmɑːk/ **I** *n* **1** Comm marque *f* (de fabrique); **2** (also **Trademark, Registered Trademark**) marque *f* déposée; **3** fig (of person) signe *m* particulier; **the professionalism which is his ~** le professionalisme qui le caractérise.

II *vtr* Comm (label) apposer une marque sur [*product*]; (register) déposer une marque sur [*product*].

trade: **Trade Minister** *n* GB Pol ministre *m* du commerce; **~ mission** *n* mission *f* commerciale; **~ name** *n* Comm nom *m* (de marque).

trade-off /'treɪdɒf/ *n* **1** (balance) compromis *m* (**between** entre); **2** (exchange) échange *m* (**between** entre).

trade pattern *n* Comm structure *f* des échanges.

trader /'treɪdə(r)/ *n* **1** Comm commerçant/-e *m/f*; **2** Fin (at Stock Exchange) opérateur/-trice *m/f* (en Bourse); **3** Naut navire *m* marchand.

tradescantia /ˌtrædɪ'skæntɪə/ *n* tradescantia *m*.

trade: **~ secret** *n* secret *m* de fabrication; hum secret *m* d'État; **Trade Secretary** *n* GB Pol = **Trade Minister**; **~sman** *n* (delivery man) livreur *m*; (person rendering service) ouvrier *m*; Tax (on official form) artisan *m*; **~sman's entrance** *n* entrée *f* de service, entrée *f* des fournisseurs; **~s union** *n* GB ▶ **trade union**; **Trades Union Congress, TUC** *n* GB Confédération *f* des syndicats (britanniques).

trade union I *n* Ind syndicat *m*.

II *modif* Ind [*activist, card, leader, headquarters, movement, subscription*] syndical.

trade: **~ union member** *n* syndiqué/-e *m/f*; **~ war** *n* guerre *f* commerciale; **~ wind** *n* Meteorol alizé *m*.

trading /'treɪdɪŋ/ *n* **1** Comm commerce *m*; **2** Fin (at Stock Exchange) transactions *fpl* (boursières); **~ was quiet/heavy** la Bourse était calme/agitée; **at the end of ~** à la fermeture du marché; **most favoured**

nation ~ status statut *m* de nation favorisée.

trading: **~ account** *n* Accts compte *m* d'exploitation; **~ company** *n* société *f* commerciale; **~ day** *n* Fin séance *f* (boursière); **~ estate** *n* GB zone *f* industrielle; **~ loss** *n* Accts pertes *fpl*; **~ nation** *n* nation *f* commerçante; **~ partner** *n* partenaire *m* commercial.

trading post *n* **1** (shop) poste *m* d'approvisionnement (*dans une région isolée*); **2** Fin (at Stock Exchange) corbeille *f*, poste *m* de négociation.

trading: **~ profit** *n* Accts bénéfices *mpl*; **~ stamp** *n* Comm point *m*; **Trading Standards Department** *n*: *direction régionale de la protection des consommateurs*; **Trading Standards Officer** *n*: *fonctionnaire de la direction régionale de la protection des consommateurs*.

tradition /trəˈdɪʃn/ *n* tradition *f* (**of** de; **to do** de faire); **by ~** par tradition; **in the ~ of** dans la tradition de; **to break with ~** rompre avec la tradition.

traditional /trəˈdɪʃənl/ *adj* traditionnel/-elle.

traditionalism /trəˈdɪʃənəlɪzəm/ *n* traditionalisme *m*.

traditionalist /trəˈdɪʃənəlɪst/ *n, adj* traditionaliste (*mf*).

traditionally /trəˈdɪʃənəlɪ/ *adv* traditionnellement.

traduce /trəˈdju:s, US -ˈdu:s/ *vtr* sout diffamer.

traducer /trəˈdju:sə(r), US -ˈdu:-/ *n* sout diffamateur/-trice *m/f*.

traffic /ˈtræfɪk/ **I** *n* **1** (road vehicles in street, town) circulation *f*; **to direct the ~** régler la circulation; **heavy ~** circulation dense; **the volume of ~ has doubled** la circulation a doublé de volume; **~ into/out of London** la circulation vers/en sortant de Londres; **~ is being diverted** il y a une déviation; **to hold up the ~** provoquer un bouchon; **2** (movement of planes, ships, trains, cars, people) trafic *m*; **freight/passenger ~** trafic de fret/voyageurs; **air ~** trafic aérien; **cross-Channel ~** trafic *m* transmanche; **3** (dealings) (in drugs, arms, slaves, goods) trafic *m* (**in** de); (in ideas) mouvement *m* (**in** de); **a one-way/two-way ~** un trafic unilatéral/dans les deux sens.

II *modif* [*accident, density, noise, problem, regulations*] de la circulation; **~ hold-up** embouteillage *m*; **~ flow** circulation *f*; **~ tailback** bouchon *m*.

III *vi* (*p prés etc* **-ck-**) **to ~ in** faire du trafic de [*drugs, cocaine, arms, stolen goods*].

traffic calming I *n* mesures *fpl* pour ralentir la circulation.

II *modif* [*measures, scheme*] pour ralentir la circulation.

traffic: **~ circle** *n* US rond-point *m*; **~ cop** ▶ 1692 *n* US agent *m* de la circulation; **~ court** *n* US cour *f* des contraventions routières.

traffic duty *n* **to be on ~** faire la circulation.

traffic: **~ engineer** ▶ 1692 *n* technicien *m* de la circulation routière; **~ engineering** *n* gestion *f* de la circulation routière; **~-free** *adj* libre de toute circulation; **~ island** *n* Transp refuge *m*; **~ jam** *n* embouteillage *m*.

trafficker /ˈtræfɪkə(r)/ *n* trafiquant/-e *m/f* (**in** de).

traffic: **~ light** *n* (*souvent pl*) feux *mpl* de signalisation or tricolores; **~ offence** *n* infraction *f* au Code de la route; **~ pattern** *n* US Aviat circuit *m* d'aérodrome; **~ police** *n* police *f* de la route; **~ policeman** *n* agent *m* de la circulation; **~ signal** *n* = **traffic light**; **~ system** *n* système *m* de circulation; **~ warden** ▶ 1692 *n* GB contractuel/-elle *m/f*.

tragedian /trəˈdʒi:dɪən/ *n* **1** (author) auteur *m* de tragédies; **2** (actor) tragédien *m*.

tragedienne /trəˌdʒi:dɪˈen/ *n* tragédienne *f*.

tragedy /ˈtrædʒədɪ/ *n* gen, Theat tragédie *f*; **it's a ~ that** c'est une tragédie que (+ *subj*); **the ~ of it is that** le (plus) tragique, c'est que; **the ~ of war is that** le plus tragique dans les guerres, c'est que.

tragic /ˈtrædʒɪk/ *adj* gen, Theat tragique; **it is ~ that** il est tragique que (+ *subj*).

tragically /ˈtrædʒɪklɪ/ *adv* tragiquement.

tragicomedy /ˌtrædʒɪˈkɒmədɪ/ *n* Theat, fig tragi-comédie *f*.

tragicomic /ˌtrædʒɪˈkɒmɪk/ *adj* tragicomique.

trail /treɪl/ **I** *n* **1** (path) chemin *m*, piste *f*; **to set off on the ~ to** se mettre en route or en chemin pour; **2** (trace, mark) (blood, dust, slime) traînée *f*, trace *f* (**of** de); **jet ~** sillage *m* d'avion; **he left a ~ of clues behind him** il a laissé des traces derrière lui; **to leave a ~ of destruction behind one** tout détruire sur son passage; **3** (trace) gen, Hunt trace *f*, piste *f* (**of** de); **to pick up/lose sb's ~** retrouver/perdre la trace de qn; **to be on sb's ~** être sur la trace de qn; **the police are on his ~** la police est sur sa trace; **they were hot on our ~** ils étaient sur nos talons○; **4** (circuit) **to be on the campaign ~** Pol être en campagne électorale; **to follow the hippy ~ to Nepal** suivre la route des hippies jusqu'au Népal.

II *vtr* **1** (follow) [*animal, person*] suivre la piste de; [*car*] suivre; **they are being ~ed by the police** la police est sur leur trace; **we ~ed him to his front door** nous l'avons suivi à la trace jusqu'à sa porte d'entrée; **the hounds ~ed the fox to his den** les chiens ont suivi la piste du renard jusque dans son terrier; **2** (drag along) traîner; **to ~ one's hand in the water** laisser traîner sa main dans l'eau; **to ~ sth along the ground** faire traîner qch sur le sol.

III *vi* **1** (hang, droop) [*skirt, scarf*] traîner; [*plant*] pendre; **your belt is ~ing along the ground** votre ceinture traîne par terre; **2** (lag, dawdle) **they ~ed back after dark** ils sont revenus péniblement après la tombée de la nuit; **the children ~ed back into the classroom** les enfants sont rentrés dans la salle de classe en traînant les pieds; **3** (fall behind) **he was ~ing far behind the rest of the group** il traînait loin derrière le reste du groupe; **our team were ~ing by 3 goals to 1** Sport notre équipe avait un retard de 2 buts; **to ~ badly** [*racehorse, team*] être à la traîne; **they are ~ing in the polls** Pol ils sont à la traîne dans les sondages; **the company is ~ing behind its European competitors** la société est à la traîne derrière ses concurrents européens.

■ **trail away, trail off** [*person, voices*] se taire (peu à peu); [*music*] s'arrêter (peu à peu); [*signature, writing*] s'effacer.

trail: **~ bike** *n* moto *f* tout-terrain; **~ blazer** *n* pionnier/-ière *m/f*; **~-blazing** *adj* innovateur/-trice.

trailer /ˈtreɪlə(r)/ *n* **1** (vehicle, boat) remorque *f*; **2** US (caravan) caravane *f*; **3** Cin bande-annonce *f*.

trailer: **~ park** *n* US terrain *m* de caravaning; **~ tent** *n* GB tente *f* remorque.

trailing /ˈtreɪlɪŋ/ *adj* [*plant*] rampant.

train /treɪn/ **I** *n* **1** Rail train *m*; (underground) rame *f*; **on** ou **in the ~** dans le train; **fast/slow ~** train *m* rapide/omnibus; **the London/Paris ~** le train de Londres/Paris; **a ~ to London/Paris** un train pour Londres/Paris; **the morning/5 o'clock ~** le train du matin/de 5 heures; **an up/down ~** GB (in commuter belt) un train à destination de/en provenance de Londres; **to take/catch/miss the ~** prendre/attraper/manquer le train; **to send sth by ~** ou **on the ~** expédier qch par le train; **to go to Paris by ~** aller à Paris en train; **it's five hours by ~ to Geneva** Genève est à cinq heures de train; **the ~ now standing at platform 6** le train au quai numéro 6; **the ~ is running late** le train a du retard; **2** (succession) (of events) série *f*; (of ideas) enchaînement *m*; **to set off a ~ of events** déclencher une série d'événements; **a ~ of thought** un raisonnement; **the bell interrupted my/John's ~ of thought** la sonnette a interrompu le fil de mes pensées/a distrait John de ses pensées; **3** (procession) gen (of animals, vehicles, people) file *f*; (of mourners) cortège *m*; Mil train *m*; **4** (of gunpowder) traînée *f* (de poudre); **5** (motion) **to be in ~** être en train or en marche; **to set** ou **put sth in ~** mettre qch en train; **6**† (retinue) suite *f*; **the war brought famine in its ~** fig la guerre a entraîné la famine dans son sillage; **7** (on dress) traîne *f*; **8** Tech **a ~ of gears** un train d'engrenages.

II *modif* Rail [*crash, service, station*] ferroviaire; [*times, timetable*] des trains; [*driver, ticket*] de train; [*traveller*] en train; [*strike*] des chemins de fer.

III *vtr* **1** gen, Mil, Sport (instruct professionally) former [*staff, worker, musician*] (**to do** à faire); (instruct physically) entraîner [*athlete, player*] (**to do** à faire); dresser [*circus animal, dog*]; **these men are ~ed to kill** ces hommes sont entraînés à tuer; **to be ~ed on the job** être formé sur le tas; **to ~ sb for/in sth** former qn pour qch; **she is being ~ed for the Olympics/in sales techniques** on la forme pour les jeux Olympiques/aux techniques commerciales; **to ~ sb as a pilot/engineer** donner à qn une formation de pilote/d'ingénieur; **she was ~ed as a linguist** elle a reçu une formation de linguiste; **a Harvard-~ed economist** un économiste formé à Harvard; **an Irish-~ed horse** un cheval entraîné en Irlande; **he's ~ing his dog to sit up and beg** il apprend à son chien à faire le beau; **she has her husband well-~ed** hum elle a bien dressé son mari; **2** (aim, focus) **to ~ X on Y** pointer or braquer X sur Y; **she ~ed the gun/binoculars on him** elle a braqué le fusil/les jumelles sur lui; **the firemen ~ed the hose on the fire** les pompiers ont dirigé le tuyau sur les flammes; **3** Hort palisser [*plant, tree*].

IV *vi* **1** gen (for profession) être formé, étudier; **he ~ed at the Language Institute** il a été formé or il a étudié à l'Institut des Langues; **he's ~ing for the ministry** il étudie pour être pasteur; **I ~ed on a different type of machine** j'ai été formé sur un autre type de machine; **he's ~ing to be/he ~ed as a doctor** il suit/il a reçu une formation de docteur; **2** Sport s'entraîner (**for** pour); **I ~ by running 15 km** je m'entraîne en courant 15 km.

■ **train up**○: **~ up [sb], ~ [sb] up** former [*employee, staff, soldier*]; entraîner [*athlete*].

trainbearer /ˈtreɪnbeərə(r)/ *n* (female) demoiselle *f* or dame *f* d'honneur; (male) garçon *m* d'honneur.

trained /treɪnd/ *adj* [*staff, workforce, worker*] qualifié; [*professional*] diplômé; [*mind, voice*] exercé; [*singer, actor*] professionnel/-elle; [*animal*] dressé; **highly ~** hautement qualifié; **well** ou **properly ~** bien formé; [*animal*] bien dressé; **to the ~ eye/ear** pour un œil/une oreille exercé/-e; **when will you be fully ~?** quand est-ce que tu auras fini ta formation?

trainee /treɪˈni:/ *n, modif* stagiaire (*mf*).

traineeship /treɪˈni:ʃɪp/ *n* poste *m* de stagiaire.

trainer /ˈtreɪnə(r)/ *n* **1** Sport, Turf (of athlete, horse) entraîneur/-euse *m/f*; (of circus animal, dogs) dresseur/-euse *m/f*; **2** Aviat (simulator) simulateur *m* de vol; (aircraft) avion-école *m*; **3** GB (shoe) basket *f*.

train ferry *m* ferry-boat *m*.

training /ˈtreɪnɪŋ/ **I** *n* **1** gen formation *f* (**as** de); (less specialized) apprentissage *m* (**in** de); **secretarial/staff ~** formation de secrétaire/du personnel; **skills/technical ~** formation spécialisée/technique; **on-the-job ~** formation sur le tas; **~ in publish-**

ing/medicine formation à l'édition/à la médecine; **a good ~ for life/for running one's own business** un bon apprentissage de la vie/pour diriger sa propre entreprise; **'~ will be given'** (job advertisement) 'formation assurée'; **2** Mil, Sport, Equit entraînement *m*; **to be in ~** gen s'entraîner; (following specific programme) suivre un entraînement; **to break ~** interrompre l'entraînement; **to be out of ~** manquer d'entraînement; **the horse/athlete recorded an excellent time in ~** le cheval/l'athlète a fait un excellent temps à l'entraînement.
II *modif* **1** (instruction) [*course, period, scheme, method, package, agency*] de formation; [*manual*] d'instruction; [*requirements*] de qualification; **2** Mil, Sport [*course, exercise, method, facilities, mission*] d'entraînement.

training: **~ camp** *n* Mil, Sport camp *m* d'entraînement; **~ centre** *n* centre *m* de formation; **~ college** *n* GB gen école *f* professionnelle; (for teachers) centre *m* de formation pédagogique; **~ ground** *n* Sport terrain *m* d'entraînement; fig filière *f*; **~-plane** *n* avion-école *m*; **~ ship** *n* navire-école *m*; **~ shoe** *n* basket *f*.

train: **~man** ▶**1692** *m* US cheminot *m*; **~ oil** *n* huile *f* de baleine; **~ set** *n* petit train *m*; **~ spotter** *m* passionné/-e *m/f* de trains; **~ spotting** *n*: *loisir consistant à observer et répertorier les trains.*

traipse /treɪps/ *vi* traîner; **to ~ around the world** se traîner à travers le monde; **I've been traipsing around town all day** j'ai passé ma journée à traîner partout dans la ville; **to ~ in and out** entrer et sortir.

trait /treɪ, treɪt/ *n* **1** (of personality, family) trait *m*; **personality ~** trait de caractère; **2** (genetic) caractéristique *f*.

traitor /'treɪtə(r)/ *n* traître/traîtresse *m/f* (**to** à); **to turn ~** trahir; **to be a ~ to oneself** trahir sa propre cause.

traitorous /'treɪtərəs/ *adj* sout traître/traîtresse.

traitorously /'treɪtərəslɪ/ *adv* sout traîtreusement.

traitress /'treɪtrɪs/ *n* sout traîtresse *f*.

trajectory /trə'dʒektərɪ/ **I** *n* trajectoire *f*.
II *modif* [*calculation, reconstruction*] de trajectoire.

tram /træm/ **I** *n* **1** GB Transp (also **tramcar**†) tramway *m*, tram *m*; **2** Mining berline *f*; **3** Tech (adjustment) ajustage *m*.
II *modif* [*driver, rails, stop*] de tramway.
III *vtr* (*p prés etc* **-mm-**) Tech ajuster.

tramline /'træmlaɪn/ **I** *n* Transp (track) rail *m* du tramway; (route) ligne *f* de tramway.
II **tramlines** *npl* (in tennis) lignes *fpl* de côté.

trammel /'træml/ **I** *n* Equit entrave *f* also fig.
II **trammels** *npl* Tech compas *m* à ellipse.
III *vtr* **1** Tech ajuster; **2** (hamper) entraver.

tramp /træmp/ **I** *n* **1** (vagrant) (rural) vagabond *m*; (urban) clochard/-e *m/f*; **2** (sound of feet) bruit *m*; **I heard the ~ of feet** j'ai entendu un bruit de pas; **the ~ of soldiers' feet** le bruit des pas des soldats; **3** (hike) marche *f*; **4**○ injur (promiscuous woman) traînée○ *f* offensive; **5** Naut (also **~ steamer**) tramp *m*.
II *vi* **1** (hike) marcher; **2** (walk heavily) marcher à pas lourds; **to ~ up/down the stairs** monter/descendre l'escalier à pas lourds; **to ~ the streets** courir les rues.

trample /'træmpl/ **I** *vtr* lit piétiner; fig fouler [qch/qn] aux pieds; **to ~ sth underfoot** piétiner qch; **to be ~d to death** être piétiné à mort.
II *vi* **to ~ on** lit piétiner; fig fouler [qn/qch] aux pieds.

trampoline /'træmpəli:n/ **I** *n* trampoline *m*.
II *vi* faire du trampoline.

trampolining /'træmpəli:nɪŋ/ ▶**1282** *n* trampoline *m*.

tramway /'træmweɪ/ *n* ligne *f* de tramway.

trance /trɑ:ns, US træns/ *n* (in hypnosis, spiritualism etc) transe *f*; fig état *m* second; **to be in a ~** lit être en transe; fig être dans un état second; **to go into a ~** lit entrer en transe; **to put sb into a ~** faire entrer qn en transe.

trance-like /'trɑ:nslaɪk, US træns-/ *adj* [*calm, silence*] surnaturel/-elle; **to be in a ~ state** être dans un état second.

tranche /trɑ:nʃ/ *n* Fin tranche *f*.

trannie○†, **tranny**○† /'trænɪ/ *n* GB (*abrév* = **transistor**) transistor *m*, radio *f*.

tranquil /'træŋkwɪl/ *adj* tranquille.

tranquillity, **tranquility** US /ˌtræŋ'kwɪlətɪ/ *n* tranquillité *f*.

tranquillize, **tranquilize** US /'træŋkwɪlaɪz/ *vtr* mettre [qn] sous tranquillisants.

tranquillizer, **tranquilizer** US /'træŋkwɪlaɪzə(r)/ *n* tranquillisant *m*; **to be on ~s** être sous tranquillisants.

tranquillizer dart *n* Vet fléchette *f* (*pour calmer un animal*).

tranquilly /'træŋkwɪlɪ/ *adj* (calmly) tranquillement; (peacefully) paisiblement.

transact /træn'zækt/ *vtr* négocier [*business, rights*]; **to ~ a deal** passer un accord.

transaction /træn'zækʃn/ **I** *n* **1** (piece of business) gen, Comm, Fin transaction *f*; (on stock exchange) opération *f*; **legal ~** procédure *f* légale; **cash/credit card ~** transaction en liquide/effectuée avec une carte de crédit; **foreign exchange ~** opération de change; **2** (negotiating) **the ~ of business** les relations *fpl* d'affaires; **3** Comput transaction *f*.
II **transactions** *npl* (proceedings) (of society etc) actes *mpl*.

transactional /træn'zækʃənl/ *adj* transactionnel/-elle.

transactional analysis, **TA** *n* analyse *f* transactionnelle.

transalpine /trænz'ælpaɪn/ *adj* transalpin.

transatlantic /ˌtrænzət'læntɪk/ *adj* [*crossing, flight*] transatlantique; [*attitude, accent*] d'outre-atlantique *inv*.

Transcaucasia /ˌtrænzkɔ:'keɪzjə/ *pr n* Transcaucasie *f*.

Transcaucasian /ˌtrænzkɔ:'keɪzjən/ *adj* transcaucasien/-ienne.

transceiver /træn'si:və(r)/ *n* émetteur-récepteur *m*.

transcend /træn'send/ *vtr* **1** (go beyond) transcender [*barrier, reason*]; **2** (surpass) surpasser [*performance, quality*]; **3** Relig, Philos transcender.

transcendence /træn'sendəns/ *n* transcendance *f*.

transcendent /træn'sendənt/ *adj* transcendant.

transcendental /ˌtrænsen'dentl/ *adj* transcendantal.

transcendentalism /ˌtrænsen'dentəlɪzəm/ *n* transcendantalisme *m*.

transcendentalist /ˌtrænsen'dentəlɪst/ *n, adj* transcendantaliste (*mf*).

transcendental meditation, **TM** *n* méditation *f* transcendantale.

transcontinental /ˌtrænzkɒntɪ'nentl/ *adj* transcontinental.

transcribe /træn'skraɪb/ *vtr* **1** gen, Mus (by writing) transcrire (**into** en); **2** Radio (by recording) enregistrer [*concert, programme*]; **3** Comput transcrire (**onto** sur).

transcript /'trænskrɪpt/ *n* **1** (copy) transcription *f*; **2** US Sch duplicata *m* de livret scolaire.

transcription /ˌtræn'skrɪpʃn/ *n* gen, Phon transcription *f*.

transduce /træns'dju:s, US -'du:s/ *vtr* Biol transformer (**into** en).

transducer /træns'dju:sə(r), US -'du:-/ *n* Elec transducteur *m*.

transduction /træns'dʌkʃn/ *n* Biol transduction *f*.

transect /træn'sekt/ *vtr* couper (transversalement).

transept /'trænsept/ *n* transept *m*.

transfer **I** /'trænsfɜ:(r)/ *n* **1** (transmission) (of information, technology, skills, feelings, power, heat, goods, ownership, shares) transfert *m* (**from** de; **to** à); (of property, debt) cession *f* (**from** de; **to** à); (of funds) virement *m*, transfert *m*; (of a right) transmission *m*; **file/heat ~** transfert de fichier/chaleur; **2** (relocation) (of employee, player, patient, prisoner) transfert *m* (**from** de; **to** à); (of civil servant) mutation *f* (**from** de; **to** à); (of proceedings) renvoi *m* (**from** de; **to** devant); **3** GB Art, Fashn (on skin, china, paper) décalcomanie *f*; (on T-shirt) transfert *m*; **4** Sewing décalque *m*; **5** Tourism transfert *m*; **bus ~** transfert en car; **6** US Rail billet *m* de correspondance; **7** Ling, Biol, Chem, Psych transfert *m*.
II /træns'fɜ:(r)/ *vtr* (*p prés etc* **-rr-**) **1** (move) transférer [*data, luggage, prisoner*] (**from** de; **to** à); **to ~ data onto hard disc** transférer les données sur disque dur; **2** (recopy) reporter [*details, information*] (**from** de; **onto** sur); **3** (hand over) transférer [*land, ownership*]; virer [*money*]; céder [*property, power*]; transmettre [*right*]; reporter [*allegiance, support*]; **4** (relocate) transférer [*employee, office, prisoner*]; muter [*civil servant*]; **5** Telecom faire passer [*call*]; **I'm ~ing you to reception** je vous passe la réception; **6** Sport transférer [*player*]; **7** Math transférer [*term*]; **8** (translate) **to ~ an idea onto paper** mettre une idée sur le papier.
III /træns'fɛ:(r)/ *vi* (*p prés etc* **-rr-**) **1** (relocate) [*employee, player, passenger*] être transféré; [*civil servant*] être muté; **I'm ~ring to the Boston office** on me transfère au bureau de Boston; **2** Aviat [*traveller*] changer d'avion; **3** Univ [*student*] (change university) changer d'université; (change course) changer de cours; **to ~ from Bath to York** faire un transfert de Bath à York; **4** (adapt) **the novel didn't ~ well to the stage** le roman ne passait pas bien à la scène.

transferable /træns'fɜ:rəbl/ *adj* **1** Fin [*security, value*] négociable; **2** Jur, gen [*right, vote, debt, expertise, skill*] transmissible.

transfer: **~ certificate** *n* certificat *m* de transfert; **~ deed** *n* acte *m* de cession; **~ desk** *n* Aviat guichet *m* de correspondance; **~ duty** *n* droit *m* de mutation.

transferee /ˌtrænsfɜ:'ri:/ *n* **1** Jur (of goods, property) cessionnaire *mf*; **2** (of letter of credit) bénéficiaire *mf*.

transference /'trænsfərəns, US træns'fɜ:rəns/ *n* **1** (transfer) (of blame, responsibility) transfert *m*; (of power, thought) transmission *f*; **2** Psych transfert *m*.

transfer: **~ fee** *n* Sport prix *m* du transfert; **~ form** *n* Fin acte *m* de cession; **~ income** *n* revenu *m* de transfert; **~ list** *n* Sport liste *f* des transferts; **~ lounge** *n* Aviat salle *f* de transit.

transferor /træns'fɜ:rə(r)/ *n* Jur cédant/-e *m/f*.

transfer: **~ passenger** *n* passager/-ère *m/f* en transit; **~ payment** *n* transfert *m* social; **~red charge call** *n* Telecom appel *m* en PCV; **~ season** *n* Sport période *f* des transferts; **~ time** *n* Tourism durée *f* du transfert.

transfiguration /ˌtrænsfɪgə'reɪʃn, US -gjə'r-/ *n* sout, Relig transfiguration *f*.

transfigure /træns'fɪgə(r), US -gjər/ *vtr* transfigurer.

transfix /træns'fɪks/ *vtr* **1** (render motionless) (*gén au passif*) [*horror, fear*] paralyser (**with** de; **by** par); [*beauty, gaze*] stupéfier; **2** (impale) transpercer.

transform /træns'fɔ:m/ **I** *vtr* (all contexts) transformer (**from** de; **into** en); **to be ~ed into** se transformer en.
II *v refl* **to ~ oneself** se transformer (**into** en).

transformation /ˌtrænsfə'meɪʃn/ *n* (all contexts) transformation *f* (**from** de; **into** en).

transformational /ˌtrænsfə'meɪʃənl/ *adj* transformationnel/-elle.

transformational grammar *n* grammaire *f* transformationnelle.

transformer /træns'fɔ:mə(r)/ *n* transformateur *m*.

transformer station *n* poste *m* de transformation.

transfuse /træns'fju:z/ *vtr* **1** Med transfuser; **2** littér **to be ~d with** être empli de [*joy, excitement*]; être pris de [*sorrow*].

transfusion /træns'fju:ʒn/ *n* transfusion *f*; **to give sb a ~** faire une transfusion à qn.

transgenic /træns'dʒenɪk/ *adj* transgénique.

transgress /trænz'gres/ **I** *vtr* transgresser.
II *vi* **1** Jur commettre une infraction; **2** Relig commettre un péché.

transgression /trænz'greʃn/ *n* **1** Jur transgression *f* (**against** de); **2** Relig péché *m*.

transgressor /trænz'gresə(r)/ *n* **1** Jur transgresseur *m* (**against** de); **2** Relig pécheur/pécheresse *m/f*.

tranship *vtr* ▶ **transship**.

transhipment *n* ▶ **transshipment**.

transience /'trænzɪəns/ *n* caractère *m* éphémère.

transient /'trænzɪənt, US 'trænʃnt/ **I** *n* US personne *f* de passage.
II *adj* [*phase*] transitoire; [*emotion, beauty*] éphémère; [*population*] de passage.

transistor /træn'zɪstə(r), -'sɪstə(r)/ *n* **1** (radio) transistor *m*, radio *f*; **2** Electron (semiconductor) transistor *m*.

transistorize /træn'zɪstəraɪz, -'sɪst-/ *vtr* transistoriser.

transit /'trænzɪt, -sɪt/ **I** *n* **1** gen transit *m*; **in ~** en transit; **2** Astron passage *m*.
II *modif* [*camp, lounge*] de transit; [*passenger*] en transit.

transition /træn'zɪʃn, -'sɪʃn/ **I** *n* **1** gen transition *f* (**from** de; **to** à); **in a state of ~** dans une phase transitoire; **2** Mus (between keys) modulation *f*; (between sections) transition *f*.
II *modif* [*period, point*] de transition.

transitional /træn'zɪʃənl, -'sɪʃənl/ *adj* [*arrangement, measure*] transitoire; [*economy, period*] de transition.

transitive /'trænzətɪv/ *adj* transitif/-ive.

transitively /'trænzətɪvlɪ/ *adv* transitivement.

transitivity /ˌtrænzə'tɪvətɪ/ *n* transitivité *f*.

transitoriness /'trænsɪtrɪnɪs, US -tɔ:rɪnɪs/ *n* caractère *m* passager.

transitory /'trænsɪtrɪ, US -tɔ:rɪ/ *adj* [*stage*] transitoire; [*hope, pain*] passager/-ère.

transit van *n* camionnette *f* (de transport).

Transkei /træns'kaɪ/ *pr n* Transkei *m*.

translatable /trænz'leɪtəbl/ *adj* traduisible.

translate /trænz'leɪt/ **I** *vtr* **1** Ling traduire (**from** de; **into** en); fig interpréter [*gesture, remark*]; traduire [*theory, idea, principle*] (**into** en); **to ~ theory into practice** traduire la théorie en pratique; **2** (convert) convertir [*measurement, temperature*] (**into** en); **3** Math translater.
II *vi* **1** gen [*person*] traduire; [*word, phrase, text*] se traduire; **his poetry does not ~ well** sa poésie ne se traduit pas bien; **this word does not ~** ce mot est intraduisible; **2** Comput traduire.

translation /trænz'leɪʃn/ *n* (all contexts) traduction *f* (**from** de; **into** en; **of** de); **in ~** en traduction; **the play loses a lot in ~** la pièce perd beaucoup à la traduction.

translator /trænz'leɪtə(r)/ *n* **1** (person) traducteur/-trice *m/f*; **2** Radio réémetteur *m*.

transliterate /trænz'lɪtəreɪt/ *vtr* translittérer.

transliteration /ˌtrænzlɪtə'reɪʃn/ *n* translittération *f*.

translucence /ˌtrænz'lu:sns/ *n* translucidité *f*.

translucent /trænz'lu:snt/ *adj* translucide.

transmigrate /ˌtrænzmaɪ'greɪt/ *vi* [*person, animal*] migrer; [*soul*] transmigrer.

transmigration /ˌtrænzmaɪ'greɪʃn/ *n* (of people, animals) migration *f*; (of souls) transmigration *f*.

transmissible /trænz'mɪsəbl/ *adj* transmissible (**to** à).

transmission /trænz'mɪʃn/ *n* (all contexts) transmission *f*.

transmission: **~ belt** *n* courroie *f* de transmission; **~ cable** *n* câble *m* de transmission; **~ chain** *n* chaîne *f* de transmission; **~ line** *n* ligne *f* de transport (d'énergie); **~ shaft** *n* arbre *m* de transmission; **~ tunnel** *n* tunnel *m* de la transmission.

transmit /trænz'mɪt/ (*p prés etc* **-tt-**) **I** *vtr* (all contexts) transmettre (**from** de; **to** à).
II *vi* émettre.

transmittance /trænz'mɪtns/ *n* transmittance *f*.

transmitter /trænz'mɪtə(r)/ *n* Radio, TV émetteur *m*; Telecom capsule *f* microphonique; **short/long wave ~** émetteur *m* à ondes courtes/longues; **radio ~** émetteur *m* radio.

transmogrify /trænz'mɒgrɪfaɪ/ sout **I** *vtr* transformer (**into** en).
II *v refl* se métamorphoser (**into** en).

transmutable /trænz'mju:təbl/ *adj* sout transmuable (**into** en).

transmutation /ˌtrænzmju:'teɪʃn/ *n* Chem, fig transformation *f*.

transmute /trænz'mju:t/ *vtr* Chem, fig transmuer (**into** en).

transom /'trænsəm/ *n* **1** Archit traverse *f*; **2** Naut tableau *m* arrière; **3** US (fanlight) imposte *f*.

transonic *adj* ▶ **transsonic**.

transparency /træns'pærənsɪ/ *n* **1** ¢ gen, fig transparence *f*; **2** Phot diapositive *f*; **colour ~** diapositive *f* en couleur; **3** (for overhead projector) transparent *m*.

transparent /træns'pærənt/ *adj* lit, fig transparent.

transparently /træns'pærəntlɪ/ *adv* (obviously) manifestement.

transpierce /træns'pɪəs/ *vtr* littér transpercer.

transpiration /ˌtrænspɪ'reɪʃn/ *n* transpiration *f*.

transpire /træn'spaɪə(r), trɑ:-/ *vi* **1** (be revealed) apparaître; **it ~d that** il est apparu par la suite que; **2** (occur) usage critiqué se produire; **3** Bot, Physiol transpirer.

transplant /træns'plɑ:nt, US -'plænt/ **I** *n* (operation) transplantation *f*; (organ, tissue transplanted) transplant *m*; **to have a heart/lung ~** subir une transplantation cardiaque/pulmonaire.
II *modif* **~ operation** transplantation *f*; **~ patient** transplanté/-e *m/f*; **heart ~ patient** transplanté/-e *m/f* cardiaque.
III *vtr* **1** Hort transplanter [*plant, tree*]; repiquer [*seedlings*]; **2** Med transplanter; **3** fig transplanter [*person, custom etc*] (**to** en).

transplantation /ˌtrænsplɑ:n'teɪʃn, US -plænt-/ *n* transplantation *f*.

transponder /træn'spɒndə(r)/ *n* transpondeur *m*.

transport /træns'pɔ:t/ **I** *n* **1** (of goods, passengers) transport *m*; **air/rail/road ~** transport aérien/ferroviaire/par route; **to travel by public ~** utiliser les transports en commun; **Transport Secretary**, **Secretary of State for Transport** GB ministre *m* des Transports; **Ministry** GB ou **Department of Transport** ministère *m* des Transports; **2** (means of travelling) moyen *m* de locomotion; **I haven't got any ~ at the moment** je n'ai pas de moyen de locomotion en ce moment; **3** Mil (ship) (navire *m* de) transport *m* de troupes; (aircraft) (avion *m* de) transport *m* de troupes; **4** littér (rapture) transport *m*; **to go into ~s of delight** tomber dans des transports de joie.
II *modif* [*costs, facilities, ship*] de transport; [*industry, strike, system*] des transports.
III *vtr* **1** transporter [*passengers, goods*] (**from** de; **to** à); **to be ~ed back to one's childhood** fig être ramené à son enfance; **2** Hist (deport) transporter.

transportable /træns'pɔ:təbl/ **I** *n* Telecom transportable *m*.
II *adj* transportable.

transportation /ˌtrænspɔ:'teɪʃn/ *n* **1** US = **transport I 1, 2, II**; **2** (of passengers, goods) transport *m*; **3** Hist transport *m*.

transport café *n* GB café *m* de routiers.

transporter /træns'pɔ:tə(r)/ *n* **1** Mil (for troops, planes) transport *m*; **tank ~** porte-char *m*; **2** ▶ **car transporter**.

Transport Police *n* GB ≈ la police des chemins de fer.

transpose /træn'spəʊz/ *vtr* **1** intervertir [*pages, arguments*]; **2** Math, Mus transposer.

transposition /ˌtrænspə'zɪʃn/ *n* **1** (of pages, arguments) interversion *f*; **2** Math, Mus transposition *f*.

transputer /træns'pju:tə(r), -z'pju:tə(r)/ *n* transordinateur *m*.

transsexual /trænz'sekʃʊəl/ *n, adj* transsexuel/-elle (*m/f*).

transsexualism /trænz'sekʃʊəlɪzəm/ *n* transsexualisme *m*.

transship /træn'ʃɪp/ *vtr* transborder.

transshipment /træn'ʃɪpmənt/ *n* transbordement *m*.

Trans-Siberian /ˌtrænsaɪ'bɪərɪən/ *adj* transsibérien/-ienne.

transsonic /træn'sɒnɪk/ *adj* transsonique.

transubstantiate /ˌtrænsəb'stænʃɪeɪt/ *vtr, vi* transsubstantier.

transubstantiation /ˌtrænsəbˌstænʃɪ'eɪʃn/ *n* transsubstantiation *f*.

Transvaal /'trænzvɑ:l/ *pr n* Transvaal *m*.

transversal /trænz'vɜ:sl/ **I** *n* (intersecting triangle) transversale *f*; (intersecting hyperbola) axe *m* transverse; (intersecting parallel lines) droite *f* sécante.
II *adj* transversal.

transversally /trænz'vɜ:səlɪ/ *adv* transversalement.

transverse /'trænzvɜ:s/ **I** *n* partie *f* transversale.
II *adj* transversal.

transversely /'trænzvɜ:slɪ/ *adv* transversalement.

transvestism /trænz'vestɪzəm/ *n* travestisme *m*.

transvestite /trænz'vestaɪt/ *n* travesti/-e *m/f*.

Transylvania /ˌtrænsɪl'veɪnɪə/ *pr n* Transylvanie *f*.

Transylvanian /ˌtrænsɪl'veɪnɪən/ *adj* transylvanien/-ienne.

trap /træp/ **I** *n* **1** Hunt, fig (snare) piège *m*; **to set a ~ for** poser un piège pour [*animals*]; tendre un piège à [*humans*]; **to fall into a ~** tomber dans un piège; **to fall into the ~ of doing** fig commettre l'erreur de faire; **2** (vehicle) cabriolet *m*; **3** (in plumbing) siphon *m*; **4** Sport (in shooting) ball-trap *m*; **5** (in dog racing) stalle *f* de départ; **6**◐ (mouth) gueule◐ *f*; **shut your ~!** ta gueule◐!
II *vtr* (*p prés etc* **-pp-**) **1** Hunt prendre [qch] au piège [*animal*]; **2** (catch, immobilize) coincer [*person, finger*]; **to be ~ped in an elevator** être coincé dans un ascenseur; **he ~ped a nerve in his back** Med il s'est coincé un nerf du dos; **3** (prevent from escaping) retenir [*heat*]; empêcher [qch] de fuir [*gas*]; **there was air ~ped in the pipe** il y avait de l'air dans le tuyau; **4** fig (emprison) prendre [qn] au piège; **to ~ sb into doing** amener qn à faire; **to be/feel ~ped (in a situation/a marriage)** être/se sentir piégé or coincé (dans une situation/un mariage).
III *vi* (*p prés etc* **-pp-**) Hunt braconner.

trapdoor /'træpdɔ:(r)/ *n* trappe *f*.

trapeze /trə'pi:z, US træ-/ *n* **1** (also **flying ~**) (in circus) trapèze *m*; **to perform on a ~** faire du trapèze; **2** Naut trapèze *m*.

trapeze: **~ act** *n* numéro *m* de trapèze; **~ artist** *n* ▶1692 trapéziste *mf*.

trapezist /trəˈpiːzɪst, US træ-/ ▶1692 *n* trapéziste *mf*.

trapezium /trəˈpiːzɪəm/ *n* (*pl* **-ium** ou **-ia**) **1** GB Math trapèze *m*; **2** Anat os *m* trapèze.

trapezius /trəˈpiːzɪəs/ *n* (*pl* **~es**) (muscle *m*) trapèze *m*.

trapezoid /ˈtræpɪzɔɪd/ *n* US Math trapèze *m*.

trapezoidal /ˈtræpɪzɔɪdl/ *adj* trapézoïde.

trapper /ˈtræpə(r)/ *n* trappeur *m*.

trappings /ˈtræpɪŋz/ *npl* **1** péj (outer signs) attributs *mpl*; **the ~ of** les signes *mpl* extérieurs de [*wealth, power, success*]; **2** (harness) caparaçon *m*; **3** (ceremonial dress) apparat *m*.

Trappist /ˈtræpɪst/ **I** *n* trappiste *m*.
II *adj* **~ monk** trappiste *m*; **~ monastery** monastère *m* de la Trappe.

trap shooting *n* (tir *m* au) ball-trap *m*.

trash /træʃ/ **I** *n* ¢ **1** US (refuse) (in streets) déchets *mpl*; (household) ordures *fpl*; (garden) détritus *mpl*; **to put the ~ out** sortir les poubelles; **2**○ péj (goods) camelote○ *f*; **3**○ péj (nonsense) âneries *fpl*; **to talk ~** dire or débiter des âneries; **the book/film is (absolute) ~** le livre/film est (complètement) nul○; **4**○ (person) injur minable○ *mf* offensive.
II○ *vtr* US **1** (vandalize) saccager [*vehicle, building*]; **2** (criticize) descendre [qch/qn] en flammes○ [*person, performance*].

trashcan /ˈtræʃkæn/ *n* US poubelle *f*.

trashed○ /træʃt/ *adj* bourré◑, ivre; **to get ~** se soûler la gueule◑.

trash heap /ˈtræʃ hiːp/ *n* lit tas *m* d'ordures; **to throw sb/sth on the ~** fig mettre qn/qch au rancart.

trash man ▶1692 *n* US éboueur *m*.

trashy○ /ˈtræʃɪ/ *adj* péj [*novel, film, magazine*] nul/nulle○; [*souvenirs*] de pacotille pej.

trauma /ˈtrɔːmə, US ˈtraʊ-/ *n* (*pl* **-as, -ata**) Med, Psych traumatisme *m*; **what a ~!** fig quelle horreur!

trauma centre *n* centre *m* d'aide psychologique (*pour victimes de catastrophes*).

traumatic /trɔːˈmætɪk, US traʊ-/ *adj* Psych, fig traumatisant; Med traumatique.

traumatism /ˈtrɔːmətɪzəm, US ˈtraʊ-/ *n* traumatisme *m*.

traumatize /ˈtrɔːmətaɪz, US ˈtraʊ-/ *vtr* (all contexts) traumatiser.

travail /ˈtræveɪl, US trəˈveɪl/ *n* littér **1** (work) dur labeur *m*; **2** (of childbirth) travail *m*.

travel /ˈtrævl/ **I** *n* **1** gen, Tourism voyages *mpl*; (one specific trip) voyage *m*; **air/sea/space ~** voyages aériens/par mer/spatiaux; **business/holiday ~** voyages d'affaires/d'agrément; **overseas** ou **foreign ~** voyages à l'étranger; **~ by road/train/car** voyages par la route/en train/en voiture; **~ to Italy/Canada/the Far East** des voyages en Italie/au Canada/en Extrême-Orient; **after 27 hours' ~, he was exhausted** après 27 heures de voyage, il était épuisé; **~ is easy/expensive/dangerous in those parts** il est facile/cher/dangereux de voyager dans cette région; **the job involves a lot of ~** le poste exige beaucoup de déplacements; **2** Tech course *f*.
II travels *npl* voyages *mpl*; **on** ou **in the course of my ~s** au cours de mes voyages; **he's off on his ~s again** il repart en voyage.
III *modif* [*book, grant, plans, service*] de voyage; [*brochure, company, firm, magazine*] de voyages; [*allowance, voucher, expenses*] de déplacement; [*business*] de tourisme; [*writer*] de récits de voyage; [*ban*] de déplacements à l'étranger; **~ regulations** règlement de passage à l'étranger; **'~ time: 3 hours'** 'durée du trajet: 3 heures'.
IV *vtr* (*p prés etc* **-ll-**, US **-l-**) parcourir [*country, district, road, distance*].
V *vi* (*p prés etc* **-ll-**, US **-l-**) **1** (journey) [*person*] voyager; **to ~ by bus/car etc** voyager en bus/voiture etc; **their teacher is ~ling with them** leur professeur voyage avec eux; **he ~s widely** il voyage beaucoup; **to ~ on a season ticket/German passport** voyager avec un abonnement/un passeport allemand; **to ~ in style** voyager princièrement; **they were ~ling abroad** ils étaient en voyage à l'étranger; **to ~ abroad/to Brazil** aller à l'étranger/au Brésil; **to ~ light** voyager léger; **this is the way to ~!** c'est comme ça que je comprends les voyages!; **2** (move) [*person, news, object, plane, boat*] aller; [*car, lorry, train*] aller, rouler; Phys [*light, sound, wave*] se propager; [*moving part*] se déplacer; **bad news ~s fast** les mauvaises nouvelles vont vite; **the washing machine ~s when it spins** la machine à laver se déplace pendant l'essorage; **to ~ at 50 km/h** rouler à 50 km/h, faire du 50 km/h; **the train was ~ling through a tunnel/up a hill** le train traversait un tunnel/montait une pente; **the car/motorbike was really ~ling**○ la voiture/moto roulait à toute vitesse; **to ~ faster than the speed of sound** dépasser la vitesse du son; **a bullet ~s at a tremendous speed** une balle file à une vitesse impressionnante; **to ~ a long way** [*person*] faire beaucoup de chemin; [*arrow*] aller très loin; **to ~ back in time** remonter le temps; **to ~ forward in time** se projeter dans l'avenir; **her mind ~led back to her youth** elle s'est reportée en esprit à sa jeunesse; **his eye ~led along the line of men** il a promené son regard sur la rangée d'hommes; **3** Comm (as sales rep) **to ~ in** être représentant en [*product*]; **he ~s in encyclopedias** il est représentant en encyclopédies; **to ~ for** être représentant de [*company, firm*]; **4 to ~ well** [*cheese, fruit, vegetable, wine*] supporter le transport or bien voyager; **5** Sport (in netball) *faire plus de pas qu'il n'est autorisé*.
VI -travelled GB, **-traveled** US (*dans composés*) **much-** ou **well-~led** [*road, route*] fréquenté; **much-** ou **widely-~led person** personne qui a beaucoup voyagé.
IDIOMS **~ broadens the mind** ≈ les voyages forment la jeunesse.

travel: **~ agency** *n* agence *f* de voyages; **~ agent** ▶1692, 1692 *n* agent *m* de voyages; **~ agent's** ▶1692 *n* agence *f* de voyage.

travelator /ˈtrævəleɪtə(r)/ *n* tapis *m* roulant, trottoir *m* roulant.

travel bureau *n* = **travel agency**.

travel card *n* GB carte *f* de transport; **weekly/monthly/one-day ~** carte de transport hebdomadaire/mensuelle/valable une journée.

travel: **~ flash** *n* TV, Radio flash *m* d'information routière; **~ insurance** *n* assurance *f* voyage.

traveller GB, **traveler** US /ˈtrævlə(r)/ *n* **1** (voyager) (on business, holiday) voyageur/-euse *m/f*; (regular passenger) usager/-ère *m/f*; **~s to Moscow/Russia** les voyageurs pour Moscou/la Russie; **air/rail ~** usager/-ère de l'air/des chemins de fer; **a frequent ~ by air** un usager régulier de l'avion; **2** (commercial) représentant *m* de commerce; **3** GB (gypsy) nomade *mf*.

traveller: **~'s cheque** GB, **traveler's check** US *n* chèque-voyage *m*; **~'s joy** *n* clématite *f* des haies; **~'s tale** *n* récit *m* de voyage enjolivé.

travelling GB, **traveling** US /ˈtrævlɪŋ/ **I** *n* gen voyages *mpl*; (on single occasion) voyage *m*; **~ is tiring** les voyages sont fatigants; **to go ~** partir en voyage; **the job involves ~** le poste exige des déplacements; **~ in Britain is expensive** voyager en Grande Bretagne coûte cher.
II *adj* **1** (mobile) [*actor, company, circus, exhibition*] itinérant; [*bank*] mobile; **the ~ public** les usagers des transports; **2** (for travellers) [*companion, gadget, game, rug*] de voyage; [*conditions*] (on road) de route; **3** (for travel purposes) [*grant, fellowship, scholarship*] de voyage; [*allowance, expenses*] de déplacement.

travelling: **~ clock** *n* réveil *m* de voyage; **~ library** *n* bibliobus *m*; **~ salesman** ▶1692 *n* voyageur *m* de commerce.

travelogue /ˈtrævəlɒg/ GB, **travelog** US /ˈtrævəlɔːg/ *n* (film) film *m* de voyage; (talk) conférence *f* sur son voyage or ses voyages.

travel-sick /ˈtrævlsɪk/ *adj* **to be** ou **get ~** souffrir du mal des transports.

travel: **~-sickness** *n* mal *m* des transports; **~-sickness pills** *npl* médicament *m* contre le mal des transports; **~ warrant** *n* Mil feuille *f* de route.

traverse /trəˈvɜːs/ **I** *n* **1** (in climbing, skiing) traversée *f*; **2** Jur contestation *f*; **3** Constr traverse *f*; **4** Mil pare-éclats *m inv*.
II *vtr* **1** sout franchir [*ocean, desert*]; [*comet, route*] traverser; **2** (in climbing, skiing) traverser; **3** Jur contester.
III *vi* (in skiing) descendre en zig-zag.

travesty /ˈtrævəstɪ/ pej **I** *n* **1** Art, Literat farce *f*; **2** (distortion) travestissement *m* (**of** de); **the trial was a ~ of justice** c'était une parodie de procès, le procès était une farce.
II *vtr* (all contexts) travestir.

trawl /trɔːl/ **I** *n* **1** Fishg (net) chalut *m*; (line) palangre *f*; **2** fig (action, result) pêche *f* (**for** à).
II *vtr* **1** Fishg pêcher dans [*water, bay*]; **2** fig (also **~ through**) écumer [*place*]; éplucher [*papers*].
III *vi* **1** Fishg pêcher au chalut; **to ~ for herring** pêcher le hareng au chalut; **2** fig **to ~ for information** aller à la pêche aux renseignements.

trawler /ˈtrɔːlə(r)/ **I** *n* chalutier *m*.
II *modif* [*crew*] de chalutier; [*fleet*] de chalutiers.

trawlerman /ˈtrɔːləmən/ ▶1692 *n* chalutier *m*.

trawling /ˈtrɔːlɪŋ/ *n* pêche *f* au chalut.

tray /treɪ/ *n* gen plateau *m*; **baking ~** plaque *f* à pâtisserie; **ice ~** bac *m* à glaçons; **oven ~** plaque *f* de four; **in-/out-~** corbeille *f* arrivée/départ; **seed ~** germoir *m*.

traycloth /ˈtreɪklɒθ/ *n* napperon *m*.

treacherous /ˈtretʃərəs/ *adj* [*person, weather, ice, current, quicksand*] traître/traîtresse; [*road, driving conditions*] traître/traîtresse, très dangereux/-euse.

treacherously /ˈtretʃərəslɪ/ *adv* [*act, betray*] traîtreusement.

treachery /ˈtretʃərɪ/ *n* traîtrise *f*.

treacle /ˈtriːkl/ **I** *n* GB (black) mélasse *f*; (golden syrup) mélasse *f* raffinée.
II *modif* [*tart, pudding*] à la mélasse raffinée.

treacly /ˈtriːklɪ/ *adj* GB sirupeux/-euse also fig.

tread /tred/ **I** *n* **1** (footstep) pas *m*; **2** (of stair) dessus *m* (d'une marche); **3** (of tyre) (pattern) sculptures *fpl*; (outer surface) chape *f*; **there's almost no ~ left** les sculptures sont presque complètement usées.
II *vtr* (*prét* **trod**; *pp* **trodden**) fouler [*street, path, area*]; **to ~ grapes** fouler du raisin; **to ~ water** nager sur place; **to ~ sth underfoot** piétiner qch; **to ~ mud indoors** traîner de la boue dans la maison; **to ~ mud into the carpet** écraser de la boue sur la moquette; **to ~ a path across the hillside** tracer un chemin à flanc de colline; **she's ~ing a dangerous path** elle s'engage sur une voie dangereuse; **to ~ the same path as** fig marcher sur les pas de; **a well-trodden path** lit, fig une voie très empruntée.
III *vi* (*prét* **trod**; *pp* **trodden**) (walk) marcher; **to ~ on** (walk) marcher sur; (squash) piétiner; **to ~ carefully** ou **warily** fig être or se montrer prudent.

■ **tread down**: **~ [sth] down**, **~ down [sth]** piétiner [*earth, plant*].

■ **tread in**: **~ [sth] in**, **~ in [sth]** tasser la terre sur [*plant, root*].

treadle /ˈtredl/ **I** *n* pédale *f*.
II *modif* [*sewing machine, loom*] à pédale.
III *vi* pédaler.

treadmill /ˈtredmɪl/ *n* **1** (for hamster, mouse) roue *f*; **2** Hist (worked by animal) trépigneuse *f*; (worked by people) roue *f* à cheville; **3** fig (dull routine) train-train *m*; (which one can't break) engrenage *m*.

treas *abrév écrite* = **treasurer**.

treason /ˈtriːzn/ *n* trahison *f* (**against** envers); **high ~** haute trahison; **that would be ~** ce serait une trahison.

treasonable /ˈtriːzənəbl/ *adj* [*act, offence*] qui constitue une trahison.

treasure /ˈtreʒə(r)/ **I** *n* **1** (hoard of valuables) trésor *m*; **to find buried ~** trouver un trésor enfoui; **2** (precious object) trésor *m*; **art/national ~s** trésors artistiques/nationaux; **3** (prized person) (woman) perle *f*; (man) homme *m* en or.
II *vtr* **1** (cherish) chérir [*person, memory, keepsake, gift*]; **2** (prize) tenir beaucoup à [*independence, friendship*]; adorer [*person*]; tenir beaucoup à [*object, possession*].
III treasured *pp adj* [*memory, possession*] précieux/-ieuse.

treasure house *n* (building) musée *m*; **a ~ of information** fig une mine d'informations.

treasure: **~ hunt** *n* chasse *f* au trésor; **~ hunter** *n* chasseur/-euse *m/f* de trésor.

treasurer /ˈtreʒərə(r)/ *n* **1** (on committee) trésorier/-ière *m/f*; **to act** ou **serve as ~** être trésorier; **2** US Comm, Fin (in company) directeur *m* financier.

treasure trove *n* (all contexts) trésor *m*.

treasury /ˈtreʒərɪ/ *n* **1** (state, company revenues) trésorerie *f*; **2** fig (anthology) trésor *m*; **3** (in cathedral) trésor *m*; (in palace) musée *m*.

Treasury /ˈtreʒərɪ/ Fin, Pol **I** *n* ministère *m* des finances.
II *modif* [*figures, official, policy*] du ministère des finances.

Treasury bench *n* GB banc *m* du gouvernement.

Treasury bill *n* **1** GB billet *m* or bon *m* du Trésor; **2** US bon *m* du Trésor en comptes courants (*à court terme*).

Treasury bond *n* **1** GB bon *m* du Trésor; **2** US bon *m* du Trésor (*à long terme*).

Treasury: **~ Department** *n* US ministère *m* des finances; **~ Minister** *n* GB ministre *m* des finances; **~ note** *n* US obligation *f* du Trésor; **~ Secretary** *n* US ministre *m* des finances; **~ warrant** *n* mandat *m* du Trésor.

treat /triːt/ **I** *n* **1** (pleasure) (petit) plaisir *m*; (food) gâterie *f*; **to give sb a ~** offrir un petit plaisir à qn; **I gave myself a ~** je me suis offert un petit plaisir; **I took them to the museum as a ~** je les ai emmenés au musée pour leur faire plaisir; **it was a ~ to see you looking well/to get your letter** ça m'a fait vraiment plaisir de te voir aussi bonne mine/de recevoir ta lettre; **oysters! what a ~!** des huîtres! vous nous gâtez!; **she gets lots of ~s from her grandmother** elle se fait beaucoup gâter par sa grand-mère; **as a special ~ I was allowed to stay up late** exceptionnellement on m'a permis de me coucher plus tard; **her birthday ~ was a trip to the zoo** pour son cadeau d'anniversaire, on l'a emmenée au zoo; **a ~ in store** une bonne surprise; **2**○ **it's my/Henry's ~** c'est moi/Henry qui paie; (food, drink) c'est moi/Henry qui régale○; **to stand sb a ~**○ offrir or payer qch à qn; **he stood us a ~ in the pub/the restaurant** il nous a payé une tournée au pub/un repas au restaurant.
II○ **a treat** *adv phr* GB **the plan worked a ~** le projet a marché comme sur des roulettes○; **the car works a ~ now** la voiture tourne rond○ maintenant; **the cake/present/show went down a ~ with the children** les enfants ont adoré le gâteau/cadeau/spectacle; **the room looks a ~ now you've redecorated it** la pièce est superbe, maintenant que tu l'as refaite.
III *vtr* **1** (act towards, handle) gen traiter [*person, animal, object, topic*]; **to ~ sb well/badly** bien traiter/maltraiter qn; **that's no way to ~ a child!** on ne traite pas un enfant comme ça!; **to ~ sb/sth with** traiter qn avec [*care, contempt, kindness, suspicion*]; **to ~ sb like a child/fool** traiter qn comme un enfant/idiot; **we were ~ed as if...** on nous a traités comme si...; **to ~ sb as an enemy** traiter qn en ennemi; **to ~ sth as** considérer qch comme [*idol, shrine*]; **they ~ the house like a hotel** ils prennent la maison pour un hôtel; **to ~ a remark as a joke** ne pas prendre une remarque au sérieux; **to ~ the whole thing as a joke** prendre toute l'affaire à la plaisanterie; **to ~ a request seriously** prendre une requête au sérieux; **2** Med traiter [*patient, casualty*]; traiter [*disease*] (**with** avec); **to ~ sb with** traiter qn à [*drug*]; traiter qn par [*method*]; **3** Chem, Constr, Ind traiter [*chemical, fabric, problem, rot, sewage, water*] (**with** à); **to ~ sth against** traiter qch contre [*damp, infestation, rot*]; **4** (pay for) payer or offrir qch à [*person*]; **go on, have it, I'll ~ you** prends-le, c'est moi qui paie; **to ~ sb to sth** payer or offrir qch à qn; **he ~ed us to a trip to the concert/ice creams all round** il nous a payé une soirée au concert/une tournée de glaces; **he ~ed us to a lecture on personal hygiene/a description of his symptoms** iron il nous a gratifié d'un sermon sur l'hygiène corporelle/d'une description de ses symptômes iron; **we were ~ed to the unusual spectacle of a minister in disgrace** nous avons eu le privilège d'assister au spectacle insolite d'un ministre en disgrâce.
IV *v refl* **to ~ oneself** s'offrir un petit plaisir; **to ~ oneself to** s'offrir [*holiday, hairdo*].

treatise /ˈtriːtɪs, -ɪz/ *n* traité *m* (**on** sur).

treatment /ˈtriːtmənt/ *n* **1** gen (of person) traitement *m* (**of** de); **preferential ~** traitement de faveur; **special ~** (preferential) traitement de faveur; (unusual) traitement spécial; **it won't stand up to rough ~** ça ne résistera pas aux mauvais traitements; **her husband's ~ of her was cruel** la façon dont son mari la traitait était cruelle; **her ~ of her staff was appalling** elle traitait ses employés de façon odieuse; **2** (analysis) **the question gets** ou **is given a more extended ~ in...** cette question est traitée plus longuement dans...; **3** Med (by specific drug, method) traitement *m*; (general care) soins *mpl*; **a course of ~** un traitement; **cancer ~** traitement contre le cancer; **dental/hospital/veterinary ~** soins dentaires/hospitaliers/vétérinaires; **medical ~** traitement médical, soins médicaux; **preventive ~** traitement préventif, soins préventifs; **urgent ~** traitement or soins d'urgence; **people requiring ~ should...** les gens ayant besoin de soins or d'un traitement devraient...; **to receive ~ for sth** être sous traitement pour qch, recevoir des soins pour qch; **to undergo ~** être en traitement; **the infection is/isn't responding to ~** le traitement agit/n'agit pas sur l'infection; **drug ~ is preferable to radiotherapy** l'emploi des médicaments est préférable à la radiothérapie; **4** Chem, Constr, Ind traitement *m* (**against** contre; **with** à); **timber ~** traitement du bois.
IDIOMS **to give sb the full ~**○ (indulge, flatter) sortir or jouer le grand jeu○ à qn; (grill, chide) faire passer un mauvais quart d'heure○ à qn.

treatment: **~ plant** *n* usine *f* de traitement; **~ room** *n* salle *f* de soins.

treaty /ˈtriːtɪ/ **I** *n* **1** Pol traité *m* (**for** sur); **peace ~** traité de paix; **the Treaty of Rome** le traité de Rome; **to draw up/sign a ~** rédiger/signer un traité; **a ~ banning chemical weapons** un traité interdisant les armes chimiques; **2** Comm Jur accord *m*, contrat *m*; **for sale by private ~** à vendre de gré à gré.
II *modif* [*provision, signatory*] d'un traité; [*obligation*] conventionnel/-elle.

treble /ˈtrebl/ **I** *n* **1** Audio aigus *mpl*; **2** Mus (voice) soprano *m* (*de garçon avant la mue*); (boy) soprano *m*; **3** Sport Turf triple victoire *f*; (in darts) triple *m*; **4** (drink) triple *m*.
II *adj* **1** (three times) triple; **~ nine five six (99956)** quatre-vingt-dix-neuf, neuf cent cinquante-six; **to reach ~ figures** atteindre la centaine; **2** Mus [*voice*] de soprano (*avant la mue*); **~ part** partie *f* pour soprano.
III *det* trois fois; **~ the amount** trois fois la quantité; **~ the size** (town, house) trois fois plus grand; (heap, swelling) trois fois plus gros/grosse.
IV *vtr, vi* tripler; **to ~ in size** [*town*] devenir trois fois plus grand; [*heap, swelling*] devenir trois fois plus gros/grosse.

treble: **~ chance** *n* GB *système de pari sur les matchs de football*; **~ clef** *n* Mus clé *f* de sol.

trebly /ˈtreblɪ/ *adv* [*difficult, demanding*] triplement; **to work ~ hard** travailler trois fois plus dur.

tree /triː/ **I** *n* arbre *m*; **an apple/a cherry ~** un pommier/un cerisier; **the ~ of life** l'arbre de vie; **the ~ of knowledge** l'arbre de la connaissance. ▶ **pear etc.**
II *vtr* US lit poursuivre [qch] jusqu'en haut d'un arbre [*animal*]; fig mettre [qn] dans une situation délicate [*person*].
IDIOMS **he can't see the wood** GB ou **forest** US **for the ~s** il se perd dans les détails; **money doesn't grow on ~s** l'argent ne se trouve pas sous les sabots d'un cheval; **to be out of one's ~**○ être cinglé○; **to be up a tree** US être dans le pétrin○; **to get to/be at the top of the ~** arriver/être arrivé au sommet.

tree: **~-covered** *adj* boisé; **~ creeper** *n* Zool grimpereau *m*; **~ diagram** *n* gen, Admin organigramme *m*; Ling arbre *m*, arborescence *f*; **~ fern** *n* Bot fougère *f* arborescente; **~ frog** *n* rainette *f*, grenouille *f* arboricole; **~house** *n* cabane *f* dans un arbre.

treeless /ˈtriːlɪs/ *adj* dénué d'arbres.

tree: **~ line** *n* limite *f* supérieure de la forêt; **~-lined** *adj* bordé d'arbres; **~ of heaven** *n* Bot ailante *m*; **~ ring** *n* cerne *m*; **~ rose** *n* US rose *f* sur tige; **~ snake** *n* Zool serpent *m* arboricole; **~ stump** *n* souche *f*; **~ surgeon** *n* arboriculteur/-trice *m/f*; **~ surgery** *n* arboriculture *f*; **~top** *n* cime *f* (d'un arbre); **~ trunk** *n* tronc *m* d'arbre.

trefoil /ˈtrefɔɪl/ *n* Bot, Archit trèfle *m*.

trek /trek/ **I** *n* **1** (long journey) randonnée *f*; **to make a ~** faire une randonnée; **mule ~** randonnée à dos de mulet; **2** (laborious trip) randonnée *f* pénible; **it's a bit of a ~**○ ça fait une trotte○; **3** Hist (migration) migration *f* des Boers.
II *vtr* (*p prés etc* **-kk-**) **to ~ the same distance/12 kilometres** se taper○ le même parcours/les 12 kilomètres.
III *vi* (*p prés etc* **-kk-**) **1** (journey) **to ~ across/through** cheminer à travers, traverser péniblement [*desert, jungle*]; **2**○ (go far) **to ~ to** faire le trajet jusqu'à [*shop, office*]; **I had to ~ into town** je me suis tapé○ le trajet à pied jusqu'à la ville.

trekking /ˈtrekɪŋ/ ▶ **1282** *n* (on foot) randonnée *f* pédestre; **to go ~** faire de la randonnée pédestre.

trellis /ˈtrelɪs/ **I** *n* treillis *m*; (sturdier) treillage *m*.
II *vtr* treillisser; (sturdier) treillager.
III trellised *pp adj* [*wall*] avec treillage; [*pattern*] à croisillons.

trelliswork /ˈtrelɪswɜːk/ *n* treillage *m*.

tremble /ˈtrembl/ **I** *n* tremblement *m*.
II *vi* [*person, body, leaves*] trembler, frémir (**with** de); [*voice, hand, lip, building*] trem-

bler (**with** de); **how much does he owe?—I ~ to think!** il doit combien?—je tremble rien que d'y penser!

trembling /ˈtremblɪŋ/ **I** *n* (of person, body, leaves) tremblement *m*, frémissement *m*; (of voice, hand, lip, building) tremblement *m*.

II *adj* [*person, body, leaves*] tremblant, frémissant; [*voice, hand, lip, building*] tremblant.

tremendous /trɪˈmendəs/ *adj* **1** (great, intense) [*effort, improvement, contrast*] énorme; [*pleasure*] immense; [*storm, blow, explosion*] violent; [*speed, success*] fou/folle○; **a ~ amount of sth** une énorme quantité de qch; **it costs a ~ amount** ça coûte un prix fou; **2**○ (marvellous) formidable○.

tremendously /trɪˈmendəslɪ/ *adv* [*exciting, important, rich*] extrêmement; [*grow, vary*] énormément.

tremolo /ˈtreməl əʊ/ *n* trémolo *m*.

tremor /ˈtremə(r)/ *n* **1** (in body, voice) tremblement *m*; (of delight, fear) frisson *m*; **2** Geol secousse *f*.

tremulous /ˈtremjʊləs/ *adj* [*voice*] (with anxiety, tension) tremblant; (from weakness) tremblotant; (with excitement) frémissant; [*sound*] tremblotant; [*smile*] timide.

tremulously /ˈtremjʊləslɪ/ *adv* [*say*] d'une voix tremblante; **she smiled ~** un sourire trembla sur ses lèvres.

trench /trentʃ/ **I** *n* tranchée *f*; **to dig/fill in a ~** creuser/combler une tranchée; **in the ~es** Mil dans les tranchées.

II *vi* creuser des tranchées.

trenchant /ˈtrentʃənt/ *adj* incisif/-ive.

trenchantly /ˈtrentʃəntlɪ/ *adv* [*speak, retort*] d'un ton incisif.

trench coat *n* imperméable *m*, trench-coat *m*.

trencher /ˈtrentʃə(r)/ *n* **1** (machine) excavateur *m*; (person) terrassier *m*; **2** Hist (for food) tranchoir *m*.

trencherman /ˈtrentʃəmən/ *n* (*pl* **-men**) gros mangeur *m*.

trench: **~ fever** ▶ **1354** *n* fièvre *f* des tranchées; **~ warfare** *n* guerre *f* de tranchées.

trend /trend/ **I** *n* **1** (tendency) tendance *f*; **an upward/downward ~** un tendance à la hausse/à la baisse; **if the present ~ continues** si la tendance actuelle persiste; **a ~ in** une tendance dans le domaine de [*legislation, medicine, education*]; **a ~ towards doing** une tendance à faire; **the ~ is towards democracy** la tendance est à la démocratie; **a ~ away from** un désintérêt pour [*arts studies*]; **2** (fashion) mode *f* (**for** de); **a fashion ~** une mode; **to set a new ~** lancer une nouvelle mode; **to follow the ~** suivre la mode.

II *vi* Econ, Fin **to ~ up/lower** tendre à la hausse/à la baisse.

trendiness○ /ˈtrendɪnɪs/ *n* souvent péj (of dress, district, shops) aspect *m* branché○.

trendsetter /ˈtrendsetə(r)/ *n* innovateur/-trice *m/f*; **to be a ~** lancer des modes.

trend-setting /ˈtrendsetɪŋ/ *adj* [*film, album*] innovateur/-trice.

trendy○ /ˈtrendɪ/ **I** *n* souvent péj branché/-e○ *m/f*.

II *adj* souvent péj [*clothes, styles, district*] branché○, à la mode; [*film, opinion*] branché○; [*politician, lecturer*] branché○.

trepan /trɪˈpæn/ **I** *n* Med, Tech trépan *m*.

II *vtr* (*p prés etc* **-nn-**) Tech forer; Med trépaner.

trephine /trɪˈfiːn, US -ˈfaɪn/ **I** *n* Med trépan *m*.

II *vtr* trépaner.

trepidation /ˌtrepɪˈdeɪʃn/ *n* appréhension *f*; **it was with some ~ that** c'est avec une certaine appréhension que.

trespass /ˈtrespəs/ **I** *n* **1** (unlawful entry) gen intrusion *f*; Jur violation *f* de propriété; **2** (unlawful act) transgression *f*; **3** Relig (sin) offense *f*, péché *m*.

II *vi* **1** (enter unlawfully) gen s'introduire illégalement; Jur se rendre coupable d'une violation de propriété; **to ~ on** gen pénétrer illégalement dans, Jur violer [*property*]; **'no ~ing'** 'défense d'entrer'; **2** (commit unlawful act) commettre un délit; **3** fig, sout **to ~ on** abuser de [*time, generosity*]; enfreindre [*rights, liberty*]; **4** Relig **to ~ against** offenser.

trespasser /ˈtrespəsə(r)/ *n* intrus/-e *m/f*; **'~s will be prosecuted'** 'défense d'entrer sous peine de poursuites'.

tress /tres/ littér **I** *n* boucle *f* (de cheveux).

II tresses *npl* chevelure *f*.

trestle /ˈtresl/ **I** *n* tréteau *m*.

II *modif* [*table*] à tréteaux.

trews /truːz/ *npl* Scot pantalon *m* de tartan.

triad /ˈtraɪæd/ *n* gen, Chem triade *f*; Literat trio *m*; Mus accord *m* parfait.

Triad /ˈtraɪæd/ *n*: *société secrète chinoise, surtout criminelle*.

trial /ˈtraɪəl/ **I** *n* **1** Jur procès *m*; **murder/embezzlement ~** procès *m* pour meurtre/pour détournement de fonds; **to be on ~** être jugé (**for sth** pour qch; **for doing** pour avoir fait); **to go to ~** [*case*] être jugé; **to bring sb for ~** amener qn devant la justice; **to go on ~, to stand ~** passer en jugement; **to come up for ~** [*person*] comparaître en justice; [*case*] être jugé; **to put sb on ~** lit juger qn; fig [*press, person, public*] condamner qn; **to send sb for trial, to commit sb to ~** faire passer qn en jugement; **without ~** sans jugement; **to conduct a ~** diriger les débats (d'un procès); **to be awaiting ~** être en instance de jugement; **~ by jury** jugement par jury; **~ by media** procès médiatique; **2** (test) (of applicant, machine, recruit, vehicle) essai *m*; (of drug, new product, process) test *m*; **to put sth through ~s** soumettre qch à des essais or tests; **(to be) on ~** (être) à l'essai; **take it on ~** prenez-le à l'essai; **to carry out** ou **conduct** ou **run/undergo ~s** effectuer/subir des tests or essais (**on** sur); **to give sb a ~** faire faire un essai à qn; **medical/clinical ~s** tests *mpl* médicaux/cliniques; **by ~ and error** par expérience; **3** Mus, Sport (*gén pl*) épreuve *f*; **football/horse ~s** épreuves *fpl* de football/d'équitation; **voice ~s** essais *mpl* de voix; **a ~ of strength** une épreuve de force; **to hold ~s** organiser des épreuves; **4** (trouble, difficulty) épreuve *f*; (less strong) difficulté *f*; **the ~s of old age/of being a mother** les épreuves or difficultés du grand âge/qu'il y a à être mère; **to be a ~** [*person*] être pénible à supporter (**to sb** pour qn).

II *modif* gen [*arrangement, flight, offer, period, sample, separation*] d'essai; **for ~ purposes** à titre d'essai; **on a ~ basis** à titre expérimental; **for a ~ period** pour une période d'essai.

III *vtr* tester [*method, system*].

trial: **~ attorney** *n* US avocat *m* plaidant; **~ balance** *n* Fin bilan *f* de vérification; **~ balloon** *n* US lit, fig ballon *m* d'essai; **~ court**, **~ division** *n* tribunal *m* de première instance; **~ judge** *n* juge *m*; **~ jury** *n* US Jur jury *m* (dans un procès).

trial run *n* **1** Aut, Ind, Tech essai *m*; **to give sth a ~** faire faire un essai à qch; **to take a car for a ~** essayer une voiture; **2** Theat rodage *m*.

triangle /ˈtraɪæŋgl/ *n* gen, Math, Mus triangle *m*; **(red) warning ~** triangle *m* de présignalisation; ▶ **eternal triangle**.

triangular /traɪˈæŋgjʊlə(r)/ *adj* gen triangulaire; Sport [*contest*] entre trois équipes.

triangular file *n* tiers-point *m*.

triangulate /traɪˈæŋgjʊleɪt/ *vtr* trianguler.

triangulation /traɪˌæŋgjʊˈleɪʃn/ *n* (all contexts) triangulation *f*.

triangulation station *n* (on hill) borne *f* géodésique; (on map) point *m* géodésique.

Triassic /traɪˈæsɪk/ Geol **I** *n* **the ~** le trias.

II *adj* triasique.

triathlon /traɪˈæθlɒn/ *n* triathlon *m*.

triatomic /ˌtraɪəˈtɒmɪk/ *adj* triatomique.

tribal /ˈtraɪbl/ *adj* (all contexts) tribal.

tribalism /ˈtraɪbəlɪzəm/ *n* Anthrop tribalisme *m*; fig esprit *m* de tribu.

tribe /traɪb/ *n* Anthrop, Zool, fig tribu *f*.

tribesman /ˈtraɪbzmən/ *n* membre *m* d'une tribu.

triboelectricity /ˌtrɪbəʊˌɪlekˈtrɪsətɪ, ˌtraɪbəʊ-/ *n* triboélectricité *f*.

triboluminescence /ˌtrɪbəʊˌluːmɪˈnesns, ˌtraɪ-/ *n* triboluminescence *f*.

tribulation /ˌtrɪbjʊˈleɪʃn/ **I** *n* tourment *m*.

II tribulations *npl* souvent iron tribulations *fpl* fml; **trials and ~** tribulations *fpl*.

tribunal /traɪˈbjuːnl/ *n* tribunal *m*.

tribune /ˈtrɪbjuːn/ *n* **1** Antiq (person) **~ of the people** tribun *m* du peuple; **2** (platform) tribune *f*.

tributary /ˈtrɪbjʊtərɪ, US -terɪ/ **I** *n* **1** gen, Geog affluent *m*; **2** sout (owing tribute) tributaire *m*.

II *adj* **1** [*stream*] tributaire; [*road*] secondaire; **2** sout [*nation*] tributaire.

tribute /ˈtrɪbjuːt/ *n* **1** (hommage) hommage *m*; **to pay ~ to** rendre hommage à; **as a ~ to** en hommage à; **floral ~** gen fleurs *fpl*; (spray) gerbe *f*; (wreath) couronne *f*; **2** (credit) **it is a ~ to their determination that we have succeeded** le fait que nous avons réussi fait honneur à leur détermination; **3** (payment) tribut *m*.

trice /traɪs/ **I** *n* **in a ~** en un rien de temps.

II *vtr* Naut hisser [*sail*].

Tricel® /ˈtraɪsel/ *n* Tex Tricel® *m*.

tricentenary /ˌtraɪsenˈtiːnərɪ/ *n, adj* tricentenaire (*m*).

tricentennial /ˌtraɪsenˈtiːnɪəl/ *n, adj* US tricentenaire (*m*).

triceps /ˈtraɪseps/ *n* (*pl* **~**) Anat triceps *m*.

trichinosis /ˌtrɪkɪˈnəʊsɪs/ ▶ **1354** *n* trichinose *f*.

trichloride /traɪˈklɔːraɪd/ *n* trichlorure *m*.

trick /trɪk/ **I** *n* **1** (thing that deceives or outwits) combine *f*, truc○ *m*; **it's all a ~!** il y a un truc!; **a mean ~** un sale tour; **a clever ~** un tour habile; **it's the oldest ~ in the book** c'est le tour classique; **I've tried every ~ in the book** j'ai tout essayé; **to play a ~ on sb** jouer un tour à qn; **my mind/my memory plays ~s on me** mon esprit/ma mémoire me joue des tours; **grief can play ~s with the mind** le chagrin peut jouer des tours à notre imagination; **a ~ of the light** un effet de lumière; **2** (by magician, conjurer, dog, horse) tour *m*; **to do/perform a ~** faire/exécuter un tour; **my dog does ~s** mon chien sait faire des tours; **3**○ (mischievous behaviour) tour *m*; **he always pulls that ~** il joue toujours ce tour-là; **don't you ever try that ~ with me!** si jamais tu essaies de me jouer ce tour-là!; **he/the computer is up to his/its ~s again** il/l'ordinateur continue à faire des siennes; **4** (knack, secret) astuce *f*, truc○ *m*; **the ~ is to do** l'astuce c'est de faire; **the ~ in doing sth is to do** l'astuce pour faire qch c'est de faire; **there's no special ~ to it** il n'y a pas d'astuce; **to have a ~ of doing sth** avoir le chic pour faire qch; **to know a ~ or two** ou **a few ~s** s'y connaître (**about** en); **5** (habit, mannerism) manie *f*; **to have a ~ of doing** avoir la manie de faire; **6** (in cards) pli *m*; **to take** ou **win a ~** faire un pli; **7**◑ (prostitute's client) micheton◑ *m*, client *m*; **to turn ~s** racoler des clients; **8**◑ (bout of casual sex) passe *f*◑.

II *modif* [*photo, shot, pack of cards*] truqué; **~ photography** ou **camerawork** truquages *mpl*.

III *vtr* duper, rouler○; **to ~ sb into doing** amener qn par la ruse à faire; **to ~ sb into thinking that...** duper qn en lui faisant croire que...; **to ~ sb out of £10/her inheritance** escroquer qn de 10 livres/son héritage; **I've been ~ed!** on m'a roulé○ or eu○!

IDIOMS **how's ~s**○**?** ça boume○?; **the ~s of the trade** les ficelles du métier; **to do the ~** marcher, faire l'affaire; **not/never to miss a ~** ne pas/ne jamais rater un détail, ne pas/ne jamais en rater une○.

■ **trick out**: **~ out** [**sb**], **~** [**sb**] **out** attifer (**in** de); **to be ~ed out** être attifé, s'être pomponné○.

trick cyclist *n* acrobate *mf* cycliste.

trickery /ˈtrɪkərɪ/ *n* tromperie *f*.

trickiness /ˈtrɪkɪnɪs/ *n* difficulté *f*.

trickle /ˈtrɪkl/ **I** *n* **1** lit (of liquid) filet *m*; (of powder, sand) écoulement *m*; **the stream is reduced to a ~** le torrent n'est plus qu'un mince filet d'eau; **2** (tiny amount) (of investment, orders) petite quantité *f*; (of information) bribes *fpl*; (of people) petit nombre *m*; **a steady ~ of orders** une quantité minime mais constante de commandes; **the ~ back to work became a flood** le retour lent et réduit au travail s'est accru considérablement; **the number of refugees is down to** ou **has slowed to a ~** le nombre de réfugiés s'est considérablement réduit.

II *vtr* faire couler [*liquid*] (**into** dans; **onto** sur).

III *vi* **to ~ down** dégouliner le long de [*pane, wall*]; **blood ~d down his cheek/chin** le sang lui dégoulinait sur la joue/le menton; **to ~ from** couler de [*tap, spout*]; **to ~ into** [*liquid*] s'écouler dans [*container, channel*]; [*people*] s'infiltrer dans [*country, organization*]; [*ball*] rouler dans [*net*]; [*golf ball*] tomber dans [*hole*]; **to ~ out of** [*liquid*] suinter de [*crack, wound*]; [*people*] commencer à quitter [*building*].

■ **trickle away** [*water*] s'écouler lentement; [*people*] s'éloigner lentement.

■ **trickle back** [*people*] retourner lentement (**to** à).

■ **trickle in** arriver au compte-gouttes.

■ **trickle out** [*information, rumours*] filtrer.

trickle: **~ charger** *n* chargeur *m*; **~ down theory** /ˌtrɪkəːrˈtriːt/ *n*: *théorie selon laquelle la richesse de quelques-uns aura un effet positif sur toutes les couches sociales.*

trick or treat *n*: *collecte de bonbons et d'argent faite par les enfants le soir du 31 octobre*; **'~!'** 'des bonbons ou des sous, sinon gare à vous!'

trick question *n* question *f* piège.

trickster /ˈtrɪkstə(r)/ *n* escroc *m*.

tricky /ˈtrɪkɪ/ *adj* **1** [*decision, business, job, task*] difficile (**for** pour); [*problem, question*] épineux/-euse; [*situation*] délicat; **it is ~ to do** il est délicat de faire; **to be ~ to operate/produce** être difficile à manier/produire; **2** (sly, wily) malin/-igne.

tricolour GB, **tricolor** US /ˈtrɪkələ(r), US ˈtraɪkʌlə(r)/ *n* drapeau *m* tricolore; **the ~** le drapeau français.

tricorne /ˈtraɪkɔːn/ *n* tricorne *m*.

tricot /ˈtrɪkəʊ, ˈtriː-/ *n* Tex tissu *m* tricoté.

trictrac /ˈtrɪktræk/ ▶ **1282** *n* Games trictrac *m*.

tricuspid /traɪˈkʌspɪd/ *adj* Anat tricuspide.

tricycle /ˈtraɪsɪkl/ *n* (cycle) tricycle *m*.

trident /ˈtraɪdnt/ *n* trident *m*.

Trident /ˈtraɪdnt/ **I** *n* Mil Trident *m*.

II *modif* [*missile, submarine*] Trident.

tridimensional /ˌtraɪdɪˈmenʃənl/ *adj* tridimensionnel/-elle.

tried /traɪd/ **I** *prét, pp* ▶ **try** II, III.

II *pp adj* **a ~ and tested remedy/method** un médicament/une méthode infaillible.

triennial /traɪˈenɪəl/ **I** *n* troisième anniversaire *m*.

II *adj* [*festival*] triennal.

triennially /traɪˈenɪəlɪ/ *adv* tous les trois ans.

trier○ /ˈtraɪə(r)/ *n* **to be a ~** s'accrocher○, faire des efforts.

trifle /ˈtraɪfl/ **I** *n* **1 a ~** (slightly) légèrement, un tantinet iron; **a ~ dull/long** légèrement ennuyeux/long; **a ~ breathlessly** légèrement essoufflé; **to speed up/slow down a ~** accélérer/ralentir légèrement; **2** (triviality) (gift, money) bagatelle *f*; (matter, problem) détail *m*, chose *f* sans importance; **to waste time on ~s** perdre son temps à des broutilles; **3** GB Culin ≈ diplomate *m*.

II *vi* **to ~ with** jouer avec [*feelings, affections*]; **to ~ with sb** traiter qn à la légère; **she's not someone to be ~d with!** ce n'est pas une femme qu'on traite à la légère or avec qui l'on badine!

trifling /ˈtraɪflɪŋ/ *adj* [*sum, cost*] insignifiant; [*detail, concern*] sans importance; [*error*] léger/-ère (*before n*); **~ matters** des broutilles.

trifocal /traɪˈfəʊkl/ **I trifocals** *npl* lunettes *fpl* à triple foyer.

II *adj* [*lens*] à triple foyer.

trifoliate /traɪˈfəʊlɪət/ *adj* trifolié.

triforium /traɪˈfɔːrɪəm/ *n* triforium *m*.

triform /ˈtraɪfɔːm/ *adj* à trois parties.

trigger /ˈtrɪgə(r)/ **I** *n* **1** (on gun) gâchette *f*; **to pull** ou **squeeze the ~** appuyer sur la gâchette; **2** (starting mechanism) (on machine) manette *f*; **3** fig **to act as** ou **to be the ~ for sth** déclencher qch.

II *vtr* = **trigger off**.

■ **trigger off**: **~ off** [**sth**] déclencher.

trigger-happy○ /ˈtrɪgəhæpɪ/ *adj* **1** lit à la gâchette facile; **to be ~** avoir la gâchette facile; **2** fig impulsif/-ive.

trigonometrical /ˌtrɪgənəˈmetrɪkl/ *adj* trigonométrique.

trigonometry /ˌtrɪgəˈnɒmətrɪ/ *n* trigonométrie *f*.

trigram /ˈtraɪgræm/ *n* trigramme *m*.

trigraph /ˈtraɪgrɑːf, US -græf/ *n* trigramme *m*.

trike○ /traɪk/ *n* tricycle *m*.

trilateral /ˌtraɪˈlætərəl/ *adj* trilatéral.

trilby /ˈtrɪlbɪ/ *n* GB chapeau *m* en feutre, feutre *m*.

trilingual /ˌtraɪˈlɪŋgwəl/ *adj* trilingue.

trilith /ˈtraɪlɪθ/ *n* trilithe *m*.

trilithic /ˌtraɪˈlɪθɪk/ *adj* trilithique.

trilithon /ˈtraɪlɪθən/ *n* trilithe *m*.

trill /trɪl/ **I** *n* **1** Mus trille *m*; **2** Ling r roulé *m*.

II *vtr* **1** Mus triller; **2** Ling rouler.

III *vi* triller.

trillion /ˈtrɪlɪən/ *n* **1** GB trillion *m*; **2** US billion *m*.

trilobite /ˈtraɪləbaɪt/ *n* trilobite *m*.

trilogy /ˈtrɪlədʒɪ/ *n* trilogie *f*.

trim /trɪm/ **I** *n* **1** (cut) (of hair) coupe *f* d'entretien; (of hedge) taille *f*; **to have a ~** se faire faire une coupe d'entretien; **to give sb** ou **sb's hair a ~** faire une coupe d'entretien à qn; **to give one's beard a ~** se tailler la barbe; **to give the lawn a ~** tondre l'herbe; **the hedge needs a ~** la haie a besoin d'être taillée; **2** (good condition) **to be in (good) ~** être en bonne forme physique; **to keep oneself in ~** se maintenir en bonne forme physique; **to get the garden in ~** mettre le jardin en état; **3** (border) (on clothing) bordure *f*; (of braid) galon *m*; (on woodwork) moulure *f*; (on furniture, work surface) baguette *f*; (on soft furnishings) frange *f*; **4** Aut finition *f*; **exterior ~** finition *f* extérieure; **interior ~** garniture *f* intérieure; **side ~** baguette *f* de protection; **5** Naut (of ship) assiette *f*; (of sails) gréement *m*; **to be out of ~** ne pas avoir d'assiette.

II *adj* **1** (neat) [*appearance, garden, person*] soigné; [*boat, house*] en bon état; [*outline*] net/nette; **to be neat and ~** être très soigné; **2** (slender) [*figure*] svelte; [*waist*] fin.

III *vtr* (*p prés etc* **-mm-**) **1** (cut) couper [*branch, hair, grass, material, paper*]; tailler [*beard, moustache, hedge*]; tondre [*lawn*]; émarger [*page*]; ébouter [*wood*]; **to ~ (the wick of) a lamp** moucher (la mèche d')une lampe; **2** (reduce) réduire [*budget, expenditure, workforce*] (**by** de); raccourcir [*article, speech*] (**by** de); **to ~ 5% off the budget** réduire le budget de 5%; **3** Culin dégraisser [*meat*]; ébarber [*fish*]; parer [*vegetable*]; **4** (decorate) décorer [*tree, furniture*] (**in** en; **with** avec); border [*dress, curtain, handkerchief*] (**with** de); **5** Naut arrimer [*ship*]; gréer [*sails*]; **6** (modify) ajuster [*opinion, utterances*].

■ **trim away**, **trim off**: **~ away** [**sth**], **~** [**sth**] **away** tailler [*hair, fabric, branches*]; enlever [*fat*].

■ **trim down**: **~ down** [**sth**] réduire [*budget, spending, workforce*]; réviser [qch] à la baisse [*estimate, plans*].

trimaran /ˈtraɪməræn/ *n* trimaran *m*.

trimester /traɪˈmestə(r)/ *n* US trimestre *m*.

trimmer /ˈtrɪmə(r)/ *n* **1** (cutting tool) (for hedges) taille-haies *m*; (for hair) tondeuse *f*; (for lawn) taille-bordures *m*; (for carpets) ébarbeuse *f*; (for timber) ébouteuse *f*; **2** Electron condensateur *m* ajustable d'appoint; **3** Constr chevêtre *m*; **4** (expedient person) opportuniste *mf*; **5** Print massicot *m* de rognage.

trimming /ˈtrɪmɪŋ/ **I** *n* (on clothing) garniture *f*; (on soft furnishings) passementerie *f*.

II trimmings *npl* **1** Culin accompagnements *mpl* traditionnels; **with all the ~s** avec tous les accompagnements traditionnels; **2**○ (extra items) **the basic car without the ~s** la voiture telle quelle sans aucune option; **a church wedding with all the ~s** un mariage à l'église avec tout le tralala○; **3** (offcuts) (of pastry) rognures *fpl*; (of fish, meat) parures *fpl*; (of fabric) chutes *fpl*.

trimness /ˈtrɪmnɪs/ *n* **1** (neatness) (of person) netteté *f*; (of house, boat) bon état *m*; **2** (slimness) minceur *f*.

trim size *n* Print, Publ format *m* façonné.

trinary /ˈtraɪnərɪ/ *adj* ternaire.

Trinidad /ˈtrɪnɪdæd/ ▶ **1381** *pr n* (l'île *f* de) la Trinité *f*.

Trinidad and Tobago /ˌtrɪnɪdæd ən təˈbeɪgəʊ/ ▶ **1131** *pr n* Trinité-et-Tobago *f*.

Trinidadian /ˌtrɪnɪˈdædɪən/ ▶ **1486** **I** *n* (inhabitant) Trinidadien/-ienne *m/f*.

II *adj* trinidadien/-ienne.

trinitrotoluene /traɪˌnaɪtrəˈtɒljʊiːn/ *n* trinitrotoluène *m*.

trinity /ˈtrɪnətɪ/ *n* trinité *f*.

Trinity /ˈtrɪnətɪ/ *n* **the ~** la Trinité *f*; **the Holy ~** ou **Blessed ~** la Sainte Trinité.

Trinity: **~ Sunday** *n* le dimanche *m* de la Trinité; **~ term** *n* GB Univ troisième trimestre *m*.

trinket /ˈtrɪŋkɪt/ *n* babiole *f*.

trinomial /traɪˈnəʊmɪəl/ *n, adj* Math trinôme (*m*).

trio /ˈtriːəʊ/ *n* (all contexts) trio *m* (**of** de); **piano/jazz ~** trio *m* pour piano/de jazz.

triode /ˈtraɪəʊd/ *n* triode *f*.

triolet /ˈtriːəlɪt/ *n* triolet *m*.

trip /trɪp/ **I** *n* **1** (journey) (abroad) voyage *m*; (excursion) excursion *f*; **to go on** ou **take a ~** faire un voyage; **a ~ to Greece** un voyage en Grèce; **a ~ to the seaside** une excursion au bord de la mer; **business ~** voyage d'affaires; **boat ~** excursion en bateau; **to be away on a ~** être en voyage; **a 12 day/200 km ~** un voyage de 12 jours/de 200 km; **we did the ~ in five hours** nous avons fait le trajet en cinq heures; **it's only a short ~ into London** c'est juste un petit tour à Londres; **it's a two hour ~ from here** c'est à deux heures d'ici; **2** (visit) tour *m*; **a ~ to the toilet/bar** un tour aux toilettes/au bar; **to make a ~ into town** faire un tour en ville; **to make three ~s a week to London** aller à Londres trois fois par semaine; **3** Electron déclenche *f*; **4**○ argot des drogués trip○ *m*; **to have a good/bad ~** faire un bon/mauvais trip○; **an acid ~** un trip○ d'acide.

II *vtr* (*p prés etc* **-pp-**) **1** (cause to stumble) gen faire trébucher [*person*]; (with foot) faire

un croche-pied à [*person*]; **2** Electron [*person*] couper [*switch*]; [*power surge*] déclencher [*circuit breaker*].
III *vi* (*p prés etc* **-pp-**) **1** (stumble) trébucher, faire un faux pas; **to ~ on** ou **over** trébucher sur [*step, rock*]; se prendre les pieds dans [*hem, scarf, rope*]; **to ~ over one's own feet** trébucher; **you can't move in here without ~ping over a celebrity** on ne fait pas deux pas ici sans tomber sur une célébrité; **2** (move jauntily) **to ~ along** [*child*] gambader; [*adult*] marcher d'un pas léger; **to ~ into/out of the room** entrer dans/sortir de la pièce d'un pas léger; **3**○ argot des drogués tripper○, être sous l'effet du LSD.
■ **trip over**: ¶ **~ over** trébucher, faire un faux pas; ¶ **~ [sb] over** gen faire trébucher; (with one's foot) faire un croche-pied à.
■ **trip out**○ planer○.
■ **trip up**: ¶ **~ up 1** (stumble) trébucher, faire un faux pas; **2** (make an error) se tromper; ¶ **~ [sb] up, ~ up [sb] 1** (cause to stumble) gen faire trébucher; (with foot) faire un croche-pied à; **2** (catch out) désarçonner [*witness, candidate*].

tripartite /ˌtraɪˈpɑːtaɪt/ *adj* **1** [*agreement, alliance, system*] tripartite; **2** [*document, study*] en trois parties.

tripe /traɪp/ *n* ¢ **1** Culin tripes *fpl*; **2**○ (nonsense) foutaises○ *fpl*.

triphase /ˈtraɪfeɪz/ *adj* triphasé.

triphthong /ˈtrɪfθɒŋ/ *n* triphtongue *f*.

triplane /ˈtraɪpleɪn/ *n* triplan *m*.

triple /ˈtrɪpl/ **I** *n* triple *m*.
II *adj* **1** gen triple; **2** Mus **in ~ time** à trois temps.
III *vtr* tripler.
IV *vi* tripler; **to ~ in volume/value** tripler de volume/valeur; **to ~ in height/width** devenir trois fois plus haut/large; **to ~ in size** [*town*] devenir trois fois plus grand; [*heap, swelling*] devenir trois fois plus gros/grosse.

triple A *n* US Aut (*abrév* = **American Automobile Association**) association *f* américaine des automobilistes.

Triple Alliance *n* **the ~** la Triple-Alliance *f*.

triple: **~ jump** *n* triple saut *m*; **~ jumper** *n* spécialiste *mf* du triple saut; **~ somersault** *n* triple saut *m* périlleux.

triplet /ˈtrɪplɪt/ *n* **1** (child) triplé/-e *m/f*; **a set of ~s** des triplés; **2** Mus triolet *m*; **3** Literat tercet *m*.

Triplex® /ˈtrɪpleks/ *n* triplex® *m*.

triplicate /ˈtrɪplɪkət/: **in ~** *adv phr* en trois exemplaires.

triploid /ˈtrɪplɔɪd/ *adj* triploïde.

triply /ˈtrɪplɪ/ *adv* triplement.

trip meter *n* Aut compteur *m* de kilomètres.

tripod /ˈtraɪpɒd/ *n* Sci, Phot trépied *m*.

tripper /ˈtrɪpə(r)/ *n* excursionniste *mf*, touriste *mf*.

trip switch *n* Electron commutateur *m* à bascule.

triptych /ˈtrɪptɪk/ *n* triptyque *m*.

trip wire *n* fil *m* de détente.

trireme /ˈtraɪriːm/ *n* trirème *f*.

trisect /traɪˈsekt/ *vtr* diviser [qch] en trois parties égales.

trisyllabic /ˌtraɪsɪˈlæbɪk/ *adj* [*word*] tris(s)yllabe; (in prosody) [*foot, line*] tris(s)yllabique.

trisyllable /ˌtraɪˈsɪləbl/ *n* tris(s)yllabe *m*.

trite /traɪt/ *adj* banal; **~ comments** banalités *fpl*.

tritely /ˈtraɪtlɪ/ *adv* de manière banale.

triteness /ˈtraɪtnɪs/ *n* banalité *f*.

tritium /ˈtrɪtɪəm/ *n* tritium *m*.

triton /ˈtraɪtn/ *n* (mollusc, newt) triton *m*.

Triton /ˈtraɪtn/ *pr n* Mythol Triton.

tritone /ˈtraɪtəʊn/ *n* Mus triton *m*.

triturate /ˈtrɪtjʊreɪt/ *vtr* triturer.

trituration /ˌtrɪtjʊˈreɪʃn/ *n* **1** (action) trituration *f*; **2** Pharm mélange *m* (*de substances broyées*).

triumph /ˈtraɪʌmf/ **I** *n* **1** ¢ (satisfaction) triomphe *m*; **in ~** en triomphe; **an air of ~** un air triomphant; **2** (victory) triomphe *m* (**over** sur; **of** de; **for** pour); **3** (Roman ceremony) triomphe *m*.
II *vi* triompher (**over** de).

triumphal /traɪˈʌmfl/ *adj* [*entry, tour, procession*] triomphal; **~ arch** Archit arc *m* de triomphe.

triumphalism /traɪˈʌmfəlɪzəm/ *n* triomphalisme *m*.

triumphalist /traɪˈʌmfəlɪst/ *n* triomphaliste *mf*.

triumphant /traɪˈʌmfnt/ *adj* [*person, team*] triomphant; [*expression*] de triomphe; [*return, production, success, summit*] triomphal; **to feel ~** avoir un sentiment de triomphe; **to return ~** retourner en triomphe.

triumphantly /traɪˈʌmfntlɪ/ *adv* [*declare, affirm, march, return*] triomphalement; [*stride*] d'un pas triomphant; [*say*] d'une voix triomphante.

triumvirate /traɪˈʌmvɪrət/ *n* triumvirat *m*.

triune /ˈtraɪjuːn/ *adj* trin.

trivet /ˈtrɪvɪt/ *n* (at fire) trépied *m*; (on table) dessous-de-plat *m*.
IDIOMS **to be as right as a ~** être en pleine forme.

trivia /ˈtrɪvɪə/ *npl* (+ *v sg* ou *pl*) **1** (irrelevancies) futilités *fpl*; **2** (unusual facts) faits *mpl* insolites.

trivial /ˈtrɪvɪəl/ *adj* **1** (unimportant) [*matter, scale, film*] insignifiant; [*error, offence*] léger/-ère; **2** (of no interest) [*conversation, argument, person*] futile.

triviality /ˌtrɪvɪˈælətɪ/ *n* **1** (banality) banalité *f*; **2** (irrelevance) futilité *f*, détail *m* insignifiant; **to waste time on trivialities** perdre son temps en futilités.

trivialization /ˌtrɪvɪəlaɪˈzeɪʃn, US -lɪˈz-/ *n* banalisation *f*.

trivialize /ˈtrɪvɪəlaɪz/ *vtr* banaliser [*debate, comparison*]; minimiser [*rôle, art*].

trivially /ˈtrɪvɪəlɪ/ *adv* banalement.

Trivial Pursuit® *n* Trivial Pursuit® *m* (*jeu de société portant sur le savoir général*).

trivia quiz *n* jeu-test *m*.

triweekly /ˌtraɪˈwiːklɪ/ **I** *adj* **his ~ visits** les visites qu'il fait/faisait toutes les trois semaines.
II *adv* (in one week) trois fois par semaine; (every three weeks) toutes les trois semaines.

trochaic /trəʊˈkeɪɪk/ *adj* trochaïque.

trochee /ˈtrəʊkiː, -kɪ/ *n* trochée *m*.

trod /trɒd/ *prét* ▶ **tread** II, III.

trodden /ˈtrɒdn/ *pp* ▶ **tread** II, III.

troglodyte /ˈtrɒglədaɪt/ *n* troglodyte *mf*.

troika /ˈtrɔɪkə/ *n* troïka *f* also Pol.

Trojan /ˈtrəʊdʒən/ **I** *n* **1** Hist Troyen/-enne *m/f*; **2 Trojan**® US (condom) préservatif *m*.
II *adj* troyen/-enne; **the ~ War** la guerre de Troie.
IDIOMS **to work like a ~** GB travailler comme un forçat.

Trojan horse *n* **1** Hist cheval *m* de Troie; **2** Comput cheval *m* de Troie (*programme infiltré dans un autre pour le détruire*).

troll /trəʊl/ *n* troll *m*.
■ **troll along**○ [*person*] faire une trotte○ (**to** jusqu'à).

trolley /ˈtrɒlɪ/ *n* **1** GB (on wheels) chariot *m*; **dessert/drinks ~** chariot *m* à desserts/à boissons; **luggage ~** chariot *m* (à bagages); **2** US tramway *m*.
IDIOMS **to be off one's ~**○ être givré○ or cinglé○.

trolley: **~ bus** *n* trolleybus *m*; **~ car** *n* tramway *m*, tram *m*.

trollop◑ /ˈtrɒləp/ *n* péj traînée◑ *f* pej.

trombone /trɒmˈbəʊn/ ▶ **1481** *n* trombone *m*.

trombonist /trɒmˈbəʊnɪst/ ▶ **1692**, **1481** *n* tromboniste *mf*.

troop /truːp/ **I** *n* (all contexts) troupe *f*.
II troops *npl* Mil troupes *fpl*.
III *modif* [*movements*] de troupes; [*train, plane*] de transport de troupes.
IV *vtr* **to ~ the colour** GB effectuer une parade militaire (*à l'occasion de l'anniversaire officiel du souverain*).
V *vi* **to ~ in/out/off** entrer/sortir/partir en masse; **to ~ over to** ou **towards sth** se diriger en masse vers qch.

troop carrier *n* transporteur *m* de troupes.

trooper /ˈtruːpə(r)/ *n* **1** Mil homme *m* de troupe; **2** US (policeman) policier *m*.
IDIOMS **to swear like a ~** jurer comme un charretier or troupier.

trooping /ˈtruːpɪŋ/ *n* **the Trooping of the Colour** GB parade *f* militaire (*effectuée à l'occasion de l'anniversaire officiel du souverain*).

troopship /ˈtruːpʃɪp/ *n* transport *m* de troupes.

trope /trəʊp/ *n* trope *m*.

trophy /ˈtrəʊfɪ/ *n* trophée *m* also fig.

tropic /ˈtrɒpɪk/ *n* tropique *m*; **the ~ of Cancer/of Capricorn** le tropique du Cancer/du Capricorne; **in the ~s** sous les tropiques.

tropical /ˈtrɒpɪkl/ *adj* tropical.

tropism /ˈtrəʊpɪzəm/ *n* tropisme *m*.

troposphere /ˈtrɒpəsfɪə(r), US ˈtrəʊ-/ *n* troposphère *f*.

trot /trɒt/ **I** *n* **1** (of horse) trot *m*; **at a** ou **the ~** au trot; **to break into a ~** [*animal*] se mettre au trot, prendre le trot; [*person*] se mettre à trotter or à trottiner; **her children followed at a ~** ses enfants trottinaient derrière elle; **to have a ~ round the shops**○ courir les magasins○; **2**○ (run of luck) **to have** ou **be on a good/bad ~** être dans une bonne/mauvaise période; **3**○ US Sch, Univ antisèche○ *f*.
II the trots○ *npl* la courante◑, la diarrhée.
III *vtr* (*p prés etc* **-tt-**) faire trotter [*horse*].
IV *vi* (*p prés etc* **-tt-**) **1** [*horse, animal, rider*] trotter; **to ~ away/past** partir/passer au trot; **2** [*person*] (run, move briskly) courir, trotter○; [*child, woman in heels*] trottiner; **to ~ down the road/along/away** descendre la rue/passer/partir en trottinant; **~ next door and borrow some tea!**○ cours vite emprunter du thé chez la voisine!
IDIOMS **to be on the ~**○ être toujours en train de courir; **to keep sb on the ~**○ ne pas laisser de répit à qn; **on the ~**○ (one after the other) coup sur coup; (continuously) d'affilée.
■ **trot out**○: **~ out [sth]** débiter [*excuse, explanation, argument*].

Trot○ /trɒt/ *n* péj trotskard/-e○ *m/f* pej.

troth‡ /trəʊθ, US trɔːθ/ *n* **1** (oath) serment *m*; **2** (fidelity) foi *f*; **by my ~!** sur ma foi†!

Trotsky /ˈtrɒtskɪ/ *pr n* Trotski *m*.

Trotskyism /ˈtrɒtskɪɪzəm/ *n* trotskisme *m*.

Trotskyist /ˈtrɒtskɪɪst/ *n, adj* trotskiste (*mf*).

Trotskyite /ˈtrɒtskɪaɪt/ *n, adj* péj trotskard/-e○ (*m/f*) pej.

trotter /ˈtrɒtə(r)/ *n* **1** (of animal) pied *m*; **pigs'/sheeps' ~s** pieds de cochon/de mouton; **2** Equit (horse) trotteur/-euse *m/f*.

trotting /ˈtrɒtɪŋ/ *n* Equit trot *m*; **bred for ~** dressé pour le trot.

trotting race *n* course *f* de trot.

troubadour /ˈtruːbədɔː(r), US -dʊər/ *n* troubadour *m*.

trouble /ˈtrʌbl/ **I** *n* **1** ¢ (problems) (gen) problèmes *mpl*; (specific) problème *m*; (personal) ennuis *mpl*; **that's the ~** là est le problème; **engine ~** problèmes mécaniques; **to cause** ou **give sb ~** [*exam question*] poser des problèmes à qn; [*person*] créer des ennuis à qn; **his leg/car is giving him ~** il a des problèmes avec sa jambe/sa voiture; **this car has been nothing but ~**

cette voiture ne m'a apporté que des ennuis; **to get sb into ~** créer des ennuis à qn; **to get** ou **run into all sorts of ~** [*person, business*] connaître ennui sur ennui; **to make ~ for oneself** s'attirer des ennuis; **to be asking for ~** chercher des ennuis; **the/my etc ~ is that...** le/mon etc problème c'est que...; **the ~ with you/them etc is that...** l'ennui avec toi/eux etc c'est que...; **heart/kidney ~** ennuis *mpl* cardiaques/rénaux; **back ~** mal *m* de dos; **what's the ~?** qu'est-ce qui ne va pas?; **to have man** ou **woman ~**○ avoir des problèmes de cœur; **2** (difficulties) (specific) difficulté *f*; gen difficultés *fpl*; **without too much ~** sans trop de difficultés; **to be in** ou **get into ~** gen [*person*] avoir des ennuis; [*company, business*] avoir des difficultés; [*climber, competitor*] se trouver en difficulté; **to have ~ doing** avoir du mal à faire; **you'll have no ~ finding a job** tu n'auras aucun mal à trouver un emploi; **to get out of ~** se tirer d'affaire; **to get sb out of ~** tirer qn d'affaire; **to stay out of ~** éviter des ennuis; **in times of ~** dans les moments difficiles; **3** (effort, inconvenience) peine *f*; **it's not worth the ~** cela n'en vaut pas la peine; **to take the ~ to do** se donner la peine de faire; **to go to the ~ of doing** se donner le mal de faire; **to save sb/oneself the ~ of doing** épargner à qn/s'épargner la peine de faire; **he put me to the ~ of doing** à cause de lui j'ai été obligé de faire; **to go to a lot of ~** se donner beaucoup de mal; **I don't want to put you to any ~** je ne veux pas te déranger; **it's no ~** cela ne me dérange pas; **to be more ~ than it's worth** donner plus de mal qu'il n'en vaut la peine; **not to be any ~** [*child, animal*] être sage; [*task*] ne poser aucun problème; **all that ~ for nothing** tout ce mal pour rien; **it was a lot of ~** cela n'a pas été facile; **it's less/more ~ to do it this way** c'est moins/plus compliqué de faire ça comme ça; **nothing is too much ~ for him** il est très serviable; **leave it, it's too much ~** laisse, c'est trop pénible; **if it's too much ~, say so** si c'est trop ennuyeux, dis-le-moi; **all the ~ and expense** tous les dérangements et toutes les dépenses; **4** (discord) (gen) problèmes *mpl*, histoires○ *fpl*; (with personal involvement) ennuis *mpl*; (between groups) conflits *mpl*; (disturbance) incidents *mpl*; (reaction of displeasure) remous *m*; **to cause ~ between the two factions** créer des conflits entre les deux factions; **I don't want any ~** je ne veux pas d'ennuis; **there'll be ~** il y aura du remous; **to expect ~** [*police, pub landlord*] s'attendre à des incidents; **to be looking for ~** [*agitator, thug*] chercher les ennuis; **to get into ~** [*schoolchild, employee*] s'attirer des ennuis; **to make ~** faire des histoires; **it will lead to ~** ça va mal finir; **here comes ~!** hum voilà les ennuis qui arrivent!; **he looks like ~**○ il a une sale gueule◑; **to get into ~ with** avoir des démêlés avec [*police*]; avoir des ennuis avec [*authorities, taxman*]; **at the first sign of ~** au moindre signe d'agitation; **there's ~ brewing** il y a de l'orage dans l'air fig.

II troubles *npl* **1** (worries) soucis *mpl*; **to tell sb one's ~s** faire part à qn de ses soucis; **tell me your ~s** dis-moi ce qui ne va pas; **your ~s are over** c'est la fin de tes soucis; **it's the least of my ~s** c'est le cadet de mes soucis; **money ~s** problèmes *mpl* d'argent; **2 the Troubles** (in Ireland) les troubles *mpl* (*en Irlande*).

III *vtr* **1** (bother) [*person*] déranger [*person*]; **sorry to ~ you** désolé de vous déranger; **to ~ sb for sth** déranger qn pour lui demander qch; **may I ~ you for the butter?** puis-je vous demander le beurre?; **may** ou **could I ~ you to do?** puis-je vous demander de faire?; **to ~ sb with** ennuyer qn avec [*problem, question*]; **I won't ~ you with the details** je te fais grâce des détails; **to ~ to do** se donner la peine de faire; **don't ~ to knock will you?** iron ne te donne surtout pas la peine de frapper!; **2** (worry) tracasser [*person*]; tourmenter [*mind*]; **don't let that ~ you** ne te tracasse pas pour cela; **3** (harass) [*person*] harceler [*person*]; **4** (cause discomfort) [*tooth, cough, leg*] faire mal à [*person*]; **to be ~d by** être incommodé par [*cough, pain*]; **5** (agitate) littér [*breeze, wake*] troubler [*water*].

IV *v refl* **to ~ oneself to do** se donner la peine de faire; **don't ~ yourself!** iron ne vous dérangez surtout pas!

IDIOMS **to get a girl into ~** euph mettre une fille enceinte.

troubled /ˈtrʌbld/ *adj* **1** (worried) [*person, expression*] soucieux/-ieuse; [*mind*] inquiet/-iète; **to be ~ about** être préoccupé par [*problem, concern*]; s'inquiéter pour [*future*]; **to be ~ in spirit** littér avoir l'esprit inquiet; **2** (disturbed) [*sleep, times, area*] agité; littér [*waters*] troublé; **3** (having problems) [*company, economy*] en difficultés; **~ by** incommodé par [*injury*].

troublefree /ˌtrʌblˈfriː/ *adj* [*period, operation*] sans problèmes; **to be ~** [*machine*] marcher sans problème; [*meeting*] avoir lieu sans aucun problème; **the school has been ~ since...** il n'y a plus eu de problème à l'école depuis...

troublemaker /ˈtrʌblmeɪkə(r)/ *n* fauteur/-trice *m/f* de troubles.

troubleshoot /ˈtrʌblʃuːt/ *vi* gen intervenir pour régler les problèmes; Tech localiser une panne.

troubleshooter /ˈtrʌblʃuːtə(r)/ *n* (dealing with people) conciliateur/-trice *m/f*; Tech expert *m*; (in business, industry) consultant/-e *m/f* en gestion des entreprises.

troubleshooting /ˈtrʌblʃuːtɪŋ/ *n* diagnostic *m* des anomalies; **to do some ~** intervenir pour régler les problèmes; **hints for ~** conseils en cas de panne.

troubleshooting guide *n* manuel *m* de dépannage.

troublesome /ˈtrʌblsəm/ *adj* [*person*] ennuyeux/-euse; [*problem, objection*] gênant; [*aspect*] pénible; [*cough, pain*] désagréable.

trouble spot *n* point *m* chaud.

trough /trɒf, US trɔːf/ *n* **1** (for drinking) abreuvoir *m*; (for animal feed) auge *f*; (for plants) bac *m*; **2** (channel) chenal *m*; **3** (depression) (between waves, hills) creux *m*; (on graph) creux *m*; Econ creux *m*; **to have peaks and ~s** avoir des hauts et des bas; **4** Meteorol dépression *f*. ▶ **snout**.

trounce○ /traʊns/ *vtr* flanquer une raclée○ à [*team, competitor*].

troupe /truːp/ *n* troupe *f*.

trouper○ /ˈtruːpə(r)/ *n* Theat **an old ~** un/une artiste *m/f* de métier.

trouser /ˈtraʊzə(r)/ **▶ 1703** **I** *modif* [*belt, leg, pocket*] de pantalon; **my ~ leg** la jambe de mon pantalon.

II trousers *npl* pantalon *m*; **short ~s** short *m*; **long ~s** pantalon *m* long.

IDIOMS **to catch sb with their ~s down** prendre qn en flagrant délit; **to wear the ~s** GB porter la culotte○.

trouser: ~ press *n* presse-pantalon *m*; **~ suit** *n* GB ensemble-pantalon *m*.

trousseau /ˈtruːsəʊ/ *n* trousseau *m* (de mariage).

trout /traʊt/ **I** *n* (*pl* **~**) **1** (fish) truite *f*; **2** GB péj (woman) **an old ~** une vieille mégère.

II *modif* [*fishing*] à la truite; [*farm, fisherman*] de truites; [*stream*] à truites.

trove /trəʊv/ *n* ▶ **treasure trove**.

trowel /ˈtraʊəl/ *n* **1** (for cement) truelle *f*; **2** (for gardening) déplantoir *m*.

IDIOMS **to lay it on with a ~**○ mettre le paquet○.

troy /trɔɪ/ *n* troy *m*.

Troy /trɔɪ/ **▶ 1818** *pr n* Troie.

truancy /ˈtruːənsɪ/ *n* absentéisme *m*.

truant /ˈtruːənt/ *n* (child) enfant *mf* qui fait l'école buissonnière; **to play ~** faire l'école buissonnière.

truant officer *n* Sch *personne chargée de combattre l'absentéisme*.

truce /truːs/ *n* trêve *f*; **to call a ~** demander une trêve.

truck /trʌk/ **I** *n* **1** (lorry) camion *m*; **2** (rail wagon) wagon *m* de marchandises.

II *modif* [*deliveries*] (by road) par camion; (by rail) par wagon.

III *vtr* camionner.

IV *vi* US conduire un camion.

IDIOMS **to have no ~ with sb/sth** GB ne rien avoir à faire avec qn/qch; **keep on ~ing**○! US bon courage!

■ **truck on down**○ US aller tranquillement (**to** à).

truckage /ˈtrʌkɪdʒ/ *n* transport *m* routier.

truck driver **▶ 1692** *n* routier *m*; **she's a ~** elle est routier.

trucker /ˈtrʌkə(r)/ **▶ 1692** *n* **1**○ (lorry driver) routier *m*; **2** US Agric maraîcher/-ère *m/f*.

truck: ~ farm *n* US exploitation *f* maraîchère; **~ farmer** **▶ 1692** *n* US maraîcher/-ère *m/f*; **~ farming** *n* US maraîchage *m*.

trucking /ˈtrʌkɪŋ/ *n* **1** (transporting) transport *m* routier; **2** US Agric maraîchage *m*.

truckle /ˈtrʌkl/ *vi* s'abaisser (**to** devant).

truckle bed /ˈtrʌklbed/ *n* GB lit *m* gigogne.

truckload /ˈtrʌkləʊd/ *n* (of goods, produce) chargement *m* (**of** de); (of soldiers, refugees) camion *m* (**of** de); **by the ~** en grand nombre.

truck stop *n* (restaurant *m*) routier *m*.

truculence /ˈtrʌkjʊləns/ *n* agressivité *f*.

truculent /ˈtrʌkjʊlənt/ *adj* agressif/-ive.

truculently /ˈtrʌkjʊləntlɪ/ *adv* [*behave*] de façon agressive; [*say*] avec agressivité.

trudge /trʌdʒ/ **I** *n* **it's quite a ~ to my house** il y a un bon bout de chemin jusqu'à chez moi.

II *vi* marcher d'un pas lourd; **to ~ through the snow** marcher péniblement dans la neige; **to ~ up the stairs** monter péniblement l'escalier; **to ~ round the shops** se traîner de magasin en magasin.

true /truː/ **I** *adj* **1** (based on fact, not a lie) [*account, news, rumour, fact, story*] vrai; (from real life) [*story*] vécu; **~ or false?** vrai ou faux?; **it is quite/only too ~ that...** il est exact/il n'est que trop vrai que...; **it is simply not ~ that...** ce n'est pas vrai que...; **it is ~ to say that...** on peut dire que...; **to ring ~** sonner vrai; **the same is** ou **holds ~ of the new party** cela est vrai aussi or il en va de même pour le nouveau parti; **what is ~ of adults is ~ of children** ce qui est vrai pour les adultes l'est aussi pour les enfants; **to prove ~** se révéler exact; **this allegation, if ~...** si cette allégation est fondée, elle...; **it can't be ~!** ce n'est pas possible!; **that's ~** (when agreeing) c'est juste; **too ~**○! je ne vous/te le fais pas dire!; **~, we shall miss her but...** c'est vrai qu'elle va nous manquer mais...; **2** (real, genuine) [*god, democracy, American, worth*] vrai; [*identity, age*] véritable; [*cost, meaning, nature, value*] vrai; **to come ~** se réaliser; **it is hard to get the ~ picture** il est difficile de savoir ce qui se passe vraiment or en réalité; **an artist in the ~ sense of the word** un artiste dans toute l'acception du terme; **3** (heartfelt, sincere) [*feeling, repentance, understanding*] sincère; **to feel ~ remorse** éprouver un remords sincère; **to be a ~ believer** avoir la foi; **~ love** le véritable amour; **4** (accurate) [*copy*] conforme; [*assessment*] correct, juste; **is the photo a ~ likeness?** cette photo estelle vraiment ressemblante? ; **to be ~ to life** [*film, novel, book*] être vrai; **5** (faithful, loyal) [*servant, knight*] fidèle; **to be ~ to** être fidèle à [*beliefs, word*]; **6** Constr **to be/to be out of ~** [*window, post, frame*] être/ne pas être d'aplomb; **7** Mus [*note, instrument*] juste; **8** Geog **~ north** le nord géographique.

II *adv* **1** (straight) [*aim, fire*] juste; **2†** littér **to speak ~** être sincère.

IDIOMS **to be too good to be ~** être trop beau pour être vrai; **~ to form, he...** égal à lui-même, il...; **to be/remain ~ to type** [*person*] être/rester semblable à lui-même.

true: **~-blue** *adj* [*conservative, loyalist*] bon teint *inv*; [*friend*] fidèle; **~-born** *adj* [*Englishman etc*] de souche; **True Cross** *n* vraie Croix *f*; **~-false test** *n* US questionnaire *m* (*où il faut cocher 'vrai' ou 'faux'*); **~-life** *adj* [*adventure, saga, story*] vécu; **~love‡** *n* littér bien-aimé/-e *m/f*.

truffle /ˈtrʌfl/ *n* (all contexts) truffe *f*.

trug /trʌg/ *n* panier *m* de jardinage.

truism /ˈtruːɪzəm/ *n* truisme *m*.

truly /ˈtruːlɪ/ *adv* **1** (extremely) [*amazing, delighted, sorry, horrendous*] vraiment; **he's a ~ great photographer** c'est vraiment un très grand photographe; **a ~ dreadful piece of news** une nouvelle vraiment terrible; **2** (really, in truth) [*be, belong, think*] vraiment; **really and ~?** vraiment?; **well and ~** carrément; **it is ~ a celebration/a great leap forward** c'est vraiment une fête/un bond en avant; **England is where I ~ belong** l'Angleterre est ma vraie patrie; **3** (in letter) **yours ~** (to man) je vous prie d'agréer l'expression de mes sentiments distingués fml; (to woman) je vous prie d'agréer l'expression de mes respectueux hommages fml; **...and who got it all wrong? yours ~!** (referring to oneself) ...et qui s'est trompé? mézigue○!

trump /trʌmp/ **I** *n* **1** Games atout *m*; **2‡** ou littér trompette *f*; **the last ~** les trompettes du jugement dernier.
II trumps *npl* Games atout *m*; **spades are ~s** atout pique; **what's ~s?** quel est l'atout?
III *vtr* **1** Games couper; **2** (beat) battre [*person, rival*].
IDIOMS **to come** ou **turn up ~s** sauver la situation.

trump card *n* atout *m*; **to play one's ~** jouer son atout also fig.

trumped-up /ˌtrʌmptˈʌp/ *adj* [*charge*] forgé de toutes pièces; [*lawyer, doctor*] marron/-onne.

trumpet /ˈtrʌmpɪt/ **▶1481** **I** *n* **1** Mus (instrument, player) trompette *f*; **Woody Shaw on ~** Woody Shaw à la trompette; **2** (elephant call) barrissement *m*; **3** littér (of daffodil) trompette *f*.
II *modif* Mus [*solo*] de trompette; [*concerto*] pour trompette; **~ call** fig vibrant appel *m*.
III *vtr* [*group, party*] vanter les mérites de [*lifestyle, success*]; [*newspaper*] claironner.
IV *vi* [*elephant*] barrir.
IDIOMS **to blow one's own ~** vanter ses propres mérites.

trumpeter /ˈtrʌmpɪtə(r)/ **▶1692**, **1481** *n* trompettiste *mf*.

trumpeter swan *n* cygne *m* trompette.

trumpeting /ˈtrʌmpɪtɪŋ/ *n* (of elephant) barrissement *m*.

trumpet: **~ major** *n* trompette-major *m*; **~ player ▶1481** *n* trompettiste *mf*.

truncate /trʌŋˈkeɪt, US ˈtrʌŋ-/ *vtr* **1** tronquer [*text*]; écourter [*process, journey, event*]; **2** Comput, Math tronquer.

truncated /trʌŋˈkeɪtɪd, US ˈtrʌŋ-/ *adj* **1** [*text*] tronqué; [*process, journey, event*] écourté; **2** Comput, Math tronqué.

truncation /ˌtrʌŋˈkeɪʃn/ *n* **1** (of text) réduction *f*; (of word) troncation *f*; **2** Comput, Math troncature *f*.

truncheon /ˈtrʌntʃən/ *n* matraque *f*.

trundle /ˈtrʌndl/ **I** *vtr* pousser; **to ~ sth out** sortir qch; **to ~ sth in** entrer en poussant qch.
II *vi* [*vehicle*] avancer lourdement; **the lorries were trundling up and down the street** les camions montaient et descendaient lourdement la rue; **he ~d off○ to the station** hum il est parti à la gare.

trundle bed /ˈtrʌndlbed/ *n* US lit *m* gigogne.

trunk /trʌŋk/ **I** *n* **1** (of tree, body) tronc *m*; **2** (of elephant) trompe *f*; **3** (for travel) malle *f*; **4** US (car boot) coffre *m*; **5** (duct) conduite *f*.
II trunks *npl* (also **swimming trunks**) maillot *m* de bain (*pour hommes*).

trunk call† *n* communication *f* à longue distance.

trunking /ˈtrʌŋkɪŋ/ *n* (for liquid, cables) canalisations *fpl*; (for air) conduites *fpl*.

trunk: **~ line** *n* Transp, Telecom ligne *f* principale; **~ road** *n* Transp grand axe *m*.

trunnion /ˈtrʌnjən/ *n* tourillon *m*.

truss /trʌs/ **I** *n* **1** (of hay) botte *f*; **2** Med bandage *m* herniaire; **3** Constr armature *f*, ferme *f*.
II *vtr* **1** (bind) = **truss up**; **2** Constr armer.
■ **truss up**: **~ up [sth]** brider, trousser [*chicken*]; ligoter [*person*]; botteler [*hay*].

trust /trʌst/ **I** *n* **1** (faith) confiance *f*; **to betray sb's ~** trahir la confiance de qn; **a breach of ~** un abus de confiance; **a position of ~** un poste de confiance; **to have complete ~ in** avoir une confiance absolue en; **to put one's ~ in** se fier à; **to take sth on ~** croire qch sur parole; **you'll have to take it on ~** il va falloir que tu me croies sur parole; **2** Jur (set up by donor, testator) (arrangement) fidéicommis *m*; (property involved) propriété *f* fiduciaire; **to set up a ~ for** instituer un fidéicommis à l'intention de; **to hold sth in ~ for** tenir qch par fidéicommis pour; **to leave a sum in ~ for** laisser une somme en fidéicommis pour; **3** Fin (large group of companies) trust *m*; **4** Fin **▶ investment trust**.
II *vtr* **1** (believe) se fier à [*person, judgment*]; **who can we ~?** à qui pouvons-nous nous fier?; **2** (rely on) faire confiance à; **she's not to be ~ed** on ne peut pas lui faire confiance; **~ me** fais-moi confiance; **they ~ each other** ils se font confiance; **~ her!** (amused or annoyed) tu peux compter sur elle pour ça!; **I wouldn't ~ him anywhere near my car** dès que il s'agit de ma voiture, je ne lui fais pas confiance; **children cannot be ~ed with matches** on ne peut pas laisser d'allumettes entre les mains des enfants; **I wouldn't ~ him further than I could throw him** je n'ai pas la moindre confiance en lui; **3** (entrust) **to ~ sb with sth** confier qch à qn; **I would ~ you with my life** je te fais entièrement confiance; **4** (hope) espérer (**that** que); **I ~ not/so** j'espère bien que non/que oui.
III *vi* **to ~ in** faire confiance à [*person*]; croire en [*God, fortune*]; **to ~ to luck** se fier au hasard.
IV trusted *pp adj* [*friend*] fidèle; **a ~ colleague** un collègue en qui on a confiance; **tried and ~ed methods** des méthodes fiables.
V *v refl* **to ~ oneself to do** être sûr de pouvoir faire; **I couldn't ~ myself not to cry** je n'étais pas sûr de pouvoir m'empêcher de pleurer; **I couldn't ~ myself to speak** j'ai préféré me taire.

trust: **~ account** *n* compte *m* en fidéicommis; **~buster** *n* US *fonctionnaire fédéral chargé de veiller à l'application des lois antitrusts*; **~ company** *n* société *f* fiduciaire; **~ deed** *n* acte *m* fiduciaire.

trustee /trʌsˈtiː/ *n* **1** (who administers property in trust) fidéicommissaire *m*, fiduciaire *m*; **2** (who administers a company) administrateur/-trice *m/f* (**of** de); **3** (of trust territory) pays *m* applicant le régime de tutelle.

trusteeship /trʌsˈtiːʃɪp/ *n* **1** (of inheritance) fidéicommis *m*; **2** Pol (of territory) tutelle *f*; **to be under the ~ of the UN** être sous la tutelle de l'ONU.

trustful /ˈtrʌstfl/ *adj* = **trusting**.

trust fund *n* fonds *m* en fidéicommis.

trusting /ˈtrʌstɪŋ/ *adj* [*person*] qui fait facilement confiance aux gens; **you're too ~** tu es trop naïf/naïve.

trust: **~ instrument** *n* acte *m* fiduciaire; **~ territory** *n* territoire *m* sous tutelle.

trustworthiness /ˈtrʌstwɜːðɪnɪs/ *n* (of company, employee) sérieux *m*; (of sources, evidence) fiabilité *f*.

trustworthy /ˈtrʌstwɜːðɪ/ *adj* [*staff, firm*] sérieux/-ieuse; [*source*] fiable; [*confidante, lover*] digne de confiance.

trusty /ˈtrʌstɪ/ **I** *n* prisonnier/-ière *m/f* privilégié/-e.
II *adj* †hum fidèle.

truth /truːθ/ *n* **1** (real facts) **the ~** la vérité (**about** concernant, à propos de); **to face/tell the ~** faire face à/dire la vérité; **the whole ~** toute la vérité; **'...the ~, the whole ~ and nothing but the ~'** Jur '...toute la vérité, rien que la vérité'; **the ~ is beginning to dawn** (on oneself) je commence à entrevoir la vérité; (on others) la vérité commence à percer; **in ~** sout en vérité; **the ~ is that...** la vérité, c'est que...; **whatever the ~ of the matter** quoi qu'il en soit; **to tell you the ~○, I've no idea** à vrai dire, je n'en ai aucune idée; **nothing could be further from the ~** c'est absolument faux; **I can't take one more day of this, and that's the ~○!** je ne peux plus supporter cette situation, un point c'est tout!; **2** (accuracy) **to confirm/deny the ~ of sth** confirmer/nier l'exactitude de qch; **3** Philos, Relig vérité *f*; **a universal ~** une vérité universelle; **4** (foundation) **there is no ~ in that** c'est absolument faux; **there is not a word** ou **shred of ~ in that** il n'y a pas un mot or grain de vérité là-dedans or dans tout cela; **there is some/a great deal of ~ in that** il y a du vrai dans cela/une grande part de vérité fml là-dedans.
IDIOMS **~ will out** la vérité se fera jour; **~ is stranger than fiction** la réalité dépasse la fiction; **to tell sb a few home ~s** dire à qn ses quatre vérités.

truth drug, **truth serum** *n* sérum *m* de vérité.

truthful /ˈtruːθfl/ *adj* [*person*] honnête, franc/franche; [*account, version*] vrai; **to be absolutely** ou **perfectly ~...** en toute franchise, franchement...; **give me a ~ answer** réponds-moi franchement.

truthfully /ˈtruːθfəlɪ/ *adv* [*answer, testify*] sans mentir.

truthfulness /ˈtruːθflnɪs/ *n* véracité *f*.

truth value *n* Philos valeur *f* de vérité.

try /traɪ/ (*pl* **tries**) **I** *n* **1** (attempt) essai *m*; **after three/a few tries** après trois/quelques essais; **to have a ~ at doing** essayer de faire; **I'll give it a ~** je vais essayer; **I had a ~ at water skiing** j'ai essayé le ski nautique; **it's worth a ~** cela vaut la peine d'essayer; **nice ~!** bel essai!; iron bel effort!; **to have a good ~** faire tout ce qu'on peut; **2** Sport (in rugby) essai *m*; **to score a ~** marquer un essai.
II *vtr* (*prét, pp* **tried**) **1** (attempt) essayer de répondre à [*exam question*]; **to ~ doing** ou **to do** essayer de faire; **~ telling that to the judge/my wife!** essaie de faire croire cela au juge/à ma femme!; **to ~ hard to do** faire de gros efforts pour faire; **to ~ one's hardest** ou **best to do** faire tout son possible or tout ce que l'on peut pour faire; **it's ~ing to rain/snow** il a l'air de vouloir pleuvoir/neiger; **2** (test out) essayer [*recipe, tool, product, method, activity*]; prendre [qn] à l'essai [*person*]; [*thief*] essayer d'ouvrir [*door, window*]; tourner [*door knob*]; **~ the back door** essaie la porte de derrière; **you should ~ it for yourself** tu devrais l'essayer; **to ~ one's hand at pottery/weaving** s'essayer à la poterie/au tissage; **to ~ sth on sb/sth** proposer [qch] à qn/qch [*idea, possibility*]; donner [qch] à qn/qch pour voir [*food*]; **~ that meat on the dog** donne cette viande au chien pour voir; **~ that for size** ou **length** essaie pour voir si ça te va; **you should ~ it** tu devrais essayer; **I'll ~ anything once** je suis toujours prêt à faire de nouvelles expériences; **'I bet you don't know the answer'—'~ me!'** 'je parie que tu ne sais

pas la réponse!'—'vas-y!'; **3** (taste, sample) goûter; **~ a piece/the carrots** goûte un morceau/les carottes; **go on, ~ some** vas-y, goûte; **4** (consult) demander à [*person*]; consulter [*book*]; **~ the encyclopedia** consulte l'encyclopédie; **~ the library/the house next door** demandez à la bibliothèque/la maison d'à côté; **we tried all the shops** nous avons demandé dans tous les magasins; **5** (subject to stress) mettre [qch] à rude épreuve [*tolerance, faith*]; **to ~ sb's patience to the limit** pousser qn à bout; **6** Jur juger [*case, criminal*]; **to ~ sb for murder/fraud** juger qn pour meurtre/ fraude.

III *vi* (*prét, pp* **tried**) **1** (make attempt) essayer; **he didn't even ~** il n'a même pas essayé; **I'd like to ~** j'essaierais bien; **to ~ again** (to perform task) recommencer; (to see somebody) repasser; (to phone) rappeler; **to ~ and do** essayer de faire; **~ and relax** essaie de rester calme; **to ~ for** essayer d'obtenir [*loan, university place*]; essayer de battre [*world record*]; essayer d'avoir [*baby*]; **just you ~!** (as threat) essaie un peu○!; **just let him ~!** qu'il essaie seulement!; **keep ~ing!** essaie encore!; **I'd like to see you ~!** j'aimerais bien t'y voir!; **she did it without even ~ing** elle l'a fait sans le moindre effort; **~ harder!** fais plus d'effort!; **at least you tried** tu as fait tout ce que tu as pu; **2** (enquire) demander; **I've tried at the news agent's** j'ai demandé au marchand de journaux.

IDIOMS **these things are sent to ~ us** hum tout ça c'est pour notre bien.

■ **try on**: **~ [sth] on, ~ on [sth]** essayer [*hat, dress*]; **to ~ it on**○ fig bluffer; **they're just ~ing it on**○**!** c'est du bluff!; **don't ~ anything on with me**○ ne fais pas le malin○ avec moi; **to ~ it on with sb's husband/wife**○ essayer de séduire le mari/la femme de qn.

■ **try out**: ¶ **~ out** [*sportsman*] faire un essai; [*actor*] auditionner; **to ~ out for** [*player*] essayer d'entrer dans [*team*]; [*actor*] essayer d'obtenir le rôle de [*Othello, Don Juan*]; ¶ **~ [sth] out, ~ out [sth]** essayer [*machine, theory, drug, language, recipe*] (**on** sur); ¶ **~ [sb] out, ~ out [sb]** prendre [qn] à l'essai.

trying /ˈtraɪɪŋ/ *adj* [*person*] pénible; [*experience*] éprouvant; **it's all terribly ~** c'est terriblement éprouvant.

try-on○ /ˈtraɪɒn/ *n* **it's a ~** c'est du bluff○.

try-out /ˈtraɪaʊt/ *n* **1** Sport essai *m*; **to have a ~** faire un essai; **we gave him a ~** on lui a fait faire un essai; **2** US Theat audition *f*.

tryst /trɪst/ *n* littér rendez-vous *m* galant.

tsar /zɑː(r)/ *n* tsar *m*.

tsarevitch /ˈzɑːrəvɪtʃ/ *n* tsarévitch *m*.

tsarina /zɑːˈriːnə/ *n* tsarine *f*.

tsarist /ˈzɑːrɪst/ *adj* tsariste.

tsetse fly /ˈtsetsɪ flaɪ/ *n* mouche *f* tsé-tsé.

t: **T-shaped** *adj* en (forme de) T; **T-shirt** *n* T-shirt *m*, tee-shirt *m*.

tsp *abrév écrite* = **teaspoonful**.

T-square /ˈtiːskweə(r)/ *n* équerre *f* en T.

TSS *n*: *abrév* ▶ **toxic shock syndrome**.

tsunami /tsuːˈnɑːmi/ *n* tsunami *m*, raz-de-marée *m*.

TT *adj*: *abrév* ▶ **teetotal**.

tub /tʌb/ *n* **1** (large) (for flowers, water) bac *m* (**of** de); (small) (for ice cream, pâté) pot *m* (**of** de); **2** (contents) pot *m* (**of** de); **3** US (bath) baignoire *f*; **she's in the ~** elle est dans son bain; **4**○ (boat) rafiot○ *m*.

tuba /ˈtjuːbə, US ˈtuː-/ ▶ **1481** *n* Mus tuba *m*.

tubby○ /ˈtʌbɪ/ *adj* grassouillet/-ette○.

tube /tjuːb, US ˈtuːb/ **I** *n* **1** (cylinder) tube *m*; **2** (container for toothpaste, glue etc) tube *m*; **3**○ GB Transp métro *m* (londonien); **4**○ US (TV) télé○ *f*; **5** (in TV set) tube *m* cathodique.

II tubes○ *npl* Med bronches *fpl*.

III *modif* [*line, station, ticket*] de métro.

IDIOMS **to go down the ~s** [*plans*] tomber à l'eau; [*economy*] tomber en ruines; **she's had her ~s tied**○ on lui a fait une ligature des trompes.

tubeless /ˈtjuːblɪs, US ˈtuːb-/ *adj* [*tyre*] sans chambre à air.

tuber /ˈtjuːbə(r), US ˈtuː-/ *n* tubercule *m*.

tubercle /ˈtjuːbəkl, US ˈtuː-/ *n* Bot, Med tubercule *m*.

tubercular /tjuːˈbɜːkjʊlə(r), US ˈtuː-/ *adj* tuberculeux/-euse.

tuberculin /tjuːˈbɜːkjʊlɪn, US ˈtuː-/ *n* tuberculine *f*.

tuberculin-tested *adj* [*cattle*] tuberculisé.

tuberculosis /tjuːˌbɜːkjʊˈləʊsɪs, US ˈtuː-/ ▶ **1354** **I** *n* tuberculose *f*.

II *modif* [*sufferer, patient*] tuberculeux/-euse.

tuberculous /tjuːˈbɜːkjʊləs, US tuː-/ ▶ **1354** *adj* tuberculeux/-euse.

tube top *n* Fashn bustier *m*.

tubing /ˈtjuːbɪŋ, US ˈtuː-/ *n* tuyauterie *f*; **a length** ou **piece of ~** un tuyau.

tub-thumping /ˈtʌbθʌmpɪŋ/ **I** *n* éloquence *f* de bas étage.

II *adj* [*orator*] de bas étage.

tubular /ˈtjuːbjʊlə(r), US ˈtuː-/ *adj* tubulaire.

tubular: **~ bells** ▶ **1481** *npl* cloches-tubes *fpl*; **~ steel chair** *n* chaise *f* tubulaire.

tubule /ˈtjuːbjuːl, US ˈtuː-/ *n* tubule *m*.

TUC *n*: *abrév* ▶ **Trades Union Congress**.

tuck /tʌk/ **I** *n* Sewing pli *m*; (to shorten) pli *m* horizontal.

II *vtr* **to ~ sth between/into/ under/behind** (of flat object) glisser qch entre/dans/sous/derrière; **to ~ a card into a pocket** glisser une carte dans une poche; **to ~ sb's arm into yours** glisser le bras de qn sous le tien; **to ~ one's shirt into one's trousers** rentrer sa chemise dans son pantalon; **to ~ one's trousers into one's boots** enfiler son pantalon dans ses bottes; **to ~ one's hands into one's sleeves** enfiler les mains dans ses manches; **to ~ a blanket under sb** plier une couverture sous qn; **to ~ one's hair under one's hat** rentrer ses cheveux sous son chapeau; **she ~ed her feet up under her** elle a ramené ses pieds sous elle; **it ~ed its head under its wing** il a enfoui la tête sous son aile; **to ~ a flower behind one's ear** se mettre une fleur derrière l'oreille; **to ~ a blanket around sb** envelopper qn dans une couverture.

III tucked *pp adj* Fashn, Sewing plissé.

■ **tuck away**: **~ [sth] away, ~ away [sth]** **1** (safely, in reserve) enfouir [*object*]; mettre en sécurité [*money, valuable*]; **to have £5,000 ~ed away** avoir 5 000 livres sterling en sécurité; **2** (hard to find) **to be ~ed away** [*village, document, object*] se nicher; [*person*] s'isoler.

■ **tuck in**: ¶ **~ in** (start eating) attaquer; **to ~ into a meal** attaquer un repas; **~ in, everybody!** allez-y, attaquez!; ¶ **~ in [sth], ~ [sth] in** rentrer [*garment, shirt*]; border [*bedclothes*]; **to ~ the flap in** glisser le rabat dans l'enveloppe; ¶ **~ [sb] in, ~ in [sb]** border.

■ **tuck up**: **~ up [sb], ~ [sb] up** border; **to be ~ed up in bed** être bordé dans son lit.

tuck box† *n* GB Sch réserve *f* de friandises (*donnée aux pensionnaires par leurs parents*).

tucker /ˈtʌkə(r)/: IDIOMS **in one's best bib and ~** sur son trente et un○.

■ **tucker out**○: **~ [sb] out** claquer○; **to be ~ed out** être claqué○.

tuck: **~ jump** *n* Sport saut *m* groupé; **~ shop** *n* GB Sch *boutique où les élèves achètent des friandises*.

Tudor /ˈtjuːdə(r), US ˈtuː-/ **I** *pr n* Tudor *inv*.

II *modif* [*times, rose*] des Tudor.

Tue(s) *abrév écrite* = **Tuesday**.

Tuesday /ˈtjuːzdeɪ, -dɪ, US ˈtuː-/ ▶ **1883** *n* mardi *m*.

tufa /ˈtjuːfə, US ˈtuː-/ *n* Geol tuf *m*.

tuffet /ˈtʌfɪt/ *n* littér petite touffe *f*.

tuft /tʌft/ *n* touffe *f*.

tufted /ˈtʌftɪd/ *adj* [*grass*] en touffes; [*bird*] huppé; [*carpet*] tufté.

tufted duck *n* fuligule *m* morillon.

tug /tʌg/ **I** *n* **1** (pull) (on rope, in sails) résistance *f*; (on fishing line) secousse *f*; **to give sth a ~** tirer sur qch; **the ~ of old habits** fig la force des habitudes; **to feel a ~ of loyalties** se sentir partagé; **2** Naut (also **tug boat**) remorqueur *m*.

II *vtr* (*p prés etc* **-gg-**) **1** (pull) tirer [*object, hair*]; **2** Naut remorquer [*boat*].

III *vi* (*p prés etc* **-gg-**) **to ~ at** ou **on** tirer sur [*rope, hair*]; **to ~ at sb's sleeve** tirer qn par la manche; **to ~ at one's moustache/lip** se tirer la moustache/la lèvre.

tug-of-love /ˌtʌgəvˈlʌv/ **I** *n* GB Journ *lutte entre les parents pour la garde de l'enfant*.

II *modif* [*child*] dont les parents se disputent la garde.

tug-of-war /ˌtʌgəvˈwɔː(r)/ *n* **1** Sport gagne-terrain *m*; **2** fig lutte *f* (**between** entre).

tuition /tjuːˈɪʃn, US tuː-/ *n* cours *mpl*; **private ~** cours privés.

tuition fees *npl* frais *mpl* pédagogiques.

tulip /ˈtjuːlɪp, US ˈtuː-/ *n* tulipe *f*.

tulip tree *n* tulipier *m*.

tulle /tjuːl, US tuːl/ *n* tulle *m*.

tum○ /tʌm/ *n* lang enfantin ventre *m*.

tumble /ˈtʌmbl/ **I** *n* **1** (fall) chute *f*; **to take a ~** lit faire une chute; fig [*price, share, market*] chuter; **shares took a 50-point ~** les actions ont chuté de 50 points; **they had a ~ in the hay** ils ont batifolé dans le foin; **2** (of clown, acrobat) culbute *f*; **3** (jumble) tas *m*.

II *vi* **1** (fall) [*person, object*] tomber (**off, out of** de); **to ~ several metres** tomber de plusieurs mètres; **to ~ out of bed** bondir du lit; **to ~ over** ou **off** tomber de [*cliff, roof*]; **to ~ down the stairs** dégringoler dans l'escalier; **to ~ down sth** [*water, stream*] dévaler qch en cascade; **curls ~d about her shoulders** les boucles lui tombaient sur les épaules; **2** Fin [*price, share, currency*] chuter; **3** Sport [*clown, acrobat, child*] faire des culbutes; **4**○ **to ~ to sth** (understand) piger○, comprendre [*fact, plan*].

■ **tumble down** [*wall, building*] s'écrouler; **the walls came tumbling down** les murs se sont écroulés.

■ **tumble out** [*contents*] se renverser; [*words, feelings*] jaillir en désordre.

tumble: **~down** *adj* délabré; **~-drier**, **~-dryer** *n* sèche-linge *m inv*.

tumble-dry /ˌtʌmblˈdraɪ/ *vtr* sécher (*dans un sèche-linge*); **'do not ~'** 'ne pas sécher en machine'.

tumbler /ˈtʌmblə(r)/ *n* **1** (glass) verre *m* droit; **2** (acrobat) acrobate *mf*; (gymnast) tumbler *m*; **3** (of lock) gorge *f*; **4** (drier) sèche-linge *m inv*.

tumbler: **~ drier** *n* = **tumble-drier**; **~ful** *n* verre *m*; **~ pigeon** *n* pigeon *m* culbutant.

tumbleweed /ˈtʌmblwiːd/ *n* amarantacée *f*.

tumbling /ˈtʌmblɪŋ/ **I** *n* ▶ **1282** tumbling *m*.

II *adj* [*water*] qui tombe en cascade; fig [*shares, prices*] en chute libre; **a mass of ~ curls** une masse de cheveux bouclés.

tumbrel, **tumbril** /ˈtʌmbrəl/ *n* charrette *f*, tombereau *m*.

tumefaction /ˌtjuːmɪˈfækʃn, US ˌtuː-/ *n* tuméfaction *f*.

tumescence /tjuːˈmesns, US tuː-/ *n* tumescence *f*.

tumescent /tjuːˈmesnt/ *adj* tumescent.

tumid /ˈtjuːmɪd, US ˈtuː-/ *adj* [*body part*] tuméfié; [*prose*] ampoulé.

tummy○ /ˈtʌmɪ/ *n* lang enfantin ventre *m*.

tummyache○ /ˈtʌmɪeɪk/ *n* lang enfantin mal *m* au ventre.

tumour GB, **tumor** US /ˈtju:mə(r), US ˈtu:-/ *n* tumeur *f*; **secondary ~** métastase *f*.

tumuli /ˈtju:mjʊlaɪ/ *pl* ▶ **tumulus**.

tumult /ˈtju:mʌlt, US ˈtu:-/ *n* **1** (noisy chaos) tumulte *m*; **to be in ~** [*hall, meeting*] être en tumulte; [*feelings*] être en émoi; **2** (disorder) agitation *f*.

tumultuous /tju:ˈmʌltjʊəs, US ˈtu:-/ *adj* tumultueux/-euse.

tumultuously /tju:ˈmʌltjʊəslɪ, US tu:-/ *adv* tumultueusement.

tumulus /ˈtju:mjʊləs/ *n* (*pl* **-li**) tumulus *m*.

tun /tʌn/ *n* fût *m*.

tuna /ˈtju:nə, US ˈtu:-/ **I** *n* Zool, Culin thon *m*.
II *modif* [*fishing, sandwich*] au thon; [*canning*] du thon.

tuna fish *n* Culin thon *m*.

tundra /ˈtʌndrə/ *n* toundra *f*.

tune /tju:n, US tu:n/ **I** *n* **1** Mus air *m*; **to dance/sing sth to the ~ of sth** danser/chanter qch sur l'air de qch; **2** Mus (accurate pitch) **to be in/out of ~** Mus être accordé/désaccordé (**with** avec); fig être/ne pas être en accord (**with** avec); **to sing in/out of ~** chanter juste/faux; **an out-of-~ piano/violin** un piano/violon désaccordé; **3**○ (amount) **to the ~ of** pour un montant de; **to be in debt/have costs to the ~ of £50,000** avoir des dettes/des frais pour un montant de 50 000 livres.
II *vtr* accorder [*musical instrument*] (**to** à); régler [*car engine, radio, TV, signal*] (**to** sur); **stay ~d!** restez à l'écoute!
IDIOMS **to call the ~** mener la danse; **to change one's ~, to sing a different ~** changer d'avis; **to dance to sb's ~** se plier aux exigences de qn.
■ **tune in** ¶ mettre la radio; **to ~ in to** se mettre à l'écoute de [*programme*]; régler sur [*channel*] ; ¶ **~ [sth] in** régler (**to** sur).
■ **tune out**○ US: ¶ **~ out** décrocher○; ¶ **~ [sb] out** ne pas écouter.
■ **tune up** ¶ [*musician*] s'accorder; ¶ **~ up [sth], ~ [sth] up** accorder [*musical instrument*]; régler [*engine*].

tuneful /ˈtju:nfl, US ˈtu:-/ *adj* mélodieux/-ieuse.

tunefully /ˈtju:nfəlɪ, US ˈtu:-/ *adv* mélodieusement.

tuneless /ˈtju:nlɪs, US ˈtu:-/ *adj* dépourvu de mélodie.

tunelessly /ˈtju:nlɪslɪ, US ˈtu:-/ *adv* **to sing ~** chantonner; **to whistle ~** siffloter.

tuner /ˈtju:nə(r), US ˈtu:-/ *n* **1** ▶ **1692** Mus accordeur *m*; **organ/piano ~** accordeur *m* d'orgues/de piano; **2** Audio (unit) tuner *m*; (knob) (bouton *m* de) réglage.

tuner amplifier *n* tuner *m* amplificateur.

tungsten /ˈtʌŋstən/ **I** *n* tungstène *m*.
II *modif* [*filament, steel*] au tungstène.

tunic /ˈtju:nɪk, US ˈtu:-/ *n* **1** (classical, fashion, for gym) tunique *f*; **2** (uniform) (for nurse, schoolgirl) blouse *f*; (for policeman) tunique *f*; (for soldier) vareuse *f*.

tuning /ˈtju:nɪŋ, US ˈtu:-/ **I** *n* (of musical instrument, choir) accord *m*; (of radio, TV, engine) réglage *m*.
II *modif* **1** Mus [*key, pin*] d'accord; **2** Audio, TV [*dial, knob*] de réglage.

tuning fork *n* Mus diapason *m*.

Tunis /ˈtju:nɪs/ ▶ **1818** *pr n* Tunis.

Tunisia /tju:ˈnɪzɪə, US tu:-/ ▶ **1131** *pr n* Tunisie *f*.

Tunisian /tju:ˈnɪzɪən, US tu:-/ ▶ **1486** **I** *n* Tunisien/-ienne *m/f*.
II *adj* tunisien/-ienne.

tunnel /ˈtʌnl/ **I** *n* tunnel *m*; **to use a ~** emprunter un tunnel.
II *vtr, vi* (*prés p etc* **-ll-** GB, **-l-** US) creuser.
IDIOMS **to see (the) light at the end of the ~** voir le bout du tunnel.

tunnel effect *n* effet *m* tunnel.

tunnel vision *n* **1** Med rétrécissement *m* (tubulaire) du champ visuel; **2** fig **to have ~** avoir des œillères.

tunny /ˈtʌnɪ/ *n* = **tuna**.

tuppence /ˈtʌpəns/ *n* deux pence; **it's not worth ~**○ ça ne vaut pas un rond○.
IDIOMS **not to care ~ for sb/sth** se moquer éperdument de qn/qch.

tuppeny-ha'penny /ˌtʌpənɪˈheɪpənɪ/ *adj* (*tjrs épith*) péj minable○.

turban /ˈtɜ:bən/ *n* turban *m*.

turbaned /ˈtɜ:bənd/ *adj* enturbanné.

turbid /ˈtɜ:bɪd/ *adj* littér turbide liter, trouble.

turbidity /tɜ:ˈbɪdətɪ/ **I** *n* turbidité *f*.
II *modif* [*current*] de turbidité.

turbine /ˈtɜ:baɪn/ *n* turbine *f*; **gas/steam ~** turbine à gaz/à vapeur.

turbo /ˈtɜ:bəʊ/ *n* (engine) turbo *m*; (car) turbo *f*.

turbocharged /ˌtɜ:bəʊˈtʃɑ:dʒd/ *adj* [*engine*] turbo *inv*; [*car, vehicle*] à moteur turbo.

turbocharger /ˈtɜ:bəʊtʃɑ:dʒə(r)/ *n* turbocompresseur *m*.

turbofan /ˈtɜ:bəʊfæn/ *n* turbosoufflante *f*.

turbogenerator /ˌtɜ:bəʊˈdʒenəreɪtə(r)/ *n* turbo-alternateur *m*.

turbojet /ˈtɜ:bəʊdʒet/ **I** *n* turboréacteur *m*.
II *modif* [*plane*] à turboréacteurs.

turboprop /ˈtɜ:bəʊprɒp/ **I** *n* turbopropulseur *m*.
II *modif* [*plane*] à turbopropulseur.

turbot /ˈtɜ:bət/ **I** *n* turbot *m*.
II *modif* [*fishing*] au turbot; [*steak*] de turbot.

turbotrain /ˈtɜ:bəʊtreɪn/ *n* turbotrain *m*.

turbulence /ˈtɜ:bjʊləns/ *n* ¢ **1** (of air) turbulences *fpl*; (of waves) turbulence *f*; **2** (turmoil) agitation *f*; (unrest) perturbations *fpl*.

turbulent /ˈtɜ:bjʊlənt/ *adj* **1** [*water*] agité; [*air current*] turbulent; **2** [*times, situation*] agité; [*career, history*] mouvementé; [*passions, character, faction*] turbulent.

turbulently /ˈtɜ:bjʊləntlɪ/ *adv* avec turbulence.

turd /tɜ:d/ *n* **1**○ (faeces) crotte *f*; **2**● (person) merdeux/-euse● *m/f*.

tureen /təˈri:n/ *n* soupière *f*.

turf /tɜ:f/ **I** *n* (*pl* **~s, turves**) **1** (grass) gazon *m*; (peat) tourbe *f*; (piece of peat) motte *f* de tourbe; **to lay ~** poser du gazon; **2** (horseracing) **the ~** le turf *m*, les courses *fpl*; **3**○ (territory) (of gang) territoire *m*; (of busker, prostitute) secteur *m*; **to be back on one's own ~** se retrouver chez soi.
II *vtr* **1** gazonner [*lawn, patch, pitch*]; **2**○ (throw) **~ that dog off the sofa** vire ce chien du divan○.
■ **turf out**: **~ out [sb/sth], ~ [sb/sth] out** virer○.

turf accountant ▶ **1692** *n* bookmaker *m*.

Turgenev /tɜ:ˈgeɪnjev/ *pr n* Tourgueniev.

turgid /ˈtɜ:dʒɪd/ *adj* sout [*style*] boursouflé; littér [*water*] gonflé.

turgidity /tɜ:ˈdʒɪdətɪ/ *n* (of style) boursouflure *f*; littér (of waters) gonflement *m*.

Turin /tjʊˈrɪn/ ▶ **1818** *pr n* Turin.

Turin shroud *n* saint suaire *m* de Turin.

Turk /tɜ:k/ ▶ **1486** *n* **1** (person) Turc/Turque *m/f*; **2**○ péj (brute) tyran *m*. ▶ **Young Turk**.

turkey /ˈtɜ:kɪ/ *n* **1** Culin dinde *f*; **2**○ US péj Theat, Cin (flop) bide○ *m*; (bad film) navet○ *m*; **3**○ US (person) cloche○ *f*.
IDIOMS **to talk ~**○ passer aux choses sérieuses.

Turkey /ˈtɜ:kɪ/ ▶ **1131** *pr n* Turquie *f*.

turkey buzzard *n* vautour *m* d'Amérique.

turkey cock *n* **1** (bird) dindon *m*; **2**○ (young man) m'as-tu-vu *m*, plastronneur *m*.

turkey: **~ trot** *n* Hist (dance) turkey-trot *m*; **~ vulture** *n* = **turkey buzzard**.

Turkish /ˈtɜ:kɪʃ/ ▶ **1486**, **1402** **I** *n* Ling turc *m*.
II *adj* turc/turque.

Turkish: **~ bath** *n* bain *m* turc; **~ coffee** *n* café *m* turc; **~ delight** *n* loukoum *m*; **~ tobacco** *n* tabac *m* turc; **~ towel** *n* serviette *f* éponge; **~ towelling** *n* tissu *m* éponge épais.

Turkmen /ˈtɜ:kmən/ ▶ **1486**, **1402** **I** *n* **1** (inhabitant) Turkmène *mf*; **2** (language) turkmène *m*.
II *adj* turkmène.

Turkmenistan /ˌtɜ:kmenɪˈstɑ:n/ ▶ **1131** *pr n* Turkménistan *m*.

Turkoman /ˈtɜ:kəʊmən/ ▶ **1486**, **1402** **I** *n* **1** (person) Turkmène *mf*; **2** Ling turkmène *m*.
II *adj* turkmène.

turmeric /ˈtɜ:mərɪk/ *n* **1** Bot curcuma *m*; **2** (spice) safran *m* des Indes.

turmoil /ˈtɜ:mɔɪl/ *n* (political, emotional) désarroi *m*; **in ~** dans le désarroi.

turn /tɜ:n/ ▶ **1173** **I** *n* **1** (opportunity, in rotation) tour *m*; **to wait one's ~** attendre son tour; **it's my ~** gen c'est mon tour; (in game) c'est à moi de jouer; **whose ~ is it?** gen c'est à qui le tour?; (in game) c'est à qui de jouer?; **'miss a ~'** 'passez votre tour'; **to be sb's ~ to do** être à qn or au tour de qn de faire; **it's your ~ to make the coffee** c'est à toi or à ton tour de faire le café; **it was his ~ to feel rejected** il se sentait rejeté à son tour; **to have a ~ on** or **at** or **with the computer** utiliser l'ordinateur à son tour; **to have a ~ at driving** prendre son tour de conduite; **to take ~s at doing, to take it in ~s to do** faire qch à tour de rôle; **to do sth ~ and ~ about** faire qch à tour de rôle; **take it in ~s!** chacun son tour!; **by ~s** tour à tour; **to feel happy and depressed by ~s** être tour à tour heureux et malheureux; **to speak out of ~** fig commettre un impair; **I hope I haven't spoken out of ~** j'espère ne pas avoir commis d'impair; **2** (circular movement) tour *m*; **to give sth a ~** tourner qch; **to give sth half a ~ to the left** faire tourner qch d'un demi-tour vers la gauche; **to do a ~** [*dancer*] faire un tour; **to take a ~ in the park** faire un tour dans le parc; **3** (in vehicle) virage *m*; **a 90° ~** un virage à 90°; **to make** ou **do a left/right ~** tourner à gauche/à droite; **to do a ~ in the road** faire un demi-tour; **'no left ~'** 'défense de tourner à gauche'; **4** (bend, side road) tournant *m*, virage *m*; **there's a left ~ ahead** il y a un tournant or virage à gauche plus loin; **brake before you go into the ~** freinez avant de prendre le virage; **take the next right ~, take the next ~ on the right** prenez la prochaine (rue) à droite; **5** (change, development) tournure *f*; **the ~ of events** la tournure des événements; **this is an extraordinary ~ of events** les événements ont pris une tournure extraordinaire; **to take an encouraging/a worrying ~** [*events*] prendre une tournure encourageante/inquiétante; **to take a ~ for the better** [*person, situation*] s'améliorer; [*things, events*] prendre une meilleure tournure; **to take a ~ for the worse** [*situation*] se dégrader; [*health*] s'aggraver; **she has taken a ~ for the worse** elle va de plus en plus mal; **to be on the ~** [*luck, milk*] commencer à tourner; [*tide*] commencer à changer; ▶ **century**; **6**○ GB (attack) crise *f*, attaque *f*; **she's had one of her ~s again** elle a eu une nouvelle crise or attaque; **a giddy** ou **dizzy ~** un vertige; **to have a funny ~** se sentir tout/-e chose○; **it gave me quite a ~, it gave me a nasty ~** ça m'a fait un coup○; **7** (act) numéro *m*; **a comic/variety ~** un numéro comique/de variété; **to do a/one's ~** faire un/son numéro.
II in turn *adv phr* **1** (in rotation) [*answer, speak*] à tour de rôle; **she spoke to each of us in ~** elle nous a parlé chacun à notre tour; **2** (linking sequence) à son tour; **this in ~ leads to higher inflation** ceci à son tour fait augmenter l'inflation; **I invited Andrew who in ~ invited Robert** j'ai invité Andrew qui à son tour a invité Robert.

III *vtr* **1** (rotate) [*person*] tourner [*knob, wheel, handle*]; serrer [*screw*]; [*mechanism*] faire tourner [*cog, wheel*]; **to ~ sth to the right/left** tourner qch vers la droite/gauche; **to ~ sth to 'on'/'off'** tourner qch sur (la position) 'marche'/'arrêt'; **to ~ a switch through 90 degrees** faire tourner un sélecteur de 90 degrés ; **to ~ sth halfway/the wrong way** tourner qch d'un demi-tour/dans le mauvais sens; **to ~ the key in the door** ou **lock** (lock up) fermer la porte à clé; (unlock) tourner la clé dans la serrure; **to ~ the key on sb** enfermer qn à clé; **2** (turn over, reverse) retourner [*mattress, soil, steak, collar*]; tourner [*page*]; **to ~ sb onto his side/back** retourner qn sur le côté/dos; **to ~ one's ankle** se tordre la cheville; **it ~s my stomach** cela me soulève le cœur, cela m'écœure; **3** (change direction of) tourner [*chair, head, face, car*]; **to ~ a picture to the wall** tourner un tableau face au mur; **to ~ one's face towards** tourner le visage vers; **to ~ one's steps towards** tourner or diriger ses pas vers; **to ~ one's attention** ou **mind to** tourner son attention vers; **to ~ one's back on** lit tourner le dos à [*group, place*]; fig laisser tomber [*friend, ally*]; abandonner [*homeless, needy*]; **as soon as my back is ~ed** lit, fig dès que j'ai le dos tourné; **to ~ one' s back on the past** tourner la page; **to ~ sb from one's door** chasser qn; **4** (focus, direction of) **to ~ sth on sb** braquer qch sur qn [*gun, hose, torch*]; fig diriger qch sur qn [*anger, scorn*]; **5** (transform) **to ~ sth white/black** blanchir/noircir qch; **to ~ sth milky/opaque** rendre qch laiteux/opaque; **to ~ sth into** transformer qch en [*office, car park, desert*]; **to ~ water into ice/wine** changer de l'eau en glace/vin; **to ~ a book into a film** adapter un livre pour l'écran; **~ your old newspapers into cash!** convertissez vos vieux journaux en argent!; **to ~ sb into** [*magician*] changer qn en [*frog*]; [*experience*] faire de qn [*extrovert, maniac*]; **it ~ed him from a normal child into a delinquent** cela a transformé l'enfant normal qu'il était en délinquant; **to stand there as if ~ed to stone** rester là comme pétrifié; **6** (deflect) détourner [*person, conversation*]; **to ~ the conversation towards** ou **onto sth** détourner or faire dévier la conversation vers qch; **to ~ sb from a course of action/from her purpose** détourner qn d'une ligne de conduite/de son but; **7**○ (pass the age of) **he has ~ed 50** il a 50 ans passés; **she has just ~ed 20/30** elle vient d'avoir 20/30 ans; **as soon as I ~ 18** dès que j'aurai mes 18 ans; **it's just ~ed five o'clock** il est cinq heures passées; **8** Ind (on lathe) tourner [*wood, piece, spindle*]; **9** fig (fashion) **to ~ an elegant sentence** tourner une phrase élégante; **10** (in espionage) retourner [*spy, agent*].

IV *vi* **1** (change direction) [*person, car, plane, road*] tourner; [*ship*] virer; **to ~ (to the) left/right** tourner à gauche/droite; **to ~ to the east/the west** tourner à l'est/l'ouest; **to ~ down** ou **into** tourner dans [*street, alley*]; **to ~ off** quitter [*main road, street*]; **to ~ towards** tourner en direction de [*village, mountains*]; **I ~ed towards home** j'ai repris le chemin de la maison; **her thoughts ~ed to her family** ses pensées se sont tournées vers sa famille; **the conversation ~ed to Ellie** on en est venu/ils en sont venus à parler d'Ellie; **he later ~ed to teaching** plus tard il s'est tourné vers l'enseignement; **2** (reverse direction) [*person, vehicle*] faire demi-tour; [*tide*] changer; [*luck*] tourner; **there's no room for the bus to ~** le bus n'a pas assez de place pour faire demi- tour; **'no ~ing'** (in driveway) 'propriété privée, défense d'entrer'; ▶ **turn around**; **3** (revolve) [*key, wheel, planet*] tourner; [*person*] se tourner (**to, towards** vers); **to ~ on its axis** tourner sur son axe; **a key ~ed in the lock** une clé a tourné dans la serrure; **to ~ in one's chair** se retourner dans sa chaise; **to ~ and face the camera** se tourner vers la caméra; **to ~ and walk out of the room** faire demi-tour et sortir de la pièce; **to ~ to do** se retourner pour faire; **to ~ to face sth** se retourner vers qch; **to ~ and fight** se retourner pour se battre; **to ~ to lie on one's side** se tourner pour se mettre sur le côté; **I ~ed once again to my book/my work** j'ai repris encore une fois ma lecture/mon travail; **4** fig (hinge) **to ~ on** [*argument*] tourner autour de [*point, issue*]; [*outcome*] dépendre de [*factor*]; **5** (spin round angrily) **to ~ on sb** [*dog*] attaquer qn; [*person*] se retourner contre qn; **6** fig (resort to, rely on) **to ~ to** se tourner vers [*person, religion*]; **to ~ to drink** se mettre à boire; **to ~ to drugs** commencer à se droguer; **to ~ to sb for** se tourner vers qn pour demander [*help, advice, money*]; **I don't know who to ~ to for advice** je ne sais vers qui me tourner pour demander conseil; **I don't know where** ou **which way to ~** je ne sais plus où donner la tête○; **7** (change) **to ~ into** [*tadpole*] se transformer en [*frog*]; [*sofa*] se transformer en [*bed*]; [*situation, evening*] tourner à [*farce , disaster*]; [*conversation*] tourner à [*shouting match*]; (magically) [*person*] se transformer en [*animal, prince etc*]; **to ~ to** [*substance*] se changer en [*ice, gold etc*]; [*fear, surprise*] faire place à [*horror, relief*]; **his hopes had ~ed to dust** ses espoirs étaient réduits en poussière; **8** (become by transformation) devenir [*pale, cloudy, green*]; **to ~ white/black/red** gen blanchir/noircir/rougir; Chem virer au blanc/noir/rouge; **the weather is ~ing cold/warm** le temps se rafraîchit/se réchauffe; **events ~ed tragic** les événements ont tourné au tragique; **9**○ (have change of heart) devenir [*Conservative, Communist*]; **business-woman ~ed politician** ancienne femme d'affaires devenue politicienne; **to ~**○ **Catholic/Muslim** se convertir au catholicisme/à l'islam; **to ~ traitor** se mettre à trahir; **10** (go sour) [*milk*] tourner; **11** [*trees, leaves*] jaunir.

IDIOMS at every ~ à chaque instant, à tout moment; **one good ~ deserves another** Prov c'est un prêté pour un rendu; **to be done to a ~** être cuit à point; **to do sb a good ~** rendre un service à qn; **to feel another ~ of the screw** sentir la pression augmenter encore.

■ **turn about** faire demi-tour; **about ~!** Mil demi-tour droite!

■ **turn against**: ¶ **~ against [sb/sth]** se retourner contre; ¶ **~ [sb] against** retourner [qn] contre [*person, ideology*].

■ **turn around**: ¶ **~ around 1** (to face other way) [*person*] se retourner, faire demi-tour (**to do** pour faire); [*bus, vehicle*] faire demi-tour; **2** fig **you can't just ~ around and say you've changed your mind** tu ne peux pas tout simplement dire que tu as changé d'avis; **what if he just ~s around and says no?** et si jamais il disait non?; **3** (revolve, rotate) [*object, windmill, dancer*] tourner; **4** (change trend) **the market has ~ed around** il y a eu un renversement de situation sur le marché; **sales have ~ed round** il y a eu un renversement de tendance dans les ventes; **5** Transp (unload and reload) décharger et charger; ¶ **~ [sth] around, ~ around [sth] 1** (to face other way) tourner [qch] dans l'autre sens [*car, chair, piano, head, baby*]; **2** (reverse decline in) redresser [*situation, economy, company*]; redresser la situation de [*political party, factory*]; **3** Transp (unload and reload) décharger et mettre en état de repartir [*plane , ship*]; **the plane can be ~ed around in an hour** l'avion peut être déchargé et prêt à reprendre l'air en une heure; **4** (rephrase) reformuler [*question, sentence*].

■ **turn aside** se détourner (**from** de).

■ **turn away**: ¶ **~ away** se détourner; **to ~ away in disgust/horror** se détourner avec dégoût/horreur; ¶ **~ [sth] away, ~ away [sth]** détourner [*head, torch*]; ¶ **~ [sb] away, ~ away [sb]** refuser [*spectator, applicant*]; ne pas laisser entrer [*salesman, caller*]; chasser [*beggar*]; **I was ~ed away from the Ritz** on ne m'a pas laissé entrer au Ritz.

■ **turn back**: ¶ **~ back 1** (turn around) (usu on foot) rebrousser chemin; (usu in vehicle) faire demi-tour; **it's too late to ~ back** lit il est trop tard pour faire demi-tour; fig il est trop tard pour revenir en arrière; **there's no ~ing back** fig il n'est pas question de revenir en arrière; **2** (in book) revenir (**to** à); ¶ **~ [sth] back, ~ back [sth] 1** (rotate backwards) reculer [*dial, clock*]; **to ~ one's watch back five minutes** retarder sa montre de cinq minutes; **2** (fold back) rabattre [*sheet, lapel*]; replier [*corner, page*]; ¶ **~ [sb] back, ~ back [sb]** faire faire demi-tour à, refouler [*marchers, refugees, heavy vehicles*]; **to be ~ed back at the border** être refoulé à la frontière.

■ **turn down**: ¶ **~ down** [*graph, curve*] descendre; **his mouth ~s down at the corners** il a une bouche aux commissures tombantes; ¶ **~ [sth] down, ~ down [sth] 1** (reduce) baisser [*volume, radio, heating, light, gas*]; **2** (fold over) rabattre [*sheet, collar*]; retourner [*corner of page*]; corner [*page*]; ¶ **~ [sb/sth] down, ~ down [sb/sth]** refuser [*suitor, candidate, request, application*]; rejeter [*offer, suggestion*].

■ **turn in**: ¶ **~ in 1**○ (go to bed) aller se coucher; **2** (point inwards) **his toes ~ in** il a les pieds tournés en dedans; **to ~ in on itself** [*leaf, page*] se recroqueviller; **to ~ in on oneself** fig se replier sur soi-même; ¶ **~ in [sth], ~ [sth] in**○ **1** (hand in) rendre [*membership, badge, homework*]; **2** (produce) **to ~ in a profit** rapporter un bénéfice; **to ~ in a good performance** [*player*] bien jouer; [*company*] avoir de bons résultats; [*currency, share*] augmenter; **3** (give up, stop) laisser tomber○ [*job, activity*]; ¶ **~ [sb] in, ~ in [sb]** livrer [*suspect*] (**to** à); ¶ **~ oneself in** se livrer.

■ **turn off**: ¶ **~ off 1** (leave road) tourner; **~ off at the next exit** prends la prochaine sortie; **2** [*motor, fan*] s'arrêter; **where does the light ~ off?** où est-ce qu'on éteint la lumière?; ¶ **~ off [sth], ~ [sth] off** éteindre [*light, oven, TV, radio, computer*]; fermer [*tap*]; couper [*water, gas, electricity, engine*]; **~ that rubbish off!**○ éteins-moi ça!○; ¶ **~ [sb] off**○ rebuter, dégoûter○; **to ~ sb off sth** dégoûter qn de [*sex, food*].

■ **turn on**: ¶ **~ on** [*oven, device*] s'allumer; ¶ **~ on [sth], ~ [sth] on** allumer [*light, oven, TV, radio, computer, gas, electricity*]; ouvrir [*tap*]; **to ~ the water back on** rouvrir l'eau; **to ~ the electricity back on** rétablir le courant; **to ~ sth on like a tap** fig faire qch sur commande; **to ~ on the pressure** fig mettre la pression; ▶ **charm, heat**; ¶ **~ [sb] on, ~ on [sb]**○ exciter; **to be ~ed on** être excité (**by** par); **to ~ sb on to sth**○ brancher○ qn sur [*drug*].

■ **turn out**: ¶ **~ out 1** (be eventually) **to ~ out well/badly** bien/mal se terminer; **to ~ out differently** prendre une tournure différente; **to ~ out all right** s'arranger; **it depends how things ~ out** cela dépend de la façon dont les choses vont tourner; **that child will ~ out badly** cet enfant tournera mal; **to ~ out to be** (prove to be) se révéler, s'avérer être; **to ~ out to be wrong** se révéler faux; **the job ~ed out (to be) difficult** finalement le travail a été difficile, le travail s'est avéré difficile fml; **it ~ed out to be a good decision** finalement cela a été une bonne décision, cela s'est avéré être une bonne décision fml; **it ~s out that** il se trouve que, il s'avère que; **it ~ed out (that) she knew him** il s'est trouvé qu'elle le connaissait; **as it ~ed out** en fin de compte; **2** (come out) [*crowd, people*] venir (**to do** pour faire; **for** à); **the fans ~ out every Saturday** les fans sont là tous les samedis; **we had to ~**

out at six GB il fallait être là à six heures; **3** (point outwards) **his toes** ou **feet ~ out** il a les pieds tournés en dehors; ¶ **~ [sth] out, ~ out [sth] 1** (turn off) éteindre [*light*]; **2** (empty) retourner, vider [*pocket, bag*]; Culin démouler [*mousse, mould*]; **3** (produce) fabriquer [*goods*]; former [*scientists, graduates*]; sortir [*novel, script, poem*]; **4 to ~ one's toes** ou **feet out** marcher en canard; ¶ **~ [sb] out, ~ out [sb] 1** (evict) mettre [qn] à la porte; **to ~ sb out into the street** jeter qn à la rue; **2** GB (send) envoyer [*guard, police, troops*].

■ **turn over**: ¶ **~ over 1** (roll over) [*person*] se retourner; [*car*] se retourner, faire un tonneau; [*boat*] se retourner, chavirer; **to ~ over and over** [*person, object*] faire plusieurs tours; [*car*] faire plusieurs tonneaux; **2** (turn page) tourner la page; **3** [*engine*] se mettre en marche; ¶ **~ [sth/sb] over, ~ over [sth/sb] 1** (turn) tourner [*page, paper*]; retourner [*card, object, mattress, soil, baby, patient*]; faire chavirer [*ship*]; **he ~ed the car over** sa voiture a fait un tonneau; **2** (hand over) remettre [*object, money, find, papers*] (**to** à); livrer [*person, fugitive*] (**to** à); remettre la succession de [*company, business*] (**to** à); transmettre [*control, power*] (**to** à); **I'm ~ing the new recruits over to you** les nouvelles recrues sont à vous; **3** (reflect) **I've been ~ing it over in my mind** j'y ai bien réfléchi; **4**○ GB (rob) cambrioler [*shop, place*]; **I have been ~ed over** on m'a cambriolé; **5** Fin (have turnover of) [*company*] faire un chiffre d'affaires de [*amount*]; **6** [*battery, starter motor*] faire tourner [*engine*].

■ **turn round** GB = **turn around**.

■ **turn to**† GB se mettre au travail, s'y mettre.

■ **turn up**: ¶ **~ up 1** (arrive, show up) arriver, se pointer ○ (**to, at** à; **for** pour); **to ~ up late** arriver en retard; **to ~ up in jeans** se pointer○ en jean; **she didn't ~ up** elle ne s'est pas pointée○; **guess who ~ed up at the station** devine qui s'est pointé○ à la gare; **2** (be found) **don't worry—it will ~ up** ne t'inquiète pas—tu finiras par le retrouver; **3** (present itself) [*opportunity, job*] se présenter; **something will ~ up (for me/for you etc)** je finirai/tu finiras etc par trouver quelque chose; **4** (point up) [*corner, edge*] se remonter, être relevé; **his nose ~s up** il a le nez retroussé; **5** (take upturn) [*economy, market*] se redresser; [*investment, sales, profits*] remonter; ¶ **~ up [sth], ~ [sth] up 1** (increase, intensify) augmenter [*heating, lighting, volume, gas*]; mettre [qch] plus fort [*TV, radio, music*]; **2** (point up) remonter, relever [*collar*]; **a ~ed-up nose** un nez retroussé; ▶ **nose**; **3** (discover) déterrer [*buried object*]; [*person*] dénicher○ [*discovery, information*]; **facts ~ed up by the inquiry** faits révélés ou mis au jour par l'enquête.

turnabout /ˈtɜːnəbaʊt/ *n* revirement *m*.

turnaround /ˈtɜːnəraʊnd/ *n* **1** (reversal of attitude) revirement *m*; **2** (reversal of fortune) revirement *m* (**in** de); (for the better) redressement *m* (**in** de); **3** (of ship, plane etc) rotation *f*.

turn: **~around time** *n* Transp, Mil temps *m* de rotation; Admin délai *m* d'exécution; **~coat** *n* gen, Pol renégat/-e *m/f*, personne *f* qui retourne sa veste○; **~cock** *n* robinet *m*; **~down** *n* baisse *f*.

turned-out /ˌtɜːndˈaʊt/ *adj* **to be well ~** être élégant; **to be immaculately ~** être d'une mise irréprochable.

turner /ˈtɜːnə(r)/ *n* tourneur *m*; **metal/wood ~** tourneur sur métal/sur bois.

turnery /ˈtɜːnərɪ/ *n* **1** ¢ (finished articles) articles *mpl* tournés; **2** (also **turning**) tournage *m*; **3** (workshop) atelier *m* de tourneur.

turning /ˈtɜːnɪŋ/ **▶ 1173** *n* **1** GB (in road) virage *m*; **to take a ~ too quickly** prendre un virage trop vite; **to take a wrong ~** tourner au mauvais endroit; **a ~ off the main street** une rue latérale qui donne sur la rue principale; **the second next ~ on the right** la deuxième prochaine à droite; **I've missed my ~** j'aurais dû tourner plus tôt; **here's our ~** c'est ici que nous devons tourner; **2** (work on lathe) tournage *m*.

turning: **~ circle** *n* rayon *m* de braquage; **~ lathe** *n* tour *m*.

turning point *n* tournant *m* (**in, of** de); **to be at a ~** être à un tournant.

turnip /ˈtɜːnɪp/ *n* navet *m*.

turnip moth *n* agrotis *m*.

turnkey /ˈtɜːnkiː/ **I** *n*‡ geôlier/-ière *m/f*.
II *modif* Civ Eng, Comput [*contract, project, system*] clés en main *inv* (*after n*).

turnoff /ˈtɜːnɒf/ *n* **1** (in road) embranchement *m*; **the Slough ~** l'embranchement où il faut tourner pour Slough; **2**○ (passion-killer) **to be a real ~** être vraiment repoussant, être un vrai tue-l'amour○.

turn: **~ of mind** *n* tournure *f* d'esprit; **~ of phrase** *n* (expression) expression *f*; (way of expressing oneself) façon *f* de parler.

turn-on○ /ˈtɜːnɒn/ *n* **to be a real ~** être vachement○ excitant.

turnout /ˈtɜːnaʊt/ *n* **1** (to vote, strike, demonstrate) taux *m* de participation (**for** à); **a 75% ~** un taux de participation de 75%; **a high/low ~ for the election** un fort/faible taux de participation électorale; **there was a magnificent ~ for the parade** beaucoup de gens sont venus voir le défilé; **what sort of ~ do you expect?** combien de personnes attendez-vous?; **2** (clearout) nettoyage *m*; **to need a good ~** avoir besoin d'un bon nettoyage; **3**○ (appearance) tenue *f*.

turnover /ˈtɜːnəʊvə(r)/ *n* **1** Accts chiffre *m* d'affaires; **2** (rate of replacement) (of stock) rotation *f*; (of staff) turnover *m*, rotation *f* de personnel; **the staff ~ in this school is 25%** le taux de renouvellement des professeurs dans cette école est de 25%; **3** Culin chausson *m*; **apple ~** chausson aux pommes.

turn: **~pike** *n* (tollgate) barrière *f* de péage; US (toll expressway) autoroute *f* à péage; **~ signal** *n* clignotant *m*; **~stile** *n* gen tourniquet *m*; (to count number of visitors) compteur *m* pour entrées.

turntable /ˈtɜːnteɪbl/ *n* **1** (on record player) platine *f*; **2** Rail, Aut plaque *f* tournante.

turntable ladder *n* échelle *f* pivotante.

turnup /ˈtɜːnʌp/ *n* GB (of trousers) revers *m*.
IDIOMS **a ~ for the books** GB une grande surprise.

turpentine /ˈtɜːpəntaɪn/ *n* térébenthine *f*.

turpitude /ˈtɜːpɪtjuːd, US -tuːd/ *n* turpitude *f*.

turps○ /tɜːps/ *n* = **turpentine**.

turquoise /ˈtɜːkwɔɪz/ **▶ 1104** *n, adj* turquoise (*f*).

turret /ˈtʌrɪt/ *n* (all contexts) tourelle *f*.

turreted /ˈtʌrɪtɪd/ *adj* à tourelles.

turret: **~ lathe** *n* tour *m* revolver; **~-mounted** *adj* [*gun*] monté sur tourelle.

turtle /ˈtɜːtl/ *n* GB tortue *f* marine; US tortue *f*.
IDIOMS **to turn ~** se retourner.

turtle: **~ dove** *n* tourterelle *f*; **~ neck** *n* (neckline) col *m* montant; (sweater) pull-over *m* à col montant; **~-necked** *adj* [*sweater*] à col montant; **~ soup** *n* soupe *f* de tortue.

turves /tɜːvz/ *pl* ▶ **turf**.

Tuscan /ˈtʌskən/ **I** *n* **1** (person) Toscan/-e *m/f*; **2** Ling toscan *m*.
II *adj* toscan.

Tuscany /ˈtʌskənɪ/ *pr n* Toscane *f*.

tush /tʌʃ/ **I**○ *n* US (buttocks) derrière○ *m*.
II‡ *excl* bah!

tusk /tʌsk/ *n* (of elephant, walrus) défense *f*; (of wild boar) dague *f*.

tusker /ˈtʌskə(r)/ *n* animal *m* à défenses.

tussle /ˈtʌsl/ **I** *n* **1** (struggle) empoignade *f* (**for** pour); **2** (wrangle) **verbal/legal ~** empoignade verbale/légale (**over** à propos de).
II *vi* être aux prises (**for** pour, pour avoir); **to ~ with sb** être aux prises avec qn (**over** au sujet de).

tussock /ˈtʌsək/ *n* touffe *f* d'herbe.

tut /tʌt/ **I** *excl* tss-tss!
II *vi* (*p prés etc* **-tt-**) produire un tss-tss de désapprobation.

Tutankhamen, Tutankhamun /ˌtuːtəŋˈkɑːmən/ *pr n* Hist Toutankhamon.

tutee /tjuːˈtɪ, US tuː-/ *n* gen étudiant/-e *m/f*; (individual) élève *mf* particulier/-ière.

tutelage /ˈtjuːtɪlɪdʒ, US tuː-/ *n* sout tutelle *f*.

tutelary /ˈtjuːtɪlərɪ, US tuː-/ *adj* sout tutélaire.

tutor /ˈtjuːtə(r), US tuː-/ **▶ 1692** **I** *n* **1** (private teacher) professeur *m* particulier; **2** GB Univ (teacher) chargé/-e *m/f* de travaux dirigés; (for general welfare) conseiller/-ère *m/f* d'éducation; **3** US Univ assistant/-e *m/f*; **4** GB Sch (of class) professeur *m* principal; (of year group) responsable *mf* pédagogique d'année; (for general welfare) conseiller/-ère *m/f* d'éducation; **5** Mus (instruction book) méthode *f*.
II *vtr* donner des leçons particulières à (**in** de).
III *vi* donner des cours (**in** de).

tutor group *n* Univ ≈ groupe *m* de travaux dirigés.

tutorial /tjuːˈtɔːrɪəl, US tuː-/ **I** *n* Univ (group) classe *f* de travaux dirigés; (private) cours *m* privé.
II *modif* [*system*] de travaux dirigés; **~ duties** obligations *fpl* d'encadrement.

tutoring /ˈtjuːtərɪŋ, US ˈtuː-/ *n* **1** Univ enseignement *m* (par petits groupes); **2** (to individuals) leçons *fpl* particulières.

tutor period *n* Sch, Univ tranche *f* horaire consacrée au tutorat.

tutti frutti /ˌtuːtɪˈfruːtɪ/ **I** *n* (also **~ ice cream**) glace *f* tutti frutti.
II *adj* tutti frutti.

tutu /ˈtuːtuː/ *n* tutu *m*.

Tuvalu /ˌtuːvəˈluː/ **▶ 1131** *pr n* Tuvalu *m*.

tu-whit tu-whoo /ˌtʊˈwɪt ˌtʊˈwuː/ *n* onomat hou hou.

tuxedo /tʌkˈsiːdəʊ/ *n* US smoking *m*.

tuyère /twiːˈjeə(r), tuː-/ *n* tuyère *f*.

TV○ *n* (*abrév* = **television**) télé○ *f*.

TV dinner *n* plateau *m* télé.

TVEI *n* GB Sch (*abrév* = **Technical and Vocational Educational Initiative**) *réforme de l'enseignement professionnel axée sur le contact avec le monde du travail.*

TVP *n*: *abrév* = **textured vegetable protein**.

TV screen *n* écran *m* télé.

twaddle○ /ˈtwɒdl/ *n* balivernes *fpl*.

twain‡ /tweɪn/ *npl* **the ~** les deux; **never the ~ shall meet** les deux sont inconciliables.

twang /twæŋ/ **I** *n* (of string, wire) vibration *f*; (of tone) ton *m* nasillard.
II *vtr* pincer [*instrument*].
III *vi* [*string, wire*] produire une vibration; [*instrument*] vibrer.

twangy○ /ˈtwæŋɪ/ *adj* [*instrument*] au son pincé; [*accent*] nasillard.

'twas /twɒz, twəz/ littér or dial *abrév* = **it was**.

twat● /twɒt/ *n* **1** (female genitals) chatte○ *f*, sexe *m* de la femme; **2** péj (person) con/conne◑ *m/f*.

tweak /twiːk/ **I** *n* **1** (tug) coup *m* sec; **2** Comput amélioration *f*.
II *vtr* **1** tordre [*ear, nose*]; tirer [*hair, moustache*]; **2** (in car racing) gonfler [*engine*].
III *vi* **1** Comput fignoler; **2**○ argot des drogués être dans un état fébrile.

twee○ /twiː/ *adj* GB péj [*house, décor*] mièvre, mignard; [*manner*] emprunté; **to find sb/sth rather ~** trouver qn/qch un peu mièvre.

tweed /twiːd/ **I** *n* (cloth) tweed *m*.

II **tweeds** *npl* (clothes) vêtements *mpl* en tweed.
III *modif* [*clothing*] en tweed.

tweedy /ˈtwiːdɪ/ *adj* **1** [*material*] genre tweed; **2** hum ou péj style gentleman-farmer.

'tween /twiːn/ *prep* littér entre.

tweet /twiːt/ I *n* (chirp) pépiement *m*.
II *excl* onomat **~ ~** cui-cui!

tweeter /ˈtwiːtə(r)/ *n* Audio haut-parleur *m* d'aigus, tweeter *m*.

tweeze /twiːz/ *vtr* Cosmet épiler.

tweezers /ˈtwiːzəz/ *npl* gen pincettes *fpl*; (for eyebrows) pince *f* à épiler.

twelfth /twelfθ/ ▶ 1505, 1150 I *n* **1** (in order) douzième *mf*; **2** (of month) douze *m inv*; **the glorious ~** GB Hunt le douze août; **3** (fraction) douzième *m*; **4** Mus douzième *f*.
II *adj* douzième.
III *adv* [*come, finish*] douzième, en douzième position.

twelfth: **~ man** *n* (in cricket) joueur *m* de réserve; **Twelfth Night** *n* fête *f* des Rois, Épiphanie *f*.

twelve /twelv/ ▶ 1505, 971, 1096 I *n* douze *m*.
II *adj* douze *inv*; **the Twelve** Bible les douze apôtres.

twelve: **~ mile limit** *n* limite *f* des douze milles; **~ month**‡ *n* année *f*; **~ tone** *adj* Mus dodécaphonique.

twentieth /ˈtwentɪəθ/ ▶ 1505, 1150 I *n* **1** (in order) vingtième *mf*; **2** (of month) vingt *m*; **3** (fraction) vingtième *m*.
II *adj* vingtième.
III *adv* [*come, finish*] vingtième, en vingtième position.

twenty /ˈtwentɪ/ ▶ 1505, 971, 1096 *n, adj* vingt (*m*) *inv*.

twenty: **~-one** ▶ 1282 *n* Games (in cards) vingt-et-un *m*; **~ twenty** *adj* [*vision*] de dix à chaque œil; **~-two metre line** *n* (in rugby) ligne *f* des vingt-deux mètres.

twerp○ /twɜːp/ *n* péj crétin/-e○ *m/f*.

twice /twaɪs/ *adv* deux fois; **~ a day/ week/month, ~ daily/weekly/monthly** deux fois par jour/semaine/mois; **he's ~ as big as you** il est deux fois plus grand que toi; **she's ~ his age** elle a le double de son âge; **~ as much, ~ as many** deux fois plus; **she earns ~ as much as me** elle gagne deux fois plus que moi; **~ as many people** deux fois plus de monde; **to be ~ as likely to be elected** avoir deux fois plus de chances d'être élu; **~ over** à deux reprises, deux fois; **you should think ~ about it** tu devrais y réfléchir à deux fois; **you need to be ~ as careful/vigilant** il faut redoubler de prudence/vigilance.
IDIOMS **once bitten ~ shy** Prov chat échaudé craint l'eau froide Prov.

twice-laid /ˌtwaɪsˈleɪd/ *adj* tortillé.

twiddle /ˈtwɪdl/ I *n* **to give sth a ~** donner un petit tour à qch.
II *vtr* tripoter [*hair*]; tourner [*knob*]; **to ~ one's thumbs** lit, fig se tourner les pouces.

twiddly○ /ˈtwɪdlɪ/ *adj* **~ bits** fioritures *fpl*.

twig /twɪg/ I *n* brindille *f*.
II○ *vtr, vi* (*p prés etc* **-gg-**) piger○.

twilight /ˈtwaɪlaɪt/ I lit, fig *n* crépuscule *m*; **in the ~, at ~** au crépuscule; **in the ~ of his career** au crépuscule de sa carrière.
II *modif* **1** lit [*hours*] du crépuscule; **2** fig [*world*] énigmatique; **~ years** dernières années.

twilight: **~ sleep** *n* Med demi-sommeil *m* provoqué; **~ zone** *n* zone *f* d'ombre.

twill /twɪl/ I *n* sergé *m*.
II **twills** *npl* pantalon *m* en sergé.
III *modif* [*clothing*] en sergé.

twilled /twɪld/ *adj* [*fabric*] en sergé.

twin /twɪn/ I *n* **1** (one of two children) jumeau/-elle *m/f*; **a pair** ou **set of ~s** des jumeaux/-elles *mpl/fpl*; **2** (one of two objects) **this candlestick has lost its ~** ce chandelier n'a plus son pendant; **this vase is the ~ to yours** ce vase est celui qui va avec le tien; **3** (room) chambre *f* à deux lits.
II **twins** *npl* **1** (pair of children) jumeaux/-elles *mpl/fpl*; **2** Astrol **the Twins** les Gémeaux *mpl*.
III *modif* **1** (related) [*brother, sister, lamb*] jumeau/-elle; **my ~ sons/daughters** mes fils jumeaux/filles jumelles; **2** (two) [*masts, propellors, towers, taps*] jumeaux/-elles (*after n*); [*speakers*] jumelés; **3** (combined) double; **the ~ aims/problems/roles of** le double but/problème/rôle de.
IV *vtr* (*p prés etc* **-nn-**) (link) jumeler; **to ~ Oxford with Bonn** jumeler Oxford et Bonn.

twin: **~-bedded** *adj* [*room*] avec lits jumeaux; **~ beds** *npl* lits *mpl* jumeaux; **~ bill** *n* US (of films) *programmation de deux films l'un à la suite de l'autre*; (of games) *deux matchs qui se déroulent l'un à la suite de l'autre*.

twine /twaɪn/ I *n* ficelle *f*.
II *vtr* **1** (coil) enrouler [*rope*] (**around** autour de); **she ~d her arms around him** elle l'a enlacé; **2** (interweave) entrelacer [*flowers, ribbon*] (**through** dans).
III *vrefl* **to ~ itself** [*snake, vine*] s'enrouler (**around** autour de).

twin-engined /ˌtwɪnˈendʒɪnd/ *adj* [*plane*] bimoteur (*after n*); **~ jet** biréacteur *m*.

twinge /twɪndʒ/ *n* (of pain) élancement *m*; (of conscience, doubt) accès *m*; (of regret, jealousy) pointe *f*.

twining /ˈtwaɪnɪŋ/ *adj* Bot volubile.

twinkle /ˈtwɪŋkl/ I *n* (of light, jewel) scintillement *m*; (of eyes) pétillement *m*.
II *vi* [*light, star, jewel*] scintiller; [*eyes*] pétiller (**with** de).
IDIOMS **when you were just** ou **still a ~ in your daddy's eye** quand tu n'étais pas encore dans le ventre de ta mère.

twinkling /ˈtwɪŋklɪŋ/ I *n* scintillement *m*; **in the ~ of an eye** en un clin d'œil.
II *adj* [*light, star, eyes*] scintillant.

twinning /ˈtwɪnɪŋ/ *n* jumelage *m*.

twin: **~ set** *n* GB Fashn twin-set *m*; **~ town** *n* ville *f* jumelle; **~-track recorder** *n* magnétophone *m* bi-piste; **~ tub** *n* machine *f* à laver à deux tambours.

twirl /twɜːl/ I *n* **1** (spin) tournoiement *m*; **to do a ~** [*person*] tournoyer; **to give sth a ~** faire tournoyer qch; **2** (spiral) volute *f*.
II *vtr* **1** (spin) faire tournoyer [*baton, lasso, partner*]; **2** (twist) tortiller [*hair, moustache*]; entortiller [*ribbon, vine*] (**around** autour de).
III *vi* **1** (spin) [*dancer, wheel*] tournoyer; **to ~ round and round** virevolter; **2** (twist) [*vine, rope*] s'enrouler (**around** autour de).
■ **twirl round** (turn round) [*person*] se retourner brusquement; **he ~ed round to face her** il s'est retourné brusquement vers elle.

twirler○ /ˈtwɜːlə(r)/ *n* US majorette *f*.

twist /twɪst/ I *n* **1** (action) **he gave the cap a ~** (to open) il a dévissé le bouchon; (to close) il a vissé le bouchon; **with a couple of ~s she unscrewed the lid** en deux tours de poignet elle a dévissé le couvercle; **he gave his ankle a nasty ~** il s'est tordu la cheville; **2** (bend, kink) (in rope, cord, wool) tortillon *m*; (in road) zigzag *m*; (in river) coude *m*; **the road is full of ~s and turns** la route est pleine de zigzags; **there's a ~ in the hosepipe** le tuyau est entortillé; **I've got my wool into a real ~** ma laine est complètement emmêlée; **3** fig (unexpected change of direction) (in play, story) coup *m* de théâtre; (episode in crisis, events) rebondissement *m*; **a strange ~ of fate** un étrange coup du sort; **the ~s and turns of the argument/the plot** le fil tortueux de l'argumentation/de l'intrigue; **to give sth a new ~** donner un tour nouveau à qch; **events took an unexpected ~** les événements ont pris un tour inattendu; **4** (small amount) (of yarn, thread, hair) torsade *f*; **a ~ of paper** une papillote; **a ~ of lemon** une tranche de citron; **5** Sport **to put some ~ on the ball** donner de l'effet à la balle; **6** Sewing (thread) cordonnet *m*; **7** Dance **the ~** le twist; **to do the ~** danser le twist.
II *vtr* **1** (turn) tourner [*knob, handle*]; (open) dévisser [*top, cap, lid*]; (close) visser [*top, cap, lid*]; **to ~ sth off** dévisser qch [*cap, top, lid*]; arracher qch (en tordant) [*piece, branch*]; **he ~ed the neck of the bag to close it** il a tortillé le haut du sac pour le fermer; **to ~ one's head around** tourner la tête; **to ~ one's head away** tourner la tête; **he ~ed around in his chair** il s'est retourné dans son fauteuil; **~ it round sideways to get it through the door** tournez-le de côté pour le faire passer par la porte; **to ~ sb's arm** lit tordre le bras à qn; fig forcer la main à qn; **2** (wind, twine) **to ~ X and Y together** torsader X et Y; **to ~ the threads together** torsader les fils; **to ~ X round Y** enrouler X autour de Y; **she ~ed the scarf (round) in her hands** elle tortillait l'écharpe entre ses doigts; **to ~ a rope around sth** passer une corde autour de qch; **they ~ed a sheet (up) into a rope** ils ont entortillé un drap pour en faire une corde; **to ~ one's hair up into a bun** se faire un chignon torsadé; **3** (bend, distort) lit tordre [*metal, rod, branch*]; **his face was ~ed with pain/rage** son visage était tordu de douleur/de rage; **she ~ed her mouth into a smile** elle a grimacé un sourire; **4** fig déformer [*words, statement, facts*]; **you're trying to ~ my meaning** vous essayez de déformer mes paroles; **5** (injure) **to ~ one's ankle/wrist** se tordre la cheville/le poignet; **to ~ one's neck** attraper un torticolis; **6** Sport donner de l'effet à [*ball*].
III *vi* **1** [*person*] **he ~ed free of her grasp** il s'est dégagé d'un mouvement brusque; **the wounded man lay ~ing and writhing on the ground** le blessé se tordait et se contorsionnait sur le sol; **his face ~ed into a smile** il a grimacé un sourire; **to ~ round** (turn round) se retourner; **2** [*rope, flex, coil*] s'entortiller; [*river, road*] serpenter; **to ~ and turn** [*road, path*] serpenter; **3** Dance danser le twist; **4** (in cards) tirer une carte.
IDIOMS **(to have a) ~ in the tail** (avoir un) dénouement inattendu; **to get oneself into a ~**○ se tracasser○; **to be round the ~**○ être dingue○ or fou/folle; **to go round the ~**○ devenir fou/folle; **to drive sb round the ~**○ rendre qn fou/folle.

twist drill *n* mèche *f* hélicoïdale, foret *m* à spire.

twisted /ˈtwɪstɪd/ *adj* **1** gen [*wire, metal, rod*] tordu; [*rope, cord*] entortillé; [*ankle, wrist*] tordu; **2** pej [*logic, argument*] faux/fausse; [*outlook, viewpoint*] bizarre; **to have a ~ mind** avoir l'esprit tordu; **a ~ sense of humour** un sens de l'humour très spécial; **a bitter and ~ person** une personne aigrie.

twister○ /ˈtwɪstə(r)/ *n* **1** (swindler) escroc *m*; **2** US (tornado) tornade *f*.

twist grip *n* (of motorbike) poignée *f*.

twisting /ˈtwɪstɪŋ/ *adj* [*road, path, course*] sinueux/-euse.

twist-off /ˈtwɪstɒf/ *adj* [*cap, top, lid*] dévissable.

twisty /ˈtwɪstɪ/ *adj* = **twisting**.

twit○ /twɪt/ *n* idiot/-e *m/f*.

twitch /twɪtʃ/ I *n* **1** (tic) tic *m*; **to have a ~ in the corner of one's eye/mouth** avoir un tic à l'œil/la bouche; **2** (spasm) soubresaut *m*; **to give a ~** avoir un soubresaut; **3** (sudden jerk) **to give the fabric/curtain a ~** réajuster le tissu/rideau d'un coup sec.
II *vtr* **1** (tug) tirer sur [qch] d'un coup sec [*fabric, curtain*]; **2** (cause to quiver) **to ~ one's nose** [*person*] froncer le nez; [*animal*] froncer le museau.
III *vi* **1** (quiver) [*person, animal*] trembloter; [*mouth*] trembler; [*eye*] cligner nerveusement; [*limb, muscle*] tressauter; [*fishing line*] vibrer; **the dog's nose ~ed with excitement** le museau du chien remuait d'excitation; **to ~ in one's sleep** tressauter dans

son sommeil; **2** (tug) **to ~ at** [*person*] tirer d'un coup sec sur [*curtain, tablecloth*]; [*fish*] taquiner [*bait*].

twitcher○ /ˈtwɪtʃə(r)/ *n* **1** (fidgety person) agité/-e *m/f*; **2** GB (birdwatcher) observateur/-trice *m/f* d'oiseaux.

twitchiness /ˈtwɪtʃɪnɪs/ *n* agitation *f*.

twitchy /ˈtwɪtʃɪ/ *adj* agité.

twitter /ˈtwɪtə(r)/ **I** *n* gazouillement *m*; **to be all of a ~** hum être excité.
II *vi* [*bird*] gazouiller; [*person*] babiller.
■ **twitter on** péj jacasser (**about** sur).

twittery○ /ˈtwɪtərɪ/ *adj* [*person*] excité; **~ state** état *m* d'excitation.

'twixt‡ /twɪkst/ *prep* littér entre.
IDIOMS **there's many a slip ~ cup and lip** Prov il y a loin de la coupe aux lèvres Prov.

two /tuː/ **▶1505**, **971**, **1096** **I** *n* deux *m inv*; **in ~s** par deux; **in ~s and threes** par deux ou trois, deux ou trois à la fois.
II *det* deux *inv*.
III *pron* deux *inv*; **I bought ~ of them** j'en ai acheté deux; **to break/cut sth in ~** casser/couper qch en deux; **in a day or ~** dans un jour ou deux.
IDIOMS **that makes ~ of us** on est tous les deux dans le même cas; **'I'm fed up○!'—'that makes ~ of us'** 'j'en ai marre○!'—'moi aussi'; **to be in ~ minds about doing** hésiter à faire; **to be in ~ minds about sth** être partagé au sujet de qch; **to put ~ and ~ together** faire le rapprochement; **~ hearts that beat as one** deux cœurs qui battent à l'unisson; **there are ~ sides to every story** ≈ autant d'hommes, autant d'avis.

two: **~-bit**○ *adj* péj US [*person*] médiocre, à la gomme○; **~ bits**○ *npl* US 25 cents *mpl*; **~-by-four** *n*: *morceau de bois de deux pouces sur quatre*; **~-chamber system** *n* Pol système *m* bicaméral.

twocker○ /ˈtwɒkə(r)/ *n* GB voleur/-euse *m/f* de voiture.

twocking○ /ˈtwɒkɪŋ/ *n* GB vol *m* de voitures.

two: **~-dimensional** *adj* lit en deux dimensions; fig [*character*] insipide; **~-edged** *adj* fig à double tranchant; **~-faced** *adj* péj hypocrite, fourbe.

twofold /ˈtuːfəʊld/ **I** *adj* double.
II *adv* doublement.

two-four time *n* Mus mesure *f* à deux-quatre; **in ~** à deux quatre.

two-handed /ˌtuːˈhændɪd/ *adj* **1** gen Sport [*sword, backhand*] à deux mains; [*saw*] à deux poignées; **2** (ambidextrous) ambidextre.

two: **~-hander** *n* Theat pièce *f* pour deux personnages; **~-party system** *n* Pol système *m* bipartite or à deux partis; **~pence** *n* GB deux pence; **▶tuppence**; **~penny** *adj* [*piece*] de deux pence; [*stamp*] à deux pence; **~penny-halfpenny**○ *adj* GB péj de rien du tout, à la gomme○; **~-phase** *adj* Elec diphasé.

two-piece /ˌtuːˈpiːs/ *n* **1** (also **~ suit**) (woman's) tailleur *m* (deux-pièces); (man's) costume *m* (deux-pièces); **2** (also **~ swimsuit**) (maillot *m* de bain à) deux-pièces *m inv*.

two: **~-pin** *adj* [*plug, socket*] à deux fiches; **~-ply** *adj* [*rope, wool, yarn*] à deux fils; [*wood*] contreplaqué à double épaisseur.

two-seater /ˌtuːˈsiːtə(r)/ **I** *n* Aut voiture *f* à deux places; Aviat avion *m* à deux places, (avion *m*) biplace *m*.
II *adj* à deux places.

two-sided /ˌtuːˈsaɪdɪd/ *adj* **1** gen [*tablemat, covering etc*] réversible; **2** (debatable) [*argument*] discutable.

two: **~some** *n* (two people) couple *m*; (game) jeu *m* pour deux joueurs; **~-star (petrol)** *n* GB (essence *f*) ordinaire *f*; **~-star hotel** *n* hôtel *m* deux étoiles; **~-step** *n* Mus pas *m* de deux; **~-storey** *adj* à deux étages; **~-stroke** *adj* [*engine, cycle*] à deux temps; **~-tier** *adj* [*bureaucracy*] à deux niveaux or étages; pej (unequal) [*society, health service etc*] à deux vitesses.

two-time○ /ˈtuːtaɪm/ **I** *vtr* être infidèle envers, tromper [*partner*].
II *vi* être infidèle.

two-timer○ /ˈtuːtaɪmə(r)/ *n* (double-crosser) gen traître *m*; **to be a ~** [*partner*] être infidèle.

two: **~-timing** *adj* infidèle; **~-tone** *adj* (in hue) de deux tons; (in sound) à deux tons or timbres.

two-way /ˌtuːˈweɪ/ *adj* **1** [*street*] à double sens; [*traffic*] dans les deux sens; **2** [*communication process, exchange*] bilatéral; **friendship should be a ~ thing** une relation d'amitié doit fonctionner dans les deux sens; **3** Elec [*wiring, switch*] va-et-vient *inv*.

two: **~-way mirror** *n* glace *f* sans tain; **~-way radio** *n* émetteur-récepteur *m*; **~-way switch** *n* (interrupteur *m* de) va-et-vient *m*; **~-wheeler**○ *n* (vehicle, bicycle) deux-roues *m inv*.

TX US Post *abrév écrite* = **Texas**.

tycoon /taɪˈkuːn/ *n* magnat *m*; **oil/property/publishing ~** magnat du pétrole/de l'immobilier/de l'édition.

tyke○ /taɪk/ *n* **1** péj (boor) pignouf *m*; **2** (mongrel) clébard◑ *m*, chien *m* bâtard; **3** US (child) coquin/-e *m/f*.

tymbal *n* = **timbal**.

tympan /ˈtɪmpən/ *n* (all contexts) tympan *m*.

tympani *npl* = **timpani**.

tympanic /tɪmˈpænɪk/ *adj* Anat [*bone*] tympanal; [*artery, cavity*] tympanique; **~ membrane** tympan *m*.

tympanist *n* Mus = **timpanist**.

tympanum /ˈtɪmpənəm/ **▶1481** *n* (*pl* **-pani**) **1** Anat, Archit tympan *m*; **2** Mus timbale *f*.

Tyne and Wear /ˌtaɪn ən ˈwɪə(r)/ **▶1624** *pr n* Tyne and Wear *m*.

type /taɪp/ **I** *n* **1** (variety, kind) type *m*, genre *m* (**of** de); **main ~** type principal; **hair/skin ~** type de cheveux/de peau; **what ~ of person/car/problem?** quel type or genre de personne/voiture/problème?; **he's an army ~** il a le genre militaire; **you're not my ~** tu n'es pas mon genre; **they're our ~ of people** c'est le genre de personnes que nous aimons bien; **I'm not that ~, I don't go in for that ~ of thing** ce n'est pas mon genre; **is she the right ~ for this job?** est-elle bien le genre de personne qui convient pour ce travail?; **he's all right if you like that ~** il n'est pas mal mais ce n'est pas mon genre; **he's the introspective ~** il est du genre introspectif; **she's not the ~ to fuss** elle n'est pas du genre à faire des histoires; **they' re the ~ who** c'est le genre d'individus qui; **he's one of those pretentious university ~s** c'est un de ces individus prétentieux de l'université; **a very special ~ of person** quelqu'un de bien particulier; **I know his ~** péj je connais les gens de son espèce; **her ~ always get what they want** péj ce genre de fille obtient toujours ce qu'elle veut; **you know the ~ of thing I mean** vous voyez à peu près ce que je veux dire; **2** (archetype) archétype *m*; **the characters in this novel are only ~s** les personnages dans ce roman ne sont que des archétypes; **he's/she's etc reverted to ~** le naturel a pris le dessus; **to play** ou **be cast against ~** Cin, Theat jouer à contre-emploi; **3** Print caractères *mpl*; **bold/italic/large ~** caractères *mpl* gras/italiques/gros; **metal ~** caractères *mpl* en plomb; **printed in small ~** imprimé en petits caractères; **to set up ~** composer; **to set sth in bold ~** composer qch en caractères gras; **4** Ling type *m*.
II *modif* **1** Bot, Med **~ A and B cells** cellules de type A et de type B; **2**○ **a documentary-~ film** un film du genre documentaire; **a Regency-~ table** une table de type Régence.
III *vtr* **1** (on typewriter) taper (à la machine) [*text, word, letter, line*]; **to ~ 60 words a minute** taper 60 mots à la minute; **to have sth ~d** faire taper qch; **a ~d letter** une lettre dactylographiée; **2** (classify) classifier [*blood sample*]; cataloguer [*person*] (**as** comme); **he was ~d as an avant-garde poet** il a été catalogué comme poète d'avant-garde.
IV *vi* taper (à la machine); **can you ~?** (est-ce que) vous savez taper à la machine or dactylographier fml?; **I was typing away** je tapais sans arrêt.
■ **type in**: **~ in [sth]**, **~ [sth] in** taper [*word, character*].
■ **type out**: **~ out [sth]**, **~ [sth] out** taper (à la machine).
■ **type over**: **~ over [sth]** (erase) effacer; **I ~d over my error** j'ai effacé ma faute de frappe.
■ **type up** taper, dactylographier fml.

type: **~cast** *vtr* (*prét, pp* **-cast**) Theat, fig cataloguer [*person*] (**as** comme); **~casting** *n* Theat, fig catalogage *m* dans un rôle; **~face** *n* police *f* (de caractères).

typescript /ˈtaɪpskrɪpt/ *n* texte *m* dactylographié; **several pages of ~** plusieurs pages dactylographiées.

type: **~set** *vtr* composer; **~setter** *n* typographe *mf*; **~setting** *n* composition *f*.

typewriter /ˈtaɪpraɪtə(r)/ **I** *n* machine *f* à écrire; **manual/electronic/portable ~** machine à écrire mécanique/électronique/portative.
II *modif* [*ribbon, keyboard*] de machine à écrire.

typewritten /ˈtaɪprɪtn/ *adj* tapé (à la machine), dactylographié fml.

typhoid /ˈtaɪfɔɪd/ **▶1354** **I** *n* (also **~ fever**) (fièvre *f*) typhoïde *f*.
II *modif* [*epidemic, victim, symptom*] de typhoïde; **~ scare** alerte à la typhoïde.

Typhoid Mary○ *n* US péj être *m* pernicieux.

typhoon /taɪˈfuːn/ *n* typhon *m*.

typhus /ˈtaɪfəs/ **▶1354** *n* (also **~ fever**) typhus *m*.

typical /ˈtɪpɪkl/ *adj* [*case, example, day, village*] typique; [*tactlessness, compassion*] caractéristique; **he's a ~ civil servant** c'est un fonctionnaire typique; **a ~ feature** une caractéristique (principale); **to be ~ of** être typique de [*period, species*]; **it's (all too) ~ of him to be late** cela ne m'étonne pas (du tout) de lui qu'il soit en retard; **'I've left my keys behind'—'~○!'** 'j'ai oublié mes clés'—'ça ne m'étonne pas!'

typically /ˈtɪpɪklɪ/ *adv* [*behave*] (of person) comme à mon/ton etc habitude; **in a ~ evasive reply, he said...** refusant comme à son habitude de prendre position, il a dit...; **that was a ~ inept remark from Anne** Anne a fait une remarque stupide, comme à son habitude; **they assumed, ~, that** ils supposaient comme à leur habitude que; **~ English** [*place, atmosphere, behaviour*] typiquement anglais; **she's ~ English** c'est l'Anglaise type; **it's ~ Australian to do that** c'est bien typique des Australiens de faire ça; **it was a ~ warm, sunny day** c'était une journée chaude et ensoleillée, comme d'habitude; **~, it was left to us to organize everything** comme d'habitude, c'est nous qui avons dû tout organiser.

typify /ˈtɪpɪfaɪ/ *vtr* [*quality, feature, condition, behaviour, work*] caractériser; [*person, institution*] être le type même de; **as typified by the EC** comme le représente la CE.

typing /ˈtaɪpɪŋ/ **I** *n* **1** (skill) dactylo *f*, dactylographie *f*; **to learn ~** apprendre la dactylo; **'good ~ essential'** Journ 'bonne pratique de la dactylo essentielle'; **my ~ is slow** ma frappe est lente; **2** (typed material) **two pages of ~** deux pages dactylographiées; **check the ~** vérifiez ce qui a été dactylographié; **I've got some ~ to do** j'ai quelque chose à taper; **she does academic ~** elle tape des textes universitaires.

II *modif* [course] de dactylo(graphie).

typing: **~ error** *n* faute *f* de frappe; **~ paper** *n* papier *m* pour machine à écrire.

typing pool *n* **to work in the ~** travailler au service dactylo°.

typing skills *npl* pratique *f* de la dactylo; **good ~** une bonne pratique de la dactylo.

typing speed *n* vitesse *f* de frappe; **she has a ~ of 80** elle tape 80 mots à la minute.

typist /ˈtaɪpɪst/ *n* dactylo *mf*.

typo° /ˈtaɪpəʊ/ *n* Print coquille° *f*.

typographer /taɪˈpɒgrəfə(r)/ ▶1692 *n* typographe *mf*.

typographic(al) /ˌtaɪpəˈgræfɪk(l)/ *adj* typographique.

typography /taɪˈpɒgrəfɪ/ *n* typographie *f*.

typology /taɪˈpɒlədʒɪ/ *n* typologie *f*.

tyrannic(al) /tɪˈrænɪk(l)/ *adj* tyrannique.

tyrannically /tɪˈrænɪklɪ/ *adv* [act] en tyran; [cruel, strict] tyranniquement.

tyrannicide /tɪˈrænɪsaɪd/ *n* (act, person) tyrannicide *m*.

tyrannize /ˈtɪrənaɪz/ **I** *vtr* tyranniser.
II *vi* tyranniser; **to ~ over sb** tyranniser qn.

tyrannosaurus (rex) /tɪˌrænəˈsɔːrəs/ *n* tyrannosaure *m*.

tyrannous /ˈtɪrənəs/ *adj* = **tyrannic(al)**.

tyrannously /ˈtɪrənəslɪ/ *adv* = **tyrannically**.

tyranny /ˈtɪrənɪ/ *n* **1** (despotism) tyrannie *f* (**over** sur); **2** (tyrannical act) abus *m* de pouvoir; **3** (country) dictature *f*.

tyrant /ˈtaɪərənt/ *n* tyran *m*.

tyre GB, **tire** US /ˈtaɪə(r)/ *n* pneu *m*; **back/front ~** pneu *m* arrière/avant; **burst/flat ~** pneu *m* crevé/à plat; **spare ~** lit pneu *m* de rechange; fig hum (fat) pneu *m*.

tyre: **~ centre** *n* centre *m* de vente et de réparation de pneus; **~ lever** *n* démonte-pneu *m*; **~ pressure** *n* pression *f* des pneus; **~ pressure gauge** *n* manomètre *m* (pour pneus).

tyro /ˈtaɪərəʊ/ *n* débutant/-e *m/f*.

Tyrol /tɪˈrəʊl/ *pr n* Tyrol *m*.

Tyrolean /ˌtɪrəˈliːən/ **I** *n* Tyrolien/-ienne *m/f*.
II *adj* tyrolien/-ienne.

Tyrone /tɪˈrəʊn/ ▶1624 *pr n* comté *m* de Tyrone.

Tyrrhenian Sea /tɪˌriːnɪən ˈsiː/ *pr n* mer *f* Tyrrhénienne.

tzar *n* = **tsar**.

tzarina *n* = **tsarina**.

Uu

u, U /juː/ *n* **1** (letter) u, U *m*; **2** GB Cin (*abrév* = **universal**) ≈ tous publics.

UAE *pr npl* (*abrév* = **United Arab Emirates**) EAU *m*.

U-bend *n* (in pipe) courbure *f* en U; Aut virage *m* en épingle à cheveux.

ubiquitous /juːˈbɪkwɪtəs/ *adj* omniprésent.

ubiquity /juːˈbɪkwətɪ/ *n* omniprésence *f*.

U bolt *n* boulon *m* étrier.

UCCA /ˈʌkə/ *n* GB (*abrév* = **Universities Central Council on Admissions**) centre *m* national des inscriptions en faculté.

UDA *n* (*abrév* = **Ulster Defence Association**) UDA *f* (*organisation paramilitaire loyaliste en Irlande du Nord*).

UDC *n* GB *abrév* ▸ **Urban District Council**.

udder /ˈʌdə(r)/ *n* pis *m*.

UDI *n* (*abrév* = **unilateral declaration of independence**) déclaration *f* unilatérale d'indépendance.

UDR *n*: *abrév* ▸ **Ulster Defence Regiment**.

UEFA /juːˈiːfə/ *n* (*abrév* = **Union of European Football Associations**) UEFA *f*.

UFO *n* (*abrév* = **unidentified flying object**) ovni *m inv*.

ufologist /juːˈfɒlədʒɪst/ *n* spécialiste *mf* des ovni.

ufology /juːˈfɒlədʒɪ/ *n* étude *f* des ovni.

Uganda /juːˈgændə/ ▸ **1131** *pr n* Ouganda *m*.

Ugandan /juːˈgændən/ ▸ **1486** **I** *n* Ougandais/-e *m/f*.
II *adj* ougandais/-e.

ugh /ʌg/ *excl* berk!

ugli (fruit) /ˈʌglɪ/ *n* tangelo *m*.

uglify /ˈʌglɪfaɪ/ *vtr* enlaidir.

ugliness /ˈʌglɪnɪs/ *n* (of person, object, place) laideur *f*.

ugly /ˈʌglɪ/ *adj* **1** (hideous) [*person, appearance, furniture, building, place*] laid; [*sound*] désagréable; **to be an ~ sight** être hideux/-euse à voir; [*wound*] vilain (*before n*); **2** (vicious) [*situation, conflict*] dangereux/-euse; [*tactics, campaign*] bas/basse; [*accusation*] vicieux/-ieuse; [*passion, violence*] effroyable; **the situation turned ~** la situation a dégénéré; **to give sb an ~ look** regarder qn d'un sale œil; **he had an ~ expression on his face/an ~ look in his eye** il avait l'air méchant/l'œil méchant; **to be in an ~ mood** [*group, mob*] gronder; [*individual*] être d'humeur massacrante; **the ~ face of** l'aspect inacceptable de; **3** (repugnant) [*incident, scene, crime*] déplorable.
IDIOMS **an ~ customer**○ un sale type○; **he looks like an ~ customer**○ il a une sale tronche○; **as ~ as sin** laid comme un pou; **racism/elitism rears its ~ head** on voit surgir le spectre du racisme/de l'élitisme.

ugly duckling *n* fig vilain petit canard *m*.

UHF *n* (*abrév* = **ultra-high frequency**) UHF *f*.

uh-huh /ˌʌˈhʌ/ *excl* oui, oui.

UHT *adj* (*abrév* = **ultra heat treated**) UHT; **~ milk** lait *m* UHT, lait *m* à longue conservation.

UK ▸ **1131** **I** *pr n* (*abrév* = **United Kingdom**) Royaume-Uni *m*; **in/to the ~** dans le/au Royaume-Uni.
II *modif* [*citizen, passport*] britannique.

uke○ /juːk/ ▸ **1481** *n* ukulélé *m*.

Ukraine /juːˈkreɪn/ *pr n* **the ~** l'Ukraine *f*; **in/to the ~** en Ukraine.

Ukrainian /juːˈkreɪnɪən/ ▸ **1486**, **1402** **I** *n* **1** (person) Ukrainien/-ienne *m/f*; **2** (language) ukrainien *m*.
II *adj* ukrainien/-ienne.

ukulele /ˌjuːkəˈleɪlɪ/ ▸ **1481** *n* ukulélé *m*.

ulcer /ˈʌlsə(r)/ *n* ulcère *m*; **stomach ~** ulcère à l'estomac.

ulcerate /ˈʌlsəreɪt/ **I** *vtr* ulcérer.
II *vi* s'ulcérer.

ulceration /ˌʌlsəˈreɪʃn/ *n* ulcération *f*.

ulcerative /ˈʌlsərətɪv/ *adj* ulcératif/-ive.

ulcerous /ˈʌlsərəs/ *adj* ulcéreux/-euse.

ulna /ˈʌlnə/ *n* (*pl* **-nae** ou **~s**) cubitus *m*.

Ulster /ˈʌlstə(r)/ **I** *pr n* Ulster *m*.
II *modif* [*people, landscape, accent, dialect*] d'Irlande du Nord, de l'Ulster.

Ulster: **~ Defence Regiment**, **UDR** *n*: *régiment de l'armée britannique chargé du maintien de l'ordre en Ulster*; **~man** *n* Ulstérien *m*; **~woman** *n* Ulstérienne *f*.

ult.† *adv* Admin (*abrév écrite* = **ultimo**) du mois dernier.

ulterior /ʌlˈtɪərɪə(r)/ *adj* **1** (hidden) [*motive, purpose*] inavoué; **without any ~ motive** sans arrière-pensée; **2** (subsequent) ultérieur.

ultimata /ˌʌltɪˈmeɪtə/ *npl* ▸ **ultimatum**.

ultimate /ˈʌltɪmət/ **I** *n* nec plus ultra *m inv*; **the ~ in** le nec plus ultra de [*comfort, luxury*].
II *adj* (*épith*) **1** (final) [*accolade, achievement, ambition, challenge, deterrent, power, responsibility, sacrifice, success, victory, weapon*] suprême (*after n*); [*aim, conclusion, decision, defeat, destination, effect, failure, purpose, result*] ultime (*after n*); [*loser, beneficiary*] au bout du compte; **carried to the ~ extreme** poussé à l'extrême; **2** (fundamental) [*principle, question, truth*] fondamental; [*cause, origin, source*] premier/-ière (*after n*); **3** (unsurpassed) [*insult, luxury, refinement*] suprême (*after n*); [*car, holiday, product, stereotype*] dernier cri○ *inv*.

ultimate constituent *n* Ling constituant *m* ultime.

ultimately /ˈʌltɪmətlɪ/ *adv* en fin de compte, au bout du compte.

ultimate strength *n* Tech limite *f* de rupture.

ultima Thule /ˌʌltɪmə ˈθuːliː/ *n* lit Thulé *f* hyperboréenne; fig l'autre bout *m* du monde.

ultimatum /ˌʌltɪˈmeɪtəm/ *n* (*pl* **~s** ou **-mata**) ultimatum *m*; **to issue** ou **deliver** ou **give an ~** adresser un ultimatum (**to** à); **cease-fire ~** ultimatum de cessez-le-feu.

ultra /ˈʌltrə/ **I** *n* ultra *mf*.
II○ **ultra+** (*dans composés*) hyper-○.

ultraconservative /ˌʌltrəkənˈsɜːvətɪv/ *adj* ultraconservateur/-trice.

ultrahigh /ˌʌltrəˈhaɪ/ *adj* [*risk, crime rates*] très élevé.

ultra-left /ˌʌltrəˈleft/ **I** *n* **the ~** l'extrême gauche *f*.
II *adj* d'extrême gauche.

ultramarine /ˌʌltrəməˈriːn/ *n, adj* outremer (*m*) (*inv*).

ultramodern /ˌʌltrəˈmɒdən/ *adj* ultramoderne.

ultramontane /ˌʌltrəˈmɒnteɪn/ Relig *n, adj* ultramontain/-e (*m/f*).

ultramontanism /ˌʌltrəˈmɒntənɪzəm/ *n* ultramontanisme *m*.

ultra-right /ˌʌltrəˈraɪt/ **I** *n* **the ~** l'extrême droite *f*.
II *adj* d'extrême droite.

ultrasonic /ˌʌltrəˈsɒnɪk/ **I** *adj* ultrasonique.
II ultrasonics *n* (+ *v sg*) science *f* des ultrasons.

ultrasound /ˈʌltrəsaʊnd/ *n* ultrasons *mpl*; **he received** ou **was given ~ (treatment)** Med on lui a fait des ultrasons.

ultrasound scan *n* échographie *f*; **to give sb an ~** faire une échographie à qn; **to have an ~** se faire faire une échographie.

ultrasound scanner *n* échographe *m*.

ultraviolet /ˌʌltrəˈvaɪələt/ *adj* ultraviolet/-ette; **~ ray** rayon *m* ultraviolet.

ultra vires /ˌʌltrə ˈvaɪəriːz, ˌʊltrɑː ˈviːreɪz/ **I** *adj* **to be ~** [*individual*] commettre un excès de pouvoir; [*proclamation, action*] constituer un excès de pouvoir; [*company*] être en dehors des statuts.
II *adv* **to act ~** commettre un excès de pouvoir.

ululate /ˈjuːljʊleɪt/ *vi* sout [*mourner*] pousser des youyous.

ululation /ˌjuːljʊˈleɪʃn/ *n* sout **the ~ of the women** les youyous des femmes.

Ulysses /ˈjuːlɪsiːz/ *pr n* Ulysse.

umber /ˈʌmbə(r)/ *n* Art terre *f* d'ombre.

umbilical /ʌmˈbɪlɪkl, ˌʌmbɪˈlaɪkl/ **I** *n* = **umbilical cord**.
II *adj* Anat, Physiol [*area, function*] ombilical; **~ ties** fig liens très étroits.

umbilical cord *n* **1** Anat, fig cordon *m* ombilical; **to cut/tie the ~** couper/nouer le cordon ombilical; **2** Aerosp, Naut câble *m* de liaison.

umbilicus /ʌmˈbɪlɪkəs, ˌʌmbɪˈlaɪkəs/ *n* (*pl* **-lici**) ombilic *m*.

umbrage /ˈʌmbrɪdʒ/ *n* **to take ~** prendre ombrage (**at** de).

umbrella /ʌmˈbrelə/ *n* **1** lit parapluie *m*; **folding ~** parapluie pliant; **2** fig **under the ~ of** (protection) sous la protection de; (authority) sous l'égide *f* de; **3** Zool ombrelle *f*.

umbrella: **~ bird** *n* oiseau-ombrelle *m*, céphaloptère *m* spec; **~ group** *n* collectif *m*, association *f* de tutelle; **~ organization** *n* = **umbrella group**; **~ stand** *n* porte-parapluies *m inv*; **~ term** *n* terme *m* générique; **~ tree** *n* magnolier *m* parasol.

Umbria /ˈʌmbrɪə/ *pr n* Ombrie *f*.

Umbrian /ˈʌmbrɪən/ **I** *n* Ombrien/-ienne *m/f*.
II *adj* (all contexts) ombrien/-ienne.

umlaut /ˈʊmlaʊt/ *n* tréma *m*.

ump○ /ʌmp/ US *abrév* ▶ **umpire**.

umpire /ˈʌmpaɪə(r)/ **I** *n* Sport, fig arbitre *m*; **to act as an ~ between two parties** fig servir d'arbitre entre deux parties.
II *vtr* Sport arbitrer.
III *vi* Sport être l'arbitre; **to ~ at a match** arbitrer un match.

umpteen○ /ʌmpˈtiːn/ **I** *adj* des tas de○; **I've told you ~ times** je te l'ai dit trente-six fois.
II *pron* des tas○; **I have ~ at home** j'en ai des tas○ chez moi, j'en ai je ne sais combien chez moi; **there are ~ of us** on est nombreux.

umpteenth○ /ʌmpˈtiːnθ/ *adj* énième.

'un○ /ən/ *pron* (*abrév* = **one**) **come here, little ~** viens ici, mon petit; **that's a good ~!** (joke) elle est bonne, celle-là○; **he caught a big ~** (fish) il en a pris un gros.

UN I *n* (*abrév* = **United Nations**) ONU *f*; **the ~** l'ONU.
II *modif* [*conference, forces, General Assembly, resolution, Security Council*] de l'ONU; [*ambassador*] à l'ONU.

unabashed /ˌʌnəˈbæʃt/ *adj* [*curiosity*] sans retenue; [*celebration*] sans réserve; **they were ~ by anything we said** rien de ce que nous avons dit ne les a décontenancés; **he seemed quite ~** il ne semblait aucunement décontenancé.

unabated /ˌʌnəˈbeɪtɪd/ *adj* **to continue ~** [*industrial growth*] continuer avec la même vigueur; [*fighting, storm*] continuer avec la même violence; **the discussion continued ~** la discussion continua toujours aussi animée.

unable /ʌnˈeɪbl/ *adj* **1** (lacking the means or opportunity) **to be ~ to do** ne pas pouvoir faire; **I wanted to come, but I was ~ (to)** je voulais venir mais je n'ai pas pu; **2** (lacking the knowledge or skill) **to be ~ to do** ne pas savoir faire; **children ~ to read** les enfants qui ne savent pas lire; **3** (incapable, not qualified) **to be ~ to do** être incapable de faire; **she tried to answer, but she was ~ to** elle a essayé de répondre, mais elle en était incapable.

unabridged /ˌʌnəˈbrɪdʒd/ *adj* intégral; **the ~ version of the book** le texte intégral du livre.

unaccented /ˌʌnækˈsentɪd/ *adj* non accentué.

unacceptable /ˌʌnəkˈseptəbl/ *adj* [*proposal, suggestion*] inacceptable; [*behaviour, situation*] inadmissible; **it is ~ that** il est inadmissible que (+ *subj*); **the ~ face of capitalism** la face répugnante du capitalisme.

unacceptably /ˌʌnəkˈseptəblɪ/ *adv* [*high, low, long, expensive*] beaucoup trop; [*classify, describe*] de façon inacceptable.

unaccompanied /ˌʌnəˈkʌmpənɪd/ *adj* **1** (alone) non accompagné; **~ children/minors** des enfants/mineurs non accompagnés; **an ~ young woman** une jeune femme seule; **2** Mus [*cello suite, song, singing*] sans accompagnement.

unaccomplished /ˌʌnəˈkʌmplɪʃt/ *adj* **1** [*work*] inachevé; **2** [*performer*] sans talent.

unaccountable /ˌʌnəˈkaʊntəbl/ *adj* **1** [*phenomenon, feeling*] inexplicable; **for some ~ reason** pour une raison incompréhensible; **2** (not answerable) **to be ~ to sb** ne pas avoir à répondre devant qn.

unaccountably /ˌʌnəˈkaʊntəblɪ/ *adv* [*vanish, appear, late, absent*] inexplicablement; **quite ~,...** sans qu'on sache pourquoi,...

unaccounted /ˌʌnəˈkaʊntɪd/ *adj* **to be ~ for** [*sum, documents*] être introuvable; **two of the crew are still ~ for** deux membres de l'équipage sont toujours portés disparus.

unaccustomed /ˌʌnəˈkʌstəmd/ *adj* [*luxury, speed, position*] inhabituel/-elle; **to be ~ to sth/to doing** ne pas avoir l'habitude de qch/de faire; **~ as I am to public speaking...** hum bien qu'il ne soit pas dans mes habitudes de prendre la parole en public...

unacknowledged /ˌʌnəkˈnɒlɪdʒd/ *adj* [*genius, inventor, contribution*] non reconnu; [*leader*] non reconnu officiellement; [*terror, taboo*] qu'on ne veut pas admettre; [*epidemic*] qui n'est pas reconnu officiellement; **her letter remained ~** on n'a pas accusé réception de sa lettre.

unacquainted /ˌʌnəˈkweɪntɪd/ *adj* **to be ~ with sth/sb** ne pas connaître qch/qn; **he is ~ with computing** il ne connaît rien à l'informatique; **to be ~ with the facts/situation** ne pas être au courant des faits/de la situation; **to be ~ with one another** ne pas se connaître.

unadapted /ˌʌnəˈdæptɪd/ *adj* non adapté.

unaddressed /ˌʌnəˈdrest/ *adj* sans adresse.

unadopted /ˌʌnəˈdɒptɪd/ *adj* **1** GB **~ road**: *chemin dont l'entretien n'est pas assuré par la commune*; **2** [*child*] non adopté.

unadorned /ˌʌnəˈdɔːnd/ *adj* [*walls, building*] sans ornement; [*manner, style*] sans fioritures; **the plain ~ facts** les faits tout simples.

unadulterated /ˌʌnəˈdʌltəreɪtɪd/ *adj* **1** (pure) [*water*] pur; [*food*] naturel/-elle; [*wine*] non frelaté; **2** (emphatic) [*pleasure, misery*] pur (*before n*); **this is ~ nonsense** ce sont des bêtises pures et simples.

unadventurous /ˌʌnədˈventʃərəs/ *adj* [*meal, menu, choice*] pas très original; [*decor, production, style*] qui manque d'audace; [*person*] conventionnel/-elle.

unadventurously /ˌʌnədˈventʃərəslɪ/ *adv* [*dressed, presented*] de manière conventionnelle.

unadvertised /ʌnˈædvətaɪzd/ *adj* [*visit, sale*] sans publicité; **it was an ~ post** il n'y avait pas eu d'annonce pour ce poste.

unaesthetic, unesthetic US /ˌʌniːsˈθetɪk/ *adj* [*thing*] inesthétique; [*person*] qui manque de sens esthétique.

unaffected /ˌʌnəˈfektɪd/ *adj* **1** (untouched) **to be ~** ne pas être affecté (**by** par); **2** (natural, spontaneous) tout simple.

unaffectedly /ˌʌnəˈfektɪdlɪ/ *adv* sans affectation.

unaffiliated /ˌʌnəˈfɪlɪeɪtɪd/ *adj* non affilié (**to** à).

unafraid /ˌʌnəˈfreɪd/ *adj* [*person*] sans peur; **to be ~ of sth/of doing** ne pas avoir peur de qch/de faire.

unaided /ʌnˈeɪdɪd/ **I** *adj* [*work, intuition*] personnel/-elle; **~ by sth** sans l'aide de qch; **to do sth by one's own ~ efforts** faire qch sans aide extérieure.
II *adv* [*stand, sit, walk*] sans aide extérieure.

unaired /ʌnˈeəd/ *adj* **1** [*room, sheets, bed*] non aéré; **2** (undiscussed) **to remain ~** [*objections, issues*] rester sous silence.

unalike /ˌʌnəˈlaɪk/ *adj* dissemblable; **they are not ~** ils ne sont pas dissemblables.

unalloyed /ˌʌnəˈlɔɪd/ *adj* **1** [*pleasure, success*] sans mélange; **2** [*metal*] pur.

unalterable /ʌnˈɔːltərəbl/ *adj* inaltérable.

unaltered /ʌnˈɔːltəd/ *adj* inchangé; **to remain ~** rester inchangé.

unambiguous /ˌʌnæmˈbɪgjʊəs/ *adj* sans équivoque.

unambiguously /ˌʌnæmˈbɪgjʊəslɪ/ *adv* [*define, deny*] sans équivoque; [*interpret*] sans ambiguïté.

unambitious /ˌʌnæmˈbɪʃəs/ *adj* [*person*] sans ambition; [*reform*] modeste; [*novel*] sans prétention.

un-American /ˌʌnəˈmerɪkən/ *adj* anti-américain.

unamused /ˌʌnəˈmjuːzd/ *adj* **to be ~** rester froid; **he was ~ by your joke** votre plaisanterie l'a laissé froid.

unanimity /ˌjuːnəˈnɪmətɪ/ *n* unanimité *f* (**between, among** entre); **to be based on ~** être basé sur le principe de l'unanimité; **to reach ~** parvenir à l'unanimité.

unanimous /juːˈnænɪməs/ *adj* [*members, agreement, support*] unanime; **to be ~ in doing** être unanime à faire; **to be ~ that** estimer unanimement que.

unanimously /juːˈnænɪməslɪ/ *adv* [*agree, condemn, approve*] unanimement; [*vote, acquit*] à l'unanimité; **to be ~ against/in favour of sth** être unanimement contre/en faveur de qch.

unannounced /ˌʌnəˈnaʊnst/ **I** *adj* [*visit, changes*] non annoncé.
II *adv* [*arrive, call*] sans prévenir.

unanswerable /ʌnˈɑːnsərəbl, US ˌʌnˈæn-/ *adj* [*question*] à laquelle il n'y a pas de réponse possible; [*remark, case*] irréfutable.

unanswered /ʌnˈɑːnsəd, US ʌnˈæn-/ *adj* [*letter, question, query*] resté sans réponse.

unappealing /ˌʌnəˈpiːlɪŋ/ *adj* [*title, name, person, mannerism*] peu attrayant; [*food*] peu appétissant.

unappetizing /ʌnˈæpɪtaɪzɪŋ/ *adj* peu appétissant.

unappreciated /ˌʌnəˈpriːʃɪeɪtɪd/ *adj* [*work of art, status, value*] non reconnu; **to feel ~** se sentir sous-estimé.

unappreciative /ˌʌnəˈpriːʃətɪv/ *adj* [*person, audience, public*] ingrat; **to be ~ of sth** être insensible à qch.

unapproachable /ˌʌnəˈprəʊtʃəbl/ *adj* inaccessible.

unappropriated /ˌʌnəˈprəʊprɪeɪtɪd/ *adj* [*funds*] disponible, sans affectation; [*profits*] non réparti.

unapt /ʌnˈæpt/ *adj* sout **1** (dull) [*student, pupil*] peu doué; **2** (unsuited) inapte (**for** à).

unarguable /ʌnˈɑːgjʊəbl/ *adj* [*sovereignty, rights*] incontestable; Jur [*defence*] inattaquable.

unarguably /ʌnˈɑːgjʊəblɪ/ *adv* [*true, best*] incontestablement; **they were ~ the winners** ils étaient sans conteste les vainqueurs.

unarmed /ʌnˈɑːmd/ *adj* [*police, civilians*] non armé; [*combat*] sans armes.

unary /ˈjuːnərɪ/ *adj* Comput unaire.

unashamed /ˌʌnəˈʃeɪmd/ *adj* [*admirer, joy*] sincère; (more informal) sans complexes; [*belief*] assuré; **to be ~ of sth** être dénué de complexes quant à qch.

unashamedly /ˌʌnəˈʃeɪmɪdlɪ/ *adv* ouvertement.

unasked /ʌnˈɑːskt, US ʌnˈæskt/ *adv* [*come, attend*] sans être invité; **to do sth ~** faire qch spontanément.

unaspirated /ʌnˈæspəreɪtɪd/ *adj* non aspiré.

unassailable /ˌʌnəˈseɪləbl/ *adj* **1** gen [*position*] invulnérable; [*reputation*] inattaquable; [*optimism, case*] à toute épreuve; **to have an ~ lead** Sport avoir un avantage décisif; (in market, elections) avoir une supériorité décisive; **2** Mil [*stronghold*] imprenable.

unassisted /ˌʌnəˈsɪstɪd/ **I** *adj* **it's her own ~ work** c'est son travail personnel.
II *adv* [*stand, walk, sit*] sans assistance.

unassuming /ˌʌnəˈsjuːmɪŋ, US ˌʌnəˈsuː-/ *adj* [*person, manner*] modeste; [*building*] sans prétention.

unassumingly /ˌʌnəˈsjuːmɪŋlɪ, US ˌʌnəˈsuː-/ *adv* [*speak, behave*] avec modestie.

unattached /ˌʌnəˈtætʃt/ *adj* **1** (single) célibataire; **'are you ~?'** 'est-ce que vous vivez seul/-e?'; **2** [*part, element*] détaché; [*building, organization*] indépendant.

unattainable /ˌʌnəˈteɪnəbl/ *adj* (all contexts) inaccessible.

unattended /ˌʌnəˈtendɪd/ *adj* [*vehicle, dog, child*] laissé sans surveillance; **patrons are advised not to leave their baggage ~** nous conseillons à nos clients de surveiller leurs bagages.

unattractive /ˌʌnəˈtræktɪv/ *adj* **1** (ugly) [*furniture, characteristic*] peu attrayant; [*person*] peu attirant; **I find him ~** il ne m'attire pas; **2** (not appealing) [*career, idea*] peu attrayant (**to** à); [*bid, proposition*] peu intéressant (**to** pour); **economically ~** peu intéressant du point de vue économique; **an**

~ prospect une perspective peu attrayante.

unattractiveness /ˌʌnəˈtræktɪvnɪs/ *n* (of building) laideur *f*; (of landscape) manque *m* d'attrait; **the ~ of his appearance** son extérieur peu séduisant.

unauthenticated /ˌʌnɔːˈθentɪkeɪtɪd/ *adj* [*signature, document*] non authentifié; [*evidence*] non établi; [*story*] non confirmé.

unauthorized /ʌnˈɔːθəraɪzd/ *adj* [*disclosure, reproduction, building work*] fait sans autorisation; [*phone tapping*] non autorisé; **no ~ access** accès interdit aux personnes sans autorisation; **~ access** Comput accès *m* non autorisé.

unavailable /ˌʌnəˈveɪləbl/ *adj* **to be ~** [*person*] ne pas être disponible; **Mr Hill is ~ for comment** M. Hill se refuse à tout commentaire; **medical treatment/information is ~** on ne peut pas obtenir de traitement médical/de renseignements.

unavailing /ˌʌnəˈveɪlɪŋ/ *adj* sout [*efforts, search, battle*] vain.

unavailingly /ˌʌnəˈveɪlɪŋlɪ/ *adv* sout vainement.

unavoidable /ˌʌnəˈvɔɪdəbl/ *adj* inévitable.

unavoidably /ˌʌnəˈvɔɪdəblɪ/ *adv* **I shall be ~ detained** j'ai un empêchement; **he was ~ absent** il ne pouvait pas être présent; **their failure was ~ public** leur échec fut connu de tous, ce qui était inévitable.

unaware /ˌʌnəˈweə(r)/ *adj* **1** (not informed) **to be ~ of sth** ne pas être au courant de qch; **to be ~ that** ne pas savoir que; **2** (not conscious) **to be ~ of sth** ne pas être conscient de qch; **she was ~ of all the noise around her** elle ne remarquait pas tout le bruit autour d'elle; **she was ~ of his presence** elle ne savait pas qu'il était là; **to be politically ~** ne pas être politisé; **to be blissfully ~ of sth** être parfaitement ignorant de qch.

unawares /ˌʌnəˈweəz/ *adv* **to catch** ou **take sb ~** prendre qn au dépourvu.

unbacked /ʌnˈbækt/ *adj* Fin [*account*] non soldé.

unbalance /ʌnˈbæləns/ *vtr* déséquilibrer.

unbalanced /ʌnˈbælənst/ *adj* **1** [*person, mind*] instable; **mentally ~** instable; **2** (biased) [*reporting*] partial; **3** (uneven) [*diet, economy, load*] pas équilibré; **4** [*accounts*] non soldé.

unbaptized /ˌʌnbæpˈtaɪzd/ *adj* non baptisé.

unbearable /ʌnˈbeərəbl/ *adj* insupportable.

unbearably /ʌnˈbeərəblɪ/ *adv* **1** [*hurt, tingle*] de manière insupportable; **2** (emphatic) [*hot, cynical, tedious*] incroyablement.

unbeatable /ʌnˈbiːtəbl/ *adj* **1** (excellent) [*quality, price*] imbattable; **it's ~ value** le rapport qualité-prix est imbattable; **the food is ~** la nourriture est la meilleure; **2** [*opponent, team, record*] imbattable.

unbeaten /ʌnˈbiːtn/ *adj* [*player, team*] invaincu; [*score, record*] qui n'a pas été battu.

unbecoming /ˌʌnbɪˈkʌmɪŋ/ *adj* sout [*colour*] difficile à porter; [*garment*] peu seyant; **conduct ~ to a soldier** un comportement qui ne sied pas à un militaire liter; **it is ~ to do** il est inconvenant de faire fml.

unbeknown /ˌʌnbɪˈnəʊn/ *adv* **~ to sb** à l'insu de qn; **~ to me** à mon insu.

unbelief /ˌʌnbɪˈliːf/ *n* Relig incroyance *f*.

unbelievable /ˌʌnbɪˈliːvəbl/ *adj* incroyable; **it is ~ that** il est incroyable que (+ *subj*).

unbelievably /ˌʌnbɪˈliːvəblɪ/ *adv* incroyablement.

unbeliever /ˌʌnbɪˈliːvə(r)/ *n* incroyant/-e *m/f*.

unbelieving /ˌʌnbɪˈliːvɪŋ/ *adj* [*look, tone*] incrédule; Relig incroyant.

unbelievingly /ˌʌnbɪˈliːvɪŋlɪ/ *adv* [*stare, exclaim*] d'un air incrédule.

unbend /ʌnˈbend/ **I** *vtr* (straighten) détordre. **II** *vi* devenir moins inflexible.

unbending /ʌnˈbendɪŋ/ *adj* [*person, attitude*] inflexible; **an ~ will** une volonté de fer.

unbias(s)ed /ʌnˈbaɪəst/ *adj* [*advice, newspaper, person*] impartial; **to be ~ in one's opinions** être sans parti pris.

unbidden /ʌnˈbɪdn/ *adv* littér **to do sth ~** faire qch sans en être prié; **to come ~ into one's mind** venir spontanément à l'esprit.

unbind /ʌnˈbaɪnd/ *vtr* (*prét, pp* **-bound**) délier [*string, rope,prisoner*].

unbleached /ʌnˈbliːtʃt/ *adj* [*cloth*] écru; [*hair*] non décoloré; [*paper, flour*] non blanchi; [*nappies, coffee filters*] sans chlore.

unblemished /ʌnˈblemɪʃt/ *adj* [*reputation, record*] sans tache; [*career*] impeccable.

unblinking /ʌnˈblɪŋkɪŋ/ *adj* **to stare ~ at sb** fixer qn sans ciller; **he stood there ~** il est resté là, impassible.

unblinkingly /ʌnˈblɪŋkɪŋlɪ/ *adv* **to stare at sb ~** fixer qn sans ciller.

unblock /ʌnˈblɒk/ *vtr* déboucher [*pipe, sink*].

unblushing /ʌnˈblʌʃɪŋ/ *adj* sout [*admission, lie*] sans vergogne.

unblushingly /ʌnˈblʌʃɪŋlɪ/ *adv* sout [*lie, deny sth*] sans vergogne.

unbolt /ʌnˈbəʊlt/ **I** *vtr* déverrouiller [*door*]. **II unbolted** *pp adj* **to be ~ed** ne pas être verrouillé.

unborn /ʌnˈbɔːn/ *adj* **1** lit **~ child** enfant *mf* à naître; **her ~ child** l'enfant qu'elle porte/portait etc; **2** fig **yet ~** [*party, idea*] qui n'a/n'avait pas encore vu le jour; **generations yet ~** les générations à venir.

unbosom /ʌnˈbʊzəm/ *v refl* littér **to ~ oneself** se confier (**to** à).

unbound /ʌnˈbaʊnd/ *adj* [*book*] non relié.

unbounded /ʌnˈbaʊndɪd/ *adj* [*joy, optimism, gratitude*] sans bornes; [*love*] démesuré; [*relief*] immense (*before n*).

unbowed /ʌnˈbaʊd/ *adj* littér **she/the nation remains ~** elle/la nation demeure non vaincue; **bloody but ~** blessé mais non vaincu.

unbreakable /ʌnˈbreɪkəbl/ *adj* incassable.

unbreathable /ʌnˈbriːðəbl/ *adj* irrespirable.

unbribable /ʌnˈbraɪbəbl/ *adj* incorruptible.

unbridle /ʌnˈbraɪdl/ *vtr* débrider [*horse*].

unbridled /ʌnˈbraɪdld/ *adj* (*épith*) [*imagination, sexuality*] débridé; [*power*] illimité; [*emotion*] non contenu; [*optimism*] effréné.

unbroken /ʌnˈbrəʊkən/ *adj* **1** (uninterrupted) [*series, sequence, silence*] ininterrompu; [*view*] ininterrompu; [*curve*] parfait; **in an ~ line** en ligne directe; **2** (intact) [*pottery*] intact; **the ~ surface of the lake** l'eau du lac que rien ne troublait en surface; **3** (unsurpassed) **it's an ~ record** le record n'a pas été battu.

unbuckle /ʌnˈbʌkl/ *vtr* défaire [*strap*]; déboucler [*belt*]; défaire la boucle de [*shoe*].

unbuilt /ʌnˈbɪlt/ *adj* [*house, land*] non construit.

unbundle /ʌnˈbʌndl/ *vtr* **1** Comput facturer séparément; **~d software** logiciels *mpl* non fournis avec l'ordinateur; **2** Fin, Econ dépecer, démanteler [*company, group*].

unburden /ʌnˈbɜːdn/ *v refl* sout **to ~ oneself** se confier à qn; **to ~ oneself of** confier [*worries, secret*]; se libérer de [*guilt*].

unburied /ʌnˈberɪd/ *adj* non enterré; **the ~ dead** les morts qui n'ont pas été enterrés.

unbusinesslike /ʌnˈbɪznɪslaɪk/ *adj* [*method, conduct*] peu acceptable dans le monde des affaires.

unbutton /ʌnˈbʌtn/ **I** *vtr* déboutonner. **II unbuttoned** *pp adj* fig [*attitude*] détendu.

uncalled-for /ʌnˈkɔːldfɔː(r)/ *adj* [*remark, behaviour*] déplacé.

uncannily /ʌnˈkænɪlɪ/ *adv* (very much) incroyablement; (surprisingly) étrangement.

uncanny /ʌnˈkænɪ/ *adj* **1** (strange) [*resemblance, way*] étrange; [*accuracy, success*] étonnant; **to bear an ~ resemblance to sth/sb** ressembler étrangement à qch/qn; **2** (frightening) troublant.

uncap /ʌnˈkæp/ *vtr* (*p prés etc* **-pp-**) retirer le capuchon de [*pen*]; décapsuler [*beer bottle*].

uncared-for /ʌnˈkeədfɔː(r)/ *adj* [*house*] mal entretenu; [*pet*] mal soigné; **an ~ child** un enfant dont on s'occupe mal.

uncaring /ʌnˈkeərɪŋ/ *adj* [*world*] indifférent; **an ~ society** une société qui se soucie peu du bien-être de chacun.

uncarpeted /ʌnˈkɑːpɪtɪd/ *adj* sans tapis.

uncashed /ʌnˈkæʃt/ *adj* non encaissé.

uncatalogued /ʌnˈkætəlɒgd/ *adj* non catalogué.

unceasing /ʌnˈsiːsɪŋ/ *adj* ininterrompu.

unceasingly /ʌnˈsiːsɪŋlɪ/ *adv* sans cesse.

uncensored /ʌnˈsensəd/ *adj* [*film, book*] non censuré; fig [*version*] intégral.

unceremonious /ˌʌnˌserɪˈməʊnɪəs/ *adj* [*departure, end*] précipité.

unceremoniously /ˌʌnˌserɪˈməʊnɪəslɪ/ *adv* [*dismiss*] sans cérémonie.

uncertain /ʌnˈsɜːtn/ **I** *adj* **1** [*person*] (unsure) incertain; **to be ~ about** ne pas être certain de; **to be ~ about what to do** ne pas être certain de ce que l'on doit faire; **to be ~ whether to stay or to leave** ne pas savoir si l'on doit partir ou rester; **2** (not predictable, not known) [*future, market, outcome*] incertain; **it is ~ whether there will be a chairperson** il n'est pas certain qu'il y ait un président; **3** (changeable) [*temper, economic conditions*] instable; [*weather*] variable. **II in no ~ terms** *adv phr* [*state*] en termes on ne peut plus clairs; [*express oneself*] de façon très directe.

uncertainly /ʌnˈsɜːtnlɪ/ *adv* [*approach*] avec hésitation; [*smile, look*] d'un air hésitant.

uncertainty /ʌnˈsɜːtntɪ/ *n* incertitude *f* (**about** en ce qui concerne); **there is some ~ surrounding the project** l'avenir du projet est quelque peu incertain; **the uncertainties of life/of the market** les incertitudes de la vie/du marché.

uncertainty principle *n* principe *m* d'incertitude.

uncertified /ʌnˈsɜːtɪfaɪd/ *adj* Admin [*document*] non certifié.

unchallengeable /ʌnˈtʃælɪndʒəbl/ *adj* [*power, authority*] incontestable; [*judgment*] inattaquable; [*argument, reason*] indiscutable.

unchallenged /ˌʌnˈtʃælɪndʒd/ *adj* **to win ~** être le vainqueur incontesté; **to go ~** [*statement, decision*] ne pas être récusé.

unchangeable /ʌnˈtʃeɪndʒəbl/ *adj* [*existence, system, routine*] immuable.

unchanged /ʌnˈtʃeɪndʒd/ *adj* inchangé; **to remain ~** [*landscape, team, system*] demeurer inchangé; [*orders*] rester les mêmes; [*medical condition*] rester stationnaire; **the shares remain ~ at 480p** Fin les actions restent fixées à 480p.

unchanging /ʌnˈtʃeɪndʒɪŋ/ *adj* [*beliefs, customs, beauty*] immuable.

uncharacteristic /ˌʌnkærɪktəˈrɪstɪk/ *adj* [*generosity*] peu habituel/-elle; **it was ~ of him to leave like that** ce n'est pas son genre de partir comme ça.

uncharacteristically /ˌʌnkærɪktəˈrɪstɪklɪ/ *adv*: **she was ~ quiet/irritable** elle était silencieuse/irritable, ce qui ne lui est pas habituel.

uncharitable /ʌnˈtʃærɪtəbl/ *adj* peu charitable (**to do** de faire).

uncharted /ʌnˈtʃɑːtɪd/ *adj* **1** (not explored) [*territory, island*] inexploré; **to sail in ~ waters** lit naviguer dans des eaux inexplorées; fig être en terrain inconnu; **2** (not mapped) [*island*] qui n'apparaît pas sur les cartes.

unchaste /ʌn'tʃeɪst/ *adj* [*thought, deed*] impur.

unchecked /ʌn'tʃekt/ **I** *adj* **1** (uncontrolled) [*development, proliferation*] incontrôlé; **the wave of crime which had gone ~** cet accroissement de la criminalité qu'on n'a pu maîtriser; **2** (unverified) non vérifié.
II *adv* [*to develop, grow, spread*] de manière incontrôlée.

unchristian /ʌn'krɪstʃən/ *adj* **1** (uncharitable) [*person, attitude, life*] peu charitable; **2** (not Christian) peu chrétien/-ienne.

uncial /'ʌnsɪəl, -ʃl/ **I** *n* onciale *f*.
II *adj* oncial.

uncircumcised /ʌn'sɜ:kəmsaɪzd/ **I** *n* **the ~** (+ *v pl*) les incirconcis *mpl*.
II *adj* incirconcis.

uncivil /ʌn'sɪvl/ *adj* discourtois (**to** envers).

uncivilized /ʌn'sɪvɪlaɪzd/ *adj* **1** (inhumane) [*treatment*] inhumain; **in ~ conditions** dans des conditions inhumaines; **2** (uncouth, rude) grossier/-ière; **3** (barbarous) [*people, nation*] non civilisé; **at an ~ hour** à une heure indue.

unclad /ʌn'klæd/ *adj* sout nu.

unclaimed /ʌn'kleɪmd/ *adj* [*lost property, reward*] non réclamé; **an ~ allocation** une allocation qui n'a pas été touchée; **to go** ou **remain ~** ne pas être réclamé.

unclasp /ʌn'klɑ:sp, US -'klæsp/ *vtr* dégrafer [*brooch*]; **to ~ one's hands** desserrer ses mains.

unclassified /ʌn'klæsɪfaɪd/ *adj* [*document, information, waste*] non classifié; [*road*] non classé; **to get an ~ grade** GB Sch être reçu avec de très médiocres résultats.

uncle /'ʌŋkl/ *n* oncle *m*.
IDIOMS **Bob's your ~!** GB c'est simple comme bonjour!; **to cry ~** US demander grâce.

unclean /ʌn'kli:n/ *adj* **1** [*water, beaches*] sale; **2** Relig impur.

unclear /ʌn'klɪə(r)/ *adj* **1** (not evident) (*après v*) [*motive, reason, circumstances*] peu clair; [*future*] incertain; **it is ~ whether the government will support him** on ne sait pas très bien si le gouvernement l'appuiera; **it is ~ how successful the reforms will be** on ne sait pas très bien quel sera le succès des réformes; **it is ~ how he managed to escape** on ne sait pas très bien comment il a réussi à s'échapper; **2** (not comprehensible) [*instructions, voice, delivery*] pas clair; [*answer*] peu clair; [*handwriting*] difficile à lire; **3** (uncertain) [*person*] **to be ~ about sth** ne pas être sûr de qch.

uncleared /ʌn'klɪəd/ *adj* [*cheque*] non compensé; [*goods*] non dédouané; [*road*] (after snow) enneigé.

unclench /ʌn'klentʃ/ *vtr* desserrer [*fist, jaw*].

uncle: **Uncle Sam** *pr n* l'oncle Sam (*personnification des États-Unis*); **Uncle Tom** *pr n* péj bon nègre *m*.

unclimbed /ʌn'klaɪmd/ *adj* [*mountain*] invaincu.

uncloak /ʌn'kləʊk/ *vtr* sout démasquer.

unclog /ʌn'klɒg/ *vtr* (*p prés etc* **-gg-**) déboucher [*pipe*]; débloquer [*mechanism*].

unclothed /ʌn'kləʊðd/ *adj* sout nu.

unclouded /ʌn'klaʊdɪd/ *adj* **1** lit [*liquid*] limpide; [*mirror*] sans buée; **2** fig [*happiness*] sans nuages; [*future*] souriant.

uncoded /ʌn'kəʊdɪd/ *adj* [*message, radio signal*] non chiffré; [*TV signal*] non crypté.

uncoil /ʌn'kɔɪl/ **I** *vtr* dérouler.
II *vi* [*spring*] se détendre; [*rope, snake*] se dérouler.

uncollected /ˌʌnkə'lektɪd/ *adj* [*mail, luggage, lost property*] non réclamé; [*benefits*] non réclamé; [*taxes*] non perçu; [*refuse*] non ramassé.

uncombed /ʌn'kəʊmd/ *adj* [*hair*] non peigné.

uncomely‡ /ʌn'kʌmlɪ/ *adj* [*person*] laid; [*sight*] peu attrayant.

uncomfortable /ʌn'kʌmftəbl, US -fərt-/ *adj* **1** (physically) [*shoes, garment, seat, accommodation*] inconfortable; [*journey, heat, position, conditions*] pénible; **we spent an ~ few days there** nous y avons passé quelques jours peu agréables; **to be ~ doing** trouver inconfortable de faire; **it's ~ doing** c'est inconfortable de faire; **you look ~ in those clothes/in that chair** tu n'as pas l'air à l'aise dans ces vêtements/dans ce fauteuil; **the bed/jacket feels ~** le lit/la veste n'est pas confortable; **2** (emotionally) [*feeling, silence, situation, presence*] pénible; **to be/feel ~** être/se sentir gêné or mal à l'aise; **to make sb (feel) ~** mettre qn mal à l'aise; **to be ~ about** se sentir gêné par [*rôle, decision, fact*]; **to be ~ with** être gêné par [*situation, attitude, behaviour*]; **to be ~ with sb** se sentir mal à l'aise avec qn; **I feel ~ talking about it** ça me gêne d'en parler; **to make life** ou **things ~ for sb** rendre la vie difficile à qn; **3** (unpalatable) [*issue, position, reminder, thought*] pénible.

uncomfortably /ʌn'kʌmftəblɪ, US -fərt-/ *adv* **1** (unpleasantly) [*loud, bright, cramped*] désagréablement; **it's ~ hot** il fait une chaleur pénible; **~ seated** inconfortablement assis; **2** (awkwardly) [*say, laugh, glance*] d'un air gêné; **to be ~ aware of sth** se rendre compte avec gêne de qch; **the exam is ~ near** ou **close** l'approche de l'examen devient angoissante; **to sit ~ with** s'accommoder mal de [*belief, position*].

uncommitted /ˌʌnkə'mɪtɪd/ *adj* **1** [*delegate, member*] non engagé; [*voter*] non décidé; **2** [*funds*] non engagé.

uncommitted logic *n* Comput réseau *m* logique programmable.

uncommon /ʌn'kɒmən/ *adj* **1** (rare, unusual) [*occurrence, word, plant*] rare; **it is/is not ~ to do** il est/il n'est pas rare de faire; **2** (exceptional) [*capacity, gift, intelligence, beauty*] rare.

uncommonly /ʌn'kɒmənlɪ/ *adv* **1** (very) [*advanced, gifted, hot*] exceptionnellement; **~ clever** d'une intelligence exceptionnelle; **~ well** extraordinairement bien; **2** (rarely) **not ~** assez souvent.

uncommunicative /ˌʌnkə'mju:nɪkətɪv/ *adj* peu communicatif/-ive; **to be ~ about sth** se montrer réservé sur qch.

uncomplaining /ˌʌnkəm'pleɪnɪŋ/ *adj* [*patience, acceptance*] résigné; [*person*] qui ne se plaint pas.

uncomplainingly /ˌʌnkəm'pleɪnɪŋlɪ/ *adv* sans se plaindre.

uncompleted /ˌʌnkəm'pli:tɪd/ *adj* inachevé.

uncomplicated /ʌn'kɒmplɪkeɪtɪd/ *adj* [*person*] peu compliqué; [*plot*] pas compliqué; [*meal*] simple; **my life is ~** ma vie est toute simple; **totally ~** pas compliqué du tout.

uncomplimentary /ˌʌnkɒmplɪ'mentrɪ, US -terɪ/ *adj* peu flatteur/-euse.

uncomprehending /ˌʌnkɒmprɪ'hendɪŋ/ *adj* [*person*] complètement perplexe; **with an ~ stare** avec le regard de quelqu'un qui ne comprend pas.

uncomprehendingly /ˌʌnkɒmprɪ'hendɪŋlɪ/ *adv* [*listen, stare*] sans rien comprendre.

uncompromising /ʌn'kɒmprəmaɪzɪŋ/ *adj* [*person, attitude, stance*] intransigeant; [*integrity*] absolu; [*standards*] sans concession; [*terms, reply*] catégorique; [*system, strategy*] inflexible; [*socialist, conservative*] irréductible; Art, Literat [*representation*] sans concession.

uncompromisingly /ʌn'kɒmprəmaɪzɪŋlɪ/ *adv* [*reply, state*] catégoriquement; [*harsh*] implacablement; **~ loyal/honest** d'une loyauté/honnêteté absolue.

unconcealed /ˌʌnkən'si:ld/ *adj* [*emotion*] non déguisé; [*appetite*] non caché.

unconcern /ˌʌnkən'sɜ:n/ *n* (lack of care) insouciance *f*; (lack of interest) indifférence *f*; **with a look of apparent ~** sans trouble apparent.

unconcerned /ˌʌnkən'sɜ:nd/ *adj* **1** (uninterested) indifférent (**with** à); **totally ~, quite ~** complètement indifférent; **she is ~ with her own image** son image la laisse indifférente; **2** (not caring) insouciant; **3** (untroubled) imperturbable; **he seems ~ about the debt** la dette n'a pas l'air de l'inquiéter; **he went on, ~** il continua, imperturbable.

unconditional /ˌʌnkən'dɪʃənl/ *adj* [*obedience*] inconditionnel/-elle; [*credits, offer*] sans condition; [*surrender, withdrawal*] sans condition; **to be released on ~ bail** Jur être mis en liberté provisoire.

unconditionally /ˌʌnkən'dɪʃənəlɪ/ *adv* [*support, surrender*] inconditionnellement; [*promise, lend*] sans condition.

unconditioned /ˌʌnkən'dɪʃnd/ *adj* Psych inconditionné.

unconfined /ˌʌnkən'faɪnd/ *adj* [*space*] ouvert; [*joy*] sans borne.

unconfirmed /ˌʌnkən'fɜ:md/ *adj* non confirmé.

unconformity /ˌʌnkən'fɔ:mətɪ/ *n* Geol discordance *f*.

uncongenial /ˌʌnkən'dʒi:nɪəl/ *adj* [*atmosphere, surroundings, job*] peu agréable; [*person*] peu sympathique.

unconnected /ˌʌnkə'nektɪd/ *adj* **1** gen [*incidents, facts*] sans lien entre eux/elles; **the two events are ~** il n'y a aucun rapport entre les deux événements; **to be ~ with** [*event, fact*] n'avoir aucun rapport avec; [*person*] n'avoir aucun lien avec; **not to be ~ with** ne pas être sans rapport avec; **2** Elec, Telecom pas branché.

unconquerable /ʌn'kɒŋkərəbl/ *adj* (all contexts) invincible.

unconquered /ʌn'kɒŋkəd/ *adj* (all contexts) invaincu.

unconscionable /ʌn'kɒnʃənəbl/ *adj* sout excessif/-ive.

unconscious /ʌn'kɒnʃəs/ **I** *n* **the ~** l'inconscient *m*; **deep in her ~** profondément enfoui dans son inconscient.
II *adj* **1** (insensible) sans connaissance; **to knock sb ~** faire perdre connaissance à qn; **he was knocked ~ by a stone** un coup de pierre lui a fait perdre connaissance; **to lie ~** rester sans connaissance; **to fall ~** perdre connaissance; **she remained ~ for several hours** elle ne reprit pas connaissance pendant quelques heures; **2** (unaware) **to be ~ of sth/of doing** ne pas être conscient de qch/de faire; **3** (unintentional) [*bias, impulse, hostility*] inconscient.

unconsciously /ʌn'kɒnʃəslɪ/ *adv* [*conform, absorb, cause, desire etc*] inconsciemment; **she patted his arm ~** elle lui tapota le bras sans être consciente de ce qu'elle faisait.

unconsciousness /ʌn'kɒnʃəsnɪs/ *n* **1** (comatose state) inconscience *f*; **to lapse into ~** perdre connaissance; **2** (unawareness) inconscience *f*.

unconsidered /ˌʌnkən'sɪdəd/ *adj* **1** [*words, remark*] irréfléchi; **2** (disregarded) [*species, aspect*] négligé.

unconstitutional /ˌʌnkɒnstɪ'tju:ʃənl/ *adj* [*action, proposal, law*] inconstitutionnel/-elle.

unconstitutionally /ˌʌnkɒnsti:'tju:ʃənəlɪ/ *adv* inconstitutionnellement.

unconstrained /ˌʌnkən'streɪnd/ *adv* (spontaneous) [*expression, generosity*] spontané; (uncontrolled) [*emotions, violence*] débridé.

uncontaminated /ˌʌnkən'tæmɪneɪtɪd/ *adj* lit, fig non contaminé.

uncontested /ˌʌnkənˈtestɪd/ *adj* gen incontesté; Pol [*seat*] non disputé.

uncontrollable /ˌʌnkənˈtrəʊləbl/ *adj* gen incontrôlable; [*tears*] qu'on ne peut retenir.

uncontrollably /ˌʌnkənˈtrəʊləblɪ/ *adv* [*laugh, sob*] sans pouvoir se contrôler; [*increase, decline*] irrésistiblement; **his hand shook ~** sa main tremblait de manière incontrôlable.

uncontrolled /ˌʌnkənˈtrəʊld/ *adj* **1** (not supervised) [*drainage, felling, use*] non réglementé; **2** (unrestrained) [*price rises, immigration*] incontrôlé; [*costs*] non maîtrisé; [*anger, fear*] non maîtrisé.

uncontroversial /ˌʌnkɒntrəˈvɜːʃl/ *adj* anodin.

unconventional /ˌʌnkənˈvenʃənl/ *adj* peu conventionnel/-elle.

unconventionality /ˌʌnkənˌvenʃəˈnælətɪ/ *n* originalité *f*.

unconventionally /ˌʌnkənˈvenʃənəlɪ/ *adv* [*dress, live*] de façon peu conventionnelle.

unconverted /ˌʌnkənˈvɜːtɪd/ *adj* **1** Relig non converti; **2** Sport (in rugby) [*try*] non transformé.

unconvinced /ˌʌnkənˈvɪnst/ *adj* pas convaincu; **to be ~ of sth** ne pas être convaincu de qch; **to be ~ that** ne pas être convaincu que.

unconvincing /ˌʌnkənˈvɪnsɪŋ/ *adj* peu convaincant.

unconvincingly /ˌʌnkənˈvɪnsɪŋlɪ/ *adv* de façon peu convaincante.

uncooked /ʌnˈkʊkt/ *adj* non cuit.

uncool° /ʌnˈkuːl/ *adj* pas cool°.

uncooperative /ˌʌnkəʊˈɒpərətɪv/ *adj* peu coopératif/-ive.

uncooperatively /ˌʌnkəʊˈɒpərətɪvlɪ/ *adv* [*respond*] de façon peu coopérative; **to behave ~** être peu coopératif/-ive.

uncoordinated /ˌʌnkəʊˈɔːdɪneɪtɪd/ *adj* [*effort, performance, service*] désordonné; [*person*] (clumsy) manquant de coordination; **to be ~** [*person*] manquer de coordination.

uncork /ʌnˈkɔːk/ *vtr* déboucher [*bottle, wine*].

uncorrected /ˌʌnkəˈrektɪd/ *adj* [*error, proofs*] non corrigé; [*meter reading*] non rectifié; **the errors went ~** les erreurs n'avaient pas été corrigées.

uncorroborated /ˌʌnkəˈrɒbəreɪtɪd/ *adj* non corroboré; **~ evidence** Jur preuve *f* par présomption.

uncorrupted /ˌʌnkəˈrʌptɪd/ *adj* non corrompu.

uncountable /ʌnˈkaʊntəbl/ *adj* Ling indénombrable, non comptable.

uncounted /ʌnˈkaʊntɪd/ *adj* **1** (not counted) [*money, votes*] non compté; **2** (innumerable) innombrable.

uncount noun *n* nom *m* non comptable.

uncouple /ʌnˈkʌpl/ *vtr* détacher [*wagon*]; découpler [*locomotive*]; Hunt découpler [*dogs*].

uncouth /ʌnˈkuːθ/ *adj* [*person, manner*] grossier/-ière, rustre; [*accent*] peu raffiné.

uncover /ʌnˈkʌvə(r)/ *vtr* **1** (expose) dévoiler [*plot, fraud, scandal*]; **2** (discover) découvrir [*evidence, treasure, weapons*]; **3** (remove covering from) découvrir [*face, body*].

uncovered /ʌnˈkʌvəd/ *adj* **1** gen non couvert; **leave the saucepan ~** ne couvre pas la casserole; **2** Fin découvert.

uncritical /ʌnˈkrɪtɪkl/ *adj* peu critique; **to be ~ of sb/sth** ne pas être critique envers qn/qch.

uncritically /ʌnˈkrɪtɪklɪ/ *adv* [*accept, endorse*] sans se poser de questions; [*regard*] sans faire preuve d'esprit critique.

uncross /ʌnˈkrɒs, US -ˈkrɔːs/ *vtr* décroiser [*legs, arms*].

uncrowded /ʌnˈkraʊdɪd/ *adj* agréablement vide.

uncrowned /ʌnˈkraʊnd/ *adj* [*king, queen*] non couronné; **the ~ king** fig le roi sans couronne.

uncrushable /ʌnˈkrʌʃəbl/ *adj* [*fabric*] infroissable.

UNCTAD /ˈʌŋktæd/ *n* (*abrév* = **United Nations Conference on Trade and Development**) CNUCED *f*.

unction /ˈʌŋkʃn/ *n* **1** (unctuousness) manières *fpl* onctueuses; **2** Relig ▶ **extreme unction**.

unctuous /ˈʌŋktjʊəs/ *adj* onctueux/-euse, mielleux/-euse.

unctuously /ˈʌŋktjʊəslɪ/ *adv* avec onction.

unctuousness /ˈʌŋktjʊəsnɪs/ *n* manières *fpl* onctueuses.

uncultivated /ʌnˈkʌltɪveɪtɪd/ *adj* (all contexts) inculte.

uncultured /ʌnˈkʌltʃəd/ *adj* [*person, society*] inculte; [*voice, accent, manners*] peu raffiné.

uncurl /ʌnˈkɜːl/ **I** *vtr* déplier [*fingers, legs*]; dérouler [*tendrils*].
II *vi* [*snake*] se dérouler; [*cat*] s'étirer.
III *v refl* **to ~ oneself** [*person, animal*] s'étirer.

uncut /ʌnˈkʌt/ *adj* **1** [*branch, hair, crops*] non coupé; **2** [*film, version, text*] intégral; **3** [*book*] aux pages non coupées; [*page*] non coupé; **4** [*gem*] non taillé; **5**° US (not circumcised) non circoncis.

undamaged /ʌnˈdæmɪdʒd/ *adj* [*flowers, crops*] non endommagé; [*vehicle, building, reputation, confidence*] intact; **psychologically ~** psychologiquement indemne.

undated /ʌnˈdeɪtɪd/ *adj* [*letter, painting*] non daté; [*bond*] Fin perpétuel/-elle.

undaunted /ʌnˈdɔːntɪd/ *adj* imperturbable; **~ by her fall/by criticism, she...** nullement ébranlée par sa chute/par les critiques, elle...

undeceive /ˌʌndɪˈsiːv/ littér **I** *vtr* détromper.
II undeceived *pp adj* **1** (freed from error) détrompé; **2** (not deceived) pas dupe; **to be ~d by sth** ne pas se laisser duper par qch.

undecided /ˌʌndɪˈsaɪdɪd/ *adj* [*person*] indécis; [*outcome*] incertain; **the ~ voters** les (électeurs) indécis; **the ~ fixture dates** Sport les dates des rencontres qui n'ont pas encore été décidées; **they are ~ as to whether he is a genius** ils n'arrivent pas à décider si c'est un génie; **I am ~ about which dress to wear** je ne sais pas quelle robe mettre; **to be ~ whether to go abroad** ne pas savoir si l'on va aller à l'étranger; **the jury is ~** le jury n'a pas encore décidé.

undeclared /ˌʌndɪˈkleəd/ *adj* **1** (illegal) [*income, payments, imports*] non déclaré; **2** (unspoken) [*ambition, love*] inavoué.

undefeated /ˌʌndɪˈfiːtɪd/ *adj* invaincu.

undefended /ˌʌndɪˈfendɪd/ *adj* **1** [*frontier, citizens*] non défendu; [*chess piece*] non protégé; **2** Jur [*case*] non contesté.

undefiled /ˌʌndɪˈfaɪld/ *adj* littér [*altar, temple*] non souillé; [*morals*] non corrompu.

undefined /ˌʌndɪˈfaɪnd/ *adj* **1** [*work, powers, objective*] non défini; [*nature*] indéterminé; [*space*] vague; **2** Comput [*term, error, macro*] indéfini.

undelivered /ˌʌndɪˈlɪvəd/ *adj* [*mail*] non distribué.

undemanding /ˌʌndɪˈmɑːndɪŋ, US -ˈmænd-/ *adj* [*job, task*] peu fatigant; [*relative, pupil, colleague*] peu exigeant; **he was ~ of her attention/affection** sout il ne réclamait pas son attention/affection.

undemocratic /ˌʌndeməˈkrætɪk/ *adj* antidémocratique.

undemonstrative /ˌʌndɪˈmɒnstrətɪv/ *adj* peu démonstratif/-ive.

undeniable /ˌʌndɪˈnaɪəbl/ *adj* [*truth, fact, feeling, affection*] indéniable; **it is ~ that** (irrefutable) il est indéniable que; (clear) il est incontestable que; **that they have charm is ~** on ne saurait nier qu'ils ont du charme.

undeniably /ˌʌndɪˈnaɪəblɪ/ *adv* **1** [*deserve, need*] incontestablement; [*superb, powerful, beautiful*] indiscutablement; **it's ~ true/correct** c'est incontestablement vrai/correct; **2** [*sentence adv*] incontestablement.

undependable /ˌʌndɪˈpendəbl/ *adj* (all contexts) peu fiable.

under /ˈʌndə(r)/

■ **Note** When *under* is used as a straightforward preposition in English it can almost always be translated by *sous* in French: *under the table* = sous la table; *under a sheet* = sous un drap; *under a heading* = sous un titre.
– *under* is often used before a noun in English to mean *subject to* or *affected by* (*under control, under fire, under oath, under review etc*). For translations, consult the appropriate noun entry (***control, fire, oath, review*** etc).
– *under* is also often used as a prefix in combinations such as *undercooked, underfunded, underprivileged* and *undergrowth, underpass, underskirt*. These combinations are treated as headwords in the dictionary.
– For particular usages, see the entry below.

I *prep* **1** (physically beneath or below) sous; **~ the bed/chair** sous le lit/la chaise; **~ it** en dessous; **it's ~ there** c'est là-dessous; **to come out from ~ sth** sortir de dessous qch; **2** (less than) **~ £10/two hours** moins de 10 livres sterling/deux heures; **children ~ five** les enfants de moins de cinq ans or en dessous de cinq ans; **a number ~ ten** un nombre inférieur à dix; **temperatures ~ 10°C** des températures inférieures à 10°C; **those ~ the rank of** ceux qui ont un rang inférieur à celui de; **3** (according to) **~ the law/clause 5** selon la loi/l'article 5; **fined ~ a rule** condamné à une amende en vertu d'une règle; **4** (subordinate to) sous; **I have 50 people ~ me** j'ai 50 employés sous mes ordres; **5** (in classification) **do I look for Le Corbusier ~ 'le' or 'Corbusier'?** est-ce que je dois chercher Le Corbusier sous 'le' ou 'Corbusier'?; **you'll find it ~ 'Problems'** tu le trouveras à la rubrique 'Problèmes'.
II *adv* **1** (physically beneath or below something) [*crawl, sit, hide*] en dessous; **to go/stay ~** [*diver, swimmer*] disparaître/rester sous l'eau; **2** (less) moins; **£10 and ~** 10 livres sterling et moins; **children of six and ~** des enfants de six ans et moins; **to run five minutes ~** [*event, programme*] durer cinq minutes de moins que prévu; **3** (anaesthetized) **to put sb ~** endormir qn; **to stay ~ for three minutes** être endormi pendant trois minutes; **4** (subjugated) **to keep sb ~** opprimer qn; **5** (below, later in text) **see ~** voir ci-dessous.

underachieve /ˌʌndərəˈtʃiːv/ *vi* Sch ne pas obtenir les résultats dont on est capable; [*team, player etc*] ne pas faire aussi bien qu'on aurait pu espérer.

underachiever /ˌʌndərəˈtʃiːvə(r)/ *n* Sch sous-performant/-e *m/f*; (generally) personne *f* qui reste en deçà de ses possibilités.

underage /ˌʌndərˈeɪdʒ/ *adj* **~ drinker/driver** personne qui consomme de l'alcool/conduit sans avoir atteint l'âge légal; **to be ~** être mineur/-e.

underarm /ˈʌndərɑːm/ **I** *adj* [*deodorant*] pour les aisselles; [*perspiration*] aux aisselles; [*hair*] des aisselles; [*service, throw*] à la cuillère.
II *adv* Sport [*serve, throw*] à la cuillère.

underbelly /ˈʌndəbelɪ/ *n* **1** lit bas-ventre *m*; **2** fig (vulnerable part) point *m* névralgique; (unattractive part) côté *m* peu reluisant.

underbid I /ˈʌndəbɪd/ *n* **1** (in cards) contrat *m* inférieur au potentiel de jeu; **2** Comm offre *f* au-dessous de l'enchère.
II /ˌʌndəˈbɪd/ *vtr* (*p prés* **-dd-**; *prét, pp* **-bid**) **1** Comm faire une soumission moins élevée que; **2** (in cards) **to ~ one's hand** annoncer en dessous de sa main.
III /ˌʌndəˈbɪd/ *vi* (*p prés* **-dd-**; *prét, pp* **-bid**) **1** Comm faire une soumission plus avantageuse pour l'acheteur; **2** (in cards) annoncer de petits contrats.

underbody /ˈʌndəbɒdɪ/ *n* Aut dessous *m* de la caisse.

underbrush /ˈʌndəbrʌʃ/ *n* US = **undergrowth**.

undercapitalize /ˌʌndəˈkæpɪtəlaɪz/ *vtr* sous-investir dans.

undercapitalized /ˌʌndəˈkæpɪtəlaɪzd/ *adj* [*business*] sous-capitalisé.

undercarriage /ˈʌndəkærɪdʒ/ *n* Aviat train *m* d'atterrissage.

undercharge /ˌʌndəˈtʃɑːdʒ/ **I** *vtr* ne pas faire payer assez à [*person*]; faire porter un débit moindre à [*account*]; **she ~d me by £1** elle aurait dû me faire payer une livre de plus; **he ~d me for the wine** il m'a fait payer le vin moins cher qu'il n'aurait dû.
II *vi*: **he ~d for the wine** il a fait payer le vin moins cher qu'il n'aurait dû.

under: **~class** *n* classe *f* sous-prolétariat *m*; **~classman** *n* US Sch, Univ étudiant *m* de première année; **~clothes** *npl* sous-vêtements *mpl*.

undercoat /ˈʌndəkəʊt/ **I** *n* **1** (of paint, varnish) couche *f* de fond; **2** US Aut peinture *f* antirouille pour châssis.
II *vtr* passer une couche de fond sur.

undercook /ˌʌndəˈkʊk/ **I** *vtr* ne pas faire assez cuire.
II undercooked *pp adj* pas assez cuit.

undercover /ˌʌndəˈkʌvə(r)/ **I** *adj* [*activity, organization*] clandestin; **~ agent** agent *m* secret.
II *adv* clandestinement.

undercurrent /ˈʌndəkʌrənt/ *n* **1** (in water) gen courant *m* profond; (in sea) courant *m* sous-marin; **2** fig (in relationship, situation, conversation) courant *m* sous-jacent.

undercut **I** /ˈʌndəkʌt/ *n* **1** GB Culin filet *m*; **2** Sport balle *f* coupée.
II /ˌʌndəˈkʌt/ *vtr* (*p prés* **-tt-**; *prét, pp* **-cut**) **1** Comm (set prices lower than) concurrencer [qn] en offrant des prix plus intéressants; concurrencer [*prices*]; **2** (cut away) miner [*cliff, bank*]; **3** fig (undermine) saper [*position, efforts, image*]; couler○ [*person*]; **4** Econ réduire [*inflation*]; **5** Sport couper.
III /ˌʌndəˈkʌt/ *adj* [*cliff*] miné.

underdeveloped /ˌʌndədɪˈveləpt/ *adj* [*country, economy etc*] sous-développé; [*person, physique, muscles*] peu développé; Phot pas assez développé.

underdog /ˈʌndədɒg, US -dɔːg/ *n* **1** (in society) opprimé/-e *m/f*; **to side with the ~** prendre le parti du plus faible; **2** (in game, contest) (loser) perdant/-e *m/f*.

underdone /ˌʌndəˈdʌn/ *adj* [*food*] pas assez cuit; [*steak*] GB saignant.

underdrawers /ˈʌndədrɔːz/ *npl* US (men's) caleçon *m*; (women's)† dessous *mpl*.

underdressed /ˌʌndəˈdrest/ *adj* qui n'a pas la tenue de rigueur.

underemphasize /ˌʌndərˈemfəsaɪz/ *vtr* ne pas donner assez d'importance à.

underemployed /ˌʌndərɪmˈplɔɪd/ *adj* [*person*] sous-employé; [*resources, equipment etc*] sous-exploité.

underemployment /ˌʌndərɪmˈplɔɪmənt/ *n* (of person) sous-emploi *m*; (of resources, equipment) sous-exploitation *f*; (of building) sous-utilisation *f*.

underequipped /ˌʌndərɪˈkwɪpt/ *adj* sous-équipé.

underestimate **I** /ˌʌndərˈestɪmət/ *n* sous-estimation *f*.
II /ˌʌndərˈestɪmeɪt/ *vtr* sous-estimer.

underestimation /ˌʌndərestɪˈmeɪʃn/ *n* sous-estimation *f*.

underexpose /ˌʌndərɪkˈspəʊz/ *vtr* Phot sous-exposer.

underexposed /ˌʌndərɪkˈspəʊzd/ *adj* Phot sous-exposé.

underexposure /ˌʌndərɪkˈspəʊʒə(r)/ *n* Phot sous-exposition *f*.

underfed /ˌʌndəˈfed/ **I** *prét, pp* ▶ **underfeed**.
II *adj* sous-alimenté.

underfeed /ˌʌndəˈfiːd/ *vtr* (*prét, pp* **-fed**) sous-alimenter.

underfeeding /ˌʌndəˈfiːdɪŋ/ *n* sous-alimentation *f*.

underfelt /ˈʌndəfelt/ *n* Tex thibaude *f*.

underfinanced /ˌʌndəˈfaɪnænst/ *adj* qui ne dispose pas de fonds suffisants.

underfloor /ˈʌndəflɔː(r)/ *adj* [*pipes, wiring*] (wooden floor) situé sous le plancher; (concrete floor) situé sous le sol; **~ heating** chauffage par le sol.

underflow /ˈʌndəfləʊ/ *n* **1** = **undercurrent**; **2** Comput dépassement *m* de capacité négatif.

underfoot /ˌʌndəˈfʊt/ *adv* sous les pieds; **the ground was wet ~** le sol était humide; **to trample sb/sth ~** lit, fig fouler qn/qch aux pieds.

underframe /ˈʌndəfreɪm/ *n* châssis *m*.

underfunded /ˌʌndəˈfʌndɪd/ *adj* insuffisamment financé.

underfunding /ˌʌndəˈfʌndɪŋ/ *n* manque *m* de fonds.

undergarment† /ˈʌndəgɑːmənt/ *n* sous-vêtement *m*.

undergo /ˌʌndəˈgəʊ/ *vtr* (*prét* **-went**, *pp* **-gone**) subir [*change, test, alteration*]; subir [*operation*]; suivre [*treatment, training*]; endurer [*hardship, suffering*]; **to ~ surgery** subir une intervention chirurgicale; **to be ~ing renovations/repairs** être en rénovation/réparation.

undergraduate /ˌʌndəˈgrædʒʊət/ **I** *n* ≈ étudiant/-e *m/f* (*de premier ou de deuxième cycle*).
II *modif* [*course, studies*] pour étudiants de premier ou de deuxième cycle; [*club, society*] d'étudiants; [*accommodation*] pour étudiants; [*life*] estudiantin, étudiant.

underground **I** /ˈʌndəgraʊnd/ *n* **1** GB Transp métro *m*; **on the ~** dans le métro; **2** (secret movement) mouvement *m* clandestin; **3** Art, Mus, Theat underground *m*.
II /ˈʌndəgraʊnd/ *modif* GB Transp [*network, station, train*] de métro; [*map, staff, strike*] du métro.
III /ˈʌndəgraʊnd/ *adj* **1** (below ground) [*tunnel, shelter*] souterrain; **2** (secret) [*newspaper, movement, activity*] clandestin; **3** Art, Mus, Theat [*art, film, movement*] underground *inv*; [*artist*] de l'underground.
IV /ˌʌndəˈgraʊnd/ *adv* **1** (below ground) [*lie, live, tunnel, work*] sous terre; **it is two metres ~** c'est à deux mètres sous terre; **2** (secretly) **to go/stay ~** passer/rester dans la clandestinité; **to drive sb ~** obliger qn à passer dans la clandestinité.

underground railroad *n* US Hist réseau *m* clandestin d'aide aux esclaves fugitifs.

undergrowth /ˈʌndəgrəʊθ/ *n* sous-bois *m*.

underhand /ˌʌndəˈhænd/ **I** *adj* **1** péj [*person, method, behaviour*] sournois; **an ~ trick** un sale coup○; **~ dealings** magouilles○ *fpl*; **2** (in tennis) **to have an ~ serve** servir à la cuillère.
II *adv* Sport [*throw, serve*] à la cuillère.

underhanded /ˌʌndəˈhændɪd/ *adj* US = **underhand** I 1.

underhandedly /ˌʌndəˈhændɪdlɪ/ *adv* sournoisement.

underinsure /ˌʌndərɪnˈʃɔː(r), US -ɪnˈʃʊər/ **I** *vtr* sous-assurer [*person, object*].
II *v refl* **to ~ oneself** se sous-assurer.

underinvest /ˌʌndərɪnˈvest/ *vi* sous-investir (**in** dans).

underinvestment /ˌʌndərɪnˈvestmənt/ *n* sous-investissement *m*.

underlay /ˌʌndəˈleɪ/ **I** *prét* ▶ **underlie**.
II *n* Constr thibaude *f*.
III *vtr* (*prét, pp* **-laid**) **to be underlaid by** avoir une sous-couche de [*gravel, rock*].

underlie /ˌʌndəˈlaɪ/ *vtr* (*p prés* **-lying**; *prét* **-lay**; *pp* **-lain**) **1** lit [*rock*] être sous [*topsoil*]; **2** fig [*philosophy, theory*] sous-tendre [*principle, view, work*]; **underlying these terms/beliefs is...** sous ces conditions/croyances il y a...

underline /ˌʌndəˈlaɪn/ *vtr* lit, fig souligner.

underling /ˈʌndəlɪŋ/ *n* péj subordonné/-e *m/f*.

underlining /ˌʌndəˈlaɪnɪŋ/ *n* soulignage *m*, soulignement *m*.

underlying /ˌʌndəˈlaɪɪŋ/ **I** *p prés* ▶ **underlie**.
II *adj* [*claim, liability*] prioritaire; [*infection, inflation, problem, tension, trend*] sous-jacent.

undermanager /ˌʌndəˈmænɪdʒə(r)/ ▶ **1692** *n* sous-directeur/-trice *m/f*.

undermanned /ˌʌndəˈmænd/ *adj* [*factory, industry*] en sous-effectif *inv*.

undermanning /ˌʌndəˈmænɪŋ/ *n* sous-effectif *m*.

undermentioned /ˌʌndəˈmenʃnd/ **I** *n* **the ~** la personne *f* nommée ci-après.
II *adj* [*item, list*] ci-dessous; [*person*] nommé ci-dessous; [*name*] cité ci-dessous.

undermine /ˌʌndəˈmaɪn/ *vtr* **1** Civ Eng saper [*cliff, foundations, road*]; **2** fig (shake, subvert) saper [*authority, efforts, foundations*]; ébranler [*confidence, organization, position, value*]; **stop undermining me!** arrête de saper ce que je fais!

undermost /ˈʌndəməʊst/ *adj* **1** (lowest) [*part*] le plus bas/la plus basse; **2** (last) [*sheet, layer*] dernier/-ière.

underneath /ˌʌndəˈniːθ/ **I** *n* dessous *m*.
II *adj* d'en dessous; **the apartment ~** l'appartement d'en dessous.
III *adv* lit, fig dessous, en dessous.
IV *prep* lit, fig sous, au-dessous de; **she took out some papers from ~ a pile of books** elle a sorti des papiers de dessous une pile de livres.

undernourish /ˌʌndəˈnʌrɪʃ/ *vtr* sous-alimenter.

undernourished /ˌʌndəˈnʌrɪʃt/ *adj* sous-alimenté.

undernourishment /ˌʌndəˈnʌrɪʃmənt/ *n* sous-alimentation *f*.

underpaid /ˌʌndəˈpeɪd/ **I** *prét, pp* ▶ **underpay**.
II *adj* [*person, worker*] sous-payé (**for** pour).

underpants /ˈʌndəpænts/ *npl* slip *m*; **a pair of ~** un slip.

underpart /ˈʌndəpɑːt/ *n* partie *f* inférieure.

underpass /ˈʌndəpɑːs, US -pæs/ *n* **1** (for traffic) voie *f* inférieure (*dans un échangeur*); **2** (for pedestrians) passage *m* souterrain.

underpay /ˌʌndəˈpeɪ/ *vtr* (*prét, pp* **-paid**) **1** (pay badly) sous-payer [*employee*]; **2** (pay too little) **I was underpaid this month** je n'ai pas eu mon salaire intégral ce mois-ci; **you have underpaid me by £5** vous me devez cinq livres.

underperform /ˌʌndəpəˈfɔːm/ *n* Fin [*stock*] faire une contre-performance; **~ing businesses** entreprises peu rentables.

underpin /ˌʌndəˈpɪn/ *vtr* (*p prés etc* **-nn-**) **1** Constr étayer [*wall*]; reprendre [qch] en sous-œuvre, étayer [*building*]; **2** fig (strengthen) [*honesty, morality*] être à la base de [*religion, society*]; étayer [*currency, economy, power, theory*].

underpinning /ˌʌndəˈpɪnɪŋ/ **I** *n* Civ Eng reprise *f* en sous-œuvre.
II underpinnings *npl* fig fondements *mpl*.

underplay /ˌʌndəˈpleɪ/ *vtr* **1** gen minimiser [*aspect, impact, severity*]; **2** Theat jouer [qch] de façon plate [*role*].

underpopulated /ˌʌndəˈpɒpjʊleɪtɪd/ *adj* sous-peuplé.

underpowered /ˌʌndəˈpaʊəd/ *adj* [*vehicle*] peu puissant; **to be ~** manquer de puissance.

underprice /ˌʌndəˈpraɪs/ *vtr* Comm afficher un prix trop bas pour [*goods, product*].

underpriced /ˌʌndəˈpraɪst/ *adj* [*goods*] vendu en dessous de leur valeur; **petrol/their cleaning service is ~** le prix de l'essence/leur tarif de nettoyage est beaucoup trop bas; **this car is ~** cette voiture est vendue à un prix trop bas.

underprivileged /ˌʌndəˈprɪvəlɪdʒd/ **I** *n* **the ~** (+ *v pl*) les déshérités *mpl*.
II *adj* [*area, background, person*] défavorisé.

underproduce /ˌʌndəprəˈdjuːs, US -ˈduːs/ **I** *vtr* Mus **to ~ a record** produire un disque sans fioritures.
II *vi* Comm, Ind sous-produire.

underproduction /ˌʌndəprəˈdʌkʃn/ *n* sous-production *f*.

underrate /ˌʌndəˈreɪt/ *vtr* sous-estimer.

underrated /ˌʌndəˈreɪtɪd/ *adj* sous-estimé.

underreact /ˌʌndərɪˈækt/ *vi* réagir mollement (**to** à).

underripe /ˌʌndəˈraɪp/ *adj* (fruit) pas mûr; (cheese) pas fait.

underscore /ˌʌndəˈskɔː(r)/ *vtr* lit, fig souligner.

underscoring /ˌʌndəˈskɔːrɪŋ/ *n* **1** lit (line) soulignement *m*; **2** fig (emphasis) insistance *f* (**of** sur).

undersea /ˈʌndəsiː/ *adj* sous-marin.

underseal /ˈʌndəsiːl/ Aut **I** *n* (peinture *f*) antirouille *m*.
II *vtr* traiter [qch] contre la rouille.

undersealing /ˈʌndəsiːlɪŋ/ *n* = **underseal I**.

under-secretary /ˌʌndəˈsekrətrɪ, US -terɪ/ *n* (also **~ of state**) GB Pol sous-secrétaire *mf* d'État (**at** auprès de).

undersell /ˌʌndəˈsel/ (*prét, pp* **-sold**) **I** *vtr* **1** (undercut) vendre moins cher que [*competitor*]; **we ~ our competitors by £10 a crate** nous vendons le cageot à dix livres sterling de moins que nos concurrents; **2** (sell discreetly) pratiquer une publicité trop discrète pour [*product*].
II *vi* vendre à bas prix.
III *v refl* **to ~ oneself** se dévaloriser.

undersexed /ˌʌndəˈsekst/ *adj* **to be ~** [*person*] avoir un faible appétit sexuel.

undershirt /ˈʌndəʃɜːt/ *n* US maillot *m* de corps.

undershoot /ˌʌndəˈʃuːt/ (*prét, pp* **-shot**) Aviat **I** *vtr* [*aircraft, pilot*] se poser avant [*runway*].
II *vi* [*aircraft*] atterrir trop court; [*pilot*] se présenter trop court.

undershorts /ˈʌndəʃɔːts/ *npl* US caleçon *m*.

undershot /ˌʌndəˈʃɒt/ **I** *prét, pp* ▶ **undershoot**.
II *adj* **1** (of jaw) proéminent; **2** (of water wheel) entraîné par un courant par en dessous.

underside /ˈʌndəsaɪd/ *n* **1** (bottom) dessous *m*; **2** fig (dark side) face *f* cachée.

undersigned /ˌʌndəˈsaɪnd/ **I** *n* soussigné/-e *m/f*; **the ~ confirms that** le soussigné affirme que; **we, the ~** nous, soussignés.
II *adj* [*person*] soussigné.

undersized /ˌʌndəˈsaɪzd/ *adj* [*person*] chétif/-ive; [*portion, ration*] maigre (*before n*); [*animal, plant*] rachitique.

underskirt /ˈʌndəskɜːt/ *n* jupon *m*.

underslung /ˈʌndəslʌŋ/ *adj* [*chassis*] surbaissé; [*load*] suspendu.

undersoil /ˈʌndəsɔɪl/ *n* = **subsoil**.

underspend /ˌʌndəˈspend/ *vi* (*prét, pp* **-spent**) Admin, Fin dépenser moins que les crédits disponibles.

underspending /ˌʌndəˈspendɪŋ/ *n* Admin, Fin dépenses *fpl* inférieures aux crédits disponibles.

understaffed /ˌʌndəˈstɑːft, US -ˈstæft/ *adj* **to be ~** manquer de personnel.

understaffing /ˌʌndəˈstɑːfɪŋ, US -ˈstæfɪŋ/ *n* manque *m* d'effectif.

understand /ˌʌndəˈstænd/ (*prét, pp* **-stood**) **I** *vtr* **1** (intellectually) comprendre [*question, language, concept*]; **is that understood?** c'est compris?; **I just don't ~ it** je n'arrive vraiment pas à comprendre; **to ~ that** comprendre que; **to ~ how/why** comprendre comment/pourquoi; **I can't ~ why** je n'arrive pas à comprendre pourquoi; **to make oneself understood** se faire comprendre; **2** (emotionally) comprendre [*person, feelings*]; **I don't ~ you** je ne te comprends pas; **to ~ sb doing** comprendre que qn fasse; **I can ~ her being upset** je comprends qu'elle soit bouleversée; **3** (interpret) comprendre [*person, statement*]; **do I ~ you correctly?** vous ai-je bien compris?; **what do you ~ by this?** qu'est-ce que tu comprends par ceci?; **as I ~ it** si je comprends bien; **I understood him to say** ou **as saying that**... j'ai compris qu'il disait que...; **I think we ~ each other** je pense que nous nous comprenons; **4** (believe) **to ~ that** croire que; **I understood (that) I was to wait** je croyais que je devais attendre; **it is/was understood that** on pense/pensait que; **he was/they were given to ~ that** on lui/leur a donné à entendre que; **you won I ~** vous avez gagné si je comprends bien; **'he's dead'—'so I ~'** 'il est mort'—'c'est ce que j'ai cru comprendre'; **5** (accept mutually) **to be understood** être entendu; **I thought that was understood** je pensais que c'était entendu; **it must be understood that** il faut qu'il soit bien entendu que; **6** Ling (imply) **to be understood** [*subject*] être sous-entendu.
II *vi* **1** (comprehend) comprendre (**about** à propos de); **no slip-ups, (do you) ~?** et pas de gaffes, d'accord?; **2** (sympathize) comprendre; **I quite/fully ~** je comprends tout à fait/parfaitement.

understandable /ˌʌndəˈstændəbl/ *adj* (all contexts) compréhensible; **it is ~ that** il est compréhensible que (+ *subj*); **it's ~** ça se comprend.

understandably /ˌʌndəˈstændəblɪ/ *adv* naturellement; **he is ~ disappointed** il est déçu, c'est normal.

understanding /ˌʌndəˈstændɪŋ/ **I** *n* **1** (grasp of subject, issue) compréhension *f*; **to show an ~ of** faire preuve d'une bonne compréhension de; **2** (perception, interpretation) interprétation *f*; **to my ~** d'après ce que j'ai/j'avais compris; **our ~ was that** nous avions compris que; **3** (arrangement) entente *f* (**about** sur; **between** entre); **there is an ~ that** il est entendu que; **on the ~ that** étant entendu que; **on that ~** sur cette base; **4** (sympathy) compréhension *f*; **love and ~** amour et compréhension; **5** (powers of reason) entendement *m*; **to pass human ~** dépasser l'entendement.
II *adj* [*tone, glance*] bienveillant; [*person*] compréhensif/-ive (**about** au sujet de).

understandingly /ˌʌndəˈstændɪŋlɪ/ *adv* [*smile, reply*] avec bienveillance.

understate /ˌʌndəˈsteɪt/ *vtr* **1** (say with reserve) exprimer [qch] de façon réservée [*feeling, opinion, reaction*]; **2** (play down) minimiser [*cost, danger, quantity, severity*].

understated /ˌʌndəˈsteɪtɪd/ *adj* [*charm, design, effect, style, tone*] discret/-ète; [*dress*] d'une élégance discrète; [*performance*] sobre.

understatement /ˈʌndəsteɪtmənt/ *n* **1** (remark) litote *f*, euphémisme *m*; **that's an ~!, that's the ~ of the year!** c'est le moins qu'on puisse dire!; **2** ₵ (style) (of person) réserve *f*, sens *m* de la litote; **he said with typical ~ that** il a dit avec cette réserve qui le caractérise que; **3** (subtlety) (of dress, decor) discrétion *f*.

understood /ˌʌndəˈstʊd/ *prét, pp* ▶ **understand**.

understudy /ˈʌndəstʌdɪ/ **I** *n* Theat doublure *f* (**to** de); gen suppléant/-e *m/f* (**to** de).
II *vtr* Theat doubler [*role, actor*].

undertake /ˌʌndəˈteɪk/ *vtr* (*prét* **-took**; *pp* **-taken**) **1** (carry out) entreprendre [*search, study, trip, work*]; occuper [*function*]; se charger de [*mission, offensive*]; **2** (guarantee) **to ~ to do** s'engager à faire.

undertaker /ˈʌndəteɪkə(r)/ ▶ **1692** *n* **1** (person) entrepreneur *m* de pompes funèbres; **2** (company) entreprise *f* de pompes funèbres; **at the ~'s** aux pompes funèbres.

undertaking /ˌʌndəˈteɪkɪŋ/ *n* **1** (venture) entreprise *f*; **joint ~** joint-venture *m*; **2** (promise) garantie *f* (**from sb** de la part de qn); **to give sb an ~ to do/that** promettre à qn de faire/que; **to give a written ~ to do sth** s'engager par écrit à faire qch; **3** (company) entreprise *f*; **4** (funeral business) pompes *fpl* funèbres.

undertax /ˌʌndəˈtæks/ *vtr* Fin [*tax office*] sous-évaluer le montant de l'impôt de [*tax payer*]; **~ed goods** marchandises insuffisamment taxées.

under-the-counter I *adj* [*goods, supply, trade*] illicite; [*payment*] sous le manteau.
II under the counter *adv* [*buy, obtain, sell*] sous le manteau, clandestinement.

undertone /ˈʌndətəʊn/ *n* **1** (low voice) voix *f* basse; **to speak in an ~** parler à voix basse; **2** (undercurrent) **an ~ of chaos/jealousy** un relent de chaos/jalousie; **comic/dark ~s** un côté comique/sombre; **the music has African/classical ~s** la musique a des résonances Africaines/classiques; **3** (hint) nuance *f*.

undertow /ˈʌndətəʊ/ *n* **1** (of wave) reflux *m*; **2** (at sea) contre-courant *m*; **3** (influence) influence *f* sous-jacente.

underuse /ˌʌndəˈjuːz/ *vtr* ne pas exploiter [qch] au mieux [*equipment, facility, land*]; sous-utiliser [*expression*].

underused /ˌʌndəˈjuːzd/ *adj* [*land*] sous-exploité; [*equipment, facility, resource, technique*] sous-utilisé; [*expression*] insuffisamment employé.

underutilize /ˌʌndəˈjuːtəlaɪz/ *vtr* = **underuse**.

undervalue /ˌʌndəˈvæljuː/ *vtr* **1** Fin, Insur sous-évaluer [*building, contribution, company, currency, painting*]; **to ~ sth by £1,000** sous-évaluer qch de 1 000 livres; **2** (not appreciate) sous-estimer [*employee, friend, honesty, patience*]; ne pas apprécier [qch] à sa juste valeur [*opinion, theory*].

undervalued /ˌʌndəˈvæljuːd/ *adj* **1** Fin [*artwork, company, contribution, currency, share*] sous-évalué; **2** (not appreciated) [*person, quality*] sous-estimé; [*opinion, theory*] non apprécié à sa juste valeur.

undervest /ˈʌndəvest/ *n* maillot *m* de corps.

undervoltage /ˈʌndəvəʊltɪdʒ/ *n* Elec sous-tension *f*.

underwater /ˌʌndəˈwɔːtə(r)/ **I** *adj* [*cable, exploration, test, world*] sous-marin; [*lighting, swimmer*] sous l'eau; [*birth*] dans l'eau.
II *adv* sous l'eau.

underway /ˌʌndəˈweɪ/ *adj* **to be ~** [*vehicle*] être en route; [*filming, rehearsals, talks, work*] être en cours; **to get ~** [*vehicle*] se mettre en route; [*preparation, show, season, work*] commencer; **to get sth ~** mettre qch en route.

underwear /ˈʌndəweə(r)/ *n* sous-vêtements *mpl*.

underweight /ˌʌndəˈweɪt/ *adj* [*baby, person*] maigre; **this child is four kilos ~** il manque quatre kilos à cet enfant.

underwent /ˌʌndəˈwent/ *prét* ▶ **undergo**.

underwhelm /ˌʌndəˈwelm/ hum **I** *vtr* décevoir franchement.
II underwhelming *pres p adj* franchement décevant.

underwired /ˌʌndəˈwaɪəd/ *adj* [*bodice, bra*] à armature.

underworld /ˈʌndəwɜːld/ **I** *n* **1** (criminal world) milieu *m*, pègre *f*; **the criminal ~** le milieu; **2** Mythol **the ~** les enfers *mpl*; **in the ~** aux enfers.
II *modif* [*character, activity, gang*] du milieu; [*killing*] organisé par le milieu.

underwrite /ˌʌndəˈraɪt/ *vtr* (*prét* **-wrote**; *pp* **-written**) **1** Insur garantir, souscrire [*policy, share issue, flotation*]; souscrire [*risk*]; assurer [*boat, property*]; **2** Fin financer [*project, scheme*]; prendre en charge [*cost,* expense, loss]; **3** (approve) donner son accord à [*decision*]; soutenir [*proposal, theory*].

underwriter /ˈʌndəraɪtə(r)/ *n* **1** Fin (of share issue) soumissionnaire *m*; **a company of ~s** une compagnie de soumissionnaires; **to act as ~ for sth** se porter garant de qch; **2** Insur assureur *m*, souscripteur *m*; **marine ~** assureur *m* maritime.

underwriting /ˈʌndəraɪtɪŋ/ *n* **1** Fin (of share issue) prise *f* ferme, garantie *f* d'émission; **2** Insur (of policy, risk) souscription *f*.

underwriting: **~ agent** ▶ **1692** *n* Insur agent *m* souscripteur; **~ contract** *n* Fin contrat *m* de garantie; **~ syndicate** *n* Fin syndicat *m* financier.

undeserved /ˌʌndɪˈzɜːvd/ *adj* immérité.

undeservedly /ˌʌndɪˈzɜːvɪdlɪ/ *adv* [*blame, punish*] injustement; [*praise, reward, win*] de façon imméritée.

undeserving /ˌʌndɪˈzɜːvɪŋ/ *adj* **~ of attention/praise/support** indigne d'attention/de louanges/de soutien; **he was an ~ winner** il n'a pas mérité de gagner.

undesirable /ˌʌndɪˈzaɪərəbl/ **I** *n* indésirable *mf*.
II *adj* [*aspect, effect, habit, practice, result*] indésirable; [*influence*] néfaste; [*friend*] peu recommandable; **it is ~ for sb to do** il n'est pas souhaitable que qn fasse; **it is ~ that he should know** il n'est pas souhaitable qu'il sache; **it is ~ to do** il n'est pas souhaitable de faire; **~ alien** Jur étranger/-ère *m/f* indésirable.

undesirably /ˌʌndɪˈzaɪərəblɪ/ *adv* [*hot, long, obvious, small*] beaucoup trop.

undetected /ˌʌndɪˈtektɪd/ **I** *adj* [*intruder, observer*] inaperçu; [*cancer, fracture*] non décelé; [*bug, error, flaw, movement*] non détecté; [*crime, fraud*] non découvert.
II *adv* [*break in, listen, steal, watch*] sans être aperçu; **to go** ou **remain ~** [*person*] rester inaperçu; [*cancer*] rester non décelé; [*crime, error*] rester non découvert.

undetermined /ˌʌndɪˈtɜːmɪnd/ *adj* **1** (unknown) indéterminé; **2** (unresolved) [*matter, problem*] indéterminé; [*outcome*] inconnu.

undeterred /ˌʌndɪˈtɜːd/ **I** *adj* **to be ~** ne pas être découragé; **to be ~ by sth/sb** ne pas se laisser démonter par qn/qch; **~, she resumed her speech** en rien démontée, elle continua son discours.
II *adv* [*continue, persevere, set out*] résolument.

undeveloped /ˌʌndɪˈveləpt/ *adj* [*person, fruit*] chétif/-ive; [*limb, muscle, organ*] atrophié; [*land, resource*] inexploité; [*film*] pas encore développé; [*idea, theory*] en état de germe; [*country*] sous-développé.

undeviating /ʌnˈdiːvɪeɪtɪŋ/ *adj* [*course, path*] sans détours; fig [*belief, loyalty*] immuable.

undiagnosed /ʌnˈdaɪəgnəʊzd/ *adj* **to be** ou **go ~** [*disease*] ne pas être diagnostiqué.

undid /ʌnˈdɪd/ *prét* ▶ **undo**.

undies○ /ˈʌndɪz/ *npl* sous-vêtements *mpl*, dessous *mpl*.

undigested /ˌʌndaɪˈdʒestɪd/ *adj* [*food*] qui n'a pas été digéré.

undignified /ʌnˈdɪgnɪfaɪd/ *adj* [*behaviour, fate, failure, name, person*] indigne; [*haste, language*] choquant; [*position*] inélégant; **it is ~ to do** il est indigne de faire.

undiluted /ˌʌndaɪˈljuːtɪd/ *adj* [*liquid, solution, version*] non dilué; fig [*admiration, pleasure*] sans retenue; [*contempt, hostility, passion*] sans mélange; [*nonsense*] pur et simple; [*Christianity, Marxism*] à l'état pur.

undiminished /ˌʌndɪˈmɪnɪʃt/ *adj* [*courage, enthusiasm, intelligence, power, stature*] intact; [*appeal*] toujours aussi fort; **he remains ~ by criticism** les critiques ne l'atteignent pas.

undimmed /ʌnˈdɪmd/ *adj* [*beauty, memory, mind, splendour*] intact; [*eyesight*] parfait; **her beauty is ~ by age/time** sa beauté est intacte malgré son âge/les années.

undiplomatic /ˌʌndɪpləˈmætɪk/ *adj* **he is ~** il manque de diplomatie; **his remark was ~** il n'a pas été très diplomate en disant cela; **it was ~ of you to say that** ce n'était pas diplomatique de votre part de dire cela.

undipped /ʌnˈdɪpt/ *adj* Aut **on** ou **with ~ headlights** en pleins phares.

undiscerning /ˌʌndɪˈsɜːnɪŋ/ *adj* qui manque de discernement (*after n*).

undischarged /ˌʌndɪsˈtʃɑːdʒd/ *adj* [*debt, fine*] non acquitté.

undischarged bankrupt *n* Jur failli/-e *m/f* non réhabilité/-e.

undisciplined /ʌnˈdɪsɪplɪnd/ *adj* indiscipliné.

undisclosed /ˌʌndɪsˈkləʊzd/ *adj* gen non révélé; Jur [*evidence*] non divulgué.

undisclosed principal *n* Jur commettant *m* dont le nom ne doit pas être divulgué.

undiscovered /ˌʌndɪsˈkʌvəd/ *adj* [*identity, secret*] non révélé; [*area, land*] inexploré; [*species*] inconnu; [*crime, document, hiding place*] non découvert; [*artist, talent*] méconnu; **to lie** ou **remain ~** rester sans être découvert.

undiscriminating /ˌʌndɪˈskrɪmɪneɪtɪŋ/ *adj* [*customer, observer, reader*] sans discernement; **to be ~** manquer de discernement.

undisguised /ˌʌndɪsˈgaɪzd/ *adj* [*anger, curiosity, envy, passion*] non déguisé (*after n*); **his envy/contempt was ~** il ne cachait pas son envie/mépris.

undismayed /ˌʌndɪsˈmeɪd/ *adj* **to be ~ at** ou **by sth** ne pas être découragé par qch; **~, she continued to speak** en rien découragée, elle a continué à parler.

undisputed /ˌʌndɪˈspjuːtɪd/ *adj* [*capital, champion, leader*] incontesté; [*fact, right*] incontestable.

undistinguished /ˌʌndɪˈstɪŋgwɪʃt/ *adj* [*achievement, career, building*] médiocre; [*appearance, person*] insignifiant.

undistributed /ˌʌndɪˈstrɪbjuːtɪd/ *adj* Comm, Fin non réparti.

undisturbed /ˌʌndɪˈstɜːbd/ **I** *adj* **1** (untouched) [*countryside*] inviolé; [*village*] paisible; **the ship had lain** ou **remained ~ for many years** le navire n'avait pas été dérangé pendant très longtemps; **2** (peaceful) [*sleep, night*] paisible, tranquille; **to work/play ~ by the noise** travailler/jouer sans être dérangé par le bruit.
II *adv* [*play, sleep, work*] tranquillement, paisiblement.

undivided /ˌʌndɪˈvaɪdɪd/ *adj* [*opposition*] unanime; [*loyalty*] entier/-ière; **to give sb one's ~ attention** accorder à qn toute son attention.

undo /ʌnˈduː/ *vtr* (*3ᵉ pers sg prés* **-does**; *prét* **-did**; *pp* **-done**) **1** (unfasten) défaire [*fastening, sewing, lock*]; ouvrir [*zip, parcel*]; **2** (cancel out) détruire [*good, work, effort*]; réparer [*harm*]; **3** (be downfall of) déconsidérer [*person*]; **4** Comput annuler.
IDIOMS **what's done cannot be undone** ce qui est fait est fait.

undocumented /ʌnˈdɒkjʊmentɪd/ *adj* **1** [*event*] sur lequel il n'existe pas de document; **2** US [*alien*] sans papiers.

undoing /ʌnˈduːɪŋ/ *n* littér perte *f*; **it proved to be his ~** cela a causé sa perte.

undone /ʌnˈdʌn/ **I** *pp* ▶ **undo**.
II *adj* **1** (not fastened) [*parcel, button, knot*] défait; **to come ~** [*buttons, laces*] se défaire; **2** (not done) **to leave sth ~** ne pas faire qch; **3**‡ ou littér (ruined) **I am ~!** je suis perdu!

undoubted /ʌnˈdaʊtɪd/ *adj* indubitable.

undoubtedly /ʌnˈdaʊtɪdlɪ/ *adv* indubitablement.

undramatic /ˌʌndrəˈmætɪk/ *adj* peu marquant.

undreamed-of /ʌnˈdriːmd ɒv/ *adj* gen inimaginable; **an ~ opportunity** une occasion rêvée.

undress /ˌʌnˈdres/ **I** *n* **in a state of ~** en petite tenue.
II *vtr* déshabiller.
III *vi* se déshabiller.
IV *v refl* **to ~ oneself** se déshabiller.

undressed /ʌnˈdrest/ *adj* **1** [*person*] déshabillé; **to get ~** se déshabiller; **2** Culin [*salade*] sans assaisonnement; **3** Constr [*metal, stone*] à nu.

undrinkable /ʌnˈdrɪŋkəbl/ *adj* **1** (unpleasant) imbuvable; **2** (dangerous) non potable.

undue /ʌnˈdjuː, US -ˈduː/ *adj* excessif/-ive.

undulate /ˈʌndjʊleɪt, US -dʒʊ-/ **I** *vi* onduler.
II undulating *pres p adj* [*movement*] sinueux/-euse; [*surface, landscape*] onduleux/-euse; [*plants*] ondoyant.

undulation /ˌʌndjʊˈleɪʃn, US -dʒʊ-/ *n* **1** (bump) courbe *f*; **2** (wavy motion) ondulation *f*.

undulatory /ˈʌndjʊlətərɪ, US ˈʌndʒʊlətɔːrɪ/ *adj* oscillant.

unduly /ˌʌnˈdjuːlɪ, US -ˈduːlɪ/ *adv* [*affected, concerned, optimistic, surprised, inclined*] excessivement; [*flatter, favour, neglect, worry*] outre mesure.

undying /ʌnˈdaɪɪŋ/ *adj* [*love*] éternel/-elle.

unearned /ʌnˈɜːnd/ *adj* **1** (undeserved) immérité; **2** Tax **~ income** rentes *fpl*.

unearth /ʌnˈɜːθ/ *vtr* **1** Archeol exhumer [*remains, pottery*]; **2** fig (find) dénicher [*person, object*]; découvrir [*fact, evidence*].

unearthly /ʌnˈɜːθlɪ/ *adj* **1** [*apparition, light*] surnaturel/-elle; [*cry, silence*] étrange; [*beauty*] immatériel/-ielle; [*sight*] irréel/-elle; **2** (unreasonable) **at an ~ hour** à une heure indue.

unease /ʌnˈiːz/ *n* ¢ **1** (worry) inquiétude *f*, appréhension *f* (**about, at** au sujet de); **2** (dissatisfaction) malaise *m*; **social/economic ~** un malaise social/économique.

uneasily /ʌnˈiːzɪlɪ/ *adv* **1** (anxiously) avec inquiétude; **2** (uncomfortably) avec gêne; **3** (with difficulty) avec difficulté.

uneasiness /ʌnˈiːzɪnɪs/ *n* **1** (worry) appréhension *f* (**about** au sujet de); **2** (dissatisfaction) malaise *m*; **there is some ~** il y a un certain malaise (**about** en ce qui concerne).

uneasy /ʌnˈiːzɪ/ *adj* **1** (worried) [*person*] inquiet/-iète (**about, at** au sujet de) [*conscience*] pas tranquille; **to grow ~** s'inquiéter; **2** (precarious) [*compromise*] difficile; [*alliance, balance, peace*] boiteux/-euse; [*combination, mixture*] indigeste; [*silence*] gêné; **3** (worrying) [*feeling, suspicion*] de malaise; [*night, sleep*] agité; **an ~ feeling** ou **sense of danger** un sentiment désagréable de danger; **4** (ill at ease) mal à l'aise.

uneatable /ʌnˈiːtəbl/ *adj* immangeable.

uneaten /ʌnˈiːtn/ *adj* non mangé.

uneconomic /ˌʌnˌiːkəˈnɒmɪk, -ˌekə-/ *adj* pas rentable.

uneconomical /ˌʌnˌiːkəˈnɒmɪkl, -ˌekə-/ *adj* **1** (wasteful) [*person, use*] pas économique; **2** (not profitable) pas rentable.

unedifying /ʌnˈedɪfaɪɪŋ/ *adj* peu édifiant.

unedited /ʌnˈedɪtɪd/ *adj* inédit.

uneducated /ʌnˈedʒʊkeɪtɪd/ *adj* **1** (without education) [*person*] sans instruction; **2** (vulgar) péj [*person, speech, writing*] inculte; [*accent, tastes*] commun.

unemotional /ˌʌnɪˈməʊʃənl/ *adj* [*person, approach, face*] impassible, insensible pej; [*reunion*] froid; [*account, analysis*] qui n'appelle pas aux sentiments.

unemotionally /ˌʌnɪˈməʊʃənəlɪ/ *adv* [*say, behave*] avec indifférence; [*analyse, describe*] froidement.

unemployable /ˌʌnɪmˈplɔɪəbl/ *adj* incapable d'assurer un emploi.

unemployed /ˌʌnɪmˈplɔɪd/ **I** *n* **the ~** (+ *v pl*) les chômeurs *mpl*.
II *adj* **1** (out of work) au chômage, sans emploi; **~ people** chômeurs *mpl*; **to register oneself as ~** s'inscrire au chômage; **2** Fin [*capital*] inutilisé.

unemployment /ˌʌnɪmˈplɔɪmənt/ *n* chômage *m*; **seasonal/youth ~** chômage *m*

saisonnier/des jeunes; **with ~ at 20%** avec un chômage de 20%.
unemployment: **~ benefit** GB, **~ compensation** US allocations *fpl* de chômage; **~ figures** *npl* chiffres *mpl* du chômage; **~ level**, **~ rate** *n* taux *m* de chômage.
unencumbered /ˌʌnɪnˈkʌmbəd/ *adj* pas encombré (**by, with** par).
unending /ʌnˈendɪŋ/ *adj* sans fin.
unendorsed /ˌʌnɪnˈdɔːst/ *adj* [*cheque*] non endossé.
unendurable /ˌʌnɪnˈdjʊərəbl, US -ˈdʊər-/ *adj* intolérable.
unenforceable /ˌʌnɪnˈfɔːsəbl/ *adj* inapplicable.
un-English /ʌnˈɪŋglɪʃ/ *adj* peu anglais.
unenlightened /ˌʌnɪnˈlaɪtnd/ *adj* borné.
unenterprising /ʌnˈentəpraɪzɪŋ/ *adj* [*person, organization, behaviour*] sans initiative; [*decision, policy*] timide.
unenthusiastic /ˌʌnɪnˌθjuːzɪˈæstɪk, US -ˌθuːz-/ *adj* peu enthousiaste (**about** au sujet de).
unenthusiastically /ˌʌnɪnˌθjuːzɪˈæstɪklɪ, US -ˌθuːz-/ *adv* sans enthousiasme.
unenviable /ʌnˈenvɪəbl/ *adj* peu enviable.
unequal /ʌnˈiːkwəl/ *adj* **1** (not equal) [*amounts, parts, size, contest, pay, struggle, division*] inégal; **2** (inadequate) **to be ~ to** ne pas être à la hauteur de [*task*].
unequalled, **unequaled** US /ʌnˈiːkwəld/ *adj* [*achievement, quality, record*] inégalé; [*person*] incomparable (**as** en tant que).
unequally /ʌnˈiːkwəlɪ/ *adv* de manière inégale.
unequivocal /ˌʌnɪˈkwɪvəkl/ *adj* [*person, declaration*] explicite; [*attitude, answer, belief, meaning, pleasure, support*] sans équivoque.
unequivocally /ˌʌnɪˈkwɪvəkəlɪ/ *adv* explicitement.
unerring /ʌnˈɜːrɪŋ/ *adj* infaillible.
unerringly /ʌnˈɜːrɪŋlɪ/ *adv* [*accurate*] de manière infaillible; [*judge*] de manière infaillible; [*aim, go, head for*] droit.
Unesco, UNESCO /juːˈneskəʊ/ *pr n* (*abrév* = **United Nations Educational, Scientific and Cultural Organization**) UNESCO *f*.
unescorted /ˌʌnɪˈskɔːtɪd/ *adj* gen, Naut sans escorte.
unesthetic US *adj* = **unaesthetic**.
unethical /ʌnˈeθɪkl/ *adj* **1** gen, Comm contraire à la morale (**to do** de faire); **2** Med contraire à la déontologie (**to do** de faire).
unethically /ʌnˈeθɪklɪ/ *adv* de façon malhonnête.
uneven /ʌnˈiːvn/ *adj* **1** (variable) [*colouring, hem, pattern, pressure, results, rhythm, speed, teeth*] irrégulier/-ière; [*contest, performance, quality, surface*] inégal; [*voice*] tremblant; **2** Sport **~ bars** barres *fpl* asymétriques.
unevenly /ʌnˈiːvnlɪ/ *adv* [*distribute, affect, cover*] de façon inégale; [*hang, function, develop*] de façon irrégulière.
unevenness /ʌnˈiːvənnɪs/ *n* (of surface, edge, rhythm) irrégularité *f*; (of voice) tremblement *m*; (of contest) inégalité *f*.
uneventful /ˌʌnɪˈventfl/ *adj* [*day, occasion, life, career*] ordinaire; [*journey, period*] sans histoires; [*place*] où il ne se passe rien.
uneventfully /ʌnɪˈventfəlɪ/ *adv* sans incident.
unexcelled /ˌʌnɪkˈseld/ *adj* sans égal.
unexceptionable /ˌʌnɪkˈsepʃənəbl/ *adj* [*behaviour, attitude*] irréprochable; [*remark*] indiscutable.
unexceptionably /ˌʌnɪkˈsepʃənəblɪ/ *adv* sout de façon irréprochable.
unexceptional /ˌʌnɪkˈsepʃənl/ *adj* qui n'a rien d'exceptionnel.
unexciting /ˌʌnɪkˈsaɪtɪŋ/ *adj* sans intérêt.
unexpected /ˌʌnɪkˈspektɪd/ **I** *n* **the ~** l'imprévu *m*.
II *adj* [*arrival, development, danger, event, expense, question, success*] imprévu; [*ally, choice, gift, outcome, announcement*] inattendu; [*death, illness*] inopiné.
unexpectedly /ˌʌnɪkˈspektɪdlɪ/ *adv* [*happen*] à l'improviste; [*large, small, fast*] étonnamment; **~, the phone rang** de façon inattendue, le téléphone a sonné.
unexplained /ˌʌnɪkˈspleɪnd/ *adj* inexpliqué.
unexploded /ˌʌnɪkˈspləʊdɪd/ *adj* [*bomb*] qui n'a pas explosé.
unexploited /ˌʌnɪkˈsplɔɪtɪd/ *adj* inexploité.
unexplored /ˌʌnɪkˈsplɔːd/ *adj* inexploré.
unexposed /ˌʌnɪkˈspəʊzd/ *adj* Phot vierge.
unexpressed /ˌʌnɪkˈsprest/ *adj* inexprimé.
unexpurgated /ʌnˈekspəgeɪtɪd/ *adj* non expurgé.
unfading /ʌnˈfeɪdɪŋ/ *adj* qui ne meurt pas.
unfailing /ʌnˈfeɪlɪŋ/ *adj* [*support*] fidèle; [*kindness, good temper, optimism*] à toute épreuve; [*efforts*] constant; [*source*] intarissable; [*supply*] inépuisable.
unfair /ʌnˈfeə(r)/ *adj* [*person, action, decision, advantage, comparison, treatment*] injuste (**to, on** envers; **to do** de faire); [*play, tactics*] irrégulier/-ière; Comm [*trading*] frauduleux/-euse; [*competition*] déloyal; **it is ~ that he should go** ou **for him to go** ce n'est pas juste qu'il aille.
unfair dismissal *n* Jur licenciement *m* abusif.
unfairly /ʌnˈfeəlɪ/ *adv* [*treat, condemn*] injustement; [*play*] irrégulièrement; [*critical*] injustement; **rates are ~ high** les loyers sont excessivement chers; **to be ~ dismissed** Jur faire l'objet d'un licenciement abusif.
unfairness /ʌnˈfeənɪs/ *n* injustice *f*.
unfaithful /ʌnˈfeɪθfl/ *adj* [*partner*] infidèle (**to** à).
unfaithfully /ʌnˈfeɪθfəlɪ/ *adv* de façon déloyale.
unfaithfulness /ʌnˈfeɪθflnɪs/ *n* infidélité *f*.
unfaltering /ʌnˈfɔːltərɪŋ/ *adj* [*step, voice*] assuré; [*devotion, loyalty*] à toute épreuve.
unfalteringly /ʌnˈfɔːltərɪŋlɪ/ *adv* sans hésitation.
unfamiliar /ˌʌnfəˈmɪlɪə(r)/ *adj* **1** (strange) [*face, name, place, surroundings*] pas familier/-ière (**to** à); [*appearance, concept, feeling, problem, situation*] inhabituel/-elle (**to** à); [*artist, book, music, subject*] mal connu; **it's not ~ to me** ça me dit quelque chose; **2** (without working knowledge) **to be ~ with sth** ne pas être familiarisé avec qch.
unfamiliarity /ˌʌnfəmɪlɪˈærətɪ/ *n* **1** (strangeness) caractère *m* insolite, caractère *m* peu familier; **2** (lack of knowledge) **his ~ with sth** sa mauvaise connaissance de qch.
unfashionable /ʌnˈfæʃənəbl/ *adj* qui n'est pas à la mode; **it's ~ to do** ce n'est pas chic de faire.
unfasten /ʌnˈfɑːsn/ *vtr* défaire [*clothing, button*]; ouvrir [*bag, zip*]; **to ~ sth from sth** détacher qch de qch; **to come ~ed** se défaire.
unfathomable /ʌnˈfæðəməbl/ *adj* littér insondable liter.
unfathomed /ʌnˈfæðəmd/ *adj* [*ocean*] insondé; [*motive, mystery*] inexpliqué.
unfavourable /ʌnˈfeɪvərəbl/ *adj* défavorable (**for sth** à qch; **to** à); Fin [*rate*] désavantageux/-euse.
unfavourably /ʌnˈfeɪvərəblɪ/ *adv* de façon défavorable.
unfazed○ /ʌnˈfeɪzd/ *adj* imperturbable (**by** devant).
unfeeling /ʌnˈfiːlɪŋ/ *adj* [*person*] insensible (**towards** envers); [*remark*] dépourvu de tact; [*attitude, behaviour*] froid.
unfeelingly /ʌnˈfiːlɪŋlɪ/ *adv* froidement.
unfeigned /ʌnˈfeɪnd/ *adj* sincère.
unfeignedly /ʌnˈfeɪnɪdlɪ/ *adv* [*delighted, distressed*] sincèrement.
unfeminine /ʌnˈfemɪnɪn/ *adj* pas féminin.
unfettered /ʌnˈfetəd/ *adj* [*liberty, right, competition, market*] sans entraves; [*emotion, expression, power*] sans retenue.
unfilial /ʌnˈfɪlɪəl/ *adj* peu filial.
unfilled /ʌnˈfɪld/ *adj* [*post*] à pourvoir, vacant; **~ vacancy** poste *m* à pourvoir ou vacant.
unfinished /ʌnˈfɪnɪʃt/ *adj* [*work, product, music, novel*] inachevé; [*matter*] en cours; **we still have some ~ business** nous avons encore des choses à régler.
unfit /ʌnˈfɪt/ **I** *adj* **1** (unhealthy) (ill) malade; (out of condition) **I'm ~** physiquement, je ne suis pas en forme; **2** (sub-standard) [*housing*] inadéquat; [*pitch, road*] impraticable (**for** à); **~ for human habitation/consumption** impropre à l'habitation/la consommation humaine; **the field is ~ for play** le terrain est impraticable; **~ to eat** (dangerous) impropre à la consommation; **3** (unsuitable) [*parent*] inapte; **~ for work/military service** inapte au travail/au service militaire; **~ to run the country** inapte à gouverner le pays; **he's ~ to be a teacher** il ne devrait pas être professeur; **4** Jur incapable; **to be ~ to plead/give evidence** être inapte à se défendre/témoigner.
II *vtr* (*p prés etc* **-tt-**) sout **to ~ sb for sth** rendre qn inapte à qch.
unfitness /ʌnˈfɪtnɪs/ *n* Jur incapacité *f* (**to do** à faire).
unfitted /ʌnˈfɪtɪd/ *adj* sout **to be ~ for sth** ne pas être fait pour qch.
unfitting /ʌnˈfɪtɪŋ/ *adj* sout [*conduct, end, language*] inadapté; **it's ~ that** c'est inconvenant que (+ *subj*).
unflagging /ʌnˈflægɪŋ/ *adj* [*energy, attention*] infatigable; [*interest*] inlassable.
unflaggingly /ʌnˈflægɪŋlɪ/ *adv* inlassablement.
unflappable○ /ʌnˈflæpəbl/ *adj* imperturbable.
unflattering /ʌnˈflætərɪŋ/ *adj* [*clothes, hairstyle, portrait, description*] peu flatteur/-euse; **to be ~ to sb** [*clothes, hairstyle*] ne pas avantager qn; [*portrait, description*] ne pas flatter qn.
unflatteringly /ʌnˈflætərɪŋlɪ/ *adv* [*describe, portray*] d'une manière peu flatteuse.
unfledged /ʌnˈfledʒd/ *adj* **1 ~ bird** oisillon *m* sans duvet; **2** fig [*person*] sans expérience; [*movement, project*] à ses débuts.
unflinching /ʌnˈflɪntʃɪŋ/ *adj* **1** (steadfast) [*stare*] impassible; [*courage, determination*] à toute épreuve; [*commitment, person*] inébranlable; **2** (merciless) [*account*] impitoyable.
unflinchingly /ʌnˈflɪntʃɪŋlɪ/ *adv* [*fight*] sans flancher; [*persevere*] inébranlablement; **~ determined/resolute** d'une détermination/d'une fermeté à toute épreuve.
unflyable /ʌnˈflaɪəbl/ *adj* [*aircraft*] incapable de voler.
unfold /ʌnˈfəʊld/ **I** *vtr* **1** (open) déplier [*paper, cloth, chair*]; déployer [*wings*]; décroiser [*arms*]; **2** fig (reveal) dévoiler [*plan, intention*].
II *vi* **1** [*deckchair, map*] se déplier; [*flower, leaf*] s'ouvrir; **2** fig [*scene*] se dérouler; [*plot, mystery*] se dévoiler; [*beauty*] s'épanouir.
unforced /ʌnˈfɔːst/ *adj* [*style, humour*] spontané; [*error*] injustifié.
unforeseeable /ˌʌnfɔːˈsiːəbl/ *adj* imprévisible.
unforeseen /ˌʌnfɔːˈsiːn/ *adj* imprévu.
unforgettable /ˌʌnfəˈgetəbl/ *adj* inoubliable.
unforgettably /ˌʌnfəˈgetəblɪ/ *adv* mémorablement.
unforgivable /ˌʌnfəˈgɪvəbl/ *adj* impardonnable; **it was ~ of them to do** il était impardonnable de leur part de faire.
unforgivably /ˌʌnfəˈgɪvəblɪ/ *adv* [*forget, attack*] de manière impardonnable; **~**

rude/biased d'une grossièreté/d'un parti-pris impardonnable.

unforgiven /ˌʌnfəˈgɪvn/ *adj* impardonné.

unforgiving /ˌʌnfəˈgɪvɪŋ/ *adj* impitoyable.

unforgotten /ˌʌnfəˈgɒtn/ *adj* inoublié.

unformed /ʌnˈfɔːmd/ *adj* [*character*] non encore formé; [*idea, belief*] informe; **his personality is still ~** sa personnalité n'est pas encore formée.

unforthcoming /ˌʌnfɔːθˈkʌmɪŋ/ *adj* [*person, reply*] réservé; **to be ~ about** se montrer réservé au sujet de [*changes, money*].

unfortified /ʌnˈfɔːtɪfaɪd/ *adj* non fortifié.

unfortunate /ʌnˈfɔːtʃənət/ **I** *n* malheureux/-euse *m/f*.
II *adj* **1** (pitiable) [*person, situation*] malheureux/-euse; **2** (regrettable) [*matter, incident, choice*] malencontreux/-euse; [*remark*] fâcheux/-euse; **it was ~ that** il était malheureux que (+ *subj*); **how ~** comme c'est dommage; **3** (unlucky) [*person, loss, attempt*] malchanceux/-euse; **to be ~ enough to do** avoir la malchance de faire.

unfortunately /ʌnˈfɔːtʃənətlɪ/ *adv* [*begin, end*] fâcheusement; [*worded*] malencontreusement; **~, she forgot** malheureusement, elle a oublié; **~ not** il semblerait que non.

unfounded /ʌnˈfaʊndɪd/ *adj* sans fondement.

unframed /ʌnˈfreɪmd/ *adj* sans cadre.

unfreeze /ʌnˈfriːz/ (*prét* **-froze**; *pp* **-frozen**) **I** *vtr* **1** faire dégeler [*lock, pipe*]; **2** Fin libérer [*prices*]; débloquer [*assets, loan*]; **3** Comput libérer.
II *vi* [*pipe, lock*] dégeler.

unfreezing /ʌnˈfriːzɪŋ/ *n* Fin (of prices) libération *f*; (of assets, loan) déblocage *m*.

unfrequented /ˌʌnfrɪˈkwentɪd/ *adj* peu fréquenté.

unfriendliness /ʌnˈfrendlɪnɪs/ *n* (of person) froideur *f*; (of place) caractère *m* inhospitalier.

unfriendly /ʌnˈfrendlɪ/ **I** *adj* [*person, attitude, behaviour*] peu amical, inamical; [*reception*] hostile; [*place, climate*] inhospitalier/-ière; [*remark*] malveillant; [*product, innovation*] nocif/-ive; **it was ~ of him to do** c'était de la malveillance de sa part de faire; **to be ~ towards sb** faire preuve d'hostilité à l'égard de qn.
II -unfriendly (*dans composés*) **environmentally-~** nuisible à l'environnement; **user-~** d'utilisation difficile.

unfrock /ʌnˈfrɒk/ *vtr* défroquer.

unfroze /ʌnˈfrəʊz/ *prét* ▶ **unfreeze**.

unfrozen /ʌnˈfrəʊzn/ *pp* ▶ **unfreeze**.

unfruitful /ʌnˈfruːtfl/ *adj* infructueux/-euse.

unfruitfully /ʌnˈfruːtfəlɪ/ *adv* de façon infructueuse.

unfruitfulness /ʌnˈfruːtflnɪs/ *n* (of discussion, land) stérilité *f*.

unfulfilled /ˌʌnfʊlˈfɪld/ *adj* [*ambition, potential*] non réalisé; [*desire, need*] inassouvi; [*promise*] non tenu; [*condition*] non rempli; [*prophecy*] inaccompli; **to feel ~** [*person*] se sentir insatisfait.

unfulfilling /ˌʌnfʊlˈfɪlɪŋ/ *adj* [*occupation*] ingrat.

unfunny /ʌnˈfʌnɪ/ *adj* [*humour, joke, comedian*] qui ne fait rire personne; **I find that distinctly ~** je ne trouve pas ça drôle du tout.

unfurl /ʌnˈfɜːl/ littér **I** *vtr* dérouler [*banner, sail*]; ouvrir [*parasol*].
II *vi* se déployer.

unfurnished /ʌnˈfɜːnɪʃt/ *adj* [*accommodation*] non meublé; **the house is ~** la maison n'est pas meublée.

ungainliness /ʌnˈgeɪnlɪnɪs/ *n* gaucherie *f*.

ungainly /ʌnˈgeɪnlɪ/ *adj* gauche, maladroit.

ungallant /ʌnˈgælənt/ *adj* peu galant; **it was ~ of him to do it** ce n'était pas très galant de sa part de le faire.

ungenerous /ʌnˈdʒenərəs/ *adj* **1** (mean) [*person*] peu généreux/-euse (**to** envers); **2** (unsympathetic) [*person, attitude*] dur (**towards** envers); **it was ~ of you to do** ce n'était pas très charitable de ta part de faire.

ungenerously /ʌnˈdʒenərəslɪ/ *adv* **1** (meanly) par manque de générosité; **2** (unkindly) durement.

ungentlemanly /ʌnˈdʒentlmənlɪ/ *adj* discourtois (**of** de la part de).

ungetatable○ /ˌʌngetˈætəbl/ *adj* inaccessible.

unglazed /ʌnˈgleɪzd/ *adj* **1** [*window*] sans vitres; **2** [*pottery*] non vernissé.

unglue /ʌnˈgluː/ *vtr* **1** (unstick) décoller [*envelope, stamp*]; **to come ~d** se décoller; **2**○ US (upset) mettre [qn] dans tous ses états; **to come ~d** craquer○.

ungodliness /ʌnˈgɒdlɪnɪs/ *n* impiété *f*; **despite the ~ of the hour** hum en dépit de l'heure.

ungodly /ʌnˈgɒdlɪ/ *adj* [*person, act, behaviour*] impie; **at some ~ hour** à une heure indue.

ungovernable /ʌnˈgʌvənəbl/ *adj* **1** [*country, people*] ingouvernable; **2** [*desire, anger*] indomptable.

ungracious /ʌnˈgreɪʃəs/ *adj* désobligeant (**of** de la part de).

ungraciously /ʌnˈgreɪʃəslɪ/ *adv* de manière désobligeante.

ungraciousness /ʌnˈgreɪʃəsnɪs/ *n* désobligeance *f*.

ungrammatical /ˌʌngrəˈmætɪkl/ *adj* incorrect.

ungrammatically /ʌngrəˈmætɪklɪ/ *adv* de manière incorrecte.

ungrateful /ʌnˈgreɪtfl/ *adj* ingrat (**of** de la part de; **towards** envers).

ungratefully /ʌnˈgreɪtfəlɪ/ *adv* de manière ingrate.

ungreen /ʌnˈgriːn/ *adj* Ecol [*person*] peu sensibilisé aux problèmes de l'environnement; [*product*] nuisible à l'environnement.

ungrudging /ʌnˈgrʌdʒɪŋ/ *adj* [*support*] inconditionnel/-elle; [*praise*] sincère.

ungrudgingly /ʌnˈgrʌdʒɪŋlɪ/ *adv* [*support*] inconditionnellement; [*praise*] sincèrement, avec sincérité; [*help*] sans rechigner.

unguarded /ʌnˈgɑːdɪd/ *adj* **1** (unprotected) [*prisoner, frontier*] sans surveillance; **2** (careless) [*remark, criticism*] irréfléchi; **in an ~ moment** dans un moment d'inattention.

unguent /ˈʌŋgwənt/ *n* littér onguent *m*.

ungulate /ˈʌŋgjʊlət/ *n, adj* ongulé/-e (*m/f*).

unhallowed /ʌnˈhæləʊd/ *adj* [*ground, union*] non consacré.

unhampered /ʌnˈhæmpəd/ *adj* [*narrative*] dégagé (**by** de); **~ by** sans être encombré par [*luggage*]; sans être gêné or entravé par [*protocol, red tape*].

unhand /ʌnˈhænd/ *vtr* littér ou hum lâcher.

unhappily /ʌnˈhæpɪlɪ/ *adv* **1** (miserably) [*say, stare, walk*] d'un air malheureux; **~ married** malheureux/-euse en mariage; **2** (unfortunately) malheureusement; **3** (inappropriately) malencontreusement.

unhappiness /ʌnˈhæpɪnɪs/ *n* **1** (misery) tristesse *f*; **2** (dissatisfaction) mécontentement *m* (**about, with** au sujet de).

unhappy /ʌnˈhæpɪ/ *adj* **1** (miserable) [*person, childhood*] malheureux/-euse; [*face, occasion*] triste; **2** (dissatisfied) [*person, government, company*] mécontent; **to be ~ about** ou **with sth** ne pas être satisfait de qch; **3** (concerned) inquiet/-iète (**about** à propos de); **to be ~ about doing** ne pas aimer faire; **to be ~ at the idea/suggestion that** être contrarié par l'idée/la suggestion que; **4** (unfortunate) [*situation, coincidence, remark, choice*] malheureux/-euse.

unharmed /ʌnˈhɑːmd/ *adj* [*person*] indemne; [*building, object*] intact.

unharness /ʌnˈhɑːnɪs/ *vtr* dételer [*horse*] (**from** de).

unhealthy /ʌnˈhelθɪ/ *adj* **1** Med, fig [*person, complexion, cough*] maladif/-ive; [*economy, climate, diet*] malsain; [*conditions*] insalubre; **2** (unwholesome) [*interest, desire*] malsain.

unheard /ʌnˈhɜːd/ *adv* **we entered/left ~** nous sommes entrés/partis sans qu'on nous entende; **her pleas went ~** ses prières restèrent lettre morte.

unheard-of /ʌnˈhɜːdɒv/ *adj* **1** (shocking) [*behaviour, suggestion*] inouï; **2** (previously unknown) [*levels, proportions, price*] record *inv*; [*actor, brand, firm*] inconnu; **to be previously ~** être inconnu jusqu'alors.

unheated /ʌnˈhiːtɪd/ *adj* non chauffé.

unhedged /ʌnˈhedʒd/ *adj* sans haies.

unheeded /ʌnˈhiːdɪd/ *adj* **to go ~** [*warning, plea*] rester vain.

unheeding /ʌnˈhiːdɪŋ/ *adj* littér [*world, crowd*] indifférent; **they went by, ~** ils passaient, indifférents.

unhelpful /ʌnˈhelpfl/ *adj* [*assistant, employee*] peu serviable; [*witness*] peu coopératif/-ive; [*advice, remark*] qui n'apporte rien d'utile; [*attitude*] peu obligeante; **it is ~ of him to do** ce n'est guère serviable de sa part de faire.

unhelpfully /ʌnˈhelpfəlɪ/ *adv* de manière peu coopérative.

unheralded /ʌnˈherəldɪd/ **I** *adj* [*arrival*] inopiné.
II *adv* [*arrive*] sans tambour ni trompette.

unhesitating /ʌnˈhezɪteɪtɪŋ/ *adj* spontané.

unhesitatingly /ʌnˈhezɪteɪtɪŋlɪ/ *adv* sans hésiter.

unhide /ʌnˈhaɪd/ *vtr* (*prét* **-hid**; *pp* **-hidden**) Comput afficher [*window*].

unhindered /ʌnˈhɪndəd/ **I** *adj* [*access*] libre; [*freedom*] total; **~ by** sans être entravé par [*rules, regulations*]; sans être encombré par [*luggage*].
II *adv* [*work, continue*] librement.

unhinge /ʌnˈhɪndʒ/ *vtr* (*p prés* **-hingeing**) **1** lit enlever [qch] de ses gonds [*door*]; **2**○ fig déstabiliser [*person, mind*].

unhinged○ /ʌnˈhɪndʒd/ *adj* [*person, mind*] dérangé.

unhitch /ʌnˈhɪtʃ/ *vtr* dételer [*horse*]; détacher [*rope*].

unholy /ʌnˈhəʊlɪ/ *adj* **1** (shocking) [*alliance, pact*] contre nature; **2** (horrendous) [*din, mess, row*] épouvantable; **3** (profane) [*behaviour, thought*] impie.

unhook /ʌnˈhʊk/ *vtr* dégrafer [*bra, skirt*]; décrocher [*picture, coat*] (**from** de); **to come ~ed** [*clothing*] se dégrafer; [*picture*] se décrocher.

unhoped-for /ʌnˈhəʊptfɔː(r)/ *adj* inespéré.

unhopeful /ʌnˈhəʊpfl/ *adj* [*person*] pessimiste; [*situation*] guère encourageant; [*outlook, start*] guère prometteur/-euse.

unhorse /ʌnˈhɔːs/ *vtr* désarçonner [*rider*].

unhurried /ʌnˈhʌrɪd/ *adj* [*person, manner, voice*] posé; [*journey, pace, meal*] tranquille.

unhurriedly /ʌnˈhʌrɪdlɪ/ *adv* [*walk, prepare*] sans se presser; [*discuss*] posément.

unhurt /ʌnˈhɜːt/ *adj* indemne.

unhygienic /ˌʌnhaɪˈdʒiːnɪk/ *adj* [*conditions*] insalubre; [*way, method*] peu hygiénique.

unicameral /juːnɪˈkæmərəl/ *adj* Pol monocaméral.

UNICEF /ˈjuːnɪsef/ *n* (*abrév* = **United Nations Children's Fund**) UNICEF *m*, FISE *m*.

unicellular /juːnɪˈseljʊlə(r)/ *adj* unicellulaire.

unicorn /ˈjuːnɪkɔːn/ *n* licorne *f*.

unicycle /ˈjuːnɪsaɪkl/ *n* monocycle *m*.

unidentified /ˌʌnaɪˈdentɪfaɪd/ *adj* non identifié.

unidirectional /juːnɪdɪˈrekʃənl, juːnɪdaɪ-/ *adj* unidirectionnel/-elle.

unification /juːnɪfɪˈkeɪʃn/ *n* unification *f* (**of** de).

UNIFIL /ˈjuːnɪfɪl/ *n* (*abrév* = **United Nations International Force in Leba-**

non) FINUL *f*, Force *f* intérimaire des Nations unies au Liban.

uniform /ˈjuːnɪfɔːm/ **I** *n* uniforme *m*; **out of ~** gen en tenue de ville; Mil en civil.
II *adj* [*temperature, acceleration*] constant; [*shape, size, colour*] identique; **~ in appearance** d'apparence identique.
III *modif* [*jacket, trousers etc*] d'uniforme.

uniformed /ˈjuːnɪfɔːmd/ *adj* en uniforme.

uniformity /ˌjuːnɪˈfɔːmətɪ/ *n* uniformité *f*.

uniformly /ˈjuːnɪfɔːmlɪ/ *adv* uniformément.

unify /ˈjuːnɪfaɪ/ *vtr* unifier.

unifying /ˈjuːnɪfaɪɪŋ/ *adj* [*factor, feature, principle*] de cohésion.

unilateral /ˌjuːnɪˈlætrəl/ *adj* unilatéral.

unilateralism /ˌjuːnɪˈlætrəlɪzəm/ *n* politique *f* du désarmement unilatéral.

unilateralist /ˌjuːnɪˈlætrəlɪst/ **I** *n* partisan/-e *m/f* du désarmement unilatéral.
II *adj* **~ policy** politique *f* de désarmement unilatéral.

unilaterally /ˌjuːnɪˈlætrəlɪ/ *adv* unilatéralement.

unimaginable /ˌʌnɪˈmædʒɪnəbl/ *adj* inimaginable.

unimaginably /ˌʌnɪˈmædʒɪnəblɪ/ *adv* incroyablement.

unimaginative /ˌʌnɪˈmædʒɪnətɪv/ *adj* [*person*] sans imagination; [*style, production*] sans originalité; **to be ~** [*person, style*] manquer d'imagination.

unimaginatively /ˌʌnɪˈmædʒɪnətɪvlɪ/ *adv* [*talk, write, describe*] platement; [*captain, manage*] sans brio.

unimaginativeness /ˌʌnɪˈmædʒɪnətɪvnɪs/ *n* (of style, speech) platitude *f*; (of leadership) manque *m* d'imagination.

unimpaired /ˌʌnɪmˈpeəd/ *adj* intact.

unimpeachable /ˌʌnɪmˈpiːtʃəbl/ *adj* [*morals, character*] irréprochable; Jur [*witness*] non récusable.

unimpeded /ˌʌnɪmˈpiːdɪd/ *adj* [*access, influx*] libre; **the work continued ~** le travail a continué sans entraves; **to be ~ by sth** ne pas être entravé par qch.

unimportant /ˌʌnɪmˈpɔːtnt/ *adj* [*question, feature*] sans importance (**for, to** pour).

unimposing /ˌʌnɪmˈpəʊzɪŋ/ *adj* [*person, personality*] effacé; [*building*] ordinaire.

unimpressed /ˌʌnɪmˈprest/ *adj* (by person, performance) peu enthousiaste; (by argument) guère convaincu; **to be ~ by** être peu impressionné par [*person, performance*]; n'être guère convaincu par [*argument*].

unimpressive /ˌʌnɪmˈpresɪv/ *adj* [*sight, building, person*] quelconque; [*figures, start, performance*] médiocre.

unimproved /ˌʌnɪmˈpruːvd/ *adj* **1** gen **to be** ou **remain ~** [*situation, health*] rester stationnaire; [*outlook*] rester sombre; [*team, work*] rester médiocre; **2** Agric [*land, pasture*] non amendé.

unincorporated /ˌʌnɪnˈkɔːpəreɪtɪd/ *adj* [*society, business*] non incorporé.

uninfluential /ˌʌnɪnflʊˈenʃl/ *adj* [*person, viewpoint*] sans influence; **to be ~** ne pas avoir d'influence.

uninformative /ˌʌnɪnˈfɔːmətɪv/ *adj* [*report, reply*] qui n'apporte rien; **to be ~** ne rien apporter.

uninformed /ˌʌnɪnˈfɔːmd/ **I the ~** (+ *v pl*) le profane (+ *v sg*).
II *adj* [*person*] sous-informé (**about** quant à); **the ~ reader** le non-spécialiste.

uninhabitable /ˌʌnɪnˈhæbɪtəbl/ *adj* inhabitable.

uninhabited /ˌʌnɪnˈhæbɪtɪd/ *adj* inhabité.

uninhibited /ˌʌnɪnˈhɪbɪtɪd/ *adj* [*attitude*] direct; [*person*] sans complexes (**about** en ce qui concerne); [*dance, performance*] sans retenue; [*remarks*] sans retenue; [*sexuality*] débordant; [*outburst*] incontrôlé; [*desire, impulse*] non refréné; **to be ~ about doing** n'avoir aucun complexe à faire.

uninhibitedly /ˌʌnɪnˈhɪbɪtɪdlɪ/ *adv* sans retenue.

uninitiated /ˌʌnɪˈnɪʃɪeɪtɪd/ **I** *n* **the ~** (+ *v pl*) le profane (+ *v sg*).
II *adj* [*person*] non initié (**into** dans).

uninjured /ʌnˈɪndʒəd/ *adj* indemne; **to escape ~** sortir indemne.

uninspired /ˌʌnɪnˈspaɪəd/ *adj* [*approach, team, times*] terne; [*performance*] honnête; [*budget, syllabus*] sans imagination; **to be ~** [*writer, team*] manquer d'inspiration; [*strategy, project*] manquer d'imagination.

uninspiring /ˌʌnɪnˈspaɪərɪŋ/ *adj* [*person, performance, prospect*] terne.

uninsured /ˌʌnɪnˈʃɔːd, US ˌʌnɪnˈʃʊərd/ *adj* non assuré; **to be ~** ne pas être assuré.

unintelligent /ˌʌnɪnˈtelɪdʒənt/ *adj* inintelligent.

unintelligently /ˌʌnɪnˈtelɪdʒəntlɪ/ *adv* sans intelligence.

unintelligible /ˌʌnɪnˈtelɪdʒəbl/ *adj* incompréhensible (**to** pour).

unintelligibly /ˌʌnɪnˈtelɪdʒəblɪ/ *adv* inintelligiblement.

unintended /ˌʌnɪnˈtendɪd/ *adj* [*slur, irony*] involontaire; [*consequence*] non voulu; **to be ~** [*outcome*] ne pas être voulu.

unintentional /ˌʌnɪnˈtenʃənl/ *adj* involontaire.

unintentionally /ˌʌnɪnˈtenʃənəlɪ/ *adv* involontairement.

uninterested /ʌnˈɪntrəstɪd/ *adj* indifférent (**in** à).

uninteresting /ʌnˈɪntrəstɪŋ/ *adj* sans intérêt.

uninterrupted /ˌʌnɪntəˈrʌptɪd/ *adj* ininterrompu.

uninterruptedly /ˌʌnɪntəˈrʌptɪdlɪ/ *adv* sans interruption.

uninvited /ˌʌnɪnˈvaɪtɪd/ **I** *adj* **1** (unsolicited) [*attentions*] non sollicité; [*remark*] gratuit; **2** (without invitation) **~ guest** intrus/-e *m/f*.
II *adv* [*arrive*] sans avoir été invité; **to do sth ~** faire qch sans y avoir été invité.

uninviting /ˌʌnɪnˈvaɪtɪŋ/ *adj* [*place, prospect*] rébarbatif/-ive; [*food*] peu appétissant.

union /ˈjuːnɪən/ **I** *n* **1** (also **trade ~**) Ind syndicat *m*; **to join a ~** se syndiquer; **2** Pol union *f*; **political/economic ~** union politique/économique; **3** (uniting) union *f*; (marriage) union *f*, mariage *m*; **4** (also **student ~**) GB Univ (building) maison *f* des étudiants; (organization) syndicat *m* d'étudiants; **5** Tech raccord *m*.
II Union *pr n* US Pol États-Unis *mpl*; US Hist Union *f*.
III *modif* Ind [*card, leader, movement, headquarters*] syndical.

union: **~ bashing** *n* Ind attaques *fpl* contre le pouvoir des syndicats; **~ catalog** *n* US catalogue *m* collectif; **~ dues** *npl* cotisation *f* syndicale.

unionism /ˈjuːnɪənɪzəm/ *n* Ind syndicalisme *m*.

Unionism /ˈjuːnɪənɪzəm/ *n* **1** GB Pol (in Northern Ireland) unionisme *m*; **2** US Hist unionisme *m*.

unionist /ˈjuːnɪənɪst/ *n* Ind syndiqué/-e *m/f*.

Unionist /ˈjuːnɪənɪst/ **I** *n* **1** GB Pol (in Northern Ireland) unioniste *mf*; **2** US Hist unioniste *mf*.
II *modif* [*party, politician*] unioniste.

unionization /ˌjuːnɪənaɪˈzeɪʃn, US -nɪˈz-/ *n* Ind syndicalisation *f*.

unionize /ˈjuːnɪənaɪz/ *vtr* Ind syndicaliser.

union: **Union Jack** *n* drapeau *m* du Royaume-Uni; **~ member** *n* Ind syndiqué/-e *m/f*.

union membership *n* **1** (members) membres *mpl* syndiqués; **2** (state of being member) adhésion *f* à un syndicat; **3** (number of members) nombre *m* d'adhérents au syndicat.

union: **Union of Soviet Socialist Republics, USSR** *pr n* Hist Union *f* des républiques socialistes soviétiques, URSS *f*; **~ shop** *n* US, Ind *établissement dont tous les employés doivent être ou devenir membres d'un même syndicat*; **~ suit** *n* US sous-vêtement *m* (*en une pièce comportant gilet et caleçon long*).

uniparous /juːˈnɪpərəs/ *adj* unipare.

unique /juːˈniːk/ *adj* **1** (sole) [*example, characteristic*] unique (**in that** en ce que); **to be ~ in doing** être seul/-e à faire; **to be ~ to** être particulier/-ière à; **2** (remarkable) [*individual, skill, performance*] unique, exceptionnel/-elle.

uniquely /juːˈniːklɪ/ *adv* **1** (exceptionally) éminemment; **2** (only) exclusivement.

uniquely abled *adj* handicapé.

uniqueness /juːˈniːknɪs/ *n* **1** (singularity) caractère *m* unique; **2** (special quality) caractère *m* exceptionnel.

unique selling proposition, USP *n* USP *f*, choix *m* et valorisation *f* d'un argument publicitaire.

unisex /ˈjuːnɪseks/ *adj* unisexe.

unison /ˈjuːnɪsn, ˈjuːnɪzn/ *n* **in ~** [*say, recite, sing*] à l'unisson; **to act in ~ with** agir de concert avec.

unit /ˈjuːnɪt/ *n* **1** (whole) unité *f*; **2** (group with specific function) gen groupe *m*; (in army, police) unité *f*; **research ~** groupe de recherche; **3** (building, department) gen, Med service *m*; Ind unité *f*; **casualty/intensive care ~** service des urgences/soins intensifs; **manufacturing ~** unité de fabrication; **production ~** unité de production; **4** Math, Meas unité *f*; **a ~ of measurement** une unité de mesure; **monetary ~** unité monétaire; **5** (part of machine) unité *f*; **6** (piece of furniture) élément *m*; **to buy furniture in ~s** acheter du mobilier par éléments; **7** Univ (credit) unité *f* de valeur; **8** Sch (in textbook) unité *f*; **9** US (apartment) appartement *m*.

Unitarian /ˌjuːnɪˈteərɪən/ *n, adj* unitarien/-ienne (*m/f*).

Unitarianism /ˌjuːnɪˈteərɪənɪzəm/ *n* unitarisme *m*.

unitary /ˈjuːnɪtrɪ, US -terɪ/ *adj* unitaire.

unit cost *n* Comm prix *m* de revient unitaire.

unite /juːˈnaɪt/ **I** *vtr* unir (**with** à).
II *vi* s'unir (**with** à; **in doing** en faisant; **to do** pour faire); **environmentalists ~!** écologistes, unissez-vous!

united /juːˈnaɪtɪd/ *adj* [*groups, front, nation*] uni (**in** dans); [*attempt, effort*] conjoint.
IDIOMS **~ we stand, divided we fall** Prov l'union fait la force Prov.

united: **United Arab Emirates** ▶ 1131 *pr npl* Émirats *mpl* arabes unis; **United Kingdom (of Great Britain and Northern Ireland)** ▶ 1131 *pr n* Royaume-Uni *m* (de Grande-Bretagne et d'Irlande du Nord); **United Nations (Organization)** *n* (Organisation *f* des) Nations *fpl* unies; **United States (of America)** ▶ 1131 *pr n* États-Unis *mpl* (d'Amérique).

unit: **~ furniture** *n* mobilier *m* en éléments; **~ price** *n* Comm prix *m* unitaire; **~ rule** *n* US, Pol règle *f* de vote unitaire; **~ trust** *n* GB Fin ≈ société *f* d'investissement à capital variable, SICAV *f*; **~ value** *n* valeur *f* unitaire.

unity /ˈjuːnətɪ/ *n* unité *f*; Theat **~ of place/time/action** unité de lieu/de temps/d'action.
IDIOMS **~ is strength** Prov l'union fait la force Prov.

Univ *abrev écrite* = **University**.

univalent /ˌjuːnɪˈveɪlənt/ *adj* monovalent.

univalve /ˈjuːnɪvælv/ **I** *n* mollusque *m* univalve.
II *adj* univalve.

universal /ˌjuːnɪˈvɜːsl/ **I** *n* Philos universel *m*.
II universals *npl* Philos universaux *mpl*.
III *adj* **1** (general) [*acclaim, complaint, reaction, solution*] général; [*education, health*

care] pour tous; [*principle, law, truth, remedy, message*] universel/-elle; [*use*] généralisé; **~ suffrage** suffrage *m* universel; **the suggestion gained ~ acceptance** la suggestion a été acceptée par tout le monde; **the practice soon became ~** la pratique s'est bientôt généralisée partout; **his type of humour has ~ appeal** son style d'humour est universel; **2** Ling universel/-elle.

universal coupling, **universal joint** *n* joint *m* de cardan.

universality /ˌjuːnɪvɜːˈsælətɪ/ *n* universalité *f*.

universalize /ˌjuːnɪˈvɜːsəlaɪz/ *vtr* rendre [qch] universel/-elle.

universally /ˌjuːnɪˈvɜːsəlɪ/ *adv* [*believed, accepted, perceived, criticized*] par tous, universellement; [*known, loved*] de tous; **this system is ~ used throughout the country/company** ce système est utilisé dans tout le pays/toute la société.

universal: **~ motor** *n* Tech moteur *m* universel; **Universal Product Code** *n* US Comm code *m* (à) barres; **~ time** *n* temps *m* universel.

universe /ˈjuːnɪvɜːs/ *n* univers *m*.

university /ˌjuːnɪˈvɜːsətɪ/ **I** *n* université *f*.

II *modif* [*lecturer*] d'université; [*degree, town*] universitaire; [*place*] à l'université; **~ entrance** entrée *f* à l'université; **~ education** formation *f* universitaire.

unjust /ʌnˈdʒʌst/ *adj* injuste (**to** envers); **it is/was ~ of them to do** c'est/c'était injuste de leur part de faire.

unjustifiable /ʌnˈdʒʌstɪfaɪəbl/ *adj* injustifiable.

unjustifiably /ʌnˈdʒʌstɪfaɪəblɪ/ *adv* [*claim, condemn*] sans justification; [*act*] d'une manière injustifiable; **to be ~ anxious/critical** être nerveux/critique de façon injustifiée.

unjustified /ʌnˈdʒʌstɪfaɪd/ *adj* injustifié.

unjustly /ʌnˈdʒʌstlɪ/ *adv* [*condemn, favour*] d'une manière injuste; **~ accused/slandered** injustement accusé/calomnié.

unkempt /ʌnˈkempt/ *adj* [*person, appearance*] négligé; [*hair*] ébouriffé; [*beard*] peu soigné; [*garden, home*] mal tenu.

unkind /ʌnˈkaɪnd/ *adj* [*person, thought, act*] pas très gentil/-ille; [*remark*] hostile; [*climate, environment*] rude; [*fate*] littér cruel/-elle; **it was a bit ~** ce n'était pas très gentil; **it is/was ~ of her to do** ce n'est/n'était pas très gentil de sa part de faire; **to be ~ to sb** (by deed) ne pas être gentil avec qn; (verbally) être méchant avec qn.

IDIOMS **the ~est cut of all** le coup le plus perfide.

unkindly /ʌnˈkaɪndlɪ/ *adv* [*think, say, compare*] durement; **my advice was not meant ~** mon avis ne se voulait pas hostile.

unkindness /ʌnˈkaɪndnɪs/ *n* (of person, remark, act) dureté *f*; littér (of fate) cruauté *f*.

unknot /ʌnˈnɒt/ *vtr* (*p prés etc* **-tt-**) dénouer.

unknowable /ʌnˈnəʊəbl/ *adj* inconnaissable.

unknowing /ʌnˈnəʊɪŋ/ *adj* inconscient.

unknowingly /ʌnˈnəʊɪŋlɪ/ *adv* sans le savoir.

unknown /ʌnˈnəʊn/ **I** *n* **1** (unfamiliar place or thing) inconnu *m*; **journey into the ~** voyage dans l'inconnu; **2** (person not famous) inconnu/-e *m/f*; **3** Math inconnue *f*.

II *adj* [*actor, band, force, threat, country*] inconnu; **the man/place was ~ to me** l'homme/l'endroit m'était inconnu; **~ to me, they had already left** à mon insu, ils étaient déjà partis; **it is not ~ for sb to do** il arrive à qn de faire; **it's not ~ for him to be late** ça lui arrive d'être en retard; **~ quantity** Math inconnue *f*; **he/she is an ~ quantity** il/elle représente une inconnue; **murder by person or persons ~** Jur meurtre dont l'auteur ou les auteurs sont inconnus; **Mr X, address ~** M. X, adresse inconnue; **Stephen King, whereabouts ~** Stephen King, dont on ignore où il se trouve.

Unknown Soldier, **Unknown Warrior** *n* Soldat *m* inconnu.

unlace /ʌnˈleɪs/ *vtr* délacer.

unladen /ʌnˈleɪdn/ *adj* à vide.

unladylike /ʌnˈleɪdɪlaɪk/ *adj* [*female, behaviour*] inélégant (**to do** de faire).

unlamented /ˌʌnləˈmentɪd/ *adj* sout **her death was ~** personne ne pleura sa mort.

unlatch /ʌnˈlætʃ/ **I** *vtr* soulever le loquet de [*door, gate*]; **to leave the door/window ~ed** laisser la porte/fenêtre sans (mettre le) loquet.

II *vi* [*door, window etc*] s'ouvrir.

unlawful /ʌnˈlɔːfl/ *adj* [*activity, possession*] illégal; [*violence, killing*] indiscriminé; [*contract*] sans valeur légale; [*detention*] arbitraire.

unlawful: **~ arrest** *n* Jur (without cause) arrestation *f* arbitraire; (with incorrect procedure) arrestation *f* sommaire; **~ assembly** *n* Jur rassemblement *m* de nature à troubler l'ordre public; **~ detention** *n* Jur détention *f* arbitraire.

unlawfully /ʌnˈlɔːfəlɪ/ *adv* **1** Jur de façon criminelle; **~ detained** détenu arbitrairement; **2** gen illégalement.

unlawfulness /ʌnˈlɔːflnɪs/ *n* caractère *m* illégal.

unleaded /ʌnˈledɪd/ *adj* [*petrol*] sans plomb.

unlearn /ʌnˈlɜːn/ *vtr* (*prét, pp* **-learned** ou **-learnt**) désapprendre [*fact*]; se défaire de [*habit*].

unleash /ʌnˈliːʃ/ *vtr* **1** (release) lâcher [*animal*]; libérer [*aggression, market*]; déchaîner [*violence, passion*]; déverser [*torrent*]; **2** (trigger) déclencher [*wave, boom, war*]; **3** (launch) lancer [*force, campaign, attack*] (**against** contre).

unleavened /ʌnˈlevnd/ *adj* sans levain.

unless /ənˈles/ *conj* **1** (except if) à moins que (+ *subj*), à moins de (+ *infinitive*), sauf si (+ *indic*); **he won't come ~ you invite him** il ne viendra pas à moins que tu (ne) l'invites or sauf si tu l'invites; **she can't take the job ~ she finds a nanny** elle ne peut pas accepter le poste à moins de trouver or à moins qu'elle (ne) trouve une nourrice; **I'll have the egg, ~ anyone else wants it?** je mangerai l'œuf, à moins que quelqu'un d'autre (ne) le veuille?; **~ I get my passport back, I can't leave the country** si je ne récupère pas mon passeport je ne pourrai pas quitter le pays; **he threatened that ~ they agreed to pay him he'd reveal the truth** il a menacé de révéler la vérité s'ils refusaient de le payer; **it won't work ~ you plug it in!** ça ne marchera pas si tu ne le branches pas!; **she wouldn't go ~ she was accompanied by her mother** elle ne voulait y aller que si elle était accompagnée par sa mère; **~ I'm very much mistaken, that's Jim** si je ne m'abuse fml or à moins que je (ne) me trompe, c'est Jim; **~ I hear to the contrary** sauf contrordre; **~ otherwise agreed/stated** sauf accord/avis contraire; **2** (except when) sauf quand; **we eat out on Fridays ~ one of us is working late** nous mangeons au restaurant le vendredi sauf quand l'un de nous travaille tard.

unlettered /ʌnˈletəd/ *adj*‡ illettré.

unliberated /ʌnˈlɪbəreɪtɪd/ *adj* non libéré.

unlicensed /ʌnˈlaɪsnst/ *adj* [*activity*] non autorisé; [*vehicle*] non immatriculé; [*transmitter*] sans licence.

unlicensed premises *npl* GB établissement *m* sans licence de débit de vins et spiritueux.

unlikable *adj* = **unlikeable**.

unlike /ʌnˈlaɪk/ **I** *prep* **1** (in contrast to) contrairement à, à la différence de; **~ me, he likes sport** contrairement à moi, il aime le sport; **2** (different from) différent de; **the house is (quite) ~ any other** la maison ne ressemble à aucune autre; **they are quite ~ each other** ils ne se ressemblent pas du tout; **3** (uncharacteristic of) **it's ~ her (to be so rude)** ça ne lui ressemble pas or ce n'est pas du tout son genre (d'être aussi impolie); **how ~ John!** on ne s'attendait pas à cela de la part de John!, ce n'est pas du tout le style de John!

II *adj* (*jamais épith*) **the two brothers are ~ in every way** les deux frères ne se ressemblent pas du tout.

unlikeable /ʌnˈlaɪkəbl/ *adj* [*person*] antipathique; [*place*] désagréable.

unlikelihood /ʌnˈlaɪklɪhʊd/ *n* improbabilité *f*.

unlikely /ʌnˈlaɪklɪ/ *adj* **1** (unexpected) improbable, peu probable; **highly** ou **most ~** extrêmement improbable; **it is ~ that** il est peu probable que (+ *subj*); **they are ~ to succeed** il est peu probable qu'ils réussissent; **it's not ~ that** il n'est pas impossible que (+ *subj*); **2** (strange) [*partner, marriage, choice, situation*] inattendu; **3** (probably untrue) [*story*] invraisemblable; [*excuse, explanation*] peu probable.

unlimited /ʌnˈlɪmɪtɪd/ *adj* illimité.

unlined /ʌnˈlaɪnd/ *adj* **1** [*garment, curtain*] sans doublure; **2** [*paper*] non réglé; **3** [*face*] sans rides.

unlisted /ʌnˈlɪstɪd/ *adj* **1** gen [*campsite, hotel*] non homologué; **2** Fin [*account*] ne figurant pas sur les registres; [*company, share*] non coté; **3** Telecom [*number*] qui n'est pas dans l'annuaire; **her number is ~** elle n'est pas dans l'annuaire; **4** Constr, Jur [*building*] non classé.

Unlisted Securities Market *n* Fin marché *m* hors-cote.

unlit /ʌnˈlɪt/ *adj* **1** (without light) [*room, street, area*] non éclairé; **to be ~** ne pas être éclairé; **2** (without flame) [*cigarette, fire*] non allumé; **to be ~** ne pas être allumé.

unload /ʌnˈləʊd/ **I** *vtr* **1** Transp décharger [*goods, materials, vessel*]; **2** Tech décharger [*gun, camera*]; **3** Comm déverser [*stockpile, goods*] (**on(to)** sur); **4** Fin **to ~ shares** liquider des actions; **5** fig **to ~ one's problems** s'épancher (**on(to)** auprès de).

II *vi* [*truck, ship*] décharger.

unloaded /ʌnˈləʊdɪd/ *adj* **1** [*cargo, goods*] déchargé; **2** [*gun, camera*] non chargé; **to be ~** ne pas être chargé.

unloading /ʌnˈləʊdɪŋ/ *n* déchargement *m*; **ready for ~** prêt à être déchargé.

unlock /ʌnˈlɒk/ *vtr* **1** (with key) ouvrir [*door, casket*]; **to be ~ed** ne pas être fermé à clé; **2** fig ouvrir [*heart*]; révéler [*secrets*]; libérer [*emotions*]; résoudre [*mysteries*].

unlooked-for /ʌnˈlʊktfɔː(r)/ *adj* [*success, compliment*] non sollicité.

unlovable /ʌnˈlʌvəbl/ *adj* rebutant.

unloved /ʌnˈlʌvd/ *adj* [*product, practice*] impopulaire; **to look ~** [*house, room*] avoir l'air négligé; **to feel ~** [*person*] se sentir délaissé.

unlovely /ʌnˈlʌvlɪ/ *adj* disgracieux/-ieuse.

unloving /ʌnˈlʌvɪŋ/ *adj* [*person, behaviour*] peu affectueux/-euse.

unluckily /ʌnˈlʌkɪlɪ/ *adv* malheureusement (**for** pour).

unluckiness /ʌnˈlʌkɪnɪs/ *n* malchance *f*.

unlucky /ʌnˈlʌkɪ/ *adj* **1** (unfortunate) [*person*] malchanceux/-euse; [*coincidence, event*] malencontreux/-euse; [*day*] de malchance; **to be ~ enough to do** avoir la malchance de faire; **it was ~ for you that they rejected the offer** malheureusement pour toi, ils ont rejeté l'offre; **you were ~ not to get the job** c'est pure malchance que tu n'aies pas obtenu le poste; **he is ~ in love** il n'a jamais de chance en amour; **2** (causing bad luck) [*number, colour, combination*] néfaste, maléfique; **it's ~ to walk under a ladder** ça porte malheur de marcher sous une échelle; **red is an ~ colour for me** la couleur rouge me porte malheur.

IDIOMS **lucky at cards, ~ in love** heureux au jeu, malheureux en amour.

unmade /ʌnˈmeɪd/ **I** *prét, pp* ▸ **unmake.**
II *adj* [*bed*] défait; [*road*] non encore goudronné.

unmake /ʌnˈmeɪk/ *vtr* (*prét, pp* **-made**) défaire.

unmanageable /ʌnˈmænɪdʒəbl/ *adj* [*child, animal*] farouche; [*prison, system*] ingérable; [*hair, problem*] rebelle; [*size, number*] démesuré.

unmanly /ʌnˈmænlɪ/ *adj* pusillanime.

unmanned /ʌnˈmænd/ *adj* [*flight, rocket*] non habité; [*train, crossing*] automatique; **to leave the desk ~** laisser le bureau sans personne.

unmannerly /ʌnˈmænəlɪ/ *adj* [*person*] rustre; [*behaviour*] fruste.

unmapped /ʌnˈmæpt/ *adj* non cartographié.

unmarked /ʌnˈmɑːkt/ *adj* **1** (not labelled) [*container*] sans étiquette; [*linen*] non marqué; [*police car*] banalisé; **2** (unblemished) [*skin*] sans marques; **3** Ling non marqué; **4** Sport [*player*] démarqué.

unmarketable /ʌnˈmɑːkɪtəbl/ *adj* non commercialisable.

unmarried /ʌnˈmærɪd/ *adj* [*person*] célibataire; **~ mother** mère *f* célibataire.

unmask /ʌnˈmɑːsk, US -ˈmæsk/ **I** *vtr* lit, fig démasquer.
II *vi* ôter son masque.

unmatched /ʌnˈmætʃt/ *adj* inégalé.

unmentionable /ʌnˈmenʃənəbl/ **I unmentionables**○† *npl* hum (underwear) petits dessous *mpl.*
II *adj* **1** (improper to mention) [*desire, activity*] inracontable; [*subject*] tabou; **2** (unspeakable) [*suffering*] indescriptible.

unmerciful /ʌnˈmɜːsɪfl/ *adj* sans merci (**towards** pour).

unmercifully /ʌnˈmɜːsɪfəlɪ/ *adv* [*beat, scold*] sans merci.

unmerited /ʌnˈmerɪtɪd/ *adj* immérité.

unmet /ʌnˈmet/ *adj* [*condition, requirement*] non satisfait.

unmindful /ʌnˈmaɪndfl/ *adj* sout **~ of** (not heeding) inattentif/-ive à; (not caring) insouciant de.

unmistakable /ˌʌnmɪˈsteɪkəbl/ *adj* **1** (recognizable) [*voice, writing, smell*] caractéristique (**of** de); **2** (unambiguous) [*message, meaning*] sans ambiguïté; **3** (marked) [*atmosphere, desire*] net/nette.

unmistakably /ˌʌnmɪˈsteɪkəblɪ/ *adv* [*smell, hear*] distinctement; [*his, hers*] indubitablement.

unmitigated /ʌnˈmɪtɪgeɪtɪd/ *adj* [*disaster, boredom*] complet/-ète; [*harshness, cruelty*] non tempéré; [*terror, nonsense*] absolu; [*liar, rogue*] fini.

unmixed /ʌnˈmɪkst/ *adj* [*feeling*] sans mélange.

unmodified /ʌnˈmɒdɪfaɪd/ *adj* [*version, machine*] sans altération.

unmolested /ˌʌnməˈlestɪd/ *adj* (undisturbed) sans encombre.

unmortgaged /ʌnˈmɔːgɪdʒd/ *adj* [*property*] libre de toute hypothèque.

unmotivated /ʌnˈməʊtɪveɪtɪd/ *adj* **1** (lacking motive) [*crime, act*] gratuit; **2** (lacking motivation) [*person*] non motivé.

unmounted /ʌnˈmaʊntɪd/ *adj* [*painting*] non monté; [*gem*] non serti; [*stamp*] non placé dans un album.

unmourned /ʌnˈmɔːnd/ *adj* sout [*person, death*] non regretté; **she died ~** elle est morte sans qu'on la pleure.

unmoved /ʌnˈmuːvd/ *adj* **1** (unperturbed) indifférent (**by** à); **2** (not moved emotionally) insensible (**by** à).

unmusical /ʌnˈmjuːzɪkl/ *adj* [*sound*] discordant; [*person*] peu musicien/-ienne.

unnameable /ʌnˈneɪməbl/ *adj* innommable.

unnamed /ʌnˈneɪmd/ *adj* **1** (name not divulged) [*company, buyer, source*] dont le nom n'a pas été divulgué; **2** (without name) [*club, virus*] **as yet ~** encore à la recherche d'un nom.

unnatural /ʌnˈnætʃrəl/ *adj* **1** (affected) [*style, laugh, voice*] affecté; **2** (unusual) [*silence, colour*] insolite; **3** (unhealthy) [*desire, interest*] dénaturé.

unnaturally /ʌnˈnætʃrəlɪ/ *adv* [*laugh, smile*] avec affectation; [*quiet, dark, low*] anormalement; **not ~** fort naturellement.

unnavigable /ʌnˈnævɪgəbl/ *adj* non navigable.

unnecessarily /ˌʌnˈnesəsərəlɪ, US ˌʌnˌnesəˈserəlɪ/ *adv* inutilement.

unnecessary /ʌnˈnesəsrɪ, US -serɪ/ *adj* **1** (not needed) [*expense, effort, treatment*] inutile; **it is ~ to do** il est inutile de faire; **it is ~ for you to do** il est inutile que tu fasses; **2** (uncalled for) [*remark, jibe*] déplacé.

unneighbourly GB, **unneighborly** US /ʌnˈneɪbəlɪ/ *adj* **1** (unhelpful) [*person*] désobligeant; **2** (unlike good neighbour) [*act, behaviour*] allant à l'encontre des rapports de bon voisinage.

unnerve /ʌnˈnɜːv/ *vtr* décontenancer, rendre [qn] nerveux/-euse; **I was ~d by the creaking sounds** les craquements m'ont rendu nerveux.

unnerving /ʌnˈnɜːvɪŋ/ *adj* déroutant.

unnervingly /ʌnˈnɜːvɪŋlɪ/ *adv* [*reply, smile*] de manière déroutante; **~ calm** d'une tranquillité déroutante.

unnoticed /ʌnˈnəʊtɪst/ *adj* inaperçu; **to go** ou **pass ~** passer inaperçu; **to slip in ~** entrer sans être vu.

unnumbered /ʌnˈnʌmbəd/ *adj* **1** [*house*] sans numéro; [*page, ticket, seat*] non numéroté; **2** littér (countless) innombrable.

UNO /ˈjuːnəʊ/ *n* (*abrév* = **United Nations Organization**) ONU *f.*

unobjectionable /ˌʌnəbˈdʒekʃənəbl/ *adj* inoffensif/-ive.

unobservant /ˌʌnəbˈzɜːvənt/ *adj* peu perspicace.

unobserved /ˌʌnəbˈzɜːvd/ *adj* inaperçu; **to go** ou **pass ~** passer inaperçu; **to slip out ~** s'esquiver sans être vu.

unobstructed /ˌʌnəbˈstrʌktɪd/ *adj* [*view, exit, road*] dégagé.

unobtainable /ˌʌnəbˈteɪnəbl/ *adj* **1** Comm [*item, supplies*] introuvable; **oysters are ~ in summer** on ne peut pas trouver d'huîtres en été; **2** Telecom [*number*] impossible à obtenir.

unobtrusive /ˌʌnəbˈtruːsɪv/ *adj* [*person*] effacé; [*site, object, noise*] discret/-ète.

unobtrusively /ˌʌnəbˈtruːsɪvlɪ/ *adv* discrètement.

unobtrusiveness /ˌʌnəbˈtruːsɪvnɪs/ *n* discrétion *f.*

unoccupied /ʌnˈɒkjʊpaɪd/ *adj* **1** [*house, block, shop*] inoccupé; [*seat*] libre; **2** Mil [*territory*] libre.

unofficial /ˌʌnəˈfɪʃl/ *adj* [*result, figure*] officieux/-ieuse; [*candidate*] indépendant; [*industrial action, biography*] non autorisé; **~ strike** grève *f* sauvage.

unofficially /ˌʌnəˈfɪʃəlɪ/ *adv* [*tell, estimate*] officieusement.

unopened /ʌnˈəʊpənd/ *adj* [*bottle, packet*] non entamé; [*package*] non ouvert; **to return a letter ~** renvoyer une lettre sans l'avoir ouverte.

unopposed /ˌʌnəˈpəʊzd/ *adj* [*bill, reading*] accepté sans opposition; **to be elected ~** être élu sans opposition.

unorganized /ʌnˈɔːgənaɪzd/ *adj* **1** [*labour, worker*] non syndiqué; **2** (disorganized) [*event*] mal organisé; [*group*] qui ne sait pas s'organiser; **3** Biol inorganisé.

unoriginal /ˌʌnəˈrɪdʒənl/ *adj* [*idea, plot, style*] sans originalité; **totally ~** sans aucune originalité; **to be ~** manquer d'originalité.

unorthodox /ʌnˈɔːθədɒks/ *adj* **1** (unconventional) [*approach, opinion, teacher*] peu orthodoxe; **2** Relig hétérodoxe.

unostentatious /ˌʌnɒstenˈteɪʃəs/ *adj* discret/-ète.

unpack /ʌnˈpæk/ **I** *vtr* défaire [*luggage, suitcase*]; déballer [*clothes, books, belongings*].
II *vi* défaire sa valise, déballer ses affaires.

unpacking /ʌnˈpækɪŋ/ *n* déballage *m*; **to do the ~** déballer ses affaires.

unpaid /ʌnˈpeɪd/ *adj* [*bill, tax*] impayé; [*debt*] non acquitté; [*work, volunteer*] non rémunéré; **~ leave** congé *m* sans solde.

unpainted /ʌnˈpeɪntɪd/ *adj* [*wall, wood*] non peint.

unpalatable /ʌnˈpælətəbl/ *adj* **1** fig [*truth, statistic*] inconfortable; [*advice*] dur à avaler; **2** [*food*] qui n'a pas bon goût.

unparalleled /ʌnˈpærəleld/ *adj* **1** (unequalled) [*strength, wisdom, luxury*] sans égal; [*success, achievement*] hors pair; **2** (unprecedented) [*rate, scale*] sans précédent.

unpardonable /ʌnˈpɑːdənəbl/ *adj* impardonnable; **it was ~ of you to do** vous êtes impardonnable d'avoir fait.

unpardonably /ʌnˈpɑːdənəblɪ/ *adv* [*behave, insult*] de manière inexcusable; [*rude, arrogant*] inexcusablement.

unparliamentary /ˌʌnˌpɑːləˈmentrɪ, US -terɪ/ *adj* [*behaviour*] inacceptable au parlement.

unpasteurized /ʌnˈpɑːstʃəraɪzd/ *adj* [*milk*] cru; [*cheese*] au lait cru.

unpatented /ʌnˈpeɪtəntɪd, ʌnˈpæt-/ *adj* non breveté.

unpatriotic /ˌʌnpætrɪˈɒtɪk, US ˌʌnpeɪt-/ *adj* [*person*] peu patriote; [*attitude, act*] antipatriotique.

unpatriotically /ˌʌnpætrɪˈɒtɪklɪ, US ˌʌnpeɪt-/ *adv* [*behave, react*] avec antipatriotisme.

unpaved /ʌnˈpeɪvd/ *adj* [*way*] non pavé.

unperceived /ˌʌnpəˈsiːvd/ *adj* inaperçu.

unperforated /ʌnˈpɜːfəreɪtɪd/ *adj* non perforé.

unperturbed /ˌʌnpəˈtɜːbd/ *adj* imperturbable; **to be** ou **remain ~** rester imperturbable (**by** devant).

unpick /ʌnˈpɪk/ *vtr* **1** (undo) défaire [*stitching, hem*]; **2** (sort out) démêler [*truth, facts*] (**from** de).

unpin /ʌnˈpɪn/ *vtr* (*p prés etc* **-nn-**) **1** (remove pins from) enlever les épingles de [*sewing, hair*]; **2** (unfasten) détacher [*brooch*] (**from** de).

unplaced /ʌnˈpleɪst/ *adj* [*competitor*] non classé; [*horse, dog*] non placé.

unplanned /ʌnˈplænd/ *adj* [*stoppage, increase*] imprévu; [*pregnancy, baby*] non prévu.

unplayable /ʌnˈpleɪəbl/ *adj* Sport [*ball, shot*] injouable; [*pitch*] impraticable.

unpleasant /ʌnˈpleznt/ *adj* désagréable.

unpleasantly /ʌnˈplezntlɪ/ *adv* [*smile, behave*] de manière désagréable; [*hot, cold, close*] désagréablement.

unpleasantness /ʌnˈplezntnɪs/ *n* **1** (disagreeable nature) (of odour, experience, remark) caractère *m* désagréable; **such ~ was unnecessary** il n'était pas nécessaire d'être si désagréable; **2** (bad feeling) dissensions *fpl* (**between** entre); **in order to avoid ~** pour éviter toute dissension.

unpleasing /ʌnˈpliːzɪŋ/ *adj* déplaisant; **~ to the eye** désagréable à l'œil.

unplug /ʌnˈplʌg/ *vtr* (*p prés etc* **-gg-**) débrancher [*appliance*]; déboucher [*sink*].

unplumbed /ʌnˈplʌmd/ *adj* inexploré.

unpoetic(al) /ˌʌnpəʊˈetɪk(l)/ *adj* peu poétique; **to be ~** manquer de poésie.

unpolished /ʌnˈpɒlɪʃt/ *adj* **1** lit [*floor*] non ciré; [*silver*] non astiqué; [*glass, gem*] non poli; **2** fig [*person*] gauche; [*manners*] fruste; [*state, form*] ébauché.

unpolluted /ˌʌnpəˈluːtɪd/ *adj* [*water, air*] non pollué; [*mind*] non contaminé.

unpopular /ʌnˈpɒpjʊlə(r)/ *adj* impopulaire (**with** auprès de); **to make oneself ~** se rendre impopulaire; **I'm rather ~ with the boss at the moment** je n'ai pas la cote○ auprès du patron en ce moment.

unpopularity /ˌʌnˌpɒpjʊˈlærətɪ/ *n* impopularité *f*.

unpopulated /ʌnˈpɒpjʊleɪtɪd/ *adj* non peuplé.

unpractised /ʌnˈpræktɪst/ *adj* [*person*] novice; [*ear*] inexercé.

unprecedented /ʌnˈpresɪdentɪd/ *adj* sans précédent.

unprecedentedly /ʌnˈpresɪdentɪdlɪ/ *adv* **~ brave/large** d'une bravoure/d'une taille sans précédent.

unpredictability /ˌʌnprɪˌdɪktəˈbɪlətɪ/ *n* imprévisibilité *f*.

unpredictable /ˌʌnprɪˈdɪktəbl/ *adj* [*event, result*] imprévisible; [*weather*] incertain; **he's ~** on ne sait jamais à quoi s'attendre avec lui.

unpredictably /ˌʌnprɪˈdɪktəblɪ/ *adv* de façon imprévisible.

unprejudiced /ʌnˈpredʒʊdɪst/ *adj* [*person*] sans préjugés; [*opinion, judgment*] impartial.

unpremeditated /ˌʌnpriːˈmedɪteɪtɪd/ *adj* non prémédité.

unprepared /ˌʌnprɪˈpeəd/ *adj* **1** (not ready) [*person*] pas préparé (**for** pour); **to be ~ to do** ne pas être disposé à faire; **to catch sb ~** prendre qn au dépourvu; **they were ~ financially** ils n'étaient pas prêts financièrement; **2** [*speech, performance*] improvisé; [*translation*] non préparé.

unpreparedness /ˌʌnprɪˈpeədnɪs/ *n* manque *m* de préparation.

unprepossessing /ˌʌnˌpriːpəˈzesɪŋ/ *adj* peu avenant.

unpretentious /ˌʌnprɪˈtenʃəs/ *adj* sans prétention.

unpretentiously /ˌʌnprɪˈtenʃəslɪ/ *adv* sans prétention.

unpretentiousness /ˌʌnprɪˈtenʃəsnɪs/ *n* simplicité *f*.

unpriced /ʌnˈpraɪst/ *adj* [*item, goods*] non étiqueté; **certain items were ~** certains articles n'étaient pas étiquetés.

unprincipled /ʌnˈprɪnsəpld/ *adj* [*person*] sans principes; [*act, behaviour*] peu scrupuleux/-euse.

unprintable /ʌnˈprɪntəbl/ *adj* **1** (unpublishable) impubliable; **2** (outrageous) outrancier/-ière; **her answer was quite ~** hum sa réponse n'était pas faite pour des oreilles chastes.

unprivileged /ʌnˈprɪvɪlɪdʒd/ *adj* défavorisé.

unproductive /ˌʌnprəˈdʌktɪv/ *adj* [*capital, work*] improductif/-ive; [*discussion, land*] stérile, improductif/-ive.

unproductively /ˌʌnprəˈdʌktɪvlɪ/ *adv* de façon peu productive.

unprofessional /ˌʌnprəˈfeʃənl/ *adj* qui témoigne d'un manque de conscience professionnelle.

unprofessionally /ˌʌnprəˈfeʃənəlɪ/ *adv* [*behave*] de manière peu professionnelle.

unprofitable /ʌnˈprɒfɪtəbl/ *adj* **1** Fin [*company, venture*] non rentable; **2** fig[*investigation, discussion*] improductif/-ive.

unprofitably /ʌnˈprɒfɪtəblɪ/ *adv* **1** Fin [*trade*] de façon non rentable; **2** (uselessly) [*continue, drag on*] stérilement.

unpromising /ʌnˈprɒmɪsɪŋ/ *adj* peu prometteur/-euse.

unpromisingly /ʌnˈprɒmɪsɪŋlɪ/ *adv* de façon peu prometteuse.

unprompted /ʌnˈprɒmptɪd/ *adj* non sollicité.

unpronounceable /ˌʌnprəˈnaʊnsəbl/ *adj* imprononçable.

unprotected /ˌʌnprəˈtektɪd/ *adj* **1** (unsafe) [*person, area, sex*] sans protection (**from** contre); **2** (bare) [*wood, metal*] sans revêtement.

unprotesting /ˌʌnprəˈtestɪŋ/ *adj* docile, consentant.

unprovided-for /ˌʌnprəˈvaɪdɪdfɔː(r)/ *adj* sans ressources.

unprovoked /ˌʌnprəˈvəʊkt/ **I** *adj* [*attack, aggression*] délibéré; **the attack was ~** l'attaque n'avait pas été provoquée.
II *adv* [*flare up*] sans raison.

unpublishable /ʌnˈpʌblɪʃəbl/ *adj* impubliable.

unpublished /ʌnˈpʌblɪʃt/ *adj* non publié.

unpunctual /ʌnˈpʌŋktjʊəl/ *adj* [*arrival, person*] tardif/-ive; **to be ~** ne pas être très ponctuel/-elle.

unpunctuality /ˌʌnˌpʌŋktjʊˈælətɪ/ *n* manque *m* de ponctualité.

unpunished /ʌnˈpʌnɪʃt/ *adj* [*crime, person*] impuni; **to go** ou **remain ~** rester impuni.

unputdownable○ /ˌʌnpʊtˈdaʊnəbl/ *adj* [*book*] impossible à lâcher.

unqualified /ʌnˈkwɒlɪfaɪd/ *adj* **1** (without qualifications) [*doctor, teacher, assistant*] non qualifié; **to be ~** ne pas être qualifié (**for** pour; **to do** pour faire); **medically ~ people** des personnes sans qualifications médicales; **I am ~ to judge** je ne suis pas qualifié pour juger; **2** (total) [*support, respect*] inconditionnel/-elle; [*ceasefire*] sans condition; **the evening was an ~ success** la soirée a été une grande réussite.

unquenchable /ʌnˈkwentʃəbl/ *adj* [*thirst, fire*] inextinguible.

unquenched /ʌnˈkwentʃt/ *adj* inassouvi.

unquestionable /ʌnˈkwestʃənəbl/ *adj* incontestable.

unquestionably /ʌnˈkwestʃənəblɪ/ *adv* incontestablement.

unquestioned /ʌnˈkwestʃənd/ *adj* incontesté.

unquestioning /ʌnˈkwestʃənɪŋ/ *adj* inconditionnel/-elle.

unquestioningly /ʌnˈkwestʃənɪŋlɪ/ *adv* [*follow, accept, obey*] aveuglément, inconditionnellement.

unquiet /ʌnˈkwaɪət/ littér **I** *n* tourment *m*.
II *adj* [*spirit*] tourmenté.

unquote /ʌnˈkwəʊt/ *adv* fin de citation.

unquoted /ʌnˈkwəʊtɪd/ *adj* Fin [*company, share*] non coté (en Bourse).

unravel /ʌnˈrævl/ **I** *vtr* (*p prés etc* **-ll-** GB, **-l-** US) défaire [*knitting*]; démêler [*thread, mystery*]; dénouer [*intrigue*].
II *vi* (*p prés etc* **-ll-** GB, **-l-** US) [*knitting*] se défaire; [*mystery, thread*] se démêler; [*plot*] se dénouer.

unread /ʌnˈred/ *adj* non lu; **she returned the book ~** elle a rendu le livre sans l'avoir lu.

unreadable /ʌnˈriːdəbl/ *adj* [*book, writing*] illisible.

unreadiness /ʌnˈredɪnɪs/ *n* **1** (lack of preparation) manque *m* de préparation; **2** (unwillingness) mauvaise volonté *f*.

unready /ʌnˈredɪ/ *adj* **1** (not ready) pas prêt (**to do** à faire); **to be ~ for sth** ne pas être préparé pour qch; **2** (not willing) non disposé (**to do** à faire).

unreal /ʌnˈrɪəl/ *adj* **1** (not real) [*situation, conversation*] irréel/-éelle; **it seemed a bit ~ to me** j'avais un peu l'impression de rêver; **2**○ péj (unbelievable in behaviour) incroyable; **he's ~!** il est incroyable!; **3**○ (amazingly good) incroyable, fabuleux/-euse; **the experience was ~!** ça a été une expérience fabuleuse!

unrealistic /ˌʌnrɪəˈlɪstɪk/ *adj* [*expectation, aim*] irréalisable; [*character, presentation*] peu réaliste; [*person*] qui manque de réalisme; **it is ~ to suggest that** il n'est pas réaliste de suggérer que.

unrealistically /ˌʌnrɪəˈlɪstɪklɪ/ *adv* [*high, low, short, optimistic*] invraisemblablement.

unreality /ˌʌnrɪˈælətɪ/ *n* irréalité *f*; **to have a sense of ~** avoir l'impression de rêver.

unrealizable /ʌnˈrɪəlaɪzəbl/ *adj* irréalisable.

unrealized /ʌnˈrɪəlaɪzd/ *adj* [*ambition, potential*] non réalisé; **to be** ou **remain ~** ne pas être réalisé.

unreason /ʌnˈriːzn/ *n* sout déraison *f*.

unreasonable /ʌnˈriːznəbl/ *adj* **1** (not rational) [*views, behaviour, expectation*] irréaliste; **it's not ~** ce n'est pas déraisonnable; **it's not ~ to expect prices to remain static** on peut raisonnablement espérer que les prix ne vont pas bouger; **it's ~ for them to claim that they are superior** ils ont tort de prétendre qu'ils sont supérieurs; **he's being very ~ about it** il n'est vraiment pas raisonnable; **2** (excessive) [*price*] excessif/-ive; [*demand*] irréaliste; **at an ~ hour** à une heure indue.

unreasonableness /ʌnˈriːznəblnɪs/ *n* caractère *m* déraisonnable.

unreasonably /ʌnˈriːznəblɪ/ *adv* [*behave, act*] de façon peu raisonnable; **~ high rents/prices** des loyers/prix excessifs; **not ~** à juste titre; **consent shall not be ~ withheld** Jur l'accord ne doit pas être refusé de façon déraisonnable.

unreasoning /ʌnˈriːzənɪŋ/ *adj* [*panic, person, response*] irrationnel/-elle.

unreceptive /ˌʌnrɪˈseptɪv/ *adj* peu réceptif/-ive (**to** à).

unreclaimed /ˌʌnrɪˈkleɪmd/ *adj* [*land*] non défriché; [*marsh*] non asséché; **to be ~** ne pas être défriché or asséché.

unrecognizable /ʌnˈrekəgnaɪzəbl/ *adj* méconnaissable.

unrecognized /ʌnˈrekəgnaɪzd/ *adj* **1** [*significance, talent*] méconnu (**by** de); **to go ~** rester méconnu; **2** Pol [*regime, government*] non reconnu; **3** [*person*] **he crossed the city ~** il a traversé la ville sans être reconnu.

unreconstructed /ˌʌnriːkənˈstrʌktɪd/ *adj* (all contexts) irréductible.

unrecorded /ˌʌnrɪˈkɔːdɪd/ *adj* non répertorié; **to go ~** ne pas être répertorié.

unredeemed /ˌʌnrɪˈdiːmd/ *adj* **1** Relig, hum [*sinner*] non racheté; **2** Comm, Fin [*mortgage*] non purgé; [*debt*] non remboursé; [*pledge*] non retiré; **3** [*ugliness, stupidity*] total.

unrefined /ˌʌnrɪˈfaɪnd/ *adj* **1** [*flour, sugar*] non raffiné; [*oil*] brut, non raffiné; **2** [*person, manners, style*] peu raffiné.

unreflecting /ˌʌnrɪˈflektɪŋ/ *adj* irréfléchi.

unreformed /ˌʌnrɪˈfɔːmd/ *adj* **1** [*character*] incorrigible; **2** [*church, system, institution*] non réformé.

unregarded /ˌʌnrɪˈgɑːdɪd/ *adj* peu considéré; **to pass** ou **go ~** passer inaperçu.

unregenerate /ˌʌnrɪˈdʒenərət/ *adj* **1** (unrepentant) éhonté; **2** (obstinate) obstiné.

unregistered /ʌnˈredʒɪstəd/ *adj* [*claim, firm, animal*] non enregistré; [*birth*] non déclaré; [*letter*] non recommandé; [*vehicle*] non immatriculé; **to go ~** passer inaperçu.

unregretted /ˌʌnrɪˈgretɪd/ *adj* [*action, past*] que l'on ne regrette pas; **he will die ~** il mourra sans inspirer de regret.

unrehearsed /ˌʌnrɪˈhɜːst/ *adj* [*response, action, speech*] impromptu; [*play*] sans répétitions.

unrelated /ˌʌnrɪˈleɪtɪd/ *adj* **1** (not logically connected) sans rapport (**to** avec); **his success is not ~ to the fact that he has money** son succès n'est pas sans rapport avec sa fortune; **2** (as family) **the two families/boys are ~** les deux familles/garçons n'ont pas de lien de parenté.

unrelenting /ˌʌnrɪˈlentɪŋ/ *adj* [*heat, stare, person*] implacable; [*pursuit, zeal, position*] acharné.

unreliability /ˌʌnrɪˌlaɪəˈbɪlətɪ/ *n* (of person) manque *m* de sérieux; (of machine, method, technique) manque *m* de fiabilité.

unreliable /ˌʌnrɪˈlaɪəbl/ *adj* [*evidence, fig-*

ures] douteux/-euse; [*method, scheme, employee*] peu sûr; [*equipment*] peu fiable; **the method is highly ~** la méthode est très discutable.

unrelieved /ˌʌnrɪˈliːvd/ *adj* [*substance, colour*] uniforme; [*darkness, gloom, anxiety*] permanent; [*boredom*] mortel/-elle; **a blank wall ~ by any detail** un mur aveugle que rien n'égayait.

unremarkable /ˌʌnrɪˈmɑːkəbl/ *adj* quelconque.

unremarked /ˌʌnrɪˈmɑːkt/ *adj* [*leave, enter*] sans être remarqué; **to go** ou **pass ~** passer inaperçu.

unremitting /ˌʌnrɪˈmɪtɪŋ/ *adj* [*boredom, flow, drudgery*] incessant; [*hostility*] implacable; [*pressure, effort*] continu; [*fight, struggle*] sans relâche.

unremittingly /ˌʌnrɪˈmɪtɪŋlɪ/ *adv* inlassablement.

unremunerative /ˌʌnrɪˈmjuːnərətɪv/ *adj* [*work, investment*] non rémunérateur/-trice.

unrepaid /ˌʌnrɪˈpeɪd/ *adj* Fin non remboursé; **the sum remains ~** la somme n'a toujours pas été remboursée.

unrepealed /ˌʌnrɪˈpiːld/ *adj* Jur [*legislation*] non abrogé; **statutes that remain ~** statuts qui ne sont toujours pas abrogés.

unrepeatable /ˌʌnrɪˈpiːtəbl/ *adj* **1** (unique) [*bargain, sight*] unique en son genre; [*offer*] exceptionnel/-elle; **2** (vulgar) [*language*] pas répétable; **his comment/language was ~** son commentaire/langage était du genre à ne pas répéter.

unrepentant /ˌʌnrɪˈpentənt/ *adj* impénitent; **to remain ~** n'avoir aucun repentir (**about** au sujet de).

unreported /ˌʌnrɪˈpɔːtɪd/ *adj* [*incident, attack*] non déclaré; **to go ~** ne pas être déclaré.

unrepresentative /ˌʌnreprɪˈzentətɪv/ *adj* non représentatif/-ive.

unrepresented /ˌʌnreprɪˈzentɪd/ *adj* [*person, area*] non représenté; **some areas were ~** certaines régions n'étaient pas représentées; **the accused appeared before the bench ~** l'accusé a comparu devant le tribunal sans être représenté.

unrequited /ˌʌnrɪˈkwaɪtɪd/ *adj* [*love*] sans retour.

unreserved /ˌʌnrɪˈzɜːvd/ *adj* **1** (free) [*seat*] non réservé; **2** (whole-hearted) [*support, admiration, welcome*] sans réserve.

unreservedly /ˌʌnrɪˈzɜːvɪdlɪ/ *adv* sans réserve.

unresisting /ˌʌnrɪˈzɪstɪŋ/ *adj* sans résistance.

unresolved /ˌʌnrɪˈzɒlvd/ *adj* irrésolu.

unresponsive /ˌʌnrɪˈspɒnsɪv/ *adj* [*person, audience*] peu réceptif/-ive (**to** à).

unrest /ʌnˈrest/ *n* ¢ **1** (dissatisfaction) malaise *m*; **2** (agitation) troubles *mpl*.

unrestrained /ˌʌnrɪˈstreɪnd/ *adj* [*growth, proliferation*] effréné; [*delight, emotion*] non contenu; [*freedom*] sans limites.

unrestricted /ˌʌnrɪˈstrɪktɪd/ *adj* [*access, power*] illimité; [*testing, disposal*] incontrôlé; [*warfare*] à outrance; [*roadway*] dégagé.

unrevealed /ˌʌnrɪˈviːld/ *adj* **1** (undetected) insoupçonné; **2** (kept secret) maintenu/-e secret/-ète; **~ religion** religion *f* non révélée.

unrevised /ˌʌnrɪˈvaɪzd/ *adj* non révisé.

unrewarded /ˌʌnrɪˈwɔːdɪd/ *adj* [*research, efforts*] infructueux/-euse; **to go ~** [*patience, talent*] ne pas être récompensé.

unrewarding /ˌʌnrɪˈwɔːdɪŋ/ *adj* [*job, task*] (unfulfilling) peu gratifiant; (thankless) ingrat; **financially ~** peu rémunérateur/-trice.

unrighteous /ʌnˈraɪtʃəs/ **I** *n* **the ~** (+ *v pl*) les impies.
II *adj* Relig inique.

unripe /ʌnˈraɪp/ *adj* [*fruit*] pas mûr; [*wheat*] en herbe.

unrivalled /ʌnˈraɪvld/ *adj* sans égal.

unroadworthy /ʌnˈrəʊdwɜːðɪ/ *adj* [*vehicle*] hors d'état de rouler.

unroll /ʌnˈrəʊl/ **I** *vtr* dérouler.
II *vi* se dérouler.

unromantic /ˌʌnrəˈmæntɪk/ *adj* peu romantique; **to be ~** manquer de romantisme.

unrope /ʌnˈrəʊp/ *vtr, vi* Sport décrocher.

UNRRA *n* (*abrév* = **United Nations Relief and Rehabilitation Administration**) UNRRA *f*, Administration *f* des Nations unies pour les secours et la reconstruction.

unruffled /ʌnˈrʌfld/ *adj* **1** (calm) [*person, demeanour*] imperturbable; **to be ~** ne pas être perturbé (**by** par); **2** (smooth) [*water, surface, hair*] lisse.

unruled /ʌnˈruːld/ *adj* [*paper*] non réglé.

unruly /ʌnˈruːlɪ/ *adj* [*crowd, behaviour, hair*] indiscipliné.

unsaddle /ʌnˈsædl/ *vtr* **1** desseller [*horse*]; **2** (unseat) désarçonner [*person*].

unsafe /ʌnˈseɪf/ *adj* **1** [*environment*] malsain; [*drinking water*] non potable; [*goods, furniture*] dangereux/-euse; [*working conditions, sex*] risqué; **the car is ~ to drive** il est dangereux de conduire cette voiture; **the premises are ~ for normal use** les locaux ne sont pas sûrs pour une utilisation normale; **the building was declared ~** l'édifice a été déclaré dangereux; **2** (threatened) **to feel ~** [*person*] ne pas se sentir en sécurité; **3** Jur [*conviction, verdict*] douteux/-euse; **~ and unsatisfactory** douteux/-euse.

unsaid /ʌnˈsed/ **I** *pp* ▶ **unsay**.
II *adj* **to be** ou **go ~** être passé sous silence; **to leave sth ~** passer qch sous silence.

unsalaried /ʌnˈsælərɪd/ *adj* non rémunéré.

unsaleable /ʌnˈseɪləbl/ *adj* invendable.

unsalted /ʌnˈsɔːltɪd/ *adj* non salé.

unsatisfactorily /ˌʌnsætɪsˈfæktərəlɪ/ *adv* [*start, end*] de façon peu satisfaisante.

unsatisfactory /ˌʌnsætɪsˈfæktərɪ/ *adj* insatisfaisant.

unsatisfied /ʌnˈsætɪsfaɪd/ *adj* [*person*] insatisfait; [*need, desire*] inassouvi; **she remains ~** elle n'est toujours pas satisfaite (**with** de).

unsatisfying /ʌnˈsætɪsfaɪɪŋ/ *adj* peu satisfaisant.

unsaturated /ʌnˈsætʃəreɪtɪd/ *adj* [*fat, oil*] non saturé.

unsavoury GB, **unsavory** US /ʌnˈseɪvərɪ/ *adj* [*business, individual*] louche, répugnant; [*object, smell*] peu appétissant; **it's all very ~** c'est assez répugnant.

unsay /ʌnˈseɪ/ *vtr* (*prét, pp* **-said**) effacer; **what's said cannot be unsaid** ce qui est dit est dit.

unscathed /ʌnˈskeɪðd/ *adj* (all contexts) indemne.

unscented /ʌnˈsentɪd/ *adj* non parfumé.

unscheduled /ʌnˈʃedjuːld, US ʌnˈskedʒʊld/ *adj* [*appearance, performance, speech*] surprise (*after n*); [*flight*] supplémentaire; [*break, stop*] qui n'a pas été prévu.

unscholarly /ʌnˈskɒləlɪ/ *adj* [*person, approach*] peu érudit; [*work, analysis*] dénué d'érudition.

unschooled /ʌnˈskuːld/ *adj* **1** [*person*] inculte; **he's ~ed in the art of conversation** il n'a jamais été initié à l'art de la conversation; **2** Equit [*horse*] indompté.

unscientific /ˌʌnsaɪənˈtɪfɪk/ *adj* [*theory, approach*] non scientifique; [*nonsense*] illogique; **to be ~** [*method, theory*] ne pas être scientifique; [*person*] ne pas avoir l'esprit scientifique.

unscramble /ʌnˈskræmbl/ *vtr* déchiffrer [*code, words*]; remettre de l'ordre dans [*ideas, thoughts*].

unscratched /ʌnˈskrætʃt/ *adj* [*car, paintwork*] intact.

unscrew /ʌnˈskruː/ **I** *vtr* dévisser.
II *vi* se dévisser.

unscripted /ʌnˈskrɪptɪd/ *adj* improvisé.

unscrupulous /ʌnˈskruːpjʊləs/ *adj* [*person*] sans scrupules; [*tactic, method*] peu scrupuleux/-euse; **she is completely ~** elle n'a aucun scrupule.

unscrupulously /ʌnˈskruːpjʊləslɪ/ *adv* [*behave*] sans scrupules.

unscrupulousness /ʌnˈskruːpjʊləsnɪs/ *n* manque *m* de scrupules.

unseal /ʌnˈsiːl/ *vtr* desceller [*container*]; décacheter [*envelope, parcel*].

unsealed /ʌnˈsiːld/ *adj* [*envelope*] décacheté; **by ~ writing** Jur dans une enveloppe décachetée.

unseasonable /ʌnˈsiːznəbl/ *adj* [*food, clothing*] hors de saison; **the weather is ~** ce n'est pas un temps de saison.

unseasonably /ʌnˈsiːznəblɪ/ *adv* **it is ~ hot/cold** il fait chaud/froid pour la saison.

unseasoned /ʌnˈsiːznd/ *adj* **1** [*food*] non assaisonné; **2** [*wood*] vert.

unseat /ʌnˈsiːt/ *vtr* **1** Equit désarçonner [*rider*]; **2** Pol faire perdre son siège à; **the MP was ~ed** le député a perdu son siège; **3** Tech déloger [*washer*].

unseaworthy /ʌnˈsiːwɜːðɪ/ *adj* hors d'état de naviguer.

unsecured /ˌʌnsɪˈkjʊəd/ *adj* Fin [*loan*] non garanti; [*creditor*] sans garantie.

unseeded /ʌnˈsiːdɪd/ *adj* Sport non classé.

unseeing /ʌnˈsiːɪŋ/ littér **I** *adj* [*eyes*] aveugle.
II *adv* [*gaze*] sans voir.

unseemliness /ʌnˈsiːmlɪnɪs/ *n* sout inconvenance *f* fml.

unseemly /ʌnˈsiːmlɪ/ *adj* sout inconvenant fml.

unseen /ʌnˈsiːn/ **I** *n* GB Sch devoir *m* non préparé; **a French ~** une version française non préparée.
II *adj* **1** [*figure, orchestra, assistant, hands*] invisible; **2** Sch [*translation*] non préparé.
III *adv* [*escape, slip away*] sans être vu.

unselfconscious /ˌʌnselfˈkɒnʃəs/ *adj* [*person*] (natural, spontaneous) naturel/-elle; (uninhibited) sans complexes; **she was quite ~ about it** elle a fait ça sans la moindre gêne.

unselfconsciously /ˌʌnselfˈkɒnʃəslɪ/ *adv* avec naturel.

unselfconsciousness /ˌʌnselfˈkɒnʃəsnɪs/ *n* naturel *m*.

unselfish /ʌnˈselfɪʃ/ *adj* [*person*] qui pense aux autres; [*act*] désintéressé.

unselfishly /ʌnˈselfɪʃlɪ/ *adv* de façon désintéressée.

unselfishness /ʌnˈselfɪʃnɪs/ *n* désintéressement *m*.

unsentimental /ˌʌnsentɪˈmentl/ *adj* [*speech, account, documentary*] qui ne donne pas dans la sensiblerie; [*film, novel*] qui ne tombe pas dans le mélo○; [*person*] qui ne fait pas de sentiment.

unserviceable /ʌnˈsɜːvɪsəbl/ *adj* inutilisable.

unsettle /ʌnˈsetl/ *vtr* troubler [*person, audience*]; perturber [*discussions, economy, process*].

unsettled /ʌnˈsetld/ *adj* **1** [*weather, economic climate*] instable; **2** (not paid) [*bill, account*] impayé; **3** (disrupted) [*schedule*] perturbé; **4 to feel ~** [*person*] être mal dans sa peau.

unsettling /ʌnˈsetlɪŋ/ *adj* [*question, implications, experience*] troublant; [*work of art*] dérangeant; **psychologically ~** traumatisant.

unsexed /ʌnˈsekst/ *adj* [*animal*] dont le sexage n'a pas encore été effectué.

unsexy /ʌnˈseksɪ/ *adj* peu sexy.

unshackle /ʌnˈʃækl/ *vtr* désenchaîner [*prisoner*]; fig (free) libérer.

unshaded /ʌnˈʃeɪdɪd/ *adj* **1** [*bulb*] sans abat-jour; [*place*] non ombragé; **2** Art [*drawing*] non ombré.

unshak(e)able /ʌnˈʃeɪkəbl/ *adj* inébranlable.

unshak(e)ably /ʌnˈʃeɪkəblɪ/ *adv* inébranlablement.

unshaken /ʌnˈʃeɪkən/ *adj* [*person*] imperturbable (**by** devant); [*belief, spirit*] inébranlable.

unshaven /ʌnˈʃeɪvn/ *adj* pas rasé.

unsheathe /ʌnˈʃiːð/ *vtr* dégainer.

unship /ʌnˈʃɪp/ *vtr* (*p prés etc* **-pp-**) débarquer.

unshockable /ʌnˈʃɒkəbl/ *adj* **she's quite ~** rien ne peut la choquer.

unshod /ʌnˈʃɒd/ *adj* [*person*] déchaussé; [*horse*] déferré.

unshrinkable /ʌnˈʃrɪŋkəbl/ *adj* irrétrécissable.

unsighted /ʌnˈsaɪtɪd/ *adj* Sport [*person*] au champ de vision bouché (**by** par).

unsightliness /ʌnˈsaɪtlɪnɪs/ *n* laideur *f*.

unsightly /ʌnˈsaɪtlɪ/ *adj* [*scar, blemish*] disgracieux/-ieuse; [*building*] laid.

unsigned /ʌnˈsaɪnd/ *adj* [*document, letter*] non signé; **the letter was ~** la lettre n'était pas signée.

unsinkable /ʌnˈsɪŋkəbl/ *adj* **1** [*ship, object*] insubmersible; **2** fig, hum [*personality*] que rien ne peut atteindre.

unskilful, **unskillful** US /ʌnˈskɪlfl/ *adj* maladroit.

unskilfully, **unskillfully** US /ʌnˈskɪlfəlɪ/ *adv* maladroitement.

unskilled /ʌnˈskɪld/ *adj* [*worker, labour*] non qualifié; [*job, work*] qui n'exige pas de qualification professionnelle.

unskimmed /ʌnˈskɪmd/ *adj* [*milk*] non écrémé.

unsliced /ʌnˈslaɪst/ *adj* [*loaf*] non découpé.

unsmiling /ʌnˈsmaɪlɪŋ/ *adj* [*person*] qui ne sourit pas; [*face, eyes*] grave.

unsnarl /ʌnˈsnɑːl/ *vtr* démêler [*threads*]; débloquer [*traffic jam*].

unsociability /ˌʌnˌsəʊʃəˈbɪlətɪ/ *n* insociabilité *f*.

unsociable /ʌnˈsəʊʃəbl/ *adj* [*person*] peu sociable; **to work ~ hours** travailler à des heures indues.

unsocial /ʌnˈsəʊʃl/ *adj* **~ hours** heures *fpl* indues.

unsold /ʌnˈsəʊld/ *adj* invendu.

unsolicited /ˌʌnsəˈlɪsɪtɪd/ *adj* non sollicité.

unsolvable /ʌnˈsɒlvəbl/ *adj* insoluble.

unsolved /ʌnˈsɒlvd/ *adj* [*problem*] non résolu; [*murder, mystery*] non éclairci; **the mystery remains ~** le mystère reste entier.

unsophisticated /ˌʌnsəˈfɪstɪkeɪtɪd/ **I** *n* **the philosophically/politically ~** (+ *v pl*) les gens sans culture philosophique/politique.
II *adj* [*person*] sans façons; [*tastes, mind*] simple; [*analysis*] simpliste.

unsought /ʌnˈsɔːt/ *adj* [*opinion, presence*] non sollicité.

unsound /ʌnˈsaʊnd/ *adj* [*roof, timbers, ship*] en mauvais état; [*argument*] peu valable; [*credits, investment, loan*] Fin douteux/-euse; **politically/economically ~** impraticable sur le plan politique/économique; **to be of ~ mind** Jur ne pas jouir de toutes ses facultés mentales.

unsparing /ʌnˈspeərɪŋ/ *adj* **1** [*efforts, devotion*] prodigue; **to be ~ in one's efforts to do sth** ne pas ménager ses efforts pour faire qch; **2** (merciless) impitoyable.

unsparingly /ʌnˈspeərɪŋlɪ/ *adv* **1** [*give, devote oneself*] sans compter; [*strive*] de tout son être; **2** [*critical, harsh*] implacablement.

unspeakable /ʌnˈspiːkəbl/ *adj* **1** (dreadful) [*pain, sorrow*] inexprimable; [*noise*] épouvantable; **what he did is ~** ce qu'il a fait est innommable; **2** (inexpressible) [*joy, pleasure*] indescriptible.

unspeakably /ʌnˈspiːkəblɪ/ *adv* **1** (dreadfully) épouvantablement; **2** (inexpressibly) **~ beautiful/romantic** d'une beauté/d'un romantisme indescriptible.

unspecifically /ˌʌnspəˈsɪfɪklɪ/ *adv* de façon peu explicite.

unspecified /ʌnˈspesɪfaɪd/ *adj* non spécifié.

unspectacular /ˌʌnspekˈtækjʊlə(r)/ *adj* peu spectaculaire.

unspent /ʌnˈspent/ *adj* **1** lit [*money*] non dépensé; **the grant remains ~** la subvention n'a pas encore été dépensée; **2** fig [*rage*] toujours vivace.

unspoiled /ʌnˈspɔɪld/ *adj* [*landscape, town*] préservé intact; [*person*] non gâté; **she was ~ by fame** la célébrité ne l'avait pas changée.

unspoilt /ʌnˈspɔɪlt/ *adj* [*island, area*] préservé.

unspoken /ʌnˈspəʊkən/ *adj* **1** (secret) [*desire, fear, question*] inexprimé; **2** (implicit) [*agreement, threat, plea*] tacite.

unsporting /ʌnˈspɔːtɪŋ/ *adj* [*behaviour*] peu sportif/-ive; **it was ~ of you to complain about the decision** ce n'était pas très sportif de ta part de contester la décision.

unsportsmanlike /ˌʌnˈspɔːtsmənlaɪk/ *adj* Sport **~ conduct** conduite indigne d'un sportif.

unspotted /ʌnˈspɒtɪd/ *adj* littér [*character, reputation*] non entaché (**by** par).

unstable /ʌnˈsteɪbl/ *adj* (all contexts) instable.

unstained /ʌnˈsteɪnd/ *adj* **1** [*wood, glass*] non teinté; [*material*] immaculé; **2** fig (unsullied) [*character, reputation*] pur et sans tache; **to be ~** ne pas être entaché (**by** par).

unstamped /ʌnˈstæmpt/ *adj* [*form, passport*] non tamponné; [*envelope*] non timbré.

unstated /ʌnˈsteɪtɪd/ *adj* [*violence, assumption*] tacite; [*policy, conviction*] inexprimé.

unstatesmanlike /ʌnˈsteɪtsmənlaɪk/ *adj* indigne d'un homme d'État.

unsteadily /ʌnˈstedɪlɪ/ *adv* [*walk, stand, rise*] en chancelant; **she swayed ~ forwards** elle s'est penchée en avant de façon mal assurée.

unsteadiness /ʌnˈstedɪnɪs/ *n* instabilité *f*.

unsteady /ʌnˈstedɪ/ *adj* **1** (wobbly) [*steps, legs, voice*] chancelant; [*ladder*] instable; [*hand*] tremblant; **to be ~ on one's feet** marcher de façon mal assurée; **2** (irregular) [*rhythm, speed*] irrégulier/-ière.

unstick /ʌnˈstɪk/ *vtr* (*prét, pp* **-stuck**) décoller.

unstinted /ʌnˈstɪntɪd/ *adj* [*admiration*] sans réserve; [*generosity*] sans bornes.

unstinting /ʌnˈstɪntɪŋ/ *adj* [*effort*] soutenu; [*support*] généreux/-euse; **to be ~ in one's efforts to do sth** ne pas ménager ses efforts pour faire qch; **to be ~ in one's praise of sb** se répandre en louanges sur qn.

unstitch /ʌnˈstɪtʃ/ *vtr* découdre; **to come ~ed** se découdre.

unstop /ʌnˈstɒp/ *vtr* (*p prés etc* **-pp-**) déboucher.

unstoppable /ʌnˈstɒpəbl/ *adj* [*force, momentum*] irrésistible; [*athlete, leader*] imbattable.

unstrap /ʌnˈstræp/ (*p prés etc* **-pp-**) **I** *vtr* **1** (undo) défaire les sangles de [*suitcase*]; **2** (detach) détacher [*case, bike*] (**from** de).
II *v refl* **to ~ oneself** détacher sa ceinture de sécurité.

unstressed /ʌnˈstrest/ *adj* Ling [*vowel, word*] non accentué.

unstring /ʌnˈstrɪŋ/ *vtr* (*prét, pp* **-strung**) enlever les cordes de [*racket, instrument*]; désenfiler [*beads*].

unstructured /ʌnˈstrʌktʃəd/ *adj* [*article, speech*] décousu; [*data, task*] non structuré.

unstrung /ʌnˈstrʌŋ/ **I** *prét, pp* ▸ **unstring**.
II *adj* [*violin, racket*] désencordé; **to come ~** [*racket, instrument*] se détendre; [*beads*] se désenfiler.

unstuck /ʌnˈstʌk/ **I** *prét, pp* ▸ **unstick**.
II *adj* **1** lit **to come ~** [*stamp, glue*] se décoller; **2**○ fig [*person, organization*] connaître un échec, aller à vau l'eau; [*plans*] tomber à l'eau; **to come ~ in one's exams/attempt** échouer à ses examens/dans sa tentative.

unstudied /ʌnˈstʌdɪd/ *adj* [*elegance, charm*] non affecté, naturel/-elle.

unsubdued /ˌʌnsəbˈdjuːd, US -ˈduːd/ *adj* indompté.

unsubsidized /ʌnˈsʌbsɪdaɪzd/ *adj* [*performance, activity*] non subventionné.

unsubstantial /ˌʌnsəbˈstænʃl/ *adj* [*argument*] mal étayé; [*structure*] fragile.

unsubstantiated /ˌʌnsəbˈstænʃɪeɪtɪd/ *adj* [*claim, rumour*] non corroboré.

unsuccessful /ˌʌnsəkˈsesfl/ *adj* **1** [*attempt, bid, campaign*] infructueux/-euse; [*run, production, novel, film*] sans succès; [*lawsuit*] perdu; [*love affair*] malheureux/-euse; [*effort, search*] vain; **to be ~** [*attempt, effort*] échouer; **2** [*candidate*] (for job) malchanceux/-euse; (in election) malheureux/-euse; [*businessperson*] malchanceux/-euse; [*artist*] inconnu; [*bidder*] malheureux/-euse; **to be ~ in doing** ne pas réussir à faire; **she was ~ with her application** sa candidature n'a pas été retenue.

unsuccessfully /ˌʌnsəkˈsesfəlɪ/ *adv* [*try, urge*] en vain; [*challenge, bid*] sans succès.

unsuitability /ˌʌnˌsuːtəˈbɪlətɪ/ *n* (of building, location, site) inadéquation *f* (**for** pour); **his ~ for the job** le fait qu'il n'est pas fait pour ce travail.

unsuitable /ʌnˈsuːtəbl/ *adj* [*location, equipment, clothing, accommodation, date, time*] inapproprié; [*moment*] inopportun; [*friend*] peu convenable; **to be ~** ne pas convenir (**for sb** à qn); **~ for young children** (film) déconseillé pour de jeunes enfants; **to be ~ for a job** ne pas être fait pour un travail.

unsuitably /ˈʌnˈsuːtəblɪ/ *adv* **he was ~ dressed** sa tenue était inappropriée; **to be ~ matched** [*people*] ne pas être du tout assortis.

unsuited /ʌnˈsuːtɪd/ *adj* [*place, person*] inadapté (**to** à); **posts ~ to their talents** des postes qui ne conviennent pas à leurs aptitudes; **she was ~ to country life** elle n'était pas faite pour la vie à la campagne; **they're ~ (as a couple)** ils sont mal assortis.

unsullied /ʌnˈsʌlɪd/ *adj* littér [*person*] pur et sans tache; [*reputation, innocence*] sans tache; **to be ~** ne pas être souillé (**by** par).

unsung /ʌnˈsʌŋ/ *adj* littér [*hero, achievement*] méconnu.

unsupervised /ʌnˈsuːpəvaɪzd/ *adj* [*activity*] non encadré; [*child*] laissé sans surveillance.

unsupported /ˌʌnsəˈpɔːtɪd/ **I** *adj* **1** [*allegation, hypothesis*] non confirmé; **2** Mil [*troops*] sans renfort; **3** [*family, mother*] sans soutien de famille.
II *adv* [*stand*] sans être soutenu.

unsure /ʌnˈʃɔː(r), US -ˈʃʊər/ *adj* peu sûr (**of** de); **to be ~ about how/why/where** ne pas savoir très bien comment/pourquoi/où; **to be ~ about going/staying** ne pas savoir très bien si on doit partir/rester; **to be ~ of oneself** manquer de confiance en soi.

unsurpassable /ˌʌnsəˈpɑːsəbl, US -ˈpæs-/ *adj* insurpassable.

unsurpassed /ˌʌnsəˈpɑːst, US -ˈpæst/ *adj* [*beauty*] sans égal; **to be ~** être inégalé (**in** dans; **as** comme).

unsurprising /ˌʌnsəˈpraɪzɪŋ/ *adj* **it is ~ that** il n'y a rien d'étonnant à ce que (+ *subj*); **an ~ reaction** une réaction prévisible.

unsurprisingly /ˌʌnsəˈpraɪzɪŋlɪ/ *adv* comme on peut/pouvait s'y attendre.

unsuspected /ˌʌnsəˈspektɪd/ *adj* insoupçonné.

unsuspecting /ˌʌnsəˈspektɪŋ/ *adj* [*person*] naïf/-ïve, sans méfiance; [*public*] non averti;

completely ~ sans aucune méfiance; **the stranger, ~** ... l'étranger qui ne se doutait de rien...

unswayed /ʌnˈsweɪd/ *adj* **to be ~** ne pas se laisser influencer (**by** par).

unsweetened /ʌnˈswiːtnd/ *adj* sans sucre, non sucré.

unswept /ʌnˈswept/ *adj [floor, leaves]* non balayé; *[chimney]* non ramoné.

unswerving /ʌnˈswɜːvɪŋ/ *adj* inébranlable.

unswervingly /ʌnˈswɜːvɪŋlɪ/ *adv [persist, continue]* de façon inébranlable; **~ faithful** d'une fidélité absolue (**to** envers).

unsymmetrical /ˌʌnsɪˈmetrɪkl/ *adj* asymétrique.

unsympathetic /ˌʌnsɪmpəˈθetɪk/ *adj* **1** (uncaring) *[person, attitude, manner, tone]* peu compatissant; **to be ~ to sb** se montrer peu compatissant envers qn; **2** (unattractive) *[person, character]* antipathique; *[environment, building]* peu attirant; **3** (unsupportive) **to be ~ to** ne pas soutenir *[cause, movement, policy]*; **she is ~ to the cause/to the right** elle ne sympathise pas avec la cause/la droite; **4** Ecol *[policy, measure]* qui nuit à l'environnement.

unsympathetically /ˌʌnsɪmpəˈθetɪklɪ/ *adv* avec peu de compassion.

unsystematic /ˌʌnsɪstəˈmætɪk/ *adj* peu méthodique.

unsystematically /ˌʌnsɪstəˈmætɪklɪ/ *adv* de façon peu méthodique.

untainted /ʌnˈteɪntɪd/ *adj [food]* non avarié; *[reputation]* non entaché; *[mind]* non corrompu.

untamable /ʌnˈteɪməbl/ *adj* **1** lit *[lion, tiger]* indomptable; *[bird, fox]* indressable; **2** fig *[passion, spirit]* indomptable.

untamed /ʌnˈteɪmd/ *adj [passion, person, lion]* indompté; *[garden, beauty]* (à l'état) sauvage; *[bird, fox]* non dressé.

untangle /ʌnˈtæŋgl/ **I** *vtr* démêler *[threads]* also fig; élucider *[difficulties, mystery]*.
II *v refl* **to ~ oneself** (from net, wire, situation) se dégager (**from** de).

untanned /ʌnˈtænd/ *adj [hide]* non tanné.

untapped /ʌnˈtæpt/ *adj* inexploité.

untarnished /ʌnˈtɑːnɪʃt/ *adj [reputation, sheen]* non terni; **to be ~** ne pas être terni (**by** par).

untasted /ʌnˈteɪstɪd/ *adj [food]* qui n'a pas été goûté; **she left the meal ~** elle a laissé le repas sans l'avoir goûté.

untaught /ʌnˈtɔːt/ *adj [skill, genius]* inné.

untaxable /ʌnˈtæksəbl/ *adj [income]* non imposable; *[goods]* non taxable.

untaxed /ʌnˈtækst/ *adj* **1** Tax *[income]* non soumis à l'impôt; *[goods]* non taxé; **2** GB Aut *[car]* sans vignette.

unteachable /ʌnˈtiːtʃəbl/ *adj [person]* réfractaire à l'enseignement; *[subject, skill]* qui ne se prête pas à l'enseignement.

untempered /ʌnˈtempəd/ *adj* **1** lit *[steel]* non revenu; **2** fig **to be ~** *[justice, pleasure]* ne pas être tempéré (**by** par).

untenable /ʌnˈtenəbl/ *adj [position, standpoint]* intenable; *[claim, argument]* indéfendable.

untenanted /ʌnˈtenəntɪd/ *adj [flat]* non loué.

untended /ʌnˈtendɪd/ *adj [flock]* sans surveillance; *[garden]* non entretenu.

Unterwalden **▶1776** *pr n* **the canton of ~** le canton d'Unterwald.

untested /ʌnˈtestɪd/ *adj* **1** *[theory, assertion]* non vérifié; *[method, system, drug]* non testé; **2** Psych *[person]* non testé.

unthinkable /ʌnˈθɪŋkəbl/ *adj [prospect, action]* impensable; **it is ~ that** il est impensable que (+ *subj*).

unthinking /ʌnˈθɪŋkɪŋ/ *adj [person]* irréfléchi; *[remark, criticism]* inconsidéré.

unthinkingly /ʌnˈθɪŋkɪŋlɪ/ *adv [behave, react]* sans réfléchir; *[cruel, stupid]* inconsidérément.

unthought-of /ʌnˈθɔːtɒv/ *adj* original, inédit; **hitherto ~** encore inédit.

unthread /ʌnˈθred/ *vtr* désenfiler.

untidily /ʌnˈtaɪdɪlɪ/ *adv [kept, scattered, strewn]* en désordre; **~ dressed** habillé de façon débraillée.

untidiness /ʌnˈtaɪdɪnɪs/ *n* (all contexts) désordre *m*.

untidy /ʌnˈtaɪdɪ/ *adj [person]* (in habits) désordonné; (in appearance) peu soigné; *[habits, clothes]* négligé; *[room]* en désordre; **he looks very ~** il a l'air très négligé; **the garden looks ~** le jardin a l'air peu entretenu; **his clothes lay in an ~ heap** ses vêtements formaient un tas désordonné.

untie /ʌnˈtaɪ/ *vtr* (*p prés* **-tying**) défaire, dénouer *[knot, rope, laces]*; défaire *[parcel]*; délier *[hands, hostage]*; **to come ~d** *[laces, parcel]* se défaire; *[hands]* se délier.

until /ənˈtɪl/

■ **Note** When used as a preposition in positive sentences *until* is translated by *jusqu'à*: *they're staying until Monday* = ils restent jusqu'à lundi.
– Remember that *jusqu'à* + *le* becomes *jusqu'au* and *jusqu'à* + *les* becomes *jusqu'aux*: *until the right moment* = jusqu'au bon moment; *until the exams* = jusqu'aux examens.
– In negative sentences *not until* is translated by *ne...pas avant*: *I can't see you until Friday* = je ne peux pas vous voir avant vendredi.
– When used as a conjunction in positive sentences *until* is translated by *jusqu'à ce que + subjunctive*: *we'll stay here until Maya comes back* = nous resterons ici jusqu'à ce que Maya revienne.
– In negative sentences where the two verbs have different subjects *not until* is translated by *ne...pas avant que + subjunctive*: *we won't leave until Maya comes back* = nous ne partirons pas avant que Maya revienne.
– In negative sentences where the two verbs have the same subject *not until* is translated by *pas avant de + infinitive*: *we won't leave until we've seen Claire* = nous ne partirons pas avant d'avoir vu Claire.
– For more examples and particular usages see the entry ***until.***

I *prep* **1** (also **till**) (up to a specific time) jusqu'à; (after negative verb) avant; **~ Tuesday** jusqu'à mardi; **~ the sixties** jusqu'aux années soixante; **~ very recently** il n'y a encore pas si longtemps; **~ a year ago** jusqu'à il y a un an; **~ now** jusqu'à présent; **~ then** jusqu'à ce moment-là, jusque-là; **(up) ~ 1901** jusqu'en or jusqu'à 1901; **valid (up) ~ April 1993** valable jusqu' en avril 1993; **you have ~ the end of the month** vous avez jusqu'à la fin du mois (**to do** pour faire); **~ the day he died** jusqu'à sa mort; **~ well after midnight** bien au-delà de minuit; **to wait ~ after Easter** attendre après Pâques; **from Monday ~ Saturday** du lundi au samedi; **put it off ~ tomorrow** remets-le à demain; **~ such time as you find work** jusqu'à ce que tu trouves (*subj*) du travail, en attendant que tu trouves (*subj*) du travail; **it won't be ready ~ next week** ça ne sera pas prêt avant la semaine prochaine; **I won't know ~ Tuesday** je n'aurai pas la réponse avant mardi; **they didn't ring ~ the following day** ils n'ont pas appelé avant le lendemain; **it wasn't ~ the 50's that...** ce n'est qu'à partir des années cinquante que...; **nothing changed ~ after the war** ce n'est qu'après la guerre que les choses ont commencé à changer; **2** (as far as) jusqu'à; **stay on the bus ~ Egham** ne descends pas du bus avant Egham.
II *conj* (also **till**) (*with past and present tenses*) jusqu'à ce que (+ *subj*); (in negative constructions) avant que (+ *subj*), avant de (+ *infinitive*); **we'll stay ~ a solution is reached** nous resterons jusqu'à ce que nous trouvions une solution; **and so it continued ~ they left** et cela a continué jusqu'à ce qu'ils partent or jusqu'à leur départ; **let's watch TV ~ they arrive** regardons la télévision en attendant qu'ils arrivent (*subj*); **things won't improve ~ we have democracy** la situation ne s'améliorera pas tant que nous ne serons pas en démocratie; **stir mixture ~ (it is) smooth** Culin mélangez bien jusqu'à obtenir une pâte lisse; **~ you are dead** Jur jusqu'à ce que mort s'ensuive; **wait ~ I get back** attends que je rentre (*subj*); **I'll wait ~ I get back** j'attendrai d'être rentré (**before doing** pour faire); **wait ~ I tell you!** attends! il faut que je te raconte!; **she waited ~ she was alone/they were alone** elle a attendu d'être seule/qu'ils soient seuls; **don't look ~ I tell you to** ne regarde pas avant que je te le dise; **you can't leave ~ you've completed the course** tu ne peux pas partir avant d'avoir fini le stage; **don't ring me ~ you know for sure** ne m'appelle pas avant d'être sûr; **we can't decide ~ we know the details** nous ne pouvons pas prendre de décision tant que nous n'avons pas de précisions; **not ~ then did she realize that** ce n'est qu'à ce moment-là qu'elle s'est rendu compte que; ▶ **death**.

untilled /ʌnˈtɪld/ *adj [land, field]* non labouré, en friche; **to leave sth ~** laisser qch en friche.

untimely /ʌnˈtaɪmlɪ/ *adj* littér *[arrival, announcement, intervention]* inopportun; *[death]* prématuré; **to come to an ~ end** *[person, activity, project]* connaître une fin prématurée.

untiring /ʌnˈtaɪərɪŋ/ *adj [person, enthusiasm]* infatigable (**in** dans).

untiringly /ʌnˈtaɪərɪŋlɪ/ *adv* inlassablement.

unto‡ /ˈʌntʊ/ *prep* = **to**.

untold /ʌnˈtəʊld/ *adj* **1** (not quantifiable) **~ millions** des millions et des millions; **~ quantities of tranquillizers** des quantités phénoménales de tranquillisants; **~ damage** d'énormes dégâts; **2** (endless) *[misery, damage, joy]* indicible; **3** littér (not told) **no event is left ~** on ne nous épargne aucun détail.

untouchable /ʌnˈtʌtʃəbl/ **I** *n* Relig intouchable *mf*.
II *adj [criminal]* intouchable; *[sportsman, feat]* imbattable.

untouched /ʌnˈtʌtʃt/ *adj* **1** (unchanged, undisturbed) intact; **2** (unscathed) indemne; **3** (unaffected) non affecté (**by** par); **4** (uneaten) intact; **to leave/send back a meal ~** laisser/renvoyer un repas sans y toucher.

untoward /ˌʌntəˈwɔːd, US ʌnˈtɔːrd/ *adj* **1** (unforeseen) *[happening]* fâcheux/-euse; **nothing/something ~** rien/quelque chose de fâcheux; **2** (unseemly) *[glee]* inconvenant.

untraceable /ʌnˈtreɪsəbl/ *adj* introuvable.

untraced /ʌnˈtreɪst/ *adj [descendant, survivor]* qui n'a pas encore été retrouvé; *[mail]* égaré.

untrained /ʌnˈtreɪnd/ *adj* **1** *[workers, school leavers]* sans formation; **2** *[voice]* non travaillé; *[eye]* inexercé; *[artist, actor]* non formé; **to be ~ in sth** n'avoir aucune formation en qch; **3** *[horse, dog]* non dressé.

untrammelled GB, **untrameled** US /ʌnˈtræmld/ *adj* non entravé.

untranslatable /ˌʌntrænzˈleɪtəbl/ *adj* intraduisible (**into** en).

untravelled GB, **untraveled** US /ʌnˈtrævld/ *adj [person]* qui a peu voyagé; *[land, road]* non fréquenté; **largely ~** très peu fréquenté.

untreatable /ʌnˈtriːtəbl/ *adj* incurable.

untreated /ʌnˈtriːtɪd/ *adj [sewage, water]* non traité; *[illness]* non soigné; *[road]* non sablé.

untried /ʌnˈtraɪd/ *adj* **1** *[recruit, beginner]* inexpérimenté; *[method, technology]* non essayé; *[product]* non testé; **2** Jur *[prisoner]* non jugé.

untrodden /ʌnˈtrɒdn/ *adj* littér *[snow, territory]* vierge; *[path]* non foulé.

untroubled /ʌnˈtrʌbld/ *adj [face, water,*

life] paisible; [*person*] serein; **to be ~** (by doubt) ne pas être perturbé (**by** par); (by news) ne pas être troublé (**by** par).

untrue /ʌn'tru:/ *adj* **1** (false) [*allegation, report*] faux/fausse; **2** (inaccurate) inexact; **it is ~ to say that** il est faux or inexact de dire que; **3**‡ [*sweetheart*] infidèle.

untrustworthy /ʌn'trʌstwɜ:ðɪ/ *adj* [*source, information*] douteux/-euse; [*person*] indigne de confiance; [*witness*] non digne de foi.

untruth /ʌn'tru:θ/ *n* contre-vérité *f*; (less strong) inexactitude *f*.

untruthful /ʌn'tru:θfl/ *adj* [*person*] menteur/-euse; [*account*] mensonger/-ère.

untruthfully /ʌn'tru:θfəlɪ/ *adv* [*say, report*] de façon mensongère.

untruthfulness /ʌn'tru:θflnɪs/ *n* (of remark) caractère *m* mensonger; (of person) tendance *f* à mentir.

untutored /ʌn'tju:təd, US -'tu:-/ *adj* [*eye, ear*] inexercé; [*mind*] non averti.

untwine /ʌn'twaɪn/ **I** *vtr* désentortiller.
II *vi* se désentortiller.

untwist /ʌn'twɪst/ **I** *vtr* dévisser [*lid*]; démêler [*rope, wool*].
II *vi* [*ribbon*] se dénouer.

untypical /ʌn'tɪpɪkl/ *adj* [*person, behaviour*] hors du commun; **to be ~ of sb** ne pas ressembler à qn (**to do** de faire).

unusable /ʌn'ju:zəbl/ *adj* inutilisable.

unused[1] /ʌn'ju:st/ *adj* (unaccustomed) **to be ~ to sth/to doing** ne pas être habitué à qch/à faire.

unused[2] /ʌn'ju:zd/ *adj* (not used) [*machine, building, site*] inutilisé; [*stamp, stationery*] neuf/neuve; **'computer, ~'** (in ad) 'ordinateur, état neuf'.

unusual /ʌn'ju:ʒl/ *adj* [*colour, animal, flower*] peu commun; [*case, circumstances, feature, occurrence, skill*] peu commun, inhabituel/-elle; [*dish, dress, jewellery, mixture, person*] original; **of ~ beauty** d'une rare beauté; **of ~ intelligence/charm** d'une intelligence/d'un charme hors du commun; **from an ~ angle** sous un angle inhabituel; **to have an ~ way of doing** avoir une manière originale de faire; **to take the ~ step of doing** prendre l'inhabituelle mesure de faire; **it is/is not ~ to find/see** il est/n'est pas rare de trouver/voir; **it's ~ for sb to do** il est rare que qn fasse; **to be ~ in doing** avoir la particularité de faire; **there's nothing ~ about it** cela n'a rien d'extraordinaire.

unusually /ʌn'ju:ʒəlɪ/ *adv* **1** (exceptionally) [*large, difficult, talented*] exceptionnellement; **2** (surprisingly, untypically) exceptionnellement; **~ for this time of year, the streets are very crowded** exceptionnellement pour cette époque de l'année, les rues sont noires de monde; **~, they have been awarded damages** exceptionnellement, on leur a accordé des dommages et intérêts; **~ for her, she made several mistakes** chose rare, elle a fait quelques erreurs.

unutterable /ʌn'ʌtərəbl/ *adj* indicible.

unutterably /ʌn'ʌtərəblɪ/ *adv* indiciblement.

unvaried /ʌn'veərɪd/ *adj* [*routine, diet*] monotone; [*style*] plat.

unvarnished /ʌn'vɑ:nɪʃt/ *adj* **1** [*wood*] non verni; **2** fig [*account, truth*] franc/franche et direct.

unvarying /ʌn'veərɪŋ/ *adj* [*habits, routine*] invariable; [*goodness, patience*] constant.

unvaryingly /ʌn'veərɪŋlɪ/ *adv* invariablement.

unveil /ʌn'veɪl/ *vtr* dévoiler [*statue, details*].

unveiled /ʌn'veɪld/ *adj* Relig **to go ~** ne pas porter le voile.

unveiling /ʌn'veɪlɪŋ/ *n* **1** (of statue) dévoilement *m*; **2** (official ceremony) inauguration *f*; **3** (of latest model, details) annonce *f*.

unventilated /ʌn'ventɪleɪtɪd/ *adj* [*room, area*] non ventilé.

unverifiable /ʌn'verɪfaɪəbl/ *adj* invérifiable.

unverified /ʌn'verɪfaɪd/ *adj* [*fact, rumour*] non vérifié.

unversed /ʌn'vɜ:st/ *adj* **to be ~ in sth** être peu versé dans qch.

unvoiced /ʌn'vɔɪst/ *adj* **1** (private) [*suspicion, opinion*] inexprimé; **2** Ling [*consonant*] non voisé.

unwaged /ʌn'weɪdʒd/ **I** *n* **the ~** (+ *v pl*) les non salariés.
II *adj* [*work, worker*] non salarié.

unwanted /ʌn'wɒntɪd/ *adj* [*appliance, furniture, goods, produce*] superflu; [*pet*] abandonné; [*visitor*] indésirable; [*child, pregnancy*] non souhaité; **removal of ~ hair** épilation *f*; **to feel ~** se sentir de trop.

unwarlike /ʌn'wɔ:laɪk/ *adj* peu belliqueux/-euse.

unwarrantable /ʌn'wɒrəntəbl, US -'wɔ:r-/ *adj* [*interference*] injustifiable; **it is ~ that sb should do** il est injustifiable de la part de qn de faire.

unwarrantably /ʌn'wɒrəntəblɪ, US -'wɔ:r-/ *adv* [*interfere*] de façon injustifiable; [*late, expensive*] injustifiablement.

unwarranted /ʌn'wɒrəntɪd, US -'wɔ:r-/ *adj* [*action, concern*] injustifié.

unwary /ʌn'weərɪ/ **I** *n* **the ~** (+ *v pl*) les imprudents.
II *adj* [*person*] sans méfiance.

unwashed /ʌn'wɒʃt/ *adj* [*clothes, dishes, feet*] sale, pas lavé; [*person*] qui ne s'est pas lavé; **the Great Unwashed** péj, hum la Populace.

unwavering /ʌn'weɪvərɪŋ/ *adj* [*devotion*] inébranlable; [*gaze*] résolu.

unwaveringly /ʌn'weɪvərɪŋlɪ/ *adv* [*gaze, follow*] résolument; **~ loyal/determined** d'une loyauté/détermination à toute épreuve.

unweaned /ʌn'wi:nd/ *adj* [*baby, animal*] non sevré.

unwearable /ʌn'weərəbl/ *adj* (not suitable) immettable; (not comfortable) impossible à porter.

unwearied /ʌn'wɪərɪd/ *adj* littér non lassé (**by, in** par).

unwearying /ʌn'wɪərɪɪŋ/ *adj* [*fighter*] infatigable; [*patience*] inlassable.

unwelcome /ʌn'welkəm/ *adj* **1** [*visitor, guest, presence, interruption*] importun; **she felt most ~** elle ne se sentait pas la bienvenue; **to make sb feel ~** faire sentir à qn qu'il n'est pas le bienvenu; **2** [*news, attention*] fâcheux/-euse; [*truth*] gênant; [*bid, proposition*] inopportun.

unwelcoming /ˌʌn'welkəmɪŋ/ *adj* [*atmosphere*] peu accueillant; **most ~** particulièrement peu accueillant.

unwell /ʌn'wel/ *adj* souffrant; **he is feeling ~** il ne se sent pas très bien; **are you ~?** vous êtes souffrant?

unwholesome /ʌn'həʊlsəm/ *adj* malsain.

unwieldy /ʌn'wi:ldɪ/ *adj* [*weapon, tool*] peu maniable; [*parcel*] encombrant; [*bureaucracy, organization*] lourd.

unwilling /ʌn'wɪlɪŋ/ *adj* [*attention, departure*] forcé; **he is ~ to do it** il n'est pas disposé à le faire; (stronger) il ne veut pas le faire; **~ accomplice** complice malgré moi/lui etc.

unwillingly /ʌn'wɪlɪŋlɪ/ *adv* à contrecœur.

unwillingness /ʌn'wɪlɪŋnɪs/ *n* réticence *f*; **her ~ to adapt cost her the job** sa réticence à s'adapter lui a fait perdre son emploi; **the border exists because of their ~ to live together** la frontière existe parce qu'ils n'étaient pas disposés à vivre ensemble.

unwind /ʌn'waɪnd/ (*prét, pp* **-wound**) **I** *vtr* dérouler.
II *vi* **1** [*tape, cable, scarf*] se dérouler; **2** (relax) se relaxer.

unwise /ʌn'waɪz/ *adj* [*choice, loan, decision*] peu judicieux/-ieuse; [*person*] imprudent; **it is ~ to do** il est imprudent de faire; **it would be ~ to invest now** il serait malavisé d'investir maintenant.

unwisely /ʌn'waɪzlɪ/ *adv* imprudemment.

unwitting /ʌn'wɪtɪŋ/ *adj* involontaire.

unwittingly /ʌn'wɪtɪŋlɪ/ *adv* **1** (innocently) [*remark*] innocemment; **2** (without wanting to) [*contribute, provide, reveal*] involontairement; **3** (accidentally) [*stumble upon*] accidentellement.

unwomanly /ʌn'wʊmənlɪ/ *adj* peu féminin.

unwonted /ʌn'wəʊntɪd/ *adj* littér inhabituel/-elle.

unworkable /ʌn'wɜ:kəbl/ *adj* impraticable; **to prove ~** s'avérer impraticable.

unworkmanlike /ʌn'wɜ:kmənlaɪk/ *adj* indigne d'un professionnel/d'une professionnelle.

unworldly /ʌn'wɜ:ldlɪ/ *adj* **1** (not materialistic) [*person, existence*] détaché de ce monde; **2** (naive) [*person, argument*] naïf/naïve; **3** (spiritual) [*beauty, beings*] surnaturel/-elle.

unworthiness /ʌn'wɜ:ðɪnɪs/ *n* absence *f* de mérite.

unworthy /ʌn'wɜ:ðɪ/ *adj* indigne (**of** de).

unwound /ʌn'waʊnd/ *prét, pp* ▶ **unwind**.

unwrap /ʌn'ræp/ (*p prés etc* **-pp-**) *vtr* déballer [*parcel*]; **to come ~ped** se défaire.

unwritten /ʌn'rɪtn/ *adj* **1** (tacit) [*rule, agreement*] tacite; **2** (not written) [*story, song*] non écrit; [*tradition*] oral; **the letter remained ~** la lettre n'a jamais été écrite.

unyielding /ʌn'ji:ldɪŋ/ *adj* **1** [*person, rule*] inflexible; **2** [*surface, barrier*] rigide.

unyoke /ʌn'jəʊk/ *vtr* **1** lit dételer [*animal*]; **2** fig libérer [*nation, person*] (**from** de).

unzip /ʌn'zɪp/ (*p prés etc* **-pp-**) **I** *vtr* défaire la fermeture à glissière de [*dress, trousers*]; **could you ~ me?** est-ce que tu peux défaire ma fermeture à glissière?
II *vi* s'ouvrir.

up /ʌp/

■ **Note** *up* appears frequently in English as the second element of phrasal verbs (*get up, pick up etc*). For translations, consult the appropriate verb entry (***get, pick*** etc).

I *adj* **1** (out of bed) **she's ~** elle est levée; **they're often ~ early/late** ils se lèvent souvent tôt/tard; **we were ~ very late last night** nous nous sommes couchés très tard hier soir; **they were ~ all night** ils ont veillé toute la nuit; **she was ~ all night waiting for them** elle a passé toute la nuit à les attendre; **I was still ~ at 2 am** j'étais toujours debout à 2 heures du matin; **John isn't ~ yet** John n'est pas encore levé; **we arrived before anyone was ~** quand nous sommes arrivés, personne n'était encore levé or tout le monde dormait encore; **2** (higher in amount, level) **sales/prices/interest rates are ~ (by 10%)** les ventes/les prix/les taux d'intérêt ont augmenté (de 10%); **shares/numbers of students are ~** les actions sont/le nombre d'étudiants est en hausse; **tourism/production is ~ (by) 5%** le tourisme/la production a augmenté de 5%; **his temperature is ~ 2 degrees** sa température a augmenté de 2°; **oranges/carrots are ~ again** le prix des oranges/carottes augmente de nouveau; **sales/prices are 10% ~ on last year** les ventes/les prix ont augmenté de 10% par rapport à l'an dernier; **I came out of the deal £5,000 ~** j'ai fait 5 000 livres sterling de bénéfice dans cette affaire; **3**○ (wrong) **what's ~?** qu'est-ce qui se passe?; **what's ~ with him?** qu'est-ce qu'il lui arrive?; **is there something ~?** est-ce qu'il y a quelque chose qui ne va pas?; **there's something ~** il y a quelque chose qui ne va pas; **there's something ~ with him/your dad** il/ton père n'a pas l'air bien; **what's ~ with the TV?** qu'est-ce qu'elle a la télé?; **what's ~ with your arm?** qu'est-ce que tu as au bras?; **there's something ~ with the brakes** il y a un problème avec les freins; **there's something ~ with my back** mon dos me fait mal; **4** (erected, affixed) **the notice/the photograph is ~ on the board** l'annonce/la photographie est affichée sur le panneau; **is the tent ~?** est-ce que la tente est déjà montée?; **the building will be ~ in three months time** le bâtiment sera terminé dans trois mois; **how long have those curtains been ~?** depuis quand est -ce que ces rideaux sont pendus or là?; **he had his hand ~ for five minutes** il a gardé la main levée pendant cinq minutes; **5** (open) **he had his umbrella ~** il avait son parapluie ouvert; **the hood** GB **of the car was ~** la capote de la voiture était fermée; **the blinds were ~** les stores étaient levés; **when the switch/lever is ~ the machine is off** si le bouton/levier est vers le haut la machine est arrêtée; **when the barrier is ~ you can go through** quand la barrière est levée vous pouvez passer; **6** (finished) **'time's ~!'** 'le temps est épuisé!'; **his leave/military service is almost ~** son congé/service militaire est presque terminé; **when the four days/months were ~** à la fin des quatre jours/mois; **it's all ~**○ **with this government** c'est la fin du gouvernement; **it's all ~**○ **with him** il est fini○; **7** (facing upwards) **'this side ~'** (on parcel, box) 'haut'; **he was lying/floating face ~** il était allongé/flottait sur le dos; **the bread landed with the buttered side ~** la tartine est tombée côté beurré vers le haut; **8** (rising) **the river is ~** la rivière est en crue; **the wind is ~** le vent est fort; **his colour's ~** il est tout rouge; **his blood's ~** fig la moutarde lui monte au nez; **9** (pinned up) **her hair was ~** elle avait les cheveux relevés; **10** (cheerful) **he's ~ at the moment** il est en forme en ce moment; **11** (being repaired) **the road is ~** la route est en travaux; **'Road ~'** (on sign) 'Travaux'; **12** (in upward direction) **the ~ escalator** l'escalator® qui monte; **13** (on trial) **to be ~ before a judge** passer devant le tribunal; **he's ~ for murder/fraud** il est accusé de meurtre/fraude; **14** Sport (in tennis, badminton) **not ~!** faute!; **15**○ GB (ready) **tea ~!** le thé est prêt!

II *adv* **1** (high) **~ here/there** là-haut; **~ on the wardrobe/the top shelf/the hill** sur l'armoire/l'étagère la plus haute/la colline; **~ in the tree/the clouds** dans l'arbre/les nuages; **~ at the top of the house** tout en haut de la maison; **~ on top of the mountain** au sommet de la montagne; **~ in London** à Londres; **~ to/in Scotland** en Écosse; **~ to Aberdeen** à Aberdeen; **~ North** au nord; **four floors ~ from here** quatre étages au- dessus; **I live two floors ~** j'habite au deuxième étage; **he lives ten floors ~ from her** il habite dix étages au-dessus d'elle; **on the second shelf ~** sur la deuxième étagère en partant du bas; **I'm on my way ~** je monte; **I'll be right ~** je monte tout de suite; **he's on his way ~ to see you/to the fifth floor** il est en train de monter vous voir/au cinquième étage; **it needs to be a bit further ~** (picture etc) il faut le mettre un peu plus haut; **all the way ~** jusqu'en haut, jusqu'au sommet; **2** (ahead) d'avance; **to be four points ~ (on sb)** avoir quatre points d'avance (sur qn); **they were two goals ~** ils menaient avec deux buts d'avance; **she's 40–15 ~** (in tennis) elle mène 40–15; **3** (upwards) **t-shirts from £2 ~** des t-shirts à partir de deux livres; **from (the age of) 14 ~** à partir de 14 ans; **everyone in the company from the cleaning lady ~** tout le monde dans l'entreprise, de la femme de ménage au patron; **4** (at, to high status) **to be ~ with** ou **among the best/the leaders** faire partie des meilleurs/des leaders; **~ the workers!** vive les travailleurs!; **'~ with Manchester United'** 'vive Manchester United'.

III *prep* **1** (at, to higher level) **~ the tree** dans l'arbre; **~ a ladder** sur une échelle; **the library is ~ the stairs** la bibliothèque se trouve en haut de l'escalier; **he ran ~ the stairs** il a monté l'escalier en courant; **the road ~ the mountain** la route qui gravit la montagne; **the spider crawled ~ my back** l'araignée a grimpé le long de mon dos; **the pipe runs ~ the front of the house** le tuyau monte le long de la façade de la maison; **2** (in direction) **the shops are ~ the road** les magasins sont plus loin dans la rue; **she lives ~ that road there** elle habite dans cette rue; **he lives just ~ the road** il habite juste à côté; **the boathouse is further ~ the river** le hangar à bateaux est plus loin au bord de la rivière; **his office is ~ the corridor from mine** son bureau est dans le même couloir que le mien; **he walked ~ the road singing** il a remonté la rue en chantant; **the car drove ~ the road** la voiture a remonté la rue; **I saw him go ~ that road there** je l'ai vu partir dans cette rue; **she's got water ~ her nose** elle a de l'eau dans le nez; **he put it ~ his sleeve** il l'a mis dans sa manche; **3**○ GB (at, to) **he's ~ the pub** il est au pub.

IV up above *adv phr, prep phr* gen au-dessus; Relig au ciel; **~ above sth** au-dessus de qch.

V up against *prep phr* lit **~ against the wall** contre le mur; fig **to be ~** ou **come ~ against difficulties/opposition** rencontrer des difficultés/de l'opposition; **they're ~ against a very strong team** ils sont confrontés à une équipe très forte; **it helps to know what you are ~ against** il faut savoir ce contre quoi on se bat; **we're really ~ against it** on a vraiment des problèmes.

VI up and about *adv phr* (out of bed) debout, réveillé; (after illness) **to be ~ and about again** être de nouveau sur pied.

VII up and down *adv phr, prep phr* **1** (to and fro) **to walk** ou **pace ~ and down** aller et venir, faire les cent pas; **he was walking ~ and down the garden** il faisait les cent pas dans le jardin; **they travelled ~ and down the country** ils ont sillonné le pays; **she's been ~ and down all night** (in and out of bed) elle n'a pas arrêté de se lever pendant la nuit; **he's a bit ~ and down at the moment** fig (depressed) il n'a pas le moral en ce moment; (ill) il n'est pas en forme en ce moment; **2** (throughout) **~ and down the country/region** dans tout le pays/toute la région.

VIII up and running *adj phr, adv phr* **to be ~ and running** [*company, project*] bien marcher; [*system*] bien fonctionner; **to get sth ~ and running** faire marcher or fonctionner qch.

IX up for *prep phr* **he's ~ for election** il se présente aux élections; **the subject ~ for discussion/consideration is...** le sujet qu'on aborde/considère est...

X up to *prep phr* **1** (to particular level) jusqu'à; **~ to here** jusqu'ici; **~ to there** jusque là; **I was ~ to my knees in water** j'étais dans l'eau jusqu'aux genoux; **2** (as many as) jusqu'à, près de; **~ to 20 people/50 dollars** jusqu'à 20 personnes/50 dollars; **~ to 500 people arrive every day** près de 500 personnes arrivent tous les jours; **reductions of ~ to 50%** des réductions qui peuvent atteindre 50%; **tax on profits of ~ to £150,000** les impôts sur les bénéfices de moins de 150 000 livres sterling; **to work for ~ to 12 hours a day** travailler jusqu'à 12 heures par jour; **a hotel for ~ to 500 people** un hôtel qui peut accueillir jusqu'à 500 personnes; **3** (until) jusqu'à; **~ to 1964** jusqu'en 1964; **~ to 10.30 pm** jusqu'à 22 h 30; **~ to now** jusqu'à maintenant; **~ to chapter two** jusqu'au chapitre deux; **4** (good enough for) **I'm not ~ to it** (not capable) je n'en suis pas capable; (not well enough) je n'en ai pas la force; **I'm not ~ to going to London/going back to work** je n'ai pas le courage d'aller à Londres/de retourner travailler; **I'm not ~ to writing a book** je ne suis pas capable d'écrire un livre; **the play wasn't ~ to much** la pièce n'était pas formidable; **this piece of work wasn't ~ to your usual standard** ce travail n'est pas au niveau de ce que vous faites d'habitude; **5** (expressing responsibility) **it's ~ to you/him to do** c'est à toi/lui de faire; **'shall I leave?'—'it's ~ to you!'** 'est-ce que je devrais partir?'—'c'est à toi de décider!'; **if it were ~ to me/him** si ça dépendait de moi/de lui; **6** (doing) **what is he ~ to?** qu'est-ce qu'il fait?; **what are those children ~ to?** qu'est-ce qu'ils fabriquent○ ces enfants?; **they're ~ to something** ils mijotent○ quelque chose.

XI *vtr* (*p prés etc* **-pp-**) (increase) augmenter [*price, interest rate, wages*].

XII○ *vi* (*p prés etc* **-pp-**) **he ~ped and left/hit him** tout d'un coup il s'est levé et est parti/l'a frappé; **she ~ped and married someone else** elle a épousé quelqu'un d'autre sans attendre.

IDIOMS **the company is on the ~ and ~** ça marche très bien pour l'entreprise; **to be one ~ on sb** faire mieux que qn; **to be (well) ~ on** s'y connaître en [*art, history etc*]; être au courant de [*news, developments, changes*]; **the ~s and downs** les hauts et les bas **(of** de); **~ yours◑!** va te faire foutre◑!

up and coming *adj* [*person, company*] qui monte/montait, prometteur/-euse.

upbeat /ˈʌpbiːt/ **I** *n* Mus levé *m*.
II *adj* fig optimiste.

up-bow /ˈʌpbəʊ/ *n* Mus poussé *m*.

upbraid /ˌʌpˈbreɪd/ *vtr* sout reprocher à **(for, about** de; **for doing** de faire).

upbringing /ˈʌpbrɪŋɪŋ/ *n* éducation *f*.

upchuck○ /ˈʌptʃʌk/ *vtr, vi* US dégueuler◑.

upcoming /ˌʌpˈkʌmɪŋ/ *adj* (forthcoming) prochain.

upcountry /ˌʌpˈkʌntrɪ/ **I** *adj* [*town, place*] de l'arrière-pays.
II *adv* [*return, travel*] vers l'arrière-pays.

update I /ˈʌpdeɪt/ *n* mise *f* à jour **(on** de); **news ~** dernières nouvelles *fpl*.
II /ˌʌpˈdeɪt/ *vtr* **1** (revise) mettre or remettre [qch] à jour [*database, information, catalogue, figure*]; actualiser [*price, value*]; **2** (modernize) moderniser [*machinery, method*]; remettre [qch] au goût du jour [*image, style*]; **3** mettre [qn] au courant [*person*] **(on** de).

updraught /ˈʌpdrɑːft/ GB, **updraft** /ˈʌpdræft/ US *n* courant *m* d'air ascendant.

upend /ˌʌpˈend/ *vtr* **1** (turn upside down) retourner [*container*]; mettre [qn] la tête en bas [*person*]; **2** (stand upright) mettre debout [*box, barrel*].

upfront○ /ˌʌpˈfrʌnt/ **I** *adj* **1** (frank) franc/franche; **2** (conspicuous) en vue; **3** [*money*] payé d'avance.
II *adv* [*pay*] d'avance.

upgrade I /ˈʌpgreɪd/ *n* **1** (upward gradient) montée *f*; **to be on the ~** gen être en progrès; [*prices*] être en hausse; [*sick person*] être en voie de guérison; **2** Tourism surclassement *m*.
II /ˈʌpgreɪd/ *adv* US = **uphill**.
III /ˌʌpˈgreɪd/ *vtr* **1** (modernize) moderniser; (improve) améliorer [*product*]; **2** Comput augmenter [*memory*]; améliorer [*system, software, hardware*]; **3** (raise) promouvoir [*person*]; revaloriser [*job, position, skill*]; **4** Tourism surclasser [*passenger*].

upheaval /ˌʌpˈhiːvl/ *n* **1** (disturbance) **C** (political, emotional) bouleversement *m*; (physical) (in house etc) remue-ménage *m inv*; **2 ¢** (instability) (political, emotional) bouleversements *mpl*; (physical) remue-ménage *m inv*; **political/social ~** bouleversements politiques/sociaux; **emotional ~** un bouleversement affectif; **3** Geol surrection *f*.

uphill /ˌʌpˈhɪl/ **I** *adj* **1** lit [*road, slope*] qui monte; **2** fig (difficult) [*task*] difficile; **it will be an ~ struggle** ou **battle** cela va être difficile.
II *adv* [*go, walk*] en montée; **the path led** ou **ran ~** le sentier montait; **she can't walk ~** elle ne peut pas marcher dans les montées; **the house is ~ from here** la

maison est dans la montée par rapport à ici; **it's ~ all the way** lit ça monte tout le temps; fig ce n'est pas tâche facile.

uphold /ˌʌp'həʊld/ *vtr* (*prét, pp* **-held**) **1** gen soutenir [*right, principle, belief, institution*]; faire respecter [*law*]; **2** Jur confirmer [*sentence, decision*].

upholder /ˌʌp'həʊldə(r)/ *n* défenseur *m* (**of** de).

upholster /ˌʌp'həʊlstə(r)/ **I** *vtr* rembourrer [*chair, sofa etc*].

II upholstered *pp adj* **1** [*furniture*] rembourré; **2**○ hum **well ~** [*person*] bien rembourré○.

upholsterer /ˌʌp'həʊlstərə(r)/ ▶ **1692** *n* tapissier/-ière *m/f*.

upholstery /ˌʌp'həʊlstərɪ/ *n* **1** (covering) revêtement *m*; **2** (stuffing) rembourrage *m*; **3** (technique) tapisserie *f*.

upkeep /'ʌpkiːp/ *n* **1** (care) (of house, garden) entretien *m* (**of** de); [*of animal*] garde *f* (**of** de); **2** (cost of care) frais *mpl* d'entretien.

upland /'ʌplənd/ **I** *n* **the ~s** les hautes terres.

II *adj* [*area, farm, river*] des hautes terres.

uplift I /'ʌplɪft/ *n* **1** (of person, spirits) tonus *m*; (of career) nouvel essor *m*; **2** (of prices, market) nouvelle envolée *f*; (of living standards) amélioration *f*; **3** Geol soulèvement *m*.

II /ˌʌp'lɪft/ *vtr* remonter [*person, spirits*].

uplift bra *n* soutien-gorge *m* pigeonnant.

uplifted /ˌʌp'lɪftɪd/ *adj* [*face, limb*] levé; **to feel ~** fig se sentir remonté.

uplifting /ˌʌp'lɪftɪŋ/ *adj* tonique.

up-market /ˌʌp'mɑːkɪt/ *adj* [*clothes, car, hotel, restaurant*] haut de gamme; [*district, area*] riche.

upmost /'ʌpməʊst/ *adj* ▶ **uppermost**.

upon /ə'pɒn/ *prep* = **on** I.

upper /'ʌpə(r)/ **I** *n* **1** (of shoe) empeigne *f*; **'leather ~'** 'dessus cuir'; **2**○ US Rail couchette *f* supérieure; **3**○ US argot des drogués stimulant *m*.

II *adj* **1** (in location) [*shelf, cupboard*] du haut; [*floor, deck*] supérieur; [*jaw, eyelid, lip*] supérieur; [*teeth*] du haut; **the ~ body** la partie supérieure du corps; **2** (in rank) supérieur; **3** (on scale) [*register, scale*] supérieur; **the ~ limit** la limite maximale (**on** de); **temperatures are in the ~ twenties** les températures dépassent 25°; **4** Geog (*epith*) [*valley, region*] plus au nord; **the Upper** (**reaches of the**) **Thames** la haute Tamise; **5** Archeol, Geol [*period*] supérieur.

IDIOMS **to be on one's ~s**○ être dans la dèche○; **to have the ~ hand** avoir le dessus; **to get the ~ hand** prendre le dessus. ▶ **stiff**.

upper: **~ arm** *n* bras *m*, humérus *m* spec; **~ atmosphere** *n* couches *fpl* supérieures de l'atmosphère.

upper case I *n* haut *m* de casse; **in ~** en haut de casse. **II** *adj*: **~ letters** (lettres *fpl*) majuscules *fpl*.

upper circle *n* Theat deuxième balcon *m*.

upper class I *n* **the ~**, **the ~es** l'aristocratie *f*.

II upper-class *adj* [*accent, background, person*] distingué; **in ~ circles** dans la haute société.

upper classman *n* US Univ étudiant/-e *m/f* de troisième ou quatrième année.

upper crust○ hum **I** *n* **the ~** le gratin○ *m*.

II upper-crust *adj* [*accent, family*] de la haute○.

upper: **~cut** *n* Sport uppercut *m*; **Upper Egypt** *pr n* Haute-Egypte *f*; **Upper House** *n* Chambre *f* haute; **~-income bracket** *n* tranche *f* des revenus élevés.

upper middle class I *n* **the ~**, **the ~es** la haute bourgeoisie *f*.

II *adj* de la haute bourgeoisie.

uppermost /'ʌpəməʊst/ *adj* **1** (highest) [*deck, peak, branch*] le plus haut; (in rank) [*echelon, position*] le plus élevé; **2** (to the fore) **to be ~** être prédominant; **to be ~ in sb's mind** être au premier plan des pensées de qn.

upper school *n* GB Sch **1** (school) *établissement scolaire de second degré* (*pour élèves de 13 à 18 ans*); **2** (within school) **the ~** les grandes classes *fpl*.

upper: **Upper Silesia** *pr n* Haute Silésie *f*; **~ sixth** *n* GB Sch cf (classe *f*) terminale *f*; **Upper Volta** *pr n* Hist Haute-Volta *f*.

uppish○ /'ʌpɪʃ/ *adj* GB **1** = **uppity**; **2** Sport haut.

uppity○ /'ʌpətɪ/ *adj* arrogant; **to get ~ about sth** prendre qch de haut.

uprate /ˌʌp'reɪt/ *vtr* augmenter [*benefit, pension*]; améliorer [*version, performance*]; Phot pousser [*film*].

uprating /ˌʌp'reɪtɪŋ/ *n* (of benefit) augmentation *f*.

upright /'ʌpraɪt/ **I** *n* **1** Constr montant *m*; **2** (in football) montant *m* de but; **3** Mus piano *m* droit.

II *adj* lit, fig droit; **to have an ~ bearing** se tenir très droit; **to stay ~** [*person*] rester debout; **'keep ~'** (on package) 'ne pas retourner'.

III *adv* **to stand ~** se tenir droit; **to sit ~** (action) se redresser.

upright: **~ chair** *n* chaise *f*; **~ freezer** *n* congélateur *m* armoire.

uprightly /'ʌpraɪtlɪ/ *adv* honnêtement.

uprightness /'ʌpraɪtnɪs/ *n* droiture *f*.

upright: **~ piano** ▶ **1481** *n* piano *m* droit; **~ vacuum cleaner** *n* aspirobatteur *m*.

uprising /'ʌpraɪzɪŋ/ *n* soulèvement *m* (**against** contre).

upriver /ˌʌp'rɪvə(r)/ **I** *adj* en amont.

II *adv* vers l'amont.

uproar /'ʌprɔː(r)/ *n* **1** (violent indignation) indignation *f*; **to cause an international ~** soulever une indignation internationale; **2** (noisy reaction) tumulte *m*; **to cause** (**an**) **~** déclencher un tumulte de protestations; **3** (chaos) **to be in ~** être dans la plus vive agitation.

uproarious /ʌp'rɔːrɪəs/ *adj* **1** (funny) désopilant; **2** (rowdy) [*behaviour*] tapageur/-euse; [*laughter*] tonitruant.

uproariously /ʌp'rɔːrɪəslɪ/ *adv* [*laugh*] aux éclats; **~ funny** désopilant.

uproot /ˌʌp'ruːt/ *vtr* lit, fig déraciner.

upsa-daisy /'ʌpsədeɪzɪ/ *excl* hop là.

upscale /'ʌpskeɪl/ *adj* US chic *inv*.

upset I /'ʌpset/ *n* **1** (surprise, setback) Pol, Sport revers *m*; **to suffer an ~** subir un revers; **big Conservative ~** journ sérieux revers pour les conservateurs; **to cause an ~** causer la surprise; **2** (upheaval) bouleversement *m*; **3** (distress) peine *f*; **4** Med **to have a stomach ~** avoir un problème d'estomac.

II /ˌʌp'set/ *vtr* (*p prés* **-tt-**; *prét, pp* **-set**) **1** (distress) [*sight, news*] retourner; [*person*] faire de la peine à; **2** (annoy) contrarier; **you'll only ~ her** tu ne feras que la contrarier; **3** fig (throw into disarray) bouleverser [*plan*]; déjouer [*calculations, forecast*]; affecter [*pattern, situation*]; **4** (destabilize) rompre [*balance*]; (knock over) renverser; **5** Pol, Sport (topple) déloger [*leader, party in power*]; **6** Med rendre malade [*person*]; perturber [*digestion*].

III○ /ˌʌp'set/ *v refl* (*p prés* **-tt-**; *prét, pp* **-set**) **to ~ oneself** se tracasser○; **don't ~ yourself** ne te tracasse donc pas.

IV /ˌʌp'set/ *pp adj* [*person*] **to be** ou **feel ~** (distressed) être très affecté (**at, about** par); (annoyed) être contrarié (**at, about** par); **to get ~** (angry) se fâcher (**about** pour); (distressed) se tracasser (**about** pour).

upset price US Comm mise *f* à prix.

upsetting /ˌʌp'setɪŋ/ *adj* (distressing) [*sight, story, news*] navrant (**to do** de faire); affligeant (**to do** de faire); (annoying) contrariant (**to do** de faire).

upshot /'ʌpʃɒt/ *n* résultat *m*; **the ~ is that** le résultat, c'est que.

upside○ /'ʌpsaɪd/ US **I** *n* haut *m*.

II *prep* sur le côté de.

upside down /ˌʌpsaɪd 'daʊn/ **I** *adj* lit à l'envers; fig sens dessus dessous; **~ cake** Culin gâteau *m* renversé.

II *adv* **1** lit à l'envers; **bats hang ~** les chauves-souris s'accrochent la tête en bas; **2** fig **to turn the house ~** mettre la maison sens dessus dessous; **to turn sb's life ~** bouleverser la vie de qn.

upstage /ˌʌp'steɪdʒ/ **I** *adj* Theat [*entrance*] situé au fond de la scène.

II *adv* Theat [*stand*] au fond de la scène; [*move*] vers le fond de la scène; **to be ~ of sb/sth** être plus au fond de la scène que qn/qch.

III *vtr* Theat, fig éclipser.

upstairs /ˌʌp'steəz/ **I** *n* haut *m*; **the ~ is much nicer** le haut est beaucoup plus joli; **there is no ~ in this house** il n'y a pas d'étage dans cette maison; **~ and downstairs** fig (masters and servants) maîtres *mpl* et valets *mpl*.

II *modif* [*room*] du haut; [*neighbours*] du dessus; **an ~ bedroom** une chambre à l'étage; **the ~ bedroom** la chambre du haut; **the ~ flat** GB l'appartement du haut or d'en haut; **with ~ bathroom** avec salle de bains à l'étage.

III *adv* en haut; **to go ~** monter (l'escalier); **a noise came from ~** il y a eu un bruit venant d'en haut.

IDIOMS **he hasn't got much ~**○ il n'a pas grand-chose dans le ciboulot○ or dans la tête; **to be kicked ~**○ recevoir une promotion placard.

upstanding /ˌʌp'stændɪŋ/ *adj* lit bien bâti; fig plein de probité; **to be ~** sout se lever.

upstart /'ʌpstɑːt/ *n, adj* arriviste (*mf*).

upstate /'ʌpsteɪt/ **I** *adj* **~ New York** la partie nord de l'État de New York.

II *adv* **to go/come from ~** (north) aller vers le/venir du nord (*d'un État*); (rural) aller au/venir du fin fond d'un État.

upstream /ˌʌp'striːm/ **I** *adj* en amont.

II *adv* [*travel*] vers l'amont; **~ from here** en amont d'ici.

upstretched /ˌʌp'stretʃt/ *adj* [*arms*] tendu.

upstroke /'ʌpstrəʊk/ *n* **1** (in handwriting) délié *m*; **2** Tech mouvement *m* ascensionnel.

upsurge /'ʌpsɜːdʒ/ *n* (of violence) montée *f* (**of** de); (in debt, demand, industrial activity) augmentation *f* (**in** de).

upswept /'ʌpswept/ *adj* [*hairstyle*] en hauteur; [*tail fin*] qui remonte.

upswing /'ʌpswɪŋ/ *n* (improvement) reprise *f* (**in** de); (increase) augmentation *f* (**in** de).

uptake /'ʌpteɪk/ *n* **1** Tech (shaft) carneau *m*; **2** Biol, Med (absorption) assimilation *f*.

IDIOMS **to be quick/slow on the ~**○ comprendre/ne pas comprendre vite.

up-tempo /ˌʌp'tempəʊ/ *adj* au rythme enlevé.

upthrust /'ʌpθrʌst/ *n* **1** Tech poussée *f* ascendante; **2** Geol soulèvement *m*.

uptick /'ʌptɪk/ *n* US **1** Fin *transaction boursière à un prix plus élevé que la précédente*; **2** gen augmentation *f*.

uptight○ /ˌʌp'taɪt/ *adj* (tense) tendu; péj (reserved) coincé○.

up-to-date /ˌʌptə'deɪt/ *adj* **1** (modern, fashionable) [*music, clothes*] à la mode; [*equipment*] moderne; **2** (containing latest information) [*brochure, records, accounts, map, timetable*] à jour; [*information, news*] récent; **to keep sth up to date** tenir qch à jour [*records, list, accounts*]; **3** (informed) [*person*] au courant; **to keep up to date with** se tenir au courant de [*developments*]; être au courant de [*gossip*]; **to bring/keep sb up to date** mettre/tenir qn au courant (**about** de); **to keep up to date** être bien informé.

up-to-the-minute *adj* [*information, account*] dernier/-ière.

uptown /ˌʌp'taʊn/ US **I** *adj* **in the ~**

section of New York au nord de New York; fig (smart) [*girl, restaurant*] chic.
II *adv* **1** (upmarket) **to move ~** (residence) aller habiter dans un quartier résidentiel chic; (shop) transférer son magasin dans un quartier chic; fig réussir socialement; **2** (central) **to go ~** aller dans le centre.

upturn I /ˈʌptɜ:n/ *n* reprise *f*.
II **upturned** *pp adj* posé à l'envers; [*brim*] remonté; [*soil*] retourné; [*nose*] retroussé.

upward /ˈʌpwəd/ **I** *adj* [*glance, push, movement*] vers le haut; [*path, road*] qui monte; **an ~ slope** une montée; **an ~ trend** fig Fin une tendance à la hausse.
II *adv* ▶ **upwards**.

upwardly mobile *adj* en pleine ascension sociale.

upward mobility *n* ascension *f* sociale.

upwards /ˈʌpwədz/ **I** *adv* **1** lit [*look, point*] vers le haut; **to go** ou **move ~** monter; **to glide ~** remonter or glisser vers le haut; **he was lying face ~** il était allongé sur le dos; **2** fig **to push prices ~** faire monter les prix; **to revise one's forecasts ~** réviser ses prévisions à la hausse; **from five years/£10 ~** à partir de cinq ans/10 livres sterling; **she's moving ~ in her profession** elle avance dans sa carrière.
II **upwards of** *prep phr* plus de; **~ of £50/20%** plus de 50 livres sterling/20%.

upwind /ˌʌpˈwɪnd/ **I** *adj* sous le vent; **to be ~ of sth** être dans le vent de qch.
II *adv* [*sail*] contre le vent.

uraemia, **uremia** US /jʊˈri:mɪə/ ▶ **1354** *n* urémie *f*.

Ural /ˈjʊərəl/ *pr n* **the ~s** l'Oural *m*.

uranium /jʊˈreɪnɪəm/ **I** *n* uranium *m*.
II *modif* [*reserves, producer*] d'uranium.

uranium series *n* famille *f* radioactive de l'uranium 238.

Uranus /ˈjʊərənəs, jʊˈreɪnəs/ *pr n* **1** Mythol Ouranos *m*; **2** Astron Uranus *f*.

urban /ˈɜ:bən/ *adj* [*environment, landscape, life, transport, area*] urbain; [*school*] en ville; **~ dweller** citadin/-e *m/f*.

urban: **~ blight** *n* dégradation *f* urbaine; **~ conservation area** *n* GB secteur *m* sauvegardé; **~ decay** *n* dégradation *f* urbaine; **~ development zone** *n* cf zone *f* à urbaniser en priorité; **Urban District Council**, **UDC** *n* GB conseil *m* de district urbain.

urbane /ɜ:ˈbeɪn/ *adj* [*person*] plein de savoir-faire; [*grace, style*] raffiné.

urbanism /ˈɜ:bənɪzəm/ *n* US **1** (way of life) vie *f* citadine; **2** (urban studies) études *fpl* d'urbanisme; (town planning) urbanisme *m*.

urbanist /ˈɜ:bənɪst/ *n* US urbaniste *mf*.

urbanite /ˈɜ:bənaɪt/ *n* US citadin/-e *m/f*.

urbanity /ɜ:ˈbænətɪ/ *n* urbanité *f*.

urbanization /ˌɜ:bənaɪˈzeɪʃn, US -nɪˈz-/ *n* urbanisation *f*.

urbanize /ˈɜ:bənaɪz/ *vtr* urbaniser; **to become ~d** s'urbaniser.

urban: **~ planner** ▶ **1692** *n* urbaniste *mf*; **~ planning** *n* urbanisme *m*; **~ renewal** *n* rénovation *f* urbaine; **~ sprawl** *n* péj (phenomenon) étalement *m* de la ville; (buildings) agglomération *f*; **~ studies** *npl* études *fpl* d'urbanisme.

urchin /ˈɜ:tʃɪn/ **I** *n* gamin *m*; **street ~** gamin des rues.
II *modif* [*smile, haircut*] gamin.

Urdu /ˈʊədu:/ ▶ **1402** *n* urdu *m*.

urea /ˈjʊərɪə, US ˈjʊrɪə/ *n* (all contexts) urée *f*.

ureter /jʊəˈri:tə(r)/ *n* uretère *m*.

urethra /jʊəˈri:θrə/ *n* urètre *m*.

urge /ɜ:dʒ/ **I** *n* **1** désir *m*, forte envie *f*; **to feel** ou **have an ~ to do** avoir une forte envie de faire; **2** (sexual) pulsion *f* sexuelle.
II *vtr* **1** (encourage) conseiller vivement, préconiser [*caution, restraint, resistance*]; **to ~ sb to do** conseiller vivement à qn de faire; (stronger) pousser or exhorter qn à faire; **we ~d her to go to the police** nous lui avons vivement conseillé d'aller à la police; **I ~d them not to go** je leur ai vivement déconseillé d'y aller; **to ~ that sth (should) be done** insister pour que qch soit fait; **'go and ask him again,' she ~d** 'va lui redemander,' insista-t-elle; **to ~ patience/restraint on sb** exhorter qn à la patience/modération; **they needed no urging** ils ne se sont pas fait prier; **2** (goad) faire avancer, pousser [*horse, herd*]; **he ~d the sheep through the gate** il a fait passer les moutons de l'autre côté de la barrière.
■ **urge on**: **~ on [sb]**, **~ [sb] on** **1** (encourage) encourager [*person, team etc*]; **to ~ sb on to do** inciter or pousser qn à faire; **2** (make go faster) talonner [*horse*]; faire avancer [*herd, crowd*].

urgency /ˈɜ:dʒənsɪ/ *n* (of situation, appeal, request) urgence *f*; (of voice, tone) insistance *f*; **a matter of ~** une affaire urgente; **to do sth as a matter of ~** faire qch d'urgence; **there's no ~** ce n'est pas urgent; **there was a note of ~ in his voice** il y avait une note d'insistance dans sa voix.

urgent /ˈɜ:dʒənt/ *adj* **1** (pressing) [*case, need*] urgent, pressant; [*message, letter, demand*] urgent; [*meeting, investigation, measures*] d'urgence; **to be in ~ need of** avoir un besoin urgent de; **it is ~ that you (should) leave as soon as possible** il est urgent que vous partiez le plus vite possible; **it is most ~ that we (should) find a solution** il est vraiment urgent que nous trouvions une solution; **it's ~!** c'est urgent!; **it requires your ~ attention** il faut que vous vous en occupiez d'urgence; **2** (desperate) [*plea, entreaty, request, tone, voice*] insistant, pressant.

urgently /ˈɜ:dʒəntlɪ/ *adv* [*request*] d'urgence; [*plead*] instamment; **books are ~ needed** il y a un besoin urgent de livres.

urging /ˈɜ:dʒɪŋ/ *n* incitation *f*; **to do sth at sb's ~** faire qch devant l'insistance or sur les instances de qn.

Uri ▶ **1776** *pr n* **the canton of ~** le canton d'Uri.

uric /ˈjʊərɪk/ *adj* urique.

urinal /jʊəˈraɪnl, ˈjʊərɪnl/ *n* (place) urinoir *m*; (fixture) urinal *m*.

urinary /ˈjʊərɪnərɪ, US -nerɪ/ *adj* urinaire.

urinate /ˈjʊərɪneɪt/ *vi* uriner.

urine /ˈjʊərɪn/ *n* urine *f*.

urinogenital /ˌjʊərɪnəʊˈdʒenɪtl/ *adj* urogénital/-e.

urn /ɜ:n/ *n* urne *f*.

urological /ˌjʊərəˈlɒdʒɪkl/ *adj* urologique.

urologist /jʊəˈrɒlədʒɪst/ ▶ **1692** *n* urologue *mf*.

urology /jʊəˈrɒlədʒɪ/ *n* urologie *f*.

Ursa Major /ˌɜ:sə ˈmeɪdʒə(r)/ *pr n* la Grande Ourse *f*.

Ursa Minor /ˌɜ:sə ˈmaɪnə(r)/ *pr n* la Petite Ourse *f*.

urticaria /ˌɜ:tɪˈkeərɪə/ ▶ **1354** *n* urticaire *f*.

Uruguay /ˈjʊərəgwaɪ/ ▶ **1131** *pr n* Uruguay *m*; **to ~** en Uruguay.

Uruguayan /ˌjʊərəˈgwaɪən/ ▶ **1486** **I** *n* Uruguayen/-enne *m/f*.
II *adj* uruguayen/-enne.

us /ʌs, əs/

■ **Note** The direct or indirect object pronoun *us* is always translated by nous: *she knows us* = elle nous connaît. Note that both the direct and the indirect object pronouns come before the verb in French and that in compound tenses like the present perfect and past perfect, the past participle agrees in gender and number with the direct object pronoun: *he's seen us* (*masculine or mixed gender object*) il nous a vus; (*feminine object*) il nous a vues.
– In imperatives *nous* comes after the verb: *tell us!* = dis-nous!; *give it to us or give us it* = donne-le-nous (note the hyphens).
– After the verb *to be* and after prepositions the translation is also *nous*: *it's us* = c'est nous.
– For expressions with *let us* or *let's* see the entry ***let***.
– For particular usages see the entry below.

pron nous; **both of ~** tous/toutes les deux; **both of ~ like Balzac** nous aimons Balzac tous/toutes les deux; (more informally) on aime Balzac tous/toutes les deux; **every single one of ~** chacun/-e d'entre nous; **people like ~** des gens comme nous; **some of ~** quelques-uns/-unes d'entre nous; **she's one of ~** elle est des nôtres; **give ~ a hand, will you**○**?** tu peux me donner un coup de main s'il te plait?; **oh give ~ a break**○**!** fiche-moi la paix○!; **give ~ a look**○**!** fais voir!

US I *pr n* (*abrév* = **United States**) USA *mpl*.
II *adj* américain.

USA *pr n* **1** (*abrév* = **United States of America**) USA *mpl*; **2** (*abrév* = **United States Army**) armée *f* des États-Unis.

usable /ˈju:zəbl/ *adj* utilisable; **no longer ~** hors d'usage.

USAF (*abrév* = **United States Air Force**) *n* armée *f* de l'air des États-Unis.

usage /ˈju:sɪdʒ, ˈju:zɪdʒ/ *n* **1** (custom) usage *m*, coutume *f*; **2** Ling usage *m*; **in ~** en usage; **3** (way sth is used) utilisation *f*; **4** (amount used) consommation *f*.

USCG *n* (*abrév* = **United States Coast Guard**) (body) garde *f* côtière *m* des États-Unis.

USDA *n* US (*abrév* = **United States Department of Agriculture**) ministère *m* de l'agriculture.

USDAW *n* GB (*abrév* = **Union of Shop, Distributive and Allied Workers**) *syndicat des commerçants, distributeurs et professions apparentées*.

USDI *n* US (*abrév* = **United States Department of the Interior**) ministère *m* de l'intérieur.

use I /ju:s/ *n* **1** ¢ (act of using) (of substance, object, machine) emploi *m*, utilisation *f* (**of** de); (of word, expression, language) emploi *m*, usage *m* (**of** de); **the ~ of force/diplomacy** le recours à la force/la diplomatie, l'usage de la force/la diplomatie; **the ~ of sth as/for sth** l'emploi or l'utilisation de qch comme/pour qch; **for ~ as/in** pour être utilisé comme/dans; **for the ~ of sb**, **for ~ by sb** (customer, staff) à l'usage de qn; **for my own ~** pour mon usage personnel; **to make ~ of sth** utiliser qch; **to make good/better/the best ~ of sth** tirer parti/un meilleur parti/le meilleur parti (possible) de qch; **to get** ou **have good** ou **a lot of ~ out of sth** se servir beaucoup de qch, faire grand usage de qch; **to put sth to good ~** tirer bon parti de qch; **the car gets regular ~** la voiture est utilisée régulièrement; **the room/photocopier is in ~ at the moment** la pièce/la photocopieuse est occupée en ce moment; **while the machine is in ~** lorsque la machine est en service or en fonctionnement; **for external ~ only** Pharm usage externe; **a word in common** ou **general ~** un mot d'usage courant; **out of** ou **no longer in ~** [*machine*] (broken) hors service; (because obsolete) plus utilisé; [*word, expression*] plus en usage; **worn/stained with ~** râpé/taché par l'usage; **this machine came into ~ in the 1950s** cette machine a fait son apparition pendant les années cinquante; **the bridge/new system comes into ~ next year** le pont/le nouveau système entrera en service l'année prochaine; **2** C (way of using) (of resource, object, material) utilisation *f*; (of term) emploi *m*, **the many ~s of a hairpin** les nombreux usages d'une épingle à cheveux; **she has her ~s** elle a son utilité; **to find a ~ for sth** trouver une utilisation pour qch; **to have no further ~ for sth/sb** ne plus avoir besoin de qch/qn; **I've no ~ for that sort of talk** fig je ne veux pas entendre parler de ça; **3** ¢ (right to use) **to have the ~ of** avoir l'usage de [*house, car, kitchen*]; avoir la jouissance de [*garden*]; **to**

let sb have the ~ of sth permettre à qn de se servir de qch; **to lose/still have the ~ of one's legs** perdre/conserver l'usage de ses jambes; **with ~ of** avec usage de [*kitchen, bathroom*]; **4** ¢ (usefulness) **to be of ~** être utile (**to** à); **to be (of) no ~** [*object*] ne servir à rien; [*person*] n'être bon/bonne à rien; **to be (of) no ~ to sb** [*object*] ne pas servir à qn; [*person*] n'être d'aucune utilité à qn; **he's no ~**○ **at cards** il est nul○ aux cartes; **what ~ is a wheel without a tyre?** à quoi sert une roue sans pneu?; **what's the ~ of crying?** à quoi bon pleurer?; **oh, what's the ~?** oh, et puis à quoi bon?; **is it any ~ asking him?** est-ce que cela vaut la peine de lui demander?; **it's no ~ asking me** inutile de me demander; **it's no ~ (he won't listen)** c'est inutile (il n'écoutera pas); **it's no ~, we'll have to start** rien à faire, il faut s'y mettre.

II /ju:z/ *vtr* **1** (employ) se servir de, utiliser [*object, car, room, money, tool, telephone*]; employer, utiliser [*method, technique*]; employer [*word, expression*]; se servir de [*language, metaphor*]; profiter de, saisir [*opportunity*]; se servir de, faire jouer [*influence*]; avoir recours à [*blackmail, force, power*]; utiliser [*knowledge, information, talent*]; **to ~ sth/sb as sth** se servir de qch/qn comme qch; **to ~ sth for sth/to do** se servir de or utiliser qch pour qch/pour faire; **to be ~d for sth/to do** servir à qch/à faire, être utilisé pour qch/pour faire; **we only ~ local suppliers** nous achetons tous nos produits à des fournisseurs locaux; **somebody's using the toilet** il y a quelqu'un dans les toilettes; **can I ~ you** ou **your name as a reference?** est-ce que je peux donner votre nom comme référence?; **to ~ one's initiative** faire preuve d'initiative; **~ your initiative!** allez, un peu d'initiative!; **~ your head** ou **loaf**○**!** fais marcher un peu ta cervelle!○; **I could ~**○ **a drink/bath!** j'aurais bien besoin d'un verre/bain!; **2** (also **~ up**) (consume) consommer [*fuel, food*]; **he's ~d all the water** il a utilisé toute l'eau; **~ the leftovers** utilisez les restes; **3** (exploit) péj se servir de [*person*]; **4** (take habitually) prendre [*drugs*]; **5**‡ (treat) **to ~ sb well** bien traiter qn; **to ~ sb ill** maltraiter qn.

III /ju:z/ *vi* (take drugs) se droguer.

IV used *pp adj* [*car*] d'occasion; [*container*] vide; [*crockery, cutlery*] sale; [*condom*] usagé.

■ **use up**: **~ [sth] up, ~ up [sth]** finir, utiliser [*remainder, food*]; dépenser [*money, savings*]; épuiser [*supplies, fuel, energy*].

used[1]

■ **Note** To translate *used to do*, use the imperfect tense in French: *he used to live in York* = il habitait York. To stress that something was done repeatedly, you can use *avoir l'habitude de faire*: *she used to go out for a walk in the afternoon* = elle avait l'habitude de sortir se promener l'après-midi.
– To emphasize a contrast between past and present, you can use *avant*: *I used to love sport* = j'adorais le sport avant.
– For more examples and particular usages, see the entry below.

I /ju:st/ *modal aux* **I ~ to do** je faisais; **what did he ~ to** ou **what ~ he to look like then?** comment était-il à cette époque?; **he didn't ~ to** ou **he ~ not to smoke** il ne fumait pas avant; **didn't she ~ to smoke?** est-ce qu'elle ne fumait pas, avant?; **she ~ to smoke, didn't she?** elle fumait avant, non?; **she doesn't smoke now, but she ~ to** elle ne fume plus maintenant, mais elle fumait avant; **it ~ to be thought that** avant on pensait que; **there ~ to be a pub here** il y avait un pub ici (dans le temps); **didn't there ~ to be** ou **~ there not to be a pub here?** est-ce qu'il n'y avait pas un pub ici?

II /ju:st/ *adj* (accustomed) **to be ~ to sth** avoir l'habitude de qch, être habitué à qch; **I'm not ~ to this sort of treatment** je n'ai pas l'habitude qu'on me traite (*subj*) ainsi; **to be ~ to sb** être habitué à qn; **to get ~ to** [*person, eyes, stomach*] s'habituer à; **to be ~ to doing** avoir l'habitude de faire; **to get ~ to doing** s'habituer à faire; **she's been ~ to having her own office** jusqu'à maintenant, elle avait l'habitude d'avoir son propre bureau; **to be ~ to sb doing** être habitué à ce que qn fasse; **I'm not ~ to it** je n'ai pas l'habitude; **you'll get ~ to it** tu t'y habitueras; **it takes a bit/a lot of getting ~ to** ça prend du temps/beaucoup de temps pour s'y habituer.

used[2] /ju:zd/ *prét, pp, pp adj* ▶ **use** II III, IV.

useful /'ju:sfl/ *adj* **1** (helpful) [*object, information, book, work, contact*] utile; [*discussion, meeting*] utile, profitable; **~ for doing** utile pour faire; **to be ~ to sb** être utile à qn; **it is ~ to do** il est utile de faire; **to make oneself ~** se rendre utile; **2**○ (competent) [*footballer, cook etc*] bon/bonne (*before n*); **to be ~ with a gun/paintbrush** savoir se servir d'un fusil/d'un pinceau, savoir manier un fusil/un pinceau; **to be ~ at cooking/football** savoir cuisiner/jouer au football.

usefully /'ju:sfəlɪ/ *adv* utilement.

usefulness /'ju:sflnɪs/ *n* utilité *f*.

useless /'ju:slɪs/ *adj* **1** (not helpful) [*object, machine, information*] inutile; **it's ~ to do** ou **doing** il est inutile de faire; **2** (not able to be used) [*object, limb*] inutilisable; **3**○ (incompetent) [*person*] incapable, nul/nulle○; **to be ~ at sth/doing** être nul en qch/pour (ce qui est de) faire; **he's a ~ cook/driver** il ne vaut rien comme cuisinier/conducteur.

uselessly /'ju:slɪslɪ/ *adv* inutilement.

uselessness /'ju:slɪsnɪs/ *n* **1** (lack of practical use) (of object, machine, effort, information) inutilité *f*; **2** (incompetence) (of person) incompétence *f*.

usen't /'jʊ:snt/ GB = **used not**.

user /'ju:zə(r)/ *n* **1** (person who makes use of) (of road, public transport, service, electricity) usager *m*; (of product, credit card, book, computer, machine) utilisateur/-trice *m/f*; **road ~** usager de la route; **dictionary ~** utilisateur/-trice de dictionnaires; **library ~** usager de bibliothèques; **2** (also **drug ~**) toxicomane *mf*; **cocaine ~** cocaïnomane *mf*; **heroin ~** heroïnomane *mf*; **3** US (exploiter) homme/femme *m/f* intéressé/-e.

user: **~-defined key** *n* Comput touche *f* définissable par l'utilisateur; **~ friendliness** *n* Comput convivialité *f*; gen facilité *f* d'emploi; **~-friendly** *adj* Comput convivial; gen facile à utiliser; **~ group** *n* groupe *m* d'utilisateurs.

USES *n* US (*abrév* = **United States Employment Service**) agence *f* fédérale d'emploi; cf ANPE.

Ushant /'ʌʃənt/ ▶ **1381** *pr n* **(the Isle of) ~** (l'île *f* d')Ouessant *m*.

U-shaped *adj* en (forme de) U.

usher /'ʌʃə(r)/ ▶ **1692** **I** *n* (at function, lawcourt) huissier *m*; (in theatre, church) placeur *m*.

II *vtr* conduire, escorter; **to ~ sb in/out** faire entrer/sortir qn; **to ~ sb to the door** conduire qn à la porte.

■ **usher in**: **~ in [sth]** ouvrir la voie à [*era, negotiations*]; introduire [*scheme, reforms*].

usherette /,ʌʃə'ret/ ▶ **1692** *n* ouvreuse *f*.

USIA *n* (*abrév* = **United States Information Agency**) *agence de propagande proaméricaine.*

USM *n* **1** US (*abrév* = **United States Mint**) hôtel *m* de la Monnaie; **2** (*abrév* = **underwater to surface missile**) missile *m* mer-sol.

USMC *n* US (*abrév* = **United States Marine Corps**) corps *m* des marines américains.

USN *n* US (*abrév* = **United States Navy**) marine *f* des États-Unis.

USNG *n* US (*abrév* = **United States National Guard**) Garde *f* Nationale des États-Unis.

USO *n* US (*abrév* = **United Service Organizations**) centre *m* d'accueil pour les militaires américains.

USP *n*: *abrév* ▶ **unique selling proposition**.

USPS *n* US (*abrév* = **United States Postal Service**) services *mpl* postaux américains; cf PTT.

USS *n* US **1** (*abrév* = **United States Ship**) navire *m* américain; **2** (*abrév* = **United States Senate**) Sénat *m* des États-Unis.

USSR ▶ **1131** *pr n* Hist (*abrév* = **Union of Soviet Socialist Republics**) URSS *f*.

usual /'ju:ʒl/ **I**○ *n* **the ~** la même chose que d'habitude; **'what did he say?'—'oh, the ~'** 'qu'est-ce qu'il a dit?'—'oh, toujours la même chose'; **your ~, sir?** (in bar) comme d'habitude, monsieur?

II *adj* [*attitude, behaviour, form, procedure, problem, route, place, time*] habituel/-elle; [*word, term*] usuel/-elle; **available at the ~ price** disponible au prix habituel; **roast beef with all the ~ trimmings** un rôti de bœuf avec la garniture traditionnelle; **it is ~ for sb to do** c'est normal pour qn de faire; **they left earlier than was ~ for them** ils sont partis plus tôt que d'habitude; **it is ~ to do, the ~ practice is to do** il est d'usage de faire; **they did/said all the ~ things** ils ont fait/dit tout ce qu'il est d'usage de faire/dire; **she was her ~ cheerful self** elle était gaie, comme d'habitude; **as ~** comme d'habitude; **'business as ~'** 'la vente continue'; **it was business as ~ at the school** on travaillait comme d'habitude à l'école; **as ~ with such accidents** comme toujours dans ces accidents; **as is ~ at this time of year/at these events** comme il est d'usage à cette époque de l'année/dans ces occasions; **more/less than ~** plus/moins que d'habitude; **he is better prepared/less awkward than ~** il est mieux préparé/moins mal à l'aise que d'habitude; **as ~ with Max, everything has to be perfect!** comme d'habitude avec Max, tout doit être parfait!

usually /'ju:ʒəlɪ/ *adv* d'habitude, normalement; **'does he eat here?'—'not ~'** 'est-ce qu'il mange ici?'—'normalement non'; **more ~** plus souvent; **he was more than ~ friendly** il était plus aimable que d'habitude; **I ~ arrive at seven** d'habitude ou normalement j'arrive à sept heures.

usufruct /'ju:zju:frʌkt/ *n* Jur usufruit *m*.

usufructary /'ju:zju:frʌktrɪ, US -terɪ/ *n, adj* Jur usufruitier/-ière (*m/f*); **~ right** droit *m* d'usufruit.

usurer /'ju:ʒərə(r)/ *n* usurier/-ière *m/f*.

usurious /ju:'ʒʊərɪəs/ *adj* sout usuraire.

usurp /ju:'zɜ:p/ *vtr* usurper.

usurpation /,ju:zə'peɪʃn/ *n* sout usurpation *f*.

usurper /ju:'zɜ:pə(r)/ *n* usurpateur/-trice *m/f*.

usurping /ju:'zɜ:pɪŋ/ *adj* usurpateur/-trice.

usury /'ju:ʒərɪ/ *n* Fin usure *f*.

UT US Post *abrév écrite* = **Utah**.

Utah /'ju:tɑ:/ ▶ **1744** *pr n* Utah *m*.

utensil /ju:'tensl/ *n* ustensile *m*.

uterine /'ju:təraɪn/ *adj* utérin.

uterus /'ju:tərəs/ *n* utérus *m*.

utilitarian /,ju:tɪlɪ'teərɪən/ **I** *n* Philos utilitariste *mf*.

II *adj* **1** Philos [*doctrine, ideal*] utilitariste; **2** (practical) [*object, vehicle*] utilitaire; [*building*] fonctionnel/-elle; [*clothing*] pratique.

utilitarianism /,ju:tɪlɪ'teərɪənɪzəm/ *n* Philos utilitarisme *m*.

utility /ju:'tɪlətɪ/ **I** *n* **1** (usefulness) utilité *f*; **2** (also **public ~**) (service) service *m* public, commodité *f*.

II utilities *npl* US factures *fpl*.

III *modif* **1** (functional) [*vehicle*] tous usages *inv*; [*object*] utilitaire; **2** (multi-skilled) [*player*] polyvalent; **3** Agric [*breed, animal*] d'exploitation.

utility: **~ bond** *n* obligation *f* (émise par une société gérant un service public); **~ company** *n* société *f* chargée d'assurer un service public; **~ furniture** *n* GB meubles *mpl* de série (*fabriqués pendant la deuxième guerre mondiale*); **~ programme** GB, **~ program** US *n* Comput programme *m* utilitaire; **~ room** *n* buanderie *f*.

utilizable /'ju:təlaɪzəbl/ *adj* utilisable.

utilization /ˌju:təlaɪ'zeɪʃn/ *n* utilisation *f*.

utilize /'ju:təlaɪz/ *vtr* utiliser [*object, idea, materials*]; exploiter [*resource*].

utmost /'ʌtməʊst/ **I** *n* **to do** ou **try one's ~ to come/help** faire tout son possible pour venir/aider; **to do sth to the ~ of one's abilities** faire qch au maximum de ses capacités; **at the ~** au maximum, au plus; **that's the ~ we can do** c'est le maximum que nous puissions faire.

II *adj* **1** (greatest) [*caution, discretion, ease, secrecy*] le plus grand/la plus grande (*before n*); [*limit*] extrême; **with the ~ care** avec le plus grand soin; **it is of the ~ importance that she should come** il est extrêmement important qu'elle vienne; **with the ~ haste** aussi vite que possible; **2** (furthest) **the ~ ends of the earth** les confins de la terre.

Utopia /ju:'təʊpɪə/ *n* utopie *f*.

Utopian /ju:'təʊpɪən/ **I** *n* utopiste *mf*.

II *adj* utopique.

Utopianism /ju:'təʊpɪənɪzəm/ *n* utopisme *m*.

utricle /'ju:trɪkl/ *n* utricule *m*.

utter /'ʌtə(r)/ **I** *adj* [*failure, disaster, amazement, boredom, despair etc*] total; [*honesty, sincerity*] absolu; [*fool, scoundrel*] fieffé (*before n*); [*stranger*] parfait (*before n*); **~ rubbish!** pure sottise *f*!

II *vtr* **1** prononcer [*word, curse*]; pousser [*cry*]; émettre [*sound, warning*]; **I couldn't ~ a word** j'étais incapable de prononcer une parole; **2** Jur répandre [*libel, slander*]; mettre en circulation [*forged banknotes*].

utterance /'ʌtərəns/ *n* **1** (statement, remark) parole *f*; **public ~s** interventions *fpl* publiques; **2** sout (word, remark) formulation *f*, énonciation *f*; (of opinion) expression *f*; **to give ~ to** exprimer, formuler; **3** Ling énoncé *m*.

utterly /'ʌtəlɪ/ *adv* complètement; **we ~ condemn this action** nous condamnons cette action jusqu'au bout; **I ~ detest her** je la déteste au plus haut point.

uttermost† /'ʌtəməʊst/ *n, adj* = **utmost**.

U-turn *n* demi-tour *m*; fig volte-face *f inv*; **'no ~s'** 'défense de faire demi-tour'; **to do a ~** fig faire volte-face (**on** sur).

UV *adj* (*abrév* = **ultraviolet**) [*light, ray, radiation*] ultraviolet/-ette.

UVF *n* GB Pol (*abrév* = **Ulster Volunteer Force**) UVF *f* (*organisation paramilitaire loyaliste en Irlande du Nord*).

uvula /'ju:vjʊlə/ *n* (*pl* **-lae**) luette *f*.

uvular /'ju:vjʊlə(r)/ *adj* Anat, Phon uvulaire.

uxorious /ʌk'sɔ:rɪəs/ *adj* hum ou péj [*husband*] soumis.

uxoriousness /ʌk'sɔ:rɪəsnɪs/ *n* hum ou péj soumission *f* excessive devant sa femme.

Uzbek /'ʊzbek, 'ʊz-/ ▶ 1486, 1402 **I** *n* **1** (person) Ouzbek/-èke *m/f*; **2** Ling ouzbek *m*.

II *adj* [*culture, land*] ouzbek/-èke.

Uzbekistan /ˌʌzbekɪ'stɑ:n, ˌʊz-/ ▶ 1131 *pr n* Ouzbékistan *m*.

Vv

v, V /viː/ *n* **1** (letter) v, V *m*; **2 v** (*abrév écrite* = **versus**) contre; **3 v** (*abrév écrite* = **vide**) voir; **4 V** Elec (*abrév écrite* = **volt**) V, volt *m*.

VA US **1** Mil *abrév* ▶ **Veterans Administration**; **2** Post *abrév écrite* = **Virginia**.

vac○ /væk/ *n* GB (*abrév* = **vacation**) vacances *fpl*; **the long ~** les grandes vacances.

vacancy /ˈveɪkənsɪ/ *n* **1** (free room) chambre *f* libre; **'vacancies'** (on sign) 'chambres libres'; **'no vacancies'** 'complet'; **2** (on campsite) emplacement *m* libre; **3** (unfilled job, place) poste *m* à pourvoir, poste *m* vacant; **a ~ for an accountant** un poste de comptable à pourvoir; **to fill/create a ~** pourvoir/libérer un poste (**for** de); **to advertise a ~** faire paraître une offre d'emploi; **'no vacancies'** (on sign) 'pas d'embauche'; **4** (dreaminess) air *m* absent; **5** (stupidity) stupidité *f*.

vacancy rate *n* Tourism coefficient *m* d'occupation.

vacant /ˈveɪkənt/ *adj* **1** (unoccupied) [*flat, room, seat, place*] libre, disponible; [*office, land*] inoccupé; (on toilet door) libre; **2** (available) [*job, post*] vacant, à pourvoir; **to become** ou **fall ~** se libérer; **'Situations ~'** (in newspaper) 'offres d'emploi'; **3** (dreamy) [*look, stare*] absent; [*expression*] vide; [*face, smile*] vide d'expression; **he looks ~** il a l'air absent; **he gave me a ~ stare** ou **look** il m'a regardé d'un air absent; **4** (stupid) stupide.

vacant lot *n* US terrain *m* vague.

vacantly /ˈveɪkəntlɪ/ *adv* **1** (absently) [*answer, stare*] d'un air absent; **2** (stupidly) [*smile, stare*] d'un air stupide.

vacant possession *n* GB Jur jouissance *f* immédiate.

vacate /vəˈkeɪt, US ˈveɪkeɪt/ *vtr* quitter [*house, premises, job*]; libérer [*room, seat*].

vacation /vəˈkeɪʃn, US veɪ-/ **I** *n* gen, Univ vacances *fpl*; Jur vacances *fpl* judiciaires; **the long ~** GB, **the summer ~** les grandes vacances; **on ~** en vacances; **to take a ~** prendre des vacances; **during** ou **over** ou **in the ~** pendant les vacances; **did you have a good ~?** as-tu passé de bonnes vacances?

II *modif* [*date, course, job, trip*] de vacances.

III *vi* US passer des vacances; **they're ~ing in Miami** ils passent leurs vacances à Miami.

IV vacationing *pres p adj* US en vacances.

vacationer /vəˈkeɪʃənə(r), US veɪ-/ *n* US vacancier/-ière *m/f*.

vaccinate /ˈvæksɪneɪt/ *vtr* vacciner (**against** contre).

vaccination /ˌvæksɪˈneɪʃn/ **I** *n* vaccination *f* (**against, for** contre); **polio/smallpox ~** vaccination contre la polio/la variole; **to have a ~** se faire vacciner.

II *modif* [*clinic, programme, campaign*] de vaccination.

vaccine /ˈvæksiːn, US vækˈsiːn/ *n* vaccin *m* (**against, for** contre); **tetanus/polio ~** vaccin contre le tétanos/la polio.

vacillate /ˈvæsəleɪt/ *vi* hésiter (**between** entre; **over** au sujet de).

vacillation /ˌvæsəˈleɪʃn/ *n* indécision *f*, hésitations *fpl*.

vacuity /vəˈkjuːətɪ/ *n* sout **1** (inanity) vacuité *f*; **2** (empty space) vide *m*.

vacuous /ˈvækjʊəs/ *adj* sout [*person, look, expression*] niais; [*optimism, escapism*] béat pej.

vacuum /ˈvækjʊəm/ **I** *n* **1** Phys vide *m*; **partial ~** vide partiel; **to create a ~** faire le vide; **to observe an effect in a ~** observer un effet sous vide; **2** (lonely space) vide *m*; **emotional/intellectual ~** vide affectif/intellectuel; **it left a ~ in our lives** ça a fait un grand vide dans notre vie; **I'm in a ~** je n'ai pas de points de repère; **3** (also **~ cleaner**) aspirateur *m*; **4** (also **~ clean**) **to give [sth] a ~** passer un coup d'aspirateur sur [*sofa, carpet*]; passer l'aspirateur dans [*room*].

II *vtr* (also **~ clean**) passer [qch] à l'aspirateur [*carpet, upholstery*]; passer l'aspirateur dans [*room, house*].

vacuum: **~ bottle** *n* US = **vacuum flask**; **~ brake** *n* frein *m* à vide; **~ cleaner** *n* aspirateur *m*; **~ flask** *n* bouteille *f* thermos®; **~ gauge** *n* vacuomètre *m*.

vacuum pack I *n* emballage *m* sous vide.

II *vtr* emballer [qch] sous vide.

III vacuum packed *pp adj* emballé sous vide.

vacuum: **~ pump** *n* pompe *f* à vide; **~ sweeper** *n* US = **vacuum cleaner**; **~ tube** *n* tube *m* à vide.

vade mecum /ˌvɑːdɪ ˈmeɪkʊm, ˌveɪdɪ ˈmiːkəm/ *n* vade-mecum *m inv*.

vagabond /ˈvægəbɒnd/ *n, adj* vagabond/-e (*m/f*).

vagal /ˈveɪgl/ *adj* vagal.

vagary /ˈveɪgərɪ/ *n* sout caprice *m*.

vagi /ˈveɪgaɪ/ *npl* ▶ **vagus**.

vagina /vəˈdʒaɪnə/ *n* (*pl* **-nas** ou **-nae**) vagin *m*.

vaginal /vəˈdʒaɪnl/ *adj* vaginal; **~ discharge** pertes *fpl* blanches.

vagrancy /ˈveɪgrənsɪ/ **I** *n* gen, Jur vagabondage *m*.

II *modif* [*act, law*] sur le vagabondage.

vagrant /ˈveɪgrənt/ *n, adj* gen, Jur vagabond/-e (*m/f*).

vague /veɪg/ *adj* **1** (imprecise) [*person, account, idea, memory, rumour, term*] vague; **2** (evasive) **to be ~ about** rester vague sur ou évasif/-ive au sujet de [*plans, intentions, past, role*]; **3** (distracted) [*person, state, expression*] distrait; [*gesture*] vague; **to look ~** avoir l'air distrait; **4** (faint, slight) [*sound, smell, taste*] vague, imprécis; [*fear, embarrassment, disgust, unease*] vague (*before n*); [*doubt*] léger/-ère (*before n*); **a ~ sense of guilt** un vague sentiment de culpabilité; **5** (unsure) **I am (still) a bit ~ about events** je ne sais (toujours) pas très bien ce qui s'est passé; **we're rather ~ about his plans** nous ne connaissons pas très bien ses projets.

vaguely /ˈveɪglɪ/ *adv* **1** (faintly) [*sinister, amusing, classical*] vaguement; [*resemble*] vaguement; **it feels ~ like a bee sting** cela fait un peu comme une piqûre d'abeille; **it seems ~ familiar** cela me dit vaguement quelque chose; **2** (slightly) [*embarrassed, insulting, irritated*] vaguement; **3** (distractedly) [*smile, gaze, say, gesture*] d'un air distrait or vague; [*wander, move about*] distraitement; **4** (imprecisely) [*remember, understand, imagine, reply*] vaguement; [*describe*] de manière vague or imprécise; [*defined, formulated*] vaguement.

vagueness /ˈveɪgnɪs/ *n* **1** (imprecision) (of wording, proposals) flou *m*; (of thinking) imprécision *f*; (of outline, image) manque *m* de netteté; **2** (absent-mindedness) distraction *f*.

vagus /ˈveɪgəs/ *n* (*pl* **-gi**) (also **vagus nerve**) nerf *m* vague.

vain /veɪn/ **I** *adj* **1** (conceited) vaniteux/-euse, vain (*after n*); **to be ~ about sth** tirer vanité de qch; **2** (futile) [*attempt, promise, hope*] vain (*before n*); [*demonstration, show*] futile; **in a ~ attempt** ou **effort to do** dans une vaine tentative de faire.

II in vain *adv phr* en vain.

IDIOMS **to take sb's name in ~** hum parler de qn (derrière son dos); **to take God's name in ~** blasphémer le nom de Dieu.

vainglorious /ˌveɪnˈglɔːrɪəs/ *adj* littér [*person*] suffisant, vain (*after n*); [*boast, assessment, ambition*] plein de suffisance.

vainly /ˈveɪnlɪ/ *adv* **1** (futilely) [*try, wait, struggle*] vainement, en vain; **2** (conceitedly) [*look, stare*] avec vanité; [*admire oneself*] avec complaisance.

Valais ▶ **1776** *pr n* **the (canton of) ~** le (canton de) Valais.

valance /ˈvæləns/ *n* (on bed base) tour *m* de lit; (round canopy) lambrequin *m*; (above curtains) cantonnière *f*.

Val-de-Marne ▶ **1163** *pr n* Val-de-Marne *m*; **in/to ~** dans le Val-de-Marne.

Val-d'Oise ▶ **1163** *pr n* Val-d'Oise *m*; **in/to ~** dans le Val-d'Oise.

vale /veɪl/ *n* littér val *m* liter, vallée *f*; **~ of tears** vallée de larmes.

valediction /ˌvælɪˈdɪkʃn/ *n* sout **1** (farewell) adieu *m*; **2** (farewell speech) discours *m* d'adieu; **funeral ~** oraison *f* funèbre.

valedictorian /ˌvælɪdɪkˈtɔːrɪən/ *n* US Sch Univ major *m* d'une promotion (*qui prononce le discours d'adieu*).

valedictory /ˌvælɪˈdɪktərɪ/ *adj* sout [*speech*] d'adieu.

valence /ˈveɪləns/ *n* Chem valence *f*.

Valencia /vəˈlensɪə/ ▶ **1818** *pr n* Valence; **in ~** à Valence.

Valencian /vəˈlensɪən/ **I** *n* Valencien/-ienne *m/f*.

II *adj* [*custom, identity*] de Valence.

valency /ˈveɪlənsɪ/ **I** *n* Chem, Ling valence *f*.

II *modif* Chem [*electron*] de valence; Ling [*grammar*] de la valence.

valentine /ˈvæləntaɪn/ *n* **1** (also **~ card**) carte *f* de la Saint-Valentin; **2** (sweetheart) **who is your ~?** qui est-ce que tu aimes?; **be my ~** veux-tu m'aimer?

Valentine('s) Day *n* la Saint-Valentin.

valerian /və'lɪərɪən/ **I** *n* Bot, Pharm valériane *f*.
II *modif* [*flower, tablet*] de valériane; [*mixture*] à la valériane.

valet /'vælɪt, -leɪ/ ▶ 1692 **I** *n* **1** (employee) valet *m* de chambre; **2** US (rack) valet *m* de nuit.
II *vtr* nettoyer [*clothes, car interior*].
III *vi* être valet de chambre.

valet parking *n* service *m* de voiturier.

valet service *n* **1** (car-cleaning) service *m* de nettoyage de voitures; **2** (clothes repair) service *m* d'entretien.

valetudinarian /ˌvælɪtju:dɪ'neərɪən/ *n, adj* sout valétudinaire (*mf*); hum hypocondriaque (*mf*).

Valhalla /væl'hælə/ *pr n* Walhalla *m*.

valiant /'vælɪənt/ *adj* [*soldier*] vaillant; [*attempt*] courageux/-euse; **to make a ~ attempt to do** tenter courageusement de faire; **to make a ~ effort to smile** s'efforcer bravement de sourire; **despite their ~ efforts** malgré tous leurs efforts.

valiantly /'vælɪəntlɪ/ *adv* [*fight*] vaillamment; [*try*] courageusement.

valid /'vælɪd/ *adj* **1** (still usable) [*passport, visa, licence*] valide; [*ticket, voucher, offer*] valable (**for** pour); **2** (well-founded, reasonable) [*argument, reason, excuse, method*] valable; [*complaint, objection*] fondé; [*point, comment*] pertinent; [*comparison*] légitime; **3** (in law) [*consent, defence*] valable, valide; **4** (in logic) [*inference, proposition*] valide.

validate /'vælɪdeɪt/ *vtr* **1** prouver le bien-fondé de [*claim, theory, conclusion*]; **2** valider [*document, passport*].

validation /ˌvælɪ'deɪʃn/ *n* validation *f* (**of** de).

validity /və'lɪdətɪ/ *n* **1** Jur (of ticket, document, consent) validité *f*; **2** (of argument, excuse, method) validité *f*; (of complaint, objection) bien-fondé *m*.

valise† /və'li:z, US və'li:s/ *n* nécessaire *m* de voyage.

Valium® /'vælɪəm/ *n* Pharm valium® *m*.

Valkyrie /væl'kɪərɪ/ *pr n* Valkyrie *f*.

valley /'vælɪ/ *n* (*pl* **~s**) vallée *f*; (small) vallon *m*; **the Thames ~** la vallée de la Tamise.

valor *n* US = **valour**.

valorous /'vælərəs/ *adj* littér valeureux/-euse liter.

valour GB, **valor** US /'vælə(r)/ *n* littér valeur *f* liter, bravoure *f*; **for ~** Mil pour la valeur militaire.
IDIOMS **discretion is the better part of ~** Prov prudence est mère de sûreté Prov.

valuable /'væljʊəbl/ *adj* **1** [*commodity, asset*] de valeur; **to be ~** avoir de la valeur; **a very ~ ring** une bague de grande valeur; **2** [*advice, information, lesson, member*] précieux/-ieuse; **to be ~ in treating** être précieux dans le traitement de [*illness*].

valuables /'væljʊəblz/ *npl* objets *mpl* de valeur; **'do not leave ~in your car'** 'ne laissez aucun objet de valeur dans votre voiture'.

valuation /ˌvæljʊ'eɪʃn/ *n* (of house, land, company) évaluation *f*; (of antique, art) expertise *f*; **to have a ~ done on sth** faire évaluer qch; **a ~ of £50** une valeur estimée de £50; **to take sb at his own ~** juger qn selon l'opinion qu'il a de lui-même.

valuator /'væljʊeɪtə(r)/ ▶ 1692 *n* expert *m*.

value /'vælju:/ **I** *n* **1** (monetary worth) valeur *f*; **of little/great ~** de peu de/de grande valeur; **of no ~** sans valeur; **to have a ~ of £5** valoir 5 livres sterling; **it has a ~ of £50** cela vaut 50 livres sterling; **to the ~ of** pour une valeur de; **40% by ~** 40% en valeur réelle; **you can't put a ~ on loyalty** la loyauté n'a pas de prix; **2** (usefulness, general worth) valeur *f*; **to have** ou **be of educational ~** avoir une valeur éducative; **to set great ~ on sth** attacher une grande valeur à qch; **the ~ of sb as** la valeur de qn en tant que; **the ~ of doing** l'importance de faire; **novelty/entertainment ~** caractère nouveau/divertissant; **3** (worth relative to cost) **to be good/poor ~** avoir un bon/mauvais rapport qualité-prix; **to be good ~ at £5** ne pas être cher/chère à 5 livres sterling; **you get good ~ at Buymore** on en a pour son argent à Buymore; **he's always good ~ for satirists** fig c'est toujours une mine d'or pour les satiristes; **the set menu offers good ~** ou **~ for money** avec le menu vous en avez pour votre argent; **to get ~ for money** en avoir pour son argent; **a ~-for-money product** un produit qui vous en donne pour votre argent; **4** (standards, ideals) valeur *f*; **puritan/family ~s** valeurs puritaines/familiales; **5** Maths, Music, Ling valeur *f*.
II *vtr* **1** (assess worth of) évaluer [*house, asset, company*]; expertiser [*antique, jewel, painting*]; **to have sth ~d** faire évaluer or expertiser qch; **to ~ sth at £150** évaluer qch à 150 livres sterling; **2** (esteem, appreciate) apprécier [*person, friendship, advice, opinion, help*]; tenir à [*reputation, independence, life*]; **to ~ sb as a friend** apprécier qn en tant qu'ami; **if you ~ your freedom** si tu tiens à ta liberté.

value-added tax, **VAT** *n* taxe *f* à la valeur ajoutée, TVA *f*.

valued /'vælju:d/ *adj* [*colleague, customer, employee, member*] apprécié; [*contribution, opinion*] précieux/-ieuse.

value: **~ date** *n* Fin date *f* de valeur; **~-free** *adj* objectif/-ive; **~ judgment** *n* jugement *m* de valeur.

valueless /'væljʊlɪs/ *adj* sans valeur (*after n*); **to be quite ~** n'avoir aucune valeur.

value pack *n* Comm lot *m* économique.

valuer /'væljʊə(r)/ ▶ 1692 *n* expert *m*.

valve /vælv/ *n* **1** (in machine, engine) soupape *f*; (on tyre, football) valve *f*; **2** Anat (of organ) valvule *f*; **3** (of mollusc, fruit) valve *f*; **4** (on brass instrument) piston *m*; **5** GB Electron lampe *f*.

valve: **~ gear** *n* distribution *f*; **~ house** *n* bâtiment *m* à vannes; **~-in-head engine** *n* US moteur *m* à soupape en tête; **~ spring** *n* ressort *m* de soupape.

valvular /'vælvjʊlə(r)/ *adj* (all contexts) valvulaire.

vamoose○ /və'mu:s/ *vi* US filer○.

vamp /væmp/ **I** *n* **1**† péj (woman) vamp *f*; **2** (on shoe) empeigne *f*; **3** Mus improvisation *f*.
II *vi* **1** Mus plaquer des accords; **2**† péj (seduce) jouer les vamps.
■ **vamp up**: **~ [sth] up, ~ up [sth]** rafraîchir [*clothing*]; remettre [qch] au goût du jour [*story*]; remanier [*written notes*].

vampire /'væmpaɪə(r)/ *n* vampire *m*.

vampire bat *n* Zool vampire *m*.

van /væn/ *n* **1** Aut (small, for deliveries etc) fourgonnette *f*, camionnette *f*; (larger, for removals etc) fourgon *m*; **2** US (camper) autocaravane *f*, camping-car *m*; **3** (vanguard) avant-garde *f*; **to be in the ~ of** être à l'avant-garde de.

vanadium /və'neɪdɪəm/ **I** *n* vanadium *m*.
II *modif* [*atom*] de vanadium; [*compound*] du vanadium; [*steel*] au vanadium.

Vancouver /væn'ku:və/ ▶ 1818 *pr n* Vancouver.

Vancouver Island ▶ 1381 *pr n* île *f* de Vancouver.

V and A *pr n* (*abrév* = **Victoria and Albert Museum**) *musée des arts décoratifs à Londres*.

vandal /'vændl/ **I** *n* (hooligan) vandale *mf*.
II Vandal *pr n* Hist Vandale *mf*.

vandalism /'vændəlɪzəm/ *n* vandalisme *m*.

vandalize /'vændəlaɪz/ *vtr* gen vandaliser; Jur **to ~ a building/telephone** commettre des déprédations dans un bâtiment/sur un téléphone.

van driver ▶ 1692 *n* chauffeur *m* de camionnette.

vane /veɪn/ *n* **1** (also **weather ~**) girouette *f*; **2** (blade of windmill) aile *f*; **3** (on turbine, pump, projectile) ailette *f*; (of feather) barbe *f*; **4** (of quadrant, compass) pinnule *f*.

vanguard /'vængɑ:d/ *n* Mil, fig avant-garde *f*; **to be in the ~** être à l'avant-garde (**of** de).

vanilla /və'nɪlə/ **I** *n* Culin, Bot vanille *f*.
II *modif* [*sauce, ice cream*] à la vanille; [*pod, plant*] de vanille.

vanilla: **~ essence** *n* extrait *m* de vanille; **~-flavoured** *adj* (aromatisé) à la vanille; **~ sugar** *n* sucre *m* vanillé.

vanish /'vænɪʃ/ *vi* (all contexts) disparaître (**from** de); **to ~ into the distance** disparaître au loin.
IDIOMS **to ~ into thin air** se volatiliser.

vanishing /'vænɪʃɪŋ/ **I** *n* disparition *f*.
II *adj* [*species, environment*] en voie de disparition.
IDIOMS **to do a ~ act** se volatiliser.

vanishing: **~ cream** *n* crème *f* de jour; **~ point** *n* point *m* de fuite; **~ trick** *n* tour *m* de passe-passe.

vanity /'vænətɪ/ *n* **1** (quality) vanité *f*; **all is ~** tout n'est que vanité; **2** (dressing table) coiffeuse *f*; **3** (basin) = **vanity unit**.

vanity: **~ bag**, **~ case** *n* vanity-case *m*; **~ mirror** *n* Aut miroir *m* de courtoisie; **~ plate** *n* Aut plaque *f* minéralogique personnalisée; **~ press** *n* maison *f* d'édition publiant à compte d'auteur; **~ unit** *n* meuble *m* sous-vasque.

vanload *n* fourgonnette *f* (**of** de).

vanquish /'væŋkwɪʃ/ *vtr* littér défaire liter, vaincre [*enemy*]; surmonter [*doubt, prejudice, fear*].

vantage /'vɑ:ntɪdʒ, US 'væn-/ *n*‡ avantage *m*.

vantage point *n* **1** gen, Mil point *m* de vue, position *f* élevée; **from my ~ I could see...** de ma position je voyais...; **from the ~ of** du haut de; **2** fig (point of view) perspective *f*.

Vanuatu /'vænu:ætu:/ ▶ 1131 *pr n* Vanuatu *m*.

vapid /'væpɪd/ *adj* [*person, expression, remark, debate*] mièvre, fade; [*style, novel*] insipide, fade.

vaporize /'veɪpəraɪz/ **I** *vtr* vaporiser [*liquid*].
II *vi* se vaporiser.

vaporizer /'veɪpəraɪzə(r)/ *n* (all contexts) vaporisateur *m*.

vaporous /'veɪpərəs/ *adj* vaporeux/-euse.

vapour GB, **vapor** US /'veɪpə(r)/ **I** *n* vapeur *f*; **water ~** vapeur d'eau.
II vapours† *npl* **to have a fit of the ~s** avoir des vapeurs *fpl*.

vapour: **~ lock** *n* bouchon *m* de vapeur; **~ pressure** *n* pression *f* de vapeur; **~ trail** *n* traînée *f* de condensation, traînée *f* d'un avion.

Var ▶ 1163 *pr n* Var *m*; **in/to the ~** dans le Var.

variability /ˌveərɪə'bɪlətɪ/ *n* variabilité *f*.

variable /'veərɪəbl/ **I** *n* gen, Comput, Math variable *f*; **dependent/free/random ~** variable dépendante/libre/aléatoire.
II *adj* gen, Comput variable.

variable: **~ pitch propellor** *n* hélice *f* à pas variable; **~ star** *n* étoile *f* variable.

variance /'veərɪəns/ *n* **1** gen désaccord *m* (**between** entre); **to be at ~ with** être en désaccord avec [*evidence, facts*]; **my views are at ~ with his** mes opinions divergent des siennes; **that is at ~ with what you said yesterday** cela ne concorde pas avec ce que vous avez dit hier; **2** Math, Phys, Stat variance *f*; **3** Jur (discrepancy) discordance *f* (**between** entre).

variance analysis *n* analyse *f* de variance.

variant /'veərɪənt/ **I** *n* variante *f* (**of** de; **on** par rapport à).

II *adj* [*colour, species, strain*] différent; **~ reading** ou **text** ou **version** variante *f*; **~ form** Bot variante *f*.

variation /ˌveərɪˈeɪʃn/ *n* **1** (change) variation *f*, différence *f* (**in, of** de); **regional/seasonal ~** variations régionales/saisonnières; **~ between A and B** différence entre A et B; **subject to considerable/slight ~** sujet à des variations importantes/à de légères variations; **2** (version) version *f* (**of** de); (new version) variante *f* (**of** de); **what he said was just a ~ on the same theme** il n'a rien dit de nouveau; **3** Mus variation *f* (**on** sur).

varicose /ˈværɪkəʊs/ *adj* variqueux/-euse; **~ veins** varices *fpl*.

varied /ˈveərɪd/ *adj* varié; **her talents are many and ~** ses talents sont divers et variés.

variegated /ˈveərɪgeɪtɪd/ *adj* **1** gen [*assortment, landscape*] varié; **2** Bot, Zool [*leaf, animal's coat*] panaché.

variegation /ˌveərɪˈgeɪʃn/ *n* **1** (diversity) diversité *f*; **2** Bot, Zool panachure *f*.

variety /vəˈraɪətɪ/ **I** *n* **1** (diversity, range) variété *f* (**in, of** de); **wide ~** grande variété; **for a ~ of reasons** pour diverses raisons; **the dresses come in a ~ of sizes/colours** ces robes existent dans un grand choix de tailles/de coloris; **2** (type) gen type *m*; Bot variété *f*; **new ~** Bot nouvelle variété; **lighters of the disposable/refillable ~** des briquets jetables/rechargeables; **3** ¢ Theat, TV variétés *fpl*.

II *modif* Theat, TV [*artist, act, show*] de variétés.

variety: **~ meats** *npl* US abats *mpl*; **~ show** *n* spectacle *m* de variétés; **~ store** *n* US bazar *m*.

variola /vəˈraɪələ/ ▶ **1354** *n* variole *f*.

various /ˈveərɪəs/ *adj* **1** (different) différents (*before n*); **at their ~ addresses** à leurs différentes adresses; **2** (several) divers; **at ~ times** à diverses reprises; **in ~ ways** de diverses manières.

variously /ˈveərɪəslɪ/ *adv* (in different ways) [*arranged, decorated*] de différentes manières; (by different people) [*called, described, estimated*] à tour de rôle.

varmint○† /ˈvɑːmɪnt/ *n* péj vermine *f*.

varnish /ˈvɑːnɪʃ/ **I** *n* vernis *m*.

II *vtr* vernir [*woodwork, painting*]; **to ~ one's nails** GB se vernir les ongles.

III **varnished** *pp adj* [*woodwork, nail*] verni.

varnishing /ˈvɑːnɪʃɪŋ/ *n* vernissage *m*.

varsity /ˈvɑːsətɪ/ **I** *n* **1**† GB université *f*; **2** US Sport première équipe *f*.

II *modif* **1** (university) [*match, sports*] universitaire; **2** US (first) [*team*] premier/-ière (*before n*).

vary /ˈveərɪ/ **I** *vtr* varier [*food, menu, programme*]; faire varier [*flow, temperature*]; changer de [*approach, method, pace, route*].

II *vi* [*objects, people, tastes*] varier (**with, according to** selon); **to ~ from sth** différer de qch; **to ~ from X to Y** varier de X à Y; **it varies from one town/child to another** cela varie d'une ville/d'un enfant à l'autre; **they ~ in cost/size** ils varient quant au coût/à la taille; **to ~ greatly** varier considérablement.

varying /ˈveərɪŋ/ *adj* [*amounts, degrees, opinions*] variable; [*circumstances*] varié; **with ~ (degrees of) success** avec plus ou moins de succès.

vascular /ˈvæskjʊlə(r)/ *adj* Anat, Bot vasculaire.

vase /vɑːz, US veɪs, veɪz/ *n* vase *m*; **flower ~** vase à fleurs.

vasectomy /vəˈsektəmɪ/ *n* vasectomie *f*.

Vaseline® /ˈvæsɪliːn/ *n* vaseline® *f*.

vasoconstrictor /ˌveɪzəʊkənˈstrɪktə(r)/ *n* Med, Anat vasoconstricteur *m*.

vasodilator /ˌveɪzəʊdaɪˈleɪtə(r)/ *n* Med, Anat vasodilatateur *m*.

vasomotor /ˈveɪzəʊməʊtə(r)/ *adj* vasomoteur/-trice.

vassal /ˈvæsl/ *n* Hist, fig vassal/-e *m/f*.

vassalage /ˈvæsəlɪdʒ/ *n* vassalité *f*.

vast /vɑːst, US væst/ *adj* **1** (quantitatively) [*amount, sum, improvement, difference*] énorme; [*number*] très grand; [*knowledge*] extrêmement étendu; **the ~ majority** la très grande majorité; **2** (spatially) [*room, area, plain*] vaste (*before n*), immense.

vastly /ˈvɑːstlɪ, US væstlɪ/ *adv* [*improved, increased, overrated, superior*] considérablement, infiniment; [*complex, popular*] terriblement; [*different*] complètement.

vastness /ˈvɑːstnɪs, US ˈvæstnɪs/ *n* immensité *f*.

vat /væt/ *n* cuve *f*; **beer/wine ~** cuve à bière/vin.

VAT (*abrév* = **value-added tax**) **I** *n* GB TVA *f*.

II *modif* GB [*return, rate*] de TVA; [*payment*] de la TVA.

Vatican /ˈvætɪkən/ *pr n* (palace, governing body) Vatican *m*.

Vatican: **~ City** ▶ **1131**, **1818** *pr n* Vatican *m*; **~ Council** *n* concile *m* du Vatican.

Vaucluse ▶ **1163** *pr n* Vaucluse *m*; **in/to the ~** dans le Vaucluse.

Vaud ▶ **1776** *pr n* **the (canton of) ~** le (canton de) Vaud.

vaudeville /ˈvɔːdəvɪl/ **I** *n* ¢ Theat variétés *fpl*.

II *modif* [*act, star*] de variétés.

vaudevillian /ˌvɔːdəˈvɪlɪən/ **I** *n* (performer) artiste *mf* de variétés.

II *adj* [*style*] digne des variétés.

vault /vɔːlt/ **I** *n* **1** (roof) voûte *f*; **the ~ of heaven** la voûte céleste; **2** (underground room) (of house, hotel) cave *f*; (of church, monastery) caveau *m*; (of bank) chambre *f* forte; (for safe-deposit boxes) salle *f* des coffres; **wine ~** cave *f* à vin; **family ~** caveau *m* de famille; **3** Anat voûte *f*; **4** (jump) saut *m*.

II *vtr* gen, Sport sauter par-dessus [*fence, bar*].

III *vi* gen, Sport sauter (**over** par-dessus).

vaulted /ˈvɔːltɪd/ *adj* Archit voûté.

vaulting /ˈvɔːltɪŋ/ **I** *n* **1** ¢ Archit voûtes *fpl*; **2** ▶ **1282** (in gymnastics) saut *m*; **3** Equit voltige *f*.

II *adj* [*ambition, arrogance*] démesuré.

vaulting: **~ horse** *n* cheval *m* de saut; **~ pole** *n* perche *f*.

vaunt /vɔːnt/ *vtr* vanter.

vaunted /ˈvɔːntɪd/ *adj* vanté; **much ~** tant vanté.

VC *n* **1** (*abrév* = **vice chairman**) vice-président/-e *m/f*; **2** GB Univ (*abrév* = **vice chancellor**) ≈ président/-e *m/f* d'université; **3** (*abrév* = **vice consul**) vice-consul *m*; **4** GB Mil *abrév* ▶ **Victoria Cross**; **5** US Mil (*abrév* = **Vietcong**) Viêt-cong *mpl*.

VCR (*abrév* = **video cassette recorder**) **I** *n* magnétoscope *m*.

II *vtr* US enregistrer [qch] en vidéo.

VD ▶ **1354** (*abrév* = **venereal disease**) **I** *n* MST *f*.

II *modif* [*clinic*] de vénérologie.

VDT *n* (*abrév* = **visual display terminal**) = **VDU**.

VDU (*abrév* = **visual display unit**) **I** *n* écran *m* de visualisation.

II *modif* [*screen*] de visualisation; [*operator*] de terminal de visualisation.

veal /viːl/ **I** *n* veau *m*.

II *modif* [*stew, cutlet*] de veau; [*pie*] au veau; [*rearing*] des veaux.

veal: **~ calf** *n* veau *m* de boucherie; **~ crate** *n* batterie *f* (d'élevage) pour veaux.

vector /ˈvektə(r)/ **I** *n* **1** Biol, Math vecteur *m*; **2** Aviat trajectoire *f*.

II *modif* Math [*product, sum*] vectoriel/-ielle; [*field*] de vecteurs.

vectorial /ˌvekˈtɔːrɪəl/ *adj* Math vectoriel/-ielle.

veep○ /viːp/ *n* US vice-président/-e *m/f*.

veer /vɪə(r)/ **I** *vtr* **1** Naut (alter direction of) faire virer [*ship*]; **2** (slacken) filer [*rope, chain*].

II *vi* **1** lit (change direction) [*ship*] virer; [*person, road, wind*] tourner; **to ~ away from/towards sth** se détourner de/vers qch; **to ~ off the road** s'éloigner de la route; **to ~ away** ou **off** s'éloigner; **to ~ off course** dévier de sa route; **the car ~ed across the road** la voiture a traversé la route; **2** fig [*person, opinion, emotion*] changer; **to ~ (away) from sth** se détourner de qch; **to ~ towards sth** se tourner vers qch; **to ~ between depression and elation** osciller entre le découragement et l'allégresse.

veg○ /vedʒ/ *n* GB (*abrév* = **vegetables**) légumes *mpl*.

vegan /ˈviːgən/ *n, adj* végétalien/-ienne (*m/f*).

veganism /ˈviːgənɪzəm/ *n* végétalisme *m*.

vegeburger /ˈvedʒɪbɜːgə(r)/ *n* croquette *f* pour végétariens.

vegetable /ˈvedʒtəbl/ **I** *n* **1** (edible plant) légume *m*; **2** (as opposed to mineral, animal) végétal *m*; **the ~ kingdom** le règne végétal; **3**○ fig **to become a ~** être réduit à l'état de légume.

II *modif* [*knife, dish, rack*] à légumes; [*soup, plot, patch*] de légumes; [*fat, oil, matter*] végétal.

vegetable: **~ garden** *n* potager *m*; **~ marrow** *n* GB courge *f*; **~ peeler** *n* épluche-légumes *m*.

vegetarian /ˌvedʒɪˈteərɪən/ *n, adj* végétarien/-ienne (*m/f*).

vegetarianism /ˌvedʒɪˈteərɪənɪzəm/ *n* végétarisme *m*.

vegetate /ˈvedʒɪteɪt/ *vi* (all contexts) végéter.

vegetation /ˌvedʒɪˈteɪʃn/ *n* végétation *f*.

vegetative /ˈvedʒɪtətɪv/ *adj* végétatif/-ive.

veggie○ /ˈvedʒɪ/ *n* **1** (vegetarian) végétarien/-ienne *m/f*; **2** (vegetable) légume *m*.

vehemence /ˈviːəməns/ *n* (of speech, action) véhémence *f*; (of feelings) intensité *f*.

vehement /ˈviːəmənt/ *adj* [*tirade, gesture, attack*] véhément; [*dislike, disapproval*] violent.

vehemently /ˈviːəməntlɪ/ *adv* [*speak, react*] avec véhémence; **to be ~ opposed** s'opposer avec véhémence.

vehicle /ˈvɪəkl, US ˈviːhɪkl/ *n* **1** Aut véhicule *m*; **'closed to ~s'** 'interdit à la circulation'; **'unsuitable for wide/high ~s'** interdit aux véhicules larges/hauts; **2** Pharm, Chem véhicule *m*; **3** (medium of communication) véhicule *m* (**for** de); **4** Cin, Theat (showcase) **to be a ~ for sb** être destiné à mettre en valeur qn.

vehicular /vɪˈhɪkjʊlə(r), US viː-/ *adj* **'no ~ access'**, **'no ~ traffic'** 'circulation interdite'.

veil /veɪl/ **I** *n* **1** Fashn, Relig voile *m*; (on hat) voilette *f*; **to take the ~** prendre le voile; **2** fig voile *m*; **a ~ of secrecy** le voile du secret; **let's draw a ~ over that episode** oublions cet épisode.

II *vtr* **1** [*mist, material, cloud*] voiler; **2** fig (conceal) dissimuler [*emotion*].

III **veiled** *pp adj* **1** [*person*] voilé; **2** (indirect) [*hint, threat*] voilé; **a thinly ~ed allusion** une allusion à peine voilée.

vein /veɪn/ *n* **1** (blood vessel) veine *f*; **2** (on insect wing, leaf) nervure *f*; **3** (thread of colour) (in marble) veine *f*; (in cheese) veinure *f*; **4** (of ore) veine *f*; **to work a ~** exploiter une veine; **5** (theme) veine *f*; **to continue in a similar ~** continuer dans la même veine; **a ~ of nostalgia runs through his work** on retrouve un élément de nostalgie à travers toute son œuvre; **in the same ~, she criticized the town council** dans le même esprit, elle a critiqué le conseil municipal.

veined /veɪnd/ *adj* [*hand, marble, rock, cheese*] veiné (**with** de); [*leaf, wing*] nervuré.

veinule /ˈveɪnjuːl/ *n* veinule *f*.

velar /ˈviːlə(r)/ *adj* Phon, Anat vélaire.

Velcro® /ˈvelkrəʊ/ **I** *n* velcro® *m*.
II *modif* [*strip, fastener*] velcro.

veld(t) /velt/ *n* veld *m*.

vellum /ˈveləm/ *n* vélin *m*; **in/on ~** en/sur vélin.

velocipede /vɪˈlɒsɪpiːd/ *n* Hist vélocipède *m*.

velocity /vɪˈlɒsətɪ/ *n* **1** Tech vitesse *f*; **2** fml vélocité *f*.

velocity of circulation *n* US Fin vitesse *f* de circulation.

velodrome /ˈvelədrəʊm/ *n* vélodrome *m*.

velour(s) /vəˈlʊə(r)/ **I** *n* **1** (material) velours *m*; **2** (also **~ hat**) feutre *m*.
II *modif* [*curtain, seat*] de velours.

velum /ˈviːləm/ *n* (*pl* **-la**) Anat voile *m* du palais.

velvet /ˈvelvɪt/ **I** *n* **1** (fabric) velours *m*; **crushed ~** velours frappé; **2** (on antler) peau *f* veloutée.
II *modif* [*garment, curtain, cushion*] en velours.
III *adj* [*skin, paw, tread, eyes*] de velours; [*tones, softness*] velouté.
IDIOMS **to be in ~**† avoir la belle vie.

velveteen /ˌvelvɪˈtiːn/ **I** *n* velvet *m*.
II *modif* [*garment, curtain, upholstery*] en velvet.

velvet: **~ glove** *n* gant *m* de velours also fig; **~ revolution** *n* Pol révolution *f* de velours.

velvety /ˈvelvətɪ/ *adj* velouté.

vena cava /ˌviːnə ˈkeɪvə/ *n* (*pl* **venae cavae**) veine *f* cave.

venal /ˈviːnl/ *adj* vénal.

venality /viːˈnælətɪ/ *n* vénalité *f*.

vend /vend/ *vtr* †ou Jur vendre.

vendee /venˈdiː/ *n* Jur acheteur/-euse *m/f*.

Vendée ▶ 1163 *pr n* Vendée *f*; **in/to the ~** en Vendée.

vendetta /venˈdetə/ *n* vendetta *f* (**between** entre; **against** contre).

vending /ˈvendɪŋ/ *n* vente *f*.

vending machine *n* distributeur *m* automatique.

vendor /ˈvendə(r)/ *n* **1** (in street, kiosk) marchand/-e *m/f*; **2** (as opposed to buyer) vendeur/-euse *m/f*; **3** US (machine) distributeur *m* automatique.

veneer /vɪˈnɪə(r)/ *n* **1** (on wood) placage *m*; **2** fig (surface show) vernis *m*.

venerable /ˈvenərəbl/ *adj* vénérable.

venerate /ˈvenəreɪt/ *vtr* vénérer.

veneration /ˌvenəˈreɪʃn/ *n* vénération *f* (**for** pour).

venereal /vəˈnɪərɪəl/ ▶ 1354 *adj* vénérien/-ienne; **~ disease** maladie *f* vénérienne.

venereology /vəˌnɪərɪˈɒlədʒɪ/ *n* vénérologie *f*.

Venetian /vɪˈniːʃn/ **I** *n* Vénitien/-ienne *m/f*.
II *adj* [*custom, church*] vénitien/-ienne; [*inhabitant, carnival*] de Venise.

Venetian: **~ blind** *n* store *m* vénitien; **~ glass** *n* verre *m* de Venise.

Veneto /ˈvenetəʊ/ *pr n* Vénétie *f*.

Venezuela /ˌvenɪˈzweɪlə/ ▶ 1131 *pr n* Venezuela *m*.

Venezuelan /ˌvenɪˈzweɪlən/ ▶ 1486 **I** *pr n* Vénézuélien/-ienne *m/f*.
II *adj* [*town, river, politician*] vénézuélien/-ienne; [*embassy*] du Venezuela.

vengeance /ˈvendʒəns/ *n* vengeance *f*; **to take ~ (up)on sb** se venger de qn (**for** pour); **with a ~** de plus belle.

vengeful /ˈvendʒfl/ *adj* sout [*person, act*] vengeur/-eresse; [*desire, need*] de vengeance.

vengefully /ˈvendʒfəlɪ/ *adv* sout vindicativement.

venial /ˈviːnɪəl/ *adj* sout véniel/-ielle.

Venice /ˈvenɪs/ ▶ 1818 *pr n* Venise.

venison /ˈvenɪsn, -zn/ **I** *n* (viande *f* de) chevreuil *m*.
II *modif* [*stew, steak*] de chevreuil; [*pie*] au chevreuil.

Venn diagram /ven/ *n* diagramme *m* de Venn.

venom /ˈvenəm/ *n* Zool, fig venin *m*.

venomous /ˈvenəməs/ *adj* Zool, fig venimeux/-euse.

venomously /ˈvenəməslɪ/ *adv* fielleusement.

venous /ˈviːnəs/ *adj* veineux/-euse.

vent /vent/ **I** *n* **1** (outlet for gas, pressure) bouche *f*, conduit *m*; **air ~** bouche d'aération; **to give ~ to** fig décharger [*anger, feelings*]; **2** (of volcano) cheminée *f*; **3** Fashn (slit) fente *f*; **4** US (window) déflecteur *m*; **5** Zool orifice *m* anal.
II *vtr* **1** fig (release) décharger [*anger, spite, frustration*] (**on** sur); **2** (air) aborder publiquement [*question, topic*]; **3** (let out) évacuer [*gas, smoke*].
III *vi* [*gas, chimney, volcano*] s'évacuer.

vent glass *n* Aut déflecteur *m*.

ventilate /ˈventɪleɪt/ **I** *vtr* **1** (provide with air) aérer [*room, office*]; **2** Med ventiler [*patient, lungs*]; **3** fig (air) exprimer [qch] publiquement [*idea, opinion*].
II ventilated *pp adj* **1** [*room, building, tunnel*] aéré; **well/badly ~d** bien/mal aéré; **2** Aut [*disc brakes*] ventilé; **3** (slatted) à lames.

ventilation /ˌventɪˈleɪʃn/ *n* **1** aération *f*, ventilation *f*; **2** Med (of patient) ventilation *f* artificielle.

ventilation: **~ shaft** *n* puits *m* d'aérage; **~ system** *n* système *m* de ventilation.

ventilator /ˈventɪleɪtə(r)/ *n* **1** Med respirateur *m* artificiel; **to switch** ou **turn off the ~** arrêter l'assistance respiratoire; **2** Constr (opening) aérateur *m*; (fan) ventilateur *m*.

ventricle /ˈventrɪkl/ *n* ventricule *m*.

ventriloquism /venˈtrɪləkwɪzəm/ *n* ventriloquie *f*.

ventriloquist /venˈtrɪləkwɪst/ ▶ 1692 *n* ventriloque *mf*.

ventriloquist's dummy *n* pantin *m* de ventriloque.

ventriloquy /venˈtrɪləkwɪ/ *n* = **ventriloquism**.

venture /ˈventʃə(r)/ **I** *n* **1** Comm, Fin (undertaking) aventure *f*, entreprise *f*; **a publishing/media ~** une aventure éditoriale/médiatique; **her first ~ into marketing** sa première expérience dans le marketing; **2** gen, Sci (experiment) essai *m*; **a scientific ~** un coup d'essai en matière scientifique; **his first ~ into fiction** son premier essai dans le domaine littéraire; **3** sout (journey) voyage *m* d'aventure (**to** à).
II *vtr* **1** (offer) hasarder [*opinion, remark, suggestion*]; **to ~ the opinion that** hasarder l'opinion selon laquelle; **might I ~ a suggestion?** puis-je me permettre une suggestion?; **'maybe she's right' he ~d** 'il se peut qu' elle ait raison' se hasarda-t-il de dire; **to ~ to do** se risquer à faire; **I ~ to suggest that…, I would ~ that…** sout je me permets de suggérer que… fml; **2** (gamble) risquer [*bet, money*] (**on** sur).
III *vi* **1** (go) **to ~ into** s'aventurer dans [*place, street, city*]; **to ~ out (doors)** s'aventurer dehors; **to ~ downstairs/further** s'aventurer en bas/plus loin; **2** Comm (make foray) **to ~ into** se lancer dans [*retail market, publishing*].
IDIOMS **nothing ~d nothing gained** Prov qui ne risque rien n'a rien Prov.
■ **venture forth** littér se risquer à sortir.

venture: **~ capital** *n* capital-risque *m*; **~ scout** *n* GB routier *m*, scout *m* de la branche aînée.

venturesome /ˈventʃəsəm/ *adj* littér aventureux/-euse.

venue /ˈvenjuː/ *n* **1** gen lieu *m*; **a change of ~** un changement de lieu; **the ~ for the match was/will be** le match a eu lieu/aura lieu à; **2** Jur lieu *m* du jugement.

Venus /ˈviːnəs/ *pr n* (planet, goddess) Vénus *f*.

Venus fly-trap *n* Bot dionée *f*.

Venusian /vɪˈnjuːzɪən/ *adj* vénusien/-ienne.

veracious /vəˈreɪʃəs/ *adj* sout [*statement*] véridique.

veracity /vəˈræsətɪ/ *n* sout véracité *f*.

veranda(h) /vəˈrændə/ *n* véranda *f*; **on the ~** sous la véranda.

verb /vɜːb/ *n* verbe *m*.

verbal /ˈvɜːbl/ *adj* gen, Ling (all contexts) verbal.

verbal abuse *n* Jur emploi *m* de propos injurieux.

verbalize /ˈvɜːbəlaɪz/ *vtr, vi* verbaliser.

verbally /ˈvɜːbəlɪ/ *adv* verbalement.

verbal reasoning *n* raisonnement *m* verbal.

verbatim /vɜːˈbeɪtɪm/ **I** *adj* [*report, account*] textuel/-elle.
II *adv* [*describe, record*] mot pour mot.

verbena /vɜːˈbiːnə/ *n* verveine *f*; **lemon ~** verveine citronnelle.

verbiage /ˈvɜːbɪɪdʒ/ *n* sout verbiage *m*.

verbless /ˈvɜːblɪs/ *adj* sans verbe.

verbose /vɜːˈbəʊs/ *adj* sout verbeux/-euse fml.

verbosity /vɜːˈbɒsətɪ/ *n* sout verbosité *f* fml.

verb phrase, **VP** *n* syntagme *m* verbal.

verdant /ˈvɜːdnt/ *adj* littér verdoyant liter.

verdict /ˈvɜːdɪkt/ *n* **1** Jur verdict *m*; **to return a ~** rendre un verdict; **to reach a ~** arriver au verdict; **a ~ of guilty/not guilty** un verdict positif/négatif; **the ~ was suicide/accidental death** l'enquête a conclu au suicide/à une mort accidentelle; **2** fig (opinion) verdict *m*; **well, what's the ~?**○ eh bien, qu'est-ce que tu en penses?; **to give one's ~ on sth** se prononcer sur qch.

verdigris /ˈvɜːdɪgrɪs, -griːs/ *n* vert-de-gris *m inv*.

verdure /ˈvɜːdʒə(r)/ *n* littér verdure *f*.

verge /vɜːdʒ/ *n* **1** GB (by road) accotement *m*, bas-côté *m*; **grass ~** accotement herbeux; **soft ~** accotement non stabilisé; **2** (brink) **on the ~ of** au bord de [*tears*]; au seuil de [*adolescence, old age, death*]; **on the ~ of success** sur le point de réussir; **on the ~ of doing** sur le point de faire; **on the ~ of sleep/a discovery** sur le point de s'endormir/de faire une découverte; **to bring** ou **drive sb to the ~ of** amener qn au bord de [*bankruptcy, despair, revolt, suicide*]; **to bring** ou **drive sb to the ~ of doing** amener qn au point de faire.
■ **verge on**: **~ on [sth]** friser [*panic, stupidity, contempt*]; **to be verging on the ridiculous/the illegal** friser le ridicule/l'illégal.

verger /ˈvɜːdʒə(r)/ ▶ 1692 *n* Relig (caretaker) bedeau *m*; (in ceremony) huissier *m* à verge.

verifiable /ˈverɪfaɪəbl/ *adj* vérifiable.

verification /ˌverɪfɪˈkeɪʃn/ **I** *n* (of claim, facts) vérification *f*; (as procedure) contrôle *m*; Mil vérification *f*.
II *modif* [*measure, process, technique*] de vérification, de contrôle.

verify /ˈverɪfaɪ/ *vtr* vérifier.

verily‡ /ˈverɪlɪ/ *adv* en vérité.

verisimilitude /ˌverɪsɪˈmɪlɪtjuːd, US -tuːd/ *n* sout vraisemblance *f*.

veritable /ˈverɪtəbl/ *adj* sout véritable.

verity /ˈverətɪ/ *n* littér vérité *f*.

vermicelli /ˌvɜːmɪˈselɪ, -ˈtʃelɪ/ *n* ₵ (pasta, chocolate) vermicelle *m*.

vermicide /ˈvɜːmɪsaɪd/ *n* vermicide *m*.

vermifugal /ˌvɜːmɪˈfjuːgl/ *adj* vermifuge.

vermifuge /ˈvɜːmɪfjuːdʒ/ *n* vermifuge *m*.

vermilion /vəˈmɪlɪən/ ▶ 1104 *n, adj* vermillon (*m*) *inv*.

vermin /ˈvɜːmɪn/ *n* **1** ₵ (rats etc) animaux *mpl* nuisibles; **2** (lice, insects) vermine *f*; **3** péj (person) canaille *f*.

verminous /ˈvɜːmɪnəs/ *adj* (infested) (with

rats) infesté de rats; (with lice) infesté de vermine.

Vermont /vɜːˈmɒnt/ ▶1744 *pr n* Vermont *m*.

vermouth /ˈvɜːməθ, US vərˈmuːθ/ *n* vermouth *m*.

vernacular /vəˈnækjʊlə(r)/ I *n* **1** (language) **the ~** la langue vulgaire; **in the ~** (not Latin) dans la langue vulgaire; (in local dialect) en dialecte; **2** (jargon) jargon *m*; **3** (common name) nom *m* vernaculaire.

II *adj* [*architecture, building*] en style local; [*writing*] dans la langue vulgaire.

vernal /ˈvɜːnl/ *adj* littér printanier/-ière.

vernal equinox *n* équinoxe *m* de printemps.

Verona /vəˈrəʊnə/ ▶1818 *pr n* Vérone.

veronica /vəˈrɒnɪkə/ *n* véronique *f*.

verruca /vəˈruːkə/ *n* (*pl* **-cae** ou **-cas**) verrue *f* plantaire.

versatile /ˈvɜːsətaɪl/ *adj* **1** (flexible) [*person*] plein de ressources, aux talents divers (*after n*); [*mind*] souple; **2** (with many uses) [*vehicle*] polyvalent; [*equipment*] à usages multiples; **3** Zool (movable) [*antenna*] orientable; [*anther*] flottant.

versatility /ˌvɜːsəˈtɪlətɪ/ *n* **1** (flexibility) (of person) adaptabilité *f*; (of mind) souplesse *f*; **2** (of equipment) polyvalence *f*.

verse /vɜːs/ *n* **1** (poems) poésie *f*; **a book of ~** un livre de poésie; **to write ~** faire de la poésie; **2** (form) vers *mpl*; **in ~** en vers; **blank ~** vers blancs; **3** (part of poem) strophe *f*; (of song) couplet *m*; **4** Bible verset *m*; **5** (single line) vers *m*.

versed /vɜːst/ *adj* (also **well-versed**) versé (**in** dans).

versification /ˌvɜːsɪfɪˈkeɪʃn/ *n* versification *f*.

versifier /ˈvɜːsɪfaɪə(r)/ *n* rimailleur/-euse *m/f*.

version /ˈvɜːʃn, US -ʒn/ *n* (all contexts) version *f* (**of** de).

verso /ˈvɜːsəʊ/ *n* (*pl* **-sos**) verso *m*.

versus /ˈvɜːsəs/ *prep* contre; **Brazil ~ Argentina** Sport le Brésil contre l'Argentine; **Crane ~ Conroy** Jur Crane contre Conroy; **it's integration ~ independence** c'est l'intégration contre l'indépendance.

vertebra /ˈvɜːtɪbrə/ *n* (*pl* **-brae**) vertèbre *f*.

vertebral /ˈvɜːtɪbrəl/ *adj* vertébral; **the ~ column** la colonne vertébrale.

vertebrate /ˈvɜːtɪbreɪt/ *n, adj* vertébré (*m*).

vertex /ˈvɜːteks/ *n* (*pl* **-tices**) **1** gen, Math sommet *m*; **2** Anat vertex *m*.

vertical /ˈvɜːtɪkl/ I *n* verticale *f*; **out of the ~** pas d'aplomb.

II *adj* [*line, column, take-off*] vertical; [*cliff*] à pic; **a ~ drop** un à-pic.

vertical: **~ hold** *n* TV, Comput commande *f* de synchronisation verticale; **~ integration** *n* Comm intégration *f* verticale.

vertically /ˈvɜːtɪklɪ/ *adv* [*draw, divide*] verticalement; [*drop, climb*] à la verticale.

vertiginous /vəˈtɪdʒɪnəs/ *adj* lit, fig vertigineux/-euse.

vertigo /ˈvɜːtɪgəʊ/ *n* (*pl* **-goes** ou **-gines**) vertige *m*; **to get ~** avoir le vertige.

verve /vɜːv/ *n* brio *m*, verve *f*.

very /ˈverɪ/ I *adj* **1** (actual) même (*after n*); **the ~ words** les paroles mêmes; **this ~ second** à la seconde même; **2** (ideal) **the ~ person I need** exactement la personne qu'il me faut; **the ~ thing I need** exactement ce qu'il me faut; **3** (ultimate) tout; **from the ~ beginning** depuis le tout début; **at the ~ front/back/top** tout devant/au fond/en haut; **to the ~ end** jusqu'au bout; **to the ~ top of her profession** jusqu'au sommet de sa profession; **on the ~ edge** à l'extrême bord; **4** (mere) [*mention, thought, word*] seul (*before n*); **the ~ idea!** quelle idée!

II *adv* **1** (extremely) [*hot, cold, good, bad*] très; **I'm ~ sorry** je suis vraiment désolé; **how ~ sad** comme c'est triste; **~ well** très bien; **you know ~ well why** tu sais très bien pourquoi; **she couldn't ~ well do that** elle ne pouvait pas vraiment faire cela; **that's all ~ well but** c'est fort bien mais; **~ much** beaucoup; **to like sth ~ much** aimer beaucoup qch; **~ much better** beaucoup mieux; **I didn't eat/find ~ much** je n'ai pas mangé/trouvé grand-chose; **to be ~ much a city dweller** être un vrai citadin; **it's ~ much a question of** c'est vraiment une question de; **the Very Reverend** le Très Révérend; **2** (absolutely) **the ~ best/worst thing** de loin la meilleure/pire chose; **the ~ best hotels** les meilleurs hôtels; **in the ~ best of health** en pleine santé; **at the ~ latest/earliest** au plus tard/tôt; **at the ~ least** tout au moins; **the ~ first/last** le tout premier/dernier; **3** (actually) **the ~ same words** exactement les mêmes mots; **the ~ next day** le lendemain même; **the ~ next person I met** la toute première personne que j'ai rencontrée ensuite; **a car of your ~ own** ta propre voiture.

very high frequency, VHF I *n* très haute fréquence *f*.

II *modif* [*broadcast*] à très haute fréquence.

Very light *n* Naut fusée *f* éclairante.

very low frequency, VLF I *n* très basse fréquence *f*.

II *modif* [*broadcast*] à très basse fréquence.

Very pistol *n* Naut pistolet *m* lance-fusées.

vesicle /ˈvesɪkl/ *n* vésicule *f*.

vespers /ˈvespəz/ *n* (+ *v sg ou pl*) vêpres *fpl*.

vessel /ˈvesl/ *n* **1** Naut, Transp vaisseau *m*; **2** Anat vaisseau *m*; **blood ~** vaisseau sanguin; **3** (container) vase *m*; (for liquids only) coupe *f*; **4** fig (person) instrument *m* (**for** de).

vest /vest/ ▶1703 I *n* **1** (underwear) maillot *m* de corps; **2** (for sport, fashion) débardeur *m*; **3** US gilet *m*.

II *vtr* conférer [*authority, power*] (**in** à); **to ~ the ownership of sth in sb** transférer qch à la propriété de qn; **to ~ a right in sb** investir qn d'un droit.

vestal /ˈvestl/ *adj* littér chaste.

vestal virgin *n* vestale *f*.

vested interest *n* **1** gen intérêt *m* personnel; **to have a ~** être personnellement intéressé (**in** dans); **2** Jur droit *m* acquis.

vestibular /veˈstɪbjʊlə(r)/ *adj* Anat vestibulaire.

vestibule /ˈvestɪbjuːl/ *n* Anat, Archit vestibule *m*.

vestige /ˈvestɪdʒ/ *n* **1** (trace) (*gén pl*) (of civilization, faith, system) vestige *m*; (of emotion, truth, stammer) trace *f*; **2** Anat, Zool vestige *m*.

vestigial /veˈstɪdʒɪəl/ *adj* **a ~ memory/headache** un vestige de souvenir/de mal de tête; Anat, Zool **~ tail** vestige *m* de queue.

vestment /ˈvestmənt/ *n* habit *m* sacerdotal.

vest pocket US I *n* poche *f* de gilet.

II **vest-pocket** *adj* [*dictionary, calculator*] de poche.

vestry /ˈvestrɪ/ *n* Relig (place) sacristie *f*; (meeting) réunion *f* paroissiale; (members) responsables *m/fpl* paroissiaux/-iales.

vesture /ˈvestʃə(r)/ *n* littér vêture *f* liter.

Vesuvius /vɪˈsuːvɪəs/ *pr n* Vésuve *m*.

vet /vet/ I *n* ▶1692 **1** (*abrév* = **veterinary surgeon**) vétérinaire *mf*; **to take an animal to the ~'s** emmener un animal chez le vétérinaire; **2**○ US Mil ancien combattant *m*, vétéran *m*.

II *vtr* (*p prés etc* **-tt-**) mener une enquête approfondie sur [*person*]; passer [qch] en revue [*plan, accommodation*]; approuver [*teaching material, publication*]; **he has been ~ted for the Civil Service** on a mené une enquête approfondie sur lui en vue de son entrée dans la fonction publique.

vetch /vetʃ/ *n* vesce *f*.

veteran /ˈvetərən/ I *n* gen vétéran *m*; Mil ancien combattant *m*, vétéran *m*.

II *modif* [*actor, sportsman, politician*] chevronné; [*championship, division, marathon*] vétéran; [*ship, bicycle*] antique (*before n*); **a ~ peace campaigner** un vieux routier de la campagne pour la paix.

veteran: **~ car** *n* GB voiture *f* ancienne (*construite avant 1905*); **Veterans Administration, VA** *n* US Administration *f* des anciens combattants; **Veterans Day** *n* US jour *m* des anciens combattants.

veterinarian /ˌvetərɪˈneərɪən/ ▶1692 *n* US vétérinaire *mf*.

veterinary /ˈvetrɪnrɪ, US ˈvetərmerɪ/ ▶1692 *n, adj* vétérinaire (*mf*).

veterinary: **~ surgeon** ▶1692 *n* vétérinaire *mf*; **~ surgery** *n* (for consultation) clinique *f* vétérinaire.

vetiver /ˈvetɪvə(r)/ *n* vétyver *m*.

veto /ˈviːtəʊ/ I *n* (*pl* **-toes**) **1** (practice) veto *m*; **2** (right) droit *m* de veto (**over, on** sur); **to use/exercise one's ~** user de/exercer son droit de veto; **3** US Pol (president's) *message justifiant le veto présidentiel*.

II *vtr* (*prés* **-toes**; *prét, pp* **-toed**) gen, Pol mettre or opposer son veto à.

vetting /ˈvetɪŋ/ I *n* contrôle *m*; **security ~** enquête *f* de sécurité; **to give sb a ~** mener une enquête sur qn.

II *modif* [*procedure, service, system*] de contrôle.

vex /veks/ *vtr* (annoy) contrarier; (worry) tracasser.

vexation /vekˈseɪʃn/ *n* (annoyance) contrariété *f*; (worry) tracas *m*.

vexatious /vekˈseɪʃəs/ *adj* [*situation*] contrariant; [*person*] agaçant.

vexed /vekst/ *adj* **1** (annoyed) mécontent (**with** de); **2** (problematic) [*question, issue, situation*] épineux/-euse.

vexing /ˈveksɪŋ/ *adj* = **vexatious**.

VFR *n* Aviat (*abrév* = **Visual Flight Rules**) navigation *f* à vue.

vg (*abrév* = **very good**) TB.

VG *n* Relig *abrév* ▶ **vicar general**.

VHF I *n* (*abrév* = **very high frequency**) VHF.

II *modif* [*transmitter, radio*] VHF.

VI *npl*: *abrév* ▶ **Virgin Islands**.

via /ˈvaɪə/ *prep* **1** (by way of) gen en passant par; (on ticket, timetable) via; **we came ~ Paris** nous sommes venus en passant par Paris; **2** (by means of) par; **transmitted ~ satellite** transmis par satellite; **to get into politics ~ the trade unions** entrer dans la vie politique par le syndicalisme.

viability /vaɪəˈbɪlətɪ/ *n* **1** (feasibility) (of company, government, farm) viabilité *f*; (of project, idea, plan) validité *f*; **2** Biol, Zool, Med (of foetus, egg, plant) viabilité *f*.

viable /ˈvaɪəbl/ *adj* **1** (feasible) [*company, government, farm*] viable; [*project, idea, plan*] réalisable, valable; **politically ~** réalisable or valable sur le plan politique; **2** Biol, Zool, Med [*foetus, egg, plant*] viable.

viaduct /ˈvaɪədʌkt/ *n* viaduc *m*.

vial /ˈvaɪəl/ *n* littér gen fiole *f*; Pharm ampoule *f*.

viands‡ /ˈviːəndz/ *npl* mets‡ *mpl*.

viaticum /vaɪˈætɪkəm/ *n* viatique *m*.

vibe○ /vaɪb/ I *n* **1** (atmosphere) (in place) atmosphère *f*; (in situation) ambiance *f*; **2** (from music, group) courant *m*.

II **vibes**○ *npl* **1** (feeling) **to have good/bad ~s** dégager de bonnes/mauvaises vibrations○; **2** ▶1481 Mus vibraphone *m*.

vibrancy /ˈvaɪbrənsɪ/ *n* **1** (liveliness) (of person) vitalité *f*; (of place) vie *f*, trépidation *f*; (of colour) éclat *m*; **2** (of voice, instrument) sonorité *f*.

vibrant /ˈvaɪbrənt/ *adj* **1** (lively) [*person, place, personality*] plein de vie; [*colour*] éclatant; **to be ~ with health** éclater de santé; **2** (resonant) [*voice, instrument*] sonore; **a voice ~ with emotion** une voix vibrante d'émotions.

vibrantly /ˈvaɪbrəntlɪ/ *adv* [*speak, say*] d'un ton vibrant; [*smile*] avec éclat.

vibraphone /ˈvaɪbrəfəʊn/ ▶ 1481 *n* vibraphone *m*.

vibrate /vaɪˈbreɪt, US ˈvaɪbreɪt/ **I** *vtr* faire vibrer.
II *vi* vibrer (**with** de).

vibration /vaɪˈbreɪʃn/ *n* vibration *f*.

vibrato /vɪˈbrɑːtəʊ/ *n* (*pl* **-tos**) vibrato *m*; **to play/sing (with) ~** faire du vibrato en jouant/en chantant.

vibrator /vaɪˈbreɪtə(r)/ *n* **1** (sex aid) vibromasseur *m*; **2** Elec vibrateur *m*.

vibratory /vaɪˈbreɪtərɪ, US -tɔːrɪ/ *adj* vibratoire.

viburnum /vaɪˈbɜːnəm/ *n* viorne *f*.

vicar /ˈvɪkə(r)/ ▶ 1268 *n* pasteur *m* (*anglican ou de l'Église épiscopale*).

vicarage /ˈvɪkərɪdʒ/ *n* presbytère *m*.

vicar: **~ apostolic** *n* vicaire *m* apostolique; **~ general**, **VG** *n* vicaire *m* général.

vicarious /vɪˈkeərɪəs, US vaɪˈk-/ *adj* **1** (indirect) [*pleasure, knowledge*] indirect; **to get a ~ thrill from** ou **out of sth** ressentir un frisson par l'intermédiaire de qch; **2** (delegated) [*authority, power*] délégué; **~ liability** Jur responsabilité *f* du fait d'autrui.

vicariously /ˈvɪkeərɪəslɪ, US vaɪˈk-/ *adv* (indirectly) [*enjoy, experience, live*] par personne interposée, indirectement; **to live ~ through sb** vivre par l'intermédiaire de qn; **~ liable** Jur responsable du fait d'autrui.

Vicar of Christ *n* vicaire *m* de Jésus-Christ.

vice /vaɪs/ **I** *n* **1** (failing) vice *m*; hum faiblesse *f*; **2** (corruption) vice *m*; **3** (also **vise** US) Tech (clamp) étau *m*.
II *modif* [*laws*] sur les mœurs; [*scandal*] de mœurs.

vice: **Vice-Admiral** ▶ 1612 *n* vice-amiral *m*; **~-captain** *n* Sport capitaine *m* en second; **~-chair** *n* vice-président/-e *m*/*f*; **~-chairman** *n* vice-président/-e *m*/*f*; **~-chairmanship** *n* vice-présidence *f*; **~-chairperson** *n* vice-président/-e *m*/*f*; **~-chairwoman** *n* vice-présidente *f*; **~-chancellor** ▶ 1692 *n* GB Univ président/-e *m*/*f* d'Université; US Jur *juge assistant(e)*; **~-chancellorship** *n* GB Univ présidence de l'Université; **~-chief** *n* sous-chef *m*; **~-consul** *n* vice-consul *m*; **~-director** *n* vice-directeur/-trice *m*/*f*; **~-like** GB, **vise-like** US *adj* [*grip*] comme un étau; **~-presidency** *n* vice-présidence *f*; **~-president**, **VP** *n* vice-président/-e *m*/*f*; **~-presidential** *adj* [*candidate, race*] à la vice-présidence; [*residence*] vice-présidentiel/-ielle; **~-principal** *n* Sch (of senior school) proviseur *m* adjoint; (of junior school, college) directeur/-trice *m*/*f* adjoint/-e; **~regal** *adj* [*duties*] du vice-roi; **~roy** *n* vice-roi *m*; **~ squad** *n* brigade *f* des mœurs.

vice versa /ˌvaɪsɪ ˈvɜːsə/ *adv* vice versa.

vichyssoise /ˌviːʃiːˈswɑːz/ *n* Culin vichyssoise *f* (*soupe froide aux poireaux et pommes de terre avec de la crème*).

vicinity /vɪˈsɪnətɪ/ *n* voisinage *m*, environs *mpl*; **in the ~** dans le voisinage or les environs; **in the (immediate) ~ of Oxford/the explosion** à proximité (immédiate) d'Oxford/de l'explosion; **in the ~ of £30,000/10,000 people** environ 30 000 livres/10 000 personnes.

vicious /ˈvɪʃəs/ *adj* [*person, animal, power, system*] malfaisant; [*speech, attack, price cut, revenge*] brutal; [*rumour, sarcasm, version, lie*] malveillant.

vicious circle *n* cercle *m* vicieux.

viciously /ˈvɪʃəslɪ/ *adv* **1** (savagely) brutalement; **2** (perversely) méchamment.

viciousness /ˈvɪʃəsnɪs/ *n* **1** (physical) (of person) brutalité *f*; (of attack) sauvagerie *f*; **2** (verbal) méchanceté *f*.

vicissitude /vɪˈsɪsɪtjuːd, US -tuːd/ *n* sout vicissitude *f* fml.

victim /ˈvɪktɪm/ *n* lit, fig victime *f*; **a ~ of rape/one's own success** une victime du viol/de son propre succès; **murder/polio/earthquake ~** victime d'un meurtre/de la polio/d'un tremblement de terre; **a rape ~** la victime d'un viol; **to fall ~ to** être victime de [*disease, disaster*]; succomber à [*charm, unscrupulousness*].

victimization /ˌvɪktɪmaɪˈzeɪʃn/ *n* persécution *f*.

victimize /ˈvɪktɪmaɪz/ *vtr* persécuter.

victimless /ˈvɪktɪmlɪs/ *adj* [*crime*] sans victime.

Victim Support *n* GB *organisme d'aide aux victimes de crime*.

victor /ˈvɪktə(r)/ *n* vainqueur *m*.

victoria /vɪkˈtɔːrɪə/ *n* Hist Transp victoria *f*.

Victoria /vɪkˈtɔːrɪə/ *pr n* **1** (name) Victoria; **Queen/Lake ~** la reine/le lac Victoria; **2** (state) Victoria *m*.

Victoria: **~ Cross**, **VC** *n* GB Mil Victoria Cross *f*; **~ Falls** *npl* chutes *fpl* Victoria.

Victorian /vɪkˈtɔːrɪən/ **I** *n* homme/femme *m*/*f* de l'époque victorienne.
II *adj* [*building, furniture, period, attitude*] victorien/-ienne; [*writer, poverty*] de l'époque victorienne.

Victoriana /vɪkˌtɔːrɪˈɑːnə/ *npl* objets *mpl* d'art de l'époque victorienne.

victorious /vɪkˈtɔːrɪəs/ *adj* [*troops, team, campaign*] victorieux/-ieuse (**over** sur); **to be ~ in the election/match** remporter les élections/le match.

victoriously /vɪkˈtɔːrɪəslɪ/ *adv* victorieusement.

victory /ˈvɪktərɪ/ *n* victoire *f*; **to win a ~** remporter une victoire (**over** sur).

victual /ˈvɪtl/ **I victuals** *npl* victuailles *fpl*.
II *vtr* (*p prés etc* **-ll-**, **-l-** US) approvisionner.

victualler /ˈvɪtlə(r)/ ▶ 1692 *n* (also **victualer** US) fournisseur/-euse *m*/*f* en alimentation générale.

vid° /vɪd/ *n* US vidéo *f*.

vide /ˈvɪdeɪ, ˈvaɪdiː/ *v imper* sout (in book) voir, v.

videlicet /vɪˈdiːlɪset/ *adv* sout à savoir.

video /ˈvɪdɪəʊ/ **I** *n* (*pl* **~s**) **1** (also **~ recorder**) magnétoscope *m*; **2** (also **~ cassette**) vidéo(cassette) *f*; **on ~** en vidéo(cassette); **3** (also **~ film**) vidéo *f*; **promotional/training ~** vidéo publicitaire/d'entraînement; **4** US (television) télévision *f*.
II *modif* [*company, footage*] de vidéo; [*age, market*] de la vidéo; [*channel, evidence, link, equipment, graphics, recording*] vidéo; [*interview*] en vidéo; [*producer*] de vidéos.
III *vtr* (*prés* **~s**; *prét, pp* **~ed**) **1** (from TV) enregistrer [qch]; **2** (on camcorder) filmer [qch] en vidéo.

video: **~ art** *n* art *m* vidéo; **~ book** *n* livre *m* vidéo; **~ camera** *n* caméra *f* vidéo; **~ clip** *n* clip *m*; **~ club** *n* vidéo-club *m*; **~conference** *n* vidéoconférence *f*; **~conferencing** *n* vidéoconférence *f*; **~disc** *n* vidéodisque *m*; **~fit** *n* portrait *m* robot; **~ frequency** *n* vidéofréquence *f*; **~ game** *n* jeu *m* vidéo; **~ jock**, **VJ** *n* US vidéo jockey *mf*; **~ library** *n* vidéothèque *f*; **~ nasty** *n* GB vidéo *f* représentant des violences véritables; **~phone** *n* vidéophone *m*; **~ shop** GB, **~ store** US ▶ 1692 *n* magasin *m* (de) vidéo.

videotape /ˈvɪdɪəʊteɪp/ **I** *n* bande *f* vidéo.
II *vtr* enregistrer [qch] en vidéo.

video: **~tape recording** *n* enregistrement *m* en vidéo; **~taping** *n* enregistrement *m* en vidéo.

videotex® /ˈvɪdɪəʊteks/ *n* vidéotex® *m*.

videotext /ˈvɪdɪəʊtekst/ *n* vidéotexte *m*.

vie /vaɪ/ *vi* (*p prés* **vying**) rivaliser (**with** avec; **for** pour; **to do** pour faire); **children vying (with each other) for attention** des enfants qui rivalisent (entre eux) pour attirer l'attention.

Vienna /vɪˈenə/ ▶ 1818 *pr n* Vienne.

Vienne ▶ 1163 *pr n* Vienne *f*; **in/to ~** dans la Vienne.

Viennese /vɪəˈniːz/ **I** *npl* **the ~** les Viennois.
II *adj* viennois.

Vietcong /ˌvjetˈkɒŋ/ *pr n* Viêt-cong *m*.

Vietnam /ˌvjetˈnæm/ ▶ 1131 *pr n* Viêt Nam *m*.

Vietnamese /ˌvɪetnəˈmiːz/ ▶ 1486, 1402 **I** *n* **1** (person) Vietnamien/-ienne *m*/*f*; **2** Ling vietnamien *m*.
II *adj* [*people, language, government*] vietnamien/-ienne; [*embassy*] du Vietnam.

view /vjuː/ **I** *n* **1** lit (of landscape, scene) vue *f*; fig (of situation) vue *f*; **a sea/mountain ~** une vue de la mer/des montagnes; **a room with a ~ (of the sea)** une chambre avec vue (sur la mer); **the trees cut off/break up the ~** la vue est cachée/est en partie cachée par les arbres; **you're blocking my ~!** tu me bouches la vue!; **the window gives you a good ~ of the church** de la fenêtre on a très bonne vue de l'église; **we had a good ~ of the stage from our seats** de nos sièges nous avions une bonne vue de la scène; **ten ~s of Paris** (on postcard, painting) dix vues de Paris; **we moved forward to get a better ~** nous nous sommes avancés pour mieux voir; **all I got was a back ~ of sb's head** tout ce que je voyais c'était la nuque de quelqu'un devant moi ; **to have a front/back/side ~ of sth** voir qch de face/de derrière/de côté; **she painted a side ~ of the building** elle a peint le bâtiment vu de côté; **an overall ~ of the situation** une vue d'ensemble de la situation; **an inside ~ of the situation** une idée or un aperçu de la situation vue de l'intérieur; **to take the long(-term)/short (-term) ~ of sth** avoir une vision à long terme/à court terme de qch; **in the long ~ he could be right** à long terme il a peut-être raison; **2** (field of vision, prospect) lit, fig vue *f*; **there wasn't a single house within ~** il n'y avait pas une seule maison en vue; **the lake was within ~ of the house** on pouvait voir le lac de la maison; **to do sth in (full) ~ of sb** faire qch devant qn or sous les yeux de qn; **in full ~ of the neighbours' windows** (en plein) devant les fenêtres des voisins; **to be in ~** lit [*coast, house*] être en vue; **what do you have in ~?** fig qu'est-ce que vous pensez faire?; **with the future in ~** en pensant l'avenir; **to keep sth in ~** lit, fig ne pas perdre qch de vue; **to disappear from** ou **be lost to ~** lit disparaître; **their original aims were soon lost from ~** ils ont vite perdu de vue leurs objectifs d'origine; **to hide sth from ~** cacher qch, dissimuler qch aux regards; **to be on ~** [*exhibition*] être présenté; Comm [*new range, clothes collection*] être exposé; **the house and contents will be on ~ the day before the sale** la maison et son contenu pourront être vus la veille de la vente; **3** (personal opinion, attitude) avis *m*, opinion *f*; **point of ~** point *m* de vue; **the scientific/medical/legal ~ is that** l'avis or l'opinion des scientifiques/des médecins/des juristes est que; **the widely-/generally-accepted ~** l'opinion largement/généralement répandue; **the majority ~** l'opinion la plus répandue; **the official/government ~** le point de vue officiel/du gouvernement; **my ~ is that** mon avis est que, à mon avis; **in his ~** à son avis; **in the ~ of Mr Jones/many experts** selon M. Jones/de nombreux spécialistes; **4** (visit, inspection) (of exhibition, house) visite *f*; (of film) projection *f*; Comm (of new range, clothes collection) présentation *f*.
II in view of *prep phr* (considering) vu, étant donné [*situation, facts, problem*]; **in ~ of his refusal, I...** vu or étant donné son refus, je...; **in ~ of this, they...** cela étant, ils...
III with a view to *prep phr* **with a ~ to sth** en vue de qch; **with a ~ to doing** en

vue de faire, afin de faire; **with a ~ to sb** ou **sb's doing** afin que qn fasse.
IV *vtr* **1** (regard, consider) considérer; (envisage) envisager; **to ~ the future with optimism** envisager or considérer l'avenir avec optimisme; **how do you ~ the situation?** comment envisages-tu la situation?, que penses-tu de la situation?; **to ~ sb with suspicion** être méfiant à l'égard de qn; **to ~ sb/sth as sth** considérer qn/qch comme qch; **the evening was ~ed as a success** la soirée a été considérée comme une réussite; **she ~ed him as an enemy** elle le considérait comme un ennemi; **the reforms are ~ed as not going far enough** on considère que les réformes ne vont pas assez loin; **2** (look at) gen voir [*scene, building*]; (inspect) visiter [*house, castle*]; voir, regarder [*collection, exhibition*]; visionner [*slide, microfiche*]; examiner [*documents*]; **the building ~ed from the side** le bâtiment vu de côté; **3** (watch) regarder [*television, programme*].
V *vi* TV regarder la télévision.

viewdata /ˈvjuːdeɪtə/ *n* Comput vidéographie *f* interactive.

viewer /ˈvjuːə(r)/ *n* **1** (person) (of TV) téléspectateur/-trice *m/f*; (of exhibition, property) visiteur/-euse *m/f*; **2** Phot visionneuse *f*.

viewership /vjuːəʃɪp/ *n* US audience *f*.

viewfinder /ˈvjuːfaɪndə(r)/ *n* viseur *m*.

viewing /ˈvjuːɪŋ/ **I** *n* **1** TV **we plan our ~ ahead** nous choisissons à l'avance ce que nous allons regarder (à la télévision); **'and that concludes Saturday night's ~'** 'et avec ceci se termine votre programme du samedi soir'; **essential ~ for teachers** à voir impérativement par les enseignants; **a programme scheduled for late-night/prime-time ~** une émission programmée en fin de soirée/aux heures de grande écoute; **the film makes compulsive ~** le film est captivant; **2** (visit, inspection) (of exhibition, house) visite *f*; (of film) projection *f*; Comm (of new range, clothes collection) présentation *f*; **'early ~ recommended'** (estate agent's notice) 'à visiter d'urgence'; **'~ by appointment only'** 'visite sur rendez-vous uniquement'.
II *modif* TV [*trends, patterns*] d'écoute; [*habits, preferences*] des téléspectateurs; **~ figures** taux *m* d'écoute; **the ~ public** les téléspectateurs *mpl*.

viewing panel, **viewing window** *n* (in oven, washing machine) hublot *m*.

view: **~phone** *n* vidéophone *m*, visiophone *m*; **~point** *n* (all contexts) point *m* de vue.

vigil /ˈvɪdʒɪl/ *n* gen veille *f*; (by sickbed, deathbed) veillée *f*; Relig vigile *f*; Pol manifestation *f* silencieuse; **to keep a ~ (over sb)** veiller (qn); **to hold** ou **stage a ~** Pol manifester silencieusement; **an all-night ~** une nuit de veille.

vigilance /ˈvɪdʒɪləns/ *n* vigilance *f*.

vigilance committee *n* groupe *m* d'autodéfense.

vigilant /ˈvɪdʒɪlənt/ *adj* vigilant.

vigilante /ˌvɪdʒɪˈlæntɪ/ **I** *n* membre *m* d'un groupe d'autodéfense.
II *modif* [*group, protection, attack, role*] d'autodéfense.

vigilantism /ˌvɪdʒɪˈlæntɪzəm/ *n* US *méthodes, comportement, idées propres aux groupes d'autodéfense*.

vigilantly /ˈvɪdʒɪləntlɪ/ *adv* avec vigilance.

vignette /viːˈnjet/ *n* **1** (drawing) vignette *f*; **2** Cin, Literat, Theat tableau *m*; **3** Phot photographie *f* aux bords estompés; **4** Art tableau *m* aux bords estompés.

vigor *n* US = **vigour**.

vigorous /ˈvɪgərəs/ *adj* [*person, plant, attempt, exercise*] vigoureux/-euse; [*campaign, campaigner*] énergique; [*denial*] catégorique; [*defender, supporter*] ardent.

vigorously /ˈvɪgərəslɪ/ *adv* [*push, stir, exercise, grow*] vigoureusement; [*defend, campaign, deny*] énergiquement.

vigour GB, **vigor** US /ˈvɪgə(r)/ *n* **1** (of person, plant) vigueur *f*; **2** (of argument, denial) vigueur *f*; **with great ~** avec une grande vigueur; **3** (of campaign, efforts) énergie *f*.

Viking /ˈvaɪkɪŋ/ **I** *n* Viking *mf*.
II *adj* viking.

vile /vaɪl/ *adj* **1** (wicked) [*crime, slander, traitor*] vil, ignoble; **2** (unpleasant) [*smell, taste, food*] infect; [*weather*] abominable; [*place, experience, colour*] horrible; [*mood, behaviour*] exécrable.

vilely /ˈvaɪlɪ/ *adv* honteusement, vilement.

vileness /ˈvaɪlnɪs/ *n* **1** (of crime, person) vilenie *f*; **2** (of smell, place, weather) horreur *f*.

vilification /ˌvɪlɪfɪˈkeɪʃn/ *n* diffamation *f* (**of** de).

vilify /ˈvɪlɪfaɪ/ *vtr* diffamer.

villa /ˈvɪlə/ *n* (large) (in town) pavillon *m*; (in country, for holiday) villa *f*.

village /ˈvɪlɪdʒ/ **I** *n* (place, community) village *m*; **fishing/mining ~** village de pêcheurs/de mineurs.
II *modif* [*shop, fête, school*] du village.

village: **~ green** *n* terrain *m* communal; **~ hall** *n* salle *f* des fêtes; **~ idiot** *n* idiot *m* du village.

villager /ˈvɪlɪdʒə(r)/ *n* villageois/-e *m/f*.

villain /ˈvɪlən/ *n* (scoundrel) canaille *f*; (criminal) bandit *m*; (in book, film) méchant *m*, traître *m* hum; (child) coquin/-e *m/f*; **the ~ of the piece** hum le méchant.

villainous /ˈvɪlənəs/ *adj* [*person, behaviour, action*] infâme; [*plot, expression, look, smile*] diabolique.

villainously /ˈvɪlənəslɪ/ *adv* [*behave*] d'une manière infâme; [*smile, look*] d'un air mauvais.

villainy /ˈvɪlənɪ/ *n* infamie *f*, vilenie *f* liter.

villein /ˈvɪleɪn/ *n* vilain/-e *m/f*.

villus /ˈvɪləs/ *n* (*pl* **-li**) villosité *f*.

vim /vɪm/ *n* allant *m*; **full of ~ and vigour** plein d'allant et d'énergie.

vinaigrette /ˌvɪnɪˈgret/ *n* (also **vinaigrette dressing**) vinaigrette *f*.

vindaloo /ˌvɪndəˈluː/ *n* (also **vindaloo curry**) *curry très épicé*.

vindicate /ˈvɪndɪkeɪt/ *vtr* gen donner raison à; Jur innocenter [*person*]; justifier, montrer le bien-fondé de [*action, claim, judgment*]; **the report ~d the doctor's decision** le rapport a montré le bien-fondé de la décision du médecin or a confirmé que le médecin avait pris la bonne décision.

vindication /ˌvɪndɪˈkeɪʃn/ *n* gen justification *f*; Jur (of person) disculpation *f*; **in ~ of** en justification de [*action, behaviour*]; à l'appui de [*decision*].

vindictive /vɪnˈdɪktɪv/ *adj* [*person, behaviour*] vindicatif/-ive (**towards** envers); [*decision, action*] revanchard.

vindictively /vɪnˈdɪktɪvlɪ/ *adv* vindicativement.

vindictiveness /vɪnˈdɪktɪvnɪs/ *n* esprit *m* de vengeance.

vine /vaɪn/ *n* **1** (producing grapes) vigne *f*; **2** (climbing plant) plante *f* grimpante.

vinegar /ˈvɪnɪgə(r)/ *n* vinaigre *m*; **cider/wine ~** vinaigre de cidre/de vin.

vinegary /ˈvɪnɪgərɪ/ *adj* [*taste, odour*] de vinaigre; [*remark, temper*] acide.

vine leaf *n* feuille *f* de vigne.

vinery /ˈvaɪnərɪ/ *n* (vineyard) vignoble *m*; (building) serre *f* (où on cultive la vigne).

vine stock *n* cep *m* de vigne.

vineyard /ˈvɪnjəd/ *n* vignoble *m*.

viniculture /ˈvɪnɪkʌltʃə(r)/ *n* viticulture *f*.

vino○ /ˈviːnəʊ/ *n* vin *m*.

vinous /ˈvaɪnəs/ *adj* sout [*colour*] lie-de-vin *inv*; [*taste, smell*] vineux/-euse.

vintage /ˈvɪntɪdʒ/ **I** *n* **1** Wine millésime *m*; **the 1986 ~** le millésime 1986; **the great ~s** les grands millésimes; **2** (era, date) époque *f*; **a pupil of (a) more recent ~** un élève d'une époque plus récente; **a dress of pre-war ~** une robe de l'époque d'avant-guerre.
II *adj* **1** Wine [*wine, champagne*] millésimé; [*port*] vieux/vieille (*before n*); **2** (classic) [*performance, comedy*] classique; **it's ~ Armstrong** c'est du Armstrong du meilleur cru; **3**○ (ancient) [*machine, model*] antique.

vintage: **~ car** *n* voiture *f* d'époque (*construite entre 1917 et 1930*); **~ year** *n* lit, fig grande année *f*.

vintner /ˈvɪntnə(r)/ ▶ 1692 *n* marchand *m* de vin.

vinyl /ˈvaɪnl/ **I** *n* **1** Tex vinyle *m*; **2** (record) disque *m* noir.
II *modif* [*cover, wallpaper, upholstery*] en vinyle; [*paint*] vinylique.

viol /ˈvaɪəl/ ▶ 1481 *n* viole *f*.

viola[1] /vɪˈəʊlə/ ▶ 1481 *n* (violon *m*) alto *m*.

viola[2] /ˈvaɪələ/ *n* Bot (genus) violacée *f*; (flower) pensée *f*.

viola /vɪˈəʊlə/: **~ da gamba** ▶ 1481 *n* viole *f* de gambe; **~ d'amore** ▶ 1481 *n* viole *f* d'amour; **~ player** ▶ 1481 *n* altiste *mf*.

violate /ˈvaɪəleɪt/ *vtr* **1** (infringe) violer [*law, agreement, constitution, cease-fire, right, privacy*]; transgresser [*criteria, duty, taboo*]; Jur enfreindre [*rule, regulation*]; **2** (desecrate) profaner [*sacred place*]; (disturb) troubler [*peace*]; **3** sout ou† (rape) violer.

violation /ˌvaɪəˈleɪʃn/ *n* **1** (of law, agreement, constitution, ceasefire, right, privacy) violation *f*; (of criteria, duty, taboo) transgression *f*; **in ~ of** en violation de; **2** (desecration) (of sacred place) profanation *f*; **3** Jur (minor offence) infraction *f*; **traffic ~** infraction au code de la route; **signal/safety ~** non-respect *m* de la signalisation/des règles de sécurité; **4** sout ou† (rape) viol *m*.

violator /ˈvaɪəleɪtə(r)/ *n* violateur/-trice *m/f*.

violence /ˈvaɪələns/ *n* **1** (physical aggression) violence *f* (**against** contre); **to resort to/use ~** recourir à/user de la violence; **an outbreak of ~** une flambée de violence; **two days of ~** deux jours d'incidents violents; **football ~** la violence lors des matchs de football; **2** (force) (of storm, feelings, reaction) violence *f*; **he hit the table with such ~ that** il a heurté la table avec une violence telle que; **3** (distortion) **to do ~ to sth** faire violence à [*text, truth*].

violent /ˈvaɪələnt/ *adj* **1** [*crime, behaviour, film, temper*] violent; **a ~ attack** (physical) une attaque violente; (verbal) une attaque virulente; **2** (sudden) [*acceleration, braking*] soudain; [*change, contrast*] brutal; **3** (powerful) [*wind, storm, explosion, emotion, fit, headache*] violent; **4** (harsh) [*colour*] criard; [*light*] cru.

violently /ˈvaɪələntlɪ/ *adv* **1** [*push, attack*] violemment; [*struggle*] furieusement; [*assault*] sauvagement; **he was ~ kicked** on lui a donné de violents coups de pied; **to die ~** mourir de mort violente; **2** (dramatically) [*brake, swerve, alter, swing*] brusquement; **3** (vehemently) [*respond, react, object*] violemment; **to be ~ opposed to** être violemment opposé à; **4** [*blush, cough, shake*] violemment; **to be ~ ill** ou **sick** GB avoir de violentes nausées.

violet /ˈvaɪələt/ ▶ 1104 **I** *n* **1** Bot violette *f*; **2** (colour) violet *m*.
II *adj* violet/-ette.

violin /ˌvaɪəˈlɪn/ ▶ 1481 **I** *n* violon *m*; **the first/second ~** le premier/second violon.
II *modif* [*concerto, sonata*] pour violon; [*teacher*] de violon.

violin case *n* étui *m* à violon.

violinist /ˌvaɪəˈlɪnɪst/ ▶ 1692, 1481 *n* violoniste *mf*.

violin player *n* = **violinist**.

violist /ˈvaɪəlɪst/ ▶ 1692, 1481 *n* **1** US (viola player) altiste *mf*; **2** (viol player) violiste *mf*.

violoncellist /ˌvaɪələnˈtʃelɪst/ ▶ 1692, 1481 *n* violoncelliste *mf*.

violoncello /ˌvaɪələn'tʃeləʊ/ ▶1481 *n* violoncelle *m*.

VIP (*abrév* = **very important person**) **I** *n* personnalité *f* (en vue), VIP *m inv*, personnage *m* de marque.
II *adj* [*area, tent, facility*] réservé aux personnalités; **~ guest** hôte *mf* de marque; **~ lounge** salon *m* réservé aux personnalités; **to give sb (the) ~ treatment** recevoir qn en hôte de marque; **to get (the) ~ treatment** être reçu en hôte de marque.

viper /'vaɪpə(r)/ *n* Zool, fig vipère *f*.
IDIOMS **to nurse a ~ in one's bosom** littér réchauffer un serpent dans son sein; **a nest of ~s, a ~s' nest** fig un panier de crabes.

viperish /'vaɪpərɪʃ/ *adj* péj de vipère.

virago /vɪ'rɑːgəʊ/ *n* (*pl* **-goes** ou **-gos**) péj mégère *f*, virago *f* pej.

viral /'vaɪərəl/ *adj* viral.

Virgil /'vɜːdʒɪl/ *pr n* Virgile.

virgin /'vɜːdʒɪn/ **I** *n* (woman) vierge *f*; (man) puceau° *m*, homme *m* vierge; **to be a ~** être (encore) vierge.
II Virgin *pr n* **the Virgin** Relig la Vierge *f*; **the Virgin Mary** la Vierge Marie; **the Virgin and Child** la Vierge et l'Enfant.
III *adj* (all contexts) vierge.

virginal /'vɜːdʒɪnl/ **I** *n* Mus virginal *m*.
II *adj* [*smile, expression, woman*] innocent; [*white, innocence*] virginal.

Virgin Birth *n* **the ~** Relig la conception virginale.

virgin forest *n* forêt *f* vierge.

Virginia /və'dʒɪnɪə/ ▶1744 *pr n* **1** Geog Virginie *f*; **in ~** en Virginie; **2** = **Virginia tobacco**.

Virginia creeper *n* vigne *f* vierge.

Virginian /və'dʒɪnɪən/ **I** *n* Virginien/-ienne *m/f*.
II *adj* de Virginie.

Virginia tobacco *n* tabac *m* blond.

Virgin Islands, **VI** ▶1381 *n* îles *fpl* Vierges.

virginity /və'dʒɪnətɪ/ *n* virginité *f*; **to lose one's ~** perdre sa virginité.

Virgo /'vɜːgəʊ/ ▶1916 *n* Vierge *f*.

Virgoan /vɜː'gəʊən/ *n* Astrol **to be a ~** être (du signe de la) Vierge.

virgule /'vɜːgjuːl/ *n* Print barre *f* oblique.

virile /'vɪraɪl, US 'vɪrəl/ *adj* lit, fig viril.

virility /vɪ'rɪlətɪ/ *n* virilité *f*.

virologist /vaɪə'rɒlədʒɪst/ ▶1692 *n* virologue *mf*, virologiste *mf*.

virology /vaɪə'rɒlədʒɪ/ *n* virologie *f*.

virtual /'vɜːtʃʊəl/ *adj* **1** (almost complete) [*collapse, failure, disappearance, standstill*] quasi-total (*after n*); **the ~ disappearance of this custom** la disparition quasi-totale or la quasi-disparition de cette coutume; **he was a ~ prisoner** il était quasiment° or pratiquement prisonnier; **it's ~ slavery** c'est presque de l'esclavage; **she is the ~ ruler of the country** de fait c'est elle qui dirige le pays; **2** Comput, Phys virtuel/-elle.

virtually /'vɜːtʃʊəlɪ/ *adv* pratiquement, presque; **~ anywhere** presque or pratiquement partout; **it's ~ impossible** c'est quasiment° impossible; **~ every household has one** chaque ménage ou presque en a un; **there is ~ no public transport** les transports en commun sont quasiment° inexistants.

virtual reality *n* réalité *f* virtuelle.

virtue /'vɜːtʃuː/ **I** *n* **1** (goodness, good quality, chastity) vertu *f*; **to lose/preserve one's ~** perdre/préserver sa vertu; **a woman of easy ~** une femme de petite vertu; **2** (advantage) avantage *m*; **to have the ~ of convenience** ou **of being convenient** avoir l'avantage d'être pratique; **to extol the ~s of sth** vanter les mérites de qch.
II by virtue of *prep phr* en raison de.
IDIOMS **~ is its own reward** Prov la vertu est sa propre récompense; **to make a ~ of necessity** faire de nécessité vertu.

virtuosity /ˌvɜːtʃʊ'ɒsətɪ/ *n* virtuosité *f*.

virtuoso /ˌvɜːtjʊ'əʊsəʊ, -zəʊ/ **I** *n* (*pl* **-sos** ou **-si**) virtuose *mf* (**of** de); **piano/violin ~** virtuose du piano/violon.
II *adj* de virtuose.

virtuous /'vɜːtʃʊəs/ *adj* vertueux/-euse; **~ indignation** indignation outragée.

virtuously /'vɜːtʃʊəslɪ/ *adv* **1** (morally) [*behave, live*] de façon vertueuse; [*help, act*] vertueusement; **2** (self-righteously) avec satisfaction.

virulence /'vɪrʊləns/ *n* gen, Med virulence *f*.

virulent /'vɪrʊlənt/ *adj* Med, fig virulent.

virulently /'vɪrʊləntlɪ/ *adv* avec virulence.

virus /'vaɪərəs/ ▶1354 *n* Med, Comput virus *m*; **the flu/rabies/Aids ~** le virus de la grippe/de la rage/du sida.

visa /'viːzə/ *n* visa *m*; **entry/tourist ~** visa d'entrée/de touriste.

vis-à-vis /ˌviːzɑː'viː/ **I** *n* (person) homologue *m*.
II *prep* (in relation to) par rapport à, vis-à-vis de; (concerning) en ce qui concerne.

viscera /'vɪsərə/ *npl* viscères *mpl*.

visceral /'vɪsərəl/ *adj* Anat viscéral; fig (instinctive) [*feeling, reaction*] viscéral; (raw) [*power, performance*] qui vous prend aux tripes°.

viscid /'vɪsɪd/ *adj* visqueux/-euse, gluant.

viscose /'vɪskəʊz, -kəʊs/ **I** *n* viscose *f*.
II *modif* Tex [*garment*] en viscose.

viscosity /vɪ'skɒsətɪ/ *n* viscosité *f*.

viscount /'vaɪkaʊnt/ ▶1268 *n* vicomte *m*.

viscountcy /'vaɪkaʊntsɪ/ *n* vicomté *f*.

viscountess /'vaɪkaʊntɪs/ ▶1268 *n* vicomtesse *f*.

viscounty /'vaɪkaʊntɪ/ *n* = **viscountcy**.

viscous /'vɪskəs/ *adj* visqueux/-euse, gluant.

vise /vaɪs/ *n* US étau *m*.

visé /'viːzeɪ/ *n* US visa *m*.

visibility /ˌvɪzə'bɪlətɪ/ *n* **1** (clarity, ability to see) visibilité *f*; **~ is good/poor** il y a une bonne/mauvaise visibilité; **~ is below 150 metres** la visibilité est inférieure à 150 mètres; **to have restricted ~** avoir une visibilité limitée; **2** (ability to be seen) visibilité *f*; **light clothes improve your ~** des vêtements clairs vous rendent plus visible la nuit.

visible /'vɪzəbl/ *adj* **1** (able to be seen) visible; **clearly ~** bien visible; **to be ~ from** être visible de; **to be ~ for miles around** être visible à des kilomètres à la ronde; **2** (concrete) [*improvement, sign*] évident; [*evidence*] flagrant; **with no ~ means of support** sans ressources apparentes.

visibly /'vɪzəblɪ/ *adv* **1** (to the eye) [*shrinking, ill, paler*] visiblement; **2** (clearly) [*annoyed, moved, relieved*] manifestement.

Visigoth /'vɪzɪgɒθ/ *pr n* Wisigoth/-e *m/f*.

vision /'vɪʒn/ **I** *n* **1** (mental picture, hallucination) vision *f*; **to have ~s** avoir des visions; **to appear to sb in a ~** apparaître à qn; **2** (conception, idea) vision *f*; **her ~ of Europe in the 21st century** sa vision de l'Europe au XXIe siècle; **Rousseau's ~ of the ideal society** l'idée de la société idéale selon Rousseau; **3** (imaginative foresight) sagacité *f*; **to have/lack ~** avoir de la/manquer de sagacité; **a man of ~** un visionnaire; **4** (ability to see) vue *f*; **to have poor/good ~** avoir une mauvaise/bonne vue; **to have blurred ~** avoir la vue trouble; **to come into ~** devenir visible; **5** (sight, visual image) image *f*; **a ~ of loveliness/hell** l'image de la beauté/de l'enfer; **6** TV (picture) image *f*; **sound and ~** le son et l'image.
II *vtr* US imaginer.

visionary /'vɪʒənrɪ, US 'vɪʒənerɪ/ *n, adj* visionnaire (*mf*).

vision mixer *n* (person) réalisateur *m* de direct; (equipment) mélangeur *m* d'images.

visit /'vɪzɪt/ **I** *n* **1** (call) visite *f*; **an official** ou **state ~** une visite officielle; **a home ~** une visite à domicile; **a flying ~** une visite éclair; **on her first/last ~ to China, she**... la première/dernière fois qu'elle est allée en Chine, elle...; **he is on an official ~ to Canada** il est en visite officielle au Canada; **to pay a ~ to sb, pay sb a ~** (to friend) aller voir qn, rendre visite à qn; (on business) aller voir qn, aller chez qn; **I'll have to pay a ~ to the dentist** il faudra que j'aille chez le dentiste; **to have a ~ from** recevoir la visite de [*parents, friend, nurse, police*]; **to make a ~ to** visiter, inspecter [*premises, venue*]; **to make home ~s** [*doctor etc*] faire des visites à domicile; **2** (stay) séjour *m*; **a ~ to France** un séjour en France; **it's my first ~ to this country** c'est la première fois que je viens dans ce pays; **to go on a ~ to** faire un séjour à [*town*].
II *vtr* **1** (call on) aller voir, rendre visite à [*family, friend*]; aller voir, aller chez [*doctor, dentist, solicitor, client*]; **when can I come and ~ you?** quand est-ce que je peux venir te voir?; **2** (see) visiter, aller voir [*monument, exhibition, region*]; **3** (inspect) inspecter [*school, workplace, premises*]; **4** (on holiday etc) **to ~ sb** venir chez qn; **to ~ a country** faire un séjour ou séjourner dans un pays; **come and ~ us for a few days** venez passer quelques jours avec nous; **they often come to ~ (us)** ils viennent souvent chez nous; **5** (affect) sout **to be ~ed by** être éprouvé par [*disaster, difficulty*]; **6**† (inflict) **to ~ sth (up) on sb** infliger qch à qn; **7** US (socially) **to ~ with** aller voir, rendre visite à [*family, friend*].

visitation /ˌvɪzɪ'teɪʃn/ **I** *n* **1** (supernatural sign) signe *m* (**from** de); **2** (punishment) châtiment *m* (**from** de); **3** (by official person) visite *f* (**from** de).
II Visitation *pr n* Relig Visitation *f*.

visiting /'vɪzɪtɪŋ/ *adj* (*épith*) [*statesman, stateswoman*] en visite; [*athlete*] visiteur/-euse; [*orchestra*] invité.

visiting: **~ card** *n* US carte *f* de visite; **~ fireman** *n* US visiteur *m* de marque; **~ hours** *npl* heures *fpl* de visite; **~ lecturer** *n* (short term) maître *m* de conférence invité; (long term) maître *m* de conférence associé; **~ nurse** ▶1692 *n* US infirmier/-ière *m/f* à domicile; **~ professor** *n* (short term) professeur *m* invité; (long term) professeur *m* associé; **~ room** *n* parloir *m*; **~ teacher** ▶1692 *n* US Sch enseignant/-e *m/f* à domicile; **~ team** *n* visiteurs/-euses *m/fpl*; **~ time** *n* heures *fpl* de visite.

visitor /'vɪzɪtə(r)/ *n* **1** (caller) invité/-e *m/f*; **we have ~s** nous avons de la visite; **she didn't often have ~s** elle ne recevait pas beaucoup de visites; **they were frequent ~s to our house** ils venaient souvent chez nous; **2** (tourist) visiteur/-euse *m/f*; **I've been a regular ~ to this country/to the museum** je viens souvent dans ce pays/au musée; **3** (animal bird) migrateur *m*; **a summer ~** un migrateur d'été.

visitor: **~ centre** *n* centre *m* d'accueil et d'information des visiteurs; **~s' book** *n* (in museum, exhibition) livre *m* d'or; (in hotel) registre *m*.

visor /'vaɪzə(r)/ *n* **1** (part of helmet, eyeshade) visière *f*; **2** Aut pare-soleil *m inv*.

vista /'vɪstə/ *n* lit panorama *m*; fig perspective *f*; **to open up new ~s** ouvrir de nouvelles perspectives.

visual /'vɪʒʊəl/ **I visuals** *npl* (photographs, pictures) images *fpl*; Cin (visual effects) effets *mpl* visuels; Sch (visual aids) supports *mpl* visuels.
II *adj* (all contexts) visuel/-elle.

visual: **~ aid** *n* support *m* visuel; **~ artist** ▶1692 *n* plasticien/-ienne *m/f*; **~ arts** *npl* arts *mpl* plastiques; **~ display terminal**, **VDT**, **~ display unit**, **VDU** *n* Comput écran *m* de visualisation; **~ field** *n* champ *m* visuel.

visualize /'vɪʒʊəlaɪz/ *vtr* **1** (picture) s'imaginer, se représenter [*person, scene*]; **she had ~d the house as more modern** elle

The human voice

Voices and singers

		voice	singer
soprano	=	soprano *m*	soprano *m* or *f* (*depending on whether a boy soprano or a woman*)
mezzo-soprano	=	mezzo-soprano *m*	mezzo-soprano *f*
contralto	=	contralto *m*	contralto *f*
alto	=	alto *m*	alto *m*
counter-tenor	=	haute-contre *f*	haute-contre *m*
tenor	=	ténor *m*	ténor *m*
baritone	=	baryton *m*	baryton *m*
bass-baritone	=	baryton-basse *m*	baryton-basse *m*
bass	=	basse *f*	basse *f*

In the following examples tenor *and* ténor *stand for any of the above voices:*

he's a tenor	=	il est ténor *or* c'est un ténor
he sings tenor	=	il chante ténor
a tenor voice	=	une voix de ténor
the tenor part	=	la partie ténor
a tenor solo	=	un solo de ténor

s'était imaginée que la maison serait plus moderne; **I met him once, but I can't ~ his face** je l'ai rencontré une fois, mais je n'arrive pas à me rappeler sa tête; **2** (envisage) envisager.

visually /ˈvɪʒʊəlɪ/ *adv* visuellement.

visually handicapped **I** *n* **the ~** (+ *v pl*) (partially-sighted) les malvoyants/-es *m/f pl*; (non-sighted) les non-voyants/-es *m/f pl*.
II *adj* (partially-sighted) malvoyant; (non-sighted) nonvoyant.

visually impaired **I** *n* **the ~** (+ *v pl*) les malvoyants/-es *m/f pl*.
II *adj* malvoyant.

vital /ˈvaɪtl/ *adj* **1** (essential) [*asset, document, expenditure, information, research, industry, supplies*] essentiel/-ielle, primordial; [*role, issue, need, interest*] fondamental, primordial; [*match, point, support, factor*] décisif/-ive; [*service, help*] indispensable; [*treatment, importance*] vital; **it is ~ that, it is of ~ importance that** il est indispensable or vital que (+ *subj*); **~ to sb/sth** indispensable à qn/qch; **it is ~ to do** il est indispensable de faire; **of ~ importance** d'une importance capitale; **to play a ~ role** ou **part** jouer un rôle capital; **2** (essential to life) [*organ, force*] vital; **3** (lively) [*person*] plein de vie or de vitalité; [*culture, music*] vivant.

vitality /vaɪˈtælətɪ/ *n* vitalité *f*.

vitally /ˈvaɪtəlɪ/ *adv* [*important*] extrêmement; [*necessary, needed*] absolument.

vital statistics *n* **1** Stat données *fpl* démographiques; **2** hum gen informations *fpl* essentielles; (of woman's body) mensurations *fpl*.

vitamin /ˈvɪtəmɪn, US ˈvaɪt-/ **I** *n* vitamine *f*; **~ A/B/C** vitamine A/B/C; **with added ~s, ~ enriched** vitaminé.
II *modif* [*requirements*] en vitamines; **to have a high/low ~ content** être riche/pauvre en vitamines.

vitamin: **~ deficiency** *n* carence *f* en vitamines; **~ pill, ~ tablet** *n* comprimé *m* de vitamines.

vitiate /ˈvɪʃɪeɪt/ *vtr* sout gen, Jur vicier.

viticulture /ˈvɪtɪkʌltʃə(r)/ *n* viticulture *f*.

vitreous /ˈvɪtrɪəs/ *adj* **1** Tech [*enamel*] vitrifié; [*rock, china*] vitreux/-euse; **2** Anat [*body, humour*] vitré.

vitrification /ˌvɪtrɪfɪˈkeɪʃn/ *n* vitrification *f*.

vitrify /ˈvɪtrɪfaɪ/ **I** *vtr* vitrifier.
II *vi* se vitrifier.

vitriol /ˈvɪtrɪəl/ *n* Chem, fig vitriol *m*.

vitriolic /ˌvɪtrɪˈɒlɪk/ *adj* Chem de vitriol; fig au vitriol.

vitriolize /ˈvɪtrɪəlaɪz/ *vtr* vitrioler.

vitro ▸ **in vitro**.

vituperate /vɪˈtjuːpəreɪt, US vaɪˈtuː-/ **I** *vtr* vitupérer contre.
II *vi* vitupérer (**against** contre).

vituperation /vɪˌtjuːpəˈreɪʃn, US vaɪˌtuː-/ *n* ¢ vitupérations *fpl*.

vituperative /vɪˈtjuːpərətɪv, US vaɪˈtuː-pəreɪtɪv/ *adj* injurieux/-ieuse.

viva **I** /ˈvaɪvə/ *n* GB Univ oral *m*.
II /viːvə/ *excl* vive!; **~ freedom!** vive la liberté!

vivacious /vɪˈveɪʃəs/ *adj* [*person, performance, manner*] plein de vivacité.

vivaciously /vɪˈveɪʃəslɪ/ *adv* [*speak, behave*] avec vivacité.

vivacity /vɪˈvæsətɪ/ *n* vivacité *f*.

vivarium /vaɪˈveərɪəm, vɪ-/ *n* (*pl* **-riums** ou **-ria**) vivarium *m*.

viva voce /ˌvaɪvə ˈvəʊtʃɪ, ˈvəʊsɪ/ **I** *n, modif* GB = **viva I**.
II *adv* Jur [*testify*] viva voce.

vivid /ˈvɪvɪd/ *adj* **1** (bright) [*colour, light*] vif/vive; [*garment*] aux couleurs vives; [*sunset*] éclatant; **2** (graphic) [*imagination*] vif/vive; [*memory, picture*] (très) net/nette; [*dream, impression*] frappant; [*description, example, language, imagery*] vivant, frappant; **to describe sth in ~ detail** faire une description vivante et détaillée de qch.

vividly /ˈvɪvɪdlɪ/ *adv* [*shine, glow*] d'une lumière éclatante; [*picture, dream*] de façon très nette; [*describe*] de façon très vivante or frappante; **~ coloured** aux couleurs vives; **I remember it ~!** je m'en souviens très bien!

vividness /ˈvɪvɪdnɪs/ *n* (of colour, light, sunset, garment) éclat *m*; (of memory, dream, description) netteté *f*; (of language, imagery) richesse *f*; (of style) vigueur *f*.

vivify /ˈvɪvɪfaɪ/ *vtr* vivifier.

viviparous /vɪˈvɪpərəs, US vaɪ-/ *adj* (all contexts) vivipare.

vivisect /ˈvɪvɪsekt/ *vtr* pratiquer une vivisection sur.

vivisection /ˌvɪvɪˈsekʃn/ *n* vivisection *f*.

vivisectionist /ˌvɪvɪˈsekʃənɪst/ *n* (practiser) vivisecteur/-trice *m/f*; (supporter) partisan *m* de la vivisection.

vixen /ˈvɪksn/ *n* **1** Zool renarde *f*; **2** péj (woman) mégère *f*.

viz /vɪz/ *adv* sout (*abrév* = **videlicet**) à savoir.

vizier /vɪˈzɪə(r)/ *n* vizir *m*.

VLF *n*: *abrév* ▸ **very low frequency**.

V: **V-neck** *n* (neck) encolure *f* en V; (sweater) pull *m* en V; **V-necked** *adj* à encolure *f* en V.

vocabulary /vəˈkæbjʊlərɪ, US -lerɪ/ **I** *n* **1** (of person, group, language) vocabulaire *m*; **2** (list, glossary) lexique *m*.
II *modif* [*book, test*] de vocabulaire.

vocal /ˈvəʊkl/ **I vocals** *npl* chant *m*; **'with Mick Jagger on ~s'** 'avec Mick Jagger au chant'; **who did the ~s?** qui a assuré la partie vocale?; **to do the backing ~s** faire les chœurs.
II *adj* **1** [*organs, range, music, sound*] vocal; **2** (vociferous) [*person, group*] qui se fait entendre, pej bruyant; **an increasingly ~ minority** une minorité qui se fait entendre de plus en plus; **one of her most ~ critics** un de ses critiques les plus intarissables.

vocal c(h)ords *n* cordes *fpl* vocales.

vocalic /vəˈkælɪk/ *adj* vocalique.

vocalist /ˈvəʊkəlɪst/ *n* chanteur/-euse *m/f* (*dans un groupe pop*).

vocalization /ˌvəʊkəlaɪˈzeɪʃn/ *n* Phon, Mus vocalisation *f*.

vocalize /ˈvəʊkəlaɪz/ **I** *vtr* **1** Phon vocaliser; **2** Ling marquer les voyelles de [*text*]; **3** fig exprimer [*thought, emotion, opposition*].
II *vi* Mus vocaliser, faire des vocalises.

vocally /ˈvəʊkəlɪ/ *adj* **1** Mus vocalement; **2** (vociferously) haut et fort.

vocal: **~ organs** *npl* organes *mpl* vocaux; **~ tract** *n* appareil *m* vocal.

vocation /vəʊˈkeɪʃn/ *n* vocation *f*; **to find/miss one's ~** trouver/rater sa vocation; **to have a ~ for sth** avoir la vocation de qch; **to have a ~ to do** ou **for doing** avoir une vocation pour faire.

vocational /vəʊˈkeɪʃənl/ *adj* gen professionnel/-elle; [*syllabus, approach*] à orientation professionnelle.

vocational: **~ course** *n* stage *m* de formation professionnelle; **~ education** *n* enseignement *m* professionnel; **~ guidance** *n* orientation *f* professionnelle; **~ training** *n* formation *f* professionnelle.

vocative /ˈvɒkətɪv/ **I** *n* Ling vocatif *m*.
II *adj* [*form*] du vocatif; **in the ~ case** au vocatif.

vociferate /vəˈsɪfəreɪt, US vəʊ-/ *vtr, vi* sout vociférer.

vociferous /vəˈsɪfərəs, US vəʊ-/ *adj* [*person, protest*] véhément.

vociferously /vəˈsɪfərəslɪ, US vəʊ-/ *adv* avec véhémence.

vodka /ˈvɒdkə/ *n* vodka *f*; **to order two ~s** commander deux vodkas.

vogue /vəʊg/ **I** *n* vogue *f*, mode *f* (**for** de); **to come into/be in ~** entrer/être en vogue or à la mode; **to go out of ~** se démoder; **to be out of ~** être démodé.
II *modif* [*word, expression*] en vogue, à la mode.

voice /vɔɪs/ **I** *n* **1** (speaking sound) voix *f*; **to hear a ~** entendre une voix; **in a loud ~** à haute voix; **in a low ~** à voix basse; **in a cross ~** d'une voix irritée; **to have a high/low(-pitched) ~** avoir une voix aiguë/grave; **to raise/lower one's ~** élever/baisser la voix; **keep your ~ down!** baisse la voix or le ton! **his ~ is breaking/has broken** sa voix mue/a mué; **to lose one's ~** (when ill) perdre la voix; (when afraid) perdre la parole; **to give ~ to sth** exprimer qch; **at the top of one's ~** à tue-tête; **2** (for singing) voix *f*; **to have a good ~** avoir une belle voix; **to be in fine ~** être en voix; **in superb ~** superbement en voix; **for four ~s** pour quatre voix; **3** (opinion, expression) voix *f*; **to have a ~** avoir voix au chapitre (**in sth** en or dans qch; **in doing** pour faire); **the ~ of reason/dissent** la voix de la raison/dissidence; **to add one's ~ to sth** unir sa voix à qch; **~s have been raised against** plusieurs voix se sont élevées contre; **to reply with one ~** répondre d'une seule voix; **to demand sth with one ~** exiger unanimement qch; **the ~ of the people** la voix du peuple; **4** (representative organization, newspaper) porte-parole *m* (**of** de); **5** Literat (of writer, poet) style *m*; **narrative ~** voix *f* du narrateur; **6** Ling voix *f*; **in the active/passive ~** à la voix active/passive; **7** Phon voix *f*.
II -voiced (*dans composés*): **hoarse-/deep-~d** à la voix rauque/grave; **a shaky-~d reply** une réponse donnée d'une voix tremblante.
III *vtr* **1** (express) exprimer [*concern, grievance*]; **2** Phon sonoriser [*consonant*].
IDIOMS **to like the sound of one's own ~** s'écouter parler; **the still small ~ of conscience** la voix de la conscience.

voice: **~ box** *n* larynx *m*; **~d consonant** *n* consonne *f* sonore.

voiceless /ˈvɔɪslɪs/ *adj* **1** Phon sourd; **2** [*minority, group*] privé de la parole; **3** littér (silent) sans voix.

voice: **~ mail, ~ messaging** *n* messagerie *f* vocale; **~-over** *n* voix-off *f*; **~ print** *n* empreinte *f* vocale; **~ recognition** *n* reconnaissance *f* vocale; **~ training** *n* entraînement *m* de la voix; **~ vote** *n* US vote *m* par acclamation.

void /vɔɪd/ **I** *n* lit, fig vide *m*; **to fill the ~** combler le vide.
II *adj* **1** Jur [*contract, agreement*] nul/nulle; [*cheque*] annulé; **to make** ou **render ~** annuler; **2** (empty) vide; **~ of** dépourvu de.
III *vtr* Jur annuler.

voidable /ˈvɔɪdəbl/ *adj* [*contract, policy*] résiliable; [*marriage*] annulable.

voile /vɔɪl/ **I** *n* voile *m*.
II *modif* [*garment*] en voile.

vol /vɒl/ *n* (*pl* **-s**) *abrév* = **volume**.

volatile /ˈvɒlətaɪl, US -tl/ *adj* **1** Chem volatil; **2** fig [*situation*] explosif/-ive; [*market, exchange rate*] instable; [*person*] lunatique, versatile; [*mood*] changeant.

volatility /ˌvɒləˈtɪlətɪ/ *n* **1** Chem volatilité *f*; **2** fig (of situation) caractère *m* explosif; (of market, exchange rate) instabilité *f*; (of person) versatilité *f*.

volatilize /vəˈlætɪlaɪz/ **I** *vtr* volatiliser.
II *vi* se volatiliser.

volcanic /vɒlˈkænɪk/ *adj* volcanique.

volcano /vɒlˈkeɪnəʊ/ *n* (*pl* **-noes** ou **-nos**) volcan *m*.

volcanology /ˌvɒlkəˈnɒlədʒɪ/ *n* volcanologie *f*.

vole /vəʊl/ *n* **1** Zool campagnol *m*; **2** (in card games) vole *f*.

Volga /ˈvɒlgə/ **▶ 1644** *pr n* Volga *f*.

volition /vəˈlɪʃn, US vəʊ-/ *n* volonté *f*; **of one's own ~** de son propre gré.

volley /ˈvɒlɪ/ **I** *n* **1** Sport (in tennis) volée *f*; (in soccer) reprise *f* de volée; **to miss a ~** (in tennis) rater une volée; **to practise one's ~s** (in tennis) s'entrainer à la volée; **to hit** ou **kick the ball on the ~** frapper la balle de volée; **2** Mil (of gunfire) salve *f* (**of** de); (of missiles) volée *f* (**of** de); **3** fig (series) **a ~ of** un feu roulant de [*questions, words*]; une bordée de [*insults, oaths*].
II *vtr* Sport (in tennis) prendre [qch] de volée; (in soccer) reprendre [qch] de volée.
III *vi* Sport (in tennis) jouer à la volée.

volleyball /ˈvɒlɪbɔːl/ **▶ 1282** **I** *n* volley (-ball) *m*.
II *modif* [*match, court*] de volley(-ball); **~ player** volleyeur/-euse *m/f*.

volleyer /ˈvɒlɪə(r)/ *n* (in tennis) volleyeur/-euse *m/f*.

volt /vəʊlt/ *n* volt *m*; **nine-~ battery** pile de neuf volts.

voltage /ˈvəʊltɪdʒ/ *n* tension *f*; **high-/low-~ cable** câble de haute/basse tension.

voltage surge *n* surtension *f*.

voltaic /vɒlˈteɪɪk/ *adj* voltaïque.

voltaic pile *n* pile *f* de Volta.

volte-face /ˌvɒltˈfɑːs/ *n* volte-face *f inv*; **to perform a ~** faire volte-face.

voltmeter *n* voltmètre *m*.

volubility /ˌvɒljʊˈbɪlətɪ/ *n* volubilité *f*.

voluble /ˈvɒljʊbl/ *adj* volubile.

volubly /ˈvɒljʊblɪ/ *adv* avec volubilité.

volume /ˈvɒljuːm, US -jəm/ **▶ 1869** **I** *n* **1** Meas, Phys (of gas, liquid, object) volume *m* (**of** de); (of container) capacité *f*; **by ~** au volume; **2** (amount) volume *m*; **~ of** volume de [*traffic, sales, production, trade*]; quantité de [*work*]; **3** (book) volume *m*; (part of complete work) tome *m*; **a ten-~ set** un ensemble de dix volumes; **in ten ~s** en dix volumes; **4** Audio (sound quantity) volume *m*, puissance *f*; **to adjust the ~** régler le volume.

Volume measurement

For pints, gallons, litres etc. **▶ 1068**.
Note that French has a comma where English has a decimal point.

1 cu in = 16,38 cm³
1 cu ft = 0,03 m³
1 cu yd = 0,76 m³

There are three ways of saying 16,38 cm³, *and other measurements like it:* seize virgule trente-huit centimètres cubes *or* (*less formally*) seize centimètres cubes virgule trente-huit *or* seize centimètres cubes trente-huit. *For more details on how to say numbers,* **▶ 1505**.

what is its volume?	= quel est son volume?
its volume is 200 cubic metres	= ça fait 200 mètres cubes
it's 200 cubic metres	= ça fait 200 mètres cubes
it's one metre by two metres by three metres	= ça mesure un mètre sur deux mètres sur trois mètres
sold by the cubic metre	= vendu au mètre cube
A has a greater volume than B	= le volume de A est supérieur à celui de B
B has a smaller volume than A	= le volume de B est inférieur à celui de A

Note the use of de *in this construction.*

there are a million cubic centimetres in a cubic metre	= il y a un million de centimètres cubes dans un mètre cube
a million cubic centimetres make one cubic metre	= un million de centimètres cubes font un mètre cube

Note the French construction with de, *coming after the noun it describes:*
a 200-cubic-metre tank = un réservoir de 200 mètres cubes

II *modif* Comm (bulk) [*production, purchasing, sales*] en nombre.
IDIOMS **to speak ~s (about sth)** en dire long (sur qch).

volume: **~ control** *n* Audio (bouton *m* de) réglage *m* du volume; **~ discount** *n* Comm remise *f*, ristourne *f* (sur quantité).

volumetric /ˌvɒljʊˈmetrɪk/ *adj* volumétrique.

voluminous /vəˈluːmɪnəs/ *adj* volumineux/-euse.

voluntarily /ˈvɒləntrəlɪ/ *adv* de plein gré, volontairement.

voluntary /ˈvɒləntrɪ, US -terɪ/ **I** *n* Mus voluntary *m*.
II *adj* **1** (not imposed) [*consent, control, recruit, euthanasia*] volontaire; [*statement*] spontané; [*agreement, ban*] librement consenti; [*participation, attendance*] facultatif/-ive; [*sanction*] non obligatoire; **on a ~ basis** sur une base volontaire; **to resolve sth by ~ means** résoudre qch en faisant appel à la bonne volonté; **2** (unpaid) [*work, organization, agency, sector*] bénévole; **~ worker** travailleur/-euse *m/f* bénévole; **to work on a ~ basis** travailler bénévolement; **3** (done by will) [*movement*] volontaire.

voluntary: **~ hospital** *n* US ≈ hôpital *m* privé; **~ liquidation** *n* Comm liquidation *f* volontaire; **~ manslaughter** *n* Jur homicide *m* volontaire; **~ redundancy** *n* GB départ *m* volontaire; **~ repatriation** *n* rapatriement *m* volontaire; **~ school** *n* GB ≈ école *f* libre.

volunteer /ˌvɒlənˈtɪə(r)/ **I** *n* **1** gen, Mil volontaire *mf*; **2** (unpaid worker) bénévole *mf*.
II *modif* **1** (unpaid) [*driver, fire brigade, helper, work*] bénévole; **2** Mil [*force, division*] de volontaires.
III *vtr* **1** (offer willingly) offrir [*help, advice*]; **to ~ to do** offrir de faire, se porter volontaire pour faire; **2** (divulge willingly) fournir [qch] spontanément [*information, explanation*]; **'it was me,' he ~ed** 'c'était moi,' dit-il de lui-même.
IV *vi* **1** gen se porter volontaire (**for** pour); **2** Mil s'engager comme volontaire; **to ~ for military service/the army** s'engager (comme volontaire) pour le service militaire/dans l'armée.

voluptuous /vəˈlʌptʃʊəs/ *adj* voluptueux/-euse.

voluptuously /vəˈlʌptʃʊəslɪ/ *adv* voluptueusement.

voluptuousness /vəˈlʌptjʊəsnɪs/ *n* volupté *f*.

volute /vəˈluːt/ *n* **1** (spiral) Archit volute *f*; (on shell) spire *f*; **2** Zool (mollusc) volute *f*.

voluted /vəˈluːtɪd/ *adj* [*shell*] en spire; [*pattern*] en volute.

vomit /ˈvɒmɪt/ **I** *n* vomi *m*.
II *vtr, vi* vomir.

vomiting /ˈvɒmɪtɪŋ/ *n* vomissement *m*; **repeated ~** des vomissements répétés.

voodoo /ˈvuːduː/ *n, modif* vaudou (*m*).

voracious /vəˈreɪʃəs/ *adj* vorace.

voraciously /vəˈreɪʃəslɪ/ *adv* avec voracité.

voracity /vəˈræsətɪ/ *n* voracité *f*.

vortex /ˈvɔːteks/ *n* (*pl* **~es** ou **-tices**) lit, fig tourbillon *m*.

Vosges **▶ 1163** *pr n* Vosges *fpl*; **in/to the ~** dans les Vosges.

votary /ˈvəʊtərɪ/ *n* Relig fervent/-e *m/f*.

vote /vəʊt/ **I** *n* **1** (choice) vote *m*; **to cast one's ~** voter; **to get 100 ~s** obtenir 100 votes; **one man one ~** ≈ suffrage universel; **that gets my ~!** fig moi je suis pour!; **2** (franchise) **the ~** le droit de vote; **to get the ~** obtenir le droit de vote; **3** (ballot) vote *m*; **to have a ~** voter; **to take a ~ on** voter sur; **to put sth to the ~** mettre qch aux voix; **4** (body of voters) voix *fpl*; **the teenage/Scottish ~** les voix des jeunes/des Écossais; **to receive 60% of the ~** obtenir 60% des voix; **by a majority ~** à la majorité des voix; **to increase one's ~ by 10%** recevoir 10% de voix en plus.
II *vtr* **1** (affirm choice of) voter [*Liberal, yes*]; **what** ou **how do you ~?** pour qui est-ce que tu votes?; **to ~ sb into/out of office** ou **power** élire/ne pas réélire qn; **to ~ sb into the White House** élire qn à la Maison Blanche; **to be ~d best film/Miss World** être élu meilleur film/Miss Monde; **2** (authorize) **to ~ sb sth** accorder qch à qn; **to ~ oneself a pay rise** s'accorder une augmentation de salaire; **3**° (propose) proposer; **I ~ we all go** je propose que nous y allions tous.
III *vi* voter (**on** sur; **for sb** pour qn; **against** contre); **to ~ for reform** voter en faveur de la réforme; **to ~ on whether** voter pour décider si; **let's ~ on it** mettons-le aux voix; **to ~ to join the EEC/to strike** voter l'adhésion à la CEE/voter la grève.
IDIOMS **to ~ with one's feet** (by leaving) quitter le navire°; (by other action) montrer sa désapprobation par des actes.
■ **vote down**: **~ [sb/sth] down, ~ down [sb/sth]** battre [qn] aux voix [*person, group*]; rejeter [*motion*].
■ **vote in**: **~ [sb] in, ~ in [sb]** élire [*person, party*].
■ **vote out**: **~ [sb/sth] out, ~ out [sb/sth]** ne pas réélire [*person*]; rejeter [*motion*].
■ **vote through**: **~ [sth] through, ~ through [sth]** faire adopter [*bill, proposal*].

vote of censure *n* Pol vote *m* sur une motion de censure.

vote of confidence *n* Pol, fig vote *m* de confiance (**in** en); **to win a ~** se voir accorder la confiance.

vote of thanks *n* discours *m* de remerciement.

voter /ˈvəʊtə(r)/ *n* Pol électeur/-trice *m/f*.

voter: **~ registration** *n* US inscription *f* sur les listes électorales; **~ registration card** *n* US carte *f* d'électeur.

voting /ˈvəʊtɪŋ/ **I** *n* (procedure, ballot) scrutin *m*; **second round of ~** second tour de scrutin; **~ is by secret ballot** le vote se fait au scrutin secret.
II *modif* [*patterns, intentions, rights*] de vote.

voting age *n* majorité *f* électorale; **people of ~** personnes ayant la majorité électorale.

voting: **~ booth** *n* isoloir *m*; **~ machine** *n* US machine *f* à voter; **~ paper** *n* bulletin *m* de vote; **~ precinct** *n* US circonscription *f* électorale; **~ record** *n* US antécédents *mpl* de vote; **~ share** *n* Fin action *f* avec droit de vote.

votive /ˈvəʊtɪv/ *adj* Relig votif/-ive.

vouch /vaʊtʃ/ *vtr* **to ~ that** garantir que.
■ **vouch for**: **~ for [sb/sth] 1** (informally) répondre de [*person*]; témoigner de [*fact*]; **2** (officially) se porter garant de [*person, fact*].

voucher /ˈvaʊtʃə(r)/ *n* **1** (for gift, concession) bon *m*; **2** (receipt) reçu *m*.

vouchsafe /vaʊtʃˈseɪf/ *vtr* sout **1** (grant) **to ~ sb sth** gratifier qn de qch; **we have been ~d a glimpse** on nous a gratifiés d'un aperçu; **2** (promise) octroyer [*support*]; garantir [*peace*]; **to ~ to do** s'engager à faire.

vow /vaʊ/ **I** *n* (religious) vœu *m*; (of honour) serment *m*; **a ~ of silence/poverty** un vœu de silence/pauvreté; **to take** ou **make a ~** faire un vœu; **to make a ~ to do** faire le vœu de faire; **to be under a ~ of silence** (secrecy) avoir fait le serment de garder le secret.
II vows *npl* **1** Relig vœux *mpl*; **to take one's ~s** prononcer ses vœux; **2 marriage** ou **wedding ~s** serments *mpl* du mariage.
III *vtr* faire vœu de [*revenge, love, allegiance*]; **to ~ to do** jurer de faire; (privately) se jurer de faire; **he ~ed that he would never return** il a juré de ne plus jamais revenir; **'I will succeed,' she ~ed** 'je réussirai,' se jura-t-elle.

vowel /ˈvaʊəl/ **I** *n* voyelle *f*.
II *modif* [*sound*] vocalique; **~ shift** mutation *f* vocalique.

vox pop○ /ˌvɒks ˈpɒp/ *n* **1** (also **vox populi**) opinion *f* publique; **2** TV, Radio (street interviews) interviews *mpl* pris dans la rue.

voyage /ˈvɔɪɪdʒ/ **I** *n* Naut voyage *m* (en mer), traversée *f*; fig voyage *m*; **on the ~** pendant le voyage; **to go on a ~** partir en voyage; **a ~ of discovery** ou **exploration** un voyage d'exploration; **the outward/homeward ~** le voyage aller/de retour.
II *vi* littér voyager; **to ~ across** traverser.

voyager /ˈvɔɪɪdʒə(r)/ *n* littér voyageur/-euse *m/f*.

voyeur /vɔɪˈɜː(r)/ *n* voyeur/-euse *m/f*.

voyeurism /vɔɪˈɜːrɪzəm/ *n* voyeurisme *m*.

voyeuristic /ˌvwɑːjəˈrɪstɪk/ *adj* voyeuriste.

VP *n* **1** Pol *abrév* ▶ **vice-president**; **2** Ling *abrév* ▶ **verb phrase**.

vs *prep* (*abrév* = **versus**) contre.

V-shaped *adj* en (forme de) V.

V-sign /ˈviːsaɪn/ *n* (victory sign) V *m* de la victoire; (offensive gesture) GB geste *m* obscène.

VSO *n* GB (*abrév* = **Voluntary Service Overseas**) coopération *f* civile; **to do ~** travailler comme coopérant civil.

VSOP (*abrév* = **very special** ou **superior old pale**) VSOP.

Vt, VT *abrév écrite* = **Vermont**.

VTOL *n* (*abrév* = **vertical takeoff and landing**) (plane) VTOL *m*, aéronef *m* à décollage vertical.

Vulcan /ˈvʌlkən/ *pr n* Vulcain *m*.

vulcanite /ˈvʌlkənaɪt/ *n* ébonite *f*.

vulcanize /ˈvʌlkənaɪz/ *vtr* vulcaniser.

vulcanology /ˌvʌlkəˈnɒlədʒɪ/ *n* = **volcanology**.

vulgar /ˈvʌlgə(r)/ *adj* **1** (tasteless) [*furniture, clothes, building*] de mauvais goût; [*behaviour, curiosity*] déplacé; [*taste*] douteux/-euse; [*person*] vulgaire, qui a mauvais goût; **2** (rude) grossier/-ière, vulgaire; **3** Ling [*Latin*] vulgaire.

vulgar fraction *n* Math fraction *f* ordinaire.

vulgarism /ˈvʌlgərɪzəm/ *n* Ling vulgarisme *m*.

vulgarity /vʌlˈgærətɪ/ *n* **1** (tastelessness) (of furniture, clothes) mauvais goût *m*; (of person, behaviour) vulgarité *f*; **2** (rudeness) grossièreté *f*.

vulgarization /ˌvʌlgəraɪˈzeɪʃn, US -rɪˈz-/ *n* vulgarisation *f*.

vulgarize /ˈvʌlgəraɪz/ *vtr* **1** (popularize) populariser [*place, activity*]; vulgariser [*book, art etc*]; **2** (make rude) rendre [qch] vulgaire [*situation, story*].

vulgarly /ˈvʌlgəlɪ/ *adv* **1** (tastelessly) [*dressed, furnished*] avec mauvais goût; [*behave*] avec vulgarité; **2** (rudely) [*say, gesture, express oneself*] avec grossièreté.

vulgate /ˈvʌlgeɪt/ **I** *n* vulgate *f*.
II Vulgate *pr n* (Bible) Vulgate *f*.

vulnerability /ˌvʌlnərəˈbɪlətɪ/ *n* vulnérabilité *f*.

vulnerable /ˈvʌlnərəbl/ *adj* (all contexts) vulnérable (**to** à).

vulture /ˈvʌltʃə(r)/ *n* lit, fig vautour *m*.

vulva /ˈvʌlvə/ *n* (*pl* **-vae** ou **-vas**) vulve *f*.

vying /ˈvaɪɪŋ/ *p prés* ▶ **vie**.

w, W /ˈdʌbljuː/ *n* **1** (letter) w, W *m*; **2 W** Elec *abrév écrite* = **watt**; **3 W** Geog *abrév écrite* = **West**.

WA *n* US Post *abrév écrite* = **Washington**.

wack○ /wæk/ *adj* US nul/nulle○, insensé.

wacky○ /ˈwækɪ/, **wacko**○ /ˈwækəʊ/ *adj* farfelu○.

wacky (ta)backy○ /ˌwækɪˈbækɪ/ *n* hum herbe○ *f*, marijuana *f*.

wad /wɒd/ **I** *n* **1** (bundle) (of banknotes, money, papers) liasse *f* (**of** de); **2** (lump) (of cotton wool, padding) balle *f* (**of** de); **a ~ of tobacco** une chique; **a ~ of chewing gum** un chewing-gum mâché; **3**○ (large amount of money) grosse somme *f*, paquet *m*○; **4** (plug) (for cannon, shotgun) bourre *f*.
II wads *npl* US **~s of**○ des tas○ de.
III *vtr* (also **~ up**) (*p prés etc* **-dd-**) ouater [*garment*]; faire un bouchon de [*paper*].
IDIOMS **to shoot one's ~**● US tirer son coup●, éjaculer.

wadding /ˈwɒdɪŋ/ *n* **1** (padding) ouatage *m*; **2** (for gun) bourre *f*.

waddle /ˈwɒdl/ **I** *n* dandinement *m*.
II *vi* [*duck, person*] se dandiner; **to ~ in/out** entrer/sortir en se dandinant.

wade /weɪd/ *vi* **1** (in water) **to ~ into the water** entrer dans l'eau; **to ~ ashore** regagner la rive à pied; **to ~ across** traverser à gué; **to go wading** [*child*] barboter; **2** (proceed with difficulty) **to ~ through sth** lit se frayer un chemin pour traverser qch; **I managed to ~ through the book/work** j'ai réussi péniblement à terminer le livre/le travail; **he was wading through his work/a long novel** il s'échinait sur son travail/sur un long roman.
■ **wade in**○ **1** (start with determination) se mettre au travail; **2** (attack) passer à l'attaque.
■ **wade into**○: ¶ **~ into [sth]** se mettre à [*task*]; ¶ **~ into [sb]** (attack) se jeter sur [*person, crowd*].

wader /ˈweɪdə(r)/ *n* **1** Zool échassier *m*; **2** US personne *f* en train de barboter.

waders /ˈweɪdəz/ *npl* cuissardes *fpl*.

wadi /ˈwɒdɪ/ *n* (*pl* **~s**) oued *m*.

wading pool *n* US **1** (in swimming baths) petit bassin *m* (*d'une piscine*); **2** (inflatable pool) piscine *f* gonflable.

wafer /ˈweɪfə(r)/ *n* **1** Culin gaufrette *f*; **2** Relig hostie *f*; **3** Electron (of silicon) tranche *f* (de silicium); **4** (on letter, document) cachet *m*.

wafer-thin /ˌweɪfəˈθɪn/ *adj* ultrafin, mince comme du papier à cigarette.

wafery /ˈweɪfərɪ/ *adj* [*texture, consistency*] qui ressemble à de la gaufrette.

waffle /ˈwɒfl/ **I** *n* **1** Culin gaufre *f*; **2**○ péj (wordy speech) verbiage *m*, blablabla○ *m*; (in essay) remplissage *m*; (in book) verbiage *m*.
II *vi*○ (also **~ on**) (when speaking) bavasser○ (**about** sur), parler pour ne rien dire; (in writing) faire du remplissage (**about** sur).
III waffled *pp adj* US gaufré.

waffle iron *n* Culin gaufrier *m*.

waffler○ /ˈwɒflə(r)/ *n* GB **he's such a ~** il parle pour ne rien dire.

waffly○ /ˈwɒflɪ/ *adj* verbeux/-euse.

waft /wɒft, US wæft/ **I** *n* (of air) souffle *m*; (of smell) bouffée *f*.
II *vtr* **to ~ sth through/towards** [*wind*] apporter qch dans/vers.
III *vi* **to ~ towards** [*smell, sound*] flotter dans la direction de; **to ~ up** monter; **to ~ through the house** flotter dans toute la maison.

wag /wæg/ **I** *n* **1** (movement) (of tail) frétillement *m*; **2**○† (joker) farceur/-euse *m/f*.
II *vtr* (*p prés etc* **-gg-**) remuer [*tail*]; hocher [*head*]; **to ~ one's finger at sb** agiter son doigt (en signe de reproche) dans la direction de qn.
III *vi* (*p prés etc* **-gg-**) [*tail*] remuer, frétiller; [*head*] s'agiter; **tongues will ~** fig ça va faire jaser.
IDIOMS **it's the tail ~ging the dog** c'est le monde à l'envers.

wage /weɪdʒ/ **I** *n* (also **~s**) salaire *m*; **high ~(s)** salaire élevé; **low ~(s)** bas salaire; **my ~s are £140 a week** mon salaire est de 140 livres par semaine; **~s and conditions** les salaires et les conditions.
II *modif* [*agreement, claim, inflation, negotiations, rate, settlement, talks*] salarial; [*increase, rise*] de salaire; [*policy, restraint, freeze*] des salaires.
III *vtr* mener [*campaign*]; **to ~ (a) war against sth/sb** lit, fig faire la guerre contre qch/qn.
IDIOMS **the ~s of sin is death** Bible la mort est le prix du péché.

wage: **~ bargaining** *n* négociations *fpl* salariales; **~ bill**, **~s bill** *n* facture *f* salariale; **~ costs** *npl* coûts *mpl* salariaux.

waged /weɪdʒd/ **I** *n* **the ~** (+ *v pl*) les salariés *mpl*.
II *adj* salarié.

wage earner *n* **1** (person earning a wage) salarié/-e *m/f* (hebdomadaire); **2** (breadwinner) soutien *m* de famille.

wage packet *n* **1** lit (envelope) enveloppe *f* de paie; **2** (money) paie *f*.

wager /ˈweɪdʒə(r)/ **I** *n* pari *m*; **to make** ou **lay a ~** parier (**on** sur; **that** que).
II *vtr* parier [*money, property*] (**on** sur; **that** que); **I'd be willing to ~ that**... je suis prêt à parier que...

wage: **~ round** *n* réajustement *m* des salaires; **~s clerk** ▶**1692** *n* préposé/-e *m/f* aux salaires; **~s council** *n* ≈ commission *f* des salaires; **~ sheet**, **~ slip** *n* feuille *f* de paie; **~ structure** *n* échelle *f* salariale; **~ worker** *n* US = **wage earner**.

waggish /ˈwægɪʃ/ *adj* facétieux/-ieuse.

waggishly /ˈwægɪʃlɪ/ *adv* [*smile*] avec facétie; [*say*] d'un ton facétieux.

waggle /ˈwægl/ **I** *vtr* remuer [*tail*]; faire bouger [*tooth, ear, object*]; (shake) agiter [*object*]; **to ~ one's hips** rouler des hanches.
II *vi* (also **~ around**, **~ about**) remuer.

waggon *n* GB = **wagon**.

Wagner /ˈvɑːgnə/ *pr n* Wagner.

Wagnerian /vɑːgˈnɪərɪən/ *adj* wagnérien/-ienne.

wagon /ˈwægən/ *n* **1** (horse-drawn, ox-drawn) chariot *m*; **2** GB Rail wagon *m* (de marchandises); **3**○ GB Aut (lorry) camion *m*; **4** US = **station wagon**; **5** US (toy) (petit) chariot *m* (*jouet*).
IDIOMS **to be on the ~** être au régime sec; **to fix sb's ~**○ US chercher à se venger de qn.

wagoner /ˈwægənə(r)/ *n* roulier *m*.

wagonette /ˌwægəˈnet/ *n* break *m*.

wagonload /ˈwægənləʊd/ *n* **1** (in horse-drawn vehicle) charretée *f* (**of** de); **2** GB Rail wagon *m* (**of** de).

wagon train *n* US Hist convoi *m* de chariots.

wagtail /ˈwægteɪl/ *n* Zool bergeronnette *f*; **pied ~** bergeronnette d'Yarrell; **yellow ~** bergeronnette flavéole; **grey ~** bergeronnette des ruisseaux.

waif /weɪf/ *n* enfant *m* abandonné; **~s and strays** (children) enfants abandonnés; (animals) animaux *mpl* perdus.

waif-like /ˈweɪflaɪk/ *adj* [*person*] à l'air famélique; [*looks*] famélique.

wail /weɪl/ **I** *n* (of person, wind) gémissement *m*; (of siren) hurlement *m*; (of musical instrument) son *m* plaintif.
II *vtr* **'oh no!' he ~ed** 'oh non!' gémit-il.
III *vi* [*person, wind*] gémir; [*siren*] hurler; [*musical instrument*] pleurer.

wailing /ˈweɪlɪŋ/ **I** *n* (of person) gémissements *mpl*; (of wind) gémissement *m*; (of siren) hurlement *m*; (of music) son *m* plaintif.
II *adj* [*voice, sound, music, instrument*] plaintif/-ive; [*siren*] strident.

Wailing Wall *pr n* Mur *m* des Lamentations.

wain /weɪn/ *n* littér chariot *m*.

wainscot /ˈweɪnskət/ **I** *n* = **wainscot(t)ing**.
II *vtr* lambrisser.

wainscot(t)ing /ˈweɪnskətɪŋ/ *n* lambris *m* d'appui.

waist /weɪst/ ▶**1703** *n* **1** Anat, Fashn taille *f*; **to have a 70 cm ~** [*skirt, person*] avoir un tour de taille de 70 cm; **to be tight around the ~** serrer à la taille; **to put/have one's arm around sb's ~** prendre/tenir qn par la taille; **to be ~-deep in water** avoir de l'eau jusqu'à la taille; **2** (of insect) taille *f*; **3** (of ship) embelle *f*; **4** (of violin) échancrure *f*.

waist: **~band** *n* ceinture *f*; **~coat** *n* GB gilet *m*.

waisted /ˈweɪstɪd/ *adj* [*jacket, coat*] cintré; **a high/low-~ dress** une robe à taille haute/basse; **a narrow-~ girl** une fille à la taille fine.

waist: **~line** /ˈweɪstlaɪn/ *n* ligne *f*; **~ measurement** ▶**1703** *n* tour *m* de taille; **~ slip** *n* jupon *m*.

wait /weɪt/ **I** *n* attente *f*; **an hour's ~** une heure d'attente; **to be worth the ~** valoir l'attente; **to have a long ~** devoir attendre longtemps; **you'll have a long ~** iron tu peux attendre toute ta vie; **it will only be a short ~** ce ne sera pas long.
II *vtr* **1** (await) attendre [*turn, chance*]; **don't ~ dinner for me**○ US ne m'attendez pas pour dîner; US **to ~ table** servir à table.

III *vi* **1** (remain patiently) attendre; **please ~ here** veuillez attendre ici; **to keep sb ~ing** faire attendre qn; **to ~ for sb/sth** attendre qn/qch; **it was worth ~ing for** cela valait la peine d'attendre; **to ~ for sb/sth to do** attendre que qn/qch fasse; **we ~ed for the car to stop** nous avons attendu que la voiture s'arrête (*subj*); **to ~ and see how/why** attendre de voir comment/pourquoi; **to ~ to do** attendre de faire; **I'm ~ing to use the phone** j'attends de pouvoir me servir du téléphone; **I/you can't ~ to do** j'ai/tu as hâte de faire; **she can't ~ to start** elle a hâte de commencer; **I/you can hardly ~ to do** je/tu meurs d'impatience de faire; **I can hardly ~ to see him** je meurs d'impatience de le voir; **you'll just have to ~ and see** attends et tu verras; **(just you) ~ and see** tu verras bien; **just you ~!** (as threat) tu vas voir○!; **~ for it!** tiens-toi bien○!; Mil pas encore!; **2** (be left until later) [*object, meal, action*] attendre; **the goods are ~ing to be collected** les marchandises attendent d'être réclamées; **it can/can't ~** cela peut/ne peut pas attendre; **3** (server) **to ~ at** ou **on table** être serveur/-euse *m/f*; **who's ~ing on table 16?** qui sert à la table 16?

IDIOMS **everything comes to him who ~s** tout vient à point à qui sait attendre; **to lie in ~** être à l'affût; **to lie in ~ for sb** [*troops, ambushers*] guetter qn; [*reporter, attacker*] tendre une embuscade à qn.

■ **wait around, wait about** GB attendre; **to ~ around** ou **about for sb** attendre qn; **to ~ around** ou **about for sb/sth to do** attendre que qn/qch fasse.

■ **wait behind** attendre un peu; **to ~ behind for sb** attendre qn.

■ **wait in** GB rester à la maison; **to ~ in for sb** rester à la maison pour attendre qn.

■ **wait on**: ¶ **~ on** GB Dial attendre; **~ on!** attends!; ¶ **~ on [sb] 1** (serve) servir; **to be ~ed on** être servi; **to ~ on sb hand and foot** être aux petits soins pour qn; **I'm tired of ~ing on you hand and foot!** je ne suis pas ta bonne!; **2**† sout (visit formally) venir présenter ses respects à; ¶ **~ on**○ **[sb/sth]** attendre [*result, permission*].

■ **wait out**: **~ [sth] out, ~ out [sth]** attendre la fin de [*crisis, storm, recession*].

■ **wait up 1** (stay awake) veiller; **to ~ up for sb** veiller jusqu'au retour de qn; **2** US (stay patiently) **~ up!** attends!

■ **wait upon** = **wait on**.

waiter /ˈweɪtə(r)/ **▶ 1692** *n* serveur *m*; **'~!'** 'monsieur!'

waiter service *n* service *m* à table.

waiting /ˈweɪtɪŋ/ **I** *n* **1** (staying) attente *f*; **'no ~'** 'arrêt et stationnement interdits'; **2** sout **to be in ~ on** être attaché au service de [*King, lady*].

II *adj* (*épith*) [*ambulance, taxi, crowd*] qui attend (*after n*); [*ambush*] sur le point d'être déclenché; [*troops*] sur le qui-vive; [*reporter*] à l'affût; **sb's ~ arms** les bras ouverts de qn.

waiting game *n* attentisme *m*; **to play a ~** faire de l'attentisme.

waiting: **~ list** *n* liste *f* d'attente; **~ room** *n* salle *f* d'attente.

waitress /ˈweɪtrɪs/ **▶ 1692** *n* serveuse *f*; **'~!'** 'madame!','mademoiselle!'

waive /weɪv/ *vtr* gen, Jur déroger à [*regulation, rule*]; renoncer à [*claim, demand, privilege, right*]; supprimer [*fee, condition, requirement*]; **to ~ one's claim to sth** renoncer à ses droits sur qch.

waiver /ˈweɪvə(r)/ *n* **1** Jur renonciation *f*; **visa ~** exemption *f* de visa; **2** Insur rachat *m*.

waiver clause *n* **1** Jur (in contract) clause *f* libératoire; (in treaty) clause *f* de dénonciation; **2** Insur clause *f* de rachat.

wake /weɪk/ **I** *n* **1** (track) Naut sillage *m*; fig sillage *m*, suite *f*; **in the ~ of sb/sth** dans le sillage de qn/qch, à la suite de qn/qch; **the war brought many changes in its ~** la guerre a apporté de nombreux changements dans son sillage; **to follow in sb's ~** lit marcher dans le sillage de qn; fig être dans le sillage de qn, suivre les traces de qn; **2** (over dead person) veillée *f* funèbre (*accompagnée de célébrations*).

II *vtr* (also **~ up**) (*prét* **woke**, **waked**†, *pp* **woken**, **waked**†) réveiller [*person*] (**from** de); fig réveiller [*desires, memories, feelings*]; **to ~ sb from sleep** réveiller qn, tirer qn du sommeil; **to ~ sb from a dream** tirer qn d'un rêve; **they were making enough noise to ~ the dead!** ils faisaient un bruit à réveiller les morts!

III *vi* (also **~ up**) (*prét* **woke**, **waked**†, *pp* **woken**, **waked**†) se réveiller; **I woke (up) to find him gone** à mon réveil, il était parti; **to ~ (up) from a deep sleep/a dream** sortir d'un profond sommeil/d'un rêve; **she finally woke (up) from her illusions/to her responsibilities** elle est finalement revenue de ses illusions/à ses responsabilités.

■ **wake up**: ¶ **~ up** se réveiller; **~ up!** lit réveille-toi!; fig ouvre les yeux!; **it's about time you woke up and realized the damage you are doing!** il serait temps que tu ouvres les yeux et que tu prennes conscience du mal que tu fais!; **to ~ up to sth** fig prendre conscience de qch; ¶ **~ up [sb], ~ [sb] up** = **wake** II.

wakeful /ˈweɪkfl/ *adj* [*person*] (not sleeping) éveillé; (vigilant) éveillé, vigilant; **to have a ~ night** passer une nuit blanche.

wakefulness /ˈweɪkflnɪs/ *n* (insomnia) insomnie *f*; (vigilance) vigilance *f*.

waken /ˈweɪkən/ *vtr, vi* = **wake II, III**.

waker /ˈweɪkə(r)/ *n* **to be an early/late ~** se réveiller tôt/tard.

wake-up call *n* réveil *m* téléphoné.

wakey-wakey○ /ˈweɪkɪweɪkɪ/ *excl* debout!

waking /ˈweɪkɪŋ/ **I** *n* (état *m* de) veille *f*; **between sleeping and ~** dans un demi-sommeil.

II *adj* **in** ou **during one's ~ hours** pendant la journée; **she spends most of her ~ hours at work** elle passe la plus grande partie de sa journée au travail.

wale /weɪl/ *n* US = **weal 1**.

Wales /weɪlz/ **▶ 1131** *pr n* Pays *m* de Galles.

walk /wɔːk/ **I** *n* **1** promenade *f*; (shorter) tour *m*; (hike) randonnée *f*; **country ~** promenade dans la campagne; **morning/evening ~** promenade du matin/du soir; **long ~** longue or grande promenade; **short ~** courte or petite promenade; **a 12 km ~** une promenade de 12 km; **a hotel five minutes' ~ away from the station** un hôtel à cinq minutes à pied de la gare; **it's about ten minutes' ~/four hours' ~** c'est environ à dix minutes à pied/à quatre heures de marche; **on the ~ home** en rentrant à pied à la maison; **a ~ to/beside the sea** une promenade jusqu'à/au bord de la mer; **to go for** ou **on a ~** (aller) faire une promenade, se promener; **I've been out for a ~** je suis sorti me promener or faire une promenade; **to have** ou **take a ~** faire une promenade, se promener; (shorter) faire un tour; **to take sb for a ~** emmener qn faire une promenade or (shorter) un tour; **to take the dog for a ~** promener or sortir le chien; **has the dog had his ~?** est-ce qu'on a sorti le chien?; **it's a short ~ to the station** on est à quelques minutes à pied de la gare; **it's a long ~ back to the hotel** il y a une longue marche d'ici à l'hôtel; **it seemed a very long ~ to the podium** l'estrade avait l'air d'être très loin; **2** (gait) démarche *f*; **I knew him by his ~** je l'ai reconnu à sa démarche; **3** (pace) pas *m*; **he set off at a brisk ~** il est parti d'un pas vif; **to slow down to a ~** se mettre à marcher (*après avoir couru*); **4** (path) gen, Hort allée *f*; (trail in forest) sentier *m*; **people from all ~s of life** des gens de tous les milieux; **5** Sport épreuve *f* de marche; **the 10 km ~** l'épreuve de marche de 10 km; **6** Equit pas *m*.

II *vtr* **1** (cover on foot) faire [qch] à pied [*distance, path, road*]; parcourir [qch] à pied [*district, countryside*]; (patrol) parcourir; **I can't ~ another step** je ne peux pas faire un pas de plus; **to ~ the streets** [*tourist*] parcourir les rues; [*homeless person*] errer dans les rues; [*prostitute*] faire le trottoir; **to ~ the ramparts/walls** [*soldier*] arpenter les remparts/murs; **shall we take the bus or ~ it?** on prend le bus ou on y va à pied?; **we ~ed it in 20 minutes** nous l'avons fait à pied en 20 minutes; **to ~ it**○ Sport gagner haut la main; **2** (escort on foot, lead) accompagner [*friend*]; promener [*tourist*]; conduire [*horse, mule etc*]; promener [*dog*]; **I ~ed her home** je l'ai accompagnée chez elle; **the guide ~ed us all over Bonn** le guide nous a promenés dans tout Bonn; **the guards ~ed him back to his cell** les gardiens l'ont reconduit à sa cellule.

III *vi* **1** (in general) marcher; (for pleasure) se promener; (not run) aller au pas; (not ride or drive) aller à pied; **the baby's learning to ~** le bébé apprend à marcher; **you should be ~ing again soon** vous devriez recommencer à marcher bientôt; **he'll never ~ again** il ne pourra plus jamais marcher; **to ~ with a stick** marcher avec une canne; **to ~ with a limp/a swing** boiter/se dandiner en marchant; **don't run, ~!** ne cours pas, marche!; **'~'** US (at traffic lights) ≈ traversez; **it's not very far, let's ~** ce n'est pas très loin, allons-y à pied; **we ~ed all day** nous avons marché toute la journée; **we've missed the bus, we'll have to ~** nous avons manqué le bus, il va falloir marcher; **we go on holiday to ~** nous allons en vacances pour faire de la marche; **to ~ across** ou **through sth** traverser qch (à pied) (*see note*); **she ~ed across the room** elle a traversé la pièce; **she ~ed across France** elle a traversé la France à pied; **a policeman ~ed by** un policier est passé; **he ~ed up/down the road** il a remonté/descendu la rue (à pied) (*see note*); **we've been ~ing round in circles for hours** nous tournons en rond depuis des heures; **someone was ~ing around** ou **about upstairs** quelqu'un allait et venait à l'étage; **there's no lift, you'll have to ~ up** il n'y a pas d'ascenseur, tu devras monter à pied; **I'd just ~ed in at the door when...** je venais à peine de passer la porte, quand...; **suddenly in ~ed my father** soudain voilà que mon père est entré; **to ~ in one's sleep** (habitually) être somnambule; **he was ~ing in his sleep** il marchait en dormant; **she ~s to work/home** elle se rend à son travail/rentre chez elle à pied; **we ~ed all the way back** nous avons fait tout le chemin du retour à pied; **to ~ up and down** faire les cent pas; **to ~ up and down a room** arpenter une pièce; **shall I ~ with you to the bus?** veux-tu que je t'accompagne au bus?; **I'll ~ some of the way with you** je vais faire un bout de chemin avec toi; **he ~ed under a bus** il est passé sous un bus; **the ghost ~s at midnight** le fantôme apparaît à minuit; **2**○ hum (disappear) [*possession*] se faire la malle○.

IDIOMS **take a ~**○! US dégage○!; **that was a ~**○! US c'était simple comme bonjour○!; **you must ~ before you can run** il ne faut pas brûler les étapes; **to ~ sb off their feet** mettre qn sur les rotules○.

■ Note *à pied* is often omitted with movement verbs if we already know that the person is on foot. If it is surprising or ambiguous, *à pied* should be included.

■ **walk across**: ¶ traverser; **to ~ across to sth/sb** s'approcher de qch/qn; ¶ **~ across [sth]** traverser.

■ **walk around**: ¶ **~ around** lit se promener; (aimlessly) traîner; **you can't ~**

around in the rain without an umbrella tu ne peux pas traîner sous la pluie sans parapluie; ¶ **~ around [sth]** (to and fro) faire un tour dans [*city, streets, garden*]; (make circuit of) faire le tour de [*building, space*]; **he ~ed around the lake** il a fait le tour du lac (à pied); **we ~ed around Paris for hours** nous nous sommes promenés dans Paris pendant des heures.
■ **walk away 1** lit s'éloigner (**from** de); **2** fig (avoid involvement) **to ~ away from a problem/one's responsibilities** fuir un problème/ses responsabilités; **3** fig (survive unscathed) sortir indemne (**from** de); **she ~ed away from the accident** elle est sortie indemne de l'accident; **4 to ~ away with** (win easily) gagner [qch] haut la main [*game, tournament*]; remporter [qch] haut la main [*election*]; (carry off) décrocher [*prize, honour*]; ▶ **walk off 2**; **5** Sport **to ~ away from sb/sth** laisser qn/qch loin derrière [*team*].
■ **walk back** revenir sur ses pas (**to** jusqu'à); **we ~ed back (home)** nous sommes rentrés à pied.
■ **walk in** entrer; **he simply ~ed in as if he owned the place** il est carrément entré comme s'il était chez lui; **who should ~ in but my husband!** devine qui est arrivé?—mon mari!; **'please ~ in'** (sign) 'entrez sans frapper'.
■ **walk into**: **~ into [sth] 1** (enter) entrer dans [*room, house*]; **she ~ed into that job** fig (acquired easily) elle a eu ce poste sans lever le petit doigt; **2** (become entangled in) tomber dans [*trap, ambush*]; se fourrer dans [*tricky situation*]; **you ~ed right into that one**○! tu es tombé dans le panneau○!; **3** (bump into) rentrer dans [*wall, door, person*].
■ **walk off**: ¶ **~ off 1** lit partir brusquement; **2**○ fig **to ~ off with sth** (take) (innocently) partir avec qch; (as theft) filer○ avec qch; **3** (carry off) ▶ **walk away 4**; ¶ **~ off [sth]**, **~ [sth] off** se promener pour faire passer [*headache, hangover, large meal*]; **she ~ed off eight pounds** elle a perdu 4 kilos en faisant de la marche.
■ **walk on 1** (continue) continuer à marcher; **2** Theat être figurant.
■ **walk out 1** lit sortir (**of** de); **2** fig (desert) [*lover, partner, servant, collaborator*] partir; **to ~ out on** laisser tomber○ [*lover, partner*]; rompre [*contract, undertaking*]; **3** (as protest) [*negotiator, committee member*] partir en signe de protestation; (on strike) [*workers*] se mettre en grève; **they ~ed out of the meeting** ils ont quitté la réunion en signe de protestation; **4**† GB [*lovers*] se fréquenter; **to be ~ing out with sb** fréquenter qn.
■ **walk over**: ¶ **~ over** (a few steps) s'approcher (**to** de); (a short walk) faire un saut○ (**to** à); **he ~ed over to her/the window** il s'est approché d'elle/de la fenêtre; **he ~ed over to see her/to the farm** il a fait un saut pour la voir/à la ferme; ¶ **~ over [sb]**○ **1** (defeat) gen, Sport battre [qn] à plates coutures; **2** (humiliate) marcher sur les pieds de; **he'll ~ all over you if you let him** il te marchera sur les pieds si tu le laisses faire; **he lets her ~ all over him** elle le mène par le bout du nez.
■ **walk round**: ¶ **~ round** faire le tour; **no-one answered so I ~ed round to the garden** personne n'a répondu alors je suis passé par le jardin; ¶ **~ round [sth]** (round edge of) faire le tour de [*lake, stadium, garden, building*]; (through) visiter [*exhibition, historic building*].
■ **walk through**: ¶ **~ through** lit traverser; ¶ **~ through [sth] 1** lit traverser [*town, field, forest*]; passer [*door, gate*]; marcher dans [*deep snow, mud, grass*]; **2** Theat répéter les déplacements de [*scene, act*]; **to ~ sb through a scene** faire répéter les déplacements d'une scène à qn.
■ **walk up 1 to ~ up to** s'approcher de [*person, building, object*]; **2** (in market, fairground) s'approcher; **~ up, ~ up!** approchez, approchez!

walkabout /'wɔ:kəbaʊt/ *n* **1** gen (among crowd) bain *m* de foule; **to go on (a) ~** prendre un bain de foule; **2** Austral **to go ~** Anthrop [*aborigine*] partir dans le désert; fig hum [*person, object*] disparaître dans la nature.

walkathon /'wɔ:kəθɒn/ *n* marathon *m* de marche.

walker /'wɔ:kə(r)/ *n* **1** (for pleasure) promeneur/-euse *m/f*; (for exercise, sport) marcheur/-euse *m/f*; **she's a fast ~!** elle marche vite!; **2** (device) (for invalid) déambulateur *m*; (for baby) trotteur *m*.

walkie-talkie /ˌwɔ:kɪ'tɔ:kɪ/ *n* talkie-walkie *m*.

walk-in /'wɔ:kɪn/ **I** *n* US client/-e *m/f* sans rendez-vous.
II *adj* **1** [*cupboard, closet*] où l'on peut tenir debout; **2** US [*apartment*] de plain-pied sur la rue; **3** US [*clinic*] qui reçoit les clients sans rendez-vous.

walking /'wɔ:kɪŋ/ **I** *n* (for pleasure) promenades *fpl* à pied; (for exercise, sport) marche *f* à pied; **I enjoy ~** j'aime me promener; **there's some lovely ~ around here** il y a de belles promenades à faire aux alentours.
II *adj* hum **she's a ~ dictionary** c'est un dictionnaire ambulant.

walking boots *npl* chaussures *fpl* de marche.

walking distance *n* **to be within ~** être à quelques minutes de marche (**of** de).

walking: **~ frame** *n* Med déambulateur *m*; **~ holiday** *n* vacances *fpl* de randonnée.

walking pace *n* pas *m*; **at a ~** au pas.

walking papers *npl* US fig **to get** ou **be given one's ~**○ se faire flanquer○ à la porte.

walking: **~ race** *n* épreuve *f* de marche; **~ shoes** *npl* chaussures *fpl* de marche; **~ stick** *n* canne *f*; **~ tour** *n* randonnée *f* à pied; **~ wounded** *npl* Mil blessés *mpl* capables de marcher; fig (victims) victimes *fpl*; (survivors) rescapés *mpl*.

walkman® /'wɔ:kmən/ *n* (*pl* **-mans**) walkman® *m*, baladeur *m*.

walk-on /ˌwɔ:k'ɒn/ **I** *n* Theat figurant/-e *m/f*.
II *adj* [*role*] de figurant.

walkout /'wɔ:kaʊt/ *n* (from conference, meeting) départ *m* en signe de protestation; (strike) grève *f* surprise; **to stage a ~** [*delegates, members*] partir en signe de protestation; [*workers*] faire une grève surprise.

walk: **~over** /'wɔ:kəʊvə(r)/ *n* gen, Sport victoire *f* facile (**for** pour); Turf walk-over *m*; **~-up** *n* US immeuble *m* sans ascenseur; **~way** *n* allée *f*.

Walkyrie *n* = **Valkyrie**.

wall /wɔ:l/ **I** *n* **1** gen, Constr, Archit mur *m*; **on the ~** (on vertical face) au mur; (on top) sur le mur; **the back/front ~** (of house) le mur arrière/de façade; **my secret must not go beyond these four ~s** mon secret ne doit pas sortir de ces murs; **2** (of cave, tunnel) paroi *f*; **3** Anat, Biol paroi *f*; **the cell/stomach ~** la paroi cellulaire/stomacale; **4** Aut (of tyre) flanc *m*; **5** fig mur *m*; **a ~ of silence/of incomprehension** un mur de silence/d'incompréhension; **a ~ of water/of flame** un mur d'eau/de flammes; **a tight ~ of security around the President** une barrière de sécurité autour du Président.
II *modif* [*heater, light*] mural.
IDIOMS **to be a fly on the ~** être une mouche; **to be off the ~**○ [*person*] être dingue○; [*comment*] être incohérent; **to drive sb up the ~**○ exaspérer qn, rendre qn fou/folle; **to go to the ~** faire faillite; **to have one's back to the ~** avoir le dos au mur; **to push** ou **drive sb to the ~**, **to have sb up against the ~** mettre qn au pied du mur; **~s have ears** les murs ont des oreilles.
■ **wall in**: ¶ **~ in [sth]**, **~ [sth] in** entourer; **the valley is ~ed in by mountains** la vallée est entourée de montagnes; ¶ **~ [sb] in**, **~ in [sb]** emprisonner; **to feel ~ed in** se sentir emprisonné.
■ **wall off**: **~ off [sth]**, **~ [sth] off** (block up, block off) condamner [*room, wing, area*]; (separate by wall) séparer [qch] par un mur.
■ **wall up**: **~ up [sb/sth]**, **~ [sb/sth] up** emmurer.

wallaby /'wɒləbɪ/ *n* Zool wallaby *m*.

wallah† /'wɒlə/ *n* **tea/kitchen ~** préposé *m* au thé/à la cuisine.

wall: **~bars** *npl* espalier *m*; **~board** *n* cloison *f* sèche; **~ chart** *n* affiche *f*; **~ covering** *n* revêtement *m* mural; **~ cupboard** *n* élément *m* (mural).

walled /wɔ:ld/ *adj* [*city*] fortifié; [*garden*] clos; **a white-~ house** une maison aux murs blancs.

wallet /'wɒlɪt/ *n* (for notes) portefeuille *m*; (for cards) porte-cartes *m inv*; (for documents) porte-documents *m inv*; **kind to your ~** Advertg bon marché.

walleyed○ /'wɔ:laɪd/ *adj* **to be ~** loucher.

wallflower /'wɔ:lflaʊə(r)/ *n* Bot giroflée *f*.
IDIOMS **to be a ~** faire tapisserie.

wall: **~ hanging** *n* tapisserie *f*, tenture *f*; **~ light** *n* applique *f* murale; **~-mounted** *adj* [*radiator, television*] fixé au mur.

Walloon /wɒ'lu:n/ ▶ **1486**, **1402** **I** *n* **1** (person) Wallon/-onne *m/f*; **2** Ling wallon *m*.
II *adj* wallon/-onne.

wallop○ /'wɒləp/ **I** *n* **1** (punch) beigne○ *f*, grand coup *m*; **to give sb a ~** donner un grand coup à qn; **to give sth a ~** frapper qch d'un grand coup; **this vodka packs a ~**○ elle arrache, cette vodka○; **2** (loud noise) (as onomatopoeia) vlan!; **to hit sth with a ~** faire bang en touchant qch; **3** (speed) **to go at a tremendous ~** aller à fond de train○; **4**○ GB (beer) mousse○ *f*, bière *f*.
II *vtr* **1** (hit) flanquer une raclée à○, taper [*person*]; taper dans [*ball, punchbag*]; **to ~ sb in the stomach** filer○ un coup dans l'estomac de qn; **to get ~ed** recevoir une raclée○, se faire taper; **2** (defeat) battre [qn] à plates coutures [*person, team*]; **to get ~ed** se faire battre à plates coutures.

walloping○ /'wɒləpɪŋ/ **I** *n* raclée *f*; **to get a ~** recevoir une raclée○; **to give sb a ~** donner une raclée○ à qn.
II *adj* (huge) [*building, mistake*] super (*before n*).
III *adv* super; **a ~ great** ou **big fine/kiss** une super grosse amende/bise.

wallow /'wɒləʊ/ **I** *n* **1** (action) **to have a ~** [*person, animal*] se vautrer; **2** (place) bauge *f*.
II *vi* **1 to ~ in** se vautrer dans [*mud, morass, luxury*]; se complaire dans [*self-pity, nostalgia*]; **2** Naut [*ship*] ballotter.

wall painting *n* peinture *f* murale.

wallpaper /'wɔ:lpeɪpə(r)/ **I** *n* papier *m* peint.
II *vtr* tapisser [*room*].

wallpaper stripper *n* décolleuse *f* (de papier peint).

Wall Street /'wɔ:l stri:t/ *pr n* US Fin Wall Street; **on ~** à Wall Street.

wall-to-wall /ˌwɔ:ltə'wɔ:l/ *adj* **1 ~ carpet** moquette *f*; **2** fig **the ~ silence of large art galleries** le silence complet des grandes galeries d'art; **we don't want ~ junk food outlets** nous ne voulons pas voir des fast-foods partout.

wally○ /'wɒlɪ/ *n* GB andouille○ *f*, idiot/-e *m/f*.

walnut /'wɔ:lnʌt/ **I** *n* **1** (nut) noix *f*; **2** (tree, wood) noyer *m*.
II *modif* [*cake, yoghurt*] aux noix; [*oil, shell*] de noix; [*furniture*] en noyer.

walrus /'wɔ:lrəs/ *n* morse *m*; **~ moustache** moustache *f* à la gauloise.

Walter Mitty /ˌwɔ:ltə 'mɪtɪ/ *pr n* **to be a ~ (character)** vivre dans un monde de fantasmes.

waltz /wɔ:ls, US wɔ:lts/ I *n* valse *f*; **to do** ou **dance a ~** danser la valse.
II *vtr* **to ~ sb around** entraîner qn dans une valse autour de [*room, garden*].
III *vi* **1** (dance) danser la valse (**with** avec); **2** (walk jauntily) **to ~ into/out of sth** entrer dans/sortir de qch d'un pas désinvolte; **to ~ up to sb** s'approcher de qn d'un pas désinvolte; **3** (get easily) **to ~ off with sth** gagner qch haut la main○ [*prize, award*]; **to ~ into a job** trouver du travail sans se forcer; **to ~ through an exam** réussir un examen facilement.

wampum /'wɒmpəm/ *n* **1** (beads) wampum *m*; **2**○ US hum (money) fric○ *m*.

wan /wɒn/ *adj* blême.

WAN *n* Comput *abrév* ▶**wide area network**.

wand /wɒnd/ I *n* (all contexts) baguette *f*.
II **wands** *npl* (in tarot) bâtons *mpl*.

wander /'wɒndə(r)/ I *n* promenade *f*, balade○ *f*; **to go for a ~** partir en balade○; **to have** ou **take a ~** faire une balade○; **a ~ round the park** une balade○ dans le parc; **to have a ~ round the shops** faire un tour dans les magasins.
II *vtr* parcourir [*countryside, town*]; **to ~ the world** courir le monde; **to ~ the streets** traîner dans la rue.
III *vi* **1** (walk, stroll) se promener, se balader○; **the patients/the chickens are free to ~** les patients/les poulets sont libres d'aller et de venir; **to ~ around town/in the park/along the beach** se balader en ville/dans le parc/sur la plage; **to ~ in and out of the shops** flâner dans les magasins; **2** (stray) [*animal, lost person*] errer; **to ~ up and down the road** errer dans la rue; **to ~ into the next field** s'égarer dans le champ voisin; **to ~ away** s'éloigner (**from** de); **I had ~ed into the wrong room** j'étais entré sans faire attention dans la mauvaise pièce; **3** (arrive nonchalantly) **to ~ in** se pointer○, arriver tranquillement; **he ~ed into work two hours late** il s'est pointé○ or est arrivé tranquillement au travail avec deux heures de retard; **to ~ over to** ou **up to sb** s'approcher tranquillement de qn; **4** (drift) [*mind, thoughts, attention*] (through boredom, inattention) s'égarer; (through age, illness) divaguer; [*eyes, gaze, hands*] errer (**over** sur); **her mind ~ed back to** son esprit revenait sur; **let your mind ~** laisse ton esprit errer; **to ~ off the point** ou **subject** s'éloigner du sujet, faire des digressions; **her eyes ~ed along the row/among the crowd** son regard a erré sur la rangée/sur la foule.
■ **wander about, wander around** (stroll) se balader, flâner; (when lost) errer.
■ **wander off 1** [*child, animal*] s'éloigner; **2** hum [*object, belongings, scissors*] disparaître.

wanderer /'wɒndərə(r)/ *n* voyageur/-euse *m/f*; **the ~ returns!** un revenant!

wandering /'wɒndərɪŋ/ *adj* **1** (nomadic) [*person, tribe, minstrel, poet*] itinérant, vagabond liter or pej; [*animal*] voyageur/-euse; **2** (roving) [*gaze, eye*] qui s'égare; [*attention, thoughts, mind*] vagabond; **~ hands** hum mains *fpl* baladeuses.

wandering Jew *n* **1** Bot misère *f*, tradescantia *m* spec; **2** Bible, Literat Juif *m* errant.

wanderings /'wɒndərɪŋz/ *npl* **1** (journeys) vagabondages *mpl*; **2** (confusion) divagations *fpl*.

wanderlust /'wɒndəlʌst/ *n* envie *f* de voyager.

wane /weɪn/ I *n* **to be on the ~** être sur le déclin.
II *vi* **1** Astron [*moon*] décroître; **2** [*enthusiasm, popularity*] diminuer, être sur le déclin.

wangle○ /'wæŋgl/ I *n* (trick) combine○ *f*.
II *vtr* carotter○ [*gift*]; réussir à obtenir [*leave, meeting*]; **to ~ sth out of sb** soutirer qch à qn [*job, money, promise*]; **he ~d £10 out of me** il m'a soutiré 10 livres; **to ~ sth for sb** arranger qch à qn○; **can you ~ me a ticket?** est-ce que tu peux m'avoir un ticket?; **she ~d me an invitation** elle a réussi à m'avoir une invitation; **to ~ it for sb to do** s'arranger pour que qn fasse; **can you ~ it for me?** tu peux m'arranger ça○?; **to ~ sb into doing** persuader qn de faire; **to ~ one's way into** réussir à s'introduire dans [*club, building*].

wangler○ /'wæŋglə(r)/ *n* combinard/-e○ *m/f*.

waning /'weɪnɪŋ/ I *n* **1** Astron déclin *m*, décours *m*; **2** (lowering) baisse *f* (**of** de); (weakening, fading) déclin *m* (**of** de).
II *adj* **1** Astron [*moon*] décroissant; **2** [*enthusiasm, popularity*] en baisse, sur le déclin.

wank● /wæŋk/ GB I *n* **1** (masturbation) **to have a ~** se faire une branlette●; **2** (rubbish) **a load of ~** un tas de conneries●.
II *vi* se branler●.
■ **wank off●**: ¶ **~ off** se branler●; ¶ **~ [sb] off, ~ off [sb]** branler●.

wanker● /'wæŋkə(r)/ *n* GB péj branleur/-euse● *m/f*.

wanking● /'wæŋkɪŋ/ *n* GB branlette● *f*.

wanly /'wɒnlɪ/ *adv* **1** [*smile*] d'un air las; **2** littér [*shine*] d'une lueur blême.

wanna○ /'wɒnə/ = **want to, want a**.

wannabe(e)○ /'wɒnəbi:/ I *n*: *personne qui rêve d'être célèbre*.
II *modif* **~ American/star** personne *f* qui rêve d'être Américain/vedette.

wanness /'wɒnnɪs/ *n* pâleur *f*.

want /wɒnt/ I *n* **1** (need) besoin *m*; **my ~s are few** j'ai peu de besoins; **to be in ~ of** avoir besoin de; **the tower is in ~ of repair** la tour a besoin d'être restaurée; **2** (deprivation) littér indigence *f*; **war on ~** journ lutte contre la pauvreté; **3** (lack) défaut *m*; **~ of discipline** défaut de discipline; **for ~ of** à défaut or faute de; **it's not for ~ of trying** ce n'est pas faute d'avoir essayé; **for ~ of a better word** à défaut d'un meilleur mot; **there is no ~ of candidates** on ne manque pas de candidats.
II *vtr* **1** (desire) vouloir; **I ~** (as general statement) je veux; (would like) je voudrais; (am seeking) je souhaite; **they ~ peace/money** ils veulent la paix/de l'argent; **we want cooperation/understanding** nous souhaitons la coopération/la compréhension; **how many do you ~?** combien en voulez-vous?; **where do you ~ this desk?** où est-ce que tu veux ce bureau?; **what** ou **how much do you ~ for this chair?** combien voulez-vous pour ce fauteuil?; **I ~ the walls blue/my steak rare/the job finished** je voudrais les murs bleus/mon steak saignant/que ce travail soit fini; **to ~ to do** vouloir faire; **do you ~ to come with us?** tu veux venir avec nous?; **I don't ~ to** je n'ai pas envie; **to ~ sb to do** vouloir que qn fasse; **when/why does she ~ me to come?** quand/pourquoi veut-elle que je vienne?; **to ~ sb/sth doing** vouloir que qn/qch fasse; **I ~ the machine working by 11 o'clock** je veux que la machine soit en état de marche d'ici onze heures; **where do you ~ me?** où voulez-vous que je me mette?; **he doesn't ~ much does he?** iron il est toujours aussi peu exigeant! iron; **they just don't ~ to know** ils préfèrent ne rien savoir; **to ~ an end to sth** vouloir que qch prenne fin; **2**○ (need) avoir besoin de; **you won't ~ your overcoat** tu n'auras pas besoin de ton manteau; **you won't be ~ed at the meeting** on n'aura pas besoin de vous à la réunion; **I take it he'll not be ~ing this book any more** je suppose qu'il n'aura plus besoin de ce livre; **do you ~ anything from town?** tu as besoin de quelque chose en ville?; **what we ~ is to do** ce dont nous avons besoin c'est de faire; **to ~ to do** devoir faire; **you ~ to watch out** tu devrais faire attention; **what do they ~ with all those machines?** pourquoi est-ce qu'ils ont besoin de toutes ces machines? ; **what do you ~ with me?** qu'est-ce que vous me voulez?; **all that's ~ed is your signature** il ne manque plus que ta signature; **several jobs ~ doing** GB il y a plusieurs tâches à faire; **3** (require presence of) demander; **if anyone ~s me** si quelqu'un me demande; **he/she is ~ed** on le/la demande; **you're ~ed on the phone** on vous demande au téléphone; **'gardener ~ed'** 'on demande un jardinier'; **I ~ my mummy!** GB ou **mommy!** US je veux ma maman!; **the boss ~s you** le patron veut te voir; **to be ~ed by the police** être recherché par la police; **I know when I'm not ~ed** souvent hum je sens bien que je suis de trop; **4** (desire sexually) vouloir [*person*].
III *vi* **to ~ for** manquer de; **you will never ~ for anything** tu ne manqueras jamais de rien.
■ **want in**○ **1** (asking to enter) vouloir entrer; **2** (asking to participate) vouloir participer; **I ~ in on the deal** je veux être dans le coup○.
■ **want out**○ **1** (asking to exit) vouloir sortir; **2** (discontinuing participation) vouloir laisser tomber○; **to ~ out of** vouloir se retirer de [*contract, deal*].

want ad *n* US petite annonce *f*.

wanted /'wɒntɪd/ *adj* **1** (sought by police) [*fugitive*] recherché par la police; **'~ for armed robbery'** 'recherché pour vol à main armée'; **~ poster** avis *m* de recherche; **2** (loved) **to be (very much) ~** (of child) (before birth) être (très) désiré; (after birth) être (très) aimé.

wanted list *n* liste *f* des suspects; **to be on a ~** être recherché par la police.

wanting /'wɒntɪŋ/ *adj* **1** (lacking) **to be ~** faire défaut; **what was ~ was a little understanding** ce qui faisait défaut, c'était un peu de compréhension; **to be ~ in** manquer de; **a speech ~ in fervour** un discours manquant d'ardeur; **2** Relig (failing expectation) **to be found ~** être réprouvé.

wanton /'wɒntən, US 'wɔ:n-/ I† *n* dévergondé/-e *m/f*.
II *adj* **1** (malicious) [*cruelty, damage, waste*] gratuit; [*disregard*] délibéré; **2** littér (playful) [*mood*] joueur/-euse; [*breeze*] capricieux/-ieuse; **3**† (immoral) dévergondé.

wantonly /'wɒntənlɪ, US 'wɔ:n-/ *adv* **1** (gratuitously) [*attack, destroy, ignore*] sans raison, gratuitement: [*cruel, destructive*] sans raison; **2** littér (playfully) de façon capricieuse; **3**† (provocatively) [*act, pose, smile*] de façon dévergondée.

wantonness /'wɒntənnɪs, US 'wɔ:n-/ *n* **1** (gratuity) caractère *m* gratuit (**of** de); **2** (playfulness) exubérance *f*; **3**† (provocativeness) impudeur *f*.

war /wɔ:(r)/ I *n* **1** (armed conflict) guerre *f*; **the horrors of ~** les horreurs de la guerre; **the day ~ broke out** le jour où la guerre a éclaté; **in the ~** à la guerre; **between the ~s** (world wars) entre les deux guerres; **a state of ~ now exists between our two countries** nos deux pays sont désormais en état de guerre; **to win/lose a ~** gagner/perdre une guerre; **to go off to the ~** partir à la guerre; **to go to ~ against** entrer en guerre contre [*country*]; **to wage ~ on** faire la guerre contre [*country*]; **to be at ~ with a country** être en guerre avec un pays; **a ~ over** ou **about** une guerre pour [*land, independence*]; une guerre sur [*issue, problem*]; **2** fig (fierce competition) guerre *f*; **price/ trade ~** guerre des prix/commerciale; **a state of ~ now exists between the two departments/companies** c'est la guerre entre les deux services/sociétés; **a ~ of words** un conflit verbal; **3** fig (to eradicate sth) lutte *f* (**against** contre); **the ~ against drug traffickers** la lutte contre les narco-trafiquants; **to wage ~ on** ou **against** mener une lutte contre [*poverty, crime*].
II *modif* [*debts, correspondent, crime, criminal, effort, film, historian, medal, photogra-*

pher, widow, wound] de guerre; [*cemetery, leader, grave, zone*] militaire; [*hero*] de la guerre; **~ deaths** victimes *fpl* de la guerre; **he has a good ~ record** il a de bons états de service.
III *vi* (*p prés etc* **-rr-**) **to ~ with a country/one's neighbours** être en guerre contre un pays/ses voisins (**over** à cause de).
IDIOMS **you look as if you've been in the ~s** on dirait qu'il t'est arrivé des malheurs.

warble /'wɔ:bl/ I *n* **1** (of bird) gazouillis *m*; **2** Vet (on cattle) varron *m*.
II *vi* **1** [*bird*] gazouiller; **2** péj [*singer*] roucouler.

warbler /'wɔ:blə(r)/ *n* **1** (bird) fauvette *f*; **2** péj (singer) roucouleur/-euse *m/f*.

war: **~ bond** *n* titre *m* d'emprunt de guerre; **~ cabinet** *n* conseil *m* de guerre; **~ chest** *n* caisse *f* (du parti) (*servant à financer ses campagnes électorales*); **~ cry** *n* cri *m* de guerre also fig.

ward /wɔ:d/ *n* **1** (in hospital) (unit) service *m*; (room) unité *f*; (separate building) pavillon *m*; **he's in ~ 3** il est à l'unité 3; **to work on a ~** travailler dans un service; **maternity/pediatric ~** service de maternité/pédiatrie; **hospital ~** salle *f* d'hôpital; **2** Pol circonscription *f* électorale; **3** (also **~ of court**) Jur pupille *m*; **to be made a ~ of court** être placé sous tutelle judiciaire; **a child in ~** un enfant sous tutelle judiciaire.
■ **ward off**: **~ off [sth]** chasser [*evil, predator*]; faire taire [*accusations, criticism*]; écarter [*attack, threat*]; éviter [*bankruptcy, disaster*].

war dance *n* danse *f* de guerre.

warden /'wɔ:dn/ ▶ **1692** *n* (of institution, college) directeur/-trice *m/f*; (of park, estate) gardien/-ienne *m/f*; US (of prison) directeur/-trice *m/f*; ▶ **traffic warden etc**.

warder /'wɔ:də(r)/ *n* GB gardien/-ienne *m/f*.

ward heeler *n* US Pol péj homme *m* à tout faire (d'un parti).

wardrobe /'wɔ:drəʊb/ *n* **1** (furniture) armoire *f*; **built-in ~** armoire encastrée; **double ~** grande armoire; **2** (set of clothes) garde-robe *f*; **I need a new ~** il faut que je renouvelle ma garde-robe; **3** Theat costumes *mpl*.

wardrobe: **~ assistant** ▶ **1692** *n* assistant/-e *m/f* costumier/-ière; **~ director** *n* costumier/-ière *m/f*; **~ mistress** ▶ **1692** *n* costumière *f*; **~ trunk** *n* malle-penderie *f*.

ward: **~room** *n* Mil Naut carré *m* (des officiers); **~ round** *n* Med visite *f* (*du médecin hospitalier*).

wardship /'wɔ:dʃɪp/ *n* Jur placement *m* sous tutelle judiciaire.

ward sister *n* GB Med infirmière *f* en chef.

ware /weə(r)/ I *n* ¢ articles *mpl*; **leather/wooden ~** articles de cuir/de bois. ▶ **kitchenware etc**.
II **wares** *npl* marchandises *fpl*; **to sell one's ~s** vendre sa marchandise.

warehouse /'weəhaʊs/ I *n* entrepôt *m*.
II *vtr* entreposer.

warehouseman /'weəhaʊsmən/ ▶ **1692** *n* manutentionnaire *m*.

warehousing /'weəhaʊzɪŋ/ *n* entreposage *m*.

warfare /'wɔ:feə(r)/ *n* **the art of ~** l'art *m* de la guerre; **modern ~** conflits *mpl* modernes; **chemical ~** guerre *f* chimique.

war: **~ game** /'wɔ:geɪm/ *n* Mil manœuvre *f* militaire; Games (with models) jeu *m* de stratégie (militaire); **~ games** *npl* Games (with nonmilitary participants) guerre *f* simulée; **~head** *n* ogive *f*.

war horse *n* lit cheval *m* de bataille; fig (campaigner) vétéran *m*; **an old ~** fig un vétéran.

warily /'weərɪlɪ/ *adv* **1** (cautiously) avec prudence; **2** (mistrustfully) avec méfiance.

wariness /'weərɪnɪs/ *n* **1** (caution) prudence *f* (**of** à l'égard de); **2** (distrust) méfiance *f* (**of** à l'égard de); **his ~ about doing** sa réticence à faire.

warlike /'wɔ:laɪk/ *adj* [*leader, people, tribe*] guerrier/-ière; [*mood, words*] belliqueux/-euse.

warlock /'wɔ:lɒk/ *n* sorcier *m*.

warlord *n* Hist seigneur *m* de la guerre; fig chef *m* militaire.

warm /wɔ:m/ I° *n* **1** GB **the ~** (warm place) le chaud; **to be in/come into the ~** être/entrer au chaud; **2 to give sth a ~** chauffer [*dish, plate, implement*]; réchauffer [*part of body*].
II *adj* **1** (not cold) [*place, bed, clothing, food, temperature, air, water, day, climate, fire, sun*] chaud; [*scent, trail*] (encore) frais/fraîche; **in ~ weather** quand il fait chaud; **to be ~** [*person*] avoir chaud; [*weather*] faire chaud; **it's ~ today** il fait bon or chaud aujourd'hui; **it's nice and ~ in here** on est bien au chaud ici; **are you ~ enough?** as-tu assez chaud?; **in a ~ oven** Culin à four très doux; **'serve ~'** Culin 'servir tiède'; **this soup is only ~, not hot** cette soupe est tiède, pas chaude; **it's ~ work** c'est un travail qui donne chaud; **to get ~** [*person, weather, object*] se réchauffer; **you're getting ~er!** (in guessing game) tu chauffes!; **to get sb/sth ~** réchauffer qn/qch; **to get oneself ~** se réchauffer; **to keep (oneself) ~** (wrap up) ne pas prendre froid; (take exercise) se tenir chaud; (stay indoors) rester au chaud; **to keep sb ~** [*extra clothing, blanket*] tenir chaud à qn; [*nurse*] tenir qn au chaud; **to keep sth ~** tenir [qch] au chaud [*food*]; chauffer [qch] (en permanence) [*room*]; **we got the sitting-room ~** nous avons chauffé le salon; **2** (cordial, enthusiastic) [*person, atmosphere, applause, congratulations, feeling, reception, smile, thanks, welcome*] chaleureux/-euse; [*admiration, support*] enthousiaste; **to have a ~ heart** être chaleureux/-euse; **~(est) regards** meilleures amitiés; **to give sb/get a ~ welcome** accueillir qn/être accueilli chaleureusement; **3** (mellow) [*colour*] chaud; [*sound*] chaleureux/-euse.
III *vtr* chauffer [*plate, dish, food, water*] chauffer; réchauffer [*implement*]; réchauffer [*bed*]; se réchauffer [*part of body*]; **she was ~ing her hands by the fire** elle se réchauffait les mains près du feu; **to ~ sb's heart** réchauffer le cœur de qn.
IV *vi* [*food, liquid, object*] chauffer.
V *v refl* **to ~ oneself** se réchauffer.
IDIOMS **to make things ~ for sb**° en faire voir de toutes les couleurs° à qn.
■ **warm to, warm towards**: **~ to [sb/sth]** se prendre de sympathie pour [*acquaintance*]; s'enthousiasmer pour [*artist, idea, cause*]; commencer à apprécier [*artistic, literary style*]; s'attaquer avec enthousiasme à [*task, work*]; **'and then,' he said, ~ing to his theme,...** 'ensuite,' dit-il, de plus en plus enthousiaste,...
■ **warm up** ¶ **1** [*person, room, house*] se réchauffer; [*food, liquid*] chauffer; Aut, Elec [*car, engine, radio*] chauffer; **2** fig (become lively) [*discussion, campaign, party, audience*] s'animer; **things ~ed up when the band arrived** ça s'est animé quand le groupe est arrivé; **it took the audience a while to ~ up** il a fallu du temps pour chauffer° la salle; **3** Sport [*athlete, player*] s'échauffer; Mus [*singer*] s'échauffer la voix; [*orchestra, musician*] se préparer; ¶ **~ up [sth], ~ [sth] up** **1** (heat) réchauffer [*room, bed, person*]; faire réchauffer [*food*]; **2** (prepare) Theat chauffer° [*audience*]; Sport échauffer [*athlete, player*]; Mus [*singer*] s'échauffer [*voice*]; [*musician*] chauffer [*instrument*].

warm-blooded /ˌwɔ:m'blʌdɪd/ *adj* Zool à sang chaud; fig ardent.

war memorial *n* monument *m* aux morts.

warm: **~ front** *n* front *m* chaud; **~-hearted** *adj* chaleureux/-euse.

warming /'wɔ:mɪŋ/ I *n* réchauffement *m*.
II *adj* [*drink, sunlight*] qui réchauffe; fig [*relations*] de plus en plus chaleureux/-euse.

warming: **~ oven** *n* four *m* à réchauffer; **~ pan** *n* bassinoire *f*; **~-up exercises** *npl* Mus, Sport, Theat exercices *mpl* d'échauffement.

warmly /'wɔ:mlɪ/ *adv* **1** lit [*dress, wrap up*] chaudement; **the sun shone ~** le soleil était chaud; **2** fig [*greet, smile, recommend, thank*] chaleureusement; [*speak, praise*] avec enthousiasme.

warmonger /'wɔ:mʌŋgə(r)/ *n* belliciste *mf*.

warmongering /'wɔ:mʌŋgərɪŋ/ I *n* propagande *f* belliciste.
II *adj* [*person, article*] belliciste.

warmth /wɔ:mθ/ *n* lit, fig chaleur *f*; **they huddled round the fire for ~** ils se sont serrés autour du feu pour se tenir chaud; **he replied with some ~ that** il a répondu vivement que.

warm-up /'wɔ:mʌp/ I *n* Mus, Sport, Theat échauffement *m*.
II *modif* [*exercise, routine*] d'échauffement.

warn /wɔ:n/ I *vtr* avertir, prévenir [*person, government, authority*]; **to ~ that** dire or annoncer que; **to ~ sb that** avertir or prévenir qn que; **to ~ sb about** ou **against sth** mettre qn en garde contre qch; **to ~ sb about** ou **against doing** déconseiller à qn de faire; **to ~ sb to do** conseiller or dire à qn de faire; **to ~ sb not to do** déconseiller à qn de faire; **I'm ~ing you!** je te préviens!; **you have been ~ed!** tu es prévenu!; **I shan't ~ you again** c'est la dernière fois que je te le dis.
II *vi* **to ~ of sth** annoncer qch.
■ **warn away**: **~ [sb] away, ~ away [sb]** détourner [qn]; **to ~ sb away from** déconseiller à qn d'aller dans [*district, nightclub*]; déconseiller à qn de fréquenter [*person*].
■ **warn off**: **~ [sb] off, ~ off [sb]** décourager; **to ~ sb off doing** déconseiller à qn de faire; **to ~ sb off sth** déconseiller qch à qn [*alcohol, drugs*]; **to ~ sb off one's land** demander à qn de quitter ses terres.

warning /'wɔ:nɪŋ/ I *n* gen avertissement *m*; (of danger) mise *f* en garde, avertissement *m*; (by an authority) avis *m*; (by light, siren) signal *m*; **a ~ that** un avertissement que; **a ~ against sth** une mise en garde contre qch; **a ~ about** ou **on sth** une mise en garde à propos de qch; **to give sb a ~ not to do** déconseiller à qn de faire; **to give sb ~** avertir qn (**of** de); **advance ~** préavis *m*; **health ~** mise en garde; **flood/gale ~** avis de crue/de coup de vent; **let that be a ~ to you!** que cela te serve d'avertissement!; **to sound a note of ~** donner un avertissement; **the storm started without ~** la tempête a commencé soudainement or sans avertissement; **to be attacked without ~** être attaqué sans avertissement; **to be sacked without ~** être licencié sans préavis; **an official/a written ~** un avis officiel/écrit; **the police let her off with a ~** la police l'a laissée partir avec un avertissement; **'~! Fire risk!'** 'attention! risque d'incendie!'
II *modif* **1** (giving notice of danger) [*siren, bell, device*] d'alarme; [*notice*] d'avertissement; **~ light** voyant *m* d'alarme; **~ shot** lit, fig coup *m* de semonce; **~ sign** lit (on board) panneau *m* d'avertissement; fig (of illness, stress etc) signe *m* annonciateur; **~ signal** fig signe *m* annonciateur; **2** (threatening) [*glance, gesture, tone, voice*] de mise en garde; (stronger) menaçant.

war: **War Office** *n* GB ministère *m* de la Guerre; **War of Independence** *n* US Hist Guerre *f* d'Indépendance.

warp /wɔ:p/ I *n* **1** (deformity) (in wood, metal) déformation *f*, voilure *f* spec (**in** de); (in record) déformation *f*, voile *m* spec; **2** Tex chaîne *f*; **3** fig (essence) **the ~ (and woof) of sth** l'étoffe *f* dont qch est fait; **4** Naut aussière *f*.

II *vtr* **1** (deform) déformer, voiler [*metal, wood, record*]; **2** fig (distort) pervertir [*mind, personality*]; fausser [*judgment, outlook, thinking*].
III *vi* se déformer, se voiler spec.

warpaint /ˈwɔːpeɪnt/ *n* Mil peinture *f* de guerre; hum (make-up) peintures *fpl* de guerre.

warpath /ˈwɔːpɑːθ/ *n*:
IDIOMS **to be on the ~** être sur le sentier de la guerre.

warped /wɔːpt/ *adj* **1** (deformed) [*metal, plane, record*] déformé, voilé; **to become ~** se déformer, se voiler; **2** fig (distorted) [*mind, humour*] tordu; [*personality, sexuality*] perverti; [*account, judgment, view*] faussé; **to become ~** [*judgment*] se fausser; [*personality*] se pervertir; [*mind*] devenir perturbé.

warplane /ˈwɔːpleɪn/ *n* avion *m* militaire.

warp thread *n* Tex fil *m* de chaine.

warrant /ˈwɒrənt, US ˈwɔːr-/ **I** *n* **1** Jur mandat *m*; **to issue a ~** établir un mandat; **arrest/search ~** mandat d'arrêt/de perquisition; **a ~ to do** un mandat pour faire; **a ~ for sb's arrest** un mandat d'arrêt contre qn; **a ~ is out for his arrest** un mandat a été lancé contre lui; **2** Fin (for shares) bon *m* de souscription; **dividend ~** coupon *m* de dividende; **3** GB Comm (receipt) récépissé *m*, warrant *m*; **4** (legitimate right) droit *m*; **to be without ~** ne pas être justifié; **5** Mil brevet *m*.
II *vtr* **1** (justify) justifier [*action, investigation, measure*]; **2** (guarantee) garantir [*equipment, goods*]; **3** (bet) parier (**that** que); **he'll be back, I ~ you** je parie qu'il reviendra.
III *vi* parier; **she's married I'll ~** je parie qu'elle est mariée.
IV warranted *pp adj* **1** (justified) justifié; **2** (guaranteed) garanti.

warrantable /ˈwɒrəntəbl, US ˈwɔːr-/ *adj* (justifiable) légitime.

warrant card *n* plaque *f* (de police).

warrantee /ˌwɒrənˈtiː, US ˌwɔːr-/ *n* Comm receveur/-euse *m/f* d'une garantie.

warranter /ˈwɒrəntɔː(r), US ˈwɔːr-/ *n* Comm garant/-e *m/f*.

warrant officer, **WO** ▶ **1612** *n* Mil adjudant *m*.

warranty /ˈwɒrəntɪ, US ˈwɔːr-/ *n* **1** Comm garantie *f*; **under ~** sous garantie; **a 12-month ~** une garantie de douze mois; **2** Jur simple garantie *f*; **3** Insur condition *f* d'application.

warren /ˈwɒrən, US ˈwɔːrən/ *n* **1** (rabbits') (whole area) garenne *f*; (tunnels only) terriers *mpl*; **2** (building, maze of streets) labyrinthe *m*.

warring /ˈwɔːrɪŋ/ *adj* [*factions, parties, nations*] en conflit.

warrior /ˈwɒrɪə(r), US ˈwɔːr-/ *n, adj* guerrier/-ière (*m/f*).

Warsaw /ˈwɔːsɔːw/ ▶ **1818** *pr n* Varsovie.

Warsaw Pact **I** *n* Mil, Hist pacte *m* de Varsovie.
II *modif* [*troops, countries*] du pacte de Varsovie.

warship /ˈwɔːʃɪp/ *n* navire *m* de guerre.

wart /wɔːt/ *n* **1** (on skin) verrue *f*; **2** (on plant) excroissance *f*.
IDIOMS **to describe sb ~s and all, to give a ~s-and-all description of sb** décrire qn avec tous ses défauts.

warthog /ˈwɔːthɒg/ *n* phacochère *m*.

wartime /ˈwɔːtaɪm/ **I** *n* **in ~** en temps de guerre.
II *modif* [*economy, memories, rationing*] de guerre; **a story set in ~ Berlin** une histoire qui se passe à Berlin pendant la guerre.

war-torn *adj* déchiré par la guerre.

warty /ˈwɔːtɪ/ *adj* **1** [*skin*] couvert de verrues; **2** [*stem, vegetable*] verruqueux/-euse.

war-weary /ˈwɔːwɪərɪ/ *adj* las/lasse de la guerre.

Warwickshire /ˈwɒrɪkʃə(r)/ ▶ **1624** *pr n* Warwickshire *m*.

wary /ˈweərɪ/ *adj* **1** (cautious) [*attitude, manner, reply*] prudent; **to be ~** montrer de la circonspection (**of** vis à vis de); **2** (distrustful) [*animal, look, movement, person*] méfiant; **to be ~** se méfier (**of** de).

was /wɒz/ *prét* ▶ **be**.

wash /wɒʃ/ **I** *n* **1** ¢ (by person) **to give [sth] a ~** laver [*window, floor*]; nettoyer [*object*]; lessiver [*paintwork, walls*]; se laver [*hands, face*]; **to give sb a ~** débarbouiller [*child*]; **you need a good ~** tu as besoin d'un bon débarbouillage; **to have a quick ~** faire un brin de toilette○; **these curtains/your feet need a ~** ces rideaux/tes pieds ont besoin d'être lavés; **2** (laundry process) lavage *m*; **weekly ~** lessive *f* hebdomadaire; **after only two ~es** après deux lavages seulement; **in the ~** (about to be cleaned) au sale; (being cleaned) au lavage; **3** (movement) (from boat, aircraft) remous *m*; **4** (coating) gen couche *f* (de peinture); (with whitewash) badigeon *m*; Art lavis *m*; **5** Pharm lotion *f*; **6** (swill) pâtée *f*.
II *modif* **frequent ~ shampoo** shampooing *m* pour lavages fréquents; **pen and ~ drawing** dessin *m* à la plume et au lavis.
III /wɒʃ, US wɔːʃ/ *vtr* **1** (clean) laver [*person, clothes, floor*]; nettoyer [*object, wound*]; lessiver [*paintwork, surface*]; **to get ~ed** se laver; **to ~ everything by hand/in the machine** laver tout à la main/à la machine; **to ~ one's hands/face** se laver les mains/le visage; **to ~ sth clean** laver [*hands, clothes, floor*]; lessiver [*paintwork*]; nettoyer [*cut*]; **to ~ the dishes** faire la vaisselle; **2** (carry along) [*tide, current*] entraîner [*silt, debris*]; **to be ~ed out to sea** être entraîné vers le large; **to be ~ed along by the tide** être entraîné par la marée; **to be ~ed downstream** être entraîné en aval; **to ~ sb/sth ashore** rejeter qn/qch sur le rivage; **to ~ sb/sth overboard** emporter qn/qch par-dessus bord; **3** littér (lap against) lécher [*rock, shore*]; **4** (dig out) creuser; **the water had ~ed a hole in the bank** les inondations avaient creusé un trou dans le talus; **5** (coat) Art laver [*drawing*]; gen, Constr passer une légère couche de peinture sur [*wall*]; (with whitewash) badigeonner [*wall*]; **to ~ a wall in pink** passer une légère couche de rose sur un mur; **to ~ sth with gold** dorer qch au trempé [*metal, coin*]; **6** Chem, Miner, Mining (purify by separation) épurer [qch] par lavage [*gas*]; laver [*ore*].
IV *vi* **1** (clean oneself) [*person*] se laver, faire sa toilette; [*animal*] faire sa toilette; **2** (clean clothes) faire la lessive; **I ~ on Mondays** je fais la lessive le lundi; **Whizzo ~es whiter** Advertg Whizzo lave plus blanc; **3** (become clean) se laver; **to ~ easily/well** se laver facilement/bien; **4**○ (be believed) **his explanation won't ~ with the electorate** son explication ne satisfera pas l'électorat; **that excuse won't ~ with me** cette excuse ne me satisfait pas.
V *v refl* **to ~ oneself** [*person*] se laver; [*animal*] se nettoyer.
IDIOMS **it will all come out in the ~** (be revealed) tout finira bien par se savoir; (be resolved) tout finira par s'arranger; **to ~ one's hands of** se laver les mains de [*matter*]; se désintéresser de [*person*].
■ **wash away**: ¶ **~ [sth] away, ~ away [sth]** **1** (clean) faire partir [*dirt*]; Relig laver [*sins*]; **2** (carry off) [*flood, tide, current*] emporter [*structure, debris*]; (by erosion) [*sea*] éroder [*cliff, bank*]; ¶ **~ [sb] away** [*wave, tide*] emporter [*person*].
■ **wash down**: **~ [sth] down, ~ down [sth]** **1** (clean) laver [qch] à grande eau [*surface, vehicle*]; lessiver [*paintwork*]; **2**○ (help to swallow) faire descendre [*pill*]; faire passer [*unpleasant food*]; arroser [*food*]; **a good steak ~ed down with a glass of claret** un bon steak arrosé d'un verre de bordeaux.
■ **wash off**: ¶ **~ off** [*mark*] partir au lavage; ¶ **~ [sth] off, ~ off [sth]** **1** (clean off) faire partir [qch] à l'eau [*dirt, mark*]; **to ~ the mud off the car** laver la voiture pour faire partir la boue; **go and ~ that dirt off your face** débarbouille-toi la figure; **2** (carry off) drainer [*topsoil*].
■ **wash out**: ¶ **~ out** **1** (disappear by cleaning) [*stain*] partir au lavage; [*colour*] passer; **stains that won't ~ out** Advertg taches rebelles; **2**○ US (fail to reach standard for) **she ~ed out of college** elle s'est fait recaler aux examens d'entrée en fac○; ¶ **~ [sth] out, ~ out [sth]** **1** (remove by cleaning) faire partir [qch] au lavage [*stain*]; faire passer [*colour*]; **2** (rinse inside) rincer [*cup, inside*]; **3** (clean quickly) passer [qch] à l'eau [*dishcloth, brush*]; **4** (rain off) (*gén au passif*) **the first day's play was ~ed out** la première journée a été annulée à cause de la pluie; **5** Miner, gen extraire [*precious metal*]; (from mud) débourber [*precious metal*].
■ **wash over**: [*water*] balayer [*deck*]; **everything I say just ~es over him** tout ce que je dis glisse sur lui; **a great feeling of relief ~ed over me** un immense soulagement m'a envahi.
■ **wash through**: **~ [sth] through** passer [qch] à l'eau.
■ **wash up**: ¶ **~ up** **1** GB (do dishes) faire la vaisselle; **2** US (clean oneself) [*person*] faire un brin de toilette○; ¶ **~ [sth] up, ~ up [sth]** **1** (clean) laver [*plate*]; nettoyer [*pan*]; **2** (bring to shore) [*tide*] rejeter [*body, debris*].

washable /ˈwɒʃəbl, US ˈwɔːʃ-/ *adj* [*material, paint, ink*] lavable.

wash: **~-and-wear** *adj* [*fabric, clothes*] d'entretien facile; **~basin** *n* lavabo *m*; **~board** *n* planche *f* à laver; **~bowl** *n* US lavabo *m*; **~cloth** *n* US lavette *f*; **~day** *n* jour *m* de lessive.

wash down○ /ˈwɒʃdaʊn, US ˈwɔːʃ-/ *n* **to give sth a ~** laver [qch] à grande eau [*vehicle*]; lessiver [*wall, paintwork*].

washed-out /ˌwɒʃtˈaʊt, US ˌwɔːʃ-/ *adj* **1** (faded) [*colour, jeans*] délavé; **2** (tired) lessivé○, épuisé; **the ~ look on his face** son air épuisé.

washed-up○ /ˌwɒʃtˈʌp, US ˌwɔːʃ-/ *adj* **1** (finished) fichu○, foutu◑; **2** US (tired) lessivé○, épuisé.

washer /ˈwɒʃə(r), US ˈwɔːʃər/ *n* **1** Tech (to spread load) rondelle *f*; (as seal) joint *m*; **2**○ (washing machine) machine *f* à laver.

washer-dryer /ˌwɒʃəˈdraɪə(r), US ˌwɔːʃ-/ *n* lave-linge/sèche-linge *m*.

washer-up(per)○ /ˌwɒʃəˈʌp(ə(r)), US ˌwɔːʃ-/ *n* (in restaurant) plongeur/-euse *m/f*; **who's going to be the ~?** hum qui va faire la plonge?

washerwoman /ˈwɒʃəwʊmən, US ˈwɔːʃ-/ ▶ **1692** *n* lavandière *f*.

wash: **~-hand basin** *n* lavabo *m*; **~house** *n* buanderie *f*.

washing /ˈwɒʃɪŋ, US ˈwɔːʃɪŋ/ *n* **1** (act) (of oneself) toilette *f*; (of clothes) lessive *f*; **2** (laundry) (to be cleaned) linge *m* sale; (when clean) linge *m*; **to do the ~** faire la lessive; **to hang out the ~** étendre le linge; **to take in ~** faire des lessives chez soi (*comme métier*).

washing: **~ day** *n* jour *m* de lessive; **~ facilities** *npl* douches-lavabos *fpl*; **~ line** *n* corde *f* à linge; **~ machine** *n* machine *f* à laver; **~ powder** *n* GB lessive *f* (en poudre); **~ soda** *n* soude *f* ménagère.

Washington /ˈwɒʃɪŋtən, US ˈwɔːʃ-/ ▶ **1818**, **1744** *pr n* (city, state) Washington *m*.

washing: **~-up** *n* GB vaisselle *f*; **~-up bowl** *n* GB cuvette *f* (pour la vaisselle); **~-up cloth** *n* GB lavette *f*; **~-up liquid** *n* GB liquide *m* à vaisselle; **~-up water** *n* GB eau *f* de vaisselle.

wash: **~ leather** *n* peau *f* de chamois; **~load** *n* capacité *f* de lavage; **~out** *n* fiasco *m* dû à la pluie; **~-rag** *n* US lavette *f*; **~room** *n* toilettes *fpl*; **~ sale** *n* US Fin (on Stock Exchange) vente *f* fictive; **~-stand** *n* US (washbasin) lavabo *m*; (table) table *f* de toilette; **~ symbol** *n* symbole *m* de lavage; **~ trough** *n* (for gold) batée *f*; **~tub** *n* bassine *f*; **~-wipe** *n* Aut lavage *m* du pare-brise.

wasn't /ˈwɒznt/ = **was not**.

wasp /wɒsp/ *n* guêpe *f*.

WASP /wɒsp/ *n* US (*abrév* = **White Anglo-Saxon Protestant**) *membre de l'élite des blancs protestants d'origine anglo-saxonne*.

waspish /ˈwɒspɪʃ/ *adj* acerbe.

waspishly /ˈwɒspɪʃlɪ/ *adv* d'un ton acerbe.

wasp-waisted /ˌwɒspˈweɪstɪd/ *adj* [*person*] à taille de guêpe; [*clothing*] cintré à la taille.

wassail‡ /ˈwɒseɪl/ **I** *n* (merry-making) ribote‡ *f*, beuverie *f* (*surtout à Noël*).
II *vi* GB (sing carols) **to go ~ing** aller de maison en maison en chantant des chants de Noël.

wastage /ˈweɪstɪdʒ/ *n* **1** (of money, resources, talent) gaspillage *m*; (of heat, energy) déperdition *f*; **through ~** par gaspillage; **2** (also **natural ~**) Sociol, Econ élimination *f* naturelle.

wastage rate *n* Sociol, Econ taux *m* d'abandon.

waste /weɪst/ **I** *n* **1** ¢ (squandering) (of commodity, food, resources, money, energy, opportunity) gaspillage *m* (**of** de); (of time) perte *f* (**of** de); **that was a complete ~ of an afternoon** l'après-midi a été perdu complètement inutilement; **what a ~!** quel gaspillage!; **don't throw it away, it's a ~** ne le jette pas, c'est du gaspillage; **it's a ~ of her talents** elle gaspille ses talents (**doing** en faisant); **a ~ of effort** un effort inutile; **taking taxis is a ~ of money** prendre des taxis c'est jeter l'argent par les fenêtres; **that car was a complete ~ of money** cette voiture est de l'argent complètement gaspillé; **it's a ~ of time and money** c'est une perte de temps et d'argent; **it's a ~ of time trying to explain it** on perd son temps à essayer de l'expliquer; **to go to ~** être gaspillé; **that's another good opportunity gone to ~** et voilà encore une bonne occasion de perdue; **to let sth go to ~** gaspiller qch; **there is no ~, every part is used** il n'y a pas de déchets, chaque élément est utilisé; **2** ¢ (detritus) gen, Ind déchets *mpl* (**from** de); **chemical/nuclear ~** déchets chimiques/nucléaires; **household** ou **kitchen ~** déchets domestiques, ordures *fpl* ménagères; **industrial ~** déchets industriels; **the burning of hazardous ~s** l'incinération des déchets dangereux; ▶ **nuclear waste**; **3** (wasteland) désert *m*.
II wastes *npl* **1** (wilderness) étendues *fpl* sauvages; **the frozen ~s of the Arctic** les étendues glacées de l'Arctique; **2** US = **waste** I 2.
III *adj* **1** (discarded) [*food*] inutilisé; [*heat, energy*] perdu, gaspillé; [*water*] usé; **~ materials** ou **matter** déchets *mpl*; **~ products** Ind déchets *mpl* de fabrication; Physiol, Med déchets *mpl*; **~ gases** déchets *mpl* gazeux; **~ plastics** plastiques *mpl* de rebut; **2** (unused) [*land, ground*] inculte; **3** (destruction) **to lay ~ (to)** dévaster.
IV *vtr* **1** (squander) gaspiller [*food, resources, energy, money, talents*]; perdre [*time, opportunity*]; user [*strength*]; **there's no time to ~** il n'y a pas de temps à perdre; **I won't ~ my time on her/administration** je ne vais pas perdre mon temps avec elle/l'administration; **I ~ed a whole morning looking for it** j'ai perdu une matinée entière à le chercher; **he ~d his youth** il a gâché sa jeunesse; **all our efforts/sacrifices were ~d** tous nos efforts/sacrifices ont été vains; **he didn't ~ words** il a été franc et direct; **she didn't ~ any time in trying to explain** (pointlessly) elle n'a pas perdu son temps à essayer d'expliquer; **she ~ed no time in contacting the police** (acted at once) elle n'a pas perdu de temps pour contacter la police; **he certainly didn't ~ any time!** iron il n'a pas perdu de temps!; **subtlety is ~d on her** la subtilité lui passe au-dessus de la tête; **good wine is ~d on him** il n'est pas capable d'apprécier un bon vin; **2** (make thinner) décharner [*person, body, limb*]; (make weaker) atrophier [*person, body, limb*]; **3**○ US (kill) supprimer○.
V *vi* se perdre.
IDIOMS **~ not want not** Prov l'économie protège du besoin.
■ **waste away** dépérir.

waste: **~basket** *n* corbeille *f* à papier; **~bin** *n* GB (for paper) corbeille *f* à papier; (for rubbish, scraps) poubelle *f*.

wasted /ˈweɪstɪd/ *adj* **1** (squandered) [*care, effort, expense, life, vote*] inutile; [*commodity, energy, years*] gaspillé; **another ~ opportunity** encore une occasion de perdue; **2** (fleshless) [*body, limb*] décharné; [*face*] émacié; (weak) [*body, limb*] atrophié, malingre; **~ by disease** ravagé par la maladie; **3**○ (drunk) bourré○; **to get ~** se bourrer○.

waste depository *n* entrepôt *m* de déchets.

waste disposal I *n* traitement *m* des déchets.
II *modif* [*company, industry, system*] de traitement des déchets.

waste: **~ disposal unit** *n* GB broyeur *m* d'ordures; **~ dump** *n* dépotoir *m*.

wasteful /ˈweɪstfl/ *adj* [*product, machine*] qui consomme beaucoup; [*method, process*] peu économique; [*person*] gaspilleur/-euse; (of money) dépensier/-ière; **to be ~ of** gaspiller [*commodity, resources, energy*]; perdre beaucoup de [*space, time*]; **our way of life is so ~** notre mode de vie implique tant de gaspillage.

wastefully /ˈweɪstfəlɪ/ *adv* [*spend, produce, package*] inutilement; **to use ~** gaspiller.

wastefulness /ˈweɪstflnɪs/ *n* (extravagance) gaspillage *m*; (inefficiency) manque *m* de rentabilité.

waste: **~land** *n* (urban) terrain *m* vague; (rural) terre *f* à l'abandon; fig désert *m*; **~ management** *n* traitement *m* des déchets; **~paper** *n* ¢ vieux papiers *mpl*; **~paper basket**, **~paper bin** GB *n* corbeille *f* à papier; **~ pipe** *n* tuyau *m* de vidange.

waster○ /ˈweɪstə(r)/ *n* péj dépensier/-ière *m/f*.

waste: **~ recycling** *n* recyclage *m* des déchets; **~ service** *n* service *m* de voirie.

wasting /ˈweɪstɪŋ/ *adj* [*disease*] débilitant.

wastrel† /ˈweɪstrəl/ *n* **1** (spendthrift) péj dépensier/-ière *m/f*; **2** (idler) vaurien *m*.

watch /wɒtʃ/ **I** *n* **1** (timepiece) montre *f*; **my ~ is slow/fast** ma montre retarde/avance; **by my ~ it's three o'clock** à ma montre il est trois heures; **to set one's ~** mettre sa montre à l'heure; **you can set your ~ by him** vous pouvez vous régler sur lui; **2** (lookout, surveillance) gen, Mil surveillance *f* (**on** sur); **to keep ~** [*sentry, police, watcher*] monter la garde; **to keep (a) ~ on sb/sth** lit, fig surveiller qn/qch; **keep a close ~ on expenditure** surveillez les dépenses de près; **to keep ~ over sb/sth** monter la garde auprès de qn/près de qch; **to be on the ~** être sur ses gardes; **to be on the ~ for sb/sth** lit guetter qn/qch; fig être à l'affût de qn/qch; **to set a ~ on sb/sth** tenir qn/qch à l'œil; **badger/fox ~** observation *f* des blaireaux/renards; **tornado ~** Meteorol surveillance *f* des cyclones; **3** Naut (time on duty) quart *m*; (crew on duty) (one person) homme *m* de quart; (several) quart *m*; **the port/starboard ~** les bâbordais *mpl*/tribordais *mpl*; **to be/go on ~** être de quart/prendre le quart; **to come off ~** rendre le quart; **4** Mil, Hist (patrol) **the ~** le guet.
II *modif* [*chain, spring, strap*] de montre.
III *vtr* **1** lit (look at) regarder [*event, entertainment, object, sport, television*]; (observe) observer [*behaviour, animal*]; **she ~es three hours of television a day** elle regarde la télévision trois heures par jour; **is there anything worth ~ing on television?** y a-t-il quelque chose à voir à la télévision?; **I ~ed them with binoculars** je les ai observés avec des jumelles; **he ~ed them run** ou **running** il les a regardés courir; **she's a pleasure to ~** c'est un vrai plaisir de la regarder; **the match, ~ed by a huge crowd...** le match, suivi par une foule immense...; **I've ~ed these children grow up** j'ai vu grandir ces enfants; **2** fig (monitor) suivre [*career, progress, development*]; surveiller [*situation*]; **a young artist/a name to ~** un jeune artiste/un nom à suivre; **we had to sit by and ~ the collapse of all our hopes** nous avons dû assister impuissants à l'effondrement de tous nos espoirs; **3** lit (keep under surveillance) surveiller [*building, suspect, troublemaker, movements*]; **we're having him ~ed** nous le faisons surveiller; **to ~ the clock** fig surveiller la pendule; **~ the local press/this noticeboard for further details** lire la presse locale/ce panneau d'affichage pour plus de détails; **4** (pay attention to) faire attention à [*dangerous object, obstacle, unreliable person, thing*]; surveiller [*language, manners, money, weight*]; **~ that car/that child!** (fais) attention à cette voiture/cet enfant!; **~ your arm/your big feet!** fais attention à ton bras/tes grands pieds!; **are you ~ing the time?** est-ce que tu surveilles l'heure?; **~ you don't spill it** fais attention à ne pas le renverser; **~ that she doesn't go out alone** veille à ce qu'elle ne sorte pas seule; **~ where you're going!** regarde devant toi!; **~ where you put that paint-brush!** ne mets pas ce pinceau n'importe où!; **~ it**○**!** fais gaffe○!; **to ~ one's step** lit, fig regarder où on met les pieds; **~ your back**○**!** lit attention devant!; fig surveille tes arrières; **5** (look after) garder [*property, child, dog*].
IV *vi* **1** (look on) regarder (**from** de); **as she ~ed the plane exploded** alors qu'elle regardait l'avion a explosé; **they are ~ing to see what will happen next** ils attendent pour voir ce qui va se passer maintenant; **he could only ~ helplessly as the disease advanced** il ne pouvait que suivre impuissant le progrès de la maladie; **2**† (keep vigil) veiller.
V *v refl* **to ~ oneself 1** lit (on film, TV) se regarder; **2** fig (be careful) faire attention.
IDIOMS **in the long ~es of the night** littér durant les longues heures de la nuit.
■ **watch for**: **~ for [sb/sth]** guetter [*person, event, chance, moment*]; surveiller l'apparition de [*symptom, phenomenon, risk*]; **~ for the scene where...** regardez bien la scène où...
■ **watch out** (be careful) faire attention (**for** à); (keep watch) guetter; **~ out!** attention!; **to ~ out for** faire attention à [*features, events*]; guetter [*person, development, problem*]; **I'll ~ out for her when I'm in town** je guetterai si je la vois quand je serai en ville; **~ out for trouble!** gare aux ennuis!; **~ out for our next issue!** ne ratez pas notre prochain numéro!
■ **watch over**: **~ over [sb/sth]** veiller sur [*person*]; veiller à [*interests, rights, welfare*].

watchable /ˈwɒtʃəbl/ *adj* [*film, programme*] qui se laisse regarder.

watchband /ˈwɒtʃbænd/ *n* US bracelet *m* de montre.

watchdog /ˈwɒtʃdɒg/ **I** *n* **1** (dog) chien *m* de garde; **2** Admin, Econ (monitor) (person) observateur *m*; (organization) organisme *m* de surveillance, observateur *m*; **financial ~** observateur économique; **consumer ~** service de protection du consommateur.
II *modif* [*committee, group*] de surveillance.

watcher /ˈwɒtʃə(r)/ *n* (at event, entertainment) spectateur/-trice *m/f*; (hidden) guetteur/-euse *m/f*; (monitoring event, developments) observateur/-trice *m/f*; **fashion/industry ~** spécialiste *mf* de la mode/de l'industrie; **television ~** téléspectateur/-trice *m/f*.

watch fire *n* littér feu *m* de camp (*pour monter la garde*).

watchful /ˈwɒtʃfl/ adj vigilant; **to keep a ~ eye on sb/sth** garder qn/qch à l'œil.

watch: **~maker** ▶1692 n horloger/-ère m/f; **~making** n horlogerie f.

watchman /ˈwɒtʃmən/ ▶1692 n **1** Hist (night) ~ veilleur m (de nuit); **2** (guard) gardien m.

watch: **~-night service** n messe f de minuit de la Saint-Sylvestre; **~tower** n Hist tour f de guet; Mil mirador m; **~word** n gen (slogan) slogan m; Mil (password) mot m de passe.

water /ˈwɔːtə(r)/ **I** n eau f; **drinking/running ~** eau potable/courante; **tap/washing-up ~** eau du robinet/de vaisselle; **by ~** par bateau; **under ~** (submerged) sous l'eau; (flooded) inondé; **at high/low ~** à marée haute/basse; **to let in ~** [shoe, boat] prendre l'eau; **to make ~** [ship] faire eau; **to pass ~** uriner; **to turn the ~ on/off** ouvrir/fermer le robinet; **he lives across the ~ on the mainland** il habite sur le continent; **our French colleagues across the ~** nos collègues français de l'autre côté de la Manche; **the wine was flowing like ~** le vin coulait à flots; **to keep one's head above ~** lit garder la tête hors de l'eau; fig (financially) faire face à ses engagements.
II waters npl **1** Naut eaux fpl; **enemy/international ~s** eaux (territoriales) ennemies/internationales; **2** (spa water) **to take the ~s** faire une cure thermale; **to drink the ~s** prendre les eaux fpl; **3** Med (in obstetrics) eaux fpl; **her ~s have broken** elle a perdu les eaux.
III modif [glass, jug, tank] à eau; [snake, shrew] d'eau; [filter, pump] à eau; [pipe, pressure, shortage] d'eau; [industry] de l'eau.
IV vtr Hort arroser [lawn, plant]; Agric irriguer [crop, field]; abreuver [horse, livestock]; **a country ~ed by many rivers** littér un pays arrosé par de nombreuses rivières.
V vi **the smell of cooking makes my mouth ~** l'odeur de cuisine me fait venir l'eau à la bouche; **the smoke/onion made her eyes ~** la fumée/l'oignon l'a fait pleurer.
IDIOMS **to spend money like ~** jeter l'argent par les fenêtres; **not to hold ~** [theory, argument] ne pas tenir debout; **I can't walk on ~!** je ne peux pas faire de miracles!; **he's a cheat/liar of the first ~** c'est un menteur/lâche de la pire espèce.
■ **water down**: **~ down [sth] 1** (dilute) couper [qch] d'eau [beer, milk]; diluer [syrup]; **2** (tone down) atténuer [criticism, effect, plans, policy]; édulcorer [description, story]; **3** Fin diluer [capital, stock].

waterage /ˈwɔːtərɪdʒ/ n Comm, Transp prix m du transport par voie d'eau.

water: **~ authority** n compagnie f des eaux; **~ bailiff** ▶1692 n GB Hunt garde-pêche m (inv); **~ bath** n Chem, Culin bain m marie; **~ bed** n matelas m d'eau; **~ beetle** n Zool coléoptère m aquatique; **~ bird** n oiseau m aquatique; **~ biscuit** n Culin biscuit sec sans matière grasse; **~ blister** n Med ampoule f, phlyctène f spec; **~ board** n compagnie f des eaux; **~ boatman** n Zool notonecte f; **~ bomb** n bombe f à eau.

water-borne /ˈwɔːtəbɔːn/ adj **1** Biol, Med d'origine hydrique; **2** Transp transporté par voie d'eau; **3** Naut à flot.

water bottle n (for traveller) gourde f; (for cyclist) bidon m; (for warmth) bouillotte f.

water: **~ buffalo** n buffle m (d'Asie); **~ butt** n citerne f; **~ cannon** n canon m à eau.

water-carrier /ˈwɔːtəkærɪə(r)/ n **1** (person) porteur/-euse m/f d'eau; **2** (container) bidon m à eau; **3** Astrol Verseau m.

water: **~ chestnut** n Bot, Culin chataîgne f d'eau; **~ clock** n horloge f à eau, clepsydre f; **~ closet**† GB n toilettes fpl.

watercolour GB, **watercolor** US /ˈwɔːtəkʌlə(r)/ Art **I** n **1** (paint) peinture f pour aquarelle; **a landscape painted in ~** un paysage peint à l'aquarelle; **2** (painting) aquarelle f.
II modif [landscape, painting] à l'aquarelle.

water: **~colourist** GB, **~colorist** US ▶1692 n Art aquarelliste mf; **~-cooled** adj Ind, Nucl à refroidissement à eau; **~-cooler** n distributeur m d'eau réfrigérée; **~-cooling** n Ind, Nucl refroidissement m par eau; **~ course** n cours m d'eau; **~cress** n Bot, Culin cresson m (de fontaine); **~ diviner** ▶1692 n sourcier/-ière m/f, radiesthésiste mf; **~ divining** n radiesthésie f.

watered-down /ˌwɔːtəd'daʊn/ adj **1** (diluted) [beer, milk, wine] coupé d'eau; **2** fig (scaled-down) [legislation, measures, policies] atténué; [version] édulcoré.

water: **~ed silk** n Tex soie f moirée; **~ed stock** n Fin actions fpl émises pour diluer le capital; **~fall** n cascade f, chute f d'eau; **~ filter** n filtre m à eau; **~fowl** n Zool oiseau m d'eau; Hunt gibier m d'eau.

waterfree /ˈwɔːtəfriː/ adj [substance] anhydre; [area, container] sec/sèche.

waterfront /ˈwɔːtəfrʌnt/ **I** n (on harbour) front m de mer; (by lakeside, riverside) bord m de l'eau; **on the ~** (on harbour) sur le front de mer; (by lakeside, riverside) au bord de l'eau.
II modif [cafe, development, hotel] au bord de l'eau.

water gas n gaz m à l'eau.

Watergate /ˈwɔːtəgeɪt/ pr n lit, fig Watergate m.

water: **~ glass** n silicate m de potasse; **~-heater** n chauffe-eau m (inv); **~ hen** n poule f d'eau; **~ hole** n Geog, Zool point m d'eau; **~ ice** n Culin sorbet m.

watering /ˈwɔːtərɪŋ/ n Hort arrosage m; Agric irrigation f.

watering can n arrosoir m.

watering hole n **1** Geog point m d'eau; **2**○ (bar) bar m.

watering place n **1**† (resort) station f balnéaire; **2**† (spa) station f thermale; **3**○ (pub) bar m.

water: **~ jacket** n Tech, Aut chemise f d'eau; **~ jump** n Sport, Equit rivière f; **~ level** n niveau m d'eau; **~ lily** n nénuphar m; **~ line** n Naut ligne f de flottaison; **~logged** adj [ground, pitch] détrempé; [carpet] plein d'eau; [ship] plein d'eau.

Waterloo /ˌwɔːtə'luː/ pr n Waterloo; **battle of ~** bataille f de Waterloo.
IDIOMS **to meet one's ~** trouver son maître.

water main n canalisation f d'eau.

watermark /ˈwɔːtəmɑːk/ **I** n **1** (indication of highest level) (of sea) laisse f; (of river) ligne f des hautes eaux; **2** Naut = **water line**; **3** Print (on paper, banknote) filigrane m.
II vtr Print filigraner.

water: **~ meadow** n Geog prairie f inondable; **~melon** n pastèque f, melon m d'eau; **~ mill** n moulin m à eau; **~ nymph** n Mythol Naïade f; **~ on the brain** ▶1354 n Med hydrocéphalie f.

water on the knee ▶1354 n Med épanchement m de synovie; **to have ~** avoir un épanchement de synovie.

water: **~ pistol** n pistolet m à eau; **~ polo** ▶1282 n Sport water-polo m; **~ power** n énergie f hydraulique.

waterproof /ˈwɔːtəpruːf/ **I** n (coat) imperméable m.
II waterproofs npl vêtements mpl imperméables.
III adj [material, coat] imperméable; [watch, make-up] résistant à l'eau.
IV vtr imperméabiliser.

water: **~proofing** n imperméabilisation f; **~ purifying tablet** n pastille f pour purifier l'eau; **~ rail** n râle m (d'eau); **~ rat** n rat m d'eau; **~ rates** npl GB Admin taxe f sur l'eau; **~-repellent** adj [fabric, coat, spray] imperméable; **~-resistant** adj qui resiste à l'eau (after n); **~ retention** n Med (inability to pass water) rétention f d'urines; (bloating) rétention f d'eau; **~scape** n Art paysage m d'eau; **~shed** n Geog ligne f de partage des eaux; fig (turning point) tournant m; **~shed hour** n GB TV heure après laquelle les émissions déconseillées aux enfants peuvent être diffusées.

waterside /ˈwɔːtəsaɪd/ **I** n bord m de l'eau.
II modif [cafe, hotel, house] au bord de l'eau; [plant, wildlife] du bord de l'eau.

water-ski /ˈwɔːtəskiː/ Sport **I** n ski m nautique.
II vi faire du ski nautique.

water-skier /ˈwɔːtəskiːə(r)/ n skieur/-euse m/f nautique.

water-skiing /ˈwɔːtəskiːɪŋ/ ▶1282 n ski m nautique; **to go ~** faire du ski nautique.

water: **~ slide** n toboggan m de piscine; **~ softener** n (equipment) adoucisseur m (d'eau); (substance) adoucissant m; **~-soluble** adj soluble dans l'eau; **~ spaniel** n water spaniel m, épagneul m d'eau; **~ spider** n argyronète f; **~ sport** ▶1282 n sport m nautique; **~spout** n Meteorol trombe f; (pipe) tuyau m de descente.

water supply n **1** (service) (in an area, region) approvisionnement m en eau; (to a building) alimentation f en eau; **they've cut off our ~** ils ont coupé l'eau; **2** (ration) provision f d'eau.

water system n **1** Geog réseau m hydrographique; **2** (network of pipes) (for town) système m d'approvisionnement en eau; (for building) système m d'alimentation en eau.

water table n Geog niveau m hydrostatique.

watertight /ˈwɔːtətaɪt/ adj **1** lit [container, joint, seal] étanche; **2** fig (perfect) [cordon, defence system] infaillible; **3** fig (irrefutabe) [argument, case] incontestable; [alibi] irréfutable.

water: **~ tower** n château m d'eau; **~ treatment** n traitement m des eaux; **~ trough** n abreuvoir m; **~way** n Geog, Transp voie f navigable; **~weed** n Bot plante f aquatique; **~ wheel** n roue f hydraulique; **~ wings** npl bracelets mpl de natation.

waterworks /ˈwɔːtəwɜːks/ n **1** Tech station f de pompage; **2**○ euph voies fpl urinaires; **3** US (distribution network) système m hydraulique.
IDIOMS **she turned on the ~** c'était les grandes eaux.

watery /ˈwɔːtərɪ/ adj **1** (too dilute) [coffee] trop léger/-ère; [consistency, paint, sauce] trop liquide; **2** (insipid) [colour, moon, sun, smile] pâle; **3** (full of tears) [eye] plein de larmes; **4** (secreting liquid) [eye] qui pleure; [wound] qui suinte; **5** (badly drained) [vegetables] mal égoutté.
IDIOMS **he/the Titanic is lying in a ~ grave** il/le Titanic gît au fond des mers.

watt /wɒt/ n watt m; **100-~ bulb** ampoule de 100 watts.

wattage /ˈwɒtɪdʒ/ n puissance f en watts.

wattle /ˈwɒtl/ n **1** Hist, Constr clayonnage m; **2** Zool (skin flap) caroncule f; **3** Bot (tree) acacia m.

wattle and daub /ˌwɒtl ən 'dɔːb/ n Hist, Constr clayonnage m enduit de torchis.

wave /weɪv/ **I** n **1** (hand gesture) signe m (de la main); **to give sb a ~** faire un signe de la main à qn; **she gave him a ~ from the bus** elle lui a fait signe du bus; **with a ~, she disappeared** après un signe (de la main) elle a disparu; **to greet sb with a ~** accueillir qn d'un signe de la main; **to dismiss objections with a ~** balayer des objections d'un geste; **with a ~ of his wand** d'un coup de baguette magique; **2** (of water) vague f; **a 10-metre ~** une vague de 10 mètres; **to make ~s** [wind] faire des vagues; fig (cause a stir) faire du bruit; (cause trouble) créer des histoires; **3** (outbreak) vague f; **a ~ of arrests/sympathy/strikes** une vague d'arrestations/de solidarité/de grèves; **to occur in ~s** se produire par vagues; **4** (surge) vague *f*; **a ~ of heat/settlers** une vague de chaleur/colons; **5** (in hair) cran *m*; **6** Phys onde *f*; **radio/light ~s** ondes radio/lumineuses; **7** (in sand etc) ondulation *f*.

II waves *npl* littér **the ~s** les flots *mpl*.

III *vtr* **1** (move from side to side) agiter [*ticket, banknote, piece of paper, flag, handkerchief*]; brandir [*umbrella, stick, gun*]; **to ~ sth at sb** agiter qch devant qn [*ticket, flag*]; brandir qch en direction de qn [*gun, stick*]; **to ~ one's magic wand** donner un coup de baguette magique (**over** à); **2 to ~ goodbye to** faire au revoir de la main à [*person*]; fig **you can ~ goodbye to your chances of winning** tu peux dire adieu à tes chances de gagner; **3** (direct) **they ~ed us on/away/through** ils nous ont fait signe d'avancer/de nous éloigner/de passer; **4** (at hairdresser's) **to have one's hair ~d** se faire faire une mise en plis.

IV *vi* **1** (with hand) **to ~ to** ou **at sb** saluer qn de la main; **to ~ to sb to do** faire signe à qn de faire; **to ~ frantically at sb** gesticuler en direction de qn; **2** (move gently) [*branches*] onduler; [*corn*] ondoyer; [*flag*] flotter au vent.

■ **wave around, wave about**: ¶ **~ around** [*flag, washing*] flotter; ¶ **~ [sth] around** brandir [*stick, umbrella, gun*]; **don't ~ that gun around!** ne jouez pas avec cette arme! ; **to ~ one's arms around** agiter les bras dans tous les sens.

■ **wave aside**: ¶ **~ [sth] aside, ~ aside [sth]** repousser [qch] d'un geste [*suggestion, offer*]; ¶ **~ [sb] aside** écarter qn.

■ **wave off**: **~ [sb] off, ~ off [sb]** faire au revoir de la main à qn.

wave: **~ action** *n* action *f* des vagues; **~ band** *n* bande *f* de fréquence; **~ energy** *n* = **wave power**; **~ form** *n* forme *f* d'onde.

wavelength /'weɪvleŋθ/ *n* Phys, Radio longueur *f* d'onde.

IDIOMS **to be on the same ~ as sb** être sur la même longueur d'onde que qn.

wavelet /'weɪvlɪt/ *n* littér vaguelette *f*.

wave: **~ mechanics** *n* mécanique *f* ondulatoire; **~ power** *n* énergie *f* des vagues.

waver /'weɪvə(r)/ **I** *vi* **1** (wobble, weaken) [*person, stare, look*] vaciller; [*courage, determination, faith, love*] faiblir; [*voice*] trembler; **to ~ from** changer [*decision, stance*]; **2** (flicker) [*flame, light*] vaciller; [*needle*] osciller; **3** (hesitate) hésiter; **to ~ over** hésiter sur [*decision, choice*]; **to ~ between** hésiter entre; **4** (change) [*health, fortunes*] avoir des hauts et des bas; **to ~ between** balancer entre.

II wavering *pres p adj* [*person, politician, voice*] hésitant; [*voter*] indécis; [*confidence, courage, faith, flame*] vacillant.

waverer /'weɪvərə(r)/ *n* indécis/-e *m/f*.

wavering /'weɪvərɪŋ/ *n* **1** (hesitation) hésitation *f*; **2** (wobble) (of flame) vacillement *m*; (of voice) tremblement *m* (**of** dans).

wavy /'weɪvɪ/ *adj* [*hair, line*] ondulé.

wax /wæks/ **I** *n* **1** gen (for candle, sealing, polishing, records) cire *f*; **2** (for skis) fart *m*; **3** Chem, Tech (mineral wax) paraffine *f*; **4** (in ear) cérumen *m*.

II *modif* [*candle, figure, polish, seal*] en cire.

III *vtr* **1** (polish) cirer [*floor, table*]; lustrer [*car*]; farter [*ski*]; **2** Cosmet épiler [qch] à la cire [*leg*].

IV *vi* **1** Astron [*moon*] croître; **to ~ and wane** Astron, fig croître et décroître; **2** (speak) **to ~ eloquent/indignant** se montrer éloquent/indigné (**about, over** à propos de); **to ~ lyrical** disserter avec lyrisme (**about, over** à propos de).

V waxed *pp adj* [*fabric, floor, moustache, table*] ciré; [*paper*] paraffiné; [*thread*] poissé; **~ed jacket** GB ciré *m*.

wax bean *n* US Culin, Bot haricot *m* beurre.

waxen /'wæksn/ *adj* littér [*face, skin*] cireux/-euse.

waxing /'wæksɪŋ/ *n* **1** (of floor, table) cirage *m*; **2** (of car) lustrage *m*; **3** (of skis) fartage *m*; **4** Cosmet épilation *f* à la cire.

wax: **~ museum** *n* musée *m* de cire; **~ paper** *n* papier *m* paraffiné.

waxwing /'wækswɪŋ/ *n* Zool jaseur *m*.

wax: **~work** *n* personnage *m* en cire; **~works** *n* (+ *v sg* ou *pl*) musée *m* de cire.

waxy /'wæksɪ/ *adj* [*skin, texture*] cireux/-euse; [*potato*] ferme.

way /weɪ/ **I** *n* **1** (route, road) chemin *m* (**from** de; **to** à); **a paved ~** un chemin pavé; **to live over the ~**○ habiter en face; **the quickest ~ to town** le chemin le plus court pour aller en ville; **if we go this ~ we avoid the traffic** si nous prenons cette route nous éviterons la circulation; **to ask the ~ to** demander le chemin pour aller à; **which is the best ~ to the station?** quel est le meilleur chemin or le chemin le plus court pour aller à la gare?; **can you tell me the ~ to the museum?** pouvez-vous m'indiquer le chemin pour aller au musée?; **to find one's ~** trouver son chemin; **how did that find its ~ in here?** comment est-ce que c'est arrivé ici?; **the ~ ahead** lit le chemin devant moi/eux etc; **the ~ ahead looks difficult** fig l'avenir s'annonce difficile; **a ~ around** lit un chemin pour contourner [*obstacle*]; **there is no ~ around the problem** il n'y a pas moyen de contourner le problème; **to take the long ~ around** prendre le chemin le plus long; **the ~ back to** le chemin pour retourner à; **I telephoned on the ~ back** j'ai téléphoné sur le chemin du retour; **on the ~ back from the meeting** en revenant de la réunion; **the ~ down** le chemin pour descendre, la descente; **she was hurt on the ~ down** elle s'est blessée en descendant; **the ~ forward** fig la clé de l'avenir; **the ~ forward is to...** la clé de l'avenir consiste à...; **the ~ in** l'entrée (**to** de); **'~ in'** 'entrée'; **the ~ out** la sortie (**of** de); **the quickest ~ out is through here** c'est par ici que l'on sort le plus vite; **there's no ~ out** fig il n'y a pas d'échappatoire; **a ~ out of our difficulties** un moyen de nous sortir de nos difficultés or de nous en sortir; **the ~ up** la montée; **on the ~** en route; **we're on the ~ to Mary's** nous allons chez Mary; **I did it on the ~ here** je l'ai fait en venant ici; **I stopped on the ~** je me suis arrêté en (cours de) route; **on the ~ past** en passant; **I'm on my ~** j'arrive; **she's on her ~ over** elle arrive; **on your ~ through town, look out for the cathedral** en traversant la ville essaie de voir la cathédrale; **the shop is on the/my ~** le magasin est sur le/mon chemin; **his house is on your ~ to town** tu passes devant chez lui en allant au centre-ville; **it's not on my ~** ce n'est pas sur mon chemin; **I must be on my ~** il faut que je parte; **to go on one's ~** se remettre en route; **to send sb on his ~** (tell to go away) envoyer promener qn○; **she sent him on his ~ with an apple** elle lui a donné une pomme pour la route; **to be on one's ~ to victory** être sur le chemin de la victoire; **to be on the ~ to disaster** aller à la catastrophe; **to be well on the** ou **one's ~ to doing** être bien parti pour faire; **to be on the ~ out** fig passer de mode; **she's got four kids and another one on the ~**○ elle a quatre gosses et un autre en route○; **to be out of sb's ~** ne pas être sur le chemin de qn; **sorry to have taken you out of your ~** désolé de t'avoir fait faire un détour; **don't go out of your ~ to do** ne t'embête pas à faire; **to go out of one's ~ to make sb feel uncomfortable** tout faire pour que qn se sente mal à l'aise; **out of the ~** (isolated) isolé; (unusual) extraordinaire; **along the ~** lit en chemin; fig en cours de route; **by ~ of** (via) en passant par; **to go one's own ~** fig suivre son chemin; **they decided to go their separate ~s** (of couple) ils ont décidé de suivre chacun son chemin; **there we went our separate ~s** là chacun est parti de son côté; **to go the ~ of sb/sth** finir comme qn/qch; **to make one's ~ towards** se diriger vers; **to make one's ~ along** avancer le long de; **the procession makes its solemn ~ through London** la procession avance solennellement dans Londres; **to make one's own ~ there/home** se débrouiller seul pour y arriver/pour rentrer; **to make one's own ~ in life** faire son chemin tout seul dans la vie; **to push one's ~ through sth** se frayer un chemin à travers qch; **to argue/lie one's ~ out of trouble** se sortir d'affaire en argumentant/en mentant; **2** (direction) direction *f*, sens *m*; **which ~ is the arrow pointing?** quelle direction indique la flèche?; **which ~ did he go?** dans quelle direction est-il parti?; **he went that ~** il est parti par là; **south is that ~** le sud est dans cette direction or par là; **come** ou **step this ~** suivez-moi, venez par ici; **can we get to the park this ~?** est-ce que l'on peut aller au parc par ici?; **'this ~ for the zoo'** 'vers le zoo'; **she's heading this ~** elle vient par ici; **'this ~ up'** 'haut'; **look/turn this ~** regarde/tourne-toi par ici; **to look this ~ and that** regarder dans toutes les directions; **to run this ~ and that** courir dans tous les sens; **to look both ~s** regarder des deux côtés ; **to look the other ~** (to see) regarder de l'autre côté; (to avoid seeing unpleasant thing) détourner les yeux; fig (to ignore wrong doing) fermer les yeux; **to go every which ~** partir dans tous les sens; **the other ~ up** dans l'autre sens; **the right ~ up** dans le bon sens; **the wrong ~ up** à l'envers; **to turn sth the other ~ around** retourner qch; **to do it the other ~ around** faire le contraire; **I didn't ask her, it was the other ~ around** ce n'est pas moi qui lui ai demandé, c'est l'inverse; **the wrong/right ~ around** dans le mauvais/bon sens; **to put one's skirt on the wrong ~ around** mettre sa jupe à l'envers; **you're Ben and you're Tom, is that the right ~ around?** tu es Ben, et toi tu es Tom, c'est bien ça?; **you're going the right ~** tu vas dans le bon sens or la bonne direction; **you're going the right ~ to get a smack** tu es bien parti pour te prendre une claque; **are you going my ~?** est-ce que tu vas dans la même direction que moi?; **if you're ever down our ~** si jamais tu passes près de chez nous; **over Manchester ~** du côté de Manchester; **she's coming our ~** elle vient vers nous; **an opportunity came my ~** une occasion s'est présentée; **to put sth sb's ~**○ filer qch à qn○; **everything's going my/his ~** tout me/lui sourit; **3** (space in front, projected route) passage *m*; **to bar/block sb's ~** barrer/bloquer le passage à qn; **to be in sb's ~** empêcher qn de passer; **to be in the ~** gêner le passage; **am I in your ~ here?** est-ce que je te gêne comme ça?; **to get in sb's ~** [*hair, clothing*] gêner qn; [*children*] être dans les jambes de qn; **anyone who gets in his ~ gets knocked down** fig quiconque se met en travers de son chemin se fait envoyer au tapis○; **she won't let anything get in the ~ of her ambition** elle ne laissera rien entraver son ambition; **to get out of the ~** s'écarter (du chemin); **to get out of sb's ~** laisser passer qn; **put that somewhere out of the ~** mets ça quelque part où ça ne gêne pas; **she couldn't get out of the ~ in time** elle n'a pas pu s'écarter à temps; **out of my ~!** pousse-toi!; **get your car out of my ~!** pousse ta voiture!; **get him out of the ~ before the boss gets here!** fais-le disparaître d'ici avant que le patron arrive!; **if only he were out of the ~...** si seulement on pouvait se débarrasser de lui...; **let me get lunch out of the ~** laisse-moi en terminer avec le déjeuner; **once the election is out of the ~**

une fois les élections passées; **to keep out of the ~** rester à l'écart; **to keep out of sb's ~** éviter qn; **to keep sb out of sb's ~** (to avoid annoyance) tenir qn à l'écart de qn; **to keep sth out of sb's ~** (to avoid injury, harm) garder qch hors de portée de qn; **to shove/pull sb out of the ~** écarter qn; **to make ~** s'écarter; **to make ~ for sb/sth** faire place à qn/qch; **make ~ for the mayor!** place au maire!; **make ~! make ~!** place! place!; **it's time he made ~ for someone younger** il est temps qu'il laisse la place à quelqu'un de plus jeune; **4** (distance) distance *f*; **it's a long ~** c'est loin (to jusqu'à); **it's not a very long ~** ce n'est pas très loin; **to be a short ~ off** lit être près; **my birthday is still some ~ off** mon anniversaire est encore loin; **we still have some ~ to go before doing** lit, fig nous avons encore du chemin à faire avant de faire; **to go all the ~ on foot/by bus** faire tout le chemin à pied/en bus; **to go all the ~ to China with sb** faire tout le voyage jusqu'en Chine avec qn; **there are cafés all the ~ along the road** il y a des cafés tout le long de la rue; **I'm with you** ou **behind you all the ~** je suis de tout cœur avec toi, je te soutiendrai jusqu'au bout; **to go all the ~**○ (have sex) [*two people*] coucher ensemble; **to go all the ~ with sb**○ coucher avec qn; **5** (manner of doing something) façon *f*, manière *f*; **do it this/that ~** fais-le comme ceci/cela; **you won't convince her that ~** tu ne vas pas la convaincre de cette façon or manière; **which ~ shall I do it?** de quelle façon or manière dois-je le faire?; **let me explain it another ~** laisse-moi t'expliquer autrement; **to do sth the French ~** faire qch comme les Français; **to do sth the right/wrong ~** faire bien/mal qch; **you're going about it the wrong ~** tu t'y prends très mal; **he said it in such a hostile ~ that...** il l'a dit de façon tellement hostile que...; **in the usual ~** de la façon habituelle; **let her do it her ~** laisse-la faire à sa façon or manière; **that's not her ~** ce n'est pas sa façon de faire; **try to see it my ~** mets-toi à ma place; **in his/her/its own ~** à sa façon; **they're nice people in their own ~** ce sont des gens sympathiques à leur façon; **to have a ~ with sth** s'y connaître en qch; **to have a ~ with children** savoir s'y prendre avec les enfants; **she certainly has a ~ with her**○ GB elle sait décidément s'y prendre avec les gens; **a ~ of doing** (method) une façon or manière de faire; (means) un moyen de faire; **there's no ~ of knowing/judging** il n'y a pas moyen de savoir/juger; **to my ~ of thinking** à mon avis; **that's one ~ of looking at it** c'est une façon de voir les choses; **a ~ to do** une façon or manière de faire; **what a horrible ~ to die** quelle façon horrible de mourir; **that's the ~ to do it!** voilà comment il faut s'y prendre!; **that's the ~!** voilà, c'est bien!; **~ to go**○! US voilà qui est bien○!; **that's no ~ to treat a child** ce n'est pas une façon de traiter les enfants; **what a ~ to run a company!** en voilà une façon de gérer une entreprise! ; **the ~ (that) sb does sth** la façon or manière dont qn fait qch; **I like the ~ he dresses** j'aime la façon dont il s'habille, j'aime sa façon de s'habiller; **I like the ~ you blame me!** iron c'est toi qui me fais des reproches!; **that's not the ~ we do things here** ce n'est pas notre façon de faire ici; **whichever ~ you look at it** de quelque façon que tu envisages les choses; **either ~, she's wrong** de toute façon, elle a tort; **one ~ or another** d'une façon ou d'une autre; **one ~ and another it's been rather eventful** tout compte fait ça a été assez mouvementé; **I don't care one ~ or the other** ça m'est égal; **no two ~s about it** cela ne fait aucun doute; **you can't have it both ~s** on ne peut pas avoir le beurre et l'argent du beurre; **no ~**○! pas question○!; **no ~ am I doing that**○! pas question que je fasse ça○!; **6** (respect, aspect) sens *m*; **in a ~ it's sad** en un sens or d'une certaine façon c'est triste; **in a ~ that's true/she was responsible** dans une certaine mesure c'est vrai/elle était responsable; **can I help in any ~?** puis-je faire quoi que ce soit?; **would it make things easier in any ~ if...** est-ce que cela simplifierait un peu les choses si...; **without wanting to criticize in any ~** sans vouloir le moins du monde critiquer; **it was unforgivable in every ~** c'était impardonnable à tous points de vue; **in every ~ possible** dans la mesure du possible; **in many ~s** à bien des égards; **in more ~s than one** à plus d'un égard; **in some ~s** à certains égards; **in that ~ you're right** à cet égard or en ce sens tu as raison; **in no ~, not in any ~** aucunement, en aucune façon; **in no ~ are you to blame** ce n'est aucunement ta faute; **this is in no ~ a criticism** cela n'est en aucune façon une critique; **not much in the ~ of news/work** il n'y a pas beaucoup de nouvelles/travail; **what have you got in the ~ of drinks?** qu'est-ce que vous avez comme boissons or à boire?; **by ~ of light relief** en guise de divertissement; **in a general ~** (generally) en général; **in the ordinary ~** (ordinarily) d'ordinaire; **7** (custom, manner) coutume *f*, manière *f*; **you'll soon get used to our ~s** tu t'habitueras vite à nos coutumes; **the old ~s** les coutumes d'autrefois; **that's the modern ~** c'est la coutume d'aujourd'hui, c'est comme ça de nos jours; **I know all her little ~s** je connais toutes ses petites habitudes; **he's rather strange in his ~s** il a des habitudes un peu bizarres; **she's got a funny ~ of suddenly raising her voice** elle a une façon curieuse d'élever brusquement la voix; **that's just his ~** il est comme ça; **it's not my ~ to complain but...** ce n'est pas mon genre or dans mes habitudes de me plaindre mais...; **it's the ~ of the world** c'est la vie, ainsi va le monde; **8** (will, desire) **to get one's ~, to have one's own ~** faire à son idée; **she likes (to have) her own ~** elle aime n'en faire qu'à sa tête; **if I had my ~...** si cela ne tenait qu'à moi...; **have it your (own) ~** comme tu voudras; **she didn't have it all her own ~** elle n'a pas pu en faire qu'à son idée; **Leeds had things all their own ~** Sport Leeds a complètement dominé le match; **to have one's (wicked) ~ with sb**† ou hum arriver à ses fins avec qn.

II *adv* **to live ~ beyond one's means** vivre largement au-dessus de ses moyens; **we went ~ over budget** le budget a été largement dépassé; **to be ~ out** (in guess, estimate) [*person*] être loin du compte; **to be ~ more expensive/dangerous** être bien plus coûteux/dangereux; **to go ~ beyond what is necessary** aller bien au-delà de ce qui est nécessaire; **that's ~ out of order** je trouve ça un peu fort.

III by the way *adv phr* [*tell, mention*] en passant; **by the ~,...** à propos,...; **what time is it, by the ~?** quelle heure est-il, au fait?; **and she, by the ~, is French** et elle, à propos, est française; **but that's just by the ~** mais ce n'est qu'une parenthèse.

way: **~bill** *n* lettre *f* de voiture; **~farer** *n* littér voyageur/-euse *m/f*.

waylay /ˌweɪˈleɪ/ *vtr* (*prét, pp* **-laid**) [*bandit, attacker*] attaquer; [*beggar, questioner, friend*] arrêter, harponner○ hum.

way: **~ of life** *n* mode *m* de vie; **Way of the Cross** *n* chemin *m* de Croix.

way-out○ /ˌweɪˈaʊt/ *adj* **1** (unconventional) excentrique; **2**† (great) super○, formidable.

way: **~s and means** *npl* moyens *mpl*; **Ways and Means (Committee)** *n* Pol Commission *f* des Finances.

wayside /ˈweɪsaɪd/ **I** *n* littér bord *m* de la route; **at/by the ~** au bord de la route.

II *modif* [*inn, café, flowers*] au bord de la route.

IDIOMS **to fall by the ~** (stray morally) quitter le droit chemin; (fail, not stay the course) être éliminé; (be cancelled, fall through) tomber à l'eau.

way station *n* **1** lit petite gare *f*; **2** fig étape *f*.

wayward /ˈweɪwəd/ *adj* [*child, person, nature*] difficile, rétif/-ive; [*missile, horse*] incontrôlable; [*husband, wife*] volage.

waywardness /ˈweɪwədnɪs/ *n* (wilfulness) naturel *m* difficile; (capriciousness) inconstance *f*.

wazzock○ /ˈwæzək/ *n* GB imbécile○ *m*.

WC *n* GB (*abrév* = **water closet**) WC *mpl*.

WCC *n*: *abrév* ▶ **World Council of Churches.**

we /wiː, wɪ/

■ **Note** In standard French, *we* is translated by *nous* but in informal French *on* is frequently used: *we're going to the cinema* = nous allons au cinéma *or* (*more informally*) on va au cinéma.

– *on* is also used in correct French to refer to a large, vaguely defined group: *we shouldn't lie to our children* = on ne devrait pas mentir à ses enfants. For particular usages see the entry below.

pron nous; **~ saw her yesterday** nous l'avons vue hier; **~ left at six** gen nous sommes partis à six heures; (informal) on est partis○ à six heures; **~ Scots like the sun** nous autres Écossais, nous aimons le soleil; WE **didn't say that** gen nous, nous n'avons pas dit cela; (informal) nous, on n'a pas dit ça○; **~ four are agreed that** nous quatre sommes convenus que; **~ all make mistakes** tout le monde peut se tromper.

WEA *n* GB (*abrév* = **Workers' Educational Association**) *association britannique pour l'éducation populaire.*

weak /wiːk/ **I** *n* **the ~** (+ *v pl*) les faibles *mpl*.

II *adj* **1** (in bodily functions) [*person, animal, muscle, limb*] faible; [*health, ankle, eyes, chest, bladder, nerves*] fragile; [*digestion*] difficile; [*stomach*] délicat; [*intellect*] médiocre; [*memory*] défaillant; [*chin*] fuyant; [*mouth*] tombant; **to have a ~ heart** avoir le cœur fragile; **to be ~ with** ou **from** être affaibli par [*hunger, excitement, fear*]; **to grow** ou **become ~(er)** [*person*] s'affaiblir; [*pulse, heartbeat*] faiblir; **2** Constr [*beam, support*] peu solide; [*structure*] fragile; **to have a ~ leg** [*chair*] avoir un pied qui n'est pas très solide; **3** (lacking authority, strength) [*government, team, president, army*] faible; [*parent, teacher*] (not firm) qui manque de fermeté; (poor) piètre (*before n*); [*essay, pupil, performance*] faible; [*script, novel*] inconsistant; [*plot*] mince; [*actor, protest, excuse, argument*] peu convaincant; [*evidence*] peu concluant; **~ link** ou **point** ou **spot** lit, fig point *m* faible; **he's ~ in** ou **at French, his French is ~** il est faible en français; **to grow** ou **become ~er** [*government, team*] s'affaiblir; [*position*] devenir de plus en plus précaire; **in a ~ moment** dans un moment de faiblesse; **4** (faint, lacking substance) [*light, current, signal, lens, concentration, acid, sound, laugh*] faible; [*tea, coffee*] léger/-ère; [*solution*] dilué; **to give a ~ smile** faire un faible sourire; **5** Econ, Fin [*market, economy, demand, dollar*] faible (**against** par rapport à); [*share*] à bas prix; **6** Ling (regular) faible; (unaccented) inaccentué; **7** Games (in cards) [*hand, card*] mauvais; [*suit*] faible.

weaken /ˈwiːkən/ **I** *vtr* **1** [*illness, climate*] affaiblir [*person, heart, system*]; saper [*stamina*]; diminuer [*resistance*]; **2** [*explosion, stress*] affaiblir [*structure, beam*]; rendre [qch] moins solide [*joint, bank, wall*]; **3** [*event, discovery*] nuire à l'autorité de [*government, president*]; affaiblir [*team, company, authority, resolve, cause, defence*]; diminuer [*support, influence*]; amoindrir [*argument, power*]; nuire à [*morale*]; ébranler [*will*]; **4** (dilute) diluer [*solution, concentration*]; **5** Econ, Fin affaiblir [*economy,*

currency]; faire baisser [*prices, demand, shares*].
II *vi* **1** (physically) [*person, muscles*] s'affaiblir; [*grip*] se relâcher; **2** (lose power) [*government, president, country, resistance, resolve*] fléchir; [*support, alliance*] se relâcher; [*friendship, love*] faiblir; **3** Econ, Fin [*economy, market, currency*] être en baisse.

weakening /'wi:kənɪŋ/ *n* **1** (physical) (of person, health, eyesight) affaiblissement *m*; (of structure) dégradation *f*; **2** (loss of power) (of government, company, authority, resolve, cause) affaiblissement *m*; (of ties, alliance, friendship) relâchement *m*; **3** Fin (of market, economy, currency) affaiblissement *m*.

weak-kneed /ˌwi:k'ni:d/ *adj* [*person, agreement*] faible, pusillanime.

weakling /'wi:klɪŋ/ *n* **1** (person) (physically) gringalet *m*; (morally) mauviette *f*; **2** (animal) animal *m* chétif.

weakly /'wi:klɪ/ *adv* **1** (without physical force) [*move, struggle*] faiblement; **2** (ineffectually) [*smile, say, protest*] mollement; **a ~-worded protest** une vague protestation.

weak-minded /ˌwi:k'maɪndɪd/ *adj* **1** (indecisive) irrésolu; **2** euph (simple) faible d'esprit.

weakness /'wi:knɪs/ *n* **1** (weak point) (of person, argument, institution) point *m* faible; **2** (liking) faible *m*, penchant *m* (**for** pour); **3** (physical) (of person, limb, eyesight, heart, memory) faiblesse *f*; (of stomach, digestion) délicatesse *f*; (of beam, structure) fragilité *f*; **4** (lack of authority) (of government, army, teacher, plot, argument, protest) faiblesse *f*; (of evidence, position) fragilité *f*; **5** (faintness, dilution) (of light, current, sound, lens, smile, voice) faiblesse *f*; (of tea, solution, concentration) légèreté *f*; **6** Econ, Fin (of economy, pound, dollar) faiblesse *f*.

weak-willed /ˌwi:k'wɪld/ *adj* **to be ~** manquer de fermeté.

weal /wi:l/ *n* **1** (mark) marque *f* (*de coup*); **2‡ the public** ou **common ~** le bien commun.

wealth /welθ/ *n* **1** (possessions) fortune *f*, richesses *fpl*; **2** (state) richesse *f*; **national ~** richesse nationale; **'The Wealth of Nations'** 'La Richesse des Nations'; **3** (resources) richesses *fpl*, ressources *fpl*; **mineral ~** richesses ou ressources minières; **4** (large amount) **a ~ of** une mine de [*information, opportunity*]; une profusion de [*detail, ideas*]; énormément de [*experience, talent*]; un grand nombre de [*books, documents*].

wealth tax *n* GB impôt *m* sur la fortune.

wealthy /'welθɪ/ *adj* riche.

wean /wi:n/ **I** *vtr* **1** lit sevrer [*baby*]; **to ~ a baby onto solids** sevrer un bébé et lui donner une alimentation solide; **2** fig **to ~ sb away from** ou **off sth** détourner qn de qch; **to ~ sb from/onto sth** faire passer qn de/à qch; **to be ~ed on sth** être nourri de qch.
II *v refl* **to ~ oneself off sth** se sevrer de qch.

weaning /'wi:nɪŋ/ *n* sevrage *m*; **early ~** sevrage rapide.

weapon /'wepən/ **I** *n* lit, fig arme *f*; **to use sth as a ~** utiliser qch comme arme.
II *modif* (also **weapons**) [*capability, factory, manufacturer, system*] d'armes.

weaponry /'wepənrɪ/ *n* ¢ matériel *m* de guerre; **antisatellite ~** armement *m* antisatellite.

wear /weə(r)/ **I** *n* ¢ **1** (clothing) vêtements *mpl*; **children's/beach ~** vêtements pour enfants/de plage; **in beach/sports ~** en tenue *f* de plage/de sport; **2** (use) **for everyday ~** de tous les jours; **for summer ~** pour l'été; **to stretch with ~** [*shoes*] s'assouplir à l'usage; **I've had three years' ~ out of these boots** ces bottes m'ont duré trois ans; **there's some ~ left in these tyres** ces pneus ne sont pas encore usés; **there's still a few months' ~ in this shirt** cette chemise peut encore servir quelques mois; **3** (damage) usure *f* (**on** de); **~ and tear** usure *f*; **fair** ou **normal ~ and tear** usure normale; **to stand up to ~** résister à l'usure; **to get hard** ou **heavy ~** servir beaucoup; **there are signs of ~ on the brake linings** les garnitures de freins sont un peu usées; **to show signs of ~** commencer à être usé; **to look the worse for ~** (damaged) être abîmé; **to be somewhat the worse for ~** (drunk) être ivre; (tired) être épuisé.
II *vtr* (*prét* **wore**; *pp* **worn**) **1** (be dressed in) porter [*garment, jewellery, earphones etc*]; **to ~ blue** s'habiller en bleu; **to ~ one's hair long/short** avoir les cheveux longs/courts; **to ~ one's hair in a bun** porter un chignon; **to ~ a ribbon in one's hair** avoir un ruban dans les cheveux; **to ~ one's skirts long** s'habiller long; **to ~ one's clothes loose** aimer les vêtements lâches; **2** (put on) mettre [*garment, jewellery etc*]; **what are you ~ing tonight?** qu'est-ce que tu vas mettre ce soir?; **what should I ~?** qu'est-ce que je devrais mettre?; **I haven't got a thing to ~** je n'ai rien à me mettre; **3** (use) mettre [*perfume, sun-cream*]; **to ~ make-up** se maquiller; **she's ~ing make-up** elle est maquillée; **4** (display) **he** ou **his face wore a puzzled frown** il fronçait les sourcils d'un air perplexe; **her face wore a smug expression** elle avait un air plein de suffisance; **5** (damage by use) user [*carpet, clothes, clutch, component*]; **to be worn to a thread** être usé jusqu'à la corde; **to ~ a hole in** trouer [*garment, sheet*]; **to ~ a track/a groove in** creuser un sentier/une rigole dans; **6**○ (accept) tolérer [*behaviour, attitude*]; accepter [*excuse*].
III *vi* (*prét* **wore**; *pp* **worn**) **1** (become damaged) [*carpet, garment, shoes*] s'user; **my patience is ~ing thin** je commence à être à bout de patience; **2** (withstand use) **a carpet/fabric that will ~ well** un tapis/tissu solide; **he's worn very well** fig il est encore bien pour son âge.
■ **wear away**: ¶ **~ away** [*inscription*] s'effacer; [*tread, cliff, façade*] s'user; ¶ **~ away [sth], ~ [sth] away** [*water*] ronger; [*footsteps, friction, rubbing*] user.
■ **wear down**: ¶ **~ down** [*heel, step, tread*] s'user; **to be worn down** être usé; ¶ **~ down [sth], ~ [sth] down 1** (damage) [*friction, person, water*] user; **2** fig (weaken) saper [*resistance, resolve, will*]; ¶ **~ [sb] down** épuiser.
■ **wear off**: ¶ **~ off 1** (lose effect) [*anaesthetic, drug, effect*] se dissiper; [*feeling, sensation*] passer; **the novelty will soon ~ off** ça n'aura bientôt plus l'attrait de la nouveauté; **2** (come off) [*paint, gold plate*] s'effacer; ¶ **~ [sth] off, ~ off [sth]** faire partir [*paint, varnish*]; effacer [*inscription*].
■ **wear on** [*day, evening*] s'avancer; **as the evening wore on** à mesure que la soirée s'avançait.
■ **wear out**: ¶ **~ out** [*clothes, shoes, equipment*] s'user; **my patience is beginning to ~ out** je commence à perdre patience; ¶ **~ out [sth], ~ [sth] out** user [*clothes, shoes, mechanism*]; **to ~ out one's welcome** lasser l'amabilité de ses hôtes; ¶ **~ [sb] out** épuiser.
■ **wear through**: **~ through** [*elbow, trousers*] se trouer; [*sole, metal, fabric*] se percer.

wearable /'weərəbl/ *adj* mettable.

wearer /'weərə(r)/ *n* **do the clothes suit the ~?** est-ce que ces vêtements vont bien à la personne qui les porte?; **~s of glasses/wigs** les personnes *fpl* qui portent des lunettes/une perruque.

wearily /'wɪərɪlɪ/ *adv* [*sigh, smile, gesture*] d'un air las; [*say, ask, explain*] d'un ton las; **she got ~ to her feet** elle s'est mise debout péniblement; **they trudged ~ home** ils sont rentrés chez eux d'un pas traînant.

weariness /'wɪərɪnɪs/ *n* lassitude *f*.

wearing /'weərɪŋ/ *adj* **1** (exhausting) [*day, job, journey*] fatigant; **it can be ~ doing** c'est parfois fatigant de faire; **2** (irritating) [*behaviour, person*] pénible.

wearing: **~ course** *n* couche *f* de roulement; **~ plate** *n* plaque *f* d'usure.

wearisome /'wɪərɪsəm/ *adj* sout [*task, process*] fastidieux/-ieuse; [*child, day*] pénible; [*complaints, demands, opposition*] lassant; **it's a ~ business** c'est vraiment pénible.

weary /'wɪərɪ/ **I** *adj* **1** (physically) [*person*] las/lasse; [*eyes, limbs, mind*] fatigué; **to feel ~** se sentir las; **to look ~** avoir l'air fatigué; **they are ~ from lack of sleep** le manque de sommeil les a fatigués; **2** (showing fatigue) [*smile, sigh, voice, gesture*] las/lasse; **3** (mentally) [*person*] las/lasse (**of** de; **of doing** de faire); **to be ~ of being alone** être las/lasse de la solitude; **to grow ~** se lasser (**of** de; **of doing** de faire); **4** (tiresome) [*journey, task, day*] fatigant; [*routine*] lassant.
II *vtr* lasser, fatiguer.
III *vi* se lasser (**of** de; **of doing** de faire).

weasel /'wi:zl/ **I** *n* **1** Zool belette *f*; **2** péj (sly person) sournois/-e *m/f*.
II *adj* (also **weaselly**) péj [*face, features, manner*] chafouin; [*argument*] retors; **~ words** mots *mpl* équivoques.
III *vtr* (*p prés etc* **-ll-** GB, **-l-** US) **to ~ one's way into** s'insinuer dans; **to ~ sth out of sb** soutirer qch de qn.
IV *vi* (*p prés etc* **-ll-** GB, **-l-** US) **to ~ out of a responsibility** se défiler○; **to ~ out of doing** se débrouiller pour ne pas faire.

weather /'weðə(r)/ **I** *n* temps *m*; **good/bad ~** beau/mauvais temps; **wet/hot/wintry ~** temps humide/chaud/d'hiver; **what's the ~ like?** quel temps fait-il? **the ~ here is hot** il fait chaud ici; **in hot/cold ~** quand il fait chaud/froid; **you can't go out in this ~!** tu ne peux pas sortir par un temps pareil!; **a change in the ~** un changement de temps; **when the good ~ comes** quand il fera beau; **if the ~ breaks** si le temps change; **if the ~ clears up** si le temps s'arrange; **perfect ~ for** un temps idéal pour [*picnics, skiing*]; **~ permitting** si le temps le permet; **in all ~s** par tous les temps; **whatever the ~** lit par tous les temps; fig qu'il pleuve ou qu'il vente.
II *modif* [*chart, check, conditions, map, pattern, satellite, station*] météorologique; [*centre, bureau, study*] de météorologie.
III *vtr* **1** (withstand, survive) essuyer [*gale, storm*]; se tirer de [*crisis, upheaval, recession, bad patch*]; **to ~ the storm** fig surmonter la crise; **2** [*elements, wind, rain*] éroder [*rocks, stone*]; battre [*landscape, hills*]; [*rain, wind*] hâler [*face*].
IV *vi* [*rocks, landscape*] s'éroder; **this stone ~s well** cette pierre prend une belle patine; **he has not ~ed well** fig il n'a pas bien vieilli.
V weathered *pp adj* [*stone, rock, finish, wood*] patiné; [*face, skin*] hâlé.
IDIOMS **to be under the ~** ne pas se sentir bien; **to be ~-wise** flairer d'où vient le vent; **to keep a ~ eye on sb/sth** avoir qn/qch à l'œil; **to keep a** ou **one's ~ eye open** veiller au grain; **to make heavy ~ of sth** avoir du mal à faire qch; **to make heavy ~ of doing** faire toute une histoire pour faire○; **he made heavy ~ of it** il en a fait tout un plat○.

weather balloon *n* ballon-sonde *m* météorologique.

weatherbeaten /'weðəbi:tn/ *adj* [*face, features, skin*] hâlé; [*building, stone, brick*] érodé; [*rocks, cliffs, landscape*] battu (par les vents).

weatherboard /'weðəbɔ:d/ *n* **1** (clapboard) bordage *m* à clins; **2** (fitted to door) planche *f* de recouvrement.

weather: **~cock** *n* girouette *f*; **~ forecast** *n* bulletin *m* météorologique, météo *f*; **~ forecaster** ▶ 1692 *n* (on TV) présentateur/-trice *m/f* de la météo; (in weather centre) météorologue *mf*, météorologiste *mf*;

~glass *n* baromètre *m*; **~ house** *n* baromètre *m* suisse; **~man**○ *n* (on TV) = **weather forecaster**.

weatherproof /ˈweðəpru:f/ **I** *adj* [*garment, shoe*] imperméable; [*shelter, door*] étanche.
II *vtr* imperméabiliser [*fabric, garment*].

weather: **~ report** *n* = **weather forecast**; **~ ship** *n* navire *m* météo.

weatherstrip /ˈweðəstrɪp/ US **I** *n* bourrelet *m* (*contre les courants d'air*).
II *vtr* mettre du bourrelet à [*door, window*].

weather vane *n* girouette *f*.

weave /wi:v/ **I** *n* tissage *m*; **open ~**, **loose ~** tissage lâche; **close ~**, **fine ~** tissage serré or fin.
II *vtr* (*prét* **wove** ou **weaved**; *pp* **woven** ou **weaved**) **1** Tex tisser [*thread, fabric, blanket, rug*]; **to ~ sth on a loom** tisser qch sur un métier; **to ~ silk into cloth**, **to ~ cloth out of silk** tisser de l'étoffe de soie; **2** (interlace, make by interlacing) tresser [*cane, raffia, flowers, basket, garland, wreath*]; [*spider*] tisser [*web*]; **to ~ sth out of sth** tresser qch de qch; **to ~ flowers into a garland** tresser une guirlande de fleurs; **3** fig (create) inventer [*story, narrative, plot*]; **to ~ the plot around one's own experience** inventer l'intrigue à partir de sa propre expérience; **to ~ sth into sth** introduire qch dans qch; **to ~ together sth and sth** mêler qch à qch; **to ~ two things together** mêler deux choses; **the writer ~s a spell** l'écrivain nous tient sous le charme; **4** (move) **to ~ one's way through/around sth** se faufiler entre/autour de qch; **to ~ a path through sth** s'ouvrir un chemin à travers qch.
III *vi* (*prét* **wove** ou **weaved**; *pp* **woven** ou **weaved**) **to ~ in and out** se faufiler (**of** entre); **he was weaving in and out of the traffic** il se faufilait entre les voitures; **to ~ between** se faufiler entre; **to ~ towards sth** (drunk) s'approcher en titubant de qch; (avoiding obstacles) se frayer un chemin vers qch; **he was weaving unsteadily** il titubait.
IV woven *pp adj* [*cloth, jacket*] tissé.
IDIOMS **to get weaving on** ou **with sth** se mettre à qch; **get weaving!** remue-toi!

weaver /ˈwi:və(r)/ **▶ 1692** *n* **1** (person) tisserand/-e *m/f*; **2** = **weaverbird**.

weaverbird /ˈwi:vəbɜ:d/ *n* tisserin *m*.

weaving /ˈwi:vɪŋ/ **I** n tissage *m*; **to do ~** faire du tissage.
II *modif* [*frame, machine, machinery*] à tisser; [*workshop, factory, mill*] de tissage; [*trade, industry*] du tissage.

web /web/ *n* **1** (also **spider's ~**) toile *f* (d'araignée); **2** fig **a ~ of** un réseau de [*ropes, lines*]; un écheveau de [*laws, regulations, interests*]; **a ~ of lies** ou **deceit** un tissu de mensonges; **3** Anat, Zool (in animals) palmure *f*; (in humans) palmature *f*.

Web /web/ Comput **I** *n* Web *m*.
II *modif* [*page, site, server*] Web.

webbing /ˈwebɪŋ/ *n* ¢ **1** (material) sangles *fpl*; **2** Anat, Zool (of bird, animal) palmure *f*; (of human) palmature *f*.

web: **~-fed** *adj* Print alimenté par bobine; **~ foot** *n* (*pl* **web feet**) patte *f* palmée.

Webmaster /webmɑ:stə(r)/ *n* administrateur/-trice *m/f* de site Internet.

web: **~ offset** *n* Print impression *f* offset en continu; **~ press** *n* rotative *f* à bobine.

wed /wed/ **I** *n* **the newly ~s** les jeunes mariés *mpl*.
II *vtr* (*p prés etc* **-dd-**; *prét, pp* **wedded** ou **wed**) **1** (get married to) épouser [*man, woman*]; **to get wed** se marier; **to be wed** être marié; **2** (marry) [*priest*] unir [*couple*]; **3** fig (unite) allier [*qualities*]; **in him are ~ded charm and ambition** il allie le charme à l'ambition; **to ~ sth with** allier qch à; **to be ~ded to** être attaché à.
III *vi* (*p prés etc* **-dd-**; *prét, pp* **wedded** ou **wed**) se marier.
IV wedded *pp adj* [*man, woman*] marié; **~ded bliss** hum bonheur *m* conjugal; **my lawful ~ded wife** mon épouse légitime.

we'd /wi:d/ = **we had**, **we would**.

Wed *abrév écrite* = **Wednesday**.

wedding /ˈwedɪŋ/ **I** *n* **1** (marriage) mariage *m*; **a church ~** un mariage religieux; **2** (also **~ anniversary**) noces *fpl*; **our silver ~** nos noces d'argent.
II *modif* [*anniversary, cake, ceremony, feast, present*] de mariage.

wedding band† *n* = **wedding ring**.

wedding bells *npl* lit cloches *fpl*; **I can hear ~** fig je crois qu'il y a un mariage dans l'air.

wedding: **~ breakfast** *n* repas *m* de mariage; **~ day** *n* jour *m* des noces; **~ dress**, **~ gown** *n* robe *f* de mariée; **~ guest** *n* invité/-e *m/f* au mariage; **~ invitation** *n* invitation *f* à un mariage; **~ march** *n* marche *f* nuptiale; **~ night** *n* nuit *f* de noces; **~ reception** *n* repas *m* de mariage; **~ ring** *n* alliance *f*; **~ vows** *n* vœux *mpl*.

wedge /wedʒ/ **I** *n* **1** (block) (to insert in rock, wood etc) coin *m*; (to hold sth in position) cale *f*; (in rockclimbing) piton *m*; (of cake, pie, cheese) morceau *m*; **a ~ of lemon** une tranche de citron; **a ~ of high pressure** Meteorol une dorsale barométrique; **a ~ of geese** un vol d'oies; **2** Sport (in golf) cocheur *m* de sable; **3** Fashn (heel) semelle *f* compensée; (shoe) chaussure *f* à semelle compensée.
II *modif* **1** Fashn [*shoe*] à semelle compensée; **~-heeled** à semelle compensée; **2** gen [*shape*] de coin; **~-shaped** en forme de coin.
III *vtr* **1** (make firm) **to ~ sth in** ou **into place** caler qch; **to ~ a door open/shut** caler une porte pour la tenir ouverte/fermée; **the door is ~d shut** (stuck) la porte est coincée; **2** (jam) **to ~ sth into** enfoncer or faire rentrer qch dans [*gap, hole*]; **to be ~d against/between** être coincé contre/entre.
IV *v refl* **to ~ oneself** se coincer (**between** entre; **in** dans); **to get oneself ~d** se coincer.
IDIOMS **to drive a ~ between X and Y** monter X contre Y; **it's (only) the thin end of the ~** ce n'est qu'un début.
■ **wedge in**: **~ [sb/sth] in**, **~ in [sb/sth]** coincer [qn/qch].

wedlock† /ˈwedlɒk/ *n* mariage *m*; **to enter into ~** contracter mariage; **to be born in/out of ~** naître de parents mariés/non mariés; **to have a child out of ~** avoir un enfant sans être marié.

Wednesday /ˈwenzdeɪ, -dɪ/ **▶ 1883** *n* mercredi *m*.

wee /wi:/ **I** *n*○ GB pipi○ *m*; **to do** ou **have a ~** faire pipi.
II *adj* (tout) petit; **a ~ bit** un (tout) petit peu; **(in the) ~ small hours** (aux) petites heures.
III *vi*○ GB faire pipi.

weed /wi:d/ **I** *n* **1** Bot (wild plant) mauvaise herbe *f*; **overgrown with ~s** envahi de mauvaises herbes; **to pull up ~s** enlever les mauvaises herbes; **2** ¢ Bot (in water) herbes *fpl* aquatiques; **3**○ GB péj (weakling) mauviette○ *f* pej; **don't be such a ~!** quelle vraie mauviette○!; **4**○ hum (tobacco) **the ~** le tabac; **5**○ (marijuana) herbe○ *f*, marijuana *f*; **▶ widow's weeds**.
II *vtr* désherber.
III *vi* désherber.
■ **weed out**: ¶ **~ [sb] out**, **~ out [sb]** éliminer [*candidate, client, dissident*]; se débarrasser de [*employee*]; ¶ **~ [sth] out**, **~ out [sth]** se débarrasser de [*stock, items*]; arracher [*dead plants*].

weeding /ˈwi:dɪŋ/ *n* désherbage *m*; **to do some ~** désherber.

weedkiller /ˈwi:dkɪlə(r)/ *n* désherbant *m*, herbicide *m*.

weedy /ˈwi:dɪ/ *adj* **1**○ péj [*person, build*] malingre; [*character, personality*] faible; **2** (full of weeds) [*garden*] envahi de mauvaises herbes; [*pond*] envahi d'herbes aquatiques.

week /wi:k/ *n* **▶ 1807** semaine *f*; **what day of the ~ is it?** quel jour de la semaine sommes-nous?; **this ~** cette semaine; **last/next ~** la semaine dernière/prochaine; **the ~ before last** il y a deux semaines; **the ~ after next** dans deux semaines; **every ~** toutes les semaines; **every other ~** tous les quinze jours; **twice a ~** deux fois par semaine; **for ~s** pendant des semaines; **I'll do it some time this ~** je le ferai dans le courant de la semaine; **~s and ~s** des semaines et des semaines; **~ in ~ out** toutes les semaines; **a ~ today/on Monday** GB, **a ~ from today/Monday** US, **today/Monday ~** aujourd'hui/lundi en huit; **a ~ yesterday** GB, **a ~ from yesterday** US il y a eu huit jours or une semaine hier; **a ~ (ago) last Saturday** il y a eu huit jours or une semaine samedi; **six ~s ago** il y a six semaines; **~s ago** il y a des semaines; **in three ~s time** dans trois semaines; **a six-~-old baby** un bébé de six semaines; **a six-~ contract** un contrat de six semaines; **a ~'s wages/rent** une semaine de salaire/de loyer; **to pay by the ~** payer à la semaine; **during the ~** gen pendant la semaine; (Monday to Friday) en semaine; **a 40-hour ~** une semaine de 40 heures; **the working** ou **work** US **~** la semaine de travail; **the ~ ending June 10** la semaine du 3 au 10 juin.
IDIOMS **he doesn't know what day of the ~ it is** il est complètement dans les nuages; **to knock sb into the middle of next ~**○ flanquer une bonne raclée à qn○.

weekday /ˈwi:kdeɪ/ **I** *n* jour *m* de (la) semaine, jour *m* ouvrable; **on ~s** en semaine.
II *modif* [*evening, morning, programme*] de la semaine; [*train*] circulant du lundi au vendredi; [*flight*] assuré du lundi au vendredi; [*timetable*] valable du lundi au vendredi.

weekend /ˌwi:kˈend, US ˈwi:k-/ **I** *n* week-end *m*, fin *f* de semaine; **last/next ~** le week-end dernier/prochain; **this ~** ce week-end; **for the ~** pour le week-end; **the ~ after (that)** le week-end suivant; **a long ~** un long week-end; **at the ~** GB, **on the ~** US pendant le week-end; **at ~s** GB, **on ~s** US le week-end.
II *modif* [*break, excursion*] de week-end; [*performance, programme*] du samedi et du dimanche; **~ bag** petit sac *m* de voyage; **~ cottage** résidence *f* secondaire; **~ ticket** ticket *m* valable (uniquement) le week-end.
III *vi* passer le week-end.

weekender /ˌwi:kˈendə(r), US ˈwi:k-/ *n* **1** (person) **houses owned by ~s** des maisons appartenant à des gens qui viennent passer le weekend; **2** US (bag) petit sac *m* de voyage.

weekly /ˈwi:klɪ/ **I** *n* (newspaper) journal *m* hebdomadaire; (magazine) (revue *f*) hebdomadaire *m*.
II *adj* [*visit, service, payment, shopping*] hebdomadaire; **on a ~ basis** à la semaine.
III *adv* [*pay*] à la semaine; [*check*] chaque semaine; [*meet, leave*] une fois par semaine.

ween○ /wi:n/ *n* US péj bûcheur/-euse○ *m/f*.

weenie○ /ˈwi:nɪ/ *n* US **1** péj (weak person) lavette○ *f*; **2** lang enfantin (penis) zizi○ *m*.

weeny○ /ˈwi:nɪ/ *adj* **1** (tiny) tout petit; **2** US = **weenie**.

weep /wi:p/ **I** *n* **to have a little ~** verser quelques larmes.
II *vtr* (*prét, pp* **wept**) **to ~ tears of joy** verser des larmes de joie.
III *vi* (*prét, pp* **wept**) **1** (cry) pleurer (**over** sur); **to ~ with** pleurer de [*relief, joy, exhaustion*]; **to ~ for sb** pleurer sur le sort de qn; **it's enough to make you ~!** c'est à pleurer!; **2** (ooze) [*wound, wall, joint*] suinter.

The days of the week

Note that the French uses lower-case letters for the names of days; also, French speakers normally count the week as starting on Monday.

Write the names of days in full; do not abbreviate as in English (Tues, Sat *and so on*). *The French only abbreviate in printed calendars, diaries etc.*

Monday = lundi
Tuesday = mardi
Wednesday = mercredi
Thursday = jeudi
Friday = vendredi
Saturday = samedi
Sunday = dimanche

What day is it?

(Lundi *in this note stands for any day; they all work the same way; for more information on dates in French* ▶ **1150**.)

what day is it? = quel jour sommes-nous? *or* (*very informally*) on est quel jour?
it is Monday = nous sommes lundi
today is Monday = c'est lundi aujourd'hui

Note the use of French le *for regular occurrences, and no article for single ones.* (*Remember: do not translate* on.)

on Monday = lundi
on Monday, we're going to the zoo = lundi, on va au zoo
I'll see you on Monday morning = je te verrai lundi matin

but

on Mondays = le lundi
on Mondays, we go to the zoo = le lundi, on va au zoo
I see her on Monday mornings = je la vois le lundi matin

Specific days

Monday afternoon = lundi après-midi
one Monday evening = un lundi soir
that Monday morning = ce lundi matin-là
last Monday night = la nuit de lundi dernier *or* (*if evening*) lundi dernier dans la soirée
early on Monday = lundi matin de bonne heure
late on Monday = lundi soir tard
this Monday = ce lundi
that Monday = ce lundi-là
that very Monday = précisément ce lundi-là
last Monday = lundi dernier
next Monday = lundi prochain
the Monday before last = l'autre lundi
a month from Monday = dans un mois lundi
in a month from last Monday = dans un mois à dater de lundi dernier
finish it by Monday = termine-le avant lundi
from Monday on = à partir de lundi

Regular events

every Monday = tous les lundis
each Monday = chaque lundi
every other Monday = un lundi sur deux
every third Monday = un lundi sur trois

Sometimes

most Mondays = presque tous les lundis
some Mondays = certains lundis
on the second Monday in the month = le deuxième lundi de chaque mois
the odd Monday *or* the occasional Monday = le lundi de temps en temps

Happening etc. on that day

Monday's paper = le journal de lundi *or* de ce lundi
the Monday papers = les journaux du lundi
Monday flights = les vols du lundi
the Monday flight = le vol du lundi
Monday closing (*of shops*) = la fermeture du lundi
Monday's classes = les cours de lundi *or* de ce lundi
Monday classes = les cours du lundi
Monday trains = les trains du lundi

Weight measurement

Note that French has a comma where English has a decimal point.

1 oz = 28,35 g* (*grammes*)
1 lb† = 453,60 g
1 st = 6,35 kg (*kilos*)
1 cwt = 50,73 kg
1 ton = 1014,60 kg

* *There are three ways of saying 28,35 g, and other measurements like it:* vingt-huit virgule trente-cinq grammes, *or* (*less formally*) vingt-huit grammes virgule trente-cinq, *or* vingt-huit grammes trente-cinq.
For more details on how to say numbers, ▶ **1505**.

† *English* a pound *is translated by* une livre *in French, but note that the French* livre *is actually 500 grams* (*half a kilo*).

People

what's his weight? = combien pèse-t-il?
how much does he weigh? = combien pèse-t-il?
he weighs 10 st (*or* 140 lbs) = il pèse 63 kg 500 (soixante-trois kilos et demi)
he weighs more than 20 st = il pèse plus de 127 kilos

Things

what does the parcel weigh? = combien pèse le colis?
how heavy is it? = quel poids fait-il?
it weighs ten kilos = il pèse dix kilos
about ten kilos = environ dix kilos
it was 2 kilos over weight = il pesait deux kilos de trop
A weighs more than B = A pèse plus lourd que B
A is heavier than B = A est plus lourd que B
B is lighter than A = B est plus léger que A
A is as heavy as B = A est aussi lourd que B
A is the same weight as B = A a le même poids que B
A and B are the same weight = A et B ont le même poids
6 lbs of carrots = six livres de carottes
2 kilos of butter = deux kilos de beurre
1½ kilos of tomatoes = un kilo cinq cents de tomates
sold by the kilo = vendu au kilo
there are about two pounds to a kilo = il y a à peu près deux livres anglaises dans un kilo

Note the French construction with de, *coming after the noun it describes:*

a 3-lb potato = une pomme de terre de trois livres
a parcel 3 kilos in weight = un colis de trois kilos

weepie○ /ˈwiːpɪ/ *n* (film) mélo○ *m*.

weeping /ˈwiːpɪŋ/ **I** *n* ₵ pleurs *mpl*.
II *adj* (*épith*) **1** [*person*] qui pleure; **2** [*wound*] qui suinte.

weeping willow *n* saule *m* pleureur.

weepy /ˈwiːpɪ/ **I** *n* = **weepie**.
II *adj* [*person*] au bord des larmes; [*mood, voice, book, film*] larmoyant.

weever /ˈwiːvə(r)/ *n* vive *f*.

weevil /ˈwiːvɪl/ *n* charançon *m*.

weewee /ˈwiːwiː/ *n, vi* lang enfantin = **wee** I, III.

weft /weft/ *n* trame *f*.

weigh /weɪ/ **I** *vtr* **1** lit peser [*object, person, quantity*]; **to ~ 10 kilos** peser 10 kilos; **how much** ou **what do you ~?** combien pèses-tu?; **to ~ sth in one's hand** soupeser qch; **2** (consider carefully) évaluer [*advantages, arguments, evidence, factors, options, points*]; peser [*consequences, risk, words*]; **to ~ the pros and cons** peser le pour et le contre; **to ~ sth against sth** mettre en balance qch et qch; **to ~ sth in the balance** évaluer soigneusement qch; **to be ~ed in the balance and found wanting** être jugé et ne pas résister à l'examen; **3** Naut **to ~ anchor** lever l'ancre.
II *vi* **1** (have influence) **to ~ with sb** compter pour qn; **to ~ heavily/very little with sb** compter beaucoup/ très peu pour qn; **to ~ against sb** faire du tort à qn; **to ~ in sb's favour** jouer en faveur de qn; **2** (be a burden) **to ~ on sb** peser sur qn; **the responsibility ~s heavily on her** la charge lui pèse; **to ~ on sb's conscience** peser sur la conscience de qn; **to ~ on sb's mind** préoccuper qn.
III *v refl* **to ~ oneself** se peser.
■ **weigh down**: ¶ **~ down on [sb/sth]** peser sur [*person, object*]; ¶ **~ down [sth/sb], ~ [sth/sb] down** lit surcharger [*vehicle, boat*]; faire plier [*branches, tree*]; bloquer [*papers, sheet*]; fig [*responsibility, anxiety, debt*] accabler [*person*]; **to be ~ed down with** [*person*] crouler sous le poids de [*luggage*]; être comblé de [*gifts, prizes*]; être accablé de [*worry , guilt*].
■ **weigh in 1** [*boxer, wrestler*] se faire peser; [*jockey*] aller au pesage; **to ~ in at 60 kg** peser 60 kilos (*avant la course ou le combat*); **2** (contribute to appeal, effort) contribuer; **to ~ in with sth** donner qch; **3** (intervene in debate) intervenir; **to ~ in with one's opinion** intervenir en donnant son opinion.
■ **weigh out** peser [*ingredients, quantity*].
■ **weigh up**: **~ up [sth/sb], ~ [sth/sb] up 1** fig évaluer [*prospects, situation*]; juger [*stranger, opponent*]; mettre [qch] en balance [*options, benefits, risks*]; **after ~ing things up, I decided**... tout bien pesé, j'ai décidé...; **2** lit peser [*fruit, coal*].

weigh: **~bridge** *n* pont-bascule *m*; **~-in** *n* Sport pesage *m*.

weighing machine /ˈweɪɪŋ məʃiːn/ *n* **1** (for people) balance *f*; **2** (for luggage, freight) bascule *f*.

weighing scales *n* balance *f*.

weight /weɪt/ **I** *n* **1** (heaviness) poids *m*; **to lose/put on ~** perdre/prendre du poids; **to be under/over 1 kilo in ~** avoir un poids inférieur/supérieur à 1 kilo; **by ~** au poids; **what is your ~?** combien pesez-vous?; **to be twice sb's ~** peser deux fois plus que qn; **they're the same ~** ils font le même poids; **to put one's full ~ on/against sth** appuyer de tout son poids sur/contre qch; **to put one's full ~ behind**

a blow frapper de toutes ses forces; **he's quite a ~!** il est drôlement lourd!; **2** (system of measurement) poids *m*; **unit of ~** unité *f* de poids; **3** (object of a fixed heaviness) poids *m*; **a 25 gramme ~** un poids de 25 grammes; **to lift ~s** soulever des poids; **what a ~!** quel poids! **the ~ of responsibility** le poids des responsabilités; **to sink under the ~ of sth** fig crouler sous le poids de qch; **to carry ~** [*horse*] être handicapé; **4** fig (credibility, influence) poids *m*; **of some intellectual ~** d'un certain poids intellectuel; **to add** ou **give** ou **lend ~ to sth** ajouter or donner du poids à qch; **not to carry much ~** ne pas peser lourd (**with** pour); **what she says carries ~** elle a du poids or de l'influence (**with** auprès de); **to add one's ~ to sth** faire jouer son influence en faveur de qch; **to throw one's ~ behind sth** soutenir qch à fond; **5** fig (importance, consideration) **to give due ~ to a proposal** accorder à une proposition l'importance qu'elle mérite; **to give equal ~ to** accorder une importance égale à; **6** (in statistics) coefficient *m* pondérateur.

II *vtr* **1** (put weight(s) on) lester [*net, hem, dart, arrow, boat*]; **2** (bias) **to ~ sth against sb/sth** faire jouer qch contre qn/qch; **to ~ sth in favour of sb/sth** faire jouer qch en faveur de qn/qch; **3** (in statistics) pondérer [*index, variable, average, figure*].

IDIOMS **by (sheer) ~ of numbers** par la force du nombre; **to be a ~ off one's mind** être un grand soulagement; **to pull one's ~** faire sa part de travail; **to take the ~ off one's feet** s'asseoir, se reposer; **to throw one's ~ about** ou **around** faire l'important/-e *m/f*.

■ **weight down**: **~ down [sth]**, **~ [sth] down** retenir [qch] avec un poids [*paper, sheet*] (**with** avec); lester [*body*].

weightiness /ˈweɪtɪnɪs/ *n* importance *f* (**of** de).

weighting /ˈweɪtɪŋ/ *n* (of index, variable) pondération *f*; **London ~** indemnité *f* pour résidence à Londres.

weightless /ˈweɪtlɪs/ *adj* **1** lit [*state, environment*] d'apesanteur (*after n*); [*body, object in space*] en apesanteur (*after n*); **2** fig [*grace, movement*] léger/-ère.

weightlessness /ˈweɪtlɪsnɪs/ *n* **1** (in space) apesanteur *f*; **2** (of dancer, dance) légèreté *f* aérienne.

weight: **~-lifter** *n* haltérophile *m*; **~-lifting ▶1282** *n* haltérophilie *f*; **~ loss** *n* perte *f* de poids; **~ machine** *n* appareil *m* de musculation; **~ problem** *n* problème *m* de poids; **~ training ▶1282** *n* musculation *f* (en salle); **~watcher** *n* gen personne *f* qui surveille son poids; (member of group) personne *f* qui suit un régime amaigrissant.

weighty /ˈweɪtɪ/ *adj* **1** (serious) [*problem, consideration, reason, question*] de grand poids; **2** (large) [*book, treatise*] monumental; **3** (heavy) [*object, responsibility*] lourd.

weir /wɪə(r)/ *n* **1** (dam) barrage *m*; **2** (for trapping fish) écluse *f* à poissons.

weird /wɪəd/ *adj* **1** (strange) bizarre; **it's ~ that** c'est bizarre que (+ *subj*); **~ and wonderful** étrange et merveilleux/-euse; **2** (eerie) mystérieux/-ieuse.

weirdly /ˈwɪədlɪ/ *adj* **1** (strangely) bizarrement; **2** (eerily) mystérieusement.

weirdo° /ˈwɪədəʊ/ *n* loufoque° *mf*.

welcome /ˈwelkəm/ **I** *n* accueil *m*; **to give sb a warm ~, to extend a warm ~ to sb** fml faire un accueil chaleureux à qn.

II *modif* [*speech*] de bienvenue.

III *adj* **1** (gratefully received) [*boost, initiative, relief, news*] bienvenu; **that's a ~ sight/sound!** ça fait plaisir à voir/entendre!; **nothing could be more ~!** rien ne pourrait tomber plus à propos!; **thank you for your most ~ gift** sout merci de votre cadeau des plus opportuns fml; **2** (warmly greeted) **to be ~, to be a ~ guest** ou **visitor** être le bienvenu; **'children ~'** (on sign) 'les enfants sont les bienvenus'; **I never feel very ~ at their house** je ne me sens jamais le bienvenu chez eux; **to make sb ~** (on arrival) réserver un bon accueil à qn; (over period of time) accueillir qn à bras ouverts; **3** (warmly invited) **you are ~ to spend a few days with us** si vous voulez passer quelques jours chez nous, n'hésitez pas or vous êtes le bienvenu; **if you want to finish my fries you're ~ to them** (politely) si tu veux finir mes frites, ne te gêne pas; **if you want to watch such rubbish you're ~ to it!** (rudely) si tu veux regarder ces idioties, libre à toi!; **you're ~** (acknowledging thanks) de rien, je vous en prie fml.

IV *excl* **~!** (to respected guest) soyez le bienvenu chez nous!; (greeting friend) entre donc!; **~ back, ~ home!** je suis content que tu sois de retour!; **~ on board/to the United States!** bienvenu à bord/aux États-Unis!

V *vtr* accueillir [*person*]; se réjouir de [*news, decision, intervention, change*]; être heureux/-euse de recevoir [*donation, contribution*]; accueillir favorablement [*initiative, move*]; **they said they would ~ a meeting** ils ont dit qu'ils souhaiteraient une rencontre; **we would ~ your view on this matter** nous aimerions savoir ce que vous pensez de cette affaire; **I ~ this opportunity to express my thanks** je suis heureux/-euse d'avoir l'occasion d'exprimer ma gratitude; **'please ~ our guest tonight, Willie Mays'** 'applaudissons notre invité d'honneur, Willie Mays'; **I'd ~ a hot drink** je prendrais bien une boisson chaude.

IDIOMS **to put out the ~ mat for sb** fig faire un accueil chaleureux à qn; **to wear out one's ~** abuser de l'hospitalité de qn; **to ~ sb with open arms** accueillir qn à bras ouverts.

■ **welcome back**: **~ back [sb]**, **~ [sb] back** accueillir [qn] à son retour; (more demonstratively) faire fête à [qn] à son retour.

■ **welcome in**: **~ in [sb]**, **~ [sb] in** faire entrer [qn] chez soi.

welcoming /ˈwelkəmɪŋ/ *adj* **1** (warm) [*atmosphere, smile, person*] accueillant; **2** (reception) [*ceremony, committee*] d'accueil.

weld /weld/ **I** *n* soudure *f*.

II *vtr* **1** lit souder [*metal, joint*] (**on, to** à); **2** fig souder [*team, nation, workforce*].

III *vi* [*metal, joint*] être soudé ensemble.

■ **weld together**: **~ [sth] together** lit, fig souder.

welded /ˈweldɪd/ *adj* lit, fig soudé.

welder /ˈweldə(r)/ **▶1692** *n* **1** (person) soudeur/-euse *m/f*; **2** (tool) appareil *m* à souder.

welding /ˈweldɪŋ/ *n* **1** lit soudage *m*; **2** fig union *f*.

welfare /ˈwelfeə(r)/ **I** *n* **1** gen (well-being) bien-être *m inv*; (interest) intérêt *m*; **national ~** intérêt national; **student ~** intérêts *mpl* des étudiants; **to be concerned about sb's ~** se faire du souci pour le sort de qn; **to be responsible for sb's ~** avoir la responsabilité de qn; **2** (state assistance) assistance *f* sociale; (money) aide *f* sociale; **to go on ~** US demander l'aide sociale; **to be (living) on ~** US vivre de l'aide sociale.

II *modif* [*system*] de protection sociale; US [*meal*] gratuit; **~ cuts** réductions *fpl* dans les dépenses sociales; **~ spending** dépenses *fpl* sociales.

welfare: **~ adviser** *n* US = **welfare rights adviser**; **~ assistant ▶1692** *n* GB Sch ≈ femme *f* de service; **~ benefit** *n* prestation *f* sociale; **~ department** *n* service *m* d'aide sociale; **~ hotel** *n* US foyer *m* d'accueil; **~ mother** *n* US *mère seule bénéficiant de l'aide sociale*; **~ officer ▶1692** *n* GB conseiller/-ère *m/f* en matière d'assistance sociale; US employé/-e *m/f* des services sociaux; **~ payment** *n* = **welfare benefit**; **~ recipient** *n* bénéficiaire *mf* de l'aide sociale; **~ rights adviser ▶1692** *n* GB conseiller/-ère *m/f* en matière d'assistance sociale; **~ services** *n* services *mpl* sociaux.

welfare state *n* (as concept) État-providence *m*; (stressing state assistance) protection *f* sociale; **to be dependent on the ~** survivre grâce à l'aide sociale; **a ~ mentality** péj une mentalité d'assisté.

welfare: **~ work** *n* assistance *f* sociale; **~ worker ▶1692** *n* employé/-e *m/f* des services d'assistance sociale.

welfarism /ˈwelfeərɪzəm/ *n* doctrine *f* de l'État-providence.

welfarist /ˈwelfeərɪst/ *n* apôtre *m* de la protection sociale.

welfarite° /ˈwelfeəraɪt/ *n* US péj assisté/-e *m/f*.

welkin /ˈwelkɪn/ *n* littér voûte *f* céleste.

well[1] /wel/ **I** *adj, comp* **better**, *superl* **best** **1** (in good health) **to feel ~** se sentir bien; **are you ~?** vous allez bien?, tu vas bien?; **I'm very ~, thank you** je vais très bien, merci; **she's not ~ enough to travel** elle n'est pas en état de voyager; **he's not a ~ man** il a des problèmes de santé; **people who are ~ don't need doctors** les gens qui se portent bien n'ont pas besoin de médecin; **she doesn't look at all ~** elle n'a pas l'air en forme du tout; **to get ~** se rétablir; **get ~ soon!** rétablis-toi vite!; **'how is he?'—'as ~ as can be expected'** 'comment va-t-il?'—'pas trop mal étant donné les circonstances'; **2** (in satisfactory state, condition) bien; **all is ~** tout va bien; **she began to fear that all was not ~** elle commençait à craindre qu'il y eût un problème; **all is not ~ in their marriage** il y a des problèmes dans leur mariage; **I hope all is ~ with you** j'espère que tout va bien pour vous; **all being ~, I'll be home before six** si tout va bien, je serai à la maison avant six heures; **that's all very ~, but** tout ça c'est bien beau or joli, mais; **it's all very ~ to go on strike, but** c'est bien beau or joli de faire la grève, mais; **it's all very ~ for you to laugh, but** tu peux rire, mais; **that's all very ~ for him, but some of us have to work for a living** tant mieux pour lui, mais certains d'entre nous doivent gagner leur vie; **if you think you can cope on your own, ~ and good** si tu penses que tu peux te débrouiller tout seul, c'est très bien; **3** (advisable, prudent) **it would be just as ~ to check** il vaudrait mieux vérifier; **it would be as ~ for you not to get involved** tu ferais mieux de ne pas t'en mêler; **it might be as ~ to telephone first** il vaudrait mieux téléphoner d'abord, ce serait peut-être aussi bien de téléphoner d'abord; **4** (fortunate) **it was just as ~ for him that the shops were still open** il a eu de la chance que les magasins étaient encore ouverts; **it's just as ~ you're not hungry, because I didn't buy any food** c'est aussi bien que tu n'aies pas faim, parce que je n'ai rien acheté à manger; **the flight was delayed, which was just as ~** le vol a été retardé, ce qui n'était pas plus mal.

II *adv*, (*comp* **better**, *superl* **best**) **1** (satisfactorily) [*treat, behave, feed, eat, sleep, perform etc*] bien; **to work ~** [*person*] bien travailler, [*system*] bien marcher; **these scissors cut ~** ces ciseaux coupent bien; **he isn't eating very ~** il ne mange pas beaucoup; **she can play the piano as ~ as her sister** elle joue du piano aussi bien que sa sœur; **that boy will do ~** ce garçon ira loin; **he hasn't done as ~ as he might** il n'a pas réussi aussi bien qu'il aurait pu; **I did ~ in the general knowledge questions** je me suis bien débrouillé pour les questions de culture générale; **to do ~ at school** être bon/bonne élève; **mother and baby are both doing ~** la mère et l'enfant se portent bien; **the operation went ~** l'opération s'est bien passée; **you did ~ to tell me** tu as bien fait de me le dire; **he would do ~ to remember that** il ferait bien de se rappeler que; **we'll be doing ~ if we get there on time** on aura de la chance si on arrive à l'heure; **if all goes ~** si tout va bien; **all went ~ until** tout allait bien jusqu'à ce que; **~ done!** bravo!; **~ played!** bien joué!; **he has done very ~ for himself since he became self-employed** il s'en tire très bien depuis qu'il travaille à son compte; **to do oneself ~** bien se soigner; **to do ~ by sb** se montrer généreux/-euse avec qn; **they're doing quite ~ out of the mail-order business** leur affaire de vente par correspondance marche très bien; **some businessmen did quite ~ out of the war** certains hommes d'affaires se sont enrichis pendant la guerre; **she didn't come out of it very ~** (of situation) elle ne s'en est pas très bien sortie; (of article, programme etc) ce n' était pas très flatteur pour elle; **as I know only too ~** comme je ne le sais que trop bien; **he is ~ able to look after himself** il est assez grand pour se débrouiller tout seul; **2** (used with modal verbs) **you may ~ be right** il se pourrait bien que tu aies raison; **I might ~ go there** il se pourrait bien que j'y aille, je pourrais bien y aller; **the concert might very ~ be cancelled** il est bien possible que le concert soit annulé; **I can ~ believe it** je veux bien le croire, je n'ai pas de mal à le croire; **it may ~ be that** il se pourrait bien que (+ *subj*), il est bien possible que (+ *subj*); **I couldn't very ~ say no** je pouvais difficilement dire non; **you may ~ ask!** je me le demande bien!, alors ça, si je le savais!; **we might just as ~ have stayed at home** on aurait aussi bien fait de rester à la maison; **we may as ~ go home** on ferait aussi bien de rentrer; **one might ~ ask why the police were not informed** on est en droit de se demander pourquoi la police n'a pas été informée; **'shall I shut the door?'—'you might as ~'** 'est-ce que je ferme la porte?'—'pourquoi pas'; **he offered to pay for the damage, as ~ he might!** il a proposé de payer pour les dégâts, c'était la moindre des choses!; **she looked shocked, as ~ she might** elle a eu l'air choquée, ce qui n'avait rien d'étonnant; **we didn't panic, as ~ we might (have done)** nous n'avons pas paniqué, alors qu'il y avait de quoi; **3** (intensifier) bien, largement; **to be ~ over the speed limit** être bien au-dessus de la vitesse autorisée, avoir largement dépassé la vitesse autorisée; **she is ~ over 30** elle a bien plus de 30 ans; **she looks ~ over 30** elle fait largement 30 ans; **there were ~ over a hundred people** il y avait largement plus de cent personnes; **the house is ~ over a hundred years old** la maison a bien plus de cent ans; **the museum is ~ worth a visit** le musée mérite vraiment la visite; **it was ~ worth waiting for** ça valait vraiment la peine d'attendre; **the weather remained fine ~ into September** le temps est resté au beau fixe pendant une bonne partie du mois de septembre; **she was active ~ into her eighties** elle était toujours active même au-delà de ses quatre-vingts ans; **temperatures are ~ up in the twenties** les températures dépassent largement vingt degrés; **profits are ~ above/below average** les bénéfices sont nettement supérieurs/inférieurs à la moyenne; **stand ~ back from the kerb** tenez-vous bien à l'écart du bord du trottoir; **the house is situated ~ back from the road** la maison est située bien à l'écart de la route; **it was ~ after midnight** il était bien après minuit; **it went on until ~ after midnight** ça s'est prolongé bien au-delà de minuit; **the party went on ~ into the night** la soirée a continué tard dans la nuit; **4** (approvingly) **to speak/think ~ of sb** dire/penser du bien de qn; **5 to wish sb ~** souhaiter beaucoup de chance à qn; **I wish you ~ of it!** iron je vous souhaite bien du plaisir! iron; **6 as ~** (also) aussi; **as ~ as** (in addition to) aussi bien que; **is Tom coming as ~?** est-ce que Tom vient aussi?; **you know as ~ as I do why he left** tu sais aussi bien que moi pourquoi il est parti; **he is studying Italian as ~ as French** il étudie à la fois l'italien et le français; **I worked on Saturday as ~ as on Sunday** j'ai travaillé samedi et dimanche; **they have a house in the country as ~ as an apartment in Paris** ils ont une maison à la campagne ainsi qu'un appartement à Paris; **by day as ~ as by night** de jour comme de nuit; **7**○ GB **it was ~ good!** ou **~ bad!** (in approval) c'était d'enfer○!

III *excl* **1** (expressing astonishment) eh bien!; (expressing indignation, disgust) ça alors!; (expressing disappointment) tant pis!; (after pause in conversation, account) bon; (qualifying statement) enfin; **~, who would have thought it!** eh bien, qui aurait pu croire ça!; **~, I think so** eh bien, je crois; **~, you may have a point, but** bon or d'accord, ce que tu dis est peut-être vrai, mais; **~, you may be right** après tout, tu as peut-être raison; **~, as I was saying** bon, comme je disais; **~, that's too bad** c'est vraiment dommage; **~ then, what's the problem?** alors, quel est le problème?; **they've gone already? oh ~!** ils sont déjà partis? tant pis!; **oh ~, there's nothing I can do about it** ma foi, je n'y peux rien; **~, ~, ~, if it isn't my aunt Violet!** ma parole, c'est ma tante Violet!; **~, ~, ~, so you're off to America?** alors comme ça, tu pars aux États-Unis!; **the weather was good, ~, good for March** il faisait beau, enfin beau pour un mois de mars; **'he said he'd kill himself'—'~, did he?'** 'il a dit qu'il se tuerait'—'eh bien or et alors, est-ce qu'il l'a fait?'; **very ~ then** très bien.

IDIOMS **all's ~ that ends ~** Prov tout est bien qui finit bien; **to be ~ in with sb**○ être bien avec qn○; **to be ~ up in sth** s'y connaître en qch; **to leave ~ alone** GB ou **~ enough alone** US (not get involved) ne pas s'en mêler; **I would leave ~ alone if I were you** moi à ta place je ne m'en mêlerais pas; **you're ~ out of it**○**!** heureusement que tu n'as plus rien à voir avec ça!; **~ and truly** bel et bien; **~ and truly over/lost** bel et bien fini/perdu.

well² /wel/ **I** *n* **1** (sunk in ground) puits *m*; **to get one's water from a ~** tirer son eau d'un puits; **2** (pool) source *f*; **3** Constr (shaft for stairs, lift) cage *f*; **4** GB Jur (in law court) barreau *m*.

II *vi* = **well up**.

■ **well up** monter; **tears ~ed up in my eyes** les larmes me sont montées aux yeux; **anger ~ed up inside me** j'ai senti la colère monter en moi.

we'll /wi:l/ = **we shall**; **we will**.

well-appointed /wel/ *adj* [*room, house*] bien amenagé.

well-attended *adj* **the meeting was ~** il y avait beaucoup de monde à la réunion.

well /wel/: **~-balanced** *adj* [*person, meal, diet*] équilibré; **~-behaved** *adj* [*child*] sage, bien élevé; [*animal*] bien dressé; **~-being** *n* bien-être *m inv*; **~-born** *adj* bien né, de bonne famille.

well-bred /ˌwel'bred/ *adj* **1** [*person*] (of good birth) bien né; (having good manners) bien élevé; **2** [*animal*] gen de pure race; [*horse*] pur sang.

well-built /ˌwelbɪlt/ *adj* [*person*] bien bâti, solide; [*building*] solide, bien construit.

well-chosen /ˌwel'tʃəʊzn/ *adj* bien choisi; **a few ~ words** quelques mots bien choisis.

well-defined /ˌweldɪ'faɪnd/ *adj* [*shape, outline, image*] net/nette; [*role, boundary*] bien défini.

well-developed /ˌweldɪ'veləpt/ *adj* **1** Anat bien développé; **2** [*instinct*] très développé; [*structure, system*] très développé, très évolué; [*plan, argument*] solide.

well-disposed /ˌweldɪ'spəʊzd/ *adj* **to be ~ towards** être bien disposé envers [*person*]; être favorable à [*regime, idea, policy*].

well-done /ˌwel'dʌn/ *adj* **1** Culin bien cuit; **2** (well performed) [*task, job*] bien fait.

well /wel/: **~-earned** *adj* bien mérité; **~-educated** *adj* (having a good education) instruit; (cultured) cultivé; **~-favoured** *adj* †ou hum beau/belle; **~-fed** *adj* bien nourri.

well-formed /ˌwel'fɔ:md/ *adj* **1** [*mouth, nose, features*] bien modelé; **2** Ling syntaxiquement correct.

well /wel/: **~-founded** *adj* [*rumour, assumption*] fondé; **~-groomed** *adj* [*person, appearance*] soigné; [*hair*] bien coiffé; [*horse*] bien pansé.

wellhead /wel/ *n* source *f*.

well /wel/: **~-heeled**○ *adj* riche, aisé; **~-hung**◑ *adj* hum [*man*] bien monté◑.

well-informed /ˌwelɪn'fɔ:md/ *adj* [*person*] bien informé (**about** sur); **he's very ~** (knows a lot about current affairs) il est très au courant de l'actualité; **~ source** Journ source *f* sérieuse.

wellington (boot) /'welɪŋtən/ *n* GB botte *f* de caoutchouc.

Wellington /'welɪŋtən/ **▶1818** *pr n* Wellington.

well /wel/: **~-intentioned** *adj* bien intentionné; **~-judged** *adj* [*statement, phrase*] bien senti; [*performance*] intelligent; **~-kept** *adj* [*house, garden, village*] bien entretenu, bien tenu; **~-knit** *adj* [*body, frame*] solide, bien bâti; fig [*argument, plan, plot*] bien construit.

well-known /ˌwel'nəʊn/ *adj* **1** (famous) [*person, place, work of art*] célèbre, connu; **she's not very ~** elle n'est pas très connue; **to be ~ to sb** être connu de qn; **2** (widely known) **it is ~ that, it is a ~ fact that** il est bien connu que.

well-liked /ˌwel'laɪkt/ *adj* [*person*] très apprécié.

well /wel/: **~-made** *adj* bien fait; **~-mannered** *adj* bien élevé, poli; **~-meaning** *adj* [*person*] bien intentionné; [*advice, suggestion, gesture*] qui part d'une bonne intention.

well-meant /ˌwel'ment/ *adj* **his offer was ~, but she was too proud to accept it** sa proposition partait d'une bonne intention, mais elle était trop fière pour l'accepter; **my remarks were ~, but I offended her** je ne voulais pas être désagréable dans ce que je disais, mais je l'ai offensée.

well-nigh /ˌwel'naɪ/ *adv* sout pratiquement, presque; **~ impossible** quasiment impossible.

well-off /ˌwel'ɒf/ **I** *n* (+ *v pl*) **the well-off** les gens *mpl* aisés, les riches *mpl*; **the less well-off** les plus défavorisés *mpl*.

II *adj* **1** (wealthy) [*person, family, neighbourhood*] aisé; **2** (fortunate) **you don't know when you're ~** tu ne connais pas ton bonheur; **3 to be ~ for** avoir beaucoup de [*space, provisions etc*].

well-oiled /ˌwel'ɔɪld/ *adj* **1** lit [*machine, engine*] bien graissé; fig (smooth-running) [*department, organization*] bien au point; **2**○ (drunk) bien parti○, soûl.

well /wel/: **~-padded**○ *adj* hum [*person*] bien rembourré○, bien en chair; **~-paid** *adj* [*person, job*] bien payé, bien rémunéré; **~-preserved** *adj* bien conservé; **~-read** *adj* cultivé, instruit.

well-respected /ˌwelrɪ'spektɪd/ *adj* [*person*] très respecté.

well-rounded /ˌwel'raʊndɪd/ *adj* **1** [*education, programme, life*] complet/-ète; [*individual*] qui a reçu une éducation complète; **2** (shapely) [*figure*] harmonieux/-ieuse; [*cheeks*] bien rond.

well /wel/: **~-set** *adj* [*person*] bien bâti; **~-spoken** *adj* [*person*] qui parle bien.

well-spoken-of *adj* **he's very ~** on dit beaucoup de bien de lui.

well /wel/: **~-tempered** *adj* Mus bien tempéré; **~-thought-of** *adj* [*person,* *product*] apprécié; **~-thought-out** *adj* [*plan, theory, plot etc*] bien élaboré.

well-timed /ˌwelˈtaɪmd/ *adj* [*remark, takeover*] qui tombe/tombait à point; **that was ~!** (of entrance, phonecall etc) c'est bien tombé!

well-to-do I *n* **the ~** (+ *v pl*) les gens *mpl* aisés.
II *adj* aisé.

well-tried /wel/ *adj* [*method, remedy*] éprouvé.

well-trodden /ˌwelˈtrɒdn/ *adj* **a ~ path** lit, fig une voie très empruntée, un chemin battu.

well-turned /ˌwelˈtɜːnd/ *adj* **1** [*phrase, remark, compliment etc*] bien tourné; **2†** [*ankle, leg*] galbé.

well-upholstered /wel/○ *adj* hum = **well padded**.

well-wisher /ˈwelwɪʃə(r)/ *n* gen personne *f* qui veut témoigner sa sympathie; Pol sympathisant/-e *m/f*; **'from a ~'** (as signature) 'un ami qui vous veut du bien'.

well-woman clinic /wel/ *n* centre *m* de conseils médicaux pour les femmes.

well-worn /wel/ *adj* [*carpet, garment*] élimé, usé jusqu'à la corde; [*steps, floorboards*] usé; fig [*joke, theme, phrase*] rebattu.

welly○ /ˈwelɪ/ *n* GB **1** (*abrév* = **wellington (boot)**) botte *f* en caoutchouc; **2** fig (acceleration) reprises *fpl*.
IDIOMS **to give it some ~** appuyer sur le champignon○.

welsh /welʃ/ *vi* **to ~ on** faire faux bond à [*person*]; manquer à [*promise, deal*].

Welsh /welʃ/ ▶1486, 1402 I *n* **1** (nation) **the ~** (+ *v pl*) les Gallois *mpl*; **2** Ling gallois *m*.
II *adj* gallois.

Welsh: **~ dresser** *n* GB vaisselier *m*; **~ harp** ▶1481 *n* harpe *f* galloise; **~man** *n* Gallois *m*; **~ mountain pony** *n* poney *m* welsh; **~ Office** *n* in GB ministère *m* des Affaires galloises; **~ rarebit**, **~ rabbit** *n* toast *m* au fromage; **~ secretary** *n* GB Pol ministre *m* des Affaires galloises; **~ terrier** *n* welsh-terrier *m*; **~woman** *n* Galloise *f*.

welt /welt/ *n* **1** (on shoe) trépointe *f*; **2** (on knitted garment) brodure *f* à côtes; **3** (on skin) marque *f* (de coup).

welter /ˈweltə(r)/ I *n* **a ~ of** un fatras de [*objects, fragments*]; un bain de [*blood, water*]; un déferlement de [*emotions, criticism, influences*].
II *vi* **to ~ in** baigner dans [*blood, water, emotion*].

welterweight /ˈweltəweɪt/ I *n* poids *m* welter.
II *modif* [*boxer, champion*] poids welter *inv*; [*fight, competition*] dans la catégorie welter.

wen /wen/ *n* Med loupe *f*; **the great ~** fig hum Londres.

wench‡ /wentʃ/ also hum I *n* gigolette† *f*.
II *vi* courir la gueuse.

wend /wend/ *vtr* **to ~ one's way** cheminer (**to, towards** vers); **to ~ one's way home** prendre la route du retour.

Wendy house /ˈwendɪ haʊs/ *n* GB cabane *f* (*pour les enfants*).

went /went/ *prét* ▶ **go**.

wept /wept/ *prét, pp* ▶ **weep**.

were /wɜː(r), wə(r)/ *prét* ▶ **be**.

we're /wɪə(r)/ = **we are**.

weren't /wɜːnt/ = **were not**.

werewolf /ˈwɪəwʊlf/ *n* (*pl* **-wolves**) loup-garou *m*.

Wesleyan /ˈwezlɪən/ I *n* Wesleyen/-enne *m/f*.
II *adj* wesleyen/-enne.

west /west/ ▶1568 I *n* ouest *m*.
II **West** *n* **1** Pol, Geog **the West** l'Ouest *m*, l'Occident *m*; **2** (in cards) ouest *m*.
III *adj* (*épith*) [*side, bank, face, coast, wall*] ouest *inv*; [*wind*] d'ouest.
IV *adv* [*move*] vers l'ouest; [*lie, live*] à l'ouest (**of** de); **to go ~ of sth** passer à l'ouest de qch.
IDIOMS **to go ~** (die) euph passer l'arme à gauche; (get lost) se perdre; **there's another glass gone ~!** voilà encore un verre de cassé!

west: **West Africa** *pr n* Afrique *f* de l'Ouest; **West African** *adj* [*person, culture etc*] de l'Afrique occidentale; **West Bank** *pr n* Cisjordanie *f*.

West Bengal /ˌwest benˈgɔːl/ *pr n* Bengale-Occidental *m*.

westbound /ˈwestbaʊnd/ *adj* [*carriageway, traffic*] en direction de l'ouest; **the ~ platform/train** GB (in underground) le quai/la rame direction ouest.

West Country *pr n* GB **the ~** le Sud-Ouest (de l'Angleterre).

West End *pr n* GB **the ~** le West End *m* (*quartier de théâtres et de boutiques chic au centre ouest de Londres*).

westerly /ˈwestəlɪ/ I *n* vent *m* d'ouest.
II *adj* [*wind*] d'ouest; [*point*] à l'ouest; [*area*] de l'ouest; [*breeze*] venant de l'ouest; **in a ~ direction** en direction de l'ouest.

western /ˈwestən/ ▶1568 I *n* Cin western *m*.
II *adj* (*épith*) **1** Geog [*coast, boundary*] ouest *inv*; [*town, region, custom, accent*] de l'ouest; **~ France** l'ouest de la France; **2** Pol occidental.

western: **Western (omelet)** *n* US Culin *omelette au jambon, aux poivrons et aux oignons*; **Western Australia** *pr n* Australie *f* occidentale.

westerner /ˈwestənə(r)/ *n* Occidental/-e *m/f*.

western: **Western Europe** *pr n* Europe *f* de l'Ouest, Europe *f* occidentale; **Western Isles** ▶1381 *pr npl* îles *fpl* Hébrides occidentales.

westernization /ˌwestənaɪˈzeɪʃn, US -nɪˈz-/ *n* occidentalisation *f*.

westernize /ˈwestənaɪz/ *vtr* occidentaliser; **to become ~d** s'occidentaliser.

western: **~most** *adj* à l'extrême ouest, le/la plus à l'ouest; **~ roll** *n* Sport saut *m* en rouleau ventral; **Western saddle** *n* US Equit selle *f* américaine; **Western Sahara** *pr n* Sahara *m* Occidental; **Western Samoa** ▶1131 *pr n* Samoa *fpl* Occidentales.

west-facing /ˈwestfeɪsɪŋ/ *adj* exposé à l'ouest.

West German /ˌwest ˈdʒɜːmən/ ▶1486 I *n* Hist Allemand/-e de l'Ouest *m/f*.
II *adj* Hist ouest-allemand.

West Germany /ˌwest ˈdʒɜːmənɪ/ ▶1131 *pr n* Hist Allemagne *f* de l'Ouest.

West Glamorgan /ˌwest gləˈmɔːgən/ ▶1624 *pr n* West Glamorgan *m*.

West Indian /ˌwest ˈɪndɪən/ ▶1486 I *n* Antillais/-e *m/f*.
II *adj* antillais.

West Indies /ˌwest ˈɪndiːz/ ▶1131, 1381 *pr npl* Antilles *fpl*.

West Midlands /ˌwest ˈmɪdləndz/ ▶1624 *pr n* West Midlands *fpl*.

Westminster /ˈwestmɪnstə(r)/ *n* Westminster (*siège du parlement de Grande-Bretagne*); **to be elected to ~** être élu au Parlement (de Grande-Bretagne).

West Point *n* US West Point *m* (*académie militaire américaine*).

West Sussex /ˌwest ˈsʌsɪks/ ▶1624 *pr n* West Sussex *m*.

West Virginia /ˌwest vɜːˈdʒɪnɪə/ ▶1744 *pr n* Virginie *f* occidentale.

westward /ˈwestwəd/ ▶1568 I *adj* [*side*] ouest *inv*; [*wall, slope*] du côté ouest; [*journey, route, movement*] vers l'ouest; **in a ~ direction** en direction de l'ouest, vers l'ouest.
II *adv* (also **~s**) vers l'ouest.

West Yorkshire /ˌwest ˈjɔːkʃə(r)/ ▶1624 *pr n* West Yorkshire *m*.

wet /wet/ I *n* **1** (dampness) humidité *f*; **this plant is tolerant of the ~** cette plante tolère l'humidité; **ducks like the ~** les canards aiment l'eau; **the car won't start in the ~** la voiture ne veut pas démarrer par temps humide; **the tyre performs well in the ~** le pneu a de bons résultats sur terrain mouillé; **2**○ GB (feeble person) péj chiffe *f* molle○ pej; **3** GB Pol conservateur/-trice *m/f* modéré/-e.
II *adj* **1** (damp) [*clothing, hair, hand, grass, road, surface, patch*] mouillé; **~ with rain/urine** mouillé par la pluie/l'urine; **~ with blood/tea** mouillé de sang/de thé; **~ with tears** [*hanky*] humide de larmes; **her face was ~ with tears** son visage était baigné de larmes; **~ with sweat** trempé de sueur; **to get ~** se faire mouiller; **to get one's feet/clothes ~** se mouiller les pieds/les vêtements; **to get the floor/the towel ~** tremper le sol/la serviette; **~ through** trempé; **2** (freshly applied) [*cement, clay, plaster, varnish*] humide; [*paint*] frais/fraîche; **'~ paint'** 'peinture fraîche'; **the ink is still ~** l'encre n'est pas encore sèche; **to keep sth ~** empêcher qch de sécher; **3** (rainy) [*weather, climate, season, day, night, area*] humide; [*conditions*] d'humidité; [*spell*] de pluie; **tomorrow, the North will be ~** demain, il pleuvra dans le nord; **when it's ~** quand il pleut; **4** GB péj [*person*] qui manque de caractère; [*remark, action*] sans intérêt; **don't be so ~!** du nerf!; **5** GB Pol [*Tory, minister, cabinet, MP*] modéré; **6**○ (where alcohol is sold) [*state, country*] où l'on peut acheter des boissons alcoolisées.
III *vtr* **1** (*prés* **-tt-**; *prét, pp* **wet**) (with water, blood, sweat, tea) mouiller [*floor, object, clothes*]; **2** (urinate in or on) **to ~ one's pants/the bed** [*adult*] mouiller sa culotte/le lit; [*child*] faire pipi dans sa culotte/dans son lit.
IV *v refl* **to ~ oneself** gen mouiller sa culotte; [*child*] faire pipi dans sa culotte. ▶ **ear**, **whistle**.

wet: **~back**○ *n* US *ouvrier agricole mexicain entré clandestinement aux États-Unis*; **~ blanket**○ *n* éteignoir *m*, rabat-joie *mf inv*; **~ cell (battery)** *n* pile *f* à liquide.

wet dream *n* (dream) rêve *m* érotique; (emission) éjaculation *f* nocturne.

wet fish *n* GB poisson *m* frais.

wether /ˈweðə(r)/ *n* bélier *m* (châtré).

wetland /ˈwetlənd/ I *n* terres *fpl* marécageuses.
II *modif* [*bird, plant, wildlife*] des terres marécageuses; [*area, site*] marécageux/-euse.

wet-look /ˈwetlʊk/ *adj* Fashn [*plastic, leather*] luisant; [*hair gel*] à effet mouillé.

wetly /ˈwetlɪ/ *adv* [*glisten, gleam*] d'humidité.

wetness /ˈwetnɪs/ *n* (of climate, weather, soil, garment) humidité *f*.

wetnurse /ˈwetnɜːs/ I *n* nourrice *f*.
II **wet-nurse** *vtr* **1** lit allaiter [*baby*]; **2** fig dorloter [*person*]; mitonner [*project*].

wet: **~ rot** *n* carie *f* aqueuse; **~ suit** *n* combinaison *f* de plongée.

wetting /ˈwetɪŋ/ *n* **to get a ~** se faire mouiller; **to give sth a ~** faire tremper qch.

wetting agent *n* mouillant *m*.

we've /wiːv/ *abrév* = **we have**.

W Glam *n* GB Post *abrév écrite* ▶ **West Glamorgan**.

whack /wæk, US hwæk/ I *n* **1** (blow) (grand) coup *m*; **to give sth/sb a ~** donner un grand coup dans qch/à qn; **2**○ (share) part *f*; **to get one's ~** recevoir sa part; **to do one's ~** faire ce qu'on doit; **to pay one's ~** payer sa quote-part; **3** GB○ (wage) **to pay/earn top ~** payer/recevoir un très gros salaire; **to pay top ~** payer le maximum; **4**○ (try) essai *m*; **to have** ou **take a ~ at (doing) sth** essayer (de faire) qch; **to get first ~ at sth/at doing** avoir la primeur de qch/de faire.

what

As a pronoun

In questions

When used in questions as an object pronoun, *what* is translated by *que* or *qu'est-ce que*.

After *que* the verb and subject are inverted and a hyphen is placed between them:

what is he doing? = que fait-il? *or* qu'est-ce qu'il fait?

When used in questions as a subject pronoun, *what* is translated by *qu'est-ce qui*:

what happened? = qu'est-ce qui s'est passé?

Used with preposition

After a preposition the translation is *quoi*.

Unlike in English, the preposition must always be placed immediately before *quoi*:

with what did she cut it? *or what did she cut it with?* = avec quoi l'a-t-elle coupé?

To introduce a clause

When used to introduce a clause as the object of the verb, *what* is translated by *ce que* (*ce qu'* before a vowel):

I don't know what he wants = je ne sais pas ce qu'il veut

When *what* is the subject of the verb it is translated by *ce qui*:

tell me what happened = raconte-moi ce qui s'est passé

For particular usages see **I** in the entry ***what***.

As a derterminer

what used as a determiner is translated by *quel*, *quelle*, *quels* or *quelles* according to the gender and number of the noun that follows:

what train did you catch? = quel train as-tu pris?
what books do you like? = quels livres aimes-tu?
what colours do you like? = quelles couleurs aimes-tu?

For particular usages see **II** in the entry ***what***.

II *excl* paf!

III *vtr* **1** (hit) battre [*person, animal*]; frapper [*ball*]; **2**○ GB (defeat) piler○; **3** fig **to ~ £10 off the price** réduire le prix de dix livres.

IDIOMS **out of ~**○ US [*cupboard*] mal foutu○; [*arm, leg*] blessé.

■ **whack off**● se branler●.

whacked○ /wækt, US hwækt/ *adj* (*jamais épith*) (tired) vanné○; (stoned) US défoncé◐.

whacking○ /ˈwækɪŋ, US ˈhwæk-/ **I** *n* raclée○ *f*.

II *adj* GB énorme.

III *adv* GB **~ great, ~ big** énorme.

whacky○ /ˈwækɪ, US ˈhwækɪ/ *adj* [*person*] dingue○; [*sense of humour, joke*] farfelu○; [*party, clothes*] délirant○.

whale /weɪl, US hweɪl/ **I** *n* **1** Zool baleine *f*; **2**○ **a ~ of a difference/story** une super○ différence/histoire; **to have a ~ of a time** s'amuser comme un fou.

II○ *vtr* US (thrash) lit, fig donner une raclée○ à.

whale: **~boat** *n* baleinière *f*; **~bone** *n* (in corset etc) baleine *f*; **~ calf** *n* baleineau *m*; **~man** ▶**1692** *n* US pêcheur *m* de baleines; **~ oil** *n* huile *f* de baleine.

whaler /ˈweɪlə(r), US ˈhweɪlər/ ▶**1692** *n* **1** (ship) baleinier *m*; **2** (person) pêcheur *m* de baleines.

whaling /ˈweɪlɪŋ, US ˈhweɪlɪŋ/ *n* **1** (whale fishing) pêche *f* à la baleine; **to go ~** aller pêcher la baleine; **2**○ US (thrashing) lit, fig raclée○ *f*.

wham /wæm, US hwæm/ **I** *n* grand coup *m*.

II *excl* vlan!

III *vtr* (*p prés etc* **-mm-**) frapper [qch] avec force.

whammy○ /ˈwæmɪ, US ˈhwæmɪ/ *n* US poisse *f*.

whang○ /wæŋ, US hwæŋ/ **I** *n* coup *m* retentissant.

II *vtr* jeter.

wharf /wɔːf, US hwɔːf/ **I** *n* (*pl* **wharves**) quai *m*.

II *vi* [*boat*] se mettre à quai.

wharfage /ˈwɔːfɪdʒ, US ˈhwɔːfɪdʒ/ *n* **1** (accommodation) emplacement *m* à quai; **2** (fee) droits *mpl* de bassin.

wharves /wɔːvz, US hwɔːvz/ *npl* ▶**wharf**.

what /wɒt, US hwɒt/ **I** *pron* **1** (what exactly) (as subject) qu'est-ce qui; (as object) que, qu'est-ce que; (with prepositions) quoi; **~ is happening?** qu'est-ce qui se passe, qu'est-ce qui arrive?; **~ are you doing/up to**○**?** qu'est-ce que tu fais/fabriques○?; **with/about ~?** avec/de quoi?; **or ~?** ou quoi?; **and ~ else?** et quoi d'autre?; **~ is to be done?** que faire?; **~ do six and four add up to?** que font six et quatre?; **~ is up there?** qu'est-ce qu'il y a là-haut?; **~'s wrong?**, **~'s the matter?**, **~'s up?** qu'est-ce qu'il y a?, qu'est-ce qui ne va pas?; **~ does it matter?** qu'est-ce que ça peut faire?; **~'s that machine?** qu'est-ce que c'est que cet appareil?; **~'s her telephone number?** quel est son numéro de téléphone?; **~'s that button for?** à quoi sert ce bouton?; **~ did he do that for?** pourquoi est-ce qu'il a fait ça?; **~ for?** (why) pourquoi?; (concerning what) à propos de quoi?, à quel sujet?; **'I'm going to the shops'—'~ for?'** 'je vais aux magasins'—'qu'est-ce que tu veux?'; **~'s it like?** comment c'est?; **~'s it like having an older brother?** comment c'est d'avoir un grand frère?; **~'s this called in Flemish**, **~'s the Flemish for this?** comment dit-on cela en flamand?; **~ did it cost?** combien est-ce que ça a coûté?; **2** (in rhetorical questions) **~'s life without love?** que serait la vie sans l'amour?; **~'s the use?** (enquiringly) à quoi bon?; (exasperatedly) à quoi ça sert?; **~ does he care?** qu'est-ce que ça peut bien lui faire?; **~ can anyone do?** qu'est-ce qu'on peut faire?; **3** (whatever) **do ~ you want/have to** fais ce que tu veux/as à faire; **4** (in clauses) (as subject) ce qui; (as object) ce que, (*before vowel*) ce qu'; **to wonder/know ~ is happening** se demander/savoir ce qui se passe; **to ask/guess ~ sb wants** demander/deviner ce que qn veut; **they had everything except ~ I wanted** ils avaient tout sauf ce que je voulais; **this is ~ is called a 'monocle'** c'est ce qu'on appelle un 'monocle'; **do you know ~ that device is?** sais-tu ce que c'est que cet appareil?; **and ~ is equally surprising is that** et ce qui est tout aussi étonnant, c'est que; **she's not ~ she was** elle n'est plus ce qu'elle était; **~ I need is** ce dont j'ai besoin c'est; **a hammer, a drill and I don't know ~** un marteau, une perceuse et je ne sais quoi encore; **drinking ~ looked like whisky** buvant quelque chose qui ressemblait à du whisky; **and ~'s more** et en plus; **and ~'s worse** ou **better** et en plus; **5**○ (when guessing) **it'll cost, ~, £50** ça coutera, quoi ou combien, dans les 50 livres?; **6** (inviting repetition) **~'s that, ~ did you say?** quoi? qu'est-ce que tu as dit?; **he earns ~?** il gagne combien?; **he did ~?** il a fait quoi?; **George ~?** George comment?; **7** (expressing surprise) **and ~ it must have cost!** combien ça a dû coûter!; **8**† GB (as question tag) **a good dinner, ~?** c'était un bon dîner, non?

II *det* **1** (which) quel/quelle; **~ magazines do you read?** quels magazines est-ce que tu lis?; **~ time is it?** quelle heure est-il?; **do you know ~ train he took?** est-ce que tu sais quel train il a pris?; **2** (in exclamations) quel/quelle; **~ a nice dress/car!** quelle belle robe/voiture!; **~ a lovely apartment!** quel bel appartement!; **~ a strange thing to do!** quelle drôle d'idée!; **~ use is that?** lit, fig à quoi ça sert?; **3** (the amount of) **~ money he earns he spends** tout ce qu'il gagne, il le dépense; **~ little she has** le peu qu'elle a, tout ce qu'elle a; **~ belongings she had she threw away** elle a jeté tout ce qui lui appartenait or toutes ses affaires; **~ few friends she had** les quelques amis qu'elle avait.

III what about *phr* **1** (when drawing attention) **~ about the letter they sent?** et la lettre qu 'ils ont envoyée, alors?; **~ about the children?** et les enfants (alors)?; **2** (when making suggestion) **~ about a meal out?** et si on dinait au restaurant?; **~ about Tuesday? OK?** qu'est-ce que tu dirais de mardi? ça te va?; ▶**about**; **3** (in reply) **'~ about your sister?'—'~ about her?'** 'et ta sœur?'—'quoi ma sœur?'

IV what if *phr* et si; **~ if I bring the dessert?** et si j'apportais le dessert?

V what of *phr* **~ of Shakespeare and Lamb?** littér qu'en est-il de Shakespeare et de Lamb?; **~ of it**○**!** et puis quoi○!

VI what with *phr* **~ with her shopping bags and her bike** avec ses sacs à provisions et son vélo en plus; **~ with the depression and unemployment** entre la dépression et le chômage ; **~ with one thing and another** avec ceci et cela.

VII *excl* quoi!, comment!

IDIOMS **I'll tell you ~** tu sais quoi; **to give sb ~ for**○ GB passer un savon○ à qn; **to know ~'s ~** s'y connaître; **he doesn't know ~'s ~** il n'y connaît rien; **well, ~ do you know** iron tout arrive; **~ do you think I am**○**!** tu me prends pour quoi!; **~'s it to you**○**?** en quoi ça vous regarde?, qu'est-ce que ça peut bien vous faire?; **~'s yours**○**?** qu'est-ce que tu bois?; **you know ~ he/she etc is!** on le/la etc connait!

what: **~-d'yer-call-her**○, **~'s-her-name**○ *n* Machine○ *f*; **~-d'yer-call-him**○, **~'s-his-name**○ *n* Machin○ *m*; **~-d'yer-call-it**○, **~'s-its-name**○ *n* machin○ *m*, truc○ *m*.

whatever /wɒtˈevə(r), US hwɒt-/ **I** *pron* **1** (that which) (as subject) ce qui; (as object) ce que; **to do ~ is expedient/required** faire ce qui est nécessaire/exigé; **2** (anything that) (as subject) tout ce qui; (as object) tout ce que; **do ~ you like** fais tout ce que tu veux; **~ you can afford to give is welcome** tous les dons même les plus modestes seront les bienvenus; **~ he says goes** c'est lui qui décide; **~ you say** (as you like) tout ce qui vous plaira; **3** (no matter what) quoi que (+ *subj*); **~ happens** quoi qu'il arrive; **~ I do, it's wrong** quoi que je fasse, j'ai tort; **~ he says, don't pay any attention** quoi qu'il dise, n'y fais pas attention; **~ it costs it doesn't matter** quel que soit le prix, ça n'a pas d'importance; **4** (what on earth) (as subject) qu'est-ce qui; (as object) qu'est-ce que; **~'s the matter?** qu'est-ce qui ne va pas?; **~ do you mean?** qu'est-ce que tu veux dire par là?; **~ did he say?** qu'est-ce qu'il a bien pu dire?; **~'s that!** qu'est-ce que c'est que ça!; **'let's go'—'~ for?'** 'allons-y'—'pour quoi faire?'; **'I've bought some caviar'—'~ for?'** 'j'ai acheté du caviar'—'quelle idée!'; **~ next!** qu'est-ce que ça sera la prochaine fois?; **5**○ (the like) **curtains, cushions and ~** des rideaux, des coussins et toutes sortes de choses; **to the cinema or ~** au cinéma ou n'importe où ailleurs; **you add it or subtract it or ~** vous l'ajoutez ou le soustrayez ou n'importe quoi d'autre.

when

when can very often be translated by *quand* in time expressions:

when did she leave? = quand est-ce qu'elle est partie?
or elle est partie quand?
or quand est-elle partie?

Note that in questions *quand* on its own requires inversion of the verb and subject:

when are they arriving? = quand arrivent-ils?

but when followed by *est-ce que* needs no inversion: *quand est-ce qu'ils arrivent?*

Occasionally a more precise time expression is used in French:

when's your birthday? = quelle est la date de ton anniversaire?
when did he set off? = à quelle heure est-il parti?

Remember that the future tense is used after *quand* if future time is implied:

tell him when you see him = dis-le-lui quand tu le verras

It is often possible to give a short neat translation for a *when* clause if there is no change of subject in the sentence:

when I was very young, I lived in Normandy = tout jeune, j'habitais en Normandie
when he was leaving, he asked for my address = en partant, il m'a demandé mon adresse

In expressions such as *the day when, the year when, où* is used:

the day when we got married = le jour où nous nous sommes mariés

For examples of the above and further uses of *when*, see the entry ***when***.

II *det* **1** (any) **~ hope he once had** tous les espoirs qu'il avait; **they eat ~ food they can get** ils mangent tout ce qu'ils trouvent à manger; **~ items you've bought, return them** il faut rendre tous les articles que vous avez achetés; **2** (no matter what) **~ the events/their arguments** quels que soient les événements/leurs arguments; **~ the reason** quelle que soit la raison; **for ~ reason** pour je ne sais quelle raison; **any race of ~ creed** toutes les races quelles que soient leurs croyances; **3** (expressing surprise) **~ idiot forgot the key?** quel est l'imbécile qui a oublié la clé?; **~ video was that?** qu'est-ce que c'était que cette vidéo?
III *adv* (at all) **no evidence ~** pas la moindre preuve; **to have no idea ~** ne pas avoir la moindre idée; **'any chance?'—'none ~'** 'il y a une chance?'—'pas la moindre'; **'any petrol?'—'none ~'** 'il y a de l'essence?'—'pas du tout'; **anything ~** n'importe quoi; **is there any possibility ~ that you can come?** y a-t-il la moindre chance que tu puisses venir?

whatnot /'wɒtnɒt, US 'hwɒt-/ *n* **1** (furniture) étagère *f*; **2**○ (unspecified person or thing) machin○ *m*; **3**○ (and so on) **...and ~...** et ainsi de suite.

whatsit○ /'wɒtsɪt, US 'hwɒt-/ *n* (thingummy) machin○ *m*, truc○ *m*; **Mr/Mrs Whatsit** M./Mme Machin.

whatsoever /ˌwɒtsəʊ'evə(r), US 'hwɒt-/ **I**‡ *pron* = **whatever I**.
II *adv* = **whatever III**.

wheat /wi:t, US hwi:t/ **I** *n* blé *m*.
II *modif* [*field, sheaf*] de blé.
IDIOMS **to separate the ~ from the chaff** séparer le bon grain de l'ivraie.

wheatear /'wi:tɪə(r), US 'hwi:t-/ *n* Zool cul-blanc *m*.

wheaten /'wi:tn, US 'hwi:tn/ *adj* de blé.

wheat: **~ flour** *n* farine *f* de blé, farine *f* de froment; **~ germ** *n* germe *m* de blé; **~meal** *n* farine *f* complète; **~meal bread** *n* pain *m* complet; **~ rust** *n* rouille *f* du blé.

wheedle /'wi:dl, US 'hwi:dl/ *vtr* **to ~ sth out of sb** soutirer qch à qn par la cajolerie; **to ~ sb into doing sth** amener qn à faire qch par la cajolerie.

wheedling /'wi:dlɪŋ, US 'hwi:dlɪŋ/ **I** *n* cajoleries *fpl*.
II *adj* [*voice, tone, person*] cajoleur/-euse.

wheel /wi:l, US hwi:l/ **I** *n* **1** (on vehicle) roue *f*; (on trolley, piece of furniture) roulette *f*; **front/back ~** roue avant/arrière; **2** (for steering) (in vehicle) volant *m*; Naut roue *f* (de gouvernail); **to be at** ou **behind the ~** être au volant; **to take the ~** (in vehicle) prendre le volant; Naut tenir la roue; **to fall asleep at the ~** s'endormir au volant; **3** (in watch, mechanism, machine) rouage *m*; **the ~s of government** fig les rouages du gouvernement; **4** (for pottery) tour *m*; **5** Hist (instrument of torture) roue *f*; **6** Games (in roulette) roue *f*.
II○ **wheels** *npl* (car) bagnole○ *f*, voiture *f*; **are these your new ~s?** c'est ta nouvelle bagnole○?; **have you got ~s**○**?** tu es motorisé○?
III *vtr* pousser [*bicycle, barrow, pram*]; **to ~ a child in a pram** promener un enfant dans sa poussette; **they ~ed me into the operating theatre** ils m'ont emmené dans la salle d'opération sur un chariot.
IV *vi* **1** (also **~ round**) (circle) [*bird*] tournoyer; **2** (turn sharply) [*person, regiment*] faire demi-tour; [*car, motorbike*] braquer fortement; [*ship*] virer de bord; **to ~ to the right** [*person, regiment*] faire demi-tour à droite; **right/left ~!** Mil demi-tour droite/gauche!
V -wheeled (*dans composés*) **a three-/four-~ed vehicle** un véhicule à trois/quatre roues.
IDIOMS **to ~ and deal** magouiller○; **the ~ of fortune** la roue de la fortune; **it's ~s within ~s** l'affaire est plus compliquée qu'elle n'en a l'air; **to reinvent the ~** réinventer la roue; **to be fifth ~** US être la cinquième roue du carrosse.
■ **wheel in** = **wheel out**.
■ **wheel out**: **~ [sth] out, ~ out [sth]** remettre [qch] sur le tapis [*argument, story*]; ressortir [*excuse, statistics*].

wheel: **~ alignment** *n* Aut parallélisme *m*; **~barrow** *n* brouette *f*; **~base** *n* Aut écartement *m* des essieux; **~chair** *n* fauteuil *m* roulant.

wheelclamp /'wi:lklæmp, US 'hwi:l-/ **I** *n* Aut sabot *m* de Denver.
II *vtr* mettre un sabot de Denver à [*car*].

-wheeler /'wi:lə(r), US 'hwi:lər/ (*dans composés*) **it's a two/three-~** (vehicle) il/elle a deux/trois roues.

wheel: **~er dealer**○ *n* péj magouilleur/-euse○ *m/f*; **~house** *n* timonerie *f*.

wheeling and dealing *n* (+ *v sg*) péj (intrigue) gen manigances *fpl*; micmacs○ *mpl*; (during negotiations) tractations *fpl*.

wheelwright /'wi:lraɪt, US 'hwi:l-/ *n* charron *m*.

wheeze /wi:z, US hwi:z/ **I** *n* **1** (breathing) respiration *f* sifflante; **2**○ †GB **a good ~** une idée géniale; **3** US (cliché) adage *m*; (joke) blague○ *f*.
II *vtr* dire d'une voix rauque.
III *vi* [*person, animal*] ahaner; [*engine, machine, organ*] crachoter.

wheezy /'wi:zɪ, US 'hwi:zɪ/ *adj* [*person*] qui a la respiration sifflante; [*voice, cough*] rauque; [*chest*] qui siffle.

whelk /welk, US hwelk/ *n* buccin *m*.

whelp /welp, US hwelp/ **I** *n* **1** (of dog) chiot *m*; (of wolf) louveteau *m*; **2**○ †péj (young man) garnement† *m*.
II *vi* mettre bas.

when /wen, US hwen/ **I** *pron* **1** (with prepositions) quand; **by ~?** avant quand?; **from ~ until ~?** de quand à quand?; **since ~?** depuis quand? also iron; **2** (the time when) **that was ~ it all started to go wrong** c'est à ce moment-là que tout a commencé à mal aller; **that's ~ I was born** (day) c'est le jour où je suis né; (year) c'est l'année où je suis né; **now is ~ we must act** c'est maintenant qu'il faut agir; **he spoke of ~ he was a child** il a parlé de l'époque où il était enfant.
II *adv* **1** (as interrogative) quand (est-ce que); **~ are we leaving?** quand est-ce qu'on part?; **~ is the concert?** c'est quand le concert?; **~ is it possible to say/use...?** quand est-ce qu'on peut dire/utiliser...? ; **~ do the first rains come?** quand commence la saison des pluies?; **~ was it that he died?** quand est-ce qu'il est mort?; **2** (as indirect interrogative) quand; **ask him ~ he wrote the letter** demande-lui quand il a écrit la lettre; **I wonder ~ the film starts** je me demande à quelle heure commence le film; **I forget exactly ~** (time) j'ai oublié l'heure exacte; (date) j'ai oublié la date exacte; **there was some disagreement as to ~...** tout le monde n'était pas d'accord sur la date à laquelle...; **tell me ou say ~** (pouring drink) dis-moi d'arrêter; **3** (as relative) **on Monday/in 1993 ~** lundi/en 1993 quand; **at the time ~** (precise moment) au moment où; (during same period) à l'époque où; **the week ~ it all happened** la semaine où tout s'est passé; **on those rare occasions ~** les rares fois où; **there are times ~** il y a des moments où; **it's times like that ~** c'est dans ces moments-là que; **it's the time of year ~** c'est la période de l'année où; **one morning ~ he was getting up, he...** un matin en se levant, il...; **4** (then) **she resigned in May, since ~ we've had no applicants** elle a démissionné en mai, et depuis (lors) nous n'avons reçu aucune candidature; **until ~ we must stay calm** d'ici là nous devons rester calmes; **by ~ we will have received the information** d'ici là nous aurons reçu toutes les informations; **5** (whenever) quand; **he's only happy ~ he's moaning** il n'est content que quand il rouspète; **~ on holiday you should relax** quand on est en vacances il faut se détendre; **~ I sunbathe, I get freckles** chaque fois que je prends un bain de soleil, j'ai des taches de rousseur; **~ necessary** quand c'est nécessaire; **~ possible** dans la mesure du possible.
III *conj* **1** (at the precise time when) quand, lorsque; **~ she reaches 18** quand elle aura 18 ans; **2** (during the period when) quand, lorsque; **~ he was at school/just a trainee** quand il était à l'école/simplement stagiaire; **~ you're in your teens** quand on est adolescent; **~ sailing, always wear a lifejacket** quand on fait de la voile, il faut toujours porter un gilet de sauvetage; **3** (as soon as) quand, dès que; **~ he arrives, I'll tell him** quand or dès qu'il arrivera, je le lui dirai; **~ drawn up, the plan...** quand le projet sera rédigé, il..., une fois rédigé, le projet...; **4** (when simultaneously) quand; **I was in the bath ~ the phone rang** j'étais dans mon bain quand le téléphone a sonné; **5** (when suddenly) quand; **I was strolling along ~ all of a sudden...** je marchais tranquillement quand tout d'un coup...; **hardly** ou **scarcely** ou **barely had I sat down ~** je venais à peine de m'asseoir quand; **6** (once, after) quand, une fois que; **~ you've been to Scotland, you'll want to go again and again** quand or une fois que vous aurez visité l'Écosse, vous aurez forcément envie d'y retourner; **7** (when it is the case that) alors que; **why buy their products ~ ours are cheaper?** pourquoi acheter leurs produits alors que les nôtres sont moins chers?; **8**

(whereas) alors que; **she became a nun ~ she could have been an actress** elle est devenue religieuse alors qu'elle aurait pu devenir actrice; **he refused ~ I would have gladly accepted** il a refusé alors que j'aurais été ravi d'accepter.

whence‡ /wens, US hwens/ *adv, conj* d'où.

whene'er *adv* littér = **whenever**.

whenever /wen'evə(r), US hwen-/ *adv* **1** (as interrogative) **~ will he arrive?** quand est-ce qu'il va finir par arriver?; **~ did she find the time?** comment est-ce qu'elle a bien pu trouver le temps?; **2** (no matter when) **~ you want** quand tu veux; **till ~ you like** aussi longtemps que tu veux; **~ he does it, it won't matter** il peut le faire quand il veut, ça n'a pas d'importance; **I'll come ~ it is convenient** je viendrai quand cela vous arrangera; **3**○ (some time) **or ~** ou n'importe quand; **'how long are you staying?'—'till ~'** 'combien de temps est-ce que tu vas rester?'—'on verra bien'; **4** (every time that) chaque fois que; **~ I see a black cat, I make a wish** chaque fois que je vois un chat noir, je fais un vœu; **~ he sees a spider, he trembles** il suffit qu'il voie une araignée pour qu'il tremble; **~ (it is) necessary** quand c'est nécessaire; **~ (it is) possible** dans la mesure du possible; **5** (expressing doubt) **she promised to return them soon, ~ that might be!** elle a promis de les rendre bientôt, mais je ne sais pas quand.

where /weə(r), US hweər/

■ **Note** *where* is generally translated by *où*: *where are the plates?* = où sont les assiettes?; *do you know where he's going?* = est-ce que tu sais où il va?; *I don't know where the knives are* = je ne sais pas où sont les couteaux.
– Note that in questions *où* on its own requires inversion of the verb: *where are you going?* = où allez-vous? but *où* followed by *est-ce que* needs no inversion: où est-ce que vous allez?

I *pron* **1** (with prepositions) où; **from ~?** d'où?; **near ~?** près d'où?; **to go up to ~ sb is standing** s'approcher de qn; **to go past ~ sb is standing** passer devant qn; **not from ~ I'm standing** lit pas de là où je suis; fig ce n'est pas mon avis; **2** (the place or point where) là que; **this is ~ it happened** c'est là que c'est arrivé; **this is ~ we're at** c'est là que nous en sommes; **that is ~ he's mistaken** c'est là qu'il se trompe; **so that's ~ I put them** c'était là que je les avais mis; **here's ~ we learn the truth** voilà enfin la vérité; **France is ~ you'll find good wine** c'est en France que vous trouverez du bon vin.
II *adv* **1** (as interrogative) où (est-ce que); **~ is my coat/do you work?** où est mon manteau/est-ce que tu travailles?; **~ would I be if...?** où est-ce que je serais si...?; **~ does Martin figure in all this?** qu'est-ce que Martin vient faire dans tout ça?; **~'s the harm?** quel mal y a-t-il à ça?; **~'s the problem?** je ne vois pas le problème; **~ have you got to in your book?** où est-ce que vous en êtes dans votre lecture?; **2** (as indirect interrogative) où; **ask him/I wonder ~ he's going** demande-lui/je me demande où il va; **I told him ~ he could put them** lit je lui ai dit où les mettre; ◑fig je lui ai dit qu'il pouvait se les mettre où je pense◑; **to know ~ one is going** savoir où on va; fig savoir ce qu'on veut; **you don't know ~ it's been!** tu ne sais pas où ça a traîné!; **I forget exactly ~ it is** j'ai oublié où c'est exactement; **3** (as relative) où; **the village ~ we live** le village où nous habitons; **at the spot ~ he died** à l'endroit où il est mort; **up there ~ there's a branch** là-haut à l'endroit où il y a une branche; **near ~ she lived** près de l'endroit où or près de là où elle habitait; **to lead to a situation ~** aboutir à une situation où; **to reach the stage ~** arriver au stade où; **in several cases ~** dans plusieurs cas où; **4** (here where, there where) **stay/go ~ it's dry** reste/mets-toi à l'abri; **it's cold ~ we live** il fait froid là où nous habitons; **it's ~ the Indre meets the Loire** c'est au confluent de l'Indre et de la Loire; **it's not ~ you said** (not there) ça n'y est pas; (found elsewhere) ce n'est pas là où tu crois; **5** (wherever) où; **put them/go ~ you want** mets-les/va où tu veux; **6** (whenever) quand; **~ necessary** si nécessaire; **she's stupid ~ he's concerned** elle se conduit toujours de façon stupide quand il s'agit de lui; **~ children are at risk** quand les enfants sont menacés de violence; **~ there's a scandal there's a reporter** dès qu'il y a un scandale il y a des journalistes; **~ possible** dans la mesure du possible.
III *conj* = **whereas**.

whereabouts I /'weərəbaʊts, US 'hweər-/ *n* **do you know his ~?** savez-vous où il est?
II /ˌweərə'baʊts/ *adv* gen où; **'I've put them in the living room'—'~?'** 'je les ai mis dans le salon'—'où ça?'

whereas /ˌweər'æz, US ˌhweər-/ *conj* **she likes dogs ~ I prefer cats** elle aime les chiens mais moi je préfère les chats; **he chose to stay quiet ~ I would have complained** il a choisi de ne rien dire alors que moi je me serais sûrement plaint.

whereby /weə'baɪ, US hweər-/ *conj* **a system ~ all staff will carry identification** un système qui prévoit que tous les membres du personnel auront une carte; **the criteria ~ allowances are allocated** les critères selon lesquels les allocations sont attribuées.

wherefore /'weəfɔ:(r), US 'hweər-/ **I** *adv* littér pourquoi.
II‡ *conj* donc.
IDIOMS **the whys and ~s** le pourquoi et le comment.

wherein /weər'ɪn, US hweər-/ *pron, adv* sout où.

whereof /weər'ɒv, US hweər-/ *pron* Jur en témoignage or en foi de quoi.

wheresoever‡ /ˌweəsəʊ'evə(r), US ˌhweər-/ *adv* = **wherever**.

whereupon /ˌweərə'pɒn, US ˌhweər-/ *conj* sout sur quoi.

wherever /weər'evə(r), US hweər-/ *adv* **1** (as interrogative) **~ did you put them?** où est-ce que tu as bien pu les mettre?; **~ has he got to?** où est-ce qu'il a bien pu passer?; **~ did she get that from?** où est-ce qu'elle a bien pu trouver ça?; **2** (anywhere) **~ she goes I'll go** où qu'elle aille, j'irai; **~ you want** où tu veux; **~ you put the painting it won't look right** tu peux mettre le tableau où tu veux, de toute façon il ne rendra pas bien; **we'll meet ~'s convenient for you** nous nous retrouverons là où ça t'arrange; **3**○ (somewhere) **or ~** ou n'importe où ailleurs; **4** (whenever) **~ there's an oasis, there's a settlement** dès qu'il y a une oasis, il y a une implantation; **~ necessary** quand c'est nécessaire ; **~ possible** dans la mesure du possible; **5** (expressing doubt) **she's from Vernoux ~ that is!** elle vient de Vernoux mais ne me demande pas où c'est!

wherewithal /'weəwɪˌðɔ:l/ *n* **the ~** les moyens *mpl* (**to do** de faire).

whet /wet, US hwet/ *vtr* (*p prés etc* **-tt-**) **1** (stimulate) **to ~ the appetite** stimuler l'appétit; **the book ~ted his appetite for travel** les livres lui donnèrent envie de voyager; **2**‡ (sharpen) aiguiser [*tool, knife*].

whether /'weðə(r), US 'hweðər/

■ **Note** When *whether* is used to mean *if*, it is translated by *si*: *I wonder whether she got my letter* = je me demande si elle a reçu ma lettre. See 1 in the entry below.
– *whether* often occurs after verbs such as *ask, doubt, decide, know, say, see* and *wonder*, with adjectives such as *doubtful, sure*, and with nouns like *doubt, question*. You can find further examples at these entries.
– In *whether...or not* sentences *whether* is translated by *que* and the verb that follows is in the subjunctive: *whether you agree or not* = que vous soyez d'accord ou non. See 2 in the entry below.

conj **1** (when outcome is uncertain: if) si; **I wasn't sure ~ to answer or not** ou **~ or not to answer** je ne savais pas s'il fallait répondre, je n'étais pas sûr qu'il fallait répondre; **I wonder ~ it's true** je me demande si c'est vrai; **you can't tell ~ she's joking or not** c'est impossible de savoir si elle plaisante; **they can't decide ~ to buy or rent** ils n'arrivent pas à décider s'ils doivent acheter ou louer; **can you check ~ it's cooked?** est-ce que tu peux vérifier si c'est cuit?; **it's not clear ~ they've reached an agreement** c'est difficile de savoir s'ils sont tombés d'accord; **the question is ~ anyone is interested** le problème est de savoir si quelqu'un est intéressé; **she was worried about ~ to invite them** elle se demandait si elle devait les inviter; **2** (when outcome is fixed: no matter if) **you're going to school ~ you like it or not!** tu iras à l'école que cela te plaise ou non!; **~ you have children or not , this book should interest you** que vous ayez des enfants ou non, ce livre devrait vous intéresser; **~ or not people are happy is of little importance** que les gens soient heureux ou non ce n'est pas très important; **they need an adult ~ it be a parent or teacher** ils ont besoin d'un adulte que ce soit un parent ou un professeur; **everyone, ~ students or townspeople, celebrates** tout le monde, que ce soient les étudiants ou les habitants de la ville, fait la fête.

whetstone /'wetstəʊn, US 'hwet-/ *n* pierre *f* à aiguiser.

whew /fju:/ *excl* (in relief) ouf!; (in hot weather) pff!; (in surprise) hein!

whey /weɪ, US hweɪ/ *n* petit-lait *m*, lactosérum *m* spec.

whey: **~-faced** *adj* au teint blême; **~ powder** *n* lactosérum *m* en poudre.

which /wɪtʃ, US hwɪtʃ/ **I** *pron* **1** (also **~ one**) lequel *m*, laquelle *f*; **~ do you want, the red skirt or the blue one?** laquelle est-ce que tu veux, la jupe rouge ou la bleue?; **~ of the groups...?** (referring to one) lequel des groupes...?; (referring to several) lesquels des groupes ...? ; **~ of you...?** lequel/laquelle etc de vous or d'entre vous...?; **I know ~ you'd like** je sais lequel/laquelle etc tu voudrais; **show her ~ you mean** montre-lui celui/celle etc dont tu parles; **~ is the best/the shortest route?** quel est le meilleur chemin/le chemin le plus court?; **do you mind ~ you have?** est-ce que tu as une préférence?; **I don't mind ~** ça m'est égal; **can you tell ~ is ~?** peux-tu les distinguer?; **2** (relative to preceding noun) (as subject) qui; (as object) que; (after prepositions) lequel/laquelle/lesquels/lesquelles; **the painting ~ hangs in the sitting room** le tableau qui est accroché dans le salon; **you'll see some crates behind ~ I've placed...** tu verras des caisses derrière lesquelles j'ai mis...; **the contract ~ he's spoken about** ou **about ~ he's spoken** le contrat dont il a parlé; **3** (relative to preceding clause or concept) (as subject) ce qui; (as object) ce que; **he said he hadn't done it, ~ may be true/~ he can't prove** il a nié l'avoir fait, ce qui est peut-être vrai/ce qu'il ne peut pas prouver; **~ reminds me...** ce qui me fait penser que...; **upon ~ she disappeared** littér sur quoi elle a disparu; **we'll be moving, before ~ we need to...** nous allons déménager mais avant il faut que nous...; **he's resigned, from ~ we must assume that** il a démissionné, d'où on peut déduire que.
II *det* **1** (interrogative) quel/quelle/quels/quelles (*before n*); **~ books?** quels livres?; **~ medals did he win?** quelles médailles a-t-il gagnées?; **he told me ~ jacket he'd like** il m'a dit quelle veste il aimerait avoir ; **she asked me ~ coach was leaving first** elle

which

As a pronoun

In questions

When *which* is used as a pronoun in questions it is translated by *lequel, laquelle, lesquels* or *lesquelles* according to the gender and number of the noun it is referring to:

there are three peaches, which do you want? = il y a trois pêches, laquelle veux-tu?
'Lucy's borrowed three of your books' 'which did she take?' = 'Lucy t'a emprunté trois livres' 'lesquels a-t-elle pris?'

The exception to this is when *which* is followed by a superlative adjective, when the translation is *quel, quelle, quels* or *quelles*:

which is the biggest (apple)? = quelle est la plus grande?
which are the least expensive (books)? = quels sont les moins chers?

In relative clauses as subject or object

When *which* is used as a relative pronoun as the subject of a verb, it is translated by *qui*:

the book which is on the table = le livre qui est sur la table
the books which are on the table = les livres qui sont sur la table

When *which* is the object of a verb it is translated by *que* (*qu'* before a vowel or mute 'h'):

the book which Tina is reading = le livre que lit Tina

Note the inversion of subject and verb; this is the case where the subject is a noun but not where the subject is a pronoun:

the book which I am reading = le livre que je lis

In compound tenses such as the present perfect and past perfect, the past participle agrees in gender and number with the noun *que* is referring to:

the books which I gave you = les livres que je t'ai donnés
the dresses which she bought yesterday = les robes qu'elle a achetées hier

In relative clauses after a preposition

Here the translation is *lequel, laquelle, lesquels* or *lesquelles* according to the gender and number of the noun referred to:

the road by which we came or *the road which we came by* = la route par laquelle nous sommes venus
the expressions for which we have translations = les expressions pour lesquelles nous avons une traduction

Remember that if the preposition would normally be translated by *à* in French (*to, at* etc.), the preposition + *which* is translated by *auquel, à laquelle, auxquels* or *auxquelles*:

the addresses to which we sent letters = les adresses auxquelles nous avons envoyé des lettres

With prepositions normally translated by *de* (*of, from* etc.) the translation of the preposition *which* becomes *dont*:

a blue book, the title of which I've forgotten = un livre bleu dont j'ai oublié le titre

However, if *de* is part of a prepositional group, as for example in the case of *près de* meaning *near*, the translation becomes *duquel, de laquelle, desquels* or *desquelles*:

the village near which they live = le village près duquel ils habitent
the houses near which she was waiting = les maisons près desquelles elle attendait

The translation *duquel* etc. is also used where a preposition + noun precedes *of which*:

a hill at the top of which there is a house = une colline au sommet de laquelle il y a une maison

As a determiner

In questions

When *which* is used as a determiner in questions it is translated by *quel, quelle, quels* or *quelles* according to the gender and number of the noun that follows:

which car is yours? = quelle voiture est la vôtre?
which books did he borrow? = quels livres a-t-il empruntés?

Note that in the second example the object precedes the verb so that the past participle agrees in gender and number with the object.

For translations of *which* as a determiner in relative clauses see **II 2** in the entry ***which***.

m'a demandé lequel des cars allait partir le premier; **~ one of the children...?** lequel or laquelle des enfants...?; **2** (relative) **he left the room, during ~ time**... il a quitté la pièce et pendant ce temps-là...; **you may wish to join, in ~ case**... vous voulez peut-être vous inscrire, auquel cas...; **he failed to apologize, for ~ mistake he paid dearly** sout il ne s'est même pas excusé, (c'est une) erreur qu'il a payée cher.

whichever /wɪtʃ'evə(r), US hwɪtʃ-/ **I** *pron* **1** (the one that) (as subject) celui *m* qui, celle *f* qui; (as object) celui *m* que, celle *f* que; **'which restaurant?'—'~ is nearest/you prefer'** 'quel restaurant?'—'celui qui est le plus proche/que tu préfères'; **come at 2 or 2.30, ~ suits you best** viens à 14 h ou 14 h 30, comme cela te convient le mieux; **choose either alternative, ~ is the cheaper** choisis la moins chère des deux solutions; **2** (no matter which one) (as subject) quel *m* que soit celui qui (+ *subj*), quelle *f* que soit celle qui (+ *subj*); (as object) quel *m* que soit celui que (+ *subj*), quelle *f* que soit celle que (+ *subj*); **both courses are worthwhile ~ you choose** les deux cours sont aussi intéressants quel que soit celui que tu choisisses; **~ of the techniques is used, the result will be the same** quelle que soit la technique utilisée, le résultat sera le même; **'do you want the big piece or the small piece?'—'~'** 'est-ce que tu veux le gros ou le petit morceau?'—'n'importe'; **3** (which on earth) **~ did he choose in the end?** qu'est-ce qu'il a fini par choisir?
II *det* **1** (the one that) **let's go to ~ station is nearest** allons à la gare la plus proche; **you may have ~ dress you prefer** tu peux avoir la robe que tu préfères; **underline ~ answer you consider correct** soulignez la réponse que vous jugez bonne; **2** (no matter which) **it won't matter ~ hotel we go to** peu importe l'hôtel où nous irons; **I'll be happy ~ horse wins** quel que soit le cheval qui gagne je serai content; **~ way you look at things** quelle que soit la façon dont tu envisages le problème; **3** (which on earth) **~ one do you mean?** mais duquel/de laquelle est-ce que tu peux bien parler?

whiff /wɪf, US hwɪf/ *n* (smell) (of perfume, food) odeur *f* also pej (**of** de); (of smoke, garlic) bouffée *f* (**of** de); fig (of danger, failure, controversy) relent *m* (**of** de); **to get** ou **catch a ~ of** sentir l'odeur de.

whiffy○ /'wɪfɪ, US hwɪfɪ/ *adj* GB puant.

whig /wɪg, US hwɪg/ *n, adj* Pol Hist whig *mf*.

while /waɪl, US hwaɪl/ **I** *conj* **1** (although) bien que (+ *subj*), quoique (+ *subj*); **~ the house is big, it is not in a very good state** bien que or quoique la maison soit grande, elle n'est pas en très bon état; **the peaches, ~ being ripe, had little taste** les pêches, quoique mûres, avaient peu de goût; **2** (as long as) tant que; **~ there's life there's hope** tant qu'il y a de la vie, il y a de l'espoir; **3** (during the time that) (with different subjects) pendant que; (with the same subject) alors que; **sit there ~ I speak to Brigitte** asseyez-vous là pendant que je parle à Brigitte; **he made a sandwich ~ I phoned** il a fait un sandwich pendant que je téléphonais; **he met her ~ on holiday** il l'a rencontrée pendant qu'il était en vacances; **~ in Spain I visited Madrid** pendant que j'étais en Espagne j'ai visité Madrid; **he collapsed ~ mowing the lawn** il a eu un malaise alors qu'il tondait le gazon; **4** (at the same time as) en; **I fell asleep ~ watching TV** je me suis endormi en regardant la télé; **this eliminates draughts ~ allowing air to circulate** cela élimine les courants d'air tout en permettant à l'air de circuler; **close the door ~ you're about** ou **at it** ferme la porte pendant que tu y es; **'MOT ~ you wait'** 'contrôle technique express'; **'heels repaired ~ you wait'** 'talons minute'; **5** (whereas) tandis que.
II *n* **a ~ ago** ou **back**○ il y a quelque temps; **a ~ later** quelque temps plus tard; **a good** ou **long ~ ago** il y a longtemps; **for a good ~** pendant longtemps; **a good ~ later** longtemps après, beaucoup plus tard; **a short** ou **little ~ ago** il y a peu de temps; **a short ~ later, after a short ~** peu de temps après; **it will be** ou **take a ~** cela va prendre un certain temps; **it takes a ~ to cook** cela prend un certain temps à cuire; **it may take a ~** ça risque de prendre un certain temps; **to wait a ~ longer** attendre encore un peu; **to stop/rest for a ~** s'arrêter/se reposer un peu or un moment; **after a ~ he fell asleep** au bout d'un moment il s'est endormi; **after a ~ I started to trust him** au bout d'un moment or au bout d'un certain temps j'ai commencé à lui faire confiance; **he worked, humming all the ~** ou **the whole ~** il travaillait tout en chantonnant; **and all the ~** ou **the whole ~, he was cheating on her** et depuis le début , il la trompait; **once in a ~** de temps en temps; **in between ~s** entre-temps. ▸ **worth**.
■ **while away**: **~ away [sth]** tuer [*hours, minutes*] (**doing, by doing** en faisant); **to ~ away the time by playing cards** tuer le temps en jouant aux cartes.

whilst /waɪlst, US hwaɪlst/ *conj* = **while** I.

whim /wɪm, US hwɪm/ *n* caprice *m*; **on a ~** sur un coup de tête.

whimper /'wɪmpə(r), US 'hwɪm-/ **I** *n* gémissement *m* (**of** de).
II *vtr* **'I'm cold,' she ~ed** 'j'ai froid,' ditelle en gémissant.
III *vi* **1** [*person, animal*] gémir; **2** péj (whinge) [*person*] pleurnicher.
IDIOMS **to end, not with a bang, but a ~** finir sans éclat.

whimpering /'wɪmpərɪŋ, US hwɪm-/ **I** *n* (of person, puppy) gémissements *mpl*; pej (of person) geignements *mpl*.
II *adj* [*voice*] geignard; pej [*person*] pleurnicheur/-euse; **a ~ sound** ou **noise** un gémissement.

whimsical /'wɪmzɪkl, US 'hwɪm-/ *adj* [*person*] fantasque; [*play, tale, manner, idea*] saugrenu; Fin [*market*] capricieux/-ieuse.

whimsicality /ˌwɪmzɪ'kælətɪ, US 'hwɪm-/ *n* fantaisie *f*.

whimsically /'wɪmzɪklɪ, US 'hwɪm-/ *adv* [*remark, write*] de façon saugrenue; [*decide*] sur un coup de tête.

whimsy /'wɪmzɪ, US 'hwɪm-/ *n* littér fantaisie *f*.

whimwhams○ /ˈwɪmwæms, US ˈhwɪm-/ *npl* US frousse○ *f*; **to get the ~** avoir la frousse○.

whine /waɪn, US hwaɪn/ **I** *n* (of person, animal) geignement *m*; (of engine) plainte *f*; (of bullet) sifflement *m*; **her voice had a nasal ~** elle parlait d'une voix nasillarde.
II *vtr* **'I'm hungry,' he ~d** 'j'ai faim,' dit-il d'une voix geignarde.
III *vi* (complain) se plaindre, geindre (**about** de); (snivel) pleurnicher; [*dog*] gémir.

whinge○ /wɪndʒ/ *vi* râler○.

whingeing○ /ˈwɪndʒɪŋ/ GB **I** *n* plaintes *fpl*.
II *adj* [*person*] geignard.

whining /ˈwaɪnɪŋ, US ˈhwaɪn-/ **I** *n* (complaints) jérémiades *fpl*, geignements *mpl*; (of engine) gémissements *mpl* aigus; (of dog) gémissements *mpl*.
II *adj* [*voice*] (complaining, high-pitched) geignard; [*child*] pleurnicheur/-euse; [*letter*] de réclamation.

whinny /ˈwɪnɪ, US ˈhwɪnɪ/ **I** *n* faible hennissement *m*.
II *vi* [*horse*] hennir doucement; fig péj [*person*] hennir.

whinnying /ˈwɪnɪɪŋ, US ˈhwɪnɪɪŋ/ **I** *n* (of horse) (faible) hennissement *m*; fig péj (of person) hennissement *m*.
II *adj* péj [*voice, sound*] hennissant.

whip /wɪp, US hwɪp/ **I** *n* **1** (for punishment) fouet *m*; (for horse) cravache *f*; **2** GB Pol (official) *député chargé d'assurer la discipline de vote des membres de son parti*, chef *m* de file; (notice, summons) convocation *f* (*envoyée aux membres d'un parti lors d'une séance de Parlement importante*); **three-line ~** convocation *f* urgente (*pour assister à une séance de vote*); **to resign the party ~** démissionner du groupe parlementaire; **3** Culin mousse *f*; **strawberry ~** mousse aux fraises; **instant ~** dessert *m* instantané.
II *vtr* (*p prés etc* **-pp-**) **1** (beat) fouetter [*person, animal*]; **the wind ~ped our faces** le vent nous fouettait le visage; **2** Culin fouetter [*cream*]; battre [qch] en neige [*egg whites*]; **3**○ (remove quickly) **she ~ped the newspaper from under his nose** elle lui a chipé○ le journal sous le nez; **I ~ped the key out of his hand** je lui ai arraché la clé des mains; **he ~ped the plates off the table** il a prestement retiré les assiettes de la table; **4** GB (steal) piquer○, chiper○ (**from sb** à qn); **5** surfiler [*fabric*]; surlier [*rope*]; **6** US (defeat) battre.
III○ *vi* (*p prés etc* **-pp-**) (move fast) **to ~ in/out** entrer/sortir précipitamment; **he ~ped into a shop to buy a paper** il est entré rapidement dans un magasin pour acheter un journal; **I'll just ~ out to get some milk** je sors juste une minute pour aller acheter du lait; **she's just ~ped over** ou **round to the neighbours** elle est juste allée faire un saut○ chez les voisins; **to ~ round** se retourner brusquement.
■ **whip away**: **~ away [sth], ~ [sth] away** [*person*] retirer or enlever prestement [*plate, book*]; [*wind*] faire voler, emporter brusquement [*hat, scarf*].
■ **whip back**: ¶ **~ back** [*branch, wire*] revenir brusquement en arrière; ¶ **~ back [sth], ~ [sth] back** récupérer [qch] brusquement [*object*]; **I wanted to read the letter, but he ~ped it back** je voulais lire la lettre mais il me l'a arrachée des mains.
■ **whip in**: ¶ **~ in** Hunt être piqueur; ¶ **~ in [sth], ~ [sth] in 1** Hunt rassembler [*hounds*]; **2** Culin incorporer [qch] (*avec un fouet*) [*cream*]; ¶ **~ in [sb], ~ [sb] in** US Pol rallier [*party members*].
■ **whip off**: **~ off [sth], ~ [sth] off** enlever or ôter [qch] à toute vitesse [*garment, shoes*].
■ **whip on**: **~ on [sth], ~ [sth] on 1** enfiler [qch] à toute vitesse [*garment*]; **2** (urge on) cravacher [*horse*].
■ **whip out**: **~ out [sth]** sortir [qch] brusquement [*wallet, gun*].
■ **whip through** expédier [*task, book*].
■ **whip up**: **~ up [sth] 1** (incite) attiser [*hatred, enthusiasm*]; provoquer [*fear*]; ranimer [*indignation, hostility*]; éveiller, stimuler [*interest*]; rallier [*support*]; inciter, provoquer [*strike, unrest*]; **to ~ the crowd up into a frenzy** mettre la foule en délire; **2** Culin battre [qch] au fouet, fouetter [*cream, eggs*]; **3** (produce quickly) préparer [qch] en vitesse [*snack, meal, report*].

whipcord /ˈwɪpkɔːd, US hwɪp-/ *n* **1** Tex whipcord *m*; **2** (part of whip) mèche *f* de fouet.

whip hand *n* **to have the ~** avoir le dessus; **to have the ~ over sb** l'emporter sur qn.

whip: **~lash** *n* coup *m* de fouet; **~lash injury** *n* Med coup *m* du lapin, traumatisme *m* cervical; **~ped cream** *n* crème *f* fouettée; **~per-in** *n* Hunt piqueur *m*.

whippersnapper† /ˈwɪpəsnæpə(r), US ˈhwɪpə-/ *n* freluquet† *m*.

whippet /ˈwɪpɪt, US ˈhwɪpɪt/ *n* Zool whippet *m*.

whipping /ˈwɪpɪŋ, US ˈhwɪp-/ *n* **1** correction *f* (*au fouet*); **to give sb a ~** donner le fouet à qn, fouetter qn; **2** (stitching on fabric, rug) surfilage *m*.

whipping: **~ boy** *n* souffre-douleur *m inv*; **~ cream** *n* crème *f* fraîche (*à fouetter*); **~ post** *n* poteau *m* (*des condamnés au fouet*); **~ top** *n* toupie *f*.

whippoorwill /ˈwɪpʊəwɪl, US ˈhwɪp-/ *n* engoulevent *m*.

whip: **~-round**○ *n* GB collecte *f*; **~saw** *n* ≈ scie *f* à ruban; **~snake** *n* couleuvre *f*; **~stitch** *n* surfil *m*.

whir *n, vi* = **whirr**.

whirl /wɜːl, US hwɜːl/ **I** *n* **1** fig (of activity, excitement) tourbillon *m* (**of** de); **the social ~** le tourbillon social; **to be in a ~** vivre dans un tourbillon; **my head's in a ~** tout tourbillonne dans ma tête; **2** (swirl of dust, air, leaves etc) tourbillon *m*; **3** (spiral motif) spirale *f*.
II *vtr* **1** (swirl, turn) faire tournoyer [*sword, flag, leaves, snowflakes, dust*]; **2** (whisk, hurry) **to ~ sb along/away** entraîner/emmener qn à toute vitesse.
III *vi* **1** (swirl, turn) [*dancer*] tournoyer; [*blade, propeller*] tourner; [*snowflakes, dust, mind, thoughts*] tourbillonner; **2** (move quickly, whizz) **to ~ in/past** [*person, vehicle*] entrer/filer à toute vitesse.
IDIOMS **to give sth a ~**○ essayer qch.
■ **whirl round**: ¶ **~ round** [*person*] se retourner brusquement; [*blade, rotor, clock hand*] tourner brusquement; ¶ **~ [sth] round** faire tournoyer [*sword, rope*].

whirligig /ˈwɜːlɪgɪg, US ˈhwɜːl-/ *n* **1** (merry-go-round) manège *m*; **2** (spinning top) toupie *f*; **3** fig (whirl) tourbillon *m*.

whirligig beetle *n* Zool gyrin *m*, tourniquet *m*.

whirl: **~pool** *n* tourbillon *m*, remous *m*; **~pool bath** *n* bain *m* bouillonnant; **~wind** *n* tourbillon *m*.

whirlybird○ /ˈwɜːlɪbɜːd, US ˈhwɜːl-/ *n* US hélico○ *m*.

whirr /wɜː(r), US hwɜːr/ **I** *n* (of propeller, motor) vrombissement *m*; (of toy, camera, insect) bourdonnement *m*; (of wings) bruissement *m*.
II *vi* [*motor, propeller*] vrombir; [*camera, fan*] tourner; [*insect*] bourdonner; [*wings*] bruire.

whisk /wɪsk, US hwɪsk/ **I** *n* **1** Culin (also **egg ~**) (manual) fouet *m*; (mechanical, electric) batteur *m*; **2 with a ~ of its tail** d'un coup de queue.
II *vtr* **1** Culin (beat) battre [*sauce, mixture, eggs*]; **~ the eggs and cream together** battre les œufs avec la crème; **2** (transport, move quickly) **he was ~ed off to meet the president** on l'a emmené sur le champ rencontrer le président; **she was ~ed off to hospital** elle a été emmenée d'urgence à l'hôpital; **she ~ed open the gate** elle a ouvert rapidement le portail; **he ~ed the plates off the table** il a enlevé les assiettes de la table d'un geste rapide; **3** (flick) **the cow ~ed its tail** la vache fouettait l'air de sa queue; **she ~ed the fly away with her hand** elle a chassé la mouche d'un geste rapide de la main.
III *vi* **she ~ed into the room** elle est entrée précipitamment dans la pièce; **he ~ed off in his long cloak** il est parti rapidement, vêtu de sa longue cape; **he ~ed around the room with a duster** il a donné un rapide coup de chiffon dans la pièce.

whisker /ˈwɪskə(r), US ˈhwɪ-/ **I** *n* **1** lit (of animal) moustache *f*; **2** fig **to lose/win by a ~** perdre/gagner d'un poil○ or de justesse; **to come within a ~ of victory/of winning** être à deux doigts de la victoire/de gagner.
II whiskers *npl* (of animal) moustaches *fpl*; (of man) (side-whiskers) favoris *mpl*; (beard) barbe *f*; (moustache) moustache *f*.

whiskery /ˈwɪskərɪ, US ˈhwɪ-/ *adj* [*chin*] poilu.

whisky GB, **whiskey** US, Ir /ˈwɪskɪ, US ˈhwɪ-/ **I** *n* (*pl* **-kies** GB, **~s** US, Ir) whisky *m*; **~ and soda** ≈ whisky-Perrier®.
II *modif* [*bottle, glass*] à whisky; [*sauce*] au whisky.

whisky mac *n* cocktail *m*.

whisper /ˈwɪspə(r), US ˈhwɪs-/ **I** *n* (of person, voices) chuchotement *m*; fig (rustling sound) (of trees, leaves, wind) chuchotement *m*, bruissement *m*; (of water) murmure *m*; fig (rumour) bruit *m*, rumeur *f*; **to speak in a ~** ou **in ~s** parler à voix basse; **to say in a ~** dire à voix basse; **her voice hardly rose above a ~** sa voix était à peine plus forte qu'un chuchotement; **his voice dropped to a ~** il a baissé la voix et s'est mis à chuchoter; **I don't want to hear a ~ out of you** je ne veux pas t'entendre; **there is a ~ going round that** fig le bruit court que.
II *vtr* chuchoter (**to** à); **to ~ sth to sb** chuchoter qch à qn, dire qch à voix basse à qn; **'she's asleep,' he ~ed** 'elle dort,' dit-il en chuchotant; **she ~ed sth in his ear** elle lui a chuchoté qch à l'oreille; **it is ~ed that** fig on dit que, le bruit court que.
III *vi* [*person*] chuchoter, parler à voix basse; [*leaves, trees, wind*] chuchoter; [*water*] murmurer; **to ~ to sb** parler à voix basse à qn; **it's bad manners to ~** c'est impoli de faire des messes basses○.

whispering /ˈwɪspərɪŋ, US ˈhwɪ-/ **I** *n* ₵ (of voices) chuchotement *m*; (of leaves, trees, wind) chuchotement *m*, murmure *m*, bruissement *m*; (of water) murmure *m*; fig (rumours) rumeurs *fpl* insidieuses.
II *adj* [*person*] qui chuchote; [*leaves, trees, wind*] chuchotant, murmurant; [*water*] murmurant; **~ voices** chuchotements *mpl*.

whispering: **~ campaign** *n* campagne *f* de diffamation; **~ gallery** *n* galerie *f* à écho.

whist /wɪst, US hwɪst/ ▶ **1282** *n* whist *m*.

whist drive *n* tournoi *m* de whist.

whistle /ˈwɪsl, US ˈhwɪ-/ **I** *n* **1** (small pipe) sifflet *m*; (siren) sirène *f*; **the factory ~ goes at 5 pm** la sirène de l'usine sonne à 17 h; **to blow the** ou **one's ~** donner un coup de sifflet; **to blow the ~ for half time** siffler la mi-temps; **2** (sound) (made by mouth, kettle, train, wind) sifflement *m*; (made with a small pipe) coup *m* de sifflet; **to give a ~ of surprise** pousser un sifflement de surprise; **3** Mus flageolet *m*.
II *vtr* gen siffler [*tune, command*]; (casually) siffloter [*melody*].
III *vi* **1** (make noise) [*bird, person, kettle, train, wind*] siffler; **to ~ at sb/sth** siffler qn/qch; **to ~ for** siffler [*dog*]; **he ~d to us to come** il nous a sifflés pour nous faire venir; **2** (move fast) **to ~ past** ou **by** [*arrow, bullet*] passer en sifflant; [*train*] passer à toute vitesse; **the arrows ~d past our heads/through the air** les flèches sifflaient au-dessus de nos têtes/dans l'air.
IDIOMS **to blow the ~ on sb** dénoncer

qn; **to blow the ~ on sth** révéler qch; **(as) clean as a ~** propre comme un sou neuf; **you can ~ for it**○! tu peux toujours courir○!; **to wet one's ~**○ se rincer le gosier○; **to ~ in the dark** essayer de se donner du courage.

■ **whistle up**○: **~ up [sth]** dégoter○ [*object, volunteer*].

whistle-blower○ /ˈwɪslbləʊə(r), US ˈhwɪsl-/ *n* dénonciateur/-trice *m/f*.

whistle-stop /ˈwɪslstɒp, US ˈhwɪsl-/ US Rail **I** *n* gare *f* à arrêt facultatif.
II *vi* (*p prés etc* **-pp-**) s'arrêter dans les petites gares.

whistle-stop tour *n* (by diplomat, president) tournée *f* éclair *inv* (**of** de); (by candidate on campaign) tournée *f* électorale (**of** de).

whit† /wɪt, US hwɪt/ *n* brin *m*; **not a ~** pas un brin; **it bothered him not a ~** ça ne l'ennuyait pas le moins du monde.

Whit /wɪt, US hwɪt/ *n*: *abrév* ▶ **Whitsun**.

white /waɪt, US hwaɪt/ ▶ **1104** **I** *n* **1** (colour) blanc *m*; **I like ~** j'aime le blanc; **in ~** en blanc; **a shade of ~** un ton de blanc; **2** (part of egg, eye) blanc *m*; **the ~s of sb's eyes** le blanc des yeux de qn; **3** (also **White**) (Caucasian) Blanc/Blanche *m/f*; **4** (white ball) bille *f* blanche (*de billard/snooker*); **5** (wine) blanc *m*; **6** (in chess, draughts) blancs *mpl*; **I'll be ~** je prends les blancs; **~ wins** les blancs gagnent; **7** (also **White**) Pol (reactionary) Blanc/Blanche *m/f*.
II whites *npl* **1** (clothes) **cricket/tennis/chef's ~s** tenue *f* de cricket/ de tennis/de chef-cuisinier; **2** Med (leucorrhoea) pertes *fpl* blanches.
III *adj* **1** [*paint, tooth, flower, hair*] blanc/blanche; **bright/cool ~** blanc éclatant/glacial inv; **to go** ou **turn ~** devenir blanc, blanchir; **to turn sth ~** faire blanchir qch; **to paint/colour sth ~** peindre/colorer qch en blanc; **2** (Caucasian) [*race, child, skin*] blanc/blanche; [*area*] habité par des Blancs; [*culture, prejudice, fears*] des Blancs; **a ~ man/woman** un Blanc/une Blanche; **an all-~ jury** un jury exclusivement composé de Blancs; **3** (pale) [*face, person, cheek*] pâle (**with** de); **to go** ou **turn ~** pâlir (**with** de).
IDIOMS **he would swear black was ~** il a l'esprit de contradiction; **the men in ~ coats** hum les infirmiers psychiatriques; **two blacks don't make a ~** on n'efface pas un tort par un autre; **whiter than ~** [*reputation, person*] plus blanc/blanche que neige.

■ **white out**: **~ out [sth], ~ [sth] out** effacer [qch] (avec du blanc).

whitebait /ˈwaɪtbeɪt, US ˈhwaɪt-/ *npl* **1** (raw) blanchaille *f*; **2** (fried) petite friture *f*.

white: **~beam** *n* Bot alisier *m* blanc; **~ blood cell, ~ blood corpuscle** *n* globule *m* blanc; **~board** *n* tableau *m* blanc; **~ book** *n* US livre *m* blanc, rapport *m* officiel (**on** sur); **~ bread** *n* pain *m* blanc; **~cap** *n* mouton *m*; **~ cedar** *n* cèdre *m* blanc; **White Christmas** *n* Noël *m* avec de la neige; **~ coffee** *n* (at home) café *m* au lait; (in café) café *m* crème.

white-collar /ˌwaɪtˈkɒlə(r), US ˌhwaɪt-/ *adj* [*job, work*] d'employé de bureau, de col blanc; [*staff*] de bureau; [*vote*] des cols blancs; [*neighborhood*] US résidentiel/-ielle.

white: **~-collar crime** *n* délinquance *f* en col blanc; **~-collar union** *n* syndicat *m* des employés de bureau; **~-collar worker** *n* employé/-e *m/f* de bureau, col *m* blanc; **~d sepulchre** *n* péj hypocrite *mf*; **~ dwarf** *n* naine *f* blanche.

white elephant *n* péj **1** (item, knicknack) bibelot *m*; **2** (public project) réalisation *f* coûteuse et peu rentable.

white: **~ elephant stall** *n* stand *m* de bibelots; **White Ensign** *n* pavillon *m* blanc (*de la marine de guerre britannique*); **~-faced** *adj* [*person*] pâle; [*animal*] à tête blanche.

white feather *n*: *symbole de reddition, avec connotation de poltronnerie.*
IDIOMS **to show the ~** se rendre comme un poltron.

white: **~ fish** *n* poisson *m* blanc; **~ flag** *n* drapeau *m* blanc; **~fly** *n* aleurode *m*; **~ fox** *n* (animal) renard *m* polaire; (fur) renard *m* blanc; **~ friar** *n* carme *m*; **~ gasoline** *n* US essence *f* sans plomb; **~ gold** *n* or *m* blanc.

white goods *n* **1** (appliances) gros électroménager *m*; **2** (linens) blanc *m* ¢.

white-haired /ˌwaɪtˈheəd, US ˌhwaɪt-/ *adj* aux cheveux blancs.

Whitehall /ˈwaɪthɔːl, US ˈhwaɪt-/ *pr n* GB Pol *avenue à Londres où sont concentrés les principaux ministères et les principales administrations publiques.*

Whitehall farce *n* GB Theat *genre comique créé par le Théâtre de Whitehall.*

white-headed /ˌwaɪtˈhedɪd, US ˌhwaɪt-/ *adj* [*person*] aux cheveux blancs; [*animal*] à tête blanche.

white heat *n* **1** Phys rouge *m* blanc; **2** (intense heat) chaleur *f* accablante; **3** (of emotion) chaleur *f*.

white: **~ hope** *n* espoir *m*; **~ horse** *n* (wave) mouton *m*.

white hot *adj* **1** lit [*metal*] chauffé à blanc, incandescent; **2** fig incandescent.

White House **I** *n* Maison *f* Blanche.
II *modif* [*aide, adviser, chief of staff, spokesman*] de la Maison Blanche.

White knight *n* **1** gen sauveur *m*; **2** Fin chevalier *m* blanc.

white: **~-knuckle ride** *n* tour *m* de manège qui fait peur; **~ lead** *n* blanc *m* de céruse; **~ lie** *n* pieux mensonge *m*; **~ light** *n* lumière *f* blanche; **~ line** *n* Transp ligne *f* blanche; **~-livered** *adj* poltron/-onne; **~ magic** *n* magie *f* blanche; **~ meat** *n* viande *f* blanche; **~ metal** *n* métal *m* blanc; **~ meter** *n* GB Elec compteur *m* 'heures creuses'; **~ mouse** *n* souris *f* blanche.

whiten /ˈwaɪtn, US ˈhwaɪtn/ **I** *vtr* blanchir [*shoes, wall, face, skin*].
II *vi* [*sky, face, cheeks*] pâlir; [*knuckles*] blanchir.

whitener /ˈwaɪtnə(r), US ˈhwaɪt-/ *n* **1** (for clothes) agent *m* blanchissant; **2** (for shoes) produit *m* pour blanchir; **3** (for coffee, tea) succédané *m* de lait en poudre.

whiteness /ˈwaɪtnɪs, US ˈhwaɪt-/ *n* blancheur *f*.

White Nile *pr n* Nil *m* blanc.

whitening /ˈwaɪtnɪŋ, US ˈhwaɪt-/ *n* **1** (act of turning sth white) blanchiment *m*; **2** (process of becoming white) blanchissement *m*; **3** (substance) agent *m* blanchissant.

white: **~ noise** *n* bruit *m* blanc; **~ oak** *n* chêne *m* blanc; **~out** *n* Meteorol voile *m* blanc; **White Paper** *n* GB Pol Admin livre *m* blanc, rapport *m* officiel (**on** sur); **~ pepper** *n* poivre *m* blanc; **~ pine** *n* pin *m* blanc; **~ plague** *n* US tuberculose *f* pulmonaire; **~ poplar** *n* peuplier *m* blanc; **~ rhino(ceros)** *n* rhinocéros *m* blanc; **~ room** *n* Ind salle *f* blanche.

White Russian *n* **1** (Tsarist) Russe *mf* blanc/blanche; **2** (Byelorussian) Biélorusse *mf*.

white: **~ sale** *n* vente *f* de blanc; **~ sauce** *n* sauce *f* blanche; **~ shark** *n* requin *m* blanc; **~-skinned** *adj* à peau blanche; **~ slave** *n* victime *f* de la traite des Blanches; **~ slavery** *n* traite *f* des Blanches; **~ slave trade** *n* traite *f* des Blanches; **~s-only** *adj* réservé aux Blancs; **~ spirit** *n* white-spirit *m*; **~ stick** *n* canne *f* blanche; **~ supremacist** *n* partisan/-e *m/f* de la suprématie blanche; **~ supremacy** suprématie *f* blanche; **~tail, ~-tailed deer** *n* cerf *m* de Virginie; **~-tailed eagle** *n* pygargue *m* à queue blanche; **~ tea** *n* thé *m* au lait; **~thorn** *n* aubépine *f*; **~throat** *n* fauvette *f* grisette.

white tie **I** *n* **1** (tie) nœud *m* papillon blanc; **2** (formal dress) habit *m*; **~ and tails** queue *f* de pie.
II white-tie *modif* [*dinner, occasion*] habillé.

white: **~ trash** *n* (+ *v pl*) US péj petits Blancs *mpl*; **~wall (tyre)** GB, **~wall (tire)** US *n* pneu *m* à flanc blanc.

whitewash /ˈwaɪtwɒʃ, US ˈhwaɪt-/ **I** *n* **1** (for walls) lait *m* de chaux; **2** fig (cover-up) mise *f* en scène, camouflage *m*; **3**○ Sport déculottée○ *f*.
II *vtr* **1** lit blanchir [qch] à la chaux, chauler [*wall, step*]; **2** (also **~ over**) fig (conceal) blanchir, camoufler [*action, truth*]; **3**○ Sport flanquer une déculottée à○ [*team*]; **4** Fin réhabiliter [*company*].

white water **I** *n* eau *f* vive.
II white-water *modif* [*canoeing, rafting*] en eau vive.

white: **~ wedding** *n* mariage *m* en blanc; **~ whale** *n* baleine *f* blanche; **~ wine** *n* vin *m* blanc; **~ witch** *n* bonne sorcière *f*; **~wood** *n* bois *m* blanc.

whitey /ˈwaɪtɪ, US ˈhwaɪtɪ/ **I**○ *n* péj Blanc/Blanche *m/f*.
II *adj* [*blue, green*] laiteux/-euse.

whither /ˈwɪðə(r), US ˈhwɪðər/ *adv* littér où; **~ goest thou?** où te rends-tu de ce pas?; **~ modern architecture?** Journ où va l'architecture moderne?

whiting /ˈwaɪtɪŋ, US ˈhwaɪt-/ *n* **1** (*pl* **~**) Zool merlan *m*; **2** (whitener) agent *m* blanchissant, blanc *m*.

whitish /ˈwaɪtɪʃ, US ˈhwaɪt-/ *adj* blanchâtre.

whitlow /ˈwɪtləʊ, US ˈhwɪt-/ *n* panaris *m*.

Whit Monday *n* le lundi de Pentecôte.

Whitsun /ˈwɪtsn, US hwɪ-/ *n* (also **Whitsuntide**) Pentecôte *f*; **at ~** à la Pentecôte.

Whit Sunday *n* Pentecôte *f*.

whittle /ˈwɪtl, US ˈhwɪt-/ *vtr* tailler [qch] au couteau.

■ **whittle away**: ¶ **~ away [sth]** fig réduire [*advantage, lead*]; ¶ **~ away at [sth]** lit tailler [*stick*]; fig réduire [*advantage, lead, profits*].

■ **whittle down**: **~ down [sth], ~ [sth] down** réduire [*number*] (**to** à); **we've ~d the number of applicants down to three** on a réduit le nombre de candidats à trois.

whiz○ *n* = **whizz I 1**.

whizz /wɪz, US hwɪz/ **I** *n* **1**○ (expert) as○ *m* (**at** en); **computer ~** as en informatique; **2** (whirr) sifflement *m*; **3**○ (quick trip) tour *m* rapide (**around** de); **4**○ Culin **give the mixture a ~ in the blender** faites passer rapidement le mélange au mixer.
II○ *vtr* (deliver quickly) filer○; **I'll ~ round the contract to you** je te filerai le contrat.
III *vi* **to ~ by** ou **past** [*arrow, bullet*] passer en sifflant; [*car, bicycle*] passer à toute allure; [*person*] passer rapidement; **to ~ through the air** [*arrow, bullet*] fendre l'air; **to ~ along the road** [*car*] filer à toute allure le long de la route.

■ **whizz up** Culin: **~ up [sth]** réduire [qch] en purée.

whizz-bang○ /ˈwɪzbæŋ, US ˈhwɪz-/ **I** *n* (shell) obus *m*; (firework) pétard *m*.
II *adj* super○.

whizz-kid○ /ˈwɪzkɪd, US ˈhwɪz-/ *n* jeune prodige *m*.

whizzo○† /ˈwɪzəʊ, US ˈhwɪz-/ *excl* super○.

who /huː/

■ **Note** *who* is translated by *qui*.
– In questions *qui* on its own as the object of a verb requires inversion of the verb: *who did he call?* = qui a-t-il appelé? but *qui* followed by *est-ce que* or *est-ce qui* needs no inversion: qui est-ce qu'il a appelé? Note, however, that the form *il a appelé qui?* is also used in spoken French.
– For particular usages see the entry below.

pron **1** (interrogative) (as subject) qui (est-ce qui); (as object) qui (est-ce que); (after prepositions) qui; **~ knows the answer?** qui connaît la réponse?; **~ did you invite?** qui est-ce que tu as invité?, qui as-tu invité?; **~'s going to be there?** qui sera là?; **behind/next to ~?** derrière/à côté de qui?; **~ was she with?** elle était avec qui?, avec qui était-elle?; **~ does he live with?** il habite avec qui?, avec qui est-ce qu'il habite?; **~ did you buy it for?** pour qui l'as-tu acheté?; **~ did you get it from?** qui te l'a donné?; **'I gave it away'—'~ to?'** 'je l'ai donné'—'à qui?'; **do you know ~'s ~?** est-ce que tu sais qui est qui?; **I was strolling along when ~ should I see but Diane** je me promenais et devine qui j'ai rencontré...Diane; **~ shall I say is calling?** (on phone) 'c'est de la part de qui?'; **2** (relative) (as subject) qui; (as object) que; (after prepositions) qui; **his friend ~ lives/~ he sees** son ami qui habite/qu'il voit; **he/she ~** celui/celle qui; **they** ou **those ~** ceux/celles qui; **those ~ have something to say should speak up now** quiconque a quelque chose à dire doit le dire or ceux qui ont quelque chose à dire doivent le dire maintenant; **3** (whoever) **bring ~ you like** tu peux amener qui tu veux; **~ do you think you are?** tu te prends pour qui?; **~ do you think you're talking to?** à qui est-ce que tu crois parler?; **~'s he to tell you what to do?** de quel droit est-ce qu'il te donne des ordres?

WHO *n* (*abrév* = **World Health Organization**) OMS *f*.

whoa /wəʊ/ *excl* ho (là).

who'd /hu:d/ = **who had, who would**.

whodun(n)it /ˌhu:ˈdʌnɪt/ *n* roman *m* policier, polar○ *m*.

whoe'er /hu:ˈeə(r)/ *pron* littér = **whoever**.

whoever /hu:ˈevə(r)/ *pron* **1** (the one that) **~ wins the election will have to deal with the problem** celui ou celle qui gagnera les élections devra faire face au problème; **2** (anyone that) qui; **invite ~ you like** invite qui tu veux; **show it to ~ you want** montre-le à qui tu veux; **~ saw the accident should contact the police** quiconque a assisté à l'accident devrait contacter la police, tout témoin est prié de prendre contact avec la police; **3** (all who) tous ceux qui; **tell ~ you know** dis-le à tous ceux que tu connais; **they're providing cars for ~ comes** ils fournissent des voitures à tous ceux qui viennent; **4** (no matter who) **come out ~ you are** qui que vous soyez, sortez de là; **~ he saw, it makes no difference** quelle que soit la personne qu'il ait vue, ça ne change rien; **write to the minister or ~** écris au ministre ou à n'importe qui d'autre; **5** (who on earth) qui; **~ did that to you?** mais qui a bien pu te faire ça?; **~ did he speak to?** à qui est-ce qu'il a bien pu parler?; **~ do you think you are?** tu te prends pour qui?

whole /həʊl/ **I** *n* **1** (total unit) tout *m*; **to consider the ~** considérer le tout or l'ensemble *m*; **as a ~** (not in separate parts) en entier, en bloc; (overall) dans l'ensemble; **to sell sth as a ~** vendre qch en bloc; **taken as a ~** pris dans l'ensemble; **for the country as a ~** pour le pays dans son ensemble; **this will benefit society as a ~** ceci profitera à l'ensemble de la société; **2** (all) **the ~ of** tout/-e; **the ~ of London is talking about it** tout Londres en parle; **the ~ of the weekend/morning** tout le week-end/toute la matinée; **the ~ of the time** tout le temps; **the ~ of August** tout le mois d'août; **nearly the ~ of Berlin was destroyed** Berlin a été presque entièrement détruit.

II *adj* **1** (entire) tout, entier/-ière; (more emphatic) tout entier/-ière; **her ~ attention** toute son attention; **his ~ body** tout son corps; **to be aware of the ~ person** être conscient de la personne sous tous ses aspects; **his ~ life** toute sa vie, sa vie entière; **I've never been so insulted in my ~ life!** de toute ma vie je n'ai jamais été insulté comme ça!; **to search the ~ country** chercher dans tout le pays or dans le pays tout entier; **the ~ world** le monde entier; **the most beautiful city in the ~ world** la plus belle ville du monde or qui existe au monde; **for three ~ weeks** pendant trois semaines entières; **a ~ hour** une heure entière; **a ~ day** toute une journée; **~ cities were devastated** des villes entières ont été dévastées; **she drank a ~ bottle of gin** elle a bu toute une bouteille de gin; **the ~ story** toute l'histoire; **the ~ truth** toute la vérité; **this doesn't give the ~ picture** ceci ne dit pas tout; **let's forget the ~ thing!** oublions tout ça!; **she made the ~ thing up** elle a tout inventé; **2** (emphatic use) **he looks a ~ lot better** il a vraiment bien meilleure mine; **she's a ~ lot nicer** elle est vraiment beaucoup plus sympathique; **there were a ~ lot of them** [*objects*] il y en avait tout un tas; [*people*] il y en avait toute une bande; **a ~ lot of money** un tas○ d'argent; **that goes for the ~ lot of you!** ça s'applique à vous tous!; **a ~ new way of life** un mode de vie complètement différent; **a ~ new era** une époque complètement nouvelle; **that's the ~ point of the exercise** c'est tout l'intér êt de l'exercice; **the ~ idea is to do** toute l'idée est de faire; **I find the ~ idea absurd** je trouve cette idée complètement absurde; **3** (intact) intact, complet/-ète; **there wasn't a plate left ~** il n'y avait plus une assiette intacte; **to make sb ~** guérir qn.

III *adv* [*swallow, cook*] tout entier; **to swallow a story ~** gober une histoire.

IV on the whole *adv phr* dans l'ensemble; **on the ~ I agree** dans l'ensemble je suis d'accord; **the film is on the ~ good** le film est bon dans l'ensemble.

whole blood *n* **1** Med sang *m* total; **2** Jur **of the ~** du même sang.

whole: **~food** *n* GB produits *mpl* biologiques; **~food shop** ▶1692 *n* GB magasin *m* de produits diététiques; **~ gale** *n* Meteorol tempête *f* (*selon l'échelle de Beaufort*); **~grain** *adj* complet/-ète.

wholehearted /ˌhəʊlˈhɑ:tɪd/ *adj* [*approval, agreement, support*] sans réserve; **to be in ~ agreement with** être en accord total avec.

whole: **~heartedly** *adv* [*approve, support*] sans réserve, totalement; **~ holiday** *n* GB journée *f* de congé; **~meal** *adj* complet/-ète; **~ milk** *n* lait *m* entier; **~ note** *n* US Mus ronde *f*; **~ number** *n* (nombre *m*) entier *m*.

wholesale /ˈhəʊlseɪl/ **I** *n* vente *f* en gros; **by ~** en gros.

II *adj* **1** Comm [*price, company, trade, market*] de gros; **2** (large-scale) [*destruction, alteration*] total, massif/-ive; [*acceptance, rejection, adoption*] en bloc; [*commitment*] total; [*attack*] sur tous les fronts.

III *adv* **1** Comm [*buy, sell*] en gros; **I can get it for you ~** je peux vous l'avoir au prix de gros; **2** fig [*accept, reject, copy*] en bloc.

wholesale price index *n* indice *m* des prix de gros.

wholesaler /ˈhəʊlseɪlə(r)/ *n* grossiste *mf*, marchand/-e *m/f* en gros; **wine ~** marchand de vin en gros.

wholesome /ˈhəʊlsəm/ *adj* **1** (healthy) [*diet, food, air*] sain; **good ~ home cooking** de la bonne cuisine de famille; **2** (decent) [*person, appearance*] bien propre; [*entertainment, era*] innocent.

whole: **~ step, ~ tone** *n* US Mus ton *m*; **~-tone scale** *n* US Mus gamme *f* pentatonique; **~wheat** *adj* = **wholemeal**.

who'll /hu:l/ = **who will, who shall**.

wholly /ˈhəʊllɪ/ *adv* entièrement, tout à fait.

wholly-owned subsidiary *n* Econ filiale *f* à cent pour cent.

whom /hu:m/

■ **Note** In questions, *qui* on its own requires inversion of the verb: *whom do you wish to see?* = qui voulez-vous voir? but *qui* followed by *est-ce que* needs no inversion: qui est-ce que vous voulez voir?

pron **1** (interrogative) qui (est-ce que); (after prepositions) qui; **~ did she meet?** qui a-t-elle rencontré?, qui est-ce qu'elle a rencontré?; **to ~ are you referring?** à qui est-ce que vous faites allusion?; **the article is by ~?** de qui est l'article?; **2** (relative) que; (after prepositions) qui; **the minister ~ he'd seen** le ministre qu'il avait vu; **the person to ~/of ~ I spoke** la personne à qui/de qui or dont j'ai parlé; **those ~ he baptized** ceux qu'il a baptisés; **...four of ~ are young and all of ~ are single** ...dont quatre sont jeunes et qui sont tous célibataires; **Kirsten and Matthew, both of ~ had ridden before** Kirsten et Matthew, qui avaient déjà fait du cheval tous les deux; **she pointed to the boys, one of ~ was laughing** elle a indiqué le groupe de garçons dont un riait; **he was particular about ~ he chose** il était exigeant quant à ceux qu'il choisissait; **3** (whoever) qui; **you may invite ~ you wish** vous pouvez inviter qui vous voulez.

whom(so)ever /hu:mˈevə(r), hu:səʊˈevə(r)/ *pron* sout qui; **to arrest/support etc ~ one wishes** arrêter/soutenir etc qui on veut; **for ~ shall find them** pour ceux qui les trouveront; **to ~ it may concern** à qui de droit.

whomp○ /wɒmp, US hwɒmp/ *vtr* US **1** (hit) cogner○; **2** Sport (beat) défoncer○.

whoop /hu:p, wu:p, US hwu:p/ **I** *n* **1** (shout) cri *m*; **2** Med toux *f* de coqueluche.

II *vi* **1** (shout) pousser des cris (**with** de); **2** Med émettre une quinte de coqueluche.

■ **whoop it up**○ s'éclater○.

whoopee○ /ˈwʊpi:, US ˈhwʊ-/ **I** *n* **to make ~** hum (make love) faire l'amour; (have fun) faire la foire○.

II *excl* youpi!

whoopee cushion *n* coussin-péteur *m*.

whoop: **~er swan** *n* cygne *m* sauvage; **~ing cough** ▶1354 *n* coqueluche *f*.

whoops /wʊps, US hwʊps/ *excl* (on avoiding accident) oups!; (on realizing mistake) oh là là!; **~ a daisy!** houp-là!

whoosh○ /wʊʃ, US hwʊʃ/ **I** *n* **~ of a train/of a car going by** bruit *m* d'un train/d'une voiture qui passe à toute allure; **~ of skis on the snow** crissement *m* de skis sur la neige.

II *excl* zoum!

III *vi* **to ~ in/out/past** entrer/sortir/passer à toute allure.

whop○ /wɒp, US hwɒp/ *vtr* (*p prés etc* **-pp-**) **1** (hit) cogner; **to ~ sb one**○ flanquer une mandale○ à qn; **2** (beat in game) défoncer○.

whopper○ /ˈwɒpə(r), US ˈhwɒpər/ *n* **1** gen (large thing) monstre *m*; (hamburger) hamburger *m* géant; **2** (lie) bobard *m* gros comme une maison○.

whopping○ /ˈwɒpɪŋ, US ˈhwɒpɪŋ/ **I** *n* (beating) tripotée○ *f*.

II *adj* (also **~ great**) monstre○.

whore /hɔ:(r)/ **I** *n* injur prostituée *f*, pute◑ *f*.

II *vi* péj **1** [*man*] fréquenter les prostituées; **2** [*woman*] être prostituée; **to ~ around**○ coucher avec n'importe qui.

who're /ˈhu:ə(r)/ = **who are**.

whorehouse /ˈhɔ:haʊs/ *n* bordel◑ *m*.

whoremonger /ˈhɔ:mʌŋgə(r)/ *n*‡ péj micheton◑ *m*.

whorish /ˈhɔ:rɪʃ/ *adj* injur putassier/-ière◑.

whorl /wɜ:l, US hwɜ:l/ *n* (of cream, chocolate etc) spirale *f*; (on fingerprint) volute *f*; (shell pattern) spire *f*; (of petals) verticille *m*.

whortleberry /ˈwɜ:tlberɪ, US ˈhwɜ:rtlberɪ/ **I** *n* myrtille *f*.

II *modif* [*pie, sauce*] aux myrtilles; [*bush, flower*] de myrtille.

who's /hu:z/ = **who is, who has**.

whose /hu:z/ **I** *pron* à qui; **~ is this?** à qui

est ceci?; **we don't know ~ it is** nous ne savons pas à qui c'est; **~ did you take?** tu as pris celui/celle etc de qui?; **I wonder ~ he'll prefer** je me demande celui/celle etc de qui il va préférer.

II *adj* **1** (interrogative) **~ pen is that?** à qui est ce stylo?; **do you know ~ car was stolen?** est-ce que tu sais à qui appartient la voiture volée?; **~ coat did you take?** tu as pris le manteau de qui?; **~ party did you go to?** tu es allé à la fête de qui?; **with ~ permission?** avec la permission de qui?; **2** (relative) **the boy ~ dog/books etc** le garçon dont le chien/les livres etc; **the one ~ name is drawn out first** celui or celle dont le nom sera tiré au sort en premier; **the man ~ daughter he was married to** l'homme dont il avait épousé la fille.

whosoe'er, whosoever /huːsəʊ'evə(r)/ *pron* littér = **whoever**.

whosoever† /ˌhuːsəʊ'evə(r)/ *pron* = **whoever**.

Who's Who *n* ≈ bottin® *m* mondain.

who've /huːv/ = **who have**.

why /waɪ, US hwaɪ/

■ **Note** *why* translates as *pourquoi* in French, but see II, III below for exceptions.
– As with other words such as *où, quand, comment etc*, questions are formed by inserting *est-ce que* after the question word: *why did you go?* = pourquoi est-ce que tu y es allé? or by inverting the subject and verb after the question word, which is slightly more formal: pourquoi y es-tu allé? In spoken French the question word can be put at the end: *tu y es allé pourquoi?*
– *why* occurs with certain reporting verbs such as *ask, explain, know, think* and *wonder.* For translations, see these entries.

I *adv* **1** (in questions) pourquoi; **~ do you ask?** pourquoi est-ce que tu me poses la question?, pourquoi me poses-tu la question?; **~ didn't she tell us?** pourquoi est-ce qu'elle ne nous l'a pas dit?, pourquoi ne nous l'a-t-elle pas dit?; **~ risk everything?** pourquoi tout risquer?; **~ bother?** pourquoi se tracasser?; **'I'm annoyed'—'~ is that?'** 'je suis vexé'—'pourquoi?'; **~ all the fuss?** pourquoi tout ce remue-ménage?; **~ the delay?** pourquoi ce retard?; **~ me?** pourquoi moi?; **oh no, ~ me?** oh non, pourquoi est-ce que ça me tombe dessus?; **~ not somebody else?** pourquoi pas quelqu'un d'autre?; **'it's not possible'—'~ not?'** 'ce n'est pas possible'—'pourquoi pas?'; **'would you be interested?'—'~ not?'** 'ça t'intéresserait?'—'pourquoi pas?'; **'can I apply?'—'I don't see ~ not'** 'est-ce que je peux m'inscrire?'—'je ne vois pas pourquoi tu ne pourrais pas'; **2** (when making suggestions) pourquoi; **~ don't you apply for the job?** pourquoi est-ce que tu ne poses pas ta candidature?; **~ don't we go away for the weekend?** pourquoi ne pas partir quelque part pour le week-end?; **~ don't I invite them for dinner?** et si je les invitais à manger?; **~ not sell the car?** pourquoi ne pas vendre la voiture?; **~ not send off now for our brochure?** pourquoi ne pas demander dès maintenant notre brochure?; **~ not a mix of traditional and modern?** pourquoi pas un mélange de classique et de moderne?; **3** (expressing irritation, defiance) pourquoi; **~ don't they mind their own business?** pourquoi est-ce qu'ils ne s'occupent pas de leurs affaires?; **~ can't you be quiet?** tu ne peux pas te taire deux minutes?; **~ do I bother?** à quoi ça sert que je me donne du mal?; **~ should they get all the praise?** pourquoi est-ce que c'est eux qui auraient tous les compliments?; **'tell them'—'~ should I?'** 'dis- leur'—'et pourquoi est-ce que je devrais le faire?'; **4** (also **~ever**) (expressing surprise) **~ever not?** GB pourquoi pas?; **~ever did you say that?** pourquoi donc as-tu dit cela?

II *conj* pour ça; **that is ~ they came** c'est pour ça qu'ils sont venus; **that's not ~ I asked** ce n'est pas pour ça que j'avais posé la question; **is that ~ she telephoned?** est-ce que c'est pour ça qu'elle a téléphoné?; **so that's ~!** (finally understanding) ah, c'est pour ça!; **'~?'—'because you're stubborn, that's ~!'** 'pourquoi?'—'parce que tu es têtu, c'est tout!'; **the reason ~** la raison pour laquelle; **one of the reasons ~ they left** une des raisons pour lesquelles ils sont partis; **I need to know the reason ~** j'ai besoin de savoir pourquoi; ▶ **reason I 2**.

III *n* **the ~** le pourquoi *m*; ▶ **wherefore**.

IV† *excl* mais; **~, we've just arrived!** mais nous venons d'arriver!

WI *n* **1** GB *abrév* ▶ **Women's Institute**; **2** US Post *abrév écrite* = **Wisconsin**; **3** *abrév écrite* = **West Indies**.

wick /wɪk/ *n* (of candle, lamp etc) mèche *f*.
IDIOMS **to get on sb's ~**○ GB taper sur les nerfs de qn○.

wicked /'wɪkɪd/ *adj* **1** (evil) [*person*] méchant; [*heart, deed*] cruel/-elle; [*plot*] pernicieux/-ieuse; [*intention*] mauvais; **it is ~ to do** c'est méchant de faire; **it was ~ of him** c'était méchant de sa part; **that was a ~ thing to do** c'est méchant d'avoir fait cela; **2** (mischievous) [*grin, humour, stare, wink*] malicieux/-ieuse; **3** (naughty) [*thoughts*] pervers; **sb's ~ ways** hum les mauvais penchants de qn; **go on, be ~!** allons, laisse-toi tenter!; **4** (nasty, vicious) [*wind*] méchant (*before n*); [*weapon*] redoutable; [*sarcasm*] cinglant; **a ~ tongue** une mauvaise langue; **5**○ (terrible) **a ~ waste** un sale○ gâchis; **it was a ~ shame** c'était vraiment une honte; **6**○ (great) super○; **he plays a ~ game of chess** il est super aux échecs.
IDIOMS **no peace** ou **rest for the ~** pas de repos pour les braves○.

wickedly /'wɪkɪdlɪ/ *adv* **1** [*smile, say, chuckle, wink*] avec malice; **~ satirical** satirique et malicieux/-ieuse; **~ accurate** juste et malicieux/-ieuse; **2** [*act, lie, plot*] avec méchanceté.

wickedness /'wɪkɪdnɪs/ *n* **1** (evil) (of person, deed, regime, heart) cruauté *f*; **the ~ of all that waste** le scandale de tout ce gâchis; **2** (of grin, wink, joke) malice *f*; **the ~ of chocolate cake** hum le côté tentant du gâteau au chocolat.

wicker /'wɪkə(r)/ **I** *n* (also **wickerwork**) osier *m*.
II *modif* [*basket, furniture*] en osier.

wicket /'wɪkɪt/ *n* **1** (field gate) portillon *m*; (sluice gate) petite porte *f* d'écluse; **2** US (transaction window) guichet *m*; **3** (in cricket) (stumps) guichet *m*; (pitch) terrain *m* entre les guichets; **4** (in croquet) arceau *m*.
IDIOMS **to be on a sticky ~**○ être dans le pétrin○.

wicket keeper *n* (in cricket) gardien *m* de guichet.

wickiup○ /'wɪkɪʌp/ *n* US hutte *f* de branchages.

wide /waɪd/ **I** *adj* **1** (broad) [*river, opening, mouth*] large; [*margin*] grand; **how ~ is your garden?** quelle est la largeur de votre jardin?; **it's 30 cm ~** il fait 30 cm de large; **the river is 1 km across at its ~st** le fleuve a 1 km de large au point le plus large; **they're making the street ~r** ils élargissent la rue; **her eyes were ~ with fear** ses yeux étaient agrandis par la peur; **2** (immense) [*ocean, desert, sky*] vaste; **he had no-one to talk to in the whole ~ world** il n'avait personne à qui parler en ce monde; **3** (extensive) [*variety, choice*] grand; [*market*] vaste; **a woman of ~ interests** une femme qui s'intéresse à beaucoup de choses; **a ~ range of products** une vaste gamme de produits; **a ~ range of opinions/interests** une grande variété d'opinions/de centres d'intérêt; **in the ~ European context** dans le plus vaste contexte européen; **in the ~st sense of the word** au sens le plus large du mot; **4** Sport [*ball, shot*] perdu.
II *adv* **to open one's eyes ~** ouvrir grand les yeux; **his eyes are (set) ~ apart** il a les yeux très écartés; **open ~!** ouvrez grand la bouche!; **to be ~ of the mark** [*ball, dart*] être à côté; fig [*guess*] être loin de la vérité.
III -wide (*dans composés*) **a country~ search** une recherche menée dans tout le pays; **a nation~ survey** un sondage à l'échelle nationale.

wide: **~-angle lens** *n* objectif *m* à grand angle, grand angle *m*; **~ area network, WAN** *n* Comput grand réseau *m*; **~ awake** *adj* complètement éveillé.

wideboy○ /'waɪdbɔɪ/ *n* GB péj escroc *m*.

wide-eyed /ˌwaɪd'aɪd/ *adj* aux yeux écarquillés.

widely /'waɪdlɪ/ *adv* **1** (commonly) [*acknowledged, accepted, used*] largement; **it is ~ accepted that** il est largement admis que; **it is ~ believed that** beaucoup de gens pensent que; **a country ~ admired for its technology** un pays qui fait l'admiration générale pour sa technologie; **this product is now ~ available** ce produit est maintenant en vente libre; **to be ~ known** être bien connu (**for** pour); **she is ~ regarded as an expert in her field** elle est considérée par beaucoup comme étant un expert dans son domaine; **these are not ~ held views** ce ne sont pas des opinions très répandues; **2** (at a distance) [*spaced, planted*] à de grands intervalles; (over a large area) [*travel*] beaucoup; **to be ~ travelled** avoir beaucoup voyagé; **copies of the magazine circulate ~** les exemplaires du magazine ont une grande diffusion; **3** (significantly) [*differ, vary*] beaucoup; [*different*] radicalement.

widely-read /ˌwaɪdlɪ'red/ *adj* [*student*] qui lit beaucoup; [*author*] beaucoup lu.

widen /'waɪdn/ **I** *vtr* **1** élargir [*road, path, gap*]; **2** fig élargir [*debate*]; étendre [*powers*]; **to ~ the scope of an enquiry** élargir le champ d'une enquête; **this has ~ed their lead in the opinion polls** ceci a renforcé leur position dominante dans les sondages.
II *vi* **1** [*river, road*] s'élargir; **his eyes ~ed** il a ouvert grand or écarquillé les yeux; **2** (increase) **the gap is ~ing between rich and poor** le fossé entre riches et pauvres s'élargit.
III widening *pres p adj* [*division*] de plus en plus grand; [*gap*] qui s'élargit de plus en plus; **the ~ing perception that** la conviction de plus en plus répandue que.

wide open *adj* **1** [*door, window etc*] grand ouvert; **her eyes were ~** ses yeux étaient grand ouverts; **2** [*competition*] ouvert à tous.

wide-ranging /ˌwaɪd'reɪndʒɪŋ/ *adj* [*poll, report, enquiry*] de grande envergure; **a ~ discussion** une discussion couvrant un grand nombre de sujets.

wide screen *n* Cin grand écran *m*.

widescreen TV *n* téléviseur *m* à grand écran.

widespread /'waɪdspred/ *adj* [*epidemic*] généralisé; [*devastation*] étendu; [*belief*] très répandu.

widgeon /'wɪdʒən/ *n* canard *m* siffleur.

widget○ /'wɪdʒɪt/ *n* hum bidule○ *m*, petite pièce *f*.

widow /'wɪdəʊ/ **I** *n* gen, Print veuve *f*; **golf ~** hum femme *f* délaissée par son mari golfeur; **war ~** veuve de guerre.
II *vtr* **to be ~ed** devenir veuf/veuve *m/f*; **she has been ~ed for two years** elle est veuve depuis deux ans; **my ~ed mother** ma mère devenue veuve.

widower /'wɪdəʊə(r)/ *n* veuf *m*.

widowhood /'wɪdəʊhʊd/ *n* veuvage *m*.

widow: **~'s mite** *n* Bible, fig denier *m* de la veuve; **~'s peak** *n* implantation *f* des cheveux en V sur le front; **~'s pension** *n* allocation *f* veuvage; **~'s walk** *n* US belvédère *m*; **~'s weeds†** *npl* vêtements *mpl* de deuil; **~ woman†** *n* veuve *f*.

width /wɪdθ, wɪtθ/ ▶ **1412** *n* **1** Meas largeur *f*; **it is 30 metres in ~** il fait or mesure 30 mètres de large, sa largeur est de 30 mètres; **2** Tex lé *m*; **3** (of swimming pool) largeur *f*.

widthways, **widthwise** /ˈwɪdθweɪz, ˈwɪtθ-, ˈwɪdθwaɪz, ˈwɪtθ-/ *adv* dans la largeur.

wield /wiːld/ *vtr* **1** (brandish) brandir [*weapon, tool*]; **2** fig (exercise) exercer [*influence, authority*] (**over** sur).

wiener /ˈwiːnə(r)/ *n* US **1** (also **~wurst**) Culin saucisse *f* de Francfort; **2**○ lang enfantin (penis) zizi○ *m*.

wiener schnitzel *n* escalope *f* panée.

wienie○ *n* US = **wiener**.

wife /waɪf/ *n* (*pl* **wives**) **1** (spouse) gen femme *f*; Admin, Jur épouse *f*; **she was his second ~** c'était sa deuxième femme; **he had three children by his first ~** il a eu trois enfants de sa première femme; **she will make him a good ~** elle fera une bonne épouse pour lui; **many wives would disagree** beaucoup de femmes mariées ne seraient pas d'accord; **the baker's/farmer's/butcher's ~** la boulangère/la fermière/la bouchère; **to take sb as one's ~** sout, **to take sb to ~**‡ prendre qn pour femme†; **the ~**○ hum la régulière○ hum; **2**‡ (woman) bonne femme *f*.

wife batterer *n* mari *m* violent.

wife battering *n* violence *f* corporelle contre les femmes; **the problem of ~** le problème des femmes battues.

wifely /ˈwaɪflɪ/ *adj* sout ou hum [*virtues, duties*] conjugal; [*loyalty, concern*] qui convient à une bonne épouse.

wife: **~'s equity** *n* US Jur *partie des biens communs qui revient à la femme après un divorce*; **~-swapper** *n* échangiste *m*; **~-swapping** *n* échange *m* de partenaires, échangisme *m*.

wig /wɪg/ *n* **1** (false hair) (whole head) perruque *f*; (partial) postiche *m*; **2**○ péj (hairdo) tignasse○ *f* pej.

wigeon *n* = **widgeon**.

wigging○† /ˈwɪgɪŋ/ *n* **to give sb a ~** gronder qn; **to get a ~** se faire gronder.

wiggle○ /ˈwɪgl/ **I** *n* **a ~ of the hips** un roulement des hanches; **to give sth a ~** faire bouger qch.
II *vtr* faire bouger [*tooth, wedged object*]; **to ~ one's hips** rouler des hanches; **to ~ one's fingers/toes** agiter les doigts/orteils; **to ~ one's ears** remuer les oreilles.
III *vi* [*snake, worm*] se tortiller; [*road, river*] faire des zigzags.

wiggly○ /ˈwɪglɪ/ *adj* [*road, line*] sinueux/-euse.

wigwam /ˈwɪgwæm, US -wɑːm/ *n* wigwam *m*.

wilco /ˈwɪlkəʊ/ *excl* Telecom message reçu.

wild /waɪld/ **I** *n* **in the ~** [*conditions, life*] en liberté; **to grow in the ~** pousser à l'état sauvage; **the call of the ~** l'appel de la nature.
II wilds *npl* **to live in the ~s of Arizona** habiter au fin fond de l'Arizona; **they live out in the ~s** ils vivent en pleine cambrousse○.
III *adj* **1** (in natural state) [*creature, plant, person*] sauvage; **~ bird/animal** oiseau/animal sauvage; **~ beast** bête fauve; **the pony is still quite ~** le poney est encore assez farouche; **2** (desolate) [*hill, landscape*] sauvage; **3** (turbulent) [*wind*] violent; [*sea*] agité; **it was a ~ night** c'était une nuit de tempête; **4** (unrestrained) [*party, laughter*] fou/folle; [*person*] fou/folle, dévergondé pej; [*imagination*] délirant; [*applause*] déchaîné; **to go ~** [*fans, audience*] se déchaîner; **she led a ~ life in her youth** elle a fait les quatre cents coups or elle s'est dévergondée pej dans sa jeunesse; **we had some ~ times together** on s'est bien marré○ ensemble; **his hair was ~ and unkempt** il avait les cheveux en bataille; **there was a ~ look in her eyes** elle avait un regard de folle, il y avait une lueur insensée dans son regard; **~ mood swings** changements d'humeur brutaux; **5**○ (furious) furieux/-ieuse; **he'll go** ou **be ~!** il sera hors de lui!; **6**○ (enthusiastic) **to be ~ about** être un fana○ de [*computers, films*]; **I'm not ~ about him/it** il/ça ne m'emballe○ pas; **7** (outlandish) [*idea , plan, scheme*] fou/folle; [*claim, promise, accusation*] extravagant; [*story*] farfelu○, dingue○; **all this ~ talk** tous ces propos exagérés; **8**○ (very good) **the concert was really ~**○**!** c'était un concert d'enfer○!
IV *adv* **1** [*grow*] à l'état sauvage; **the garden had run ~** le jardin était devenu sauvage, le jardin avait été laissé à l'abandon; **those children are allowed to run ~!** on permet à ces enfants de faire n'importe quoi!; **to let one's imagination run ~** laisser son imagination se débrider.
IDIOMS **to walk on the ~ side** vivre en marge.

wild: **~ boar** *n* sanglier *m*; **~ brier** *n* = **wild rose**.

wild card *n* **1** (in cards) joker *m*; **2** fig (unpredictable element) élément *m* imprévisible; **3** Sport wild-card *f* (*droit de participer à un tournoi sans s'être qualifié*); **4** (also **wildcard**) Comput joker *m*.

wildcat /ˈwaɪldkæt/ **I** *n* **1** Zool chat *m* sauvage; **2** fig (woman) furie *f*; **3** (oil well) puits *m* d'exploration; **4**○ US (unsound business scheme) entreprise *f* risquée.
II *adj* US [*scheme, venture*] risqué.
III *vi* (*p prés etc* **-tt-**) (drill for oil) faire un forage d'exploration.

wildcat strike *n* grève *f* sauvage.

wild: **~ cherry** *n* merisier *m*; **~ dog** *n* dingo *m*; **~ duck** *n* canard *m* sauvage.

wildebeest /ˈwɪldɪbiːst/ *n* gnou *m*.

wilderness /ˈwɪldənɪs/ *n* **1** (barren area, wasteland) étendue *f* sauvage et désolée; Bible désert *m*; **a ~ of factories** un paysage désolé d'usines; **2** Ecol (uncultivated, wild area) étendue *f* sauvage; **the world's great ~es** les grandes étendues sauvages du monde; **the garden has become a ~** le jardin est devenu une vraie jungle.
IDIOMS **to be in the ~** [*person*] faire sa traversée du désert; **he spent ten years in the ~** sa traversée du désert a duré dix ans; **to be a voice crying in the ~** prêcher dans le désert.

wild-eyed /ˌwaɪldˈaɪd/ *adj* au regard égaré.

wildfire /ˈwaɪldfaɪə(r)/ *n* **to spread like ~** se répandre comme une traînée de poudre.

wild flower *n* fleur *f* des champs, fleur *f* sauvage.

wildfowl /ˈwaɪldfaʊl/ *n* **1** (wild bird) oiseau *m* sauvage; (birds collectively) oiseaux *mpl* sauvages; **2** Hunt (game) gibier *m* à plume.

wild: **~fowler** *n* chasseur *m* de gibier à plume; **~fowling** *n* chasse *f* du gibier à plume.

wild-goose chase /ˌwaɪldˈguːs tʃeɪs/ *n* **it turned out to be a ~** ça n'a abouti à rien; **to send sb on a ~** faire chercher qn partout pour rien; **to lead sb on a ~** mettre qn sur une mauvaise piste.

wild: **~ hyacinth** *n* jacinthe *f* des bois; **~life** *n* (animals) faune *f*; (animals and plants) faune *f* et flore *f*; **~life conservation** *n* préservation *f* de la faune et de la flore; **~life park**, **~life reserve**, **~life sanctuary** *n* réserve *f* naturelle.

wildly /ˈwaɪldlɪ/ *adv* **1** (recklessly) [*invest, spend*] de façon insensée; [*fire, shoot*] au hasard; **to hit out/run ~** envoyer des coups/courir dans tous les sens; **to talk ~ of revenge** tenir des propos insensés de vengeance; **2** (violently, energetically) [*wave, gesture*] de manière très agitée; [*applaud*] à tout rompre; **to fluctuate ~** subir des fluctuations violentes; **his heart was beating ~** son cœur battait à tout rompre; **3** (extremely) [*enthusiastic, optimistic, successful*] extrêmement; **the news is not ~ encouraging** les nouvelles ne sont pas follement encourageantes.

wildness /ˈwaɪldnɪs/ *n* **1** (of landscape, mountains) aspect *m* sauvage; **2** (of wind, waves, weather) violence *f*; **3** (disorderliness) (of person, behaviour) caractère *m* débridé; (of appearance) désordre *m*; (of evening, party) folie *f*; **to have a reputation for ~** avoir la réputation de mener une vie débridée; **4** (extravagance) (of idea, plan, scheme) extravagance *f*; (of imagination) délire *m*.

wild: **~ rice** *n* riz *m* sauvage; **~ rose** *n* rosier *m* sauvage, églantier *m*; **~ water rafting** ▶ **1282** *n* rafting *m* sur rapides; **Wild West** *n* Far West *m*; **Wild West show** *n* US spectacle *m* inspiré du Far West.

wiles /waɪlz/ *npl* ruses *fpl*.

wilful GB, **willful** US /ˈwɪlfl/ *adj* **1** (headstrong) [*person, behaviour*] volontaire; **2** (deliberate) [*damage, disobedience*] délibéré; **3** Jur [*murder, misconduct*] volontaire.

wilfully GB, **willfully** US /ˈwɪlfəlɪ/ *adv* **1** (in headstrong way) obstinément, sciemment; **2** (deliberately) délibérément.

wilfulness GB, **willfullness** US /ˈwɪlflnɪs/ *n* **1** (of character) entêtement *m*; **2** (of act) caractère *m* délibéré.

wiliness /ˈwaɪlmɪs/ *n* (of character) astuce *f*; (of plan) subterfuge *m*.

will[1] /wɪl, əl/ **I** *modal aux* **1** (to express the future) **she'll help you** elle t'aidera; (in the near future) elle va t'aider; **the results ~ be announced on Monday** les résultats seront communiqués lundi; **I haven't read it yet, but I ~** je ne l'ai pas encore lu, mais je vais le faire; **must I phone him or ~ you?** est-ce que je dois lui téléphoner ou est-ce que tu vas le faire?; **I've said I'll repay you and I ~** j'ai dit que je te rembourserai et je le ferai; **2** (expressing consent, willingness) **'~ you help me?'—'yes, I ~'** 'est-ce que tu m'aideras?'—'oui, bien sûr'; **he won't cooperate/agree** il ne veut pas coopérer/donner son accord; **'have a chocolate'—'thank you, I ~'** 'prends un chocolat'—'volontiers, merci'; **I ~ not be talked to like that** je n'accepte pas qu'on me parle sur ce ton; **I won't have it said of me that I'm mean** il ne sera pas dit que je suis mesquin; **~ you or won't you?** c'est oui ou c'est non?; **do what** ou **as you ~** fais ce que tu veux; **ask who you ~** demande à qui tu veux; **call it what you ~** appelle ça comme tu veux; **it's a substitute, if you ~, for a proper holiday** ça remplace les vraies vacances en quelque sorte; **~ do**○**!** d'accord!; **3** (in commands, requests) **~ you pass the salt, please?** est-ce que tu peux me passer le sel, s'il te plaît?; **open the door ~ you** tu peux ouvrir la porte, s'il te plaît; **'I can give the speech'—'you ~ not!'** 'je peux faire le discours'—'pas question!'; **you ~ say nothing to anybody** ne dis rien à personne; **'I'll do it'—'no you won't'** 'je vais le faire'—'il n'en est pas question'; **~ you please listen to me!** est-ce que tu vas m'écouter!; **wait a minute ~ you!** attends un peu!; **4** (in offers, invitations) **~ you have a cup of tea?** est-ce que vous voulez une tasse de thé?; **~ you marry me?** est-ce que tu veux m'épouser?; **won't you join us for dinner?** est-ce que tu veux dîner avec nous?; **you'll have another cake, won't you?** vous prendrez bien un autre gâteau?; **5** (expressing custom or habit) **they ~ usually ask for a deposit** ils demandent généralement une caution; **any teacher ~ tell you that** n'importe quel professeur te dira que; **these things ~ happen** ce sont des choses qui arrivent; (in exasperation) **she ~ keep repeating the same old jokes** elle n'arrête pas de répéter les mêmes blagues; **if you ~ talk in class then he's bound to get cross** si tu n'arrêtes pas de bavarder pendant les cours, c'est logique qu'il se mette en colère; **6** (expressing a conjecture or assumption) **that ~ be my sister** ça doit être ma sœur; **they won't be aware of what has happened** ils ne doivent pas savoir ce qui s'est passé; **that ~ have been last month** ça devait être le mois dernier; **he'll be about 30 now** il doit

will¹

The future tense

When *will* is used to express the future in English, the future tense of the French verb is generally used:

he'll come = il viendra

In spoken and more informal French or when the very near future is implied, the present tense of *aller + infinitive* can be used:

I'll do it now = je vais le faire tout de suite

If the subject of the modal auxiliary *will* is *I* or *we*, *shall* is sometimes used instead of *will* to talk about the future. For further information, consult the entry ***shall*** in the dictionary.

Note that ***would*** and ***should*** are treated as separate entries in the dictionary.

Tag questions

French has no direct equivalent of tag questions like *won't he?* or *will they?* There is a general tag question *n'est-ce pas?* which will work in many cases:

you'll do it tomorrow, won't you? = tu le feras demain, n'est-ce pas?

In cases where an opinion is being sought, *non?* meaning *is that not so?* can be useful:

that will be easier, won't it? = ce sera plus facile, non?

In many other cases the tag question is simply not translated at all and the speaker's intonation will convey the implied question.

Short answers

Again, there is no direct equivalent for short answers like *no she won't, yes they will* etc. Where the answer *yes* is given to contradict a negative question or statement, the most useful translation is *si*:

'they won't forget' 'yes they will' = 'ils n'oublieront pas' 'si' *or (for more emphasis)* bien sûr que si

Where the answer *no* is given to contradict a positive question or statement the most useful translation is *bien sûr que non*:

'she'll post the letter, won't she?' 'no she won't' = 'elle va poster la lettre?' 'bien sûr que non'

In reply to a standard enquiry the tag will not be translated:

'you'll be ready at midday then?' 'yes I will' = 'tu seras prêt à midi?' 'oui'

For more examples and other uses, see the entry ***will***.

avoir 30 ans maintenant; **you'll be tired I expect** tu dois être fatigué je suppose; **you'll have gathered that** vous aurez compris que; **7** (expressing ability or capacity to do) **the lift ~ hold 12** l'ascenseur peut transporter 12 personnes; **that jug won't hold a litre** ce pichet ne contient pas un litre; **the car ~ do 120 km/h** la voiture peut faire 120 km/h; **this chicken won't feed six** ce poulet n'est pas assez gros pour six personnes; **oil ~ float on water** l'huile flotte sur l'eau; **the car won't start** la voiture ne veut pas démarrer.

II *vtr* **1** (urge mentally) **to ~ sb's death/downfall** souhaiter ardemment la mort/chute de qn; **to ~ sb to do** supplier mentalement qn de faire; **to ~ sb to live** prier pour que qn vive; **2** (wish, desire) vouloir; **fate/God ~ed it** le destin/Dieu l'a voulu ainsi; **3** Jur léguer (**to** à).

III *v refl* **he ~ed himself to stand up** au prix d'un effort surhumain il a réussi à se lever; **she ~ed herself to finish the race** au prix d'un effort surhumain elle a terminé la course.

■ **will on**: **~ [sb/sth] on** encourager.

will² /wɪl/ **I** *n* **1** (mental power) volonté *f* (**to do** de faire); **to have a strong/weak ~** avoir beaucoup/peu de volonté; **to have a ~ of one's own** faire ce qu'on a envie de faire; **strength of ~** force de caractère; ▶ **battle, effort, free will, iron**; **2** (wish, desire) volonté *f*, désir *m* (**to do** de faire); **it's the ~ of the people** c'est la volonté du peuple; **it's the ~ of the nation that** le pays souhaite que (+ *subj*); **Thy ~ be done** que ta volonté soit faite; **to impose one's ~ on sb** imposer sa volonté à qn; **it's my ~ that** c'est ma volonté que (+ *subj*); **to do sth against one's...** faire qch contre sa volonté; **he made me drink it against my ~** il me l'a fait boire contre mon gré; **to do sth with a ~** faire qch de bon cœur; **to lose the ~ to live** ne plus avoir envie de vivre; ▶ **goodwill, ill will**; **3** Jur testament *m*; **to make one's ~** faire son testament; **the last ~ and testament of** les dernières volontés de; **to leave sb sth in one's ~** léguer qch à qn; **to mention sb in one's ~** mettre qn sur son testament.

II at will *adv phr* **1** (as much as one likes) [*select, take*] à volonté; **2** (whenever you like) **you can change it at ~** tu peux le changer quand tu veux; **3** (freely) **they can wander about at ~** ils peuvent se promener comme ils veulent.

IDIOMS **where there's a ~ there's a way** Prov quand on veut on peut Prov; ▶ **world**.

willful *adj* US = **wilful**.

William /ˈwɪlɪəm/ *pr n* Guillaume; **~ the Conqueror** Guillaume le Conquérant.

willie○ /ˈwɪlɪ/ *n* lang enfantin zizi○ *m*.

IDIOMS **to have** ou **get the ~s**○ avoir la trouille○ or les chocottes○; **to give sb the ~s**○ ficher la frousse○ à qn.

willing /ˈwɪlɪŋ/ *adj* **1** (prepared) **to be ~ to do** être prêt or disposé à faire; **I'm quite ~** je veux bien; **if she's ~** si elle veut bien; **whether he's ~ or not** qu'il veuille ou non; **God ~** si Dieu le veut; **I'm more than ~ to help you** j'accepte volontiers de vous aider; **2** (eager) [*pupil, helper, friend*] de bonne volonté; [*slave*] consentant; [*recruit, victim*] volontaire; **to show ~** faire preuve de bonne volonté; **we need some ~ hands to clean up** nous avons besoin de volontaires pour nettoyer; **you were a ~ accomplice in the deception** tu as pris part volontairement à la tromperie; **3** (voluntary) [*donation*] bénévole; [*sacrifice*] volontaire.

IDIOMS **the spirit is ~ but the flesh is weak** l'esprit est ardent mais la chair est faible.

willingly /ˈwɪlɪŋlɪ/ *adv* [*accept, help*] volontiers; [*work*] avec bonne volonté; **'will you come?'—'~'** 'viendras-tu?'—'volontiers'; **did she go ~, or did you have to call the police?** est-elle partie de son propre gré, ou a-t-il fallu appeler la police?; **they went ~ to their death** ils sont allés à la mort de plein gré.

willingness /ˈwɪlɪŋnɪs/ *n* **1** (readiness) volonté *f* (**to do** de faire); **2** (helpfulness) bonne volonté *f*.

will-o'-the-wisp /ˌwɪləðəˈwɪsp/ **I** *n* feu *m* follet also fig.

II *modif* [*person, tendency*] fuyant.

willow /ˈwɪləʊ/ **I** *n* **1** (also **~ tree**) saule *m*; **2** (wood) (bois *m* de) saule *m*; **3** (for weaving) osier *m*; **4** (cricket bat) batte *f* (en saule).

II *modif* [*leaf*] de saule; [*bat*] en saule; [*basket, crib*] en osier; **~ plantation** oseraie *f*, saulaie *f*.

willow: **~ grouse** *n* lagopède *m* des saules; **~herb** *n* (also **rosebay ~herb**) épilobe *m*.

willow pattern I *n* motif *m* chinois (*bleu sur fond blanc*).

II *modif* [*dinner service*] au motif chinois.

willow: **~ tit** *n* mésange *f* des saules; **~ warbler** *n* pouillot *m* fitis.

willowy /ˈwɪləʊɪ/ *adj* [*person, figure*] élancé.

will power /wɪl/ *n* volonté *f* (**to do** de faire).

willy○ /ˈwɪlɪ/ *n* = **willie**.

willy-nilly /ˌwɪlɪˈnɪlɪ/ *adv* **1** (regardless of choice) bon gré mal gré; **2** (haphazardly) au hasard.

wilt /wɪlt/ **I**‡ *deuxième personne du singulier de* **will**.

II *n* Bot, Hort flétrissement *m*.

III *vtr* faire dépérir [*plant*].

IV *vi* lit [*plant, flower*] se faner; fig [*person*] (from heat, fatigue) flancher○, se sentir faible; (at daunting prospect) perdre courage.

V wilted *pp adj* [*leaves, lettuce*] fané.

Wilts *n* GB Post *abrév écrite* ▶ **Wiltshire**.

Wiltshire /ˈwɪltʃə(r)/ ▶ **1624** *pr n* Wiltshire *m*.

wily /ˈwaɪlɪ/ *adj* [*person, animal, plot*] rusé; **~ old bird**○ roublard/-e○ *m/f*; **~ old fox**○ vieux renard○ *m*.

IDIOMS **as ~ as a fox** rusé comme un renard.

wimp○ /wɪmp/ *n* péj (ineffectual person) lavette○ *f*; (fearful person) poule *f* mouillée.

■ **wimp out** se défiler○.

wimpish○ /ˈwɪmpɪʃ/ *adj* péj [*person*] mollasson/-onne○; [*behaviour, act*] mou/molle○.

wimple /ˈwɪmpl/ *n* guimpe *f*.

wimpy○ /ˈwɪmpɪ/ *adj* = **wimpish**○.

win /wɪn/ **I** *n* **1** (victory) gen, Pol, Sport victoire *f* (**over** sur); **to have a ~ over sb in sth** Pol, Sport remporter une victoire sur qn dans qch; **2** Games, Turf (successful bet) pari *m* gagnant; **to have a ~ on the horses** gagner sur un cheval.

II *vtr* (*p prés* **-nn-**; *prét, pp* **won**) **1** Games, Mil, Sport gagner [*battle, victory, competition, match, bet, money, prize*]; Pol gagner [*election, votes*] (**from sb** aux dépens de qn); gagner les élections dans [*region, city*] (**from sb** aux dépens de qn); **to ~ a (parliamentary) seat** être élu député (**from sb** aux dépens de qn); **2** (acquire) obtenir [*delay, reprieve*] (**from** de); gagner [*friendship, heart*] (**from** de); s'attirer [*sympathy*]; s'acquérir [*support*] (**of** de); **it won him the admiration of his colleagues** cela lui a valu l'admiration de ses collègues; **to ~ sb's love/respect** se faire aimer/respecter de qn; **to ~ one's way to sth** parvenir à qch; **to ~ sb's hand**† ou littér obtenir la main de qn.

III *vi* (*p prés* **-nn-**; *prét, pp* **won**) gagner; **to ~ against sb** l'emporter sur qn; **to ~ by a length/by two goals** gagner d'une longueur/de deux buts; **to play to ~** lit, fig jouer pour gagner; **go in and ~!** vas-y, tu l'auras!; **you ~!** (in argument) je m'incline!; **I've done my best to please her, but you just can't ~** j'ai tout fait pour lui plaire, mais rien à faire; **~ or lose, I shall enjoy the game** gagnant ou perdant, je jouerai avec plaisir; **~ or lose, the discussions have been valuable** quoi qu'il arrive, les discussions ont été profitables; **it's a ~ or lose situation** tout se joue là-dessus.

IDIOMS **~ some, lose some** on ne peut pas gagner à tous les coups.

■ **win back**: **~ [sth] back, ~ back [sth]** récupérer [*majority, support, votes*] (**from sb** sur qn); regagner [*affection, respect*]; reprendre [*prize, title, territory*] (**from** à).

■ **win out** l'emporter; **to ~ out over sth** vaincre qch.

■ **win over, win round**: **~ over [sb], ~ [sb] over** convaincre; **to ~ sb over to** convaincre qn de [*point of view*]; **can we ~ her over to our side?** pouvons-nous la convaincre de se joindre à nous?

■ **win through** finir par gagner; **to ~ through to** Sport se qualifier pour [*semifinal etc*].

wince /wɪns/ **I** *n* grimace *f*.

II *vi* grimacer, faire une grimace; **to ~ with pain/disgust** grimacer de douleur/dégoût.

winch /wɪntʃ/ **I** *n* treuil *m*.
II *vtr* **1** = **winch down**; **2** = **winch up**.
■ **winch down**: **~ [sth/sb] down**, **~ down [sth/sb]** descendre [qch/qn] au treuil.
■ **winch up**: **~ [sth/sb] up**, **~ up [sth/sb]** hisser [qch/qn] au treuil.

Winchester /ˈwɪntʃɪstə(r)/ *n* **1** Comput (also **~ disk**) disque *m* dur; **2** ®Mil (also **~ rifle**) fusil *m* à répétition Winchester; **3** (also **winchester (jar)**) Chem bocal *m* de chimiste.

wind[1] /wɪnd/ **I** *n* **1** Meteorol vent *m*; **North/East ~** vent du nord/d'est; **the ~ is blowing** il y a du vent; **which way is the ~ blowing?** d'où vient le vent?; **a high ~** un vent fort, un grand vent; **to have the ~ at one's back** ou **to have the ~ behind one** avoir le vent pour soi; **2** Naut vent *m*; **fair ~** bon vent; **to sail** ou **run before the ~** lit, fig avoir le vent en poupe; **to sail into the ~** naviguer contre le vent, avoir le vent debout; **to sail close to the ~** Naut serrer le vent; fig jouer avec le feu; **3** (breath) souffle *m*; **to knock the ~ out of** couper le souffle à; **to get one's ~** reprendre souffle; **to get one's second ~** fig reprendre ses forces; **4** fig (current) vent *m*; **the ~ of change** le vent du changement; **the cold ~s of recession** le spectre de la récession; **there is something in the ~** il y a quelque chose dans l'air, il se prépare quelque chose; **5** (flatulence) vents *mpl*, gaz *mpl* intestinaux; **to break ~** lâcher un vent; **to suffer from ~** avoir des gaz; **to bring up ~** roter; **that's a lot of ~**○! c'est du vent○!; **6** Mus **the ~(s)** les instruments *mpl* à vent.
II *vtr* **1** (make breathless) [*blow, punch*] couper la respiration or le souffle à; [*climb, exertion*] essouffler, mettre [qn] hors d'haleine; **2** (burp) faire faire son rot○ à [*baby*]; **3** Hunt (scent) avoir un vent de, flairer.
IDIOMS **to get ~ of** avoir vent de, apprendre; **to get the ~ up**○ avoir la trouille○ or la frousse○ (**about** à cause de); **to put the ~ up sb**○ flanquer la trouille○ à qn, faire une peur bleue à qn; **to go/run like the ~** aller/filer comme le vent; **it's (like) pissing**● ou **whistling in the ~** c'est comme si on pissait● dans un violon; **to see which way the ~ blows** prendre le vent; **you'll be stuck like that if the ~ changes!** (to child pulling faces) arrête ou tu vas rester comme ça!

wind[2] /waɪnd/ **I** *n* **1** (bend) (of road) tournant *m*; **2** (movement) (of handle) tour *m*; **to give a clock a ~** remonter une pendule.
II *vtr* (*prét, pp* **wound**) **1** (coil up) enrouler [*hair, rope, string, tape, wire*] (**on, onto** sur; **round** autour de); **he wound a scarf round his neck** il s'est enroulé or passé une écharpe autour du cou; **she wound her arms around him** elle l'a enlacé; **to ~ wool** faire une pelote de laine; **2** (set in motion) (also **~ up**) remonter [*watch, clock, toy*]; **3** (turn) donner un tour de [*handle*]; **4** (move sinuously) **to ~ one's** ou **its way** [*procession, road, river*] serpenter.
III *vi* (*prét, pp* **wound**) [*road, river, procession*] serpenter (**along** le long de); [*stairs*] tourner; **a queue ~ing round the theatre** une queue qui tournait au coin du théâtre.
■ **wind down**: ¶ **~ down 1** (end) [*organization*] réduire ses activités, ralentir; [*activity, production*] toucher à sa fin; [*person*] (relax) se détendre; **2** [*clockwork*] être sur le point de s'arrêter; ¶ **~ down [sth]**, **~ [sth] down 1** (open) baisser [*car window*]; **2** (prepare for closure) mettre fin à [*activity, organization*]; **the business is being wound down** on est en train de mettre fin à l'entreprise.
■ **wind in**: **~ in [sth]**, **~ [sth] in** remonter [*cable, line, fish*].
■ **wind off**: **~ off [sth]**, **~ [sth] off** dérouler [*thread, rope*].
■ **wind on**: ¶ **~ on** [*film*] s'enrouler, s'embobiner; ¶ **~ on [sth]**, **~ [sth] on** enrouler [*thread, rope*]; enrouler, embobiner [*film*].
■ **wind up**: ¶ **~ up 1** (finish) [*event*] se terminer (**with** par); [*speaker*] conclure; **2**○ (end up) finir, se retrouver; **we wound up at Louise's house/sleeping in a barn** on a fini chez Louise/par dormir dans une grange; **the car wound up in the ditch** la voiture s'est retrouvée dans le fossé; **she wound up as a dancer in Tokyo** elle s'est retrouvée danseuse à Tokyo; ¶ **~ up [sth]**, **~ [sth] up 1** (terminate) liquider [*business*]; fermer [*account , club*]; mettre fin à [*campaign, career, debate, meeting, project, tour*]; Jur régler [*estate*]; **2** (cause to move) remonter [*clock, watch, toy, car window*]; ¶ **~ [sb] up**, **~ up [sb] 1** (tease) faire marcher [*person*]; **2** (annoy, make tense) énerver; **to be wound up about sth** être énervé à cause de qch.

wind /wɪnd/: **~bag**○ *n* péj moulin *m* à paroles; **~blown** *adj* [*hair*] ébouriffé par le vent; [*tree*] fouetté par le vent; **~borne** *adj* apporté par le vent; **~bound** *adj* [*ship*] retenu par des vents défavorables; **~break** *n* (natural) brise-vent *m inv*; (on beach) pare-vent *m inv*; **Windbreaker** *n* US coupe-vent *m inv*, anorak *m*; **~burn** *n* brûlure *f* superficielle (due au vent), érythème *m* solaire spec; **~cheater** *n* GB coupe-vent *m inv*, anorak *m*; **~-chill factor** *n* facteur *m* de refroidissement de la température dû au vent; **~ chimes** *npl* carillon *m* éolien; **~ cone** *n* manche *f* à air; **~ deflector** *n* Aut déflecteur *m*; **~ energy** *n* énergie *f* éolienne.

winder /ˈwaɪndə(r)/ *n* **1** (object) (for watch) remontoir *m*; (for wool, thread) dévidoir *m*; (for window) lève-glace *m inv*; **2** Ind (person) dévideur/-euse *m/f*.

windfall /ˈwɪndfɔːl/ **I** *n* **1** lit fruit *m* tombé par terre; **2** fig aubaine *f*.
II *modif* [*apple*] tombé par terre.

wind /wɪnd/: **~fall profit** *n* profit *m* inattendu; **~flower** *n* anémone *f* des bois; **~ gap** *n* couloir *m*, défilé *m*; **~ gauge** *n* anémomètre *m*; **~ generator** *n* aérogénérateur *m*; **~ harp** ▶ **1481** *n* harpe *f* éolienne; **~hover** *n* GB littér ou dial crécerelle *f*.

winding /ˈwaɪndɪŋ/ **I** *n* **1** (of road, river) sinuosité *f*; **2** Elec bobinage *m*.
II *adj* [*path, road, river, valley, course*] sinueux/-euse; [*stairs*] en spirale.

winding: **~ coil** *n* Elec bobine *f*; **~ drum** *n* tambour *m* d'enroulage; **~ gear** *n* matériel *m* de hissage; **~ sheet** *n* linceul *m*.

winding-up /ˌwaɪndɪŋˈʌp/ **I** *n* (of business, affairs) clôture *f*.
II *modif* [*order, petition*] de clôture.

wind instrument /wɪnd/ ▶ **1481** *n* instrument *m* à vent.

windjammer /ˈwɪnddʒæmə(r)/ *n* **1** Naut grand voilier *m* (commercial); **2** GB coupe-vent *m inv*, anorak *m*.

windlass /ˈwɪndləs/ *n* gén treuil *m*; Naut guindeau *m*.

windless /ˈwɪndləs/ *adj* sans vent.

wind machine /wɪnd/ *n* machine *f* à vent.

windmill /ˈwɪndmɪl/ *n* **1** moulin *m* à vent; **2** (toy) moulinet *m*.
IDIOMS **to tilt at ~s** se battre contre des moulins à vent.

window /ˈwɪndəʊ/ *n* **1** (to look through) (of house, room) fenêtre *f*; (of shop, public building) vitrine *f*, devanture *f*; (of train) vitre *f*, fenêtre *f*; (of car) vitre *f*, glace *f*, fenêtre *f*; (of plane) hublot *m*; (stained-glass) vitrail *m*; **to sit at** ou **by the ~** (in room) s'asseoir à la fenêtre; (in train, car) s'asseoir près de la fenêtre; **I'd like a seat by a ~** Aviat j'aimerais une place côté fenêtre; **to look out of** ou **through the ~** regarder par la fenêtre; **if you look out of the ~ you will see Paris** Aviat si vous regardez par le hublot vous verrez Paris; **to lean out of the ~** se pencher par la fenêtre; **'do not lean out of the ~'** (in train) 'ne pas se pencher au dehors'; **to break a ~** casser une vitre or un carreau; **to clean** ou **wash the ~s** laver les vitres or les carreaux; **how much is the jacket in the ~?** Comm combien coûte la veste dans la vitrine?; **a ~ on the world** fig une fenêtre sur le monde; **to provide a ~ on what goes on behind the scenes** fig ouvrir une fenêtre sur ce qui se passe dans les coulisses; **2** (for service at bank or post-office) guichet *m*; **3** (of envelope) fenêtre *f*; **4** Comput fenêtre *f*; **5** (space in diary, time) créneau *m*; **we've missed our ~** nous avons raté notre créneau; **to provide a ~ of opportunity for sb to do** fournir un créneau à qn pour faire; **launch ~** créneau de lancement.
IDIOMS **to go** ou **fly out the ~**○ [*plans*] tomber à l'eau; [*hopes*] s'écrouler; **the eyes are the ~s of the soul** Prov les yeux sont le miroir de l'âme.

window: **~ blind** *n* store *m*; **~ box** *n* jardinière *f*, bac *m* à fleurs; **~ cleaner** *n* (person) laveur/-euse *m/f* de carreaux; (product) produit *m* pour nettoyer les vitres or les carreaux; **~ display** *n* Comm vitrine *f*; **~ dresser** ▶ **1692** *n* étalagiste *mf*.

window dressing *n* **1** lit composition *f* de vitrines; **2** fig **it's all ~** fig, péj c'est de la poudre aux yeux○, c'est pour épater la galerie○ **3** Fin habillage *m* de bilan.

window: **~ envelope** *n* enveloppe *f* à fenêtre; **~ frame** *n* châssis *m* de fenêtre; **~ glass** *n* verre *m* à vitres; **~ ledge** *n* appui *m* de fenêtre; **~pane** *n* carreau *m*, vitre *f*.

window seat *n* **1** (in room) banquette *f* (*encastrée sous une fenêtre*); **2** (in plane, bus, train) place *f* côté fenêtre.

window-shopping *n* **to go ~** faire du lèche-vitrines *m inv*.

window: **~sill** *n* rebord *m* de fenêtre; **~ winder** *n* Aut lève-glace *m inv*.

wind /wɪnd/: **~pipe** *n* Anat trachée-artère *f*; **~-pollinated** *adj* fécondé par du pollen porté par le vent; **~power** *n* énergie *f* éolienne; **~proof** *adj* qui protège du vent, qui ne laisse pas passer le vent; **~screen** *n* GB Aut pare-brise *m inv*; **~screen washer** *n* GB Aut lave-glace *m*; **~screen wiper** *n* GB Aut essuie-glace *m inv*; **~ section** *n* instruments *mpl* à vent; **~shield** *n* US Aut = **windscreen**; **~-sleeve**, **~-sock** *n* manche *f* à air; **~speed** *n* vitesse *f* du vent; **~speed indicator** *n* anémomètre *m*; **~storm** *n* tempête *f*, tourbillon *m*; **~surf** *vi* faire de la planche à voile; **~surfer** *n* (person) véliplanchiste *mf*; (board) planche *f* à voile; **~surfing** ▶ **1282** *n* planche *f* à voile; **~ surge** *n* élévation *f* du niveau de l'eau due au vent; **~swept** *adj* [*moor, hillside, coast*] venteux/-euse, balayé par le vent.

wind tunnel /wɪnd/ *n* **1** Tech tunnel *m* aérodynamique; **2** (windy gap or passage) couloir *m* venté.

wind turbine /wɪnd/ *n* moteur *m* éolien.

windward /ˈwɪndwəd/ **I** *n* côté *m* du vent; **to sail to ~** naviguer contre le vent, avoir le vent debout.
II *adj, adv* contre le vent.

windward: **Windward Islands** *pr npl* îles *fpl* du Vent; **Windward Passage** *pr n* canal *m* au Vent.

windy /ˈwɪndɪ/ *adj* **1** [*place*] venteux/-euse, balayé par le vent; [*day*] de vent; **it** ou **the weather was very ~** il faisait beaucoup de vent; **2** péj (verbose) [*person, speech*] verbeux/-euse; **3**† ○GB (scared) **to get ~ about**○ avoir la frousse○ à propos de.

Windy City *pr n* US Chicago.

wine /waɪn/ ▶ **1104** **I** *n* **1** (drink) vin *m*; **2** (colour) lie-de-vin *m*, bordeaux *m*.
II *modif* [*production*] de vin; [*cellar, cask*] à vin.
III *adj* (also **~-coloured**) lie-de-vin *inv*, bordeaux *inv*.
IDIOMS **to ~ and dine** manger dans les

bons restaurants; **she's always being ~d and dined** elle se fait toujours inviter dans les bons restaurants.

■ **wine up**○ US se cuiter○.

wine: **~ bar** *n* bar *m* à vin; **~bibber** *n* hum bon buveur *m*; **~ bottling** *n* mise *f* en bouteilles du vin; **~ box** *n* = cubitainer® *m*; **~ cask** *n* tonneau *m* à vin; **~ cellar** *n* cave *f*.

wine cooler *n* **1** (ice bucket) seau *m* à rafraîchir; **2** US (drink) *boisson légèrement alcoolisée.*

wined **(up)**○ /ˌwaɪnd (ˈʌp)/ *pp adj* US cuité○.

wine: **~ glass** *n* verre *m* à vin; **~ grower** *n* viticulteur/-trice *m/f*.

wine growing I *n* viticulture *f*.
II *modif* [*region*] vinicole.

wine: **~ gum** *n* GB gomme *f* acidulée; **~ list** *n* carte *f* des vins; **~ merchant** ▶ 1692 *n* négociant *m* en vins; **~ press** *n* pressoir *m*; **~ producer** ▶ 1692 *n* viticulteur/-trice *m/f*.; **~ rack** *n* cellier *m*.

winery /ˈwaɪnərɪ/ *n* US entreprise *f* vinicole.

wine shop ▶ 1692 *n* marchand *m* de vin; **he owns a ~** il tient un commerce de vin.

wine: **~ skin** *n* outre *f* à vin; **~ taster** ▶ 1692 *n* (person) dégustateur/-trice *m/f* de vins; (cup) taste-vin *m*; **~ tasting** *n* dégustation *f* de vins; **~ vinegar** *n* vinaigre *m* de vin; **~ waiter** ▶ 1692 *n* sommelier/-ière *m/f*.

wing /wɪŋ/ I *n* **1** Zool (of bird, insect) aile *f*; **to be on the ~** être en vol; **to catch insects on the ~** attraper des insectes au vol; **2** (of building, plane, car) aile *f*; (of armchair) oreille *f*; **3** Mil, Pol (of army, party) aile *f*; (unit in air force) escadre *f*; **4** Sport (player) ailier *m*; (side of pitch) aile *f*, côté *m*; **to play on the right ~** être ailier droit.
II **wings** *npl* **1** Theat **the ~s** les coulisses *fpl*; **to be waiting in the ~s** Theat attendre dans les coulisses; fig attendre son heure; **2** Aviat **to get one's ~s** obtenir l'insigne de pilote.
III *vtr* **1 to ~ one's way to** [*plane, pasenger, letter*] voler vers; **2** (injure) [*bullet*] érafler.
IV *vi* (fly) voler; **the geese are ~ing into the estuary/back to their winter home** les oies volent vers l'estuaire/repartent pour l'hiver.
IDIOMS **to clip sb's ~s** rogner les ailes à qn; **to spread one's ~s** (entering adult life) voler de ses propres ailes; (entering wider career) voir autre chose; **to take sb under one's ~s** prendre qn sous son aile; **to take ~** littér [*thoughts*] s'envoler; **to ~ it**○ US improviser.

wing: **~ case** *n* élytre *m*; **~ chair** *n* fauteuil *m* à oreilles; **~ collar** *n* col *m* cassé; **~ commander** ▶ 1612 *n* lieutenant-colonel *m* de l'armée de l'air; **~-ding**○ *n* US nouba○ *f*, fête *f*.

winge *vi* = **whinge**.

winged /wɪŋd/ *adj* [*cupid, horse, creature*] ailé; [*insect*] volant; **a blue-~ bird** un oiseau aux ailes bleues.

winger○ /ˈwɪŋə(r)/ *n* GB ailier *m*.

wing: **~ flap** *n* aileron *m*; **~-footed** *adj* littér (swift) au pied léger; **~ forward** *n* (in rugby) avant *m* troisième ligne; **~ half** *n* (in soccer) demi-droit *m*, demi-gauche *m*; **~ mirror** *n* GB rétroviseur *m* extérieur; **~ nut** *n* écrou *m* à oreilles; **~span** *n* envergure *f*; **~ three-quarter** *n* (in rugby) trois-quarts aile *m*, ailier *m*; **~ tip** *n* bout *m* de l'aile.

wink /wɪŋk/ I *n* clin *m* d'œil; **to give sb a ~** faire un clin d'œil à qn; **we didn't get a ~ of sleep all night** nous n'avons pas fermé l'œil de la nuit.
II *vtr* **to ~ one's eye** cligner de l'œil; **he ~ed his eye at me** il m'a fait un clin d'œil.
III *vi* **1** [*person*] cligner de l'œil; **to ~ at sb** faire un clin d'œil à qn; **to ~ at sth** fig fermer les yeux sur qch; **2** [*light*] clignoter; [*jewellery*] briller.
IDIOMS **a nod is as good as a ~ to a blind horse** ou **man** c'est bien, on a compris; **as quick as a ~, in the ~ of an eye** en un clin d'œil; **to tip sb the ~**○ avertir qn.

winker○ /ˈwɪŋkə(r)/ *n* GB Aut clignotant *m*.

winking /ˈwɪŋkɪŋ/ I *n* (of eye) clignement *m*; (of light) clignotement *m*.
II *adj* [*light*] clignotant.
IDIOMS **as easy as ~**○ simple comme bonjour○.

winkle /ˈwɪŋkl/ *n* (also **periwinkle**) Zool bigorneau *m*.

■ **winkle out**○: **~ [sth/sb] out**, **~ out [sth/sb]** dénicher [*person, objet*] (**of** de); soutirer [*truth, confession*] (**of** de).

winkle-pickers /ˌwɪŋklˈpɪkəz/ *npl* chaussures *fpl* à bout pointu.

winner /ˈwɪnə(r)/ *n* **1** (victor) gagnant/-e *m/f*; **to be the ~(s)** Sport, Turf finir gagnant; **to be on to a ~** Turf, fig jouer gagnant; **to back the ~** parier sur le gagnant; **he certainly backed a ~ when he married her** il a vraiment joué gagnant en l'épousant; **to pick** ou **spot the ~** Turf jouer le gagnant; **~ takes all** Games le gagnant rafle tout; **that shot was a ~!** c'était un coup gagnant!; **2** (success) **to be a ~** [*film, book, play, design, song*] avoir un gros succès; **he's a ~** tout lui réussit.

winning /ˈwɪnɪŋ/ I *n* réussite *f*.
II **winnings** *npl* gains *mpl*.
III *adj* **1** (victorious) [*competitor, car, horse, team, entry, shot*] gagnant; **2** (charming) [*smile*] engageant; **to have a ~ way** ou **~ ways** avoir du charme.

winningly /ˈwɪnɪŋlɪ/ *adj* d'un air engageant; **to smile ~** faire un sourire engageant.

winning post *n* poteau *m* d'arrivée.

winning streak *n* Sport, fig **to be on a ~** être dans une bonne période.

winnow /ˈwɪnəʊ/ *vtr* **1** Agric vanner; **2** fig démêler [*truth, facts*] (**from** de).

■ **winnow down**: **~ [sth] down**, **~ down [sth]** réduire [qch] par tri.

winnower /ˈwɪnəʊə(r)/ *n* Agric **1** (person) vanneur/-euse *m/f*; **2** (machine) tarare *m*.

wino○ /ˈwaɪnəʊ/ *n* péj poivrot/-ote○ *m/f* pej.

winsome /ˈwɪnsəm/ *adj* [*person*] charmant, accort; [*smile*] engageant.

winsomely /ˈwɪnsəmlɪ/ *adv* d'un air engageant.

winsomeness /ˈwɪnsəmnɪs/ *n* charme *m*.

winter /ˈwɪntə(r)/ ▶ 1671 I *n* hiver *m*.
II *modif* [*activity, clothes, weather*] d'hiver; [*ascent*] hivernal.
III *vtr* Agric, Hort hiverner.
IV *vi* passer l'hiver.

winter: **~ aconite** *n* eranthis hyemalis *m*; **~ cherry** *n* alkékenge *m*, amour-encage *m*; **~ feed** *n* fourrage *m* d'hiver; **~ garden** *n* Hort jardin *m* d'hiver; **~green** *n* wintergreen *m*.

winterize /ˈwɪntəraɪz/ *vtr* US préparer [qch] pour l'hiver.

winter: **~ jasmine** *n* jasmin *m* d'hiver; **~kill** *n* US gel *m*; **Winter Olympics** *npl* jeux *mpl* Olympiques d'hiver; **~ quarters** *npl* quartiers *mpl* d'hiver; **~ sleep** *n* hibernation *f*; **~ sports** *npl* sports *mpl* d'hiver; **~time** *n* hiver *m*; **~ wheat** *n* blé *m* d'hiver.

wintry /ˈwɪntrɪ/ *adj* **1** lit hivernal; **2** fig [*smile, welcome*] glacé.

wipe /waɪp/ I *n* **1** (act of wiping) (with dry cloth) coup *m* de torchon; (with wet cloth) coup *m* d'éponge; **to give sth a ~** essuyer qch [*table, work surface*]; nettoyer qch [*bath, sink*]; **2** Cosmet lingette *f*; Med tampon *m*; **antiseptic ~** tampon *m* aseptique; **baby ~s** lingettes *fpl* de bébé; **3** Cin effaçage *m*.
II *vtr* **1** (mop) essuyer [*part of body, crockery, surface*] (**on** sur; **with** avec); **she ~d her eyes** elle s'est essuyé les yeux; **he ~d the sweat from his eyes** il s'est essuyé la sueur qui lui coulait dans les yeux; **to ~ one's nose** se moucher; **she ~d the baby's nose** elle a mouché le bébé; **she ~d the baby's bottom** elle a essuyé les fesses du bébé; **to ~ sth clean** essuyer qch; **'please ~ your feet'** (sign) 'prière de s'essuyer les pieds'; **~ that smile/grin off your face!** cesse de sourire/de ricaner!; **2** Cin, Comput, Radio, TV effacer.

■ **wipe away**: **~ away [sth]**, **~ [sth] away** essuyer [*tears, sweat*]; faire partir [*dirt, mark*].

■ **wipe down**: **~ down [sth]**, **~ [sth] down** nettoyer [*wall, floor*].

■ **wipe off**: **~ off [sth]**, **~ [sth] off** **1** faire partir [*dirt, mark*]; **2** Audio, Cin, Comput, Video effacer.

■ **wipe out**: **~ out [sth]**, **~ [sth] out** **1** lit (clean) nettoyer [*container, cupboard*]; **2** Audio, Cin, Comput, Video effacer; **3** fig (cancel) effacer [*memory, past*]; liquider [*debt*]; annuler [*chances, inflation, gains, losses*]; (kill) anéantir [*species, enemy, population*]; **4**○ Sport (defeat) lessiver○.

■ **wipe up**: ¶ **~ up** essuyer la vaisselle; ¶ **~ up [sth]**, **~ [sth] up** essuyer.

wipe: **~-clean** *adj* facile à nettoyer; **~-down** *n* (coup *m* de) nettoyage *m*.

wiper /ˈwaɪpə(r)/ *n* **1** Aut (also **windscreen ~** GB, **windshield ~** US) essuie-glace *m inv*; **2** (cloth) torchon *m*.

wiper: **~ arm** *n* Aut bras *m* d'essuie-glace; **~ blade** *n* Aut balai *m* d'essuie-glace; **~ motor** *n* Aut moteur *m* d'essuie-glace.

wire /ˈwaɪə(r)/ I *n* **1** (length of metal) fil *m*; **copper ~** fil de cuivre; **electric/telephone ~** fil électrique/téléphonique; **a length/coil of ~** un bout/rouleau de fil; **loose ~s** (from wall) des fils qui dépassent; (on floor) des fils qui traînent; (from plug) des fils qui sortent; **2** US (telegram) télégramme *m*; **to get a ~ from sb** recevoir un télégramme de qn; **to send sb a ~** envoyer un télégramme à qn; **3** US (in horseracing) ligne *f* d'arrivée.
II *vtr* **1** Elec **to ~ a house** installer l'électricité dans une maison; **to ~ a plug/a lamp** connecter une prise/une lampe; **the oven had been incorrectly ~d** le four avait été mal connecté; **the house is ~d for television** la maison peut capter la télévision; **2** (send telegram to) télégraphier à [*person*]; **he ~d us his answer immediately** il nous a immédiatement télégraphié sa réponse; **3** (stiffen) renforcer [qch] avec un fil métallique [*stem, flower, bodice*].
IDIOMS **down to the ~** US jusqu'au tout dernier moment; **to get in under the ~** US (arrive) arriver de justesse; (accomplish sth) finir qch de justesse; **to pull ~s** US se faire pistonner○; **to get one's ~s** ou **lines crossed** se comprendre de travers; **~d up**○ énervé.

■ **wire up**: **~ [sth] up to sth** relier [qch] à qch; **the TV is ~d up to the speakers** la télé est reliée aux haut-parleurs.

wire: **~ brush** *n* brosse *f* métallique; **~ cloth** *n* toile *f* métallique; **~ cutters** *npl* cisailles *fpl*; **~ gauge** *n* calibreur *m* à fil métallique; **~ gauze** *n* toile *f* métallique; **~ glass** *n* verre *m* armé.

wireless /ˈwaɪəlɪs/ *n* GB **1**† (radio set) poste *m* de radio; **on the ~** à la T.S.F.; **2** (transmitter, receiver) radio *f*; **by ~** par radio; **to receive a message over the ~** recevoir un message par radio.

wireless: **~ message** *n* message *m* radio(phonique); **~ operator** ▶ 1692 *n* radiotélégraphiste *mf*; **~ room** *n* cabine *f* radio; **~ set**† *n* poste *m* de radio; **~ telegraphy** *n* télégraphie *f* sans fil.

wire: **~man**○ ▶ 1692 *n* US (electrician) électricien *m*; (phone tapper) *technicien spécialisé dans l'espionnage électronique*; **~ mesh** *n* treillis *m* métallique; **~ netting** *n* grillage *m*.

wirepuller○ /ˈwaɪəpʊlə(r)/ *n* US **he's a ~** il a du piston○.

wire service *n* (agency) agence *f* de presse; (facility) lignes *fpl* d'une agence de presse.

wire tap I *n* 1 (device) (on phone, in room) micro *m*; 2 (occurrence) mise *f* sur écoute.
II *vtr* (*p prés etc* **-pp-**) mettre [qn/qch] sur écoute [*person, room, phone line*].

wire: **~ tapping** *n* espionnage *m* électronique; **~ wool** *n* paille *f* de fer; **~worm** *n* (in crops) ver *m* de fer.

wiriness /ˈwaɪərɪnɪs/ *n* (of dog's hair) dureté *f* de poil; (of build) maigreur *f*.

wiring /ˈwaɪərɪŋ/ *n* (in house) installation *f* électrique; (in appliance) circuit *m* (électrique); **to redo the ~** refaire l'installation électrique; **faulty ~** (in house) installation électrique défectueuse; (in appliance) circuit (électrique) défectueux; **the ~ in the oven is faulty** le four est mal connecté.

wiry /ˈwaɪərɪ/ *adj* 1 [*person, body*] maigre; **a ~ little man** un petit homme sec et nerveux; 2 [*hair*] raide; [*grass*] dru; **to have a ~ coat** [*animal*] avoir le poil raide.

Wisconsin /ˌwɪsˈkɒnsɪn/ **▶ 1744** I *pr n* (state, river) Wisconsin *m*.
II *modif* [*climate, border etc*] du Wisconsin.

wisdom /ˈwɪzdəm/ *n* (of action, decision, person) sagesse *f*; **to doubt** ou **question the ~ of doing** douter qu'il soit sage de faire; **in his ~** iron dans son infinie sagesse; **with the ~ of hindsight** avec une sagesse rétrospective.

wisdom tooth *n* dent *f* de sagesse.

wise /waɪz/ I sout† *n* (way) façon *f*; **in no ~** en aucune façon, aucunement.
II *adj* 1 (prudent) [*person*] sage, prudent; [*action, advice, decision, precaution*] sage; [*choice*] judicieux/-ieuse; **it is ~ of sb to do** il est prudent de la part de qn de faire; **you would be ~ to do** tu ferais bien de faire; **I think it ~ that you should do** je pense qu'il serait sage de ta part de faire; **to be ~ enough to do** avoir le bon sens de faire; **the ~st thing (to do) would be to** le plus sage serait de; **was that ~?** était-ce bien raisonnable?; 2 (learned) [*academic, book, speech*] pertinent; **to be ~ after the event** être sage après coup; **to be none the ~r** (understand no better) ne pas être plus avancé; (not realize) ne s'apercevoir de rien; **to be sadder and ~r** tirer la leçon de la triste expérience; 3○ (aware) **to be ~ to** être au courant de [*facts*]; **to get ~ to** prendre le coup de [*situation*]; **to get ~ to sb** saisir à qui on a affaire; **to put sb ~ to** mettre qn au courant de, affranchir○ qn de [*facts*].
III **-wise** (*dans composés*) 1 (direction) dans le sens de; **length-/width-~** dans le sens de la longueur/de la largeur; 2 (with regard to) pour ce qui est de; **time-/work-~** pour ce qui est du temps/du travail.
IDIOMS **a word to the ~**:... en tout cas un conseil:...
■ **wise up**○ se mettre au courant (**to** de).

wise: **~acre**† *n* puits *m* de science; **~-ass**◑ *n* US petit malin○ *m*.

wisecrack /ˈwaɪzkræk/ I *n* vanne○ *f*.
II *vi* balancer des vannes○.

wise: **~cracking** *adj* vanneur/-euse○; **~ guy**○ *n* gros malin○ *m*.

wisely /ˈwaɪzlɪ/ *adv* [*choose, decide*] judicieusement; **~, he decided to**... il a judicieusement décidé de...

Wise Men *npl* **the three ~** les (trois) Rois *mpl* Mages.

wise woman *n* sorcière *f*.

wish /wɪʃ/ I *n* (desire) désir *m* (**for** de; **to do** de faire); (in fairy story) souhait *m* (**for** de); **her ~ came true** son souhait s'est réalisé; **the fairy gave her three ~es** la fée lui a accordé trois souhaits; **a ~ for freedom/to be free** un désir de liberté/d'être libre; **to make a ~** faire un vœu; **to have/express/cherish a ~** avoir/exprimer/caresser un désir; **to grant sb's ~** [*monarch, official, authority, parent*] accéder au désir de qn; [*fairy*] exaucer le souhait de qn; **I have no ~ to disturb you/talk to you** sout je n'ai pas l'intention de vous déranger/de vous parler; **at his wife's/boss's ~** selon la volonté de sa femme/de son chef; **to do sth against sb's ~es** faire qch à l'encontre des désirs de qn; **it is my dearest ~ to visit Capri** mon vœu le plus cher est de visiter Capri; **you will get your ~** vous aurez ce que vous désirez.
II **wishes** *npl* vœux *mpl*; **good** ou **best ~es** meilleurs vœux; (ending letter) bien amicalement; **best ~es on your birthday/engagement** meilleurs vœux pour votre anniversaire/vos fiançailles; **to offer/give/send good ~es** (for specific event) formuler/faire/envoyer ses meilleurs vœux; **please give him my best ~es** je vous prie de lui faire toutes mes amitiés; (**with**) **all good ~es for Christmas** avec tous mes or nos meilleurs vœux pour Noël.
III *vtr* 1 (expressing longing) **I ~ he were here/had been here** si seulement il était ici/avait été ici; **I just ~ we lived closer** si seulement nous habitions plus près; **I ~ you hadn't told me that** si seulement tu ne m'avais pas dit cela; **he ~ed he had written** il aurait voulu avoir écrit; **he ~ed she had written** il aurait voulu qu'elle ait écrit; **he wishes his mother would write** il voudrait que sa mère écrive; **he bought it and then ~ed he hadn't** il l'a acheté et puis a regretté de l'avoir fait; **I ~ed him dead/myself single again** j'aurais voulu le voir mort/être à nouveau célibataire; 2 (express congratulations, greetings) souhaiter; **I ~ you Happy Birthday/a pleasant journey/good luck** je vous souhaite un bon anniversaire/un bon voyage/bonne chance; **to ~ sb joy** ou **happiness** souhaiter à qn d'être heureux; **to ~ sb joy with sth/sb** iron souhaiter bien du plaisir à qn avec qch/qn; **he ~ed her good day**† il lui a souhaité le bonjour; **we ~ed each other goodbye and good luck** nous nous sommes dit au revoir et bonne chance; **I ~ed him well** j'espérais que tout irait bien pour lui; 3 (want) sout souhaiter, vouloir; (weaker) désirer; **he ~es an audience with you** sout il désire or il souhaite avoir un entretien avec vous; **that was what your father would have ~ed** c'est ce que ton père aurait voulu; **you will do it because I ~ it** vous le ferez parce que je le veux; **to ~ to do** vouloir or souhaiter or désirer faire; **I ~ to leave at once** je souhaite partir sur le champ; **she ~es to be alone/excused** elle désire être seule/se faire excuser; **I do not ~ to seem unkind but**... je ne veux pas avoir l'air antipathique mais...; **I ~ you to leave** je veux que vous partiez; **I ~ it to be clear that**... je veux qu'il soit bien clair que...
IV *vi* 1 (desire, want) vouloir; **just as you ~** comme vous voudrez; **spend it as you ~** dépense-le comme tu voudras; **to ~ for** souhaiter, espérer; **they wished for an end to the war** ils souhaitaient la fin de la guerre; **what more could one ~ for?** qu'est-ce qu'on pourrait espérer or souhaiter de plus?; 2 (in fairy story or ritual) faire un vœu.
IDIOMS **your ~ is my command** hum vos désirs sont des ordres.
■ **wish away**: **~ away [sth]**, **~ [sth] away** souhaiter que [qch] n'existe pas.
■ **wish on**: **~ [sth] on sb** fourguer○ [qch] à qn; **it's a job I wouldn't ~ on anyone** c'est un boulot que je ne fourguerais○ à personne.

wish: **~bone** *n* bréchet *m*; **~bone boom** *n* Naut Sport wishbone *m*; **~ fulfilment** *n* Psych assouvissement *m* du désir.

wishful thinking /ˌwɪʃfl ˈθɪŋkɪŋ/ *n* **that's ~** c'est prendre ses désirs pour des réalités.

wish: **~ing well** *n* puits *m* aux vœux; **~ list** *n* liste *f* des choses qu'on souhaite.

wishy-washy○ /ˈwɪʃɪwɒʃɪ/ *adj* 1 [*colour*] délavé; 2 péj [*person, approach*] incolore et inodore○.

wisp /wɪsp/ *n* (of hair) mèche *f*; (of straw) brin *m*; (of smoke, cloud) volute *f*; (of flame) langue *f*; **a ~ of a girl** un petit bout de fille.

wispy /ˈwɪspɪ/ *adj* [*hair, beard*] fin; [*cloud, smoke*] léger/-ère; [*piece, straw*] menu.

wisteria /wɪˈstɪərɪə/ *n* glycine *f*.

wistful /ˈwɪstfl/ *adj* (sad) mélancolique; (nostalgic) nostalgique.

wistfully /ˈwɪstfəlɪ/ *adv* (sadly) avec mélancolie; (nostalgically) avec nostalgie.

wistfulness /ˈwɪstflnɪs/ *n* (sadness) mélancolie *f*; (nostalgia) nostalgie *f*.

wit /wɪt/ I *n* 1 (humour, sense of humour) esprit *m*; **to have a quick/ready ~** avoir la repartie facile/l'esprit d'à-propos; **to have a dry ~** être pince-sans-rire; 2 (witty person) personne *f* spirituelle; **he is a ~** il est spirituel.
II **wits** *npl* (intelligence) intelligence *f*; (presence of mind) présence *f* d'esprit; **to have the ~s to do** avoir la présence d'esprit de faire; **to have** ou **keep (all) one's ~s about one** (vigilant) rester attentif; (levelheaded) conserver sa présence d'esprit; **to collect** ou **gather one's ~s** rassembler ses esprits; **to sharpen one's ~s** se dégourdir l'esprit; **to frighten/startle/terrify sb out of their ~s** faire une peur/surprise/terreur épouvantable à qn; **to pit one's ~s against sb** se mesurer (intellectuellement) à qn; **to live by one's ~s** vivre d'expédients; **to lose one's ~s** ne plus savoir où on est; **a battle of ~s** une joute verbale.
III **to wit** *adv phr* sout à savoir.
IDIOMS **to be at one's ~s' end** ne plus savoir quoi faire.

witch /wɪtʃ/ *n* sorcière *f*; fig (bewitching woman) ensorceleuse *f*; péj (**old**) **~** (vieille) sorcière *f*.

witch: **~craft** *n* sorcellerie *f*; **~ doctor** *n* shaman *m*.

witchery /ˈwɪtʃərɪ/ *n* sorcellerie *f*.

witch: **~es' brew** *n* bouillon *m* de sorcière also fig; **~es' Sabbath** *n* sabbat *m* (*de sorcières*).

witch hazel /ˈwɪtʃ heɪzl/ I *n* Bot, Med hamamélis *m*.
II *modif* [*twig, solution*] d'hamamélis *m*.

witch: **~-hunt** *n* lit, fig chasse *f* aux sorcières; **~-hunter** *n* chasseur/-euse *m/f* de sorcières; **~-hunting** *n* chasse *f* aux sorcières; **~ing hour** *n* littér heure *f* de minuit; fig hum moment *m* fatal; **~like** *adj* de sorcière.

with /wɪð, wɪθ/

■ **Note** If you have any doubts about how to translate a phrase or expression beginning with *with* (*with a vengeance, with all my heart, with luck, with my blessing etc*) you should consult the appropriate noun entry (***vengeance***, ***heart***, ***luck***, ***blessing*** etc).
– *with* is often used after verbs in English (*dispense with, part with, get on with etc*). For translations, consult the appropriate verb entry (***dispense***, ***part***, ***get*** etc).
– This dictionary contains Usage Notes on such topics as the human body and illnesses, aches and pains which use the preposition *with*. For the index to these Notes **▶ 1919**.
– For further uses of *with*, see the entry below.

1 (in descriptions) **a girl ~ black hair** une fille aux cheveux noirs; **a child ~ blue eyes** un enfant aux yeux bleus; **the boy ~ the broken leg** le garçon à la jambe cassée; **a boy ~ a broken leg** un garçon avec une jambe cassée; **a dress ~ a large collar** une robe avec un large col; **a TV ~ remote control** une télévision avec télécommande; **a room ~ a sea view** une chambre avec vue sur la mer; **furnished ~ antiques** décoré avec des meubles anciens; **covered ~ mud** couvert de boue; **wet ~ dew** mouillé par la rosée; **to lie ~ one's eyes closed** être allongé les yeux fermés; **to**

stand ~ one's arms folded se tenir les bras croisés; **filled/loaded ~ sth** rempli/chargé de qch; **covered/surrounded ~** couvert/entouré de; **2** (involving, concerning) avec; **a treaty/a discussion /a meeting ~ sb** un traité/une discussion/un rendez-vous avec qn; **3** (indicating an agent) avec; **to hit sb ~ sth** frapper qn avec qch; **to walk ~ a stick** marcher avec une canne; **to open/cut sth ~ a penknife** ouvrir/couper qch avec un canif; **4** (indicating manner, attitude) **~ difficulty/pleasure/care** avec difficulté/plaisir/soin; **to be patient ~ sb** être patient avec qn; **'OK,' he said ~ a smile/sigh** 'd'accord,' a-t-il dit en souriant/soupirant; **delighted/satisfied ~ sth** ravi/satisfait de qch; **5** (according to) **to increase ~ time** augmenter avec le temps; **to improve ~ age** [*wine*] se bonifier avec l'âge; **to expand ~ heat** se dilater sous l'action de la chaleur; **to vary ~ the temperature** varier selon la température; **6** (accompanied by, in the presence of) avec; **to travel/dance ~ sb** voyager/ danser avec qn; **go out ~ sb** sortir avec qn; **bring a friend ~ you** viens avec un ami; **she's got her brother ~ her** (on one occasion) elle est avec or accompagnée de son frère; (staying with her) son frère est chez elle; **to live ~ sb** (in one's own house) vivre avec qn; (in their house) vivre chez qn; **I'll be ~ you in a second** je suis à vous dans un instant; **take your umbrella ~ you** emporte ton parapluie; **bring the books back ~ you** ramène les livres; **7** (owning, bringing) **passengers ~ tickets** les passagers munis de billets; **people ~ qualifications** les gens qualifiés; **somebody ~ your experience** quelqu'un qui a ton expérience; **have you got the report ~ you?** est-ce que tu as (amené) le rapport?; **~ a CV** GB ou **resumé** US **like yours you're sure to find a job** avec un CV comme le tien, tu es sûr de trouver du travail; **8** (in relation to, as regards) **the frontier ~ Belgium** la frontière avec la Belgique; **problems ~ the computer** des problèmes avec l'ordinateur; **remember what happened ~ Bob's kids** rappelle-toi ce qui est arrivé aux enfants de Bob; **how are things ~ you?** comment ça va?; **what's up ~ Amy?, what's ~ Amy?** US qu'est-ce qui ne va pas avec Amy?; **what do you want ~ another car?** qu'est-ce que tu veux faire d'une deuxième voiture?; **it's a habit ~ her** c'est une habitude chez elle; ▶**matter**, **trouble**, **what**, **wrong**; **9** (showing consent, support) **I'm ~ you on this matter** je suis tout à fait d'accord avec toi là-dessus; **I'm ~ you 100%** ou **all the way** je suis avec toi; **10** (because of) **sick ~ worry** malade or mort d'inquiétude; **white ~ fear** blanc de peur; **to blush ~ embarrassment** rougir d'embarras; **to scream ~ laughter** hurler de rire; **to tremble ~ fear** trembler de peur; **he can see better ~ his glasses on** il voit mieux avec ses lunettes; **~ six kids, it's impossible** avec six enfants, c'est impossible; **I can't do it ~ you watching** je ne peux pas le faire si tu me regardes; **~ summer coming** avec l'été qui approche; **I can't go out ~ all this work to do** avec tout le travail que j'ai à faire, je ne peux pas sortir; ▶**what**; **11** (remaining) **~ only two days to go before the election** alors qu'il ne reste plus que deux jours avant les élections; **he pulled out of the race ~ 100 metres to go** il a abandonné la course 100 m avant l'arrivée; **12** (suffering from) **people ~ Aids/leukemia** les personnes atteintes du sida/de la leucémie, les personnes qui ont le sida/la leucémie; **to be ill ~ flu** avoir la grippe; **to be in bed ~ chickenpox** être au lit avec la varicelle; **13** (in the care or charge of) **you're safe ~ us** tu es en sécurité avec nous; **the blame lies ~ him** c'est de sa faute; **is Paul ~you?** est-ce que Paul est avec vous?; **14** (against) avec; **to fight ~ sb** se bagarrer avec qn; **the war ~ Germany** la guerre avec l'Allemagne; **to have an argument ~ sb** se disputer avec qn; **to be in competition ~ sb** être en concurrence avec qn; **15** (showing simultaneity) **~ the approach of spring** à l'approche du printemps; **~ the introduction of the reforms** avec l'introduction des nouvelles réformes; **~ that, he left** sur ce, il est parti; **16** (employed by, customer of) **a reporter ~ the Gazette** un journaliste de la Gazette; **he's ~ the UN** il travaille pour l'ONU; **I'm ~ Chemco** je travaille chez Chemco; **we're ~ the National Bank** nous sommes à la National Bank; **17** (in the same direction as) **to sail ~ the wind** naviguer dans le sens du vent; **to drift ~ the tide** dériver avec le courant; **18** (featuring, starring) **Casablanca ~ Humphrey Bogart** Casablanca avec Humphrey Bogart.

IDIOMS **to be ~ it**○ (on the ball) être dégourdi or capable; (trendy) être dans le vent or le coup; **I'm not really ~ it today**○ j'ai l 'esprit ailleurs aujourd'hui; **get ~ it**○! (wake up) réveille-toi!; (face the facts) redescends sur terre!; **I'm not ~ you, can you repeat?** je ne te suis pas, tu peux répéter?

withal /wɪ'ðɔ:l/ *adv*‡ ou littér (besides) en outre; (therewith) sur le champ; (nevertheless) ce nonobstant liter.

withdraw /wɪð'drɔ:, wɪθ'd-/ (*prét* **-drew**; *pp* **-drawn**) **I** *vtr* retirer [*hand, money, support, application, offer*] (**from** de); retirer [*aid, permission*] (**from** à); renoncer à, retirer [*claim*]; rétracter [*allegation, accusation, statement*]; Mil retirer [*troops*] (**from** de); Pol rappeler [*ambassador, diplomat*]; **to ~ a product from sale** Comm retirer un produit de la vente; **to ~ money from circulation** retirer de l'argent de la circulation; **to ~ one's labour** GB Ind faire un arrêt de travail.
II *vi* **1** [*person, troops*] se retirer (**from** de); [*applicant, candidate*] se retirer, se désister; **to ~ from a game/tournament** se retirer d'un jeu/d'un tournoi; **to ~ to one's room** se retirer dans sa chambre; **to ~ from one's position** Mil abandonner sa position; **2** Psych [*person*] se replier; **to ~ into oneself** se replier sur soi-même.

withdrawal /wɪð'drɔ:əl, wɪθ'd-/ *n* **1** gen, Fin, Mil retrait *m* (**of, from** de); (of accusation, statement) rétractation *f*, retrait *m* (**of** de); (of applicant, candidate, competitor) désistement *m*, retrait *m*; Pol (of ambassador) rappel *m*; **he has made several ~s from his account recently** il a effectué plusieurs retraits de son compte récemment; **~ of labour** GB Ind arrêt *m* de travail; **2** Psych (introversion) repli *m* sur soi-même; **3** Med (of drug addict) état *m* de manque.

withdrawal slip *n* bordereau *m* de retraite.

withdrawal symptoms *npl* symptômes *mpl* de manque or de l'état de manque; **to be suffering from ~** être en état de manque.

withdrawn /wɪð'drɔ:n, wɪθ'd-/ **I** *pp* ▶**withdraw**.
II *adj* (introverted) [*person*] renfermé, replié sur soi-même.

wither /'wɪðə(r)/ **I** *vtr* **1** flétrir [*plant*]; **2** littér flétrir [*face, feelings*].
II *vi* [*plant*] se flétrir.
■ **wither away** [*spirit*] s'atrophier; [*hope, interest*] s'évanouir.

withered /'wɪðəd/ *adj* [*plant, skin, cheek*] flétri; [*arm*] atrophié; [*emotions*] dépéri.

withering /'wɪðərɪŋ/ *adj* [*look*] plein de mépris; [*contempt, comment*] cinglant.

witheringly /'wɪðərɪŋlɪ/ *adv* [*speak*] d'un ton cinglant; [*look, glare*] avec mépris.

withers /'wɪðəz/ *npl* garrot *m*.

withhold /wɪð'həʊld/ *vtr* (*prét, pp* **-held**) différer [*payment*]; retenir [*tax, grant, rent*]; refuser [*consent, permission*]; ne pas divulguer [*information*]; **to be accused of ~ing information from the police** être accusé de rétention d'informations.

withholding tax *n* US retenue *f* à la source.

within /wɪ'ðɪn/ **I** *prep* **1** (enclosed in) **~ the city walls** dans l'enceinte de la ville; **~ the boundaries of the estate** dans l'enceinte de la propriété; **to lie ~ Italy's borders** être en Italie; **2** (inside) **~ the government/party** au sein du gouvernement/parti; **countries ~ the EC** les pays qui font partie de la CEE; **conditions ~ the camp/the prison** les conditions de vie dans le camp/la prison; **candidates from ~ the company** les candidats internes; **it appeals to something deep ~ us all** cela touche quelque chose de profond en nous; **3** (in expressions of time) **I'll do it ~ the hour** je le ferai en moins d'une heure; **he did it ~ the week** il l'a fait en moins d'une semaine; **15 burglaries ~ a month** 15 cambriolages en moins d'un mois; **'please reply ~ the week'** 'prière de répondre dans la semaine'; **'use ~ 24 hours of purchase'** 'à consommer dans les 24 heures'; **to finish ~ the time limit** finir dans les temps impartis; **~ minutes he was back** quelques minutes plus tard il était de retour; **~ a week of his birth** moins d'une semaine après sa naissance; **they died ~ a week of each other** ils sont morts à une semaine d'intervalle; **4** (not more than) **to be ~ several metres of sth** être à quelques mètres seulement de qch; **to live ~ minutes of the station** habiter à quelques minutes de la gare; **it's accurate to ~ a millimetre** c'est exact à un millimètre près; **to be ~ a day's drive of the mountains** être à une journée en voiture de la montagne; **to be ~ a 12 km radius** être dans un rayon de 12 km; **to fill a bucket to ~ 10 cm of the brim** remplir un seau jusqu'à 10 cm du bord; ▶**inch**; **5** (not beyond the range of) **to be ~ sight** lit [*coast, town*] être en vue; fig [*end*] être proche; **stay ~ sight of the car** ne vous éloignez pas de la voiture; **to be ~ range of** être à portée de [*enemy guns*]; **he's ~ shouting distance** il est suffisamment près pour nous entendre crier; ▶**earshot**, **grasp**, **hearing**, **reach**; **6** (not beyond a permitted limit) **to stay ~ budget** ne pas dépasser le budget; **to live ~ one's income** ou **means** vivre selon ses moyens; **~ the limitations of the treaty** dans les limites du traité; ▶**jurisdiction**, **law**, **limit**, **reason**, **right**; **7** (inside the scope of) **it lies ~ the Impressionist tradition** ça s'inscrit dans la tradition impressionniste; **it's a play ~ a play** c'est une pièce en abyme; ▶**brief**, **confines**, **framework**, **scope**.
II *adv* à l'intérieur; **seen from ~** vu de l'intérieur; **~ and without** à l'intérieur comme à l'extérieur; ▶**apply**, **enemy**, **inquire**.

without /wɪ'ðaʊt/ **I** *prep* **1** (lacking, not having) sans; **~ a key** sans clé; **~ any money/help** sans argent/aide; **to be ~ friends** ne pas avoir d'amis; **to be ~ shame** n'avoir aucune honte; **she left ~ it** elle est partie sans; **they went ~ me** ils sont partis sans moi; **~ end** sans fin; **not ~ difficulty** non sans difficulté; **to manage** ou **make do ~ sth** se débrouiller sans qch; **I'll just have to manage ~** il va falloir que je me débrouille sans; ▶**do**[1], **doubt**, **fail**, **foundation**, **get**, **go**; **2** (not) sans; **~ doing** sans faire; **~ looking/paying attention** sans regarder/faire attention; **do it ~ him noticing** fais-le sans qu'il s'en aperçoive ; **~ saying a word** sans mot dire; **it goes ~ saying that** il va de soi or sans dire que; **~ so much as asking permission** sans même demander la permission.
II *adv* (on the outside) à l'extérieur; **from ~** de l'extérieur.

with-profits *adj* Fin [*endowment assurance, policy*] avec participation aux bénéfices.

withstand /wɪð'stænd/ *vtr* (*prét, pp* **-stood**) résister à.

withy /ˈwɪðɪ/ *n* brin *m* d'osier.
witless /ˈwɪtlɪs/ *adj* stupide; **to be scared ~** avoir une peur bleue; **to be bored ~** s'ennuyer à mourir.
witness /ˈwɪtnɪs/ **I** *n* **1** gen, Jur (person) témoin *m*; **she was a ~ to the accident** elle a été témoin de l'accident; **~ for the prosecution/the defence, prosecution/defence ~** témoin à charge/à décharge; **to call sb as a ~** citer qn comme témoin; **I have been called as a ~ in the Mulloy case** j'ai été appelé à témoigner dans l'affaire Mulloy; **to sign a document in the presence of a ~** signer un document en présence d'un témoin; **to be a ~ to sb's will** servir de témoin lors de la signature du testament de qn; **2** (testimony) témoignage *m*; **to be** ou **bear ~ to sth** témoigner de qch; **his expensive cars are** ou **bear ~ to his wealth** ses voitures de luxe témoignent de sa richesse; **the dilapidation of the school bears ~ to the lack of funds** la dégradation de l'école est une preuve évidente du manque de fonds; **to bear false ~** Jur faire un faux témoignage; **3** Relig ¢ témoignage *m*.
II *vtr* **1** (see) être témoin de, assister à [*attack, incident, burglary*]; **they ~ed the murder/the accident** ils ont été témoins du meurtre/de l'accident; **2** (at official occasion) servir de témoin lors de la signature de [*document, treaty*]; être témoin à [*marriage*]; **3** fig **we are about to ~ a transformation of the world economy** nous sommes sur le point d'assister à une transformation de l'économie mondiale; **the last decade has ~ed tremendous advances in technology** la dernière décennie a vu des progrès considérables dans le domaine de la technologie; **his hard work has paid off, (as) ~ his exam results** son travail acharné a payé, comme en témoignent ses résultats d'examen; **this house has ~ed many historic events** cette maison a été le théâtre de beaucoup d'événements historiques, beaucoup d'événements historiques se sont déroulés dans cette maison.
witness box GB, **witness stand** US *n* barre *f* des témoins; **in the ~** à la barre des témoins.
witter○ /ˈwɪtə(r)/ *vi* GB = **witter on**○.
■ **witter on**○ GB parler sans arrêt (**about** de).
wittering○ /ˈwɪtərɪŋ/ *n* GB bavardage *m*.
witticism /ˈwɪtɪsɪzəm/ *n* bon mot *m*.
wittily /ˈwɪtɪlɪ/ *adv* avec esprit.
wittingly /ˈwɪtɪŋlɪ/ *adv* littér sciemment.
witty /ˈwɪtɪ/ *adj* spirituel/-elle.
wives /waɪvz/ *pl* ▶ **wife**.
wiz○ /wɪz/ *n* crack○ *m* (**at** en).
wizard /ˈwɪzəd/ **I** *n* **1** (magician) magicien *m*; **2** fig (expert) **to be a ~ with a needle** être un as de l'aiguille; **to be a ~ at** avoir le génie de [*chess, computing etc*]; **to be a ~ at doing** être très fort pour faire.
II *adj*○† GB super.
wizardry /ˈwɪzədrɪ/ *n* magie *f* also fig.
wizened /ˈwɪznd/ *adj* ratatiné.
wk *abrév écrite* = **week**.
WLM *n*: *abrév* ▶ **Women's Liberation Movement**.
W Midlands *n* GB Post *abrév écrite* ▶ **West Midlands**.
w/o 1 *abrév* = **without**; **2** *abrév* = **written off**.
WO *n* Mil *abrév* ▶ **Warrant Officer**.
woad /wəʊd/ *n* Bot guède *f*, herbe *f* de Saint-Philippe.
wobble /ˈwɒbl/ **I** *n* (in voice) tremblement *m*; (of chair, table) branlement *m*; (in movement) oscillation *f*; fig vacillation *f*.
II *vtr* faire bouger [*table, tooth*].
III *vi* [*table, chair*] branler; [*pile of books, plates etc*] osciller; [*voice*] trembler; [*person*] (on bicycle) osciller; (on ladder, tightrope) chanceler; **the chair was wobbling** la chaise branlait; **this chair is inclined to ~** cette chaise est branlante or bancale; **she ~d down the street on her bicycle** elle a descendu la rue en zigzagant sur sa bicyclette; **his legs were wobbling under him** ses jambes flageolaient; **the front wheels are wobbling** Aut il y a du jeu dans les roues avant.
wobbly /ˈwɒblɪ/ *adj* [*table, chair*] bancal; [*tooth*] branlant; [*chin, voice, jelly*] tremblotant; [*handwriting, line*] tremblant; fig [*theory, plot*] boiteux/-euse; **she still feels a bit ~ after her illness** elle se sent toujours un peu chancelante or faible après sa maladie; **he is still a bit ~ on his legs** il est encore un peu chancelant (sur ses jambes); **she's still a bit ~ on her new bicycle** elle n'est pas encore très stable sur sa nouvelle bicyclette.
IDIOMS **to throw a ~**○ GB piquer une crise○.
wodge○ /wɒdʒ/ *n* GB **a ~ of** un tas○ de [*papers, money*]; un gros morceau de [*cake, bread*].
woe /wəʊ/ **I** *n* **1** littér (sorrow) chagrin *m*; **a tale of ~** hum une jérémiade; **2** hum (misfortune) malheur *m*.
II *excl*‡ ou hum quel malheur!; **~ betide him if he's late** gare à lui s'il est en retard; **~ betide the person who...** gare à celui qui...; **~ is me!** pauvre de moi!
woebegone /ˈwəʊbɪgɒn, US -gɔːn/ *adj* abattu.
woeful /ˈwəʊfl/ *adj* **1** (mournful) [*look, smile*] affligé; [*story, sight*] affligeant; **2** (deplorable) [*lack, way*] déplorable.
woefully /ˈwəʊfəlɪ/ *adv* **1** (mournfully) [*say, look*] tristement; **2** (very) [*inadequate, underfunded*] déplorablement.
wog◑ /wɒg/ *n* GB injur métèque *mf* offensive.
wok /wɒk/ *n* wok *m*.
woke /wəʊk/ *prét* ▶ **wake**.
woken /ˈwəʊkən/ *pp* ▶ **wake**.
wold /wəʊld/ *n* Geog plateau *m*.
wolf /wʊlf/ **I** *n* (*pl* **wolves**) **1** loup *m*; **she-~** louve *f*; **the big bad ~** le grand méchant loup; **2**○ fig (womanizer) cavaleur○ *m*.
II *vtr* = **wolf down**.
IDIOMS **to cry ~** crier au loup; **to be a ~ in sheep's clothing** être un loup déguisé en brebis; **to keep the ~ from the door** mettre qn à l'abri du besoin; **a lone ~** un/une solitaire *m/f*; **to throw sb to the wolves** jeter qn dans la gueule du loup.
■ **wolf down**: **~ down [sth]**, **~ [sth] down** engloutir, dévorer [*food*].
wolf: **~ call** *n* US = **wolf-whistle**; **~ cub** *n* louveteau *m*; **~ dog** US, **~hound** GB *n* chien-loup *m*.
wolfish /ˈwʊlfɪʃ/ *adj* [*appetite*] vorace, féroce; [*grin*] féroce.
wolfishly /ˈwʊlfɪʃlɪ/ *adv* voracement.
wolf-man /ˈwʊlfmæn/ *n* homme-loup *m*.
wolfram /ˈwʊlfrəm/ *n* tungstène *m*.
wolfsbane /ˈwʊlfsbeɪn/ *n* aconit *m*.
wolf-whistle /ˈwʊlfwɪsl, US -hwɪ-/ **I** *n* sifflement *m* (*au passage d'une femme*).
II *vi* siffler (*au passage d'une femme*); **to ~ at sb** siffler qn.
wolverine /ˈwʊlvəriːn/ **I** *n* Zool glouton *m*.
II Wolverine *n* US (native) natif/-ive *m/f* du Michigan; (resident) habitant/-e *m/f* du Michigan.
wolves /wʊlvz/ *pl* ▶ **wolf**.
woman /ˈwʊmən/ **I** *n* (*pl* **women**) femme *f*; **the working ~** la femme active; **~ as portrayed in the Victorian novel** la femme telle qu'elle est représentée dans le roman victorien; **a ~ of letters** une femme de lettres; **a ~ of the streets**† euph une prostituée; **I've never even spoken to the ~!** péj je n'ai même jamais parlé à cette femme!; **a ~ comes in to clean twice a week** une femme de ménage vient deux fois par semaine; **she's her own ~** elle est maîtresse de sa vie; **to talk about sth ~ to ~** parler de qch entre femmes; **for heaven's sake, ~!** mais enfin tu es idiote ou quoi?; **my good ~** ma petite dame; **the little ~**† péj ma petite femme; **the other ~** péj l'autre.
II *modif* **a ~ Prime Minister** un premier ministre femme ; **she asked for a ~ doctor** elle a demandé un médecin femme; **women doctors were not so common then** les femmes médecins n'étaient pas très nombreuses à cette époque; **he's always criticizing ~ drivers** il est toujours en train de critiquer les femmes au volant; **the women members of staff** les membres féminins du personnel; **he has lots of women friends** il a beaucoup d'amies; **women voters** électrices *fpl*; **women writers** femmes *fpl* écrivains; **a six-~ team** une équipe composée de six femmes.
IDIOMS **a ~'s place is in the home** la place d'une femme est au foyer; **a ~'s work is never done** une femme a toujours à faire dans sa maison.
woman-hater○ *n* mysogyne *m*.
womanhood /ˈwʊmənhʊd/ *n* (state of being a woman) féminité *f*; (women collectively) les femmes *fpl*; **to reach ~** devenir femme.
womanish /ˈwʊmənɪʃ/ *adj* péj efféminé.
womanize /ˈwʊmənaɪz/ *vi* courir les femmes.
womanizer /ˈwʊmənaɪzə(r)/ *n* coureur *m* de jupons or de femmes.
womankind /ˈwʊmənkaɪnd/ *n* sout les femmes *fpl*.
womanliness /ˈwʊmənlɪnɪs/ *n* féminité *f*.
womanly /ˈwʊmənlɪ/ *adj* féminin.
woman police constable, WPC *n* GB femme *f* agent de police.
womb /wuːm/ *n* Anat ventre *m*, utérus *m*; **the child in the ~** l'enfant dans le ventre de sa mère.
wombat /ˈwɒmbæt/ *n* wombat *m*.
women /ˈwɪmɪn/ *pl* ▶ **woman**.
womenfolk /ˈwɪmɪnfəʊk/ *n* **the ~** les femmes *fpl*.
women: **~'s group** *n* groupe *m* féministe; **Women's Institute, WI** *n* GB *association de femmes qui s'intéresse aux problèmes du foyer et qui organise des œuvres de bienfaisance*; **Women's Libber**○ *n* péj féministe *f*; **Women's Liberation Movement, Women's Lib**○**, WLM** *n* mouvement *m* de libération de la femme, MLF *m*.
women's magazine *n* magazine *m* féminin; **~s** la presse féminine.
women: **~'s movement** *n* mouvement *m* des femmes; **~'s page** *n* Journ page *f* des lectrices; **~'s refuge** *n* foyer *m* pour femmes battues; **~'s rights** *npl* droits *mpl* de la femme; **~'s shelter** = **women's refuge**; **~'s studies** *npl* études *fpl* féministes; **~'s suffrage** *n* droit *m* de vote pour les femmes.
won /wʌn/ *prét, pp* ▶ **win**.
wonder /ˈwʌndə(r)/ **I** *n* **1** (miracle) merveille *f*; **it's a ~ that** c'est extraordinaire que (+ *subj*); **(it's) no ~ that** (ce n'est) pas étonnant que (+ *subj*); **small** ou **little ~ that** ce n'est guère étonnant que (+ *subj*); **to be a ~ with** savoir comment s'y prendre avec [*children, dogs*]; **to be a ~ with engines/computers** s'y connaître en mécanique/informatique; **to do** ou **work ~s** faire des merveilles (**for** pour; **with** avec); **he's/she's a ~** il/elle est merveilleux/-euse!; **the ~s of modern medicine/technology** les prodiges de la médecine/technologie moderne; **2** (amazement) émerveillement *m*; **in ~** avec émerveillement; **a sense** ou **feeling of ~** une sensation d'émerveillement; **lost in ~** émerveillé.
II *modif* [*cure, drug*] miracle (*after n*).
III *vtr* **1** (ask oneself) se demander; **I ~ how/why** je me demande comment/pourquoi; **I ~ if** ou **whether** je me demande si; (as polite request) **I ~ if you could help me/give me some information?** peut-être

pourriez-vous m'aider/me fournir des renseignements?; **it makes you ~** on peut se poser des questions; **it makes you ~ why/if/how** c'est à se demander pourquoi/si/comment; **'why are we here?' he ~ed** 'pourquoi sommes-nous là?' se demandait-il; **one ~s what he is trying to achieve** on se demande où il veut en arriver; **2** (be surprised) **I ~ that** cela m'étonne que (+ *subj*).
IV *vi* **1** (think) **to ~ about sth** penser or songer à qch; **to ~ about doing** penser or songer à faire; **2** (be surprised) **to ~ at sth** s'étonner de qch; (admiringly) s'émerveiller de qch; **they'll be late again, I shouldn't ~** cela ne m'étonnerait pas qu'ils soient encore en retard.

wonderful /'wʌndəfl/ *adj* [*book, film, meal, experience, holiday*] merveilleux/-euse, magnifique; [*musician, teacher*] excellent (*before n*); [*achievement*] beau/belle (*before n*); **to be ~ with** savoir comment s'y prendre avec [*children, animals*]; **to be ~ with computers/engines** s'y connaître en informatique/mécanique; **I feel ~** je suis en pleine forme; **you look ~!** (healthy) tu as l'air en pleine forme!; (attractive) tu es superbe!

wonderfully /'wʌndəfəlɪ/ *adv* **1** (very) [*funny, clever, generous, exciting*] très; **2** (splendidly) [*cope, behave, perform, work*] admirablement.

wondering /'wʌndərɪŋ/ *adj* **1** (full of wonder) [*look, expression*] émerveillé; **2** (puzzled) [*look, expression*] étonné.

wonderingly /'wʌndərɪŋlɪ/ *adv* **1** (in wonder) [*look, say*] avec émerveillement; **2** (in puzzlement) [*look, say*] d'un air étonné.

wonderland /'wʌndəlænd/ *n* pays *m* enchanté.

wonderment /'wʌndəmənt/ *n* **1** (wonder) émerveillement *m*; **in ~** avec émerveillement; **2** (puzzlement) étonnement *m*; **in ~** avec étonnement.

wondrous /'wʌndrəs/ *adj* littér merveilleux/-euse.

wondrously /'wʌndrəslɪ/ *adv* littér merveilleusement.

wonk° /wɒŋk/ *n* US bûcheur/-euse *m/f*.

wonky° /'wɒŋkɪ/ *adj* GB **1** (crooked) de traviole°; **2** (wobbly) [*furniture*] bancal; [*legs*] flageolant; **3** (faulty) **the television is a bit ~** la télé est un peu détraquée°; **he has a ~ knee** il a un genou déglingué°.

wont /wəʊnt, US wɔ:nt/ *adj* **to be ~ to do** avoir coutume de faire; **as is his/their ~** comme à son/leur habitude.

won't /wəʊnt/ = **will not**.

wonted /'wəʊntəd/ *adj* sout coutumier/-ière.

woo /wu:/ *vtr* **1**† (court) courtiser [*lady*]; **2** fig (curry favour with) courtiser [*voters, company, country*]; **to ~ mothers back to work** encourager les mères à reprendre la vie professionnelle.

wood /wʊd/ **I** *n* **1** (fuel, timber) bois *m*; **ash/beech ~** bois de frêne/de hêtre; **made of solid ~** en bois massif; **a piece of ~** un morceau de bois; **2** Wine (barrel) fût *m*; **aged in the ~** vieilli en fût; (**drawn**) **from the ~** tiré du fût; **3** (forest) bois *m*; **birch/oak ~** bois *m* de bouleaux/de chênes; **4** Sport (in bowls) boule *f* (*en bois*); (in golf) bois *m*; **a** (**number**) **three ~** un bois trois; **to hit a ball off the ~** (in tennis) faire un bois.
II woods *npl* **1** (forest) bois *mpl*; **2** Mus bois *mpl*.
III *modif* [*fire, smoke, shavings*] de bois; **~ floor** plancher *m*.
IDIOMS **touch ~!** GB, **knock on ~!** US touchons du bois! or je touche du bois!; **we are not out of the ~ yet** on n'est pas encore sorti de l'auberge.

wood: **~ alcohol** *n* alcool *m* méthylique; **~ anemone** *n* anémone *f* des bois; **~ ant** *n* fourmi *f* fauve.

woodbine /'wʊdbaɪn/ *n* **1** (honeysuckle) chèvrefeuille *m* (des bois); **2** US (Virginia creeper) vigne *f* vierge.

wood: **~block** *n* (for flooring) latte *f*; US Art planche *f*; **~-block floor** *n* parquet *m*; **~-burning stove** *n* = **wood stove**; **~ carver** ▶1692 *n* sculpteur/-trice *m/f* sur bois; **~carving** *n* sculpture *f* sur bois; **~chuck** *n* marmotte *f* d'Amérique; **~cock** *n* bécasse *f*; **~craft** *n* connaissance *f* des bois; **~cut** *n* (block) planche *f*; (print) xylographie *f*; **~cutter** ▶1692 *n* bûcheron/-onne *m/f*; **~cutting** *n* abattage *m* des arbres.

wooded /'wʊdɪd/ *adj* boisé; **heavily** ou **thickly ~** très boisé.

wooden /'wʊdn/ *adj* **1** [*furniture, implement, house, floor*] en bois; [*leg*] de bois; **~ shoe** sabot *m*; **2** fig [*acting, expression*] figé.

wood engraving *n* gravure *f* sur bois.

wooden: **~headed** *adj* borné; **~ horse** *n* cheval *m* de Troie also fig; **~ nickel** *n* US objet *m* sans valeur; **~ spoon** *n* cuillère *f* de bois; fig prix *m* de consolation.

woodland /'wʊdlənd/ **I** *n* bois *m*.
II *modif* [*animal, plant*] des bois; [*scenery*] boisé; [*walk*] dans les bois; **~ management** exploitation *f* forestière.

wood: **~lark** *n* alouette *f* des bois; **~louse** *n* cloporte *m*; **~man** GB, **~sman** US ▶1692 *n* (woodcutter) forestier *m*; (versed in woodcraft) homme *m* des bois; **~ nymph** *n* nymphe *f* des bois; **~pecker** *n* pic *m*; **~ pigeon** *n* pigeon *m* ramier; **~pile** *n* tas *m* de bois; **~ pulp** *n* pâte *f* à papier; **~screw** *n* vis *f* à bois; **~ shavings** *npl* copeaux *mpl*; **~shed** *n* remise *f* à bois; **~ sorrel** *n* oxalis *m*, petite oseille *f*; **~ stove** *n* poêle *m* à bois.

woodsy° /'wʊdzɪ/ *adj* US [*atmosphere*] sylvestre; [*person*] qui aime la verdure.

wood trim *n* boiserie *f*.

woodwind /'wʊdwɪnd/ **I** *npl* bois *mpl*.
II *modif* [*instrument*] à bois; [*player*] d'instrument à bois; [*section*] des bois.

woodwork /'wʊdwɜ:k/ **I** *n* **1** (carpentry) menuiserie *f*; **2** (doors, windows etc) boiseries *fpl*; **3**° GB Sport (goalpost) poteaux *mpl*.
II *modif* [*teacher, class*] de menuiserie; [*student*] en menuiserie.
IDIOMS **to come** ou **crawl out of the ~**° hum surgir d'un peu partout°.

woodworm /'wʊdwɜ:m/ *n* **1** (animal) ver *m* à bois; **2** (disease) maladie *f* du ver à bois; **to have ~** être vermoulu.

woody /'wʊdɪ/ *adj* [*hill, landscape*] boisé; [*plant, stem*] ligneux/-euse; [*smell*] de bois.

woof /wʊf/ **I** *n* **1**° (bark) aboiement *m*; **2** onomat ouah; **3** /wu:f/ Tex (weft) trame *f*.
II *vi*° aboyer.

woofer /'wʊfə(r)/ *n* Audio haut-parleur *m* de graves, woofer *m*.

wool /wʊl/ **I** *n* laine *f*; **pure** (**new**) **~** pure laine (vierge); **knitting/baby ~** laine à tricoter/pour bébé.
II *modif* [*carpet, coat, shop*] de laine; [*trade*] lainier/-ière.
IDIOMS **to pull the ~ over sb's eyes** duper qn; **you can't pull the ~ over my eyes** je ne suis pas dupe.

wool: **~ fat** *n* suint *m*; **~gathering** *n* rêvasserie *f*; **~ grease** *n* = **wool fat**; **~grower** ▶1692 *n* éleveur/-euse *m/f* de moutons.

woollen GB, **woolen** US /'wʊlən/ **I** *n* **1** (garment) lainage *m*; **2** (piece of cloth) tissu *m* en laine.
II *adj* [*garment*] de laine.

woollen mill *n* lainerie *f*.

woolliness, **wooliness** US /'wʊlɪnɪs/ *n* **1** (of cloth) nature *f* laineuse; (of animal's coat) épaisseur *f* laineuse; **2** fig (of thinking) imprécision *f* (**of** de).

woolly GB, **wooly** US /'wʊlɪ/ **I** *n*° lainage *m*.
II *adj* **1** [*garment*] de laine; [*animal coat, hair*] laineux/-euse; [*cloud*] cotonneux/-euse; **2** fig (vague) [*thinking*] flou.
IDIOMS **wild and ~** [*person*] fruste, barbare; [*plan, theory*] primitif/-ive, rudimentaire.

woolly-headed, **woolly-minded** *adj* aux idées floues.

wool: **~ merchant** ▶1692 *n* Hist lainier/-ière *m/f*; **Woolsack** *n* GB *siège du Grand Chancelier à la chambre des Lords*; **~shed** *n* lainerie *f*.

woops *excl* = **whoops**.

woozy° /'wu:zɪ/ *adj* **to feel ~** avoir la tête qui tourne.

wop /wɒp/ **I** *n*◐ injur (Italian) rital/-e◐ *m/f* offensive.
II *vtr*° = **whop**.

Worcester sauce /'wʊstə(r)/ GB, **Worcestershire sauce** /'wʊstəʃə(r)/ US *n*: *sauce épicée au soja et vinaigre*.

Worcestershire /'wustəʃə(r)/ ▶1624 *pr n* Worcestershire *m*.

Worcs *n* GB Post *abrév écrite* ▶**Worcestershire**.

word /wɜ:d/ **I** *n* **1** (verbal expression) mot *m*; **to say a few ~s about** dire quelques mots sur; **those were his very ~s** ce sont ses propres mots; **to have no ~s to express sth** ne pas trouver les mots pour exprimer qch; **idle/well-chosen ~s** mots en l'air/choisis; **long ~s** mots savants; **in 120 ~s** en 120 mots; **in a ~, no** en un mot, non; **there is no other ~ for it** il n'y a pas d'autre mot (pour le dire); **with these ~s he left** sur ces mots il est parti; **in your own ~s** avec tes propres mots; **I don't think 'aunt' is quite the right ~** je ne suis pas sûr que 'tante' soit le mot qui convienne; **the last ~** lit le dernier mot; fig le dernier cri (**in** en); **to get a ~ in** placer un mot; **not in so many ~s** pas exactement ; **in other ~s** en d'autres termes; **the spoken ~** la langue parlée; **the written ~** la langue écrite; **to put one's feelings** ou **thoughts into ~s** exprimer ce qu'on ressent; **there's no such ~ as 'can't'** 'impossible' n'est pas français; **what's the Greek ~ for 'table'?** comment dit-on 'table' en grec?; **a ~ of warning** un avertissement; **a ~ of advice** un conseil; **kind ~s** paroles aimables; **vulgar is hardly the ~ for it** vulgaire est trop peu dire; **lazy is a better ~ for him** je dirais plutôt qu'il est paresseux; **I've said my last ~ on the subject** j'ai dit tout ce que j'avais à dire sur le sujet; **too funny/sad for ~s** trop drôle/triste; **in the ~s of Washington** pour reprendre l'expression de Washington; **I believed every ~ he said** je croyais tout ce qu'il me disait; **I mean every ~ of it** je pense ce que je dis; **a ~ to all those who...** quelques conseils pour tous ceux qui...; **a man of few ~s** un homme peu loquace; **2** (anything, something) mot *m*; **without saying a ~** sans dire un mot; **I couldn't get a ~ out of her** je n'ai pas réussi à tirer un mot d'elle; **not to believe/hear/understand a ~ of sth** ne pas croire/entendre/comprendre un mot de qch; **not a ~ to anybody** pas un mot à qui que ce soit; **I don't believe a ~ of it** je n'en crois pas un mot; **not to have a good ~ to say about sb/sth** n'avoir rien de bon à dire de qn/sur qch; **I want to say a ~ about honesty** je voudrais dire quelque chose au sujet de l'honnêteté; **I didn't say a ~!** je n'ai pas ouvert la bouche; **he won't hear a ~ against her** il ne supporte pas qu'on dise quoi que ce soit contre elle; **the article didn't say a ~ about it** l'article n'en a pas parlé; **3** ¢ (information) nouvelles *fpl* (**about** concernant); **we are waiting for ~** nous attendons des nouvelles; **there is no ~ of the missing climbers** on est sans nouvelles des alpinistes disparus; **we are hoping for ~ that all is well** nous espérons des bonnes nouvelles; **~ got out that...** la nouvelle a transpiré que...; **to bring ~ of sth** annoncer qch; **to bring/send ~ that** annoncer/faire savoir que; **he left ~ at the desk that...** il a laissé un message à la réception disant que...; **to spread the ~** faire circuler la nouvelle; **4** (promise, affirmation) parole *f*; **he gave me his ~** il m'a donné sa parole; **to keep/break one's ~** tenir/ne pas tenir parole; **it's his ~ against mine** c'est sa parole contre la mienne; **to hold sb to his/her ~** obliger qn à tenir parole; **a woman of her ~** une femme de parole; **to take sb's ~ for it** croire qn sur parole; **to take sb at his/her ~** prendre qn au mot; **I've only got her ~ for it** je n'ai que sa parole; **to doubt/question sb's ~** douter/mettre en doute les paroles de qn; **take my ~ for it!** crois-moi!; **to go back on one's ~** revenir sur sa promesse; **to be as good as one's ~** tenir parole; **to be better than one's ~** faire plus que ce qu'on a promis; **5** (rumour) **~ has it that he's a millionaire** on dit qu'il est millionnaire; **~ got round** ou **around that...** le bruit a couru que...; **6** (command) ordre *m*; **to give the ~ to do** donner l'ordre de faire; **if you need anything just say the ~** si tu as besoin de quoi que ce soit, dis-le; **just say the ~ and I'll come** tu n'as qu'un mot à dire et je viendrai; **at** ou **on the ~ of command, present arms** à mon commandement, présentez armes; **their ~ is law** ils font la loi; **7** (key word) maître mot *m*; **the ~ now is devolution** le maître mot est maintenant la décentralisation; **8** Relig **the Word** Relig gen la bonne parole; (of Trinity) le Verbe; **to preach the Word** prêcher la bonne parole; **the Word of God** la parole de Dieu; **9** Comput mot *m*.

II words *npl* **1** (oratory) paroles *fpl*; **show your support by deeds not ~s** montrez votre soutien par des actes et non par des paroles; **empty ~s** paroles vides de sens; **2** Theat, Mus (of play) texte *m*; (of song) paroles *fpl*; **to forget one's ~s** oublier son texte; **I'll sing the ~s** je vais chanter les paroles; **to set the ~s to music** mettre un texte en musique.

III -worded (*dans composés*) **a carefully-~ed letter** une lettre soigneusement formulée; **a strongly-~ed statement** un communiqué ferme; **a sarcastically-~ed reply** une réponse caustique.

IV *vtr* formuler [*reply, letter, statement*].

IDIOMS **my ~!** (in surprise) ma parole!; (in reproof) tu vas voir!; **right from the ~ go** dès le départ; **to have a ~ with sb about sth** parler (un peu) à qn à propos de qch; **to have ~s with sb** s'accrocher avec qn; **to put in a good ~ for sb** glisser un mot en faveur de qn; **upon my ~†!** (in surprise) ma parole!; (confirming truth) parole d'honneur!

word: **~ association** *n* Psych association *f* de mots; **~ blindness** *n* dyslexie *f*; **~book** *n* Mus livret *m* (d'opéra); **~break** *n* Print coupure *f* (du mot); **~ class** *n* Ling partie *f* du discours; **~count** *n* Comput nombre *m* de mots; **~ deaf** *adj* aphasique sensoriel/-ielle; **~ deafness** *n* aphasie *f* sensorielle.

word-for-word /ˌwɜːdfəˈwɜːd/ **I** *adj* mot à mot *inv*.

II word for word *adv* mot à mot.

word game *n* jeu *m* de lettres.

wordiness /ˈwɜːdɪnɪs/ *n* verbosité *f*.

wording /ˈwɜːdɪŋ/ *n* formulation *f*.

wordlist *n* gen liste *f* de mots; (in dictionary) nomenclature *f*.

word-of-mouth I *adv* [*promise*] verbal.

II by word of mouth *adv phr* verbalement.

word order *n* Ling ordre *m* des mots.

word-perfect /ˌwɜːdˈpɜːfɪkt/ *adj* [*recitation*] parfait; **to be ~** [*recitation*] être parfait; [*person*] connaître son texte sur le bout des doigts.

word: **~ processing, WP** *n* Comput traitement *m* de texte; **~ processor** *n* Comput machine *f* à traitement de texte.

wordsmith /ˈwɜːdsmɪθ/ *n* **to be an accomplished ~** avoir le génie des mots.

word: **~ stress** *n* Ling accentuation *f*; **~ wrapping** *n* Comput retour *m* à la ligne automatique.

wordy /ˈwɜːdɪ/ *adj* verbeux/-euse.

wore /wɔː(r)/ *prét* ▶ **wear**.

work /wɜːk/ **I** *n* **1** (physical or mental activity) travail *m* (**on** sur); **to be at ~ on sth** être en train de travailler à qch; **to watch sb at ~** regarder qn (en train de) travailler; **to go to** ou **set to** ou **get to ~** se mettre au travail; **to go to** ou **set to** ou **get to ~ on sth** se mettre à travailler à or faire qch; **to set to ~ doing** se mettre à faire; **to put a lot of ~ into** travailler [*essay, speech*]; passer beaucoup de temps sur [*meal, preparations*]; **to put a lot of ~ into doing** passer beaucoup de temps à faire; **to put** ou **set sb to ~** faire travailler qn; **we put him to ~ doing** nous lui avons donné pour tâche de faire; **it was hard ~ doing** ça a été dur de faire; **to be hard at ~** travailler consciencieusement; **your essay needs more ~** tu dois travailler davantage ta rédaction; **there's still a lot of ~ to be done** il reste encore beaucoup à faire; **I've got ~ to do** j'ai du travail à faire; **to make short** ou **light work of sth** expédier qch; **to make short ~ of sb** envoyer promener qn; **it's all in a day's ~** c'est une question d'habitude; **'good** ou **nice ~'** (on written work) 'bon travail'; (orally) 'c'est bien!'; **it's hot/thirsty ~** ça donne chaud/soif; **2** (occupation) travail *m*; **to be in ~** avoir du travail or un emploi; **to look for ~** chercher du travail; **day/night ~** travail de jour/nuit; **place of ~** lieu *m* de travail; **to start** ou **begin ~** (daily) commencer le travail; (for the first time) commencer à travailler; **to stop ~** (at the end of the day) terminer son travail; (on retirement) cesser de travailler; **to be off ~** (on vacation) être en congé; **to be off ~ with flu** être en arrêt de travail parce qu'on a la grippe; **to be out of ~** être au chômage; **nice ~ if you can get it○!** c'est une bonne planque○!; **3** (place of employment) (office) bureau *m*; (factory) usine *f*; **to go to ~** aller au travail; **don't phone me at ~** ne me téléphone pas à mon travail; **there's a canteen at ~** il y a une cantine à mon travail; **4** (building, construction) travaux *mpl* (**on** sur); **5** (papers) **to take one's ~ home** lit emporter du travail chez soi; fig ramener ses soucis professionnels à sa famille; **spread your ~ out on the table** étale tes papiers sur la table; **6** (achievement, product) (essay, report) travail *m*; (artwork, novel, sculpture) œuvre *f* (**by** de); (study) ouvrage *m* (**by** de; **on** sur); **an exhibition of ~ by young artists** une exposition d'œuvres de jeunes artistes; **he sells his ~ to tourists** il vend ses créations aux touristes; **is this all your own ~?** est-ce que vous l'avez fait tout seul?; **to mark students' ~** noter les devoirs des étudiants; **his ~ isn't up to standard** son travail n'a pas le niveau requis; **the research was the ~ of a team** la recherche était l'œuvre d'une équipe; **a ~ of genius** une œuvre de génie; **a ~ of fiction** une œuvre de fiction; **a ~ of reference** un ouvrage de référence; **this attack is the ~ of professionals** l'attaque est l'œuvre de professionnels; **I hope you're pleased with your ~!** iron j'espère que tu es fier de ton œuvre! iron; **the ~s of Shakespeare/Flaubert** l'œuvre *m* de Shakespeare/Flaubert; **7** Phys travail *m*; **8** (research) recherches *fpl* (**on** sur); **there is still a lot of ~ to be done on the virus** il y a encore beaucoup de recherches à faire sur le virus; **9** (effect) **to go to ~** [*drug, detergent*] agir; **the weedkiller has done its ~** l'herbicide a été efficace.

II works *npl* **1** (factory) usine *f*; **~s canteen** cantine *f* de l'usine; **2** (building work) travaux *mpl*; **public ~s** travaux publics; **3○** (everything) **the** (**full** ou **whole**) **~s** toute la panoplie○.

III *modif* [*clothes, shoes*] de travail; [*phone number*] au travail.

IV *vtr* **1** (drive) **to ~ sb hard** surmener qn; **2** (labour) **to ~ shifts** travailler en équipes (de travail posté); **to ~ days/nights** travailler de jour/de nuit; **to ~ one's passage** Naut travailler pour payer son voyage; **to ~ one's way through university** travailler pour payer ses études; **to ~ one's way through a book/document** lire un livre/document; **to ~ a 40 hour week** faire la semaine de 40 heures; **3** (operate) se servir de [*computer, equipment, lathe*]; **4** (exploit commercially) exploiter [*oilfield, land, mine, seam*]; **5** (have as one's territory) [*representative*] couvrir [*region*]; **beggars/ prostitutes ~ the streets around the station** les mendiants/prostituées occupent les rues autour de la gare; **6** (consume) **to ~ one's way through** (use) utiliser [*amount, quantity*]; **to ~ one's way through two whole cakes** manger deux gâteaux entiers; **7** (bring about) **to ~ wonders/miracles** lit, fig faire des merveilles/miracles; **the landscape started to ~ its magic on me** la magie du paysage a commencé à faire effet; **8** (use to one's advantage) **to ~ the system** profiter du système; **can you ~ it for me to get tickets?** peux-tu t'arranger pour m'avoir des billets?; **how did you manage to ~ it?** comment as-tu pu arranger ça?; **I've ~ed things so that...** j'ai arrangé les choses de sorte que... (+ *subj*); **9** (fashion) travailler [*clay, dough, gold, iron*]; **to ~ sth to a soft consistency** travailler qch pour le rendre malléable; **to ~ gold into jewellery** travailler l'or pour en faire des bijoux; **10** (embroider) broder [*design*] (**into** sur); **to be ~ed in blue silk** être brodé à la soie bleue; **11** (manoeuvre) **to ~ sth into** introduire qch dans [*slot, hole*]; **to ~ a lever up and down** actionner un levier; **12** (exercise) faire travailler [*muscles, biceps*]; **13** (move) **to ~ one's way through** se frayer un passage à travers [*crowd*]; **to ~ one's way along** avancer le long de [*ledge, sill*]; **to ~ one's hands free** se libérer les mains; **to ~ the rope loose** desserrer la corde; **it ~ed its way loose, it ~ed itself loose** il s'est desserré peu à peu; **to ~ its way into** passer dans [*bloodstream, system, food, chain*]; **start at the top and ~ your way down** commencez par le haut et continuez jusqu'en bas.

V *vi* **1** (engage in activity) travailler (**doing** à faire); **to ~ at the hospital/the factory** travailler à l'hôpital/l'usine; **to ~ at home** travailler à domicile; **to ~ as a midwife/teacher** travailler comme sage-femme/professeur; **to ~ for sb** travailler pour qn; **to ~ for Grant and Company** travailler pour la Société Grant; **to ~ in advertising/publishing** travailler dans la publicité/l'édition; **to ~ with young people** travailler avec les jeunes; **to ~ for a living** gagner sa vie; **to ~ in oils/watercolours** [*artist*] travailler à l'huile/l'aquarelle; **2** (strive) lutter (**against** contre; **for** pour; **to do** pour faire); **to ~ against corruption** lutter contre la corruption; **to ~ towards** se diriger vers [*solution*]; s'acheminer vers [*compromise*]; négocier [*agreement*]; **3** (function) [*equipment, machine*] fonctionner, marcher; [*institution, system, heart, brain*] fonctionner; **to ~ on electricity/on gas** marcher or fonctionner à l'électricité/au gaz; **to ~ off the mains** marcher sur le secteur; **the washing machine isn't ~ing** la machine à laver est en panne or ne marche pas; **4** (act, operate) **it doesn't** ou **things don't ~ like that** ça ne marche pas comme ça; **to ~ on the assumption that** présumer que; **to ~ in sb's favour, to ~ to sb's advantage** tourner à l'avantage de qn; **to ~ against sb, to ~ to sb's disadvantage** jouer en la défaveur de qn; **5** (be successful) [*treatment*] avoir de l'effet; [*detergent, drug*] agir (**against** contre; **on** sur);

[*spell*] agir; [*plan, plot*] réussir; [*argument, hypothesis*] tenir debout; **flattery won't ~ with me** la flatterie ne marche pas avec moi; **the adaptation really ~s** l'adaptation est vraiment réussie; **I didn't think the novel would ~ as a film** je ne pensais pas qu'on pouvait tirer un bon film de ce roman; **6** (move) [*face, features*] se contracter.

VI *v refl* **1** (labour) **to ~ oneself too hard** se surmener; **to ~ oneself to death** se tuer à la tâche; **2** (rouse) **to ~ oneself into a rage** se mettre en colère; **to ~ oneself into a frenzy** (with anger) se mettre en rage; (with hysteria) devenir hystérique.

IDIOMS **to ~ one's way up** gravir tous les échelons; **to ~ one's way up the company** faire son chemin dans l'entreprise.

■ **work around**: **~ around to [sth]** aborder [*subject*]; **it took him ages to ~ around to what he wanted to say** il lui a fallu un temps fou pour exprimer ce qu'il avait à dire; **to ~ the conversation around to sth** faire tourner la conversation autour de qch; **to ~ around to telling sb sth** parvenir à dire qch à qn.

■ **work in**: **~ in [sth], ~ [sth] in 1** (incorporate) glisser [*joke, reference*]; mentionner [*fact, name*]; **2** Culin incorporer [*ingredient*].

■ **work off**: **~ [sth] off, ~ off [sth] 1** (remove) retirer [*lid*]; **to ~ a ring off one's finger** ôter une bague avec difficulté; **2** (repay) travailler pour rembourser [*loan, debt*]; **3** (get rid of) se débarrasser de [*excess weight*]; dépenser [*excess energy*]; passer [*anger, frustration*].

■ **work on**: ¶ **~ on** continuer à travailler; ¶ **~ on [sb]** travailler○; ¶ **~ on [sth]** travailler à [*book, report*]; travailler sur [*project*]; s'occuper de [*case, problem*]; chercher [*cure, solution*]; examiner [*idea, theory*]; **I'm ~ing on a way of doing** je cherche une façon de faire; **'have you found a solution?'—'I'm ~ing on it'** 'as-tu trouvé une solution?'—'j'y réfléchis'; **he's ~ing on his French** il travaille son français; **we've got no clues to ~ on** nous n'avons aucun indice.

■ **work out**: ¶ **~ out 1** (exercise) s'entraîner; **2** (go according to plan) [*plan, marriage*] marcher; **I hope things ~ out for them** j'espère que ça marchera pour eux; **3** (add up) **to ~ out at** GB ou **to** US [*total, share*] s'élever à [*amount, proportion*]; ¶ **~ out [sth], ~ [sth] out 1** (calculate) calculer [*answer, average, total*]; **2** (solve) trouver [*answer, reason, culprit*]; résoudre [*riddle, problem*]; comprendre [*clue*]; **to ~ out why/when/where** comprendre pourquoi/quand/où; **to ~ out what sth means** comprendre qch; **3** (devise) concevoir [*plan, scheme*]; trouver [*route*]; **4** Admin **to ~ out one's notice** faire son mois de préavis; **5** (exhaust) épuiser [*mine, soil*]; ¶ **~ [sb] out** comprendre; **I can't ~ her out** je ne la comprendrai jamais.

■ **work over**○: **~ [sb] over** passer [qn] à tabac○.

■ **work to**: **~ to [sth]** s'astreindre à [*budget*]; **to ~ to deadlines** travailler avec des objectifs; **to ~ to tight deadlines** avoir des délais très serrés.

■ **work up**: ¶ **~ up [sth]** développer [*interest*]; accroître [*support*]; **to ~ up the courage to do** trouver le courage de faire; **to ~ up some enthusiasm for** s'enthousiasmer pour; **to ~ up an appetite** s'ouvrir l'appétit; ¶ **~ up to [sth]** se préparer à [*announcement, confession, confrontation*]; **the music is ~ing up to a climax** la musique va crescendo pour finir en apothéose; ¶ **~ up [sb], ~ [sb] up 1** (excite) exciter [*child, crowd*]; **to ~ sb up into a frenzy** rendre qn énervé; **to ~ sb up into a rage** mettre qn en colère; **2** (annoy) énerver; **to get ~ed up** s'énerver; **to ~ oneself up** s'énerver; **to ~ oneself up into a state** se mettre dans tous ses états; **to get oneself all ~ed up over** ou **about** se mettre dans tous ses états au sujet de.

workable /'wɜːkəbl/ *adj* **1** (feasible) [*idea, plan, suggestion*] réalisable; [*system*] pratique; [*arrangement, compromise*] possible; **2** Agric, Ind [*land, mine, quarry*] exploitable; **3** Constr [*cement*] maniable.

workaday /'wɜːkədeɪ/ *adj* [*matters*] de routine; [*clothes, life, writing*] ordinaire.

workaholic○ /ˌwɜːkə'hɒlɪk/ *n* bourreau *m* de travail.

work: **~ basket** *n* corbeille *f* à ouvrage; **~bench** *n* établi *m*; **~book** *n* (blank) cahier *m*; (with exercises) livre *m* d'exercices; **~box** *n* boîte *f* à ouvrage; **~ camp** *n* chantier *m* (de bénévoles); **~day** *n* gen jour *m* de travail; Comm jour *m* ouvrable; **~desk** *n* bureau *m*.

worker /'wɜːkə(r)/ **I** *n* **1** (employee) (in manual job) ouvrier/-ière *m/f*; (in white-collar job) employé/-e *m/f*; **agricultural ~** ouvrier/-ière agricole; **office ~** employé/-e de bureau; **she's a good/slow ~** elle travaille bien/lentement; **2** (proletarian) prolétaire *mf*; **~s' revolution** révolution *f* prolétarienne; **3** Zool ouvrière *f*.

II *modif* [*ant, bee*] ouvrier/-ière.

worker: **~ director** *n* ouvrier/-ière *m/f* qui siège au conseil de direction; **~ participation** *n* participation *f* des travailleurs à la gestion, co-gestion *f*; **~-priest** *n* prêtre-ouvrier *m*; **~s' control** *n* autogestion *f*.

work: **~ ethic** *n* culte *m* puritain du travail; **~ experience** *n* stage *m*.

workfare /'wɜːkfeə(r)/ *n* GB *politique exigeant que les bénéficiaires de l'allocation de chômage fournissent un travail en échange.*

work: **~force** *n* (+ *v sg ou pl*) (in industry) main-d'œuvre *f*; (in service sector) effectifs *mpl*; **~horse** *n* Agric cheval *m* de trait; fig (person) bête *f* de travail; **~house** *n* GB Hist asile *m* des pauvres; US Hist maison *f* de correction; **~-in** *n* occupation *f* du lieu de travail (sans arrêt de la production).

working /'wɜːkɪŋ/ **I** *n* **1** (functioning) fonctionnement *m*; **2** (shaping, preparation) travail *m* (**of** de); **3** (draft solution) calculs *mpl*; **candidates must show all ~** les candidats doivent montrer leurs calculs; **4** Ind (mine) chantier *m* de mine; (quarry) chantier *m* de carrière.

II workings *npl* lit, fig rouages *mpl*; **the ~s of the human mind** les rouages de l'esprit humain.

III *adj* **1** (professional) [*parent, woman, mother*] qui travaille; [*conditions, environment, methods*] de travail; [*population*] actif/-ive; [*life*] actif/-ive, professionnel/-elle; [*breakfast, lunch, day, week*] de travail; **during ~ hours** (in office) pendant les heures de bureau; (in shop) pendant les heures de travail; **the ~ woman** la femme active; **~ mothers** les mères qui travaillent; **we have a good ~ relationship** nous avons de bons rapports professionnels; **2** (provisional) [*document, hypothesis*] de travail; [*definition, title*] provisoire; **3** (functional) [*model*] qui fonctionne; [*farm, mine*] en exploitation; **to have a ~ knowledge of** connaître les éléments de base de; **in full ~ order** en parfait état de marche; **4** Accts [*expenses, plant, ratio, stock*] d'exploitation.

working: **~ account** *n* Fin compte *m* d'exploitation; **~ agreement** *n* modus *m* vivendi; **~ balance** *n* Fin fonds *mpl* de roulement; **~ capital** *n* Fin fonds *m* de roulement.

working class **I** *n* classe *f* ouvrière; **the ~es** les classes *fpl* laborieuses.

II *adj* [*area, background, childhood, family, life*] ouvrier/-ière; [*culture, London*] prolétarien/-ienne; [*person*] de la classe ouvrière.

working: **~ dog** *n* chien *m* d'utilité; **~ drawing** *n* épure *f*.

working girl *n* **1**† lit femme *f* active; **2** euph (prostitute) professionnelle○ *f* euph, prostituée *f*.

working: **~ group** *n* groupe *m* de travail; **~ majority** *n* majorité *f* suffisante.

working-over○ /ˌwɜːkɪŋ'əʊvə(r)/ *n* passage *m* à tabac○; **to give sb a ~** passer qn à tabac○.

working: **~ party** *n* Admin groupe *m* de travail; Mil escouade *f*; **~ substance** *n* fluide *m* de travail; **~ week** *n* semaine *f* (de travail).

workload /'wɜːkləʊd/ *n* charge *f* de travail; **to have a light/heavy ~** avoir peu/beaucoup de travail; **to reduce/increase sb's ~** donner moins/plus de travail à qn.

workman /'wɜːkmən/ *n* ouvrier *m*.

IDIOMS **a bad ~ blames his tools** un mauvais ouvrier a toujours de mauvais outils Prov.

workmanlike /'wɜːkmənlaɪk/ *adj* **1** (effective) [*job, repair*] soigné; **2** péj (uninspired) [*performance, effort*] honnête.

workmanship /'wɜːkmənʃɪp/ *n* (skill) habileté *f*; **that's a fine piece of ~** c'est du beau travail; **a company famous for sound ~** une compagnie réputée pour la qualité de sa fabrication.

work: **~mate** *n* collègue *mf* de travail; **~ of art** *n* œuvre *f* d'art; **~out** *n* séance *f* de mise en forme; **~pack** *n* fiches *fpl* de travail; **~ permit** *n* permis *m* de travail.

workplace /'wɜːkpleɪs/ **I** *n* lieu *m* de travail.

II *modif* [*creche, nursery*] d'entreprise; **~ pressures** les tensions *fpl* liées au travail.

work: **~ prospects** *npl* possibilités *fpl* de carrière; **~room** *n* atelier *m*; **~s committee, ~ council** *n* GB Ind comité *m* d'entreprise; **~-sharing** *n* partage *m* du travail; **~sheet** *n* Ind feuille *f* d'opérations; Sch feuille *f* de questions.

workshop /'wɜːkʃɒp/ *n* **1** Ind atelier *m*; **2** (training session) atelier *m* (**on** consacré à); **drama ~** atelier de théâtre.

work: **~shy** *adj* péj paresseux/-euse; **~s manager** ▶ 1692 *n* directeur *m* d'usine; **~space** *n* Comput espace *m* de travail; **~ station** *n* Comput poste *m* de travail; **~ study** *n* étude *f* ergonomique; **~ surface** *n* plan *m* de travail; **~table** *n* table *f* de travail; **~top** *n* plan *m* de travail; **~-to-rule** *n* grève *f* du zèle; **~wear** *n* vêtements *mpl* de travail; **~ week** *n* US semaine *f* de travail; **~-worn** *adj* usé par le travail.

world /wɜːld/ **I** *n* **1** (planet) monde *m*; **the whole ~** le monde entier; **throughout the ~** dans le monde entier; **to go round the ~** faire le tour du monde; **the biggest/smallest in the ~** le plus grand/petit du monde; **no-one in the ~** personne au monde; **more than anything in the ~** plus que tout au monde; **this ~ and the next** le monde d'ici-bas et l'au-delà; **the things of this ~** les choses d'ici-bas; **the next** ou **other ~** l'autre monde; **'~ without end'** Relig 'pour les siècles des siècles'; **to lead the ~ in electronics** être à la pointe de l'électronique; **to bring sb into the ~** [*mother*] donner le jour à qn; [*doctor, midwife*] mettre qn au monde; **to come into the ~** [*baby*] voir le jour; **2** (group of people) monde *m*; **the art/business/medical ~** le monde de l'art/des affaires/médical; **the ~ of politics/music** le monde de la politique/de la musique; **the whole ~ knows/is against me** tout le monde le sait/est contre moi; **who cares what the ~ thinks?** on se moque bien de ce que pensent les autres!; **to make one's way in the ~** faire son chemin dans le monde; **in the eyes of the ~** aux yeux du monde; **to go up in the ~** faire chemin; **to go down in the ~** déchoir; **for all the ~ to see** devant tout le monde; **the outside ~** le reste du monde; **the ~ in general** tout le monde; **3** (section of the earth) pays

mpl; **the Eastern/Western ~** les pays de l'Est/occidentaux; **the developed ~** les pays développés; **4** (person's environment) monde *m*, univers *m*; **the ~ of the child** le monde or l'univers de l'enfant; **his death has shattered her ~** sa mort a basculé son univers; **he lives in a ~ of his own** ou **a private ~** il vit dans un monde à part.
II *modif* [*agenda, events, climate, market, leader, politics, proportions, prices, rights, scale*] mondial; [*record, tour, championship*] du monde; [*cruise*] autour du monde.
IDIOMS **(all) the ~ and his wife** hum tout le monde; **a ~ away from sth** très éloigné de qch; **to be all the ~ to sb** représenter tout pour qn; **to be on top of the ~** être aux anges; **for all the ~ like/as if** exactement comme/comme si; **he's one of the Rasputins/Don Juans of this ~** c'est un véritable Raspoutine/Don Juan; **the Pauls/Annes of this ~** les gens de cette espèce; **how in the ~ did you know ?** comment diable l'as-tu su?; **to get the best of both ~s** gagner sur les deux tableaux; **he wants to get the best of both ~s** il veut tout avoir, il veut le beurre et l'argent du beurre; **I'd give the ~ to**... je donnerais n'importe quoi pour...; **it's a small ~!** le monde est petit; **it's not the end of the ~!** ce n'est pas la fin du monde!; **a man/woman of the ~** un homme/une femme d'expérience; **not for (all) the ~** pas pour tout l'or du monde; **out of this ~** extraordinaire; **that's the way of the ~** c'est la vie; **the ~'s worst cook/correspondent** le pire chef/correspondant du monde entier; **the ~, the flesh and the devil** les tentations du monde, de la chair et du diable; **there's a ~ of difference** il y a une différence énorme; **it did him/them the** ou **a ~ of good** ça lui/leur a fait énormément de bien; **to have the ~ at one's feet** avoir le monde à ses pieds; **to set the ~ on fire** épater le monde°; **to think the ~ of sb** penser le plus grand bien de qn; **to think the ~ owes you a living** penser que le monde vous doit quelque chose; **to watch the ~ go by** regarder le monde s'agiter; **what/where/who etc in the ~?** que/où/qui etc diable?; **with the best will in the ~** avec la meilleure volonté du monde; **~s apart** diamétralement opposé; **the two sides are ~s apart** les deux parties ont un point de vue diamétralement opposé. ▶ **oyster**.

world: **World Bank** *n* Banque *f* mondiale; **World Bank Group** *n* Groupe *m* de la Banque mondiale.

world-beater *n* (person) personne *f* qui surpasse les autres; (product) produit *m* qui se vend le mieux.

world: **~-beating** *adj* qui surpasse les autres; **~-class** *adj* de niveau mondial; **World Council of Churches, WCC** *n* Conseil *m* œcuménique des Églises; **World Cup** *n* (in football) Coupe *f* du Monde; **World Fair** *n* Exposition *f* universelle; **~-famous** *adj* mondialement connu; **World Health Organization, WHO** *n* Organisation *f* mondiale de la santé; **~ language** *n* langue *f* parlée dans le monde entier.

world leader *n* **1** Pol chef *m* d'État; **2** (best in the world) Sport meilleur/-e *m/f* du monde; Comm [*company*] leader *m* mondial; **this company/country is (a) ~ in the field of information technology** cette compagnie/ce pays est un des leaders mondiaux de l'informatique.

world-line /ˈwɜːldlaɪn/ *n* Phys ligne *f* d'univers.

worldliness /ˈwɜːldlɪnɪs/ *n* matérialisme *m*.

worldling /ˈwɜːldlɪŋ/ *n* matérialiste *mf*.

worldly /ˈwɜːldlɪ/ *adj* **1** gen, Relig (not spiritual) matériel/-ielle; **~ goods** les biens matériels; **~ wisdom** la sagesse des nations; **2** (materialistic) péj matérialiste.

worldly-wise /ˌwɜːldlɪˈwaɪz/ *adj* avisé, qui a de l'expérience.

world: **World Music** *n* musiques *fpl* du monde; **~ power** *n* Pol puissance *f* mondiale; **World Series** *n* US Sport championnat *m* national de base-ball; **World Service** *n* GB Radio service *m* international de la BBC; **World Trade Organization, WTO** *n* Organisation *f* mondiale du commerce, OMC; **~view** *n* vision *f* du monde.

world war *n* guerre *f* mondiale; **World War I/II, the First/Second World War** la Première/Seconde Guerre mondiale.

world: **~-weariness** *n* dégoût *m* de la vie; **~-weary** *adj* fatigué de la vie.

world(-)wide /ˌwɜːldˈwaɪd/ **I** *adj* mondial.
II *adv* dans le monde entier.

World Wide Web, WWW *n* Comput World Wide Web *m*.

worm /wɜːm/ **I** *n* **1** Fishg, Zool ver *m*; **2** Med, Vet ver *m* (intestinal); **to have/get ~s** avoir/attraper des vers; **a dog with ~s** un chien infesté de vers; **3**° (wretch) vermine° *f*; **4** Comput (disk) (*abrév* = **write-once read many times**) disque *m* inscriptible une seule fois; **5** Comput (virus) virus *m*; **6** Tech vis *f* sans fin.
II *vtr* **1** Med, Vet donner un vermifuge à [*person, animal*]; **2** (wriggle) **to ~ one's way** lit se faufiler (**along** le long de; **through** à travers); fig s'insinuer (**into** dans); **to ~ one's way into sb's affections** gagner les bonnes grâces de qn.
IDIOMS **the ~ has turned** la situation s'est renversée; **the ~ in the bud** le ver dans le fruit; **a can of ~s** un sac de nœuds.
■ **worm out**: **~ [sth] out** arracher [*truth, facts*] (**of sb** à qn).

worm: **~-eaten** *adj* [*fruit*] véreux/-euse; [*wood*] vermoulu; **~ gear** *n* engrenage *m* à vis sans fin; **~hole** *n* (in fruit, plant) trou *m* de ver; (in wood) vermoulure *f*.

worm's eye view *n* Phot contre-plongée *f*; fig hum point *m* de vue de l'humble spectateur.

wormwood /ˈwɜːmwʊd/ *n* armoise *f*.

wormy /ˈwɜːmɪ/ *adj* **1** (full of worms) [*soil*] plein de vers; [*wood*] vermoulu; [*fruit*] véreux/-euse; **2** US (grovelling) [*person*] servile.

worn /wɔːn/ **I** *pp* ▶ **wear II, III.**
II *adj* [*carpet, clothing, shoe, tyre*] usé; [*façade, stone*] abîmé; [*tread*] lisse.

worn-out /ˌwɔːnˈaʊt/ *adj* **1** [*carpet, brake*] complètement usé; **2** [*person*] épuisé.

worried /ˈwʌrɪd/ *adj* soucieux/-ieuse; **to be ~** être soucieux/-ieuse; **to look ~** avoir l'air soucieux; **to be ~ about sb/sth** se faire du souci or s'inquiéter pour qn/qch; **to be ~ about doing** avoir peur de faire; **to be ~ that** avoir peur que (+ *subj*).

worrier /ˈwʌrɪə(r)/ *n* anxieux/-ieuse *m/f*; **don't be such a ~!** ne sois pas si anxieux!

worrisome /ˈwʌrɪsəm/ *adj* [*matter, situation*] préoccupant; [*person*] qui cause des soucis (*after n*).

worry /ˈwʌrɪ/ **I** *n* **1** ¢ (anxiety) soucis *mpl* (**about, over** à propos de) **her disappearance caused him a lot of ~** sa disparition lui a causé beaucoup de soucis; **2** (problem) souci *m* (**about, over** au sujet de); **to have financial worries** avoir des soucis financiers; **that's the least of my worries** c'est le dernier de mes soucis; **my only/main ~ is that** mon seul/principal souci est que; **he's a ~ to his parents** il cause des soucis à ses parents.
II *vtr* **1** (concern) [*fact, rumour*] inquiéter [*person*]; **I ~ that** j'ai peur que (+ *subj*); **it worries me that** ça m'inquiète que (+ *subj*); **it worried him that he couldn't find the keys** ça l'a inquiété de ne pas trouver les clés; **2** (alarm) tracasser [*person*]; **I don't want to ~ you, but** je ne veux pas vous tracasser, mais; **3** (bother) ennuyer [*person*]; **would it ~ you if I opened the window?** est-ce que ça vous ennuie que j'ouvre la fenêtre?; **4** (chase) [*dog*] harceler [*sheep*]; **5** (toss about) [*cat, dog*] secouer [qch] entre les dents.
III *vi* (be anxious) s'inquiéter; **to ~ about** ou **over sth/sb** s'inquiéter ou se faire du souci pour qch/qn; **to ~ about doing** avoir peur de faire; **I ~ for his sanity sometimes** je me fais parfois du souci pour sa santé mentale; **there's nothing to ~ about** il n'y a pas lieu de s'inquiéter; **not to ~, I'll get a taxi** ne t'inquiète pas, je vais appeler un taxi; **don 't ~ about me, I'm OK** ne t'inquiète pas pour moi, je vais bien; **he'll be punished, don't you ~!** il sera puni, tu peux en être sûr!; **he said it's nothing to ~ about** il a dit qu'il n'y avait là rien d'inquiétant.
IV *v refl* **to ~ oneself** s'inquiéter, se faire du souci (**about sb** au sujet de qn; **about sth** à propos de qch); **to ~ oneself sick over sth** se ronger les sangs au sujet de qch.
■ **worry at**: **~ at [sth]** lit [*dog*] secouer [qch] entre les dents [*toy*]; fig [*person*] retourner [qch] dans tous les sens [*problem*].

worry beads *npl* chapelet *m* antistress.

worrying /ˈwʌrɪɪŋ/ **I** *n* **all this ~ is making you ill** tout ce souci que tu te fais te rend malade; **stop your ~!** arrête de te faire du souci!
II *adj* inquiétant; **the ~ thing is that** ce qu'il y a d'inquiétant c'est que.

worry: **~ line** *n* ride *f* (*causée par les soucis*); **~wart**° /ˌwʌrɪˈwɔːt/ *n* US bileux/-euse° *m/f*.

worse /wɜːs/ **I** *adj* (comparative of **bad**) **1** (more unsatisfactory, unpleasant) pire; **the next day was ~** le lendemain a été pire; **there's nothing ~ than** il n'y a rien de pire que; **there's only one thing ~ than** il n'y a qu'une chose qui soit pire que; **they're ~ than children!** ils sont pires que des enfants!; **she can't be ~ than her predecessor** elle ne peut pas être pire que son prédécesseur; **you're ~ for encouraging them to lie!** tu es encore pire puisque tu les as poussés à mentir!; **he got ~ as the years went on** il est devenu pire avec l'âge; **the regime is no ~ than that in many other countries** le régime n'est pas pire que celui de beaucoup d'autres pays; **there are ~ things in life than losing sleep** il y a pire dans la vie que de perdre le sommeil; **the noise is ~** il y a plus de bruit; **to get ~** [*pressure, noise*] augmenter; [*conditions, weather*] empirer; **'you missed the bus'—'yes ~ luck!'** 'tu as raté le bus'—'oui pas de veine°!'; **2** (more serious, severe) pire (**than** que); **it looks ~ than it is!** ça a l'air pire que ça ne l'est en vérité; **the situation is even ~ now/is ~ than ever** la situation est encore pire maintenant/est pire que jamais; **it could have been ~** ça aurait pu être pire; **it couldn't be ~!** ça ne pourrait pas être pire!; **and what is ~, she doesn't care** et le pire, c'est que ça lui est égal; **to go from bad to ~** aller de pire en pire; **to get ~ (and ~)** [*illness, conflict*] s'aggraver, empirer; [*patient*] aller de plus en plus mal; **to be made ~** être aggravé (**by** par) ; **you'll only make things** ou **it ~!** tu ne feras qu'empirer les choses!; **and to make matters ~, he lied** et pour ne rien arranger, il a menti; **3** (of lower standard) pire (**than** que); **the film is ~ than the book** le film est pire que le livre; **this essay is bad but his is even ~** cette rédaction est mauvaise mais la sienne est encore pire; **~ than usual** pire que d'habitude; **to be even ~ at languages** être encore plus mauvais en langues; **4** (more unwell, unhappy) **he's getting ~** il va plus mal; **the cough is getting ~** la toux empire; **to feel ~** (more ill) se sentir plus malade; (more unhappy) aller moins bien; **his death made me feel ~** sa mort m'a démoralisé encore plus; **the more you move about, the ~ it gets** plus on bouge pire c'est; **he is none the ~ for the experience** il ne se porte pas plus mal après cette expérience; **it was a hard life but they're**

none the ~ for it c'était une vie dure mais ils ne s'en portent pas plus mal; **so much the ~ for them!** tant pis pour eux!; **5** (more inappropriate) **he couldn't have chosen a ~ place to meet** il n'aurait pas pu choisir un lieu de rendez-vous moins approprié; **the decision couldn't have come at a ~ time** la décision n'aurait pas pu arriver à un moment plus inopportun.

II *n* **there is ~ to come** ce n'est pas encore le pire; **~ was to follow** ce n'était pas encore le pire; **to change for the ~** empirer; **things took a turn for the ~** les choses ont empiré; **it could mean prison or ~** ça pourrait entraîner la prison ou pire.

III *adv* (*comparative of* **badly**) **1** (more unsatisfactorily, incompetently) moins bien (**than** que); **he plays the piano ~ than you!** il joue moins bien au piano que toi!; **to behave ~** se conduire plus mal; **you could do ~ than take early retirement** ce ne serait pas si mal de partir en préretraite; **she could do ~ than follow his example** ce ne serait pas si mal si elle suivait son exemple; **2** (more seriously, severely) [*cough, bleed, vomit*] plus; **~ still, there are signs of unrest** pire encore, il y a des signes d'agitation; **she could complain or ~, report you to the police** elle pourrait se plaindre ou pire, te dénoncer à la police.

worsen /ˈwɜːsn/ **I** *vtr* aggraver [*situation, problem*].

II *vi* [*condition, health, weather, situation*] se détériorer; [*problem, crisis, shortage, flooding*] s'aggraver.

worsening /ˈwɜːsnɪŋ/ **I** *n* aggravation *f* (**of** de).

II *adj* [*situation*] en voie de détérioration; [*problem, shortage*] en voie d'aggravation.

worse off *adj* **1** (less wealthy) **to be ~** avoir moins d'argent (**than** que); **to end up ~** finir avec moins d'argent; **we're no ~ now than before the recession** nous n'avons pas moins d'argent maintenant qu'avant la crise; **I'm £10 a week ~** j'ai dix livres de moins par semaine; **2** (in a worse situation) **to be ~** être dans une situation pire; **to be no ~ without sth** pouvoir parfaitement se passer de qch.

worship /ˈwɜːʃɪp/ **I** *n* **1** (veneration) gen vénération *f*; Relig culte *m*; **nature/ancestor ~** culte de la nature/des ancêtres; **that car has become an object of ~ for her** cette voiture est devenue pour elle un objet de vénération; **2** (religious practice) pratique *f* religieuse; **public ~ is forbidden** la pratique religieuse publique est interdite; **freedom of ~** liberté *f* de culte; **place of ~** lieu *m* de culte; **an act of ~** un acte de dévotion; **a service of divine ~** un office religieux or divin; **hours of ~** (Christian, Jewish) heures des offices; (Moslem) heures des prières.

II **Worship** *pr n* GB ▶ 1268 (for man) monsieur *m*; (for woman) madame *f*; **his Worship the mayor** Monsieur le maire.

III *vtr* (*p prés etc* **-pp-**) **1** Relig (venerate) adorer, vénérer [*Buddha, God*]; (give praise) rendre hommage à; **2** (idolize) lit vénérer [*person*]; fig être en adoration devant [*animal, person*]; **to ~ money/fame** avoir le culte de l'argent/la renommée.

IV *vi* (*p prés etc* **-pp-**) pratiquer sa religion; **to ~ at the altar of** élever des autels à la gloire de [*money, fame*].

IDIOMS **to ~ the ground sb walks** ou **treads on** vénérer jusqu'au sol que qn foule.

worshipful /ˈwɜːʃɪpfl/ *adj* **1** (respectful) révérencieux/-ieuse; **2** GB Hist [*company, guild*] honorable (*before n*); **3** (in freemasonry) **Worshipful Master** Vénérable *m*.

worshipper /ˈwɜːʃɪpə(r)/ *n* (in established religion) fidèle *mf*; (in nonestablished religion) adorateur/-trice *m/f*; **to be a nature ~** vouer un culte à la nature.

worst /wɜːst/ **I** *n* **1** (most difficult, unpleasant) **the ~** le/la pire *m/f*; **the storm was one of the ~ in recent years** la tempête était parmi les pires qu'il y ait eu ces dernières années; **last year was the ~ for strikes** du point de vue des grèves l'année dernière a été la pire; **they're the ~ of all** (people) c'est eux les pires; (things, problems, ideas) c'est ce qu'il y a de pire; **wasps are the ~ of all** les guêpes, c'est ce qu'il y a de pire; **he's not the ~** il y a pire que lui; **we're over the ~ now** nous avons passé le pire; **the ~ was yet to come** le plus dur était encore à venir; **the ~ of it is, there's no solution** le pire c'est qu'il n'y a pas de solution; **to get the ~ of all** or **both worlds** se retrouver avec tous les inconvénients à la fois; **that's the ~ of waiting till the last minute** c'est ça l'inconvénient d'attendre jusqu'à la dernière minute; **during the ~ of the riots/of the recession** au plus fort des émeutes/de la crise; **the ~ of the heat is over** les plus fortes chaleurs sont passées; **we escaped the ~ of the tremors** nous avons échappé aux secousses les plus violentes; **do your ~!** essaie un peu pour voir!; **let them do their ~!** qu'ils essaient un peu pour voir!; **2** (expressing the most pessimistic outlook) **the ~** le pire *m*; **to fear the ~** craindre le pire; **to expect the ~** s'attendre au pire; **to think the ~ of sb** avoir une mauvaise opinion de qn; **the ~ that can happen is that** le pire qui puisse arriver ce serait que (+ *subj*); **if the ~ were to happen**, **if the ~ came to the ~** (in serious circumstances) dans le pire des cas; (involving fatality, death) si le pire devait arriver; **at ~** au pire; **at best neutral, at ~ hostile** au mieux neutre, au pire hostile; **3** (most unbearable) **to be at its ~** [*relationship, development, tendency, economic situation*] aller au plus mal; **when things were at their ~** lorsque les choses allaient au plus mal; **at its ~, the noise could be heard everywhere** quand le bruit était à sa puissance maximum, on l'entendait partout; **when the heat is at its ~** au plus fort de la chaleur; **this is media hype**○ **at its ~** c'est le battage○ publicitaire dans ce qu'il a de pire; **these are fanatics at their ~** ce sont des fanatiques dans ce qu'ils ont de pire; **when you see people at their ~** quand on voit les gens sous leur plus mauvais jour; **I'm at my ~ in the morning** (in temper) c'est le matin que je suis de plus mauvaise humeur; **at her ~ she's totally unbearable** dans ses plus mauvais jours elle est vraiment insupportable; **4** (most negative trait) **to exploit the ~ in people** exploiter ce qu'il y a de plus mauvais or bas chez les gens; **to bring out the ~ in sb** mettre à jour ce qu'il y a de plus mauvais or de pire chez qn; **5** (of the lowest standard, quality) **the ~** le plus mauvais/la plus mauvaise *m/f*; **they're the ~ in the group** ce sont les plus mauvais du groupe; **he's one of the ~** c'est un des plus mauvais; **the country's economic record is one of the ~ in Europe** le pays a l'un des plus mauvais bilans économiques d'Europe; **the film is certainly not her ~** ce n'est sûrement pas son plus mauvais film; **to be the ~ at French/rugby** être le plus mauvais en français/rugby; **she must be the world's ~ at cooking** c'est la plus mauvaise cuisinière qui soit, pour la cuisine elle a le pompon○.

II *adj* (*superlative of* **bad**) **1** (most unsatisfactory, unpleasant) plus mauvais; **the ~ book I've ever read** le plus mauvais livre que j'aie jamais lu; **it's the ~ meal we've ever eaten** c'est le plus mauvais repas que nous ayons jamais mangé; **hypocrites of the ~ kind** des hypocrites de la pire espèce; **the ~ thing about the film/about being blind is** ce qu'il y a de pire dans le film/lorsqu'on est aveugle c'est; **the ~ thing about him is his temper** ce qu'il y a de pire chez lui c'est son mauvais caractère; **and the ~ thing about it is** (**that**) et le pire c'est que; **2** (most serious) plus grave; **the ~ air disaster in years** la plus grave catastrophe aérienne depuis des années; **one of the ~ recessions** une des crises les plus graves; **one of the ~ things anyone has ever done** une des choses les plus graves qu'on ait jamais faites; **the ~ mistake you could have made** la pire erreur possible; **the ~ victims were children** ce sont les enfants qui ont été les plus touchés; **3** (most inappropriate) pire; **the ~ possible place to do** le pire endroit pour faire; **the ~ possible environment for a child** le pire milieu qu'on puisse imaginer pour un enfant; **she rang at the ~ possible time** elle a téléphoné au plus mauvais moment; **the ~ thing** (**to do**) **would be to ignore it** le pire serait de ne pas en tenir compte; **it would be ~ if they forgot** le pire serait qu'ils oublient (*subj*); **it's the ~ thing you could have said!** c'était vraiment la chose à ne pas dire!; **4** (of the poorest standard) pire, plus mauvais; **the ~ hotel in town** le pire hôtel de la ville; **the world's ~ chef** le plus mauvais cuisinier du monde.

III *adv* **the children suffer** (**the**) **~** ce sont les enfants qui souffrent le plus; **they were** (**the**) **~ affected** ou **hit by the strike** ce sont eux qui ont été les plus touchés par la grève; **to smell the ~** sentir le plus mauvais; **to come off ~** perdre le plus; **the ~-off groups in society** les groupes les plus démunis de la société; **the ~-behaved child he'd ever met** l'enfant le plus mal élevé qu'il ait jamais rencontré; **~ of all,...** le pire de tout, c'est que...; **they did** (**the**) **~ of all the group in the exam** ce sont eux qui ont le moins bien réussi l'examen.

IV *vtr* sout **to be ~ed** être battu (**by** par).

worsted /ˈwʊstɪd/ **I** *n* tissu *m* en laine peignée.

II *modif* [*trousers, jacket*] en laine peignée.

worth /wɜːθ/ **I** *n* ₵ **1** Fin (measure, quantity) **five/a hundred pounds' ~ of sth** pour cinq/cent livres de qch; **thousands of pounds' ~ of damage** des milliers de livres de dégâts; **a day's ~ of fuel** un jour de combustible; **a week's ~ of supplies** une semaine de provisions; **to get one's money's ~** en avoir pour son argent; **2** (value, usefulness) (of object, person) valeur *f*; **what's its precise ~?** quelle est sa valeur précise?; **of great ~** de grande valeur; **of little ~** de peu de valeur; **of no ~** sans valeur; **people of ~ in the community** des gens de valeur dans la communauté; **what is its ~ in pounds?** combien cela fait-il en livres sterling?; **to prove one's ~** démontrer sa valeur; **to see the ~ of sth** voir ce que vaut qch.

II *adj* (*jamais épith*) **1** (of financial value) **to be ~ sth** [*object*] valoir qch; **the pound is ~ 10 francs** la livre vaut 10 francs; **the land is ~ millions** les terres valent des millions; **what** ou **how much is it ~?** combien cela vaut-il?; **it's not ~ much** ça ne vaut pas grand-chose; **it's ~ a lot/more** ça vaut beaucoup/plus; **he is ~ £50,000** sa fortune s'élève à 50 000 livres; **2** (of abstract value) **to be ~ sth** valoir qch; **two hours' solid work is ~ a day's discussion** deux heures de travail intensif valent une journée de discussion; **an experienced worker is ~ three novices** un travailleur expérimenté vaut trois débutants; **unsubstantiated reports are not ~ much/are ~ nothing** les rapports sans fondement concret ne valent pas grand-chose/ ne valent rien; **it's as much as my job's ~ to give you the keys** je risque mon emploi si je te donne les clés; **it's more than my life's ~ to...** hum je ne vais pas risquer ma peau pour...; **the contract isn't ~ the paper it's written on** le contrat ne vaut pas le papier sur lequel il est écrit; **the house/car is only ~ what you can get for it** la maison/voiture ne vaut que ce qu'elle vaut; **to be ~ a mention** mériter une mention ou d'être mentionné; **to be ~ a try** valoir la peine d'essayer; **to be ~ a visit/the time/the effort** valoir une visite/le temps/l'effort; **to be ~ it** valoir la peine; **it**

was a long journey/a lot of money: **was it ~ it?** c'était un long voyage/ça a coûté cher: est-ce que ça en valait la peine?; **I won't pay the extra/complain, it's not ~ it** je ne paierai pas le supplément/je ne me plaindrai pas, ça n'en vaut pas la peine; **don't get upset, he's not ~ it** ne te fâche pas, il n'en vaut pas la peine; **to be ~ doing** valoir la peine d'être fait; **the book is/isn't ~ reading** le livre vaut/ne vaut pas la peine d'être lu; **is life ~ living?** est-ce que la vie vaut la peine d'être vécue?; **that suggestion/idea is ~ considering** la suggestion/l'idée mérite réflexion; **that's ~ knowing** cela est utile à savoir; **everyone ~ knowing had left town** tous ceux qui comptaient avaient quitté la ville; **what he doesn't know about farming isn't ~ knowing** il sait tout ce qu'on peut savoir sur le travail à la ferme; **those little pleasures that make life ~ living** ces petits plaisirs qui donnent un sens à la vie; **it is/isn't ~ doing** ça vaut/ne vaut pas la peine de faire; **is it ~ paying more?** vaut-il la peine de payer plus ?; **it's ~ knowing that**... il est utile de savoir que...; **it could be ~ consulting your doctor** ça vaudrait peut-être la peine de consulter votre médecin.

IDIOMS **for all one is ~** de toutes ses forces; **for what it's ~** pour ce que cela vaut; **and that's my opinion for what it's ~** et voilà mon avis, prenez-le pour ce qu'il vaut; **to be ~ sb's while** valoir le coup; **I decided it was/wasn't ~ my while to**... j'ai décidé que ça valait/ne valait pas le coup de...; **if you come I'll make it ~ your while** si tu viens, tu ne le regretteras pas; **if a job's ~ doing it's ~ doing well** ce qui vaut la peine d'être fait vaut la peine d'être bien fait; ▶ **bush**, **candle**.

worthily /ˈwɜːðɪlɪ/ *adv* dignement.

worthiness /ˈwɜːðɪnɪs/ *n* **1** (respectability) dignité *f*; **2** (merit) (of candidate) mérite *m*; (of cause, charity) dignité *f*.

worthless /ˈwɜːθlɪs/ *adj* [*contract, currency, object, idea, theory, promise*] sans valeur; **he's ~** c'est un bon à rien.

worthlessness /ˈwɜːθlɪsnɪs/ *n* **1** (of object, coin, currency) absence *f* de valeur; **2** (of person, advice, contract, promise) nullité *f*; (of character) immoralité *f*.

worthwhile /wɜːθˈwaɪl/ *adj* [*discussion, undertaking, visit*] qui en vaut la peine; [*career, project*] intéressant; **to be ~ doing** valoir la peine de faire; **it's been well ~** cela en valait vraiment la peine.

worthy /ˈwɜːðɪ/ **I** *n* notable *m*.

II *adj* **1** (*jamais épith*) (deserving) **to be ~ of sth** mériter qch, être digne de qch; **that's not ~ of mention/of your attention** cela ne mérite pas d'être mentionné/de retenir votre attention; **is he ~ of the honour?** mérite-t-il cet honneur?; **the idea's not ~ of your consideration** l'idée ne mérite pas réflexion; **~ of note** digne d'intérêt; **to be ~ of doing** mériter d'être fait; **the matter's/he's not ~ of being taken seriously** l'affaire/il ne mérite pas qu'on la/le prenne sérieusement; **to be ~ to do** être digne de faire; **2** (admirable) [*cause*] noble; [*citizen, friend*] digne; **3** (appropriate) **~ of sth/sb** digne de qn/qch; **a performance ~ of a champion** une performance digne d'un champion; **a speech ~ of the occasion** un discours adapté aux circonstances.

wot○ /wɒt/ *excl* GB = **what**.

wotcher○ /ˈwɒtʃə(r)/ *excl* (also **wotcha**) GB salut!

would /wʊd, wəd/

■ **Note** When *would* is used with a verb in English to form the conditional tense, *would + verb* is translated by the present conditional of the appropriate verb in French and *would have + verb* by the past conditional of the appropriate verb: *I would do it if I had time* = je le ferais si j'avais le temps; *I would have done it if I had had time* = je l'aurais fait si j'avais eu le temps; *he said he would fetch the car* = il a dit qu'il chercherait la voiture.
– For more examples, particular usages and all other uses of *would* see the entry below.

modal aux (aussi **'d**; *nég* **wouldn't**) **1** (in sequence of past tenses, in reported speech) **she said she wouldn't come** elle a dit qu'elle ne viendrait pas; **we thought we ~ be late** nous avons pensé que nous serions en retard; **I was sure you'd like it** j'étais sûr que ça te plairait; **we were wondering if he'd accept** nous nous demandions s'il accepterait; **they promised that they'd come back** ils ont promis de revenir; **soon it ~ be time to get up** ce serait bientôt l'heure de se lever; **it was to be the last chance we ~ have to leave** ça devait être la dernière chance que nous aurions de partir; **he thought she ~ have forgotten** il pensait qu'elle aurait oublié; **I wish he ~ shut the door!** il pourrait fermer la porte!; **I wish you'd be quiet!** tu ne pourrais pas te taire!; **2** (in conditional statements) **it ~ be wonderful if they came** ce serait merveilleux s'ils venaient; **I'm sure she ~ help if you asked her** je suis sûr qu'elle t'aiderait si tu le lui demandais; **if we'd left later we ~ have missed the train** si nous étions partis plus tard nous aurions raté le train; **we wouldn't be happy anywhere else** nous ne serions heureux nulle part ailleurs; **what ~ be the best way to approach him?** quel serait le meilleur moyen de l'aborder?; **who ~ ever have believed it?** qui l'aurait cru?; **you wouldn't have thought it possible!** on n'aurait jamais cru que c'était possible!; **I ~ have found out sooner or later** je l'aurais découvert tôt ou tard; **wouldn't it be nice if**... ce serait bien si...; **we wouldn't have succeeded without his help** nous n'aurions jamais réussi sans son aide; **it wouldn't be the same without them** ça ne serait pas la même chose sans eux; **it cost far less than I ~ have expected** ça a coûté beaucoup moins cher que je n'aurais pensé; **3** (expressing willingness to act) **do you know anyone who ~ do it?** est-ce que tu connais quelqu'un qui le ferait?; **they couldn't find anyone who ~ take the job** ils n'arrivaient pas à trouver quelqu'un qui accepte (*subj*) le poste; **he wouldn't hurt a fly** il ne ferait pas de mal à une mouche; **she just wouldn't listen** elle ne voulait rien entendre; **after that I wouldn't eat any canned food** après cela je ne voulais plus manger de conserves; **he wouldn't do a thing to help** il n'a rien voulu faire pour aider; **the police wouldn't give any further details** la police a refusé de donner plus de détails; **they asked me to leave but I wouldn't** ils m'ont demandé de partir mais j'ai refusé; **4** (expressing inability to function) **the door wouldn't close** la porte ne voulait pas se fermer; **the brakes wouldn't work** les freins ne marchaient pas; **5** (expressing desire, preference) **we ~ like to stay another night** nous aimerions rester une nuit de plus; **we'd really love to see you** nous aimerions vraiment te voir; **I ~ much rather travel alone** je préfèrerais nettement voyager seul; **she ~ have preferred a puppy** elle aurait préféré un chiot; **which film ~ you rather see?** quel film est-ce que tu préfèrerais voir?; **I wouldn't mind another slice of cake** je prendrais bien un autre morceau de gâteau; **it's what he ~ have wanted** c'est ce qu'il aurait voulu; **6** (in polite requests or proposals) **~ you like something to eat?** voudriez-vous quelque chose à manger?; **~ you like some more tea?** voulez-vous encore du thé?; **~ you help me set the table?** est-ce que tu pourrais m'aider à mettre la table?; **switch off the radio, ~ you?** éteins la radio, tu veux bien?; **~ you be interested in buying a vacuum cleaner?** est-ce que vous seriez intéressé par un aspirateur?; **~ you like to go to a concert** est-ce que tu aimerais aller à un concert?; **~ you give her the message?** est-ce que vous voulez bien lui transmettre le message?; **~ you mind not smoking please?** est-ce que ça vous ennuyerait de ne pas fumer s'il vous plaît?; **~ you please be quiet** un peu de silence s'il vous plaît; **~ you be so kind as to leave?** sout auriez-vous l'obligeance de partir d'ici? fml; **7** (used to attenuate statements) **it ~ seem that he was right** il semblerait qu'il avait raison; **so it ~ seem** c'est ce qu'il semble; **you ~ think they'd be satisfied with the results!** on aurait pu penser qu'ils seraient satisfaits des résultats!; **I wouldn't say that** je ne dirais pas ça; **I ~ have thought it was obvious** j'aurais pensé que c'était évident; **I wouldn't know** je ne pourrais pas vous le dire; **8** (when giving advice) **I wouldn't do that if I were you** je ne ferais pas ça à ta place or si j'étais toi; **I really wouldn't worry** à ta place je ne m'en ferais pas; **I ~ check the timetable first** tu ferais bien de vérifier l'horaire d'abord; **I'd give her a ring now** tu devrais lui téléphoner maintenant; **wouldn't it be better to write?** est-ce que ce ne serait pas mieux d'écrire?; **9** (expressing exasperation) **'he denies it'—'well he ~, wouldn't he?'** 'il le nie'—'évidemment!'; **of course you ~ contradict him!** bien sûr il a fallu que tu le contredises!; **'she put her foot in it○'—'she ~!'** 'elle a mis les pieds dans le plat○'—tu m'étonnes!', 'c'est bien d'elle!'; **10** (expressing an assumption) **what time ~ that be?** c'était vers quelle heure?; **I suppose it ~ have been about 3 pm** je pense qu'il était à peu près 15h 00; **being so young, you wouldn't remember the war** étant donné ton âge tu ne dois pas te rappeler la guerre; **let's see, that ~ be his youngest son** voyons, ça doit être son plus jeune fils; **it ~ have been about five years ago** ça devait être il y a environ cinq ans; **you'd never have guessed she was German** on n'aurait jamais cru qu'elle était allemande; **11** (indicating habitual event or behaviour in past: used to) **she ~ sit for hours at the window** elle passait des heures assise à la fenêtre; **every winter the fields ~ be flooded** tous les hivers les champs étaient inondés; **the children ~ be up at dawn** les enfants étaient toujours debout à l'aube; **12** sout (if only) **~ that it were true!** si seulement c'était vrai! ; **~ to God that**... pl ût à Dieu que (+ *subj*) fml.

would-be /ˈwʊdbiː/ *adj* **1** (desirous of being) **~ emigrants/investors** des émigrés/investisseurs en puissance; **~ intellectuals** péj des soi-disant or prétendus intellectuels pej; **2** (having intended to be) **the ~ thieves were arrested** les voleurs ont été arrêtés avant qu'ils aient pu passer à l'acte.

wouldn't /ˈwʊd(ə)nt/ = **would not**.

would've /wʊdəv/ = **would have**.

wound¹ /wuːnd/ **I** *n* **1** (injury) blessure *f*; **a ~ to** ou **in the head** une blessure à la tête; **to die from** ou **of one's ~s** succomber à ses blessures; **2** (cut, sore, incision) plaie *f*; **an open ~** une plaie ouverte; **3** fig blessure *f*; **it takes time for the ~s to heal** il faut longtemps pour que les plaies se cicatrisent; **4** Bot entaille *f*.

II *vtr* (all contexts) blesser; **to ~ sb in the leg/stomach** blesser qn à la jambe/au ventre.

IDIOMS fig **to lick one's ~s** panser ses blessures; **to reopen old ~s** rouvrir de vieilles blessures; **to rub salt into the ~** remuer le couteau dans la plaie.

wound² /waʊnd/ *prét, pp* ▶ **wind**² II, III.

wounded /ˈwuːndɪd/ **I** *n* **the ~** (+ *v pl*) les blessés/-es *m/f*.

II *adj* [*person*] blessé; **~ in the arm** blessé au bras; **~ in action** blessé en service commandé.

wounding /ˈwuːndɪŋ/ *adj* [*sarcasm, comment*] blessant.

wove /wəʊv/ *prét* ▶ **weave**.

woven /ˈwəʊvn/ *pp, pp adj* ▶ **weave**.

wow○ /waʊ/ **I** *n* **1** (success) succès *m*; **2** Audio (distortion) pleurage *m*.
II *excl* hou la!
III *vtr* (enthuse) emballer○ [*person*].

WOW (*abrév* = **waiting on weather**) en fonction du temps.

WP 1 *abrév* = **weather permitting**; **2** *abrév* = **word processing**.

WPC *n*: *abrév* ▶ **woman police constable**.

wpm (*abrév* = **words per minute**) mots/min.

WRAC *n* Mil (*abrév* = **Women's Royal Army Corps**) *services féminins de l'armée britannique*.

wrack /ræk/ **I** *n* (seaweed) varech *m*.
II *vtr* **1** (torment) [*pain*] tourmenter [*body*]; **to be ~ed with** ou **by guilt** être tenaillé par le remords; **to be ~ed with grief** être accablé de chagrin; **2** (ravage) ravager [*land*].

WRAF *n* (*abrév* = **Women's Royal Air Force**) *services féminins de l'armée de l'air britannique*.

wraith /reɪθ/ *n* littér apparition *f*.

wraithlike /ˈreɪθlaɪk/ *adj* fantomatique.

wrangle /ˈræŋgl/ **I** *n* querelle *f* (**over** à propos de; **between** entre; **with** avec).
II *vi* **1** se quereller (**over, about** sur, à propos de; **with** avec); **2** US (herd) conduire [*livestock*].

wrangler /ˈræŋglə(r)/ *n* US cowboy *m*.

wrangling /ˈræŋglɪŋ/ *n* tractations *fpl* (**over** à propos de).

wrap /ræp/ **I** *n* **1** Fashn (shawl) châle *m*; (stole) étole *f*; **2** (dressing-gown) peignoir *m*; **3** (packaging) emballage *m*; **4** Cin **it's a ~** c'est dans la boîte.
II *vtr* (*p prés etc* **-pp-**) lit (in paper) emballer (**in** dans); (in blanket, garment) envelopper (**in** dans); **to ~ X in Y, to ~ Y round X** envelopper X dans Y; **I ~ped a handkerchief around my finger** je me suis noué un mouchoir autour du doigt; **he ~ped his arms around her** il l'a enlacée; **the child ~ped its legs around my waist** l'enfant a noué ses jambes autour de ma taille; **to ~ tape around a join** enrouler du ruban adhésif autour d'une jointure; **he ~ped the car round a lamppost**○ hum il a embrassé○ un réverbère; **to be ~ped in** lit (for warmth, protection) être emmitouflé dans [*blanket, coat*]; (for disposal) être enveloppé dans [*newspaper*]; fig être enveloppé de [*mystery*]; être plongé dans [*silence*]; être absorbé dans [*thoughts*]; **would you like it ~ped?** je vous fais un paquet?
III *v refl* (*p prés etc* **-pp-**) **to ~ oneself in sth** s'envelopper dans qch.
IV -wrapped (*dans composés*) **foil-/plastic-~ped** emballé dans du papier d'aluminium/du plastique.
IDIOMS **to keep sth/to be under ~s** garder qch/être secret; **to take the ~s off sth** dévoiler qch.
■ **wrap up**: ¶ **~ up 1** (dress warmly) s'emmitoufler; **~ up well** ou **warm!** couvre-toi bien!; **2**○ GB (shut up) la fermer○; **~ up!** ferme-la!○; ¶ **~ up** [**sth**], **~** [**sth**] **up 1** lit faire [*parcel*]; envelopper [*gift, purchase*]; emballer [*rubbish*]; **it's cold, ~ the children up warm!** il fait froid, couvre bien les enfants!; **well ~ped up against the cold** bien emmitouflé contre le froid; **it's a disco and sports club all ~ped up in one** c'est une discothèque et un club sportif à la fois; **2** fig (terminate) conclure [*project, event*]; **3** (settle) régler [*project, event*]; conclure [*deal, negotiations*]; s'assurer [*championship, title, victory*]; **4** (involve) **to be ~ped up in** ne s'occuper que de [*person, child*]; être absorbé dans [*activity, hobby, work*]; être absorbé par [*problem*]; **they are completely ~ped up in each other** ils ne vivent que l'un pour l'autre; **he is ~ped up in himself** il est replié sur lui-même; **there is £50,000 ~ped up in the project** il y a 50 000 livres sterling d'investies dans le projet; **5** (conceal) fig dissimuler [*meaning, facts, ideas*] (**in** derrière); **tell me the truth, don't try to ~ it up** dites-moi la vérité, allez droit au but.

wrap: **~-around** *adj* [*window, windscreen*] panoramique; [*skirt*] portefeuille; **~-over** *adj* Fashn [*skirt*] portefeuille; [*dress*] croisé.

wrapper /ˈræpə(r)/ *n* **1** (of sweet, chocolate etc) papier *m*; (of package) emballage *m*; (of newspaper) bande *f*; **sweet ~** papier *m* de bonbon; **2** (dressing-gown) peignoir *m*.

wrapping /ˈræpɪŋ/ *n* emballage *m*.

wrapping paper *n* (brown) papier *m* d'emballage; (decorative) papier *m* cadeau.

wrap: **~ top** *n* Fashn cache-cœur *m*; **~-up**○ *n* US résumé *m*.

wrath /rɒθ, US ræθ/ *n* littér courroux *m* liter, colère *f*.

wrathful /ˈrɒθfl, US ˈræθ-/ *adj* littér courroucé liter.

wreak /ri:k/ *vtr* assouvir [*revenge*] (**on** sur); **to ~ havoc** ou **damage** infliger des dégâts; **to ~ havoc** ou **damage on sth** dévaster qch.

wreath /ri:θ/ *n* **1** (of flowers, leaves) couronne *f*; **funeral ~** couronne mortuaire; **to lay a ~** déposer une gerbe; **2** (of smoke) ruban *m*; (of cloud) couronne *f*.

wreathe /ri:ð/ **I** *vtr* (weave, fashion) lisser.
II wreathed *pp adj* **~d in** enveloppé de [*mist, smoke*]; **to be ~d in smiles** être tout sourire.
III *vi* **to ~ upwards** monter en spirales.

wreath-laying (**ceremony**) *n* dépôt *m* de gerbes.

wreck /rek/ **I** *n* **1** (car, plane) (crashed) épave *f*; (burnt out) carcasse *f*; **2**○ (old car) tas *m* de ferraille○; **3** (sunken ship) épave *f*; **4** (sinking, destruction) (of ship) naufrage *m*; fig **the ~ of sb's hopes/dreams** le naufrage des espoirs/rêves de qn; **5** (person) épave *f*, loque *f*; **a human ~** une épave, une loque humaine.
II *vtr* **1** lit [*explosion, fire, vandals, looters*] dévaster [*building, home, hotel, machinery*]; [*person, driver, crash, impact*] détruire [*car, plane, vehicle*]; **to be completely ~ed by fire** être entièrement dévasté par un incendie; **2** fig ruiner, détruire [*career, chances, future, health, life, marriage*]; gâcher [*holiday, weekend*]; faire échouer [*talks, deal, negotiations*].

wreckage /ˈrekɪdʒ/ *n* **1** lit (of plane, car) épave *f*; (of building) décombres *mpl*; **to pull sth from the ~** retirer qch de l'épave; **2** fig (of hopes, plan, attempt) naufrage *m*; **to salvage sth from the ~ of one's marriage** sauver qch du naufrage de son mariage.

wrecked /rekt/ *adj* **1** lit [*car, plane*] accidenté; [*ship*] naufragé; [*building*] démoli; **2** fig [*plan, hope, life, marriage, career*] ruiné; **3**○ (exhausted) [*person*] claqué○, épuisé; **4**○ (drunk) paf○, ivre.

wrecker /ˈrekə(r)/ *n* **1** (destroyer of marriage, plans) destructeur/-trice *m/f*; **2** (saboteur of machinery, talks) saboteur/-euse *m/f*; **3** (who causes shipwrecks) naufrageur *m*; **4** US (demolition worker) démolisseur *m*; **5** US (salvage truck) camion-remorque *m*.

wrecking /ˈrekɪŋ/ *n* **1** (destruction) destruction *f*; **2** (sabotage) sabotage *m*; **3** US (demolition) démolition *f*.

wrecking: **~ ball** *n* US boulet *m* de démolition; **~ bar** *n* pince *f* à levier.

wren /ren/ *n* **1** Zool roitelet *m*; **2 Wren** volontaire *f* du WRNS (*corps féminin de la Marine royale britannique*).

wrench /rentʃ/ **I** *n* **1** (tool) tourne-à-gauche *m inv*; **2** (movement) (of handle, lid) mouvement *m* brusque (tournant); **she pulled the lid off with a ~** elle a dévissé le couvercle d'un mouvement brusque; **to give one's ankle a ~** se tordre la cheville; **3** fig déchirement *m*; **it was a real ~ leaving** c'était un vrai déchirement de partir.
II *vtr* tourner [qch] brusquement [*handle*]; **to ~ one's ankle/knee** se tordre la cheville/le genou; **to ~ sth from sb** arracher qch à qn; **she ~ed the bag from my hands** elle m'a arraché le sac des mains; **to ~ sth away from** ou **off sth** arracher qch de qch; **he ~ed the handle off the door** il a arraché la poignée de la porte; **to ~ a door open** ouvrir une porte d'un mouvement brusque.
III *vi* **to ~ at sth** tirer sur qch.
IV wrenching *pres p adj* [*anguish, sorrow, poignancy*] à fendre l'âme.
V *v refl* **to ~ oneself free** se dégager d'un mouvement brusque.
IDIOMS **to throw a ~ in the works** US créer des difficultés; **this will throw a ~ into the economy** cela portera un coup dur à l'économie.

wrest /rest/ *vtr* (all contexts) arracher (**from sb** à qn); **to ~ sth from sb's hands** arracher qch des mains de qn.

wrestle /ˈresl/ **I** *vtr* **to ~ sb for sth** lutter contre qn pour qch; **to ~ sb to the ground** terrasser qn; **to ~ sth into place** se battre avec qch pour le mettre en place.
II *vi* **1** Sport faire du catch; **2** (struggle) **to ~ with** se débattre avec [*person, problem, homework, conscience*]; se battre avec [*controls, zip, suitcase*]; lutter contre [*temptation*]; **to ~ to do** se débattre pour faire.

wrestler /ˈreslə(r)/ *n* **1** Sport catcheur/-euse *m/f*; **2** Antiq lutteur *m*.

wrestling /ˈreslɪŋ/ ▶ **1282** **I** *n* **1** Sport catch *m*; **2** Antiq lutte *f*.
II *modif* [*match, champion, hold*] de catch.

wretch /retʃ/ *n* **1** (unlucky) miséreux/-euse *m/f*; **those poor ~es!** ces pauvres miséreux!; **2** (evil) misérable *mf* also hum; (child) hum coquin/-e *m/f*.

wretched /ˈretʃɪd/ *adj* **1** (miserable) [*person*] infortuné; [*existence, appearance, conditions*] misérable; [*weather*] affreux/-euse; [*accommodation*] minable; [*amount*] dérisoire; **to feel ~** (due to illness) être à plat; (due to hangover) se sentir abruti; **to feel ~ about** être honteux/-euse de [*behaviour*]; **'flu makes you feel ~**○ la grippe vous met à plat; **things are ~ for her** elle est dans une situation désespérante; **what ~ luck!** quelle malchance!; **2**○ (damned) [*animal, machine*] fichu○, satané○; **it's a ~ nuisance** c'est une vraie galère.

wretchedly /ˈretʃɪdlɪ/ *adv* **1** (badly, pitifully) [*organize, behave, treat*] très mal; [*clothed, furnished*] misérablement; [*paid, small*] dérisoirement; **2** (unhappily) [*say, gaze, weep*] piteusement.

wretchedness /ˈretʃɪdnɪs/ *n* **1** (unhappiness) détresse *f*; **2** (poverty) misère *f*.

wrick /rɪk/ *vtr* GB = **rick II**.

wriggle /ˈrɪgl/ **I** *vtr* **to ~ one's toes/fingers** remuer les orteils/doigts; **to ~ one's way out of sth** lit se sortir or se dégager de qch; fig se sortir de qch.
II *vi* [*person*] s'agiter, gigoter; [*snake, worm*] se tortiller; **he was wriggling with embarrassment/excitement** il gigotait d'embarras/d'excitation; **to ~ along the ground** ramper en se tortillant; **to ~ through a hole in the fence** se glisser par un trou dans la clôture; **to ~ under sth** se glisser sous qch; **to ~ free** arriver à se dégager; **to ~ off the hook** lit [*fish*] se décrocher de l'hameçon; fig [*person*] se tirer d'affaire.
■ **wriggle about, wriggle around** [*fish*] frétiller; [*worm, snake*] se tortiller; [*person*] s'agiter, se tortiller.
■ **wriggle out** se dégager or se sortir en se tortillant; **to ~ out of sth** lit se dégager or se sortir de qch en se tortillant; fig se défiler devant [*task, duty*]; **you can't ~ out of it, you'll have to tell them the truth** tu ne peux pas te défiler, il faudra que tu leur dises la vérité.

wriggler /ˈrɪglə(r)/ *n* **he's a ~** il ne tient pas en place.

wriggly /ˈrɪglɪ/ *adj* [*snake, worm*] frétillant; [*person*] remuant.

wring /rɪŋ/ **I** *n* **to give sth a ~** essorer qch.
II *vtr* (*prét, pp* **wrung**) **1** (also **~ out**) (squeeze) (by twisting) tordre; (by pressure, centrifugal force) essorer; **'do not ~'** (on label) 'ne pas essorer'; **2** fig (extract) arracher [*confession, information, money*] (**from, out of** à); **3** (twist) **to ~ sb's/sth's neck** lit, fig tordre le cou à qn/qch; **to ~ one's hands** se tordre les mains; fig se lamenter.
III wringing *adv* **~ing wet** trempé.
IDIOMS **to be wrung out**○ être lessivé○; **to ~ sb's heart** serrer le cœur à qn.
■ **wring out**: **~ [sth] out, ~ out [sth]** tordre [*cloth, clothes*]; **to ~ the water out from one's clothes** essorer ses vêtements.

wringer /ˈrɪŋə(r)/ *n* essoreuse *f*.
IDIOMS **to put sb through the ~** mettre qn sur la sellette.

wrinkle /ˈrɪŋkl/ **I** *n* **1** (on skin) ride *f*; **it gives you ~s** ça donne des rides; **2** (in fabric) pli *m*; **to iron out the ~s** lit enlever les plis au fer à repasser; fig aplanir les difficultés.
IDIOMS **he knows a ~ or two** il est loin d'être bête.
II *vtr* **1** rider [*skin*]; **to ~ one's nose** faire la grimace (**at** a); **to ~ one's forehead** plisser le front; **2** froisser [*fabric*].
III *vi* **1** [*skin*] se rider; **2** [*fabric*] se froisser; [*wallpaper*] se gondoler.
■ **wrinkle up** [*rug, mat*] faire des plis.

wrinkled /ˈrɪŋkld/ *adj* **1** [*face, skin*] ridé; [*brow*] froncé; [*apple*] fripé; **2** [*fabric, clothing*] froissé; [*stockings*] qui font des plis.

wrinklies○ /ˈrɪŋklɪz/ *npl* péj ou hum (older people) vioques○ *mpl*, petits vieux/petites vieilles *mpl/fpl*.

wrinkly○ /ˈrɪŋklɪ/ *adj* = **wrinkled**.

wrist /rɪst/ **▶ 1037** *n* poignet *m*.
IDIOMS **to get a slap on the ~** se faire taper sur les doigts.

wrist: **~band** *n* (for tennis) poignet *m*; (on sleeve) poignet *m*; (on watch) bracelet *m* (de montre); **~watch** *n* montre-bracelet *f*.

writ /rɪt/ **I** *n* Jur assignation *f* (**for** pour); **to issue** ou **serve a ~ against sb, to serve sb with a ~** assigner qn en justice.
II‡ ou Dial *vtr* (*prét, pp désuets du verbe* **write**) **to be ~ large** lit être écrit en grosses lettres; fig **disappointment was ~ large across his face** la déception se lisait sur son visage; **it wasn't champagne, just sparkling wine ~ large** ce n'était pas du champagne, ce n'était rien d'autre que du vin mousseux.

write /raɪt/ (*prét* **wrote**; *pp* **written**) **I** *vtr* **1** (put down on paper) écrire [*letter, poem, novel*] (**to** à); composer [*song, symphony*]; rédiger [*business letter, article, essay, report*]; faire [*cheque, prescription*]; écrire [*software, program*]; élaborer [*legislation*]; **she wrote that she was changing jobs** elle a écrit qu'elle changeait de travail; **it is written that** sout il est écrit que; **he wrote me a cheque for 100 francs** il m'a fait un chèque de 100 francs; **it's written in Italian** c'est écrit en italien; **I wrote home** j'ai écrit à ma famille; **guilt was written all over her face** fig la culpabilité se lisait sur son visage; **he had 'policeman' written all over him** fig ça crevait les yeux qu'il était policier; **2** US (compose a letter to) écrire à [*person*]; **~ me when you get to Rome** écris-moi quand tu arriveras à Rome.
II *vi* **1** (form words) écrire; **to learn to ~** apprendre à écrire; **to ~ in pencil/pen** écrire au crayon/stylo; **to ~ neatly/badly** écrire bien/mal; **this pen doesn't ~** ce stylo n'écrit pas; **I have nothing to ~ with** je n'ai rien pour écrire; **give me something to ~ on** donne-moi un papier pour écrire; **to ~ sth into a contract** inclure qch dans un contrat; **2** (compose professionally) écrire (**for** pour); **I ~ for a living** je suis écrivain de métier; **to ~ about** ou **on** traiter de [*current affairs, ecology*]; **3** (correspond) écrire (**to sb** à qn); **I'll try to ~ every week** j'essaierai d'écrire chaque semaine.
■ **write away** écrire (**to** à); **to ~ away for sth** demander qch par écrit [*catalogue, details*].
■ **write back**: ¶ **~ back** répondre (**to** à); ¶ **~ [sth] back** Accts, Fin réévaluer [*asset*]; ¶ **~ back [sth]** écrire [*letter*].
■ **write down**: **~ [sth] down, ~ down [sth]** **1** (note) noter [*details, name*]; mettre [qch] par écrit [*ideas, suggestions*]; **2** (record) consigner [qch] par écrit [*information, findings, adventures*]; **3** Comm, Fin (reduce) réduire [*price*]; dévaluer [*stocks*]; amortir [*debt*].
■ **write in**: ¶ **~ in** écrire (**to sb** à qn; **to do** pour faire) ; **please ~ in with your suggestions** vous êtes invités à nous envoyer vos suggestions; **to ~ in to** écrire une lettre à [*TV show, presenter*]; ¶ **~ [sb] in** US Pol inscrire le nom de [*candidate*].
■ **write off**: ¶ **~ off** écrire une lettre (**to** à); **to ~ off for** écrire pour demander [*catalogue, information*]; ¶ **~ [sth/sb] off 1** (wreck) gen bousiller○ complètement [*car*]; Insur mettre [qch] en épave [*car*]; **2** Accts passer [qch] par pertes et profits [*bad debt, loss*]; amortir [*capital*]; **3** (end) annuler [*debt, project, operation*]; **4** (dismiss) [*critic*] enterrer○ [*person , athlete*]; **to ~ sb off for dead** tenir qn pour mort.
■ **write out**: ¶ **~ [sth] out, ~ out [sth] 1** (put down on paper) écrire [*instructions, list*]; **2** (copy) copier [*lines, words*]; **~ it out again neatly** recopie-le au propre; ¶ **~ [sb] out** TV, Radio supprimer [*character*] (**of** de).
■ **write up**: **~ [sth] up, ~ up [sth] 1** (produce in report form) rédiger [*findings, notes*]; **2** Accts, Fin réévaluer [*asset*].

write: **~ head** *n* Comput tête *f* d'enregistrement; **~-in** *n* US Pol vote *m* par correspondance.

write-off /ˈraɪtɒf/ *n* **1** US Tax somme *f* déductible de la déclaration des revenus; **2** Insur, fig (wreck) épave *f*.

write: **~ once read many disk** *n* Comput disque *m* inscriptible une seule fois; **~ protect** *n* Comput protection *f* en mode écriture; **~ protection** *n* Comput protection *f* contre l'écriture; **~-protect notch** *n* Comput encoche *f* de protection contre l'écriture.

writer /ˈraɪtə(r)/ **▶ 1692** *n* (author) (professional) écrivain *m*; (nonprofessional) auteur *m*; **the ~ of the letter** l'auteur de la lettre; **she's a ~** elle est écrivain; **sports/travel/cookery ~** journaliste *mf* spécialisé/-e en sport/voyages/gastronomie; **he's a neat/messy ~** il écrit avec/sans soin.

writer: **~'s block** *n* angoisse *f* de la page blanche; **~'s cramp** *n* crampe *f* de l'écrivain.

write-up /ˈraɪtʌp/ *n* **1** (review) critique *f*; **2** (account) rapport *m* (**of** sur); **3** US Accts fausse déclaration *f* (dans un bilan).

writhe /raɪð/ *vi* (also **~ about, ~ around**) se tortiller; **to ~ in agony** se tordre de douleur; **to ~ with embarrassment** se tortiller de gêne.

writing /ˈraɪtɪŋ/ **I** *n* **1** ¢ (activity) **~ is her life** écrire, c'est sa vie; **2** (handwriting) écriture *f*; **his ~ is poor/good** il écrit mal/bien; **3** (words and letters) écriture *f*; **to put sth in ~** mettre qch par écrit; **4** (literature) littérature *f*; **modern/American ~** littérature moderne/américaine; **the ~s of Colette** l'œuvre *f* de Colette; **selected ~s of Oscar Wilde** morceaux *mpl* choisis d'Oscar Wilde; **it was an excellent piece of ~** c'était très bien écrit.
II *modif* **a ~ career** une carrière d'écrivain.
IDIOMS **the ~ is on the wall** la catastrophe est imminente; **the ~ is on the wall for the regime** la fin du régime est imminente.

writing: **~ case** *n* nécessaire *m* de correspondance; **~ desk** *n* secrétaire *m*; **~ materials** *npl* matériel *m* pour écrire; **~ pad** *n* bloc *m* de papier à lettres; **~ paper** *n* papier *m* à lettres; **~ table** *n* bureau *m*.

writ: **~ of attachment** *n* Jur commandement *m* de saisie; **~ of execution** *n* Jur titre *m* d'exécution; **~ of subpoena, ~ of summons** *n* Jur citation *f* en justice.

written /ˈrɪtn/ **I** *pp* ▶ **write**.
II *adj* [*exam, guarantee, reply*] écrit; **I'm better at oral work than ~ work** je suis meilleur à l'oral qu'à l'écrit; **he failed the ~ paper** il a échoué à l'écrit; **~ evidence/proof** Admin pièces *fpl* justificatives; Jur preuves *fpl* écrites; **the ~ word** l'écriture.

WRNS *n* GB (*abrév* = **Women's Royal Naval Service**) *services féminins de la Marine royale britannique*.

wrong /rɒŋ, US rɔːŋ/ **I** *n* **1** ¢ (evil) mal *m*; **no sense of right or ~** aucun sens du bien ou du mal; **she could do no ~** elle était incapable de faire du mal; **in their eyes, she could do no ~** pour eux, tout ce qu'elle faisait était parfait; **2** (injustice) tort *m*; **to right a ~** réparer un tort; **to do sb ~/a great ~** sout faire du tort/beaucoup de tort à qn; **the rights and ~s of the matter** les aspects moraux de la question; **3** Jur délit *m*; **private/public ~** délit civil/pénal.
II *adj* **1** (incorrect) (ill-chosen) mauvais; (containing errors) [*total*] erroné; [*note, forecast, hypothesis*] faux/fausse, erroné; **in the ~ place at the ~ time** au mauvais endroit au mauvais moment; **he picked up the ~ key** il a pris la mauvaise clé; **it's the ~ wood/glue for the purpose** ce n'est pas le bois/la colle qu'il faut; **she was the ~ woman for you** ce n'était pas la femme qu'il te fallait; **to prove to be ~** [*forecast, hypothesis*] se révéler faux; **to go the ~ way/to the ~ place** se tromper de chemin/d'endroit; **to take the ~ road/train** se tromper de route/train; **to take the ~ turning** GB ou **turn** US ne pas tourner au bon endroit; **to give the ~ password/answer** ne pas donner le bon mot de passe/la bonne réponse; **confrontation is the ~ approach** l'affrontement n'est pas la bonne méthode; **everything I do is ~** je ne fais jamais rien de bon; **it was the ~ thing to say/do** c'était la chose à ne pas dire/faire; **to say the ~ thing** faire une gaffe, dire ce qu'il ne faut/fallait etc pas dire; **don't get the ~ idea** ne te méprends pas; **you've got the ~ number** (on phone) vous faites erreur; **2** (reprehensible, unjust) **it is ~ to do** c'est mal de faire; **it's ~ to cheat** c'est mal de tricher; **she hasn't done anything ~** elle n'a rien fait de mal; **it was ~ of me/you to do** je/tu n'aurais pas dû faire; **it is ~ for sb to do** ce n'est pas juste que qn fasse; **it's ~ for her to have to struggle alone** ce n'est pas juste qu'elle soit obligée de lutter seule; **it is ~ that** c'est injuste que (+ *subj*); **it is ~ that the poor should go hungry** c'est injuste que les pauvres aient faim; **there's nothing ~ with** ou **in sth** il n'y a pas de mal à qch; **there's nothing wrong with** ou **in doing** il n'y a pas de mal à faire; **what's ~ with trying?** quel mal y a-t-il à essayer?; (**so**) **what's ~ with that?** où est le mal?; **3** (mistaken) **to be ~** [*person*] avoir tort, se tromper; **that's where you're ~** c'est là que tu te trompes; **can you prove I'm ~?** est-ce que tu peux prouver que j'ai tort?; **how ~ can you be!** comme on peut se tromper!; **I might be ~** il se peut que je me trompe; **to be ~ about** se tromper sur [*person, situation, details*]; **she was ~ about him** elle s'est trompée sur son compte; **to be ~ to do** ou

in doing sout avoir tort de faire; **you are ~ to accuse me** vous avez tort de m'accuser; **am I ~ in thinking that...?** ai-je tort de penser que...?; **to prove sb ~** donner tort à qn; **4** (not as it should be) **to be ~** ne pas aller; **there is something** (**badly**) **~** il y a quelque chose qui ne va pas (du tout); **what's ~?** qu 'est-ce qui ne va pas?; **what's ~ with the machine/clock?** qu'est-ce qui ne va pas avec la machine/pendule?; **there's something ~ with this computer** cet ordinateur a quelque chose qui ne va pas; **the wording is all ~** la formulation ne va pas du tout; **what's ~ with your arm/leg?** qu'est-ce que tu as au bras/à la jambe?; **what's ~ with you?** (to person suffering) qu'est-ce que tu as?; (to person behaving oddly) qu'est-ce qui t'arrive or te prend?; **your clock is ~** votre pendule n'est pas à l'heure; **nothing ~ is there?** tout va bien?
III *adv* **to get sth ~** se tromper de qch [*date, time, details*]; se tromper dans qch [*calculations*]; **I think you've got it ~** je pense que tu te trompes; **to go ~** [*person*] se tromper; [*machine*] ne plus marcher; [*plan*] ne pas marcher; **what's gone ~ between them?** qu'est-ce qui n'a pas marché entre eux?; **you won't go far ~ if**... vous ne risquez pas de faire fausse route si...; **you can't go ~** (in choice of route) tu ne peux pas te tromper; (are bound to succeed) tu peux être tranquille.
IV *vtr* **1** (treat unjustly) faire du tort à [*person, family*]; **2** sout (judge unfairly) mésestimer.
IDIOMS don't get me ~ ne le prends pas mal; **to be in the ~** être dans mon/ton etc tort; **to be ~ in the head**○ être dérangé○, avoir une case en moins○; **to get into the ~ hands** tomber dans de mauvaises mains; **to get on the ~ side of sb** se faire mal voir de qn; **to go down the ~ way** [*food, drink*] passer de travers; **to jump to the ~ conclusions** tirer des conclusions hâtives; **two ~s don't make a right** on ne répare pas une injustice avec une autre; **you've got me all ~** vous ne m'avez pas du tout compris; ▶ **stick**.

wrong: **~doer** *n* malfaiteur *m*; **~doing** *n* méfait *m*; **~foot** *vtr* Sport prendre [qn] à contre-pied [*opponent, adversary*]; fig prendre [qn] au dépourvu.

wrongful /ˈrɒŋfl, US ˈrɔːŋ-/ *adj* Jur [*dismissal, arrest, imprisonment*] arbitraire.

wrongfully /ˈrɒŋfəlɪ, US ˈrɔːŋ-/ *adv* Jur [*dismiss, convict, arrest*] injustement.

wrong-headed /ˌrɒŋˈhedɪd, US ˌrɔːŋ-/ *adj* **1** (stubborn) [*person*] buté; **2** (perverse) [*policy, decision*] aveugle.

wrongly /ˈrɒŋlɪ, US ˈrɔː-/ *adv* [*word, position, translate, connect*] mal; **he concluded, ~, that**... il a conclu, à tort, que...; **rightly or ~** à tort ou à raison.

wrote /rəʊt/ *prét* ▶ **write**.

wrought /rɔːt/ **I** *prét, pp* littér ou journ **it ~ havoc** ou **destruction** il a fait des ravages; **the changes ~ by sth** les changements apportés par qch.
II *pp adj* **1** [*silver, gold*] travaillé; **2** (devised) **finely/carefully ~** [*plot, essay*] finement/soigneusement travaillé.

wrought iron I *n* fer *m* forgé.
II *modif* [*gate, grill*] en fer forgé.

wrought iron work *n* ferronnerie *f*.

wrought-up /ˌrɔːtˈʌp/ *adj* [*person*] dans tous ses états.

wrung /rʌŋ/ *prét, pp* ▶ **wring**.

WRVS *n* GB (*abrév* = **Women's Royal Volunteer Service**) *service féminin royal bénévole*.

wry /raɪ/ *adj* **1** (ironic) [*look, comment, amusement*] narquois; **to have a ~ sense of humour** être pince-sans-rire; **2** (disgusted) **to make a ~ face** faire une drôle de tête.

wryly /ˈraɪlɪ/ *adv* [*smile, grin*] d'un air narquois; [*comment*] narquoisement.

W Sussex *n* GB Post *abrév écrite* ▶ **West Sussex**.

wt *n*: *abrév écrite* = **weight**.

WTO *n* (*abrév* = **World Trade Organization**) OMC *f*.

WV *n* US *abrév écrite* = **West Virginia**.

WWI *n*: *abrév écrite* = **World War One**.

WWII *n*: *abrév écrite* = **World War Two**.

WWW *n* Comput (*abrév* = **World Wide Web**) WWW *m*, Web *m*.

WY *n* US *abrév écrite* = **Wyoming**.

wych elm /ˈwɪtʃ elm/ *n* orme *m* blanc.

wynd /waɪnd/ *n* Scot venelle *f*.

Wyoming /ˌwaɪˈəʊmɪŋ/ ▶ **1744** *pr n* Wyoming *m*.

W Yorkshire *n* GB Post *abrév écrite* ▶ **West Yorkshire**.

WYSIWYG /ˈwɪzɪwɪg/ Comput (*abrév* = **what you see is what you get**) tel-tel *inv*.

x, **X** /eks/ **I** *n* **1** (letter) x, X *m*; **2 x** Math x *m*; **3 x** (unspecified place) x *m*; **for x people**, **for x number of people** pour x personnes; **4 X** (anonymous person, place) X *m*; **Ms X** Mme X; **5 X** (on map) croix *f*; **X marks the spot** l'endroit est marqué d'une croix; **6 x** (at end of letter) **x x x** grosses bises; **7 X** (as signature) croix *f*.
II x *vtr* (*prét, pp* **x-ed**) cocher [qch] d'une croix.

X certificate GB **I** *n* **the film was given an ~** le film a été classé X.
II *modif* [*film*] classé X.

xenon /ˈziːnɒn/ *n* xénon *m*.

xenophobe /ˈzenəfəʊb/ *n* xénophobe *mf*.

xenophobia /ˌzenəˈfəʊbɪə/ *n* xénophobie *f*.

xenophobic /ˌzenəˈfəʊbɪk/ *adj* xénophobe.

Xenophon /ˈzenəfən/ *pr n* Xénophon.

xerography /zɪəˈrɒgrəfɪ/ *n* xérographie® *f*.

xerox, **Xerox**® /ˈzɪərɒks/ **I** *n* **1** (machine) photocopieuse *f*; **2** (process) (procédé de) photocopie *f*; **3** (copy) (photo)copie *f*.
II *vtr* photocopier.

Xerxes /ˈzɜːksiːz/ *pr n* Xerxès.

XL **▶ 1703** *n* (*abrév écrite* = **extra-large**) XL.

Xmas *n*: *abrév écrite* = **Christmas**.

X rated *adj* [*film, video*] interdit aux moins de 18 ans.

X rating *n* **to have an ~** [*film, video*] être interdit aux moins de 18 ans.

X-ray /ˈeksreɪ/ **I** *n* **1** (ray) rayon *m* X; **2** (photo) radiographie *f*, radio○ *f*; **3** (process) radiographie *f*, radioscopie *f*; **to have an ~** se faire radiographier, se faire faire une radio○; **to give sb an ~** faire une radiographie or radio○ à qn.
II *vtr* radiographier.

X-ray: **~ machine** *n* générateur *m* à rayons X; **~ radiation** *n* rayonnement *m* X; **~ unit** *n* service *m* de radiologie.

xylograph /ˈzaɪləgrɑːf, US -græf/ *n* xylographie *f*.

xylographic /ˌzaɪləˈgræfɪk/ *adj* xylographique.

xylography /zaɪˈlɒgrəfɪ/ *n* xylographie *f*.

xylophone /ˈzaɪləfəʊn/ **▶ 1481** *n* xylophone *m*.

xylophonist /zaɪˈlɒfənɪst/ **▶ 1692**, **1481** *n* xylophoniste *mf*.

y, Y /waɪ/ *n* **1** (lettre) y, Y *m*; **2 y** Math y *m*.

yacht /jɒt/ **I** *n* yacht *m*.
II *modif* [*crew*] de yacht; [*race*] de yachts; **~ club** yacht-club *m*.
III *vi* faire du yachting.

yachting /ˈjɒtɪŋ/ **▶ 1282** **I** *n* yachting *m*; **to go ~** faire du yachting.
II *modif* [*clothes*] de yachtman; [*enthusiast*] du yachting; [*course*] de yachting; [*holiday*] en yacht.

yacht: **~sman** *n* yachtman *m*; **~swoman** *n* yachtwoman *f*.

yack○ /jæk/ **I** *n* **1** (also **yackety-yak**) (chat) **to have a ~** papoter; **2** US (loud laugh) éclat *m* de rire; **3** US (joke) gag *m*.
II *vi* (also **yackety-yak**) papoter.
▪ **yack at** US tarabuster [*person*].

yah○ /jɑː/ **I** *n* péj (person) snob *mf*.
II *particle* oui certes.

yahoo /jəˈhuː/ **I** *n* abruti/-e○ *m/f*.
II *excl* hourra!

yak /jæk/ *n* **1** Zool yack *m*; **2**○ = **yack**○.

Yale® /jeɪl/ *n* (also **Yale lock**) serrure *f* de sûreté.

Yale key® *n* clé *f* de sûreté.

yam /jæm/ *n* **1** (tropical) igname *f*; **2** US (sweet potato) patate *f* douce.

yammer○ /ˈjæmə(r)/ **I** *vtr* marmonner.
II *vi* = **yammer on**.
▪ **yammer on**○ rouspéter○ (**about** sur).

yang /jæŋ/ *n* yang *m*.

yank /jæŋk/ **I** *n* coup *m* sec; **to give sth a ~** tirer sur qch d'un coup sec.
II *vtr* tirer [*person*]; **he ~ed me into his office** il me tira brutalement dans son bureau.
▪ **yank off**: **~** [**sth**] **off**, **~ off** [**sth**] arracher [*tie, scarf*]; **to ~ off the bedcovers** arracher les couvertures du lit.
▪ **yank out**: **~** [**sth**] **out**, **~ out** [**sth**] arracher [*tooth, gun*].

Yank○ /jæŋk/ *n* injur Yankee *mf* offensive.

Yankee /ˈjæŋkɪ/ *n* **1** US (inhabitant of New England) habitant/-e *m/f* de la Nouvelle Angleterre; **2** US (inhabitant of North) habitant/-e *m/f* du Nord (des États-Unis); **3** Hist (soldier) Nordiste *m*; **4** injur (North American) yankee *m* offensive.

Yankee doodle *n*: *air symbolisant l'Indépendance américaine.*

yap /jæp/ **I** *n* jappement *m*; **~ ~!** onomat (dog) ouah ouah!; (person) bla bla!
II *vi* **1** [*dog*] japper (**at** après); **2** péj [*person*] piailler.

yapping /ˈjæpɪŋ/ **I** *n* ₵ jappements *mpl*.
II *adj* [*dog*] jappeur/-euse.

Yarborough /ˈjɑːbrə/ *n* (in bridge) main *f* sans honneurs.

yard /jɑːd/ *n* **1** **▶ 1412** Meas yard *m* (= *0.9144*); **2** fig **you've got ~s of room!** tu as plus de place qu'il n'en faut!; **she writes poetry by the ~, she writes ~s and ~s of poetry** elle écrit des pages et des pages de poésie; **3** (of house, farm, prison, hospital) cour *f*; **4** US (garden) jardin *m*; **5** Comm, Constr (for storage) dépôt *m*; (for construction) chantier *m*; **builder's ~** dépôt *m* de matériaux de construction; **6** Naut vergue *f*.
II Yard *pr n* GB **the ~** *police judiciaire britannique.*

yardage /ˈjɑːdɪdʒ/ *n* longueur *f* en yards, ≈ métrage *m*.

yardarm /ˈjɑːdɑːm/ *n* bout *m* de vergue.

yardbird○ /ˈjɑːdbɜːd/ *n* **1** (prisoner) taulard○ *m*; **2** US argot des militaires (soldier) recrue *f* qui est souvent de corvée.

Yardie○ /ˈjɑːdiː/ *pr n* GB truand *m* d'origine jamaïquaine.

yard: **~master** *n* US Rail chef *m* de triage; **~ sale** *n* US brocante *f* (*tenue dans sa propre cour*); **~stick** *n* fig point *m* de référence (**for** pour).

yarn /jɑːn/ *n* **1** Tex fil *m* (à tricoter); **polyamide/cotton ~** fil *m* polyamide/de coton; **2** (tale) histoire *f*; **to spin a ~** raconter des histoires.

yarrow /ˈjærəʊ/ *n* achillée mille-feuille *f*.

yashmak /ˈjæʃmæk/ *n* voile *m* islamique.

yaw /jɔː/ *vi* Naut, Aviat dévier.

yawl /jɔːl/ *n* (sailing boat) yawl *m*; (ship's boat) chaloupe *f*; (fishing boat) yole *f*.

yawn /jɔːn/ **I** *n* **1** (physical action) bâillement *m*; **to give a ~** bâiller; **2** fig (bore) **what a ~**○! que c'est barbant○!
II *vtr* **'See you tomorrow,' he ~ed** 'à demain,' dit-il en bâillant.
III *vi* **1** [*person*] bâiller; **2** fig (gape) [*tunnel*] s'ouvrir béant; [*abyss, chasm*] béer.

yawning /ˈjɔːnɪŋ/ **I** *n* bâillements *mpl*.
II *adj* [*abyss, chasm*] béant; fig **a ~ gap in the market/law** un vide dans le marché/la loi; **the ~ gap between promises and performance** le décalage entre les promesses et la réalisation; **the ~ gap between the two countries** l'abîme qui sépare les deux pays.

yawp○ /jɔːp/ US **I** *n* braillement *m*.
II *vi* brailler.

yaws /jɔːz/ *n* (+ *v sg*) pian *m*.

yd *abrév écrite* = **yard** 1.

ye‡ /jiː/ **I** *pers pron* vous.
II *article* le/la/les.
IDIOMS **~ gods**○! dieux du ciel!

yea /jeɪ/ **I**‡ *particle* oui *m*.
II *n* Pol **the ~s and the nays** les oui et les non.
III‡ *adv* (indeed) voire.

yeah○ /jeə/ *particle* ouais○, oui; **oh ~?** vraiment? also iron.

year /jɪə(r), jɜː(r)/ **▶ 1807** **I** *n* **1** (period of time) an *m*, année *f*; **in the ~ 1789/2000** en 1789/l'an 2000; **every ~/every other ~** tous les ans/tous les deux ans; **two ~s ago** il y a deux ans; **all (the) year round** toute l'année; **during the ~** au cours de l'année; **over the ~s** au cours des ans or des années; **the ~ before last** il y a deux ans; **~ by ~** d'année en année; **three ~s running** trois ans or années d'affilée or de suite; **~ in ~ out** tous les ans, chaque année; **in ~s to come** dans les années à venir; **at the end of the ~** à la fin de l'année; **I shall retire in two ~s** je prendrai ma retraite dans deux ans; **we hope to build the bridge in two ~s** nous espérons construire le pont en deux ans; **they have been living in Paris for ~s** ils habitent Paris depuis des années, il y a des années qu'ils habitent Paris; **they lived in Paris for ~s** ils ont habité Paris pendant des années; **they will probably live there for ~s** ils y habiteront sans doute pendant des années; **for the first time in ~s** pour la première fois depuis des années; **it was a ~ ago last October that I heard the news** il y a eu un an en octobre que j'ai appris la nouvelle; **it will be four ~s in July since he died** cela fera quatre ans en juillet qu'il est mort; **it's a ~ since I heard from him** je n'ai plus de ses nouvelles depuis un an or il y a un an que je n'ai plus de nouvelles de lui; **from one ~ to the next** d'une année à l'autre; **in all my ~s as a journalist** dans toute ma carrière de journaliste; **to earn £30,000 a ~** gagner 30000 livres sterling par an; **2** (indicating age) **to be 19 ~s old** ou **19 ~s of age** avoir 19 ans; **a two-~-old child** un enfant de deux ans; **he's in his fiftieth ~** il est dans sa cinquantième année; **3** Sch, Univ année *f*; **to be in one's first ~ at Cambridge** être en première année à Cambridge; **is that boy in your ~?** est-ce que ce garçon est dans la même année que toi?; **4** GB Sch (pupil) **first/second-~** ≈ élève *mf* de sixième/cinquième; **5** (prison sentence) an *m*; **to get 15 ~s** être condamné à 15 ans de prison.
II years *npl* **1** (age) âge *m*; **from her earliest ~s** dès son plus jeune âge; **a man of your ~s and experience** un homme de votre âge et de votre expérience; **2**○ (a long time) (used in exaggeration) **but that would take ~s!** ça prendrait une éternité or un siècle!; **it's ~s since we last met!** ça fait un siècle qu'on ne s'est pas vus!
IDIOMS **this job has put ~s on me!** ce travail m'a vieilli de 10 ans!; **losing weight takes ~s off you** perdre du poids, ça rajeunit!; **I gave you the best ~s of my life** je t'ai sacrifié les plus belles années de ma vie.

yearbook /ˈjɪəbʊk, ˈjɜː-/ *n* **1** (directory) annuaire *m*; **2** US Sch, Univ album *m* de promotion.

year-end Accts **I** *n* fin *f* or clôture *f* de l'exercice.
II *modif* [*adjustment, audit, dividend*] de fin d'exercice.

yearling /ˈjɪəlɪŋ, ˈjɜː-/ *n* gen animal *m* d'un an; (horse) yearling *m*.

yearlong /ˈjɪəlɒŋ, US -lɔːŋ/ *adj* [*stay, course, absence*] d'un an, d'une année.

yearly /ˈjɪəlɪ, ˈjɜː-/ **I** *adj* [*visit, account, income*] annuel/-elle.
II *adv* annuellement.

yearn /jɜːn/ *vi* **1** (desire) **to ~ for** désirer (avoir) [*child, food*]; aspirer à [*freedom, unity*]; attendre [*era, season, event*]; **to ~ for sb** désirer qn; **to ~ to do** avoir très envie de faire; **2** (miss) **she ~s for her son/her homeland** son fils/sa patrie lui manque terriblement.

yearning /ˈjɜːnɪŋ/ **I** *n* désir *m* ardent (**for** de; **to do** de faire).
II yearnings *npl* aspirations *fpl*.
III *adj* [*expression*] plein de désir.

yearningly /ˈjɜːnɪŋlɪ/ *adv* [*gaze*] avec des yeux pleins de désir.

year-round *adj* [*resident, supply, source*] permanent; **designed for ~ use** conçu pour être utilisé toute l'année.

year tutor *n* GB *professeur responsable de toutes les classes d'un même niveau.*

yeast /jiːst/ *n* levure *f*.

yeasty /ˈjiːstɪ/ *adj* **1** [*smell, taste*] de levure; [*bread, wine*] qui a un goût de levure; **2** (frothy) mousseux/-euse.

yecch○ US *excl* = **yuck**.

yec(c)hy○ *adj* US = **yucky**.

yegg○† /jeg/ *n* US (also **yegg man**) cambrioleur *m*.

yell /jel/ **I** *n* (shout) cri *m*; (of rage, pain) hurlement *m*; **to give** ou **let out a ~ of delight** pousser un cri de joie.
II *vtr* crier [*warning*]; (louder) hurler [*insults*]; **'I can't hear you,' he ~ed** 'je ne t'entends pas,' cria-t-il.
III *vi* (shout) crier; **to ~ at sb** crier après qn.

yelling /ˈjelɪŋ/ **I** *n* cris *mpl*.
II *adj* [*mob, crowd*] vociférant.

yellow /ˈjeləʊ/ ▶ 1104 **I** *n* jaune *m*.
II *adj* **1** lit jaune; **to go** ou **turn ~** jaunir; **the lights are on ~** les feux sont à l'orange; **2**○ (cowardly) [*person*] trouillard○; **to have a ~ streak** être une poule mouillée○.
III *vtr, vi* jaunir.

yellow: **~-belly**○ *n* trouillard/-e○ *m/f*; **~ brick road** *n* route *f* du bonheur; **~ card** *n* Sport carton *m* jaune; **~ fever** ▶ 1354 *n* fièvre *f* jaune; **~ flag** *n* Naut pavillon *m* de quarantaine; **~hammer** *n* bruant *m* jaune.

yellowish /ˈjeləʊɪʃ/ ▶ 1104 *adj* jaunâtre, tirant sur le jaune.

yellowish brown ▶ 1104 **I** *n* brun *m* tirant sur le jaune.
II *adj* d'un brun tirant sur le jaune.

yellow jacket *n* **1** Zool guêpe *f*; **2**○ argot des drogués capsule *f* de barbiturique.

yellow: **~ jersey** *n* (in cycling) maillot *m* jaune; **~ line** *n* ligne *f* jaune; **~ metal** *n* (brass) cuivre *m* jaune; (gold) métal *m* jaune.

yellowness /ˈjeləʊnɪs/ *n* **1** (of hue) jaune *m*; (of white) jauni *m*; **2**○ (cowardice) trouillardise○ *f*.

yellow: **~ ochre** ▶ 1104 *n* (colour) jaune *m* d'ocre; (substance) ocre *m* jaune; **Yellow Pages**® *pr npl* pages *fpl* jaunes®; **~-painted** *adj* peint en jaune; **~ peril** *n* injur péril *m* jaune offensive; **~ press**† *n* presse *f* à sensations†; **Yellow River** ▶ 1644 *pr n* fleuve *m* Jaune; **Yellow Sea** ▶ 1511 *pr n* mer *f* Jaune; **~-skinned** *adj* à la peau jaune; **~ soap** *n* ≈ savon *m* de Marseille; **~ spot** *n* tache *f* jaune; **~ wagtail** *n* bergeronnette *f* flavéole.

yellowy /ˈjeləʊɪ/ ▶ 1104 *adj* jauni.

yelp /jelp/ **I** *n* (of person) glapissement *m*; (of animal) (of pain, fear) glapissement *m*; (of happiness) jappement *m*.
II *vi* [*person*] glapir (**with** de); [*animal*] [*with pain, fear*] glapir; (with happiness) japper.

yelping /ˈjelpɪŋ/ **I** *n* ₵ (of animal) (with pain, fear) glapissements *mpl*; (with happiness) jappements *mpl*; (of person) glapissements *mpl*.
II *adj* [*animal*] (with pain, fear) qui glapit; (with happiness) qui jappe.

Yemen /ˈjemən/ ▶ 1131 *pr n* Yémen *m*; **North/South ~** Hist Yémen *m* du Nord/du Sud.

Yemeni /ˈjemənɪ/ ▶ 1486 **I** *n* Yéménite *mf*.
II *adj* yéménite.

yen /jen/ ▶ 1143 **I** *n* **1** Fin yen *m*; **2**○ (craving) **to have a ~ for sth/to do** avoir grande envie de qch/de faire.
II *modif* [*trading, value*] du yen; [*broker*] des yens.
III○ *vi* (*p prés etc* **-nn-**) **to ~ for sth/to do** avoir très envie de qch/de faire.

yenta○ /ˈjentə/ *n* US pej (gossip) commère *f*.

yeoman /ˈjəʊmən/ *n* (*pl* **-men**) **1** (also **~ farmer**) GB Hist franc tenancier *m*; **2** GB Mil Hist cavalier *m* (*volontaire*); **3** = **yeoman of the guard**; **4** GB Mil sous-officier *m* de la marine (*chargé de la signalisation*); US Mil sous-officier de la marine (*affecté au travail de bureau*).

yeoman of the guard *n* GB gen membre *m* de la garde royale.

yeomanry /ˈjəʊmənrɪ/ *n* ₵ **1** (freeholders) francs tenanciers *mpl*; **2** GB Mil Hist corps *m* de cavalerie (*constitué de volontaires*).

yep○ /jep/, **yup**○ /jʌp/ *particle* US ouais○, oui.

yes /jes/

■ **Note** *yes* is translated by *oui*, except when used in reply to a negative question when the translation is *si* or, more emphatically *si, si* or *mais si*: *'did you see him?'—'yes (I did)'* = 'est-ce que tu l'as vu?'—'oui (je l'ai vu)'; *'you haven't seen him, have you?'—'yes (I have)'* = 'tu ne l'as pas vu?'—'si, si (je l'ai vu)'
– Note that there are no direct equivalents in French for tag questions and short replies such as *yes I did, yes I have*.
– For some suggestions on how to translate these, see the notes at ***do*** and ***have***.

particle, n oui; (in reply to negative question) si; **to say ~** dire oui; **she always says ~ to everything** elle dit toujours oui à tout; **10 points for a ~** 10 points pour un oui; **the ~es and the nos** les oui et les non.

yeshiva /jəˈʃɪvə/ *n* (*pl* **-vahs** ou **-voth**) yeshiva *f*, école *f* hébraïque.

yes-man○ /ˈjesmæn/ *n* (*pl* **-men**) péj lèche-bottes *m inv*.

yes-no question *n* Ling question *f* fermée.

yesterday /ˈjestədeɪ, -dɪ/ ▶ 1150, 1883 **I** *n* **1** lit hier *m*; **~ was Friday** hier c'était vendredi; **~'s newspaper** le journal d'hier; **~ was a sad day for all of us** la journée d'hier a été triste pour nous tous; **~ was the fifth of April** hier nous étions le cinq avril; **what was ~'s date?** quel jour étions-nous hier, on était le combien hier○?; **the day before ~** avant-hier; **2** fig (the past) **~'s fashions** la mode d'hier; **~'s men** péj hommes *mpl* du passé; **all our ~s** tout notre passé.
II *adv* **1** lit hier; **it snowed ~** il a neigé hier; **I saw her only ~** je l'ai vue pas plus tard qu'hier; **all day ~** toute la journée d'hier; **a week ago ~** il y a une semaine hier; **it was ~ week** ou **a week ~** cela fait une semaine hier; **early/late ~** tôt/tard dans la journée d' hier; **I remember it as if it was ~** je m'en souviens comme si c'était hier; **only ~ he was saying to me**... hier encore il me disait...; **2** fig (in the past) hier, autrefois.
IDIOMS **I wasn't born ~** je ne suis pas né d'hier.

yesterday: **~ afternoon** *n, adv* hier après-midi; **~ evening** *n, adv* hier soir; **~ morning** *n, adv* hier matin.

yesteryear /ˈjestəjɪə(r)/ littér *n* temps *m* jadis; **the fashions of ~** la mode du temps jadis or d'antan.

yes-vote *n* oui *m inv*.

yet /jet/ **I** *conj* (nevertheless) pourtant; **he was injured, (and) ~ he still won** il était blessé, et pourtant il a gagné; **so strong (and) ~ so gentle** si fort (et) pourtant si doux.
II *adv* **1** (up till now, so far: with negatives) encore jusqu'à présent; (in questions) déjà; (with superlatives) jusqu'ici; **it's not ready ~, it's not ~ ready** ce n'est pas encore prêt; **she hasn't ~ arrived, she hasn't arrived ~** elle n'est pas encore arrivée; **has he arrived ~?** est-il (déjà) arrivé?; **not ~** pas encore, pas pour l'instant; **this is his best/worst ~** c'est ce qu'il a fait de mieux/de pire jusqu'ici; **her most ambitious/dangerous project ~** le projet le plus ambitieux/dangereux qu'elle ait entrepris jusqu'ici; **it's the best ~** jusqu'ici, c'est le mieux; **2** (also **just ~**) (now) tout de suite, encore; **don't start (just) ~** ne commence pas tout de suite; **we don't have to leave (just) ~** nous ne sommes pas obligés de partir tout de suite; **3** (still) encore; **they may ~ come, they may come ~** ils pourraient encore arriver; **she might ~ decide to leave** elle pourrait encore décider de partir; **he'll finish it ~** il va le finir; **you're young ~** tu es encore jeune; **the campaign has ~ to begin** il faut encore que la campagne démarre, reste encore à démarrer la campagne; **the news has ~ to reach them** il faut encore que la nouvelle leur parvienne, reste encore à leur faire parvenir la nouvelle; **the as ~ unfinished building** le bâtiment encore inachevé; **there is a year to go ~ before**... il reste encore un an avant...; **it'll be ages ~ before**... il va encore falloir des siècles avant...; **he won't come for hours ~** il ne viendra pas avant quelques heures; **there are three more packets ~** il reste encore trois paquets; **4** (even, still: with comparatives etc) encore; **~ more cars** encore plus de voitures; **~ louder/more surprising** encore plus fort/plus surprenant; **~ another attack/question** encore une autre attaque/question; **~ again** encore une fois.

yeti /ˈjetɪ/ *n* yéti *m*.

yew /juː/ **I** *n* **1** (also **~ tree**) if *m*; **2** (wood) bois *m* d'if.
II *modif* [*hedge*] d'ifs.

Y-fronts *npl* GB slip *m* ouvert.

YHA GB (*abrév* = **Youth Hostels Association**) association *f* des auberges de jeunesse.

Yid◑ /jɪd/ *n* injur youpin/-e◑ *m/f* offensive.

Yiddish /ˈjɪdɪʃ/ ▶ 1402 *n, adj* yiddish (*m inv*).

yield /jiːld/ **I** *n* **1** gen (product, amount produced) production *f*, rendement *m*; (of tree, field, farm) rendement *m*, récolte *f*; **the annual milk ~** la production laitière annuelle; **a good/poor ~ of wheat** une bonne/mauvaise récolte de blé; **a high ~ variety** une variété à fort rendement; **2** Fin (of shares, investments) rendement *m*, rapport *m* (**from, on** de); **a ~ of 8%** un rendement de 8%; **a high ~ bond** une obligation à haut rendement.
II *vtr* **1** (produce, bear) [*crop, animal, land*] rendre, produire; [*mine, quarry*] produire; **2** Fin rapporter; **to ~ 25% over 10 years** rapporter 25% sur 10 ans; **to ~ millions in taxes** rapporter des millions en taxes; **3** (provide) donner, fournir [*information, result, meaning*]; produire [*clue*]; livrer [*secret*]; **to ~ new insights into** apporter de nouvelles perspectives quant à; **4** (surrender) céder (**to** à); **to ~ ground to** Mil, fig céder du terrain à; **to ~ a point to sb** céder à qn sur un point, concéder un point à qn; **she refused to ~ this point** elle a refusé de céder sur ce point; **to ~ the floor to** donner or céder la parole à.
III *vi* **1** (give in) (to person, temptation, pressure, threats) céder (**to** à); (to army, arguments) se rendre (**to** à); **to ~ to force** céder devant la force; **to ~ to persuasion** se laisser persuader; **I ~ to no-one in my admiration for her work** personne plus que moi n'admire son œuvre; **2** (under weight, physical pressure) [*lock, door, shelf, bridge*] céder (**under** sous); **3** (be superseded) **to ~ to** [*technology, phenomenon*] céder le pas à; [*land, countryside*] céder la place à; **4** (be productive) **to ~ well/poorly** avoir un bon/mauvais rendement; **the cow ~s well** la vache produit une bonne quantité de lait; **5** US Aut céder le passage (**to** à); **'~'** (on sign) 'cédez le passage'.
■ **yield up** livrer [*secret, treasure*].

yield: **~ criterion** *n* critère *m* de rentabilité; **~ curve** *n* courbe *f* de rentabilité; **~ gap** *n* Fin différence *f* de rendement.

yielding /ˈjiːldɪŋ/ *adj* **1** [*person*] (accommo-

you

In English *you* is used to address everybody, whereas French has two forms: *tu* and *vous*. The usual word to use when you are speaking to anyone you do not know very well is *vous*. This is sometimes called the *polite form* and is used for the subject, object, indirect object and emphatic pronoun:

would you like some coffee? = voulez-vous du café?
can I help you? = est-ce que je peux vous aider?
what can I do for you? = qu'est-ce que je peux faire pour vous?

The more informal pronoun *tu* is used between close friends and family members, within groups of children and young people, by adults when talking to children and always when talking to animals; *tu* is the subject form, the direct and indirect object form is *te* (*t'* before a vowel) and the form for emphatic use or use after a preposition is *toi*:

would you like some coffee? = veux-tu du café?
can I help you? = est-ce que je peux t'aider?
there's a letter for you = il y a une lettre pour toi

As a general rule, when talking to a French person use *vous*, wait to see how they address you and follow suit. It is safer to wait for the French person to suggest using *tu*. The suggestion will usually be phrased as *on se tutoie?* or *on peut se tutoyer?*

Note that *tu* is only a singular pronoun and *vous* is the plural form of *tu*.

Remember that in French the object and indirect object pronouns are always placed before the verb:

she knows you = elle vous connaît *or* elle te connaît

In compound tenses like the present perfect and the past perfect, the past participle agrees in number and gender with the direct object:

I saw you on Saturday
(to one male: polite form) = je vous ai vu samedi
(to one female: polite form) = je vous ai vue samedi
(to one male: informal form) = je t'ai vu samedi
(to one female: informal form) = je t'ai vue samedi
(to two or more people, male or mixed) = je vous ai vus samedi
(to two or more females) = je vous ai vues samedi

When *you* is used impersonally as the more informal form of *one* it is translated by *on* for the subject form and by *vous* or *te* for the object form, depending on whether the comment is being made amongst friends or in a more formal context:

you can do as you like here = on peut faire ce qu'on veut ici
these mushrooms can make you ill = ces champignons peuvent vous rendre malade *or* ces champignons peuvent te rendre malade
you could easily lose your bag here = on pourrait facilement perdre son sac ici

Note that *your* used with *on* is translated by *son*/*sa*/*ses* according to the gender and number of the noun that follows.

For verb forms with *vous*, *tu* and *on* see the French verb tables.
For particular usages see the entry ***you***.

dating) accommodant; (submissive) soumis; **2** [*material*] mou/molle, élastique.

yikes○ /jaɪks/ *excl* US aïe!

yin /jɪn/ *n* yin *m*; **~ (and) yang** le yin et le yang.

yip○ /jɪp/ US = **yelp**.

yipe(s)○ US = **yikes**.

yippee○ /'jɪpi:/ *excl* hourra○!

YMCA (*abrév* = **Young Men's Christian Association**) ≈ Union *f* Chrétienne des Jeunes Gens.

yob○ /'jɒb/, **yobbo**○ /'jɒbəʊ/ *n* GB péj loubard○ *m*, voyou *m*.

yock○ /jɒk/ US *n* (laugh) gros rire *m*; (joke) grosse plaisanterie *f*; **to have a ~** rire un bon coup○.

yod /jɒd/ *n* yod *m*.

yodel /'jəʊdl/ **I** *n* hurlement *m*.
II *vi* (*p prés etc* **-ll-**) jodler, iodler.

yoga /'jəʊgə/ ▶ 1282 **I** *n* yoga *m*.
II *modif* [*class, teacher*] de yoga.

yoghurt /'jɒgət, US 'jəʊgərt/ *n* yaourt *m*, yoghourt *m*; **natural ~** yaourt nature.

yogi /'jəʊgɪ/ *n* yogi *mf*.

yo-heave-ho /jəʊhi:v'həʊ/ *excl* oh! hisse!

yoke /jəʊk/ **I** *n* **1** lit (for oxen) joug *m*; (for person) palanche *f*; fig joug *m*; **to throw off the ~** briser le joug; **2** (pair of oxen) attelage *m* de bœufs; **3** Sewing empiècement *m*; **4** Constr (framework) armature *f*; (tie beam) moise *f*.
II *vtr* **1** (also **~ up**) atteler [*ox, horse*]; **2** (also **~ together**) fig joindre.

yokel /'jəʊkl/ *n* pej péquenaud/-e○ *m/f*, plouc○ *mf*.

yoke oxen *npl* bœufs *mpl* d'attelage.

yolk /jəʊk/ *n* jaune *m* (d'œuf).

yomp○ /jɒmp/ *vtr, vi* GB argot des militaires crapahuter○ (*avec un lourd équipement*).

yon /jɒn/ *adj* ‡ ou dial = **yonder** II.

yonder /'jɒndə(r)/‡ ou littér **I** *adj* (this, that) ce/cet/cette...là.
II *adv* là-bas; **up ~** là -haut; **over ~** là-bas (au loin).
IDIOMS **to disappear into the (wide) blue ~** s'évanouir dans la nature.

yonks○ /jɒŋks/ *npl* GB **I haven't seen him for ~** ça fait une éternité que je ne l'ai pas vu.

Yonne ▶ 1163 *pr n* Yonne *f*; **in/to the ~** dans l'Yonne.

yoo-hoo /'ju:hu:/ *excl* ohé!

yore /jɔ:(r)/ *n* littér **of ~** d'antan liter; **in days of ~** jadis.

Yorkshire /'jɔ:kʃə/ ▶ 1624 *pr n* Yorkshire *m*.

Yorkshire: **~ pudding** *n* GB Yorkshire pudding *m* (*pâte à crêpe cuite au four accompagnant le rôti de bœuf*); **~ terrier** *n* Yorkshire-terrier *m*.

you /ju:, jʊ/ *pron* **1** (addressing sb) **I saw ~ on Saturday** (one person) (polite) je vous ai vu samedi; (informal) je t'ai vu samedi; (more than one person) je vous ai vus samedi; **are ~ busy?** (one person) (polite) vous êtes occupé?; (informal) tu es occupé?; (more than one person) vous êtes occupés?; **oh, it's ~** ah, c'est vous or c'est toi; **it's for ~** c'est pour vous or pour toi; **~ who...** vous qui..., toi qui...; YOU **would never do that** (polite) vous, vous ne feriez jamais cela; (informal) toi tu ne ferais jamais ça; **there's a manager for ~**○! iron ça c'est un patron!; **~ English** vous autres Anglais; **don't ~ talk to me like that!** ne me parle pas sur ce ton!; **~ idiot**○! espèce d'imbécile○!; **~ two can stay** vous deux vous pouvez rester; **do ~ people smoke?** vous fumez?; **2** (as indefinite pronoun) (subject) on; (object, indirect object) vous, te; **~ never know!** on ne sait jamais!; **they say sweets give ~ spots** on dit que les bonbons vous or te donnent des boutons.

you-all○ *pron pl* US vous.

you'd /ju:d/ **1** = **you had**; **2** = **you would**.

you: **~-know-what**○ *pron* vous-savez-quoi, tu-sais-quoi; **~-know-who**○ *pron* qui-vous-savez, qui-tu-sais.

you'll /ju:l/ = **you will**.

young /jʌŋ/ **I** *n* **1** (young people) **the ~** (+ *v pl*) les jeunes *mpl*, la jeunesse *f*; **for ~ and old (alike)** pour les jeunes comme les vieux, pour jeunes et vieux; **2** (animal's offspring) (+ *v pl*) petits *mpl*; **to be with ~** être pleine.
II *adj* (not very old) [*person, tree, animal, plant*] jeune (*before n*); [*nation, organization*] jeune (*before n*); **~ at heart** jeune de cœur; **he's ~ for his age** il est jeune pour son âge; **she is ten years ~er than him** elle a dix ans de moins que lui; **I feel ten years ~er** j'ai l'impression d'avoir rajeuni de dix ans; **in my ~er days** quand j'étais jeune; **you're only ~ once!** on n'est jeune qu'une fois; **children as ~ as five years old** des enfants dont certains n'avaient que cinq ans; **to marry/die ~** se marier/mourir jeune; **the ~ moon** la lune nouvelle; **the night is ~** la nuit ne fait que commencer; **Mr Brown the ~er** ou **the ~er Mr Brown** M. Brown le jeune; (Mr Brown's son) M. Brown fils; **~ Jones** le jeune Jones; **they are aiming at a ~ audience** ils visent un public jeune; **to have a ~ outlook** être jeune d'esprit; **~ fashion** mode *f* jeunes; **~ lady** jeune femme *f*; **what did you say, ~ lady?** (patronizingly) qu'est-ce que vous avez dit, mademoiselle?; **~ man** jeune homme *m*; **her ~ man**† son (petit) ami; **~ people** jeunes gens *mpl*; **~ person** jeune *m*; **the ~er generation** la jeune génération; **her ~er brother** son frère cadet; **her ~er sister** sa sœur cadette; **the two ~er children** les deux cadets; **I'm not as ~ as I used to be** je n'ai plus 20 ans; **we're not getting any ~er** nous ne rajeunissons pas.

young blood *n* sang *m* neuf.

youngish /'jʌŋɪʃ/ *adj* assez jeune.

young-looking *adj* **to be ~** faire (très) jeune.

young: **~ offender** *n* délinquant/-e *m/f*; **~ offenders' institution** *n* GB centre *m* de détention pour les délinquants (*âgés de 14 à 21 ans*); **~ professional** *n* jeune salarié/-e *m/f*.

youngster /'jʌŋstə(r)/ *n* **1** (young person) jeune *m*; **2** (child) enfant *mf*.

Young Turk *n* (male) jeune turc *m*; (female) jeune turque *f*.

your /jɔ:(r), jʊə(r)/ *det* votre/vos; (more informally) ton/ta/tes; (with impersonal pronoun) son/sa/ses.

you're /jʊə(r), jɔ:(r)/ = **you are**.

yours /jɔ:z, US jʊərz/

■ **Note** For a full note on the use of the *vous* and *tu* forms in French, see the entry ***you***.
– In French, possessive pronouns reflect the gender and number of the noun they are standing for. When *yours* is referring to only one person it is translated by *le vôtre, la vôtre, les vôtres* or, more familiarly, *le tien, la tienne, les tiens, les tiennes*. When *yours* is referring to more than one person it is translated by *le vôtre, la vôtre, les vôtres*.
– For examples and particular usages see the entry below.

pron **my car is red but ~ is blue** ma voiture est rouge mais la vôtre or la tienne est bleue; **which house is ~?** votre maison c'est laquelle, ta maison c'est laquelle?; **he's a colleague of ~** c'est un de vos or tes collègues ; **it's not ~** ce n'est pas à vous or à toi; **the money wasn't ~ to give away** vous n'aviez pas à donner cet argent; **~ was not an easy task** votre tâche n'était pas facile; **I'm fed up**○ **with that dog of ~!** j'en ai marre de ton sale chien○!

yourself /jɔːˈself, US jʊərˈself/

■ **Note** For a full note on the use of the *vous* and *tu* forms in French, see the entry ***you***.
– When used as a reflexive pronoun, direct and indirect, *yourself* is translated by *vous* or familiarly *te* or *t'* before a vowel: *you've hurt yourself* = vous vous êtes fait mal *or* tu t'es fait mal.
– In imperatives, the translation is *vous* or *toi*: *help yourself* = servez-vous *or* sers-toi.
– When used in emphasis the translation is *vous-même* or *toi-même*: *you yourself don't know* = vous ne savez pas vous-même *or* tu ne sais pas toi-même.
– After a preposition the translation is *vous* or *vous-même* or *toi* or *toi-même*: *you can be proud of yourself* = vous pouvez être fier de vous *or* vous-même, tu peux être fier de toi *or* toi-même.

pron **1** (refl) vous, te, (*before vowel*) t'; **have you hurt ~?** est-ce que tu t'es fait mal?; **2** (in imperatives) vous, toi; **3** (emphatic) vous-même, toi-même; **you ~ said that...** vous avez dit vous-même que..., tu as dit toi-même que...; **4** (after prep) vous, vous-même, toi, toi-même; **5** (expressions) (**all**) **by ~** tout seul/toute seule; **you're not ~ today** tu n'as pas l'air dans ton assiette aujourd'hui.

yourselves /-ˈselvz/

■ **Note** When used as a reflexive pronoun, direct and indirect, *yourselves* is translated by *vous*: *help yourselves* = servez-vous.
– When used as an emphatic, the translation is *vous-mêmes*: *do it yourselves* = faites-le vous-mêmes.
– After a preposition the translation is *vous* or *vous-mêmes*: *did you buy it for yourselves?* = est-ce que vous l'avez acheté pour vous *or* pour vous-mêmes?

pron **1** (refl) vous; **2** (emphatic) vous-mêmes; **3** (after prep) vous, vous-mêmes; **all by ~** tous seuls/toutes seules.

youth /juːθ/ **I** *n* (*pl* **~s** /juːðz/) **1** (young man) jeune homme *m*; **a gang of ~s** péj une bande de jeunes gens; **2** (period of being young) jeunesse *f*; **in my ~** dans ma jeunesse; **3** (state of being young) jeunesse *f*; **because of/despite his ~** à cause de/malgré son jeune âge; **4** (young people) jeunes *mpl*.
II *modif* [*club, organization*] de jeunes; [*TV programme, magazine, theatre*] pour les jeunes or la jeunesse; **~ culture** culture *f* des jeunes.

youthful /ˈjuːθfl/ *adj* **1** (young) [*person, team, population*] jeune; **2** (typical of youth) [*enthusiasm, confusion, freedom*] de la jeunesse; **his ~ looks** ou **appearance** son air jeune; **she's very ~ for 65, she's a very ~ 65** elle fait très jeune pour ses 65 ans.

youthfulness /ˈjuːθfəlnɪs/ *n* jeunesse *f*.

youth: **~ hostel** *n* auberge *f* de jeunesse; **~ hostelling** *n* randonnée *f* avec logement en auberges de jeunesse; **~ leader** ▶ 1692 *n* animateur/-trice *m/f* de groupe de jeunes; **~ work** *n* travail *m* social auprès des jeunes; **~ worker** ▶ 1692 *n* éducateur/-trice *m/f*.

you've /juːv/ = **you have**.

yowl /jaʊl/ **I** *n* (of person, dog) hurlement *m*; (of cat) miaulement *m*; (of baby) braillement *m*.
II *vi* [*person, dog*] hurler (**with** de); [*cat*] miauler (**with** de); [*baby*] brailler (**with** de).

yo-yo® /ˈjəʊjəʊ/ **I** *n* **1** gen yo-yo® *m*; **2**○ US péj (fool) abruti/-e○ *m/f*.
II *modif* [*market*] instable.
III○ *vi* [*prices, inflation*] fluctuer.

yr *abrév écrite* = **year**.

Y-shaped *adj* en (forme de) Y.

YTS GB (*abrév écrite* = **Youth Training Scheme**) *programme de formation professionnelle pour les jeunes quittant le système scolaire à 16 ans*.

ytterbium /ɪˈtɜːbɪəm/ *n* ytterbium *m*.

yttrium /ˈɪtrɪəm/ *n* yttrium *m*.

yucca /ˈjʌkə/ *n* yucca *m*.

yuck○ /jʌk/ *excl* GB berk○!

yucky○ /ˈjʌkɪ/ *adj* GB dégueulasse◑, dégoûtant.

Yugoslav /ˈjuːgəʊslɑːv/ ▶ 1486, 1402 **I** *n* Yougoslave *mf*.
II *adj* yougoslave.

Yugoslavia /juːgəʊˈslɑːvɪə/ ▶ 1131 *pr n* Yougoslavie *f*.

Yugoslavian /juːgəʊˈslɑːvɪən/ *n, adj* = **Yugoslav**.

yuk○ GB *excl* = **yuck**.

yukky○ *adj* GB = **yucky**.

Yukon /ˈjuːkɒn/ *pr n* Yukon *m*.

Yule† /juːl/ *n* Noël *m*.

Yule log *n* bûche *f* de Noël.

Yuletide† /ˈjuːltaɪd/ **I** *n* (période *f* de) Noël *f*.
II *modif* [*festivities, greetings, spirit*] de Noël.

your

For a full note on the use of the *vous* and *tu* forms in French, see the entry ***you***.

In French, determiners agree in gender and number with the noun they qualify. So *your*, when addressing one person, is translated by *votre*, or more familiarly *ton*, + masculine singular noun (*votre chien* or *ton chien*), by *votre* or *ta* + feminine singular noun (*votre maison* or *ta maison*) and by *vos* or *tes* + plural noun (*vos enfants* or *tes enfants*). Note that *ton* is used with a feminine noun beginning with a vowel or mute 'h' (*ton adresse*).

When addressing more than one person, the translation is *votre* + singular noun and *vos* + plural noun. When *your* is stressed, *à vous* or *à toi* is added after the noun:

your house = votre maison à vous

When used impersonally to mean *one's*, *your* is translated by *son*, *sa* or *ses* when *you* is translated by *on*:

you buy your tickets at the door = on prend ses billets à l'entrée

The translation after an impersonal verb in French is *son, sa, ses*:

you have to buy your tickets at the door = il faut prendre ses billets à l'entrée

Note, however the following:

sweets are bad for your teeth = les bonbons sont mauvais pour les dents
your average student = l'étudiant moyen

For *your* used with parts of the body ▶ 1037.

yum○ = **yummy** II.

yummy○ /ˈjʌmɪ/ **I** *adj* délicieux/-ieuse.
II *excl* miam-miam○!

yum-yum /jʌmˈjʌm/ *excl* = **yummy** II.

yup /jʌp/ *particle* US = **yep**.

yuppie /ˈjʌpɪ/ péj **I** *n* jeune cadre *m* dynamique, yuppie *m* pej.
II *modif* [*image, style, fashion*] de jeune cadre dynamique, de yuppie pej.

yuppie flu ▶ 1354 *n* péj syndrome *m* de la fatigue chronique, encéphalomyélite *f* myalgique spec.

Yvelines ▶ 1163 *pr n* Yvelines *fpl*; **in/to ~** dans les Yvelines.

YWCA (*abrév* = **Young Women's Christian Association**) ≈ Union *f* Chrétienne des Jeunes Femmes.

Zz

The signs of the Zodiac

Aries	= le Bélier	[belje]	21 mars–20 avril
Taurus	= le Taureau	[tɔʀo]	21 avril–20 mai
Gemini	= les Gémeaux	[ʒemo]	21 mai–21 juin
Cancer	= le Cancer	[kɑ̃sɛʀ]	22 juin–22 juillet
Leo	= le Lion	[ljɔ̃]	23 juillet–22 août
Virgo	= la Vierge	[vjɛʀʒ]	23 août–22 septembre
Libra	= la Balance	[balɑ̃s]	23 septembre–23 octobre
Scorpio	= le Scorpion	[skɔʀpjɔ̃]	24 octobre–21 novembre
Sagittarius	= le Sagittaire	[saʒitɛʀ]	22 novembre–21 décembre
Capricorn	= le Capricorne	[kapʀikɔʀn]	22 décembre–19 janvier
Aquarius	= le Verseau	[vɛʀso]	20 janvier–18 février
Pisces	= les Poissons	[pwasɔ̃]	19 février–20 mars

I'm Leo	= je suis Lion
I'm Gemini	= je suis Gémeaux
born in Leo *or* under the sign of Leo	= né sous le signe du Lion
born in Gemini	= né sous le signe des Gémeaux
Leos/Ariens are very generous	= les Lions/les Béliers sont très généreux
what's the horoscope for Leos?	= que dit l'horoscope pour les Lions?
the sun is in Leo	= le soleil est au Lion

All the signs work in the same way in French.

z, Z /zed, US ziː/ *n* z, Z *m*.

Zacharias /ˌzækəˈraɪəs/ *pr n* Zacharie.

Zaire /zɑːˈɪə/ **▶ 1131◀** *pr n* Zaïre *m*.

Zairean /zɑːˈɪən/ **▶ 1486◀** **I** *n* Zaïrois/-e *m/f*.
II *adj* zaïrois.

Zambesi, Zambezi /zæmˈbiːzɪ/ **▶ 1644◀** *pr n* Zambèze *m*.

Zambia /ˈzæmbɪə/ **▶ 1131◀** *pr n* Zambie *f*.

Zambian /ˈzæmbɪən/ **▶ 1486◀** **I** *n* Zambien/-ienne *m/f*.
II *adj* zambien/-ienne.

zany /ˈzeɪnɪ/ **I** *n* Hist Theat bouffon *m*.
II *adj* loufoque○.

Zanzibar /ˌzænzɪˈbɑː/ **▶ 1381◀** *pr n* Zanzibar *m*.

zap○ /zæp/ **I** *n* (energy) tonus *m*.
II *excl* paf!
III *vtr* (*p prés etc* **-pp-**) **1** (destroy) détruire [*town*]; tuer [*person, animal*]; **2** (fire at) tirer sur [*person*]; **3** (stun) assommer; **4** (treat) traiter; **to ~ a tumour with a laser** traiter une tumeur au laser; **to ~ food with radiation** irradier la nourriture; **5** Comput (delete) supprimer [*word, data*].
IV *vi* (*p prés etc* **-pp-**) (move quickly) **to ~ into town/a shop** faire un saut○ en ville/dans un magasin; **to ~ from channel to channel** zapper○.

zapper○ /ˈzæpə(r)/ *n* télécommande *f*.

z: **Z-bed** *n* GB lit *m* pliant; **Z-bend** *n* zigzag *m*.

zeal /ziːl/ *n* **1** (fanaticism) gen zèle *m*; (religious) ferveur *f*; **2** (enthusiasm) ardeur *f*, zèle *m*; **~ to do** empressement *m* à faire.

zealot /ˈzelət/ **I** *n* gen, pej fanatique *mf*.
II Zealot *pr n* zélote *mf*.

zealotry /ˈzelətrɪ/ *n* zèle *m*.

zealous /ˈzeləs/ *adj* [*supporter, missionary*] zélé; [*determination*] acharné; **to be ~ to do** avoir très envie de faire.

zealously /ˈzeləslɪ/ *adv* avec zèle.

zebra /ˈzebrə, ˈziː-/ *n* zèbre *m*.

zebra crossing *n* GB passage *m* (protégé) pour piétons.

zebu /ˈziːbuː/ *n* zébu *m*.

Zechariah /ˌzekəˈraɪə/ *pr n* Zacharie.

Zen /zen/ **I** *n* Zen *m*.
II *modif* [*Buddhism, Buddhist, philosophy*] zen.

zenana /zeˈnɑːnə/ *n* zénana *f*.

zenith /ˈzenɪθ/ *n* Astron zénith *m*; fig apogée *m*.

zephyr /ˈzefə(r)/ *n* littér zéphyr *m*.

zeppelin /ˈzepəlɪn/ *n* zeppelin *m*.

zero /ˈzɪərəʊ/ **▶ 1505◀** **I** *n* gen, Math, Meteorol zéro *m*; **at/above/below ~** à/au-dessus de/au-dessous de zéro.
II *modif* [*altitude, growth, inflation, voltage*] zéro *inv*; [*confidence, interest, involvement, development*] nul/nulle; **at sub-~ temperatures** à des températures en dessous de zéro.
■ **zero in** Mil viser; **to ~ in on sth** Mil viser [*target*]; fig (pinpoint) cerner [*key issue, problem*]; se rabattre sur [*option*]; foncer droit sur [*person*]; repérer [*place*].

zero: **~-based** *adj* à base zéro; **~ gravity** *n* apesanteur *f*; **~ hour** *n* Mil, fig heure *f* H; **~ option** *n* option *f* zéro; **~ point** *n* zéro *m*; **~-rated** *adj* GB exempté de TVA; **~ rating** *n* GB exemption *f* de TVA; **~ sum** *n* somme *f* nulle.

zest /zest/ *n* **1** (enthusiasm) entrain *m*; **a ~ for sth** un goût prononcé pour qch; **his ~ for life** sa joie de vivre; **2** (piquancy) piquant *m*; **to add ~ to sth** ajouter du piquant à qch; **3** (of citrus fruit) zeste *m*.

zestful /ˈzestfʊl/ *adj* [*person, performance, participation*] plein d'entrain.

zestfully /ˈzestfʊlɪ/ *adv* avec entrain.

Zeus /zjuːs/ *pr n* Zeus.

zigzag /ˈzɪɡzæɡ/ **I** *n* zigzag *m*; **there are ~s in the road** la route fait une série de zigzags; **to run in ~s** courir en zigzag.
II *modif* [*design, pattern*] à zigzags; [*route, road*] en zigzag.
III *vi* (*p prés etc* **-gg-**) [*person, vehicle, road*] zigzaguer; [*river, path*] serpenter; **to ~ up/down** monter/descendre en zigzag.

zilch○ /zɪltʃ/ *n* (nothing) que dalle◑, rien; **he's a real ~** c'est un zéro○.

zillion○ /ˈzɪlɪən/ *n* **a ~ things, ~s of things** des millions *mpl* (et des millions) de choses.

Zimbabwe /zɪmˈbɑːbwɪ, -weɪ/ **▶ 1131◀** *pr n* Zimbabwe *m*.

Zimbabwean /zɪmˈbɑːbwɪən/ **▶ 1486◀** **I** *n* Zimbabwéen/-enne *m/f*.
II *adj* zimbabwéen/-enne.

zimmer® /ˈzɪmə(r)/ *n* (also **zimmer aid, zimmer frame**) GB déambulateur *m*.

zinc /zɪŋk/ *n* zinc *m*.

zinc: **~ blende** *n* blende *f*; **~ chloride** *n* chlorure *m* de zinc; **~ dust** *n* limaille *f* de zinc; **~ ointment** *n* pommade *f* à l'oxyde de zinc; **~ oxide** *n* oxyde *m* de zinc; **~ sulphate** *n* sulfate *m* de zinc; **~ white** *n* = **zinc oxide**.

zing○ /zɪŋ/ **I** *n* **1** (sound) sifflement *m*; **2** (energy) entrain *m*.
II *vtr* US (strike) impressionner; fig (criticize) démolir○.
III *vi* siffler.
■ **zing along**○ US [*car*] filer○ à toute allure.

zingy○ /ˈzɪŋɪ/ *adj* dynamique.

zinnia /ˈzɪnɪə/ *n* zinnia *m*.

Zion /ˈzaɪən/ *pr n* Sion *f*.

Zionism /ˈzaɪənɪzəm/ *n* sionisme *m*.

Zionist /ˈzaɪənɪst/ *n, adj* sioniste *mf*.

zip /zɪp/ **I** *n* **1** (also **zipper, zip fastener**) fermeture *f* à glissière, fermeture *f* éclair®; **to do up/undo a ~** fermer/ouvrir une fermeture à glissière; **the ~ is stuck** la fermeture à glissière est coincée; **a side/full-length ~** une fermeture à glissière latérale/sur toute la longueur; **2**○ (energy) tonus *m*; **3** (sound) sifflement *m*; **4** US Post = **zip code**; **5**○ US (zero) zéro *m*; **to know ~ about sb/sth** savoir que dalle◑ sur qn/qch.
II *vtr* (*p prés etc* **-pp-**) **to ~ sth open/shut** ouvrir/fermer la fermeture à glissière de qch.
III○ *vi* (*p prés etc* **-pp-**) **to ~ along, to ~ past** filer à toute allure; **to ~ past sb/sth** dépasser qn/qch à toute allure.
■ **zip in**: **~ [sb] in** fermer sa fermeture à glissière à qn; **I ~ped the baby into his sleeping bag** j'ai fermé la fermeture à glissière du sac de couchage du bébé.
■ **zip on**: ¶ **~ on** [*sleeve, hood*] s'attacher par une fermeture à glissière; ¶ **~ [sth] on, ~ on [sth]** remonter la fermeture à glissière de qch; **I ~ped on my anorak** j'ai remonté la fermeture à glissière de mon anorak.
■ **zip through**: **~ through [sth] to ~ through one's book/marking** lire son livre/corriger les copies en diagonale○.
■ **zip up**: ¶ [*garment, bag*] se fermer par une fermeture à glissière; **to ~ up at the back/front/side** se fermer par une fermeture à glissière dans le dos/sur le devant/sur le côté; ¶ **~ [sb /sth] up, ~ up [sb/sth]** remonter la fermeture à glissière de qn/qch; **can you ~ me up please?** tu peux me remonter ma fermeture à glissière?

zip: **~ code** *n* US Post code *m* postal; **~ fastener** *n* = **zip**; **~-in, ~-on, ~-up**

adj [*jacket, hood, sleeve*] à fermeture à glissière, zippé.

zipper /ˈzɪpə(r)/ *n* US = **zip**.

zippered /ˈzɪpəd/ *adj* US à fermeture à glissière.

zippily○ /ˈzɪpɪlɪ/ *adv* [*move*] en pétant le feu○.

zip pocket *n* poche *f* à fermeture à glissière, poche *f* zippée.

zippy○ /ˈzɪpɪ/ *adj* [*vehicle*] qui pète le feu○.

zircon /ˈzɜːkɒn/ *n* zircon *m*.

zirconium /zəˈkəʊnɪəm/ *n* zirconium *m*.

zit○ /zɪt/ *n* bouton *m*.

zither /ˈzɪðə(r)/ ▶ 1481 *n* cithare *f*.

zodiac /ˈzəʊdɪæk/ *n* zodiaque *m*.

zombie /ˈzɒmbɪ/ *n* Relig zombi(e) *m*; fig abruti/-e○ *m/f*.

zonal /ˈzəʊnl/ *adj* [*administration*] par zone; [*boundary, organizer*] de zone; [*soil, climate*] zonal.

zone /zəʊn/ **I** *n* (all contexts) zone *f*; **neutral/postal ~** zone neutre/postale.
II *vtr* **1** (divide) diviser [qch] en zones or secteurs; **2** (assign) réserver; **to be ~d for enterprise/housing** être réservé à l'entreprise/au logement.

zone defence *n* défense *f* de zone.

zoning /ˈzəʊnɪŋ/ *n* (in urban planning) découpage *m* par zones, zonage *m* spec.

zonk○: ■ **zonk out**○ s'endormir.

zonked○ /zɒŋkt/ *adj* (also **zonked out**) (tired) crevé○; (drunk) bourré○; (on drugs) défoncé○.

zonk out○ s'endormir.

zoo /zuː/ *n* zoo *m*.

zoo keeper ▶ 1692 *n* gardien/-ienne *m/f* de zoo.

zoological /ˌzəʊəˈlɒdʒɪkl/ *adj* zoologique.

zoological gardens *n* jardins *mpl* zoologiques.

zoologist /zəʊˈɒlədʒɪst/ ▶ 1692 *n* zoologue *mf*, zoologiste *mf*.

zoology /zəʊˈɒlədʒɪ/ *n* zoologie *f*.

zoom /zuːm/ **I** *n* **1** (of traffic, aircraft) vrombissement *m*, vacarme *m*; **2** Phot (also **~ lens**) zoom *m*.
II *vi* **1**○ (move quickly) **to ~ past** passer en trombe; **I saw you ~ing past** je t'ai vu passer en trombe; **to ~ around** passer à toute vitesse dans [*streets, region*]; **the motorcyclist went ~ing off down the road** le motocycliste a démarré sur les chapeaux de roues; **he's ~ed off to Paris** il a foncé○ à Paris; **I'll just ~ out to the shop** je vais faire un saut○ au magasin; **2**○ (rocket) [*prices, profits*] monter en flèche; **3** Aviat [*plane*] monter en chandelle.
■ **zoom in** Cin, Phot faire un zoom (**on** sur).
■ **zoom out** Cin, Phot faire un zoom arrière.

zoomorphic /ˌzəʊəˈmɔːfɪk/ *adj* zoomorphe.

zoot suit○ /zuːt/ *n* costume *m* zazou (*des années 40*).

Z-shaped *adj* en (forme de) Z.

zucchini /zuːˈkiːnɪ/ *n* (*pl* **~** ou **~s**) US courgette *f*.

Zug ▶ 1818, 1776 *pr n* Zoug; **the canton of ~** le canton de Zoug.

Zuider Zee /ˈzaɪdə ˈziː/ *pr n* Zuiderzee *m*.

Zulu /ˈzuːluː/ ▶ 1486, 1402 **I** *n* (person) Zoulou *mf*; Ling zoulou *m*.
II *adj* zoulou.

Zulu land *pr n* Zoul(o)uland *m*.

Zurich /ˈzjʊərɪk/ ▶ 1818, 1400, 1776 *pr n* (town) Zurich; (canton) canton *m* de Zurich; **Lake ~** le lac *m* de Zurich; **the canton of ~** le canton de Zurich.

zwieback /ˈzwiːbæk, ˈtsviːbɑːk/ *n* US ≈ biscotte *f*.

zygote /ˈzaɪgəʊt/ *n* zygote *m*.

Index of English lexical usage notes

Liste des notes d'usage lexicales françaises

French verbs

Standard verb endings

INDICATIVE Present

		-er	-ir	-r, -re
Singular	**1**	-e	-is	-s *or* -e
	2	-es	-is	-s *or* -es
	3	-e	-it	-t *or* -e
Plural	**1**	-ons	-(iss)ons	-ons
	2	-ez	-(iss)ez	-ez
	3	-ent	-(iss)ent	-ent

INDICATIVE Imperfect

		-er	-ir	-r, -re
Singular	**1**	-ais	-(iss)ais	-ais
	2	-ais	-(iss)ais	-ais
	3	-ait	-(iss)ait	-ait
Plural	**1**	-ions	-(iss)ions	-ions
	2	-iez	-(iss)iez	-iez
	3	-aient	-(iss)aient	-aient

INDICATIVE Past historic

		-er	-ir	-r, -re
Singular	**1**	-ai	-is	-s
	2	-as	-is	-s
	3	-a	-it	-t
Plural	**1**	-âmes	-îmes	-mes
	2	-âtes	-îtes	-tes
	3	-èrent	-irent	-rent

INDICATIVE Future

		-er	-ir	-r, -re
Singular	**1**	-erai	-rai	-rai
	2	-eras	-ras	-ras
	3	-era	-ra	-ra
Plural	**1**	-erons	-rons	-rons
	2	-erez	-rez	-rez
	3	-eront	-ront	-ront

INFINITIVE

	-er	-ir	-r, -re
Present	-er	-ir	-r *or* -re

SUBJUNCTIVE Present

		-er	-ir	-r, -re
Singular	**1**	-e	-(iss)e	-e
	2	-es	-(iss)es	-es
	3	-e	-(iss)e	-e
Plural	**1**	-ions	-(iss)ions	-ions
	2	-iez	-(iss)iez	-iez
	3	-ent	-(iss)ent	-ent

SUBJUNCTIVE Imperfect

		-er	-ir	-r, -re
Singular	**1**	-asse	-sse	-sse
	2	-asses	-sses	-sses
	3	-ât	-ît	-ît *or* -ût
Plural	**1**	-assions	-ssions	-ssions
	2	-assiez	-ssiez	-ssiez
	3	-assent	-issent	-ssent

IMPERATIVE Present

		-er	-ir	-r, -re
Singular				
	3	-e	-s	-s
Plural	**1**	-ons	-(iss)ons	-ons
	2	-ez	-(iss)ez	-ez

CONDITIONAL Present

		-er	-ir	-r, -re
Singular	**1**	-erais	-rais	-rais
	2	-erais	-rais	-rais
	3	-erait	-rait	-rait
Plural	**1**	-erions	-rions	-rions
	2	-eriez	-riez	-riez
	3	-eraient	-raient	-raient

PARTICIPLE

	-er	-ir	-r, -re
Present	-ant	-(iss)ant	-ant
Past	-é	-i	-i *or* -u

1 aimer

INDICATIVE

Present

j'	aim**e**
tu	aim**es**
il	aim**e**
nous	aim**ons**
vous	aim**ez**
ils	aim**ent**

Imperfect

j'	aim**ais**
tu	aim**ais**
il	aim**ait**
nous	aim**ions**
vous	aim**iez**
ils	aim**aient**

Past historic

j'	aim**ai**
tu	aim**as**
il	aim**a**
nous	aim**âmes**
vous	aim**âtes**
ils	aim**èrent**

Future

j'	aim**erai**
tu	aim**eras**
il	aim**era**
nous	aim**erons**
vous	aim**erez**
ils	aim**eront**

Perfect

j'	ai	aim**é**
tu	as	aim**é**
il	a	aim**é**
nous	avons	aim**é**
vous	avez	aim**é**
ils	ont	aim**é**

Pluperfect

j'	avais	aim**é**
tu	avais	aim**é**
il	avait	aim**é**
nous	avions	aim**é**
vous	aviez	aim**é**
ils	avaient	aim**é**

Past anterior

j'	eus	aim**é**
tu	eus	aim**é**
il	eut	aim**é**
nous	eûmes	aim**é**
vous	eûtes	aim**é**
ils	eurent	aim**é**

Future perfect

j'	aurai	aim**é**
tu	auras	aim**é**
il	aura	aim**é**
nous	aurons	aim**é**
vous	aurez	aim**é**
ils	auront	aim**é**

IMPERATIVE

Present aim**e**
aim**ons**
aim**ez**

Past aie aim**é**
ayons aim**é**
ayez aim**é**

SUBJUNCTIVE

Present

(que) j'	aim**e**
(que) tu	aim**es**
(qu')il	aim**e**
(que) nous	aim**ions**
(que) vous	aim**iez**
(qu')ils	aim**ent**

Imperfect

(que) j'	aim**asse**
(que) tu	aim**asses**
(qu')il	aim**ât**
(que) nous	aim**assions**
(que) vous	aim**assiez**
(qu')ils	aim**assent**

Perfect

(que) j'	aie	aim**é**
(que) tu	aies	aim**é**
(qu')il	ait	aim**é**
(que) nous	ayons	aim**é**
(que) vous	ayez	aim**é**
(qu')ils	aient	aim**é**

Pluperfect

(que) j'	eusse	aim**é**
(que) tu	eusses	aim**é**
(qu')il	eût	aim**é**
(que) nous	eussions	aim**é**
(que) vous	eussiez	aim**é**
(qu')ils	eussent	aim**é**

CONDITIONAL

Present

j'	aim**erais**
tu	aim**erais**
il	aim**erait**
nous	aim**erions**
vous	aim**eriez**
ils	aim**eraient**

Past I

j'	aurais	aim**é**
tu	aurais	aim**é**
il	aurait	aim**é**
nous	aurions	aim**é**
vous	auriez	aim**é**
ils	auraient	aim**é**

Past II

j'	eusse	aim**é**
tu	eusses	aim**é**
il	eût	aim**é**
nous	eussions	aim**é**
vous	eussiez	aim**é**
ils	eussent	aim**é**

PARTICIPLE

Present aim**ant**

Past aim**é, -e**
ayant aim**é**

INFINITIVE

Present aim**er**

Past avoir aim**é**

2 plier

INDICATIVE

Present

je	pli**e**
tu	pli**es**
il	pli**e**
nous	pli**ons**
vous	pli**ez**
ils	pli**ent**

Imperfect

je	pli**ais**
tu	pli**ais**
il	pli**ait**
nous	pli**ions**
vous	pli**iez**
ils	pli**aient**

Past historic

je	pli**ai**
tu	pli**as**
il	pli**a**
nous	pli**âmes**
vous	pli**âtes**
ils	pli**èrent**

Future

je	pli**erai**
tu	pli**eras**
il	pli**era**
nous	pli**erons**
vous	pli**erez**
ils	pli**eront**

Perfect

j'	ai	pli**é**
tu	as	pli**é**
il	a	pli**é**
nous	avons	pli**é**
vous	avez	pli**é**
ils	ont	pli**é**

Pluperfect

j'	avais	pli**é**
tu	avais	pli**é**
il	avait	pli**é**
nous	avions	pli**é**
vous	aviez	pli**é**
ils	avaient	pli**é**

Past anterior

j'	eus	pli**é**
tu	eus	pli**é**
il	eut	pli**é**
nous	eûmes	pli**é**
vous	eûtes	pli**é**
ils	eurent	pli**é**

Future perfect

j'	aurai	pli**é**
tu	auras	pli**é**
il	aura	pli**é**
nous	aurons	pli**é**
vous	aurez	pli**é**
ils	auront	pli**é**

IMPERATIVE

Present pli**e**
pli**ons**
pli**ez**

Past aie pli**é**
ayons pli**é**
ayez pli**é**

SUBJUNCTIVE

Present

(que) je	pli**e**
(que) tu	pli**es**
(qu')il	pli**e**
(que) nous	pli**ions**
(que) vous	pli**iez**
(qu')ils	pli**ent**

Imperfect

(que) je	pli**asse**
(que) tu	pli**asses**
(qu')il	pli**ât**
(que) nous	pli**assions**
(que) vous	pli**assiez**
(qu')ils	pli**assent**

Perfect

(que) j'	aie	pli**é**
(que) tu	aies	pli**é**
(qu')il	ait	pli**é**
(que) nous	ayons	pli**é**
(que) vous	ayez	pli**é**
(qu')ils	aient	pli**é**

Pluperfect

(que) j'	eusse	pli**é**
(que) tu	eusses	pli**é**
(qu')il	eût	pli**é**
(que) nous	eussions	pli**é**
(que) vous	eussiez	pli**é**
(qu')ils	eussent	pli**é**

CONDITIONAL

Present

je	pli**erais**
tu	pli**erais**
il	pli**erait**
nous	pli**erions**
vous	pli**eriez**
ils	pli**eraient**

Past I

j'	aurais	pli**é**
tu	aurais	pli**é**
il	aurait	pli**é**
nous	aurions	pli**é**
vous	auriez	pli**é**
ils	auraient	pli**é**

Past II

j'	eusse	pli**é**
tu	eusses	pli**é**
il	eût	pli**é**
nous	eussions	pli**é**
vous	eussiez	pli**é**
ils	eussent	pli**é**

PARTICIPLE

Present pli**ant**

Past pli**é, -e**
ayant pli**é**

INFINITIVE

Present pli**er**

Past avoir pli**é**

3 finir

INDICATIVE

Present	
je	fin**is**
tu	fin**is**
il	fin**it**
nous	fin**issons**
vous	fin**issez**
ils	fin**issent**

Imperfect	
je	fin**issais**
tu	fin**issais**
il	fin**issait**
nous	fin**issions**
vous	fin**issiez**
ils	fin**issaient**

Past historic	
je	fin**is**
tu	fin**is**
il	fin**it**
nous	fin**îmes**
vous	fin**îtes**
ils	fin**irent**

Future	
je	fin**irai**
tu	fin**iras**
il	fin**ira**
nous	fin**irons**
vous	fin**irez**
ils	fin**iront**

Perfect		
j'	ai	fini
tu	as	fini
il	a	fini
nous	avons	fini
vous	avez	fini
ils	ont	fini

Pluperfect		
j'	avais	fini
tu	avais	fini
il	avait	fini
nous	avions	fini
vous	aviez	fini
ils	avaient	fini

Past anterior		
j'	eus	fini
tu	eus	fini
il	eut	fini
nous	eûmes	fini
vous	eûtes	fini
ils	eurent	fini

Future perfect		
j'	aurai	fini
tu	auras	fini
il	aura	fini
nous	aurons	fini
vous	aurez	fini
ils	auront	fini

IMPERATIVE

Present	fin**is**	
	fin**issons**	
	fin**issez**	
Past	aie	fini
	ayons	fini
	ayez	fini

SUBJUNCTIVE

Present	
(que) je	fin**isse**
(que) tu	fin**isses**
(qu')il	fin**isse**
(que) nous	fin**issions**
(que) vous	fin**issiez**
(qu')ils	fin**issent**

Imperfect	
(que) je	fin**isse**
(que) tu	fin**isses**
(qu')il	fin**ît**
(que) nous	fin**issions**
(que) vous	fin**issiez**
(qu')ils	fin**issent**

Perfect		
(que) j'	aie	fini
(que) tu	aies	fini
(qu')il	ait	fini
(que) nous	ayons	fini
(que) vous	ayez	fini
(qu')ils	aient	fini

Pluperfect		
(que) j'	eusse	fini
(que) tu	eusses	fini
(qu')il	eût	fini
(que) nous	eussions	fini
(que) vous	eussiez	fini
(qu')ils	eussent	fini

CONDITIONAL

Present	
je	fin**irais**
tu	fin**irais**
il	fin**irait**
nous	fin**irions**
vous	fin**iriez**
ils	fin**iraient**

Past I		
j'	aurais	fini
tu	aurais	fini
il	aurait	fini
nous	aurions	fini
vous	auriez	fini
ils	auraient	fini

Past II		
j'	eusse	fini
tu	eusses	fini
il	eût	fini
nous	eussions	fini
vous	eussiez	fini
ils	eussent	fini

PARTICIPLE

Present	fin**issant**
Past	fin**i, -e**
	ayant fini

INFINITIVE

Present	fin**ir**
Past	avoir fini

4 offrir

INDICATIVE

Present	
j'	offr**e**
tu	offr**es**
il	offr**e**
nous	offr**ons**
vous	offr**ez**
ils	offr**ent**

Imperfect	
j'	offr**ais**
tu	offr**ais**
il	offr**ait**
nous	offr**ions**
vous	offr**iez**
ils	offr**aient**

Past historic	
j'	offr**is**
tu	offr**is**
il	offr**it**
nous	offr**îmes**
vous	offr**îtes**
ils	offr**irent**

Future	
j'	offr**irai**
tu	offr**iras**
il	offr**ira**
nous	offr**irons**
vous	offr**irez**
ils	offr**iront**

Perfect		
j'	ai	offert
tu	as	offert
il	a	offert
nous	avons	offert
vous	avez	offert
ils	ont	offert

Pluperfect		
j'	avais	offert
tu	avais	offert
il	avait	offert
nous	avions	offert
vous	aviez	offert
ils	avaient	offert

Past anterior		
j'	eus	offert
tu	eus	offert
il	eut	offert
nous	eûmes	offert
vous	eûtes	offert
ils	eurent	offert

Future perfect		
j'	aurai	offert
tu	auras	offert
il	aura	offert
nous	aurons	offert
vous	aurez	offert
ils	auront	offert

IMPERATIVE

Present	offr**e**	
	offr**ons**	
	offr**ez**	
Past	aie	offert
	ayons	offert
	ayez	offert

SUBJUNCTIVE

Present	
(que) j'	offr**e**
(que) tu	offr**es**
(qu')il	offr**e**
(que) nous	offr**ions**
(que) vous	offr**iez**
(qu')ils	offr**ent**

Imperfect	
(que) j'	offr**isse**
(que) tu	offr**isses**
(qu')il	offr**ît**
(que) nous	offr**issions**
(que) vous	offr**issiez**
(qu')ils	offr**issent**

Perfect		
(que) j'	aie	offert
(que) tu	aies	offert
(qu')il	ait	offert
(que) nous	ayons	offert
(que) vous	ayez	offert
(qu')ils	aient	offert

Pluperfect		
(que) j'	eusse	offert
(que) tu	eusses	offert
(qu')il	eût	offert
(que) nous	eussions	offert
(que) vous	eussiez	offert
(qu')ils	eussent	offert

CONDITIONAL

Present	
j'	offr**irais**
tu	offr**irais**
il	offr**irait**
nous	offr**irions**
vous	offr**iriez**
ils	offr**iraient**

Past I		
j'	aurais	offert
tu	aurais	offert
il	aurait	offert
nous	aurions	offert
vous	auriez	offert
ils	auraient	offert

Past II		
j'	eusse	offert
tu	eusses	offert
il	eût	offert
nous	eussions	offert
vous	eussiez	offert
ils	eussent	offert

PARTICIPLE

Present	offr**ant**
Past	offert, -e
	ayant offert

INFINITIVE

Present	offr**ir**
Past	avoir offert

5 recevoir

INDICATIVE

Present

je	reç**ois**
tu	reç**ois**
il	reç**oit**
nous	rec**evons**
vous	rec**evez**
ils	reç**oivent**

Imperfect

je	rec**evais**
tu	rec**evais**
il	rec**evait**
nous	rec**evions**
vous	rec**eviez**
ils	rec**evaient**

Past historic

je	reç**us**
tu	reç**us**
il	reç**ut**
nous	reç**ûmes**
vous	reç**ûtes**
ils	reç**urent**

Future

je	rec**evrai**
tu	rec**evras**
il	rec**evra**
nous	rec**evrons**
vous	rec**evrez**
ils	rec**evront**

Perfect

j'	ai	reç**u**
tu	as	reç**u**
il	a	reç**u**
nous	avons	reç**u**
vous	avez	reç**u**
ils	ont	reç**u**

Pluperfect

j'	avais	reç**u**
tu	avais	reç**u**
il	avait	reç**u**
nous	avions	reç**u**
vous	aviez	reç**u**
ils	avaient	reç**u**

Past anterior

j'	eus	reç**u**
tu	eus	reç**u**
il	eut	reç**u**
nous	eûmes	reç**u**
vous	eûtes	reç**u**
ils	eurent	reç**u**

Future perfect

j'	aurai	reç**u**
tu	auras	reç**u**
il	aura	reç**u**
nous	aurons	reç**u**
vous	aurez	reç**u**
ils	auront	reç**u**

IMPERATIVE

Present reç**ois**, rec**evons**, rec**evez**

Past aie reç**u**, ayons reç**u**, ayez reç**u**

SUBJUNCTIVE

Present

(que) je	reç**oive**
(que) tu	reç**oives**
(qu')il	reç**oive**
(que) nous	rec**evions**
(que) vous	rec**eviez**
(qu')ils	reç**oivent**

Imperfect

(que) je	reç**usse**
(que) tu	reç**usses**
(qu')il	reç**ût**
(que) nous	reç**ussions**
(que) vous	reç**ussiez**
(qu')ils	reç**ussent**

Perfect

(que) j'	aie	reç**u**
(que) tu	aies	reç**u**
(qu')il	ait	reç**u**
(que) nous	ayons	reç**u**
(que) vous	ayez	reç**u**
(qu')ils	aient	reç**u**

Pluperfect

(que) j'	eusse	reç**u**
(que) tu	eusses	reç**u**
(qu')il	eût	reç**u**
(que) nous	eussions	reç**u**
(que) vous	eussiez	reç**u**
(qu')ils	eussent	reç**u**

CONDITIONAL

Present

je	rec**evrais**
tu	rec**evrais**
il	rec**evrait**
nous	rec**evrions**
vous	rec**evriez**
ils	rec**evraient**

Past I

j'	aurais	reç**u**
tu	aurais	reç**u**
il	aurait	reç**u**
nous	aurions	reç**u**
vous	auriez	reç**u**
ils	auraient	reç**u**

Past II

j'	eusse	reç**u**
tu	eusses	reç**u**
il	eût	reç**u**
nous	eussions	reç**u**
vous	eussiez	reç**u**
ils	eussent	reç**u**

PARTICIPLE

Present rec**evant**

Past reç**u, -e**, ayant reç**u**

INFINITIVE

Present rec**evoir**

Past avoir reç**u**

6 rendre

INDICATIVE

Present

je	rend**s**
tu	rend**s**
il	rend
nous	rend**ons**
vous	rend**ez**
ils	rend**ent**

Imperfect

je	rend**ais**
tu	rend**ais**
il	rend**ait**
nous	rend**ions**
vous	rend**iez**
ils	rend**aient**

Past historic

je	rend**is**
tu	rend**is**
il	rend**it**
nous	rend**îmes**
vous	rend**îtes**
ils	rend**irent**

Future

je	rend**rai**
tu	rend**ras**
il	rend**ra**
nous	rend**rons**
vous	rend**rez**
ils	rend**ront**

Perfect

j'	ai	rend**u**
tu	as	rend**u**
il	a	rend**u**
nous	avons	rend**u**
vous	avez	rend**u**
ils	ont	rend**u**

Pluperfect

j'	avais	rend**u**
tu	avais	rend**u**
il	avait	rend**u**
nous	avions	rend**u**
vous	aviez	rend**u**
ils	avaient	rend**u**

Past anterior

j'	eus	rend**u**
tu	eus	rend**u**
il	eut	rend**u**
nous	eûmes	rend**u**
vous	eûtes	rend**u**
ils	eurent	rend**u**

Future perfect

j'	aurai	rend**u**
tu	auras	rend**u**
il	aura	rend**u**
nous	aurons	rend**u**
vous	aurez	rend**u**
ils	auront	rend**u**

IMPERATIVE

Present rends, rend**ons**, rend**ez**

Past aie rend**u**, ayons rend**u**, ayez rend**u**

SUBJUNCTIVE

Present

(que) je	rend**e**
(que) tu	rend**es**
(qu')il	rend**e**
(que) nous	rend**ions**
(que) vous	rend**iez**
(qu')ils	rend**ent**

Imperfect

(que) je	rend**isse**
(que) tu	rend**isses**
(qu')il	rend**ît**
(que) nous	rend**issions**
(que) vous	rend**issiez**
(qu')ils	rend**issent**

Perfect

(que) j'	aie	rend**u**
(que) tu	aies	rend**u**
(qu')il	ait	rend**u**
(que) nous	ayons	rend**u**
(que) vous	ayez	rend**u**
(qu')ils	aient	rend**u**

Pluperfect

(que) j'	eusse	rend**u**
(que) tu	eusses	rend**u**
(qu')il	eût	rend**u**
(que) nous	eussions	rend**u**
(que) vous	eussiez	rend**u**
(qu')ils	eussent	rend**u**

CONDITIONAL

Present

je	rend**rais**
tu	rend**rais**
il	rend**rait**
nous	rend**rions**
vous	rend**riez**
ils	rend**raient**

Past I

j'	aurais	rend**u**
tu	aurais	rend**u**
il	aurait	rend**u**
nous	aurions	rend**u**
vous	auriez	rend**u**
ils	auraient	rend**u**

Past II

j'	eusse	rend**u**
tu	eusses	rend**u**
il	eût	rend**u**
nous	eussions	rend**u**
vous	eussiez	rend**u**
ils	eussent	rend**u**

PARTICIPLE

Present rend**ant**

Past rend**u, -e**, ayant rend**u**

INFINITIVE

Present rend**re**

Past avoir rend**u**

7 être

INDICATIVE

Present

je suis
tu es
il est

nous sommes
vous êtes
ils sont

Imperfect

j' étais
tu étais
il était

nous étions
vous étiez
ils étaient

Past historic

je fus
tu fus
il fut

nous fûmes
vous fûtes
ils furent

Future

je serai
tu seras
il sera

nous serons
vous serez
ils seront

Perfect

j' ai été
tu as été
il a été

nous avons été
vous avez été
ils ont été

Pluperfect

j' avais été
tu avais été
il avait été

nous avions été
vous aviez été
ils avaient été

Past anterior

j' eus été
tu eus été
il eut été

nous eûmes été
vous eûtes été
ils eurent été

Future perfect

j' aurai été
tu auras été
il aura été

nous aurons été
vous aurez été
ils auront été

IMPERATIVE

Present sois
soyons
soyez

Past aie été
ayons été
ayez été

SUBJUNCTIVE

Present

(que) je sois
(que) tu sois
(qu')il soit

(que) nous soyons
(que) vous soyez
(qu')ils soient

Imperfect

(que) je fusse
(que) tu fusses
(qu')il fût

(que) nous fussions
(que) vous fussiez
(qu')ils fussent

Perfect

(que) j' aie été
(que) tu aies été
(qu')il ait été

(que) nous ayons été
(que) vous ayez été
(qu')ils aient été

Pluperfect

(que) j' eusse été
(que) tu eusses été
(qu')il eût été

(que) nous eussions été
(que) vous eussiez été
(qu')ils eussent été

CONDITIONAL

Present

je serais
tu serais
il serait

nous serions
vous seriez
ils seraient

Past I

j' aurais été
tu aurais été
il aurait été

nous aurions été
vous auriez été
ils auraient été

Past II

j' eusse été
tu eusses été
il eût été

nous eussions été
vous eussiez été
ils eussent été

PARTICIPLE

Present étant

Past été (invariable)
ayant été

INFINITIVE

Present être

Past avoir été

8 avoir

INDICATIVE

Present

j' ai
tu as
il a

nous avons
vous avez
ils ont

Imperfect

j' avais
tu avais
il avait

nous avions
vous aviez
ils avaient

Past historic

j' eus
tu eus
il eut

nous eûmes
vous eûtes
ils eurent

Future

j' aurai
tu auras
il aura

nous aurons
vous aurez
ils auront

Perfect

j' ai eu
tu as eu
il a eu

nous avons eu
vous avez eu
ils ont eu

Pluperfect

j' avais eu
tu avais eu
il avait eu

nous avions eu
vous aviez eu
ils avaient eu

Past anterior

j' eus eu
tu eus eu
il eut eu

nous eûmes eu
vous eûtes eu
ils eurent eu

Future perfect

j' aurai eu
tu auras eu
il aura eu

nous aurons eu
vous aurez eu
ils auront eu

IMPERATIVE

Present aie
ayons
ayez

Past aie eu
ayons eu
ayez eu

SUBJUNCTIVE

Present

(que) j' aie
(que) tu aies
(qu')il ait

(que) nous ayons
(que) vous ayez
(qu')ils aient

Imperfect

(que) j' eusse
(que) tu eusses
(qu')il eût

(que) nous eussions
(que) vous eussiez
(qu')ils eussent

Perfect

(que) j' aie eu
(que) tu aies eu
(qu')il ait eu

(que) nous ayons eu
(que) vous ayez eu
(qu')ils aient eu

Pluperfect

(que) j' eusse eu
(que) tu eusses eu
(qu')il eût eu

(que) nous eussions eu
(que) vous eussiez eu
(qu')ils eussent eu

CONDITIONAL

Present

j' aurais
tu aurais
il aurait

nous aurions
vous auriez
ils auraient

Past I

j' aurais eu
tu aurais eu
il aurait eu

nous aurions eu
vous auriez eu
ils auraient eu

Past II

j' eusse eu
tu eusses eu
il eût eu

nous eussions eu
vous eussiez eu
ils eussent eu

PARTICIPLE

Present ayant

Past eu, -e
ayant eu

INFINITIVE

Present avoir

Past avoir eu

9 aller

INDICATIVE

Present		
je	vais	
tu	vas	
il	va	
nous	allons	
vous	allez	
ils	vont	

Imperfect		
j'	all**ais**	
tu	all**ais**	
il	all**ait**	
nous	all**ions**	
vous	all**iez**	
ils	all**aient**	

Past historic		
j'	all**ai**	
tu	all**as**	
il	alla	
nous	all**âmes**	
vous	all**âtes**	
ils	all**èrent**	

Future		
j'	**irai**	
tu	**iras**	
il	**ira**	
nous	**irons**	
vous	**irez**	
ils	**iront**	

Perfect		
je	suis	all**é**
tu	es	all**é**
il	est	all**é**
nous	sommes	all**és**
vous	êtes	all**és**
ils	sont	all**és**

Pluperfect		
j'	étais	all**é**
tu	étais	all**é**
il	était	all**é**
nous	étions	all**és**
vous	étiez	all**és**
ils	étaient	all**és**

Past anterior		
je	fus	all**é**
tu	fus	all**é**
il	fut	all**é**
nous	fûmes	all**és**
vous	fûtes	all**és**
ils	furent	all**és**

Future perfect		
je	serai	all**é**
tu	seras	all**é**
il	sera	all**é**
nous	serons	all**és**
vous	serez	all**és**
ils	seront	all**és**

IMPERATIVE

Present		
	va	
	allons	
	allez	

Past		
	sois	all**é**
	soyons	all**és**
	soyez	all**és**

SUBJUNCTIVE

Present		
(que) j'	aill**e**	
(que) tu	aill**es**	
(qu')il	aill**e**	
(que) nous	all**ions**	
(que) vous	all**iez**	
(qu')ils	aill**ent**	

Imperfect		
(que) j'	allass**e**	
(que) tu	allass**es**	
(qu')il	all**ât**	
(que) nous	allass**ions**	
(que) vous	allass**iez**	
(qu')ils	allass**ent**	

Perfect		
(que) je	sois	all**é**
(que) tu	sois	all**é**
(qu')il	soit	all**é**
(que) nous	soyons	all**és**
(que) vous	soyez	all**és**
(qu')ils	soient	all**és**

Pluperfect		
(que) je	fusse	all**é**
(que) tu	fusses	all**é**
(qu')il	fût	all**é**
(que) nous	fussions	all**és**
(que) vous	fussiez	all**és**
(qu')ils	fussent	all**és**

CONDITIONAL

Present		
j'	**irais**	
tu	**irais**	
il	**irait**	
nous	**irions**	
vous	**iriez**	
ils	**iraient**	

Past I		
je	serais	all**é**
tu	serais	all**é**
il	serait	all**é**
nous	serions	all**és**
vous	seriez	all**és**
ils	seraient	all**és**

Past II		
je	fusse	all**é**
tu	fusses	all**é**
il	fût	all**é**
nous	fussions	all**és**
vous	fussiez	all**és**
ils	fussent	all**és**

PARTICIPLE

Present all**ant**

Past all**é**, **-e**
étant all**é**

INFINITIVE

Present aller

Past être all**é**

10 faire

INDICATIVE

Present		
je	fais	
tu	fais	
il	fait	
nous	faisons	
vous	faites	
ils	font	

Imperfect		
je	fais**ais**	
tu	fais**ais**	
il	fais**ait**	
nous	fais**ions**	
vous	fais**iez**	
ils	fais**aient**	

Past historic		
je	fis	
tu	fis	
il	fit	
nous	fîmes	
vous	fîtes	
ils	firent	

Future		
je	fe**rai**	
tu	fe**ras**	
il	fe**ra**	
nous	fe**rons**	
vous	fe**rez**	
ils	fe**ront**	

Perfect		
j'	ai	fait
tu	as	fait
il	a	fait
nous	avons	fait
vous	avez	fait
ils	ont	fait

Pluperfect		
j'	avais	fait
tu	avais	fait
il	avait	fait
nous	avions	fait
vous	aviez	fait
ils	avaient	fait

Past anterior		
j'	eus	fait
tu	eus	fait
il	eut	fait
nous	eûmes	fait
vous	eûtes	fait
ils	eurent	fait

Future perfect		
j'	aurai	fait
tu	auras	fait
il	aura	fait
nous	aurons	fait
vous	aurez	fait
ils	auront	fait

IMPERATIVE

Present		
	fais	
	faisons	
	faites	

Past		
	aie	fait
	ayons	fait
	ayez	fait

SUBJUNCTIVE

Present		
(que) je	fass**e**	
(que) tu	fass**es**	
(qu')il	fasse	
(que) nous	fass**ions**	
(que) vous	fass**iez**	
(qu')ils	fass**ent**	

Imperfect		
(que) je	**fisse**	
(que) tu	**fisses**	
(qu')il	**fît**	
(que) nous	**fissions**	
(que) vous	**fissiez**	
(qu')ils	**fissent**	

Perfect		
(que) j'	aie	fait
(que) tu	aies	fait
(qu')il	ait	fait
(que) nous	ayons	fait
(que) vous	ayez	fait
(qu')ils	aient	fait

Pluperfect		
(que) j'	eusse	fait
(que) tu	eusses	fait
(qu')il	eût	fait
(que) nous	eussions	fait
(que) vous	eussiez	fait
(qu')ils	eussent	fait

CONDITIONAL

Present		
je	fe**rais**	
tu	fe**rais**	
il	fe**rait**	
nous	fe**rions**	
vous	fe**riez**	
ils	fe**raient**	

Past I		
j'	aurais	fait
tu	aurais	fait
il	aurait	fait
nous	aurions	fait
vous	auriez	fait
ils	auraient	fait

Past II		
j'	eusse	fait
tu	eusses	fait
il	eût	fait
nous	eussions	fait
vous	eussiez	fait
ils	eussent	fait

PARTICIPLE

Present faisant

Past fait, -e
ayant fait

INFINITIVE

Present faire

Past avoir fait

PASSIVE être aimé

INDICATIVE

Present

je suis aim**é**
tu es aim**é**
il est aim**é**
nous sommes aim**és**
vous êtes aim**és**
ils sont aim**és**

Imperfect

j' étais aim**é**
tu étais aim**é**
il était aim**é**
nous étions aim**és**
vous étiez aim**és**
ils étaient aim**és**

Past historic

je fus aim**é**
tu fus aim**é**
il fut aim**é**
nous fûmes aim**és**
vous fûtes aim**és**
ils furent aim**és**

Future

je serai aim**é**
tu seras aim**é**
il sera aim**é**
nous serons aim**és**
vous serez aim**és**
ils seront aim**és**

Perfect

j' ai été aim**é**
tu as été aim**é**
il a été aim**é**
nous avons été aim**és**
vous avez été aim**és**
ils ont été aim**és**

Pluperfect

j' avais été aim**é**
tu avais été aim**é**
il avait été aim**é**
nous avions été aim**és**
vous aviez été aim**és**
ils avaient été aim**és**

Past anterior

j' eus été aim**é**
tu eus été aim**é**
il eut été aim**é**
nous eûmes été aim**és**
vous eûtes été aim**és**
ils eurent été aim**és**

Future perfect

j' aurai été aim**é**
tu auras été aim**é**
il aura été aim**é**
nous aurons été aim**és**
vous aurez été aim**és**
ils auront été aim**és**

IMPERATIVE

Present sois aim**é**
soyons aim**és**
soyez aim**és**

Past *(obsolete)*

SUBJUNCTIVE

Present

(que) je sois aim**é**
(que) tu sois aim**é**
(qu')il soit aim**é**
(que) nous soyons aim**és**
(que) vous soyez aim**és**
(qu')ils soient aim**és**

Imperfect

(que) je fusse aim**é**
(que) tu fusses aim**é**
(qu')il fût aim**é**
(que) nous fussions aim**és**
(que) vous fussiez aim**és**
(qu')ils fussent aim**és**

Perfect

(que) j' aie été aim**é**
(que) tu aies été aim**é**
(qu')il ait été aim**é**
(que) nous ayons été aim**és**
(que) vous ayez été aim**és**
(qu')ils aient été aim**és**

Pluperfect

(que) j' eusse été aim**é**
(que) tu eusses été aim**é**
(qu')il eût été aim**é**
(que) nous eussions été aim**és**
(que) vous eussiez été aim**és**
(qu')ils eussent été aim**és**

CONDITIONAL

Present

je serais aim**é**
tu serais aim**é**
il serait aim**é**
nous serions aim**és**
vous seriez aim**és**
ils seraient aim**és**

Past I

j' aurais été aim**é**
tu aurais été aim**é**
il aurait été aim**é**
nous aurions été aim**és**
vous auriez été aim**és**
ils auraient été aim**és**

Past II

j' eusse été aim**é**
tu eusses été aim**é**
il eût été aim**é**
nous eussions été aim**és**
vous eussiez été aim**és**
ils eussent été aim**és**

PARTICIPLE

Present étant aim**é**

Past été aim**é**
ayant été aim**é**

INFINITIVE

Present être aim**é**

Past avoir été aim**é**

REFLEXIVE s'adonner

INDICATIVE

Present

je m' adonn**e**
tu t' adonn**es**
il s' adonn**e**
nous nous adonn**ons**
vous vous adonn**ez**
ils s' adonn**ent**

Imperfect

je m' adonn**ais**
tu t' adonn**ais**
il s' adonn**ait**
nous nous adonn**ions**
vous vous adonn**iez**
ils s' adonn**aient**

Past historic

je m' adonn**ai**
tu t' adonn**as**
il s' adonn**a**
nous nous adonn**âmes**
vous vous adonn**âtes**
ils s' adonn**èrent**

Future

je m' adonn**erai**
tu t' adonn**eras**
il s' adonn**era**
nous nous adonn**erons**
vous vous adonn**erez**
ils s' adonn**eront**

Perfect

je me suis adonn**é**
tu t' es adonn**é**
il s' est adonn**é**
nous nous sommes adonn**és**
vous vous êtes adonn**és**
ils se sont adonn**és**

Pluperfect

je m' étais adonn**é**
tu t' étais adonn**é**
il s' était adonn**é**
nous nous étions adonn**és**
vous vous étiez adonn**és**
ils s' étaient adonn**és**

Past anterior

je me fus adonn**é**
tu te fus adonn**é**
il se fut adonn**é**
nous nous fûmes adonn**és**
vous vous fûtes adonn**és**
ils se furent adonn**és**

Future perfect

je me serai adonn**é**
tu te seras adonn**é**
il se sera adonn**é**
nous nous serons adonn**és**
vous vous serez adonn**és**
ils se seront adonn**és**

IMPERATIVE

Present adonn**e** - toi
adonn**ons** - nous
adonn**ez** - vous

Past *(obsolete)*

SUBJUNCTIVE

Present

(que) je m' adonn**e**
(que) tu t' adonn**es**
(qu')il s' adonn**e**
(que) nous nous adonn**ions**
(que) vous vous adonn**iez**
(qu')ils s' adonn**ent**

Imperfect

(que) je m' adonn**asse**
(que) tu t' adonn**asses**
(qu')il s' adonn**ât**
(que) nous nous adonn**assions**
(que) vous vous adonn**assiez**
(qu')ils s' adonn**assent**

Perfect

(que) je me sois adonn**é**
(que) tu te sois adonn**é**
(qu')il se soit adonn**é**
(que) ns ns soyons adonn**és**
(que) vs vs soyez adonn**és**
(qu')ils se soient adonn**és**

Pluperfect

(que) je me fusse adonn**é**
(que) tu te fusses adonn**é**
(qu')il se fût adonn**é**
(que) ns ns fussions adonn**és**
(que) vs vs fussiez adonn**és**
(qu')ils se fussent adonn**és**

CONDITIONAL

Present

je m' adonn**erais**
tu t' adonn**erais**
il s' adonn**erait**
nous nous adonn**erions**
vous vous adonn**eriez**
ils s' adonn**eraient**

Past I

je me serais adonn**é**
tu te serais adonn**é**
il se serait adonn**é**
nous nous serions adonn**és**
vous vous seriez adonn**és**
ils se seraient adonn**és**

Past II

je me fusse adonn**é**
tu te fusses adonn**é**
il se fût adonn**é**
nous nous fussions adonn**és**
vous vous fussiez adonn**és**
ils se fussent adonn**és**

PARTICIPLE

Present s'adonn**ant**

Past s'étant adonn**é**

INFINITIVE Present

Present s'adonn**er**

Past s'être adonn**é**

INFINITIVE	Rules	INDICATIVE Present	Imperfect	Past Historic	Future
11 créer	*always* é	je crée, -es, -e, -ent nous créons, -ez	je créais …	je créai …	je créerai …
12 placer	c	je place, -es, -e, -ez, -ent	nous placions, -iez	ils placèrent	je placerai …
	ç *before* a *and* o	nous plaçons	je plaçais, -ais, -ait, -aient	je plaçai, -as, -a, -âmes, -âtes	
13 manger	g	je mange, -es, -e, -ez, -ent	nous mangions, -iez	ils mangèrent	je mangerai …
	ge *before* a *and* o	nous mangeons	je mangeais, -eais, -eait, -eaient	je mangeai, -as, -a, -âmes, -âtes	
14 céder	è *before silent final syllable*	je cède, -es, -e, -ent			
	é	nous cédons, -ez	je cédais …	je cédai …	je céderai …
15 assiéger	è *before silent final syllable*	j'assiège, -es, -e, -ent			
	ge *before* a *and* o	nous assiégeons	j'assiégeais, -eais, -eait, -eaient	j'assiégeai	
	é *before silent syllable*				j'assiégerai …
16 lever	è *before silent syllable*	je lève, -es, -e, -ent			je lèverai …
	e	nous levons, -ez	je levais …	je levai …	
17 geler	è *before silent syllable*	je gèle, -es, -e, -ent			je gèlerai …
	e	nous gelons, -ez	je gelais …	je gelai …	
18 acheter	è *before silent syllable*	j'achète, -es, -e, -ent			j'achèterai …
	e	nous achetons, -ez	j'achetais …	j'achetai …	
19 appeler	ll *before mute* e	j'appelle, -es, -e, -ent			j'appellerai …
	l	nous appelons, -ez	j'appelais …	j'appelai …	
20 jeter	tt *before mute* e	je jette, -es, -e, -ent			je jetterai …
	t	nous jetons, -ez	je jetais …	je jetai …	
21 payer	i *before mute* e	je paie, -es, -e, -ent			je paierai …
	or y	je paye, -es, -e, -ent nous payons, -ez	je payais …	je payai …	je payerai …

CONDITIONAL	SUBJUNCTIVE		IMPERATIVE	PARTICIPLE		
Present	**Present**	**Imperfect**		**Present**	**Past**	
je créerais …	que je crée …	que je créasse …	crée	créant	créé, -e	**11**
			créons, -ez			
je placerais …	que je place …		place, -ez		placé, -e	**12**
		que je plaçasse …	plaçons	plaçant		
je mangerais …	que je mange …		mange, -ez		mangé, -e	**13**
		que je mangeasse …	mangeons	mangeant		
	que je cède, -es, -e, -ent		cède			**14**
je céderais …	que nous cédions, -iez	que je cédasse …	cédons, -ez	cédant	cédé, -e	
	que j'assiège …		assiège			**15**
j'assiégerais …	que nous assiégions , -iez	que j'assiégeasse …	assiégeons	assiégeant	assiégé, -e	
je lèverais …	que je lève, -es, -e, -ent		lève			**16**
	que nous levions, -iez	que je levasse …	levons, -ez	levant	levé, -e	
je gèlerais …	que je gèle, -es, -e, -ent		gèle			**17**
	que nous gelions, -iez	que je gelasse …	gelons, -ez	gelant	gelé, -e	
j'achèterais …	que j'achète, -es, -e, -ent		achète			**18**
	que nous achetions, -iez	que j'achetasse …	achetons, -ez	achetant	acheté, -e	
j'appellerais …	que j'appelle, -es, -e, -ent		appelle			**19**
	que nous appelions, -iez	que j'appelasse …	appelons, -ez	appelant	appelé, -e	
je jetterais …	que je jette, -es, -e, -ent		jette			**20**
	que nous jetions, -iez	que je jetasse …	jetons, -ez	jetant	jeté, -e	
je paierais …	que je paie, -es, -e, -ent		paie			**21**
je payerais …	que je paye, -es, -e, -ent	que je payasse …	paye			
	que nous payions, -iez		payons, -ez	payant	payé, -e	

INFINITIVE	Rules	INDICATIVE			
		Present	Imperfect	Past Historic	Future
22 essuyer	i *before mute* e	j'essuie, -es, -e, -ent			j'essuierai …
	y	nous essuyons, -ez	j'essuyais	j'essuyai …	
23 employer	i *before mute* e	j'emploie, -es, -e, -ent			j'emploierai …
	y	nous employons, -ez	j'employais …	j'employai …	
24 envoyer	i *before mute* e	j'envoie, -es, -e, -ent			
	y	nous envoyons, -ez	j'envoyais …	j'envoyai …	
	err				j'enverrai …
25 haïr	i	je hais, -s, -t			
	ï	ns haïssons, -ez, -ent	je haïssais …	je haïs … (haïmes, haïtes)	je haïrai …
26 courir		je cours …	je courais …	je courus …	je courrai …
27 cueillir		je cueille, -es, -e, nous cueillons …	je cueillais …	je cueillis …	je cueillerai …
28 assaillir		j'assaille, -es, -e, nous assaillons, -ez, -ent	j'assaillais …	j'assaillis …	j'assaillirai …
29 fuir	i *before consonants and* e	je fuis, -s, -t, -ent		je fuis …	je fuirai …
	y *before* a, ez, i, o	nous fuyons, -ez	je fuyais …		
30 partir	*without* t	je pars …			
	with t	il part …	je partais …	je partis …	je partirai …
31 bouillir	ou	je bous, s, t			
	ouill	nous bouillons …	je bouillais …	je bouillis …	je bouillirai …
32 couvrir		je couvre, -es, -e, nous couvrons …	je couvrais …	je couvris …	je couvrirai
33 vêtir		je vêts …	je vêtais …	je vêtis …	je vêtirai …
34 mourir	eur	je meurs, -s, -t, -ent			
	our	nous mourons, -ez	je mourais …	je mourus …	je mourrai …
35 acquérir	quier	j'acquiers, -s, -t, -ièrent			
	quer	nous acquérons -ez	j'acquérais …		j'acquerrai …
	qu			j'acquis …	

CONDITIONAL	SUBJUNCTIVE		IMPERATIVE	PARTICIPLE		
Present	Present	Imperfect		Present	Past	
j'essuierais …	que j'essuie, -es, -e, -ent		essuie			22
	que nous essuyions, -iez	que j'essuyasse…	essuyons, -ez	essuyant	essuyé, e	
j'emploierais …	que j'emploie, -es, -e, -ent		emploie			23
	que nous employions, -iez	que j'employasse …	employons, -ez	employant	employé, -e	
	que j'envoie, -es, -e, -ent		envoie			24
	que nous envoyions, -iez	que j'envoyasse …	envoyons, -ez	envoyant	envoyé, -e	
j'enverrais …						
			hais			25
je haïrais …	que je haïsse, qu'il haïsse	que je haïsse, qu'il haït	haïssons, haïssez	haïssant	haï, -e	
je courrais …	que je coure …	que je courusse …	cours, courons, -ez	courant	couru, -e	26
je cueillerais …			cueille			27
	que je cueille …	que je cueillisse …	cuillons, -ez	cueillant	cueilli, -e	
			assaille			28
j'assaillirais …	que j'assaille …	que j'assaillisse	assaillons, -ez	assaillant	assailli, -e	
je fuirais …	que je fuie, -es, -e, -ent	que je fuisse	fuis		fui, -e	29
	que nous fuyions, -iez		fuyons, -ez	fuyant		
			pars			30
je partirais …	que je parte …	que je partisse …	partons, -ez	partant	parti, -e	
			bous			31
je bouillirais …	que je bouille …	que je bouillisse …	bouillons, -ez	bouillant	bouilli, -e	
	que je couvre, -es, -e,		couvre			32
je couvrirais …	que nous couvrions …	que je couvrisse …	couvrons, -ez	couvrant	couvert, -e	
je vêtirais …	que je vête …	que je vêtisse …	vêts vêtons, vêtez	vêtant	vêtu, -e	33
	que je meure …		meurs		mort, -e	34
je mourrais …		que je mourusse …	mourons, -ez	mourant		
	que j'acquière, -es, -e, -ent		acquiers			35
j'acquerrais …	que nous acquérions, -iez		acquérons, -ez	acquérant		
		que j'acquisse …			acquis, -e	

INFINITIVE	Rules	INDICATIVE Present	Imperfect	Past Historic	Future
36 venir	i	je viens, -s, -t, -nent		je vins … ils vinrent	je viendrai …
	e	nous venons, -ez	je venais …		
37 gésir	*Defective*	je gis, tu gis, il gît, nous gisons, -ez, -ent	je gisais …		
38 ouïr	*Archaic*	j'ois … nous oyons …	j'oyais …	j' ouïs …	j' ouïrai …
39 pleuvoir		il pleut	il pleuvait	il plut	il pleuvra
		ils pleuvent	ils pleuvaient	ils plurent	ils pleuvront
40 pourvoir	i	je pourvois, -s, -t, -ent			je pourvoirai …
	y	nous pourvoyons, -ez	je pourvoyais …		
	u			je pourvus …	
41 asseoir	ie	j'assieds, -ds, -d			j' assiérai …
	ey	nous asseyons, -ez, -ent	j' asseyais …		
	i			j'assis …	
asseoir (oi/oy *replace* ie/ey)	oi	j'assois, -s, -t, -ent			j' assoirai …
	oy	nous assoyons, -ez	j' assoyais …		
42 prévoir	oi	je prévois, -s, -t, -ent			je prévoirai …
	oy	nous prévoyons, -ez	je prévoyais …		
	i/u			je prévis …	
43 mouvoir	eu	je meus, -s, -t, -vent			
	ou	nous mouvons, -ez	je mouvais …		mouvrai …
	u			je mus, -s, -t, -(û)mes, -(û)tes, -rent	
44 devoir	û *in the past participle masc. sing.*	je dois, -s, -t -vent		je dus …	
		nous devons, -ez	je devais …		je devrai …
45 valoir	au, aille	je vaux, -x, -t			je vaudrai …
	al	nous valons, -ez, -ent	je valais …	je valus …	
prévaloir					

CONDITIONAL	SUBJUNCTIVE		IMPERATIVE	PARTICIPLE		
Present	Present	Imperfect		Present	Past	
je viendrais …	que je vienne, -es, -e, -ent	que je vinsse …	viens			36
	que nous venions, -iez		venons, -ez	venant	venu, -e	
				gisant		37
j' ouïrais …	que j'oie …	que j'ouïsse …	ois		ouï, -e	38
	nous oyions …		oyons, -ez	oyant		
il pleuvrait	qu'il pleuve	qu'il plût		pleuvant	plu	39
ils pleuvraient	qu'ils pleuvent	qu'ils plussent				
je pourvoirais …	que je pourvoie, -es, -e, -ent		pourvois			40
	que nous pourvoyions, -iez		pourvoyons, -ez	pourvoyant		
		que je pourvusse …			pourvu, -e	
je assiérais …			assieds			41
	que j' asseye … que nous asseyions …		asseyons, -ez	asséyant		
		que j'assisse …			assis, -e	
j' assoirais …	que j'assoie, -es, -e, -ent		assois			
	que nous assoyions, -iez		assoyons, -ez	assoyant		
je prévoirais …	que je prévoie, -es, -e, -ent		prévois			42
	que ns prévoyions, -iez		prévoyons, -ez	prévoyant		
		que je prévisse …			prévu, -e	
	que je meuve, -es, -e, -ent		meus			43
je mouvrais …	que nous mouvions, -iez		mouvons, -ez	mouvant		
		que je musse …			mû, mue	
	que je doive, -es, -e, -ent	que je dusse …	dois		dû, due	44
je devrais …	que nous devions, -iez		devons, -ez	devant		
je vaudrais …	que je vaille, -es, -e, -ent		vaux			45
	que nous valions, -iez	que je valusse …	valons, -ez	valant	valu, -e	
	que je prévale, -es, -e					

INFINITIVE	Rules	INDICATIVE Present	Imperfect	Past Historic	Future
46 voir	oi	je vois, -s, -t, -ent			
	oy	nous voyons, -ez	je voyais …		
	i/e/u			je vis …	je verrai …
47 savoir	5 forms	je sais, -s, -t, nous savons, ez, -ent	je savais …	je sus …	je saurai …
48 vouloir	veu/veuil	je veux, -x, -t, veulent			
	voul/voudr	nous voulons, -ez	je voulais …	je voulus …	je voudrai …
49 pouvoir	eu/u(i)	je peux, -x, -t, peuvent		je pus …	
	ouv/our	nous pouvons, -ez	je pouvais …		je pourrai …
50 falloir	*Impersonal*	il faut	il fallait	il fallut	il faudra
51 déchoir	choir *and* échoir *are defective*	je déchois, -s, -t, -ent nous déchoyons, -ez	je déchoyais …	je déchus …	je décherrai …
52 prendre	prend	je prends, -ds, -d			je prendrai …
	pren	nous prenons, -ez ils prennent	je prenais …		
	pri(s)			je pris …	
53 rompre		je romps, -ps, -pt, nous rompons …	je rompais …	je rompis …	je romprai …
54 craindre	ain/aind	je crains, -s, -t			je craindrai …
	aign	nous craignons, -ez, -ent	je craignais …	je craignis …	
55 peindre	ein	je peins, -s, -t			je peindrai …
	eign	nous peignons, -ez, -ent	je peignais …	je peignis …	
56 joindre	oin/oind	je joins, -s, -t			je joindrai …
	oign	nous joignons, -ez, -ent	je joignais …	je joignis …	
57 vaincre	ainc	je vaincs, -cs, -c			je vaincrai …
	ainqu	nous vainquons, -ez, -ent	je vainquais …	je vainquis …	
58 traire	i	je trais, -s, -t, -ent		(*obsolete*)	je trairai …
	y	nous trayons, -ez	je trayais …		

CONDITIONAL	SUBJUNCTIVE		IMPERATIVE	PARTICIPLE		
Present	**Present**	**Imperfect**		**Present**	**Past**	
je verrais …	que je voie, -es, -e, -ent que nous voyions, -iez	que je visse …	vois voyons, -ez	voyant	vu, -e	**46**
je saurais …	que je sache …	que je susse …	sache, -ons, -ez	sachant	su, -e	**47**
je voudrais …	que je veuille, -es, -e, -ent que nous voulions, -iez	que je voulusse …	veux (veuille) voulons, -ez (veuillez)	voulant	voulu, -e	**48**
je pourrais …	que je puisse …	que je pusse …	(*obsolete*)	pouvant	pu	**49**
il faudrait	qu'il faille	qu'il fallût	(*no form*)	(*obsolete*)	fallu	**50**
je décherrais …	que je déchoie, -es, -e, -ent que nous déchoyions, -iez	que je déchusse …	déchois déchoyons, -ez	(*no form but* échéant)	déchu, -e	**51**
je prendrais …	que je prenne …	que je prisse …	prends prenons, -ez	prenant	pris, -e	**52**
je romprais …	que je rompe …	que je rompisse …	romps -pons, -pez	rompant	rompu, -e	**53**
je craindrais …	que je craigne …	que je craignisse …	crains craignons, -ez	craignant	craint, -e	**54**
je peindrais …	que je peigne …	que je peignisse …	peins peignons, -ez	peignant	peint, -e	**55**
je joindrais …	que je joigne …	que je joignisse …	joins joignons, -ez	joignant	joint, -e	**56**
je vaincrais …	que je vainque …	que je vainquisse …	vaincs vainquons, -ez	vainquant	vaincu, -e	**57**
je trairais …	que je traie, -es, -e, -ent que nous trayions, -yiez	(*obsolete*)	trais trayons, -ez	trayant	trait, -e	**58**

INFINITIVE	Rules	INDICATIVE Present	Imperfect	Past Historic	Future
59 plaire	ai	je plais, tu plais, il plaît (*but* il tait) nous plaisons …	je plaisais …		je plairai …
	u			je plus …	
60 mettre	met	je mets, nous mettons	je mettais …		je mettrai …
	mis			je mis …	
61 battre	t	je bats, -ts, -t			
	tt	nous battons …	je battais …	je battis …	je battrai …
62 suivre	ui	je suis, -s, -t			
	uiv	nous suivons …	je suivais …	je suivis …	je suivrai …
63 vivre	vi/viv	je vis, -s, -t, nous vivons …	je vivais …		je vivrai …
	véc			je vécus …	
64 suffire		je suffis, -s, -t, nous suffisons …	je suffisais …	je suffis …	je suffirai …
65 médire		je médis, -s, -t, nous médisons, vous médisez (*but* vous dites, redites)	je médisais …	je médis …	je médirai …
66 lire	i	je lis, -s, -t			je lirai …
	is	nous lisons, -ez, -ent	je lisais …		
	u			je lus …	
67 écrire	i	j'écris, -s, -t			j' écrirai …
	iv	nous écrivons, -ez, -ent	j' écrivais …	j' écrivis …	
68 rire		je ris, -s, -t, nous rions …	je riais … nous riions, -iez	je ris … nous rîmes …	je rirai …
69 conduire		je conduis …	je conduisais …	je conduisis…	je conduirai …
70 boire	oi	je bois, -s, -t, -vent			je boirai …
	u(v)	nous buvons, -ez	je buvais …	je bus …	
71 croire	oi	je crois, -s, -t, ils croient			je croirai …
	oy	nous croyons, -ez	je croyais …		
	u			je crus …	

CONDITIONAL	SUBJUNCTIVE		IMPERATIVE	PARTICIPLE		
Present	Present	Imperfect		Present	Past	
je plairais …	que je plaise …		plais plaisons, -ez	plaisant		59
		que je plusse …			plu	
je mettrais …	que je mette …		mets mettons, -ez	mettant		60
		que je misse …			mis, -e	
			bats			61
je battrais …	que je batte …	que je battisse …	battons, -ez	battant	battu, -e	
			suis			62
je suivrais …	que je suive …	que je suivisse …	suivons, -ez	suivant	suivi, -e	
je vivrais …	que je vive …		vis vivons, -ez	vivant		63
		que je vécusse …			vécu, -e	
je suffirais …	que je suffise …	que je suffisse …	suffis suffisons, -ez	suffisant	suffi (*but* confit, déconfit, frit, circoncis)	64
je médirais …	que je médise … que nous médisions, -iez	que je médisse …	médis médisons médisez (but dites, redites)	médisant	médit	65
je lirais …			lis			66
	que je lise …		lisons, -ez	lisant		
		que je lusse …			lu, -e	
j'écrirais …			écris		écrit, -e	67
	que j'écrive …	que j'écrivisse …	écrivons, -ez	écrivant		
je rirais …	que je rie …	que je risse …	ris, rions, riez	riant	ri	68
	que nous riions, -iez	que nous rissions …				
je conduirais …	que je conduise …	que je conduisisse …	conduis conduisons, -ez	conduisant	conduit, -e (*but* lui, nui)	69
je boirais …	que je boive, -es, -e, -ent		bois			70
	que nous buvions, -iez	que je busse …	buvons, -ez	buvant	bu, -e	
je croirais …	que je croie …		crois			71
			croyons, -ez	croyant		
		que je crusse …			cru, -e	

INFINITIVE	Rules	INDICATIVE			
		Present	**Imperfect**	**Past Historic**	**Future**
72 croître	oî	je croîs, -s, -t			je croîtrai …
	oiss	nous croissons, -ez, -ent	je croissais …		
	û			je crûs …	
73 connaître		je connais, -s, -ssons, -ssez, -ssent	je connaissais …	je connus …	
	î *before* t	il connaît			je connaîtrai …
74 naître		je nais, nais,			
	î *before* t	naît			je naîtrai ...
	naisse	nous naissons, -ez, -ent	je naissais …		
	naqu			je naquis …	
75 résoudre	ou/oudr	je résous, -s, -t		(absoudre *and* dissoudre *have no past historic*)	je résoudrai...
	ol/olv	nous résolvons, -ez, -ent	je résolvais …		
	olu			je résolus …	
76 coudre	oud	je couds, -ds, -d			je coudrai …
	ous	nous cousons, -ez, -ent	je cousais …	je cousis …	
77 moudre	moud	je mouds, -ds, -d			je moudrai …
	moul	nous moulons, -ez, -ent	je moulais …	je moulus …	
78 conclure		je conclus, -s, -t, nous concluons, -ez, -ent	je concluais …	je conclus …	je conclurai …
79 clore	*Defective*	je clos, -os, -ôt ils closent	(*obsolete*)	(*obsolete*)	je clorai …
80 maudire		je maudis, -s, -t nous maudissons, -ez, -ent	je maudissais ...	je maudis ...	je maudirai ...

CONDITIONAL	SUBJUNCTIVE		IMPERATIVE	PARTICIPLE		
Present	Present	Imperfect		Present	Past	
je croîtrais…	que je croisse …	que je crûsse …	croîs croissons, -ez	croissant	crû, crue (*but* accru, -e)	**72**
je connaîtrais …	que je connaisse …	que je connusse …	connais, -ssons, -ssez	connaissant	connu, -e	**73**
je naîtrais ...	que je naisse …	que je naquisse …	nais naissons, -ez	naissant	né, -e	**74**
je résoudrais …	que je résolve …	que je résolusse …	résous résolvons, -ez	résolvant	(absous, -oute; dissous, -oute) résolu, -e	**75**
je coudrais …	que je couse …	que je cousisse …	couds cousons, -ez	cousant	cousu, -e	**76**
je moudrais …	que je moule …	que je moulusse …	mouds moulons, -ez	moulant	moulu, -e	**77**
je conclurais …	que je conclue …	que je conclusse …	conclus concluons, -ez	concluant	conclu, -e (*but* inclus, -e)	**78**
je clorais …	que je close …	(*obsolete*)	clos	closant	clos, -e	**79**
je maudirais ...	que je maudisse qu'il maudisse	que je maudisse qu'il maudît	maudis -ssons, -ssez	maudissant	maudit, -e	**80**

Verbes irréguliers anglais

Vous trouverez ci-après la liste des formes irrégulières des verbes qui figurent dans le dictionnaire, à l'exception :

- des verbes composés s'écrivant avec un trait d'union et dont l'un des éléments est un verbe irrégulier (ex. *baby-sit*) ;
- des verbes dont on double la dernière consonne au prétérit et au participe passé (ex. *spot*) (la conjugaison est indiquée dans le dictionnaire pour cette catégorie) ;
- des verbes dont le *y* final devient *-ie* dès que l'on ajoute la désinence *-d* ou *-s* (ex. *try*).

Les verbes dont les formes irrégulières ne s'appliquent qu'à certains sens sont signalés par un astérisque (*) (ex. *costed*).

Infinitif	Prétérit	Participe Passé
abide	abode, abided	abode, abided
arise	arose	arisen
awake	awoke	awoken
be	was/were	been
bear	bore	borne
beat	beat	beaten
become	became	become
befall	befell	befallen
beget	begot, begat††	begotten
begin	began	begun
behold	beheld	beheld
bend	bent	bent
beseech	beseeched, besought	beseeched, besought
beset	beset	beset
bespeak	bespoke	bespoke, bespoken
bet	bet, betted	bet, betted
bid	bade, bid	bidden, bid
bind	bound	bound
bite	bit	bitten
bleed	bled	bled
blow	blew	blown
break	broke	broken
breed	bred	bred
bring	brought	brought
broadcast	broadcast	broadcast
browbeat	browbeat	browbeaten
build	built	built
burn	burned, burnt *GB*	burned, burnt *GB*
bust	bust, busted *GB*	bust, busted *GB*
buy	bought	bought
cast	cast	cast
catch	caught	caught
choose	chose	chosen
cleave	clove, cleaved	cleft, cleaved, cloven
cling	clung	clung
come	came	come
cost	cost, *costed	cost, *costed
creep	crept	crept
crow	crowed, crew††	crowed
cut	cut	cut
deal	dealt	dealt
dig	dug	dug
dive	dived *GB*, dove *US*	dived
do	did	done
draw	drew	drawn
dream	dreamed, dreamt *GB*	dreamed, dreamt *GB*
drink	drank	drunk
drive	drove	driven
dwell	dwelt	dwelt
eat	ate	eaten
fall	fell	fallen
feed	fed	fed
feel	felt	felt
fight	fought	fought
find	found	found
flee	fled	fled
fling	flung	flung
floodlight	floodlit	floodlit
fly	flew	flown
forbear	forbore	forborne
forbid	forbade, forbad	forbidden
forecast	forecast	forecast
foresee	foresaw	foreseen
foretell	foretold	foretold
forget	forgot	forgotten
forgive	forgave	forgiven
forsake	forsook	forsaken
forswear	forswore	forsworn
freeze	froze	frozen
gainsay	gainsaid	gainsaid

Infinitif	Prétérit	Participe Passé
get	got	got, gotten *US*
give	gave	given
go	went	gone
grind	ground	ground
grow	grew	grown
hamstring	hamstrung	hamstrung
hang	hung, *hanged	hung, *hanged
have	had	had
hear	heard	heard
heave	heaved, *hove	heaved, *hove
hew	hewed	hewn, hewed
hide	hid	hidden
hit	hit	hit
hold	held	held
hurt	hurt	hurt
inlay	inlaid	inlaid
inset	inset	inset
interweave	interwove	interwoven
keep	kept	kept
kneel	kneeled, knelt	kneeled, knelt
knit	knitted, knit	knitted, knit
know	knew	known
lay	laid	laid
lead	led	led
lean	leaned, leant *GB*	leaned, leant *GB*
leap	leaped, leapt *GB*	leaped, leapt *GB*
learn	learned, learnt *GB*	learned, learnt *GB*
leave	left	left
lend	lent	lent
let	let	let
lie	lay	lain
light	lit, *lighted	lit, *lighted
lose	lost	lost
make	made	made
mean	meant	meant
meet	met	met
miscast	miscast	miscast
misdeal	misdealt	misdealt
mishear	misheard	misheard
mislay	mislaid	mislaid
mislead	misled	misled
misread /ˌmɪsˈriːd/	misread /ˌmɪsˈred/	misread /ˌmɪsˈred/
misspell	misspelled, misspelt *GB*	misspelled, misspelt *GB*
misspend	misspent	misspent
mistake	mistook	mistaken
misunderstand	misunderstood	misunderstood
mow	mowed	mowed, mown
outbid	outbid	outbid, outbidden *US*
outdo	outdid	outdone
outgrow	outgrew	outgrown
output	output, outputted	output, outputted
outrun	outran	outrun
outsell	outsold	outsold

Infinitif	Prétérit	Participe Passé
outshine	outshone	outshone
overbid	overbid	overbid
overcome	overcame	overcome
overdo	overdid	overdone
overdraw	overdrew	overdrawn
overeat	overate	overeaten
overfly	overflew	overflown
overhang	overhung	overhung
overhear	overheard	overheard
overlay	overlaid	overlaid
overlie	overlay	overlain
overpay	overpaid	overpaid
override	overrode	overridden
overrun	overran	overrun
oversee	oversaw	overseen
overshoot	overshot	overshot
oversleep	overslept	overslept
overtake	overtook	overtaken
overthrow	overthrew	overthrown
partake	partook	partaken
pay	paid	paid
plead	pleaded, pled *US*	pleaded, pled *US*
prove	proved	proved, proven
put	put	put
quit	quit, quitted	quit, quitted
read /riːd/	read /red/	read /red/
rebuild	rebuilt	rebuilt
recast	recast	recast
redo	redid	redone
rehear	reheard	reheard
remake	remade	remade
rend	rent	rent
repay	repaid	repaid
reread /-riːd/	reread /-red/	reread /-red/
rerun	reran	rerun
resell	resold	resold
reset	reset	reset
resit	resat	resat
retake	retook	retaken
retell	retold	retold
rewrite	rewrote	rewritten
rid	rid	rid
ride	rode	ridden
ring	rang	rung
rise	rose	risen
run	ran	run
saw	sawed	sawed, sawn *GB*
say	said	said
see	saw	seen
seek	sought	sought
sell	sold	sold
send	sent	sent
set	set	set
sew	sewed	sewn, sewed
shake	shook	shaken
shear	sheared	shorn, *sheared
shed	shed	shed

Infinitif	Prétérit	Participe Passé
shine	shone, *shined	shone, *shined
shit	shat	shat
shoe	shod	shod
shoot	shot	shot
show	showed	shown
shrink	shrank	shrunk, shrunken
shrive	shrived, shrove	shrived, shriven
shut	shut	shut
sing	sang	sung
sink	sank	sunk
sit	sat	sat
slay	slew	slain
sleep	slept	slept
slide	slid	slid
sling	slung	slung
slink	slunk	slunk
slit	slit	slit
smell	smelled, smelt *GB*	smelled, smelt *GB*
smite	smote	smitten
sow	sowed	sowed, sown
speak	spoke	spoken
speed	sped, *speeded	sped, *speeded
spell	spelled, spelt *GB*	spelled, spelt *GB*
spend	spent	spent
spill	spilled, spilt *GB*	spilled, spilt *GB*
spin	spun, span††	spun
spit	spat	spat
split	split	split
spoil	spoiled, spoilt *GB*	spoiled, spoilt *GB*
spotlight	spotlit, spotlighted	spotlit, spotlighted
spread	spread	spread
spring	sprang	sprung
stand	stood	stood
stave	staved, stove	staved, stove
steal	stole	stolen
stick	stuck	stuck
sting	stung	stung
stink	stank	stunk
strew	strewed	strewed, strewn
stride	strode	stridden
strike	struck	struck
string	strung	strung
strive	strove	striven
sublet	sublet	sublet
swear	swore	sworn
sweep	swept	swept

Infinitif	Prétérit	Participe Passé
swell	swelled	swollen, swelled
swim	swam	swum
swing	swung	swung
take	took	taken
teach	taught	taught
tear	tore	torn
tell	told	told
think	thought	thought
thrive	thrived, throve	thrived, thriven††
throw	threw	thrown
thrust	thrust	thrust
tread	trod	trodden
underbid	underbid	underbid
undercut	undercut	undercut
undergo	underwent	undergone
underlie	underlay	underlain
underpay	underpaid	underpaid
undersell	undersold	undersold
understand	understood	understood
undertake	undertook	undertaken
underwrite	underwrote	underwritten
undo	undid	undone
unfreeze	unfroze	unfrozen
unlearn	unlearned, unlearnt *GB*	unlearned, unlearnt *GB*
unstick	unstuck	unstuck
unwind	unwound	unwound
uphold	upheld	upheld
upset	upset	upset
wake	woke	woken
waylay	waylaid	waylaid
wear	wore	worn
weave	wove, weaved	woven, weaved
wed	wedded, wed	wedded, wed
weep	wept	wept
wet	wet, wetted	wet, wetted
win	won	won
wind /waɪnd/	wound /waʊnd/	wound /waʊnd/
withdraw	withdrew	withdrawn
withhold	withheld	withheld
withstand	withstood	withstood
wring	wrung	wrung
write	wrote	written

La Constitution française

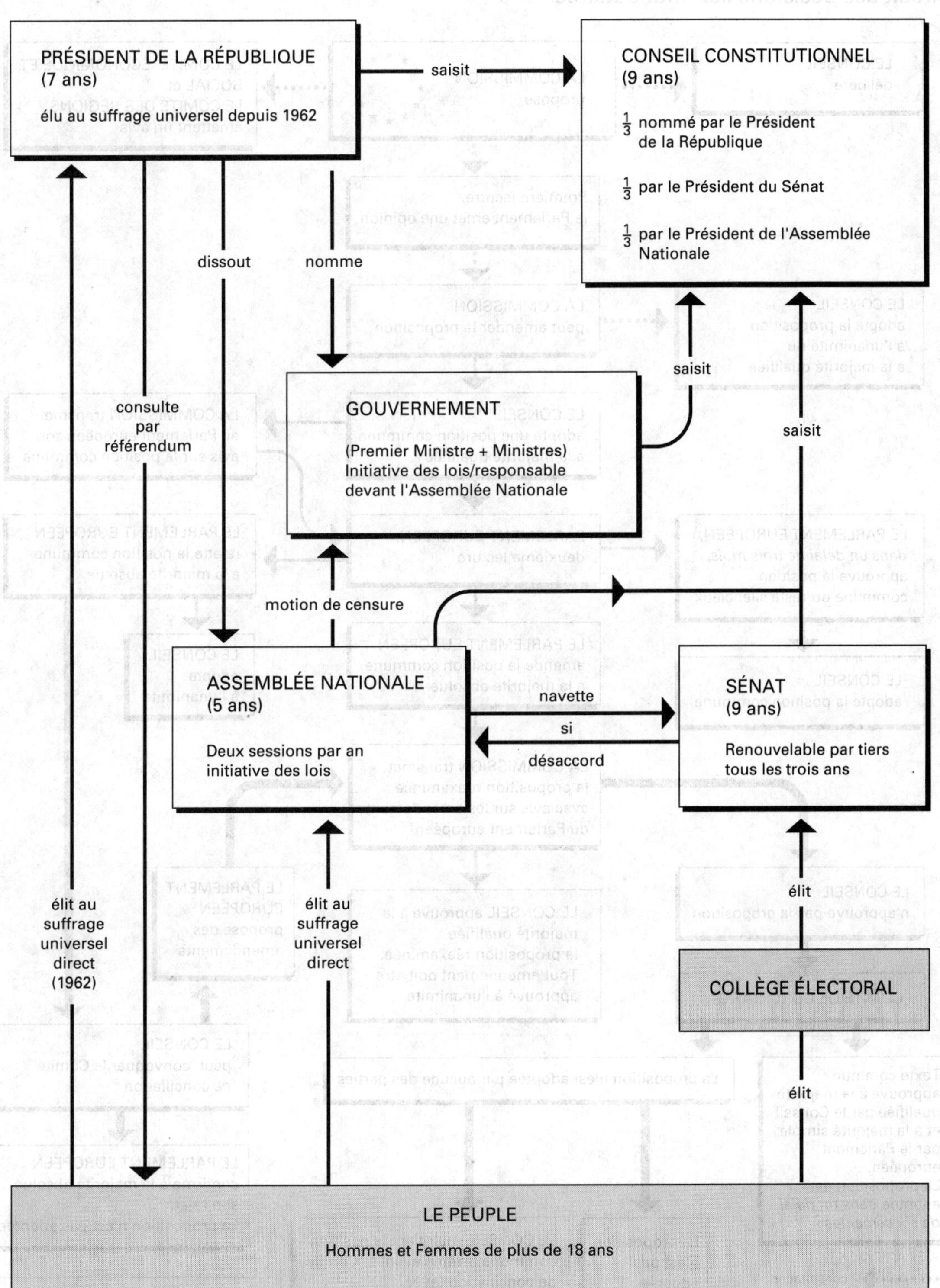

Le droit de vote (antérieurement à 21 ans) est fixé à 18 ans depuis 1974

Circuit des décisions communautaires

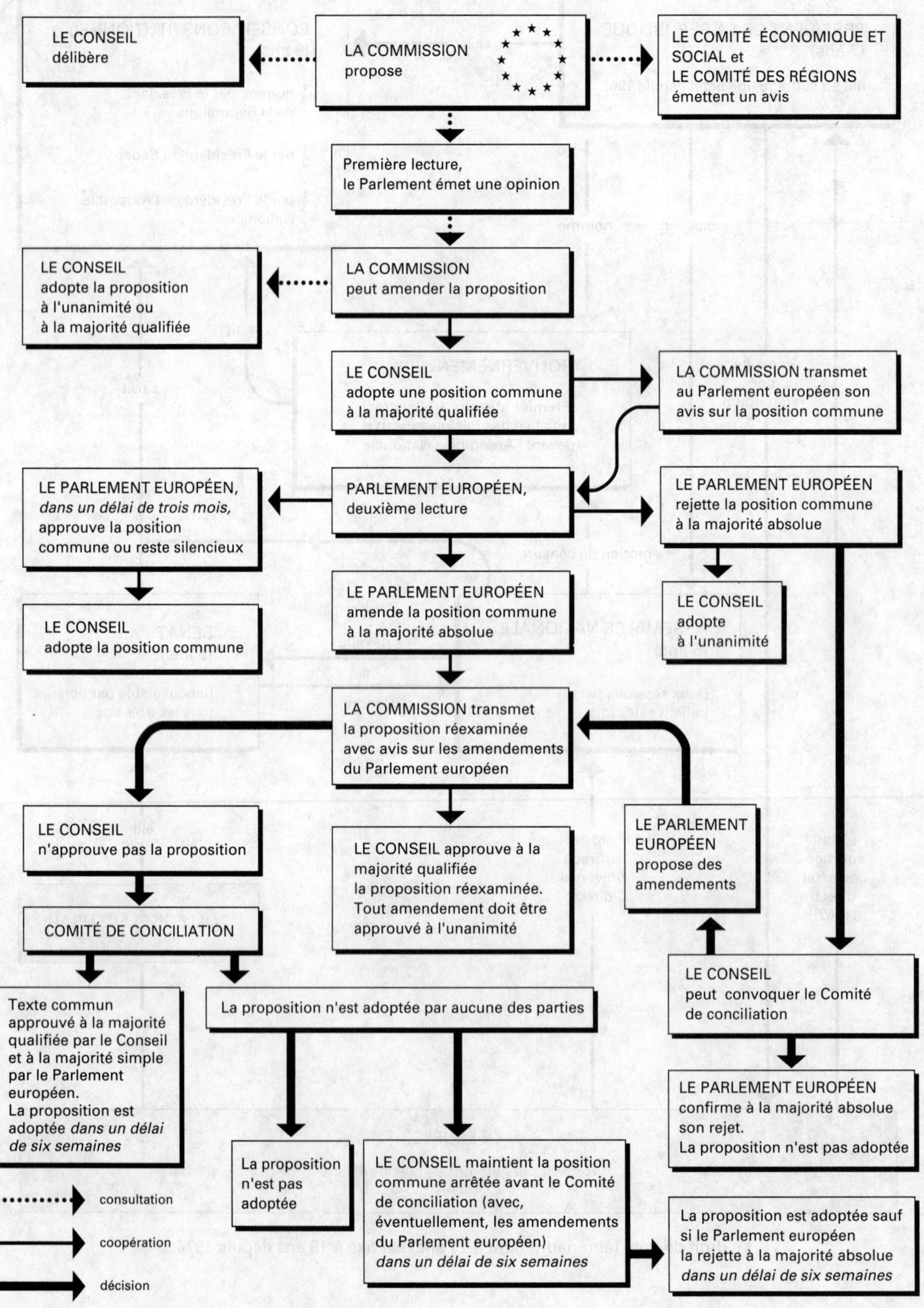

Procedure for legislation

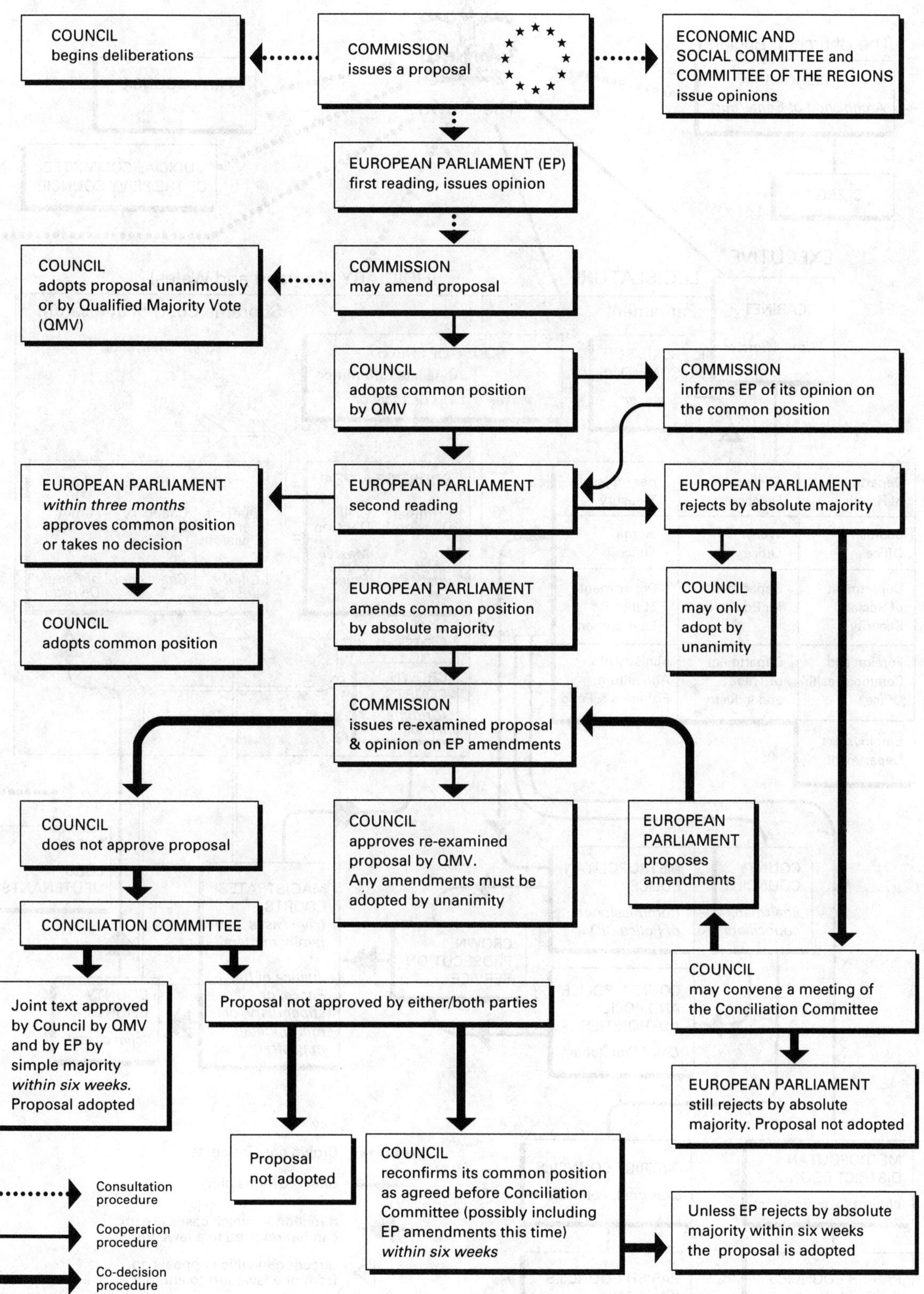

Reproduced with permission from the Local Government International Bureau's European Information Service.

The constitution in the United Kingdom

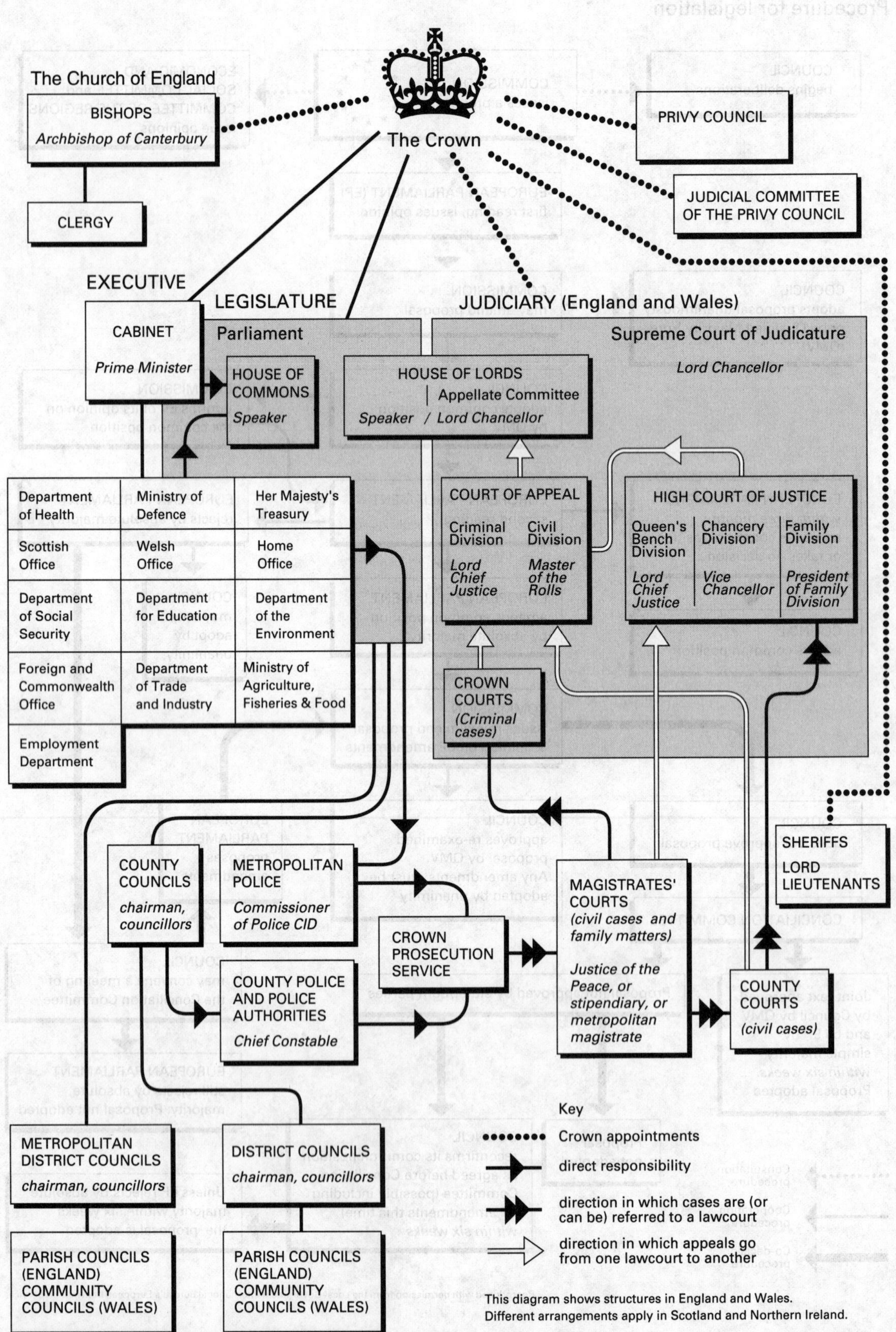

This diagram shows structures in England and Wales.
Different arrangements apply in Scotland and Northern Ireland.

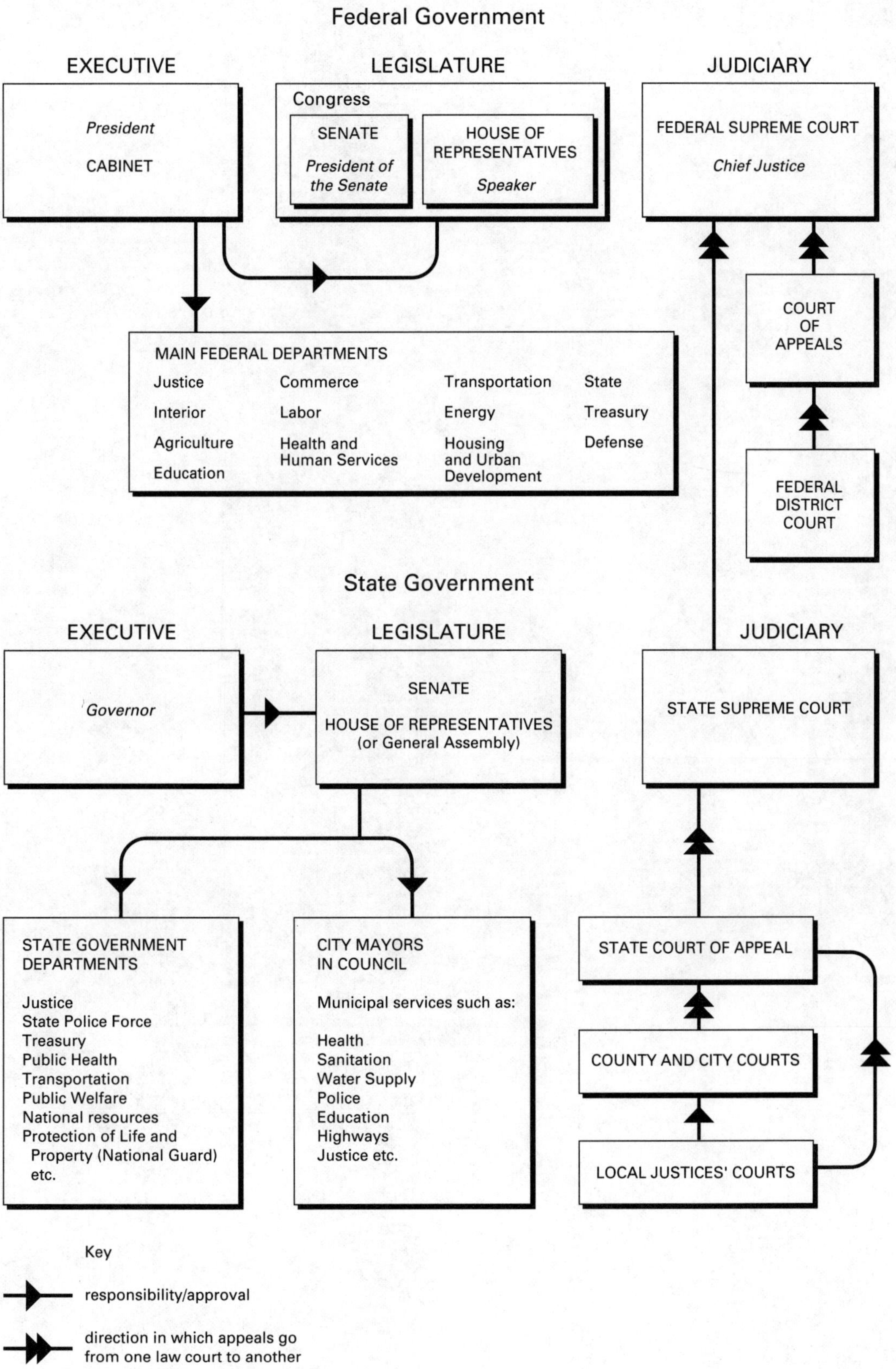

Federal Government
EXECUTIVE
President
CABINET
LEGISLATURE
Congress
SENATE
President of the Senate
HOUSE OF REPRESENTATIVES
Speaker
JUDICIARY
FEDERAL SUPREME COURT
Chief Justice
COURT OF APPEALS
FEDERAL DISTRICT COURT
MAIN FEDERAL DEPARTMENTS
Justice
Interior
Agriculture
Education
Commerce
Labor
Health and Human Services
Transportation
Energy
Housing and Urban Development
State
Treasury
Defense
State Government
EXECUTIVE
Governor
LEGISLATURE
SENATE
HOUSE OF REPRESENTATIVES (or General Assembly)
JUDICIARY
STATE SUPREME COURT
STATE GOVERNMENT DEPARTMENTS
Justice
State Police Force
Treasury
Public Health
Transportation
Public Welfare
National resources
Protection of Life and Property (National Guard) etc.
CITY MAYORS IN COUNCIL
Municipal services such as:
Health
Sanitation
Water Supply
Police
Education
Highways
Justice etc.
STATE COURT OF APPEAL
COUNTY AND CITY COURTS
LOCAL JUSTICES' COURTS
Key
responsibility/approval
direction in which appeals go from one law court to another

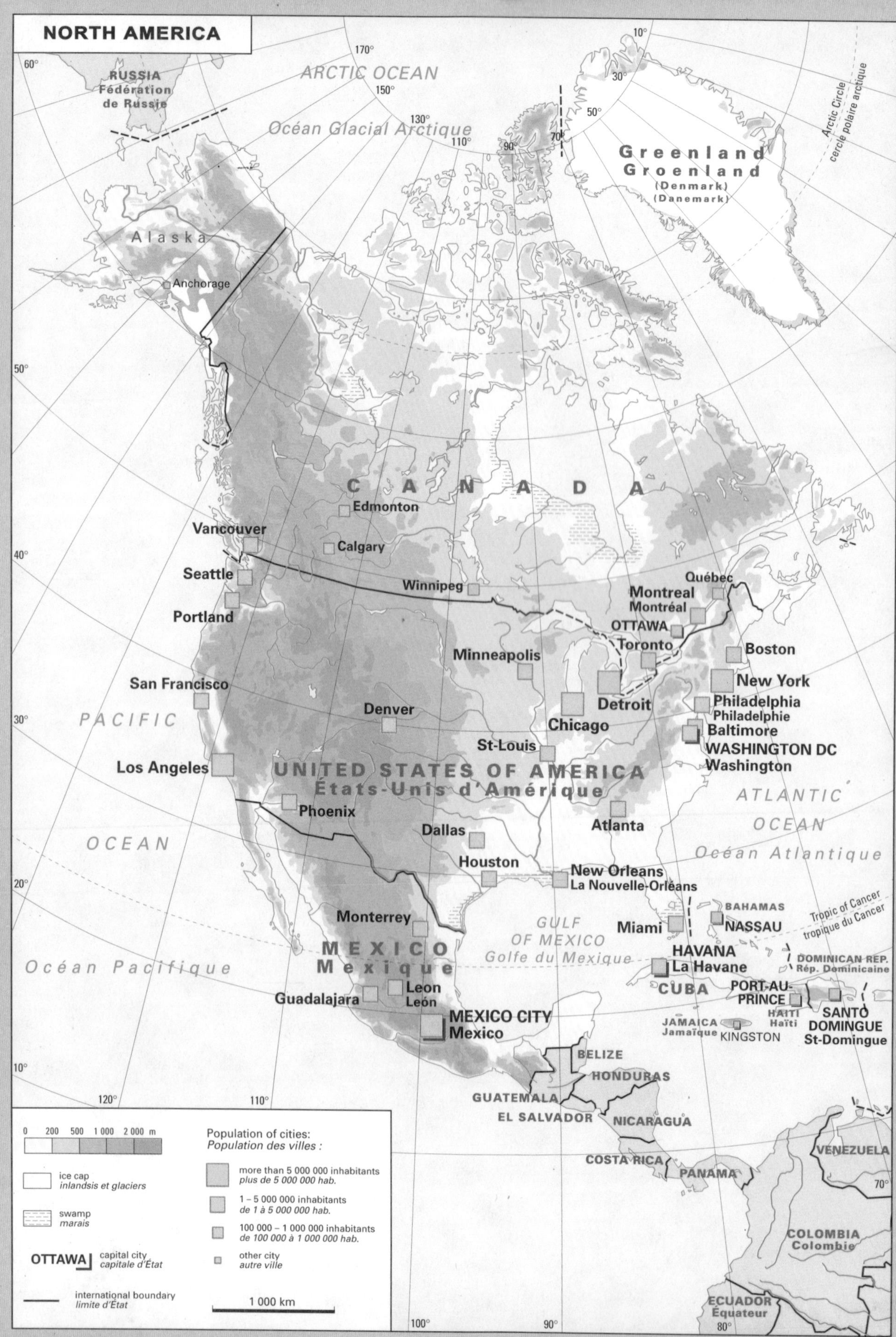
NORTH AMERICA
ARCTIC OCEAN
Océan Glacial Arctique
RUSSIA
Fédération de Russie
Greenland
Groenland
(Denmark)
(Danemark)
Arctic Circle
cercle polaire arctique
Alaska
Anchorage
CANADA
Edmonton
Calgary
Vancouver
Seattle
Portland
Winnipeg
Québec
Montreal
Montréal
OTTAWA
Toronto
Boston
Minneapolis
New York
Detroit
Chicago
Philadelphia
Philadelphie
Baltimore
WASHINGTON DC
Washington
San Francisco
Denver
St-Louis
Los Angeles
UNITED STATES OF AMERICA
États-Unis d'Amérique
Phoenix
Dallas
Atlanta
Houston
New Orleans
La Nouvelle-Orléans
PACIFIC
OCEAN
Océan Pacifique
ATLANTIC
OCEAN
Océan Atlantique
GULF OF MEXICO
Golfe du Mexique
Tropic of Cancer
tropique du Cancer
Monterrey
MEXICO
Mexique
Guadalajara
Leon
León
MEXICO CITY
Mexico
Miami
BAHAMAS
NASSAU
HAVANA
La Havane
CUBA
DOMINICAN REP.
Rép. Dominicaine
PORT-AU-PRINCE
HAITI
Haïti
SANTO DOMINGUE
St-Domingue
JAMAICA
Jamaïque
KINGSTON
BELIZE
HONDURAS
GUATEMALA
EL SALVADOR
NICARAGUA
COSTA RICA
PANAMA
VENEZUELA
COLOMBIA
Colombie
ECUADOR
Équateur
0 200 500 1 000 2 000 m
ice cap
inlandsis et glaciers
swamp
marais
OTTAWA capital city
capitale d'État
international boundary
limite d'État
Population of cities:
Population des villes :
more than 5 000 000 inhabitants
plus de 5 000 000 hab.
1 – 5 000 000 inhabitants
de 1 à 5 000 000 hab.
100 000 – 1 000 000 inhabitants
de 100 000 à 1 000 000 hab.
other city
autre ville
1 000 km